THE PUBLISHER'S PAGE

It encourages us at Chambers to see a positive response to the US directory. The American market was skeptical at first – and for good reason. 'Pay-to-play' publications had given directories a bad name. We had to prove ourselves.

In this third edition, we have made improvements. Firstly, we have increased the number of interviews with lawyers and clients by 40%. Client interviews – the ones we value most – have more than doubled in number. They include influential General Counsel at Fortune 100 companies, high-profile entrepreneurs building up their own private corporations, and significant purchasers of legal services.

Another change, as readers will see, is the expansion of our 'national' section. Last year it covered only four practice areas: this year it covers eleven.

In the individual states, we have added to the practice areas we cover. New coverage includes healthcare, white-collar crime, Native American law, ERISA litigation, zoning and land use, employee benefits and natural resources.

Our research this year has delved deeper into the legal market, not just in New York City, Chicago or San Francisco, but in the smaller jurisdictions where quality practices and individuals find it more difficult to gain recognition. We aim to provide clients not only with the established names but also the next generation of outstanding practitioners.

Michael Chambers

Published by **Chambers & Partners Publishing**
(a division of Orbach & Chambers Ltd)
23 Long Lane, London EC1A 9HL
Tel +44 207 606 1300
Fax +44 207 600 3191

ISBN 0-85514-422-X
Copyright © 2005 Michael Chambers and Orbach and Chambers Ltd

Publisher Michael Chambers
Managing Editor Fiona Boxall
Editors Thao Hua, Rieta Ghosh
Contributing Editors Ross Cogan, Anna Williams
Assistant Editor Tom Stevens
Editorial Assistant Joanne Grote
Profiles Editor Richard Pettet
Profiles Assistants Jill Tugwell, Sarah Tilling, Michelle Lemonius, Lydia Baillie

Production Team Jasper John, Paul Cummings, John Osborne, Jane Walker
Business Development Manager Brad Sirott
Business Development Team Richard Ramsay, Neil Murphy, Janene Warren
Distribution Marli Enslin

Orders to: Chambers & Partners Publishing
Printed in the USA by R R Donnelley

www.ChambersandPartners.com

NATIONAL RANKINGS & TABLES

BPO 9
Capital Markets: Northeast 13
Capital Markets: Midwest 21
Capital Markets: Southeast 22

Capital Markets: West Coast . . .23
ERISA Litigation 25
Government Contracts 26
Healthcare 29

International Arbitration 32
International Trade 39
Products Liability 48
Project Finance 52

Sports 55
Transportation 57

STATE RANKINGS & COMMENTARY

Alabama **111**
Corporate 111
Employment 113
Litigation 115
Real Estate 119
Alaska **133**
Bankruptcy 133
Corporate 134
Employment 135
Environment, ...136
Litigation 138
Native Law 140
Real Estate 140
Arizona **146**
Corporate 146
Employment 148
Environment 149
Litigation 151
Real Estate 153
Arkansas **168**
Corporate 168
Employment 169
Litigation 171
Real Estate 174
California **183**
Antitrust 183
Banking 187
Bankruptcy 190
Construction 193
Corporate 195
Employment 201
Energy 204
Environment 206
Healthcare 209
Insurance 212
IP .215
IT & IT Outsourcing 221
Litigation 223
Media 229
Projects 235
Real Estate 237
Tax 241
Colorado **303**
Corporate 303
Employment 305
Environment 307
IP .309
Litigation 310
Real Estate 313

Connecticut **327**
Corporate 327
Employment 329
Litigation 331
Real Estate 333
Delaware **341**
Bankruptcy 341
Chancery/Litigation 343
Corporate 346
Employment 347
IP .348
Real Estate 349
District of Columbia . .**366**
Antitrust 366
Bankruptcy 371
Construction 373
Corporate 376
Employee Benefits 378
Employment 379
Energy 381
Environment 390
Healthcare 397
Insurance 400
IP .403
Investment Management 405
Litigation 407
Media & Entertainment .413
Projects 415
Real Estate 417
Tax 422
Telecom, Broadcast & Sat 425
Florida **498**
Antitrust 498
Banking 500
Bankruptcy 501
Construction 505
Corporate 509
Employment 511
Environment 515
Healthcare 517
Insurance 519
Litigation 520
Real Estate 525
Tax 529
Georgia **578**
Antitrust 578
Banking 580
Bankruptcy 582
Construction 584

Corporate 586
Employment 589
Energy 591
Environment 592
Healthcare 594
IP .595
Litigation 598
Real Estate 601
Tax 603
Hawaii **640**
Bankruptcy 640
Corporate 641
Employment 642
Land Use 643
Litigation 644
Real Estate 646
Idaho **655**
Corporate 655
Employment 656
Litigation 657
Real Estate 658
Illinois **661**
Antitrust 661
Banking 664
Bankruptcy 668
Construction 672
Corporate 674
Employment 679
Energy 685
Environment 686
Healthcare 690
Insurance 692
IP .695
Litigation 699
Media 702
Real Estate 705
Tax 709
Technology 712
Indiana **781**
Corporate 781
Employment 783
Litigation 785
Real Estate 787
Iowa **802**
Corporate 802
Employment 804
Litigation 806
Real Estate 809

Kansas **816**
Corporate 816
Employment 817
Litigation 819
Real Estate 821
Kentucky **827**
Corporate 827
Employment 829
Litigation 834
Real Estate 837
Louisiana **857**
Banking 857
Corporate 858
Employment 860
Energy & Nat. Resources .862
Gaming & Licensing 864
Litigation 864
Real Estate 867
Maine **888**
Corporate 888
Employment 890
Environment 892
Litigation 893
Real Estate 895
Maryland **909**
Corporate 909
Employment 911
Litigation 914
Real Estate 916
Massachusetts **930**
Antitrust 930
Banking 931
Bankruptcy 934
Corporate 937
Employment 938
Environment 942
Healthcare 946
IP .947
Litigation 949
Private Equity 952
Real Estate 956
Tax 959
Michigan **987**
Banking 987
Corporate 988
Employment 991
Litigation 993
Real Estate 994

CONTENTS

INDEX TO ALL LAW FIRMS 1845
INDEX TO INDIVIDUAL LAWYERS 1869

Minnesota **1005**
Corporate 1004
Employment 1007
Litigation 1010
Real Estate 1014

Mississippi **1024**
Corporate 1024
Employment 1026
Litigation 1028
Real Estate 1031

Missouri **1042**
Corporate 1042
Employment 1045
Litigation 1048
Real Estate 1052

Montana **1072**
Corporate 1072
Employment 1073
Litigation 1074
Natural Resources 1077
Real Estate 1078

Nebraska **1082**
Corporate 1082
Employment 1083
Litigation 1084
Real Estate 1086

Nevada **1089**
Corporate 1089
Employment 1091
Environment 1093
Gaming 1094
Litigation 1095
Real Estate 1098

New Hampshire **1107**
Corporate 1107
Employment 1109
Litigation 1111
Real Estate 1114

New Jersey **1123**
Corporate 1123
Employment 1126
Environment 1128
Litigation 1130
Real Estate 1134

New Mexico **1155**
Corporate 1155
Employment 1156
Litigation 1159

Natural Resources 1157
Real Estate 1161

New York **1169**
Antitrust 1169
Banking 1173
Bankruptcy 1177
Construction 1185
Corporate 1187
Employment 1199
Energy 1201
Environment 1205
Healthcare 1209
Insurance 1211
IP 1216
Litigation 1220
Media 1231
Private Equity 1237
Projects 1242
Real Estate 1247
Tax 1254
Technology & IT 1259

North Carolina **1381**
Banking & Finance ...1381
Bankruptcy 1382
Capital Markets 1383
Corporate 1383
Employment 1385
Environment 1387
Litigation 1389
Real Estate 1392

North Dakota **1403**
Corporate 1403
Employment 1405
Litigation 1406
Real Estate 1408

Ohio **1411**
Banking 1411
Bankruptcy 1413
Construction 1416
Corporate 1419
Employment 1421
Environment 1424
IP 1427
Litigation 1430
Real Estate 1434

Oklahoma **1459**
Corporate 1459
Employment 1460
Litigation 1462
Real Estate 1463

Oregon **1471**
Corporate 1471
Employment 1473
Litigation 1475
Real Estate 1478

Pennsylvania **1489**
Antitrust 1489
Banking 1492
Bankruptcy 1494
Corporate 1497
Employment 1500
Environment 1504
IP 1507
Litigation 1510
Real Estate 1515

Rhode Island **1564**
Corporate 1564
Employment 1565
Litigation 1566
Real Estate 1568

South Carolina **1572**
Corporate 1572
Employment 1574
Litigation 1575
Real Estate 1577

South Dakota **1587**
Corporate 1587
Employment 1589
Litigation 1589
Real Estate 1591

Tennessee **1594**
Corporate 1594
Employment 1596
Litigation 1598
Media 1602
Real Estate 1603

Texas **1622**
Antitrust 1622
Banking 1624
Bankruptcy 1626
Construction 1629
Corporate 1631
Employment 1633
Energy 1637
Environment 1642
Healthcare 1645
Insurance 1647
IP 1649
Litigation 1655

Projects 1659
Real Estate 1661
Tax 1664
Technology 1667

Utah **1727**
Corporate 1727
Employment 1729
Litigation 1731
Real Estate 1733

Vermont **1743**
Corporate 1743
Employment 1744
Litigation 1745
Real Estate 1747

Virginia **1750**
Construction 1750
Corporate 1752
Employment 1755
Environment 1757
IP 1758
Litigation 1762
Real Estate 1765

Washington **1776**
Bankruptcy 1776
Corporate 1777
Employment 1780
Environment 1782
IP 1783
Litigation 1785
Real Estate 1787

West Virginia **1798**
Corporate 1798
Employment 1800
Litigation 1802
Real Estate 1805

Wisconsin **1817**
Corporate 1817
Employment 1819
Litigation 1820
Real Estate 1822

Wyoming **1832**
Corporate 1832
Employment 1833
Litigation 1834
Real Estate 1836

THE RESEARCH TEAM 2005

Thao Hua (Editor)
Graduated in History at the University of North Texas and later completed a one-year law research fellowship for journalists at the University of Michigan. Worked as a legal affairs writer for the Los Angeles Times.

Ross Cogan (Editor)
Studied Law and Philosophy at Nottingham University. M Phil from St John's College, Cambridge. PhD in Logic from Bristol University. Taught at several universities and previously worked in underwriting.

Sarah Brown (Head of Client Research)
Solicitor. Graduated in Law at Newnham College, Cambridge. Trained and practiced at a magic circle firm. Specialized in corporate finance and insolvency law.

Rieta Ghosh (Editor)
Graduated in Ancient History at University of Durham. Former client information manager with European market research agency. Previously worked at a leading business advisory company.

Anna Williams (Contributing Editor)
Solicitor. Graduated in Human Sciences at St Anne's College, Oxford. Practiced commercial property and social housing at a leading London firm for eight years. Editor of Chambers Student Guide.

● **James Cowdell (Deputy Editor)**
Barrister. Graduated in Modern History at The Queen's College, Oxford. Practiced at the Criminal Bar for five years and was a fee-earner in the family department of a leading London law firm.

● **Michael Leigh (Deputy Editor)**
Gained a First in Philosophy from Bristol University, where he also completed a doctorate in modern social contract theory. Has taught ethics and political philosophy and undertaken freelance satire for local newspapers.

● **Edward Bannell (Research Manager)**
Graduated in Law at London School of Economics. Worked as a Legal Executive for a leading Australian law firm. Has worked in legal publishing and legal recruitment.

● **Eleni Chalkidou (Senior Researcher)**
MA in Journalism from Westminster University. Worked as a journalist for BBC News Online, International Financial Law Review and Corporate Finance magazine. Also journalist for Commercial Lawyer magazine. Fluent in Greek, German, Spanish and Krio (spoken in Sierra Leone).

● **Ben Tendler (Senior Researcher)**
Graduated from the University of Bristol with a First in English Literature. Previously worked as a freelance market researcher.

● **Kerrie Taylor (Senior Researcher)**
Non-practicing Solicitor. Graduated in Spanish at University of St Andrews and University of Salamanca, Spain. Trained with leading Inns of Court law firm in London.

● **Pippa Grèze (Deputy Editor)**
Solicitor. Graduated in Law at UCW Aberystwyth. LL.M in European and International Trade Law from Leicester University. Trained with a major law firm, subsequently qualifying into commercial property law. Previously worked as a translator and guide in Poitiers, France.

● **Naomi Lawson (Deputy Editor)**
Graduated in German at Lady Margaret Hall, Oxford. Worked in Germany for a year as an English teaching assistant before gaining experience in various areas of publishing.

● **Richard James (Senior Researcher)**
Graduated in English Literature at the University of Wales, Cardiff. Former paralegal and recently published author.

● **Robert Wainwright (Senior Researcher)**
Solicitor. Graduated in Law and English at University of Queensland, Australia. Trained at leading niche litigation firm and wrote for a national legal journal. Has also written for Chambers Student Guide.

● **Mark Knowles (Senior Researcher)**
Graduated in Classics followed by Management Studies at Downing College, Cambridge. Worked as a preparatory school teacher, sports journalist with a published book on the 2002 FIFA World Cup, and a headhunter.

● **Abigail Rochford (Senior Researcher)**
Graduated with a Master's in American Studies from the University of Edinburgh. Previously worked for an independent publisher and traveled extensively before going in to research.

● **Ignacio Abella** BA in English Language and Literature from Universidad de Oriente in Cuba. Freelance translator/interpreter. Worked as project manager for a local branch of the Ministry of Culture, started an MA in Caribbean Studies before relocating to the UK. Extensive experience in market research having worked for an information and communication technology advisory company and for a major data analysis group in London.

● **Jodi Bartle** Studied English and Law at the University of Auckland, New Zealand. Worked as a researcher for a film company and as a barrister and solicitor.

● **Rupert Candy** Graduated in Modern Languages and Law at Selwyn College, Cambridge. Previously worked at a City firm. Fluent in French.

● **Louise Carr** Graduated in American and English Studies at the University of Nottingham. Previously worked in consumer magazine publishing and in information management for the insurance and financial services industry.

● **Shivali Chaudhry** Graduated in Law at University College London. Completed the LPC at the College of Law. Has studied in Singapore.

● **Romila Chowdhury** Graduated in Law at the School of Oriental and African Studies.

● **Jessica Culpan** Studied English and Law at the University of Otago in New Zealand. Has worked as a press officer and private secretary in the New Zealand House of Representatives, and subsequently as a researcher in both the public and private sectors.

● **Kate Fitzgerald** Solicitor. Graduated in Law and English at the University of New South Wales, Australia. Worked in human rights and international relations in Geneva and Australia.

● **Ed Frettingham** Graduated with a First in History with European Study from the University of Exeter, before gaining an MScEcon with Distinction in International Politics at the University of Wales, Aberystwyth. Has studied in Germany and worked in Italy.

● **Amanda Howe** Graduated from University of Leeds with a First in German and Russian and is currently studying for Graduate Diploma in Law. Previously worked in the conference industry, organizing and producing business seminars in Moscow.

● **Julia Kelk** Graduated in English and Spanish at McGill University, Canada and Université de Paris 4-Sorbonne, France. MA in English from King's College London. Worked in Mexico and Ireland as well as teaching in a Colombian university. Fluent in French and Spanish.

● **Claire Leach** Graduated in Law at the University of Warwick. Lived and studied in Houston, Texas, for two years and attained the Certificate of French Law while living in Bordeaux for a year. Previously has undertaken legal placements in San Francisco and London.

● **John Lucarotti** Barrister. Graduated in French from Royal Holloway, University of London, before taking the CPE at City University and the BVC at ICSL. Has worked at CAB as an immigration adviser and is also a Free Representation Unit employment representative. Fluent in French.

● **Michelle Madsen** Graduated in English Language and Literature at Balliol College, Oxford. Has written for the Guardian and the Guardian Weekly during an internship. Fluent in Spanish.

● **Senja Malone-Lee** Graduated in German and English at the University of Belgrade. MA in German from University College, London. Completed internship at the Institute for Public Policy Research. During the Yugoslav crisis worked as a freelance media researcher for the Guardian and as a translator for the BBC. Fluent in German and Serbo-Croat.

● **Joanna Mason** Awarded first-class honours in English Literature from University of East Anglia. Graduated from King's College, Cambridge with an M.Phil in Eighteenth-Century British Literature. Has completed several placements with UK law firms.

● **Beth McMillan** Graduated in Law with French Law at UCL. Fluent French speaker.

● **Daniela Nadj** Studied English and European Law at Queen Mary College, University of London. Completed a Master's degree (LL.M.) in International Law at Cornell Law School (USA). Previously worked as paralegal and legal translator in the USA and as an English language teacher in Italy. Fluent in German, Serbo-Croat, Italian, Spanish and French.

● **Alexandra Quilici** Graduated in Politics at the American University in Paris. Completed a Master's in Modern History and an MA in Political and Social Communications at Université Paris 1 Panthéon-Sorbonne. Has worked in business research, advertising sales and financial information. Bilingual.

● **Catherine Rodgers** Graduated from King's College London with a First in English Language and Literature. Completed two mini-pupillages with sets of barristers, gaining experience in aspects of criminal law.

● **Anna Saunders** Graduated in English Literature and Language at Pembroke College, Oxford, before training and working as a fine art auctioneer.

● **Lee Saunders** Graduated in French and History at University of Leeds. Worked as an English teacher in Paris, France, and subsequently as a research analyst in London for an American media company.

● **Steven Sharman** Graduated with first-class honours in Law from the University of Greenwich, London. Subsequently awarded a Diploma in Legal Practice with Commendation from the College of Law and has worked for a solicitors firm in South London.

● **Edward Shum** Graduated in Law at Magdalene College, Cambridge. Previously worked at a South London law firm.

● **Amy Stroud** Graduated in English at Queens' College, Cambridge. Worked as a business journalist and paralegal at a City law firm before being called to the Bar in Autumn 2004.

● **Douglas Watson** Graduated in Jurisprudence at The Queen's College, Oxford. Completed the Diploma of Legal Practice at the Oxford Institute of Legal Practice in 2004.

● **Andrew Watts** Graduated in Literae Humaniores at Merton College, Oxford. Taught in a Japanese University before studying law and working as a legal consultant in the construction industry.

● **Philippe Weyland** Completed the Legal Practice Course at the College of Law in London. Earned Maîtrise en Droit Privé in Strasbourg. Developed Intellectual Property and EU law expertise during legal placements in London. Has also completed a publishing and business internship in large music company. Fluent in French, Luxembourgeois and German.

● **Tom Wicker** Graduated in English Language and Literature at Corpus Christi College, Oxford. Worked in the editorial department of a London-based literary magazine after completing an MPhil in British Studies at Cambridge. Has also been involved in the research for a biography to be published in 2005.

● **Karen Williams** Graduated in politics at Glasgow University. Previously worked as a parliamentary researcher at the House of Commons and as a paralegal at a New York law firm.

● **Christine Yung** Graduated in Law from Christ's College, University of Cambridge.

The Rankings

This guide – like Chambers UK and Chambers Global – is designed to reflect market opinion.

Entry in the guide is based on market recommendations. Our researchers canvass clients and lawyers across the USA to obtain a consistent market view of which firms and attorneys are considered leaders in the field. Over 10,000 telephone interviews – about half of which involved clients – were conducted, from Maine to Hawaii. These resulted in the rankings.

We accept that there is ultimately no strict scientific basis on which to compare the value and quality of lawyers. What appeals to one client may not appeal to another. But by interviewing enough sources, a ranking does emerge – a ranking shaped by the market. Not everyone will agree with it, but clients will be interested to see if their own preferences are shared by others.

In addition to a maximum of six tiers in the Chambers' tables, there are three additional categories in which attorneys might be ranked. They are as follows:

Senior Statesman

How should we rank those distinguished older partners – often name partners – who are admired throughout the profession and who are still, in their senior years, the principal point of contact with major clients? In the very top band? But they are no longer seen around so much on everyday transactions. Their role has changed. As leading practitioners doing the deals they are being overtaken by the next generation. Logically, then, they should be demoted to the band below. But given their immense prestige, this would look wrong. It would also be inaccurate. They are not exactly 'declining': their contribution is as valuable as ever.

We resolved this dilemma with the 'senior statesman' category. They are the sages of their particular legal markets and beyond. Among them is Marty Lipton, one of the global giants of M&A and the main architect of the 'poison pill' defense. Another legal virtuoso is Jack Levin, hailed for his contribution to the development of private equity law, not just in Illinois but across the world.

Star

These players are the first names that roll off everyone's lips, the standard by which others are judged. Beyond that, these attorneys operate in a 'right here, right now' mode, immersing themselves in the most significant work around. At the top of their game, they also bring to the negotiating table a certain degree of gravitas – the kind of influence that sends shivers down the spine of the opposing side. The star category is reserved for those individuals whose profile is far ahead of the pack.

This marketplace authority is cultivated through a long history of excellence, and it usually manifests in the research process through the sheer weight of recommendations compared with their peers. Additionally, they've also managed to change the legal landscape in dramatic ways. For example, rainmaker Larry Sonsini of Wilson Sonsini Goodrich & Rosati is not only a catalyst in the success of his own firm, but also consistently sets industry records for the number of IPOs to his name. In New York, Wolcott Dunham of Debevoise & Plimpton has helped engineer legislation that affects the entire insurance industry.

Up-and-Coming Individual

If the senior statesmen are the brains of a firm, then this 'bubbling-under' set is its added brawn. Yet, while these individuals do not make or break a firm, they do fuel the firm's growth. This next generation of talent doesn't necessarily have the industry reputation to warrant a numeric ranking, which is reserved for those with an already established profile. But what they lack in experience, they make up for in energy.

They are the young dynamos that give an operation extra edge. More importantly, they bridge the practice's present and its future. These operators range in age, but are generally in their 30s and early 40s, partly depending on their areas of specialty; certain fields require more 'seasoning' than others.

NATIONAL

As a result of the continuing efforts to better reflect the legal market-place, *Chambers USA* has significantly increased the number of practice areas covered in the national category. In this edition, there are 11 sections, compared with four in the previous directory.

National sections concern the nature of the practice areas. Products liability, for example, casts a wide net across the country. Therefore, to place this section in any one state would misrepresent the essence of the practice, which is all-encompassing in terms not only of the law that guides it, but also of jurisdiction.

In other areas, the focus is less about boundaries and more about the way clients choose to retain law firms. They look for the ability to weave together various networks of resources to deliver adroit services throughout the country. The broader scope of expertise affords a seamlessness that provides a distinct legal advantage. For example, there's such an amalgamation of the various specialist issues affecting healthcare that a national focus makes sense to certain clients. In this case and others, the teams are examined not only on a national scale, but also on a state-by-state basis in order to differentiate the subtleties

that together, round out the entire practice. Therefore, it is not unusual for firms to be ranked in both the national and state categories.

Some sections mirror more recent trends in the domestic market, for example ERISA litigation. Spurred by a bevy of corporate scandals recently, the practice has become a more distinct specialty on a national scale.

Another feature of the national rankings is that they take into account the nature and scope of the practice areas rather than the geographic reach of the firms. Indeed, many of the firms here are not necessarily national in terms of spread and a significant portion of those ranked on the state side have offices all over the country. The other element of the national rankings is that they are fundamentally different from the state tables and the two are not comparable. In other words, a firm ranked in the national division is not necessarily 'better' than a firm ranked on the state side in terms of quality; it simply addresses different requirements from a client's standpoint. In future editions, we plan to add even more practice areas to this category, depending on what clients tell us they need and our own resources, so as to ensure that the research is satisfactory.

BUSINESS PROCESS OUTSOURCING

National
Leading firms
(Business Process Outsourcing)

1 MAYER, BROWN, ROWE & MAW LLP
  MILBANK, TWEED, HADLEY
  SHAW PITTMAN LLP

2 ALSTON & BIRD LLP
  BAKER BOTTS LLP
  BROWN RAYSMAN MILLSTEIN
  HUGHES & LUCE LLP
  JONES DAY
  LATHAM & WATKINS LLP
  MORGAN, LEWIS & BOCKIUS LLP
  SONNENSCHEIN NATH & ROSENTHAL

3 ARNOLD & PORTER LLP
  HUNTON & WILLIAMS
  KING & SPALDING LLP
  O'MELVENY & MYERS LLP

4 BAKER & MCKENZIE
  BIERCE & KENERSON, PC
  KIRKLAND & ELLIS LLP
  SKADDEN, ARPS, SLATE, MEAGHER

Firms are listed alphabetically in each band.

Band 1

Mayer, Brown, Rowe & Maw LLP

See firm details p.771

The Firm: This "*world-class*" team has historically been noted for its supplier work on behalf of such clients as Anderson and Accenture, particularly in the IT sphere. However, peers note that it has also "*built a formidable presence on the customer side*" in recent times. Clients were full of praise for a team of attorneys who they believe "*understand the industry well*" and are "*really helpful in focusing us on issues we would have missed otherwise!*" As one satisfied customer put it, the group is "*professional, willing to be flexible and turn things around quickly – it's obvious that they've gained the respect of everyone they deal with.*"

The Lawyers: Dan Masur (see p.455), in the firm's DC office, is renowned in the market as the architect of the firm's outsourcing practice. Clients keep returning to him because he "*has a deep knowledge of the law, market conditions and the state of the industry overall – he spends a lot of time on background and theory.*" Despite this academic approach, he "*can be a bulldog for his client*" if needs be. In Chicago, the "*talented*" **Brad Peterson** (see p.746) "*has a great sense of urgency*" sources say. Clients note he has "*great experience on both the buyer side and the provider side, so he can judge issues from varying perspectives.*" He recently represented Aon Corporation in the outsourcing of finance and accounting functions to Accenture, and advised CNA Financial Corporation on outsourcing its insur-

ance underwriting, claims management and care management functions. Also in Chicago, "*hard-working*" Rebecca Eisner (see p.725) is admired for her "*good substantive knowledge.*" She was also said to be an "*excellent negotiator who is patient with clients who require an explanation of the process.*" She recently advised The Williams Companies on the combination of its IT, finance and accounting and HR functions under one seven-year outsourcing agreement with IBM. Meanwhile, **Paul Roy** (see p.749) "*knows the important variables to be addressed in every agreement – he's fair but forceful if necessary.*" His highlights from the year include acting for Procter & Gamble in connection with a global outsourcing transaction with Hewlett-Packard for the provision of accounts payable services. **Nigel Howard** (see p.1288) in New York is noted for his technology work and "*does a good job of analyzing issues and pushing the transaction along.*" Also in New York, the "*tenacious but never unpleasant*" **David Hudanish** (see p.1289) "*brings a fair perspective to the deal.*" Clients recommend him as "*always accessible and accommodating to our needs.*" He advised TXU on a ten-year $3.5 billion BPO transaction with Capgemini, which included revenue management, finance and accounting, procurement, HR, customer care/call centers and IT.

The Clients: TXU; Procter & Gamble; Fifth Third Bank; Aon Corporation; CNA Financial Corporation; IndyMac Bank; OneChicago and The Williams Companies.

Milbank, Tweed, Hadley & McCloy

The Firm: Milbank Tweed is not merely "*one of the foremost outsourcing firms in the country,*" it is also "*truly multinational in scope*" according to interviewees. Everyone agrees that this customer-focused practice remains a "*dominant and entrenched player*" in the sector. Much of its profile is felt to be due to the outstanding reputation of New York-based practice head John Halvey, and many leading names in the field were "*trained by him at Milbank before going out on their own.*"

The Lawyers: "*Phenomenal on the customer side,*" **John Halvey** literally wrote the book on outsourcing – it's entitled 'Business Process Outsourcing Transactions: Process, Strategies and Contracts.' Peers note that "*you can't talk about outsourcing without talking about Halvey – he's played perhaps the leading role in the development of the industry,*" while clients value him because "*he's a deep thinker and looks at deals with incredible focus like an investor would.*" A recent highlight was representing Deutsche Bank in a major outsourcing deal with Accenture. This was the largest procurement outsourcing deal to date in the financial services sector, involving the out-

sourcing by Deutsche Bank of its worldwide corporate purchasing and accounts payable services. He also represented the purchasers, General Atlantic Partners and Oak Hill Capital Partners, in the $500 million sale by GE of a majority stake in its global outsourcing business GE Capital International Services (Gecis). The "*accomplished*" **Rob Finkel** was described to researchers as having "*really taken the number two spot in Milbank's outsourcing practice.*"

The Clients: DuPont; AT&T; Cendant; Pepsi-Co; BellSouth; GM; Alcatel; Xerox; Boeing; Hughes; Bombardier; General Atlantic and the Commonwealth Bank of Australia.

Shaw Pittman LLP

See firm details p.490

The Firm: This "*trend-setting*" group was roundly praised by interviewees for its impressive track record of industry leadership. As one source put it, the firm has been involved in "*the majority of the large-scale outsourcings that have been done since the late '80s, starting with IT but evolving into BPO.*" Clients and peers agree the team has been successful in "*leveraging off being a tremendous procurement contract practice,*" which has helped propel it to the top of the tree, and maintains it as "*one of the serious players in the market,*" notwithstanding the recent departures of key New York personnel Akiba Stern and Ed Hansen for Morgan Lewis. The team is focused on customer representation, and also boasts a number of in-house strategic consulting personnel. At the time of going to press the firm announced its merger with Pillsbury Winthrop LLP to form Pillsbury Winthrop Shaw Pittman.

The Lawyers: Bob Zahler (see p.108) is said to be particularly active on the customer side. Peers described him as "*one of the early pioneers,*" and paid tribute to the "*great amount he's done to advance the industry.*" Clients, meanwhile, keep returning to him for his ability to "*analyze transactions and get them concluded in the most efficient way.*" LA-based **Michael Murphy** (see p.264) was particularly rated by sources for his "*ability to build strong partnering deals.*" He recently advised a client in the electronics manufacturing field on an international facilities management outsourcing project. Other highlights include assisting a client to negotiate a business transformation contract with a major service provider in the energy sector. In the firm's DC office, **Trevor Nagel** (see p.96) was commended for his "*wonderful international practice,*" and indeed he has recently been advising on two of the largest current global outsourcings, namely Ahold's outsourcing of all 'towers' in its IT environment and PepsiCo's outsourcing of its global network.

www.ChambersandPartners.com

All quotes in the text are from interviews with clients and competitors.

9

National

Leading individuals

(Business Process Outsourcing)

★ **HALVEY John** *Milbank Tweed*, New York

[1] **DOCKSEY Ross** *Sonnenschein Nath*, Chicago

FUNK John *Jones Day*, Dallas

HOWELL John *Hughes & Luce*, Dallas

MASUR Daniel *Mayer Brown*, Washington, DC

ZAHLER Robert *Shaw Pittman*, Washington, DC

[2] **FORD Christopher** *Alston & Bird*, Washington, DC

GUEDRY David *Hughes & Luce*, Dallas

HUDANISH David *Mayer Brown*, New York

KIMBALL George *Arnold & Porter*, Los Angeles

MARTIN John *Baker Botts*, Dallas

MELBY Barbara *Morgan Lewis*, Philadelphia

MILLSTEIN Julian *Brown Raysman*, New York

MUMMERY Dan *Latham & Watkins*, Menlo Park

PETERSON Brad *Mayer Brown*, Chicago

[3] **BIERCE William** *Bierce & Kenerson*, New York

EISNER Rebecca *Mayer Brown*, Chicago

FINKEL Robert *Milbank Tweed*, New York

GULLIKSON Rosemary *Sonnenschein Nath*, Chicago

HARVEY James *Alston & Bird*, Atlanta

HOBBY Scott *Hunton & Williams*, Atlanta

HOWARD Nigel *Mayer Brown*, New York

KIRCHHOEFER Gregg *Kirkland & Ellis*, Chicago

KLEIN Allen *Latham & Watkins*, Washington, DC

MENSIK Michael *Baker & McKenzie*, Chicago

MURPHY Michael *Shaw Pittman*, Los Angeles

NAGEL Trevor *Shaw Pittman*, Washington, DC

PETERS William *O'Melveny & Myers*, Los Angeles

RAYSMAN Richard *Brown Raysman*, New York

REYNOLDS Robert *Alston & Bird*, Atlanta

ROCHE William *King & Spalding*, Atlanta

ROY Paul *Mayer Brown*, Chicago

SHOCKRO Michael *Latham & Watkins*, Los Angeles

STERN Akiba *Morgan Lewis*, New York

Individuals are listed alphabetically in each band.

The Clients: The group recently advised GE Capital on a data management outsourcing transaction, and acted for CheckFree in the offshore outsourcing of applications, maintenance and development functions. Other clients include: Merrill Lynch; Sprint; Capital One; Telus; Solectron and McDonald's.

Band 2

Alston & Bird LLP

See firm details p.626

The Firm: The firm's outsourcing team "*generates a lot of publicity*" say peers, who note its involvement in a series of important transactions. It also attracted attention for "*actively seeking work on both sides*" and appearing regularly for both customers and service providers. Clients, meanwhile, appreciate the way that "*during the deals, we see them not just focusing on legal issues, but integrating business issues too.*" The team's expertise in the outsourcing field spans human resources, check and credit card

processing, telecommunications and networking, and logistics and fulfilment.

The Lawyers: Chris Ford (see p.83) in the firm's DC office was recommended by peers for his work on the customer side, where he is "*a real player in the industry.*" His recent work has included advising ING America on the $600 million outsourcing of its IT infrastructure to IBM, and representing Sabre in the renegotiation of its outsourcing agreement with American Airlines. He has also acted for a number of international financial institutions in the outsourcing of their back-office and IT functions. In the firm's Atlanta office, **Jim Harvey** (see p.87) is a respected adviser whose clients include both customers and suppliers, while **Bob Reynolds**' (see p.101) practice is focused on strategic corporate projects involving significant outsourcing, technology or information components.

The Clients: Assurant; Sabre; Six Continents Hotels; UnumProvident; UPS and WebMD.

Baker Botts LLP

See firm details p.1708

The Firm: According to interviewees, this practice is known for being "*historically supplier focused.*" It still has a superb supplier client base, and over the past year has represented various suppliers in relation to outsourcings involving call center operations, HR and benefits administration, customer care (particularly in the utilities sector), billing, account termination, procurement and F&A. However, it is increasingly building a reputation among customers from a range of sectors. Clients themselves value the team for its "*strength across the board in outsourcing matters.*" As one noted, "*whether it's regulatory, corporate or just about any issue that pops up, they can bring the strength to bear on it and staff the deals well.*" In this, its success is said to be founded on a solid base of attorneys who are "*smart, personable and hard working*" with the "*ability to articulate complex legal issues to business people.*"

The Lawyers: Interviewees enthusiastically recommended Dallas-based practice head **John Martin** (see p.1690) for his "*terrific negotiating skills*" and his "*knack for understanding the business itself and making it primary to the transaction.*" As one appreciative client noted, "*the rigour and experience he and his team bring to bear in analyzing transactions is invaluable.*"

The Clients: The team has been representing a number of suppliers, as well as customers from sectors such as utilities, energy, real estate management, financial services, healthcare, chemicals and telecommunications. Examples include: EDS; ACS; Accenture; Deloitte Consulting; Perot Systems and First Data.

Brown Raysman Millstein Felder & Steiner LLP

See firm details p.1338

The Firm: This "*top-quality*" New York firm has built on its traditional expertise in technology and IP, and now advises on a range of outsourcing transactions. Typical examples of its work include tax compliance, purchasing, human resources, facilities and real property operations and manufacturing, packaging, and logistics. While the practice is increasingly customers-oriented, peers note that it retains "*a good spread of vendor clients too,*" in particular long-term client AT&T Solutions.

The Lawyers: "*Big-name player*" **Julian Millstein** (see p.1302) is renowned as a "*first-rate technology and outsourcing lawyer,*" and is especially highly rated by competitors for his vendor-side work. He has recently been handling a finance and accounting outsourcing for a large retailer. He has also been busy representing one of the big four accounting firms in an outsourcing transaction concerning financial work being done in India, and advising on an application, development and maintenance outsourcing involving a major global insurance company. Described by sources as a "*class act,*" **Richard Raysman** (see p.1311) has recently advised a healthcare provider, a data analysis company and a venture investment fund on various outsourcing matters.

The Clients: Clients include commercial and investment banks, hospitals, insurance companies and data companies. AT&T Solutions is the best-known example.

Hughes & Luce LLP

The Firm: This Texas-based outfit has a particular niche in the technology field. It is especially well regarded by competitors for service provider representation, where its name is closely connected with that of long-term client EDS. As one peer noted, "*on the vendor side they're as good as it gets.*" Clients themselves value the lawyers here because they are "*good at the details of transactions and able to gauge the skill level of attorneys at outside firms.*" The group's work in recent times has included HR and finance and accountancy outsourcings, and it has also seen increasing activity on the customer side.

The Lawyers: John Howell was described by one admiring commentator as "*probably the longest tenured outsourcing lawyer in the world.*" As one satisfied client commented: "*The first thing you realize is that he's been down this road many times before, so he can help us anticipate the issues and can gauge what is a reasonable outcome to negotiations.*" He has recently advised a couple of investment management firms on the outsourcing of various back-office operations. He also acted for an oil and gas exploration company in the outsourcing of its revenue accounting, royalty disbursement and other financial operations. The transportation area is a particular niche, and he has helped a number of airlines with the outsourcing of their reservations processes and other IT and administrative activities. His historical relationship with EDS was also noted. **David Guedry** is appreciated by clients for "*his great competence and skills.*" As one put it, "*he got the project so under control that I felt I could work on other priorities.*" Although traditionally active for suppliers, such as Hewitt Associates, he has been handling an increasing amount of work for customers such as Ericsson, Blockbuster and Worldspan.

The Clients: EDS; Worldspan; PIMCO; RCM Capital Management; Ericsson and Blockbuster.

Jones Day
See firm details p.485

The Firm: The firm is admired by peers and valued by clients for its extensive national and international network. In the outsourcing arena, however, its strength is concentrated in Texas. In recent years, the group has been especially active in the financial services and healthcare arenas. An increasing volume of HR outsourcings swells a practice that also includes customer care, finance and accountancy, and real estate operations.

The Lawyers: "*Seasoned veteran*" **John Funk** (see p.1680) was described by peers as "*one of the premier providers on the customer side.*" The department head picked up much of his trade while an in-house lawyer at EDS, and then worked with fellow luminaries John Howell and John Halvey, from Hughes & Luce and Milbank Tweed respectively, before returning to his traditional stomping grounds in the Lone Star State. Recent highlights include advising Washington Mutual on a seven-year business outsourcing transaction with Unisys for a new check processing operation. He also assisted Hewitt Associates, as subcontractor for HR outsourcing services, in relation to Capgemini's BPO and IT outsourcing agreement with TXU.

The Clients: The team recently advised on a complex transaction combining the sale of AEP's IT services, call center and customer care subsidiary to outsourcer Alliance Data Systems (ADS). This involved a contemporaneous master services outsourcing agreement for ADS to provide these services to various AEP business units. Other clients include Washington Mutual and Hewitt Associates.

Latham & Watkins LLP

The Firm: Having "*got into this industry in a big way in recent years*" with the recruitment of key personnel like Dan Mummery and Allen Klein, this practice is "*becoming an effective force on the customer side.*" Observers particularly commended the group's strength on the West Coast. Its outsourcing expertise spans finance and accounting, human resources, procurement, credit card processing, back-office functions,

asset management, logistics, insurance applications, underwriting and claims processing, and wired and wireless communications IT systems.

The Lawyers: Another Milbank Tweed alumnus, **Dan Mummery**, in the firm's Silicon Valley office "*has enhanced the value of the firm*" since moving from Cooley Godward at the beginning of 2004. He recently represented Levi Strauss in an $85 million HR outsourcing to Accenture, and advised Gateway on the restructuring of a $400 million outsourcing transaction with ACS, including HR, finance and accounting functions. In DC, **Allen Klein** joined the firm from Shaw Pittman in the middle of 2003. His BPO expertise spans call centers, credit card processing, item processing, and insurance claims processing transactions. His highlights from the year include assisting F&G Life Insurance Company (the US life and annuity affiliate of Old Mutual) in negotiating an insurance product design and distribution outsourcing with Legacy Marketing. He also negotiated a billing and customer care arrangement for CenturyTel, the country's largest rural telecommunications company, with AMDOCS. LA-based **Michael Shockro** chairs the firm's technology transactions practice group, and was described by interviewees as "*a dignified and skilful diplomat*" who is particularly "*knowledgeable in e-commerce.*"

The Clients: The firm represented Hawaiian Telecom in a series of BPO transactions for directory printing, supply chain services, wireless carrier services and wireless billing services. Other clients include: Old Mutual Life Insurance; F&G Life Insurance; Gateway; CenturyTel and Beverly Enterprises.

Morgan, Lewis & Bockius LLP
See firm details p.1556

The Firm: Morgan Lewis "*certainly has offices everywhere,*" say market sources, and these offices are full of "*skilled and practical*" attorneys. The biggest news for the practice this year has been the arrival of Akiba Stern and colleague Ed Hansen from Shaw Pittman's New York office. Peers believe this move "*signals that the firm is making further investments in the practice,*" as does the recent elevation to partner of Barbara Murphy Melby.

The Lawyers: **Barbara Murphy Melby** (see p.95) is known in the market as a former protégée of John Halvey at Milbank Tweed, and wrote the famous 'Business Process Outsourcing' text with him. A "*superb, tough*" attorney, she is also noted for her work with the firm's institutional clients. **Akiba Stern** (see p.1324) brought the majority of his individual client base over with him from Shaw Pittman, helping to "*add an outsourcing capability*" to the firm's New York office.

The Clients: Clients come from a range of industries, including life sciences, energy and financial services.

Sonnenschein Nath & Rosenthal LLP
See firm details p.779

The Firm: The practice enjoys a "*national presence,*" and is especially active on the vendor side for clients such as Accenture, ACS and Aon. Its lawyers are respected by peers for the "*scope of their knowledge of the industry.*" Clients, meanwhile, recommended them because they are "*careful in long negotiations to serve not only our interests but also those of the other side and the relationship itself.*" One particularly praised their great expertise: "*They're good at advising on things that might become issues down the road, and often things we didn't even know we need to think about.*"

The Lawyers: **Ross Docksey** (see p.724) was especially rated for his work on the supplier side, and his "*courteous, disciplined and efficient*" approach. Clients note his "*long history of dealing with complicated outsourcing contracts,*" and particularly appreciate the way that he "*brings to the table a great amount of credibility and persuasiveness.*" As one put it, "*he's old school in a positive way, in that he's interested in reaching a win-win situation for the customer and the provider.*" **Rosemary Gullikson** (see p.86) is "*a pleasure to deal with*" say interviewees. In the words of one client: "*She's got a good sense of business practicalities – she doesn't chase ghosts by advising on the vagaries of what could happen in the next few years, she tries to bring the opposing counsel back to earth.*"

The Clients: The team has recently advised Accenture on outsourcings involving a chemical company, a financial services company and an insurance company. It assisted Hyrian in a recruiting outsourcing transaction with United-Health Group, and has been handling various applications maintenance and development deals on the customer side. Other clients include: Affiliated Computer Services; Aon Consulting/Aon HR Outsourcing; IBM; Outsource Partners International; Hewitt; Sara Lee; Wipro Technologies; City of Chicago; APAC Customer Service; DSC Logistics and Trident Capital.

Band 3

Arnold & Porter LLP
See firm details p.478

The Firm: In this firm's Washington DC and Northern Virginia offices, outsourcing work is conducted as part of a broader technology transactions practice for long-standing corporate clients. On the West Coast, meanwhile, the practice represents both suppliers and users of outsourced services. Important work for the practice from the past year has included negotiating contracts to outsource clinical trials, and advising a major consumer finance company on the outsourcing of various back-office finance, accounting and banking operations.

The Lawyers: In the firm's Los Angeles office, the *"knowledgeable"* **George Kimball** (see p.260) is especially noted by interviewees for his top-notch work for suppliers. Recent examples include advising a leading services provider on potential HR outsourcing opportunities and acting for a startup supplier of procurement services. He is also said to be *"pretty active on the speaking circuit,"* where his wisdom and clarity are appreciated.

The Clients: The team represented the Southern California-based IndyMac Bank in the renegotiation of a major contract to outsource some key retail banking functions. Other clients include Ascension Health, Chiron and Herbalife.

Hunton & Williams
See firm details p.1775

The Firm: Described by peers as a *"smaller but high-quality shop,"* this team has expertise in a range of outsourcing work, including accounting data center operations, employee welfare and benefit programs, foreign operations, human resources, information services and logistics manufacturing. Recent highlights include helping to manage the transition of more than 500 employees to an outsourcing vendor. The group also advised on the transfer of title/use of equipment and real property to an outsourcing vendor, while another transaction involved transferring a lease of more than 150,000 sq ft.

The Lawyers: In the firm's Atlanta office, **Scott Hobby** (see p.87) advises on both domestic and offshore outsourcing services arrangements for Fortune 1000 companies. His broad experience spans integrated banking and financial operations, human resources and benefits administration, finance and accounting services, and applications development and maintenance services.

The Clients: Clients are drawn from a range of industries, such as financial institutions, healthcare, online information services, restaurants, retailing, telecommunications and software.

King & Spalding LLP
See firm details p.635

The Firm: The firm was lauded by clients for its *"business-based expertise."* Peers, meanwhile, admire its vendor work, especially for key client Accenture. The group has been active in the healthcare sector in recent times, advising a number of hospital chains on the outsourcing of various functions. It also handles work on the customer side for a range of institutional clients.

The Lawyers: **Bill Roche** (see p.101) coordinates the firm's outsourcing group from Atlanta. He was praised by clients as *"an effective force"* on the vendor side, with one noting that *"he's pragmatic and can easily differentiate issues that will affect our business."*

The Clients: Accenture; EDS; SAIC; Total Systems; Sprint; Home Depot; UPS; SunTrust; Coca-Cola; Georgia-Pacific; GM and ChevronTexaco.

O'Melveny & Myers LLP
See firm details p.294

The Firm: The team here is said by observers to be *"increasingly getting into the business."* Over the past year, this West Coast firm has advised on, inter alia, outsourcings of HR, finance and accounting, facilities management, procurement and logistics, and legal services. Important recent examples have included outsourcing some of the banking functions of Toyota Financial Services.

The Lawyers: Another Milbank alumnus, LA-based **Bill Peters** was described by peers as *"one of Halvey's incredible stable of stars."* He has advised clients from industries as diverse as financial services, retailing, logistics, distribution, aerospace, pharmaceuticals, telecommunications, oil and gas, and electricity utilities.

The Clients: The team advised Federal-Mogul on outsourcing some of its finance and accounting functions abroad. It has also been advising on outsourcing the claims processing functions of various healthcare companies, and the outsourcing of construction engineering services by various construction companies. Other clients include: Toyota; Goodyear; Marriott; Washington Group International; Allianz; Unical; Fireman's Fund; Nissan and Rockwell.

Band 4

Baker & McKenzie
See firm details p.761

The Firm: This team has been especially active of late in HR administration outsourcing transactions. It has historically been most visible on the provider side; however it is also increasingly representing users. Recent highlights include acting for Orbitz in negotiations with a Fortune 100 company to become that company's exclusive provider of travel services. The group has also assisted Robert Half with a number of voiceover IP trials involving local and long-distance telecom services and data, which are anticipated to be worth $40-60 million for five years. Clients return to the team because *"there's no need to babysit"* its lawyers, who *"perform well both technically and practically."*

The Lawyers: Chicago-based **Michael Mensik** (see p.741) is a *"nice guy,"* say interviewees, as well as being *"a fine lawyer for outsourcings with complex global issues."*

The Clients: The team assisted Rohm & Haas with a 20-plus jurisdiction HR outsourcing transaction involving outsourced administrative services (call centers and benefits administration). It also advised the Saudi Arabian Stock Exchange on offshoring its software development and maintenance with an Indian outsourcer. Other clients include: CSG; Hewlett-Packard; Kanbay; Orbitz; Robert Half; Towers Perrin and Turtle Wax.

Bierce & Kenerson, P.C.

The Firm: This New York-based international business boutique concentrates on outsourcing of all varieties. It was recommended by clients for being *"completely wired into the global 1000 client marketplace and the tier-one HR outsourcing provider market."*

The Lawyers: **Bill Bierce** has a well-established practice, which clients describe as *"truly multinational in scope."* He was recommended to researchers for *"producing strong and reliable results"* across the spectrum of BPO, HR and IT outsourcing.

The Clients: Clients are drawn from a range of sectors, such as banking and finance, health, insurance, real estate, manufacturing, mining, power, accounting and financial advice, consumer goods, publishing, educational, nonprofit and inter-governmental organizations.

Kirkland & Ellis LLP
See firm details p.770

The Firm: Market sources particularly note this practice for its customer-side work, although it also represents service providers. It built a historical presence in *"some of the earliest outsourcing transactions,"* say observers, and continues to handle major work. Recent examples include advising a large financial institution on various outsourcing agreements relating to call centers, HR and finance and accountancy. It has also been acting for a Canadian-based manufacturer of technology equipment in relation to an agreement with a Swedish company concerning the outsourcing of a range of services critical to the business, including manufacturing and accounting.

The Lawyers: **Gregg Kirchhoefer** (see p.735) heads the firm's IP/technology transactions practice group in Chicago. A *"knowledgeable"* technology lawyer, his practice encompasses the outsourcing of business processes, IT, applications processing and application service providers.

The Clients: The team acts for service providers and customers in manufacturing, financial services and other business sectors seeking to outsource critical functions. It has been advising a service provider on an outsourcing deal with a financial services institution.

Skadden, Arps, Slate, Meagher & Flom LLP & Affiliates
See firm details p.1372

The Firm: Skadden Arps is *"obviously known more as an M&A shop,"* but competitors acknowledge that it has *"been successful in leveraging its phenomenal corporate base to get into some sophisticated outsourcing transactions,"* on both the vendor and the customer side. Recent examples include representing Capgemini North America in its agreements with TXU Energy and ONCOR Electronic Delivery to form a joint venture to provide IT and other outsourcing services to TXU.

The Lawyers: Stuart Levi heads the firm's IT and e-commerce practice, while Rita Rodin is another key member of the outsourcing group.

The Clients: The firm advised Cendant on its agreement with United Airlines to operate United's internal airline reservation system and build an Internet booking agent for its United.com website. It also assisted FleetBoston Financial in connection with outsourcing its payroll processing and human resource administration services to Fidelity Employers Services. As well as Capgemini, the team acts for clients in such industries as financial services, transportation, manufacturing, publishing, entertainment and retailing.

CAPITAL MARKETS

NORTHEAST REGION

DEBT & EQUITY

National: Northeast Region
Leading firms
(Capital Markets: Debt & Equity)
[1] CRAVATH, SWAINE & MOORE LLP
DAVIS POLK & WARDWELL
SULLIVAN & CROMWELL LLP
[2] CLEARY GOTTLIEB STEEN & HAMILTON
SHEARMAN & STERLING LLP
SIMPSON THACHER & BARTLETT LLP
[3] CAHILL GORDON & REINDEL
LATHAM & WATKINS LLP
SKADDEN, ARPS, SLATE, MEAGHER
[4] FRIED, FRANK, HARRIS, SHRIVER
SIDLEY AUSTIN BROWN & WOOD LLP
WEIL, GOTSHAL & MANGES LLP
Firms are listed alphabetically in each band.

Band 1

Cravath, Swaine & Moore LLP

See firm details p.1344

The Firm: Known as the "*Rolls Royce*" of securities practices, the 20-partner firm commands respect across the range of debt and equity products. A deep bench means that clients are offered varying levels of expertise. Its focus has swayed toward equity work, with substantial pending IPOs originating from an impeccable client roster that includes DreamWorks Animation and IBM. Other transactions include representing lead underwriters Goldman Sachs and JPMorgan in the $144 million IPO of Archipelago Holdings, which owns and operates the Archipelago ExchangeSM (ArcaEx(r)) – the nation's first totally open, all-electronic stock market. The firm also represented DreamWorks Animation in connection with its IPO. A strong debt practice continues to thrive, for example, acting for initial purchasers CSFB and JPMorgan in connection with Borden Chemical's $475 144A offering.

The Lawyers: John White (see p.108) is lauded both for his acuity with regard to accounting matters and "*sophisticated understanding of disclosure issues at the heart of securities.*" He acted for CSFB and Merrill Lynch as underwriters of DuPont's $1.4 billion debt offering in addition to separately working on the Archipelago and DreamWorks deals. High-yield specialist **Kris Heinzelman** (see p.87) is "*just a gem,*" according to commentators, who also praise his innovation and technical excellence. His "*calm, results-oriented, non-combative philosophy*" enables him to excel on matters such as the Borden Chemical transaction. He also represented CSFB and Citigroup as initial purchasers for PanAmSat's $1 billion 144A debt offering. "*Smart, considerate and helpful*" **Marc Rosenberg** (see p.101) concentrates on advising companies involved in SEC investigations, while the "*fabulous*" **Stephen Burns** (see p.77) advised Goldman Sachs, Deutsche Bank and JPMorgan in relation to Goodyear's $300 million 144A debt offering. **William Whelan** (see p.108) is "*absolutely terrific*" on the underwriting side. Clients added: "*From day one he's accessible, and attuned to all levels.*" Advising Goldman Sachs and Morgan Stanley, he handled the $1.4 billion Conseco offering of preferred and common insurance stock.

The Clients: CSFB; Citigroup; Deutsche Bank; DreamWorks Animation; Goldman Sachs; JPMorgan; Lehman Brothers; Merrill Lynch and Morgan Stanley.

Davis Polk & Wardwell

See firm details p.1345

The Firm: A phalanx of solid players "*tops the tables in convertibles and equity-linked work.*" Its appetite for the "*sophisticated and cutting edge*" has enabled the team to undertake sizable and innovative debt and equity transactions. The firm boasts particular strength in convertibles. For example, it advised underwriters Morgan Stanley and Goldman Sachs on the $3.5 billion Genworth Financial offering – one of the largest IPOs of the year. It also represented New York boutique financial adviser Greenhill on its challenging $101 million IPO, which concerns such issues as employee retention and SEC approval. Debt work includes involvement in two separate $4 billion debt offerings for lead manager Morgan Stanley and underwriter GMAC, respectively.

The Lawyers: "*In a class of his own,*" head of the firm's global capital markets group **Richard Sandler** (see p.102) oversaw the Genworth Financial offering. He also handled GE's $3.8 billion offering on behalf of lead managers Morgan Stanley, Citigroup, Goldman Sachs and JPMorgan Securities. Clients also praise **Jeffrey Small** (see p.104), who helped orchestrate the Greenhill IPO, and **Winthrop Conrad** (see p.79), who is "*highly rated in emerging markets.*" He worked on the GE offering as well as assisting in representing the underwriters of Canadian aluminum producer Alcan's $1.25 billion notes offering. "*Wonderful, smart and capable,*" **Sarah Beshar** (see p.76) advised GMAC on its substantial debt offering.

The Clients: ABN AMRO; Citigroup; Deutsche Bank; GMAC; Genworth Financial; Goldman Sachs; Greenwich Capital Markets; ICI; JPMorgan; Lehman Brothers; Morgan Stanley; Royal Bank of Scotland; RBC Dominion Securities and Telecom Italia.

Sullivan & Cromwell LLP

See firm details p.1373

The Firm: The firm's New York team is described as being at "*the top of the game.*" The practice earned client respect for its sheer quality and international strength as well as its "*responsiveness*" and "*team ethos.*" Its reputation for taking a somewhat conservative approach to legal advice was also noted by clients. One of its most fruitful relationships is with Goldman Sachs, and the team also experienced an increase in high yield output. The firm acted on a $2 billion refinancing for a New York cable television company and a separate $1.25 billion high yield component of electronics company Freescale's $1.8 billion IPO. Equity work includes Chicago satellite mapping company NAVTEQ's $1 billion IPO and a separate $250 million IPO for real estate investment trust Strategic Hotel. A substantial portion of the firm's securities work is for non-US entities, including Latin American sovereign financing.

National Northeast
Leading individuals
(Capital Markets: Debt & Equity)

Senior Statesmen

MALLOW Matthew *Skadden Arps*, New York
WILLIAMS William *Sullivan*, New York

[1] HARTNETT William *Cahill Gordon*, New York
HEINZELMAN Kris *Cravath Swaine*, New York
SANDLER Richard *Davis Polk*, New York
WHITE John *Cravath Swaine*, New York

[2] BOSTELMAN John *Sullivan & Cromwell*, New York
DAVENPORT Kirk *Latham & Watkins*, New York
FORD Paul *Simpson Thacher*, New York
SILVERMAN Leslie *Cleary Gottlieb*, New York
SMALL Jeffrey *Davis Polk*, New York
SPERLING Allan *Cleary Gottlieb*, New York

[3] BUCKHOLZ Robert *Sullivan & Cromwell*, New York
CLARK James *Cahill Gordon*, New York
CONRAD Winthrop *Davis Polk*, New York
EVANS III Robert *Shearman & Sterling*, New York
HARMS David *Sullivan & Cromwell*, New York
KORFF Phyllis *Skadden Arps*, New York
PISANO Vincent *Kirkland & Ellis*, New York
REITER Glenn *Simpson Thacher*, New York
SLONAKER Norman *Sidley Austin*, New York
TEHAN John *Simpson Thacher*, New York
WEERASINGHE Rohan *Shearman* New York

[4] BESHAR Sarah *Davis Polk*, New York
BURNS Stephen *Cravath Swaine*, New York
FORD JACOB Valerie *Fried Frank*, New York
GANNETT William *Cahill Gordon*, New York
GOLDSCHMIDT David *Skadden Arps*, New York
JAFFE Marc *Latham & Watkins*, New York
KANTER Stacy *Skadden Arps*, New York
KROUSE George *Simpson Thacher*, New York
LEFKOWITZ David *Weil Gotshal*, New York
LOBRANO John *Simpson Thacher*, New York
ROSENBERG Marc *Cravath Swaine*, New York
SCHAFFZIN Jonathan *Cahill Gordon*, New York
SMITH Mark *Skadden Arps*, New York
SOUSSLOFF Andrew *Sullivan & Cromwell*, New York
SUTHERLAND Susan *Skadden Arps*, New York
TOLLEY III Edward *Simpson Thacher*, New York
WHELAN William *Cravath Swaine*, New York

Up-and-coming individuals

CORRALES Carmen *Cleary Gottlieb*, New York

Individuals are listed alphabetically in each band.

The Lawyers: John Bostelman (see p.76) attracts a loyal client for his market knowledge and ability to parlay the information into "*good flexible answers at short notice.*" He was involved in the NALCO IPO. Commended for his good sense of the law and judgment calls, **David Harms** (see p.87) represented underwriters in financial advisor Greenhill's $101 million IPO. The "*phenomenal*" **Robert Buckholz** (see p.77) is a "*tremendous negotiator,*" especially on complex high yield bond offerings. One client's wish was to "*replicate him and locate him nearer me and at half-price.*" **Andrew Soussloff** (see p.105) is active in the firm's Latin American sovereign financing work as part of a broader practice. He advised on Asbury Automotive's high yield offering. "*One of the really all-time greats,*" **Bill Williams** "*has the experience that sets the top firms apart.*"

The Clients: BP; British Airways; Citigroup; China Telecom; Deutsche Bank; Goldman Sachs; JPMorgan; RR Donnelley; Strategic Hotel Capital; UBS; Vertis; Vodafone and Wachovia.

Band 2

Cleary Gottlieb Steen & Hamilton
See firm details p.1342

The Firm: Though its tremendous international clout may have sometimes overshadowed its domestic strength, this cadre of "*high-octane lawyers*" shouldn't be overlooked, sources said. It remains popular among clients, particularly in the areas of IPO and converts. In addition, the firm's incisive experience on the issuer side has enhanced its underwriting expertise. Advising CSFB as underwriters, the team handled a $1.35 billion SEC-registered notes offering. It also represented Petroleos Mexicanos on its $1.75 billion issuance of perpetual bonds. Other emerging markets work includes representing America Movil in its $1.3 billion Rule 144A notes offering – the company's first ever international offering.

The Lawyers: "*Impressive*" **Allan Sperling** (see p.105) concentrates on advising underwriters and is, for many of his clients, the "*first call if anything sticky happens.*" Of **Les Silverman** (see p.104) sources said: "*Lawyers don't come up much better than him.*" He devotes about a quarter of his time to issuer work, increasingly advising a stellar list of underwriters. He also represented GlaxoSmithKline in its $2 billion SEC-registered notes offering. Rounding out the practice is **Carmen Corrales** (see p.80), who is "*highly rated*" for her flourishing sovereign financing practice.

The Clients: America Movil; Barclays Capital; CSFB; Citigroup; HSBC; GlaxoSmithKline; Goldman Sachs; Lehman Brothers; Merrill Lynch; Morgan Stanley; Petroleos Mexicanos and Rand Merchant Bank.

Shearman & Sterling LLP
See firm details p.1369

The Firm: "*An exceptionally good, broad practice able to bring other disciplines to bear on its work,*" this 15-partner team in New York maintains its robust high-yield experience along with a burgeoning equity practice that involves significant IPOs. It has also tempered its traditional investment bank strength with notable issuer work, including handling Viacom's $2 billion sale of its subsidiary Blockbuster to Viacom's existing shareholders. On the underwriter's side, the firm was involved in advertising agency company Interpublic Group's $625 million common and preferred stock offering.

The Lawyers: Rohan Weerasinghe (see p.107) won client confidence for his "*level-headed and even-keeled*" approach, while the "*awesome*" **Robert Evans** (see p.82) is the firm's lead securities partner and "*carries that banner admirably.*"

The Clients: The team advises private and public companies, including investment banks.

Simpson Thacher & Bartlett LLP
See firm details p.1370

The Firm: Described by clients as "*superb in every way,*" this group of "*erudite and intuitive*" partners has a strong tradition of issuer-side work. One client added: "*It's the only firm I would jump up and down to use.*" It often wins work through private equity contacts and LBO houses, and "*the fact that it gets some underwriter work is a testament to its strength.*" Its formidable financial sponsor experience is highlighted by such work as NALCO's $2 billion buyout and the acquisition of Warner Music Group by Thomas H Lee Partners. Its IPO strength is illustrated by its representation of the underwriter for DreamWorks' offering. It also advised underwriters Citigroup, Merrill Lynch and UBS Investment Bank in relation to a $2.1 billion offering for Calamos Strategic Total Return Fund. The firm has also continued a respectable high-yield practice.

The Lawyers: "*Leading light*" **Paul Ford** (see p.83) "*can run circles around some of his peers*" and is a mainstay of the firm's international practice, particularly in relation to matters in Latin America. **John Tehan** (see p.106) is a go-to expert who balances a mixture of company and banking work. One client particularly admired his ability to "*persuade the other side.*" **Glenn Reiter** (see p.100) has cultivated strong relationships with US retail clients, and is often praised for his careful analysis. For example, he acted as underwriter counsel in transactions involving Wal-Mart and Toys 'R' Us. "*Smart and practical*" **George Krouse** (see p.91) represents mostly underwriters, while "*stalwart*" **John Lobrano** (see p.93) impresses a varied clientele that includes both private equity sponsors and investment banks. "*He has a good sense of what is really important,*" sources said. **Edward Tolley** (see p.106) represented The Blackstone Group in its complicated acquisition of chemical company Celanese. Clients value his "*unparalleled insights into the high-yield market.*"

The Clients: American Electric Power; The Blackstone Group; DreamWorks; Duke Energy; KKR; Lehman Brothers; Philip Morris; Kraft Foods; Thomas H Lee Partners; Vodafone and Wal-Mart.

Band 3

Cahill Gordon & Reindel

The Firm: The firm's distinguished high-yield practice continues to win enthusiastic clients who are attracted to the "*top-notch*" service. Nearly three-quarters of its practice is devoted to high yield, and it has carried out sterling equity work such as representing Goldman Sachs as underwriter in an IPO for Spectrasite valued at more than $1 billion. It also advised on an IPO for mobile phone gaming company Jemdat Mobile. However, its heavy leaning toward high yield has led to criticisms that its overall versatility in the wider capital markets arena is somewhat limited, particularly on the loan side. Nevertheless, it continues to gain respect in the more narrow area of high-yield transactions, including the $1.78 billion Quest Communications deal, which required complicated financial restatements to comply with SEC regulations. The firm also advised on the $2 billion Crown Cork restructuring.

The Lawyers: Described as "*the street expert for bond securities*," **Bill Hartnett** brings stature to any transaction. "*He is always involved in the bidding stage*," sources said. "*He doesn't recede into the woodwork*." A feather in his cap is representing Citigroup in NALCO's $2 billion buyout. **James Clark** is praised for complex cases including the Quest Communications transaction, while the "*experienced and communicative*" **William Gannett** works closely with Deutsche Bank. He also concentrates on debt financing and restructuring for chemical companies, including Crompton Corporation's $600 million refinancing. Clients praise his "*impressive technical acumen.*" **Jonathan Schaffzin** is applauded as hard working and knowledgeable, characteristics that are parlayed in transactions such as the Quest Communications and Jemdat Mobile deals.

The Clients: Bank of America; CIBC World Markets Corporation; CSFB; Citigroup Global Markets; Deutsche Bank Securities; Goldman Sachs; JPMorgan; Merrill Lynch; Royal Bank of Scotland and UBS Securities.

Latham & Watkins LLP

The Firm: With "*exceptional financing ability*" and "*some extraordinary lawyers,*" the firm is among the elite in national high-yield work. It is also credited with substantially broadening its agenda in recent months to make its mark in the equity field. Its sparkling clientele is formed from a substantial corporate base, with one praising the practice's "*excellent recommendations on appropriate levels of disclosure.*" However, other clients have questioned the consistency in the quality of work from associates. The firm has undertaken LBO work for borrowers such as Carlyle and Apollo, in addition to advising Goldman Sachs in relation to Knoll's IPO. Its debt ventures include representing underwriter Merrill Lynch in Calpine's first secured bond offering valued at $785 million. It also acted for a clutch of underwriters including CSFB and Lehman Brothers in connection to Midwest Generation's $1.25 billion notes issuance.

The Lawyers: "*Astute*" **Kirk Davenport** is the lodestone of the practice, impressing clients with a "*combination of competence and style*" as well as "*knowledge of where to push resources.*" He is recognized for "*developing a phenomenal high-yield practice*" due partly to his "*knowledge of both sides of the equation,*" clients said. His recent focus on the energy sector is illustrated by the Calpine transaction. **Marc Jaffe** led the online learning company Blackboard's IPO, representing CSFB, Bank of America and Merrill Lynch as underwriters.

The Clients: Citigroup; CSFB; Goldman Sachs; JPMorgan; Lehman Brothers; Merrill Lynch; Odyssey Investment Partners; Morgan Stanley and UBS Investment Bank.

Skadden, Arps, Slate, Meagher & Flom LLP & Affiliates

See firm details p.1372

The Firm: The firm's clutch of "*prescient*" lawyers is often suitably placed to structure bespoke transactions such as advising on a $1.2 billion three-tranche IPO. Another jewel in its crown has been China Life's $3.46 billion IPO, in which the firm's New York office worked in conjunction with Hong Kong and Beijing colleagues to represent the underwriters. This transaction also reinforces the firm's dedication to the underwriting market. In terms of debt work, the firm represented fallen angel issuer Crompton Corporation in its $600 million high-yield restructuring and separately advised Morgan Stanley as initial purchaser of E*TRADE Finance's $400 million debt offering. The firm has also been at the forefront of Income Deposit Securities (IDS) development, representing CSFB in connection with UAP Holding's portfolio.

The Lawyers: "*Respected*" rainmaker **Matthew Mallow** (see p.94) has been advising Putnam Investment in relation to SEC investigations of the mutual fund industry. **Phyllis Korff** (see p.91), who is a contender in both the IPO and high-yield arenas, represented Crompton Corporation in its restructuring. The "*doughty*" **David Goldschmidt** (see p.85) has taken the lead in the newly emergent IDS deals, while **Stacy Kanter** (see p.90) is commended for her issuer-side work. Her long-standing relationship with Revlon has yielded a debt-for-equity exchange transaction and related restructuring. **Mark Smith** (see p.105) is "*particularly adept*" in a predominantly debt-driven practice balanced between issuers and underwriters. He advised on the financing of Graham Packaging's $1.2 billion acquisition of plastic container com-pany Owens. **Susan Sutherland** (see p.106) held the reins representing institutional investors in China Life's landmark IPO.

The Clients: Bank of America; The Blackstone Group; CSFB; Citigroup; Crompton Corporation; Elite; Goldman Sachs; Host Marriott; Kuwait Petroleum; Morgan Stanley; NASDAQ; Revlon and UBS.

Band 4

Fried, Frank, Harris, Shriver & Jacobson LLP

See firm details p.1349

The Firm: The firm continues to benefit from its association with Merrill Lynch, completing both high yield and IPO work while furnishing its bantam team with additional firepower in the marketplace. It has been active in pharmaceutical transactions, advising Goldman Sachs, JPMorgan and Merrill Lynch as lead managers in the $1.2 billion issuance of notes by Procter & Gamble. Again on behalf of underwriters, the team handled the $563 million sale of Class A common stocks by Estée Lauder. Elsewhere the firm also advised on Citadel Broadcasting's $450 million offering and separately represented Medco Health Solutions' $500 million senior notes issuance.

The Lawyers: Managing partner **Valerie Ford Jacob** (see p.83) is the turbine within this enduring practice, helping to drive the firm's profile with her long-standing reputation for high-yield work.

The Clients: Bank of America; Citigroup Global Markets; CSFB; Goldman Sachs; JPMorgan; Medco Health Solutions; Merrill Lynch; Methanex; Morgan Stanley; ntl; Noranda and The Rouse Company.

Sidley Austin Brown & Wood LLP

See firm details p.778

The Firm: Praised for its "*breadth of practice*" and "*capable lawyers,*" the firm offers both issuer and underwriter advice with a preponderance of structured and convertible debt work. The firm has advised on several large monetization programs, representing among others Merrill Lynch and Bank of America. Other notable transactions include Australia and New Zealand Banking Group's (ANZ) issuance that raised $1.25 billion, where Deutsche Bank underwrote the transaction. In another deal, the firm advised the Government of China in its bond offering.

The Lawyers: Few are more adept in securities law than **Norman Slonaker** (see p.104), according to competitors, who also praise the established practitioner for his deep-rooted experience in the industry.

The Clients: ANZ; Apache Oil & Gas; Bank of New York; Deutsche Bank; GB Insurance; JPMorgan; Lehman Brothers; Merrill Lynch; Morgan Stanley; Qantas and Wachovia.

Weil, Gotshal & Manges LLP

See firm details p.1378

The Firm: The firm's New York practice is pitched as "*absolutely the best you can imagine,*" said clients, who also described it as "*thrilling*" and "*outstanding.*" Though the team suffered a blow in 2004 with Stephen Cooper's retirement and Jeremy Dickens's transfer to the London office, it also tempered the setbacks with the hiring of Alex Lynch, former managing partner of Wilson Sonsini's New York office. The firm's traditional bankruptcy strengths also make it "*especially useful on the loan side,*" although its breadth of practice across the gamut of issuer and underwriter work is also acknowledged. Highlights include representing Genworth Financial in its $3.5 billion IPO and separately advising Estée Lauder in its $500 million offering.

The Lawyers: Clients "*cannot say enough about how good he is,*" referring to **David Lefkowitz** (see p.92). His "*commercial finesse*" and "*broad perspective, which does not prevent him focusing well on the key issue,*" attracts praise. In contrast to the niche expertise of some high-yield lawyers, Lefkowitz possesses an "*overall sagacity*" that contributes to a more varied diet of transactions. He masterminded the firm's involvement in the Genworth Financial and Lipman Electronics IPOs.

The Clients: Citigroup; CSFB; Estée Lauder; Elizabeth Arden; Genworth Financial; Getty Images; Lehman Brothers; Merrill Lynch; Premier Foods; Quanta Services and WellChoice.

Other Notable Practitioners

Vincent Pisano (see p.98) of Kirkland & Ellis is credited with extending the firm's capital markets capabilities beyond its traditional issuer strength – mainly through his dominance in underwriter representation. "*I would use him again in a heartbeat,*" a client said of the practitioner, who advised on Conseco's high-profile $800 million IPO, its first such transaction since emerging from bankruptcy. Other work includes representing Goldman Sachs in relation to Jackson Hewitt Tax Service's $900 million spin-off IPO.

NORTHEAST REGION

DERIVATIVES

National: Northeast Region

Leading firms
(Capital Markets: Derivatives)

1. CLEARY GOTTLIEB STEEN & HAMILTON
   SULLIVAN & CROMWELL LLP
2. ALLEN & OVERY
   CADWALADER, WICKERSHAM & TAFT LLP
   DAVIS POLK & WARDWELL
   STROOCK & STROOCK & LAVAN LLP
3. MAYER, BROWN, ROWE & MAW LLP
   SHEARMAN & STERLING LLP
   SIDLEY AUSTIN BROWN & WOOD LLP
   SKADDEN, ARPS, SLATE, MEAGHER

Leading individuals
(Capital Markets: Derivatives)

1. BRANDOW John *Davis Polk*, New York
   CUNNINGHAM Daniel *Allen & Overy*, New York
   OSBORN John *Skadden Arps*, New York
   RAISLER Kenneth *Sullivan & Cromwell*, New York
   ROSEN Edward *Cleary Gottlieb*, New York
2. COHN Joshua *Allen & Overy*, New York
   DAYAN Michael *Cleary Gottlieb*, New York
   GILBERG David *Sullivan & Cromwell*, New York
   GROSSHANDLER Seth *Cleary Gottlieb*, New York
   HEFTLER Thomas *Stroock & Stroock*, New York
   MITCHELL David *Cadwalader Wickersham*, New York
3. BUDOFSKY Daniel *Davis Polk*, New York
   GOLDSTEIN Marvin *Stroock & Stroock*, New York
   JOHNSON Philip *Skadden Arps*, Washington, DC
   REEDER Robert *Sullivan & Cromwell*, New York
   ROTHWELL James *Davis Polk*, New York
   STROMFELD Lary *Cadwalader Wickersham*, New York

Up-and-coming individuals

GANDHI Samir *Sidley Austin*, New York

Firms and individuals are listed alphabetically in each band.

Band 1

Cleary Gottlieb Steen & Hamilton

See firm details p.1342

The Firm: This firm is in the vanguard of the industry thanks to its breadth of practice and enduring relationships with the likes of Citigroup. Its "*prodigious team of lawyers*" includes about nine partners who work on a mixture of fixed income and equity derivatives. Experience includes assisting the Bond Market Association in its establishment of new capital rules for banks. The team has also advised Lehman Brothers, Goldman Sachs and Bank of Montreal in the ongoing Enron litigation in connection with retrieving payments made shortly before the Houston-based energy trader filed for bankruptcy in 2001. Transactional highlights include representing Citigroup and Merrill Lynch in Citigroup's issuance and underwriting of $7.2 million SynDECS variable rate exchangeable notes. The group also acted for Citigroup as lead manager of a $400 million offering linked to The Williams Companies.

The Lawyers: "*Smart, terrific*" **Ed Rosen** (see p.101) "*brings a very sophisticated view to the table,*" commentators said. Gravitating toward the regulatory side, he is respected among clients because "*he really understands how federal regulators think.*" He represented the Joint Market Practices Forum drafting its statement of principles and recommendations regarding the use of certain nonpublic information by credit market participants. Active on the insolvency side, "*bright and judicious*" **Seth Grosshandler** (see p.86) is "*really just one of the best people at this,*" said commentators. He advised Citigroup in its management of The Williams Companies' $400 million offering and separately represented XL Financial Solutions in its provision of credit protection for the financing of Three Rivers Securi-

ties. "*One of the most detail-oriented lawyers I've ever come across*" is how one client described **Michael Dayan** (see p.80), who is also praised for being "*incredibly reachable and reliable.*" In addition to his substantial credit derivatives work for Citigroup, Dayan assisted the CDO index consortium in developing a single tranche CDO.

The Clients: BrokerTec Futures Exchange; Citigroup; Merrill Lynch and XL Financial Solutions.

Sullivan & Cromwell LLP

See firm details p.1373

The Firm: "*Everyone beats a path to its door,*" clients said of Sullivan & Cromwell. The firm's derivatives group is integrated within its banking and securities forces, yet has sufficient vigor to attract standalone clients for its structured derivatives products. Wachovia, ING and Bear Stearns are fans of the team, which is renowned for its expertise in commodities. It is also energetic in the trading derivatives sector, working with the Chicago Climate Exchange. The firm assisted in developing a volatility index product with the Chicago Board Options Exchange (CBOE). Representing Goldman Sachs, it was involved in energy trading on the New York Mercantile Exchange where it cleared options through a unique auction pricing system.

The Lawyers: "*Leading lawyer*" **Kenneth Raisler** (see p.100) is prized for his intelligent approach particularly as regards to regulatory issues. He has concentrated on hedge funds, for example, negotiating with the SEC on behalf of the Managed Funds Association with regards to hedge fund regulations. Clients seeking equity derivatives expertise applaud the "*responsive*" **David Gilberg** (see p.85), who "*always knows the answers.*" The practice is further enhanced by the "*highly esteemed*" **Robert Reeder** (see p.100), who garnered respect for his "*good* judgment and understanding of how to interact with the SEC."

The Clients: Bear Stearns; CBOE; Chicago Climate Exchange; Managed Funds Association; Goldman Sachs and Wachovia.

Band 2

Allen & Overy

See firm details p.1335

The Firm: Consistent quality of work attracts clients to the firm, which impresses the marketplace with a prestigious role as chief external advisory counsel to ISDA. For example, the team assisted in ISDA's campaign to persuade Congress to pass bankruptcy legislation favorable to the derivatives industry. Again displaying its negotiating dexterity, another highlight involved the National Association of Insurance Commissioners after its attempts to bring weather derivatives within the ambit of insurance regulations. Clients also comment favorably on the firm's *"strength in credit-linked notes and general credit derivatives."* The group has arranged complex netting structures for insolvency purposes and is gradually dispelling perceptions in the market that it lacks transactional brawn and patronage from the major investment banks. The team structured total return swap arrangements for clients Highbridge, Barclays and Lehman Brothers.

The Lawyers: *"A clear thinker and good strategist,"* **Daniel Cunningham** (see p.80) *"is one of the most effective lawyers I've ever utilized,"* one client said. Peers have a *"formidable respect"* for his regulatory knowledge, while **Joshua Cohn** won client acclaim for combining *"encyclopedic knowledge with the ability to give practical advice."* A technical authority, he delivers *"solutions that accommodate to what the market might need."* Recent experience includes swaps of asset-backed securitizations.

The Clients: Barclays; Highbridge; Lehman Brothers and ISDA.

Cadwalader, Wickersham & Taft LLP

See firm details p.1339

The Firm: Clients have *"nothing but great things to say"* about this group which is rated particularly for its structured credit derivatives, exchange-rated derivatives and municipal products capability. It has an established fixed-income derivatives practice, but is also adventurous in evolving new structures; new cash and synthetic CDOs involving municipal and tax-advantaged over the counter (OTC) products are examples. Another gem is the first tax-exempt variable rate funding of a prepaid gas contract. It also works with commercial and investment banks to develop joint ventures for marketing derivatives with regional and minority-owned banks. An industry luminary, the

firm is designated counsel to the Bond Market Association's new municipals products committee and separately represents ISDA in its development of a new credit derivative product linked to the municipal markets.

The Lawyers: *"Painstakingly detailed"* **Lary Stromfeld** (see p.106) has been instrumental in adopting corporate structures to fit the municipal markets. *"He has expertise in the municipal world that we couldn't get anywhere else,"* said a client. *"Thorough and smart,"* **David Mitchell** (see p.95) is *"simply one of the most visible guys."* His practice centers on fixed income and commodity derivatives as well as some equity.

The Clients: Ambac Assurance; Barclays Capital; ISDA; Morgan Stanley and Société Générale.

Davis Polk & Wardwell

See firm details p.1345

The Firm: The firm is regarded as *"the premier equity derivatives shop"* with about six dedicated derivatives partners in New York. They cultivate specialist expertise as well as benefiting from a more generalist approach attuned to derivative components within the broader capital markets sphere. Some clients would prefer a more responsive approach, but overall, its *"lock-in"* concerning the equity market still ensures a loyal following in the convertibles and exchanges market. It represented underwriter Deutsche Bank in independent power producer Calpine's notable $725 million offering, which required the use of a stock loaning agreement. The firm's OTC practice remains robust with its representation of Citigroup and CIBC World Markets in relation to electronic transfer processing provider Global Payments' $351 million stock offering. Also tucked under its belt is hedge fund expertise, and the firm advised lead manager JPMorgan on Microsoft's $8.8 billion secondary offering.

The Lawyers: *"Major player"* **John Brandow** (see p.77) has a stellar reputation for equity derivatives, advising JPMorgan, Lehman Brothers and Merrill Lynch in American Express' $2 billion Rule 144A offering. His ability to *"think of things you'd never think of"* garnered market respect, commentators said. *"He could run circles around some of the top derivatives lawyers."* **Daniel Budofsky** (see p.77) is responsible for much of the firm's hedge fund work. Described as *"bright and energetic,"* he deftly balances the business interests of clients and the potentially risky issues. *"He goes out of his way to identify related concerns not part of his remit,"* one client said. Commentators also enjoy working with **James Rothwell** (see p.101) who *"has a knack with equity derivatives."*

The Clients: Citigroup; CIBC World Markets; Comcast; CSFB; Deutsche Bank; Goldman Sachs; JPMorgan; Lehman Brothers; Merrill Lynch; Morgan Stanley and US Bancorp Piper Jaffray.

Stroock & Stroock & Lavan LLP

The Firm: Clients are attracted to the firm's dominance in the physical commodities sector. For example, it advised GC Power Acquisition in its $3.65 billion takeover of Texas Genco Holdings, a wholesale electric power generation company, from CenterPoint Energy. The transaction, pitched as one of the largest energy deals in the past year, is also testimony to the affiliation between the derivatives team, nestled in the firm's corporate wing, and the firm's M&A profile. Other highlights involved a natural gas contract for the North American Energy Standards Board and separately assisting ISDA regarding US tax treatment for energy initiatives. The group also has expertise in hedge funds and enjoys a burgeoning credit derivatives practice, which focuses on protection sellers in the insurance sector such as Raytheon and Aleon.

The Lawyers: Managing partner **Thomas Heftler** is widely regarded as a kingpin of the industry. Clients describe him as *"an unusually good commercial lawyer,"* while **Marvin Goldstein** earned his stripes as a *"longtime participant in the market place."*

The Clients: Constellation Power Source; Hess Energy Trading; Goldman Sachs and Texas Pacific Group.

Band 3

Mayer, Brown, Rowe & Maw LLP

See firm details p.771

The Firm: Earning *"great respect"* for its New York profile, this *"outstanding"* firm has a broad derivatives practice that fortifies its structured finance and fixed-income CDO work. A clutch of standalone clients are attracted to its New York strength, further enhanced by a wealth of resources from its base in Chicago and across the Atlantic. Its work includes simple fixed and floating interest rate swaps, offshore hedge funds, emerging market structured products, and listed futures and options. The team is often retained to structure complex instruments.

The Lawyers: Pamela Sackmann and John Hewitt are key players on the firm's derivatives team.

The Clients: Its clientele are derived from investment banks, traders, hedge funds and international corporations among others.

Shearman & Sterling LLP

See firm details p.1369

The Firm: *"A capable firm with transactional strength,"* Shearman & Sterling wields its expertise in this field as an adjunct to its securitization practice. Though that hasn't diminished the firm's strength in pure derivatives work, as illustrated by its involvement in various global transactions. Its hedge fund deals are well regarded, and the group also delivers a gamut of products including fixed income, credit and commodity-linked instruments.

The Lawyers: Following the departure of Holland West, Robert Zochowski is the contact partner here.

The Clients: The firm acts for traders, investment banks and hedge funds among others.

Sidley Austin Brown & Wood LLP

See firm details p.778

The Firm: The firm's credit derivatives expertise serves as an extension of its structured finance and securities practices, enabling it to structure highly sophisticated financial instruments for the securities market. Swaps constitute a large portion of the group's work, especially those involving preferred stock or prepaid forwards. The group also benefits from a resourceful overseas network, which attracts a luminous international clientele.

The Lawyers: "*Smart, sensible*" **Samir Gandhi** (see p.84) is underwriter counsel for Freddie Mac's debt issuance, straddling the securities and derivatives spheres in arranging complex financial products for an illustrious clientele.

The Clients: Bank of America; Deutsche Bank; Dresdner Bank; Merrill Lynch; Société Générale and WestLB.

Skadden, Arps, Slate, Meagher & Flom LLP & Affiliates

See firm details p.1372

The Firm: The team applies its strong regulatory and technical grasp of the market within the firm's wider corporate ambit, particularly as related to real estate financings, monetizations and various dispute resolutions. It is also in demand for cross-border financing and such

products as catastrophe bonds for insurance companies. In an advisory capacity it has represented stock and commodity exchange users including Cinergy, the Chicago Mercantile Exchange, the Natural Gas Exchange and both the Korea Stock and Futures Exchanges.

The Lawyers: **John Osborn**'s (see p.97) "*technical acuity*" makes some of his peers' capabilities look "*like cocktail party knowledge*," industry sources said. Eschewing transactional work for regulatory work, **Philip McBride Johnson** (see p.89) is a cynosure for stock and commodity exchanges, corporations and agencies around the world.

The Clients: Cinergy; Natural Gas Exchange; the Sydney Futures Exchange; Western Gas Resources; Korea Stock Exchange and Korea Futures Exchange.

NORTHEAST REGION

SECURITIZATION

National: Northeast Region
Leading firms
(Capital Markets: Securitization)
[1] ORRICK, HERRINGTON & SUTCLIFFE
SIDLEY AUSTIN BROWN & WOOD LLP
SKADDEN, ARPS, SLATE, MEAGHER
[2] CADWALADER, WICKERSHAM & TAFT LLP
MAYER, BROWN, ROWE & MAW LLP
MCKEE NELSON LLP
[3] CLEARY GOTTLIEB STEEN & HAMILTON
SIMPSON THACHER & BARTLETT LLP
THACHER PROFFITT & WOOD LLP
WEIL, GOTSHAL & MANGES LLP
[4] CRAVATH, SWAINE & MOORE LLP
DEWEY BALLANTINE LLP
LATHAM & WATKINS LLP
Firms are listed alphabetically in each band.

Band 1

Orrick, Herrington & Sutcliffe

See firm details p.295

The Firm: Favored for its "*pragmatism*" and "*refusal to cut corners*," the firm's northeast practice is divided between DC and New York. Its dedicated structured finance partners maintain a formidable presence in credit card securitization, fostered partly by its ongoing relationship with Capital One. However, it also boasts a "*soup-to-nuts diversity*," engaging in conduit work with, among others, the Royal Bank of Canada, Merrill Lynch and Citigroup. Other examples include truck and equipment leasing transactions, mortgage deals involving Wachovia and plenty of CDO work. Recent transactions include the MBBA 2003-A issuance of $15.1 million tax lien collateralized bonds.

The Lawyers: Peers credited the "*intelligent, technical and hard-working*" **Cam Cowan** (see p.80) with having enhanced the firm's regulatory presence through such roles as outside counsel to the American Securitization Forum (ASF). The Forum has contributed to the SEC's efforts to structure comprehensive regulations for ABS. **Joshua Raff** (see p.100) "*deserves credit for completing some very complicated transactions*," commentators said. Focusing chiefly on CDOs and CMBS, he completed the first real estate CDO containing underlying assets composed primarily of subordinate real estate interests. "*Effective*" **Katherine Crost** (see p.80), who co-heads the firm's structured finance practice, won respect for such work as the MBBA 2003-A transaction. Her forte is ABS, particularly those involving mortgage loans. She has also helped structure innovative transactions linked to the tobacco litigation settlement funds, tax liens, utility stranded costs, and student loans.

The Clients: Bear Stearns; Capital One; Citigroup; Deutsche Bank; GMAC Commercial Mortgage; JPMorgan Chase; Lehman Brothers; Merrill Lynch; Washington Mutual and WestLB.

Sidley Austin Brown & Wood LLP

See firm details p.778

The Firm: With "*probably one of the broadest practices in the world*," the group garnered praise for the diversity of its securitization practice, which is touted by clients as "*the go-to firm across all asset chains*." The merger of Sidley & Austin and Brown & Wood has created a dazzling presence, particularly on the international stage. In addition to enabling the firm to expand beyond its traditional banking arena, the merger has allowed it to make a concerted push to develop publicly registered expertise.

The Lawyers: Considered one of the "*best securitization lawyers in the business*," according to some market commentators, **Renwick Martin** (see p.94) inspires respect throughout the industry as a "*tireless, practical*" attorney armed with "*immaculate technical abilities*." Meanwhile, **Cathy Kaplan** (see p.90) is "*a dream to work with on complex transactions*." She has substantial CLO experience. "*Smart and incredibly detail-oriented*" **William Cullen** (see p.80) has made a name for himself in the CMBS market, while **Arthur Hickok** (see p.87) is praised for his aptitude in the area of commercial paper conduits. Commentators also appreciate his "*ability to represent his client well without grandstanding*."

The Clients: The firm has advised a number of significant investment banks including Lehman Brothers.

Skadden, Arps, Slate, Meagher & Flom LLP & Affiliates

See firm details p.1372

The Firm: Clients relish the firm's score of "*smart and talented lawyers*," who often eschew the conveyor-belt transactions in favor of "*the innovative, private and interesting*" deals. About ten New York partners cover a gamut of securitization transactions, including auto receivables and lease work for Ford and Mitsubishi. On the subject of CMBS and RMBS, the team has represented underwriters including Deutsche Bank and Goldman Sachs. Other features of the practice involve the more esoteric insurance products and CAT bonds. Representing Deutsche Bank, the firm advised on the underwriting of the hybrid CDO secured by ABS. Another highlight involved Clout Financial Services' $110 million note issuance.

18   All quotes in the text are from interviews with clients and competitors.

CHAMBERS USA 2005

National: Northeast Region
Leading individuals
(Capital Markets: Securitization)

Senior Statesman
KRAVITT Jason *Mayer Brown*, New York

[1] **COWAN Cameron** *Orrick Herrington*, Washington, DC
DE SEAR Edward *McKee Nelson*, New York
KUNZ C Thomas *Skadden Arps*, New York
MARTIN Renwick *Sidley Austin*, New York

[2] **AUERBACH Reed** *McKee Nelson*, New York
CURTIS Susan *Skadden Arps*, New York
GLICK Anna *Cadwalader Wickersham*, New York
ISAACSON Laurence *McKee Nelson*, New York
SCHETMAN Richard *Cadwalader Wickersham*, New York

[3] **ARNHOLZ John** *McKee Nelson*, Washington, DC
CITRON Diane *Mayer Brown*, New York
DIANGELO Christopher *Dewey Ballantine*, New York
EISENBERG David *Simpson Thacher*, New York
FAULKNER Andrew *Skadden Arps*, New York
KAPLAN Cathy *Sidley Austin*, New York
KUDENHOLDT Stephen *Thacher Proffitt*, New York
NOCCO Frank *Weil Gotshal*, New York
PALMA Laura *Simpson Thacher*, New York
RAFF Joshua *Orrick Herrington*, New York
STRINGFELLOW James *Skadden Arps*, New York
WIPPERMAN Robert *McKee Nelson*, New York

[4] **BLAUCH Kevin** *Latham & Watkins*, New York
BRYAN Charles *Cadwalader Wickersham*, DC
BUCKLEY Kevin *Hunton & Williams*, Richmond
CROST Katherine *Orrick Herrington*, New York
CULLEN William *Sidley Austin*, New York
GAMBRO Michael *Cadwalader Wickersham*, New York
GLASS Adam *Linklaters*, New York
HOROWITZ Richard *Thacher Proffitt*, New York
KADLICK Richard *Skadden Arps*, New York
SCHACTER Ira *Cadwalader Wickersham*, New York
SCHWARTZ Jordan *Cadwalader*, New York

Up-and-coming individuals
HICKOK Arthur *Sidley Austin*, New York
SMITH Jason *Weil Gotshal*, New York

Individuals are listed alphabetically in each band.

The Lawyers: *"Innovative"* **Thomas Kunz** (see p.92) is hailed as a dynamic leader who *"gives discipline to deals,"* industry sources said. Those who have come across him respect his *"strong views"* and ability to see the big picture, which *"ensures that he is not intimidated by new structures."* He often acts as an overseer on high-profile transactions, for example advising Goldman Sachs in purchasing a prominent power contracts portfolio. **Susan Curtis** (see p.80) is *"hands-on, smart and helpful,"* regularly advising powerhouses such as Ford. She also represented The Putnam Advisory Company as an issuer in connection with a CLO secured by a diversified loan portfolio. *"Excellent deal facilitator"* **James Stringfellow** (see p.106) *"represents his clients zealously."* His drawing card is CDOs: he masterminded the hybrid CDO. *"Diligent hard worker"* **Andrew Faulkner** (see

p.83) has built a reputation for his credit card expertise and was responsible for the Clout Financial Services transaction. **Richard Kadlick** (see p.90) led the representation of Lehman Brothers in relation to the Eaton Vance CDO 2003-1. He is viewed as an *"effective negotiator"* who *"knows his stuff."*

The Clients: Clout Financial Services; Deutsche Bank; Ford; Goldman Sachs; Lehman Brothers; MACRO Securities; Mitsubishi and The Putnam Advisory Company.

Cadwalader, Wickersham & Taft LLP
See firm details p.1339

The Firm: Regarded by peers as the *"giants of the CMBS market,"* the firm *"has so many deals because it's good at what it does,"* said industry sources. Also commended for its RMBS work, the group represents issuers and underwriters across a spectrum of real estate financings and asset-backed transactions such as equipment leases and home equity loans. In particular the firm has capitalized on the growth of CDO work, completing more than 100 CDO transactions in the past seven years. Perhaps as a result of such volume, the level of innovation and complexity of its mortgage-backed commitments have been somewhat curtailed, clients said.

The Lawyers: *"One of the best in the business,"* **Richard Schetman** (see p.103) combines a mixture of securitization and derivatives to provide specialized expertise in synthetic CDOs. He represented CSFB on its first managed synthetic CDO and is also involved in credit card securitization for the likes of Citibank. Lehman Brothers and Bank of America have both sought his experience on repackaging. With her *"strong intellectual contribution,"* **Anna Glick** (see p.85) is lauded as *"one of the stars of the industry."* She advised on federal securities law in addition to an extensive mortgage-backed practice. **Michael Gambro**'s (see p.84) work includes representing Bear Stearns in the $2.6 billion securitization for Extended Stay America. Also advising Goldman Sachs and Greenwich Capital, he helped implement a $2.8 billion CMBS. *"A fine lawyer,"* **Jordan Schwartz** (see p.103) is noted for his experience in the RMBS market, while the *"sharp, innovative"* **Ira Schacter** (see p.102) is hailed as *"outstanding for complex derivative-based cutting-edge work."* A substantial portion of his practice involves domestic and cross-border lease finance deals. DC-based **Charlie Bryan** (see p.77) is *"practical, effective and thorough."* Peers praise his *"willingness to work out points lawyer-to-lawyer"* without letting his ego get in the way.

The Clients: The group's clients include: AIG Trading Group; Bank of America; CSFB and Lehman Brothers.

Mayer, Brown, Rowe & Maw LLP
See firm details p.771

The Firm: *"Good across the board,"* the firm is praised for its diversity and established national strength throughout its New York, Chicago and Charlotte offices. Providing *"spectacular client service"* and *"depth at both associate and partner level,"* the group boasts a portfolio that includes MBS, credit card dealings and trade receivables transactions. On behalf of Lehman Brothers, it marshaled the $5 billion Thornburg Mortgage and separately structured the $500 million Orbian program, issuing term notes with less than a year's maturity. The team also advised ABN AMRO in its North Sea Funding arbitrage conduit with an issuance capacity of approximately $10 billion.

The Lawyers: *"Wonderful"* **Jason Kravitt**'s (see p.91) increasing work with the ASF and regulatory bodies *"taps the pulse of where the industry is going."* Despite his stature as a senior statesman, he has still *"rolled up his sleeves"* to represent Orbian as well as JPMorgan Chase, CSFB and Deutsche Bank in their $300 million trade receivables securitization for the $4.2 billion acquisition of INVISTA. **Diane Citron** (see p.78) is *"cooperative"* and *"technically very good."* Her work includes representing the Commonwealth Bank of Australia in several offerings.

The Clients: The team has undertaken an array of CDOs including the CapitalSource Commercial Loan Trust 2004-1, representing arrangers Citigroup and Wachovia Securities. Other clients include: Merrill Lynch; ABN AMRO; Bank of America; CSFB; Commonwealth Bank of Australia; Deutsche Bank; GE Capital; GMAC Commercial Mortgage Corporation; Lehman Brothers and JPMorgan Chase.

McKee Nelson LLP
See firm details p.489

The Firm: The firm's rapid growth is further illustrated by the relocation of its New York office to larger premises as well as several new additions, including former Weil Gotshal & Manges partner Eugene Ferrer and co-head of structured finance William Gray. The team's *"host of talented people"* earned a reputation for understanding *"both business and law,"* sources said. Clients appreciate the team's ability *"to do with three lawyers what some firms would do with eight."* McKee Nelson has increased its market share of CDO and ABS work while still undertaking securitization of credit cards, mortgages and commodities such as timber. On behalf of Lehman Brothers it marshaled the $500 million IndyMac Home Equity Loan asset-backed notes securitization. Other notable transactions involve Sallie Mae in its Student Loan Trust 2003-10 transaction, which exceeded $3 billion.

The Lawyers: *"Talented"* **Ed De Sear** (see p.81) combines a statesmanlike image with sophisticated securitization expertise such as the monetization of tobacco litigation fees. He also advised Merrill Lynch on an innovative life insurance structure based primarily on mortality analysis. The *"charismatic"* **Reed Auerbach** (see p.75) boasts a *"well-rounded and mature"* portfolio of work involving student loans, auto loans, equipment contracts and conduits. DC-based **John Arnholz** (see p.75) is a *"bright"* practitioner who's squarely *"at the top of his game."* Benefiting from a fruitful relationship with Lehman Brothers, he co-heads the practice with **Robert Wipperman** (see p.108), who garnered praise for his mortgage work. The *"knowledgeable"* **Laurence Isaacson** (see p.89) continues to fortify the firm's reputation in cash and synthetic CDOs.

The Clients: HSBC; Lehman Brothers; Merrill Lynch and Sallie Mae.

Band 3

Cleary Gottlieb Steen & Hamilton
See firm details p.1342

The Firm: The firm's domestic securitization practice – which is integrated into its global profile – spreads between New York and DC. The group's flair for bespoke structures demonstrates *"real quality across the board,"* peers said. The group represented Fannie Mae, Ginnie Mae and Freddie Mac in their structured offerings amounting to $489 billion in 2003 and 2004. On behalf of Goldman Sachs, the group handled a $1.1 billion CMBS and separately acted for Korea First Bank in its $449 million RMBS – the first transaction of its kind in Korea. The team has also been linked to an abundance of synthetic CDOs for Citigroup among other clients, totaling more than $10 billion in 2003 and 2004 combined.

The Lawyers: Andrea Podolsky heads the securitization practice. Her work often pertains to technology, e-commerce and electronic trading ventures.

The Clients: Abbey National; BBVA Bancomer; Citigroup Global Markets; Excel Capital; Fannie Mae; Freddie Mac; Ginnie Mae; Korea First Bank; MasterCard International; South Street Securities; Visa International Service Association and XL Financial Solutions.

Simpson Thacher & Bartlett LLP
See firm details p.1370

The Firm: In contrast to many of its competitors, this coterie of three partners is prized for an eclectic mix of *"excellently lawyered"* non-commoditized work. *"Everything they do is top quality,"* say clients. The team takes pride in its generalist approach, pursuing high-end work as a strong component of its overall capital markets practice. Recent deals include acting for the underwriters on fleet financing linked to Avis and Hertz car rental companies. Another similar transaction involved Vanguard Car Rental's $4 billion asset-backed fleet financing program.

The Lawyers: *"Terrific"* **David Eisenberg** (see p.82) undertakes credit card and CDO transactions, and is known for *"always doing a thoughtful job."* **Laura Palma** (see p.97) delivers *"documents that are impeccable,"* commentators said. *"Everything works."* She was responsible for the restructuring of Alamo's fleet financing.

The Clients: Clients include car rental companies such as Avis, Hertz and Vanguard Car Rental.

Thacher Proffitt & Wood LLP
See firm details p.1374

The Firm: A bastion for mortgage-backed work, this firm bases its *"talent"* almost entirely in New York with a scattered few in Washington. About 21 structured finance partners have undertaken considerable securitization backed by home equity loans as well as subprime mortgage financing. The firm's expansion in this field is illustrated by the hiring of Christopher Lewis from Simmons & Simmons in London and Robert Villani from Fried, Frank, Harris, Shriver & Jacobson. The recruits have enabled the firm to meet the increased demand for synthetic CDO experience as well as enhance the less sturdy areas of its practice, such as securitization of auto loans and trade receivables. The group advised on a $2.3 billion securitization of Alt-A mortgage loans originated by Impac Mortgage Holdings and separately acted on Countrywide Home Loans' $980 million subprime mortgage securitization.

The Lawyers: *"Smart and cooperative"* **Stephen Kudenholdt** (see p.91) *"protects his clients without over-lawyering"* and receives plaudits from his peers for his work for the ASF and other industry matters. **Richard Horowitz** (see p.88) also receives praise, representing issuer clients on subprime and home equity loan transactions.

The Clients: The firm was involved in Bear Stearns' $1 billion mortgage securitization. Other clients include Citigroup and Ameriquest Mortgage.

Weil, Gotshal & Manges LLP
See firm details p.1378

The Firm: This *"transaction-oriented"* practice benefits from dedicated attorneys "handpicked" for their structured finance capabilities, clients said. The group "does a good job of delivering" a combination of securitization and derivatives expertise. Advising Vanguard Car Rental, it helped orchestrate a $4 billion asset-backed fleet financing program and related restructuring in connection with Vanguard's purchase of ANC assets. The firm also advised Merrill Lynch/Orion in a $2.25 billion portfolio investment of high-grade assets. Its CDO experience includes a $270 million synthetic structure organized as three funded credit default swap transactions.

The Lawyers: **Frank Nocco** (see p.97), who masterminds the firm's practice, was hailed by

commentators as *"a great negotiator"* who *"understands the risks."* Clients also praise his thoroughness and ability to bring a fresh perspective to novel issues. Working closely with him on the Vanguard Car Rental transaction, the *"exceptional"* **Jason Smith** (see p.105) displays judgment and confidence beyond his years. He was made partner in 2004.

The Clients: Financial Security Assurance; Hudson Castle Group; Lehman Brothers; MBIA Insurance; Rabobank; Wachovia and WestLB.

Band 4

Cravath, Swaine & Moore LLP
See firm details p.1344

The Firm: Despite the transfer of linchpin partner Gregory Shaw to London, the team's domestic practice remained buoyant. For example, it advised Canada Mortgage and Housing with regard to its $4.25 billion issuance of mortgage bonds. The group comprises two securitization partners working alongside two tax partners to deliver top-quality advice for anchor clients such as Citibank. The firm represented Providian National Bank on a $900 million credit card issuance and separately advised IBM in connection with its $500 million receivables securitization.

The Lawyers: Neil Westreich leads the practice, while David Mercado predominantly handles South American receivables work.

The Clients: Ambac Assurance; Canada Mortgage and Housing; Citibank; Hertz; Providian National Bank and Vitro America.

Dewey Ballantine LLP
See firm details p.1347

The Firm: Clients value the *"top notch"* practice for the elegant intellect of its five core US partners. *"They know the answers on some very complex points and don't disappear for three days to do research,"* another client added. In addition to carrying out mortgage and auto work, the firm has made forays into the insurance field, advising Goldman Sachs on a complex note issuance; the transaction involves Forethought Life Assurance dividend funds. Its issuer work includes representing AmeriCredit Financial Services in connection with a $400 million facility to provide funding for certain auto loan receivables. Advising on Freedom Park Capital, the group handled a $2 billion multiseller commercial paper facility without any liquidity facility support. In addition, the firm's emerging markets practice has acted for underwriter Merrill Lynch in the $500 million Brazilian Merchant Voucher Receivables issuance.

The Lawyers: **Christopher DiAngelo** (see p.81), who heads the practice, *"is technically as good as it gets,"* clients said. He is also prized for his *"great business acumen"* and *"excellent client rapport."* In addition to the AmeriCredit transaction, he also oversaw Accredited Home

Lenders Holding Company's $85 million accredited REIT preferred shares issue.
The Clients: Accredited Home Lenders Holding Company; AmeriCredit Financial Services; Citigroup; Goldman Sachs; Merrill Lynch and Promontory Asset Finance.

Latham & Watkins LLP
The Firm: A group of five partners form the New York arm of the firm's structured finance practice, which is bifurcated between CDO work and real estate securitization. Its established profile, combined with the efficiency of a generalist approach, won a loyal client following that includes Morgan Stanley, Deutsche Bank

and JPMorgan. The firm has advised on an ongoing program jointly administered by Bear Stearns and Morgan Stanley with issuances of more than $1 billion on a regular basis.
The Lawyers: *"A good solid lawyer,"* **Kevin Blauch** heads the MBS team and is *"one of the few"* who excels in commercial securitization. Laura DeFelice heads the CDO practice.
The Clients: Bear Stearns; Deutsche Bank; JPMorgan; Merrill Lynch and Morgan Stanley.

Other Notable Practitioners
Adam Glass of Linklaters *"is highly thought of"* in synthetic securitization. In addition to rental car transaction work his specific areas of exper-

tise include commercial paper funded financing of securities, CDOs, net lease properties, franchise and mortgage loans, and trade receivables. *"Exceptional"* **Kevin Buckley** (see p.1768) of Hunton & Williams LLP focuses on mortgage and asset-backed securitization. *"Not only does he have a complete mastery of the law,"* one client said, *"but he is also sensitive to the business requirements of any transaction."* Co-head of the firm's asset securitization group, he has represented issuers, underwriters, trustees, master servicers and insurers among others.

CAPITAL MARKETS: MIDWEST REGION

National: Midwest Region
Leading firms (Capital Markets)

1	MAYER, BROWN, ROWE & MAW LLP
	SIDLEY AUSTIN BROWN & WOOD LLP
2	KIRKLAND & ELLIS LLP
	WINSTON & STRAWN LLP

Leading individuals
(Capital Markets: Securitization)

★	HUGI Robert *Mayer Brown*, Chicago
1	ALBRECHT Thomas *Sidley Austin*, Chicago
	HITSELBERGER Carol *Mayer Brown*, Chicago
	LITWIN Stuart *Mayer Brown*, Chicago
	MORRISON Kenneth *Kirkland & Ellis*, Chicago
	PECOULAS George *Mayer Brown*, Chicago
	STERN Gary *Sidley Austin*, Chicago
2	BUCK Willis *Sidley Austin*, Chicago
	FONTAINE Mary *Mayer Brown*, Chicago
	GALAINENA David *Winston & Strawn*, Chicago
	HOCHBERG Kevin *Sidley Austin*, Chicago

Up-and-coming individuals

	VAN GORP Jon *Mayer Brown*, Chicago

Leading individuals
(Capital Markets: Derivatives)

1	COLLINS Joseph *Mayer Brown*, Chicago
	HARRISON Joseph *Sidley Austin*, Chicago
	SALZMAN Jerrold *Freeman Freeman*, Chicago
	SAWYIER David *Sidley Austin*, Chicago

Firms and individuals are listed alphabetically in each band.

Band 1

Mayer, Brown, Rowe & Maw LLP
See firm details p.771
The Firm: *"Strong and capable,"* say clients, the firm has *"seen it all and done it all."* The Chicago office, which is its largest with about 20 partners, is a structured finance powerhouse

spanning the girth of the industry; it is considered a market leader in developing conduits. Tasks at hand involve mortgage-backed, auto loan, and trade receivables structures as well as credit card programs and CDOs. It represented GE Capital in a Rule 144A $450 million securitization of its first restaurant franchise portfolio. It also advised Volkswagen and WestLB as underwriters in an auto lease securitization program totaling about €1 billion. The team is also lauded for its derivatives work, which includes representing electronic broker Ameritrade in its acquisitions of other brokers including InvesTech, Bidwell and American Brokerage. The firm launched the first publicly registered managed futures fund index in 2004.
The Lawyers: The *"wonderful"* and *"enterprising"* **Robert Hugi** (see p.89), according to clients, *"makes you feel as though you are his only client."* Combining practical business sense with an *"inside-out knowledge of the market,"* the *"great intellect"* concentrates on credit card receivables. He represented GE Capital in connection with its $952 million master note trust. *"Technically phenomenal,"* **Carol Hitselberger** (see p.87) *"knows her stuff forward and backwards."* Her breadth of practice recently involved JPMorgan Chase, CSFB and Deutsche Bank as underwriters in the $300 million trade receivables transaction. She also advised GE Capital in its restaurant securitization. *"Nationally recognized for his penetrating understanding of the market,"* **Stuart Litwin** (see p.93) is an *"auto-leasing virtuoso."* In addition to advising on the Volkswagen deal, he represented Goldman Sachs in a $1.25 billion auto loan securitization. **George Pecoulas** (see p.98) specializes in commercial paper conduits and is acclaimed for his bedside manners on behalf of clients: *"He doesn't waste your time nitpicking."* He advised the Bank of Montreal and Harris Nesbitt on the $3 billion PIN Capital program. *"Tough, practical*

and exceptionally organized," **Mary Fontaine** (see p.83) demonstrated flair in advising Winmark Equipment Finance in its £300 million secondary syndication transaction. A *"resilient negotiator,"* she is experienced in CDOs as well as the more unconventional asset classes. **Joseph Collins** divides his time between New York and Chicago, winning respect along the way for advisory work on derivatives matters. In addition to the Ameritrade transaction, he also represented Merrill Lynch in its acquisition of ABN AMRO's professional clearing business. **Jon Van Gorp's** (see p.107) *"hands-on, amenable"* style wins favor among clients and peers alike. His practice combines auto loan receivables, mortgage-backed and derivatives transactions.
The Clients: Ameritrade; CSFB; Deutsche Bank; GE; GM; Goldman Sachs; JPMorgan Chase; Lehman Brothers; Merrill Lynch; Revco; Volkswagen; WestLB and Winmark Finance.

Sidley Austin Brown & Wood LLP
See firm details p.778
The Firm: *"One of the big guns on the scene,"* the firm has forged strong relationships with prominent financial institutions as part of a broader clientele. A group of about ten securitization lawyers consistently delivers an impressively broad compass of structured finance expertise. As well as trade receivables and commercial paper conduit securitization, the group's transactions involve student loans, CDOs, insurance, auto loans and credit card programs among others; the firm also has expertise in sports-related structures. An enviable appetite for the esoteric such as its film revenue financing work and railcar securitization places the firm on center stage nationwide. For example, it represented the Municipal Bond Insurance Association as guarantor in a complex transaction requiring SPVs in Canada and Mexico. Its *"fantastic*

reputation" for derivatives is illustrated with significant work on monoline wraps, involving the credit risk transferred to the insurance companies. **The Lawyers:** Co-head of the firm's global securitization and structured finance practice group, **Thomas Albrecht** (see p.74) is a much-vaunted rainmaker. *"A problem-solving expert,"* **Gary Stern** (see p.105) earned high marks for his practical approach to deals. He masterminded the firm's involvement in film revenue financing and separate IP transactions related to music copyright. **Willis Buck** (see p.77) is lauded as being *"smart, bright and careful,"* winning particular praise for his credit card and auto loan work. *"Pragmatic"* **Kevin Hochberg** (see p.88) numbers Wachovia and Raytheon among his clients. His practice is heavily geared toward monoline insurance, conduits and utility stranded costs. He oversaw the operating assets transaction involving railcars. Another highlight involved a container transaction combining traditional asset-backed securities with a leverage lease structure. **Joseph Harrison** is as polished handling a futures-related litigation as he is on the regulatory side, while **David Sawyier** often advises on futures, commodity pools and hedge funds. **The Clients:** Barclays Capital; Citicorp; GE Capital; MBIA Insurance; Merrill Lynch; Radian Asset Assurance; Raytheon and Wachovia.

Band 2

Kirkland & Ellis LLP
See firm details p.770
The Firm: Its traditional private equity and bankruptcy strengths provide a sturdy foundation for its structured finance practice, especially in its representation of issuers. Market sources praise its credentials for auto and equipment lease work. The team of about seven partners – fortified by the arrival of Todd Miller from Mayer Brown Rowe & Maw – has undertaken considerable work for GMAC, including its public offerings of securities backed by retail auto loans. Other asset-related transactions include distressed, commercial and industrial debt. Also on offer is a budding CDO practice. **The Lawyers:** Tending to his long-standing relationships with issuers, **Kenneth Morrison** (see p.96) heads the firm's asset finance and securitization practice. He is considered *"at the top of the mountain,"* according to market sources. **The Clients:** Its clientele includes issuers, underwriters, principal finance groups and conduit sponsors.

Winston & Strawn LLP
See firm details p.780
The Firm: A handful of partners turn a deft hand toward a hybrid of securitization and capital markets transactions. The group predomi-

nantly represents issuers as well as collateral managers such as Columbia and Deerfield Capital in a string of CLOs. It is mostly associated with the more traditional asset types, amassing a generous number of transactions. The team participated in the $3 billion shelf registration of brokerage company Aon. Representing Harley-Davidson, it handled about $9 billion worth of publicly issued transactions backed by loans secured by the company's motorcycles. A recent innovation was the $200 million securitization of membership fees of Bally Total Fitness. **The Lawyers:** **David Galainena** (see p.84) is praised for his pragmatism on behalf of both public and private companies. A former investment banker at CSFB, his structure finance experience has included asset-backed and mortgage-backed transactions. **The Clients:** American Capital Strategies; Aon; Bally Total Fitness; CSFB; Harley-Davidson Financial Services; Heller Financial; JPMorgan Chase and Wachovia.

Other Notable Practitioners
"Superlative" **Jerrold Salzman** of Freeman, Freeman & Salzman won respect as principal outside counsel for the Chicago Mercantile Exchange on regulatory and litigation matters. He often defends clients before federal agencies and similar regulatory organizations.

CAPITAL MARKETS: SOUTHEAST REGION
SECURITIZATION

National: Southeast Region
Leading firms
(Capital Markets: Securitization)

1	CADWALADER WICKERSHAM
2	HUNTON & WILLIAMS
	MAYER BROWN
3	MOORE & VAN ALLEN

Leading individuals
(Capital Markets: Securitization)

1	CARROLL James *Cadwalader Wickersham*, Charlotte
	COHEN Steven *Cadwalader Wickersham*, Charlotte
2	BRADY Christopher *Mayer Brown*, Charlotte
	GOLDSTEIN Stuart *Cadwalader Wickersham*, Charlotte
	HAHN Robert *Hunton & Williams*, Charlotte
	MURPHY Paul *Moore & Van Allen*, Charlotte
	NEDZBALA Michael *Hunton & Williams*, Charlotte
	OBERKFELL Keith *Mayer Brown*, Charlotte

Firms and individuals are listed alphabetically in each band.

Band 1

Cadwalader, Wickersham & Taft LLP
See firm details p.1339
The Firm: The group enjoys a steady influx of cash and synthetic CDO work, often with commercial real estate products to take advantage of the firm's mastery of CMBS. Though its influence spans nationwide, its Charlotte base ensures proximity to two of its burliest issuers clients – Bank of America and Wachovia. Another strength is in interim asset financing, in addition to a taste for the esoteric, such as the $50 million securitization of legal fees for tobacco litigation. **The Lawyers:** **Stuart Goldstein** (see p.85) works extensively with Wachovia and is at the vanguard of the firm's CDO and CLO work, while **Jim Carroll** (see p.78) focuses primarily on CMBS, particularly the inception of the loan structuring process. **Steven Cohen** (see p.79), who divides his time between the New York and Charlotte offices, earned his spurs on a variety of structures. His expertise includes commodity financing, hedge fund financings and debt trading among others.

The Clients: Bank of America; Dubuque Bank & Trust; Royal & SunAlliance and Wachovia.

Band 2

Hunton & Williams
See firm details p.1775
The Firm: Divided between the firm's North Carolina and Virginia offices, the team covers the spectrum of securitization work including MBS, ABS commercial paper transactions, credit card programs and securitization of auto loans. The firm's industry and resourcefulness is a particular attraction among clients, who also seek its expertise on such matters as foreign trade receivables and risk transfer insurance deals. The Charlotte office has the distinction of participating in the first auto loan transaction involving debt securities and preferred shares. The team also handled the first synthetic deal for a North Carolina-based insurance company. **The Lawyers:** **Robert Hahn** (see p.86) possesses *"incisive business acumen"* and a natural aptitude for transaction-driven work, say market sources. **Michael Nedzbala**'s (see p.96) *"large book of business"* includes a variety of

sophisticated synthetic work as well as some heavy-duty MBS transactions.

The Clients: Clients include Bank of America, GE and Wells Fargo.

Mayer, Brown, Rowe & Maw LLP

See firm details p.771

The Firm: The firm's national strength in structured finance is naturally extended to its North Carolina satellite office, from which the team has undertaken a raft of substantial projects. On behalf of CSFB, it structured a $900 million subprime mortgage-backed transaction and a separate $1.5 billion CP conduit. The team also advised on a letter-of-credit facility supporting ten separate student loan deals. Other notable work includes a challenging MTN conduit unwrapped by monoline insurers.

The Lawyers: **Keith Oberkfell** (see p.97) won respect for his work on behalf of New York financial institutions, handling a variety of work. His recent transactions have involved CDOs, though his broader practice also includes CLOs and derivatives. **Chris Brady** (see p.77) cultivates a hefty CMBS practice in addition to some novel structures including single-seller conduits with various funding options.

The Clients: Bank of America; CSFB; Deutsche Bank; Ginnie Mae; Sallie Mae; Société Générale and Wachovia.

Band 3

Moore & Van Allen, PLLC

The Firm: The team cut its teeth on private and public transactions such as those involving trade and healthcare receivables, commercial and residential mortgage loans. Other interests involve credit card debt, auto loans, student loans and municipal leases. Synthetics and tobacco-related fees also have featured in its portfolio.

The Lawyers: **Paul Murphy** delivers adroit performances on a wide variety of work, including container transactions, shelf registrations and CP conduits.

The Clients: The team's array of clients includes underwriters, issuers and financial guarantors. One of its principal clients is Wachovia.

CAPITAL MARKETS: WEST COAST

<table>
<tr><td colspan="2">

National: West Coast Region
Leading firms (Capital Markets)

</td></tr>
<tr><td>1</td><td>DAVIS POLK & WARDWELL
SIMPSON THACHER & BARTLETT LLP
SKADDEN, ARPS, SLATE, MEAGHER</td></tr>
<tr><td>2</td><td>LATHAM & WATKINS LLP
SULLIVAN & CROMWELL LLP
WILSON SONSINI GOODRICH</td></tr>
<tr><td>3</td><td>GIBSON, DUNN & CRUTCHER LLP
MILBANK, TWEED, HADLEY & MCCLOY
SIDLEY AUSTIN BROWN & WOOD</td></tr>
</table>

<table>
<tr><td colspan="2">

Leading individuals (Capital Markets)

</td></tr>
<tr><td>1</td><td>DALLAS Bruce Davis Polk, Menlo Park
HINMAN William Simpson Thacher, Palo Alto
SAGGESE Nicholas Skadden Arps, Los Angeles</td></tr>
<tr><td>2</td><td>DENENBERG Alan Davis Polk, Menlo Park
EDMONSON Tracy Latham & Watkins, San Francisco
FORE John Wilson Sonsini, Palo Alto
RESSLER Alison Sullivan & Cromwell, Los Angeles</td></tr>
<tr><td>3</td><td>BARONSKY Kenneth Milbank Tweed, Los Angeles
KILB Brian Gibson Dunn, Los Angeles
KING Kenton Skadden Arps, Palo Alto
MOTTESI Marcello Milbank Tweed, Palo Alto
PRINGLE Paul Sidley Austin, San Francisco
SAPER Jeff Wilson Sonsini, Palo Alto</td></tr>
<tr><td colspan="2">Firms and individuals are listed alphabetically in each band.</td></tr>
</table>

Band 1

Davis Polk & Wardwell

See firm details p.1345

The Firm: The firm's entrenched West Coast practice no doubt reaps the benefits of its invaluable New York profile, consistently proving that it is *"adept at the complex,"* market sources said. Its innovation and depth is instilled from a strong tradition of underwriter representation, though the group has made a conscious effort to increase its representation of issuers. Acting for E*TRADE, it handled a $400 million high-yield senior note offering, which was underwritten by Morgan Stanley and CSFB among others. Westar Energy has been another loyal issuer client, turning to the team to handle recent offerings worth about $885 million. On behalf of Comcast, the group marshaled the monetization of a $1 billion stake in Liberty media common stock.

The Lawyers: **Bruce Dallas** (see p.80) has a *"mighty reputation in the market,"* further enhanced by an easygoing manner that proved effective in negotiations. He oversaw the Comcast monetization transaction and separately represented lead managers Citigroup, Goldman Sachs and Morgan Stanley in Providian's $250 million convertible notes offering with an embedded call option. Clients praise **Alan Denenberg**'s (see p.81) *"winning combination of experience and involvement"* in complex deals, particularly those fraught with political repercussions. He delicately *"balances competing interests"* to obtain favorable results for clients.

The Clients: Banc of America Securities; Citigroup; E*TRADE; Goldman Sachs; JPMorgan Chase; UltraClean Technologies; Vitesse Semiconductors and Westar Energy.

Simpson Thacher & Bartlett LLP

See firm details p.1370

The Firm: Pitched as the *"cream of the crop,"* the firm has been noted for its convertibles and equity work. Benefiting from the firm's international brand of *"business acumen coupled with extensive legal expertise,"* the California team garnered respect in a variety of areas, including biopharmaceutical, healthcare and technology among others. It enjoys a steady stream of work on behalf of issuers and underwriters.

The Lawyers: Touted as *"first-choice lawyer"* by several clients, **William Hinman** (see p.87) is respected for his industry experience as well as his prowess in the equity sphere.

The Clients: Blue-chip investment banks and other corporations are among its clients.

Skadden, Arps, Slate, Meagher & Flom LLP & Affiliates

See firm details p.1372

The Firm: The group commands attention both in the Bay Area and Southern California, offering a combination of capital markets and M&A expertise. Branded as *"one of the big high-yield players,"* it has an assiduous underwriting presence that has enabled it to evolve, particularly in the LA area, beyond institutional work. Its northern contingent services a staunch flock of technology companies in their convertible and follow-on offerings. These include a series of deals for medical devices company Kinetic Concepts, including a $1 billion recapitalization and a $621 million IPO. The firm also undertook the restructuring of broadband operator UnitedGlobalCom's subsidiary UPC in a deal valued at more than $5 billion.

The Lawyers: **Nicholas Saggese** (see p.102) enjoys a diet of general corporate transactions with a leaning toward capital markets. He helped shape the team's profile in the area, along with **Kenton King** (see p.91), who leads the corporate team in the Bay Area. His repertoire also includes cross-border transactions, particularly those linked to Japan.

The Clients: The firm has counseled highfliers including top international investment banks, manufacturers, technology companies and others.

Band 2

Latham & Watkins LLP

The Firm: The firm's national reputation for high-yield investments is no less glittering on the West Coast, where the practice is amalgamated with substantial M&A work. Three California offices – Los Angeles, San Francisco and the Silicon Valley – contain a wealth of talented lawyers who *"have their eye on getting the deal done rather than raising road blocks,"* commentators said. Its debt work has predominated, leading the team to participate in such deals as the financing for glass manufacturer Owens-Illinois' $1.2 billion acquisition of GlassMac; the cross-border transaction involved complex jurisdictional requirements.

The Lawyers: **Tracy Edmonson** *"knows her stuff,"* say industry sources, and does *"a fabulous job on debt."* She attracted the limelight with the novel structuring of a convertible debt exchange so as to enable her client to avoid SEC filings.

The Clients: The team has advised major investment banks, private equity companies and prominent manufacturers among others.

Sullivan & Cromwell LLP

See firm details p.1373

The Firm: Esteemed for its breadth of practice and *"skilful lawyers,"* the firm compensates for its modest size in LA by producing the highest caliber of work. This encompasses high-yield transactions, IPOs and other offerings such as those involving convertible and exchangeable securities. True to its *"smart and sophisticated"* character, the team has cultivated a loyal following in underwriter representation.

The Lawyers: **Alison Ressler** (see p.100) is *"always impressive"* on securities work, which she ably combines with her management duties as leader of the firm's West Coast practice, sources said.

The Clients: Among its high-profile clients are Goldman Sachs and Nokia.

Wilson Sonsini Goodrich & Rosati

See firm details p.302

The Firm: Despite the repercussions of a fitful market, the firm has maintained sizable clout in the equity markets, leading one commentator to describe it as *"the big gorilla in the Bay Area."*

Some eye-catching transactions include wireless company Callwave's $50 million public offering, in which the firm represented Deutsche Bank and Piper Jaffrey as underwriters. *"They have a name that opens doors I wish I could open,"* said one industry source. On behalf of shoe manufacturer Converse, the team handled a $100 million IPO and its sale to Nike for $300 million. Its debt transactions include a $250 million high-yield transaction for technology company Amkor. The firm is also cutting a dash with contingently convertible debt offerings structured simultaneously with derivative transactions to provide huge tax advantages.

The Lawyers: **John Fore** (see p.84) is touted as one of a handful of lawyers who *"can understand and do the sophisticated deals."* according to market sources. He masterminded Amkor's high-yield transaction and separately advised underwriters Citigroup and Deutsche Bank in offerings for biotechnology company CB Therapeutics. **Jeff Saper** (see p.102) is respected for his equity work, and earned commendation for the Converse and Callwave offerings.

The Clients: Amkor; Bank of America; Citigroup; Lehman Brothers; Merrill Lynch; Morgan Stanley; Solectron and UBS Warburg.

Band 3

Gibson, Dunn & Crutcher LLP

See firm details p.285

The Firm: *"A distinguished presence"* in Southern California, the firm devotes itself chiefly to large structured transactions for its stock of private equity clients and related institutions. Issuers dominate its client roster as does debt securities work, typically in high-yield Rule 144A transactions and often with a cross-border and Regulation S component. Recent deals include representing sports equipment company K2 in a $350 million high-yield financing linked to its European acquisitions.

The Lawyers: *"Sharp"* **Brian Kilb** (see p.91) is *"a good negotiator with excellent attention to detail,"* say clients. He oversaw the K2 transaction and obtains vital capital markets expertise from his strong relationships with clients such as MGM and electronics distributor Avnet.

The Clients: These include Avnet and MGM, among others.

Milbank, Tweed, Hadley & McCloy

The Firm: Clients relish the firm's *"wealth of experience"* and commercial perspective. It is active principally in the LA market, engaging in debt financing with an M&A component. It also has its foot in the door in Palo Alto's technology sector, partly due to burgeoning relationships with the likes of Lehman Brothers. This has led to transactions such as healthcare company Beverly Enterprise's $215 million Rule 144A offering, in which it represented the bank as underwriter. It also represented Lehman Brothers in Ormat Funding Corporation's $190 million Rule 144A offering. On the issuer side, among its credentials is a $1.3 billion refinancing of Station Casino's long-term capital.

The Lawyers: **Kenneth Baronsky** continues to win recognition in the market; he oversaw the Station Casino's refinancing. Clients also praise the *"commercial agility"* of **Marcello Mottesi**, who was responsible for the Beverly Enterprise's deal.

The Clients: Citigroup; Deutsche Bank; JPMorgan Chase; Lehman Brothers; Morgan Stanley; Station Casinos and Wells Fargo.

Sidley Austin Brown & Wood LLP

See firm details p.778

The Firm: The firm's team is commended for its orthodox securities practice representing underwriters on debt public offerings, mortgage-backed securitization and municipal finance. The San Francisco office is viewed as the strongest on the West Coast, though the LA contingent also won commendation for its extensive issuer-directed work. Highlights include advising underwriters Citigroup and Deutsche Bank in Safeway's $750 million debt offering. In the same capacity, it also represented Citigroup, JPMorgan Chase and Morgan Stanley in Sempra Energy's $450 million common stock offering.

The Lawyers: *"Seasoned"* **Paul Pringle** (see p.99) is always *"extremely willing to pitch in,"* observers said. He oversaw the Sempra Energy and Safeway deals.

The Clients: Citigroup; Deutsche Bank; JPMorgan Chase and Morgan Stanley.

ERISA LITIGATION

Passed in 1974, the Employee Retirement Income Security Act has been pushed to the fore in the past five to ten years, when various factors have contributed to create a 'perfect storm' in ERISA litigation. A federal law with broad provisions that set the minimum standards for pension and health plans in private industry, ERISA is designed to protect the millions of employees participating in these plans; it does not require employers to establish pension plans, only that they follow certain guidelines when they do. Further enhancing ERISA is the Retirement Protection Act of 1994, which assists employees by increasing funding of underfunded pension plans and strengthens the pension insurance program.

Given that pension plans represent one of the driving financial forces on Wall Street – with trillions of dollars under management – it's little wonder that much attention has been devoted to the management of these plans. ERISA provides such broad rights to employees that some specialists believe "it is tailor-made for class actions." Many see the Enron scandal as a watershed, in view of the fact that fiduciary activity was brought under the national microscope for the first time. Inextricably tied up with fraud and securities claims, this was a major 'stock drop' case, where employees chose to invest company stock in a 401(k) plan and suffered huge losses. Enron precipitated a big wave of cases alleging breach of fiduciary duty, though this is by no means the only type of ERISA litigation.

For example, retiree welfare coverage and health benefits are also more under scrutiny. In addition, employers have increasingly swapped certain defined plans in favor of cash-balance schemes. Added to this mix is an ever-expanding and entrepreneurial plaintiffs Bar, which continues to thrive. To the contrary, it still remains to be seen how efforts such as President Bush's campaign to overhaul Social Security will affect employee pension plans.

The lawyers highlighted in this section are considered ERISA litigation defense specialists. They combine the technical intricacies of the law with dazzling courtroom performances, lending cachet to their firms – which can also be said to display real dedication to the overall employee benefits arena.

National
Leading firms (ERISA Litigation)

1 MORGAN, LEWIS & BOCKIUS LLP
O'MELVENY & MYERS LLP
PROSKAUER ROSE LLP
STEPTOE & JOHNSON LLP

2 ALSTON & BIRD LLP
GROOM LAW GROUP
MCDERMOTT WILL & EMERY
NIXON PEABODY LLP
VEDDER, PRICE, KAUFMAN & KAMMHOLZ
WEIL, GOTSHAL & MANGES LLP

Leading individuals (ERISA Litigation)

1 ECCLES Bob *O'Melveny & Myers*, Washington, DC
ONDRASIK Paul *Steptoe & Johnson*, Washington, DC
SHAPIRO Howard *Proskauer Rose*, New Orleans

2 BRADEN Gregory *Alston & Bird*, Atlanta
GALLAGHER Robert *Groom Law Group*, Washington, DC
KALLSTROM D Ward *Morgan Lewis*, San Francisco
ROSS Nancy *McDermott Will*, Chicago
SPENCER Steven *Morgan Lewis*, Philadelphia
ULTERINO Eugene *Nixon Peabody*, New York
WOLF Charles *Vedder Price*, Chicago

Firms and individuals are listed alphabetically in each band.

Band 1

Morgan, Lewis & Bockius LLP
See firm details p.1556
The Firm: Well-regarded by market sources for its traditional labor and employment practice, the firm has secured another string to its bow by investing in a dedicated ERISA litigation task force. The team has handled numerous multistate ERISA class actions. Also on offer is their familiarity of issues such as ERISA exemption, fiduciary standards compliance and retiree medical benefits.

The Lawyers: The nationwide group commands a strong hold on the market, with Philadelphia-based **Steve Spencer** (see p.105) and San Francisco-based **Ward Kallstrom** (see p.90) leading the charge. Both were distinguished as much for their technical ability as their courtroom prowess, with observers stating: *"These excellent lawyers deserve to be on the list."*

O'Melveny & Myers LLP
See firm details p.294
The Firm: *"A leading firm that pulls ahead of the others due to its breadth and depth,"* and that houses one of the best Title I litigation practices in the country, clients said. The firm's workload spans a wide array of claims under ERISA. Recent Supreme Court appearances include CIGNA Healthcare of Texas v Ruby Calad; the case examines whether ERISA preempts state law and concerns the patient's right to sue an HMO under state law. The team also demonstrated expertise in such areas as breach of fiduciary duty, securities-related cases and other claims pertaining to employee benefits.
The Lawyers: Its historic emphasis on this area of law is largely due to **Bob Eccles,** a former ERISA attorney for the Department of Labor (DOL). Described as the *"premier ERISA litigator in the country,"* he blends *"exceptional knowledge of the law with superb judgment."*

Proskauer Rose LLP
See firm details p.1365
The Firm: A nationally established employee benefits and executive compensation group, Proskauer Rose has made strides in ERISA litigation with the recruitment of seasoned practitioner Howard Shapiro and his team from Shook, Hardy & Bacon in October 2004. This lateral move is more than likely to pay off given the current trend for major class actions, and ensures that Proskauer's marquee clients don't have to look elsewhere for expert ERISA litigation experience.
The Lawyers: **Howard Shapiro** (see p.103) brings more than 25 years of experience to the firm and is unequivocally regarded as a *"top-class"* player. In addition to ERISA class actions, he has also represented management in such matters as preemption issues, fiduciary duty, ESOP litigation and 401(k) disputes among others.

Steptoe & Johnson LLP
See firm details p.492
The Firm: Early involvement in the industry is a characteristic found in Steptoe & Johnson, a firm that orchestrates a *"crème de la crème"* practice. The firm has advised on ERISA matters for close to 30 years. Particular experience includes lawsuits concerning breach of fiduciary duty, which are generally bought alongside securities fraud allegations. High-profile instructions include acting for members of the administrative committee of the Enron plans. The team has also taken a lead defense role in ERISA litigation on behalf of The Williams Companies, Qwest and Dynegy.
The Lawyers: Much of its reputation for quality lies with its *"multifaceted"* team leader **Paul Ondrasik** (see p.460). A jewel in his crown is Albrecht v Committee on Employee Benefits of the Federal Reserve Employee Benefits System, in which he successfully defended claims of fiduciary breach linked to mandatory employee contribution.

www.ChambersandPartners.com

All quotes in the text are from interviews with clients and competitors.

25

Band 2

Alston & Bird LLP

See firm details p.626

The Firm: A firm that deserves its share of the limelight, Alston & Bird has also had the foresight to cultivate a group of trained ERISA practitioners and experienced trial lawyers.

The Lawyers: The Georgia-based team is admirably led by **Greg Braden** (see p.77), an operator with a growing track record in ERISA litigation. Braden has led on headline-grabbing cases such as Franklin v First Union, a class action concerning the use of a proprietary mutual fund in the company's 401(k) plan. He is also lead defense counsel in the Goodyear ERISA litigation and is separately representing several individual defendants in the Health-South litigation.

Groom Law Group

The Firm: Altogether a different model compared to other ranked firms, the Groom Law Group is branded a *"premier employee benefits boutique in the USA,"* clients said. It offers *"the whole package,"* combining *"incredible expertise with fabulous service."* The team specializes in employer stock litigation, mutual fund disputes and the treatment of employee benefit plans in bankruptcies. In this context, it has played an important role in the bankruptcies involving many old legacy airline carriers.

The Lawyers: One of the most accomplished in the firm's ERISA litigation team is DOL alumnus **Bob Gallagher,** who tried the first ever case bought by the DOL under ERISA in 1976. He has been called upon to testify as an expert witness in ERISA cases due to his superb technical expertise and sophisticated understanding of the law.

McDermott Will & Emery

See firm details p.773

The Firm: The firm's ability to devote enormous resources to major class actions is a trait valued by clients entangled in difficult situations. The firm boasts one of the largest employee benefits departments in the USA, and is a magnet for clients who value its predilection for *"effective strategy planning."*

The Lawyers: Within this top-notch coterie is a handful of specialist ERISA litigators, including the *"first-rate"* **Nancy Ross** (see p.749). Recent successes include Keach v US Trust, a multimillion ERISA class action in which Ross defended the chairman and CEO of Foster & Gallagher. She also won a $60 million victory on behalf of Avondale Industries, representing the plan's fiduciaries and trustees.

Nixon Peabody LLP

See firm details p.1361

The Firm: On behalf of Fortune 500 clients, the firm has proven that it has ample capacity to take on high-level ERISA defense litigation. A dedicated group of 11 attorneys concentrates on fiduciary and benefits litigation. The team gained recognition for its role in advising sponsors and fiduciaries in federal trial and appellate courts throughout the nation, including the Supreme Court. Important rulings include Crowley v Corning, in which a judge dismissed claims against ERISA fiduciaries in connection to badly performing stock invested in a 401(k) plan.

The Lawyers: Leading the case was **Eugene Ulterino** (see p.107), who is noted by peers for his consistently *"fabulous work."* He has handled a range of cases involving fiduciary, benefit claims, and preemption issues under ERISA.

Vedder, Price, Kaufman & Kammholz

The Firm: Sharing the same stomping ground is this Chicago-based firm. Although it may not have the international strength of some of its competitors, what it lacks in geographic spread it makes up for in quality.

The Lawyers: Well-experienced in ERISA litigation, **Chuck Wolf** leads the charge at Vedder Price. He is credited with developing case law concerning the employer's right to terminate retiree welfare benefits in accordance with plan documents. Recent victories include defeating an ERISA class action on behalf of Amsted Industries, a corporation that is entirely owned through an ESOP.

Weil, Gotshal & Manges LLP

See firm details p.1378

The Firm: In a different vein, Weil Gotshal & Manges takes a slice of the action based on its strength as a killer bankruptcy firm. In both the WorldCom and the Enron cases, the team provided counseling with respect to breach of fiduciary duty involving 401(k) and pension plans. Such cases are often bought in tandem with securities claims; herein is another of the firm's drawing cards. Other high-level instructions include representing UnitedHealth Group in the numerous class actions ravaging the managed care industry. In McRaney v UnitedHealthcare, the team defeated class certification in a case alleging RICO and ERISA violations.

GOVERNMENT CONTRACTS

National
Leading firms (Government Contracts)

1. CROWELL & MORING LLP
   DLA PIPER RUDNICK GRAY CARY
   MCKENNA LONG & ALDRIDGE LLP
2. FRIED, FRANK, HARRIS, SHRIVER
   ROGERS JOSEPH O'DONNELL
   VENABLE LLP
   WILEY REIN & FIELDING LLP
3. GARDERE WYNNE SEWELL LLP
   GIBSON, DUNN & CRUTCHER LLP
   JENNER & BLOCK LLP
   MAYER, BROWN, ROWE & MAW LLP
4. MILLER & CHEVALIER
   SHEPPARD, MULLIN, RICHTER
   THELEN REID & PRIEST LLP
   VINSON & ELKINS LLP

Firms are listed alphabetically in each band

Band 1

Crowell & Moring LLP

See firm details p.482

The Firm: A long history in the government contracts sector and the commitment of vast resources combine to make this practice a major force. Attorneys here possess *"comprehensive tactical skills and a real understanding of how the agencies react,"* sources said. The group of more than 50 dedicated attorneys advises clients on challenges to contract awards and related proceedings before such bodies as the Government Accountability Office (GAO) and the US Federal Claims Court. Counseling and litigation across a range of industries fall into the firm's remit, including supply and service contracts arising out of the defense and healthcare sectors.

The Lawyers: The group is home to some of the sector's longest standing players. **Stan Johnson** (see p.89) is an extremely established attorney whose gravitas in court and before the agencies has won a loyal following. His trial skills are *"second to none"* and his recent experience has included contract award litigation involving both contractor and government claims. **Terry Albertson** is a skilled negotiator and an effective trial lawyer whose work, particularly in the field of contract cost and accounting, is widely recognized. Over the past year, he has counseled companies with contracts relating to Iraq and the issue of cost allowability.

DLA Piper Rudnick Gray Cary US LLP

See firm details p.765

The Firm: According to clients, this firm's *"army of experts"* is able to cover a range of specialist

All quotes in the text are from interviews with clients and competitors.

National
Leading individuals
(Government Contracts)

Senior Statesman
DEES Stanley *McKenna Long*, Washington, DC

[1] **DOKE Jr** Marshall *Gardere Wynne*, Dallas
JOHNSON Stanfield *Crowell & Moring*, Washington, DC
JOSEPH Allan *Rogers Joseph*, San Francisco
MADDEN Thomas *Venable LLP*, Washington, DC
VACKETTA Carl *DLA Piper*, Washington, DC

[2] **ALLEN** Rand *Wiley Rein*, Washington, DC
CHIERICHELLA John *Sheppard Mullin*, Washington, DC
CHURCHILL David *Jenner & Block*, Washington, DC
MADSEN Marcia *Mayer Brown*, Washington, DC
MCCULLOUGH James *Fried Frank*, Washington, DC

[3] **ALBERTSON** Terry *Crowell & Moring*, Washington, DC
CHARNESS Michael *Vinson & Elkins*, Washington, DC
DEVECCHIO Jay *Miller & Chevalier*, Washington, DC
GALLAGHER James *McKenna Long*, Los Angeles
O'DONNELL Neil *Rogers Joseph*, San Francisco
RECTOR Richard *DLA Piper*, Washington, DC
WEST Joseph *Gibson Dunn*, Washington, DC

Individuals are listed alphabetically in each band.

issues related to government contracts. Property rights, contract costs and procurement integrity are just some of the niches that this *"responsive and knowledgeable"* group inhabits. Clients also value the firm's commitment to the business development issues surrounding this field, describing its attorneys as *"generous with their time and their devotion."* Geographic spread and the depth of resources available to clients are also defining features of this practice. The group is well equipped to advise on general counseling related to an award, bid protests, and dispute resolution before the Department of Defense, the DOI, the GAO and the US Federal Claims Court.

The Lawyers: *"A master in the field,"* **Carl Vacketta** (see p.107) possesses such a breadth of knowledge and *"an innate sense of the practicalities facing clients in negotiations"* that he is regularly a first port of call for many major companies. His clients are household names from the aerospace, construction, technology and telecom fields as well as smaller businesses with preferential treatment concerns. His work in the field of multiple award schedule (MAS) schemes is widely recognized. Market observers also identified **Richard Rector** (see p.100) as a member of the next generation helping to define the sector. Clients appreciate his expertise in procurement integrity and ethics issues, claiming: *"He is technically superb and is always on top of the issues."*

McKenna Long & Aldridge LLP
See firm details p.636
The Firm: One of the largest government contracts groups in the USA, this firm is *"a real pow-*erhouse, pioneering the field from the start."* The group's deep coverage has led clients to claim: *"They have seen everything."* Among the group's specialist expertise is the development of antiterror products arising out of the defense industry, and incentives and protections for the pharmaceutical industry. Attorneys also advised on privatization and performance contracts, and matters related to fraud and Qui Tam cases. Recent highlights include the representation of contractors working with the Department of Energy on issues relating to toxic materials, proceedings related to the Safety Act and matters concerning multiple award schedule (MAS) programs. Bid protests before the GAO and the US Federal Claims Court continue to account for a large portion of the practice. While the majority of this team's members are based in DC, it can also draw on the support of attorneys in Denver and Los Angeles. They are talented litigators and *"sensitive counselors"* able to undertake the most complex of matters.

The Lawyers: Stanley Dees (see p.81) is a *"legend"* whose deep knowledge of the law and vast experience continues to hold sway over the marketplace. For many observers, he is so closely associated with government contracts that he is *"the first name that springs to mind and best choice if you need a sounding board on any matter."* His clients include Lockheed Martin and AT&T, representing the latter alongside Lucent Technologies in a case concerning proper remedy for contractors over issues of realistic pricing. Based in LA, **Jay Gallagher** (see p.84) has cultivated a national reputation for his work on fraud investigations, terminations, bid protests and issues of costs and accounting. Cochair of the firm, he combines his managerial duties with litigation on a range of government contract issues.

Band 2

Fried, Frank, Harris, Shriver & Jacobson LLP
See firm details p.1349
The Firm: With a practice spanning about 40 years, the firm has broadened its reach to advise on a range of issues related to the bids for government contracts, and related corrective actions and litigation. Such expertise has attracted clients from the top end of the defense and aerospace industry as well as major construction companies and accounting firms. Dedicated specialists are housed in this firm's DC and LA offices, while attorneys in New York advise on associated M&A issues. Clients described this firm as *"one of the preeminent players for bid protests – they have the experience and expertise to answer unique questions."* The team is also well versed in contract interpretation and performance, pricing issues and export controls. The group is able to advise on fraud and Qui Tam claims, and works well with attorneys in the white-collar crime and arbitration departments.

The Lawyers: According to clients, **James McCullough** (see p.94) provides *"responsive, practical advice tailored to our needs."* His experience is so far-reaching that *"whenever novel questions pop up, he'll have dealt with the issue in some capacity."* McCullough is head of the government contracts practice in DC and frequently appears in bid protests before the GAO and the US Federal Claims Court. He recently represented Science Applications International Corp in a challenge to the EPA's award to Lockheed Martin of a $706 million contract to provide IT support services. Other clients include AT&T, Northrop Grumman and Level 3 Communications.

Rogers Joseph O'Donnell & Phillips
The Firm: A litigation boutique, it was founded nearly 25 years ago by a small group of government contract specialists and general business trial lawyers, and has since expanded to field more than 30 dedicated attorneys. One of seven distinct practice areas undertaken by the firm, government contracts law is undoubtedly the highest in profile. A group of *"broadly trained and incredibly wise"* lawyers has cultivated a reputation for dominating the West Coast market. Sources also commended the team's sensible approach to litigation and its *"extensive experience of the idiosyncrasies of the process."* The firm is conversant in matters such as bid protests, procurement integrity, MAS programs, fraud and IP issues.

The Lawyers: Allan Joseph is *"an extremely intelligent attorney who analyzes cases thoroughly and can spot the details."* Cochair of the group with **Neil O'Donnell**, he is widely respected for his advice on Qui Tam actions and allegations relating to the False Claims Act. O'Donnell is a specialist in construction and public contract law. Interviewees endorsed him as a *"fine litigator who knows how to run smooth proceedings."*

Venable LLP
The Firm: The sizable team possesses both the technical legal skills and an understanding of the nuances in government contracts to secure its place as a national leader in the field. The group advises on costs and accounting, bid protests, suspension and debarment issues as well as a growing volume of MAS contract matters. Attorneys attract mandates from the defense industry, as well as technology, construction and service maintenance companies. They also advise smaller – often minority businesses – on issues of ethics and procurement.

The Lawyers: *"A real expert with a unique practice"* **Thomas Madden**'s background in IP (he has a degree in electrical engineering) is widely regarded as his core strength. Among recent highlights, he advised on a patent infringement case arising out of the aerospace industry. He also represented Raytheon Technical Services in a challenge made by the incumbent contractor to its award of a multimillion-dollar, ten-year facilities management contract for the US Antarctic Program.

Wiley Rein & Fielding LLP
See firm details p.496

The Firm: This team of 25 talented attorneys has displayed expertise in both their written briefs and powerful advocacy skills in proceedings before the agencies. Attorneys advise on bid protests and contract claims, procurement fraud and IP rights protection. The group has attracted clients of the caliber of Boeing, Hewlett-Packard, EDS and BAE SYSTEMS. In line with its firm-wide reputation for telecom work, the team has advised on spin-offs in this sector. The firm also counseled EDS in its billion-dollar contract to outsource Internet functions to the Navy-Marine Corps following unexpected delays.

The Lawyers: Rand Allen (see p.74) is perhaps best known for his high-quality work with key client Boeing, recently advising the company in a dispute with the Air Force over the suspension of three Boeing units from government contracts. Sources credited him with being the driving force behind the practice, and endorsed his pragmatic approach to negotiations. *"He has huge experience – he knows it all."*

Band 3

Gardere Wynne Sewell LLP
See firm details p.1718

The Firm: While this firm is clearly the dominant player in the Texas market, its influence is not limited by such geographic boundaries. The firm is a major player on the national scene, often advising Texas-based contractors on proceedings before the GAO and the US Federal Claims Court. Its attorneys bring *"a broad set of skills"* to procurement, contract compliance and claims, and government investigations.

The Lawyers: *"Highly accomplished"* **Marshall Doke** (see p.81) has developed a national practice that has attracted marquee clients such as Texas Instruments. He is an expert on defective pricing and cost accounting issues, particularly proceedings under the Truth in Negotiations Act.

Gibson, Dunn & Crutcher LLP
See firm details p.285

The Firm: Clients highlighted this practice for its pragmatic approach to problem solving and its high level of support and client service. Its attorneys are *"timely and thorough in their responses"* and focused on building strong relationships. Perhaps best known for its work in construction-related issues, the group has devel-

oped a broad offering. Among its recent caseload are contract award disputes, terminations and suspensions, and costs and pricing issues. Recent highlights include representing Mellon Bank in its agreement with the US Treasury to provide cash management services.

The Lawyers: According to clients, **Joseph West** (see p.475) is one of the most sophisticated government contracts lawyers around. He is *"completely conversant with the body of the law and finds creative solutions to problems that don't fit into boxes."* He represented Northrop Grumman in a dispute with subcontractors over the design and development of the B-2 Stealth Bomber.

Jenner & Block LLP
See firm details p.768

The Firm: Market observers commended this firm for its success in attracting attorneys who are steeped in the sector. The key focus of the practice resides in the defense and aerospace industry, and it has developed long-standing relationships with large contractors such as General Dynamics. The team successfully represented this client on protests surrounding its multimillion-dollar development and production contract with the US Army for the Joint Tactical Radio System. Attorneys also advise on federal procurement issues, ethics and compliance, and cost allowability. The group is also supported by a sophisticated appellate practice with experience before the US Supreme Court.

The Lawyers: **David Churchill** (see p.78) has impressed clients with his understanding of a client's business needs and a practical approach to the negotiating table. He possesses a clear focus on the aerospace and defense industry and is *"a key player with a deep legal knowledge,"* agree sources. His clients include General Dynamics and GE, advising the latter on federal cost principles and internal investigations. **Jay DeVecchio** recently moved from Miller & Chevalier Chartered. He is an *"extremely knowledgeable attorney – the kind I would want fighting my corner,"* acknowledged one client. He is articulate, has real presence in court and is an expert on IP-related issues.

Mayer, Brown, Rowe & Maw LLP
See firm details p.771

The Firm: *"Long-time credentials"* and a real understanding of how government works have made this practice a true national player. Sources credited the firm with building up the practice through lateral hires from leading DC firms, and clients appreciate the level of resources fielded here. The group's broad coverage has ensured familiarity with a range of issues including negotiations with the Department of Defense, the Department of Energy and NASA, as well as bid protest proceedings before the

GAO and the US Federal Claims Court. Its clients include Lockheed Martin, BAE SYSTEMS and a host of technology vendors and pharmaceutical companies. Other areas of practice include the healthcare sector and the federal requirements surrounding Medicare and Medicaid. The group recently advised Lockheed Martin in its successful challenge to the award of an Army contract relating to mortar munitions.

The Lawyers: **Marcia Madsen** (see p.93) wins sustained plaudits for her *"sound judgment and responsible advice."* One of the leading figures nationally, she is best known for her effective handling of bid protests and her work on homeland security issues. She successfully represented Data Enterprises in a breach of contract claim arguing that the Navy had wrongfully disclosed proprietary software documentation to a rival company.

Band 4

Miller & Chevalier Chartered
The Firm: *"Historically a player on the scene,"* this firm has a long track record of representing some of the USA's leading aerospace and defense companies, as well as IT firms and healthcare businesses. The group is well versed in fraud investigations conducted by the government including Qui Tam claims, bid protests and performance and suspension issues. Among recent highlights, the group has litigated a $350 million claim concerning the launch of communications satellites on the space shuttle in proceedings before the US Federal Claims Court.

Sheppard, Mullin, Richter & Hampton LLP
The Firm: This practice spans both sides of the country, with about ten attorneys on the East Coast working alongside a group of 26 on the West Coast. In what is a constantly evolving market, these attorneys win plaudits for their *"flexibility and desire to grow the practice."* Their approach is *"always realistic and technically sound,"* and clients particularly value the group's skills in handling MAS contracts. Much of its caseload relates to bid challenges before the GAO and the US Federal Claims Court, often relating to matters arising out of the aerospace and technology sector. Attorneys also advise on procurement ethics and handle dispute resolution.

The Lawyers: **John Chierichella** has been a *"leading player in this area for an age,"* agreed sources. His recent caseload has included advice to Northrop Grumman in a bid protest over a contract to create an automated travel management system for the Department of Defense.

Thelen Reid & Priest LLP
See firm details p.300

The Firm: The breadth of the firm's experience

has impressed sources, as has its expertise in related construction matters. A discrete group of government contract attorneys can also draw upon the firm's respected construction specialists, government affairs attorneys and general commercial litigators. Among the group's recent workload is the representation of contractors in protesting the Army's decision to retain services and logistical functions in-house. The firm was successful on behalf of its client following cost appeal proceedings and a protest to the GAO, and further defended it against subsequent challenges to its contract agreements. Alongside its

bid protest work, the team also advises on contract negotiations and performance issues, pricing, ethics and fraud claims.
The Lawyers: Stuart Nibley is the key contact in the dedicated government contracts group.

Vinson & Elkins LLP
See firm details p.1724
The Firm: The government and international procurement practice of this global law firm remains best known for its ability to handle complex litigation before the federal agencies. According to clients, its attorneys are able to

"*present their advice in a way that's clearly understandable to the layman,*" and they adopt a proactive approach to contract negotiations. Alongside a steady diet of bid challenges and performance-related litigation, the team also counsels clients on privatization issues and related corporate transactions.
The Lawyers: Clients commended **Michael Charness** (see p.78) for his responsive service and technical expertise. He "*always goes the extra mile to meet deadlines*" and has a practical understanding of possible courses of action and their consequences.

HEALTHCARE

<table>
<tr><td colspan="2">**National**</td></tr>
<tr><td colspan="2">Leading firms (Healthcare)</td></tr>
<tr><td>1</td><td>BAKER, DONELSON, BEARMAN</td></tr>
<tr><td></td><td>DAVIS WRIGHT TREMAINE LLP</td></tr>
<tr><td></td><td>EPSTEIN BECKER & GREEN PC</td></tr>
<tr><td></td><td>FOLEY & LARDNER</td></tr>
<tr><td></td><td>FULBRIGHT & JAWORSKI LLP</td></tr>
<tr><td></td><td>GARDNER CARTON & DOUGLAS LLP</td></tr>
<tr><td></td><td>HALL, RENDER, KILLIAN, HEATH</td></tr>
<tr><td></td><td>HOGAN & HARTSON LLP</td></tr>
<tr><td></td><td>HOOPER LUNDY & BOOKMAN INC</td></tr>
<tr><td></td><td>JONES DAY</td></tr>
<tr><td></td><td>LATHAM & WATKINS LLP</td></tr>
<tr><td></td><td>MCDERMOTT WILL & EMERY</td></tr>
<tr><td></td><td>OBER KALER GRIMES & SHRIVER</td></tr>
<tr><td></td><td>REED SMITH LLP</td></tr>
<tr><td></td><td>ROPES & GRAY LLP</td></tr>
<tr><td></td><td>SONNENSCHEIN NATH & ROSENTHAL</td></tr>
<tr><td></td><td>VINSON & ELKINS LLP</td></tr>
<tr><td colspan="2">Firms are listed alphabetically in each band.</td></tr>
</table>

Band 1

Baker, Donelson, Bearman, Caldwell & Berkowitz, PC
See firm details p.1613
The Firm: The opening of an outpost in New Orleans means this firm now has ten offices devoted to healthcare. Inevitably, these branches have their own individual slant. The DC office, for example, tackles a good deal of public policy work, while its sister in Nashville is more transactional in tone. But between them they cover the full spectrum of healthcare work. All corporate, regulatory and litigation needs are met for an impressive client base that can rely on a set of attorneys who form "*a vital regional and increasingly national presence.*" The team includes Dick Cowart, "*a major deal-maker with strong ties to the present political administration.*" A former president of the American Health Lawyers Association, he has now been joined by Donna Fraische, the first woman ever to occupy that role. She is fully expected to add luster to a

practice already involved in the largest matters. These include acting on the sale of the National Nephrology Association to the Renal Care Group, and separately representing King Pharmaceuticals on Office of Inspector General and SEC investigations. It also worked on a large IPO for Medical Properties Trust worth $233 million.
The Clients: Adventist Health System; Cardiology Associates; Franciscan Missionaries of Our Lady Health System; Renal Care Group; National Nephrology and University Health Systems.

Davis Wright Tremaine LLP
See firm details p.1796
The Firm: Satisfied customers from every corner of the market spoke of a firm whose "*reading of a situation is second to none. Nothing is allowed to fall through the cracks.*" Their delight springs from access to a team with real strength across the board. Clients are able to call upon a team strong in regulatory, reimbursement, corporate organization, compliance programs and medical staffing issues. Though medical malpractice suits do not figure, elsewhere, scarcely an area of the market is neglected. The practice itself is heavily into the technical side of affairs but has achieved diversity through some shrewd lateral hires and strategic moves over the years. One of the most recent recruits is Kathleen Drummy – a regulatory, transactional and litigation expert now installed in the California office. Her arrival marks more good news for a firm that is already happily hosting Bob Homchick, "*a lawyer of considerable enterprise*" best known for his fraud and abuse expertise.

Epstein Becker & Green PC
The Firm: Epstein Becker succeeds in servicing a full range of organizations that form part of the expanding US healthcare system. Relying on lawyers who cross every specialty, it tackles all regulatory, corporate, tax exemption and litigation matters including employment issues. Its

team operates from a network of eight offices although more than half its members are stationed in the flagship DC office. It was from here in the 1970's that the practice rose from humble beginnings to form the hundred plus taskforce that is in existence today. One of the architects of it all, Steve Epstein, is still in situ and continues to enjoy the respect of his peers. An attorney who "*has cast an eye on the unfurling tapestry of healthcare law for three decades,*" he is credited with nurturing a team of some distinction. Perhaps the most famous among this group is Doug Hastings, a transactional expert who "*sits at the very top table of healthcare lawyers nationwide.*" He stands as an invaluable part of a team whose particular knowledge of reimbursement was vividly illustrated in its involvement in Baystate Medical Center v Thompson, a case that affected 600 Medicare hospitals.

Foley & Lardner
See firm details p.1828
The Firm: With the absorption of Epstein, Becker & Green's Boston office earlier this year, Foley & Lardner sent out another stark reminder to its rivals of its continuing robustness. Aside from adding another cadre of talented attorneys to its already swelling ranks, this move has now afforded the firm a presence in all five of the major US lifescience markets: Boston, DC, Silicon Valley, San Diego and Madison. This presents further living proof of Foley's position in the top flight of health law nationally. Its team is one of the largest in the market with tentacles in all areas of the discipline. Medicare reimbursement, where it first came to prominence, remains a central part of the practice, but its hospital work generally is also commanding attention. "*Comfortable in everything it handles,*" the group led by George Root particularly shines in the nonprofit sphere and wins approval for its "*long reach and dedication to service.*"
The Clients: The firm's clients include hospitals, physician groups, managed care institutions and outpatient centers.

Fulbright & Jaworski LLP

See firm details p.1715

The Firm: The six attorneys on board at the birth of this firm's dedicated healthcare practice in the late 1970s can look on the development of the practice with glowing pride. Then, the idea of a specialist group was a relatively radical notion. Now, not only have other firms followed their model but the Fulbright team itself has gone from strength to strength. At present the team comprises over 80 attorneys spread across various offices and can be justly said to have transcended its regional roots to occupy a berth on the national scene. Bursting with vibrancy across the board, it has tangible transactional, regulatory and litigation capability as well as a taste for professional liability and medical malpractice suits. Jerry Bell directs operations from the Houston office, presiding over a group that recently represented Ilex Oncology in its sale to Genzyme. The group also acted for the University of Texas System in its acquisition of Zale Lipshy Hospital in Dallas.

The Clients: The firm's clients range from multihospital systems, healthcare finance authorities, universities and trade associations to nurses and individual physicians.

Gardner Carton & Douglas LLP

See firm details p.767

The Firm: Over its 90-year history in the healthcare sector, Gardner Carton & Douglas has stood firm as *"a byword for excellence."* Inevitably, it has experienced its vicissitudes, the most recent of which was the loss of some of its team members to great rival McDermott Will & Emery. These are but minor blips though in an unbroken record of service few can match. The operation represents huge swathes of hospitals and all other sectors of the industry. Its main platform is to be found in Chicago, where the legendary Ed Bryant continues to practice. But its pioneering spirit has taken it much further afield to places such as DC, where it impresses as one of the finest in the nation's capital. Prominent among its full complement of work is a solid showing in fraud and abuse, reimbursement and nonprofit work with the efforts of TJ Sullivan on the tax front being especially well received. Beyond this the firm's transactional skills are self evident and were recently showcased when it represented Jewish Hospital in its functional merger with Barnes Hospital. In other notable matters it has served as transaction counsel in the combination of Providence Seattle Medical Center with Swedish Health Services.

The Clients: Its client base comprises academic medical centers, foundations, hospital systems, long-term care providers, managed care organizations, medical schools, pharmaceuticals, physician groups and hospitals.

Hall, Render, Killian, Heath & Lyman Professional Services Corporation

The Firm: Perhaps not the first name on everybody's lips when it comes to leading healthcare practices, this firm's counsel is nonetheless *"always worth seeking out."* Its 50 lawyers act both regionally and nationally, mainly in antitrust, fraud and abuse, M&A and tax; reimbursement and regulatory compliance also play a significant role in the firm's portfolio. The vast majority of this work is undertaken for healthcare providers although some lobbying work is handled for pharmaceutical companies. Interviewees backed a practice that, while not up with the market leaders in terms of size and reach, is still *"a significant healthcare boutique not to be sniffed at."* William Thompson is the main contact at the firm, which boasts a clientele that mainly includes providers such as Ascension Health, Michigan Hospital Association and the Indiana Health & Hospital Association.

Hogan & Hartson LLP

See firm details p.484

The Firm: Hogan & Hartson is *"one of the true big daddies in healthcare law"* offering blanket coverage of the sector. All angles are tackled from business and finance matters to litigation and IP issues, but it scores highest on the regulatory front working at the interface between government and business. Here, its attorneys, many of whom have served in government, are expertly prepared to assist the firm's glut of clients in all federal regulation and legislative issues. Fraud and abuse, and reimbursement questions form a particularly fertile seam of work. For example, the Fred Hutchinson Cancer Research Center has placed its faith in the group for some time and recently hired it in the bone marrow clinical trials litigation. Transactionally the firm is no slouch either, and it has advised the City of Minneapolis on the spin-off of Hennepin County Medical Center into a separate public benefit corporation. With such vibrancy in so many different areas, it will come as no surprise that the team, under the stewardship of Ann Morgan Vickery, is looking beyond the horizon of the USA and increasingly participating in matters on an international scale. Europe and the rest of the world are finding out what the USA already knows: *"Hogan & Hartson has what it takes in the competitive world of health law."* Academic health centers, ambulance services, biotech companies, hospitals, pharmaceutical manufacturers and physician groups are just some of the clients on its prestigious roster.

Hooper Lundy & Bookman Inc

The Firm: Hooper Lundy is a true boutique that believes specialization is the key to this most convoluted and fluctuating of practice areas. About 40 lawyers devote themselves exclusively to the cause, providing a service that one client described as *"intimate and reassuringly so."* The firm is yet to make the impact on the larger scene of some of its more exalted rivals, but is commended for its efforts and is home to the eminent John Hellow. Hellow is an expert in Medicare/Medicaid reimbursement matters, an area in which the firm as a whole flourishes. In this context it is respected as an effective force that has represented 1,300 hospitals in the national 'outlier' Medicare appeal, having participated in such cases as Alhambra Hospital v Thompson. The rest of the practice is wide enough to take in all areas including transactions, litigation, managed care, and fraud and abuse. The team acts in the main for health providers but takes in some pharmaceutical clients.

Jones Day

See firm details p.485

The Firm: Jones Day's 70 attorneys nationwide may not be formed into a department as others are, but they nevertheless provide a cohesive force in the market. *"Sophisticated operators – beyond improvement,"* one client said – they truly straddle the market from state to state, inching their way into every nook and cranny of healthcare law. Interviewees were as one in suggesting that their best work is done on the transactional side. Deals such as the firm's representation of Caremark Rx in its $6 billion acquisition of AdvancePCS highlight its profile; its work on a variety of mergers and takeovers for Bon Secours Health System also underlines the suggestion. However, all avenues are trod from fraud and abuse to tax and antitrust matters. The team's work on behalf of MedStar Health involves corporate, regulatory and antitrust matters. Ross Stromberg is at the helm of a team that also made noteworthy appearances on behalf of MedStar and University Hospitals of Cleveland in the Jung v AAMC National Residency Match Program litigation.

The Clients: Clients include healthcare providers, banks, insurance companies and technical companies who service the health industry.

Latham & Watkins LLP

The Firm: A practice both *"excellent in terms of quality and wide in scope,"* it has the resources to throw at any problem however complex or substantial. Some 50 specialists are on hand at any time as well as another 100 attorneys who can turn their hands to this type of work in the context of their broader practices. With such riches, it is not surprising that most of the major bases are covered, with medical malpractice suits being the only notable omission from the firm's caseload. Amid this welter of work the team impresses most readily on transactional and litigation matters. It has represented The Carlyle

30   All quotes in the text are from interviews with clients and competitors.

CHAMBERS USA 2005

Group on major healthcare transactions for several years, most recently advising on the sale of Empi, a medical device manufacturer, to Encore Medical. It also represented Renovis in its $75.9 million IPO. Its litigation triumphs include advising Tenet Healthcare in a series of investigations brought by the DOJ. Acting for TAP Pharmaceutical Products, it marshaled a dispute with the government over whether the company conspired with doctors to bill government insurers for free samples of the company's prostate cancer drug Lupron. Though less conspicuous, the team also offers some DC regulatory capability. Roger Goldman, Stuart Kurlander and Daniel Settelmayer are global cochairs of the group. The firm has represented hospitals, pharmaceutical and biotech companies, medical devices manufacturers, physician organizations, hospices and healthcare trade associations.

McDermott Will & Emery
See firm details p.773
The Firm: In an era of frantic competition McDermott Will & Emery is still the one by which others are judged. In terms of breadth of scope and size of resources, it is difficult to look beyond a firm whose skills have been crafted over a period of 50 years in the market. The firm is, in fact, something of a rarity in that it has consolidated itself into a discrete health department comprising at least 100 specialist lawyers. These are spread across its Boston, Chicago, Los Angeles, Miami, New York and DC offices, each of which has its own character but contributes to an excellent whole. From these locations the team is able to offer advice on every aspect of the market, bar medical malpractice, thus affording the client *the confidence of knowing his every difficulty can be addressed.* Distinct amongst the team's attributes is its flair in transactional, regulatory and qui tam cases defending against whistle-blowers. In these contexts, observers say, the firm is *capable of trading punch for punch with any pretenders to its throne.* Examples of the firm's recent work include representing Tenet Healthcare on the disposition of 27 hospitals and separately advising Hillcrest on the disposal of ten of its Oklahoma hospitals to Ardent Health Services. The team, led by Monte Dube, also features transactional expert Mike Anthony and reimbursement guru Tim Blanchard. A strong litigation arm is illustrated by its defense of over 800 class actions in the Fen-Phen diet drug litigation. The team has an exceptionally wide client base comprising providers, payers, insurers and manufacturers.

Ober Kaler Grimes & Shriver
The Firm: The nerve center of this midsized healthcare practice is to be found in Baltimore. Here, three quarters of the available team tackles a general caseload, further benefiting from a DC

office strong on antitrust, white-collar and tax issues. The practice dates back to the 1970's when Leonard Homer started out representing academic hospitals, health systems and physician organizations. Much has changed since then: the firm remains provider-based, but also counsels pharmaceutical companies and trade organizations. In the midst of a broad practice it stands out *as good as anyone in the field,* particularly in reimbursement proceedings. This is due in great part to the presence of a bevy of attorneys who have had experience in government. Foremost among these is Sanford Teplitsky, an alumnus of the Office of General Counsel of the Department of Health, Education and Welfare. He is pitched as *one of the most accessible and adept practitioners in the country.* A performer who *knows everything there is to know about Medicare and Medicaid issues,* he is part of a team that enjoys a place in the front rank of leading healthcare firms. Cases of note include the defense of 40 major hospitals in a suit alleging improper billing of the Medicare program in relation to investigative devices. The team represents health systems, academic and community hospitals, physician organizations and other providers. Pharmacy and biotech firms also feature in the client base.

Reed Smith LLP
See firm details p.1560
The Firm: Up to 40 attorneys staff a fine practice with aggressive expansionist ambitions. The firm has a 30-year history in this field, leading the charge mainly from a DC office that is highly regarded for its reimbursement practice. Nowadays, while DC remains the hub, it is taking its message across the country, winning converts as it goes. The emphasis is on the pharmaceutical side, with the firm representing nine out of the top ten pharmaceutical giants and 50 of the world's leading drug and device manufacturers. However, all areas are delved into and transactional work is well catered for. By way of illustration, Eugene Tillman led a team of 20 lawyers representing AdvancePCS in its $6 billion sale to a leading prescription benefits manager. Another eventful year has seen the group, which also includes Elizabeth Carder-Thompson, act for 120 hospitals seeking to reopen Medicare reimbursement decisions dating back at least a decade. The firm represents clients from across the spectrum of health law including GlaxoSmithKline, Inspire Pharmaceuticals and Bristol-Myers Squibb.

Ropes & Gray LLP
See firm details p.985
The Firm: This *exceptionally strong New England firm* has, over three decades, exported its expertise out of its traditional stronghold and into the national consciousness. People still immediately associate it with its powerhouse

Boston office but acknowledge the spread of its influence across America, citing it as *one to watch.* Its increasingly busy team, headed up by Michele Garvin, is diverse in its approach but is most heartily endorsed for its regulatory skills, advising on research trials and work with academic medical centers. A strong litigation bent is evidenced by its recent representation of 50 Massachusetts hospitals in the defense of a class action involving hospital medical records. It also engaged in groundbreaking policy litigation regarding a patient's right to refuse treatment under Massachusetts law.
The Clients: Its clients have included hospitals, pharmaceutical companies, managed care organizations, physician groups and academic medical centers.

Sonnenschein Nath & Rosenthal LLP
See firm details p.779
The Firm: Many of the established players have nervously been peering over their shoulders as Sonnenschein has come up on the rails. Of all the firms seeking to gain a greater share of the multitrillion-dollar healthcare market, it has probably made up the most ground through a policy of shrewd expansion. With no helter-skelter approach, the firm has made incremental gains and can now look with satisfaction on a practice with a definite national reach. Seven out of its nine offices play host to healthcare attorneys who as a team cover financing, reimbursement, compliance, M&A, antitrust and managed care issues. But it is the practice's fraud and abuse profile that is featured in the shop window due to the presence of Mac Thornton, former Chief Counsel to the Inspector General of the HHS. He is a definite drawing card to some of the big names in the business, and has helped to buttress an already impressive client base. This includes the likes of Pharmacy Care Alliance and Tenet Healthcare, which the firm acts as primary compliance counsel.
The Clients: Other clients include healthcare systems, academic medical centers, hospitals, physician groups, hospices and many other healthcare providers.

Vinson & Elkins LLP
See firm details p.1724
The Firm: More than 80 lawyers are available to assist a glittering client base of healthcare providers. The team, universally touted as *one of the unquestionable industry leaders,* has a distinguished pedigree dating back to the 1960s. It was then that *grandfather of the healthcare Bar* Jon David Epstein began a practice that he continues to oversee. In that time, he and others of his ilk have laid the foundation of a team noted for its *astoundingly good nuts to soup service.* Operating chiefly from the firm's headquarters in Houston but with attorneys liberally sprinkled in offices nationwide, the group takes

versatility as its watchword. "*If you want straightforward answers to difficult questions this is the place to go,*" clients said. All angles are covered but critics reserve special praise for its strong regulatory practice and reimbursement prowess. In this regard it can rely on Dennis Barry, a regulatory expert who works from the DC office. Countless hospitals and health systems have looked to him and his colleagues for proper reimbursement of their Medicare payments, and the firm gets involved in some significant litigation as a result. Only recently the team's appearance in Baystate Medical Center v Thompson attested to this fact. Clients spoke with discernible affection of attorneys who "*are very professional in getting to the heart of an issue but who lace their work with humor and good cheer.*" A host of healthcare providers turn to the firm for assistance. These include academic medical centers, physician groups and hospitals. The firm has also recently been appointed interim general counsel of the Parkland Health and Hospital System in Dallas.

INTERNATIONAL ARBITRATION

National
Leading firms
(International Arbitration)
[1] DEBEVOISE & PLIMPTON LLP
WHITE & CASE LLP
[2] COVINGTON & BURLING
HUGHES HUBBARD & REED LLP
SHEARMAN & STERLING LLP
SIDLEY AUSTIN BROWN
SIMPSON THACHER & BARTLETT LLP
SKADDEN, ARPS, SLATE, MEAGHER
SULLIVAN & CROMWELL LLP
[3] BAKER & MCKENZIE
BOIES, SCHILLER & FLEXNER
CLEARY GOTTLIEB STEEN & HAMILTON
CLIFFORD CHANCE US LLP
FRESHFIELDS BRUCKHAUS DERINGER
FULBRIGHT & JAWORSKI LLP
KING & SPALDING LLP
VINSON & ELKINS LLP
WINSTON & STRAWN
[4] ASTIGARRAGA DAVIS
GREENBERG TRAURIG LLP
HOGAN & HARTSON LLP
HOLLAND & KNIGHT LLP
KIRKLAND & ELLIS LLP
MAYER, BROWN, ROWE & MAW LLP
MORGAN, LEWIS & BOCKIUS LLP
O'MELVENY & MYERS LLP
WEIL, GOTSHAL & MANGES LLP
WILMER CUTLER PICKERING HALE
Firms are listed alphabetically in each band.

Band 1

Debevoise & Plimpton LLP

See firm details p.1346

The Firm: Lawyers and clients alike from both sides of the Atlantic discerned this firm to be "*a towering presence*" in the field. Its New York office is perceived as the firm's international arbitration powerhouse. The team here is "*outstanding in every sense, from overall strategy to the nuts and bolts of a case.*" The workload involves bilateral investment treaties and sovereign debt; power and energy disputes; construction and engineering; insurance and reinsurance; political risk issues and IP. The team is further distinguished by an increasing emphasis on public international law. Interviewees indicated that Barton Legum rejoining the firm's Paris office would strengthen the firm's already formidable global profile due to his experience gained as the first chief of the NAFTA Arbitration Division at the US Department of State. Other recent developments include the increased insurance arbitration resources in London, as well as supporting practice groups in Moscow and Hong Kong. The team's involvement in bilateral investment treaty-related international arbitration has led to some of the largest awards obtained from sovereigns, including approximately $370 million for Central European Media Enterprises and $75 million for Occidental Petroleum. Further highlights include successfully representing Autopista Concesiondada de Venezuela ('Aucoven') in an ICSID arbitration against the Republic of Venezuela over the breach of a concession agreement for a toll road in Venezuela.

The Lawyers: When interviewees considered the combined talents of **Donald Donovan** (see p.81) and **David Rivkin** (see p.101) they typically commented that the team constituted a "*step up from almost any other.*" Donovan was cast as a "*visionary and aggressive strategist*" while Rivkin came in for praise as a "*brilliant technician.*" Both are considered major authorities in their field.

White & Case LLP

See firm details p.1379

The Firm: According to commentators, no other practice could claim to be "*quite so thoroughly international.*" As a firm it combines worldwide coverage superior to almost any other US operation with a powerful contingent in Washington DC and a thriving New York practice. Other domestic offices involved include those in California and Florida. Equally impressive credentials, both in terms of counsel and arbitrators, give the practice an extra edge in the market place. ICSID cases are a particularly strong specialty, while copious ICC and AAA experience is also clearly in evidence. Such deeply rooted expertise guarantees the firm an undisputed top-flight presence even after the departure of Ronald Goodman to Winston & Strawn. Around 80 practitioners work in the field throughout the USA, Europe and Asia. Outside of the USA, London, Stockholm, Moscow and Hong Kong are the principal offices involved.

The Lawyers: The "*superb leadership qualities*" of **Carolyn Lamm** (see p.92) "*inspire great confidence and achieve great results.*" **Abby Cohen Smutny** (see p.105) was described as "*already a brilliant and wise lawyer.*" These are the stars of the firm's DC practice, which revolves around ICSID and investor-state disputes. Based in New York, co-head of international arbitration **Paul Friedland** (see p.84) continues to impress. Under his auspices the office concentrates on construction, oil and gas, and power sector disputes that often relate to Latin America and East Asia. Cases are generally manned by a mostly non-US set of lawyers, giving the team a heightened awareness of the cultural sensitivities that arise in international business. As for arbitrators, special counsel **Charles Brower** (see p.77) is considered among the very best US arbitrators in the ICSID arena. Given the rich blend of Brower's public and private law experience, he is uniquely qualified to preside over such disputes and as a result they form a central strand in his practice. Brower is also a member of the London chambers, 20 Essex Street and a regular judge on the Iran-United States Claims Tribunal in The Hague. According to sources, **Horacio Grigera Naón** possesses a "*tremendous range of knowledge,*" which he applies via a "*great manner*" whether as chair or as party-appointed arbitrator. His Argentinean background makes him particularly well suited to handling Latin American disputes. However the scope of his experience is immense, with his previous positions including senior counsel to the IFC and secretary general of the International Court of Arbitration of the ICC in Paris.

National
Leading individuals
International Arbitration

1 CARTER James *Sullivan & Cromwell*, New York
DONOVAN Donald *Debevoise & Plimpton*, New York
REED Lucy *Freshfields Bruckhaus*, New York
RIVKIN David *Debevoise & Plimpton*, New York
TOWNSEND John *Hughes Hubbard*, Washington, DC

2 ASTIGARRAGA José *Astigarraga Davis*, Miami
BISHOP Doak *King & Spalding*, Houston
FREYER Dana *Skadden Arps*, New York
GARFINKEL Barry *Skadden Arps*, New York
KERR John *Simpson Thacher*, New York
LAMM Carolyn *White & Case*, Washington, DC
PRICE Daniel *Sidley Austin*, Washington, DC
SCHILLER Jonathan *Boies Schiller*, Washington, DC
SHEPPARD Ben *Vinson & Elkins*, Houston
SMIT Robert *Simpson Thacher*, New York
SMUTNY Abby Cohen *White & Case*, Washington, DC
WEISBURG Henry *Shearman & Sterling*, New York

3 ALEXANDROV Stanimir *Sidley Austin*, Washington, DC
BAKER Mark *Fulbright & Jaworski*, Houston
BOWMAN John *Fulbright & Jaworski*, Houston
DAVIS Fred *Shearman & Sterling*, New York
FRIEDLAND Paul *White & Case*, New York
FRIEDMAN Lawrence *Cleary Gottlieb*, New York
GARIBALDI Oscar *Covington & Burling*, Washington, DC
GOODMAN Ronald *Winston & Strawn*, Washington, DC
GULLAND Eugene *Covington & Burling*, Washington, DC
HORNICK Robert *Morgan Lewis*, New York
LINDSEY David *Clifford Chance*, New York
LOFTIS James *Vinson & Elkins*, Houston
NEUHAUS Joseph *Sullivan & Cromwell*, New York
NEWMAN Lawrence *Baker & McKenzie*, New York
ROVINE Arthur *Baker & McKenzie*, New York

4 DAVIS Platt *Vinson & Elkins*, Houston
FELLAS John *Hughes Hubbard*, New York
GARDINER John *Skadden Arps*, New York
GONZALEZ Daniel *Hogan & Hartson*, Miami
HAMMOND Steven *Hughes Hubbard*, New York
ISAACSON William *Boies Schiller*, Washington, DC
JOHNSON Jr O Thomas *Covington*, Washington, DC
KIMMELMAN Louis *O'Melveny & Myers*, New York
MARTINEZ-FRAGA Pedro *Greenberg Traurig*, Miami
ORDWAY Eric *Weil Gotshal*, New York
POLEBAUM Elliot E *Fried Frank*, Washington, DC
RODRIGUEZ Wilfredo A *Holland & Knight*, Miami
RUBINSTEIN Javier H *Mayer Brown*, Chicago
SCHNABL Marco E *Skadden Arps*, New York
WEINER Daniel H *Hughes Hubbard*, New York

Up-and-coming individuals
DI ROSA Paolo *Winston & Strawn*, Washington, DC
PIERCE John *Wilmer Cutler*, New York
RUSSELL William *King & Spalding*, Houston

Individuals are listed alphabetically in each band.

Band 2

Covington & Burling
See firm details p.481

The Firm: Such is the extent of the firm's resources that it is "*always a likely candidate for*

instructions*," acknowledged clients. "*Brilliant performances*" and "*spectacular results*" have won this international arbitration practice admirers globally. The team handles both private and public international law issues making it well positioned to handle an increasing volume of ICSID instructions. Heavy involvement in insurance sector matters gives it a natural advantage in related international arbitration, especially when it comes to representing Fortune 100 companies in large claims against insurers. An increasing diet of litigation surrounding questions of arbitrability and enforcement of awards further contributes to the workload. Washington DC and London are the principal offices involved.

The Lawyers: Few lawyers make for "*tougher or more pleasant opposition*" than **Eugene Gulland** (see p.86), the firm's most established practitioner in the field. He is experienced in AAA, LCIA, ICC, ICSID and UNCITRAL matters. Born in Argentina, **Oscar Garibaldi** (see p.85) enters the table having established an envied Latin American practice. His investor-state disputes prowess has been rewarded with an appointment by the United States to ICSID's Panel of Conciliators. Both attorneys are based in DC. The duo represented Malaysia-based MTD Equity in an ICSID dispute with the Republic of Chile relating to a Chilean real estate development project. Gulland also represented Telkom, the principal South African telecom company, in successfully blocking enforcement of an ICC arbitration award. **Thomas Johnson** (see p.89) is best known for his involvement in international boundary disputes but is also heavily involved in international arbitration relating to foreign investment. He led advice to a multinational group of institutional investors in an ICC arbitration concerning the management of a company that built and operated power plants throughout Asia. The case included parallel shareholder derivative litigation in New York's state court. The firm's active clients also include: Bacardi; Cardinal Health; ExxonMobil; Kingdom of Jordan; LG&E Energy; Owens Corning and State of Eritrea.

Hughes Hubbard & Reed LLP
See firm details p.1353

The Firm: This firm continues to enjoy a rising profile in the field: its Washington DC and Paris offices are traditionally considered the firm's strongest, while the New York-based contingent develops at a pace. Observers noted an increasingly integrated operation with Los Angeles and Miami offices also becoming involved as required. The firm is well equipped to deal with proceedings under the rules of most leading institutions worldwide.

The Lawyers: Chair of arbitration and alternative dispute resolution, **John Townsend** (see p.106) remains by far the best-known practi-

tioner at the firm and is deemed critical to its success in international arbitration. He is "*just a master,*" who "*understands international ADR better than any other in the market*" and anchors the team in DC. Townsend is involved in international arbitration at a policy level in addition to acting as counsel and arbitrator. He assisted ALSTOM Power with an appeal to the First Circuit Court of Appeals against an order of a federal judge denying an order to compel arbitration of a claim brought against ALSTOM by InterGen. Three New York-based practitioners join the table in this edition. Sources credited **John Fellas** (see p.83) with an increasingly high profile in the field. He represented MacGregor (FIN) Oy as respondent in an appeal to the Texas Supreme Court by Kellogg, Brown & Root against a Texas Court of Appeals decision compelling KBR to arbitrate a cruise ship elevator construction dispute with MacGregor. This will determine the extent to which a subcontractor can be compelled to arbitrate a dispute with a top-level contractor where top-level and second-level contractors are parties to an ICC arbitration agreement, but the subcontractor is not. Former president of the Union Internationale des Avocats, **Steven Hammond** (see p.86) was identified as growing in stature both as counsel and arbitrator in ICC, AAA and ad hoc matters. He is experienced in procedures conducted in English, French and Spanish. **Daniel Weiner** (see p.107) also won recognition as a key player in both national and international arbitration. He won a $94 million arbitration award for Merck against a major European-based pharmaceutical company arising from a joint venture dispute. Weiner also represented a partnership of HBO, Disney and Sony in an ICC arbitration involving a dispute with a European cable and satellite television distributor.

Shearman & Sterling LLP
See firm details p.1369

The Firm: This "*absolutely first-rate team*" continues to rest easily among the upper echelons of the market. Clients paid testament to "*the level of detail it masters,*" making the firm "*among the top five nationally with which to go to war*" in any dispute, not least international arbitration. While Paris continues to be perceived as its true center of excellence, the firm's New York litigation team can boast a heavy-hitting duo backed up by considerable worldwide resources. International coverage incorporating offices in Abu Dhabi, Beijing, Frankfurt, London, Singapore and Washington DC makes for a force to be reckoned with. Oil and gas and construction remain core focus areas.

The Lawyers: **Henry Weisburg** (see p.107) possesses an "*electric intellect*" that enables him to deal with the most complex disputes. His involvement in multiple ad hoc international reinsurance arbitrations relating to Unicover is

National

Leading individuals

(International Arbitration: Arbitrators)

1 **AKSEN Gerald** *Sole Practitioner,* New York
  BERMANN George *Sole Practitioner,* New York
  BROWER Charles *White & Case,* Washington, DC
  CARON David *C. William Maxeiner,* Berkeley
  GRIGERA NAÓN Horacio *White & Case,* Washington, DC
  PARK William *Sole Practitioner,* Boston
  REISMAN W Michael *Sole Practitioner,* New Haven
  RENFREW Charles *Sole Practitioner,* San Francisco
  SCHWEBEL Judge Stephen *Sole Practitioner,* Washington, DC
  VON MEHREN Robert *Sole Practitioner,* New York

Individuals are listed alphabetically in each band.

a case in point. These involved US, Canadian and English parties, cross-border discovery issues and witnesses from several jurisdictions. Substantial ICSID and ICC matters have further contributed to Weisburg's workload. In addition to achieving excellence as a commercial litigator, **Fred Davis** (see p.1274) has made a name for himself through the representation of the likes of GE in international arbitration. He recently handled a series of ICC arbitrations arising from the Hamaca project in Venezuela.

Sidley Austin Brown & Wood LLP
See firm details p.778

The Firm: Clients are *"enormously pleased"* with the firm, discerning a *"superb knowledge of substantive legal issues, finely honed litigation skills and a keen sense of political strategy."* Add to this the *"seamless coordination among team members,"* and it is no surprise that clients branded its international trade and dispute resolution attorneys *"among the best external legal counsel, not only within the specific discipline of international arbitration, but overall."* One further key strength is a consistency of performance *"from lead counsel down to research assistants."* The government experience of lead attorneys was also remarked upon as a distinct advantage. While the department is DC-based a substantial proportion of matters undertaken have no US nexus. It can call on resources in numerous locations, from Los Angeles to Hong Kong. The firm is best known for ICSID and World Trade Organization (WTO) disputes. Additional experience is strongly in evidence for UNCITRAL, ICC, AAA, China International Economic and Trade Arbitration Commission (CIETAC), China Maritime Arbitration Commission (CMAC) and the London Maritime Arbitrators Association (LMAA). ICC highlights include advising ITOCHU Corporation in a dispute over $350 million worth of damages following a catastrophic fire at a steel mill in Northern California.

The Lawyers: Practice chair **Dan Price** (see p.99) was billed as *"truly world class."* Clients repeatedly praised his *"tremendous experience,*

intelligence and creativity." As one commentator noted: *"When governments know that you are represented by Dan, they pay attention."* Meanwhile, his *"unique breadth of international experience"* makes **Stanimir Alexandrov** (see p.74), former Vice Minister of Foreign Affairs of Bulgaria, the principal practitioner developing a profile in the field beyond Price. Their respective heads of state appointed the pair to the ICSID panel of arbitrators and conciliators. Price serves as chair of the US Department of State Advisory Committee on investment treaties and arbitration. Together they advised Vivendi Universal on an investor-state case involving a water services concession in Argentina, securing the fourth ever annulment decision in ICSID history. A further highlight for the duo was representing an Italian investor in a dispute relating to a $500 million long-term construction project in Pakistan.

The Clients: Other notable clients include Cargill International; Fireman's Fund/Allianz; Goldman Sachs; Government of Peru; Government of Turkey; ILJIN Corporation; Impregilo; LG Electronics and LG Life Sciences.

Simpson Thacher & Bartlett LLP
See firm details p.1370

The Firm: This remains *"a genuinely serious and committed firm in the field,"* agree observers. With an established track record of appearances in some of the largest international arbitrations to date, the practice continues to prosper. Members of the team have partaken in cases sited in Geneva, Paris, London, Amsterdam, Hong Kong, Buenos Aires, New York and Washington DC. The New York office is easily the firm's strongest in this area and the international arbitration practice is housed within a top-tier litigation outfit. A major highlight was successfully representing Andersen Consulting (now Accenture) in achieving an alimony-free divorce from the global Andersen organization. This included relieving it firstly of an obligation to pay hundreds of millions of dollars in transfer payments annually and secondly to make a multibillion-dollar liquidated damages payment upon leaving the organization. The process incorporated one of the largest ICC arbitrations ever filed, involving 140-member firm parties from 60 countries worldwide, over $14 billion in claims, and ancillary judicial proceedings in various national courts around the world. Other significant matters include ongoing representation of GE and Bechtel in two bilateral investment treaty arbitrations under UNCITRAL rules against the Government of India, seeking in excess of $6 billion for the expropriation of the Dabhol power project. Successful representations in international arbitration of DHL, relating to a dispute under a shareholders agreement, and of Ford, over high-level excess insurance claims against Bermuda insurers ACE and XL,

also contribute to the firm's profile.

The Lawyers: Observers praised **John Kerr** (see p.90) for his *"immovable focus on the matter in hand"* while **Robert Smit** (see p.104) is cast as *"utterly dependable."* Kerr is experienced in UNCITRAL, ICC, AAA, Netherlands Arbitration Institute (NAI) and ad hoc arbitrations while Smit is one of three US members of the ICC International Court of Arbitration.

Skadden, Arps, Slate, Meagher & Flom LLP & Affiliates
See firm details p.1372

The Firm: This continually expanding practice has attracted a multinational client base of considerable distinction that guarantees the firm an enviable workload. It acts both for and against non-US entities in a range of industry sectors, and its overwhelming corporate might is matched by the sophistication of its specialists. New York forms the hub of the operation while the firm's London office also fields internationally recognized leaders. Of its West Coast locations, Los Angeles was pointed to as the strongest with a particularly impressive track record in the oil sector. The team can also call at will on the resources of its worldwide network incorporating Beijing, Brussels, Frankfurt, Hong Kong, Moscow, Paris, Singapore, Sydney, Tokyo, Toronto and Vienna. Highlights include acting for CTF Hotel Holdings and Hotel Property Investments before the International Center for Dispute Resolution (ICDR) in New York. This concerned Marriott International's alleged breaches of contract and violations of fiduciary duty as agent for Hotel Property's 44 hotels in North America, Europe and Australia operating under the 'Renaissance' and 'Ramada' brands.

The Lawyers: The *"intellectually agile"* **Dana Freyer** (see p.84) *"commands instant recognition internationally."* The firm's foremost US-based practitioner in the field heads its arbitration and alternative dispute resolution groups as well as being heavily engaged in international arbitration. Various cutting-edge issues of jurisdiction together with enforcing an ICSID award in multiple states have occupied Freyer recently. Head of international litigation and arbitration **Barry Garfinkel** (see p.85) remains a popular choice internationally both as counsel and arbitrator. **John Gardiner** (see p.85) was identified as an emerging star of the practice. He has made an impact early in his career as an arbitrator with *"exactly the right searching and insightful questions that go to the heart of a case."* Gardiner is equally well received as counsel – he recently cooperated with the firm's London office, representing the respondent in ICC arbitration arising from a dispute over the value of certain businesses that Avis Group Holdings sold to BNP Paribas. **Marco Schnabl** (see p.103) sustains a wide-ranging international practice including specialized Latin American experience. He retains a profile in international arbitration having recently acted with Garfinkel in ICSID arbitration in Singapore. The duo represented a claimant seeking rescission of the contract under which CEMEX invested in cement facilities in Indonesia, with over $250 million at issue. Schnabl also acted with Freyer for a respondent in the ICDR under Mexican law concerning corporate governance rights and corporate control in a Mexican telecommunications company.

Sullivan & Cromwell LLP
See firm details p.1373

The Firm: Billed as an "*absolutely first-class practice,*" it has the expertise "*to make a critical difference to the outcome of a case.*" While the profile of the firm has its foundations in the outstanding practice of James Carter, interviewees agreed that the overall team has the broad experience to justify its high standing in the market. Joint ventures together with trade and investment issues provide this lean team with the majority of its international arbitration workload. The practice excels at every stage of consultation, from drafting mediation and arbitration clauses in commercial agreements to advising on business risks and representing clients in all forms of dispute resolution.

The Lawyers: James Carter (see p.78) continues to attract a greater part of the most effusive praise from lawyers and clients alike. A member of the AAA board of directors and of the LCIA, he is in constant demand whether as counsel or arbitrator. Although a considerable portion of his practice takes **Joseph Neuhaus** (see p.96) outside the field, numerous interviewees "*think the world of him.*" In one instance Neuhaus was described as "*just a dynamo.*" Carter and Neuhaus coordinate the firm's distinctly global international arbitration practice.

Band 3

Baker & McKenzie
See firm details p.761

The Firm: While the principal US offices involved are New York and Chicago, the firm can draw on the resources of over 200 lawyers in 38 countries globally. It is therefore well positioned to deal with cases in virtually any fora including major AAA, ICC, LCIA and UNCITRAL matters. Recent areas of focus include international arbitrations relating to power projects, finance and IP. The Chicago practice offers specialist expertise in international arbitration affecting German, Swiss and Austrian clients. Highlights for the team include advice to Petrobras in a major dispute with Kellogg, Brown & Root where the contract calls for UNCITRAL arbitration. The dispute relates to the engineering and construction of two floating production, storage and off-loading vessels.

The Lawyers: Long-standing leaders in the field **Lawrence Newman** (see p.1305) and **Arthur Rovine** (see p.101) continue to dominate as the figureheads of the practice and "*true senior statesmen in the field.*" Both are based in New York and increasingly practice as arbitrators. Newman is a founding partner of the office's litigation department and is considered highly influential in shaping its revered market profile. Rovine defended the Taiwan High Speed Rail Corporation (THSRC) in major ICC arbitration relating to a claim brought by Franco-German joint venture Eurotrain.

Boies, Schiller & Flexner
See firm details p.1337

The Firm: "*Would certainly use the firm again, no doubt about it*" was the verdict returned by clients, who appreciated the diligence and technical expertise provided by its attorneys. The practice centers on the firm's DC office. Members have experience in ICC, LCIA, UNCITRAL, ICSID, AAA, NASD and ad hoc arbitration. It has represented clients before tribunals in Paris, Geneva, London, Zurich and Hong Kong, not to mention throughout the USA. Indeed, given its considerable commercial litigation capabilities, the firm is well positioned to tackle parallel US actions in addition to its assured international arbitration touch. Highlights include winning an arbitration award in ICC arbitration vacating a $1.4 billion default judgment against Siemens Westinghouse obtained in Pakistan. It also won an LCIA award affirming the contractual rights of Lasmo and Khaleej Petroleum in arbitration against BP Amoco under a joint bidding agreement for a $7 billion oil field modernization project in north Kuwait. Further success was achieved in obtaining an arbitral award for YES Network, a regional sports network owned by Goldman Sachs, the New York Yankees and Providence Equity Partners, leading to a long-term carriage agreement with Cablevision increasing enterprise value by $1.5 billion for YES.

The Lawyers: Clients from both sides of the Atlantic admitted they "*couldn't have asked for any one better*" than **Jonathan Schiller** in major international arbitration matters. A member of the Milan Chamber of National and International Arbitration Club of Arbitrators, he is particularly admired for being a "*smooth operator in both American and European circles.*" The same clients pinpointed Schiller's "*rare and outstanding forensic skills*" together with his "*first-rate advocacy*" as accounting for some impressive victories. **William Isaacson** was also identified as being "*key to developing mightily effective lines of argument.*"

Cleary Gottlieb Steen & Hamilton
See firm details p.1342

The Firm: A stellar corporate profile puts the firm in line for a portion of major international arbitration in which it generally represents an element of its "*spectacular client base.*" According to observers, "*a number of exceedingly brilliant attorneys*" are able to "*handle such matters beautifully.*" The team has impressed with its high-profile appearances on behalf of foreign and domestic corporations, international bodies such as the Bank for International Settlements and financial institutions. Sources also acknowledged an extensive track record of representing foreign sovereigns. With an integrated worldwide partnership at its disposal, particularly strong suits are to be found in Paris, Brussels and Rome, alongside the New York and DC centers. ICC arbitration has been a particular focus of recent activity.

The Lawyers: **Lawrence Friedman** (see p.84) in New York sustains a wide-ranging disputes practice and "*makes an excellent ship's captain*" when it comes to managing large international arbitrations. With significant public international law expertise, Robert Greig in Paris was also mentioned as being a driving force for the firm in the area.

Clifford Chance US LLP
See firm details p.1343

The Firm: The New York office is perceived as an integral part of the firm's formidable international arbitration armory, whereby expertise is on hand to cover AAA, ICC, LCIA and UNCITRAL matters involving a range of industries, jurisdictions and laws. Energy sector matters have dominated the workload for the US team of late, though not exclusively. It acted for the subsidiary of a US-based fund manager in ICC arbitration in New York involving a claim against a former Argentine investment partner. New York-based attorneys also advised a European energy company in an ICC matter against a joint venture partner arising from a dispute over preemptive rights provisions relating to an oil and gas concession in Venezuela. The Madrid office is on hand to provide support in the event of proceedings being conducted in Spanish.

The Lawyers: Opposing counsel and arbitrators alike cast **David Lindsey** (see p.93) as "*the model of a gentleman.*" He is internationally renowned for involvement in procedures relating to Latin America. He acted for a major US energy company in ICSID arbitration stemming from claims against Argentina following the 2002 economic crisis, with approximately $600 million damages at stake. Lindsey also advised a European energy company with global operations on a dispute against other joint venture parties in an LNG project in Latin America under ICDR rules. Work in other continents involved Lindsey acting for a US multinational energy company in a dispute defending claims brought by a state-owned joint venture partner in an electricity distribution company in India. This has led to involvement in two related cases in the Indian Supreme Court.

Freshfields Bruckhaus Deringer LLP

The Firm: Excellence in the field is just as much in evidence in the firm's New York office as in the highly developed Paris, Frankfurt and London components of the practice. Specialist resources in a further ten offices worldwide can be called upon as necessary. Clients were generous in their commendation of the US team consisting of one partner and five associates, which is deemed to employ the "*culturally aware approach*" of the firm generally.

The Lawyers: New York head of international arbitration **Lucy Reed** (see p.100) was credited with "*tremendous intelligence and a great demeanor.*" She is in high demand both as counsel and arbitrator – she acts as one of five arbitrators on the Eritrea-Ethiopia Claims Commission. As one observer pointed out: "*Reed could leave Freshfields tomorrow and have more than a full plate of appointments as arbitrator.*" She represented CMS Gas Transmission in its $260 million dispute with the Government of Argentina over its stake in Argentine gas transportation company TGN. The outcome confirmed that a minority shareholder in a corporation can bring a claim under a bilateral investment treaty for losses incurred as a result of measures taken against the entity in which shares are held. Reed also acted for an Italian construction company in an ICC matter in Miami relating to a Venezuelan joint venture company. Further ICC highlights include acting for the respondent in a dispute arising out of the construction of a 700 km gas pipeline in Peru pursuant to an engineering, procurement and construction (EPC) contract. Other significant active clients serviced by the team include ArcLight Capital Partners, Sangemini and Gas Natural.

Fulbright & Jaworski LLP

See firm details p.1715

The Firm: Recognized as a national force, it is best known for energy sector international arbitration. While Houston continues to be perceived as the hub of the practice, New York is also an important office for the firm's practice. Meanwhile investment in expanding its expertise elsewhere has focused on London and DC, where Michael Collins QC acts as special legal consultant and the likes of Andres Rigo boast senior-level World Bank experience. Further resources can be employed as required whether located in the firm's other US offices, its second European office in Munich or the public international law expertise of its Hong Kong office. A premium is placed on the diversity of the firm's team, which incorporates ten nationalities and fluency in over a dozen languages. LCIA, ICC, AAA, ICSID, UNCITRAL and Inter-American Arbitration Commission procedures are all covered by the practice.

The Lawyers: Observers identified both **Mark Baker** (see p.1671) and **John Bowman** (see p.1673) as "*practitioners of genuine distinction*" whether acting in the capacity of counsel or arbitrator. Both devote the great majority of their time to the field. Baker is both co-head of the firm's 11-office international department and co-head with Bowman of its arbitration and alternative dispute resolution practice group. Admired for the "*vigor with which he sustains a vibrant practice,*" Baker's many recent appointments have included acting as arbitrator in an ICC intellectual property dispute between Mexican and Spanish parties. As counsel he represented a multinational energy company in UNCITRAL arbitration against the El Salvadorian governmental energy agency concerning long-term electric power purchase agreements. Meanwhile Bowman represented an oil terminal operator in ICC arbitration with a state oil company over expropriation of contract rights. He also acted for a European oil company in ICC arbitration over voting rights governing operations in Latin America.

King & Spalding LLP

See firm details p.635

The Firm: This compact team caught the attention of interviewees largely on the basis of its representation in international arbitration of a selection of the world's top energy players. Energy disputes, investment state disputes and Latin American projects form the three major strands in this respect. Beyond the concentration of specialist expertise in Houston the firm benefits from being able to call on the capacities of Atlanta, New York and London. Highlights include involvement in Azurix Corp v Argentina, featuring a $400 million claim in an ICSID arbitration under a bilateral investment treaty (BIT). In SBD v Turkey the team obtained a $28 million award in ICC arbitration concerning the power sector.

The Lawyers: Head of international arbitration **Doak Bishop** (see p.1672) has made a name for himself that "*rings real bells outside the USA,*" particularly when it comes to BIT and ICSID matters relating to Latin America. **William Russell** (see p.102) came in for praise as a "*junior but also extremely promising*" member of the team. He featured in the team led by Bishop assisting Texaco in obtaining an award of $71.2 million following AAA international rules arbitration involving a project in China.

Vinson & Elkins LLP

See firm details p.1724

The Firm: This was perceived as among the most expansive Houston-based offerings in the field, with a respected London arm in addition to its long established roots in Texas. Beyond this, the DC office also provides substantial input to the combined international arbitration and litigation operation. A distinct emphasis on the combination of energy and construction expertise helps to distinguish the practice further. A portion of general commercial international arbitration also contributes to its activity. Other offices with strategic significance for the firm's profile in the field are New York and Dallas on the domestic front while Dubai and Beijing provide further depth internationally. An increasingly strong public international law flavor to the firm's workload was also noted.

The Lawyers: **Ben Sheppard** (see p.1700) is the firm's foremost international arbitration practitioner as well as a seasoned litigator. Cochair of international dispute resolution **James Loftis** (see p.93) was credited with a "*powerful reputation*" especially when it comes to investor-state disputes. **Platt Davis** (see p.1676) also comes highly recommended for his ICC, AAA and UNCITRAL experience.

Winston & Strawn

See firm details p.780

The Firm: The firm enters the table upon supplementing already formidable disputes expertise with the recruitment of two high-profile specialists in the field who brought with them a substantial portion of international arbitration. Clients described the result in terms of a "*profoundly hard-working team*" that operates with "*diligence, focus and resourcefulness.*" Members of the firm fluent in Spanish make it well placed for the construction and energy sector cases concerning Latin America that have been the focus of much recent activity. The workload also relates to matters in Europe and the Far East. The DC-based outfit benefits from expertise stationed overseas, especially in Geneva.

The Lawyers: Principal partner **Ronald Goodman** (see p.86) is commended for his "*sense of leadership*" combined with a "*perfect knowledge of ICSID procedures.*" Clients recognize that this enables him to provide "*strategic advice par excellence, not to mention highly persuasive performances before tribunals.*" Goodman is also experienced in ICC, UNCITRAL and LCIA procedures. Partner **Paolo Di Rosa** (see p.81) is also recognized as integral to the team's success. Clients announced "*the birth of a new rising star*" in praise of "*a talent able rapidly to win the total confidence of witness and experts alike.*" Di Rosa is said to benefit from experience in both federal government and the private sector as well as from speaking English and Spanish fluently. The duo joined the firm from White & Case in 2004. Clients include both domestic and foreign corporations as well as sovereign entities.

36   All quotes in the text are from interviews with clients and competitors.

CHAMBERS USA 2005

Band 4

Astigarraga Davis

See firm details p.556

The Firm: This Miami-based, 16-lawyer litigation and arbitration boutique is a major force in Latin American disputes. AAA, ICC, IACAC, UNCITRAL and ICSID matters form the core of the international arbitration strand of the practice. Members of the firm are also heavily involved in litigation relating to international arbitration. It was often remarked that the firm has been instrumental in establishing Miami as a major international arbitration center.

The Lawyers: One interviewee described **José Astigarraga** (see p.75) as "*the patrician of international arbitration.*" Research indicates that this is particularly the case when it comes to Latin American matters. "*Always precise and polite in equal measure,*" Astigarraga is fluent in Spanish. He is experienced acting as both arbitrator and counsel and is a member of several arbitral institutions including the LCIA.

Greenberg Traurig LLP

See firm details p.564

The Firm: Interviewees recognized the fruits born of the firm's "*concerted effort to reach out into the international arbitration arena.*" Miami is considered the stronghold in its network of over 20 offices throughout the USA and Europe, including an Amsterdam arm with specialist expertise in the field. That the firm has significant resources for involvement in ICC, AAA and UNCITRAL matters was never in doubt.

The Lawyers: National cochair of international litigation and arbitration **Pedro Martinez-Fraga** (see p.94) is widely regarded as the firm's key player in the field. International arbitration constitutes an important strand of his wide-ranging disputes expertise. Martinez-Fraga is considered to offer a considerable depth of experience in matters relating to Latin America, not to mention the Spanish-speaking world in general. An ICC-approved arbitrator, the Miami-based practitioner is noted for acting as counsel in AAA and ICC arbitrations.

Hogan & Hartson LLP

See firm details p.484

The Firm: Clients praised the team's "*celerity in solving matters the moment they arose*" and emphasized its "*technical, commercial and legal rigorousness.*" The "*instant rapport*" it managed to establish with clients also impressed interviewees. Technology sector matters have kept members involved in the operation particularly busy. Centers of activity in the USA are New York, Washington DC and, with a strong Latin American orientation to its workload, Miami. Given that around half the firm's clients in the field are based outside the USA, its international network stretching throughout Europe and Asia was held to be a considerable boon. As a result, commentators sensed that lawyers alive to the cultural nuances of a given case were in plentiful supply. Advice to the likes of Mitsubishi, Black & Veatch, AES and Alcatel Space gives an indication of the caliber of the client base.

The Lawyers: Director of international litigation and arbitration **Daniel Gonzalez** (see p.85) was classed as a "*bright and aggressive emerging talent.*" He has been heavily involved in ICC and AAA matters of late, relating to business throughout South America and the Caribbean including Venezuela, El Salvador, Argentina and Puerto Rico.

Holland & Knight LLP

See firm details p.1352

The Firm: The firm's international litigation practice is principally involved in international arbitration through the Miami and New York offices, where members of the firm have won considerable respect among interviewees. Latin American matters have particular prominence in the firm's workload, and the team possesses a highly developed capacity to deal with negotiations in both Spanish and English. Attorneys are well equipped for ICC, AAA, UNCITRAL, LCIA and ICSID proceedings as well as having experience of matters before institutions in China, Japan and Chile.

The Lawyers: Chair of international litigation **Wilfredo Rodriguez** (see p.101) is well renowned nationally for his broad-based international disputes experience, which incorporates a rich vein of international arbitration. He is based in Miami.

Kirkland & Ellis LLP

See firm details p.770

The Firm: The international arbitration practice received praise for a number of consistently brilliant performances. Highlights included successfully representing GM in an ICC proceeding where Inversora sought substantial damages for alleged fraud and breach of fiduciary duty relating to a Venezuelan joint venture. The team also represented SC Johnson in ICC arbitration arising out of a post-closing dispute concerning the purchase of a worldwide business. Attorneys from Chicago, where the firm is already outright leader in commercial litigation, are most heavily involved in the field. Members of the practice are also on hand in New York, Los Angeles and London. In addition to ICC matters the workload also commonly includes LCIA, AAA, UNCITRAL and ad hoc proceedings.

The Lawyers: Partner James Schink is a senior trial counsel in Chicago spending a considerable portion of his time on international arbitration.

Mayer, Brown, Rowe & Maw LLP

See firm details p.771

The Firm: The firm is increasingly a force to be reckoned with and commentators agreed that no table of this kind would be complete without it. Its powerful Chicago base boasts a substantial concentration of international arbitration practitioners able to provide existing multinational clients headquartered in the region with specialist expertise. Meanwhile New York, Houston and DC also contribute significant firepower. The firm's European network further enhances its coverage and aids its ability to bridge the common law-civil law divide. It is felt to have a distinct advantage when it comes to matters involving oil and gas (the team has acted on one of the largest ICC arbitrations to date), and construction.

The Lawyers: Chicago partner **Javier Rubinstein** (see p.102) has made a considerable impact as an emerging talent in the field. His "*marvelous ability to translate the client's position into the language of international arbitration*" particularly impressed interviewees. Being fluent in Spanish accentuates the decidedly international edge to Rubinstein's practice, whereby he has acted for US, Latin American, European and Asian clients.

Morgan, Lewis & Bockius LLP

See firm details p.1556

The Firm: Through a mixture of international arbitration and international business litigation this firm has carved an enviable position in the market. On the basis of the reputation of its leading lawyer the New York office attracted the most praise. The firm also benefits from specialist resources in DC, London and San Francisco, as well as offering Spanish-speaking capabilities in Miami. The team has experience in proceedings before the major international arbitration institutions as well as in numerous ad hoc matters.

The Lawyers: **Robert Hornick** (see p.88) in New York was described by one commentator as being "*among the top minds in the field.*" He is "*spectacular both orally and on paper.*" Hornick's recent work has centered on UNCITRAL, ICC and ICSID matters. He is experienced in advising both investors and governments especially when it comes to Asia and particularly Indonesia.

O'Melveny & Myers LLP

See firm details p.294

The Firm: Its international arbitration capacity stems from a broad-based international disputes resolution practice that has won the firm a name as an emerging force in the market. The New York and San Francisco offices form the principal axis on which it operates. Branches in Beijing and Shanghai aid members of the firm in matters relating to Asia. The team is experienced in appearing before such fora as the ICC, AAA and Kuala Lumpur Regional Centre for Arbitration.

The Lawyers: Co-chair of international dispute resolution **Benno Kimmelman** is based in New York and said to treat each case with an "*energetic academicism.*" He successfully represented two international financial institutions in ICC arbitration against the Republic of Uruguay, winning a tribunal award of $100 million damages. Kimmelman also acted for a European telecom company and its subsidiary in another ICC matter relating to control of Brasil Telecom, one of four major fixed-line telecom operators in Brazil. Further highlights for Kimmelman include successfully acting for a major hotel operator in two parallel arbitrations concerning its investment in a luxury hotel project in Panama City. He also chairs the Arbitration Committee of the United States Council for International Business.

Weil, Gotshal & Manges LLP
See firm details p.1378

The Firm: The firm possesses a sophisticated network of offices on both sides of the Atlantic and a track record of appearing in disputes that have been known to involve multibillion-dollar stakes. New York, DC, Houston and Dallas all contribute to the stature of the practice in the Americas, while operations in Europe and Asia also feature pockets of expertise from Warsaw to Shanghai. Such resources ensure that the firm is well placed to handle complex multijurisdictional matters spanning a broad range of major commercial and financial sectors on behalf of both corporations and governments. Claims worth hundreds of millions of dollars concerning the construction of steel plants in Venezuela have been the subject of ICC arbitration in which the firm successfully represented Grupo Industrial Alfa's steel company, Hylsa. Further ICC highlights include successfully defending Samsung Electronics against InterDigital against a claim relating to a patent license for wireless telecommunications technology. In a separate matter, the team and its Spanish co-counsel succeeded in dismissing a $167 million fraud claim against a Spanish manufacturer. Further successes include defending Reuters in AAA international arbitration where the claimant sought the termination of a long-term contract worth over $250 million.

The Lawyers: **Eric Ordway** (see p.97) is recognized as a leader in the field having focused increasingly on international arbitration. Cochair of global dispute resolution, he is fluent in French and Spanish. Ordway divides his time between New York and Paris.

Wilmer Cutler Pickering Hale and Dorr LLP
See firm details p.497

The Firm: While the heart of the firm's international arbitration practice is perceived to lie in London, its New York office was highlighted as playing an increasingly critical role in major cases. Clients said every practitioner here seems to act as a "*model of calm even under excruciating pressure.*" The DC branch was also acknowledged as a traditional stronghold for the firm in the field. These resources are widely acknowledged as making the firm an attractive option on a global basis for ICC, AAA, LCIA, UNCITRAL and ICSID arbitration.

The Lawyers: Counsel **John Pierce** (see p.98) is the firm's principal contact in New York for international arbitration. He has experience of acting in proceedings in both the USA and Europe, whether for US or foreign entities.

Other Notable Practitioners
Elliot Polebaum (see p.98) of Fried, Frank, Harris, Shriver & Jacobson LLP is praised for having cultivated a "*great ICC practice.*" Fluent in French, he is also experienced in LCIA, UNCITRAL and ICSID matters. Polebaum leads the firm's international arbitration practice, dividing his time between the firm's DC and Paris offices.

Other Notable Arbitrators
Declared as the "*doyen of the US international arbitration community,*" **Gerald Aksen** (see p.74) is deemed to be "*in great shape*" and "*feverishly busy.*" His practice is equally split between ICC and AAA matters with LCIA, UNCITRAL and ad hoc proceedings yielding yet more appointments. Aksen is a retired Thelen Reid & Priest partner. **George Bermann** is renowned for his "*thoughtful and meticulous approach,*" particularly in ICC cases. He is a professor of law at Columbia Law School and also a noted US

adviser on EU law. Professor of law at Berkeley **David Caron** was described as "*absolutely superb*" with regard to his involvement in ICSID and NAFTA arbitrations. Special mention was made of his expertise in environmental law. **William Park** (see p.98) is professor of law at Boston University School of Law and came highly recommended for ICC and AAA matters. He is also making his mark on ICSID procedures. Park has presided over proceedings conducted in English and in French. "*Equally strict application of both common sense and analytical thinking*" was pointed to as the signature of his work whether as chair or party-appointed arbitrator. One commentator declared he would entrust his life to **Michael Reisman**, professor of law at Yale University. He was remarked upon as a "*man of great energy*" and is particularly renowned for his investor-state dispute expertise. He is president of the Arbitration Tribunal of the Bank for International Settlements. A former president of the Inter-American Committee on Human Rights, Reisman is also perceived as being among America's premier public international lawyers. Sole practitioner and former district judge **Charles Renfrew** is credited with being "*a permanent fixture on numerous short lists.*" Though heavily involved in both domestic arbitration and mediation, Renfrew also wins his fair share of major international arbitration appointments. Most of these are ICC matters with some LCIA, UNCITRAL and ad hoc proceedings also contributing to his workload. America's "*true superstar in the field,*" former president of the International Court of Justice **Stephen Schwebel** received praise from market observers on both sides of the Atlantic. Credited with "*true gravitas*" he is involved in international arbitration arising from both commercial, including BIT-related, and interstate disputes. In addition to acting as arbitrator, often but not exclusively in London, Schwebel also occasionally acts as co-counsel. Retired Debevoise & Plimpton partner **Robert von Mehren** has experience of most major arbitral institutions as well as ad hoc arbitration. "*A high-quality operator of considerable distinction,*" the octogenarian continues to be in demand.

INTERNATIONAL TRADE

National
Leading firms (International Trade)

1 STEPTOE & JOHNSON LLP
WILMER CUTLER PICKERING HALE

2 DEWEY BALLANTINE LLP
HOGAN & HARTSON LLP
SIDLEY AUSTIN BROWN
WHITE & CASE LLP
WILLKIE FARR & GALLAGHER

3 AKIN GUMP STRAUSS HAUER
ARNOLD & PORTER LLP
COLLIER SHANNON SCOTT
COVINGTON & BURLING
GIBSON, DUNN & CRUTCHER LLP
KAYE SCHOLER LLP
KING & SPALDING LLP
MAYER, BROWN, ROWE & MAW LLP
MILLER & CHEVALIER CHARTERED
SKADDEN, ARPS, SLATE, MEAGHER
WEIL, GOTSHAL & MANGES LLP

4 MCDERMOTT WILL & EMERY
VINSON & ELKINS LLP
WILEY REIN & FIELDING LLP

5 ADDUCI, MASTRIANI
CROWELL & MORING LLP
DAVIS POLK & WARDWELL
O'MELVENY & MYERS LLP
PAUL, HASTINGS, JANOFSKY
SANDLER, TRAVIS & ROSENBERG
STEWART & STEWART

Firms are listed alphabetically in each band.

Band 1

Steptoe & Johnson LLP

See firm details p.492

The Firm: Sources acknowledge that this firm is able to "*achieve amazing results,*" not least by "*throwing a huge amount of resources at every case it handles.*" In addition to boasting one of the larger international trade practices in the world, the core team of about 35 lawyers and other professionals is considered to have "*its fair share of the field's true stars.*" A number of these benefit from senior government experience with the Office of the United States Trade Representative, the ITC and the departments of Commerce, State, Defense, Justice, and Treasury. With a London office and an expanding operation in Brussels, EU law resources are available as required. Most of its activity centers on international trade litigation for a balanced client base, comprising respondents and petitioners. Industry sectors in which the team has had major cases in recent years include steel, lumber, wheat and uranium. The representation of domestic and foreign interests in safeguard cases in the USA and abroad also features in the workload. The firm covers the full spectrum of specialties including trade policy, WTO, export

controls, customs and Section 337 issues. International arbitration and public international law expertise also contributes to its profile, along with supporting expertise in areas such as immigration. Other related areas include Foreign Corrupt Practices Act matters, where the team benefits from significant white-collar crime expertise.

The Lawyers: Senior international trade partner **Richard Cunningham** (see p.80) possesses "*not only the irreplaceable weight of authority but also a great force of a personality.*" He is viewed by many commentators as "*the leading light at the trade bar,*" having secured lead roles in many of the major US antidumping and countervailing duty cases of the past 20 years. Cunningham also handles trade policy and WTO matters as well as advising corporate clients on developing international trade strategies. On the export controls and particularly the economic sanctions front, **Edward Krauland** (see p.91) was credited with "*a rare level of sophistication combined with an equal depth of experience.*" His Foreign Corrupt Practices Act expertise also received special acknowledgement. Further practice areas in which Krauland is involved include administrative litigation and international arbitration. He advised Ampex on developing a strategy for filing Section 337 cases at the ITC that has led to Ampex netting over $65 million in up-front royalty payments from the successful enforcement of several patents. **Mark Moran** (see p.96) is a "*terrific litigator*" with a "*sharp, analytical and perceptive approach*" to trade remedy cases. He is particularly adept in proceedings before the ITC, and also has extensive experience of matters involving the Department of Commerce, the Office of the United States Trade Representative, the US Court of International Trade, the North American Free Trade Agreement and the WTO. On behalf of Canadian industry, Moran was heavily involved at the injury phase of the antidumping and countervailing duty cases against imports of softwood lumber from Canada. He also advises domestic and foreign clients on trade policy issues and international arbitration. Sources recognized that **Susan Esserman** (see p.82), chair of the firm's international trade and investment department, has "*broadened her horizons no end*" following senior level posts at the Office of the United States Trade Representative and the Department of Commerce during the Clinton administration. There was strong consensus that she is now "*set for great things.*" As well as possessing expertise in US trade laws and trade policy, Esserman is well known for her WTO expertise. She specializes in US-Europe and US-India trade matters, among others. Esserman successfully defended the US-based National Oilseed Processors Association and its Brazilian

and Argentinean counterparts against the imposition of safeguard duties by the Government of India on imports of soybean oil. **George Grandison** (see p.86) is an outstanding trade remedies practitioner, who also offers expertise in customs and export controls. He too was involved in the USA-Canada softwood lumber trade disputes. According to clients, **Sheldon Hochberg** (see p.88) "*gives the highly nuanced court performance of a model appellate lawyer.*" He benefits from wide-ranging international and administrative law experience. Hochberg is widely respected for his impressive appearances before the Department of Commerce, the US Court of International Trade and the Federal Court of Appeals, often in cases that go to the heart of the fundamental principles of trade law. **Eric Emerson** (see p.82) was identified as an up-and-coming lawyer who "*already operates at a level well beyond the mechanics of even the most complex cases.*" Antidumping and countervailing duty proceedings form the core of his practice. Cunningham, Hochberg and Emerson all assisted USEC, the only US producer of enriched uranium, with a number of court appeals arising from highly complex antidumping and countervailing duty matters. This work has included successful actions against imports of nuclear fuel from the Russian Federation.

The Clients: Canadian Wheat Board; Canadian Lumber Trade Alliance and British Columbia Lumber Trade Council; Corn Refiners Association; National Association of Animal Breeders; Corus Group; Bechtel; Mitsubishi Heavy Industries; Norsk Hydro; Reliance Industries; Occidental Chemical; Outokumpu; Raytheon; BAT; New Skies BV; Syngenta; Yahoo!; Electronic Data Systems; Elementis; Harley-Davidson; Homer Laughlin China and ISPAT Mexicana/Caribbean ISPAT.

Wilmer Cutler Pickering Hale and Dorr LLP

See firm details p.497

The Firm: Billed as "*a bit of a powerhouse,*" this firm is clearly at the forefront of the market. Above all it was deemed to have "*the deepest bench of high-level lawyers,*" providing "*superb assistance*" in the form of "*definitive advice that is crisp, direct and to the point.*" Overwhelming firepower means that the team's expertise goes some way to "*penetrating the politics surrounding it.*" Interviewees declared that this was a "*one-stop shop for pretty much any issue in any part of the world,*" from US domestic policy to WTO matters concerning China, India or Central America. "*Maximum counseling*" meant clients said they "*would not hesitate using it repeatedly, no matter how sensitive the matter.*" The team includes top former government officials and is therefore particularly well renowned

National

Leading individuals (International Trade: Trade Remedies and Trade Policy)

1

ANDERSON M Jean *Weil Gotshal*, Washington, DC	BARSHEFSKY Charlene *Wilmer Cutler*, Washington, DC
CUNNINGHAM Richard *Steptoe & Johnson*, DC	HORLICK Gary *Wilmer Cutler*, Washington, DC
NOVICK Robert *Wilmer Cutler*, Washington, DC	

2

BARRINGER William *Willkie Farr*, Washington, DC	CAMERON Donald *Kaye Scholer*, Washington, DC
CONNELLY Warren *Akin Gump*, Washington, DC	ESSERMAN Susan *Steptoe & Johnson*, Washington, DC
GREENWALD John *Wilmer Cutler*, Washington, DC	KANTOR Michael *Mayer Brown*, Washington, DC
LEIBOWITZ Lewis *Hogan & Hartson*, Washington, DC	MCCONNELL Mark *Hogan & Hartson*, Washington, DC
MORAN Mark *Steptoe & Johnson*, Washington, DC	PRICE Daniel *Sidley Austin*, Washington, DC
ROSENTHAL Paul *Collier Shannon*, Washington, DC	SCHER Peter *Mayer Brown*, Washington, DC
WOLFF Alan *Dewey Ballantine*, Washington, DC	

3

CLARK Matthew *Arent Fox*, Washington, DC	DORN Joseph *King & Spalding*, Washington, DC
DURLING James *Willkie Farr*, Washington, DC	EIZENSTAT Stuart *Covington & Burling*, Washington, DC
GRANDISON W George *Steptoe & Johnson*, DC	HARTQUIST David *Collier Shannon*, Washington, DC
KAPLAN Gilbert *King & Spalding*, Washington, DC	LIGHTHIZER Robert *Skadden Arps*, Washington, DC
MENDOZA Julie *Kaye Scholer*, Washington, DC	PIERCE Kenneth *Willkie Farr*, Washington, DC
PLAINE Daniel *Gibson Dunn*, Washington, DC	READE Claire *Arnold & Porter*, Washington, DC
ROSEN Stuart *Weil Gotshal*, New York	SHOYER Andrew *Sidley Austin*, Washington, DC
SLATER Valerie *Akin Gump*, San Francisco	SPAK Walter *White & Case*, Washington, DC
STEWART Terence *Stewart & Stewart*, Washington, DC	

4

ADDUCI II V James *Adduci Mastriani*, Washington, DC	APPLEBAUM Harvey *Covington & Burling*, DC
ARCHIBALD Jeanne *Hogan & Hartson*, Washington, DC	BERG Gracia *Gibson Dunn*, Washington, DC
CLINTON William *White & Case*, Washington, DC	DEMPSEY Kevin *Dewey Ballantine*, Washington, DC
DUNN Christopher *Willkie Farr*, Washington, DC	GRIFFITH Spencer *Akin Gump*, Washington, DC
HOCHBERG Sheldon *Steptoe & Johnson*, DC	HOUSE Michael *McDermott Will*, Washington, DC
KAPLAN H Deen *Hogan & Hartson*, Washington, DC	LEVINE David *McDermott Will*, Washington, DC
LEVY Charles *Wilmer Cutler*, Washington, DC	MANGAN John *Skadden Arps*, Washington, DC
MOYER E Homer *Miller & Chevalier*, Washington, DC	PORTER Daniel *Willkie Farr*, Washington, DC
ROH Charles *Weil Gotshal*, Washington, DC	SCHNEIDER Lawrence *Arnold & Porter*, Washington, DC
SHOR Michael *Arnold & Porter*, Washington, DC	STOKES Christopher *Hogan & Hartson*, Washington, DC
VERRILL Charles *Wiley Rein*, Washington, DC	WARD Bradford *Dewey Ballantine*, Washington, DC

5

CORR Christopher *White & Case*, Washington, DC	CURTISS Catherine *Hughes Hubbard*, Washington, DC
PORGES Amelia *Sidley Austin*, Washington, DC	PRICE Joseph *Gibson Dunn*, Washington, DC
RAGOSTA John *Dewey Ballantine*, Washington, DC	SAMET Andrew *Sandler Travis*, Washington, DC
SCHAGRIN Roger *Schagrin Associates*, Washington, DC	SPAK Gregory *White & Case*, Washington, DC

Up-and-coming individuals

EMERSON Eric *Steptoe & Johnson*, Washington, DC	NICELY Matthew *Willkie Farr*, Washington, DC
SHAPIRO Hal *Miller & Chevalier*, Washington, DC	

Individuals are listed alphabetically in each band.

for its trade policy prowess, as well as its trade remedies representations. The workload incorporates WTO, market access and legislative matters, not to mention wide-ranging trade negotiations at the highest levels. Section 337 cases and export control matters also contribute to the firm's activity in the field. A substantial Brussels operation provides the firm with additional resources and a broad base of technical expertise.

The Lawyers: Senior international partner **Charlene Barshefsky** (see p.76) was "*always among the top five lawyers in the field*" even before becoming US Trade Representative in 1997, a post she held until 2001. "*When Barshefsky is involved in a case, there is no better lawyer to have on your side,*" according to sources. Another colossus in the field, **Gary Horlick** (see p.88) was described as "*a broad thinker with a phenomenal international reputation.*" He was responsible for the administration of US

antidumping and countervailing duty laws while in government, and has been involved in cases in the USA and Europe and further afield. According to commentators, Horlick's capacity to bridge trade remedy and trade policy areas is his greatest strength, while GATT, WTO and FTA negotiation expertise is a major component in his armory. He represented the Government of El Salvador in Central America Free Trade Agreement negotiations. The fact that **Robert Novick** (see p.97), chair of the trade department, was General Counsel in the Office of the US Trade Representative under Barshefsky means the duo possesses unparalleled expertise on matters relating to China, having been prime negotiators of China's WTO agreement. Clients report that they have "*never found anyone easier to work with than Novick,*" who was also credited with "*leverage in all areas – law, policy and politics.*" Barshefsky and Novick represented Boeing in connection with European subsidies

to Airbus, including in WTO proceedings. They also advised Cisco on its activities in China, including IP issues involving a Chinese competitor. Novick also assisted Cargill with market access barriers in China and India, and advised the Cosmetic, Toiletry, and Fragrance Association on an import ban relating to BSE issues, successfully negotiating a solution allowing the resumption of exports. **John Greenwald** (see p.86) is active on trade policy matters at both executive and legislative levels, while sustaining a high profile in trade remedies. All four attorneys so far mentioned have represented various Quebec and British Columbia industry interests in the USA-Canada softwood lumber dispute, involving WTO, NAFTA and administrative litigation. Further highlights for Greenwald included involvement in the Chinese wooden bedroom furniture antidumping investigation, incorporating a Court of International Trade and a Department of Commerce proceeding. He also won a victory in a Court of International Trade proceeding and appeal relating to the Chinese ball-bearing industry. Given the unique blend of his government and corporate connections, **Charles Levy** (see p.93) is a valuable resource for the firm, particularly when it comes to US trade policy. Clients deemed Levy to have "*continuously shined, having been instrumental in developing the position of US business in the worldwide arena.*" Advice to the Business Roundtable on a range of trade policy issues, including FTA implementation legislation has contributed to his workload recently. Levy also represented a coalition of technology companies on international trade and export control matters.

The Clients: The firm successfully represented ASML Holding in a Section 337 action brought by Nikon alleging infringement of seven patents. In addition, it represented Wolfson Microelectronics in a Section 337 investigation involving patent infringement claims against certain of the company's semiconductor products. Further highlights include providing a due diligence review and transactional advice to Danaher for the acquisition of a major European medical products supplier with operations in countries subject to US embargoes. The team also advised Parker Hannifin in negotiations with the US government over a major flight controls systems project in China and on a related technology control plan.

Band 2

Dewey Ballantine LLP

See firm details p.1347

The Firm: Highly rated for "*pulling out all the stops*" on behalf of petitioners in trade remedy cases, this is generally considered the foremost firm for such specialist advice. Its much envied track record incorporates appearances in the

National

Leading individuals

(International Trade: Export Controls and Economic Sanctions)

1
BERLACK Evan *Baker Botts*, Washington, DC
FLOWE Benjamin *Berliner Corcoran*, Washington, DC
HOFFMAN William *Davis Polk*, Washington, DC
KRAULAND Edward *Steptoe & Johnson*, Washington, DC
LITTLE Kathleen *Vinson & Elkins*, Washington, DC
MCGLONE William *Miller & Chevalier*, Washington, DC
RUBINOFF Edward *Akin Gump*, Washington, DC
SNYDER Jeffrey *Crowell & Moring*, Washington, DC
TROOBOFF Peter *Covington & Burling*, Washington, DC
WALL Christopher *Pillsbury Winthrop*, Washington, DC

2
AYRES Margaret *Davis Polk*, Washington, DC
BARKER John *Arnold & Porter*, Washington, DC
CLEMENTS William *Foley & Lardner*, Washington, DC
FLANAGAN Peter *Covington & Burling*, Washington, DC
JOHNSON David *Vinson & Elkins*, Washington, DC
LEVINE David *McDermott Will*, Washington, DC
LICHTENBAUM Greta *O'Melveny*, Washington, DC
MCFADDEN II W Clark *Dewey*, Washington, DC
REYNOLDS III John *Wiley Rein*, Washington, DC
SEGALL Wynn *Akin Gump*, Washington, DC

Up-and-coming individuals

DAYANIM Behnam *Paul Hastings*, Washington, DC
MABERRY Scott *Fulbright & Jaworski*, Washington, DC

Individuals are listed alphabetically in each band.

largest cases before the Department of Commerce. As such the international trade department can be relied upon "*to fight every case as if it was a question of life or death.*" In addition to advising on international trade litigation, the team advises on policy and legislative initiatives. Its experience of advocating for client interests in the most significant trade agreements over the past quarter of a century commands great respect from interviewees. It is particularly valued for its involvement in those cases resulting from the Uruguay Round and from the accession of China and Taiwan to the WTO. The practice also covers export controls, economic sanctions, defense industry security issues and government contract regulations.

The Lawyers: Practice leader and managing partner of the DC office **Alan Wolff** (see p.108) was described as the "*mastermind behind the operation and a political strategist par excellence.*" Commentators agree that Wolff's experience as US Deputy Special Representative for Trade Negotiations in the Carter administration provides a good complement to the department's emerging talents. Of these **Kevin Dempsey** (see p.81) was considered one of the most promising. He is best known as an international trade litigator and has worked with Wolff on behalf of the US Semiconductor Industry Association to resolve market access restrictions imposed by the Government of China. The case involved the first WTO dispute settlement case brought to obtain China's compliance with its WTO oblig-

ations. Wolff and Dempsey also cooperated on representing the same association in negotiations between the US government and the Government of China over the adoption of international encryption standards for wireless local area networks in China. **Bradford Ward** (see p.107) was commended as an "*excellent technician*" on the trade remedies front. He led the firm's team representing the Southern Shrimp Alliance in an ongoing antidumping duty investigation of shrimps imported from Brazil, Ecuador, India, China, Vietnam and Thailand. At stake in the case are the interests of 70,000 jobs dependent on the domestic shrimp industry with an economic impact of over $3.5 billion. Wolff, Dempsey and Ward cooperated in representing Mercury Marine in antidumping litigation against Japanese outboard engine exports to the USA worth $670 million. **John Ragosta** (see p.100) was also identified as making a name for himself in GATT and NAFTA-related advice and trade remedy cases. **Clark McFadden** (see p.95) is an acknowledged export controls leader benefiting from US Department of Defense and National Security Council experience. Observers valued McFadden's ability to fuse a shrewd understanding of foreign affairs with international trade law expertise.

The Clients: Important long-term representations for the team include assisting the Coalition for Fair Lumber Imports in the USA-Canada softwood lumber dispute. Export control review highlights include advising SEMI, an alliance of equipment and materials suppliers for the semiconductor industry, on persuading the US government to support the elimination of most automated test equipment from export controls.

Hogan & Hartson LLP

See firm details p.484

The Firm: "*An excellent practice sustaining a relentlessly high quality and diversity of trade litigation, policy matters and Section 337 cases*" remarked one interviewee, who accurately summed up the considerable volume of market recommendation for Hogan & Hartson. A core team of almost 40 lawyers has an outstanding track record of representing respondents in trade remedy cases. It benefits from its members having held positions such as head of the EC's Washington delegation, EC deputy director-general for external relations and senior director for the Middle East Initiative at the National Security Council. Clients acknowledged that the high-level connections established by such lawyers were instrumental in the outcome of both trade remedy cases and trade policy issues.

The Lawyers: **Mark McConnell** (see p.294) is well known for the depth and range of his experience particularly on matters relating to Canada. USA-China trade matters are another area in which he is experienced. **Lewis Leibowitz** (see

p.92) "*commands tremendous respect on all sides.*" He represented the Consuming Industries Trade Action Coalition in working toward the repeal of steel safeguard tariffs. This involved close cooperation with allied groups including the Emergency Committee for American Trade, members of Congress and the administration and governments bringing WTO cases against the steel tariffs. Head of department **Jeanne Archibald** (see p.75) also comes highly recommended. She has acted for the Government of Japan in bringing about an Eighth Circuit ruling allowing it to file a high-profile amicus curiae brief. The case may determine whether countermeasures permitted by the WTO can be taken against the USA in relation to a $31.5 million award of damages against a Japanese company made under the 1916 Antidumping Act. Research indicated the increasing market prominence of **Deen Kaplan** (see p.90) and **Christopher Stokes** (see p.105). Kaplan worked with McConnell representing the Government of Ontario in the ongoing Canada-USA softwood lumber dispute. A Portuguese speaker, Stokes is also known for his involvement in Latin American issues, particularly those relating to Brazil.

The Clients: Work highlights accomplished in conjunction with the firm's government relations group include a role in re-establishing congressional commitment to the Berry Amendment, including successfully seeking the revocation of an unfair trade preference for Russian titanium. Further clients include: Accenture; University of Southern California; Agilent; Amgen; Becton Dickinson; Embassy of Japan; Ministry of Commerce of the Republic of China; DuPont Photomasks; Pharmaceutical Research and Manufacturers of America; GE Medical Systems; Hughes Network Systems; Network Appliance; DIRECTV Group; INVISTA; LeapFrog Enterprises; MeadWestvaco; Mexinox; Companhia Siderurgica Belgo-Mineira; Asocaña; Ontario Pork Producers' Marketing Board; Univar; Caterpillar; Nissan; Toyota; Chubb; Freightliner and Unocal.

Sidley Austin Brown & Wood LLP

See firm details p.778

The Firm: The international trade and dispute resolution team's overwhelming strength in WTO matters has led some commentators to consider it to be "*in a field of its own.*" Its preeminence rests on the "*highly sophisticated sense of international trade policy and related political processes*" that won the firm such substantial praise. An intimate knowledge of all types of international trade negotiations, such as the Doha round, WTO accession and regional free trade agreements, and insight into US government agencies are regarded as core features of this practice. Clients further discerned "*a truly impressive ability to forecast the impact of WTO* rulings" on a range of regulated industry sectors including capital markets and financial services. They commented that these attributes were "*critical in improving the client's ability to compete globally.*" In addition to its DC stronghold and clutch of international trade lawyers in San Francisco, the firm benefits from the expertise of recognized leaders in the field based in Brussels and Geneva. Such resources allow it to offer "*distinct breadth and depth in EU trade-related expertise.*" The Geneva and DC offices recently advised the Brazilian cotton industry in its complaint against the USA on cotton subsidies. Brazil estimates damage of $500 million in lost revenue for Brazilian exporters, resulting from subsidies worth $2.5 billion. With more than 50 practitioners worldwide, the firm has an almost unparalleled depth of resources to assist multinational corporations, trade associations and governments. Its long-established customs practice also came in for praise. Other areas of major activity include trade remedy proceedings, the trade related aspects of IP rights, export controls, embargos and economic trade sanctions compliance.

The Lawyers: Put simply, practice chair **Dan Price** (see p.99) makes for "*an outstanding lead counsel and first-class litigator.*" A hugely influential figure, Price is former principal deputy general counsel of the Office of the United States Trade Representative, in which role he negotiated trade and investment agreements with Eastern Europe, Latin America and the former Soviet Union. That he also served as the US Trade Representative's lead negotiator on investment issues in the NAFTA talks and as legal adviser on the GATT Uruguay round investment agreement gives further weight to his authority. Although his workload has recently been biased in favor of investor-state arbitration, Price remains a force to be reckoned with in international trade. **Andrew Shoyer** (see p.104) impresses as a "*formidable legal talent,*" particularly when it comes to the firm's true forte, matters relating to the WTO. While at the US Trade Representative, he was legal adviser to the US mission to the WTO in Geneva. He recently worked alongside the Geneva office assisting the US biotech industry in a dispute arising out of a US challenge to the EU's moratorium on the approval of biotech agricultural products. According to commentators, the table would not be complete without counsel **Amelia Porges** (see p.99). Her lengthy US Trade Representative experience saw her involved with the WTO and GATT during the formative years of both. Investor-state arbitration has also recently contributed to Porges' workload.

The Clients: Evidence of the diversity of the firm's client base includes recent activity on behalf of the likes of: Caterpillar; Goldman Sachs; Anheuser-Busch; Monsanto; Nike; Airbus; Pharmaceutical Research and Manufactur-

ers of America; Severstal; the Government of Peru and the Government of Colombia.

White & Case LLP
See firm details p.1379

The Firm: The traditional trade remedy aspects of the firm's international trade practice are widely recognized in the market. It is credited with having made particular inroads into matters relating to China, not to mention numerous other Asian countries. Latin American matters are also a major focus, and the firm benefits from having a presence in Mexico city. With a more extensive global network than most, including an operation in Geneva, the firm is also considered adept in WTO matters across many jurisdictions. Offices in 11 countries boast specialist international trade expertise, and attract a broad spread of clients, including governments, which the firm often advises on the drafting of trade laws. A wide range of trade negotiation, transactional support, export control and national security issues are also dealt with. Former Court of International Trade administrative law judge D R Terrill joined the team as counsel at the beginning of 2005, a move set to bolster the firm's already significant Section 337 practice.

The Lawyers: International trade head **Walter Spak** (see p.105) was widely recommended as a leading trade lawyer. He has acted in matters affecting companies and governments throughout Asia and Latin America. **William Clinton** (see p.79) is particularly well known for representing Chinese respondents in the US and other import markets. Like Spak, he also advises a number of sovereigns on trade law drafting and implementation along with WTO accession issues. **Christopher Corr** (see p.79) has sustained an impressive hybrid practice incorporating international trade remedy cases and IP issues. He cooperated with partners in Palo Alto in representing the Taiwan semiconductor industry during various trade disputes in the USA. Most recently, the team acted for Taiwan Semiconductor Manufacturing Company in a court action filed against China's Semiconductor Manufacturing International Corporation for theft of trade secrets, patent infringement and unfair trade. Corr was also involved in high-profile antidumping cases, including lumber from Canada, shrimp from Thailand, and antifriction bearings from Singapore. He successfully led advice to Duferdofin in Italy and Nizhny Tagil Iron & Steel Works in Russia in an antidumping investigation into structural steel beams. Corr also heads the trade group's export control and national security practice. **Gregory Spak** (see p.105) was recommended for the decidedly international nature of his trade remedy-oriented practice. The Spak brothers represented GCC Cementos in several aspects of the USA-Mexico trade dispute over cement. This

included pursuing one of the largest WTO challenges to the US government antidumping laws and practice.

The Clients: Further highlights for the team include being retained by Tenaris to represent its interest in two separate WTO dispute settlement proceedings involving oil country tubular goods exported from Argentina and Mexico. This meant providing advice to Argentinean and Mexican governments at every phase of both disputes. Other clients include: the Buchanan Group; Federal Express; Fuji Film; Industrias Monterrey; Novartis and Unisource/Georgia-Pacific.

Willkie Farr & Gallagher LLP
See firm details p.1380

The Firm: Armed with "*great expertise and resources,*" this firm will pursue clients' interests "*even to the ends of the earth.*" Typically clients commented on the energy channeled into understanding their business, so that members of the firm "*hit the ground running like few others can.*" One said its approach is "*to take the intricacies of the industry by the scruff of the neck until the lawyers know it better than three-quarters of our company.*" The team came in for further praise for "*talking to people working in the trenches*" and its ability to communicate on all levels. The "*great political antennae*" cultivated by its lawyers provide added value in this respect. The firm has a particularly good name for representing respondents, especially Far Eastern and Canadian interests, in trade remedy matters. Latin American issues are also often a source of income. The firm is acknowledged as having a high profile in the steel sector among others. Related areas in which it has significant expertise include Foreign Corrupt Practices Act issues. Beyond the firm's DC stronghold, the New York-based IP team also handles Section 337 matters.

The Lawyers: Viewed as something of an elder statesman, **William Barringer** (see p.76), who holds the reigns of the firm's international trade practice, brings "*a sea of calm*" to his negotiations. He advised the Vietnamese industry in the shrimp antidumping investigation. **James Durling** (see p.82) and **Kenneth Pierce** (see p.98) are two key members of the team also developing excellent profiles for themselves. Durling has recently been involved in high-profile WTO proceedings, including on behalf of the Government of Japan in a dispute arising from US safeguard measures on steel products. Barringer acted for the Government of Brazil in a related matter that included appearing at meetings with the WTO panel and appellate body. Pierce has a particular depth of experience in matters relating to Thailand, most recently having represented the Thai Frozen Food Association and Rubicon Resources in the shrimp antidumping investigation. He also advised on the formation of the Shrimp Task Force of the Consuming Industries Trade Action Coalition, and subsequently on media and political strategies to neutralize the efforts of the petitioners, the Southern Shrimp Alliance. "*A passionate advocate*," **Daniel Porter** (see p.99) was credited with "*an enthusiasm that proved to be critical to getting people to get things done*." He represented Hynix Semiconductor in Court of International Trade proceedings arising from countervailing duty investigations into whether the financial restructuring of Hynix constituted countervailable subsidies. Porter also represented the Manitoba Pork Council and three of the four mandatory respondents in the antidumping investigation and the entire Canadian industry in the countervailing duty investigation into live swine from Canada. **Christopher Dunn** (see p.82) is also highly respected for his trade remedies expertise and has dealt substantially with cases relating to Latin America, particularly Brazil. With regard to the outboard engines from the Japan antidumping case, he advised on the US side of the Department of Commerce investigation and is heavily involved in the related Court of International Trade investigation. Durling advised on the Japan side of the Department of Commerce investigation while Barringer acted as overall lead partner in the matter. **Matthew Nicely** (see p.97) received plaudits from market observers in the USA and overseas for his role in relation to the Vietnamese shrimp industry during the antidumping investigation into the sector. He is widely respected for his work on developing surrogate values on which normal value is ultimately based.

Band 3

Akin Gump Strauss Hauer & Feld LLP
See firm details p.477
The Firm: The international trade department received much praise for its balanced approach to litigation, trade policy, customs, export controls and economic sanctions. A thriving Korea practice, with bilingual lawyers at its disposal, is a focus for activity. Experience of assisting clients based in Canada, China, France, Germany, Japan, Mexico, the former Soviet Union, Taiwan, Thailand and the UK is also in evidence. In addition to the DC office, the firm's Moscow, Brussels, and London offices offer specialist trade expertise.
The Lawyers: According to sources, **Warren Connelly** (see p.79) possesses "*deep insight into the intricacies of ITC proceedings*" in particular and trade remedy matters generally. He successfully acted for Samsung in the US countervailing duty investigation of dynamic random access memory semiconductors from Korea. Samsung was the only Korean producer to receive de minimis margins and be excluded

from the countervailing duty order. He won further success assisting Funai Electric with a US antidumping duty investigation involving color televisions from Malaysia. Chair of international trade **Valerie Slater** (see p.104) was commended for her "*forensic analysis*" in trade remedy matters. She successfully represented the Catfish Farmers of America in the first US antidumping action against a product of Vietnam. **Spencer Griffith** (see p.86) impresses as one "*doing an admirable job of strategically running negotiations*." He represented the Government of British Columbia in the USA-Canada lumber dispute. Head of the export control and economic sanctions practice **Edward Rubinoff** (see p.101) comes highly rated, particularly in the field of trade embargoes concerning countries like Cuba. He assists a wide range of hi-tech and other companies on such matters. In the same practice, **Wynn Segall** (see p.103) was commended for his expertise in export controls, IP and economic sanctions.
The Clients: Archer Daniels Midland; UPS; POSCO; Ad Hoc Committee of Domestic Nitrogen Producers; Hyundai Hysco; American Seafood Distributors Association; Fujitsu; Tyson Foods; Chilean Salmon Association; Baker Hughes and Pier 1 Imports.

Arnold & Porter LLP
See firm details p.478
The Firm: One commentator described the typical international trade lawyer at this firm as a "*walking encyclopedia with contacts everywhere who leaves no stone unturned*." The responsiveness of team members who "*can be relied upon in case of a crisis day or night*" also came in for praise. Recent trade remedy successes included representing Hulett Aluminium and Empire Resources in an antidumping investigation into aluminum plate imports from South Africa. The petition was filed by Alcoa. The Court of International Trade voted four to two in favor of the firm's clients. With regard to export controls the team's contacts in government mean it "*can get questions answered you couldn't get answered any other way*." Members of the firm received praise whether it was for filing export licenses or discussing philosophical and policy-oriented aspects of export controls. The presence of the likes of former CIA general counsel Jeffrey Smith was considered to add further weight to the firm's profile in this respect.
The Lawyers: **Claire Reade** (see p.100) was identified as the firm's foremost trade remedies lawyer. Clients remarked, "*She is one of the most talented and inventive lawyers I've seen*." Of a similar ilk, **Lawrence Schneider** (see p.103) was complimented for his familiarity with the workings of Congress. Interviewees praised **Michael Shor** (see p.103) for his wide-ranging disputes practice in which international trade matters feature heavily. **John Barker** (see p.75) was iden-

tified as "*one of the best in Washington*" on the export front and is particularly well known for his advice to universities, an increasingly important area. His ability to "*supply quick and complete answers on technical matters*" means several clients have Barker's telephone number memorized. His extensive experience of having worked in the US Department of State is thought to hold him in good stead.
The Clients: Long-term clients include the Government of Alberta, which the firm represented in US countervailing duty cases on imports from Canada such as softwood lumber (of which Alberta is one of the four major producers), wheat and live swine. Further clients include the Chilean Salmon Association, various individual Chilean salmon producers and exporters, and the governments of Israel and Abitibi Consolidated.

Collier Shannon Scott
The Firm: This international trade and customs practice comes highly recommended by market commentators as a "*technically accomplished outfit, expert in representing domestic industry in trade remedy cases*." Matters relating to China have been a focus of recent activity. Export controls, economic sanctions, the Foreign Corrupt Practices Act and customs matters are also covered. In-house economic experts bolster an already substantial team of lawyers.
The Lawyers: Chairman of the firm **Paul Rosenthal** is "*one of the best petitioner lawyers in town*." His outstanding presentation of matters before US trade agencies and courts, not to mention Congress and the Executive Branch, won Rosenthal much praise. WTO and NAFTA matters are also part of his practice. He successfully represented the National Pork Producers Council in filing antidumping and countervailing duty cases against live hog imports from Canada. **David Hartquist** is also a highly respected member of the trade bar, who is strongly associated with the steel sector. He is viewed as particularly influential when it comes to trade legislation and policy. Hartquist successfully represented Five Rivers Electronic Innovations and two unions in the first case involving US importers seeking protection from unfairly priced Chinese imports where the product in question was a mainstream consumer product. The case was notable for the unprecedented move by certain US retailers that are major importers of television sets testifying against the US manufacturer. Hartquist also assisted with the filing of an unprecedented unfair trade action charging that China's manipulation of its currency amounted to an export subsidy and therefore contravened global trading rules.
The Clients: Specialty Steel Industry of North America; National Pork Producers Council; Five Rivers Electronic Innovations; Petroleo de

www.ChambersandPartners.com

All quotes in the text are from interviews with clients and competitors.

43

Venezuela, South America; Copper and Brass Fabricators Council; Chocolate Manufacturers Association; Juice Products Association; Seaman Paper Company of Massachusetts; Yum! Brands/Long John Silver's; The Garlic Company; Christopher Ranch; Giorgio Foods and FMC.

Covington & Burling
See firm details p.481

The Firm: Sources provided equally favorable reviews for both this firm's import and its export work. High-level trade policy appointments are a distinctive feature of the workload. Other areas of expertise include sanctions, export controls, antiboycott and Foreign Corrupt Practices Act issues relating to clients in energy, life sciences, hi-tech and commodities sectors. Exon-Florio amendment transactional support has punctuated recent work. The firm's alliance with the strategic consultancy Kissinger McLarty Associates, led by former US Secretary of State Henry Kissinger and former White House Chief of Staff and Special Envoy for the Americas Thomas McLarty, gives clients the benefit of access to lawyers, diplomats, lobbyists, intelligence analysts and others. A presence in Brussels was pointed to as a further advantage for the firm, while lawyers in New York, San Francisco and London are on hand as required. Related areas of strength include ICSID arbitration.

The Lawyers: "*A driving force,*" interviewees found **Peter Trooboff** (see p.106) to be both "*personable and scholarly.*" He is best known for his trade compliance expertise, particularly when it comes to sanctions. Trooboff's practice in this area dovetails with his involvement in international arbitration. Co-vice chair of the department **Peter Flanagan** (see p.83) was tipped as following in the footsteps of the likes of Trooboff. He is one of a select group of lawyers esteemed for his ability to tailor export controls and economic sanctions advice to the needs of financial institutions. However, Flanagan also acts for clients in a range of industry sectors. Research clearly indicated that no list of this kind would be complete without the firm's head of international practice, **Stuart Eizenstat** (see p.82). His experience of working in government leaves him well positioned in dealing with trade policy matters. Eizenstat's past posts have included Under Secretary of Commerce for International Trade in the Clinton administration and Ambassador to the European Union. **Harvey Applebaum** (see p.75) is well respected as a long-standing figure in the field, who developed an international trade practice out of an initial focus on antitrust. Court of International Trade, Department of Commerce and US Trade Representative proceedings continue to feature in his workload, alongside WTO and NAFTA matters.

The Clients: Boeing; BT; Canon; Council of the European Union; Global Crossing; Medtronic; Microsoft; Motorola; Pacific Telecom; Vodafone and leading pharmaceutical and energy sector corporations.

Gibson, Dunn & Crutcher LLP
See firm details p.285

The Firm: Clients associate the firm with its ability to handle "*massive cases*" and to be of correspondingly "*enormous assistance.*" The international trade and customs practice also received praise for "*outstanding teamwork*" and "*willingness to work 24 hours for a solution.*" The Japanese steel sector provides it with a considerable portion of work representing the likes of Nippon Steel. Matters relating to Canada form another strand, whereby the firm acts for West Fraser in the USA-Canada softwood lumber dispute. A sophisticated customs practice contributes further to the firm's profile. Expertise on issues relating to the USA Patriot Act, economic sanctions, trade embargoes and export controls is also offered. The department can draw on the firm's antitrust, IP, government contracts and litigation resources as required. European offices, including one in Brussels, enhance this firm's standing in the field.

The Lawyers: Clients cast **Daniel Plaine** (see p.98) above all as a strategist with "*profound insight relating to law, politics and business.*" Ex-Steptoe & Johnson attorney **Gracia Berg** (see p.76) was singled out as a leading trade remedies practitioner with experience of working at the Court of International Trade. **Joseph Price** (see p.99) also attracted commendation for his hybrid export and import practice.

The Clients: Clients include Nissan North America, First Data Corporation and Jazz Semiconductor.

Kaye Scholer LLP
See firm details p.1354

The Firm: This high-quality operation was praised by commentators for its "*profoundly knowledgeable lawyers.*" The team of lawyers and trade analysts is steeped in trade policy and trade remedy experience. It is also involved in WTO, Section 337, customs and export licensing and control matters. In addition to serving its distinctly international corporate client base, the firm runs training seminars on international trade issues for the governments of Mexico, Taiwan, Uruguay, Venezuela, Indonesia, El Salvador and Argentina.

The Lawyers: According to sources, cochairs of international trade **Donald Cameron** (see p.77) and **Julie Mendoza** (see p.95) work together seamlessly. Cameron is renowned as a "*flamboyant trade remedies litigator able to take complete control of a case*" who is "*as smart as they come and will give his all for the client.*" Mendoza was extolled as a "*critical component of the practice*" and is fluent in Spanish, making her well placed for dealing with matters relating to Latin America. The duo successfully represented one of Canada's largest lumber producers in a US investigation into and administrative review of alleged dumping and subsidization. They also represented an Argentinean honey producer in an antidumping administrative review, successfully warding off a Department of Commerce cost of production investigation. Further highlights include representing Korean steel producers and advising the Korean government in a successful WTO challenge to US safeguards on steel products. As a result, the USA terminated steel safeguard duties of up to 30% on imports of flat-rolled steel 15 months before they were scheduled to expire.

The Clients: POSCO; Korea Iron and Steel Association; Pusan Pipe America; Terminal Forest Products; SIVENSA; Brookstone and NEXCO.

King & Spalding LLP
See firm details p.635

The Firm: A highly respected practice, it owes part of its success to its skill in developing "*a body of highly conscientious junior lawyers*" operating under established leaders in the field. Interviewees also noted the group's recent hires and agreed that a "*team of real depth and substance*" now resided at the firm. It covers all facets of international trade but is best known for acting on behalf of US petitioners in a great range of industries including key activity relating to semiconductors. Expertise in trade policy and legislation, market access issues, WTO dispute settlement proceedings, Section 337 cases, export controls and customs is also an important facet of the practice. Highlights include successfully negotiating a price undertaking agreement suspending a Chinese antidumping case against US exports of chloroform to China, on behalf of Dow Chemical.

The Lawyers: **Joseph Dorn** (see p.82) is the firm's most respected practitioner in the field. He is best known for advising the American Furniture Manufacturers Committee for Legal Trade, a coalition of US furniture producers, in the largest US antidumping case pursued against China. He won another US antidumping case against plastic retail carrier bags from China on behalf of the Polyethylene Retail Carrier Bag Committee, a coalition of US plastic bag producers. Further highlights for Dorn included representing the US magnesium industry in the first US antidumping case against Russia as a market economy. Former head of international trade at Hale & Dorr **Gilbert Kaplan** (see p.90) joined the firm in 2004. While at the Department of Commerce during the 1980's, he was in charge of administering US antidumping and countervailing duty laws, giving him special insight in the field. WTO and GATT expertise constitutes another string to Kaplan's bow.

44   All quotes in the text are from interviews with clients and competitors.

CHAMBERS USA 2005

The Clients: GE; Lockheed Martin; DuPont Dow; Boise Cascade; US Magnesium; Dow Agro Sciences; American Forest & Paper Association; Southern Tier Cement Committee; USA Rice Federation and Bassett Furniture.

Mayer, Brown, Rowe & Maw LLP
See firm details p.771

The Firm: Clients hold the firm's global trade group in high esteem, not least for the "*great sway its lawyers hold among international institutions,*" whether the WTO or EU. It advises some of the world's top corporations on trade policy at the highest level, and is renowned for its treatment of market access issues. The group attracted much praise for its "*ability to connect the dots within international trade law and simultaneously understand the implications for business activities in a given country.*" With seven US and six European offices, the firm is able to supply expertise for most jurisdictions. Brussels, London and Chicago offices all possess specialist international trade expertise in addition to Washington, DC. An additional consulting office in China and the presence of a former deputy chief negotiator for China's accession to the WTO mean that Asian matters are also well understood within the firm. Expertise in export controls, trade embargoes, antiboycott, Foreign Corrupt Practices Act and trade remedy matters is also offered by this group.

The Lawyers: One commentator described **Michael Kantor** as "*arguably the finest trade negotiator in the world and a terrific resource for the firm.*" He served in the Clinton cabinet from 1993 to 1997, first as US Trade Representative and later as Secretary of Commerce. **Peter Scher** was commended for his "*depth of understanding*" particularly with regard to financial institutions competing in international markets. He received similarly emphatic praise from clients in other industry sectors, who valued his advice on US-European trade relations as well as Asian and Latin American issues. Like Kantor, he knows "*how to engage with the US government at all levels – whether from an executive, legislative and regulatory viewpoint.*" Scher heads the government and global trade practice. His extensive government experience includes being a former US Special Trade Negotiator, with the rank of Ambassador, in the Office of the US Trade Representative. As a result, food, agriculture and biotechnology sectors are all ones in which Scher has specialist expertise.

Miller & Chevalier Chartered
The Firm: Interviewees credited this group with an "*eclectic range of expertise.*" It is best known for success in trade policy and Section 337 maneuvers but also offers specialist trade remedy, export controls and Foreign Corrupt Practices Act expertise. International trade accounts for around one third of the firm's busi-

ness, with tax and government contracts being its two other principal spheres of activity. Each department can call on the resources of about 40 professionals.

The Lawyers: Many of the firm's achievements in this sector are attributed to the "*capable and convincing*" **Homer Moyer** who founded the practice. He is a former Department of Commerce general counsel and has been involved in precedent setting WTO and NAFTA disputes. "*An outstanding legislative lawyer,*" **Hal Shapiro** represented a coalition of leading corporations including Boeing, Caterpillar, Microsoft, and UTC seeking the amendment of the US tax code following a WTO ruling that deemed US tax provisions benefiting exporters to be inconsistent with WTO rules. Another of his highlights involved advising a coalition of major corporations seeking passage of legislation to implement multiple changes to the US tariff system. Companies such as Honeywell, Dow Chemical, DuPont, Bayer, BASF and Eastman were party to the action. **William McGlone** received enormous praise as an export controls and economic sanctions lawyer. "*A true understanding of business-minded clients operating in heavily regulated industry environments*" distinguished him from peers. McGlone focuses on the hi-tech and oil and gas industries.

The Clients: The team represented Weyerhaeuser in the USA-Canada softwood lumber dispute. Section 337 highlights included acting for Nikon against ASML in a case involving technology used in the manufacture of semiconductors. Representing Corn Products International in one of the largest arbitrations brought under NAFTA Chapter 11 against the Government of Mexico was another highlight. The firm also represented Acres International in one of the first sanction proceedings conducted by the World Bank based on an alleged foreign corrupt practice.

Skadden, Arps, Slate, Meagher & Flom LLP & Affiliates
See firm details p.1372

The Firm: A track record of being "*intricately involved in every facet of international trade law and policy*" means the firm is widely sought after and highly respected among US petitioners. Much of its expertise evolved in the steel sector. The practice is built around a "*cadre of tenacious partners and a strong supporting cast*" including accountants, economists and trade analysts. The workload also involves lobbying Congress and the administration as well as advising on US export controls and trade embargoes. Highlights include assisting the US government in successfully defending five-year review determinations made by the Department of Commerce and Court of International Trade following challenges before a WTO panel and WTO appellate body. As a result of the favorable outcome, the

antidumping order on certain imports of steel from Japan was upheld. Members of the team have also recently been involved in Court of International Trade and Federal Circuit Court of Appeals, WTO and OECD procedures.

The Lawyers: "*Politically savvy*" head of international trade **Robert Lighthizer** (see p.93) was described as having a "*golden touch for orchestrating trade policy.*" He is increasingly involved in market opening trade actions. Lighthizer has extensive government experience, including as Deputy US Trade Representative with the rank of Ambassador under the Reagan administration. Observers also identified **John Mangan** (see p.94) as a "*formidable force.*" His considerable depth of experience of the steel industry is partly derived from having been chief international trade attorney at USX for a decade before joining the firm. Mangan remains active in trade remedy cases and legislative initiatives.

The Clients: The client base consists of large US corporations and coalitions including US producers of steel, enriched uranium, optical fibers, furniture, agricultural products and office machinery.

Weil, Gotshal & Manges LLP
See firm details p.1378

The Firm: On the trade remedy front, the firm has attracted much envied instructions on the largest and most complex cases. In addition to winning lead roles in a range of sophisticated international trade disputes, members of the firm are able to advise on export issues including economic sanctions, antiboycott actions and Foreign Corrupt Practices Act matters. The firm is involved in cases relating to industry sectors as diverse as electronics, steel and textiles. Washington DC and Brussels are the primary offices of this global firm involved in this sector. However, with USA-China trade relations being a major area of activity, it is also worth noting the firm recently opened offices in Shanghai.

The Lawyers: It is with "*the superb*" **Jean Anderson** (see p.74) that a number of interviewees "*would rather work above any other.*" She has provided ongoing advice to the Government of Canada, coordinating the joint Canadian defense among counsel for the Canadian provinces and industry associations, in the USA-Canada softwood lumber dispute. This has led to the largest antidumping and countervailing duty cases in history, involving about $7 billion in annual trade, not to mention litigation before the Department of Commerce and Court of International Trade, appeals to NAFTA panels and multiple WTO proceedings. New York-based **Stuart Rosen** (see p.105) has also impressed many market observers. He represented Eurodif of France in major US antidumping and countervailing duty proceedings brought by sole US uranium enricher USEC. The litigation involves appeals before the

All quotes in the text are from interviews with clients and competitors.

US Court of International Trade and Federal Court of Appeals challenging the applicability of the trade remedy laws to uranium enrichment. **Charles Roh** (see p.74) received praise for the diversity of his practice, which bridges international trade and international arbitration areas. He is best known for involvement in investor-state arbitrations, under Chapter 11 of NAFTA and bilateral investment treaties. Roh represented a private investor in arbitration under NAFTA and UNCITRAL concerning Mexico's expropriation of sugar mills.

Band 4

McDermott Will & Emery

See firm details p.773

The Firm: A mixture of trade remedy proceedings and export issues, as well as customs advice, account for the bulk of the practice. Immigration matters also contribute to the workload. Sources agreed that the firm has made a concerted effort in this market, making lateral hires from Kaye Scholer. Highlights for the group include representing Illinois Tool Works and its Korean subsidiary, ITW Specialty Films, in antidumping proceedings brought by another US producer against ITW Specialty Films' imports from Korea. The team also assisted Renesas Technology America with litigation in the Court of International Trade and Court of Appeals for the Federal Circuit in a case against the Department of Commerce seeking a refund of antidumping duty deposits. It is involved in WTO matters, and, as with other international trade disciplines, it is particularly well equipped in the agricultural sector. Its capacity for dealing with matters relating to China was recently enhanced with the recruitment of a former director in the Ministry of Foreign Trade and Economic Cooperation in Beijing.

The Lawyers: **Michael House** (see p.88) was identified as an "*extraordinarily impressive operator.*" He is the most prominent of two lateral hires from Kaye Scholer and is considered to provide the group with a "*massive boost.*" House focuses on China as well as Korea. Described as a "*fantastic lawyer heavily involved in international trade matters,*" **David Levine** (see p.92) spends most of his time on trade remedy matters with export controls and sanctions, together with customs matters, accounting for the rest.

The Clients: Other significant clients include Owens Corning.

Vinson & Elkins LLP

See firm details p.1724

The Firm: Clients and peers alike endorsed this firm's thriving export controls and sanctions practice. Its attorneys have represented clients before all federal agencies regulating exports, including the departments of State, Defense, Commerce and Treasury. Matters involving

NASA and the intelligence agencies are also covered. The group is also well equipped to advise on the aerospace, electronics, computer hardware and software, and telecom markets. Expert advice on economic sanctions is also offered, and the group is experienced in public policy matters.

The Lawyers: **Kathleen Little** (see p.93) was described as the "*best all-round export controls lawyer*" clients had come across. She combines expert knowledge with "*great energy and outstanding client skills.*" Little has special expertise in the International Traffic in Arms Regulations and the Export Administration Regulations as well as sanctions regulations linked to the Office of Foreign Assets Control and the Foreign Corrupt Practices Act. **David Johnson** (see p.89) was tipped as "*heading for the top rung of his profession.*" His practice combines government contract and export controls matters.

Wiley Rein & Fielding LLP

See firm details p.496

The Firm: Commentators recognized this outfit as holding a firm position amid elite international trade practices. In trade remedy cases, it acts mostly, though not exclusively, for respondents. Aerospace, defense, distribution and manufacturing constitute the core industry areas where members of the firm are involved. The team also covers issues arising from the intermingling of trade, foreign policy and national security controls.

The Lawyers: Chair of international trade **Charles Verrill** is widely recognized as an international trade lawyer who has long enjoyed a high standing in his field. Trade policy matters are viewed as his true forte, though Verrill's practice incorporates expertise in most areas within the field and as well as such disciplines as alternative dispute resolution. Clients commended **John Reynolds** for being "*equally comfortable whether dealing with Wall Street investment banks or branches of government.*" He is often seen to "*perform as an invaluable interface between the two,*" particularly on sanctions issues. A rare combination of transactional and regulatory acumen distinguishes him in the marketplace. Reynolds also benefits from experience of government service as a former attorney in the Department of State who subsequently held high-profile ABA positions. Other areas in which he offers expertise include Foreign Corrupt Practices Act and defense sector issues.

The Clients: Recent work highlights include a Section 337 action on behalf of a major pharmaceutical corporation. The team secured victory on behalf of a French producer in a Court of International Trade antidumping investigation into imports of certain wax and wax/resin thermal transfer ribbons from France and Japan. Further active clients include: Natural

Resources Council of Maine; Nucor; Chaparral Steel and Goss.

Band 5

Adduci, Mastriani & Schaumberg LLP

The Firm: Section 337 cases are the arena in which this boutique firm is considered to excel. Recent highlights have involved encapsulated integrated circuit devices, zero-mercury-added alkaline batteries, sortation systems, gel-filled wrist rests and set-top boxes. One case recently included successfully appearing before the Federal Court of Appeals. The team's lawyers are also experienced in trade remedy matters, including antidumping and countervailing duty investigations, making it a "*genuine force in the field.*" Customs is another area that generates a significant flow of work for the operation.

The Lawyers: "*First-rate adviser*" **James Adduci** caught the attention of peers and clients alike. He benefits from experience of working at the Court of International Trade and with the US Trade Representative.

Crowell & Moring LLP

See firm details p.482

The Firm: An emerging force in international trade, this firm has successfully built on a traditional government contracts profile. Trade remedy highlights include assisting US hand truck manufacturer Gleason with obtaining an antidumping order on imports of hand trucks from China. Further success was achieved on behalf of NSK in a case before the Federal Court of Appeals concerning how antidumping margins are calculated. The firm has a growing presence in London and Brussels, and benefits from its affiliation with C&M International, an international trade policy consultancy. Other areas of activity include advising on the investigation of US exports to China and the impact of China sourcing on government contracts under the Buy American Act. Issues relating to transfer of technical data and foreign nationals under International Traffic in Arms Regulations also contribute to the workload, along with numerous customs cases.

The Lawyers: An "*expert client relationship manager*" and "*brilliant adviser,*" head of the international practice **Jeffrey Snyder** received outstanding praise from peers and clients alike. He is best known for his export work and often advises on transactions involving assets in countries against which the USA has sanctions, particularly when it comes to the oil and gas sector. However Snyder is "*super-versatile*" and maintains a diverse practice that has included successful representation of DuPont in a recent antidumping case involving polyvinyl alcohol from Taiwan.

The Clients: AstraZeneca; Avecia; SAP Amer-

46   All quotes in the text are from interviews with clients and competitors.

CHAMBERS USA 2005

ica; Tomen; TDK USA; Elementis; Metal One; Hitachi Metals America and Levi Strauss.

Davis Polk & Wardwell

See firm details p.1345

The Firm: Its Washington DC office houses specialists advising on international trade regulation of considerable stature, who practice within the firm's corporate department. As a result, it wins a position in the table, albeit as rather a different animal from many of the other firms. Given the group's cutting-edge cross-border transactional work, the section would hardly be complete without featuring this small team that acts for some of the largest companies in the world on issues critical to global trade.

The Lawyers: The "*consummately careful*" **William Hoffman** (see p.88) can boast extensive State and Treasury Department experience, including having been Chief Counsel to the Office of Foreign Assets Control. Together with **Margaret Ayres** (see p.75), he is considered among the foremost economic sanctions experts in the country. Meanwhile, Ayres won especial market recommendation for her Foreign Corrupt Practices Act expertise.

O'Melveny & Myers LLP

See firm details p.294

The Firm: Lawyers with experience of working in the firm's Tokyo and Beijing offices are considered to contribute much to the firm's profile in the field. Members of the team have advised the likes of ConocoPhillips, Amerada Hess, Marathon Oil and Occidental Petroleum on the removal of US economic sanctions against Libya and re-entering the country. The firm has also served as special counsel on US economic sanctions to a major international oil company in matters relating to the development of oil reserves in and transportation of oil from the Caspian Sea region. Further recent highlights include successfully defending Delta EMD, a South African and Australian producer of manganese dioxide, against allegations that its exports to the USA were being sold at less than fair value.

The Lawyers: According to sources, **Greta Lichtenbaum** is key player in the sanctions field, where she adopts an "*extremely smart and conscientious approach.*"

The Clients: Further clients of the group include: Goldman Sachs; Nippon Steel; Macsteel International; Cargill; Nachi-Fujikoshi; Bohler Uddeholm and GlobalSantaFe.

Paul, Hastings, Janofsky & Walker LLP

See firm details p.297

The Firm: This firm has cultivated a track record in representing respondents in trade remedy cases as well as advising on export controls and sanction matters. Section 337 pro-

ceedings are also a major focus for the practice. Many of the matters undertaken by members of the firm have related to the hi-tech sector. It has acted on behalf of interests based throughout South East Asia as well as Canada. Instructions from sovereigns have accounted for a large portion of the group's recent workload.

The Lawyers: **Behnam Dayanim** (see p.80) emerged as a favorite of clients. He covers US embargoes, antiboycott regulations and sanctions as they relate to hi-tech products. Dayanim's involvement in trade dispute resolution focuses on USA-Japan and USA-Canada relations.

The Clients: The team represented the Government of Quebec in numerous proceedings including a recent success in a NAFTA Extraordinary Challenge Committee proceeding. Advice to the Government of China in Section 421 safeguard proceedings under the new China WTO accession agreement has been a major highlight of recent work relating to China. Others include advising SMIC on a Court of International Trade Section 337 proceeding with TSMC seeking to block imports by SMIC on the basis of alleged trade secret and patent violations. Further clients include Tokio Marine & Fire Insurance and the Japan Non-Life Insurance Association; Dai Nippon Printing; Government of Canada and Fujitsu IT Holdings.

Sandler, Travis & Rosenberg

The Firm: Though much of the firm's market profile is based on its customs work, these lawyers are also esteemed for their skill in taking on important trade negotiation roles. Clients judged the group to have particular depth in textile matters. Trade remedy and trade policy matters also enter into the workload. An affiliation with the customs and international trade consultancy Sandler & Travis Trade Advisory Services is considered to provide the firm with added depth.

The Lawyers: **Andrew Samet** advises domestic and international clients on legislation in the Congress and decisions by the Executive Branch that affect global trade interests. A former Deputy Under Secretary for International Affairs at the Department of Labor, Samet also has specialist international labor expertise.

Stewart & Stewart

The Firm: The firm is best known as a perennial performer in steel sector antidumping, countervailing duties and safeguards cases. There is no area of trade remedies and safeguards with which the firm is unfamiliar. Expertise extends even to measures relating to China. Customs is also a major focus. Outside DC, the firm benefits from a rich network of contacts including correspondent offices in Brussels and Moscow.

The Lawyers: As a US petitioner going into any substantial trade remedy case "*you'd certain-*

ly want to talk to" **Terence Stewart**, claimed market observers. The highest profile figure at the firm, he has acted in many senior advisory capacities, and is currently a member of the Permanent Group of Experts of the WTO Committee on Subsidies and Countervailing Measures. Stewart has considerable depth of knowledge on GATT issues.

Other Notable Practitioners

Trade Remedies and Trade Policy

Matthew Clark of Arent Fox PLLC was identified as an outstanding trade remedies lawyer credited with both "*clarity and precision.*" Involvement in the Canadian softwood lumber case features as a recent highlight from a track record that includes a number of high-profile cases including WTO and NAFTA procedures. **Catherine Curtiss** (see p.80) of Hughes Hubbard & Reed LLP also came highly recommended for trade remedy matters, particularly those relating to Canada. **Roger Schagrin** of Schagrin Associates is considered an important player in the market acting for US steel manufacturers, steel product manufacturers, iron ore manufacturers, coke manufacturers, iron foundries and abrasives manufacturers. A small portion of customs work and federal lobbying complements an otherwise overwhelmingly trade remedy-oriented practice. This has led Schagrin to appear in forums ranging from the Court of International Trade to the Federal Court of Appeals.

Export Controls and Sanctions

Market commentators respect **Evan Berlack** (see p.76) of Baker Botts LLP as a well-seasoned practitioner, who is able to operate in a diverse range of contexts whether dealing with financial institutions or multinational oil companies. Despite being best known for the export controls and economic sanctions work on which he spends most time, Berlack maintains a wide-ranging practice that includes trade remedies. It is unusual for a lawyer to be included in Chambers' tables so soon after leaving a corporation for private practice. However, former GE international trade regulation counsel **William Clements** (see p.79) is so well regarded in the field that it would be "*unreasonable not to include him*" according to interviewees. Now at Foley & Lardner, he focuses on export controls, economic sanctions and Foreign Corrupt Practices Act issues. **Benjamin Flowe** of Berliner, Corcoran & Rowe, LLP is best known for his export controls work in hi-tech and finance sector settings and is among the most revered lawyers in the field. **Christopher Wall** (see p.107) of Pillsbury Winthrop LLP was identified as one of a handful of practitioners adept in advising on both transactional and regulatory matters. He was noted for excelling in the service of clients with substantial acquisition programs. Interviewees cast **Scott Maberry** of Fulbright &

www.ChambersandPartners.com

All quotes in the text are from interviews with clients and competitors.

47

Jaworski LLP as *"the young buck of the elite."* Clients and peers alike noted that no table of this kind would be complete without the Chairman of the ABA Export Controls & Economic Sanctions Committee.

PRODUCTS LIABILITY

National
Leading firms (Products Liability)
1 ARNOLD & PORTER LLP
DECHERT LLP
JONES DAY
KING & SPALDING LLP
KIRKLAND & ELLIS LLP
SKADDEN, ARPS, SLATE, MEAGHER
2 LATHAM & WATKINS LLP
MAYER, BROWN, ROWE & MAW LLP
O'MELVENY & MYERS LLP
ORRICK, HERRINGTON & SUTCLIFFE
SHOOK, HARDY & BACON LLP
SIDLEY AUSTIN BROWN & WOOD LLP
3 CHADBOURNE & PARKE LLP
DLA PIPER RUDNICK GRAY CARY
FULBRIGHT & JAWORSKI LLP
GIBSON, DUNN & CRUTCHER LLP
HOLLAND & KNIGHT LLP
HUGHES HUBBARD & REED LLP
KAYE SCHOLER LLP
PEPPER HAMILTON LLP
REED SMITH LLP
SIMPSON THACHER & BARTLETT LLP
WHEELER TRIGG KENNEDY LLP
WILLIAMS & CONNOLLY LLP
4 BUTLER, SNOW, O'MARA, STEVENS
HOGAN & HARTSON LLP
NELSON MULLINS RILEY
Firms are listed alphabetically in each band.

Band 1

Arnold & Porter LLP
See firm details p.478
DC-based but nationally renowned, this firm has really come to the fore in this area over the past ten to 15 years. Much of its progress has been the result of a strong showing in the FDA regulatory arena and, as a result, its bank of pharmaceutical and medical clients has come to rely on it for products liability expertise. The consequence has been the representation of Hoffman-La Roche and Pfizer on cases involving prescription drugs and artificial heart valves; its profile is also sustained as a result of its advice to the American Red Cross in the blood transfusion litigation. The team, led by Ellen Reisman, is displaying its pulling power by acting as national counsel for Wyeth in the mammoth Phen-Fen drug litigation. This has involved the coordinated defense of thousands upon thousands of suits against the pharmaceutical giant, confirming the belief that this is an outfit that has *"much more than a trial presence."* Interestingly, the practice is far from confined to the drugs and medical device field. Its talented attorneys straddle many industry sectors; the advocates have acted as national counsel on numerous occasions for tobacco supremo Philip Morris, appeared in suits relating to radiation exposure and defended ARCO in its lead paint litigation. Other clients include: Wyeth; Pfizer; American Red Cross and ARCO.

Dechert LLP
See firm details p.1547
With the deft footwork of a Nijinsky, Dechert has positioned itself in all of the major products liability markets in double quick time. Always strong in tobacco, it is representing Philip Morris on significant class actions, individual cases and litigation over Lights cigarettes. Of late, however, it has expanded its horizons to the health and pharmaceutical sector with ease. Its representations in this field include involvement in the Fen-Phen litigation, the defense of Merck in personal injury cases relating to Vioxx and advising GlaxoSmithKline in resisting lawsuits concerning the drugs Baycol and Paxil. Its medical device clients further include Stryker, which it is assisting in a class action relating to the company's Trident artificial hip system. This relentless expansion is all the more remarkable in that it has been achieved in just over a decade or so. In that time, Sean Wajert's team of 15 partners has come to be recognized as a *"uniformly impressive unit deep enough to tackle the largest litigation."* Clients were particularly impressed at the team's *"readiness to go the distance"* and the perception that the team *"comes guaranteed as fully tried and tested in the courtroom."* Clients include: Cardinal Health; Baxter Healthcare; BP and Rhodia.

Jones Day
See firm details p.485
Directed by Robert Weber, 45 partners and another 100 or so attorneys devote the majority of their efforts to products liability. Just as well when one considers the *"widespread and mightily impressive caseload"* tackled by this *"hot team."* Historically, the firm focused on cases relating to mechanical products in the heartland of the country and this tradition has endured. The firm's involvement as lead counsel for Bridgestone/Firestone in the tire litigation confirms the fact, as does the attraction of new manufacturing clients such as Colt's Manufacturing. Increasingly, though, the firm has crafted a strong reputation in tobacco litigation, acting in numerous matters for key client RJ Reynolds. One of the most recent of these saw the team triumph in Conley v RJ Reynolds, the first West Coast win for a tobacco firm since 1985. Commentators widely admired a team whose ability to get to the cutting edge has been further illustrated by its front-line involvement in toxic tort cases. The team has confronted a spate of silica claims and won a unanimous verdict for IBM in the first toxic tort case involving the microelectronics industry to go to trial anywhere in the nation. The firm is not as fully locked into the pharmaceutical scene as some of its competitors, but the representation of TAP Pharmaceutical Product – producers of the hormone treatment Lupron – suggests a remedy to this situation.

King & Spalding LLP
See firm details p.635
King & Spalding is thriving in a climate where pharmaceutical companies are increasingly under attack. The firm's strong FDA practice has been a considerable draw to large drug companies looking for legal saviors boasting both regulatory and litigation skills. Its team, led by Robert Hays, has accordingly signed up some of the big names in the field acting as coordinating counsel for Purdue Pharma in the OxyContin saga. Another high point involved GlaxoSmithKline in the Paxil antidepressant litigation. Such attention-grabbing matters have ensured a national profile for a firm too often dismissed as rooted to its Southeast origins. In fact, the team's endeavors have taken it right across the country on matters that stretch beyond the pharmaceutical realm. On the tobacco front the team demonstrated its credentials acting for Brown & Williamson Tobacco in hundreds of smoking class actions, while its toxic tort capability and geographical reach were both amply illustrated by its representation of Union Carbide in more than 50 individual and class actions in ten states. Its satisfied clients are drawn from a whole host of industries and are happy to rely on lawyers seen as *"honest, above board, friendly and smart."* The presence of Chilton Varner, a top female attorney in a field dominated by men, was the cause of especial glee to many of those interviewed. Other clients include 3M, Merck and GM.

Kirkland & Ellis LLP
See firm details p.770
This firm's products liability and mass tort attorneys add luster to the legend of the practice's notoriously brilliant litigation capability. Gener-

ally retained on bet-the-company cases, its team displays the usual Kirkland hallmarks – *"hard-headedness, coruscating intelligence and an unswerving will to win."* It has involved itself in a diverse mix of prominent disputes of recent years including those referring to breast implants, cell phones, lead paint, tobacco and car seat belts. It has probably gained most publicity, though, in asbestos cases where David Bernick has gone a long way to shaping accepted strategies for coping with such matters. Always ready to litigate, this is *"a group with a very impressive culture"* that *"guarantees, above all, professionalism."* The firm represents leading companies across numerous industries including Dow Chemical and GM.

Skadden, Arps, Slate, Meagher & Flom LLP & Affiliates
See firm details p.1372
Skadden Arps has a rich history of success in this most fluctuating of legal areas. Its practice grew up more than 20 years ago on the back of standard cases in the automobile industry, where it advised Chrysler and Ford. This traditional work was then superseded as the firm graduated into the sphere of complex class actions. Its success in this area brought it cross-industry favor and a reputation as *"one of the most strategically sound practices around."* Its continued fame today is such that it has secured involvement in cases of the utmost importance. Its role in State Farm v Campbell (the case which set constitutional limits on punitive damages awards) has covered it in glory of late. Much of the work at present is drawn from the drugs, medical device and biotech sectors, evidence of which is supplied by the firm's appearances in the Fen-Phen diet drug, silicon gel breast implant and Albuterol litigation. Tobacco, silica, asbestos and other toxic tort cases are far from neglected, however, as the team pursues *"a practice branded through and through with legal analysis of the first water."* Sheila Birnbaum directs matters and is ascribed much of the credit for making this *"a natural choice as national coordinating counsel."* The firm acts for a legion of Fortune 500 companies in all of the usual industry sectors.

Band 2

Latham & Watkins LLP
A strong toxic tort tinge permeates the caseload here. The firm has built up a strong reputation in this area representing clients from differing industries all over the country. Its representations include acting for PepsiAmericas on allegations of harmful exposure at the firm's former chrome plating facility and advising National Semiconductor on allegations of injury to employees brought about by exposure to solvents. Its good name in the area looks set to be further confirmed with its ongoing appearance

in the Agent Orange litigation. Here, it is representing Monsanto in what is the largest toxic tort case in US history. Such publicity should, however, not detract from the fact that at heart this is a varied practice. Partner Beth Wilkinson's work for Philip Morris in the Altria Group litigation is evidence, for example, of a strong standing within the tobacco industry. Furthermore, her retention by Pfizer to defend cases involving hormone replacement therapy hints at greater involvement in pharmaceutical work, an area that has previously proved more elusive to the firm. This *"diverse but inclusive"* team rests under the guidance of Ernie Getto, among others, and was commended to researchers for its *"creative and innovative approach to the most difficult and challenging of cases."* Clients include: ChevronTexaco; National Semiconductor; Altria Group; ConocoPhillips and PG&E.

Mayer, Brown, Rowe & Maw LLP
See firm details p.771
This firm, like Skadden Arps, proves particularly adept in the development of national mass tort strategies. It has the manpower, spread across seven offices, and the requisite *"wealth of highly cerebral attorneys"* to offer *"an unusually high degree of strategic sophistication."* Whether it be marshaling expert evidence, picking through discovery or managing MDL procedures, this is a team with a very steady hand on the tiller. Added to this is its appellate practice, whose challenges on the admissibility of expert opinions (the team has participated in all three post-Daubert Supreme Court decisions) and punitive damages (the firm had a role in State Farm v Campbell) mark it out as *"professorial in its knowledge base."* Much of the caseload is environmental litigation and toxic tort work involving asbestos, silica, heavy metals, chemicals and others. The team recently defended BP/Burmah Castrol Holdings in suits arising from alleged exposure to the company's products and separately advised various chemical companies such as Chevron. It is also serving as national counsel for Union Carbide in its ongoing asbestos litigation. On a more traditional level, the group has appeared in automobile cases for industry leaders like Mercedes and DaimlerChrysler and enjoys a significant role on Philip Morris's punitive damages committee. Commentators agreed, therefore, that this is a firm *"more than capable of taking in the bigger picture."* Herb Zarov won particular praise for a broad practice that embraces noted specialization in asbestos litigation. Clients include: Dow Chemical; Union Carbide; Novartis; BASF and Abbott Laboratories.

O'Melveny & Myers LLP
See firm details p.294
Researchers unearthed palpable respect for a firm that *"has reached out beyond its corporate core to take in appreciable amounts of mass tort*

work." Its attorneys are renowned for their *"tactical acumen"* in negotiating cases of great magnitude across America for manufacturing clients. Pharmaceutical work is less pronounced but the team scores well, especially in automobile litigation, where it has appeared in the Ford ignition switch litigation. The team, which includes Rich Goetz and John Beisner, prides itself on its class action know-how and has played a key role in advising on actions brought by welders alleging neurological injuries brought on by exposure to manganese from welding rods. The firm's clients are drawn from a wide pool of manufacturing companies.

Orrick, Herrington & Sutcliffe
See firm details p.295
Products liability work forms a significant proportion of the work handled by Orrick's 125-attorney litigation team. With capacity on both the East and West coasts the firm has consistently improved in this area and was congratulated for producing a practice both *"wide in scope and tailored to quality cases."* Initially, it was occupied with tobacco litigation but it has turned to other grazing fields. Chief among these are pharmaceutical, chemical and medical device matters. The team, under Daniel Thomasch, currently serves as national counsel for Wyeth and Lederle Laboratories in separate childhood vaccination cases and has acted for Cytec Industries in class actions claiming personal injury resulting from the use of paints containing lead pigment. Asbestos also looms large with the firm representing Union Carbide in two related matters. To all this work its attorneys, according to clients, bring *"great articulation, an excellent rapport with judges and the guarantee that all bases are being covered."* Rival lawyers, too, were keen to point out the constructive nature of the firm's collegial approach to litigation. Clients include: Dow Chemical, American Cyanamid and Dana.

Shook, Hardy & Bacon LLP
See firm details p.1067
Always the go-to firm in Kansas for products liability, Shook Hardy & Bacon long ago reached out from its regional base to impose itself on the national scene. This it achieved largely through tobacco litigation and the market perception is that it was Philip Morris' No. 1 in the beauty parade. Tobacco remains a huge constituent of its lifeblood but the practice has turned to other forms of sustenance in recent years. Most strikingly, it has engendered a strong reputation in pharmaceutical and medical device work, undertaking such matters as the vaccine and diet drug litigations. Orchestrated by Harvey Kaplan the team has further defended cases involving antidepressants, acne drugs, heart valves and bone screws. Its determination to capture a burgeoning slice of the market has been further pinpointed through its involvement in the

www.ChambersandPartners.com

All quotes in the text are from interviews with clients and competitors.

49

automobile and alcohol sectors, where it has acted for the likes of Miller Brewing. Such versatility should ensure bountiful times ahead. Multiple tobacco firms including Philip Morris, automobile companies, vaccine manufacturers and others form the core of its client roster.

Sidley Austin Brown & Wood LLP
See firm details p.778

Interviewees acknowledged a firm that has *"done everything there is to do for a host of major companies."* Under the guidance of Michael Davis, more than 20 partners operate primarily out of Chicago and LA, upholding a firm-wide reputation for litigation excellence. The core of the work is based on pharmaceutical and medical device products, but the team can claim involvement with a range as eclectic as cell phones, breast implants, vinyl chloride and sports utility vehicles. Particular praise was reserved for the team's efforts on behalf of Aventis/Armour in the Hemophilia/AIDS imbroglio and for its advice to American Cyanamid in the lead paint litigation. In other scenarios, the firm has acted for Bayer over the withdrawal of its cholesterol reducing medicine Baycol and separately defended Suzuki over suits claiming its Samurai model was liable to roll over. These and many other representations have led to an inundation of acclaim for *"a firm whose strategy and execution, absolute dedication to the client and, above all, appellate capability are second to none."* Its clientele includes AstraZeneca Pharmaceuticals, Aventis and Pfizer.

Band 3

Chadbourne & Parke LLP
See firm details p.1341

Tobacco litigation constitutes the central prop of this 35-lawyer team led by Thomas Bezanson. The firm's expertise in this area is, according to interviewees, *"right up there with the best,"* a fact illustrated by its appointment as international counsel by both BAT and Gallagher. On the domestic front its strongest ally is Brown & Williamson Tobacco, which it has successfully defended in jurisdictions as far apart as New York, Louisiana and Texas. Suggestions in some quarters that it owes its fame in the products liability/mass tort pantheon to tobacco alone are countered by its appearances in matters relating to alcohol, dietary supplements, military weapons and pesticides, as well as its work on behalf of Purdue in the OxyContin litigation and in relation to suits arising from the laxative Senokot. Indeed, as some commentators noted, the firm is *"ever ready to take the initiative and try the more interesting cases."* This is perhaps best illustrated by its representation of a nuclear bomb manufacturer in the defense of claims by residents of the Marshall Islands contingent upon the testing of the first hydrogen bomb in 1954. Clients include: BAT; Gallagher; Jim Beam;

Purdue and Brown & Williamson Tobacco.

DLA Piper Rudnick Gray Cary US LLP
See firm details p.765

"Nothing if not consistent," Piper Rudnick may not be one of the real superstars of this field but it does keep perpetually busy. This it achieves through adaptability. All of the major fields have the firm's imprint upon them with pharmaceutical, automotive and tobacco cases proving particularly lucrative areas. The team, well marshaled by Amy Schulman, defended Wyeth in the Fen-Phen litigation and has represented a leading manufacturer in MDL relating to hormone replacement medication. It has also acted as national or regional counsel for international as well as domestic automotive manufacturers and has advised numerous companies in national asbestos cases. Clients include: Harley Davison; Brown & Williamson Tobacco; University of Pennsylvania and Kawasaki Motors.

Fulbright & Jaworski LLP
See firm details p.1715

From the inception of manufacturers' liability cases in the 1960s, Fulbright & Jaworski has been involved in some of the nation's most significant disputes. Its cause in this regard has been advanced by virtue of it being one of the most renowned firms in the litigation hotbed that is Texas. From this base it draws in a number of regional matters and does extend a sizable proportion of these matters nationally. In so doing it relies on a network of seven offices housing more than 50 attorneys who are proficient in all the major industries. Foremost among these is the pharmaceutical world but the team is regularly involved in aerospace, automotive, tobacco, farm equipment and recreational vehicle cases. Vince Walkowiak is a major force in the team. He is defending GlaxoSmithKline over allegations relating to its diabetes drug Avandia and has handled class action litigation for Sony Electronics and Sony America involving a $100 million purported recall of televisions.

Gibson, Dunn & Crutcher LLP
See firm details p.285

Gibson Dunn's rise to prominence in this field has been gradual but relentless. It has generally garnered marketplace attention for its environmental litigation and toxic torts work, an area where Raymond Ludwiszewski has pushed the firm onward. Familiar with contaminated community cases, he has served as lead trial counsel for a major company in groundwater contamination suits, while also demonstrating an affinity with asbestos-related cases by acting as national coordinating counsel for Tyco and Oldcastle. Quite apart from this, the firm has dazzled in automotive cases, an area in which its lawyers showcase their much vaunted appellate skills. Involved in

important pleadings at this level, they combine *"thorough analysis with outstanding oral and written presentation."* Theodore Boutrous takes much of the strain in this respect and has appeared in a number of the biggest products liability cases in history. Examples include acting for Ford in the appeal against a $290 million punitive damages award arising out of the rollover litigation. He also appeared for DaimlerChrysler in the appeal of a $53 million verdict in Arizona. The team of 23 attorneys acts for household names such as Ford, DaimlerChrysler and Dow Corning.

Holland & Knight LLP
See firm details p.1352

Among the many positive characteristics attached to this practice, the most immediate is its diversity. Its team of more than 100 attorneys is large enough to involve itself in almost every corner of the market appearing in alcohol, asbestos, aviation, chemical, firearms, industrial machinery and pharmaceutical cases to name but a few. Such an approach dictates that the firm tends to have a mass of clients rather than just one or two huge concerns feeding it a steady flow of work. This does not mean, however, that the practice is not associated with some big names and, indeed, it appears in the occasional headline case. Its status is founded on such work as sole representation of aircraft giant BAE Systems, advice on behalf of ExxonMobil regarding contamination issues and an appearance alongside Jones Day in the Bridgestone/Firestone litigation. Randal Craft of the firm's New York office is an integral part of a collection of lawyers spread across some 25 offices. Texas Instruments, ExxonMobil and GlaxoSmithKline are featured among its prominent clientele.

Hughes Hubbard & Reed LLP
See firm details p.1353

The group here, comprising some 65 attorneys, can expect to attract greater interest in the future. Already well known as national counsel in the blood and dietary supplement cases, it is now fulfilling a similar role for long-standing client Merck in the Vioxx litigation. Its appointment is consistent with a recognized aptitude in the pharmaceutical and medical devices arena, but the firm's capabilities extend beyond this. It is also interested in the railway, shipping and automotive industries and is building a strong platform for itself in toxic workplace exposure cases. Since acting for Rockwood Specialties in a matter involving the chemical effects of wood treatment it has flourished in this area, picking up a number of coal mining exposure cases, as well as securing a plum role as national coordinating counsel for a large chemical group regarding its asbestos litigation. These matters should assist the team, which includes Robb Patryk and Theodore Mayer, in its ambitions to seize a greater slice of the market. A roster of large pharmaceutical, chemical and automotive manufacturers includes Merck and DaimlerChrysler.

Kaye Scholer LLP
See firm details p.1354

While Kaye Scholer may not match some of the others in our tables for variety, it takes its place there due to its connection with one very big and very litigious client. The firm is principal outside counsel to Pfizer, an appointment that has ensured its participation in some of the most high-profile matters of late. It has represented the company in the Viagra and Rezulin defenses and has advised it in the hormone replacement therapy litigation. As a result it can claim *"complete familiarity with all aspects of high-stakes litigation"* and *"a proven track record in dealing with the onslaught of multiple plaintiffs."* These qualities have further surfaced in the team's other, non-Pfizer-related, appearances. These include acting for Baxter Healthcare in the silicone breast implant case and advising on toxic injury cases for welding industry manufacturers. Cochair of the department Jay Mayesh stands out as the man most likely to impel the practice to further glory. Clients include Navistar International and various automobile manufacturers.

Pepper Hamilton LLP
See firm details p.1558

Pepper Hamilton has proved itself highly competent in a number of products liability arenas, including automotive work, but is indelibly linked with one area and one area alone – the defense of pharmaceutical and medical device manufacturers. Its prowess here is beyond doubt, as attested by its inclusion in some highly important cases. Its defense of Sofamor Danek in the Orthopedic Bone Screw litigation really brought it to the attention of the market, marking it out as a practice *"capable of tackling a hugely complex matter and producing a watertight defense strategy."* Since then, despite being marginally weakened by the departure of figures such as Jim Beck, it has consolidated its position. Still attracting good work and *"hitting the mark every time,"* it has appeared in the Prozac litigation and acted for Eli Lilly. It is currently national counsel in a diabetes medication case and MDL counsel for a number of phentermine manufacturers. Interviewees backed a team known for its courtroom abilities and its additional strength in environmental, chemical and radiation exposure cases. Nina Gussack of the Philadelphia office chairs the health effects litigation practice group. The majority of the firm's clients are to be found in the pharmaceutical, chemical and medical device fields.

Reed Smith LLP
See firm details p.1560

The market has followed Reed Smith's progress with interest and now pronounces it *"ready to emerge as a considerable force."* The firm started as a go-to local counsel before working its way up to be regional counsel. Now it has its sights firmly set on a consistent role on the national stage. That it can aim in this direction is due in part to its alliance with other legal entities, not least Crosby Heafey whose absorption, observers feel, has afforded the practice further consolidation within the lucrative pharmaceutical field. Already effective here, the firm has undertaken extensive activities on behalf of Wyeth, including the diet drug litigation. Strong mass tort capability is also at hand with Steven Kohn who heads the products liability practice group. Many of the firm's clients derive from the pharmaceutical and medical device sectors.

Simpson Thacher & Bartlett LLP
See firm details p.1370

Although ineluctably associated with corporate work and corporate-related litigation, Simpson Thacher does have a relatively fat finger in the products liability pie. It has, since the 1960s, appeared in some substantial matters for some prominent names such as Ford. Happy to delve into most areas, it acted as national coordinating counsel for BAT, the London-based parent of Brown & Williamson Tobacco, in tobacco litigation across the USA. Representing Intel, it handled the litigation surrounding the Pentium microprocessor. Interest in the pharmaceutical world was confirmed by its appointment by American Home Products (now Wyeth) to coordinate its Fen-Phen diet drug litigation in New York; a vibrant showing in the alcohol industry is indicated by its representation of Diageo North America. The firm has also distinguished itself acting for Travelers Indemnity in resisting thousands of asbestos claims. Mark Cunha plays an influential part in a team that continues to include litigation legend Roy Reardon. The firm acts for Wyeth and other manufacturers from a host of different industries.

Wheeler Trigg Kennedy LLP

This firm is built on a much smaller scale than many of the others in the tables but wins loyalty through the quality of work it attracts. Devoting some 80% of its resources to this type of work, the group snaffles some enviable clients due to its success record. By way of illustration it has been involved in rollover work for Ford, acted as national franchise counsel for DaimlerChrysler and appeared for Whirlpool in 12 class actions. In addition, it has undertaken a large volume of cases spanning 17 states on behalf of Guidant. The secret of its success is, aside from its ability to work well with other firms, the presence of Malcolm Wheeler. A nationally known figure and one of the gurus of this field, he has appeared in the US Supreme Court. *"Smart and innovative,"* he has recently tackled a constituency of work for Pfizer that has included litigation regarding its antidepressant Zoloft. Attorneys act for a large body of manufacturers many of which are found in the automotive and pharmaceutical industries.

Williams & Connolly LLP

This high-octane litigation group is also a contending force in products liability, particularly when it involves the pharmaceutical arena. Its *"strong FDA capability"* is effectively blended with its trademark courtroom pugnacity to deliver star performances for an eminent clientele. The team is participating in the Vioxx litigation, in addition to a range of other disputes involving such products as the cholesterol-reducing drug Baycol, childhood vaccines and Prempro, which alleviates menopausal symptoms. A conscious decision to expand in this practice area in recent times has been met with enthusiasm in the marketplace, and sources said they now consider the team as *"increasingly a viable option."* The firm's success is partly due to its enduring relationship with Wyeth, led by the *"terrific"* John Vardaman. Other key players include qualified physician David Kiernan, whose legal vocation is concentrated on pharmaceutical class actions among other medical-related issues. He served as lead trial counsel in the Baycol litigation. Clients include GE, Bell Sports and American Cyanamid.

Band 4

Butler, Snow, O'Mara, Stevens & Cannada, PLLC
See firm details p.1038

Butler Snow is becoming *"indispensable local and regional counsel in some tough jurisdictions,"* observers said. Its stomping ground is Tennessee but its influence extends far beyond this, and it is increasingly ratifying its status as a player on the national stage. Over the course of a rich history it has come to the assistance of manufacturers in many sectors including the pharmaceuticals, medical devices, aviation, agricultural and firearms industries. Known for its shrewd strategy, it lends credence to the suggestion that its star is in the ascendancy by its recent appointment by Wyeth to advise on its hormone replacement therapy litigation. Christy Jones is the chair of a litigation department that also received applause for its toxic tort capabilities.

Hogan & Hartson LLP
See firm details p.484

Hogan & Hartson started off in this game doing traditional manufacturers work for companies such as DaimlerChrysler, a company the firm continues to act for. It was, however, when the pharmaceutical area exploded that the firm came more to the fore. Able to exploit its internationally recognized FDA practice, it began to entice more and more producers in this sector to repose their trust in it for general products liability work. Some of its greatest benefactors have been the most recognizable names in the pharmaceutical field. Prominent among a raft of issues handled for these concerns is the defense against claims stemming from a counterfeit version of a client's pharmaceutical product. Such engagements have forced the market to sit up and take notice of *"a team with a bright future ahead of it."* The group, of which Mark Gately is a vital part, works generally out of DC but has capability in other locations including Baltimore, Denver, Miami and LA. The team represents an eclectic mix of manufacturers a preponderance of which are in the automotive and pharmaceutical industries.

Nelson Mullins Riley & Scarborough LLP
See firm details p.1584
Our interviewees identified this practice as *"definitely in the one-to-watch category."* Its team has handled matters in a multitude of differing areas including asbestos, automobiles, blood products, bicycles and chemicals. Most of its activities have been confined to its Carolina strongholds but observers note a perceptible shift to the national theater. Engagements such as the appointment to be national counsel to Wyeth in the PPA (phenylpropanolamine) litigation bode well for a group with *"a pretty strong bench and the will to succeed."* Richard Farrier, managing partner of the Charleston office, maintains a keen interest in the area.

PROJECTS

National
Leading firms (Projects)
1. LATHAM & WATKINS LLP
2. MILBANK, TWEED, HADLEY & MCCLOY
   SKADDEN, ARPS, SLATE, MEAGHER
   WHITE & CASE LLP
3. CHADBOURNE & PARKE LLP
   SULLIVAN & CROMWELL LLP
   VINSON & ELKINS LLP
4. BAKER BOTTS LLP
   SHEARMAN & STERLING LLP

Leading individuals (Projects)
1. **BILGER Bruce** *Vinson & Elkins*, Houston
   COGAN JR John *Akin Gump*, Houston
   DESANTIS Victor *White & Case*, Washington, DC
   FEO Edwin *Milbank Tweed*, Los Angeles
   FITZGERALD Peter *Chadbourne & Parke*, Washington, DC
   GORDON David *Latham & Watkins*, New York
   GREEN Jonathan *Milbank Tweed*, New York
   MOORE Harold *Skadden Arps*, New York
   RICH Frederic *Sullivan & Cromwell*, New York
   SCAVONE Arthur *White & Case*, New York
   SHUTRAN Richard *Dewey Ballantine*, New York
   SINGER Andrew *Latham & Watkins*, San Diego
   VOGE William *Latham & Watkins*, New York
2. **ALEXANDER Troy** *White & Case*, New York
   ASMUS David *Baker Botts*, Houston
   BRACH Richard *Milbank Tweed*, New York
   BURKE Ted *Freshfields Bruckhaus*, New York
   GALVIS Sergio *Sullivan & Cromwell*, New York
   HARRIS L Douglas *Milbank Tweed*, New York
   KLEPPER Martin *Skadden Arps*, Washington, DC
   MARTIN Keith *Chadbourne & Parke*, Washington, DC
   ROD Jonathan *Latham & Watkins*, New York
   SACHS John *Latham & Watkins*, Washington, DC
   UNGER Timothy *Andrews Kurth*, Houston
   WACHSBERGER Chaim *Chadbourne & Parke*, New York

Firms and individuals are listed alphabetically in each band.

Band 1

Latham & Watkins LLP
The Firm: According to market sources, this is indisputably the most prolific projects practice in the USA. Its *"heavyweight team"* received substantial praise. Lawyers in San Diego, Washington DC and New York can call on the firm's resources in Asia and Europe as required. Observers remarked: *"It's not just the senior partners that are good; they have surrounded themselves with talented people."* It is therefore perceived to offer unrivalled depth and breadth. The firm's commitment to this area of law was strongly attested to, with commentators saying: *"It's focused on the field like a laser beam and throws real firepower at it."* The strong domestic practice features cutting-edge capital markets work in the power sector on behalf of financial institutions and project companies. Heavy involvement in the high-profile M&A and restructuring transactions that currently characterize the domestic projects market also marks it out. A *"formidable"* international practice based in Washington DC and New York is particularly renowned for its experience in the Middle East. Its current international workload includes some of the most talked about projects in the industry. Highlights include acting for project companies in the enormous Ras Laffan II project and in the Q-Chem petrochemicals project, both in Qatar. Further work on behalf of the project companies includes the Uch power project in Pakistan and the Nigerian NGL expansion project in Africa. It is also representing Ex-Im Bank in the Qatargas II project, and the lenders in the Tengiz Chevron project in Kazakhstan.
The Lawyers: Interviewees discerned a distinctive brand of lawyer, and uniformly praised practitioner's commercial acumen and problem-solving approach. Practice chair **Andrew Singer** divides his time between San Diego and New York, specializing in domestic capital markets with an emphasis on Rule 144A offerings. He is renowned for *"finding solutions to issues and focusing on results,"* not to mention being *"one of the brightest lawyers in the market."* **David Gordon** in New York has a similar practice. Another of the firm's top-tier practitioners, observers describe him as *"practical, constructive, pragmatic and pleasant."* **William Voge** is the team's leading international practitioner and *"a great business-getter."* He *"excels in building client relationships."* Clients praise *"his practical approach and great negotiating style."* Key lawyer **Jonathan Rod** comes from a capital markets background and is currently working on the Qatargas II project. Clients describe him as *"responsive and wonderfully analytical as well as creative."* **John Sachs** focuses on representing the sponsors. Complimentary client feedback stated that he is *"a high-quality lawyer with great connections and experience in the power industry."*
The Clients: Financial institution clients include: Société Générale; Goldman Sachs; CSFB; Citibank; Lehman Brothers; Morgan Stanley; ING; Nord/LB and Bank of Nova Scotia. In terms of multilateral agencies it represents the likes of Inter-American Development Bank and Ex-Im Bank. Sponsors such as Chevron Phillips; Qatar Petroleum; Nigerian National Petroleum; ExxonMobil; CDC Globeleq; Jamaican Government; Dynegy; Pennsylvania Power & Light Global; United Technologies; Marubeni Power; GWS Energy and Ormat are also clients.

Band 2

Milbank, Tweed, Hadley & McCloy
The Firm: It is undoubtedly among the leading US operations representing lenders and uniformly named as one of the industry's *"core firms."* The outfit has capitalized on having established fruitful relationships with major banks when projects markets first opened. It is now increasingly representing private equity firms as the field evolves to include a wider range of investors. Indeed, its reputation among financial institutions is so favorable that peers

52   All quotes in the text are from interviews with clients and competitors.

CHAMBERS USA 2005

comment: "*It can be difficult to compete with Milbank in New York.*" There are few sectors in which the team does not represent lenders, with focus areas including power, LNG, renewable energy, transportation and mining projects throughout the USA and the world. However, the firm's considerable work for sponsors is not to be overlooked, where the New York and Los Angeles offices are particularly notable for the "*sheer breadth of their practice, extending throughout the western hemisphere.*" Overall the firm's foremost areas of expertise are considered to be renewable energy projects and Latin American mining projects.

The Lawyers: California-based **Edwin Feo** has one of the highest profiles in the industry. Clients say he is "*very knowledgeable, very experienced, and knows the business inside out.*" He has particular depth of experience when it comes to representing financial institutions in renewable energy projects. **Jonathan Green** is another "*headline name,*" especially in the context of representing financial institutions in domestic projects. He was praised as a "*practical and efficient*" lawyer who has the ability to "*sift through to the important issues.*" He is also noted as "*a tough negotiator.*" **Richard Brach** is renowned as the firm's mining projects specialist and was billed as "*a leader for Latin American work.*" **Douglas Harris** comes highly recommended as a "*consummate technician and brilliant draftsman.*" Clients rely on him for "*very smart analysis*" and "*detailed knowledge of the project.*"

The Clients: ANZ; Fortis; Dexia; BayernLB; BNP Paribas; Matlin Patterson; CSFB; Citigroup; JBIC; OPIC; Mitsubishi; Diamond Energy; Cap Rock Energy; Leucadia National; Total and Tractebel.

Skadden, Arps, Slate, Meagher & Flom LLP & Affiliates
See firm details p.1372
The Firm: Another of the traditional leaders in the field, it is particularly well known for involvement in multibillion-dollar Middle East projects. Clients report it is "*one of the truly elite firms in terms of international experience on a variety of different energy projects.*" Its projects lawyers reside in Washington DC, New York and Houston. Envious peers bill the operation as "*a real powerhouse; a formidable competitor with a lot of reach.*" Domestic prominence is perceived as stemming principally from heavy involvement in M&A and restructuring transactions with an emphasis on power and natural gas sectors. A diverse mix of clients includes developers, investors and lenders. However, having started out as a developer's firm peers still see it as "*the quintessential sponsor's operation – aggressive, tough, relentless and thorough.*" Both developer and lender clients state that the firm "*is particularly efficient in anticipating unforeseen issues.*"

The Lawyers: The success of the projects practice is virtually synonymous with **Harold Moore** (see p.1302) himself. He is universally heralded as "*a tremendously talented projects lawyer*" by both peers and his "*large client following.*" Described as "*the go-to person for the big issues,*" Moore has also proved himself "*an extremely capable technician.*" Washington DC practice head **Martin Klepper** (see p.451) enthralled clients who say he has "*more experience in international projects than any other attorney we've used.*" Many made special mention of his ability to effectively manage large groups of lawyers and his "*calm, unshakeable negotiating style.*"

The Clients: Too lengthy to reproduce here in full, the client list includes: Ex-Im Bank; ArcLight Capital Partners; Enron; KBC; Nevada Power; Edison Mission Energy; CEMEX; Excelerate Energy; Sempra Energy; Goldman Sachs and BHP Billiton.

White & Case LLP
See firm details p.1379
The Firm: There was a consensus that this firm houses a cadre of specialists all with decidedly international practices. A remarkably good reputation for representing commercial banks and multilateral agencies in established and emerging markets is especially marked in the context of oil and gas, power, and toll road projects. Clients say the firm has "*good experienced lawyers we can trust*" who "*combine excellent legal knowledge with canny business sense.*" Peers acknowledge the firm's "*real dedication to the sector.*" Its US projects hubs are New York and Washington DC, part of an international network of offices that spans Europe, Asia and Latin America. This makes it a natural choice in landmark deals globally. The team represented the lender consortium in the $11.3 billion Sakhalin LNG project in Russia, and is representing Qatar Petroleum and ExxonMobil in the $11billion Qatargas II project.

The Lawyers: It was unanimously agreed that DC-based **Victor DeSantis** (see p.439) is "*doing a stunning job representing multilateral agencies.*" Clients report he is "*calm under fire and can resolve difficult issues in a nonconfrontational manner.*" The "*bright and practical*" **Art Scavone** (see p.1317) in New York was declared "*very good at analyzing potential risks*" and rated as "*a hands-on lawyer who combines strong legal knowledge with great business sense.*" He is considered to excel in the representation of all parties and offers experience in both international and domestic projects. Peers and clients alike enjoy working with **Troy Alexander** (see p.1262). A "*terrific talent,*" he is said to "*concentrate on getting the deal done instead of scoring points.*" Like DeSantis, Alexander is best known for representing multilateral agencies. He is also representing the sponsors in the massive Qatar-

gas II project. The trio are jointly responsible for overseeing the work of the department.
The Clients: Saudi Aramco; Abu Dhabi Water and Electricity Authority; CSFB; Lehman Brothers; Amerada Hess; Deutsche Bank; Ex-Im Bank; Inter-American Development Bank; IFC; JBIC; MidAmerican Holdings; OPIC; BNP Paribas; Société Générale; Bancomext and Unocal.

Band 3

Chadbourne & Parke LLP
See firm details p.1341
The Firm: As one of the early pioneers, it is historically a major player in the field. This practice can proudly flaunt 25 years experience, highly seasoned practitioners and "*a well-established name universally recognized in the sector.*" Its lawyers are especially well renowned as "*power infrastructure experts.*" The recent workload has been heavily punctuated by asset sales and purchases, M&A and restructuring advice for developer companies in the domestic market. The firm also has expertise in the LNG, gas pipeline and transportation sectors. Despite having a relatively compact practice, clients claim it is "*qualitatively comparable to the top firms.*" On top of well-established New York and Washington DC teams, the firm has a burgeoning presence in Texas. Its domestic offices work closely with London and Moscow branches. On the international front, the CIS, Africa and Latin America have been focus points for substantial activity of late.

The Lawyers: **Peter Fitzgerald** (see p.442) is a leading light in the field of political risk insurance where he boasts a highly impressive track record. Clients report his "*outstanding technical skills*" coupled with "*incredible interpersonal skills*" make Fitzgerald stand out from the pack. **Keith Martin** (see p.455) is another leading specialist in project-related tax issues, for which peers say he is "*absolutely top.*" Clients respect him as "*a good lawyer but also a good businessman.*" **Chaim Wachsberger** (see p.1329) has a long-standing reputation, and as the head of the practice he balances his management duties with time in the trenches. He is rated as "*a savvy practitioner who knows the points to make and understands what clients need.*"

The Clients: El Paso; Royal Bank of Scotland; GE Energy; AES; CSFB; Citibank; Union Bank of California; Duke Energy; Tractebel; IFC; Inter-American Development Bank; Sovereign Risk Insurance; Greka Energy and Interconexión Eléctrica (ISA) Bolivia.

Sullivan & Cromwell LLP
See firm details p.1373
The Firm: The Wall Street giant has acquired a magnificent reputation for winning mandates in the largest, highest value and most complex projects. It is true that the firm does not have the

www.ChambersandPartners.com

All quotes in the text are from interviews with clients and competitors.

53

same day-in day-out presence in the projects arena as it enjoys in corporate terms, and that its team is comparatively lean. However, qualitatively speaking it is without doubt *"a premier projects practice."* Lawyers concentrate on major international oil and gas projects in Latin America, Central Asia and the former Soviet Union. It has a particularly fine reputation among peers for its strength in Latin American matters, recently having begun work on major mining projects in the region. Market observers also praised the team's *"very commercial"* approach and point out that *"its members don't indulge in endless pedantic exercises but instead concentrate on getting the deal done."*

The Lawyers: Frederic Rich (see p.1312) is *"an oil and gas expert"* who is *"very experienced in working on major projects."* His colleague Sergio Galvis (see p.1281) is hailed as *"great for Latin American deals."* Sources report : *"His reputation in that region is gold."*

The Clients: Petrobras; Barrack Gold; Baku-Tbilisi-Ceyhan Pipeline; BP; ExxonMobil; Kenmare Resources; Camisea Pipeline Consortium; Autoridad del Canal de Panam·; Occidental Petroleum; Pacific Hydro and Lihir Gold.

Vinson & Elkins LLP
See firm details p.1724

The Firm: In the context of America's leading oil and gas law firms it is judged to lead the pack, representing oil and gas majors in projects around the world. The firm is steeped in energy expertise and clients rave about its *"bottomless depth of experience in the industry."* The heart of the operation lies in Houston, but important outposts include New York and Washington DC. Its diversity is considerable, incorporating upstream, midstream and downstream projects, including a number of large petrochemicals facilities. The firm has benefited from a robust LNG industry, in relation to which it is involved in developing upstream facilities internationally as well as receiving terminals domestically. Although traditionally known as a developer's firm, it also has a vibrant lenders practice and represented the lenders in the El Cajon hydroelectric plant in Mexico. This example highlights the firm's involvement in the power sector. Commentators widely praised its high-quality lawyers, particularly *"the hands-on approach of partners"* and their cultivation of a *"practical and result-oriented attitude."*

The Lawyers: With five Houston-based lawyers and one DC practitioner identified as leaders in the field, the firm boasts a considerable depth of practice. However, projects head Bruce Bilger (see p.1672) stands out as *"a particularly impressive, top-tier practitioner."* He received considerable praise as *"the classic Texas energy lawyer,"* with interviewees particularly valuing his *"practical approach to closing deals."*

The Clients: BG Group; Chevron Phillips Chemical; JPMorgan Chase; WestLB; AES; PSEG Global; Bank of Nova Scotia; Calyon; WestLB; Bank of Montréal; Burmeister & Wein; AIG and Allied Irish Banks.

Band 4

Baker Botts LLP
See firm details p.1708

The Firm: Another Texas law firm synonymous with brilliance in energy sector projects was the verdict returned by the market. It has long-established relations with energy companies, and is generally recognized as an outstanding developer's firm for oil and gas projects. The practice was pronounced *"top notch"* in the development of upstream projects, including some high-profile LNG export facilities, pipelines and oil platforms. US branches of the practice, especially the Houston hub, work on a number of domestic projects, especially in the Gulf of Mexico. The firm benefits from a London office that has also contributed its fair share to major international projects where the firm is involved.

The Lawyers: David Asmus (see p.1670) was identified as standing out from a whole raft of experienced and talented energy project lawyers. He has a stellar reputation for both upstream and LNG projects. Clients also say: *"He is able to apply the experience gained from an oil industry background admirably,"* having developed *"great technical skills."*

The Clients: The firm represents large oil companies such as BP; ExxonMobil; Marathon; Hunt Oil and ConocoPhillips.

Shearman & Sterling LLP
See firm details p.1369

The Firm: Interviewees declared this firm enjoys one of the best reputations in the business for restructuring projects that have fallen on hard times. The practice is also renowned as a leading force in the Latin American market in which it has worked for 50 years and developed an expert awareness of local legal issues. The firm recently enhanced its projects capacity by opening a São Paulo office that works closely with New York. Sustained involvement in the power sector is complemented by advice on a number of metals and mines projects. Clients stress the firm's ability to *"come up with appropriate solutions amid contentious circumstances and concentrate on finding a route through the problems to getting the deal signed."*

The Lawyers: Market observers reported that a typical Shearman & Sterling lawyer has *"great technical ability"* and is *"very strong at handling complicated financings."* Prominent names include co-head of project development Cynthia Urda Kassis and Jeanne Olivier, an expert in multiple-risk insurance.

The Clients: Mizuho Bank; CSFB; Citigroup; ABN Amro; Barclays; Crédit Lyonnais; Central American Bank for Economic Integration (CABEI); Netherlands Development Finance (FMO); Deutsche Investitions und Entwicklungsgesellschaft (DEG), BNP Paribas; PSEG Global and Placer Dome.

Other Notable Practitioners

John Cogan (see p.1675) at Akin Gump Strauss Hauer & Field LLP is *"a leader in the LNG field"* and praised as *"a very accomplished international lawyer,"* not to mention *"an extremely intelligent practitioner."* Richard Shutran (see p.1321) is the leading light of Dewey Ballantine's LLP projects practice. He is recommended as *"a very experienced, smart and results-oriented lawyer."* Many observers also noted his *"great demeanor during negotiations."* Ted Burke (see p.1269) is Freshfields' key US projects lawyer and clients like to use him because of his *"fantastic commercial acumen"* and *"creative solutions."* The *"eminent and experienced"* Timothy Unger (see p.1704) of Andrews Kurth LLP has been a prominent presence on the Texas scene for years. He is currently concentrating on wind and LNG projects.

SPORTS LAW

OVERVIEW: Some of America's highest profile legal proceedings relate to sports, often engaging some of the most popular organizations and their equally prominent owners and athletes. In addition there is a proliferation of work involving media outlets, sponsorship and commercial opportunities – all of which require an ability to combine the nuances of sports law with agility in commercial contracts, antitrust, media law and employment among other areas.

The field also demands a certain finesse in execution, particularly when navigating through the political ramifications of headline issues; the proposed New York Jets stadium, for instance, is to be located four blocks down from Madison Square Gardens. Other matters involve locking horns over issues with much wider ramifications. One such dispute is the NHL lockout, which led to the cancellation of the entire 2004-2005 season.

The legal advisers who specialize in this field tend to be of a select breed, delivering corporate polish along with an instinct for the jugular in equal measure. Only a few firms and practitioners are able to offer the range of skills, knowledge, expertise and contacts to succeed on a national basis.

National

Leading firms (Sports Law)

1	PROSKAUER ROSE LLP
2	COVINGTON & BURLING
	DEWEY BALLANTINE LLP
	SKADDEN, ARPS, SLATE, MEAGHER
3	BINGHAM MCCUTCHEN LLP
	MILLER, CANFIELD, PADDOCK
	WEIL, GOTSHAL & MANGES LLP

Leading individuals (Sports Law)

1	GANZ Howard *Proskauer Rose*, New York
	GOLDFEIN Shepard *Skadden Arps*, New York
	KESSLER Jeffrey *Dewey Ballantine*, New York
	LECCESE Joseph *Proskauer Rose*, New York
	LEVY Gregg *Covington & Burling*, Washington, DC
	MISHKIN Jeffrey *Skadden Arps*, New York
2	ALKALAY Peter *McLaughlin & Stern*, New York
	ANDREOZZI Bradley *Mayer Brown*, Chicago
	FEHER David *Dewey Ballantine*, New York
	FRIEDMAN Andrew *Covington & Burling*, Washington, DC
	GOLDBERG Daniel *Bingham McCutchen*, Boston
	HOLBREICH Curt *Howard Rice*, San Francisco
	QUINN James *Weil Gotshal*, New York
	RUSKIN Bradley *Proskauer Rose*, New York

Firms and individuals are listed alphabetically in each band.

Band 1

Proskauer Rose LLP

See firm details p.1365

The Firm: The nation's leading sports practice earns praise for its work for the National Hockey League, National Basketball Association and Major League Baseball. Its experience spans across a range of disciplines, including football, soccer, tennis and golf. Peers hail the group as "*a superbly rounded practice, with great people, great skills and a great knowledge of the field.*" The group has acted for the New York Jets in matters concerning its proposed $1.3 billion stadium in New York. The project has been further complicated by a campaign against it, led by the owners of Madison Square Gardens – which is located four blocks from the site. It is in these difficult situations where the team thrives, with clients adding: "*It understands our needs and what we want, and knows when to play a tactical game and when to hit a home run.*" The team has also been involved in the ongoing litigation concerning the ownership swap of the Montreal Expos and the Florida Marlins. "*It's not just a great law firm,*" a client said; "*it's a business partner.*"

The Lawyers: This "*dream team*" of lawyers is said to parlay some of "*the finest skills in the country*" into successful results. Employment and labor expert **Howard Ganz** (see p.1282) was recommended as "*a superb, knowledgeable lawyer, with a delicate and agile touch.*" He represented the NHL in its dispute with the player's union over compensation; the case led to a prolonged lockout and cancellation of the season. He also represents the NBA and the MLB in employment matters and various collective bargaining issues. "*Corporate guru*" **Joe Leccese** (see p.92) was praised as "*a terrific lawyer – one of the best in the business.*" Combining professionalism with "*excellent judgment,*" he advised on the structure of NBA's $1 billion league-wide credit facility. He also has participated in sports-related M&A. **Bradley Ruskin** (see p.102) heads the litigation section of the sports practice, and is endorsed as "*a deep-thinking lawyer with his finger on the pulse.*"

The Clients: The group has represented three of the four major US sports leagues, including the NHL, NBA and MLB. It also undertakes work for various NFL teams and advises ATP Tour and Major League Soccer.

Band 2

Covington & Burling

See firm details p.481

The Firm: This highly rated firm is primarily known for its representation of the NFL, and is hailed for its skills in sports-related litigation, corporate, tax and antitrust matters. It is described as "*a careful and precise practice,*" often participating on considerable matters for the four main sports leagues. Ownership issues, restraint of trade and funding programs also feature in its portfolio. Other items on the menu dovetail with the group's well-regarded media and entertainment practice. For example, the team has negotiated broadcasting and new media deals for both major sports leagues and professional clubs.

The Lawyers: **Gregg Levy** (see p.93) is pitched as "*a real go-to guy,*" clients said. "*He's a smart lawyer whom you can genuinely trust.*" A top contender in all things concerning football, he is particularly distinguished as an expert litigator and a superb antitrust specialist. He successfully represented the NFL in a case concerning Ohio State University running back Maurice Clarett, who attempted to enter the NFL draw without conforming to certain requirements. Levy is also acting in two major lawsuits tinged with antitrust issues brought by the stadium landlord of an NFL club. Tax expert **Andrew Friedman** (see p.84) wins client endorsements as "*a man who can get things done.*" He handles tax work for all four major sports leagues, as well as structuring tax-exempt bonds, stadium financings and other proceedings. He is also advising clients with regards to an IRS audit of sports teams. One of his headline cases involved the US Tennis Association in the organization of the new US Open Series, which links ten summer hard-court tournaments beginning after Wimbledon and leading up to the US Open.

The Clients: The group handles matters for all four major sports leagues as well as individual clubs.

Dewey Ballantine LLP

See firm details p.1347

The Firm: This strong litigation-focused practice has represented the five leading players' unions, cities and sponsors, mainly in disputes against sports leagues, colleges and owners among others. It is regarded as "*probably the top sports litigation practice in the country,*" winning praise by clients as "*a collection of experts and enthusiasts.*" It has been involved in some of the most high-profile sports disputes in America, including matters relating to the NHL lockout. It has also handled legal battles concerning individual players and sports agents.

The Lawyers: The arrival of **Jeff Kessler** (see p.1293) from Weil Gotshal & Manges is seen as

www.ChambersandPartners.com

All quotes in the text are from interviews with clients and competitors.

55

a huge boost to Dewey Ballantine's practice. Peers hail him as "*a smart and aggressive litigator who should never be underestimated.*" He also won confidence as a "*sharp*" operator "*with a mind that works at breakneck speed,*" clients said. "*He has a great understanding of what a judge or arbiter wants.*" His practice primarily revolves around players' unions, for example, advising them on collective bargaining issues. Highlights include representing the Metropolitan Intercollegiate Basketball Association against the National Collegiate Athletic Association in antitrust litigation. Clients commended **David Feher** (see p.83) as "*a highly effective and astute litigator.*" He is known for his skills in collective bargaining, and has expertise in salary caps and team revenues.

The Clients: National Football League Players Association; National Basketball Players Association; Arena Football League Players Association; National Hockey League Players Association; Major League Baseball Players Association; North American Soccer League; United States Football League; NHL Coaches Association and SFX.

Skadden, Arps, Slate, Meagher & Flom LLP & Affiliates
See firm details p.1372

The Firm: This "*smart, aggressive*" firm earns endorsement as "*an incredibly professional outfit,*" clients said. "*There's none better in terms of body of experience and expertise.*" Its lawyers are "*a dedicated group of sports fans which is knowledgeable across the board.*" Its skills in commercial matters, litigation, antitrust, media and employment are all commended by the marketplace. The group is best known for its work in basketball and hockey, but also represents the NFL on some litigation. It has represented the NHL in its negotiations with the NHLPA, and helped marshal the same client through the lockout that led to the cancellation of the league in the 2004-2005 season. It is participating in the Big East litigation, where it represents four universities in connection with the planned move of several schools to the Atlantic Coast Conference. The group also draws enthusiastic plaudits for its corporate and transactional work. It has acted on the sale and purchase of a number of sports teams. Overall, it was pitched as "*a firm you can trust as it has done it all before and knows all the angles.*"

The Lawyers: Clients praise antitrust expert **Shep Goldfein** (see p.1284) as "*a capable professional and a good sounding board for a range of*

sporting problems." He is best known for his work for the NHL, but has also been involved in an important antitrust case involving the PGA Tour. **Jeffrey Mishkin** (see p.95) garnered acclaim for his strong links to the NBA. "*A smart, aggressive lawyer who gives good and sound advice,*" he has represented the NBA in litigation, labor, commercial and IP protection matters.

The Clients: The group recently acted for the United States Tennis Association with regards to the new US Open Series tournament. Other clients include the four major sports leagues, particularly the NHL and the NBA, and individual sporting teams. It has also represented large corporate clients with an interest in sport.

Band 3

Bingham McCutchen LLP
The Firm: This Boston-based team earns plaudits for its transactional aptitude, particularly in sports-related financing. Applauded as "*a knowledgeable group who are tough in negotiations but experts to deal with,*" the team is often retained on complex transactions. For example, it acted for Frank McCourt in his purchase of the LA Dodgers from Fox. This $430 million deal involved a number of intricate maneuverings involving such issues as television rights, real estate law and other corporate matters.

The Lawyers: **Daniel Goldberg** is perceived as a distinguishing figure in the firm's sports law profile. Cochair of the antitrust and trade regulation practice group, his generalist repertoire also involves prominent sports-related cases. For example, he has participated in IP-related litigation involving professional sports teams.

The Clients: The group's strengths are seen to derive from its Boston base, and it is especially distinguished for its work on behalf of the New England Patriots and New England Revolution. It also represents the LA Dodgers and has carried out antitrust matters for the NFL. Another client is MLB, for which the team has counseled on IP and licensing issues.

Miller, Canfield, Paddock and Stone, PLC
See firm details p.1004

The Firm: This well-regarded firm is best known in the marketplace for its work for the National Collegiate Athletic Association. On behalf of the NCAA, it has engaged in litigation and antitrust matters among other issues. For example, the team is acting in Worldwide Bas-

ketball et al v NCAA, which involves preseason tournaments. In another case, it is handling a dispute in Seattle involving scholarships.

The Lawyers: Gregory Curtner is a key member of the team.

The Clients: Among others, the NCAA is a principal client.

Weil, Gotshal & Manges LLP
See firm details p.1378

The Firm: Its experience in sports law is vast, though the team remains best known for its litigation skills. Its niche in new media is also commended; in this respect, the group recently advised the NFL on the licensing of names and images on cards, video games and the Internet. It has also represented ESPN on a number of different broadcasting issues, including cable rights relating to cricket in India. Regarding labor and employment, the team has participated in a number of arbitrations between players and leagues, as well as being involved in collective bargaining with the NFL.

The Lawyers: The group may have suffered from the departure of Jeff Kessler to Dewey Ballantine, commentators said, but there are plenty of talented attorneys left to sustain the team's success. Among them is **Jim Quinn** (see p.1310), who is generally regarded as "*a highly effective operator*" whose litigation skills are much prized by clients. He is experienced on labor and collective bargaining issues – typically for the players' unions. He has acted in football, baseball, basketball, hockey and soccer interests.

The Clients: The group's range of clients includes sports leagues, professional teams, players' unions, individual players and broadcasters.

Other Notable Practitioners
Peter Alkalay of McLaughlin & Stern LLP won praise from clients as "*an outstanding lawyer.*" "*We like everything he does and have never been less than pleased by him.*" His practice is largely related to matters concerning the Olympics, and he has represented athletic organizations on sensitive issues such as illegal doping methods. **Curt Holbreich** of Howard, Rice, Nemerovski, Canady, Falk & Rabkin is praised as "*a terrific lawyer who understands track and field issues.*" **Brad Andreozzi** (see p.74) of Mayer, Brown, Rowe & Maw LLP is commended for his work for USA Track and Field. He also worked for the Court of Arbitration in Sport during the Athens Olympics.

TRANSPORTATION

This year, Chambers and Partners introduces a national transportation category split into four sections – aviation, rail, road carriage and shipping. The latter subdivision includes an extended entry for the largest maritime US market, the already established New York Shipping sector.

Several factors led to the introduction of this section. Global multimodal commerce in containers has become the ubiquitous standard for carriage around the world, as each mode of transport becomes increasingly part of an integral, overall system for transportation clients. "The various modes are becoming more dependent and interlinked," says one leading transportation attorney. Homeland security and related aspects have refocused attention on infrastructure, and we wanted to reflect these changes. According to one industry leader: "The targeting of infrastructure has changed the transportation landscape and what it means to financial institutions and companies."

Consolidation has continued in many subsectors, with the shipping and trucking markets proving particularly dynamic. As a result, there are many fewer genuine legal boutiques in the market compared to only a few years ago. However, with one or two exceptions, law firms in general are still best known for their focus on one main area of expertise, such as Vedder, Price, Kaufman & Kammholz's work in aviation. Alternatively, others have abandoned sector expertise in favor of a cross-departmental approach, as DC's Arnold & Porter has done. This is due, in part, to the singular nature of some transportation work, such as aviation defense. This contrasts with the lower value, higher volume work often seen in the rail and trucking sectors.

Nevertheless, emerging in the marketplace are identifiable, nascent, fuller service transportation departments. Practices are responding to industry trends such as Public Private Partnerships (PPPs) and complex financing arrangements of the sort that larger, cross-departmental firms are more able to provide. Most importantly, clients are increasingly demanding a greater breadth and depth of transportation capability. Industry analysts said this continuing tension between specialist firms and those that go all out in an effort to supply a one-stop shop shows no sign of abating.

AVIATION

OVERVIEW: The events of September 11, 2001, still cast a long shadow over the industry. Increased government safety and security regulations, and subsequent enforcement actions, have been on the rise. Firms holding themselves out as leaders in the field must be conversant on such matters as the unlawful transport of hazardous goods, violations of no fly regulations and lawsuits by passengers claiming invasion of privacy and discrimination because of security procedures. As one partner noted "Although deregulation has been in effect in the US for more than 20 years, the trend has in fact been inclined toward the regulatory side where consumer issues and safety and security are concerned."

Unfortunately for the market, this is only one of its concerns. "The aircraft market is in turbulence, with 9/11, economic downturn and legacy airlines on grave financial footings, plus there is the onslaught of low-cost carriers," according to one industry expert. However, a positive development is a recent upturn in aviation capital markets transactions, which some herald as the start of a new industry cycle. Furthermore, the increasing numbers of companies purchasing corporate jets to address security issues and also attain productivity gains has fostered a new field for attorneys; as such, business assets create enormous liability exposures through their ownership and operation, as well as taxation concerns.

In other developments, the ratification of the Montreal Convention by the US in 2003 is perceived to lead to a substantial decrease in certain types of litigation. Cargo damages, for example, are limited by the Convention. The Cape Town Convention, dealing with protocols for aircraft equipment, railway rolling stock and space assets, was ratified by the US in 2004 and will likely play an important role; the Convention is expected to result in significant changes in aircraft and aircraft engine financing. The only thing certain about the future of the industry is its uncertainty, sources said, but there are encouraging signs that a difficult corner may have been turned.

National
Leading firms (Aviation)

[1]	MILBANK, TWEED, HADLEY & MCCLOY
	SHEARMAN & STERLING LLP
	VEDDER, PRICE, KAUFMAN & KAMMHOLZ
[2]	CADWALADER, WICKERSHAM & TAFT
	CONDON & FORSYTH LLP
	CROWELL & MORING LLP
	FULBRIGHT & JAWORSKI LLP
	HOGAN & HARTSON LLP
	HOLLAND & KNIGHT LLP
[3]	GAROFALO GOERLICH HAINBACH PC
	MILLER, CANFIELD, PADDOCK
	PERKINS COIE LLP
	PILLSBURY WINTHROP LLP
	SHAW PITTMAN LLP
	SIMPSON THACHER & BARTLETT LLP

Firms are listed alphabetically in each band.

Band 1

Milbank, Tweed, Hadley & McCloy

The Firm: In an industry that has been embattled in recent years, this primarily New York-based practice has unsurprisingly concentrated on restructuring, making good use of its leading insolvency practice. In addition, the market's partial recovery has led to an increase in capital markets and securitization transactions, further benefiting the firm. It regularly undertakes big-ticket work via its existing clientele of top investment banks, utilizing a familiarity with issuers, rating agencies and the nuances of the sector. One interviewee went as far as to venture that when it came to loan, debt and structured finance matters for aircraft and equipment, the firm was "*possibly the most experienced in the world.*" Truly national and international in scope, it acts on behalf of some of the leading underwriters globally. Clients particularly highlighted the group's work in Asia, as well as its technical nous. Another stated that the group's "*deep bench and client-driven staff are more interested in solving problems than talking about them.*"

The Lawyers: Elliot Gewirtz heads the firm's global transportation finance department and is involved in many of its most prominent deals for marquee clients. His traditional focus is on capital markets transactions, representing underwriters on airline deals or portfolio securitization. Commentators variously described him as "*the complete package*" and "*the godfather*" for this work. He represents bondholders' groups and ad hoc committees on various insolvency proceedings, lease financings and cross-border tax leases. Peers spoke highly of his "*terrific capability to take a mammoth structure and describe it in simple terms so that it can be understood by virtually anyone.*" His intellectual approach is allied with a decisive pragmatism; "*he will look to successfully close the transaction with his client protected.*" **Drew Fine** is respected

National
Leading individuals (Aviation)

1 GERBER Dean *Vedder Price*, Chicago
GEWIRTZ Elliot *Milbank Tweed*, New York
HONG Ji *Shearman & Sterling*, New York
SCHEINBERG Ronald *Vedder Price*, New York

2 ABORN Richard *Cadwalader Wickersham*, New York
BARRY Desmond *Condon & Forsyth*, New York
KATZ Donald *Miller Canfield*, Detroit
PIELS William *Holland & Knight*, San Francisco
PRITCHARD John *Holland & Knight*, New York
TUSSING James *Fulbright & Jaworski*, New York

3 BOGAARD Jonathan *Vedder Price*, Chicago
BOWERS William *Pillsbury Winthrop*, New York
CARNEAL George *Hogan & Hartson*, Washington, DC
COHN Robert *Hogan & Hartson*, Washington, DC
COLEMAN Payson *Pillsbury Winthrop*, New York
FINE Drew *Milbank Tweed*, New York
GAROFALO Gary *Garofalo Goerlich*, Washington, DC
HOWITT John *Paul Hastings*, New York
JACOBSON Martin *Simpson Thacher*, New York
KEINER, Jr R. Bruce *Crowell & Moring*, Washington, DC
ROBERTSON Elihu *Milbank Tweed*, New York

Up-and-coming individuals

GENTNER Joshua *Vedder Price*, Chicago
LEONG Alvin *Milbank Tweed*, New York

Individuals are listed alphabetically in each band.

for his blend of technical aptitude and client responsiveness. He is skilled in international finance transactions relating to aircraft, other types of vessels and rolling stock. **Hugh Robertson** primarily advises on banking and securities matters within transportation, including domestic and cross-border lease financings and enhanced equipment trust certificates (EETCs). Commentators also recognize his inclination toward the more esoteric side of aviation law, and those transactions with a Brazilian flavor. Partner **Alvin Leong** advises on aircraft finance, leasing and securitization on behalf of commercial and investment banks. Quick to understand structural issues, he "*looks for solutions and does not highlight problems,*" clients said.
The Clients: Among the firm's distinguished clientele are some of the world's most prominent investment banks.

Shearman & Sterling LLP

See firm details p.1369
The Firm: The bulk of the firm's transportation work is focused on aviation, especially on behalf of airlines. Clients recommended the practice for its broad corporate finance portfolio, which is considered to be "*pound for pound, the best law firm out there in this field.*" Its technical proficiency attracts clients, particularly when dealing with EETCs – an area in which the firm is considered a pioneering authority. Another instrumental factor for the group's success is its burgeoning strength in capital markets and structured finance as related to transportation.

It has advised on a large proportion of the IPOs linked to domestic airlines. This included assistance to underwriters led by Morgan Stanley on the IPO of Pinnacle, formerly a regional carrier subsidiary of Northwest Airlines. Although still primarily a New York-based team, it uses its global reach to expand into new areas, including the Asian market. The department also runs a rail sector practice of some note with a strong European focus.
The Lawyers: Ji Hoon Hong (see p.88), a partner in the firm's securitization and derivatives group, combines excellent business sense with "*qualitative skill sets,*" clients said. He has "*an exemplary understanding of capital markets and a good grasp of how to structure transactions.*" His expertise encompasses capital markets and structured equipment finance work within transportation, particularly in the airlines sector. "*Commercial, but not afraid to state his position,*" he brings a hard-working style and "*objective, thoughtful analysis*" to transactions. He advises on portfolio acquisitions of aircraft owned by leasing companies and undertakes EETCs work.
The Clients: The team notably advises on the ongoing restructuring of the public debt of Delta Air Lines, working for the solicitation agents and dealer managers, led by Merrill Lynch. It represents the underwriters on an offering of EETCs by JetBlue Airways, incorporating several structural refinements and innovations to the standard EETC format. It worked with a number of additional underwriter clients in connection with offerings of convertible debt by AMR/American Airlines, NWA/Northwest Airlines and Delta Air Lines.

Vedder, Price, Kaufman & Kammholz

The Firm: A "*well-rounded practice*" best known for its expertise on workouts and restructurings within the aircraft industry, it is historically associated with United Airlines, having counseled on its financing activity for over a decade. Several competitors considered the group to be "*probably the leading firm specializing in airline finance representation.*" Clients praised the balanced approach adopted by the team: "*They put their case forward and get people to agree in a businesslike fashion.*"
The Lawyers: Dean Gerber is the chair of the firm's "*broad and deep*" equipment finance group. Clients and competitors alike applauded his "*innovative and highly skilled*" technique and "*straight arrow*" style. A "*terrific lawyer, he doesn't leave bodies strewn in his wake*" and is "*not interested in drama or theatrics, just in a rational solution.*" He concentrates on aircraft work, chiefly representations on behalf of United Airlines. He represents the Export-Import Bank of the United States (Ex-Im Bank) on a $341 million export credit financing to Pakistan International Airlines in relation to three wide-body

aircraft. **Ron Scheinberg** primarily acts on behalf of banks, for example, advising Royal Bank of Scotland on the financing of ten narrow-body aircraft for a US air carrier. Well versed in equipment financing, he also demonstrates proficiency in structured capital markets transactions. "*The kind of guy who can get things done in an effective fashion, even if matters are difficult,*" he garnered client confidence for his "*calm, rational and bottom line-oriented*" style. Another attractive element of his practice is "*a personality that puts everyone at ease in negotiations.*" **Jonathan Bogaard** often works with Gerber on a significant portion of the United Airlines matters. "*Smart, quick and practical,*" he acted as special aircraft finance counsel in connection with the airline's Chapter 11 fleet restructuring. His focus is frequently on corporate and related tax matters, although he also advises on some rail financings. Senior associate **Joshua Gentner** "*knows his stuff as well as anybody*" and is tipped as a considerable talent among the next generation of aviation finance attorneys. Among others, he has assisted Ex-Im Bank and United. He also works with Scheinberg on public debt work, representing JetBlue Airways in a $930 million EETC financing for 28 aircraft.
The Clients: The group advised ABN AMRO as agent on behalf of a bank syndicate in connection with the management of a fleet of 15 wide-body repossessed aircraft. It also represented several French banks in connection with the leveraged lease financing of aircraft for a US air carrier.

Band 2

Cadwalader, Wickersham & Taft LLP

See firm details p.1339
The Firm: Key facets of the firm's transportation work relate to advising airline clients on maintaining liquidity and negotiating financing to acquire new planes or to refinance old ones. It also represents some non-airlines bidding on portfolios or planes. New York lawyers primarily handle its aviation work, with complimentary assistance from the firm's Charlotte office. In addition, tax-related advice is provided via its DC outpost.
The Lawyers: Richard Aborn (see p.74) deals with the financing of aircraft for the firm's two blue-chip clients, namely Northwest Airlines and Delta Air Lines. A "*real old hand,*" he earned respect as an easygoing and effective advocate. His knack for team management and talent for finding solutions among complicated issues were also underlined.
The Clients: The group represented Delta Air Lines' wholly-owned subsidiaries Atlantic Southeast Airlines and Comair in an innovative loan transaction involving UK lender Halifax

and the UK's Export Credit Guarantee Department as guarantor; the transaction resulted in each airline securing its loans with six Bombardier regional jet aircraft. It further represented Comair on debt financings involving 18 Canadair regional jets. It advised on leveraged lease financings involving 39 Canadair regional jets as well as debt financings involving ten Airbus A330 aircraft. The firm acts on the financing of all new aircraft acquired by Northwest Airlines and separately represented a major US airline on debt financing for the acquisition of a number of Boeing 747 aircraft.

Condon & Forsyth LLP

The Firm: The vast majority of this firm's lawyers practice some aviation law. It is best known for representing major airlines on matters arising from disasters, but its range is wider. Other prominent areas of practice include leading cases on the interpretation of the Warsaw Convention and the handling of hazardous materials in transport. Other interests relate to disabled passenger regulatory issues and various security concerns related to travel. It obtained operating authority for several non-US airlines to fly to the United States. Another specialty is advising airlines on economic sanctions concerning aircraft sales and products originating from the USA, particularly as related to countries such as Cuba, Sudan and Iran.

The Lawyers: **Desmond Barry** is the firm's most notable name in this practice area. Interviewees spoke of a respected strategist whose name alone is sufficiently powerful to attract clients. He represents American Airlines in litigation arising out of the 9/11 terrorist attacks. His colleague, Thomas Whalen, is also noted for counseling Saudi Arabian pilots in litigation over the revocation of their pilot certificates by the US government on grounds that they were a risk to US national security.

The Clients: The firm successfully defended Air New Zealand against a passenger's claim that she allegedly suffered deep vein thrombosis (DVT) following a long flight on the airline. It defended Singapore Airlines in US-related claims by the families of those killed in a plane crash in Taiwan on October 30, 2000. It also represents Lufthansa in litigation against Wayne County Airport, Detroit, regarding a claim that negligent snow removal damaged the engines of one of its aircraft. Other clients include American Airlines and Olympic Airways.

Crowell & Moring LLP
See firm details p.482

The Firm: The firm's portfolio splits broadly into two main areas – airline-related economic regulatory counseling, and business aircraft work and related transactions. The group serves as lead counsel for Continental Airlines on all of its aviation economic regulatory work in addi-

tion to some litigation. It represented the Regional Airline Association, groups of individual airlines and the Helicopter Association International in proceedings relating to airport access and pricing policies that allegedly discriminate against operators of small aircraft. Other expertise involves appellate proceedings as related to aviation law. Another area where the firm has demonstrated flair is in legislative advice.

The Lawyers: **Bruce Keiner** is advising Continental in proceedings before the US Department of Transportation in relation to airline routes and flight frequencies between the USA and China; such advice resulted from a breakthrough aviation agreement in 2004 between the two countries. He provided similar counsel to Continental on its efforts to secure the right to operate between various locations in the USA and throughout Latin America, enabling the client to become the second largest US airline in South America. His "*terrific reputation in the field*" is also gained through his advice on airline alliances matters, including code sharing.

The Clients: The team assisted Continental Express (now ExpressJet) in defending its right to operate regional jets from Love Field in Dallas. Aer Lingus also sought the team's advice in two federal court cases, fighting attempts by global airline reservation systems operators Sabre and Galileo to force the airline to offer its low web fares through their systems. Other clients include Continental Airlines, First Choice, Helicopter Association International, the Regional Airline Association and other US and foreign airlines. Airfreight forwarders, tour operators and manufacturer associations also feature on its roster.

Fulbright & Jaworski LLP
See firm details p.1715

The Firm: The practice operates primarily from offices in Houston, New York and DC, conducting airline regulatory work out of the latter two. Its commanding national presence is further enhanced by its international strength; around half of its work is conducted abroad. Activity since 9/11 has been dominated by insolvencies, consolidations and restructurings, but other transactional work is now on the upswing. The firm engages in general corporate aircraft transactions for clients acquiring or trading up its aircraft. It assists on financing for regional aircraft in the USA and Europe, as the movement towards smaller, regional jets on shorter haul destinations in preference to larger aircraft gathers pace. Clients endorsed its thorough understanding of financial and regulatory spheres. Personal injury and product liability counsel to air carriers also plays a significant part of the firm's aviation activity. Rounding out the practice is advice related to commercial litigation, regulatory proceedings, licensing and trademark law.

The Lawyers: **James Tussing** (see p.107), who heads the equipment finance section, regularly marshals clients through debt and lease equipment financings, as well as related workouts, reorganizations and litigation. "*Commercial and experienced*," he earns plaudits for finding solutions through a "*solid understanding of where everyone is coming from.*" His clientele is a mixture of US and foreign commercial banks, credit companies, high-yield funds and airlines.

The Clients: The team represented the Bank of New York in the ongoing United Airlines bankruptcy, and advised Japan's largest leasing company ORIX on substantial restructuring with Air Canada and United Airlines. It represented the equity participant in a US-leveraged lease transaction using an EETC structure covering 32 aircraft on lease to American Airlines. The firm successfully undertook air carrier litigation on behalf of a major airline regarding a plane crash that resulted in fatalities, injuries and property damages. It also acted for Visteon in a dispute against Ameristar Jet Charter relating to breach of contract and antitrust/price fixing allegations stemming from an agreement linked to air charter requirements. Diageo is another client.

Hogan & Hartson LLP
See firm details p.484

The Firm: A prominent focus on security and related projects is a leading drawing card for the team. Flourishing in an area that has become increasingly important to many of its clients, the group advises on regulatory issues concerning commercial litigation, aircraft and project financings among others. Similarly, the same clients are seeking assistance on economic and safety matters relating to European requirements as regulations there become more stringent. It also advises on the rising trend for the fractional ownership of corporate aircraft, and offers counseling in connection with air accident investigations. Another attractive feature is its strong links to Congress. Clients also praise the firm's "*uniform standard across the board,*" as well as its excellence "*in terms of customer service and promptness to respond.*"

The Lawyers: **George Carneal** (see p.78) chiefly engages in economic and regulatory advice. He has represented a consortium of the networks and television stations that formerly broadcast from the North Tower of the World Trade Center on a proposal to build a 2000-foot replacement tower in the vicinity of Newark Airport; this required an airspace study by the FAA and aircraft hazard determination. Market feedback also underscored Carneal's thoroughness and efficiency. The arrival of **Robert Cohn** (see p.79) from Shaw Pittman's aviation team greatly increases the extent of the firm's aviation expertise. He previously served as principal outside regulatory counsel to Delta Air Lines and Republic Airways Holdings, among others.

Alexander Van der Bellen, also from Shaw Pittman, is another addition to the team.

The Clients: The practice serves as US counsel to Air Canada in its restructuring and refinancing. It provides aviation regulatory advice to NetJets, the creator of the corporate aircraft fractional ownership concept; this includes assistance on issues related to the FAA, the Department of Transportation (DOT) and international aviation economic regulations. It has represented the Government of The Bahamas since July 1991 in litigation concerning alleged bribery-related aircraft purchases from a certain manufacturer. It also works for the Zero-Gravity Corporation on aviation regulatory and commercial approvals as well as ongoing issues relating to parabolic flight services in the USA. Other clients include: Air Jamaica; China Airlines; China Southern Airlines; FedEx; GE Capital Aviation Services; Honeywell International; Lee County Port Authority; Menlo Worldwide; Metropolitan Washington Airports Authority; National Aeronautical Association; National Business Aviation Association; Rolls-Royce North America; Toyota Industries and Vietnam Airlines.

Holland & Knight LLP

See firm details p.1352

The Firm: This national aviation practice balances between aviation finance assistance and crash litigation counsel. On the finance side, workouts, defaults and bankruptcies predominate in a broader practice that also features advice on lending and operating leases. Litigation advice centers on the defense of manufacturers of aircraft and its components, and US and foreign airlines, usually in matters arising from plane accidents and related investigations. Illustrative of this is its advice to American Airlines regarding claims arising out of the deaths of 251 passengers on the Flight 587 crash near Kennedy Airport in New York City in 2001.

The Lawyers: **William Piels** (see p.98) frequently works with large financial institutions on aviation finance matters. In addition, he has also worked with lessees and enjoys a recognized understanding from both sides of the transaction. He "*has a terrific personality for this work – great market knowledge but a low-key style,*" ideal for negotiation in complicated transactions, interviewees said. He represented the Royal Bank of Scotland and its affiliated leasing company, RBS Aviation Capital, on the sale, leaseback and predelivery financing of ten new Boeing 737 aircraft, valued in excess of $300 million. Group leader **John Pritchard** (see p.98) carries out a lot of work with foreign airlines on the operating lease side. "*He can be tough, and you have to credit him with his excellent knowledge of the area.*" Thorough with his documentation and adopting a "*diligent and understated approach,*" he represents clients in both financ-

ing and lending transactions. Piels and Pritchard are the leading names in a national team that revealed a deep bench of attorneys, many of whom enjoy prominent market profiles.

The Clients: The firm advised purchaser/lessor GE Capital Aviation Services on the sale and leaseback of six new aircraft engines and 22 new Boeing 737 aircraft, with an equipment value of more than $800 million. Babcock & Brown Aircraft Management retained the firm on the lease of a Boeing 737-200 aircraft to an English charter operator First Choice Airways and on the purchase of a Boeing 757-200 aircraft from Aviation Capital Group. Other clients include GATX Financial, GE Capital, RBS Aviation Capital and the Royal Bank of Scotland.

Band 3

Garofalo Goerlich Hainbach PC

The Firm: These aviation specialists advise in particular on the purchase and sale of aircraft, regulatory requirements and compliance, and matters relating to export and import. Peers identified the group as being especially well positioned to serve clients with regulatory issues that require an appeal or official hearing in front of the National Transportation safety Board (NTSB).

The Lawyers: **Gary Garofalo** often represents clients involved in financing operations. A long-time practitioner in the sector, interviewees highlighted his enduring connections with the Federal Aviation Administration (FAA).

The Clients: The firm's clientele includes carriers and business companies among others.

Miller, Canfield, Paddock and Stone, PLC

See firm details p.1004

The Firm: A large proportion of this Michigan-based team's activity is centered on transactional work for clients looking to acquire business jets, usually in response to security issues and to attain productivity gains. Such clients require assistance on multiple taxation issues, and the firm has responded by developing services that aim to link the tax and corporate aspects of aviation work. Clients of the group describe a "*timely and practical*" service often within short time frames while others commend its "*diligent*" manner. One of its leading specialties is in municipal finance, working with borrowers to finance projects such as the construction of airports, runways and related projects.

The Lawyers: **Donald Katz** principally acts on aviation matters, although he does undertake a degree of motor carrier and supply chain management advice. A "*thoughtful and responsive lawyer,*" he is valued by clients for his expertise in aviation regulations and working knowledge of the tax and business laws related to such transactions.

The Clients: The practice assisted Aerodynamics Inc (ADI) in a transaction to run Intel's regional flight department, which involves what is essentially a regional airline for its employees and transporting about 200,000 passengers a year; this included aviation regulations, contract negotiations and tax matters. The team also worked with defense contractor General Dynamics on complex, jurisdictional tax and risk management issues surrounding its purchase and operation of a Gulfstream G200 and the sale of a Citation X to an affiliated company.

Perkins Coie LLP

The Firm: The aviation group advises on equipment and leasing transactions, and aircraft finance. It represents clients on the purchase, sale and leasing of aircraft, notably for corporate planes owned by non-carrier companies, an area that has expanded. It is best known for its decades-long assistance to aerospace giant Boeing, but is also counsel to other domestic and foreign entities on the negotiation and structuring of cross-border transactions.

The Lawyers: For more than two decades, Keith Gerrard has been defending Boeing in aviation accident cases as part of a broader practice that also includes representing manufacturers on products liability litigation. Colleague Peter Archie deals with air carrier restructuring and aircraft purchase and sale.

The Clients: The group remains Boeing's largest outside counsel, but it also represents several smaller carriers. It has negotiated the debt and aircraft lease restructuring on behalf of both a US and a Caribbean carrier. It also obtains breach of warranty endorsements on aircraft liability policies, using a specific structure to reduce tax burdens for clients in the corporate jet business.

Pillsbury Winthrop LLP

See firm details p.1364

The Firm: Regulatory and insolvency concerns are two of the firm's leading aspects. In one prominent case, the firm is defending key client Airbus in ongoing litigation with about $500 million at stake concerning the crash of American Airlines Flight 587 over New York in 2001. Counsel includes assistance regarding the concurrent NTSB investigation. Other activities target equipment finance and advice to clients in the travel and leisure industries. Clients primarily recommend the firm for its breadth and available resources on larger transactions.

The Lawyers: **William Bowers** (see p.76) works primarily on transportation finance and asset-backed securitizations. He employs a conciliatory approach, getting to the heart of structural issues with "*a way of explaining esoteric tax matters that everyone can understand,*" according to clients. **Payson Coleman** (see p.79) heads the firm's equipment finance team. Clients noted a measurable progress in his style and approach, which is allied to a "*deep knowledge of the business.*" The transportation team is led by Thad Dameris. At time of press the firm announced its merger with Shaw Pittman LLP to form Pillsbury Winthrop Shaw Pittman.

The Clients: The team acted on behalf of Gemini Air Cargo in the $200 million restructuring of its long-term debt, aircraft leases and third-party maintenance agreements; the proceedings were in conjunction with preserving the principal shareholders' control of the company. It is acting as counsel to a group of lenders, led by BayernLB, with exposure in excess of $1 billion in the Air Canada bankruptcy. Working with other clients, it is advising on the United Airlines and US Airways insolvencies. It is also representing lenders on Ex-Im Bank's supported financings of Boeing aircraft for a large number of foreign carriers. Other clients include: Airbus; Avion Capital; Citibank; Gemini Air Cargo; Helaba; Mitsubishi; Mitsui; Sabre Holdings and Skylink Airways.

Shaw Pittman LLP
See firm details p.490
The Firm: The practice aims to provide assistance across a diverse range of aviation-related issues, but it is in the regulatory and litigation spheres where it gained prominence. It represented Delta Air Lines in securing DOT approval for a breakthrough alliance among Delta, Northwest and Continental airlines in the Asian airline regulatory arena. In the disputes resolution arena, the group successfully challenged a court and FAA decision to authorize $250 million in passenger facility charge funding for Chicago's O'Hare International Airport modernization project. At time of going to press

the firm announced its merger with Pillsbury Winthrop LLP to form Pillsbury Winthrop Shaw Pittman.

The Lawyers: The 2005 departure of Robert Cohn to Hogan & Hartson leaves the department under a degree of uncertainty, observers said. However, the practice does have the support of other notable practitioners, including former FAA chief counsel Sandy Murdock.

The Clients: The group is working with start-up POGO Jet – a company planning a nationwide, budget air taxi service – on its corporate and regulatory interests. Other clients includes: Air Foyle; Air Transport Association of America; Antonov Airlines; Atlantic Southeast Airlines; Austrian Airlines; Big Sky Airlines; Chautauqua Airlines; City of Kansas City; City of San Jose; Comair; DaimlerChrysler Aviation; Delta Air Lines; Embraer; Israel Aircraft Industries; Mesa Airlines; National Air Transportation Association; Peninsula Airways; Republic Airlines and the South Suburban Airport Commission.

Simpson Thacher & Bartlett LLP
See firm details p.1370
The Firm: This sizable practice leans toward larger, more complex transactions. Though not organized along industry lines compared to some of its competitors, it nevertheless gained commendation in aviation-related corporate activities for areas such as capital markets, M&A and other financing-related structures. This includes transportation equipment financing and EETC work. The team worked with Virgin America on its orders for $600 million of Airbus aircraft, having advised the company since its conceptual stage. It also assists the same client on aircraft leases, corporate finance and other

startup activities.

The Lawyers: Martin Jacobson (see p.1290) dedicates most of his time to transportation concerns, representing international clients doing business in the USA on their aircraft finance requirements, including derivatives transactions. He is considered to be "*maybe the best in the business*" by some interviewees for his "*tremendous*" technically ability, although others felt that this could sometimes be overly detailed.

The Clients: The group represents RBS Aviation Capital in connection with aircraft leasing and finance, and structured aircraft finance in North America. The firm has also participated in various bank credit facilities involving Northwest Airlines and Southwest Airlines among others. On behalf of Brazilian development bank BNDES, it handled export financings of Embraer regional jet aircraft with US air carriers. On a more general basis, it counsels banks in connection with capital market transactions, and aircraft portfolio acquisitions and dispositions. Other clients include: Citibank; City of Leipzig; City of Zurich; JPMorgan Chase; Lehman Brothers; Northwest Airlines and Virgin America.

Other Notable Practitioners

John Howitt (see p.88) of Paul, Hastings, Janofsky & Walker LLP deals with aviation finance, advising on operating and leveraged leases for aircraft lessors. Loan portfolio purchases, sales and securitization feature prominently in his portfolio, which is further enhanced by his expertise on financial restructuring. Clients are attracted to an effective combination of considerable experience and a "*high-quality and constructive approach.*"

RAIL

OVERVIEW: As a result of significant consolidation in the industry, there are fewer Class One railroads in the US than at any time in the previous 20 years. For the first time, the rail sector is facing capacity constraints, rather than having to

deal with excess capacity. One of the main new battlegrounds is in differential rates litigation, while the industry also has to deal with increased congestion caused by trucking companies turning to the railroads to escape gridlocks.

The legal market for rail is a relatively small one, with the pie divided between specialist operations and some of the most significant players in the transportation sector.

Band 1

Covington & Burling
See firm details p.481
The Firm: A major player in the rail sector, the practice is sustained by the central pillars of regulatory compliance, legislative advice and transactional assistance. Much of its activity relates to DC-based regulatory agencies, while transactional work is conducted primarily from its New York branch. Rail emerged to the fore of the firm's transportation group, illustrated by its work on behalf of trophy clients such as Union

Pacific. It maintains client satisfaction via a "*deep bench of talented railroad lawyers*" who "*always perform at a high level.*" It is frequently seen on the larger, more complicated cases. Legislative advice on highway funding is also of import, while aviation and port-related work play smaller roles in the department.

The Lawyers: Group chair **Linda Morgan** (see p.96) leads a "*thorough and careful*" team of "*highly principled and zealous*" advocates. She was previously the chair of the Surface Transportation Board (STB) and handles rail and other transportation matters across the board.

"*Extremely able,*" she demonstrates detailed knowledge of both the industry and agencies, further bolstered by her enduring links to Capitol Hill. She is judged by the market as a "*bright light with a good reputation in terms of ability and ethics.*" Interviewees recommended her for major mergers and various issues with national significance. **David Meyer** (see p.95) is an antitrust lawyer with expertise in the transportation sector. "*Smart and good on his feet,*" he parlays "*strategic sense*" into successful results in litigation. He is also involved in railroad control transactions before the STB and related pro-

National
Leading firms (Rail)

[1] COVINGTON & BURLING
SIDLEY AUSTIN BROWN & WOOD, LLP
STEPTOE & JOHNSON LLP

[2] ARNOLD & PORTER LLP
MAYER, BROWN, ROWE & MAW
SLOVER & LOFTUS

[3] DEORCHIS HILLENBRAND & WIENER, LLP
THOMPSON HINE LLP
ZUCKERT, SCOUTT & RASENBERGER, LLP

Leading individuals (Rail)

[1] MOATES G Paul *Sidley Austin*, Washington, DC
MORGAN Linda *Covington & Burling*, Washington, DC
SIPE JR. Samuel *Steptoe & Johnson*, Washington, DC

[2] CHRISTIAN Betty *Steptoe & Johnson*, Washington, DC
JENKINS III Robert *Mayer Brown*, Washington, DC
JONES Erika *Mayer Brown*, Washington, DC
LOFTUS C. Michael *Slover & Loftus*, Washington, DC

[3] ALLEN Richard *Zuckert Scoutt*, Washington
DIMICHAEL Nicholas *Thompson Hine*, Washington, DC
HILLENBRAND Hyman *DeOrchis Hillenbrand*, Miami
MCBRIDE Michael *LeBoeuf Lamb*, Washington, DC
MEYER David *Covington & Burling*, Washington, DC

Firms and individuals are listed alphabetically in each band.

ceedings, including challenges to the reasonableness of rates and disputes over trackage rights compensation.

The Clients: The group acts on behalf of Union Pacific on a wide range of high-profile agency matters, as well as day-to-day operations, regulatory concerns and legislative issues. This client "*is just a behemoth in terms of revenue, mileage, and political influence,*" rivals said. "*It's not the only client they have, but it's the only one they need.*" The firm's broader clientele also includes rail car pooling company TTX, for which it advised on a request from the STB for the renewal of its industry car-pooling agreement. It counsels on antitrust matters for certain individual railroads and a major railroad trade association. On behalf of the same client, it also advises on a broad array of regulatory and legislative issues related to the safety and security of hazardous materials transportation. The team successfully settled a lawsuit filed by a shipper against a railroad client for breach of contract and other service-related complaints. The department also undertakes legislative and government affairs proceedings for United Airlines.

Sidley Austin Brown & Wood LLP
See firm details p.778

The Firm: The practice has a long history of work in this area and is heavily focused on North American railways, primarily advising out of offices in DC, New York and Chicago. It demonstrates depth with its familiarity with rail and related motor carriage issues affecting an industrial manufacturing client base, including ad hoc loss and damage matters. Peers recognize its litigation fortitude, particularly on the freight side. Likewise, clients are attracted to its "*high degree of expertise and tremendous resources*" for specialized litigation. It does act on a considerable proportion of work in the shipping sector, and also represents air carriers on a limited number of matters.

The Lawyers: Paul Moates (see p.95) effectively blends a "*forceful*" demeanor in litigation with an ability to "*keep an eye on the larger picture,*" commentators said. "*He doesn't get lost on the details.*" He led a team representing the two major Eastern railway systems – Norfolk Southern Railway Company and CSX Transportation – in three large coal rate complaint cases before the STB. These concerned increases of up to 50% in the rates charged for transporting coal from mines in the Central Appalachian region to electricity generating facilities in the Carolinas.

The Clients: The group represents Canadian Pacific Railway on the restructuring of its Delaware and Hudson Railway Company affiliate's operations in the Northeast. It has also been advising these clients on subsequent negotiations with Norfolk Southern relating to certain track and haulage rights over their respective lines in New York State, as well as some terminal services. It served as both regulatory and special bankruptcy counsel to Norfolk Southern and CSX in connection with a complicated spin-off of the assets of the former Consolidated Rail Corporation (Conrail). It further represented Norfolk Southern in numerous disputes arising under the Railway Labor Act, including recent litigation stemming from the railway's decision to expand its purchasing of signal devices from outside suppliers and to discontinue operations at its centralized signal shop. Another client is Burlington Northern Santa Fe Railway (BNSF).

Steptoe & Johnson LLP
See firm details p.492

The Firm: Rail advice comprises the biggest component of the firm's transportation work, with key clients including two of the nation's largest freight railways. The practice advises on coal rate disputes before the STB to determine reasonable rates for coal transportation. Interviewees praise its "*effective and less confrontational*" approach. It offers expertise related to policy and legislative proceedings, and also assists on cases relating to the extent to which railroads are preempted of regulation by the state, as opposed to the federal government. Land use and environmental regulations also feature on its menu. Rail construction work, often linked to this environmental element and subject to review by the STB, is another aspect of the practice.

The Lawyers: Group head **Sam Sipe** (see p.104) advises on large-scale, high-stakes commercial litigation that regularly involves economic issues, particularly coal contracts. He has earned respect as a hard-nosed negotiator. He adopts a "*convincing but low-key demeanor when appropriate,*" often wielding "*a sound grasp of economics for the regulated portion of the work,*" observers said. He "*knows the nuts and bolts of these issues to an extraordinary degree.*" **Betty Jo Christian** (see p.78) applies her "*good skills and pedigree*" primarily on rail matters. A former head of the STB, she delivers "*first-rate and methodical*" work.

The Clients: The firm is lead counsel to the BNSF on significant commercial disputes. It also counsels clients including CSX Transportation and Riverview Trenton Railroad Company on preemption matters.

Band 2

Arnold & Porter LLP
See firm details p.478

The Firm: This DC-based practice touches on various sectors that cut across the transportation industry, rather than organizing its team along strict industry lines. Corporate, M&A and securities matters are particularly prevalent. Environmental and compliance requirements such as Sarbanes-Oxley also play a considerable role. The firm operates a strong rail practice, with CSX as one of its most significant clients. Much of its recent activities focus on operational issues, following the considerable consolidation that has occurred in the market in recent times. The practice embraces not only railroad law but also other aspects of transportation, such as matters relating to cruise lines, trucking, and airlines. The increase in homeland security concerns affects all of the firm's transportation work and the department is uniquely situated to help clients in this area. Among its DC-based cadre are the former general counsels of both the Central Intelligence Agency and the National Security Agency, and the firm can call on the services of additional leading, former government agency figures on this issue.

The Lawyers: Corporate and securities partner Richard Baltz advises on regulatory and FCC matters for CSX, as well as a degree of dispute resolution. DC-based corporate and transactional partner Steven Kaplan has advised on container shipping issues, while Mary Gabrielle Sprague offers environmental proficiency.

The Clients: In addition to ongoing regulatory matters before the STB arising from the merger of Conrail and CSX, it assists the latter on a broad range of transportation issues. This includes advice to its global container-shipping subsidiary on dispute resolution and transactional matters.

Mayer, Brown, Rowe & Maw LLP

See firm details p.771

The Firm: A chiefly national group, the firm is renowned for its rail and road expertise, including a noticeable trucking practice. Clients identified the *"well-developed practice"* as being *"close to the railroads,"* viewing the team as *"underwriters' counsel of choice."* The firm additionally handles related environmental matters at the regional level.

The Lawyers: **Robert Jenkins** (see p.89) represents BNFS and the Association of American Railroads in national regulatory proceedings. He is respected for his *"careful and sound"* approach and deep knowledge of the sector. Among a *"broad and esoteric"* range of work, he also conducts some work for Conrail and CSX. **Erika Jones** (see p.89) carries out safety and economic regulation advice, primarily at the national level. She offers some state-level rail regulatory advice, and also undertakes a significant amount of automobile and truck regulatory proceedings.

The Clients: The firm is one of the lead regulatory counsels for BNSF and its primary outside counsel for economic regulatory matters. It also advises the same client in connection with rail line construction matters, obtaining approvals from numerous federal and state authorities to build and operate a 12.8-mile rail line into Bayport Industrial District in Harris County, Texas, dubbed as the largest petrochemical area in the USA.

Slover & Loftus

The Firm: Rail transportation is the primary area of expertise for this prominent, mainly plaintiff's litigation practice, although it also gained recognition for its transactional commercial work. It has appeared before US district courts on behalf of shippers, electric utilities and other plaintiffs embroiled in arbitration or litigation. The group is best known for coal rate regulation advice, and also demonstrates proficiency on other matters regarding rail-dependent commodities, such as municipal solid waste and fertilizer. It is also involved in motor carrier work on occasions. Satisfied clients spoke of a firm that's *"just excellent in our area of the law."* Its advocates are *"knowledgeable on the issues,"* and benefit from their connections with the agencies and *"good abilities at negotiating contracts."*

The Lawyers: **Michael Loftus** handles litigation before the STB and conducts commercial transactions involving contracts between major coal shippers and prominent railroads. He employs *"excellent judgment"* and *"a trial lawyer's charm,"* commentators said. *"He doesn't come across as a technician and is good at developing client relationships as a result."*

The Clients: The group marshaled several complex disputes before the STB, acting for plaintiffs suing railroads regarding rates considered to exceed a maximum, reasonable level. It regularly assists on the negotiation of rail transportation contracts as well as on issues that arise under such contracts, including demurrage and damage to equipment. Clients include: AEP; APS; Carolina Power & Light; Duke Energy and the Western Fuels Association.

Band 3

DeOrchis Hillenbrand & Wiener, LLP

The Firm: This firm splits its practice between ocean, road and rail transportation law, in addition to a smaller proportion of aviation work. The Florida branch maintains strong, ongoing links with its New York counterpart, enabling continuous assistance on matters relating to the loss and damage of cargo. It particularly focuses on insurance work for state and national companies regarding land, sea and air transportation. It advises on contracts in multi and intermodal work, affecting a wide range of transactions for the transportation of goods.

The Lawyers: Managing partner **Hyman Hillenbrand** advised Norfolk Southern in a $1.7 million matter concerning alleged transit damage caused by a derailment. The case hinged upon whether a foreign shipper is bound to the terms of an ocean bill of lading limiting its liability when a freight forwarder arranges the deal; the matter also examines whether a US rail carrier can assert such a limitation. Hillenbrand impresses with his broad experience and straightforward style.

The Clients: The firm's multimodal expertise is illustrated by its assistance to Trailer Bridge in its successful defense of a claim by Vals Transport for damages arising from breach of a contract of carriage between the parties. It represents some of the nation's largest railroads, as well as trucking companies and third party vendors such as freight forwarders and brokers. Norfolk Southern Railway Company is also a client.

Thompson Hine LLP

See firm details p.1457

The Firm: The department's main focus is on assistance to transportation systems users, representing shippers and some intermediaries. The team is representing utility company Otter Tail Power Company in an important proceeding before the STB to determine the proper level of rail rates for its coal transportation. It also carries out a significant volume of contract drafting advice and negotiation for a wide variety of clients.

The Lawyers: **Nicholas DiMichael** (see p.81) cuts a broad swath across the transportation sector, handling rail and also maritime matters as well as a considerable proportion of roadwork. *"He epitomizes the lawyer who may have, at one time, predominantly focused on rail but has now branched out."* A successful and highly regarded attorney with an academic bent, he represents trade association National Industrial Transportation League. His colleague, DC-based Jeffrey Moreno, assists clients on rail and motor carrier issues.

The Clients: The group dealt with an application for a rail construction project by Holcim, one of the world's leading suppliers of cement, aggregates (gravel and sand), concrete and construction-related services. The group was also retained by the North Dakota Public Service Commission to undertake a study on grain rates and to appear before the STB regarding the possibility of relief for alleged unreasonably high rates.

Zuckert, Scoutt & Rasenberger, LLP

The Firm: A DC-based boutique, it offers extensive firmwide experience of transportation matters throughout the country, particularly in the regulatory and legislative spheres and on dispute resolution. The firm received recommendations across the transportation sector, including aviation, though commentators most associate it with the rail industry. It represents clients on economic regulatory matters and undertakes a broad range of advice on surface transportation matters.

The Lawyers: **Richard Allen** specializes in transportation-related disputes, including appellate work. He chiefly advises on railroads and other surface transportation matters, but also carries out some shipping and motor carrier work. He has worked with Norfolk Southern on federal economic regulatory matters. He has also developed a niche specialty in assisting clients challenging certain aspects of state transportation taxes; this has included the constitutional grounds.

The Clients: The group is working on a case involving a railroad seeking authority to abandon one of its lines in California. It also provides assistance to a Mexican railroad and its Texas subsidiary in a property dispute over a railroad line purchase in Texas. Other clients include: brokers and various intermediaries; carriers; shippers; financial institutions; leasing companies; trade associations; and state and local government units.

Other Notable Practitioners

Michael McBride (see p.94) heads LeBoeuf, Lamb, Greene & MacRae, LLP's national practice, with strengths in coal transportation contracts and railroad services. Well known for his established role in legislative and regulatory proceedings, he combines a *"conciliatory style"* with *"a lot of strategic sense"* to deliver effective advice to clients such as electrical group Edison Electric Institute, one of the largest customers carried by US railroads. His wide-ranging practice also covers regulatory and legislative matters relating to shippers. Particularly dazzling in the appellate arena, "*his sense of what is the key point to be argued is excellent,*" observers said. He advised the Virginia Electric & Power Company in its dispute against Norfolk Southern over the rail costs adjustment factors that apply to the carriage of coal.

ROAD CARRIAGE

OVERVIEW: Carriage by road is currently suffering from oversubscribed highways and a tendency to focus intently at the local level. Clients are often divided between carriage companies and associations, and their insurance underwriters. However, the national elements of this sector are increasingly coming to the fore.

Infrastructure continues its rise as a key aspect of road carriage work. New toll roads and financing techniques, including public/private collaborations, are breathing some new life into the sector. Law firms are diversifying, advising on transport considerations for the construction of new airports and other major projects, and several firms have considerably blurred the distinction between their projects and infrastructure work.

National
Leading firms Road Carriage

1	MAYER, BROWN, ROWE & MAW LLP
	MILBANK, TWEED, HADLEY & MCCLOY
	ORRICK, HERRINGTON & SUTCLIFFE
2	DENNIS, CORRY, PORTER & SMITH LLP
	DEORCHIS HILLENBRAND & WIENER, LLP
	HUNTON & WILLIAMS LLP
	MCGUIREWOODS LLP
	THOMPSON HINE LLP

Leading individuals Road Carriage

1	FEO Edwin *Milbank Tweed*, Los Angeles
	MATHEWS Daniel *Orrick Herrington*, New York
2	CHUSED Wesley *Looney & Grossman*, Boston
	COGBILL III John *McGuireWoods*, Richmond
	DIMICHAEL Nicholas *Thompson Hine*, Washington, DC
	HILLENBRAND Hyman *DeOrchis Hillenbrand*, Miami
	JONES Erika *Mayer Brown*, Washington, DC
	MARKS Allan *Milbank Tweed*, Los Angeles
	PORTER R. Clay *Dennis Corry*, Atlanta
	PULLEY III J Waverly *Hunton & Williams*, Richmond

Firms and individuals are listed alphabetically in each band.

Band 1

Mayer, Brown, Rowe & Maw LLP
See firm details p.771
The Firm: This respected practice combines its road carriage abilities with a noted rail expertise. The main focus here is automotive assistance, with trucking advice also prevalent, helping clients on a national basis. Attorneys counsel on interstate matters as well as on environmental considerations with local entities. They also represent major automobile and equipment manufacturers on their compliance with federal motor vehicle safety and consumer laws. Interviewees contend that few can match the firm's abilities on the vehicle regulatory side.
The Lawyers: Washington DC-based **Erika Jones** (see p.89) also features in the rail sector table, but it is on road matters that this star shines brightest. She advises on safety and economic regulation, primarily on a national basis, and won plaudits for her "*pugnacious, hard-*

charging" style. Jones is busiest on automobile and truck regulation at the state level, and represents most of the main auto manufacturers. DaimlerChrysler hired her to successfully defend a class action alleging that certain safety belt buckles violated federal safety standards. She also currently represents the Alliance of Automobile Manufacturers in defense of a new regulation governing the confidentiality of business information submitted to the National Highway Traffic Safety Administration (NHTSA). Her colleague Philip Recht in Los Angeles counsels on highway safety and related matters on behalf of automakers and manufacturers of vehicles and products. Both Jones and Recht are former NHTSA heads.
The Clients: The team continues to assist the Alliance of Automobile Manufacturers on several disputes. These include the defense of new regulations on advanced airbags and issues related to new regulations to protect the confidentiality of automakers' information on early warning of possible safety defects. Consumer groups have challenged this latter case and the firm has been retained as ongoing counsel. It is also working with American Trucking Associations on safety and tax issues; these touch on matters relating to the taxation of interstate road carriage and on compliance with safety and national policy issues, including litigation challenging the rules on the number of hours they may work.

Milbank, Tweed, Hadley & McCloy
The Firm: Road carriage matters are conducted by a subgroup under the firm's larger project finance and development department. Attorneys assist on private transactions outside of public finance and governmental arenas, often driven by the need for government entities to raise capital. The attorneys are technically strong regarding the nuances of toll roads and related financings, and its direct, commercial style was a favorite of clients. Clients also appreciated the breadth of this practice, which incorporates environmental and real estate matters. In addition, the group has notably acted on a number of privatizations in the Americas, representing sponsors and investment banks.
The Lawyers: Respected for his abilities in energy and projects work, Los Angeles-based **Ed Feo** also spends an equal proportion of his time on road-related transportation matters. This is at least in part due to his lead on sizable transactions such as the Chicago Skyway and California State Route 125 South (SR125) toll roads. A "*high-quality, practical and experienced attorney,*" he conveys a "*calm manner and is quick to absorb issues,*" say sources. He is recommended for complex multiparty deals that require tactical ability and business acumen. **Allan Marks** also hails from the Los Angeles office and spends the majority of his time in this area. He worked on the initial SR125 toll road deal and continues to assist in ongoing matters arising from the project. He also worked on the high-value bond financing of a Mexican toll road on behalf of the State of Nuevo Leon and a special purpose trust. The transaction was unusual in permitting the state government to monetize future toll revenues without a private concession, retaining full ownership and control of the road throughout the term of the debt. He also assisted on several other road transactions in Latin America and a rail project in Mexico.
The Clients: The team represents the Cintra-Macquarie consortium as winning bidders on the $1.82 billion, 99-year agreement to acquire the concession to toll and operate the eight-mile elevated Chicago Skyway toll road. This included negotiation of project contracts with the City of Chicago and subsequent financing. Lawyers from the firm represented project sponsor Macquarie Infrastructure Group (MIG) and its subsidiaries on the landmark $773 million project financing of the SR125 private toll road in Southern California. It is one of the first private toll roads to be financed in the USA in recent years via a European-style public-private partnership (PPP). The group further acted for underwriters Citigroup on the issuance of two tranches of bonds for the Autopista Central in Chile, one of the main toll highways in Santiago. This was Chile's first simultaneous offering

of local and global bonds sharing common collateral and the largest infrastructure bond offering in Chile at the time.

Orrick, Herrington & Sutcliffe

See firm details p.295

The Firm: A strong project finance team coupled with a robust public finance group ensures this firm a prominence in the roads sector. Historically finance led, the firm now leads in terms of both equity and debt on matters relating to bridges and roads. It advises on PPPs, including construction and operation issues, as well as on changes in tax laws impacting on the leasing industry. Clients praised a team that "*showed a lot of depth in the project finance market and a European model regarding PPP-style work.*" Others underlined its versatility and efficient, commercial aptitude: "*It finds the middle ground, rather than erects boundaries.*"

The Lawyers: Global finance partner **Dan Mathews** (see p.94) brings his knowledge of infrastructure and project finance together with his experience in tax structures and energy projects to good effect in the development of roads and bridges. He represented the mandated lead arrangers – Spanish bank Banco Bilbao Vizcaya Argentaria and counterpart DEPFA Bank – on the $400 million construction and term senior loans for the SR125 toll road project, the first application of the PPP principle to this sector of the US market. Clients say: "*His focus is on achieving the best outcome for his client and ensuring we get over any hurdles.*" Viewed by many in the market as a "*practical and commercial facilitator,*" he advances "*a softly-softly approach but manages to hit the nail on the head when it comes to key commercial issues.*" He represents the senior debt providers on the Chicago Skyway project. He also undertakes a small amount of aviation work and is active on corporate and financial transactions in the energy and infrastructure industries. Roger Davis in San Francisco represents a number of transport and major airport authorities on public finance issues.

The Clients: The group acted on behalf of the senior debt providers on the Cintra-Macquarie joint bid to purchase a concession for the Chicago Skyway. It counseled mandated lead arranger HSH Nordbank on the financing of the Baldwin County Bridge crossing the intracoastal waterway on the southern edge of Alabama. It also worked with both HSH Nordbank and Macquarie Bank on the senior secured acquisition financing of the owner and operator of fixed base operations businesses at airports throughout the USA. Clients include Banco Bilbao Vizcaya Argentaria, DEPFA Bank, and Macquarie Corporate Finance (USA).

Band 2

Dennis, Corry, Porter & Smith LLP

The Firm: This long-term defender of motor carriers and truck insurers acts on nationwide matters from its Atlanta base. As well as its commended trial expertise, the practice impresses with its sound counsel on the federal regulations applicable to motor carriers. Notably, it has also authored a standard industry treatise relating to motor carrier liability to address recurring problems in the trucking industry.

The Lawyers: Founding partner **Clay Porter** is dedicated to motor carrier defence work and also undertakes a significant volume of matters relating to truck insurance coverage.

DeOrchis Hillenbrand & Wiener, LLP

The Firm: A practice as equally recommended for its road and trucking service as for its railroads assistance and marine counsel. The firm is proficient in cargo and intermodal matters, as well as comprehensive liability exposures and products liability in general. Long-term clients attested to the enduring quality of its work and ability to achieve results.

The Lawyers: Managing partner **Hyman Hillenbrand** acted for brokers Trans American Trucking and motor carrier United Express Service in defence of an action for damage to cargo sustained in a motor vehicle accident. Clients attributed his "*first-class, tremendous results*" to an "*engaging personality,*" that combines with his "*high intelligence and extremely skilful handling of complex matters.*" Others noted his broad spectrum of knowledge and high degree of responsiveness.

The Clients: Operating primarily from its Florida base, the firm advised the motor carrier and freight forwarder in defense of a $1.7 million claim brought by the subrogated insurer of a Swedish shipper concerning the loss of a shipment from Texas to Colorado when a truck struck an overpass.

Hunton & Williams LLP

See firm details p.1775

The Firm: A niche transportation infrastructure practice that handles statutory reform and advises on public-private arrangements. The work targets highways and toll roads, concentrating in the main in the southeastern USA. However, the firm is better known in some quarters for its assistance relating to airports and on light rail projects. Counseling is provided by dedicated teams that draw from the firm's finance, corporate environment and real estate attorneys.

The Lawyers: Richmond partner **Waverly Pulley** (see p.1772) is a capital finance lawyer with particular expertise in commercial lending, leasing and public-private infrastructure projects. Interviewees highlighted his skills as a draftsman and negotiator.

The Clients: The department acted for Kellogg Brown & Root on the more than $10 billion widening of I81 for safety reasons, as it is heavily used by truckers. The deal was financed through federal grants and tax-exempt bonds and backed by a stream of toll revenues. Fluor Corporation and developer Washington Group International continue to engage the firm on the $360 million Pocahontas Parkway (I-895), most recently on a combination bridge and toll road over the James River in Richmond. In the transportation infrastructure sphere, the group represented an equity investor in a leveraged lease transaction involving the Metropolitan Atlanta Rapid Transit Authority (MARTA). In a similar vein, its DC office has been asked to assist on ways to produce revenue to support Washington Metropolitan Area Transit Authority's (WMATA) mass transport system.

McGuireWoods LLP

The Firm: National products liability assistance to automotive clients is a key feature of the practice. Additionally, the group has been at the forefront of the governments-led initiatives in the USA and abroad to privatize and introduce tolling facilities on many roads. For example, it is advising a major Bulgarian construction company forming a number of joint ventures with Western partners to build toll roads in Bulgaria, while it is pursuing similar projects in Jamaica.

The Lawyers: **John Cogbill** has a noted pedigree in real estate and land use law, including environmental matters. However, he was also recommended for his activity in transportation-related projects, which included advice on the drafting of Virginia's Public Private Transportation Act. Interviewees stated that he possesses "*a fair amount of polish and great common sense.*"

The Clients: The group represented Koch Performance Roads on the I-81 project, a $7 billion plus joint venture with Kellogg Brown & Root, including environmental assessments. It is also advising the early planning stages for the proposed Route 95 high-occupancy toll (HOT) lanes from Virginia to Washington on behalf of Clarke Construction and Shirley Contracting. Maryland Transport Authority is another client of the firm.

Thompson Hine LLP

See firm details p.1457

The Firm: The practice is primarily focused on servicing the users of transportation systems, such as shippers and some transportation intermediaries. It tends not to represent carriers, unless they are subsidiaries of shippers. As well as its respected rail expertise, the group undertakes a large amount of contract drafting advice in the roads sector. This includes the drafting of a model contract for shipper carriers on behalf of two national motor transport associations.

The Lawyers: **Nicholas DiMichael** (see p.81)

represents clients across many facets of transportation work, with rail and maritime work featuring as well as roads advice. For some interviewees "*he would really be the first choice for leading road carriage in economic regulatory proceedings.*"

Other Notable Practitioners

Wesley Chused of Looney & Grossman LLP specializes in defending motor carriers in cargo claim cases, PI liability cases and contract disputes. He also represents motor carrier insurers in Massachusetts and across New England, with occasional representations elsewhere in the country. Of particular import is his counsel on interstate truck transportation, as well as intrastate transportation and issues under the Uniform Commercial Code.

SHIPPING

OVERVIEW: Having focused only on the New York market in previous years, we are introducing an additional national shipping table for firms operating outside of the Big Apple this year. The New York section remains on its own, because in many ways, it stands apart from the rest of the country. Unlike our aviation table, where comparisons between firms on opposite sides of the country were frequently made, the shipping sector outside of New York tends to have more of a regional feel.

Outside of New York, the most active markets are to be found in Louisiana, California, Florida, Texas and Washington state. DC remains the main hub for regulatory work, while Florida and Texas boast fairly active ports. Miami is the center of the cruise line sector.

Firms serving this industry must be able to advise on security regulations among a broad array of work, while the continued criminalization of maritime accidents and pollution events has added further considerations for clients choosing their legal representation. The clamor of clients for firms to provide financial and corporate-related advice has, in many ways, reshaped the marketplace.

SHIPPING

NEW YORK

New York
Leading firms (Shipping)
[1] **FREEHILL HOGAN & MAHAR LLP**
HEALY & BAILLIE LLP
HOLLAND & KNIGHT LLP
[2] **BURKE & PARSONS**
HILL RIVKINS & HAYDEN LLP
SEWARD & KISSEL
[3] **CARTER LEDYARD & MILBURN LLP**
DEORCHIS & PARTNERS, LLP
GILMARTIN, POSTER & SHAFTO
NICOLETTI HORNIG CAMPISE AND SWEENEY
NOURSE & BOWLES LLP
WATSON, FARLEY & WILLIAMS
[4] **BADIAK WILL & RUDDY**
CICHANOWICZ, CALLAN, KEANE
CLARK, ATCHESON & REISERT
DONOVAN PARRY MCDERMOTT & RADZIK
KENNEDY LILLIS SCHMIDT & ENGLISH
THACHER PROFFITT & WOOD LLP
Firms are listed alphabetically in each band.

Band 1

Healy & Baillie LLP

See firm details p.1351

The Firm: A large, dedicated shipping practice with a significant body of casualty work, the firm has had prominent roles in many of the most high-profile cases of recent years. Peers agreed that "*the collective experience at the firm is hard to beat.*" The group's work on the transactional side is buoyant, in contrast to its charter party work, which has not been as prevalent compared to previous years. Bankruptcy and insurance coverage matters continue to bring a steady stream of work, while the firm's debtor/creditor litigation capability – including asset recovery cases – is also noteworthy. Shipping-related criminal proceedings have become more prominent, and the firm can call on lawyers skilled in both criminal and marine matters. Clients were quick to praise its "*ability to defend us rigorously in court with clean tactics.*" Although the team is more visible on litigation, it also offers expertise on marine finance. Efforts to expand in this arena have met with some success, and the firm's understanding of the operating side of shipping work enabled it to be "*effective on the financing side of transactions, particularly if negotiating non-standard commercial contracts.*" It is occasionally involved in trucking and freight forwarding matters, while its Hong Kong office maintains working relations with international shipping concerns and various Chinese companies in New York.

The Lawyers: John Kimball (see p.91) leads a deep, balanced team comprising a "*core group of experienced partners with diverse skills.*" He tends to be inclined toward the heavyweight matters, with a broad scope that includes a singular reputation for charter party work. One commentator said: "*He is the top dog, no question. When the big issues come up, he is always the man on the case.*" He combines a "*hard-nosed, yet thoroughly professional*" approach. Clients described an "*extremely knowledgeable, well-versed and articulate*" attorney who has "*an excellent feel for the law and what we are trying to achieve.*" **Jack Greenbaum** (see p.86) was similarly commended for his charter party aptitude and "*thorough and tenacious*" method. **LeRoy Lambert** (see p.92) is primarily concerned with bills of lading and charter party work. He built a respected profile based on solid knowledge of the market. "*He can be trusted at his word when he makes a commitment,*" peers said. **William France** (see p.84) was strongly recommended for his sharp technical proficiency on issues of design, based on his uncommon background in naval architecture.

The Clients: Casualty work includes continuing assistance to the owners of the 'Kariba' following its 2002 collision in the English Channel with the 'Tricolor.' The team continues to represent Marathon Ashland Petroleum on an ongoing multimillion-dollar dispute involving the termination of a long-term bareboat charter. It advised on the 'Global Natali' matter, which concerned an attempt to enforce a multimillion-dollar default judgment. On the bankruptcy side, the practice aids Steamship Mutual on both the Reliance Insurance and American Classic Voyages liquidations. The group also continues to act for various creditors on the Millennium Seacarriers and long-running US Lines and Lykes bankruptcies. It assisted Hellenic Mutual War Risk Club on an insurance coverage dispute between the owners of the 'Athena' on an insurance claim arising out of the ship's bombing in Sri Lanka. It has also advised the Estate of Anders Jahre in its legal efforts to collect assets around the world. Other clients include liability insurers of non-vessel owning common carriers (NVOCCs) and freight forwarders, Britannia and Standard Club.

Freehill Hogan & Mahar LLP

The Firm: Significant casualties are the mainstay of this dedicated, medium-sized maritime practice. The firm advised on the 'Sealand Express' and 'Bow Mariner' cases among others in a busy period, resulting in a significantly

New York
Leading individuals
(Shipping: Litigation)

1. **KIMBALL John** *Healy & Baillie*, New York
2. **BURKE Jr Raymond** *Burke & Parsons*, New York
   GUTOWSKI Peter *Freehill Hogan*, New York
   HAYDEN Raymond *Hill Rivkins*, New York
   HONAN III William *Holland & Knight*, New York
   HOOPER Chester *Holland & Knight*, New York
   NOURSE David *Nourse & Bowles*, New York
3. **BURRELL Lizabeth** *Levy Phillips*, New York
   CLARK Peter *Clark Atcheson*, New York
   COHEN Michael *Nicoletti Hornig*, New York
   DEORCHIS Vincent *DeOrchis & Partners*, New York
   GREENBAUM Jack *Healy & Baillie*, New York
   HEARD Keith *Burke & Parsons*, New York
   KEANE Paul *Cichanowicz Callan*, New York
   KENNEDY Donald *Carter Ledyard*, New York
   LAMBERT LeRoy *Healy & Baillie*, New York
   MEEHAN Wayne *Freehill Hogan*, New York
   PARÉ Jay *Nourse & Bowles*, New York
4. **ENGLISH Craig** *Kennedy Lillis*, New York
   FRANCE II William *Healy & Baillie*, New York
   GINOS Geoffrey *Nicoletti Hornig*, New York
   MURNANE Don *Freehill Hogan*, New York
   PRUZINSKY Anthony *Hill Rivkins*, New York
   RADZIK Edward *Donovan Parry*, New York
   SHIRLEY James *Holland & Knight*, New York
   STARER Brian *Holland & Knight*, New York
   SWEENEY III James *Nicoletti Hornig*, New York
   WOODS John *Thacher Proffitt*, New York

Leading individuals (Shipping: Finance)

1. **HENGEN Nancy** *Holland & Knight*, New York
   RUTKOWSKI Larry *Seward & Kissel*, New York
   WHALEN Thomas *Carter Ledyard*, New York
   WOLFE Gary *Seward & Kissel*, New York
2. **CHANG Leo** *Watson Farley*, New York
   POSTER Robert *Gilmartin Poster*, New York
   TENEV Jovi *Holland & Knight*, New York

Individuals are listed alphabetically in each band.

raised market profile. Another feather in its hat is advising on the Staten Island ferry crash. Clients recognize the practice's ability to punch above its weight, while peers often turn to the team in conflict situations. "*They are to be admired as adversaries,*" commentators said. The encroachment of criminal law into the sector continues apace, as prosecutors seek to criminalize aspects of maritime casualties. The firm makes good use of its lawyers with expertise in both areas, advising clients in related major disputes and preventative counsel. The increase in shipping regulatory work also has affected the team, and it continues to counsel on post-9/11 security measures. For example, the International Group of P&I Clubs and others have retained the group to advise regarding their ongoing legal and contractual issues pertaining to such regulations.

The Lawyers: Peter Gutowski is the most prominent name in a team of relatively young but considerably experienced lawyers, a proportion of whom possess practical merchant marine or US Navy experience. Gutowski is commended as an "*aggressive, clear-minded and decisive*" attorney who can navigate "*tough cases.*" New to the tables this year, **Wayne Meehan**'s (see p.95) involvement in some major casualty matters has markedly raised his profile. He is acting on the Staten Island ferry crash on behalf of the City of New York, following the fatal collision of the ferry 'Andrew J. Barbieri' with its berth in October 2003. "*Competent and hard working,*" he is also pitched as a leader among the next generation of practitioners. **Don Murnane**'s (see p.96) star was viewed as on the rise. He acts on litigations and arbitrations concerning cargo loss and contamination cases, as well as collisions and groundings, explosions and fires.

The Clients: The department represents Maersk Sealand, the charterers of the 'Sealand Express' that was blown off its anchorage during a storm in 2003 and ran aground; claims for salvage and cargo loss and delay exceed $12 million. It is retained by the owners of the 'Bow Mariner' and its P&I Club on a case concerning a tanker that exploded at sea off the coast of Virginia, with the loss of 18 lives and the total loss of the vessel and its cargo. The owners and insurers of the 'DG Harmony' also engage the firm on matters arising out of a fire at sea on board a container ship. The team also defended the underwriters of the vessels in an oil spill class action filed by fishermen, beachfront residents, vacationers and businesses arising out of the collision of a freighter and two barges in Tampa Bay, Florida.

Holland & Knight LLP
See firm details p.1352

The Firm: The work of this considerable powerhouse remains focused mainly on casualty matters. The firm's rise into the top band is a reflection of its depth and range. It is also emblematic of both the consolidation in the market and the increasing demand by marine clients for large, dynamic firms with not only shipping but also related finance and M&A resources. Clients described a firm with prompt response times and "*the ability to identify issues rapidly and respond without undue or unnecessary research.*" The continuing 'Prestige' case has been an important element of the firm's work in recent years – indeed, some commentators attributed this case alone to the firm's heightened profile. But the group also featured in several other leading casualty cases of recent years. Clients were happy to report that the firm wields "*power and influence*" in the marketplace. Its practice is national, with a strong Florida base, and also includes a notable aviation finance and litigation group. Some rail and road carriage work is also featured.

The Lawyers: Bill Honan (see p.88), head of the firm's maritime litigation group, has a tendency to "*produce thorough, high-quality and goal-oriented*" transactional work. He concentrates on marine contracts and arbitrations. He represented two different charterers of Silversea cruise vessels for use during the 2004 Athens Olympics. "*Smart and aggressive, you have to be on your toes against him,*" said competitors. **Chet Hooper** (see p.88) benefits from an ascending profile, not only due to his academic strengths, but also for his efforts to assist on a wide range of issues, including his development of new multimodal regimes for cargo. He garners considerable respect in New York and the wider market. "*Every one of his trials is a well-planned, well-executed affair,*" stated one client. Peers said his encyclopedic knowledge of this area was "*an invaluable resource.*" A "*formidable litigator,*" **Brian Starer** (see p.105) continues to impress as lead partner in the 'Prestige' case, representing the Kingdom of Spain in its efforts to recover $1 billion in damages. **Nancy Hengen** (see p.87) is the practice's senior lawyer on the ship finance side and appears on a number of transactions on behalf of significant clients. The ability of the firm to straddle several areas of transportation is most evident in her advice as maritime counsel to a Canadian railroad regarding its $230 million acquisition of a Great Lakes transportation company with both shipping and rail assets. **Jovi Tenev** (see p.106) continues to be recommended for his ship finance assistance and expertise on maritime contracts, while **James Shirley** (see p.103) impresses with "*a combination of practical experience and solid lawyering.*" He specializes primarily in salvage cases.

The Clients: The group continues to represent shipowner Wallenius-Wilhelmsen and its P&I club, Gard, in the ongoing 'Tricolor' case; at stake is about $200 million in claims. However, its net is cast wider than ship casualties. It represented AT&T in a significant arbitration concerning damages to one of its fiber optic submarine cables. On behalf of the Long Island Power Authority, it advised on claims stemming from damages to undersea electrical cabling caused by the construction of a natural gas pipeline. Similarly acting for the New York Power Authority, it handled a dispute involving an anchor drag incident. The team also assisted a lending bank as US counsel in connection with the transfer of a foreign-built cruise vessel under a unique federal statute. Finally, it undertakes freight defense and demurrage (FD&D) work for a broad spread of clients.

Band 2

Burke & Parsons

The Firm: This practice is composed of maritime and naval specialists whose inclination toward casualty cases has paid off handsomely. It advises on oil-water separator cases, in part as a response to the DOJ's increased scrutiny on the practice of false entries in ships' record books. Observers perceive the firm to be primarily a litigation practice, but it also generates transactional work due to a general trend toward consolidation. In this sphere, it represents clients on both sides of deals and also handles business reviews of potential acquisition targets for those considering amalgamation.

The Lawyers: Raymond Burke is lead maritime counsel for the American Bureau of Shipping (ABS) on the long-running 'Prestige' case, with claims totaling more than $700 million. This was filed in New York by the Spanish government for pollution damage and cleanup costs related to the sinking of the Bahamian-flagged tanker off the coast of Spain in November 2002. Interviewees credited him with having *"built up a pretty good group of people with some success in getting notable cases."* A capable trial lawyer with astute judgment, he is *"generally recognized in New York as one of the more able lawyers in the admiralty field,"* competitors said. **Keith Heard** is more often seen in arbitration and litigation than in a transactional role. He advises on the grounding of the 'Sealand Express' near Cape Town, South Africa, on behalf of US Ship Management, the vessel's bareboat charterer.

The Clients: The team continues to represent South Korea's Hyundai Mipo Dockyard in connection with litigation arising out of the breakup of the 'MSC Carla', a container ship that split in half and sank during a storm in the Atlantic Ocean in November 1997. It also represented a shipowner in a general average case arising out of crankshaft failure on a very large crude carrier (VLCC).

Hill Rivkins & Hayden LLP

The Firm: The practice is one of the largest specifically structured around admiralty and related issues, except marine finance. Half of its regular activity is casualty related, while charter party work and disputes also feature prominently. *"A pleasure to work with and also against,"* it carries out insurance defense work for underwriters and marine work relating to the energy sector. The firm additionally offers expertise in the aviation, rail and motor carriage sectors.

The Lawyers: Raymond Hayden has played a leading and influential role in the market for many years and remains the firm's best-known player, while **Anthony Pruzinsky** was commended for his participation in the 'DG Harmony' trial. He led for the cargo interests against the manufacturer of the chemicals that allegedly exploded on board the ship.

The Clients: The group advised as lead cargo counsel on a number of significant casualty matters, including those involving the 'MSC Carla,' 'APL China' and 'DG Harmony.' The team also conducted insurance defense proceedings for the underwriters of an oilrig in Brazil.

Seward & Kissel

See firm details p.1368

The Firm: The practice was historically a financial services firm that developed a maritime practice and, as such, it excels in transportation finance. Shipping is the busiest and largest area, followed by aviation. It is engaged in a number of large syndicated bank financings, high-yield offerings and some IPOs. *"The law firm of choice for the ship finance community,"* the practice thrives on *"a high caliber of clients and volume"* of deals, commentators said. Clients highlighted its capital markets penetration, and ability to combine maritime law and securities and corporate finance. To a lesser degree, litigation is an additional element to the practice; and the firm also undertakes major charter party matters. Clients lauded a practice *"quite willing to invest time and effort with us – it's more like a partnership."*

The Lawyers: Larry Rutkowski (see p.102) spends much of his time on lending transactions, with the remainder focused on capital markets and M&A. His understated, even-tempered strategy *"puts commercial considerations and client objectives first."* **Gary Wolfe** (see p.108) undertakes corporate and securities-related maritime work. *"Successful and effective, he is viewed by his peers as a good businessman,"* said one interviewee. The practice can also call on a number of bankruptcy lawyers who engage in shipping work.

The Clients: Ship finance activity includes counsel to DnB NOR Bank and others in connection with the $56 million refinancing of Stolt-Nielsen Transportation Group's obligations. It also aided Nordic American Tankers and Knightsbridge Tankers in connection with their conversion from passive foreign investment company status to operating company status. It appeared as special US counsel to the coordinating committee of banks in the Stolt Offshore restructuring. It assisted Top Tankers in its IPO, and separately acted for Frontline on the creation of Ship Finance International and its Rule 144A offering of high-yield notes. Maritime M&A includes representations on behalf of Ultrapetrol (Bahamas) on its purchase of the Latin American barge business of American Commercial Lines. General Maritime Corporation employed the firm on its acquisition of the fleet and technical operations of Portuguese shipping group Soponata, while ING retained the firm on the acquisition of Bank of New York's shipping portfolio. Other clients include: The Carlyle Group; Castle Harlan; Deutsche Bank; Deutsche Schiffsbank; DVB Bank; First Ship Lease; Fortis Capital; KfW; Lasco Shipping; Nordea Bank; RBS Lombard and Stelmar Shipping.

Band 3

Carter Ledyard & Milburn LLP

See firm details p.1340

The Firm: A predominantly shipping-focused firm with robust sidelines in related bankruptcy, environment and tax work. Litigation work for the group has increased, primarily as a result of bankruptcy and antitrust matters. The bulk of its activity is for clients outside the New York region, including foreign-based clients with needs in the USA, although the firm maintains more than a passing interest in local work. Attorneys here are also involved in rail financing and container leasing work and carry out some work in the aviation sector, particularly bankruptcy-related matters.

The Lawyers: Thomas Whalen busies himself with advice to the reviving New York ferry industry, representing Sea Containers and its high-speed ferry subsidiary SeaStreak, as well as the Governor's Island ferry service. He also provides legal opinions for foreign banks on ship mortgage and flag of convenience matters and assists on restructurings and bankruptcies, such as the Navigator Gas and President Casinos proceedings. Market observers acclaimed his representation of debenture trusts. **Don Kennedy** is involved in the Renaissance Cruise Lines bankruptcy litigation in Florida and also brings his *"tremendous experience"* to bear on various matters on behalf of Bowater. His colleague Gary Sesser is chiefly a commercial litigator with expertise in a number of areas, including antitrust and shipping.

The Clients: The group advises shipping companies on US antitrust investigations and assists clients on antitrust compliance, as well as adherence to the Foreign Corrupt Practices Act. It defended French shipbroker Barry Rogliano Salles in a $100 million lawsuit arising out of claims by the trustee in the bankruptcy of Renaissance Cruises Line. It is conducting environmental work for the Metropolitan Transportation Authority (MTA) in connection with its No. 7 subway line extension project on the west side of Manhattan. The group also continues to work with the mortgagee of the five Navigator Gas carrier vessels regarding the possible restructuring of a $304 million debt issue in the related proceedings. Clients include: ABN AMRO; Bank of New York; Bowater; Commerzbank; Euromar Shipping; Frachtcontor Junge; First Toronto Group; The Government of Guyana; Governors Island Preservation and Educational Corporation (GIPEC); Interpool;

KfW; Nordisk Skibsrederforening; Norwegian Hull Club; Polish Steamship Company; Sea Containers; SeaStreak America; Stolt-Nielsen Transportation Group and United States Steel Corporation.

DeOrchis & Partners, LLP

The Firm: Maritime remains the firm's largest and most concentrated area of work, but it is spending increasing time on the broader transportation sector. It is increasing its activity in insurance matters, and has recently filed suit against marine insurance brokers where there was no pay off on a large shipment that disappeared. Combined with its offices in Florida and Boston, the firm is progressively amassing a comprehensive East Coast presence. Although well known for cargo work, clients were pleased to report that the firm has expanded into other areas of marine law and transportation, such as freight forwarding and assistance regarding US customs regulations, toxic torts and insurance coverage disputes. Satisfied clients believed the practice had *"filled the gap where other firms have not,"* advancing *"a rare, personalized approach to law and a relaxed manner."* This partnership style impresses clients – one said: *"My admiration for that firm will always be there, they have acted above and beyond the call of duty."*

The Lawyers: **Vincent DeOrchis** is experienced in advising clients on issues involving deviation, damages, collisions and arbitrations. His focused, deal-oriented approach was a regular topic among interviewees. *"Thorough, detailed, reliable and punchy when he needs to be,"* he represented the North of England P&I Club and other cargo interests in a $154 million lawsuit against both the shipbuilder contracted to elongate the ship 'MSC Carla' and also the dockyard that actually performed the work. The containership broke in half off the Azores in November 1997 during a severe storm. The court ruled that the shipbuilder and the dockyard were both strictly liable for defects in the welding and design on the midsection, even though 13 years had gone by since completion of the work and the vessel had since been sold to a new owner. A balanced and well-settled team can also call on the services of one of its lawyers now working in Shanghai for a local firm.

The Clients: The team took on a class action for private pleasure yachts and major retailers in New Jersey against a paint manufacturer involving hull paint that failed. It also pursued a similar claim regarding people affected by toxic fumes from the painting of party boats alongside a pier. Its class action against Lloyd's Register relating to the 'MSC Carla' is still ongoing and may attract more work for the practice in the form of products liability claims involving manufacture of components for ships. The group also successfully acted on behalf of pur-

chasers PRA World Wide Trading against a beer company, regarding a shipment of over two million cans of beer that spoiled before reaching them. It further assisted trucker United Express Service concerning damage to a cargo of heavy machinery in New Jersey en route from Germany to Nebraska under a bill of lading. The court ruled that a one-year statute of limitations under the Carriage of Goods by Sea Act applied, rather than the Carmack Amendment or New York state law.

Gilmartin, Poster & Shafto

The Firm: Refinancings are a key aspect of the practice, with ship sale and purchase also prominent. The lion's share of its work is out of state, particularly on West Coast and international matters. For example, it provided advice on the construction of vessels in a Korean shipyard and the security-related refund from the Export-Import Bank of Korea. The practice also acted in the acquisition of new build container vessels from a Chinese shipyard and counsels on operating and holding company arrangements among South American and German investors and operators.

The Lawyers: **Robert Poster** advises on bankruptcy-related maritime matters and secured vessel financing. Technically proficient, he *"can see the forest for the trees and is more commercial"* than many in the market, according to interviewees. He worked on the extension and recasting of Crowley Maritime Corporation's $95 million secured revolving credit agreement with a Citibank-led syndicate, as well as a secured $115 million term loan facility for one of its affiliates. Frequently put forward as point of referral in conflict situations, he also acts as maritime counsel to the official committee of creditors in the ongoing Navigator Gas bankruptcy proceedings.

The Clients: Among the firm's highlights are its advice to a major LNG carrier in refinancing a large LNG vessel at the end of its original charter term and guiding financial institutions in mortgage and lease financing of US flag barge and towing vessels. Clients include Citibank, Ermis Maritime Holdings and Fleet National Bank.

Nicoletti Hornig Campise and Sweeney

The Firm: Insurance-related work is the keystone of the practice, often involving the defense of underwriters' interests in coverage disputes. Cargo subrogation also forms a significant part of the caseload. The firm's contacts are with American underwriters for the most part, with the additional ongoing links with the London market. The firm adopts an aggressive approach to negotiations, and clients proclaimed it to be a *"quite formidable firm, with experienced litigators"* contributing to an excellent legal product.

The Lawyers: **Michael Marks Cohen** is applauded for his litigation skills and comprehensive sector knowledge, as well as his capacity to deal with large workloads – *"God gave him 48 hours a day,"* said one interviewee. **Geoff Ginos** was similarly praised for his litigious ability in marine and related commercial and environment matters. Competitors said that they enjoyed their *"hard-fought battles"* with **James Sweeney**, a *"knowledgeable, no-nonsense lawyer who likes to get to the result."*

The Clients: The team represented cargo owners Morgan Stanley on the collision of the 'Vicky' with the stricken 'Tricolor' in the English Channel. It is also assisting Petróleos Mexicanos (Pemex) in a long-running arbitration concerning the Baku-Tbilisi-Ceyhan pipeline project. Other clients include chemical group Celanese and ConocoPhillips.

Nourse & Bowles LLP

The Firm: The firm is best known for its expert assistance on admiralty litigation including defense-oriented charter party work. It fields *"uniformly very capable"* attorneys, whose caseload has a heavy international element. Attorneys are well versed in charter party disputes, casualty claims and environmental regulatory compliance. The group is also on hand to advise on commercial and corporate issues arising out of the sector.

The Lawyers: Founding partner **David Nourse** heads this respected team. His strategic and tactical skills were much in evidence from interviewees, who depicted a *"canny, comprehensively wise and shrewd"* attorney with excellent judgment. His main focus is on maritime contract dispute resolution, especially under charter parties, bills of lading and contracts of affreightment. His colleague **Jay Paré**'s reputation is of a lawyer focused on protecting his clients' interests, and one particularly skilled in maritime and related insurance and international trade cases.

Watson, Farley & Williams
See firm details p.1377

The Firm: The practice remains a leading player in the maritime finance sector, handling ship finance and leasing work in addition to general litigation and restructurings within the sector. The structural and financial requirements of US and international flagship owners and financial institutions are its principal areas of focus. *"Professional and competent, but also commercially reasonable,"* the firm as a whole assists the LNG industry, often for carriers, and deals with additional rail-related matters and some aviation work.

The Lawyers: The sad death of John Osborne at the beginning of 2005 deprived the firm of one of its leading stars and the market of someone it *"could always trust and go to for any mat-*

ter that was at all delicate." Of this highly regarded team, **Leo Chang** (see p.78) stands out. He has won a following among clients for his "*expert documentation skills and understanding of the complexities of ship finance.*" He primarily assists financial institutions and operating companies and is recommended for his corporate capabilities in documenting both traditional and more complex maritime financings.

The Clients: The firm acted for the Clipper Group on its acquisition of bulk carrier Lasco Shipping, and represented a Great Lakes shipowner on its restructuring and refinancing. It also worked as maritime counsel to Nordea in connection with an $825 million syndicated facility for General Maritime and another large such facility for Ship Finance International. Citibank enlisted the firm's advice on financing the acquisition of a US flag operator and other similar ship financings.

Band 4

Badiak Will & Ruddy

The Firm: This relatively small plaintiff firm deals chiefly with major cargo losses and personal injury defenses for insurance companies. The team maintains involvement in a number of major casualty matters. It represents various underwriters, through London solicitors, on limitation proceedings on the 'Kariba' collision and also represents cargo interests for the recovery. It advises American underwriters on the 'DG Harmony' matters and works with cargo underwriters on the 'MSC Carla'. The group also carries out insurance and cargo recovery claims in related modes of transportation, frequently against truckers and railroads on interstate claims.

The Lawyers: Lead lawyer Roman Badiak previously headed a subrogation firm, a background that contributes not only to a thorough understanding of the insurance industry but also the needs of the client.

The Clients: Norsk Hydro is also a client of the firm, via its captive insurance companies.

Cichanowicz, Callan, Keane, Vengrow & Textor LLP

The Firm: This defense-oriented firm undertakes contract negotiations on behalf of cargo shippers and owners, helping to resolve performance issues resulting from such contracts. Added to this capacity is the group's expertise in advising on the requirements of the Jones Act and the Longshore and Harbor Workers' Compensation Act. Attorneys also advise workers injured at sea either on navigable waters or while working in harbor. Clients additionally noted its abilities on customs matters, including those relating to the importation of contraband.

The Lawyers: A "*super lawyer*" **Paul Keane**, is the senior member of the team. He is considered

an expert in litigation and bills of lading and is often consulted by P&I clubs keen to draw from his broad experience.

The Clients: Evergreen Marine Corp; Hanjin Shipping; Hyundai Merchant Marine; Laurin Maritime and SK Shipping Company.

Clark, Atcheson & Reisert

The Firm: A specialist maritime boutique with leading technical and engineering expertise. It also works on collisions, cargo defense and charter party disputes as well as some brown water work, including tugboat and barge defense. The majority of its activity in this sector is national in scope.

The Lawyers: **Peter Clark** is renowned for his ability on engineering matters, while all members of his team have served on ships in either an engineering capacity or as deck officers. Such technical aptitude is combined with waterfront experience to good effect. The practice also has a command of work concerning refrigeration ships and commodities.

The Clients: The group was appointed as an arbitrator on a matter concerning claims by a vessel owner that there had been overly strict interpretation of regulations. These related to taking one of its ships abroad to have it repaired at a lower price than in the USA, as it had believed immediate action was required. The practice was involved in another major arbitration in a technical case concerning engine problems with a ship and its watertight integrity. A further highlight includes a case concerning the contamination of high-premium gasoline through the pumping, piping and segregation of the cargo. The firm undertakes much technical and engineering work for P&I clubs, particularly those from the UK, and carries out a substantial degree of assistance in New Jersey relating to Port Newark/Port Elizabeth.

Donovan Parry McDermott & Radzik

The Firm: Originally a cargo recovery practice, the firm has expanded from these roots to deal with commercial insurance and maritime disputes, as well as those issues related to the aviation, rail and road sector. Such disputes center on the insurance aspects of marine casualties, as well as personal injury defense and the prosecution or defense of cargo claims for freight forwarders or NVOCCs.

The Lawyers: **Edward Radzik** most recently advised on several cargo-related cases, but he also deals with a wider range of shipping matters and intermodal work. Peers highlighted his London connections, aggressive style and thorough preparation. "*He understands the business.*"

The Clients: The team acted on the major 'MSC Carla' case on the cargo side, working closely with other firms. It advised the charterers and cargo interests on the 'San Sebastian'

tanker explosion in the Red Sea. The group represents a large number of American insurance companies involved in the maritime sector and receives a proportion of referrals from counsel in Europe and the Far East.

Kennedy Lillis Schmidt & English

The Firm: The majority of the firm's transportation work revolves around shipping litigation, although it does maintain its experience in related inland aviation work and general transportation maters within the USA. Long-held clients attested to its responsiveness and capabilities on particularly difficult matters.

The Lawyers: **Craig English** defends various liability matters for New York marine insurers involving shipyards, mariners and fishing boats. He also prosecutes some matters involving damage to goods moved by air, including both marine and air subrogation matters.

The Clients: The firm defended a charter fishing boat against a claim that its wake had caused the death of a 14-year-old child and serious injuries to a 3-year-old child. It represented a cargo interest regarding the fire and explosion of the 'San Sebastian' in the Red Sea. The client sought to obtain recovery via securing the assets of the shipowner, namely, freight money owed by those for whom it was carrying the cargo. The team also provides opinions and assistance on matters involving mega-yachts for a major US marine insurer.

Thacher Proffitt & Wood LLP

See firm details p.1374

The Firm: A large firm with a relatively small but ever increasing marine component, the practice comes to the sector from the insurance and reinsurance side and is also recommended for its maritime securities work. It concentrates on representing marine insurers and underwriters both in the USA and Europe, while broadening its appeal to include some shipowners, charterers and survey companies. The firm's involvement on the Kirby v Norfolk Southern Railway case was a leading aspect of its work in 2004. It submitted an amicus brief on behalf of two trade groups in a Supreme Court case. The decision held that there is federal admiralty jurisdiction over mixed contracts referring to both ocean and inland components, as opposed to state law. Much of its transportation work is litigation-oriented, but the team also provides ship finance counsel to banks and other lenders. Attorneys are also well equipped to provide environmental risk assessment and advice on liabilities arising out of oil and hazardous substance spills. Much of its transportation work is litigation-oriented, but the team also provides ship finance counsel to banks and other lenders. Attorneys are also well equipped to provide environmental risk assessment and advice on liabilities arising out of oil and hazardous substance spills.

The Lawyers: Senior marine partner and litigation chair **John Woods** (see p.108) is "*a force in the marine insurance market,*" advising on disputes both in New York and around the USA. He works with both US and foreign insurers and is also experienced in matters concerning oil spills and hazardous substance discharges.

The Clients: The group represented a geopositioning company on its role in a claim concerning the severing of power cables in Long Island Sound by a vessel's anchor. It acted for the hull insurer on a claim involving a vessel that sank off the coast of Brazil, and separately advised on a couple of pollution liability cases pertaining to Water Quality Insurance Syndicate. The firm's burgeoning client base is also reflected in its work on behalf of a bunker fuel supplier; the case involved an explosion and fire on a container ship.

Other Notable Practitioners

The work of **Liz Burrell** at Levy Phillips & Konigsberg LLP stands out as she is the only maritime practitioner and an appellate lawyer at a firm known for its trial work but not for its marine assistance. She does not deal with finance/transactional matters, instead acts on the private carriage of goods by charter for charterers and commodities clients on a national basis. She also advises prospective charterers, assists on resolving charter disputes and acts on a small number of substantial maritime litigations. Specific highlights include advice to a mining company on its charter parties, including those of carriage between South America and the USA. She represented a Chinese shipowner in trans atlantic litigation and arbitration revolving around the differences between US and English charter formation law.

SHIPPING

OUTSIDE NEW YORK

National (outside New York)
Leading firms (Shipping)

1. AKERMAN SENTERFITT
BLANK ROME LLP
DEORCHIS HILLENBRAND & WIENER LLP
FOWLER, WHITE, BURNETT PA
HOLLAND & KNIGHT LLP
KEESAL YOUNG & LOGAN PC
LAU, LANE, PIEPER, CONLEY
MOSELEY PRICHARD PARRISH KNIGHT
PHELPS DUNBAR LLP
SHER & BLACKWELL
TROUTMAN SANDERS LLP
WINSTON & STRAWN

Leading individuals (Shipping)

1. BENNER C Jonathan *Troutman Sanders*, Washington, DC
CUVA Anthony *Akerman Senterfitt*, Tampa
HILLENBRAND Hyman *DeOrchis Hillenbrand*, Miami
KEESAL Jr Samuel *Keesal Young*, Long Beach
MOSELEY James *Moseley Prichard*, Jacksonville
PAPAVIZAS Constantine *Winston & Strawn*, DC
PIEPER Nathaniel *Lau Lane*, Tampa
SHER Stanley *Sher & Blackwell*, DC
SUNG Audrey *Holland & Knight*, San Francisco

Firms and individuals are listed alphabetically in each band.

Band 1

Akerman Senterfitt
See firm details p.555

The Firm: This Florida-based practice counsels on maritime and related commerce matters. It also works with lenders, pension funds and other shipowners on ship finance and construction. The department increasingly undertakes maritime-related commercial litigation, including mediations and arbitrations, as traditional collisions and cargo damage cases taper off. Another feature is its extensive track record in representing clients in administrative hearings at the federal, state and local levels. Although most of the firm's work is deliberately centered in the Florida region, its merger with Katz, Kutter, Alderman & Bryant has bolstered its capability in government relations and helped boost its profile in the DC market. In addition, the group benefits from its cultivated referral relationships with firms outside Florida, who turn to the team's "*bright*" cadre on "*substantial*" issues.

The Lawyers: **Anthony Cuva** (see p.80) in Tampa is the firm's leading maritime attorney. He has litigated some of the firm's most important cases, including those related to vessel collisions. He also spends a proportion of his time on trucking work, often involving subrogation actions for insurers or cargo damage. He is ably supported by a team boasting extensive maritime sector backgrounds, including a former chief trial counsel to the United States Maritime Administration.

The Clients: The firm advises Rolls-Royce regarding its propulsion systems on cruise ships. It also works with harbor pilots on their licenses and advises mariners and other parties on coastguard proceedings, including those that involve the parasail industry. Another client is a Greek shipping company, and recent work includes representation on matters arising from the grounding of a ship.

Blank Rome LLP
See firm details p.1542

The Firm: The burgeoning area of law linked to the criminalization of pollution is a focus for this DC-based maritime practice, which often represents clients before government agencies on a variety of matters. Rather than deal with traditional admiralty matters, the phalanx of "*quality individuals*" represents shipyards and other companies on government contracts, international trade and related disputes. Clients frequently enlist the firm's help on Jones Act compliance among other vessel documentation issues. The changing US regulatory and legislative climate also has spurred the firm's ascendancy, and it has deftly combined such areas as environmental law, securities-related issues and regulatory enforcement to gain favorable outcomes for clients. The group is also a "*leader in the country*" when it comes to advising on high-speed ferry operations, including Hawaii and the Great Lakes.

The Lawyers: Practice group chair John Waldron handles pollution and citizenship issues. He also deals with much of the firm's high-speed ferry matters, representing US ports and Canadian vessels on matters such as security concerns.

The Clients: The firm has advised cruise lines, tanker operators, shipbuilders, ports and terminal operators, ferry operators, and financing institutions among others.

DeOrchis Hillenbrand & Wiener, LLP

The Firm: The firm remains rooted in its maritime core, which has been established through a strong track record in a broad array of work, including disputes involving collisions, casualty investigations, cargo and charter party issues. Its "*broad spectrum of knowledge*" also covers maritime-related insurance battles, further sustained by a varied diet of specialty expertise in such areas as products liability, government regulations and personal injury. "*Quality of work, prices and results are all there,*" one client said. "*They have good experience and knowledge of the industry.*" The firm successfully defended Italian yacht builder Cantieri di Baia against alleged breaches of two contracts, obtaining dismissals based upon the doctrine of forum non conveniens despite the fact that the plaintiff was a Florida corporation. On the transactional side, its corporate experience involves contracts, financing, and sales and purchases. It has also handled bills of lading and vessel sharing agreements, crewing contracts and vessel arrests and attachments. Though comprising a significantly smaller proportion of its practice, the team also handles matters relating to rail and road.

The Lawyers: Managing partner **Hyman Hillenbrand** "*gets tremendous results*" as one the most "*engaging*" advocates in this practice area. He combines a "*highly intelligent and extremely skillful*" approach to maritime law with a "*likeable*" personality. A leader in his field, the Florida-based operator has cultivated a "*fantastic*" practice through his work on behalf of common carriers and insurance companies among others. David Farrell of the firm's Boston office also undertakes maritime work, underlining the firm's successful East Coast coverage. He conducts insurance defense on behalf of P&I clubs and domestic underwriters.

The Clients: Vessel owners and operators, P&I clubs and underwriters are among the firm's clientele.

Fowler, White, Burnett PA

The Firm: A full-service firm with a proclivity toward maritime law, the firm often defends insurers, and owners and operators against claims related to collisions, liability issues and regulatory matters among others. The firm has represented ocean carriers in various high-profile disputes, including those relating to cargo liability. Other matters relate to service contracts, for example, those between shippers and carriers. In addition, a significant proportion of its workload is on behalf of P&I clubs, and the team is also fluent in matters pertaining to recreational vessels, usually advising insurers and builders. Working in tandem with the firm's environmental experts, it proved successful on matters linked to oil spills, hazardous discharges and damage to natural resources. Its work in the shipping sector is further supplemented by its expertise in aviation and motor carriage issues. It also gained respect for its work in Latin America, particularly as it relates to major claims or casualties.

The Lawyers: Charles De Leo is a key partner in the marine section. His practice encompasses transactional and litigation skills, and also includes an environmental aspect of maritime law.

The Clients: ACE, CNA, and Fireman's Fund Insurance are among the firm's prominent clientele. It also represents vessel owners, operators and charterers among others.

Holland & Knight LLP

See firm details p.1352

The Firm: The firm often takes its cue from P&I clubs among other clients, marshaling them through disputes such as those related to collisions, dock and cargo damages and insurance coverage. Its broader strength in litigation is aptly showcased in an initiative dubbed the Rapid Response Team – a group of experienced advocates able to quickly respond to major maritime casualties and marine environmental incidents. "*They do not dwell on legal irrelevancies,*"

one client said. "*They point out risks, help the client evaluate them and then suggest fair allocations of the identified risks.*" Another drawing card is its authority on shipping finance, including raising private equity related to The World of ResidenSea, a luxury 'floating apartment' vessel. "*It produces thorough, high-quality and goal-oriented transactional work,*" clients said. It consistently attracts clients who also value the geographic spread of the firm, which boasts 25 offices nationwide and overseas satellites. Rounding out the practice is the firm's expertise on maritime regulatory and compliance issues.

The Lawyers: San Francisco-based partner **Audrey Sung**'s (see p.106) corporate practice contains a considerable maritime aspect, particularly as related to financing structures such as leveraged leases and sales. She exhibits "*calm professionalism and engineered [the transaction] to a successful conclusion in what easily could have resulted in a failure,*" one client said, referring to a particularly thorny problem. The firm's widespread expertise includes Jacksonville's George Gabel and DC-based Michael Cavanaugh.

The Clients: P&I clubs, financial institutions, vessel owners, charterers, underwriters, carriers and shippers are among the firm's clients.

Keesal Young & Logan PC

The Firm: Portrayed as "*one of the best on the West Coast,*" the firm gained particular commendation for its dominance in admiralty work. Some of the most prestigious companies depend on the firm's experience on maritime transportation, including issues linked to the transfer of nuclear waste and massive oil spills. Its authority is also noted on related litigation such as disputes pertaining to pollution, collisions and employment matters. A phalanx of "*knowledgeable, hard-working*" operators inspires confidence among industry analysts, who also credit the group for its excellent representation of oil and gas concerns. The practice's success also derives from its strength in advising cruise lines, and it boasts a Southeast Alaska satellite office to meet the seasonal needs of such clients among others.

The Lawyers: Founder **Skip Keesal** is a generalist litigator who often helps maritime clients through a variety of complex disputes. An "*exceptional*" advocate, he is "*excellent in front of a jury, extremely focused and believes in preparation, preparation and more preparation.*" Though he also has transactional experience, he is seen less frequently in this capability.

The Clients: The firm has counseled owners, operators and charterers of ships, in addition to a significant contingent of oil and gas clients.

Lau, Lane, Pieper, Conley & McCreadie

The Firm: A cultivated reputation in defending casualty, personal injury and wrongful death claims has made an impact in the maritime sector, where the firm often represents clients embroiled in related disputes. Its work in this area also intersects with other specialty niches in such areas as insurance and maritime pollution, and the specialist firm is a considerable force in mediation, arbitration and litigation before state and federal courts. Due to the nature of the firm's boutique profile, it is perceived to be more "*conscious of costs*" to clients while delivering an "*extremely thorough*" product that "*unturns every stone,*" observers said. The team also helps steer clients through regulatory proceedings concerning customs, immigration and labor relations.

The Lawyers: **Nathaniel Pieper** won applause as a hard-nosed warrior who can be "*calm under fire,*" sources said. "*He is someone who looks to the end result but is conscious of the strengths and weaknesses of the client's position.*" Foremost a litigator, his experience includes disputes relating to cruise ship passengers.

The Clients: The firm has advised vessel owners and operators among others.

Moseley Prichard Parrish Knight & Jones

The Firm: The Jacksonville boutique delivers a concentrated punch in all things concerning transportation law, which includes a considerable amount of maritime advice. The cadre of "*crackerjack*" advocates also fold their insurance expertise into the mix, culminating in a dynamic defense practice that often participates in some of the region's most high-profile disputes. "*They have pretty much cornered the market in Jacksonville with some great attorneys,*" commentators said. The team commands confidence with its ability to accurately assess the market and make "*smart decisions from there.*" On offer is the usual array of dispute resolution skills relating to such areas as cargo liability, collisions and insurance claims. In addition, the group also handles bills of lading and maritime contracts among other shipping documents.

The Lawyers: **James Moseley** impresses with his "*energetic*" and forceful advocacy skills, which have been parlayed into legal victories in some "*really tough cases,*" observers said. "*He's not afraid to roll up his sleeves and tackle difficult problems.*"

The Clients: The group offers expertise in personal injury and debt in addition to an established collision practice. It additionally advises on products liability defense and oil pollution matters. The firm maintains decades old relationships with both P&I clubs and owners, and has also advised insurance concerns and associated shipping interests.

Phelps Dunbar LLP

See firm details p.886

The Firm: The broad regional coverage provided by this practice is a key defining feature. While the group is centered in New Orleans, it can call on specialist attorneys from its offices in Tampa and Houston. Market observers commended the *"thorough, articulate advice"* provided by these attorneys and their *"quick-witted"* approach to litigation. The group has cultivated a healthy balance between maritime litigation, including casualty defense, collisions and claims under environmental law, with general business counseling and transportation regulation. Its noncontentious workload of late has included the negotiation of multi-million-dollar credit facilities and acting as admiralty counsel in a merger. In the litigation sphere, attorneys here successfully defended a ship owner in a $43 million vessel construction dispute and acted for a vessel owner/operator in a multi-million dollar recovery case against an international diesel engine manufacturer. Well versed in the nuances of environmental law, the group has also advised on claims arising out of a 30,000 gallon fuel spill in the Mississippi River following a ship collision.

The Lawyers: George Gilly coordinates the firm's admiralty practice across the firm's offices. His practice encompasses maritime, oil field and insurance matters. This respected group also fields a host of experienced litigators and transportation specialists and has recently been joined by Anne-Gwin Duval, formerly in-house with Bollinger Shipyards.

The Clients: The group acts for a substantial number of international P&I clubs; insurers such as ACE and CNA; cruise ship clients such as Radisson and Carnival; trucking companies such as Landstar, Contract Freighters and Crete Carriers and underwriters focused on the sector.

Sher & Blackwell

The Firm: Market observers highlighted this DC-based practice for its expertise in maritime regulation, particularly issues brought before the Federal Maritime Association. It fields *"a sizable core of excellent lawyers,"* whose approach is *"careful and thorough."* *"They know the market very well"* and understand the intricacies that are brought to play in complex proceedings. A broad practice can support clients across a range of commercial, regulatory and legislative issues. Among its regulatory experience, the group has counseled clients on embargo laws, taxation issues, the formation of consortia and rate agreements. Much of the caseload here has an international dimension and the attorneys are well equipped to advise on issues related to competition law outside of the USA as well as in the domestic market. The group also brings its keen business sense and understanding of the market to commercial issues such as corporate acquisitions and shipping finance.

The Lawyers: The *"superb and extensive expertise"* displayed by **Stanley Sher** has impressed many market sources. Founding partner of the firm, he can count among his loyal clients some of the market's leading international ocean carriers. He advises clients before the federal agencies, courts and Congress.

The Clients: The firm's broad client base includes owners, operators and financiers in the cargo and passenger transportation industry, maritime construction, offshore energy and fisheries markets.

Troutman Sanders LLP

The Firm: The firm houses a broad transportation practice in which maritime and rail issues feature heavily. The group is best known for its work on regulatory issues before the Federal Maritime Commission, and is respected for its smooth handling of collisions, cargo damage and personal injury litigation. The group has recently bolstered its capacity to handle casualty disputes and security issues arising out of the mid-Atlantic through the recruitment of specialists to its office in Norfolk, Virginia. Customs, trade embargo and export control counseling also form part of the practice. The group has provided legislative and policy counsel to international marine insurers, and represented groups of vessel owners on issues of environment regulation. Its attorneys have testified before state legislatures on marine safety matters and provided ship owners in the USA and abroad with advice on US antitrust and trade restrictions.

The Lawyers: According to observers, **Jonathan Benner** stands out as a *"highly knowl-*edgeable attorney who is thoroughly respected"* for his contribution to the sector. A key player in the DC market, he is a personable attorney, who *"handles people and cases well."* He has successfully challenged the constitutionality of state regulations that govern shipping operations and has advised on proceedings before the Federal Maritime Commission and other agencies.

The Clients: The firm has acted for a major domestic container operator in disputes with shippers and local government over rate levels in the domestic offshore trades, including markets such as Hawaii, Alaska and Puerto Rico. Its client base features ship owners, vessel operators, insurers and maritime trade associations.

Winston & Strawn

See firm details p.780

The Firm: A broad understanding of the admiralty and maritime sector coupled with an insight into the workings of Washington, DC has ensured this firm a prominence in the sector. Although DC remains its hub, and regulatory issues its staple diet, this group can also call upon the resources of a full-service, national operation for related corporate, tax and financing issues to name but a few. Attorneys here are well versed in regulatory compliance, products liability and environmental law issues and have experience in proceedings before the federal agencies and before Congress.

The Lawyers: **Charlie Papavizas** has impressed market sources with his detailed understanding of regulatory issues facing the sector and his commitment to the market. As part of his broad maritime transportation practice, he has advised clients in proceedings before the federal agencies and Congress, as well as advising clients on corporate and securities transactions.

The Clients: The group recently assisted First American Bulk Carrier Corporation in the successful reversal of the US Department of Transportation Maritime Administration's denial of permission concerning the assignment of three maritime security program operating agreements from Lykes Brothers Steamship Company. This involved the restructuring of charter and financial arrangements and the negotiation of vessel management agreements.

National Leaders

ABORN, Richard A
Cadwalader, Wickersham & Taft LLP,
New York 212 504 6188
richard.aborn@cwt.com
Recommended in Aviation
Practice Areas: Practice focuses on leveraged lease, aircraft, vessel and other equipment and project financings. Since mid-1980s, primarily involved in aircraft financing transactions. Primary aircraft clients include Northwest Airlines and Delta Air Lines. Also represented equity investors and lenders in aircraft financing transactions with major air carriers. Since 1984, has participated in aircraft financing transactions aggregating more than $20 billion.
Personal: BA Williams College 1965, JD Boston College 1969. Member of the Boston College Industrial and Commercial Law Review, Order of the Coif. Chosen as a "Recommended High Flyer" in Aviation Counsel's elite peer-group survey of the world's leading aviation law practitioners. Member, Association of the Bar of the City of New York and New York State Bar Association.

ADDUCI II, James
Adduci, Mastriani & Schaumberg LLP,
Washington, DC 202 467 6300
Recommended in International Trade

AKSEN, Gerald
Gerald Aksen - Sole Practitioner, New York 212 603 2174
gaksen@thelenreid.com
Recommended in Arbitration
Practice Areas: Full time arbitrator and mediator. Retired Partner of Thelen Reid & Priest LLP where he specialized in international arbitration and alternative dispute resolution. Has represented American, English, French, German, Japanese and Korean clients in arbitrations in eighteen different countries. Has served as an arbitrator under the rules of leading arbitral institutions such as American Arbitration Association (AAA), International Chamber of Commerce (ICC), Japan Commercial Arbitration Association, London Court of International Arbitration, Stockholm Chamber of Commerce, and under UNCITRAL Arbitration Rules. Speaker at many conferences and seminars.
Prof. Memberships: College of Commercial Arbitrators, President, 2002-03, ICC International Court of Arbitration, Vice-Chairman 2000 -02, American Bar Association, Chairman, Section of International Law & Practice, 1982-83, Member House of Delegates 1985-88; Association of the Bar of the City of New York, Chairman of Arbitration Committee 1970-72 and ADR Committee 1993-94.
Career: City College of New York (BA 1951); Columbia University (MA 1952); US Army 1st LT (1952-55); NYU School of Law (JD 1958); Admitted to NY Bar in 1959; Flood & Purvin, litigation asso-

ciate, 1958-60; AAA, Assistant to President and General Counsel 1961-80; Reid & Priest LLP, Partner 1981; became Thelen Reid & Priest LLP in 1998. Adjunct Professor of Law at NYU School of Law teaching course on international arbitration (1970-2000).
Personal: Born February 16, 1930. Interests include travel and sports. Resides in NY City.

ALBERTSON, Terry
Crowell & Moring LLP, Washington, DC
202 624 2635
talbertson@crowell.com
Recommended in Government Contracts
Practice Areas: Terry Albertson is a Partner in Crowell & Moring's Government Contracts Group and member of the firm's management board. He focuses on government procurement law, including contract, cost accounting, pricing and termination issues. He has tried numerous important cases concerning defective pricing, Cost Accounting Standards, multiple award contracts, terminations, and more.
Career: Selected by Legal Times as a leading Washington government contracts lawyer; received Bronze Star for service in Vietnam War for service in US Army. Bachelor's degree from Georgetown University, magna cum laude,1968; MA from Yale University, 1969; JD from Harvard Law School, cum laude, 1974.

ALBRECHT, Thomas W
Sidley Austin Brown & Wood LLP,
Chicago 312 853 7213
talbrecht@sidley.com
Recommended in Capital Markets
Practice Areas: Partner in Chicago office of Sidley Austin Brown & Wood LLP. Practice includes domestic and international securitisations and structured finance. Head of firm's securitisation practice area. Member of the firm's Management and Executive Committees and Co-Chair of its International Operations Committee. Frequent lecturer at securitisation industry conferences.
Prof. Memberships: Member, American Bar Association.
Career: University of Dayton, BA, 1975; University of Chicago Law School, JD, 1979. Bar Admission: Illinois, 1979.
Publications: Co-author, 'Corporate Loan Securitisation: Selected Legal and Regulatory Issues' (Duke Journal of Comparative & International Law, Spring 1998).

ALEXANDER, Troy
White & Case LLP, New York
212 819 8200
Recommended in Projects
Please see New York for profile

ALEXANDROV, Stanimir A
Sidley Austin Brown & Wood LLP, Washington, DC 202 736 8115
salexandrov@sidley.com
Recommended in Arbitration
Practice Areas: Stanimir Alexandrov practices in the areas of international business transactions, trade and investment policy and international dispute resolution. He has advised and represented private-sector clients in arbitration with host governments in expropriation disputes, and private parties and governments in WTO disputes. He advises foreign clients on capital markets transactions, EU law, trademark protection and expanding distribution and sales networks. He is appointed to the Panel of Arbitrators and the Panel of Conciliators of the World Bank's International Centre for Settlement of Investment Disputes (ICSID). His publications have been cited by parties to disputes before the International Court of Justice and by Judges of the Court.
Prof. Memberships: Senior Fellow at the International Rule of Law Institute; member of the American Bar Association, where he provides legislative analysis to the ABA's Central and Eastern European Law Initiative (CEELI).
Career: He served as Vice Minister of Foreign Affairs of Bulgaria, and was responsible for relations with the European Union, the United Nations, the OSCE and NATO. He lectures at the George Washington School of Law on international law. He holds both Russian and U.S. law degrees. Moscow Institute of International Relations, JD, 1981; The George Washington University Law School, LL.M., 1992, S.JD, 1994. Bar Admissions: New York, 1999 and District of Columbia, 2005.
Publications: 'Inducing Compliance in WTO Dispute Settlement, in The Political Economy of International Trade: Essays in Honor of Robert E. Hudec' (Kennedy and Southwick, Eds.), Cambridge University Press 2002, with David Palmeter, and numerous articles and lectures.

ALKALAY, Peter
McLaughlin & Stern LLP, New York
212 448 1100
Recommended in Sport

ALLEN, Rand L
Wiley Rein & Fielding LLP,
Washington, DC 202 719 7329
rallen@wrf.com
Recommended in Government Contracts
Practice Areas: Chairs firm's 25-attorney Government Contracts Practice, representing many of the nation's largest government contractors, and the 'go-to' counsel for industry on some of the highest-profile matters. Named the Washington, DC area's Top Government

Contracts Lawyer by 'Legal Times.' Handles full range of contracting issues, including bid protests, contract claims and disputes litigation, terminations, mergers and acquisitions, procurement fraud/False Claims Act investigations, and suspension/debarment.
Prof. Memberships: American Bar Association, Past Chair, Section of Public Contract Law.
Personal: Georgetown University Law Center (JD); United States Military Academy at West Point (AB).

ALLEN, Richard
Zuckert, Scoutt & Rasenberger, LLP,
Washington 202 298 8660
Recommended in Transport

ANDERSON, M Jean
Weil, Gotshal & Manges LLP, Washington, DC 202 682 7217
jean.anderson@weil.com
Recommended in International Trade
Practice Areas: International trade, litigation.
Career: Ms Anderson co-chairs Weil Gotshal's International Trade Practice, providing strategic trade policy advice. She represents companies and governments in complex, high-profile trade proceedings, including groundbreaking WTO cases and as lead counsel in the largest trade dispute on record. Formerly Chief Counsel for International Trade at the US Department of Commerce; was a principal negotiator of trade agreements involving industry sectors, trade remedies and dispute settlement. Oversaw all Commerce legal work on antidumping and subsidies, safeguards and Section 301, market access, trade negotiations, legislative implementation and export controls.
Personal: Georgetown University, JD; Northwestern University, BA.

ANDREOZZI, Bradley J
Mayer, Brown, Rowe & Maw LLP,
Chicago 312 701 8564
bandreozzi@mayerbrown.com
Recommended in Sport
Practice Areas: Represents sports federations and athletes in litigation and international arbitration concerning governance issues, drug testing, eligibility, regulatory compliance, and other matters, including before the Court of Arbitration for Sport (CAS) in Lausanne, Switzerland and CAS' ad hoc division at the Olympics. Represents corporations, banks, insurance companies and accounting firms before trial and appellate courts throughout the U.S., including class action defense, and claims involving securities, accountant liability, lender liability, and constitutional law issues. Conducts internal investigations and advises clients regarding remedial measures to avoid or limit claims.

Career: Mayer, Brown, Rowe & Maw LLP, Chicago, 1998 to date; Partner, 2000; Counsel, 1998. Mayer, Brown, Rowe & Maw LLP, New York, 1991-98. Reboul, MacMurray, Hewitt, Maynard & Kristol, New York, 1986-91. Hughes, Hubbard & Reed, New York, 1983-86. **Publications:** 'Arbitration and Dispute Resolution in the Olympics,' 2005 Annual Winter Sports Law Symposium, DePaul University College of Law; Co-Author: 'Lender's 'Right to be Wrong' on Material Adverse Change Affirmed,' Lender Liability News, August 11, 1995. **Personal:** JD, University of Chicago Law School, 1983. BA (magna cum laude), Yale College, 1980.

APPLEBAUM, Harvey M
Covington & Burling, Washington, DC
202.662.5626
happlebaum@cov.com
Recommended in International Trade
Practice Areas: Handles International Trade Commission, Commerce Department and U.S. Trade Representative proceedings under the antidumping and countervailing duty laws, Section 201 of the Trade Act and other trade laws, and WTO and NAFTA dispute matters. Also has an active practice in customs law matters, including classification, valuation, foreign origin, compliance reviews, NAFTA, and penalty proceedings.
Career: Former Chairman of the American Bar Association Antitrust Law Section; First Chairman of the Editorial Board of ABA Antitrust Law Developments; Former Chairman of the Section's Robinson-Patman Act Committee; Current Member of the Section's International Antitrust Advisory Committee.
Personal: Harvard University, (JD, 1962, magna cum laude); Yale University (BA, 1959, summa cum laude).

ARCHIBALD, Jeanne S
Hogan & Hartson LLP, Washington, DC
202 637 5740
jsarchibald@hhlaw.com
Recommended in International Trade
Practice Areas: Jeanne Archibald, director of Hogan & Hartson's International Trade Group, has more than 25 years of experience in a broad range of international trade law matters. Her practice focuses on international trade negotiations and dispute settlement under the World Trade Organization, North American Free Trade Agreement, and other international trade agreements; compliance counseling and enforcement proceedings with respect to economic sanctions and export controls; national security reviews relating to foreign direct investment in the United States; customs and legislative proposals affecting trade; and strategic trade counseling for multinational companies.
Career: Before joining Hogan & Hartson Jeanne served as general counsel of the United States Department of the

Treasury, where she served as the Chief Legal Officer of the department and all of its 10 subordinate bureaus. She provided legal and policy advice to the secretary of the treasury and other senior officials on the full range of issues under the Treasury Department's jurisdiction. Before joining the Treasury Department, Jeanne served in the Office of the United States Trade Representative. She also served on the staff of the Ways & Means Committee of the U.S. House of Representatives.
Publications: 'Final Rule: Advance Electronic Presentation of Cargo Manifest Information', International Trade and U.S. Homeland Security Update, Hogan & Hartson L.L.P. (12/12/2003).
Personal: Georgetown University Law Center (JD); Member of the District of Columbia Bar.

ARNHOLZ, John
McKee Nelson LLP, Washington, DC
202 775 4138
jarnholz@mckeenelson.com
Recommended in Capital Markets
Practice Areas: Securitization and structured finance, corporate/securities. Represents issuers and underwriters in securitization transactions with a significant emphasis on cross-border and global offerings. Works with a broad range of financial assets, including residential mortgage loans, debt obligations, home equity loans, auto loans, franchise loans, and high LTV loans. Has been active in structured finance transactions in international markets. Has represented underwriters and issuers in many significant securitization programmes.
Career: Prior to joining McKee Nelson, was a Partner at the Washington, DC office of Sidley Austin Brown & Wood. At McKee Nelson, heads the DC office's Structured Finance Group. Received a JD from the Georgetown University Law Center in 1985.

ASMUS, David
Baker Botts LLP, Houston
713 229 1234
Recommended in Energy, Projects
Please see Texas for profile

ASTIGARRAGA, José I
Astigarraga Davis, Miami
305 372 8282
jia@astidavis.com
Recommended in Arbitration
Practice Areas: José Astigarraga focuses his practice on international litigation and arbitration, primarily representing multinational companies in disputes emanating from international business transactions.
Prof. Memberships: All Florida courts; United States Supreme Court; Circuit Courts of Appeal for the Eleventh and Fifth Circuits.
Career: Astigarraga is a Founding Shareholder at Astigarraga Davis. He litigates cases in courts in the United States

and in arbitral tribunals in the United States and abroad. Astigarraga has supervised a multitude of legal proceedings throughout Latin America in the course of his 26 year career. In 2004 he became one of only four Americans on the 35-member worldwide London Court of International Arbitration. He has served as sole arbitrator, co-arbitrator or chair of arbitral panels of the International Chamber of Commerce, the American Arbitration Association and other arbitral institutions. Astigarraga is the Vice-Chair of the International Bar Association's worldwide International Arbitration Committee and was one of the ten Americans initially appointed by the US Government to advise the NAFTA Commission on arbitration and dispute resolution in private commercial disputes. He was appointed by the United States Department of State to serve as an expert at the Organization of American States' Interamerican Conference on Private International Law. He is Vice-Chair of the National Law Center for Inter-American Free Trade, and a Member of the Executive Council of the American Law Institute, publishers of the Restatements of Law.
Publications: Co-author, 'Latin American Insolvency Systems', World Bank 1999.
Personal: Fluent Spanish, born July 20, 1953. University of Miami (1975 BBA summa cum laude; 1978 JD magna cum laude).

AUERBACH, Reed
McKee Nelson LLP, New York
917 777 4400
rauerbach@mckeenelson.com
Recommended in Capital Markets
Practice Areas: Practice focused on structured finance and derivative transactions. Represents underwriters and issuers in connection with public and private offerings of asset-backed and mortgage-backed securities and related interim warehouse financings, whole loan purchases, repurchase agreements and residual financings. Has broad-based experience with a wide variety of assets, including student loans, prime and non-prime auto loans, auto leases, equipment leases, royalty streams and other intellectual property rights, dealer floor plan receivables, telecommunication receivables, litigation settlement fees, Australian mortgage loans, manufactured housing contracts, recreational vehicle loans, boat loans, home equity loans, credit card receivables, and insurance premium finance agreements.
Career: Prior to joining McKee Nelson, was a Partner at the New York office of Stroock & Stoock & Lavan LLP (Jan. 1994 – May 2001). At McKee Nelson, is Managing Partner of the firm's New York office.
Personal: JD from the Columbia University School of Law in 1985, where he was a Harlan Fiske Stone Scholar, editor for The Journal of Transactional Law,

and received a Certificate with Honors from the Parker School of International and Comparative Law. Received a Master's degree in International Affairs from Columbia University's School of International Affairs in 1982, where he was named an International Fellow. Received a Bachelor's degree, magna cum laude, from Franklin & Marshall College in 1980, where he was elected to membership in Phi Beta Kappa.

AYRES, Margaret M
Davis Polk & Wardwell, Washington, DC
202 962 7000
margaret.ayres@dpw.com
Recommended in International Trade
Practice Areas: Counsel in Davis Polk & Wardwell's Corporate Department, concentrating in US trade and investment laws applicable to cross-border transactions, including the Exon-Florio statute; the Foreign Corrupt Practices Act; US economic sanctions; and US anti-boycott laws and laws restricting foreign investment in the US communications, shipping, aviation, nuclear and defense industries. She has assisted US and international clients in connection with their filings under the Exon-Florio national security statute; advised a number of US investment banks in connection with various transactions involving foreign investments in protected US industries; and advised many industrial and investment banking clients of the firm on US sanctions against foreign countries and on the Foreign Corrupt Practices Act.

BAKER, Mark
Fulbright & Jaworski LLP, Houston
713 651 5151
Recommended in Arbitration, Energy
Please see Texas for profile

BARKER, John
Arnold & Porter LLP, Washington, DC
202 942 5328
John.Barker@aporter.com
Recommended in International Trade
Practice Areas: Mr Barker's practice focuses on national security matters including export controls, international technology transfers, trade sanctions administered by the Office of Foreign Assets Control at the US Treasury (OFAC), as well as compliance with the Foreign Corrupt Practices Act (FCPA). He helps companies and institutions establish compliance plans, obtain export authorizations and provides representation in enforcement proceedings. Mr Barker came to the firm from the US Department of State, where he served as the Deputy Assistant Secretary for Nonproliferation Controls and, prior to that, as Deputy Assistant Secretary for Export Controls.
Career: In his most recent position at the State Department, Mr Barker supervised the development and implementation of US policy on multilateral nonproliferation and security regimes, and nonproliferation sanctions. As the

Deputy Assistant Secretary for Export Controls, he supervised the US munitions licensing and defense trade compliance system including imposing sanctions on companies for violation of US export control law and overseeing the US government's nonproliferation review of dual-use exports. Mr Barker testified frequently before Congress on a wide variety of export control matters including trade sanctions, preventing the transfer of arms and dual-use technology to state sponsors of terrorism, the Export Administration Act, export licensing and compliance, and regulation of the aerospace industry.
Publications: Co-author, Stanford University study on ballistic missile proliferation.
Personal: Mr Barker received his JD from the University of Michigan Law School in 1986, where he was managing editor of the Journal of Law Reform.

BARONSKY, Kenneth
Milbank, Tweed, Hadley & McCloy, Los Angeles 213 892 4000
Recommended in Capital Markets

BARRINGER, William H
Willkie Farr & Gallagher LLP, Washington, DC 202 303 1101
wbarringer@willkie.com
Recommended in International Trade
Practice Areas: Partner and Chair of the International Trade Department, specializing in all aspects of international trade law, with particular emphasis on defending antidumping and countervailing duty investigations and advising on international trade negotiations and trade policy disputes. He has significant experience defending Japanese and other foreign interests in trade disputes with the United States and representing clients in WTO dispute settlement proceedings. Has been involved in some of the most significant international trade disputes over the last several decades, including among others, disputes between the US and Japan involving autos, film, and steel. He has been the lead counsel on more than 50 antidumping investigations, more than a dozen safeguards investigations, and numerous investigations under section 301 of US trade law. Frequently advises foreign industries and governments on bilateral and multilateral trade issues and was actively involved in this capacity during the Uruguay Round negotiations. He has also advised governments and industries extensively on WTO disputes, including the ongoing proceeding challenging US payment of antidumping duties to petitioning parties under the Byrd Amendment.
Prof. Memberships: Member of the American Bar Association.
Career: Admitted to the Bar of the District of Columbia.
Publications: Has lectured and written extensively on a wide variety of trade law and trade policy issues. He recently

authored a book published under the auspices of the American Institute for International Steel entitled 'Paying the Price for Big Steel: 30 Years of the Integrated Steel Companies' Capture of U.S. Trade Policy'.
Personal: Received an LLM in 1976 and a JD in 1973 from Georgetown University Law Center, and an AB from Brown University in 1970.

BARRY, Desmond
Condon & Forsyth LLP, New York 212 370 4453
Recommended in Aviation

BARSHEFSKY, Charlene
Wilmer Cutler Pickering Hale and Dorr LLP, Washington, DC 202 663 6130
charlene.barshefsky@wilmerhale.com
Recommended in International Trade
Practice Areas: Senior International Partner. Practice centers on international business transactions, the structuring and negotiation of commercial agreements and the removal of trade and regulatory impediments to exporting to or investing in markets throughout Asia, Europe and Latin America.
Prof. Memberships: Chairman's Forum of the Council on Foreign Relations; Board of the America-China Society; American Academy of Diplomacy and the Trilateral Commission; Boards of Directors of American Express Company, The Estée Lauder Companies Inc., Intel Corporation and Starwood Hotels & Resorts Worldwide, Inc.
Personal: Catholic University, Columbus School of Law (JD 1975); University of Wisconsin, 1972.

BENNER, Jonathan
Troutman Sanders LLP, Washington, DC 202 274 2950
Recommended in Shipping

BERG, Gracia
Gibson, Dunn & Crutcher LLP, Washington, DC 202 887 3644
gberg@gibsondunn.com
Recommended in International Trade
Practice Areas: Extensive experience in international trade and customs law, including trade disputes under the antidumping and countervailing duty laws, the escape clause, Section 301, and general fact-finding investigations. Represents domestic and multinational companies on trade matters before US administrative agencies and Congress.
Prof. Memberships: Past Chair, ABA Administrative Law and Practice Section's Committee on International Trade Regulation.
Career: Served as Deputy General Counsel and Assistant General Counsel for Antidumping and Countervailing Duty Investigations at the International Trade Commission.
Personal: JD, University of Notre Dame,1980, year in London and diploma from Institute Internationale des Droits de L'Homme, Strasbourg, France.

BERLACK, Evan R
Baker Botts LLP, Washington, DC 202 639 7771
evan.berlack@bakerbotts.com
Recommended in International Trade
Practice Areas: Evan Berlack's practice involves a broad and diverse range of transactional/governmental regulatory matters. His industry experience includes forest products, steel, rail passenger cars, computers/related peripherals, encryption software, liquefied natural gas (LNG).
Prof. Memberships: District of Columbia Bar; New York State Bar; United States Court of International Trade
Career: His transactional experience over a period of many years includes turnkey contracts, joint ventures, project finance in which he works with the US Export-Import Bank, the International Finance Corporation, the US Overseas Private Investment Corporation (OPIC).
Personal: JD, Harvard Law School, 1962; AB (magna cum laude), government, Harvard University, 1956.

BERMANN, George
George A Bermann, New York 212 854 2680
Recommended in Arbitration

BESHAR, Sarah
Davis Polk & Wardwell, New York 212 450 4000
sarah.beshar@dpw.com
Recommended in Capital Markets
Practice Areas: Member of Davis Polk & Wardwell's Corporate Department and represents clients in equity, debt and other securities offerings, and advises on general securities and corporate issues. Among her specialties is corporate finance in the retailing industry. Has taken a leading role in the initial public offerings on behalf of many companies. Also, has represented investment banks in many initial public offerings and other financing transactions. Advises generally on corporate issues.

BIERCE, William
Bierce & Kenerson, P.C., New York 212 840 0080
Recommended in Business Process Outsourcing

BILGER, Bruce
Vinson & Elkins LLP, Houston 713 758 2222
Recommended in Energy, Projects Please see Texas for profile

BISHOP, Doak
King & Spalding LLP, Houston 713 751 3200
Recommended in Arbitration, Energy Please see Texas for profile

BLAUCH, Kevin
Latham & Watkins LLP, New York 212 906 1200
Recommended in Capital Markets

BOGAARD, Jonathan
Vedder, Price, Kaufman & Kammholz, Chicago 312 609 7500
Recommended in Aviation

BOSTELMAN, John T
Sullivan & Cromwell LLP, New York 212 558 4000
bostelmanj@sullcrom.com
Recommended in Capital Markets
Practice Areas: Coordinates S&C's Global Securities Practice. Focuses on public and private securities offerings, corporate governance, investment management, commodities and derivatives and broker-dealer regulation. Broad securities experience includes SEC-registered public offerings, unregistered Rule 144A offerings and Regulation S offerings for issuers in a broad range of industries.
Prof. Memberships: ABA (Chair, Securities Registration Subcommittee, Federal Regulation of Securities Committee); ABCNY; NYSBA.
Career: Partner since 1986.
Publications: 'The Sarbanes-Oxley Deskbook' (Practising Law Institute, 2003).
Personal: Yale University (BA, 1975); Columbia Law School (JD, 1979).

BOWERS, William C
Pillsbury Winthrop LLP, New York 212 858 1106
wbowers@pillsburywinthrop.com
Recommended in Aviation
Practice Areas: Mr Bowers works in the field of transportation and structured finance, representing arrangers, issuers, lenders and liquidity providers in a variety of securitized debt offerings, loan transactions, leveraged and single investor leases and other financings involving aircraft and other transportation assets, including ships, railroad rolling stock and aircraft engines. As general counsel of GPA Capital and Associate General Counsel at GE Capital Aviation Services, he was the in-house legal counsel responsible for developing the first securitization of a portfolio of aircraft on operating leases to a variety of unrated airlines as well as the first SEC registered aircraft portfolio securitization. He also represented GE Capital as the liquidity provider on the first airline enhanced equipment trust certificate financing. More recently, he has represented arrangers and liquidity providers in asset-backed commercial paper financings of transportation assets and portfolio securitizations of transportation assets other than aircraft. He has been a frequent speaker on structured finance and related topics and has published a number of articles on securitization structures.
Prof. Memberships: American Bar Association, Georgia State Bar, New York State Bar Association.
Career: Admitted to practice: New York, Georgia.
Personal: JD, Emory University, 1975 (with distinction); AB, Princeton University, 1968 (Politics)

BOWMAN, John
Fulbright & Jaworski LLP, Houston
713 651 5151
Recommended in Arbitration, Energy
Please see Texas for profile

BRACH, Richard
Milbank, Tweed, Hadley & McCloy, New York 212 530 5000
Recommended in Projects
Please see New York for profile

BRADEN, Gregory C
Alston & Bird LLP, Atlanta
404 881 7497
gbraden@alston.com
Recommended in Litigation
Practice Areas: ERISA Litigation; Employee Benefits and Executive Compensation; ESOP transactions.
Prof. Memberships: Fellow, American College of Employee Benefits Counsel; Member, American Bar Association (Tax and Labor sections), State Bars of Georgia and Wisconsin, ESOP Association, Southern Employee Benefits Conference (Treasurer).
Career: Represented defendants in several major ERISA class action lawsuits; extensive courtroom experience in ERISA cases; represented clients on benefits issues in corporate transactions.
Publications: Published and lectured extensively, including in 'Benefits Law Journal' and 'Journal of Compensation' Planning and Compliance.'
Personal: BA, with honors, University of Wisconsin-Milwaukee (1979); JD, with honors, University of Wisconsin-Madison (1982)

BRADY, Christopher J
Mayer, Brown, Rowe & Maw LLP, Charlotte 704 444 3511
cbrady@mayerbrownrowe.com
Recommended in Capital Markets
Practice Areas: Specializes in securitization and other structured finance products. Represents issuers, underwriters, placement agents, servicers and trustees in private and public executions in term securitizations of a range of asset types, including commercial mortgages, residential mortgages, auto loans, aircraft loans and student loans. Also represent two of the largest servicers of commercial mortgage-backed securities, including in connection with acquisitions of servicing rights. Represent program sponsor in connection with the establishment of commercial paper program and mortgage originator in connection with warehouse facility.
Career: Mayer, Brown, Rowe & Maw LLP, Charlotte, 1999 to date; Partner, 2002. Kilpatrick Stockton LLP, 1993-99.
Personal: JD, University of North Carolina School of Law, 1993; Order of the Coif, Dean's List; North Carolina Law Review. BS, (cum laude) University of North Carolina at Charlotte, 1983.

BRANDOW, John M
Davis Polk & Wardwell, New York
212 450 4000
john.brandow@dpw.com
Recommended in Capital Markets
Practice Areas: Member of Davis Polk & Wardwell's Corporate Department and heads the firm's Equity Derivatives Group. The group advises a wide variety of market participants - commercial and investment banks, issuers, hedge funds and institutional and individual holders of equity positions - on a complex array of equity-related transactions. Has been actively involved in the design of exchangeable securities containing imbedded options or forward contracts on the underlying equities, the development of mandatory and optional convertible securities that are issued in tax or accounting-driven capital-raising transactions, and the structuring of public and private hedging transactions using collars and variable prepaid forward contracts.

BROWER, Charles
White & Case LLP, Washington, DC
202 626 3600
cbrower@whitecase.com
Recommended in Arbitration
Practice Areas: Counsel and advocate or arbitrator in international arbitrations including commercial and state parties, especially investment disputes.
Prof. Memberships: DC and New York Bars.
Career: White & Case LLP since 1961. US State Department Acting Legal Adviser; Judge, Iran-United States Claims Tribunal in The Hague; Judge Ad Hoc, Inter-American Court of Human Rights; co-arbitrator/chairman, arbitral tribunals under AAA rules, ICC International Court of Arbitration, UN Commission on International Trade Law, ICSID. Register of Experts of the UN Compensation Commission Member, Institute for Transnational Arbitration Chair. Book: 'The Iran-United States Claims Tribunal'.
Publications: Listed at www.whitecase.com.
Personal: Listed at www.whitecase.com.

BRYAN, Charles E
Cadwalader, Wickersham & Taft LLP, Washington, DC 202 862 2212
charlie.bryan@cwt.com
Recommended in Capital Markets
Practice Areas: Concentrates in the areas of securities, structured finance, financings and commercial transactions. Has acted as issuer's or underwriter's counsel on several thousand securitized offerings, involving both mortgage and asset-backed securities. Has extensive experience with mortgage pass-throughs, CMOs and REMICs, as well as ABS backed by student loans, auto loans and other financial instruments. Represents investment banks, banks, government-sponsored enterprises and other

financial institutions. Has supervised and participated in acquisitions, divestitures and reorganizations.
Personal: A Phi Beta Kappa graduate of the University of Virginia, (bachelor's degree with highest distinction, 1970), and JD from Yale Law School (1974).

BUCK, Willis
Sidley Austin Brown & Wood LLP, Chicago 312 853 7819
wbuck@sidley.com
Recommended in Capital Markets
Practice Areas: Willis R Buck specializes in securitization and structured finance. His practice includes term and conduit executions involving a variety of assets, including trade receivables, automobile loans and leases, taxi medallion loans, aircraft leases, floorplan loans and home equity loans, with an emphasis over the past 10 years on credit card receivables and other consumer assets. Transaction structures have included, among others, direct asset purchases, master trusts and master note trusts (including de-linked structures). He has been involved in the structuring and formation of several asset-backed commercial paper conduits, including conduits issuing extendible and callable paper and eurocommercial paper. Clients include Bank of America, Barclays Capital, Citigroup, ING, JPMorgan Chase, MBIA, Societe Generale and Wheels, Inc. (a national automobile fleet leasing company).
Career: The University of Chicago Law School, JD, 1984; Yale University, M.Phil., 1979; Williams College, BA, 1973; Oxford University, BA, 1975. Clerked for Judge Milton I Shadur of the Northern District of Illinois from 1984-85. Bar Admission: Illinois, 1985.

BUCKHOLZ Jr, Robert E
Sullivan & Cromwell LLP, New York
212 558 4000
buckholzr@sullcrom.com
Recommended in Capital Markets
Practice Areas: Head of the firm's Corporate and Finance Group, focusing on capital markets transactions. Has handled a wide range of public and private debt and equity financings for US and foreign issuers, including initial public offerings, privatisations and high-yield financings. Also has extensive experience advising on equity derivatives matters, in both the capital markets and over-the-counter contexts.
Prof. Memberships: ABA; ABCNY; NYSBA.
Career: Partner since 1987.
Personal: Columbia Law School (JD, 1979); Dartmouth College (AB, 1976).

BUCKLEY, Kevin J
Hunton & Williams LLP, Richmond
804 788 8200
Recommended in Capital Markets, Corporate/M&A
Please see Virginia for profile

BUDOFSKY, Daniel
Davis Polk & Wardwell, New York
212 450 4000
daniel.budofsky@dpw.com
Recommended in Capital Markets
Practice Areas: Member of Davis Polk & Wardwell's Derivatives and Financial Institutions Groups. Advises financial institutions, corporations, hedge funds and individuals on innovative financial products in domestic and international transactions and has worked on numerous convertible, exchangeable and private equity derivatives transactions. Also advises underwriters and issuers on public securities offerings and acquisitions involving derivatives.

BURKE Jr, Raymond
Burke & Parsons, New York
212 354 3800
Recommended in Shipping

BURKE, Ted
Freshfields Bruckhaus Deringer LLP, New York 212 277 4000
Recommended in Projects
Please see New York for profile

BURNS, Stephen
Cravath, Swaine & Moore LLP, New York 212 474 1146
sburns@cravath.com
Recommended in Capital Markets
Practice Areas: Represents investment banking firms and issuers in connection with public and private offerings of securities. Represents various corporations on general corporate matters.
Career: Partner since 1998.
Personal: University of Texas School of Law (JD, with honors, 1990; associate editor of the 'Law Review'; Chancellors); University of Oklahoma (BBA, with distinction, 1987).

BURRELL, Lizabeth
Levy Phillips & Konigsberg LLP, New York 212 605 6200
Recommended in Shipping

CAMERON Jr, Donald B
Kaye Scholer LLP, Washington, DC
202 682 3630
dcameron@kayescholer.com
Recommended in International Trade
Practice Areas: Partner and Co-Chair, international trade. During his career of more than 25 years, Mr Cameron has represented foreign manufacturers, foreign governments, trade associations and US importers in various trade actions arising under the US countervailing duty law, the anti-dumping law, Sections 201 and 301, and various provisions of the customs laws and the export control law. Mr Cameron has represented foreign producers and importers in a number of product sectors including footwear, lumber, textiles, electronic products, and steel products. He regularly practices before the US Department of Commerce, the US International Trade Commission, the Office of the US. Trade Representative, the US Court

of International Trade and the US Court of Appeals for the Federal Circuit. In addition, Mr Cameron advises clients on World Trade Organization (WTO) proceedings and has participated in WTO Panel and Appellate Body proceedings on behalf of clients and their member governments.

Prof. Memberships: American Bar Association.

Career: LLM, Program on International Legal Cooperation, Vrije Universiteit Brussels, 1975. JD, Vanderbilt University, 1974. BA, Kenyon College, 1971.

CARNEAL, George U
Hogan & Hartson LLP, Washington, DC
202 637 6546
gucarneal@hhlaw.com
Recommended in Aviation

Practice Areas: Aviation, all segments.
Prof. Memberships: General Counsel, National Aeronautic Association; ABA (Forum Committee on Air and Space Law); Aero Club of Washington (past President); Princeton Club of Washington, DC (past President); Board of Governors (past), Flight Safety Foundation.
Career: 1961-62 law clerk, Honorable E. Barrett Prettyman, U.S. Court of Appeals for the District of Columbia Circuit; 1962-68 Hogan & Hartson, associate; 1969-70 special assistant, secretary of transportation; 1970-72 general counsel, Federal Aviation Administration; 1973-present Hogan & Hartson, Partner.
Personal: University of Virginia School of Law (LLB, Order of the Coif, 1961); Princeton University (AB, 1957).

CARON, David
C. William Maxeiner Distinguished Professor of International Law, Berkeley
510 642 7249
Recommended in Arbitration

CARROLL, James P
Cadwalader, Wickersham & Taft LLP, Charlotte 704 348 5116
james.carroll@cwt.com
Recommended in Capital Markets

Practice Areas: Managing Partner of Cadwalader's Charlotte office and a member of the firm's Management Committee. Concentrates in the areas of real estate finance and securitization. Represents national, international, and regional financial institutions, investment banks, pension funds, and investors in the financing, acquisition, disposition and leasing of commercial office buildings, shopping centers, hotels, industrial warehouses, merchandise marts, multifamily housing, residential and planned unit developments, including golf course developments. Has an active capital markets practice in mortgage loan conduit programs, mortgage pool purchases and sales as well as multiple property and single asset real estate securitizations.
Personal: Served from 1985-96 as adjunct Professor of Law at George

Washington University, where he lectured in the area of real estate finance. Serves as Chairman of the Real Estate Securitization Section of the American Bar Association's Real Property Division. Received his BA, with honors, from Georgetown University, and his JD, with honors, from The Catholic University of America. Chairman of ABA Section on Real Estate Securitization (2001-present).

CARTER, James H
Sullivan & Cromwell LLP, New York
212 558 4000
carterj@sullcrom.com
Recommended in Arbitration

Practice Areas: Coordinator of firm's Arbitration Practice. Principal area of practice is international arbitration, as counsel and arbitrator, in ICC, LCIA, AAA, CPR, ICSID, CAS, ad hoc proceedings and other fora. Typical cases are international joint venture, investment and intellectual property licensing disputes.
Prof. Memberships: AAA Chair of the Board of Directors. Member, AAA and CPR Arbitration Rules Revisions committees; LCIA Court; Court of Arbitration for Sport; Japan Commercial Arbitration Association Arbitrator Panel; Swiss Arbitration Association; International Arbitration Institute; President, American Society of International Law.
Career: Partner since 1977.
Publications: 30 arbitration articles and book chapters.
Personal: Graduate, Yale College and Yale Law School; Fulbright Scholar, Cambridge University.

CHANG, Leo
Watson, Farley & Williams, New York
212 922 2210
lchang@wfw.com
Recommended in Shipping

Practice Areas: Shipping, ship finance, general corporate and commercial transactions.
Prof. Memberships: Association of the Bar of the City of New York, the American Bar Association and the Maritime Law Association of the United States.
Career: Associate and Partner at Burlingham, Underwood & Lord in New York City (1978-90); Partner Watson, Farley & Williams since 1990. He is a graduate of Pennsylvania State University (BA, 1973) and of Columbia University (JD, 1978).

CHARNESS, Michael
Vinson & Elkins LLP, Washington, DC
202 639 6780
mcharness@velaw.com
Recommended in Government Contracts

Practice Areas: Government contracts.
Prof. Memberships: Section of Public Contract Law, American Bar Association; National Contract Management Association; National Council of Public-Private Partnerships.

Career: University of Pennsylvania, BA. magna cum laude, 1976; Georgetown University, JD, 1979. Admitted to practice: District of Columbia, 1979; District Court of Maryland; U.S. Court of Federal Claims; U.S. Courts of Appeal for the District of Columbia and the Federal Circuit. Extensive experience with domestic and international government claims and disputes; due diligence in mergers and acquisitions; bid protests; defense of Qui Tam actions; and internal investigations involving false claims and statements and Foreign Corrupt Practices Act violations.
Publications: Numerous articles on government contracts, privatization and outsourcing, and construction law. Frequent public and in-house lecturer on government and international procurement issues.

CHIERICHELLA, John
Sheppard, Mullin, Richter & Hampton LLP, Washington 202 218 0000
Recommended in Government Contracts

CHRISTIAN, Betty Jo
Steptoe & Johnson LLP, Washington, DC 202 429 8113
bchristian@steptoe.com
Recommended in Transport

Practice Areas: Practices extensively before the US Supreme Court, US Courts of Appeals, state supreme courts and federal regulatory agencies, primarily in cases involving railroads and other regulated industries. Recent cases include Commerce Clause and other federal constitutional issues, federal preemption, statutory interpretation, and administrative procedure issues. Also represents companies in connection with the regulatory aspects of a wide variety of transactions, including railroad mergers and acquisitions, tender offers, and equipment financing.
Personal: LLB, University of Texas, 1960; BA, University of Texas, 1957.

CHURCHILL, David
Jenner & Block LLP, Washington, DC
202 639 6056
dchurchill@jenner.com
Recommended in Government Contracts

Practice Areas: David A Churchill is a Partner in Jenner & Block's Washington, DC office. He is Chair of the firm's Government Contracts Practice, Co-Chair of the Defense & Aerospace Practice, and a member of its Arbitration: Domestic and International Practice. Mr Churchill practices before the major forums for resolution of federal contract award and performance disputes, including the Court of Federal Claims, the agency boards of contract appeals and the General Accounting Office. He also counsels in matters involving the award and performance of international public contracts under the U.S. Foreign Military Sales and Foreign Military

Finance programs. He has experience in conducting domestic and international arbitration proceedings and various types of alternative dispute resolution techniques. He was lead counsel in Thomson CSF v Lockheed Martin Corporation, an ICC international arbitration brought by a French company against Lockheed Martin involving the development and testing of a short range antiaircraft missile. In Norden Systems, Inc. v General Dynamics Corporation he represented General Dynamics in a suit brought by a subcontractor involving termination of a large, classified avionics subcontract. Mr Churchill has an active counseling practice in proposal and award-related matters involving government contracts, including domestic preference requirements, such as Buy American and Trade Agreements Acts, independent price determination and antitrust issues, Truth in Negotiations Act requirements, and suspension and debarment of prime and subcontractors. He counsels regularly in issues arising during performance of government contracts and subcontracts, such as changes, delays and claims preparation.
Personal: Cornell University, JD, 1979.

CHUSED, Wesley
Looney & Grossman LLP, Boston
617 951 2800
Recommended in Transport

CITRON, Diane
Mayer, Brown, Rowe & Maw LLP, New York 212 506 2520
dcitron@mayerbrownrowe.com
Recommended in Capital Markets

Practice Areas: Partner and Co-Head of the firm's Securitization Practice. Represents investment banks and financial institutions in structuring and developing foreign and domestic residential and commercial mortgage-backed programs and conduits for the issuance of MBS and CMBS in the United States and global markets; underwriters and issuers in public and private offerings of asset-backed securities; represents financial institutions, corporations, and development companies in issuance of corporate debt, limited partnerships, initial public offerings, thrift mergers and acquisitions, and acquisitions of commercial and residential real estate portfolios as well as portfolios of other financial assets. Previous Federal Agency and government experience.
Career: Joined Mayer, Brown, Rowe & Maw LLP as a Partner (1992); Skadden, Arps, Slate, Meagher & Flom (1987-92); Brown & Wood (1985-87); Orrick, Herrington & Sutcliffe (1984-85); and Wasserman, Orlow, Ginsberg & Rubin (1977-80). Staff Attorney, SEC, Division of Enforcement (1980-83) and Senior Counsel, Federal Home Loan Mortgage Corporation (1983-84).

Publications: Author, 'The Legal Aspects of Lease Securitization', Banking and Financial Services Reporter, Vol. 9, No. 16, September 29, 1993. Lectures widely on securitization at industry-related conferences.
Personal: JD, Case Western Reserve University School of Law, 1978; BA, Franklin and Marshall College, 1975. Fluent in Spanish.

CLARK, James
Cahill Gordon & Reindel, New York
212 701 3900
Recommended in Capital Markets

CLARK, Matthew
Arent Fox PLLC, Washington, DC
202 857 6000
Recommended in International Trade

CLARK, Peter
Clark, Atcheson & Reisert, New York
212 297 0257
Recommended in Shipping

CLEMENTS, William L
Foley & Lardner, Washington, DC
202 295 4615
wclements@foley.com
Recommended in International Trade
Career: William L Clements is a Partner with Foley & Lardner's Washington, DC office. A member of the Litigation Department (White Collar Defense & Corporate Compliance Practice Group), he counsels foreign and domestic parties regarding international business regulatory matters, particularly export controls, economic sanctions and the Foreign Corrupt Practices Act. He leads internal investigations of potential violations of the US Export Administration Regulations, the International Traffic in Arms Regulations, Office of Foreign Assets Control regulations and the Foreign Corrupt Practices Act. He received his JD from Suffolk University Law School.

CLINTON, William J
White & Case LLP, Washington, DC
202 626 3620
wclinton@whitecase.com
Recommended in International Trade
Practice Areas: A recognized authority on legal developments related to the WTO, NAFTA and other multilateral trade arrangements. Has extensive experience in representing parties in import trade investigations under the antidumping, countervailing duty, safeguards and customs laws of many jurisdictions. Also advises sovereign governments on multilateral dispute settlements and negotiations related to these laws.
Prof. Memberships: District of Columbia Bar, US Court of International Trade, US Court of Appeals for the Federal Circuit.
Career: Speaks and reads Chinese, taught writing at Tunghai University and Tamkang University in Taiwan.
Personal: JD, Georgetown University, 1982; BS, Georgetown University, 1976.

COGAN Jr, John
Akin Gump Strauss Hauer & Feld LLP,
Houston 713 220 5800
*Recommended in Energy, Projects
Please see Texas for profile*

COGBILL III, John
McGuireWoods LLP, Richmond
804 775 1000
Recommended in Real Estate, Transport

COHEN, Michael
Nicoletti Hornig Campise and Sweeney,
New York 212 220 3830
Recommended in Shipping

COHEN, Steven N
Cadwalader, Wickersham & Taft LLP,
Charlotte 704 348 5176
steven.cohen@cwt.com
Recommended in Capital Markets
Practice Areas: Partner resident in Cadwalader's New York, NY and Charlotte, NC offices. Represents domestic and foreign commercial banks, investment banks and other financial institutions in a wide variety of financing transactions, including leveraged finance and other syndicated bank loan transactions, the financing of financial assets, structured finance transactions, cross-border financings, commodity finance transactions, hedge fund financings, credit enhancement transactions, workouts and debtor-in-possession financings, the trading of distressed debt, and various innovative financing transactions. Serves as a member of Cadwalader's Legal Opinions Committee.
Personal: Law clerk to the Honorable Max Rosenn, Senior Circuit Judge, United States Court of Appeals for the Third Circuit. Graduated magna cum laude in 1976 from Wesleyan University and received his JD degree in 1981 from New York University School of Law, where he was Note and Comment Editor of the New York University Law Review. Also attended the Lycée Classique Mixte, in Saintes, France, from which he received a baccalauréat with high honors (mention bien) in 1971. Member of the American Bar Association (including the Section of Business Law).

COHN, Joshua
Allen & Overy, New York
212 610 6300
joshua.cohn@allenovery.com
Recommended in Capital Markets
Practice Areas: Derivatives.
Career: JD, New York University School of Law 1980. Admitted to the New York Bar 1981. Partner, Allen & Overy, 2001.

COHN, Robert
Hogan & Hartson LLP, Washington, DC
202 637 4999
recohn@hhlaw.com
Recommended in Aviation
Practice Areas: Counseling and representation of airlines and airports on regulatory and transactional matters, including licensing, certification, compliance, safety, security, environmental,

airport rates and charges and revenue use issues, aircraft acquisitions/finance/leasing, airport use and lease agreements, domestic and international air service development, FAA funding, legislation, litigation before federal courts, international trade, mergers and acquistions.
Prof. Memberships: American Bar Association; Federal Bar Association; International Aviation Club; Aero Club.
Career: Mr Cohn has specialized in aviation law for over 35 years. Prior to joining Hogan & Hartson, Mr Cohn was Chairman of the Aviation Practice Group of a major Washington DC law firm and was outside general counsel to one of the largest post-deregulation airlines. Prior to entering private practice he held a number of senior policy positions at the Civil Aeronautics Board, including executive assistant to three board members, including the Chairman and Vice-Chairperson of the CAB.
Personal: Georgetown University Law Center (JD, 1969); Syracuse University (BA, 1966).

COLEMAN, Payson
Pillsbury Winthrop LLP, New York
212 858 1426
pcoleman@pillsburywinthrop.com
Recommended in Aviation
Practice Areas: Mr Coleman represents aircraft and equipment financiers and owners in a broad range of domestic and international lease, finance, purchase and remarketing transactions and related repossession, restructuring and work-out activities. He is the leader of the firm's Equipment Finance Practice Team, a Member of the Aviation Working Group appointed by Boeing and Airbus to advise on the implementation of the Capetown Convention, has been listed in the Best Lawyers in America for more than twenty years, and was named in 2004 as the Best of the Best among Aviation lawyers in The Experts Guide to the World's Aviation Lawyers (4th Edition). Recent assignments include transactions for several billion dollars of new aircraft for Air Canada, Lufthansa, China Airlines, EgyptAir, United Airlines, Northwest Airlines, and others. Mr Coleman has supervised the repossession and remarketing of well over one hundred aircraft and advised creditors in the bankruptcies of Air Canada, US Airways, United Airlines, TWA, Continental, Eastern, PanAm and others.
Career: Mr Coleman is admitted to practice in the State of New York, is a member of the American Bar Association (Aircraft Financing Sub-Committee) and of the Association of the Bar of the City of New York.

CONNELLY, Warren E
Akin Gump Strauss Hauer & Feld LLP,
Washington, DC 202 887 4046
wconnelly@akingump.com
Recommended in International Trade
Practice Areas: Warren Connelly rep-

resents clients in proceedings before the Department of Commerce, International Trade Commission, Office of the U.S. Trade Representative, Customs Service, Court of International Trade and U.S. Court of Appeals for the Federal Circuit. He handles a wide variety of import- and export-related matters, including trade policy, WTO dispute resolution proceedings, export controls, import licensing, sanctions, antiboycott and customs. He has been extensively involved in a variety of administrative and civil court litigation.
Personal: AB, Dartmouth College (1968); JD, Georgetown University Law Center (1973).

CONRAD Jr, Winthrop B
Davis Polk & Wardwell, New York
212 450 4000
winthrop.conrad@dpw.com
Recommended in Capital Markets
Practice Areas: Member of Davis Polk & Wardwell's Corporate Department. Has extensive experience in securities offerings of all types, as well as mergers and acquisitions. Recent experience includes numerous initial public offerings representing underwriters, including Morgan Stanley, Bank of America Securities, and CSFB; and issuers, such as Canadian National Railway and Pepsi Bottling Group. Represented PepsiCo in its $13.5 billion acquisition of Quaker Oats. Has also worked on numerous restructuring transactions, including high-yield financings, debt tender offers and exchange offers, as well as cross-border transactions.

CORR, Christopher F
White & Case LLP, Washington, DC
202 626 3613
ccorr@whitecase.com
Recommended in International Trade
Practice Areas: International trade matters, including antidumping, countervailing duty and intellectual property actions before the ITC and DOC; trade litigation before US Federal Courts; Section 337 investigations; WTO and NAFTA rules governing goods, services, investment and intellectual property; export control; national security controls; customs matters; Section 301; and GSP proceedings. He has served as counsel in numerous trade cases including those concerning semiconductors, computers and other electronics, steel products, lumber, seafood, agricultural products, chemicals, pharmaceuticals and technology transfer, as well as the negotiation of government-to-government agreements.
Publications: Listed at www.whitecase.com.
Personal: Listed at www.whitecase.com.

CORRALES, Carmen Amalia
Cleary Gottlieb Steen & Hamilton LLP,
New York 212 225 2982
ccorrales@cgsh.com
Recommended in Capital Markets
Practice Areas: Sovereign transactions, including securities offerings by sovereign issuers and sovereign debt restructuring. International finance transactions, including representing public and private issuers and underwriters in equity and debt offerings in international markets and in the legal structuring and documentation of derivative transactions and complex commercial bank lending transactions.
Prof. Memberships: Member of the Bar in New York and New Jersey.
Career: Joined firm, 1990; became Partner, 1998. JD, Harvard Law School (1989); BA, University of Pennsylvania (1986).

COWAN, Cameron
Orrick, Herrington & Sutcliffe,
Washington, DC 202 339 8488
ccowan@orrick.com
Recommended in Capital Markets
Practice Areas: Represents financial institutions, investment banks, and companies with particular expertise in the structuring, issuance, and purchase of asset-backed, mortgage-backed, and derivative products.
Career: Founder of Orrick's Washington, DC, office (1993); Managing Partner of the firm's East Coast offices (1998-2000); Managing Director of Orrick's Finance Division (2001-04); Member of Orrick's Executive Committee (2001-present); University of Virginia School of Law (JD, 1981); Columbia University Graduate School of Business (MBA); Syracuse University, magna cum laude (BS); Partner, Milbank, Tweed, Hadley, & McCloy (1990-93). Member, Executive and Management Committees of the American Securitization Forum, as well as Chair of its Legislative and Judicial Subcommittee.
Publications: Co-author of 'Mortgage-Backed Securities: Developments and Trends in the Secondary Mortgage Market.'

CROST, Katharine I
Orrick, Herrington & Sutcliffe, New York
212 506 5070
kcrost@orrick.com
Recommended in Capital Markets
Practice Areas: Represents issuers, underwriters, servicers, institutional purchasers, and credit enhancers in securitization transactions involving a wide variety of assets, including all types of mortgage loans. She has helped develop innovative structures for the securitization of assets such as mortgages, tobacco litigation settlement funds, tax liens, utility stranded costs, and student loans.
Career: Co-Head of Orrick's Structured Finance Group; served six years on the firm's Executive Committee; Partner

since 1986; University of Virginia School of Law (JD, 1978); Michigan State University, cum laude, (BM, 1974).

CULLEN, William J
Sidley Austin Brown & Wood LLP,
New York 212 839 7376
wcullen@sidley.com
Recommended in Capital Markets
Practice Areas: William J Cullen is a Partner in the New York office in the securitization group. His practice is focused on securities and corporate finance, with an emphasis on securitization of financial assets and, in particular, commercial mortgage assets.
Career: University of Pennsylvania Law School, JD, 1985; Colgate University, BA, 1982, summa cum laude, Phi Beta Kappa. Bar Admission: New York, 1986.

CUNNINGHAM, Daniel P
Allen & Overy, New York
212 610 6300
daniel.cunningham@allenovery.com
Recommended in Capital Markets
Practice Areas: Acquisitions, mergers and disposals, securities, and derivatives.
Career: JD Harvard Law School 1975. Admitted to the New York Bar 1980. Partner, Allen & Overy, 2001.

CUNNINGHAM, Richard
Steptoe & Johnson LLP, Washington,
DC 202 429 6434
rcunningham@steptoe.com
Recommended in International Trade
Practice Areas: Senior Partner, Steptoe & Johnson LLP, Washington, DC. Focuses on US import relief laws, trade policy issues, WTO matters, and international trade strategies. Advises and represents foreign and domestic clients in matters involving market access negotiations, US antidumping and countervailing duty laws, bilateral and multilateral trade negotiations, and trade-related IP policy and litigation. Represented clients in the Tokyo Round and the Uruguay Round of Multilateral Trade Negotiations, and governments and corporations in WTO dispute resolution proceedings. Advised Congressional committees and governmental agencies on trade issues.
Personal: JD, George Washington University, 1968; AB, George Washington University, 1964.

CURTIS, Susan M
Skadden, Arps, Slate, Meagher & Flom
LLP & Affiliates, New York
212 735 2119
scurtis@skadden.com
Recommended in Capital Markets
Practice Areas: Represents underwriters, placement agents, issuers and banks in asset-backed securities transactions and other financings. Acts as counsel in public offerings and private placement and Regulation S transactions involving the issuance of asset-backed notes, asset-backed certificates, preferred stock, commercial paper and medium-term

notes. Has represented underwriters and collateral managers in the collateralized bond obligation market from its inception. Acts as deal counsel in cash-flow CBOs and market value CBOs and in the repackaging of bonds, asset-backed securities, swaps and other derivative instruments.
Career: JD, Vanderbilt University, 1981; BA, University of Tennessee, 1977 (summa cum laude; Phi Beta Kappa).

CURTISS, Catherine
Hughes Hubbard & Reed LLP,
Washington, DC 202 721 4660
curtiss@hugheshubbard.com
Recommended in International Trade
Practice Areas: Countervailing duty; antidumping; customs; NAFTA; WTO Agreement.
Career: Partner, Washington, DC since 1997. Chair, firm's International Trade Group. Private practice since 1981, Partner since 1990.
Publications: 'Against the Grain: U.S.-Canada Wheat Trade Dispute,' in The First Decade of NAFTA (2004); 'U.S. Customs Law and Compliance,' in Corporate Legal Departments (2004); 'Agreement on Trade-Related Investment Measures: A Five-Year Review,' in The Comparative Law Yearbook of International Business (2003); 'Antidumping As An International Corporate Strategy,' Canadian International Lawyer (2001).
Personal: Born 1950. University of Michigan BA (1972), MA (1973 cum laude), Georgetown University Law Center JD (1980 cum laude).

CUVA, Anthony J
Akerman Senterfitt, Tampa
813 223 7333
anthony.cuva@akerman.com
Recommended in Shipping
Career: Anthony Cuva is a Board Certified Specialist in Admiralty and Maritime Litigation by the Florida Bar. He has extensive experience representing maritime clients in federal courts, Florida state courts, arbitrations and administrative hearings. For the past 15 years, he has been actively involved in traditional maritime litigation pertaining to collisions, personal injuries, cargo damage and salvage cases. A complete biography can be found at www.akerman.com.

DALLAS, Bruce
Davis Polk & Wardwell, Menlo Park
650 752 2000
bruce.dallas@dpw.com
Recommended in Capital Markets
Practice Areas: Member of Davis Polk & Wardwell's global Technology Group. Advises and represents clients in public and private securities offerings, including equity derivatives, high-yield debt and initial public offerings. Also advises clients on general corporate matters, including SEC and Sarbanes-Oxley compliance, and audit committees in

connection with Securities Exchange Act Section 10A(b) investigations. Has been the primary capital markets Partner for Comcast, E*Trade and Oracle, among others, regularly represents Morgan Stanley and J.P. Morgan, among others, as underwriters' counsel, and has been lead partner on a number of technology, telecommunications and biotechnology public offerings, PIPES transactions and Rule 144A private placements.

DAVENPORT, Kirk
Latham & Watkins LLP, New York
212 906 1200
Recommended in Capital Markets

DAVIS, Fred
Shearman & Sterling LLP, New York
212 848 4000
Recommended in Arbitration, Litigation
Please see New York for profile

DAVIS, Platt W
Vinson & Elkins LLP, Houston
713 758 2222
Recommended in Arbitration, Energy
Please see Texas for profile

DAYAN, Michael D
Cleary Gottlieb Steen & Hamilton LLP,
New York 212 225 2382
mdayan@cgsh.com
Recommended in Capital Markets
Practice Areas: Structuring and documenting complex over-the-counter and capital markets derivative products; regulatory analysis of securities, margin, commodities, banking and insolvency issues relating to derivative products.
Prof. Memberships: Member New York Bar; Global Documentation Steering Committee; ISDA Equity Derivatives and Credit Derivatives Committees.
Career: Joined firm, 1993; became Partner, 2003. Law clerk, Honorable Jon O Newman, US Court of Appeals, Second Circuit (1992-93). JD, magna cum laude, Law Review, Harvard Law School (1992); BS, summa cum laude, Wharton School, University of Pennsylvania (1986).
Publications: 'Raising Capital Through OTC Equity Derivatives: The Goldman, Sachs & Co. Interpretive Letter,' FDLR; Securities Reporter.

DAYANIM, Behnam
Paul, Hastings, Janofsky & Walker LLP,
Washington, DC 202 551 1737
bdayanim@paulhastings.com
Recommended in International Trade
Practice Areas: Advises on international trade, export controls and technology transfer issues, representing clients in enforcement investigations, counseling and developing compliance programs. Also advises in privacy and information security; electronic financial services, gaming and commerce; IT outsourcing; and false advertising and intellectual property. His work in each area includes counseling, compliance, litigation, licensing and related transactional representations.

Prof. Memberships: American Bar Association; Computer Law Association.
Publications: He has published extensively in law reviews, magazines and newspapers on trade, information technology and public international law issues.
Personal: Harvard Law School, JD cum laude 1993; Yeshiva University, BA summa cum laude 1989.

DEORCHIS, Vincent
DeOrchis & Partners, LLP, New York
212 344 4700
Recommended in Shipping

DE SEAR, Edward
McKee Nelson LLP, New York
917 777 4565
edesear@mckeenelson.com
Recommended in Capital Markets
Practice Areas: Specialises in asset-backed securities, both in the US and abroad. Particular expertise in the areas of securitisation of credit card receivables, auto loans, leases, trade receivables, mutual fund fees, bank loans, tobacco company payments, and catastrophe risk coverage assets. Represents issuers, underwriters, credit enhancers, placement agents, and trustees.
Career: Partner at Orrick from 1993 to 2003. Partner at Milbank, Tweed, Hadley & McCloy from 1988-93.
Personal: University of Virginia School of Law, JD, 1973. Columbia University, AB.

DEES, Stanley C
McKenna Long & Aldridge LLP, Washington, DC 202 496 7628
sdees@mckennalong.com
Recommended in Government Contracts
Practice Areas: Practice encompasses counseling and litigation in the field of government contracts and related areas, including: contract formation and negotiation; bid protests; issues in commercialization and privatization; rights in technical data; schedule contracts; claims preparation under supply, construction, and shipbuilding contracts; debarment and suspension proceedings; procurement fraud investigations and qui tam cases; contractor self-governance and compliance programs; defective pricing; cost recovery under contracts and grants; equitable adjustments; and remedies under illegal contract provisions. Authored articles on antitrust in government contracts, defective specifications, contract interpretation, delays, recovery of unabsorbed overhead, recovery of attorneys' fees, disputes and remedies, competition in service contracting, contract financing, and contractor self-governance.
Prof. Memberships: Member and officer of: Public Contract Law Section of American Bar Association (Chair 1987-88); District of Columbia Bar; National Contract Management Association; Council of Defense and Space Industry Associations; honorary faculty member,

U. S. Army JAG School.
Personal: University of Virginia (LLB, 1963); Princeton University (AB, 1960)

DEMPSEY, Kevin M
Dewey Ballantine LLP, Washington, DC
202 862 3676
kdempsey@deweyballantine.com
Recommended in International Trade
Practice Areas: Kevin Dempsey represents corporations and trade associations on a wide variety of international trade matters, including antidumping and countervailing duty litigation, safeguards actions under Section 201, trade policy and international negotiations, e-commerce issues and legislative matters. He has considerable experience in US law and international agreements relating to subsidies, antidumping, safeguards market access, investment and dispute settlement as well as legislative procedures for authorizing and implementing international trade agreements.
Career: Partner, Dewey Ballantine LLP.
Personal: Born January 29, 1962. AB, Washington University, 1984. JD, Harvard Law School, 1987.

DENENBERG, Alan
Davis Polk & Wardwell, Menlo Park
650 752 2000
alan.denenberg@dpw.com
Recommended in Capital Markets
Practice Areas: Member of Davis Polk & Wardwell's Global Technology Group. Has extensive experience in capital markets and mergers and acquisitions transactions. Practice includes general corporate representations, as well as a broad range of public and private financings, including convertible debt, high-yield debt, equity and initial public offerings, representing both domestic and foreign issuers and underwriters. In the mergers and acquisitions area, has represented both acquirer and target companies in a variety of public and private transactions.

DESANTIS, Victor J
White & Case LLP, Washington, DC
202 626 3600
Recommended in Projects
Please see District of Columbia for profile

DEVECCHIO, Jay
Jenner & Block LLP, Washington, DC
Recommended in Government Contracts

DI ROSA, Paolo
Winston & Strawn, Washington, DC
202 371 5700
pdirosa@winston.com
Recommended in Arbitration
Practice Areas: International arbitration and litigation; public international law. Specializes in disputes between investors and sovereign States, particularly pursuant to Bilateral Investment Treaties, and represents both Claimants and Respondent States in arbitral fora such as the International Centre for Set-

tlement of Investment Disputes (ICSID). Extensive experience in public international law and sovereign representation, including treaty issues, extradition, sovereign immunity, and human rights.
Prof. Memberships: President, Chilean-American Chamber of Commerce (Washington DC); Member, International Law Association; American Society of International Law; Inter-American Bar Association; American Bar Association; District of Columbia Bar Association
Career: Partner at Winston & Strawn since 2004. Former Head of Office of Legal Adviser for Western Hemisphere Affairs, US Department of State; Chief US negotiator for numerous treaties and international agreements
Publications: Speaker/panelist at conferences sponsored by, inter alia, International Chamber of Commerce (ICC), American Arbitration Association (AAA), Institute of Transnational Arbitration (ITA); New York State Bar Association. Author, 'The Recent Wave of Arbitrations Against Argentina Under Bilateral Investment Treaties: Background and Principal Legal Issues' (U. of Miami Inter-American Law Review, vol 36 no 1 (Fall 2004)).
Personal: Harvard Law School, JD cum laude (1991); Harvard College, BA magna cum laude (1987). Languages: Spanish (native fluency).

DIANGELO, Christopher
Dewey Ballantine LLP, New York
212 259 6718
cdiangelo@deweyballantine.com
Recommended in Capital Markets
Practice Areas: Focuses his practice on financial services/structured finance. With more 20 years' experience in the financial services industry, Mr DiAngelo represents a wide variety of clients in the industry, including issuers, lenders, underwriters and bond insurers on a variety of programs and projects, including asset-backed debt, municipal debt, straight corporate debt and equity, warehouse lines, regulatory matters and acquisitions.
Career: Joined Dewey Ballantine in 1984, and has been a Partner since 1992.
Personal: Born March 24, 1957. Columbia University Law School, JD, 1984; City University of New York, Economics, MA, 1987; Williams College, Economics and Religion, BA, 1979.

DIMICHAEL, Nicholas
Thompson Hine LLP, Washington, DC
202 263 4103
Nick.DiMichael@ThompsonHine.com
Recommended in Transport
Career: Nick is partner-in-charge of the Washington office of Thompson Hine LLP. He focuses on assisting companies in developing arrangements to satisfy their domestic and international transportation needs and in complex transportation-related litigation. Nick repre-

sents numerous industrial concerns and utility companies, and serves as the general counsel to The National Industrial Transportation League, the nation's oldest and largest transportation trade association. Nick has participated in many major proceedings before the Surface Transportation Board and its predecessor, the Interstate Commerce Commission, as well as proceedings before the Department of Transportation, the Federal Maritime Commission and other agencies concerned with transportation.

DOCKSEY, Ross
Sonnenschein Nath & Rosenthal LLP, Chicago 312 876 8000
Recommended in Business Process Outsourcing, Technology
Please see Illinois for profile

DOKE Jr, Marshall J
Gardere Wynne Sewell LLP, Dallas
214 999 4733
mdoke@gardere.com
Recommended in Government Contracts
Practice Areas: Government contracts litigation and counseling.
Prof. Memberships: US OMB Acquisition Advisory Panel for Federal Procurement; American Bar Association (former Board of Governors, House of Delegates, Chairman of Section of Public Contract Law, Co-Chair of National Council of Lawyers and Certified Public Accountants, and current Standing Committee on Audit); Board of Governors and former President of both US Court of Claims Bar Association and Boards of Contract Appeals Bar Association; American Arbitration Association's Commercial Panel of National Roster of Neutrals.
Career: Marshall Doke represents clients in counseling and litigation involving federal, state, and local public contracts, including procurement protests, changes and termination claims, defective pricing cost and accounting issues, compliance matters, and false claims allegations. He also has extensive experience in international transactional issues related to government contracts, including the Buy American and Trade Agreements Acts, the Foreign Corrupt Practices Act, license agreements, and export controls.
Publications: 'Government Procurement Chapter,' American Bar Association's International Lawyer's Desk Book 2003.
Personal: LLB with high honors, Southern Methodist University School of Law, 1959; BA, Hardin Simmons University, magna cum laude, 1956.

DONOVAN, Donald
Debevoise & Plimpton LLP, New York
212 909 6000
Recommended in Arbitration

DORN, Joseph W

King & Spalding LLP, Washington, DC
202 626 5445
jdorn@kslaw.com
Recommended in International Trade

Practice Areas: International trade regulation, customs law and complex business litigation. Substantial experience in trade remedy actions on behalf of US industries against imports from other countries. Extensive experience in NAFTA and WTO dispute settlement proceedings, appeals before the U.S. Court of International Trade and the U.S. Court of Appeals for the Federal Circuit.

Prof. Memberships: American Bar Association; I.T.C. Trial Lawyers Association; International Bar Association; State Bar of Georgia; The District of Columbia Bar; U.S. Court of International Trade, U.S. Court of Appeals for the Federal Circuit.

Personal: BA, University of North Carolina, 1970; JD, University of Virginia, 1973.

DUNN, Christopher A

Willkie Farr & Gallagher LLP,
Washington, DC 202 303 1108
cdunn@willkie.com
Recommended in International Trade

Practice Areas: Partner in the International Trade Department, specializing in antidumping, subsidies, and safeguards cases as well as customs matters. With a client base that includes Asian and Latin American governments and companies, he has significant experience representing actions before the World Trade Organization. Recent significant matters include the high-profile, antidumping defense of outboard motors from Japan and orange juice from Brazil.

Prof. Memberships: Member of the Bar Association of the District of Columbia and the American Bar Association.

Career: Admitted to the District of Columbia Bar.

Publications: Author of 'The Buy American Act and Other Buy National Programs', 'A Lawyers Guide to International Transactions', ALI/ABA, 1977 and 'Antidumping and Countervailing Duty Investigations Under the Trade Agreements Act of 1979', 'George Washington Journal of Law and Economics', 1979. He is the co-author of 'Trade Agreement Program of the United States, A Lawyer's Guide to International Business Transactions', ALI/ABA, 1977 and a treatise entitled 'International Trade Practice' (Clark Boardman Callaghan, 1977).

Personal: Received a JD from the Georgetown University Law Center in 1975, where he served as student editor in chief of The Tax Lawyer, and an AB from Brown University in 1972.

DURLING, James P

Willkie Farr & Gallagher LLP, Washington, DC 202 303 1109
jdurling@willkie.com
Recommended in International Trade

Practice Areas: Partner in the International Trade Department, specializing in defending foreign companies and governments in antidumping, countervailing duty and other trade remedy investigations, and providing advice on parties' obligations under World Trade Organization agreements. Additionally, he has significant experience litigating WTO disputes and trade policy disputes between the US and foreign parties. Handles a wide range of customs matters, export control issues, including transfer pricing issues, and regularly works with economic experts. He has a significant practice representing Asian, particularly Japanese and Korean, companies and has also worked with clients in Thailand, Malaysia, Singapore, Taiwan, Indonesia, and the Philippines. Has worked with clients on a wide range of high-profile trade policy disputes, including the trade policy battles over automobiles, semiconductors, and color film, and has been actively involved in the related WTO proceedings arising out of these trade policy battles. His recent major matters include defending foreign steel companies in dumping and safeguard actions, prosecuting several WTO challenges to US trade remedies, and coordinating the presentation of complex economic expert testimony. He has also been called upon to provide advice on launching a new round of WTO trade talks and on negotiating strategies for the round.

Prof. Memberships: Member of the American Bar Association, the DC Bar Association and the American Economics Association.

Career: Admitted to the District of Columbia Bar.

Publications: Regularly writes and has spoken frequently at trade association groups around the world about U.S. international trade laws, transfer pricing laws, and trade policy issues. He authored the following books: 'A Business Guide to U.S. Trade Remedy Laws' (2003); 'Understanding the WTO Antidumping Agreement: Negotiating History and Subsequent Interpretation' (2002) (co-author), and 'Anatomy of a Trade Dispute: A Documentary History of the Kodak-Fujifilm Dispute' (2000).

Personal: Received a JD from New York University School of Law in 1984, where he was an articles editor of the New York University Law Review, an MPA from the Woodrow Wilson School at Princeton University in 1984, where he studied applied microeconomics and international economics, and a BA from Haverford College in 1980, where he was elected to Phi Beta Kappa.

ECCLES, Bob

O'Melveny & Myers LLP, Washington, DC 202 383 5300
Recommended in Employee Benefits, Litigation

EDMONSON, Tracy

Latham & Watkins LLP, San Francisco
415 391 0600
Recommended in Capital Markets

EISENBERG, David

Simpson Thacher & Bartlett LLP, New York 212 455 2000
deisenberg@stblaw.com
Recommended in Capital Markets

Practice Areas: A Partner at Simpson Thacher & Bartlett and member of the firm's Corporate Department, concentrating on banking and corporate law and asset-backed securities transactions.

Prof. Memberships: Association of the Bar of the City of New York.

Career: Member of the firm since 1984.

Personal: Received a BA, summa cum laude, in 1974 from Duke University and a JD in 1977 from Duke University School of Law.

EISNER, Rebecca

Mayer, Brown, Rowe & Maw LLP, Chicago 312 782 0600
Recommended in Business Process Outsourcing, Technology
Please see Illinois for profile

EIZENSTAT, Stuart

Covington & Burling, Washington, DC
seizenstat 202 662 5745
Recommended in International Trade

Practice Areas: Heads Covington's International Practice, focusing on international business transactions and regulations and on resolving international trade problems.

Career: Ambassador to the European Union (1993-96); Deputy Treasury Secretary; Under Secretary of State for Economic, Business and Agricultural Affairs; Under Secretary of Commerce for International Trade; Chief Domestic Policy Adviser and Executive Director of the White House Domestic Policy Staff (1977-81). During the Clinton administration, Eizenstat had a prominent role in the development of key international initiatives, including the negotiation of the Transatlantic Agenda with the European Union; the development of the Transatlantic Business Dialogue among European and US CEOs; the negotiation of agreements with the European Union regarding the Helms-Burton Act and the Iran-Libya Sanctions Act; the negotiation of the Japan Port Agreement; and the negotiation of the Kyoto Protocol on global warming. He acted as the Administration's lead official in anti-money laundering initiatives.

Publications: Author of 'Imperfect Justice: Looted Assets, Slave Labor and the Unfinished Business of World War II'.

Personal: Harvard University (JD, 1967).

EMERSON, Eric

Steptoe & Johnson LLP, Washington, DC 202 429 8076
eemerson@steptoe.com
Recommended in International Trade

Practice Areas: Partner, Steptoe & Johnson LLP, Washington, DC. Focuses on international trade regulation and trade policy, with particular emphasis on US antidumping and countervailing duty law. Represents US and foreign companies across a wide range of industries. Appears before US government agencies and federal courts in trade litigation proceedings. Assists clients in developing pricing strategies to minimize antidumping risks. Experienced with both market and non-market economy based antidumping investigations. Counsels clients on their rights and obligations under the WTO agreements. Participated in Steptoe's export control and immigration practices.

Personal: JD, University of Virginia, 1991; BA, University of Iowa, 1986.

ENGLISH, Craig

Kennedy Lillis Schmidt & English, New York 212 430 0800
Recommended in Shipping

ESSERMAN, Susan

Steptoe & Johnson LLP, Washington, DC 202 429 6753
sesserman@steptoe.com
Recommended in International Trade

Practice Areas: Heads Steptoe & Johnson LLP's International Department. Advises on expanding access to foreign markets, WTO policy, trade litigation and dispute resolution. Former Deputy US Trade Representative (with ambassadorial rank) responsible for trade policy and negotiations with Europe, India, Russia, the former Soviet Union, Africa, the Middle East, and in the WTO. Served as USTR General Counsel devising US litigation strategy in the early years of WTO dispute resolution. Decision maker in hundreds of antidumping and countervailing duty cases as Assistant Secretary of Commerce for Import Administration.

Personal: JD, University of Michigan Law School, 1977; BA, Wellesley College, 1974.

EVANS III, Robert

Shearman & Sterling LLP, New York
212 848 8830
revans@shearman.com
Recommended in Capital Markets

Practice Areas: Co-Head of Shearman & Sterling's Capital Markets-Americas Group. Specializes in corporate and securities law. Works extensively with investment banks as underwriters in securities offerings, particularly involving complex transactions such as convertible securities issuances, initial public offerings and tender/exchange offers. Advises corporate clients on offerings and corporate and securities law matters.

Prof. Memberships: American Bar Association, New York State Bar Association, New York County Lawyer's Association, admitted to the New York bar.

Career: Joined Shearman in 1990 and became partner in 1996.

Personal: AB, cum laude, Harvard College (1982); JD, cum laude, Boston University School of Law (1985).

FAULKNER, Andrew M
Skadden, Arps, Slate, Meagher & Flom LLP & Affiliates, New York
212 735 2853
afaulkne@skadden.com
Recommended in Capital Markets
Practice Areas: Represents issuers, underwriters, credit enhancers and lenders in asset-backed and mortgage-backed securities transactions and credit-enhanced securities issuances. Has a broad securitization practice with emphasis on credit card transactions. Helped establish credit card master trusts for many major issuers, and has represented issuers and the underwriters of securities backed by bank VISA and MasterCard receivables and retailer private label credit card receivables. Worked on the first public trade receivables securitization as well as many other innovative structured transactions.
Career: JD, Columbia University School of Law, 1985 (Harlan Fiske Stone Scholar); BA, Cornell University, 1981 (magna cum laude).

FEHER, David G
Dewey Ballantine LLP, New York
212 259 8070
dfeher@deweyballantine.com
Recommended in Sport
Practice Areas: Mr Feher is one of the leading sports lawyers in the country. He is one of the principal negotiators of the CBAs in the NFL, NBA and AFL, and is an expert on the Salary Cap in each of those sports. He has litigated numerous matters in those and other sports, including the Terrell Owens proceeding and the Joe Smith circumvention case.
Prof. Memberships: Sports Lawyers Association, ABA Antitrust Section.
Career: Partner, Dewey Ballantine LLP. Admitted to practice 1984, New York.
Personal: AB, magna cum laude, Georgetown University, 1980. JD, Duke University School of Law, 1984.

FELLAS, John
Hughes Hubbard & Reed LLP, New York
212 837 6075
fellas@hugheshubbard.com
Recommended in Arbitration
Practice Areas: International arbitration and litigation. Has acted as counsel, and served as sole arbitrator, co-arbitrator and chair, in cases under, eg, ICC, AAA and UNCITRAL Rules. Has been retained to act as expert witness on US law in foreign courts, most recently by the US Department of Justice. Regularly represents foreign clients involved in litigation in US courts and advises foreign and US clients on global litigation strategy.
Prof. Memberships: American Law Institute; American Society for International Law; International Bar Association; London Court of International Arbitration.

Career: Admitted in New York; Solicitor of Supreme Court of England and Wales.
Publications: Numerous publications on issues on international arbitration and litigation, including, Transatlantic Commercial Litigation and Arbitration (Oceana 2004) (editor).
Personal: University of Durham, BA (Hons) (Law), 1983; Harvard Law School, LLM, 1985; SJD 1989.

FEO, Edwin
Milbank, Tweed, Hadley & McCloy, Los Angeles 213 892 4000
Recommended in Energy, Projects, Transport

FINE, Drew
Milbank, Tweed, Hadley & McCloy, New York 212 530 5000
Recommended in Aviation

FINKEL, Robert
Milbank, Tweed, Hadley & McCloy, New York 212 530 5000
Recommended in Business Process Outsourcing

FITZGERALD, Peter
Chadbourne & Parke LLP, Washington, DC 202 974 5600
*Recommended in Projects
Please see District of Columbia for profile*

FLANAGAN, Peter L
Covington & Burling, Washington, DC
202 662 5163
pflanagan@cov.com
Recommended in International Trade
Practice Areas: Counsels clients on compliance requirements involving questions of national security, most notably including export controls, economic sanctions constraints, defense trade limitations, and the implications of related non-US requirements. Also advises on other international regulatory requirements bearing on cross-border trade and investment. Clients include leading companies in the oil and gas sector, software and high-technology concerns, pharmaceutical and biotechnology companies, defense contractors, manufacturing entities, financial institutions, and university-affiliated laboratories.
Career: Co-Vice Chair of Covington & Burling's International Trade and Finance Group. Prior employment with Federal Reserve Board's International Finance Division.
Personal: Former Term Member of the Council on Foreign Relations. Graduate of New York University (JD, 1993, magna cum laude and Order of the Coif); Princeton University (MPA, 1993); and University of Wisconsin (BA, 1987, with distinction).

FLOWE Jr, Benjamin
Berliner, Corcoran & Rowe, LLP, Washington, DC 202 293 5555
Recommended in International Trade

FONTAINE, Mary C
Mayer, Brown, Rowe & Maw LLP, Chicago 312 701 7106
mfontaine@mayerbrownrowe.com
Recommended in Capital Markets
Practice Areas: Represents commercial banks, investment banks, issuers, and insurance and reinsurance companies in securitizations of financial assets in the term and commercial paper markets; synthetic risk transfer products, including credit derivatives and reinsurance arrangements; CDO transactions; establishment of single-seller and multi-seller asset securitization conduits, including hybrid and arbitrage conduits; domestic and cross-border medium-term note issuances in the public and private markets; securitization workouts; currency and interest rate hedge facilities; asset swap transactions; secured and unsecured lending. Foreign and domestic assets financed include credit cards, trade receivables, insurance receivables, leases, timeshare loans, franchise loans, corporate and asset-backed bonds, other commercial and consumer debt, e-commerce receivables, future cash flows and operating assets.
Prof. Memberships: American Bar Association, Section on Business Law; New York State Bar Association, Section on Business Law.
Career: Joined Mayer, Brown, Rowe & Maw LLP, Chicago, in 1981; became Partner, 1988; served at Tokyo affiliate office, April - May 1987 and London affiliate office, September 1985 - March 1986.
Publications: Frequent speaker at securitization industry conferences.
Personal: University of Chicago Law School, JD, 1981. Syracuse University, BA summa cum laude, 1978.

FORD, Christopher D
Alston & Bird LLP, Washington, DC
202 756 3371
cford@alston.com
Recommended in Business Process Outsourcing
Practice Areas: Business process outsourcing, information technology outsourcing, technology, telecommunications, electronic commerce
Prof. Memberships: State Bar of Georgia; District of Columbia Bar; Executive Committee, Potomac Counsel of the American Electronics Association
Career: Extensive experience advising clients on technology transactions, including information technology outsourcing, business process outsourcing, strategic alliances, and joint ventures. Frequent speaker on outsourcing and technology-related legal issues.
Publications: Authored numerous articles in such publications as TPI's 'Journal of Sourcing Leadership,' 'Finance Today,' and the Sourcing Interest Group's 'Inside Sourcing Newsletter.'
Personal: BS, University of Virginia (1987); JD, Emory University (1993)

FORD, Paul
Simpson Thacher & Bartlett LLP, New York 212 455 2000
pford@stblaw.com
Recommended in Capital Markets
Practice Areas: A senior partner at Simpson Thacher & Bartlett LLP. Has extensive experience in Europe, Asia and Latin America and has advised on capital raisings, joint ventures, strategic alliances and acquisitions during a 35 year career, representing a broad range of financial institutions and multinational corporations. Was instrumental in establishing the firm's offices in Tokyo, Hong Kong and Singapore.
Prof. Memberships: Chairman from 1993 through 2000 of the United States Foreign Policy Association, the nation's oldest and largest non-partisan foreign policy organisation. A Member of the Council on Foreign Relations, The Japan Society, where he serves on the Corporate Council, The Korea Society and the National Committee on US-China Relations. A Member of the Association of the Bar of the City of New York, the American Bar Association, Union Internationale des Avocats and the International Bar Association, serving as Co-Chairman of the Business Organizations Committee from 1996 to 2000.
Career: Has written and lectured extensively on international legal matters.
Personal: Received a BA from Boston College in 1965, magna cum laude, and a JD in 1968 from Duke University School of Law where he was an editor of the 'Duke Law Journal'.

FORD JACOB, Valerie
Fried, Frank, Harris, Shriver & Jacobson LLP, New York 212 859 8158
valerie.jacob@friedfrank.com
Recommended in Capital Markets
Practice Areas: Corporate Partner. Ms Jacob is Chairperson of Fried Frank and Head of the Global Capital Markets Group. She acts as counsel to both issuers and underwriters in domestic and international financings and represents her clients in all types of securities offerings, including initial public offerings, secondary offerings, high-yield offerings, mezzanine and bridge financings, investment-grade debt offerings, acquisition financings and recapitalizations. She also counsels corporations on corporate governance and securities regulation.
Prof. Memberships: Ms Jacob chaired an IBC SEC conference entitled 'SEC Regulation for Non-US Companies'. Ms Jacob has spoken at a number of Practising Law Institute sessions, including 'Understanding the Securities Laws' in 1997, 1998, 1999, 2000, 2001 and 2002 and 'Conducting Due Diligence' in 2000, 2001, 2002, 2003 and 2004. She is a frequent contributor to legal and other periodicals on securities laws and financing topics. In 1995, Ms Jacob was named one of the '45 Top Lawyers

Under 45' by 'The American Lawyer'. Ms Jacob is a Member of the American Bar Association and the Association of the Bar of the City of New York.
Career: Admitted to practice in New York. Joined Fried Frank in 1978 and became a Partner in 1986.
Personal: Born 1952. Received JD in 1978 from Cornell University and BS 1975 from Boston University.

FORE, John
Wilson Sonsini Goodrich & Rosati, Palo Alto 650 493 9300
jfore@wsgr.com
Recommended in Capital Markets
Practice Areas: Extensive experience with a variety of debt transactions, including secured/unsecured bank financings, private placements, acquisition finance, project finance, leveraged leasing, senior, subordinated and convertible note sales, multicurrency loans, letter of credit facilities, interest rate caps, collars and swaps, off-balance sheet financings, 144A and Regulation S transactions and public offerings of investment grade and non-investment grade notes and convertible subordinated debt securities.
Prof. Memberships: Admitted to practice in California and New York.
Career: Became WSGR Partner, 1991. Member, WSGR Policy Committee.
Personal: JD, New York University School of Law, 1983; BA (cum laude), Yale University, 1979.

FRANCE II, William N
Healy & Baillie LLP, New York
212 709 9226
wfrance@healy.com
Recommended in Shipping
Practice Areas: All maritime casualty and related commercial litigation and arbitration with focus on naval architecture, marine engineering, design, safety, surveying, classification, construction, and operational liabilities, and cargo claims of any kind.
Prof. Memberships: Society of Naval Architects and Marine Engineers; ASME; Maritime Law Association.
Career: Naval architect/marine engineer, Esso International 1972-76; admitted NY Bar 1978; joined Healy & Baillie 1977, Partner 1983; licensed professional engineer.
Publications: 'An Investigation of Head-Sea Parametric Rolling and its Influence on Container Lashing Systems,' 40 Marine Technology 1 (SNAME 2003).
Personal: BSc. NA & ME, Webb Institute 1972; JD NYU Law School 1977.

FREYER, Dana H
Skadden, Arps, Slate, Meagher & Flom LLP & Affiliates, New York
212 735 2506
dfreyer@skadden.com
Recommended in Arbitration
Practice Areas: Heads the firm's Arbitration and Alternative Dispute Resolu-

tion Practices and is a member of the firm's International Arbitration Group. Represents clients in all types of US and international commercial litigation and arbitration, including international arbitrations under the ICC, ICSID, AAA International, UNCITRAL, Stockholm Chamber of Commerce and other arbitration rules, and in mediations and other ADR proceedings. Serves as chair and member of arbitration panels. Also heads the firm's Corporate Compliance Program Practice. Advises clients on the development and implementation of ethics, compliance and corporate governance programs.
Career: JD, Columbia University, 1971; BA, Connecticut College, 1965.

FRIEDLAND, Paul
White & Case LLP, New York
212 819 8917
pfriedland@whitecase.com
Recommended in Arbitration
Practice Areas: Co-Head of firm's International Arbitration Practice Group. Counsel/arbitrator in international commercial arbitrations.
Prof. Memberships: NYS Bar; Paris Bar; US District Courts for Southern and Eastern Districts of NY; US Court of Appeals for the Second Circuit; US Supreme Court; AAA Arbitration Practice Committee (Chairman); AAA (Board of Directors); Institute for Transnational Arbitration (Executive Committee, Board of Trustees, Programs Co-Chair); US Council for International Business (Board of Trustees, Arbitration Committee); World Arbitration and Mediation Reporter (International Editor).
Publications: Include 'Arbitration Clauses for International Contracts' (2000).
Personal: Yale University (BA, 1976); Columbia Law School (JD, 1980), Law Review, Kent Scholar.

FRIEDMAN, Andrew
Covington & Burling, Washington, DC
202 662 5466
afriedman@cov.com
Recommended in Sport
Practice Areas: Primary tax counsel to all four United States major professional sports leagues: Major League Baseball, National Basketball Association, National Football League, National Hockey League as well as the United States Tennis Association and professional sports clubs such as the Boston Red Sox. Lead industry representative in dealings with the Internal Revenue Service professional sports audit task force.
Career: Highlights include John Henry's sale of the Florida Marlins baseball club and the purchase of the Boston Red Sox and related entities; the NFL's expansion to Cleveland and Houston; the financing structures for the stadium in Cleveland and other sports facilities; the NFL and NHL credit facilities; and

Buffalo Bills v United States.
Personal: Harvard University (JD, 1980, cum laude); Trinity College (BA, 1977, summa cum laude, as valedictorian).

FRIEDMAN, Lawrence B
Cleary Gottlieb Steen & Hamilton LLP, New York 212-225-2840
lfriedman@cgsh.com
Recommended in Arbitration
Practice Areas: Domestic and international commercial litigation and arbitration involving multijurisdictional litigation in M&A, joint venture and licensing agreements, securities law and international banking regulation. Intellectual property disputes, including trademark, trade dress, patent and copyright infringement and misappropriation of trade secrets.
Prof. Memberships: Member, New York Bar; Inaugural Chair, International Commercial Dispute Resolution Committee of Association of the Bar of the City of New York; Secretary, Association's Committee to Enhance Diversity in the Legal Profession.
Career: Joined firm, 1983; became Partner, 1991. JD, cum laude, Harvard Law School (1982); BSFS, summa cum laude, Georgetown University School of Foreign Service (1979).

FUNK, John A
Jones Day, Dallas 214 220 3939
Recommended in Business Process Outsourcing, Technology
Please see Texas for profile

GALAINENA, David
Winston & Strawn LLP, Chicago
312 558 7442
dgalainena@winston.com
Recommended in Capital Markets
Practice Areas: Partner in the firm's Corporate Department. His practice concentrates in asset securitization/structured finance including the asset-backed and mortgage-backed markets.
Career: Admitted to Illinois Bar in 1983. Joined Winston & Strawn LLP, 1995 as Partner. Member, Diversity Committee. Member, firm's Executive Committee.
Personal: Born November 11, 1957. Received BA, magna cum laude, Phi Beta Kappa 1980, Tulane University; JD from University of Notre Dame 1983.

GALLAGHER, James J
McKenna Long & Aldridge, Los Angeles
213 688 6165
jgallagher@mckennalong.com
Recommended in Government Contracts
Practice Areas: Has represented government contractors, including many of the largest aerospace companies, for over three decades. Experience includes the full range of government contract financial issues, including civil and criminal fraud investigations and litigation, defective pricing, terminations, claims, breach of contract and cost allowability.

Has served as lead counsel in more than 20 False Claims Act cases, most of which were qui tam matters. Four of those cases have been heard by the United States Court of Appeals for the Ninth Circuit, including the highly publicized US ex rel Schumer v Hughes case. Has also argued more than a dozen cases at the federal appellate courts.
Prof. Memberships: Public Contract Law Section of the American Bar Association; District of Columbia Bar; Federal Bar Association; National Contract Management Association; State Bar of California.
Personal: Georgetown University Law Center (LLB, 1965); University of Notre Dame (BBA, 1961).

GALLAGHER, Robert
Groom Law Group, Washington, DC
202 857 0620
Recommended in Employee Benefits, Litigation

GALVIS, Sergio J
Sullivan & Cromwell LLP, New York
212 558 4000
Recommended in Projects
Please see New York for profile

GAMBRO, Michael S
Cadwalader, Wickersham & Taft LLP, New York 212 504 6825
michael.gambro@cwt.com
Recommended in Capital Markets
Practice Areas: Corporate and securities lawyer who primarily represents financial institutions in the financing, purchase and sale, and securitization of financial assets. Has represented some of the largest financial institutions in the country in noteworthy securitization transactions, including: representation of Lehman Brothers and Goldman Sachs as underwriters for the largest single borrower commercial mortgage loan securitization, for General Growth Properties; representation of Confederation Life Insurance Company (US) in Rehabilitation and the underwriters in Confederation Life's securitization of commercial mortgage loans, at the time the largest CMBS transaction in history and one of the Institutional Investor deals of the year; representation of The Prudential Insurance Company of America in a securitization of loans secured by life insurance policies, which is the only transaction of its kind and was recognized as one of the Investment Dealer's Digest deals of the year.
Personal: JD Columbia 1980 (Harlan Fiske Stone Scholar); BS Tufts University, summa cum laude and Phi Beta Kappa. Frequently lectures and writes articles on numerous business law topics.

GANDHI, Samir A
Sidley Austin Brown & Wood LLP, New York 212 839 5684
sgandhi@sidley.com
Recommended in Capital Markets
Practice Areas: Samir A Gandhi is a

Partner in the New York office whose practice focuses on structured finance and capital markets offerings. He concentrates on corporate finance and the development of new financial products, representing domestic and foreign issuers and underwriters in capital markets activities, with particular emphasis on structured corporate finance transactions. He handles complex financial structures, domestic and international Tier-1 capital raising transactions, convertible securities, debt- and equity-linked products and preferred securities products, and represents underwriters in a variety of securities offerings by US government sponsored entities and multilateral development banks.
Prof. Memberships: Serves on the Board of Directors of Lawyers Alliance for New York.
Career: The George Washington University Law School (JD, 1993) University of Chicago (AB, 1990). Bar Admission: New York, 1994.

GANNETT, William
Cahill Gordon & Reindel, New York
212 701 3900
Recommended in Capital Markets

GANZ, Howard
Proskauer Rose LLP, New York
212 969 3000
Recommended in Employment, Sport
Please see New York for profile

GARDINER, John L
Skadden, Arps, Slate, Meagher & Flom LLP & Affiliates, New York
212 735 2442
jgardine@skadden.com
Recommended in Arbitration
Practice Areas: Represents clients in commercial disputes in both federal and state courts in the US, as well as before domestic and international arbitration tribunals such as the International Chamber of Commerce and the American Arbitration Association. Involved in allegations of fraud, breach of contract, theft of trade secrets and other related matters as both plaintiff's counsel and as defendant's counsel. Has advised clients in corporate litigations including takeover contests, related shareholder litigation, and class actions involving the federal securities laws.
Career: Roll of Solicitors, Republic of Ireland, 1988; Roll of Solicitors, England and Wales; LLB, University College, Dublin, 1984.

GARFINKEL, Barry H
Skadden, Arps, Slate, Meagher & Flom LLP & Affiliates, New York
212 735 2500
bgarfink@skadden.com
Recommended in Arbitration
Practice Areas: Heads Skadden's international Litigation and Arbitration Practice. Lead many of the firm's more significant trials, appeals and major international arbitrations. Acted as arbi-

trator in ICC, UNCITRAL, and AAA arbitrations. Advised major US and foreign companies on transnational arbitration matters.
Prof. Memberships: Chairman and trustee, Practising Law Institute; Advisory Committee, Institute for Transnational Arbitration; International Arbitration Committee, American Arbitration Association; American Arbitration Association (Complex Cases), London Court of International Arbitration and ICC; Fellow, American College of Trial Lawyers.
Career: LLB, Yale University, 1955 (Managing Editor, Yale Law Journal); BSS, College of the City of New York, 1950.

GARIBALDI, Oscar M
Covington & Burling, Washington, DC
202 662 5624
ogaribaldi@cov.com
Recommended in Arbitration
Practice Areas: International arbitration (investor-state and international commercial arbitration); international trade; public and private international law.
Prof. Memberships: Member of the ICSID Panel of Conciliators (appointed by the United States).
Career: Trained in both the civil-law and common-law systems; taught public international law at the Cornell and Virginia Law Schools; representative clients include ExxonMobil Corporation; LG&E Energy LLC; MTD Equity Sdn. Bhd.; Bacardi Ltd.; Newmont Mining Company; Southern Peru Copper Corporation; and Amoco Oil Company.
Publications: Several articles on issues of public international law.
Personal: University of Buenos Aires Law School (Procurador [LLB], 1971, Abogado [JD], 1972, Diploma de Honor); Harvard Law School (LLM, 1975); studied at Harvard towards SJD (1975-76 and 1978-79).

GAROFALO, Gary
Garofalo Goerlich Hainbach PC, Washington, DC 202 776 3970
Recommended in Aviation

GENTNER, Joshua
Vedder, Price, Kaufman & Kammholz, Chicago 312 609 7500
Recommended in Aviation

GERBER, Dean N
Vedder, Price, Kaufman & Kammholz, Chicago 312 609 7500
Recommended in Aviation

GEWIRTZ, Elliot
Milbank, Tweed, Hadley & McCloy, New York 212 530 5000
Recommended in Aviation

GILBERG, David J
Sullivan & Cromwell LLP, New York
212 558 4000
gilbergd@sullcrom.com
Recommended in Capital Markets

Practice Areas: Practice involves broad range of derivatives and related matters, including development of electronic trading facilities for trading of securities and derivatives; structuring of indexed products, over-the-counter derivatives and other financial instruments; and development of structured transactions, private funds and other managed trading vehicles. Also advises clients on legal and regulatory issues related to the trading of securities and derivatives.
Career: Partner since 1996.
Personal: University of Pennsylvania (BA, MA, 1978) and Harvard Law School (JD, 1981).

GLASS, Adam
Linklaters, New York
212 424 9130
Recommended in Capital Markets

GINOS, Geoffrey
Nicoletti Hornig Campise and Sweeney, New York 212 220 3830
Recommended in Shipping

GLICK, Anna
Cadwalader, Wickersham & Taft LLP, New York
212 504 6309
anna.glick@cwt.com
Recommended in Capital Markets
Practice Areas: Concentrates in multi-class securitization, structured mortgage finance, securitization of commercial mortgage loans, mezzanine debt and other financings of mortgage-related assets, federal securities laws issues particular to securitizations, and related securities compliance matters. Also works in CBOs (particularly those backed by asset and mortgage securities). Represents issuers, underwriters and institutional investors active in the primary and secondary capital markets. Works closely with real estate attorneys to advise on rating agency and securitization issues (origination of large and conduit-size mortgage loans pending securitization). Concentrates on federal securities law, registration of public securities, financings, and other business arrangements for closely-held corporations.
Career: JD, New York University School of Law (1982); Member of the Law Review and Order of the Coif.

GOLDBERG, Daniel
Bingham McCutchen LLP, Boston
617 951 8000
Recommended in Antitrust, Sport

GOLDFEIN, Shepard
Skadden, Arps, Slate, Meagher & Flom LLP & Affiliates, New York
212 735 3000
Recommended in Antitrust, Sport
Please see New York for profile

GOLDSCHMIDT, David J
Skadden, Arps, Slate, Meagher & Flom LLP & Affiliates, New York
212 735 3574
dgoldsch@skadden.com

Recommended in Capital Markets
Practice Areas: Represents investment banks and US and international issuers in a variety of financing matters, including public offerings and private placement of debt and equity securities, and international securities offerings. Focuses primarily on offerings for technology companies as well as REITs. Involved in developing new products, such as the Income Deposit Security.
Career: JD, New York University School of Law, 1987 (Member, Review of Law and Social Change); BA, New York University, 1984 (magna cum laude).

GOLDSTEIN, Marvin
Stroock & Stroock & Lavan LLP, New York 212 806 5400
Recommended in Capital Markets

GOLDSTEIN, Stuart N
Cadwalader, Wickersham & Taft LLP, Charlotte 704 348 5258
stuart.goldstein@cwt.com
Recommended in Capital Markets
Practice Areas: Partner in the Capital Markets Department, resident in Cadwalader's Charlotte and New York offices. Concentrates on structured finance, structured products and the federal securities laws. Practices primarily in the areas of commercial mortgage and asset securitization, representing issuers, underwriters, institutional investors, servicers and trustees in both public and private transactions. Has extensive experience analyzing and structuring securities, collateralized debt obligations and other instruments and products, as well as structuring transactions involving interest rate swaps, caps, floors and other derivative instruments. Also represents clients in the purchase and sale of commercial and multifamily mortgage loans, mezzanine debt, subordinate debt and residential first and second mortgage loans (including FHA, VA, conventional and manufactured housing) in whole loan and participation structures. Has additional extensive experience in secured lending and represents lenders in structuring and negotiating finance facilities.
Personal: Received a BS from Cornell University and his JD from Boalt Hall School of Law at the University of California at Berkeley. Member of the New York State Bar Association.

GONZALEZ, Daniel E
Hogan & Hartson LLP, Miami
305 459 6649
degonzalez@hhlaw.com
Recommended in Arbitration
Practice Areas: Chairman of the firm's International Litigation and Arbitration Practice Group. Practices principally in the areas of international complex commercial litigation and arbitration, having tried and arbitrated cases in English and Spanish throughout the United States, Latin America, and Europe. With both civil and common law experience,

and an accounting background, he handles matters involving all aspects of commercial disputes, including securities, construction and product defects, insurance coverage disputes, distributorship rights, environmental liability and professional malpractice.

Prof. Memberships: Member, American Bar Association; International Bar Association; International Chamber of Commerce; American Arbitration Association.

Publications: Author and speaker on a number of topics involving international litigation and arbitration.

Personal: University of Miami School of Law (JD, Summa Cum Laude).

GOODMAN, Ronald
Winston & Strawn, Washington, DC
202 371 5718
rgoodman@winston.com
Recommended in Arbitration

Practice Areas: Heads Washington, DC office's International Arbitration Practice. Specialises in investment, commercial and construction disputes involving State and commercial parties before international courts, tribunals and commissions, including: ICSID, ICC, LCIA, AAA, United Nations Compensation Commission, and ad hoc arbitration (UNCITRAL Rules and others).

Prof. Memberships: New York State Bar, admitted 1987; District of Columbia Bar, admitted 1989; Paris Bar, admitted 1992.

Career: Previously Partner at White & Case (DC, Paris and Johannesburg offices). Prior to joining W&C, he was a legal adviser at the Iran-United States Claims Tribunal.

Personal: English, French (fluent), Dutch (proficient), Spanish (legal reading proficiency).

GORDON, David
Latham & Watkins LLP, New York
212 906 1200
Recommended in Projects

GRANDISON, W George
Steptoe & Johnson LLP,
Washington, DC 202 429 6447
wgrandison@steptoe.com
Recommended in International Trade

Practice Areas: Partner, International Trade Group, Steptoe & Johnson LLP, Washington, DC. Work has encompassed major cases under the antidumping and countervailing duty laws, WTO agreements, and the customs and export control laws. Represented and advised clients in matters involving a variety of products from agricultural and forestry products to high technology equipment and materials. Extensive experience in cases involving the valuation and pricing of natural resources, subsidy aspects of export restrictions and imports of complex, high technology equipment and high volume commercial products.

Personal: JD, Yale Law School, 1972; BS, United States Military Academy, 1966.

GREEN, Jonathan
Milbank, Tweed, Hadley & McCloy,
New York 212 530 5000
Recommended in Projects

GREENBAUM, Jack A
Healy & Baillie LLP, New York
212 943 3980
jgreenbaum@healy.com
Recommended in Shipping

Practice Areas: Maritime law; commercial law; litigation; maritime arbitration; best known for charter party and bill of lading disputes, as advocate and arbitrator, but experience extends to litigation involving commodity contracts, letters of credit, and general commercial disputes. Clients include P&I and FD&D associations, shipowners, operators, charterers, brokers, and commodity traders. Admitted 1971, New York; 1983, New Jersey.

Prof. Memberships: The Maritime Law Association of the United States.

Career: Joined Healy & Baillie 1971; became Partner 1977; Executive Committee 1990 to present.

Personal: Born: Brooklyn, New York, October 26, 1947. Brooklyn Law School, 1971, JD Brooklyn College, 1967, BS.

GREENWALD, John D
Wilmer Cutler Pickering Hale and Dorr
LLP, Washington, DC
202 663 6743
john.greenwald@wilmerhale.com
Recommended in International Trade

Practice Areas: Represents various clients in matters arising under the trade laws of the United States, the Commission of the European Communities and other foreign jurisdictions. Advises and represents various clients on trade legislation in Congress and/or trade policy issues under review in the Executive branch of the US government.

Career: Attorney in the Office of the US Trade Representative in 1974, then served as Deputy General Counsel of that office; 1980-81, served as the first Head of the Commerce Department's Import Administration.

Personal: Columbia University School of Law (JD 1972); University of North Carolina at Chapel Hill (BA 1967).

GRIFFITH, Spencer S
Akin Gump Strauss Hauer & Feld LLP,
Washington, DC 202 887 4575
sgriffith@akingump.com
Recommended in International Trade

Practice Areas: Partner, International Trade practice. Handles international trade litigation in US and international fora. Handles countervailing duty, antidumping and other trade remedy matters, and provides trade policy advice. Regularly appears before US agencies and courts handling trade remedy proceedings, including Office of the United States Trade Representative, US Department of Commerce and US International Trade Commission. Routinely handles complex appeals to US

courts and to international tribunals, including NAFTA and WTO Panels. Also provides advice on WTO matters and WTO litigation.

Personal: AB (honors), Brown University; JD, New York University School of Law.

GRIGERA NAÓN, Horacio
White & Case LLP, Washington, DC
202 626 3600
Recommended in Arbitration

GROSSHANDLER, Seth
Cleary Gottlieb Steen & Hamilton LLP,
New York 212 225 2542
sgrosshandler@cgsh.com
Recommended in Capital Markets

Practice Areas: Creditors' rights, derivative products, securities transactions, financial institutions and structured finance, with particular emphasis on risks to counterparties and investors in the event of insolvency.

Prof. Memberships: Member of the Bar in New York.

Career: Joined firm,1983; became Partner, 1992. JD, 'Law Review' - editorial board, cum laude, Order of the Coif, Northwestern University School of Law (1983); BA, Phi Beta Kappa, Reed College (1979).

Publications: Mr Grosshandler lectures and is widely published on various aspects of creditors' rights and derivative products and securities transactions.

GUEDRY, David
Hughes & Luce LLP, Dallas
214 939 5500
Recommended in Business Process Outsourcing, Technology

GULLAND, Eugene D
Covington & Burling, Washington, DC
202 662 5504
egulland@cov.com
Recommended in Arbitration

Practice Areas: Extensive experience in international and domestic commercial arbitration, and in judicial actions seeking or resisting enforcement of arbitration awards. Practice has included cases before the ICC, LCIA, ICSID, AAA, CPR, CAS (Court for Arbitration of Sport) and disputes conducted under UNCITRAL Rules.

Prof. Memberships: Member of the District of Columbia and Virginia bars, the US Supreme Court, ten federal courts of appeals, and many federal district courts. Also a Member of the LCIA, the American Judicature Society, USCIB (arbitration committee), and Faculty Member of the National Institute for Trial Advocacy (NITA).

Career: Joined Covington & Burling as an associate in 1973, parter 1980 to date. Captain, US Army Infantry, 1972-73.

Personal: Born 27 August 1947. JD Yale Law School (1972) and AB Princeton University (1969).

GULLIKSON, Rosemary L
Sonnenschein Nath & Rosenthal LLP,
Chicago 312 876 8963
rgullikson@sonnenschein.com
Recommended in Business Process Outsourcing

Practice Areas: A transactional lawyer focusing on strategic alliances, complex technology development and implementation projects, and outsourcing transactions. Negotiates global and cross border services, licensing and technology arrangements, and healthcare industry IT and financial/investment industry IT transactions.

Prof. Memberships: Director and President, Tim & Tom Gullikson Foundation, a not-for-profit corporation, funding support programs for brain tumor patients and their families.

Personal: Northwestern University, JD, cum laude; Northern Illinois University, BS, Nursing, summa cum laude.

GUTOWSKI, Peter
Freehill Hogan & Mahar LLP, New York
212 425 1900
Recommended in Shipping

HAHN, Robert J
Hunton & Williams, Charlotte
704 378 4764
rhahn@hunton.com
Recommended in Capital Markets

Practice Areas: Practice focuses on asset securitization, primarily in non-mortgage assets, including synthetic securitizations. Represents financial institutions, issuers, underwriters, credit enhancers, liquidity providers, asset-backed commercial paper conduits and other securitization participants in issuing, administering, servicing and underwriting asset-backed securities. Extensive experience in structuring securitizations, including public and 144A/Reg S offerings, asset-backed commercial paper conduits and synthetic structures. Active in structuring transactions involving a wide variety of financial assets, including vehicle loans, credit card receivables, trade receivables, HELOCs, home equity loans, equipement leases, aircraft and charged-off loans and receivables. Member of Hunton & Williams' pro bono committee.

HALVEY, John
Milbank, Tweed, Hadley & McCloy,
New York 212 530 5000
Recommended in Business Process Outsourcing, Technology

HAMMOND, Steven A
Hughes Hubbard & Reed LLP, New York
212 837 6253
hammond@hugheshubbard.com
Recommended in Arbitration

Practice Areas: Specializes in international arbitration and litigation, with service as counsel or arbitrator in dozens of international commercial arbitrations under ICC, UNCITRAL, AAA, and IACAC rules, including proceedings conducted in English, Spanish and French. Also experienced in sovereign claims and defense, extraterritorial application of US laws, foreign discovery, parallel proceedings, and enforcement of foreign arbitral awards and judgments.

Prof. Memberships: Union Internationale des Avocats (President d'Honneur); International Bar Association; American Bar Association; The Association of the Bar of the City of New York; Judicial Conference of the US Court of Appeals for the Second Circuit (Executive Secretary, Planning Committee) (1992-99).

Career: Partner since 1986.

Publications: Published work has appeared in 'The Journal of International Arbitration' and Graham & Trotman's 'Pre-Trial and Pre-Hearing Procedures Worldwide.'

Personal: Honors graduate: Free University of Brussels (LLM, 1979); Maine Law School (JD, 1977); Bowdoin College (AB, 1974). Institut d'Etudes Sciences Politique, Faculté de Droit, Paris 1 (1972-73). Fluent in French, Spanish.

HARMS, David B
Sullivan & Cromwell LLP, New York
212 558 4000
harmsd@sullcrom.com
Recommended in Capital Markets

Practice Areas: Focuses on wide variety of capital markets and corporate law matters, including public and private offerings by US and non-US issuers, securities trading practices, corporate governance and derivative securities. Also focuses on broker-dealer regulation. Co-coordinator of S&C's securities finance practice; coordinator of broker-dealer regulation practice.

Career: Partner since 1992. Judicial Clerk to Hon. Edward Weinfeld, US District Court (SDNY), 1984-85.

Publications: Numerous articles on securities regulatory matters. Co-chairman, PLI's 35th Annual Institute on Securities Regulation (2003). 2002 winner, Burton Award for Legal Achievement, for 'Integration Under the 1933 Act: The SEC Provides New Safe Harbors,' in 'The Review of Securities & Commodities Regulation.'

Personal: SUNY Purchase (BA, 1978); New York University Law School (JD, 1984; editor in chief, 'NYU Law Review').

HARRIS, L Douglas
Milbank, Tweed, Hadley & McCloy, New York 212 530 5000
Recommended in Projects

HARTNETT, William
Cahill Gordon & Reindel, New York
212 701 3900
Recommended in Capital Markets

HARTQUIST, David
Collier Shannon Scott, Washington, DC
202 342 8400
Recommended in International Trade

HARVEY, James
Alston & Bird LLP, Atlanta
404 881 7328
jharvey@alston.com
Recommended in Business Process Outsourcing

Practice Areas: Outsourcing, privacy, technology

Prof. Memberships: Member, Board of Editors, 'The Internet and Computer Lawyer' and 'GigaLaw.com;' member, Computer Law Association; member, Sourcing Interests Group.

Career: Complex practice focused on technology and related issues, including IT and business process outsourcing, M&A, finance and litigation.

Publications: Numerous articles in such publications as 'The Privacy and Information Law Report,' 'The Electronic Commerce and Banking Law Report,' 'EuroWatch,' 'The Computer and Internet Litigation Journal,' 'The Georgia Bar Journal,' and 'The International Computer Lawyer.'

Personal: BA, University of Arkansas (1983); JD, with honors, University of North Carolina (1988).

HAYDEN, Raymond
Hill Rivkins & Hayden LLP, New York
212 669 0600
Recommended in Shipping

HEARD, Keith
Burke & Parsons, New York
212 354 3800
Recommended in Shipping

HEFTLER, Thomas
Stroock & Stroock & Lavan LLP, New York 212 806 5400
Recommended in Capital Markets

HEINZELMAN, Kris
Cravath, Swaine & Moore LLP, New York 212 474 1336
kris.heinzelman@cravath.com
Recommended in Capital Markets

Practice Areas: Head of the Corporate Department. Domestic and international corporate finance transactions, including public and private offering of debt and equity securities. Routinely represents underwriters and has extensive experience representing issuers in IPOs. Has served as Recruiting Partner, Corporate, and Managing Partner, Corporate.

Prof. Memberships: ABA; NYSBA; ABCNY.

Career: Partner since 1983.

Personal: Yale Law School (JD, 1976); Brown University (MA, AB, magna cum laude, 1973; Phi Beta Kappa).

HENGEN, Nancy
Holland & Knight LLP, New York
212 513 3200
nancy.hengen@hklaw.com
Recommended in Shipping

Practice Areas: Partner in firm's Business Law Section. She represents clients in secured and unsecured financing transactions in connection with com-

mercial vessels and other 'big ticket' equipment financing, including leveraged and single-investor leases, synthetic leases, loan agreements and related security documentation, ship mortgages, Title XI financing, and other US governmental financing programs and vessel construction contracts. She has represented US and foreign banks, financial institutions and other investors, as well as borrowers and lessees in loan and leasing transactions involving equipment and facilities. Her practice includes mergers and acquisitions in the shipping industry and corporate transactions.

HICKOK, Arthur
Sidley Austin Brown & Wood LLP, New York 212 839 5318
ahickok@Sidley.com
Recommended in Capital Markets

Practice Areas: Arthur F Hickok focuses on the representation of commercial and investment banks, monoline insurers and other financial institutions participating in securitisation and structured finance transactions as underwriters, placement agents, providers of credit enhancement and investors. Transactions include the securitisation of corporate loans and bonds (CLOs and CBOs), mortgage loans, premium finance loans, trade receivables, commodities, guaranteed investment contracts, intellectual property and other financial assets, financed through a variety of means including the issuance of term securities and commercial paper. Mr Hickok has also assisted clients in establishing commercial paper conduits and other investment vehicles.

Career: The University of Chicago Law School, JD, 1994; Princeton University, AB, 1990. Bar Admission: Illinois, 1994; New York, 2001.

HILLENBRAND, Hyman
DeOrchis Hillenbrand & Wiener, LLP, Miami 305 571 9200
Recommended in Shipping, Transport

HINMAN Jr, William
Simpson Thacher & Bartlett LLP, Palo Alto 650 251 5000
whinman@stblaw.com
Recommended in Capital Markets

Practice Areas: Corporate Partner at Simpson Thacher & Bartlett. His area of concentration is corporate finance, advising both issuers and underwriters in capital-raising transactions with a particular emphasis on public and private financings and initial public offerings. He has been involved with debt and equity offerings of high technology, healthcare, and biopharmaceutical companies as well as a variety of offerings and general corporate work for a wide range of issuers and underwriters. His practice has had a strong international focus. He also has significant experience regarding convertible offerings, derivatives, novel securities, and private placements. Has represented boards of direc-

tors and their audit committees on a number of governance matters.

Prof. Memberships: Member, Bar Association of the State of California, Association of the Bar of the City of New York; Advisory Board Member, Latin American Law and Business Report edited by WorldTrade Executive, Inc.

Career: Joined the firm in 2000 as a Partner. Prior to coming to Simpson Thacher, he was the Managing Partner of Shearman & Sterling's San Francisco and Menlo Park offices.

Personal: Cornell University Law School, JD, 1980; Editorial Board, Cornell Law Review. Michigan State University, BA (with honours), 1977.

HITSELBERGER, Carol A
Mayer, Brown, Rowe & Maw LLP, Chicago 312 701 7740
chitselberger@mayerbrownrowe.com
Recommended in Capital Markets

Practice Areas: Specializes in securitization, including structuring domestic and cross-border commercial paper funded securitization vehicles and securitizing trade receivables, credit card receivables, auto and equipment leases and loans, corporate loans and various other financial assets in private placements, public offerings and Rule 144A/Regulation S offerings. Advises on leveraged buyout financings; restructurings of troubled credits; and synthetic leases. She has been at the forefront of several initiatives in the asset backed securities market, including accounting and regulatory developments affecting the industry.

Prof. Memberships: Membership Committee, American Securitization Forum.

Career: Joined Mayer, Brown, Rowe & Maw LLP, Chicago, 1989; Partner, 1998.

Publications: Is a contributing author to the two-volume treatise, 'Securitization of Financial Assets', Aspen Law & Business (2nd ed. 2004). Regularly speaks at professional seminars and conferences, including at the American Securitization Forum and Information Management Network industry conferences.

Personal: University of Pennsylvania Law School, JD cum laude, 1989. Bryn Mawr College, AB magna cum laude, 1986.

HOBBY, Scott M
Hunton & Williams, Atlanta
404 888 4263
shobby@hunton.com
Recommended in Business Process Outsourcing

Practice Areas: Scott Hobby's practice focus is in three areas: multinational business process, information technology and application service provider outsourcing arrangements; enterprise resource platform level systems development and integration transactions; and corporate finance including public and private offerings, mergers and acquisitions and corporate governance. Listed in 'Best Lawyers in America' 2003-04 and 2005-06, named one of Georgia's 2003 and 2004 Legal Elite, selected by Georgia attorneys and published in 'Georgia Trend Magazine', December 2003 and December 2004, named a Corporate Finance Super Lawyer, as published in 'Atlanta Magazine' and 'Georgia Super Lawyers' magazine, March 2004 and March 2005.

HOCHBERG, Kevin J
Sidley Austin Brown & Wood LLP, Chicago 312 853 2085
khochberg@sidley.com
Recommended in Capital Markets
Practice Areas: Kevin Hochberg's practice focuses on structured finance, asset securitization, merger and acquisition financing, restructurings and bankruptcies, and other secured and unsecured lending transactions. He represents issuers, monoline insurance companies, underwriters and investors in both public and private offerings of asset-backed securities, including commercial paper conduit transactions, Rule 144A and public offerings. His practice has covered a wide range of asset classes, including trade receivables, auto loans, equipment leases, rental car fleets, shipping containers, container chassis, railcars, utility stranded costs and relocation company receivables.
Prof. Memberships: Member of the Chicago and American Bar Associations and the American College of Commercial Finance Lawyers.
Career: The University of Chicago Law School, JD, 1984; University of Chicago, MA, 1978; University of Maryland, BA, 1977. Bar Admission: Illinois, 1984.

HOCHBERG, Sheldon
Steptoe & Johnson LLP, Washington, DC 202 429 6218
shochberg@steptoe.com
Recommended in International Trade
Practice Areas: Partner in the Washington office of Steptoe & Johnson LLP. Focuses on international trade and administrative law matters, particularly judicial review of federal agency determinations. Has extensive experience on some of the most complex and important issues related to countervailing duty and antidumping laws. He is also a recognized expert in the Real Estate Settlement Procedures Act, the Fair Credit Reporting Act, and privacy issues relating to financial/insurance institutions. Clients include foreign and domestic industries in trade matters, as well as the title, and property/casualty, insurance industries.
Personal: LLB, Harvard University, 1967; AB, Columbia College, 1964

HOFFMAN, William
Davis Polk & Wardwell, Washington, DC 202 962 7000
william.hoffman@dpw.com

Recommended in International Trade
Practice Areas: Counsel in Davis Polk & Wardwell's Washington office, advising financial institutions and other clients on economic sanctions issues and certain money laundering, terrorist financing and other regulatory matters.

HOLBREICH, Curt
Howard, Rice, Nemerovski, Canady, Falk & Rabkin, San Francisco
415 434 1600
Recommended in Sport

HONAN III, William J
Holland & Knight LLP, New York
212 513 3200
bill.honan@hklaw.com
Recommended in Shipping
Practice Areas: Partner in the Litigation Section. He has extensive experience in arbitration, mediation and maritime law, especially as to maritime contracts. He is Vice-Chairman of the Documentary Committee of Intertanko, an entity that represents most of the privately owned tanker owners in the world. He is also a member of the Arbitration Committee of the ABA Section of Dispute Resolutions, the Committee on Arbitration and ADR of the International Bar Association and the Committee on Maritime Arbitration of the Maritime Law Association of the United States.

HONG, Ji Hoon
Shearman & Sterling LLP, New York
212 848 7417
jhong@shearman.com
Recommended in Aviation
Practice Areas: Partner in the Structured Finance Group at Shearman & Sterling. Experience includes structured finance transactions, capital markets transactions, sovereign debt restructurings and general corporate practice.
Career: Joined Shearman in 1986 and became Partner in 1996.
Personal: Mr Hong is a native speaker of Korean and studied at Seoul National University in 1977 before immigrating to the United States. SB in economics, Massachusetts Institute of Technology, (1983); JD, Harvard Law School (1986).

HOOPER, Chester D
Holland & Knight LLP, New York
212 513 3200
chester.hooper@hklaw.com
Recommended in Shipping
Practice Areas: Partner in the Litigation Section, practice involves the defense of vessel interests against claims for cargo damage, multimodal carriage of cargo and drafting bills of lading. Has tried numerous cargo cases on behalf of vessel interests. Was president of The Maritime Law Association of the United States from 1994-96 and is a Titulary member of the Comitè Maritime International. He is a member of the United States delegation to the United Nations Commission on International Trade Law Working Group that is drafting a

new treaty to govern the international carriage of goods that includes an international sea leg.

HORLICK, Gary N
Wilmer Cutler Pickering Hale and Dorr LLP, Washington, DC 202 663 6050
gary.horlick@wilmerhale.com
Recommended in International Trade
Practice Areas: Provides global business, investment, regulatory and negotiating advice to US and international clients. Has handled antidumping and countervailing duty cases in the US and Europe and ten other countries; GATT and WTO cases; and GATT, WTO and FTA negotiations for governments and businesses.
Prof. Memberships: ABA International Section Committee on International Trade, the Executive Council of the American Branch of the International Law Association, the Council on Foreign Relations and the Trade Policy Subcouncil of the Competitiveness Policy Council.
Personal: Yale Law School (JD 1973); Cambridge University (MA); Cambridge University (BA 1970); Dartmouth College (AB 1968).

HORNICK, Robert
Morgan, Lewis & Bockius LLP, New York 212 309 6945
rhornick@morganlewis.com
Recommended in Arbitration
Practice Areas: Robert Hornick is a Partner in the Litigation Practice. He concentrates on international commercial arbitration, with special emphasis on Asia. His arbitration work has included representation both of investors and governments, including the foreign investors in the four Amco arbitrations against the Government of Indonesia during the 1980s and early 1990s and a South Asian government in the first ICSID claim ever brought under a bilateral investment treaty. His other cases have involved inter alia disputes about power projects, international distributorships and joint ventures, engineering, procurement and construction contracts, licenses, patents and other intellectual property, acquisition agreements and services agreements.

HOROWITZ, Richard M
Thacher Proffitt & Wood LLP, New York 212 912 7828
rhorowitz@tpw.com
Recommended in Capital Markets
Practice Areas: Mr Horowitz concentrates in mortgage-backed securities. He has represented various investment banking firms as issuers and underwriters, sellers, servicers and financial guarantors, among others, in public offerings and private placements of pass-through and debt transactions. Mr Horowitz has experience in residential, multifamily and commercial loan securitizations.
Career: Mr Horowitz graduated from Hamilton College in 1983 and the University of Pennsylvania Law School in 1986.

HOUSE, Michael
McDermott Will & Emery, Washington, DC 202 756 8626
mhouse@mwe.com
Recommended in International Trade
Practice Areas: Member of International Trade Group. Focuses on import relief measures, multilateral trade disputes, and export controls. Represents multinational clients in trade actions arising under antidumping and countervailing duty laws, unfair trade and import practices laws, safeguards proceedings, GSP program and export controls. Represents clients before US Department of Commerce, US Trade Representative, US International Trade Commission, Customs and Border Protection, and other agencies. Advises and represents clients in export licensing and foreign availability proceedings before US Department of Commerce and in export transactions before the Treasury Department's Office of Foreign Assets Control. Advises clients with regard to entry, classification, valuation and other customs issues involving US Customs and Border Protection. Lead counsel in numerous international trade proceedings that have presented some of the most complex and novel substantive and procedural issues to arise.
Prof. Memberships: Member of American Bar Association and American Society of International Law.
Career: Admitted in District of Columbia, and before US Court of International Trade, US Supreme Court and US Court of Appeals for the Federal Circuit.
Personal: Earned JD (magna cum laude) from University of Texas School of Law, JD in 1981 and BFA (magna cum laude) from Southern Methodist University in 1978.

HOWARD, Nigel
Mayer, Brown, Rowe & Maw LLP, New York 212 506 2500
Recommended in Business Process Outsourcing, Technology
Please see New York for profile

HOWELL, John
Hughes & Luce LLP, Dallas
214 939 5500
Recommended in Business Process Outsourcing, Communications, Technology

HOWITT, John P
Paul, Hastings, Janofsky & Walker LLP, New York 212 318 6005
johnhowitt@paulhastings.com
Recommended in Aviation
Practice Areas: General finance practice, specializing in aircraft finance, including securitisations; leveraged and single-investor leases; operating leases; purchases, sales; loans secured by aircraft; engines, parts; enhanced equipment trust certificate financings; airline restructurings; airline bankruptcies; and manufacturer support arrangements.
Prof. Memberships: Admitted to prac-

tice in New York and California.

Career: Paul, Hastings, Janofsky & Walker (1978-present; Partner 1986-present; seconded to Nagashima & Ohno, Tokyo, Japan 1981-83).

Publications: Spoken and written on aircraft leasing, aircraft financing and operating leases.

Personal: UCLA (BA 1975, magna cum laude, Phi Beta Kappa); UCLA (JD 1978, Order of the Coif).

HUDANISH, David
Mayer, Brown, Rowe & Maw LLP, New York 212 506 2500
Recommended in Business Process Outsourcing, Technology
Please see New York for profile

HUGI, Robert F
Mayer, Brown, Rowe & Maw LLP, Chicago
312 701 7121
rhugi@mayerbrownrowe.com
Recommended in Capital Markets

Practice Areas: Has represented issuers, underwriters and conduit administrators in public and private issuances of asset-backed securities, principally backed by credit card and equipment contract receivables. Has represented the American Securitization Forum and other industry groups in commenting on various accounting and bank regulatory proposals.

Career: Joined Mayer, Brown, Rowe & Maw LLP, Chicago, 1986. Served with London office, 1989-91; Partner, 1995.

Publications: Co-author: 'Registration Under the Investment Company Act of 1940,' Securitization of Financial Assets, Prentice Hall Law & Business, 1993. 'Hidden Liens: A Trap for the Unwary,' Banking Law Journal, 1989. 'Recent Regulatory Developments Affecting Sales of Strip Participations,' Journal of International Banking Law, 1988.

Personal: University of Chicago, JD cum laude, 1986. Northwestern University, BS with highest distinction, 1980.

ISAACSON, Laurence B
McKee Nelson LLP, New York
917 777 4500
lisaacson@mckeenelson.com
Recommended in Capital Markets

Practice Areas: Corporate Partner. Concentrates practice in structured finance, particularly in complex securitisations, and the development, offering and sale of structured products. Clients include commercial and investment banks, insurance companies and other institutional investors and participants in the structured finance market. Has assisted Bear, Stearns & Co., CSFB, Deutsche Bank AG, Goldman, Sachs & Co., JP Morgan Chase, Merrill Lynch, Morgan Stanley & Co., and UBS AG in the structuring and offering of collateralized debt obligations, credit linked transactions and other structured products.

Career: Qualified in 1987. Previously he was the Head of Fried Frank's structured Finance Practice. He began his career at Milbank, Tweed, Hadley & McCloy.

Personal: Born 1963. Received JD from Duke University in 1987 and BA from Cornell University in 1984.

ISAACSON, William
Boies, Schiller & Flexner, Washington, DC 202 237 2727
Recommended in Arbitration

JACOBSON, Martin
Simpson Thacher & Bartlett LLP, New York 212 455 2000
Recommended in Aviation, Projects
Please see New York for profile

JAFFE, Marc
Latham & Watkins LLP, New York 212 906 1200
Recommended in Capital Markets

JENKINS III, Robert M
Mayer, Brown, Rowe & Maw LLP, Washington, DC 202 263 3261
rmjenkins@mayerbrown.com
Recommended in Transport

Practice Areas: Counsels and representats corporate clients and trade associations in all aspects of economic regulation, including rulemaking proceedings, agency and court litigation, appellate proceedings, and counseling; specific experience in: design, implementation, and defense of regulated rate structures, service design, investment-based valuation, cost of capital calculation, new construction, abandonments; mergers and acquisitions; claims of monopolization, predation, discrimination, foreclosure, unreasonable practices; deregulation of previously regulated entities or services.

Career: Mayer, Brown, Rowe & Maw LLP, Washington, DC, 1998 to date. Harkins Cunningham, 1992-98. Pepper, Hamilton & Scheetz, 1980-92. Covington & Burling, 1975-80. Law Clerk to the Honorable Malcolm R Wilkey, US Court of Appeals for the D.C. Circuit, 1974-75. Peace Corps Volunteer (Peru), 1969-71.

Personal: JD (honors), University of California at Berkeley, 1974; Order of the Coif; Editor, 'Law Review.' BA (honors), Harvard College,1969.

JOHNSON, David R
Vinson & Elkins LLP, Washington, DC
202 639 6706
drjohnson@velaw.com
Recommended in International Trade

Practice Areas: US export controls, including technology and defense sector export controls work. Engagements include counseling, compliance and enforcement work involving the US International Traffic in Arms Regulations (ITAR), Export Administration Regulations (EAR), and Office of Foreign Assets Control (OFAC) economic sanctions regulations. Represents US and non-US companies and individuals

in US courts and before US regulatory agencies.

Prof. Memberships: ABA (International Section; Public Contracts Section); DC Bar; Virginia State Bar.

Career: Partner.

Publications: Written and lectured extensively on US export controls and economic sanctions.

Personal: College of William & Mary (JD, 1989); University of Virginia (BA, 1986).

JOHNSON, Philip McBride
Skadden, Arps, Slate, Meagher & Flom LLP & Affiliates, Washington, DC
202 371 7340
pjohnson@skadden.com
Recommended in Capital Markets

Practice Areas: Served as Chairman of the US Commodity Futures Trading Commission in Reagan Administration, author of the dominant US legal treatise on derivatives regulation (Derivatives Regulation, 3 vol Aspen Law & Business 2004), founded the derivatives law committees for both American and International Bar Associations, served on five CFTC advisory committees, New York Stock Exchange Regulatory Advisory Committee, first public director of Futures Industry Association, heads exchange-traded derivatives law practice at Skadden with extensive international practice.

Career: LLB, Yale University, 1962 (Managing Editor, 'Yale Law Journal'); BA, Indiana University, 1959 (with honors).

JOHNSON, W Stanfield
Crowell & Moring LLP, Washington, DC
202 624 2520
wjohnson@crowell.com
Recommended in Government Contracts

Practice Areas: W Stanfield Johnson served four times as Crowell & Moring's Chairman. As a senior member of the firm's Government Contracts Group, he focuses on counseling, litigation and resolution of contract issues. He recently helped secure a victory in the 'Great Engine War', a dispute between United Technologies Corp.'s Pratt & Whitney and the Air Force over a jet engine contract awarded in the 1980s. He has negotiated settlements of numerous government claims, including cost disallowances, defective pricing, and false claims allegations. He has counseled and represented a substantial portion of the defense industry and other contractors.

Personal: Undergraduate with great distinction, Stanford University,1960; JD, Harvard Law School, 1963. He is a member of Phi Beta Kappa.

JOHNSON Jr, O Thomas
Covington & Burling, Washington, DC
202.662.5170
ojohnson@cov.com
Recommended in Arbitration

Practice Areas: Handles international

litigation, including land and maritime boundary disputes, international trade disputes, claims by and against foreign governments, and commercial arbitrations; advises clients concerning the application of the Foreign Corrupt Practices Act. Served as counsel to Eritrea in negotiating the peace treaty that ended its two-year border war with Ethiopia and in the arbitration of the underlying boundary dispute (2002). Represented Amoco in its claim against Iran before the Iran-US Claims Tribunal (1990) — which resulted in that tribunal's largest award to any claimant.

Career: Co-Chair of firm's Arbitration Practice Group; appointed by President Bush to the United States Panel of Arbitrators for ICSID arbitrations (2003); previously worked in the Office of the Legal Adviser, US Department of State (1971-75) and served as special assistant to the Legal Adviser (1973-75).

Publications: Writes and speaks frequently on matters related to international dispute resolution and the Foreign Corrupt Practices Act.

Personal: Stanford University (JD, 1971; AB, 1968).

JONES, Erika
Mayer, Brown, Rowe & Maw LLP, Washington, DC 202 263 3232
ejones@mayerbrownrowe.com
Recommended in Transport

Practice Areas: Federal regulation: represent clients before Federal regulatory agencies, including: National Highway Traffic Safety Administration, Federal Motor Carrier Safety Administration, Surface Transportation Board; Federal Communications Commission; Consumer Product Safety Commission; Environmental Protection Agency and others. Federal information law: issues related to Federal information laws, including: Freedom of Information Act; the Privacy Act; Federal Advisory Committee Act; Government in the Sunshine Act. Legislation: pending Federal legislative proposals, including strategic advice, testimony preparation, and legislative drafting. Litigation: judicial review of federal regulatory agency decisions; federal regulatory issues in product liability actions; federal preemption of state or local laws.

Career: Mayer, Brown, Rowe & Maw LLP, Washington, DC, 1989 to date; Partner, 1991. National Highway Traffic Safety Administration, US Department of Transportation, Washington, DC: Chief Counsel, 1985-89; Special Counsel to the Administrator, 1981-85. Attorney/Regulatory Policy Analyst, Office of Management and Budget, Washington, DC, 1980-81. Staff, Federal Communications Commission, Washington, DC, 1976-80.

Personal: JD, Georgetown University Law Center, 1980; Dean's List. BA (magna cum laude), Georgetown University, 1976; Phi Beta Kappa.

JOSEPH, Allan
Rogers Joseph O'Donnell & Phillips,
San Francisco 415 956 2828
*Recommended in Government
Contracts*

KADLICK, Richard F
Skadden, Arps, Slate, Meagher & Flom
LLP & Affiliates, New York
212 735 2716
rkadlick@skadden.com
Recommended in Capital Markets
Practice Areas: Represents principally
underwriters, financial institutions,
banks and borrowers in mortgage-
backed and asset-backed securities
transactions, and credit enhancers in
credit-enhanced securities issuances.
Has acted as counsel in a variety of public offerings, private placements and
transactions in which structured securities instruments have been backed by
single-family and commercial mortgage
loans, credit card receivables, under-per-
forming and non-performing assets,
home equity loan receivables, auto loan
receivables, boat loan receivables, federal
agency securities, auto and equipment
leases and various other assets.
Career: JD, Georgetown University,
1982; BA, Hamilton College, 1979
(summa cum laude; Phi Beta Kappa).

KALLSTROM, D Ward
Morgan, Lewis & Bockius LLP,
San Francisco 415 442 1308
dwkallstrom@morganlewis.com
Recommended in Litigation
Practice Areas: D Ward Kallstrom is a
Partner in the Labor and Employment
Law Practice. He focuses his practice on
employee benefits counseling and litiga-
tion. He is a nationally known labor and
employment attorney, named in 1998 by
The National Law Journal as one of the
top management side benefits litigators
in the nation. Mr Kallstrom lectures and
publishes frequently.
Prof. Memberships: Governor and
Charter Fellow, American College of
Employee Benefits Counsel. Fellow, Col-
lege of Labor and Employment Lawyers.
Member, American Employment Law
Council. Management Member, Council of the ABA Section of Labor and
Employment Law.

KANTER, Stacy J
Skadden, Arps, Slate, Meagher & Flom
LLP & Affiliates, New York
212 735 3497
skanter@skadden.com
Recommended in Capital Markets
Practice Areas: Represents corporate
clients and investment banks in a variety
of transactions, including public and
private offerings of equity and debt
securities, initial public offerings,
exchange offers, consent solicitations,
restructurings and mergers and acquisitions. Counsels corporate clients on an
ongoing basis, assisting with the review
and preparation of SEC filings.
Career: JD, Brooklyn Law School, 1984

(cum laude; Managing Editor, Brooklyn
Law Review); BS, State University of
New York at Albany, 1979 (magna cum
laude).

KANTOR, Michael
Mayer, Brown, Rowe & Maw LLP,
Washington, DC
202 263 3295
mkantor@mayerbrownrowe.com
Recommended in International Trade
Practice Areas: Corporate and financial international transactions. Specializes in: market access issues; expanding
client activities in foreign markets
through trade, direct investment, joint
ventures and strategic business alliances.
Former Secretary of Commerce and US
Trade Representative in Clinton Administration.
Career: Mayer, Brown, Rowe & Maw
LLP, Washington, 1997-present; Partner,
1997. Senior Advisor, Morgan Stanley &
Co., 1997-present. Distinguished Lecturer, Annenberg School of Communications, University of Southern California, 1997-present. US Secretary of Commerce, 1996-97. US Trade Representa-
tive, Washington, 1993-96. Manatt,
Phelps, Phillips & Kantor, Los Angeles,
1976-93.
Personal: JD, Georgetown University,
1968. BA, Vanderbilt University, 1961.
Directorships: Board Member, CB
Richard Ellis; International Advisory
Board, Fleishman-Hillard; Board Mem-
ber, ING Americas; Korea First Bank;
National Association of Public Interest
Lawyers. Order of the Southern Cross
Award by The Government of Brazil,
2001. William O. Douglas Award by the
Constitutional Rights Foundation.
Thomas Jefferson Distinguished Public
Service Medal from the Center for the
Study of the Presidency. The Albert
Schweitzer Leadership Award from the
Hugh O'Brien Youth Foundation. Elihu
Root Distinguished Lecturer, Council
on Foreign Relations. International
Commercial Diplomacy Project,
Trustee. Council on Foreign Relations,
Member. Clinton/Gore '92 Campaign,
National Chair, 1991-92. Legal Services
Corporation, Board Member, 1978-81.

KAPLAN, Cathy
Sidley Austin Brown & Wood LLP,
New York 212 839 5531
ckaplan@sidley.com
Recommended in Capital Markets
Practice Areas: Cathy Kaplan serves as
Co-Head of the New York office's Securitization Practice, is a member of the
firm's Executive Committee and is Co-
Chair of the firm's Finance Committee.
Ms Kaplan practice focuses on asset
backed securitizations, with particular
concentration on cross border transactions, CLOs and CDOs. Developed the
first receivables program backed by
healthcare receivables. Ms Kaplan represents numerous issuers and underwriters on structured finance transactions

involving many types of receivables,
including mobile home receivables, consumer loan receivables and trade receivables, and also works on international
securitizations involving export receivables, natural resource assets and trade
receivables in Asia, Europe and Latin
America.
Career: Columbia University School of
Law, JD, 1977; Yale University, BA, 1974.
Bar Admission: New York, 1978.

KAPLAN, Gilbert
King & Spalding LLP, Washington, DC
202 661 7981
gkaplan@kslaw.com
Recommended in International Trade
Practice Areas: International trade and
trade policy issues focusing on
antidumping (price discrimination),
countervailing duties (subsidies), Section 337, (intellectual property infringement), and other trade matters. Substantial experience with international
transactions, market access, trade negotiation, export matters, and legislative
and trade policy matters. Extensive work
in connection with WTO matters.
Prof. Memberships: Massachusetts Bar
Association; District of Colombia Bar
Association.
Personal: BA, Harvard College, 1973;
JD, Harvard Law School, 1977.

KAPLAN, H Deen
Hogan & Hartson LLP, Washington, DC
202 637 5799
hdkaplan@hhlaw.com
Recommended in International Trade
Practice Areas: Deen Kaplan's areas of
concentration include World Trade
Organization policy and dispute resolution, subsidy law policy, homeland security and trade, antidumping and countervailing duty litigation, customs, specialized trade sector analysis, immigration, and trade in technology products.
Prof. Memberships: Member, International Law & Practice Section, American
Bar Association.
Career: Prior to joining Hogan & Hartson, Deen worked with a series of international non-profits, and served as an
executive with computer hardware, software development and consulting businesses. He lectures regularly on international trade issues and teaches international trade law at the University of
Maryland School of Law as a member of
the adjunct faculty.
Publications: Leibowitz, Lewis E.,
Chandri Navarro-Bowman, Craig A.
Lewis, Teresa M. Polino, H. Deen
Kaplan, Erika L. Moritsugu. 'World Customs Organization Commits to Global
Trade Security and Facilitation Standards', Customs & International Trade
Update, Hogan & Hartson L.L.P.
(12/20/04). Archibald, Jeanne S. and
Kaplan, H. Deen. 'Final Rule: Advance
Electronic Presentation of Cargo Mani-
fest Information', International Trade
and US Homeland Security Update,

Hogan & Hartson L.L.P. (12/12/03)
Personal: Georgetown University Law
Center (JD, magna cum laude, Order of
the Coif). Member, District of Columbia and Virginia Bars.

KATZ, Donald
Miller, Canfield, Paddock and Stone,
P.L.C., Detroit 313 963 6420
Recommended in Aviation

KEANE, Paul
Cichanowicz, Callan, Keane, Vengrow &
Textor LLP, New York 212 344 7042
Recommended in Shipping

KEESAL Jr, Samuel
Keesal Young & Logan PC, Long Beach
562 436 2000
Recommended in Shipping

KEINER Jr, R Bruce
Crowell & Moring LLP, Washington, DC
202 624 2615
rbkeiner@crowell.com
Recommended in Aviation
Practice Areas: Bruce Keiner is Chair
of Crowell & Moring's Aviation Group.
Since 1970, his practice has focused on
domestic and international aviation
matters. He advises clients on matters
involving international passenger and
cargo aviation, fares and rates, regulation of air freight forwarders, airline
charters, enforcement issues, and control relationships involving the airline
industry.
Personal: Bachelor of Laws, University
of Virginia Law School, Editorial Board,
Virginia Journal of International Law,
1966-67; BA, Dickinson College, 1964.

KENNEDY, Donald
Carter Ledyard & Milburn LLP,
New York 212 732 3200
Recommended in Shipping

KERR, John
Simpson Thacher & Bartlett LLP,
New York 212 455 2000
jkerr@stblaw.com
Recommended in Arbitration
Practice Areas: Partner, member of
Litigation Department and Head of
Arbitration Group. Advises clients in
general litigation before the state courts
of New York, the federal courts nation-
wide and the US Supreme Court
(recently, New Jersey v New York).
Advises clients in arbitrations, ICC,
AAA, UNCITRAL, LCIA, NAI and CPR
cases, and serves as arbitrator.
Prof. Memberships: American Arbitra-
tion Association (director); American
Bar Association (Litigation Section and
International Litigation Committee; for-
mer Chair, Jury Trials Committee);
International Bar Association (Business
Section and Arbitration/ADR Commit-
tees), Federal Bar Council, Association
of the Bar of the City of New York and
American Foreign Law Association
(director); Member, Columbia Law
School Board of Visitors.
Career: Joined firm 1978; became Part-

ner 1983. Law Clerk to Honourable Gus J Solomon, US District Court (District of Oregon).

Publications: Author, 'Court Jurisdiction and Arbitration over Misrepresentation in US Securities Transactions' (Sweet & Maxwell, London, 1999); 'A Chart Comparing International Commercial Arbitration Rules', published in collaboration with Parker School of Comparative Law, Columbia Law School (Juris Publishing, 1998; 2d ed 2003).

Personal: Boston College (AB, 1972, summa cum laude); Columbia Law School (JD, 1976), (Stone Scholar; International Fellow; National Scholar (7th Circuit); editor in chief, 'Columbia Journal of Environmental Law').

KESSLER, Jeffrey L
Dewey Ballantine LLP, New York
212 259 8000
Recommended in Antitrust, Sport
Please see New York for profile

KILB, Brian
Gibson, Dunn & Crutcher LLP,
Los Angeles 310 551 8871
bkilb@gibsondunn.com
Recommended in Banking & Finance,
Capital Markets

Practice Areas: Partner in the firm's Global Finance Group. Mr Kilb's practice includes representation of private equity groups and other borrowers, and banks and other capital sources, in leveraged acquisition financings and other secured and unsecured senior, mezzanine and subordinated lending transactions, second lien financings, asset securitizations and other financing transactions, and credit and equity derivatives transactions. Mr Kilb also represents issuers and underwriters in debt capital markets transactions. Mr Kilb's finance practice covers many industries, including gaming, media and entertainment, lodging and real estate.

Personal: JD, Harvard Law School, 1983.

KIMBALL, George
Arnold & Porter LLP, Los Angeles
213 243 4000
Recommended in Business Process
Outsourcing, IT Outsourcing
Please see California for profile

KIMBALL, John D
Healy & Baillie LLP, New York
212 709 9241
jkimball@healy.com
Recommended in Shipping

Practice Areas: Chairman. Main area of work is maritime law, including casualties, charterparty disputes, insurance, creditors rights, insolvency. Adjunct professor of Law at NYU Law School (1986-present).

Prof. Memberships: Maritime Law Association of the United States; Fellow of the American Bar Association; Federal Bar Council.

Career: Joined Healy & Baillie in 1975. Graduate of Duke University (BA 1971); Georgetown University Law School (1975).

Publications: Co-author, 'Time Charters' (5th ed. 2003); co-author, 'Voyage Charters' (2d ed. 2001); co-author, 'The Law of Salvage, 3A Benedict on Admiralty' (2003).

KIMMELMAN, Louis
O'Melveny & Myers LLP, New York
212 408 2400
Recommended in Arbitration

KING, Kenton J
Skadden, Arps, Slate, Meagher & Flom
LLP & Affiliates, Palo Alto
650 470 4530
kking@skadden.com
Recommended in Capital Markets,
Corporate/M&A

Practice Areas: Head of Skadden's Palo Alto and San Francisco offices and Corporate Group in the Bay Area. Has extensive experience in a broad range of corporate and securities law matters, including US and cross-border M&A, joint ventures, investment and capital markets transactions, and restructurings. Has worked on several high-profile transactions, including representing Compaq Computer Corporation in several transactions, including its $25 billion merger with Hewlett-Packard Company, its transfer of proprietary Alpha microprocessor technology to Intel Corporation, and its $2.3 billion sale of Alta Vista Comapny to CMGI, Inc.; Ascend Communications, Inc. in its $20 billion acquisition by Lucent Technologies, Inc.; and Yahoo! Inc. in its $436 million unsolicited takeover proposal for HotJobs.com, Ltd, its $1.6 billion acquisition of Overture Services, Inc. and its $750 million zero coupon convertible note offering.

Career: JD, Boalt Hall School of Law at the University of California at Berkeley, 1987 (Editor in Chief, California Law Review; Order of the Coif); BA, Stanford University, 1977.

KIRCHHOEFER, Gregg
Kirkland & Ellis LLP, Chicago
312 861 2000
Recommended in Business Process
Outsourcing, Technology
Please see Illinois for profile

KLEIN, Allen
Latham & Watkins LLP,
Washington, DC 202 637 2200
Recommended in Business Process
Outsourcing

KLEPPER, Martin
Skadden, Arps, Slate, Meagher & Flom
LLP & Affiliates, Washington, DC
202 371 7000
Recommended in Projects
Please see District of Columbia for
profile

KORFF, Phyllis G
Skadden, Arps, Slate, Meagher & Flom
LLP & Affiliates, New York
212 735 2694
pkorff@skadden.com
Recommended in Capital Markets

Practice Areas: Represents US and international issuers and investment banks in a variety of financing matters. Has worked on equity and debt financings, both investment grade and high-yield, in the US and international markets. Has worked on numerous initial public offerings and other offerings registered with the Securities and Exchange Commission, as well as offerings exempt from SEC registration pursuant to Rule 144A and Regulation S. Has extensive experience in representing Israeli and Canadian companies.

Career: JD, New York University School of Law, 1981 (Notes Editor, NY University Law Review); EdM, Boston University, 1967; BA, Brooklyn College, 1964.

KRAULAND, Edward
Steptoe & Johnson LLP,
Washington, DC 202 429 8083
ekrauland@steptoe.com
Recommended in International Trade

Practice Areas: Partner in Steptoe & Johnson LLP's Washington office. 23 years of experience. Advises on requirements in export control, economic sanctions, anticorruption, counter money laundering, and foreign investment/national security (NISPOM) restrictions in the US (transactions, corporate structures, mergers and acquisitions, and intra-corporate supply relationships). Handles internal investigations, enforcement actions by US government authorities, and compliance programs enhancements. Represents US and non-US multinationals, businesses, and individuals in aerospace and defense, energy, oil field services, information management, electronics, telecommunications, consumer products, e-commerce, engineering, professional services, chemicals, industrial equipment, and financial services.

Personal: JD, University of Michigan, 1980; AB, Princeton University, 1976.

KRAVITT, Jason H P
Mayer, Brown, Rowe & Maw LLP,
New York 212 262 2622
jkravitt@mayerbrownrowe.com
Recommended in Capital Markets

Practice Areas: Founder of the firm's Securitisation Practice and Senior Partner in that practice. Variety of finance and regulatory related practices. Represents industry groups with regard to securitisation regulatory initiatives, including the Bank for International Settlements' risk-based capital consultative papers, the FFIEC's risk-based capital projects, FASB's Standards on Securitization and Consolidation, SEC initiatives.

Prof. Memberships: Adjunct professor of Law at Northwestern University Law

School, an adjunct professor of Finance at the Kellogg Graduate School of Management of Northwestern University, and a Fellow in the American College of Commercial Finance Lawyers. One of three founding Members, secretary, and Chair of Legal, Regulatory, Accounting and Tax Committee, American Securitization Forum and Executive Committee Member, European Securization Forum.

Career: Joined Mayer, Brown, Rowe & Maw LLP, 1973; became Partner, 1979. Co-Chairman of the firm in 1998-2001.

Publications: Editor of, and contributing author to, 'Securitization of Financial Assets', Aspen Law & Business, 1996 (2nd Ed).

Personal: Born 19 January 1948. Phi Beta Kappa graduate of The Johns Hopkins University (member of the Advisory Board to the Dean of School of Arts & Sciences). JD, cum laude, Harvard Law School, 1972; diploma in comparative law, Cambridge University, 1973. Chairman, The Cameron Kravitt Foundation.

KROUSE Jr, George R
Simpson Thacher & Bartlett LLP,
New York 212 455 2730
gkrouse@stblaw.com
Recommended in Capital Markets

Practice Areas: A Partner at Simpson Thacher & Bartlett LLP, specialising in corporate, securities law and mergers and acquisitions. From 1991 through 2002, served as Head of the firm's Corporate Department. Also a member of the Executive Committee, the firm's management body, and the firm's senior administrative partner. Has principal responsibility for some of the firm's most important client relationships, including Lehman Brothers, which the firm represents as issuer of its own securities, underwriter or placement agent for offerings in the domestic and international capital markets, financial adviser and principal in merchant banking transactions.

Prof. Memberships: Association of the Bar of the City of New York; the New York State and American Bar Associations.

Career: Has been a member of the firm since 1979. Received AB degree cum laude from Brown University in 1967 and graduated with distinction in 1970 from Duke University School of Law, where he was articles editor of the 'Duke Law Journal' and elected to Order of the Coif. Admitted to practise law in New York in 1971.

KUDENHOLDT, Stephen S
Thacher Proffitt & Wood LLP, New York
212 912 7450
skudenholdt@tpw.com
Recommended in Capital Markets

Practice Areas: Mr Kudenholdt serves as Chairman of the firm's Structured Finance Practice Group. His practice includes residential and commercial mortgage-backed securities, and other asset-related securities (ABS), primarily focusing on residential mortgage loan securitization as well as resecuritization transactions involving various classes of MBS. He has helped develop many transaction structures and formats that have become industry standards, including shifting interest subordination techniques. He represents issuers, underwriters, loan sellers and other entities in public offerings and private placements and has represented several major investment banks in a variety of mortgage securitization transactions, including subprime and home equity loans, commercial and multifamily mortgage loan securitizations and in connection with new product and structure development and joint ventures.

KUNZ, C Thomas
Skadden, Arps, Slate, Meagher & Flom LLP & Affiliates, New York
212 735 3240
ckunz@skadden.com
Recommended in Capital Markets
Practice Areas: Represents underwriters, issuers, depository institutions and credit enhancers in asset-backed securities transactions and credit-enhanced securities issuances. Counsels in public offerings and private placement transactions involving the issuance of pass-through certificates, asset-backed notes and bonds, commercial paper notes and participation certificates. Worked on transactions in which structured finance techniques were utilized to enable non-traditional financings to access the capital markets.
Career: JD, Cornell University, 1975 (magna cum laude; Order of the Coif; Phi Kappa Phi; Editor, Cornell Law Review); BA, Colgate University, 1972 (magna cum laude; Phi Beta Kappa).

LAMBERT, LeRoy
Healy & Baillie LLP, New York
212 709 9274
llambert@healy.com
Recommended in Shipping
Practice Areas: Maritime (charter parties, bills of lading, liens, arrests, attachments); general litigation; arbitration; international law; bankruptcy.
Prof. Memberships: American Bar Association, New York State Bar Association, Maritime Law Association of the United States.
Career: Joined Healy & Baillie 1984; Partner 1991. Member, Executive Committee, 2001-present.
Publications: Co-author, 'Voyage Charters' (2d ed 2001); 'Damages Arising from Breach of Contract, Loss of Revenue, and 'Indirect' Damages', 72 'Tulane Law Review' 759 (1997), among others.
Personal: Born 13 April 1954. JD, 1983, Tulane University School of Law; University of Tuebingen, Germany, 1976-78; BA, Louisiana State University, 1976. Foreign language: German.

LAMM, Carolyn
White & Case LLP, Washington, DC
202 626 3605
clamm@whitecase.com
Recommended in Arbitration
Practice Areas: Concentrates on international: arbitration (counsel or arbitrator) or litigation, including ICSID, AAA, ICC and Stockholm chamber arbitration. Lead counsel representing foreign corporations and sovereigns. Frequent speaker on international litigation and arbitration issues.
Prof. Memberships: ABA, Board of Governors; DC Bar, President (1997-98); US Secretary of State's Advisory Committee on Private International Law; Secretary of State's working group on proposed Hague Convention on Jurisdiction and the Enforcement of Judgements; American College of Trial Lawyers, Fellow; American Law Institute, Council Member; AAA Executive Committee; NAFTA 2022 Committee; ICSID Panel of Arbitrators.

LECCESE, Joseph M
Proskauer Rose LLP, New York
212 969 3238
jleccese@proskauer.com
Recommended in Sport
Practice Areas: A Partner in Proskauer Rose LLP's Corporate Department, he has a broad-based corporate practice with particular emphasis on the representation of professional sports leagues and teams and companies engaged in various media and communications businesses including numerous matters for the National Basketball Association, the National Hockey League, and ATP Tour, as well as a number of individual sports teams and other sports-related entities, including the NBA's recently completed $1 billion League-wide credit facility; the NBA's expansion in 2002 to Charlotte; North Carolina, and the related arena lease and development negotiations; the lease, development and financing of the Philadelphia Eagles' new football-based stadium; the ATP Tour's $1.2 billion transaction with ISL relating to the worldwide television and marketing rights to the ATP World Championships and Super 9 Tournaments; the formation and structuring of the Women's National Basketball Association. His media and communications experience includes numerous acquisitions, dispositions and private and public financings relating to cable television systems, network and independent television stations, radio stations, magazines and other publishing, and trade shows.
Personal: University of Virginia Law School, JD, 1985 Member, Virginia Law Review, 1983-85. Georgetown University, BA, cum laude, 1982.

LEFKOWITZ, David
Weil, Gotshal & Manges LLP, New York
212 310 8850
david.lefkowitz@weil.com
Recommended in Capital Markets
Practice Areas: Mr Lefkowitz has a diverse corporate finance practice representing issuers and investment banks in a variety of public and private equity and debt offerings and bridge financings.
Career: He is Co-Head of the Global Capital Markets Practice and has represented issuers and investment banks in offerings with aggregate proceeds in excess of $20 billion. He led GE's representation in the spin-off of its life and mortgage insurance business (now known as Genworth Financial) in a $2.8 billion IPO - the largest IPO of a US company since 2002. His representation of GE in this transaction earned him selection as a top 'Dealmaker of the Year' for 2004 by The American Lawyer. Mr Lefkowitz frequently represents Citigroup in a wide range of high-yield and other leveraged finance transactions, including a $1.4 billion high-yield offering for Novelis Inc. and a $400 million high-yield offering for Sanmina –SCI, and has represented a variety of large and small issuers across a broad range of industries. IPO Vital Signs ranked him the #1 IPO lawyer in 2004, based on total offering amount. At age 35, he was selected by The National Law Journal for its '40 Under Forty' listing of 40 rising stars in the law under age 40. In 1996, Mr. Lefkowitz moved to London to help open the firm's office there and lead its US.Securities Practice. He was active in the management and development of that office as it grew to more than 85 US and English lawyers in just over three years. He returned to the New York office and its Capital Markets practice in 1999.
Personal: Georgetown University Law Center, JD; Northwestern University, BS.

LEIBOWITZ, Lewis E
Hogan & Hartson LLP, Washington, DC
202 637 5638
leleibowitz@hhlaw.com
Recommended in International Trade
Practice Areas: Lewis Leibowitz practices in the areas of international trade law, customs law and international commercial transactions. He represents clients before all agencies and courts dealing with international trade matters, including the Department of Commerce, the office of the US Trade Representative, the International Trade Commission, and US Customs and Border Protection, the Court of International Trade and the Court of Appeals for the Federal Circuit.
Prof. Memberships: Board Member, Consumers for World Trade; Counsel, Consuming Industries Trade Action Coalition; Member, National Foreign Trade Council; Member, American Association of Exporters and Importers; Customs and International Trade Bar Association; National Association of Foreign Trade Zones.
Career: As a leading attorney in trade law matters under United States and international law, Lewis advises and assists clients in actual and potential antidumping and countervailing duty proceedings. In addition, he works with clients on proceedings under Section 201 and 301 of the Trade Act of 1974 and Section 337 of the Tariff Act of 1930. He is also active in dispute settlement activities involving the World Trade Organization (WTO), advising clients in private industry and government on all these matters. Lewis specializes in representing downstream industries in trade cases.
Publications: 'WTO Negotiations on Rules: Prospects for Reform 'From the Centre", 'The World Trade Brief' (9/1/2003).
Personal: University of Maryland School of Law (JD, with honors, Order of the Coif). He is admitted to practice before the Court of International Trade.

LEONG, Alvin
Milbank, Tweed, Hadley & McCloy, New York 212 530 5000
Recommended in Aviation

LEVINE, David J
McDermott Will & Emery, Washington, DC 202 756 8153
dlevine@mwe.com
Recommended in International Trade
Practice Areas: Partner in the International Trade Group. Practices before international trade organizations, federal agencies and courts regarding international trade and related regulatory matters. Has represented a variety of industries in trade proceedings, including antidumping and countervailing duty cases and related federal appellate litigation, Section 301 cases involving foreign unfair trade practices, NAFTA procedures, World Trade Organization disputes, legislative and rulemaking proceedings, and multilateral and bilateral trade negotiations. Counsels clients on customs, export controls, trade sanctions, US Foreign Corrupt Practices Act, antiboycott, business immigration (visa) matters, and related trade laws and procedures.
Prof. Memberships: Serves on the Advisory Board of the Washington University Global Studies Law Review. Listed on the US NAFTA Chapter 19 Roster of prospective panelists who hear appeals of final antidumping and countervailing duty determinations by the US, Canada and Mexico.
Career: Prior to joining McDermott, served as international trade analyst with US Department of Commerce and before working at the Commerce Department, he was a law clerk in the Office of the US Trade Representative.
Personal: Earned JD in 1985 from Washington University School of Law.

Earned MA in 1985 from University of Denver Graduate School of International Studies, and BA from Colorado College.

LEVY, Charles S
Wilmer Cutler Pickering Hale and Dorr LLP, Washington, DC 202 663 6400
charles.levy@wilmerhale.com
Recommended in International Trade
Practice Areas: Advises corporations and business associations on international trade, financial and investment issues, including the Business Roundtable, the Coalition of Service Industry/Financial Services Group, the Intellectual Property Committee, Burlington Industries, and the Information Technology Industry Council (ITIC). Was Counsel to USA*NAFTA and GATT*NOW, the national coalitions that successfully supported implementation of NAFTA and the Uruguay Round of Multilateral Trade Agreements by the Congress.
Prof. Memberships: Board of directors of Transparency International USA, a non-governmental organization dedicated to combating bribery and corruption in international business transactions.
Personal: George Washington University Law School (JD 1970); Boston College (BA 1967).

LEVY, Gregg
Covington & Burling, Washington, DC 202 662 5292
glevy@cov.com
Recommended in Sport
Practice Areas: Sports law and Litigation. Emphasis on antitrust and competition-related issues; extensive experience in complex, multi-party litigation, including trial-level, appellate, and arbitral proceedings; broad expertise with respect to legal issues affecting amateur and professional sports leagues. Co-Chair of Covington's Litigation Group.
Prof. Memberships: CPR Institute's Panel of Distinguished Neutrals.
Career: Principal outside counsel for the National Football League for over a decade. Lead role in each of the major trial and appellate victories for the NFL during that period, including: Brown v Pro-Football, Inc., 518 US 231 (1996); Clarett v National Football League, 369 F.3d 124 (2d Cir. 2004); VKK Corp. v National Football League, 244 F.3d 114 (2d Cir. 2001); St. Louis Convention & Visitors Comm'n v NFL, 154 F.3d 851 (8th Cir. 1998); Oakland Raiders v National Football League, No. B163115 (Cal. Ct. App. Feb. 23, 2005). See also Jung v American Association of Medical Colleges, 2004 US Dist. LEXIS 16099 (D.D.C. Aug. 12, 2004) (securing dismissal of class action antitrust claims against America's leading medical schools).
Personal: Harvard Law School (JD, 1977); Harvard College (AB, 1974).

LICHTENBAUM, Greta
O'Melveny & Myers LLP, Washington, DC 202 383 5300
Recommended in International Trade

LIGHTHIZER, Robert E
Skadden, Arps, Slate, Meagher & Flom LLP & Affiliates, Washington, DC 202 371 7770
rlighthi@skadden.com
Recommended in International Trade
Practice Areas: Leads the firm's International Trade Department. Clients include large US corporations and coalitions. Represents heavy manufacturing, agricultural and high-tech companies, as well as financial services institutions. Has been lead counsel in scores of antidumping and countervailing duty cases during the last several years and is currently active in numerous pending cases and administrative reviews. Also focuses on market-opening trade actions on behalf of US companies seeking access to foreign markets.
Career: JD, Georgetown University Law Center, 1973; BA, Georgetown University, 1969.

LINDSEY, David
Clifford Chance US LLP, New York 212 878 8019
david.lindsey@cliffordchance.com
Recommended in Arbitration
Practice Areas: New York Partner and leader of the Clifford Chance International Arbitration group in the Americas. Currently represents clients in an ICSID arbitration against Argentina, an arbitration seated in India against a state-owned utility, and an ICDR New York arbitration regarding tax issues in Trinidad. Focus is international commercial contracts, power/energy projects, and reinsurance in arbitrations under the rules of the major international arbitral institutions and ad hoc rules. Experienced in US federal and state court litigation. Frequent lecturer and co-editor/author of International Arbitration in Latin America (Kluwer, December 2002). Co-Chair, Dispute Resolution Interest Group of ASIL.

LITTLE, Kathleen C
Vinson & Elkins LLP, Washington, DC 202 639 6663
klittle@velaw.com
Recommended in International Trade
Practice Areas: Export controls (ITAR and EAR), OFAC sanctions, FCPA, Foreign Military Sales and Foreign Military Financed Direct Sales, Government Contracts. Work includes criminal and civil enforcement matters, compliance, counseling, training and audits. Represents both domestic and foreign companies.
Prof. Memberships: ABA, SIA.
Career: Partner since 1988.
Publications: Has lectured and written extensively on Export Controls and related topics.

LITWIN, Stuart M
Mayer, Brown, Rowe & Maw LLP, Chicago 312 701 7373
slitwin@mayerbrownrowe.com
Recommended in Capital Markets
Practice Areas: Co-Head of firm's global Securitization Group. Among leading lawyers in representing originators, investment banks, ABCP conduit sponsors, commercial banks and investors in structuring, negotiating and documenting US and international asset-backed and other securities transactions. Emphasis on auto loan, auto lease, equipment lease, cross border, synthetic risk transfer and transactions in which auto and equipment finance, leasing, structured finance and the capital markets come together. Substantial experience representing lessees, equity investors and debt investors in leveraged and synthetic lease transactions. Experienced in securitization of virtually all asset types. Recognized expert in the securitization and financing of equipment and auto leases, auto loans, dealer floorplan receivables, synthetic risk transfers and the creation of asset-backed securities for money market funds.
Prof. Memberships: Former Chairman of the Securities Law Committee of the Chicago Bar Association.
Career: Mayer, Brown, Rowe & Maw LLP, 1985-present; Partner, 1994.
Publications: Frequent lecturer on securitization. Author: 'Equipment and Auto Lease Financing: Securitization, Leveraged Leasing and Titling Trusts', Aspen Law and Business.
Personal: JD, University of Chicago Law School. MBA, University of Chicago Graduate School of Business. Certified Public Accountant.

LOBRANO, John D
Simpson Thacher & Bartlett LLP, New York 212 455 2890
jlobrano@stblaw.com
Recommended in Capital Markets
Practice Areas: A Partner in the firm's Corporate Department and Member of the Capital Markets and Mergers and Acquisitions Practice Groups. Regularly represents investment banking clients, such as JP Morgan Securities, Lehman Brothers and Bear Stearns, and issuers in domestic and international securities offerings, with a particular specialization in offerings of convertible securities and high yield debt securities. These activities are complemented by his liability management practice, representing dealer managers and issuers in tender offers and consent solicitations, as well as merger and acquisition representations.
Prof. Memberships: Association of the Bar of the City of New York, New York Bar Association, American Bar Association, International Bar Association.
Career: Member of the firm since 1990. A member of the firm's International Practice Group and practiced in the firm's London office for seven years. He

has advised on securities offerings and corporate matters all over the world.
Personal: Graduate of New York University School of Law (JD, 1983) and Amherst College (BA, magna cum laude, 1979).

LOFTIS, James
Vinson & Elkins LLP, Houston 713 758 1024
jloftis@velaw.com
Recommended in Arbitration
Practice Areas: Arbitration of international disputes, particularly state contracts, investment agreements, foreign investment laws and investment treaties. Has handled arbitrations under all major arbitration rules and in most major arbitral venues. Represents clients in a broad range of areas, including oil and gas and energy, construction, technology, environment, and finance.
Prof. Memberships: ICC Commission on Arbitration; LCIA; Chartered Institute of Arbitrators; Vice-Chair, International Law Section, Texas Bar.
Career: Partner since 2000. Senior Legal Officer, Energy Sector Panel, UN Compensation Commission, Geneva, 1997-2000.
Publications: Co-Editor, International Litigation Quarterly; "Advocacy Before International Claims Resolution Bodies", The Art of Advocacy in International Arbitration.

LOFTUS, Michael
Slover & Loftus, Washington, DC 202 347 7170
Recommended in Transport

MABERRY, John Scott
Fulbright & Jaworski LLP, Washington, DC 202 662 4693
smaberry@fulbright.com
Recommended in International Trade
Practice Areas: International law; international trade; sanctions; export controls; anti-bribery; white collar crime; and government investigations and enforcement.
Prof. Memberships: New York, District of Columbia, and American Bar Associations; ABA Export Controls & Economic Sanctions Committee, Chairman.
Career: J Scott Maberry is a Partner in Fulbright's International Law Department. Prior to entering private practice he was Law Clerk to Arlin M Adams, US Independent Counsel.
Personal: BS - Northwestern University (1988); MS - Georgetown University (1993); JD - Georgetown University (1993).

MADDEN, Thomas
Venable LLP, Washington, DC 202 962 4800
Recommended in Government Contracts

MADSEN, Marcia
Mayer, Brown, Rowe & Maw LLP, Washington, DC 202 263 3274
mgmadsen@mayerbrownrowe.com
Recommended in Government Contracts

Practice Areas: Advises on government contract formation, teaming and strategic alliances, contract and subcontract negotiations, performance disputes, audits, terminations, cost accounting and allowability, technical data rights and trade secrets, and fraud/false claims investigations. Litigates bid protests and claims and disputes before the GAO, the Boards of Contract Appeals, the Court of Federal Claims, and other courts. Numerous ADR and mediation proceedings. Areas of concentration: aerospace and defense contracts, systems integration, information systems and telecommunications contracts, health care and bio-technology, homeland security contracts; environmental remediation, and research and development contracts.

Prof. Memberships: Chair, Federalist Society Government Contracts Committee; Past Chair, ABA Section of Public Contract Law; Past President, Board of Contract Appeals Bar Association.

Career: Mayer, Brown, Rowe & Maw LLP, Washington, DC, 2001 to date (Chair, Homeland Security Practice Group). Miller & Chevalier, 1996-2001 (Chair, Government Contracts Department). Morgan, Lewis & Bockius, 1980-96.

Publications: Published numerous articles on government contracts issues in Government Contract Litigation Reporter, BNA Federal Contracts, West Briefing Papers Series, and many similar publications.

Personal: JD, American University, Washington College of Law, 1976. LLM, Georgetown University Law Center, 1980. BA, University of Utah, 1972.

MALLOW, Matthew J
Skadden, Arps, Slate, Meagher & Flom LLP & Affiliates, New York
212 735 3930
mmallow@skadden.com
Recommended in Capital Markets
Practice Areas: Head of firm's Corporate Finance Department. Represents investment banks, issuers and corporations in a variety of financing matters, including initial public offerings and insurance company offerings.
Prof. Memberships: Board of Trustees, Brown University, Member (1990-present), Treasurer (1999-present).
Career: LLM, New York University, 1968; LLB, New York University, 1967; AB, Brown University, 1964.

MANGAN, John J
Skadden, Arps, Slate, Meagher & Flom LLP & Affiliates, Washington, DC
202 371 7775
jmangan@skadden.com
Recommended in International Trade
Practice Areas: Focuses on antidumping and countervailing duty matters. A part of his practice has been in the legislative arena. Has testified before key congressional committees, including the Senate Finance Committee and the Sen-

ate Judiciary Committee, on various trade bills. Other areas of his practice include customs matters, Section 301 cases and the Generalized System of Preferences program. Has represented respondents in antidumping proceedings in Europe and in Mexico.
Career: JD, Cornell University, 1967; B Civil Eng., Cornell University, 1964.

MARKS, Allan
Milbank, Tweed, Hadley & McCloy, Los Angeles 213 892 4000
Recommended in Projects, Transport

MARTIN, John
Baker Botts LLP, Dallas
214 953 6500
Recommended in Business Process Outsourcing, Communications, Technology
Please see Texas for profile

MARTIN, Keith
Chadbourne & Parke LLP, Washington, DC 202 974 5600
Recommended in Projects
Please see District of Columbia for profile

MARTIN, Renwick
Sidley Austin Brown & Wood LLP, New York 212 839 5319
rmartin@sidley.com
Recommended in Capital Markets
Practice Areas: Renwick D Martin is Co-Head of the global Securitisation Practice and a member of the firm's Management and Executive Committees. Mr Martin has worked in the mortgage-backed area since 1977 when he participated in the Bank of America pass-through transaction, which was the first publicly-offered conventional pass-through transaction. Since 1984, Mr Martin has concentrated on mortgage-backed and asset-backed financings of all types.
Career: Harvard Law School, JD, 1972; Stanford University, AB, 1969. Bar Admission: New York, 1974

MARTINEZ-FRAGA, Pedro J
Greenberg Traurig LLP, Miami
305 579 0595
martinep@gtlaw.com
Recommended in Arbitration
Practice Areas: International litigation.
Prof. Memberships: ICC approved arbitrator; Member, Board of Directors of Editorial Cubana, Inc.; Member, The Florida Bar Federal Court Practice Committee; Member, Consultative Group on ALI/Unidroit working group: Principles and Rules of Transnational Civil Procedure; Adjunct Professor of Law, University of Miami School of Law, International Litigation and International Arbitration (2002-04).
Publications: Co-author, 'Forum Non Conveniens and the Foreign Forum: a Defense Perspective,' 35 U. Miami Inter-Am. L. Rev. 1 (2004); author/editor, Chapter 2, 'Organization and Development of the Case,' Florida Civil Practice

Before Trial; author/editor, Chapter on Venue, Florida Civil Practice Before Trial.

MASUR, Daniel A
Mayer, Brown, Rowe & Maw LLP, Washington, DC 202 263 3000
Recommended in Business Process Outsourcing, IT Outsourcing
Please see District of Columbia for profile

MATHEWS, Daniel A
Orrick, Herrington & Sutcliffe, New York
212 506 5050
dmathews@orrick.com
Recommended in Transport
Practice Areas: Represents lenders, developers and investors in the development, construction, and financing of complex infrastructure projects, with expertise in the transportation, energy, and telecommunications sectors. In over 25 years of practice, he has acted as lead counsel on numerous project financings, acquisitions, divestitures, privatizations and restructurings, including representation of the mandated lead arrangers for Project Finance Magazine's North American Transport Deals of the Year for 2003 and 2004. He has significant experience in corporate and asset acquisitions and other investment-related transactions, debt restructurings, and commercial finance.
Career: University of California, Hastings College of Law (JD, 1975); Occidental College (AB).

MCBRIDE, Michael F
LeBoeuf, Lamb, Greene & MacRae, LLP, Washington, DC
202 986 8050
mfmcbrid@llgm.com
Recommended in Transport
Practice Areas: Counsel to utilities involved in litigation at the Interstate Commerce Commission (now known as Surface Transportation Board) and in court cases concerning transportation of nuclear materials, coal and oil. As special assistant attorney general of the Commonwealth of Massachusetts, he litigated at the STB and courts on railroad-related transportation matters.
Prof. Memberships: District of Columbia Bar; Association for Transportation Law, Logistics and Policy (President, 1994-95, 2004-05).
Career: Joined LeBoeuf, 1976; Oak Ridge National Laboratory, Environmental Sciences Division, Research Associate 1972.
Personal: University of Wisconsin - Madison (JD)1976; California Institute of Technology (MS)1973; University of Wisconsin - Milwaukee (BS)1972.

MCCONNELL, Mark S
Hogan & Hartson LLP, Washington, DC
202 637 5796
msmcconnell@hhlaw.com
Recommended in International Trade
Practice Areas: Mark McConnell rep-

resents a broad range of clients in international trade litigation and disputes, and regularly advises public policy coalitions created to express views on US international trade and foreign policy issues. He frequently assists clients on strategic matters that involve a blend of litigation, policy and diplomatic activity.
Career: Mark joined Hogan & Hartson in 1979 and is one of the founders of the firm's international trade practice. He served on President-elect Reagan's Presidential Transition Team in 1980-81, and in 2000-01 served President-elect Bush as a member of his Transition Advisory Committee for the US Trade Representative.
Publications: Mark has written a number of articles on international trade and investment regulation, and speaks frequently on US trade policy and political developments.
Personal: Stanford Law School (JD, Associate Editor of the Law Review, 1979); Stanford Graduate School of Business, (MBA). He is admitted to practice in the District of Columbia.

MCCULLOUGH, James
Fried, Frank, Harris, Shriver & Jacobson LLP, Washington, DC
202 639 7130
James.McCullough@friedfrank.com
Recommended in Government Contracts
Practice Areas: Litigation Partner. Head of Fried Frank's Government Contracts Practice in Washington, DC. Practice includes pre-award litigation and counseling on contract formation issues, post-award disputes and litigation and representation of government contractors in various civil proceedings, including Procurement Integrity Act and Freedom of Information Act disputes, and enforcement matters involving voluntary disclosure and suspension and debarment. He has been lead counsel in numerous bid protests before the General Accounting Office, the United States Court of Federal Claims and the federal district courts, and he has extensive litigation experience involving claims and terminations at various Boards of Contract Appeals and the Court of Federal Claims. In addition, he has frequently participated in the resolution of government contract disputes through the use of alternative dispute resolution techniques, including mediation and arbitration.
Prof. Memberships: Chair of the Public Contract Committee of the Dispute Resolution Section of the American Bar Association, Vice-Chairman of the Procurement Planning Committee of the National Defense Industrial Association; Advisory Board of the National Veterans Business Development Corporation, Advisory Board of The Government Contractor, and the US Chamber of Commerce Privatization and Procurement Council. Selected in 2004 as one of

the 'Leading Lawyers' in Government procurement by the 'Legal Times of Washington.'

Career: Joined Fried Frank in 1980 and became a Partner in 1985. Previously served as a trial attorney and assistant to the general counsel in the Office of the General Counsel of the Navy (1976-79). Also served on active duty as an officer of the United States Navy from 1969-73. Admitted to the Bar in the District of Columbia and Virginia.

Publications: Lectured extensively on government contracts, and regularly speaks at continuing legal education programs and government contracts-related conferences. Has written extensively on government contract matters. In addition, has co-authored a book entitled 'Contracting with the RTC and FDIC' (Prentice Hall Law and Business 1991), and has co-authored a chapter on bid protests in 'Multiple Award Schedule Contracting' (Xlibris Corporation 2002).

Personal: Born 1947. Received JD from the University of Virginia School of Law in 1976 and BA, cum laude, from Villanova University in 1969.

MCFADDEN II, W Clark
Dewey Ballantine LLP, Washington, DC
202 429 2333
cmcfadden@deweyballantine.com
Recommended in International Trade
Practice Areas: W Clark McFadden II represents corporate clients in international trade, encompassing work in litigation, regulation and legislation. He has conducted numerous international investigations and defended clients in enforcement proceedings. He also specializes in international corporate transactions, especially the formation of joint ventures and consortia. Mr McFadden has a broad background in foreign affairs and international trade, having experience with Congressional committees, the US Department of Defense and the National Security Council.
Career: Partner, Dewey Ballantine LLP.
Personal: Born July 28, 1946. BA, Williams College, 1968. MBA, Harvard Business School, 1972. JD, Harvard Law School, 1972.

MCGLONE, William
Miller & Chevalier Chartered, Washington, DC 202 626 5800
Recommended in International Trade

MEEHAN, Wayne D
Freehill Hogan & Mahar LLP, New York
212 425 1900
meehan@freehill.com
Recommended in Shipping
Practice Areas: Areas of expertise are collisions and all types of marine casualties, including groundings, allisions, sinkings, and fires. Is well-versed in casualty related issues such as limitation of liability, general average and navigation. Holds US Coast Guard Unlimited Chief Mate's license. Has considerable

experience in cargo loss and damage cases and in charter party disputes. Has tried cargo, collision and total loss cases in various Federal courts.
Prof. Memberships: Maritime Law Association of the United States; Association of Average Adjusters of the United States; New York State Bar Association.
Career: Joined Freehill Hogan & Mahar as an associate in 1984 and became a Partner in 1992; admitted to Bar, 1985, New York and New Jersey.
Personal: Born 1954, New York; United States Merchant Marine Academy at Kings Point, BS, With Honors, 1976; Boston University, JD, 1984.

MELBY, Barbara Murphy
Morgan, Lewis & Bockius LLP, Philadelphia 215 963 5053
bmelby@morganlewis.com
Recommended in Business Process Outsourcing
Practice Areas: Ms Melby is a Partner in the Global Outsourcing Practice focusing on US based and international outsourcing and technology-related transactions, including information technology, human resources, finance and accounting, logistics, call center, claims processing and various other business process outsourcing; offshore outsourcing; licensing and hosting agreements; joint ventures and strategic alliances. Ms Melby has authored several books on outsourcing, including Information technology outsourcing transactions and business process outsourcing transactions.
Prof. Memberships: Editor, Boston University Law Review Distinguished Scholar.

MENDOZA, Julie C
Kaye Scholer LLP, Washington, DC
202 682 3640
jmendoza@kayescholer.com
Recommended in International Trade
Practice Areas: Partner, Co-Chair, International Trade. Ms Mendoza has worked as an international trade lawyer for more than 15 years representing foreign manufacturers and governments in various types of trade actions, including anti-dumping and countervailing duty cases, Section 201 and 301 actions, customs issues and GSP petitions. Fluent in Spanish, she has led training seminars on trade law administration and its practical applications for foreign governments throughout Latin America. She has also conducted such seminars for the governments of Indonesia and Taiwan. Ms Mendoza routinely practices before the US Department of Commerce, the US International Trade Commission, the Office of the US. Trade Representative, and the US Bureau of Customs and Border Protection, as well as other agencies of the federal government, and the US Court of International Trade and the US Court of Appeals for the Federal Circuit. In addition, Ms

Mendoza advises clients on World Trade Organization (WTO) proceedings and has participated in WTO Panel and Appellate Body proceedings on behalf of clients and their member governments.
Career: JD, University of Chicago. BA (summa cum laude), Tufts University. Harvard University. Universidad Nacional Autónoma de México.

MENSIK, Michael S
Baker & McKenzie, Chicago
312 861 8000
Recommended in Business Process Outsourcing, Technology
Please see Illinois for profile

MEYER, David L
Covington & Burling, Washington, DC
202 662 5582
dmeyer@cov.com
Recommended in Transport
Practice Areas: Vice-Chair of Covington's Antitrust Practice Group. Broad and deep experience in antitrust (counseling, litigation, government investigations) and railroad matters (including control cases, rate regulation, contract arbitration, and others). Represents a broad array of rail clients, including the Association of American Railroads, Union Pacific Railroad Company, and TTX Company. Representative transportation matters include Surface Transportation Board railroad merger proceedings and rulemakings (including UP/CNW, UP/SP, CN/IC, KCS/Tex Mex), trackage rights compensation disputes, rate reasonableness challenges (including AEPCO v BNSF/UP), TTX's 2004 flatcar pooling reauthorization, and the proceeding that addressed Amtrak's authority to carry 'express' shipments. Outside the rail field, counsels clients on all manner of antitrust issues and successfully defends them in antitrust litigation (covering both state and federal claims, class actions and individual plaintiff suits, and conspiracy and monopolization theories) and government investigations (including the Antitrust Division's Section 2 investigation of PPL Corp. and FTC's consent decree in the Exxon-Mobil merger case).
Prof. Memberships: ABA Antitrust Section Leadership - Associate Editor of Antitrust Magazine.
Career: Special Assistant to the Assistant Attorney General, Antitrust Division, US Department of Justice (1987-89).
Publications: Numerous publications in the antitrust field.
Personal: Yale University (JD, 1986); Amherst College (BA, 1983, magna cum laude).

MILLSTEIN, Julian
Brown Raysman Millstein Felder & Steiner LLP, New York 212 895 2000
Recommended in Business Process Outsourcing, Technology
Please see New York for profile

MISHKIN, Jeffrey A
Skadden, Arps, Slate, Meagher & Flom LLP & Affiliates, New York
212 735 3230
jmishkin@skadden.com
Recommended in Sport
Practice Areas: Practice centers on all aspects of sports law, and includes antitrust, intellectual property, labor and a wide range of trial and appellate business litigation. Serves the NBA as its chief outside counsel. Has participated in every major legal decision that has affected the NBA in the past 30 years. Has been involved in every round of collective bargaining negotiations between the NBA and the NBA Players Association. Has acted as lead litigation counsel in numerous major sports litigations.
Career: JD, Cornell Law School, 1972; BA, State University of New York at Albany, 1969.

MITCHELL, David S
Cadwalader, Wickersham & Taft LLP, New York 212 504 6285
david.mitchell@cwt.com
Recommended in Capital Markets
Practice Areas: Concentrates on all aspects of the derivatives markets, including providing regulatory, transactional and litigation advice relating to sales and trading activities and formation of funds. Represents a diverse group of clients, including broker-dealers, commercial and investment banks, trading companies, hedge funds, investment managers, and corporate and institutional end-users of derivative products. Practice includes advice concerning the development and offering of complex structured products and managed fund products, regulatory and compliance issues, and insolvency matters. Has authored numerous articles on derivatives law issues and is a frequent speaker at industry conferences.
Personal: BA, City College (1976) (summa cum laude, Phi Beta Kappa); JD, New York Law School (1979) (magna cum laude); LLM, New York University School of Law (1980). Member, American Bar Association, Association of the Bar of the City of New York, New York State Bar Association, and Member, Board of Directors, Futures Industry Association.

MOATES, G Paul
Sidley Austin Brown & Wood LLP, Washington, DC 202 736 8175
pmoates@sidley.com
Recommended in Transport
Practice Areas: Paul Moates leads the firm's transportation practice, is a member of Sidley's Executive Committee, and Co-Chair of the firm's Accounting and Finance Committee. His practice includes representation of large railroads, railroad holding companies, and the railroad industry's national trade association. He has tried contract and antitrust cases in the federal courts,

argued appeals of decisions of federal regulatory agencies in several of the United States Court of Appeals, represented various railroad clients in rate cases and commercial disputes, and has served as lead litigation counsel in many of the largest railroad merger and intermodal consolidation cases before the now Surface Transportation Board of the Department of Transportation. He played a prominent role in the Surface Transportation Board's decision to declare a moratorium on major railroad consolidations, and in the subsequent development of rules for adjudicating major rail merger applications.

Career: Admitted to US Supreme Court; DC and Illinois Bars.

Publications: He has written numerous transportation-related articles in professional journals and is a respected speaker at conferences and symposia relating to developments in the transportation industry.

MOORE, Harold F
Skadden, Arps, Slate, Meagher & Flom LLP & Affiliates, New York
212 735 3000
Recommended in Projects
Please see New York for profile

MORAN, Mark
Steptoe & Johnson LLP,
Washington, DC 202 429 6292
mmoran@steptoe.com
Recommended in International Trade
Practice Areas: International Partner, Steptoe & Johnson LLP, Washington, DC. Litigation-based trade practice concentrating on US antidumping, countervailing duty, and safeguards actions, and WTO dispute resolution proceedings. Advises on WTO agreements, market access issues, and negotiation of bilateral trade agreements. Represents trade associations, governments, and domestic and foreign corporations in the forest products, steel, agricultural, semiconductor, and uranium sectors. Diverse international arbitration experience under ICC, AAA, Stockholm, and UNCITRAL Rules involving turn-key construction projects, oil and gas concession agreements, aircraft services agreements, telecommunications joint ventures, and electric power projects.
Personal: JD, University of Michigan, 1986; AB, University of Michigan, 1979

MORGAN, Linda
Covington & Burling, Washington, DC
202.662.5214
lmorgan@cov.com
Recommended in Transport
Practice Areas: Chair of the Transportation Practice Group, and core member of the Legislative Practice Group. Handles a broad range of railroad and other transportation regulatory and legislative matters, as well as general governmental and policy issues. Has 25 years of in-depth regulatory and legislative experience with the transporta-

tion sector.
Career: Originally appointed Chairman of the former Interstate Commerce Commission (ICC) by President Clinton in 1995, and then of the successor agency, the Surface Transportation Board (1996-2002, spanning two different Administrations). During that time, presided over numerous regulatory proceedings, including the significant restructuring of the rail freight industry. Prior to that, served for 15 years as counsel with the Senate Committee on Commerce, Science, and Transportation, including 7 years as General Counsel. During that time, was instrumental in the passage of several major pieces of transportation reform legislation.
Publications: Numerous speeches and guest columns on transportation and public policy.
Personal: Georgetown University (JD, 1976); Vassar College (AB, 1973); Harvard's John F. Kennedy School of Government Senior Managers Program, 1991. Specific recognition by the Georgetown University Law Center, the University of Maryland's School of Business, and The Washington Post for her contributions to transportation and the legal profession. Member, Board of Visitors, the Georgetown University Law Center.

MORRISON, Kenneth P
Kirkland & Ellis LLP, Chicago
312 861 2347
kmorrison@kirkland.com
Recommended in Capital Markets
Practice Areas: Ken Morrison is the partner in charge of Kirkland's rapidly growing asset securitization practice. Since 1990, he has handled securitizations involving a variety of asset classes on behalf of originators, underwriters, and conduit sponsors. Mr. Morrison is particularly known for his work with first time issuers and his handling of novel transactional structures. He speaks widely on securitization topics. Since 1994, he has taught 'The Law of Securitization' at Northwestern University Law School.
Personal: Yale University, BA, 1977; Massachusetts Institute of Technology, MSM, 1983; Boston University School of Law, JD, 1983.

MOSELEY, James
Moseley Warren Prichard & Parish,
Jacksonville 904 356 1306
Recommended in Shipping

MOTTESI, Marcello
Milbank, Tweed, Hadley & McCloy,
Palo Alto 650 739 7000
Recommended in Capital Markets

MOYER Jr, Homer
Miller & Chevalier Chartered,
Washington, DC 202 626 5800
Recommended in International Trade

MUMMERY, Dan
Latham & Watkins LLP, Menlo Park
650 328 4600
Recommended in Business Process Outsourcing, IT Outsourcing

MURNANE, Don P
Freehill Hogan & Mahar LLP, New York
212 425 1900
murnane@freehill.com
Recommended in Shipping
Practice Areas: Areas of expertise are maritime litigation and arbitration of contractual and tort disputes including cargo, charter party, collisions and casualties. Has a significant amount of experience with cases involving bulk and product tanker disputes including product contamination and loss. Has also handled major cases involving vessel purchase and sale, liner service contract disputes and issues involving electronic bills of lading. Bar Admissions: New York (State and Federal); District of Columbia.
Prof. Memberships: Maritime Law Association of the United States (Arbitration Committee Member); Society of Maritime Arbitrators - MLA Liaison Committee Member; New York State Bar Association.
Career: Joined Freehill Hogan & Mahar as a Partner in 1997 having been associated with Haight, Gardner, Poor & Havens from 1986-97; admitted to Bar, 1986, New York.
Personal: Born 1960; United States Merchant Marine Academy at Kings Point, BS, 1982 (Salutatorian); Georgetown University Law Center, JD, 1986.

MURPHY, Michael
Shaw Pittman LLP, Los Angeles
310 551 4500
Recommended in Business Process Outsourcing, IT Outsourcing
Please see California for profile

MURPHY, Paul
Moore & Van Allen, PLLC, Charlotte
704 331 1000
Recommended in Capital Markets

NAGEL, Trevor
Shaw Pittman LLP, Washington, DC
202 663 8417
trevor.nagel@shawpittman.com
Recommended in Business Process Outsourcing
Practice Areas: He has advised both public and private sector clients on legal and commercial issues on a wide-range of large-scale global outsourcing and complex technology transactions. He represents clients in structuring, negotiating and implementing IT infrastructure projects, business process outsourcing, innovative co-marketing arrangements and other strategic alliances.
Prof. Memberships: International Bar Association, Vice-Chair, Committee on Technology and e-Commerce; American Bar Association, Section of International and Practice

Career: Head, Global Technology Practices; Partner since 1989
Publications: 'She Blinded Me With Science' Reflections on Changes in Practicing Technology Law in a World of Changing Technology, Reflections on the International Practice of Law (N. Vogt, ed., 2004); Structuring Outsourcing Transactions, IT-Outsourcing (R. Weber et al, eds., 2003); Structuring Technology Outsourcing Relationships: Customer Concerns, Strategies and Processes, International Journal of Law & Information Technology, Vol. 4, No. 2, 1996; Convergence of Technologies and Complex Transfer Structures, International Technology Transfers (H. Rubin, ed., 1995). He is a frequent speaker at business and legal conferences on technology, outsourcing and global firm management issues.
Personal: Harvard Law School (SJD, 1984); Chicago Law School (LLM, 1981); University of Adelaide (LLB(Hons), 1980; Dip. Ed., 1974; BA(Hons), 1973); Knox Fellow, Harvard Law School, 1981-84.

NEDZBALA, Michael
Hunton & Williams, Charlotte
704 378 4703
mnedzbala@hunton.com
Recommended in Capital Markets
Practice Areas: Mr Nedzbala's practice focuses on structured finance, securitization and other capital markets transactions. He is Co-Head of the firm's Asset Securitization Group and a member of the Global Capital Markets Team.

NEUHAUS, Joseph E
Sullivan & Cromwell LLP, New York
212 558 4000
neuhausj@sullcrom.com
Recommended in Arbitration
Practice Areas: International commercial litigation in arbitral and court settings.
Prof. Memberships: Program Chair, Institute for Transnational Arbitration; NYSBA Committee on Professional Ethics; ABCNY Professional and Judicial Ethics Committee.
Career: Partner since 1992. Law Clerk, Justice Lewis F Powell, Jr of US Supreme Court and for the Iran-United States Claims Tribunal.
Publications: Guide to the UNCITRAL Model Law on International Commercial Arbitration: Legislative History and Commentary (Kluwer, 1989); 'Settlement and Release' in Commercial Contracts: Strategies for Drafting and Negotiating (Aspen 2001).
Personal: Dartmouth College; Columbia University Law School.

NEWMAN, Lawrence W
Baker & McKenzie, New York
212 891 3970
lawrence.w.newman@bakernet.com
Recommended in Arbitration
Practice Areas: Partner in Litigation Department of New York office. Areas of

work are litigation in the United States of transnational commercial disputes and international commercial arbitration, to a great extent in matters involving foreign languages (French, Spanish, Portuguese) and law. Lead attorney for BellSouth International in an arbitration (1994-99) that resulted in an award of $19.5 million against a French telecommunications company on the basis of fraudulent concealment of information in the sale of shares in a cellular telephone company. Was also lead attorney in arbitration between US and Mexican companies in which client obtained an award based on breach of contract and fraud.

Prof. Memberships: Member of various Bar organizations including the American Law Institute; former Chairman of the United States Iranian Claimants Committee (USICC), the national organisation of US businesses with claims arising out of the Iranian revolution.

Career: Member of the Bar since 1961. Attorney, US Securities & Exchange Commission's Special Study of Securities Markets, 1961-63; Assistant US Attorney, Southern District of New York, 1964-69. Associate and Partner, Baker & McKenzie New York office 1969 to present.

Publications: Co-author of 'Litigating International Disputes' (West Group 1996) 'The Practice of International Litigation' (Juris Publishing, 2d Ed 1999); general editor of a series of books on international litigation, including 'Enforcement of Foreign Judgments' and 'Attachment of Assets'. Since 1982 the author of column in the New York Law Journal 'International Litigation'.

Personal: Born July 1935. Harvard College 1957; Harvard Law School 1960. Leisure interests include writing, publishing, travel and golf.

NICELY, Matthew R
Willkie Farr & Gallagher LLP, Washington, DC 202 303 1113
mnicely@willkie.com
Recommended in International Trade

Practice Areas: Special counsel in the International Trade Department, specializing in trade remedy laws, WTO dispute settlement, and other trade policy disputes. He regularly represents respondents in antidumping (AD), countervailing duty (CVD), Section 201 safeguards, and Section 301 market access litigation before US agencies, US courts, and the European Commission. He has managed all aspects of the defense in investigations/reviews before the US Department of Commerce (DOC) and International Trade Commission (ITC) on behalf of producers, exporters, importers, and users of steel, agricultural, and other products from various countries including Australia, Brazil, Canada, Korea, Japan, Thailand, and Vietnam. He also advises govern-

ments on WTO agreements compliance and dispute settlement, with a focus on trade remedy matters. Recently represented the Thai and Vietnamese shrimp industries in high-profile antidumping actions.

Prof. Memberships: A Member of the American Bar Association.

Career: Admitted to the District of Columbia Bar.

Publications: Publications include Understanding the WTO Anti-Dumping Agreement: Negotiating History and Subsequent Interpretation (2002) (co-author); Textiles and Apparel: The New Protectionism - Primer on Antidumping Duties, Countervailing Duties, and Safeguard Measures (January 2001, co-author); 'International Legal Developments in Review: 2000 - International Trade,' The International Lawyer (Summer 2001); 'Thailand's Application of Post-Uruguay Round Antidumping Procedures,' Trade Balance, a legal journal of the Royal Thai Government, Ministry of Justice (April-June 1997, co-author).

Personal: Received a JD (cum laude) from the American University Law School in 1991 and a BA from Oberlin College in 1987.

NOCCO, Frank
Weil, Gotshal & Manges LLP, New York
212 310 8918
frank.nocco@weil.com
Recommended in Capital Markets

Practice Areas: Structured finance and derivatives: concentrates in representing issuers, underwriters, and credit enhancers in structured and corporate securities offerings worldwide.

Career: Head of the firm's Structured Finance and Derivatives Practice. Has worked on ground-breaking transactions, including: first asset-backed medium term note offering to be effected by a bankrupt company before filing of emergence plan; development of "rental car fleet financing structure," regularly used to raise billions of dollars of financing for rental car companies; first cross-border securitization involving Hong Kong dollar denominated credit card receivables; and first securitization of airline ticket receivables.

Personal: Columbia University, JD; Columbia College, BA.

NOURSE, David
Nourse & Bowles LLP, New York
212 952 6200
Recommended in Shipping

NOVICK, Robert T
Wilmer Cutler Pickering Hale and Dorr LLP, Washington, DC 202 663 6140
robert.novick@wilmerhale.com
Recommended in International Trade

Practice Areas: Chair of the firm's Trade Department. Represents clients in international business, trade, negotiation and dispute resolution matters, with particular emphasis on developing

and implementing market penetration strategies and securing market access opportunities. Representations include companies and associations in the aerospace, agriculture, hi-tech, consumer goods and services sectors.

Career: Counselor and General Counsel in the Office of the US Trade Representative from 1997 to 2001. Served as a Commissioner on the 19-member Advisory Commission on Electronic Commerce.

Personal: American University, Washington College of Law (JD 1983); Bucknell University (BA 1980).

OBERKFELL, Keith F
Mayer, Brown, Rowe & Maw LLP, Charlotte 704 444 3549
koberkfell@mayerbrownrowe.com
Recommended in Capital Markets

Practice Areas: Specializes in securitization and other structured finance products, including CDOs, CLOs and derivatives. Advises foreign and domestic financial institutions, underwriters, placement agents, liquidity providers and issuers in private, public and Rule 144A/Regulation S executions in securitizations of a wide range of asset types, including trade receivables; aircraft, container and other equipment loan and lease portfolios; student loans; credit card receivables; automobile loans and other financial assets. Represents program sponsors with respect to the development of novel multi-seller commercial paper and medium term note conduit structures.

Prof. Memberships: Admitted: North Carolina, 2000; Illinois, 1993.

Career: Mayer, Brown, Rowe & Maw LLP, Charlotte, 1999 to date; Chicago, 1996-99; Partner, 2002. Vedder Price Kaufman and Kammholz, Chicago, 1994-96. Chapman and Cutler, Chicago, 1993-94.

Personal: Harvard Law School, JD cum laude, 1993. University of Virginia, BA with highest distinction, 1990; Phi Beta Kappa, Dean's List.

O'DONNELL, Neil
Rogers Joseph O'Donnell & Phillips, San Francisco 415 956 2828
Recommended in Government Contracts

ONDRASIK, Paul
Steptoe & Johnson LLP, Washington, DC 202 429 3000
Recommended in Employee Benefits, Litigation
Please see District of Columbia for profile

ORDWAY, Eric
Weil, Gotshal & Manges LLP, New York
212 310 8609
eric.ordway@weil.com
Recommended in Arbitration

Practice Areas: Arbitration, litigation.

Career: Mr Ordway co-chairs Weil Gotshal's Global Dispute Resolution Prac-

tice. He specializes in international commercial and investor state arbitration, representing companies and foreign governments in disputes concerning various sectors. These have recently included nuclear power, oil and gas, real estate, financial services and banking, food and others. Mr Ordway has handled international arbitrations before the ICC, AAA, LCIA, International Arbitration Center of Austrian Federal Economic Chamber, Arbitration Court of Hungarian Chamber of Commerce, and investor-state arbitrations under UNCITRAL rules.

Personal: Brooklyn Law School, JD; New York University, MA; Princeton University, AB; Institut d'Etudes Politiques, CEP.

OSBORN, John W
Skadden, Arps, Slate, Meagher & Flom LLP & Affiliates, New York
212 735 3270
josborn@skadden.com
Recommended in Capital Markets

Practice Areas: Head of Derivative Financial Products Practice. In OTC derivatives practice represents commercial and investment banks and other dealers as well as major corporations, hedge funds, high net worth individuals and other end-users of the products; has analyzed, developed, negotiated and documented full range of transaction types. In securities-related financial products practice represents issuers, underwriters, placement agents and other parties in a wide range of convertible securities, equity securities units and other complex debt and equity securities. Strong new product development focus.

Career: JD, University of Pennsylvania School of Law, 1975; BA, Michigan State University, 1972.

PALMA, Laura
Simpson Thacher & Bartlett LLP, New York 212 455 2000
lpalma@stblaw.com
Recommended in Capital Markets

Practice Areas: A Partner at Simpson Thacher & Bartlett LLP and a member of the firm's Corporate Department. Concentrates on general corporate finance matters, with a particular focus on the representation of sponsors, underwriters and credit enhancement providers in a variety of structured finance transactions, including rental car fleet financings, intellectual property securitizations, auto loan and lease securitizations, equipment lease securitizations and other receivable financings.

Prof. Memberships: Bar Association of the City of New York.

Career: A Partner at the firm since 1995.

Personal: Received a BA magna cum laude in 1980 from Dartmouth College, and was elected to Phi Beta Kappa. Received a JD in 1983 from Columbia University Law School.

PAPAVIZAS, Constantine
Winston & Strawn, Washington, DC
202 371 5700
Recommended in Shipping

PARÉ, Jay
Nourse & Bowles LLP, New York
212 952 6200
Recommended in Shipping

PARK, William W
William W. Park - Sole Practitioner,
Boston 617 353 3149
wwpark@bu.edu
Recommended in Arbitration
Practice Areas: Chairman, sole arbitrator and party-nominated arbitrator in ICC, AAA, ICSID, LCIA, UNCITRAL and IACAC arbitrations, concerning inter alia joint ventures, expropriation, political risk insurance, corporate acquisitions, insurance coverage, LNG pricing, construction, financial transactions, securities, biotech licenses, letters of credit, technology transfer, agency and distribution contracts. Arbitrator and Senior Claims Judge, Claims Resolution Tribunal for Dormant Accounts in Switzerland. Appeals Tribunal, International Commission on Holocaust Era Insurance Claims.
Prof. Memberships: Editor, Arbitration International. NAFTA Financial Services Roster. Vice President, London Court of International Arbitration. Co-Chairman, ABA International Commercial Dispute Resolution Committee. Fellow, College of Commercial Arbitrators. Chartered Arbitrator and Fellow, Chartered Institute of Arbitrators. Admitted to Bar, Massachusetts (1972) and DC (1980).
Career: Practised in Paris from 1972-79. Since 1979, Professor of Law at Boston University and Director of Boston University Centre for Banking and Financial Law Studies. Other academic appointments have included Cambridge University, Fletcher School of Law and Diplomacy, University of Dijon, Geneva's Institut Universitaire de Hautes Etudes Internationales and University of Hong Kong.
Publications: Published works include 'International Chamber of Commerce Arbitration' (with Craig and Paulsson), 'International Commercial Arbitration' (with Reisman, Craig and Paulsson), 'International Forum Selection', 'Arbitration in Finance and Banking' and 'Income Tax Treaty Arbitration' (with Tillinghast).
Personal: Yale, BA; Columbia, JD; Cambridge, MA. Fluent in written and spoken French.

PECOULAS, George A
Mayer, Brown, Rowe & Maw LLP,
Chicago 312 701 7956
gpecoulas@mayerbrownrowe.com
Recommended in Capital Markets
Practice Areas: Specializes in representing commercial banks, issuers, underwriters and placement agents in structured securities offerings. Participation in the securitization of trade receivables and retail installment contracts, including auto loans and equipment loans, credit card receivables, equipment and vehicle leases, commercial loans, insurance premium finance contracts and intellectual property. Experience structuring single-seller and multi-seller commercial paper vehicles, owner trusts, master trusts, grantor trusts, and domestic special purpose corporation vehicles that can issue a variety of debt and equity securities.
Career: Joined Mayer, Brown, Rowe & Maw LLP, Chicago, 1990; Partner, 1996. Schiff Hardin & Waite, Chicago, 1987-90.
Personal: The John Marshall Law School, JD summa cum laude, 1987; first in class; 'Law Review'. Southern Illinois University, BA, 1971; Dean's List.

PETERS, William
O'Melveny & Myers LLP, Los Angeles
213 430 6000
Recommended in Business Process Outsourcing, IT Outsourcing
Please see California for profile

PETERSON, Brad L
Mayer, Brown, Rowe & Maw LLP,
Chicago 312 782 0600
Recommended in Business Process Outsourcing, Technology
Please see Illinois for profile

PIELS, William
Holland & Knight LLP, San Francisco
415 743 6900
william.piels@hklaw.com
Recommended in Aviation
Practice Areas: Partner in the firm's Structured Finance Group, he has a broad range of experience in general corporate, partnership and securities law matters, as well as more than 20 years of experience in asset-based financing. His practice is focused on aviation finance and includes representation of financial institutions, airlines, shipping lines, manufacturers and investors in a variety of domestic and cross-border equipment financing transactions, operating leases, joint ventures, workouts and repossessions. He is a member of the State Bar of California and the American Bar Association. He is an author and frequent lecturer on commercial law topics.

PIEPER, Nathaniel
Lau, Lane, Pieper, Conley & McCreadie,
Tampa 813 229 2121
Recommended in Shipping

PIERCE, John V H
Wilmer Cutler Pickering Hale and Dorr
LLP, New York 212 230 8829
john.pierce@wilmerhale.com
Recommended in Arbitration
Practice Areas: Has a diverse practice focusing on international arbitration and litigation, complex commercial litigation, securities enforcement and litigation, and internal corporate investigations.

Prof. Memberships: American Bar Association; International Bar Association; Association of the Bar of the City of New York.
Publications: 'The Haitian Crisis and the Future of Collective Enforcement of Democratic Governance,' 27 Law and Policy in International Business 477 (1996); co-author, 'Trade Finance Fraud: Understanding the Threats and Reducing the Risk', ICC Commercial Crime Services, April 2002.
Personal: Georgetown University Law Center (JD 1996); Georgetown University, School of Foreign Service (BSFS. 1992).

PIERCE, Kenneth J
Willkie Farr & Gallagher LLP,
Washington, DC 202 303 1114
kpierce@willkie.com
Recommended in International Trade
Practice Areas: Partner in the International Trade Department, specializing in the full range of US unfair trade actions, such as antidumping and countervailing duty, and Sections 301 and 201 actions. He has extensive experience in customs matters including audits, valuation and classification investigations, and Foreign Trade Zones applications, operations, and audits. Regularly handles the litigation and policy aspects of such matters at the agency, legislative, and judicial levels. Additionally, he represents clients in connection with World Trade Organization complaints and in antidumping investigations by European and other non-US national authorities. Clients include major foreign manufacturers (including their US-based operations), foreign governments, trading houses, and US importers. Has recently been active in seeking to revoke antidumping and countervailing duty orders through new sunset review procedures, particularly concerning steel products. He represents the Thai, Vietnamese, and Indian shrimp industries in the recent high-profile antidumping actions and has been lead counsel for respondents in dozens of other antidumping and countervailing duty investigations in the United States and other countries.
Prof. Memberships: Member of the American Bar Association and the International Trade Steering Committee.
Career: Admitted to the Washington, DC Bar. He is also admitted to practice before the United States Court of International Trade, the United States Court of Appeals for the Federal Circuit, and various other federal courts. Legislative Assistant to US Senator Patrick Leahy, 1978-81.
Publications: Writes and lectures frequently on international trade law issues in diverse forums in the United States and abroad.
Personal: Received a JD (cum laude) from Cornell Law School in 1984, where he was a lead Editor for the Cornell International Law Journal and was awarded the 1984 Earl Warren Prize for writing, and a BA (magna cum laude) from the University of Vermont in 1978, where he was elected to Phi Beta Kappa and received several scholastic awards.

PISANO, Vincent
Kirkland & Ellis LLP, New York
212 446 4980
vpisano@kirkland.com
Recommended in Capital Markets
Practice Areas: Extensive experience with public and private debt and equity issues, representing major US and foreign corporations, leveraged buyout groups, and US investment banks. He frequently represents major corporate issuers or has been designated by them as underwriters' counsel in a variety of financing situations. For example, for the last 17 years, he has represented the underwriters in capital market transactions for The News Corporation Limited. Has also represented the underwriters in a number of significant initial public offerings, including those of Fox Entertainment and Infinity Broadcasting.
Personal: Vassar College, BA, 1975; St. John's University, JD, 1978.

PLAINE, Daniel
Gibson, Dunn & Crutcher LLP,
Washington, DC 202 955 8286
dplaine@gibsondunn.com
Recommended in International Trade
Practice Areas: Extensive experience in international law, including trade disputes, antidumping and countervailing duty cases, and matters involving economic sanctions, foreign corrupt practice issues, antiboycott law compliance and US export control regulation. Represents clients in civil and criminal fraud investigations, in foreign sovereign claims litigation, and in antitrust issues. Advises both domestic and overseas clients in establishing transnational mergers, acquisitions and joint ventures.
Prof. Memberships: Member of the American Society of International Law and the Washington Institute of Foreign Affairs.
Personal: JD, Yale Law School, 1970; LLB, International Law, Cambridge University, 1967; BA, magna cum laude, Williams College, 1965.

POLEBAUM, Elliot E
Fried, Frank, Harris, Shriver & Jacobson
LLP, Washington, DC 202.639.7067
Elliot.Polebaum@friedfrank.com
Recommended in Arbitration
Practice Areas: Partner, Litigation. Leads Fried Frank's International Arbitration Practice. Specializes in international arbitration (handling cases throughout the world) and complex civil litigation in US courts.
Prof. Memberships: Member of the Institut pour L'Arbitrage International, the Arbitration Committee of the US Council for International Business (the US affiliate of the ICC), the LCIA, and

the International Centre for Dispute Resolution. Member of the CPR Institute for Dispute Resolution Panel of Distinguished Neutrals, and a Fellow of the College of Commercial Arbitrators.
Career: Joined Fried Frank in 1986 and became a Partner in 1989. Served as law clerk to Supreme Court Justice William J Brennan, Jr and United States Circuit Judge James L Oakes. Admitted to the bar in the District of Columbia, New York and Massachusetts. Adjunct Professor of Law, Georgetown University Law Center (teaching International Arbitration).
Publications: Written extensively on a variety of international arbitration and litigation issues and regularly speaks at professional programs in the United States and Europe.
Personal: Born 1950. Received JD, cum laude, in 1977 from New York University School of Law, MPA in 1975 from Harvard University and AB, magna cum laude, in 1972 from Middlebury College, where he was elected to Phi Beta Kappa. Languages: English; French.

PORGES, Amelia
Sidley Austin Brown & Wood LLP, Washington, DC 202 736 8361
aporges@sidley.com
Recommended in International Trade
Practice Areas: Amy Porges has 20 years experience with the Office of the US Trade Representative, the WTO and the GATT, advising businesses, trade associations and governments on the use of these and other trade rules to solve market access problems. She counsels governments and companies in WTO and dispute settlement proceedings and advises on the law of international organizations, US legislation and bilateral trade agreements. She served as the Senior Counsel for Dispute Settlement and head of enforcement at USTR where she briefed and argued WTO cases before dispute settlement panels and the Appellate Body, guided US WTO litigation efforts in over 120 government-to-government disputes, and negotiated on reform of the WTO's dispute settlement rules. She helped draft the Japan-US agreements on beef and citrus liberalization and on trade in automobiles, and the first US proposal for a General Agreement on Trade in Services.
Prof. Memberships: Member: American Bar Association, Section of International Law and Practice International Trade Steering Committee; American Society of International Law; Trade Policy Forum; US Roster of Dispute Settlement Panelists, NAFTA Chapter 19.
Career: Teaches WTO law at the Johns Hopkins University School of Advanced International Studies. Harvard Law School, JD, 1980; Harvard University - John F. Kennedy School of Government, MPP, 1980; Cornell University, BA, 1973. Bar Admissions: US Court of

International Trade, 1985; District of Columbia, 1980
Publications: Ms Porges is the principal author of the leading current work on GATT law, the 'Guide to GATT Law and Practice' published by the WTO.

PORTER, Daniel L
Willkie Farr & Gallagher LLP, Washington, DC 202 303 1115
dporter@willkie.com
Recommended in International Trade
Practice Areas: Daniel L Porter is a partner in the International Trade Department, specializing in a variety of US laws that affect the cross-border shipment of goods, including antidumping, countervailing duty, market access (Section 301), escape clause relief (Section 201), customs, and the various US laws imposing economic sanctions. His practice also includes assisting exporters and governments in World Trade Organization (WTO) Panel proceedings. Has developed particular expertise representing the interests of foreign exporters in US antidumping proceedings. On behalf of foreign exporters, he appears regularly before the US Commerce Department, the US International Trade Commission (ITC), the US Court of International Trade, the US Court of Appeals, and NAFTA Bi-National Panels. In antidumping cases he has represented clients from a wide variety of industries such as various steel products, semiconductors, and consumer goods, and from diverse economies such as Japan, Thailand, Korea, Brazil, Thailand, Canada, and India. He has significant expertise in preparing defenses for ITC injury proceedings and minimizing the dumping margin in Commerce Department proceedings. Recent significant matters include representing Japanese and Brazilian steel mills in US (Section 201) proceedings to restrict imports of steel; assisting Hynix Semiconductor's successful efforts to terminate antidumping duties through a sunset review; providing counsel to the Korean government on a possible WTO subsidies case; and a successful court appeal to overturn an ITC ruling.
Career: Admitted to the Bars of Maryland, Virginia and the District of Columbia.
Publications: Co-author of a book-length treatise entitled 'US Trade Remedies: A Guide for Foreign Businesses,' (2002), among other publications.
Personal: Received a JD (with a specialization in international legal affairs) from Cornell Law School in 1985, where he was an Articles Editor for the 'Cornell International Law Journal', and a BA from Columbia University in 1982.

PORTER, Clay
Dennis, Corry, Porter & Smith LLP, Atlanta 404 365 0102
Recommended in Transport

POSTER, Robert
Gilmartin, Poster & Shafto, New York 212 425 3220
Recommended in Shipping

PRICE, Daniel M
Sidley Austin Brown & Wood LLP, Washington, DC 202 736 8226
dmprice@sidley.com
Recommended in Arbitration, International Trade
Practice Areas: Daniel Price chairs the firm's International Trade and Dispute Resolution practice. He counsels multinational companies, financial institutions and trade associations on market access, services, investment and sanctions issues, and matters arising in intergovernmental negotiations. He advises parties in disputes under international trade agreements and investment treaties. He served as counsel or arbitrator in disputes under the UNCITRAL, AAA, ICC, ICSID, and Stockholm Chamber rules. He was appointed by President George W. Bush to the ICSID Panel of Arbitrators.
Prof. Memberships: Mr Price is a member of the Department of State's Advisory Committee on International Economic Policy, the Council on Foreign Relations, the Advisory Board of the European Institution, the Advisory Board of Georgetown University Law Center's Institute of International Economic Law, the Advisory Board of the Canada-United States Law Institute, the Executive Council of the ABA Section on International Law and the Advisory Board of the British Institute of International and Comparative Law.
Career: He served as USTR Principal Deputy General Counsel, negotiating trade and investment agreements with the former Soviet Union, Eastern Europe and Latin America; served as USTR's lead negotiator on investment issues in the NAFTA talks and as legal adviser on the GATT Uruguay Round investment agreement. He earlier served as a State Department lawyer and as Deputy Agent to the Iran-US Claims Tribunal in The Hague, representing the US government and advising US business in arbitrating multi-million dollar claims against Iran stemming from the Iranian revolution. Harvard Law School, JD, 1981; University of Cambridge, Diploma in Law, 1979; Haverford College, BA, 1977. Admitted to US Supreme Court; DC and PA Bars.

PRICE, Joseph
Gibson, Dunn & Crutcher LLP, Washington, DC 202 955 8500
jprice@gibsondunn.com
Recommended in International Trade
Practice Areas: Extensive experience in international trade regulatory matters, foreign investments (including OPIC financing and insurance), antidumping and countervailing duty cases, trade sanctions and country embargoes,

export controls and the Foreign Corrupt Practices Act. Has tried numerous cases before Commerce Department, International Trade Commission, US Court of International Trade and Court of Appeals for the Federal Circuit.
Career: Law clerk to Supreme Justice Hugo Black, 1967-68.
Publications: Frequent speaker on international trade and author of 'The Trade and Tariff Act of 1984: An Analytical Overview.'
Personal: JD, Harvard Law School, 1964; Knox Scholar - London School of Economics.

PRINGLE, Paul C
Sidley Austin Brown & Wood LLP, San Francisco 415 772 1249
ppringle@sidley.com
Recommended in Capital Markets
Practice Areas: Paul C Pringle is the Managing Partner for the San Francisco office and practices in corporate securities and REIT transactions. He has worked on a wide range of transactions and served as underwriters' counsel on financings by: Beverly Enterprises, Inc.; Del Monte Foods Company; Global Marine, Inc.; Hilton Hotels Corporation; KB Home; Nike, Inc.; Occidental Petroleum Corporation; Questar Gas Company; Robert Half International, Inc.; Safeway Inc.; Sempra Energy; Southern California Gas Company; The Walt Disney Company and Wells Fargo & Company. REIT representations include financings by Bedford Property Investors, Inc., BRE Properties, Inc., Health Care Property Investors, Inc. and Nationwide Health Properties, Inc.
Career: The University of Michigan Law School (JD, 1968). Dartmouth College (AB, 1965). Bar Admissions: California, 1972 and New York, 1969.

PRITCHARD, John
Holland & Knight LLP, New York 212 513 3200
john.pritchard@hklaw.com
Recommended in Aviation
Practice Areas: Partner in the firm's Business Law Section, concentrates on the representation of lessees, lessors, lenders, borrowers, and government guarantors in domestic and cross-border financings, securitizations, workouts and foreclosures. He has over 20 years experience in aircraft, equipment and facility finance and is knowledgeable in all areas of asset-based financing. He has given many speeches on aircraft and equipment financing. Pritchard is an active Member of the American Bar Association and served as Chairman of the Subcommittee on Aircraft Financing from 1987-94. He is also a member of the American College of Finance Lawyers.

PRUZINSKY, Anthony
Hill Rivkins & Hayden LLP, New York 212 669 0600
Recommended in Shipping

PULLEY III, Waverly
Hunton & Williams LLP, Richmond
804 788 8200
Recommended in Real Estate, Transport
Please see Virginia for profile

QUINN, James W
Weil, Gotshal & Manges LLP, New York
212 310 8000
Recommended in Litigation, Sport
Please see New York for profile

RADZIK, Edward
Donovan Parry McDermott & Radzik, New York 212 376 6400
Recommended in Shipping

RAFF, Joshua E
Orrick, Herrington & Sutcliffe, New York
212 506 5090
jraff@orrick.com
Recommended in Capital Markets
Practice Areas: Represents issuers, underwriters, institutional investors, investment advisors, credit enhancement providers, and other market participants in the structuring, issuance, distribution, and purchase of asset-backed and mortgage-backed securities. He has experience in transactions involving a wide variety of structures and asset types, including residential and commercial mortgage loans, home equity loans and lines of credit, high yield bonds, bank loans, auto and truck loans, trade receivables, lease receivables, credit card receivables, perpetual floating rate notes, and other assets. He currently focuses on CBOs and CLOs and commercial mortgage-backed securities. Over the course of his career, he has participated in many novel transactions and in the development of innovative structures for existing and new asset types. He has lectured and participated in panels on topics such as CBOs and CLOs and international real estate securitizations.
Career: University of Maryland School of Law, with honors, Order of the Coif, (JD, 1977); Columbia University (BA).

RAGOSTA, John A
Dewey Ballantine LLP, Washington, DC
202 862 1025
jragosta@deweyballantine.com
Recommended in International Trade
Practice Areas: John Ragosta advises clients concerning World Trade Organization and North American Free Trade Agreement issues, including: subsidies; dispute settlement; dumping; and intellectual property. Mr Ragosta counseled sector and policy advisory groups on the NAFTA and WTO drafts. The US government has designated him as a possible NAFTA dispute panelist. He has been lead counsel in many of the largest trade litigations of the past several decades and publishes extensively on trade and other topics.
Career: Of Counsel, Dewey Ballantine LLP.

Personal: BS, Grove City College, 1981. JD, University of Virginia Law School, 1984. MA, George Washington University, 2004.

RAISLER, Kenneth M
Sullivan & Cromwell LLP, New York
212 558 4000
raislerk@sullcrom.com
Recommended in Capital Markets
Practice Areas: Head, Commodities, Futures and Derivatives Group, which renders a full range of regulatory, transactional and litigation advice in the commodities, securities and banking areas to brokerage, fund, investment banking, banking and commercial clients.
Prof. Memberships: ABA; ABCNY (Chairman, Committee on Futures Regulation, 1988-91).
Career: Judicial Clerk to Hon. Lee P. Gagliardi, US District Court (S.D.N.Y.) Asst. US Attorney D.C. 1977-82. General Counsel, Commodity Futures Trading Commission 1983-87.
Personal: Yale University (BS, 1973); NYU School of Law (JD, 1976). Working Group of The Group of Thirty Derivatives Project, 1992-93; Board of Directors, Futures Industry Association.

RAYSMAN, Richard
Brown Raysman Millstein Felder & Steiner LLP, New York
212 895 2000
Recommended in Business Process Outsourcing, Technology
Please see New York for profile

READE, Claire E
Arnold & Porter LLP, Washington, DC
202 942 5566
Claire.Reade@aporter.com
Recommended in International Trade
Practice Areas: Claire Reade represents foreign and domestic clients on international trade, customs, legislative, and business issues. Her work includes NAFTA and WTO-related matters and 'trade-plus' questions, including labor, environment, and international business practices.
Publications: She is the author of numerous articles addressing international trade questions, including '1995-96 Developments in International Trade Disputes,' 'Fair Value Investigations Under the Antidumping Statute,' and an article on NAFTA dispute settlement in Mexico.
Personal: Sheldon Fellow, Harvard University, 1979-80; MALD, Fletcher School of Law and Diplomacy, 1979; JD, Harvard Law School, 1979, cum laude; BA, Wesleyan University, 1973, magna cum laude.

RECTOR, Richard
DLA Piper Rudnick Gray Cary US LLP, Washington, DC 202 861 6426
richard.rector@dlapiper.com
Recommended in Government Contracts

Practice Areas: Government contracts; government affairs.
Career: His practice is focused on federal and state procurement issues, including IT contracts and transactions, homeland security, entry to the federal market, state procurement laws and issues, terminations for convenience, US Postal Service procurement, and compliance with procurement integrity and ethics laws. He has litigated contract actions and bid protests before various courts and other jurisdictions and has represented prime contractors and subcontractors in breach-of-contract and protest actions, as well as prepared contract claims and requests for equitable adjustment.
Personal: JD, University of Maryland; BA, University of Maryland.

REED, Lucy
Freshfields Bruckhaus Deringer LLP, New York 212 277 4000
Recommended in Arbitration

REEDER, Robert W
Sullivan & Cromwell LLP, New York
212 558 4000
reederr@sullcrom.com
Recommended in Capital Markets
Practice Areas: Provides wide array of corporate and securities advice to public companies. Advises commercial and investment banks on derivative instruments and 'restricted' and 'control' securities. Has acted in many significant IPOs, including the Goldman Sachs IPO. Has advised on numerous unique and complex securities offerings, including the German Government's innovative monetization of the debt it holds under Paris Club agreements with Russia. Has established AAA-rated structured derivative products ompanies such as GS Financial Products US (the only SEC-registered derivatives product company).
Prof. Memberships: ABA; ABCNY; NYSBA.
Career: Partner since 1993. Judicial Clerk to Hon. Anthony J. Celebrezze, US Court of Appeals (6th Circuit), 1984-86.
Personal: Youngstown State University (BS, 1981); Ohio State University Law School (JD, 1984).

REISMAN, Michael
W. Michael Reisman - Sole Practitioner, New Haven
Recommended in Arbitration

REITER, Glenn M
Simpson Thacher & Bartlett LLP, New York 212 455 2000
greiter@stblaw.com
Recommended in Capital Markets
Practice Areas: Corporate Partner at Simpson Thacher & Bartlett LLP. Advises clients on a broad range of capital markets transactions, including domestic US securities offerings, cross-border securities offerings and international corporate finance transactions. Has sig-

nificant experience in merger and acquisition transactions. Represents US and non-US corporations, government-related entities and leading investment banks in equity offerings (including IPOs and follow-on offerings), debt offerings (including investment grade, high-yield, Yankee bond, Eurobond and sovereign bond offerings), structured financings, liability management transactions, merger and acquisition transactions, outsourcing transactions and other types of corporate transactions. In recent years, active in transactions involving Latin America, the Caribbean, Canada and Europe in addition to the United States.
Prof. Memberships: American Bar Association, Association of Bar of The City of New York and International Bar Association.
Career: Joined the firm 1978; became Partner 1984. Managing Partner of London office, 1986-90.
Publications: Regularly lectures and publishes articles on US federal securities laws-related topics.
Personal: BA, Yale College, 1973 (summa cum laude, Phi Beta Kappa). JD, Yale Law School, 1976 (Note Editor of 'Yale Law Journal'). Law Clerk, 1976-77, The Honorable Arlin M Adams, United States Court of Appeals, Third Circuit.

RENFREW, Charles
Law Offices of Charles B. Renfrew, San Francisco 415 397 3933
Recommended in Arbitration

RESSLER, Alison S
Sullivan & Cromwell LLP, Los Angeles
310 712 6600
resslera@sullcrom.com
Recommended in Capital Markets
Practice Areas: Broad experience in M&A, corporate finance, and private equity investments in regulated and unregulated industries. Corporate finance experience includes complex transactions involving secured and unsecured equity and debt securities, such as principal equity investments, acquisition financing, equity and debt securities offerings for real estate investment trusts, rights offerings, and offerings of convertible and exchangeable securities. Also has worked on IPOs for diverse companies, including Asia Global Crossing, Exelixis, Tibco Software, Korn/Ferry International, Microsoft and Spieker Properties. Advised on multiple offerings for Chiron Corporation, Tenet Healthcare and Western Wireless, and significant offerings by Mission Energy and Sunstone Hotel Investors.
Prof. Memberships: ABA; CSBA; LACBA.
Career: Partner since 1991. Member, Management Committee; Co-Head, Private Equity Group.
Personal: Columbia Law School (JD, 1983); Brown University (BA, 1980).

REYNOLDS, Robert
Alston & Bird LLP, Atlanta
404 881 7560
rreynolds@alston.com
*Recommended in Business Process
Outsourcing*
Practice Areas: Technology, outsourcing, information systems, business model innovation activities, privacy, M&A.
Prof. Memberships: American Bar Association; State Bar of Georgia.
Career: Frequent speaker at professional seminars on such topics as strategic alliances, outsourcing arrangements, and emerging business models
Personal: BA, University of Virginia (1981); JD, Vanderbilt University (1984).

REYNOLDS III, John
Wiley Rein & Fielding LLP,
Washington, DC 202 719 7000
Recommended in International Trade

RICH, Frederic C
Sullivan & Cromwell LLP, New York
212 558 4000
*Recommended in Projects
Please see New York for profile*

RIVKIN, David
Debevoise & Plimpton LLP, New York
212 909 6000
Recommended in Arbitration

ROBERTSON, Elihu
Milbank, Tweed, Hadley & McCloy,
New York 212 530 5000
Recommended in Aviation

ROCHE, William G
King & Spalding LLP, Atlanta
404 572 4936
broche@kslaw.com
*Recommended in Business Process
Outsourcing*
Practice Areas: Private Equity and Intellectual Property focusing primarily on the computer software and telecommunications industries. Extensive experience in transactions involving intellectual property and technology based assets and services, including information technology outsourcing transactions. Substantial experience in acquisition, development, marketing and protection of intellectual property and technology assets through merger and acquisition transactions, development agreements, licensing, joint ventures, strategic alliances and other arrangements.
Prof. Memberships: American Bar Association; State Bar of Georgia.
Personal: BA, Notre Dame, 1980; JD, Stanford University, 1983.

ROD, Jonathan
Latham & Watkins LLP, New York
212 906 1200
Recommended in Projects

RODRIGUEZ, Wilfredo A
Holland & Knight LLP, Miami
305 374 8500
fred.rodriguez@hklaw.com

Recommended in Arbitration
Practice Areas: Partner in the Litigation Section, specializing in international litigation and arbitration. Rodriguez serves as the firm's Chair of the International Litigation Team consisting of more than 25 specialized legal practitioners. With over 20 years of experience, Rodriguez has defended, prosecuted and tried numerous complex international business disputes in various courts. He also routinely acts as advocate and legal counsel in a wide variety of international arbitrations conducted in the United States and in several foreign jurisdictions. Rodriguez is a member of the Advisory Board of the Institute for Transnational Arbitration and is a regular speaker on international litigation.

ROH, Charles E
Weil, Gotshal & Manges LLP,
Washington, DC 202 682 7100
chip.roh@weil.com
Recommended in International Trade
Practice Areas: International trade, arbitration.
Career: Mr Roh co-heads Weil Gotshal's International Trade Practice, representing businesses, associations and governments in international dispute settlement proceedings, international arbitrations and negotiations, and compliance issues under US laws pertaining to economic sanctions, export controls, customs, national security, and antibribery. Roh served as Assistant US Trade Representative for North America, was Deputy Chief Negotiator of NAFTA for the US, and litigated numerous international disputes for the United States. Roh serves by presidential appointment on the Panel of Conciliators of the International Center for the Settlement of Investment Disputes.
Personal: Harvard University, JD; Princeton University, BA.

ROSEN, Edward J
Cleary Gottlieb Steen & Hamilton LLP,
New York 212 225 2820
erosen@cgsh.com
Recommended in Capital Markets
Practice Areas: Structuring and regulatory analysis of complex securities and derivatives transactions and US securities and commodities law regulation. Clients include Securities Industry Association, International Swaps and Derivatives Association and Futures Industry Association, The Bond Market Association, major commercial and investment banks, exchanges, and clearinghouses.
Prof. Memberships: Member ISDA Regulatory Advisory Committee, FIA Board of Directors, CFTC Technology Advisory Committee. Chair, Practicing Law Institute Annual Conference on Swaps and Derivatives.
Career: JD, Columbia University School of Law (1982) (Stone Scholar); BA, MA (Hon), Oxford University (1975).
Publications: Co-author 'US Regula-

tion of the International Securities and Derivatives Markets' (seventh edition, 2003).

ROSEN, Stuart M
Weil, Gotshal & Manges LLP, New York
212 310 8660
stuart.rosen@weil.com
Recommended in International Trade
Practice Areas: International trade, litigation/regulatory.
Career: Mr Rosen specializes in international trade litigation, regulatory and commercial matters. He has extensive experience in all types of trade proceedings, including anti-dumping, countervailing duty, escape clause and other proceedings, customs valuation, classification, penalty and enforcement matters, commercial transactions, regulatory matters, retailing and distribution, insurance, credit and finance. He Co-chairs the New York State Bar Association Customs and International Trade Committee; is a Member of the Customs and International Trade Bar Association's Customs and Tariffs Committee; and a member of the American Association of Exporters and Importers.
Personal: Harvard University, JD; Dickinson College, BA.

ROSENBERG, Marc
Cravath, Swaine & Moore LLP,
New York 212 474 1676
mrosenberg@cravath.com
Recommended in Capital Markets
Practice Areas: Securities, mergers and acquisitions. Counseling boards of directors, audit committees and senior management in connection with SEC investigations and other special situations.
Prof. Memberships: ABCNY.
Career: Partner since 1990. Clerkship: Hon. Walter R. Mansfield (US Court of Appeals for the Second Circuit).
Personal: Harvard Law School (JD, magna cum laude, 1983; Sears Prize; editor, 'Law Review'); Princeton University (AB, summa cum laude, 1980; Phi Beta Kappa).

ROSENTHAL, Paul
Collier Shannon Scott, Washington, DC
202 342 8400
Recommended in International Trade

ROSS, Nancy
McDermott Will & Emery, Chicago
312 372 2000
*Recommended in Employee Benefits,
Litigation
Please see Illinois for profile*

ROTHWELL, James T
Davis Polk & Wardwell, New York
212 450 4000
james.rothwell@dpw.com
Recommended in Capital Markets
Practice Areas: Member of Davis Polk & Wardwell's Corporate Department. Represents investment banks, corporations, and individuals regarding equity derivatives and other structured equity

financial products. Has been involved in the original design of many innovative financial products that have become staples of the equity derivatives marketplace. Also advises underwriters and issuers in securities offerings, specializing in convertible and equity-linked securities in the public, Rule 144A and Regulation S capital markets.

ROVINE, Arthur
Baker & McKenzie, New York
212 891 3550
arthur.w.rovine@bakernet.com
Recommended in Arbitration
Practice Areas: International commercial arbitration involving complex contracts and investment disputes under US, foreign and international law. Represents many major corporate clients and has handled cases for and against governments. Previously served in the Office of the Legal Adviser in the Department of State as Assistant Legal Adviser for Treaty Affairs and then as the first US Agent to the Iran-US Claims Tribunal.
Prof. Memberships: Past President, American Society of International Law (2000-02); Former Chair, American Bar Association International Law Section (1985-86), Section Delegate to ABA House of Delegates (1986-87); Member, Council on Foreign Relations, the American Arbitration Association (Panel of Arbitrators), the Association of the Bar of the City of New York, the Center for Public Resources (Panel on the Settlement of Transnational Business Disputes), and US Council for International Business (Arbitration Committee).
Career: Taught international law and organization at Cornell and later at Georgetown while in the Department of State. Visiting Lecturer in Law at Yale in 1998, teaching international arbitration. Currently Adjunct Professor of Law at Fordham Law School, teaching international commercial arbitration.
Publications: Has written widely on international law and international arbitration, and has given many addresses on these topics. Served for 10 years as a Member of the Board of Editors of the 'American Journal of International Law'.

ROY, Paul J N
Mayer, Brown, Rowe & Maw LLP,
Chicago 312 782 0600
*Recommended in Business Process
Outsourcing, Technology
Please see Illinois for profile*

RUBINOFF, Edward L
Akin Gump Strauss Hauer & Feld LLP,
Washington, DC 202 887 4026
erubinoff@akingump.com
Recommended in International Trade
Practice Areas: Heads firm's Export Trade Practice. Is a recognized authority on US export controls, trade embargoes, economic sanctions, antiboycott regulations, CFIUS reviews and foreign cor-

rupt practices. Advises domestic, foreign and multinational companies in all business sectors on compliance with US export control and sanctions laws; structures export compliance programs; performs audits and internal investigations; conducts international trade due diligence for mergers, acquisitions and joint ventures; and represents clients in civil and criminal export enforcement cases.
Prof. Memberships: President's Export Council Subcommittee on Export Administration; ABA, Section of International Law.
Personal: BA, University of Pennsylvania; JD, George Washington University.

RUBINSTEIN, Javier H
Mayer, Brown, Rowe & Maw LLP, Chicago 312 701 7781
jrubinstein@mayerbrownrowe.com
Recommended in Arbitration
Practice Areas: Represents clients from Latin America, Europe, North America and Asia in international commercial arbitrations before the world's leading arbitral institutions, including the ICC International Court of Arbitration, the London Court of International Arbitration, the Court of Arbitration for Sport, the American Arbitration Association, and the Arbitration Institute of the Stockholm Chamber of Commerce.
Career: Mayer, Brown, Rowe & Maw LLP, Chicago, 1989 to date; Partner, 1998; Chicago Litigation Practice Leader, 2003 to date. University of Chicago Law School, Lecturer in Law, 1996 to date. Teaching courses in International Commercial Arbitration and Litigation and US Supreme Court Litigation.
Publications: International Commercial Arbitration: Reflections at the Crossroads of the Common Law and Civil Law Traditions, 5 Chi J Intl L 303 (2004). The Attorney-Client Privilege and International Arbitration, 18 J. Intl. Arb. 587 (Dec. 2001).
Personal: JD (cum laude), Georgetown University Law Center, 1989; Dean's List; Member, Law and Policy in International Business; Member, National Moot Court Team. Master of Public Policy, Harvard University, John F. Kennedy School of Government, 1986. BA (magna cum laude; Dean's List), University of Michigan, 1984. Born, Buenos Aires, Argentina. Native fluency in Spanish.

RUSKIN, Bradley I
Proskauer Rose LLP, New York
212 969 3465
bruskin@proskauer.com
Recommended in Sport
Practice Areas: A Partner in Proskauer Rose LLP's Litigation and Dispute Resolution Department and a member of the firm's Executive Committee. A significant portion of his practice is dedicated to litigating issues and counseling clients active in the sports business. Among the league clients for whom he performs

services are the National Hockey League, Major League Soccer, the National Basketball Association, the ATP, and the WTA. In addition, he has represented ownership groups and clubs in each of the major US sports (including the Florida Marlins, the New York Jets, the Philadelphia Eagles and the New Jersey Devils), and media companies in sports-related disputes.
Career: He also regularly handles a wide range of litigated matters for media and entertainment companies, and financial services companies, including contract, fraud, licensing, antitrust, trademark, franchising, partnership, intra-corporate, bankruptcy, unfair competition, and other commercial disputes. He has also litigated trust matters throughout the country in various federal and state courts and in domestic and international arbitral forums, and has handled proceedings (along with foreign counsel) before the European Commission and the Office of Fair Trading.
Personal: New York University School of Law, JD, 1981. Brown University, AB, 1978.

RUSSELL, William
King & Spalding LLP, Houston
713 751 3237
wrussell@kslaw.com
Recommended in Arbitration
Practice Areas: Fluent in Spanish with extensive experience in international litigation and arbitration, complex commercial litigation and professional liability.
Prof. Memberships: State Bar of Texas, Grievance Committee; advisory board of the Southwest Legal Foundation's Institute for Transnational Arbitration; Houston International Arbitration Club.
Personal: BA, Southern Methodist University, 1992; JD, South Texas College of Law, 1995.

RUTKOWSKI, Larry
Seward & Kissel, New York
212 574 1206
rutkowski@sewkis.com
Recommended in Shipping
Practice Areas: Mr Rutkowski is Head of the firm's Transportation Finance Group, a cross section of attorneys within the firm from the Corporate Finance, Corporate Securities, Litigation and Tax Departments with expertise on matters of interest to clients in the transportation industry. In such capacity, Mr Rutkowski has worked on matters ranging from the formation of joint ventures, asset finance transactions, registered and unregistered securities transactions and cross border leases to restructurings and bankruptcy. In addition to representing clients in the transportation industry, Mr Rutkowski's practice has included considerable experience in equipment finance and in the energy and mining fields.
Prof. Memberships: Mr Rutkowski is a Member of the Association of the Bar of

the City of New York (former Chair, Maritime Law Committee), the American Bar Association (the Air and Space Law Forum, Business Law Section, International Law and Practice Section), the Association for Transportation Law, Logistics and Policy, the Maritime Law Association of the United States (Maritime Finance Committee) and the City Bar Association Committee on Aeronautics.
Career: Mr Rutkowski received a BA degree, magna cum laude, from College of the Holy Cross, in 1975, and a JD degree, from Columbia University in 1978. Mr Rutkowski is a Partner in Seward & Kissel's Corporate Finance Group. Mr Rutkowski has practiced law since 1979. He joined Seward & Kissel as a Partner in 1992.

SACHS, John
Latham & Watkins LLP, Washington, DC 202 637 2200
Recommended in Projects
Please see District of Columbia for profile

SAGGESE, Nicholas P
Skadden, Arps, Slate, Meagher & Flom LLP & Affiliates, Los Angeles
213 687 5550
nsaggese@skadden.com
Recommended in Capital Markets, Corporate/M&A
Practice Areas: Has been involved with numerous mergers and acquisitions, securities offerings and corporate restructurings. Examples of recent transactions include: Vulcan Energy Corporation's acquisition of Plains Resources Inc., the sale of Hotwire.com by Texas Pacific Group, UnitedGlobal-Com Inc.'s acquisition of the minority shares of UGC Europe; and the acquisition of PETCO Animal Supplies by Leonard Green & Partners and Texas Pacific Group. Also advised on the IPOs of DreamWorks Animation SKG, Inc., Herbalife International, Inc. and FTD Group, Inc., the initial listing of UGC Europe as a NASDAQ national markets security and numerous high-yield bond offerings.
Prof. Memberships: Board member for LA Regional Foodbank and Member, Board of Overseers, Loyola Law School.
Career: JD, Loyola Law School of Los Angeles, 1980 (cum laude; Member, Loyola Law Review, St. Thomas More Law Honor Society); MBA, University of California at Los Angeles, 1973 (Beta Gamma Sigma Honor Society); BA, University of California at Los Angeles, 1969.

SAMET, Andrew
Sandler, Travis & Rosenberg, Washington, DC 202 216 9307
Recommended in International Trade

SANDLER, Richard J
Davis Polk & Wardwell, New York
212 450 4000
richard.sandler@dpw.com
Recommended in Capital Markets
Practice Areas: Head of Davis Polk & Wardwell's Global Capital Markets Practice, with extensive experience advising on corporate governance matters, securities regulatory matters and all aspects of public and private securities offerings, including initial public offerings, spin-offs, high-yield debt securities, venture capital and leveraged investments, restructurings, exchange offers and new financial products. Regularly represents Morgan Stanley, JP Morgan Securities, Credit Suisse First Boston and other corporate clients on US and international transactions.

SAPER, Jeff
Wilson Sonsini Goodrich & Rosati, Palo Alto 650 493 9300
jsaper@wsgr.com
Recommended in Capital Markets, Corporate/M&A
Practice Areas: Corporate Law and Governance. Also specializes in public and private financings of high technology, telecommunications and retail and consumer products companies; corporate partnership transactions; representation of investment banks and corporate issuers in connection with public offerings, mergers and acquisitions.
Prof. Memberships: Admitted to practice in New York and California.
Career: Joined WSGR as Partner, 1980. Member, WSGR, Executive Management Committee and Policy Committee. Represents over 20 public companies, numerous private companies and several leading investment banks and venture capital funds. Has managed more than 100 public offerings.
Personal: JD, 1974 and BA (summa cum laude), 1968, New York University.

SCAVONE, Arthur
White & Case LLP, New York
212 819 8200
Recommended in Projects
Please see New York for profile

SCHACTER, Ira
Cadwalader, Wickersham & Taft LLP, New York 212 504 6035
ira.schacter@cwt.com
Recommended in Capital Markets
Practice Areas: Practice consists principally of creating and structuring complex financial solutions and the formation, acquisition and capital raising activities of businesses that issue, underwrite, trade or invest in financial products. Frequently called upon to develop unique financial solutions for corporate and financial institutions that bridge traditional finance with structured finance. Involved in virtually all aspects of the structured finance business and with almost every type of securitization including insurance risk, whole-compa-

ny and CDO's and with assets from the traditional to the varied, including corporate loans, swap receivables, repo and other financial assets, as well as a variety of other unique assets, such as franchise royalties and shipping containers. Has extensive experience counseling monolines and representing them in their transactions.

Personal: BA in Economics from the State University of New York at Stony Brook; JD from the Nova Center for the Study of Law; LLM in Corporations Law from the New York University School of Law.

SCHAFFZIN, Jonathan
Cahill Gordon & Reindel, New York
212 701 3900
Recommended in Capital Markets

SCHAGRIN, Roger
Schagrin Associates, Washington, DC
202 223 1700
Recommended in International Trade

SCHEINBERG, Ronald
Vedder, Price, Kaufman & Kammholz, New York 212 407 7700
Recommended in Aviation

SCHER, Peter L
Mayer, Brown, Rowe & Maw LLP, Washington, DC 202 263 3360
pscher@mayerbrown.com
Recommended in International Trade

Practice Areas: Represents companies on a worldwide basis, assisting clients in addressing regulatory and other governmental issues and expanding their business activities in foreign markets. Specializes in: Market access issues - expanding client activities in foreign markets through trade and strategic business alliances. Provides advice and counsel on federal legislative and regulatory affairs in international trade, tax policy, environmental policy, copyright and intellectual property.

Career: Mayer, Brown, Rowe & Maw LLP, Washington, DC, 2000 to date; Partner 2000. United States Special Trade Negotiator, 1997-2000. Chief of Staff, United States Department of Commerce, 1996-97. Chief of Staff, Office of the United States Trade Representative, 1995-96. Staff Director, US Senate Committee on Environment and Public Works, 1993-95. Chief of Staff to US Senator Max Baucus, 1991-93. Keck, Mahin & Cate, Washington, DC, 1989-91.

Publications: Auhor: 'The WTO and America's Agricultural Trade Agenda,' Minnesota Journal of Global Trade, Winter 2000, Volume 9, Issue 1. Atlantic Council of the United States, Working Group on US-EU Trade and Economic Issues, 2000-01. German Marshall Fund, Guest Lecturer, 2000.

Personal: JD, American University, Washington College of Law, 1987. BA, The American University, 1983.

SCHETMAN, Richard
Cadwalader, Wickersham & Taft LLP, New York 212 504 6906
richard.schetman@cwt.com
Recommended in Capital Markets

Practice Areas: Concentrates in structured finance, derivative products, other types of financing, and the federal securities laws. Represents underwriters, credit enhancers, issuers, institutional investors, sponsors, and swap counterparties in a wide range of matters, including the securitization of cash flows from such assets as credit card receivables, auto loans, trade receivables, wholesale auto dealer notes, leases, tobacco settlements, and airplane contracts. Extensive experience in structuring commercial paper vehicles and CDOs, synthetic CDOs and vehicles for repackaging corporate, asset-backed and non-US securities. Speaker at various conferences on CDOs, repackagings and other securitization issues.

Personal: BA, Brown University 1980; JD, The University of Pennsylvania School of Law 1983 (cum laude, member of Moot Court Board). Member, The Association of the Bar of the City of New York and the American Bar Association.

SCHILLER, Jonathan
Boies, Schiller & Flexner, Washington, DC 202 237 2727
Recommended in Arbitration

SCHNABL, Marco E
Skadden, Arps, Slate, Meagher & Flom LLP & Affiliates, New York
212 735 2312
mschnabl@skadden.com
Recommended in Arbitration

Practice Areas: Handles international and domestic litigations and arbitrations. Represents clients in litigations stemming from US and international M&A and changes in corporate control. Worked on securities class actions for US and foreign clients, contested proceedings before administrative agencies, SEC investigations, contract disputes and other commercial litigations. Represented underwriters and Latin American issuers in debt and equity offerings in the industrial, telecommunications, banking and energy sectors.

Career: JD, Columbia University School of Law, 1981; MPhil, Economics, Columbia University, 1977; MS, Management, Sloan School of Management, Massachusetts Institute of Technology, 1973; Lic., Economics, University of Buenos Aires, 1971.

SCHNEIDER, Lawrence
Arnold & Porter LLP, Washington, DC
202 942 5694
Lawrence.Schneider@aporter.com
Recommended in International Trade

Practice Areas: Lawrence Schneider is a Senior Partner who heads the firm's international Trade Practice. He handles a full range of international trade, customs, legislative and policy matters,

including disputes under import laws. He has more than two decades of experience representing companies, trade associations, and governments in antidumping, countervailing duty, and other international trade proceedings before administrative agencies, courts, and international dispute settlement panels.

Prof. Memberships: He has served as President and member of the Board of Directors of the Washington Council of Lawyers.

Personal: JD, Harvard Law School, 1974, cum laude; BA, Yale University, 1971, cum laude.

SCHWARTZ, Jordan
Cadwalader, Wickersham & Taft LLP, New York 212 504 6136
jordan.schwartz@cwt.com
Recommended in Capital Markets

Practice Areas: Has been lead counsel in hundreds of public and private securitization transactions, involving over $100 billion in securities and a wide array of asset classes. Clients include major mortgage banks, investment banks, commercial banks, insurance companies and institutional investors. Has many years experience as corporate lawyer and business advisor and has participated in a variety of corporate transactions, including mergers and acquisitions, leveraged buyouts, initial public offerings, leveraged aircraft leasing, and computer hardware and software development, acquisition and licensing arrangements.

Personal: BA, Stanford University (1978); JD University of Chicago Law School (1981). Member, American Bar Association and the Secondary and Capital Markets Committee of the Mortgage Bankers Association.

SCHWEBEL, Stephen
Judge Stephen M. Schwebel, Washington, DC 202 736 8328
Recommended in Arbitration

SEGALL, Wynn H
Akin Gump Strauss Hauer & Feld LLP, Washington, DC 202 887 4573
wsegall@akingump.com
Recommended in International Trade

Practice Areas: Mr Segall assists clients with national security and foreign policy-based trade controls and policy, and restricted market access. Widely recognized for work on export controls and economic sanctions. Work includes international corporate compliance, risk assessment, licensing, enforcement, government affairs. Experience with companies in aerospace, agriculture, construction, electronics, energy, entertainment, financial services, medical products, telecommunications, transportation industries.

Publications: Running on Empty: US Economic Sanctions and Export Controls; Employment of Foreign Nationals: The Deemed Export Rule; The UN Debate on Iraq.

Personal: AB (cum laude), University of Pennsylvania (1983); MPhil, Oxford University (St. Antony's) (1985); JD, University of Chicago (1989).

SHAPIRO, Hal
Miller & Chevalier Chartered, Washington, DC 202 626 5800
Recommended in International Trade

SHAPIRO, Howard
Proskauer Rose LLP, New Orleans
504 310 4085
howshapiro@proskauer.com
Recommended in Litigation

Practice Areas: Partner at Proskauer Rose LLP. National ERISA litigation practice focuses on defending matters raising sophisticated preemption issues; fiduciary issues; fiduciary misrepresentation claims; ESOP litigation issues; 401(k) plan issues; blackout period cases; plan asset diversification issues; prohibited transaction allegations; directed trustee issues; cash balance cases; independent contractor litigation; 'serious consideration' cases; retiree rights litigation; severance pay cases; executive compensation/'top hat' litigation; Section 510 cases; benefit claims cases; ERISA class actions; and class-wide challenges to plans that do not offer contraception benefits. He has appeared in federal courts from coast to coast, maintaining an active national ERISA litigation practice.

Prof. Memberships: Chair of the Section of Labor and Employment Law, American Bar Association. Past Chair of the Joint Committee on Employee Benefits (ABA). Also past Chair of the Employee Benefits Committee, Section of Labor and Employment Law (ABA).

Personal: BA Tulane University, New Orleans, LA, May 1972; MA History, McGill University, Montreal, Quebec, November 1975; JD Loyola University of New Orleans, LA, May 1979.

SHEPPARD, Ben
Vinson & Elkins LLP, Houston
713 758 2222
Recommended in Arbitration, Energy
Please see Texas for profile

SHER, Stanley
Sher & Blackwell, Washington
202 463 2500
Recommended in Shipping

SHOCKRO, Michael
Latham & Watkins LLP, Los Angeles
213 485 1234
Recommended in Business Process Outsourcing, IT Outsourcing

SHOR, Michael T
Arnold & Porter LLP, Washington, DC
202 942 5732
Michael.Shor@aporter.com
Recommended in International Trade

Practice Areas: Michael Shor has over 20 years experience representing private companies, trade associations, and foreign governments in international trade matters, including antidumping and countervailing duty investigations, reviews and appeals, sunset reviews, WTO disputes, and US Customs proceedings. Mr Shor also has extensive experience with appeals of trade cases, including involvement as counsel in some 40 decisions issued by courts and binational panels. He has also assisted foreign governments in dispute settlement proceedings before the World Trade Organization.

Career: Legal Assistant, Iran-United States Claims Tribunal, 1984-86.

Personal: JD, Harvard Law School, 1983; AB, Dartmouth College, 1980.

SHOYER, Andrew W
Sidley Austin Brown & Wood LLP, Washington, DC 202 736 8326
ashoyer@sidley.com
Recommended in International Trade

Practice Areas: Andrew Shoyer focuses on the implementation and enforcement of international trade and investment agreements. He advises companies, trade associations and governments on the use of WTO, NAFTA and other trade rules to address market access barriers and unfair conditions of competition. Client representations range from representing US manufacturers in WTO claims against a government using legislation to restrict imports, to the representation of financial institutions and trade associations in the use of bilateral treaties and WTO rules to gain market access. Mr Shoyer spent seven years at the Office of the US Trade Representative, and with the WTO, serving most recently as Legal Advisor in the US Mission to the WTO in Geneva. He was the principal negotiator for the United States of the rules implementing the WTO Dispute Settlement Understanding, and briefed and argued numerous WTO cases before dispute settlement panels and the WTO Appellate Body. He served as legal counsel on the $500 billion global Information Technology Agreement concluded in 1996 and on customs-related matters during the GATT Uruguay Round. In Washington, he served as Assistant General Counsel at USTR where he was principal legal counsel in the negotiation of the market access rules of the NAFTA, as well as the framework agreements with various Latin American countries. He worked on numerous trade policy issues with Congress and the economic agencies of the Executive Branch, including the drafting of the Andean Trade Preference Act.

Prof. Memberships: Member of the American Bar Association SLIP International Trade Committee (Steering Committee) and the American Society of International Law.

Career: Georgetown University Law Center, JD, 1986; Georgetown University School of Foreign Service, MS in For-

eign Services, 1986; University of Pennsylvania, BA, 1981. Bar Admission: District of Columbia, 1987.

SHUTRAN, Richard
Dewey Ballantine LLP, New York
212 259 8000
Recommended in Projects
Please see New York for profile

SILVERMAN, Leslie N
Cleary Gottlieb Steen & Hamilton LLP, New York 212 225 2380
lsilverman@cgsh.com
Recommended in Capital Markets

Practice Areas: Domestic and international capital markets, particularly cross-border offerings and development of new financial products, and corporate counseling regarding compliance with the Sarbanes-Oxley Act and related governance matters.

Prof. Memberships: Member of the Bar in New York. Admitted to practice before US Court of Appeals (Second Circuit) and US District Court (Southern District of New York).

Career: Joined firm, 1974; became Partner, 1982. JD, 'Law Journal' editor, Yale Law School (1973); BS, summa cum laude, Wharton School of the University of Pennsylvania (1969).

Publications: The SEC's Securities Offering Reform Proposals: Will This Ship Sail? The Review of Securities and Commodities Regulation (March 2005); Raising Capital Through OTC Equity Derivatives: The Goldman, Sachs & Co. Interpretive Letter, Futures and Derivatives (January 2004); Co-author of US Regulation of the International Securities and Derivatives Markets (Seventh edition, 2003); and The Sarbanes-Oxley Act: Analysis and Practice (2003).

SINGER, Andrew
Latham & Watkins LLP, San Diego
619 236 1234
Recommended in Projects

SIPE Jr, Samuel
Steptoe & Johnson LLP, Washington, DC 202 429 6486
ssipe@steptoe.com
Recommended in Transport

Practice Areas: Partner in the Washington office of Steptoe & Johnson LLP. Represented railroads in merger cases, rate cases, rulemakings, and other proceedings before the Surface Transportation Board as well as in litigation in the federal courts and commercial arbitrations. Advises non-railroad clients, including municipalities and port authorities, regarding commercial and regulatory issues arising from their dealings with the rail industry. Extensive background in antitrust law and economic regulation encompassing the communications and petroleum industries as well as railroads.

Personal: JD, Yale University, 1978; PhD., State University of New York - Buffalo, 1973.

SLATER, Valerie A
Akin Gump Strauss Hauer & Feld LLP, San Francisco 202 887 4112
vslater@akingump.com
Recommended in International Trade

Practice Areas: Extensive experience in prosecuting and defending antidumping, countervailing duty, safeguard and other trade remedy investigations; particular expertise with suspension agreements and non-market economy cases. Handles appeals before Court of International Trade and Court of Appeals for the Federal Circuit. Practices before Office of the US Trade Representative and other federal agencies in connection with trade policy and WTO matters, including accessions and dispute settlements. Experienced with NAFTA panel proceedings.

Prof. Memberships: Member, Advisory Committee on Rules, US Court of International Trade.

Personal: BA, Allegheny College (magna cum laude, Phi Beta Kappa); JD, Catholic University of America.

SLONAKER, Norman
Sidley Austin Brown & Wood LLP, New York 212 839 5356
nslonaker@sidley.com
Recommended in Capital Markets

Practice Areas: Norman D Slonaker is co-head of the Corporate Securities Practice in New York and is a member of the firm's Management and Executive Committees. He has extensive experience in all aspects of capital markets transactions, with particular emphasis on structured securities, investment grade debt securities, medium-term note programs, Rule 144A offerings and convertible and exchangeable securities. Mr Slonaker was a member of the ABA Task Force on Sellers' Due Diligence and Similar Defenses under the Federal Securities Laws and is currently a member of the Financial Reporting Committee of the Association of the Bar of the City of New York. He has been a speaker at seminars on new financial instruments and techniques and other aspects of the federal securities laws. He has also co-authored articles on bank notes and deposit notes and innovative debt securities.

Career: Harvard Law School (LLB, 1965) University of Washington (BS, 1962) Bar Admission: New York, 1966.

SMALL, Jeffrey
Davis Polk & Wardwell, New York
212 450 4000
jeffrey.small@dpw.com
Recommended in Capital Markets

Practice Areas: Co-Head of Davis Polk & Wardwell's global Capital Markets Group. Advises US and non-US clients on a variety of transactions, including initial public offerings, spinoffs, other securities underwritings, corporate finance, foreign asset privatisations, and international corporate and sovereign offerings. Advises numerous US compa-

nies in conjunction with capital-raising transactions and corporate governance, and has been a principal legal adviser to Morgan Stanley for many years. Also a principal adviser to Telefonica, Banco Santander Central Hispano and Repsol YPF.

SMIT, Robert
Simpson Thacher & Bartlett LLP, New York 212 455 2000
rsmit@stblaw.com
Recommended in Arbitration

Practice Areas: Litigation Partner at Simpson Thacher & Bartlett LLP specialising in international arbitration and litigation. Represents clients and serves as arbitrator in a wide range of complex commercial arbitrations, concentrating in the areas of bilateral investment treaty arbitrations, joint venture, agency, distributorship and construction disputes as well as insurance matters. Recent engagements include counsel to General Electric Capital Corporation in various arbitrations arising out of India's expropriation of the Dabhol Power Plant in Maharashtra, India, and counsel to Andersen Consulting in one of the largest ever ICC arbitrations, based in Geneva, Switzerland.

Prof. Memberships: US member of ICC Court of Arbitration, and Chair of CPR Arbitration Committee.

Career: Has been a Partner at the firm since 1997.

Personal: JD from Columbia Law School; DEA in private international law and international arbitration from the Sorbonne in Paris; clerked in the SDNY Federal courts; taught US Commercial Law at the Sorbonne.

SMITH, Jason
Weil, Gotshal & Manges LLP, New York
212 310 8914
jason.smith@weil.com
Recommended in Capital Markets

Practice Areas: Structured finance and derivatives: represents issuers, financial institutions, credit enhancers and investors worldwide in various capacities in structured transactions and securities offerings.

Career: Experienced in structuring rental car fleet financings, establishing single-seller and multi-seller commercial paper vehicles (including vehicles issuing secured liquidity notes and extendible commercial paper and employing various synthetic liquidity alternatives), as well as CBOs/CDOs/CLOs, synthetic securities and credit default swaps. Proficient with a wide variety of assets, including auto loans, commercial loans, student loans, equipment loans, credit card receivables, trade receivables, equipment/vehicle leases, corporate bonds and loans.

Personal: New York University, JD; Columbia College, BA.

SMITH, Mark C
Skadden, Arps, Slate, Meagher & Flom LLP & Affiliates, New York
212 735 3330
msmith@skadden.com
Recommended in Capital Markets
Practice Areas: Has an active acquisition, financial sponsor and capital markets practice. Regularly represents private equity firms, issuers and underwriters in a wide variety of acquisition transactions, leveraged recapitalizations, high-yield debt financings and intial public offerings.
Career: JD, Fordham University School of Law, 1982 (cum laude; Articles Editor, Fordham Law Review); BA, Middlebury College, 1978 (cum laude).

SMUTNY, Abby Cohen
White & Case LLP, Washington, DC
202 626 3600
asmutny@whitecase.com
Recommended in Arbitration
Practice Areas: International dispute resolution through arbitration or litigation; disputes involving State parties, disputes under investment treaties, claims of expropriation and political risk insurance. Counsel in ICSID, ICSID Additional Facility, ICC, UNCITRAL and other ad hoc proceedings, and cases before US courts.
Prof. Memberships: NY State Bar, 1990; Washington DC Bar, 1992; Member of Executive Council and Executive Committee, American Society of International Law; Chair, International Law Section of DC Bar; ABA; IBA; LCIA; Institute for Transnational Arbitration; International Law Association.
Personal: AB, cum laude, Vassar College; London School of Economics; Université de Grenoble ; JD, University of Chicago.

SNYDER, Jeffrey L
Crowell & Moring LLP, Washington, DC
202 624 2790
jsnyder@crowell.com
Recommended in International Trade
Practice Areas: Jeffrey L Snyder is Chair of Crowell & Moring's International Group and focuses on the US regulation of international trade. With clients in the chemical, electronics, pharmaceuticals, and insurance industries, he advises on Customs law, antidumping, and other import laws. Creating strategies to eliminate, minimize, or manage the burden on imports is a feature of his practice. He has developed approaches for multinationals to manage the impact of US extraterritorial regulations, such as sanctions administered by the Office of Foreign Assets Control.
Personal: BA from American University, 1980; JD from American University, 1983; LLM from Columbia University, 1984.

SOUSSLOFF, Andrew D
Sullivan & Cromwell LLP, New York
212 558 4000
soussloffa@sullcrom.com
Recommended in Capital Markets

Practice Areas: Capital markets transactions, securities law and corporate governance matters. He has represented industrial companies, financial institutions and sovereign governments in debt and equity financings in US and international markets, and he advises multinational companies on public disclosure, securities law and corporate governance issues.
Prof. Memberships: Legal Practice Division Council of the International Bar Association (2005-); Co-Chairman, Securities Law Committee of the International Bar Association (2000-2003).
Career: Partner since 1986. Co-Managing Partner of General Practice Group.
Personal: University of Pennsylvania (BA, MA, 1975); University of Pennsylvania Law School (JD, 1979).

SPAK, Gregory J
White & Case LLP, Washington, DC
202 626 3641
gspak@whitecase.com
Recommended in International Trade
Practice Areas: International trade regulation at all levels, including national administrative bodies, reviewing courts, regional arbitral panels, and all levels of WTO dispute resolution.
Prof. Memberships: American Bar Association.
Career: Partner since 1995.
Publications: Multiple publications on international business and trade regulation.
Personal: Georgetown University (BSFS, 1984); Georgetown University Law Center (JD, 1987).

SPAK, Walter J
White & Case LLP, Washington, DC
202 626 3606
wspak@whitecase.com
Recommended in International Trade
Practice Areas: Practice emphasizes the US and third country trade proceedings, customs issues, bilateral and multilateral trade negotiations, dispute resolution under NAFTA and the WTO and sector specific trade policy issues. Has been involved in over 100 original investigations and reviews under the US trade laws and the trade laws of third countries. His experience in customs law includes criminal and civil customs fraud investigations, valuation issues, classifications issues, customs audit, country-of-origin matters, marking requirements and general customs advice.
Personal: JD, Georgetown University, 1977; BA, University of Notre Dame, 1973; Sophia University (Japan), 1971.

SPENCER, Steven D
Morgan, Lewis & Bockius LLP, Philadelphia 215 963 5714
sspencer@morganlewis.com
Recommended in Litigation
Practice Areas: Steven D Spencer is a Partner in the Labor and Employment Law and Employee Benefits and Executive Compensation Practices. Mr

Spencer regularly advises plan sponsors, multiemployer and single employer pension and welfare plans and fiduciaries with respect to federal and state statutes, including ERISA, ADEA, ADA, and Title VII. He has handled numerous lawsuits involving ERISA, fiduciaries, discrimination, withdrawal liability and preemption. He is currently a Lecturer at the University of Pennsylvania School of Law and an Adjunct Professor at the Villanova University Law School.
Prof. Memberships: Charter Fellow, American College of Employee Benefits Counsel. Member, ABA.

SPERLING, Allan G
Cleary Gottlieb Steen & Hamilton LLP, New York 212 225 2260
asperling@cgsh.com
Recommended in Capital Markets
Practice Areas: Securities, financial, and corporate matters. Extensive experience representing underwriters, issuers and investors in public and private debt and equity financings, advising financial institutions on securities law and counseling businesses on corporate legal matters.
Prof. Memberships: Bar in New York. Admitted to practice before US Court of Appeals (Second Circuit), US District Court (Southern and Eastern Districts of New York), Member of New York State Bar Association.
Career: Joined firm, 1968; became Partner, 1976. LLB, Law Journal Editor, Order of the Coif, Yale Law School (1967); AB, cum laude, Phi Beta Kappa, Columbia University (1964).

STARER, Brian
Holland & Knight LLP, New York
212 513 3200
brian.starer@hklaw.com
Recommended in Shipping
Practice Areas: Partner and National Practice Leader for Maritime Group and Head of Rapid Response Team. Over 30 years experience in admiralty practice focused primarily on marine casualties including groundings, sinkings, fires, collisions and environmental pollution. Starer regularly advises ship owners, international Protection and Indemnity Clubs and hull underwriters on worldwide basis. Starer has investigated and advised on all aspects of maritime and environmental casualties, including property damage, cargo loss, personal injury and death claims, natural resource and other environmental damage. Starer has served as casualty counsel on more than 100 ship disasters worldwide including Exxon Valdez and Prestige.

STERN, Akiba
Morgan, Lewis & Bockius LLP, New York 212 309 6000
Recommended in Business Process Outsourcing, Technology
Please see New York for profile

STERN, Gary
Sidley Austin Brown & Wood LLP, Chicago 312 853 7267
gstern@sidley.com
Recommended in Capital Markets
Practice Areas: Partner in the Banking and Securitisation Group in Chicago. Represents investors, issuers, placement agents, credit enhancers and liquidity providers in securitisation transactions involving a variety of asset types, including, credit cards, auto loans, equipment leases, student loans, consumer loans, trade receivables, sports related revenue streams and entertainment royalties and distribution revenues. Transaction structures include multi-seller and single-seller commercial paper conduit deals, private placements and 144A issuances.
Prof. Memberships: American and Chicago Bar Associations.
Career: Northwestern University School of Law, JD, 1982; University of Michigan, BA, 1979. Bar Admission: Illinois, 1982.

STEWART, Terence
Stewart & Stewart, Washington, DC
202 785 4185
Recommended in International Trade

STOKES, Christopher S
Hogan & Hartson LLP, Washington, DC
202 637 5495
csstokes@hhlaw.com
Recommended in International Trade
Practice Areas: Christopher Stokes has more than 17 years of experience in international trade law, policy, and regulatory issues. He represents clients before all federal agencies regulating international trade matters, including the US Department of Commerce, the International Trade Commission, the US Trade Representative's office, and the US Customs Service. He also has extensive experience in representing companies and governments in World Trade Organization (WTO) disputes and negotiations, and has appeared before the WTO Appellate Body.
Personal: Georgetown University Law Center (JD, cum laude). He is admitted to practice before the Court of International Trade.

STRINGFELLOW, James S
Skadden, Arps, Slate, Meagher & Flom LLP & Affiliates, New York
212 735 3405
jstringf@skadden.com
Recommended in Capital Markets
Practice Areas: Represents issuers, underwriters, placement agents, lenders, agents, managers, investors and other participants in a variety of public and private structured finance transactions. Experience includes credit card, auto loan and other receivable securitizations; collateralized debt obligation issuances (including cash flow, market value, synthetic and hybrid type transactions) and other investment funds; com-

mercial and residential mortgage loan securitizations; asset-backed commercial paper transactions; and resecuritizations and repackagings of various securities and other financial assets and derivative products.

Career: JD, New York University School of Law, 1987; AB, Columbia College, 1983.

STROMFELD, Lary
Cadwalader, Wickersham & Taft LLP, New York 212 504 6291
lary.stromfeld@cwt.com
Recommended in Capital Markets

Practice Areas: Expertise in OTC fixed income products, credit derivatives, and municipal finance. Represents numerous commercial banks, bond insurers, derivative product companies, broker-dealers, hedge funds, and other financial institutions. Develops, negotiates and documents financial products, including credit derivatives, total return swaps, currency swaps, and fixed income swaps. Assists clients in the creation of structured derivative products that combine securitization techniques and derivative products. Extensively involved in developing and utilizing financial products in the primary and secondary municipal markets, including tender option programs, swaps, repurchase agreements, and other investment products.

Personal: BA, Brandeis University (1977); JD, University of Pennsylvania Law School (1981). Credit Derivatives and General Documentation Committees of the International Swaps and Derivatives Association, Inc.; National Association of Bond Lawyers.

SUNG, Audrey L
Holland & Knight LLP, San Francisco 415 743 6900
audrey.sung@hklaw.com
Recommended in Shipping

Practice Areas: Partner in the firm's Business Law Section, practices general corporate and commercial law, with a particular emphasis on asset-based financing for assets ranging from commercial jet aircraft to turboprop aircraft and from oil drilling rigs to private yachts. She represents financial institutions as well as borrowers and operators in a variety of financing structures. She also has extensive experience representing financial institutions and operating lessors in a wide range of domestic and cross-border leasing transactions (including sale-leasebacks), in asset acquisitions and dispositions in the secondary market, and in negotiations with manufacturers and vendors of new equipment.

SUTHERLAND, Susan J
Skadden, Arps, Slate, Meagher & Flom LLP & Affiliates, New York
212 735 2388
ssutherl@skadden.com
Recommended in Capital Markets

Practice Areas: Has over 20 years of experience representing US and international issuers and underwriters in a wide variety of capital markets transactions, including public offerings and private placements of debt and equity securities. Practice focuses on transactions involving US and international insurance and reinsurance companies in all lines of business. Has also worked on merger and acquisition transactions, leveraged buyouts, exchange offers and restructurings, and corporate governance and securities law disclosure matters.

Career: JD, New York University School of Law, 1982 (Root-Tilden Scholar; Member, Review of Law and Social Change); BA, Denison University, 1979 (highest honors; Phi Beta Kappa).

SWEENEY III, James
Nicoletti Hornig Campise and Sweeney, New York
212 220 3830
Recommended in Shipping

TEHAN, John
Simpson Thacher & Bartlett LLP, New York 212 455 2000
jtehan@stblaw.com
Recommended in Capital Markets

Practice Areas: Corporate Partner at Simpson Thacher & Bartlett LLP and Chairman of the firm's Opinions Committee. Concentrates in corporate finance advising both issuers and underwriters in capital raising transactions with emphasis on public and private high-yield financings and initial public offerings. Also designated by investment grade and other corporate issuers to act as underwriters counsel on an ongoing basis in connection with the offering by such issuers of their debt and equity securities. Regularly advises KKR and its portfolio companies in connection with their high yield debt and initial public offerings. On the underwriting side, primarily represents Lehman Brothers, J.P. Morgan Chase, Merrill Lynch, Morgan Stanley and Goldman Sachs. Acts as underwriters counsel for corporate issuers such as Anadarko Petroleum Corporation, Textron, MBNA Corporation, Halliburton Corporation, Georgia-Pacific Corporation, The Ryland Group and Owens-Illinois.

Prof. Memberships: Member of the Association of the Bar of the City of New York.

Career: Member of the firm since 1982. Admitted to the New York Bar in 1974.

Personal: Received AB from LeMoyne College in 1970 and JD from Catholic University School of Law in 1973 where he was the Recent Developments Editor of The Catholic University Law Review from 1972 to 1973.

TENEV, Jovi
Holland & Knight LLP, New York
212 513 3200
jovi.tenev@hklaw.com
Recommended in Shipping

Practice Areas: Partner in the firm's Business Law Section. He has extensive experience representing financial institutions, investment banks, foreign and domestic companies, and airlines in a wide variety of transactions. He practices in all areas of corporate finance, including finance projects in the US and international aerospace, shipping, offshore drilling and rail industries, utilizing complex syndicated loan, leveraged and single-investor leasing structures, and capital markets. He has been involved in domestic and foreign mergers and acquisitions, portfolio purchases, workouts, bankruptcies, restructurings, enforcement and foreclosures, and in US regulatory proceedings.

TOLLEY III, Edward P
Simpson Thacher & Bartlett LLP, New York 212 455 3189
etolley@stblaw.com
Recommended in Capital Markets

Practice Areas: Partner in the Corporate Department. Represents several of the country's largest private equity sponsors in connection with their securities financing matters. Recent experience includes representing Blackstone in connection with bridge and high yield financings for its $3 billion acquisition of Celanese; THLee, Bain and Providence Equity in connection with bridge and high yield financings for their $2.6 billion acquisition of Warner Music; Blackstone and Apollo in connection with $1.6 billion in high yield financings for their $4.2 billion acquisition of Ondeo Nalco in November 2003; THLee, Bain and Blackstone in connection with bridge and $1 billion in high yield financings for their $1.8 billion acquisition of Houghton Mifflin in January 2003; KKR in connection with financings for Sealy, Wincor-Nixdorf, Willis Group and Rockwood Specialties; and Blackstone in connection with multiple financings. Equity experience includes representing Celanese, Nalco, Alpha National Resources, Foundation Coal, Premcor and Willis Group in their IPOs and underwriters in various IPOs, including the $8.6 billion IPO of Kraft Foods in 2001.

Career: Joined Simpson Thacher in 1990 and became a Partner in January 1999.

Personal: BA, 1984, Dartmouth College (Phi Beta Kappa, magna cum laude); JD, 1990, University of Virginia School of Law.

TOWNSEND, John M
Hughes Hubbard & Reed LLP, Washington, DC 202 721 4640
townsend@hugheshubbard.com
Recommended in Arbitration

Practice Areas: Partner; Chair, Arbitration and ADR Group. International disputes; competition law.

Prof. Memberships: Board of Directors, Chairman of Executive Committee, American Arbitration Association; Trustee, Arbitration and Competition Law Committees, US Council for International Business; Chair, Mediation Committee, International Bar Association; Challenge Review Board, CPR Institute for Dispute Resolution; American Law Institute; College of Commercial Arbitrators.

Career: Hughes Hubbard & Reed since 1971, New York, Paris and Washington. Admitted New York 1972; District of Columbia 1990.

Publications: Include 'Revised AAA-ABA Code of Ethics for Arbitrators Explained' (with Bruce Meyerson), Dispute Resolution Journal, Feb./April 2004; 'Drafting Arbitration Clauses: Avoiding the 7 Deadly Sins', Dispute Resolution Journal, Feb./April 2003; 'Arbitration Across the Civil Law—Common Law Divide' (with Siegfried Elsing), Arbitration International, Feb. 2002; 'The Case for Site Licenses', ECLR, March 1999; 'Nonsignatories and Arbitration', ADR Currents, Sept. 1998.

Personal: Born 21 March, 1947. BA Yale University 1968; JD Yale University 1971. Fluent French.

TROOBOFF, Peter D
Covington & Burling, Washington, DC 202 662 5512
ptrooboff@cov.com
Recommended in International Trade

Practice Areas: Handles foreign investment, foreign trade and export controls, foreign trade sanctions, international investments, foreign assets control, and international litigation and arbitration. For over 30 years, he has advised US and non-US companies on a wide range of legal issues arising from the application to them of US laws and regulations affecting trade and investment.

Career: Served as counsel on Grand Duchy of Luxembourg in Whitehead v Grand Duchy of Luxembourg, et al., US District Court, Eastern District of Virginia; and as one of the three arbitrators in a claim before the International Centre for the Settlement of Investment Disputes (ICSID), Compañia de Aguas del Aconquija, S.A. & Compagnie Générale des Eaux v Argentine Republic (Case No. ARB/97/3).

Personal: Harvard University (LLB, 1967, cum laude); London School of Economics, London, England (LLM, 1968); Hague Academy of International Law, (Diploma, 1968, cum laude); Columbia University (AB, 1964, cum laude); Institut d' Études Européennes, Paris (1962-63).

TUSSING, James D
Fulbright & Jaworski L.L.P., New York 212 318 3024
jtussing@fulbright.com
Recommended in Aviation

Practice Areas: Aviation Law and Equipment Finance.

Prof. Memberships: Mr Tussing is the Chairman of the Aircraft Financing Subcommittee of the American Bar

Association. He joined the US Civil Aeronautics Board in Washington, DC, in 1976 and served as trial attorney and senior trial attorney from 1977-82.
Career: James D Tussing is a Partner in the New York office of Fulbright and heads the firm's Equipment Finance Practice Group. He has nearly 30 years of experience in aircraft financing.
Personal: BA, cum laude, Yale University (1973); JD, Boston University School of Law (1976). Mr Tussing is admitted to practice in Massachusetts, Washington, DC, and New York.

ULTERINO, Eugene D.
Nixon Peabody LLP, Rochester
585 263 1580
eulterino@nixonpeabody.com
Recommended in Litigation
Practice Areas: Practice concentrates on Labor and Employment Law. He has extensive litigation experience in state and federal courts, in matters pertaining to employment-at-will issues; fiduciary, benefit claims and pre emption issues under ERISA; discrimination issues arising under state and federal statutes and overtime claims under state and federal law. Litigation matters have ranged from single plaintiff claims to class actions involving thousands of claimants.
Prof. Memberships: Admitted to practice in New York; NY State (Labor and Employment Law Section) and American (Labor Law Section) Bar Associations.
Personal: Georgetown University, LLB; University of Rochester, BA.

UNGER, Timothy
Andrews Kurth LLP, Houston
713 220 4200
Recommended in Energy, Projects
Please see Texas for profile

VACKETTA, Carl Lee
DLA Piper Rudnick Gray Cary US LLP, Washington, DC 202 861 6460
carl.vacketta@dlapiper.com
Recommended in Government Contracts
Practice Areas: Government affairs; government contracts.
Career: He has more than 38 years of experience in government contracts law. He has represented companies selling information technology, telecommunications equipment, and professional and technical services to the government. He has also led teams of attorneys, accountants, and engineers in the investigation and preparation of multimillion-dollar claims for major shipyards, aerospace, power generating, electronics, and telecommunication companies. He has in depth experience in the General Services Administration's Multiple Award Schedule Contract (MASC) program.
Personal: JD, University of Illinois at Urbana-Champaign; BS, University of Illinois at Urbana-Champaign.

VAN GORP, Jon D
Mayer, Brown, Rowe & Maw LLP, Chicago 312 701 7091
jvangorp@mayerbrownrowe.com
Recommended in Capital Markets
Practice Areas: Concentrates on structured finance transactions, with an emphasis on asset-backed securities offerings in the public and private markets. Experience securitizing virtually all types of financial assets, and is a recognized expert in the securitization of mortgage loans and auto receivables.
Prof. Memberships: New York, 2004. Illinois, 1998. Texas, 1994.
Career: Mayer, Brown, Rowe & Maw LLP, Chicago, 1997 to date; Partner, 2003. Thompson & Knight, LLP, Associate, Dallas, 1994-97.
Publications: Recent articles: "Funding Mortgage Loans With Extendible Note Funding Facilities," Journal of Structured Finance, Fall 2004. Recent Presentations: "IMN 2005 ABS West," Phoenix, Arizona, February 2005. "IMN 2004 ABS East," Boca Raton, Florida, October 2004. " Structured Finance Institute Introduction to Securitization Transactions," Chicago, Illinois, June and October 2004. "Structured Finance Institute Introduction to Securitization Transactions," Chicago, Illinois, June 2004.
Personal: JD (cum laude), Southern Methodist University School of Law, 1994; Staff Editor, The International Lawyer. BA, Calvin College, 1991. Member, 2005 Leadership Greater Chicago Fellows Class.

VERRILL Jr, Charles
Wiley Rein & Fielding LLP, Washington, DC 202 719 7000
Recommended in International Trade

VOGE, William
Latham & Watkins LLP, New York
212 906 1200
Recommended in Projects

VON MEHREN, Robert
Robert B von Mehren - Sole Practitioner, New York 212 909 6588
Recommended in Arbitration

WACHSBERGER, Chaim
Chadbourne & Parke LLP, New York
212 408 5100
Recommended in Projects
Please see New York for profile

WALL, Christopher
Pillsbury Winthrop LLP, Washington, DC
202 775 9850
cwall@pillsburywinthrop.com
Recommended in International Trade
Practice Areas: Export controls; economic sanctions; national security reviews; Foreign Corrupt Practices Act; import proceedings; NAFTA and WTO dispute resolution; investor-state arbitration; antiboycott regulation; trade policy. International litigation and commercial transactions. Work with the US Departments of Commerce, State, Treasury and Defense, US Trade Representa-

tive, Committee on Foreign Investment in the US, Customs and Border Protection, US International Trade Commission, and other agencies.
Career: Admitted to practice in New York (1980), District of Columbia (1986), Court of International Trade (1985), Court of Appeals for the Federal Circuit (2002).
Publications: Pillsbury Winthrop International Trade New Briefs - 'President Implements Sanctions Against Syria,' May 18, 2004; 'US Ends Libya Sanctions,' April 29, 2004; 'New Economic Sanctions Imposed Against Burma,' July 30, 2003;' U.N. Security Council Removes Sanctions Against Iraq,' May 23, 2003; 'International Convention Prohibits Bribery of Public Officials,' Metropolitan Corporate Counsel, October 1998; 'Cross-Border Dilemma: EU Action Over Helms-Burton Would Be A Mistake,' Financial Times, July 16, 1996; 'US Foreign Investment Regulations,' Financial Times, December 12, 1991; 'Exon-Florio and the Myth of CFIUS,' FT Mergers & Acquisitions, August 1989.
Personal: Yale College, BA 1974 (Summa cum laude, Phi Beta Kappa), Oxford University, BA 1976, University of Virginia Law School, JD 1979.

WARD, Bradford L
Dewey Ballantine LLP, Washington, DC
202 429 2342
bward@deweyballantine.com
Recommended in International Trade
Practice Areas: Mr Ward has specialized in international trade law and particularly antidumping matters since 1984. His recent activities have included litigation before NAFTA panels, advising the US government in WTO litigation, management of numerous antidumping procedings before US government agencies, litigation before the US Court of International Trade, preparation of extensive antidumping, analyses for use during consideration of the Uruguay Round Agreements Act and implementing regulations, and client counseling regarding business negotiations and public and political relations.
Career: Partner, Dewey Ballantine LLP.
Personal: BS, University of Oregon, 1980. JD, American University, 1983.

WEERASINGHE, Rohan
Shearman & Sterling LLP, New York
212 848 7088
rweerasinghe@shearman.com
Recommended in Capital Markets
Practice Areas: Partner in Shearman & Sterling's Capital Markets Group. Specializes in corporate and securities law. Regularly represents both underwriters and issuers in public offering transactions, especially involving complex transactions such as those involving leveraged buyouts, high yield debt issuances, initial public offerings and cross-border offerings.
Prof. Memberships: Member, New York State Bar Association.

Career: Joined Shearman in 1977 and became Partner in 1985.
Personal: BA, summa cum laude, Harvard College (1972); MBA, Baker Scholar, Harvard Business School (1977); JD, Harvard Law School (1977).

WEINER, Daniel H
Hughes Hubbard & Reed LLP, New York
212 837 6874
weiner@hugheshubbard.com
Recommended in Arbitration
Practice Areas: Partner, New York. Concentrates on international and domestic arbitration and litigation. Dan has served as counsel in numerous arbitrations under ICC and AAA rules including matters involving joint ventures, licensing and other contractual disputes.
Career: Hughes Hubbard & Reed LLP since 1984. Admitted in New York 1985.
Personal: Born January 20, 1960. Princeton University AB cum laude 1981; New York University JD 1984.

WEISBURG, Henry
Shearman & Sterling LLP, New York
212 848 4193
hweisburg@shearman.com
Recommended in Arbitration
Practice Areas: Partner at Shearman & Sterling specializing in international arbitration and litigation, particularly in the area of international financial, investment and insolvency disputes; also active in handling complex international insurance matters, particularly involving political risk insurance.
Prof. Memberships: Member of the Committee on International Commercial Dispute Resolution, the Association of the Bar of the City of New York; Member of the American Bar Association; Member of the American Society of International Law.
Career: Joined Shearman in 1977 and became Partner in 1986.
Personal: BA, Trinity College (1973); JD, New York University School of Law (1977).

WEST, Joseph D
Gibson, Dunn & Crutcher LLP, Washington, DC 202 955 8500
Recommended in Construction, Government Contracts
Please see District of Columbia for profile

WHALEN, Thomas
Carter Ledyard & Milburn LLP, New York 212 732 3200
Recommended in Shipping

WHELAN, William
Cravath, Swaine & Moore LLP, New York 212 474 1644
wwhelan@cravath.com
Recommended in Capital Markets
Practice Areas: High-yield offerings, initial public offerings and follow-on equity offerings. Head of Cravath's internal continuing legal education program for corporate lawyers.

Prof. Memberships: ABA (Negotiated Covenant Task Force of the Trust Indenture Subcommittee); ABCNY (Securities Regulation Committee).
Career: Partner since 1998. Clerkship: Hon. William H. Timbers (US Court of Appeals for the Second Circuit).
Publications: Chair, 'Securities Offerings 2005: What Issuers' & Underwriters' Counsel Need to Know Now', Practising Law Institute, April 2005.
Personal: Fordham University School of Law (JD, cum laude, 1983; Managing Editor, 'Fordham Law Review'); University of Virginia (BA, with distinction, 1980).

WHITE, John
Cravath, Swaine & Moore LLP, New York 212 474 1732
jwhite@cravath.com
Recommended in Capital Markets
Practice Areas: Corporate finance, securities offerings, IPOs, corporate governance. Managing Partner, Finance. Has served as Recruiting Partner, Managing Partner and Head of the Corporate Department.
Prof. Memberships: New York Stock Exchange (member, Legal Advisory Committee); Practising Law Institute (Board of Directors; past Co-Chair Annual Institute of Securities Regulation); Securities Regulation Institute (Vice Chairman).
Career: Partner since 1980. Clerkship: US Court of Appeals for the Third Circuit.
Publications: Frequent speaker on securities, public financings, accounting and corporate governance issues.
Personal: New York University School of Law (JD 1973; Managing Editor, 'Law Review'); University of Virginia (BS 1970).

WILLIAMS Jr, William
Sullivan & Cromwell LLP, New York 212 558 4000
Recommended in Capital Markets

WIPPERMAN, Robert
McKee Nelson LLP, New York 917 777 4600
rwipperman@mckeenelson.com
Recommended in Capital Markets
Practice Areas: Since 1986 has concentrated exclusively in structured finance transactions. Regularly represents originators, servicers, issuers, purchasers, and underwriters in public offerings and private placements of mortgaged-backed

and asset-backed securities, as well as originators in both on-balance-sheet and off-balance-sheet warehouse arrangements. Established and maintained securitization programs for several issuers.
Career: Prior to joining McKee Nelson, was a Partner in the New York Office of Stroock & Stroock & Lavan LLP. At McKee Nelson, heads the firm's Structured Finance Group. Received a JD from Boston College Law School in 1979.

WOLF, Charles B
Vedder, Price, Kaufman & Kammholz, Chicago 312 609 7500
Recommended in Employee Benefits, Litigation

WOLFE, Gary
Seward & Kissel, New York 212 574 1223
wolfe@sewkis.com
Recommended in Shipping
Practice Areas: Securities, capital markets, corporate finance, shipping and environmental, cross-boarder transactions and maritime lease finance.
Prof. Memberships: Association of the Bar of the City of New York (Admiralty Committee); New York County Lawyers Association (former Chairman, Maritime Law Committee); US Business Council for Southern Europe (former President).
Career: Partner,Seward & Kissel LLP, since 1992; associate then Partner, Hill, Betts & Nash , 1980-91; associate, Cahill Gordon & Reindel, 1977-80; Fulbright Dissertation Fellowship, Ljubljana, Slovenia, Belgrade, Yugoslavia (1975-76).
Personal: Yale Law School (JD 1975); Cornell University (six-year PhD Program, AB 1971); AIESEC Exchange, Maribor, Slovenia, Zagreb, Croatia (1971).

WOLFF, Alan
Dewey Ballantine LLP, Washington, DC 202 429 2352
awolff@deweyballantine.com
Recommended in International Trade
Practice Areas: Alan Wolff is a member of Dewey Ballantine's Management Committee and Managing Partner of the firm's Washington, DC office. He also leads Dewey Ballantine's International Trade Practice Group.
Career: Partner, Dewey Ballantine LLP.

Mr Wolff served as United States Deputy Special Representative for Trade Negotiations (1977-79) in the Carter Administration, holding the rank of ambassador, after having served as General Counsel of the agency from 1974-77.
Personal: Born June 12, 1942. BA, Harvard College, 1963. LLB, Columbia Law School, 1966.

WOODS, John
Thacher Proffitt & Wood LLP, New York 212 912 7672
jwoods@tpw.com
Recommended in Shipping
Practice Areas: John Woods concentrates his practice in maritime law and insurance and reinsurance litigation and arbitration. He principally represents US and foreign insurers (and their assureds) in the areas of maritime hull, liability, cargo, pollution, war risk, loss of earnings, general average and environmental law. His practice also includes arbitration and mediation of maritime disputes, handling of offshore and onshore energy claims and losses, and review and advising on shipbuilding contracts and related disputes. Mr. Woods has handled litigations involving major maritime casualties and claims in courts across the United States, and has counseled clients involved in litigations in foreign courts, principally in Europe. He has argued appeals in the New York appellate courts (including the New York Court of Appeals) and five of the US Courts of Appeal.

ZAHLER, Robert
Shaw Pittman LLP, Washington, DC 202 663 8130
robert.zahler@shawpittman.com
Recommended in Business Process Outsourcing: National, IT Outsourcing
Practice Areas: Robert Zahler, a Partner and Founder of Shaw Pittman's Global Sourcing Practice Group and Lead Director of the firm's Management Board, has been practicing law for 30 years. He participates in a wide range of legal and business consulting work, with special emphasis on sourcing, both information technology outsourcing (ITO) and business process outsourcing (BPO). This work includes business process and information technology outsourcing arrangements (both onshore and offshore and covering data center operations, distributed comput-

ing, desktop support, and applications development and maintenance), the structuring of telecommunications and managed network services transactions, the development of systems integration and custom system development contracts, the protection of intellectual property rights, the licensing of computer software and, over the last five years, significant business process outsourcing relationships focusing on human resources, finance and accounting, procurement and supply chain management, among others. His work includes cutting-edge transactions across most major industries and in the United States, Canada, Latin and South America, Europe, South Africa and Australia. During the past 20 years, Mr Zahler and his colleagues at Shaw Pittman have represented more than 450 corporations and governmental entities on strategic sourcing initiatives with a total contract value in excess of $350 billion.
Prof. Memberships: Society of Sigma Xi (scientific honorary); admitted to practice: District of Columbia (1975); District of Columbia Court of Appeals; US Supreme Court; US Court of Appeals for the First, Third, Fourth and District of Columbia Circuits; US District Court for the District of Columbia.
Publications: Mr Zahler has written widely on the subjects of outsourcing and procuring complex information technology and business process services. He was a key contributor to the Global Sourcing group's MOSAIC framework and VALUECHAIN methodology. He is a frequent speaker on the subject having appeared at conferences sponsored by CIO, Fortune and Forbes magazines, the Society of Information Management (SIM), the Sourcing Interests Group, the Outsourcing Institute, the Information Technology Association of American (ITAA), Digital Consulting, Inc., and the Yankee Group.
Personal: Harvard Law School, J.D., cum laude, 1975; Massachusetts Institute of Technology, SB, Physics, 1972. (At press time, Shaw Pittman LLP had entered into a merger agreement with Pillsbury Winthrop LLP. The merger is expected to close by April 2005. Post-closing, the name of the firm will be Pillsbury Winthrop Shaw Pittman LLP.)

RANKINGS AND COMMENTARY

CONTENTS: Corporate/M&A p.111; Employment: p.113; Litigation: p.115; Real Estate p.119; Individuals' Profiles p.121; Firms' Profiles p.127.

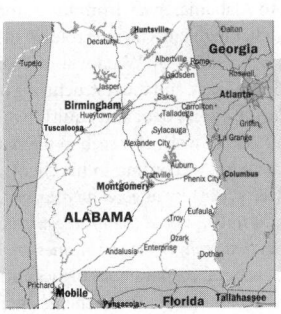

How lawyers are ranked

The opinions we gather from clients — mainly from in-house lawyers but also from other purchasers of legal services — are balanced by opinions from colleagues and competitors. Together, they provide two different perspectives — an all-round view — and biased viewpoints cancel each other out.

CORPORATE/M&A

Alabama
Leading firms (Corporate/M&A)

1 BALCH & BINGHAM *Birmingham*
  BRADLEY ARANT ROSE & WHITE LLP *Birmingham*
  BURR & FORMAN LLP *Birmingham*

2 BAKER, DONELSON, BEARMAN *Birmingham*
  MAYNARD, COOPER & GALE PC *Birmingham*

3 JOHNSTON BARTON PROCTOR *Birmingham*
  SIROTE & PERMUTT PC *Birmingham*

Leading individuals (Corporate/M&A)

1 CARRUTHERS Thomas *Bradley Arant*, Birmingham
  CURRAN Gregory *Maynard Cooper*, Birmingham
  GRENIER John *Bradley Arant*, Birmingham
  HUGHEY Jr James *Balch & Bingham*, Birmingham
  KUSHNER Harold *Baker Donelson*, Birmingham
  PRICE Gene *Burr & Forman*, Birmingham
  THUSTON Lee *Burr & Forman*, Birmingham

2 BEALE Walter *Balch & Bingham*, Birmingham
  BROCKMAN Richard *Johnston Barton*, Birmingham
  COOPER John *Sirote & Permutt*, Birmingham
  DREW Mark *Maynard Cooper*, Birmingham
  HARMON Christopher *Maynard Cooper*, Birmingham
  MINISMAN B G *Baker Donelson*, Birmingham
  ROSE Jr J William *Johnston Barton*, Birmingham
  STEPHENSON Jack *Burr & Forman*, Birmingham
  TRACY Timothy *Balch & Bingham*, Birmingham

Firms and Individuals are listed alphabetically in each band.

Band 1

Balch & Bingham
See firm details p.127

The Firm: This *"impressive full-service law firm"* is historically known for its work for Alabama Power. These days, over half of its work is for major public companies, including a number of household names, and the firm is increasingly recognized in the market as a true corporate heavyweight. It fields separate corporate and securities, M&A and corporate governance practice groups, which between them, clients agree, *"have it all covered."* On the securities side,

for example, the firm recently handled the $250 million IPO of the Vesta Insurance Group. It has also been heavily involved in the project to build HealthSouth's digital hospital, and in subsequent ventures connected to this.

The Lawyers: *"One of the leaders in the state,"* managing partner **Jim Hughey** (see p.123) continues to impress clients and attorneys alike. Over the past year he has been heavily involved in providing corporate governance advice to public and closely held companies. Clients were also impressed by *"fine securities and general corporate"* practitioner, **Mac Beale** (see p.121), and drew particular attention to his intricate knowledge of the Alabama securities statutes. He is especially well regarded for his expertise in corporate finance transactions connected with public utilities. A new addition to the tables this year is the *"exceptionally thorough and hardworking"* **Timothy Tracy** (see p.126). Described as *"a good lawyer for complicated transactions,"* he is particularly noted for his *"intricate knowledge of complex financial arrangements."*

The Clients: Southern Company; Compass Bank; AmSouth Bank; Regions; Vesta Insurance; Intergraph; Wolverine Tube; Alfa Insurance and Alabama Power.

Bradley Arant Rose & White LLP
See firm details p.128

The Firm: When it comes to sheer quality, for many commentators this is *"the finest firm in the state,"* as well as being the largest in Birmingham. It continues to be *"the firm of choice"* for a number of major public and private companies for transactions at both state and national levels. Covering all aspects of M&A, securities law, banking and finance, bankruptcy, and general commercial advice, this full-service corporate group is also able to draw on advice from other equally impressive departments when necessary. With all this expertise, it's hardly surprising that the firm recently landed roles in some of the largest corporate projects ever seen in the state, notably the $14.3 billion acquisition by Wachovia

of Alabama-based SouthTrust, and the $1.35 billion sale of Blount International to Lehman Brothers Merchant Banking Partners and its co-investors. The firm also represents a number of educational and nonprofit enterprises.

The Lawyers: Tom Carruthers (see p.121) is widely regarded as *"the dean of the Bar and the master counselor."* He continues to employ his vast experience, contacts and knowledge to oversee major transactions and bring in substantial amounts of new international work to the firm. He also provides intricate estate planning advice, often involving properties or assets valued at over $500 million. **Beau Grenier** (see p.122) chairs the firm's executive committee and is managing partner of its corporate group. He was described as *"a deal-maker not a deal-breaker,"* and many fellow attorneys agreed that he would be their corporate lawyer of choice. Clients, meanwhile, value the *"consistent sage advice he provides,"* and appreciate that he is *"still one of the hardest working people in existence."*

The Clients: The firm recently acted for REVCO in its $380 million acquisition of drug company, Big B. Other clients include: SouthTrust; Hyundai; University of Alabama in Birmingham; Heritage Bank; Vulcan Materials Company; EBSCO Industries; BE&K; Torchmark; Russell; Energen and James Wilson and Associates.

Burr & Forman LLP
See firm details p.129

The Firm: Consistently referred to as *"one of the preeminent business firms in Alabama,"* Burr & Forman's general corporate practice continues to excel in a range of areas. It is held in particularly high regard, however, for its specialist experience in the automotive industry and, especially, branch relocations. For example, the firm was recently appointed primary counsel to Mercedes-Benz US International, to advise on its plant relocation to Alabama, and has also overseen the site selection, incentives negotiation and economic development packages for many other leading automotive companies relocating to Alabama. Away from the automotive sector, other highlights include roles in the $14.3 billion acquisition by Wachovia of Alabama-based SouthTrust, and the restructuring of Citation Corporation's debt and equity, two of the largest pieces of work ever seen in the state.

The Lawyers: According to his clients, **Gene Price** (see p.124) is "*as good an attorney as you will get in town, with a technical competency in the issues that really affect our business on a daily basis.*" A general corporate, securities and M&A lawyer, he has a particular niche in the IT and healthcare industries, and has worked on many transactions for physicians' groups over the year. Price was also the lead attorney representing Gestamp in connection with Oxford Automotive's Chapter 11 filing and the sale of its facility in McCalla, the purchase price of which was in the $100 million range. A "*big rainmaker and successful corporate lawyer,*" **Lee Thuston** (see p.125) represents major automotive companies and is well known for his specialist expertise in automotive plant relocation work. The president-elect of the Birmingham Bar Association, he was also described as "*an asset to the community.*" "*Strong technician*" **Jack Stephenson** (see p.125) is the lead securities lawyer at the firm. During the year he has been busy developing his niche in nursing home acquisitions and financing.

The Clients: Mercedes-Benz; ProAssurance; Vulcan Engineering; SouthTrust Bank; ACIPCO; Honda; Citation Corporation and USX.

Band 2

Baker, Donelson, Bearman, Caldwell & Berkowitz, PC
See firm details p.1613

The Firm: This large, full-service firm was described by clients as "*one of the best corporate law firms in the southeast.*" The consensus of opinion is that its recent merger has created a force to reckon with, bolstering the firm's profile and capacity in a variety of key areas. The corporate team enjoys a tradition of handling top-quality securities work, and has also been continuing to provide advice on corporate governance issues post-Sarbanes-Oxley. It represents both private and public companies from a diverse range of industries, such as manufacturing, retail, healthcare, software and technology. Highlights from the year include working on a financial package to aid the growth of a steel company, and advising on the formation of many new healthcare entities.

The Lawyers: "*One of the absolute star corporate lawyers in Alabama,*" **Harold Kushner** (see p.123) continues to impress clients by "*striving to truly understand our business in order to reach the best overall solution,*" and for his meticulous attention

to detail. Although active in a broad range of corporate and transactional matters, he is most closely associated with advice to private companies. In the past year he has worked on the acquisition and disposal of a number of software companies. He is also currently chair of the Alabama Securities Commission, a position which, clients agree, gives him a rounded understanding of all aspects of securities law. A new entrant to the tables this year, **BG Minisman** (see p.124) was recommended as being "*extremely knowledgeable in the securities field, particularly in the healthcare arena.*" Admiring sources noted that: "*He really does have this thing airtight for publicly held companies.*" Recent highlights include working on a private offering of 25.3 million common shares for Medical Properties Trust, as part of a scheme to acquire or develop over $500 million of healthcare facilities across the country.

The Clients: Express Oil Change; SouthTrust Bank; Daniel Realty; The Colonial Company; Hanna Steel; Bayer Properties and Southern Pipe and Supply Co.

Maynard, Cooper & Gale PC
The Firm: According to one client – and echoing a wider market view – this is "*one of the best firms I've worked with: it's dedicated to clients and very responsive.*" M&A, securities regulation, venture capital financings, general corporate work and private investment fund creation form the core of the corporate, securities and banking practice. Recent highlights include the formation of three new banks in Alabama, and working on a cross-border finance project for McWane Cast Iron Pipe. Private investment fund formation has been a growing area for the group, and it completed around ten fund formation transactions during the past year.

The Lawyers: The "*calm, level-headed*" **Greg Curran** was described to researchers as a fine attorney and a well-respected member of the Alabama Bar. As well as M&A and securities work, he provides general strategic business advice. During the past year he has been busy working on the creation of a number of private investment funds. According to peers, "*main point guy*" **Mark Drew** enjoys "*great relationships with his clients,*" and these include McWane Cast Iron Pipe. Among his recent highlights are a substantial cross-border joint venture, and he has also been representing financial institutions in M&As. Following market approval, securities specialist **Christopher Harmon** enters this year's tables. Heavily involved with Alabama National BanCorporation, he is probably best known for his securities compliance work and received numerous recommendations as "*a quality general corporate and securities regulation attorney.*"

The Clients: Alabama National BanCorporation; Protective Life Corporation; Torchmark Corporation; Baptist Health System; Computer Pro-

grams and Systems; Harbert Management; Drummond Company and McWane Cast Iron Pipe.

Band 3

Johnston Barton Proctor & Powell LLP
The Firm: The corporate and securities group of this full-service firm enters the tables this year following enthusiastic market endorsement. The group represents public and private corporations in a range of matters, including M&A, joint ventures, reorganizations and the public and private sales of securities. At present the firm is perhaps better known for its commercial practice rather than its corporate work, however observers agree that the general corporate practice is rapidly gaining ground. Clients drew particular attention to the firm's burgeoning expertise in corporate tax and M&A in the healthcare sector.

The Lawyers: "*A pleasure to deal with and a great lawyer,*" **William Rose** is highly admired for his transactional acumen, but has also enjoyed success in building corporate tax and business organization practices. "*If a case involves nursing homes,*" say peers, **Richard Brockman** "*will inevitably be on the other side.*" His "*tremendous expertise and stable of clients, particularly in the nursing home arena,*" are widely admired in the market.

The Clients: Clients include public and private corporations and partnerships from a variety of sectors, including healthcare.

Sirote & Permutt PC
The Firm: This corporate team advises clients on all areas of corporate and commercial law, including M&A, securities issues and joint ventures. However, it is historically best known for its tax expertise and boasts one of the largest tax practices in the southeast. Interviewees were full of praise for the quality of the specialist tax advice on offer to both individuals and public and private companies. As well as representing clients involved in tax controversies, the group also has the ability to deal with tax abatements and tax exempt financings. Other work undertaken includes business reorganizations and creating structures for new business ventures.

The Lawyers: "*A fine, experienced lawyer with a glowing reputation,*" **John Cooper** advises on general corporate and tax issues, securities transactions and M&A. He offers notable experience in a number of sectors, such as the pharmaceutical, retail and technology industries.

The Clients: Tax-exempt organizations and public and private companies make up the client base.

EMPLOYMENT

MAINLY DEFENDANT

Alabama
Leading firms
(Employment: Mainly Defendant)

1 BRADLEY ARANT ROSE & WHITE LLP *Birmingham*
2 BURR & FORMAN LLP *Birmingham*
  LEHR MIDDLEBROOKS PRICE *Birmingham*
  MAYNARD, COOPER & GALE PC *Birmingham*
3 BALCH & BINGHAM *Montgomery*
  CABANISS, JOHNSTON, GARDNER, *Birmingham*
  CONSTANGY, BROOKS & SMITH, LLC *Birmingham*
  JOHNSTON BARTON PROCTOR *Birmingham*
  OGLETREE, DEAKINS, NASH, SMOAK *Birmingham*

Leading individuals
(Employment: Mainly Defendant)

1 ALEXANDER James *Bradley Arant*, Birmingham
  GARDNER William *Cabaniss Johnston*, Birmingham
2 INGRAM Fredric *Burr & Forman*, Birmingham
  LEE Jeffrey *Maynard Cooper*, Birmingham
  MAY James *Bradley Arant*, Birmingham
  MIDDLEBROOKS David *Lehr Middlebrooks*, Birmingham
  MITCHELL Chris *Maynard Cooper*, Birmingham
  NELSON Carol *Maynard Cooper*, Birmingham
  POWELL Charles *Johnston Barton*, Birmingham
3 BROWN Stephen *Maynard Cooper*, Birmingham
  COLEMAN John *Burr & Forman*, Birmingham
  DAVIS Thomas *Constangy Brooks*, Birmingham
  DEBRUGE Marcel *Burr & Forman*, Birmingham
  DOBBS Tammy *Constangy Brooks*, Birmingham
  FRAZIER Sydney *Cabaniss Johnston*, Birmingham
  HANCOCK William *Adams and Reese*, Birmingham
  JOHNSON E Barry *Johnston Barton*, Birmingham
  LACY Peyton *Ogletree Deakins*, Birmingham
  LEHR Richard *Lehr Middlebrooks*, Birmingham
  SINGER Fern *Baker Donelson*, Birmingham
  SMITH David *Maynard Cooper*, Birmingham
  ST CLAIR Jay *Bradley Arant*, Birmingham
  VREELAND Albert *Lehr Middlebrooks*, Birmingham

Firms and Individuals are listed alphabetically in each band.

Band 1

Bradley Arant Rose & White LLP
See firm details p.128
The Firm: This well-established team was described to researchers as "*one of the sharpest groups around, with lawyers who are the best in the business.*" From cutting-edge employment litigation to traditional labor law, the firm has it covered, and it was particularly recommended for its ability to handle large, complex class actions. Recent examples include acting for US Pipe & Foundry Company in the settlement of a class action by African American employees of several facilities. The settlement affected all of US Pipe's operations in the eastern half of the country, and provided for a restructured promotion system. Another highlight was negotiating a settlement in a multiplaintiff, gender

discrimination case. The team is committed to alternative methods of dispute resolution, and acted in around 20 mediations and alternative dispute resolution proceedings over the past year. **The Lawyers:** "*First and foremost, you have to mention*" **Jim Alexander** (see p.121) "*if you're discussing great attorneys*" was a typical response during research. Often described as "*the lawyers' lawyer who stands head and shoulders above the rest,*" he advises employers on both labor and employment law issues and litigates on their behalf. As well as the US Pipe case described above, his recent highlights include advising on the lawsuit between the Steelworkers Union and Sloss Industries. This case ended with a summary judgment in favor of Sloss on procedural grounds, avoiding the need to litigate the substantive facts. **Jim May** (see p.123) is said to be "*an attorney of great judgment, good reasoning and practical advice.*" He is prime counsel on employment matters for such companies as BE&K. His workload includes defending major class action discrimination cases, EEOC charges and OFCCP proceedings. Following strong market recommendation, **Jay St Clair** (see p.125) enters the table this year. Described by clients as "*an absolute star of an attorney who really gets involved in our business needs,*" he was also said in some quarters to have "*the advantage of being smarter than everyone else practicing in this area*" – a claim that derives some support from his position as an adjunct professor at the Cumberland School of Law. He represents employers in virtually all matters arising in the workplace and has been lead trial attorney on a number of multiplaintiff discrimination cases during the year.
The Clients: US Pipe & Foundry Company; EBSCO Industries; State Farm; Chubb Group; Brasfield & Gorrie; Vulcan Materials Company and United Technologies.

Band 2

Burr & Forman LLP
See firm details p.129
The Firm: This large, high-class law firm boasts a full-service, cross-departmental labor and employment group. According to clients, it is well integrated with the rest of the firm, and its ability to draw on the support of other departments where necessary is a distinct advantage. The firm houses some of the most experienced and respected employment attorneys in the state, and also fields attorneys with a long track record in traditional labor issues. Employers are full of praise for the team's expertise in litigation and investigations before various courts and bodies. However, they also rely on its preventative advice and appreciate the employment audits, seminars and training it offers.

The Lawyers: "*One of the most senior and respected employment lawyers around,*" **Fred Ingram** (see p.123) successfully obtained two summary judgments in the federal court this year. As well as being an important rainmaker for the firm, he continues to lecture widely in the field of labor and employment law. His broad practice spans the range from union avoidance to employment discrimination litigation. "*Real fine attorney,*" **John Coleman** (see p.122) was particularly recommended for his experience in bench and jury trials and discrimination class actions. A certified mediator, his work this year includes obtaining summary judgment in a case concerning the alleged rape of an underage employee. He also acted in a number of cases involving alleged race and sex discrimination, and provided employment law training for a household name client. **Marcel Debruge** (see p.122) was hailed as "*doing a marvelous job for his clients.*" He tends to work more in the labor law issues, such as union avoidance and elections, but also has extensive experience of defending complex discrimination class actions and conducts training seminars for supervisors and other professionals.
The Clients: Sara Lee; Honda; US Steel; PPG Industries; Sears Roebuck; 3M; MeadWestvaco; CLP; UnitedHealthcare and Mercedes-Benz.

Lehr Middlebrooks Price & Vreeland, P.C.
The Firm: "*If I had something in Alabama that involved employment law I would use them for sure,*" said one client, echoing a general conviction that, in Alabama, this is as good as it gets. "*In the Southern regions, this boutique labor and employment firm has really got it covered,*" added another client, and it was particularly commended for running cases "*lean and mean.*" The team practices labor and employment law exclusively on behalf of management. Its client base includes many impressive names, such as BP America Inc, which the firm advised on its first strike in North America in the last 24 years. It is also held in very high regard for its track record of success in jury trials involving discrimination claims, and was hailed as being particularly good at defeating claims at the decertification stage.
The Lawyers: Even though David Proctor has been appointed as a federal judge and Barry Frederick has left the firm to practice plaintiff work, commentators agree that this "*great labor and employment law boutique*" has not been knocked off its stride. For example, it still boasts the services of **David Middlebrooks**, described as "*one of the leading employment attorneys in Alabama,*" with "*a quiet confidence that allows him to forge great relationships.*" He focuses primarily on employment litigation, and this year has successfully defended Allstate in several

critical cases involving, inter alia, discrimination claims. Also top of the tree is **Richard Lehr**, a "*really knowledgeable labor relations specialist*" and "*an exceptional negotiator with an unflappable style.*" More of a traditional labor lawyer, Lehr has led the firm as chief outside counsel to BP, assisting the company in traditional labor law matters throughout the USA, including union-organizing efforts at its largest refinery. **Al Vreeland** was referred to as "*a first-rate lawyer, hard working, academic and with a laid back, gentlemanly way of doing things.*" Appreciating his firm grasp of local conditions, commentators noted that: "*Al is certainly with the Southern way of doing things.*" His work over the year has included representing Benchmark Medical in federal litigation and two arbitrations over disputes arising from a $30 million acquisition.

The Clients: BP; Allstate; BellSouth; O'Neal Steel; Kellwood Company; Alyeska Pipeline Service; Aviagen; BAE Systems; Circuit City Stores; Dean Foods; ITT Technical Institute; JVC America; Liberty Mutual; Ogihara America Corp; Wal-Mart and Xerox.

Maynard, Cooper & Gale PC

The Firm: The labor and employment practice group of this full-service firm continues to expand, and the high-profile recent additions to the team are universally seen as strengthening it. As commentators noted: "*The addition of such fine attorneys can only mean that a fuller service will be provided to a wider client base.*" The group represents management in virtually every phase of employment law and labor relations, gaining praise from clients for its "*responsive and dedicated*" service. This year it has fully lived up to its reputation for handling the more complex employment cases, with work including Groover v Michelin North America, a nationwide class action involving approximately 10,000 class members. The firm also successfully defended 36 individual 'racially hostile work environment' claims, totaling over $33 million, in a complex, month-long trial.

The Lawyers: "*Exceptional attorney*" **Stephen Brown** heads the firm's labor and employment practice group. He was widely admired for his breadth of expertise and the "*good workmanlike approach he adopts to cases.*" He was involved in the two highlight matters listed above. According to his clients, **Jeff Lee** "*really has been the key to our legal successes over the years: he is a great litigator and arbitrator and has grown with us.*" He has a diverse practice, mostly defending management in a range of employment actions, but also doing some large commercial plaintiff work. Formerly with Constangy, Brooks & Smith, **Chris Mitchell** and **Carol Sue Nelson** are notable additions to the team this year. Mitchell is described by clients as being "*the pizzazz of the office – good on his feet with sound*

practical judgment that we always trust and run with.*" He represents employers in all sorts of discrimination claims, and also handles union contract negotiation and union arbitration issues, having been involved in 12 arbitrations over the past year. Carol Sue Nelson, meanwhile, is "*particularly well known for her sex discrimination practice*" but also has wide experience defending other forms of discrimination claim. She was appointed chair of the Governor's Alabama Womens Commission and is an approved mediator for the northern district of Alabama. **David Smith** continues to enjoy a fine reputation for his labor and employment litigation practice and is an original member of the firm's labor group. A keen author and speaker for the legal profession, Smith continues to be roundly applauded for "*his successful litigation practice.*"

The Clients: Michelin; Movie Gallery; Pemco Aeroplex; Boeing; BellSouth; Gulf States Paper Corporation and AmSouth Bank.

Band 3

Balch & Bingham
See firm details p.127

The Firm: This Montgomery-based team enters our table of leading firms this year following enthusiastic endorsement from clients for "*the proactive nature of the advice provided.*" The labor and employment group advises on a broad spectrum of matters for both private and public employers. Areas covered include labor-management relations, employee benefits work, and OSHA training and representation, and the group regularly represents employers before the NLRB and the EEOC. Recent highlights include successfully defending a number of class and collective race and other discrimination cases, and the firm has also tried numerous sexual harassment cases during the year.

The Lawyers: The group includes David Boyd and Jefferson Starling.

The Clients: The client base of this group is comprised of employers of a variety of sizes. Commentators particularly noted the group's work for Compass Bank and Southern Company.

Cabaniss, Johnston, Gardner, Dumas & O'Neal

The Firm: The labor and employment group here is known for the traditional virtues of technical excellence, clarity and service – high-quality attorneys provide academically strong but business-focused advice. The team has a long track record in the traditional labor arena, but is also witnessing considerable growth in its employment law practice, where it represents management in, among other matters, state and federal discrimination and harassment cases.

The Lawyers: **Bill Gardner** continues to be described as "*one of the icons of the area.*" According to interviewees, he is "*definitely one of*

the best in the business,*" and clients expressed their complete trust in his advice. As one said: "*If Bill tells you in the vernacular, you can just go straight ahead and run with it.*" Another well-respected labor and employment lawyer and "*one of the old school*" is **Sydney Frazier**. He was noted both for his employment litigation and traditional labor law experience, and boasts a long record of success before bodies such as the NLRB.

The Clients: The firm represents some major national and international companies as well as many local private companies.

Constangy, Brooks & Smith, LLC

The Firm: This "*boutique firm is well known in the employment arena,*" according to interviewees, where it is dedicated to representing management in labor and employment claims. The team is divided into separate departments specializing in all facets of employer representation, including employment litigation, labor relations, wage and hour disputes and workers' compensation defense. A recent highlight includes acting in a racial discrimination class action against a large retailer, involving over 40 individual claims. The team also successfully defended a nationwide discrimination class action for Target Stores and subsequently developed policies and procedures to help train employees and supervisors.

The Lawyers: **Thomas Davis**' practice encompasses all aspects of employment law. This includes not just the preparation for and participation in jury and non-jury trials and arbitrations, but helping to create preventative strategies. He was described to researchers as leading a good team and working well alongside **Tammy Dobbs**. "*A terrific all-rounder,*" she debuts in the tables following enthusiastic praise for her "*ability to really fashion an argument well.*" Dobbs undertakes both labor and employment litigation and is widely noted for her expertise in FMLA matters. The team did, however, lose several rated lawyers this year – it is considered too early to say whether this will affect it.

The Clients: SouthTrust Bank; AmSouth Bank; Gulf States Paper Corporation; Sara Lee; Advance Auto; Target Stores; Alfa Insurance; Asplundh and Winn-Dixie.

Johnston Barton Proctor & Powell LLP

The Firm: This single site firm has around 12 dedicated labor and employment lawyers providing a full spectrum of workplace representation. The group handles administrative and judicial litigation, including labor and employment arbitration, for national, regional and local clients. It was particularly noted for its ability to effectively handle wage and hour cases and discrimination litigation. For example, it recently conducted the defense in EEOC v R.P.H.

114   All quotes in the text are from interviews with clients and competitors.

CHAMBERS USA 2005

Management (trading as McDonald's), which involved alleged discrimination and constructive dismissal of an employee with the congenital disorder known as Sturge-Weber Syndrome. Another recent highlight for the team includes successfully getting a wage and hour case dismissed for a major retailer. The group also helps management to develop effective employment policies, and its 'client alert' e-mails were described by clients as *"informative on the topical issues that matter."*

The Lawyers: *"An absolutely first-class labor and employment attorney,"* **Butch Powell** was applauded by clients for his *"knack of efficiently resolving cases by obtaining summary judgment."* He is a founding member of the American Employment Law Council and a former president of the labor and employment law section of the Alabama State Bar. Another *"fantastic employment lawyer,"* **Barry Johnson** makes her debut in the tables. She represents management in all aspects of employment law counseling but was particularly highlighted for her litigation expertise.

The Clients: Important clients include Delphi, Coors Brewing Company and O'Charley's.

Ogletree, Deakins, Nash, Smoak & Stewart, PC
See firm details p.638

The Firm: This huge national outfit is among the largest specialist labor and employment law firms in the USA. Twenty-one offices spread around the country service a client base that includes over half of the Fortune 50. In Alabama itself, the firm is clearly going from strength to strength. *"In a few years the firm has virtually doubled in size,"* note observers, largely as a result of its recent merger with Haynsworth Baldwin Johnson & Greaves. At this rate, they agree, *"the visibility and depth of the firm can only increase."* The Birmingham office handles a volume of traditional labor work, such as representing clients before the NLRB, and was widely admired for the depth of its experience in employment litigation and preventative counseling.

The Lawyers: A *"well-respected traditional labor lawyer and a real smart attorney,"* **Peyton Lacy** (see p.123) is widely considered *"one of the bet-*

ter traditional labor lawyers in the state." He also undertakes employment litigation and counseling, and is held in high regard for his class action defense work.

The Clients: Mercedes-Benz; Regions; University of North Alabama and Vulcan Group.

Other Notable Practitioners
Will Hancock (see p.123) of Adams and Reese LLP was labeled *"really good on the big picture, with the ability to see the forest and not get caught up in the trees."* Sources also refer to his *"ability to get the best deal for his client"* and his *"hard-working self-motivation."* He has represented management in the labor and employment field for many years, and has notable experience of planning and defending employment policies and procedures in the healthcare and telecommunications sectors. **Fern Singer** (see p.125), at Baker, Donelson, Bearman, Caldwell & Berkowitz, PC is considered by some to be *"the best mediator in Birmingham."* Her work over the year includes obtaining summary judgment for a client in a case where the plaintiff had alleged race and gender discrimination.

LITIGATION

Alabama
Leading firms
(Litigation: General Commercial)

1	**BRADLEY ARANT ROSE & WHITE LLP** Birmingham
	CUNNINGHAM, BOUNDS, YANCE Mobile
	LIGHTFOOT, FRANKLIN & WHITE, LLC Birmingham
	STARNES & ATCHISON LLP Birmingham
2	**BALCH & BINGHAM** Birmingham
	HARE, WYNN, NEWELL & NEWTON LLP Birmingham
	HELMSING, LEACH, HERLONG, NEWMAN Mobile
	RUSHTON, STAKELY, JOHNSTON Montgomery
3	**BAINBRIDGE, MIMS, ROGERS** Birmingham
	BEASLEY, ALLEN, CROW Montgomery
	CABANISS, JOHNSTON, GARDNER Birmingham
	CHRISTIAN & SMALL LLP Birmingham
	LANIER FORD SHAVER & PAYNE Huntsville
	MAYNARD, COOPER & GALE PC Birmingham
	MCDOWELL KNIGHT ROEDDER Mobile

Firms are listed alphabetically in each band.

Band 1

Bradley Arant Rose & White LLP
See firm details p.128

The Firm: This *"wonderful and highly skilled litigation group"* is full of *"excellent, top-notch lawyers,"* according to the market. With its great bench strength and experience, it can effectively handle the most complex, high-profile litigation. Clients enthused about the team's efforts to forge close business links with them, and about the seamless skill with which it pulls together cross-

departmental groups to best serve their interests. Highlights from among the many notable cases the group has handled in the past year include successfully representing Torchmark in multistate litigation, which led to a $45 million jury verdict. It also successfully represented, inter alia, a magazine against a defamation lawsuit filed by a former football coach of the University of Alabama. In the area of construction litigation *"this construction group has no peer in the state,"* say market sources. It is felt to host *"some of the best construction lawyers in the country – in fact, even internationally,"* and represents clients at every stage from negotiating contracts through to resolving disputes. Clients themselves were full of praise for the group's practical approach, which they say is based on the fact that many of its lawyers have practical experience in the construction industry.

The Lawyers: **James Gewin** (see p.122) is universally acknowledged to be *"one of the premier trial attorneys in Alabama."* Clients recommended him as *"a top litigator for bet-the-company matters"* because of his talent, experience and track record of success in major litigation. His practice encompasses products liability and insurance disputes, often for large corporate defendants, and he enjoys a particularly good reputation in the pharmaceuticals industry. He was recently successful as co-lead counsel on behalf of Torchmark in multistate litigation lasting several years. *"Top-flight litigator"* **John Morrow** (see p.124) is held in high regard for his extensive experience. He is

GENERAL COMMERCIAL

seen as being a major client-winner for the firm with an impressive reputation forged through success in substantial litigation. Described as a *"super-smart and effective attorney,"* **Hobart McWhorter**'s (see p.124) advisory skills are a hit with clients. Along with Gewin, he was heavily involved in the Torchmark litigation. A new addition to this year's tables is *"effective trial attorney"* **Mike McKibben** (see p.124), the chair of the firm's general litigation practice group. Clients keep returning to him because *"he really does have significant trial experience and the ability to use his knowledge of the trial process for our benefit."* He regularly represents healthcare providers in commercial litigation, professional negligence and products liability cases. **Mabry Rogers** (see p.125) was singled out as *"one of the best construction lawyers in the US."* As one client put it: *"His cross-examination of the plaintiff's case was so masterful that we knew we'd won there and then."*

The Clients: Jim Walter Resources; Dryvit Systems; SouthTrust Bank; Pfizer; Torchmark; Synovus; Bayer; Cooper Tire & Rubber Company; 3M and University of Alabama Health Services Foundation. Major construction clients include BE&K Construction Company and Blount International.

Cunningham, Bounds, Yance, Crowder & Brown, LLC
The Firm: According to interviewees, there is *"real depth at this firm: lots of talented attorneys and good work."* The Mobile-based outfit has a

Alabama
Leading individuals
(Litigation: General Commercial)

[1] **ASHFORD Leon** *Hare Wynn*, Birmingham
CUNNINGHAM Robert *Cunningham, Bounds*, Mobile
FRANKLIN Samuel *Lightfoot Franklin*, Birmingham
GEWIN James *Bradley Arant*, Birmingham
KEENE Thomas *Rushton Stakely*, Montgomery
LIGHTFOOT Warren *Lightfoot Franklin*, Birmingham
MCGIVAREN Crawford *Cabaniss Johnston*, Birmingham
STARNES Stancil *Starnes & Atchison*, Birmingham

[2] **ATCHISON W Michael** *Starnes & Atchison*, Birmingham
BEASLEY Jere *Beasley Allen*, Montgomery
EDWARDS Michael *Balch & Bingham*, Birmingham
MARSH David *Marsh Rickard*, Birmingham
MCKIBBEN Michael *Bradley Arant*, Birmingham
MORROW John *Bradley Arant*, Birmingham
WHITE Jere *Lightfoot Franklin*, Birmingham
YANCE James *Cunningham Bounds*, Mobile

[3] **BOYD David** *Balch & Bingham*, Birmingham
BREEDLOVE Gregory *Cunningham Bounds*, Mobile
CHRISTIAN Thomas *Christian & Small*, Birmingham
GILL Richard *Copeland Franco*, Montgomery
HELMSING Frederick *Helmsing Leach*, Mobile
KNIGHT Michael *McDowell Knight*, Mobile
LEACH John *Helmsing Leach*, Mobile
MCDOWELL Jerry *McDowell Knight*, Mobile
MCWHORTER Hobart *Bradley Arant*, Birmingham
NOVAK Tabor *Ball Ball*, Montgomery
RODGERS Stanley *Lanier Ford*, Huntsville
ROGERS Alan *Balch & Bingham*, Birmingham
ROGERS Bruce *Bainbridge Mims*, Birmingham
SELLERS Randal *Starnes & Atchison*, Birmingham
TOZZI Rik *Starnes & Atchison*, Birmingham

Leading individuals
(Litigation: Construction)

★ **ROGERS E Mabry** *Bradley Arant*, Birmingham

Firms and individuals are listed alphabetically in each band.

---

national reputation for class action litigation, having handled major class actions involving such things as consumer fraud, medical malpractice, securities and defective products. A particular recent highlight was the Forestex hardboard siding case. The settlement of this will affect all those who have owned or own property on which Forestex siding has been installed in the western USA. The verdict was originally a record $11.9 billion, but was later reduced to $3.6 billion in line with US Supreme Court guidelines.

The Lawyers: Robert Cunningham commands the universal respect of clients and peers alike. "*A good guy and an excellent advocate,*" he is held in extremely high regard for his wealth of knowledge and broad practice, which spans general negligence, products liability, personal injury, medical negligence, insurance fraud and other complex litigation. His efforts have helped many plaintiffs to win some of the largest verdicts ever seen in Alabama. Of counsel, **Jim**

Yance ("*a great, successful attorney*"), continues to garner praise for his personal injury, medical malpractice and products liability practice. Joining them in this year's tables is **Greg Breedlove**, "*an excellent younger attorney who is especially good on the plaintiff side in medical-related work.*" He concentrates on products liability, medical negligence and other, more general plaintiff litigation, and notably acted in the Amtrak 'Sunset Limited' case, following the worst disaster in US rail history.

The Clients: A notable client is the State of Alabama. The firm assisted it recently in achieving a $3.6 billion verdict in a natural gas royalty dispute with ExxonMobil.

Lightfoot, Franklin & White, LLC

The Firm: "*In terms of the time spent in trial and the success rate, this firm is unsurpassed,*" according to many sources. Often referred to as "*one of the best litigation firms in the state,*" this excellent group is always right in the middle of substantive, high-stakes litigation. With around 54 lawyers dedicated to litigation, this firm has the expertise and capacity to cover all the bases, including products liability, environmental toxic tort class actions, securities fraud and complex business litigation. Examples from the past year include successfully obtaining a multimillion-dollar verdict for Hyundai. It is also defending a number of high-stakes securities class actions. For the immediate future, a focus for the firm will be to spread the practice to the Southeast, enabling it to cover a wider area for its national clients.

The Lawyers: Samuel Franklin was hailed by clients as "*a real skillful man with a calm demeanor. He has an ability to get along with people, which is useful in negotiations, and he is one fine trial attorney.*" His main areas of focus include complex business litigation, products liability and toxic torts. **Warren Lightfoot** continues to garner praise for his great skill and wide experience. Although now working on more of a consultancy basis, he continues to appear in court and advise clients, and is admired for his "*high degree of professionalism.*" **Jere White**, referred to simply as a "*great attorney,*" enjoys an expanding practice that increasingly includes major business litigation, such as class actions in securities matters. He was also lead counsel in the Hyundai case mentioned above.

The Clients: Over the past year the firm has acted for a number of household name clients, including: Hyundai; Volkswagen; General Electric; AIG; General Motors; Avondale Mills; USX and ExxonMobil.

Starnes & Atchison LLP

See firm details p.132

The Firm: According to its clients, this is "*one of the best pure litigation firms in the state,*" and is "*particularly strong on medical malpractice litigation.*" With around 54 "*damn fine trial attor-*

neys" dedicated to litigation, four of them fellows of the Association of Trial Lawyers of America, this large and experienced team covers all areas of litigation. It does indeed excel in medical malpractice cases and class action defense; however, it is equally adept at securities cases, professional negligence, products liability and anything else complex and challenging. Recent examples of headline-grabbing work include the WorldCom securities litigation and the HealthSouth corporate derivative litigation. It also played a part in the derivative action concerning the proposed acquisition of SouthTrust by Wachovia, and acted in the high-profile, multimillion-dollar case involving the dismissal of the former coach at the University of Alabama.

The Lawyers: "*One of the most distinguished trial lawyers in Alabama,*" **Stancil Starnes** (see p.125) continues to impress market sources. Commended for his "*extensive experience and impeccable judgment,*" he is described by peers as "*a serious force to contend with*" and is felt to be held in high regard by the bench. His name is closely associated with that of ProAssurance, which insures the state's doctors, and he also acts for many of the state's larger investment banks and represents the University of Alabama in all of its significant litigation. **Michael Atchison** (see p.121) is acknowledged as an "*impressive attorney with a fine reputation.*" "*Often seen doing superb work in the courtroom,*" his range of experience and effective presentation of cases have impressed sources. The past year has seen him work on the WorldCom and Caremark disputes, and represent all the individual members of SouthTrust in the derivative action involving its proposed acquisition by Wachovia. Class action securities litigation is a particularly important part of his practice, though he also does some personal injury work. **Rik Tozzi** (see p.126) debuts in the tables this year, following enthusiastic client recommendations. He "*gets superb results*" they say, and "*has a class action defense practice that is comparable to any lawyer in the southern USA.*" **Randal Sellers** (see p.125) also enters the table this year. An "*excellent malpractice lawyer,*" he "*really stands out*" for his litigation skills, say clients.

The Clients: Medical Assurance/ProNational; GE Capital; University of Alabama System; Caremark; Protective Life; Honda North America; Drummond Company and Citigroup.

Band 2

Balch & Bingham

See firm details p.127

The Firm: This firm is among the largest in the state, and covers the region from six offices in Alabama, Georgia and Mississippi. Impressed sources noted that it fields "*a large litigation group with lots of top-notch attorneys.*" This is felt to be particularly obvious in the area of securities litigation, where its expertise has been evident in a number of high-profile actions, and it also boasts a distinct insurance industry litigation group. However, the firm also fields skilled attorneys in a range of other areas, from civil rights disputes to energy and utilities litigation.

The Lawyers: Michael Edwards (see p.122) *"continues to rise above the crowd,"* according to interviewees. He was especially noted for his *"superb defense of accounting cases and securities claims."* A devoted business litigator, he regularly represents financial institutions, accounting firms and energy companies, as well as individuals. He is a partner in the firm's technology law group, and has experience in trademark and computer litigation. He is joined in this year's tables by the *"intelligent and well-regarded"* David Boyd (see p.121). Boyd divides his time between commercial litigation and labor and employment, as well as being managing partner of the Montgomery office. Clients also praised *"real smooth operator"* Alan Rogers (see p.124) for *"his great performances in court and general professionalism."*

The Clients: Compass Bank; AmSouth Bank; ExxonMobil; Alabama Power and Regions Bank.

Hare, Wynn, Newell & Newton LLP

The Firm: Hare Wynn is best known as the state's oldest plaintiff's firm. Although not the largest outfit in Alabama, commentators agree that what the firm lacks in size it more than makes up for in the quality of its work. It houses *"some of the top personal injury plaintiff attorneys in the state,"* who were particularly praised for the *"thoroughness with which they prepare their cases."* The firm handles a wide variety of litigation, spanning general commercial disputes, business litigation and personal injury. Some more unusual niche areas include railroad cases and whistle-blower litigation arising under the Federal False Claims Act. During the past year it was retained as lead counsel in a fraudulent representation class action lawsuit against Caremark et al, in which damages of $3.2 billion were sought.

The Lawyers: The *"exceptionally talented"* Leon Ashford was commended to researchers for being *"a thorough and knowledgeable attorney, particularly in medical defense and personal injury cases."* His practice covers a broad spectrum of complex litigation, including medical malpractice, professional negligence, personal injury and wrongful death cases. Among his highlights from the year is his success in securing a $5.5 million settlement for a client in a tractor-trailer wrongful death suit.

The Clients: As a plaintiff firm, many of its clients are private individuals, though it also represents companies as plaintiffs.

Helmsing, Leach, Herlong, Newman & Rouse, PC

See firm details p.131

The Firm: The litigation group of this mid-sized, full-service firm is well regarded in the market. A sizable team of *"good defendant litigators"* handles a broad mix of business and general commercial litigation for companies and individual professionals. Peers singled it out in particular as *"a firm that you will see in pharmaceutical cases and on res ipsa issues."* Other areas of litigation, meanwhile, include personal injury, property damage, tax, probate and condemnation cases.

The Lawyers: Fred Helmsing was recommended to researchers as *"an effective attorney,"* with an *"excellent defense practice and good experience."* He practices in a variety of areas, which include white-collar crime, tax and fraud, products liability and aviation litigation, as well as his stock-in-trade commercial defense work. Another of the firm's effective and pragmatic litigators, John Leach is a fellow of the American College of Trial Lawyers. He handles a variety of cases from business litigation to professional liability defense.

The Clients: GlaxoSmithKline; Alabama Power; Hunt Petroleum and Montgomery Aviation.

Rushton, Stakely, Johnston & Garrett

The Firm: This firm was described by clients as *"excellent, thorough and quick to respond if we have a problem."* It is held in particularly high regard for its healthcare litigation practice, and its growing business and antitrust litigation arm is becoming a force to contend with. Other typical work includes professional liability, products liability and insurance disputes.

The Lawyers: Medical malpractice specialist Thomas Keene is widely regarded as being virtually unsurpassed in his field. Described as *"the guy in central Alabama for medical defense work,"* he is *"an outstanding lawyer, period,"* agree commentators. Keene represents doctors and hospitals as well as defending other professionals, such as accountants and lawyers in professional liability litigation.

The Clients: The client base includes corporations, individuals, hospitals, insurance agents, architects and other professionals.

Band 3

Bainbridge, Mims, Rogers & Smith, LLP

The Firm: This *"excellent boutique firm"* joins the rankings this year following sustained market applause. Although smaller than many of its competitors, it fields a *"wealth of talented attorneys"* who *"really know how to handle complex commercial litigation."* The group undertakes

both plaintiff and defense work, and is widely considered to be a firm of choice to represent the larger law firms themselves in disputes. Typical work spans a variety of litigation, including employment and products liability cases.

The Lawyers: A *"group of lawyers' lawyers"* includes Bruce Rogers. He was described as having a good, solid general commercial disputes practice and being *"really good in the courtroom."* Rogers is a recent president of the Birmingham Bar Association. He concentrates on shareholder and business litigation, and is often involved in business torts and insurance matters.

The Clients: The firm represents businesses and individuals. Notable clients include: BE&K; Dow Chemical; HealthSouth; First Commercial Bank and Ansell.

Beasley, Allen, Crow, Methvin, Portis & Miles, PC

The Firm: This *"great plaintiff firm"* is widely admired for *"picking its venues carefully and getting great results."* Clients value the firm for housing *"some of the state's top personal injury attorneys,"* and sources agree that it *"has tremendous resources and staffs its cases more carefully than many others."* The Montgomery-based outfit is home to over 40 lawyers. It specializes in products liability, personal injury, consumer fraud, business litigation, and mass and toxic torts. Highlights of the year include representing the State of Alabama in the record $11.8 billion punitive damages award against ExxonMobil (later reduced to $3.6 billion) for breach of contract and fraud. It also helped to negotiate the $700 million global settlement of the PCB damage claims of over 20,000 residents of Calhoun County against Monsanto, Pharmacia, and their subsidiary company, Solutia.

The Lawyers: Jere Beasley is said to be *"one of the most successful lawyers in the South by a long stretch."* Noted by peers for his *"careful selection of venues,"* clients also value the 'Jere Beasley Report,' a monthly newsletter dealing with consumer issues that is sent to over 25,000 households. He is currently involved in the review of claims related to the drug Vioxx, which has been voluntarily recalled from the market due to concerns of an increased risk of cardiovascular problems in users.

The Clients: As well as acting for the State of Alabama, the firm represents individual plaintiffs and large plaintiff groups.

Cabaniss, Johnston, Gardner, Dumas & O'Neal

The Firm: The litigation group here is well respected not just for the amount of work it handles but for the variety of cases that it can take on. Expertise is readily available in a wide range of complex litigation, spanning antitrust, environmental, IP, personal injury, professional liability and securities regulation disputes. Although it isn't the largest team in the state, it is also more than capable of advising on large, complex derivative cases and major class actions.

The Lawyers: Crawford McGivaren moves up into pole position this year following overwhelming market approval. A "*well-prepared, intense and immensely experienced*" attorney, according to clients "*nobody out-works or out-thinks him, period.*" Commentators note that he has a "*more aggressive and forthright style than most,*" but they agree that this is an effective approach when backed up by his "*smartness and capability.*" McGivaren is especially well known for his work in the area of business litigation, and also handles medical malpractice defense, products liability class actions defense and some employment disputes.

The Clients: The firm represents local and national clients, including both public and privately held companies.

Christian & Small LLP
See firm details p.130
The Firm: Interviewees spoke enthusiastically about the "*great lawyers doing really good work*" at this 31-lawyer, Birmingham-based firm. It handles a volume of corporate, bankruptcy, environmental and tax advice, but particularly stands out for litigation. In this area, it has established a strong track record of success before a variety of courts and tribunals, and can handle practically any area of litigation.

The Lawyers: Tom Christian (see p.121) is "*a real good lawyer with a strong reputation*" according to market sources. He enjoys extensive experience as a trial attorney and is primarily known for defending physicians charged with medical malpractice, and insurance companies and manufacturers in products liability cases, although his practice spans a variety of other complex business disputes.

The Clients: St Vincent's Hospital; Community Health Systems; AstraZeneca; Ingersoll-Rand; Medical Assurance and Caremark.

Lanier Ford Shaver & Payne
The Firm: This full-service firm, based in Huntsville, has "*an excellent reputation*" and is praised by clients for having "*a thriving litiga-*

tion practice.*" With more than 40 lawyers, it is the largest law firm in northern Alabama, and regularly appears on the biggest and juiciest cases in the area. These include construction, products liability, professional malpractice and technology litigation, as well as the range of general corporate, commercial and securities disputes.

The Lawyers: Stanley Rodgers was described as "*a well-informed attorney,*" who "*has it pretty much covered in terms of litigation in the north of the state.*" He tends to concentrate on professional liability and products liability litigation, but he also has a substantial involvement in healthcare and insurance litigation.

The Clients: Clients include manufacturers, financial institutions, healthcare providers, professionals, insurance companies, government contractors and agencies and charitable and public service organizations.

Maynard, Cooper & Gale PC
The Firm: The firm is new to the tables this year, having impressed onlookers with its "*expertise in complicated, multidistrict class actions and litigation with a national impact.*" Clients were particularly impressed with the "*wide variety of cases undertaken and the ability to handle almost any type of litigation*". This firm handles cases in both the state and federal courts, regularly defending fraud, *male fides* and other punitive damage cases for a number of major insurance companies. Along with its diet of general commercial disputes, the firm undertakes a volume of securities litigation and class actions in fields like products liability, environmental tort and consumer finance, drawing on the expertise available within its special class action and complex litigation group.

The Lawyers: This firm "*boasts many great litigation attorneys,*" according to the market, although it was the team that stood out, rather than any one individual. The chair of the litigation and arbitration department is Lee Cooper.

The Clients: The firm acts for national brokerages, investment banks and major life insurance companies. The litigation group also advises many Fortune 500 companies throughout the Southeast on major consumer and environmental matters.

McDowell Knight Roedder & Sledge LLC
The Firm: This Mobile-based firm is described as having "*quite a deep well of talent*" in the litigation field. In particular, peers noted that it is "*always turning up in the pharmaceutical and res ipsa type cases.*" The team covers a range of business and commercial litigation, with particular emphasis on contractual disputes, bankruptcy and the defense of state and nationwide class actions. Its sure handling of products liability, pharmaceutical liability, and claims relating to railroads and medical devices were particularly noted.

The Lawyers: Michael Knight, described simply as being "*a very very talented attorney,*" regularly defends personal injury and products liability cases, typically for the manufacturer or seller of products. He also acts for corporate clients in class actions and other business litigation. **Jerry McDowell** was recommended to researchers for his "*tremendous talent and extensive experience in handling really complicated matters.*" His practice spans general corporate litigation, products and professional liability, and insurance disputes, and he is also well known for representing corporate clients caught up in class actions.

The Clients: Clients include large and small public and private companies.

Other Notable Practitioners
"*By far and away the best plaintiff lawyer in the state of Alabama*" is **David Marsh** of Marsh, Rickard & Bryan P.C. He was described as "*an extraordinarily gifted attorney with a great manner of presentation,*" combined with "*hard work and natural ability – the jury loves him.*" Although probably best known for his personal injury work, business litigation also forms a part of his practice. **Richard Gill** of Copeland, Franco, Screws & Gill in Montgomery is described as having "*a strong reputation in appellate work.*" Gill covers most areas of litigation from antitrust to wrongful death plaintiff work. Another highly respected attorney is **Tabor Novak** at the Montgomery firm Ball, Ball, Matthews & Novak. He was recommended to researchers as "*strong, hard-working and not one to make mistakes.*" His practice is largely devoted to litigation, with civil defense and medical malpractice defense among the core elements.

REAL ESTATE

Alabama
Leading firms (Real Estate)

1. **BRADLEY ARANT ROSE & WHITE LLP** *Birmingham*
   BURR & FORMAN LLP *Birmingham*
2. **BALCH & BINGHAM** *Birmingham*
   LEITMAN, SIEGAL & PAYNE, PC *Birmingham*
3. **BAKER, DONELSON, BEARMAN** *Birmingham*
   CORRETTI, NEWSOM & HAWKINS *Birmingham*
   MAYNARD, COOPER & GALE PC *Birmingham*
   SIROTE & PERMUTT PC *Birmingham*
   WALSTON, WELLS, ANDERSON *Birmingham*

Leading individuals (Real Estate)

1. **BEAVERS Charles** *Bradley Arant*, Birmingham
   POWELL Fred *Burr & Forman*, Birmingham
2. **BAINS Kay** *Bradley Arant*, Birmingham
   CORRETTI Douglas *Corretti Newsom*, Birmingham
   DE BUYS Jr John *Burr & Forman*, Birmingham
   ISOM Chervis *Baker Donelson*, Birmingham
   LANIER Randolph *Balch & Bingham*, Birmingham
   MIXSON Dwight *Burr & Forman*, Birmingham
   MONK Stephen *Bradley Arant*, Birmingham
   SEXTON Robert *Maynard Cooper*, Birmingham
   SIEGAL Don *Leitman Siegal*, Birmingham
   SMITH Felton *Balch & Bingham*, Birmingham
3. **BOLES H Hampton** *Balch & Bingham*, Birmingham
   BRICKMAN Steven *Sirote & Permutt*, Birmingham
   DRESHER J David *Bradley Arant*, Birmingham
   HELD Jerry *Sirote & Permutt*, Birmingham
   MILLS Gail *Burr & Forman*, Birmingham
   SIEGAL Bradley *Leitman Siegal*, Birmingham
   STEWART Carol *Burr & Forman*, Birmingham
   SYLVESTER William *Walston Wells*, Birmingham

Firms and Individuals are listed alphabetically in each band.

Band 1

Bradley Arant Rose & White LLP
See firm details p.128

The Firm: For its fans, "*this is the finest firm in the state.*" Satisfied clients make that judgment partly because "*it is a full-service firm, meaning that there are capable, experienced lawyers in all areas of practice and the real estate group is no exception.*" This full-service ethos is obvious from its range of work, which includes acquisitions, development, land use and zoning, leasing and construction, as well as "*a lot of quality financing work.*" Its premier position is also evident in the many notable projects the team has worked on during the year, including the sale of SouthTrust Tower, the tallest office building in Alabama, to an Atlanta real estate company for over $50 million. Other highlights include the successful defense of a lawsuit relating to the rezoning of a Home Depot center, and handling the sale of luxury apartments valued at around $100 million.

The Lawyers: Charles Beavers (see p.121) is an "*excellent real estate lawyer, deserving of his*

position at number one," say commentators. A leading figure in the market, he is involved in much of the firm's most cutting-edge work, such as the mixed-use, town center development in Homewood. He also acted for the developer of a public site in Mountain Brook in a controversial rezoning case. As a former general counsel of Daniel Realty, **Stephen Monk** (see p.124) "*has a unique view of both sides of the fence, and an excellently balanced practice,*" according to clients. He was particularly noted for his planned unit development work. "*Phenomenal lawyer*" **Kay Bains** (see p.121 is described by clients as being "*as high quality a lawyer as you will ever want to work with.*" Bains is regarded as "*top notch on the lending side*" with a large volume of real estate finance for state and national banks. However, she also represents a host of buyers and sellers as part of a broad commercial real estate practice. **David Dresher** (see p.122) is perhaps best known for his banking work, but he is also acknowledged to be a "*good practical real estate lawyer.*" He represents a roster of banks and other lenders as well as serving as counsel to various companies in Alabama engaged in real estate activities.

The Clients: Daniel Realty; Hyundai; Graham & Company; EBSCO Properties; SouthTrust Bank; Honda; Mercedes-Benz; Toyota; Jim Wilson & Associates; Stonegate Realty; The Birmingham News; Home Depot and CarMax.

Burr & Forman LLP
See firm details p.129

The Firm: According to the market, this is an "*outstanding law firm made up of dedicated and professional lawyers.*" Its "*excellent real estate practice*" is probably best known for advising leading lenders on real estate finance; however, the firm also regularly assists with real estate developments and leasing. It also works on landlord and tenant, land use and zoning issues, and is hailed as doing "*a good job for its developer clients.*" During the year it has played an important role in some notable timber-related transactions; namely the purchase and financing of large tracts of timber yards in the South and Canada. Other recent highlights include a number of acquisitions and disposals of 'Power Center' developments throughout the country.

The Lawyers: According to clients, the whole team here is "*diligent in its legal efforts, responsible and well informed on business matters.*" Still topping the tables is the "*outstanding*" **Fred Powell** (see p.124), who is acknowledged to have been "*a leading guy for many years.*" Commentators value his input because "*he is there to accomplish the goal and make the deal happen.*" He is involved in many of the firm's important deals, including acting for major institutional lenders in the timber transactions mentioned above. "*Excellent real*

estate attorney" **Dwight Mixson** (see p.124) continues to impress for both his out-of-state and local work. He concentrates on out-of-state lender representation and is particularly noted for his mezzanine and retail financing advice. Within the state, he also handles a volume of commercial sales and leasing. **John De Buys** (see p.122) is noted by market sources for being "*especially good on land use and zoning,*" and is also roundly admired for his real estate litigation practice. **Gail Mills** (see p.124) debuts in this year's tables, following enthusiastic praise from the market. A "*great lawyer, careful and creative,*" she has represented the developers of shopping centers in many states, and has been busy this year with a large volume of Alabama real estate work for DR Horton. Also joining the tables is **Carol Stewart** (see p.125), described as "*one of the best condominium lawyers in the state.*" "*There is no one in this area who knows condominium law like she does*" added one client. Her practice focuses on condominium law, but also involves complex commercial litigation.

The Clients: Colonial Properties Trust; JPMorgan; United Systems; SouthTrust Bank and Lawrence Arendall Humphries Real Estate.

Band 2

Balch & Bingham
See firm details p.127

The Firm: This sizable regional firm covers the ambit of real estate law, but is best known for its financial services practice. Indeed, the real estate group acts out of the financial services department, serving a client base of regional banks and financial institutions. As well as its burgeoning lender practice, which provides finance for office, retail, residential and other government supported projects, the group regularly advises on acquisitions and sales, leasing and land use regulations.

The Lawyers: "*Fine attorney*" **Randolph Lanier** (see p.123) is a big name on the true real estate side, say peers, with a practice concentrated on commercial lending and commercial development. He acts for lenders and borrowers, developers and utility companies in a variety of real estate transactions, and has assisted a number of banks that have acquired properties in the Southwest of the country. **Felton Smith** (see p.125) is an "*easy-going, extremely capable real estate lawyer*" who "*does a good job for his clients.*" The bulk of his practice concerns the acquisition, sale and leasing of commercial and industrial real estate for users and investors. He is also involved on the financial side of transactions, an area in which the firm can also call on the services of **Hampton Boles** (see p.121). Better known as a banking lawyer, Boles also advises developers on corporate, financial and regulatory matters, impressing them with his *"professionalism and performance."*

The Clients: Compass Bank; AmSouth Bank; SouthTrust Bank; Regions Bank; US Steel and Harbert Management.

Leitman, Siegal & Payne, PC

The Firm: A third of the firm's attorneys concentrate primarily on real estate, giving it the resources to handle even the largest projects within the state. Its lawyers are highly recommended by clients *"for the fantastic services they provide"* in a range of areas, including development, acquisitions and disposal, leasing, financings and, to a lesser extent, land use and zoning. Highlights of the year include negotiating a lifestyle shopping center development in Knoxville, Tennessee, and handling the major refinancing of a large industrial park. The firm is well known for acting for local REIT, Colonial Properties Trust, and also acts for two of the largest banks in the state.

The Lawyers: Don Siegal is *"professional, practical and easy to get along with"* say sources. His practice spans general business law as well as real estate. This is important when it comes to cutting-edge work like the complex joint venture between a REIT and local Tennessee residents, involving unique tax and business issues, which he worked on this year. **Brad Siegal** is an aggressive lawyer who is *"doing a fine job and continues to impress"* according to interviewees. He is involved in co-ownership ventures for large numbers of tenants, and represents developers of all types of commercial properties through all stages of a transaction. Leasing, the acquisition and development of land and commercial retail and shopping center work also form a large part of his practice.

The Clients: Colonial Properties Trust; DR Horton; RTM Restaurant Group and Polar-BEK.

Band 3

Baker, Donelson, Bearman, Caldwell & Berkowitz, PC

See firm details p.1613

The Firm: According to long-standing clients, the firm's recent merger *"has been good for the team; it now has an even deeper practice."* The group covers the range of real estate law, though leasing and shopping center-related work are particular strengths. Historically, it established a good reputation in Alabama's real estate circles with its work on the development, financing and leasing of Birmingham's Summit Shopping Center, an 800,000 sq ft lifestyle center. More recent highlights include work on a 250,000 sq ft mixed-use development with a residential component. The firm also has a flourishing refinancing practice, which has completed over a dozen refinancings over the year, for the developers and owners of properties.

The Lawyers: Chervis Isom (see p.123) is the *"thorough, experienced and knowledgeable"* head of the real estate group here. Clients particular-ly like the fact that he *"has the distinct advantage of having represented both the large retail companies as well as the tenants, and so has experience on both sides of a transaction."* His practice is concentrated in the areas of real estate and capital finance, with a slant towards the development of commercial real estate projects.

The Clients: Bayer Properties and Daniel Realty Company are key clients of the firm, among a host of other developers, owners and borrowers.

Corretti, Newsom & Hawkins

The Firm: This *"small but highly respected"* boutique continues to house *"some great real estate attorneys."* It debuts in this year's tables following enthusiastic market recommendations for the skills and experience of its lawyers. In particular, it was recognized for the extent to which it had *"developed on the lending and acquisition side."* The group now has credible finance capacity as well as the range of transactional experience and a respected niche land use practice. It is often seen acting for mortgage companies and financial institutions.

The Lawyers: Doug Corretti was described by some sources as *"the dean of real estate in Birmingham, particularly in terms of land use and zoning."* He remains as active as ever, and peers agree that he *"is a worthy adversary and a tough guy to come up against."* He advises on most aspects of real estate law, but has a particular name for land use and zoning. This year he has been involved in many cases concerning the religious use of land and eminent domain law.

The Clients: Notable clients continue to include Wal-Mart, the City of Hoover and Grimmer Realty.

Maynard, Cooper & Gale PC

The Firm: The real estate group at this full-service firm covers the spectrum of real property work; however, commentators believe that its strength lies on the finance side. It splits into commercial real estate lending and pure real estate work, with the lending department representing many of the state's biggest banks, as well as out-of-state lenders. Other typical work includes low-income housing developments in many states.

The Lawyers: The *"excellent"* **Robert Sexton** continues to be the highlight name in this department. Described to researchers as *"having many strengths,"* he is perhaps best known for representing lenders in real estate finance transactions, though he also advises borrowers and assists in acquisition, development and leasing issues.

The Clients: US Steel; AmSouth Bank; Alabama Teachers' Retirement System; Blue Cross and Blue Shield of Alabama; Collateral Mortgage Capital and New South Federal Savings Bank.

Sirote & Permutt PC

The Firm: This is *"one of the most respected law firms in Alabama,"* according to sources, *"with*

attorneys specializing in all areas of the law and a strong reputation for knowledge and professionalism." The full-service practice boasts a sizable real estate group, which covers all aspects of real estate including finance, land use and zoning, environmental law and eminent domain work. In terms of financial advice, for example, clients agree: *"This firm meets time frames in pressure situations."* Recent transactional highlights include working on a multi-parcel development in Pelham and its ultimate sale to the retail developer, and working on a major real estate purchase for Lowes Homes Centers in Alabama.

The Lawyers: According to clients, **Steven Brickman**'s *"experience, personality, integrity and attention to detail are second to none."* Others added that *"he is a real asset to our business and a pleasure to deal with: you know a transaction will get done the right way with Steven."* His practice spans commercial real estate development and transactions, and more general corporate acquisitions and disposals. Recent work includes the multi-parcel development in Pelham and the purchase of a company in Huntsville. Clients also recommended **Jerry Held** for his *"prompt and accurate advice on foreclosure, bankruptcy, litigation or title issues."* Held has a national foreclosure practice and provides a full range of services to mortgage lenders. Clients also commented favorably on the *"really prompt responses of the well-staffed and sophisticated group."*

The Clients: The client base includes public companies, landlords, developers and financial institutions.

Walston, Wells, Anderson & Bains

The Firm: This firm continues to command a place among the leaders following warm recommendations from clients and peers alike for the quality of its attorneys and real estate practice. The team is perhaps best known for representing banks and financial institutions in real estate lending, and clients were quick to endorse its expertise in this area. However, it is also known for advising on multifamily residential developments and commercial and leisure schemes, and offers expertise in the acquisition, disposal and leasing of property, including related construction issues.

The Lawyers: Bill Sylvester was given high marks by commentators, with the consensus being that *"he is a great real estate banking lawyer – on the lending side of commercial deals he is just excellent."* His caseload has included residential developments, retail projects and hotels.

The Clients: Public companies, landlords, developers and financial institutions form the backbone of the client base. As well as representing a number of major financial institutions, the team also assists several of Birmingham's largest real estate development companies.

Leaders in Alabama

ALEXANDER, James P
Bradley Arant Rose & White LLP,
Birmingham 205 521 8348
jalexander@bradleyarant.com
Recommended in Employment
Practice Areas: Defends employment
discrimination cases; advises employers
on efficacious policies and practices to
manage risks; also handles traditional
management labor disputes.
Prof. Memberships: Admitted to prac-
tice in Alabama (1969); adjunct profes-
sor of law at the University of Alabama
Law School teaching employment dis-
crimination (1981-2003); Member of
American and Alabama Bars; Arbitrator,
American Arbitration Association;
Employment Disputes and Commercial
Panels.
Career: Joined Bradley Arant Rose &
White LLP in 1969; became a Partner in
1975.
Personal: Born 14 October 1944, JD
Duke University 1969; AB Duke Univer-
sity 1966.

ASHFORD, Leon
Hare, Wynn, Newell & Newton LLP,
Birmingham 205 328 5330
Recommended in Litigation

ATCHISON, W Michael
Starnes & Atchison LLP, Birmingham
205 868 6015
matchison@starneslaw.com
Recommended in Litigation
Practice Areas: He has been lead
defense counsel in a wide variety of civil
trials and appeals spanning more than
35 years of practice. Included are cases
involving securities; antitrust; ERISA;
legal, accounting and medical malpractice; commerical airline crashes; prod-
ucts liability; complex civil litigation;
class actions; copyright infringement
and prescription drugs.
Prof. Memberships: Fellow, American
College of Trial Lawyers; Advocate,
American Board of Trial Advocates;
Member, Birmingham, Alabama and
American Bar Associates; Federation of
Insurance and Corporate Counsel.
Career: Admitted 1968. Law Clerk, US
District Court 1968 - 69, Partner at
Starnes & Atchison LLP; Adjunct Profes-
sor, University of Alabama School of
Law, 2003 to present.
Publications: Co-author, 'Proving
Damages in Mass Tort Litigation', 1982;
co-author, 'Alabama Damages', 1985; co-
author, 'Medical Practice in Alabama',
1986; author, 'Medical Malpractice: A
Defense Attorney's Perspective', 1994;
co-author, 'The Professional Liability of
Attorneys in Alabama', 2000.
Personal: Born April 13, 1941. Graduat-
ed with an AB Degree from Birming-
ham Southern College in 1965 and Juris
Doctorate Degree from Cumberland
School of Law Samford University in
1968.

BAINS, Kay
Bradley Arant Rose & White LLP,
Birmingham 205 521 8220
kbains@bradleyarant.com
Recommended in Real Estate
Practice Areas: Commercial real estate,
including advice regarding title issues,
access, zoning, permitting and usage.
Has represented lenders in loans secured
by real estate in multiple states. Has rep-
resented regional banks in acquiring and
disposing sites in multistate market.
Prof. Memberships: ABA; Alabama Bar
Association; Member, American College
of Mortgage Attorneys
Career: Has been in private practice,
concentrating in real estate, for 25 years.
Personal: Auburn University, magna
cum laude, 1969; Cumberland School of
Law, summa cum laude, 1980.

BEALE, Walter
Balch & Bingham, Birmingham
205 226 3436
mbeale@balch.com
Recommended in Corporate/M&A
Practice Areas: Corporate and securities; energy regulation and transactions;
mergers and acquisitions; corporate
governance.
Prof. Memberships: Birmingham Bar
Association; Alabama State Bar; American Bar Association
Career: Mr Beale's practice is devoted
primarily to corporate finance transactions and advising publicly held corporations. He has over 30 years' experience
in these areas and has represented
issuers in both initial and secondary
public offerings, public and private
offerings of debt securities and offerings
of "hybrid" securities, such as trust preferred securities. Mr Beale also advises
publicly held corporations regarding
compliance with federal and state securities laws and regularly advises boards
of directors of publicly held corporations on their duties and responsibilities.
Mr Beale represents corporations with
securities listed on the New York Stock
Exchange and the NASDAQ National
Market System. In addition to his corporate and securities practice, Mr Beale
serves as a member of the Executive
Committee and as co-chairman of the
Corporate, Tax and Finance section. Mr
Beale is listed in 'The Best Lawyers in
America', 2003 Edition - Present.
Personal: Born: October 30, 1945; Edu-
cation: Cumberland School of Law (JD,
1970); Auburn University (BS, 1967).

BEASLEY, Jere
Beasley, Allen, Crow, Methvin, Portis &
Miles, PC, Montgomery 334 269 2343
Recommended in Litigation

BEAVERS, Charles
Bradley Arant Rose & White LLP,
Birmingham 205 521 8620
cbeavers@bradleyarant.com
Recommended in Real Estate

Practice Areas: Real estate practice
concentrated in the acquisition, sale and
development of commercial, office, residential and mixed-use properties. Experienced in representing developers and
neighborhood associations in the rezoning and subdivision of real properties.
Prof. Memberships: Admitted to practice in Alabama (1977). Member, Alabama Law Institute, American College of
Mortgage Attorneys, American Bar
Association, Alabama State Bar and
Birmingham Bar Association.
Career: Has practiced law in Birmingham, Alabama for the past 27 years, he
joined Bradley Arant Rose & White LLP
as a Partner in 1985.
Personal: Born 19 June 1952; JD, University of Alabama School of Law, 1977.

BOLES, H Hampton
Balch & Bingham, Birmingham
205 226 3471
hboles@balch.com
Recommended in Real Estate
Practice Areas: Banking law; commercial and residential lending and closings
law; real estate-commercial law.
Career: H Hampton Boles is Chairman
of the Financial Services and Transactions section. Mr Boles' practice consists
primarily of advising banks and other
creditors, insurance companies and real
estate developers in corporate, financial
and regulatory matters. Mr Boles is a
member of the American College of Real
Estate Lawyers, and has served on the
Alabama Law Institute UCC Articles 2A, 3,
4, 4A and Revised Article 9 Committees.
He has been listed in 'The Best Lawyers in
America', 1995 Edition - Present.
Personal: Born: November 27, 1942;
Education: Tulane University School of
Law (JD, 1967); Auburn University (BS,
1965); Military: US Navy Reserve, active
duty 1968-1971.

BOYD, David R
Balch & Bingham, Birmingham
205 226 3485
dboyd@balch.com
Recommended in Litigation
Practice Areas: Business litigation; civil
rights litigation; class action litigation;
education; financial services litigation;
labor and employment litigation; state
governmental relations; state and local
government litigation; appellate.
Prof. Memberships: Alabama Board of
Bar Examiners, Former Chairman;
Alabama Law Institute, Executive Committee; American Bar Foundation, Fellow; Alabama Law Foundation, Fellow;
Multistate Bar Examination Committee,
Chairman; National Conference of Bar
Examiners, Chair of Board of Trustees
Career: Mr Boyd's practice focuses primarily on commercial litigation,
employment law, and constitutional and
civil rights litigation, where he has
extensive trial and appellate experience

in the state and federal courts. Mr
Boyd's practice also includes education
law and state government matters.
Among other state and national professional involvements, he is a member of
the Lawyer's Advisory Committee in the
Middle District of Alabama, Chair of the
National Conference of Bar Examiners,
and Chair of the Multistate Bar Examination Committee. Mr Boyd has been
listed for the last ten years in the 'Best
Lawyers in America'.
Personal: Born: October 2, 1950; Education: University of Alabama (JD,
1976); University of Alabama (BA,
1973).

BREEDLOVE, Gregory
Cunningham, Bounds, Yance, Crowder
& Brown, LLC, Mobile
251 471 6191
Recommended in Litigation

BRICKMAN, Steven
Sirote & Permutt PC, Birmingham
205 930 5100
Recommended in Real Estate

BROCKMAN, Richard
Johnston Barton Proctor & Powell LLP,
Birmingham 205 458 9400
Recommended in Corporate/M&A

BROWN, Stephen
Maynard, Cooper & Gale PC,
Birmingham 205 254 1000
Recommended in Employment

CARRUTHERS, Thomas Neely
Bradley Arant Rose & White LLP,
Birmingham 205 521 8263
tcarruthers@bradleyarant.com
Recommended in Corporate/M&A
Practice Areas: Specializes in M&A,
estate planning and corporate taxation.
In January 2005, he handled a thorny
change of management of a public
banking corporation.
Prof. Memberships: Named 2001 Out-
standing Lawyer of the Year, Birming-
ham Bar Association. American Law
Institute, American Bar Association,
American College of Tax Counsel, Alaba-
ma Bar Foundation Fellow, International
Law Association, Birmingham Rotary
Club, Children's Hospital Board, The
Community Foundation, Chairman
Alabama Academy of Honor, Past Chair-
man Birmingham Museum of Art.
Awarded Spain-Hickman Award, Medal
of Honor Birmingham-Southern College.
Career: Partner and former Managing
Partner of Bradley Arant. Graduate of
Princeton University and Yale Law
School.

CHRISTIAN, Thomas
Christian & Small LLP, Birmingham
205 250 6611
twchristian@csattorneys.com
Recommended in Litigation
Practice Areas: Accomplished litigation attorney, representing an extensive

list of clients in most areas of tort litigation, government contract litigation and construction litigation. His practice is primarily devoted to the defense of physicians and hospitals charged with medical malpractice and the defense of manufacturers and insurance companies in product liability cases.

Prof. Memberships: Admitted to the Alabama State Bar, 1965. Admitted to practice in all state and federal trial courts in Alabama, the Supreme Court of Alabama, the Courts of Appeals for the Fifth and Eleventh Circuits and the Supreme Court of the United States. Fellow of the American College of Trial Lawyers, the International Academy of Trial Lawyers, the American Board of Trial Advocates, and the American Bar Foundation. Member of the American Bar Association, Birmingham Bar Association (President, 1984), and Alabama State Bar. Member of the Alabama Defense Lawyers Association (President, 1978); International Association of Defense Counsel.

Career: Associate and Partner with Balch & Bingham, 1965-81; partner with Rives & Peterson, 1981-2000; a founding Partner of Christian & Small LLP, 2000-present.

COLEMAN, John
Burr & Forman LLP, Birmingham
205 458 5167
jcoleman@burr.com
Recommended in Employment

Practice Areas: Labor and employment law, including litigation defense, counseling and rulemaking representation respecting disability discrimination and FMLA issues as well as race, sex, color, religion, age and national origin discrimination cases; whistle blower defense and counseling; ULP defense, collective bargaining and arbitrations; union avoidance and policy advice.

Prof. Memberships: ABA (member, Labor and Employment Law Section and Occupational Safety and Health Subcommittee), Alabama State Bar (Chair, Labor & Employment Section 1997-98; annual speaker, annual section seminar for past twenty years), State Bar of Georgia (member), State Bar of Texas (member), Management Labor & Employment Roundtable (member).

Career: Past chair, Labor & Employment section; partner, Labor & Employment section; Law Clerk, US Circuit Judge Donald Russell, US Court of Appeals for the Fourth Circuit (1981-82).

Publications: 'Disability Discrimination in Employment' (West 2005); Contributor, '2004 Supplement to Occupational Safety & Health Law' (BNA 2004); 'Employment Discrimination in Alabama' (Southern University Press 1991; supplements for 1991 and 1992 years); 'Alabama Workers Compensation Practice Guide' (Guide Pub. 1994)

Personal: Duke University School of

Law (JD 1981); Duke University (AB, magna cum laude, and with departmental distinction, 1978); member, Board of Directors, Industrial Health Council of Alabama, Inc

COOPER, John
Sirote & Permutt PC, Birmingham
205 930 5100
Recommended in Corporate/M&A

CORRETTI, Douglas
Corretti, Newsom & Hawkins, Birmingham 205 251 1164
Recommended in Real Estate

CUNNINGHAM, Robert
Cunningham, Bounds, Yance, Crowder & Brown, LLC, Mobile
251 471 6191
Recommended in Litigation

CURRAN, Gregory
Maynard, Cooper & Gale PC, Birmingham 205 254 1000
Recommended in Corporate/M&A

DAVIS, Thomas
Constangy, Brooks & Smith, LLC, Birmingham 205 323 7676
Recommended in Employment

DE BUYS Jr, John
Burr & Forman LLP, Birmingham
205 458 5200
jdebuys@burr.com
Recommended in Real Estate

Practice Areas: Land use and development including planning and zoning, construction, condemnation, transactions and negotiations; Litigation involving land use, zoning, variances, condemnation, engineering, boundary lines, adverse possession, sale and division, construction (residential and commercial) and surface water drainage and control; Clients also include entities involved in coal mining and extraction.

Prof. Memberships: American Bar Association, Alabama State Bar and the Birmingham Bar Association. Served as president of the Young Lawyers Section of the Birmingham Bar Association and served on various committees of that association, including the Executive Committee (1979-81). He is a member of the American Academy of Attorney-Mediators, and has been appointed to the Alternative Dispute Resolution Panel of Neutrals.

Career: Practiced law since 1967.
Personal: Vanderbilt University School of Law (BA 1964); University of Alabama (JD 1967); Youth basketball and baseball coach; Formation of Alabama I Can Through Education Foundation, Monday Morning Quarterback Club in Birmingham (member), past board member of Girl's Club, Inc. and Magic Moments.

DEBRUGE, Marcel
Burr & Forman LLP, Birmingham
205 458 5263
mdebruge@burr.com
Recommended in Employment

Practice Areas: Representing employers in labor and employment-related disputes, class action litigation, employment discrimination cases, sexual harassment claims, National Labor Relations Board matters, arbitrations, OSHA matters, Wage/Hour matters and OFCCP compliance.

Prof. Memberships: Alabama State Bar; Georgia State Bar; Texas State Bar; Chairman, Alabama State Bar Labor and Employment Law Section.

Personal: BA, Louisiana State University, 1987; JD, University of Alabama, 1991

DOBBS, Tammy
Constangy, Brooks & Smith, LLC, Birmingham 205 323 7676
Recommended in Employment

DRESHER, J David
Bradley Arant Rose & White LLP, Birmingham 205 521 8605
ddresher@bradleyarant.com
Recommended in Real Estate

Practice Areas: Representing real estate and commercial lenders in loans and workouts; residential mortgage lenders in regulatory compliance and structuring issues; and closely-held businesses in real estate and business issues.

Prof. Memberships: ABA, Alabama Bar, MBA, Alabama Consumer Finance Association (Counsel).

Career: Firm leader for Banking and Finance Group; Partner since 1990; Best Lawyers in America since 2000.

Publications: Frequent lecturer and writer on lending and regulatory matters for legal and trade groups.

Personal: Samford University (JD summa cum laude 1983); Auburn University (BS Economics 1977); editor in chief: Cumberland Law Review.

DREW, Mark
Maynard, Cooper & Gale PC, Birmingham 205 254 1000
Recommended in Corporate/M&A

EDWARDS, Michael
Balch & Bingham, Birmingham
205 226 3401
medwards@balch.com
Recommended in Litigation

Practice Areas: Banking; business litigation; financial services litigation; alternative dispute resolution.

Prof. Memberships: Fellow, American College of Trial Lawyers; Master, Birmingham Inns of Court (President, 2001-2003); Birmingham Bar Association; Birmingham Bar Foundation; Alabama State Bar; Fellow, Alabama Law Foundation; American Arbitration Association, Arbitrator - Commercial Panel; Mediator.

Career: Michael L Edwards' practice is concentrated in business litigation. He has represented financial institutions, accounting firms, manufacturing, mining and energy companies, as well as individuals. He also has experience in trademark, patent, trade secret, and computer litigation. Mr Edwards has written

and lectured on a variety of legal topics, including trial of complex cases, appellate practice, enforcement of agreements to arbitrate, class actions, lender liability, securities litigation, accountantsi liability, shareholder liability for corporate debt, covenants not to compete, and the attorney-client privilege. Mr Edwards is listed in 'The Best Lawyers in America'.

Personal: Born: September 10, 1942;Education: University of Alabama (LLB, 1966); University of Alabama (AB, 1964)Military: United States Army, Judge Advocate General's Corps, 1966 - 1971.

FRANKLIN, Samuel
Lightfoot, Franklin & White, LLC, Birmingham 205 581 0700
Recommended in Litigation

FRAZIER, Sydney
Cabaniss, Johnston, Gardner, Dumas & O'Neal, Birmingham 205 716 5200
Recommended in Employment

GARDNER, William
Cabaniss, Johnston, Gardner, Dumas & O'Neal, Birmingham 205 716 5200
Recommended in Employment

GEWIN, James
Bradley Arant Rose & White LLP, Birmingham 205 521 8352
jgewin@bradleyarant.com
Recommended in Litigation

Practice Areas: General civil litigation. Extensive experience centering around representation of corporate defendants, including clients who are claimants in commercial disputes.

Prof. Memberships: Admitted, Alabama (1966). Member, American College of Trial Lawyers; Alabama Law Foundation; Fellow, American Bar Foundation; Alabama Bar Association, Board of Bar Examiners (1976-80), Bar Commissioners (1991-2000); United States Court of Appeals (11th Circuit), Lawyers Qualifications and Conduct Committee.

Career: Joined Bradley Arant, 1967; Partner, 1973. 'The Best Lawyers in America'; 'Chambers USA - America's Leading Business Lawyers'.

Personal: Born 9 November 1940. LLB, University of Alabama School of Law, 1966, AB, editor in chief, Alabama Law Review; Princeton University, 1963.

GILL, Richard
Copeland, Franco, Screws & Gill, Montgomery 334 834 1180
Recommended in Litigation

GRENIER, John B
Bradley Arant Rose & White LLP, Birmingham 205 521 8355
bgrenier@bradleyarant.com
Recommended in Corporate/M&A

Practice Areas: Practices in general corporate and securities law, corporate finance, and mergers and acquisitions. Has been the responsible partner for the public and private offering of securities and acquisitions and divestitures in various industries.

Prof. Memberships: Admitted to practice in Alabama (1982). Member, American and Birmingham Bar Associations. Planning Committee, Southeastern Corporate Law Institute.
Career: Joined Bradley Arant Rose & White LLP in 1983; became Partner in 1990; Chairman of the Executive Committee of the firm, 2001 to present.
Personal: Born 28 April 1956. JD, Vanderbilt University, 1982; BA, with High Distinction, University of Virginia, 1978. Phi Beta Kappa.

HANCOCK, William K
Adams and Reese LLP, Birmingham
205 250 5007
will.hancock@arlaw.com
Recommended in Employment
Practice Areas: Partner, Special Business Services Practice Group; labor and employment; management counseling; forestry.
Prof. Memberships: Alabama Bar Association; American Bar Association.
Career: Has represented management in the labor and employment field and has handled ERISA litigation matters since 1989, assisting healthcare, telecommunications, and poultry processing clients plan, implement, and defend employment policies and procedures.
Personal: JD from the Cumberland School of Law, Alabama, in 1989, Dean's Scholar and editor of the Cumberland Law Review. BA from the University of the South, Sewanee, Tennessee in 1986.

HARMON, Christopher B
Maynard, Cooper & Gale PC, Birmingham 205 254 1000
Recommended in Corporate/M&A

HELD, Jerry
Sirote & Permutt PC, Birmingham 205 930 5100
Recommended in Real Estate

HELMSING, Frederick
Helmsing, Leach, Herlong, Newman & Rouse, PC, Mobile 251 432 5521
Recommended in Litigation

HUGHEY Jr, James F
Balch & Bingham, Birmingham
305 226 3469
jhughey@balch.com
Recommended in Corporate/M&A
Practice Areas: Corporate and securities; employee benefits and executive compensation; wills, trusts, estates and wealth management; tax; healthcare; mergers and acquisitions; corporate governance.
Prof. Memberships: Alabama Board of Bar Examiners; American Bar Foundation, Fellow; Alabama Law Foundation, Fellow; Alabama Law Institute, Member
Career: James F Hughey Jr's practice relates primarily to corporate and securities transactions and general representation of business entities, including wealth preservation planning for business owners and executives. He has extensive experience advising both pri-

vate and publicly held companies regarding corporate governance matters, business planning, mergers and acquisitions, compliance with federal and state securities laws and general corporate matters.In addition to his corporate and securities practice, Mr Hughey serves as Chairman of the firm's Executive Committee. Mr Hughey is listed in 'The Best Lawyers in America'.
Personal: Born: August 15, 1945;Education: New York University (LLM in Taxation, 1972); University of Alabama (JD, 1970); University of Alabama (BA, 1967)

INGRAM, Fredric
Burr & Forman LLP, Birmingham
205 458 5237
fingram@burr.com
Recommended in Employment
Practice Areas: Defense of equal employment litigation including individual and class actions. Representing employers in proceedings before the National Labor Relations Board. Representing employers before the Department of Labor in FLSA and OSHA matters. Collective bargaining and arbitrations, representing employers.
Prof. Memberships: American Bar Association (Labor & Employment Section); Alabama State Bar (Past Chair, Labor & Employment Section); Fellow, The College of Labor and Employment Lawyers, Inc.; Past President and Member, and Executive Committee Member, Birmingham Bar Association; Past President and Board Member, Birmingham Bar Foundation.
Career: Associate and Partner, Burr & Forman, 1967 to present; admitted to practice before the United States Supreme Court, the 11th and 5th Circuit Courts of Appeal, and the Northern, Middle and Southern US District Courts of Alabama.
Personal: University of Alabama (BA 1960), University of Alabama (LLB 1962), Phi Beta Kappa.

ISOM, Chervis
Baker, Donelson, Bearman, Caldwell & Berkowitz, PC, Birmingham
205 250 8302
cisom@bakerdonelson.com
Recommended in Real Estate
Practice Areas: Chair of Baker Donelson's Real Estate Group. Practice concentrated in real estate and capital finance, with emphasis on the legal aspects of the development of commercial real estate including retail, office, industrial and apartment properties.
Prof. Memberships: Member, American College of Mortgage Attorneys. Member, American and Birmingham Bar Associations. Associate Member, International Council of Shopping Centers.
Career: Licensed in Alabama since 1967.
Personal: Birmingham-Southern Col-

lege, BA, 1962. Cumberland School of Law of Samford University, JD, 1967. Member, Curia Honoris.

JOHNSON, E Barry
Johnston Barton Proctor & Powell LLP, Birmingham 205 458 9400
Recommended in Employment

KEENE, Thomas
Rushton, Stakely, Johnston & Garrett, Montgomery 334 834 8480
Recommended in Litigation

KNIGHT, Michael
McDowell Knight Roedder & Sledge LLC, Mobile 251 432 5300
Recommended in Litigation

KUSHNER, Harold
Baker, Donelson, Bearman, Caldwell & Berkowitz, PC, Birmingham
205 250 8303
hkushner@bakerdonelson.com
Recommended in Corporate/M&A
Practice Areas: Practice concentrated in the areas of tax and corporate law, including mergers and acquisitions, securities, estate and trust planning and employer resources. Represents clients in diverse industries including steel, manufacturing, retail, technology and software, real estate development and health care, with an emphasis on representation of closely held corporations.
Prof. Memberships: Chair, Alabama Securities Commission. Member, American and Birmingham Bar Associations. Member, American Bar Association Personal Services Organizations Committee. Representative of the Alabama Bar Association to the Internal Revenue Service Practitioner's Council.
Career: Licensed in Louisiana since 1971 and Alabama since 1975.

LACY, Jr, Peyton
Ogletree, Deakins, Nash, Smoak & Stewart, PC, Birmingham
205 328 1900
peyton.lacy@ogletreedeakins.com
Recommended in Employment
Practice Areas: Labor Relations and Employment Law.
Prof. Memberships: Alabama, American and District of Columbia Bar Associations. National Association of College and University Attorneys.
Career: Admitted to practice in Alabama, District of Columbia, US Supreme Court, US Court of Appeals (Fifth, Eighth and Eleventh Circuits), and US District Courts (Western District of Louisiana; Northern, Middle and Southern Districts of Alabama; Northern District of Mississippi; and Northern District of Florida). Adjunct professor of labor law at the University of Alabama (1987-88).
Publications: Co-authored the 'Alabama Employers Handbook'.
Personal: University of Alabama (BA, 1962), University of Alabama School of Law (LLB, 1965).

LANIER, Randolph
Balch & Bingham, Birmingham
205 226 3487
rlanier@balch.com
Recommended in Real Estate
Practice Areas: Construction; real estate; finance, lending and leasing.
Prof. Memberships: Birmingham Bar Association; Alabama State Bar; American Bar Association; International Council of Shopping Centers; National Association of Industrial and Office Properties.
Career: Randolph H. Lanier is an attorney with over 25 years' experience practicing in the real estate and financial services industries, with emphasis on commercial lending and commercial real estate development. Prior to joining Balch & Bingham LLP, Mr Lanier served as Clerk to the Honorable James H. Hancock, United States District Judge, Northern District of Alabama. Mr Lanier has also been listed in 'The Best Lawyers in America' from the 1987 Edition - present.
Personal: Born: August 26, 1949;Education: Vanderbilt University (JD, 1974); University of Alabama (BS, 1971).

LEACH, John
Helmsing, Leach, Herlong, Newman & Rouse, PC, Mobile 251 432 5521
Recommended in Litigation

LEE, Jeffrey
Maynard, Cooper & Gale PC, Birmingham 205 254 1000
Recommended in Employment

LEHR, Richard
Lehr Middlebrooks Price & Vreeland, P.C., Birmingham 205 326 3002
Recommended in Employment

LIGHTFOOT, Warren
Lightfoot, Franklin & White, LLC, Birmingham 205 581 0700
Recommended in Litigation

MARSH, David
Marsh, Rickard & Bryan P.C., Birmingham 205 879 1981
Recommended in Litigation

MAY, James
Bradley Arant Rose & White LLP, Birmingham 205 521 8324
jmay@bradleyarant.com
Recommended in Employment
Practice Areas: Practices labor and employment. Extensive experience in individual and major class action employment discrimination cases, collective actions under the FLSA. Defends EEOC charges and OFCCP proceedings.
Prof. Memberships: Admitted to Practice in Alabama (1980). Past Chair of the Alabama Bar's Labor Section. Has appeared in a leading legal publication in America since 1995-96 and Member of the College of Labor and Employment Lawyers.
Career: Joined Bradley Arant in 1980; Partner in 1987.

Personal: Born 7 Jan 1949. BS University of Mississippi (Mathematics), 1971; JD University of Virginia 1980. LT, USN 1971-1977.

MCDOWELL, Jerry
McDowell Knight Roedder & Sledge LLC, Mobile 251 432 5300
Recommended in Litigation

MCGIVAREN, Crawford
Cabaniss, Johnston, Gardner, Dumas & O'Neal, Birmingham 205 716 5200
Recommended in Litigation

MCKIBBEN, Michael D
Bradley Arant Rose & White LLP, Birmingham 205 521 8421
mmckibben@bradleyarant.com
Recommended in Litigation
Practice Areas: Chairs firm's Litigation Group. Represents clients in a variety of areas, including medical, manufacturing, and computer industries. Subject matters include contracts and business torts, professional negligence, and products liability disputes.
Prof. Memberships: ABA; DRI; International Association of Defense Counsel (Drug and Medical Device and Medical Defense Committees); Alabama Defense Lawyers Association. Alabama State Bar (Character & Fitness Committee); Birmingham Bar (Medical Liaison Committee).
Publications: 'The Resale Price Maintenance Compromise', 38 Vand. L. Rev. 163.
Personal: JD (Patrick Wilson Scholar), Vanderbilt University, 1985; BS (magna cum laude), Spring Hill College, 1981. Associate editor, Vanderbilt Law Review.

MCWHORTER, Hobart
Bradley Arant Rose & White LLP, Birmingham 205 521 8241
hmcwhorter@bradleyarant.com
Recommended in Litigation
Practice Areas: Senior Partner, general civil litigation. Extensive experience securities fraud, commercial litigation, construction, environmental, product liability, and insurance defense.
Prof. Memberships: Admitted, Alabama (1958). Fellow, American College of Trial Lawyers; International Association of Defense Counsel; International Association of Railroad Trial Counsel; American Board of Trial Advocates; American Bar Association.
Career: Joined Bradley Arant Rose & White LLP, 1958; Partner, 1963; Litigation Practice Group.
Personal: Born 24 December 1931. LLB, University of Virginia Law School 1958; BA, Yale University, 1953.

MIDDLEBROOKS, David
Lehr Middlebrooks Price & Vreeland, P.C., Birmingham 205 326 3002
Recommended in Employment

MILLS, Gail L
Burr & Forman LLP, Birmingham 250 458 5300
gmills@burr.com
Recommended in Real Estate
Practice Areas: Commercial Real Estate Law: representation of lenders in commercial mortgage lending, including retail developments, multifamily, residential and golf course developments, office, industrial, and healthcare properties, and workouts, restructures, and foreclosures of defaulted loans; representation of commercial developers in retail developments, including municipal incentive transactions; representation of residential developers in land acquisition and entitlement issues.
Prof. Memberships: American College of Real Estate Lawyers; Birmingham Bar Association; Alabama Bar Association.
Career: Partner since 1991.
Personal: BS, magna cum laude, Birmingham-Southern College, 1982; JD, University of Alabama School of Law, 1985 (member of Law Review).

MINISMAN, B G
Baker, Donelson, Bearman, Caldwell & Berkowitz, PC, Birmingham 205 250 8305
bminisman@bakerdonelson.com
Recommended in Corporate/M&A
Practice Areas: Practice concentrated in corporate, securities and health law. Extensive experience in representing public companies regarding compliance with proxy solicitation and periodic reporting requirements of the 1934 Act, tender offers, corporate governance, going private transactions and mergers and acquisitions. Practice also includes representation of a variety of closely-held companies in private debt placement and equity securities.
Prof. Memberships: Member, American, Alabama and Birmingham Bar Associations. Member, Order of the Coif.
Career: Licensed in Alabama since 1970.
Personal: Unviersity of North Carolina, BA, 1967.Emory University School of Law, JD, 1970, with distinction.

MITCHELL, Chris
Maynard, Cooper & Gale PC, Birmingham 205 254 1000
Recommended in Employment

MIXSON, Dwight
Burr & Forman LLP, Birmingham 205 458 5280
dmixson@burr.com
Recommended in Real Estate
Practice Areas: Specializes in the financing, acquisition, development and leasing of commercial real estate and health care properties. He has significant experience representing lenders in all types of construction and permanent financing of real estate, including securitized lending and mezzanine financing. His clients also include owners and leas-

ing firms involved in the development and leasing of office and retail properties.
Prof. Memberships: ABA, Alabama Bar Association.
Personal: BS, summa cum laude, The University of Alabama, 1979; JD, Order of the Coif, The University of Alabama, 1982.

MONK, Stephen
Bradley Arant Rose & White LLP, Birmingham 205 521 8429
smonk@bradleyarant.com
Recommended in Real Estate
Practice Areas: Partner in Birmingham office specializing in representation of real estate development clients. Extensive experience in large-scale residential, retail, office, golf and mixed-use developments, including annexation and planned unit development matters and formulation of restrictive covenants and residential, office and mixed use condominiums .
Prof. Memberships: Admitted to practice in Alabama (1980). Member, American, Alabama and Birmingham Bar Associations.
Career: Joined Bradley Arant Rose & White LLP in 1996 as partner; 1983-96: General Counsel of Daniel Corporation, Birmingham, Alabama.
Personal: Born 28 February 1955; JD (cum laude), Cumberland School of Law (Birmingham, Alabama) (1980); BS (Accounting), Auburn University (1977).

MORROW, John H
Bradley Arant Rose & White LLP, Birmingham 205 521 8212
jmorrow@bradleyarant.com
Recommended in Litigation
Practice Areas: General civil litigation, including commercial litigation, product and personal injury defense.
Prof. Memberships: Member, American College of Trial Attorneys; listed: 'Chambers USA' 2003 and 2004, Alabama, one of top four general commercial litigation attorneys; listed: 'The Best Lawyers in America', Business Litigation, Personal Injury Litigation, First Amendment Law, since inception; Birmingham Bar Association, President, 1981.
Career: Joined Bradley Arant Rose & White LLP, 1958; became Partner, 1963.
Personal: Born July 15, 1931. Order of the Coif, JD, University of Michigan Law School, 1958; AB, Princeton University, (magna cum laude), Phi Beta Kappa, 1953.

NELSON, Carol Sue
Maynard, Cooper & Gale PC, Birmingham 205 254 1000
Recommended in Employment

NOVAK, Tabor
Ball, Ball, Matthews & Novak, Montgomery 334 387 7680
Recommended in Litigation

POWELL, Charles
Johnston Barton Proctor & Powell LLP, Birmingham 205 458 9400
Recommended in Employment

POWELL, Fred
Burr & Forman LLP, Birmingham 205 458 5228
fpowell@burr.com
Recommended in Real Estate
Practice Areas: Commercial real estate law, representing life insurance companies, banks, pension funds, individuals, and businesses in secured financings and equity investments in income properties, including large timber tracts, office buildings, shopping centers, hotels, apartments, and industrial properties.
Prof. Memberships: American College of Real Estate Lawyers; Fellow, American College of Mortgage Attorneys; Birmingham Bar Association; State Bar of Alabama (former Chairman, Real Property Section).
Personal: BS, University of Alabama, 1957; LLB, University of Alabama, 1959

PRICE, Gene
Burr & Forman LLP, Birmingham 205 458 5328
gprice@Burr.com
Recommended in Corporate/M&A
Practice Areas: Mergers and acquisitions, securities, intellectual property and general corporate representing domestic and international clients in transactions throughout the US. Has extensive experience in the technology and health care industries.
Prof. Memberships: ABA, Birmingham Bar Association, the Alabama State Bar, the New York State Bar; serves on the Board of Directors of the Alabama Information Technology Association, Tech Birmingham, the Entrepreneurial Center, Operation New Birmingham and the Birmingham Area Chamber of Commerce; past president of the Birmingham Venture Club; member of the Rotary Club of Birmingham.
Career: Associate at Milbank, Tweed, Hadley & McCloy 1983-1988, Partner at Burr & Forman since 1990.
Personal: BA, cum laude, the University of the South, 1979 JD and MBA, Vanderbilt University, 1983.

RODGERS, Stanley
Lanier Ford Shaver & Payne, Huntsville 256 535 1100
Recommended in Litigation

ROGERS, Alan T
Balch & Bingham, Birmingham 205 226 3486
arogers@balch.com
Recommended in Litigation
Practice Areas: Energy and utility litigation; insurance industry litigation; financial services litigation; business litigation; appellate.
Prof. Memberships: Federation of

Insurance and Corporate Counsel; Alabama State Bar; Alabama Defense Lawyers Association; Louisiana State Bar; American Bar Association; Rotary International; Newcomen Society; American Inns of Court.
Career: Alan T Rogers is Chairman of the firm's Litigation Section. He has substantial experience presenting cases to juries, arbitrators and appellate courts. His cases and legal counseling work have involved the energy industry, the commercial insurance industry, the financial services industry and others. Mr Rogers also has experience in representing a variety of other businesses and professionals in civil litigation. Alan is also listed in 'The Best Lawyers in America,' 2005 - 2006 Edition.
Personal: Born: March 10, 1954; Education: Tulane University School of Law (JD, cum laude, 1980); Birmingham-Southern College (BA, 1977).

ROGERS, Bruce
Bainbridge, Mims, Rogers & Smith, LLP, Birmingham
205 879 1100
Recommended in Litigation: Construction

ROGERS, E Mabry
Bradley Arant Rose & White LLP, Birmingham 205 521 8225
mrogers@bradleyarant.com
Recommended in Litigation
Practice Areas: Construction contract negotiation, advice and litigation, all over the world. Familiar with virtually all ADR methods, US and international. Frequent speaker on construction topics.
Prof. Memberships: American College of Construction Lawyers; American Bar Association; Forum on the Construction Industry.
Career: Partner since 1980.
Publications: Frequently published on various construction topics.
Personal: JD, (cum laude, class secretary), Harvard Law School, 1974; BA (cum laude, Honors English), Yale University, 1969.

ROSE Jr, J William
Johnston Barton Proctor & Powell LLP, Birmingham 205 458 9400
Recommended in Corporate/M&A

SELLERS, Randal H
Starnes & Atchison LLP, Birmingham
205 868 6019
rsellers@starneslaw.com
Recommended in Litigation
Practice Areas: 24 years of experience dedicated to civil litigation in state and federal courts.
Prof. Memberships: Fellow, American College of Trial Lawyers; Advocate, American Board of Trial Advocates; Member, Defense Lawyers Association; Member, Birmingham, Alabama and American Bar Association; Listed Best Lawyers in America.
Career: Admitted to practice in 1981

and has since tried cases in state and federal courts throughout Alabama.
Personal: Graduated from Vanderbilt University, cum laude, with a BA degree. Graduated from Vanderbilt University, School of Law in 1981.

SEXTON, Robert
Maynard, Cooper & Gale PC, Birmingham 205 254 1000
Recommended in Real Estate

SIEGAL, Bradley
Leitman, Siegal & Payne, PC, Birmingham 205 251 5900
Recommended in Real Estate

SIEGAL, Don
Leitman, Siegal & Payne, PC, Birmingham 205 251 5900
Recommended in Real Estate

SINGER, Fern
Baker, Donelson, Bearman, Caldwell & Berkowitz, PC, Birmingham
205 250 3801
fsinger@bakerdonelson.com
Recommended in Employment
Practice Areas: Chair of Baker Donelson's Labor & Employment Group. Practice concentrated in labor and employment, commercial litigation, alternative dispute resolution and fair housing litigation.
Prof. Memberships: Charter Member, Alabama Academy of Mediators. Former Adjunct Faculty Member, University of Alabama School of Law. Former Chair, Employment Law Section of the Alabama Defense Lawyers Association. Member, American Bar Association.
Career: Licensed in New York since 1981 and Alabama since 1987.
Personal: State University of New York at Stony Brook, BA, 1973. St. John's University School of Law, JD, 1980.

SMITH, David
Maynard, Cooper & Gale PC, Birmingham 205 254 1000
Recommended in Employment

SMITH, Felton
Balch & Bingham, Birmingham
205 226 3458
fsmith@balch.com
Recommended in Real Estate
Practice Areas: Real estate; finance, lending and leasing; real property/title insurance litigation; condemnation, land use and water rights.
Prof. Memberships: American Bar Association; Alabama State Bar; Birmingham Bar Association
Career: Felton Smith practices primarily in the areas of real estate and finance and represents a range of clients from large corporations to individual owners and investors. The largest part of Mr Smith's practice is acquisitions, sales, operation, management and leasing of commercial and industrial real estate for users and investors. He also represents lenders and borrowers in various types of in-state and multistate financing

transactions. Prior to joining Balch & Bingham LLP, Mr Smith worked as a banker for a number of years in the areas of branch banking, investment services, correspondent banking and commercial lending and is a graduate of the Stonier Graduate School of Banking.
Personal: Born: March 29, 1955;Education: University of Alabama (JD, 1990); Colorado University (BA, 1977).

ST CLAIR, Jay D
Bradley Arant Rose & White LLP, Birmingham 205 521 8344
jstclair@bradleyarant.com
Recommended in Employment
Practice Areas: Labor and employment.
Prof. Memberships: ABA, Sections on Labor and Employment and Litigation.
Career: Partner since 1990. Adjunct professor, Cumberland School of Law, 1999 to present.
Publications: Has lectured and written extensively on labor and employment matters.
Personal: Yale Law School (JD, 1983), University of Tennessee (BA, 1980).

STARNES, Stancil
Starnes & Atchison LLP, Birmingham
205 868 6014
sstarnes@starneslaw.com
Recommended in Litigation
Practice Areas: For over 30 years, he has represented local and national clients in a wide range of civil trials, appeals,and litigation in state and federal courts, including antitrust, securities, defense of major law firms, professional liability, RICO, insurance and complex civil litigation.
Prof. Memberships: Fellow, American College of Trial Lawyers; Advocate, American Board of Trial Attorneys; Chair, Alabama Supreme Court Advisory Committee on Alabama Rules of Civil Procedure; Member, Alabama Law Institute.
Career: Admitted in 1972. Formed current firm in 1975, specializing in civil litigation. Firm has grown from two lawyers in 1975 to over 60 lawyers in 2005.
Personal: Graduated from University of Alabama with BS in Business Administration in 1969 and Cumberland School of Law at Samford University, summa cum laude, in 1972.

STEPHENSON, Jack
Burr & Forman LLP, Birmingham
205 458 5201
jstephen@burr.com
Recommended in Corporate/M&A
Practice Areas: Experienced in the areas of securities and insurance regulation, corporate and partnership taxation, mergers and acquisitions and real estate development. A substantial part of his practice involves corporate and tax planning for transactions involving business, insurance, real estate and health care entities and the negotiation and implementation of such transactions.

Prof. Memberships: American Bar Association (Committee on Partnerships and Unincorporated Business Organizations), Alabama State Bar, Birmingham Bar Association.
Career: Partner since 1979. Adjunct faculty member of The University of Alabama School of Law from 1980-2000 teaching Securities Regulation; Business Planning; and Corporate Finance.
Personal: BA, the University of the South, 1970; JD, The University of Alabama School of Law, 1973.

STEWART, Carol
Burr & Forman LLP, Birmingham
205 458 5219
cstewart@burr.com
Recommended in Real Estate
Practice Areas: Condominium Law representing developers in creating condominiums and representing associations in management issues.
Prof. Memberships: ABA, Alabama State Bar (Board of Bar Commissioners, Executive committee, Disciplinary Commission, MCLE Commission), The Florida Bar, Georgia State Bar, Alabama Law Institute (Real Estate), Birmingham Bar Association (Executive Committee).
Career: Partner since 1990. Law Clerk to Chief Judge Sam C. Pointer, Jr. 1982.
Personal: Cumberland School of Law at Samford University (magna cum laude); University of North Carolina at Charlotte (BS Chemistry); University of Alabama in Birmingham (MS Forensic Sciences).

SYLVESTER, William
Walston, Wells, Anderson & Bains, Birmingham 205 244 5200
Recommended in Real Estate

THUSTON, Lee
Burr & Forman LLP, Birmingham
205 458 5143
lthuston@burr.com
Recommended in Corporate/M&A
Practice Areas: Corporate Law, economic development and taxation. Frequently advises clients relocating to the South regarding the process of site selection, incentives negotiation and implementation.
Prof. Memberships: ABA (Sections on Taxation and Business Law); the Alabama State Bar; Birmingham Bar Association (Secretary/Treasurer - 1995, President - 2005).
Career: Managing Partner since January 2005, Alabama Automobile Manufacturers Association (Board of Directors).
Publications: Co-author 'Alabama Limited Liability Company Forms and Practice Manual'.
Personal: BA University of Virginia, 1971; JD, Cumberland School of Law at Samford University, 1974; LLM in Taxation, New York University, 1977; Law Clerk to Associate Justice Richard L. Jones of the Alabama Supreme Court.

TOZZI, Rik S

Starnes & Atchison LLP, Birmingham
205 868 6088
rtozzi@starneslaw.com
Recommended in Litigation

Practice Areas: His practice involves representing a wide range of commercial entities and financial institutions including national banks, state chartered banks, broker-dealers, and insurance companies in both state and federal litigation throughout the country. He has served as lead counsel in numerous class and mass actions as well as cases involving FCRA, FDCPA, privacy claims, RICO, unfair competition and allegations of fraud or bad faith. A significant portion of his practice focuses on enforcing arbitration agreements and arbitrating before the NASD, AAA, JAMS and NAF.

Prof. Memberships: Member, Birmingham, Alabama, Fifth Circuit Court of Appeals, and American Bar Associations.

Career: Admitted 1993. Burr and Forman, associate, 1993-95; Deputy Attorney General, State of Alabama, 1995; Starnes & Atchison LLP, Partner and Associate, 1995 - present.

Personal: Graduated with honors degree from Oxford University (Mansfield College) with BA/MA in 1990; JD cum laude from Tulane University School of Law in 1993. Certificate in Environmental Law from Tulane University School of law in 1993.

TRACY, Timothy J

Balch & Bingham, Birmingham
205 226 3456
ttracy@balch.com
Recommended in Corporate/M&A

Practice Areas: Corporate & Securities; Tax; Mergers & Acquisitions.

Prof. Memberships: Birmingham Bar Association; Alabama State Bar; American Bar Association.

Career: Timothy J. Tracy's practice is devoted primarily to mergers and acquisitions, corporate and project finance, and corporate and partnership taxation. He has structured, negotiated and documented numerous acquisitions of stock and assets of both public and private companies, project finance transactions for independent power production facilities, steel production facilities and pulp and paper facilities, leveraged lease financings of equipment and industrial facilities, and secured and unsecured corporate borrowings. Mr Tracy also regularly advises and counsels companies regarding a variety of federal and state taxation matters, including obtaining from the Internal Revenue Service private letter rulings on tax issues and consequences of multiparty business transactions.

Personal: Born: Alabama, September 1, 1956; Education: New York University (LLM in Taxation, 1985); Cumberland School of Law (JD, cum laude, 1984); University of Alabama (BS, 1979).

VREELAND, Albert

Lehr Middlebrooks Price & Vreeland, P.C., Birmingham 205 326 3002
Recommended in Employment

WHITE, Jere

Lightfoot, Franklin & White, LLC, Birmingham
205 581 0700
Recommended in Litigation

YANCE, James

Cunningham, Bounds, Yance, Crowder & Brown, LLC, Mobile
251 471 6191
Recommended in Litigation

BALCH & BINGHAM LLP

THE FIRM

Managing Partner & Chairman, Executive Committee: James F Hughey, Jr

Number of partners: 129
Number of other lawyers: 88

AREAS OF PRACTICE:

Litigation	30%
Financial Services & Transactions	19%
Utility, Legislative & Regulatory	18%
Corporate, Tax & Finance	17%
Labor & Employment	9%
Environmental & Natural Resources	7%

FIRM OVERVIEW: Founded in 1922, Balch & Bingham LLP is one of the largest law firms in Alabama with offices in Birmingham, Montgomery, and Huntsville, Alabama, Gulfport and Jackson, Mississippi, and Washington, DC, Balch & Bingham LLP serves a diverse group of clients in business and litigation matters.

MAIN AREAS OF PRACTICE:

Litigation: Attorneys in this group handle trial and appellate practice before federal and state courts, administrative agencies and arbitration panels. The litigation attorneys handle cases in the areas of antitrust, professional liability, consumer finance, insurance, personal injury and property damage, securities, accounting, construction, products liability, intellectual property and trade secrets, computers and technology, First Amendment and media. This group supports the litigation needs of the firm's other practice groups, including banking, healthcare, ERISA and managed care litigation, environmental, labor and commercial disputes.

Financial Services & Transactions: The firm represents financial institutions in bank and bank holding formations, mergers and acquisitions, establishing branches, interstate banking, and compliance with state and federal regulatory matters. In the area of commercial real estate, developers, owners and mortgage lenders are represented in the many aspects of project development. The firm has played a major role in significant real estate projects throughout the State of Alabama. The firm's Bankruptcy Practice is devoted to creditors' rights, debt restructuring, workouts, debt collection and bankruptcy.

Utility, Legislative & Regulatory: The Utility, Legislative and Regulatory Practice handles legal issues associated with every energy option. In addition to being active in the field of utility regulation and rate making, these attorneys handle contract work, including drafting, negotiation and administration and have particular expertise with contracts relating to the purchase, sale and transportation of coal, natural gas and other energy resources. Attorneys are also actively involved in the drafting and evaluating of proposed federal and state legislation and regulations.

Corporate, Tax & Finance: The firm's Corporate and Securities Practice provides business planning and counseling services to corporations, partnerships and individuals, including structuring and restructuring business organizations and preparing agreements for corporate and partnership governance, shareholder and partnership relationships and employment arrangements. The firm assists clients with public and private securities offerings, corporate transactions and finance, project finance, intellectual property, and antitrust matters. This group also includes attorneys practicing in the following areas: (1) general taxation, including tax planning and representation in complex business transactions involving publicly traded and closely held corporations, general and limited partnerships, joint ventures, proprietorships, and charitable and other tax-exempt organizations, tax litigation, and representation before the Internal Revenue Service and state and local administrative bodies; (2) estate planning and administration, including preparation of wills and trusts and counseling

and representation in gift and estate tax matters; and (3) governmental and public authority finance, in which area the firm's attorneys serve as bond counsel, underwriter's counsel and issuer's counsel in tax-exempt and taxable financing on behalf of the State of Alabama, agencies and departments of the State, municipalities and counties and numerous public authorities, boards and corporations at the State and local levels.

Labor & Employment: Attorneys in this group advise clients on employment and labor issues and represent clients in administrative proceedings, elections, arbitrations, and jury and non-jury trials in state and federal forums. Development of effective employment policies, testing and other employee selection procedures, employee manuals, and programs to control drug and alcohol abuse are among the services offered. Industries served by the firm's labor and employment attorneys include utility, construction, manufacturing, retail, banking and financial organizations as well as municipalities, school boards and universities.

Environmental & Natural Resources: The Environmental and Natural Resources Group provides representation and counseling on environmental and natural resource issues to clients ranging from individuals and small businesses to large corporations. Attorneys are actively engaged in state and federal legislation processes and the related administrative rule-making proceedings. Using their knowledge of the laws, regulations and political climate, the attorneys provide direction on compliance issues, applications for environmental permits, and the appeal and litigation defense of state and federal environmental issues.

INTERNATIONAL WORK: The firm has assisted its clients from time to time in transactions in foreign countries.

HEAD OFFICE

ALABAMA
1710 Sixth Avenue North, **Birmingham**, AL 35203
Tel: 205 251 8100   **Fax:** 205 226 8798
Email: nyardley@balch.com
Website: www.balch.com

BRANCH OFFICES

ALABAMA
2 Dexter Avenue, **Montgomery**, AL 36104
Tel: 334 834 6500   **Fax:** 334 269 3115

655 Gallatin Street, **Huntsville**, AL 35801
Tel: 256 551 0171   **Fax:** 256 512 0119

DISTRICT OF COLUMBIA
1275 Pennsylvania Avenue, NW, **Washington, DC** 20004
Tel: 202 347 6000   **Fax:** 202 347 6001

GEORGIA
14 Piedmont Center, Suite 1100, 3535 Piedmont Rd, NE, **Atlanta, GA** 30305
Tel: 404 261 6020   **Fax:** 404 261 3656

MISSISSIPPI
1310 Twenty Fifth Avenue, **Gulfport**, MS 39501
Tel: 228 864 9900   **Fax:** 228 864 8221

401 East Capitol Street, Suite 200, **Jackson**, MS 39201
Tel: 212 751 5700   **Fax:** 212 759 9133

CONTACTS

Litigation	Alan T Rogers
Financial Services & Transactions	H Hampton Boles
Utility, Legislative & Regulatory	DH McCrary
	M Stanford Blanton
Labor & Employment	M Jefferson Starling, III
Environmental & Natural Resources	William H Satterfield

BRADLEY ARANT ROSE & WHITE LLP

THE FIRM

Executive Committee Chairman: John B Grenier

Number of partners: 120
Number of other lawyers: 92

FIRM OVERVIEW: More than 200 Bradley Arant Rose & White LLP lawyers resident in six offices located in the Southeastern United States provide clients with a broad range of legal experience and business resources. Since its founding in Birmingham, Alabama, in 1871, the firm has remained committed to providing the highest quality legal services to its clients, understanding and addressing their needs, and doing so in a timely and cost-effective manner. The firm's offices are located in Birmingham, Huntsville and Montgomery, Alabama, Jackson, Mississippi, Charlotte, North Carolina and Washington, DC.

Bradley Arant's practice groups work closely together, sharing information and lending expertise as needed. This team approach ensures that each matter is handled by the lawyers whose skill and experience are best suited for the clients' particular needs.

MAIN AREAS OF PRACTICE: Practice areas include alternative dispute resolution; antitrust and trade regulation; appellate litigation; banking and financial services; bankruptcy, reorganization, restructuring and insolvency; complex and multi-district litigation; construction and procurement and government contracts; corporate and securities; energy; environmental law and litigation; ERISA and ERISA litigation; general litigation; governmental affairs; healthcare; healthcare fraud and abuse; intellectual property (copyrights, patents, trademarks and trade secrets); international law and transactions; labor and employment; media law; mergers and acquisitions; partnership law; private equity, venture capital and investment funds; products liability; public finance; public utility law; real estate law, finance and development; tax exempt entities; taxation (federal, state and local) and tax litigation; trusts and estates and white collar crime.

CLIENTS: Aker Kvaerner; Alabama Municipal Electric Authority; Associated Builders and Contractors, Inc.; Associated Grocers of Alabama, Inc.; AT&T; Auburn University; Bayer; BE&K, Inc.; BioCryst Pharmaceuticals; BP/Amoco; Bridgestone/Firestone, Inc.; Champion International Corp.; Chevron/Texaco; Chicago Bridge & Iron; Children's Health System of Alabama; Coca-Cola Bottling Company United, Inc.; ComFrame Software Corporation; Daniel Realty; Ductile Iron Pipe Research Association; EBSCO Industries, Inc.; EBSCO Realty; Energen/Alagasco; Financial Investors of the South; First Commercial Bank; Graham & Company; B.L. Harbert International LLC; Hunt Refining Co.; Hyundai Motor Manufacturing of Alabama, LLC; Jim Walter Resources, Inc.; MeadowBrook Healthcare, Inc. and its subsidiaries; Michelin Tire Corp.; MONY Life Insurance Co.; National Cement; Pfizer; Principal Life Insurance Co.; Progressive Casualty Insurance; Randall Publishing Company; Retirement Systems of Alabama; Russell Corporation; Shoney's; Southern Applied Technologies, Inc.; Southern BioSystems, Inc.; Southern Progress Corporation; SouthTrust Bank; SouthTrust Corporation; Sprint; Synovus Financial Corp.; The Clark Construction Group; The Goodyear Tire & Rubber Co.; The Huntsville Times; The New York Times Co. ; 3M Company; Torchmark; U.S. Pipe and Foundry Co.; University of Alabama; University of Alabama at Birmingham; University of Alabama Health Services Foundation, P.C.; University of South Alabama; Vulcan Materials Comany.

HEAD OFFICE

ALABAMA
One Federal Place, 1819 Fifth Avenue North, **Birmingham**, 35203-2104
Tel: 205 521 8000   **Fax:** 205 521 8800
Email: info@bradleyarant.com
Website: www.bradleyarant.com

BRANCH OFFICES

ALABAMA
200 Clinton Avenue West, Suite 900, **Huntsville**, AL, 35801-4900
Tel: 256 517 5100   **Fax:** 256 517 5200

Alabama Center for Commerce, 401 Adams Avenue, Suite 780,
Montgomery, AL, 36104
Tel: 334 956 7700   **Fax:** 334 956 7701

MISSISSIPPI
188 East Capital Street, Suite 450, **Jackson**, MS, 39201
Tel: 601 948 8000   **Fax:** 601 948 3000

DISTRICT OF COLUMBIA
1200 G Street NW, Suite 550, **Washington**, DC, 20005
Tel: 202 393 7150   **Fax:** 202 347 1684

NORTH CAROLINA
Bank of America Corporate Center, 100 N Tyron Street, Suite 2690,
Charlotte, NC 28202
Tel: 704 332 8842   **Fax:** 704 332 8858

CONTACTS

Birmingham Office	John B Grenier
Charlotte Office	John D Bond
Huntsville Office	Gary C Huckaby
Montgomery Office	Philip H Butler
Jackson Office	Margaret O Cupples
Washington, DC Office	Jeffrey D Komarow

Banking & Financial Services	J David Dresher (Birmingham)
Competitive Practices & IP	Thad G Long (Birmingham)
Construction & Procurement	Walter J Sears (Birmingham)
Corporate & Securities	Virginia C Patterson (Birmingham)
Energy	John G Harrell (Birmingham)
Environmental	Sid J Trant (Birmingham)
Government Affairs	Luther J Strange (Birmingham)
Healthcare	Deane K Corliss (Birmingham)
International	Douglas E Eckert (Birmingham)
Labor & Employment	James P Alexander (Birmingham)
Litigation	Michael D McKibben (Birmingham)
Public Finance	P Nicholas Greenwood (Birmingham)
Real Estate	John E Hagefstration (Birmingham)
Reorganization, Restructuring & Bankruptcy	J Patrick Darby (Birmingham)
Tax, Trusts & Estates, & ERISA	K Wood Herren (Birmingham)

Bradley Arant
BRADLEY ARANT ROSE & WHITE LLP

BURR & FORMAN LLP

THE FIRM

Managing Partner: W Lee Thuston
Senior Partner: William C Knight

Number of partners: 93
Number of other lawyers: 72

FIRM OVERVIEW: Founded in 1905, Burr & Forman LLP's experienced legal team serves clients in several industries including real estate, banking, healthcare, construction and automotive. With 165 attorneys in Atlanta, Georgia, Birmingham and Montgomery, Alabama and Jackson and Laurel, Mississippi, the firm draws from a diverse range of resources and expertise to help clients achieve their goals.

MAIN AREAS OF PRACTICE:

Banking & Finance: The firm's practice includes traditional asset-based and commercial lending activities, as well as syndicated and participated credit facilities and bond financings relating to real estate, healthcare, manufacturing and other industries. Burr attorneys stay updated on the latest trends in creditors' rights, lender liability and litigation, advising clients on the prevailing federal and state regulatory aspects of commercial banking.

Construction: The firm represents general contractors, subcontractors, suppliers, owners, developers and design professionals in counseling, planning and negotiating during the construction process. During the planning and negotiation phases of the construction process, attorneys work to obtain the most advantageous contractual position possible. During construction, attorneys anticipate, evaluate and handle a wide range of day-to-day legal issues to avoid and minimize potential conflicts.

Corporate: Corporate services to clients include reviewing, negotiating and preparing various corporate, commercial, construction, real estate, insurance, shareholder, employment and financial transactions and agreements. Attorneys regularly represent individuals, corporations and other business entities in acquiring and selling both private and public companies. Attorneys provide counsel and services related to federal and state securities laws and regulations for public and privately owned companies, individual investors, investment advisors, broker-dealers, insurance companies and corporate officers.

Creditors' Rights, Workouts & Insolvency: Attorneys protect and enforce creditors' interests in debt enforcement and collection and in bankruptcy and non-bankruptcy workouts across the United States. The firm has extensive experience in real estate workouts and in representing lenders in a broad range of industries.

Economic Development: The firm has extensive experience with all legal issues relating to the site selection process, incentive negotiation and implementation. Attorneys work with site selection teams to analyze various legal issues and negotiate with state and local governments considered for plant sites. The firm advises clients in choice-of-entity and tax structure issues and assists with all aspects of environmental permitting and the construction process. Additionally, attorneys guide clients with new hire concerns and supplier contracts.

Healthcare: The firm represents hospitals, physicians and other health care providers in the primary legal and regulatory aspects of healthcare, including fraud and abuse, antitrust, licensure, Medicare certification, medical staff credentialing, certificate of need issues, reimbursement and potential tort liability resulting from the physician-patient relationship.

Labor & Employment: Attorneys advise clients on improving day-to-day operations such as employment and disengagement agreements, policies and procedures, regulatory compliance, employment publications and employee training. The firm represents employers in disputes including individual and class action employment discrimination cases, workplace safety actions and workers' compensation claims.

Litigation: Almost half of the firm's attorneys practice dispute resolution and have vast experience in areas such as commercial, financial services, insurance, securities, antitrust, toxic tort, class actions and franchising.

Real Estate: The firm has broad capabilities in real estate development, leasing and land use. Representing both developers and lenders, attorneys provide counsel from the initial steps of planning and zoning through the completion of the project. The firm routinely handles the purchase and sale of commercial buildings, shopping centers, multi-family properties, office and industrial projects and large tracts of land, as well as land-use planning for major residential subdivisions, condominiums and other commercial and residential real estate developments.

CLIENTS: American Cast Iron Pipe Company; SouthTrust Bank; Mercedes Benz USI; Honda Motor Company.

HEAD OFFICE

ALABAMA
420 North Twentieth Street, Suite 3100, **Birmingham, AL** 35203
Tel: 205 251 3000 **Fax:** 205 458 5100
Website: www.burr.com

BRANCH OFFICES

ALABAMA
201 Monroe Street, Suite 1950, **Montgomery, AL** 36104
Tel: 334 241 7000 **Fax:** 334 262 0200

GEORGIA
171 Seventeenth Street NW, Suite 1100, **Atlanta, GA** 30363
Tel: 404 815 3000 **Fax:** 404 817 3244

MISSISSIPPI
210 East Capitol Street, Suite 2120, **Jackson,** MS 39201
Tel: 601 355 3434 **Fax:** 601 355 5150

535 North Fifth Avenue, **Laurel,** MS 39441
Tel: 601 425 0400 **Fax:** 601 649 0088

BURR & FORMAN LLP

CHRISTIAN & SMALL LLP

THE FIRM

Managing Partner: Richard E Smith

Number of partners: 17
Number of other lawyers: 14

AREAS OF PRACTICE:

Litigation	80%
Corporate & Business Transactions	15%
Mediation	5%

HEAD OFFICE

ALABAMA
505, North 20th Street, Suite 1800, **Birmingham**, AL 35203
Tel: 205 795 6588 **Fax:** 205 328 7234
Website: www.csattorneys.com

CONTACTS

Litigation	Duncan Y Manley
Corporate & Business Transactions	Steven A Benefield
Mediation	Kenneth O Simon

FIRM OVERVIEW: Christian & Small is a full-service law firm representing a diverse clientele throughout Alabama, the Southeast and across the nation. Founded in July 2000 by partners Thomas W Christian and Clarence M Small, formerly with Rives & Peterson, the firm has a solid foundation and an impressive history. Four partners are Fellows of the American College of Trial Lawyers; four are Fellows of the International Academy of Trial Lawyers; four are members of the American Board of Trial Advocates; four are Fellows of the American Bar Foundation; and two have served as President of the Alabama State Bar. Each of the firm's attorneys is committed to providing the most vigorous, effective and cost-efficient representation available, with a continual focus on building enduring client relationships and exceeding client expectations. Christian & Small has proven itself as a leader among Birmingham law firms, offering the high quality of legal representation expected from the larger firms and the client focused attention that distinguishes the best small firms. The firm's team approach, recruitment of top level attorneys, and investment in the most advanced technology enhances our success and efficiency. Zealous client advocacy tempered by a commitment to the highest ethical standards has secured the superior reputation in every representation the firm undertakes. These guiding principles have earned the firm a distinguished place among Alabama's elite law firms.

MAIN AREAS OF PRACTICE: Christian & Small's diverse practice enables the firm to provide the broad range of capabilities that clients expect from a full- service law firm. By working in practice teams, the lawyers are able to deliver innovative solutions to the legal and business problems facing their clients. The firm's practice groups are primarily divided into the areas of litigation, corporate and business transactions, and mediation.
Litigation: Christian & Small's trial lawyers have an impressive history of earning defense verdicts. Extensive experience in a variety of state and judicial forums nationwide combined with the firm's reputation for creative and zealous client advocacy has earned Christian & Small a distinguished place in Alabama's Trial Bar. The firm matches highly experienced litigators with specific client needs so that the most innovative, effective and efficient solutions can be achieved. The firm assists clients in all stages of litigation from preventative strategies to avoid potential liability, pre-transaction counseling, and alternative dispute proceedings, trial and, if necessary, appeal. Christian & Small's litigation practice encompasses virtually every area of the law including: labor and employment; medical/professional malpractice defense; product liability; business and commercial; transportation, including trucking and aviation; bankruptcy; environmental and toxic tort; construction; white collar criminal defense; domestic relations; insurance and first party insurance defense; bad faith and fraud; briefing and appellate.
Corporate & Business Transactions: The corporate and business lawyers at Christian & Small handle all aspects of a business' operations through all stages of development, including real estate acquisition. They also have substantial experience managing the legal needs of individuals with small business, estate planning and tax needs. The firm's corporate and business lawyers routinely handle legal matters in the following areas: business and tax planning; business organization and reorganization; corporate and business transactions; contract disputes; employer/employee relationship agreements; real estate; wills, estate and trust planning.
Mediation: The firm has several attorneys who routinely participate in a variety of ADR proceedings as mediators and arbitrators. Consistently recognized by their peers for the strength and effectiveness of their mediation skills, the firm's attorney mediators' comprehensive knowledge of litigation, claims and the judicial process allows them to provide meaningful insight and assessment to the involved parties throughout the negotiation.

CLIENTS: Christian & Small represents a diverse clientele, ranging from individuals and closely-held businesses to Fortune 500 corporations. The firm's list of clients includes manufacturers, banks and financial institutions, hospitals, nursing homes and assisted living facilities, physicians, accountants, retail companies, technology companies, insurance companies, and trucking companies.

HELMSING, LEACH, HERLONG, NEWMAN & ROUSE, PC

THE FIRM

Managing Partner: James B Newman
Senior Partner: Frederick G Helmsing
Number of partners: 11
Number of other lawyers: 5

AREAS OF PRACTICE:

Commercial Litigation 60%
Banking & Finance 20%
M&A 20%

FIRM OVERVIEW: The firm was founded in 1976 when successful partners of large firms joined forces to create a firm that could offer a diverse array of legal services with enthusiasm, expertise, and confidence. As a full service firm of medium size, Helmsing, Leach, Herlong, Newman & Rouse, PC combines the characteristics of smaller firms' vigor and personality with the quality and efficiency attributed to larger groups. Since 1976, the firm has been dedicated to providing quality legal services to business, professionals, families and individuals.

MAIN AREAS OF PRACTICE:

Banking & Finance: The firm is routinely involved in all phases of banking and financial transactions as counsel for both borrowers and lenders. Its representation of banks, other financial institutions and borrowers includes negotiating and structuring loans, analyzing loan terms and conditions, and developing and drafting loan documents and agreements.

Bankruptcy: The firm has engaged in the active practice of all creditors' rights, workouts and insolvency litigation. This practice group offers a comprehensive array of services regarding the protection and enforcement of creditors' interests in bankruptcy and non-bankruptcy workouts. The firm has extensive experience in representing asset-based lenders and financial service institutions, including local, regional and national banks. The firm also has significant experience involving representation of bankruptcy trustees, examiners and other fiduciaries. The firm represents both creditors and corporate debtors faced with the numerous issues that accompany business insolvencies.

Business & Corporate Matters: The firm regularly performs the functions involved in modern corporate law. It creates, maintains, reorganizes, liquidates and dissolves corporations, partnerships, limited liability companies, joint ventures, and professional corporations and associations. The firm has significant experience in the resolution and litigation of business and corporate disputes. It administers corporate acquisitions and mergers, and works out corporate structural changes among stockholders, partners, and other business owners.

Taxation & Tax Planning: Several of the firm's lawyers have received advanced training in taxation. The firm regularly advises its clients on individual and corporate tax matters spanning the total spectrum of State and Federal taxation.

White Collar Criminal Defense: The firm has broad experience in white collar criminal practice, including tax crimes, fraud, health fraud, RICO, anti-trust, bank and credit charges, embezzlement and other economic crimes. The firm provides representation for those undergoing criminal investigation by the Internal Revenue Service and other governmental agencies, as well as grand jury investigation. The firm handles the case in every phase of investigation, trial and appellate proceedings.

Litigation: The firm conducts a substantial Litigation Practice. It has tried major cases in all surrounding State and Federal courts and has handled appeals to the highest levels of the State and Federal judicial systems. The firm is known for successfully handling complicated and significant cases and disputes. The firm has extensive experience in virtually all types of business litigation, whether involving breach of contract, tortious conduct, equitable or extraordinary remedies, or statutory relief.

HEAD OFFICE

ALABAMA
150 Government Street, Suite 2000, **Mobile**, AL 36602
Tel: 251 432 5521   **Fax:** 251 432 0633
Website: www.helmsinglaw.com

CONTACTS

Banking & Financing . . . . .Robert H Rouse
Litigation/White Collar Criminal Practice . . . . .Frederick G Helmsing
M&A . . . . Robert H Rouse

Eminent Domain & Condemnation: For more than 20 years the firm has engaged in the practice of eminent domain law. It represents landowners and condemning agencies throughout the State of Alabama in a wide variety of takings, both direct and inverse, at the local, state, and federal level in administrative, trial and appellate proceedings.

Product Liability: The firm has extensive and significant experience in representing manufacturers, component part suppliers, distributors, and individuals in product liability cases. Products the firm has defended include aircraft, aviation equipment, aircraft engines, helicopters, automobiles, automobile parts, seatbelts, boats, marine products, chainsaws, household appliances, power tools, drugs, pharmaceutical products, medical devices and equipment, surgical supplies, tires, motor homes, water heaters, paper-making machinery, wire rope and other steel products and heavy machinery and engines. The firm has also represented manufacturers and distributors of chemicals and other products in toxic tort cases and class actions. Recently, a team of its lawyers successfully represented Kumho Tire Company in the United States Supreme Court landmark decision clarifying that the trial court's gatekeeping duty under Federal Rule of Evidence 702 applies to all experts and not just scientific experts (Kumho Tire Co. v Carmichael), 119 S.CT.1167 (1999).

Real Estate Law: The firm has a broad Real Estate Practice, representing clients engaged in all areas of the real estate industry. Its clients include residential and commercial buyers and sellers, shopping center owners and tenants, apartment complex and condominium owners and developers, brokerage companies, residential and commercial contractors, real estate investment trusts, title companies, and banks and other financial institutions who lend money secured by real estate.

Government Relations: The firm has full scale capability in handling matters arising from the regulation of business affairs by the government at all levels. Such activities include the regulation of pharmaceutical products, the environment, healthcare facilities, public utilities, zoning and matters involving the licensure of businesses, professions and contractors.

Health Law: The firm maintains an active Health Law Section dedicated to serving the healthcare community in administrative, regulatory and compliance matters. The firm has represented clients' interests in matters involving Medicare, Medicaid, HCFA, the United State Department of Justice and the Alabama Attorney General's office, in successfully defending clients accused of Medicare and Medicaid fraud and abuse.

Employment Law: The firm is engaged, primarily by employers, in employment-related transactions and disputes. The firm's attorneys assist its business clients in dealing with a wide range of employment matters, including employment contracts, arbitration agreements, day-to-day employment issues with the goal of avoiding or minimizing conflicts, and responses to EEOC or other complaints. The firm also has an extensive Litigation Practice in this area of law.

STARNES & ATCHISON LLP

THE FIRM

Managing Partner: W Michael Atchison

Number of partners: 27
Number of other attorneys: 30

FIRM OVERVIEW: Founded in 1975, Starnes & Atchison LLP has always been a firm devoted exclusively to litigation. Today, Starnes & Atchison LLP is made up of over 50 attorneys and continues to be committed to a civil litigation practice. The firm's distinguished list of clients includes physicians, attorneys, architects, accountants and other professionals, as well as corporations, hospitals, long-term care facilities, nursing homes and insurance companies. Starnes & Atchison LLP has its main office in Birmingham, with a second office in Mobile. The firm handles litigation matters throughout Alabama and serves as lead counsel in a number of cases pending around the United States. The attorneys who make up Starnes & Atchison LLP are recognized as ranking among the most experienced trial lawyers in the state - four of the firm's partners are Fellows of the American College of Trial Lawyers, five of its partners are members of the American Board of Trial Advocates and four of its attorneys are listed in the Best Lawyers in America. Starnes & Atchison LLP is a young and energetic firm which holds a respected position in the legal community. The firm maintains substantial legal and medical libraries and utilizes state of the art computer technology so as to provide clients with excellent resources and professional legal expertise.

CLIENTS:

Corporations & Institutions: University of Alabama; Salomon Smith Barney, Inc.; General Electric Capital Corporation; City of Mountain Brook; ACE USA; Consolidated Construction Co.; First American Bank; Bancorp South; UBS Securities, LLC; Burk-Kleinpeter, Inc.; Gold-Cup Coffee Services, Inc.; SPX Corporation; Primeamerica; AT&T Universal Card Services; National Bank of Commerce; Citigroup, Inc.; Bancorp South, Inc.; Alabama National Bancorporation; Verizon; Verizon Wireless; International Paper; Capital One; Caremark RX, Inc.; American Mining, Co.; National Service Industries; Murphy Oil USA, Inc.; Lowes; Drummond Company, Inc.; American Arbitration Association; American Honda; Auburn University; GTE Mobilnet; Mercedes Benz of North America, Inc.; Home Depot; Kohlberg, Kravits & Roberts; Fluke Corp.; Aero-Global, Inc.; Hennessy Industries, Inc.; Bonds Development Co.
Medical: ProNational Inc; ProAssurance Inc; American Health Insurance Company; Brookwood Medical Center, Inc.; Glaxo Wellcome, Inc.; HealthPartners of Alabama, Inc.; Hoffman-LaRoche, Inc.; Med Partners, Inc.; Medical Care International; Mobile Infirmary Medical Center; Medical Assurance, Inc.; Podiatry Insurance Company of America; St. Vincent's Hospital; University of Alabama at Birmingham; University of Alabama Health Services Foundation; Tenet Health Systems; Woodcrest

HEAD OFFICE

ALABAMA
100 Brookwood Place, 7th Floor, P.O. Box 598512, **Birmingham**, AL 35259
Tel: 205 868 6000   **Fax:** 205 868 6099
Website: www.starneslaw.com

BRANCH OFFICES

ALABAMA
Riverview Plaza, Suite 1106, 63 S. Royal Street, **Mobile**, AL 36602
Tel: 251 433 6049

Service, Inc.; Ascension Health Care; Mariner Health Care; Caronia Corp.
Insurance: Protective Life Insurance Co.; Alabama Municipal Insurance Corp.; Markel Insurance Co.; American National Insurance Company; American Heritage Insurance Company; Associated Aviation Underwriters; Attorneys Insurance Mutual; Attorneys Liability Assurance Society; Chubb Group Insurance; CNA Insurance Company; Farmers Insurance Company; Fidelity and Deposit Company of Maryland; The Fidelity and Casualty Company of New York; Great American Insurance Company; International Fidelity Insurance Company; J. C. Penney Life Insurance Company; Reliance Insurance Company; St. Paul Fire and Marine Insurance Company; State Farm Insurance Company; Travelers Insurance Company; Western Surety Company; Zurich Insurance Company; Kemper Insurance Co.; PMA Insurance Co.; AIG; Allstate Insurance Co.; Meadowbrook ASI Insurance Group.

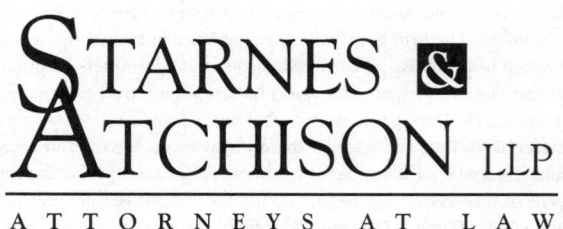

CONTENTS: Bankruptcy p.133; Corporate/M&A p.134; Employment p.135; Environment, Natural Resources & Regulated Industries p.136; Litigation: p.138; Native American Law p.140; Real Estate p.140; Individuals' Profiles p.141; Firm's Profiles p.145.

How lawyers are ranked

The opinions we gather from clients — mainly from in-house lawyers but also from other purchasers of legal services — are balanced by opinions from colleagues and competitors. Together, they provide two different perspectives — an all-round view — and biased viewpoints cancel each other out.

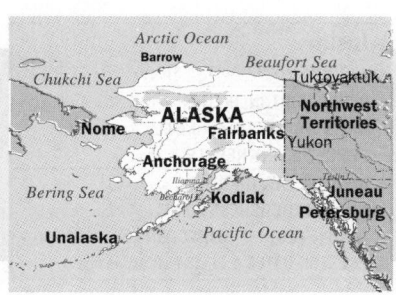

BANKRUPTCY

Alaska
Leading firms (Bankruptcy)

1. CHRISTIANSON, BOUTIN & SPRAKER *Anchorage*
2. DAVIS WRIGHT TREMAINE LLP *Anchorage*
   DORSEY & WHITNEY LLP *Anchorage*

Leading individuals (Bankruptcy)

1. BUNDY David *Sole Practitioner, Anchorage*
   CHRISTIANSON Cabot *Christianson Boutin, Anchorage*
   MILLS Michael *Bankston Gronning, Anchorage*
   PARISE Michael *Birch Horton, Anchorage*
   SIEMERS John *Burr Pease, Anchorage*
   SNEED Spencer *Dorsey & Whitney, Anchorage*
2. BOUTIN Michelle *Christianson Boutin, Anchorage*
   DAWSON Jon *Davis Wright, Anchorage*
   OESTING David *Davis Wright, Anchorage*
   SPRAKER Gary *Christianson Boutin, Anchorage*
   TRAVOSTINO Joan *Preston Gates, Anchorage*

Firms and Individuals are listed alphabetically in each band.

Band 1

Christianson, Boutin & Spraker

The Firm: This small practice won wide market acclaim as an *"excellent bankruptcy boutique."* Each of the three name partners is a specialist in this field, and offers advice to debtors and creditors on financial workouts, business reorganizations and Chapter 7 and 11 matters.

The Lawyers: With his many years of experience, interviewees distinguish **Cabot Christianson** as *"one of the best bankruptcy attorneys in the state."* Notably, he was involved in the Compton v Chatanika Gold Camp Properties case. Following in his wake, and equally devoted to this area of work, are **Michelle Boutin** and **Gary Spraker**, both of whom were identified as *"top-notch bankruptcy specialists"* and important contributors to the success of the firm.

The Clients: Clients include both debtors and creditors.

Band 2

Davis Wright Tremaine LLP
See firm details p.1796

The Firm: This multioffice, commercial player has achieved recognition as a leading force in bankruptcy work in the state. The Anchorage office acts for lenders and creditors on workouts, and in collection matters driven by litigation. Attorneys have counseled in some of the most significant bankruptcy cases in Alaska.

The Lawyers: Litigator **David Oesting** (see p.143) has an impressive track record in acting for secured and unsecured creditors in bankruptcy proceedings. He represented MarkAir in a major Alaska airline Chapter 11 bankruptcy, and was also involved in University Savings Bank v Kenai Professional Associates in the US Bankruptcy Court. Transactional specialist **Jon Dawson** (see p.142) acts for businesses and financial institutions on maritime foreclosure actions and creditors in bankruptcy proceedings. He is felt to be a particularly adept draftsman and negotiator of workouts, but also has ample trial experience.

The Clients: The firm counts as clients some of the largest companies in the USA and globally; it represents both creditors and debtors.

Dorsey & Whitney LLP

The Firm: The bankruptcy attorneys of the Anchorage branch of this international firm represent debtors, creditors and boards of directors in reorganization, liquidation and workout proceedings, as well as advising solvent businesses on capital and corporate restructuring. Like many of their peers, lawyers here have niche expertise in maritime bankruptcy.

The Lawyers: **Spencer Sneed** impresses all those who encounter him. Clients say he is both *"tenacious"* and *"effective;"* rival attorneys are equally favorable in their comments on his handling of commercial bankruptcy litigation.

Other Notable Practitioners

David Bundy of David H Bundy PC is deemed a *"superb"* creditors' attorney, who also handles a steady diet of debtors work and counsels businesses in workouts. His key client is Wells Fargo in Anchorage. **Michael Mills** of Bankston, Gronning, O'Hara, PC has built a name as *"a stellar bankruptcy attorney."* He advises debtors, trustees and creditors on financial restructurings and in Chapter 7 and Chapter 11 proceedings. He notably represented MarkAir and software company Martech in some of the most prominent reorganization cases in Alaska. Clients recognize **Michael Parise** (see p.144) of Birch, Horton, Bittner & Cherot, for his *"exceptional knowledge of bankruptcy issues and effective negotiation skills."* According to rivals: *"He is very calm and issues are never blown out of proportion when dealing with him."* Representative clients include KeyBank National Association, the Alaska Industrial Development and Export Authority, National Bank of Alaska and Thor Gold Alaska. **John Siemers** of Burr, Pease & Kurtz, PC attracted high praise for his work advising financial institutions on Chapter 7 and Chapter 11 representations. He has served as bankruptcy examiner and boasts extensive experience in advising bankruptcy trustees and creditors' committees on US Bankruptcy Code issues. **Joan Travostino** of Preston Gates & Ellis LLP is admired for her versatility in handling commercial and bankruptcy matters. She acts for creditors, and has particular expertise in the mining and fishing industries. She also counsels clients on real estate-related bankruptcies.

CORPORATE/M&A

Alaska
Leading firms (Corporate/M&A)

[1] BIRCH, HORTON, BITTNER & CHEROT *Anchorage*
DAVIS WRIGHT TREMAINE LLP *Anchorage*
DORSEY & WHITNEY LLP *Anchorage*

[2] DURRELL LAW GROUP, PC *Anchorage*
HUGHES THORSNESS POWELL *Anchorage*
LANDYE BENNETT BLUMSTEIN LLP *Anchorage*
PRESTON GATES & ELLIS LLP *Anchorage*

Leading individuals (Corporate/M&A)

[1] BLACK Kathryn *Birch Horton*, Anchorage
DAWSON Jon *Davis Wright*, Anchorage
DURRELL Brian *Durrell Law Group*, Anchorage
KRAFT Barbara Simpson *Davis Wright*, Anchorage
ROSSTON Richard *Dorsey & Whitney*, Anchorage

[2] BLUMSTEIN Philip *Landye Bennett*, Anchorage
CYPHERS Christopher *Preston Gates*, Anchorage
ODSEN Frederick *Hughes Thorsness*, Anchorage
RECKMEYER Peter *Heller Ehrman*, Anchorage
REECE Joseph *Davis Wright*, Anchorage
SAUER Jane *Perkins Coie*, Anchorage

Firms and Individuals are listed alphabetically in each band.

Band 1

Birch, Horton, Bittner & Cherot

See firm details p.145

The Firm: Clients distinguish this practice as one to turn to for complex deals. Its banking experience and corporate know-how combine with particular expertise in drafting and negotiating agreements in oil, gas and regulated industries to produce an obviously dominant force in commercial law in Alaska. The firm also benefits from an office in Washington DC, providing clients with access to advice on federal legislative and regulatory affairs in the telecom and natural resources sectors.

The Lawyers: Interviewees say the way **Kathryn Black** (see p.141) handles transactions is "*superb.*" According to one client, she is "*very capable of putting complex matters into terms easily understood by clients.*" Black "*knows her stuff*" when it comes to regulated industry-related commercial issues, and her recent key deals include representing the Municipality of Anchorage in its purchase of oil and gas leases in the Beluga Field, and acting for Alaska Communications Systems in the purchase of facilities throughout the state.

The Clients: KeyBank National Association; Wells Fargo; Alaska Industrial Development and Export Authority; Encore Credit; St. Mary's Episcopal Church and Northwest Farm Credit Services.

Davis Wright Tremaine LLP

See firm details p.1796

The Firm: This firm's transactional group can, whenever necessary, draw upon an extensive network of offices on the West Coast and in New York, DC and China. It focuses on the energy, healthcare and defense sectors, and maintains a growing niche in advising oil, gas and computer companies on IP and licensing issues. Clients praise the firm's attorneys for "*clarifying the commercial issues and responding to our deadlines.*"

The Lawyers: The firm continues to house some of the state's leading transactional lawyers, including the "*superlative*" **Barbara Simpson Kraft** (see p.143). According to one major client: "*Her knowledge is so sound that she is the face I would send to the board of directors.*" She recently acted as local counsel to Yukon Fuel in the sale of its assets to Crowley Marine Services. Clients acknowledge **Jon Dawson** (see p.142) to be "*a jack of all trades,*" though far from a master of none. He is "*as sharp as a knife, very honest and always quick in coming back with precise answers.*" Dawson's practice centers on corporate finance, real estate-driven transactions and IP. He represented Alaska Industrial Resources, one of the world's leading suppliers of fabric-covered buildings, in several foreign and domestic military and commercial sales agreements, including contracts with the UK's Ministry of Defence. Interviewees confirm that **Joe Reece** (see p.144) is "*a first-class corporate specialist.*" He advises on corporate acquisitions and sales, and the transfer of real estate portfolios. He represented Unique Machine in the $10 million sale of its oil field services business to Sumitomo. This major deal involved the transfer of licenses, patented processes and real estate interests.

The Clients: Unique Machine; Valley Hospital Association; Flint Hills Resources; Alaska Industrial Resources; Eklutna; Providence Anchorage Anaesthesia Medical Group; Alaska Native Tribal Health Consortium and Yukon Fuel.

Dorsey & Whitney LLP

The Firm: Attorneys in the Anchorage office of Dorsey & Whitney derive strength from the firm's national and international network of offices. The corporate and commercial group advises on business mergers, acquisitions, joint ventures and restructurings as well as a range of commercial contracts. It further advises companies on real estate, natural resources and regulated industry issues. According to clients, attorneys "*work very hard and handle transactions without the flash and the dash.*"

The Lawyers: Singled out, in part, for his skill in negotiations, **Richard Rosston** exceeds client expectations in providing "*high-quality work and superb attention to detail.*" One general counsel for a leading national company revealed: "*His legal judgment is so acute that he is the quarterback you want on the team.*"

The Clients: Denali Foods; Doyon; Fred Meyer Stores; Morrison Auto Group and Waipono.

Band 2

Durrell Law Group, PC

The Firm: Clients appreciate this firm's "*quality-oriented approach*" to business transactions. The practice particularly excels where there are real estate, estate planning and taxation matters to consider.

The Lawyers: Interviewees place **Brian Durrell** at "*the top of the totem pole*" in Anchorage for advice to small and medium-sized businesses on mergers, acquisitions, tax and estate planning. His experience as a CPA is deemed an asset to his practice.

The Clients: This practice's clients stem from the transportation, construction and tourism industries.

Hughes Thorsness Powell Huddleston & Bauman LLC

The Firm: The firm undertakes transactions in all areas of banking and finance, corporate, tax and real estate, and advises several large, Alaska-based companies on acquisitions and lending.

The Lawyers: Peers view **Fred Odsen** as "*a first-class*" corporate and commercial specialist. He handles a steady flow of banking, real property and loan workout instructions, and comes with a wealth of experience in oil and gas.

The Clients: First Interstate Bank of Alaska; Fisher-Price; Fleetwood Enterprises; Harley-Davidson and State Farm.

Landye Bennett Blumstein LLP

See firm details p.1488

The Firm: This firm remains a preeminent name in Alaska for commercial transactions. It counsels businesses on the full range of M&A, securities and bankruptcy matters, and maintains a niche in acting for regional Alaska Native corporations in negotiating natural resource-driven transactions.

The Lawyers: **Phil Blumstein** (see p.142) is the firm's front runner. Peers value his "*breadth of experience*" in corporate and real estate formations.

The Clients: Chugach Alaska; Northwest Arctic Borough; Ilisagvik College; Alaska Native Heritage Center and Bering Straits Native.

Preston Gates & Ellis LLP

The Firm: Preston Gates is developing a growing profile in corporate finance, advising several emerging companies on joint ventures, strategic business alliances and equity investments. The practice benefits from offices throughout the West Coast and an international presence in Hong Kong, Taiwan and Beijing.

The Lawyers: Interviewees were impressed with **Chris Cyphers**, who they saw as "*a thorough and tenacious go-getter.*" Cyphers advises many clients in the oil and gas and hi-tech sectors.
The Clients: The client base encompasses local, national and international clients.

Other Notable Practitioners

Peter Reckmeyer, from the Anchorage office of Heller Ehrman White & McAuliffe LLP is said to display finesse in negotiating and drafting agreements in the areas of life sciences, IP and technology. Interviewees have a high opinion of

Jane Sauer at Perkins Coie LLP. She is recognized as "*a meticulous and thoughtful*" business lawyer, specializing in corporate and commercial transactions as well as estate planning.

EMPLOYMENT

MAINLY DEFENDANT

Alaska
Leading firms
(Employment: Mainly Defendant)

[1] **DAVIS WRIGHT TREMAINE LLP** *Anchorage*
PERKINS COIE LLP *Anchorage*
PRESTON GATES & ELLIS LLP *Anchorage*

[2] **BIRCH, HORTON, BITTNER & CHEROT** *Anchorage*
DORSEY & WHITNEY LLP *Anchorage*
TINDALL BENNETT & SHOUP PC *Anchorage*
TURNER & MEDE, PC *Anchorage*

Leading individuals
(Employment: Mainly Defendant)

[1] **DANIEL Thomas** *Perkins Coie*, Anchorage
GROVER Parry *Davis Wright*, Anchorage
PARKER Douglas *Preston Gates*, Anchorage

[2] **BENNETT Wilfred** *Tindall Bennett*, Anchorage
COLBO Kimberlee *Hughes Thorsness*, Anchorage
EVANS William *Dorsey & Whitney*, Anchorage
HALL Helena *Perkins Coie*, Anchorage
JULIUSSEN James *Davis Wright*, Anchorage
LIMERES Amy *Preston Gates*, Anchorage
MEDE William *Turner & Mede*, Anchorage
ROHLF Joan *Guess & Rudd*, Anchorage
STEWART Robert *Davis Wright*, Anchorage

Up-and-coming individuals
ALEXANDER Jennifer *Birch Horton*, Anchorage

Firms and individuals are listed alphabetically in each band.

Band 1

Davis Wright Tremaine LLP
See firm details p.1796
The Firm: "*Very knowledgeable, has depth and is easy to work with*" sums up the market view of this five-star labor and employment practice. Its representation of management in employment discrimination and collective bargaining matters is perceived to be among the very best in the state.
The Lawyers: Clients describe **Parry Grover** (see p.142) as "*the godfather of employment law*" in Alaska. He is said to combine the perfect balance of "*cool intellect with a human touch.*" Grover acts for Alaska-based clients; a recent highlight was assisting an Alaska hospital, newly merged with a national healthcare company, in the renegotiation of its collective bargaining agreement with a union. He also defended an

Alaska employer in litigation filed by a former employee alleging unfair discharge in retaliation for making safety complaints about crane operations on Alaska's North Slope oil fields. **James Juliussen** (see p.143) is acknowledged to be a "*very sound and capable*" employment benefits attorney. He also represents management in wage and hour class actions, and has served as hearing officer in unfair labor practice and representational proceedings before the Anchorage Municipal Employee Relations Board. Clients distinguish newcomer to the table, **Robert Stewart** (see p.144), as "*very helpful*" and "*very thorough*" in his advice on personnel issues, especially where these converge with Indian Protection law.
The Clients: Peak Oilfield Service; Usibelli Coal Mine; Central Peninsula General Hospital; Chugach Electric Association; CSK Auto and Valley Hospital Association.

Perkins Coie LLP
The Firm: Perkins Coie's Anchorage branch is just one piece in a large jigsaw of 15 offices, with nearly 600 lawyers, across the USA and China. According to clients, this firm's employment attorneys are "*potent advocates, user-friendly and highly knowledgeable.*" They handle a steady stream of cases for management, including wrongful terminations, wage and hour issues and conduct investigations on claims of employment discrimination and environmental whistle-blowing. The team successfully defended Kiewit Construction in a lawsuit filed by an alleged whistle-blower over his termination, and acted for BP Exploration (Alaska) in a wrongful termination and slander suit filed by a former employee.
The Lawyers: Clients highlight **Thomas Daniel** as a star performer, saying: "*He is thoroughly pleasant, insightful and drafts so well that he knows how to keep us out of litigation.*" According to one local company: "*He is smart and has a tenacious style, which means he's always on the ball.*" Daniel is heavily involved in FMLA issues and wrongful discharge litigation. His trusty number two, **Helena Hall**, is coming along nicely, interviewees report. Clients view her as "*just superb*" on human resources issues, including employee benefits, and internal investigations on discrimination claims.

The Clients: BP Exploration (Alaska); NANA Development; Norton Sound Health; Era Aviation; Hertz; Northwest Airlines; Tanana Chiefs Conference; University of Alaska and Princess Cruise Lines.

Preston Gates & Ellis LLP
The Firm: This full-service firm impresses clients with its "*thorough and responsive*" approach to handling labor and employment matters. The practice defends management in state and federal employment litigation, and in unfair labor proceedings before the NLRB. It has successfully defended several wrongful termination cases, including Jepson v American Red Cross, and represented Alaska Petroleum Contractors in an FMLA and wrongful termination case.
The Lawyers: **Doug Parker** is "*incredibly practical and extremely well versed*" in employment discrimination issues. His practice revolves around wrongful discharge and associated torts, and complex class action litigation. He also advises employers on union avoidance, wage and hour issues and in the drafting of personnel policies. **Amy Limeres** is known for her prowess in employee benefits issues. She has special expertise in regulatory compliance and taxation matters surrounding retirement and welfare benefit plans following M&A activity.
The Clients: ConocoPhillips; Era Aviation; Municipality of Anchorage; Artic Slope Regional and Cook Inlet Region.

Band 2

Birch, Horton, Bittner & Cherot
See firm details p.145
The Firm: This firm is a growing force in employment law. It represents employers in sexual harassment, and race, age and gender discrimination cases. Its attorneys also handle collective bargaining, grievance arbitrations and unfair labor practice and wage and hour claims.
The Lawyers: Interviewees recognize **Jennifer Alexander** (see p.141) as someone with "*a bright future ahead of her.*" She acts for employers in all areas of employment discrimination and collective bargaining.
The Clients: The firm represents local and

national companies and Alaskan native corporations. Sample clients include Chenega and Alaska Communications Systems.

Dorsey & Whitney LLP

The Firm: A major name in corporate and commercial matters in Alaska, this firm also offers representation in employment litigation and has plenty of experience in traditional labor law. It represented the employer in the collective bargaining agreement lawsuit International Longshore and Warehouse Union v Alaska Maritime Employers Association. In another prominent case, Hughes v Alaska Petroleum Contractors and Natchiq Corp, it acted for the defendants in a sex, marital status and breach of contract claim.

The Lawyers: "*A consummate professional,*" **William Evans** can be invaluable on traditional labor law matters. According to interviewees, he drafts exceptionally well and is "*the person to bring in when things get political.*"

The Clients: The firm represents a broad range of local, national and international companies.

Tindall Bennett & Shoup PC

The Firm: Interviewees have a high opinion of this firm's labor and employment team. It advises companies and institutions on employment discrimination, contracts and personnel policies. It also has a particularly potent reputation for its work on traditional labor matters.

The Lawyers: Spearheading the group is **Wilfred Bennett**. Clients praise his traditional labor skills and advice; peers refer to him as "*a big player*" on employment issues.

The Clients: Alaska Development Group; Carr-Gottstein Properties; Chugach Electric Association; Northrim Bank and Norton Sound Health.

Turner & Mede, PC

The Firm: Described as "*an important port of call*" for traditional labor law matters, Turner & Mede handles all aspects of labor and employment-driven work, including public and private employment relations, public and private sector collective bargaining and wage and hour law.

The Lawyers: **William Mede** is the team's frontrunner for litigation and advisory work. He has plenty of experience representing employers before the NLRB, the Alaska Labor Relations Agency and the National Mediation Board.

The Clients: Arctic Slope Regional; Basic Industries; Alaska Housing Finance; Alaska Pacific University; Alaska Railroad and Aleutian Development.

Other Notable Practitioners

Newcomer to the tables **Kimberlee Colbo** from the firm of Hughes Thorsness Powell Huddleston & Bauman LLC achieved market commendations for her employee benefits work. She also assists management in drafting personnel policy handbooks, and conducts wage and hour and other employment litigation. **Joan Rohlf** of Guess & Rudd PC continues to impress with her knowledge and long experience in general employment matters.

ENVIRONMENT, NATURAL RESOURCES & REGULATED INDUSTRIES

Alaska
Leading firms
(Environment, Natural Resources and Regulated Industries)

1	**DORSEY & WHITNEY LLP** Anchorage
	GUESS & RUDD PC Anchorage
	PERKINS COIE LLP Anchorage
2	**ASHBURN & MASON, PC** Anchorage
	FOSTER PEPPER RUBINI & REEVES PLLC Anchorage
	HARTIG RHODES HOGE & LEKISCH PC Anchorage
	HELLER EHRMAN WHITE Anchorage
	HUGHES THORSNESS POWELL Anchorage
	PATTON BOGGS LLP Anchorage
	REGES & BOONE LLC Juneau

Firms are listed alphabetically in each band.

Band 1

Dorsey & Whitney LLP

The Firm: This commercial dynamo achieves consistent market recognition for its natural resource and environmental regulatory work, especially in the areas of public land and utility matters. The Anchorage attorneys have "*good contacts with regulators and are top-notch litigators.*" The practice also benefits from an international network of offices, which attorneys can rely upon for additional resources.

The Lawyers: Market sources distinguish **Heather Grahame** as "*one of the top utilities specialists in the state.*" She acts for telecom, refuse, and oil and gas companies in proceedings before state public utility commissions, the FCC and state and federal courts. She cochairs the firm-wide telecom practice group, and clients appreciate her "*very effective style*" when dealing with federal and state telecom commissions. One representative of a major national utility company concluded that Grahame was "*always consistent in her research and is just superb in educating in-house counsel on utility law and FCC regulations.*" **James Reeves** is the firm's managing partner in Anchorage. According to clients and peers alike, he is "*an excellent environmental litigator, who knows everyone.*" Mining and natural resource law are particular fortes.

The Clients: United Utilities; Waste Management; TelAlaska; Safeway; Ketchikan Public Utilities and BP.

Guess & Rudd PC

The Firm: Set up in 1961, soon after Alaska achieved statehood in 1959, this full-service player is one of the oldest and most established names for natural resource law. The practice's center of gravity remains its expertise in environmental insurance issues, particularly insofar as they impact on mining and oil and gas extraction business.

The Lawyers: Interviewees love working with "*down-to-earth*" **James Linxwiler**. According to rivals: "*He has a lot of integrity and means exactly what he says.*" His litigation-driven practice encompasses both environmental and Alaska Native Claims Settlement Act issues. **George Lyle** has diverse interests in natural resource, oil and gas and general commercial law. He also undertakes a steady diet of work pertaining to contaminated properties insurance defense. **Joseph Perkins** specializes in natural resource and mining transactions. Sources highlight his good relationships with regulators in the public utilities sector. **Louis Veerman**, meanwhile, "*brings that wow factor to public utilities law.*" Rivals laud him as "*a very ethical, knowledgeable and thorough trial attorney.*" His practice emphasizes litigation, administrative law and public utilities matters.

The Clients: The firm acts for all manner of companies involved in exploring, acquiring, developing, producing and promoting Alaska's natural resources.

Perkins Coie LLP

The Firm: Perkins Coie's reputation for undiluted quality extends to its environment and natural resource group, which clients describe as "*superb.*" There is an emphasis on land use and defense of government enforcement actions, with attorneys advising oil and gas companies, public utilities and Alaska native corporations on air, water and hazardous waste.

The Lawyers: Clients adore **Eric Fjelstad**, who they say is "*an ultra-competent, helpful and exceptional*" environmental regulatory specialist. He is primary outside counsel to BP Exploration (Alaska) on compliance advice relating to air,

Alaska
Leading individuals
(Environment, Natural Resources and Regulated Industries)

Senior Statesman
MASON III Julian *Ashburn & Mason, Anchorage*

[1] FJELSTAD Eric *Perkins Coie, Anchorage*
GRAHAME Heather *Dorsey & Whitney, Anchorage*
REEVES James *Dorsey & Whitney, Anchorage*
TORGERSON James *Heller Ehrman, Anchorage*

[2] BAUMAN Carl *Hughes Thorsness, Anchorage*
HARTIG Lawrence *Hartig Rhodes, Anchorage*
REEVES Susan *Foster Pepper, Anchorage*
ROZELL William *Sole Practitioner, Juneau*
SAUPE A William *Ashburn & Mason, Anchorage*
STOLLER Robert *Sole Practitioner, Anchorage*

[3] GROVIER Tina *Birch Horton, Anchorage*
LINXWILER James *Guess & Rudd, Anchorage*
LYLE George *Guess & Rudd, Anchorage*
MORAN Joseph *DeLisio Moran, Anchorage*
PERKINS Joseph *Guess & Rudd, Anchorage*
REGES Robert *Reges & Boone, Juneau*
SERDAHELY Douglas *Patton Boggs, Anchorage*
VEERMAN Louis *Guess & Rudd, Anchorage*

Leading individuals
(Regulated Industries)

Senior Statesman
MASON III Julian *Ashburn & Mason, Anchorage*

[1] GRAHAME Heather *Dorsey & Whitney, Anchorage*
SAUPE A William *Ashburn & Mason, Anchorage*
STOLLER Robert *Sole Practitioner, Anchorage*

[2] GROVIER Tina *Birch Horton, Anchorage*
MORAN Joseph *DeLisio Moran, Anchorage*
VEERMAN Louis *Guess & Rudd, Anchorage*

Individuals are listed alphabetically in each band.

waste, water and oil spill contingency plans, and represents Ketchikan Pulp in settlement negotiations regarding contaminated sites claims at 25 of the company's logging camps. He is also acting for Flint Hills Resources Alaska in its clean fuels project at the North Pole Refinery.

The Clients: BP Exploration; Flint Hills Resources Alaska; Ketchikan Pulp; Cook Inlet Region; Ketchikan Public Utilities and NANA.

Band 2

Ashburn & Mason, PC

The Firm: Already a prominent name in litigation and in real estate, the firm also achieves high marks as "*a quality performer on public utility matters.*" It further advises in the areas of telecom and fisheries.

The Lawyers: The firm's reputation is attributable to "*first-class litigator*" **William Saupe**. According to interviewees he is "*one of the best public utilities and telecom specialists in the state.*" **Julian Mason** is recognized by many as a leading light on public utility-related arbitrations. This

"*gentleman of the profession*" has a great deal of experience in all areas of public utilities, oil and gas and commercial contracts law.

The Clients: AT&T Alascom; Crowley Maritime Services; Prince William Sound Aquaculture and Semco Energy.

Foster Pepper Rubini & Reeves PLLC

The Firm: Clients in the Pacific Northwest have the advantages of local expertise and the resources of an international law firm since Foster Pepper – with its offices in Anchorage, Seattle, Spokane and Portland – entered into an alliance with US giant Akin Gump. The Alaska environmental group's expertise lies in federal environmental and health and safety compliance, and attorneys have experience litigating in federal and state courts.

The Lawyers: Much of the firm's reputation in environmental law is linked to that of **Susan Reeves**, who can handle the full range of environmental issues at national, state and local level.

The Clients: The firm acts for local, national and international clients.

Hartig Rhodes Hoge & Lekisch PC

The Firm: Commentators acknowledge that this firm is "*doing a very good job*" for clients on environmental issues. The team assists with obtaining air, water and other government permits for natural resource development projects, and provides commercial entities with input on environmental compliance and cleanup, acting in administrative proceedings before federal and state authorities.

The Lawyers: John Norman's recent departure to take up an appointment by Governor Frank Murkowski to head the Alaska Oil and Gas Conservation Commission has not harmed the practice's standing. **Lawrence Hartig** impresses as "*a very thorough and astute adviser*" on environmental regulatory issues that impact on real estate transactions.

The Clients: Alpine Pipeline; Anadarko Petroleum; Forest Oil; Matanuska Telephone Association; Kuparuk Pipeline; Forest Oil and Taiga Mining.

Heller Ehrman White & McAuliffe LLP

See firm details p.288

The Firm: With offices in 13 US and international locations, this well-respected firm is making an impact in Alaska. Its Anchorage office places emphasis on litigation for oil, gas and energy producers and environmental advice. It also acts for financial institutions and other commercial entities in all legal aspects of natural resource matters.

The Lawyers: **James Torgerson** is the administrative shareholder of the Anchorage office.

"*He strikes the perfect balance of first-class legal brains with quality people skills and achieves cost-effective results.*" One very impressed in-house counsel appreciated his "*24/7 availability and knack for placing the client above his ego in litigation trials.*" Prior to joining the practice, Torgerson was special assistant attorney general for the State of Alaska in Washington, DC. He now focuses on environmental and other litigation at both state and federal level.

The Clients: Chugach Electric Association; Deloitte Touche Tohmatsu; NANA Regional; CenturyTel of the Northwest and Peak Oilfield.

Hughes Thorsness Powell Huddleston & Bauman LLC

The Firm: This local outfit is considered a mover and shaker in Alaska on environmental and natural resource law. Attorneys handle oil and gas matters, mining claims, Superfund issues and hazardous waste management issues. The team also counsels on public lands and natural resource development.

The Lawyers: Market observers distinguish **Carl Bauman** as "*one smart cookie and a one-man stop for defendant natural resource work.*" He is chairman of the firm's management group and his practice includes oil and gas and environmental/coastal zone litigation.

The Clients: Municipality of Anchorage; Tongass Federal Credit Union; Denali Borough; Amerada Hess and Anadrill Schlumberger.

Patton Boggs LLP

The Firm: This national and international player is building a solid presence in Alaska. The Anchorage office has 13 attorneys specializing in all areas of civil, commercial and white-collar crime litigation. Environmental and antitrust matters are particular strengths of the practice, largely attributable to the firm's clout on Capitol Hill and partners' strong ties to federal agencies.

The Lawyers: **Douglas Serdahely** is famed for "*his top-drawer political litigation and lobbying skills.*" He has represented several energy, transportation and fuel companies in Alaska and notably acted as counsel in Alaska to ExxonMobil in the Exxon Valdez oil spill litigation.

The Clients: ExxonMobil Production; Sea River Maritime; Safeway; Tesoro Alaska; Marathon Oil and Matanuska Electric Association.

Reges & Boone LLC

The Firm: This small yet high-quality Juneau-based law firm is recognized as a prominent name for environmental law. Attorneys counsel businesses on natural resource extraction permits and EPA and local and state environmental compliance laws.

The Lawyers: **Robert Reges** is well known and admired for his dogged persistence in obtaining permits and in tackling environmental regulations and litigation.

www.ChambersandPartners.com

All quotes in the text are from interviews with clients and competitors.

137

Other Notable Practitioners

Juneau-based **William Rozell** is a sole practitioner who "*remains impressive*" on issues impacting the oil and gas industry. **Robert Stoller**, also a sole practitioner and based in Anchorage, maintains a rock-solid reputation for public utility matters. According to rivals, he is "*really smart and quick on his feet.*" **Tina Grovier** (see p.143) of Birch, Horton, Bittner & Cherot is "*part of a rising talent pool*" of public utility specialists in the state. She is recognized as an intelligent and consistent performer on regulatory matters, and notably acts for clients such as Alaska Communication Systems and Koch Pipeline. **Joseph Moran** of DeLisio Moran Geraghty & Zobel, PC is singled out as a great corporate lawyer who advises a number of Alaska public utility companies. He is said to be "*a steady ship*" when it comes to dealing with telecom regulators.

LITIGATION

Alaska
Leading firms
(Litigation: General Commercial)

1. **ASHBURN & MASON, PC** *Anchorage*
   DORSEY & WHITNEY LLP *Anchorage*
   FELDMAN & ORLANSKY *Anchorage*
2. **ATKINSON, CONWAY & GAGNON** *Anchorage*
   BANKSTON, GRONNING, O'HARA *Anchorage*
   BIRCH, HORTON, BITTNER & CHEROT *Anchorage*
   PATTON BOGGS LLP *Anchorage*
3. **LANE POWELL PC** *Anchorage*

Leading individuals
(Litigation: General Commercial)

1. **ASHBURN Mark** *Ashburn & Mason, Anchorage*
   BUNDY Robert *Dorsey & Whitney, Anchorage*
   FELDMAN Jeffrey *Feldman & Orlansky, Anchorage*
   GAGNON Bruce *Atkinson Conway, Anchorage*
2. **BANKSTON William** *Bankston Gronning, Anchorage*
   GILMORE Patrick *Atkinson Conway, Anchorage*
   OESTING David *Davis Wright, Anchorage*
   ORLANSKY Susan *Feldman & Orlansky, Anchorage*
   PETUMENOS Timothy *Birch Horton, Anchorage*
   SNEED Spencer *Dorsey & Whitney, Anchorage*
   SPAAN Michael *Patton Boggs, Anchorage*
3. **COUGHLIN Jennifer** *Preston Gates, Anchorage*
   DICKSON Robert *Atkinson Conway, Anchorage*
   HUTCHINGS Stephen *Birch Horton, Anchorage*
   JAMIESON Brewster *Lane Powell, Anchorage*
   SERDAHELY Douglas *Patton Boggs, Anchorage*
   TORGERSON James *Heller Ehrman, Anchorage*

Leading individuals
(Litigation: Construction)

1. **DICKSON Robert** *Atkinson Conway, Anchorage*
   HUTCHINGS Stephen *Birch Horton, Anchorage*
   KREGER Michael *Perkins Coie, Anchorage*
   WATTS Grant *Holmes Weddle, Anchorage*

Firms and individuals are listed alphabetically in each band.

Band 1

Ashburn & Mason, PC
The Firm: According to clients, this firm "*consistently delivers top-notch advocacy*" and "*accurate advice.*" Its breadth of experience extends from general civil actions to white-collar crime, antitrust and all areas of business and products liability litigation. Significant highlights include representing Crowley Maritime in an antitrust matter, State of Alaska v Crowley, and continuing to defend the University of Alaska in a number of grievances, arbitrations and various other contentious issues.

The Lawyers: Much of the practice's success is attributed to **Mark Ashburn**, "*one of the top litigators in the state.*" Clients expressed admiration for his "*amazing analytical and drafting skills*" and "*finesse in understanding the heart of an issue.*"

The Clients: First National Bank of Alaska; AT&T Alascom; Alaska Marine Pilots; University of Alaska; Prince William Sound Aquaculture and Crowley Maritime.

Dorsey & Whitney LLP
The Firm: Heavily litigation-oriented, with more than half of its attorneys active in contentious matters, sources claim Dorsey & Whitney to be "*one of the top firms in Alaska for litigation.*" Underscoring its popularity is an institutional client base in the banking and insurance sectors, with many companies eager to secure the services of a stellar roster of trial attorneys. The Anchorage office handles civil, healthcare and commercial litigation, and criminal litigation in the areas of white-collar and environmental matters. The group also benefits from the resources of a national network of offices together with offices in Canada, Asia and Europe.

The Lawyers: Clients and rivals distinguish former US Attorney for the District of Alaska **Robert Bundy** as "*a number-one trial attorney.*" Local sources acclaim his "*superb know-how*" in handling insurance, complex litigation and public sector matters. He was notably involved in a pro bono case that successfully overturned a US District Court death penalty ruling in Texas. His practice spans all areas of business, white-collar and environmental litigation. **Spencer Sneed** continues to attract attention for his top-level business and bankruptcy litigation work. He represents Alaska North Slope oil field operators in disputes with working interest owners.

The Clients: ExxonMobil; Cook Inlet Region (CIRI); CNA Insurance and Xerox.

GENERAL COMMERCIAL

Feldman & Orlansky
The Firm: The firm's reputation for excellence in litigation is, say clients, due to its habit of "*offering Cadillac service by nationally renowned experts who are detail-oriented and attack like bull dogs to win your case.*" Although small compared to some of its competitors, Feldman & Orlansky has consistently enjoyed involvement in headline matters, such as successfully defending US fish processor giant Trident Seafoods in a $2 million antitrust case. The team also advantageously represented a large commercial real estate owner in a complex lease dispute with its major tenant, Safeway. In another coup, it achieved a favorable trial verdict for automobile manufacturer DaimlerChrysler in a $20 million lawsuit alleging breach of contract.

The Lawyers: **Jeffrey Feldman** (see p.143) is a name on everybody's lips when thinking of leading trial attorneys in Alaska. According to clients, he has achieved this status through "*hard work, follow-through and the ability to saliently pinpoint the Achilles' heel of an opponent's case.*" He defended the state's largest healthcare provider, Providence Alaska Medical Center, in a significant medical malpractice action, and continues to handle a wide variety of commercial, environmental, white-collar and products liability cases. His outstanding partner **Susan Orlansky** (see p.143) is widely recognized as "*one of the most brilliant and talented litigators and appellate specialists*" in the state. She often works with Feldman on high-profile cases, such as the aforementioned Trident Seafoods case.

The Clients: Trident Seafoods; BP Exploration (Alaska); DaimlerChrysler; Carr-Gottstein Properties and Providence Alaska Medical Center.

Band 2

Atkinson, Conway & Gagnon
The Firm: This firm is famed for combining a first-class transactions capability with a top-grade litigation practice. Since its inception in 1962, the practice has maintained a strong client following of Alaska-based companies and financial and insurance institutions.

The Lawyers: The firm's leading light in litigation is **Bruce Gagnon**. His advocacy skills are well known in professional liability and general litigation circles, though he also undertakes

138

All quotes in the text are from interviews with clients and competitors.

CHAMBERS USA 2005

transactional work. Another good all-rounder, **Patrick Gilmore** has impressed the market with his performance in commercial and bankruptcy litigation, while **Robert Dickson** has chalked up a great reputation in medical malpractice defense. His practice also incorporates construction claims.

The Clients: Ahtna; Alaska Telecom; Alaska Industrial Development and Export Authority; Baugh Construction & Engineering; Chugach Electric Association; Cook Inlet Region, (CIRI); Crowley Maritime; Doyon; Holland American Line and Wells Fargo.

Bankston, Gronning, O'Hara,

The Firm: This firm is active in commercial litigation, with areas of expertise in class actions, securities, employment and breach of contract claims. Highlights include acting for Alaska Fiber Star in a significant dispute between its owners, and for Carr-Gottstein Foods in an antitrust investigation. It successfully defended the State of Alaska in a class action securities litigation involving investors' claims that it is responsible for their $50 million loss in the World Plus/Bonham Ponzi scheme.

The Lawyers: **William Bankston** is the firm's front runner and has lengthy experience in the areas of real estate and corporate litigation. Not limited to litigation, he has experience representing developers, bankers and other commercial entities on transactions.

The Clients: Alaska Fiber Star; The State of Alaska; ANCSA Native village; Carr-Gottstein Foods and ALLTEL Publishing.

Birch, Horton, Bittner & Cherot
See firm details p.145

The Firm: Acclaimed as an accomplished litigation firm, it encompasses a broad range of commercial areas, including banking, government contracts, employment and creditors' rights. Attorneys also act for large corporations and small businesses on construction matters. The Alaska practice benefits from the presence of the firm's Washington DC office, which provides its lawyers with access to the federal courts and regulatory bodies.

The Lawyers: According to client feedback, **Timothy Petumenos** (see p.144) offers "*concise*

and clear representation that achieves cost-effective results." Petumenos has been involved in many of the state's most prominent litigations: he represented several of the Alaska Native Corporations that owned beaches affected by the Exxon Valdez oil spill in the Prince William Sound, and he acted for the Williams Companies in a case involving a claim concerning environmentally contaminated property. **Stephen Hutchings** (see p.143) brings his considerable experience to bear in a variety of commercial and construction claims and wrongful termination defense.

The Clients: Baranof Island Housing Authority; Alaska Energy Commission/AIDEA; Yukon-Kuskokwim Health; Association Village Council Presidents Regional Housing Authority; The Williams Companies and JLT Risk Solutions.

Patton Boggs LLP

The Firm: The Anchorage office of Patton Boggs is advantaged by the profile surrounding the firm's national practice in federal and state government litigation. With equivalent litigation practices in Washington DC, Dallas, Denver and Northern Virginia, the Alaska team can rely upon a network of attorneys with backgrounds in federal agencies and federal and state courts. The in-state group handles the full gamut of business, oil and gas, telecom and emerging technology work, with numerous energy, transportation and fuel distribution entities on its books.

The Lawyers: **Michael Spaan** provides expertise in complex commercial litigation and white-collar cases, additionally offering experience in conducting internal corporate investigations. He had previously served as US Attorney for the District of Alaska, handling federal investigations. Rivals acknowledge that **Douglas Serdahely**, the managing partner of Patton Boggs' Anchorage office, is "*a potent litigator*" on environmental cases. He acts for ExxonMobil in the Exxon Valdez oil spill litigation and is counsel to more than 40 defendants in a $1 billion class action brought by 4,000 Alaska fisheries.

The Clients: ExxonMobil Production; Sea River Maritime; Safeway; Tesoro Alaska Company; Marathon Oil; Travelers; Matanuska Electric Association.

Band 3

Lane Powell PC
See firm details p.1797

The Firm: The team here distinguishes itself in maritime and energy-related disputes, handling complex cases with "*great aplomb.*" Beyond this, it acts for companies in securities, banking, healthcare, antitrust and IP litigation.

The Lawyers: Clients single out **Brewster Jamieson** (see p.143) as a "*personable and productive attorney with a fantastic track record of results in litigation.*" He specializes in insurance, maritime and products litigation.

The Clients: The practice represents local, national and international companies.

Other Notable Practitioners

Clients recognize **David Oesting** (see p.143) from the firm of Davis Wright Tremaine LLP as "*doing a very good job*" on litigation matters. He is the lead counsel for the 30,000 fishermen, seafood processing companies, Alaska Natives, landowners and other commercial entities filing a series of class action lawsuits against Exxon, as a result of the damages incurred during the 11.8 million gallon North Slope oil spill by Exxon Valdez. His impressive client roster additionally includes: AT&T/Alascom; Holland America (USA); Bank of America and Artic Slope Regional. **Jennifer Coughlin** of Preston Gates & Ellis LLP is recommended by clients as "*a top-dog litigator*" who pleads very well and understands the commercial realities of a case. According to one leading local institution, she is "*a knowledgeable, assertive and charming litigator.*" Market sources recommend **James Torgerson** of Heller Ehrman White & McAuliffe LLP for his expertise in litigating products liability, insurance coverage and white-collar crime matters. He also defends several clients in the energy sector. **Michael Kreger** of Perkins Coie LLP and **Grant Watts** from Holmes Weddle & Barcott, A Professional Corporation, have both achieved prominence in construction law and related litigation.

NATIVE AMERICAN LAW

Alaska
Leading firms (Native American Law)

[1] **LANDYE BENNETT BLUMSTEIN LLP** *Anchorage*
SONOSKY, CHAMBERS, SACHSE, *Anchorage*
[2] **GUESS & RUDD PC** *Anchorage*

Leading individuals (Native Law)

[1] **BLUMSTEIN Philip** *Landye Bennett, Anchorage*
CASE David *Landye Bennett, Anchorage*
LINXWILER James *Guess & Rudd PC, Anchorage*
MILLER Lloyd *Sonosky Chambers, Anchorage*
MUNSON Myra *Sonosky Chambers, Anchorage*

Firms and individuals are listed alphabetically in each band.

Band 1

Landye Bennett Blumstein LLP

See firm details p.1488

The Firm: This full-service firm has represented regional, village and urban Alaska Native Corporations since 1976. A multifaceted practice encompasses negotiations on real estate transactions and land disputes with the DOI, guidance on business formations and organizational advice. It also assists with natural resource management issues, bankruptcy and tax expertise.

The Lawyers: Corporate player **Phil Blumstein** (see p.142) impresses many with his *"genuine understanding of the commercial interests of Alaska Native law."* He is additionally well versed on financial transactions and municipal law. **David Case** (see p.142) is also considered *"a well-respected"* specialist with *"excellent knowledge"* of rural business and municipal laws and policies.

The Clients: The firm acts for a variety of Alaska Native Corporations.

Sonosky, Chambers, Sachse, Miller & Munson LLP

The Firm: Market sources agree that this is *"the big firm in Alaska when it comes to native law issues."* Dedicated to representing Native American interests in health, corporate, tax and natural resource and land claims, the firm is additionally experienced in matters of self-determination and self-governance as well as hunting, fishing and gaming rights. The offices in Anchorage and Juneau benefit from the resources on offer in Washington DC, Albuquerque, and San Diego. According to those Alaska Native Corporations interviewed, this boutique is *"first class,"* and particularly valuable in handling lobbying and funding agreements that are specific to Alaska native health law.

The Lawyers: Clients and peers alike distinguish **Lloyd Miller** as *"a preeminent specialist."* His wealth of experience in tribal jurisdiction litigation serves clients well, and he has the role of general counsel to a large number of tribal governments, Alaska Native Claims Settlement Act (ANCSA) corporations, and tribal health and social service providers. Clients also recognize **Myra Munson** as *"one of the best native law healthcare experts in the country."* Prior to joining the firm, she served as commissioner of the Alaska Department of Health and Social Services. Her practice focuses on Medicare/Medicaid, lobbying and regulatory issues affecting the Alaska native community.

The Clients: This practice only represents tribal interests and will not act for gaming management companies or oil and gas developers on Indian law matters.

Band 2

Guess & Rudd PC

The Firm: Famed for its strength in natural resource and environmental law, this firm is also recognized as a potent force for ANCSA issues. Attorneys have a particular strength in negotiating mining and natural resource agreements between native corporations and commercial entities.

The Lawyers: **James Linxwiler** impresses many with his knowledge of ANCSA matters. He additionally practices commercial law and litigation.

The Clients: The firm represents Alaska Native Corporations and other local and national commercial entities.

REAL ESTATE

Alaska
Leading firms (Real Estate)

[1] **ASHBURN & MASON, PC** *Anchorage*
[2] **DAVIS WRIGHT TREMAINE LLP** *Anchorage*
DORSEY & WHITNEY LLP *Anchorage*
[3] **ATKINSON, CONWAY & GAGNON** *Anchorage*
FOSTER PEPPER RUBINI & REEVES PLLC *Anchorage*
PRESTON GATES & ELLIS LLP *Anchorage*
TINDALL BENNETT & SHOUP PC *Anchorage*

Firms are listed alphabetically in each band.

Band 1

Ashburn & Mason, PC

The Firm: According to clients and peers, this firm remains the uncontested *"heavyweight champion of real estate law"* in Alaska. Its muscle is to be found in general real estate, property finance and land use matters. Highlights include several rural Alaska Native design projects and corporate headquarters projects, and advising Venture Development in a joint venture concerning the new Anchorage Convention Center, which relied on bed tax bonds. In a recent coup, the firm won a significant superior court decision in a land use appeal involving a 600+ residential unit development.

The Lawyers: *"Deal-maker par excellence"* **Donald McClintock** is credited by clients as *"one of the practice's most significant go-getters, imbued with an unlimited capacity to handle work."* He specializes in real estate finance and land use. Another real estate finance specialist, **William Cummings** is perceived to be a master at closing land use deals. He has been involved in several appellate matters pertaining to sovereign immunity of the Alaska Railroad from local land use regulation, and has advised on a major leaseback deal with Renal Care Group.

The Clients: Carr-Gottstein; Venture Development; Renal Care Group and Alaska Association of Realtors.

Band 2

Davis Wright Tremaine LLP

See firm details p.1796

The Firm: This firm achieves market-wide acclaim for its real estate and finance advice. Attorneys from its transactions department act for companies, financial institutions and non-profit entities on sales, leasing, acquisitions and land use planning of development projects. The group notably acted for Anchorage Global Logistics Airpark Development in the construction of a $22 million air cargo facility at Ted Stevens Anchorage International Airport, and represented Valley Hospital Association in the $120 million joint venture for the construction of a new hospital in the Mat-Su Valley.

The Lawyers: Much of the firm's stellar reputation is linked to transactions specialist **Joseph Reece** (see p.144). This *"cool-headed operator"* worked on the aforementioned deals and acted as local counsel in Alaska on Flint Hills Resources' purchase of the North Pole oil refinery and two petroleum terminals from the Williams Companies.

The Clients: Valley Hospital Association; Weyerhaeuser Financial Investments; Natives of Kodiak; Bank of America; Eklutna; Flint Hills Resources and Koch Pipeline.

Alaska
Leading individuals (Real Estate)

1 MCCLINTOCK Donald *Ashburn & Mason*, Anchorage
ROSSTON Richard *Dorsey & Whitney*, Anchorage

2 CHEROT Suzanne *Birch Horton*, Anchorage
CUMMINGS William *Ashburn & Mason*, Anchorage
HEAPHEY Christopher *Bankston Gronning*, Anchorage
MCCOLLUM James *James McCollum LLC*, Anchorage
REECE Joseph *Davis Wright*, Anchorage
STANLEY James *Foster Pepper*, Anchorage
TINDALL John *Tindall Bennett*, Anchorage
TRAVOSTINO Joan *Preston Gates*, Anchorage

Individuals are listed alphabetically in each band.

Dorsey & Whitney LLP

The Firm: As a national commercial giant, Dorsey & Whitney is renowned for its real estate transactions capability. With 20 offices in North America, Asia and Europe, the Anchorage office benefits from a deep well of support and resources. In Alaska, its real estate department operates from within the corporate team in handling commercial acquisitions, leases and sales.
The Lawyers: The firm's front runner is commercial transactions star **Richard Rosston**. He recently advised on the purchase of Sheraton Anchorage Hotel and various fast food franchises in the state.
The Clients: Fred Meyer Stores, Doyon and Tanana Chiefs Conference are among the clients.

Band 3

Atkinson, Conway & Gagnon

The Firm: While the firm is well known for its litigation work, a number of its attorneys practice in real estate, advising a variety of developer clients. They are regarded as having particular expertise in the financing of commercial and residential projects. Bruce Gagnon is the point of contact for real estate matters.

Foster Pepper Rubini & Reeves PLLC

The Firm: This full-service firm offers advice on the entire range of real estate activities in the state, with key strengths in finance, land use and environmental regulatory matters. Since its strategic alliance with international powerhouse Akin Gump Strauss Hauer & Feld, the firm has broadened its outlook in terms of clients and work.
The Lawyers: James Stanley is a member of Alaska's real estate glitterati. Rivals single him out as "*a sterling land use and real estate finance attorney.*" He acts for developers on transactions and land use zoning and regulatory issues.
The Clients: Clients include local, national and international oil and gas companies as well as real estate developers.

Preston Gates & Ellis LLP

The Firm: This Seattle firm is building a significant reputation for itself in Alaska. Full service and visible in many transactions and litigations on a local, state and federal level, it is going from strength to strength in real estate. The group's puissance in banking and bankruptcy matters makes it a first port of call for lenders seeking representation in real estate financings and workouts of prior loans.
The Lawyers: The bedrock of the practice is **Joan Travostino**, who "*gets the big picture and can negotiate with finesse.*" Her time is occupied by a blend of real estate transactions and bankruptcy work. She recently represented a client in the sale of a $3.2 million apartment building and acted as local counsel to a lender on the $22 million refinancing of an Anchorage hotel.

The Clients: The firm's client base encompasses several local and national financial institutions as well as commercial and residential developers.

Tindall Bennett & Shoup PC

The Firm: Having picked up steam, this firm is a welcome newcomer to the real estate rankings. It is already a force to be reckoned with in employment law and is now carving out a place for itself in the world of real estate-driven M&A.
The Lawyers: **John Tindall** is the practice's fulcrum. He is described as "*on the ball*" when it comes to acquisitions, sales and joint ventures, and also undertakes work in telecom, banking and corporate law.
The Clients: Alaska Development Group; Carr-Gottstein Properties; Northrim Bank; The Williams Companies; Eagle Crossing Development; Spinell Homes and Hultquist Homes.

Other Notable Practitioners

Suzanne Cherot (see p.142) is the managing partner of Birch, Horton, Bittner & Cherot. She enjoys a prominence for her transactional real estate work. **Christopher Heaphey** of Bankston, Gronning, O'Hara, PC is endorsed by peers as "*a quality real estate litigator.*" His practice emphasizes construction, environmental and real estate disputes, notably representing the Municipality of Anchorage in three lawsuits on the design and construction of the Anchorage Performing Arts Center. **James McCollum** at Law Offices of James McCollum LLC is "*a vastly experienced negotiator*" and advises local and national developers, financial institutions and title insurance companies on land use, planning and sales and acquisitions.

Leaders in Alaska

ALEXANDER, Jennifer C
Birch, Horton, Bittner & Cherot, Anchorage 907 276 1550
jalexander@bhb.com
Recommended in Employment
Practice Areas: Ms Alexander's practice focuses on representation of union and non-union employers in all areas of labor and employment law. Ms Alexander represents employers in matters concerning wrongful discharge, discrimination, sexual harassment, grievance arbitration, unfair labor practices, contract negotiation, and wage and hour claims. Her experience includes proceedings in trial and appellate courts; before the National Labor Relations Board, Equal Employment Opportunity Commission, Alaska State Commission for Human Rights, Department of Labor; and before labor and employment arbitrators. She counsels employers concerning unfair labor practices, grievance arbitration, settlement agreements, disciplinary matters, confidentiality agreements, wage and hour compliance, race and age discrimination, sexual harassment, the Americans with Disabilities Act, the Family and Medical Leave Act, substance abuse and drug testing, employment policies and handbooks, employment contracts, covenants not to compete, collective bargaining and contract interpretation.
Prof. Memberships: Alaska Bar Association.

Career: Ms Alexander received a JD from the University of San Francisco in 1995, and a BA from the University of Colorado in 1992. Ms Alexander was admitted to practice in Alaska in 1995.

ASHBURN, Mark
Ashburn & Mason, PC, Anchorage 907 276 4331
Recommended in Litigation

BANKSTON, William
Bankston, Gronning, O'Hara, PC, Anchorage 907 276 1711
Recommended in Litigation

BAUMAN, Carl
Hughes Thorsness Powell Huddleston & Bauman LLC, Anchorage 907 274 7522
Recommended in Environment, Natural Resources

BENNETT, Wilfred
Tindall Bennett & Shoup PC, Anchorage 907 278 8533
Recommended in Employment

BLACK, Kathryn
Birch, Horton, Bittner & Cherot, Anchorage 907 276 1550
kblack@bhb.com
Recommended in Corporate/M&A
Practice Areas: Banking, finance, corporate, real estate, business. Extensive

www.ChambersandPartners.com
All quotes in the text are from interviews with clients and competitors.
141

experience representing financial institutions in relation to bankruptcies, repossessions, commercial loans, secured transactions, and real estate financings. M&A; complex real estate transactions; corporate and business advice.
Prof. Memberships: Alaska State Bar Association (1980); American Bar Association (1980); California State Bar Association (inactive) (1979-2000).
Career: Joined Birch, Horton, Bittner, and Cherot 1984; made shareholder 1987.
Publications: Co-author: 'Emerging Doctrine of Fiduciary Responsibility of Credit Union Officials,' The Business Lawyer, Vol 40, Issue 3, May, 1985; 'When Worlds Collide: Alaska Native Corporations and the Bankruptcy Code,' Alaska Law Review, Vol. VI, Issue 1, June, 1989.
Personal: JD (magna cum laude), University of Santa Clara, Santa Clara, California (1979); BA, Anthropology, University of Colorado, Boulder, Colorado (1973).

BLUMSTEIN, Philip
Landye Bennett Blumstein LLP, Anchorage 907 276 5152
philb@lbblawyers.com
Recommended in Corporate/M&A, Native Law
Practice Areas: Alaska Native law, municipal law, business formations and transactions and banking and finance.
Prof. Memberships: Member of the Bar of the United States Supreme Court, State of Alaska, and United States District Court for the District of Alaska. Also Member of the United States Court of Appeals for the Ninth Circuit, the United States Court of International Trade, and the United States Claims Court.
Personal: BA from the State University of New York at Binghamton in 1979, and JD from Boston University Law School in 1982. Mr Blumstein has been on the Alaska Fee Arbitration Committee since 1990.

BOUTIN, Michelle
Christianson, Boutin & Spraker, Anchorage 907 258 6016
Recommended in Bankruptcy

BUNDY, David
David H Bundy PC, Anchorage
907 248 8431
Recommended in Bankruptcy

BUNDY, Robert
Dorsey & Whitney LLP, Anchorage
907 276 4557
Recommended in Litigation

CASE, David
Landye Bennett Blumstein LLP, Anchorage 907 276 5152
dcase@lbblawyers.com
Recommended in Native Law
Practice Areas: Alaska Native law and policy, rural business law and policy and rural municipal law and policy.
Prof. Memberships: Affiliated with Lewis & Clark Law School, Board of Visitors since 1994, the Anchorage Opera, Board of Directors since 1998 (Secretary 1999-2001), and Alaska Federation of Natives, Denali Award (1998).
Personal: BA from Whitman College in 1966. JD from the University of Washington in 1974. Authored 'Alaska Natives and American Laws,' recognized as the authoritative treatise on the subject. From 1978-82, Unites States Department of the Interior, Alaska Regional Solicitor's office.

CHEROT, Suzanne
Birch, Horton, Bittner & Cherot, Anchorage 907 276 1550
scherot@bhb.com
Recommended in Real Estate
Practice Areas: Real estate and corporate. Extensive experience in representation of owners and developers in complex real estate transactions and purchases, sales and financings of business assets.
Prof. Memberships: Alaska Bar Association (1972).
Career: Joined Birch, Horton, Bittner and Cherot in 1973; Managing shareholder 1995-97, and 1999 to present. JD, University of Kansas (1972); BA, University of Kansas (1970).

CHRISTIANSON, Cabot
Christianson, Boutin & Spraker, Anchorage 907 258 6016
Recommended in Bankruptcy

COLBO, Kimberlee
Hughes Thorsness Powell Huddleston & Bauman LLC, Anchorage
907 274 7522
Recommended in Employment

COUGHLIN, Jennifer
Preston Gates & Ellis LLP, Anchorage
907 276 1969
Recommended in Litigation

CUMMINGS, William
Ashburn & Mason, PC, Anchorage
907 276 4331
Recommended in Real Estate

CYPHERS, Christopher
Preston Gates & Ellis LLP, Anchorage
907 276 1969
Recommended in Corporate/M&A

DANIEL, Thomas
Perkins Coie LLP, Anchorage
907 279 8561
Recommended in Employment

DAWSON, Jon S
Davis Wright Tremaine LLP, Anchorage
907 257 5330
jondawson@dwt.com
Recommended in Bankruptcy, Corporate/M&A
Practice Areas: Partner, commercial and general corporate law, intellectual property and internet law, real estate, and litigation. Experience representing businesses and financial institutions in complex commercial transactions and disputes; in real estate transactions and disputes; in trademark, trade secrets, and copyright matters and disputes; as creditors in bankruptcy; and as general counsel.
Prof. Memberships: Alaska State and American Bar Associations.
Career: Admitted to Alaska Bar, 1984. Admitted to Washington State Bar, 1983. Joined firm, 1983; named Partner, 1989.
Personal: JD, University of California - Berkeley, 1983 (Order of the Coif). BA, (Highest Distinction), University of Kansas, 1980.

DICKSON, Robert
Atkinson, Conway & Gagnon, Anchorage 907 276 1700
Recommended in Litigation

DURRELL, Brian
Durrell Law Group, PC, Anchorage
907 258 3224
Recommended in Corporate/M&A

EVANS, William
Dorsey & Whitney LLP, Anchorage
907 276 4557
Recommended in Employment

FELDMAN, Jeffrey M
Feldman & Orlansky, Anchorage
907 272 3538
Feldman@frozenlaw.com
Recommended in Litigation
Practice Areas: Complex civil and criminal litigation, trials and appeals.
Prof. Memberships: Admitted to practice in Alaska and Rhode Island; fellow, American Academy of Appellate Lawyers; member, American Law Institute; Woodrow Wilson Fellow; Association of Trial Lawyers of America; American Board of Trial Advocates; American Judicature Society National Association of Criminal Defense Lawyers; member, Alaska, and Rhode Island Bar Associations.
Career: Prior to entering private practice, served as Assistant Public Defender, Alaska Public Defender Agency (1976-78), and as law clerk to Justice Edmond W Burke of the Alaska Supreme Court (1975-76).
Publications: 'Justice Rabinowitz And Personal Freedom: Evolving A Constitutional Framework,' 'Report Of The Civil Justice Advisory Group For The United States District Court For The District Of Alaska,' 'Compelling Testimony In Alas-

ka: The Coming Rejection Of Use And Derivative Use Immunity,' 'The Fifth Amendment, Self-Incrimination And Foreign Prosecution: The Saga Of The Ryuyo Maru,' 'Certifying Professional Competence: The Alaska Experiment,' 'Criminal Procedure In Alaska,' 'Search And Seizure In Alaska: A Comprehensive Review,' and 'Pre-Trial Diversion Of The Mentally Retarded Offender.'
Personal: Born 7 November 1949; BA degree with honors (1972) and a JD degree (1975) from Northeastern University in Boston, Massachusetts.

FJELSTAD, Eric
Perkins Coie LLP, Anchorage
907 279 8561
Recommended in Environment, Natural Resources

GAGNON, Bruce
Atkinson, Conway & Gagnon, Anchorage 907 276 1700
Recommended in Litigation

GILMORE, Patrick
Atkinson, Conway & Gagnon, Anchorage 907 276 1700
Recommended in Litigation

GRAHAME, Heather
Dorsey & Whitney LLP, Anchorage
907 276 4557
Recommended in Environment, Regulated Industries

GROVER, Parry
Davis Wright Tremaine LLP, Anchorage
907 257 5341
parrygrover@dwt.com
Recommended in Employment
Practice Areas: Partner, employment and labor law. Experience includes representing management in employment discrimination/wrongful discharge litigation; and labor relations matters including representation, unfair labor practices, collective bargaining, arbitration and wage/hour cases.
Prof. Memberships: Alaska State and American Bar Associations. Operations Board Member, The Foraker Group (2002-present). Commissioner, Anchorage Parks & Recreation Commission (1994-2000).
Career: Admitted to Alaska Bar, 1980. Joined DWT, 1976; became Partner, 1984.
Publications: Co-author/editor, 'Alaska Employment Law Deskbook'. Frequent speaker on employment law and labor relations matters.
Personal: JD, (honors), University of Washington, 1976 (Order of the Coif). BA, (magna cum laude), University of Washington, 1969.

GROVIER, Tina M
Birch, Horton, Bittner & Cherot, Anchorage
907 276 1550
tgrovier@bhb.com
Recommended in Environment, Regulated Industries
Practice Areas: Ms Grovier's practice focuses on representation of telecommunications public utilities in litigation, regulatory proceedings and commercial transactions, and general civil litigation.
Prof. Memberships: Alaska Bar Association; Anchorage Association of Women Lawyers; YWCA.
Career: Ms Grovier received a JD from Washington University School of Law in 1993, and a SB from Southwest Missouri State University in 1990. Ms Grovier was admitted to practice in Alaska in 1994. She also is admitted to practice before the United States District Court for the District of Alaska and the United States Court of Appeals for the Ninth Circuit. Ms Grovier represents telecommunications clients before the Regulatory Commission of Alaska, and the trial and appellate courts in Alaska. Ms Grovier's experience also includes representation of telecommunications public utilities and other clients in commercial transactions, oil and gas law (including pipelines), and commercial litigation, including construction and employment law. Her practice also includes participation in arbitrations and mediations. Before joining Birch, Horton, Bittner and Cherot, Ms Grovier served as law clerk for Chief Judge Brynner of the Alaska Court of Appeals.

HALL, Helena
Perkins Coie LLP, Anchorage
907 279 8561
Recommended in Employment

HARTIG, Lawrence
Hartig Rhodes Hoge & Lekisch PC, Anchorage 907 276 1592
Recommended in Environment, Natural Resources

HEAPHEY, Christopher
Bankston, Gronning, O'Hara, PC, Anchorage 907 276 1711
Recommended in Real Estate

HUTCHINGS, Stephen H
Birch, Horton, Bittner & Cherot, Anchorage 907 276 1550
shutchings@bhb.com
Recommended in Litigation
Practice Areas: Senior litigation Partner. Practice focused primarily on corporate law and commercial and construction litigation. Mr Hutchings serves as general corporate counsel to a number of Alaska Native corporations. His construction law representation includes major private and public sector owners as well as companies engaged in design, construction and construction management.

Prof. Memberships: Alaska Bar Association, 1976; United States District Court for the District of Alaska, 1986; Ninth Circuit Court of Appeals, 1986; Alaska Bar Association Board of Law Examiners.
Career: Admitted to Iowa Bar, 1976, and Alaska Bar, 1977; Assistant District Attorney, Anchorage, Alaska; District Attorney at Bethel and Sitka, Alaska; Instructor at Alaska State Trooper Academy; Lead trial counsel for Alaska Attorney General's Office, Torts and Special Litigation Section at Anchorage; Private practice with Birch, Horton, Bittner and Cherot since 1989.
Personal: BA, Grinnell College, 1971; Commercial Fisherman, 1971-73, Puget Sound; JD, Washington University, St Louis, Missouri, 1976. Fluent Spanish.

JAMIESON, Brewster
Lane Powell PC, Anchorage
907 264 3325
jamiesonb@lanepowell.com
Recommended in Litigation
Practice Areas: Admiralty law, insurance coverage, accident and personal injury, products liability law, employment litigation, and commercial litigation. Has received favorable verdicts in a wide variety of maritime, construction, aviation, commercial, and professional negligence matters.
Prof. Memberships: International Association of Defense Counsel; The Maritime Law Association of the United States; American Bar Association, Torts and Insurance Practice Section.
Career: Partner since 1991. Law Clerk, Alaska Supreme Court, 1984-85.
Personal: Willamette University (JD, magna cum laude, 1984; BS, 1980).

JULIUSSEN, James H
Davis Wright Tremaine LLP, Anchorage
907 257 5338
jimjuliussen@dwt.com
Recommended in Employment
Practice Areas: Partner, employment and labor law, and related litigation. Representative experience includes discrimination, wrongful discharge, breach of contract, wage and hour disputes before Alaska State and Federal courts. Provides counsel to employers on wage and hour, discrimination, sexual harassment, drug policies, privacy, ADA and FMLA issues. Lead negotiator for employers in collective bargaining negotiations. Counseled Anchorage Employee Relations Board in unfair labor practices.
Prof. Memberships: Member, American, Alaska State and Anchorage Bar Associations.
Career: Joined firm, 1992; named Partner, 2000.
Personal: JD, Willamette University School of Law, 1992. BA, University of Alaska at Anchorage, 1989.

KRAFT, Barbara Simpson
Davis Wright Tremaine LLP, Anchorage
907 257 5324
barbarasimpsonkraft@dwt.com
Recommended in Corporate/M&A
Practice Areas: Partner, corporate law. Practice includes advising Alaska entities on their complex transactions, including issues relating to real estate, financing options and structure of acquisition.
Prof. Memberships: Alaska and Anchorage Bar Associations.
Career: Admitted to Alaska Bar, 1988. Joined firm, 1988; became Partner, 1998.
Publications: 'The State and Local Tax Lawyer' (ABA), 'State and Local Tax Important Developments', 1995-2000.
Personal: JD, University of Washington School of Law, 1988 (Order of the Coif). BA, with honors, Oregon State University, 1982. Member, Board of Directors, Anchorage Historic Properties, Inc. and Alaska Dance Theatre.

KREGER, Michael
Perkins Coie LLP, Anchorage
907 279 8561
Recommended in Litigation

LIMERES, Amy
Preston Gates & Ellis LLP, Anchorage
907 276 1969
Recommended in Employment

LINXWILER, James
Guess & Rudd PC, Anchorage
907 793 2200
Recommended in Environment, Native Law, Natural Resources

LYLE, George
Guess & Rudd PC, Anchorage
907 793 2200
Recommended in Environment, Natural Resources

MASON, Julian
Ashburn & Mason, PC, Anchorage
907 276 4331
Recommended in Environment, Regulated Industries

MCCLINTOCK, Donald
Ashburn & Mason, PC, Anchorage
907 276 4331
Recommended in Real Estate

MCCOLLUM, James
Law Offices of James McCollum LLC, Anchorage 907 770 7773
Recommended in Real Estate

MEDE, William
Turner & Mede, PC, Anchorage
907 276 3963
Recommended in Employment

MILLER, Lloyd
Sonosky, Chambers, Sachse, Miller & Munson LLP, Anchorage
907 258 6377
Recommended in Native Law

MILLS, Michael
Bankston, Gronning, O'Hara, PC, Anchorage 907 276 1711
Recommended in Bankruptcy

MORAN, Joseph
DeLisio Moran Geraghty & Zobel, P.C., Anchorage 907 279 9574
Recommended in Environment, Regulated Industries

MUNSON, Myra
Sonosky, Chambers, Sachse, Miller & Munson LLP, Anchorage
907 258 6377
Recommended in Native Law

ODSEN, Frederick
Hughes Thorsness Powell Huddleston & Bauman LLC, Anchorage
907 274 7522
Recommended in Corporate/M&A

OESTING, David W
Davis Wright Tremaine LLP, Anchorage
907 257 5323
daveoesting@dwt.com
Recommended in Bankruptcy, Litigation
Practice Areas: Partner, litigation, bankruptcy and commercial transactions. Practice focused primarily upon commercial and maritime litigation. Court-appointed lead counsel in the Exxon Valdez oil spill litigation for roughly 32,000 plaintiffs, which include fishermen, communities, Alaska Natives, businesses and landowners.
Prof. Memberships: American, Alaska and Washington State Bar Associations.
Career: Admitted to Washington State Bar, 1970, and Alaska Bar, 1981. Joined firm, 1970; became Partner, 1976. Partner-in-charge, Anchorage office, 1980-present.
Personal: JD, with honors, Washington University School of Law, 1970, (Order of the Coif). BA, Earlham College, 1967. Member, Board of Directors for the Alaska Native Heritage Center.

ORLANSKY, Susan
Feldman & Orlansky, Anchorage
907 272 3538
orlansky@frozenlaw.com
Recommended in Litigation
Practice Areas: Complex civil and criminal litigation, trials and appeals.
Prof. Memberships: Admitted to practice in Alaska; Attorney Member, Alaska Judicial Council; member, Alaska Bar Association, Alaska Academy of Trial Lawyers, Association of Trial Lawyers of America, National Association of Criminal Defense Lawyers, and the Anchorage Bar Association.
Career: Before entering private practice, served as Assistant Public Defender (Appellate Supervisor) for the Alaska Public Defender Agency, as Staff Attorney for the Alaska Appellate Courts, and as Law Clerk to the Honorable John Dooling, United States District Court for the Eastern District of New York.
Publications: 'Justice Rabinowitz And Personal Freedom: Evolving A Constitutional Framework,' 'Developments in the Law - Corporate Crime: Regulating Corporate Behavior Through Criminal Sanctions,' 'Comment, Affirmative

Action - Regents of the University of California v Bakke,' and 'Developments in the Law - Zoning.'

Personal: Born 13 September 1953; BA degree from Reed College (1975) (Phi Beta Kappa); JD degree from Harvard University (Magna Cum Laude).

PARISE, Michael J
Birch, Horton, Bittner & Cherot, Anchorage 907 276 1550
mparise@bhb.com
Recommended in Bankruptcy

Practice Areas: Specializing in bankruptcy practice, secured lending, commercial paper, banking, real estate finance, out-of-court restructuring, commercial litigation under the Uniform Commercial Code, and defense of lender liability claims. Representative clients include KeyBank National Association, Alaska Industrial Development and Export Authority, General Electric Capital Corporation, Regions Bank, AutoNation Financial Services.

Prof. Memberships: Member, Alaska Bar Association (Bankruptcy Section) and Massachusetts Bar Association. Admitted in Alaska and Massachusetts, 1979.

Career: Served as firm's Managing Shareholder.

Publications: Lecturer in 'Representing Secured Creditors in Bankruptcy Proceedings,' National Business Institute.

Personal: BA, cum laude, Williams College, 1975 (Phi Beta Kappa). JD Boston University, 1978.

PARKER, Douglas
Preston Gates & Ellis LLP, Anchorage 907 276 1969
Recommended in Employment

PERKINS, Joseph
Guess & Rudd PC, Anchorage 907 793 2200
Recommended in Environment, Natural Resources

PETUMENOS, Timothy J
Birch, Horton, Bittner & Cherot, Anchorage 907 276 1550
tpetumenos@bhb.com
Recommended in Litigation

Practice Areas: Mr Petumenos specializes in the trial of cases before juries. Generally speaking, Mr Petumenos does both plaintiff work and defense work where the amounts in controversy are substantial and the facts are complex. Mr Petumenos and his staff have expertise in utilizing advanced computerized evidentiary presentations that effectively present complex evidence in a compelling and persuasive manner and in a way the minimizes the cost of preparation for trial.

Prof. Memberships: Certified Faculty, National Institute for Trial Advocacy (NITA). Advocate, American Board of Trial Advocates. Alaska Bar Association, 1976; United States District Court for the District of Alaska; Ninth Circuit; United States Supreme Court.

Career: Mr Petumenos graduated from Georgetown University Law Center, Washington DC with a Juris Doctorate in 1976. After serving as an Assistant District Attorney in Fairbanks, Mr Petumenos was selected to be the first attorney at the newly formed Office of Special Prosecutions with the Alaska Attorney General's Office where it fell upon Mr Petumenos to supervise and conduct the state's most complex commercial and public corruption trials. In 1983, Mr Petumenos joined the law firm of Birch Horton Bittner and Cherot, one of Alaska's leading law firms, where he is currently its senior trial lawyer. Over the course of his career at Birch Horton, Mr Petumenos has handled many of Alaska's most celebrated cases, including serving as lead trial counsel in the three month jury trial in state court representing that Native Corporation owners of the Prince William Sound beaches in the Exxon Valdez Oil Spill Litigation. Mr Petumenos has taught trial advocacy to practicing lawyers for the State of Alaska Attorney General's Office, the Alaska Bar Association, the National Institute for Trial Advocacy, the Honolulu District Attorney's Office and the Alaska Trial Lawyers Association.

Personal: In addition to trial work, Mr Petumenos has done work on the interface between the mental health profession and the law, having served, in the past, as counsel to the Alaska Psychiatric Institute. Mr Petumenos also has an interest in aviation law which was brought about by his personal interest in aviation. Mr Petumenos is a land and seaplane private pilot with an instrument rating who has flown airplanes all over the North American continent and in Latin America. He speaks fluent Spanish.

RECKMEYER, Peter
Heller Ehrman White & McAuliffe LLP, Anchorage 907 277 1900
Recommended in Corporate/M&A

REECE, Joseph
Davis Wright Tremaine LLP, Anchorage 907 257 5325
josephreece@dwt.com
Recommended in Corporate/M&A, Real Estate

Practice Areas: Partner, real property and commercial transactions. Focuses practice on commercial and real estate transactions including: mergers and acquisitions; financing; corporate law; real estate purchases and sales; leasing; commercial and residential development; and environmental issues.

Prof. Memberships: American and Alaska State Bar Associations.

Career: Admitted to the Alaska Bar, 1981. Joined firm, 1987; became Partner, 1990.

Publications: Frequent lecturer at CLE seminars on commercial and real estate law.

Personal: JD, (cum laude), Gonzaga University School of Law, 1981. BA, (magna cum laude), Loyola University, New Orleans, 1970.

REEVES, James
Dorsey & Whitney LLP, Anchorage 907 276 4557
Recommended in Environment, Natural Resources

REEVES, Susan
Foster Pepper Rubini & Reeves PLLC, Anchorage 907 222 7100
Recommended in Environment, Natural Resources

REGES, Robert
Reges & Boone LLC, Juneau 907 790 2777
Recommended in Environment, Natural Resources

ROHLF, Joan
Guess & Rudd PC, Anchorage 907 793 2200
Recommended in Employment

ROSSTON, Richard
Dorsey & Whitney LLP, Anchorage 907 276 4557
Recommended in Corporate/M&A, Real Estate

ROZELL, William
William Rozell - Sole Practitioner, Juneau 907 586 0142
Recommended in Environment, Natural Resources

SAUER, Jane
Perkins Coie LLP, Anchorage 907 279 8561
Recommended in Corporate/M&A

SAUPE, William
Ashburn & Mason, PC, Anchorage 907 276 4331
Recommended in Environment, Regulated Industries

SERDAHELY, Douglas
Patton Boggs LLP, Anchorage 907 277 4900
Recommended in Environment, Litigation, Natural Resources

SIEMERS, John
Burr, Pease & Kurtz, PC, Anchorage 907 276 6100
Recommended in Bankruptcy

SNEED, Spencer
Dorsey & Whitney LLP, Anchorage 907 276 4557
Recommended in Bankruptcy, Litigation

SPAAN, Michael
Patton Boggs LLP, Anchorage 907 277 4900
Recommended in Litigation

SPRAKER, Gary
Christianson, Boutin & Spraker, Anchorage 907 258 6016
Recommended in Bankruptcy

STANLEY, James
Foster Pepper Rubini & Reeves PLLC, Anchorage 907 222 7100
Recommended in Real Estate

STEWART, Robert K
Davis Wright Tremaine LLP, Anchorage 907 257 5336
bobstewart@dwt.com
Recommended in Employment

Practice Areas: Partner, labor and employment law. Representative experience includes civil litigation, public procurement, construction and personal injury law. Relative labor matters include wrongful termination, Davis-Bacon Act, Fair Labor Standards Act and OSHA. Representative Clients include Chugach Electric Association, Iditarod Trail Committee and Doyon Limited.

Prof. Memberships: Member, American Bar Association, Alaska and Washington State Bar Associations.

Career: Joined firm, 1983. Named Partner, 1989. Immediate past Chair, firm's Pro Bono Committee. Previously served as Extern to Hon. William Orrick, US District Court, Northern District of California.

Personal: JD, Stanford, 1983. BS (magna cum laude), Western Washington University, 1980.

STOLLER, Robert
Robert Stoller - Sole Practitioner, Anchorage 907 522 2299
Recommended in Environment, Regulated Industries

TINDALL, John
Tindall Bennett & Shoup PC, Anchorage 907 278 8533
Recommended in Real Estate

TORGERSON, James
Heller Ehrman White & McAuliffe LLP, Anchorage 907 277 1900
Recommended in Environment, Litigation, Natural Resources

TRAVOSTINO, Joan
Preston Gates & Ellis LLP, Anchorage 907 276 1969
Recommended in Bankruptcy, Real Estate

VEERMAN, Louis
Guess & Rudd PC, Anchorage 907 793 2200
Recommended in Environment, Regulated Industries

WATTS, Grant
Holmes Weddle & Barcott, A Professional Corporation, Anchorage 907 274 0666
Recommended in Litigation

BIRCH, HORTON, BITTNER AND CHEROT

THE FIRM

Firmwide Managing Shareholder: Suzanne Cherot
Senior Partners: Ronald G Birch & William H Bittner

Number of shareholders: 19
Number of other lawyers: 10

FIRM OVERVIEW: Founded in Alaska in 1971, Birch, Horton, Bittner and Cherot maintains a national, full-service law practice with offices in Anchorage, Alaska, and Washington, DC. The firm has earned widespread recognition of its performance in serving the needs of clients located in over 30 states and foreign countries, in all areas of business and individual representation. The firm's practice mirrors the varied nature of Alaska's economy, its cultural richness, and the vastness of its natural resources.

MAIN AREAS OF PRACTICE

Banking & Financial Services: The firm's core commercial practice centers around the representation of financial institutions. Transactions include the origination and documentation of loans, closing of complex loans, and advice regarding enforcement of remedies, from bankruptcy options to repossessions and foreclosures.

Commercial Transactions/Corporate & Business Transactions: The firm's attorneys advise clients on the formation, organization, and day-to-day operation of enterprises, with a focus on meeting immediate challenges and preventing future disputes. The firm serves as corporate counsel to several Alaska Native corporations.

Employment: The firm handles all types of employment disputes, including wrongful discharge and defamation claims, and claims based upon federal, state, and local statutes.

Land, Wildlife, Natural Resources & Energy: The firm practices in these areas in the administrative, judicial, and legislative arenas. The firm's expertise in wildlife law is widely respected. The firm represents clients before the Federal Energy Regulatory Commission on hydroelectric licensing, electric and gas utility rates, and rulemaking.

Legislative & Regulatory Affairs: The firm maintains continuing relationships with high-level Executive branch officials and key Republican and Democratic members of Congress. The firm strategically combines comprehension of political issues, familiarity and relationships with major policymakers, and our experience in making and executing federal, state, and municipal laws and regulations to assist clients.

Litigation: The firm has decades of litigation and trial practice in Alaska with an impressive record of success. The firm has conducted many of Alaska's largest and most well-known trials. The firm represents clients in federal and state trial and appellate courts around the country, in administrative tribunals, state human rights agencies, and state public service commissions. The firm has a robust personal injury/plaintiff practice.

Native Law: An important part of the Alaska experience is the Alaska Native community. The firm has in-depth knowledge and expertise in representing Alaska Native corporations, Indian housing authorities, and Native not-for-profit health corporations in issues unique to conducting business under the Alaska Native Claims Settlement Act and other federal and state laws. The firm also assists private business entities interested in working cooperatively with Native corporations on important projects around the country.

Public Finance: The firm has served as bond counsel in connection with tax-exempt obligations of Alaska municipalities and state agencies. Such services have been provided in connection with over $1.3 billion of tax-exempt bonds.

US OFFICES

ALASKA
1127 W 7th Avenue, **Anchorage**, AK 99501 3399
Tel: 907 276 1550 **Fax:** 907 276 3680
E-mail: info@bhb.com
Website: www.birchhorton.com

DISTRICT OF COLUMBIA
1155 Connecticut Avenue, NW, Suite 1200,
Washington, DC 20036 4306
Tel: 202 659 5800 **Fax:** 202 6591027 **Toll Free:** 888 482 4724
E-mail: inquiries@dc.bhb.com

CONTACTS

Banking & Financial Services	Kathryn A Black (Anchorage)
Bankruptcy	Michael J Parise (Anchorage)
Commercial, Corporate, Business	Kathryn A Black (Anchorage)
	Harvey A Levin (DC)
Employment	Stanley T Lewis (Anchorage)
	Jennifer C Alexander (Anchorage)
Land, Wildlife, Natural Resources, Energy	William P Horn (DC)
Legislative & Regulatory	William P Horn (DC)
	William H Bittner (Anchorage)
Litigation	Timothy J Petumenos (Anchorage)
	Harvey A Levin (DC)
	Stephen H Hutchings (Anchorage)
Native Law (Corporate)	Kathleen Erb (Anchorage)
Native Law (Health, Housing)	Stephen H Hutchings (Anchorage)
Public Finance	Thomas F Klinkner (Anchorage)
	Kenneth E Vassar (Anchorage)
Public Law & Policy	Ronald G Birch (DC)
	William H Bittner (Anchorage)
Real Property	Suzanne Cherot (Anchorage)
Telecommunications	Tina M Grovier (Anchorage)
	Elisabeth H Ross (DC)

Public Law & Policy: The firm assists clients with federal issues, in addition to seeking solutions at the state or local government levels.

Real Property: The firm represents all parties to commercial real estate transactions. The firm's attorneys are skilled at attending to the complexities of purchasing, owning, leasing, developing, and financing real property.

Telecommunications: The firm represents state commissions, independent local exchange carriers, and competitive inter-exchange carriers, in common carriers, wireless, rulemaking, and licensing cases before the FCC and state public utilities commissions. The firm has extensive expertise in telecommunications, legislative, and regulatory issues, including interpretation of the Telecommunications Act of 1996.

CLIENTS: The firm provides representation to a broad base of clients, including state, local, and territorial governments, major universities, state public utility commissions, multinational industrial companies, large financial institutions, Alaska Native corporations, telecommunications, technology, and media companies, and physicians and other medical groups.

INTERNATIONAL WORK: William H Bittner serves as the Honorary Consulate to South Korea. Timothy J Petumenos speaks Spanish.

CONTENTS: Corporate/M&A p.146; Employment: p.148; Environment p.149; Litigation: p.151; Real Estate p.153; Individuals' Profiles p.156; Firms' Profiles p.164.

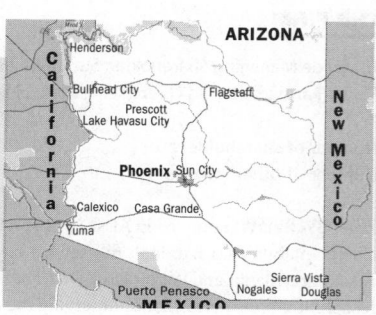

How lawyers are ranked

The opinions we gather from clients — mainly from in-house lawyers but also from other purchasers of legal services — are balanced by opinions from colleagues and competitors. Together, they provide two different perspectives — an all-round view — and biased viewpoints cancel each other out.

CORPORATE/M&A

Arizona
Leading firms (Corporate/M&A)

1. SNELL & WILMER LLP *Phoenix*
2. BRYAN CAVE LLP *Phoenix*
   FENNEMORE CRAIG *Phoenix*
   OSBORN MALEDON PA *Phoenix*
   SQUIRE, SANDERS & DEMPSEY LLP *Phoenix*
3. GREENBERG TRAURIG LLP *Phoenix*
   QUARLES & BRADY STREICH LANG LLP *Phoenix*
4. JENNINGS, STROUSS & SALMON, PLC *Phoenix*
   LEWIS AND ROCA *Phoenix*
   PERKINS COIE LLP *Phoenix*
5. RYLEY CARLOCK & APPLEWHITE *Phoenix*
   TITUS, BRUECKNER & BERRY PC *Scottsdale*

Leading individuals (Corporate/M&A)

1. CURZON Thomas *Osborn Maledon, Phoenix*
   JOHNSON Christopher *Squire Sanders, Phoenix*
   MCCONNELL Karen *Fennemore Craig, Phoenix*
   PIDGEON Steven *Snell & Wilmer, Phoenix*
2. COHEN Jon *Snell & Wilmer, Phoenix*
   FEENEY Matthew *Snell & Wilmer, Phoenix*
   KANT Robert *Greenberg Traurig, Phoenix*
   PLACENTI Frank *Bryan Cave, Phoenix*
3. HARDIN William *Osborn Maledon, Phoenix*
   HOFFMANN Christian *Quarles & Brady, Phoenix*
   RICHARDSON Joseph *Bryan Cave, Phoenix*
   WILLIAMS Quinn *Greenberg Traurig, Phoenix*
4. BERRY Charles *Titus Brueckner, Scottsdale*
   BROPHY James *Ryley Carlock, Phoenix*
   CRABB Joseph *Quarles & Brady, Phoenix*
   DEWALD Scott *Lewis and Roca, Phoenix*
   EMERICK Steven *Quarles & Brady, Phoenix*
   HACKETT Robert *Jennings Strouss, Phoenix*
   ROMAN Terry *Snell & Wilmer, Phoenix*
   STRUNK Sarah *Fennemore Craig, Phoenix*
   WEISS Judith *Perkins Coie, Phoenix*

Firms and individuals are listed alphabetically in each band.

Band 1

Snell & Wilmer LLP
See firm details p.167

The Firm: This firm remains at the top of the table this year, due to its continued work on large and sophisticated deals. The corporate group, described by competitors as "*the biggest, broadest and best,*" is well versed in a range of transactional matters, particularly M&A, bankruptcy and securities law. The quality of clientele – this firm represents 17 of the 27 corporate headquarters located in Arizona as well as a number of Fortune 500 companies – attests to its strength as a corporate powerhouse.

The Lawyers: Clients endorsed **Steven Pidgeon** (see p.161) as "*probably the premier securities lawyer in Arizona*" and pointed to his technical understanding and responsive service. He advises on M&A and venture capital investments for clients from a wide range of industries. Chair of the group **Jon Cohen** (see p.157) has established a general corporate practice, which of late has included a large number of public offerings and M&A deals. Sources also endorsed the IPO and M&A advice of **Matthew Feeney** (see p.158), "*a smart and capable attorney, who understands the issues and gets the job done.*" **Terry Roman** (see p.161) is admired for her work representing companies in their SEC reporting and M&A activity.

The Clients: The client list includes Pinnacle West and Arizona Public Service.

Band 2

Bryan Cave LLP
The Firm: The Phoenix-based attorneys benefit from the greater resources provided by the firm's national and international capabilities. Such expertise is particularly evident in securities law advice, M&A and corporate governance matters. According to clients, the team provides a prompt, technically excellent service and is mindful of staffing matters appropriately.

Clients describe the firm as "*in tune with our business; they understand our needs.*"

The Lawyers: "*Rainmaker*" **Frank Placenti** impresses clients with his personable style, legal knowledge and strong advocacy skills. They report: "*If he moved, we'd move with him.*" His practice encompasses M&A, private equity and SEC dealings. **Joseph Richardson** is respected as one of the market's leading securities experts. He is "*great at making sure the transaction is done right and on time.*"

The Clients: Clients include regional and national corporates including a number of Fortune 500 entities.

Fennemore Craig
See firm details p.164

The Firm: This 22-strong team is the second largest corporate group in Arizona. Its attorneys possess a wealth of experience in transactional matters such as the formation of companies and partnerships, private equity M&A and securities law. The firm also serves as counsel for numerous software development companies, both local and national, advising on both corporate and intellectual property issues.

The Lawyers: **Karen McConnell** (see p.160) has attracted much respect from commentators as a "*wonderful deal-doer,*" whose pragmatic approach makes for a smooth transaction. Sources also appreciated the negotiation and strategic skills of **Sarah Strunk** (see p.162). Chair of the firm's business and finance practice, she possesses a "*bottom-line effectiveness*" that has impressed clients. Strunk has recently advised sports franchises and natural resource companies.

The Clients: Clients include Arizona-based public companies, and public entities such as the Arizona Sports & Tourism Authority

Osborn Maledon PA
See firm details p.165

The Firm: While this corporate group is well equipped to handle all aspects of corporate work, it has had a particular impact in the growth company arena, providing venture capital, angel financing and M&A services to technology companies. Clients agree that the firm commands the *"highest respect,"* fielding talented attorneys, who *"appreciate the nuances of the venture capital sector."*

The Lawyers: According to clients, **Tom Curzon** (see p.157) is *"skilled at bringing along emerging companies."* They also value his comprehensive service and describe him as *"a very creative thinker and a great advocate for his clients".* **Bill Hardin** (see p.159) primarily works with growth companies, advising them on efforts to establish strategic relationships and joint ventures as well as handling licensing and employment issues.

The Clients: AZDB Baseball; NetPro Computing; SiVerion and Andigilog.

Squire, Sanders & Dempsey LLP

The Firm: Part of a national and international giant, the Phoenix-based corporate group of 13 provides the full range of transactional advice with a respected reputation for bankruptcy and Chapter 11 proceedings. Clients claim that the team *"brings a high level of expertise to any matter, be it local or national,"* and they endorsed the M&A and private financing experience of its attorneys.

The Lawyers: The *"very savvy"* **Christopher Johnson** is highly respected and was described as *"results-oriented and effective".* His specialty is bankruptcy and refinancing, and this *"clearly excellent"* attorney recently completed a complex, multiparty restructuring of $1.2 billion of debt for a large national client.

The Clients: AMERCO and U-Haul International are clients of the firm.

Band 3

Greenberg Traurig LLP

See firm details p.564

The Firm: This national firm is developing *"a growing presence in the community,"* acknowledge sources, and the corporate practice is carving itself a niche in capital formation. Phoenix-based attorneys also work on private stock offerings and M&A. They have successfully won the loyalty of a large number of Arizona's public companies and hi-tech corporations.

The Lawyers: **Robert Kant** (see p.159) has cultivated a busy practice that incorporates finance, securities and public offerings as well as venture capital. He recently advised on the acquisition of 20 dealerships for the world's largest boat dealer. Clients respect him as *"a powerful negotiator."* According to some commentators, **Quinn Williams** (see p.162) is *"almost a spokesman on*

the topic of enhancing capital formation in Arizona." His M&A experience has involved work with Fortune 500 and other midmarket companies in the technology, retail, media and manufacturing sectors.

The Clients: Brillian Corporation, MarineMax and Synaptics are examples of the firm's client base.

Quarles & Brady Streich Lang LLP

The Firm: A national corporate services group fields a team of some 120 attorneys providing a full range of corporate law advice. Offices in Phoenix and Tucson service clients based in Arizona and from the southwest region on debt offerings, refinancing, M&A and venture capital work. The client roster includes public companies and private entities, and the group recently represented ASM International in its $60 million acquisition of a semiconductor company.

The Lawyers: Observers commended **Christian Hoffmann** for his work for issuers and underwriters in public and private offerings. His pragmatic deal-making skills ensure that he is a *"highly valuable adviser"* to have on your side, claimed clients. **Steven Emerick** undertakes corporate finance and securities, including venture capital as well as equipment finance. **Joseph Crabb** has used his broad mix of M&A and securities skills to attract clients from the manufacturing, distribution and hi-tech arenas.

Band 4

Jennings, Strouss & Salmon, PLC

The Firm: This respected Phoenix firm is continuing to make its mark in the corporate sector. Twelve corporate attorneys represent both public and private companies on general corporate matters, with particular emphasis on IPOs, M&A and venture capital. The group also advises on the legal structure for newly formed entities and provides dispute resolution advice in contested transactions. Clients find the firm *"suitably client-focused."*

The Lawyers: Joining the firm in May 2004 from Fennemore Craig, **Robert Hackett** brings with him a strong corporate and finance practice. Loyal clients, including Fortune 500 companies and local midsized entities, hailed his *"creative solutions and groundbreaking approaches."*

Lewis and Roca

The Firm: This regional firm continues to provide a range of corporate services, focusing on securities (private and public offerings), corporate structuring and M&A. The transactional attorneys work closely with their IP counterparts in the firm and have a number of hi-tech

clients. The client base is drawn from industries as varied as construction, cable and atomic microscopy.

The Lawyers: **Scott DeWald** handles corporate matters, and particularly venture capital and M&A, for clients often drawn from the e-commerce and emerging markets.

Perkins Coie LLP

The Firm: Before its merger with the Seattle-headquartered giant, this firm was best known for its litigation and IP capabilities. Its transactional attorneys can now count themselves as part of a 200-strong corporate practice group that can draw on further resources provided by this national firm. The corporate team continues to offer the full range of corporate and commercial advice, with traditional strengths in banking, M&A and IP transactional work. Sources remarked that this team *"certainly has the capability to be a strong corporate contender in Phoenix."*

The Lawyers: **Judith Weiss** works on both general corporate and IP transactional matters, focusing on M&A and public and private offerings in the corporate sector. Clients include hi-technology corporations.

The Clients: Vitesse Semiconductor and Phelps Dodge are examples of the firm's clients.

Band 5

Ryley Carlock & Applewhite

See firm details p.166

The Firm: This local firm continues to impress the market in a number of practice areas, including corporate, in which it handles domestic and international transactions. It has a dedicated business practice, which is involved in the earliest stages of formation and financing of entities through to devising strategies for mature businesses.

The Lawyers: **Jim Brophy** (see p.157) practices in securities and employee benefits law. Sources respect his *"ability to provide sound advice"* and describe him as a pleasure to work with.

Titus, Brueckner & Berry PC

The Firm: This Scottsdale firm received praise for its corporate law advice, particularly securities matters. The firm also handles M&A and broker/dealer investment work, in addition to serving the transactional needs of the firm's real estate, insurance and IP practices.

The Lawyers: Interviewees endorsed **Charles Berry** for his focus on the conclusion of a deal. His practice extends to capital formation, business management and M&A

EMPLOYMENT

Arizona
Leading firms
(Employment: Mainly Defendant)

[1] STEPTOE & JOHNSON LLP *Phoenix*

[2] BRYAN CAVE LLP *Phoenix*
FENNEMORE CRAIG *Phoenix*
LEWIS AND ROCA *Phoenix*
RYLEY CARLOCK & APPLEWHITE *Phoenix*
SNELL & WILMER LLP *Phoenix*

[3] BROCKELMAN FATICA PLC *Tempe*
GREENBERG TRAURIG LLP *Phoenix*
PERKINS COIE LLP *Phoenix*
QUARLES & BRADY STREICH LANG LLP *Phoenix*
STINSON MORRISON HECKER LLP *Phoenix*

Leading individuals
(Employment: Mainly Defendant)

[1] COHEN Richard *Lewis and Roca, Phoenix*
KATZ Lawrence *Steptoe & Johnson, Phoenix*
STOLKIN Ronald *Fennemore Craig, Tucson*

[2] CLEES Joseph *Bryan Cave, Phoenix*
GOEBEL Monica *Steptoe & Johnson, Phoenix*
PETTIBONE Jon *Quarles & Brady, Phoenix*
SELDEN David *Stinson Morrison, Phoenix*
WILLIAMS Jr Lonnie *Quarles & Brady, Phoenix*

[3] HAYDEN William *Snell & Wilmer, Phoenix*
HERF Charles *Quarles & Brady, Phoenix*
MOBERLY Michael *Ryley Carlock, Phoenix*
WINTERSCHEIDT Rebecca *Snell & Wilmer, Phoenix*

[4] BARR Daniel *Perkins Coie, Phoenix*
BERMAN Michael *Perkins Coie, Phoenix*
BROCKELMAN Kent *Brockelman Fatica, Tempe*
DORAN John *Greenberg Traurig, Phoenix*
GILBERT Donald *Fennemore Craig, Phoenix*
GITTLER Amy *Frazer Ryan, Phoenix*
MORALES Gerard *Snell & Wilmer, Phoenix*
NIEMUTH Nathan *Ryley Carlock, Phoenix*
REDDIN Jane *Lewis and Roca, Phoenix*
ROSENFELD Lawrence *Greenberg Traurig, Phoenix*

Firms and individuals are listed alphabetically in each band.

Band 1

Steptoe & Johnson LLP
See firm details p.492
The Firm: This team maintains its position as a leading employment and labor relations practice, with sources highlighting its "*strength and commitment right at the top*" and "*quality throughout*." The 12-strong group handles the full gamut of employment-related work including counseling and litigation at federal and state levels, as well as appellate matters. Commentators admired the group's ability to settle matters quickly and keep a lid on litigation expenses.
The Lawyers: With his extensive experience and expertise, "*top-notch*" **Larry Katz** (see p.159) heads the department. His practice encompasses equal opportunity and wrongful

discharge litigation, labor relations and union avoidance, and HR counseling. Protégé **Monica Goebel** (see p.158) defends employers, among them retailers, manufacturers and insurance companies, in all areas of employment law.

Band 2

Bryan Cave LLP
The Firm: The labor and employment group, which works out of five US offices and a UK base in London, provides a network of attorneys well-versed in employment and labor law. This employment powerhouse represents employers at tribunals and all levels of federal and state courts, and has developed a particular reputation for defending large class actions. The 15-strong team in Phoenix was described as "*extremely responsive and very knowledgeable*," handling matters for a range of clients, regionally and nationally, across many industry sectors.
The Lawyers: **Joseph Clees**, who heads the firm's national employment practice, represents employers in discrimination and wrongful discharge, as well as providing employment counseling to clients primarily from the financial, hospitality, hi-tech and public utility sectors. One client reported that Clees' knowledge of their business and key staff, and his sensitivity, meant it was "*as though he works with us*." His presentation skills and sense of humor were also applauded.

Fennemore Craig
See firm details p.164
The Firm: Boasting 16 specialist attorneys between its Tucson and Phoenix offices, this firm advises and defends management on all employment and labor matters, including workers' compensation to which it dedicates a team of five. The firm represents employers in litigation before the Industrial Commission of Arizona and Arizona's appellate courts. It also services clients on employment-related immigration issues, assisting domestic and international companies with their foreign national employees. Peers admire these attorneys for their "*good judgment*" and acknowledge that they "*really know their subject matter*."
The Lawyers: Cochair of the practice, **Ronald Stolkin** (see p.162) is known to be "*upfront and realistic*" in his advice. He counsels employers on personnel practices, employee discipline and labor relations, and is a respected litigator at both administrative tribunals and courts. Clients commend him for being "*responsive and very knowledgeable*." Cochair **Donald Gilbert** (see p.158) represents clients in a broad range of employment-related issues before the NLRB, the EEOC, the DOL, the Arizona Civil Rights Division and the Arizona Department of Economic Security.

Lewis and Roca
The Firm: This firm is a major player in the southwest, operating from both Phoenix and Tucson. It fields a dedicated team that counsels employers and defends them at administrative proceedings and state and federal courts. Areas of expertise include wrongful termination suits and individual or class actions, including those under civil rights laws, ADEA, ERISA and other employment statutes, as well as unfair labor practice, job safety and health matters. Competitors admired this group for its direct approach and strong client relationships.
The Lawyers: **Richard Cohen**'s extensive experience in employment law has earned him a first-tier reputation among peers and clients. His litigation record is complemented by a healthy mediation and arbitration practice, and researchers were told that he is "*sensible, very capable, responsive and client-friendly*." "*Proactive*" **Jane Reddin** enters the table in recognition of her respected practice advising individuals and defending employers in discrimination and wrongful termination claims, particularly focusing on sex, race, age and disability cases.
The Clients: The firm's clients include large public employers as well as regional and national corporations.

Ryley Carlock & Applewhite
See firm details p.166
The Firm: As one of the oldest firms in the state, this Phoenix outfit has a long and proven track record. Serving clients from a range of industries and of varying size, and boasting a reputation that is particularly strong on the labor law side, the group deals with all aspects of employment and labor law, in arbitration and litigation, collective bargaining and union relations.
The Lawyers: **Mike Moberly** (see p.160) is head of the firm's labor and employment law practice. Moberly represents management in civil rights and employment-related litigation, the arbitration of collective bargaining agreement disputes, and administrative proceedings involving statutory discrimination claims. Peers describe this attorney as "*technically excellent, very scholarly, with strong intellectual skills*." "*One of the best*," **Nate Niemuth** (see p.160) is a nationally recognized authority on labor relations law. He represents major enterprises from a range of industries including manufacturing, mining and utilities, and, for many, serves as the principal architect of their labor relations strategies.

148   All quotes in the text are from interviews with clients and competitors.

CHAMBERS USA 2005

Snell & Wilmer LLP

See firm details p.167

The Firm: The labor and employment law group offers clients expertise in all areas including discrimination, wrongful discharge and breach of contract. With attorneys in both Phoenix and Tucson, the firm has developed a reputation for helping clients to avoid litigation, offering counseling and investigation services to employers. Sources also highlighted the superb corporate practice housed at this firm and envied the strong corporate client relationships that the firm has successfully developed. However, the team has had to weather the departure of trial lawyer and employment law specialist Lonnie Williams to Quarles & Brady.

The Lawyers: Interviewees confirmed **William Hayden**'s (see p.159) strong presence in both employment and labor law in the state. This "*knowledgeable*" attorney advises management clients on all aspects of personnel administration and the avoidance of personnel-related litigation, representing them, when necessary, before all state and regulatory agencies. **Rebecca Winterscheidt** (see p.163) enters the table this year, attracting praise for a practice that centers on advice to management clients on all areas of personnel administration. She also represents employers and individuals in immigration matters. Labor law is the primary focus of **Gerard Morales**' (see p.160) practice, encompassing collective bargaining and proceedings before the NLRB, as well as policy advice and the drafting of handbooks.

Band 3

Brockelman Fatica PLC

The Firm: With its compact team, this Tempe-based boutique earned high praise for its work in the employment arena. Market recognition is backed by a roster of large, national and Fortune 500 companies.

The Lawyers: **Kent Brockelman** was described to researchers as "*very bright, very professional*" and handles all aspects of employment law. Recent highlights include counseling a publicly traded company with respect to reductions in force and WARN Act obligations, and representing a national accounting firm in the

enforcement of restrictive covenants and litigation of trade secret matters.

Greenberg Traurig LLP

See firm details p.564

The Firm: The Phoenix office of this major national player is key to its nationwide labor and employment practice. Eight attorneys offer clients a full range of services, including compliance advice, policy development and preventive counseling.

The Lawyers: **Lawrence Rosenfeld** (see p.161) is cochair of the group, and was described as a "*quality attorney*," earning respect for his employment expertise and litigation capabilities. He is joined in this year's rankings by **John Doran** (see p.158). "*An enthusiastic courtroom litigator*," Doran possesses "*a real understanding of the issues.*"

Perkins Coie LLP

The Firm: In July 2004, local firm Brown & Bain merged with Seattle-headquartered giant Perkins Coie, boosting the former's capabilities in the labor and employment area. While the team can naturally draw upon a broad, national base of resources, the most immediate impact appears to be its ability to handle class actions. The Phoenix team of eight attorneys also provides preventive counseling measures and a full litigation and arbitration service, handling discrimination and wage and hour cases.

The Lawyers: First Amendment guru **Daniel Barr** combines a media law practice with employment work that focuses on wrongful termination and discrimination cases. Sources also commended **Mike Berman** for his great employment expertise as well as his general commercial litigation skills.

The Clients: Clients include hi-tech, sports and hospitality companies, and general commercial concerns.

Quarles & Brady Streich Lang LLP

The Firm: This large national player services the state and southwest region from its Phoenix and Tucson offices, providing management clients with expertise in both employment and labor law. The firm provides a raft of strategic anti-litigation solutions, and when necessary fields a

strong litigation team which represents clients at all administrative and formal courts, including the NLRB.

The Lawyers: The employment team this year scored a coup with the recruitment of litigator **Lonnie Williams**. Although a portion of his time is dedicated to general commercial matters, Williams' track record and understanding of employment litigation has made him a prominent figure in this market. According to sources, "*when a case is destined for trial, Lonnie should be your first port of call.*" **Jon Pettibone** advises management clients on labor and employment strategies and represents them before federal and state courts and agencies, and in arbitration and in collective bargaining. Technically astute and blessed with ample common sense, Pettibone "*focuses on getting good results.*" **Charles Herf** is described as "*a wonderful lawyer*" who has carved a niche in the education and public sectors.

Stinson Morrison Hecker LLP

See firm details p.1069

The Firm: The Phoenix office of this full-service commercial and corporate firm is recognized for its employment and litigation prowess. The employment group consists of 11 attorneys, five of whom are exclusively dedicated to all areas of employment law including employment policies and practices, discrimination, employee benefits, wage and hour, discipline and termination, government regulatory compliance and administrative proceedings. The team is bolstered by the broader litigation capabilities of the firm.

The Lawyers: **David Selden** (see p.161) is "*the real deal*," according to interviewees. Active at the Arizona legislature, drafting state employment laws, he is said to have "*a good intellectual approach, and is very astute.*" Selden represents management in a wide variety of employment law matters including human resources counseling, investigation and training as well as litigation.

Other Notable Practitioners

Interviewees endorsed the employment practice of **Amy Gittler** of Frazer Ryan Goldberg Arnold & Gittler LLP, describing her as a "*smart adviser and a tough lawyer.*"

ENVIRONMENT

Band 1

Fennemore Craig

See firm details p.164

The Firm: This firm offers a comprehensive environment practice, encompassing natural resources, endangered species, and ground and surface water issues. Sources described the attor-

neys here as "*thoroughly knowledgeable and well-connected,*" noting also the firm's relationship and constructive interaction with the governor and environmental department. The group, which also provides environmental litigation expertise, serves clients in manufacturing, industry, mining, real estate development, utility and agriculture industries.

The Lawyers: **Phillip Fargotstein** (see p.158) chairs the environmental and natural resources practice and possesses "*superb*" litigation ability, particularly in environmental and toxic tort matters. Rivals have "*no hesitation in referring a client*" to this attorney, particularly in his specialist field of air quality compliance, permitting and enforcement. **John Pearce** (see p.161) is a

Arizona
Leading firms
Environment

1. FENNEMORE CRAIG *Phoenix*
   GALLAGHER & KENNEDY PA *Phoenix*
2. BRYAN CAVE LLP *Phoenix*
   LEWIS AND ROCA *Phoenix*
   MOYES STOREY *Phoenix*
   QUARLES & BRADY STREICH LANG LLP *Phoenix*
   RYLEY CARLOCK & APPLEWHITE *Phoenix*
   SNELL & WILMER LLP *Phoenix*
   SQUIRE, SANDERS & DEMPSEY LLP *Phoenix*
   STEPTOE & JOHNSON LLP *Phoenix*

Leading individuals
Environment

1. BROPHY Michael *Ryley Carlock, Phoenix*
   FERLAND Roger *Quarles & Brady, Phoenix*
   KIMBALL David *Gallagher & Kennedy, Phoenix*
   PORTER Amy *Lewis and Roca, Phoenix*
2. CURRY Stanton *Gallagher & Kennedy Phoenix*
   DEROUIN James *Steptoe & Johnson, Phoenix*
   FARGOTSTEIN Phillip *Fennemore Craig, Phoenix*
   NARDUCCI Lucas *Bryan Cave, Phoenix*
   PETERS Karen *Squire Sanders, Phoenix*
   THOMAS Christopher *Squire Sanders, Phoenix*
3. ANDERSON Robert *Withey Anderson, Phoenix*
   CASTER Lauren *Fennemore Craig, Phoenix*
   DAY Barton *Bryan Cave, Phoenix*
   HAMULAR James *Gallagher & Kennedy, Phoenix*
   MOELLENBERG Dalva *Gallagher & Kennedy, Phoenix*
   MOYES Jay *Moyes Storey, Phoenix*
   PEARCE John *Fennemore Craig, Phoenix*
   STOREY Lee *Moyes Storey, Phoenix*
   WOLF Van *Snell & Wilmer, Phoenix*

Firms and individuals are listed alphabetically in each band.

"details-oriented attorney," whose work in environmental and natural resources regulatory compliance and permitting is widely respected. Sources also endorsed his lobbying efforts and his familiarity with the regulators and government bodies. He represents clients in Arizona and Nebraska, and recently advised a major pipeline company in relation to a gasoline pipeline release. Water rights specialist, **Lauren Caster** (see p.157) is *"a very sharp attorney."* He represents clients in state and federal courts and at proceedings before the Department of Water Resources.

Gallagher & Kennedy PA

The Firm: Among this firm's broad environmental practice can be found expertise in air and water quality, water rights and management, solid and hazardous waste management and Superfund exposure and liability. *"They have a breadth that other firms can't match,"* reported sources. Attorneys here assist clients with compliance and permitting work at all state and federal environmental agencies. The firm

works closely with clients from the mining, as well as industrial, commercial and manufacturing industries.

The Lawyers: David Kimball heads the firm's environmental and natural resources practice, and, according to commentators, *"has created the deepest competitive environment practice group."* Well-known for his environmental legislative activities, Kimball concentrates on surface and groundwater quality issues, water rights, and matters arising from the mining industry. *"If I wanted the best technical advice, I would go to **Stanton Curry**",* is the view of a number of peers. Curry's practice features air quality, Superfund, water quality and environmental auditing. **James Hamular** serves clients in a range of areas including compliance counseling, strategic planning, permitting, lobbying and litigation on solid and hazardous waste and Superfund issues. Interviewees hold this attorney in high esteem, describing him as *"very knowledgeable and highly principled."* **Dal Moellenberg** is a *"skilled adviser"* whose work on water quality and water rights and hazardous waste issues is applauded. He works closely with mining clients, and handles compliance counseling, permitting, legislation and litigation.

Band 2

Bryan Cave LLP

The Firm: The environmental practice of this national firm is making significant inroads into the Arizona market, with commentators noting that *"it seems to be rapidly expanding and performing well."* A team of 17 attorneys is dedicated to environmental and natural resources matters. Litigation and insurance, as well as compliance and regulatory matters, are on the agenda. The natural resources team works closely with mining and industrial clients.

The Lawyers: According to observers, **Lucas Narducci**, head of the environmental client service group, is *"putting this group on the map."* He advises on toxic tort litigation, insurance coverage and air, water and waste regulation counseling and permitting. **Barton Day** transferred to Phoenix from the Washington DC office five years ago. He has steadily built up a loyal client following for his work in the regulated hazardous waste area. His practice involves compliance and enforcement matters under the RCRA and Underground Injection Control programs.

Lewis and Roca

The Firm: With offices in Phoenix and Tucson, this group is admired for the *"incredible depth and breadth of its capabilities."* These offices form a network across the southwest with counterparts in Las Vegas and Albuquerque. The group represents manufacturing entities, government bodies and, in particular, mining companies, in a range of environmental matters.

The Lawyers: Head of the environmental group, **Amy Porter** is renowned throughout the market for her work on air quality and rights. Her clients are drawn from mining and industrial entities, Fortune 500 companies and smaller businesses. Environmental regulation litigation at state and federal levels is a staple part of her practice.

Moyes Storey

The Firm: This boutique Phoenix firm serves clients throughout Arizona and the southwest, across a range of practice areas. **Jay Moyes** is highly regarded by the market for his environmental practice, and particularly his work in water law, in which he is said to be *"the best of the best."* Interviewees also commended **Lee Storey**'s detailed knowledge of water and Indian law issues.

Quarles & Brady Streich Lang LLP

The Firm: This group can draw on the strong loyalties created by the firm's 30-year history of environmental practice in order to serve clients from a range of industries, particularly the hi-tech markets. The group offers a full environmental practice, and is particularly recognized for its air and water quality work.

The Lawyers: Peers admire **Roger Ferland**'s legal acumen and describe him as *"the best-known environment attorney across the board."* Viewed as an air quality specialist, he works primarily with hi-tech clients.

Ryley Carlock & Applewhite

See firm details p.166

The Firm: This firm's environmental practice encompasses water law and regulation and natural resources. One commentator told researchers: *"I don't know one lawyer there that isn't wonderful!"* The team handles all environment regulation and litigation work, and has developed a concerted legislation policy practice that is involved in lobbying government at state and federal levels.

The Lawyers: Managing partner **Michael Brophy** (see p.157) advises on water issues, representing clients in Arizona general stream adjudications and in the development of interstate water banking arrangements. He also advises on the negotiation and implementation of Indian water rights settlements. Brophy possesses *"a gravitas that makes people listen,"* and is hugely respected for his lobbying efforts.

Snell & Wilmer LLP

See firm details p.167

The Firm: This firm advises clients on all aspects of environment and natural resource matters, from due diligence to negotiating Superfund settlements. This concentrated team is *"full of experienced attorneys,"* according to commentators, and serves a diverse array of

150   All quotes in the text are from interviews with clients and competitors.

CHAMBERS USA 2005

clients from both the public and private sectors. Among its clients are hi-tech and manufacturing companies, financial institutions, real estate developers and large electric utilities.

The Lawyers: Sources described **Van Wolf** (see p.163) as the figurehead of the group, and praised his national profile on environmental matters. He practices at federal, state and local levels, and his work focuses on compliance, liability counseling and dispute resolution. Market sources were quick to emphasize his litigation capabilities.

Squire, Sanders & Dempsey LLP

The Firm: The local environmental practice group of this international firm is forging a presence with its work across a range of environmental sectors. Experienced with regulatory bodies and courts at state and federal levels, this group is noted for its work in hazardous waste and water rights. Among its recent clients are MeadWestvaco, GE and the City of Phoenix.

The Lawyers: Christopher Thomas is "*a skilled litigator and a very smart attorney,*" agree sources. He possesses extensive experience in hazardous waste, groundwater contamination and industrial compliance, advising clients from industries such as paper, semiconductor and manufacturing. Water quality, water rights and permitting are key aspects of **Karen Peters'** practice. Sources endorsed her government relations and lobbying prowess. Recent notable successes include providing assistance to a rural Arizona county in the creation of a public-private partnership to develop a state-of-the-art solid waste disposal facility.

Steptoe & Johnson LLP

See firm details p.492

The Firm: This large international firm has a prominent environmental and chemical litigation practice, spanning its Washington DC, Brussels, London and Phoenix offices. The Phoenix office works on a range of issues

including groundwater contamination, surface water discharges, and solid and hazardous waste disposal. It also assists clients in the mining industry with permitting issues.

The Lawyers: James Derouin (see p.158) is leader of the environmental and natural resources group. An experienced and well-respected member of the local legal community, he is "*a talented adviser and an honorable person,*" agreed observers. His recent work has included two Superfund matters, each involving over $100 million in cleanup efforts, and the successful defense of a chemical manufacturer. His practice also includes groundwater and regulatory work.

Other Notable Practitioners

At Withey Anderson & Morris PLC **Robert Anderson** has attracted recommendations for his knowledge of groundwater and endangered species issues.

LITIGATION

GENERAL COMMERCIAL

Arizona
Leading firms
(Litigation: General Commercial)

1	**OSBORN MALEDON PA** *Phoenix*
2	**FENNEMORE CRAIG** *Phoenix*
	LEWIS AND ROCA *Phoenix*
	PERKINS COIE LLP *Phoenix*
	SNELL & WILMER LLP *Phoenix*
3	**GALLAGHER & KENNEDY PA** *Phoenix*
	MARISCAL, WEEKS, MCINTYRE *Phoenix*
	MEYER, HENDRICKS & BIVENS PA *Phoenix*
	QUARLES & BRADY STREICH LANG LLP *Tuscon*
4	**HARALSON, MILLER, PITT & MCANALLY** *Tuscon*
	RUSING & LOPEZ PLLC *Tuscon*
	RYLEY CARLOCK & APPLEWHITE *Phoenix*

Firms are listed alphabetically in each band.

Band 1

Osborn Maledon PA

See firm details p.165

The Firm: Closely focused on litigation, this firm's lawyers are thought by some commentators to be "*out on their own*" in terms of market profile and breadth of coverage. Their commercial work encompasses class actions, white-collar criminal defense, multidistrict litigation and appellate matters. The "*first-rate*" attorneys often work in relatively small teams to defend clients in various industries on matters including antitrust, bankruptcy, environmental claims, insurance and securities.

The Lawyers: "*Combining great depth of intelligence with a great deal of street smarts,*" **William Maledon** (see p.160) handles trial and appellate

cases at both state and federal levels. He is "*world-class,*" said one client: "*He is one of the best civil litigators in the country – professional, poised and very much a presence in the courtroom.*" Maledon's areas of particular expertise include antitrust and trade regulation, securities and sports law. **David Rosenbaum** (see p.161) was described by commentators as "*efficient, smart and persuasive.*" His areas of specialty include employment, securities, intellectual property and technology. **Mark Harrison** (see p.159) is particularly well thought of in the field of professional liability, and a number of attorneys reported that he was the man to whom they would turn should such a problem arise. He is seen not only as an "*outstanding*" lawyer, but a man for whom peers have a great deal of admiration on a personal level. In the sphere of white-collar criminal defense, peers were quick to sing the praises of **Lawrence Hammond** (see p.159). This highly respected trial lawyer is a "*very bright, hard-working*" attorney, whose articulate courtroom presence has won him a strong following.

The Clients: Boeing; Gore; Arizona Public Service and Continental Airlines.

Band 2

Fennemore Craig

See firm details p.164

The Firm: In one of the oldest and largest firms in the southwest, the commercial litigation department extends beyond traditional trial law to alternative dispute resolution and litigation prevention. Areas of activity include appellate

work, bankruptcy, insurance, products liability and securities disputes.

The Lawyers: Kenneth Sherk (see p.162) is a long-standing name in this litigation group, and has extensive experience in business litigation as well as personal injury and products liability. Focusing on insurance and products liability, **Andrew Federhar** (see p.158) is cochair of the practice group. Clients were impressed by his "*responsiveness, efficiency and cost-effectiveness,*" as well as his knowledge of the Phoenix courts. Practicing in a variety of areas, particularly securities litigation, environmental and lender liability issues, **John Everroad** (see p.158) is a new entrant to the table following market commendation. **William Thorpe** (see p.162) also cochairs the group and received strong praise for his products liability work, in which he represents a range of clients including manufacturers of rough terrain forklifts, aerial work platforms, earth-moving equipment, exercise equipment, child restraint seats and various other consumer products. Chair of the firm's litigation practice, **Jordan Green** (see p.158) represents business entities and individuals involved in criminal investigations and prosecutions involving the SEC and the IRS, in addition to internal investigations. Peers applauded him for being "*extremely well-prepared*" and described him as "*a bright man with a wide range of experience.*" Head of the Tucson office, **Bates Butler** (see p.157) focuses on white-collar crime defense and civil and environmental matters. An "*extremely thorough attorney,*" he "*cares about his clients and has huge credibility with the court.*" "*Politically well-connected*" **Lee Stein** (see p.162)

Arizona
Leading individuals
(Litigation: General Commercial)

1 BAIRD Peter *Lewis and Roca*, Phoenix
ECKSTEIN Paul *Perkins Coie*, Phoenix
MALEDON William *Osborn Maledon*, Phoenix

2 BIRNBAUM Gary *Mariscal Weeks*, Phoenix
BIVENS Donald *Meyer Hendricks*, Phoenix
BOUMA John *Snell & Wilmer*, Phoenix
CABOT Howard *Perkins Coie*, Phoenix
MALTZ Gerald *Haralson Miller*, Tucson
SHERK Kenneth *Fennemore Craig*, Phoenix

3 EVERROAD John *Fennemore Craig*, Phoenix
HENDRICKS Jr Ed *Meyer Hendricks*, Phoenix
MEEHAN Michael *Meehan LLP*, Tucson
ROSENBAUM David *Osborn Maledon*, Phoenix
WILLIAMS Jr Lonnie *Quarles & Brady*, Phoenix

4 BEUS Leo *Beus Gilbert*, Scottsdale
CONDO James *Snell & Wilmer*, Phoenix
DANNEMAN Dale *Lewis and Roca*, Phoenix
FEDERHAR Andrew *Fennemore Craig*, Phoenix
HARRISON Mark *Osborn Maledon*, Phoenix
KENNEDY Michael *Gallagher & Kennedy*, Phoenix
MITCHELL Barry *Gallagher & Kennedy*, Phoenix
O'MALLEY Kevin *Gallagher & Kennedy*, Phoenix
RAUCH David *Snell & Wilmer*, Phoenix
RUSING Michael *Rusing & Lopez*, Tucson
THORPE William *Fennemore Craig*, Phoenix

Individuals are listed alphabetically in each band.

is also gaining in prominence for his white-collar criminal defense and environmental law practice.

Lewis and Roca

The Firm: This firm's litigation practice is recognized for its ability to conduct complex commercial litigation involving a variety of issues and across a number of jurisdictions. The firm fields a team of attorneys seasoned in both state and federal trials, and in a range of commercial litigation, insurance and tort defense, appellate and white-collar crime work.

The Lawyers: **Peter Baird** boasts an impressive list of appearances at the Supreme Court, the Seventh and Ninth Circuits Courts of Appeals and all Arizona appellate courts. The past year has seen him litigate bankruptcy cases and the gamut of commercial litigation, including bad faith, antitrust and corporate transaction disputes. Widely seen as *"an excellent lawyer,"* **Scott Bales** handles appellate work and public law litigation, recently representing the Governor of Arizona over the state budget, and the State of Arizona in a class action concerning the operation of its retirement system. **Dale Danneman** is a pragmatic attorney who combines white-collar criminal matters with broader civil litigation. Cochair of the firm's white-collar and corporate criminal defense group, **James Belanger** is held in high regard. Clients and peers rated his versatility and described him as

"responsive, smart and down-to-earth."
The Clients: Clients include the State of Arizona, Royal Insurance, CIT Group and a host of multinational, national and local companies.

Perkins Coie LLP

The Firm: Since merging with national player Perkins Coie in July 2004, the Phoenix firm Brown & Bain has been bolstered by new nationwide capability. In addition to traditional strengths in commercial, IP and hi-tech litigation, the team of about 50 attorneys is rated for its products liability, malpractice and securities work.

The Lawyers: **Paul Eckstein** has developed a practice that encompasses appellate, media law, gaming and antitrust matters. Having established a reputation as a well-respected litigator he has now moved into mediation and arbitration. Invariably described as *"highly capable"* and *"one of the best,"* he has earned respect from clients and competitors alike. **Howard Cabot**'s expertise lies in intellectual property, class-action defense and complex commercial litigation.
The Clients: Clients include Honda, Honeywell, IBM and other Fortune 500 companies.

Snell & Wilmer LLP

See firm details p.167
The Firm: One of the largest full-service firms in the southwest, the litigation department provides great depth and experience across the board, including antitrust, class actions, identity theft and professional malpractice. Its products liability team is recognized for its high-profile work in the automobile industry. Interviewees invariably described the firm as *"talented and experienced,"* particularly in handling large-scale litigation, and pointed to the large number of good attorneys within the group.
The Lawyers: **John Bouma** (see p.157), who heads the group, has had a full year, with notable cases in antitrust, and professional and products liability. Colleagues admired his ability to take on and manage mammoth cases. **James Condo** (see p.157) is a skilled trial lawyer whose core strength lies in products liability litigation. **David Rauch** (see p.161) garnered praise as a *"wonderful, fine young lawyer,"* with a practice focusing on general commercial cases and media law.
The Clients: The firm's roster of big-name corporate clients, many of them Fortune 500 companies, attests to its quality of service.

Band 3

Gallagher & Kennedy PA

The Firm: This firm, founded in 1978, continues to serve national and local businesses at trial in state and federal courts. It has substantial complex litigation experience in all areas, including construction, professional malpractice and public liability. With *"top-notch litigators,*

and growing," it serves as national coordinating counsel for toxic tort litigation for a Fortune 500 corporation.
The Lawyers: Cofounder **Michael Kennedy** practices in general commercial litigation, and was viewed as a well-respected member of the Arizona legal community. Rivals described him as *"a trusted figure at the Bar."* There are those who *"think the world"* of litigation cochair **Kevin O'Malley**. His clients include the Phoenix Home Builders Association and a software development company. Much of **Tom Henze**'s white-collar defense work arises from allegations across most industries including utilities' regulations, trademark violations, Federal Aviation Administration regulations and corporate fraud. Interviewees described him as *"an excellent trial lawyer,"* skilled in handling the business end of trials *"where the rubber meets the road."* **Barry Mitchell** is *"a splendid lawyer,"* whose defense of individuals and corporations facing criminal investigations is combined with advice on compliance programs for companies.

Mariscal, Weeks, McIntyre & Friedlander PA

The Firm: Commercial and real estate cases are at the core of the litigation practice of this well-respected local firm. The practice has a sterling reputation in the real estate sector and handles all manner of disputes, including escrow liability, eminent domain and title insurance. The litigation team consists of approximately 30 attorneys, mostly partners, and was described by competitors as *"focused on the speedy resolution of disputes."*
The Lawyers: Managing partner **Gary Birnbaum** has a broad, general commercial litigation practice. Clients and peers alike were quick to stress this attorney's intellect, with rivals describing him as a *"smart, top-notch litigator."* Echoing their sentiments, one claimed he'd turn to Birnbaum *"in a heartbeat."*
The Clients: U-Haul International, Vestar, First American Title Insurance Company and a full roster of banks and real estate-related organizations and enterprises.

Meyer, Hendricks & Bivens PA

The Firm: This firm focuses almost exclusively on commercial litigation, including insurance defense and intellectual property cases. Rivals admire its attorneys' ability to achieve big-firm results with boutique-sized resources.
The Lawyers: **Don Bivens** covers all areas of commercial litigation and has built a niche in hi-tech and intellectual property cases. His trial skills and understanding of the law garnered high praise from peers, who described him as *"one of the best-prepared and most articulate adversaries."* **Ed Hendricks** impresses with his broad experience of general commercial disputes.

152   All quotes in the text are from interviews with clients and competitors.

CHAMBERS USA 2005

Arizona
Leading firms (Litigation: White-Collar Crime & Government Investigations)

1. **FENNEMORE CRAIG** *Phoenix*
2. **GALLAGHER & KENNEDY PA** *Phoenix*
   LEWIS AND ROCA *Phoenix*
   OSBORN MALEDON PA *Phoenix*
   QUARLES & BRADY STREICH LANG LLP *Phoenix*
3. **KARP, HEURLIN & WEISS PC** *Tucson*
   PICCARRETA & DAVIS PC *Tucson*

Leading individuals (Litigation: White-Collar Crime & Government Investigations)

1. **GREEN Jordan** *Fennemore Craig, Phoenix*
   HAMMOND Lawrence *Osborn Maledon, Phoenix*
   HENZE Tom *Gallagher & Kennedy, Phoenix*
2. **BELANGER James** *Lewis and Roca, Phoenix*
   BUTLER III A Bates *Fennemore Craig, Tucson*
   PICCARRETA Michael *Piccarreta & Davis, Tucson*
3. **BUDOFF Marc** *Budoff & Ross, Phoenix*
   KIMERER Mike *Kimerer & Derrick, Phoenix*
   NOVAK Edward *Quarles & Brady, Phoenix*
   PETTI Fred *Lewis & Roca, Phoenix*
   STEIN Lee *Fennemore Craig, Phoenix*
   WEISS Stephen *Karp Heurlin, Tucson*

Leading individuals
(Litigation: Appellate)

1. **BALES Scott** *Lewis and Roca, Phoenix*

Firms and individuals are listed alphabetically in each band.

Quarles & Brady Streich Lang LLP

The Firm: This firm, with offices in Phoenix and Tucson, fields an impressive team of attorneys and services clients of all sizes on a range of commercial litigation including antitrust, insurance and products liability.

The Lawyers: A recent recruit from Snell & Wilmer, **Lonnie Williams** focuses on employment, tort, banking and real estate disputes. Although perhaps more closely associated with employment law disputes, his mastery of the courtroom has ensured that Williams is a popular choice for any commercial dispute. **Ed Novak** specializes in white-collar crime, and has extensive jury and appellate experience in criminal defense matters. Peers highlighted his ability to handle large cases and commended his thorough knowledge of the local legal system.

Band 4

Haralson, Miller, Pitt & McAnally PLC

The Firm: Handling commercial litigation as well as personal injury and malpractice suits, this small but talented team has built a fine reputation in Tucson.

The Lawyers: **Gerald Maltz** was described as "*superb*" by attorneys who had appeared against him.

Rusing & Lopez PLLC

The Firm: This Tucson firm enjoys a healthy reputation in commercial litigation, serving local and some international clients in various areas, particularly employment, business torts,

real estate, contract disputes, trade secrets and construction matters.

The Lawyers: Cofounder **Michael Rusing** is, according to peers, "*a dedicated lawyer.*" He handles a wide range of litigation matters including construction, tort and real estate.

Ryley Carlock & Applewhite
See firm details p.166

The Firm: A new entry to the tables, this firm is a real presence in the Arizona market. Its commercial litigation clients come from the banking, oil, mining and real estate sectors.

Other Notable Practitioners

Cofounder of Tucson firm Piccarreta & Davis PC **Michael Piccarreta** has forged a strong presence in the Arizona community for his corporate criminal defense work. Colleagues admired his ability to handle challenging cases. **Michael Meehan**'s robust performances in court are not to every commentator's liking, but there is no question as to his effective handling of complex disputes. Market sources endorsed the trial skills of **Leo Beus** of Beus Gilbert PLLC, particularly in the field of accounting malpractice. **Marc Budoff** of Budoff & Ross PC was singled out for his "*practical and efficient*" handling of white-collar criminal matters. At Kimerer & Derrick, P.C. **Mike Kimerer** practices in criminal and white-collar crime litigation, and is well respected among interviewees who said that "*his integrity is valued.*" At Karp, Heurlin & Weiss PC, **Stephen Weiss** was reported to be a "*good, bright lawyer*" who handles a wide variety of criminal defense matters at this Tucson firm.

REAL ESTATE

Arizona
Leading firms (Real Estate)

1. **MARISCAL, WEEKS, MCINTYRE** *Phoenix*
2. **BRYAN CAVE LLP** *Phoenix*
   FENNEMORE CRAIG *Phoenix*
   GALLAGHER & KENNEDY PA *Phoenix*
   SNELL & WILMER LLP *Phoenix*
3. **QUARLES & BRADY STREICH LANG LLP** *Phoenix*
   SQUIRE, SANDERS & DEMPSEY LLP *Phoenix*
   STOREY & BURNHAM PLC *Phoenix*
4. **LEWIS AND ROCA** *Phoenix*
   OSBORN MALEDON PA *Phoenix*
   PERKINS COIE LLP *Phoenix*
   SACKS TIERNEY PA *Scottsdale*

Firms and individuals are listed alphabetically in each band.

Band 1

Mariscal, Weeks, McIntyre & Friedlander PA

The Firm: Market sources commended this firm as "*the best for its broad coverage of real estate.*" The depth of skill and expertise housed in this practice has ensured its prominence and, as the cornerstone of the firm, its commitment to the market is never in doubt. A team of 20 attorneys represents an enviable portfolio of clients including developers, homeowner associations and contractors. Acquisitions, sale and leasebacks, mortgage lending and ground lease transactions all form part of the workload here.

The Lawyers: **David Lansky** is a "*terrific attorney,*" whose retail development expertise has impressed commentators to the extent that they proclaim: "*There is nobody better.*" **Fred Fathe** is "*a strong technical lawyer,*" whose broad commercial practice incorporates a range of real

estate financing transactions. Sources also admired "*tough attorney*" **Peter Winkler** for his technical abilities across a range of real estate finance and development transactions.

The Clients: Vestar Development and Levine Investments feature on the firm's client list.

Band 2

Bryan Cave LLP

The Firm: The attorneys fielded by this Phoenix-based practice have won the loyalty of clients through their "*detailed and professional advice.*" The practice continues to secure prominence with its work on the development, purchase and sale of retail, commercial and residential projects. Interviewees report that the group "*does a fine job and provides sensible advice.*" The group serves clients such as major home builders and developers.

The Lawyers: Sources applauded **Steven**

Leading individuals (Real Estate)
1 LANSKY David *Mariscal Weeks*, Phoenix
MAST Gregory *Gallagher & Kennedy*, Phoenix
POKORSKI Jody *Snell & Wilmer*, Phoenix
2 FATHE Fred *Mariscal Weeks*, Phoenix
HALLER Diane *Quarles & Brady*, Phoenix
LISKER Steven *Bryan Cave*, Phoenix
MAY Bruce *Jennings Strouss*, Phoenix
STOREY Lesa *Storey & Burnham*, Phoenix
VAN WINKLE Kenneth *Lewis and Roca*, Phoenix
3 BISKIND Neil *Biskind Hunt*, Phoenix
BROADFOOT Alexander *Gallagher*, Phoenix
KRAMER Jay *Fennemore Craig*, Phoenix
ROBINSON Robert *Fennemore Craig*, Phoenix
STOKES Randall *Lewis and Roca*, Phoenix
WINKLER Peter *Mariscal Weeks*, Phoenix
WRIGHT Joyce *Snell & Wilmer*, Phoenix
4 BATES Robert *Snell & Wilmer*, Phoenix
BURNHAM Beckey *Storey & Burnham*, Phoenix
HENDERSON Scott *Squire Sanders*, Phoenix
HINK John *Ryley Carlock*, Phoenix
OSBORN II Jones *Osborn Maledon*, Phoenix
SACKS Seymour *Sacks Tierney*, Scottsdale
SORENSON Derek *Bryan Cave*, Phoenix
WILEY Jay *Snell & Wilmer*, Phoenix
Firms and individuals are listed alphabetically in each band.

Lisker for his residential home-building expertise in a practice that also encompasses commercial development. He is "*a great lawyer and a pleasure to deal with.*" **Derek Sorenson's** practice concentrates on a range of commercial real estate transactions. Clients were impressed with his "*timely service and attention to detail.*"

The Clients: Clients include Westfund LLC, Gateway American Properties and Harris Bank.

Fennemore Craig

See firm details p.164

The Firm: The firm fields the largest real estate team in the Southwest, with 26 attorneys dedicated to real estate. Competitors endorsed its "*good all-round practice and high-caliber attorneys.*" Developers and large landowners such as public utilities are all found among the firm's clients. The team also advises mining companies in all real estate transactions involving the Arizona State Land Department, the Arizona Department of Real Estate and the Indian nations.

The Lawyers: Market commentators endorsed **Robert Robinson** (see p.161) for his real estate finance practice, in which he represents both lenders and borrowers, and his work on the acquisition and development of land. **Jay Kramer** (see p.160) is "*a force to be reckoned with*" and his distinctive style combined with his real estate transactional skills keeps clients – such as home builders and multifamily developers – very satisfied.

Gallagher & Kennedy PA

The Firm: This firm continues to forge a presence in the local market, representing landowners, developers and home builders in all real estate development and finance matters. Commentators described the team of 14 attorneys as "*sharp, dedicated and very experienced.*" In a testament to its success in establishing a powerful client base, the team acts for four of the largest home builders in Arizona.

The Lawyers: **Gregory Mast** is well-respected by clients and peers alike. He represents home builders and developers on commercial, residential and retail projects. Clients say that he is so dedicated that they consider him "*a close member of our team,*" while competitors note that he is "*very knowledgeable and a true gentleman.*" **Sandy Broadfoot** has "*hit a lot of high marks*" in his practice of late. Development, acquisitions, and leasing feature in his practice, and he represents the regional office of one of the nation's largest developers.

The Clients: Clients include Arizona Cardinals, Opus West and the Pederson Group.

Snell & Wilmer LLP

See firm details p.167

The Firm: A recognized player in the busy Arizona market, this firm provides a team of 34 attorneys that works on all real estate transactions. Its wide-ranging expertise has ensured a loyal following among developer, builder and investor clients of all sizes. Interviewees were happy to tell us that this firm "*does a fine job, fulfills all of our needs and deserves recognition*" for its large real estate and commercial finance practice.

The Lawyers: **Jody Pokorski** (see p.161) "*leaves no stone unturned*" and has a healthy transactional practice including acquisition and leasing work for builders, developers and master-planned communities. Commentators reported that she is "*excellent at reaching the goal line.*" **Joyce Wright** (see p.163) is involved in all areas of real estate development, including master-planned, resort and golf course developments. Rivals told us that she is "*technically skilled.*" A "*smart, thorough and careful attorney,*" **Jay Wiley** (see p.162) has built up a following among sellers, investors, landlords and tenants. **Robert Bates** (see p.156) is a certified real estate law specialist and was recommended for his work in master-planning strategy, acquisitions and sales of large tracts of undeveloped property.

Quarles & Brady Streich Lang LLP

The Firm: With offices in Phoenix and Tucson, this firm offers a full transactional service to a predominantly commercial clientele and is involved in single and multifamily homes, office, retail and industrial projects. Interviewees told researchers this firm "*does a fine job,*" particularly in the financing area. The firm this year faced the departure of key team member Bruce May, who joined the firm of Jennings, Strouss & Salmon PLC. Commentators await the impact of this move on the team.

The Lawyers: **Diane Haller** is seen as the "*quiet achiever*" at this firm. She represents an enviable roster of clients on the acquisition, disposition, sale, leaseback and financing of developments. Her practice crosses both commercial and residential developments as well as leisure facilities.

Squire, Sanders & Dempsey LLP

The Firm: This large international firm is "*highly skilled across the board*" for real estate in Arizona. Sources agree that the team has shown a commitment to the local market as well as assisting clients on developments across the region. The firm has a long history of representing the hospitality industry worldwide.

The Lawyers: **Scott Henderson** has extensive experience in development, construction, leasing and management of multifamily and master-planned communities, commercial and leisure projects. Clients report that they enjoy his personable style.

Storey & Burnham PLC

The Firm: This boutique real estate firm climbs the table this year due to unequivocal praise from commentators, who admire its "*efficient and focused approach.*" Rivals said they would happily refer a client to this firm, which handles all commercial real estate matters.

The Lawyers: **Lesa Storey** garnered praise from competitors and clients for her "*ability to get deals done.*" She is "*an absolute pleasure to deal with*" and highly respected for her drafting skills. "*Incredibly bright*" **Beckey Burnham** is respected for her project management skills.

Lewis and Roca

The Firm: This firm's real estate practice has a national reach but a clear focus on the Southwest. Its breadth and experience of managing large projects have ensured an efficient service for clients across the USA. A team of 25 has a keen focus on tenant leasing and franchise financing as part of a broader real estate practice. Clients are drawn from the hospitality industry, institutional investors and developers.

The Lawyers: Managing partner **Kenneth Van Winkle** is a "*smart adviser*" experienced in real property acquisitions and dispositions, as well as leasing and financing issues. **Randall Stokes** is one of the "*top-notch development attorneys in town,*" according to observers. He advises on planned mixed-use communities, condominiums and shopping centers.

The Clients: Clients include America West Airlines, Sun America and Prudential.

Osborn Maledon PA

See firm details p.165

The Firm: While the traditional mainstays of this practice reside in its corporate and litigation departments, the real estate practice maintains a respected foothold in the market. It undertakes development, financing, zoning and land use regulations. Attorneys here are able to advise on both public and Indian lands.

The Lawyers: Firm president **Jones Osborn** (see p.160) incorporates real estate into a much broader corporate and commercial law practice. A transactional attorney, he has a wealth of experience in the Arizona market and is said to be "*an extremely dedicated attorney.*"

The Clients: Wells Fargo and DeRito Partners are examples of the firm's client base.

Perkins Coie LLP

The Firm: The Phoenix office of this newly merged firm (formerly Brown & Bain) has traditionally had its roots in commercial litigation. Commentators are keen to see how the real estate practice, now bolstered by national capabilities, will grow. Early signs are promising as the group wins respect for its work on development issues, serving clients such as home builders, community developers and holders of significant tracts of land.

The Lawyers: Ronald Lowe is a key member of this real estate group.

Sacks Tierney PA

The Firm: This Scottsdale-based firm continues to impress with a real estate practice that commentators agree "*punches well above its weight.*" The comparatively small team takes on acquisitions and dispositions of real property, title issues and environmental and zoning work.

The Lawyers: **Seymour Sacks**, "*a great negotiator,*" is praised for his real estate and healthcare work. He is a popular feature in the legal community, winning a following with his "*highly personable manner*" and astute legal knowledge.

Other Notable Practitioners

In early 2004, **Bruce May** moved his respected real estate practice to Jennings Strouss & Salmon PLC. His clients include Arizona State University and Baron Collier. While market sources commend May's "*energy, efficiency and deep knowledge of the law,*" they await his success in developing the practice at this firm. **Neil Biskind** of Biskind, Hunt & Taylor PLC attracted high praise from competitors, who told researchers they would not hesitate to refer clients to him. Noted for his real estate and development work, he is "*focused on getting the job done right.*" When it comes to real estate matters, **John Hink** (see p.159) at Ryley Carlock & Applewhite "*can stand up to anyone and advise on any issue*" reported commentators. Among his clients are home builders, whom he advises on the establishment of homeowner associations.

REAL ESTATE

ZONING/LAND USE

Arizona
Leading firms
(Real Estate: Zoning/Land Use)

1. BEUS GILBERT PLLC *Scottsdale*
   GAMMAGE & BURNHAM, PLC *Phoenix*
2. BRYAN CAVE LLP *Phoenix*
   BURCH & CRACCHIOLO *Phoenix*
   EARL, CURLEY & LAGARDE, PC *Phoenix*
   FENNEMORE CRAIG *Phoenix*
   GALLAGHER & KENNEDY PA *Phoenix*
   LEWIS AND ROCA *Tucson*
   SNELL & WILMER LLP *Phoenix*
   WITHEY ANDERSON & MORRIS PLC *Phoenix*

Leading individuals
(Real Estate: Zoning/Land Use)

1. BERRY John *Beus Gilbert*, Scottsdale
   GAMMAGE Grady *Gammage & Burnham*, Phoenix
   GILBERT Paul *Beus Gilbert*, Scottsdale
2. ANDERSON Stephen *Gammage & Burnham*, Phoenix
   BANGS Frank *Lewis and Roca*, Tucson
   BULL Edwin *Burch & Cracchiolo*, Phoenix
   EARL Stephen *Earl Curley*, Phoenix
   HIRSCH Stephen *Bryan Cave*, Phoenix
   KERRICK Robert *Gallagher & Kennedy*, Phoenix
   LAZARUS Larry *Lazarus & Associates*, Phoenix
   PHALEN Michael *Fennemore Craig*, Phoenix
   SCHUBART Lawrence *Stubbs & Schubart*, Phoenix
   SIMON Marc *Snell & Wilmer*, Phoenix
   TAYLOR Karrin *Biskind Hunt*, Phoenix
   WITHEY Michael *Withey Anderson*, Phoenix

Firms and individuals are listed alphabetically in each band.

Band 1

Beus Gilbert PLLC

The Firm: This firm has established itself as a major player in Arizona for zoning and land use matters. Attorneys advise on mixed-use, retail, residential and office developments. The firm is "*the best there is.*" Commentators admire this comparatively small team for the volume of work it handles.

The Lawyers: Clients endorsed **John Berry** as "*very direct and very honest, right from the beginning.*" He displays his technical prowess on all types of development projects, most notably obtaining approval for the Scottsdale Waterfront Project, which will involve the construction of the two tallest buildings in downtown Scottsdale. The well-connected and hugely knowledgeable **Paul Gilbert** is "*one of the best zoning attorneys in the state.*" Rivals highlighted his presentation skills and extensive experience in the Arizona real estate market.

The Clients: Clients include Starwood Capital Group, Banner Hospital and Starpointe Properties.

Gammage & Burnham, PLC

The Firm: Sources respect "*the phenomenal strength and depth*" of this firm's zoning and land use practice. The firm represents property owners and developers on real estate projects, as well as homeowners and community associations concerned about such proposals. The group specializes in projects involving lands owned by the Arizona State Land Department.

The Lawyers: Founding partner **Grady Gammage** has cultivated an influential practice, built on his "*great, in-depth knowledge of nearly everything,*" acknowledged observers. Alongside his fee-earning, Gammage is an adjunct professor at Arizona State University and the College of Law. **Stephen Anderson** has worked on a wide range of projects throughout the state, including major resort, commercial and residential projects.

Band 2

Bryan Cave LLP

The Firm: The team of five specialist attorneys concentrates on providing litigation support in federal and state courts as well as administrative agencies such as the Department of Real Estate and the Registrar of Contractors. The practice predominantly represents landowners involved in zoning, land use and title matters.

The Lawyers: **Stephen Hirsch** heads up the litigation group in Phoenix, and specializes in valuation, eminent domain and construction litigation. An experienced litigator, he is often called upon for his land use knowledge by the firm's existing real estate clients.

The Clients: ExxonMobil, Sempra Energy (San Diego), Arizona Water Company and a major international retailer feature on the client roster.

All quotes in the text are from interviews with clients and competitors.

Burch & Cracchiolo

The Firm: **Edwin Bull**, president of Burch & Cracchiolo, has extensive experience in all land use matters arising from projects of all sizes for clients such as commercial developers, home builders and landowners. He possesses *"immense credibility and knowledge of zoning laws"* and is admired for his *"willingness to dig into the technicalities and out-work anyone."*

Earl, Curley & Lagarde, PC

The Firm: Much of the profile belonging to this niche land use firm rests with its leading light **Stephen Earl**. He is, according to rivals, *"absolutely the best at zoning and site plan approvals."* Clients saluted him for his extensive experience and calm demeanor, telling researchers: *"He is right at the top, probably the best."*

Fennemore Craig

See firm details p.164
The Firm: The Phoenix office of this full-service firm is home to a niche land use practice. Attorneys here are well-equipped to advise developer clients in their negotiations with cities and councils in order to gain access to utilities. **The Lawyers:** **Michael Phalen** (see p.161) focuses on land use entitlements, zoning, condemnation and governmental relations. He has been involved in developing the state trust land reform proposal, representing a real estate industry group. Clients, who include master-planned community developers, commercial developers and utilities, praise him for his excellent relationships with relevant government departments.

Gallagher & Kennedy PA

The Firm: This group of six dedicated land use attorneys covers the gamut of land use matters, including zoning, as part of its full-service real estate practice. Among recent highlights, the firm advised on the development of the Glendale multipurpose stadium project and the Scottsdale Waterfront project.
The Lawyers: **Robert Kerrick** is *"a senior, respected condemnation lawyer,"* well versed in real estate valuation litigation with an emphasis on eminent domain. Recent matters include representing the City of Phoenix in the acquisition and condemnation of approximately 20 parcels of land for construction of the America West Arena, a 20,000-seat arena in downtown Phoenix.
The Clients: Bank One Ballpark; Valley Partnership; Diamond Ventures and SunCor Development.

Lewis and Roca

The Firm: The Tucson office of this firm serves clients in all aspects of land use and zoning, as well as providing finance and environmental advice. Clients report that this firm *"really goes out of its way"* and has *"excellent relationships with city government and in the business community that are very helpful."*
The Lawyers: Clients appreciate **Frank Bangs** for his ability to *"understand all the issues"* and they agree that he is *"excellent at explaining the complexities in lay terms."* His broad land use practice features experience in state and local government legislation, administrative law and related litigation.
The Clients: Clients include Town West Realty, Fannie Mae and Omni Hotels.

Snell & Wilmer LLP

See firm details p.167
The Firm: The Phoenix office of this firm forms part of one of the largest zoning and land use practices in the Western region, representing landowners, developers and builders. Clients include Fortune 100 and 500 companies, particularly those focused on the energy, resort and broadcasting sectors.
The Lawyers: Interviewees commended **Marc Simon** (see p.162) for his wealth of technical knowledge and his sound judgment on matters relating to permitting and land use as well as title insurance and construction law.

Withey Anderson & Morris PLC

The Firm: This practice is best known for its work in land use and zoning, environmental law and water and natural resources issues. Its client base comprises owners, developers and government bodies. Competitors admire **Mike Withey** for his tenacious style, telling researchers he *"really goes after his zoning cases"* and *"is a lot of fun"* to work with.

Other Notable Practitioners

Karrin Taylor of Biskind, Hunt & Taylor PLC was described to researchers as a specialist, whose knowledge and personality have won a loyal client following. At Tucson firm Stubbs & Schubart, **Lawrence Schubart** was noted for his eminent domain and condemnation work. **Larry Lazarus** of Lazarus & Associates is *"one of the deans of the zoning community."* He has many years of experience and is lauded for his local market knowledge.

Leaders in Arizona

ANDERSON, Robert
Withey Anderson & Morris P.L.C.,
Phoenix 602 230 0600
Recommended in Environment

ANDERSON, Stephen
Gammage & Burnham, P.L.C., Phoenix
602 256 0566
Recommended in Real Estate

BAIRD, Peter
Lewis and Roca, Phoenix
602 262 5311
Recommended in Litigation

BALES, Scott
Lewis and Roca, Phoenix
602 262 5311
Recommended in Litigation

BANGS, Frank
Lewis and Roca, Tucson
520 622 2090
Recommended in Real Estate

BARR, Daniel
Perkins Coie LLP, Phoenix
602 351 8000
Recommended in Employment

BATES, Robert
Snell & Wilmer LLP, Phoenix
602 382 6263
bbates@swlaw.com
Recommended in Real Estate
Practice Areas: A certified Arizona real estate law specialist engaged in all areas of real estate practice, including municipal development agreements; master planning strategy; acquisitions and sales of large tracts of undeveloped property; sale leaseback transactions; development, financing and leasing of shopping centers, office buildings and industrial, warehouse and office parks; representation of major resort hotels and international clients regarding real estate.
Prof. Memberships: Admitted to practice in Arizona and Colorado. Memberships include the State Bar of Arizona, the American Bar Association, and the Maricopa County Bar Association. Is also a Founding Fellow of the Arizona Bar Foundation.

BELANGER, James
Lewis and Roca, Phoenix
602 262 5311
Recommended in Litigation

BERMAN, Michael
Perkins Coie LLP, Phoenix
602 351 8000
Recommended in Employment

BERRY, Charles
Titus, Brueckner & Berry PC,
Scottsdale 480 483 9600
Recommended in Corporate/M&A

BERRY, John
Beus Gilbert PLLC, Scottsdale
480 429 3000
Recommended in Real Estate

BEUS, Leo
Beus Gilbert PLLC, Scottsdale
480 429 3000
Recommended in Litigation

BIRNBAUM, Gary
Mariscal, Weeks, McIntyre & Friedlander PA, Phoenix 602 285 5000
Recommended in Litigation

BISKIND, Neil
Biskind, Hunt & Taylor plc, Phoenix
602 955 3452
Recommended in Real Estate

BIVENS, Donald
Meyer, Hendricks & Bivens PA, Phoenix
602 604 2200
Recommended in Litigation

BOUMA, John J
Snell & Wilmer LLP, Phoenix
602 382 6216
jbouma@swlaw.com
Recommended in Litigation
Practice Areas: Practice concentrated in complex commercial litigation, including antitrust, commercial and business torts, financial institutions, professional malpractice defense and alternative dispute resolution.
Prof. Memberships: Admitted in Arizona, Iowa, Wisconsin, US Supreme Court; US Court of Appeals, Ninth, Tenth and District of Columbia Circuits. Memberships include American College of Trial Lawyers, Fellow; American Bar Association-Board of Governors (1998-2001), House of Delegates (1989-present); Attorneys' Liability Assurance Society (ALAS), Board of Directors (1986-present), Chairman (2002-04); State Bar of Arizona, President (1983-84); National Conference of Bar Presidents, President (1989-90); Maricopa County Bar Association, President (1977-78); Phoenix Association of Defense Counsel, President (1970-71).

BROADFOOT, Alexander
Gallagher & Kennedy PA, Phoenix
602 530 8000
Recommended in Real Estate

BROCKELMAN, Kent
Brockelman Fatica PLC, Tempe
480 731 9200
Recommended in Employment

BROPHY, James E
Ryley Carlock & Applewhite, Phoenix
602 440 4807
jbrophy@rcalaw.com
Recommended in Corporate/M&A
Practice Areas: James E Brophy has practiced as an attorney with Ryley Carlock & Applewhite since 1974, primarily in the areas of business transactions, securities, mergers and acquisitions, insurance and banking regulation, and related tax and fiduciary matters. Mr Brophy has experience in public and private securities offerings, preparation of periodic securities reports, including Forms 10-K, 10-Q and proxy solicitations. In addition, Mr Brophy has advised boards of directors concerning their fiduciary and legal obligations, including Sarbanes-Oxley compliance and executive compensation programs. Mr Brophy was the lead counsel in Trans City Life Insurance Co. v Commissioner, 106 T.C. 274 (1966), a seminal case in which the taxpayer prevailed, involving the Internal Revenue Service's application of Section 845(b) of the Internal Revenue Code to disregard reinsurance agreements.
Prof. Memberships: Mr Brophy is a Member of the American Bar Association, the Arizona State Bar, and the Tax and Securities Sections of the Arizona State Bar. Mr Brophy is past-president and a director of the Men's Arts Council

of the Phoenix Art Museum, a founder and past director of the Phoenix Chapter of the Western Pension Conference, a past director of the Phoenix Tax Workshop, a member of the Board of Directors and the Chairperson of the Finance and Human Relations Committee of The Foundation for Senior Living, and a member of the Executive Committee of Ryley Carlock & Applewhite.
Publications: Mr Brophy has lectured at various programs for the Arizona State Bar, including serving as an instructor for the State Bar's Professionalism course. Mr Brophy's publications include 'Securities Aspects of Real Estate Syndication, Real Estate Syndication Syllabus, Realty Seminar Institution'; 'Selected Tax Aspects of Real Estate Transactions'; 'Fiduciary Responsibility Under ERISA - An Update'; 'Plan Terminations and Conversions under ERISA'; the 'Sarbanes-Oxley Act of 2002 and Intellectual Property'; and 'Problems with Stock Option Exercises'.
Personal: BA, cum laude, University of Arizona (1968); JD magna cum laude, Arizona State University (1974); Articles Editor, Arizona State Law Journal, (1974).

BROPHY, Michael J
Ryley Carlock & Applewhite, Phoenix
602 440 4811
mbrophy@rcalaw.com
Recommended in Environment
Practice Areas: Natural resources, with an emphasis on water rights. Extensive experience in strategic water rights planning, major water rights acquisitions and dispositions, and the negotiated or litigated resolution of federal, state and local water rights disputes in the Southwest.
Prof. Memberships: Admitted to practice in Arizona in 1977. Admitted to practice before United States District Court for the District of Arizona (1977); United States Court of Appeals for the Ninth Circuit (1977); and the United States Supreme Court (1983). Past Chairman of the Western States Water Council.
Career: Joined Ryley Carlock & Applewhite in 1977. Became a shareholder in 1982 and has served on the firm's Management Committee and as the firm's Managing Shareholder.
Publications: Editor in chief, Arizona State University Law Journal: 'Statutes of Limitations in Civil Rights Litigation.' Numerous publications on water rights for CLE programs.
Personal: Born on May 8, 1949. BA (magna cum laude), University of Arizona (1971). JD (with distinction), Arizona State University (1977). Phi Beta Kappa.

BUDOFF, Marc
Budoff & Ross, P.C., Phoenix
602 253 9110
Recommended in Litigation

BULL, Edwin
Burch & Cracchiolo, Phoenix
602 234 9913
Recommended in Real Estate

BURNHAM, Beckey
Storey & Burnham PLC, Phoenix
602 468 0111
Recommended in Real Estate

BUTLER III, A Bates
Fennemore Craig, Tucson
520 879 6804
bbutler@fclaw.com
Recommended in Litigation
Practice Areas: White collar criminal defense; civil litigation.
Prof. Memberships: Arizona Attorneys for Criminal Justice, National Association of Former US Attorneys, National Association of Criminal Defense Lawyers, Trial Lawyers for Public Justice.
Career: Former county prosecutor and US Attorney for Arizona, and 24 years as a defense attorney. Participated in numerous multi-party complex trials. Conducts internal corporate investigations. Recently successfully defended physician charged with illegally prescribing controlled substances. Representative clients include defense contractors, accountants, economists, small businesses and business leaders.
Personal: JD, National Law Center, George Washington University, 1969; BA, Trinity University, 1966; 'Best Lawyers in America'; Rated 'AV', 'Martindale-Hubbell'.

CABOT, Howard
Perkins Coie LLP, Phoenix
602 351 8000
Recommended in Litigation

CASTER, Lauren
Fennemore Craig, Phoenix
602 916 5367
lcaster@fclaw.com
Recommended in Environment
Practice Areas: Environmental; natural resources; water.
Prof. Memberships: Vice-Chair, Section of Environment, Energy, and Resources, American Bar Association.
Career: Practices in the area of water rights. Represents clients in the general stream adjudications in Arizona courts, and in interstate stream conflicts and other water right litigation pending in federal courts. Also advises clients on water matters generally.
Personal: JD, with distinction, Order of the Coif, University of Nebraska, 1976; BA, University of Nebraska, 1973; 'Best Lawyers in America'; Rated 'AV', 'Martindale-Hubbell'.

CLEES, Joseph
Bryan Cave LLP, Phoenix
602 364 7000
Recommended in Employment

COHEN, Jon
Snell & Wilmer LLP, Phoenix
602 382 6247
jcohen@swlaw.com
Recommended in Corporate/M&A
Practice Areas: General corporate practice concentrated in the area of securities, including a large number of public offerings and mergers and acquisitions.
Prof. Memberships: Admitted to practice in Arizona. Memberships include the State Bar of Arizona and the American Bar Association. Board of Directors Memberships include: the Arizona Science Center, the Arizona Technology Council, Lincoln Laser Company, and Vika Corporation.

COHEN, Richard
Lewis and Roca, Phoenix
602 262 5311
Recommended in Employment

CONDO, James
Snell & Wilmer LLP, Phoenix
602 382 6353
jcondo@swlaw.com
Recommended in Litigation
Practice Areas: Trial practice concentrated in complex and class action business and product liability litigation.
Prof. Memberships: State Bar of Arizona; Fellow, Arizona Bar Foundation; Maricopa County Bar Association; American Bar Association; Defense Research Institute; Former Judge Pro Tempore, Arizona Court of Appeals.

CRABB, Joseph
Quarles & Brady Streich Lang LLP, Phoenix 602 229 5200
Recommended in Corporate/M&A

CURRY, Stanton
Gallagher & Kennedy PA, Phoenix
602 530 8000
Recommended in Environment

CURZON, Thomas H
Osborn Maledon PA, Phoenix
602 640 9308
tcurzon@omlaw.com
Recommended in Corporate/M&A
Practice Areas: Serves as outside general counsel to emerging, growth-oriented companies; entrepreneurial transactions, including venture capital and other private placements of securities, entity formation and transaction structuring, mergers, acquisitions and divestitures, initial public offerings, corporate governance, licensing and distribution of software and other products, employee matters, and executive compensation.
Career: Partner, Osborn Maledon, PA (and predecessor firm) since 1986; recognitions include: The Best Lawyers in America®, editions 1995-2004; Best of the Bar (Business Journal), 2004; Chambers USA, American's Leading Business Lawyers, 2003-05; Marquis' Who's Who in American Law®; Marquis' Who's Who in America®.

Publications: Arizona Legal Forms, Business Organizations (Corporations), Volumes 8 and 9, West Publishing, Second Edition, 2001-02; Presenter: 'Show Me the Money: Lecture on Intellectual Property in Business Models' (Thunderbird, the Garvin School of International Management, 2004); Presenter: 'Venture Capital Financing Recent Trends and Developments' (Enterprise Network Business Seminar Series, 2003) Presenter: 'Venture Capital Financing - Standard Terms and Recent Developments,' (Financial Executives Institute, 2002); Presenter: 'Getting Ready for the Dance: Preparing to Raise Venture Capital - A Coaching Primer' (The Seminar Group, 2001).

Personal: JD, magna cum laude, University of Texas, 1979; BA, summa cum laude, University of Kansas, 1976; Third Degree Black Belt, Taekwon-do (ITF).

DANNEMAN, Dale
Lewis and Roca, Phoenix
602 262 5311
Recommended in Litigation

DAY, Barton
Bryan Cave LLP, Phoenix
602 364 7000
Recommended in Environment

DEROUIN, James
Steptoe & Johnson LLP, Phoenix
602 257 5237
jderouin@steptoe.com
Recommended in Environment
Practice Areas: Partner, Phoenix office of Steptoe & Johnson LLP. Represents clients on environmental and natural resource issues including groundwater contamination, surface water discharges, hazardous waste, toxicology, endangered species, groundwater contaminant fate and transport modeling, civil and criminal enforcement and complex project permitting. Member: Superfund Subcommittee to EPA's National Advisory Council for Environmental Policy and Technology (2002-02). Negotiated several environmental and natural resource laws involving surface water quality, solid and hazardous waste, air quality, PCBs, dioxin, pesticides, fluorocarbons, mining reclamation, groundwater quality and interbasin water transfers.
Personal: JD, University of Wisconsin Law School, 1968; BA, University of Wisconsin-Eau Claire, 1967.

DEWALD, Scott
Lewis and Roca, Phoenix
602 262 5311
Recommended in Corporate/M&A

DORAN, John Alan
Greenberg Traurig LLP, Phoenix
602 445 8507
doranj@gtlaw.com
Recommended in Employment
Practice Areas: Labor and employment; litigation; appellate.
Prof. Memberships: Chair, Arizona

Association of Industries, HR Subcommittee. Chairman, State Bar of Arizona Employment and Labor Executive Council. National Council of Appellate Attorneys. State Bar of Arizona Appellate Section. Charter Member, Management Labor and Employment Roundtable.
Career: 'The Business Journal's' 'Best of the Bar Award', Labor and Employment Law, 2003, 2004, 2005.
Publications: Contributing Author, 'Arizona Employment Law Handbook'; 'Using Severance Agreements to Avoid Litigation,' Employer's Handbook 1998: Cutting Edge Employment Law Issues for Human Resources Professionals
Personal: JD, Vanderbilt University Law School, 1988. BA, magna cum laude, Loyola Marymount University, 1985.

EARL, Stephen
Earl, Curley & Lagarde, P.C, Phoenix
602 265 0094
Recommended in Real Estate

ECKSTEIN, Paul
Perkins Coie LLP, Phoenix
602 351 8000
Recommended in Litigation

EMERICK, Steven
Quarles & Brady Streich Lang LLP, Phoenix 602 229 5200
Recommended in Corporate/M&A

EVERROAD, John
Fennemore Craig, Phoenix
602 916 5302
jeverroad@fclaw.com
Recommended in Litigation
Practice Areas: Alternative dispute resolution; business and personal injury torts; litigation.
Prof. Memberships: Fellow, American College of Trial Lawyers; Member, American Board of Trial Advocates; Fellow, American Bar Association; Founding Fellow, Arizona and Maricopa County Bar Associations.
Career: Primarily practices in the area of general civil litigation dealing with personal injury and wrongful death, professional negligence, employment law, securities litigation, environmental and lender liability issues. Handles major medical malpractice cases, principally for hospital clients, and product liability cases principally for pharmaceutical companies.
Personal: JD, Vanderbilt University, 1969; 'Best Lawyers in America'; Rated 'AV', 'Martindale-Hubbell'.

FARGOTSTEIN, Phillip F
Fennemore Craig, Phoenix
602 916 5453
pfargots@fclaw.com
Recommended in Environment
Practice Areas: Environmental; litigation.
Prof. Memberships: State Bar of Arizona, Environmental and Natural Resources Law Section; American Bar Association, Section of Environment, Energy, and Resources; Arizona Association of Industries; Rocky Mountain

Mineral Law Institute.
Career: Chair, Environmental and Natural Resources Practice; Co-Chair Litigation Section. Former editor of State Bar environmental newsletter. Represents business and property owners relating to state and federal air quality, Superfund, underground storage tanks and waste laws. Has 23 years experience defending medical malpractice and medical device product liability claims.
Personal: JD, Harvard University, 1977; 'Best Lawyers in America'; Rated 'AV', 'Martindale-Hubbell', Colonel (USMCR Retired).

FATHE, Fred
Mariscal, Weeks, McIntyre & Friedlander PA, Phoenix 602 285 5000
Recommended in Real Estate

FEDERHAR, Andrew M
Fennemore Craig, Phoenix
602 916 5301
afederhar@fclaw.com
Recommended in Litigation
Practice Areas: Commercial litigation; product liability; professional liability; insurance coverage; government relations.
Prof. Memberships: Chairman, Supreme Court's Committee on Complex Civil Litigation and Supreme Court's Business Roundtable; Lawyer's Committee, National Center for State Courts.
Career: Chairs the firm's Commercial Litigation Practice. Represents clients in professional liability, product liability, insurance coverage matters, disputes with government, and general commercial litigation. Notable recent cases include: ChartOne v Bernini, 83 P.3d 1103 (App. 2004); Manistee Town Center v City of Glendale, 227 F.3d 1090 (9th Cir. 2000).
Personal: JD, University of Arizona, 1980; Rated 'AV', 'Martindale-Hubbell'.

FEENEY, Matthew
Snell & Wilmer LLP, Phoenix
602 382 6239
mfeeney@swlaw.com
Recommended in Corporate/M&A
Practice Areas: General corporate practice concentrated in the area of securities, including public offerings, private placements, and mergers and acquisitions.
Prof. Memberships: State Bar of Arizona; American Bar Association (Commission on Interest on Lawyer Trust Accounts, 1998-2002, and Co-Chair, Committee on Prototype Limited, Liability Company Legislation 1991-92); Board Member for the Arizona Foundation for Legal Services and Education.

FERLAND, Roger
Quarles & Brady Streich Lang LLP, Phoenix 602 229 5200
Recommended in Environment

GAMMAGE Jr, Grady
Gammage & Burnham, P.L.C., Phoenix
602 256 0566
Recommended in Real Estate

GILBERT, Donald R
Fennemore Craig, Phoenix
602 916 5306
dgilbert@fclaw.com
Recommended in Employment
Practice Areas: Labor and employment; litigation.
Prof. Memberships: Member, State Bar of Arizona; State Bar of California.
Career: Co-chairs the firm's Labor and Employment Practice and has also chaired the firm's Litigation Section. Represents clients in connection with employment-related issues in both state and federal courts including disputes over restrictive covenants, contract interpretation and discrimination. Also represents clients before the NLRB, the EEOC, the Department of Labor, and the Arizona Civil Rights Division. Has tried more than 100 labor arbitrations. Counsels clients on employment issues and policies.
Personal: JD, University of California, 1971; BA, Stanford University, 1968; Rated 'AV', 'Martindale-Hubbell'.

GILBERT, Paul
Beus Gilbert PLLC, Scottsdale
480 429 3000
Recommended in Real Estate

GITTLER, Amy
Frazer Ryan Goldberg Arnold & Gittler LLP, Phoenix 602 277 2010
Recommended in Employment

GOEBEL, Monica
Steptoe & Johnson LLP, Phoenix
602 257 5218
mgoebel@steptoe.com
Recommended in Employment
Practice Areas: Partner in Steptoe & Johnson LLP's Phoenix office. Practices employment and employee benefits law, emphasizing multi-plaintiff and class action lawsuits, discrimination and sexual harassment claims, wage-and-hour matters, non-compete agreements, and defending benefits plans and fiduciaries in ERISA litigation. Advises and defends retailers, manufacturers, and insurance companies in connection with unfair labor practice proceedings, union-avoidance efforts, union elections, matters before the National Labor Relations Board, and investigations or litigation by the EEOC and Department of Labor's Wage and Hour Division and OFCCP.
Personal: JD, Arizona State University, 1988; BS, Grand Canyon University, 1985.

GREEN, Jordan
Fennemore Craig, Phoenix
602 916 5426
jgreen@fclaw.com
Recommended in Litigation
Practice Areas: White collar criminal defense; internal investigations; commercial litigation.
Prof. Memberships: Fellow, American College of Trial Lawyers; Fellow, International Academy of Trial Lawyers;

Member, National Association of Criminal Defense Lawyers; Arizona Attorneys for Criminal Justice.

Career: Represents businesses and individuals in criminal investigations and prosecutions in matters involving, among others, the Environmental Protection Agency, Securities and Exchange Commission, Sarbanes-Oxley, Internal Revenue Service, Medicare/Medicaid, antitrust and the Department of Defense.

Personal: JD, DePaul University College of Law, 1965; 'Best Lawyers in America' (1983-2005); Rated 'AV', 'Martindale-Hubbell'.

HACKETT, Robert
Jennings, Strouss & Salmon, PLC, Phoenix 602 262 5911
Recommended in Corporate/M&A

HALLER, Diane
Quarles & Brady Streich Lang LLP, Phoenix 602 229 5200
Recommended in Real Estate

HAMMOND, Larry
Osborn Maledon PA, Phoenix
602 640 9361
lhammond@omlaw.com
Recommended in Litigation

Practice Areas: Criminal defense (including both white collar and major felony - especially capital defense); also engages in complex commercial litigation and False Claims Act litigation.

Prof. Memberships: President, American Judicature Society; Chair, Justice Project of Arizona Attorneys for Criminal Justice (Arizona's project related to questions of actual innocence); Chair, Arizona State Bar Indigent Defense Task Force; Officer, Arizona Capital Representation Project.

Career: Mr Hammond has practiced law for 35 years; five of those years were spent with the United States Department of Justice both as an Assistant Watergate Special Prosecutor and as the First Deputy Assistant Attorney General in the Office of Legal Counsel during the Carter Administration. His practice has always included both complex commercial litigation and criminal defense. Throughout his career he has devoted substantial time to cases, projects and programs designed to improve the administration of justice.

Publications: Mr Hammond has written extensively on issues associated with convictions of the wrongfully accused. A sampling of his numerous publications can be found at the website for Osborn Maledon.

Personal: Mr Hammond considers himself the most knowledgeable baseball fan in his law firm. While the claim is often disputed, it has yet to be disproved. He is also extremely proud to be able to say that all of his children have devoted their careers to public service; his eldest daughter is a social worker for an immigrant and refugee rights project;

his son is a Phoenix police officer; and his youngest daughter after returning from the Peace Corps is now enrolled as a law student at the University of Colorado.

HAMULAR, James
Gallagher & Kennedy PA, Phoenix
602 530 8000
Recommended in Environment

HARDIN, William
Osborn Maledon PA, Phoenix
602 640 9322
whardin@omlaw.com
Recommended in Corporate/M&A

Practice Areas: Business transactions practice, including outside general counsel services, mergers and acquisitions, venture capital and private equity financings, securities, intellectual property transactions and executuve compensation matters.

Prof. Memberships: State Bar of Arizona; Enterprise Network Board of Directors.

Career: Partner, Osborn Maledon, PA (and predecessor firm) since 1988. Co-Chair, Governor's Council on Innovation and Technology, 2004-05. Recognitions include: Chambers USA, American's Leading Business Lawyers, 2003-05; The Best Lawyers in America, editions 1995-2006; Best of the Bar (Business Journal), 2004. Law Clerk to Judge Thomas Gibbs Gee, United States Court of Appeals for the Fifth Circuit, 1982-83.

Publications: Arizona Legal Forms, Business Organizations, (Corporations), Volumes 8 and 9, West Publishing, 2d Edition, 2001-02. Presenter: 'Venture Capital Financing Recent Trends and Developments' (Enterprise Network Business Seminar Series, 2003); Presenter: 'Venture Capital Financing - Standard Terms and Recent Developments,' (Financial Executives Institute, 2002); Presenter: 'Getting Ready for the Dance: Preparing to Raise Venture Capital - A Coaching Primer' (The Seminar Group, 2001).

Personal: JD, with honors, University of Chicago Law School, 1982. Associate Editor, University of Chicago Law Review; Order of the Coif.

HARRISON, Mark
Osborn Maledon PA, Phoenix
602 640 9324
mharrison@omlaw.com
Recommended in Litigation

Practice Areas: Professional ethics and professional liability; consulting and testifying as an expert in matters involving legal ethics, professional liability and law firm risk management; appellate litigation; complex commercial and tort litigation; service as a mediator and arbitrator.

Prof. Memberships: Member and past President, State Bar of Arizona and Arizona Bar Foundation; Member and past President, Maricopa County Bar Association; Member and past President, Association of Professional Responsibility Lawyers; Fellow and past President,

American Academy of Appellate Lawyers; ABA (Member and Chair, Standing Committees on Professional Discipline and Professionalism; Member, Standing Committee on Ethics.

Career: Law Clerk to former Chief Justice Lorna E Lockwood, Supreme Court of Arizona; Harrison, Harper, Christian & Dichter (and predecessor firms), 1966-93; Partner, Bryan Cave LLP (1993-2004); Of Counsel, Osborn Maledon, P.A. (2004-).

Publications: Co-author, Arizona Appellate Practice; 'An Overview: The New Arizona Rules of Professional Conduct', 20 Arizona Bar Journal 8 (1985); 'LLPs Are Just Another Star Wars!' 39 S.Tex. L.R. 633 (1998); co-author, 'Ethical Implications of Partnerships and Other Associations Involving American and Foreign Lawyers', 22 Penn State Internat'l L.R. 639 (Spring 2004).

Personal: Adjunct Professor, Arizona State University Law School (Legal Ethics), 2000 -); Antioch College (BA 1957); Harvard Law School (LLB, 1960).

HAYDEN, William
Snell & Wilmer LLP, Phoenix
602 382 6329
bhayden@swlaw.com
Recommended in Employment

Practice Areas: Advises management clients regarding all phases of personnel administration and avoidance of personnel-related litigation. Represents management clients before state and federal regulatory agencies including, for example, the Equal Employment Opportunity Commission, the Arizona Civil Rights Division, the National Labor Relations Board, and the Department of Labor. Defends management clients in personnel-related litigation, including employment discrimination, wrongful discharge, breach of contract, restrictive covenants.

Prof. Memberships: Memberships include the State Bar of Arizona; the American Bar Association; Maricopa County Bar Association; District of Columbia Bar Association; the American Arbitration Association, National Panel of Arbitrators, specializing in employment dispute resolution.

HENDERSON, Scott
Squire, Sanders & Dempsey LLP, Phoenix 602 528 4000
Recommended in Real Estate

HENDRICKS Jr, Ed
Meyer, Hendricks & Bivens PA, Phoenix
602 604 2200
Recommended in Litigation

HENZE, Tom
Gallagher & Kennedy PA, Phoenix
602 530 8000
Recommended in Litigation

HERF, Charles
Quarles & Brady Streich Lang LLP, Phoenix 602 229 5200
Recommended in Employment

HINK, John
Ryley Carlock & Applewhite, Phoenix
602 440 4835
jhink@rcalaw.com
Recommended in Real Estate

Practice Areas: Real estate finance, acquisition and development, including acquisitions and sales of undeveloped property and developed property; development, financing and leasing of shopping centers, office buildings, and apartment projects.

Prof. Memberships: Admitted to practice in Arizona. Memberships include the State Bar of Arizona; Maricopa County Bar Association; Arizona Town Hall; Scottsdale Charros; Scottsdale Area Chamber.

Personal: JD, Arizona State University (1988); BA (Economics), University of Arizona (1984).

HIRSCH, Stephen
Bryan Cave LLP, Phoenix
602 364 7000
Recommended in Real Estate

HOFFMANN, Christian
Quarles & Brady Streich Lang LLP, Phoenix 602 229 5200
Recommended in Corporate/M&A

JOHNSON, Christopher
Squire, Sanders & Dempsey LLP, Phoenix 602 528 4000
Recommended in Corporate/M&A

KANT, Robert
Greenberg Traurig LLP, Phoenix
602 445 8302
kantr@gtlaw.com
Recommended in Corporate/M&A

Practice Areas: Corporate and securities/M&A.

Prof. Memberships: Member, State Bar of Arizona, Small Business Capital Formation Subcommittee of Committee on Securities Regulation; Chairman, Securities Section, 1987-88.

Career: Listed, 'Best Lawyers in America' 2003-2004 and 2005-2006; Best of the Bar, Corporate Law, 'Phoenix Business Journal', February 2003; Best of the Bar, Securities Law, 'Phoenix Business Journal', February 2004; Best Lawyer in Valley, 'Phoenix Business Journal', January 2005.

Publications: Co-author: 'Presumptive Merit-A New Era for Arizona Securities Law', 45 Bus. Law, 1347, 1990.

Personal: JD, Villanova University, 1970. BA, University of Pennsylvania, 1966.

KATZ, Lawrence
Steptoe & Johnson LLP, Phoenix
602 257 5211
lkatz@steptoe.com
Recommended in Employment

Practice Areas: Head of the Labor Relations and Employment Practice Group and Partner in the Phoenix office of Steptoe & Johnson LLP. Practice involves state and federal court litigation representing management in the defense

of lawsuits alleging violations of employment discrimination statutes, contracts, or various common-law employment rights. Further assists clients in union-avoidance efforts and represents employers in union elections, unfair labor practice proceedings, litigation related to union organizational activities, and other matters before the National Labor Relations Board.
Personal: JD, Boston College Law School, 1967; BA, Harvard University, 1960.

KENNEDY, Michael
Gallagher & Kennedy PA, Phoenix
602 530 8000
Recommended in Litigation

KERRICK, Robert
Gallagher & Kennedy PA, Phoenix
602 530 8000
Recommended in Real Estate

KIMBALL, David
Gallagher & Kennedy PA, Phoenix
602 530 8000
Recommended in Environment

KIMERER, Mike
Kimerer & Derrick, P.C., Phoenix
602 279 5900
Recommended in Litigation

KRAMER, Jay
Fennemore Craig, Phoenix
602 916 5341
jkramer@fclaw.com
Recommended in Real Estate
Practice Areas: Real estate; finance.
Prof. Memberships: Member, State Bar of Arizona; Member, Maricopa County Bar Association; President, Fennemore Craig Foundation; Board Member, Kivel Campus of Care; Board Member, Arizona Work Force Housing Task Force.
Career: Practice encompasses real estate transactions and corporate finance, including real estate acquisition, entitlements, infrastructure development and financing, and disposition, and real estate and other asset-based financing.
Personal: JD, Vanderbilt University, 1984; MBA, Vanderbilt University, 1984; BA, Georgetown University, 1980; Certified Real Estate Specialist, 1995; 'Best Lawyers in America'; Rated 'AV', 'Martindale-Hubbell'.

LANSKY, David
Mariscal, Weeks, McIntyre & Friedlander PA, Phoenix 602 285 5000
Recommended in Real Estate

LAZARUS, Larry
Lazarus & Associates, Phoenix
602 340 0900
Recommended in Real Estate

LISKER, Steven
Bryan Cave LLP, Phoenix
602 364 7000
Recommended in Real Estate

MALEDON, William
Osborn Maledon PA, Phoenix
602 640 9000
wmaledon@omlaw.com

Recommended in Litigation
Practice Areas: Complex commercial litigation, with an emphasis on antitrust, trade regulation, securities, product liability, insurance bad faith, and sports litigation.
Prof. Memberships: A member of various state and federal bar associations, a Founding Fellow of the Arizona Bar Foundation and a Life Member of the American Bar Foundation, a former Chairman of the Antitrust Section of the Arizona State Bar, and a member of various Arizona State Bar Committees.
Career: University of Notre Dame (JD 1972); Law Clerk to the Honorable William J Brennan, Jr, United States Supreme Court (1972-73).
Publications: Has lectured extensively on trade regulation matters, complex litigation, and jury trial reform issues.
Personal: Adjunct Professor of Sports Law, Arizona State University Law School.

MALTZ, Gerald
Haralson, Miller, Pitt & McAnally PLC, Tucson 520 792 3836
Recommended in Litigation

MAST, Gregory
Gallagher & Kennedy PA, Phoenix
602 530 8000
Recommended in Real Estate

MAY, Bruce
Jennings, Strouss & Salmon, PLC, Phoenix 602 262 5911
Recommended in Real Estate

MCCONNELL, Karen C
Fennemore Craig, Phoenix
602 916 5307
kmcconne@fclaw.com
Recommended in Corporate/M&A
Practice Areas: Securities; mergers and acquisitions; business law.
Prof. Memberships: Member, Securities and Business Law Sections, State Bar of Arizona; Subcommittees on 1933 Act Registration and 1934 Act Reporting Companies and Committee on Federal Regulation of Securities, Business Law Section, American Bar Association.
Career: Member, Fennemore Craig Management Committee. Represents buyers and sellers in asset and stock-based transactions, private equity and venture capital transactions, mergers, leveraged buyouts and other business acquisitions and reorganizations. Represents issuers in public offerings and private placements of debt and equity securities.
Personal: JD, University of Notre Dame, 1984; 'Best Lawyers in America'; Rated 'AV', 'Martindale-Hubbell'.

MEEHAN, Michael
Meehan LLP, Tucson
520 622 8855
Recommended in Litigation

MITCHELL, Barry
Gallagher & Kennedy PA, Phoenix
602 530 8000
Recommended in Litigation

MOBERLY, Michael D
Ryley Carlock & Applewhite, Phoenix
602 440 4821
mmoberly@rcalaw.com
Recommended in Employment
Practice Areas: Former Practice Leader of firm's Labor and Employment Group. Has extensive experience in employment and civil rights litigation, EEOC, NLRB and other agency representation, labor arbitration, and strike contingency and other employment planning issues.
Prof. Memberships: Admitted to practice in Arizona (1983). Member of Defense Research Institute; American Bar Association, Section of Labor and Employment Law; State Bar of Arizona, Employment and Labor Law Section; Arizona Industrial Relations Association. Appointment; Chairman, Arizona Agricultural Employment Relations Board.
Career: Joined Ryley Carlock & Applewhite, 1983; became shareholder, 1989. Serves as a Chairman of Ryley Carlock & Applewhite Executive Committee.
Publications: Contributing author 'Arizona Employment Law Handbook' (1998). Author of more than 30 law review articles addressing litigation and labor related topics, including 'Striking a Happy Medium: The Conversion of Unfair Labor Practice Strikes to Economic Strikes', 22 Berkeley Journal of Employment & Labor Law 131 (2001).
Personal: Born 21 November 1956. JD (with high distinction), University of Iowa (1983); BBA (with high distinction), University of Iowa (1979).

MOELLENBERG, Dalva
Gallagher & Kennedy PA, Phoenix
602 530 8000
Recommended in Environment

MORALES, Gerard
Snell & Wilmer LLP, Phoenix
602 382 6362
jmorales@swlaw.com
Recommended in Employment
Practice Areas: Labor/employment/ employee benefits include: wrongful termination, employment discrimination, arbitration, wage and hour, employment policies. Extensive experience in NLRB unfair labor practice proceedings, union elections, collective bargaining, administrative proceedings before DOL, EEOC, NLRB.
Prof. Memberships: American Bar Association; Hispanic National Bar Association; Arizona Academy; American Arbitration Association; Lex Mundi; American Law Institute; National Law Center for Inter-American Free Trade; Chair, Labor/Employment Law Council, Associated General Contractors of America.
Career: Field Attorney, National Labor Relations Board.
Publications: Contributing author/ chapter editor: 'Employee Benefits Law (ABA); How to Take a Case Before the

NLRB (ABA)'; 'Mexican/US Labor Law and Practice (NLCIFT)'; ALIABA Employee Benefits Course Materials.
Personal: Foreign languages: Spanish.

MOYES, Jay
Moyes Storey, Phoenix 602 604 2141
Recommended in Environment

NARDUCCI, Lucas
Bryan Cave LLP, Phoenix
602 364 7000
Recommended in Environment

NIEMUTH, Nathan R
Ryley Carlock & Applewhite, Phoenix
602 440 4810
nniemuth@rcalaw.com
Recommended in Employment
Practice Areas: Labor and employment. Has extensive experience in National Labor Relations Board representation and unfair labor practice proceedings, collective bargaining negotiations, strikes and lockouts, grievance and arbitration cases, union avoidance strategy, equal employment opportunity matters, wage and hour issues, drug and alcohol testing, and related federal and state labor and employment issues.
Prof. Memberships: Admitted to practice in Arizona (1976) and Wisconsin (1976). Admitted to practice before US Supreme Court, US Court of Appeals for the Fifth Circuit, US Court of Appeals for the Ninth Circuit, and US District Court, District of Arizona. Member of American Bar Association, Labor and Employment Law Section and International Law Section; State Bar of Arizona, Employment and Labor Law Section and International Law Section; Outstanding Lawyers of America; Industrial Relations Research Association; Arizona Industrial Relations Association.
Career: Joined Evans, Kitchel, & Jenckes, 1976; became Partner, 1982. Joined Ryley, Carlock & Applewhite as a shareholder, 1989. Member, Ryley, Carlock & Applewhite 401(k) Plan Trustee Committee.
Publications: 'Constitutional Law - Prejudgment Garnishment', Wisconsin Law Review.
Personal: Born 2 October 1951. JD (cum laude), University of Wisconsin, 1976; BA, University of Wisconsin, 1973.

NOVAK, Edward
Quarles & Brady Streich Lang LLP, Phoenix 602 229 5200
Recommended in Litigation

O'MALLEY, Kevin
Gallagher & Kennedy PA, Phoenix
602 530 8000
Recommended in Litigation

OSBORN II, Jones
Osborn Maledon PA, Phoenix
602 640 9338
josborn@omlaw.com
Recommended in Real Estate
Practice Areas: Commercial real estate including transactions, leasing, secured

transactions, and entitlements; entity formation and joint ventures; development; and general corporate and business law.

Career: Founding Partner and President, Osborn Maledon, P.A.; Member, Phoenix Planning Commission, 1981-85; Chairman, City of Phoenix Peripheral Planning Committee, 1986-88; and Member and past President of CoreNet Arizona (organization of corporate real estate executives).

Publications: Author of book, 'Arizona Real Estate Law'; and numerous articles in various business and legal publications.

Personal: University of Arizona (JD, 1970); law clerk to Justice James Duke Cameron, Arizona Supreme Court (1970-71).

PEARCE, John
Fennemore Craig, Phoenix
602 916 5376
jpearce@fclaw.com
Recommended in Environment

Practice Areas: Environmental; litigation; real estate.

Prof. Memberships: Member, State Bar of Arizona, State Bar of Nevada, and State Bar of Washington. Past Chairperson, Environmental and Natural Resources Law Section, State Bar of Arizona.

Career: Practices in the areas of environmental and natural resources, regulatory compliance, and regulatory interface. Litigation regarding waste facilities, underground storage tanks, pipelines, CERCLA, RCRA, toxic tort, and actions sounding in indemnity, contribution, nuisance and trespass. Experienced in all aspects of convenience store /motor fuels facilities, condemnation and real estate transactions.

Personal: JD, University of Oregon, 1988; BA, Washington State University, 1985; Rated 'AV', 'Martindale-Hubbell'.

PETERS, Karen
Squire, Sanders & Dempsey LLP,
Phoenix 602 528 4000
Recommended in Environment

PETTI, Fred
Lewis and Roca, Phoenix
602 262 5311
Recommended in Litigation

PETTIBONE, Jon
Quarles & Brady Streich Lang LLP,
Phoenix 602 229 5200
Recommended in Employment

PHALEN, Michael
Fennemore Craig, Phoenix
602 916 5415
mphalen@fclaw.com
Recommended in Real Estate

Practice Areas: Real estate; zoning; government lands.

Prof. Memberships: Member, Real Property Section, Executive Council, Treasurer, State Bar of Arizona; Member, State Bar of California; American Bar Association; Member, ULI; Member, NAIOP.

Career: Focuses on all aspects of land development, such as land use entitlements, zoning, and governmental relations, with a specialization in transactions that involve state and other government lands. Former Assistant Attorney General, Land and Natural Resources Section, Arizona Attorney General's Office (1988-94) and former Planning Director, Arizona State Land Department (1994-99).

Personal: JD, University of the Pacific, McGeorge School of Law, 1984; BA, University of Arizona, 1980.

PICCARRETA, Michael
Piccarreta & Davis PC, Tucson
520 622 6900
Recommended in Litigation

PIDGEON, Steven
Snell & Wilmer LLP, Phoenix
602 382 6252
spidgeon@swlaw.com
Recommended in Corporate/M&A

Practice Areas: Practice concentrated on securities offerings, mergers and acquisitions, and venture capital investments involving clients in a wide variety of industries including technology, financial services, healthcare, manufacturing, transportation, homebuilding and consumer goods, as well as the representation of underwriters, venture capital firms and other financial intermediaries in their underwriting, investment and advisory activities.

Prof. Memberships: 'Best Lawyers in America'; 'Who's Who in American Law'; 'National Registry of Who's Who'; State Bar of Arizona; American Bar Association; Maricopa County Bar Association.

PLACENTI, Frank
Bryan Cave LLP, Phoenix
602 364 7000
Recommended in Corporate/M&A

POKORSKI, Jody
Snell & Wilmer LLP, Phoenix
602 382 6399
jpokorski@swlaw.com
Recommended in Real Estate

Practice Areas: Practice primarily in the area of real estate transactions, finance and regulatory matters, including work relating to commercial purchase and sale transactions, real estate financing, master planned communities, subdivision matters and leasing.

Prof. Memberships: Memberships include the State Bar of Arizona; American Bar Association; Maricopa County Bar Association; Arizona Commercial Real Estate Women; Arizona Women Lawyers Association; Lambda Alpha; Urban Land Institute, full Member.

PORTER, Amy
Lewis and Roca, Phoenix
602 262 5311
Recommended in Environment

RAUCH, David
Snell & Wilmer LLP, Phoenix
602 382 6294
drauch@swlaw.com
Recommended in Litigation

Practice Areas: Practice concentrated in general commercial litigation, franchise litigation, professional malpractice defense and media law.

Prof. Memberships: Arizona Liaison For Franchise Business Network; Sandra Day O'Connor Inn of Court American Bar Association, President, 2002-03; American Bar Association, Chairman, Young Lawyer Division Corporate Counsel Committee, 1997; State Bar of Arizona; Maricopa County Bar Association.

REDDIN, Jane
Lewis and Roca, Phoenix
602 262 5311
Recommended in Employment

RICHARDSON, Joseph
Bryan Cave LLP, Phoenix
602 364 7000
Recommended in Corporate/M&A

ROBINSON, Robert P
Fennemore Craig, Phoenix
602 916 5355
rrobinson@fclaw.com
Recommended in Real Estate

Practice Areas: Commercial and real estate finance; real estate; business law.

Prof. Memberships: Fellow, American College of Mortgage Attorneys; Past Chair, Business Law Section, State Bar of Arizona; Past Chair, Real Property Section, State Bar of Arizona.

Career: Practice focuses on new corporate, asset-based and real estate finance, as well as workouts of troubled loans and the acquisition, development and sale of real estate. He is a Certified Public Accountant and Certified Real Estate Specialist.

Personal: JD, University of Arizona, 1966; MS, Arizona State University, 1963; 'Best Lawyers in America'; Rated 'AV', 'Martindale-Hubbell'.

ROMAN, Terry
Snell & Wilmer LLP, Phoenix
602 382 6293
troman@swlaw.com
Recommended in Corporate/M&A

Practice Areas: Experience in advising corporate clients in various business transactions, including healthcare and insurance regulatory issues (including captive insurance issues), securities offerings, mergers and acquisitions, and contract negotiations.

Prof. Memberships: Memberships include the State Bar of Arizona, Securities Council, Committee on Corporate, Banking and Business Law; the American Bar Association, Health Law Section; Maricopa County Bar Association; Arizona Women Lawyers Association; Arizona Health Lawyers Association; and Arizona Captive Insurance Association.

ROSENBAUM, David
Osborn Maledon PA, Phoenix
602 640 9345
drosenbaum@omlaw.com
Recommended in Litigation

Practice Areas: Complex commercial litigation in US federal and state court. He has represented public companies and their officers and directors in numerous securities fraud class actions and represented Fortune 50 companies in a wide range of complex commercial litigation. He has handled intellectual property litigation and large sales and use tax disputes.

Prof. Memberships: ABA; AZBA; DAZ; 9thCir; Former President, Federal Bar Association Phoenix Chapter; Fellow, American Bar Foundation; Charter Fellow, Treasurer, Foundation of Federal Bar Association.

Career: Partner since 1990.

Publications: He lectures frequently on litigation topics.

Personal: Georgetown Law School (JD, 1983); University of Pennsylvania (BA 1979).

ROSENFELD, Lawrence
Greenberg Traurig LLP, Phoenix
602 445 8501
rosenfeldl@gtlaw.com
Recommended in Employment

Practice Areas: Labor and employment; litigation.

Prof. Memberships: Member, Arizona State Bar; Member, Maricopa County Bar Association General Counsel, 1997 to present; Member, American Bar Association; Member, International Association of Defense Counsel; Member, American Employment Law Council.

Career: Listed, 'Best Lawyers in America.'

Publications: Co-author: 'When Mary Fires Joe: Defending Wrongful Termination Lawsuits'; Arizona Journal, June 1999; author: 'AIDS and the ADA', HRfocus, December 1998; author, '"Duffield" Puts Compulsory Arbitration in Doubt', The National Law Journal, October 5, 1998.

Personal: JD, Yale University, 1975. BA, magna cum laude, City University of New York at Queens College, 1972.

RUSING, Michael
Rusing & Lopez PLLC, Tucson
520 792 4800
Recommended in Litigation

SACKS, Seymour
Sacks Tierney PA, Scottsdale
480 425 2600
Recommended in Real Estate

SCHUBART, Lawrence
Stubbs & Schubart, Phoenix
520 623 5466
Recommended in Real Estate

SELDEN, David
Stinson Morrison Hecker LLP, Phoenix
602 212 8566
dselden@stinsonmoheck.com
Recommended in Employment

Practice Areas: Represents management in discrimination, wrongful discharge, employment contracts, workplace torts, OSHA, DOL, restrictive covenants, trade secrets, litigation, counseling, training, etc.
Prof. Memberships: Chairman, Arizona Chamber of Commerce Employment Committee, 1989-present; Board of Directors, Arizona Chamber and Phoenix Symphony; Management Labor and Employment Roundtable.
Career: Congressional aide, Washington, DC, 1971-82. Author of and lobbied to enactment several landmark Arizona employment laws to reduce employment litigation.
Publications: Editor in chief, 'Arizona and Federal Employment Law'; Board of Editors, 'Arizona Employment Law Handbook' and 'Arizona Labor Letter'.
Personal: JD, magna cum laude, Georgetown University, 1982; MA, 1976, BA, 1973, George Washington University.

SHERK, Kenneth J
Fennemore Craig, Phoenix
602 916 5383
ksherk@fclaw.com
Recommended in Litigation
Practice Areas: Civil litigation.
Prof. Memberships: Past Member, Board of Directors, Arizona Bar Foundation; Fellow, American College of Trial Lawyers and American Academy of Appellate Lawyers; Past President, State Bar of Arizona and Maricopa County Bar Association.
Career: Has extensive experience, including trial experience, in personal injury and business litigation as well as products liability, lawyer discipline, professional liability, insurance coverage and toxic tort matters. Recipient of the Walter E Craig Distinguished Service Award, Arizona Bar Foundation (1999).
Personal: JD, George Washington University, 1961; BSC, University of Iowa, 1955; 'Best Lawyers in America'; Rated 'AV', 'Martindale-Hubbell'.

SIMON, Marc
Snell & Wilmer LLP, Tucson
520 882 1233
msimon@swlaw.com
Recommended in Real Estate
Practice Areas: Areas of practice concentration include real estate, subdivision and development, title insurance, commercial finance and foreclosure, general commercial and corporate, and construction law and water law.
Prof. Memberships: American Bar Association (Business Law Section; Real Property, Probate and Trust Section); State Bar of Arizona, Member: Arizona Real Property Section, and Certified Specialist, Real Estate Law, Arizona Board of Legal Specialization; Pima County Bar Association; Arizona Planning Association.

SORENSON, Derek
Bryan Cave LLP, Phoenix
602 364 7000
Recommended in Real Estate

STEIN, Lee
Fennemore Craig, Phoenix
602 916 5337
lstein@fclaw.com
Recommended in Litigation
Practice Areas: Litigation; white collar criminal defense.
Prof. Memberships: Member, State Bar of Arizona; Member, Arizona Water Quality Assurance Revolving Fund Advisory Board; Attorney General's Capital Case Commission; Lawyer Representative to the 9th Circuit Judicial Conference.
Career: Practices in white collar criminal defense, governmental investigations, government relations and environmental law. Was Special Assistant Attorney General and Chief Counsel of the Civil Rights and Public Advocacy Division, Arizona Attorney General's Office. Also Former Assistant US Attorney.
Personal: JD, Arizona State University, 1988; BA, University of Arizona, 1983; 'Best Lawyers in America'; Rated 'AV', 'Martindale-Hubbell'.

STOKES, Randall
Lewis and Roca, Phoenix
602 262 5311
Recommended in Real Estate

STOLKIN, Ronald J
Fennemore Craig, Tucson
602 916 5321
rstolkin@fclaw.com
Recommended in Employment
Practice Areas: Labor and employment; litigation.
Prof. Memberships: Past Chairman, Labor and Employment Section, State Bar of Arizona; Judge Pro Tem, Arizona Superior Court, Pima County.
Career: Co-chairs the firm's Labor and Employment Practice. Counsels management on personnel practices, employee discipline and labor relations. Defends employers in litigation alleging employment discrimination, breach of contract, wrongful discharge and other employment related torts. Also practices in education law and complex commercial litigation.
Personal: JD, University of Arizona, 1970; BA, University of Arizona, 1967; 'Best Lawyers in America', 1983-2005; Rated 'AV', 'Martindale-Hubbell'.

STOREY, Lee
Moyes Storey, Phoenix
602 604 2141
Recommended in Environment

STOREY, Lesa
Storey & Burnham PLC, Phoenix
602 468 0111
Recommended in Real Estate

STRUNK, Sarah A
Fennemore Craig, Phoenix
602 916 5327
sstrunk@fclaw.com
Recommended in Corporate/M&A
Practice Areas: Securities; mergers and acquisitions; business law.
Prof. Memberships: Member, American Bar Association, State Bar of Arizona, State Bar of New York, State Bar of California, State Bar of Connecticut, and State Bar of Kansas; Member, Phoenix Committee on Foreign Relations; Member, Rocky Mountain Mineral Law Foundation.
Career: Chair, Commercial Section. Practice includes securities, complex corporate transactions, mergers and acquisitions, and general contracts, corporate law and governance. Experienced in derivative or commodities hedging agreements.
Personal: LLM, New York University, 1987; JD, University of Kansas School of Law, 1985; BA, Wichita State University, 1982; Rated 'AV', 'Martindale-Hubbell'.

TAYLOR, Karrin
Biskind, Hunt & Taylor plc, Phoenix
602 955 3452
Recommended in Real Estate

THOMAS, Christopher
Squire, Sanders & Dempsey LLP, Phoenix
602 528 4000
Recommended in Environment

THORPE, William L
Fennemore Craig, Phoenix
602 916 5350
wthorpe@fclaw.com
Recommended in Litigation
Practice Areas: Business and personal injury torts; product liability; litigation.
Prof. Memberships: Member, Pacific Region Executive Committee, National Association of Railroad Trial Counsel.
Career: Co-chairs the firm's Litigation Section. Has represented manufacturers of rough terrain forklifts, aerial work platforms, tires, earth-moving equipment, child restraint seats, consumer products, and exercise equipment. He also represents railroads and trucking companies engaged in interstate transportation. Mr Thorpe has extensive commercial litigation experience in the areas of securities, professional negligence, employment law and insurance bad faith.
Personal: JD, Boston College, 1978; BA, Stanford University; 'Best Lawyers in America'; Rated 'AV', 'Martindale-Hubbell'.

VAN WINKLE, Kenneth
Lewis and Roca, Phoenix
602 262 5311
Recommended in Real Estate

WEISS, Judith
Perkins Coie LLP, Phoenix
602 351 8000
Recommended in Corporate/M&A

WEISS, Stephen
Karp, Heurlin & Weiss PC, Tucson
520 325 4200
Recommended in Litigation

WILEY, Jay
Snell & Wilmer LLP, Phoenix
602 382 6261
jdwiley@swlaw.com
Recommended in Real Estate
Practice Areas: Practice areas focus on real estate and real estate finance, including the representation of buyers, sellers, investors, landlords and tenants in a wide variety of real estate transactions; representation of developers of multi-use projects and planned communities, office, retail, industrial and distribution centers and facilities, resort, recreational and hospitality projects, and multi-family and single family housing projects in all phases of such development, including acquisition, financing, obtaining entitlements, subdivision, preparation of CC&Rs and condominium documents, leasing and parcel and project sales; representation of contractors and architects; and representation of lenders in acquisition, development, construction, bridge and permanent loans.
Prof. Memberships: Memberships: State Bar of Arizona; American Bar Association; Maricopa County Bar Association; and Arizona Bar Foundation (Founding Fellow).

WILLIAMS, Quinn
Greenberg Traurig LLP, Phoenix
602 445 8343
williamsq@gtlaw.com
Recommended in Corporate/M&A
Practice Areas: Corporate and securities.
Prof. Memberships: Board Member, Governor's Council on Innovation and Technology; Board Member, Enterprise Network, 2004, President 2002, Chairman, 2003; Board, Arizona Technology Council Executive Committee, 2002 - present; Board Member, Scottsdale Chamber of Commerce, 1998 - present; Founding Chair, Governor's Small Business Executive Council.
Career: The Business Journal's 'Best of the Bar Award' for Corporate Financing, 2005.
Publications: Contributing author, 'United States Law of Trade and Investment', William S. Hein & Co., 2000. Contributing author, 'Attracting Capital From Angels', John Wiley and Sons., 2002.
Personal: JD, University of Arizona, 1975. BBA, Finance, University of Wisconsin-Madison.

WILLIAMS Jr, Lonnie
Quarles & Brady Streich Lang LLP, Phoenix 602 229 5200
Recommended in Employment, Litigation

WINKLER, Peter
Mariscal, Weeks, McIntyre & Friedlander PA, Phoenix 602 285 5000
Recommended in Real Estate

WINTERSCHEIDT, Rebecca
Snell & Wilmer LLP, Phoenix
602 382 6343
bwinterscheidt@swlaw.com
Recommended in Employment
Practice Areas: Advises employers concerning all aspects of employment law, including discrimination, harassment, wrongful discharge, breach of contract, wage and hour disputes, disability accommodation issues, family and medical leave issues, etc.
Prof. Memberships: American Bar Association; State Bar of Arizona; American Immigration Lawyers Association; American Bar Association, Labor and Employment Law Sections, Member; Committee on Immigration Law; Arizona Women Lawyers Association; National Association of Women Business Owners-Phoenix Chapter (President 1998-99).

WITHEY, Michael
Withey Anderson & Morris P.L.C,
Phoenix 602 230 0600
Recommended in Real Estate

WOLF, Van
Snell & Wilmer LLP, Phoenix
602 382 6201
vwolf@swlaw.com
Recommended in Environment
Practice Areas: Practices exclusively in environmental and natural resources law at the federal, state and local levels. Work focuses upon regulatory compliance, liability counseling, dispute resolution, enforcement response, and corporate and real estate transactions, including 'due diligence.' In addition, is experienced in legislative matters, rule-making activities, and environmental litigation. Work concentrates on federal and state Superfund laws, hazardous waste, water quality, including municipal wastewater regulation, underground storage tanks, the National Environmental Policy Act/environmental impact statement process, and natural resources issues involving public lands.
Prof. Memberships: Supreme Court of Arizona, 1982; Supreme Court of New York, First Department, 1974; United States District Court, District of Arizona, 1982, and Southern District of New York, 1974; United States Courts of Appeals, Ninth Circuit, 1982, and Second Circuit, 1974.

WRIGHT, Joyce
Snell & Wilmer LLP, Phoenix
Recommended in Real Estate
Practice Areas: Certified real estate law specialist engaged in all areas of real estate practice including: master planned developments; resort and golf course developments; subdivisions; leases; options; restrictive covenants and easements; purchase, sale and development transactions involving large tracks of undeveloped land, golf, resort and hotel properties, energy and telecommunication facilities, retail, office, industrial, residential and mixed-use projects, low income housing projects, educational facilities, agricultural and ranch land; state and federal land transactions; title examinations and insurance; real estate finance; structure and negotiation of joint venture and entity agreements; condemnation matters, nonprofit owners associations; corporate law; hospitality law; and development agreements.
Prof. Memberships: State Bar of Arizona (Real Property Section, Corporate, Banking, and Business Law Section); American Bar Association (Corporation, Banking, and Business Law Section, Real Property, Tax, and Probate Law Section); Maricopa County Bar Association; Arizona Women Lawyers Association; Maricopa County Volunteer Lawyers Program; National Network of Commercial Real Estate Women; Arizona Commercial Real Estate Women.

FENNEMORE CRAIG

THE FIRM

Chairman, Management Committee: Stephen M Savage

Number of partners: 98
Number of other lawyers: 57

FIRM OVERVIEW: Fennemore Craig is one of the largest and oldest law firms in the Southwest with over 150 attorneys. The firm recognizes that both complex challenges and straightforward legal issues require and deserve the best possible legal advice, provided as efficiently as possible. Fennemore Craig offers clients a full range of quality legal services in both litigation and commercial transactions.

MAIN AREAS OF PRACTICE:

Bankruptcy & Creditors' Rights: This practice group represents secured creditors, unsecured creditors, financial institutions, bankruptcy committees, debtors, bankruptcy trustees and purchasers of financially distressed businesses.

Business & Finance: Firm attorneys have substantial experience in a variety of corporate, commercial and securities-related transactions, including public offerings, private placements, 1934 Act reporting, corporate reorganizations, mergers and acquisitions, venture capital financing, leveraged lease financing, leveraged buyouts, and syndications.

Business & Personal Injury Torts: Fennemore Craig represents litigants in personal injury and business tort actions ranging from individual negligence actions to complex multi-party litigation.

Commercial Litigation: Fennemore Craig represents business parties in commercial disputes in federal and state courts, including cases involving white collar crime, fraud, derivative claims, lender liability, securities, corporate control, contracts, consumer statutes, insurance coverage, the UCC and eminent domain.

Estate Planning & Probate: Fennemore Craig attorneys represent individuals, business owners, nonprofit organizations, charitable foundations, and trust companies in trust, estate, probate, guardianship/conservatorship, and taxation matters.

Government Relations: For more than a century, Fennemore Craig has been deeply involved in developing and defining local and state laws affecting many of the state's major industries.

Immigration: The firm provides representation on employment-related immigration issues. This includes assisting businesses to obtain the required permits for employing foreign managers, professionals and highly skilled workers.

Intellectual Property: Fennemore Craig counsels clients on intellectual property protection, including patent prosecution, transactions, and enforcement.

Labor & Employment: The firm defends management in virtually all aspects of the employment relationship and counsels employers on employment practices. This includes personnel policies and manuals, supervisor training, employee discipline, drug and alcohol testing and sexual harassment policies, and compliance with state and federal statutes and regulations. It also counsels clients on issues relating to unions, including collective bargaining, contract interpretation and administration.

Natural Resources & Environmental: This practice includes environmental, water, mining, timber, oil and gas, energy, Indian and public land law. The firm consults with and represents clients on all aspects of permitting, planning and compliance as well as in transactions and due diligence investigations.

Real Estate: The practice encompasses all aspects of real estate investment, from acquisition and finance, through development, leasing and sale. The firm represents developers of master-planned communities, condominiums, apartment complexes, hotels, resorts, clubs, office buildings, industrial parks, shopping centers, golf courses, and other residential and commercial projects.

Tax: The firm handles tax planning for individuals, partnerships, and

HEAD OFFICE

ARIZONA
3003 North Central Avenue, Suite 2600, **Phoenix**, AZ 85012-2913
Tel: 602 916 5000 **Fax:** 602 916 5999
Website: www.fennemorecraig.com

BRANCH OFFICES

ARIZONA
1891 North Mastick Way, Suite A, **Nogales**, AZ 85621-1081
Tel: 520 761 4215 **Fax:** 520 761 3505

One South Church Avenue, Suite 1000 **Tucson**, AZ 85701-1627
Tel: 520 879 6800 **Fax:** 520 879 6899

NEBRASKA
1221 N Street, Suite 801, **Lincoln**, NE 68508-2028
Tel: 402 323 6200 **Fax:** 402 323 6210

BRANCH OFFICE CONTACTS

Nogales, AZ	Hector G Arana, Kimberly A Arana
Tucson, AZ	Richard T Coolidge
Lincoln, NE	Donald G Blankenau

CONTACTS

Bankruptcy & Creditors' Rights	Cathy L Reece
Business & Finance	Anne L Kleindienst
Business & Personal Injury Torts	Douglas C Northup
Commercial Litigation	Andrew M Federhar
Estate Planning & Probate	Louis F Comus, Jr
Government Relations	Michael Preston Green
Immigration	Nancy-Jo Merritt
Intellectual Property	Ray K Harris
Labor & Employment	Donald R Gilbert, Ronald J Stolkin
Natural Resources & Environmental	Phillip F Fargotstein
Real Estate	M Virginia Perry
Tax	Paul J Mooney
Utilities	Timothy Berg

corporations, and represents clients before the Internal Revenue Service and the courts. It also has a significant practice involving Arizona income taxation, and state and local excise and property taxation.

Utilities: Fennemore Craig represents several utilities in the telecommunications, water, sewer, and natural gas industries.

CLIENTS: 7-Eleven Inc.; Allied Waste Industries, Inc.; America West Arena; Arizona-American Water Company; Arizona State University; Arizona Sports & Tourism Authority; ASARCO Incorporated; Avnet, Inc.; Banner Health Arizona; The Burlington Northern and Santa Fe Railway Co.; Catholic Healthcare West; Cendant Corporation; Crescent Real Estate Equities Limited Partnership; DMB Associates, Inc.; D.R. Horton-Continental Series; Florida, State of; Howmedica Osteonics; Lennar Communities Development, Inc.; The Lyle Andersen Co., Inc.; National Association of Homebuilders; Nebraska, State of; Phelps Dodge Corporation; Phoenix Suns Limited Partnership; Qwest Corporation; Red Mountain Research Laboratory, Inc.; Southwest Airlines Co.; Standard Pacific Homes; Starr Pass Resort Developments LLC; Sturm, Ruger & Co.; Summit Builders; SunAmerica Securities Inc. (Royal Alliance Associates, Inc., Sentra Securities Corporation, Spelman & Co.); United Auto Group Inc.; Viad Corp.; Wachovia Corporation; Wells Fargo Bank, N.A.; Wick Communications Co.; Wyndham International, Inc.

FENNEMORE CRAIG
A HISTORY TO LEVERAGE

OSBORN MALEDON, P.A.

THE FIRM

Managing Partner: Jones Osborn II

Number of Members: 24
Number of other lawyers: 17

FIRM OVERVIEW: A leading law firm based in Phoenix, Arizona, Osborn Maledon is recognized by its clients and peers for its smart and creative litigation, business and general counsel solutions to complex problems. The firm represents a wide range of clients from sophisticated international companies in major litigation to start-up enterprises requiring all manner of counsel in launching a new venture.

MAIN AREAS OF PRACTICE:

Administrative & Regulatory: Osborn Maledon is at the forefront of administrative and regulatory work involving the telecommunications and cable industries and represents major clients in these areas before the Arizona Corporation Commission.

Antitrust & Trade Regulation: The firm provides comprehensive antitrust litigation and counseling services to its clients and has been heavily involved in a majority of the significant antitrust and trade regulation cases in Arizona and throughout the US.

Bankruptcy: The firm represents debtors, creditors, trustees, creditors' committees and purchasers of bankruptcy estate assets in commercial Chapter 11 bankruptcy reorganizations.

Corporate: Osborn Maledon's Corporate Practice serves clients ranging from venture capital-backed start-ups to publicly-held corporations. The firm has made a significant commitment to assist emerging ventures in the technology, life sciences and media industries in the Southwest and has extensive experience in the software and internet industries. The firm provides counsel and general counsel services in the areas of corporate governance, public and private equity financing, venture capital and angel financings, debt financing, mergers, acquisitions and strategic transactions, technology licensing, distribution and transactions, compliance with state and federal securities laws, public and private securities offerings, equity compensation and executive employment, compensation and severance agreements.

Employment & Labor: The firm defends employers and executives in litigation involving a wide variety of employment issues before administrative agencies such as the EEOC and in state and federal court. The firm has an extensive employment counseling practice focusing on preventative practices.

Environmental: The firm's Environmental Practice focuses on contamination issues in class action cases, regulatory agency proceedings, and CERCLA allocations. The firm handles investigations of historical site operations and defends against citizens' suits and litigates insurance coverage actions.

Ethics & Professional Liability: The firm's professional responsibility lawyers counsel clients in matters relating to complex ethics questions, Sarbanes-Oxley laws, and risk management. The firm defends lawyers and law firms and provides expert testimony in legal discipline and malpractice claims.

Indian Law: The firm represents Indian tribes in litigation, employment, business, and real estate and development matters. The firm's Indian law practice also involves assisting non-Indian clients in business dealings with Indian tribes.

Intellectual Property & Technology: Osborn Maledon's Intellectual Property and Technology Practice assists clients in acquiring, exploiting and transferring proprietary assets and businesses, and in aggressively defending proprietary positions.

HEAD OFFICE

ARIZONA
2929 North Central Avenue, Suite 2100, **Phoenix**, AZ 85012-2794
Tel: 602 640 9000 **Fax:** 602 640 9050
Email: webmaster@omlaw.com
Website: www.omlaw.com

CONTACTS

Administrative & Regulatory	Joan Burke
Antitrust & Trade Regulation	William J Maledon
Bankruptcy	James E Cross
Corporate & Mergers & Acquisitions	Thomas H Curzon
	William M Hardin, Randall C Nelson
Ethics & Professional Liability	Mark I Harrison
Environmental	Diane M Johnsen
Indian Law	Thayne Lowe
Intellectual Property & Technology	Brent L Dunkelman
	Jonathan F Ariano
Labor & Employment	Scott W Rodgers
Litigation & Appellate	William J Maledon, Diane M Johnsen
	David B Rosenbaum
Real Estate	Jones Osborn II
White Collar Criminal	Larry A Hammond

Litigation & Appellate: The firm represents clients throughout the country in complex and major litigation in class actions and multi-district matters in state and federal court and in regulatory agencies. Osborn Maledon's appellate services include pre-trial counsel on surviving appellate scrutiny, special action petitions and appeals in state and federal courts, including the United States Supreme Court. The firm has represented clients in numerous significant appeals.

Real Estate: The firm's real estate lawyers provide extensive real estate services involving real estate transactions, development, financing, zoning and land use regulations, joint ventures, leasing, brokerage, taxation and public and Indian lands.

White Collar Criminal: Osborn Maledon represents corporations and individual officers, directors or employees in matters involving securities fraud, cybercrime, health care fraud, industrial accidents, environmental crimes and financial frauds in Federal and State criminal investigations, Grand Jury inquiries and in all manner of pre-trial, trial and appellate proceedings. The firm also handles complex criminal defense matters involving non-violent and violent crimes.

CLIENTS: Altria Group, Inc.; American International Group; AT&T Communications, Inc.; AAA Arizona, Inc.; Arizona State University; Arizona Public Service Co.; The Boeing Co.; Colliers International; Cox Communications; DeRito Partners, Inc.; Diamond Animal Health, Inc.; Grand Canyon Railroad, Inc.; Grayhawk Venture Partners; Heska Corporation; Honeywell International, Inc.; Hopi Indian Tribe; MCO Properties, Inc.; Microchip Technology, Inc.; Microsoft Corporation; myGeek.com, Inc.; NetPro Computing, Inc.; PGA Tour, Inc.; Philosophy, Inc.; Pinnacle West; Quality Care Solutions, Inc.; Salt River Maricopa Indian Community; Schaller Anderson, Inc.; SunCor Development; Wells Fargo Bank; WL Gore & Associates.

INTERNATIONAL WORK: Osborn Maledon represents a wide variety of international clients in litigation and transactions in the United States and maintains collaborative relationships with premier firms outside the United States to service the intermittent needs of the firm's clients.

RYLEY CARLOCK & APPLEWHITE

THE FIRM

Executive Committee Chairman: Michael D Moberly

Number of shareholders: 40
Number of other lawyers: 27

FIRM OVERVIEW: Since being founded in Phoenix in 1948, the Ryley Carlock & Applewhite law firm has been a major player in the development of Arizona. In response to the expanding needs of its clients, the firm and its services have grown substantially. The firm now has more than 65 lawyers in Arizona and Colorado, serving clients throughout the West and beyond. The firm's phoenix office represents all segments of the Arizona business community, and some of the firm's practices take its attorneys far beyond the Arizona border. The firm's Denver office, created in 2005, is home to some of the most experienced natural resources and lending lawyers in Colorado. RC&A lawyers pride themselves on understanding clients' businesses and the business implications of legal advice. Many of the firm's lawyers have worked in-house for clients. All understand the importance of providing sound legal advice and the need to complement this advice with imagination, innovation, and creative solutions. The firm knows its clients' businesses and has helped them achieve their goals, taking them from an emerging company to listing the company on national stock exchanges. In today's environment, businesses expect their lawyers to solve problems and create value. This is where Ryley Carlock & Applewhite delivers, and that is why clients trust and rely on the firm.

MAIN AREAS OF PRACTICE:

Corporate: Banks, corporations, municipalities, partnerships, and high wealth individuals turn to RC&A for advice on business planning, formation, financing, mergers, acquisitions, securities, bonds, estate planning, wills, taxation, and intellectual property matters. The firm also has an active practice in all aspects of public finance and municipal law.

Creditors' Rights & Bankruptcy: RC&A represents a wide array of creditors, creditors committees, and trustees in bankruptcy matters. Financial institutions regularly tap into the firm's broad experience in defaults, restructuring, liquidations and reorganizations.

Environmental & Natural Resources: The firm's Environmental and Natural Resources Practice is widely-known throughout the region. RC&A provides services ranging from assistance with regulatory compliance and permitting issues associated with the handling and use of hazardous materials, water quality, hazardous and solid waste disposal and underground storage tanks to contamination cleanup, asbestos abatement and environmental real estate due diligence. RC&A has extensive experience in all aspects of water law, and is involved in water rights litigation, transactions, legislation and rule-making efforts in Arizona and throughout much of the Southwest.

Labor & Employment: RC&A advises employers and management throughout the Southwest and nationally on a comprehensive range of labor and employment law issues. The firm also maintains an active immigration law practice.

Litigation: The firm's Litigation Practice is devoted primarily to complex commercial disputes and other matters involving business interests. The diverse backgrounds of the litigators result in a diversity of substantive expertise and industry knowledge. The bulk of RC&A's trial practice is in complex litigation, with an emphasis on intellectual property, business torts and complex business transactions. RC&A's litigators collectively have conducted more than 400 civil and criminal trials.

HEAD OFFICE

ARIZONA
One North Central Avenue, Suite 1200, **Phoenix**, AZ 85004-4417
Tel: 602 258 7701 **Fax:** 602 257 9582
Website: www.rcalaw.com

BRANCH OFFICES

COLORADO
1775 Sherman Street, 21st Floor, **Denver**, CO 80203
Tel: 303 863 7500 **Fax:** 303 595 3159

CONTACTS

Corporate	Phillip P Guttilla
Creditors' Rights & Bankruptcy	John J Fries
Environmental & Natural Resources	L William Staudenmaier
Labor & Employment	Carolann E Cervetti
Litigation	Rodolfo Parga
Real Estate & Lending	Charles J Riekena

Real Estate & Lending: RC&A is actively involved in the real estate industry, a key driver of Arizona's economy. The firm provides comprehensive legal services in all aspects of real estate development, ownership, construction and financing. RC&A is conversant with the numerous federal, state and local laws and regulations affecting real estate, including those relating to water, mineral and other property rights, commercial leases, land use controls, condemnation, duties and liabilities of landlords and real property owners, subdivisions and lot sales, business planning and ownership, entity structuring, federal, state and local taxation, environmental issues, construction law, and title insurance.

CLIENTS: The firm's clients include: Arizona Public Service, Bank of America, Banner Health Arizona, Del Webb Corporation, Knight Transportation, The Industrial Authority of the County of Maricopa, PETsMART, Phelps Dodge, Pinnacle West Capital, Pulte Homes, and U-Haul International.

ATTORNEYS
Ryley Carlock & Applewhite
A PROFESSIONAL ASSOCIATION

SNELL & WILMER LLP

THE FIRM

Chairman: John J Bouma

Number of partners: 163
Number of other lawyers: 241

FIRM OVERVIEW: Snell & Wilmer has grown to become one of the largest full-service law firms in the Western United States, with more than 400 attorneys in six offices located throughout the region. Since being established in 1938 the firm's diverse client base of Fortune 500 companies, small businesses, emerging organizations, individuals and entrepreneurs has grown to more than 8,000 businesses and individuals. Over the years, Snell & Wilmer has earned a reputation for providing clients what they value - exceptional legal skills, quick response and practical solutions with the highest level of professional integrity.

Snell & Wilmer is most renowned nationally for its extensive experience in product liability litigation concentrated in the automotive industry, as well as its business litigation, intellectual property, and employee benefits. The firm's Arizona offices currently represent 17 of the 27 corporate headquarters located in the state, and provide legal advice to clients in virtually every type of industry. The long-standing relationships that the firm has established with its clients can be attributed to offering customized legal strategies to achieve the client's goals, together with cost-effective, practical solutions through an integrated team approach.

Snell & Wilmer has been recognized for its legal skills and ethical business practices with various distinguished awards, including having the most attorneys of any Arizona law firm listed in The Best Lawyers in America 2003-2004 (Woodward/White, Inc., of Aiken, S.C.); being named a winner of the 2003 Better Business Bureau's Business Ethics Awards; and named the best law firm in Phoenix to do business with by Corporate Board Member magazine for the third consecutive year. The firm is a member of LEX MUNDI, a leading association of independent law firms. Through LEX MUNDI and other international contacts, Snell & Wilmer clients have access to attorneys and law firms practicing throughout the World network.

MAIN AREAS OF PRACTICE: General practice, including trials and appeals before state and federal courts. Administrative law, alternative dispute resolution, airport, antitrust, appellate, banking, bankruptcy insolvency and business reorganization, commercial finance, commercial litigation, construction, corporate finance, corporate and securities, copyrights, emerging business, employee benefits and executive compensation, employee relations, environmental and natural resources, ERISA, estate planning and probate, financial institutions, financial services, franchising and licensing, gaming, government contracts, healthcare, hospitality, immigration, investment, insurance company regulation, insurance defense litigation, intellectual property and technology, international law, labor, legislation and government affairs, media, mergers and acquisitions, municipal finance, natural resources, partnerships, patents, probate and trust litigation, product liability litigation, professional liability litigation, public utilities and energy, real estate, retail services, securities regulation, taxation, telecommunications, transportation, water resources. Alternative dispute resolution, Latin American services, water law, venture capital and zoning and land use.

US OFFICES

ARIZONA
400 East Van Buren, One Arizona Center, **Phoenix**, AZ 85004-2202
Tel: 602 382 6000 **Fax:** 602 382 6070

One South Church Avenue, Suite 1500, **Tucson**, AZ 85701-1630
Tel: 520 882 1200 **Fax:** 520 884 1294

CALIFORNIA
1920 Main Street, Suite 1200, **Irvine**, CA 92614-7060
Tel: 949 253 2700 **Fax:** 949 955 2507

COLORADO
1200 Seventeenth Street, Suite 1900, **Denver**, CO 80202-5854
Tel: 303 634 2000 **Fax:** 303 634 2020

NEVADA
3800 Howard Hughes Parkway, Suite 1000, **Las Vegas**, NV 89109-0925. **Tel:** 702 784 5200 **Fax:** 702 784 5252

UTAH
15 West South Temple, Suite 1200, **Salt Lake City**, UT 84101-1531
Tel: 801 257 1900 **Fax:** 801 257 1800

CLIENTS: Apollo Group, Inc.; Arizona Public Service Co.; Bank of America; Chrysler Motors Corp.; CIGNA Healthcare, Inc.; Del Webb Corp.; Emerson Electric Company; Ford Motor Co.; General Motors Corp.; Honeywell, Inc.; Mayo Clinic; Mutual Insurance Company of Arizona; Nissan Motor Corp.; Perini Building Company; Pinnacle West; U-Haul International; Wells Fargo, N.A.

INTERNATIONAL WORK: For more than 30 years, Snell & Wilmer has been a leader in providing International Legal Services to businesses and individuals involved with transactions or investments in the United States and internationally. Over the years, the firm has represented clients in a wide variety of international legal matter. The firm's attorneys regularly work with clients to attract foreign capital to the Western United States and in facilitating and structuring investments and corporate transactions on behalf of international businesses and investors in foreign regions including Asia, Canada, Europe, and Latin America.

Snell & Wilmer
—— L.L.P. ——
LAW OFFICES
Character comes through.SM

CONTENTS: Corporate/M&A p.168; Employment: p.169; Litigation: p.171; Real Estate p.174; Individuals' Profiles p.175; Firm Profiles p.179.

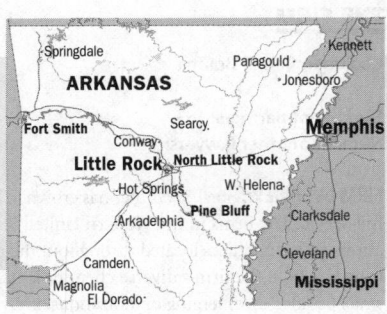

How lawyers are ranked

The opinions we gather from clients — mainly from in-house lawyers but also from other purchasers of legal services — are balanced by opinions from colleagues and competitors. Together, they provide two different perspectives — an all-round view — and biased viewpoints cancel each other out.

CORPORATE/M&A

Arkansas
Leading firms (Corporate/M&A)

1 FRIDAY, ELDREDGE & CLARK *Little Rock*
   MITCHELL WILLIAMS SELIG GATES *Little Rock*

2 KUTAK ROCK LLP *Little Rock*
   ROSE LAW FIRM *Little Rock*

3 JACK, LYON & JONES, PC *Little Rock*
   WILLIAMS & ANDERSON PLC *Little Rock*
   WRIGHT, LINDSEY & JENNINGS LLP *Little Rock*

Leading individuals (Corporate/M&A)

1 BUFORD Douglas *Mitchell Williams*, Little Rock
   GREGORY H Watt *Kutak Rock*, Little Rock
   SELIG John *Mitchell Williams*, Little Rock

2 BENHAM III Paul *Friday Eldredge*, Little Rock
   CLARK Ronald *Rose Law Firm*, Little Rock
   FLETCHER John *Kutak Rock*, Little Rock
   GARDNER Price *Friday Eldredge*, Little Rock
   JACK Donald *Jack Lyon*, Little Rock
   TISDALE John *Wright Lindsey*, Little Rock

Leading individuals
(Corporate/M&A: Tax)

Senior Statesman
   EISEMAN Byron *Friday Eldredge*, Little Rock

1 CLARK Ronald *Rose Law Firm*, Little Rock
   EBEL Walter *Friday Eldredge*, Little Rock
   GRUNDFEST Jack *Mitchell Williams*, Little Rock

Firms and Individuals are listed alphabetically in each band.

Band 1

Friday, Eldredge & Clark

The Firm: The state's largest firm boasts a strong team of high-quality lawyers. Clients were full of praise for the service they receive: "*I get great attention any time I call,*" said one; "*the attorneys are very responsive and knowledgeable, especially on Arkansas law as they helped to write a lot of it!*" The team is felt to be particularly strong in private company work. Over the past year, this has been drawn from a number of sectors, including retail, energy, healthcare and financial services. The group handles some large, multistate transactions, but most of its work is local, with a typical value of $5-30 million. An increasing volume involves complex tax issues, which are seamlessly handled by what is widely considered the deepest tax department in the state. **The Lawyers: Paul Benham** is a corporate finance and municipal bond expert. He was praised by clients as a "*responsive, honest and ethical*" adviser, while peers noted that he is also "*a good relationship guy.*" He maintains a busy practice despite his managerial responsibilities. Clients applauded **Price Gardner** for having "*excellent business sense coupled with thorough legal knowledge.*" His practice includes a mixture of M&A, real estate and healthcare work. "*The dean of tax,*" **Byron Eiseman** heads the tax department here. He can rely on the support of "*pre-eminent tax lawyer*" **Walter Ebel**, who divides his time evenly between tax and general commercial law. "*Personable and smart, not autocratic and opinionated,*" his recent highlights include advising Oaklawn Jockey Club and USA Drug on corporate tax issues.
The Clients: Entergy Arkansas; Union Pacific; Dillard's; Regions Bank; Stephens; ALLTEL and Acxiom.

Mitchell Williams Selig Gates Woodyard, PLLC
See firm details p.180
The Firm: The recent arrival of Douglas Buford and Walter May, from Wright, Lindsey & Jennings, has served to further strengthen this ten-attorney corporate practice. It will "*give the firm more of a securities outlook and a higher profile generally,*" admit market sources. Over the past year, the team has seen a number of banking sector transactions, with recent highlights including two transactions for Liberty Bancshares. Its lawyers have also been involved in take-privates and a volume of M&A, with typical deal values ranging between $25-75 million.
The Lawyers: New arrival **Douglas Buford** (see p.175) is a hit with clients because "*we like his practical side – he's a well-rounded business-man not just a by-the-book lawyer.*" His presence will considerably boost the firm's capacity in securities law, though his M&A and lobbying work was also noted. He is closely connected with high-profile clients, such as JB Hunt. **John Selig** (see p.177) is a "*real smart lawyer, but he won't beat you to death with how smart he is,*" say peers. He is known in the market as a "*good technical details man,*" and as an "*ethical and honest*" lawyer, who inspires confidence and takes care of his clients well. His practice is focused on banking and M&A. On the tax side, the firm boasts the services of **Jack Grundfest** (see p.176). His broad practice spans estate planning, tax credits and advice on corporate transactions, and he has particular expertise in the tax aspects of low-income housing projects and in advising closely held corporations on tax efficiency.
The Clients: JB Hunt Transport, American Management Corporation, Stephens and a number of the state's financial institutions feature in the client roster.

Band 2

Kutak Rock LLP
The Firm: Despite the departure of Jeffrey Gearhart to Wal-Mart, market sources acknowledge that this ten-lawyer corporate group maintains a prominent presence in the Arkansas legal market. Satisfied clients point to the team's "*national quality partners doing extraordinarily high-quality work at reasonable rates.*" This national, full-service firm has been busy helping both small and established clients with capital raising. It handles both public and private company M&A, and has also been assisting clients with Sarbanes-Oxley issues. Highlights of the past twelve months include private equity advice to the University of Arkansas biotechnology program.
The Lawyers: Watt Gregory attracts widespread praise as an "*outstanding person and an outstanding lawyer.*" According to clients, he is "*fantastic – responsive, experienced and knowl-*

edgeable with a lot of contacts in Arkansas and nationally." He handles both public company issues and private equity transactions, especially in the biotechnology field. "*Thorough and detailed*" **John Fletcher** makes his debut in the tables. According to clients he is a "*pragmatic, knowledgeable adviser who finds ways to get through problems.*" He has been advising high-profile clients, including ALLTEL, Tyson Foods, Acxiom and Wal-Mart, on multimillion-dollar transactions.

The Clients: ALLTEL; Tyson Foods; Acxiom; Wal-Mart; Bank of the Ozarks; Beverly Enterprises; Back Yard Burgers; Stephens; Arkansas BioVentures and ContourMed.

Rose Law Firm

The Firm: A team of around twelve lawyers undertakes M&A, private equity, venture capital and general commercial matters for a client base with a concentration of private companies. It has been active in a number of industry sectors, including energy, real estate and financial services, and offers one of the stronger tax groups in the state. Highlights of the past year include providing venture capital advice for a company being created in South Carolina.

The Lawyers: According to interviewees, **Ronald Clark** is "*a very balanced attorney,*" who does "*an excellent job of everything he touches.*" He has a background in tax law, which he brings to his corporate and commercial work, much of it for closely held companies. Tax still forms around a third of his practice.

The Clients: Stephens, Mountaire Corporation and White River are amongst the firm's clients.

Band 3

Jack, Lyon & Jones, PC

The Firm: Though not the biggest player in the market, the firm impressed sources with the breadth of its practice. It has "*a niche in the medical community,*" and appears in hospital transactions and financings, but it was also noted for its bank work and its "*good entertainment practice.*" Other work includes securities law, municipal finance and bankruptcy advice. Peers noted with envy its impressive client base: "*A lot of its clients are movers and shakers.*"

The Lawyers: The firm's standout name for transactional work is **Donald Jack**. "*His quality of work is great – I've not heard a bad word about him,*" said interviewees, who also noted that he is "*ethical and hardworking.*"

The Clients: The firm represents a variety of public and privately held companies, from a range of sectors, including insurance and healthcare. They range from family-run businesses to major names.

Williams & Anderson PLC

The Firm: A team of 11 lawyers advises on transactional matters. While it is not considered a first choice for straight corporate/M&A, the group is particularly noted for municipal bonds and commercial finance work. Recent examples include representing the University of Arkansas System, the state's largest bond issuing authority. It has also assisted a number of clients in drafting state legislation.

The Lawyers: Jack Williams enjoys a busy municipal finance practice and is the contact partner for this area.

The Clients: State of Arkansas, Arkansas Democrat-Gazette and WEHCO Media are among the clients.

Wright, Lindsey & Jennings LLP

See firm details p.182

The Firm: This reputable 16-lawyer corporate practice advises on the full range of corporate matters, including M&A, municipal finance, tax and intellectual property. The corporate team has been retrenching this year, following the departure of two senior members. However, it has still enjoyed a steady year, with a healthy stream of transactions and commercial projects around the region.

The Lawyers: With Douglas Buford's departure, the firm's highest profile lawyer is now **John Tisdale** (see p.178). A "*cooperative and conscientious*" adviser, he is known as a true generalist, whose practice straddles M&A, commercial work, finance, insurance and tax advice. The past year has seen him advising on a number of M&A transactions, valued between $3-69 million, for both acquirers and target companies. Other highlights include work on two ongoing IRS audits and several state tax controversies.

The Clients: QCA Heath Plan, West Tree Service and Mckimmey Associates are among the clients.

EMPLOYMENT

MAINLY DEFENDANT

Arkansas
Leading firms
(Employment: Mainly Defendant)
1 CROSS, GUNTER, WITHERSPOON *Little Rock*
FRIDAY, ELDREDGE & CLARK *Little Rock*
2 KAPLAN, BREWER, MAXEY *Little Rock*
MITCHELL WILLIAMS SELIG GATES *Little Rock*
WRIGHT, LINDSEY & JENNINGS LLP *Little Rock*
3 GILKER AND JONES PA *Mountainburg*
ROSE LAW FIRM *Little Rock*
4 QUATTLEBAUM, GROOMS, TULL *Little Rock*
RAMSAY, BRIDGFORTH, HARRELSON *Pine Bluff*
Firms are listed alphabetically in each band.

Band 1

Cross, Gunter, Witherspoon & Galchus, PC

See firm details p.179

The Firm: This boutique firm "*does more employment law than anyone,*" acknowledge local sources. However, its success is not just built on size, although at around 20 attorneys the employment and labor law practice is one of the largest in the state. It is also based on a core of "*excellent attorneys,*" who are "*laid back, reasonable and good to work with.*" Key to its success is a confident and dynamic approach to litigation. The firm handles a range of discrimination and harassment actions before a variety of courts and tribunals. For example, it successfully defended Deluxe in a case brought by an employee claiming that he was denied a promotion on racial grounds, and represented Potlatch against alleged racial harassment and sexual harassment claims. The team is also

arguably the leader in Arkansas for traditional labor work, advising on union-organizing campaigns and collective bargaining. However, it puts as much effort into keeping clients out of court, and its expertise in such areas as contract negotiations, employment audits, supervisor training and affirmative action programs is widely valued by a variety of well-known clients. Interviewees also noted the group's expertise in employee-immigration work.

The Lawyers: Interviewees describe **Carolyn Witherspoon** (see p.178) as a "*fighter*" for her clients, but note that she combines controlled aggression with a "*pleasant demeanor and great knowledge of the law.*" Best known for her labor practice, she is also a "*good rainmaker*" and an important name in the Arkansas Bar Association. **Russell Gunter** (see p.176) was credited with a "*sense of stability coupled with the gumption to make hard decisions and tell clients what they need to hear – whether they want to or not.*" Like Witherspoon, he is an "*impressive speaker,*"

Arkansas

Leading individuals

(Employment: Mainly Defendant)

[1] BOE Tim *Rose Law Firm*, Little Rock

GRAVES Kathlyn *Wright Lindsey*, Little Rock

GUNTER Russell *Cross Gunter*, Little Rock

KAPLAN Philip *Kaplan Brewer*, Little Rock

MOORE Michael *Friday Eldredge*, Little Rock

ROBINSON Spencer *Ramsay Bridgforth*, Pine Bluff

WITHERSPOON Carolyn *Cross Gunter*, Little Rock

[2] FREELAND Byron *Mitchell Williams*, Little Rock

JONES Michael *Gilker and Jones*, Mountainburg

MAXEY JoAnn *Kaplan Brewer*, Little Rock

[3] CROSS Bruce *Cross Gunter*, Little Rock

DAVIS Oscar *Friday Eldredge*, Little Rock

GALCHUS Donna *Cross Gunter*, Little Rock

LILE John *Wright Lindsey*, Little Rock

MARTIN Dave *Rose Law Firm*, Fort Smith

Up-and-coming individuals

HERRINGTON Daniel *Friday Eldredge*, Little Rock

JACKSON Stuart *Wright Lindsey*, Little Rock

SHIPLEY Benjamin *Cross Gunter*, Little Rock

Leading individuals (Employee Benefits)

[1] NISBET A Wyckliff *Friday Eldredge*, Little Rock

Individuals are listed alphabetically in each band.

with a particular name for union work, though he also handles employment litigation. **Bruce Cross** (see p.175) enjoys a good reputation for a range of work, including wage and hour cases and discrimination litigation. According to clients, he is "*extremely professional, knowledgeable and responsive – he's with us 24/7 when we need him.*" His interests in arbitration and commercial work were also noted. Clients also praised **Donna Galchus** (see p.176) as a knowledgeable and professional attorney and particularly stressed her "*skill in making employees feel comfortable.*" She is in charge of the firm's immigration practice, and also handles, inter alia, employment discrimination cases and supervisor training. **Benjamin Shipley** (see p.177) joins the tables this year, following praise from clients who rate him an "*excellent lawyer who gets results.*" His practice spans both employment and commercial litigation.

The Clients: Tyson Foods; Wal-Mart; Potlatch; Arkansas Oklahoma Gas Corporation; Arkansas ABF; Gerber; Coca-Cola and Entergy.

Friday, Eldredge & Clark

The Firm: One of the biggest firms in the state provides the closest employment law competition to Cross Gunter. "*It's a large firm so it gets a lot of business,*" say commentators, including a lot of work from its fantastic corporate client base. An experienced team of around eight attorneys covers the range of employment and labor law advice. Over the past year, this has seen it defending clients against claims involving OSHA, wage and hour, FMLA, ADA, Title VII

and ERISA issues. Its assured handling of contentious work has earned the group a reputation as "*top litigators; excellent in the courtroom,*" but the firm also works closely with clients to prevent employment law problems before they arise, as well as frequently employing alternative dispute resolution techniques to settle disputes favourably. A high-profile case from the past year involved defending Little Rock School District against a class action. The team is also acting in a case against seven salespeople and their new employer for breach of duty of loyalty and trade secrets.

The Lawyers: Clients were full of praise for **Michael Moore**'s plain-spoken style. He's "*pragmatic and unafraid to give his opinion – he'll tell you where you stand and that includes whether he thinks you're going to win.*" Sources described him as having a "*slightly intense, aggressive style,*" but agree that he is "*highly knowledgeable and honorable.*" "*Veteran labor lawyer*" **Oscar Davis** was admired for his experience in OSHA and other regulatory matters. He is considered a good choice for union avoidance and collective bargaining because he "*has the knowledge and experience to keep his client in a good position.*" "*Bright star*" **Daniel Herrington** was widely praised as a "*hard-working and highly ethical*" up-and-coming lawyer. According to clients he "*does quality legal analysis and has a great ability to just give you the facts.*" Clients and peers praised **Wyckliff Nisbet** for his "*thorough work*" in the area of employee benefits. Clients noted, in particular, that "*he is reliable and prompt.*"

The Clients: Entergy Arkansas; Union Pacific; ConAgra Foods; Liberty Mutual; Federated Rural Electric Insurance Company; Rebsamen Medical Center; Acxiom; Dillard's; Mail Contractors of America and Hi-Tech Engineering.

Band 2

Kaplan, Brewer, Maxey & Haralson

The Firm: The firm offers "*excellent trial counsel,*" according to clients. Just how good was obvious recently during the firm's successful work for the University of Arkansas in a high profile, six-week employment trial. This case was brought by former basketball coach, Nolan Richardson, who alleged that the termination of his contract was due to race discrimination. Although primarily undertaking defense work, the firm is unusual in also taking some employment cases for plaintiffs, which adds another angle to the team's experience. Typical work includes representing clients in discrimination and harassment claims, though the group also has a slice of union-related work.

The Lawyers: **Philip Kaplan** is a "*creative and polished litigator,*" according to market sources, and "*one of the top three, if not the best*" employment lawyer in the state. His profile is particularly high this year following his leading role in

the Nolan Richardson case, which he "*handled with the utmost professionalism.*" His honesty and integrity ("*he's a really smart lawyer and a gentleman*") make him popular with peers. He works closely with **JoAnn Maxey** whom interviewees noted as "*an incredibly diligent and consummate professional*" who "*works hard and does well for her clients.*"

The Clients: Arkansas Oklahoma Gas Corporation; Cingular Wireless; SBC; University of Arkansas; Wal-Mart; Stephens; Green Bay Packaging and Carlton-Bates Company.

Mitchell Williams Selig Gates Woodyard, PLLC

See firm details p.180

The Firm: According to clients, this "*absolutely excellent*" four-lawyer employment litigation practice has "*a broad and in-depth knowledge of the functions of a human services department.*" It has enjoyed a busy year defending clients against age, race and sex discrimination claims. There has also been an increase in ERISA work, with recent highlights including handling ERISA claims for MetLife.

The Lawyers: Clients say that **Byron Freeland** (see p.176) is both an "*excellent trial lawyer*" and an "*excellent counsel, especially in pre-trial negotiations,*" while a number of peers have had bruising encounters with him ("*frankly, he kicked my butt,*" said one.) Which is not to say that he is a fire breather – quite the reverse, in fact, his style is described as "*laid back and not too intense*" – just that he can be devastatingly effective on his feet. As well as employment litigation, he also handles union-related matters, negotiating contracts and representing clients before the NLRB. Interviewees were full of praise for "*thorough, knowledgeable and level-headed*" **Kathlyn Graves** (see p.176), who recently moved from Wright, Lindsey & Jennings LLP. Researchers were told that "*her real strength is on paper: she can prepare a case as well as, if not better than, anyone.*" An employment expert, she has been busy over the past year in an increasing number of class actions, including a recent FLSA claim.

The Clients: Baptist Health; Southwestern Bell; First Electric Cooperative and MetLife.

Wright, Lindsey & Jennings LLP

See firm details p.182

The Firm: Market sources agree that this team offers "*great depth and experience.*" In particular, its lawyers are said to be "*excellent on paper and in pre-litigation.*" Connected to this is its commitment to using cutting-edge alternative dispute resolution techniques to get the best solution for its clients: the team frequently employs mediation to settle disputes both before and after filing motions for summary judgment. When this fails, the highly regarded employment group has considerable experience of

170

All quotes in the text are from interviews with clients and competitors.

CHAMBERS USA 2005

defending its numerous management clients against discrimination claims based on age, race, sex, disability and national origin. Though it is less well known in traditional labor circles, it also has a share of ERISA, wage and hour, union organization and collective bargaining work, as well as providing representation before the EEOC. A recent highlight includes advising a client in an equal pay claim against Merchants and Planters Bank.

The Lawyers: "*Well-rounded trial lawyer*" **John Lile** (see p.177) divides his practice between employment defense litigation and products liability matters. His performance in court makes him a respected opponent. According to clients, **Stuart Jackson** (see p.176) is "*absolutely wonderful – always responsive and prompt.*" A talented up-and-coming employment lawyer, he was also admired for his "*thorough approach and on-target legal assessment.*"

The Clients: Weyerhaeuser; Enterprise Leasing Company; Chubb Group; Raytheon Aircraft Company; Price Companies and IC Corporation.

Band 3

Gilker and Jones PA

The Firm: Gilker and Jones is "*unusual in that they've built a boutique practice outside of Little Rock,*" say market sources. The Mountainburg-based team of four lawyers is flourishing and advises on the gamut of labor and employment law matters. This includes wage and hour and numerous Title VII cases, as well as compliance reviews. However, it is for its extensive labor law practice that the firm is probably best known. Here it advises on strategic planning for collective bargaining, union avoidance and union-organizing campaigns, and represents clients before the NLRB.

The Lawyers: **Michael Jones** (see p.177) is "*not flashy, but real tenacious: a real fighter,*" according to peers. But this aggression is never out of

control, allowing him to maintain a "*good courtroom demeanor and an excellent command of facts and theory.*" The past year has seen Jones representing Razorback Foundation in the high-profile race discrimination action brought against the University of Arkansas by Nolan Richardson, over the termination of his contract.
The Clients: Tyson Foods; Southwestern Energy Co; Rheem Manufacturing Company and Razorback Foundation.

Rose Law Firm

The Firm: This is an "*impressively broad*" practice, with a deep pool of expertise for collective bargaining, defense of discrimination and harassment cases, and OSHA claims, right through to restrictive covenant and breach of confidentiality agreements. This includes some major appellate litigation. A recent highlight was successfully representing Nucor in an important appeal case, while the team also won an OSHA penalty case on behalf of the same client concerning an employee fatality. The employer was found to have no blame.

The Lawyers: An "*exceptional lawyer: articulate, professional and thorough,*" **Tim Boe** (see p.175) received widespread praise from clients and peers. He is "*tough and tenacious; he leaves no stone unturned,*" say sources, who consider him a top choice for clients who want an aggressive and proactive counsel. His background in traditional labor law was also noted. **Dave Martin** is "*knowledgeable and prompt, and a good communicator – he gives us legal opinions we can understand,*" say clients. He was also praised for providing "*thorough, accurate information and a top-notch follow through.*" His practice spans race, sex and disability discrimination, wage and hour claims and OSHA.

The Clients: L'Oréal USA; Tyson Foods; Murphy Oil; Denver Roller and Deltic Timber.

Band 4

Quattlebaum, Grooms, Tull & Burrow PLLC
See firm details p.181

The Firm: A team of attorneys splits its time between commercial litigation and employment cases. It undertakes a range of employment law work, defending employers against race and sex discrimination, sexual harassment and wrongful dismissal claims. The team has been busy in recent months representing America's Car-Mart in a race discrimination class action concerning claims of a glass ceiling for African-American employees.

The Lawyers: Chip Chiles is the contact partner here.

The Clients: America's Car-Mart, AT&T Wireless and Concurrent Computer Corporation are among the clients.

Ramsay, Bridgforth, Harrelson & Starling LLP

The Firm: The "*most prominent firm in Pine Bluff,*" it defends employers and individuals against wrongful termination, federal and state discrimination claims, OHSA and wage and hour matters. The compact team also handles a share of traditional labor law work, appearing regularly before the NLRB. A recent highlight was the defense of a school against unfair dismissal claims made by employees, which resulted in a groundbreaking decision for Arkansas.

The Lawyers: **Spencer Robinson** (see p.177) has 27 years' experience of working with companies and union law. He defends employers against various types of commercial litigation claims, increasingly employing arbitration and mediation. Interviewees agreed that he is an "*intelligent, articulate communicator*" with a "*great courtroom presence.*"

The Clients: Washington International Group; Levi Strauss; Riceland Foods and Simmons First National Corporation.

LITIGATION

Band 1

Friday, Eldredge & Clark

The Firm: This is among the largest firms in the state and is widely admired for a great client roster and a litigation team brimming with experienced trial lawyers. The "*well-prepared and easy to work with*" group represents clients in a wide spectrum of litigation matters, from commercial and contractual disputes to products liability, antitrust, medical malpractice and large and complex class actions. Clients were full of praise for the commitment and intelligence of the litigators, and their aggressive,

proactive approach, both in court and at pre-trial hearings. The team's good political connections were also mentioned.

The Lawyers: Clients praised the "*dean of litigators*" **William Sutton** for his "*excellent courtroom demeanor and effectiveness at trial.*" His management responsibilities may have reduced his visibility at the coalface, yet sources maintain that, "*no one else compares*" to this "*legend at the Bar.*" "*First-class lawyer*" **Kevin Crass** (see p.175) is "*careful, reliable, responsive and effective.*" Peers also admire his "*high integrity, honesty and intelligence.*" His practice is focused primarily on business litigation in federal and

GENERAL COMMERCIAL

state courts, and he has defended claims in products liability, toxic torts, breach of contract, securities fraud and trade secrets. "*Talented*" **William Waddell** (see p.178) also won the approval of the market. "*Extremely thorough and methodical,*" according to one source he is "*possibly the most thoughtful lawyer I have worked with.*" He is renowned for defending banks and businesses in relation to lenders' liability claims, allegations of fraud and breach of contract. The past year has seen him successfully prevent a case against a client from being certified a class action. In the realm of medical malpractice defense, **Laura Smith** has

Arkansas

Leading firms
(Litigation: General Commercial)

1 FRIDAY, ELDREDGE & CLARK *Little Rock*
QUATTLEBAUM, GROOMS, TULL *Little Rock*
WILLIAMS & ANDERSON PLC *Little Rock*

2 KAPLAN, BREWER, MAXEY *Little Rock*
MITCHELL WILLIAMS SELIG GATES *Little Rock*
WRIGHT, LINDSEY & JENNINGS LLP *Little Rock*

3 ALLEN LAW FIRM *Little Rock*
EVERETT LAW FIRM *Fayetteville*
ROSE LAW FIRM *Little Rock*

Leading individuals
(Litigation: General Commercial)

Senior Statesman
SUTTON William *Friday Eldredge*, Little Rock

1 CRASS Kevin *Friday Eldredge*, Little Rock
KAPLAN Philip *Kaplan Brewer*, Little Rock
QUATTLEBAUM Steven *Quattlebaum*, Little Rock
SHEMIN Kenneth *Shemin & Hendren*, Fayetteville

2 ALLEN William *Allen Law Firm*, Little Rock
ANDERSON Philip *Williams & Anderson*, Little Rock
EVERETT John *Everett Law Firm*, Fayetteville
KUMPE Peter *Williams & Anderson*, Little Rock
LOWTHER Edwin *Wright Lindsey*, Little Rock
RATHER Gordon *Wright Lindsey*, Little Rock
TULL III John *Quattlebaum Grooms*, Little Rock

3 BEARD III RT *Mitchell Williams*, Little Rock
DONOVAN Richard *Rose Law Firm*, Little Rock
GATES Allan *Mitchell Williams*, Little Rock
LILE John *Wright Lindsey*, Little Rock
POWELL David *Williams & Anderson*, Little Rock
WADDELL Jr William *Friday Eldredge*, Little Rock

Up-and-coming individuals
ASKEW Jess *Williams & Anderson*, Little Rock
CHILES IV EB (Chip) *Quattlebaum*, Little Rock

Leading individuals
(Litigation: Environmental)

1 ADAMS Andy *Barrett & Deacon*, Jonesboro
GATES Allan *Mitchell Williams*, Little Rock
NESTRUD Charles *Chisenhall Nestrud*, Little Rock
PERKINS Alan *Hill Gilstrap*, Little Rock

Leading individuals
(Litigation: Medical Malpractice Defense)

1 BEARD III RT *Mitchell Williams*, Little Rock
SHULTS Robert *Shults Law Firm*, Little Rock
SMITH Laura *Friday Eldredge*, Little Rock

Firms and individuals are listed alphabetically in each band.

established an admirable reputation. Clients particularly noted her expertise in injury cases, and praised her as "*responsive and accurate with an excellent courtroom demeanor.*"

The Clients: Stephens; ALLTEL; Tyson Foods; Regions Bank; Dillard's; Union Pacific; Capital One Bank and ConAgra Foods.

Quattlebaum, Grooms, Tull & Burrow PLLC
See firm details p.181

The Firm: A team of around 12 full-time attorneys handle a substantial caseload of toxic tort and general business litigation, including some major products liability cases. Sources note that the group includes "*some of the finest trial lawyers in Arkansas,*" and clients were particularly pleased that it offers "*excellent advice in complex trials, but at reasonable rates.*" Highlights of the past year include securing an award of compensatory and punitive damages for Waste Management, in a breach of contract and business expectancy trial. It also handled a high profile Internet defamation case.

The Lawyers: "*Poised and smart,*" **Steven Quattlebaum** (see p.177) received widespread praise from both clients and peers. Clients keep returning to him because he "*thinks out of the box and always goes the extra mile.*" Although he often succeeds in keeping his commercial clients out of court, when it comes to the crunch, he "*has a real sense of what the jury is interested in and knows how to present an argument to the common man.*" Clients recommended **John Tull** (see p.178) as a "*good, smart trial lawyer with good judgment.*" Peers too acknowledge that he is an "*honorable and hard-working business lawyer,*" who is "*good in front of a jury.*" Apart from his general commercial workload, he has handled a number of libel and defamation cases. **Chip Chiles** (see p.175) makes his debut in the table. Clients praised his "*knowledgeable, hardworking and diligent*" approach, noting that he is always "*polite and on top of things – nothing falls through the cracks.*" He undertakes a mixture of general business and employment litigation. A recent highlight includes representing a group with interests in the cotton industry, who were intervening in litigation concerning the constitutionality of certain Arkansas State Plant regulations.

The Clients: America's Car-Mart; AT&T Wireless; Waste Management of Arkansas; Concurrent Computer.

Williams & Anderson PLC

The Firm: The ten-attorney litigation team continues to advise on all aspects of business and media litigation for national and statewide clients. The firm's appellant practice has been expanding substantially over the past year, with the team recently representing the plaintiffs in a nursing home case on appeal. It also has a renowned construction practice, and acts in a steady diet of contractual disputes, banking cases, tort litigation and other general business matters. Recent highlights include representing Mastercard in a class action, handling a conflict between rural and urban water utility companies and appearing in a newspaper libel case.

The Lawyers: **Philip Anderson**'s "*high-profile*

First Amendment cases for newspapers and other clients,*" along with his position at the Arkansas Bar Association, make him a well-known figure inside and outside the state. Interviewees also consider him "*a great communicator whose writing skills are beyond reproach.*" As well as his reputation for libel work, he has a strong background in antitrust and banking law. Peers described **Peter Kumpe** as "*absolutely tenacious and one of the smartest lawyers around.*" His academic skills are felt to make him "*particularly good at arguing a case before a judge,*" so he is a favorite choice for important appellate cases. **David Powell** maintains his reputation as "*the best construction lawyer in Arkansas.*" His diet of work from engineers and architects has given him outstanding experience in arbitration and mediation. He is currently mediating in a high-profile case for Chubb Group concerning the death by electrocution of an individual who was trying to save a drowning girl. **Jess Askew** joins the tables following widespread praise as an "*exceedingly bright and hard-working trial lawyer and legal writer.*"

The Clients: Baldwin & Shell Construction Company; CNA Insurance Companies; AIG; ABC; CNN; Arkansas Democrat-Gazette; Metropolitan National Bank and Potlatch.

Band 2

Kaplan, Brewer, Maxey & Haralson

The Firm: This compact but highly regarded litigation practice offers clients expertise in a range of matters, including employment, commercial and contract, and family law. A recent highlight includes defending the CEO of Rebsamen Insurance in a lawsuit by the former owners of the company alleging fraud in its sale.

The Lawyers: **Philip Kaplan** is widely acknowledged to be "*top of the ladder*" and, according to some sources, is "*one of the top three litigators in the state.*" His success is said to be based on a mixture of "*good judgment and quick-thinking intelligence*" and a "*dogged, practical*" approach. Well known for his employment practice – he handled the headline-grabbing University of Arkansas case recently – his practice also spans the commercial arena. Clients told researchers that they go to him "*when we're counting on litigation and we want a tough, aggressive lawyer.*"

The Clients: Rebsamen Insurance and the University of Arkansas feature in the client list.

Mitchell Williams Selig Gates Woodyard, PLLC
See firm details p.180

The Firm: This large and strong litigation practice places a particular emphasis on medical malpractice and environmental regulatory work. In fact, the medical malpractice is only one element of a large personal injury and professional negligence practice that constitutes the largest slice of the firm's workload. However, the litigation team, comprising around 35 practitioners, is also experienced in a wide variety of other matters, including commercial and contractual disputes and tort claims.

The Lawyers: Interviewees recommended **RT Beard** (see p.175) for his "*trial skills and good jury appeal – he does a good job in the courtroom.*" His "*accuracy and good communications skills*" were also a hit with clients. Medical malpractice is his forte, however he also has experience in personal injury, products liability, legal malpractice and other civil litigation. He has worked on four nursing home cases and brought two medical malpractice trials to conclusion in the past year. **Allan Gates** (see p.176) attracted widespread praise for his environmental practice. Clients particularly value his "*thoroughness and the energy he puts into his work.*" A recent highlight includes defending a class action brought by cotton farmers in east Arkansas to challenge fees on production.

The Clients: Beverly Enterprises; CNA Insurance Companies; Medical Assurance; State Volunteer Mutual Insurance Company and United Insurance Companies.

Wright, Lindsey & Jennings LLP

See firm details p.182

The Firm: This highly regarded litigation practice undertakes a mixture of commercial litigation, including construction disputes, toxic torts, medical malpractice and products liability. With employment and bankruptcy litigation as well, over 30 attorneys at this large firm have a hand in litigation. A recent highlight includes successfully defending Ford against a claim that a defect in one of its cars caused a driver to lose control of the vehicle, resulting in his death.

The Lawyers: "*Fine courtroom lawyer*" **Edwin Lowther** (see p.177) is best known for his expertise in products liability and medical malpractice cases. Clients seek him out because he "*has his finger on the pulse in his part of the world,*" and is "*very responsive with a good sense of humor.*" **Gordon Rather** (see p.177), meanwhile, is "*immensely prepared and exudes credibility with the jury.*" Peers described him as a talented lawyer "*in a solid, statesmanlike way that makes him effective and convincing in the commercial arena.*" His caseload encompasses contractual disputes, toxic tort and products liability litigation, with recent highlights including settling a five-year, $9 million case brought against Lion Oil for a fraction of that amount. **John Lile**'s (see p.177) practice is evenly split between products liability and employment litigation. Market sources praised him as "*excellent in the courtroom, with well-rounded experience.*"

The Clients: AT&T; Bank of America: Central Arkansas Water; Chubb Group; CNA Insurance Companies; Entergy; Ford; Ingersoll-Rand; JB Hunt Transport; Deere and Company; Murphy Oil; Pulaski County Special School District; Sisters of Mercy Health System; University of Arkansas Systems and Weyerhaeuser Company.

Band 3

Allen Law Firm

The Firm: This three-lawyer litigation team maintains an excellent reputation for handling a top-notch commercial caseload, often for major insurers. Its profile rests heavily upon the reputation of its name partner, however clients stress that this is not a one-man show: there's an "*efficient and quick*" team behind him. A recent highlight was successfully defending Wells Fargo in a trial concerning the Uniform Commercial Code in the bank's handling of cheques. The group also recently defended an important case for Medicaid Billing Company which was sued for alleged breach of contract and negligent billing of doctor's services.

The Lawyers: The standout practitioner in this team is **William Allen**. Clients raved about this "*personable, responsive and intelligent*" attorney: "*He's prompt to respond to calls and e-mails and extremely meticulous in filing court information.*" His practice encompasses banking, insurance and general business litigation.

The Clients: Concurrent Computer; Interactive Management; Medicaid Billing Company and Wells Fargo are among the clients.

Everett Law Firm

The Firm: This litigation-focused firm handles a steady stream of commercial and criminal cases, the brilliance of its attorneys ensuring it a place in numerous major trials despite its compact size. A three-lawyer team undertakes trials in the state and federal courts and before regulatory commissions. A highlight of the past year includes representing Tyson Foods against claims alleging a link between chicken litter and cancer.

The Lawyers: The lawyers here claim that they will try any case they think they are smart enough to win. And, if peers are to be believed, that will be a lot of cases as **John Everett** has "*the sharpest wits of anyone in Arkansas.*" Mesmerizing in the courtroom, he is widely considered "*the most versatile and brilliant trial lawyer*" in the state, with an ability to "*take witnesses and tear them apart.*" Unlike most in this table, however, he also tries criminal cases, including capital offences.

The Clients: The team serves a range of national corporations and individual clients across a spectrum of industries.

Rose Law Firm

The Firm: "*If you're up against them,*" say competitors, "*you know you've got a fight on your hands, but it will be a fair fight.*" This is a litigation practice that is "*doing a great job*" in defending its high-profile clients. A recent example includes successfully handling the defense of Griffin Chipping, Inc against a $2.6 million claim by Regions Bank arising from a corporate line of credit. It also managed to obtain a $1.5 million counterclaim in the same proceedings.

The Lawyers: "*Skilled and persuasive*" **Richard Donovan** was widely recommended by market sources. A "*forthright and honest advocate for his client,*" according to peers, he projects "*a good, solid presence in front of the jury.*"

The Clients: Griffin Chipping; Murphy Oil; Bank of the Ozarks and Acxiom.

Other Notable Practitioners

Kenneth Shemin of two-partner boutique, Shemin & Hendren, PLLC "*has great courage where others don't and is a genuine student of the law,*" say sources. Clients praised his "*absolute dedication and his ability to look at things from a holistic perspective – which means not always going to trial.*" This was echoed by another client, who acknowledged that "*we use him when there's a good chance of a settlement and we want a soft touch in mediation.*" However, his soft skills don't prevent him from being a formidable adversary on his feet in the courtroom. In the medical malpractice sphere, **Robert Shults** at Shults Law Firm, LLP undertakes a significant volume of malpractice and nursing home defense cases. Interviewees rate him as an "*excellent practitioner, who is extremely effective at trial.*" The state also boasts a wealth of talent in the environmental niche. **Andy Adams** of Barrett & Deacon divides his time between environmental regulatory and litigation work. Based in Northeast Arkansas, his practice focuses on water and natural resource work. Clients describe him as a "*real find, with a work ethic beyond belief.*" **Charles Nestrud** of Chisenhall, Nestrud & Julian, PA also works on both regulatory and litigation matters. Clients described him as "*just the most effective lawyer: smart, trustworthy and good value.*" A recent highlight for Nestrud includes work on an oil spill cleanup. "*Excellent lawyer*" **Alan Perkins** of Hill Gilstrap Perkins & Trotter, PC was also widely recommended for his environmental practice.

REAL ESTATE

Arkansas
Leading firms (Real Estate)

1. **FRIDAY, ELDREDGE & CLARK** Little Rock
   MITCHELL WILLIAMS SELIG GATES Little Rock
2. **DOVER DIXON HORNE** Little Rock
   HANKINS & HICKS Little Rock
   KUTAK ROCK LLP Little Rock
   QUATTLEBAUM, GROOMS, TULL Little Rock
   WRIGHT, LINDSEY & JENNINGS LLP Little Rock

Leading individuals (Real Estate)

Senior Statesman
MITCHELL Maurice *Mitchell Williams*, Little Rock

1. **BARRIER Christopher** *Mitchell Williams*, Little Rock
   GROOMS Timothy *Quattlebaum Grooms*, Little Rock
2. **DOVER Darrell** *Dover Dixon*, Little Rock
   HANKINS Stuart *Hankins & Hicks*, Little Rock
   SCHALLHORN Scott *Kutak Rock*, Little Rock
   SPIVEY III John *Wright Lindsey*, Little Rock
3. **HAMLIN Harold** *Mitchell Williams*, Little Rock
   SAXTON James *Friday Eldredge*, Little Rock
   TAYLOR Jay *Friday Eldredge*, Little Rock

Leading individuals
(Real Estate: Zoning/Land Use)

1. **FRAZIER Randy** *Quattlebaum Grooms*, Little Rock
   KEMP Hal *Kemp Duckett*, Little Rock

Firms and individuals are listed alphabetically in each band.

Band 1

Friday, Eldredge & Clark

The Firm: The firm's decision to create a formal real estate department, with around eight lawyers, reflects its increasing focus on the area. It is particularly connected with loan work and handles a variety of plain vanilla and complex real estate finance work for its impressive lender client base. For example, last year it advised on a $56 million financing for a new office and residential development in Northwest Arkansas, which involved 11 banks. The group also played a central role in the development of a planned community in Northeastern Arkansas.

The Lawyers: **James Saxton** is a new addition to this year's tables. He won plaudits from clients for his "*good connections and experience*" and his "*remarkable responsiveness.*" He has particular expertise in loan work, and is involved in matters outside, as well as inside, the state. Peers acknowledge that, despite his relative youth, **Jay Taylor** "*will clearly become one of the leaders in the area.*" Clients, meanwhile, keep returning to him because he is "*very thorough, knowledgeable in both real estate and finance, and easy to work with.*"

The Clients: Henry Corporation; Regions Bank; Dillard's; Bank of the Ozarks and Farmers Bank and Trust Company.

Mitchell Williams Selig Gates Woodyard, PLLC
See firm details p.180

The Firm: The firm is universally acknowledged to have one of the premier real estate practices in the state. "*Serious competitors with a lot of work,*" according to peers, the firm is popular with clients for the strength of its attorneys and their "*professionalism and grasp of the issues.*" Its broad experience spans real estate finance, acquisitions and disposals, leasing and development projects. Financing has been a particularly active part of the practice over the past twelve months, and it is also seeing an increase in sales and acquisitions. Recent highlights include negotiating multimillion-dollar loans documents for apartment projects in Northwest Arkansas and Oklahoma City.

The Lawyers: The dean of the real estate Bar, "*gentleman*" **Maurice Mitchell** (see p.177) is "*the most awesome attorney.*" Though he has been less visible on transactional work, he remains an enormous resource for the firm. Another highly respected real estate veteran is **Christopher Barrier** (see p.175). According to peers, he is "*a great lawyer – very thorough with a deep knowledge of the subject,*" while clients deemed him "*prompt and responsive: a real pro.*" Clients say **Harold Hamlin** (see p.176) is "*concise, succinct, to the point, extremely pleasant to work with and always arrives at the best conclusion.*"

The Clients: Bank of the Ozarks; Bailey Properties; Bank of America; BancorpSouth; MetLife and Arkansas Teacher Retirement System.

Band 2

Dover Dixon Horne

The Firm: This team maintains an excellent reputation for advising on the transactional and tax aspects of real property matters. These include acquisitions, development, leasing, title issues, loan transactions and tax-deferred exchanges. It was particularly recommended to researchers for loan work.

The Lawyers: Veteran real estate player, **Darrell Dover** is a "*capable and seasoned lawyer*" and a pleasure to deal with. Clients praised him for "*knowing the market and the laws, and having the capacity to resolve issues well.*"

The Clients: The team acts for, inter alia, the Arkansas Home Builders Association and a range of developer and lender clients.

Hankins & Hicks

The Firm: This compact but skilled group serves a "*strong client base,*" especially in the area of retail development work. It handles a range of real estate matters, including acquisitions and sales, commercial leases and real estate litigation.

The Lawyers: "*We value*" **Stuart Hankins**' "*practical, problem-solving mindset,*" said one interviewee of this highly respected real estate attorney. However, when the situation demands it, he can also be "*tenacious: effectively wearing out the other side.*" His noted experience of handling real estate litigation adds another string to his bow.

The Clients: Ashley Development; Twin City Bank; Community Bank; Apartment House Builders; National Coatings Company; Maumelle Water Management; Red Apple Enterprises and Aromatique.

Kutak Rock LLP

The Firm: This national firm maintains a significant presence in the Arkansas real estate market. Its corporate strength and superb client base ensure a healthy stream of work for its compact real estate group. Its varied expertise includes real estate finance, development work, acquisitions and disposals, advice on low-income housing credits, and the creation of efficient structures for real estate investment. Highlights of the past year include the development of a large residential golf course in Northwest Arkansas.

The Lawyers: **Scott Schallhorn** inspires confidence in both peers and clients. A "*skilled corporate and real estate lawyer,*" with a pragmatic, client-focused approach, he was also recommended for his "*good bond work.*" A feature of his practice in recent years has been the development of family housing projects, often involving complex finance issues.

The Clients: Among others, the firm represents Beverly Enterprises, as well as Fairfield Corporation and several of its sister companies.

Quattlebaum, Grooms, Tull & Burrow PLLC
See firm details p.181

The Firm: This highly regarded real estate group has been involved in numerous development projects over the past year. It advises buyers and sellers in acquisitions and disposals, combining this transactional acumen with tax, banking and regulatory expertise. It is also known for its experience in land use. Recent work includes advising on single-user developments for major retailers, as well as shopping mall and power center developments for multiusers.

The Lawyers: "*Top-notch*" **Tim Grooms** (see p.176) is "*a good lawyer with a large book of business.*" He was described to researchers as having an aggressive, high-energy style. His focus is on real estate acquisitions and disposals, however he is also involved in banking and regulatory matters and has recently expanded his lending practice. He also acts for real estate brokerage firms and state trade associations.

Randy Frazier (see p.176) advises on zoning disputes. His recent work has included matters for national and local retail and restaurant clients.

The Clients: Arkansas Community Bankers Association; Arkansas Realtors Association; Northwest Arkansas Home Builders Association; Nextel Partners; Sprint PCS; AT&T Wireless; Cricket Communications; Sonic Corporation and other retail and commercial developers.

Wright, Lindsey & Jennings LLP
See firm details p.182

The Firm: According to peers, this is one of the "*most active and significant practices*" in the state. It is best known for its high-profile bond financing, though its experience spans a variety of real estate finance and transactional work. The well-rounded, cross-departmental team also offers advice on real estate litigation, taxation and investment structures. The firm's close relationship with clients of the caliber of Cooper Realty Investments was noted.

The Lawyers: John Spivey (see p.177) was widely praised as a "*first-class municipal finance*"

lawyer with an impressive reputation in real estate-related finance transactions. Interviewees value his "*broad experience and creative approach to finding solutions.*"

The Clients: Bank of America; Cooper Realty Investments; Deltic Timber and Irwin & Saviers Company.

Other Notable Practitioners

Hal Kemp of Kemp, Duckett, Curry & Arnold was praised for his "*presentation skills and ability to evaluate a case well.*" He handles a considerable caseload of zoning work.

Leaders in Arkansas

ADAMS, Andy
Barrett & Deacon, Jonesboro
870 931 1700
Recommended in Litigation

ALLEN, William
Allen Law Firm, Little Rock
501 374 7100
Recommended in Litigation

ANDERSON, Philip
Williams & Anderson PLC, Little Rock
501 372 0800
Recommended in Litigation

ASKEW, Jess
Williams & Anderson PLC, Little Rock
501 372 0800
Recommended in Litigation

BARRIER, W Christopher
Mitchell, Williams, Selig, Gates Woodyard, PLLC, Little Rock
501 688 8806
cbarrier@mwsgw.com
Recommended in Real Estate

Practice Areas: Private practice since 1967 emphasizing real estate development, finance and litigation, land use, and municipal finance. Also, bond and conventional financing for industrial, residential, healthcare, higher education, utilities, and public improvements. Well published in these fields.

Prof. Memberships: Arkansas Bar Association - House of Delegates, Executive Council Member, Secretary-Treasurer, Executive Council Chair; Chair, Financial Institutions Law Section, 1992-93; Chair, Real Estate Law Committee, 1994-95; continuing legal education speaker (Best of CLE Award, 1996, 1997); Arkansas Bar Foundation - Board of Directors, Fellow. Best Lawyers in America (real estate law). Best Arkansas Real Estate Lawyer, Arkansas Times poll 2000.

BEARD III, RT
Mitchell, Williams, Selig, Gates Woodyard, PLLC, Little Rock
501 688 8832
rbeard@mwsgw.com
Recommended in Litigation

Practice Areas: Civil litigation, insurance defense and medical malpractice defense.

Prof. Memberships: American College of Trial Lawyers, Fellow; American Board of Trial Advocates, Member; International Association of Defense Counsel and Arkansas Association of Defense Counsel, Member; Recognized in The Best Lawyers in America; Editorial Board of Arkansas Law Review, 1970-71; Associate Editor and Editor of The Affiliate newsletter, served on Executive Council and Affiliate Outreach Team, Young Lawyers Division, American Bar Association; President of the Young Lawyers section, member of the House of Delegates and the Executive Committee, Arkansas Bar Association; Civil Procedure Committee, Member.

BENHAM, Paul
Friday, Eldredge & Clark, Little Rock
501 376 2011
Recommended in Corporate/M&A

BOE, Tim
Rose Law Firm, Little Rock
501 375 9131
Recommended in Employment

BUFORD, Douglas
Mitchell, Williams, Selig, Gates Woodyard, PLLC, Little Rock
501 688 8866
dbuford@mwsgw.com
Recommended in Corporate/M&A

Practice Areas: Corporate law; securities; mergers and acquisitions. Representing and advising clients on mergers, acquisitions, financing and other forms of business transactions. Advising and representing individuals, corporations and partnerships in all facets of securities laws before securities regulatory

agencies and self-regulatory organizations. Representing and advising banks, bank holding companies, and savings and loan associations on business and regulatory matters.

Prof. Memberships: Beta Alpha Psi; Gamma Beta Phi (President). Blue Key. Editor-in-Chief, Arkansas Law Review, 1973. CPA, Arkansas, 1973. Recipient: E. L. Cullum Award. Listed in: Who's Who in Arkansas Universities. President, Student Union Governing Board. Best Lawyers in America.

CHILES IV, EB (Chip)
Quattlebaum, Grooms, Tull & Burrow PLLC, Little Rock 501 379 1734
cchiles@qgtb.com
Recommended in Litigation

Practice Areas: Primary areas of practice include business, employment, and products liability litigation.

Prof. Memberships: DRI, Eighth Circuit Bar Association, and William R. Overton Inn of Court.

Career: Admitted to Arkansas and Tennessee Bars, Eighth and Sixth Circuits, and US Supreme Court. A Partner of Quattlebaum, Grooms, Tull & Burrow PLLC.

Publications: A Hand to Rock the Cradle: Transracial Adoption, the Multiethnic Placement Act and a Proposal for the Arkansas General Assembly, 49 Arkansas Law Review 501 (1996).

Personal: Received a JD (cum laude) from Harvard Law School in 1996 and BA (summa cum laude) from Hendrix College in 1993.

CLARK, Ronald
Rose Law Firm, Little Rock
501 375 9131
Recommended in Corporate/M&A, Tax

CRASS, Kevin
Friday, Eldredge & Clark, Little Rock
501 376 2011
Recommended in Litigation

CROSS, J Bruce
Cross, Gunter, Witherspoon & Galchus, PC, Little Rock
501 212 1800
bcross@cgwg.com
Recommended in Employment

Practice Areas: Labor and employment, Director.

Career: Mr Cross is listed in the Outstanding Lawyers of America (2004-05). The International Directory of Distinguished Leadership, Who's Who in America, Who's Who in American Law, Who's Who Legal Eagles, Who's Who in the South and Southwest, Who's Who in the United States, and International Who's Who of Professionals and in a leading US legal publication.

Publications: Contributing author to supplements to Elkouri & Elkouri, 'How Arbitration Works'.

Personal: Mr Cross received his undergraduate degree from the University of Notre Dame and his JD from the University of Arkansas School of Law.

DAVIS, Oscar
Friday, Eldredge & Clark, Little Rock
501 376 2011
Recommended in Employment

DONOVAN, Richard
Rose Law Firm, Little Rock
501 375 9131
Recommended in Litigation

DOVER, Darrell
Dover Dixon Horne, Little Rock
501 375 9151
Recommended in Real Estate

EBEL, Walter
Friday, Eldredge & Clark, Little Rock
501 376 2011
Recommended in Corporate/M&A

EISEMAN, Byron
Friday, Eldredge & Clark, Little Rock
501 376 2011
Recommended in Corporate/M&A

EVERETT, John
Everett Law Firm, Fayetteville
479 443 0292
Recommended in Litigation

FLETCHER, John
Kutak Rock LLP, Little Rock
501 975 3000
Recommended in Corporate/M&A

FRAZIER, Randy
Quattlebaum, Grooms, Tull & Burrow
PLLC, Little Rock
501 379 1771
rfrazier@qgtb.com
Recommended in Real Estate

Practice Areas: Primary areas of practice include banking law, real estate acquisitions and financing and zoning law.
Career: Admitted to the Arkansas Bar (1984).
Personal: Received a JD from University of Oklahoma School of Law in 1984 and a BA from Olivet Nazarene University (summa cum laude) in 1981.

FREELAND, Byron
Mitchell, Williams, Selig, Gates Woodyard, PLLC, Little Rock 501 688 8810
bfreeland@mwsgw.com
Recommended in Employment

Practice Areas: Civil litigation. Representation of employers, including the largest hospital system in Arkansas, in Title VII defense. Advising employers on various labor law matters, including wage and hour issues, reductions in force, termination and disciplinary issues and employee benefits issues. Litigating and arbitrating construction contract disputes. Complex commercial litigation; representation of the City of Jacksonville before Civil Commission and in Court. Attorney for Arkansas Racing Commission since 1975.
Prof. Memberships: Speaker at state and regional seminars on employment law issues sponsored by Arkansas Institute of Continuing Legal Education; Member, Arkansas Bar Association, Arkansas Hospital Association, and American Hospital Association.

GALCHUS, Donna Smith
Cross, Gunter, Witherspoon & Galchus, PC, Little Rock 501 212 1803
dgalchus@cgwg.com
Recommended in Employment

Practice Areas: Labor and employment, immigration, Director.
Prof. Memberships: American Bar Association (labor and employment, serves on Federal Labor Standards Committee), American Immigration Lawyers Association, Arkansas Bar Foundation, College of Labor and Employment Lawyers.
Career: Ms Galchus is listed in Best Lawyers in America (2004-05); Board of Directors, Arkansas Council on Economic Education; Board of Directors, Wildwood Park; member, Arkansas Hospitality Association.
Publications: Board of Editors, ABA

Section of Labor and Employment Law, The Fair Labor Standards Act (1999).
Personal: BS University of Missouri-St. Louis (cum laude), MA Economics Washington University-St. Louis, JD University of Arkansas at Little Rock.

GARDNER, Price
Friday, Eldredge & Clark, Little Rock
501 376 2011
Recommended in Corporate/M&A

GATES, Allan
Mitchell, Williams, Selig, Gates Woodyard, PLLC, Little Rock 501 688 8816
agates@mwsgw.com
Recommended in Litigation

Practice Areas: All aspects of environmental law. Counsel to private parties, public interest groups, and trade associations in nonenvironmental regulatory matters. Lead counsel in complex commercial disputes and litigation.
Prof. Memberships: Law clerk to Chief Judge Pat Mehaffy, US Court of Appeals, Eighth Circuit, and Associate Justice Harry A Blackmun, US Supreme Court; Adjunct professor, Environmental Law, UALR Law School; Guest lecturer, environmental law, University of Arkansas for Medical Sciences; Panelist and speaker in national, regional and state seminars on environmental law and litigation; American Law Institute and Environmental Law Institute, Member; Arkansas Bar Committee on Alternate Dispute Resolution, Member.

GRAVES, Kathlyn
Mitchell, Williams, Selig, Gates Woodyard, PLLC, Little Rock 501 688 8831
kgraves@mwsgw.com
Recommended in Employment

Practice Areas: Lead counsel to public and private employers in all areas of labor and employment law and litigation.
Prof. Memberships: American College of Labor and Employment Lawyers, Fellow; American Bar Association, Labor and Employment Law and Litigation Section, Member; Arkansas Bar Association, Labor and Employment Law Section, Member; Pulaski County Bar Association, Member; Arkansas Bar Foundation, Fellow; American Arbitration Association Employment Dispute Resolution Panel, Member; American Bar Association Committee for Federal Judiciary, 1989-91, Eighth Circuit Member; Southwestern Law Journal, 1973-74; Arkansas Women Leadership Forum, Member; American Employment Law Council, Member; named in Best Lawyers in America (employment law).

GREGORY, Watt
Kutak Rock LLP, Little Rock
501 975 3000
Recommended in Corporate/M&A

GROOMS, Timothy
Quattlebaum, Grooms, Tull & Burrow
PLLC, Little Rock 501 379 1713
tgrooms@qgtb.com
Recommended in Real Estate

Practice Areas: Primary areas of practice are banking law, real estate, acquisitions and financing, and he serves as General Counsel to the Arkansas REALTORS Association, Arkansas Homebuilders Association and the Arkansas Community Bankers.
Prof. Memberships: American, Arkansas and Pulaski County Bar Associations; American College of Real Estate Lawyers; International Council of Shopping Centers.
Career: Admitted to the Arkansas Bar (1984). A founding Partner of Quattlebaum, Grooms, Tull & Burrow PLLC. Licensed real estate broker, Arkansas, 1979.
Personal: Received a JD (with high honors) from the University of Arkansas at Little Rock Law School in 1984 and a BBA (magna cum laude) from the University of Arkansas at Little Rock in 1981.

GRUNDFEST, Jack
Mitchell, Williams, Selig, Gates Woodyard, PLLC, Little Rock 501 688 8878
jgrundfest@mwsgw.com
Recommended in Corporate/M&A

Practice Areas: Transactions; taxation and tax planning; real estate exchanges, acquisitions and development; estate planning. Counsel to corporations, partnerships, other entities and individuals concerning formation, reorganization, acquisitions and related tax planning matters, and drafting documents necessary to accomplish these objectives.
Prof. Memberships: American Bar Association, Member (Taxation Section); Arkansas Bar Association, Member; Pulaski County Bar Association, Member. Adjunct Professor of Law in Corporations, UALR William H. Bowen School of Law.
Career: Prior to entering the practice of law, experience in business included banking, finance, and real estate development.

GUNTER, Russell
Cross, Gunter, Witherspoon & Galchus, PC, Little Rock 501 212 1801
rgunter@cgwg.com
Recommended in Employment

Practice Areas: Labor and employment law, Director.
Prof. Memberships: Active: The American Bar Association's Committee on Practice & Procedure before the National Labor Relations Board, and the Labor & Employment Law Section. Certified by the Society for Human Resource Management, Human Resource Certification Institute as a Senior Professional in Human Resources.
Career: Licensed to practice law by the states of Arkansas and Texas, federal courts in Arkansas and Texas, Eighth and Fifth Circuit Courts of Appeals and

the United States Supreme Court. Selected for inclusion in the current and past editions of a leading US legal publication.

HAMLIN, Harold
Mitchell, Williams, Selig, Gates Woodyard, PLLC, Little Rock
501 688 8868
hhamlin@mwsgw.com
Recommended in Real Estate

Practice Areas: Counsel to developers, property managers, retailers and petroleum marketers concerning the conveyance, purchase and leasing of real property. Counsel to financial institutions on a variety of lending and transactional matters. Counsel to business entities regarding formation, merger, acquisition, and sale of business. Former Assistant Attorney General representing Arkansas Department of Parks and Tourism and Arkansas Contractors Licensing Board.
Prof. Memberships: American Bar, Arkansas Bar, and Pulaski County Bar Associations, Member. Arkansas Air National Guard, Lt. Colonel; Embry-Riddle Aeronautical University, Adjunct Faculty; Associate Survey/Comments Editor, UALR Law Journal; Assistant Research Editor, UALR Law Journal.

HANKINS, Stuart
Hankins & Hicks, Little Rock
501 371 9226
Recommended in Real Estate

HERRINGTON, Daniel
Friday, Eldredge & Clark, Little Rock
501 376 2011
Recommended in Employment

JACK Jr, Donald
Jack, Lyon & Jones, PC, Little Rock
501 375 1122
Recommended in Corporate/M&A

JACKSON, William Stuart
Wright, Lindsey & Jennings LLP, Little Rock 501 371 0808
wjackson@wlj.com
Recommended in Employment

Practice Areas: Federal and state court litigation and appeals, including claims under Title VII, ADA, FMLA, ADEA, EPA, and 42 USC Sec. 1981 and 1983, and state law claims involving trade secrets, non-compete agreements, arbitration agreements, the Arkansas Civil Rights Act, and wrongful discharge.
Prof. Memberships: American Bar Association (Labor and Employment Law Section); Arkansas Bar Association; Pulaski County Bar Association.
Career: Partner since 1998.
Personal: Duke Law School (JD 1992); Hendrix College (BA 1989, magna cum laude with distinction). Youth Opportunities Unlimited Board Member, 1995-present; American Diabetes Association (Chair of the Central Arkansas Council 2003-04; Council Member 2001-present).

JONES, Michael
Gilker and Jones PA, Mountainburg
479 369 4294
Recommended in Employment

KAPLAN, Philip
Kaplan, Brewer, Maxey & Haralson,
Little Rock
501 372 0400
*Recommended in Employment,
Litigation*

KEMP, Hal
Kemp, Duckett, Curry & Arnold, Little
Rock 501 372 7243
Recommended in Real Estate

KUMPE, Peter
Williams & Anderson PLC, Little Rock
501 372 0800
Recommended in Litigation

LILE, John G
Wright, Lindsey & Jennings LLP, Little
Rock 501 371 0808
jlile@wlj.com
*Recommended in Employment,
Litigation*
Practice Areas: Business and commercial litigation (including employment discrimination) and product liability.
Prof. Memberships: American Bar Association (Litigation and Labor and Employment Law Sections); Arkansas Bar Association (Chair, Professional Ethics Committee 2002-04; Chair, Young Lawyers Section 1971-72); Pulaski County Bar Association; Jefferson County Bar Association (President 1973); National Association of Railroad Trial Counsel; Fellow, American College of Trial Lawyers; Fellow, American Bar Foundation; Arkansas Association of Defense Counsel.
Career: Coleman, Gantt & Ramsay (1962-65); Ramsay, Cox, Lile, Bridgforth, Gilbert, Harrelson and Starling (1965-87); Partner, Wright, Lindsey & Jennings LLP since 1990.
Personal: Hendrix College (BA 1959); Duke University (LLB 1962).

LOWTHER Jr, Edwin L
Wright, Lindsey & Jennings LLP,
Little Rock 501 371 0808
elowther@wlj.com
Recommended in Litigation
Practice Areas: General litigation (including product liability), legal and medical malpractice, toxic tort, and employment litigation.
Prof. Memberships: American Bar Association (Tort and Insurance Practice and Litigation Sections); Arkansas Bar Association; Pulaski County Bar Association; American College of Trial Lawyers; American Board of Trial Advocates; Arkansas Association of Defense Counsel; International Association of Defense Counsel; Fellow, Arkansas Bar Foundation.
Career: Partner since 1987. Managing Partner (2005-).
Personal: Ouachita Baptist University (BA1975, cum laude); University of

Arkansas at Little Rock (JD 1981, with honors); UALR Law Journal (1980-81).

MARTIN, Dave
Rose Law Firm, Little Rock
501 375 9131
Recommended in Employment

MAXEY, JoAnn
Kaplan, Brewer, Maxey & Haralson,
Little Rock 501 372 0400
Recommended in Employment

MITCHELL, H Maurice
Mitchell, Williams, Selig, Gates Woodyard, PLLC, Little Rock
501 688 8801
mmitchell@mwsgw.com
Recommended in Real Estate
Practice Areas: Finance, corporate and real estate.
Prof. Memberships: Pulaski County Bar Association (President, 1990-91), Member; Arkansas Bar Association, Member (Secretary-Treasurer, member of Executive Committee, 1952-59; Senior Task Force Committee, 1994-96; Chair, Legal Services Task Force Committee, 1996-99); American Bar Association, Member; American and Arkansas Bar Foundations, Fellow; American Judicature Society, former Director.

MOORE, Michael
Friday, Eldredge & Clark, Little Rock
501 376 2011
Recommended in Employment

NESTRUD, Charles
Chisenhall, Nestrud & Julian, PA,
Little Rock 501 372 5800
Recommended in Litigation

NISBET, Wyckliff
Friday, Eldredge & Clark, Little Rock
501 376 2011
Recommended in Employee Benefits

PERKINS, Alan
Hill Gilstrap Perkins & Trotter, PC,
Little Rock
501 603 9000
Recommended in Litigation

POWELL, David
Williams & Anderson PLC, Little Rock
501 372 0800
Recommended in Litigation

QUATTLEBAUM, Steven
Quattlebaum, Grooms, Tull & Burrow
PLLC, Little Rock
501 379 1707
quattlebaum@qgtb.com
Recommended in Litigation
Practice Areas: Primary areas of practice include business, products liability, environmental and toxic tort litigation.
Prof. Memberships: International Academy of Trial Lawyers, American Board of Trial Advocates, Products Liability Advisory Council, William R Overton Inn of Court.
Career: Admitted to the Arkansas Bar (1984). A founding Partner of Quattlebaum, Grooms, Tull & Burrow PLLC.
Publications: 'Defending the Institution

of Trial by Jury', Voire Dire, Fall 2001; 'Effective Video Presentations at Trial', Arkansas Lawyer, Spring and Summer 1993.
Personal: Received a JD from the University of Arkansas in 1983 and a BA from Western State College of Colorado in 1981.

RATHER Jr, Gordon S
Wright, Lindsey & Jennings LLP,
Little Rock 501 371 0808
grather@wlj.com
Recommended in Litigation
Practice Areas: Litigation (including product liability,toxic tort, commercial issues, and maritime personal injury defense).
Prof. Memberships: American Board of Trial Advocates (National President 1996; President, Arkansas Chapter 1987-88); American College of Trial Lawyers (Fellow); International Academy of Trial Lawyers (Fellow and State Chair); Arkansas Association of Defense Counsel; Maritime Law Association of the United States (Proctor); American Bar Association (Litigation Section); Arkansas Bar Association; Pulaski County Bar Association; Arkansas Bar Foundation (Fellow); Arkansas Chapter of The Fellows of the American Bar Foundation.
Career: Partner since 1972.
Personal: Vanderbilt University (BA 1961, cum laude), Phi Beta Kappa; Duke University (JD 1968).

ROBINSON, Spencer
Ramsay, Bridgforth, Harrelson &
Starling LLP, Pine Bluff 870 535 9000
Recommended in Employment

SAXTON, James
Friday, Eldredge & Clark, Little Rock
501 376 2011
Recommended in Real Estate

SCHALLHORN, Scott
Kutak Rock LLP, Little Rock
501 975 3000
Recommended in Real Estate

SELIG, John S
Mitchell, Williams, Selig, Gates Woodyard, PLLC, Little Rock
501 688 8804
jselig@mwsgw.com
Recommended in Corporate/M&A
Practice Areas: Corporate and municipal finance, securities regulation, public utilities, banking, savings and loan and business law.
Prof. Memberships: Arkansas Liaison for State Regulation of Securities Committee, American Bar Association; Best Lawyers in America (1993 - current); former Arkansas Securities Commissioner; member, American Law Institute; Chairman of the Bank Powers Subcommittee of the Governor's Task Force For the Revision of the Arkansas State Banking Code (enacted 1997).
Publications: Author, Registration and Regulation of Broker-Dealers, Agents

and Investment Advisors, 'Blue Sky Regulation' published by Matthew Bender & Company, Inc.

SHEMIN, Kenneth
Shemin & Hendren, PLLC, Fayetteville
479 973 4442
Recommended in Litigation

SHIPLEY III, Benjamin H
Cross, Gunter, Witherspoon & Galchus,
PC, Fort Smith 479 783 8200
bshipley@cgwg.com
Recommended in Employment
Practice Areas: Labor and employment, commercial litigation, Director.
Prof. Memberships: Arkansas Bar Association (Labor and Employment, House of Delegates, Foundation Fellow and Judicial Nominations Committee), American Bar Association (Labor and Employment), Society for Human Resource Management, W.B. Putnam American Inn of Court (Master).
Career: Mr Shipley is listed in Best Lawyers in America (2004-05). He is also Chairman, Board of Directors of United Way; Board of Directors, City of Fort Smith; recipient, Distinguished Eagle Scout Award.
Personal: Mr Shipley graduated with honors from Southern Methodist University and received his JD from the University of Arkansas at Fayetteville School of Law.

SHULTS, Robert
Shults Law Firm, LLP, Little Rock
501 375 2301
Recommended in Litigation

SMITH, Laura
Friday, Eldredge & Clark, Little Rock
501 376 2011
Recommended in Litigation

SPIVEY III, John William
Wright, Lindsey & Jennings LLP,
Little Rock 501 371 0808
jspivey@wlj.com
Recommended in Real Estate
Practice Areas: Banking and finance, commercial real estate, zoning and land use, acquisitions, municipal bonds, bankruptcy, and property tax appeals.
Prof. Memberships: American Bar Association (Urban, State and Local Government Law and Real Property, Probate and Trust Law Sections); Arkansas Bar Association; Pulaski County Bar Association; National Association of Bond Lawyers.
Career: Partner since 1983.
Personal: Hendrix College Alumni Loyalty Fund (past Chair); Hendrix College Alumni Association (past member, Board of Governors); Arkansas Territorial Restoration Foundation (past President, Board Member); Westside YMCA (past member, Board of Management); Camp Aldersgate, Inc. (past Treasurer, past member, Board of Directors).

SUTTON, William
Friday, Eldredge & Clark, Little Rock
501 376 2011
Recommended in Litigation

TAYLOR, Jay
Friday, Eldredge & Clark, Little Rock
501 376 2011
Recommended in Real Estate

TISDALE, John R
Wright, Lindsey & Jennings LLP,
Little Rock 501 371 0808
jtisdale@wlj.com
Recommended in Corporate/M&A
Practice Areas: Taxation (including
tax-exempt financing, corporate and
partnership issues), corporate law,
health law and real estate.
Prof. Memberships: American Bar
Association (Taxation and Business Law
Sections); Arkansas Bar Association;
Pulaski County Bar Association; National Association of Bond Lawyers; Fellow,
Arkansas Bar Foundation.
Career: Partner since 1980.
Personal: Rhodes College (BA 1968,

with honors); Washington University
(JD 1975), Managing Editor, Washington University Law Quarterly (1974-75).
Our House (Board of Directors 1998-
present); Chancellor, Episcopal Diocese
of Arkansas; Moderator for various
American Institute of Certified Public
Accountants continuing professional
education seminars; Advisor, Tobacco
Settlement Task Force-Arkansas House
of Representatives.

TULL III, John E
Quattlebaum, Grooms, Tull & Burrow
PLLC, Little Rock 501 379 1705
jtull@qgtb.com
Recommended in Litigation
Practice Areas: Mr Tull's primary areas
of practice are commercial litigation,
media law and products liability.
Prof. Memberships: American,
Arkansas and Pulaski County Bar Associations, ABOTA, DRI and MLRC.
Career: Admitted to the Arkansas Bar
(1984). A founding Partner of Quattlebaum, Grooms, Tull & Borrow PLLC.

Personal: Received a JD (with high
honors) from the University of Arkansas
in 1984 and a BA from Vanderbilt University in 1980.

WADDELL Jr, William
Friday, Eldredge & Clark, Little Rock
501 376 2011
Recommended in Litigation

WITHERSPOON, Carolyn B
Cross, Gunter, Witherspoon & Galchus,
PC, Little Rock 501 212 1802
cspoon@cgwg.com
Recommended in Employment
Practice Areas: Employment and
labor, Director.
Prof. Memberships: Past President of
Arkansas Bar Association, former member, Executive Council of National Conference of Bar Presidents & Executive
Committee of Transportation Lawyers
Association. The American Law Institute, The House of Delegates of American Bar Association, Fellow of the College of Labor and Employment Lawyers,
TIPS, and EEO Committee (Labor Law

Section-American Bar Association).
Career: Licensed to practice law in
Arkansas, Federal Court, 8th Circuit
Court of Appeals & US Supreme Court.
Arbitrator, The Court of Arbitration for
Sport, AAA Roster of Employment
Arbitrators. Listed in 1995-2005 editions
of leading US legal publication.

CROSS, GUNTER, WITHERSPOON & GALCHUS, P.C.

THE FIRM

Managing Partner: Richard 'Rick' Roderick
Number of directors: 11
Number of associates: 8

FIRM OVERVIEW: The law firm of Cross, Gunter, Witherspoon & Galchus, P.C., represents union and non-union companies, locally, regionally and nationally, in almost every industry. From trucking to banking, manufacturing to health care, retailing to hospitality, and many others, with 100 plus years of cumulative experience, the firm's lawyers intertwine legal expertise with practical hands-on knowledge of business operations to provide its clients with successful and economical strategies.

MAIN PRACTICE AREAS:

Labor & Employment: Listed as the best management labor/employment law firm in Arkansas, the firm is well recognized with emphasis on union avoidance and NLRB matters; EEOC charges and lawsuits; arbitration, contract interpretation/negotiation of DOL-OFCCP/affirmative action matters, and general employment advice.

Employee Relations: The firm has worked for many years with a broad cross-section of companies to develop effective employee relations programs designed to attract, maintain and motivate high-quality employees. CGWG works with clients to design and implement employee compensation and benefits programs, management development programs, communications and employee motivation programs, personnel policies and practices, and seminars/training. With its extensive knowledge of labor and employment issues, CGWG also advises and counsels multinational corporations, United States corporations doing business oversees, and foreign employers with operations in the United States regarding labor and employment issues.

Construction Law: The firm handles materialman's and laborer's liens, licensing, payment and performance bond claims, construction contract drafting interpretation and disputes, and Miller Act claims.

Immigration: The firm works with employers and individuals to offer assistance in obtaining non-immigrant visas and immigrant status. It also offers employers strategic planning advice and counseling on compliance issues, including Forms I-9 and Social Security documentation.

General Litigation: CGWG handles a wide spectrum of cases in a number of diverse areas of law. Active in state and federal courts at the trial and appellate levels, the firm's lawyers are able to fully and aggressively address the litigation needs and concerns of its clients. CGWG lawyers are experienced and skilled in: products liability, professional liability, general insurance defense, commercial litigation, credit card fraud, and bankruptcy litigation.

Healthcare: The firm represents healthcare providers, including hospitals, nursing homes, and clinics in matters involving medical staff membership and credentialing; employee benefits; administrative and regulatory matters, including permits of approval, licensing and reimbursement; development of policies and procedures, including corporate compliance programs and HIPAA compliance; and general corporate matters including personal services and employment agreements, recruitment agreements, and joint ventures between providers.

Products Liability: CGWG represents insurers, manufacturers and suppliers in the defense of products liability actions involving such items as motor vehicles, heavy equipment, home appliances and medical devices, as well as other industrial and consumer products. The firm serves as local counsel for several national and international manufacturers.

HEAD OFFICE

ARKANSAS
500 President Clinton Avenue, Suite 200, **Little Rock**, Arkansas 72201
Tel: 501 371 9999 **Fax:** 501 371 0035
Website: www.cgwg.com

BRANCH OFFICES

ARKANSAS
5401 Rogers Avenue, Suite 200, **Fort Smith**, AR 72903
Tel: 479 783 8200 **Fax:** 479 783 8265

101 West Mountain Street, Suite 200, **Fayetteville**, AR 72701
Tel: 479 443 6978 **Fax:** 479 443 7697

Corporate & Business: Significant experience in business and corporate law matters including: incorporating businesses; establishing limited liability companies, partnerships and joint ventures; drafting and reviewing various types of business and commercial contracts including leases, contracts of sale, and noncompete agreements; handling all legal matters related to the acquisition and sale of businesses; and advising clients regarding debt collection methods and procedures.

CLIENTS: Categories of clients: trucking companies; retailers; banks; builders and construction companies; hospitality employers; manufacturers; retail, non-profits; utilities; municipalities; information technology companies; hospitals (general medical/surgical and behavioral); physician clinics and offices; home health agencies; hospices; nursing homes; nursing home development companies; durable medical equipment suppliers; and community mental health centers.

MITCHELL, WILLIAMS, SELIG, GATES & WOODYARD, P.L.L.C.

THE FIRM

Managing Member: Jack Grundfest

Number of Members: 37
Number of other lawyers: 27

FIRM OVERVIEW: Mitchell, Williams, Selig, Gates & Woodyard, P. L. L. C. was founded in 1954 by Maurice Mitchell. Today, Mitchell Williams is the second largest law firm in Arkansas, with more than 60 lawyers and a large staff of legal assistants and support personnel. Well known for expertise in business, regulated business, and litigation, the attorneys at Mitchell Williams are among the most respected and knowledgeable in the profession. Mitchell Williams has been providing positive and measurable results, outstanding client communication, innovative solutions, creative problem solving, and fair, flexible billing arrangements for over 50 years. The firm's achievements are evidenced by the national recognition, appointments, awards, and honors of its attorneys, many of whom are consistently listed in 'Best Lawyers in America'.

HEAD OFFICE

ARKANSAS
425 West Capitol Avenue, Suite 1800, **Little Rock,** AR 72201-3525
Tel: 501 688 8800   **Fax:** 501 688 8807
Website: www.mitchellwilliamslaw.com

BRANCH OFFICE

ARKANSAS
Northwest Arkansas Office: 5414 Pinnacle Point Drive, Suite 500
Rogers, AR 72758-8131
Tel: 479 273 9561   **Fax:** 479 273 0527

MAIN AREAS OF PRACTICE

Business: The firm has extensive experience in representing business clients in a broad range of areas. The firm represents clients in all forms of commercial transactions including transfers of intangible intellectual property. The firm structured and closed Arkansas' largest transfer of privately-held assets, including the transfer of thousands of mortgage assets representing properties in 25 states in a single transaction. The firm represents both creditors and debtors in bankruptcy and related matters. The firm has comprehensive experience working with individual and corporate clients on all forms of taxation issues, estate planning and trust administration, and transactions involving the transfer of controlling or other significant interests in business entities. The firm is an established leader in Arkansas banking law, regularly assisting banks and other financial institutions on various regulatory issues and lending transactions. The firm's attorneys have been involved in mergers and acquisitions, drawing upon their knowledge in corporate, tax, environmental, securities, antitrust, regulatory, and property law. Engagements have included acquisitions and mergers of banks and bank holding companies, hospitals, multi-state insurance companies, a multi-state cable TV system, multinational transactions including Arkansas assets, and the sale of a major Arkansas electric utility's out-of-state service area. The firm also deals regularly with tax-exempt financings of real estate projects and the necessary mortgage documents on behalf of issuers, underwriters, and utilizers of the financing, including non-profit and public institutions. The firm regularly represents diverse industries regarding SEC and state securities matters and in litigating these issues in state and federal courts and before arbitrators. The firm has worked in municipal finance and has the distinction of having acted as bond counsel for the largest tax-exempt general obligation bond issue in Arkansas history. The firm has proven experience in employee relations and negotiations. The firm represents tax-exempt entities, governmental units, privately-held companies, and publicly-traded companies with respect to all types of pension and welfare benefit plans, including ESOPs, non-qualified plans and 401(k) plans.

Litigation: The firm is equipped to handle all forms of civil litigation. The firm has a national trial practice and client base, and has served as regional coordinating counsel for large insurance carriers. The firm's attorneys have actual trial experience in every corner of Arkansas in both state and federal courts, as well as substantial appellate experience. Recognized specialities include class action defense, where the firm has acted as defense counsel for nationwide and statewide consumer, insurance and product actions; toxic tort defense of lawsuits alleging nuisance, trespass, personal injury or strict liability claims based on alleged violations of state and federal environmental laws; products liability and drug/medical defense, representing national manufacturers including chemical manufacturers, pharmaceutical firms, laboratories, medical device makers and distributors; labor/employment defense, including all forms of Title VII litigation, age discrimination, Americans With Disabilities Act, wrongful termination, wage and hour disputes and NLRB claims; insurance defense, including automobile and vehicular liability, commercial general liability, contractor's liability, and homeowner's liability; medical malpractice defense, including defense work for individual physicians, dentists, nurses, hospitals and nursing homes; insurance coverage defense, handling disputes arising directly from the insurance coverage, including ERISA issues and representation of corporate, small business and individual interests in litigation arising from a variety of corporate transactions.

Regulated Industries: The firm is unique in the number of attorneys coming from the government and private sector, bringing it invaluable experience in dealing with highly regulated businesses. The firm has extensive experience nationwide in virtually every aspect of insurance-related corporate and regulatory law. The firm engages in extensive representations before all state insurance departments and the National Association of Insurance Commissioners. The firm also handles mergers, acquisitions, self critical analyses, market conduct issues, and defense of regulatory actions. The firm has represented public utilities and has handled certification proceedings for major generation, transmission and distribution facilities, and rate cases, and has participated in many rule-making proceedings. The firm boasts a team of attorneys with over 60 years of combined experience in environmental law.

MITCHELL·WILLIAMS
SELIG • GATES • WOODYARD • PLLC

Knowledge. Experience. Results.
For Over 50 Years.

CHAMBERS USA 2005

QUATTLEBAUM, GROOMS, TULL & BURROW PLLC

THE FIRM

Number of partners: 6
Number of other lawyers: 15

FIRM OVERVIEW: Quattlebaum, Grooms, Tull & Burrow PLLC provides a full range of business-related legal services. The firm represents individuals, sole proprietorships, partnerships, limited liability companies, corporations, and government organizations. Its practice encompasses a wide variety of transactions, litigation, regulatory work, and estate planning.

MAIN AREAS OF PRACTICE

Corporate & Commercial: The firm has extensive experience in litigating complex business and commercial cases, including class actions. It has been involved in numerous matters involving multiple parties and claims pending in multiple jurisdictions. These cases have included antitrust litigation, business and commercial disputes, construction disputes, securities disputes, franchise disputes, employment discrimination and related disputes, real estate litigation, toxic tort claims, products liability claims, professional malpractice claims, libel and First Amendment claims, constitutional law claims, and insurance coverage litigation. The firm has represented corporate and individual clients, as both plaintiffs and defendants. It also has extensive litigation experience in trial and appellate courts on both the state and federal levels.

Banking & Finance: The firm has extensive experience in a wide range of banking issues for state and national banks and bank holding companies, including bank formation, holding company formation, loan transactions, representation of the bank as creditor, as well as regulatory and compliance issues involving the FDIC, the OCC, and the Federal Reserve Board. It is frequently called upon to prepare loan documentation and provide legal opinions in the areas of usury, enforceability of security interests, and choice of law issues. The firm has advised clients on issues involving financing for public and private entities. It has acted as bond counsel and trustee counsel in Arkansas Development Finance Authority bond issues. The firm has counseled issuers in numerous corporate securities offerings, including initial and secondary capital offerings for financial institutions, offerings for bank holding companies, and restricted offerings pursuant to Regulation D. Frequently in connection with securities offerings, the firm is called upon to offer professional advice on ancillary issues in securities offerings, such as taxation, real estate, banking and environmental issues.

Real Estate: The firm represents, among others, developers, lenders, investment banks, pension funds, domestic investors and major corporations in connection with real estate-related transactions involving the purchase, sale, construction, financing, development, management and operation of commercial, industrial and residential projects throughout Arkansas and the United States; the public and private offering of various types of real estate securities; securitized lending transactions; leasing on behalf of landlords and major tenants; real estate litigation; and debt restructuring transactions on behalf of lenders and borrowers.

HEAD OFFICE

ARKANSAS
111 Center Street, Suite 1900, **Little Rock**, Arkansas 72201
Tel: 501 379 1700 **Fax:** 501 379 1701
Website: www.qgtb.com

CONTACTS

Banking & Finance	Patrick A Burrow
Commercial Property	Timothy W Grooms
Environmental	Al Eckert
Litigation	Steven W Quattlebaum
	John E Tull III
	Kristine G Baker
	EB (Chip) Chiles, IV

CLIENTS: Abbott Laboratories Inc.; Acxiom Corporation; Arkansas Community Bankers; Arkansas Press Association; Arkansas REALTORS® Association; AT&T Wireless, Inc.; BancorpSouth Bank; BASF Corporation; Building & Utility Contractors, Inc.; CenterPoint Energy; DaimlerChrysler Corporation; Entergy Corporation; H&R Block, Inc.; The Phillips Companies; Koppers Industries, Inc.; Simmons First National Bank; Uniroyal; Multi-Purpose Civic Center Facility Board for Pulaski County (Alltel Arena); Moses Tucker Real Estate, Inc.; Regions Bank; Salomon Smith Barney, Inc.; Schering-Plough Corp.; US Bank; Vulcan Materials Company; and Waste Management, Inc.

QUATTLEBAUM, GROOMS, TULL & BURROW, PLLC

WRIGHT, LINDSEY & JENNINGS LLP

THE FIRM

Managing Partner: Chair of Management Committee
Number of partners: 41
Number of other attorneys: 19

FIRM OVERVIEW: Wright, Lindsey & Jennings LLP is a full service law firm with offices in Little Rock and Rogers, Arkansas, from which legal services are provided to clients based in Arkansas and across the country. Founded in 1900, the firm now consists of some 60 lawyers. Interaction among the practice groups enables the firm's members to address legal issues while remaining sensitive to the business considerations inherent in every legal matter. They strive to understand each client's particular needs and to address them in a cost-efficient and timely manner.

MAIN AREAS OF PRACTICE:

Bankruptcy & Creditors' Rights: The firm practices in all chapters and aspects of bankruptcy cases. The bankruptcy practice includes the representation of secured and unsecured creditors, creditor committees, trustees, and reorganizing and liquidating debtors. Firm members also specialize in creditors' rights issues, including 'out-of-court' restructuring and workouts, lender liability cases, replevin, foreclosure, and commercial and consumer banking matters.

Corporate & Securities: The firm advises a wide array of business clients on commercial transactions, business planning and regulatory matters. Firm members currently serve as regular counsel to a number of large multinational corporations headquartered in the state of Arkansas and work closely with management in all areas of SEC reporting, acquisitions and sales of companies, negotiation and documentation of contracts and debt facilities, debt and stock offerings, and management compensation plans.

Intellectual Property: The firm handles various aspects of intellectual property, including patents, trademarks, copyrights, trade secrets and unfair competition. Firm members litigate infringement cases in both state and federal courts and practice before the relevant administrative bodies, including the United States Patent and Trademark Office.

Labor & Employment: The firm has a management-oriented labor and employment practice covering all aspects of employee – employer relations. The firm has extensive experience in litigation of employment claims and also represents clients in labor arbitrations, union contract negotiations and in administrative investigations.

Litigation: The firm provides experienced representation in all areas of tort and commercial litigation, including medical, engineering, architect, and professional malpractice, environmental law, franchise and construction issues, maritime, railroad, personal injury, transportation, and insurance defense. Firm members represent and defend a broad range of clients, including insurance carriers, product manufacturers, professionals, individuals and businesses.

Products Liability: The firm serves as statewide counsel for one of the US 'big three' and two of the major Japanese automobile manufacturers, as well as several other manufacturers of automobiles, trucks, and recreational vehicles. Firm members also regularly defend a broad array of manufacturers of other products. In addition, the firm is active in the defense of toxic tort, environmental, and chemical exposure cases.

HEAD OFFICE

ARKANSAS
200 West Capitol Avenue, Suite 2300
Little Rock, AR 72201-3699
Tel: 501 371 0808 **Fax:** 501 376 9442
Website: www.wlj.com

BRANCH OFFICES

ARKANSAS
903 North 47th Street, Suite 101, **Rogers**, AR 72756
Tel: 476 986 0888 **Fax:** 479 986 8932

Real Estate: The firm offers a wide range of real estate related legal services and has been recognized as being one of the leading real estate law firms in the state. The practice focuses primarily upon commercial real estate and real estate finance; however, firm members also provide services for the owners of residential properties.

Regulated Industries: Many of the firm's clients are engaged in businesses or professions that are regulated by state or federal agencies and commissions. The firm offers broad expertise in the area of public utility regulation, particularly including electricity, natural gas, telecommunications and transportation. Additionally, firm members are experienced in regulatory matters involving the environment, occupational safety, labor relations and health care.

CLIENTS: The firm's corporate clients include Axiom Corp.; Amerisure Cos.; Associated Aviation Underwriters; AT&T Communications, Inc.; Bank of America Securities LLC; Bank of America N.A.; Chubb Group of Insurance Cos.; Cooper Realty Investments, Inc.; Deltic Timber Corp.; E.I. Du Pont, de Nemours and Co.; Entergy Corp.; Ford Motor Co.; General Electric Capital Corp.; Georgia Pacific Corp.; Government Employees Insurance Group; Hartford Insurance Cos., Helena Chemical Co.; Hyundai Motor America; John Deere & Co.; J.B. Hunt Transport Services, Inc.; Landstar Transportation Group; Lion Oil Co.; Mazda Motors of America, Inc.; Medmarc, Inc.; Murphy Oil USA, Inc.; Reliant Energy; Ryder Systems, Inc.; Schneider National Carriers Inc.; Sisters of Mercy Health System, St. Louis; Stephens Inc.; Synthes, Inc.; Toyota Motor Sales USA, Inc.; UST, Inc; United States Aviation Underwriters; Virco Manufacturing Co.; Wal-Mart Stores, Inc.; Weyerhaeuser Co.; and Xerox Corp.

CONTENTS: Antitrust p.183; Banking & Finance p.187; Bankruptcy p.190; Construction p.193; Corporate/M&A p.195; Employment p.201; Energy p.204; Environment p.206; Healthcare p.209; Insurance p.212; Intellectual Property p.215; IT & IT Outsourcing p.221; Litigation: p.223; Media & Entertainment p.229; Projects p.235; Real Estate p.237; Tax p.241; Individuals' Profiles p.243; Firm Profiles p.279.

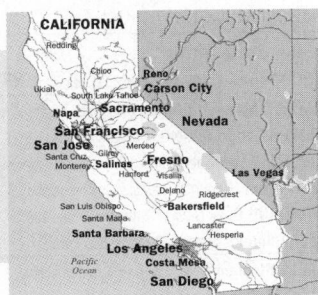

How lawyers are ranked

The opinions we gather from clients — mainly from in-house lawyers but also from other purchasers of legal services — are balanced by opinions from colleagues and competitors. Together, they provide two different perspectives — an all-round view — and biased viewpoints cancel each other out.

ANTITRUST

California
Leading firms (Antitrust)

1. **GIBSON, DUNN & CRUTCHER LLP** *Los Angeles*
   LATHAM & WATKINS LLP *Los Angeles*
2. **BINGHAM MCCUTCHEN LLP** *San Francisco*
   BLECHER & COLLINS *Los Angeles*
   HELLER EHRMAN LLP *San Francisco*
   O'MELVENY & MYERS LLP *Los Angeles*
3. **HOWREY SIMON ARNOLD & WHITE** *Los Angeles*
   MUNGER, TOLLES & OLSON LLP *Los Angeles*
   SHEPPARD, MULLIN, RICHTER *San Francisco*
4. **COOLEY GODWARD LLP** *San Francisco*
   JONES DAY *Los Angeles*
   MORRISON & FOERSTER LLP *San Francisco*
   ORRICK, HERRINGTON & SUTCLIFFE *San Francisco*
   TOWNSEND AND TOWNSEND *San Francisco*
   WILSON SONSINI GOODRICH *San Francisco*

Firms are listed alphabetically in each band.

Band 1

Gibson, Dunn & Crutcher LLP
See firm details p.285

The Firm: For many interviewees this is the state's *"premium"* antitrust outfit. The substantial yet *"seamless"* group is among the larger practices in California, and an obvious choice for the bet-the-company matter. Competitors *"doubt that anyone in LA can really match the depth and experience in antitrust that Gibson Dunn has."* Clients meanwhile value the team's *"tremendous expertise,"* particularly in huge, complicated matters, and its knowledge of government agencies. The group has a presence in Los Angeles, San Francisco, Orange County and Century City. It undertakes federal and state government investigations and litigation, private antitrust litigation, cartel investigations, criminal antitrust litigation and follow-on civil damage claims, as well as merger review and trade regulation advice. Lawyers were retained recently on appeal as co-counsel for Jostens, successfully reversing a district court decision that the company had monopoly power in the Southern

California market for high school graduation products, and also its conclusion that the client was in violation of California's unfair competition law.

The Lawyers: *"The consummate authority"* in the field, **Robert Cooper** (see p.249) enjoys a national reputation for his courtroom brilliance. As one rival commented, *"Gibson Dunn has great antitrust lawyers, but if you wanted one person to try a case he's number one on the list."* Clients meanwhile describe him as an authoritative and *"convincing"* figure: *"Right from the beginning you have the feeling you are on the safe side when you put your problems in his hands."* This year he has been acting on behalf of Sempra Energy in the California natural gas and electricity antitrust litigation. This high-profile case stems from the rise in natural gas and electricity prices between 2000 and 2001, with plaintiffs seeking billions of dollars in damages and restitution on behalf of classes of business and consumer energy customers. **Gary Spratling** (see p.273) was formerly deputy attorney general of the antitrust division of the DOJ, and is *"the father of the current cartel world."* He brings his government experience to bear in private practice, where his *"tremendous insight"* has earned him a premier position in criminal and cartel-related antitrust matters. According to admiring sources, he *"possesses superlative skill in anything you'd measure a lawyer by,"* and *"the force of his opinions, combined with his depth of integrity"* confirms him as one of the market's leading experts. **Daniel Swanson** (see p.275) cochairs the firm's antitrust group, and is a *"world-class"* practitioner, according to sources. His *"incredible academic credentials"* are balanced by an ability *"to talk to people like he's on a street corner,"* which makes him an effective adviser, say clients. His work has a considerable international element, and he spends a large chunk of time in Europe. He is currently representing Akzo Nobel in direct purchaser class actions consolidated in the Eastern District of Pennsylvania, and indirect purchaser class actions pending in many

states. Skilled litigator **Peter Sullivan** (see p.275) remains a potent force in the antitrust arena. He has been busy of late representing Nissan Motor (Japan), Nissan North America and Nissan Canada in the Canadian auto export antitrust litigation. A total of 70 class actions are ongoing around the USA, with plaintiffs contending that the major vehicle manufacturers colluded to raise prices in the USA by preventing sales of their vehicles from Canada.

The Clients: The firm has been acting for Sempra Energy, Southern California Gas and San Diego Gas & Electric in the California natural gas and electricity antitrust litigation. Other clients include: Sony Pictures; Motion Picture Association of America; DreamWorks; Flexsys NV; News Corp/Twentieth Century Fox; Cox Communications; Hillerich & Bradsby and Boehringer Ingelheim.

Latham & Watkins LLP

The Firm: If there is one firm in the California market that can effectively lock antitrust horns with Gibson Dunn, it is Latham & Watkins. *"The Latham presence is obviously big,"* acknowledge sources, pointing to its success in seamlessly organizing groups on the national and even international levels to tackle the largest and most complex cases. Antitrust proceedings are a forte, and the team has cemented its reputation of late with its high-profile defense of Oracle against an attempt to enjoin its takeover of PeopleSoft on antitrust grounds. The plaintiffs included the DOJ and ten state attorneys general. Following a month-long bench trial, the court rejected the plaintiffs' claims, concluding that they had failed to meet their burden of proof, and found in favor of Oracle. The team has particular expertise in antitrust cases involving IP, hi-tech and healthcare issues. The group is also active advising on M&A-related antitrust matters, providing general compliance counseling.

The Lawyers: Widely regarded as *"a star,"* **Tom Rosch**'s *"keen intellect"* and *"no-nonsense approach,"* teamed with *"generosity of spirit,"*

California	
Leading individuals (Antitrust)	
Senior Statesman	
LYNCH Patrick *O'Melveny & Myers*, Los Angeles	
[1] BLECHER Maxwell *Blecher & Collins*, Los Angeles	
COOPER Robert *Gibson Dunn*, Los Angeles	
POPOFSKY Laurence *Heller Ehrman*, San Francisco	
ROSCH Tom *Latham & Watkins*, San Francisco	
SPRATLING Gary *Gibson Dunn*, San Francisco	
WALL Daniel *Latham & Watkins*, San Francisco	
[2] BOMSE Stephen *Heller Ehrman*, San Francisco	
HOCKETT Christopher *Bingham*, San Francisco	
MARKHAM Jesse *Morrison & Foerster*, San Francisco	
PICKETT Donn *Bingham McCutchen*, San Francisco	
SWANSON Daniel *Gibson Dunn*, Los Angeles	
TAYLOR Robert *Howrey Simon*, Menlo Park	
[3] ALEXIS Geraldine *Bingham McCutchen*, San Francisco	
BAKER Tyler *Fenwick & West*, Mountain View	
COMPTON Charles *Wilson Sonsini*, Palo Alto	
CREW Eugene *Townsend*, San Francisco	
GOLDMAN Melvin *Morrison & Foerster*, San Francisco	
HALLING Gary *Sheppard Mullin*, San Francisco	
HUNT James *Bingham McCutchen*, San Francisco	
LEVEE Jeffrey *Jones Day*, Los Angeles	
NOLAN Thomas *Skadden Arps*, Los Angeles	
PHILLIPS Bradley *Munger Tolles*, Los Angeles	
POMERANTZ Glenn *Munger Tolles*, Los Angeles	
PREOVOLOS Penelope *Morrison*, San Francisco	
ROSENFELD Robert *Heller Ehrman*, San Francisco	
STORK Anita *Cooley Godward*, San Francisco	
SULLIVAN Peter *Gibson Dunn*, Los Angeles	
THUMANN Henry *O'Melveny & Myers*, Los Angeles	
TUBACH Michael *O'Melveny & Myers*, San Francisco	
VARNER Carlton *Sheppard Mullin*, Los Angeles	

Individuals are listed alphabetically in each band.

appeal to clients and rivals alike. His visibility on the national stage is affirmed by his involvement in the high-profile Oracle litigation. Other recent highlights include acting for HCA and St Mark's Hospital in a dispute with Rocky Mountain Medical Center (RMMC) concerning the legitimacy of one-year managed care contracts with three health insurance companies. The court held that RMMC failed to establish that any of the managed care organizations agreed not to contract with it, and so granted summary judgment in favor of St Mark's. Rosch's practice combines cartel and monopolization litigation with M&A advice and general compliance counseling. **Daniel Wall** did "*a superb job*" as lead counsel on the Oracle case, say interviewees. He cochairs the firm's antitrust practice. An "*intellectually brilliant*" strategist, according to clients, he is also skilled in "*communicating complex and esoteric issues to non-lawyers.*" He acts predominantly for clients in the computer hardware, software, biotech and other technology-related industries, and recently represented Genentech, in a dispute over a patent on a key technology employed in the production of genetically engineered antibodies. The plaintiff, MedImmune, alleged that

Genentech acquired the patent as the result of a collusive agreement between it and Celltech Group. However, a recent summary judgment found in favor of Genentech.

The Clients: Avery Dennison; Invista; Koch Industries; Toyota Motor Sales USA and Wells Fargo.

Band 2

Bingham McCutchen LLP

The Firm: According to clients, this is a group with the ability to pull "*impossible things*" out of the bag. Miracles aside, they also value the fact that they can always rely on the advice being "*top notch,*" and the lawyers being "*accessible and responsive.*" Peers meanwhile acknowledge that it is "*increasingly a force*" in the marketplace. The group is experienced in antitrust and unfair competition litigation, as well as aspects of M&A and competition counseling. This expertise was on show recently, when the team represented the McGraw Medical Center, which was sued by former medical residents, alleging antitrust violations in the way they were selected for the residency programs. On the appellate side, the team was successful on behalf of Covad Communications in getting a district court ruling in the Eleventh Circuit Court of Appeals reversed. This allowed Covad to pursue antitrust and associated claims arising from BellSouth's alleged monopolization of Internet access markets in the Southeast.

The Lawyers: **Chris Hockett** is deputy chair of the firm's litigation practice group and is, according to sources, "*a first-rate lawyer.*" His "*levelheadedness and great judgment*" have helped to win him a number of fans in the sector. His practice includes a variety of litigation – including antitrust, unfair competition and false advertising – as well as antitrust counseling and advice on the competition aspects of M&A. "*True professional*" **Donn Pickett** is a skilled antitrust litigator, as well as being the firm's vice chairman. Alongside antitrust cases, he handles securities disputes and IP litigation, and has developed particular expertise in matters involving the application of both IP and antitrust. Possessed of "*tremendous instincts,*" **Geraldine Alexis** is able to provide clients with "*high-caliber*" advice. Her practice encompasses antitrust litigation and advice on the competition aspects of M&A, and she also counsels clients on government-related investigations. Her recent highlights include advising First Data on issues connected to its $7 billion acquisition of Concord EFS. "*Fine commercial trial lawyer*" **James Hunt** is a general business litigator, and indeed chairs the firm's 400-strong litigation practice group. Antitrust forms an important element of a practice that also includes professional negligence, securities litigation and general commercial and contractual disputes.

The Clients: Western Union; AT&T Wireless; Roche Diagnostics and Oracle.

Blecher & Collins

See firm details p.282

The Firm: According to market sources, this "*brilliant*" outfit is almost unique in California's antitrust circles, as "*one of the few firms willing to prosecute an antitrust case against a big company.*" Defense attorneys commend it as a "*frequent and skilled adversary*" packed with talented courtroom performers. A well-known litigation boutique, the 14-strong firm focuses the bulk of its energy on antitrust cases, which it pursues primarily on behalf of plaintiffs. The team is currently representing Los Angeles County in a high-profile lawsuit against Sempra Energy. This alleges conspiracy to restrain pipeline activity in order to unnaturally inflate gas prices in Southern California. This follows last year's settlement with the other defendant in the action, El Paso.

The Lawyers: The credit for much of this group's superb reputation can be laid at the door of "*national institution*" **Maxwell Blecher** (see p.246). A "*phenomenal lawyer of the old school,*" his "*enormous talent and compelling persuasive power*" have made him "*a legend*" of the Los Angeles antitrust Bar. His many successes as a plaintiff's lawyer have ensured him a place in the antitrust hall of fame. As one interviewee noted: "*There are just so many decisions in the law books that have his name on them.*" A recent highlight is his ongoing work for Intertainer in a $1.6 billion case against AOL/Time Warner, Vivendi, Universal and Sony, which accuses the movie industry of conspiring to interfere with video-on-demand movie delivery.

The Clients: The practice is primarily plaintiff-oriented. Clients include Intertainer, the County of Los Angeles and Century Theatres.

Heller Ehrman LLP

See firm details p.288

The Firm: Heller Ehrman was recommended by clients as "*a first port of call for antitrust work,*" whether in California or nationwide. Rivals acknowledge the team as "*real tough competition,*" with a style that is both highly professional and academically impeccable. The group's work runs the gamut of antitrust issues, and includes price-fixing, price discrimination, monopolization, merger work and unfair competition advice and litigation. Its name is closely associated with that of Visa USA, for which it tries cases across the country; this year, for instance, that has included winning the successive dismissal of 14 indirect purchaser cases against MasterCard. Other highlights for the team include acting for Microsoft in a well-publicized case against Sun Microsystems, which settled this year.

The Lawyers: **Laurence Popofsky** is not merely one of the leading attorneys in California, but is "*someone who has most influenced the direction of antitrust in the USA over the last 30 years.*" His immense experience and knowledge make him a genuine national player, with "*enormous volumes of antitrust work.*" A pillar of the California Bar, and a "*hall of famer*" in the eyes of interviewees, he also enjoys an active and prominent appellate practice. He is currently representing Visa in a matter involving First Data. Another "*major force*" in the market, **Stephen Bomse** co-heads the firm's national antitrust group. Best known for his skill in complex litigation, he has argued over 50 federal and state appeal cases, including US Supreme Court hearings. **Robert Rosenfeld** is particularly recognized for his work on behalf of Microsoft. As well as handling antitrust litigation, he also regularly advises on the competition aspects of M&A and joint ventures, often on behalf of healthcare companies. A recent highlight was arguing an appeal on behalf of Weyerhaeuser in a predatory buying case.

The Clients: In addition to Microsoft and Visa the team represents the likes of Disney, Weyerhaeuser, Black & Decker and Mylan Laboratories.

O'Melveny & Myers LLP

See firm details p.294

The Firm: Researchers received glowing reports of this "*phenomenal practice,*" which has successfully carved out a leading place in the state's antitrust market. The large, well-established firm enjoys a particularly strong reputation in the Los Angeles financial community, and continues to expand its operations across the USA and internationally. Considerable bench strength in both Los Angeles and San Francisco enables it to handle the most complex civil and criminal antitrust proceedings "*with flying colors.*" Recent examples include representing a major DRAM manufacturer in a large criminal investigation. The group has also provided competition advice to chemical manufacturer Crompton, including assistance in investigations involving its products.

The Lawyers: **Patrick Lynch** is unanimously considered "*one of the country's premier antitrust litigators.*" A veteran in the field, his track record includes a string of highly important cases over the course of a long career. **Henry Thumann** may not devote all of his time to antitrust matters, but his status as "*an outstanding lawyer*" follows him into the antitrust arena. A sharp and technically skilled litigator, his resumé includes major pieces of work for the likes of US Airways and Southern California Gas. Joining them in this year's rankings is **Michael Tubach**. A "*growing force in the area,*" he is active in a wide range of antitrust work, but is particularly well known for his skill in criminal antitrust matters.

The Clients: The team recently represented Degussa in a series of investigations related to alleged price-fixing. Other clients include Hynix Semiconductor and Crompton.

Howrey Simon Arnold & White

The Firm: The team in California is believed to benefit from the firm's "*major presence on the national antitrust litigation scene.*" It boasts a number of talented practitioners and a considerable stand-alone practice. Although Tom Nolan's departure was seen as a blow to the group, its members remain active in major antitrust litigation, handling a range of state and federal court proceedings, including class actions. A recent example of its work was the confidential settlement that the team negotiated in a civil RICO and state antitrust case. First filed in 1994, the case was thrown out, but an appeal process began in January 2001 and the California Supreme Court reversed the previous decision. The plaintiffs were required to preview much of their expert testimony through a series of pretrial evidentiary hearings, culminating in a request to participate in mediation, which resolved the case.

The Lawyers: "*One heck of a good litigator,*" **Robert Taylor** is particularly known for his skill in the interface between antitrust and IP. The former managing partner of the firm's Northern California practice, he has experience of working in a wide range of industries, typically in the hi-tech sector. His recent highlights include acting for ARM in an antitrust dispute with Herodion which stemmed from the settlement of an earlier patent case.

The Clients: The team represents an impressive range of public and private companies, many of them from the hi-tech, biotech or healthcare sectors.

Munger, Tolles & Olson LLP

The Firm: Interviewees highlight this as "*one of the best general litigation firms*" in California, which naturally gives it a significant foothold in antitrust-related matters. Sources note that the group's strengths include not just technical skill, drive and experience, but a "*culture that they can and will do anything*" when it comes to assisting the client. The group is experienced in private claims and government investigations, among other things, and enjoys a particularly strong name among clients in the entertainment, media and computer sectors, as well as the pharmaceuticals industry. Recent successes have included acting for Universal Studios in a conspiracy case, which was brought by independent video stores alleging that the studio was conspiring to favor Blockbuster. The team has also represented Universal Music Group in various antitrust lawsuits involving the alleged price-fixing of compact discs, and in a set of suits involving advertising policies. Additional highlights included appearing for Rambus in an antitrust action before the FTC.

The Lawyers: Clients dub **Glenn Pomerantz** a

"*valuable resource*" for his "*experience and intelligent understanding of antitrust laws.*" His practice has an entertainment focus, and he recently represented Universal Studios, now NBC Universal, in a government investigation into the Movielink joint venture. The investigation was closed without the government taking action, and all the studios involved were cleared of wrongdoing. **Bradley Phillips** is another popular figure in the marketplace. A general litigator with a broad practice, his experience spans the media and entertainment, energy, publishing, utilities, aerospace, manufacturing and financial services sectors.

The Clients: The group's client base spans a range of industries, including pharmaceuticals, computers, entertainment, energy, publishing and aerospace. Examples include: Abbott Laboratories; Vivendi Universal; Southern California Edison; Alliance Entertainment and Shell.

Sheppard, Mullin, Richter & Hampton LLP

The Firm: Sheppard Mullin was perceived by interviewees to be a growing force in the practice area, and one that "*has attracted some good talent*" over the past few years. The team's clients appreciate its responsiveness and familiarity with state antitrust laws, while rivals admire its client base. Typical activity includes advice on government merger and civil conduct investigations, private civil litigation, unfair competition law, consumer protection and criminal antitrust matters.

The Lawyers: **Gary Halling** is "*among the best antitrust lawyers in California,*" say sources. He is involved in antitrust and unfair competition disputes as part of a complex business litigation practice, and offers expertise on both the civil and criminal sides of the fence. **Carlton Varner** "*has a brilliant mind*" and a "*deep understanding of antitrust law*" according to observers. He was also dubbed "*a real workhorse in the area.*" His recent workload includes a volume of IP-related antitrust matters, in addition to price-fixing, price discrimination, monopolization, merger, joint venture and unfair competition issues in a variety of industry sectors.

The Clients: The group's client base hails from a number of sectors, including healthcare, pharmaceuticals, energy, technology, financial services, aerospace, food services, publishing, distribution and transport.

Cooley Godward LLP

The Firm: This 13-attorney group is active in a range of antitrust matters, including distribution, exclusivity issues, counseling, and litigation in state and federal courts. Highlights of the year include defending Tyco Healthcare against claims of monopolization in the pulse oximetry market. This complex case involved issues of bundled rebates to hospitals and exclusive dealing arrangements. The team also recently acted for Dillard's in a consumer antitrust class action.

The Lawyers: **Anita Stork** retains a high profile in the market for antitrust litigation, counseling and agency investigations. Her name is perhaps particularly associated with work in the technology sector, though she is active in a number of other industries and recently advised Pacificare Health Systems in a civil conspiracy case.

The Clients: As well as Dillard's and Tyco Healthcare, clients include: LSI Logic; The Clorox Company; Integrated Device Technology and LeapFrog.

Jones Day

See firm details p.485

The Firm: Clients were full of praise for the "*phenomenal turnaround time*" of this high-quality, internationally focused group. The team operates from bases in Los Angeles and San Francisco, and is principally active in the fields of healthcare, manufacturing, retail and technology. Led by Jeff LeVee, it recently defended the Internet Corporation for Assigned Names and Numbers (ICANN), against claims made by VeriSign. The court ruled that VeriSign's antitrust claims could not proceed as there was no indication that its competitors had unduly influenced ICANN's board of directors or decision-making processes.

The Lawyers: "*Top-notch litigator*" **Jeff LeVee** (see p.261) is "*coming on strong in the area,*" say commentators. Clients are impressed by his powers of persuasion, his grasp of the complexities of difficult cases, and his incredible work rate. "*I don't know that he sleeps,*" remarked one. He coordinates the firm's antitrust and competition offering for the California region.

The Clients: Ricoh; Alliant Techsystems; Proctor & Gamble; Federated Department Stores; CBS Television; Sutter Health; Banner Health and Presbyterian Healthcare.

Morrison & Foerster LLP

See firm details p.293

The Firm: The growing team here is considered to be "*extremely knowledgeable about all aspects of antitrust.*" It boasts a solid reputation in the marketplace for compliance counseling, antitrust litigation and advice on regulatory investigations. This profile is only expected to rise following the high-profile recruitment last year of Jesse Markham. Recent highlights include representing JPMorgan Chase in a number of antitrust class actions brought against leading banks. The group also defended Norske Canada in connection with investigations by the DOJ and the Canadian Competition Bureau. The matter has also spawned a number of class action lawsuits alleging that the industry engaged in price-fixing and market allocation.

The Lawyers: "*Engaging*" **Jesse Markham** (see p.262), who joined the firm last year from

Orrick Herrington, is developing a name as a "*super-smart antitrust lawyer.*" "*He has the background, the experience, the demeanor and a way with people – everything's perfect,*" enthused one client. His practice covers the gamut of antitrust issues, but he pays particular attention to the interface between IP and monopoly matters. He joins intelligent and experienced **Melvin Goldman** (see p.253), who continues to impress sources with his expertise in antitrust trials and appeals, and compliance counseling. Also warmly recommended to researchers was **Penelope Preovolos** (see p.268). She boasts considerable experience with taking the lead in complex, multidefendant cases, and has recently acted as counsel to Chanel in coordinated antitrust and unfair trade practice actions, which are currently pending.

The Clients: Toshiba; Apple; Hitachi; Yahoo!; Barnes & Noble and EchoStar Systems.

Orrick, Herrington & Sutcliffe LLP

See firm details p.295

The Firm: Although the departure this year of Jesse Markham is believed to have been a blow to the group, clients remain comfortable that it can effectively advise on a range of matters, while peers agree that it "*always handles cases professionally.*" These cases include both civil and criminal cartel matters, as well as private litigation and class actions for both plaintiffs and defendants. Recent work has included advice on Robinson-Patman, state law price discrimination litigation and patent settlements.

The Clients: The team's client base includes companies from the transportation, electronics, pharmaceuticals, vitamins, securities, biotech, chemical manufacturing, technology, and financial services industries.

Townsend and Townsend and Crew LLP

The Firm: Clients enthused about this litigation practice, which focuses on handling IP and antitrust cases for both plaintiffs and defendants. Recent successes have included acting for the inventors of a patented energy-saving electronic ballast technology, which was licensed to the defendants, who then shelved it in order to eliminate competition. Here, the group won $96 million on behalf of the plaintiffs. The group also represented St Luke's Hospital in a case concerning exclusive-dealing contracts between two other competing hospitals and a physicians' independent practice association, which controlled a large share of the HMO-enrolled patients in the area. The firm obtained a settlement for St Luke's, including an affiliation agreement and payments of over $50 million.

The Lawyers: "*Phenomenal trial attorney*" **Eugene Crew** was placed by some sources among "*the first rank of plaintiffs' attorneys.*" His success rate and his involvement in a number of

high-profile antitrust cases ensure him a prominent position in the marketplace. He has acted recently on behalf of California businesses and consumers, in an antitrust and unfair competition action against Microsoft. $1.1 billion was recovered from Microsoft.

The Clients: Clients have included Sun Microsystems, Visa USA and Intergraph Corporation.

Wilson Sonsini Goodrich & Rosati

See firm details p.302

The Firm: The firm is particularly well known for its skill in the regulatory aspects of mergers, acquisitions and joint ventures, especially in the technology sector, and the group is also active counseling clients on antitrust litigation. Clients appreciate its "*flexibility and keen understanding of the factual underpinning of matters.*" A recent high point was representing JD Edwards in connection with its acquisition by PeopleSoft, a transaction that was investigated by the DOJ and the European Commission. Because of this work, the group was then retained by PeopleSoft to work alongside Cleary Gottlieb in responding to the DOJ investigation leading up to the Oracle trial.

The Lawyers: Clients expressed their admiration for **Charles Compton**'s (see p.248) ability to "*establish an immediate rapport, trust and confidence, in a nonadversarial way.*" He heads the firm's antitrust practice, and is primarily involved in M&A regulatory work and IP-related antitrust counseling.

The Clients: Brocade Communications Systems; Logitech; ScanSoft; Gardner Group; Juniper Networks; 3Com; Plantronics; Autodesk; Polycom; Hewlett-Packard; Sun Microsystems; Varian; Solectron; Dolby Laboratories; Business Objects; Apple; Synopsys; Broadcom and Cypress Semiconductor.

Other Notable Practitioners

Tyler Baker (see p.244) of Fenwick & West LLP is an active litigator, particularly for hi-tech clients at the intersection of antitrust and IP. He and his fellow group members have been defending a major leather accessories and jewelry manufacturer against claims of vertical price-fixing brought by two former retailers. **Thomas Nolan** (see p.265) of Skadden, Arps, Slate, Meagher & Flom LLP & Affiliates, also enjoys a strong reputation in the state, both in and outside of antitrust. His practice spans antitrust and IP, as well as litigation involving unfair business practices, contact disputes and class actions.

BANKING & FINANCE

California
Leading firms (Banking & Finance)

1	O'MELVENY & MYERS LLP *Los Angeles*
2	GIBSON, DUNN & CRUTCHER LLP *Los Angeles*
	LATHAM & WATKINS LLP *Los Angeles*
3	BINGHAM MCCUTCHEN LLP *San Francisco*
	MORRISON & FOERSTER LLP *Los Angeles*
	ORRICK, HERRINGTON & SUTCLIFFE *San Francisco*
	PAUL, HASTINGS, JANOFSKY *Los Angeles*
	PILLSBURY WINTHROP LLP *San Francisco*
	WHITE & CASE LLP *Los Angeles*
4	BUCHALTER NEMER FIELDS *Los Angeles; San Francisco*
	MANATT PHELPS & PHILLIPS LLP *Los Angeles*
	MCDERMOTT WILL & EMERY *Los Angeles*
	MILBANK, TWEED, HADLEY & MCCLOY *Los Angeles*
	SHEARMAN & STERLING *San Francisco*
	SHEPPARD, MULLIN, RICHTER *Los Angeles*
	SKADDEN, ARPS, SLATE, MEAGHER *Los Angeles*
	SULLIVAN & CROMWELL LLP *Los Angeles*
	WINSTON & STRAWN *Los Angeles*

Leading individuals (Banking & Finance)

	Senior Statesman
	DE MEULES James *O'Melveny & Myers, Los Angeles*
	FARRAR Stanley *Sullivan & Cromwell, Los Angeles*
1	BENJAMIN Alan *Orrick Herrington, Los Angeles*
	HILSON John *Paul Hastings, Los Angeles*
	KIRBY Matthew *O'Melveny & Myers, Los Angeles*
2	FELDSTEIN Hydee *Paul Hastings, Los Angeles*
	HISERT George *Bingham McCutchen, San Francisco*
	KILB Brian *Gibson Dunn, Los Angeles*
	MATICHAK Jill *O'Melveny & Myers, San Francisco*
	RUST Neil *White & Case, Los Angeles*
3	BERCHILD John *Sheppard Mullin, Los Angeles*
	CAIRNS James *White & Case, Los Angeles*
	COLEMAN Thomas *Orrick Herrington, San Francisco*
	MARMORSTEIN Vicki *Latham & Watkins, Los Angeles*
	MENDEZ John *Latham & Watkins, Los Angeles*
	OLSEN Christine *O'Melveny & Myers, Los Angeles*
	REAMER David *Skadden Arps, Los Angeles*
	REIMER Eric *McDermott Will, Los Angeles*
	ROSENBAUM Gary *Winston & Strawn, Los Angeles*
	SCOTT IV William *Sheppard Mullin, Los Angeles*
	SHERMAN Steven *Shearman & Sterling, San Francisco*

Firms and individuals are listed alphabetically in each band.

Band 1

O'Melveny & Myers LLP
See firm details p.294

The Firm: "*Far and away the deepest and most talented group out here,*" agreed market sources. This team has a long history of producing skilled bank lending attorneys from both its LA and San Francisco offices. The group's "*creative approach*" to its diet of leveraged finance, including acquisition finance, recapitalization and bankruptcy-related refinancings, has earned it a reputation as the go-to firm among institution-al lenders. The group acted for Citibank NA as lead arranger in the financing for the €1.3 billion acquisition of BSN Glasspack by Owens-Illinois. The team also represented Deutsche Bank in the restructuring of the company's credit facility.

The Lawyers: **James De Meules** remains an "*extremely respected*" force in the marketplace, and someone peers "*enjoy seeing on the other side of the table.*" Coordinating partner **Matthew Kirby** is a "*super lawyer*" who splits his time between California and New York. He employs his "*detail-oriented*" approach and "*flexibility in accommodating borrowers' needs*" on both coasts. Clients such as Deutsche Bank, BNP Paribas and CSFB ensure that Kirby has a heavy workload. "*Wonderful lawyer*" **Jill Matichak** has a strong client following, according to interviewees, and shares with the "*accomplished*" **Christine Olsen** an ability to develop close client relationships. Olsen's depth of experience in the finance arena was also widely commended.

The Clients: The team's clients include: Deutsche Bank; CSFB; BNP Paribas; Bank of America and Wells Fargo. For BNP Paribas the group acted on the financing for Knowledge Learning Center's acquisition of the Aramark early childhood education division, and its pending acquisition of KinderCare. The team is also representing the lead arrangers in the proposed $8.8 billion bankruptcy exit facilities for Adelphia Communications.

Band 2

Gibson, Dunn & Crutcher LLP
See firm details p.285

The Firm: Thanks to its high visibility advising borrowers in prominent transactions, the group has "*done exceedingly well in the finance arena.*" It remains a major presence in the California market, bolstered by its additional and expanding resources in New York. A healthy dose of leveraged acquisition financings for its strong stable of corporate issuer clients and private equity houses forms the bulk of the group's work. In addition, it is active in lender representation for clients such as Wells Fargo and Bank of America. The group's recent highlights have included advising Avnet in its implementation of a $5 million bank credit facility. The team also represented The Williams Companies in a number of complex bank credit facilities and high-yield issues.

The Lawyers: **Brian Kilb** (see p.91) is a player often in evidence across the table on financing transactions, and rivals approve of his ability "*to recognize the points worth fighting for.*" A generalist finance attorney, he acted for Tenet Healthcare in a restructuring of its syndicated healthcare facility.

The Clients: The firm's clients include: MGM Studios; Hilton Hotels; Leonard Green & Partners; Caesar's Entertainment; Aura Capital; Northrop Grumman; Wells Fargo and Bank of America.

Latham & Watkins LLP

The Firm: Clients applaud this "*diverse*" group for its "*practical and resourceful*" approach to difficult issues and "*devotion to client needs.*" The 75-strong team has cultivated a successful practice on behalf of institutional lenders, and is active in leveraged finance, structured finance and asset-based transactions. Peers highlight a quality mezzanine debt presence. The team acted for Morgan Stanley as placement agent in a large emerging market CDO. Other successes have included advising UBS on various acquisition financings, including facilities for Grundle/SLT Environmental, Bear Creek, CHI Door, Dresser-Rand and Sunny Delight. Other interests for this broad finance team include project finance, municipal infrastructure work and debt restructuring.

The Lawyers: Global chair of the firm's finance and real estate department, **Vicki Marmorstein** continues to impress commentators. She is particularly skilled in the documentation and negotiation of domestic and cross-border financings, including structured finance and credit transactions. A "*wonderful adviser,*" **John Mendez** has been a key arrival to the LA office from Skadden, Arps, Slate, Meagher & Flom, in what has been a dynamic year for Latham, following a number of significant hires nationally. He is particularly well versed in leveraged finance.

The Clients: American Express; AIG; Time Warner and Morgan Stanley.

Band 3

Bingham McCutchen LLP

The Firm: The practice has developed into a leading presence in the finance arena, and attracts particular plaudits for its expertise in corporate and regulatory matters. In this sphere it fields "*a terrific team*" that encapsulates "*all the things you'd like to see in a law firm,*" say commentators. It represented First Financial Bancorp in its purchase by Placer Sierra Bancshares, and also advised Union Bank of California in its acquisition of Jackson Federal Bank, and the sale of its merchant card business to NOVA Systems (US Bancorp). The group is also involved in a full range of credit work, principally for lending institutions, including regional banks, insurance companies, asset-based lenders, and investment funds. It also dabbles in borrower representation, such as advice to DaVita in a multitranche credit facility for $1.615 billion. For BNP Paribas, the group advised on a secured

California
Leading individuals
(Banking & Finance: Mainly Regulatory)

Senior statesman

FARRAR Stanley *Sullivan & Cromwell*, Los Angeles

[1] FIELDS Henry *Morrison & Foerster*, Los Angeles

PECK Rodney *Pillsbury Winthrop*, San Francisco

ROCKETT James *Bingham McCutchen*, San Francisco

[2] ELERDING Gene *Manatt Phelps*, Los Angeles

YOUNG Maureen *Bingham McCutchen*, San Francisco

Individuals are listed alphabetically in each band.

syndicated facility. Clients believe the group "*ranks with the top firms in the state and nationally*" in terms of client service and technical understanding.

The Lawyers: Clients applaud "*moral and straightforward*" **James Rockett** as "*the kind of lawyer who will tell you the pros and cons of a situation and offer a recommendation as to which way to go.*" He co-heads the firm's financial institutions, corporate and regulatory group, making him a key figure in regulatory and M&A-related work. He acted for Cathay Bancorp in its acquisition of GBC Bancorp/General Bank. Rivals paint a highly complimentary picture of **George Hisert**, who cochairs the bank, commercial and structured finance group at the firm. A "*careful and reasonable fellow,*" he is a first-rate finance lawyer with a particular emphasis on syndicated loan transactions and letter of credit work. He recently completed two syndicated asset-based credit facilities for GE Capital and represented McKesson Corporation as the borrower in a $1.3 billion syndicated credit facility. **Maureen Young** has a thorough understanding of the regulatory area, and clients appreciate her "*good bedside manner*" and knowledge of the subject.

The Clients: Union Bank of California; Capital Corp of the West; Bridge Bank; First Financial Bancorp; JPMorgan Chase; Wells Fargo; Silicon Valley Bank; Bank of New York; Allied Capital; BNP Paribas and Pacific Life Insurance.

Morrison & Foerster LLP
See firm details p.293

The Firm: "*Traditionally a long-standing banking and finance practice,*" the group is best known for its work for institutional lenders, especially Bank of America. The team is particularly skilled in agented-loan transactions, often linked to derivatives products. On the regulatory side, the group has also established a name for itself; here, it appears on behalf of domestic and international banks in connection with their strategic direction, new products, acquisition activity and the regulatory framework. For example, the team acted for Union Bank in the expanding trusts and wealth management area. Clients place the team "*at the top of the class*" for complex M&A work.

The Lawyers: Henry Fields (see p.252) is a popular figure in the marketplace for his regulatory and finance expertise. Clients claimed that "*over and over again he has demonstrated great expertise, and creativity in problem solving.*" He is active on behalf of Hong Kong and Taiwanese institutions in connection with acquisitions and large global offerings. In the M&A market, he represents the buyers and sellers of financial institutions, and advises on new bank formation. A recent highlight was his advice to Cathay Financial Holdings in a $500 million offering.

The Clients: Union Bank of California; The Bank of East Asia; Sinopac Holdings; Chinatrust Commercial Bank; DBS Bank; United Overseas Bank; Nara Bank; Bank of the West; Cathay General Bancorp and Mitsubishi Tokyo Financial Group.

Orrick, Herrington & Sutcliffe LLP
See firm details p.295

The Firm: Public and municipal finance are where the strengths of this "*exceedingly experienced*" home-grown group lies. Within this field, the team is especially skilled in Indian gaming matters, and the team has developed a number of structured products on behalf of both tribes and their lenders. The broader global finance group is occupied with large structured financings, generally for bank and institutional lender clients, including a number of money center banks, regional banks and European banks with operations in the USA. The team also acts for borrowers. Highlights have included representing Wells Fargo and Bank of America as arrangers in a five-year $200 million credit facility for the Barona Tribal Gaming Authority. The group also acted for Wells Fargo as lead arranger in the $130 million senior secured revolving credit facility for Temecula Band of Luiseño Mission Indians.

The Lawyers: Head of the firm's banking and commercial finance practice group, **Alan Benjamin** (see p.244) is a widely respected figure in the marketplace. He represented PG&E Corporation in a three-year $200 million credit facility. Although **Thomas Coleman**'s (see p.248) management duties have lowered his involvement in day-to-day matters, he remains a valuable adviser on syndicated agreements, project financings, public finance transactions and lease arrangements.

The Clients: Wells Fargo; Bank of America; JPMorgan Chase; Citibank; Calyon; Société Générale; National City Bank; KeyBank; Vivendi; Gap; Knight Ridder; Varian; Caterpillar Financial Services; Renault and NOVA Chemicals.

Paul, Hastings, Janofsky & Walker LLP
See firm details p.297

The Firm: The group continues to rise in prominence. Sources credit it with having devel-

oped a "*seasoned banking practice,*" with "*several strong leadership players.*" Its members have gained a reputation as "*problem solvers as opposed to problem creators,*" while clients endorse their "*client-friendly and enthusiastic approach.*" The practice centers on lending transactions for commercial and investment banks, with a large complement of international finance. A significant project finance component also features in the workload. The group recently represented Wells Fargo Foothill, as agent in the $100 million credit facility to Evergreen International Aviation.

The Lawyers: Clients were keen to emphasize the impressive skill set of "*thoughtful and intellectual*" **John Hilson** (see p.257), whose "*calm and even-tempered demeanor is advantageous on our side and in negotiation.*" He is, nevertheless, "*a can-do person,*" and is credited with a phenomenal grasp of leverage finance and asset-based lending. He acted for Ableco Finance in its $100 million credit facility with BlueLinx Corporation. **Hydee Feldstein** (see p.252) is another favorite among clients, who appreciate her "*enthusiasm, fire,*" and "*willingness to go to the ends of the earth to make things work.*" Her client focus, "*high level of integrity,*" and background straddling bankruptcy and banking finance also ensure that she remains a go-to figure for investment banks and borrowers alike. She acted for GE Capital in its $200 million financing of Gateway, and also represented Dymas Capital in an $87 million acquisition financing to Vitality Foodservice Holding Corporation.

The Clients: Wells Fargo; Goldman Sachs; Morgan Stanley; SilverPoint Capital; Highbridge Capital; City National Bank and Windjammer Mezzanine.

Pillsbury Winthrop LLP
See firm details p.1364

The Firm: A loyal following among regional and national clients has placed this practice on the map. The group has been heavily involved in M&A, and a centerpiece transaction this year has been representing BNP Paribas and its US operation BancWest in the acquisition of Community First Bankshares. The deal enabled the clients to acquire 160 branches in 12 states, in a transaction valued at $1.2 billion. The team also acted for ChevronTexaco in the $4.4 billion expansion of a Tengizchevroil production joint venture in Kazakhstan. The team represented ChevronTexaco as 50% partner in the joint venture, and also acted for the joint venture in negotiation of fiscal agreements with the Republic of Kazakhstan. On the securities side, the LA group represented the State of California in a $10 billion bond financing. At time of press the firm announced its merger with Shaw Pittman to form Pillsbury Winthrop Shaw Pittman.

The Lawyers: "*Terrific attorney*" **Rodney Peck**

(see p.267) is an experienced bank M&A and regulatory specialist. He co-heads the firm's financial institutions practice group.

The Clients: BNP Paribas; BancWest Corporation; Bank of New York; Citigroup; Marubeni and Union Bank of California.

White & Case LLP

See firm details p.1379

The Firm: This team of *"commercially oriented"* negotiators was applauded by clients for its ability *"to keep everyone's tempers under control."* Advice on public finance, credit and liquidity enhancement form part of a full range of bank finance matters handled by the group. For example, the team acted for Banc of America Securities as arranger, Bank of America as administrative agent and lenders, and a host of others in a $3 billion State of California financing. The group has particular expertise in asset finance, especially in the field of aircraft finance. Here, it represented Bank of America in the United Airlines and the US Airways bankruptcies, as well as in a number of operating lease transactions, and advised on the restructuring of leveraged lease transactions involving American Airlines.

The Lawyers: Clients find **Neil Rust** (see p.270) *"critical in helping move forward a deal"* and able to provide *"everything you want in a client-attorney relationship."* He is actively involved in public finance matters. He represented Deutsche Bank as issuer of a syndicated letter of credit supporting certain bonds issued on behalf of PG&E. *"Thoughtful, careful and fastidious"* **James Cairns** (see p.247) also impressed with his leasing and aircraft finance practice. He represented Boeing Capital Corporation in its financing of Boeing Business Jets.

The Clients: Allied Irish Banks; Babcock & Brown; Bank of America; Bank of New York; Delta Air Lines; CIT Group; Commerzbank; Deutsche Bank; JPMorgan Chase Bank; Mizuho Bank; WestLB and Union Bank of California.

Band 4

Buchalter Nemer Fields & Younger

The Firm: A highly visible group in the finance arena, this team is active in loan transactions, specialized industry financing and equipment leasing. Highlights have included transactions arising out of the media, healthcare, gaming, and technology as well as leasings related to the aircraft sector.

The Lawyers: Matthew Kavanaugh is the head of the banking and finance practice.

The Clients: The group's clients include regional, national and international banks, commercial finance companies, mortgage companies and equipment lessors.

Manatt Phelps & Phillips LLP

The Firm: Commentators recognize this practice for its expertise on behalf of regional and community banks, specifically its regulatory advice and involvement in bank startups. The group combines transactional work on syndicated loans, acquisition finance and structured finance with its experience in regulatory matters.

The Lawyers: **Gene Elerding** (see p.251) caught the eye of rivals in the regulatory field, who place his name among the leading regulatory attorneys in the state. He is active on behalf of financial institutions and advertisers in connection with regulatory and operational issues.

The Clients: The team's client base comprises foreign banks, savings institutions, mortgage lenders, acquirers and industrial loan companies. Examples include: Bank of America; California National Bank; Chinatrust Bank (USA); Citizens Business Bank; Silicon Valley Bank; Union Bank of California; United PanAm; US Bank; Wachovia and Bear Stearns.

McDermott Will & Emery

See firm details p.773

The Firm: Clients trust this group's ability *"to modify what they do to fit our needs,"* and are confident that *"when someone from the team is assigned to a matter they are going to be good lawyers."* Borrower-based M&A transactions form the bulk of the workload, and recent successes have included representing The Jean Coutu Group in the financing of its $2.375 billion acquisition of over 1500 drug stores. The deak related to the purchase of Eckerd's northern and mid-Atlantic drugstore business from JC Penney, and included a complex tax reorganization and notes issuance.

The Lawyers: Much of the team's reputation rests on the shoulders of **Eric Reimer** (see p.269). His ability *"to move forward a transaction and get issues resolved"* impresses clients, who also cite his *"knowledgeable, client-oriented and accessible"* style as evidence of his effectiveness in deals. His deal flow comprises work on behalf of banks, and he also has a substantial restructuring and project finance practice.

The Clients: Oaktree Capital Management; Vector Group; Bank of America and JPMorgan Chase.

Milbank, Tweed, Hadley & McCloy

The Firm: A *"responsive"* and valuable resource, this group is commended by clients for its business judgment and ability to *"act as a member of our team."* High-risk transactions, or those with a workout element, form an important part of the team's deal flow. Its lending work encompasses hi-tech related matters, representation of hedge funds, and work for institutional lenders financing Indian tribes. Recent successes have included representing Wachovia Bank as agent for a syndicate in loaning around $90 million to

Family Christian Stores. The team also acted for Station Casinos as borrower in a $750 million dollar senior working capital facility.

The Lawyers: Greg Bray is a key contact in the banking and finance department.

The Clients: Cerberus Capital Management; Trust Company of the West; GE Capital; ABN AMRO and Fleet National Bank (now Bank of America).

Shearman & Sterling

See firm details p.1369

The Firm: This San Francisco-based group is believed to benefit from the firm's sterling banking presence in New York. The California practice is nevertheless distinguished for its *"clear and decisive advice"* and *"willingness to really take a stand on behalf of clients."* The group represents both financial institutions and borrowers, and recently acted for Banc of America Securities and Bank of America in a $3 billion financing for Anthem in its merger with Wellpoint Health Networks. The group also acted for Levi Strauss in the $1.15 billion refinancing of its outstanding bank debt.

The Lawyers: *"Tenacious"* **Steven Sherman** (see p.272) is an attorney about whom one client said: *"He's aggressive in negotiations – I'd much rather have him on my side!"* An *"attentive"* figure, he combines *"approachability and creativity"* with a business mind to make himself a preferred choice for a variety of commercial finance matters. He is the manager of the firm's West Coast private financing and bankruptcy practice.

The Clients: Citibank; Bank of America; Credit Suisse; GE Capital; Wells Fargo Bank; Bechtel; BNP Paribas and ABN AMRO.

Sheppard, Mullin, Richter & Hampton LLP

The Firm: A respected regional presence, particularly for homegrown financings. Although the market profile of this team centers on its midmarket work, it is making inroads into the East Coast market and high-value transactions. Key areas for the group include representing banks and financial institutions in fully secured loan transactions, revolving credit facilities and asset-based lending as well as gaming work. The group has worked on major revolving credit facilities for manufacturers, in addition to a significant amount of debt restructuring.

The Lawyers: **John Berchild** enjoys a longstanding position in the marketplace. He concentrates on personal property secured credit facilities, while **William Scott** is recognized for his gaming practice, which involves lending to Indian tribes. He has acted in a number of multibillion-dollar loan facilities for major gaming and resort companies.

The Clients: Bank of America; Wells Fargo Bank; Union Bank of California; CIT Corporation and LaSalle Bank.

Skadden, Arps, Slate, Meagher & Flom LLP & Affiliates

See firm details p.1372

The Firm: "*An excellent team with very thorough and competent associates,*" this LA-based group concentrates on leveraged lending for noninvestment grade companies, including secured transactions. Syndicated loan work forms a significant portion of the work, as does acquisition finance. The team's broad-based clientele includes those in the gaming, private equity and REIT markets. Highlights have included representing Penn National Gaming in raising £3 billion capital for its pending acquisition of Argosy Gaming.

The Lawyers: **David Reamer** (see p.269) wins clients over on the basis of his impressive negotiating skills; "*he can be tough as nails or compromising*" as the deal requires. His practice centers on noninvestment-grade leveraged financings, with an emphasis on secured syndicated bank financings.

The Clients: The firm represents private equity companies, investment banks and growth-oriented companies, such as: The Fremont Group; Fox Paine & Company; Oaktree Capital Management; Penn National Gaming; CSFB and JPMorgan Chase.

Sullivan & Cromwell LLP

See firm details p.1373

The Firm: The West Coast operation of this Wall Street giant is a smaller presence, but packed with "*fine lawyers.*" A key strength for the group is its M&A work for financial institutions, and accompanying regulatory advice. The group also advises investment banks and corporate clients in syndicated bank lending and acquisition finance. In one of its recent highlights, the group acted for Central Pacific Financial in its $400 million acquisition of CB Bancshares. The deal involved two Hawaii-based entities.

The Lawyers: The mention of **Stanley Farrar** continues to elicit warm commendations from both clients and peers, who note his "*extraordinary talent*" in bank regulatory matters and financing transactions.

The Clients: Clients include PMI, First Community Bancorp and Zions Bank.

Winston & Strawn

See firm details p.780

The Firm: Identified as one of the market's growing groups, this firm has cultivated a broad finance practice that features senior secured lending and subordinated debt, and a substantial private equity and borrowers practice. The team's San Francisco office has also developed niche expertise in agricultural work. For instance, it advised GE Capital on the provision of a $125 million credit facility to a privately held company that is the leading producer of container grown plants. In another highlight the group represented GE Capital in its $120 million revolving credit and term facility to Western Digital Corporation.

The Lawyers: Excellent and experienced attorney **Gary Rosenbaum**'s (see p.270) deal flow encompasses work for both lender and borrower clients. He advises on asset-based and cash flow transactions, and represented Union Bank of California on over one dozen loan transactions, including credit facilities extended to a grower and wholesaler of ornamental nursery products.

The Clients: Clients have included: American AgCredit; The Travelers Insurance Company; Allied Capital; American Capital Strategies; Greyrock Capital and Wells Fargo Foothill.

BANKRUPTCY

California
Leading firms (Bankruptcy)

1
KLEE, TUCHIN, BOGDANOFF *Los Angeles*
MILBANK, TWEED, HADLEY *Los Angeles*
STUTMAN, TREISTER & GLATT *Los Angeles*

2
LATHAM & WATKINS LLP *Los Angeles*
O'MELVENY & MYERS LLP *Los Angeles*
PACHULSKI, STANG, ZIEHL, YOUNG *Los Angeles*
SIDLEY AUSTIN BROWN & WOOD LLP *Los Angeles*
SKADDEN, ARPS, SLATE, MEAGHER *Los Angeles*
WINSTON & STRAWN *San Francisco*

3
ALSCHULER GROSSMAN STEIN *Santa Monica*
GIBSON, DUNN & CRUTCHER LLP *Los Angeles*
HELLER EHRMAN LLP *San Francisco*
HENNIGAN, BENNETT & DORMAN *Los Angeles*
HOWARD, RICE, NEMEROVSKI *San Francisco*
ORRICK, HERRINGTON & SUTCLIFFE *San Francisco*
PAUL, HASTINGS, JANOFSKY *San Francisco*
PEITZMAN, GLASSMAN, WEG *Los Angeles*
SHEPPARD, MULLIN, RICHTER *Los Angeles*

Firms are listed alphabetically in each band.

Band 1

Klee, Tuchin, Bogdanoff & Stern LLP

See firm details p.292

The Firm: This boutique firm retains its position at the top of the tables, thanks to sweeping market recognition of its expertise in troubled situations. The practice is packed with "*highly intellectual attorneys,*" whose long track record means "*they have seen all situations and can handle any type of case.*" Clients and peers identified the trial skills on offer here and the creative, solutions-oriented approach adopted by the group's attorneys. A healthy mix of clients sees the group act for debtors, bondholders, acquirers, and secured and unsecured lenders. The bankruptcy specialists also work in conjunction with the firm's transactional practice, advising on debtor-in-possession lending, and the acquisition of distressed assets.

The Lawyers: "*Legendary*" **Kenneth Klee** (see p.260) takes a "*cerebral*" approach to complex matters, and is "*clearly one of the premier guys*" in the marketplace. He continues to be active as an expert witness in bankruptcy matters. "*Terrific*" **Lee Bogdanoff** (see p.246) "*will drive a hard bargain if necessary, but is always looking to get all parties to work together.*" Such "*business skill*" is combined with his commitment to the development of this market and to the community. Among his recent highlights was a Chapter 11 case for Crescent Jewelers, as well as ongoing involvement as lead attorney on the Sun World Chapter 11. "*Practical*" **Michael Tuchin** (see p.276) represented Samuels Jewelers, which operates more than 130 stores, in its successful Chapter 11 proceedings. The "*excellent and highly trusted*" bankruptcy practitioner **Tom Patterson** (see p.267) has been involved in a Chapter 7 case connected to the Brobeck Phleger & Harrison bankruptcy. Like many of the Klee, Tuchin attorneys, he is respected for his robust litigation and high-quality client service.

The Clients: The group's clients include Ableco Finance, Paramount Pictures and PG&E National Energy Group.

Milbank, Tweed, Hadley & McCloy

The Firm: Rivals place this group "*high on the list*" for the quality and volume of its caseload. Complex restructurings and Chapter 11 cases form a significant portion of the practice. A truly international practice, the attorneys based in California can call on a respected network of offices, including esteemed New York bankruptcy specialists. Highlights have included representing the noteholders in a prepackaged Chapter 11 case involving a manufacturer of industrial safety products, Jackson Products. The team acted for the holders before the bankruptcy, during the case, and in connection with the exit financing facility. Attorneys here also advise on corporate transactions related to the disposal of distressed assets.

The Lawyers: "*Bright star*" **Paul Aronzon** "*has an enormous breadth of practice*" according to

190   All quotes in the text are from interviews with clients and competitors.

CHAMBERS USA 2005

California
Leading individuals (Bankruptcy)

Senior Statesman

MURPHY Patrick *Winston & Strawn, San Francisco*

[1] ARONZON Paul *Milbank Tweed, Los Angeles*

KLEE Kenneth *Klee Tuchin, Los Angeles*

PACHULSKI Richard *Pachulski Stang, Los Angeles*

[2] GREENFIELD Robert *Stutman Treister, Los Angeles*

LEVIN Richard *Skadden Arps, Los Angeles*

LUREY Michael *Latham & Watkins, Los Angeles*

PACHULSKI Isaac *Stutman Treister, Los Angeles*

[3] BENVENUTTI Peter *Heller Ehrman, San Francisco*

BOGDANOFF Lee *Klee Tuchin, Los Angeles*

FELDSTEIN Hydee *Paul Hastings, Los Angeles*

HAVEL Richard *Sidley Austin, Los Angeles*

LOGAN III Ben *O'Melveny & Myers, Los Angeles*

LOPES James *Howard Rice, San Francisco*

NEELY Sally *Sidley Austin, Los Angeles*

PEDLAR Alan *Stutman Treister, Los Angeles*

TUCHIN Michael *Klee Tuchin, Los Angeles*

[4] AHRENS Michael *Sheppard Mullin, San Francisco*

BENNETT Bruce *Hennigan Bennett, Los Angeles*

COLEMAN Kathryn *Gibson Dunn, San Francisco*

DAVID Henry *Alschuler Grossman, Santa Monica*

GODSHALL Brad *Pachulski Stang, Los Angeles*

HOLDEN Jr Frederick *Orrick, San Francisco*

KLYMAN Robert *Latham & Watkins, Los Angeles*

KRELLER Thomas *Milbank Tweed, Los Angeles*

MILLET Craig *Gibson Dunn, Irvine*

MOORE Robert *Milbank Tweed, Los Angeles*

PATTERSON Thomas *Klee Tuchin, Los Angeles*

PEITZMAN Lawrence *Peitzman Glassman, Los Angeles*

SHENEMAN Margaret *Winston, San Francisco*

WEG Howard *Peitzman Glassman, Los Angeles*

WHITE Robert *O'Melveny & Myers, Los Angeles*

Individuals are listed alphabetically in each band.

sources, who particularly note his skill on behalf of bondholders and creditors' committees. He cochairs the firm's financial restructuring group. **Robert Moore** is an *"outstanding commercial adviser,"* whose expertise in bankruptcy and corporate reorganization has won him a loyal following. He acts on behalf of debtors, creditors and bondholders, and remains best known for his advice to the creditors' committee of PG&E in one of the largest utilities Chapter 11 proceedings ever seen. **Thomas Kreller** is making a name for himself in the workout and bankruptcy sphere through his consistently high-quality advice and practical understanding of the business issues faced in this market. He has represented debtors such as Bugle Boy Industries and MedPartners Provider Network, while his official creditors' committee work has included the Chapter 11 of McLeodUSA.

The Clients: The group's clients include debtors and official and ad hoc committees of creditors, as well as individual financial institutions, lender syndicates and equity security holders.

Stutman, Treister & Glatt Professional Corporation

See firm details p.299

The Firm: This group impressed interviewees with its technical expertise and its pragmatic approach to workout negotiations and bankruptcy litigation. The team is staffed with *"aggressive"* lawyers who are *"brilliant across the board – they have all the knowledge, insight and acumen"* befitting a leading business reorganization, bankruptcy and insolvency practice. In addition to serving its highly esteemed debtor client base, the group acts for equity and creditor committees, and is occupied with M&A issues connected to troubled companies. Recent highlights include acting for funds holding approximately $500 million dollars of bank debt connected to the Owens Corning Chapter 11 case.

The Lawyers: **Robert Greenfield** (see p.254) was roundly endorsed as one of the practice's most highly visible attorneys. He is currently representing furniture manufacturer Falcon Products in its Chapter 11 reorganization, a case that involves nine debtor entities and six foreign subsidiaries. *"Brilliant"* **Isaac Pachulski** (see p.266) is considered *"a genius"* by many peers, and one of the smartest people in the field. Over the past year, he acted for funds holding about $2 billion of Enron's bank debt in their claims against the company. While some feel that the technical expertise of **Alan Pedlar** (see p.267) makes him *"a lawyer's lawyer,"* clients were also enthusiastic in their praise for his commercial understanding of their businesses. All regard him as *"wonderfully smart, insightful and creative"* with a talent for identifying the key details in negotiations.

The Clients: Southern California Edison; Mariner; Edwards Theaters; the bondholders in Primestar; Maguire Thomas Partners-Grand Place Towers; Thrifty Oil; Lamonts Apparel; Bumble Bee Seafoods; Carter Hawley Hale; Kennetech Windpower; Public Service of New Hampshire and Standard Brands.

Band 2

Latham & Watkins LLP

The Firm: This *"highly credible practice"* has devoted substantial resources to its bankruptcy group. Attorneys here are well equipped to handle a full range of bankruptcy matters, including federal income tax consequences, corporate reorganizations and debt restructuring. Exchange and tender offers and prepackaged bankruptcies are areas of focus for the team. This expertise sits well among the team's diet of lender representation on distressed credits, and debtor and creditor advice on Chapter 11 proceedings and bankruptcy-related litigation. Key highlights have included advising Trump Casino Resorts and 28 subsidiaries and affiliates in the restructuring of about $1.9 billion debt. The team acted for Consolidated Freightways in litigation surrounding the liquidation of its assets; a Chapter 11 plan of liquidation was approved by the bankruptcy court.

The Lawyers: *"Consensus-builder"* **Michael Lurey** is *"especially effective in large lender groups,"* say clients. He cochairs the firm's insolvency practice, and this year acted for Leap Wireless International, its operating subsidiary, Cricket Communications, and 64 affiliates, in their filing for Chapter 11 bankruptcy protection. A plan to restructure about $2.5 billion in indebtedness was confirmed after a one-week trial despite opposition from a creditor and major shareholder of Leap. Lead trial attorney in the Leap Wireless International matter **Robert Klyman** is another highly regarded name in the practice area. His trial skills are matched by an *"understanding of the business practicalities,"* say clients.

The Clients: The group's clients include Consolidated Freightways, Trump Casino Resorts and Yucaipa.

O'Melveny & Myers LLP

See firm details p.294

The Firm: Clients appreciate this group's *"highly research-oriented"* approach to bankruptcy matters. The team acts for syndicated bank groups in restructuring and Chapter 11 matters, as well as debtors and an increasing number of distressed debt and hedge funds. Recent high points have included acting for hedge fund Cerberus, as the acquirer of the largest group of Burger King franchises in the USA. The team also represented two groups of lenders providing an $8.8 billion exit financing for Adelphia.

The Lawyers: *"Calming influence"* **Ben Logan** *"is constructive and laid-back without ever giving an inch,"* enthused clients. His *"keen business sense"* makes him a favorite in his mainstay practice of Chapter 11 reorganizations and out-of-court restructurings for major creditors and debtors. He cochairs the firm's finance and restructuring practice. Clients count practice group founder **Robert White** among *"the most preeminent bankruptcy partners in the USA,"* because of his *"knowledge and creativity."* Business restructurings, Chapter 11 proceedings and out-of-court reorganizations form the backbone of his practice.

The Clients: Sun Healthcare; Tower Records; Ormet; Lionel and the lenders to Horizon Coal.

Pachulski, Stang, Young, Jones & Weintraub PC

See firm details p.296

The Firm: Rivals believe this *"aggressive"* group has *"done a great job in growing and getting involved in deals,"* placing itself firmly on the list of leading practices. Business reorganizations and workouts, avoidance actions and bankruptcy litigation are all to be found in the group's portfolio. Attorneys here are also able to advise on transactions related to distressed assets.

The Lawyers: Richard Pachulski (see p.266) is an "*amazing business generator.*" He impresses many with his ability to "*really move large cases along.*" Business reorganizations and related litigation encompass the bulk of his practice, and he has acted for debtors and creditors' committees in court and in out-of-court workouts. "*Practical*" **Brad Godshall** is experienced in finance, workouts and Chapter 11 business reorganizations.

The Clients: America West Airlines; Chicago Title; Commonwealth Equity Trust; First Alliance Mortgage; Hilton Hotels and Six Continents Hotels; Loews Cineplex Entertainment; Orange County; Safeway and Xerox.

Sidley Austin Brown & Wood LLP

See firm details p.778

The Firm: This group is singled out as "*a serious player nationally*" in the bankruptcy and reorganization arena. A broad-ranging practice advises on court-supervised proceedings, insurance insolvency and out-of-court restructurings and workouts. While a respected team in California has won a following with its deep resources and "*highly practical, client-focused attorneys,*" it can call on the support of an international network of offices, particularly a strong offering in its Chicago heartland.

The Lawyers: "*First-rate*" **Richard Havel** (see p.255) heads the Los Angeles bankruptcy practice. He acts for parties in informal workouts and Chapter 11 proceedings and has counseled creditors' committees, trustees and debtors. **Sally Neely** (see p.265) is another "*excellent adviser, who always puts her client's interests first.*" She advised Bombardier and Learjet on litigation related to the airline purchase contracts that involved a Chapter 11 debtor. She has also advised Flintkote on its asbestos-related Chapter 11 proceedings.

The Clients: The team's clients include debtors, special board committees, official and unofficial creditors' and bondholders' committees, senior creditors, senior debt syndicates, unsecured creditors, subordinated debt groups, acquirers and trustees.

Skadden, Arps, Slate, Meagher & Flom LLP & Affiliates

See firm details p.1372

The Firm: Clients uphold this as "*the group you want on your side when the chips are down.*" Packed with "*super lawyers from top to bottom,*" it acts in a wide range of complex deals, in all areas of restructuring, for lenders, debtors and committees. Key matters have included advising Hollywood Casino Shreveport as debtor in a bondholder restructuring. Other successes include representing the bank group in the AMERCO restructuring.

The Lawyers: Clients applaud "*fabulous*" **Richard Levin**'s (see p.261) "*practical and solutions-driven*" approach, and speak of his thorough understanding of clients' needs. Corporate restructuring, insolvency and bankruptcy issues are his core areas of focus, and he is experienced in advising debtor and non-debtor clients. He is also involved in protecting against bankruptcy risks in securitization transactions.

The Clients: Sierra Pacific Communications; Friedman's Jewelers; Penn National Gaming; JPMorgan Chase; CNF and Indigo Partners.

Winston & Strawn

See firm details p.780

The Firm: This respected outfit has secured a strong reputation with its steady diet of bankruptcy cases, workouts and corporate reorganizations. Its dedicated attorneys have the backup of this international firm in undertaking a significant volume of cross-border and international cases. Team members are also well equipped to advise on M&A related to troubled companies

The Lawyers: Widely considered "*the dean of bankruptcy practice in California,*" **Patrick Murphy** (see p.264) retains his "*fabulous*" reputation in restructuring and insolvency work. "*Bulldog*" **Margaret Sheneman** is "*tough as nails*" when protecting her clients' interests. Her thorough and practical approach to workouts and bankruptcy litigation is respected by peers.

The Clients: American National Bank and Trust Company of Chicago; Bank One; Black Diamond; Comdisco Ventures; Deutsche Bank; LaSalle Bank; Metricom and Wells Fargo.

Band 3

Alschuler Grossman Stein & Kahan LLP

See firm details p.280

The Firm: This Santa Monica operation is well known nationally for its litigation expertise, which it translates into a respected bankruptcy and creditors' rights practice. The practice is creditor oriented, and this caseload sits alongside substantial work for commissioners as receivers in insurance matters. Highlights have included acting for a healthcare network in its efforts to buy hospitals out of bankruptcy. The team also represented a lender intending to provide exit financing in connection with a medical device company.

The Lawyers: Henry David (see p.249) acted for the California Insurance Commissioner in the prosecution of a preference and fraudulent transfer action arising from the failure of the Superior National Insurance Group. He is respected for his sound judgment and smooth handling of complex matters, particularly those requiring robust litigation skills.

The Clients: The group's clients include Epson America and Marubeni-Itochu Steel.

Gibson, Dunn & Crutcher LLP

See firm details p.285

The Firm: Commentators agree that this group has "*really established itself,*" staffing its cases with "*attentive*" attorneys, who are well versed in bankruptcy matters. Clients speak of a service that is "*invaluable to the overall strategy of a situation.*" The group advises debtors and creditor and equity committees in a full range of bankruptcy matters, including litigation. Recent highlights include representing London-based FLAG Telecom, an owner and operator of undersea fiber-optic cable networks. The matter involved litigation before the bankruptcy court in New York, arising from the performance of its Chapter 11 reorganization. The group also acted for Flowserve in the Powerplant Maintenance Specialists Chapter 11 bankruptcy case. Attorneys are also skilled in the field of professional firm insolvencies, and post-bankruptcy matters. For example, they are representing a group of lenders (led by Citibank) in the restructuring of £100 million of debt to Brobeck, Phleger & Harrison.

The Lawyers: "*Excellent litigator and strategist*" **Craig Millet** (see p.264) and **Kathryn Coleman** (see p.248), who is "*well versed in bankruptcy,*" are key members of the practice group.

The Clients: Filtration Development; Tactical Aerospace; Callaway Golf; The Irvine Company; Applied Materials; California Community Colleges; Fluor; Solutia and Merrill Lynch.

Heller Ehrman LLP

See firm details p.288

The Firm: Regarded as "*an extremely good practice,*" the team is occupied with complex bankruptcy, reorganizations and debt restructuring and related litigation. The team represented sole secured creditor Lehman Brothers Holdings in highly litigated bankruptcy cases concerning USA-based holding companies that own Polish real estate development companies. The cases concerned allegations that shortly before the appointment of a Chapter 11 trustee on Lehman's motion, the debtor's principal surreptitiously transferred a controlling interest in the Polish entities to his Polish confederate.

The Lawyers: "*Solid and well-regarded*" **Peter Benvenutti** heads the firm's bankruptcy practice. His workload features a substantial number of business reorganizations, insolvency advice and workout negotiations. He represented a Chapter 11 debtor in possession in liquidation proceedings, involving cross-border issues of US, Dutch and Swedish law.

The Clients: Clients include institutional lenders, secured and unsecured creditors, unsecured creditor committees, debtors in possession, bankruptcy trustees, lessors of real and personal property, acquirers of distressed assets and businesses, assignees for the benefit of creditors, state and federal court receivers, venture capital investors and equity holders.

192

All quotes in the text are from interviews with clients and competitors.

CHAMBERS USA 2005

Hennigan, Bennett & Dorman LLP
See firm details p.289

The Firm: Peers recognized that this group has made an impact on the market thanks to its "*standout*" attorneys. The group's representation of the Chapter 7 trustee appointed in the Brobeck, Phleger & Harrison case has helped raise its profile over the past year. However, the group is well equipped to handle a range of issues. The business reorganization and bankruptcy group works on behalf of debtors, secured and unsecured creditors and those seeking business opportunities from troubled assets.

The Lawyers: **Bruce Bennett** (see p.245) is the "*real go-to guy*" at the team, impressing interviewees as a highly professional and technically skilled bankruptcy attorney.

The Clients: Aureal; Sempra; Amoco and Equatorial Communications.

Howard, Rice, Nemerovski, Canady, Falk & Rabkin

The Firm: This firm continues to build on its high-profile appearance on behalf of PG&E, for which it successfully implemented a reorganization plan early in 2004. A talented group of San Francisco-based attorneys acts for substantial debtors, creditors' committees and Chapter 11 trustees, in addition to individual creditors. The caseload incorporates creditors' rights, bankruptcy and commercial finance issues. The breadth of experience housed in this firm has impressed market commentators, and the firm remains a trusted point of call for referrals.

The Lawyers: Practice chair **James Lopes** is among the state's most prominent bankruptcy practitioners. His workload has encompassed debtor and creditor committee representations, and representation of various parties involved in creditors' rights issues. He is a "*highly capable attorney, and quick to grasp the important issues in a case.*"

The Clients: The team's clients have included: PG&E; the creditors' committee of Media Vision Technology; Charles Schwab; the creditors' committee for Technical Equities; Osborne Computer and the Oakland Tribune.

Orrick, Herrington & Sutcliffe LLP
See firm details p.295

The Firm: A key player in the bankruptcy and debt-restructuring field, this firm is distinguished by its geographic reach and broad base of resources. The group's "*professional and talented*" attorneys advise clients in bankruptcy cases, out-of-court restructurings and recapitalizations. The caseload here also includes the representation of parties involved in law firm bankruptcies: for example, the firm is acting for former partners of the now-dissolved Lyons & Lyons. Attorneys are also acting for the official committees of retirees appointed in the unrelated Chapter 11 cases of Kaiser Aluminum and Kaiser Group International.

The Lawyers: **Frederick Holden** (see p.257) offers clients a "*constructive*" approach to bankruptcy with his "*personable and responsive*" manner.

The Clients: Wells Fargo; Bank of America; John Hancock Life Insurance; Retirement Systems of Alabama; the Reliance bondholders committee and MatlinPatterson.

Paul, Hastings, Janofsky & Walker LLP
See firm details p.297

The Firm: Clients endorse this "*strong bench*" of bankruptcy specialists for their responsive, client-focused service, while peers note its visibility on some of the state's more significant matters. Much of the group's representation is for senior secured lenders in existing secured facilities and debtor-in-possession financings. Highlights have included advising GE Capital in connection with Enron-related matters, as well as handling the sale of Distribution Dynamics for GE Capital.

The Lawyers: **Hydee Feldstein** (see p.252) is "*a creative thinker,*" whose knowledge, negotiating prowess and skill at "*reading the situation*" make her the preferred choice for many clients.

The Clients: Wells Fargo Foothill; Ableco Finance; Morgan Stanley and American Restaurant Group.

Peitzman, Glassman, Weg & Kempinski

The Firm: This popular bankruptcy, restructuring and business litigation boutique remains a force in the California marketplace. The group practices in a range of bankruptcy matters, including Chapter 11 cases and workouts, on behalf of debtors, creditors' committees, real property clients and purchasers of assets.

The Lawyers: Among the firm's nine attorneys are **Howard Weg** and "*smart*" **Lawrence Peitzman**.

The Clients: The team has acted in the Chapter 11 cases of: California Power Exchange; PG&E; Clothestime; Carolco Pictures; Enron and Granada Hills Community Hospital. Past clients have included BI Commerce Liquidation (formerly BMK).

Sheppard, Mullin, Richter & Hampton LLP

The Firm: "*Not just prominent but an active presence,*" this regional player is home to "*constructive, knowledgeable and wise*" team members. The team appears on behalf of debtors and creditors' committees and is particularly active for financial institutions. Workouts, financial restructurings, bankruptcy and other insolvency proceedings comprise the bulk of the group's activities. Notable representations include acting in the Western asbestos Chapter 11, as official counsel to the committee of asbestos claimants, resulting in a $2 billion trust for creditors. The group also represented the debtor in a Chapter 11 plan confirmation regarding Advanced Telecom Group.

The Lawyers: **Michael Ahrens** is a practical adviser, whose wealth of knowledge and long track record in the sector are widely recognized.

The Clients: Bank of America; Wells Fargo; US Bank; Union Bank of California; First Union National Bank; GE Capital; Massachusetts Mutual Life Insurance; Qwest Communications; Tower Records; Knudsen Foods; Foremost Dairies; Rusty Pelican Restaurants; Clark Construction Group and Vector Aerospace, as well as lessors, creditors' committees, franchisers, licensors, trustees, and indenture trustees.

CONSTRUCTION

Band 1

Thelen Reid & Priest LLP
See firm details p.300

The Firm: Peers agree that Thelen Reid stands out as "*the number one practice,*" while this is the firm clients turn to for "*those particularly large and complex cases.*" The expertise and industry knowledge housed in this group are absolutely exemplary because many of its "*really high-class attorneys*" have an industry or technical background, and the firm encourages in-house secondments. The main office is in San Francisco but Thelen Reid also fields construction specialists from the branch in Los Angeles and so maintains a presence throughout the state. These offices are also part of a thriving international practice that gives clients access to a worldwide set of resources. The practice is particularly renowned for its dispute resolution capabilities and it has worked on a wide range of projects in this context. For example, it is currently working on claims arising from the Coca-Cola concentrate facility in Ireland and is in mediation with steel suppliers in relation to the Tacoma Narrows Bridge in Washington state. However, the firm is also increasing its level of transactional work, and has recently been advising on the formation of a joint venture between American and Chinese engineering companies.

The Lawyers: **David Buoncristiani** is a litigator with an emphasis on construction

California
Leading firms (Construction)

1. **THELEN REID & PRIEST LLP** San Francisco
2. **FARELLA BRAUN & MARTEL LLP** San Francisco
3. **COX CASTLE & NICHOLSON LLP** Los Angeles
   GIBBS, GIDEN, LOCHER & TURNER Los Angeles
   HANSON, BRIDGETT, MARCUS San Francisco
   MONTELEONE & MCCRORY LLP Los Angeles
4. **BINGHAM MCCUTCHEN LLP** San Francisco
   HUNT, ORTMANN, BLASCO, PALFFY Pasedena
   MCKENNA LONG & ALDRIDGE San Diego
   MILLER, MORTON, CAILLAT & NEVIS San Jose
   QUINN EMANUEL URQUHART OLIVER Los Angeles

Leading individuals (Construction)

1. **BUONCRISTIANI David** Thelen Reid, San Francisco
   CLARK John Thelen Reid, Los Angeles
   HARRIS Alan Farella Braun, San Francisco
   SINK Charles Farella Braun, San Francisco
2. **BALLATI Deborah** Farella Braun, San Francisco
   GIBBS Kenneth Gibbs Giden, Los Angeles
   HEISSE II John Thelen Reid, San Francisco
   IPPOLITO Peter McKenna Long, San Diego
   MINCHELLA Michael Monteleone, Los Angeles
   O'NEAL Stephen Thelen Reid, San Francisco
   TEPLIN Lawrence Cox Castle, Los Angeles
   THUM Robert Thelen Reid, Los Angeles
3. **ASHCRAFT Howard** Hanson Bridgett, San Francisco
   BENNETT Fred Quinn Emanuel, Los Angeles
   HUGHES Frank Miller Morton, San Jose
   HUNT Gordon Hunt Ortmann, Pasedena
   MCMILLAN Daniel Jones Day, Los Angeles
   TRUAX Tim Cox Castle, Los Angeles
   TURNER III Glenn Gibbs Giden, Los Angeles
   ZOVICKIAN Stephen Bingham McCutchen, San Francisco

Firms and individuals are listed alphabetically in each band.

disputes. He is "*extremely experienced*" and has worked on many international projects that have gone into mediation or arbitration. Sources consider him "*absolutely excellent and very well respected in the field.*" The "*top-notch*" **John Clark** is a technically skilled and highly personable construction trial lawyer. "*A smart and capable senior attorney,*" he splits his practice between San Francisco and Los Angeles. **John Heisse** is lauded as a good all-round construction lawyer who is particularly strong in negotiations and in trial. He shares such a broad skill set with **Stephen O'Neal**, who is the chairman of the construction and government contracts department. **Robert Thum** was highly recommended for his dispute resolution skills. He is currently trying a large case regarding a power project in Bakersfield, California.
The Clients: The firm predominantly represents contractors, but it also handles cases on behalf of owners, subcontractors, design professionals, material suppliers and engineers. Representative clients include Homestake Mining and the University of California.

Band 2

Farella Braun & Martel LLP

The Firm: This full-service construction practice is said by one client to be "*top to bottom the most capable firm that I have dealt with.*" This success stems from the highly qualified attorneys and the "*imagination and innovation they bring to problem solving.*" The practice focuses on matters within the state of California and is particularly experienced in contentious issues. Over the past year, it has been involved in a flood of litigation arising from the False Claims Act, companies going out of business, and general contractual disputes between owners and contractors. Particularly active areas include disputes over energy facilities and hospitals.
The Lawyers: Alan Harris has long experience in both contracts and dispute resolution and peers commend his high-quality advice and ability to manage complex projects. **Charles Sink** is named as "*the first choice for complex multiparty disputes.*" Clients also praise his "*ability to communicate well with the other parties and facilitate successful settlements.*" Construction litigator **Deborah Ballati** impresses many observers with her strong work ethic. Clients enjoy working with her because of her "*bright capability and keen insights into the right issues.*"
The Clients: Clients include: City of San Francisco; University of California; InterGen and Bechtel.

Band 3

Cox Castle & Nicholson LLP

The Firm: This niche real estate firm has developed an experienced and broad-ranging construction practice that can aid clients through every stage of the construction process, from drafting agreements to dispute resolution. Client feedback on this practice was very positive, with one enthralled customer claiming, "*On a scale of ten, I'd give them a twelve.*" Key attributes include "*lots of experience and familiarity with the marketplace, a real team approach*" and the fact that the lawyers are "*always aware of the bottom line and don't waste clients' money.*" The firm has offices in San Francisco, Los Angeles and Orange County, so can handle matters arising throughout the state. Highlights from the past year include winning a case regarding entitlement to easement and representing a developer in a dispute over a right to purchase a certain tract of land.
The Lawyers: Lawrence Teplin, head of the litigation team, is a "*first-rate advocate and a great courtroom performer*" in both real estate and construction disputes. Sources agree that **Tim Truax** has talent and ability that belies his young age. He focuses exclusively on construction law, including contracts and dispute resolution.
The Clients: The firm's market reputation is largely based on its work for developers.

Gibbs, Giden, Locher & Turner
See firm details p.284

The Firm: This specialist boutique is "*very knowledgeable and well versed in construction law*" and produces "*excellent results*" for its clients. It is constantly expanding and can boast a large, well-resourced team that has attracted an impressive client list. Satisfied clients love working with the firm because "*the lawyers are just how lawyers should be – they make the process as painless as possible for everyone and solve problems in the most economical way.*" The practice covers all of California and also handles some cases in Arizona and Nevada. Representative matters include acting for the Arizona Cardinals in the construction of a new $330 million stadium and advising the University of Southern California on the development of a new sports centre.
The Lawyers: The firm has a broad-based team that can handle every issue facing the construction industry, from the early planning stages to litigation. **Kenneth Gibbs** (see p.253) stands out as "*highly experienced, well-spoken and knowledgeable.*" He is dedicating more and more of his time to mediation and is widely recognized as a leading figure in this field. **Glenn Turner** (see p.276) is popular with clients because he has a "*straightforward everyday guy demeanor*" and "*excels at making complex issues understandable to the layman.*"
The Clients: The firm works for both owners and contractors, representing a large chunk of public owners in Southern California. Clients include: City of Long Beach; City of Pasadena; City of Burbank; the Metro Water District; the Walt Disney Concert Hall; Mortensen; Swinerton Builders; the Arizona Cardinals and Centex Homes.

Hanson, Bridgett, Marcus, Vlahos & Rudy, LLP
See firm details p.287

The Firm: This strong midsized firm really excels at construction litigation and claims management. In fact, clients report that "*the quality here is better than the brand name firms.*" This is partly due to the firm's expertise in its niche and partly due to the "*responsive and really client-friendly*" service. It is very much a national practice, and the team is as likely to be found working on a project in Mexico or an arbitration in Nevada as on local matters.
The Lawyers: Clients praised **Howard Ashcraft** (see p.243) and claim that he is "*probably the best construction litigator this side of the Mississippi.*" He has an "*unbelievable grasp of technology, and ability to make these issues understandable and presentable to a jury.*"
The Clients: The firm has a broad client base that includes engineers, owners, contractors and public agencies. These clients include: Compania de Nitrogeno de Cantarell; BOC Gases;

Marubeni Corporation; CH2M HILL; URS Corporation; HDR Architecture & Engineering; ROMA Design Group; University of California; Golden Gate Bridge HTSD; San Mateo Transit; State of California, Department of Corrections; Terra Insurance; Kingston Constructors and MYR Power.

Monteleone & McCrory, LLP

The Firm: This firm has a long-established reputation as a leading adviser to contractors. The construction practice constitutes about 65% of the firm's overall business, and the firm has taken great strides to ensure that it fields resources and experience to cover all aspects of the business. This broad team is complemented by a couple of standout "*practical and talented*" attorneys. The group concentrates on local matters, and has recently been representing a number of contractors involved in building the Red Line and Green Line of the Los Angeles train system. It is also working for the two main contractors responsible for the upgrade of the Hyperion Treatment Plant in Los Angeles.

The Lawyers: Peers report that **Michael Minchella** is the firm's leading light. He specializes in representing clients in complex disputes.

The Clients: The firm works mainly for the contractors on construction projects, but the client base also includes subcontractors, suppliers, architects, engineers, construction managers, owners and public agencies.

Band 4

Bingham McCutchen LLP

The Firm: This firm was named by many sources as the "*first choice*" for representing owners, both for drafting contracts and for litigation. It is particularly experienced in class action lawsuits and also has considerable expertise in land use. The attorneys here have recently developed an affordable housing practice.

The Lawyers: The "*extremely capable*" **Stephen Zovickian** is a broadly generalist litigator who spends the vast majority of his time on construction matters.

The Clients: This firm's major clients include Bechtel.

Hunt, Ortmann, Blasco, Palffy & Rossell Inc

The Firm: This "*highly knowledgeable*" construction boutique has an active caseload covering both transactional and contentious aspects of the law. It is noted for its expertise in public works projects.

The Lawyers: Gordon Hunt is "*well renowned as an authority*" in the sector, and peers regard him as one of the market's "*senior advisers.*"

The Clients: Clients include: City of Los Angeles; Metropolitan Water District of Southern California; City of Oxford; St. John's Hospital; Charles Pankow Builders; Sachs Electric Company; ACCO Engineered Systems; Malcolm Drilling; The Converse Professional Group and Building Industry Credit Association.

McKenna Long & Aldridge
See firm details p.636

The Firm: This firm has made a name for itself in the market through its involvement in False Claims Act matters throughout the country. Additionally, the firm offers expertise in public works projects, industrial construction disputes, and advice to international companies.

The Lawyers: Market commentators endorse **Peter Ippolito** (see p.258) as an "*absolutely first-rate construction attorney.*" He has a wide international practice that encompasses all areas of construction law.

The Clients: The firm represents contractors, subcontractors, state and local governments, owners, engineers and architects.

Miller, Morton, Caillat & Nevis

The Firm: Clients regard Miller Morton as "*one of the most experienced construction law firms in California*" and are pleased with the "*many fine results*" that the firm has delivered. A large part of the practice is dedicated to large commercial contractors. For example, it is currently pursuing a complex claim against a bankrupt hi-tech company on behalf of a contractor working on 12 of its projects. An interesting development recently has been the increased representation of contractors working on casinos built on Indian reserves. The practice also has a division working on construction defect litigation. The case-

load here is varied, and ranges from representing a nonprofit housing association suing contractors to defending home builders in large multiparty claims.

The Lawyers: Frank Hughes received particularly glowing client feedback, with many appreciating his "*business-oriented approach and ability to find solutions.*"

The Clients: The firm focuses on representing contractors, but it also works for owners.

Quinn Emanuel Urquhart Oliver & Hedges, LLP
See firm details p.298

The Firm: This specialist business litigation firm is home to an army of experienced trial lawyers. It has been involved in a variety of construction litigation cases, and is expert in both defending and prosecuting claims. Peers particularly noted its experience in advising on government contracts matters.

The Lawyers: Fred Bennett (see p.245) is a highly experienced general litigator, who has particular expertise in construction matters.

The Clients: Clients include: Dinwiddie Construction; Fujita; Haseko; Jacobs Engineering; KB Home; Lewis Homes; Matt Construction; Montgomery Watson; Odebrecht Contractors of California; Samsung America; Times Mirror Company; Williams & Burroughs Construction and Zurich Group.

Other Notable Practitioners

Daniel McMillan (see p.263) from Jones Day is known for his "*skill in litigation*" and is also an expert in false claims. He is especially renowned for his representation of owners, both public and private. On the public side, he has recently been advising Los Angeles County and the Metropolitan Transportation Authority in litigation and arbitration related to a large subway project. Another highlight was defending a claim and winning a cross-claim on behalf of Chevron Texaco with regards to an offshore oil pipeline in Angola.

CORPORATE/M&A

Wilson Sonsini Goodrich & Rosati
See firm details p.302

The Firm: This Silicon Valley stalwart has historically been credited with facilitating the increasingly energetic startup market. It continues this pioneering role, committing a depth of resources to such clients and in return attracting a much envied client loyalty. However, the departure of three high-profile partners from

the corporate team in early 2005 and the stepping down of iconic Larry Sonsini as chief executive have been the cause of comment during research. While there is no doubt that the firm has a wealth of talent to withstand such losses, the move is indicative of the high-level competitive pressures faced by law firms in the California market. There is no denying the strength of this corporate group's performance over the

past year, with its representation of Juniper in its acquisition of NetScreen standing as a highlight. The firm's corporate practice concentrates on three areas: startups, corporate governance and M&A. The busy startup practice typically nurtures hi-tech and life sciences companies, and is admired by rivals for its ability to strategically expand new companies and provide them with all corporate services as they mature. The firm

California
Leading firms
(Corporate/M&A: Northern California)

1. LATHAM & WATKINS LLP *Menlo Park*
   WILSON SONSINI GOODRICH & ROSATI *Palo Alto*
2. COOLEY GODWARD LLP *Palo Alto*
   FENWICK & WEST LLP *Mountain View*
   SKADDEN, ARPS, SLATE, MEAGHER *San Francisco*
3. DAVIS POLK & WARDWELL *Menlo Park*
   DLA PIPER RUDNICK GRAY CARY US *Palo Alto*
   HELLER EHRMAN WHITE *Menlo Park*
   O'MELVENY & MYERS LLP *Menlo Park*
   PILLSBURY WINTHROP LLP *Palo Alto*
4. GUNDERSON DETTMER STOUGH *Menlo Park*
   MORGAN, LEWIS & BOCKIUS LLP *San Francisco*
   MORRISON & FOERSTER *San Francisco*

Leading firms
(Corporate/M&A: Southern California)

1. GIBSON, DUNN & CRUTCHER LLP *Los Angeles*
   LATHAM & WATKINS LLP *Los Angeles*
   SKADDEN, ARPS, SLATE, MEAGHER *Los Angeles*
2. MUNGER, TOLLES & OLSON LLP *Los Angeles*
   O'MELVENY & MYERS *Los Angeles, Newport Beach*
   PAUL, HASTINGS, JANOFSKY & WALKER *Los Angeles*
3. IRELL & MANELLA LLP *Los Angeles*
   SHEPPARD, MULLIN, RICHTER *Los Angeles*
   SIDLEY AUSTIN BROWN & WOOD *Los Angeles*

Firms are listed alphabetically in each band.

also advises a large roster of public and private companies on traditional corporate governance issues; and in M&A, the team represents mostly hi-tech clients, increasingly in cross-border transactions.
The Lawyers: Larry Sonsini (see p.273) is seen as "*overwhelmingly dominant*" in the West Coast market, and is credited with spearheading the firm's eminent hi-tech practice. A favorite of clients, he brings "*an intelligent overview and vast experience*" to the negotiating table. He is the premier deal-maker, and now presides over the firm as chairman. Among his recent highlights, Sonsini advised Juniper in its $4 billion acquisition of NetScreen and assisted longstanding client Google in its IPO. Newly minted as vice chairman, **Jeff Saper** (see p.271) commands respect for his financing and transactional work. Noted as a "*consummate relationship guy*" his recent transactions include representing Eontec in its $130 million acquisition by Siebel Systems, and advising a defense company in its acquisition by British Aerospace. He possesses deep cross-border transactional expertise, having represented Infosys Technologies, one of India's leading information technology services companies in its $1 billion equity offering. **Kenneth Clark** (see p.248) is the managing partner of the firm's technology transactions practice, and his transactional work, combined with his expertise in the life sciences

and information technology industries, is well regarded by the market. **Marty Korman** (see p.260) is a "*star among the new generation*" of attorneys at this firm, and represents public clients such as Hewlett-Packard and TIBCO Software. Although seen primarily as a litigator, **Boris Feldman**'s (see p.251) securities and corporate governance expertise sustains his presence in the tables. Rivals endorsed his sound judgment in corporate matters and highlighted his excellent work for Hewlett-Packard during its litigation against Walter Hewlett. A specialist in the startup market, **Casey McGlynn** (see p.263) is recognized for his life sciences, information technology and telecom expertise. **Mario Rosati** (see p.270) impresses with his ability to form strong client relationships, a skill shared by **Mark Bertelsen** (see p.245), whose clients include Advent Software and CSFB.
The Clients: Amid a long list of blue-chip clients can be found: Google; Juniper; Wind River; Eontec; McAfee and Lehman Brothers.

Cooley Godward LLP

The Firm: Building on its reputation in the venture capital and startup arenas, this firm has made its mark with M&A capability and a number of big-ticket deals. Expertise in life sciences and technology has made this one of the premier Silicon Valley firms. In addition to corporate and financial services, the firm offers clients a dedicated M&A group, specializing exclusively in transactions for both the bidder and target. Clients appreciate the depth of the team on offer here, which extends to the associates, who are "*technically sound and very diligent.*" Over the past year the group handled more than 70 M&A transactions. Buy-side clients include Siebel Systems, Adobe, Synopsis and eBay International, the last of which they advised at the end of 2004 on its $290 million acquisition of the Dutch Internet trading company Marktplaats. Sell-side deals include representing InVision Technologies in its $900 million acquisition by GE. In the life sciences sphere, attorneys advised Tularik in its sale to Amgen.
The Lawyers: Richard Climan heads the M&A group and is hailed by some as "*one of the best M&A attorneys in the country.*" Although his workload spans various sectors, he is particularly well versed in matters arising out of the information technology and biotech sectors. Clients include Synopsis, which he is advising on its intended acquisition of Nassda. **Mark Tanoury**'s "*outstanding reputation*" has been fostered by his work in venture capital and emerging companies. He is also well regarded for his general corporate and securities work. **Bob Jones** advised on the InVision acquisition by GE, and is especially well regarded for his expertise in the life sciences field, where clients include Exelixis and Five Prime Therapeutics.

Steering that dedicated group, **Barbara Kosacz** has a practice that encompasses general corporate matters, with an emphasis on life sciences. Garnering comments such as "*the best attorney I have ever worked with,*" **Keith Flaum** was identified by clients as their "*go-to guy.*" He is appreciated for his business sense as much as his technical abilities and noted for his dedication to client relationships. Flaum led on a number of acquisitions for eBay and Siebel Systems. Heading the San Diego office, **Fred Muto** works across corporate and securities law. He focuses on emerging and public technology growth companies. Market commentators said they respected his work in life sciences.
The Clients: Adobe; Synopsis; Applied Materials; eBay; Quest Software; Invidia; Borland; Genencor and InVision Technologies.

Fenwick & West LLP

See firm details p.283
The Firm: This indigenous firm is emerging as a real force in Northern California, impressing clients and rivals with its hi-tech focused M&A, IPO, venture capital and startup work. The team is known for having "*expertise up and down the ranks*" as well as for its efficiency. Clients, many of them Silicon Valley stars, said: "*It cannot be overemphasized that the team has accomplished extraordinary results working to very tight timeframes.*" The firm acts as outside counsel for Cisco Systems, recently advising it on its $450 million acquisition of Airespace, a leading provider of wireless local area networking systems. The firm is also representing long-time client Symantec in its proposed $13.5 billion merger with VERITAS, which would stand as the largest software merger ever. A further high-profile deal was representing NetScreen in its $4 billion acquisition by Juniper. The firm's established IPO practice continues to prosper; last year it represented Shopping.com in its IPO, which raised $123 million.
The Lawyers: Gordy Davidson (see p.249) is undoubtedly a heavy hitter in the market, helping to grow firms from their IPO and then throughout their major transactions. His success in handling the mature end of the market is illustrated with his advice to long-term client Ocular Sciences in its $1.2 billion acquisition by The Cooper Companies. Clients told researchers that "*his integrity and ability to step back and take the long-run view are extraordinary.*" He co-led on the Symantec merger agreement and, according to rivals, has firmly established a position as "*one of Silicon Valley's stars.*" **Mark Stevens** (see p.274) is warmly regarded by the market, and rated for his M&A and strategic partnership work. He acts for key clients such as Electronic Arts, and also specializes in IPOs, having directed over 25 IPOs of hi-tech companies. **Jeff Vetter** (see p.277) and **Laird Simons** (see p.273) are recommended as top securities

California
Leading individuals (Corporate/M&A)

★ SONSINI Larry *Wilson Sonsini*, Palo Alto

[1] BOGEN Andy *Gibson Dunn*, Los Angeles
DAVIDSON Gordon *Fenwick & West*, Mountain View
GALLO Greg *DLA Piper Rudnick*, Palo Alto
KAUFMAN Christopher *Latham & Watkins*, Menlo Park
KING Kenton *Skadden Arps*, Palo Alto
MCCARTHY Brian *Skadden Arps*, Los Angeles
MENDELSON Alan *Latham & Watkins*, Menlo Park
SAPER Jeff *Wilson Sonsini*, Palo Alto
TOSETTI Paul *Latham & Watkins*, Los Angeles

[2] CAMAHORT Steve *O'Melveny & Myers*, San Francisco
CLIMAN Richard *Cooley Godward*, Palo Alto
COBEN Jerome *Skadden Arps*, Los Angeles
DEL CALVO Jorge *Pillsbury Winthrop*, Palo Alto
SAGGESE Nicholas *Skadden Arps*, Los Angeles

[3] GUNDERSON Bob *Gunderson Dettmer*, Menlo Park
JOHNSON Craig *Heller Ehrman*, Menlo Park
KENNEDY Mike *O'Melveny & Myers*, San Francisco
LARSON John *Morgan Lewis*, San Francisco
LESSER Henry *DLA Piper Rudnick*, Palo Alto
ROSATI Mario *Wilson Sonsini*, Palo Alto
SMITH Gregory *Skadden Arps*, Palo Alto
STEVENS Mark *Fenwick & West*, Mountain View
TANOURY Mark *Cooley Godward*, Palo Alto
VILLENEUVE Tom *Gunderson Dettmer*, Menlo Park

[4] ADLER Robert *Munger Tolles*, Los Angeles
CLARK Kenneth *Wilson Sonsini*, Palo Alto
DENHAM Robert *Munger Tolles*, Los Angeles
FELDMAN Boris *Wilson Sonsini*, Palo Alto
JENETT Bruce *Heller Ehrman*, Menlo Park
JONES Robert *Cooley Godward*, Palo Alto
KORMAN Marty *Wilson Sonsini*, Palo Alto
KOSACZ Barbara *Cooley Godward*, Palo Alto
LAZAROW Warren *O'Melveny & Myers*, Menlo Park
RUCK Charles *Latham & Watkins*, Costa Mesa
TONSFELDT Steven *Heller Ehrman*, Menlo Park

[5] BELLAH MAGUIRE Jennifer *Gibson Dunn*, Los Angeles
BERTELSEN Mark *Wilson Sonsini*, Palo Alto
BRAUN Lawrence *Sheppard Mullin*, Los Angeles
DETTMER Scott *Gunderson Dettmer*, Menlo Park
FLAUM Keith *Cooley Godward*, Palo Alto
GIUNTA Joseph *Skadden Arps*, Los Angeles
GREEN Josh *Heller Ehrman*, Menlo Park
HALL Michael *Latham & Watkins*, Menlo Park
KELLER Don *Orrick Herrington*, Menlo Park
KNAUSS Robert *Munger Tolles*, Los Angeles
LAYNE Jonathan *Gibson Dunn*, Los Angeles
MCGLYNN Casey *Wilson Sonsini*, Palo Alto
MILLER Robert *Paul Hastings*, Los Angeles
MUTO Fred *Cooley Godward*, San Diego
NASH Glenn *Latham & Watkins*, Menlo Park
SANCHEZ Carl *Paul Hastings*, San Diego
SEGEL Alvin *Irell & Manella*, Los Angeles
SIMONS Laird *Fenwick & West*, Mountain View
SINGER Gary *O'Melveny & Myers*, Newport Beach
SMITH Douglas *Gibson Dunn*, San Francisco
SNYDER David *Pillsbury Winthrop*, San Diego
VETTER Jeff *Fenwick & West*, Mountain View

Individuals are listed alphabetically in each band.

---

lawyers, who share great experience of the market and an understanding of how businesses are run, claimed sources. Vetter led for Morgan Stanley as underwriters on the Salesforce.com and SiRF Technology IPOs. Laird Simons has built his reputation by advising on IPOs for eBay and Oracle.

The Clients: Cisco Systems; Intuit; Electronic Arts; Adaptec; Interwoven; Macromedia; Silicon Image; Symantec; Telcontar and VERITAS Software.

Davis Polk & Wardwell
See firm details p.1345

The Firm: Menlo Park hosts this national firm's only California office, and represents the firm's commitment to high-end corporate and transaction work in the technology sectors. It competes with its Silicon Valley rivals in venture capital, M&A and private equity. Despite being a relatively recent addition to the Northern Californian market, the group has been involved in three of the past year's biggest West Coast deals: advising Oracle on its successful $10.3 billion hostile takeover of PeopleSoft; assisting JPMorgan Securities as financial adviser to NetScreen Technologies on its acquisition of Juniper Networks and advising The Robert Mondavi Corporation on its $1.3 billion acquisition by Constellation Brands. The team utilized its cross-border capabilities advising on a number of international acquisitions. For example, it assisted Yahoo! in its acquisition of FareChase, an Israeli travel search engine.

The Lawyers: Clients reported that this team is "*of exceptional quality up and down the ranks.*" Daniel Kelly and William Kelly head the team.

The Clients: Oracle; JPMorgan Securities; The Robert Mondavi Corporation; ARM Holdings; Ingram Micro; NPTest; VERITAS Software; Domaines Barons de Rothschild (Lafite); Francisco Partners; Texas Pacific Group; Comcast; Novo Nordisk; Vitesse Semiconductor; Global eXchange Services; Thomas Weisel Capital Partners and Yahoo!

DLA Piper Rudnick Gray Cary US LLP
See firm details p.765

The Firm: Effective January 2005, the Gray Cary Ware & Freidenrich law firm joined forces with national giant Piper Rudnick and Europe's DLA to form a global behemoth. The sheer depth of resources and specialist capabilities provided by this turn of events looks set to afford the Silicon Valley team an even greater international and cross-border caseload. However, this should not downplay the considerable bank of knowledge and experience, and excellent market reputation that the team already brings to the deal table. It has successfully attracted a stable and loyal clientele, providing them with venture capital, startup and IPO advice. Attorneys also advise the

more mature private and public companies, offering a full range of transactional and M&A services. The firm acts for private and public companies, many of them Fortune 500, and has established a name for its expertise in both the IT and biotech spheres. A portfolio of retail clients has also been won over with focused advice on corporate and securities law. In this sphere Jack in the Box restaurants and Starbucks are among the firm's household-name clients.

The Lawyers: Greg Gallo (see p.253) is highly regarded by the market, particularly for his IPO and venture capital work. He recently advised Salesforce.com on its $114 million IPO and assisted InPhonic in its listing on Nasdaq. He also has extensive M&A experience, in addition to a healthy corporate counseling practice. Henry Lesser (see p.261) is seen as a pure M&A attorney. Researchers were told "*he is an excellent technician, with a strong command of his craft.*" He has advised a string of hi-tech companies through their M&As, as well as financial advisers such as Deutsche Bank Securities and Merrill Lynch.

The Clients: Agilent Technologies; Agile Software; Finisar; Extreme Networks; Hewlett-Packard; QUALCOMM; Dreyer's Grand Ice Cream; iManage; Immersion; InPhonic; Invitrogen; Mattson Technology; Maxtor; Morgan Stanley; Packeteer; Pinnacle Systems; Protein Design Labs; Salesforce.com; SciClone Pharmaceuticals; Signatel; Starbucks; Zhone Technologies and Zoran.

Heller Ehrman White & McAuliffe
See firm details p.288

The Firm: The Menlo Park-based corporate practice – known as the Heller Ehrman Venture Law Group following its 2003 merger – continues to carve a niche in the venture financing and startup market. The team, which sits as part of the broader corporate group, serves all types of industries, but is recognized particularly for its life sciences and hi-tech expertise. Attorneys here guide startups through their venture financing, IPOs, M&A and beyond. The team recently advised Pelikan Technologies through its preferred stock financing – one of the largest private medical device financings last year in the USA. On the M&A front, they are representing Solexa through its proposed merger with Lynx Therapeutics. At time of press in early 2005, a number of partners announced their intention to join the Silicon Valley office of Orrick, Herrington & Sutcliffe.

The Lawyers: Craig Johnson continues to impress with his hi-tech-focused corporate practice, working with clients from incorporation through to M&A and transactional work. Co-leading the firm's life sciences practice, Bruce Jenett has extensive local and international corporate and financing experience, particularly in the equity and debt financing area.

His clients include Yamanouchi Venture Capital, a subsidiary of one of Japan's largest pharmaceuticals, Pelikan and Thoratec. **Steven Tonsfeldt** is an M&A specialist and cochairs that group at the firm. Well respected by sources, he counsels publicly and privately held companies through M&A, LBOs and joint ventures. **Josh Green** wins *"very high points"* from clients for his responsiveness and negotiation skills.

The Clients: Yamanouchi Venture Capital; Pelikan Technologies; Jazz Pharmaceuticals; Digital Theater Systems; Symantec; Seattle Genetics; Yahoo!; RITA Medical Systems; Foundry Networks; RedEnvelope; Intellisync; Threshold Pharmaceuticals; IronPort Systems; Corcept Therapeutics; Depomed; At Road; Virage Logic; Impinj; OSA Technologies; Airespace; OnFiber Communications; Menlo Ventures; US Venture Partners; Kleiner Perkins Caufield & Byers; New Enterprise Associates and Sequoia Capital Partners.

Pillsbury Winthrop LLP
See firm details p.1364
The Firm: This firm continues to make headway in the market, with commentators recognizing its increasing presence in M&A and IPO work. The firm handles a broad swath of corporate matters for companies, ranging from startup to value realization, particularly those with a hi-tech and pharmaceutical bent. The team has taken a slice of the IPO market, advising on a number of transactions in 2004, including those for M-Flex and Orange 21. Clients value its cross-border capabilities; for example the group recently closed an IPO for MediciNova in Japan, raising $108 million – making it the first American company to close an IPO in Japan. On the M&A side, the Northern California team represented SICOR in its $3.4 billion acquisition by Teva Pharmaceutical Industries. Clients were happy to report that the firm fields expert and efficient teams: *"They don't bring in an army of attorneys, they pick the appropriate level of staffing."* The upcoming merger of the firm with DC-based Shaw Pittman should do nothing but strengthen the capabilities of the West Coast team, particularly with regard to major IT and business process outsourcing projects.
The Lawyers: **Jorge del Calvo** (see p.249) is a prominent player in Silicon Valley, with a focus on venture capital and securities work. His IPO expertise is widely respected and he has successfully built up strong client relationships. Among his highlights, he counseled SiRF Technology and PortalPlayer in their recent offerings. **David Snyder** (see p.273) is well equipped to handle a range of corporate and securities matters, and is said by clients to be incredibly responsive, with even time zones proving no barrier to his ability to provide timely and business-focused advice. He has a particular niche in the life sciences and pharmaceutical market, recently

counseling IDEC Pharmaceuticals in its $6.7 billion merger with Biogen. He has also acted for key client Xcel Pharmaceuticals in a range of transactions.
The Clients: BNP Paribas; Potlatch; Headwaters Incorporated; SICOR; Applied Molecular Evolution and Advanced Fibre Communications.

Gunderson Dettmer Stough Villeneuve Franklin & Hachigian
The Firm: This firm gained recognition for its venture capital and hi-tech corporate work during the tech boom, and continues to serve emerging companies in the hi-tech, life sciences and retail sectors. Its attorneys offer a mix of corporate and securities expertise, in addition to IP and strategic alliance advice. Venture capital raising and IPOs made by emerging companies comprise much of the corporate practice. Recent M&A highlights include advising Visto Corporation in its acquisition of Psion Software.
The Lawyers: **Bob Gunderson**, **Scott Dettmer** and **Tom Villeneuve** are seen as the captains of this corporate team. Bob Gunderson possesses a wealth of experience in corporate transactions related to the strategic growth of technology companies. He shares with Scott Dettmer a *"real understanding of how business is conducted."* Clients also described Tom Villeneuve as *"one of the smartest and most competent lawyers I have ever worked with."*
The Clients: Actionpoint; Blue Coat Systems; Lightspeed Venture Partners; Morgan Stanley Dean Witter Venture Partners; Merrill Lynch and Lehman Brothers are among the firm's clients.

Morgan, Lewis & Bockius LLP
See firm details p.1556
The Firm: This firm maintains its presence in the Northern California market, with the San Francisco and Palo Alto offices both serving clients predominantly from the technology sector, encompassing biotech, hardware and semiconductor manufacturers, as well as life sciences and pharmaceuticals. The emerging growth and startup advice – such as financings for strategic growth – is fast becoming a specialty of these teams. The LA office provides a more traditional transactional and securities practice. An extensive international network ensures additional resources across a range of disciplines, such as tax and capital markets financings, which has proved attractive to clients.
The Lawyers: **John Larson** (see p.260) is a partner in the business and finance group. He handles M&A, corporate governance and securities work for clients who are primarily hi-tech companies. He remains a *"trusted adviser,"* and the most prominent member of this team.
The Clients: The firm represents Fortune 500 companies, multinational financial services and investment banking organizations, as well as

leading names in the life sciences, technology and securities sectors.

Morrison & Foerster LLP
See firm details p.293
The Firm: The Northern California offices of this firm provide the full range of corporate services to clients. Riding the current upswing of M&A deals, the team advises public and private companies through a variety of transactions and financings, including strategic alliances and joint ventures. The firm's cross-border capabilities were illustrated by the San Francisco office's recent advice to China HR throughout Monster Worldwide's acquisition of 40% of its stock. The team also represented Hitachi in its $2 billion acquisition of IBM's hard disk drive business. In addition, the firm advises financial institutions in private equity and fund formations. An increasing slice of the group's practice involves providing corporate governance counseling to clients, with board committees being added to the firm's client roster. The Palo Alto office has a technology and life sciences focus, and serves companies throughout all stages of their growth cycle.
The Lawyers: William Sherman in Palo Alto and William Schwartz in San Francisco are the primary contacts. Last year William Sherman advised Credence Systems in its $660 million acquisition of NPTest Holdings.
The Clients: Pathway Capital Management; American Pharmaceutical Partners; Objective Systems Integrators; Verio; Hitachi; MarketWatch and Thomson.

Gibson, Dunn & Crutcher LLP
See firm details p.285
The Firm: This firm, according to commentators, *"has the edge in terms of talent."* Clients told researchers that this West Coast native has the depth and skill to rival its East Coast competitors in the Southern California market. The *"world-class"* corporate team concentrates on M&A and private equity, with a significant capital markets practice also attracting attention. The firm has cultivated strong relationships with investment banks, recently advising UBS and Merrill Lynch on tenders and offerings. Among recent highlights, the attorneys have represented Herbalife in its IPO, and they have displayed a particular strength in handling Rule 144A offerings. The San Francisco office has developed a significant venture capital skill set, and its M&A capability was underlined during its representation of PeopleSoft during Oracle's takeover last year.
The Lawyers: **Andy Bogen** (see p.246) has built a formidable reputation as an M&A expert, and particularly in dealing with hostile takeovers. Highly regarded for his *"business acumen and technical skill,"* his work for top clients such as Northrop Grumman and Boeing means he is recommended for complex transactions in addi-

tion to securities and bankruptcy-related matters. **Jonathan Layne** (see p.261) enters the table this year, and is noted for his M&A practice, representing mostly public and large private companies. On the securities front, he represented Herbalife in its $345 million IPO. Clients reported that he is a *"go-to"* partner, and is *"prompt, accessible, very smart and experienced."* He also has a significant capital markets practice, representing Merrill Lynch as underwriters in the public offering of senior notes by MGM Mirage. San Francisco-based partner **Douglas Smith** (see p.273) is recognized for his securities work for public companies, public debt and equity offerings and M&A. He was one of the advisers to PeopleSoft in its acquisition of JD Edwards and in its response to the successful Oracle takeover. Recently he has advised Lehman Brothers as lead agent for World Savings Bank's $8 billion bank note program. **Jennifer Bellah Maguire** (see p.244) is a capital markets specialist, but also advises on M&A, strategic alliances, financings and divestitures. She recently represented Pacific Corporate Group in a $100 million PIPE investment in WebMD. As part of her busy fund formation practice she advised Leonard Green & Partners in the formation of the $1.85 billion Green Equity Investors fund.
The Clients: A selection of the firm's impressive client portfolio are: Hewlett-Packard; Intel; Leonard Green & Partners; UBS Investment Bank; Xilinx; Lehman Brothers; Merrill Lynch; Goldman Sachs; Cadence Design Systems and Northrop Grumman.

Latham & Watkins LLP
The Firm: This international player translates its global strength to the California market, with commentators highlighting the firm's capabilities across the state and spanning the corporate spectrum. Rivals remarked that it is *"the firm we love to hate,"* due to its unshakable presence in the market. The firm fields about 150 lawyers among the six local offices dedicated to M&A, with industry specialization in life sciences, healthcare, gaming and technology. Clients reported that the team consists of great *"deal people,"* who can focus on the broader business picture for them, while still providing technically sound legal advice. The Los Angeles and Orange County offices recently advised Amgen in its acquisition of Tularik, and the team's gaming expertise was underlined by its advice to Harrah's in its acquisition of Caesars Entertainment. The firm is also well respected for its private equity capabilities.
The Lawyers: Co-head of the firm's global M&A group, LA-based **Paul Tosetti** enjoys a formidable reputation as a *"top-notch"* M&A specialist. Clients reported that in addition to being a great technical lawyer, *"he is straightforward – you believe him when he tells you something."* He recently advised Amgen on its $1.3

billion acquisition of Tularik. **Kit Kaufman** specializes in hi-tech M&A deals and corporate finance. Commentators universally praised his intellect, remarking that *"he has an intensity that has helped him develop a very loyal following."* His recent work includes representing two directors and significant stockholders of the Robert Mondavi Corporation during its acquisition by Constellation Brands, in what was the largest wine and spirit deal of the year. **Alan Mendelson**'s reputation for his work with emerging companies and venture capital, particularly in the life sciences arena, goes from strength to strength. As testament to his skill and success, rivals praised his *"impressive collection of clients."* Orange County-based **Charles Ruck** enters the table this year, making his presence felt with a string of M&A deals and his far broader corporate finance practice. Over the past year, he has been advising Harrah's Entertainment in its acquisition of Caesars Entertainment for approximately $9.44 billion, making it the largest deal ever in the gaming industry. Other clients include Amgen and Merrill Lynch. **Glenn Nash** has joined the firm's venture and technology transaction groups in Menlo Park from Cooley Godward. He brings significant IP and transactional experience to emerging and established clients. **Michael Hall** is known for his venture capital and transactional work for emerging companies, particularly those in the life sciences arena.
The Clients: Amgen; Harrah's Entertainment; Merrill Lynch and Deutsche Bank Securities.

Skadden, Arps, Slate, Meagher & Flom LLP & Affiliates
See firm details p.1372
The Firm: The New York giant continues to make inroads into the local market, led by a team of great depth and experience. Hailed for its international presence and cross-border expertise, the firm is viewed as *"hugely active and influential in California,"* through its offices in San Francisco, Palo Alto and Los Angeles. Sophisticated M&A and financing work is the order of the day here. Big-ticket clients keep the M&A team busy with work, such as advice to Yahoo! on its acquisition of Musicmatch. Drawing on its considerable resources, the firm offers corporate clients expertise in all areas including capital markets work, private equity and REITS. The firm also has an enviable client base of investment banks, which it advises on a swath of large deals.
The Lawyers: **Kenton King** (see p.260) heads up the corporate team in the Bay Area, and wins plaudits for his tech work. Interviewees were quick to point out his keen intellect and corporate and securities abilities. Key deals include his representation of NTT DoCoMo as stockholder of AT&T Wireless Services in connection with the public auction of AT&T Wireless for $41 billion. **Brian McCarthy**'s (see p.263) name was often suggested to researchers as one of the best

all-rounders for corporate work. His practice encompasses all aspects of M&A, and he is also valued for his general corporate counseling work. He is *"results oriented, honest and straightforward, and knows what the key points are,"* said clients. Over the past year, he represented Freedom Communications in its leveraged recapitalization transaction with affiliates of Blackstone Capital Partners and Providence Equity Partners. **Jerome Coben** (see p.248) focuses on corporate and securities law, representing a broad range of clients in M&A, as well as issuers and underwriters in finance deals. Last year he undertook a major refinancing of a Las Vegas casino for Wynn Resorts and advised on a number of transactions for corporate clients, including retailers such as Oakley sunglasses and Juicy Couture. A *"great client winner"* **Nick Saggese** (see p.271) is noted for the variety and volume of his work, which encompasses recapitalizations, securities offerings and restructuring. He was recently involved in UnitedGlobalCom's acquisition of the minority shares of UGC Europe and represented Providence Equity Partners in its acquisition, with others, of MGM. **Greg Smith** (see p.273) continues to impress the market with his representation of mature and growing companies in corporate and finance matters. Trusted and respected **Joseph Giunta** (see p.253) handles all types of M&A, proxy contests, tender offers, recapitalizations and LBOs. He is recognized for his high-quality work for Del Webb in its acquisition of Pulte Homes.
The Clients: Merrill Lynch; UBS Warburg; Yahoo!; Leonard Green & Partners; Deutsche Bank; Texas Pacific Group; Oakley; Del Webb; RockShox; McKesson and Openwave Systems.

Munger, Tolles & Olson LLP
The Firm: Litigation has historically been seen as this home-grown firm's strong suit, but clients report: *"There is no question that this firm has one of the leading transactional practices in California."* The firm's roster of clients includes some of the largest companies in Southern California such as KB Home, City National Bank and Edison International, and attorneys recently advised the latter on the divestiture of its energy generating plants. Clients said this team is responsive, cost effective and efficient, and that they *"don't believe there is any law firm that has the same level of extraordinary talent across the ranks."* Its securities law capability and understanding of the nuances involved in private equity work are also widely recommended. The group has advised funds such as Yucaipa Companies and Oaktree Capital Management over the past year. Attorneys have also developed strong relationships with entertainment clients, and last year represented Jeffrey Katzenberg through the DreamWorks IPO.
The Lawyers: **Robert Adler** enjoys a good rep-

www.ChambersandPartners.com

All quotes in the text are from interviews with clients and competitors.

199

utation in the market and has a diverse practice, incorporating transactional and corporate counseling. Praised for his restructuring and divestiture of Edison International, he also represented Edison Mission Energy in its $2 billion acquisition by International Power and Mitsui. According to clients, **Robert Denham** is an excellent technical attorney with "*a good, strong intellect.*" He is primary counsel to Berkshire Hathaway, and has a strong private equity practice, advising funds such as Rustic Canyon Partners. **Robert Knauss** has a broad corporate practice. He was particularly rated for his private equity and securities work, advising funds through formation and M&A of their portfolio companies. Researchers were told that he is "*easy to work with and gets the job done.*" His clients include Yucaipa Companies and Oaktree Capital Management.

The Clients: Berkshire Hathaway; Oaktree Capital Management; KB Home; Yucaipa Companies; United Talent Agency and City National Bank.

O'Melveny & Myers LLP
See firm details p.294

The Firm: This firm appears to be bolstering its corporate practice in California, poaching three partners from rival firms at the beginning of 2005. The market still sees litigation as this firm's West Coast highest profile specialty, but there is recognition that the corporate team is increasingly making an impact, in terms of the quality and quantity of recent deals. The Silicon Valley team serves technology clients through all stages of their development, from startup financing, IPOs, corporate transactions and mergers. The team also advises venture capital investors. Recent deals include representing Ask Jeeves in its $360 million acquisition of Interactive Search Holdings. On the sell-side, attorneys have represented clients through a number of acquisitions, including Mojave in its acquisition by Magma Design Automation and Twingo Systems in its acquisition by Cisco Systems. The Orange County team focuses on M&A and securities law, and has a strong midmarket client base in addition to Fortune 500 companies and high net-worth individuals.

The Lawyers: **Steve Camahort** is "*one of the stars*" to have come across to the San Francisco office from Wilson Sonsini. He is an M&A specialist, and was one of the advisers to Juniper Networks in its acquisition of NetScreen last year. At time of press, **Mike Kennedy** announced his decision to join the team. He brings with him extensive M&A experience in the technology sector. The "*impressive*" **Warren Lazarow** continues to be a mainstay of this expanding group. Based in Silicon Valley, he advises largely technology companies throughout their venture capital and startup phases and is well equipped to advise on all forms of corporate transactions. He recently advised Snap Appliance through its acquisition by Adaptec and Q Design Automation in its acquisition by Cadence Design Systems. **Gary Singer** heads up the Orange County office and is well liked by commentators. His work centers on public offerings and venture financings, in addition to M&A. Last year he represented JMP Securities as placement agent in a financing deal for ConnectivCorp.

The Clients: Ask Jeeves; Bay Partners; LightSpeed Venture Partners; NeoScale Systems; Trinity Ventures; Pacific Sun; Corinthian Colleges; New Century Financial; Security Pacific; Western Digital and Qlogic.

Paul, Hastings, Janofsky & Walker LLP
See firm details p.297

The Firm: The firm has recently reorganized its corporate practice, so that it can devote greater resources and commitment to its specialized M&A team, as well as continuing to support its startup and private equity practice groups. The San Diego team serves largely life sciences and technology clients, including semiconductor, hardware, software and telecom companies. In the past this team represented Musicmatch in its acquisition by Yahoo! In Los Angeles, the corporate group boasts a strong roster of midmarket clients, in addition to institutional investors and banks, leveraging its proximity to both the East Coast and Asia. Locally the team represented Hancock Park Capital in a combined total of $100 million worth of transactions. Attorneys also continue to represent Dole Food in its acquisitions, last year assisting it to acquire JR Wood.

The Lawyers: **Robert Miller**'s (see p.264) practice covers both corporate and securities law, with a focus on the telecom and technology industries. Last year he advised Biomarin Pharmaceutical in its acquisition of Ascent Pediatrics. In private equity, Paladin Capital Group is one of his key clients. Commended as "*a strong deal-doer,*" he is part of a team respected for the depth of experience it fields. **Carl Sanchez** (see p.271) recently moved over from another firm to head up the M&A team worldwide. He is an experienced M&A attorney, representing private and public companies across a range of West Coast industries, and has good relationships with East Coast financial services clients.

The Clients: The firm advises a mix of private equity and venture capital houses, as well as financial institutions and emerging and mature companies in the telecom and technology sector.

Irell & Manella LLP

The Firm: While commentators spoke more loudly of this firm's IP, tax and restructuring practices, the corporate group is proving an attractive draw card to a number of clients. Dedicated attorneys provide the full range of M&A and transactional capabilities, and provide clients – both public and private companies – with a broad and integrated service, drawing on the expertise of its other practice groups. The team advises clients on securities and financing matters and last year handled several billion dollars worth of debt financings on behalf of Charter Communications, the nation's third largest cable company, controlled by Paul Allen. Clients are drawn from a range of industries, with a particular niche in the gaming market, in addition to manufacturing, technology and telecom sectors.

The Lawyers: **Alvin Segel** is an "*experienced attorney and decent person,*" reported appreciative clients. He is primary counsel to Paul Allen, the cofounder of Microsoft, and last year he represented the buyer of the Milwaukee Brewers baseball team in connection with the acquisition and related financings.

The Clients: Chandler Family, Mandalay Resort Group and Pinnacle Entertainment are among the firm's clients.

Sheppard, Mullin, Richter & Hampton LLP

The Firm: The corporate practice at this indigenous firm is concentrated in three areas: M&A, securities and its specialist entertainment and media practice. The transactional team handles a range of deals of various sizes, with a focus and recognized strength in the midmarket range, recently advising Northrop Grumman and Boeing on a number of transactions. JAMDAT Mobile and Valiant Pharmaceuticals recently sought the firm's securities advice in preparation for their public offerings. While the firm does undertake international work, its focus is serving clients nationwide. To this end, last year saw the opening of offices in New York and Washington, DC.

The Lawyers: **Lawrence Braun** "*understands what clients are trying to accomplish.*" He is best known for his work on distressed company M&A transactions and 'corporate divorces' through redemptions and dissolutions. He recently represented Boeing Capital in the sale of its commercial lending and leasing business to GE Capital.

The Clients: PepsiCo; Unified Western Grocers; adidas; Alcatel; National Technical Systems; JAMDAT Mobile; Deckers Outdoor; Boeing Capital; The Copley Press and International Rectifier are clients of the corporate team.

Sidley Austin Brown & Wood LLP

See firm details p.778

The Firm: This international firm has a local presence in both Los Angeles and San Francisco and is recognized for its prowess in capital markets and private equity transactions. In the capital markets sphere, this creative and thoroughly technical team generally represents underwriters and debtors, and has advised on a number of equity issues for the real estate industry. Clients such as Wells Fargo utilize the firm's mezzanine finance expertise. On the traditional lending side, the practice is handling an increasingly international portfolio of deals, particularly in Singapore and the Philippines. Among the firm's private equity caseload is the representation of key client Century Park Capital Partners in a number of acquisitions and dispositions over the past year.

The Lawyers: Commentators reported that the California offices field a team of "*bright and capable lawyers*" which is responsive to clients' legal and business needs. Moshe Kupietzky is managing partner in Los Angeles, and heads up the corporate and finance group in that office.

The Clients: The team has been representing MGM in connection with its potential opening of a theme park in Korea; private equity clients include Century Park Capital Partners and Oaktree Capital Management.

Other Notable Practitioners

At time of press in early 2005, Orrick, Herringtno & Sutcliffe LLP a coup with the recruitment into its Menlo Park office of a number of partners from Heller Ehrman Venture Law Group. While the market awaits the impact of these moves, the initial feedback is positive as such resources are expected to provide a sound platform from which to advise the region's active corporate entities and private equity houses. Among the recruits is the respected **Don Keller**, who represents startups and mature companies, both public and private, through the full spectrum of corporate and financing services.

EMPLOYMENT

MAINLY DEFENDANT

California
Leading firms
(Employment: Mainly Defendant)

1	**PAUL, HASTINGS, JANOFSKY** *Los Angeles*
2	**GIBSON, DUNN & CRUTCHER LLP** *Los Angeles*
	ORRICK, HERRINGTON & SUTCLIFFE *Los Angeles*
	SEYFARTH SHAW LLP *Los Angeles*
3	**LATHAM & WATKINS LLP** *Los Angeles*
	MORGAN, LEWIS & BOCKIUS LLP *San Francisco*
	MORRISON & FOERSTER LLP *Los Angeles*
	WILSON SONSINI GOODRICH *San Francisco*
4	**HELLER EHRMAN LLP** *San Francisco*
	LITTLER MENDELSON PC *San Francisco*
	O'MELVENY & MYERS LLP *Los Angeles*
	SHEPPARD, MULLIN, RICHTER *Los Angeles*
5	**CARLTON, DISANTE** *Los Angeles*
	JACKSON LEWIS *Los Angeles*
	LIEBERT CASSIDY WHITMORE *Los Angeles*
	MUNGER, TOLLES & OLSON LLP *Los Angeles*

Firms are listed alphabetically in each band.

Band 1

Paul, Hastings, Janofsky & Walker LLP

See firm details p.297

The Firm: This firm has secured its place at the forefront of the market with clear endorsement among clients and peers, who say it remains "*the best employment practice in the state by some margin.*" Clients value its "*top-class, dedicated employment experts,*" who can draw resources from the firm's vast network of offices for cases that run across the USA and overseas. Such resources ensure that the firm is first port of call for multijurisdictional class actions and the most sophisticated matters, including the drafting of appellate briefs. Its recent caseload has spanned employment discrimination claims as well as union matters, bringing the firm an "*enviable blue-chip clientele.*" Commentators praised the firm's involvement in Blomgren v Weatherford Motors, in which the team won summary adjudication of the claims brought by a former salesman against the bay area's leading BMW dealership. Further highlights include the group's representation of Sprint in the Tenth Circuit Court of Appeals in a case concerning alleged age discrimination.

The Lawyers: Chair of the practice **Nancy Abell** (see p.243) is not only a highly skilled attorney but also an "*exceptional leader*" of the group. She represents private and public employers in a broad array of employment cases such as wrongful discharge, discrimination and labor-management litigation. Market commentators credited her with "*a superb job*" in Dukes v Wal-Mart. Together with the "*preeminent*" **Paul Grossman** (see p.255), she is defending one of the largest employment discrimination lawsuits in history. This case is typical of Grossman's ability to handle the most complex of cases. Sources endorsed his skill in protecting his clients' interests and ensuring the smooth running of any litigation should it need to go to court. "*Cooperative*" **Kirby Wilcox** (see p.277) is, according to clients, a "*straight shooter,*" who shares with **Paul Cane** (see p.247) a real understanding of how to litigate effectively. Cane is also endorsed as a talented attorney, who "*knows what makes his clients tick.*" He recently dealt with the case Lo v Judicial Council of the State of California, in which the California Court of Appeal affirmed a jury verdict in favor of his client following a claim of sexual harassment. **Jeffrey Wohl** (see p.278) is "*driven to produce results for his clients.*" In Syverson v IBM, he won a motion to dismiss the nationwide collective-action status of a challenge to IBM's reductions in workforce. The case centered on allegations of age discrimination and violations of ERISA.

The Clients: Clients include Target Stores, Sempra Energy and Disney.

Band 2

Gibson, Dunn & Crutcher LLP

See firm details p.285

The Firm: With over 30 lawyers in California alone, this firm is a favorite among clients for its "*top all-round quality advice*" on both labor and employment issues. It maintains a tight relationship with the firm's litigation department, which ensures it has the technical and strategic understanding to handle "*even the most intricate employment litigation issues.*" The group is frequently called upon to advise on labor relations, wage and hour litigation, discrimination and ERISA matters. Clients applauded the firm's "*superior representation – its consistently high-quality advice and service levels.*" It recently litigated an alternative workweek class action for Carlton Forge Works to settlement, and advised Sony Entertainment on wrongful termination claims brought by three former executives. The group has also defended employers such as UPS and Anheuser-Busch in OSHA matters.

The Lawyers: "*Super smart*" **Pamela Hemminger** (see p.256) is an attorney that clients "*trust implicitly.*" Of late, she has handled several class action cases, primarily in the wage and hour arena, and she has continued to litigate nationwide pattern and practice ADA cases. **William Claster** (see p.248) recently acted for Dole Food in a class action, which alleged a failure to give proper notice under the Worker Adjustment and Retraining Notification Act to a class of 1900 agricultural employees. He also represented Tenet Healthcare in a series of class actions alleging failure to adhere to California's wage and hour laws regarding meal periods and rest breaks for over 50,000 employees.

The Clients: UPS; Tenet Healthcare; Dole Foods and Callaway Golf and Washington Mutual; Mitsubishi; Standard Pacific and Tenet Healthcare.

California
Leading individuals
(Employment: Mainly Defendant)

1 **ABELL Nancy** *Paul Hastings*, Los Angeles
GROSSMAN Paul *Paul Hastings*, Los Angeles
PFISTER Thomas *Latham & Watkins*, Los Angeles
WILCOX Kirby *Paul Hastings*, San Francisco

2 **ALVAREZ Fred** *Wilson Sonsini*, Palo Alto
HERMLE Lynne *Orrick Herrington*, Menlo Park
SINISCALCO Gary *Orrick Herrington*, San Francisco

3 **CANE Paul** *Paul Hastings*, San Francisco
DIEKMANN Gilmore *Seyfarth Shaw*, San Francisco
FRIEDMAN Alan *Munger Tolles*, Los Angeles
GILLETTE Patricia *Heller Ehrman*, San Francisco
HEMMINGER Pamela *Gibson Dunn*, Los Angeles
HOWARD Jr George *Pillsbury Winthrop*, San Diego
MATHIASON Garry *Littler Mendelson*, San Francisco

4 **ADLER James** *Irell & Manella*, Los Angeles
CLASTER William *Gibson Dunn*, Irvine
DRAPKIN Steven *Sole Practitioner*, Los Angeles
EISEN Rebecca *Morgan Lewis*, San Francisco
EMANUEL William *Littler Mendelson*, San Francisco
KADUE David *Seyfarth Shaw*, Los Angeles
KEYES Judith *Morrison & Foerster*, San Francisco
KRISCHER Gordon *O'Melveny & Myers*, Los Angeles
ONCIDI Anthony *Proskauer Rose*, Los Angeles
SAXE Deborah *Heller Ehrman*, Los Angeles
SIEGEL Robert *O'Melveny & Myers*, Los Angeles
SIMMONS Richard *Sheppard Mullin*, Los Angeles
THOMPSON Tracy *Morgan Lewis*, San Francisco
TURNER Jonathan *Epstein Turner*, Los Angeles
WALTER Brian *Liebert Cassidy*, Los Angeles
WHEELER Raymond *Morrison & Foerster*, Palo Alto
WOHL Jeffrey *Paul Hastings*, San Francisco

Up-and-coming individuals
TSATALIS Marina *Wilson Sonsini*, Palo Alto

Individuals are listed alphabetically in each band.

Orrick, Herrington & Sutcliffe

See firm details p.295

The Firm: Clients and peers feel this "*formidable leader*" has secured a strong reputation for the high quality and broad range of its employment practice. Its workload encompasses areas such as protection of trade secrets, discrimination and harassment and wrongful termination claims. The group also advises on wage and hour litigation and counsels employers on employee benefits and related ERISA litigation.

The Lawyers: "*Peacemaker*" **Gary Siniscalco** (see p.273) is respected by both clients and peers because "*he doesn't need to win by thrashing the opponent.*" This "*well-prepared and highly ethical player*" focuses on his clients' business needs and long-term reputations and can see beyond the results of an individual court case. His clients include major household names such as Albertsons, which he has defended on a range of discrimination and harassment claims. According to clients, "*tenacious*" **Lynne Hermle** (see p.256) is a tough courtroom performer and, when nec-

essary, is "*a tigress of a jury litigator.*" She successfully defended Advanced Micro Devices against a $200 million claim alleging post-9/11 discrimination. She has also advised on wage and hour class actions brought against major clothing retailers.

The Clients: Advanced Micro Devices; Gap; IBM; Blockbuster; Inland Container and Burlington Coat Factory.

Seyfarth Shaw LLP

See firm details p.777

The Firm: The national strength and depth of this firm's employment practice is widely recognized and respected. Its presence on the West Coast is expanding in line with the level of resources the firm has devoted to the market. A team of over 60 attorneys now operates from the Los Angeles and San Francisco offices and is well equipped to handle a range of discrimination litigation, including appellate matters and labor relations issues. Interviewees highlighted the group's work on wage and hour issues, placing their advice at the cutting edge of the market. Rivals agreed that the team has "*gained strength and is a great competitor – it's a great choice for the biggest cases,*" particularly those that cross state lines.

The Lawyers: Clients applaud "*class action luminary*" **Gilmore Diekmann** for his "*balance and know-how.*" A consummate trial lawyer, he is quick on his feet and able to win the trust of a jury. Clients also singled out the "*gifted*" **David Kadue** for his practical approach to negotiations and litigation. He has a broad employment practice that covers all forms of litigation as well as counseling on policies and the preparation of handbooks.

The Clients: Intel; Robert Half International; Federal Express; Sun Microsystems; IKON Office Solutions; Delta Air Lines; Kellogg; Simpson Strong-Tie; Walgreen; State Compensation Insurance Fund; Lockheed Martin and Weight Watchers.

Band 3

Latham & Watkins LLP

The Firm: This international firm has impressed in many quarters for its success in developing a "*comprehensive employment group with great skill and breadth.*" Although thought to focus more on high-end matters, its specialist attorneys are well equipped to handle a range of employment and labor law disputes. The group represented the City of Garland, Texas, in a Title 7 adverse impact lawsuit brought by the DOJ challenging the city's police officer and firefighter hiring practices. It also defended Denny's in an action brought by three plaintiffs seeking to represent a class of all restaurant managers in California. The claim centered on overtime pay and the allegation that they were improperly classified as exempt employees.

The team also won an important victory for its client SAFECO Insurance.

The Lawyers: "*Dedicated player*" **Thomas Pfister** is, according to clients, "*first choice for the biggest class actions.*" Even among rivals he scores highly with one market leader saying, "*I would turn to him in a heartbeat.*" He successfully advised the cancer research and treatment center City of Hope on discrimination and wrongful discharge claims brought by a former hospital manager.

The Clients: Southern California Edison; Rent-A-Center; SAFECO Insurance; Toyota Motor Sales, USA; Allstate Insurance and Denny's.

Morgan, Lewis & Bockius LLP

See firm details p.1556

The Firm: According to clients, this firm houses "*a well-resourced practice with a friendly and dedicated employment group.*" The team's sound judgment and ability "*to get to the core of the issue*" impressed competitors and clients alike. The group has secured a place on major pieces of discrimination litigation recently and combines this caseload with advice on union issues. The group's expertise in wage and hour disputes and employee benefits is also respected.

The Lawyers: "*Vibrant litigator and adviser*" **Rebecca Eisen** (see p.251) counsels employers on a range of issues such as employment litigation, including class actions, hiring practices and terminations. Clients also praised **Tracy Thompson** (see p.275) as a "*fine litigator, able to deal with anything thrown at her.*"

The Clients: The firm has attracted major clients from a range of industries such as financial services, pharmaceuticals and the media sector.

Morrison & Foerster LLP

See firm details p.293

The Firm: A "*high-quality, national scope*" within the labor and employment law sector is the key to this firm's continued prominence. A 50-attorney team is also supported by a small group of dedicated ERISA specialists, who offer advice on a range of employee benefits counseling and litigation. While these attorneys are respected for their litigation skills, they also advise on compliance and union issues such as collective bargaining. Clients appreciate that "*it will firstly steer clear of litigation – until all other avenues are exhausted.*"

The Lawyers: "*Lawyer's lawyer*" **Raymond Wheeler** (see p.277) is the chair of the group and is considered "*a straight-talking attorney.*" Interviewees endorse his advice on complex employment litigation and his adroit counseling on traditional labor law matters. He acted for Novellus Systems in federal court wage and hour class actions and advised on union-organizing efforts by the International Association of Machinists involving facilities. **Judith Keyes** (see p.259) is renowned for "*finding solutions to intricate employment problems.*" She advised one high-pro-

202   All quotes in the text are from interviews with clients and competitors.

CHAMBERS USA 2005

file client through a major corporate restructuring involving both union and nonunion facilities, and she worked with another client on revamping all its employment and contractor agreements. Well known for her work with key client Fireman's Fund Insurance, she represented the company through a wage and hour class action trial and has handled class action and individual suits against Coca-Cola and Intel.

The Clients: Lucasfilm; Intel; Coca-Cola; Fireman's Fund Insurance; Mechanics Bank and City of Oakland

Wilson Sonsini Goodrich & Rosati
See firm details p.302
The Firm: This *"high-quality corporate powerhouse"* was particularly recommended to researchers for its advice to existing blue-chip clients on their employment issues. According to interviewees, *"its counsel, guidance and expertise are of superior quality."* The workload here spans sexual harassment, termination and discrimination issues, which the group handles with sensitivity. The team dealt recently with the jury trial Harvey v Sybase, in which a senior executive claimed retaliation against her for complaints about working conditions and discrimination in her termination. Further examples include the defense of Google over an allegation of age discrimination and the defense of a high-profile sexual harassment case for Infosys.
The Lawyers: *"Gentleman"* Fred Alvarez is a *"true expert"* on matters concerning labor, employment and equal opportunities law. Clients value that he is *"highly intelligent and always on the ball."* Rising star Marina Tsatalis (see p.275) handled the Santoro v Juniper Networks case, concerning wrongful termination and trade secrets, in a matter that settled just before a jury trial.
The Clients: Sybase; Google; Cypress Semiconductor; Juniper Networks; Network Appliance; McAfee and Business Objects.

Band 4

Heller Ehrman LLP
See firm details p.288
The Firm: This player is celebrated by market sources for its *"outstanding general litigation counsel."* It has developed a significant presence with its experienced labor and employment law practice. Discrimination and claims of wrongful discharge form the basis of this group's workload. It also offers expertise in traditional labor law such as wage and hour issues, collective bargaining and general policy counseling. Peers report, *"There is no question about the firm's growing dedication to the area."*
The Lawyers: Patricia Gillette is applauded for her *"reliability and honesty"* and her efforts to make sure her clients' best interests are upheld. Her fine trial skills combine with an ability *"to stay on top of things"* ensuring that she is a popular choice for referrals. The *"tremendously knowledgeable"* Deborah Saxe is widely respected for her litigation skills and her dedication to the profession through her work with the bar.
The Clients: Clients include major financial institutions and consumer credit providers such as Bank of America, Household International and First Nationwide Bank, as well as hospitals, hi-tech companies and utilities.

Littler Mendelson PC
The Firm: Clients endorsed this national firm's San Francisco-based attorneys as *"exceptionally responsive and creative"* even when dealing with *"the most challenging matters."* One client felt *"its strength is that it offers proactive education to customers and its lawyers know what law is relevant in different states."* Unsurprisingly given the firm's vast size, this employment practice has handled a substantial range of employment disputes. Commentators noted its expertise in union issues and specialist regulatory advice.
The Lawyers: Highly intelligent Garry Mathiason *"spends time thinking about and trying to get ahead of potential strategic issues,"* clients said. His technical strengths are recognized in the preparation of litigation strategy and policy development. The *"brilliant adviser"* William Emanuel is predominantly celebrated in the area of labor-management relations but has also dealt with sophisticated strategic business decisions, wage and hour issues, and litigated high-profile employment law claims.
The Clients: The firm's clients range from small companies to Fortune 500 companies of a regional and national scope.

O'Melveny & Myers LLP
See firm details p.294
The Firm: Market commentators believe that the firm's depth of resources ensures that it plays a part on some of the leading national cases. Clients spoke of a *"comprehensively talented and hard-working team"* that is highly experienced in dealing with class action, employment discrimination and wage and hour matters. The group is respected for its day-to-day advice on employee benefits, ERISA and general policy issues.
The Lawyers: *"Highly effective"* Robert Siegel is a leading light in the airline sector as a result of his work with marquee clients such as US Airways. For example, he represented US Airways before the Third Circuit in an action brought by the International Association of Machinists concerning the outsourcing of aircraft maintenance. The *"highly skilled"* Gordon Krischer is in demand for his litigation prowess in discrimination, ERISA and wrongful discharge claims.
The Clients: California Institute of Technology; Columbia Pictures; Ford; Lockheed Martin; Sony; US Airways and Verizon.

Sheppard, Mullin, Richter & Hampton LLP
The Firm: This firm is home to some of the state's leading trial lawyers, so it is no surprise that the firm's skill in handling complex employment disputes forms the foundation of the practice. Market observers described this group as *"efficient and accessible."* Its expert advice on wage and hour class actions and discrimination litigation is particularly noted, but the firm is also well equipped to advise on labor law and employee benefits.
The Lawyers: Clients commend Richard Simmons, saying he is a *"true connoisseur of the law"* who keeps up-to-date with developments across a range of employment issues such as wage and hour, discrimination and wrongful termination.
The Clients: The group advises a number of clients in the emerging market as well as multinational corporations.

Band 5

Carlton, DiSante & Freudenberger
The Firm: This *"superior boutique"* possesses a depth of resources across its five offices in the state that has ensured its place as a key player in the California market. Clients endorsed the wealth of experience possessed by these attorneys and their *"good, sensible rates and ability to achieve excellent results with the minimum of fuss."* The firm has acted for employers in several large wage and hour class actions concerning alleged minimum wage and overtime violations. Attorneys are also experienced in OSHA matters, wrongful discharge and discrimination litigation and proceedings before the NLRB.
The Lawyers: Founder and managing partner Christopher Carlton is a key contact for the firm.
The Clients: California Chiropractic Association; BAX Global; City of Santa Ana; City of Long Beach; Chevron Products; Brink's Home Security; American Express; Neighborhood House Association; Sysco Food Services and USA Wireless.

Jackson Lewis
The Firm: This national dedicated labor and employment firm is *"a real gem,"* claim interviewees who have seen its wide-ranging skills and ability to mobilize resources in action. One client felt that *"the breadth of knowledge on display is astounding,"* and endorsed the consistent quality of advice across the firm's many offices. Attorneys based in Los Angeles have dealt with employment discrimination and sexual harassment claims as well as OSHA and labor relations issues.
The Lawyers: Managing partner Lawrence Stone is the main contact for the Los Angeles office.
The Clients: This firm attracts a range of public and private businesses and nonprofit institutions.

Liebert Cassidy Whitmore

The Firm: Although smaller than some of its direct rivals in the labor and employment market, this firm offers "approachable and exceedingly proficient" legal advice that has won it a following among clients and peers. It combines a broad understanding of employment litigation with a niche expertise in government issues.

The Lawyers: Brian Walter "*has made a real impact in the field.*" He acts for clients in a wide array of employment and labor law issues including labor negotiations, training and presentations and litigation. Clients appreciate his particular proficiency in dealing with FLSA issues.

The Clients: The firm advises public entities and private employers throughout the State of California.

Munger, Tolles & Olson LLP

The Firm: One of the state's leading litigation firms, it is also home to respected employment law specialists. Market sources agree that this firm is an important player with its "*robust approach to litigation.*" The group has represented major studios in age discrimination claims and has advised a major financial services firm in the defense of a wage and hour lawsuit. The caseload here also features trade secrets protections and privacy issues, and labor law matters such as collective bargaining.

The Lawyers: "*Leading light*" Alan Friedman is "*experienced, energetic and smart*" and impressed clients with his strategic planning and courtroom performance.

The Clients: The firm has attracted major clients from a range of industries such as financial institutions, pharmaceuticals, media, manufacturing and retailing.

Other Notable Practitioners

The "*astute and practical*" George Howard (see p.257) of Pillsbury Winthrop LLP in San Diego provides advice that clients can "*understand and easily apply to their particular circumstances.*" He recently negotiated an initial collective bargaining agreement between Viejas Tribe and Communications Workers of America Local 9400. At Irell & Manella LLP, James Adler has developed a strong profile in the market through his "*extremely practical and tremendously helpful*" employment and labor law advice. "*Academic*" Steven Drapkin of the Law Offices of Steven Drapkin in Los Angeles is, according to one client, "*the kind of litigator who will take no prisoners.*" The "*charismatic*" Anthony Oncidi (see p.265) of Proskauer Rose LLP has a broad labor and employment practice but is renowned for his work advising the entertainment industry. Clients also highlighted the practice of Jonathan Turner of Epstein, Turner & Song. He is "*a guy who understands the entertainment labor negotiations process perfectly well.*" Interviewees also pointed to his familiarity and skill in the area of collective bargaining.

ENERGY & NATURAL RESOURCES

California
Leading firms
(Energy & Natural Resources)

1	MILBANK, TWEED, HADLEY & MCCLOY *Los Angeles*
	ORRICK, HERRINGTON & SUTCLIFFE *San Francisco*
	WHITE & CASE LLP *Los Angeles*
2	LATHAM & WATKINS LLP *San Diego*
	MORRISON & FOERSTER LLP *Walnut Creek*
3	DAVIS WRIGHT TREMAINE LLP *San Francisco*
	GOODIN MACBRIDE SQUERI RITCHIE *San Francisco*
	MUNGER, TOLLES & OLSON LLP *Los Angeles*
	PILLSBURY WINTHROP LLP *San Francisco*
4	DOWNEY, BRAND, SEYMOUR *Sacramento*
	ELLISON SCHNEIDER & HARRIS *Sacramento*

Leading individuals
(Energy & Natural Resources)

1	BLOOM Jerry *White & Case*, Los Angeles
	FEO Edwin *Milbank Tweed*, Los Angeles
	MALKIN Joseph *Orrick Herrington*, San Francisco
2	DAY Michael *Goodin MacBride*, San Francisco
	ELLISON Christopher *Ellison Schneider*, Sacramento
	GREENWALD Steve *Davis Wright*, San Francisco
	HANSCHEN Peter *Morrison & Foerster*, Walnut Creek
	KARP Joseph *White & Case*, San Francisco
3	BOOTH William *Sole Practitioner*, Walnut Creek
	ERSPAMER Gordon *Morrison & Foerster*, Walnut Creek
	FESSLER Daniel *Holland & Knight*, San Francisco
	MACK Joel *Latham & Watkins*, San Diego
	O'NEILL Edward *Davis Wright*, San Francisco
	WEISSMANN Henry *Munger Tolles*, Los Angeles

Firms and individuals are listed alphabetically in each band.

Band 1

Milbank, Tweed, Hadley & McCloy

The Firm: Milbank Tweed stands out as the top firm in California for transactional work in the energy field. As one client emphasized, "*it simply has the most experience of any law firm in this sector.*" It is particularly renowned for its prominent role in the renewable energy industry, and has represented lenders such as Fortis Bank, Dexia, and ANZ Bank in a number of wind projects, including the Brazos Wind Farm in Texas, and the Colorado Green Wind Farm. The group's renewable energy expertise also stretches to geothermal projects, and it recently represented the underwriters in the $150 million financing of a portfolio of geothermal assets by Ormat. In the traditional power market, the team has worked on a number of asset sales and disposals this year. For example, it represented KGen in the purchase of eight gas-fired generation plants from Duke Energy, a benchmark transaction in the acquisition of distressed power assets.

The Lawyers: The "*ubiquitous*" Ed Feo is one of the country's leading specialists in wind energy. First and foremost a transactional lawyer, with his focus on alternative energy and undeniable expertise, this "*extremely talented*" lawyer has been able to capture a substantial share of the renewable energy market, both in California and further afield.

The Clients: The firm has a particularly strong reputation for representing financial institutions. Examples include: ANZ; Fortis; Dexia; BayernLB and BNP Paribas. It is also assisting a number of private equity companies, such as Matlin Patterson and Oak Tree Investors. However, in recent months it has been representing more and more sponsor companies, and this year advised Mitsubishi, Diamond Energy, Cap Rock Energy and Leucadia National.

Orrick, Herrington & Sutcliffe LLP
See firm details p.295

The Firm: The firm is widely respected for its "*impressive*" work on behalf of energy companies in both transactional and regulatory matters. It has been engaged in a variety of important deals over the past year, however the clear standout for the energy team was its key role in the PG&E bankruptcy proceedings. This involved $9 billion worth of finance, and the success in getting one of the country's largest utilities out of bankruptcy marked a major step in ending the Californian energy crisis. The deal allowed the energy team to utilize both its transactional and regulatory strengths, as it was involved in both arranging the financing, and steering the settlement though regulatory proceedings. The group is also well known for representing the developers of wind farm projects.

The Lawyers: Joseph Malkin (see p.261) is one of the highest profile lawyers in California's energy Bar. Observers describe him as a "*senior, prominent and well-respected practitioner.*" His recent successes include leading on the pure energy side of the PG&E transaction.

The Clients: As well as having a long-established relationship with PG&E, the firm does a

204

All quotes in the text are from interviews with clients and competitors.

CHAMBERS USA 2005

considerable amount of work for Sempra Energy. It has been representing the company in a California Public Utilities Commission proceeding regarding gas price rises.

White & Case LLP
See firm details p.1379

The Firm: The energy group here focuses on representing independent power producers. Its diverse workload encompasses transactional and regulatory matters, and energy litigation. It is also heavily involved in the growth of competitive markets. For example, the team has been representing Calpine in a landmark case concerning the development of the competitive power market in the Southeastern USA. This involves a challenge by Calpine to Entergy's pricing methodology for purchasing power from IPPs. The practice has also been kept busy with transactional matters, and recently advised Origin Energy on its $1 billion purchase of Contact Energy from Edison Mission Energy. Another highlight of the year was representing Delta Power on the official unsecured creditor's committee in the PG&E bankruptcy.

The Lawyers: Jerry Bloom (see p.246) is renowned for representing independent generators. Peers noted that he is *"plugged into that community and knows the issues better than anyone."* Clients, meanwhile, report that he is a *"phenomenal"* practitioner who offers *"a real depth of experience in the energy sector, along with pointed and candid advice."* Joseph Karp (see p.259) is a strong regulatory lawyer with a great reputation. *"An excellent negotiator who gets good results for his clients,"* he has *"a detailed and thorough understanding of regulations and can clearly explain their financial implications."*

The Clients: The practice has represented the California Cogeneration Council in energy regulatory matters and litigation. It is currently working on a case against Southern California Edison regarding the renewal of contracts with independent generators. Other prominent clients include: Calpine; Delta Power Company; California Wind Energy Association and Temple-Inland.

Band 2

Latham & Watkins LLP
The Firm: Market observers praise this firm's *"amazing comprehensive energy practice,"* and claim that its lawyers *"do everything at a high level."* The team is particularly visible when it comes to representing energy companies in the development of new generating facilities. For example, one of this year's highlights was acting for MidAmerican Energy in the development of a geothermal project, one of very few privately sponsored projects currently under development. The firm also advised Southern California Edison on the purchase of the Mountainview power project from InterGen, a notable example of a regulated utility getting back into the generating business.

The Lawyers: San Diego-based Joel Mack is prolific in representing the developers of power projects. Indeed peers comment that *"he seems to be everywhere, representing every utility of note."* Michael Carroll chairs the environmental, land and resources department, and the firm's energy team also benefits from the support of a strong project finance group.

The Clients: MidAmerican Energy; InterGen; Southern California Edison; City of Roseville; Mirant and Pacific Gas and Electricity.

Morrison & Foerster LLP
See firm details p.293

The Firm: This *"excellent"* energy practice is well known for its twin strengths in state regulatory work and energy litigation. The regulatory team primarily works for power consumers and is hailed by its clients as having *"the preeminent experts in the area."* In recent months they have been working on challenges to rates, lobbying for direct access to the grid, and representing property owners in a number of electric transmission siting cases. The *"knowledgeable and responsive"* energy litigators, meanwhile, handle natural gas litigation for prominent client El Paso, and recently completed a major piece of antitrust litigation for the company. They are also active in the ongoing litigation following the California energy crisis.

The Lawyers: *"Well-respected"* Peter Hanschen (see p.255) is widely agreed to be the firm's most prominent regulatory lawyer. Clients particularly recommend him for his *"vast knowledge and experience in this area."* Gordon Erspamer (see p.251), meanwhile, heads the energy litigation group. As well as being a fine litigator, he was admired for his *"efficiency"* and *"real focus on client service."*

The Clients: The litigation team is defending IDACORP, Puget Sound Energy and Tucson Electric in the California Attorney General action following the energy crisis. The regulatory lawyers have been representing both Constellation NewEnergy and an agricultural energy consumers' association on direct access and rate issues. They also advised Genentech over the siting of a PG&E transmission line.

Band 3

Davis Wright Tremaine LLP
See firm details p.1796

The Firm: This is known in California as *"an excellent practice that produces work of an extraordinarily high quality."* According to peers *"its work before the California Public Utilities Commission is exemplary."* The group handles regulatory matters and litigation for a client base that consists primarily of merchant power plants and non-public utilities. Its key client is Calpine, and it handled the regulatory aspects of several billion dollars' worth of financings for the company this year. The team was also

kept busy over the past twelve months gaining approvals for the construction of new power plants. The group is frequently found representing consumer groups and local communities. For example, it is currently representing the 280 Corridor Concerned Citizens Group, in connection with the siting of a PG&E transmission line, which runs through the San Francisco peninsula.

The Lawyers: Steve Greenwald (see p.254) leads on the Calpine work and is renowned as *"an experienced and distinguished regulatory lawyer."* Edward O'Neill (see p.266) was also highly recommended by the market, and brings years of experience from his time at the California Public Utilities Commission. He was described to researchers as a *"careful, thoughtful and thorough"* lawyer.

The Clients: A highlight of the year was representing a consumer group called TURN, which came up with a proposal that saved ratepayers $1 billion off the cost of financing PG&E's bankruptcy.

Goodin MacBride Squeri Ritchie & Day LLP
The Firm: The energy practice here is largely built around a number of former state commission legal staff, so retaining its services is akin to having a walking dictionary of California Public Utilities Commission policy to hand. Clients view it as *"the best firm for energy regulatory law,"* while peers heap praise on *"outstanding and well-connected lawyers who really understand the ins and outs of the regulatory world."* The group handles a considerable amount of power work, but natural gas has been a major focus over the last year. For example, it has been working on an LNG project for Mitsubishi, and was heavily involved in efforts to revise regulations on natural gas supply for EnCana and various pipeline companies. The firm also dedicates resources to legislative work, and recently succeeded in getting a bill passed for EnCana regarding gas storage operations.

The Lawyers: As a former head of the California Public Utilities Commission, Michael Day brings great prestige and experience to the practice. He is said to excel at *"handling complex matters with favorable results,"* and one impressed client even named him *"one of the best regulatory lawyers on the continent."*

The Clients: The energy group here serves a broad array of clients, including oil and gas companies like EnCana, electricity generating companies, and customer groups like the California Retailers Association.

Munger, Tolles & Olson LLP
The Firm: This firm's prominence in the energy field is due in large part to its strong relationship with Southern California Edison, one of the largest utilities in the USA. As well as providing it with a general corporate service, Munger Tolles has been busy in recent months

www.ChambersandPartners.com

All quotes in the text are from interviews with clients and competitors.

205

representing this brand name client in a range of issues arising from the California energy crisis. These include regulatory proceedings and federal litigation against the California Public Utilities Commission.

The Lawyers: Henry Weissmann handles a large volume of regulatory and litigation work for Southern California Edison. According to market sources, he stands out as *"an excellent litigator and a strong advocate for his clients."*

Pillsbury Winthrop LLP
See firm details p.1364

The Firm: This team enjoys a broad practice that encompasses regulatory advice, energy litigation and transactional work. What shines through, according to research, is its real enthusiasm and dedication. Clients value the *"loyal and committed"* lawyers who have *"become an integral part of our team,"* and praise *"the classy and thoughtful culture."* They also appreciate the firm's *"unique strategic vision for energy companies."* An enviable client list has seen the team involved in a number of interesting projects this year. In the international arena, it has been advising marquee client ChevronTexaco on the $4.4 billion expansion of the Tengiz oil production joint venture. It has also been acting for Dynegy and Duke Energy in issues arising from the California energy crisis, including major litigation and regulatory work. At time of press the firm announced its merger with Shaw Pittman LLP to form Pillsbury Winthrop Shaw Pittman.

The Lawyers: The real selling point of this firm's Californian team is said to be the breadth of the group rather than the profile of a single attorney. The team is led by Robert James, and covers corporate, regulatory and litigation matters in the energy field.

The Clients: The California branch of the energy practice focuses on representing major industrial companies, such as: ChevronTexaco; Dynegy; PacifiCorp; Duke Energy; Valero; Headwaters; GE and Hanson.

Band 4

Downey, Brand, Seymour & Rohwer LLP

The Firm: This Sacramento-based energy practice specializes in representing clients before the California Public Utilities Commission. The team is particularly renowned for its expertise in power plant licensing, with peers commenting that *"the lawyers there are real experts on the regulatory process."*

The Lawyers: The energy group here numbers six lawyers, who were described as having *"an effective style and a good handle on the regulatory and legal requirements."*

The Clients: The group represents large industrial energy consumers, qualified facilities, private energy producers and producer groups. Examples include: California Municipal Utilities Association; Energy Bar Association; Independent Energy Producers of Northern California; Power Association of Northern California; Rocky Mountain Mineral Law Foundation and the Sacramento Petroleum Association.

Ellison Schneider & Harris

The Firm: This group is principally known in the market for representing a stellar client list of non-utility generators before the California Public Utilities Commission. Its work here covers both regulatory issues for existing power plants, and permits for new power plants. However, the team's practice also extends beyond this niche to include a range of other matters, such as advice

to customers on transmission access issues.

The Lawyers: Christopher Ellison heads the energy practice here and is named by market sources as *"a highly credible advocate with a great reputation in California."* He has achieved a considerable profile in the local market, to the extent that one interviewee claimed *"if anyone is building a power plant in this state, they are either using, or conflicted out of using, Christopher Ellison."*

The Clients: Clients in the generating community include: Calpine; Duke Energy; California Independent Energy Producers Association; the American Wind Energy Association and The California Solar Energy Industry Association. On the customer side, the firm represents: East Bay Municipal Utility District; Stanford University; California Department of General Services and the Western Electricity Coordinating Council.

Other Notable Practitioners

William Booth, of the eponymous law offices, represents large utilities such as Southern California Edison and PG&E at the California Public Utilities Commission. This year he worked on the PG&E bankruptcy, and guided both clients through the approval process for rate increases. According to interviewees he is *"a real expert in electric industry issues."* **Daniel Fessler** (see p.252) from Holland & Knight LLP is a former president of the California Public Utilities Commission. He concentrates on policy formation, and has recently been tackling the thorny issue of whether utilities or independent power producers should be building more generating facilities for California, on behalf of San Diego Gas & Electric. Other clients include Western Hub Properties and Southern California Edison.

ENVIRONMENT

California
Leading firms (Environment)

1	**LATHAM & WATKINS LLP** *Los Angeles*
2	**BINGHAM MCCUTCHEN LLP** *Los Angeles*
	MORRISON & FOERSTER LLP *San Francisco*
	PILLSBURY WINTHROP LLP *San Francisco*
3	**FARELLA BRAUN & MARTEL LLP** *San Francisco*
	WESTON BENSHOOF ROCHEFORT *Los Angeles*
4	**BEVERIDGE & DIAMOND, PC** *San Francisco*
	GIBSON, DUNN & CRUTCHER LLP *Los Angeles*
	MORGAN, LEWIS & BOCKIUS LLP *San Francisco*
	PAUL, HASTINGS, JANOFSKY *San Francisco*

Firms are listed alphabetically in each band.

Band 1

Latham & Watkins LLP

The Firm: With offices in LA, San Diego, San Francisco, and Silicon Valley, this legal behemoth dominates the state. Its broad-based environment practice spans areas such as compliance, transactional and regulatory proceedings. The practice is further bolstered by the firm's expertise in other related areas such as litigation and land use. Praised by market sources for the *"high caliber"* of its members, the group's *"uniformly strong bench"* and well-oiled administrative structure inevitably involve the team in complex cases. Furthermore, its close ties to state government officials make it a force to be reckoned with.

The Lawyers: Gene Lucero's combination of *"field experience"* and unparalleled knowledge

of the statutes wins market confidence. He is also pitched as *"one of the best in the country"* for Superfund and hazardous waste work. **Robert Wyman** is the firm's lead counsel for Clean Air Act matters. Competitors are in no doubt that he has the *"edge"* over other Southern Californian lawyers in this arena. *"Sought after by industries,"* his *"stellar"* reputation in LA is illustrated in such work as advising a union of energy providers on reducing power facility emissions throughout the USA. He has also successfully represented Oxbow in its challenge of South Coast Air Quality Management District's proposed restrictions. Another partner with a *"wonderful reputation"* when it comes to air regulation and counseling, **BJ Kirwan** also handles permitting and administrative issues. Her *"sharp and insightful instincts"* ensure that

California
Leading individuals (Environment)

1 BARR Michael *Pillsbury Winthrop, San Francisco*
CORASH Michèle *Morrison & Foerster, San Francisco*
LUCERO Gene *Latham & Watkins, Los Angeles*
WYMAN Jr Robert *Latham & Watkins, Los Angeles*

2 BRUEN James *Farella Braun, San Francisco*
DENNIS Patrick *Gibson Dunn, Los Angeles*
HERNANDEZ Jennifer *Beveridge, San Francisco*
KIRWAN BJ *Latham & Watkins, Los Angeles*
RUBALCAVA Sharon *Weston Benshoof, Los Angeles*
ZISCHKE Michael *Morrison & Foerster, San Francisco*

3 HOYE Maria *Latham & Watkins, Los Angeles*
SCHMALL Deborah *Farella Braun, San Francisco*
SHANKS Patricia *Bingham McCutchen, Los Angeles*
STEEL Michael *Pillsbury Winthrop, San Francisco*
WEINER Peter *Paul Hastings, San Francisco*

4 CARROLL Michael *Latham & Watkins, Costa Mesa*
DRAGNA James *Bingham McCutchen, Los Angeles*
GARVIN Anthony *Morgan Lewis, San Francisco*
HART Gordon *Paul Hastings, San Francisco*
ROSEGAY Margaret *Pillsbury Winthrop, San Francisco*
ROSS Jerry *Pillsbury Winthrop, San Francisco*
THOMPSON Jocelyn *Weston Benshoof, Los Angeles*

Up-and-coming individuals
NORRIS Trenton *Bingham McCutchen, San Francisco*

Firms and Individuals are listed alphabetically in each band.

she keeps abreast of market changes; interviewees spoke of her successful inroads into product regulation and Proposition 65 matters. **Maria Hoye** inspires admiration, particularly for her *"collegial and competent"* style of solving problems regarding due diligence, recovery litigation and other issues. Clients were deeply appreciative of the *"great job"* she does in tackling the intricacies of California environmental law. A *"smart, aggressive litigator,"* **Michael Carroll** chairs the Orange County Environment, Land and Resources department. Market sources highlight his strength in air and energy matters, often illustrated by his work on behalf of clients in the petroleum, automotive, entertainment and electronics industries. He has advised ChevronTexaco in a matter related to the construction of a new hydrogen plant in LA.

The Clients: ConocoPhillips; ChevronTexaco; Edison International; Fluor; Regulatory Flexibility Group; Toyota; Montrose Chemical; Oxbow Carbon and Minerals; Sempra Energy and Western States Petroleum Association.

Band 2

Bingham McCutchen LLP

The Firm: Emphasizing the regulatory aspects of environmental law – with an additional focus on litigation – the firm maintains its historical strength in advising on issues related to military bases and various contaminated properties. Operating out of five offices in California, this *"top-of-the-heap"* group displays *"strength, breadth and depth."*

The Lawyers: *"Insightful, quick to get the point and an effective thinker,"* **Patricia Shanks** is a pioneering veteran of Superfund litigation and related areas of law, including brownfield developments. In addition, she advises clients on environmental health and safety matters, and often defends them against Proposition 65 claims. *"Maverick"* **James Dragna** drew praise for his *"wonderfully innovative"* approach to Superfund litigation. Chair of the national environmental and land use group, he represents a variety of energy, aerospace and manufacturing clients in a range of matters, including air and wastewater counseling. *"Rising star"* **Trent Norris** earned plaudits for his expertise in matters relating to state toxic and labeling laws, in addition to the intricacies of Proposition 65.

The Clients: The firm's clientele is forged from prominent national and international companies in the technology, electronic, manufacturing and petroleum industries.

Morrison & Foerster LLP

See firm details p.293

The Firm: Combining land use and environment under one umbrella group, this 40-strong team represents many of California's major developers and engages in *"top-flight"* Proposition 65 matters, site cleanups, and military base closures and conversions. It is also heavily involved in state and federal level regulatory work; the team successfully resolved a federal enforcement action for violations of the Clean Air Act that could have ended in multimillion-dollar penalties. In another dispute, it is seeking contributions from the US government to pay for the cleanup of a former uranium mine. Another niche practice concerns food companies in exposure claims.

The Lawyers: In the *"higher echelons"* of Proposition 65 practitioners is the *"inimitable"* **Michèle Corash** (see p.249), a former EPA general counsel who plays a key role in some 200 cases that the firm is handling concerning that particular area of law. Opponents praise her ability to *"find the best solutions to an issue without turning it into World War III,"* while clients appreciate her *"tremendous judgment and fabulous people skills."* **Michael Zischke** (see p.278) does a *"wonderful job"* helping clients navigate the terrain of land use law. *"Extremely bright,"* commentators said: *"He is great at wrestling with cutting-edge questions."*

The Clients: The firm has advised companies from the consumer products, food and beverage, land development, petrochemical, construction, and defense industries. Examples include US Borax and Grocery Manufacturers of America.

Pillsbury Winthrop LLP

See firm details p.1364

The Firm: Founded on a bedrock of loyal clients, the environment group has expanded well beyond its traditional base to include matters relating to air, water, waste, land use and endangered species. The practice is further supplemented by government enforcement and permitting work. Its *"responsive"* members and *"excellent"* associates often prevail in legal battles. On behalf of Union Pacific Railroad, the team helped prepare an analysis of diesel emissions at one of its major rail yards. Other highlights include defending Duke Energy in an environmental releases claim and successfully appealing a permit denial on behalf of New United Motors. At time of press the firm announced its merger with Shaw Pittman LLP to form Pillsbury Winthrop Shaw Pittman.

The Lawyers: Known for his authority on air issues, **Michael Barr** (see p.244) chaired the iron, steel and natural gas industry group that participated in the last round of federal clean air amendments. The leader of the firm's land use and natural resources department specializes in permitting issues and complex regulatory matters, further bolstered by enduring political ties. He helped implement a Netherlands-based system of compliance in the USA. **Michael Steel** (see p.274) is described as a *"hands-on compliance person for operating industries."* He often defends clients against regulatory enforcement actions, for example, representing several major retailers in a case centering on the presence of lead in jewelry. *"Low-key and effective"* **Margaret Rosegay**'s (see p.270) practice revolves around water quality, and solid and hazardous waste, including permitting and compliance. In this area *"there is possibly no one better,"* commentators said. She also won client confidence for her counseling work for the oil industry. **Jerry Ross** (see p.270) divides his time between San Francisco and Texas, specializing in the defense of cost recovery and government enforcement actions. He also assists on structuring and auditing compliance programs. The environmental expert also participates in Clean Water Act litigation and Proposition 65 matters.

The Clients: PSEG; 3M; Imation; Sempra Energy; Association of American Railroads; Golden Gate National Parks Association; New United Motor Manufacturing (a joint venture between GM and Toyota); Medtronic and Union Pacific.

Band 3

Farella Braun & Martel LLP

The Firm: *"Excellent, knowledgeable and responsive,"* this 25-attorney environment group collaborates with the firm's IP and land use departments to cut a broad swath of environmental law. Excelling in litigation and regulato-

www.ChambersandPartners.com
All quotes in the text are from interviews with clients and competitors.
207

ry work, the team is national counsel for GE, defending the company against state tort claims stemming from groundwater contamination. It also acts as WC Bradley's West Coast counsel in all products liability work. Other highlights include structuring environmental cleanup agreements with the US EPA and state regulators as related to Superfund sites.

The Lawyers: James Bruen delivers a ferocious punch in legal battles, so much so that one competitor likened his courtroom performance to *"a stealth attack – people queue up to take lessons from him."* The toxic tort litigator is leading the successful defense of GE in a precedent-setting natural resource damage case in New Mexico. Regulatory compliance specialist **Deborah Schmall** is pitched as a *"fierce, wonderfully strong advocate on hazardous waste issues,"* often defending enforcement actions relating to toxic materials and air pollution. She has also advised clients such as Catellus on large brownfield developments. Acting for the University of California Los Alamos National Laboratory, she defended against a state-initiated hazardous waste enforcement action for the remediation of radionuclide releases at more than 2200 solid waste areas at the 43-sq-m facility.

The Clients: In addition to GE, Levi Strauss and the University of California, the firm's clientele comprises other companies in the manufacturing, life science, pharmaceutical, chemical and biotech sectors.

Weston Benshoof Rochefort Rubalcava MacCuish LLP

See firm details p.301

The Firm: Historically one of the state's leading lights, it remains the *"largest specialist environmental firm in Southern California."* Despite some high-profile departures in recent years, it is able to retain high-profile clients who seek its advice on fairly complex issues. For example, the team is representing Boeing in the defense of groundwater contamination actions initiated by residents of the Rancho Cordova area of Northern California. The core of its practice involves air and water issues, land use permitting and regulatory compliance; it also engages in a substantial amount of Superfund and Proposition 65 work.

The Lawyers: Sharon Rubalcava (see p.270) has cultivated an impressive reputation assisting developers in obtaining project permits in California's often difficult political climate. Peers compliment her on *"excellent negotiation and advocacy skills,"* which are effectively parlayed into legal successes. She is assisting Kinder Morgan in its expansion of a refined petroleum products storage facility. Representing Pacific Energy, she is helping to secure environmental permits for the Pier 400 project, a new supertanker offloading terminal in the Port of LA. A *"terrific"* air lawyer, **Jocelyn Niebur Thompson** (see p.275)

also advises complex industrial facilities in regulatory compliance. She assisted Mitsubishi Cement in obtaining a permit from San Bernardino's Planning Commission to expand the Cushenbury Mine from 200 to 400 acres. She has also advised BP America in defending against a civil action seeking penalties of more than $400 million for alleged air quality violations.

The Clients: Browning-Ferris Industries; Pacific Energy; FPL Energy; LAX Master Plan; Mitsubishi Cement; Stonebridge Holdings; WSPA; Boeing; BP America; ConocoPhillips and Unocal.

Band 4

Beveridge & Diamond, PC

See firm details p.480

The Firm: A *"major competitor"* in the lucrative brownfield arena, the group focuses on counseling and advising businesses on industrial site redevelopment and related expansions. Market sources gave the firm strong and consistent approval for its sophisticated knowledge of the permitting issues connected to such projects. Expertise offered to a variety of clients – including fueling stations, shipyards, manufacturing facilities, and gas production companies – provides the crucial tools needed to navigate thorny environmental problems, sources said.

The Lawyers: Jennifer Hernandez (see p.257) is an *"exceptionally bright and capable counselor"* who divides her practice between permitting and land use. Politically active in smart-growth brownfield matters, she receives market praise for being *"extremely wellversed in how to do deals from the safety and commercial perspectives."*

The Clients: Catellus and Lewis Group of Companies are counted among the firm's clients.

Gibson, Dunn & Crutcher LLP

See firm details p.285

The Firm: Having garnered a market reputation for its litigation fortitude, the environment group immerses itself in large community or class action cases, often those originating in soil and air contamination. It also specializes in regulatory challenges. Recently, the team represented three of California's largest automakers in their challenge of state regulations concerning CO_2 emissions. It has also advised Lockheed Martin on its objection to California's adoption of the perchlorate drinking water standard.

The Lawyers: Group chair **Patrick Dennis** (see p.250) is acclaimed for his *"breadth of experience"* as a counselor and litigator. His expertise in cost recovery and large complex transactions involving environmental liabilities ensures that he plays a leading role in many of California's highest profile cases. In the past year he successfully litigated on behalf of Kerr-McGee in a matter connected to the cleanup of 4000 acres of land

marked for residential development. On behalf of Northrop Grumman, he advised on possible liabilities associated with its acquisition of TRW.

The Clients: Kerr-McGee; Pacific Gulf Properties; Northrop Grumman; Lockheed Martin and Proficiency Capital.

Morgan, Lewis & Bockius LLP

See firm details p.1556

The Firm: Primarily operating out of LA, this 12-attorney practice has broadened its professional scope through collaboration with the firm's toxic tort and land use groups. Along with other firms, the team has been heavily involved in litigation related to high perchlorate levels found in the South Bay area drinking water. A large segment of the practice is also devoted to regulatory work before the EPA board and California's various air quality control districts.

The Lawyers: Anthony Garvin (see p.253) has accumulated expertise in a variety of areas, including environmental litigation, regulatory compliance and due diligence. Clients salute his *"exceptional service, guidance and practical advice"* – the product of his intimate familiarity with the inner workings of state agencies. Formerly at the EPA, he is working on a Superfund site in Hawaii for Del Monte Fresh Produce and separately representing a client in a product liability claim concerning the presence of lead in jewelry.

The Clients: The firm conducts a substantial amount of work on behalf of oil companies such as Chevron USA.

Paul, Hastings, Janofsky & Walker LLP

See firm details p.297

The Firm: Emphasizing brownfield and contaminated property redevelopment, this group specializes in a range of pollution and related environmental issues. It represents many state companies responsible for the disposal of hazardous materials, including negotiating use permits for large waste sites such as Buttonwillow. The nine-attorney team has also acted on behalf of Dow Chemical in its Title V permit litigation. On the regulatory side, it advised OSRAM SYLVANIA on the requirements necessary for the recycling of its fluorescent lamps. Proposition 65 and California Environmental Quality Act matters also provide a steady stream of work.

The Lawyers: *"Well respected by regulatory agencies,"* **Peter Weiner** (see p.277) focuses on land redevelopment. His recent participation in the acquisition of a 240-acre Sacramento rail yard also involves negotiations pertaining to a multimillion-dollar cleanup of the site. He is also assisting on another matter concerning the proposed construction of a football stadium on a former landfill site. **Gordon Hart**'s (see p.255) central focus is contaminated land – particularly the reuse of military sites, which are the most substantial source of undeveloped property in the Bay area. *"Succinct, organized and able to negotiate tough solutions in ways acceptable to governmental agencies,"* he has been leading the charge on Mare Island – a former naval base being developed by Lennar for commercial and residential use. In recent months he has also advised on a prominent Superfund matter in Montana.

The Clients: Dow Chemical; OSRAM SYLVANIA; Lennar; AMB Group and The Dewey Group.

HEALTHCARE

California
Leading firms (Healthcare)

1 **FOLEY & LARDNER** *Los Angeles*
  HOOPER LUNDY & BOOKMAN INC *Los Angeles*
  MCDERMOTT WILL & EMERY *Los Angeles*

2 **DAVIS WRIGHT TREMAINE LLP** *San Francisco*
  FULBRIGHT & JAWORSKI LLP *Los Angeles*
  LATHAM & WATKINS LLP *Los Angeles*
  MANATT PHELPS & PHILLIPS LLP *Los Angeles*

3 **HASSARD BONNINGTON LLP** *San Francisco*
  JONES DAY *San Francisco*
  PAUL, HASTINGS, JANOFSKY *San Francisco*
  SONNENSCHEIN NATH & ROSENTHAL *Los Angeles*

Leading individuals (Healthcare)

Senior Statesman
  MEMEL Sherwin *Manatt Phelps, Los Angeles*

1 **DEMETRIOU Andrew** *Fulbright & Jaworski, Los Angeles*
  HELLOW John *Hooper Lundy, Los Angeles*
  HOOPER Patric *Hooper Lundy, Los Angeles*
  KADZIELSKI Mark *Fulbright & Jaworski, Los Angeles*
  MANCINO Douglas *McDermott Will, Los Angeles*
  PETERS Gerald *Latham & Watkins, San Francisco*
  ROOT Jr George *Foley & Lardner, San Diego*
  SCHWARTZ James *Manatt Phelps, Los Angeles*
  STROMBERG Ross *Jones Day, San Francisco*

2 **BOOKMAN Lloyd** *Hooper Lundy, Los Angeles*
  DEMURO Paul *Latham & Watkins, Los Angeles*
  GIRARD Robert *Sonnenschein Nath, Los Angeles*
  GOLDMAN Donald *McDermott Will, Los Angeles*
  HIGGINS Daniel *Paul Hastings, San Francisco*
  HINKLEY Gerry *Davis Wright, San Francisco*
  LANDSBERG Barry *Manatt Phelps, Los Angeles*
  LIPTON Steven *Davis Wright, San Francisco*
  SETTELMAYER Daniel *Latham & Watkins, Los Angeles*

3 **BLANCHARD Timothy** *McDermott Will, Los Angeles*
  GOLDBERG Phillip *Hassard Bonnington, San Francisco*
  LUNDY Robert *Hooper Lundy, Los Angeles*
  PIMSTONE Gregory *Manatt Phelps, Los Angeles*
  RIOS RODRIGUEZ Denise *Foley, Los Angeles*
  SCHUCHARD Robert *Sonnenschein Nath, Los Angeles*
  SEIDEN Richard *Foley & Lardner, Los Angeles*
  SMITH Paul *Davis Wright, San Francisco*
  STANTON Clark *Davis Wright, San Francisco*
  TULLY W Bradley *Hooper Lundy, Los Angeles*
  YOOD Kenneth *Paul Hastings, Los Angeles*

Up-and-coming individuals
  HIRSCH Reece *Sonnenschein Nath, San Francisco*

Firms and individuals are listed alphabetically in each band.

Band 1

Foley & Lardner
See firm details p.1828
The Firm: This *"great"* national presence devotes one-sixth of its resources to healthcare matters. The firm particularly shines in the area of payment and regulatory compliance, and is touted as *"one of the leading practices in the state"* for Medicare and Medicaid reimbursement. Also lauded for its *"strong"* regulatory work, the team has assisted major clients such as Gambro Healthcare and the Orange County-based CalOptima. To ensure it remains up-to-date in a field defined by constant legislative change, the firm employs, in an advisory capacity, a cadre of former in-house counsels and government attorneys. It also offers business counseling and provider operations counseling.
The Lawyers: General counsel for a variety of HMOs and physician groups including CalOptima, **George Root** (see p.270) is described by observers as *"Mr. San Diego – the dean of the county"* when it comes to regulatory advice. Clients greatly appreciate the *"balance of idealism and pragmatism"* that he brings to bear on Medicaid and staff issues: *"He has a strategic sense that many attorneys lack."* The *"capable and likable"* **Richard Seiden** (see p.272) wins accolades for his healthcare business counseling practice. He has conducted major M&A transactions in Southern California, in addition to delivering expertise on a variety of venture capital and tax-exempt financing matters. He also acts as outside general counsel to a number of statewide non-profit hospital systems. **Denise Rios Rodriguez** (see p.269) drew commendation as a *"walking encyclopedia"* of Medicaid, particularly on the methods by which the state can maximize its federal share of reimbursement.
The Clients: CalOptima, Gambro Healthcare and Children's Hospital and Health Center figure prominently in the firm's clientele, which comprises HMOs, hospitals and physician groups.

Hooper Lundy & Bookman Inc
The Firm: This *"incredibly deep"* boutique firm – with three offices in California – has expertise in *"virtually every nook and cranny"* of healthcare law. Comprising about 40 lawyers, the practice is structured around regulatory and transactional matters, and related litigation. It originally *"made its mark"* in high-profile payment disputes and kickback allegation cases. Medicare/Medicaid fraud and related matters continue to figure highly in the firm's market profile. Currently, the team is defending Tenet Healthcare in a federal investigation. In a separate matter, the firm's business group is representing buyers involved in Tenet's divestiture of several hospitals.
The Lawyers: **John Hellow** has a *"national reputation"* in Medicare and Medicaid reimbursement, and fraud and abuse matters. He represents hospitals before federal and state administrative agencies, and counsels clients on general health law issues such as the disclosure and privacy of medical records. **Patric Hooper** won respect through his *"incredible"* knowledge of healthcare laws and regulations, and their application to issues such as false claims. Credited by market authorities with being one of the *"driving forces"* behind his firm's growth, he specializes in reimbursement law, often representing healthcare providers before state and federal courts. *"Probably one of the smartest and most creative reimbursement attorneys in the state,"* **Lloyd Bookman** is considered a top destination for regulatory advice. He has counseled clients in matters connected to the failure of teaching hospitals to comply with billing regulations. Former president of the California Society for Healthcare Attorneys, **Robert Lundy** is viewed as an *"excellent thinker and negotiator."* Clients said he is their *"first choice"* for transactions such as joint ventures, private placements and acquisitions. The chair of the business department also handles licensing and certification matters. **Bradley Tully** counsels hospitals, physicians and laboratories on regulatory issues and business transactions. His diversified workload also includes Medicare/Medicaid fraud and abuse, and physician self-referral issues.
The Clients: The practice represents a mixture of health providers and insurance companies, including Tenet Healthcare and HCA.

McDermott Will & Emery
See firm details p.773
The Firm: Noted for its *"complete geographic coverage"* and *"comprehensive set of services,"* this healthcare group offers expertise in M&A, product regulation, class actions and the Health Insurance Portability and Accountability Act (HIPAA), among others. In addition, an extensive IP practice has precipitated the firm's successful movement into the lucrative pharmaceutical market. Founded on an *"impressive client base"* comprising major healthcare providers, it is perceived as a *"major competitor"* within California. Statewide,

www.ChambersandPartners.com

All quotes in the text are from interviews with clients and competitors.

209

this international firm has offices in LA, Silicon Valley, Orange County and San Diego.

The Lawyers: "*Popular and creative*," **Douglas Mancino** (see p.262) has cultivated a formidable reputation as a "*nationally recognized tax law expert*." He is deemed as "*one of a few*" who can explain the vagaries of tax exemption. He puts this knowledge to practical use in his work for nonprofit organizations, advising them on IRS-related issues. Accomplished all-rounder and member of the firm's management committee, **Donald Goldman** (see p.54632) often counsels hospitals and long-term care clients in a broad span of regulatory and administrative matters. Interviewees singled out his expert handling of transactional and medical staff work, and fraud and abuse investigations involving healthcare providers. **Timothy Blanchard** (see p.245) has "*depth of expertise*" in Medicaid reimbursement. His "*broad experience*" also includes compliance programs, HIPAA privacy, and certification and licensing.

The Clients: The team serves large providers such as Henry Ford Health System and Tenet Healthcare. Several of the state's most high-profile pharmaceutical companies also feature in its clientele.

Band 2

Davis Wright Tremaine LLP
See firm details p.1796

The Firm: This firm earned its spurs on the back of its regulatory expertise, often advising public entities such as hospitals. In addition to licensing and accreditation issues, the team also marshals through the more esoteric aspects of healthcare reimbursement. The 13-attorney team specializes in essential "*nuts-and-bolts*" corporate work, including tax structuring for nonprofit healthcare providers. The group also facilitates the formation of limited liability companies. Consolidating an adjunct market reputation for undertaking cutting-edge media and technology-related work, the team assisted the California Healthcare Foundation in transferring the ownership and governance of a statewide database into the public domain; the project involved the determination of various levels of healthcare assistance.

The Lawyers: Gerry Hinkley (see p.257) is widely respected for his focus on provider transactions and his specialist knowledge of healthcare law that affects children's hospitals. "*He can walk into a board meeting and take command*," observers said. He is lead counsel for a hospital that provides neonatal services to other healthcare institutions that lack such facilities. He also devotes a significant part of his practice to the ramifications of HIPAA. **Steven Lipton** (see p.261) is "*well thought of*" in the arena of patient dumping law. A "*competent and effective communicator*," he delivers regulatory advice that

includes fraud and abuse, and provider regulation matters. His additional experience on integrated delivery systems, healthcare transactions and hospital-physician relationships further adds credence to a diverse practice. "*Well known*" as an authority on medical staffing, healthcare credentials and peer reviews, **Clark Stanton**'s (see p.274) remit extends to HIPAA, confidentiality and patient treatment matters. **Paul Smith** (see p.273) is a "*detail-oriented documenter*" regarded by clients as one of the group's "*major players*" for the sales and acquisitions of hospitals, clinics and nursing homes.

The Clients: The team focuses on hospital representation, and acts on behalf of a variety of profit and nonprofit organizations, including the California Healthcare Foundation.

Fulbright & Jaworski L.L.P.
See firm details p.1715

The Firm: This "*skilled firm, national in scope*," adopts a holistic approach to its healthcare practice, with the five-attorney California team in constant communication with another 75 attorneys throughout the country. Displaying a much appreciated ability to divine "*the essential from the peripheral*," the practice has arms in all regulatory and transactional matters; it covers all legislative changes and business arrangements that impact on physician partnerships and medical staff relationships. Clients were particularly impressed by the team's ease with navigating through the murky territory of EMTALA law.

The Lawyers: Recent addition **Andrew Demetriou** (see p.250) brings with him a glowing reputation as a corporate healthcare attorney who delivers the finer points of acquisition and divestiture, corporate governance and regulatory compliance. "*Knowledgeable and measured in his approach*," he represents a variety of institutional healthcare providers including hospital systems, physician organizations and healthcare management enterprises. **Mark Kadzielski** (see p.259) is a "*quick thinker*" who combines a "*progressive outlook*" with an "*impressive depth of knowledge*" to produce the kind of results that justify his status among clients as the firm's "*house power*." He also demonstrated thorough grounding on medical staffing and EMTALA issues, as well as winning "*trust and respect*" on regulatory compliance and policy development.

The Clients: Oriented toward the representation of managed care organizations and physician groups, the practice counts Mission Hospital among its clientele.

Latham & Watkins LLP

The Firm: Its global reach means that it is indubitably "*on the front line of the most complicated transactions in the state*." This is to a great extent the consequence of a pioneering white-collar practice that, for many observers, continues to

define the firm's character and focus in the healthcare realm. The group is lead counsel for Tenet Healthcare, the second-largest health provider in the USA, and HCA Healthcare in federal litigation involving system-wide 'kickback' allegations. The practice has not rested on its laurels, however, branching out as "*major players*" into provider payment, life sciences and regulatory compliance matters. In addition, an enduring liaison between the LA and DC offices allows for a multistate scope to this practice.

The Lawyers: Chairman of the firm's US healthcare group, **Gerald Peters** synthesizes a reputation as a "*national level*" transactional business attorney with cost-effective strategies. "*He achieves the best solution for the least amount*," observers said. Focusing on healthcare M&A, joint venture and compliance matters, he has shepherded one of the largest hospital mergers in Hawaii's history. **Paul DeMuro** garnered client confidence as a reimbursement lawyer with a background in accountancy and finance, in addition to undertaking regulatory work in major compliance investigations. He represented the management in Providence Healthcare's takeover of LifePoint and separately acted on behalf of Sheridan Healthcare in regulatory matters involving MedExpert International. Boasting a reputation for "*competence and quality*," **Daniel Settelmayer** is cochair of the firm's global healthcare practice. He specializes in the corporate elements of healthcare law. Lead counsel to clients such as Adventist Health, he advises on the formation of managed care organizations, multientity health systems, M&A and joint ventures. He is also principal architect of the firm's Internet-based compliance program, used by healthcare systems such as HCA.

The Clients: HCA Healthcare; Tenet Healthcare; Adventist Health; BlueCross BlueShield; Cedars-Sinai Medical Center; Fortress Investment Group and NorthBay Healthcare.

Manatt Phelps & Phillips LLP

The Firm: This "*superb*" healthcare practice cuts a wide swath in healthcare law, though litigation is undoubtedly one of the feathers in its California cap. The firm regularly represents industry giants like BlueCross BlueShield and Tenet in fraud and abuse claims. In addition to employing "*some of the best trial lawyers around*," the "*tremendously powerful consulting arm*" afforded by the group's close ties to government health agencies also draws client loyalty. The Sacramento office often participates in lobbying activities that have statewide ramifications, making the firm invaluable to regional hospitals, healthcare systems and pharmaceutical companies.

The Lawyers: "*Industry leader*" **James Schwartz** (see p.271) specializes in advising nonprofit organizations on partnerships and conversions. A former California Deputy Attorney General, he is respected for his 25 years of

210   All quotes in the text are from interviews with clients and competitors.

CHAMBERS USA 2005

experience in charitable trust and nonprofit corporation law. He has been likened to a "*prince*" who demonstrates a "*unique understanding*" of the complexities of corporate governance, fiduciary duties and director liability issues. Competitors happily concede that **Barry Landsberg** (see p.260) is an "*unparalleled*" litigator. "*If you want to win, hire him.*" Cochair of the firm's litigation division, he is acting on behalf of Tenet in a false claims matter pertaining to allegedly fraudulent billings. In another highlight, he is representing hospitals statewide in a series of unfair competition cases. His position as lead counsel to Catholic Healthcare West supplements an already glowing resumé. **Gregory Pimstone** (see p.267) displays a "*logical and persuasive*" style that guarantees client loyalty. With a practice that encompasses healthcare plans and related insurance issues, he "*presents complex issues in a common sense way.*" One of the undisputed "*deans*" of California healthcare, **Sherwin Memel** (see p.263) is someone who knows the law "*backwards, forwards and inside out.*" Clients value his "*collaborative, respectful nature*" and ability to adapt strategies to fit circumstance. He is also characterized as "*one of the most intelligent attorneys*" around.

The Clients: BlueCross BlueShield; Tenet Healthcare; Catholic Healthcare West; Elizabeth Glaser Pediatric Aids Foundation and the University of California.

Band 3

Hassard Bonnington LLP

The Firm: Based in San Francisco, the firm's 20 healthcare attorneys counsel professional groups, hospital medical staffs, carriers and others concerned with medical board and regulatory requirements. The weight of the practice's reputation, however, rests on physician group representation. This is often the product of referrals by many state medical malpractice insurance companies, which employ the firm as outside counsel.

The Lawyers: Phillip Goldberg is distinguished for his representation of physicians in transactional and regulatory matters. This often includes compliance, federal self-referral and anti-kickback laws. His caseload ranges from providing financial assistance for surgeon recruitment to aiding physician investors in their acquisitions.

The Clients: Hospitals and physician groups – including the California Medical Association – are among the firm's clientele.

Jones Day
See firm details p.485

The Firm: This international titan tends to make its presence felt in almost every corner of the legal world, and it's no different in this one. Though its healthcare practice may not draw the same attention as its expertise in antitrust and litigation, it nevertheless has made a significant impact. The firm's wide clientele of investment banks and insurance companies enables a complex, interdisciplinary approach to regulatory compliance, M&A, civil litigation, benefits and tax matters.

The Lawyers: "*Quick study*" **Ross Stromberg** (see p.274) is "*a futurist – someone you'd want on your transaction,*" commentators said. "*He is always anticipating the direction of business.*" Chair of the healthcare specialized industry practice, he applies this aptitude to the intricacies of integrated delivery system development, medical staffing and corporate transactions.

The Clients: Aventis Pharma; Sutter Health; Capital BlueCross and the Ophthalmic Mutual Insurance Company.

Paul, Hastings, Janofsky & Walker LLP
See firm details p.297

The Firm: The "*high-quality*" statewide presence of this firm is mainly down to the strength and diversity of its transactional repertoire. Drawing expertise from a global network of resources, the healthcare practice lends authority on a broad array of issues, including M&A, divestitures, restructurings and joint ventures. On the regulatory side, it has steered clients through various disputes and investigations related to healthcare compliance rules. The team often takes its cue from providers – including general and specialty hospitals – and healthcare companies.

The Lawyers: Daniel Higgins is often described as the face of the healthcare practice. An "*effective communicator with great presentation skills,*" he has "*commanding*" presence before the DOJ, Federal Trade Commission, Internal Revenue Service and Department of Health, which ensures his key roles in major proceedings. The group cochair also offers preventive measures for clients, including regulatory advice surrounding antifraud laws. **Kenneth Yood** (see p.278) leans toward the corporate side of healthcare, representing a broad sweep of hospital facilities, home health agencies and pharmaceutical companies. In collaboration with various healthcare systems, he uses his expertise in Medicare and Medicaid reimbursement and certification matters to develop cor-

porate programs designed to identify potential regulatory compliance issues.

The Clients: The team serves general and specialty health systems, and numerous healthcare providers throughout California.

Sonnenschein Nath & Rosenthal
See firm details p.779

The Firm: This healthcare practice is firmly located in the delivery system camp. With a "*national-level reputation*" for healthcare, it represents providers in public law, M&A, antitrust and regulatory compliance matters. The team also takes advantage of its size and national orientation to offer tax and litigation assistance that goes beyond state borders. Commentators make note of this, lauding the "*knowledge and effectiveness*" of attorneys who are "*always pleasant to deal with.*" In a similar vein, the group receives praise from clients for its "*sensitivity*" to certain political issues endemic in this market.

The Lawyers: Robert Girard (see p.253) is "*a good name to know*" in healthcare circles. "*Smart, knowledgeable and scholarly,*" he represents providers, insurance companies, HMOs, preferred provider organizations and other managed care organizations. He is working with a proprietary entity that operates an HMO limited license plan in California, and has separately orchestrated the acquisition of several financially troubled hospitals. Observers agree that "*diligent*" **Robert Schuchard** (see p.271) is "*one of the hardest working lawyers around.*" His expertise lies in transactions, contracts and financing matters. He has counseled the University of California in its divestiture of a joint venture with Tenet, and also advised on the development of a research park for a union of health systems. "*Thoughtful*" **Reece Hirsch** (see p.257) focuses on privacy issues, developing a practice in the still-embryonic area of HIPAA. A distinguished player in the health technology field, he has assisted with issues pertaining to the employee records of an optical service for a large company. He has also advised a number of clients on how to negotiate the complex technical rules that structure claim upgrades and ensure conformity with government privacy requirements.

The Clients: The practice's diverse client base includes healthcare systems, hospitals, physician organizations, insurance companies, management companies, medical schools, pharmaceutical suppliers and healthcare research foundations.

INSURANCE

California
Leading firms (Insurance)

1. HANCOCK ROTHERT & BUNSHOFT LLP *San Francisco*
   HELLER EHRMAN LLP *San Francisco*
2. BARGER & WOLEN *Los Angeles*
   LATHAM & WATKINS LLP *Los Angeles*
   SONNENSCHEIN NATH *San Francisco*
3. COVINGTON & BURLING *San Francisco*
   HOWREY SIMON ARNOLD & WHITE *Los Angeles*
   MORGAN, LEWIS & BOCKIUS LLP *San Francisco*
   O'MELVENY & MYERS LLP *San Francisco*
   SHERNOFF, BIDART & DARRAS LLP *Claremont*
4. ALSCHULER GROSSMAN STEIN *Santa Monica*
   BERKES CRANE ROBINSON & SEAL *Los Angeles*
   FARELLA BRAUN & MARTEL LLP *San Francisco*
   GIBSON, DUNN & CRUTCHER LLP *Los Angeles*
   MUNGER, TOLLES & OLSON LLP *Los Angeles*

Leading individuals (Insurance)

1. BROWN Donald *Covington & Burling, San Francisco*
   CATHCART Patrick *Cathcart Collins, Los Angeles*
   GLAD Paul *Sonnenschein Nath, San Francisco*
   GOODWIN David *Heller Ehrman, San Francisco*
   PASICH Kirk *Dickstein Shapiro, Los Angeles*
2. CHECOV Martin *O'Melveny & Myers, San Francisco*
   GOLDBERG Stephen *Heller Ehrman, Los Angeles*
   HALBREICH David *Morgan Lewis, Los Angeles*
   HOBEL Lawrence *Heller Ehrman, San Francisco*
   KELLER Kent *Barger & Wolen, Los Angeles*
   LERMAN Cary *Munger Tolles, Los Angeles*
   LEVINE Harvey *Levine Steinberg, San Diego*
   LUNDBERG G Andrew *Latham & Watkins, Los Angeles*
   MATTHEWS Philip *Hancock Rothert, San Francisco*
   SEABOLT Richard *Hancock Rothert, San Francisco*
   SHERNOFF William *Shernoff Bidart, Claremont*
   STEUBER David *Howrey Simon, Los Angeles*
3. BABBE David *Morrison & Foerster, Los Angeles*
   COHEN Nancy *Heller Ehrman, Los Angeles*
   CRANE Steven *Berkes Crane, Los Angeles*
   FRIEDRICH William *Farella Braun, San Francisco*
   HERNANDEZ Gary *Sonnenschein Nath, San Francisco*
   KAPLAN Frank *Alschuler Grossman, Santa Monica*
   KENT Ronald *Sonnenschein Nath, Los Angeles*
   LEVIN Barry *Heller Ehrman, San Francisco*
   MULLIKEN David *Latham & Watkins, San Diego*
   ROSEN Peter *Latham & Watkins, Los Angeles*
4. BAYSINGER Kara *Sonnenschein Nath, San Francisco*
   BERKES Robert *Berkes Crane, Los Angeles*
   BIDART Michael *Shernoff Bidart, Claremont*
   FRIEDMAN Bruce *Alschuler Grossman, Santa Monica*
   JUSTICE Gary *Gibson Dunn, Los Angeles*
   MCCUTCHEON Mary *Farella Braun, San Francisco*
   MOONEY Ann *Cooley Godward, San Francisco*
   OAKES Royal *Barger & Wolen, Los Angeles*
   WOOD Mark *O'Melveny & Myers, Los Angeles*

Firms and individuals are listed alphabetically in each band.

Band 1

Hancock Rothert & Bunshoft LLP

See firm details p.286

The Firm: Capitalizing on a strong reputation for "*high-quality work*" – acquired through an immensely successful clientele that historically has included Lloyd's – the firm has broadened its practice to remain apace of the insurance market. In addition to coverage litigation, its attorneys have moved into policyholder and business representation. Clients are particularly attracted to the "*absence of dilly-dallying.*" The group has advised on several high-profile cases for clients such as Shell, while continuing to be involved in ongoing coverage disputes related to the Kaiser Aluminum litigation.

The Lawyers: Despite the departure of Pat Cathcart, the firm still fields a team of strong lawyers. **Philip Matthews** (see p.262) specializes in complex insurance coverage issues throughout the USA. Combining a "*charming and gentlemanly*" style with a reputation as a "*great negotiator and facilitator,*" he is representing London market insurers in asbestos-related litigation involving Kaiser Aluminum. He has also been involved in the AP Green coverage and bankruptcy matters. Soon to be chair of the California Judicial Council's Advisory Committee on Civil Jury Instructions, **Richard Seabolt** (see p.272) gathered applause as a "*good, aggressive litigator*" and was described as the "*dean of the firm right now.*" As well as representing underwriters at Lloyd's in an issue involving US Borax, he is also advising Yahoo! in a complex Internet coverage matter arising from claims brought by a group of French students.

The Clients: Greater Insurance Company; Liberty Mutual; Equitas; Lloyd's; Kraft and Yahoo!

Heller Ehrman LLP

See firm details p.288

The Firm: The firm's "*premier*" policyholder insurance practice has rapidly outgrown the asbestos coverage cases on which it cut its teeth in the 1980's. Now it covers a gamut ranging from business interruption to environmental insurance and product liability claims. Its cadre of "*superb*" lawyers generally "*avoids bombastic or aggressive tactics costly to their cause,*" a characteristic also prized by clients. The team is marshaling Kaiser Aluminum's asbestos-related coverage disputes. In one of the most conclusive confirmations of its market reputation for undertaking "*only the most complex cases*" it is advising a major lender embroiled in the multimillion-dollar World Trade Center insurance claims.

The Lawyers: A "*scholar*" of California insurance law, **David Goodwin** is a "*first-rate technical lawyer – he's very measured in strategic and tactical thinking.*" The breadth of his practice is matched only by the geographical diversity of his cases. A legal all-rounder applauded by competitors for his skillful litigation, his work has encompassed nuclear liability coverage disputes in New Orleans and Pittsburgh. On behalf of Hewlett-Packard in New York, he has assisted on business interruption matters. He's also representing BP in claims brought by 26 offshore oil construction sites worldwide. **Stephen Goldberg**'s practice has shifted in recent years from environmental litigation to property damage and business interruption disputes, interspersed with directors and officers (D&O) insurance coverage. Clients value his ability to "*fashion an argument where there is no precedent,*" as demonstrated by his involvement in the World Trade Center litigation. In a related case, he is representing the owners of a property adjacent to the Twin Towers. "*Diligent and willing to roll up his sleeves to get the job done,*" **Lawrence Hobel** continues to be lead trial lawyer for Kaiser Aluminum in a coverage case pertaining to more than 200 policies. "*He doesn't pull punches, and really advances his clients' interests,*" competitors said. In December 2004, he settled a business interruption claim for $125 million on behalf of Freeport, one of the world's largest producers of copper and gold. Exhibiting a "*disciplined approach to horribly complex, political situations,*" practice cochair **Nancy Cohen** is lead counsel for a lender in the World Trade Center insurance coverage litigation. She has also been involved in the prosecution of claims by Holocaust survivors against insurance carriers concerning life insurance claims. **Barry Levin** is scheduled to return to full-time practice in 2005 following a successful stint as the firm's chairman. He gained credence as a "*tremendous trial lawyer*" whose practice centers on insured companies.

The Clients: Kaiser Aluminum; GMAC Commercial Mortgage; Hewlett-Packard; BP America; Freeport-McMoRan Copper & Gold and American Golf Corporation.

Band 2

Barger & Wolen

The Firm: This firm earns "*first cabin*" status for its well-respected insurance regulatory department. Benefiting from its competitive price structure, the team advises insurers on how to document and acquire approvals necessary to myriad business transactions. Peers happily concede that "*if a client wants to form a company, I refer them to this firm.*" Its attorneys are experienced in defending hostile takeovers, submitting draft legislation and handling various insurance transactions on an international stage. For example, the team often advised European and Pacific Rim insurers, reinsurers and reinsurance intermediaries.

The Lawyers: "*One of the top regulatory lawyers in the state,*" **Kent Keller** is "*exceedingly well connected*" to state regulatory agencies. The managing partner of the firm specializes in defending bad faith lawsuits and, more recently, class actions. Another specialty is his participation in lawsuits relating to the California Business and Professions Code Section 17200. **Royal Oakes** garnered acclaim for his extensive trial and appellate insurance experience; he has litigated hundreds of cases in the areas of bad faith law and punitive damages. He is also recognized as KFWB All-News Radio's on-air legal analyst.

The Clients: The firm's clientele ranges from private businesses to Fortune 500 companies in both national and internal settings.

Latham & Watkins LLP

The Firm: Regarded as a "*major competitor*" by insurance practices throughout California and beyond, the firm devotes about 20 attorneys to policyholder insurance coverage matters. The diversity of its caseload is a sign of the group's regional and global range. In December 2004, it successfully settled one of the largest clergy-related sexual abuse claims in history. Another highlight involved a $3 million professional act insurance lawsuit concerning a nickel cobalt facility in Australia owned by global mining company Anaconda; the team helped secure indemnity proceeds that covered all payouts. In addition, the firm's expertise in first party property and casualty claims has led to substantial involvement in the ongoing World Trade Center litigation and related claim adjustments.

The Lawyers: **Andrew Lundberg**, a "*smart, first-rate coverage lawyer,*" was lead counsel in the clergy-related sexual abuse case. He is also representing Guidance Corporation in hundreds of product liability cases pending across the country. Exemplifying the broad reach of his firm, he has worked for companies based in Russia and Switzerland. A "*strong and effective advocate,*" **David Mulliken** also abides by the principle that his geographical location should have no bearing on the scope of his practice. He is representing Sempra Energy in political risk insurance claims directed at AIG; the dispute stems from the company's investment in Argentina's natural gas distribution system. **Peter Rosen**, formerly of Mayer, Brown, Rowe & Maw, gathered "*great client respect*" due to his reputation as a formidable policyholder attorney. He is advising Westfield Holdings in the World Trade Center insurance litigation and separately defending the City of Beverly Hills in multiple lawsuits pertaining to an oil well situated at a city high school.

The Clients: Fluor Corporation; Silicon Valley Bank; Sempra Energy; Montrose Chemical; Westfield Holdings; Avis; Time Warner and the Californian Catholic Diocese of Orange.

Sonnenschein Nath & Rosenthal

See firm details p.779

The Firm: The firm enjoys market repute as a "*deep and sophisticated*" insurance practice, which involves coordinating two distinct insurance departments – regulation and litigation – with additional experience in bad faith, appellate and various coverage proceedings. It has represented Anthem in its merger with WellPoint and separately counseled a GA insurance company involved in the Western MacArthur bankruptcy. Peers note that the firm has developed quite a profile in the area of insolvency, for example, acting on behalf of ACE-related insurance companies.

The Lawyers: **Paul Glad** (see p.253) gets down to the "*nuts and bolts*" of insurance coverage issues, commentators said. As a measure of his authority in this area, he was retained by AIG to represent a host of insurers sued for $740 million in cleanup costs connected to the Stringfellow Acid Pits. He is also counsel to Lloyd's of London syndicates in a series of IPO laddering cases. **Gary Hernandez** (see p.256) is "*one of the leading regulatory lawyers in California.*" Formerly a deputy insurance commissioner, he was involved in the Anthem-WellPoint merger. He is also extremely knowledgeable in insurance insolvency proceedings and complex reinsurance matters. "*Quick on his feet,*" **Ronald Kent** (see p.259) specializes in representing insurance companies in every facet of their operation, ranging from claim-based class actions to underwriting and policy termination. Adding to his hectic schedule, he is national coordinating counsel for ACE entities – a responsibility that encompasses more than 1,000 lawsuits and claims nationwide. The "*charismatic*" **Kara Navarro Baysinger** (see p.265) is greatly admired for her wide range of industry contacts. A regulatory specialist, her work has included representing a large disability insurance company in dealing with California's multifarious regulatory agencies. She has also concluded several complex risk transfer arrangements and broker compensations.

The Clients: First American Capital; Fireman's Fund; AIG; ACE Limited and Bristol West Insurance Group.

Band 3

Covington & Burling

See firm details p.481

The Firm: Boasting a "*tremendous bench*" nationwide, the "*intellectual powerhouse*" set an impressive standard for "*high-quality work.*" This San Francisco-based policyholder insurance practice delivers a wide array of work, including environmental cleanup liability. In the wake of the Enron scandal, D&O liability claims also dominate the practice. The group is representing McDonald's in an insurance coverage lawsuit pending in Illinois pertaining to an earlier class action settlement. Across the Atlantic, it is currently involved in a products liability case originating in the north of the UK; the case involves £14 million worth of claims relating to the failure of hay bale plastic covers produced by Illinois Tool Works.

The Lawyers: **Donald Brown**'s (see p.247) courtroom proficiency led one commentator to place him as "*one of the best insurance coverage lawyers in the country.*" Practicing for more than 26 years, his work includes an ongoing lawsuit brought against McKesson Corporation concerning environmental contamination and cleanup in Ohio and New Jersey. "*He's clearly the smartest person in the room,*" a client said. "*When he speaks, everyone listens.*"

The Clients: McDonald's, Illinois Tool Works and ExxonMobil are among its prominent client base.

Howrey Simon Arnold & White

The Firm: This firm is noted by market sources for its policyholder practice. Its "*great national reputation*" attracts considerable work to the California office, including insurance coverage disputes as related to environmental law. Its high points usually involve acting for policyholders in insurance recovery disputes, though the team also offers counseling on various insurance products.

The Lawyers: "*Highly skilled*" and considered an "*excellent opponent,*" **David Steuber** represents a variety of companies facing significant insurance coverage disputes, particularly in connection with environmental contamination matters such as Superfund sites. His experience also covers medical devices and business interruption, among other issues.

The Clients: Coca-Cola; Sony Pictures; Southern California Gas; FMC and Union Pacific.

Morgan, Lewis & Bockius LLP

See firm details p.1556

The Firm: Its takeover of much of Brobeck, Phleger & Harrison's insurance group has added vigor to the firm's profile in this practice area. Competitors lauded the group's policyholder practice, particularly its asbestos and general environmental coverage work. A feather in its hat involved Western MacArthur in relation to its recovery of more than $2 billion in carrier settlements.

The Lawyers: **David Halbreich** (see p.255), branded as the "*star*" of the group, focuses on insurance recovery. The "*aggressive and capable*" litigator led the Western MacArthur case, earning marks for his "*top-notch*" performance.

The Clients: The practice serves companies drawn from manufacturing, financial services, energy, life sciences, property, media and technology industries.

O'Melveny & Myers LLP

See firm details p.294

The Firm: Labeled one of *"the best, most consistent insurance carrier practices in the state,"* the team is a regular destination for high-profile cases involving significant exposure. The group handles class actions brought against ACE and CIGNA-associated companies. Although this is primarily in the field of asbestos litigation, the firm's remit also includes the likes of reinsurance and accident coverage among other issues. Its litigation prowess also extends to involvement in a series of lawsuits relating to the Catholic dioceses in sexual abuse allegations.

The Lawyers: **Martin Checov** receives great praise for his ability to *"pull together the facts, and marshal in a forceful way vague principles that don't have an obvious practical application."* His appointment as the firm's risk manager is testament to his skills, which he continues to exercise in a number of high-profile matters. He is representing ACE in a challenge to its 1996 restructuring of asbestos liability. He separately settled on behalf of ACE Bermuda the last of several lawsuits arising from the 1999 Olympic pipeline explosion. Proclaimed one of *"the best carrier lawyers in the state,"* **Mark Wood** *"applies great business sense to the litigation he conducts."* The litigation department chairman specializes in insurance and reinsurance matters, class action product liability cases and major aircraft accident coverage.

The Clients: ACE; CIGNA; American Re and Zurich North America.

Shernoff, Bidart & Darras LLP

The Firm: The *"place to go"* for policyholder representation, this specialist team operates on a contingency fee basis. *"If they take your case, you're in good hands,"* commentators said. The broad sweep of its practice encompasses health and disability, HMO, life, homeowner and auto-related disputes. Other interests involve business property, natural catastrophe and Holocaust-era claims.

The Lawyers: If not *"universally feared,"* **William Shernoff** is *"certainly extremely well regarded"* by his competitors, sources said. He is credited with establishing bad faith insurance law in the late 1970's and continues to be a force to be reckoned with. An important highlight is his litigating against European life insurance companies on behalf of Holocaust survivors. **Michael Bidart** is deemed to be *"wonderful"* in court. He leads the firm's HMO litigation and property/casualty department. As befits his reputation in the field, he *"tends to make insurance companies nervous."*

The Clients: AJ Industries; AppleOne; Buenavision; City of Los Angeles; Kenco Construction; Kilroy Industries; MGM Hotels Las Vegas; Mitchell Rubber; Oakland Raiders; R&J Sheet Metal; Sierra Royal Hospital and Time Warner.

Band 4

Alschuler Grossman Stein & Kahan LLP

See firm details p.280

The Firm: The firm's 12-attorney insurance practice specializes in complex coverage litigation from an insurer's perspective. It also counsels California's insurance commissioner, John Garamendi, in regulatory litigation; the group successfully represented him after Anthem sued him for refusing to approve the company's merger with WellPoint. It also obtained favorable results in a case brought against C&A by Disney seeking insurance coverage and punitive damages. Also on behalf of C&A, the team is handling an asbestos-related appellate case concerning a lower court decision to accelerate the company's claims payout.

The Lawyers: **Frank Kaplan** (see p.259) impresses with his expertise on complex insurance and securities matters. His credibility in the field is further enhanced by his representation of the state's insurance commissioner on regulatory issues; he participated in the Anthem-WellPoint merger. **Bruce Friedman**'s (see p.252) expertise lies in the progressive arena of media insurance coverage. *"Thorough, knowledgeable and responsive,"* he helped settle a complex dispute involving a GE-owned company; the case pertains to a music composition played on ABC. Friedman also handles a substantial amount of D&O professional liability and legal malpractice insurance disputes.

The Clients: California Department of Insurance; C&A; Royal & SunAlliance; Employers Reinsurance Corporation and Lowes.

Berkes Crane Robinson & Seal, LLP

The Firm: This LA-based firm *"successfully"* occupies an insurance coverage niche oriented toward environmental law, toxic tort and product liability. Competitors point to its involvement in the Stringfellow Acid Pits cleanup as evidence of the *"strong client following"* that typifies its professional standing within California. The team also prides itself on its specialist strength in alternative dispute resolution as related to insurance law.

The Lawyers: Industry sources singled out **Steven Crane** for his *"diligence, intelligence, knowledge of the field, and reasoned approach."* He displays an *"extraordinary"* facility for *"simplifying complex points to make clear legal arguments."* **Robert Berkes** garnered praise in asbestos and toxic tort matters. *"Experienced and thoughtful,"* he is also an authority on product liability.

The Clients: The group represents a variety of clients in such sectors as insurance, energy and environment among others.

Farella Braun & Martel LLP

The Firm: Prominent in the Bay Area, the coterie of *"top-quality"* litigators works within the firm's insurance coverage department. The group represents policyholders in disputes related to such issues as construction delays and defects, product liability and environmental liabilities. Damages from natural disasters such as fires and earthquakes also feature in its repertoire. Working in tandem with other specialists at the firm, the team has helped clients recover costs stemming from antitrust and IP violations. Its reach also extends to counseling prominent clients on structuring insurance coverage programs that are acceptable to various governmental agencies.

The Lawyers: **William Friedrich**, described as a *"tenacious advocate,"* obtains *"terrific results"* in coverage and bad faith litigation. With *"great depth of knowledge"* in first party claims such as property damage and business interruption, he *"instills confidence in his clients."* **Mary McCutcheon** lends cachet on matters originating from securities fraud and insurance rescission actions. Other expertise involves civil rights, product liability, IP and environmental litigation. She has also garnered *"quite a reputation"* for her input on the jury instructions committee.

The Clients: Private entities and public businesses constitute the bulk of the firm's insurance clientele.

Gibson, Dunn & Crutcher LLP

See firm details p.285

The Firm: Boasting *"years of experience,"* this full-service insurance practice aims for complex, high-end matters, including toxic tort, bad faith claims and liquidation-related issues. Its litigation prowess also stretches to the appellate level, where the firm has played a key role in judicially limiting punitive damages. In the area of healthcare, the seven-partner group has been involved in coverage work connected to prescription drugs. Its scope of practice also involves environmental, D&O and catastrophe claims.

The Lawyers: **Gary Justice** (see p.259) offers *"responsive and efficient"* client services, regularly participating in environmental and related toxic torts litigation. Of late, he has been preoccupied by an environmental coverage case tried before the Ohio federal court. His practice also features product liability litigation including drug and medical devices, and construction defect lawsuits.

The Clients: The group acts on behalf of insurers, reinsurers and insured companies. Among them are healthcare providers such as Empire BlueCross BlueShield.

Munger, Tolles & Olson LLP

The Firm: This *"wonderful"* firm with offices in LA and San Francisco is well served by an *"excellent litigation department."* The team has handled a billion-dollar claim against a brokerage

214   All quotes in the text are from interviews with clients and competitors.

CHAMBERS USA 2005

firm in the aftermath of Orange County's unprecedented bankruptcy. In another highlight, it participated in litigation relating to possible medical cost reimbursements from cigarette producers to state governments.

The Lawyers: The "*scholarly*" **Carey Lerman** has built a reputation partly anchored in his experience in asbestos insurance coverage. His profile has now expanded to include counseling national clients on issues including D&O liability, environmental impairment and first party property damage.

The Clients: Among others, the team often handles work for companies involved in bankruptcy or bankruptcy-related matters.

Other Notable Practitioners

"*Shining light*" **Patrick Cathcart** (see p.247) recently departed Hancock Rothert & Bunshoft

LLP to found a new firm, Cathcart, Collins & Kneafsey LLP. He is lauded as both a "*great trial lawyer*" and "*wonderful tactician*," applying these skills to "*cutting-edge*" complex business litigation, especially as related to multiparty insurance coverage disputes and professional liability. **Kirk Pasich** is an unmistakable feature of California's insurance landscape. "*Bright and aggressive, he's the policyholder attorney most likely to come up with a new argument or perspective concerning policy language,*" sources said. Oriented toward studio representation and entertainment insurance, "*he really knows his stuff.*" At time of press his firm, Pasich & Kornfeld, LLP, announced its merger with Dickstein Shapiro Morin & Oshinsky LLP. Market sources draw attention to **Harvey Levine**'s "*impressive knowledge of substantive insurance law.*" Partner at Levine, Steinberg, Miller & Huver, he specializes in bad faith

and personal injury litigation. He has established himself as a "*household name*" by achieving "*huge results,*" obtaining settlements or verdicts in excess of $1 million in more than 60 cases. Observers praise the "*knowledge and depth of experience*" that Morrison & Foerster LLP's **David Babbe** (see p.244) brings to his general litigation practice. Counting St Paul Travelers among his clients, he conducts state and federal insurance coverage cases, focusing on multibillion-dollar environmental matters. Recommended by observers as a "*thoughtful lawyer with a good command of coverage issues,*" **Ann Mooney** is head of the insured's rights practice group at Cooley Godward LLP. In addition to advising on the negotiation and placement of insurance policies, she represents clients in coverage disputes arising from D&O liability, and errors and omissions legislation among other matters.

INTELLECTUAL PROPERTY

California
Leading firms (Intellectual Property)

1 IRELL & MANELLA LLP *Los Angeles*
KEKER & VAN NEST LLP *San Francisco*
MORRISON & FOERSTER LLP *San Francisco*
WEIL, GOTSHAL & MANGES LLP *Redwood Shores*

2 DAY CASEBEER MADRID & BATCHELDER *Cupertino*
FENWICK & WEST LLP *Mountain View*
KIRKLAND & ELLIS LLP *Los Angeles*
MCDERMOTT WILL & EMERY *Palo Alto*
ORRICK, HERRINGTON & SUTCLIFFE *Los Angeles*

3 COOLEY GODWARD LLP *Palo Alto*
FINNEGAN HENDERSON FARABOW *Palo Alto*
FISH & NEAVE IP GROUP *Palo Alto*
FISH & RICHARDSON *San Diego*
HELLER EHRMAN LLP *San Francisco*
HOWREY SIMON ARNOLD & WHITE *San Francisco*
KNOBBE MARTENS OLSON & BEAR *San Francisco*
LATHAM & WATKINS LLP *San Francisco*
QUINN EMANUEL URQUHART *San Francisco*
SKADDEN, ARPS, SLATE, MEAGHER *Palo Alto*
TOWNSEND AND TOWNSEND *San Francisco*
WILSON SONSINI GOODRICH & ROSATI *Palo Alto*

4 ARNOLD & PORTER LLP *Los Angeles*
DEWEY BALLANTINE LLP *Palo Alto*
FARELLA BRAUN & MARTEL LLP *San Francisco*
GIBSON, DUNN & CRUTCHER LLP *Los Angeles*
JONES DAY *Los Angeles*
O'MELVENY & MYERS LLP *Los Angeles*
PAUL, HASTINGS, JANOFSKY *San Diego*
SIMPSON THACHER & BARTLETT LLP *Los Angeles*

Firms are listed alphabetically in each band.

Band 1

Irell & Manella LLP

The Firm: Clients keep returning to this "*fantastic*" firm for the "*superb quality of its legal work*" in the areas of IP, technology and enter-

tainment. Indeed, many sources believe that Irell & Manella possesses the "*greatest depth of any law firm in the country*" in areas such as trademark analysis, copyright and patent prosecution, as well as for "*truly outstanding work in patent trials.*" The team's track record is full of firsts – such as the first trial involving a computer software patent – and big-number awards, such as Texas Instruments v Samsung. A recent highlight was settling an infringement suit over key patents for client Hewlett-Packard. In this case, Intergraph sued Hewlett-Packard, Dell and Gateway, claiming that the companies had infringed patents related to cache memory technology. Despite lacking the size and global network of some of its competitors, the team tries cases of international importance for major names in the worlds of software, semiconductors, pharmaceuticals, medical devices, telecom and e-commerce.

The Lawyers: **Morgan Chu** is firmly installed in the pantheon of the IP gods, not just in California, but internationally; a glance at a resumé that includes lead roles on the likes of Stac Electronics v Microsoft, City of Hope v Genentech and Texas Instruments v Samsung makes that clear enough, but it is confirmed by research. Acknowledged as a "*preeminent player,*" Chu is described by clients as "*in a class of his own.*" He presents cases in a "*soft spoken but compelling*" way, with the perfect combination of "*showmanship and profound understanding.*" His performances in the courtroom are spectacular enough to have won him a reputation in some quarters as "*beyond doubt the most gifted trial lawyer*" in the USA. Market sources describe **Jonathan Steinberg** as "*a fair player with a real passion for his work.*" His IP practice includes patent, copyright, trademark and trade secret litigation. His recent highlights include Edwards

Lifesciences v St Jude Medical. Here he represented St Jude Medical in connection with the alleged infringement of three patents on angioplasty devices and the treatment of porcine heart valves for humans.

The Clients: The team has tried cases for the likes of: Hewlett-Packard; AT&T; Compaq; Novellus; Broadcom; Affymetrix; Elan; Texas Instruments; Lucas Digital and St Jude Medical.

Keker & Van Nest LLP

See firm details p.290

The Firm: This solid and sizable team is considered "*at the cutting edge of whatever is happening within litigation.*" Rivals note that the name of Keker & Van Nest on the other side implies "*a hard battle that will be fought with honor and integrity.*" As one noted, the team "*has made some significant strides*" recently in the IP field, giving it a strong and rounded profile. Clients, meanwhile, see the firm as "*a highly professional and extremely strong litigation boutique.*" The team acts as counsel to both defendants and plaintiffs in trademark, copyright, patent infringement and trade secrets cases. A recent string of high-profile matters included the patent case Collaboration Properties v Polycom, in which the group advised Polycom. The group is also said to have done a superb job for Genentech in the widely reported patent case, MedImmune v Genentech.

The Lawyers: "*Energetic*" **John Keker** (see p.259) was described to researchers as a "*formidable trial lawyer and a quality human being.*" His loyal clients value his "*top-notch litigation skills*" and consider him "*the one you seek out if you're in a deep mess.*" The firm's other eponymous partner, **Robert Van Nest** (see p.276), has dealt with "*some of the toughest patent cases*" in the state. He is "*aggressive, smart, lively and hardworking,*" and can be relied upon to do "*a fine*"

www.ChambersandPartners.com

All quotes in the text are from interviews with clients and competitors.

215

California
Leading individuals
(Intellectual Property)

★ **CHU Morgan** *Irell & Manella*, Los Angeles

[1] **KRUPKA Robert** *Kirkland & Ellis*, Los Angeles
MCMAHON Terry *McDermott Will*, Palo Alto
POWERS Matthew *Weil Gotshal*, Redwood Shores

[2] **DAY Lloyd** *Day Casebeer*, Cupertino
JACOBS Michael *Morrison & Foerster*, San Francisco
KEKER John *Keker & Van Nest*, San Francisco
MCELHINNY Harold *Morrison & Foerster*, San Francisco

[3] **ANTHONY William** *Orrick Herrington*, San Francisco
BUNSOW Henry *Howrey Simon*, San Francisco
DODSON Gerald *Morrison & Foerster*, Palo Alto
ELACQUA James *Dewey Ballantine*, Palo Alto
FLAGEL Mark *Latham & Watkins*, Los Angeles
GARTMAN John *Fish & Richardson*, San Diego
GUY III G Hopkins *Orrick Herrington*, Menlo Park
HAYES David *Fenwick & West*, Mountain View
JOHNSTON Ronald *Arnold & Porter*, Los Angeles
LORIG Frederick *Bright & Lorig*, Los Angeles
MARTENS Don *Knobbe Martens*, Irvine
NEWCOMBE George *Simpson Thacher*, Palo Alto
PAGE Michael *Keker & Van Nest*, San Francisco
PASAHOW Lynn *Fenwick & West*, Mountain View
POOLEY James *Milbank Tweed*, Palo Alto
SHULMAN Ron *Wilson Sonsini*, Palo Alto
STEINBERG Jonathan *Irell & Manella*, Los Angeles
STERN Claude *Quinn Emanuel*, Redwood Shores
VAN NEST Robert *Keker & Van Nest*, San Francisco

[4] **ABEL Sally** *Fenwick & West*, Mountain View
BARSKY Wayne *Gibson Dunn*, Los Angeles
BRIDGES Andrew *Winston & Strawn*, San Francisco
DURIE Daralyn *Keker & Van Nest*, San Francisco
FELDMAN Robert *Wilson Sonsini*, Palo Alto
FRAM Robert *Heller Ehrman*, San Francisco
GOLDMAN Robert *Fish & Neave*, Palo Alto
HASLAM Robert *Heller Ehrman*, Menlo Park
HEMMINGER Steven *White & Case*, Palo Alto
PRETTY Laurence *Hogan & Hartson*, Los Angeles
PRUETZ Adrian *Quinn Emanuel*, Los Angeles
RANDALL Jeff *Skadden Arps*, Palo Alto
REINES Edward *Weil Gotshal*, Redwood Shores
SAMUELS Mark *O'Melveny & Myers*, Los Angeles
SAVIKAS Victor *Jones Day*, Los Angeles
SEKA J Georg *Townsend and Townsend*, San Francisco
SMITH Neil *Howard Rice*, San Francisco
STREETER Jon *Keker & Van Nest*, San Francisco
VERHOEVEN Charles *Quinn Emanuel*, San Francisco

Up-and-coming individuals
ELSON Vera *McDermott Will*, Palo Alto

Individuals are listed alphabetically in each band.

job for his clients." **Michael Page** (see p.266) is considered the firm's *"future star."* Interviewees note that he *"knows his way around the courtroom,"* something that was amply demonstrated recently in MGM Studios v Grokster, which concerned the entertainment industry's efforts to control copyright infringement of its works. He won the case for Grokster in the trial court and the Ninth Circuit. Also warmly recom-

mended were the *"knowledgeable"* **Jon Streeter** (see p.274), who clients say can *"handle any complex matter,"* and *"talented"* **Daralyn Durie** (see p.250), who deals with sophisticated issues on behalf of such high-profile clients as Google and Polycom.

The Clients: The team represented Google in Overture Services v Google. Other clients include: Grokster; Intel; Polycom; First Data and Genentech.

Morrison & Foerster LLP
See firm details p.293

The Firm: MoFo is celebrated for its superb general commercial litigators and its experience in the hi-tech sector, a happy combination that guarantees it a leading position in IP circles. *"One of the oldest, largest and deepest"* general IP practices in the country, with expertise in all areas of the field, the firm was enthusiastically praised by clients for *"the solid base of offices around the country,"* combined with its lawyers' *"superior perspective and awareness."* Clients were particularly impressed by the *"high number of first chair trial lawyers and famous academics"* in this team and the quality of service they provide. As one put it, they are *"high energy, responsive and thoughtful – they aren't delicate, but are really in the mix."* Recent successes include representing Syntron Bioresearch in a patent suit brought by Abbott Laboratories alleging that Syntron's test kits infringed patents Abbott had purchased from Bio-Metric Systems. It also advised Novell in SCO v Novell, which forms part of the long-running dispute over whether Linux violates IP rights.

The Lawyers: *"Tenacious"* **Michael Jacobs** (see p.28983) *"always prepares his cases as if they are going to trial."* He deals with highly intricate patent cases in the area of biotech and life sciences. **Harold McElhinny** (see p.263) is a *"trial authority"* clients keep returning to because he *"always seems to triumph in court."* Peers, meanwhile, acknowledge him as *"a superb commercial lawyer."* His recent highlights include representing EchoStar in TiVo v EchoStar. This case concerned allegations by TiVo that EchoStar had infringed a patent for the process of recording and replaying TV signals. He also recently acted for Nikon in Nikon v ASML. ASML and Carl Zeiss SMT eventually paid Nikon $146 million to settle this patent litigation in the USA, Japan, Korea and Taiwan. Clients value *"likable"* **Gerald Dodson** (see p.250) for his *"good political connections"* and his track record in high-profile cases. These have recently included University of Rochester v Pfizer.

The Clients: The team acted for BEA in Software AG v BEA, a patent case currently pending in the federal district court in Delaware. It represented Australian biotech company Peptech in a dispute with Johnson & Johnson/Centocor relating to patents in TNF-alpha. Other clients include: Kaiser Permanente; Kumon Institute; Toshiba and Yahoo!

Weil, Gotshal & Manges LLP
See firm details p.1378

The Firm: Weil Gotshal has been hugely successful of late in carving out *"an enormous footprint in the area of IP,"* both in California and across the USA. Peers acknowledge that the sizable team is increasingly *"at the forefront of the most sophisticated IP matters"* and *"does a fantastic job for its clients."* In particular, commentators praised the quality and consistency of this *"experienced and resourceful"* team, which is *"constantly called upon for challenging issues."* It has established itself as a leader in a broad range of issues, from patent litigation and prosecution to copyright and trademark matters. However, it is especially renowned as a go-to firm for IP issues concerning semiconductors, biotech and IT.

The Lawyers: *"Heavyweight patent litigator"* **Matthew Powers** (see p.268) was described by clients as *"a real success story in California."* A tremendously well-respected counselor, he is a favorite with clients because of his *"top-notch"* legal advice and measured, practical approach. They also note that he can be *"persuasive and forceful when needs be."* Peers, meanwhile, describe him as *"one of the best business generators"* in the state. **Edward Reines** (see p.269) advises on intricate patent cases. According to rivals, his *"intelligence and drive"* mean that he should *"not be underestimated"* as an opponent.

The Clients: Cisco Systems; Applied Materials; Intel; Broadcom; Applera; GlaxoSmithKline; Genentech; Matsushita and Sony Computer Entertainment.

Band 2

Day Casebeer Madrid & Batchelder LLP

The Firm: At only 27 attorneys, this is far from the largest firm in the list, but it is nonetheless regarded as having *"one of the best IP practices in the state."* The team possesses *"unmatched experience and talent,"* which it lays at the disposal of its top-class biotech and IT clients. Peers too were full of praise for *"a fantastic team with several first-rate lawyers."* Recent successes for the group include representing QUALCOMM in an important trade secrets case against Maxim Integrated Products of Sunnyvale. This concerned the use of trade secrets to make computer chips for cell phones.

The Lawyers: The *"fabulous"* **Rusty Day** is *"one of the leading and most admired patent litigators"* in the state, according to clients. Rivals acknowledge that *"he has some fine clients,"* who *"can trust him to do a great job every time."* His expertise spans copyright, trademark and trade secrets litigation, as well as patents, and he has taken the field for such clients as Sun Microsystems, Amgen, National Semiconductor and Raytheon.

The Clients: Sun Microsystems; Amgen; Lilly ICOS; SAP; Symantec; Ciphergen Biosystems; Angiotech Pharmaceuticals and QUALCOMM.

Fenwick & West LLP

See firm details p.283

The Firm: This "*detail-oriented*" team has a long history in Northern California and fields more than 225 attorneys concentrated in the region. A "*top-notch litigation firm,*" it is acknowledged by rivals to have developed into "*a serious contender that is not to be underestimated.*" Clients, meanwhile, keep returning to the team because it has the capability to deal with "*anything we throw at them*" in an efficient, responsive and practical way. The firm prides itself on its understanding of clients' technologies and businesses, and offers a wide variety of tailored services in all aspects of IP law. A recent highlight was the firm's successful patent infringement jury verdict on behalf of Macromedia against Adobe Systems. On the noncontentious side, IP attorneys advise on aspects of the firm's major transactions, such as Juniper Network's recent $4 billion acquisition of Fenwick & West client NetScreen Technologies.

The Lawyers: **David Hayes** (see p.255) is a "*methodical and thorough*" attorney with a strong profile in the sector. He advises a broad range of technology companies on whatever they require to shield their intellectual property, be that patents, copyrights, trade secrets and trademarks. **Lynn Pasahow** (see p.266) is another "*highly credible*" adviser. Though he is particularly highly recommended for his expertise in patent litigation, he boasts a broad general IP litigation practice and is renowned as "*a terrific jury trial lawyer with a fine track record.*" Other specialties of his include bioscience and Internet and software technologies. Hot on their heels is "*leading light*" **Sally Abel** (see p.243). A "*renowned trademark expert,*" she enjoys a growing profile in the field.

The Clients: Cisco Systems; Apple Computers; Electronic Arts; Intuit; Logitech; Sun Microsystems and T-Netix.

Kirkland & Ellis LLP

See firm details p.770

The Firm: Kirkland & Ellis fields about 200 IP lawyers across its network, many of them in Los Angeles and San Francisco. The firm was praised to researchers for the quality of its "*knowledgeable and gifted*" lawyers and their "*tremendous span of proficiency.*" They handle a wide range of IP disputes and counseling, but the group was particularly recommended for its "*fabulous trial work*" and its involvement in some of the "*most significant matters in the field.*" In recent years it has taken part in litigation in a wide variety of areas, ranging from DNA arrays to windshields and semiconductors to label designs. The team played a role in one of the firm's highlights of

the year, Amazon's summary judgment in a patent infringement case filed by IPXL Holdings.

The Lawyers: **Bob Krupka** (see p.260) heads the practice here and is widely considered to be "*one of the foremost IP lawyers*" in the country. According to interviewees, his position is based upon his "*remarkable knowledge and great international connections*" and his "*skill at presenting a case in an understandable way, even if it is a complex high-tech case.*" One client even went so far as to describe him as the "*best patent draftsman around.*"

The Clients: The firm's top-class client base includes: Honeywell; Motorola; Pioneer and Schering-Plough.

McDermott Will & Emery

See firm details p.773

The Firm: This "*resourceful and dynamic practice*" is a frequent participant in larger national IP cases. Clients were full of praise for the service offered by the team, and appreciated the breadth of its counsel and prosecution on both hard and soft IP matters. Researchers were told that it has had "*a succession of high-profile matters*" in recent months and "*left behind a trail of happy customers.*" An example is Intel v Broadcom. Here, the group represented Broadcom in a Delaware jury trial relating to digital video processing and computer network technology. Another headline-grabbing international matter saw the team advise Intergraph against Hewlett-Packard in five patent infringement cases in California, Texas and Germany.

The Lawyers: Clients recommend "*formidable*" **Terry McMahon** (see p.263) as a "*true IP trial expert*" with an outstanding record of success in complex litigation. Indeed, one client enthused, "*he is just brilliant; I can't think of anyone who can do a better job.*" According to peers, meanwhile, "*clients turn to him when they have serious hi-tech issues to deal with.*" He handles depositions nationwide and covers litigation, counseling and prosecution on both hard and soft IP matters. "*Rising star*" **Vera Elson** (see p.251) focuses on technology, advising on IP matters concerning computers, software and medical devices.

The Clients: Seagate Technology; Intergraph; Aureal Semiconductor; Research Corporation Technologies; Extreme Networks; Broadcom; Legato Systems; Fairchild Semiconductor and Medtronic.

Orrick, Herrington & Sutcliffe

See firm details p.295

The Firm: A major player on the West Coast with a growing international footprint and a strong client base, Orrick Herrington's IP team was praised to researchers as "*trustworthy and strong.*" Clients also appreciate the group's "*extremely hard-working*" approach. Interviewees particularly stressed the firm's "*market-*

leading qualities" in the areas of biotech and software patents. The team was also enthusiastically praised for its skill in trade secrets, copyright and trademark work. Demonstrating both its expertise in complex patents, and its national reach, it recently won a complete defense verdict for Dow AgroSciences and its affiliates in a patent infringement suit brought by Syngenta Seeds in the US District Court in Delaware.

The Lawyers: **Bill Anthony** has acquired a strong reputation in California's IP circles as "*an influential patent trial lawyer.*" He recently obtained an order granting summary judgment on behalf of Compal Electronics and its subsidiaries on four patents in LG Electronics v Compal Electronics. **Hopkins Guy** is not just "*an outstanding technical lawyer,*" according to clients; he is also a "*bold and tactically astute*" adviser. Peers praise him for his role in Cisco Systems v Huawei. Here he acted as lead counsel for Cisco Systems in obtaining a worldwide preliminary injunction against Huawei.

The Clients: Compal Electronics; Dow AgroSciences; Oracle; Inktomi; Nanya Technology and Affymetrix.

Band 3

Cooley Godward LLP

The Firm: This practice commands tremendous respect among rivals and clients alike. Although the past five years have not always been kind to Cooley Godward, it has retained a strong presence in the Californian market, and continues to pull in its share of "*sophisticated*" IP work. For example, the team was applauded for its recent involvement in the high-profile case GlaxoSmithKline v Excel, heard in the Eastern District of Virginia. The court granted a summary judgment in favor of the firm's client, Excel, on GlaxoSmithKline's patent infringement suit. This arose from Excel's intention to market a generic version of GlaxoSmithKline's Wellbutrin and Zyban products.

The Lawyers: The main contact here is Stephen Swinton, who chairs the IP litigation practice.

The Clients: Excel; eBay; Flyswat; National Semiconductor; NVIDIA; PETsMART; QUALCOMM; Gilead Sciences and Siebel Systems.

Finnegan Henderson Farabow Garrett & Dunner LLP

The Firm: This dedicated IP specialist has more than 300 lawyers nationwide, more than 200 of them licensed to practice before the PTO. It also operates internationally through its handful of global offices and a network of affiliations. In California, the growing team is increasingly visible in the market. Sources agree that its practice has developed in both size and profile during the past year. It covers a broad range of IP law, including copyright, patent, trademark and trade secrets. Patent interference is felt to have been a particular focus of the Northern Californian team, in areas such as pharmaceuticals, chemicals, software and biotechnology, and the group is also a player in such cutting-edge work as gene therapy and multimedia content delivery.

The Lawyers: Palo Alto managing partner Jerry Voight is the first point of contact for the group's patent law practice.

The Clients: Dyax; Agilent Technologies; Beckman Coulter; Biosynexus; Dade Behring Marburg GmbH; Elan; Eli Lilly and Novogen.

Fish & Neave IP Group of Ropes & Gray

The Firm: In November 2004, Boston-based Ropes & Gray merged with Fish & Neave. The "*immensely admired*" IP boutique is, at least for the moment, to retain a separate brand, appearing as Fish & Neave IP Group of Ropes & Gray. Clients certainly feel that the merger has strengthened the group, providing it with greater resources and geographical spread. One was "*looking forward to continuing top-notch service.*" Peers, meanwhile, admire this "*high-caliber and hard-hitting competitor*" for its track record of involvement in "*prestigious*" IP matters, particularly patent litigation in fields such as medical devices and electronics.

The Lawyers: **Robert Goldman** is "*unquestionably esteemed*" in IP circles, say market sources. He focuses on IP litigation, with particular emphasis on the arenas of information technology, pharmaceuticals and medical devices.

The Clients: Silicon Laboratories; Motorola; Saifun Semiconductors; Caliper; Compaq and Nestlé.

Fish & Richardson

The Firm: The firm is among the largest IP specialists in the world, with a genuinely national footprint and a case list to match. Clients were full of praise for its "*gifted*" specialists, and were particularly impressed with the team's ability to "*stay on top of issues without missing deadlines.*" The group handles the range of IP law and enjoys a particularly good track record in complex patent disputes, where it won a number of major cases last year. One of the most important of these was Arendi v Microsoft, where it represented Microsoft. This dispute involved database retrieval technology. Another highlight was its win for Genesis in Genesis Microchip v MRT, a patent infringement action concerning flat panel display controllers.

The Lawyers: Clients described **John Gartman** as an "*amazingly bright lawyer*" with a "*great deal of depth.*" He was particularly recommended to researchers for his expertise in hi-tech litigation, particularly in the areas of software, telecommunications and semiconductors.

The Clients: Microsoft; Princo and Gigastorage; Adaptec; Sensormatic and ADE.

Heller Ehrman LLP

See firm details p.288

The Firm: Clients described this as "*a go-to firm*" for biotech and life sciences issues. Interviewees note that the firm is home to a host of brilliant IP lawyers, and pay tribute to their energy, skill and commitment to the sector. Typical IP work includes complex copyright, trademarks and licensing disputes, patent infringement cases, trade secrets issues and ITC investigations. A highlight from 2004 was winning a patent trial on behalf of Syntex and Allergan in the Northern District of California against a generic pharmaceutical company.

The Lawyers: "*Quick-witted*" **Robert Haslam** is renowned for his "*genius*" in the courtroom, particularly in patent, trade secret and other hi-tech disputes. This has seen him tackle complex work in fields such as semiconductor manufacture, cryptography, microprocessors and medical devices for the likes of MCI, First Data and Atmel. Commentators value **Robert Fram** for his "*high integrity and exceptional work.*" The cochair of the IP litigation group, he boasts considerable experience in patent, trade secret and licensing cases, and has appeared on behalf of such clients as Yahoo! subsidiary Overture Services, Computer Associates, Symantec and RSA Data Security.

The Clients: Chips & Technologies; AMATI; Unitrode Corporation; Merck; Allergan; Genentech; Superconductor Technologies and ActivCard.

Howrey Simon Arnold & White

The Firm: Interviewees endorsed this team of "*fine patent litigators.*" Clients were particularly impressed by the "*wide reach*" of the firm's growing international network, and its expertise in the interface between IP and antitrust issues. In the pure IP arena, the Californian team has enjoyed a number of recent successes. For example, it recently handled a patent infringement trial for Harris against Ericsson, leading to a $61 million jury verdict. The team also appeared in two separate jury trials on behalf of ACCO Division of Fortune Brands against Belkin and Kryptonite Lock. On both occasions the jury made findings of willful infringement against the defendants and awarded damages in favor of the firm's client.

The Lawyers: A "*prominent*" figure in the state's IP bar, **Henry Bunsow** boasts "*30 years of experience up his sleeve.*" He is renowned as a talented trial attorney with a good courtroom manner, and has appeared in a variety of high-profile cases in fields such as technology patents, biotech, medical devices and consumer goods.

The Clients: Harris; Toshiba; Foundry Networks and Network Appliance.

Knobbe Martens Olson & Bear

The Firm: This "*mighty*" IP boutique retains "*a superb status and a strong firm culture,*" according to its clients. It is "*simply spectacular,*" one said: "*I never heard a bad thing against it.*" Packed with highly qualified IP attorneys, typically with scientific and technical backgrounds, the firm enjoys a wealth of expertise and a number of areas of strength. For example, it is renowned as "*really high powered in molecular biology and genetics.*" The group was also praised for its skill in patent, trademark, copyright and trade secrets litigation. Here its recent highlights include defending Ranbaxy Pharmaceuticals, a subsidiary of generics manufacturer Ranbaxy Laboratories, in a patent infringement suit brought by GlaxoSmithKline. The group also successfully handled a five-week trial resulting in a Los Angeles federal jury award of $134.5 million for Masimo Corporation.

The Lawyers: **Don Martens** was described by one client as "*the leader in one of the remaining superstar boutiques.*" Rivals agreed that he is "*one of the most respected patent lawyers in the country.*"

The Clients: Nobel Biocare USA; Mustek Systems; Masimo; Ranbaxy Pharmaceuticals; Bausch & Lomb and Winn.

Latham & Watkins LLP

The Firm: This IP group is acknowledged to be "*an enormous force*" in the marketplace and is respected for its "*professionalism and strength.*" One of the premier shops in California, with a growing profile both nationally and internationally, the firm is notable for the size of its transactional work and the quality of its litigation. In the latter field, the group recently defended Broadcom against claims by ST Microelectronics alleging infringement of six semiconductor technology patents. It also defended Conexant against claims of violation of a patent on the technology of dial-up modems.

The Lawyers: "*Terrific*" **Mark Flagel** impresses sources with his "*creativity and strategic approach.*" Clients keep returning to him because he is "*responsive and will make every effort to get a favorable result.*" The cochair of the firm's national IP and technology group, Flagel litigates patent, trademark, trade secret, copyright and false advertising cases. His record of success includes securing a $120 million verdict against Microsoft.

The Clients: The team recently secured a victory in the district court for Genentech in a dispute with antibody development company MedImmune concerning a patent on a key technology employed in the production of genetically engineered antibodies. Other clients include: Gap; Silicon Graphics; Sony; VERITAS Software; Monolithic Power Systems; J Paul Getty Trust; Directors Guild of America; Allergan; Entrepreneur Media and Sony Pictures Entertainment.

Quinn Emanuel Urquhart Oliver & Hedges, LLP

See firm details p.298

The Firm: Interviewees were quick to endorse this group of "*marvelous patent attorneys.*" Market observers note that the firm has been "*increasingly on the radar over the past few years,*" following a raft of impressive client wins and "*several high-profile successes*" in headline-grabbing disputes. One of these is David Kramer v Intuit, an unfair competition and false advertising case where the team represented Intuit. Although it offers a well-rounded basket of IP skills, it is in patent litigation that the team is particularly felt to have earned its spurs, and it is here that its "*ability to attract excellent clients*" is still considered strongest.

The Lawyers: According to sources, "*dynamic player*" **Claude Stern** (see p.274) is capable of putting in "*breathtaking*" performances in IP and technology cases. Clients value his deep knowledge and intelligent, strategic approach, while peers acknowledge that "*there is no question about his stature.*" He advises, inter alia, on matters relating to hardware and semiconductor manufacture, software development, computer and equipment leasing, and infrastructure products and systems. A "*levelheaded*" counselor, **Charles Verhoeven** (see p.277) focuses on IP as part of a broad practice that also includes entertainment, antitrust and complex commercial litigation. **Adrian Pruetz** (see p.268) is hugely respected for IP litigation and handles trademark, patent, trade secret, copyright and other complex commercial issues.

The Clients: Medo Industries; Genentech; Gap; Roche Molecular Systems; Monsanto; Nike; K & N Engineering; Applied Materials; Avery Dennison; Kaiser Permanente and Mattel.

Skadden, Arps, Slate, Meagher & Flom LLP & Affiliates

See firm details p.1372

The Firm: Skadden Arps is one of the corporate heavyweights of the Californian legal market, and as such it fields an IP team skilled at advising on the IP aspects of large transactional work. However, an active team packed with distinguished attorneys also makes this a "*go-to firm*" for stand-alone matters. Despite the departure of Ron Laurie, the team retains a strong profile in the market and continues to pull in important cases. For example, it recently represented Register.com in Wornow v Register.com, a putative class action alleging that the client's automatic renewal of domain name registrations constituted a violation of the New York General Obligations Law.

The Lawyers: "*Bright and confident*" **Jeff Randall** (see p.269) is particularly valued by clients for his "*superior-quality work.*" He represents a broad array of technology companies, and has considerable knowledge in areas such as

cellular telephony and infrastructure, enterprise and database software and servers, semiconductors, disk drives and personal computers.

The Clients: The firm's top-class client base includes: Lockheed Martin; ICN; Ribapharm and Pergo.

Townsend and Townsend and Crew LLP

The Firm: Observers highlighted the IP team at this 170-attorney firm for its "*enthusiastic*" approach and "*remarkable success in IP litigation.*" Although the firm started off as a patent prosecution boutique it has now "*broadened its wings,*" developing into an outfit "*capable of dealing with even the most intricate*" IP counseling and litigation. For example, the team successfully defended Carsem and Carsem Semiconductor in an action in the ITC brought by rival Amkor Technology, and won an important patent infringement victory for a small Denver company. Other recent highlights include defending Align in a patent infringement case filed by Ormco, which claimed that the Invisalign system infringed four of its patents.

The Lawyers: The "*exceptional*" **Georg Seka** is the standout name here, according to market sources. He was recommended to researchers as an "*extremely influential patent attorney with great international clients.*" He enjoys a good name for prosecuting patent applications in the areas of electro-mechanics, optics, hydraulics and industrial developments, and has also built a profile for negotiating licenses, and litigating patent and trademark proceedings.

The Clients: Affymetrix; Altera; Bechtel; Boeing; Dolby Laboratories and NVIDIA.

Wilson Sonsini Goodrich & Rosati

See firm details p.302

The Firm: According to market sources, this is "*a dominant player*" in California's technology circles, with a "*significant presence in some of the most important IP cases.*" While its premier position in Northern California's corporate tech market has yet to translate to hegemony in related areas such as IP, its profile is undeniably on the rise. The team provided advice recently to Williams-Sonoma in connection with a "*widely talked about*" outsourcing deal with IBM. Other noncontentious work includes assisting Yodlee with negotiating a services agreement for its bill pay service with Bank One, and advising StorCard on a strategic alliance with Upgrade International. The team is no slouch, either, when it comes to litigation. Recent examples include success for Amkor Technology in a jury trial in San Jose. The plaintiff, Philips Semiconductors, was seeking to collect nearly $25 million in damages for allegedly defective semiconductor chip packages.

The Lawyers: **Ron Shulman** (see p.272) is popular with peers because he "*plays fair without compromising his clients' best interests.*" Clients themselves consider him a talented and energetic patent expert, while one even went so far as to describe him as "*among the best patent trial lawyers in the country.*" His focus is on defending companies against infringement claims. The "*energetic*" **Robert Feldman** (see p.252) was also recommended to researchers as an "*excellent*" lawyer who does "*a terrific job*" for his clients.

The Clients: Amkor Technology; Google; Williams-Sonoma; Echelon and Yodlee.

Band 4

Arnold & Porter LLP

See firm details p.478

The Firm: This growing international firm is well known for its exceptional expertise in antitrust and biotech work, two areas of "*quality and strength*" that mesh well with its substantial IP practice. A global team that now numbers over 100 attorneys is "*greatly esteemed*" by peers and clients alike for its expertise in a range of IP disputes and advisory work and its ability to handle "*large and complex*" matters. Obviously, many of these are in the core biotech field, where the firm boasts premier league international resources. However, clients are drawn from a variety of industries, including semiconductors, software and satellites.

The Lawyers: "*Straight-shooting IP specialist*" **Ronald Johnston** (see p.258) offers strategic counseling to software, computer, entertainment and Internet businesses on a broad spectrum of IP issues. His practice encompasses a wide range of expertise, which takes in trade secrets, copyright, patent, trademark, antitrust, and unfair competition law.

The Clients: The firm's client base includes such major names as Micron Technology; Intel and Xerox.

Dewey Ballantine LLP

See firm details p.1347

The Firm: This team earns high marks from interviewees for its "*sure handling of intricate IP matters.*" It boasts the depth of resources to handle not merely the usual patent, trademark, trade secrets and copyright cases, and other complex litigation before state and federal courts, but ITC investigations and disputes before foreign tribunals. A recent high-profile example was its role in the patent infringement case MicroUnity Systems Engineering v Intel et al, where it advised client Intel.

The Lawyers: "*Preeminent patent litigator*" **Jim Elacqua** (see p.251) is dedicated to IP law. He offers particular expertise in patent trials, typically involving complex technical issues, and is considered "*in his own right a leader in the field.*"

He has advised Intel on issues involving semiconductor circuit and process technology, and represented the company in disputes with the likes of Hyundai Electronics, Hughes Aircraft Corporation, Advanced Micro Devices, Texas Instruments and Cyrix.

The Clients: Intel; Biogen IDEC; Microsoft; 3M; Com21 and Nomai.

Farella Braun & Martel LLP

The Firm: The 22-attorney team at this impressive Californian outfit enters the tables this year following recommendations from clients and peers. Sources acknowledge that, with its high-quality client base and good mix of experience, this *"skilled IP group is growing into a real presence."* The team deals with complex trade secret, patent, trademark, copyright, antitrust, technology licensing and technology-related disputes. As well as serving clients from the semiconductor, software and biotech industries, the team has particular experience of acting for major clients in motion pictures, satellites, communications equipment, and, its specialty – wine making.

The Lawyers: John Cooper is the senior member of the firm's IP litigation group and the first point of contact for complex IP matters.

The Clients: California's premier firm for the wine industry (typical clients Robert Mondavi and Opus One Winery), Farella Braun also serves an impressive roster of hi-tech clients, including: Macromedia; Chiron; Verizon; Genentech; Dolby Laboratories; Disney; VISA International and VISA USA.

Gibson, Dunn & Crutcher LLP

See firm details p.285

The Firm: Interviewees note that this well-established firm *"has an excellent thing going"* in the area of IP and offers *"consistently fine advice to its clients."* One of its strongest suits is complex patent litigation. For example, the team has been heavily involved in the Columbia University patent litigation. This comprises eight separate lawsuits seeking to nullify patents covering fundamental technology for the manufacture of proteins used by almost the entire biotech industry. Here, the team is acting for Columbia in the actions instituted by Amgen and Immunex, and is co-counsel with Irell & Manella in the actions brought by Genentech, Biogen, Genetics Institute, Abbott Laboratories, Baxter and Wyeth. Another strong area is the expanding field of video gaming, where the team assists a top-class client base. Recent highlights include American Video Graphics v Electronic Arts et al, a multimillion-dollar case concerning alleged patent infringement related to hundreds of video game titles.

The Lawyers: According to clients, the *"consistently high-class"* **Wayne Barsky** (see p.244) *"likes to take on challenges and gets remarkable*

results." His success is said to be based on a combination of *"common sense"* and *"the instinct for when to fight and when to reason."*

The Clients: Electronic Arts; Johnson & Johnson; Columbia University; NEC; Vivendi Universal; Nortel; Cingular; Atari; Sega; LucasArts; Ubisoft and Activision.

Jones Day

See firm details p.485

The Firm: According to its clients, this IP team provides *"a personalized approach,"* delivered by lawyers with *"sincerity and integrity."* As one put it, the team is *"forthright and trustworthy and possesses real passion about the field."* The expanding group offers broad expertise, advising on a wide range of IP matters encompassing semiconductors, pharmaceuticals, polymers, biogenetics and medical devises, alongside the more straightforward patent prosecution and litigation, and trademark and copyright cases. Sources were impressed by the rapid growth of the firm as a major IP player, both nationally and internationally, particularly following the addition, a year ago, of about 100 IP lawyers from Pennie & Edmonds in New York, DC and Northern California.

The Lawyers: *"Hard-working"* **Vic Savikas** (see p.271) deals with a wide range of disputes. He was noted for his expertise in patent litigation. He also boasts expertise in data rights in government contracts and professional liability. The Menlo Park office recently added James Peterson from Burns, Doane, Swecker & Mathis, LLP, as part of a strategy of aggressive growth in the Bay Area.

The Clients: DIRECTV; Mag Instrument; 3D Systems; Genentech; Cedars-Sinai Medical Center; SaluMedica LLC; Easton Sports; SP Systems; Bird Barrier America and Jesco Imports.

O'Melveny & Myers LLP

See firm details p.294

The Firm: This well-established firm enters the IP listings this year following recommendations from clients for the *"consistently impressive service"* on offer. The team – which numbers about 60 lawyers – advises a variety of well-known clients on a range of IP issues, including copyright, patent and trademark disputes, trade secrets, Internet law and unfair competition. It also assists major companies with the IP aspects of their transactions. According to interviewees, the team enjoys a particularly good name for representing medical device manufacturers and life sciences companies in their licensing and regulatory work and litigation.

The Lawyers: Los Angeles-based **Mark Samuels** offers *"outstanding"* service, according to clients. He chairs the firm's IP and technology department and has expertise in a range of complex patent, trade secret and technology litigation for such clients as IBM, Motorola, Actel,

Sempra Energy and Gemstar-TV. Sources praise him as a *"high-quality attorney who does a first-rate job"* for his clients.

The Clients: Top Victory Electronics; Gemstar-TV Guide International; Sweda; Internet Machines and Actel.

Paul, Hastings, Janofsky & Walker LLP

See firm details p.297

The Firm: This sizable group advises on a wide variety of IP issues. It can call on a substantial range of resources, and boasts offices in many of the country's technology hotspots, as well as a growing international network. The team has a good record of pursuing patent cases for generics manufacturers. For example, it effectively handled the appeal for Gensia Sicor, in RCT and Bristol Myers-Squibb v Gensia Sicor, which concerned the photochemistry of platinum complexes on Bristol-Myers' cisplatin chemotherapy patent. It has also represented SICOR Pharmaceuticals in IP disputes against well-known pharmaceutical companies.

The Lawyers: John Benassi is a member of this *"talented and proactive"* team.

The Clients: The team recently acted for ICU Medical in ICU Medical v B Braun Medical. This multipatent infringement action concerned disposable medical systems for intravenous therapies. Other names on the firm's client roster include Gensia Sicor and Sicor Pharmaceuticals.

Simpson Thacher & Bartlett LLP

See firm details p.1370

The Firm: This *"gifted and hands-on"* team covers the range of IP advice, including patents, trademarks, copyright and trade secrets. It has been involved during the year in various high-profile cases, such as Intel v Patriot Scientific. This patent dispute began as a result of numerous separate lawsuits filed around the country, which alleged that every microprocessor running at over 120 MHz infringed the patents at issue. Other high-profile patent cases include NEC v Harris. Here the team advised NEC as plaintiff in a multi-patent dispute concerning microwave technology.

The Lawyers: Clients acknowledge the *"tremendous"* assistance they have received from **George Newcombe** (see p.265) and his team. He is particularly valued for his *"immense knowledge"* of IP law, and for the efforts he takes to *"understand our business perfectly."*

The Clients: The firm serves an impressive client base, including a number of financial institutions. Other major users of the IP group include Intel and NEC.

Other Notable Practitioners

According to clients, **Frederick Lorig** of Bright & Lorig is *"one of the premier IP lawyers around."*

He concentrates on patents, antitrust and trade secret work. "*Trade secrets guru*" **Jim Pooley** of Milbank, Tweed, Hadley & McCloy is another of the field's heavy hitters. He is also admired for his expertise in patent, copyright, and technology-related litigation, which he conducts in state and federal courts and before the ITC. At White & Case LLP, **Steven Hemminger** (see p.256) has an "*exceptional*" presence. He recently acted as lead counsel for TSMC, the world's largest pure-play semiconductor foundry, in an ITC investigation filed on its behalf against Chinese competitor SMIC. Other highlights include defending Cadence Design Systems/Quickturn against a claim by Mentor Graphics alleging trade secret misappropriation and patent infringement. Sources applauded "*extremely bright and effective*" **Laurence Pretty** (see p.268) of Hogan & Hartson LLP for his consistent high quality. His impressive client base includes such names as Beckman Coulter, Catalytic Solutions, MediaTek and Sichuan Changhong Electric. "*Trademark expert*" **Neil Smith** at Howard, Rice, Nemerovski, Canady, Falk & Rabkin also picked up enthusiastic recommendations from the market. **Andrew Bridges** (see p.246), who has moved from Wilson Sonsini Goodrich & Rosati to Winston & Strawn, was recommended to researchers as an "*excellent*" lawyer who does a "*terrific*" job for his clients.

IT & IT OUTSOURCING

California
Leading firms (IT & IT Outsourcing)

[1] LATHAM & WATKINS LLP *Los Angeles*

[2] COOLEY GODWARD LLP *Palo Alto*
DLA PIPER RUDNICK GRAY CARY US LLP *Palo Alto*
SHAW PITTMAN *Los Angeles*
WILSON SONSINI GOODRICH *San Francisco*

[3] ARNOLD & PORTER LLP *Los Angeles*
MORRISON & FOERSTER LLP *San Francisco*
O'MELVENY & MYERS LLP *Los Angeles*

Leading individuals (IT & IT Outsourcing)

[1] MUMMERY Dan *Latham & Watkins, Menlo Park*

[2] BELL Suzanne *Wilson Sonsini, Palo Alto*
KIMBALL George *Arnold & Porter, Los Angeles*
KLEIN Anthony *Latham & Watkins, Menlo Park*
MURPHY Michael *Shaw Pittman, Los Angeles*
NASH Glenn *Latham & Watkins, Menlo Park*
PETERS William *O'Melveny & Myers, Los Angeles*
RADCLIFFE Mark *DLA Piper Rudnick, Palo Alto*
SHOCKRO Michael *Latham & Watkins, Los Angeles*

[3] CLARK Kenneth *Wilson Sonsini, Palo Alto*
JAHN Paul *Morrison & Foerster, San Francisco*
MOORE Gary *Cooley Godward, Palo Alto*
VILLENEUVE Tom *Gunderson Dettmer, Menlo Park*

Firms and individuals are listed alphabetically in each band.

Band 1

Latham & Watkins LLP

The Firm: IT outsourcing lies at the heart of this practice's "*time-honored track record.*" Clients believe that more than a dozen IT outsourcing and technology specialists – among them "*a recently acquired bunch of superstars*" – have made this group "*plain untouchable in the field.*" The group advises on a broad array of IT matters and has dealt with cases concerning voice and data communications, LAN and WAN management, and e-commerce hosting. The team is now "*one of the preeminent IT outsourcing firms,*" commentators said. "*They worked hard at getting there and have finally achieved it.*" The department represented Hawaiian Telecom in a $250 million supply chain services transaction with Sprint. More-over it advised Gateway in the restructuring of a $400 million IT and business process outsourcing transaction with ACS. The group was also busy representing a Fortune 100 paper products company in an offshore development transaction in Eastern and Western Europe.

The Lawyers: The "*simply spectacular*" **Dan Mummery** is said to be "*the brightest crayon in the box.*" His recent work has included infrastructure deals, complex IT and business process outsourcing transactions, including outsourcing renegotiations and restructurings. Commentators dub him "*the don*" for complex ITO work, which involves infrastructure, ADM, end-user computing and network transactions among other issues. Furthermore he is conversant on HR, finance and accounting, procurement and claims processing. He recently gained a helping hand through colleague **Glenn Nash**, formerly with Cooley Godward, who continues to advise Yahoo! on complex technology transactions and is also highly regarded for his licensing expertise. Other interests involve issues related to the software, hardware, Internet and e-commerce sectors. "*Adept*" **Anthony Klein** is renowned statewide for his transactional, licensing and outsourcing expertise. He recently advised Copper Mountain Networks in a strategic agreement with Ericsson, and offered advice to Global Locate in the licensing of AGPS technology to Nextel. "*Fantastic*" **Michael Shockro** is "*a true hi-tech specialist with gusto.*" Rivals praise his "*leading skills*" as the head of the technology department. His practice entails development, licensing, strategic alliances and outsourcing.

The Clients: American Express; AT&T; BellSouth; BT; Cable & Wireless; ChevronTexaco; DuPont; Entergy; Gateway; GM; Levi Strauss; Lucent Technologies; McGraw-Hill; Miller Brewing Company; Ryder; Tenet Healthcare; United Airlines; UnitedHealthcare; WellPoint Health Networks; Adobe Systems; Blue Martini Software; Epson America; Openwave Systems and Sun Microsystems.

Band 2

Cooley Godward LLP

The Firm: The group continues "*to be a major player*" in the technology area despite the loss of some significant IT partners. Clients praise the "*consistent high quality*" and commend the "*wonderful talent and dexterity*" of its attorneys. Even rivals felt "*its presence is still one of the most impressive*" in the technology arena. The "*outstandingly thorough*" team deals with a broad array of IT work. Representing Applied Materials, a supplier of semiconductor equipment and services, the group helped orchestrate a considerable transaction with Brooks Automation. The group was also involved in the Quest Software acquisition of Aelita Software.

The Lawyers: "*Exceptional*" **Gary Moore** is well versed in technology transactions. Also demonstrating proficiency in IP, he is primarily known for patent work, licensing and IT work. Rivals said he lends "*high integrity*" to the negotiation process.

The Clients: Applied Materials; Quest Software; Synopsys; Time Warner; Borland Software; eBay; Honeywell; NVIDIA; PeopleSoft; Siebel Systems and Yahoo!

DLA Piper Rudnick Gray Cary US LLP

See firm details p.765

The Firm: Commentators believe that Gray Cary's recent alliance with Piper Rudnick and DLA has brought "*immense depth and resources*" to its technology team. Clients felt it is now "*a different animal*" and will be able to "*compete against the very best.*" A compact team offers expertise in IP, technology and life sciences, and was also noted for its information service procurement work. It advises private and public companies, ranging from Fortune 500 companies to startups. With its newly gained strength, the group is viewed as a major contender by "*stretching its wings to the international market.*"

The Lawyers: "*Licensing guru*" **Mark Radcliffe** (see p.269) is "*a name on everybody's lips*" when it comes to prominent IT work, clients say. His practice encompasses areas such as software licensing, trademark and finance.

The Clients: R&D Pipeline; Sony; Mobileway; PortalPlayer; Eastman Chemical Company and NEC.

Shaw Pittman
See firm details p.490

The Firm: This firm has recently closed its LA office to better focus on the Northern California market from its Palo Alto office. It offers "*extensive technical expertise*" in IT and related fields. The team is further enhanced by an "*internationally distinguished*" global sourcing and technology practice out of DC. Clients remain faithful to the firm's "*great strength in breadth.*" Sources also appreciate the team's ability to "*effectively see to the heart of the matter.*" At time of press, the firm announced its merger with Pillsbury Winthrop LLP to form Pillsbury Winthrop Shaw Pittman.

The Lawyers: "*Technically outstanding*" **Michael Murphy** (see p.264) focuses on intricate technology transactions and business process outsourcing projects. Clients praise this "*articulate*" practitioner and commend his "*awe-inspiring uniformity.*" He received plaudits for his transactional experience, which covers IT outsourcing, joint ventures, strategic alliances and system licensing.

The Clients: The firm takes its cue from clients in a wide variety of industries – including financial services, life sciences, telecom and utilities. It has also advised government entities on IT-related issues.

Wilson Sonsini Goodrich & Rosati
See firm details p.302

The Firm: Primarily associated with its corporate fortitude, the group sustains a reputation as "*a go-to firm for multifaceted technology work.*" The practice entails areas such as IT outsourcing, business process outsourcing (BPO), software licensing and medical technology. In addition, its ITO practice has grown significantly and can now be considered a "*crucial contender for the big jobs,*" commentators said.

The Lawyers: Described as "*smart as a whip,*" **Suzanne Bell** (see p.244) is "*a clear*" contender for pure IT work. She handles IT and IP transactions "*professionally,*" with an emphasis on work related to outsourcing and strategic alliances. Her areas of expertise involve software, hardware, life sciences, semiconductor and

Internet companies. **Kenneth Clark** (see p.248), managing partner of the firm's technology transactions practice, specializes in life sciences and IT industries. This greatly esteemed player is particularly recognized for his "*amazing biotech capabilities.*"

The Clients: Notable outsourcing clients include Gateway, Williams-Sonoma, Infosys and the Sacramento Municipal Utility District.

Band 3

Arnold & Porter LLP
See firm details p.478

The Firm: Rivals commended this firm as "*a noteworthy player on the technology scene.*" Its "*exemplary lawyers offer superior-quality advice*" in areas like IT, BPO, licensing, technology procurements and M&A. In a recent case the team advised Herbalife, the maker of dietary supplements, concerning termination of existing relationships and new outsourcing initiatives for e-commerce distribution and other strategic systems.

The Lawyers: **George Kimball** (see p.260) is renowned for his "*excellent ties*" in IP, technology and outsourcing. He has represented key corporations as well as suppliers of IT and e-commerce in the negotiation of complicated outsourcing arrangements. Recent matters include the renegotiation of Chiron Corporation's long-term IT services contract with IBM.

The Clients: Advising a major European government, the group marshaled the outsourcing of its welfare benefits system. Moreover it negotiated a long-term contract to provide comprehensive IT services for a teaching hospital. It also renegotiated multi-year contracts to provide comprehensive IT services involving the forest products, insurance, and pharmaceutical sectors among others.

Morrison & Foerster LLP
See firm details p.293

The Firm: This team regularly "*plays with the big boys,*" flourishing in a range of complex matters, clients said. It recently advised Fujitsu in its agreement with Cisco Systems for the joint development of operating system software for high-speed routers. In a different matter it offered counsel to Fujitsu concerning its agree-

ments to jointly develop and deliver future-generation Solaris and SPARC-based systems. This group of "*effective and thorough practitioners*" also advised Novell with respect to open source software issues and separately participated in Bank One's outsourcing arrangements with Total System Services.

The Lawyers: "*Thoughtful and responsive*" **Paul Jahn** (see p.258) particularly impressed clients by linking IP and IT expertise. "*He carries a wise head on young shoulders,*" they said. He recently advised Hitachi on its $2.05 billion deal to combine its hard disk drive operations with those of IBM; the transaction involves certain technology transfer, licensing and outsourcing issues.

The Clients: Novell; EchoStar; Bank One; Nikon; Chiron; Tanox; Hitachi; AIG Technologies; Hertz and Ask Jeeves.

O'Melveny & Myers LLP
See firm details p.294

The Firm: This firm is perceived as having progressed beyond "*a one-man show,*" analysts said, offering "*an outstanding group of highly qualified IT specialists.*" The group is particularly known for its high-profile representation of Toyota Financial Services. Advising a Fortune 500 telecom services company, the team negotiated a $300 million, ten-year information technology outsourcing agreement with EDS.

The Lawyers: Standing out is "*energetic*" **William Peters**, who possesses an "*all-embracing familiarity*" of legal and business issues relating to complex technology and outsourcing matters. Clients agree that this ITO specialist "*has turned things around*" for the firm, thanks to his "*stamina and efficiency.*"

The Clients: The team has advised clients in the telecom, oil and gas, financial services, retail, logistics, distribution, aerospace and pharmaceutical industries.

Other Notable Practitioners

"*Core technology aficionado*" **Tom Villeneuve** of Gunderson Dettmer Stough Villeneuve Franklin & Hachigian impressed peers with "*superb*" representation of high-profile startup companies. This IT expert is said to offer "*effective and comprehensive*" counsel to clients such as Equinix, ActionPoint, Selectica and Ariba.

LITIGATION

GENERAL COMMERCIAL

California
Leading firms
(Litigation: General Commercial)

1 GIBSON, DUNN & CRUTCHER LLP *Los Angeles*
  KEKER & VAN NEST LLP *San Francisco*
  MORRISON & FOERSTER LLP *San Francisco*
  MUNGER, TOLLES & OLSON LLP *Los Angeles*
  O'MELVENY & MYERS LLP *Los Angeles*

2 ALSCHULER GROSSMAN STEIN *Santa Monica*
  COOLEY GODWARD LLP *Palo Alto*
  FARELLA BRAUN & MARTEL LLP *San Francisco*
  HELLER EHRMAN WHITE *Los Angeles*
  HENNIGAN, BENNETT *Los Angeles*
  IRELL & MANELLA LLP *Los Angeles*
  JONES DAY *Los Angeles; San Francisco*
  LATHAM & WATKINS LLP *Los Angeles*
  LERACH COUGHLIN STOIA GELLER *San Diego*
  QUINN EMANUEL URQUHART OLIVER *Los Angeles*

3 ARNOLD & PORTER LLP *Los Angeles*
  BINGHAM MCCUTCHEN LLP *San Francisco*
  BLECHER & COLLINS *Los Angeles*
  COTCHETT, PITRE, SIMON *Burlingame*
  HOWREY SIMON ARNOLD & WHITE *Los Angeles*
  SKADDEN, ARPS, SLATE, MEAGHER *San Francisco*
  SULLIVAN & CROMWELL LLP *Los Angeles*
  WILSON SONSINI GOODRICH & ROSATI *Palo Alto*

Firms are listed alphabetically in each band.

Gibson, Dunn & Crutcher LLP

See firm details p.285

The Firm: Clients approve of the "*deep bench strength*" of this group, which ensures that it is "*always well prepared.*" A group of approximately 200 litigators acts from bases in LA, Orange County and San Francisco, and is historically regarded as among the state's leading litigation practices. Its lawyers have appeared in a number of high-profile litigations this year, including the representation of Wal-Mart in a pending appeal to the Ninth Circuit Court of Appeals, certifying one of the largest employment classes in the USA to date. Other highlights include obtaining the dismissal of three nationwide classes for DaimlerChrysler. The group's caseload also encompasses environmental litigation, antitrust, securities, IP and professional malpractice work. Sources contend that this continues to be "*a premier litigation practice.*"

The Lawyers: **Robert Cooper** (see p.249) remains a high-profile figure in the group. Sources commend his "*willingness to take cases to trial*" and the "*quality of his experience in large, complex cases.*" Particularly recognized for his antitrust expertise, Cooper's activity extends to commercial litigation, as can be seen from his involvement as trial counsel on behalf of Callaway Golf Company. Leading the white-collar crime side of the practice, **Thomas Holliday** (see p.257) has a name as "*a terrific guy who is able to see the big picture.*" As cochair of the busi-

ness crimes and investigations practice group, he has seen an upswing in education-related investigations at the practice, as well as a number of public corruption matters.

The Clients: PwC; Tenet Healthcare Corporation; American Airlines; Hewlett-Packard; Intel; Sempra Energy; Lockheed Martin; Morgan Stanley and KPMG.

Keker & Van Nest LLP

See firm details p.290

The Firm: This 50-strong trial boutique is best known for its high-profile white-collar criminal practice, but is just as "*formidable*" in the civil arena, where the team specializes in complex civil cases, which often have a criminal aspect to them. On the civil side, the team has been involved in malpractice, securities, contract, employment and products liability disputes. Highlights include defending class actions against American Honda Finance Corporation, LSI Logic, AT&T Wireless and General Nutrition Corporation. In criminal matters, involvement has ranged from healthcare cases to foreign corrupt practices matters and criminal investigations. The group defended former CSFB investment banker Frank Quattrone, where the first trial resulted in a hung jury, and the second resulted in conviction.

The Lawyers: "*Highly sought-after*" **John Keker** (see p.259) is the central figure at the firm. Widely described as a "*world-class trial lawyer*" with a national reputation, he was one of the lead partners defending Andrew Fastow, the former CFO of Enron Corp, in connection with a 108-count indictment alleging that he organized a $68 billion fraud leading to Enron's bankruptcy. The group negotiated a plea agreement with a ten-year sentence for Fastow. Interviewees say Keker possesses "*every attribute you want in a criminal advocate.*" **Robert Van Nest** (see p.276) maintains a reputation as a skilled attorney in civil matters. His caseload includes complex business litigation and white-collar work and he often undertakes simultaneous litigation involving civil, criminal and administrative proceedings. Van Nest recently defended a Japanese automaker in class action and multidistrict litigation involving more than one hundred automobile dealerships and a class of over 1000 dealers, involving RICO, fraud and commercial bribery claims.

The Clients: Clients include American Honda Motor, AT&T Wireless, USI Logic, General Nutrition Corporation, and Hellman & Friedman.

Morrison & Foerster LLP

See firm details p.293

The Firm: Practitioners here "*take the time to learn the issues and become experts, and then look at all possible approaches,*" say enthusiastic

clients. The firm's attorneys have acted on many prominent litigation matters, where they have proved themselves to be "*practical, efficient and service-oriented*" across a range of areas. The 307-lawyer practice commands experience in securities, white-collar, antitrust, financial services and consumer class action litigation. The firm successfully represented SmithKline Beecham at the California Supreme Court in a case concerning warnings used on nicotine replacement gums and patches. The court unanimously held that California could not enforce its product labeling law over FDA labeling requirements in instances where the FDA concludes that the state's warning requirements could potentially mislead consumers. The group also successfully defended Mervyn's against allegations that its merchandise display practices were unlawful under the ADA and violated the Unfair Competition law and Business & Professions Code.

The Lawyers: "*Amazing*" **James Brosnahan** (see p.247) elicits "*terrific respect*" from peers. He divides his trial practice between civil and criminal cases, and has been active in a range of high-profile matters. Sources find him "*extremely effective in front of a jury.*" **Melvin Goldman** (see p.253) "*does a great job*" on securities litigation and antitrust cases. He has considerable experience in the defense of security-accounting class actions and derivative cases, in addition to governmental investigations and accounting and financial reporting claims. Litigation chair **Lori Schechter** (see p.271) impresses clients with her ability to "*have one hundred ideas at the same time.*" Her practice encompasses consumer litigation and antitrust work. She recently acted for LensCrafters and other defendants in a constitutional challenge to Californian laws concerning the sale of eyewear, and in a consumer class action alleging unfair competition. Cochair of the securities litigation group, **Jordan Eth** (see p.251) earns plaudits for his courtroom poise. Interviewees commend his "*crisp and to-the-point*" manner, and his ability to be "*aggressive in a thoughtful way.*" His practice includes acting for public companies and their officers and directors in securities class actions, SEC investigations and derivative suits. He provided counsel in Jacobs v Yang in which a derivative suit against Yahoo! officers was dismissed.

The Clients: GlaxoSmithKline; UPS; Chiron; Oracle; Yahoo! and El Paso.

Munger, Tolles & Olson LLP

The Firm: Housing some of the "*best trial lawyers*" in the state, this 185-strong firm boasts 126 "*accomplished*" members of its nationally renowned litigation practice. One rival observed "*it's hard to pinpoint names when there are so many excellent litigators.*" The group focuses

California
Leading individuals
(Litigation: General Commercial)

1 BRIAN Brad *Munger Tolles*, Los Angeles
GROSSMAN Marshall *Alschuler Grossman*, Santa Monica
KEKER John *Keker & Van Nest*, San Francisco

2 BROSNAHAN James *Morrison*, San Francisco
COOPER Robert *Gibson Dunn*, Los Angeles
COTCHETT Joseph *Cotchett Pitre*, Burlingame
HENNIGAN J Michael *Hennigan Bennett*, Los Angeles
LERACH William *Lerach Coughlin*, San Diego
NEAL Steve *Cooley Godward*, Palo Alto
NOLAN Thomas *Skadden Arps*, Los Angeles
OLSON Ronald *Munger Tolles*, Los Angeles
POPOFSKY Laurence *Heller Ehrman*, San Francisco
QUINN John *Quinn Emanuel*, Los Angeles
SPIEGEL John *Munger Tolles*, Los Angeles
YOUNG Douglas *Farella Braun*, San Francisco

3 ARONSON Seth *O'Melveny & Myers*, Los Angeles
BLECHER Maxwell *Blecher & Collins*, Los Angeles
FELDMAN Boris *Wilson Sonsini*, Palo Alto
FELDMAN Larry *Kaye Scholer*, Los Angeles
GOLDMAN Melvin *Morrison & Foerster*, San Francisco
PETROCELLI Daniel *O'Melveny & Myers*, Los Angeles
QUINN John *Arnold & Porter*, Los Angeles
SACKS Robert *Sullivan & Cromwell*, Los Angeles
URQUHART A William *Quinn Emanuel*, Los Angeles

4 BALABANIAN David *Bingham McCutchen*, San Francisco
BOMSE Stephen *Heller Ehrman*, San Francisco
BRODY Sara *Heller Ehrman*, San Francisco
COOK Philip *Jones Day*, Los Angeles
CRIST Paul *Jones Day*, San Francisco
ETH Jordan *Morrison & Foerster*, San Francisco
FELDMAN Robert *Wilson Sonsini*, Palo Alto
MCKNIGHT Frederick *Jones Day*, Los Angeles
RUBY Allen *Ruby & Schofield*, San José
RUTHBERG Miles *Latham & Watkins*, Los Angeles
SCHECHTER Lori *Morrison & Foerster*, San Francisco
SIEGEL David *Irell & Manella*, Los Angeles
VAN NEST Robert *Keker & Van Nest*, San Francisco
VANYO Bruce *Wilson Sonsini*, Palo Alto

Individuals are listed alphabetically in each band.

principally on defending large commercial cases spanning securities, antitrust, environment and professional malpractice suits. Attorneys also undertake occasional plaintiff work. Highlights include acting for Time Warner and several of its present and former directors and officers in connection with four securities fraud lawsuits arising from Time Warner's merger with America Online. The merger was the largest in American corporate history, and the plaintiffs collectively seek more than $1 billion in damages.

The Lawyers: "*If I were in trouble and needed a great lawyer, I'd probably call him,*" claimed one rival of **Brad Brian**. He splits his practice between major civil litigation, white-collar criminal defense and internal investigations. Researchers were told he is a "*tenacious, fair and vigorous advocate*" in both criminal and civil matters. Brian

currently acts as lead counsel for Boeing in a dispute with Lockheed Martin entailing allegations that Boeing employees stole and illegally used thousands of Lockheed's confidential trade secrets in order to outbid Lockheed on a multibillion Air Force contract. Other matters include representation of GE in a voluntary disclosure to and subsequent investigation by the DOJ and the SEC concerning alleged Foreign Corrupt Practice Act violations relating to GE's planned merger with InVision. The DOJ agreed not to prosecute InVision in exchange for the payment of a monetary fine and an agreement to integrate InVision into GE's compliance program. "*Everyone mentions*" **Ronald Olson**, a prominent figure in commercial litigation, antitrust, securities, commercial contracts and business law. Olsen also counsels clients on corporate governance matters. He is acting for Coca-Cola in shareholder class actions, pending derivative litigation, and associated criminal and regulatory investigations of allegations that the company engaged in channel-stuffing, improper earnings management and asset impairment write-offs. **John Spiegel** is "*in high demand*" for complex civil and securities class actions, say commentators. Clients admire his "*terrific integrity,*" while others call him "*an excellent trial lawyer and litigator*" visible in high-stakes matters. Spiegel obtained dismissals of securities class actions and derivatives law suits against Northrop Grumman and its board of directors in connection with a proposed merger with Lockheed Martin.

The Clients: Abbott Laboratories; Allstate Insurance; AXA Financial; Berkshire Hathaway; Charles Schwab; Delta Airlines; Disney; Edison International; Koch Industries; Mattel; Merrill Lynch; MGM; Mitsubishi; Occidental Petroleum; PETsMART; Philip Morris; Purdue Pharma; Rambus; Shell; Sun America; UBS Paine Webber; Universal Studios; Warner Bros. and Verizon.

O'Melveny & Myers LLP

See firm details p.294

The Firm: Peers uniformly describe this "*impeccable*" group as among the strongest in the state for its general litigation practice. Clients contend it has produced "*some of the best trial lawyers we've ever used,*" and its trial expertise is evident in the firm's recent string of litigation victories. The firm continues to represent ExxonMobil on litigation arising from the Exxon Valdez oil spill. The team recently won a defense verdict rejecting the plaintiffs' claim that ExxonMobil owed Alaskan communities over $30 million in damages and interest for municipal services and ancillary support costs purportedly incurred during the cleanup. The team also obtained dismissals of federal court and California state court cases against Watson Pharmaceuticals involving a securities class action and shareholder derivative action. On the white-collar

crime side, the group is acting on behalf of Jeffrey Skilling, former CEO of Enron.

The Lawyers: "*Top performer*" **Seth Aronson** is well known in the marketplace for his securities class action practice. Chair of the securities litigation practice group, he also defends corporations, and their directors and professionals in shareholder derivative actions, unfair competition, and consumer class actions, as well as RICO and various M&A claims. He is currently defending Fannie Mae against securities class actions, derivative class actions and related lawsuits connected with the company's shareholder litigation. "*Tenacious*" **Daniel Petrocelli** gets "*first-class results*" for clients. Recommended for his past involvement in high-profile cases, Petrocelli is particularly active on behalf of the entertainment industry. "*Strong, calm and smart,*" **Daniel Bookin** "*really understands how a courtroom works.*" Bookin wins plaudits for his criminal practice and related civil work. His practice has encompassed securities matters and other financial cases. Chair of the firm's global enforcement and criminal defense group, **James Asperger** ranks among the team's go-to lawyers for criminal defense work. His practice also includes internal corporate investigations, and civil RICO and fraud actions. Younger attorney **Mark Holscher** has an impressive profile representing companies and individuals in federal and state criminal and regulatory investigations.

The Clients: Unocal; Advanced Marketing Services; Disney; Guess and Skechers.

Alschuler Grossman Stein & Kahan LLP

See firm details p.280

The Firm: A group whose "*sensitivity to client objectives,*" combined with its cooperative approach to working with in-house counsel, wins fans in the marketplace. The 80-strong team focuses on professional liability defense, insurance, IP, entertainment, securities fraud, defamation and real estate litigation. Current representations include acting as co-counsel to Deloitte in connection with the Adelphia securities litigation now pending in Pennsylvania. The group is also representing the California Department of Insurance and the Insurance Commissioner with regard to a number of significant matters, including the Commissioner's objections to the merger between WellPoint and Anthem. Practitioners also appeared before the US Supreme Court in a case challenging the constitutionality of a California law requiring Holocaust-era insurance companies to disclose policyholders as a condition to doing business in California.

The Lawyers: "*Charismatic*" **Marshall Grossman** (see p.255) is the group's most high-profile name in commercial litigation, and an "*incredible generator of business*" for the team. He is defending Blockbuster against a $100 million

224 All quotes in the text are from interviews with clients and competitors.

CHAMBERS USA 2005

California
Leading firms
(Litigation: White-Collar Crime & Government Investigations)

1
BECK, DE CORSO, DALY, KREINDLER *Los Angeles*
BIRD, MARELLA, BOXER & WOLPERT *Los Angeles*
CLARENCE SNELL & DYER LLP *San Francisco*
LIGHTFOOT, VANDEVELDE, SADOWSKY *Los Angeles*
STEVENS & O'CONNELL LLP *Sacramento*
SWANSON & MCNAMARA LLP *San Francisco*
TOPEL & GOODMAN PC *San Francisco*

Leading individuals
(Litigation: White-Collar Crime & Government Investigations)

1
ARGUEDAS Cristina *Arguedas Cassman, Emeryville*
BECK Mark *Beck De Corso, Los Angeles*
BOOKIN Daniel *O'Melveny & Myers, San Francisco*
BRIAN Brad *Munger Tolles, Los Angeles*
BROSNAHAN James *Morrison, San Francisco*
GREENBERG Gordon *McDermott Will, Los Angeles*
HANDZLIK Jan *Howrey Simon, Los Angeles*
HENNIGAN Brian *Irell & Manella, Los Angeles*
HOLLIDAY Thomas *Gibson Dunn, Los Angeles*
KEKER John *Keker & Van Nest, San Francisco*
LEVINE Janet *Lightfoot Vandevelde, Los Angeles*
MARELLA Vincent *Bird Marella, Los Angeles*
O'CONNELL George *Stevens & O'Connell, Sacramento*
O'NEILL Brian *Jones Day, Los Angeles*
RUBY Allen *Ruby & Schofield, San José*
STEVENS Charles *Stevens & O'Connell, Sacramento*
SUN Brian *Jones Day, Los Angeles*
VANDEVELDE John *Lightfoot Vandevelde, Los Angeles*

2
ASPERGER James *O'Melveny & Myers, Los Angeles*
BIRD Terry *Bird Marella, Los Angeles*
BREWER Jr Robert *McKenna Long, San Diego*
BROWN Walt *Orrick Herrington, San Francisco*
CLARENCE Nanci *Clarence Snell, San Francisco*
CORBIN Robert *Corbin & Fitzgerald, Los Angeles*
GOODMAN William *Topel & Goodman, San Francisco*
HOLSCHER Mark *O'Melveny & Myers, Los Angeles*
LIGHTFOOT Michael *Lightfoot Vandevelde, Los Angeles*
LINCENBERG Gary *Bird Marella, Los Angeles*
MARMARO Richard *Proskauer Rose, Los Angeles*
MCNAMARA Mary *Swanson, San Francisco*
MILLER Stephen *Howrey Simon, Los Angeles*
NESSIM Ronald *Bird Marella, Los Angeles*
POTTER John *Covington & Burling, San Francisco*
YOUNG Douglas *Farella Braun, San Francisco*

Firms and individuals are listed alphabetically in each band.

claim brought by Disney of insufficient payment under a revenue-sharing agreement entailing the sale of Disney videos to Blockbuster.
The Clients: Johnson & Johnson; NEC; CAN; Titan Corporation; Kinkade; Arthur Andersen; Quanta; Acer; BenQ and Foxconn Electronics.

Cooley Godward LLP
The Firm: The litigation practice of this major California player is distinguished in the marketplace for its strength in securities and technology-related litigation. Rivals say the firm handles "*as many high-profile business cases as any in California.*"
The Lawyers: "*A trial lawyer of extraordinary breadth,*" **Steve Neal** is a name held in high regard by market commentators, who rate him as "*a phenomenal lawyer.*" Even rivals admire this "*unbelievably skillful*" attorney's low-key courtroom manner. "*He never breaks a sweat,*" said one, "*and he already knows how the game will end as soon as it opens.*" In addition to his roles as chairman and CEO of the firm, Neal has tried a range of civil and criminal cases for corporations, individuals, audit committees and special committees of boards. He is among "*the few people I would go to if everything depended on it,*" remarked one interviewee.

Farella Braun & Martel LLP
The Firm: Clients feel that this smaller firm "*excels in every aspect of litigation.*" White-collar and regulatory matters are an area of considerable activity for the team, and the group is said to be "*superb*" in its handling of both. Other specialties include the defense of securities class actions, IP-related matters and environmental litigation. Clients appreciate the group's "*common-sense approach to litigation,*" and willingness to "*put the client's interests over everything else.*" Highlights have included acting as part of the trial team that successfully defended GE against a groundwater pollution case brought by the State of New Mexico in the federal court. Team members also represented the City and County of San Francisco in a federal case against the contractor for the new international terminal at San Francisco Airport. The case concerned allegations of false claims of costs in the construction of the terminal and non-compliance with minority hiring requirements. The team's trial experience and "*intellectual firepower*" instills confidence in clients, who vouch for the group's ability to try significant cases.
The Lawyers: Douglas Young is a rare "*gentleman trial lawyer*" who "*doesn't take anything for granted,*" say interviewees. Clients applaud his "*high integrity*" and "*thoughtful and detailed*" approach to cases. The key figure of the firm's white-collar and regulatory defense practice, Young acts in complex civil trials and appeals and IP litigation. His experience and sound judgment in these areas have earned him his reputation as "*a dean of the San Francisco Bar.*" Young defended the former controller and acting CFO of McKesson Corporation in multiple class action securities fraud cases, and in investigations by the SEC and the DOJ.
The Clients: GE; FMC; Verizon Wireless; Yahoo!; Chiron and BHP Petroleum.

Heller Ehrman White & McAuliffe LLP
See firm details p.288
The Firm: An "*absolutely outstanding*" group for prominent IP and antitrust litigation, the firm is considered a key player in the San Francisco marketplace. In addition to these strengths, the practice also displays particular expertise in unfair competition matters, securities litigation, and the representation of policyholders in insurance coverage cases. The team is acting for Deloitte in connection with the Parmalat collapse.
The Lawyers: Prominent in the antitrust field, **Stephen Bomse** is an active force in commercial litigation on behalf of the Republic of the Philippines, for whom he successfully asserted the sovereign immunity of the Republic from US litigation. Also popular for antitrust work, **Laurence Popofsky** is an established litigator, active in securities fraud and IP matters. **Sara Brody** joins the group this year from Clifford Chance. Peers view her as one of the team's "*next generation of securities litigators.*" Her practice centers on defending issuers, officers, directors, underwriters and venture capital firms in shareholder class actions and derivative litigation.
The Clients: Philip Morris; Sony Electronics; Yahoo!; Ernst & Young; PwC; Deloitte and State Farm Insurance.

Hennigan, Bennett & Dorman LLP
See firm details p.289
The Firm: This "*first-class*" trial practice is well regarded for its expertise in a broad range of matters, encompassing complex corporate litigation, breach of fiduciary duty, bankruptcy and IT litigation, as well as fraud work. Interviewees are confident that "*any of the attorneys could try any suit and any client would be fantastically represented.*" The group undertakes both plaintiff and defense work. The firm obtained a $52 million jury verdict against CIBC World Markets on behalf of three investment fund clients in connection with common law and securities claims arising from Renaissance Cosmetics' bankruptcy. The team will also be acting for a plaintiff in a pending multibillion-dollar class action against State Farm concerning failure to pay dividends.
The Lawyers: Clients and peers endorse **Michael Hennigan** (see p.256) as a "*savvy trial lawyer*" with a reputation for complex litigation. Hennigan acts for both plaintiffs and defendants.
The Clients: Archdiocese of LA; Sempra Energy Company; Trust Company of the West; Rabobank; Kazaa; Oaktree Financial Services; Aegon Insurance and AIG.

Irell & Manella LLP
The Firm: A highly esteemed litigation practice, the team is considered to have a "*terrific hi-tech practice*" in keeping with its well-documented

strength in IP litigation. The group also handles securities, entertainment, real estate and property disputes as part of its broad commercial litigation offering. Highlights include the successful representation of City of Hope National Medical Center in obtaining a jury verdict of more than $500 million against Genentech. The team also defended Idealab in a case brought by venture capital investors who attempted to compel its dissolution and a distribution of its assets.

The Lawyers: Managing partner **David Siegel** impresses sources with his securities litigation practice. He has been active defending both corporations and individual company directors and officers against securities class and stockholder claims. SEC enforcement proceedings and contentious corporate takeovers also feature heavily in his caseload. "*Great in negotiations*" **Brian Hennigan** is also a "*formidable force in the courtroom*" where he is seen to be popular with both judges and juries. A white-collar criminal defense specialist, Hennigan is visible in criminal and civil trials, fraud and abuse claims, and internal corporate investigations. Market observers praise him as a "*warm, trustworthy and capable*" practitioner. "*He'd be on every list of people to hire when you're in trouble,*" say sources.

The Clients: The firm advises Viacom and its affiliates; Disney; Hewlett-Packard and Immersion Corporation.

Jones Day
See firm details p.485

The Firm: This "*gigantic,*" 164-strong team wins enthusiastic praise from clients, who deem it "*extremely focused and creative,*" and possessed of "*bright, diligent and effective attorneys.*" The team's willingness to "*dedicate itself totally*" to client needs also earns plaudits. The group offers a full complement of litigation services, with particular concentration in IP, construction, antitrust, products liability litigation and consumer class actions. Clients particularly emphasized the group's expertise in multiparty litigation. Recent successes have included advising IBM in a workplace contamination suit brought on behalf of former IBM employees. The team also acted for 3D Systems in patent litigation cases resulting in a royalty-bearing settlement from the opposing party. On the white-collar side the team has bolstered its practice with the recruitment of a group of lawyers from O'Neill, Lysaght & Sun.

The Lawyers: "*Low-key*" **Paul Crist** (see p.249) is "*the most doggedly determined lawyer you'll ever find,*" with "*a grasp of the facts in a way that few lawyers have,*" according to his clients. He serves as national coordinating counsel for RJ Reynolds on most of its smoking and health cases throughout the USA, and has acted in the cases of Scarlett v Pneumo Abex and Major v Raybestos Manhattan, et al. "*Top-notch litigator*" **Frederick McKnight** (see p.263) is partner-in-

charge of the Los Angeles office. Clients consider him a "*savvy and persuasive*" practitioner. He acted in Tellez et al v Dole Food Company, et al. Clients also singled out "*forthright, honest and trustworthy*" **Philip Cook** (see p.248) for commendation. Researchers were told that Cook's "*articulate and intelligent*" approach, coupled with "*a genuine passion for his work,*" enable him to "*elicit widespread support*" in complicated cases. He acted for the minority shareholder clients in a corporate governance lawsuit which resulted in a million-dollar-plus jury verdict for breach of fiduciary duty. **Brian O'Neill** (see p.266) has substantial criminal experience and "*considerable talent in litigation,*" say sources. In People v Isaac Zaharoni, he acted in the criminal prosecution of a construction contractor for alleged unlawful political contributions. A "*master of negotiations,*" **Brian Sun** (see p.275) is widely admired for his ability to "*keep people focused towards a resolution.*" He acted in United States v Rutledge, a federal tax fraud prosecution of a union leader in Hawaii.

The Clients: Experian Information Solutions; RJ Reynolds Tobacco; Parker Hannifin; DIRECTV; County of Los Angeles; Countrywide Financial; Kaiser Cement & Gypsum; Cole National; SBC; Nokia; Mellon Bank; Gap; Philippine Airlines; Helm Financial; Renault & Handley and ChevronTexaco.

Latham & Watkins LLP

The Firm: Viewed as "*an outstanding firm*" by the California market, the 250-strong group wins approval for its strong securities litigation practice. Acting from offices around California, the team also actively engages in professional liability, IP, antitrust, products liability and mass tort cases and maintains a healthy white-collar practice. The firm acted for Arthur Andersen in civil cases resulting from the collapse of Enron, much of which involved defending the company in consolidated federal securities cases. The team also represented Raychem (now Tyco Electronics) in winning a victory in the appeal of Raychem v Bourns. The matter entailed two consolidated disputes involving both IP and antitrust law.

The Lawyers: Former litigation group global chair, **Miles Ruthberg** practices in the executive and professional liability area and also represents issuers, officers and directors in securities-related civil matters and investigations. Representation of global accounting firms is a key focus for the group and Ruthberg is currently leading the team acting for Ernst & Young in connection with opinions given relating to The Williams Company's 2000 and 2001 year-end financial statements. Ernst & Young is being sued in two putative class actions brought by purchasers of stock and debt issued by The Williams Company and its former subsidiary Williams Communications Group.

The Clients: Beverley Enterprises; Tenet Healthcare; Genentech; Ford; TiVo; National Football League; Philip Morris and Safeway.

Lerach Coughlin Stoia Geller Rudman & Robbins LLP

The Firm: "*At the very top of the game in plaintiff securities matters,*" the group is credited with a "*huge market share*" in this field. The team has taken a leading role in many complex and high-profile cases. Areas of emphasis include securities, consumer, insurance, healthcare, human rights, employment discrimination and antitrust class actions.

The Lawyers: Following the firm's split with Milberg Weiss, the group is home to "*powerful*" class action litigator **William Lerach** who has "*done a magnificent job of building the practice.*" Renowned for his creativity and tenacity, Lerach can be counted on to "*raise hell and keep other firms busy.*" He acts on behalf of numerous public and multiemployer pension funds in corporate securities matters.

The Clients: The firm advises public funds, multiemployer clients and institutional investors. Examples include: California Public Employees' Retirement System, Southern California Lathing Industry Pension Fund and Standard Life Investments.

Quinn Emanuel Urquhart Oliver & Hedges, LLP
See firm details p.298

The Firm: This specialist litigation outfit has a fast-growing reputation for significant trial experience and a habit of producing "*fantastic results.*" The group has particular emphasis on IP litigation, and has this year expanded its workload in that field. Corporate fraud-related civil actions are another area of concentration. On the criminal side, the team is credited with "*a top-notch*" practice. The team divides its representation between defense and plaintiff matters and recently secured a $300 million verdict on behalf of two German entrepreneurial plaintiffs against Bertelsmann AG and its former CEO. The jury found in favor of the plaintiffs' claims of breach of oral contract, breach of written contract, breach of partnership agreement, breach of fiduciary duty and culpa in contrahendo. The group also obtained summary judgments of noninfringement in a $40 million patent infringement case for Nike, and a summary judgment of noninfringement and invalidity for IBM in a multi-million-dollar patent infringement case. "*Not just litigators,*" the team is home to "*genuine trial lawyers who try a lot of cases.*"

The Lawyers: "*Formidable*" trial attorney **John Quinn** (see p.268) acted in the case against Bertelsmann. He also obtained a broad covenant not to sue for Genentech regarding a patent for an invention in genetic engineering. Interviewees "*think the world of* " **William Urquhart** (see p.276), who concentrates on complex business litigation. Clients note the breadth of his trial experience. Urquhart represented Superior National in achieving a $137 million settlement with Health Net following allegations of fraud in the sale of a number of insurance companies.

The Clients: The firm provides counsel to IBM, Shell, DIRECTV and Fox.

Arnold & Porter LLP
See firm details p.478

The Firm: Complementing the firm's impressive East Coast practice, Arnold & Porter's LA outpost was endorsed by market commentators as a quality operation. The group commands substantial general commercial expertise and has witnessed an increase in IP and technology-related cases, products liability and antitrust matters. Attorneys have been especially visible acting within the tobacco, healthcare and IT industries. Highlights have included the firm's involvement in diet drug-related litigation and a series of cases for VeriSign concerning the proper scope of supervision over their businesses.

The Lawyers: Co-head of the California litigation practice, **John Quinn** (see p.268) has a wealth of experience in complex litigation, particularly in professional malpractice and ethics matters. Peers acknowledge him as a "*savvy*" practitioner.

The Clients: Microsoft; Wyeth; VeriSign and BP.

Bingham McCutchen LLP

The Firm: Commentators point to this group's long-standing reputation in San Francisco as evidence of a wide-ranging business litigation practice. Areas of expertise include antitrust, environmental, financial services, bankruptcy, IP, labor and employment, real estate, media, products liability and toxic tort, construction and project finance and securities disputes. The team boasts a "*multidimensional*" white-collar practice. It recently obtained the dismissal of all claims for Wells Fargo in a $5 billion reparations suit brought by Mexican workers employed in the USA as temporary agricultural and railroad laborers during World War II. On appellate matters, the team obtained a reversal of an earlier court ruling for Covad Communications, allowing the client to pursue antitrust and associated claims arising from BellSouth's alleged monopolization of Internet access markets in the Southeast.

The Lawyers: "*Warhorse litigator*" **David Balabanian** "*can handle everything under the sun,*" say commentators. His litigation practice encompasses securities disputes and antitrust matters; he recently represented Oracle in an action brought by PeopleSoft in an attempt to stave off its hostile takeover.

The Clients: The group's clients include national and multinational businesses including Fortune 500 companies, financial institutions, nonprofit organizations, sovereign nationals,

government agencies and individuals. These span industry sectors such as automotive, chemicals, biotechnology, telecom, financial services and pharmaceuticals.

Blecher & Collins
See firm details p.282

The Firm: This 14-attorney litigation boutique is best known for its strength in antitrust suits, but is also active in general business litigation with competition aspects. The group's caseload has a strong plaintiff bias, although it does take on some defense work.

The Lawyers: **Maxwell Blecher** (see p.246) is "*on anyone's top-five list of plaintiffs' lawyers and has been for decades,*" say rivals. Although known primarily for his antitrust work, he also ventures into the commercial litigation arena. In the courtroom, Blecher impresses interviewees with his eloquence and ability to "*cut to the chase and not waste time on irrelevancies.*"

The Clients: The group's plaintiff client base is supplemented by work on behalf of the County of Los Angeles.

Cotchett, Pitre, Simon & McCarthy

The Firm: A "*quality*" litigation operation, particularly for plaintiff-oriented class actions. Securities actions are a particular strong suit for the practice. Partners here "*get good results*" on a steady caseload of high-profile matters, according to interviewees. The group recently obtained a settlement of approximately $93 million in cash and stock from Homestore.com and a commitment to reform its corporate policies in a class action alleging accounting irregularities. The firm acted for the lead plaintiff, the California State Teachers' Retirement System.

The Lawyers: Well-known plaintiff attorney **Joseph Cotchett** is "*way up there,*" say clients, for his "*sophistication*" and heavy caseload. Sources singled out Cotchett's consumer rights work for particular mention. His workload includes fraud and corporate corruption matters.

The Clients: The group represents individuals, corporations, profit and nonprofit organizations, municipalities, public entities, unions and representatives, banks, doctors, professionals, policyholders, homeowners, shareholders and consumers.

Howrey Simon Arnold & White

The Firm: The firm's national antitrust presence continues to draw attention from the marketplace. The 130-strong litigation team is considered particularly dynamic in complex commercial, securities and environmental litigation. The group also undertakes a large share of insurance recovery, unfair competition and consumer class actions. The team represented International Paper and its subsidiary, The Masonite Corporation, in a multiphase insurance recovery action concerning the indemnification of dam-

ages paid by both companies to settle a major products liability class action. The team was successful in all three jury trial phases. On the white-collar crime side, the group advises on securities and tax-related fraud matters. Practitioners have represented individuals in matters involving Peregrine Systems, Motorcar Parts of America, Crédit Lyonnais and Aura/Newcom.

The Lawyers: A recent arrival from Kirkland & Ellis, **Jan Handzlik** retains his impressive white-collar practice. Civil and criminal securities fraud form a substantial portion of his caseload, and he is also involved in investigations involving healthcare fraud, environmental crimes and political corruption. "*Well-established*" **Stephen Miller** also continues to impress interviewees, who describe him as "*one of the deans of the white-collar practice in LA.*"

The Clients: WorldCom (now MCI); Genentech; Unocal; Dole Food; Occidental Petroleum; Incyte Genomics; Boeing North America; Verizon Communications; Avery Dennison; Boston Scientific; Union Pacific Railroad; Nestlé; RJ Reynolds Tobacco; US Smokeless Tobacco; Chunghwa Picture Tubes (Taiwan); Ford/Volvo Car of North America; World Trade Center Properties and United Space Alliance.

Skadden, Arps, Slate, Meagher & Flom LLP & Affiliates
See firm details p.1372

The Firm: With offices in Los Angeles, San Francisco and Palo Alto this international giant holds a significant West Coast market share. Peers hold the LA office in particular esteem.

The Lawyers: Co-head of the West Coast litigation practice, **Thomas Nolan** (see p.265) stands out as a "*terrific all-around litigator*" with "*excellent judgment and superb client skills.*" His practice covers antitrust and IP matters, in addition to class action suits, white-collar work and litigation involving contract disputes and unfair business practices.

The Clients: Warner Music Group; ConocoPhillips Alaska; Chinese National Offshore Oil; Arco China; Kuwait Foreign Petroleum Exploration; Chiron; State Farm; Intel; Anheuser-Busch and Citigroup.

Sullivan & Cromwell LLP
See firm details p.1373

The Firm: The firm's West Coast branches are said to benefit from the considerable might of the New York practice. It nevertheless maintains "*first-class quality*" in its Los Angeles and Palo Alto offices. The 19-lawyer group focuses on securities litigation and investigations, antitrust, transactional litigation and corporate disputes. Highlights have included the ongoing representation of Philips and its affiliates in a dispute relating to the manufacture and sale of defective semiconductor chips. The group also acted for UBS Securities in litigation ensuing from Enron's collapse.

The Lawyers: A "*terrific lawyer and smart operator*," **Robert Sacks** (see p.270) oversees the California litigation practice. He recently represented Morgan Stanley in litigation relating to its role as financial adviser to Time Warner in the AOL/Time Warner merger.

The Clients: Thomas Weisel Partners; Goldman Sachs; Softbank; EnCana; Interactive Corp and Espirito Santo.

Wilson Sonsini Goodrich & Rosati
See firm details p.302

The Firm: This group receives particular endorsement for its strength in securities litigation, where the group boasts 70 attorneys dedicated to this alone. The team is also experienced in consumer class actions, IP and commercial litigation and counsels a growing base of technology clients.

The Lawyers: **Bruce Vanyo** (see p.277) continues to impress in the securities arena, while **Robert Feldman** (see p.252) maintains a profile for a trial practice that encompasses IP litigation, SEC investigations and antitrust matters. "*Superb securities litigator*" **Boris Feldman** (see p.251) inspires "*complete confidence*" among clients and investigators, making him a favorite choice for dealings with government agencies. "*There is no better tactician and theoretician than Boris,*" say interviewees.

The Clients: Sun Microsystems; Broadcom; Amcor; America West; Sebal and Google.

Beck, De Corso, Daly, Kreindler & Harris
See firm details p.281

The Firm: Clients were impressed with the "*humanity and capability*" of this criminal and civil trial boutique, adding "*you get the sense that they care about you as a person.*" The ten-attorney, white-collar team continues to act on behalf of clients in the healthcare and aerospace industries. Successes have included representing the Russian Federation in litigation seeking to recover $165 million in diamonds and gems stolen and laundered in Antwerp and Liechtenstein. The team obtained a judgment for this sum and then litigated with the IRS over $50 million in property recovered on behalf of the Russian Federation.

The Lawyers: "*The cream of the crop,*" **Mark Beck** wins the trust of clients and peers who laud his "*incredible sense of decency.*" He focuses on civil and criminal fraud on behalf of companies and their principals. One loyal client described him as "*the most ethical man I've ever known.*"

The Clients: The group's clients include Evergreen Shipping, for which the team obtained a declination of prosecution following a two-year multi-agency investigation into allegations that the company illegally reimbursed campaign contributions. Other clients of the group have included senior executives at: Columbia Healthcare; Tenet Healthcare; Boeing; Teledyne; Infinion; Samsung; Matson Shipping; Texaco and Merrill Lynch.

Bird, Marella, Boxer & Wolpert PC
The Firm: This well-respected team draws praise from the market for both its white-collar criminal practice and civil litigation work. Areas of expertise include securities, mail and tax fraud, antitrust, customs and environmental cases. Attorneys counseled the president of a French mutual insurance company in connection with a US DOJ prosecution arising from the purchase of the Executive Life Insurance Company of California by a French consortium. The case revolved around allegations that the French group acquired the insurance company on behalf of Crédit Lyonnais, which was prohibited from owning an insurance company under US banking laws. The DOJ ultimately prosecuted Crédit Lyonnais, the Consortium de Réalisation SA and several individuals and entities, alleging they had defrauded the US government with respect to the purchase of Executive Life's investment portfolio.

The Lawyers: **Vincent Marella** boasts an established reputation at the white-collar Bar. Securities, tax and bankruptcy fraud are the major elements of his recent practice. He currently represents the former CFO of Qwest Communications in connection with investigations by the DOJ and SEC into the company's financial reporting following a $2 billion restatement. Commentators endorse **Ronald Nessim** for his criminal and civil litigation practice. On the criminal side, he has an emphasis on healthcare fraud matters and is often seen acting on behalf of hospitals and doctors. **Gary Lincenberg** is well regarded for his subspecialty in environmental-related criminal matters, and is active across the spectrum of white-collar issues. A "*first-rate*" practitioner, **Terry Bird** has worked in securities, mail and tax fraud and manages a full civil litigation caseload.

The Clients: Sunrider; Rx Medical; Adelphia California Cablevision; Nokia; Henry Mayo Newhall Memorial Hospital; Rockwell; Thrifty Oil; Wyle Laboratories; Citigroup and Daiwa.

Clarence Snell & Dyer LLP
The Firm: Peers applaud this five-attorney litigation boutique as a group of "*team players*" with a "*strategic approach and quick grasp of the facts.*" The group is committed to criminal defense and complex civil litigation, focusing particularly on issues of constitutional and civil rights. Activity includes internal investigations of white-collar and regulatory matters, as well as complex environmental, securities, antitrust and business fraud cases.

The Lawyers: "*Smart and tenacious*" **Nanci Clarence** attracts comment from fellow white-collar crime specialists for her dexterity in representing clients "*whose financial future and liberty is at stake.*"

The Clients: The firm acts on behalf of corporations and municipal entities facing joint DOJ and SEC investigations of accounting fraud and insider trading. The group undertakes all types of white-collar prosecution from revenue recognition fraud to theft of trade secrets and criminal and civil copyright infringement.

Lightfoot, Vandevelde, Sadowsky, Medvene & Levine
The Firm: A small but solid group of "*serious workers,*" the practice is experienced in trial and criminal litigation, particularly in the federal courts. The nine-strong team is host to a number of high-profile names, known for their "*considerable talent*" in litigation and trial work.

The Lawyers: **John Vandevelde** is widely regarded as a skilled, go-to, white-collar criminal practitioner and trial lawyer with substantial experience in the field. Much of his practice is devoted to pre-indictment investigations of business-related crimes. Former Deputy Federal Public Defender **Janet Levine** commands impressive expertise in trial and appellate work. Interviewees list her among the top white-collar practitioners in the state. **Michael Lightfoot** has a long-standing reputation within the white-collar Bar and specializes in criminal and civil rights cases.

Stevens & O'Connell LLP
The Firm: Peers "*look forward to working with*" this "*outstanding crew*" of "*serious and diligent*" attorneys. The white-collar side of the firm's complex civil litigation and business crimes investigations practice receives particular acclaim.

The Lawyers: Despite his "*low-key*" manner, **Charles Stevens** is widely regarded as the firm's major "*rainmaker.*" Interviewees attribute the practice's highly respected status largely to his "*behind-the-scenes*" involvement. "*Terrific*" **George O'Connell** handles criminal cases and business litigation for both plaintiffs and defendants.

The Clients: The group's client base includes individuals, privately owned businesses and large corporations.

Swanson & McNamara LLP
The Firm: This three-person operation is perceived to be "*gaining traction*" in the marketplace, and is tipped to emerge as a prominent force in the field. Specialties include white-collar and general criminal defense and commercial litigation matters, with the former caseload ranging from tax and structuring cases to cybercrime issues.

The Lawyers: A familiar figure in the marketplace, **Mary McNamara** focuses on trial and appellate work in the white-collar arena. Her practice encompasses criminal grand jury matters and all aspects of civil and criminal trial and appellate proceedings.

The Clients: The firm provides counsel to individuals, corporations and institutions.

Topel & Goodman PC

The Firm: Clients rate this seven-attorney group for its capable practitioners and ability to deliver a "*quality product.*" Active across the spectrum of white-collar matters, the practice takes on cases and investigations involving fraud, antitrust price-fixing, tax, environmental issues, healthcare, insider trading, money laundering and questionable market practices in the insurance industry. The group also represents clients in related civil litigation. One recent success was its representation of Reliant Energy Services in a criminal case brought by the federal authorities alleging price/market manipulation during the California energy crisis.

The Lawyers: **William Goodman** (see p.254) can be relied upon to "*add value as part of a defense team.*" Described as "*plugged in and insightful*" by clients, Goodman is known to "*take a strong position with opposing counsel.*" He is acting for the former general counsel of McKesson HCOB in a criminal accounting/securities fraud case pending in the federal court.

The Clients: The group's clients include Mosel Vitelic, Titan Kogyo and current and former executives of DuPont Dow Elastomers.

Other Notable Practitioners

A "*great trial lawyer with great experience,*" **Larry Feldman** (see p.251) is visible on high-profile plaintiff cases where he represents both individuals and businesses. He is currently representing the Oakland Raiders in their suit against the NFL. Feldman recently joined Kaye Scholer's Los Angeles practice following the dissolution of Fogel, Feldman, Ostrov, Ringler & Klevens. "*Outstanding*" **Allen Ruby** of Ruby & Schofield is once again named by interviewees as one of the leading trial lawyers in the state for both white-collar and commercial litigation. Peers put him "*right at the top*" of the list, crediting him with a "*wonderful*" practice. At Arguedas, Cassman Headley LLP, **Cristina Arguedas** is warmly endorsed by peers as an "*articulate and skilled*" attorney and a "*firebrand*" in cross-examination. Her grand jury investigation and trial practice has a strong focus on financial fraud and antitrust matters. At McDermott, Will & Emery, "*first-rate*" business crime and white-collar litigator **Gordon Greenberg** (see p.254) "*doesn't overdo it, but gets results*" say clients. He has been active internationally in foreign corrupt practices matters as well as managed earnings and political corruption issues. Greenberg acted as lead counsel for the French government in connection with allegations against Crédit Lyonnais concerning the purchase of Executive Life Insurance and in related litigation. Managing partner of the San Diego office of McKenna Long & Aldridge, **Robert Brewer** (see p.246) is a "*go-to man*" in the field,

according to rivals. His practice encompasses government contract procurement fraud, professional negligence and corporate compliance matters. Seen to be growing in visibility, Orrick, Herrington & Sutcliffe's LLP **Walt Brown** (see p.247) "*attracts a lot of business*" to the firm's burgeoning white-collar practice. He is particularly active on behalf of companies and executives in connection with investigations and proceedings in the securities and antitrust fields. Brown recently represented the former CEO of McKesson in connection with an indictment in the Northern District of California. His industry expertise extends to the telecom, construction, computer, pharmaceutical, medical equipment and apparel sectors. **Robert Corbin** at Corbin & Fitzgerald LLP has "*a New York approach to life,*" but is a "*great protector of his client's interests.*" Researchers heard that his "*faultless gut instincts*" make him a powerful weapon in the courtroom. Corbin handles parallel criminal, civil and administrative proceedings for individual and corporate clients with ongoing activities in regulated businesses. "*Knowledgeable and experienced*" **Richard Marmaro** (see p.262) at Proskauer Rose LLP is "*a good advocate for clients,*" say sources. He focuses on white-collar crime and SEC enforcement cases. He recently defended the former CFO of TV Guide in one such action. **John Potter** (see p.267) of Covington & Burling is rising in prominence in the practice area, say market observers. He has particular expertise in public integrity issues.

MEDIA & ENTERTAINMENT

California
Leading firms
(Media & Entertainment: Litigation)

[1]	**ALSCHULER GROSSMAN STEIN** *Santa Monica*
	CHRISTENSEN, MILLER, FINK *Los Angeles*
	DAVIS WRIGHT TREMAINE LLP *Los Angeles*
	GREENBERG GLUSKER FIELDS *Los Angeles*
	LAVELY & SINGER PC *Los Angeles*
[2]	**DLA PIPER RUDNICK GRAY CARY US** *Palo Alto*
	IRELL & MANELLA LLP *Los Angeles*
	MITCHELL, SILBERBERG & KNUPP *Los Angeles*
	MUNGER, TOLLES & OLSON LLP *Los Angeles*
	O'MELVENY & MYERS LLP *Los Angeles*
	WHITE O'CONNOR CURRY *Los Angeles*
[3]	**GIBSON, DUNN & CRUTCHER LLP** *Los Angeles*
	HOGAN & HARTSON LLP *Los Angeles*
	LEVY, RAM & OLSON *San Francisco*
	LOEB & LOEB LLP *Los Angeles*
	QUINN EMANUEL URQUHART OLIVER *Los Angeles*
	RIEGELS CAMPOS & KENYON *Sacramento*
	SHEPPARD, MULLIN, RICHTER *Los Angeles*
	WINN & ALEXANDER LLP *Capitola*

Firms are listed alphabetically in each band.

Band 1

Alschuler Grossman Stein & Kahan LLP
See firm details p.280

The Firm: This "*hard-hitting*" group of lawyers is "*a hugely respected entity that excels in all aspects of complex entertainment litigation,*" clients say. It is particularly renowned for its domestic and international representation on the talent side, and advises clients in the TV, music and film industries. The client roster includes A-list stars, writers, producers, directors, agents and independent production companies in mediation, arbitration and litigation proceedings. The group had an impact on the reality TV sector when it filed a copyright infringement and unfair competition suit on behalf of 'Wife Swap' producers, RDF Media.

The Lawyers: "*Entertainment litigation guru*" **Larry Stein** (see p.274) is regarded as "*king on the pure talent side.*" Offering "*consistently brilliant advice,*" he was described by interviewees as "*a litigator of the highest caliber.*" Stein was instrumental in handling Mary-Kate and Ash-

ley Olsen's buyback of an interest in Dualstar Entertainment Group from their former partner Robert Thorne. Although "*titan*" **Marshall Grossman** (see p.255) is better known for his general commercial litigation, he has regular involvement in complex entertainment disputes. Commentators view him as "*an outstanding communicator and highly efficient.*"

The Clients: Celador International; RDF Media; William Morris Agency; Castaway Television Productions; Village Roadshow; Mary-Kate and Ashley Olsen; Paris Hilton; Rick Dees; Tony Hawk; Madonna; Mel Gibson; Jennifer Lopez; David Duchovny; Jennifer Love Hewitt; RJ (Robert) Wagner; Clint Eastwood; Rob Lowe and Mariah Carey.

Christensen, Miller, Fink, Jacobs, Glaser, Weil & Shapiro, LLP

The Firm: The consensus is that this is "*one of the most sophisticated entertainment practices in the state.*" The reason is simple: it has "*outstanding breadth, which enables it to tackle the most complex of cases.*" The group recently represented Sony Pictures Entertainment and Sony Electronics in

California
Leading individuals
(Media & Entertainment: Litigation)

1
FIELDS Bertram *Greenberg Glusker*, Los Angeles
GLASER Patricia *Christensen Miller*, Los Angeles
SAGER Kelli *Davis Wright*, Los Angeles
STEIN Stanton *Alschuler Grossman*, Santa Monica

2
FRACKMAN Russell *Mitchell Silberberg*, Los Angeles
GROSSMAN Marshall *Alschuler Grossman*, Santa Monica
HEINKE Rex *Akin Gump*, Los Angeles
KENDALL Richard *Irell & Manella*, Los Angeles
LAVELY Jr John *Lavely & Singer*, Los Angeles
OLSON Ronald *Munger Tolles*, Los Angeles
PETRICH Louis *Leopold Petrich*, Los Angeles
SINGER Martin *Lavely & Singer*, Los Angeles

3
BASICH Anthony *Hogan & Hartson*, Los Angeles
BOSTWICK Gary *Sheppard Mullin*, Los Angeles
BOUTROUS Jr Theodore *Gibson Dunn*, Los Angeles
BURKE Thomas *Davis Wright*, San Francisco
CUMMINS Guylyn *Sheppard Mullin*, San Diego
EDELMAN Scott *Gibson Dunn*, Los Angeles
FELDMAN Larry *Kaye Scholer*, Los Angeles
KENYON Charity *Riegels Campos*, Sacramento
MEISINGER Louis *Sheppard Mullin*, Los Angeles
POMERANTZ Glenn *Munger Tolles*, Los Angeles
QUINN John *Quinn Emanuel*, Los Angeles
SCHWARTZ Robert *O'Melveny & Myers*, Los Angeles
WHITE Andrew *White O'Connor*, Los Angeles

4
ALEXANDER Judith *Winn & Alexander*, Capitola
BERGMAN Michael *Weissmann Wolff*, Beverly Hills
CHADWICK James *DLA Piper Rudnick*, Palo Alto
DAVIS Jr Edward *DLA Piper Rudnick*, Palo Alto
GALLO Joie *Christensen Miller*, Los Angeles
GOODKIND Jim *Loeb & Loeb*, Los Angeles
GREENSPAN Eric *Myman Abell*, Los Angeles
MARENBERG Steven *Irell & Manella*, Los Angeles
MAYER Patricia *Mitchell Silberberg*, Los Angeles
MYERS Roger *DLA Piper Rudnick*, San Francisco
OLSON Karl *Levy Ram*, San Francisco
WICKERS IV Alonzo *Davis Wright*, Los Angeles

Up-and-coming individuals
CRAVEN Erica *Levy Ram*, San Francisco

Individuals are listed alphabetically in each band.

the dispute with Marvel Characters regarding the exploitation of Spiderman character rights. It also acted for former Eagles band member Don Felder in his suit against Don Henley, Glenn Frey, manager Irving Azoff and other Eagles-related entities for various claims, including breach of fiduciary duty, constructive fraud, wrongful termination and breach of implied-in-fact contract. In a different matter attorneys represented Disney before a California appellate court where a jury trial verdict in its favor was upheld.
The Lawyers: Interviewees waxed lyrical about trial lawyer **Patricia Glaser**, who is capable of being "*tough as nails.*" According to commentators, "*once she gives you her word, her word is her bond and you can take that to the bank.*" Similarly, clients see her as "*a talented lawyer with decen-*

cy and professionalism." Moving up the ranks is newcomer **Joie Marie Gallo**, who impressed competitors as a "*hard-working rising star.*"
The Clients: Sony Pictures Entertainment; Sony Electronics; Rod Stewart; Kelsey Grammer; Nick Nolte; Bob Barker; Barbra Streisand; Elton John; Don Felder; Sean Connery and Paula Abdul.

Davis Wright Tremaine LLP
See firm details p.1796
The Firm: Davis Wright Tremaine is known nationally for its success in the world of media and entertainment law. Specialist practitioners can be found on both the East and West coasts, offering a comprehensive service for contractual disputes, IP, defamation and First Amendment issues. Attorneys represent clients in the music industry, motion pictures and TV, as well as newspapers, publishers, authors and magazines. Currently, for instance, it is representing a music publisher client in its online copyright infringement claim against the owners of the music and video file-sharing websites KaZaA, Grokster and MusicCity.
The Lawyers: "*Leader of the pack*" and "*simply superb*" **Kelli Sager** (see p.270) has years of experience in the media and entertainment world and a string of reported cases on copyright and misappropriation, privacy, court access and reporters' privilege. **Thomas Burke** (see p.247) is "*a quality lawyer*" who operates out of the San Francisco office. He deals with a broad range of "*highly sophisticated matters*" for print publishers, TV networks, Internet publishers and authors. Commentators noted his recent involvement in the summary dismissal of a libel and invasion of privacy lawsuit filed against Black Entertainment Television. In another matter he represented television networks CNN, Fox, CBS, ABC and NBC in response to a subpoena for the production of videotape concerning juror misconduct in the criminal trial of The People v Scott Peterson. "*Reliable and resourceful*" **Alonzo Wickers** (see p.277) is applauded by those who have seen him in action. He recently filed two amicus curiae briefs in the United States Supreme Court on behalf of the Los Angeles Times, The New York Times and CNN. He also obtained a decision from the California Court of Appeal affirming summary judgment for Dick Clark Productions in an idea submission lawsuit concerning daytime television talk show 'The Other Half.' Interviewees were impressed with his pre-production and pre-broadcast legal counsel, particularly the advice given on First Amendment and IP issues to Comedy Central programs such as South Park and Drawn Together.
The Clients: CNN; Los Angeles Times; The New York Times; Paramount Pictures; Condé Nast Publications; Courtroom Television Network; MTV Networks; Warner Bros; Fox; CBS; ABC and NBC.

Greenberg Glusker Fields Claman Machtinger & Kinsella LLP
The Firm: According to market sources, this is "*an extraordinarily accomplished firm which attracts an enviable client roster.*" Peers describe the attorneys against whom they have worked as "*tough and worthy opponents.*" The group represents individual talent, major studios and recording companies. Commentators noted its representation of Paramount in its appeal of the Buchwald decision, in which it successfully defended Paramount against the Garrison antitrust class action and other claims. For Twentieth Century Fox it stepped up to the plate on several matters including the defense of antitrust litigation and claims brought by Polygram over movie soundtracks. The team also advised MGM on Disney's rights to use the MGM name.
The Lawyers: Of **Bert Fields** it is said: "*Bert is a legend. Everyone respects him and knows of his work.*" This outstanding litigator certainly has "*a strong brand;*" one client even called him "*an institution.*" Fields has been trying cases since the early 1950s, with the majority of his years in practice spent representing leading names in the entertainment industry – both talent and studios. His track record for winning is well established and "*he has always electrified clients with his flair.*"
The Clients: Paramount; Twentieth Century Fox; MGM; Tom Cruise; Mike Nichols; James Cameron; Joel Silver; Dustin Hoffman and Warren Beatty.

Lavely & Singer PC
The Firm: This 25-year-old compact entertainment litigation boutique is more than well known to peers and industry figures. Some 18 attorneys "*who really know what they are talking about*" principally represent individual talent in a practice that encompasses a swath of media and new media-related work, including IP, rights of publicity and privacy, defamation, contract disputes, Internet issues and labor and employment law. If celebrities litigate then there's a good chance they'll have brought this firm in to do it for them. Said one commentator: "*Although one of the smallest players, it offers as good a service as its bigger competitors.*"
The Lawyers: Both of the firm's name partners sit high in the rankings, and each has a "*terrific*" reputation as a guardian of his client's interests. **John Lavely** is "*an extremely smart guy and always effective.*" **Martin Singer** is "*without doubt a force to reckon with,*" rivals say. Over the years, the industry has witnessed many examples of his white knight missions for troubled clients.
The Clients: The firm advises actors, recording artists, directors, producers and writers. It shies away from representing corporate clients.

Band 2

DLA Piper Rudnick Gray Cary US LLP
See firm details p.765

The Firm: At the end of 2003, the firm of Steinhart & Falconer became a part of what is viewed as a "*newly created empire*" centered around Piper Rudnick, and now Europe's DLA. Its First Amendment and media law practice group is perceived to have "*gained enormous strength and breadth*" through the tie-up and subsequent growth of the firm internationally. The group acts for television companies, key newspapers, radio networks, and online and book publishers, often dealing with intricate privacy and defamation issues. Commentators say the firm's existing and now-widened client base is "*one to be envied.*"

The Lawyers: "*Highly committed*" **James Chadwick** (see p.248) is "*awfully thorough and knows the law inside out.*" This "*well-liked and tremendously respected*" attorney "*gives clients practical advice and touches the legal basis of each problem.*" He focuses on First Amendment, trademark, privacy and white-collar crime. A former newspaper reporter, **Roger Myers** (see p.264) is immensely respected for his First Amendment work. This "*intelligent and prolific market player*" impresses with "*the expertise he brings to the table.*" Commentators also rate **Ed Davis** (see p.249), who does a "*fine job for his clients.*"

The Clients: The New York Times Company; Knight-Ridder and its California flagship publication The San Jose Mercury News; MediaNews Group; Ottaway Newspapers; Pulitzer Newspapers; Associated Press; Time Warner; Newsweek; Mother Jones; CNET; NBC; HBO; Business Wire; John Wiley & Sons and Berrett-Koehler Publishers

Irell & Manella LLP

The Firm: Although particularly well known for its IP caseload, Irell & Manella has an entertainment litigation group that has managed to "*shine through and sustain the glow.*" It advises studios, recording companies and television networks on a wide range of media issues, focusing particularly on copyright, defamation, privacy and royalty payments. According to rivals it possesses "*a strong group of highly capable people.*" The firm was involved in Streisand v Californiacoastline.org et al, where it successfully defended an environmental website in Los Angeles Superior Court against Barbra Streisand's claims that a photograph of her home in Malibu on a website that displayed photographs of the entire California coastline infringed her privacy and publicity rights.

The Lawyers: "*Fantastic*" **Richard Kendall** has "*amazing status.*" Clients say that "*to him integrity is key,*" and are impressed by his record of "*constantly winning the big cases.*" Rivals report that he is "*bright, strategic and detail oriented.*"

Steven Marenberg "*has a real passion for representing his clients.*" He is known to advise ABC, Disney, Universal Music Group and the Recording Industry Association of America.

The Clients: Paramount; Viacom Outdoor; VH1; CBS; UPN; Columbia TriStar; Universal film studios; MTV; Showtime and Nickelodeon.

Mitchell, Silberberg & Knupp LLP

The Firm: This "*spectacular contender*" has, according to interviewees, "*a vast historical reputation*" for involvement in "*intricate cases, and always provides a top-quality service.*" The team represents major producers, music companies, distributors, and video game and Internet companies in relation to wide-ranging entertainment issues. On the individual talent side, it advises producers, actors, directors and musical artists. Commentators also acknowledged its work for financial institutions.

The Lawyers: "*Music star*" **Russell Frackman** is, according to key industry sources, the "*top litigator in his field.*" Simply put, "*he knows how to win a case.*" There was praise, too, for "*brainy*" **Patricia Mayer**, who "*brings plenty to the table*" and has a "*highly approachable manner.*"

The Clients: Motion Picture Association of America; Recording Industry Association of America; BMG and Arista Records.

Munger, Tolles & Olson LLP

The Firm: "*Here is a firm that will take time out for its clients,*" one interviewee told researchers. Its media and entertainment work is "*hugely valued*" by rivals, who speak readily of "*a group of talented players with great trial expertise.*" The team represents studios and networks on complex matters, recently stepping up for a US television distributor in contract disputes with German media companies in Los Angeles and the Netherlands. Furthermore, it acted for several major studios in a class action lawsuit alleging that the studios misled the public in their use of reviews in movie advertisements.

The Lawyers: **Ronald Olson** is "*in a class of his own.*" The general view of the market is that "*he is a leader with a diverse practice*" and "*exceptional judgment.*" **Glenn Pomerantz** was also singled out for his business dispute work for entertainment companies. Commentators liked his "*solid,-non-flashy*" style.

The Clients: Universal Music Group; NBC Universal; Twentieth Century Fox; Warner Bros; Activision; Brillstein-Grey Entertainment and House of Blues

O'Melveny & Myers LLP
See firm details p.294

The Firm: Doing "*top work, day in, day out,*" this firm litigates for major studios and media entities. In the case of Metro-Goldwyn-Mayer Studios et al v Grokster et al the group represents plaintiff Time Warner as one of the studios and

record companies suing those behind the KaZaA, Grokster, and MusicCity websites over copyright infringing file sharing. In Zaentz v New Line Cinema, the firm defended New Line in a 'back end' compensation dispute arising from the contract through which New Line acquired the rights to produce the 'Lord of the Rings' trilogy.

The Lawyers: Group chair **Bobby Schwartz** has "*expertise and a down-to-earth disposition.*" He represents motion picture studios, record companies, TV and cable networks and individual producers, often on complex contractual issues.

The Clients: New Line Cinema, Time Warner and Sony Pictures are among the firm's clients.

White O'Connor Curry & Avanzado LLP

The Firm: This team is "*undoubtedly one of the names to take seriously,*" one rival conceded. With a "*fantastic group of skilled litigators*" it is "*definitely going places.*" The firm's trial attorneys offer alternative dispute resolution services, "*but are not afraid*" to litigate intricate entertainment and business disputes. Commentators are aware of the close and deep-rooted relationship with client CBS, noting how "*the firm is able to offer outstanding service for a sensible price.*"

The Lawyers: "*No-nonsense litigator*" **Andrew White** is "*the brightest crayon in the box,*" clients say. He has "*a lot of insight into the industry, knows how to try a case*" and possesses "*first-rate trial skills.*"

The Clients: The firm's client roster includes Viacom, MTV and CBS.

Band 3

Gibson, Dunn & Crutcher LLP
See firm details p.285

The Firm: In the eyes of a number of commentators, this firm "*has emerged from the chasing pack*" and "*warrants an entry in the leaders table.*" The group has shown "*commitment and enthusiasm when tackling some impressive cases this year.*" The group defended publisher Penguin Putnam in a copyright action concerning 'Zodiac Unmasked', a book about the infamous Zodiac killer. It also defended Columbia TriStar Home Video in the lawsuit brought by independent video retailers against the major studios and Blockbuster. The claim challenged the revenue-sharing model by which videotapes are distributed to the major retail and rental chains.

The Lawyers: **Ted Boutrous** (see p.246) is "*extremely responsive*" and, according to clients, "*offers spot-on written work and efficiency in terms of billing.*" He recently represented several major media organizations, including NBC, CBS, ABC, CNN, Fox, The New York Times, the Los Angeles Times, Gannett, Associated Press and The Washington Post, all of whom were seeking public access to secret judicial proceedings and records in the criminal case against Michael Jackson. "*Excellent*" **Scott Edelman** (see p.250) "*has been around forever.*" Above all, competitors admire "*the superb relationship he has with his clients.*" He represents major studios, music companies, foreign distributors and investors, licensing agents and production companies. In the matter of Intertainment Licensing v Franchise Pictures he obtained a $122 million judgment on behalf of the plaintiff.

The Clients: Sony Entertainment; Fox Broadcasting; Dow Jones; The Wall Street Journal; Sony Music; Warner Bros Records; NBC Universal; Intertainment AG; Evergreen Studios; Marching Band Productions; CNN; the Los Angeles Times and The New York Times.

Hogan & Hartson LLP

See firm details p.484

The Firm: These "*fine attorneys*" scored "*high marks*" for their victory on behalf of clients Sony Pictures Entertainment, TriStar Pictures and Columbia Pictures Industries in XL Re v Sony Pictures Entertainment. Clients found them "*straightforward and enthusiastic,*" while peers declared that "*they always have the right attitude.*" The group also represented DIRECTV in a matter whereby DIRECTV and Universal Music Group were sued by Uncensored Music Network, which alleged that the two companies stole its idea for a 24-hour channel featuring uncensored music videos.

The Lawyers: "*Celebrated litigator*" **Anthony Basich** (see p.244) is "*one of the most important media and entertainment guys in the state,*" according to clients.

The Clients: News Corporation; Fox Entertainment Group; Disney; Sony Corporation of America; DIRECTV; NDS and Overture.

Levy, Ram & Olson

The Firm: This "*vibrant*" team serves a deep client base and focuses on media law, First Amendment and public records litigation. It recently represented several newspapers seeking access to various aspects of the Scott Peterson murder trial in California, and acted for the San Francisco Chronicle in the successful defense of a libel suit brought against the newspaper and sports superstars Barry Bonds and Roger Craig by a former San Francisco podiatrist. Contra Costa Newspapers turned to the firm for its successful Public Records Act lawsuit against the City of Oakland when it sought access to information about the salaries of highly paid government workers.

The Lawyers: Name partner **Karl Olson** is "*a man who has achieved plenty*" in the industry and is respected for his long experience. Meanwhile, younger lawyer **Erica Craven** is, according to her peers, "*extremely diligent and really commands the respect of judges.*"

The Clients: The San Francisco Chronicle; the

Contra Costa Times; The Sacramento Bee and the Los Angeles Times.

Loeb & Loeb LLP

The Firm: The market continues to watch this "*capable and smart*" group with fascination. It has "*done extremely well in putting together a highly regarded practice.*" Attorneys defended Bertelsmann and former CEO Thomas Middelhoff against a $3.5 billion claim by two former executives of AOL Europe.

The Lawyers: "*Talented*" entertainment lawyer **Jim Goodkind** divides his time between litigation and transactional matters. He advises entertainment companies and executives as well as individual talent and their representation.

The Clients: Bertelsmann; Poppe Tyson; Dixie Chicks; Woody Allen; William Morris Agency; Oprah Winfrey and Regis Philbin.

Quinn Emanuel Urquhart Oliver & Hedges, LLP

See firm details p.298

The Firm: This new entry to the table "*tried hard to be a major contender and has finally come through,*" interviewees noted. The group advises major talent, production companies, networks and studios in a wide variety of contract and IP disputes, and is counsel to the Academy of Motion Picture Arts and Sciences (Oscar awards), as well as the National Academy of Recording Arts and Sciences (Grammy awards) and the Academy of Television Arts and Sciences (Emmy awards).

The Lawyers: "*Rainmaker*" **John Quinn** (see p.268) is "*an exceptional trial lawyer*" who is also recognized for his work in the field of general commercial litigation.

The Clients: Warner Bros; DIRECTV; CBS; HBO and Fox.

Riegels Campos & Kenyon

The Firm: This group of "*highly successful*" civil litigators has earned acclaim for its handling of "*significant First Amendment media matters within the state.*" It represented a coalition of news media seeking access to court documents and hearings in the Scott Peterson murder pretrial proceedings and took up the cause of The Sacramento Bee in several matters including access to juvenile court proceedings in a federal court.

The Lawyers: "*Pleasing*" **Charity Kenyon** "*wears a velvet glove over a steel fist.*" She recently represented a Solano County newspaper in the Court of Appeal in San Francisco on an appeal over an order denying an anti-SLAPP motion to strike.

The Clients: The firm has a number of newspaper clients on its books.

Sheppard, Mullin, Richter & Hampton LLP

The Firm: This firm has "*put itself on the map,*" having constructed an "*incredible practice.*" The "*ever-expanding team*" advises major motion picture studios and independent production companies; its "*dedicated department can deal with anything thrown at it, even on the transactional side,*" clients say. Areas of expertise include TV, music, home video, publishing, sports, licensing and branded entertainment.

The Lawyers: "*Highly dedicated*" **Guylyn Cummins**, who recently joined from Gray Cary Ware & Freidenrich, is "*extremely thorough and very well liked.*" Similarly, clients feel **Gary Bostwick** is "*a wonderful addition to the team,*" while "*prestigious*" **Louis Meisinger** is "*a giant in the entertainment litigation world.*" Commentators note that he is "*tremendously active and possesses good strategic judgment.*"

The Clients: Disney; Paramount; Sony; New Line Cinema and The Marketing Store Worldwide.

Winn & Alexander LLP

The Firm: Winn & Alexander is "*absolutely top drawer for media and First Amendment work,*" according to satisfied clients. Despite its size, this two-partner outfit has "*stamped its mark on the sector.*" According to commentators, it can deal "*effectively*" with issues concerning invasion of privacy, contract drafting, defamation and pre-publication questions.

The Lawyers: "*Solid*" **Judith Alexander** was rated as "*a detailed and well-prepared*" attorney who works with "*skill and determination.*"

The Clients: The Palo Alto Weekly; The Sacramento Bee; the San Jose Mercury News; the Los Angeles Times; the Monterey County Herald; the Santa Cruz Sentinel; the Spartan Daily; Capital Cities/ABC; NBC; Fox Television; Ingonish Films; San Francisco magazine; Mother Jones magazine and the Stanford Daily.

Other Notable Practitioners

"*Top-notch appellate lawyer*" **Rex Heinke** (see p.77270) of Akin Gump Strauss Hauer & Feld LLP does "*splendid work for his clients.*" He advises magazines, newspapers, TV networks, motion picture studios and websites on matters concerning First Amendment, media and IP issues. "*Bright*" **Louis Petrich** of Leopold, Petrich & Smith PA "*focuses on doing the best job for his clients and has repute as a prolific writer.*" He is "*immensely respected for his upright attitude*" and noted to be "*one of the great litigators.*" Another "*exceptional trial lawyer,*" **Larry Feldman** (see p.251) of Kaye Scholer LLP, is "*a force to reckon with.*" Previously more active in personal injury litigation, Feldman has broadened his practice recently to incorporate matters relating to business, entertainment and legal malpractice. New to the tables is "*successful*" **Michael Bergman** of Weissmann, Wolff,

Bergman, Coleman, Grodin & Evall, LLP who deals with complex IP cases and business disputes touching on many facets of the entertainment industry. **Eric Greenspan** of Myman, Abell, Fineman, Greenspan & Light LLP has "*an impressive client base*" of music and media talent. Commentators agree that he possesses "*a clear understanding of the industry and takes a commercial approach.*"

MEDIA & ENTERTAINMENT

TRANSACTIONAL

California
Leading firms
(Media & Entertainment: Transactional)

1	**GANG TYRE RAMER & BROWN** *Beverly Hills*
	HANSEN JACOBSON TELLER *Beverly Hills*
	O'MELVENY & MYERS LLP *Los Angeles*
	ZIFFREN BRITTENHAM BRANCA *Los Angeles*
2	**AKIN GUMP STRAUSS HAUER & FELD** *Los Angeles*
	IRELL & MANELLA LLP *Los Angeles*
	MANATT PHELPS & PHILLIPS LLP *Los Angeles*
	SHEPPARD, MULLIN, RICHTER *Los Angeles*
3	**BLOOM, HERGOTT AND DIEMER LLP** *Beverly Hills*
	GIBSON, DUNN & CRUTCHER LLP *Los Angeles*
	KATTEN MUCHIN ZAVIS ROSENMAN *Los Angeles*
	KAYE SCHOLER LLP *Los Angeles*
	LICHTER GROSSMAN NICHOLAS *Los Angeles*
	LOEB & LOEB LLP *Los Angeles*
	WEISSMANN, WOLFF, BERGMAN *Beverly Hills*

Leading individuals
(Media & Entertainment: Transactional)

1	**BRITTENHAM Harry** *Ziffren Brittenham, Los Angeles*
	HANSEN Tom *Hansen Jacobson, Beverly Hills*
	PASSMAN Donald *Gang Tyre, Beverly Hills*
	RAMER Bruce *Gang Tyre, Beverly Hills*
	ZIFFREN Kenneth *Ziffren Brittenham, Los Angeles*
2	**BLOOM Jacob** *Bloom Hergott, Beverly Hills*
	BRANCA John *Ziffren Brittenham, Los Angeles*
	COOPER Jay *Greenberg Traurig, Santa Monica*
	FISCHER Samuel *Ziffren Brittenham, Los Angeles*
	HIRSCH Barry *Armstrong Hirsch, Los Angeles*
	JACKOWAY James *Armstrong Hirsch, Los Angeles*
	KLEINBERG Kenneth *Kleinberg Lopez, Los Angeles*
	LICHTER Linda *Lichter Grossman, Los Angeles*
	MURRAY Christopher *O'Melveny & Myers, Los Angeles*
	PHILLIPS Lee *Manatt Phelps, Los Angeles*
	WEISSMANN Eric *Weissmann Wolff, Beverly Hills*
3	**BROWN Harald** *Gang Tyre, Beverly Hills*
	BURKE P John *Akin Gump, Los Angeles*
	COOK Melanie *Ziffren Brittenham, Los Angeles*
	FAYNE Steve *Akin Gump, Los Angeles*
	FRANKENHEIMER John *Loeb & Loeb, Los Angeles*
	JEFFREY Sheri *Kaye Scholer, Los Angeles*
	LEO Thomas *Sheppard Mullin, Los Angeles*
	MAYERSON Michael *Loeb & Loeb, Los Angeles*
	NEWMAN Jeanne *Hansen Jacobson, Beverly Hills*
	TOULON Rik *Katten Muchin, Los Angeles*
	ULMAN Lawrence *Gibson Dunn, Los Angeles*
	YOUNGBLOOD Juliette *Irell & Manella, Los Angeles*

Up-and-coming individuals

ROMAN Marissa *Akin Gump, Los Angeles*

Firms and individuals are listed alphabetically in each band.

Band 1

Gang Tyre Ramer & Brown
The Firm: A "*first-class,*" old-line Beverley Hills entertainment boutique renowned for its successful representation of "*top-notch*" stage, screen and music talent; commentators agree that this is "*without a doubt the go-to firm for unsurpassed quality on the talent side.*" On transactional and corporate matters, the firm has a very commendable reputation. It was recently involved in the DreamWorks Animation IPO and has facilitated the development of numerous TV and film productions. Meanwhile, a "*spectacular*" music team has been engaged in the sale of a multimillion-dollar record company, high-profile artist deals and mobile content matters.
The Lawyers: In the thick of things in the motion picture world, **Bruce Ramer** is "*incredibly sharp and always busy.*" Interviewees praise his "*consistency and energy,*" crediting him with being "*an honest and intelligent practitioner.*" "*Preeminent*" music specialist **Donald Passman** "*merits the top slot*" for his "*outstanding music expertise,*" while "*superb*" **Harald Brown** impresses commentators with his "*tremendous entertainment awareness*" and the great care with which he attends to business.
The Clients: Clint Eastwood; Janet Jackson; Steven Spielberg; Tina Turner and REM.

Hansen Jacobson Teller Hoberman Newman, Warren, Sloane & Richman, LLP
The Firm: This "*prominent young player*" has "*evolved well beyond its historic pursuer status into 'the firm to beat' in the fray for big talent.*" The firm constantly deals with sophisticated matters and represents several "*prestigious*" producers, writers and artists. Its attorneys are attributed with "*great business sense,*" and observers have noted a recent move into the corporate arena; they say it is "*one to watch*" for advice on reality TV issues.
The Lawyers: **Tom Hansen**'s stature is that of "*a monster in the entertainment business.*" His expertise within TV and motion pictures "*can only be compared to that of the best players in the country.*" "*Quality attorney*" **Jeanne Newman** "*does a terrific job for her clients and is always on the ball,*" sources say. She is particularly well regarded for her counsel to known Hollywood producers and TV companies.

The Clients: The group advises both prominent individual talent and key companies on film and commercial endorsement issues.

O'Melveny & Myers LLP
See firm details p.294
The Firm: This group is respected by peers for its noteworthy and "*sophisticated*" contribution to international deals in the entertainment industry. "*One of the most acknowledged firms in the area,*" it has provided outside counsel to Warner Bros, Time Warner, Turner Broadcasting, HBO, Fox, Sony and MGM. It also has more than a foothold in the advertising industry, representing agencies such as Omnicom, Dentsu and Hakuhodo.
The Lawyers: Former chairman of the group **Chris Murray** has more than 30 years of experience in all legal and business aspects of the production, financing and distribution of motion pictures and television programs. This "*outstanding*" practitioner is praised for being "*subtle and easy to deal with.*" In addition to his corporate clients he acts for an impressive roster of individuals, including Carol Burnett, James Garner and numerous producers and executives as well as directors such as George Stevens.
The Clients: Convergence PLC (UK); TeleImage and M6 Television (France); Itoh; Japan Broadcasting Corporation; Hyundai; Korakuen (Tokyo Dome International); Marubeni; NHK Enterprises and Tokyo Broadcasting Systems.

Ziffren Brittenham Branca Fischer Gilbert-Lurie & Stiffelman LLP
The Firm: Founded in 1978, this "*entrepreneurial*" firm is going "*from strength to strength*" according to leading market sources. It retains its position "*at the top of the tree*" for its work on behalf of prominent talent and companies within the motion picture, multimedia, TV and music industries. Commentators describe its attorneys as "*cutting edge and clued up,*" many believing they have a distinct advantage over competitors by clearly specializing in entertainment-oriented M&A and financing.
The Lawyers: Senior partner **Skip Brittenham** is "*in a league of his own,*" say competitors. "*He is simply perfect*" when it comes to representing some of the biggest players in television, music and motion pictures. One industry insider revealed: "*Skip is a client's dream – he's a creative thinker.*" Fellow "*leader*" **Kenneth Ziffren** earns the accolade "*one of the paramount entertainment lawyers,*" and is "*always a pleasure to deal*

with." When a competitor was asked if Ziffren deserved his band-one status, the answer was: "*Of course!*" A client explained why: "*He works miracles.*" "*Effective*" **John Branca** is regarded as "*a major force in the music industry;*" while "*intellectually focused*" **Sam Fischer** "*really understands the motion picture business and is extremely practical.*" Since her arrival, **Melanie Cook** has proved to be "*a great addition to the team*" and was said to be "*a fine personality.*"

The Clients: Clients include studio executives, actors, TV scriptwriters, broadcasters and financiers. On the individual talent side the group has advised Bruce Willis, Céline Dion, Ben Affleck, Harrison Ford and Eddie Murphy. It has also represented Liberty Media and DreamWorks.

Band 2

Akin Gump Strauss Hauer & Feld LLP
See firm details p.477

The Firm: Akin Gump has a cadre of "*solid lawyers*" advising clients in TV, film, music and multimedia, though it is principally known for its notable market share of finance work. It acts for a raft of lending institutions and has ample experience in the provision of production funding for motion pictures internationally. On behalf of Comerica Bank it was recently involved in the financing of a number of pictures for Stratus Films, and advised on the purchase of a substantial video library on behalf of Paramount Pictures Home Video. In another matter it represented TVT Records on a fraud and tortious interference claim against Island Def Jam Records.

The Lawyers: "*Extraordinary*" **Steve Fayne** (see p.251) is "*a tremendous resource*" for clients and "*gets things done.*" He is applauded for his skill on intricate motion picture and television finance transactions. **John Burke** (see p.247) is "*a rock-solid entertainment finance lawyer,*" who earns approval from clients and peers alike. Listed in the table as an up-and-comer, rising star **Marissa Roman** (see p.269) is considered "*one of the real go-getters*" at the firm.

The Clients: American Film Institute; 2929 Entertainment (Todd Wagner & Mark Cuban); Bank of Ireland; cineFinance; Comerica Bank; Bristol Bay Entertainment; Disney; JPMorgan; Lions Gate Entertainment; Natexis Banque Populaires and Paramount Pictures.

Irell & Manella LLP

The Firm: Clients confirm that dealing with this player means "*knowing you are serviced by a resourceful team with the ability to close intricate matters.*" This firm has a long history of activity in the entertainment industry, in both transactions and litigation, and represents clients from practically all quarters. On its books are talent agencies, studios, actors, producers and writers as well as financial institutions and individual financiers. Its "*enormously talented professionals*" are known for their representation of Paramount Pictures and a number of TV companies.

The Lawyers: "*Seriously talented*" **Juliette Youngblood** concentrates on entertainment and IP matters relating to the motion picture, television, multimedia and advertising industries. She represents entertainment companies in matters concerning production, financing, development and distribution and acts for major studios and production companies. She also works extensively in reality TV on shows such as 'Survivor,' 'Contender' and the upcoming Mark Burnett series 'Rockstar.'

The Clients: Paramount Pictures; Mark Burnett Productions; MTV; Nickelodeon; MGM and Lucasfilm.

Manatt Phelps & Phillips LLP

The Firm: Clients rate this firm for its "*ability to cover the full range of issues;*" rivals admire its "*outstanding strength in music.*" The team represented Concord Records in the acquisition of the record catalog of Fantasy Records, and Mel Brooks' company Brooksfilms in relation to its Broadway musical version of 'The Producers,' now being made into a new motion picture. It also advises companies such as American Express and Coca-Cola in connection with various branded entertainment activities, including a reality series and films created for Internet use. The team is additionally kept busy with the representation of ARD, a large public broadcaster in Germany and its component sales and purchasing arms, MDR, Telepool and Degeto.

The Lawyers: The "*iconic*" **Lee Phillips** (see p.267) is widely regarded as "*one of the best-known music lawyers in the state.*" This "*powerful player*" has "*good judgment and a healthy appetite for creativity in his work.*" He handled several of the top musical tours of 2004, including those of the Eagles, Cher and the Rolling Stones.

The Clients: ARD; Concord Records; American Express; Brooksfilms and Coca-Cola.

Sheppard, Mullin, Richter & Hampton LLP

The Firm: This firm is moving up the ladder, having won the trust of clients who view its attorneys as being "*utterly reliable.*" The group has been able to "*put itself on the map as a significant contender*" following the influx of several high-status partners from Hill Wynne Troop & Meisinger. Clients, however, say "*its existing lawyers were first-rate prior to the new arrivals.*" A 26-strong team represents a number of the chief studios, producers, TV networks, new media ventures, advertisers, advertising agencies, production and distribution companies. It is particularly commended for its entertainment finance practice.

The Lawyers: Clients describe **Tom Leo** as "*focused and always a pleasure to deal with.*" He advises key institutional parties in entertainment industry transactions and has represented several major studios on an array of motion picture financings.

The Clients: Société Générale; Paramount; Sony and MGM.

Band 3

Bloom, Hergott and Diemer LLP

The Firm: Although this esteemed boutique does not have the largest entertainment practice around, "*its traditional talent work ensures it remains a major player.*" The Beverley Hills firm continues to advise directors and actors, and has an affiliation with music firm Davis Shapiro Lewit Montone & Hayes.

The Lawyers: The eponymous **Jacob Bloom** is the core entertainment attorney at the firm and one of the best-known names in the business; he is admired for his contribution on the talent side.

The Clients: Clients include Nicolas Cage, Brian Grazer and Ron Howard.

Gibson, Dunn & Crutcher LLP
See firm details p.285

The Firm: According to several high-profile sources, this firm "*needs to be recognized, not least for its success story in dealing with complex entertainment matters.*" The team recently advised Volkswagen in product placement and promotional matters with Disney, and acted for Universal on deals whereby external funds are invested in major studio film projects. It also represented New Line Cinema in a film investment transaction with DaimlerChrysler. Activision turned to the firm for advice concerning the licensing of film rights from a major studio for the making of video games.

The Lawyers: **Lawrence Ulman** (see p.276) has "*a special air about him.*" Also an adjunct professor at the USC School of Cinema-Television, financing issues are at the heart of his practice.

The Clients: Universal Pictures; Twentieth Century Fox; New Line Cinema; Volkswagen and Activision.

Katten Muchin Zavis Rosenman
See firm details p.769

The Firm: The firm's name is synonymous with a "*steadfast and clearly significant force*" in entertainment law. This distinguished player fields "*exceedingly skilled*" partners who represent media and entertainment companies in a variety of transactions including M&A, licensing and joint ventures. Clients come from motion pictures and TV, publishing and distribution,

All quotes in the text are from interviews with clients and competitors.

and digital and interactive entertainment. Commentators noted the firm's growing interest in reality TV and animated firms.

The Lawyers: "*Eloquent*" **Rik Toulon** (see p.275) emerged as a popular figure in research, with one satisfied interviewee stressing his "*fine response time and follow-through service.*"

The Clients: New Line Cinema; MTV Networks; Mattel; Columbia TriStar Home Entertainment; Sony Pictures International Television; Paramount International Television; NBC Universal; Dimension Films and Miramax Film.

Kaye Scholer LLP
See firm details p.1354

The Firm: Clients treasured their strong relationships with this "*robust*" new entry to the table, remarking how it is "*packed with responsive and pleasant players.*" The firm acts for TV and motion picture production companies, record companies, new media, talent agencies, actors, writers, directors, publishers and software developers.

The Lawyers: There was fulsome praise for "*practice backbone*" **Sheri Jeffrey** (see p.258), who advises clients in a broad range of entertainment industry transactions.

Lichter Grossman Nicholas Adler & Goodman

The Firm: This is a "*small but extremely efficient*" entertainment boutique with a keen interest in talent and a reputation on both sides of the Atlantic. There was a strong consensus that this group of specialists has a certain "*honesty and uprightness.*"

The Lawyers: Interviewees commended leading entertainment practitioner **Linda Lichter**,

with one even nominating her for "*a legal Oscar.*" She is more usually associated with the representation of talent.

Loeb & Loeb LLP

The Firm: LA, New York, Chicago and Nashville firm Loeb & Loeb deals with issues in relation to entertainment finance, film and TV production and distribution, music and theater. Interviewees admire its "*dexterous handling of complex transactions*" and "*wide-ranging aptitude.*" One client commented that the firm's entertainment lawyers are "*the smartest I've ever encountered.*"

The Lawyers: Cochairman **John Frankenheimer** is said to be "*extremely responsive to clients' needs.*" He offers counsel to both institutional clients and talent. Meanwhile, "*gifted*" **Michael Mayerson** is widely recognized for his motion picture and television finance, production and distribution work. Clients praised his "*astonishing knack*" for international licensing deals.

The Clients: Diana Ross; Glenn Close; Anthony Hopkins; Gary Oldman; Elijah Wood; Woody Allen; the Dixie Chicks; the Beastie Boys; the Grateful Dead; Kid Rock; Don Murphy and Irwin Winkler.

Weissmann, Wolff, Bergman, Coleman, Grodin & Evall, LLP

The Firm: Founded in 1981, this "*talented*" boutique is now applauded for its "*versatility and strength;*" its attorneys are known to be "*a dedicated and hard-working bunch.*" Entertainment clients include financiers, writers, directors, producers, distributors, software designers,

recording artists and print publishers. The firm has been linked to motion pictures such as 'Frida,' 'The Matrix' sequels, 'Scary Movie' and 'Something's Gotta Give'.

The Lawyers: "*Terrific*" **Eric Weissmann** is frequently recommended for his representation of directors, actors, producers and financiers. Interviewees say: "*He does not shout about his practice, but still makes news for his first-rate contribution.*"

The Clients: Clients include Warner Bros, Lehman Brothers and City National Bank.

Other Notable Practitioners

Chair of the firm's LA entertainment practice and "*music connoisseur*" **Jay Cooper** (see p.249) of Greenberg Traurig LLP has a strong presence for clients from motion pictures, television, multimedia and music. A very public dispute between partners of the former firm of Armstrong Hirsch Jackoway Tyerman & Wertheimer overshadowed the feedback for **Barry Hirsch** and **James Jackoway** this year. Nonetheless, these two lawyers are each known to possess great expertise and each maintains the loyalty of an enviable clientele of celebrities and other entertainment industry figures. Each is a worthy occupant of the table. Hirsch now practices from the new firm of Hirsch Wallerstein Hayum Matlof & Fishman. Jackoway now practices from the reorganized firm of Jackoway Tyerman Wertheimer Austen Mandelbaum & Morris. Finally, **Kenneth Kleinberg** of Kleinberg, Lopez, Lange, Brisbin & Cuddy is a new entrant to the table after receiving accolades for his "*simply tremendous*" film work. One client especially admired his ability to "*look at the big picture.*"

PROJECTS

California
Leading firms (Projects)

1	LATHAM & WATKINS LLP *Los Angeles*
	MILBANK, TWEED, HADLEY & McCLOY *Los Angeles*
2	THELEN REID & PRIEST LLP *San Francisco*
3	MORGAN, LEWIS & BOCKIUS LLP *Los Angeles*
	ORRICK, HERRINGTON & SUTCLIFFE LLP *Los Angeles*
	STOEL RIVES LLP *San Francisco*

Firms are listed alphabetically in each band.

Band 1

Latham & Watkins LLP

The Firm: This San Diego-based practice stands out from the competition due to its impressive capital markets experience, particularly its considerable expertise in Rule 144A transactions. This key skill set has helped to make the firm a leading light in the current sweeping trend for refinancings of domestic power projects. The

Latham team enjoys strong relationships with the investment banks and has arranged a number of high-profile refinancings on their behalf, but also excels at handling complex financial issues for the developer companies. In addition to this the group is noted, according to the market, for the quality and pragmatic attitude of its lawyers; peers and clients alike unanimously praise their "*focus on finding solutions, keeping the momentum going, and getting the deal done.*"

The Lawyers: The "*extremely commercial*" **Andy Singer** leads the team here and is one of the firm's best-known lawyers in this sector. Universally admired by peers, clients report that they keep returning to him because he is "*smart and results oriented,*" and would not place unnecessary obstacles in front of a deal. He is ably assisted by the "*superb and analytical*" **Jeffrey Greenberg**, who was recently made partner. "*Sharp and aggressive*" **Kelley Gale** enjoys a growing reputation as a developer's counsel.

The Clients: This firm is especially noted for representing lenders. For example, the California team recently acted for CSFB in the $730 million refinancing of two Calpine power plants and worked on the $2.4 billion refinancing of 15 CalGen power plants for Morgan Stanley, a complex mix of a Rule 144A offering and loans by hedge funds. Other clients on the lender side include Goldman Sachs, Société Générale and ING. On the developer side, the team recently arranged Rule 144A financings for Ormat, a company specializing in geothermal power, and for GWS Energy.

Milbank, Tweed, Hadley & McCloy

The Firm: The Los Angeles office is a key component of the global powerhouse that is Milbank's projects group. It boasts "*a formidable practice*" that is particularly focused on representing financial institutions. Sources praise the team's "*wide knowledge of the field*" and its

California
Leading individuals (Projects)

1 FEO Edwin *Milbank Tweed*, Los Angeles
   SINGER Andrew *Latham & Watkins*, San Diego

2 SHORTZ Richard *Morgan Lewis*, Los Angeles
   SPIELBERG David *Stoel Rives*, San Francisco
   WEITZEL Mark *Thelen Reid*, San Francisco

3 GALE Kelley *Latham & Watkins*, San Diego
   GLASCOCK Thomas *Thelen Reid*, San Francisco
   MARKS Allan *Milbank Tweed*, Los Angeles

Up-and-coming individuals
   GREENBERG Jeffrey *Latham & Watkins*, Los Angeles

Individuals are listed alphabetically in each band.

"*flexibility in getting projects to completion.*" Its lawyers have been working recently on the development of several new projects, particularly in the fields of LNG, renewable energy and toll roads. It also has a strong reputation for asset acquisition and sales, mainly representing the buyers of troubled power projects. A key recent deal saw the team represent a consortium of banks in the sale of the Brazos Valley plant in Texas, one of the first examples of banks going on to sell the distressed assets they had gained through foreclosure. It also offers particular expertise in wind energy and has represented Fortis as the lead arranger in the Shell-sponsored portfolio of wind projects, as well as assisting ANZ and Dexia in the Brazos Wind project, and ANZ in the Colorado Green project.

The Lawyers: Ed Feo is not only "*one of Milbank's stars*" but, according to market sources, is also "*one of the most prominent names in the sector.*" He is widely acknowledged to be a strong projects lawyer, particularly in the field of wind energy projects, where he is a leading specialist. His colleague **Allan Marks** has been busy this year on the firm's high-profile toll road projects. He attracted considerable praise, particularly for his "*thorough and well-prepared*" approach.

The Clients: The team recently advised the State of Nuevo Leon, in Mexico, on its bond financing of the Monterrey Cadereyta toll road. It is also representing Citigroup as underwriter of a $250 million bond issue for the Autopista Costanera Norte toll road in Santiago. Within the LNG field, the group has been acting for the lenders in both the Sabine Pass and the Corpus Christi projects. It also represented KGen in the acquisition of eight generation plants from Duke Energy. This $325 million B Loan structured deal was a benchmark in the acquisition of distressed power assets. Other highlights include assisting the private equity buyers of the Batesville plant from NRG, the first acquisition to go ahead following NRG's bankruptcy.

Band 2

Thelen Reid & Priest LLP
See firm details p.300

The Firm: The firm climbs the rankings this year due to sustained market praise for the "*talented group of lawyers*" based in its San Francisco office. Peers are particularly impressed with "*the depth of quality throughout the team,*" pointing in particular to a number of solid younger partners. The team works closely with the New York office to represent sponsor companies on both domestic and international projects. This year, it has advised on the development of a number of new power projects, a rare accomplishment in a troubled market. It is also involved in the current wave of acquisitions and divestitures in the industry, often representing the buyers of troubled assets. Outside of the traditional energy field, the team has started work on a series of large-scale military base privatizations within the USA. International schemes, meanwhile, include representing project companies developing power projects in India, Morocco and the Dominican Republic, and in connection with the privatization of Lima Airport in Peru.

The Lawyers: "*Smart and capable*" **Mark Weitzel** was widely praised as an experienced and pragmatic "*deal-oriented lawyer.*" His colleague **Thomas Glascock** concentrates on the financing of projects. According to market sources, his tenacity has earned him a reputation as "*one of the most relentless negotiators around.*"

The Clients: The firm's key client is Calpine, and the team has been acting for it recently in the development of the Gilroy Peaking project in California. Also on the domestic front, the team advised Energy Investors Fund as investors in the $900 million Astoria power plant in New York City. It also represented Centennial Energy in its acquisition of wind energy assets, and assisted an affiliate of GE in the acquisition of a considerable interest in a coal-fired power plant in El Paso. Internationally, the team has advised GE and Baku as part owners of the Dabhol Power project in India, and has been involved in power restructurings in the Dominican Republic. Other clients include Actus Land Lease, ABB Energy Ventures and CMS Generation.

Band 3

Morgan, Lewis & Bockius LLP
See firm details p.1556

The Firm: This firm is perhaps best known for representing utilities in the development of domestic projects. It tends to focus on projects to the west of the Mississippi, where it is working on a number of major transactions for key clients Black Hills Corporation, Edison Mission Energy and Diamond Energy. The team concentrates mainly on power projects, including

wind energy, but has also worked on oil and gas and other energy-related projects.

The Lawyers: Richard Shortz (see p.272) is the key name in this practice. "*Extremely well known in the sector*" and "*a real client's lawyer,*" he is at the head of a large team in the state with access to considerable national resources.

The Clients: The team has worked on a number of projects for Black Hills Corporation, including the sale of its hydroelectric power projects in New York, and the acquisition of Cheyenne Light Fuel and Power in Wyoming. Work for Edison Mission Energy has included the financing of the Midway Sunset natural gas plant in California. It also represented Diamond Generating Corporation in the sale of an interest in a 1200MW combined cycle facility in Oklahoma and advised Sempra Energy on the development of a 1000MW coal-fired plant in Nevada.

Orrick, Herrington & Sutcliffe
See firm details p.295

The Firm: The California offices of this substantial projects practice are closely integrated with teams in New York and Washington, DC. The California group is particularly well known in the market for its work in wind energy projects, where it often appears on behalf of Eurus Energy. However, it is also experienced in a range of other schemes. For example, the team supported the New York office in the $900 million SR125 San Diego toll road project, representing the lead arrangers – BBVA and DEPFA Bank.

The Lawyers: Joseph Malkin, cochair of the energy and project finance group, leads the California team. The team works closely with New York-based Michael Meyers.

The Clients: The team has done a lot of work of late for Eurus Energy. This year, it represented the company in the financing of the Combine Hills 1 wind energy project in Oregon, and is also advising on the development of the Crescent Ridge wind project in Illinois. Babcock & Brown is another key client for wind energy projects.

Stoel Rives LLP

The Firm: This strong team is spread between the firm's San Francisco office and its Portland headquarters. The regional giant is hailed as a leader on the West Coast, particularly for representing developer companies in domestic power projects. Work this year has included the refinancing of a number of existing projects. The firm also boasts considerable experience in renewable energy schemes, both wind energy and geothermal.

The Lawyers: Peers rate **David Spielberg** as "*a tremendous talent.*" Clients, meanwhile, claim that he is "*priceless*" because "*unlike most lawyers he cuts through the fog and confusion instead of introducing more of it!*"

The Clients: Calpine is one of the firm's biggest clients and this year the lawyers have represented it on some large-scale refinancings, including a $2.6 billion bond refinancing of 14 power plants. The team has also acted on a number of wind energy projects for PPM Energy and regularly handles projects work for Sumitomo Mitsui Banking.

REAL ESTATE

California
Leading firms (Real Estate)

[1] **ALLEN MATKINS LECK GAMBLE** Los Angeles

[2] **COX CASTLE & NICHOLSON LLP** Los Angeles
GIBSON, DUNN & CRUTCHER LLP Los Angeles
PAUL, HASTINGS, JANOFSKY Los Angeles
PIRCHER, NICHOLS & MEEKS Los Angeles

[3] **DLA PIPER RUDNICK GRAY CARY** Los Angeles
LATHAM & WATKINS LLP Los Angeles
MAYER, BROWN, ROWE & MAW LLP Los Angeles
MORRISON & FOERSTER LLP San Francisco
MUNGER, TOLLES & OLSON LLP Los Angeles
ORRICK, HERRINGTON & SUTCLIFFE San Francisco
SHEPPARD, MULLIN, RICHTER San Francisco

[4] **COBLENTZ, PATCH, DUFFY & BASS** San Francisco
DEWEY BALLANTINE LLP Los Angeles
HELLER EHRMAN WHITE & MCAULIFFE Los Angeles
PILLSBURY WINTHROP LLP Los Angeles

Firms are listed alphabetically in each band.

Band 1

Allen Matkins Leck Gamble & Mallory LLP
See firm details p.279
The Firm: This "*fabulous*" firm commits more than half of its resources to real estate matters. Approximately 100 attorneys, operating from six offices, assist clients with a variety of issues related to acquisitions and disposals, equity and debt transactions, land use, construction, joint ventures, restructurings and workouts. Enjoying a cast-iron market reputation as the "*premier developer firm in California*," especially when it comes to leasing work, Allen Matkins has been counsel for transactions involving property in excess of 40 million sq ft over the past five years. It recently negotiated a global settlement on behalf of Trizec Real Estate with Aladdin Gaming to sell Dessert Passage to the Starwood/Planet Hollywood Bay Harbor group for $241 million. In a separate matter, the group represented Catellus in the sale of 935,000 sq ft of commercial entitlements in Mission Bay to a publicly traded investment trust, Alexandria Real Estate Equities.
The Lawyers: "*Preeminent practitioner and dealmaker*" **Michael Matkins** (see p.262) involves himself in complex, multiparty development matters. Clients claim that when it comes to applying business principles to real estate assets no other attorney matches his grasp of the "*big picture.*" He was particularly valued for possessing the happy knack of divining the balance to produce an ideal solution – "*transactional stuff*

really is his specialty.*" **Rick Mallory** (see p.262), co-manager of the San Francisco office, is renowned as a "*top-tier*" leasing lawyer, "*adept at servicing clients and finding areas of compromise.*" His work for landlords spans a range of matters, from equity issues to takeovers, renewals, purchase options, and construction contracts for tenant improvements. "*One of the top leasing lawyers in the state,*" **Tony Natsis** (see p.264) has experience that also includes purchases, sales and the development of commercial, office, retail and industrial properties. His style was described to researchers as "*tight*" and technically excellent. The combination is obviously a hit with major clients, as he has recently acted for Beacon Capital Partners, Northridge Capital and Sumitomo Realty in separate transactions, as well as advising a joint venture coordinated by JPMorgan Chase on a 200,000-sq-ft lease.
The Clients: Trizec Real Estate; Catellus; JPMorgan; Beacon Capital Partners; Northridge Capital; Sumitomo Realty; Boston Properties; Kilroy Realty; CarrAmerica; Colony Advisors and Tishman Speyer.

Band 2

Cox Castle & Nicholson LLP
The Firm: This substantial team operates out of offices in LA, San Francisco and Orange County. A highly respected, long-standing player in the California market, it divides its real estate group into finance, leasing and litigation teams, enabling it to handle a wide variety of services and transactions. Market sources praise its "*thoughtful and responsive*" approach to development work in particular, acknowledging its extensive engagement throughout the state in large-scale residential, commercial, office, and higher education projects.
The Lawyers: **Ira Waldman** once headed the finance division, and is still universally considered to be "*high on the list for commercial finance transactions.*" He has not let the grass grow under his feet though, and recently branched out into public entity ground leases. "*Terrific at the technical stuff,*" he is said to employ a "*scholarly*" approach, recognizing that the "*devil is in the detail.*" This is popular with clients, and he is a trusted counsel to a number of major developers involved in the Marina del Rey project. **Kenneth Bley** is in charge of the Century City office land use group. A "*brilliant*" litigator at all stages of the development process, his practice also includes counseling and representing devel-

opers before a variety of courts and tribunals in entitlement, planning, and zoning matters. "*One of the true deans of the real estate Bar,*" **Phillip Nicholson** was said by market sources to have been "*more influential in the marketplace than almost anyone else in the last 45 years.*"
The Clients: The firm represents clients in industries ranging from banking to pure real estate. Examples include Barker Pacific Group and MassMutual Financial Group.

Gibson, Dunn & Crutcher LLP
See firm details p.285
The Firm: This broad-based, 15-partner group has a "*great roster of clients*" that it serves in areas like property development, finance and capital market transactions. It also specializes in real estate-related workouts and debt restructuring. This year the group has conducted the acquisition of a large ski resort in Colorado, including the corporate components. In February 2004, it represented Hilton Hotels in the $500 million recapitalization of a transaction with CNL. Other recent highlights include assisting Pacific Coast Capital Partners in its acquisition of the Culver City-based Sony movie studio that provided the location for 'Gone With The Wind'.
The Lawyers: **Jesse Sharf** (see p.272) acts for private investors and other private entities, lenders and developers. Lauded by clients as "*prompt and responsive,*" he garners praise for his dynamic character and "*detail-oriented*" approach to transactions. He is currently working on the recapitalization of a hotel company with an estimated market capital of $2 billion. Tax and joint venture specialist **Michael Sfregola** (see p.272) combines "*phenomenal technical expertise with great generalship.*" His years of experience in the acquisition and financing of hotel, resort, commercial, industrial and residential properties contribute to his reputation as a "*thoughtful and talented*" attorney. Competitors credit **Dennis Arnold** (see p.243) with "*paving the way for people to deal with issues that others refuse to tackle.*" Observers were particularly impressed by his up-to-date knowledge of legislative changes. According to one client: "*Anyone can look at a set of documents and revise what's there,*" but it takes a "*detail-oriented fellow with a staggering knowledge of the law to spot what should be there.*" He has recently conducted two cutting-edge land use matters for a major developer, concerning the creation of a structure to conceal new properties from the view of surrounding national parks.

www.ChambersandPartners.com

All quotes in the text are from interviews with clients and competitors.

237

California
Leading individuals (Real Estate)

Senior Statesman

NICHOLSON Phillip *Cox Castle*, Los Angeles
PIRCHER Leo *Pircher Nichols*, Los Angeles
WAYTE Alan *DLA Piper Rudnick*, Los Angeles

[1] EATMAN Louis *Mayer Brown*, Los Angeles
FEDER Philip *Paul Hastings*, Los Angeles
MATKINS Michael *Allen Matkins*, Los Angeles
MEYER Michael *DLA Piper Rudnick*, Los Angeles
NELLIS Noel *Orrick Herrington*, San Francisco
SENEKER Carl *Morrison & Foerster*, San Francisco
SHARF Jesse *Gibson Dunn*, Los Angeles
WALKER Paul *Dewey Ballantine*, Los Angeles

[2] CAREY Stevens *Pircher Nichols*, Los Angeles
LIEVER Michael *Orrick Herrington*, San Francisco
LONERGAN James *Sheppard Mullin*, Los Angeles
MALLORY Rick *Allen Matkins*, San Francisco
MILLER O'Malley *Munger Tolles*, Los Angeles
NATSIS Tony *Allen Matkins*, Los Angeles
NICHOLS Phillip *Pircher Nichols*, Los Angeles
SFREGOLA Michael *Gibson Dunn*, Los Angeles
SMITH Brian *Heller Ehrman*, San Francisco
THORNTON Charles *Paul Hastings*, San Francisco
WALDMAN Ira *Cox Castle*, Los Angeles

[3] ARNOLD Dennis *Gibson Dunn*, Los Angeles
BERGER Don *Latham & Watkins*, Los Angeles
ELLMAN Howard *Ellman Burke*, San Francisco
FILETI Thomas *Morrison & Foerster*, Los Angeles
HAGEROTT Edward *Munger Tolles*, Los Angeles
HERR Robert *Pillsbury Winthrop*, San Francisco
MENDELSON Richard *DLA Piper Rudnick*, Los Angeles
MURRAY William *Orrick Herrington*, San Francisco
RISHWAIN James *Pillsbury Winthrop*, Los Angeles
RUTTER Paul *Gilchrist & Rutter*, Santa Monica
VOLPERT Richard *Munger Tolles*, Los Angeles

Leading individuals
(Real Estate: Zoning/Land Use)

[1] DUFFY Pamela *Coblentz Patch*, San Francisco
MIHLSTEN George *Latham & Watkins*, Los Angeles
THOMPSON Robert *Sheppard Mullin*, San Francisco
ZISCHKE Michael *Morrison & Foerster*, San Francisco

[2] BLEY Kenneth *Cox Castle*, Los Angeles
MURPHY Mary *Farella Braun*, San Francisco

Individuals are listed alphabetically in each band.

The Clients: The team serves organizations in the hospitality industry, such as Hilton Hotels and Rockpoint, as well as Pacific Coast Capital Partners, Wachovia Securities, New Millennium Homes and Lehman Brothers.

Paul, Hastings, Janofsky & Walker LLP

See firm details p.297

The Firm: Paul Hastings displays a "*breadth of practice*" that allows it to tackle transactions of a complexity beyond the reach of smaller, less national firms. Its well-integrated real estate team focuses on finding sources of capital for major developments, sales and purchases; and putting together innovative real estate transactions. Sources note that the group has established a "*formidable*" reputation in the niche, but ever-expanding, alternative lending market. To this end, it continues to represent US-based pension and opportunity funds – organizations seeking to invest in value-added transactions related to part-leased properties.

The Lawyers: Department chair **Philip Feder** (see p.251) is a "*smart, conscientious, fair and diligent*" attorney. Clients proclaim him to be "*first rate*" and "*top of the list*" for sophisticated portfolio transactions. He was recently involved in the sale by Oaktree Capital Management of around 80 acres of land, a transaction which necessitated sophisticated bond financing and the granting of a variety of agency approvals. **Charles Thornton** (see p.275) is an "*excellent, well-prepared and knowledgeable lawyer.*" He "*really knows how to negotiate,*" say observers. He immerses himself in private equity investment and substantial property developments, and also counsels on joint venture structures. He has been advising Lennar on a residential and commercial property development linked to the University of California's creation of a new, Merced-based research facility.

The Clients: Lehman Brothers; Colony Capital; Oaktree Capital Management; Morgan Stanley and GE.

Pircher, Nichols & Meeks

The Firm: This "*nimble and entrepreneurial*" firm possesses a breadth of expertise that belies its boutique status. Its impressive real estate practice encompasses, inter alia, hotel transactions, establishing joint ventures, and mezzanine financing. Clients appreciate this deliberate orientation toward corporate-related issues: the team was roundly praised for its "*business perspective*" and strong finance skills. Recent work includes representing Playa Vista in connection with a mixed-use development of retail, commercial and residential property. It also acted for Farallon Capital Management in a $343 million transaction involving the acquisition from Catellus of a volume of noncore assets.

The Lawyers: Bringing a "*mathematician's accuracy*" to the law, **Stevens Carey** is a "*brilliant and meticulous draftsman, who crafts resolutions that leave both sides happy.*" This "*superstar*" attorney specializes in tax and debt restructuring, and has a large private equity practice with national scope. **Phillip Nichols** focuses on joint ventures, acquisitions and disposals, and also offers expertise in workouts and commercial leasing. A "*tough negotiator,*" he is well regarded by commentators for his "*academic approach*" and "*great instincts.*" Widely admired real estate veteran, **Leo Pircher** completes the triumvirate. He is said to excel at transaction structuring and financing, and received praise for his "*incredible ability and great business judgment.*"

The Clients: Starwood Capital Group; Farallon Capital Management; AIG Global Real Estate Investment; Continental American Properties; Nomura Credit & Capital; Waterton Associates; Apollo Real Estate Advisors; AMB; Morgan Stanley; Oaktree Capital Management; Regent Properties; Summit Commercial Properties; Walton Street Capital; JMB Realty and Playa Vista.

Band 3

DLA Piper Rudnick Gray Cary US LLP

See firm details p.765

The Firm: This mammoth firm – the product of a high-profile 2004 merger – has made a considerable impression on the topography of the California real estate market over the past twelve months. Its description by one source as a "*collection of all-stars*" is reflective of a stunning growth spurt that has seen it acquire several of the market's most renowned attorneys. The "*fantastic*" real estate team represents a number of major Fortune 500 companies in a range of transactions, including leasing. Recent highlights include a role in the $1.2 billion sale of the Embarcadero Center in San Francisco, and the divestiture of a $150 million Superfund site in Glendale.

The Lawyers: "*One of the best known and respected leasing lawyers in the state,*" **Michael Meyer** (see p.263) acts for national financial institutions on major leasing transactions throughout the USA. His involvement in Broadcom's leasing of 680,000 sq ft of property from the Irvine Company is typical of the scale of his work, as is his conclusion in January 2004 of a 330,000-sq ft lease for National Bank. **Richard Mendelson**'s (see p.263) expertise resides in the areas of joint ventures, acquisitions and financing transactions. Peers consider him to be one of the "*key guys*" for the latter, and one source even went so far as to dub him the "*best real estate finance lawyer in Southern California.*" Historically a great transaction attorney with "*strong technical skills,*" **Alan Wayte** (see p.277) has recently joined the firm as senior counsel. A 35-year career in real estate has seen him amass a wide range of experience. For example, he has acquired railroad permits on behalf of the Southern California Regional Rail Authority and obtained leases for the Hollywood Bowl and Walt Disney Concert Hall.

The Clients: In addition to Broadcom and National Bank, the practice represents a number of Fortune 500 companies.

Latham & Watkins LLP

The Firm: This 50-strong group handles high-end real estate transactions and complex land use proceedings. It casts a long shadow throughout California; for clients it is an "*A-Team, front row and center;*" while competitors speak admiringly of the firm's "*strong and well-rounded*" practice, especially in land use. Market sources also highlight the group's "*strong bench*" and considerable expertise in REIT transactions and asset contributions. The team has recently assisted the NFL in securing a location for a new franchise, and sold a parcel of land to the state for $140 million on behalf of Playa Vista.

The Lawyers: A top finance lawyer, **Don Berger**'s practice includes the origination and restructuring of securitized and mezzanine loans, and REIT and loan portfolio financings, as well as real estate acquisitions, development, construction and leasing. He is typically visible acting for real estate funds, investment banks and other institutional organizations. **George Mihlsten** specializes in land use. "*One of the deans of the southern real estate development law Bar,*" he commands a "*first-rate*" reputation in this area, based on his involvement in such important projects as the 20,000-seat Staples Center arena. Last year he secured approval on behalf of Playa Vista for 2600 new residential units.

The Clients: NFL; Legacy Partners; Vivendi Universal; Price Legacy; Westfield Corporation and The Irvine Company.

Mayer, Brown, Rowe & Maw LLP
See firm details p.771

The Firm: Market sources agree that this firm is a "*national force*" for real estate transactions. While the Los Angeles office does not perhaps have quite the profile of its cousins in Chicago and New York, their close links enable the California real estate group to undertake large-scale development projects, frequently working across state borders. It regularly conducts financing work on behalf of Nova Scotia, most recently in relation to a large regional shopping center in receipt of multistate funding. The team also negotiates joint ventures for global real estate company CB Richard Ellis Investors.

The Lawyers: **Louis Eatman** (see p.250) employs his "*strong technical skills and big picture approach*" to great effect in his main area of expertise – real estate finance and joint venture matters. At the time of press, he was on the verge of closing a substantial acquisition for TIAA-CREF involving five trophy office properties situated around the country. He has also recently concluded condominium transactions in San Francisco and Las Vegas.

The Clients: The team acts for investors, pension funds, life assurance companies and banks, including CB Richard Ellis Investors, Nova Scotia and TIAA-CREF.

Morrison & Foerster LLP
See firm details p.293

The Firm: This talented team focuses on financing, REITs, leasing and purchase and sale transactions, and also offers a renowned land development group. Although there have been

some recent departures, the consensus of opinion is that this remains a "*top-notch*" group, packed with "*well-educated, competent and creative lawyers, functioning at the height of their powers.*" These attorneys have been channeling their energies into transactional work for homebuilders such as Windermere. They have also been busy recently with rights and document negotiation relating to the Mare Island redevelopment, and the Sacramento railroad project involving Millennia Sacramento and Union Pacific. On the investor side, the group represents such names as Divco West Properties, UBS Realty Investors and Hines on co-investment, management and leasing matters connected to their property acquisitions.

The Lawyers: A "*shining light*" of the California real estate market, **Kim Seneker** (see p.272) is credited by clients with an encyclopedic knowledge of the intricacies of private equity and finance transactions. "*Brilliant, thoughtful and careful,*" he serves a variety of large, institutional clients. Recent examples include representing Divco West Properties and Peery/Arrillaga in leasing matters, working with Bank of America on syndicated lending, and advising the Hawaii-based Bishop Estate on reworking its documentation. The dominant features of **Thomas Fileti**'s (see p.252) practice recall those of his firm; within the domain of real estate finance, he specializes in "*technically proficient and precise*" resort and hotel-associated mortgage REITs and mezzanine financing. **Michael Zischke** (see p.278) is a "*top-flight*" land use specialist. He combines this knowledge with California Environmental Quality Act expertise to provide quality counsel in a variety of matters, including the ongoing, often controversial, plans to expand LA's main port.

The Clients: Divco West Properties; UBS Realty Advisors; Peery/Arrillaga; Heinz; DRA Advisors; Hitachi; Bank of America, Deutsche Bank and Goldman Sachs.

Munger, Tolles & Olson LLP

The Firm: This well-established outfit was described by peers as one of the "*elite firms in California in a range of practice areas.*" Its midsized real estate group regularly represents financial institutions and government authorities involved in property development, advising on, inter alia, real estate acquisitions and dispositions, construction and leasing. Earlier this year, its "*high-caliber people*" advised Maguire Properties on the acquisition of Park Place, a 1.7 million-sq-ft office and retail site in Orange County. It is currently involved in a transaction related to the development of a 370,000-sq-ft entertainment center, to be located in Long Beach.

The Lawyers: According to market sources, **O'Malley Miller** is one of the "*leading lights*" of the state's real estate arena. Observers were in no doubt that he is the motivating force behind the

firm's recent advancement. This is unsurprising when his reputation as a "*smart, articulate and effective negotiator who knows how to accommodate difficult situations*" is taken into account. A member of the American College of Real Estate Lawyers, his work is rarely less than high profile. He has recently represented the Catholic Archdiocese of Los Angeles in its construction of a new cathedral, and was lead counsel to Disney in the Grand Avenue project – the redevelopment of downtown LA's remaining parcels of land. **Edward Hagerott** focuses on the formation of joint ventures and the acquisition and disposal of large tracts of land. Building on his strong market profile as a "*skilled*" technical attorney "*able to balance risks effectively,*" he played a prominent role in Tishman Speyer's recent acquisition of three office buildings in the south of the state, and undertook the restructuring of various leases for a 600-unit residential condominium project. **Richard Volpert** is founding chair of the firm's real estate department. Another member of the American College of Real Estate Lawyers, he is said to be "*one of the preeminent negotiators on behalf of government agencies.*" His "*experience and good judgment*" also make him invaluable to peers seeking independent conflict mediation.

The Clients: Maguire Properties; Catholic Archdiocese of Los Angeles; Disney; Tishman Speyer Properties; Developers Diversified Realty; Southern California Edison; Beacon Capital Partners and Hines.

Orrick, Herrington & Sutcliffe LLP
See firm details p.295

The Firm: Orrick Herrington enjoys a particularly strong reputation in the market for its expert representation of pension funds. The San Francisco-based real estate team also spends around 60% of its time structuring, and advising on, a mixture of domestic and foreign property investments – a network of international offices means that its reach extends as far as Asia. In addition, sources comment admiringly on the strength of the group's experience in real estate-related capital markets transactions.

The Lawyers: According to competitors, group chair **Noel Nellis** is the "*heart and soul*" of the practice. He combines "*great client skills*" with a "*raw intellect and great understanding of the law*" to cement a position throughout the state as a "*first-rate*" resource for transactions of all types. This includes handling negotiations and documentation in the areas of financing, leasing, construction and development. **Michael Liever** (see p.261) enjoys a "*stellar*" market reputation for pension fund and REIT work. "*Clients love him,*" admit peers, "*and, if you ask around, he tops the list in these areas.*" **William Murray** (see p.264) also specializes in financial restructuring. In addition, he has been responsible for the leasing of several large office, hotel and retail properties. His "*bright and practical*" approach and "*terrific and well-*"

rounded" expertise prompted enthusiastic applause from satisfied clients.

The Clients: Divco West Properties; RREEF Funds; Colony Capital; Catellus; SSR Realty Advisors and CalWest Industrial Properties.

Sheppard, Mullin, Richter & Hampton LLP

The Firm: This substantial firm fields around 70 real estate attorneys throughout the USA. The California practice is split into development and finance sides, but remains best known for its "*strong background*" in the latter. Recently though, the group has made concerted efforts to increase its profile in the former area – in particular undertaking a substantial amount of military base redevelopment work around San Francisco. Currently, it is representing a client in the phased transfer of 500 acres of former shipyard, to be converted into residential units. The team is also advising the Presidio Trust on its redevelopment of 700 acres of property adjacent to the Golden Gate Bridge. As part of this transaction, the firm played an important role in Lucasfilms' studio relocation into one million sq ft of space within the Presidio.

The Lawyers: Authorities hold **James Lonergan** in high regard for his "*bright, practical approach*" and "*tremendous diligence*" in real estate finance transactions. As well as assisting landlords with a variety of retail, office and industry projects, he has acted for Cineplex Odeon and Burger King in the purchase and sale of properties throughout the western USA. **Robert Thompson** is one of the firm's "*stars.*" He combines expertise in writing purchase agreements with a profound knowledge of government land use regulations. Competitors agree that he is a "*particularly adept negotiator in troublesome transactions,*" with some even going so far as to suggest that he "*has no peer*" in the field.

The Clients: A diverse client roster includes the Presidio Trust, Cineplex Odeon and Burger King.

Band 4

Coblentz, Patch, Duffy & Bass LLP

The Firm: This "*practical, extremely effective*" boutique boasts a formidable presence in San Francisco's land use circles. The team consists of 11 partners and seven associates, and focuses on commercial leasing, acquisitions and divestitures, and the formation of real estate organizations, reflecting an increased emphasis on public/private development projects over the last couple of decades. In the past year the team has advised eBay on the acquisition and entitlement of a two million sq ft campus in San Jose, and counseled the Hearst Corporation on the establishment of a

conservation easement along the California coast.

The Lawyers: **Pamela Duffy** is considered by peers and clients alike to be "*one of the best*" in the state for land use and zoning work. Lead counsel for eBay, in the above transaction, she was also involved in the Mills Peninsula hospital project – a 450,000-sq-ft medical center replacement, costing $350 million.

The Clients: Fairmont Hotels; eBay; Hearst Corporation and Kisco Corporation.

Dewey Ballantine LLP
See firm details p.1347

The Firm: The firm has suffered this year from a series of departures that have undeniably affected its real estate department. Despite this, the group still handles the gamut of real property issues, and liaises closely with the firm's tax, ERISA, litigation and environment departments to offer a comprehensive service.

The Lawyers: The reputation of the firm in California's real estate market owes much to the profile of real property star, **Paul Walker** (see p.277). He receives a wealth of enthusiastic praise from clients for the way in which he combines sophisticated legal advice with a big-picture understanding of business needs. "*Smart and entirely lacking ego,*" according to interviewees, his broad practice includes real estate lending, acquisitions and disposals, creditors' rights, capital markets advice and workouts.

The Clients: The practice services a range of municipal entities, finance houses and pension funds.

Heller Ehrman White & McAuliffe LLP
See firm details p.288

The Firm: Operating as a highly integrated group, the California team works closely with sister departments throughout the USA. The firm's real estate practice is organized as a tripartite structure, encompassing hotel, bank finance and private equity/pension fund work. In keeping with a reputation for serving large commercial entities, the firm counts Four Seasons, Fairmont and Starwood among its roster of clients. Over the past 12 months, the group has bought and sold a number of hotels on behalf of Fairmont, with a total value of approximately $350 million. It also recently concluded the formation of a $2 billion private venture between GIC and Tishman Speyer, which involves a portfolio of 12 properties in eight cities. In the finance arena, the group represents a host of heavyweights that include JPMorgan Chase and Lehman Brothers.

The Lawyers: **Brian Smith** divides his time between private equity investments and hotel

acquisition. He impresses clients with his "*superior legal and analytical skills,*" and is well regarded by peers for his "*deep understanding of the business issues involved in legal transactions.*" He was lead counsel in the GIC joint venture, and continues to represent Fairmont in all of its major sales, purchases and refinancings.

The Clients: Four Seasons Hotels and Resorts; Fairmont Hotels and Resorts; JPMorgan Chase; Lehman Brothers; GIC Real Estate and AEW Capital Management.

Pillsbury Winthrop LLP
See firm details p.1364

The Firm: The firm has experienced a number of high-profile departures this year. However its sizable and experienced real estate group has proved to be highly resilient. The group's broad base of expertise covers real estate acquisitions and disposals, financing and leasing, and it offers a particular niche in capital markets and public finance. The team has counseled Lennar on a number of projects, and specializes in affordable housing all over the country. At time of press the firm announced its merger with Shaw Pittman LLP to form Pillsbury Winthrop Shaw Pittman LLP.

The Lawyers: **Robert Herr** (see p.257) was recommended to researchers as a "*smart and quick attorney, with good experience and judgment.*" He has represented a variety of developers, managers, owners and lenders – including Shorenstein, IBM, the San Francisco Giants and Stein Kingsley Stein – in commercial and residential development, acquisition and divestiture, operation and leasing. **James Rishwain** (see p.269) is "*efficient and cooperative*" say his clients, and his work product is always "*outstanding.*" Exploiting a background in land use and public/private crossovers, he focuses on the interface between government and real estate development, and handles infrastructure financing work for clients like Lennar.

The Clients: Lennar; Shorenstein; IBM and Stein Kingsley Stein Investments.

Other Notable Practitioners

Howard Ellman of Ellman, Burke, Hoffman & Johnson enjoys a great reputation for his development practice. He has also made a name for himself in this area as a litigator. Currently, he is involved in defending an approval obtained by Lennar for a 1900-unit residential and commercial project. Interviewees also drew attention to **Paul Rutter**, at Gilchrist & Rutter Professional Corporation, for his "*excellent*" leasing and transactional work. **Mary Murphy**, a partner at Farella Braun & Martel LLP, is, market sources agree, "*an extremely good land use attorney.*"

TAX

California
Leading firms (Tax)

1. IRELL & MANELLA LLP *Los Angeles*
   LATHAM & WATKINS LLP *Los Angeles*
2. BAKER & MCKENZIE *Palo Alto*
   FENWICK & WEST LLP *Mountain View*
   MORRISON & FOERSTER LLP *San Francisco*
3. GIBSON, DUNN & CRUTCHER LLP *Los Angeles*
   LOEB & LOEB LLP *Los Angeles*
   O'MELVENY & MYERS LLP *Los Angeles*
   ORRICK, HERRINGTON & SUTCLIFFE *San Francisco*
   WILSON SONSINI GOODRICH & ROSATI *Palo Alto*
4. COOLEY GODWARD LLP *Palo Alto*
   MCDERMOTT WILL & EMERY *Los Angeles*
   MUNGER, TOLLES & OLSON LLP *Los Angeles*
   PAUL, HASTINGS, JANOFSKY *Los Angeles*
   PILLSBURY WINTHROP LLP *San Francisco*

Leading individuals (Tax)

1. CLAIR John *Latham & Watkins*, Los Angeles
   FULLER James *Fenwick & West*, Mountain View
   HYMAN Milt *Irell & Manella*, Los Angeles
   OFFER Stuart *Morrison & Foerster*, San Francisco
2. CUFF Terence *Loeb & Loeb*, Los Angeles
   DIVOLA Julie *Pillsbury Winthrop*, San Francisco
   FREIER Elliot *Irell & Manella*, Los Angeles
   HUMPHREYS Ivan *Wilson Sonsini*, Palo Alto
   PETERSON Jr John *Baker & McKenzie*, Palo Alto
   RABINOVITZ Joel *Irell & Manella*, Los Angeles
   SAX Paul *Orrick Herrington*, San Francisco
3. BEHNIA Hatef *Gibson Dunn*, Los Angeles
   BOLDING Grady *Orrick Herrington*, San Francisco
   BRYAN Karen *Latham & Watkins*, Los Angeles
   CHILTON Fred *McDermott Will*, Palo Alto
   IREDALE Nancy *Paul Hastings*, Los Angeles
   ROSE Stephen *Munger Tolles*, Los Angeles
   TOLLES Stephen *Gibson Dunn*, Los Angeles
4. BLASHEK Robert *O'Melveny & Myers*, Los Angeles
   LANGDON Larry *Mayer Brown*, Palo Alto
   MORROW Bill *Cooley Godward*, San Francisco
   RIZZI Robert *O'Melveny & Myers*, Menlo Park
   SCHUCK Edwin *McDermott Will*, Los Angeles
   SCZUDLO Paul *Loeb & Loeb*, Los Angeles
   STEIN Laurence *Latham & Watkins*, Los Angeles
   WEINER Samuel *Latham & Watkins*, Los Angeles

Up-and-coming individuals

FORST David *Fenwick & West*, San Francisco

Firms and individuals are listed alphabetically in each band.

Band 1

Irell & Manella LLP

The Firm: Ever since the firm's inception more than 50 years ago, its tax expertise has been one of its prime assets. Peers declare deep respect for its *"long history of producing excellent tax lawyers who offer a first-rate service to their clients."* The firm can also boast one of the broadest tax practices in the state, as it is well versed in local, state, federal and international tax issues. Its knowledge covers corporations, partnerships, individuals and trusts among other business entities. It is particularly renowned for its experience in complex restructurings, and also for offering a comprehensive tax planning service. Other considerations include its commercial acumen and considerable litigation experience, in addition to its history of success in tax controversy matters before the IRS, California Franchise Tax Board and other government agencies.

The Lawyers: **Milt Hyman** is an *"extremely well known"* and *"impressive"* practitioner in the tax field. He is especially noted for his skilled performances in major bankruptcy proceedings. **Elliot Freier** is also highly recommended by peers and specializes in workouts for troubled companies. **Joel Rabinovitz** won respect for his involvement in some high-profile matters, including advising Disney on tax matters related to the sale of its Disney Stores, and separately acting for the purchaser of the Milwaukee Brewers baseball team.

The Clients: Mirage Resorts; Teledyne; Charter Communications; Broadcom and Vulcan.

Latham & Watkins LLP

The Firm: This *"sophisticated"* practice has a distinctly international flavor, and a reputation as *"a large group packed with able lawyers."* It bypasses local and state tax issues, and instead directs its resources toward federal and international matters for national and multinational clients; energy companies feature highly in the firm's roster. The emphasis is on high-profile transactional and tax controversy matters, and it has a particularly fine record in complex M&A deals. The firm's distinguished REIT practice is also a drawing card. One of its highlights is the group's representation of Owens-Illinois in a significant acquisition of a company in France.

The Lawyers: As well as being managing partner of the LA office, **John Clair** has a well-established practice centered on corporate taxation, especially as related to M&A transactions. Sources comment that he is a *"solid, well-rounded and practical"* attorney. **Karen Bryan** is an *"excellent and knowledgeable"* corporate tax attorney who has a *"hard-working and no-nonsense approach."* **Laurence Stein** chairs the global tax practice and is a *"highly experienced"* practitioner. Despite being a younger member of the team, **Samuel Weiner** received considerable praise for his *"smart and practical"* approach, and peers also value his *"pleasant"* style.

The Clients: Edison International; Safeway; Irvine Company; Owens Illinois and Amgen.

Band 2

Baker & McKenzie
See firm details p.761

The Firm: This truly global tax practice has *"a worldwide network of attorneys"* spread across 69 offices. The firm naturally plays to its *"obvious global strength"* and is particularly experienced in cross-border transactions, including restructurings with an international dimension. Peers regard the practice as *"a sophisticated group of people doing high-profile work."* Meanwhile, clients are attracted to the team's *"responsiveness and strong work ethic."*

The Lawyers: **John Peterson** (see p.267) chairs the global tax practice and is *"a very dynamic international tax practitioner."* Clients reported that they rely on his *"amazing memory and planning skills,"* further bolstered by his client-handling skills, leading them to *"feel like the firm's most important case."*

The Clients: The client list is dominated by major national and multinational corporations.

Fenwick & West LLP
See firm details p.283

The Firm: This full-service firm focuses on hi-tech and life sciences clients. As a natural extension, it also offers a *"standout"* tax department that represents Fortune 500 clients throughout the USA. Three major areas of expertise include international matters, M&A transactions and tax litigation. A highlight in the latter area was representing Xilinx in a high-profile, two-week trial regarding the movement of IP offshore through cross sharing.

The Lawyers: **James Fuller** (see p.252) is consistently rated as one of the best tax lawyers in the country. *"No one does international tax as well as he does,"* sources said. **David Forst** (see p.252) is a key figure in the firm, immersing his legal skills in the thick of major transactions and litigations.

The Clients: The firm tends to advise large national companies, including 35 of the Fortune 500. It has a clear specialty in representing hi-tech companies from industries such as pharmaceuticals, electronics and automobile among others.

Morrison & Foerster LLP
See firm details p.293

The Firm: This firm has one of the broadest tax practices in the state, which is further enhanced by its international strength. It frequently represents US companies investing in China and Japan, and also Asian entities that are establishing themselves in the USA. Another area of expertise is M&A transactions, and the group recently acted for MarketWatch in its acquisition by Dow Jones. A thriving investment fund practice rounds out the firm.

The Lawyers: **Stuart Offer** (see p.265) works on both domestic M&A transactions and supplies tax advice on international transactions.
The Clients: Hawaiian Airlines; MarketWatch; McGrath and Sonic Solutions.

Band 3

Gibson, Dunn & Crutcher LLP
See firm details p.285
The Firm: The firm generated enthusiasm as a strong contender in the California tax scene. It is predominantly a transactional practice, including a significant chunk of M&A activity. For example, it has recently been working on a number of acquisitions on behalf of Interactive Corporation. Another attraction is its expertise in navigating banking clients through the arcane tax rules regarding savings and loans. The remainder of the practice is dedicated to tax controversy matters, and it has advised on a number of IRS audits and protests.
The Lawyers: **Hatef Behnia** (see p.244) is *"well-known and well-respected"* as a transactional authority among tax circles, while **Stephen Tolles**' (see p.275) insights into tax issues led commentators to describe him as a *"first-class, knowledgeable and experienced"* attorney.
The Clients: Washington Mutual; Interactive Corporation; Herbalife; Pitney Bowes; MGM; Computer Sciences Corporation; Intel; Quest; The Williams Companies; Leonard Green and Aurora Capital.

Loeb & Loeb LLP
The Firm: This firm has carved out an important role for itself in the tax market due to its leading status in certain niche areas. It is the undisputed expert in providing tax advice for partnerships and limited liability companies. The group is also particularly well versed in tax issues affecting the real estate and entertainment industries.
The Lawyers: **Terence Cuff**, managing partner of the tax department, cuts a wide swath in the practice area, illustrating particular experience in issues relating to partnerships in the real estate sector. One commentator added that he is *"monomaniacal in his love of tax law and eats, breathes and sleeps the stuff."* Also recommended is **Paul Sczudlo**, who specializes in the international dimensions of real estate tax issues.
The Clients: As well as representing clients in the real estate and entertainment industries, the firm also provides tax advice to companies in agriculture, energy and other sectors.

O'Melveny & Myers LLP
See firm details p.294
The Firm: The firm has a string of offices throughout the state – including Orange County, Los Angeles, Century City, Silicon Valley and San Francisco – and is therefore perfectly placed to respond quickly to clients' needs. Sources partic-

ularly noted its high-quality work in the M&A field, though it advises on all aspects of business tax. For example, the group recently represented DreamWorks on the tax aspects of a considerable IPO. It is also very knowledgeable in strategic partnerships, joint ventures and private equity issues.
The Lawyers: **Robert Blashek** has a general business tax practice with an inclination toward representing and forming private equity groups. **Robert Rizzi**, who splits his practice between California and DC, is rated as a *"first-class, highly knowledgeable"* attorney.
The Clients: Macerich; The Irvine Company; Clarity Partners; DreamWorks SKG; Edison Capital and Trust Company of the West (TCW).

Orrick, Herrington & Sutcliffe LLP
See firm details p.295
The Firm: Many observers commented that this is a *"world-class"* firm for supplying tax advice on financial transactions, including debentures and tax-exempt bonds. It has one of the most prolific practices in the state for tax controversy work, and its solid grounding on public finance issues also won commendation.
The Lawyers: The *"terrific"* **Paul Sax** works on both tax planning and controversies. He is pitched as *"a real controversy specialist"* and *"the go-to person for transactional problems."* **Grady Bolding** has worked on a number of high-profile M&A deals, parlaying a *"sharp, balanced, 100% reliable"* approach into huge successes for clients.
The Clients: The firm represents a range of clients, particularly in the energy and entertainment sectors.

Wilson Sonsini Goodrich & Rosati
See firm details p.302
The Firm: The firm has a fairly small tax group, consisting of seven tax attorneys who are ably supported by a larger tax and funds services department. Clients report that the team is doing *"great work"* in the transactional arena, including a lot of financings, spin-offs and acquisitions. Its lawyers are respected due to their combination of legal acumen and responsiveness. Clients said: *"They know what they're talking about."*
The Lawyers: **Ivan Humphreys** (see p.258) advises on a variety of transactional issues and *"has considerable knowledge in the acquisitions area."* His *"reasonable and even-keeled"* demeanor proved to be a significant asset on difficult tax proceedings.
The Clients: Hewlett-Packard; 3Com; Solectron; Sanmina; VISX; McAfee; Brocade and Veritas.

Band 4

Cooley Godward LLP
The Firm: The tax department is a fully integrated part of the firm's leading M&A practice, and inevitably participates on a number of high-profile transactions. Other areas of expertise

include debt and equity placements and private equity funds. Clients view it as one of *"the best stables of tax partners in the Bay Area."* It represents a bevy of hi-tech companies and is rated as *"top notch for issues affecting Silicon Valley companies."* It is also popular because of its *"thorough, responsive and pragmatic"* approach.
The Lawyers: **Bill Morrow** supplies a *"one-stop shopping experience for tax issues."* His practice centers on tax applications as related to emerging companies and investment funds.
The Clients: Borland Software; GE Capital; Siebel Systems; eBay and Venrock.

McDermott Will & Emery
See firm details p.773
The Firm: Following a year of expansion, this firm can boast a considerable state tax practice to complement its already well-established international capability. It now has 13 tax attorneys who enjoyed a successful year working on numerous acquisitions. The team has also shepherded clients through some important tax controversies involving the IRS.
The Lawyers: **Fred Chilton** (see p.248) leads the team and has *"a very loyal client following,"* while **Edwin Schuck** (see p.271) was highly praised by rivals as *"a brilliant tax lawyer with a very sophisticated business sense."*
The Clients: The practice specializes in representing large multinational companies such as Cisco Systems, Cadence Design Systems and PeopleSoft.

Munger, Tolles & Olson LLP
The Firm: The tax department is closely integrated with the firm's corporate and real estate teams, offering clients a broad array of expertise that encompasses a range of transactional matters. M&A and joint ventures are features, as is the group's key strength in real estate work. To complete the one-stop-shop service, the team also offers comprehensive advice in litigation and tax controversy matters.
The Lawyers: **Stephen Rose** is the practice's most *"prolific"* attorney and an all-around federal tax expert. Peers reveal that he has *"a can-do attitude to transactions."*
The Clients: Berkshire Hathaway; Edison Capital; NBC Universal; KB Home; The Yucaipa Companies; City National Bank; The Price Group; Oaktree Capital; Rustic Canyon and Cook Inlet Region.

Paul, Hastings, Janofsky & Walker LLP
See firm details p.297
The Firm: This practice stands out because of its substantial expertise in tax litigation and related controversy matters. Unlike many firms, it has a dedicated team of trial lawyers that work solely on tax matters, and hence it has become an authority on high-profile proceedings. Another

established niche is in representing Far Eastern companies, and the group has further developed this capability with some interesting new recruits.
The Lawyers: Nancy Iredale (see p.258) is an *"astute"* practitioner who focuses on the litigation of tax controversy matters.
The Clients: Far Eastern and Latin American companies form a substantial part of the firm's client base.

Pillsbury Winthrop LLP
See firm details p.1364
The Firm: This full-service practice encompasses transactional and litigation work in the international, federal, state and local tax realms. The practice is particularly notable because of its strong government contacts. A number of its tax litigators have been recruited from government departments, and the team retains strong links with the IRS and the Treasury. At time of press the firm announced its merger with Shaw Pittman LLP to form Pillsbury Winthrop Shaw Pittman.
The Lawyers: Julie Divola (see p.250) is a domestic transactional lawyer who is noted as a *"smart and active"* practitioner in complex M&A deals.
The Clients: The practice has a loyal client following, but is widening its base with the addition of some private equity and startup clients.

Other Notable Practitioners
Larry Langdon (see p.260), director of global tax at Mayer, Brown, Rowe & Maw LLP was formerly at the IRS. Despite having only two years in private practice under his belt, he has already gained a strong reputation for his skill in settling disputes relating to the IRS. His clients declare that he is *"a top-flight tax attorney with the utmost integrity,"* and find that *"his insight is invaluable."* They also appreciate his *"collaborative approach that avoids unnecessary bombast."*

Leaders in California

ABEL, Sally
Fenwick & West LLP, Mountain View
650 335 7212
sabel@fenwick.com
Recommended in Intellectual Property
Practice Areas: Chair of firm's Trademark Group. International trademark/domain protection, selection/acquisition, registration, litigation/dispute resolution, Internet issues and trade dress.
Prof. Memberships: Member, Board of Directors of International Trademark Association (INTA), 1998-2000; chaired INTA's Internet Subcommittee, 1996-98; recently chaired INTA's Issues and Policy Committee. Served as INTA's representative on 11 member International Ad Hoc Committee (IAHC), international body organized by Internet Society at behest of Internet Assigned Numbers Authority, to develop enhancements to Internet Domain Name System. Participated in World Intellectual Property Organization's (WIPO) First Meeting of Consultants on Trademarks and Internet Domain Names, 1997.
Career: In 2001, named one of top three most frequently nominated trademark lawyers in the world in Euromoney's 'Best of the Best' Global Guide to the World's Best Lawyers; in Euromoney's 2002 'Guide to the World's Leading Trade Mark Law Practitioners'; in Law Business Research Limited's 'International Who's Who of Business Lawyers' for 2002 and 2003-04.
Personal: University of California Los Angeles School of Law, JD, 1984; University of California, Davis, BA in history summa cum laude, 1977.

ABELL, Nancy L
Paul, Hastings, Janofsky & Walker LLP, Los Angeles 213 683 6162
nancyabell@paulhastings.com
Recommended in Employment
Practice Areas: Chair of Employment Law Department. Represents employers in employment class actions and individual discrimination, harassment, retaliation and wrongful discharge lawsuits; OFCCP affirmative action compliance reviews; unfair labor practice charges; organizing campaigns; labor negotiations; arbitrations; and EEOC proceedings.
Publications: 'An Employer's Guide for Preparing Affirmative Action Programs'; 'An Employer's Guide to the Americans with Disabilities Act' (1991); 'Federal Contractor Affirmative Action Compliance' chapter of 'Employment Discrimination Law'.
Personal: Graduated first in her class - Pitzer College of the Claremont Colleges - 1972; graduated Order of the Coif and Order of the Barristers - The UCLA School of Law -1979.

ADLER, James
Irell & Manella LLP, Los Angeles
310 277 1010
Recommended in Employment

ADLER, Robert
Munger, Tolles & Olson LLP,
Los Angeles 213 683 9100
Recommended in Corporate/M&A

AHRENS, Michael
Sheppard, Mullin, Richter & Hampton LLP, San Francisco 415 434 9100
Recommended in Bankruptcy

ALEXANDER, Judith
Winn & Alexander LLP, Capitola
831 479 3490
Recommended in Media & Entertainment

ALEXIS, Geraldine
Bingham McCutchen LLP,
San Francisco 415 393 2000
Recommended in Antitrust

ALVAREZ, Fred
Wilson Sonsini Goodrich & Rosati,
Palo Alto 650 493 9300
falvarez@wsgr.com
Recommended in Employment
Practice Areas: Heads Employment Law Litigation Practice.
Prof. Memberships: Admitted to practice in California. Member, House of Delegates of the ABA; Equal Employment Opportunity Law Committee of the ABA Labor and Employment Law Section; and Advisory Committee of the American Law Institute Restatement of Employment Law. Management Chair of the Employment Sub-Committee of the Class Actions & Derivative Suits Committee of the ABA Section of Litigation.
Career: Joined WSGR as Partner, 1997. Partner, Pillsbury Madison Sutro, 1989-97. Commissioner, US EEOC, 1984-87. Assistant Secretary of Labor of the US Department of Labor, 1987-89.
Personal: BA, Stanford, 1972 and JD, Stanford, 1975.

ANTHONY, William
Orrick, Herrington & Sutcliffe LLP,
San Francisco 415 392 1122
Recommended in Intellectual Property

ARGUEDAS, Cristina
Arguedas, Cassman & Headley, LLP,
Emeryville 510 654 2000
Recommended in Litigation

ARNOLD, Dennis
Gibson, Dunn & Crutcher LLP,
Los Angeles 213 229 7864
darnold@gibsondunn.com
Recommended in Real Estate
Practice Areas: Member of the firm's Real Estate Group, Global Finance Group and Business Restructuring and Reorganization Group. Extensive experience in all aspects of commercial and residential real estate and finance, as well as workouts, bankruptcy and debt restructuring and is a nationally recognized expert in real estate finance insolvency and commercial law. He is a noted authority on secured transactions, the law of guaranties, letters of credit, and California's one action and anti-deficiency laws.
Prof. Memberships: Member, American College of Real Estate Lawyers.
Publications: Drafted California Civil Code Section 2856.
Personal: JD, Yale University, 1975.

ARONSON, Seth
O'Melveny & Myers LLP, Los Angeles
213 430 6000
Recommended in Litigation

ARONZON, Paul
Milbank, Tweed, Hadley & McCloy,
Los Angeles 213 892 4000
Recommended in Bankruptcy

ASHCRAFT, Howard
Hanson, Bridgett, Marcus, Vlahos & Rudy, LLP, San Francisco
415 995 5073
hashcraft@hansonbridgett.com
Recommended in Construction
Practice Areas: Represents public and private owners, contractors and designers in complex construction projects. In addition to dispute resolution and litigation, he provides counsel in project formation and professional practice issues. His practice includes state and federal courts, domestic and international arbitrations.
Prof. Memberships: Fellow, American College of Construction Lawyers (Board Member); ABA, Forum on the Construction Industry (Former Governing Committee Member); Arbitrator, AAA's Large and Complex Case Program for Construction; ACEC, Legal Counsel Forum.
Career: Partner, Hanson, Bridgett, Marcus, Vlahos & Rudy (1993 - Present); Shareholder, Severson & Werson (1986-93). Selected in September 2004 as one of the top 10 lawyers in Northern California by San Francisco Magazine/Law & Politics. Admitted in California and Nevada.
Publications: 'A Matter of Consequence: Construction Law & Business', Vol. 3, No. 1 2002; 'Enforceability of Limitation of Liability Clauses', 1994) 'The Construction Lawyer,' Vol. 14, No. 2; 'CERCLA 'Arranger' Liability - Emerging Risk for Environmental Consul-

tants', 1994 'The Construction Lawyer', Vol. 14, No. 1; 'Limitation of Liability - The View After Markborough', 1991 'The Construction Lawyer', Vol. 11, No. 3; 'Volt v Board of Trustees Construction Arbitration and the Making of a Federal Case', (1988) 'The Construction Lawyer' Vol 8, No 3; 'Legal Aspects of Condition Assessment and Reporting, Structural Condition Assement', Wiley 2004;'The Expert Consultant and Witness, Forensic Structural Engineering Handbook', McGraw-Hill 2000; 'Avoiding and Managing Risk of Differing Site Conditions', chapter in Differing Site Condition Claims, Wiley 1992.
Personal: Boalt Hall (University of California at Berkeley), JD 1979; Stanford University, AB Human Biology 1974.

ASPERGER, James
O'Melveny & Myers LLP, Los Angeles
213 430 6000
Recommended in Litigation

BABBE, David B
Morrison & Foerster LLP, Los Angeles
213 892 5549
dbabbe@mofo.com
Recommended in Insurance
Practice Areas: Focused on insurance coverage, professional liability and complex banking litigation within a general business litigation practice. Has handled an array of insurance coverage litigation in both state and federal courts as well as served as liaison counsel in a multi-billion dollar environmental coverage action.
Prof. Memberships: Member, Litigation Section, American Bar Association. Member, Association of Business Trial Lawyers.
Career: Admitted to practice in California.
Personal: BA degree, magna cum laude, University of California, Irvine, 1978; JD degree, second in class, University of California, Los Angeles School of Law, 1981, Order of the Coif; Member, Moot Court Honors Board.

BAKER, Tyler A
Fenwick & West LLP, Mountain View
650 335 7624
tbaker@fenwick.com
Recommended in Antitrust
Practice Areas: Chair of firm's Antitrust and Unfair Competition Group. Complex litigation, with primary emphasis on antitrust and intellectual property law. Extensive experience in all aspects of antitrust law. Has represented both plaintiffs and defendants in civil antitrust trials, as well as individuals and companies that were targets in state and federal antitrust investigations. Has provided antitrust advice to clients on issues including distribution practices, joint ventures, pre-merger notification, and substantive merger reviews by the Department of Justice and Federal Trade Commission. Significant experience in intellectual property cases, including trade secrets, trademarks, trade dress, unfair competition, and related business

torts. Has represented clients in cases including breach of contract, fraud, misrepresentation, breach of fiduciary duty, lender liability, bankruptcy fraud, tortious interference with contract, and federal 'whistle blower' cases. Involved in numerous appeals in state and federal courts. Has argued in the United States Court of Appeals for the Fifth Circuit and several Texas state courts of appeal.
Career: Law clerk to US Judge Charles Renfrew, Northern District of California, and to Justice Lewis F Powell, Jr, United States Supreme Court, 1976. Law professor, University of Virginia School of Law, 1978-81. Special Assistant to William F Baxter, Assistant Attorney General, Antitrust Division, United States Department of Justice, 1981-82.
Personal: Stanford Law School, JD with highest honors, 1975; Oxford University, BA in jurisprudence with First Class Honors (Rhodes Scholar), 1972; Southern Methodist University, BA in economics with highest honors, 1969.

BALABANIAN, David
Bingham McCutchen LLP,
San Francisco 415 393 2000
Recommended in Litigation

BALLATI, Deborah
Farella Braun & Martel LLP,
San Francisco 415 954 4400
Recommended in Construction

BARR, Michael R
Pillsbury Winthrop LLP, San Francisco
415 983 1151
mbarr@pillsburywinthrop.com
Recommended in Environment
Practice Areas: Mr Barr is a Partner in the environment, land use and natural resources; global energy; and new ventures areas. Practices in the administrative, commercial and corporate law fields and has extensive experience assisting established and emerging ventures in the transportation, communications, computer, chemical, food products, energy, mining and manufacturing industries. He focuses on emerging issues and innovative solutions to complex regulatory, commercial and corporate matters. Has assisted public and privately held companies, associations, trade groups and other entities on many matters of first impression, such as development rights creation, banking and trading. He has served on many advisory and trade groups. He speaks often on emerging development, commercial and administrative issues to round tables, associations and foundations on subjects as diverse as homeland security, rubber manufacturing and hard rock mining. He has participated and led many teams involved in business planning, venture startup, financing, project development, strategic reorganization, long term joint ventures and many other innovative activities.
Career: Admitted to practice: State of California.

Personal: JD, Harvard University, 1973; BS, University of Washington at Seattle, 1970.

BARSKY, Wayne
Gibson, Dunn & Crutcher LLP,
Los Angeles 310 557 8183
wbarsky@gibsondunn.com
Recommended in Intellectual Property
Practice Areas: Co-Chair of the firmwide Intellectual Property Practice Group. Practices exclusively in the area of patent litigation for clients in the computer, software, biotech, and medical industries. Representative clients include Columbia University, Johnson & Johnson, Vivendi Universal, Electronic Arts, and Serono.
Prof. Memberships: Member, American Intellectual Property Law Association. Member, Patent Trials Subcommittee of the IP Section, American Bar Association.
Publications: Numerous publications and speaking engagements; frequent participant in Practising Law Institute programs on patent trial practice.
Personal: JD, UC Berkeley, Boalt Hall School of Law, 1983.

BASICH, Anthony M
Hogan & Hartson LLP, Los Angeles
310 789 5417
ambasich@hhlaw.com
Recommended in Media & Entertainment
Practice Areas: Extensive experience in commercial and general business litigation, with a focus on entertainment-related matters. Has successfully litigated copyright, trademark and contract based actions involving idea submission, accounting, vertical integration, guild, product placement, employment and rights claims on behalf of major movie studios, television production companies and television networks.
Prof. Memberships: Member, Executive Committee, California State Bar Litigation Section; Chairman, Litigation Section, California Bar Education Committee; Chairman, Litigation Section, California Bar Trial Symposium Committee; Member, Los Angeles County Bar Association.
Personal: The George Washington University, (Member, Law Review, BS); Stanford University (JD).

BECK, Mark
Beck, De Corso, Daly, Kreindler & Harris, Los Angeles 213 688 1198
Recommended in Litigation

BEHNIA, Hatef
Gibson, Dunn & Crutcher LLP,
Los Angeles 213 229 7534
hbehnia@gibsondunn.com
Recommended in Tax
Practice Areas: Specializes in tax aspects of mergers and acquisitions, spin-offs and separations, debt and equity financings, derivative securities, partnership transactions, and taxation

of financial institutions. Has successfully represented taxpayers before the Internal Revenue Service in cases involving significant audit adjustments.
Personal: JD, University of Southern California, 1981, Order of the Coif, Note and Article Editor, University of Southern California Law Review. MBA, Stanford University Graduate School of Business, 1977. BA in mathematics, Reed College, 1975.

BELL, Suzanne
Wilson Sonsini Goodrich & Rosati,
Palo Alto 650 493 9300
sbell@wsgr.com
Recommended in IT Outsourcing
Practice Areas: Co-manages WSGR's Technology Transactions Practice. Handles technology and IP-related transactions, with an emphasis on strategic alliances for high technology and life sciences companies. Also counsels such clients with respect to new business models and IP issues.
Prof. Memberships: Admitted to practice in California.
Career: Joined WSGR, 1988. Became Partner, 1995. Co-Chair, Nominating Committee, WSGR. Former member, WSGR's Operations Committee, Executive Committee, Management Committee and Strategic Planning Committee.
Personal: JD (with distinction), Stanford Law School, 1988; MS, Columbia University, 1982; BA (cum laude), Middlebury College, 1980.

BELLAH MAGUIRE, Jennifer
Gibson, Dunn & Crutcher LLP,
Los Angeles 213 229 7986
jbellah@gibsondunn.com
Recommended in Corporate/M&A
Practice Areas: Extensive experience in corporate transactions and securities work, with an emphasis on mergers and acquisitions and private equity matters. She represents private equity fund sponsors and investors in diverse fund formation matters.
Career: Joined Gibson, Dunn & Crutcher after clerking for the 9th Circuit Court of Appeals and has practiced in the firm's Los Angeles offices and Paris office. She speaks fluent French and handles cross-border transactions.
Publications: Frequent commentator on corporate and securities topics.
Personal: JD, University of California, Boalt Hall School of Law, 1982, Order of the Coif, Associate Editor, Law Review.

BENJAMIN, Alan
Orrick, Herrington & Sutcliffe,
Los Angeles 213 612 2431
abenjamin@orrick.com
Recommended in Banking & Finance
Practice Areas: Mr Benjamin heads Orrick's Banking and Commercial Finance Group worldwide. Mr Benjamin focuses on banking and capital markets transactions, including secured and unsecured loan transactions, subordinated debt and second lien transac-

tions, project financings, leveraged buy-outs, lease transactions and debt restructurings. Mr Benjamin has extensive experience in large syndicated financings and intercreditor arrangements. Recent experience includes loans to and bonds issued by Native American tribes.
Career: Orrick, Herrington & Sutcliffe LLP; Partner, 1994-present; Managing Director, 2001; Executive Committee Member, 1997-2001; Private Finance Group Chair, 1996-2000. Morrison & Foerster LLP, Partner, 1983-94; associate 1977-83.
Personal: UCLA Law School, JD 1997, Order of the Coif; UCLA School of Management, MBA in Finance 1997, Beta Gamma Sigma; UCLA, 1974 AB in Economics, Phi Beta Kappa

BENNETT, Bruce S
Hennigan, Bennett & Dorman LLP, Los Angeles 213 694 1200
bennettb@hdblawyers.com
Recommended in Bankruptcy
Practice Areas: Business Reorganization and Bankruptcy
Prof. Memberships: Fellow, American College of Bankruptcy; Member, State Bar of California Section on Commercial Law and Bankruptcy.
Career: Bruce Bennett is a Managing Partner of Hennigan, Bennett & Dorman LLP, a Los Angeles based law firm, which focuses on business reorganization, commercial litigation, and intellectual property matters. Mr Bennett is Chairman of the firm's business reorganization and bankruptcy group. His practice includes representation of debtors, creditors, equity interest holders, and trustees in major business reorganization cases. Recent assignments include representation of the Committee of Osprey Note Holders in In re Enron Corp., the Ad Hoc Committee of Adelphia Communications Corp. Senior Note Holders in In re Adelphia Communications Corp., the Senior Secured Notes (mezzanine financing) in In re Oglebay Norton Corp., the Chapter 11 trustee for In re Hawaiian Airlines, Inc., the steering committee of First Lien Lenders in In re WestPoint Stevens, Inc., and Rabobank in Rabobank v The Royal Bank of Canada (Enron related commercial litigation). Mr Bennett is a fellow the American College of Bankruptcy, an honorary member of the Commercial Bar Association in London, a Member of the State Bar of California Section on Commercial Law and Bankruptcy, and previously served as a commissioner of the Personal and Small Business Bankruptcy Advisory Commission of the California Board of Legal Specialization and a member of the Board of Governors of the Los Angeles financial lawyers conference. In 1995, Mr Bennett was named runner-up for Lawyer of the Year by the National Law Journal for his

work representing the debtor in In re County of Orange.
Personal: Mr Bennett graduated from Brown University (ScB Applied Mathematics) in 1979 and received his law degree from The Harvard Law School in 1982.

BENNETT, Fred G
Quinn Emanuel Urquhart Oliver & Hedges, LLP, Los Angeles
213 443 3000
fredbennett@quinnemanuel.com
Recommended in Construction
Practice Areas: Specializes in business litigation, international and domestic arbitration. Extensive experience in technical disputes, including satellite/aerospace litigation, construction, engineering and architectural disputes; intellectual property disputes; commercial disputes; corporate partnership disputes and dissolutions; and general business litigation. Has tried or arbitrated as lead counsel, domestically and internationally, over 30 major disputes to verdict or award.
Career: Mr Bennett has broad experience in all types of business litigation, with particular emphasis on complex technical disputes, unfair competition claims involving technical matters, construction disputes, international and domestic arbitration and mediation, and general business and real estate litigation. He has tried or arbitrated as lead counsel, domestically and internationally, over 30 major disputes to verdict or award. Included among Mr Bennett's litigation representations are representation of major real estate developers and projects in downtown Los Angeles and other major cities in the United States; representation of the Los Angeles Times in various commercial and construction matters; representations of Parsons Corporation and Jacobs Engineering in connection with major engineering/construction projects around the world; representation of aerospace companies including Northrop, TRW and Loral in commercial satellite, aerospace and IP matters; and representation of corporations, such as Mattel, in intellectual property disputes. Mr Bennett also has years of experience serving as chairman or sole arbitrator on numerous international and domestic arbitrations, including disputes involving patent infringement, trade secret, entertainment issues, technical commercial matters, major construction and engineering, and insurance coverage issues. He is a member of the American Arbitration Association National Board of Directors and Large Complex Case Panels, and the US National Committee on Arbitration for the International Chamber of Commerce. Mr Bennett is a contributing editor to the 4th edition of Redfern and Hunter's eminent treatise, the Law and Practice of International Commercial Arbitration.

Publications: 'Dispositive Motions', LCCP Continuing Education Program, American Arbitration Association (October 1996); 'Discovery', LCCP Continuing Education Program, American Arbitration Association (May 1996); 'Award and Appeal', LCCP Continuing Education Program, American Arbitration Association (October 1997); 'Handling Tough Evidentiary Objections', LCCP Continuing Education Program, American Arbitration Association (April 1998); 'Drafting Arbitration Clauses', Business Litigation Report (Newsletter of Quinn Emanuel Urquhart Oliver & Hedges, LLP), February 1998. 'Characteristics of ICC Arbitrations', ICC National Seminar, San Francisco, California (April 17, 1998); 'Obtaining the Injunctive Relief You Need When You Need it in Arbitration', Business Litigation Report, February 1999; 'Role of the Panel Chair and Conducting a Preliminary Hearing', AAA National Neutrals Conference, Orlando, Florida 1998; 'Guidelines for Preparing Reasoned Arbitration Awards', AAA Continuing Education Program (September 2000); 'Enforcing Arbitration Awards Worldwide', Quinn Emanuel Annual Arbitration Seminar (October 2001); 'Beyond the Rules: Winning International Arbitration Strategies from The Viewpoints of Arbitrators, Administrators & Advocates', Quinn Emanuel Annual Arbitration Seminar (November 2002); 'Disclosure Rules for Arbitrators', AAA Continuing Education Program (November 2002), co-editor of Redfern and Hunter's 'Law and Practice of International Commercial Arbitration', (4th edition, 2005).
Personal: UCLA (JD, 1973). Managing Editor, UCLA Law Review, 1972-73. University of Utah (HBA, 1970).

BENVENUTTI, Peter
Heller Ehrman LLP, San Francisco
415 772 6000
Recommended in Bankruptcy

BERCHILD, John
Sheppard, Mullin, Richter & Hampton LLP, Los Angeles 213 620 1780
Recommended in Banking & Finance

BERGER, Don
Latham & Watkins LLP, Los Angeles
213 485 1234
Recommended in Real Estate

BERGMAN, Michael
Weissmann, Wolff, Bergman, Coleman, Grodin & Evall, LLP, Beverly Hills
310 858 7888
Recommended in Media & Entertainment

BERKES, Robert
Berkes Crane Robinson & Seal, LLP, Los Angeles 213 955 1150
Recommended in Insurance

BERTELSEN, Mark
Wilson Sonsini Goodrich & Rosati, Palo Alto 650 493 9300
mbertelsen@wsgr.com
Recommended in Corporate/M&A
Practice Areas: Corporate law and governance, M&A, international and cross-border transactions.
Prof. Memberships: Admitted to practice in California.
Career: Joined WSGR, 1972; became Partner, 1977. Member, WSGR Policy Committee and Executive Management Committee. Former Managing Partner, 1990-96. Prior to joining firm, served two years as an officer in the US Army. Serves on a number of boards of directors and is currently a Director of Autodesk and a Trustee of The UCSB Foundation.
Personal: JD, Boalt Hall School of Law, University of California (Berkeley), 1969; BA, high honors, University of California (Santa Barbara), 1966.

BIDART, Michael
Shernoff, Bidart & Darras LLP, Claremont 909 621 4935
Recommended in Insurance

BIRD, Terry
Bird, Marella, Boxer & Wolpert PC, Los Angeles 310 201 2100
Recommended in Litigation

BLANCHARD, Timothy P
McDermott Will & Emery, Los Angeles
310 551 9320
tblanchard@mwe.com
Recommended in Healthcare
Practice Areas: Focuses on healthcare regulatory issues, including Medicare and Medicaid coverage, billing and payment rules, healthcare payment appeals, healthcare compliance programs, HIPAA privacy, fraud and abuse audits and investigations, false claims act defense, certification and licensing, and utilization review.
Prof. Memberships: Member of Board of Directors of American Health Lawyers Association (AHLA) and Vice-Chair of the AHLA Annual Institute on Medicare and Medicaid Payment Issues. Fellow of Healthcare Financial Management Association. Member of editorial review board of Healthcare Financial Management. Member of editorial Advisory Board of CCH Healthcare Compliance. Member of Legal Advisory Committee of American Academy of Professional Coders.
Personal: Earned JD (cum laude) and MHA in 1986 from Saint Louis University, and earned BS (with honors) in 1982 from Oklahoma State University. Admitted to State Bar of California, State Bar of Washington, and District of Columbia Bar.

BLASHEK, Robert
O'Melveny & Myers LLP, Los Angeles
310 553 6700
Recommended in Tax

BLECHER, Maxwell M
Blecher & Collins, Los Angeles
213 622 4222
mblecher@blechercollins.com
Recommended in Antitrust, Litigation
Practice Areas: Antitrust litigation; complex business litigation; intellectual property litigation; professional malpractice litigation; class actions.
Prof. Memberships: American Bar Association; State Bar of California; Los Angeles County Bar Association; American College of Trial Lawyers (Fellow); American Board of Trial Advocates (Fellow); Aemrican Judicature Society; Chancery Club; Association of Business Trial Lawyers.
Career: Maxwell M Blecher, the founding Partner of Blecher & Collins, is renowned for his expertise in the antitrust field. He has litigated significant cases resulting in many precedent-setting decisions in state and federal courts and the Supreme Court. He has testified before Congressional hearings; authored numerous articles on antitrust and civil litigation; and lectures extensively on antitrust and trial practice at programs sponsored by federal, state and local bar associations.

BLEY, Kenneth
Cox Castle & Nicholson LLP, Los Angeles 310 277 4222
Recommended in Real Estate

BLOOM, Jacob
Bloom, Hergott and Diemer LLP, Beverly Hills 310 859 6800
Recommended in Media & Entertainment

BLOOM, Jerry
White & Case LLP, Los Angeles
213 620 7700
jbloom@whitecase.com
Recommended in Energy
Practice Areas: Jerry Bloom engages in a broad-based regulatory, infrastructure and project finance practice, emphasizing the development and operation of independent energy projects in the United States and abroad, and electric industry restructuring and privatization. Mr Bloom represents an amalgam of energy-related clients, including power generation developers and sponsors, wholesalers, marketers, end-users and foreign governments. He also continues to be a leading advocate of diversified and competitive electric markets. Mr Bloom is Chair of White & Case's Energy Practice, which integrates firmwide energy-related services across firm practice areas, such as bankruptcy, mergers and acquisitions, project and structured finance, and litigation.

BOGDANOFF, Lee R
Klee, Tuchin, Bogdanoff & Stern LLP, Los Angeles 310 407 4070
lbogdanoff@ktbslaw.com
Recommended in Bankruptcy
Practice Areas: Is a member and Co-Manager of Klee, Tuchin, Bogdanoff &

Stern LLP. He has represented debtors in and out-of-court, often in very large and complex cases, as well as parties interested in acquiring assets from debtors. Recent debtor representations include Sun World International and Crescent Jewelers. He has also represented creditors' committees, including serving as counsel to the official noteholders' committee in National Energy & Gas Transmission. Has served as lead counsel in some of the largest Chapter 11 cases pending at the time. Recent representations include Sun World International and Crescent Jewelers. He has represented many acquirers and post-petition lenders, including in Read Rite International and International Industrial Services, Inc.

BOGEN, Andy
Gibson, Dunn & Crutcher LLP, Los Angeles 213 229 7159
abogen@gibsondunn.com
Recommended in Corporate/M&A
Practice Areas: Advises clients on matters involving corporate transactions and securities law, mergers and acquisitions, and insolvency issues. Represented special board committees and corporations in matters involving corporate governance, finance, and restructuring. Recent successes include his representation of Northrop Grumman in its acquisitions of TRW and Litton Industries, The Boeing Company in its acquisition of Hughes Satellite Corporation, Computer Science Corporation in its successful defense of a hostile tender offer, Hilton Hotels in its acquisition of Promus Group Hotels and Asia Global Crossing in its sale.
Prof. Memberships: Member of firm's Executive Committee.
Personal: LLB, Harvard University, 1966, cum laude.

BOLDING, Grady
Orrick, Herrington & Sutcliffe LLP, San Francisco 415 392 1122
Recommended in Tax

BOMSE, Stephen
Heller Ehrman LLP, San Francisco
415 772 6000
Recommended in Antitrust, Litigation

BOOKIN, Daniel
O'Melveny & Myers LLP, San Francisco
415 984 8700
Recommended in Litigation

BOOKMAN, Lloyd
Hooper Lundy & Bookman Inc, Los Angeles 310 551 8111
Recommended in Healthcare

BOOTH, William
Law Offices of William H Booth, Walnut Creek 925 296 2460
Recommended in Energy

BOSTWICK, Gary
Sheppard, Mullin, Richter & Hampton LLP, Los Angeles 213 620 1780
Recommended in Media & Entertainment

BOUTROUS Jr, Theodore
Gibson, Dunn & Crutcher LLP, Los Angeles 213 229 7804
tboutrous@gibsondunn.com
Recommended in Media & Entertainment
Practice Areas: Co-Chair of firm's Media Practice Group and Appellate and Constitutional Law Practice Group. Represents media organizations and reporters in matters involving First Amendment, access, subpoena, libel, privacy, Freedom of Information Act, prior restraint, and newsgathering. Representative clients include NBC, CBS, ABC, CNN, Fox, The New York Times, Los Angeles Times, Associated Press, Washington Post, British journalist Martin Bashir, and Tonight Show host Jay Leno.
Publications: Frequent commentator and author on media, appellate, and constitutional law.
Personal: JD, University of San Diego School of Law, 1987, summa cum laude, Valedictorian, editor in chief, Law Review.

BRANCA, John
Ziffren Brittenham Branca Fischer Gilbert-Lurie & Stiffelman LLP, Los Angeles 310 552 3388
Recommended in Media & Entertainment

BRAUN, Lawrence
Sheppard, Mullin, Richter & Hampton LLP, Los Angeles 213 620 1780
Recommended in Corporate/M&A

BREWER Jr, Robert S
McKenna Long & Aldridge, San Diego
619 595 5400
rbrewer@mckennalong.com
Recommended in Litigation
Practice Areas: Managing Partner of San Diego office. Represents officers, directors and employees in complex civil and criminal litigation cases including government contract procurement fraud; fraud and false claims and qui tam; intellectual property; securities/shareholder disputes; trade secrets; professional negligence; corporate compliance; corporate investigations; class action defense.
Prof. Memberships: Fellow of the American College of Trial Lawyers; Member of American Bar Association, Association of Business Trial Lawyers; San Diego County Bar Association; Master of Enright Inn of Court; Member of Board of Directors of Federal Defenders, Inc.; Deputy District Attorney 1975-77; Assistant United States Attorney, Criminal Division, 1977-81.
Publications: Numerous Bar publications re: business crimes and evidentiary issues.
Personal: St Lawrence University, BA,

1968; University of San Diego, JD, 1975; Captain, US Army, Infantry, active duty, 1968-72.

BRIAN, Brad
Munger, Tolles & Olson LLP, Los Angeles 213 683 9100
Recommended in Litigation

BRIDGES, Andrew
Winston & Strawn, San Francisco
415 591 1482
abridges@winston.com
Recommended in Intellectual Property
Practice Areas: Trial and appellate litigation and litigation-risk counseling for technology, e-commerce, and consumer-oriented companies, especially in trademark, copyright, advertising, publicity, trade secret, unfair competition, consumer protection, and license disputes.
Prof. Memberships: Early Neutral Evaluator, US District Court for the Northern District of California. Domain Name Panelist, WIPO Arbitration and Mediation Center. Chair, Fair Use and Other Boundaries Subcommittee of Issues and Policy Committee of International Trademark Association.
Career: Previously Partner and Head of Trademarks and Advertising Practices Group, Wilson Sonsini Goodrich & Rosati; to Winston & Strawn as Partner, 2004. Cases include the landmark 1999 victory defending Diamond Multimedia, maker of the Rio MP3 music player, against the recording industry; victory for MasterCard in a contributory copyright/trademark lawsuit by a publisher alleging MasterCard's support for infringing merchants; and victory for CNET Networks against Snap-On Tools' effort to enjoin the Snap! Online Internet portal. Other notable representations include Netscape, Napster, Digital Media Association, StreamCast Networks, eBay, ClearPlay, and Google.
Publications: Frequent lecturer on cutting-edge copyright, trademark, Internet law, and litigation topics. Taught classes at Stanford, Columbia, and Univ of Michigan law schools. Addressed conferences for Federal Judicial Center, Copyright Office of the United States, Copyright Society of USA, ABA, University of Amsterdam, International Trademark Association, and Practising Law Institute.
Personal: AB (with distinction), Phi Beta Kappa, Stanford Univ., 1976; BA (Hons.) and MA, Univ. of Oxford, 1980 and 1985; JD (cum laude) Harvard Law School, 1983. Board member, Ronald McDonald House at Stanford and TheatreWorks. Languages: Modern Greek, French, Italian.

BRITTENHAM, Harry
Ziffren Brittenham Branca Fischer Gilbert-Lurie & Stiffelman LLP, Los Angeles 310 552 3388
Recommended in Media & Entertainment

BRODY, Sara
Heller Ehrman LLP, San Francisco
415 772 6000
Recommended in Litigation

BROSNAHAN, James
Morrison & Foerster LLP, San Francisco
415 268 7189
jbrosnahan@mofo.com
Recommended in Litigation
Practice Areas: Civil and criminal trial
attorney. Approximately 137 jury cases.
Argued both civil and criminal appeals
in state and federal court, including two
cases in the United States Supreme
Court.
Career: Admitted to practice in Arizona
and California. Practiced five years as
Assistant US Attorney in Arizona and
San Francisco. Associate Member, Office
of Independent Counsel: Iran-Contra.
Lead prosecutor, US v Caspar Weinberg-
er (October-December 1992). Inducted
into: 'Trial Lawyers Hall of Fame', State
Bar of California, 1996. Received:
'Samuel E Gates Award', ACTL, 2000;
'Trial Lawyer of the Year', ABTA, 2001;
'Legend of the Law', San Francisco
Lawyers' Club, 2002; 'Top 100 Most
Influential Attorneys', Daily Journal
newspaper, 2003.
Personal: BSBA, Boston College, 1956;
LLB, Harvard Law School, 1959.

BROWN, Donald W
Covington & Burling, San Francisco
415 591 7063
dwbrown@cov.com
Recommended in Insurance
Practice Areas: Trial lawyer represent-
ing policyholders with substantial and
complex claims to coverage under all
types of policies. Companies for which
he has acted as lead trial counsel include
Exxon Mobil, Fibreboard, Imperial Oil,
McKesson, and Tosco.
Career: Brobeck, Phleger & Harrison,
1978-2003 (Partner, 1985-2003, insur-
ance practice group leader, 1998-2003);
Covington & Burling, 2003-present.
Publications: 'Manual for Complex
Insurance Coverage Litigation' (Prentice
Hall 1995) (chapter contributor).
Personal: JD, Yale Law School, 1978; AB,
Ohio University, summa cum laude,
1975.

BROWN, Harald
Gang Tyre Ramer & Brown, Beverly Hills
310 777 4800
*Recommended in Media &
Entertainment*

BROWN, Walt
Orrick, Herrington & Sutcliffe LLP,
San Francisco 415 773 5995
wbrown@orrick.com
Recommended in Litigation
Practice Areas: Mr Brown's practice
focuses on white-collar criminal defense
and complex business litigation. He represents companies and individuals in
connection with criminal and regulatory investigations, as well as parallel civil

and administrative proceedings. He has
extensive experience in cases involving
securities fraud, antitrust offenses, com-
puter crimes, healthcare fraud, defense
contractor fraud, public corruption,
environmental crimes, tax evasion and
money laundering.
Prof. Memberships: ABA Litigation
Section, ABA Antitrust Section, ABA
Criminal Justice Section, White Collar
Crime Committee California State Bar,
Antitrust & Unfair Competition Sec-
tion.
Career: Mr Brown was an Assistant
United States Attorney in the Criminal
Division of the United States Attorney's
Office for the Central District of Califor-
nia (Los Angeles) from 1989 to 1994.
During that time, he tried 20 felony
cases to verdict in United States District
Court and handled 30 appeals before
the United States Court of Appeals for
the Ninth Circuit. Before joining Orrick,
Mr Brown was a Partner at Gray Cary in
San Francisco.
Personal: Mr Brown received a JD from
the University of Notre Dame in 1985.
He earned his AB from the University of
California at Berkeley in 1982.

BRUEN, James
Farella Braun & Martel LLP,
San Francisco 415 954 4400
Recommended in Environment

BRYAN, Karen
Latham & Watkins LLP, Los Angeles
213 485 1234
Recommended in Tax

BUNSOW, Henry
Howrey Simon Arnold & White,
San Francisco 415 848 4900
Recommended in Intellectual Property

BUONCRISTIANI, David
Thelen Reid & Priest LLP,
San Francisco 415 371 1200
Recommended in Construction

BURKE, P John
Akin Gump Strauss Hauer & Feld LLP,
Los Angeles 310 229 1038
jburke@akingump.com
*Recommended in Media &
Entertainment*
Practice Areas: Represents financial
institutions, producers, high net-worth
individuals, studios and distributors in
production, financing and distribution
matters, with emphasis on complex
financing and co-production arrange-
ments worldwide.
Prof. Memberships: Officer and Corpo-
rate Counsel, American Film Institute;
Co-Chair, Advisory Committee, UCLA
Entertainment Law Symposium (2002-
04); Advisory Board Member, AFI International Film Festival (2000-03); Member, Board of Directors, Japan America
Society (1988-92); Member, Intellectual
Property & Entertainment Law Section,
Los Angeles County Bar Association;
Member, Entertainment Law Section,
Beverly Hills Bar Association.

Personal: BA, University of Southern
California (1973); JD, Southwestern
University School of Law (1976), LLM,
New York University (1977).

BURKE, Thomas
Davis Wright Tremaine LLP,
San Francisco 415 276 6552
thomasburke@dwt.com
*Recommended in Media &
Entertainment*
Practice Areas: Partner, communica-
tions/media law. Helped establish firm's
Internet/eCommerce practice. Repre-
sents publishers, television networks
and authors in defamation, invasion of
privacy, right of publicity, copyright,
trademark, false advertising and other
content-related litigation. Experienced
in a broad range of Internet-related dis-
putes.
Prof. Memberships: Lecturer in Media
Law, Graduate School of Journalism,
University of California at Berkeley.
Career: Joined firm, 1996; became Partner, 1998.
Publications: Co-editor, 'Reporter's
Handbook on Media Law' (CNPA
1999); co-author, 'Internet Law and
Practice' (West 2002).
Personal: JD (magna cum laude), Uni-
versity of San Francisco School of Law,
1989. BS (magna cum laude), Arizona
State University, 1984.

CAIRNS, James
White & Case LLP, Los Angeles
213 620 7739
jcairns@whitecase.com
Recommended in Banking & Finance
Practice Areas: Banking and finance.
Career: Mr Cairns has a bank finance
practice with an emphasis on leasing
and equipment finance. He represents
and advises lessors, lessees, lenders,
intermediaries and equity interests in a
wide variety of equipment leasing transactions and has particular experience in
domestic and cross-border aircraft leasing and financing. Recent aircraft transactions have involved many jurisdictions, including the US, Canada, India,
Indonesia and Russia. Other lease transactions have involved railcars, and
telecommunications, manufacturing
and gas production equipment. Mr
Cairns also represents US-based commercial paper conduits in making
investments and in acquiring liquidity.

CAMAHORT, Steve
O'Melveny & Myers LLP, San Francisco
415 984 8700
Recommended in Corporate/M&A

CANE, Paul
Paul, Hastings, Janofsky & Walker LLP,
San Francisco 415 856 7014
paulcane@paulhastings.com
Recommended in Employment
Practice Areas: Chair, Appellate Prac-
tice Group. Briefed cases including: Guz
v Bechtel National, Turner v Anheuser-
Busch, Foley v Interactive Data, and

Cotran v Rollins Hudig Hall.
Prof. Memberships: Fellow, College of
Labor and Employment Lawyers.
Career: Law Clerk, Hon. Carl
McGowan, US Court of Appeals for the
DC Circuit; Hon Lewis F Powell, Jr,
Supreme Court of the United States.
Publications: 'An Employer's Guide to
the Americans with Disabilities Act'
(1991); 'Employment Discrimination
Law' (3d ed. 1996); editor in chief, 'Cali-
fornia Law Review' (1978-79).
Personal: AB Dartmouth College
(1976), summa cum laude; JD Universi-
ty of California at Berkeley (1979).

CAREY, Stevens
Pircher, Nichols & Meeks, Los Angeles
310 201 8900
Recommended in Real Estate

CARROLL, Michael
Latham & Watkins LLP, Costa Mesa
714 540 1235
Recommended in Environment

CATHCART, Patrick
Cathcart, Collins & Kneafsey LLP,
Los Angeles 213 225 6600
pcathcart@cckllp.com
Recommended in Insurance
Practice Areas: Founding Partner of
Cathcart Collins & Kneafsey LLP in Los
Angeles, California, in 2005. Partner and
Co-Chair of Business Litigation Practice
Group at Hancock Rothert & Bunshoft
LLP through December 2004. Concen-
trates on complex multi-party business
litigation. Has been lead defense coun-
sel, or trial counsel, in the following
cases: Pintlar v Aetna (the Bunker Hill
litigation) (US District Court, Idaho);
Martin Marietta et al v Aetna Casualty &
Surety Co. (Los Angeles) (two jury tri-
als); FMC Corporation v Liberty Mutu-
al, et al (San Jose, California) (three
month jury trial); Rockwell International Corporation v Aetna Cas. & Surety
Co., et al (Los Angeles); Southern California Gas Co. v AEGIS, Ltd., et al (Los
Angeles); McColl-Frontenac Inc. v Adri-
atic Insurance Company et al (Los
Angeles); Armstrong v Aetna (six week
arbitration in 1998, before retired US
District Judge Nicholas Bua, Chicago,
Illinois); Golden Eagle v Associated
International Ins. Co., et al (Los Angeles)
Highlands Ins. Co. v Powerine Oil Company and related cross actions (Los
Angeles); Fuller-Austin v Fireman's
Fund (Los Angeles). Is involved in litigation on behalf of clients against Del
Monte Corporation (litigation pending
in Hawaii), IC Industries, Southern
Pacific Transportation Company. Has
represented clients before appellate
courts on a variety of issues (see Certain
Underwriters at Lloyd's, London v Superior Court 24 Cal 4th 945 (2001)), most
recently in Hool and Meeker v Village
Roadshow Pictures (unpublished opinion). Has litigated intellectual property
disputes, beginning with litigation

between 'PC Magazine' and 'PC World Magazine' over trade name infringement in 1983 and in connection with a trademark copyright dispute against the Walt Disney Company. Has represented a major contractor in two arbitrations in the Hague, Netherlands, in connection with construction disputes involving pipeline and pumping station contracts with the government of Iran, and motion picture producers in a suit against Village Roadshow Pictures (an Australian motion picture production, distribution and exhibition company). Extensive experience in handling professional liability claims against lawyers and law firms.

Prof. Memberships: American Bar Association; State Bar of California; Association of Business Trial Lawyers (member of Board of Governors, currently Treasurer); Los Angeles County Bar Association.

Career: Admitted to California Bar (1975). Partner at Hancock Rothert & Bunshoft LLP (1982), and founded the firm's Los Angeles office in 1989, Partner at Cathcart Collins & Kneafsey LLP (2005).

Personal: JD from University of California Hastings College of Law (1975); AB from Stanford University (1968); graduate, Phillips Academy, Andover (1964). Member, US Peace Corps/Iran (1969-71).

CHADWICK, James
DLA Piper Rudnick Gray Cary US LLP, Palo Alto 650 833 2293
james.chadwick@dlapiper.com
Recommended in Media & Entertainment

Practice Areas: Media and new media.
Career: He focuses on media law and media defense litigation, first amendment and privacy law, trademark and copyright law, civil litigation, and white-collar criminal defense.
Personal: JD, Santa Clara University; MA, San Francisco State University. BA, University of California, Santa Cruz.

CHECOV, Martin
O'Melveny & Myers LLP, San Francisco 415 984 8700
Recommended in Insurance

CHILTON, Fred
McDermott Will & Emery, Palo Alto 650 813 5121
fchilton@mwe.com
Recommended in Tax

Practice Areas: Partner in the firm's Tax Department. Focuses on the representation of high technology, biotechnology and other companies on complex tax matters.
Career: Law clerk for Judge Leo H Irwin, US Tax Court and a Tax Law Specialist in the Foreign Rulings Group of the Internal Revenue Service. Often speaks and serves as chair for seminars on behalf of the ATLAS, Practicing Law Institute and the Tax Executives Insti-

tute. Has written a number of articles on a variety of federal income tax issues.
Personal: Received BA in 1967 from Fresno State College. Atttended Hastings College of Law, and received JD in 1971. Earned LLM in Taxation from New York University in 1973.

CHU, Morgan
Irell & Manella LLP, Los Angeles 310 277 1010
Recommended in Intellectual Property

CLAIR, John
Latham & Watkins LLP, Los Angeles 213 485 1234
Recommended in Tax

CLARENCE, Nanci
Clarence Snell & Dyer LLP, San Francisco 415 749 1800
Recommended in Litigation

CLARK, John
Thelen Reid & Priest LLP, Los Angeles 213 576 8000
Recommended in Construction

CLARK, Kenneth
Wilson Sonsini Goodrich & Rosati, Palo Alto 650 493 9300
kclark@wsgr.com
Recommended in Corporate/M&A, IT Outsourcing

Practice Areas: Specializes in intellectual property, particularly technology transactions involving products and/or technology, from strategic alliances to license, development, supply and distribution arrangements. Regularly represents companies in M&As, spin-outs and core technology licenses.
Career: Joined WSGR as Partner, 1993. Member, WSGR Policy Committee and Executive Management Committee. Negotiated more than 50 major strategic alliance transactions in both the life sciences and information technology industries. Served as Vice President, General Counsel & Secretary of Maxtor Corporation, 1992-93.
Personal: JD (highest honors), University of Texas, 1985. Order of the Coif; BA (magna cum laude), Vanderbilt University, 1980. Phi Beta Kappa.

CLASTER, William
Gibson, Dunn & Crutcher LLP, Irvine 949 451 3804
wclaster@gibsondunn.com
Recommended in Employment

Practice Areas: Advises management in a wide array of labor and employment matters, including class actions, employment discrimination, wrongful termination, negotiations and arbitrations under collective bargaining agreements, executive employment agreements, unfair competition, ERISA, and proceedings before state and federal agencies such as the EEOC, OSHA and the NLRB. Tried numerous cases in both jury and non-jury settings and argued significant cases before appellate courts.
Publications: Frequent lecturer on

labor and employment law. Contributing author, 'Wrongful Employment Termination Practice' and 'California Practice Guide: Employment Litigation'.
Personal: BA, Stanford University, 1973; JD, UCLA, 1976, managing editor of UCLA Law Review.

CLIMAN, Richard
Cooley Godward LLP, Palo Alto 650 843 5000
Recommended in Corporate/M&A

COBEN, Jerome L
Skadden, Arps, Slate, Meagher & Flom LLP & Affiliates, Los Angeles 213 687 5010
jcoben@skadden.com
Recommended in Corporate/M&A

Practice Areas: Mr Coben is one of the founding partners of Skadden's Los Angeles office. He has a broad-based corporate and securities law practice, representing both issuers and investment banks in a variety of corporate finance, merger and acquisition and general corporate matters. Mr Coben has regularly represented, among other public companies, Oakley Inc., Occidental Petroleum Corporation and Wynn Resorts, Limited.
Prof. Memberships: Member, American and Los Angeles County Bar associations; Board Member, Constitutional Rights Foundation; Board Member, Bet Tzedek Legal Services.
Career: JD, New York University School of Law, 1969 (Root-Tilden-Kern Scholar); AB, Brown University 1966 (cum laude).

COHEN, Nancy
Heller Ehrman White & McAuliffe LLP, Los Angeles 213 689 0200
Recommended in Insurance

COLEMAN, Kathryn A
Gibson, Dunn & Crutcher LLP, San Francisco 415 393 8265
kcoleman@gibsondunn.com
Recommended in Bankruptcy

Practice Areas: Practices business restructuring and reorganization. Has extensive experience in workouts, troubled loans, creditors' rights and all phases of bankruptcy cases. Represents debtors, creditors' committees, secured creditors, and acquirers in bankruptcy cases, preparation and prosecution of creditors' plans of reorganization, and complex loan restructurings.
Career: Former clerk for the Honorable C Martin Pence, US District Judge for the District of Hawaii.
Publications: Frequent lecturer on bankruptcy law and problem loans.
Personal: JD, UC Berkeley-Boalt Hall School of Law, 1983, Senior Articles Editor of the California Law Review and a member of the Order of the Coif.

COLEMAN, Thomas
Orrick, Herrington & Sutcliffe LLP, San Francisco 415 773 5870
tycoleman@orrick.com
Recommended in Banking & Finance

Practice Areas: Represents banks and other financial institutions in a variety of transactions, including syndicated and single-lender credit agreements, both secured and unsecured; project financings; public finance transactions; and synthetic and other lease arrangements.
Career: The Honorable James C Turk, Chief Judge, United States District Court for the Western District of Virginia, Law Clerk, 1975-76; Morrison & Foerster LLP, associate, 1976-79; California First Bank (now Union Bank of California), Vice-President and Counsel, 1979-85; Clifford-Turner (now Clifford Chance), Solicitors, visiting attorney, 1984; Orrick, Herrington & Sutcliffe LLP, Partner, 1985-date. Currently, Chair of Professional Development Committee and General Counsel of Orrick.
Personal: University of Virginia, BA 1971, JD 1975.

COMPTON, Charles T
Wilson Sonsini Goodrich & Rosati, Palo Alto 650 493 9300
ccompton@wsgr.com
Recommended in Antitrust

Practice Areas: Antitrust counseling.
Prof. Memberships: Admitted to practice in California and DC, as well as in several United States District Courts, the US Court of Appeals for the Ninth Circuit, the US Court of Military Appeals and the United States Supreme Court.
Career: Partner, WSGR. Overseen the antitrust regulatory work in nearly 700 M&As and joint ventures. Handled antitrust suits involving alleged price discrimination, refusals to deal, distributor terminations, group boycotts, monopoly, state law Cartwright Act claims, grand jury investigations, and price fixing.
Personal: JD, NYU School of Law, 1968. BS (with honors), United States Air Force Academy, 1965.

COOK, Melanie
Ziffren Brittenham Branca Fischer Gilbert-Lurie & Stiffelman LLP, Los Angeles 310 552 3388
Recommended in Media & Entertainment

COOK, Philip E
Jones Day, Los Angeles 213 243 2846
pcook@jonesday.com
Recommended in Litigation

Practice Areas: Has a broad background in many substantive areas of civil litigation, and is experienced lead counsel in jury and bench trials, domestic and international arbitrations, and mediations. Has taught law school classes and seminars on deposition, advocacy, and trial techniques.
Prof. Memberships: Board of Governors of the Los Angeles Chapter of the

Association of Business Trial Lawyers. Member of the State Bar of California and the Los Angeles County Bar Association. Voluntary Settlement Officer for California Court of Appeals. Admitted to practice before all US District Courts in California and the Ninth Circuit Court of Appeals.

COOPER, Jay L
Greenberg Traurig LLP, Santa Monica 310 586 7700
cooper@gtlaw.com
Recommended in Media & Entertainment
Practice Areas: Entertainment; intellectual property.
Prof. Memberships: Former President, National Academy of Recording Arts and Sciences; Member, Los Angeles Copyright Society; Co-Chairman, Alliance of Artists & Recording Companies.
Publications: 'Withol v Crow: Fair Use Revisited', UCLA Law Review; 'Use of Fair Use', LA Bar Bulletin, Publishing Entertainment Advertising Law Quarterly; 'Acquiring Music Rights for Motion Pictures and Television', Annual Program on Legal Aspects of the Entertainment Industry, Beverly Hills Bar/USC Law School; 'Current Trends in Recording Contract Negotiation', NARAS' Institute Journal; 'The Ownership and Protection of Performers' Names - Legal Aspects Of The Entertainment Industry', Beverly Hills Bar/UCLA.

COOPER, Robert
Gibson, Dunn & Crutcher LLP, Los Angeles 213 229 7179
rcooper@gibsondunn.com
Recommended in Antitrust, Litigation
Practice Areas: Has extensive experience involving major antitrust and business tort litigation. Achieved three successive trial victories for major pharmaceuticals manufacturer in antibiotics antitrust litigation. Successfully defended American Airlines in three antitrust cases. Representative clients include Hewlett-Packard, Sempra Energy, Intel, Ticketmaster, Honeywell, Northrop, Allergan and Callaway Golf Company.
Prof. Memberships: Fellow, American College of Trial Lawyers.
Publications: Frequent lecturer on antitrust laws and trial of complex litigation.
Personal: LLB, Yale University School of Law, 1964, Order of the Coif, Article and Book Review Editor, Yale Law Journal.

CORASH, Michèle B
Morrison & Foerster LLP, San Francisco 415 268 7124
mcorash@mofo.com
Recommended in Environment
Practice Areas: Specializes in environmental law and defense of enforcement actions and class actions relating to food and consumer products. Represents companies in mining and petrochemicals, real estate transactions and land development. One of the nation's lead-

ing experts on Proposition 65.
Career: Served as General Counsel, US Environmental Protection Agency (EPA)(1979-1982) and, before that, as Deputy General Counsel, US Department of Energy. Founded Environmental Section of the Inter-Pacific Bar Association. Recent honors include being named: '100 Most Influential Lawyers in California' by Daily Journal newspaper; and the 'Go-To Environmental Defense Lawyer' by The Recorder newspaper. Heads the firm's Environmental Practice Group.
Personal: BA, Economics, Mount Holyoke College, 1967; JD, cum laude, New York University School of Law, 1970.

CORBIN, Robert
Corbin & Fitzgerald LLP, Los Angeles 213 612 0001
Recommended in Litigation

COTCHETT, Joseph
Cotchett, Pitre, Simon & McCarthy, Burlingame 650 697 6000
Recommended in Litigation

CRANE, Steven
Berkes Crane Robinson & Seal, LLP, Los Angeles 213 955 1150
Recommended in Insurance

CRAVEN, Erica
Levy, Ram & Olson, San Francisco 415 433 4949
Recommended in Media & Entertainment

CREW, Eugene
Townsend and Townsend and Crew LLP, San Francisco 415 576 0200
Recommended in Antitrust

CRIST, Paul
Jones Day, San Francisco 415 875 5722
pgcrist@jonesday.com
Recommended in Litigation
Practice Areas: Currently serves as Litigation Group coordinator for the San Francisco Office. Previously, he was in Jones Day's Cleveland office for 25 years. He represents clients in complex product liability matters throughout the US. In addition, he has been involved in takeovers, securities, general business, real estate, and class actions. He is admitted to practice in Ohio and California, including all federal district and appellate courts for those states. Named one of the top 100 lawyers in Ohio by 'Cincinnati Magazine' in 2004 and 2005.
Prof. Memberships: Fellow of the American College of Trial Lawyers.

CUFF, Terence
Loeb & Loeb LLP, Los Angeles 310 282 2000
Recommended in Tax

CUMMINS, Guylyn
Sheppard, Mullin, Richter & Hampton LLP, San Diego 858 720 8900
Recommended in Media & Entertainment

DAVID, Henry S
Alschuler Grossman Stein & Kahan LLP, Santa Monica 310 255 9167
hdavid@agsk.com
Recommended in Bankruptcy
Practice Areas: Practices complex commercial litigation concentrating on bankruptcy, insurance insolvency, creditors' rights, corporate and partnership dissolutions, and international arbitration matters.
Prof. Memberships: Member, American Bankruptcy Institute; Association of Insolvency and Restructuring Advisors; Financial Lawyers Conference; International Association of Insurance Receivers (pending). Co-founder of the Provisional and Post-Judgment Remedies Section of the Los Angeles County Bar Association (served as Chair of its Executive Committee).
Career: A Partner of Alschuler Grossman Stein & Kahan LLP. Has undertaken leadership in numerous complex matters in state, federal, and bankruptcy courts, as well as before various arbitration associations. Such matters include prosecution of a $254 million preference and fraudulent transfer action on behalf of the California Insurance Commissioner; successful representation of the New York Superintendent of Insurance in obtaining a stay of litigation in California due to the New York rehabilitation proceedings; repossession of DC10s and L1011s from failing airlines; general representation of debtors, bankruptcy trustees, and creditors' committees in Chapter 11 cases in a variety of industries, including windfarms, timeshare projects, retailers, healthcare, and oil; representation of Epson America in the bankruptcy aspects of patent infringement disputes with various debtors; successful representation of minority equity holders in various debtors; representation of purchasers of assets out of bankruptcy, including hospitals, refineries, and technology. Has tried over 50 matters to judgment or arbitral award; has handled many appeals.
Personal: Mediator, Bankruptcy Mediation Panel and the Attorney Settlement Officer Panel for the Central District of California. Co-author of the chapter regarding 'Seller's Performance' in California UCC Sales and Leases (C.E.B. 1993). California Institute of Technology (BS with honors, 1976). New York University School of Law (JD cum laude, Order of the Coif, 1979). Law Review, New York University School Law. Admitted in California and Florida.

DAVIDSON, Gordon
Fenwick & West LLP, Mountain View 650 335 7237
gdavidson@fenwick.com
Recommended in Corporate/M&A
Practice Areas: Firm Chairman. Start-up companies, venture capital financings, public securities offerings, mergers and acquisitions and strategic alliances.

Advises technology companies, including networking, computer software and electronics companies, as well as medical technology companies. Also advises investors and investment banks. Clients range from start-ups to Fortune 1000 companies. Has worked on more than 30 public offerings and has acted as lead counsel on more than 100 mergers and acquisitions valued at more than $50 billion.
Career: Recognized by National Law Journal in June 2000 as one of the 100 Most Influential Lawyers in America, by Forbes Magazine in February 2001 as one of the 50 Most Powerful Venture Capital Dealmakers, by Upside Magazine in October 2001 as one of '100 People Who Changed Our World', by California Lawyer Magazine in August 2004 as one of the 10 best corporate lawyers in California, by San Francisco Magazine in August 2004 as one of the 10 best lawyers in Northern California, and by Forbes Magazine in the February 2005 Midas List as one of the top 100 venture capital deal makers in 2004. One of only two lawyers in the United States to be named by BTI Consulting to 'All Star Team' for each of the last four years for outstanding client service based on survey of Fortune 1000 companies. Law clerk to Judge Ben C. Duniway, Ninth Circuit Court of Appeals, 1974-75.
Personal: Stanford Law School, JD, Order of the Coif, 1974; Stanford University, MS in electrical engineering, computer systems, National Science Foundation Fellow, 1971; Stanford University, BS in electrical engineering, Phi Beta Kappa, 1970.

DAVIS Jr, Edward P
DLA Piper Rudnick Gray Cary US LLP, Palo Alto 650 833 2297
edward.davis@dlapiper.com
Recommended in Media & Entertainment
Practice Areas: Media and new media; white-collar litigation.
Career: His practice is focused on media law and white-collar crime.
Personal: JD, Santa Clara University School of Law; BA, Stanford University.

DAY, Lloyd
Day Casebeer Madrid & Batchelder LLP, Cupertino 408 255 3255
Recommended in Intellectual Property

DAY, Michael
Goodin MacBride Squeri Ritchie & Day LLP, San Francisco 415 392 7900
Recommended in Energy

DE MEULES, James
O'Melveny & Myers LLP, Los Angeles 213 430 6000
Recommended in Banking & Finance

DEL CALVO, Jorge
Pillsbury Winthrop LLP, Palo Alto 650 233 4537
jorge@pillsburywinthrop.com
Recommended in Corporate/M&A

Practice Areas: Mr del Calvo's practice focuses primarily on representation of technology companies in securities and venture capital transactions, including public offerings, private placements, mergers and acquisitions and joint ventures. He has represented issuers and underwriters in hundreds of private and public offerings of equity securities, including initial public offerings, and merger and acquisition transactions. Among securities transactions, he has worked on are IPOs for PortalPlayer, Sirf, Atheros, PeopleSupport, Synnex, SupportSoft, Alliance FibreOptics, Critical Path, Network Solutions, and WebEx, as well as a number of secondary public offerings including Network Solutions' $2.2 billion follow-on public offering - the largest internet follow-on public equity offering in history. His representation of investment bankers includes work with such clients as Goldman Sachs & Co., A.G Edwards, Cowen & Co and Needham & Company, Inc.

Career: Admitted to practice: State of California. Member: American Bar Association.

Publications: Coordinating Editor of the 'Venture Capital and Public Offering Negotiation'.

Personal: JD, Harvard Law School (cum laude), 1981. MA, Harvard University (public policy), 1981. MA, University of California at Los Angeles (Latin American History), 1978. BA, Stanford University (Phi Beta Kappa, with distinction), 1977. ND, University of the Philippines, 1982.

DEMETRIOU, Andrew James
Fulbright & Jaworski L.L.P., Los Angeles
213 892 9338
ademetriou@fulbright.com
Recommended in Healthcare

Practice Areas: Mergers and acquisitions, healhcare, and corporate and securities law.

Prof. Memberships: Mr Demetriou has held leadership positions in sections of the American Bar Association, the State Bar of California, the Los Angeles County Bar Association Delegation to the State Bar Conference of Delegates, and American Health Lawyers Association.

Career: Andrew Demetriou joined the Los Angeles office of Fulbright & Jaworski L.L.P. as Partner in 2004 with more than 20 years of experience in representing a range of domestic and foreign enterprises on corporate and strategic matters. Since 1991 he has concentrated on the representation of entities that provide and finance healthcare services. He was named one of 15 Outstanding Healthcare Transaction Lawyers for 2003 by Nightingale's 'Healthcare Law News'.

Personal: AB, University of California, Los Angeles (1976); JD, University of California, Berkeley, Boalt Hall School of Law (1979).

DEMURO, Paul
Latham & Watkins LLP, Los Angeles
213 485 1234
Recommended in Healthcare

DENHAM, Robert
Munger, Tolles & Olson LLP, Los Angeles 213 683 9100
Recommended in Corporate/M&A

DENNIS, Patrick W
Gibson, Dunn & Crutcher LLP, Los Angeles 213 229 7567
pdennis@gibsondunn.com
Recommended in Environment

Practice Areas: Chair of firm's Environmental Law and Natural Resources Practice Group. Represents clients in matters including litigation, due diligence, compliance counseling, defense of environmental enforcement actions, private citizen suit claims, private party cleanup cost recovery and toxic tort lawsuits, permit requirements. Deals extensively with administering agencies for air quality, hazardous waste, and water quality. Represents buyers and sellers of major industrial facilities and real estate for development. Lead counsel for numerous federal and state Superfund matters, including one of the few natural resource damage actions brought by the United States.

Personal: JD, University of California, Los Angeles, 1982.

DETTMER, Scott
Gunderson Dettmer Stough Villeneuve Franklin & Hachigian, Menlo Park
650 321 2400
Recommended in Corporate/M&A

DIEKMANN, Gilmore
Seyfarth Shaw LLP, San Francisco
415 397 2823
Recommended in Employment

DIVOLA, Julie
Pillsbury Winthrop LLP, San Francisco
415 983 7446
julie.divola@pillsburywinthrop.com
Recommended in Tax

Practice Areas: Ms Divola heads the San Francisco Tax, Benefits and Political Law Practice. She is experienced in federal income tax planning for business and financial transactions. Her practice focuses on corporate and partnership taxation with particular emphasis on structuring mergers, acquisitions, divestitures and reorganizations; partnerships and joint ventures; financial products; project finance; and tax controversy matters. She advised Vodafone in connection with the formation of Verizon Wireless, a $70 billion joint venture, and recently advised Advanced Fibre Communications in its acquisition by Tellabs. She was recognized by International Tax Review as an expert in the area of M&A and was recently ranked as one of the Top 50 Northern California Female Super Lawyers by Law & Politics Media.

Prof. Memberships: American Bar Association (Tax Section) (Incoming Vice-Chair, Corporate Tax Committee); California Bar Association (Tax Section) (Past Chair, Corporate Tax/Corporate Tax Counsel Committee; Past Chair, Passthroughs and Real Estate Committee); San Francisco Tax Club (Past President).

Career: Admitted to practice: State of California. She has been an Adjunct Professor of Law at University of San Francisco School of Law.

Personal: JD, University of San Francisco School of Law, 1986, summa cum laude; BA, University of California at Santa Barbara, 1980.

DODSON, Gerald
Morrison & Foerster LLP, Palo Alto
650 813 5983
gdodson@mofo.com
Recommended in Intellectual Property

Practice Areas: Over 30-year career, has served as lead trial and appellate counsel in complex technology cases involving hundreds of millions of dollars. Represented electronics, biotechnology and consumer product companies on cases covering pioneering patents in the medical device, biotechnology, optical and electronic hardware, software and mechanical device fields.

Career: Admitted to practice in California and before the US Patent & Trademark Office. Served as Chief Counsel, Health and Environmental Subcommittee, US House of Representatives, and Solicitor's Office, US Department of the Interior. Headed congressional investigation of Union Carbide's pesticide plant disaster in Bhopal, India.

Personal: BSME, Lafayette College, 1969; JD, University of Maryland Law School, 1972; LLM, George Washington University Law School, 1977.

DRAGNA, James
Bingham McCutchen LLP, Los Angeles
213 680 4600
Recommended in Environment

DRAPKIN, Steven
Law Offices of Steven Drapkin, Los Angeles 310 914 7909
Recommended in Employment

DUFFY, Pamela
Coblentz, Patch, Duffy & Bass LLP, San Francisco 415 391 4800
Recommended in Real Estate

DURIE, Daralyn J
Keker & Van Nest LLP, San Francisco
415 391 5400
djd@kvn.com
Recommended in Intellectual Property

Practice Areas: Daralyn Durie has tried cases in both the state and federal courts in a wide range of areas including patent, trade secret, unfair competition. Representative clients include Comcast Cable Communications, Inc, The Gap, Inc., Genentech, Inc.

Prof. Memberships: Served as a lawyer representative to the Ninth Circuit Judi-

cial Conference and has taught on the faculty of the National Institute for Trial Advocacy; member Board of Directors of Berkeley Montessori School.

Career: Law clerk to the Honorable Douglas Ginsberg on the United States Court of Appeals for the District of Columbia Circuit (1992-93). Joined Keker & Van Nest, 1993; became Partner,1999. Frequent invited speaker on patent litigation, the DMCA, and legal ethics.

Personal: Boalt Hall School of Law, University of California (JD 1992); University of California at Berkeley (MA 1989); Stanford University (BA, 1988).

EATMAN, Louis P
Mayer, Brown, Rowe & Maw LLP, Los Angeles 213 229 5144
leatman@mayerbrownrowe.com
Recommended in Real Estate

Practice Areas: Advises on real estate finance, acquisitions and sales, workouts and restructures, foreclosures and deeds in lieu of foreclosure. Represents commercial banks, savings banks, life insurance companies, pension funds and their advisors, investment banks, real estate investment trusts, portfolio asset managers, other institutional mortgage lenders and investors, commercial property landlords and tenants.

Prof. Memberships: American College of Real Estate Lawyers. International Council of Shopping Centers. Pension Real Estate Association. Board of Directors, Constitutional Rights Foundation (President and Chair, Executive Committee, 2003-05). California Mortgage Bankers Association.

Career: Joined Mayer, Brown, Rowe & Maw LLP as Partner, 1994. Firm Practice Leader, Global Real Estate Group, 2000-04. Partner-in-Charge of Los Angeles Office. Formerly with Loeb & Loeb.

Publications: Speaker and panelist on real estate financing and workout issues. Faculty Member for the 1995 ALI-ABA Advanced Course of Study on 'Real Estate Defaults, Workouts, and Reorganizations' (1995). Speaker on 'Shopping Center Financing', 1996 International Council of Shopping Centers Annual Law Conference (October 1996).

Personal: Born 16 November 1948. Stanford Law School, JD, 1974. Stanford Graduate Business School, MBA, 1974. Georgetown University School of Foreign Service, BSFS, cum laude, 1970; Phi Beta Kappa.

EDELMAN , Scott
Gibson, Dunn & Crutcher LLP, Los Angeles 310 557 8061
sedelman@gibsondunn.com
Recommended in Media & Entertainment

Practice Areas: Co-Chair of Firm's Entertainment Practice Group. Represents major entertainment clients in matters involving profit participation, AFMA arbitrations, right of publicity, copyright and trademark infringement, misappropriation of ideas, false advertising, and royalty disputes. Other commercial litigation experience includes antitrust, product liability, employment, probate, and sports litigation, breach of contract, professional negligence, RICO, real estate and construction defects. Representative clients include Sony Pictures, Fox Broadcasting Company, Columbia TriStar Home Entertainment and Intertainment Licensing GMBH.

Publications: Contributing Author, 'Intellectual Property Law, Damages and Remedies'.

Personal: JD, University of California, Boalt Hall School of Law, 1984. Co-editor in chief, Ecology Law Quarterly.

EISEN, Rebecca
Morgan, Lewis & Bockius LLP,
San Francisco 415 442 1328
reisen@morganlewis.com
Recommended in Employment

Practice Areas: Rebecca Eisen is a Partner in the Labor and Employment Law Practice Group. Ms Eisen represents employers in all facets of employment law including hiring practices, leaves of absence, trade secrets, accommodation of disabled employees, wage and hour laws, employee discipline and sensitive terminations. Ms Eisen has litigated class actions, multiple plaintiff and collective actions in state and federal court, and actions before administrative agencies and appellate courts including the Ninth Circuit Court of Appeals and the California Supreme Court.

Prof. Memberships: American Arbitration Association; The Employers Group - Legal Advisory Board; San Francisco County Bar Association.

ELACQUA, James
Dewey Ballantine LLP, Palo Alto
650 845 7100
jelacqua@deweyballantine.com
Recommended in Intellectual Property

Practice Areas: Mr Elacqua is a member of the firm's Management Committee. His practice is devoted to intellectual property law, specializing in patent litigation in complex technical cases. He has represented clients in both jury and bench trials in federal district courts, state courts and in the International Trade Commission. His role also includes advising general counsel and the board of directors on intellectual property enforcement matters, defensive and litigation strategy, and settlement negotiations.

Career: Partner, Dewey Ballantine LLP.

Personal: Born October 28, 1950. BSEE, Clarkson University, 1972. JD, Ohio Northern University Pettit College of Law, 1976.

ELERDING, Gene R
Manatt Phelps & Phillips LLP,
Los Angeles 310 312 4158
gelerding@manatt.com
Recommended in Banking & Finance

Practice Areas: Banking law, with emphasis in regulatory and operational issues affecting financial institutions and advertisers. Represents a growing number of companies with e-commerce, online banking, check disputes, deposit agreements, information management and payment system issues. Advises on legal issues affecting product development, privacy, vendor services, cash management, consumer disclosures and compliance.

Prof. Memberships: Bank Operations Counsel Association (Co-Founder & Member); CASB (former Chair, Consumer Financial Services Committee); CBA (Vice Chair, Escheat Task Force, past member, Regulatory Compliance and Legal Affairs Committees, Contributing Member, State Government Relations Committee).

Career: Partner.

Personal: Notre Dame University (JD 1974); University of Southern California (BA 1971).

ELLISON, Christopher
Ellison Schneider & Harris,
Sacramento 916 447 2166
Recommended in Energy

ELLMAN, Howard
Ellman, Burke, Hoffman & Johnson,
San Francisco 415 777 2727
Recommended in Real Estate

ELSON, Vera M
McDermott Will & Emery, Palo Alto
650 813 5112
velson@mwe.com
Recommended in Intellectual Property

Practice Areas: Focuses on IP litigation and counseling for high-tech clients. Has tried IP cases in district courts across the United States, in the International Trade Commission (ITC) and in state courts.

Prof. Memberships: Member of Federal Circuit Bar Association. Patent attorney registered to practice before the US Patent and Trademark Office. Member of the ITC Trial Lawyers Association. Member of the Bar of the Supreme Court of the State of California, the US Court of Appeals for the Federal Circuit; the Ninth Circuit Court of Appeals; and the Northern and Central Districts of California.

Career: Worked as a high-speed digital circuit designer for Hughes Aircraft's Advanced Circuit Technology Laboratory before obtaining law degree. Interned at the Court of Appeals for the Federal Circuit in Washington, D.C. for the late Chief Judge Helen Wilson Nies.

Personal: Earned her JD from University of Southern California Law School. Earned her MSEE and BS from University of California-Los Angeles.

EMANUEL, William
Littler Mendelson PC, San Francisco
310 553 0308
Recommended in Employment

ERSPAMER, Gordon
Morrison & Foerster LLP, Walnut Creek
925 295 3341
gerspamer@mofo.com
Recommended in Energy

Practice Areas: Focus on litigation of complex civil actions in both state and federal courts. Primary concentration is on energy litigation, with emphasis on the representation of new entrants in disputes with California investor-owned utilities, and the representation of utilities located outside California in litigation throughout the Western United States. Has extensive experience in matters involving power contracts, transmission/interconnection disputes, alternative energy, and the interface between energy and antitrust/unfair business practice law. Provides strategic advice to clients on energy issues, including electric industry restructuring.

Career: Admitted to practice in California. Co-Chair, firm's Inter-Disciplinary Energy Group.

Personal: BA, Hamline University, 1975; JD, University of Michigan Law School, 1978

ETH, Jordan
Morrison & Foerster LLP, San Francisco
415 268 7126
jeth@mofo.com
Recommended in Litigation

Practice Areas: Represents public companies and their officers and directors in securities class actions, SEC investigations and derivative suits. Representations have led to significant victories for defendants, as reflected in several published judicial decisions.

Career: Admitted to practice in California. From 1980 until 1982, worked as an economist in Washington DC, first for the US Department of Energy and then for the Budget Committee of the US House of Representatives. Currently Co-Chair of the firm's Securities Litigation Group.

Personal: BA, Swarthmore College, 1980; JD, Stanford University Law School, 1985.

FARRAR, Stanley
Sullivan & Cromwell LLP, Los Angeles
310 712 6600
Recommended in Banking & Finance

FAYNE, Steve
Akin Gump Strauss Hauer & Feld LLP,
Los Angeles 310 229 1069
sfayne@akingump.com
Recommended in Media & Entertainment

Practice Areas: Media finance. Advises financial institutions regarding international film and television lending. Also counsels borrowers, distributors, completion guarantors, independent producers, equity investors and others in various aspects of financing film and television projects. Advises film and television clients re tax-advantaged financing, subsidies and co-production

arrangements worldwide.

Prof. Memberships: Adjunct Professor, UCLA School of Film and Television; former Board Member, Los Angeles Copyright Society; Member, California Bar.

Personal: BA, Kent State University; JD, Columbia Law School.

FEDER, Philip
Paul, Hastings, Janofsky & Walker LLP,
Los Angeles 213 683 6298
philipfeder@paulhastings.com
Recommended in Real Estate

Practice Areas: Chairman of Paul, Hastings, Janofsky & Walker's Real Estate Department; concentrates practice in real estate transactions, both domestic and international, with emphasis in finance, acquisitions and dispositions, and real estate loan workouts. Regularly represents investors on transactions in Asia and in Europe.

Prof. Memberships: American College of Real Estate Lawyers.

Career: Frequent speaker to attorneys and other real estate professionals.

Publications: 'The State of the North Asian Real Estate Markets', Briefings in Real Estate Finance, September 2002.

Personal: AB degree, Economics, with honors, 1976, Stanford University; JD degree, 1979, Columbia University Law School. Harlan Fiske Stone Scholar.

FELDMAN, Boris
Wilson Sonsini Goodrich & Rosati,
Palo Alto 650 493 9300
bfeldman@wsgr.com
Recommended in Corporate/M&A, Litigation

Practice Areas: Securities litigation and counseling; SEC enforcement; internal investigations; corporate law and governance.

Prof. Memberships: Admitted to practice in DC and California.

Career: Represented companies and their officers in more than 75 shareholder class actions and derivative suits throughout the US. Advised audit committees and boards of directors in internal investigations into accounting matters. Recently tried and won the case of Walter Hewlett v Hewlett-Packard Company in the Delaware Court of Chancery, on behalf of HP. Member, WSGR Executive Management Committee and Policy Committee.

Personal: JD, Yale University, 1980; BA (summa cum laude), Yale University, 1977. Phi Beta Kappa.

FELDMAN, Larry
Kaye Scholer LLP, Los Angeles
310 788 1090
larryfeldman@kayescholer.com
Recommended in Litigation, Media & Entertainment

Practice Areas: Special Counsel. Specializes in civil litigation, with primary emphasis in high stakes entertainment, business, insurance, legal malpractice, real estate and personal injury tort litigation.

Prof. Memberships: Member Bar of California.

Career: President, Los Angeles County Bar Association, 1987-88. President Los Angeles Trial Lawyers Association, 1984. Fellow, American College of Trial Lawyers. Fellow, International Academy of Trial Lawyers. Vice-President, American Board of Trial Advocates. Board of Directors, Association of Business Trial Lawyers. Board of Governors, California Trial Lawyers Association. JD (cum laude), Loyola University of Los Angeles, 1969. BS, San Fernando Valley State College, 1966.

FELDMAN, Robert
Wilson Sonsini Goodrich & Rosati, Palo Alto 650 493 9300
rfeldman@wsgr.com
Recommended in Intellectual Property, Litigation

Practice Areas: IP litigation, commercial litigation, white-collar crime and internal investigations.
Prof. Memberships: Fellow, American College of Trial Lawyers.
Career: Joined WSGR, 1984; became Partner, 1986. Assistant US Attorney and Member, Special Prosecution Unit, Northern District of California, 1979-84. Was retained by Octel Corporation two months before the start of a trial which, after six weeks, resulted in a verdict invalidating each of the three patents being asserted against Octel.
Personal: JD, Columbia University, 1975. Kent Scholar, Stone Scholar; BA (magna cum laude) State University of New York (Buffalo), 1972. Phi Beta Kappa.

FELDSTEIN, Hydee R
Paul, Hastings, Janofsky & Walker LLP, Los Angeles 213 683 6100
hydeefeldstein@paulhastings.com
Recommended in Banking & Finance, Bankruptcy

Practice Areas: Hydee Feldstein is a finance Partner specializing in all aspects of finance, lending and bankruptcy law. Ms Feldstein regularly represents secured lenders in cash flow and asset based financings, senior and subordinated debt issuances, debtor in possession lending, securitizations, workouts and bankruptcies.
Personal: Ms Feldstein received her BA from Swarthmore College in 1979 and her JD from Columbia University School of Law in 1982, where she was a Member of the 'Columbia Law Review' and a Harlan Fiske Stone Scholar.

FEO, Edwin
Milbank, Tweed, Hadley & McCloy, Los Angeles 213 892 4000
Recommended in Energy, Projects, Transport

FESSLER, Daniel
Holland & Knight LLP, San Francisco 415 743 6900
daniel.fessler@hklaw.com

Recommended in Energy

Practice Areas: Partner in the firm's Government Section, practices in the areas of energy, telecommunications law, complex contract issues and alternative dispute resolution. He currently advises government and utility clients in Asia, Africa, Europe, Latin America, and North America on restructuring options, privatization issues, infrastructure development, and project finance. Has extensive experience as both a legal academic and government official. From 1991-96, he was President of the California Public Utilities Commission, which regulates the reliability, safety, and economic terms of service provided to California's population by investor-owned utilities in the fields of energy (gas and electric), telecommunications, water and transportation.

FIELDS, Bertram
Greenberg Glusker Fields Claman Machtinger & Kinsella LLP, Los Angeles 310 553 3610
Recommended in Media & Entertainment

FIELDS, Henry M
Morrison & Foerster LLP, Los Angeles 213 892 5275
hfields@mofo.com
Recommended in Banking & Finance

Practice Areas: Has advised on banking issues for over 30 years. Engaged in a general corporate and banking practice, including domestic and international mergers and acquisitions and capital market transactions.
Prof. Memberships: Member, Board of Directors, International Financial Institutions Association of California; Member (and former Chair), Board of Directors, Institute for Corporate Counsel.
Career: Admitted to practice in California, New Jersey, and New York. Named a 'World's Leading Banking Lawyer', 'International Financial Law Review'. One of only four California attorneys to receive the highest individual rating in banking and finance by 'Global Counsel 3000' (7th edition).
Personal: BA, Harvard College, 1968, Phi Beta Kappa; JD, Yale Law School, 1972, managing editor, 'Yale Law Journal'; Federal Clerkship, 1972-73, Honorable Leonard I Garth.

FILETI, Thomas
Morrison & Foerster LLP, Los Angeles 213 892 5276
tfileti@mofo.com
Recommended in Real Estate

Practice Areas: Represents clients in connection with investments in and the financing, operation and disposition of, real estate assets. Has expertise in financing of corporate real estate facilities. Practice also emphasizes real estate financings and purchase and sale transactions, including credit leases, lease financings, mezzanine financing, and REITs representations.

Prof. Memberships: Member, American Bar Association; Member, Los Angeles County Bar Association; Member, National Association of Real Estate Investment Trusts.
Career: Admitted to practice in California. Head, Real Estate Practice Group, Los Angeles office.
Personal: AB degree, with distinction, Cornell University, 1978; JD, cum laude, University of Pennsylvania Law School, 1981.

FISCHER, Samuel
Ziffren Brittenham Branca Fischer Gilbert-Lurie & Stiffelman LLP, Los Angeles 310 552 3388
Recommended in Media & Entertainment

FLAGEL, Mark
Latham & Watkins LLP, Los Angeles 213 485 1234
Recommended in Intellectual Property

FLAUM, Keith
Cooley Godward LLP, Palo Alto 650 843 5000
Recommended in Corporate/M&A

FORST, David
Fenwick & West, San Francisco 650 335 7254
dforst@fenwick.com
Recommended in Tax

Practice Areas: International corporate and partnership taxation.
Career: Included in Euromoney's Guide to the World's Leading Tax Advisers; named one of top tax advisers in the Western US by International Tax Review. Editor of and regular contributor to Journal of Taxation. Has published articles on international joint ventures, international tax aspects of mergers and acquisitions, and business purpose and economic substance doctrines. Has chaired and spoken at numerous tax seminars, including NYU Tax Institute, TEI Chapter meetings, and San Jose State Tax Institute. Has taught law school courses on partnership taxation and Section 482 transfer pricing.
Personal: Stanford Law School, JD, with distinction, 1992; Princeton University, Woodrow Wilson School of Public and International Affairs, AB, cum laude, Phi Beta Kappa, 1989.

FRACKMAN, Russell
Mitchell, Silberberg & Knupp LLP, Los Angeles 310 312 2000
Recommended in Media & Entertainment

FRAM, Robert
Heller Ehrman LLP, San Francisco 415 772 6000
Recommended in Intellectual Property

FRANKENHEIMER, John
Loeb & Loeb LLP, Los Angeles 213 688 3400
Recommended in Media & Entertainment

FREIER, Elliot
Irell & Manella LLP, Los Angeles 310 277 1010
Recommended in Tax

FRIEDMAN, Alan
Munger, Tolles & Olson LLP, Los Angeles 213 683 9100
Recommended in Employment

FRIEDMAN, Bruce A
Alschuler Grossman Stein & Kahan LLP, Santa Monica
Recommended in Insurance

Practice Areas: Regarded as a leading insurance coverage and professional liability lawyer in California, Bruce represents insurers and policyholders with respect to coverage issues and litigation involving D&O, media, internet, entertainment, professional liability, and general liability policies. Bruce also represents the California Insurance Commissioner with respect to insolvency and regulatory litigation. Bruce defends attorneys, directors, and officers against malpractice, breach of fiduciary duty and securities claims.
Prof. Memberships: Member, Board of Governors, and past President, Association of Business Trial Lawyers. Member, Board of Trustees of Public Counsel. Member, American Bar Association Litigation Section and TIPS Section and Committees on Insurance Coverage, Professional Liability, Directors and Officers Liability and Fidelity and Surety law within those sections.
Career: Managing Partner of Alschuler Grossman Stein & Kahan LLP. In 1996, obtained one of the top 10 plaintiff's verdicts in California. In 2003, represented the Los Angeles County Bar Association as amicus curiae before the California Supreme Court in Viner v. Sweet which established the causation requirement in legal malpractice.
Publications: Co-author, 'Insurance Coverage for Patent Litigation', Patent Litigation, PLI Press, 2001; author, 'Dismissal', Civil Procedure Before Trial, Continuing Education of the Bar, 1990; co-author, 'Annotated Directors and Officers Liability Policy', American Bar Association Press, anticipated publication 2005.
Personal: Claremont Men's College (BA with honors, 1972). George Washington University (JD with honors, 1975). President, Board of Trustees, Wilshire Boulevard Temple.

FRIEDRICH, William
Farella Braun & Martel LLP, San Francisco 415 954 4400
Recommended in Insurance

FULLER, James
Fenwick & West LLP, Mountain View 650 335 7205
jpfuller@fenwick.com
Recommended in Tax

Practice Areas: Chair of firm's Tax Group. Corporate, domestic and international tax, mergers and acquisitions and joint ventures.

Career: One of Euromoney's World's Top 25 Tax Advisers (2002). Top tax adviser in western US in each of International Tax Review's ten annual surveys (1994-2003). Speaks often for TEI and other organizations (11 TEI Chapters and Annual Meeting). Taught at Stanford Law School and chaired various ABA committees. Author of widely read monthly column in Tax Notes International. Appeared in each edition of Best Lawyers in America. Admitted to and has had cases in United States Supreme Court, seven federal circuit courts of appeal, various district courts, United States Court of Federal Claims, and United States Tax Court.

Personal: New York University School of Law, Graduate Law School, 1975; New York University, LLM, in taxation, 1974; Fordham University School of Law, JD, 1970; New York University, BS, 1966.

GALE, Kelley
Latham & Watkins LLP, San Diego
619 236 1234
Recommended in Projects

GALLO, Greg
DLA Piper Rudnick Gray Cary US LLP, Palo Alto 650 833 2020
greg.gallo@dlapiper.com
Recommended in Corporate/M&A

Practice Areas: Corporate and securities; emerging growth and venture capital; mergers and acqusitiions; public company and corporate governance

Career: He has a wide-ranging venture capital, corporate and securities, M&A and capital markets practice coupled with extensive experience of acting for clients in the semiconductor, networking, telecom, enterprise software, internet, biotechnology, venture capital and investment banking sectors. For more than 30 years, he has represented clients in a variety of corporate and corporate finance matters relating to emerging growth through Fortune 500, Silicon Valley technology and biotechnology companies.

Personal: JD, Harvard University; BS, University of Wisconsin, cum laude.

GALLO, Joie Marie
Christensen, Miller, Fink, Jacobs, Glaser, Weil & Shapiro, LLP, Los Angeles 310 553 3000
Recommended in Media & Entertainment

GARTMAN, John
Fish & Richardson, San Diego
858 678 5070
Recommended in Intellectual Property

GARVIN, Anthony O
Morgan, Lewis & Bockius LLP, San Francisco 415 442 1620
agarvin@morganlewis.com
Recommended in Environment

Practice Areas: Anthony O Garvin is a

Partner in the Litigation Practice, resident in the San Francisco office with broad experience in all aspects of environmental law. He has represented corporate clients in California and the Western United States in litigation and administrative proceedings regarding federal and state environmental laws including Comprehensive Environmental Response Compensation and Liability Act (CERCLA), Resource Conservation and Recovery Act (RCRA), NPDES permits under Clean Water Act and California Porter-Cologne Water Quality Control Act, Clean Air Act, Proposition 65, Endangered Species Act, and underground tank laws.

GIBBS, Kenneth C
Gibbs, Giden, Locher & Turner, Los Angeles 310 552 3400
kgibbs@gglt.com
Recommended in Construction

Practice Areas: Kenneth C Gibbs is a Senior Partner in the Los Angeles and Las Vegas law firm of Gibbs, Giden, Locher & Turner LLP, which specializes in the representation of owners, contractors, subcontractors, material suppliers, design professionals and insurers in construction industry matters and disputes. He has specialized in construction law, arbitrations and mediations for more than 30 years. Mr Gibbs presently is a full-time mediator and arbitrator and has mediated more than 600 matters. He specializes in the mediation of construction defect, breach of contract and delay, disruption and acceleration claims. He is one of the leading mediators of complex, multi-party construction defect and breach of contract disputes and has mediated such disputes throughout the nation.

Prof. Memberships: Mr Gibbs is a Member of the Large/Complex Case Panel of the American Arbitration Association and an Arbitrator on the California Public Works Arbitration Panel.

Publications: Mr Gibbs has authored or co-authored many books and articles on construction industry and mediation related topics, including 'California Construction Law', now in its 16th edition, and 'Construction Change Order Claims'. He has been a principal speaker at many national conventions and conferences including the annual Construction Law Superconference.

GILLETTE, Patricia
Heller Ehrman LLP, San Francisco
415 772 6000
Recommended in Employment

GIRARD, Robert D
Sonnenschein Nath & Rosenthal, Los Angeles 213 892 5074
rgirard@sonnenschein.com
Recommended in Healthcare

Practice Areas: Represents institutional and professional providers, including integrated medical groups, faculty practice programs, IPAs, health insurance

companies, HMOs, PPOs and other third-party payment and managed care organizations. Experience includes medico-legal and bioethics matters, service contracts, reimbursement, corporate organizational, medical staff and general transactional matters, including handling M&A and related antitrust, tax and corporate securities issues. Has drafted regulatory legislation (including California Hospital Commission Act) and prepared and presented testimony on regulatory initiatives.

Prof. Memberships: National Health Lawyers; California Society of Health Care Attorneys; American Academy of Health Care Attorneys.

Personal: Yale Law School LLB; UCLA, AB, Phi Beta Kappa.

GIUNTA, Joseph J
Skadden, Arps, Slate, Meagher & Flom LLP & Affiliates, Los Angeles
213 687 5040
jgiunta@skadden.com
Recommended in Corporate/M&A

Practice Areas: Handles all types of merger and acquisition transactions, both friendly and hostile. He is experienced in proxy contests, tender offers, restructurings, recapitalizations and leveraged buyouts. Has represented purchasers, sellers and their financial advisors in a wide variety of merger, acquisition and disposition transactions.

Career: JD, American University, Washington College of Law, 1976 (magna cum laude); Associate Editor, American University Law Review; BS, Stanford University, 1972.

GLAD, Paul E B
Sonnenschein Nath & Rosenthal, San Francisco 415 882 5001
pglad@sonnenschein.com
Recommended in Insurance

Practice Areas: Insurance Practice Chair and San Francisco office head. Matters range from coverage issues to bad-faith claims, class actions to regulatory challenges. Co-authors West's California Insurance Laws Annotated and California Insurance Law Handbook. Editor of and frequent contributor to numerous publications, including 'Underwriters' Report' and 'Insurance Litigation Reporter'.

Prof. Memberships: Past Director, San Fransisco Bar Association; Past Chairman, San Fransisco Bar Association Insurance Law Section; Past Chairman, Endowment of San Fransisco; Faculty, Environmental Law Institute, Business Insurance Law Institute; Past Chairman, National Seminar on Advertising Injury Insurance Coverage Issues, NY.

Personal: UCLA Law School JD; Stanford University, with Distinction.

GLASCOCK, Thomas
Thelen Reid & Priest LLP, San Francisco 415 371 1200
Recommended in Projects

GLASER, Patricia
Christensen, Miller, Fink, Jacobs, Glaser, Weil & Shapiro, LLP, Los Angeles 310 553 3000
Recommended in Media & Entertainment

GODSHALL, Brad
Pachulski, Stang, Ziehl, Young, Jones & Weintraub P.C., Los Angeles
310 277 6910
Recommended in Bankruptcy

GOLDBERG, Phillip
Hassard Bonnington LLP, San Francisco 415 288 9800
Recommended in Healthcare

GOLDBERG, Stephen
Heller Ehrman White & McAuliffe LLP, Los Angeles 213 689 0200
Recommended in Insurance

GOLDMAN, Donald
McDermott Will & Emery, Los Angeles 310 551 9319
dogoldman@mwe.com
Recommended in Healthcare

Practice Areas: Has served as counsel to healthcare industry clients in a broad range of planning, regulatory, administrative and litigation matters, including hospital physician ventures, Medicare fraud and abuse defense, medical staff relations and bylaws, facilities licensing, hospital-based physician matters and certificate of need. Has concentrated practice on representing clients in Medicare fraud and abuse investigations and development of corporate compliance programs. Represented individual professionals in licensing, Medicare and joint venture matters. Representative experience includes advising DaVita Inc., a NYSE-listed company, a leading supplier of renal dialysis services, in its successful appeal of Medicare payment disputes involving approximately $80 million, and advising a large national hospital chain in a wide ranging series of government, regulatory and compliance matters.

Career: Former deputy attorney general for the State of California representing state agencies such as Department of Health Services, Board of Medical Quality Assurance and Board of Pharmacy.

Personal: Earned JD in 1972 from University of California-Los Angeles School of Law and BA in 1969 from University of California-Los Angeles.

GOLDMAN, Melvin
Morrison & Foerster LLP, San Francisco 415 268 7311
mgoldman@mofo.com
Recommended in Antitrust, Litigation

Practice Areas: Specializes in defense of antitrust actions and investigations including jury trials of antitrust lawsuits; handling appeals of antitrust judgments; and grand jury and internal investigations of antitrust matters. Has counseled corporations regarding antitrust compliance and lectured on substantive antitrust issues and trial technique in defense of antitrust lawsuits.

Prof. Memberships: Member, American College of Trial Lawyers. Past President, Bar Association of San Francisco.

Career: Admitted to practice in California and Illinois.

Personal: BA, DePaul University, 1958; JD, Northwestern University School of Law, 1961, Order of the Coif; Managing Editor, Law Review; MSL, Stanford University School of Law, 1963.

GOLDMAN, Robert J
Fish & Neave IP Group of Ropes & Gray, Palo Alto 650 617 4035
robert.goldman@ropesgray.com
Recommended in Intellectual Property

Practice Areas: IP litigator in the Fish & Neave IP Group of Ropes & Gray. 27 years of trial and appellate experience in complex patent, trade secret, copyright, trademark litigation for clients including AstraZeneca Pharmaceuticals LP, Tessera, Inc., Purdue Pharma LP, Hewlett-Packard/Compaq Computer Corporation and Nellcor, Inc. Worked on behalf of Polaroid Corporation in landmark patent infringement action against Eastman Kodak Company relating to instant photography; $873 million in damages.

Career: New York Bar (1978). California Bar (1997). Partner, Fish & Neave (1977). Partner, Ropes & Gray (2005).

Personal: JD, Columbia University (1977). BS, Operations, Software Applications, Columbia University (1977).

GOODKIND, Jim
Loeb & Loeb LLP, Los Angeles
213 688 3400
Recommended in Media & Entertainment

GOODMAN, William M
Topel & Goodman PC, San Francisco
415 421 6140
wmg@topelgoodman.com
Recommended in Litigation

Practice Areas: White collar criminal defense and related civil and administrative litigation.

Prof. Memberships: California Bar Association; American Bar Association; California Attorneys for Criminal Justice; National Association of Criminal Defense Attorneys.

Career: BA Northwestern University, 1971; JD University of California, Berkeley (Boalt Hall), 1974; Law Clerk to Chief Justice Donald R. Wright, California Supreme Court 1974-75; Assistant Federal Public Defender, Northern District of California 1975-80; Partner, Topel and Goodman 1980-present.

GOODWIN, David
Heller Ehrman LLP, San Francisco
415 772 6000
Recommended in Insurance

GREEN, Josh
Heller Ehrman White & McAuliffe, Menlo Park 650 854 4488
Recommended in Corporate/M&A

GREENBERG, Gordon A
McDermott Will & Emery, Los Angeles
310 551 9398
ggreenberg@mwe.com
Recommended in Litigation

Practice Areas: Defends clients in high stakes 'bet the company' matters that often have international components. Recent matters handled include defending a foreign government agency in criminal matter concerning alleged false statements to a US banking regulator; representation of the president of a large telecommunications company in SEC and criminal proceedings; representation of the Chairman of the Board of a public company in a Foreign Corrupt Practices Investigation; and representation of a Big Four accounting firm in a money laundering investigation.

Prof. Memberships: Active in local and national bar associations and served as the chairman of the Los Angeles County Bar Association's White Collar Crime Committee. Served as a faculty lecturer at the Federal Judicial Center, the organization that provides federal judges with continuing legal education.

Career: Served as Chief of the Financial Investigations Unit in the Los Angeles US Attorney's Office.

Personal: Received his JD with honors from the Illinois Institute of Technology/Chicago Kent College of Law in 1980, and BA from the University of Illinois in 1976. Admitted to practice in Illinois and California.

GREENBERG, Jeffrey
Latham & Watkins LLP, Los Angeles
213 485 1234
Recommended in Projects

GREENFIELD, Robert A
Stutman, Treister & Glatt Professional Corporation, Los Angeles
310 228 5630
RGreenfield@Stutman.com
Recommended in Bankruptcy

Practice Areas: Senior shareholder specializing in corporate reorganization, insolvency and bankruptcy law. Is currently acting as lead reorganization counsel for Falcon Products, Inc., whose Chapter 11 case is pending in St. Louis. Falcon is engaged in the design, manufacture, and marketing of an extensive line of furniture for the food service, contract office, hospitality, healthcare and education markets. He was lead restructuring counsel for Clark Retail Enterprises, Inc., whose Chapter 11 case was pending in Chicago, Illinois. Clark operated over 800 gasoline/convenient product stores throughout the Midwest. All of the stores were sold and the case was dismissed last year. He was lead restructuring counsel for Huntsman Corporation and its domestic sub-

sidiaries. Huntsman, which is located in Salt Lake City, Utah, is the world's largest privately owned chemical company. Huntsman was successfully reorganized out of court in September 2002. He was lead Chapter 11 counsel for Edwards Theatre Circuits, one of the largest movie exhibitors in the United States, whose Chapter 11 case is pending in Santa Ana, California. A plan of reorganization for Edwards was confirmed in late 2001. He was lead reorganization counsel for Southern California Edison. He represents Leonard Green & Partners L.P., the controlling shareholders of the debtors, and defendants in LBO litigation, in the Hechinger cases pending in Delaware. Representative engagements in which Mr Greenfield has previously been involved include: lead Chapter 11 counsel for Leasing Solutions, Inc. in San Jose, California; representing the successful purchaser of the assets of Converse, Inc. pending in Delaware; representing United Airlines in the acquisition of the Heathrow route and Latin American routes in the Pan American Airlines proceeding in New York City; lead Chapter 11 counsel for Carter Hawley Hale in Los Angeles; representing the Equity Committee in Mortgage Realty & Trust in Los Angeles; lead Chapter 11 counsel for Thrifty Oil Corporation and Golden West Refining in San Diego, California; and representing numerous companies in out-of-court workout negotiations such as Ideal Basic Industries in Denver, Petro-Lewis in Denver, and Quantel Corporation in San Francisco, The Federated Group in Los Angeles; Flying Tiger Lines, Inc. in Los Angeles, and North American Car Corporation in Chicago.

Prof. Memberships: He is very active in the legal community and serves on several committees. His affiliations include: Member, National Bankruptcy Conference, 1974-present; Chairman, Committee on Court System and Administration, 1983-present; Member, Los Angeles County Bar Association (Editor, Bankruptcy Law Matters, Commercial Law and Bankruptcy Digest, 1973-75; Member, Section on Commercial Law and Bankruptcy, 1967-present) and American Bar Association (Member, Subcommittee on Secured Transaction, Section of Business Law, 1974-present; Member, Joint Task Force on Bankruptcy Court Structure and Insolvency Process, Section of Business Law and Section of Litigation, 1989). Bar Associations: The State Bar of California (Member, Committee on Uniform Commercial Code, 1977-79; Business Law Section); Member, Leadership Subcommittee of the Long Range Plan Implementation Committee of the United States Bankruptcy Court, Central District of California; Member, Financial Lawyers Conference (1967-present; Past President); Member, Board

of Trustees of the Center for Law in the Public Interest, 1979-92 (Past Chairman); Member, Board of Trustees and Executive Committee of the Constitutional Rights Foundation, 1995-present; Member, Advisory Board, Friends of the Graphic Arts at UCLA, Grunwald Center for the Graphic Arts, 1995-present. In addition, he served as an Adjunct Professor of Law, Loyola University School of Law, 1978-83.

Career: Admitted to California Bar in 1967 and has been with the firm, 'Stutman, Triester & Glatt', since 1967. Los Angeles Magazine and Law & Politics magazine recently named Mr Greenfield a Southern California Super Lawyer 2005. In addition, he was named as one of the 'Top 100 Lawyers in Los Angeles County', the publication's list of the highest rated Super Lawyers. Mr Greenfield is also listed in the most recent edition of 'Who's Who Legal', National Register's 'Who's Who in Executive and Professionals', 'Chambers USA', a leading legal publication, the K&A Restructuring Register, and is a fellow in the American College of Bankruptcy.

Publications: Authored many articles, including 'Lines v Frederick: The Effect of Bankruptcy on a Bankrupt's Accrued Vacation Pay and Other Forms of Deferred Compensation,' 47 Los Angeles Bar Bulletin 67, 1971; 'Alternatives to Bankruptcy for the Business Debtor,' 51 Los Angeles Bar Bulletin 135, 1975; 'The Bankruptcy Code and the Article 9 Secured Creditor,' The Business Lawyer, April, 1979; 'The National Bankruptcy Conference's Position on the Court System Under the Bankruptcy Amendments and Federal Judgeship Act of 1984 and Suggestions for Rules Promulgation,' 23 Harv. J. on Legis. 357, 1986.

Personal: Attended the University of California at Los Angeles, where he graduated in 1963. He was a member of Phi Beta Kappa. Received JD (cum laude) from Harvard University in 1966.

GREENSPAN, Eric
Myman, Abell, Fineman, Greenspan & Light LLP, Los Angeles 310 820 7717
Recommended in Media & Entertainment

GREENWALD, Steven
Davis Wright Tremaine LLP, San Francisco 415 276 6528
stevegreenwald@dwt.com
Recommended in Energy

Practice Areas: Partner, Chair of Energy Department. Representation includes independent power projects and financing parties in debt/equity financing, purchasing and selling generation assets; independent power producers and marketers in state and federal regulatory proceedings; and generators and power marketers in contractual negotiations/disputes with purchasing utilities.

Prof. Memberships: California Bar Association, Power Association of

Northern California, Energy Producers Supply Association, California Conference of Public Utility Counsel.
Career: California Bar, 1975. Partner, 1993.
Publications: Frequent speaker/commentator on energy industry issues.
Personal: JD (magna cum laude), University of Michigan, 1973 (Order of the Coif; Editor, Michigan Law Review). BA, University of Pennsylvania, 1970.

GROSSMAN, Marshall
Alschuler Grossman Stein & Kahan LLP, Santa Monica
Recommended in Litigation, Media & Entertainment
Practice Areas: He both prosecutes and defends major commercial litigation. Served as lead counsel for the plaintiff classes in the Equity Funding Securities Litigation and represented the owners of Guess? Jeans in their successful litigation against the owners of Jordache. He has represented Apple Computer, Inc. and Packard Bell NEC, Inc. in the defense of patent infringement and Lanham Act litigation, including the highly publicized battle between Compaq and Packard Bell. In 1999, led Arthur Andersen's trial team to a defense jury verdict in a $1 billion securities fraud class action lawsuit. In 2004 settled on the eve of trial for client Suzuki Motor Company against Consumers Union and in 2005 successfully defended Blockbuster, Inc. in action filed by the Walt Disney Co. At this time, represents international public accounting firms in complex federal securities litigation and related federal investigations, and the Hollywood Foreign Press Association (Golden Globes).
Prof. Memberships: American, Beverly Hills (Chair, Civil Practice and Procedure Committee, 1969-70; Member, Board of Governors, 1970-76), Century City, and Los Angeles County Bar Associations; State Bar of California; Beverly Hills Barristers (President, 1972-73); Association of Business Trial Lawyers (Member, Board of Governors, 1973-75).
Career: A Partner of Alschuler Grossman Stein & Kahan LLP. Has practiced with the firm since 1964. Lecturer in Law, University of Southern California Law Center, 1966-69. In 1989 and again in 1999, was recognized by a leading US law journal as among 10 of the top trial lawyers in America. Referred to by former Los Angeles Mayor Richard J Riordan as the 'toughest litigator in Los Angeles'. 2003 and 2004 Top 10 'Super-Lawyer' vote recipient in peer survey of Southern California's 65,000 lawyers. Listed in The Best Lawyers in America. Has long been active in community affairs, having served as a Commissioner on the California Coastal Commission and on the boards of Public Counsel, and the United Way. Currently serves as Vice-Chair of the State of California

Commission on Judicial Performance, on the boards of Bet Tzedek Legal Services, Jewish Big Brothers and on the national board of the American Jewish Committee.
Personal: University of California at Los Angeles; University of Southern California (BSL and LLB, 1964). Order of the Coif. Production Editor, Southern California Law Review, 1963-64.

GROSSMAN, Paul
Paul, Hastings, Janofsky & Walker LLP, Los Angeles 213 683 6203
paulgrossman@paulhastings.com
Recommended in Employment
Practice Areas: Represents major private employers in all aspects of employment law, including class actions, wage/hour, wrongful discharge, discrimination, sexual harassment, whistleblower, and labor-management litigation.
Prof. Memberships: American Bar Association Labor and Employment Law Section and its Equal Employment Opportunity Committee.
Publications: Co-author of Lindemann & Grossman, 'Employment Discrimination Law' (Bureau of National Affairs, 1996 and 2002), the official book of the American Bar Association in its field.
Personal: BA degree in 1961 from Amherst College; JD degree in 1964 from Yale Law School; Member of the Board of Editors of the Yale Law Journal.

GUNDERSON, Bob
Gunderson Dettmer Stough Villeneuve Franklin & Hachigian, Menlo Park
650 321 2400
Recommended in Corporate/M&A

GUY III, Hopkins
Orrick, Herrington & Sutcliffe, Menlo Park 650 614 7400
Recommended in Intellectual Property

HAGEROTT, Edward
Munger, Tolles & Olson LLP, Los Angeles 213 683 9100
Recommended in Real Estate

HALBREICH, David M
Morgan, Lewis & Bockius LLP, Los Angeles
213 612 7345
dhalbreich@morganlewis.com
Recommended in Insurance
Practice Areas: David Halbreich is a Partner in the Litigation Practice. He concentrates his practice on complex litigation and insurance recovery. He has represented clients in a variety of industries including manufacturing, oil and gas, financial services, real estate development, electronics, construction and others.
Prof. Memberships: (State Bar of California, Deputy Special Trial Counsel); American Bar Association (Litigation Section, Committee on Insurance Coverage).

HALL, Michael
Latham & Watkins LLP, Menlo Park
650 328 4600
Recommended in Corporate/M&A

HALLING, Gary
Sheppard, Mullin, Richter & Hampton LLP, San Francisco 415 434 9100
Recommended in Antitrust

HANDZLIK, Jan
Howrey Simon Arnold & White, Los Angeles 213 892 1800
Recommended in Litigation

HANSCHEN, Peter
Morrison & Foerster LLP, Walnut Creek
925 295 3450
phanschen@mofo.com
Recommended in Energy
Practice Areas: Advises on all aspects of energy matters, including state and federal regulations, energy-related transactions, energy project financing and arbitrations. Has been in the forefront of electric regulation matters for 25 years.
Career: Admitted to practice in California. Began career in Pacific Gas and Electric Company's legal department. During last five years with PG&E, was responsible for all regulatory matters before the California Public Utilities Commission and other state and federal regulatory agencies. Co-Chair, Morrison & Foerster Energy Practice Group.
Personal: BA, magna cum laude, San Francisco State University, 1967; JD, University of California, Berkeley, Boalt Hall, 1971.

HANSEN, Tom
Hansen Jacobson Teller Hoberman Newman, Warren, Sloane & Richman, LLP, Beverly Hills 310 271 8777
Recommended in Media & Entertainment

HARRIS, Alan
Farella Braun & Martel LLP, San Francisco 415 954 4400
Recommended in Construction

HART, Gordon E
Paul, Hastings, Janofsky & Walker LLP, San Francisco
415 856 7017
gordonhart@paulhastings.com
Recommended in Environment
Practice Areas: Brownfields redevelopment; military base reuse; permitting, enforcement, and compliance counseling under state and federal pollution laws; state legislative lobbying.
Prof. Memberships: Environmental Law Section, California State Bar; National Association of Installation Developers.
Career: Paul Hastings Janofsky & Walker, 1997 to present; California State Legislature, 1992-97 (senior consultant, Senate Toxics and Public Safety Management Committee; counsel, Senate Judiciary Committee; counsel, Speaker of the Assembly); JD McGeorge School of Law, 1994; BA Reed College, 1984.

Publications: 'Environmental Aspects of Real Estate and Commercial Transactions', American Bar Association, 2004 (chapter author, 'Brownfields Redevelopment and Closed Military Bases').

HASLAM, Robert
Heller Ehrman White & McAuliffe LLP, Menlo Park 650 324 7000
Recommended in Intellectual Property

HAVEL, Richard W
Sidley Austin Brown & Wood LLP, Los Angeles 213 896 6017
rhavel@sidley.com
Recommended in Bankruptcy
Practice Areas: Richard W. Havel heads the Los Angeles Bankruptcy Group. He has represented parties in informal workouts and in Chapter 11 proceedings, and has served as counsel to creditors' committees, Chapter 11 trustees, debtors and other parties in interest.
Prof. Memberships: Member of the Board of Trustees for the UCLA/Jonsson Cancer Center; the Financial Lawyers Conference, where he served as an officer and director; the Board of Trustees for the UCLA Law School Alumni Association; the Board of Directors for the Industrial Development Authority for the City of Los Angeles, where he served as chairman; the Commercial Law and Bankruptcy section of the Los Angeles County Bar, serving on its Executive Committee; and is a Fellow of the American College of Bankruptcy.
Career: MrHavel was adjunct professor at Loyola School of Law. University of California at Los Angeles (UCLA) School of Law, JD, 1971, Order of the Coif, University of Notre Dame (BA, 1968). Bar Admission: California, 1972.
Publications: Mr Havel served as Articles Editor, UCLA Law Review; and is a frequent lecturer on bankruptcy and environmental law at industry and legal programs including ALI-ABA and the annual Bankruptcy Ligitation Institute.

HAYES, David
Fenwick & West LLP, Mountain View
415 875 2411
dhayes@fenwick.com
Recommended in Intellectual Property
Practice Areas: Chair of firm's Intellectual Property Group. Focuses on intellectual property counseling, litigation and audits, and technology licensing, distribution and transfer. Counsels a wide range of high technology companies on establishing and maintaining procedures to protect the company's intellectual property through copyrights, patents, trade secrets, mask works and trademarks, and on avoiding infringing the rights of others. Represents numerous clients on high profile, complex technology transactions, including patent license transactions and acquisition strategies for both component technologies and turnkey systems. Nationally recognized expert on

copyright issues related to the Internet and digital media. He has served as counsel in a number of precedent setting software copyright infringement cases, including Lotus Development Corp v Borland International, Apple Computer v Microsoft Corp and A & M Records v Napster, Inc.

Prof. Memberships: Member, State Bar of California, Bar for the District of Columbia; registered patent attorney with US Patent and Trademark Office. Member, California Bar Association section on intellectual property; American Bar Association section on intellectual property; American Intellectual Property Law Association; Computer Law Association and Institute of Electrical & Electronics Engineers. Serves on intellectual property advisory committee of Practicing Law Institute, advisory board of The Berkeley Center for Law & Technology, program committee for USC Intellectual Property Law Institute, as well as editorial boards of The Computer and Internet Lawyer, Cyberspace Lawyer, The Intellectual Property Strategist, The Journal of Internet Law, Intellectual Property Counselor and Mealey's Litigation Reports on Intellectual Property.

Career: Has testified before Congress and federal agencies concerning intellectual property issues. Law clerk to Hon. John Minor Wisdom, US Court of Appeals for the Fifth Circuit.

Publications: Has published dozens of articles and given many speeches throughout the United States and in Japan on various intellectual property topics.

Personal: Harvard Law School, JD, cum laude, Editor of the Harvard Law Review, 1984; Stanford University, MSEE, in electrical engineering, 1980; Rice University, BS, in electrical engineering, summa cum laude, 1978.

HEINKE, Rex S
Akin Gump Strauss Hauer & Feld LLP, Los Angeles 310 229 1030
rheinke@akingump.com
Recommended in Media & Entertainment

Practice Areas: Chair, national Appellate and Litigation Strategy Practice and head of Los Angeles Litigation Practice. Has handled hundreds of appeals, writs, and substantive motions in state and federal courts throughout the country involving, among other things, antitrust, attorneys' fees, bankruptcy, class actions, complex business disputes, constitutional law, contracts, copyrights, defamation, domestic and international arbitrations, environmental law, false advertising, federal preemption, federal securities, personal jurisdiction, reporters' privilege, sovereign immunity, statutory interpretation, tax, trademarks, unfair competition, wage and hour, and wrongful termination.

Prof. Memberships: Member, California Judicial Council (2004 to date); For-

mer President, Los Angeles County Bar Association (2000-01).

HEISSE, John
Thelen Reid & Priest LLP, San Francisco 415 371 1200
Recommended in Construction

HELLOW, John
Hooper Lundy & Bookman Inc, Los Angeles 310 551 8111
Recommended in Healthcare

HEMMINGER, Pamela L
Gibson, Dunn & Crutcher LLP, Los Angeles 213 229 7274
phemminger@gibsondunn.com
Recommended in Employment

Practice Areas: Counseling and litigation - individual and class cases - involving all aspects of labor/employment law. Expertise in complex, high-exposure, high-profile matters. Sub-specialties include OSHA, ERISA, wage/hour, privacy, and disability/leaves of absence.

Prof. Memberships: Fellow, College of Labor and Employment Lawyers. American Arbitration Association Arbitrator (Employment Panel-Southern California). Labor and Employment Sections: Los Angeles County Bar Association (past Chair); ABA (past Management Co-Chair, Ethics Committee; current Management Co-Chair, CLE National Programs subcommittee).

Publications: Frequent commentator including television and radio. Contributing author, 'Employment Discrimination Law', 'California Practice Guide: Employment Litigation.'

Personal: JD, Pepperdine University School of Law, magna cum laude, 1976.

HEMMINGER, Steven D
White & Case LLP, Palo Alto
650 213 0300
SHemminger@whitecase.com
Recommended in Intellectual Property

Practice Areas: Executive Partner in charge of firm's Palo Alto, California office. Practice focus includes litigating over 35 major intellectual property disputes involving high technology in all forums, nationally and internationally. Substantial expertise in patent, trademark, trade secret litigation in electronics, semiconductor, computer software and hardware fields. Has managed patent and trademark portfolios regarding wireless telephony and LANs, computers, mechanical devices, medical devices in US and foreign patent offices.

Prof. Memberships: State Bar of California, 1983; registered to practice before the U.S.P.T.O.

Personal: Southwestern University School of Law (JD, magna cum laude, 1983); Rensselaer Polytechnic Institute (BS, Mechanical Engineering, 1974).

HENNIGAN, Brian
Irell & Manella LLP, Los Angeles
310 277 1010
Recommended in Litigation

HENNIGAN, J Michael
Hennigan, Bennett & Dorman LLP, Los Angeles
213 694 1200
Hennigan@hbdlawyers.com
Recommended in Litigation

Practice Areas: Partner, Hennigan, Bennett & Dorman LLP. Practice limited to the litigation and trial of complex commercial cases. Lead counsel in more than 45 major jury trials in state and federal court. Regular representation of major developers, financial institutions and energy companies. As lead trial counsel for Plaintiff has recovered more than $7.5 billion for the clients of the firm.

Prof. Memberships: Member, Board of Visitors, University of Arizona College of Law, 1976-79; and 1990-present. Member, Board of Directors, University of Arizona Law College Association, 1983-85. Member, State Bar of Arizona. Member, State Bar of California. Chair, Litigation Section, Los Angeles County Bar Association, 1998-99. Member, American Bar Association, Sections on Antitrust Law and Litigation. Lawyer Representative, Ninth Circuit Judicial Conference, 1993-97. Member, American Board of Trial Advocates, 1992-present. Member, American Law Institute, 1993-present. Trustee, Los Angeles County Bar Association, 1996. Member, Judicial Council Task Force on Complex Civil Litigation.

Career: Trial Attorney, Antitrust Division United States Department of Justice, 1970-72. Attorney General's Citation for Outstanding Performance, 1971. Lecturer in Research and Writing, University of Arizona College of Law, 1973.

Publications: 'Dean Charles Ares: The Early Years', 35 Arizona Law Review 20 (1993); 'The Essence of Standing: The Basis of a Constitutional Right to Be Heard', 10 Arizona Law Review 438 (1969); 'In Defense of the Conscientious Objector: The Constitutional Right to a Trial de Novo', 11 Arizona Law Review, 249, 1969. Co-Author: American Bar Association Section of Antitrust Law, Monograph 3, 'Expediting Pre Trials and Trial of Antitrust Cases', 1979. Co-Author 'Deskbook on Complex Civil Litigation, Judicial Council of California', 2000.

Personal: Born Tucson, Arizona, November 2, 1943; admitted to Bar, 1970, Arizona; 1974, California. Education: University of Arizona (BA, 1966; JD, with distinction, 1970). Order of the Coif. Recipient: Charles L. Strauss Award (Outstanding Student Contribution to the Arizona Law Review 1969); Ralph W Aigler Award (Outstanding Student of the Class of 1970); Prentiss Hall Tax Award (Outstanding Student of Tax, Class of 1970). Note and Comment Editor, Arizona Law Review, 1969-70.

HERMLE, Lynne
Orrick, Herrington & Sutcliffe, Menlo Park 650 614 7422
lchermle@orrick.com
Recommended in Employment

Practice Areas: Employment trial litigation, including wrongful discharge, discrimination issues, class actions, employment counseling, and training. Ms Hermle represents large employers in wage and hour class actions, including The Gap, Sears, and several other retailers. Recently she has begun to represent Silicon Valley based high tech companies in wage and hour class action lawsuits. She also has trial expertise and, in 2003, successfully defended long-time client Advanced Micro Devices (AMD) in a high-profile racial discrimination lawsuit. The National Law Journal named her one of America's Top Fifty Women Litigators. She has repeatedly been named one of Silicon Valley's top lawyers. Legal newspaper The Recorder recently named her a top Bay Area employment lawyer.

Prof. Memberships: American Bar Association EEO Committee: Labor and Employment Section; Northern District of California: Early Neutral Evaluator; California State Bar Association: Labor and Employment Section; Faculty for National Institute for Trial Advocacy; Start-Up & Emerging Companies Strategist Newsletter: Co editor in chief. Ms Hermle teaches Continuing Education of the Bar and Practicing Law Institute classes on trial skills and employment topics.

Career: JD, University of California Hastings College of the Law, 1981. Hastings Law Journal: senior editor. BA, magna cum laude, Physical Anthropology, University of California at Santa Barbara.

HERNANDEZ, Gary A
Sonnenschein Nath & Rosenthal, San Francisco 415 882 2466
ghernandez@sonnenschein.com
Recommended in Insurance

Practice Areas: Practices insurance regulatory and administrative law on behalf of insurers and holding companies. Also handles state regulatory compliance. Experienced in insurance insolvency proceedings and insurance and reinsurance matters.

Prof. Memberships: Member, International Association of Insurance Receivers, Insurance Regulatory Examiners Society; Board member, Latino Community Foundation and Iteris, Inc.; Appointed Board Member, California Coastal Conservancy by the Speaker of the California State Assembly; Lecturer to private groups and organizations, including American Conference Institute, Defense Research Institute, American Council of Life Insurers and Pacific Claims Executives Association.

Personal: University of California-Davis, JD; University of California-Berkeley, BA.

HERNANDEZ, Jennifer
Beveridge & Diamond, P.C.,
San Francisco 415 262 4001
jhernandez@bdlaw.com
Recommended in Environment

Practice Areas: Practices environmental and land use law in California and other Western states focusing on resolving federal, state and local approvals for complex development projects. Achieved national prominence in work on Brownfield redevelopment, wetlands and endangered species development projects, advising buyers, sellers, investors, local agencies and developers. Represents a diverse group of industries on compliance, enforcement and audit issues relating to air and water quality, hazardous materials and waste, Proposition 65 and other regulatory issues.
Prof. Memberships: Board Member of the California League of Conservation Voters, California Center for Land Recycling, and Mid-Peninsula Housing. Advisory Committee Member of California Environmental Redevelopment Fund, which created and is managing California's first pooled loan program for private sector Brownfields equity and debt placements. Founded the Environmental Law Forum in San Francisco and founding member of the California State Bar's Environmental Law Section.
Career: Admitted to California Bar (1984). Director of Beveridge & Diamond, P.C. since joining firm in 1993. Taught environmental and land use law at Stanford Law School, the University of California, the California Environmental Law Institute, and other venues. Co-founder and Chairman of Board (1994-97) for LandBank, Inc., a national Brownfields redevelopment company.
Publications: Has written two books and more than 30 articles on environmental, redevelopment and land use law issues.
Personal: JD from Stanford University (1984) and AB (with honors) from Harvard University (1981).

HERR, Robert
Pillsbury Winthrop LLP, San Francisco
415 983 1038
rherr@pillsburywinthrop.com
Recommended in Real Estate

Practice Areas: Mr Herr represents developers, owners, managers and lenders in commercial and residential real estate development, acquisition, operation, leasing, sale and loan transactions. He has an active land use/governmental approvals practice, representing developers of major office, retail, residential and hotel projects. Sample transactions include acquisition or disposition of over $2 billion in Class A office buildings in major US metropolitan areas during the past year, including the disposition of the 1.8 million square foot Bank of America 555 California Street complex in San Francisco, California and the 900,000 square foot Bay Colony office complex in Waltham,

Massachusetts; multiple forward and reverse 1031 exchange transactions, together with related financings; formation of ownership partnership of the San Francisco Giants and acquisition of the team; financing and other business transactional aspects of the Giants new ballpark completed in 2000; acquisition by Chivas USA of a major league soccer franchise in Los Angeles; and mixed-use luxury hotel/residential condominium project for Carpenter/Starwood Hotels and Resorts Worldwide, Inc. in San Francisco, California.
Career: Admitted to practice: State of California.
Personal: JD, University of California at Berkeley, Boalt Hall School of Law (Order of the Coif), 1967; AB, University of California at Berkeley (great distinction), 1964.

HIGGINS, Daniel
Paul, Hastings, Janofsky & Walker LLP,
San Francisco
415 856 6000
Recommended in Healthcare

HILSON, John
Paul, Hastings, Janofsky & Walker LLP,
Los Angeles 213 683 6300
johnhilson@paulhastings.com
Recommended in Banking & Finance

Practice Areas: Complex commercial and corporate finance transactions, including asset-based structured financings, tranche A and tranche B transactions, cash flow and enterprise value financings, and mezzanine debt and equity transactions. His practice also includes specialized secured transactions, Islamic compliant financings, debtor-in-possession financings, acquisition financings, usury, and suretyship law.
Prof. Memberships: Board of Regents Member; Fellow of the American College of Commercial Finance Attorneys.
Publications: Co-author of 'Asset-Based Lending - A Practical Guide to Secured Financing', Practising Law Institute (5th Ed 2004).
Personal: University of Colorado Law School (JD, Order of the Coif, 1976); Boston University (BA, magna cum laude, 1973).

HINKLEY, Gerry
Davis Wright Tremaine LLP,
San Francisco 415 276 6530
gerryhinkley@dwt.com
Recommended in Healthcare

Practice Areas: Partner, health law. Representative experience includes mergers and acquisitions, corporate finance, joint ventures, emerging companies, facility development, corporate governance, Medicare anti-fraud/abuse, Stark/PORA, HIPAA/HIT, licensing and certification. Representative clients include hospitals and academic medical centers, children's hospitals, skilled nursing facilities, senior housing organizations, HMOs, healthcare venture funds and investors.

Prof. Memberships: Member, California and New York State Bar Associations. Director, Safety New Institute of California Association of Public Hospitals. Founder, Bay Area Health Care Breakfast Club.
Career: Joined firm as Partner, 1995.
Personal: JD, University of California, 1975. BA, University of California - Santa Barbara, 1971.

HIRSCH, Barry
Hirsch Wallerstein Hayum Matlof & Fishman, Los Angeles
310 553 0305
Recommended in Media & Entertainment

HIRSCH, Reece
Sonnenschein Nath & Rosenthal,
San Francisco 415 882 5040
rhirsch@sonnenschein.com
Recommended in Healthcare

Practice Areas: Healthcare regulatory and transactional expert who counsels and represents health plans, insurers, hospitals, physician organizations, healthcare IT companies, pharmaceutical and biotech companies and other healthcare organizations with Medicare, Medicaid, fraud and abuse, self-referral, contracting and privacy issues, including HIPAA and Gramm-Leach-Bliley Act compliance. Develops and helps implement policies and procedures for privacy and security, fraud and abuse and corporate compliance.
Prof. Memberships: California State Bar Association; ABA's Health Law Section; California Society for Healthcare Attorneys; American Health Lawyers Association; Healthcare Financial Management Association.
Personal: University of Southern California, JD, 'Southern California Law Review'; Northwestern University, BS.

HISERT, George
Bingham McCutchen LLP,
San Francisco 415 393 2000
Recommended in Banking & Finance

HOBEL, Lawrence
Heller Ehrman LLP, San Francisco
415 772 6000
Recommended in Insurance

HOCKETT, Christopher
Bingham McCutchen LLP,
San Francisco 415 393 2000
Recommended in Antitrust

HOLDEN Jr, Frederick D
Orrick, Herrington & Sutcliffe LLP,
San Francisco 415 773 5985
fholden@orrick.com
Recommended in Bankruptcy

Practice Areas: Mr Holden's practice is focused on litigation and transactions involving insolvent businesses. He represents creditors, debtors, committees and governmental interests in Chapter 11 cases, international reorganizations and asset acquisitions. He has served as general counsel to court-appointed trustees

and receivers in many large financial frauds.
Prof. Memberships: Fellow, American College of Bankruptcy. Listed in the Guide to the World's Leading Insolvency and Restructuring Lawyers, as one of the top 50 restructuring and insolvency lawyers in the US in Global Counsel directories, as among the top 10 bankruptcy lawyers in the US by The Deal, and as one of the top 100 lawyers in any field by Northern California Superlawyers. He has served as Chair of the Bar Association of San Francisco Commercial Law and Bankruptcy Section, Chair of the Bench-Bar Committee of the US Bankruptcy Court for the Northern District of California, and as a Director of the Bay Area Bankruptcy Forum and Northern California Chapter of the TMA.
Career: He is a frequent speaker for the National Conference of Bankruptcy Judges, Practicing Law Institute, American Bar Association, and numerous groups in California.
Personal: JD, 1974, University of California, Davis; BA with High Honors, University of California, Santa Barbara, 1971.

HOLLIDAY, Thomas E
Gibson, Dunn & Crutcher LLP,
Los Angeles 213 229 7370
tholliday@gibsondunn.com
Recommended in Litigation

Practice Areas: Litigation Partner, Co-Chair of the Business Crimes and Investigations Practice Group. Focuses on white collar criminal defense work and commercial fraud litigation. Defends individuals and corporate entities against charges of conspiracy to defraud the United States, fraud on federally insured institutions, false statements, bribery, money laundering, RICO and tax fraud.
Prof. Memberships: Fellow, American College of Trial Lawyers. Member, National Association of Criminal Defense Lawyers.
Publications: Editor, 'Antitrust Laws and Regulations.' Co-author, 'The Effect of Sentencing Guidelines on Organizational Defendants.'
Personal: JD, University of Southern California, 1974, Order of the Coif, Executive Editor, 'Law Review.'

HOLSCHER, Mark
O'Melveny & Myers LLP, Los Angeles
213 430 6000
Recommended in Litigation

HOOPER, Patric
Hooper Lundy & Bookman Inc,
Los Angeles 310 551 8111
Recommended in Healthcare

HOWARD Jr, George S
Pillsbury Winthrop LLP, San Diego
619 544 3286
ghoward@pillsburywinthrop.com
Recommended in Employment

Practice Areas: George Howard has practiced labor and employment law in San Diego since 1977. He has successfully tried multi-week bench and jury trials, as well as numerous shorter trials, arbitrations and administrative proceedings. He chairs the Employers' Group Legal Committee, a select group of 16 California lawyers who appear as amicus curiae in the appeals of important employment cases. He is a Senior Contributing Editor for the Rutter Group California Employment Litigation Practice Guide, a reference work widely used by practitioners and courts. He has extensive experience in union/management relations as well as all types of employment litigation. He was the lead negotiator on many significant collective bargaining agreements including, in 1999/2000, the first-ever collective bargaining agreement between an Indian tribe and a labor organization. He has been listed in The Best Lawyers in America in each edition since 1993. In 1995 he was one of three lawyers to provide sexual harassment training to the California Supreme Court and several of the Courts of Appeals.
Career: Admitted in all courts in California and United States Courts of Appeal for the Ninth and DC Circuits.
Personal: JD (1977) University of Virginia; BA (with highest distinction) (1974) University of Virginia.

HOYE, Maria
Latham & Watkins LLP, Los Angeles
213 485 1234
Recommended in Environment

HUGHES, Frank
Miller, Morton, Caillat & Nevis,
San Jose 408 292 1765
Recommended in Construction

HUMPHREYS, Ivan
Wilson Sonsini Goodrich & Rosati,
Palo Alto 650 493 9300
ihumphreys@wsgr.com
Recommended in Tax
Practice Areas: Specializes in domestic/international tax and related transactions for technology companies and financial institutions. Represents clients in transactional matters including domestic and cross border mergers and acquisitions, dispositions, spin-offs, restructurings, domestic and international debt and equity offerings, taxation of technology transfers, joint ventures, establishment of domestic and offshore investment funds, and structuring offshore sales and manufacturing operations.
Prof. Memberships: Admitted to practice in California; Member, ABA (Taxation Section).
Career: Joined WSGR as Partner, 1989.
Personal: JD (magna cum laude), Harvard University, 1982; BA (with great distinction), University of California (Berkeley), 1979. Phi Beta Kappa. Editor, 'Harvard Law Review', 1981-82.

HUNT, Gordon
Hunt, Ortmann, Blasco, Palffy & Rossell Inc, Pasedena (626) 440-5200
Recommended in Construction

HUNT, James
Bingham McCutchen LLP,
San Francisco 415 393 2000
Recommended in Antitrust

HYMAN, Milt
Irell & Manella LLP, Los Angeles
310 277 1010
Recommended in Tax

IPPOLITO, Peter J
McKenna Long & Aldridge, San Diego
619 595 5400
pippolito@mckennalong.com
Recommended in Construction
Practice Areas: International practice in areas of construction law, including architect and engineer malpractice, federal and state construction litigation, federal government and private construction claims and disputes and hearings before state and federal courts, federal, state and local Boards of Contract Appeals, administrative law judges, arbitration panels and mediators. Extensive experience on projects involving public, private, commercial, heavy, highway, industrial, institutional and residential construction, representing owners, developers, public agencies, general contractors, subcontractors and specialty contractors, architects, engineers, designers, suppliers, manufacturers, sureties and insurers.
Prof. Memberships: Member of the Judicial Arbitration Panel for the San Diego Superior Court; serves as a State of California Arbitrator for disputes involving state contracts; appointed to the American Arbitration Association's Nationwide Complex Construction Arbitration and Mediation Panels; frequent guest speaker for construction industry groups.
Publications: Mr Ippolito serves on the Board of Directors of the 'Construction Business Review'. He has published numerous articles in various construction periodicals and for seminars.
Personal: Virginia Military Institute, BA, 1963; University of Notre Dame, LLB, 1966; George Washington University, LLM in Taxation, 1975; Officer, US Army.

IREDALE, Nancy L
Paul, Hastings, Janofsky & Walker LLP,
Los Angeles 213 683 6232
nancyiredale@paulhastings.com
Recommended in Tax
Practice Areas: Tax controversy; tried/settled international, federal and state civil and criminal tax cases; 'L.A. Business Journal': "One of the most powerful women in Los Angeles law"; 'Southern California Super Lawyers/ 2005, Tax'.
Prof. Memberships: First woman elected President, Jonathan Club; Planning

Committee, USC Tax Institute; Board, California Taxpayers' Association; Fellow, American College of Tax Counsel.
Career: First woman elected Partner, Paul Hastings; legislative assistant to Bill Brock, R-Tenn, on Senate Finance (tax writing) Committee.
Personal: Graduated first in class from School of Foreign Service, Georgetown University; Phi Beta Kappa; Law degree from Yale Law School; Member, Yale Legislative Services.

JACKOWAY, James
Jackoway Tyerman & Wertheimer,
Austen Mandelbaum & Morris
Los Angeles
310 553 0305
Recommended in Media & Entertainment

JACOBS, Michael A
Morrison & Foerster LLP, San Francisco
415 268 7455
mjacobs@mofo.com
Recommended in Intellectual Property
Practice Areas: Concentrates on high-technology and intellectual property litigation matters. Work in several landmark cases has helped to shape emerging technologies laws. Has litigated a range of patent, contract, and trade secret disputes in the information technology and life sciences field. Handles high-profile arbitrations, several of which involved the interplay between arbitration and court proceedings.
Career: Admitted to practice in California. Co-founder and Co-Chair, Intellectual Property Group, 1990-2002. Firmwide Managing Partner for Operations, 1995-97.
Publications: Co-author, with Prof Donald Chisum, 'World Intellectual Property Guidebook', United States (1992, Matthew Bender & Company, New York).
Personal: BA, Stanford University, 1977, Phi Beta Kappa with honors; United States Foreign Service, assignments in Kingston, Jamaica, and Washington, DC; JD, Yale Law School, 1983.

JAHN, Paul E
Morrison & Foerster LLP, San Francisco
415 268 6387
pjahn@mofo.com
Recommended in IT Outsourcing
Practice Areas: Specializes in transactions involving development, licensing, acquisition, and sale of intellectual property and technology. Transactions typically involve strategic alliances and joint ventures; commercialization and distribution arrangements; BPO and IT sourcing, and resolution of related disputes. Frequently represents clients in adversarial patent license negotiations and portfolio acquisition. Clients generally operate in high technology, life sciences, and financial services industries.
Career: Former Co-Chair of firm's Technology Transactions Group. Formerly resident in firm's Tokyo and Brussels offices.

Admitted to practice in California.
Personal: BA, University of California, Berkeley, 1986; JD, Hastings College of the Law, 1993; Clerk to Hon Claudia Wilken, Northern District of California, 1995-96.

JEFFREY, Sheri
Kaye Scholer LLP, Los Angeles
310 788 1270
sjeffrey@kayescholer.com
Recommended in Media & Entertainment
Practice Areas: Partner, Corporate and Finance. Practice covers a wide range of entertainment matters. She represents various clients in all types of entertainment industry transactions, including for development, acquisitions, finance and production of motion pictures, television series and new technologies projects (both live action and animation).
Prof. Memberships: Member, State Bar of California.
Career: LLM, New York University, 1986. JD, Loyola Law School, 1985. BS (cum laude), Loyola Marymount University, 1982.

JENETT, Bruce
Heller Ehrman White & McAuliffe LLP,
Menlo Park 650 324 7000
Recommended in Corporate/M&A

JOHNSON, Craig
Heller Ehrman White & McAuliffe,
Menlo Park 650 854 4488
Recommended in Corporate/M&A

JOHNSTON, Ronald L
Arnold & Porter LLP, Los Angeles
213 243 4256
Ronald.Johnston@aporter.com
Recommended in Intellectual Property
Practice Areas: Mr Johnston has been a leader in the information technology and intellectual property bars for 25 years. His experience includes litigation and strategic counseling for technology and entertainment businesses, including jury and non jury trials, appeals, arbitrations, and class actions. He has represented clients in a number of leading cases at the trial and appellate levels. His practice includes copyright, patent, trade secret, trademark, right of publicity, antitrust, and forms of unfair competition law.
Prof. Memberships: Mr Johnston is the editor in chief of The Computer & Internet Lawyer and is a member of the Editorial Boards of The Journal of Proprietary Rights and The Cyberspace Lawyer; Board of Directors, Computer Law Association (1986-2002); Technology and Intellectual Property Panels, American Arbitration Association; Arbitrator, International Chamber of Commerce.
Career: Mr Johnston was the founder and continuing Chairperson of the University of Southern California Computer & Internet Law Institute (1979-2003), and co-founder of The Computer &

Internet Lawyer (1984- , Aspen Publications). He has been a frequent chairperson and speaker at national institutes in the areas of trial practice and intellectual property and technology law.
Publications: Include co-author and editor, Business & Legal Guide to Online-Internet Law (1997, Glasser Legal Works); 'The Case for Trade Secret Protection for Mass Distributed Software,' Current Developments in Computer Litigation (Prentice Hall Law & Business 1994); 'Alternative Dispute Resolution,' The Corporate Analyst (May 1994); 'Toward an Effective Strategy in Software Copyright Litigation,' 19 Rutgers Computer and Technology Law Journal 91 (1993); co-editor, Computer Law Annual 1985 (Harcourt, Brace, Jovanovich 1985); 'Product Bundling Faces Increased Specter of Illegality Under the Antitrust Laws,' 1 The Computer Lawyer 1 (1984).
Personal: Mr Johnston graduated Order of the Coif from the University of Southern California School of Law in 1973, where he served as a Note and Article Editor for the University of Southern California Law Review.

JONES, Robert
Cooley Godward LLP, Palo Alto
650 843 5000
Recommended in Corporate/M&A

JUSTICE, Gary
Gibson, Dunn & Crutcher LLP,
Los Angeles 213 229 7446
gjustice@gibsondunn.com
Recommended in Insurance
Practice Areas: Litigation and jury trial of all insurance issues, including lack of 'bad faith', primarily for carriers in property and casualty, liability insurance, and health insurance fields. Expertise includes trigger of coverage, number of occurrences, 'lost' policies, ERISA preemption, apportionment among carriers, admissibility of parol evidence, rescission based on material misrepresentation, '"advice of counsel" defense in 'bad faith' litigation, and 'advertising injury' coverages. Representative clients present and past include Travelers, Aetna U.S. Healthcare, Empire Blue Cross Blue Shield and Hartford Steam Boiler.
Personal: JD, Duke University, 1979, Order of the Coif, Editorial Board Member, 'Law Review.'

KADUE, David
Seyfarth Shaw LLP, Los Angeles
310 277 7200
Recommended in Employment

KADZIELSKI, Mark A
Fulbright & Jaworski L.L.P., Los Angeles
213 892 9306
mkadzielski@fulbright.com
Recommended in Healthcare
Practice Areas: Health law.
Prof. Memberships: Mr Kadzielski is a Member of the California Bar, the American Health Lawyers Association and the California Society for Healthcare Attorneys.
Career: Mark A. Kadzielski is the Partner in charge of Fulbright & Jaworski's Los Angeles Health Law Practice. He has been selected numerous times to be included in the Health Care Law Section of The Best Lawyers in America. Mr Kadzielski is a past member of the AHLA's Board of Directors and served on the organization's first executive committee. Recently, he was elected to the AHLA's inaugural class of Fellows, whose members are recognized for their extraordinary contributions to health law in the United States. In 2004 and 2005, he was selected as a Southern California 'Super Lawyer' in Health Law.
Personal: AB, magna cum laude- John Carroll University (1968); JD - University of Pennsylvania Law School (1976).

KAPLAN, Frank
Alschuler Grossman Stein & Kahan LLP, Santa Monica 310 255 9124
fkaplan@agsk.com
Recommended in Insurance
Practice Areas: He focuses on class action, securities, insurance coverage, unfair competition, partnership, and professional liability disputes. Represented chip manufacturer Nvidia in Microsoft dispute over Xbox game console; in 2003 argued in the US Supreme Court on behalf of the State of California in litigation over statute requiring insurance companies doing business in the state to disclose information about policies issued during the European holocaust; in 2004, represented California Insurance Commissioner in litigation brought by Anthem to compel approval of merger with WellPoint; represents insurers in major coverage litigation.
Prof. Memberships: Member, Beverly Hills, Century City, Santa Monica, Los Angeles County and American Bar Associations; State Bar of California; Association of Business Trial Lawyers.
Career: A Partner of Alschuler Grossman Stein & Kahan. Has practiced with the firm since 1972. Has served as an arbitrator for the Los Angeles Superior Court and Los Angeles County Bar Association, and as a judge pro tem.
Personal: Commissioner, California Law Revision Commission (Chair, 2003-04). Adjunct Professor of securities fraud at University of Southern California.; University of Cincinnati (BA with honors, Phi Beta Kappa, 1968). University of Michigan (JD, 1971).

KARP, Joseph
White & Case LLP, San Francisco
415 544 1103
jkarp@whitecase.com
Recommended in Energy
Practice Areas: Energy-regulatory and transactional matters, project development and operations matters for US and international natural gas and electricity concerns. Particular expertise representing end users in retail gas and electricity transactions and generators of electricity in the full range of issues affecting electricity revenues, fuel costs and ongoing operations. Active in administrative litigation, contract negotiation, dispute resolution and regulatory compliance advice and regularly represents, among others, the California Cogeneration Council and the California Wind Energy Association and their members.
Personal: JD, cum laude, Harvard Law School, 1989; BA, SUNY Binghamton, 1986 (Foundation Award for Academic Excellence, Phi Beta Kappa).

KAUFMAN, Christopher
Latham & Watkins LLP, Menlo Park
650 328 4600
Recommended in Corporate/M&A

KEKER, John
Keker & Van Nest LLP, San Francisco
415 391 5400
jwk@kvn.com
Recommended in Intellectual Property, Litigation
Practice Areas: John Keker is one of the top trial lawyers in the United States. His trials have included criminal defense, patents, contracts, securities fraud, copyright, and business torts. Cases include, in 2002, winning a jury trial for Genentech in a $300 million patent dispute with Chiron; in 2001, representing Cadence Design Systems, Inc., winning $195 million from Avant! Corporation in restitution for trade secret theft. Other notable cases: chief prosecutor, United States v Oliver North, 1989, Iran/Contra Independent Counsel's Office, Washington, DC; defense counsel US v Frank Quattrone (SDNY 2003 (hung jury), convicted 2004, on appeal); defense counsel in Ventritex v Intermedics, listed by the National Law Journal as one of the top ten defense verdicts of 1992; Plaintiff's counsel in Maglica v Maglica, listed in the National Law Journal as one of the top ten plaintiff's verdicts of 1994, and plaintiff's counsel in Xilinx v Altera, (ND Cal.)) one of the most significant patent trials of 2000.
Prof. Memberships: Fellow of the American College of Trial Lawyers, the International Academy of Trial Lawyers, the American Board of Trial Advocates, and the American Bar Foundation.
Career: Former law clerk to the Honorable Earl Warren, retired chief justice of the United States (1970-71); staff attorney at the Natural Resources Defense Council, Washington DC; Assistant Federal Public Defender for the Northern District of California (1971-73); founded Keker & Van Nest in 1978.
Publications: Co-author of 'Effective Direct and Cross Examination', California Continuing Education of the Bar, 1986.
Personal: Yale Law School (JD 1970); infantry platoon leader in Vietnam while a lieutenant in the United Sates Marine Corps (wounded and retired in 1967); Princeton University (BA, 1965).

KELLER, Don
Orrick, Herrington & Sutcliffe, Menlo Park 650 614 7400
Recommended in Corporate/M&A

KELLER, Kent
Barger & Wolen, Los Angeles
213 680 2800
Recommended in Insurance

KENDALL, Richard
Irell & Manella LLP, Los Angeles
310 277 1010
Recommended in Media & Entertainment

KENNEDY, Mike
O'Melveny & Myers LLP, San Francisco
415 984 8700
Recommended in Corporate/M&A

KENT, Ronald D
Sonnenschein Nath & Rosenthal,
Los Angeles 213 892 5030
rkent@sonnenschein.com
Recommended in Insurance
Practice Areas: Insurance litigation head in Los Angeles. Represents insurance companies and other clients on matters, including coverage and 'bad faith' actions, regulatory and related class actions, environmental claims and general disputes. Has appeared in state and federal courts throughout the US, including nearly all California District Courts of Appeal and the Ninth Circuit Court of Appeals. Experienced in issues such as alleged discriminatory underwriting practices, retrospective premiums, agents and brokers errors and omissions and surplus lines licensing.
Personal: University of California, JD, Order of the Coif, California Law Review; UCLA, BA in English, summa cum laude.

KENYON, Charity
Riegels Campos & Kenyon,
Sacramento 916 779 7114
Recommended in Media & Entertainment

KEYES, Judith Droz
Morrison & Foerster LLP, San Francisco
415 268 6638
jkeyes@mofo.com
Recommended in Employment
Practice Areas: Extensive experience counseling and training clients in all aspects of labor and employment law and representing clients before almost all California and federal labor and employment agencies as well as in negotiations, mediation, arbitration and court. Serves as an evaluator and mediator of employment cases for the US District Court, Northern District, California.
Prof. Memberships: Fellow, College of Labor & Employment Lawyers. Named a 'Best Lawyer in America'. Former Chair, Labor and Employment Law Sec-

tion, Bar Association of San Francisco, 1998-2000; Former President, Alameda County Bar Association, 1997.
Career: Admitted to practice in California.
Personal: BS, Pennsylvania State University, 1966; MA, University of Missouri, 1970; JD, University of California at Berkeley, Boalt Hall School of Law, 1975.

KIMBALL, George
Arnold & Porter LLP, Los Angeles
213 243 4160
George.Kimball@aporter.com
Recommended in Business Process Outsourcing, IT Outsourcing
Practice Areas: He his practice emphasizes complex technology transactions, including negotiation and re-negotiation of IT and business process outsourcing relationships for both customers and suppliers, in such industries as aerospace, broadcasting, chemicals, consumer products, computers, engineering, insurance, metals, pharmaceuticals, and retail, among others. These transactions have involved data centers, software development and maintenance, acquisitions and sales of facilities, network management, web development and hosting, HR, purchasing and other business functions.
Prof. Memberships: Admitted in California (1978).
Career: Regular speaker on outsourcing to trade and professional groups, including PLI, California CEB, and the Sourcing Interests Group.
Publications: Has lectured and written extensively on outsourcing and related topics.
Personal: University of Michigan (JD cum laude 1978).

KING, Kenton J
Skadden, Arps, Slate, Meagher & Flom LLP & Affiliates, Palo Alto
650 470 4530
kking@skadden.com
Recommended in Capital Markets, Corporate/M&A
Practice Areas: Head of Skadden's Palo Alto and San Francisco offices and corporate group in the Bay Area. Has extensive experience in a broad range of corporate and securities law matters, including US and cross-border M&A, joint ventures, investment and capital markets transactions, and restructurings. Has worked on several high-profile transactions, including representing Compaq Computer Corporation in several transactions, including its $25 billion merger with Hewlett-Packard Company, its transfer of proprietary Alpha microprocessor technology to Intel Corporation, and its $2.3 billion sale of Alta Vista Comapny to CMGI, Inc.; Ascend Communications, Inc. in its $20 billion acquisition by Lucent Technologies, Inc.; and Yahoo! Inc. in its $436 million unsolicited takeover proposal

for HotJobs.com, Ltd, its $1.6 billion acquisition of Overture Services, Inc. and its $750 million zero coupon convertible note offering.
Career: JD, Boalt Hall School of Law at the University of California at Berkeley, 1987 (Editor in Chief, California Law Review; Order of the Coif); BA, Stanford University, 1977.

KIRBY, Matthew
O'Melveny & Myers LLP, Los Angeles
213 430 6000
Recommended in Banking & Finance

KIRWAN, BJ
Latham & Watkins LLP, Los Angeles
213 485 1234
Recommended in Environment

KLEE, Kenneth N
Klee, Tuchin, Bogdanoff & Stern LLP, Los Angeles 310 407 4080
kklee@ktbslaw.com
Recommended in Bankruptcy
Practice Areas: A founding Member of Klee, Tuchin, Bogdanoff & Stern LLP, specializing in corporate reorganization, insolvency, and bankruptcy law. He joined the UCLA Law faculty in July 1997 after teaching bankruptcy and reorganization law as a visiting lecturer since 1979. From 1974-77, was associate counsel to the House Judiciary Committee, where he was one of the principal draftsmen of the 1978 Bankruptcy Code. He currently serves as a Director of the International Insolvency Institute. He also served as an adviser to the American Law Institute's Transnational Insolvency Project. Available as an expert witness, arbitrator, or mediator.

KLEIN, Anthony
Latham & Watkins LLP, Menlo Park
650 328 4600
Recommended in IT Outsourcing

KLEINBERG, Kenneth
Kleinberg, Lopez, Lange, Brisbin & Cuddy, Los Angeles 818 995 5500
Recommended in Media & Entertainment

KLYMAN, Robert
Latham & Watkins LLP, Los Angeles
213 485 1234
Recommended in Bankruptcy

KNAUSS, Robert
Munger, Tolles & Olson LLP, Los Angeles 213 683 9100
Recommended in Corporate/M&A

KORMAN, Marty
Wilson Sonsini Goodrich & Rosati, Palo Alto 650 493 9300
mkorman@wsgr.com
Recommended in Corporate/M&A
Practice Areas: Specializes in M&As, strategic transactions, corporate securities and general corporate representation of public and private technology companies.
Prof. Memberships: Admitted to practice in New York and California.

Career: Joined WSGR, 1993; became Partner, 1997. Represented Hewlett Packard (HP) in its merger with Compaq, and Netscape in its merger with AOL.
Personal: JD, Yale University, 1989. AB, Stanford University, 1985.

KOSACZ, Barbara
Cooley Godward LLP, Palo Alto
650 843 5000
Recommended in Corporate/M&A

KRELLER, Thomas
Milbank, Tweed, Hadley & McCloy, Los Angeles 213 892 4000
Recommended in Bankruptcy

KRISCHER, Gordon
O'Melveny & Myers LLP, Los Angeles
213 430 6000
Recommended in Employment

KRUPKA, Robert G
Kirkland & Ellis LLP, Los Angeles
213 680 8456
bkrupka@kirkland.com
Recommended in Intellectual Property
Practice Areas: Specialist in patent, trade secret, copyright, trademark, advertising, marketing, unfair competition, Internet and antitrust litigation and counseling. Extensive experience in contested intellectual property matters, trials involving technologically complex subject matter, obtaining expedited remedies, and proceedings before the International Trade Commission. Tried over 50 cases to judgment. Tried eight jury trials to verdict, all victorious. Obtained verdicts totaling over $175 million; negotiated settlements resulting in over $1 billion. Handled over two dozen expedited remedy hearings (TRO's, preliminary injunctions, temporary exclusion orders) and 20 Markman (claim interpretation) hearings.
Personal: Georgetown University, BS, 1971; University of Chicago Law School, JD, 1974.

LANDSBERG, Barry S
Manatt Phelps & Phillips LLP, Los Angeles 310 312 4259
blandsberg@manatt.com
Recommended in Healthcare
Practice Areas: Litigation with focus on complex business, commercial, unfair competition, administration law and RICO disputes. In-depth knowledge of the myriad business and regulatory issues confronting health industry clients. Litigates disputes involving hospital medical staff, licensure and certification of long-term facilities, fraud and abuse, bio-ethics, antitrust, trademark and Medicare/Medicaid reimbursements. A recognized expert in the defense of UCL cases and Co-Chairman of the firm's Litigation Division.
Prof. Memberships: American Law Institute, The American Health Lawyers Association, The California Society for Health Care Attorneys.
Career: Partner.

Publications: Has lectured and written extensively on UCL developments in Healthcare.
Personal: Emory University (JD, 1980); University of Maryland (BA, 1977); Admitted to practice before the US Supreme Court.

LANGDON, Larry R
Mayer, Brown, Rowe & Maw, Palo Alto
650 331 2075
lrlangdon@mayerbrownrowe.com
Recommended in Tax
Practice Areas: Tax Controversy and Planning. Head of firm's Global Tax Practice. Former Head of the large and midsize business division within the US Internal Revenue Service, a unit that serves 150,000 businesses that pay a total of $600 billion in taxes every year.
Career: Mayer, Brown, Rowe & Maw, LLP, Palo Alto, 2003 to date; Partner, 2003. Internal Revenue Service, Commissioner, Large & Mid-Size Business Division, 1999-2003. Hewlett-Packard Company, V.P., General Transition Manager, 1999; V.P., Tax, Licensing and Customs, 1978-99. Vetco, Inc., Director of Taxes and Corporate Secretary, 1976-78. Ford Motor Company, Office of General Counsel, Sr. Tax Attorney, 1968-76. Internal Revenue Service, Legislation and Regulations Division, Office of Counsel, 1964-68. CARE, 1962-64. Internal Revenue Service, Joint Committee Division, Office of Chief Counsel, 1961-62.
Publications: Speaker at the American Bar Association Section of Taxation, American Institute of CPAs, Manufacturers Alliance [MAPI], Tax Executives Institute and many other professional and industry groups.
Personal: JD, Ohio State University College of Law, 1961. LLM (Taxation), New York University, School of Law, 1963. BS, Ohio State University, 1959. Described by The Daily Deal (Aug 2003) as a "master of the international tax game."

LARSON, John
Morgan, Lewis & Bockius LLP, San Francisco 415 442 1123
jlarson@morganlewis.com
Recommended in Corporate/M&A
Practice Areas: Mr Larson is a Partner in the Business and Finance Practice. Mr Larson's practice involves mergers and acquisitions, corporate governance and securities laws for high technology and other companies.
Prof. Memberships: Member, Board of Trustees of the California Academy of Sciences.
Career: Mr Larson was Assistant Secretary of the US Department of Interior (1971-73) and Counselor to George P Shultz (1973).
Publications: Executive Editorial Staff, Stanford Law Review.

LAVELY JR, John
Lavely & Singer PC, Los Angeles
310 556 3501
*Recommended in Media &
Entertainment*

LAYNE, Jonathan
Gibson, Dunn & Crutcher LLP,
Los Angeles 310 552 8641
jlayne@gibsondunn.com
Recommended in Corporate/M&A
Practice Areas: Co-Chair of firm's
Corporate Transactions Practice Group.
Extensive experience in mergers and
acquisitions, public offerings of equity
and debt, corporate, corporate finance
and securities law matters. Has repre-
sented numerous Boards of Directors
and Special Board Committees.
Prof. Memberships: Member, firm's
Executive Committee. Former Member,
firm's Management Committee. Mem-
ber, Board of Directors, California
Chamber of Commerce.
Publications: Frequent lecturer on
securities law topics.
Personal: JD, Emory University School
of Law, 1979, Order of the Coif, Managing Editor, 'Emory Law Journal'. MBA,
Emory University Graduate School of
Business, 1979, Beta Gamma Sigma.

LAZAROW, Warren
O'Melveny & Myers LLP, Menlo Park
650 473 2600
Recommended in Corporate/M&A

LEO, Thomas
Sheppard, Mullin, Richter & Hampton
LLP, Los Angeles 213 620 1780
*Recommended in Media &
Entertainment*

LERACH, William
Lerach Coughlin Stoia Geller Rudman
& Robbins LLP, San Diego
619 231 1058
Recommended in Litigation

LERMAN, Cary
Munger, Tolles & Olson LLP,
Los Angeles 213 683 9100
Recommended in Insurance

LESSER, Henry
DLA Piper Rudnick Gray Cary US LLP,
Palo Alto 650 833 2425
henry.lesser@dlapiper.com
Recommended in Corporate/M&A
Practice Areas: Corporate and securities; mergers and acquisitions; private
equity; public company and corporate
governance.
Career: Co-Chair of the firm's Private
Equity Practice. He has been involved in
corporate securities practice, with a particular focus on corporate acquisitions,
corporate governance and restructuring
matters and all aspects of merger and
acquisition work involving public and
private companies, including hostile
tender offers, proxy contests, friendly
mergers, leveraged buyouts, stock acquisitions and asset sales. His clients include
a wide variety of bidders, targets, stock-

holders and financial advisors.
Personal: LLM, Harvard University
School of Law; MA, Cambridge Univer-
sity; BA, Cambridge University.

LEVEE, Jeffrey A
Jones Day, Los Angeles
213 243 2572
jlevee@jonesday.com
Recommended in Antitrust
Practice Areas: Coordinator of the
Antitrust and Competition Law Practice
in Jones Day's California region. His
practice focuses on complex business
and class action litigation, antitrust litigation, healthcare litigation, and
antitrust counseling. He has successfully
litigated matters in state and federal
courts and has been involved in arbitrations and other forms of alternative dispute resolution. Named one of 13 'Super
Lawyers' in antitrust litigation in Los
Angeles and Orange Counties.
Prof. Memberships: Co-Chair of the
ABA Antitrust Section 2005 Spring
Meeting. Prior Member of Antitrust
Section Council.

LEVIN, Barry
Heller Ehrman LLP, San Francisco
415 772 6000
Recommended in Insurance

LEVIN, Richard B
Skadden, Arps, Slate, Meagher & Flom
LLP & Affiliates, Los Angeles
213 687 5940
rlevin@skadden.com
Recommended in Bankruptcy
Practice Areas: Concentrates on corporate restructuring, insolvency and
bankruptcy issues. His practice centers
on the representation of companies in
need of financial reorganization or
restructuring. Also represents acquirors
and special creditors in troubled compa-
ny situations. Was one of the principal
authors of the US Bankruptcy Code.
Prof. Memberships: Member, National
Bankruptcy Conference (Vice-Chair);
Fellow, American College of Bankruptcy
(Regent); Representative to the Ninth
Circuit Judicial Conference, 2001-04;
Lecturer in Law, Harvard Law School;
Faculty, Federal Judicial Center Work-
shops for Bankruptcy Judges.
Career: JD, Yale Law School, 1975 (edi-
tor, Yale Law Journal); SB, Massachusetts
Institute of Technology, 1972.

LEVINE, Harvey
Levine, Steinberg, Miller & Huver,
San Diego 619 231 9449
Recommended in Insurance

LEVINE, Janet
Lightfoot, Vandevelde, Sadowsky, Medvene & Levine, Los Angeles
213 622 4750
Recommended in Litigation

LICHTER, Linda
Lichter Grossman Nicholas Adler &
Goodman, Los Angeles
310 205 6999

*Recommended in Media &
Entertainment*

LIEVER, Michael H
Orrick, Herrington & Sutcliffe LLP,
San Francisco 415 773 5808
mliever@orrick.com
Recommended in Real Estate
Practice Areas: Mr Liever has extensive
involvement in representing both for-
eign and domestic investors in the
acquisition, disposition, development,
leasing, financing, and joint venture of
office buildings, shopping centers,
hotels, industrial parks, and apartments.
Clients include: CalPERS, City and
County of San Francisco, RREEF Funds,
Deutsche Bank, DIVCO Properties,
Morgan Stanley, Anheuser-Busch, Starbucks, Cargill, Shorenstein Company
LLC, IBM, Fremont Properties, LAC-
ERA, and other institutional investors
and lenders.
Career: Prior to joining Orrick, Mr
Liever had been a Partner (1984-96) and
an associate (1978-84) at Morrison &
Foerster LLP. He was Managing Partner
for Operations for Morrison & Foerster
LLP from 1989 through 1994.
Personal: Mr Liever received his B.A.
degree, summa cum laude, in 1974 from
the University of Pennsylvania, where he
was elected to Phi Beta Kappa. He
received his JD degree, magna cum
laude, in 1978 from Harvard Law School.

LIGHTFOOT, Michael
Lightfoot, Vandevelde, Sadowsky, Medvene & Levine, Los Angeles
213 622 4750
Recommended in Litigation

LINCENBERG, Gary
Bird, Marella, Boxer & Wolpert PC,
Los Angeles 310 201 2100
Recommended in Litigation

LIPTON, M Steven
Davis Wright Tremaine LLP,
San Francisco 415 276 6550
stevenlipton@dwt.com
Recommended in Healthcare
Practice Areas: Partner, health law.
Practice focuses on integrated delivery
systems, healthcare transactions, hospi-
tal/physician relationships, medical care
foundations, joint ventures, acquisitions. Regulatory matters include
fraud/abuse, patient dumping, provider
regulation, and licensing and certification.
Prof. Memberships: Member, California State Bar Association. Regional
Chapter Liasion Representative, Healthcare Financial Management Association.
Career: Joined firm, 1995; became Partner, 1998. Adjunct professor, University
of Southern California, Public Administration Program, 1984-92. Staff counsel,
California State Assembly Health Committee, 1972-77.
Publications: Author, 'A Guide to
Patient Anti-Dumping Laws', published
by California Healthcare Association.

Personal: JD, UCLA, 1971. AB, UCLA,
1968.

LOGAN, Ben
O'Melveny & Myers LLP, Los Angeles
310 553 6700
Recommended in Bankruptcy

LONERGAN, James
Sheppard, Mullin, Richter & Hampton
LLP, Los Angeles 213 620 1780
Recommended in Real Estate

LOPES, James
Howard, Rice, Nemerovski, Canady,
Falk & Rabkin, San Francisco
415 434 1600
Recommended in Bankruptcy

LORIG, Frederick
Bright & Lorig, Los Angeles
213 627 7774
Recommended in Intellectual Property

LUCERO, Gene
Latham & Watkins LLP, Los Angeles
213 485 1234
Recommended in Environment

LUNDBERG, Andrew
Latham & Watkins LLP, Los Angeles
213 485 1234
Recommended in Insurance

LUNDY, Robert
Hooper Lundy & Bookman Inc, Los
Angeles
310 551 8111
Recommended in Healthcare

LUREY, Michael
Latham & Watkins LLP, Los Angeles
213 485 1234
Recommended in Bankruptcy

LYNCH, Patrick
O'Melveny & Myers LLP, Los Angeles
310 553 6700
Recommended in Antitrust

MACK, Joel
Latham & Watkins LLP, San Diego
619 236 1234
Recommended in Energy

MALKIN, Joseph
Orrick, Herrington & Sutcliffe LLP, San
Francisco
415 773 5505
jmalkin@orrick.com
Recommended in Energy
Practice Areas: Mr Malkin is the Partner-in-Charge of the San Francisco
office, the Head of the Litigation Practice in San Francisco, and Co-Chair of
the firm's Energy & Project Finance
Group. His energy and telecommunications regulatory and transactional practice focuses on industry restructuring,
mergers, asset dispositions, and acquisitions. Recent projects include representation of PG&E Corporation in connection with financings, utility bankruptcy,
generation sales, and proceedings before
the California Public Utilities Commission (CPUC) investigating holding
company-utility relations; representation of Sempra Energy's San Diego Gas

& Electric Company unit in CPUC proceedings concerning electric rates, industry restructuring, and procurement practices; and representation of Qwest Communications in various regulatory matters.

Prof. Memberships: Northern California SuperLawyer, 2004.

Personal: Yale Law School, JD, 1972. Claremont McKenna College, BA, 1968.

MALLORY, Richard C
Allen, Matkins, Leck, Gamble & Mallory LLP, San Francisco
415 837 1515
rmallory@allenmatkins.com
Recommended in Real Estate

Practice Areas: With a diverse practice, Rick recently represented the landlord in a lease to Century Theatres for 14 new movie theaters in Napa Valley, California, E-Loan in a sublease of 150,000 square feet from Charles Schwab in Pleasanton, California, and Cooley Godward in the relocation of its office in San Francisco, California. He is also currently representing Genitope Corporation in a 200,000-square foot headquarters facility lease in Fremont, California.

Prof. Memberships: Rick has lectured at numerous CEB, PLI, and CLE International continuing education programs and is presently counsel to the American Industrial Real Estate Association. He is a member of the American College of Real Estate Lawyers and Lambda Alpha International, and currently serves on the advisory board of the Fisher Center for Real Estate and Urban Economics, the Practising Law Institute, and the Georgetown Advanced Commercial Leasing Institute.

Career: Rick is a founding Partner of the firm and Co-Managing Partner of the San Francisco office. He has been listed in 'The Best Lawyers in America' since 1984 as a leading California real estate attorney, according to a survey of his peers. In 2004, he was also listed in 'The Recorder' as one of the top six real estate attorneys in the Bay Area.

Publications: Rick is a contributor to the 'Commercial Tenant's Lease Insider'.

Personal: BS, University of Southern California, 1966; JD, Stanford Law School, 1969.

MANCINO, Douglas M
McDermott Will & Emery, Los Angeles
310 551 9323
dmancino@mwe.com
Recommended in Healthcare

Practice Areas: Has represented all types of nonprofit organizations for 30 years on tax, business and financial matters. Represents organizations and individuals in connection with the formation of nonprofit organizations such as public charities, private foundations, corporate foundations and trade associations, corporate transactions and restructuring of corporate organizations. Has extensive experience in audit,

appeals and tax controversy matters, has served as lead tax counsel in 12 IRS audits. Has litigated several tax cases in US Tax Court and US Court of Appeals.

Prof. Memberships: President of American Health Lawyers Association (1993-94), Chair of Exempt Organizations Committee of ABA's Tax Section (1995-97), Council Director of ABA's Section of Taxation (1999-2002), member of Board of Advisors of National Center on Philanthropy and the Law (1998-2000), and Chair of Tax and Accounting Interest Group of ABA's Health Law Section (1998-2001).

Publications: Author, 'Taxation of Hospitals and Health Care Organizations,' and the co-author of 'Taxation of Exempt Organizations.' Authored more than 60 articles on various tax-exempt subjects.

Personal: Earned JD (summa cum laude) in 1974 from Ohio State University College of Law, and BA (cum laude) in 1971 from Kent State University.

MARELLA, Vincent
Bird, Marella, Boxer & Wolpert PC, Los Angeles 310 201 2100
Recommended in Litigation

MARENBERG, Steven
Irell & Manella LLP, Los Angeles
310 277 1010
Recommended in Media & Entertainment

MARKHAM, Jesse W
Morrison & Foerster LLP, San Francisco
415 268 7448
jmarkham@mofo.com
Recommended in Antitrust

Practice Areas: Recognized authority on antitrust law, handling mostly large complex litigation matters. Represents clients before enforcement agencies on civil and criminal investigations and proceedings. Primarily focused on technology clients. Participated in effort to establish antitrust enforcement mechanisms in Russia and the Ukraine. Represented clients in international cartel investigations.

Prof. Memberships: Antitrust and Trade Regulation Law Section, California State Bar: Chair, 1996-97; Co-Chair, Programs, 1995-96; Treasurer, 1994-95.

Career: Before private practice, served as Deputy Attorney General (Antitrust) for California and Massachusetts. Authored the California Attorney General's Antitrust Guidelines for the Insurance Industry. Since 1993, adjunct professor, antitrust courses, University of San Francisco Law School.

Personal: AB, cum laude, Harvard University, 1974; MA, University of Massachusetts, 1976; Boalt Hall School of Law, 1978-79, special status transfer student; JD, Vanderbilt University School of Law, 1979.

MARKS, Allan
Milbank, Tweed, Hadley & McCloy, Los Angeles 213 892 4000
Recommended in Projects, Transport

MARMARO, Richard
Proskauer Rose LLP, Los Angeles
310 284 5659
rmarmaro@prokauer.co
Recommended in Litigation

Practice Areas: White collar criminal defense, SEC litigation and complex civil litigation. He has successfully defended individuals and corporations in all phases of complex civil, criminal and regulatory matters including those involving allegations of insider trading, accounting and disclosure irregularities, market manipulation, and other financial frauds. He has also conducted numerous internal corporate investigations for Fortune 500 companies, involving issues including insider trading allegations, tax violations, and corporate opportunity issues.

Personal: Graduated with highest honors from George Washington University, where he was elected to Phi Beta Kappa. He is a graduate of New York University Law School, where he was the Executive Editor of the 'Journal of International Law and Politics.'

MARMORSTEIN, Vicki
Latham & Watkins LLP, Los Angeles
213 485 1234
Recommended in Banking & Finance

MARTENS, Don
Knobbe Martens Olson & Bear, Irvine
949 760 0404
Recommended in Intellectual Property

MATHIASON, Garry
Littler Mendelson PC, San Francisco
415 433 1940
Recommended in Employment

MATICHAK, Jill
O'Melveny & Myers LLP, San Francisco
415 984 8700
Recommended in Banking & Finance

MATKINS, Michael L
Allen Matkins Leck Gamble & Mallory LLP, Los Angeles 213 622 5555
mmatkins@allenmatkins.com
Recommended in Real Estate

Practice Areas: For more than 30 years, Mike has advised institutional investors, lenders, property owners, and developers in all aspects of purchase, sale, financing, leasing, and construction of properties ranging from office and retail to recreational and mixed-use projects. He guides institutional lenders and investors through the complexities of real estate investing, offering established knowledge in loans, joint ventures, partnerships, sale-leasebacks, and other forms of financing and investing. Mike has been involved in numerous multi-hundred million dollar real property asset portfolio acquisitions. He has also represented institutional investors in the restructuring of substantial investments

in California real property as well as institutional developers in acquiring, entitling, and developing master-planned communities. Mike has negotiated numerous hotel management contracts for various property owners with nationally known luxury hotel operators as well as advising such owners regarding the financing of the hotels.

Prof. Memberships: Mike is a frequent speaker on real estate and finance trends for various professional organizations. He is a member of the Urban Land Institute, the Executive Committee of the USC Lusk Center for Real Estate, the Pepperdine University Graziadio Board of Visitors, and the ULI-LA Executive Committee.

Career: Mike is a founding Partner of the firm. In 2004, he was recognized in the Special Report on Who's Who in Real Estate published by the 'Los Angeles Business Journal'. In August 2004, 'California Lawyer Magazine' selected Mike as Best in the West for real estate lawyers. Mike was also featured in 'The International Who's Who of Real Estate Lawyers 2004'.

Personal: AB, Stanford University, 1967; JD, University of Southern California, 1969.

MATTHEWS, Philip
Hancock Rothert & Bunshoft LLP, San Francisco 415 981 5550
pmatthews@hrblaw.com
Recommended in Insurance

Practice Areas: Partner in the San Francisco office. His practice focuses on general civil litigation and insurance counseling and litigation, with an emphasis on complex cases. He has been involved in some of the largest trials and appeals in California, including the trial and appeal of Shell Oil Co. vs Accident and Casualty Co of Winterthur (Rocky Mountain Arsenal case) and In Re Coordinated Asbestos Litigation (Manville, Fibreboard, Armstrong and GAF Coverage cases.) He also has been liaison and trial counsel in numerous complex cases such as Shell Oil Co vs Accident and Casualty Co of Winterthur (Rocky Mountain Arsenal case), In Re Coordinated Asbestos Litigation, Flintkote v American Mutual, Four Star Oil & Gas Co vs Allianz (Texaco Environmental Coverage Litigation), Texaco Refining & Marketing, Inc vs Fireman's Fund Insurance Co (Texaco Toxic Tort), Exxon vs Insurance Company of North America (Exxon Environmental Coverage Litigation) and Kaiser Aluminum & Chemical Corporation vs Certain Underwriters at Lloyds. He also has experience in bankruptcy law and litigation and corporate transactions. He has spoken at a number of forums on a variety of topics relating to complex litigation, including Mealey's Conference Re Settling Complex Insurance Coverage Cases, Mealey's Conference on Tobacco Litigation, the American Bar Association Insurance Coverage Litigation Section on Allocation Issues in

California and Mealey's Allocation Conference. He co-chaired Mealey's 2001 California Insurance Law Conference.
Prof. Memberships: American Bar Association, Bar Association of San Francisco, Trustee of the Board of the Episcopal Charities of the Diocese of California, is active in other non-profit and religious organizations.
Career: Admitted to California Bar (1978). A Partner of Hancock Rothert & Bunshoft LLP since 1985. On the Management Committee of Hancock Rothert & Bunshoft LLP during 1989-94, 1996-99, and 2004-date serving as Managing Partner of the firm's San Francisco office during several of those years and is currently Chairperson of the firm.
Personal: George Washington University (BA, 1974). University of California, Hastings College of the Law (JD, 1977).

MAYER, Patricia
Mitchell, Silberberg & Knupp LLP, Los Angeles 310 312 2000
Recommended in Media & Entertainment

MAYERSON, Michael
Loeb & Loeb LLP, Los Angeles 213 688 3400
Recommended in Media & Entertainment

MCCARTHY, Brian J
Skadden, Arps, Slate, Meagher & Flom LLP & Affiliates, Los Angeles 213 687 5070
bmccarth@skadden.com
Recommended in Corporate/M&A
Practice Areas: Concentrates on corporate and securities matters, with particular emphasis on mergers, acquisitions, corporate governance issues and restructurings. Has acted as counsel to numerous companies and investment banking firms in mergers, acquisitions and tender offers, both friendly and hostile, and has also represented several investment banking clients, buyers, sellers and management groups in leveraged buyouts and related financings.
Prof. Memberships: Member, Executive Committee, Business and Corporations Law Section, Los Angeles County Bar Association.
Career: JD, Fordham University School of Law, 1978; BA, Tufts University, 1975 (magna cum laude).

MCCUTCHEON, Mary
Farella Braun & Martel LLP, San Francisco 415 954 4400
Recommended in Insurance

MCELHINNY, Harold
Morrison & Foerster LLP, San Francisco 415 268 7265
hmcelhinny@mofo.com
Recommended in Intellectual Property
Practice Areas: A trial lawyer with a general federal and state court litigation practice emphasizing intellectual property matters: patent litigation, copyright and trade secret violations, class actions, and enforcement.
Prof. Memberships: Member: American Bar Association; Intellectual Property Law section, State Bar of California; American Intellectual Property Law Association; Federal Circuit Bar Association. Former President, Northern California Association of Business Trial Lawyers, 1996-97.
Career: Admitted to practice in California. Served as firmwide Chair, Litigation Department, 1996-99.
Personal: BA, University of Santa Clara, 1970; Peace Corps, North Africa; JD, Boalt Hall School of Law, UC Berkeley, 1975, Order of the Coif; Law Clerk, Honorable Joseph Blumenfeld, US District Court, Connecticut, 1975-76.

MCGLYNN, Casey
Wilson Sonsini Goodrich & Rosati, Palo Alto 650 493 9300
cmcglynn@wsgr.com
Recommended in Corporate/M&A
Practice Areas: Focuses on the organization, funding and corporate representation of companies in the information technology and life sciences industries. Structures and negotiates mergers and acquisitions, licensing arrangements and domestic and international strategic corporate alliances, as well as other innovative financing arrangements.
Prof. Memberships: Admitted to practice in California. Member, American Bar Association.
Career: Joined WSGR, 1978; became Partner, 1985. Member, WSGR Policy Committee.
Personal: JD, (summa cum laude), 1978 and BS (summa cum laude), 1975, University of Santa Clara.

MCKNIGHT, Frederick (Rick)
Jones Day, Los Angeles 213 243 2777
fmcknight@jonesday.com
Recommended in Litigation
Practice Areas: Partner-in-Charge of the Los Angeles office. His practice primarily involves complex business litigation. He has had an active trial docket, including successful bench and jury trials of antitrust, contract, securities, oil and gas, healthcare, fraud, intellectual property, business tort, ERISA, entertainment, product liability, bankruptcy, environmental, and tax cases. He also is active in alternative forms of dispute resolution and has both recovered and defeated the recovery of substantial punitive damages awards. He frequently lectures on trial and pretrial practice and procedures.
Prof. Memberships: Fellow of the American College of Trial Lawyers.

MCMAHON, Terry
McDermott Will & Emery, Palo Alto 650 813 5010
tmcmahon@mwe.com
Recommended in Intellectual Property
Practice Areas: Partner and head of West Coast intellectual property practice. Focuses on patent, copyright, trade secrets, trade dress, trademark and high stakes litigation. Has 28 years of litigation experience successfully representing hi-tech heavyweights on 'bet the company' cases. Acted in Airtouch v Pacbell (client); Storage Technology v EMC Corporation (client); Creative Technology Ltd. v Aureal Semiconductor, Inc.(client); Reifflin v Microsoft (client); Sun Microsystems v Microsoft (client) and Intel v Broadcom (client). Lead counsel in the representation of Advanced Micro Devices (AMD) in its extensive arbitration against Intel, and as lead counsel in AMD's victory over Intel in federal court jury trial on the right to use Intel's copyright microcode.
Prof. Memberships: Member, Santa Clara Bar Association.
Career: Admitted to practice in California, the US Court of Appeals for the Ninth and Federal Circuits, the California Supreme Court and various district courts in California, Colorado and Virginia.
Personal: Received JD cum laude and BA from the University of Santa Clara. Serves as adjunct professor teaching Intellectual Property Litigation Techniques at Santa Clara University's Law School.

MCMILLAN, Daniel D
Jones Day, Los Angeles 213 243 2582
ddmcmillan@jonesday.com
Recommended in Construction
Practice Areas: Co-Chairperson of Jones Day's international Construction Practice. Specializes in complex construction disputes, contractual disputes and claims involving federal and state RICO statutes and false claims acts. Dan has substantial trial, law and motion, and appellate experience and extensive experience with all forms of alternative dispute resolution mechanisms. He is an instructor for the National Institute of Trial Advocacy and a frequent speaker and author on subjects of interest to the construction industry.
Prof. Memberships: Disputes Review Board Foundation; ABA Forum on Construction Industry/Steering Committee for Dispute Avoidance and Resolution; Executive Director of Los Angeles Economic Development Corporation.

MCNAMARA, Mary
Swanson & McNamara LLP, San Francisco 415 477 3800
Recommended in Litigation

MEISINGER, Louis
Sheppard, Mullin, Richter & Hampton LLP, Los Angeles 213 620 1780
Recommended in Media & Entertainment

MEMEL, Sherwin L
Manatt Phelps & Phillips LLP, Los Angeles 310 312 4267
smemel@manatt.com
Recommended in Healthcare
Practice Areas: Healthcare law focused on integrated delivery organizations, hospital-physician transactions, healthcare financing, PIAs, HMOs and PPOs, healthcare joint ventures, government relations, reimbursement, financially troubled healthcare organizations. Represents hospitals, multi-hospital systems, nursing homes, residential care companies, healthcare lenders, advises health and workers' compensation insurance companies, governmental entities, biotechnology research organizations, universities, physicians group, individual physicians, trade associations, medical products and health-related services companies.
Prof. Memberships: CSBA; LA County Bar, Century City Bar, American Bar, DC Bar, Associations; National Health Lawyers Association; American Society of Law and Medicine, American Healthcare Attorneys; Pacific Public Radio; California Board Medical Quality Assurance.
Career: Partner.
Personal: UCLA, (JD, 1954); UCLA, (BA, 1951).

MENDELSON, Alan
Latham & Watkins LLP, Menlo Park 650 328 4600
Recommended in Corporate/M&A

MENDELSON, Richard C
DLA Piper Rudnick Gray Cary US LLP, Los Angeles 213 330 7745
richard.mendelson@dlapiper.com
Recommended in Real Estate
Practice Areas: Real estate.
Career: He has particular knowledge in the areas of acquisitions, joint ventures, and financing transactions, as well as in workouts and restructurings. He has extensive experience in representing both domestic and international banks and other financial institutions, insurance companies, pension funds, and major developers in all aspects of commercial residential property.
Personal: JD, University of Pennsylvania; AB, Rutgers University.

MENDEZ, John
Latham & Watkins LLP, Los Angeles 213 485 1234
Recommended in Banking & Finance

MEYER, Michael
DLA Piper Rudnick Gray Cary US LLP, Los Angeles 213 330 7777
michael.meyer@dlapiper.com
Recommended in Real Estate
Practice Areas: Real estate; landlord leasing.
Career: He has a national reputation as one of the preeminent leasing attorneys in the United States. He represents many

of America's financial institutions, accounting firms and law firms with major lease transactions, and is considered one of the country's leading authorities on Fair Market Rental Rates, the Assignment and Subleasing Provision, the Tenant Improvement Agreement and the Rent Commencement Date. He is the only real estate lawyer ranked in the Top 10 Super Lawyers in Southern California in a survey published in Los Angeles Magazine. In the past 18 months he represented Broadcom on a 650,000 RSF deal in Irvine, City National Bank on a 330,000 RSF deal in Los Angeles, and Bank of America, The Capital Group Companies and TCW on their respective Southern California headquarter deals, and was named one of Los Angeles' 100 Most Influential Lawyers in a survey published in the Los Angeles Daily Journal.

Personal: JD, University of Chicago; BS, University of Wisconsin.

MIHLSTEN, George
Latham & Watkins LLP, Los Angeles
213 485 1234
Recommended in Real Estate

MILLER, O'Malley
Munger, Tolles & Olson LLP,
Los Angeles 213 683 9100
Recommended in Real Estate

MILLER, Robert
Paul, Hastings, Janofsky & Walker LLP,
Los Angeles
213 683 6254
robertmiller@paulhastings.com
Recommended in Corporate/M&A
Practice Areas: Mr Miller concentrates his practice in corporate finance transactional work, including mergers, acquisitions, public and private placement of securities, venture capital, and investment partnerships. He also represents publicly and privately held companies on general corporate and securities matters.
Personal: Mr Miller received his BS degree in 1976 from the University of North Dakota, and his JD degree in 1983 from Loyola Law School of Los Angeles, where he was a member of the St. Thomas More Law Honor Society. He serves as Vice Chair of the firm's Corporate Department.

MILLER, Stephen
Howrey Simon Arnold & White,
Los Angeles 213 892 1800
Recommended in Litigation

MILLET, Craig
Gibson, Dunn & Crutcher LLP, Irvine
949 451 3986
cmillet@gibsondunn.com
Recommended in Bankruptcy
Practice Areas: Extensive experience in complex bankruptcy litigation, Chapter 11 reorganization cases and international and cross-border bankruptcy matters including appellate, asset acquisition through bankruptcy, representation of

both debtors and creditors, out-of-court restructuring and transactional strategic planning. Represented the Japanese administrator in In Re Ken International; Callaway Golf in the acquisition of Top Flite, FLAG Telecom in Elliott Group litigation, five major broker/dealers in In Re County of Orange; debtor in In Re Advanced Tissue Sciences and Ingram Micro in BigStore.com Litigation.
Personal: JD, summa cum laude, Pepperdine University, 1982; editor in chief, 'Pepperdine Law Review'; Best Team/Best Advocate, Dalsimer Moot Court competition.

MINCHELLA, Michael
Monteleone & McCrory, LLP,
Los Angeles 213 612 9900
Recommended in Construction

MOONEY, Ann
Cooley Godward LLP, San Francisco
415 693 2000
Recommended in Insurance

MOORE, Gary
Cooley Godward LLP, Palo Alto
650 843 5000
Recommended in IT Outsourcing

MOORE, Robert
Milbank, Tweed, Hadley & McCloy, Los Angeles
213 892 4000
Recommended in Bankruptcy

MORROW, Bill
Cooley Godward LLP, San Francisco
415 693 2000
Recommended in Tax

MOTTESI, Marcello
Milbank, Tweed, Hadley & McCloy,
Palo Alto 650 739 7000
Recommended in Capital Markets

MULLIKEN, David
Latham & Watkins LLP, San Diego
619 236 1234
Recommended in Insurance

MUMMERY, Dan
Latham & Watkins LLP, Menlo Park
650 328 4600
Recommended in Business Process Outsourcing, IT Outsourcing

MURPHY, Mary
Farella Braun & Martel LLP,
San Francisco 415 954 4400
Recommended in Real Estate

MURPHY, Michael
Shaw Pittman LLP, Los Angeles
650 833 4703
michael.murphy@shawpittman.com
Recommended in Business Process Outsourcing, IT Outsourcing
Practice Areas: Michael Murphy specializes in complex sourcing relationships including technology and business process outsourcing, business transformations, joint ventures and strategic alliances. Examples of successful sourcing transactions in which Mr Murphy has been engaged include IT infrastruc-

ture and applications outsourcing, real estate facilities management, and public utility infrastructure operations and maintenance. In addition legal counsel, Mr Murphy has acted as an outsourcing advisor in some of the world's most complex outsourcing projects.
Prof. Memberships: American Bar Association; California Bankers Association.
Career: Before joining Shaw Pittman in 1992, Mr Murphy practiced with a leading Australian firm, where he represented clients in the technology, energy, automotive and finance sectors in a range of corporate and commercial transactions.
Publications: 'Structuring Outsourcing Technology Relationships: Customer Concerns, Strategies and Processes' (International Journal of Law and Information Technology, Vol 4 No 2). 'Optimizing the Tax Function Through Strategic Sourcing' (Association for Computers and Taxation, Journal of Corporate Tax Automation, Spring 2004).

MURPHY, Patrick A
Winston & Strawn, San Francisco
415 591 1500
pmurphy@winston.com
Recommended in Bankruptcy
Practice Areas: Corporate reorganizations and insolvency law.
Prof. Memberships: California State Bar; San Francisco Bar Association; American and International Bar Associations; National Bankruptcy Conference; American College of Bankruptcy; International Insolvency Institute.
Career: National practice in restructuring and insolvency law; represented Creditors' Committee in Washington Group International.
Publications: Creditors' Rights in Bankruptcy (2d Ed, West Group). Participated in more than 50 programs in the fields of bankruptcy, commercial law, and lender liability litigation for organizations such as American Law Institute-American Bar Association and Practising Law Institute.
Personal: BA Williams College 1961; JD University of California at Berkeley, Boalt Hall, 1965.

MURRAY, Christopher
O'Melveny & Myers LLP, Los Angeles
310 553 6700
Recommended in Media & Entertainment

MURRAY JR, William G
Orrick, Herrington & Sutcliffe LLP,
San Francisco 415 773 5807
wgm@orrick.com
Recommended in Real Estate
Practice Areas: Practice focuses on negotiating and documenting acquisitions and financing transactions, fund and capital formation, including substantial work for pension fund advisors, construction and long-term lending, ground leasing, sale-leaseback financing,

synthetic leases, and development transactions. Represents numerous buyers, sellers, and developers of real property, including pension funds, individual developers, domestic institutions, and foreign investors. He has been active in numerous projects involving securitization of real estate assets, real estate investment trusts and public market financing of real estate companies.
Prof. Memberships: Mr Murray is a member of the American College of Real Estate Lawyers, Lambda Alpha National Land Economics Society and the Pension Real Estate Association. He is the former chair of the Financing Subsection to the Real Estate Section of the State Bar of California.
Career: JD, University of California, Berkeley, Boalt Hall, 1975; BA, Utah State University, 1972.
Publications: Mr Murray is the author of over 30 articles and papers on various aspects of real estate transactions.

MUTO, Fred
Cooley Godward LLP, San Diego
858 550 6000
Recommended in Corporate/M&A

MYERS, Roger
DLA Piper Rudnick Gray Cary US LLP,
San Francisco
415 659 7048
roger.myers@dlapiper.com
Recommended in Media & Entertainment
Practice Areas: Media and new media; intellectual property; litigation.
Career: His practice focuses on media, cyberspace, intellectual property, and unfair competition law, representing a melding of the old media with the new. He has litigated numerous intellectual property and unfair competition matters and has successfully represented internet access, service, and content providers in both online defamation and copyright litigation.
Personal: JD, Boalt Hall School of Law, University of California at Berkeley; BA, San Jose State University.

NASH, Glenn
Latham & Watkins LLP, Menlo Park
650 328 4600
Recommended in Corporate/M&A, IT Outsourcing

NATSIS, Anton N
Allen, Matkins, Leck, Gamble & Mallory LLP, Los Angeles 310 788 2430
tnatsis@allenmatkins.com
Recommended in Real Estate
Practice Areas: Tony practices in the area of real estate, specializing in development, leasing, asset management, and purchase and sale agreements. He is continually sought out by some of the nation's largest land owners, such as J.P. Morgan Fleming Asset Management, Boston Properties, Equity Office Properties, Kilroy Realty, Inc., Beacon Capital Partners, and Kamehameha Schools to

negotiate many of the most complex leases and purchase and sale agreements in the Southwestern United States. He is also frequently retained as counsel for major national office tenants, such as AT&T, LAUSD, Citicorp, the FDIC, and AIG. In the past 12 months, Tony has closed commercial office leases exceeding 5,000,000 square feet and has worked on real estate purchase contracts with a total consideration of over $1 billion.
Prof. Memberships: Tony is a member of the American College of Real Estate Lawyers. A frequent lecturer and author, he is the chief consultant of the recently published 'California Continuing Education of the Bar Commercial Leasing Series', the legal education reference book on leasing for California attorneys. Tony is an adjunct professor of law at Loyola Law School and has spoken before such national real estate groups as ULI and BOMA.
Career: Admitted to the state Bar of California in 1983, Tony is a Partner and co-chairman of the firm's Commercial Project Group. He was recently selected as one of the 100 Top Super Lawyers in Los Angeles County by 'Los Angeles Magazine'. Tony is one of the youngest (and the only lawyer with a specialty of 'leasing') listed in 'The Best Lawyers in America'.
Publications: Tony has written articles in the area of commercial transactions and bankruptcy issues published in the 'California Real Property Journal', 'LA Lawyers', and the 'Loyola Law Review'.
Personal: BBA, Business Administration, cum laude, University of Michigan, 1980; JD, University of Michigan, 1983.

NAVARRO BAYSINGER, Kara S
Sonnenschein Nath & Rosenthal, San Francisco 415 882 2475
knavarro@sonnenschein.com
Recommended in Insurance
Practice Areas: Insurance Practice Vice Chair. Works with insurers, agents and regulators regarding market conduct (pro-actively and reactively), government/regulatory relations, privacy, security, ebusiness, regulatory licensing and approvals, insurance entity transactions (including reinsurance), reinsurance and product and market development. Represents national insurance and reinsurance companies, insurance-related service companies and state governments.
Prof. Memberships: Illinois and California Bar Associations, California State Bar Insurance Law Committee; Past Chair, California State Bar Group Insurance Programs Committee; Panel attorney, San Francisco AIDS Legal Referral Panel; Advisory Board, National Association of Insurance Commissioners.
Personal: Loyola University School of Law, JD; University of Michigan, BA, Political Science.

NEAL, Steve
Cooley Godward LLP, Palo Alto
650 843 5000
Recommended in Litigation

NEELY, Sally S
Sidley Austin Brown & Wood LLP, Los Angeles 213 896 6024
sneely@sidley.com
Recommended in Bankruptcy
Practice Areas: Sally Neely focuses on corporate workouts and Chapter 11 reorganizations, representing debtors, committees, creditors, contract parties, purchasers and defendants in adversary proceedings. She has represented: the Creditors' Committee in the Chapter 11 case for Riviera Hotel & Casino, the $8 million judgment creditor in the Kim Basinger bankruptcy case; Visa Properties (prepackaged Chapter 11 case); the purchaser of the assets of the Canadian subsidiaries of Consolidated Freightways (Chapter 7); NewPower Co. (Chapter 11); the Creditors' Committee in the Chapter 11 Case for Franchise Pictures LLC; Flintkote Co. (Chapter 11) and Bombardier Inc. and Learjet Inc. in litigation involving an individual Chapter 11 debtor; participated in the Chrysler reorganization and the FCC's sale of 'C' Block Spectrum for Broadband Personal Communications services; and currently represents Federal Mogul Global (Chapter 11).
Prof. Memberships: Member of the National Bankruptcy Conference, Chair of its Committee on Legislation, a member of its Executive Committee and past Chair of its Committee on Partnerships. She is a Fellow of the American College of Bankruptcy, a member of its Board of Directors and Chair of its Educational Programs Committee.
Career: Ms Neely was Assistant Professor at Harvard Law School and a law clerk to the Honorable Ozell M. Trask, United States Court of Appeals, Ninth Circuit. Stanford University Law School, J.D., 1971; Stanford University, B.A., 1970. Bar Admission: California, 1977.

NELLIS, Noel
Orrick, Herrington & Sutcliffe LLP, San Francisco 415 392 1122
Recommended in Real Estate

NESSIM, Ronald
Bird, Marella, Boxer & Wolpert PC, Los Angeles 310 201 2100
Recommended in Litigation

NEWCOMBE, George
Simpson Thacher & Bartlett LLP, Palo Alto 650 251 5050
gnewcombe
Recommended in Intellectual Property
Practice Areas: Partner in the firm's Litigation Department and Head of the Palo Alto office. Mr Newcombe's practice is focused on servicing the litigation needs of companies in Silicon Valley, including patent and other intellectual property litigation, commercial arbitra-

tion, securities litigation, among other matters. Representative clients include Intel Corporation, Oracle Corporation (Special Litigation Committee), Levi Strauss & Co. (Audit Committee); JDS Uniphase, MCI/WorldCom, Inc., Agilent Technologies, Inc., NEC Corporation, Olympus Optical Co. Ltd. and Avistar Communications.
Prof. Memberships: Member, the American Law Institute, the American Intellectual Property Lawyers Association, The Association of the Bar of the City of New York, the American Bar Association, the Federal Circuit Bar Association, the Federal Bar Council and the Defense Research Institute.
Career: Partner at the firm since 1983.
Personal: Received his BS magna cum laude in Chemical Engineering in 1969 from the New Jersey Institute of Technology and his JD from Columbia University School of Law in 1975, where he was a James Kent Scholar and a founding editor of the Columbia Journal of Environmental Law.

NEWMAN, Jeanne
Hansen Jacobson Teller Hoberman Newman, Warren, Sloane & Richman, LLP, Beverly Hills
310 271 8777
Recommended in Media & Entertainment

NICHOLS, Phillip
Pircher, Nichols & Meeks, Los Angeles
310 201 8900
Recommended in Real Estate

NICHOLSON, Phillip
Cox Castle & Nicholson LLP, Los Angeles 310 277 4222
Recommended in Real Estate

NOLAN, Thomas J
Skadden, Arps, Slate, Meagher & Flom LLP & Affiliates, Los Angeles
213 687 5250
tnolan@skadden.com
Recommended in Antitrust, Litigation
Practice Areas: Co-Head of the firm's West Coast Litigation Practice. Has represented and defended corporations and individuals in significant federal, state, civil and criminal complex litigation in California and in various state and federal courts throughout the United States, the cumulative result of which is extensive trial experience in both the state and federal court systems. Represented clients involving antitrust, securities, intellectual property and white collar crime issues, as well as in class action lawsuits and litigation involving a wide variety of contract disputes, unfair business practices and federal securities issues.
Career: JD, Loyola University, 1975; BBA, Loyola University, 1971.

NORRIS, Trenton
Bingham McCutchen LLP, San Francisco 415 393 2000
Recommended in Environment

OAKES, Royal
Barger & Wolen, Los Angeles
213 680 2800
Recommended in Insurance

O'CONNELL, George
Stevens & O'Connell LLP, Sacramento
916 329 9111
Recommended in Litigation

OFFER, Stuart J
Morrison & Foerster LLP, San Francisco
415 268 7052
soffer@mofo.com
Recommended in Tax
Practice Areas: Concentrates on tax aspects of mergers, acquisitions and divestitures, specialized financings, general corporate transactions, and tax intensive corporate transactions. Handles international tax planning for US-based companies with foreign operations. Advises foreign corporations on the US tax aspects of their operations and investments.
Prof. Memberships: Taxation Section, ABA (Chair, Sarbanes-Oxley Task Force; Former Section Vice-Chair, Former Chair, Corporate Tax Committee); Trustee, American Tax Policy Institute; Regent, American College of Tax Counsel; Advisory Board, NYU Institute on Federal Taxation and Mergers and Acquisitions magazine; Member, International Fiscal Association.
Career: Admitted to practice in California and District of Columbia. Chair, Corporate and International Tax Practice Groups.
Personal: BA, University of Washington, 1964; LLB, Columbia University School of Law, 1967; Managing Editor, 'Columbia Law Review'. Law Clerk, Judge Featherston, US Tax Court, 1967-68. Active Duty, US Army Judge Advocate General's Corps, 1968-72.

OLSEN, Christine
O'Melveny & Myers LLP, Los Angeles
213 430 6000
Recommended in Banking & Finance

OLSON, Karl
Levy, Ram & Olson, San Francisco
415 433 4949
Recommended in Media & Entertainment

OLSON, Ronald
Munger, Tolles & Olson LLP, Los Angeles 213 683 9100
Recommended in Litigation, Media & Entertainment

ONCIDI, Anthony J
Proskauer Rose LLP, Los Angeles
310 284 5690
aoncidi@proskauer.com
Recommended in Employment
Practice Areas: A Partner at Proskauer Rose, and the Chair of the Labor and Employment Department in the Los Angeles office. He represents employers in all aspects of labor relations and employment law, including litigation

and preventive counseling, wrongful termination, employee discipline, Title VII and the California Fair Employment and Housing Act, union-related issues, wage and hour matters, executive employment contract disputes, employee handbooks and personnel policies, sexual harassment training and investigations, workplace violence, drug testing and privacy issues, confidential information, trade secret protection and collective bargaining. A substantial portion of his practice involves the defense of employers in class action wage and hour, employment discrimination and wrongful termination litigation in both state and federal court. He also has experience in trade secret and unfair competition litigation and the defense of sexual harassment, discrimination, breach of contract and defamation lawsuits.

Career: Co-author of the treatise entitled 'Employment Discrimination Depositions' (Juris Pub. 2004; www.jurispub.com) and, since 1990, has been a columnist for the official publication of the State Bar of California, 'The California Labor & Employment Law Review', and 'The Los Angeles Daily Journal.'

Personal: University of Chicago Law School, JD, 1984. Pomona College, BA, cum laude, 1981; Phi Beta Kappa.

O'NEAL, Stephen
Thelen Reid & Priest LLP,
San Francisco 415 371 1200
Recommended in Construction

O'NEILL, Brian
Jones Day, Los Angeles
213 243 2856
boneill@jonesday.com
Recommended in Litigation

Practice Areas: A leading California trial lawyer with extensive trial experience in civil and criminal cases in federal and state courts. He also has substantial appellate experience, arguing cases in federal appeals courts and California appellate courts. He regularly represents business entities and individuals in grand jury and administrative investigations. He has successfully defended clients in antitrust, bankruptcy, bribery, customs defense contracting, environmental, export controls, foreign corrupt practices, securities, and tax cases. Regularly listed as a leading lawyer in Los Angeles and nationally.

Prof. Memberships: Fellow of the American College of Trial Lawyers and the American Board of Criminal Lawyers.

O'NEILL, Edward
Davis Wright Tremaine LLP,
San Francisco 415 276 6582
edwardoneill@dwt.com
Recommended in Energy

Practice Areas: Partner, energy and environmental law. Represents utilities, competitive utility service providers consumers and local government on electric, natural gas, telecommunications and water matters, with emphasis on administrative law/practice before California Public Utilities Commission. Lead strategist/negotiator for State of California regarding international natural gas trade dispute with Canadian government.

Prof. Memberships: Member, California State Bar. Board of Directors, California Conference of Public Utility Counsel.

Career: Partner since 2002. California Public Utilities Commission, 1977-98 (Assistant General Counsel, 1990-98).

Publications: Frequent lecturer on California Public Utilities Commission practice.

Personal: JD, Boston College, 1976. BA, University of California - Berkeley, 1973.

PACHULSKI, Isaac M
Stutman, Treister & Glatt Professional
Corporation, Los Angeles
310 228 5655
ipachulski@stutman.com
Recommended in Bankruptcy

Practice Areas: Specializing in corporate reorganization, insolvency, and bankruptcy law, Mr Pachulski currently represents the holders of approximately $2 billion of senior unsecured debt of Enron Corp. in Enron's Chapter 11 case. He also represents the holders of approximately $500 million of debt in the Owens-Corning Chapter 11 case. Mr Pachulski recently acted as lead Chapter 11 counsel for Mariner Post-Acute Network, Inc., Mariner Health Group, Inc., and 185 affiliated entities which collectively operated approximately 400 skilled nursing and long-term acute care facilities at the time of their Chapter 11 filing and confirmed a plan of reorganization. Mr Pachulski also served as lead Chapter 11 counsel for AMC Entertainment in its successful effort to acquire General Cinemas Corporation through a plan of reorganization in General Cinemas' Chapter 11 case. Representative engagements in which Mr Pachulski has previously been involved include the representation of the debtors in the Chapter 11 cases of Doskocil, Wilson Foods, and 16 affiliated entities; the representation of Public Service Company of New Hampshire, a public utility, in its Chapter 11 case; the representation of Pizza Time Theatre, and Sambo's Restaurants (both publicly held companies at the time) in their respective Chapter 11 cases; the representation of Cherokee, Inc., and Restaurant Enterprises Group in their respective prepackaged Chapter 11 cases; representation of the trustee in the liquidation of W.S. Clearing, Inc., a clearing broker, under the Securities Investor Protection Act; representation of funds managed by Apollo Management or Apollo Advisors as a major bondholder in the Chapter 11 cases of Hayes-Lemmerz International, Gillette Holdings, Inc. and Hillsborough Holdings, Inc.; the representation of funds managed by Fidelity Investments, Apollo Advisors and Trust Company of the West as the holders of approximately $500 million in bonds in the aggregate in the Chapter 11 case of SCI Television; representation of Pennzoil in the Texaco, Inc. Chapter 11 case; and the successful defense of an appeal on behalf of a plaintiff which obtained a $22.5 million lender liability judgment against Royal Bank of Canada. Mr Pachulski has also devoted a significant portion of his practice to appellate matters.

Career: Admitted to California Bar (1974). Joined the firm Stutman Triester & Glatt in 1974 and became shareholder in 1980.

Publications: Articles include 'Levy v Cohen: Another Pitfall for Creditors in Bankruptcy Proceedings', 53 Los Angeles Bar Journal 278, 1977, and 'The Cram Down and Valuation Under Chapter 11 of the Bankruptcy Code', 58 N.C.L. Review 925 (1981). He has also lectured on topics such as appellate practice, intellectual property licenses and security interests in bankruptcy and Chapter 11 plans.

Personal: Received BA in political science (summa cum laude) from University of California at Los Angeles in 1971. Received JD (summa cum laude) from Harvard University, where he received the Faye Diploma (which is awarded to the graduate with the highest cumulative grade average) in 1974. While at Harvard, he received the Sears Prize in 1972 and again in 1973, and was a member of the Harvard Law Review for the academic year 1972-73.

PACHULSKI, Richard M
Pachulski, Stang, Ziehl, Young, Jones &
Weintraub P.C., Los Angeles
310 201 4795
rpachulski@pszyjw.com
Recommended in Bankruptcy

Practice Areas: Mr Pachulski has had extensive experience in business reorganizations and related litigation. He has represented numerous debtors and creditors' committees in both out-of-court workouts and in-court proceedings, including the debtors in the Chapter 11 cases of Peregrine Systems, Breed Technologies, Covad Communcations Group, Commonwealth Equity Trust, Sizzler International, and Toni Braxton; and the committees of unsecured creditors for First Executive Corporation and Northpoint Communications, and the trustee of Triad America Corporation.

Prof. Memberships: Fellow, American College of Bankruptcy. Member, Financial Lawyers Conference Board of Governors (1989-92).

Career: Mr Pachulski is admitted to practice in the State of California, and is a resident in the firm's Los Angeles office.

Publications: Mr Pachulski has lectured extensively on bankruptcy and related litigation issues and has written several articles, including co-author: 'Chapter 11 - The Bank of Last Resort,' 45 Bus. Law. 261, 1989; co-author: 'Plan Wars - The Use of Chapter 11 to Coax Continued Financing From A Reluctant Lender,' 738 PLI/Comm. 7 (1996).

Personal: He is a graduate of UCLA (BA 1976, summa cum laude) and Stanford University (JD 1979). Phi Beta Kappa. Pi Gamma Mu. Extern to Judge Robert M Takasugi, US District Court, Central District of California, 1978-79.

PAGE, Michael
Keker & Van Nest LLP, San Francisco
415 391 5400
mhp@kvn.com
Recommended in Intellectual Property

Practice Areas: Intellectual property litigation, with extensive experience in copyright, trade secret, trademark, and patent litigation. Recently, he received a CLAY Award (California Lawyer Attorney of the Year) for his success in obtaining a landmark decision in favor of his client Grokster in litigation against all of the major motion picture studios and record companies. That decision (currently on appeal to the United States Supreme Court) established the legality of peer-to-peer file sharing software. Significant intellectual property clients have included, Google, Cadence Design Systems, Nintendo, Electronic Arts, Sega, Intertrust, eBay, Nullsoft, Palm Computing, 3Com, Harris Corporation, Heartport, AOL, E-Loan, and Tegal Corporation.

Prof. Memberships: San Francisco Bay Area Intellectual Property Inns of Court; former Co-Chairman of the Litigation Section of the Barrister's Club.

Career: Law clerk to the Honorable Samuel Conti, United States District Court, Northern District of California; joined Keker & Van Nest, 1995; became Partner, 1999.

Publications: Co-author: 'Copyright Protection of Video Games in the United States: Galoob v Nintendo', 14 European Intellectual Property Review, January 1992; 'Add-on Infringements: When Computer Add-Ons and Peripherals Should (And Should Not) be Considered Infringing Derivative Works under Lewis Galoob Toys, Inc. v Nintendo of America, Inc., and Other Recent Decisions', Vol. 15 No. 3 Hastings Communication and Entertainment Law Journal, 1993.

Personal: Boalt Hall School of Law, University of California (JD 1991); University of Pennsylvania (BA 1975).

PASAHOW, Lynn
Fenwick & West LLP, Mountain View
650 335 7225
lpasahow@fenwick.com
Recommended in Intellectual Property

Practice Areas: Chair of firm's Litigation Group. Patent and other intellectual property litigation, counseling, licensing and mediation, principally relating to bioscience, software and Internet technologies. Led teams enforcing Amazon.com's 1-Click® patent against Barnesandnoble.com, and winning jury verdict against du Pont enforcing Cetus' patents on Nobel Prize-winning polymerase chain reaction invention. Regularly represents University of California regarding such diverse inventions as FISH DNA detection, prion detection and elimination, transgenic organisms, medical lasers and strawberries.

Prof. Memberships: Director of Bay Area Bioscience Center, Alzheimer's Association of Northern California, and Boalt Hall Alumni Association. Member, advisory board of University of California's Berkeley Center for Law and Technology.

Career: Law clerk to Honorable AJ Zirpoli, United States District Court, Northern District of California. Co-instructor of 'A Life Scientist's Guide to Intellectual Property' at University of California, San Francisco. Regularly lectures about intellectual property law subjects to groups including Federal Judicial Center, American Association for the Advancement of Science, American Law Institute, Practising Law Institute, and Boalt School of Law. Included among intellectual property lawyers in The Best Lawyers in America.

Personal: University of California, Berkeley School of Law (Boalt Hall), JD, Order of the Coif, 1972 Stanford University, BA, Phi Beta Kappa, 1969.

PASICH, Kirk
Dickstein Shapiro Morin & Oshinsky LLP, Los Angeles
Recommended in Insurance

PASSMAN, Donald
Gang Tyre Ramer & Brown, Beverly Hills
310 777 4800
Recommended in Media & Entertainment

PATTERSON, Thomas E
Klee, Tuchin, Bogdanoff & Stern LLP, Los Angeles 310 407 4035
tpatterson@ktbslaw.com
Recommended in Bankruptcy

Practice Areas: Is a member of Klee, Tuchin, Bogdanoff & Stern LLP. He has represented both debtors and creditors' committees in complex Chapter 11 and out-of-court proceedings. He has represented hospital provider groups in most of the recent HMO insolvencies pending in California (including MedPartners Provider Network, Maxicare, Wattshealth, and Lifeguard) and has also been involved in most of the significant insurer insolvencies in California in the past ten years. Recent debtor cases include All Star Gas, a multi-state propane retailer. Is a frequent speaker on bankruptcy and insolvency-related topics.

PECK, Rodney
Pillsbury Winthrop LLP, San Francisco
415 983 1516
rpeck@pillsburywinthrop.com
Recommended in Banking & Finance

Practice Areas: Mr Peck is a Partner practicing corporate, securities, finance and banking law. His practice includes mergers and acquisitions, bank transactional and regulatory matters and corporate and securities transactions and has focused on the financial services, energy and telecommunications industries. He advised Chevron Corporation in its $36 billion merger with Texaco Inc.; Pacific Telesis Group in its $17 billion merger with SBC Communications; BNP Paribas in its $2.3 billion acquisition of United California Bank and its $1.2 billion acquisition of Community First Bancshares, Inc.; and Bank of America in its $2.2 billion acquisition of Continental Bank.

Prof. Memberships: Board of Trustees, Dominican University of California; Financial Institutions Committee, California State Bar; Committee on Banking Law, American Bar Association.

Career: Admitted to practice: California; District of Columbia; New York.

Publications: 'The Non-Bank Bank Phenomenon: Recent Developments and Implications for Interstate Banking' (1984); 'The Federal Home Loan Banks and the Home Finance System' (1988), The Business Lawyer; and 'FIRREA and the New Federal Home Loan Bank System' (1992), Santa Clara Law Review.

Personal: JD, Columbia University School of Law, 1970. AB, Stanford University, 1967.

PEDLAR, Alan
Stutman, Treister & Glatt Professional Corporation, Los Angeles
310 228 5600
APedlar@Stutman.com
Recommended in Bankruptcy

Practice Areas: Representation of debtors, creditors, trustees, committees and purchasers in respect to financially troubled companies, including in cases pending under the federal bankruptcy code.

Prof. Memberships: ABA, State Bar of California (former Chairman, Debtor/Creditor Relations and Bankruptcy Committee); Fellow, American College of Bankruptcy.

Career: Senior Shareholder since 1990; former adjunct Professor of Law, Loyola University School of Law.

Publications: Contributing Author, Collier on Bankruptcy (15th ed rev) since 1991.

Personal: Boalt Hall (JD, 1976); Stanford University (MS, 1973); UCLA (BS, summa cum laude, 1971).

PEITZMAN, Lawrence
Peitzman, Glassman, Weg & Kempinski, Los Angeles 310 552 3100
Recommended in Bankruptcy

PETERS, Gerald
Latham & Watkins LLP, San Francisco
415 391 0600
Recommended in Healthcare

PETERS, William
O'Melveny & Myers LLP, Los Angeles
213 430 6000
Recommended in Business Process Outsourcing, IT Outsourcing

PETERSON JR, John M
Baker & McKenzie, Palo Alto
650 856 5538
john.m.peterson@bakernet.com
Recommended in Tax

Practice Areas: John M Peterson Jr, is a Partner in the Palo Alto office of Baker & McKenzie. Mr Peterson joined Baker & McKenzie in 1977. He practices corporate tax law, with heavy emphasis on intercompany pricing, structuring of international operations, international tax planning generally, high technology tax issues, and federal income tax controversies. Mr Peterson is currently the Chair of Baker & McKenzie's Global Tax Practice Group. He received his BBA in Accounting from University of Notre Dame in 1973 and his JD degree from Harvard Law School in 1977, graduating cum laude. Mr Peterson also is a CPA.

PETRICH, Louis
Leopold, Petrich & Smith PA, Los Angeles 310 277 3333
Recommended in Media & Entertainment

PETROCELLI, Daniel
O'Melveny & Myers LLP, Los Angeles
310 553 6700
Recommended in Litigation

PFISTER, Thomas
Latham & Watkins LLP, Los Angeles
213 485 1234
Recommended in Employment

PHILLIPS, Bradley
Munger, Tolles & Olson LLP, Los Angeles 213 683 9100
Recommended in Antitrust

PHILLIPS, Lee
Manatt Phelps & Phillips LLP, Los Angeles 310 212 4111
lphillips@manatt.com
Recommended in Media & Entertainment

Practice Areas: Leader in the music industry for over 30 years and has earned a reputation for intelligence, creativity and integrity in representing major musicians, composers and record companies with focus on contract negotiations. Advice ranging from litigation, licensing and corporate issues to copyright, privacy, tax issues and the sale of publishing catalogs.

Prof. Memberships: Alliance of Artists and Recording Companies, (BOD); Santa Barbara International Film Festival, (BOD); Rock the Vote, (BOD); City of Hope Music Divison, (former Pres. and Chair).

Career: Partner.

Publications: Lecturer on legal practice in the music industry.

Personal: Best Lawyers in America, 2000-2001; Spirit of Life Award, City of Hope Music Division; Helen King Award for Philanthropy, National Academy of Songwriters; Cornell University, (JD, 1959); Cornell University, (AB, 1957).

PICKETT, Donn
Bingham McCutchen LLP, San Francisco 415 393 2000
Recommended in Antitrust

PIMSTONE, Gregory N
Manatt Phelps & Phillips LLP, Los Angeles 310 312 4133
gpimstone@manatt.com
Recommended in Healthcare

Practice Areas: Complex litigation and advice in the healthcare area. Lead counsel for major health plans, insurers, hospitals and other healthcare entities in significant matters includng RICO, consumer and ERISA class actions, representative unfair competition actions, fraud and abuse, bad faith denial of benefits, compliance counseling and investigations, qui tam actions, HIPAA and other privacy litigation, antitrust, pharmaceutical litigation, and contract and commercial disputes, product liablity, toxic tort, unfair competition, Petroleum Marketing Practices Act, Proposition 65, antitrust, defamation and wrongful death.

Career: Partner.

Personal: UC, Boalt Hall School of Law (JD, 1990); UC Berkeley (BA, 1987).

PIRCHER, Leo
Pircher, Nichols & Meeks, Los Angeles
310 201 8900
Recommended in Real Estate

POMERANTZ, Glenn
Munger, Tolles & Olson LLP, Los Angeles 213 683 9100
Recommended in Antitrust, Media & Entertainment

POOLEY, James
Milbank, Tweed, Hadley & McCloy, Palo Alto 650 739 7000
Recommended in Intellectual Property

POPOFSKY, Laurence
Heller Ehrman LLP, San Francisco
415 772 6000
Recommended in Antitrust, Litigation

POTTER, John
Covington & Burling, San Francisco
415 591 7061
jpotter@cov.com
Recommended in Litigation

Practice Areas: Handles complex civil litigation, white-collar criminal defense, and corporate investigations. Successfully defends corporations, officers, directors, and employees in state and federal courts against civil and criminal allegations involving the False Claims Act, government contract fraud, healthcare fraud, securities fraud, environmental crimes, money laundering, customs fraud, and public corruption (United States v Tucker).

Career: Assistant United States Attorney in Los Angeles. Received professional commendations from the DOJ, FBI, IRS, Department of Defense, and US Customs Service.

Personal: Georgetown University, (JD, 1986, cum laude; BA, 1983)

POWERS, Matthew D

Weil, Gotshal & Manges LLP, Redwood Shores 650 802 3200
matthew.powers@weil.com
Recommended in Intellectual Property

Practice Areas: Intellectual property, patents, litigation.

Career: Mr Powers, who heads Weil Gotshal's 90-lawyer global Patent Litigation practice, specializes in trying patent and trade secret cases worldwide. His cases involve wide-ranging technologies like semiconductor devices, manufacturing equipment and processes, DNA sequencing, medical devices and other biotechnologies, computer hardware and software, network and telephony communications and the internet. One of the world's most accomplished patent litigators, Mr Powers consistently has been recognized as a leader in the field. In March 2005, California Lawyer Magazine named him California Attorney of the Year in Intellectual Property. He was featured in PLC Which Lawyer? Yearbook 2005 and Global 50 as a 'Star Lawyer: Individuals Ranked as 'Leading' in their Practice Areas' in US Intellectual Property practice in 2001. In 2003, The American Lawyer named him one of the 'top 45 attorneys under 45' in all fields nationwide, while the San Francisco Daily Journal named him one of California's top 25 IP lawyers and the San Francisco Chronicle named him one of the top 25 Bay Area attorneys in all fields. Other publications that have recognized Mr Powers include, in 2001, The Lawyer and, in 2002, IP Worldwide, both of which have named him among the top 10 patent litigators in the US. In June 2004, The Father's Day Council of San Francisco named Mr Powers as a '2004 Father of the Year.' Mr Powers is an editor in chief of the Intellectual Property & Technology Law Journal, and has published extensively on various aspects of intellectual property law and litigation. He is a frequent lecturer nationally and internationally on intellectual property litigation issues. Mr Powers also teaches a patent litigation course at the University of California, Berkeley's Boalt Hall School of Law, and has lectured on patent law at Stanford University and Santa Clara University. He serves on Weil Gotshal's Management Committee.

Personal: Harvard Law School, JD; Northwestern University, BS.

PREOVOLOS, Penelope A

Morrison & Foerster LLP, San Francisco 415 268 7187
ppreovolos@mofo.com
Recommended in Antitrust

Practice Areas: Has extensive experience in consumer class actions, antitrust, and false advertising/unfair trade practice litigation and counseling. Has served as lead counsel in numerous major consumer class action, antitrust, and false advertising and unfair competition cases.

Prof. Memberships: Chair, 1994-95, Secretary, 1993-94, California State Bar Antitrust Section. Member, Litigation and Antitrust Sections, American Bar Association.

Career: Admitted to practice in California. Co-Chair, Antitrust, Marketing and Distribution Practice Group 1990-2004.

Personal: AB, greatest distinction, University of California, Berkeley, 1976, Phi Beta Kappa, University Medal, English Departmental Citation; JD, cum laude, Harvard Law School, 1979, Executive Editor, 'Civil Liberties Law Review', 1978-79. Law Clerk, Honorable Charles M Merrill, US Court of Appeals, Ninth Circuit (1979-80).

PRETTY, Laurence

Hogan & Hartson LLP, Los Angeles 213 337 6812
LHPretty@hhlaw.com
Recommended in Intellectual Property

Practice Areas: First Chair in numerous bench and jury trials of patent lawsuits involving diverse technologies, including healthcare products, electronics, and mechanical devices.

Prof. Memberships: Former Chair, Intellectual Property Section, California State Bar; Director, American Intellectual Property Law Association; Co-Chair, annual patent litigation program, Practicing Law Institute.

Career: Former law clerk, US Court of Customs and Patent Appeals (predecessor of the US Court of Appeals for the Federal Circuit). Court-appointed mediator and arbitrator in disputed patent matters. Adjunct lecturer in patent law at the University of California Los Angeles Law School.

Publications: Editor and co-author of 'Patent Litigation', published by Practicing Law Institute.

Personal: Best Lawyers in America, 1993-2004.

PRINGLE, Paul C

Sidley Austin Brown & Wood LLP, San Francisco 415 772 1249
ppringle@sidley.com
Recommended in Capital Markets

Practice Areas: Paul C Pringle is the Managing Partner for the San Francisco office and practices in corporate securities and REIT transactions. He has worked on a wide range of transactions and served as underwriters' counsel on financings by: Beverly Enterprises, Inc.;

Del Monte Foods Company; Global Marine, Inc.; Hilton Hotels Corporation; KB Home; Nike, Inc.; Occidental Petroleum Corporation; Questar Gas Company; Robert Half International, Inc.; Safeway Inc.; Sempra Energy; Southern California Gas Company; The Walt Disney Company and Wells Fargo & Company. REIT representations include financings by Bedford Property Investors, Inc., BRE Properties, Inc., Health Care Property Investors, Inc. and Nationwide Health Properties, Inc.

Career: The University of Michigan Law School (JD, 1968). Dartmouth College (AB, 1965). Bar Admissions: California, 1972 and New York, 1969.

PRUETZ, Adrian

Quinn Emanuel Urquhart Oliver & Hedges, LLP, Los Angeles 213 443 3000
adrianpruetz@quinnemanuel.com
Recommended in Intellectual Property

Practice Areas: Adrian Pruetz, Co-Chair of Quinn Emanuel's Intellectual Property Litigation Practice. Ms Pruetz concentrates her civil trial practice in the areas of patent, trademark, copyright, trade secret, antitrust and complex commercial matters.

Career: Ms Pruetz has tried more than 25 jury cases and argued more than 15 appeals. She has been named one of the top 25 intellectual property lawyers in California and one of the state's most influential trial lawyers by The Daily Journal, a 'Super Lawyer' by the Los Angeles Magazine and one of five "highly recommended intellectual property practitioners in Los Angeles" by Global Counsel.

Personal: Marquette University Law School (JD magna cum laude, 1982); Loyola Graduate School of Business (1972-73); Loyola University of Chicago (BA, 1972); University of Wisconsin (1966-69).

QUINN, John

Arnold & Porter LLP, Los Angeles 213 243 4080
John.J.Quinn@aporter.com
Recommended in Litigation

Practice Areas: Specializes in complex litigation.

Prof. Memberships: He has been a Fellow of the American College of Trial Lawyers since 1977.

Career: He is a former President of the Los Angeles County Bar Association and the recipient of the Association's highest honor, the Shattuck-Price Award, for outstanding achievement in the practice of law. He has also received the Learned Hand Award from the American Jewish Committee, the Distinguished Service Award presented by the United States Courts of the Ninth Circuit and the Legal Hero Award from the Pepperdine University School of Law.

Personal: He is a 1959 graduate of the University of Southern California Law

Center, where he was a member of the Editorial Board of the 'Law Review' and received the Order of the Coif.

QUINN, John B

Quinn Emanuel Urquhart Oliver & Hedges, LLP, Los Angeles 213 443 3000
johnquinn@quinnemanuel.com
Recommended in Litigation, Media & Entertainment

Practice Areas: Managing Partner, Quinn Emanuel Urquhart Oliver & Hedges, LLP. Practice areas include general trial practice, intellectual property litigation, antitrust and unfair competition litigation, banking and financial institution litigation, real estate litigation, entertainment litigation, securities and class action litigation. Practices in all areas of business litigation.

Prof. Memberships: Lecturer, J Reuben Clark School of Law, Brigham Young University, 1977. Lecturer on Federal Practice, California Continuing Education of the Bar. Member, Los Angeles County Bar Association. Member, Federal Courts and Practices Committee. Member, American Bar Association. Member, Forum Committees on: Health Law; Construction Industry. Member, Sections on: Corporations; Public Contract Law; Banking and Business Law; Litigation; Patent, Trademark and Copyright Law. Member, The State Bar of California. Member, Committee on Federal Courts. Member, The State Bar of New York. Member, Million Dollar Advocates Forum. Director, Rose Bowl Operating Company. General Counsel, Academy of Motion Picture Arts and Sciences, 1987-present.

Career: Notable litigation resolutions: won an $295 million verdict against Bertelsmann and its former CEO on breach of contract and other claims arising out of formation of the AOL Europe joint venture. Lead trial lawyer for General Motors in its lawsuit in federal court in Detroit against Volkswagen arising out of the departure of Ignacio Lopez. General Motors received $1.1 billion in settlement. Won an $80 million verdict on behalf of Avery Dennison in theft of trade secrets and RICO case in federal court in Cleveland. Won a defense verdict after a three-month jury trial in action arising out of the sale of a subsidiary of a major defense contractor in which $20 million was at issue. Obtained a defense verdict after a two-month jury trial on behalf of a Fortune 200 company in a trade secret and unfair competition action brought by its major competitor. Obtained a jury verdict for a hospital management company in a race discrimination suit in what was the longest employment trial in California history after plaintiff rejected a $1 million settlement offer. Obtained a defense verdict for an aerospace company in a whistleblower suit after a two-month jury trial. Obtained a defense verdict for an entertainment company in a highly publicized sexual harassment suit. Was successful lead defense trial lawyer for an aerospace company in the retrial of a tortious interference suit in which the plaintiff had won $15 million in the previous trial and had rejected a $1 million settlement offer before the second trial. Obtained summary judgment on behalf of an aerospace company in an action for breach of an alleged joint venture agreement.

Personal: Harvard Law School (JD, 1976). Editor, Harvard Law Review, 1974-76. Claremont Men's College (BA, magna cum laude, 1973). Since 1987, Mr Quinn has been General Counsel of the Academy of Motion Picture Arts and Sciences. Finisher, Ironman Triathlon World Championship, Kailua Kona, Hawaii, 1999 & 2004.

RABINOVITZ, Joel
Irell & Manella LLP, Los Angeles
310 277 1010
Recommended in Tax

RADCLIFFE, Mark F
DLA Piper Rudnick Gray Cary US LLP, Palo Alto 650 833 2266
mark.radcliffe@dlapiper.com
Recommended in IT Outsourcing
Practice Areas: Banking and finance; outsourcing.
Career: He concentrates in strategic intellectual property advice; private financing; corporate partnering; software licensing; internet licensing; and copyrights and trademark.
Personal: JD, Harvard University; BS, University of Michigan.

RAMER, Bruce
Gang Tyre Ramer & Brown, Beverly Hills
310 777 4800
Recommended in Media & Entertainment

RANDALL, Jeff G
Skadden, Arps, Slate, Meagher & Flom LLP & Affiliates, Palo Alto
650 470 4580
jrandall@skadden.com
Recommended in Intellectual Property
Practice Areas: Has a national litigation practice that spans all areas of intellectual property, with an emphasis on patent litigation. Has served as lead counsel in significant patent cases throughout the country, including several in Delaware, Texas, Virginia, New York and California. Represented a wide range of technology companies, including industry leaders in the areas of cellular phones and infrastructure, speech coding and processing, graphics chips, microprocessors, personal computers, database software and servers, e-commerce and online auctions, enterprise software, CAD software and semiconductor manufacturing equipment.
Career: JD, University of California, Hastings College of Law, 1987; BS, University of Oregon, 1984.

REAMER, David C
Skadden, Arps, Slate, Meagher & Flom LLP & Affiliates, Los Angeles
213 687 5052
dreamer@skadden.com
Recommended in Banking & Finance
Practice Areas: A member of the firm's Banking and Institutional Investing Group. Has participated in numerous financing transactions, representing lenders, investors, borrowers and equity sponsors in a wide range of transactions encompassing a diversity of industries, including media, telecommunications, real estate, gaming, energy and manufacturing. Such transactions have included secured lending transactions, acquisition financings, high-yield offerings, bridge financings, restructurings and project financings.
Career: JD, Columbia University School of Law, 1989 (Harlan Fiske Stone Scholar); BA, Emory University, 1985.

REIMER, Eric R
McDermott Will & Emery, Los Angeles
310 551 9358
ereimer@mwe.com
Recommended in Banking & Finance
Practice Areas: Vice-Chair of McDermott's Finance Practice and Head of Project Finance Practice. Practice includes representation of borrowers, issuers and lenders in front end lending transactions, bridge facilities, acquisition facilities, debt issuances and restructurings, including the financing of debtors in bankruptcy, ranging from low middle market asset-based transactions to investment grade syndicated financings to private bank, high net-worth individual financings, leveraged leases and project financings, with particular experience in healthcare, retail equipment and transportation. Represents opportunity and investment funds in the acquisition and restructuring of debt and credit facilities and the ongoing general representation of portfolio companies of such funds. Eric also has substantial expertise in the liquidation of assets, including real and personal property foreclosures.
Prof. Memberships: Former Member of California State Bar Uniform Commercial Code drafting committee, and Chairman of the Article 2A subcommittee and member of the Revised Article 9 drafting subcommittee, and former program Chair of the Los Angles County Bar Association Commercial Law Committee.
Personal: JD, 1987 from University of California Hastings College of Law, and BS business administration, 1983 from University of Southern California. Admitted to practice in California, New York and Washington, DC.

REINES, Edward R
Weil, Gotshal & Manges LLP, Redwood Shores 650 802 3022
edward.reines@weil.com
Recommended in Intellectual Property

Practice Areas: Patent litigation.
Career: Extensive experience in complex, high-technology patent cases for companies including Intel, Cisco, Yahoo!, and Oracle. Secretary, Federal Circuit Bar Association. The Federal Circuit is the nation's highest patent court. Teaches patent litigation at University of California (Berkeley), the country's top I.P. program. Representative cases: US v California Institute Of Technology (lead trial counsel, dispute over patent ownership of fundamental DNA sequencing technology)(2004); Applera v MJ Research (trial counsel, patent litigation involving Nobel Prize-winning PCR technology; $20 million verdict)(2004); Techsearch v Intel (California defense win of the year for 2002).
Personal: Columbia University, JD with honors.

RESSLER, Alison S
Sullivan & Cromwell LLP, Los Angeles
310 712 6600
resslera@sullcrom.com
Recommended in Capital Markets
Practice Areas: Broad experience in M&A, corporate finance, and private equity investments in regulated and unregulated industries. Corporate finance experience includes complex transactions involving secured and unsecured equity and debt securities, such as principal equity investments, acquisition financing, equity and debt securities offerings for real estate investment trusts, rights offerings, and offerings of convertible and exchangeable securities. Also has worked on IPOs for diverse companies, including Asia Global Crossing, Exelixis, Tibco Software, Korn/Ferry International, Microsoft and Spieker Properties. Advised on multiple offerings for Chiron Corporation, Tenet Healthcare and Western Wireless, and significant offerings by Mission Energy and Sunstone Hotel Investors.
Prof. Memberships: ABA; CSBA; LACBA.
Career: Partner since 1991. Member, Management Committee; Co-Head, Private Equity Group.
Personal: Columbia Law School (JD, 1983); Brown University (BA, 1980).

RIOS RODRIGUEZ, Denise
Foley & Lardner, Los Angeles
310 975 7798
drodriguez@foley.com
Recommended in Healthcare
Career: Denise Rios Rodriguez is a Partner in Foley & Lardner's Los Angeles office. A member of the firm's Health Law Department, Ms Rodriguez serves as Co-Chair of the Payments/Compliance Practice Group. Her practice focuses on payment issues arising under government programs such as Medicare and Medicaid. She represents public and private healthcare providers in administrative hearings, and state and federal courts, and counsels clients on health-

related laws and regulations, and the complexities of federal, state and local healthcare funding. She is a graduate of the University of Michigan Law School (JD cum laude, 1979).

RISHWAIN, James
Pillsbury Winthrop LLP, Los Angeles
310 203 1111
jrishwain@pillsburywinthrop.com
Recommended in Real Estate
Practice Areas: Leader of firm's Global Real Estate Practice; co-managed the Century City office from 2001 through 2004; and Member of the Partner Compensation Committee. His practice has emphasis in real estate matters including acquisitions, development, finance, CMBS, capital markets, ground leases, leasing, exchanges, syndications, REITs, tax exempt bond, synthetic leases and participating mortgages, involving multi-family complexes, corporate headquarters, development sites, golf courses, hotels, industrial parks, office buildings, schools, residential developments, shopping centers and wineries. In 2005, he received California Lawyer Attorneys of the Year Award and was recognized by Chambers USA. In 2004, he was named one of California's 'Super Lawyers.' In 2001, California Law Business profiled him as a 'Mistmaker.'
Career: Member of the ABA, California Bar Association, LA County Bar Association, an Advisory Board to Los Angeles City Council, Century City Chamber of Commerce, ULI, CASH, and BOMA Board.
Publications: Publications include editor - Pillsbury Winthrop LLP's on Real Estate; and author - 'Protecting Possession: Subtenants Need to Know Their Rights in the Event of a Sublandlord's Bankruptcy,' Commercial Investment Real Estate, July/August 2004.
Personal: JD, Pepperdine, 1984, cum laude, Moot Court Honor Board, Note Comment Editor Pepperdine Law Review; BA, UCLA, 1981, honors.

RIZZI, Robert
O'Melveny & Myers LLP,
Washington, DC 202 383 5300
Recommended in Tax

ROCKETT, James
Bingham McCutchen LLP,
San Francisco 415 393 2000
Recommended in Banking & Finance

ROMAN, Marissa J
Akin Gump Strauss Hauer & Feld LLP, Los Angeles 310 552 6408
mroman@akingump.com
Recommended in Media & Entertainment
Practice Areas: Marissa J Román concentrates on media finance and other entertainment transactions. She represents domestic and foreign financial institutions, borrowers, distributors and others involved in various aspects of the financing, distribution and production

of film and television projects, including multinational tax and co-production arrangements.

Prof. Memberships: Co-Chair, Entertainment Law Section, Beverly Hills Bar Association.

Personal: AB, Art History, Princeton University; JD, Stanford Law School. Named a 2004 Southern California Super Lawyer in Entertainment and Media area.

ROOT JR, George L

Foley & Lardner, San Diego
619 685 6412
groot@foley.com
Recommended in Healthcare

Career: George L (Jody) Root Jr is Chair of Foley & Lardner's Health Law Department. Mr Root represents healthcare providers throughout the United States, especially in the formation of integrated delivery systems, nonprofit organizations, healthcare districts, medical staff relations, mental health law, provider relationships with third-party payors and implementation of prepaid health plans. He forms and represents health maintenance organizations, structures integrated delivery systems, and advises physicians and hospitals on how to react to the changing healthcare environment. Mr Root is general counsel to several general acute care and specialty hospitals, including Children's Hospital-San Diego.

ROSATI, Mario

Wilson Sonsini Goodrich & Rosati, Palo Alto 650 493 9300
mrosati@wsgr.com
Recommended in Corporate/M&A

Practice Areas: Corporate law and governance, corporate finance and M&A for high technology and life sciences companies.

Prof. Memberships: Admitted to practice in California.

Career: Joined WSGR, 1971; became Partner, 1975. Member, WSGR Executive Management Committee and Policy Committee. Adjunct Professor, Haas School of Business, University of California (Berkeley). Serves on Board of Advisors for the Lester Center for Entrepreneurship and Innovation.

Personal: JD, Boalt Hall, University of California (Berkeley), 1971. Recipient of Am Jur Award (Corporations). BA, University of California (Los Angeles), 1968.

ROSCH, Tom

Latham & Watkins LLP, San Francisco
415 391 0600
Recommended in Antitrust

ROSE, Stephen

Munger, Tolles & Olson LLP,
Los Angeles 213 683 9100
Recommended in Tax

ROSEGAY, Margaret

Pillsbury Winthrop LLP, San Francisco
415 983 1305
mrosegay@pillsburywinthrop.com

Recommended in Environment

Practice Areas: Ms Rosegay is a Partner in the Environment, Land Use and Natural Resources Group. Her practice focuses on the regulation of solid and hazardous waste and water quality matters, including NPDES permitting and other Clean Water Act issues relating to industrial discharges, discharges of waste to land, and soil and groundwater contamination, with particular expertise in interrelationships between federal, state and local laws. She represents a broad spectrum of companies engaged in petroleum exploration, production and refining, chemical and heavy manufacturing, commercial hazardous waste management, scrap metal recycling, electricity generation and other forms of energy production and commercial redevelopment. Types of matters handled include all aspects of compliance counseling, major project permitting, permit appeals, defense of administrative and judicial enforcement actions, negotiated settlements and mediations, contract negotiations and legislative and regulatory development.

Career: Admitted to practice: State of California. Registered lobbyist.

Publications: California Hazardous Waste Management (1998, 7th ed, CEI Publications).

Personal: JD, University of Colorado School of Law 1980; Clerk, Colorado Court of Appeals, 1980-81.

ROSEN, Peter

Latham & Watkins LLP, Los Angeles
213 485 1234
Recommended in Insurance

ROSENBAUM, Gary B

Winston & Strawn, Los Angeles
213 615 1827
grosenbaum@winston.com
Recommended in Banking & Finance

Practice Areas: Gary Rosenbaum concentrates his practice in commercial and corporate finance, private equity and mezzanine investments, workouts and restructurings, venture lending and leasing, and other commercial transactions.

Career: Extensive experience serving as lead counsel for various financial institutions on leveraged finance transactions, including senior and subordinated loans, debtor-in-possession financings, acquisition financings, and troubled loan negotiations and workouts, as well as representing borrowers in secured loan transactions, creditors and debtors in Chapter 11 cases, and buyers and sellers of distressed companies.

Personal: Northwestern University, BA, 1984; UCLA School of Law, JD, 1987, Board of Editors, UCLA Law Review.

ROSENFELD, Robert

Heller Ehrman LLP, San Francisco
415 772 6000
Recommended in Antitrust

ROSS, Jerry W

Pillsbury Winthrop LLP, San Francisco
415-983-1988
jerry.w.ross@pillsburywinthrop.com
Recommended in Environment

Practice Areas: Mr Ross has handled numerous complex groundwater matters at both the administrative and trial court level. Includes significant cost recovery action, challenges to government clean up orders and basic liability issues involving piercing the corporate veil issues. Mr Ross has defended over 50 government enforcement actions related to alleged environmental violations. These enforcement proceedings have involved both litigation and administrative adjudications related to federal and state clean water laws and to hazardous waste laws. Mr Ross has been deeply involved in the various administrative and litigation activities that have forged the current structure of the regulatory programs under the Clean Water Act, Safe Drinking Water Act and Resource Conservation and Recovery Act. Mr Ross has extensive experience handling environmental issues associated with mergers and acquisitions. He also has extensive experience handling individual property divestitures and acquisitions.

Prof. Memberships: Admitted to practice: State of California, State of Texas.

Career: Mr Ross has been practicing environmental law since 1978. Mr Ross co-leads the firm's Global Energy Industry Team.

Personal: JD, University of Notre Dame Law School, 1978; MS, University of Notre Dame, 1977; BS, Stanford University, 1973.

RUBALCAVA, Sharon

Weston Benshoof Rochefort Rubalcava MacCuish LLP, Los Angeles
213 576 1105
srubalcava@wbcounsel.com
Recommended in Environment

Practice Areas: Partner, Environmental Strategy and Litigation Department. Ms Rubalcava focuses on air and water quality, toxic emissions, and permitting of major industrial and infrastructure projects. Her practice includes counseling on rulemaking, compliance, permitting, and enforcement actions before a variety of environmental agencies. Ms Rubalcava was appointed by the Mayor of Los Angeles to the No Net Increase Task Force to reduce emissions from the Port of Los Angeles.

Career: Past Chair, Air Quality Committee, ABA Section on Natural Resources, Energy and Environmental Law.

Personal: JD, University of California, Los Angeles, 1975; AB, University of California, Los Angeles, 1968.

RUBY, Allen

Ruby & Schofield, San José
408 998 8500
Recommended in Litigation

RUCK, Charles

Latham & Watkins LLP, Costa Mesa
714 540 1235
Recommended in Corporate/M&A

RUST, Neil

White & Case LLP, Los Angeles
213 620 7748
nrust@whitecase.com
Recommended in Banking & Finance

Practice Areas: Banking and finance.

Career: Mr Rust has a broad transactional practice that emphasizes bank finance, corporate finance and M&A. Although he has a broad finance practice, representing agent banks and arrangers in secured and unsecured credit facilities, Rust is best known for expertise in credit and liquidity support facilities for governmental issuers. Rust was most recently honored as 'Dealmaker of the Year' from American Lawyer, for his representation of lenders in the issuance by the State of California of its US$3 billion aggregate principal amount of 2003-04 Revenue Anticipation Notes (RANs). Rust heads the LA office Corporate Practice.

RUTHBERG, Miles

Latham & Watkins LLP, Los Angeles
213 485 1234
Recommended in Litigation

RUTTER, Paul

Gilchrist & Rutter Professional Corporation, Santa Monica 310 393 4000
Recommended in Real Estate

SACKS, Robert A

Sullivan & Cromwell LLP, Los Angeles
310 712 6640
sacksr@sullcrom.com
Recommended in Litigation

Practice Areas: Extensive experience in a wide range of complex business disputes. Defends and advises clients in securities, M&A, antitrust, intellectual property, and class action litigation; board of director obligations; and SEC and internal corporate investigations. Appears in federal and state courts throughout California and elsewhere, in administrative proceedings before the SEC and other agencies, and in arbitrations and other types of private dispute resolution proceedings.

Prof. Memberships: ABA; LACBA; BHBA.

Career: Partner since 1990.

Personal: University of Texas Law School (JD, 1982); Harvard University (AB, 1979).

SAGER, Kelli L

Davis Wright Tremaine LLP,
Los Angeles 213 633 6821
kellisager@dwt.com
Recommended in Media & Entertainment

Practice Areas: Partner, media, entertainment, and First Amendment law, including defamation, privacy, copyright, access, shield laws. Twenty years' litigation experience representing televi-

sion networks, radio stations, studios, newspapers, authors, publishers and magazines. Clients include New York Times, Los Angeles Times, E! Entertainment Television, Paramount Pictures, MTV Networks. Represented media in high profile trials, including OJ Simpson and Winona Ryder.
Career: Among 'Top 50 Women Litigators', 'National Law Journal', December 2001. Among '100 Most Influential Lawyers in California', 'Los Angeles Daily Journal', 1998-1999; 2001-2004. Joined as Partner, 1994.
Personal: JD, (cum laude), Utah School of Law, 1985. BA, West Georgia College, 1981.

SAGGESE, Nicholas P
Skadden, Arps, Slate, Meagher & Flom LLP & Affiliates, Los Angeles
213 687 5550
nsaggese@skadden.com
Recommended in Capital Markets, Corporate/M&A
Practice Areas: Has been involved with numerous mergers and acquisitions, securities offerings and corporate restructurings. Examples of recent transactions include: Vulcan Energy Corporation's acquisition of Plains Resources Inc., the sale of Hotwire.com by Texas Pacific Group, UnitedGlobalCom Inc.'s acquisition of the minority shares of UGC Europe; and the acquisition of PETCO Animal Supplies by Leonard Green & Partners and Texas Pacific Group. Also advised on the IPOs of DreamWorks Animation SKG, Inc., Herbalife International, Inc. and FTD Group, Inc., the initial listing of UGC Europe as a NASDAQ national markets security and numerous high-yield bond offerings.
Prof. Memberships: Board member for LA Regional Foodbank and Member, Board of Overseers, Loyola Law School.
Career: JD, Loyola Law School of Los Angeles, 1980 (cum laude; Member, Loyola Law Review, St. Thomas More Law Honor Society); MBA, University of California at Los Angeles, 1973 (Beta Gamma Sigma Honor Society); BA, University of California at Los Angeles, 1969.

SAMUELS, Mark
O'Melveny & Myers LLP, Los Angeles
213 430 6000
Recommended in Intellectual Property

SANCHEZ, Carl R
Paul, Hastings, Janofsky & Walker LLP, San Diego 858 720 2810
carlsanchez@paulhastings.com
Recommended in Corporate/M&A
Practice Areas: Mr Carl R Sanchez is a Partner in the firm's Corporate Department and is the Chair of the Firm's Global Mergers & Acquisitions Practice Group. Mr Sanchez's practice is focused exclusively in the area of mergers and acquisitions, where he represents public and private companies in a wide variety

of strategic transactions. Mr Sanchez has represented numerous companies in the life sciences, biotechnology, medical device, semiconductor, software, computer hardware, information technology, telecommunications and financial services industries. Mr Sanchez is a frequent lecturer and speaker on M&A topics across the country.

SAPER, Jeff
Wilson Sonsini Goodrich & Rosati, Palo Alto 650 493 9300
jsaper@wsgr.com
Recommended in Capital Markets, Corporate/M&A
Practice Areas: Corporate Law and Governance. Also specializes in public and private financings of high technology, telecommunications and retail and consumer products companies; corporate partnership transactions; representation of investment banks and corporate issuers in connection with public offerings, mergers and acquisitions.
Prof. Memberships: Admitted to practice in New York and California.
Career: Joined WSGR as Partner, 1980. Member, WSGR, Executive Management Committee and Policy Committee. Represents over 20 public companies, numerous private companies and several leading investment banks and venture capital funds. Has managed more than 100 public offerings.
Personal: JD, 1974 and BA (summa cum laude), 1968, New York University.

SAVIKAS, Victor G
Jones Day, Los Angeles
213 243 2451
vgsavikas@jonesday.com
Recommended in Intellectual Property
Practice Areas: Specializes in handling patent litigation, disputes relating to patents and data rights in government contracts, and professional liability litigation.
Prof. Memberships: Fellow of the American College of Trial Lawyers. Member of the ABA; Illinois State Bar Association; Los Angeles County Bar Association; Los Angeles Intellectual Property Law Association, and the Federal Circuit Bar Association.
Publications: He has published and contributed articles dealing with evidence, civil procedure, patent litigation, and the liability of accountants and corporate directors and officers to the Chicago Bar Record, the Illinois Institute of Continuing Legal Education, and The National Law Journal.

SAX, Paul
Orrick, Herrington & Sutcliffe LLP, San Francisco 415 392 1122
Recommended in Tax

SAXE, Deborah
Heller Ehrman White & McAuliffe LLP, Los Angeles 213 689 0200
Recommended in Employment

SCHECHTER, Lori
Morrison & Foerster LLP, San Francisco
415 268 6355
lschechter@mofo.com
Recommended in Litigation
Practice Areas: Handles federal, state, and multidistrict class action cases involving antitrust and unfair competition claims, privacy, and false advertising, as well as other complex litigation. Also represents clients in investigations and actions brought by government officials, including the FTC, various state Attorneys General and state District Attorneys.
Career: Admitted to practice in California. In 2001, named one of the country's 'Top 50 Female Litigators' by the National Law Journal and selected by California Law Business as one of their 'Top 20 under 40 California Lawyers.' Currently Chair, Firmwide Litigation Department.
Personal: BA, Cornell University, 1983; JD, Yale University, 1987.

SCHMALL, Deborah
Farella Braun & Martel LLP, San Francisco 415 954 4400
Recommended in Environment

SCHUCHARD, Robert L
Sonnenschein Nath & Rosenthal, Los Angeles 213 892 5075
rschuchard@sonnenschein.com
Recommended in Healthcare
Practice Areas: Handles general business, M&A, contract and financing matters. His transactional and commercial practice includes private and public companies in various industries including healthcare, equipment maintenance and other service businesses. General corporate and commercial matters, include loans, employment contracts, negotiating agreements for computer and telephone systems, equipment and real property sales and leases, commercial joint ventures and structuring and negotiating limited partnerships and limited liability companies.
Prof. Memberships: Past Chair, California State Bar Committee on Revision of the Nonprofit Corporation Law.
Personal: Santa Clara University Law School, JD, Business Editor, Santa Clara Law Review; Stanford University, BA Political Science.

SCHUCK, Edwin
McDermott Will & Emery, Los Angeles
310 551 9307
eschuck@mwe.com
Recommended in Tax
Practice Areas: Concentrates on corporate, finance, partnership, real estate, executive compensation and international taxation and federal, state and local tax controversies. Has experience in tax-oriented transactional work, such as M&As, public offerings, joint ventures and alliances, start-ups, leveraged leases, project finance, real estate deals, entertainment projects, cross-border

transactions, work-outs, minerals, oil and gas, employee stock ownership plans and financial products.
Prof. Memberships: Member of Tax Sections of the American Bar Association, International Fiscal Association, International Bar Association, and Los Angeles County and California State Bars. Has been chair of Taxation Section of Los Angeles County Bar Association and a member of Executive Committee of Taxation Section of California State Bar. Fellow of American College of Tax Counsel and member of Los Angeles Association of Tax Counsel and International Tax Club.
Career: Partner, McDermott Will & Emery; admitted to New York and California Bars; adjunct professor at Golden Gate University School of Taxation and has held lecturer and adjunct professor positions at several other California and graduate tax schools.
Publications: Contributor to publications such as Tax Review, USC Tax Institute, NYU Tax Institute and The Tax Lawyer.
Personal: Earned JD in 1970 from Columbia University School of Law. Earned MBA in 1970 and BS (cum laude) in 1967 from Columbia University.

SCHWARTZ, James R
Manatt Phelps & Phillips LLP, Los Angeles 310 312 4182
jschwartz@manatt.com
Recommended in Healthcare
Practice Areas: Healthcare law focused on advising non-profit organizations on corporate governance, fiduciary duties and officer-director liability issues; on alliances and conversions in the industry, with emphasis on regulated transactions; and matters pertaining to charitable trust law. Co-Chair of the Firm's Healthcare Industry Practice Group. Former California Deputy Attorney General with over 25 years' experience in charitable trust and nonprofit corporation law.
Prof. Memberships: CA Attorney General's Task Force on Charity Care; American Health Lawyers Association; CA Society for Healthcare Attorneys; Legal Framework Work Group.
Career: Partner.
Personal: UC Berkeley, Boalt Hall School of Law, (JD, 1971); UC Berkeley, (AB, 1968).

SCHWARTZ, Robert
O'Melveny & Myers LLP, Los Angeles
310 553 6700
Recommended in Media & Entertainment

SCOTT IV, William
Sheppard, Mullin, Richter & Hampton LLP, Los Angeles 213 620 1780
Recommended in Banking & Finance

SCZUDLO, Paul
Loeb & Loeb LLP, Los Angeles
310 282 2000
Recommended in Tax

SEABOLT, Richard
Hancock Rothert & Bunshoft LLP,
San Francisco 415 981 5550
RLSeabolt@HRBLaw.com
Recommended in Insurance
Practice Areas: Partner in the San
Francisco office, Co-Chair of the firm's
Business Litigation Practice Group.
Extensive experience in complex trials
and appeals arising from commercial
disputes. Has tried to defense verdicts a
number of significant jury trials where
the plaintiffs' financial losses were in
excess of $20 million. He was lead
defense counsel in Aerojet-General
Corp. v Transport, a ten-month, four-
phase trial (two jury phases) conducted
in a specially constructed, converted
auditorium courtroom involving more
than 30 other law firms. After three
months of trial, the jury returned a
unanimous defense verdict, rejecting the
plaintiff's $500 million to $1 billion
claim. The 'National Law Journal' and
the 'California Daily Journal' highlighted the case as among the largest jury trials tried to a defense verdict in 1992. The
California Supreme Court later affirmed
the defense verdict. A later Court of
Appeal opinion confirmed the effect of
the judgment and quoted his closing
argument. Other trial and arbitration
successes include: a three-judge arbitration financial services joint venture dissolution dispute; a preliminary injunction and arbitration involving a national
accounting firm's partnership noncompetition provision; the successful
defense of the construction manager in
an advanced wastewater treatment plant
construction delay dispute; an International Chamber of Commerce-conduct-
ed Indonesian cement plant arbitration,
and Trans-Panama Pipeline construction delays claims. Frequently speaks on
civil litigation topics, including panelist
and law school guest lecturer on evaluating and proving lost profits and other
business damages and panelist on multiple programs on the California Judicial
Council's new Civil Jury Instructions.
Prof. Memberships: Vice-Chair of the
Executive Committee of the Litigation
Section of the State Bar of California,
and Chair of its Technology and the Law
Committee. Member, Board of Governors of the ABTL (Association of Busi-
ness Trial Lawyers). Member, American
Arbitration Association's Large Com-
plex Case Program and Commercial
Arbitration panels. Member, California
Judicial Council Civil Jury Instructions
Advisory Committee.
Career: Admitted in California (1975).
Partner since 1982, after joining the firm
in 1975.
Publications: Author/Editorial Consul-
tant, LexisNexis Matthew Bender Cali-

fornia Pretrial Civil Procedure and Discovery Practice Guide (four volume set,
published September 2003).
Personal: University of Michigan (BGS,
with distinction 1971). University of
California, Hastings College of the Law
(JD, 1975).

SEGEL, Alvin
Irell & Manella LLP, Los Angeles
310 277 1010
Recommended in Corporate/M&A

SEIDEN, Richard
Foley & Lardner, Los Angeles
310 975 7722
rseiden@foley.com
Recommended in Healthcare
Career: Richard F Seiden is a Partner in
Foley & Lardner's Los Angeles office and
a member of the firm's Health Law
Department. His practice focuses on all
aspects of healthcare business counseling, including formation of business
entities, general business and financing
matters, and mergers and acquisitions.
Mr Seiden serves as outside general
counsel to major nonprofit hospital systems, advising and assisting them in the
development of regional integrated
delivery systems that are positioned to
operate in a managed care environment.
Mr Seiden is a graduate of Boalt Hall
School of Law, University of California,
Berkeley (JD, 1974).

SEKA, Georg
Townsend and Townsend and Crew
LLP, San Francisco
415 576 0200
Recommended in Intellectual Property

SENEKER, Carl (Kim)
Morrison & Foerster LLP, San Francisco
415 268 6619
cseneker@mofo.com
Recommended in Real Estate
Practice Areas: Focused on, and with
extensive experience in, commercial real
estate transactions, secured debt restructuring and creditors' rights, environmental law, zoning, and land use regulation. Has appeared before government
agencies relating to real estate developments and industrial projects.
Prof. Memberships: Member and Past
President, American College of Real
Estate Lawyers; Member, American College of Mortgage Attorneys, Anglo-
American Real Property Institute,
Lambda Alpha National Land Economics Society.
Career: Admitted to practice in California.
Personal: AB, Stanford University, 1964;
JD, Boalt Hall School of Law, 1967; edi-
tor in chief, 'California Law Review'. Law
Clerk, Associate Justice William O Dou-
glas, US Supreme Court, (1967-68).

SETTELMAYER, Daniel
Latham & Watkins LLP, Los Angeles
213 485 1234
Recommended in Healthcare

SFREGOLA, Michael F
Gibson, Dunn & Crutcher LLP,
Los Angeles 213 229 7558
msfregola@gibsondunn.com
Recommended in Real Estate
Practice Areas: Extensive experience in
the structuring of the acquisition and
financing of hotel, resort, commercial,
industrial and residential properties,
including multi-jurisdiction and major
portfolio acquisitions from both private
and public sellers in the United States
and Asia. Accomplished tax lawyer, representing domestic and foreign institutional investors, including private equity
funds and REITs, in connection with
structured finance transactions, mergers, divestitures and workouts, as well as
tax planning with respect to real estate
joint ventures.
Personal: JD, University of Southern
California, 1979.

SHANKS, Patricia
Bingham McCutchen LLP, Los Angeles
213 680 4600
Recommended in Environment

SHARF, Jesse
Gibson, Dunn & Crutcher LLP, Los
Angeles
310 552 8512
jsharf@gibsondunn.com
Recommended in Real Estate
Practice Areas: Co-Chair of firmwide
Real Estate Practice. Experience includes
extensive representation of funds and
other investors, lenders and developers
in all areas related to real estate and real
estate finance, including venture formation; financing; loan restructuring and
workouts; commercial development;
acquisition and sale of residential and
commercial properties, master planned
communities, and operating companies;
environmental aspects of real estate
transactions; and acquisition, sale and
financing of loan portfolios.
Publications: Frequent lecturer on
structuring equity ownership (including
preferred equity), financing, and leasing
issues.
Personal: JD, New York University
School of Law, editor, 'Law Review'.

SHENEMAN, Margaret
Winston & Strawn, San Francisco
415 591 1000
Recommended in Bankruptcy

SHERMAN, Steven E
Shearman & Sterling, San Francisco
415 616 1260
sesherman@shearman.com
Recommended in Banking & Finance
Practice Areas: Partner at Shearman &
Sterling specializing in private financing
and bankruptcy. He has spent the
majority of his career representing
financial institutions, as well as corporate clients, in private domestic and offshore debt and equity financing transactions, with a particular emphasis in
secured financings, Chapter 11 bank-

ruptcies and out-of-court reorganizations.
Prof. Memberships: Lecturer on
financings, workouts and reorganizations at numerous PLI programs and
American Bankers Association and California State Bar Association Workshops.
Career: Joined Shearman in 1978 and
became Partner in 1984.
Personal: BS, University of Pennsylvania, Wharton School of Finance (1972);
JD, Georgetown University Law School
(1975)

SHERNOFF, William
Shernoff, Bidart & Darras LLP,
Claremont 909 621 4935
Recommended in Insurance

SHOCKRO, Michael
Latham & Watkins LLP, Los Angeles
213 485 1234
*Recommended in Business Process
Outsourcing, IT Outsourcing*

SHORTZ, Richard
Morgan, Lewis & Bockius LLP,
Los Angeles 213 612 2526
rshortz@morganlewis.com
Recommended in Projects
Practice Areas: Richard Shortz is a
Partner in the Business and Finance
Practice and Co-Chair of the Energy
Finance Group. Mr Shortz practices in
the corporate area with an emphasis on
energy and project finance; corporate
mergers, acquisitions, and other business
combinations; corporate finance; and
general representation of publicly held
companies and corporate securities.
Prof. Memberships: American Bar
Association (Business Law, Natural
Resources, Energy, and Environmental
Law Sections); Los Angeles County Bar
Association (Corporate and Banking,
and Real Property Law Sections).

SHULMAN, Ron
Wilson Sonsini Goodrich & Rosati,
Palo Alto 650 493 9300
rshulman@wsgr.com
Recommended in Intellectual Property
Practice Areas: IP Litigation, focusing
primarily on defending companies
against claims of patent infringement.
Prof. Memberships: Admitted to practice in New York & California.
Career: Joined WSGR as Partner, 1995.
Partner, Fish & Neave, 1981-95. Has represented clients in more than 50 patent
suits throughout the US, and has tried
numerous cases, all of which resulted in
victories for his clients. Most recently,
tried and won a multi-patent jury case
brought by Intel against client, Broadcom Corporation, in the United States
District Court for the District of
Delaware.
Personal: JD, Rutgers Law School, 1981;
BA, Amherst College, 1977.

SIEGEL, David
Irell & Manella LLP, Los Angeles
310 277 1010
Recommended in Litigation

SIEGEL, Robert
O'Melveny & Myers LLP, Los Angeles
213 430 6000
Recommended in Employment

SIMMONS, Richard
Sheppard, Mullin, Richter & Hampton
LLP, Los Angeles
213 620 1780
Recommended in Employment

SIMONS, Laird
Fenwick & West LLP, Mountain View
650 335 7233
lsimons@fenwick.com
Recommended in Corporate/M&A
Practice Areas: Former Chair of firm's
Securities Group and current firm Managing Partner. Focuses on initial public
offerings (for both domestic and foreign
corporations), follow-on offerings for
already public companies and ongoing
securities advice and counseling for
public companies. Has worked on more
than 75 initial public offerings for a wide
range of high technology companies
and more than 25 follow-on offerings
for the same companies. Has represented a number of underwriters in initial
public offerings and follow-on offerings.
Career: Recognized in 1999 by The
American Lawyer as one of 12 'Dealmakers of the Year' and in July 2003 San
Jose Magazine as one of Silicon Valley's
top lawyers.
Personal: Harvard Law School, JD,
1974; Harvard Business School, MBA,
with distinction, 1974; Haverford College, BA, with honors, Phi Beta Kappa,
1970.

SINGER, Andrew
Latham & Watkins LLP, San Diego
619 236 1234
Recommended in Projects

SINGER, Gary
O'Melveny & Myers LLP, Newport
Beach
949 760 9600
Recommended in Corporate/M&A

SINGER, Martin
Lavely & Singer PC, Los Angeles
310 556 3501
*Recommended in Media &
Entertainment*

SINISCALCO, Gary
Orrick, Herrington & Sutcliffe LLP,
San Francisco 415 773 5833
grsiniscalco@orrick.com
Recommended in Employment
Practice Areas: Practice focuses on
class action and complex litigation
defense. Extensive expertise in EEO,
affirmative action, wrongful discharge,
and wage-and-hour matters. Has litigated class actions and individual employment cases before federal and state
courts and administrative agencies for
leading US industrial and technology
companies. Founding Member, National
Employment Law Institute & American
Employment Law Counsel.

Prof. Memberships: College of Labor
and Employment Lawyers: Member
State Bar of California. American Bar
Association's Committees on International Labor Relations and Equal
Employment Opportunity: Past Management Co-Chair, EEO Committee.
National Employment Law Institute:
Advisory Board; American Employment
Law Council; ADR panel member for
the Northern District of California.
Career: Georgetown University Law
Center, JD, 1969. LeMoyne College, BA,
1965.
Publications: 'Employment Class
Action Institute', 2000, Glasser Legal-
Works, co-chair. 'Wrongful Employment Termination Practice', Cal. CEB
1997, contributing author. 'Manager's
Guide to Lawful Terminations', Executive Enterprises, 1983 2d ed. 1991, co-author, 'Sexual Harassment: The Flirtation That Could Cost a Fortune', 6 Emp.
Rel. L.J. 277, 1980. Employment Discrimination Law, BNA 1979, by Schlei
and Grossman, contributing author to
several editions of this widely acclaimed
text.

SINK, Charles
Farella Braun & Martel LLP,
San Francisco 415 954 4400
Recommended in Construction

SMITH, Brian
Heller Ehrman LLP, San Francisco
415 772 6000
Recommended in Real Estate

SMITH, Douglas D
Gibson, Dunn & Crutcher LLP,
San Francisco 415 393 8390
dsmith@gibsondunn.com
Recommended in Corporate/M&A
Practice Areas: Practice covers securities law compliance for public companies, public debt and equity offerings
and mergers and acquisitions. In-depth
experience in the financial services, real
estate, semiconductor and software
businesses. Has led over 200 public
offerings and 50 M&A transactions.
Represented PeopleSoft in its $1.8 billion acquisition of JD Edwards and its
response to the unsolicited offer and
subsequent $10.3 billion sale of company to Oracle.
Publications: Co-Chair, Glasser Legal-
Works Annual Institute on Proxy Statements, Annual Meetings and Disclosure
Documents, 1999-2004.
Personal: JD, Vanderbilt University
School of Law, 1979, member of the
Order of the Coif.

SMITH, Gregory C
Skadden, Arps, Slate, Meagher & Flom
LLP & Affiliates, Palo Alto
650 470 4590
grsmith@skadden.com
Recommended in Corporate/M&A
Practice Areas: Extensive experience in
the areas of mergers and acquisitions,
corporation finance, licensing and part-

nering transactions, and corporate
restructurings. Represents mature and
emerging growth technology and life
science companies in all stages of development, including venture financings,
initial public offerings, and mergers and
acquisitions. Also represents underwriters, financial advisors and venture capitalists, and advises clients involved with
international transactions.
Career: JD, Columbia Law School, 1988
(Harlan Fiske Stone Scholar); BA, Stanford University, 1985 (with distinction;
Phi Beta Kappa).

SMITH, Neil
Howard, Rice, Nemerovski, Canady,
Falk & Rabkin, San Francisco
415 434 1600
Recommended in Intellectual Property

SMITH, Paul T
Davis Wright Tremaine LLP,
San Francisco 415 276 6532
paulsmith@dwt.com
Recommended in Healthcare
Practice Areas: Partner, health law.
Representative experience includes
investigations and administrative prosecutions fraud/abuse and false claims, and
conducting successful appeals of payment denials under Medicare prospective payment system. Numerous corporate, transactional, financing, reimbursement and regulatory matters, including
mergers/affiliations, sales/acquisitions,
and formation of nonprofit and proprietary organizations for acquisition/operation of medical practices. Representative clients: hospitals, healthcare practitioners, medical groups and other
provider organizations.
Prof. Memberships: Member, California State Bar, Healthcare Financial Management Association, California Society
for Healthcare Attorneys and Medical
Group Management Association
Career: Joined firm, 1991; became Partner, 1991.
Personal: LLB (cum laude), University
of Natal School of Law, 1976.

SNYDER, David R
Pillsbury Winthrop LLP, San Diego
619 544 3369
dsnyder@pillsburywinthrop.com
Recommended in Corporate/M&A
Practice Areas: Mr Snyder has been a
practicing attorney for over 30 years,
specializing in corporate finance and
general corporate matters. Mr Snyder's
practice has involved serving as lead
counsel in numerous public offerings of
equity and debt securities, representing
NASDAQ and New York Stock
Exchange public companies in their ongoing SEC reporting obligations and
handling private placement and public
and private merger and acquisition
transactions. He has counseled boards
and special committees of directors in
contested takeovers and in stockholder
litigation in California, Delaware and
federal courts.

Prof. Memberships: Registered Foreign
Lawyer, The Law Society of England and
Wales; Admitted to practice: California.
Career: Mr Snyder has served on the
firm's Managing Board since 1998, and
was elected Executive Vice-Chair of the
firm effective January 1, 2004. Mr Snyder has been a frequent speaker on matters of corporate securities law and has
written annual updates on federal securities law matters for The Business
Lawyer since 1988. He has been profiled
in the last several editions of The Best
Lawyers in America.
Personal: JD, Cornell Law School (with
Distinction; Order of the Coif; Editor,
Cornell Law Review), 1974; BA, Michigan State University (high honors, Phi
Beta Kappa), 1971.

SONSINI, Larry W
Wilson Sonsini Goodrich & Rosati,
Palo Alto 650 493 9300
lsonsini@wsgr.com
Recommended in Corporate/M&A
Practice Areas: Corporate law and
governance; M&A; corporate finance.
Prof. Memberships: Admitted to practice in California.
Career: Chairman of Wilson Sonsini
Goodrich & Rosati. Served as a Member
of the Board of Directors of the New
York Stock Exchange from 2001-03.
Currently the NYSE's Chairman of the
Regulation, Enforcement and Listing
Standards Committee and Chairman of
the Legal Advisory Committee. Director
of the following public companies: Brocade Communications Systems, Echelon, Lattice Semiconductor, LSI Logic,
PIXAR, and Silicon Valley Bancshares.
Personal: JD, Boalt Hall School of Law,
University of California (Berkeley),
1966. AB, University of California
(Berkeley), 1963.

SPIEGEL, John
Munger, Tolles & Olson LLP,
Los Angeles 213 683 9100
Recommended in Litigation

SPIELBERG, David
Stoel Rives LLP, San Francisco
415 617 8900
Recommended in Projects

SPRATLING, Gary
Gibson, Dunn & Crutcher LLP,
San Francisco 415 393 8222
gspratling@gibsondunn.com
Recommended in Antitrust
Practice Areas: Focuses on international antitrust issues. Global expertise
regarding the anti-cartel enforcement
practices of major competition enforcement authority and development of
integrated international strategies in
response thereto. Has guided numerous
successful representations of organizations and individuals facing exposure in
multiple jurisdictions.
Career: Former US Department of Justice prosecutor. Two-time recipient of
the Presidential Rank Award, the highest

honor conferred on federal government executives. Recipient of the Antitrust Lawyer of the Year Award from the State Bar of California. Chair of the Antitrust Section's Task Force Liaison to the International Competition Network Cartel Working Group.

STANTON, W Clark
Davis Wright Tremaine LLP, San Francisco
415 276 6538
clarkstanton@dwt.com
Recommended in Healthcare
Practice Areas: Partner, health law. Representative experience includes medical staff credentialing and peer review issues, confidentiality, HIPAA, patient treatment, consent and quality assurance matters.
Prof. Memberships: Past president, California Society for Healthcare Attorneys. Past chair, Committee on Credentialing and Peer Review, American Health Lawyers Association.
Career: Joined firm as Partner, 1997. Former Partner, Musick, Peeler & Garret, 1984-1997.
Personal: JD, University of Texas, 1974. BA (magna cum laude), Notre Dame, 1968.

STEEL, Michael J
Pillsbury Winthrop LLP, San Francisco
415 983 7320
msteel@pillsburywinthrop.com
Recommended in Environment
Practice Areas: Mr Steel is a Partner in the environment, land use and natural resources practice area. He defends clients in enforcement actions brought by federal, state and local agencies as well as citizens' groups. Mr Steel is particularly well-known for his work in actions involving the Unfair Practices Act and Proposition 65. Mr Steel has defended cases alleging unsafe exposures to toxic chemicals in faucets, fine china, medical devices, building materials, diesel equipment, dietary supplements and numerous other products. He has also defended companies accused of exposing people living near their operations to unsafe emissions of pollutants, working closely with experts in medicine, epidemiology, toxicology, chemical analysis and risk assessment. He has appeared before the US Environmental Protection Agency, the Department of Toxic Substances Control, the Regional Water Quality Control Boards, and state and federal OSHA. He advises a variety of industrial companies regarding cleanups, hazardous substance/waste handling, air and water quality and employee safety. Mr Steel has provided compliance counseling to businesses in the pharmaceutical, biotech, automobile, shipbuilding, oil, electronics and retail sectors.
Career: Admitted to practice: State of California.
Personal: JD, University of California, Hastings College of the Law, 1982; BA,

University of California at Davis, 1977.

STEIN, Laurence
Latham & Watkins LLP, Los Angeles
213 485 1234
Recommended in Tax

STEIN, Stanton 'Larry'
Alschuler Grossman Stein & Kahan LLP, Santa Monica 310 907 1000
Recommended in Media & Entertainment
Practice Areas: Heads the firm's Entertainment Litigation Group, one of the largest in the country emphasizing talent representation. Focuses on film, television, and music, including copyright, trademark, and publicity rights. Renowned for pioneering success in 'vertical integration' lawsuits, representing actors, writers and producers short-changed on profits by media empire self-dealing.
Prof. Memberships: Past President, Public Counsel. Past member, Board of Directors, Bet Tzedek Legal Services. Present member of the board of directors of OPPC (homeless shelter). Present member of the Board of Directors of the Foundation of the State Bar of Carlifornia. Member, Century City, Los Angeles County, and American Bar Associations, Association of Business Trial Lawyers.
Career: A Partner of Alschuler Grossman Stein & Kahan LLP. Adjunct professor at USC School of Law and Distinguished Speaker at Harvard, Yale, Stanford, and Boalt Law Schools. Named 'Entertainment Lawyer of the Year' by the Beverly Hills and Century City Bar Associations. He was ACLU Pro Bono and Civil Liberties Award recipient for 2004. Listed in the Daily Journal (100 Most Influental Lawyers in California). Has been featured in Forbes Magazine, Variety, and on the covers of Los Angeles Magazine and the National Law Journal.
Personal: Adjunct professor of Entertainment Law at University of Southern California; University of Southern California (BA with honors, 1966; JD, 1969). Captain, USC Debate Team, winner of numerous national debate championships. Associate Editor, Southern California Law Review. Moot Court Champion.

STEINBERG, Jonathan
Irell & Manella LLP, Los Angeles
310 277 1010
Recommended in Intellectual Property

STERN, Claude M
Quinn Emanuel Urquhart Oliver & Hedges, LLP, Redwood Shores
650 801 5000
claudestern@quinnemanuel.com
Recommended in Intellectual Property
Practice Areas: Claude M Stern serves as Co-Chair of the firm's National Intellectual Property Litigation Practice. In his 25 years of practice, he has developed extensive experience in business litigation, with an emphasis in intellectual

property, technology and class action litigation. Mr Stern's representative litigation clients include businesses engaged in hardware and semi-conductor manufacture, telecom and telephony, business and consumer software publication and development, venture capital, interactive television, electronic gaming, internet infrastructure products and systems, systems integration, computer/equipment leasing, healthcare, transportation, real estate, and banking.
Personal: University of California Hastings College of Law (JD, 1980); University of California, Los Angeles Los Angeles, California (BA, 1977).

STEUBER, David
Howrey Simon Arnold & White, Los Angeles 213 892 1800
Recommended in Insurance

STEVENS, Charles
Stevens & O'Connell LLP, Sacramento
916 329 9111
Recommended in Litigation

STEVENS, Mark C
Fenwick & West LLP, Mountain View
650 335 7257
mstevens@fenwick.com
Recommended in Corporate/M&A
Practice Areas: Represents companies, ranging from newly formed start-up teams to mature public companies, venture capitalists and investment banks involved in the information technology industries, with particular focus on complex transactions. Has led teams handling merger, acquisition and divestiture transactions with total announced value in excess of $20 billion. Has directed more than 25 initial public offerings and hundreds of strategic alliance transactions, ranging from technology and distribution partnerships to multinational joint venture transactions.
Career: Former Executive Vice-President of Business and Corporate Development at Excite@Home, where he assembled team of 50 deal-making professionals who handled mergers, acquisitions, divestitures, joint ventures and strategic partnerships. Former venture Partner at Granite Global Ventures, late stage fund affiliated with Venrock. Has served on Boards of Directors, including Board of Mercator Software, where he was active in sale of Mercator to Ascential Software.
Personal: Northwestern University School of Law, JD, cum laude, Order of the Coif and Law Review, 1983; Santa Clara University, BS, in mathematics, magna cum laude, 1979.

STORK, Anita
Cooley Godward LLP, San Francisco
415 693 2000
Recommended in Antitrust

STREETER, Jon
Keker & Van Nest LLP, San Francisco
415 391 5400
jbs@kvn.com
Recommended in Intellectual Property
Practice Areas: Complex commercial civil litigation cases including intellectual property, antitrust, securities, banking and energy. He recently obtained a $41 million jury verdict in a breach of contract dispute. Representative clients include, Fresenius USA, Memorex, Oakland Alameda Coliseum Authority, PG&E, Inc., Schlumberger, and Tegal Corporation.
Prof. Memberships: President of the Association of Business Trial Lawyers of Northern California; Member of the Executive Committee of the Edward McFetridge Chapter of the American Inns of Court; Member of the California Senate Commission on the Fair Administration of Justice; Member of the American Law Institute; Member, Ninth Circuit Task Force on Self-Represented Litigants; Chair of Keker & Van Nest's Pro Bono Committee; Former President of the San Francisco Bar Association; Past chair of the Northern District of California Lawyer Representatives to the Ninth Circuit Court of Appeals.
Career: Partner, Keker & Van Nest (1997-present); Orrick, Herrington & Sutcliffe (Partner, 1989-97) (Associate 1981-82, 1983-88); Law Clerk to the Hon Harry T Edwards, United States Court of Appeals for the District of Columbia Circuit (1982-83).
Personal: Boalt Hall School of Law, University of California (JD 1981); Stanford University (AB 1978).

STROMBERG, Ross E
Jones Day, San Francisco
415 875 5724
restromberg@jonesday.com
Recommended in Healthcare
Practice Areas: Chairs the firm's Health Care Specialized Industry Practice. Has extensive national experience representing healthcare field participants in corporate transactions, mergers and acquisitions, integrated delivery system development, hospital/physician integration, managed care, and healthcare-related technology. Recognized in 'The Best Lawyers in America.'
Prof. Memberships: State Bar of California; Bar Association of San Francisco; American Health Lawyers Association; California Society for Healthcare Attorneys. Editorial board member of 'Integrated Health Care Report,' 'Medical Staff Strategy Report,' and 'Hospital Strategy Report.'
Publications: He is a frequent author and lecturer on health and hospital law and has co-authored several books.

SULLIVAN, Peter
Gibson, Dunn & Crutcher LLP,
Los Angeles 213 229 7165
psullivan@gibsondunn.com
Recommended in Antitrust

Practice Areas: Represents US/international clients in civil/criminal litigations (including class actions) as well as governmental investigations concerning cartels, mergers, distribution, pricing, exclusive dealing and all other types of vertical and horizontal arrangements. Matters encompass both jury/non-jury trials and hearings (US federal and state courts, the EC and member states) and counseling.
Publications: Co-author, 'Antitrust Laws and Trade Regulation, Second Edition'. Author, 'Pricing Practices;' 'Distribution Practices;' 'A Guide to Joint Ventures and Other Cooperative Business Endeavors'. Frequent lecturer on competition, unfair competition and class action issues.
Personal: JD, Fordham University Law School, 1977, Articles Editor, 'Law Review'.

SUN, Brian A
Jones Day, Los Angeles
213 243 2858
basun@jonesday.com
Recommended in Litigation

Practice Areas: He has earned a national reputation as a trial lawyer specializing in complex business litigation and white-collar criminal defense. He represents companies and individuals in state and federal courts and before administrative and regulatory agencies. He distinguished himself by testifying before Congress and drafting and pioneering the passage of anti-money laundering legislation while serving at the DOJ. Twice ranked among the '100 Most Influential Lawyers in California.'
Prof. Memberships: Former President of the Southern California Chinese Lawyers Association and the National Asian Pacific American Bar Association. He has served as a lawyer-delegate to the Ninth Circuit Judicial Conference.

SWANSON, Daniel G
Gibson, Dunn & Crutcher LLP,
Los Angeles 213 229 7430
dswanson@gibsondunn.com
Recommended in Antitrust

Practice Areas: Co-Chair of Firm's Antitrust Practice Group since 1996. Specializes in civil and criminal antitrust/competition law and complex business litigation for clients in the US, Europe and Asia.
Prof. Memberships: Co-Chair, ABA Antitrust Section's International Antitrust Committee. International Bar Association.
Career: Has substantial antitrust trial and appellate experience, extensive IP expertise (testified in DOJ-FTC IP/antitrust hearings) and regularly practices in the high-technology, enter-

tainment and communications sectors.
Publications: Author/editor of numerous books, chapters, articles and papers on antitrust law.
Personal: Harvard University; JD, magna cum laude, 1984; MA, 1984; and PhD, 1985.

TANOURY, Mark
Cooley Godward LLP, Palo Alto
650 843 5000
Recommended in Corporate/M&A

TAYLOR, Robert
Howrey Simon Arnold & White,
Menlo Park 650 463 8100
Recommended in Antitrust

TEPLIN, Lawrence
Cox Castle & Nicholson LLP,
Los Angeles 310 277 4222
Recommended in Construction

THOMPSON, Jocelyn Niebur
Weston Benshoof Rochefort Rubalcava
MacCuish LLP, Los Angeles
213 576 1104
jthompson@wbcounsel.com
Recommended in Environment

Practice Areas: Partner, Environmental Strategy and Litigation Department. Ms Thompson has extensive experience in environmental permitting, compliance and auditing, including matters related to air and water quality, CEQA, NEPA, coastal zones, endangered and threatened species, and California's Proposition 65.
Prof. Memberships: American Bar Association; California Bar Association (Environmental Law Section); California Mining Association (Air Quality Committee); Environmental Justice Advisory Group, South Coast Air Quality Management District.
Personal: JD, University of California, Los Angeles, 1982; BA, University of California, Santa Barbara (magna cum laude), 1978.

THOMPSON, Robert
Sheppard, Mullin, Richter & Hampton
LLP, San Francisco 415 434 9100
Recommended in Real Estate

THOMPSON, Tracy
Morgan, Lewis & Bockius LLP,
San Francisco 415 442 1758
tthompson@morganlewis.com
Recommended in Employment

Practice Areas: Tracy Thompson is Senior Counsel in the Labor and Employment Law Practice Group. Ms Thompson counsels and represents employers on all aspects of employment law, including wage and hour, non-compete agreements, trade secrets, regulatory issues, and traditional labor law. Ms Thompson has represented clients under both the National Labor Relations Act and the Railway Labor Act. Ms Thompson has also successfully litigated class actions, multiple plaintiff and collective actions, as well as single plaintiff cases, in both state and federal court.

Prof. Memberships: State Bar of California, American Bar Association, and the San Francisco Bar Association.

THORNTON, Charles
Paul, Hastings, Janofsky & Walker LLP,
San Francisco 415 856 7001
charlesthornton@paulhastings.com
Recommended in Real Estate

Practice Areas: Practice concentrated in real estate and related matters, including joint ventures, complex structures, development, acquisition, leasing and financing.
Prof. Memberships: Authored several articles on corporate and real estate matters. Member - Lambda Alpha; Vice-Chair of the Board - YMCA of San Francisco.
Career: Chair of Real Estate Department in San Francisco office; former Chair of San Francisco and Los Angeles offices.
Personal: AB degree Cornell University; JD degree University of Michigan Law School (1967); assistant editor of the 'Michigan Law Review'.

THUM, Robert
Thelen Reid & Priest LLP, Los Angeles
213 576 8000
Recommended in Construction

THUMANN, Henry
O'Melveny & Myers LLP, Los Angeles
310 553 6700
Recommended in Antitrust

TOLLES, Stephen
Gibson, Dunn & Crutcher LLP,
Los Angeles 213 229 7502
stolles@gibsondunn.com
Recommended in Tax

Practice Areas: Advises clients on a wide variety of corporate tax issues, including taxable stock and asset acquisitions, tax-free reorganizations, leveraged buyouts, liquidations, redemptions, spin-offs, public offerings of stock and debt, publicly traded partnerships, real estate investment trusts, and executive compensation. Substantial experience handling administrative appeals before Internal Revenue Service, California Franchise Tax Board, California State Board of Equalization and United States Tax Court.
Prof. Memberships: Member, Planning Committee, USC Tax Institute. Member, Board of Advisors, Graduate Tax Program, Loyola Law School.
Personal: JD, University of California Law School at Boalt Hall, 1982, Order of the Coif, Member 'Law Review'.

TONSFELDT, Steven
Heller Ehrman White & McAuliffe,
Menlo Park 650 854 4488
Recommended in Corporate/M&A

TOSETTI, Paul
Latham & Watkins LLP, Los Angeles
213 485 1234
Recommended in Corporate/M&A

TOULON, Rik
Katten Muchin Zavis Rosenman,
Los Angeles 310 788 4480
rik.toulon@kmzr.com
Recommended in Media & Entertainment

Practice Areas: Represents institutions and individuals in various transactions in connection with all aspects of the worldwide development, production, financing, promotion, distribution (all media), sale and acquisition of motion pictures, television programming, music videos, video games and other entertainment content, and the exploitation of all related ancillary rights. His broad knowledge of both the legal and business aspects of the entertainment industry allows him to provide clients with specialized services with respect to risk assessments, complex chain-of-title and rights clearance issues, the purchase and sale of literary material, films and other intellectual properties, VOD, international television licensing arrangements and co-productions, and advising on entertainment and media assets in significant M&A transactions. Most recently, he was lead entertainment counsel to NBC in its acquisition of Vivendi Universal Entertainment and to Sony in its acquisition of MGM.
Prof. Memberships: USC Law School - Beverly Hills Bar Association Institute on Entertainment Law and Business.
Career: BA degree in Economics, University of California, Los Angeles, 1990; JD, University of Southern California, 1994.

TRUAX, Tim
Cox Castle & Nicholson LLP,
Los Angeles 310 277 4222
Recommended in Construction

TSATALIS, Marina
Wilson Sonsini Goodrich & Rosati,
Palo Alto 650 493 9300
mtsatalis@wsgr.com
Recommended in Employment

Practice Areas: Counsels employers and litigates cases involving a variety of employment law issues, including employment discrimination, harassment, unfair competition, misappropriation of trade secrets, wrongful termination, contract disputes and fraud.
Prof. Memberships: Admitted to practice law in California, Pennsylvania and New Jersey.
Career: In April 2001, obtained a unanimous published decision from Court of Appeals for the Ninth Circuit recognizing, for the first time, an affirmative defense to employer liability for harassment by a supervisor under California law, Kohler v Inter-Tel Technologies.
Personal: JD, 1992, Harvard Law School (cum laude). BA, 1989, Villanova University (summa cum laude, Phi Beta Kappa).

TUBACH, Michael
O'Melveny & Myers LLP, San Francisco
415 984 8700
Recommended in Antitrust

TUCHIN, Michael L
Klee, Tuchin, Bogdanoff & Stern LLP,
Los Angeles 310 407 4040
mtuchin@ktbslaw.com
Recommended in Bankruptcy
Practice Areas: Is a member and co-manager of Klee, Tuchin, Bogdanoff & Stern LLP. On the debtor side, he currently represents Crescent Jewelers (the largest retailer of fine jewelry in California, with approximately 125 stores) and, as special counsel, American Restaurant Group (the owner of the Stuart Anderson's Black Angus chain of restaurants). He recently represented Samuels Jewelers, Inc. (retailer of fine jewelry operating more than 130 stores), Fountain View, Inc. (operator of more than 50 skilled care nursing and assisted care living facilities) and Frederick's of Hollywood, Inc (world-renowned retailer of innovative specialty apparel operating more than 150 stores, a catalogue, and an internet business) in connection with their highly successful Chapter 11 cases. Out of court, he has led successful restructurings of the Lusk Company (a large California home builder with close to $1 billion in debts), an international giftware manufacturer, an international manufacturer of computer accessories, a national express delivery business, and LA Kings, Ltd. (the then-owner of the Los Angeles Kings hockey franchise). He represents, and has represented, creditors in numerous Chapter 11 cases, including American Rice, Ameriserve, Carmike Theatres, Catapult Entertainment, Chevy's, Edwards Theatres, Fresh Choice, Kmart, Sega Gameworks, Tower Records, United Airlines, and Wherehouse Records. In addition, he represented a large equity holder of the Pittsburgh Penguins hockey team in connection with the Penguins' Chapter 11 case in Pittsburgh, Pennsylvania. He has also represented numerous purchasers of assets (including Viacom, Paramount Pictures, and The Gap). He is the President of the Los Angeles Bankruptcy Forum and a past President and member of the Board of Governors of the Financial Lawyers Conference of Los Angeles.

TULLY, Bradley
Hooper Lundy & Bookman Inc,
Los Angeles 310 551 8111
Recommended in Healthcare

TURNER, Jonathan
Epstein, Turner & Song, Los Angeles
323 634 5566
Recommended in Employment

TURNER III, Glenn E
Gibbs, Giden, Locher & Turner,
Los Angeles 310 552 3400
gturner@gglt.com
Recommended in Construction
Practice Areas: Glenn Turner is a Senior Partner of the Los Angeles and Las Vegas law firm of Gibbs, Giden, Locher & Turner which specializes in the representation of prime contractors, owners, subcontractors, design professionals and all others active in the construction industry. Mr Turner specializes in trials and arbitations of major construction disputes involving delay, disruption, extra work claims, lost productivity and abandonment of contract. Mr Turner has both prosecuted and defended major construction claims.
Prof. Memberships: Mr Turner is a member of the Los Angeles County Bar Association.
Career: Mr Turner has practiced law with his firm for over 25 years.
Publications: Mr Turner has authored numerous articles for construction industry trade publications and has conducted numerous seminars for industry and legal professionals on a broad range of construction related topics from contract intrepretation and extra work claims to mechanics liens and statutory remedies.
Personal: Mr Turner holds BS and MBA degrees from Arizona State University (1975 and 1977) and a Juris Doctorate from Pepperdine University (1980).

ULMAN, Lawrence
Gibson, Dunn & Crutcher LLP,
Los Angeles 310 551 8794
lulman@gibsondunn.com
Recommended in Media & Entertainment
Practice Areas: Co-Chair of firm's Entertainment Practice Group. Specializes in entertainment finance with significant experience representing film studios in their distribution and financial matters, including negotiating and documenting tax advantaged transactions, domestic and foreign film rights acquisitions, loan and lending arrangements, library acquisitions and sales, and negotiating output arrangements for films and television. Representative clients include Universal Pictures, New Line Cinema, Twentieth Century Fox, Miramax, Ideenkapital Media Finance AG, and Constantin Film AG.
Career: Serves as an adjunct professor at the University of Southern California School of Cinema and Television.
Personal: JD, University of Southern California School of Law, 1975.

URQUHART, A William
Quinn Emanuel Urquhart Oliver & Hedges, LLP, Los Angeles
213 443 3000
billurquhart@quinnemanuel.com
Recommended in Litigation
Practice Areas: Mr Urquhart specializes in complex business litigation. Practice areas include class action litigation, securities litigation, antitrust and trade regulation litigation, intellectual property litigation, banking and financial institution litigation, entertainment litigation, domestic and international arbitration and mediation, energy litigation.
Prof. Memberships: Speaker/Lecturer, Price Waterhouse Intellectual Property Forum; University of Southern California Business Forum; Various PLI Seminars on Complex Business Litigation. Member, American Bar Association including Committees on: Class Action and Derivative Suits; Securities Litigation; Sections on: Patent, Trademark and Copyright Law; Antitrust Law; Public Contract Law; Litigation. Member, The State Bar of California including Sections on: Intellectual Property; Litigation. Member, The State Bar of New York.
Career: Mr Urquhart specializes in complex business litigation. These matters range from class actions to theft of trade secrets cases. He has been named 'One of California's Most Successful Business Lawyers' by California Law Business, named 'One of the Most Influential Attorneys in California' by The Los Angeles Daily Journal and listed as one of the world's leading litigators in the Euromoney Guide to the World's Leading International Law Firms, repeatedly named a 'Super Lawyer' by Los Angeles Magazine. Notable litigation resolutions: obtained a $120+ million award for an aerospace company in a breach of contract/misappropriation of trade secret matter before London Court of International Arbitration. Resolved seven class actions for a major financial institution, with no cost for settlement or judgment. Obtained dismissal of 27 class actions filed against Northrop-Grumman arising out of the failure of Northrop's merger with Lockheed to close. Tried and won two class actions involving allegations of race discrimination. Obtained an injunction barring the allocation of losses as a result of defaults by major California utilities. Obtained summary judgment in a class action, the appeal of which established the California rule limiting bondholders' rights to those provided by contract. Obtained settlements of several shareholder derivative actions at no cost to company or directors. Obtained $152 million settlement for a Zurich subsidiary claiming fraud in connection with the sale of an insurance company. Obtained a $25 million settlement for a manufacturing company after court granted judgment based on a finding of literal infringement of two patents. Obtained dismissal of a $40 million breach of warranty lawsuit against IBM and obtained a $25 million judgment on a counterclaim. Obtained dismissal of a $100 million suit against an entertainment company in which plaintiff alleged the company stole trade secrets regarding computerized animation. Obtained a $6.5 million verdict for a manufacturer in a dispute concerning post-closing adjustments following the sale of a business. Obtained a defense verdict for a mortgage lender in a Lanham Act passing off suit. Obtained a $20+ million settlement of a misappropriation of trade secrets case after obtaining a preliminary injunction. Both obtained and resisted temporary restraining orders and preliminary injunctions in numerous cases involving recruitment of employees by competitors. Obtained favorable settlements in a number of multi-million dollar business disputes without resort to litigation or arbitration.
Personal: Fordham Law School (JD, cum laude, 1977). Member, Fordham Law Review. Fordham College (BA, 1969).

VAN NEST, Robert
Keker & Van Nest LLP, San Francisco
415 391 5400
rvn@kvn.com
Recommended in Intellectual Property, Litigation
Practice Areas: Practice ranges widely over the field of complex business litigation, and white-collar crime. He has tried cases involving patent infringement, securities fraud, trademarks, commercial contracts, RICO, partnership disputes, real estate, insurance bad faith, mail and wire fraud, and others. Representative clients include American Honda Motor Company, AT&T Wireless Services, Inc., Genentech, Inc., Intel Corporation, LSI Logic Corp., Pacific Gas & Electric and Xilinx, Inc.
Prof. Memberships: Served on the faculties of the Hastings College of Advocacy, the National Institute for Trial Advocacy and the Sedona Conference on Patent Litigation and has been a Lecturer in Developments in Tort Practice for the California Continuing Education of the Bar since 1985. He recently served as a member of the State Bar Commission on Mandatory Continuing Legal Education. Former director of the Association of Business Trial Lawyers (1992-2000) and chairs the Development Committee of Bay Area Legal Aid (1995-present).
Career: Law clerk to the Honorable William H Orrick in the Northern District of California (1978-79); joined Keker & Brockett, 1979; Partner since 1982.
Personal: Harvard Law School (JD, magna cum laude, 1978); Stanford University (BA, with honors, 1973). Member Phi Beta Kappa.

VANDEVELDE, John
Lightfoot, Vandevelde, Sadowsky, Medvene & Levine, Los Angeles
213 622 4750
Recommended in Litigation

VANYO, Bruce
Wilson Sonsini Goodrich & Rosati,
Palo Alto 650 493 9300
bvanyo@wsgr.com
Recommended in Litigation
Practice Areas: Securities litigation.
Career: In the last four years, has prevailed in 13 cases, including six appellate victories in five different Courts of Appeal (1st, 2nd, 4th, 8th, and 9th). Asked by technology industry, and by Congress, to provide recommendations on securities litigation reform and draft major portions of the Private Securities Litigation Reform Act of 1995 and the Securities Litigation Uniform Standards Act of 1998. Argued the two appellate cases that have interpreted the Reform Act most favorably to defendants, Silicon Graphics (Ninth Circuit) and FTP Software (First Circuit).
Personal: JD, Columbia University, 1972; BS, Miami University, 1967.

VARNER, Carlton
Sheppard, Mullin, Richter & Hampton LLP, Los Angeles 213 620 1780
Recommended in Antitrust

VERHOEVEN, Charles K
Quinn Emanuel Urquhart Oliver & Hedges, LLP, San Francisco
415 875 6600
charlesverhoeven@quinnemanuel.com
Recommended in Intellectual Property
Practice Areas: Charles K Verhoeven's practice focuses primarily on intellectual property, antitrust, entertainment and complex commercial litigation.
Career: Mr Verhoeven has been recognized by California Law Business as one of the top 20 lawyers in California under 40 years old.
Personal: University of Iowa (JD, with high distinction, 1988). Member, 1986-87, articles editor, 1987-88, 'Iowa Law Review.' University of Iowa (BBA, with distinction, 1985).

VETTER, Jeff
Fenwick & West LLP, Mountain View
650 335 7631
jvetter@fenwick.com
Recommended in Corporate/M&A
Practice Areas: Focuses on public and private offerings of securities, mergers and acquisitions, counseling public and late-stage private companies and other securities law matters. Has represented underwriters of numerous initial public offerings and other public and private offerings of debt and equity securities.
Personal: University of California, Hastings College of the Law, JD, magna cum laude, Order of the Coif, Member of the Hastings Law Journal, 1990; University of California, Berkeley, BA, with honors and with distinction, 1987.

VILLENEUVE, Tom
Gunderson Dettmer Stough Villeneuve Franklin & Hachigian, Menlo Park
650 321 2400
Recommended in Corporate/M&A, IT Outsourcing

VOLPERT, Richard
Munger, Tolles & Olson LLP,
Los Angeles 213 683 9100
Recommended in Real Estate

WALDMAN, Ira
Cox Castle & Nicholson LLP,
Los Angeles 310 277 4222
Recommended in Real Estate

WALKER, Paul
Dewey Ballantine LLP, Los Angeles
213 621 6200
pwalker@deweyballantine.com
Recommended in Real Estate
Practice Areas: Real estate debt and equity investment, workout, capital markets, acquisition, disposition, development and leasing, and creditors' rights, representing domestic and foreign capital sources, real estate funds, liquidating banks, and major real estate developers.
Career: Chair of Real Estate Practice Group, Member of the firm's Management Committee, Managing Partner, Dewey Ballantine LLP, Los Angeles.
Personal: BA, University of Notre Dame, 1966. LLB, University of Pennsylvania, 1969.

WALL, Daniel
Latham & Watkins LLP, San Francisco
415 391 0600
Recommended in Antitrust

WALTER, Brian
Liebert Cassidy Whitmore, Los Angeles
310 981 2000
Recommended in Employment

WAYTE, Alan
DLA Piper Rudnick Gray Cary US LLP,
Los Angeles 213 330 7734
alan.wayte@dlapiper.com
Recommended in Real Estate
Practice Areas: Real estate.
Career: He has experience in all aspects of real estate transactions, including real estate finance, purchases and sales, leasing, sale-leasebacks, joint ventures and other forms of partnership, workouts, and foreclosures. His experience also includes extensive work in the organization of business entities such as limited partnerships, limited liability companies, and corporations. He is a writer and frequent speaker for professional groups.
Personal: AB, Stanford University. JD, Stanford University.

WEG, Howard
Peitzman, Glassman, Weg & Kempinski, Los Angeles 310 552 3100
Recommended in Bankruptcy

WEINER, Peter
Paul, Hastings, Janofsky & Walker LLP,
San Francisco
415 856 7010
peterweiner@paulhastings.com
Recommended in Environment
Practice Areas: Heads West Coast Environmental Practice. Represents property owners, developers, manufac-

turers, retailers, waste companies, energy producers, in federal, state, and local (including water boards and air districts) environmental, energy, land use, and OSHA regulatory matters, legislation, and litigation. Areas include 'brownfields' development, environmental insurance, hazardous waste, Superfund, air and water quality, California Environmental Quality Act, Proposition 65, pesticide registration, OSHA, and California energy law. Registered lobbyist, California State government.
Personal: BA, Harvard, 1966 (magna cum laude, phi beta kappa). LLB, Yale, 1970, (member, Yale Law Journal). MScEcon, 1967, London School of Economics. Admissions: California, federal courts, US Supreme Court.

WEINER, Samuel
Latham & Watkins LLP, Los Angeles
213 485 1234
Recommended in Tax

WEISSMANN, Eric
Weissmann, Wolff, Bergman, Coleman, Grodin & Evall, LLP, Beverly Hills
310 858 7888
Recommended in Media & Entertainment

WEISSMANN, Henry
Munger, Tolles & Olson LLP,
Los Angeles 213 683 9100
Recommended in Energy

WEITZEL, Mark
Thelen Reid & Priest LLP,
San Francisco 415 371 1200
Recommended in Projects

WHEELER, Raymond
Morrison & Foerster LLP, Palo Alto
650 813 5656
rwheeler@mofo.com
Recommended in Employment
Practice Areas: Advises on all aspects of labor and employment law, including litigation before the federal and state courts and administrative agencies, like the NLRB and the EEOC. Experienced in representing corporations in collective bargaining, union organizing and decertification efforts, and labor arbitrations. Has handled employment discrimination and wage/hour class actions, hundreds of arbitrations, injunctive actions, wrongful discharge suits and administrative proceedings.
Prof. Memberships: Charter Fellow, College of Labor and Employment Lawyers; Management Co-Chair, Publications Committee of the Labor and Employment Law section, ABA; National Advisory Board, Berkeley Journal of Employment and Labor Law.
Career: Admitted to practice in California. Chair, Labor and Employment Department.
Publications: Senior Editor, 'The Developing Labor Law.' 'Mergers, Acquisitions and Takeovers: Labor Relations Consequences of Corporate Transactions', 'The

Labor Lawyer, 1991'.
Personal: BA, University of Texas at Austin, 1967; JD, Harvard Law School, 1970, Executive Editor, Harvard Law Review; Law Clerk, Honorable Irving Goldberg, US Court of Appeals, Fifth Circuit, 1970-71.

WHITE, Andrew
White O'Connor Curry & Avanzado LLP,
Los Angeles 310 712 6100
Recommended in Media & Entertainment

WHITE, Robert
O'Melveny & Myers LLP, Los Angeles
310 553 6700
Recommended in Bankruptcy

WICKERS IV, Alonzo
Davis Wright Tremaine LLP,
Los Angeles 213 633 6865
alonzowickers@dwt.com
Recommended in Media & Entertainment
Practice Areas: Partner, media and entertainment law. Representative experience includes defamation, invasion of privacy, copyright, reporter's privilege, access, public records, Brown Act and business litigation, and pre-publication and pre-broadcast counseling. Representative clients include newspaper, magazine and book publishers, television networks and news organizations, production companies and distributors, and authors.
Prof. Memberships: Named one of '20 under 40', California Law Business, May 2000.
Career: Joined firm, 1997; named Partner, 2000.
Personal: JD, University of California at Berkeley, 1993. AB, Harvard, 1989.

WILCOX, Kirby
Paul, Hastings, Janofsky & Walker LLP,
San Francisco
415 856 7002
kirbywilcox@paulhastings.com
Recommended in Employment
Practice Areas: Practice involves all aspects of employment litigation and counseling for corporations.
Prof. Memberships: Member, The College of Labor and Employment Lawyers.
Publications: Chief editorial consultant for the Matthew Bender treatise entitled 'California Employment Law' and Member of Editorial Board of the Matthew Bender legal developments service entitled 'California Labor & Employment Bulletin.'
Personal: BA, 1970 - Harvard University (cum laude); MS, 1971 - the London School of Economics; JD, 1977 - Hastings College of Law; Executive Editor of the Hastings Law Journal and externed for Federal District Judge William O Orrick.

WOHL, Jeffrey D
Paul, Hastings, Janofsky & Walker LLP,
San Francisco 415 856 7255
jeffwohl@paulhastings.com
Recommended in Employment
Practice Areas: All aspects of employment law, including litigation and trial work and counseling.
Prof. Memberships: American Bar Association; Bar Association of San Francisco.
Career: Graduated with highest honors, University of California at Berkeley (1977); graduated magna cum laude, Harvard Law School (1980); Law Clerk to US District Judge Morey L. Sear, USDC, ED La (1980-81); Orrick, Herrington & Sutcliffe, San Francisco (Associate, 1981-86; Partner, 1987-2003); Paul, Hastings, Janofsky & Walker LLP, San Francisco (Partner, 2003-present).

WOOD, Mark
O'Melveny & Myers LLP, Los Angeles
310 553 6700
Recommended in Insurance

WYMAN JR, Robert
Latham & Watkins LLP, Los Angeles
213 485 1234
Recommended in Environment

YOOD, Kenneth J
Paul, Hastings, Janofsky & Walker LLP,
Los Angeles 213 683 6110
kennethyood@paulhastings.com
Recommended in Healthcare
Practice Areas: Healthcare regulatory compliance; state and federal fraud and abuse and physician referral law limitations, medicare and medicaid fraud.
Prof. Memberships: Member, California, Massachusetts and New York bars. Member, American Health Lawyers Association and California Society of Healthcare Attorneys.
Career: 1990-93 Weissburg and Aronson, Inc.; 1993-99 McCutchen Doyle Brown & Enerson, LLP; 1999-present Paul Hastings Janofsky & Walker, LLP.
Publications: Fraud and Abuse in the Pharmaceutical Industry, 'Using Health Care Professionals as Consultants' (2004) Los Angeles County Bar Association, Healthcare Section, 'The Medicare Modernization Act: Medicare Part B.' (2004) Council of Ethical Organizations, 'Managed Care Contracting and Corporate Compliance' (2003).

YOUNG, Douglas
Farella Braun & Martel LLP,
San Francisco 415 954 4400
Recommended in Litigation

YOUNG, Maureen
Bingham McCutchen LLP,
San Francisco 415 393 2000
Recommended in Banking & Finance

YOUNGBLOOD, Juliette
Irell & Manella LLP,
Los Angeles 310 277 1010
Recommended in Media & Entertainment

ZIFFREN, Kenneth
Ziffren Brittenham Branca Fischer Gilbert-Lurie & Stiffelman LLP,
Los Angeles 310 552 3388
Recommended in Media & Entertainment

ZISCHKE, Michael H
Morrison & Foerster LLP, San Francisco
415 268 6718
mzischke@mofo.com
Recommended in Environment, Real Estate
Practice Areas: Specializes in the California Environment Quality Act (CEQA), land use litigation and compliance, covering environmental impact and land use issues. Represents public agencies, businesses, industry developers, lenders, and investors.
Prof. Memberships: Advisor, Environmental Law Section, California State Bar; Member, Association of Environmental Professionals, California Building Industry Association, Select Committee on Industry Litigation, and Construction Materials Association of California.
Career: Admitted to practice in California. Named a 'Go-To Lawyer: CEQA', The Recorder newspaper (2003).
Publications: Co-author: 'Practice Under the California Environmental Quality Act' (California Continuing Education of the Bar, two volumes, 1993 supplemented annually); 'Land Use Initiatives and Referenda in California' (Solano Press, 1990).
Personal: BA, magna cum laude, Dartmouth College, 1977; JD, Boalt Hall School of Law, 1982.

ZOVICKIAN, Stephen
Bingham McCutchen LLP,
San Francisco
415 393 2000
Recommended in Construction

ALLEN MATKINS LECK GAMBLE & MALLORY LLP

THE FIRM

Managing Partner: Brian C Leck

Number of partners: 103
Number of other lawyers: 105

FIRM OVERVIEW: Allen Matkins Leck Gamble & Mallory LLP provides clients with creative, cost-effective solutions to complex legal problems. Typically, the firm staffs matters leanly with experienced attorneys who efficiently handle transactions and cases. Allen Matkins counsels companies at multiple stages of development, from handling real estate acquisitions for established entities to assisting mid-cap companies with their corporate and securities reporting. The firm does more than resolve client problems; it brings unique value to its relationships. For example, Allen Matkins' broad based real estate practice provides clients with insight on market conditions and pricing levels, which puts clients in the most advantageous business position possible. With 208 attorneys in six locations across California, Allen Matkins represents companies operating in a wide spectrum of business sectors such as real estate, financial services, healthcare, and hospitality. In providing only the highest level of service and individualized attention, the firm's attorneys develop longstanding relationships with clients, continually seeking innovative ways of resolving client legal issues and furthering client business objectives. The efficiency and dedication of Allen Matkins' attorneys and staff enables it to exceed client expectations time and time again.

MAIN AREAS OF PRACTICE: Allen Matkins' main practice areas are real estate, litigation, corporate, labor and employment, bankruptcy, and tax.

CLIENTS: The firm's clients include American Water, Arden Realty Inc., Black & Decker, Boston Properties Inc., CB Richard Ellis Investors, CIGNA Hotel Associates, E-Loan, Inc., Federal Realty Investment Trust, Homestead Village Management, LLC, Imperial Irrigation District, Indymac Bank Corp., JP Morgan, Michael A Grassmueck, Receiver, New York State Teacher's Retirement System, RAD Management, LLC, Sares-Regis Group, Taubman Centers, Inc., The Koll Company, LLC, Thomas F Lennon, Receiver, Trammell Crow, and Tenet Healthcare Corporation.

OFFICES

CALIFORNIA
515 S. Figueroa Street, Seventh Floor, **Los Angeles,** CA 90071
Tel: 213 622 5555   **Fax:** 213 620 8816

1901 Avenue of the Stars, Suite 1800, **Los Angeles,** CA 90067
Tel: 310 788 2400   **Fax:** 310 788 2410

1900 Main Street, Fifth Floor, **Irvine**, CA 92614
Tel: 949 553 1313   **Fax:** 949 553 8354

501 West Broadway, Suite 900, **San Diego,** CA 92101
Tel: 619 233 1155   **Fax:** 619 233 1158

12348 High Bluff Drive, Suite 100, **San Diego,** CA 92130
Tel: 858 481 5055   **Fax:** 858 481 5028

Three Embarcadero Center, Twelfth Floor, **San Francisco,** CA 94111
Tel: 415 837 1515   **Fax:** 415 837 1516

Allen Matkins

ALSCHULER GROSSMAN STEIN & KAHAN LLP

THE FIRM

Chief Operating Officer: Dana Ellis

Number of partners: 55
Number of other lawyers: 43

FIRM OVERVIEW: Founded in 1952, Alschuler Grossman Stein & Kahan LLP enjoys a national reputation for vigorous and creative advocacy in complex business and entertainment litigation and business transactions. This select group of diverse professionals is committed to finding practical solutions that produce tangible and cost-effective results for clients. The firm's hands-on commitment to the practice of law sets Alschuler Grossman Stein & Kahan LLP apart from many other leading law firms. The firm's involvement in and knowledge of the business, judicial, political, and cultural characteristics unique to its hometown of Los Angeles is unparalleled. The scope of the firm's practice has led it to establish relationships with leading law firms throughout the world through its founding membership in the Association of Commercial Lawyers International. These relationships give the firm the access necessary to represent clients' interests effectively in out-of-state and foreign jurisdictions.

CLIENTS: The firm's clientele includes domestic and multinational *Fortune* 500 companies, emerging companies, and individuals in diverse areas of business and the entertainment industry.

INTERNATIONAL WORK: Alschuler Grossman Stein & Kahan LLP represents domestic and international clients in all aspects of international business, trade, and investment. It advises clients about such matters as litigation (including patent and intellectual property litigation), foreign and domestic regulatory compliance, investigations, product distribution, licensing, franchising, and contractual issues. The firm is a founding member of the Association of Commercial Lawyers International. Its Asia Pacific Group has particular experience representing US clients throughout the Pacific Rim, and representing clients in the Pacific Rim in the United States; several of the firm's lawyers are fluent in various Chinese dialects and in Japanese.

HEAD OFFICE

CALIFORNIA
The Water Garden, 1620 26th Street, Fourth Floor, North Tower,
Santa Monica, CA 90404-4060
Tel: 310 907 1000 **Fax:** 310 907 2000
Email: info@agsk.com
Website: www.agsk.com

CONTACTS

Business Litigation	Marshall B Grossman
Corporate Transactions	Robert L Kahan
Entertainment Litigation	Stanton 'Larry' Stein
Financial Institutions	William S Small
Franchise	Susan Grueneberg
Insolvency	Henry S David
Insurance/Reinsurance	Bruce A Friedman
Intellectual Property	Jeffrey C Briggs
Professional Liability Defense	Bruce A Friedman
Real Estate	James D Richman
Securities Litigation	Michael A Sherman
Taxation	M Katharine Davidson

ALSCHULER GROSSMAN STEIN & KAHAN LLP

BECK, DE CORSO, DALY, KREINDLER & HARRIS APLC

THE FIRM

Managing Shareholders: Mark E Beck, Bryan D Daly

Number of shareholders: 9
Number of other lawyers: 5

FIRM OVERVIEW: Beck, De Corso is a leading complex civil litigation and white collar criminal defense firm. It represents Fortune 500 corporations, small companies and individuals in civil and criminal trials and appeals, administrative proceedings and alternative dispute resolution proceedings, exemplifying the 'great things in small packages' paradigm. Before joining Beck, De Corso, some of its attorneys served in supervisory positions in the criminal division of the United States Attorney's office. Its attorneys have been honored with numerous awards, including the Department of Justice Director's Award and Special Achievement Award; and the title of Fellow of the American College of Trial Lawyers.

MAIN AREAS OF PRACTICE

White Collar Criminal Defense: Beck, De Corso has substantial experience in defending federal and state white-collar criminal cases. It represents individuals and businesses from the pre-indictment, investigatory phase (including grand jury and corporate internal investigations) through any sentencing and appeal. The firm is also consulted regularly by other counsel, for expert advice on criminal law issues.

Civil Litigation: Beck, De Corso represents clients in a wide array of business litigation in state and federal courts, sometimes parallel to criminal proceedings. The firm is often retained to negotiate the resolution of allegations that threaten the stability or financial integrity of the client company.

Administrative Proceedings: The firm has substantial experience representing companies and individuals before administrative tribunals in various types of proceedings, including licensing and permit revocations, forfeitures, security clearance reviews, and debarment and suspension actions.

Appellate Advocacy: Beck, De Corso has extensive experience representing companies and individuals before state and federal courts of appeal, on direct appeal, and in writ proceedings.

HEAD OFFICE

CALIFORNIA
601 West 5th Street, 12th Floor, Los Angeles, CA 90071-2025
Tel: 213 688 1198   **Fax:** 213 489 7532
Email: beckdecorso@earthlink.net
Website: www.beckdecorso.com

CLIENTS: Representative criminal defense clients include individuals as well as, multinational and Fortune 500 companies, and their officers, directors, shareholders, and employees in allegations involving the following industries and subjects: aerospace (false testing, product substitution, quality assurance fraud, mischarging, defective pricing, and violations of the Foreign Corrupt Practices Act); banking and finance (currency reporting violations, money laundering, fraud, and embezzlement); healthcare (kickbacks, state and federal fraud and abuse violations, and fraudulent insurance claims); securities (violations of various SEC regulations and related federal criminal statutes); public corruption (election campaign contribution violations, bribery, and acts of political corruption); export/import (violations of laws regulating the export and import of technology, munitions, and other items); trademark (trademark misappropriation and counterfeiting); tax (violations of state and federal tax laws and regulations); environmental (violations of state and federal environmental regulations and statutes, including RCRA, CERCLA, and the Clean Air Act); and other crimes (including mail and wire fraud, RICO claims, extortion, embezzlement, and bankruptcy fraud). Representative civil litigation clients include privately and publicly held companies, foreign sovereign interests, community organizations, lending institutions, public officials, and an array of individuals with diverse professional and business interests. Cases have included: business torts such as unfair competition, anti-trust violations, and interference with business relationships; complex RICO claims; major fraud cases; securities violations involving alleged insider trading, SEC reporting violations, and related issues; defamation cases involving public and private figures; employment termination and discrimination claims; defense and prosecution of qui tam fraud actions brought under the False Claims Act; and breach of contract claims, among others.

BLECHER & COLLINS

THE FIRM

Managing Partner: Maxwell M Blecher

Number of attorneys: 14

FIRM OVERVIEW: Founded in 1971, Blecher & Collins engages in complex litigation with emphasis on antitrust. The firm's exceptional expertise in the antitrust field has resulted in many precedent setting decisions in the US Supreme Court and several courts of appeals. Blecher & Collins has had extensive trial experience in federal and state courts on behalf of both plaintiffs and defendants for a broad spectrum of domestic and international clients. The firm has handled cases against the US Department of Justice and such companies as ARCO, AT&T, the NFL, the NBA, 3M and HBO. Small by design, Blecher & Collins consists of a team of highly skilled attorneys experienced in all aspects of complex commercial litigation. The firm strives to provide a high degree of flexibility and responsiveness to the needs of its clients.

MAIN AREAS OF PRACTICE: In addition to antitrust, the firm's litigation practice includes copyright infringement; professional negligence and malicious prosecution; complex commercial litigation; and class actions. Some of the major matters the firm has recently handled include complex commercial cases involving claims of fraud, breach of contract, breach of fiduciary duty, intentional interference with contract or prospective business advantage, as well as cases under the Federal Communications Act and numerous class actions under the California Code. The firm recently won a significant malicious prosecution case which was affirmed by the Ninth Circuit Court of Appeals.

CLIENTS: The firm's clients range from Fortune 500 companies to small and medium-sized businesses, as well as individuals across a wide range of industries including telecommunications, oil and gas, entertainment, sports, healthcare, consumer goods, automotive parts, and technological goods and services.

HEAD OFFICE

CALIFORNIA
611 West Sixth Street, Suite 2000, **Los Angeles**, CA 90017
Tel: 213 622 4222 **Fax:** 213 622 1656
Website: www.blechercollins.com
Email: info@blechercollins.com

BLECHER & COLLINS

FENWICK & WEST LLP

THE FIRM

Chairman: Gordon K Davidson
Number of partners: 83
Number of other lawyers: 149

FIRM OVERVIEW: Fenwick & West LLP provides comprehensive legal services to high technology and life sciences companies of national and international prominence. More than 230 attorneys offer corporate, intellectual property, litigation and tax services from the firm's offices in Mountain View and San Francisco, California.

MAIN AREAS OF PRACTICE:

CORPORATE GROUP: Fenwick & West services high technology and life sciences companies, from early start-ups to mature public companies.

Mergers & Acquisitions: Fenwick & West's Mergers and Acquisitions Practice is ranked among the top 25 practices in the United States according to the *American Lawyer*. The firm's lawyers understand the problems that arise in technology company acquisitions and focus their efforts on issues that are of the most value to the client. The Mergers and Acquisitions Group's expertise spans the entire spectrum of high technology, from life sciences to semiconductors, and its lawyers are equally adept at small private company transactions and multi-billion dollar public transactions. For clients involved in larger deals, the firm's antitrust lawyers are experienced in working with the Department of Justice and Federal Trade Commission in the pre-merger clearance process. Fenwick & West attorneys understand the many issues that can mean the difference between a successful transaction and a broken promise.

Public Offerings & Securities Law Compliance: Fenwick & West's extensive representation of emerging companies has given it substantial depth of experience in public offerings. In recent years, the firm has represented companies or investment banks in more than 100 initial public offerings, which, combined, have raised over $6 billion dollars. The firm has helped clients raise billions more in follow-on debt and equity offerings. The firm's counseling practice for technology companies regarding ongoing public securities law issues includes extensive Sarbanes-Oxley compliance and board or audit committee counseling.

Strategic Alliances: For many high technology companies, the path to financing and commercialization begins with their first collaboration or joint venture with an industry partner. These agreements can often make or break a young technology company. Fenwick & West attorneys help clients think through the business, intellectual property, tax and other legal issues that arise in their corporate partnering transactions and joint ventures.

Executive Compensation: As an integral part of the Corporate Practice, Fenwick & West attorneys counsel clients on a wide range of employee benefits and compensation matters.

Start-Up Companies: The firm has represented hundreds of growth-oriented companies from inception through maturity. Fenwick & West attorneys understand what it takes to start with only an idea, build a team, found a company, raise venture capital funding and grow a business. They have represented many of the nation's leading venture capital firms and do multiple deals each year with companies financed by these market leaders.

INTELLECTUAL PROPERTY GROUP: Fenwick & West delivers comprehensive, integrated advice regarding all aspects of intellectual property protection and exploitation. The firm has been consistently ranked as one of the top five West Coast firms in intellectual property litigation and protection for the past 10 years by *Euromoney's Managing Intellectual Property* publication. From providing sophisticated legal defense in precedent-setting lawsuits to crafting unique license arrangements and implementing penetrating intellectual property audits, Fenwick & West's intellectual property lawyers have pioneered and remain at the forefront of legal innovation. They are continually in sync with their clients' tech-

nological advances in order to protect their positions in this fiercely competitive marketplace. The Intellectual Property Group is comprised of approximately 80 lawyers and other professionals, a significant number of whom have technical and advanced degrees, and substantial industry work experience. More than 40 attorneys are licensed to practice before the US Patent and Trademark Office. The technical skills and industry experience of Fenwick & West's lawyers help them render sophisticated advice with respect to novel technologies and related intellectual property rights issues.

LITIGATION GROUP: The Fenwick & West Litigation Group has the range of experience and critical mass to protect clients' interests in virtually any type of dispute, large or small. While the firm's attorneys have extensive litigation experience in a wide range of industries, they have exceptional depth and breadth in the areas of the law critical to their high technology clients, including software and programming; Internet and entertainment; computer hardware; semiconductors and life sciences. Fenwick & West is regularly involved in significant cases involving intellectual property (patents, copyright, trademarks and trade secrets), employment disputes, corporate governance, securities, antitrust and general commercial litigation. In addition to civil litigation, the firm's attorneys are experienced in representing clients in civil and criminal government investigations. Using a network of experienced local counsel, they routinely represent clients in cases throughout the United States.

TAX GROUP: Fenwick & West has one of the nation's leading domestic and international tax practices. The Tax Group's unusually exciting and sophisticated practice stems from a client base that is represented in every geographic region of the United States, as well as a number of foreign countries, and has included approximately 100 Fortune 500 companies, 34 of which are in the Fortune 100. In recent surveys of 1,500 companies published in *International Tax Review*, Fenwick & West was selected as the top tax adviser in the Western United States.

INTERNATIONAL WORK: Fenwick & West routinely handles corporate transactions, venture capital financing, licensing transactions and litigation, as well as intellectual property, trademark and tax matters in foreign jurisdictions for its US clients. The firm also represents a growing number of foreign technology companies throughout Asia, Europe and the Middle East on US-related transactions.

HEAD OFFICE

CALIFORNIA
Silicon Valley Center, 801 California Street, **Mountain View**, CA 94041
Tel: 650 988 8500   **Fax:** 650 938 5200
Website: www.fenwick.com

BRANCH OFFICE

CALIFORNIA
Embarcadero Center West, 275 Battery Street, **San Francisco**, CA 94111
Tel: 415 875 2300   **Fax:** 415 281 1350

CONTACTS

Corporate Group	Matthew P Quilter
Intellectual Property Group	David L Hayes
Litigation Group	Lynn H Pasahow
Tax Group	James P Fuller

FENWICK & WEST LLP

GIBBS, GIDEN, LOCHER & TURNER LLP

THE FIRM

Managing Partner: Richard J Wittbrodt
Senior Partner: Kenneth C Gibbs

Number of partners: 23
Number of other lawyers: 19

FIRM OVERVIEW: Founded to represent and serve the unique interests of clients involved in the planning and building of construction projects, Gibbs, Giden, Locher & Turner LLP currently has one of the largest teams of attorneys dedicated to dealing with these issues in the western United States. In the process of providing full service to its construction clients, the firm's practice has expanded to include the related areas of business and commercial law, employment and labor law, real property transactions, environmental law, and title insurance, suretyship, and property, casualty and liability insurance. From offices in Los Angeles and Las Vegas, the firm's attorneys counsel clients involved in projects, transactions and litigation throughout the United States.

MAIN AREAS OF PRACTICE:

Construction & Public Contracts: The Construction and Public Contracts Department of the firm provides legal guidance and counseling to clients at every stage of a construction project. The firm's attorneys regularly draft, analyze and review procurement and custom contract documents for all forms of project delivery systems, including the traditional design-bid-build, design-build and multi-prime contracts and is well-versed and routinely works with AIA construction documents. The firm is also extensively involved in all phases of preconstruction, including bid protests and contractor substitution issues. The firm has extensive experience in virtually every type of construction project, including airports, power plants, hospitals, major sports and entertainment venues, office buildings, correctional facilities, retail locations, major residential projects, transportation projects, universities, courthouses, petrochemical plants, dams, pipelines, and wastewater and water treatment facilities. The firm has represented public and private owners, design professionals, general contractors, subcontractors and material suppliers with respect to almost every conceivable circumstance that can arise before, during and after completion of a construction project. The firm has litigated numerous delay and disruption cases, including: the construction of various Metro Rail Transit projects, the Port of Long Beach, Cedars-Sinai Medical Center in Los Angeles, San Francisco International Airport, John Wayne Airport in Orange County, Ritz-Carlton Huntington Hotel in Pasadena, Kaiser Riverside Medical Center, Los Angeles County Central Jail Expansion Project, Southeast Resource Recovery Facility in Long Beach, the Space Shuttle launch facility at Vandenberg Air Force Base, Hyperion Wastewater Treatment Plant in Los Angeles, Coso Geothermal Plant located near China Lake, the Aladdin and Venetian Hotels in Las Vegas, Nevada, and the Disney Concert Hall in Los Angeles, California.

Business & Commercial Law: The Business and Commercial Law Department of the firm originally was formed to assist the firm's construction industry clients in collection matters and the enforcement of statutory mechanic's lien, stop notice, and payment bond rights. The firm also handles all aspects of creditor representation in bankruptcy proceedings, including preference claims, motions for relief from the automatic stay, motions to assume or reject executory contracts, and non-dischargeability actions. Its litigators have substantial experience in bringing and defending business tort actions such as fraud, unfair competition, RICO antitrust, trade secrets, and business interference claims. Clients include contractors, manufacturers, distributors, technology companies, and financial institutions.

HEAD OFFICE

CALIFORNIA
2029 Century Park East, 34th Floor, **Los Angeles**, CA 90067
Tel: 310 552 3400   **Fax:** 310 552 0805
Email: postmaster@gglt.com
Website: www.gglt.com

BRANCH OFFICE

NEVADA
3993 Howard Hughes Parkway, Suite 530, **Las Vegas**, NV 89109
Tel: 702 836 9800   **Fax:** 702 836 9802

CONTACTS

Construction & Public Contracts ......Kenneth C Gibbs, Barbara Gadbois
Business & Commercial Law James D Lipschultz, Richard J Wittbrodt
Labor & Employment Law ....Gerald A Griffin, Gary E Scalabrini
Insurance & Suretyship ....Theodore L Senet, Anya Stanley
Real Estate & Environmental Law.........................William D Locher
Las Vegas Office ....William Luttrell

Labor & Employment Law: For over two decades, the attorneys of the firm's Labor and Employment Department have provided this expertise to a wide range of private businesses, municipalities and institutions. The firm's attorneys have extensive experience defending against claims of wrongful termination, retaliation, employment discrimination, harassment and are actively involved in collective bargaining, labor arbitrations, and administrative hearings. The firm has defended employers against claims filed with the National Labor Relations Board, the California Labor Commissioner, the Division of Labor Standards Enforcement, the Department of Industrial Relations, the Employment Development Department, and the Federal Department of Labor. The firm represents employers not only in federal and state court, but also before governmental agencies, such as the Equal Employment Opportunity Commission and the Department of Fair Employment and Housing. In addition, the firm frequently prosecutes and defends appeals to state and federal appellate courts.

Insurance & Suretyship: The Insurance and Suretyship Department of the firm represents both insureds and insurers in claims and coverage disputes, including first-party property losses, casualty claims, surety claims, reinsurance, excess insurance, and multi-carrier litigation. Within the practice group, the firm has expertise in risk management and the analysis, negotiation and litigation of insurance coverage issues common to the business, real estate, manufacturing and construction industries.

CLIENTS: Representative Clients Include: Alameda Corridor Transportation Authority, Arizona Cardinals, Arrow Electronics, Brinderson Corporation, Centex Corporation, City of Buena Park, City of Anaheim, City of Burbank, City of Commerce, City of Glendale, City of Huntington Beach, City of Long Beach, City of Pasadena, City of Redondo Beach, City of Reno, Nevada, County of San Bernardino, Crescent Heights of America, Dick Corporation, EQR/Equity Residential, Ferguson Enterprises, Inc., General Electric Company, Kajima Engineering & Construction, Metropolitan Water District of Southern California, Morley Construction Company, M.A. Mortenson Company, Port of Long Beach, Schuff Steel Company, Snap-On Tools, Snyder Langston Builders, State Farm Insurance Co., Swinerton Builders, University of Southern California, and Vulcan Materials Company.

GIBBS, GIDEN, LOCHER & TURNER LLP

GIBSON, DUNN & CRUTCHER LLP

THE FIRM

Managing Partner: Kenneth M Doran

FIRM OVERVIEW: With approximately 800 attorneys in 13 locations worldwide, Gibson, Dunn & Crutcher is distinctively positioned for doing business in today's global marketplace. Consistently ranked among the world's top law firms in industry surveys and major publications, Gibson Dunn represents some of the world's largest multinational corporations in all major industries, leading government entities, commercial and investment banks, start-up ventures, emerging growth businesses, partnerships and individuals.

MAIN AREAS OF PRACTICE:

Business Restructuring & Reorganization: The firm has participated in many of the most complex insolvency-related proceedings and transactions of the last decade. The attorneys regularly represent Chapter 11 debtors in possession, enterprises seeking to restructure their obligations, enterprises and individuals contemplating Chapter 11 protection, creditors' committees and individual creditors, bondholders and often lenders, acquisition candidates, potential acquirers, insurers and trustees.

Capital Markets & Finance: Gibson Dunn has a reputation for excellence and creativity as counsel to issuers, underwriters, initial purchasers and placement agents. A well-balanced practice, with an extensive representation of issuers and underwriters, combined with exceptional regulatory strength, gives Gibson Dunn the breadth and insight that few firms can match.

Commercial Litigation & Arbitration: Gibson Dunn has represented many Fortune 500 companies in cases involving securities fraud, antitrust, administrative law, accountancy defense, intellectual property, employment discrimination, environmental, entertainment, white collar crime, business torts, among many others. Many of these cases have included class action claims and involved hundreds of millions of dollars in alleged damages.

Global Finance: The firm focuses on the representation of lenders, borrowers, underwriters and issuers in a large variety of debt and structured finance transactions, including leveraged loans, high yield bond offerings, mezzanine, project finance, equipment financings, restructurings and securitizations. During 2004, Gibson Dunn attorneys handled finance transactions with an aggregate value in excess of $55 billion.

Intellectual Property: Gibson Dunn assists clients with a wide range of IP issues, including litigating critical IP disputes; negotiating licenses and joint ventures; navigating local, national and international regulations governing privacy, trade and the protection of IP; and advocating for change in IP law and policy.

Labor & Employment: Recent representations includes some of the most prominent labor relations matters in the country, high stakes wage-and-hour class actions, one of the most significant Americans with Disabilities Act cases brought by the EEOC to date, and aggressive advocacy on OSHA issues.

Mergers & Acquisitions: Gibson Dunn is one of the top-ranked M&A law firms in the world. The firm has extensive experience in all types of M&A transactions, including: mergers of public and private companies, stock and asset purchases, tender and exchange offers, restructurings and acquisitions out of bankruptcy, divestitures and spin-offs, leveraged buyouts and private equity investments, strategic investments and joint ventures, special committee representations, and cross-border M&A transactions.

Real Estate: Gibson Dunn handles a variety of sophisticated matters for clients ranging from privately held entrepreneurial developers to the owners, developers and financiers of the largest real estate projects in the US and Europe. The firm's attorneys are skilled in a broad spectrum of real estate matters including real estate finance, development, sales and acquisitions, land use and environmental, leasing and workout transactions.

CLIENTS: The firm represents many of the Fortune 100 companies in the following industries: accounting, banking, biotech/biomedical, energy, gaming, healthcare, industrial and aerospace, insurance, merchant banks/VC funds, media and entertainment, real estate/REITs, retail, sports and transportation.

INTERNATIONAL WORK: Gibson Dunn's international team consists of US, UK, French and German qualified lawyers, many of whom are dual qualified. The Paris and London offices have been open since 1967 and 1979 respectively, the firm's Munich office opened in 2002 and the Brussels office opened in 2003. This long-term European presence has given them considerable experience in representing clients with international business interests requiring a coordinated response within and across national borders, throughout Europe and beyond. The firm's international offices handle all types of corporate transactions, corporate financing, tax structuring, real estate and antitrust matters. Gibson Dunn has expanded in a way that preserves firm culture and in particular the high value we place on teamwork, top level skills and professional practice.

HEAD OFFICE

CALIFORNIA
333 S Grand Avenue, **Los Angeles**, CA 90071
Tel: 213 229 7000   **Fax:** 213 229 7520
Website: www.gibsondunn.com

BRANCH OFFICES

CALIFORNIA
Jamboree Center, 4 Park Plaza, **Irvine**, CA 92614-8557
Tel: 949 451 3800   **Fax:** 949 451 4220

2029 Century Park East, **Los Angeles**, CA 90067-3026
Tel: 310 552 8500   **Fax:** 310 551 8741

1881 Page Mill Road, Suite 3100, **Palo Alto**, CA 94304-1125
Tel: 650 849 5300   **Fax:** 650 849 5333

One Montgomery Street, Suite 3100, **San Francisco**, CA 94104-4505
Tel: 415 393 8200   **Fax:** 415 986 5309

COLORADO
1801 California Street, Suite 4200, **Denver**, CO 80202-2641
Tel: 303 298 5700   **Fax:** 303 296 5310

DISTRICT OF COLUMBIA
1050 Connecticut Avenue NW, **Washington**, DC 20036-5306
Tel: 202 955 8500   **Fax:** 202 467 0539

NEW YORK
200 Park Avenue, **New York**, NY 10166-0193
Tel: 212 351 4000   **Fax:** 212 351 4035

TEXAS
2100 McKinney Avenue, Suite 1100, **Dallas**, TX 75201-6911
Tel: 214 698 3100   **Fax:** 214 571 2900

INTERNATIONAL OFFICES

The firm also has offices in Brussels, London, Munich and Paris.

HANCOCK ROTHERT & BUNSHOFT LLP

THE FIRM

Chairman: Philip R Matthews

Number of partners: 35
Number of other lawyers: 55

FIRM OVERVIEW: Hancock Rothert & Bunshoft has more than 50 years' experience representing US and international clients in litigation and transactional matters. Equally adept in negotiations or in the courtroom, the firm excels at applying advocacy skills to advance its clients' business and litigation interests to their advantage. Based in California, the firm has an extraordinary track record in the state, federal and appellate courts.

MAIN AREAS OF PRACTICE: The firm emphasizes business litigation; construction litigation; labor and employment litigation and counseling; insurance coverage litigation; products liability and professional liability litigation; real estate litigation and transactional work; and technology-related litigation and counseling. Additionally, the firm is known for its appellate work in state and federal courts, having appeared as counsel on more than 140 published decisions.

Business Litigation: The firm handles a wide range of contract disputes and business tort claims for clients, including breach of contract, unfair business practice claims, class actions, consumer fraud, directors and officers liability, antitrust, real estate, RICO, technology-related litigation and trade secrets.

Insurance: The firm counsels and represents both insurers and others in coverage disputes arising from asbestos, health hazard, the environment and technology. The firm also has experience in subrogation, reinsurance, bad faith, and professional indemnity matters. Additionally, the firm has expertise in the drafting and negotiation of insurance policies – particularly, with respect to technology and other rapidly evolving areas of the economy.

Products Liability & Complex Torts: The firm has extensive products liability experience, particularly in the automotive, sports and exercise equipment, water craft, child equipment and toy industries. It specializes in coordinating the nationwide defense of class actions for insurers, distributors and manufacturers. The firm also assists clients with recalls when necessary and in negotiations with the US Consumer Product Safety Commission.

Professional Liability: The firm represents the following professionals and their insurers in all business liability claims: architects and engineers, contractors, real estate brokers and agents, corporate directors and officers, insurance brokers, lawyers and law firms, entertainment industry professionals and organizations, employers, and sports agents.

Sports & Recreation: The firm pioneered much of the sports and recreation practice in California, and continues to represent a wide variety of recreational interests, including ski resort owners and operators, golf course owners and operators, professional sports teams and the facilities they own or use, the makers of sporting goods and equipment, and the owners and operators of other recreational businesses, such as tour companies.

HEAD OFFICE

CALIFORNIA
San Francisco, Four Embarcadero Center, Suite 300,
San Francisco, CA 94111
Tel: 415 981 5550 **Fax:** 415 955 2599
Email: info@hrblaw.com
Website: www.hrblaw.com

BRANCH OFFICES

CALIFORNIA
515 S. Figueroa St., 17th Floor, **Los Angeles**, CA 90071
Tel: 213 623 7777 **Fax:** 213 623 5405

The Lighthouse Center, 850 N. Lake Blvd, Ste 15
PO Box 7199, **Tahoe City**, CA 96145
Tel: 530 583 7767 **Fax:** 530 581 3215

NEVADA
701 Bridger Street, Suite 670, **Las Vegas**, NV 89101
Tel: 702 385 1740 **Fax:** 702 385 6862

INTERNATIONAL OFFICES

The firm also has an office in London.

CLIENTS: The firm represents a wide variety of US and international clients, from small businesses to *Fortune* 500 firms, including US and London-based insurers. Clients receive superior service through personal contact, the latest technology and the firm's client dedicated intranet.

INTERNATIONAL WORK: The firm handles a variety of work for international clients, particularly in the fields of insurance, construction, real estate, products liability and sports and recreation. Additionally, it has relationships with lawyers around the globe through ALFA International, an invitation-only affiliation of top law firms worldwide. Languages spoken by those at the firm include: Cantonese, Farsi, French, German, Korean, Mandarin, and Spanish.

HANCOCK
ROTHERT &
BUNSHOFT
—— LLP ——
ATTORNEYS

HANSON BRIDGETT

THE FIRM

Managing Partner: Andrew G Giacomini
Senior Construction Partners: Howard W Ashcraft, Jeffrey M Chu,
Andrew G Giacomini
Of Counsel for Construction Matters: Paul J Sanner

Number of partners: 56
Number of other lawyers: 69

FIRM OVERVIEW: Hanson Bridgett is a 125-attorney firm with offices in San Francisco, the North Bay and Sacramento. Its practice encompasses traditional areas of law such as general business and corporate law, litigation, estate planning and administration, as well as major practice groups that focus on health care, senior housing and care, construction, intellectual property, labor and employment and public sector law. These areas are supplemented by refined expertise in such specialized and diverse fields as transportation, agriculture, real estate, environmental law, insurance coverage and public finance.

MAIN AREAS OF PRACTICE:

Construction Law: Hanson Bridgett has a national level construction practice focusing on complex infrastructure projects. The Construction Group attorneys participate in project formation, contracting, financing, execution and claims. Clients include public owners, 'ENR Top 50' designers, developers and contractors. The scope of projects is equally broad, encompassing the areas of clean and waste water treatment, tunnels and pipelines, highway and light rail, coastal and marine, hospital and health care, geotechnical and environmental, and commercial and industrial. The Construction Group has significant experience in alternative project delivery systems, including turnkey, design/build, build/own/ transfer and similar variants.

Hanson Bridgett's Construction Group attorneys are committed to the construction industry and are actively involved with professional associations. The firm's understanding of the design and construction professions leads to efficient, creative support of clients' business goals. Although the firm has a strong litigation practice, the Construction Group works as problem solvers, not legal technicians. The Construction Group believes that disputes are best resolved before they occur. Alternative dispute resolution (ADR) procedures are often appropriate tools for resolving claims and restoring the parties' working relationship. Hanson Bridgett has utilized mediation and other ADR techniques for over 20 years, whenever appropriate to clients' business interests.

There are times when litigation is necessary or unavoidable. In such cases, the Construction Group attorneys have defended and prosecuted major construction claims and are thoroughly familiar with delay, impact and loss of efficiency issues. They are able to efficiently analyze and organize these document-intensive claims. Its Construction Group attorneys have handled many large differing site condition claims arising from geotechnical, oceanographic and environmental conditions, as well as construction defect litigation involving structural, HVAC, electrical, architectural and geotechnical claims. Major construction litigation requires state of the art techniques. The Construction Group has complete computerized litigation management and multimedia capabilities and its attorneys understand the appropriate and efficient use of technology.

Related Capabilities: Environmental law, finance, insurance law, litigation, public agency law, real estate law. The Construction Group is complemented by individual attorneys within the Public Agency, Employment, Insurance, Business and General Litigation Sections of Hanson Bridgett. Since these attorneys regularly advise and represent construction clients, they are able to provide specialized legal services tailored to the construction industry. The Public Agency Section provides exceptional capabilities in transportation, water, solid waste and construction procurement. The Labor and Employment Section counsels engineering and construction firms and represents them in employment litigation. Hanson Bridgett's Insurance Coverage Group understands the important role insurance plays in construction projects and disputes. The Business Section represents construction clients in mergers and acquisitions, tax and general business matters. As a result of this team approach, the Construction Group is able to provide the specialized skills needed by construction clients.

INTERNATIONAL WORK: Hanson Bridgett represents multi-national corporations in disputes arising from complex infrastructure projects. Currently, the firm is involved in arbitrating design and construction deficiencies in a world class industrial project in Latin America.

HEAD OFFICE

CALIFORNIA
333 Market Street, Suite 2100
San Francisco, CA 94105
Tel: 415 777 3200 · **Fax:** 415 541 9366
Website: www.hansonbridgett.com

CONTACTS

Business	Teresa V Pahl
Estate Planning	Theodore A Hellman
Health & Senior Care	Allan D Jergesen
Intellectual Property	Susan G O'Neill
Labor & Employment	Patrick M Glenn
Litigation	Lawrence M Cirelli
Public Agency	Joan L Cassman

HELLER EHRMAN LLP

THE FIRM

Chairman: Matthew L Larrabee
Executive Director: Phyllis A Gardner

FIRM OVERVIEW: Heller Ehrman LLP has more than 730 attorneys and professionals in 12 offices worldwide (San Francisco; Silicon Valley; Los Angeles; San Diego; New York; Washington, DC; Madison, WI; Seattle; Anchorage; Hong Kong; Beijing; and Singapore). As a full-service law firm, Heller Ehrman represents a wide range of industry leaders, from entrepreneurial, technology-driven enterprises to established, global corporations. Heller Ehrman takes a multidisciplinary approach to the practice of law, drawing upon its legal, industry and technical expertise from across the firm to build the best legal teams for its clients. Through commitment to the core values of excellence, people, teamwork, innovation, community and 'one firm,' Heller Ehrman offers clients unparalleled legal service. In 2004, The American Lawyer ranked Heller Ehrman number two on its 2004 'A-List,' recognizing the best law firms in the United States based on scores for Revenue Per Lawyer, Pro Bono, Associate Satisfaction and Diversity. Heller Ehrman opened its newest office in Beijing in March 2004 and in August, the firm added 10 litigation and international arbitration attorneys to its Hong Kong office from the former Hong Kong office Denton Wilde Sapte. Six lateral shareholders joined the firm in 2004, including a former Commodity Futures Trading Commission Director of Enforcement and a former Attorney Advisor for the Office of the General Counsel at FERC, and the firm promoted 14 attorneys to Shareholder in January 2005, the largest shareholder class since 2001. In 2004, Heller Ehrman implemented an innovative Diversity Fellowship program that provides summer employment and scholarships to four first-year law students who show promise of contributing meaningfully to the diversity of the legal community. In 2005, Heller Ehrman will be moving to larger offices in New York and Washington, DC to account for its significantly expanding East Coast practice. The firm's attorneys are graduates of the country's top academic institutions and include former Rhodes Scholars, US and state Supreme Court clerks, and law review editors. Heller Ehrman attorneys also include former federal prosecutors, six fellows of the American College of Trial Lawyers, a former Federal Trade Commissioner, a former general counsel to the Department of Commerce, former Patent and Trademark Office examiners, as well as a number of attorneys who hold PhDs in disciplines such as neuroscience, microbiology, chemistry and computer science.

MAIN AREAS OF PRACTICE: Clients rely on Heller Ehrman to address their most important business issues and solve their most challenging problems.
Litigation: The firm's nationally recognized Litigation Team handles bet-the-company litigation in a range of key arenas, including antitrust, securities, intellectual property, consumer class action, insurance coverage, product liability, employment and environmental law.
Business Law: Heller Ehrman's business and transactional attorneys are leaders in corporate securities, M&A, finance, real estate, tax, corporate governance and a range of regulatory issues.
Intellectual Property: The firm's Intellectual Property Practice combines a highly reputed patent litigation team with extensive in-house patent and trademark resources.

CLIENTS: In 2004, Heller Ehrman ranked 13th nationally in number of IPOs closed in 2004, based on number of offerings and US offering amount. They were ranked 11th nationally by Thomson Financial for M&A transactions closed in 2004. The firm represented GIC Real Estate (the real estate investment arm of the Government of Singapore) in the formation of a $2 billion real estate venture with Tishman Speyer Properties. The firm assisted in the sale of Telcordia Technologies, an SAIC sub-

sidiary, for $1.35 billion to Providence Equity Partners Inc. and Warburg Pincus LLC. Heller Ehrman represented Yahoo! Inc. in high-profile patent litigation against Google. The firms represents clients VISA USA, Microsoft and Philip Morris in the largest antitrust matters in the United States, and also represent clients involved in many of the highest profile securities matters in the country, including Enron, Parmalat, Cendant and AOL Time Warner. The firm successfully obtained a dismissal in a technology dispute with Cisco Systems on behalf of client Huawei Technologies, China's largest telecommunications equipment manufacturer.

HEAD OFFICE

CALIFORNIA
333 Bush Street, **San Francisco**, CA 94104-2878
Tel: 415 772 6000   **Fax:** 415 772 6268
Email: info@hellerehrman.com
Website: www.hellerehrman.com

BRANCH OFFICES

ALASKA
510 L Street, Suite 500, **Anchorage**, AK 99501-1959
Tel: 907 277 1900   **Fax:** 907 277 1920

CALIFORNIA
601 South Figueroa Street, 40th Floor, **Los Angeles**, CA 90017-5758
Tel: 213 689 0200   **Fax:** 213 614 1868

275 Middlefield Road, **Menlo Park**, CA 94025-3506
Tel: 650 324 7000   **Fax:** 650 324 0638

2775 Sand Hill Road, **Menlo Park**, CA 94025
Tel: 650 854 4488   **Fax:** 650 324 0638

4350 La Jolla Village Drive, 7th Floor, **San Diego**, CA 92122-1246
Tel: 858 450 8400   **Fax:** 858 450 8499

DISTRICT OF COLUMBIA
1717 Rhode Island Ave, N.W., **Washington**, DC 20036-3001
Tel: 202 912 2000   **Fax:** 202 912 2020

NEW YORK
Times Square Tower, 7 Times Square, **New York**, NY 10036-6524
Tel: 212 832 8300   **Fax:** 212 763 7600

WASHINGTON
701 Fifth Avenue, Suite 6100, **Seattle**, WA 98104-7098
Tel: 206 447 0900   **Fax:** 206 447 0849

WISCONSIN
One East Main Street, Suite 201, **Madison**, WI 53703-5118
Tel: 608 663 7460   **Fax:** 608 663 7499

INTERNATIONAL OFFICES

The firm also has offices in Hong Kong, Beijing and Singapore.

CONTACTS

Managing Director - Business ....Mark B Weeks
Managing Director - Litigation.................................Marie L Fiala
Firmwide Managing Shareholder ....Robert B Hubbell
Managing Shareholder For Client Relationships ....Mark S Parris

HellerEhrman LLP

HENNIGAN, BENNETT & DORMAN LLP

THE FIRM

Managing Partner: Robert L Palmer
Senior Partners: J Michael Hennigan, Bruce S Bennett, Roderick G Dorman

Number of partners: 21
Number of other lawyers: 19

HEAD OFFICE

CALIFORNIA
601 South Figueroa Street, Suite 3300, **Los Angeles**, CA 90017
Tel: 213 694 1000   **Fax:** 213 694 1234
Website: www.hbdlawyers.com

FIRM OVERVIEW: Hennigan, Bennett & Dorman LLP (HBD) is dedicated to delivering innovative and practical legal solutions to a wide range of commercial disputes of extraordinary size and complexity. The firm consists of forty highly-credentialed, experienced lawyers who effectively resolve difficult business problems by integrating skill in complex commercial litigation, bankruptcy and reorganization matters, and intellectual property disputes. The firm and its principals have achieved unusual success for its clients in these three practices areas. The firm is entrepreneurial and frequently unconventional. It employs innovative strategies to end commercial disputes quickly and advantageously for its clients. From the very beginning of a case the firm employs a collaborative process of thesis development involving its lawyers, forensic accountants, and financial analysts. This allows the firm to penetrate complex interrelated business and legal issues and to develop a winning thesis that will resonate in an effective discovery strategy on through trial or other resolution. HBD is known for its successes in trial. Most of the firm's cases settle well because its opponents know both that the firm likes to try cases and that it wins the vast majority of those tried. All of the firm's lawyers understand that HBD sells results, not hours.

MAIN AREAS OF PRACTICE:

Complex Commercial Litigation: HBD is a trial firm with particular expertise handling individual and class actions involving financial and securities frauds, shareholder derivative claims, directors' and officers' liability claims, antitrust claims, breach of fiduciary duty claims, commercial contract disputes, and the prosecution and defense of professional liability claims. Its practice covers a broad range of industries including banking, finance, securities, high technology and the internet, energy, public accounting, real estate development, aviation, health care, pharmaceutical, and entertainment and media. In the securities law area, the firm has extensive experience representing both plaintiffs and defendants in cases involving alleged violations of the Securities Exchange Act of 1934, and under state 'blue-sky' securities laws, as well as tender offer and takeover litigation and related matters. The firm also has extensive experience representing individuals and companies involved in investigations conducted by the Securities and Exchange Commission, the Justice Department, the California Department of Corporations, and the California Attorney General's Office.

Business Reorganization & Bankruptcy: The Business Reorganization and Bankruptcy Group at HBD is a national leader in its field. Its senior members have successfully represented major positions in some of the most complex and difficult reorganization and bankruptcy cases to have been filed in the last two decades. The firm's practice encompasses representation of debtors, secured creditors, unsecured creditors and equity interest holders, and statutory committees and informal or ad hoc committees of bondholders or other creditors. It also represents persons or entities in connection with the acquisition of assets of, equity interests in or control of troubled businesses, including corporations.

Patent & Technology: The firm's Patent and Technology Group is a nationally recognized leader in successfully representing major corporations and entrepreneurs to acquire, maximize and enforce their intellectual property asset portfolio. HBD lawyers have also enjoyed extraordinary success in defending clients in technology and trade secret disputes. The senior attorneys have been and continue to be lead trial counsel in major, high stakes patent, copyright, trademark and trade secret litigation for major corporations and also for well-known inventors and entrepreneurs. The partners of the Patent and Technology Group have been lead trial counsel in over 60 patent, copyright, and trade secret cases. The firm has repeatedly and successfully handled important patent matters before the Federal Circuit Court of Appeals.

CLIENTS: Hennigan, Bennett & Dorman LLP represents clients in a wide array of industries, including banking, finance, securities, digital technology and the internet, energy, real estate development, aviation, health care, pharmaceutical, entertainment and media.

KEKER & VAN NEST LLP

THE FIRM

Managing Partner: Christopher C Kearney
Number of partners: 24
Number of attorneys: 53

AREAS OF PRACTICE:
Litigation 100%

FIRM OVERVIEW: Keker & Van Nest is a trial-practice litigation firm located in San Francisco. For more than 25 years, the firm has devoted its practice exclusively to complex civil and criminal litigation. The firm's practice is national in scope and includes trials of complex, high-stakes civil or criminal litigation cases in state and federal courts throughout California and the nation. In its January 2005 edition, *The American Lawyer Magazine* named Keker & Van Nest as the "Litigation Boutique of the Year," singling out the firm for litigation success in high stakes matters. "Keker & Van Nest lawyers handle cases of national importance...Not only do they win consistently, they do so while working in an environment that is a model for the legal industry in the areas of diversity and pro bono."

MAIN AREAS OF PRACTICE:

Intellectual Property: Keker & Van Nest represents plaintiffs and defendants in patent, trade secret, trademark, and copyright cases. The firm's clients include companies in the fields of semiconductors, medical equipment, biotech, software, networking, the internet, and consumer goods such as wineries, and include four of Wired Magazine's top ten new economy companies. *The American Lawyer Magazine,* in connection with awarding the firm with Litigation Boutique of the year honor, cited the firm for its "precedent setting copyright cases," and stated "Keker & Van Nest has been in the vanguard of emerging intellectual property precedents, winning key decisions protecting the patent rights of biotech leader Genentech and successfully defending client Grokster when it was sued by virtually the entire entertainment industry."

Antitrust: Keker & Van Nest maintains a diverse antitrust practice. On the civil side, the firm defends against and prosecutes antitrust claims. The firm represents individuals and corporations in individual and class-action suits in federal and state court, as well as federal and state administrative proceedings and investigations by federal and state enforcement authorities. On the criminal side, the firm represents individuals and corporations in investigations by both federal and state prosecutors.

White Collar Criminal: Keker & Van Nest is one of the pre-eminent federal criminal defense trial firms in the country. The firm has handled a wide variety of financial fraud cases, including allegations of securities fraud, and bank fraud, tax fraud, as well as medicare fraud, false claims act charges, foreign corrupt practices act and other transnational crimes, and environmental violations. Many of these cases are resolved during the grand jury stage with no charges being brought and thus never become public.

Contract & Commercial: Keker & Van Nest represents plaintiffs and defendants in a broad range of commercial disputes, including class actions. The firm has handled class actions relating to discrimination and other unfair business practice claims, employee claims, false advertising claims, and securities related claims.

HEAD OFFICE

CALIFORNIA
710 Sansome Street, **San Francisco,** CA 94111-1704
Tel: 415 391 5400 **Fax:** 415 397 7188
Email: info@kvn.com
Website: www.kvn.com

Professional Liability: Keker & Van Nest has been hired by major law firms, particularly those insured by Attorneys Liability Assurance Society (ALAS) and MPC Insurance, Ltd. in professional liability litigation involving claims of malpractice, malicious prosecution, allegations of fraud, conflicts of interest, and breach of fiduciary duty. In the last two years, the firm has handled more than 20 legal malpractice matters. In addition, the firm has represented two national accounting firms in defending breach of contract, professional negligence and fraud claims.

CLIENTS: The firm's corporate clients include American Honda Motor Company, Inc.; AT&T Wireless; Cadence Design Systems; Comcast Cable Communications, Inc.; eBay, Inc.; Electronic Arts, Inc.; The Gap, Inc.; Genentech, Inc.; Google, Inc.; Intel Corporation; Johnson & Johnson; Micron Technology, Inc.; National Semiconductor; Netflix, Inc.; Pacific Gas & Electric; Palm, Inc.; Taiwan Semiconductor Manufacturing Corp.

KEKER & VAN NEST LLP

KIRKPATRICK & LOCKHART NICHOLSON GRAHAM LLP

THE FIRM

Chairman of the Management Committee &
Managing Partner: Peter J Kalis
Number of partners: 323
Number of other lawyers: 627

Website: www.klng.com

FIRM OVERVIEW: Kirkpatrick & Lockhart Nicholson Graham LLP (K&LNG) – the product of one of the largest Anglo-American legal combinations in history on January 1, 2005 – comprises 950 lawyers who practice from offices throughout the US and in London, England. K&LNG represents entrepreneurs, growth and middle-market companies and leading global corporations in every major industry group. The firm practices across all legal disciplines within the corporate, litigation and regulatory fields. K&LNG's extensive knowledge about the business sectors in which our clients operate enables the practice to be at once regional, national and international in scope, cutting edge, complex, and dynamic. K&LNG was the only law firm in the world to receive the CIO Magazine CIO 100 Award for three consecutive years, while the official publication of the Minority Corporate Counsel Association selected K&LNG as one of only four American law firms to feature for their innovative diversity initiatives.

MAIN AREAS OF PRACTICE:

Corporate: K&LNG practices law on an integrated and firm-wide basis. The multi-office, International Corporate and Transactional Practice is one of the most substantial in the profession. The firm closed over 100 M&A transactions last year, and is perennially a leader as issuer's counsel in equities issued by corporate clients, both in terms of number of transactions and proceeds. K&LNG has completed hundreds of public debt and equity offerings over the last decade.

Litigation: K&LNG's litigation engagements including, among other substantive areas, insurance coverage, intellectual property, real estate, white-collar criminal, construction, professional liability, environmental, toxic tort, products liability, franchise, tax, bankruptcy and insolvency, antitrust and competition, employment, benefits, and securities fraud are among the largest and most attractive enjoyed by any law firm. The firm has been rated a leading practice in the representation of corporate policyholders in the insurance coverage area, and as a leading litigation firm for the financial sector. It is active in jurisdictions around the US and in the UK as well as in various international arbitration forums.

Regulatory: K&LNG's Regulatory Practice cuts across the many disciplines that require highly specialized knowledge and experience to address governmental regulation of the private markets. The firm's lawyers regularly represent clients before regulatory bodies in both the US and the UK. Its premier regulatory practice is in the diversified financial services area. K&LNG represents a large majority of the major financial institutions and securities firms in a variety of disciplines, and the investment management practice is a perennial leader. Many of the firm's practice leaders as well as more junior lawyers have governmental experience that enhances their ability to serve K&LNG's clients in regulatory fields, while others have held prominent positions in regulated industries.

Emerging Practices: The firm continuously allocates resources so that its capabilities reach to the forefront of emerging disciplines. K&LNG's Intellectual Property Practice, with approximately 100 practicing lawyers, and its Technology Practice, serving growth companies in disciplines such as biotechnology, internet services, medical devices, and information systems, are examples of how this investment has borne fruit. Most frequently, the firm continues to recruit lateral partners in such disparate fields as structured finance, bankruptcy, real estate, food and drug, ERISA litigation, Small Business Administration financing, telecommunications, project finance, intellectual property, private equity, trademarks, employment and public sector technology to address the evolving needs of its

OFFICES

CALIFORNIA
10100 Santa Monica Boulevard, 7th Floor, **Los Angeles**, CA 90067
Tel: 310 552 5000   **Fax:** 310 552 5001

Four Embarcadero Center, 10th Floor, **San Francisco**, CA 94111
Tel: 415 249 1000   **Fax:** 415 249 1001

DISTRICT OF COLUMBIA
1800 Massachusetts Avenue, NW, 2nd Floor, **Washington**, DC 20036-1221
Tel: 202 778 9000   **Fax:** 202 778 9100

FLORIDA
Miami Center, 201 South Biscayne Boulevard, 20th Floor,
Miami, FL 33131-2399
Tel: 305 539 3300   **Fax:** 305 358 7095

MASSACHUSETTS
75 State Street, **Boston**, MA 02109
Tel: 617 261 3100   **Fax:** 617 261 3175

NEW JERSEY
One Newark Center, 10th Floor, **Newark**, NJ 07102-5252
Tel: 973 848 4000   **Fax:** 973 848 4001

NEW YORK
599 Lexington Avenue, **New York**, NY 10022-6030
Tel: 212 536 3900   **Fax:** 212 536 3901

PENNSYLVANIA
Payne Shoemaker Building, 240 North Third Street, **Harrisburg**, PA 17101-1507
Tel: 717 231 4500   **Fax:** 717 231 4501

Henry W. Oliver Building, 535 Smithfield Street, **Pittsburgh**, PA 15222-2312
Tel: 412 355 6500   **Fax:** 412 355 6501

TEXAS
2828 North Harwood Street, Suite 1800, **Dallas**, TX 75201-6966
Tel: 214 939 4900   **Fax:** 214 939 4949

INTERNATIONAL OFFICES

The firm also has an office in London, UK

clientele. The firm strives to maintain a creative, interdisciplinary approach to the practice, as evidenced by the extraordinary convergence of disciplines that permitted its K&LNG colleague, former US Attorney General Dick Thornburgh, to act as the court appointed Examiner in the WorldCom bankruptcy proceeding – the largest bankruptcy in US history – and the firm itself to act as his counsel.

CLIENTS: K&LNG currently represents or recently has performed projects for over half of the FORTUNE 100; 21 of the 25 largest mutual fund complexes or their investment managers; and 18 of the 20 largest US bank holding companies or their affiliates. Representative clients include Alcoa, Bank of America, DuPont, Fidelity, Halliburton, Mellon, PPG, United Technologies, Wachovia, and World Wrestling Entertainment. The firm is a multiple winner of DuPont's Meeting the Challenge Award for its 'remarkable and extraordinary accomplishments' for that client, and is the only law firm on which PPG Industries has conferred its Excellent Supplier Award.

INTERNATIONAL WORK: With offices throughout the US and in London, K&LNG represents clients across North America and the United Kingdom on matters that span the globe. K&LNG's primary working language is English, but the firm has attorneys fluent in Afrikaans, Chinese (Mandarin), Farsi, French, German, Greek, Hebrew, Hindi, Italian, Japanese, Korean, Polish, Portuguese, Russian and Spanish. Various members of the firm have foreign degrees, which enable them to take into account legal and cultural differences in representing the firm's clients in international transaction and litigation matters worldwide.

KLEE, TUCHIN, BOGDANOFF & STERN LLP

THE FIRM

Co-Managing Partners: Lee R Bogdanoff, Michael L Tuchin

Number of partners: 11
Number of other lawyers: 8

HEAD OFFICE

CALIFORNIA
Fox Plaza 2121 Avenue of the Stars, 33rd Floor,
Los Angeles, CA 90067
Tel: 310 407 4000 **Fax:** 310 407 9090
Website: www.ktbslaw.com

FIRM OVERVIEW: Klee Tuchin Bogdanoff & Stern is a national, boutique law firm that specializes in business reorganizations, corporate insolvency, commercial litigation, bankruptcy-related asset acquisitions, bankruptcy litigation and appellate advocacy, and expert witness services in the bankruptcy field. KTB&S represents debtors, creditors, equity holders, committees, trustees, landlords, potential acquirers of assets, and other parties with interests in financially distressed businesses. KTB&S also provides expert witness services on matters of bankruptcy law. The members of KTB&S have decades of experience practicing in this unique area of law, and are actively involved in teaching and providing expert witness consultation and testimony in this field. KTB&S lawyers are headquartered in Los Angeles, California, but regularly handle matters and appear in bankruptcy proceedings throughout the United States. KTB&S is widely recognized as a national leader in its field.

CLIENTS: Since KTB&S was established in June 1999, the firm has attracted a notable list of clients. The nature and diversity of these representations illustrate the breadth and depth of KTB&S' expertise in all aspects of bankruptcy and insolvency practice. The firm's non-confidential representations include the following, which are listed by client categories:
DEBTORS: Anacomp, Inc.: document storage and information retrieval technology company; successfully confirmed prepackaged chapter 11 plan in 57 days. Crescent Jewelers: jewelry retailer; successful out-of-court restructuring. Custom Food Products: Processor of custom and value added meat products; successful confirmation of plan of reorganization financed by Fleet Capital Corporation, junior capital provided by Simon/Triton Partners I, LLC. Fountain View, Inc. and Affiliates: skilled nursing facilities, assisted living facilities, pharmacy and therapy businesses; chapter 11 debtors presently undergoing reorganization. Frederick's of Hollywood and Affiliates: retailers of innovative specialty apparel; chapter 11 debtors presently undergoing reorganization. Guidance Software: s oftware development company; successful chapter 11 restructuring and voluntary dismissal. Incomnet, Inc.: reseller of long distance telephone services; successful development, proposal and confirmation of a chapter 11 plan of reorganization in eight months. Matthews Studio Equipment Group, Hollywood Rental Co. LLC, FourStar Inc., Matthews Studio Sales, Inc. (a/k/a Olesen) and related entities: major sellers, lessors, and outsourcers of production equipment for the entertainment industry, including theatrical, motion picture and television production; currently chapter 11 debtors. Outsource International And Affiliates: temporary employment services; successfully preserved operations for purposes of an orderly chapter 11 sale. Pacific Gateway Exchange, Inc., International Exchange Communications, Inc., Onyx Networks, Inc. and Affiliates: international wholesaler of telecommunications services, retail long distance reseller, and internet/co-location services provider; coordinated sale of assets and negotiation of chapter 11 liquidating plan. Prime Matrix Wireless Communications: retail reseller of cellular communications capacity; successfully coordinated orderly sale of the company.
BONDHOLDERS & OTHER CREDITORS: Adelphia Communications Corporation Unsecured Creditors' Committee: KTB&S presently serves as special counsel to the official unsecured creditors' committee in this case, investigating potential claims relating to approximately $13 billion in secured and unsecured debt. Ameriserve: represented one of the largest unsecured creditors in the chapter 11 case of Ameriserve. First Alliance

Mortgage Company Official Unsecured Creditors' Committee: represent official committee of unsecured creditors in chapter 11 case of major subprime residential real estate lender. ICO Global Communications: represented bondholder group in ICO Global Communications chapter 11 case, comprised of Magten Asset Management Corp., Oaktree Capital Management, Cerberus Capital Management, LLC, Aristeia Capital LLC, Mackay Shields Financial Corporation. Iridium Official Unsecured Creditors' Committee: represented official committee of unsecured creditors in chapter 11 cases of the Iridium companies, a failed satellite enterprise involving over $3 billion in debt; KTB&S served as special litigation counsel to investigate and prosecute claims against Iridium's lenders; successfully negotiated a settlement for unsecured creditors in excess of $50 million. Maxicare Official Unsecured Creditors' Committee: represent official committee of unsecured creditors in chapter 11 case of major health maintenance organization. Paramount Studios/Viacom: major creditor in the Kmart, Carmike, Edwards Cinemas, General Cinemas and United Artists Theater bankrupties; creditor and purchaser in Weststar (Mann Theaters) chapter 11 cases. Prandium, Inc.: represent an informal group of bondholders holding a majority of approximately $120 million (principal plus interest) in outstanding bonds in connection with prepackaged chapter 11 restructuring; company engaged in the operation of restaurants in the full-service and fast-casual industry segments. ZiLOG, Inc.: represent an informal group of secured bondholders holding approximately $157 million of $280 million in outstanding bonds in connection with prepackaged chapter 11 restructuring; company designs, manufactures and markets semiconductor micro devices.
EQUITY HOLDERS: 203 North LaSalle Street Limited Partnership and Related Entities: represented investors under chapter 11 reorganization plan on remand from the United States Supreme Court in the case of 203 North LaSalle Street Partnership; subsequent plan successfully confirmed. Einstein/Noah Bagel Corporation: represented Gerald K. Smith, Trustee for the Boston Chicken Plan Trust, in the chapter 11 case filed by Einstein/Noah Bagel Corporation and Einstein/Noah Bagel Partners, L.P. Transpacific Enterprises, Inc.: represent the Joint Administrators of Ansett Holdings, Ltd., the sole shareholder of Transpacific Enterpises, Inc., a full service airline support company. Pittsburgh Penguins: represented a significant shareholder in the Pittsburgh Penguins hockey team, in connection with the chapter 11 case of that team.
ACQUIRERS & OTHERS: The Century Trust: purchaser of real estate assets in chapter 11 case of Trancas Town Ltd. Crusader Entertainment: acquirer of intellectual properties out of the Red Fern bankruptcy. GAP / Old Navy: purchaser in the Loehman's, Service Merchandise, Lauriat's, Crowley's, Steinbachs, and Caldor chapter 11 cases. The Lusk Company: landlord in numerous chapter 11 cases. Paramount Pictures and Affiliates: creditor and purchaser of the Mann Theatre chain. Starwood Ceruzzi LLC and Vornado Realty LLC: purchaser in Hechingers chapter 11 case.

Klee,
Tuchin,
Bogdanoff &
Stern
LLP

MORRISON & FOERSTER LLP

THE FIRM

Chair of the Firm: Keith C Wetmore
Managing Partners for Operations: Mark W Danis
Larren M Nashelsky
Pamela J Reed

Number of partners worldwide: 329
Number of US partners: 293
Number of other lawyers worldwide: 686
Number of other US lawyers: 613

Email: info@mofo.com **Website:** www.mofo.com

FIRM OVERVIEW: Morrison & Foerster is a widely recognized international law firm with approximately 1000 lawyers in 19 offices. Morrison & Foerster combines technology and other leading industry expertise with a global full service legal practice in key financial and technology centers around the world. The firm is experienced in domestic and international corporate and corporate finance, securities and capital markets, US antitrust competition, banking and finance law. The firm's employment, litigation and arbitration, and tax practices are widely regarded as amongst the pre-eminent practices in their respective fields.

MAIN AREAS OF PRACTICE: Antitrust, bankruptcy and restructuring, communications and media, corporate, energy, entertainment, environmental, financial services, financial transactions, government contracts, intellectual property, international, investment management, labor and employment, land use and natural resources, life sciences, litigation, privacy, project finance and development, real estate, tax and technology transactions.
Corporate: The firm's Corporate Group represents some of the most dynamic companies in the world and can provide a full range of corporate finance advice, including venture financing, public offerings, strategic alliances, technology transactions, and mergers and acquisitions.
Litigation: The firm's Litigation Department includes some of the top trial and appellate lawyers in the United States, as well as leading practitioners in the areas of antitrust, securities, financial services, criminal defense, environmental and patent litigation.
Intellectual Property: The firm has one of the largest intellectual property practices of any general practice firm, including over 80 patent and trademark lawyers.
Labor & Employment: The firm's Employment Law Group advises and represents companies in all areas of employment-related law, ranging from traditional labor to trade secret/intellectual property matters in virtually every industry.
Tax: The firm's Tax Department contains the country's leading state and local tax practice, as well as providing federal and international tax advice.

INTERNATIONAL WORK: The firm has offices in key business centers around the world including London, Brussels, Hong Kong, Beijing, Shanghai, Singapore and Tokyo, as well as a strategic alliance with Cabanellas, Etchebarne, Kelly & Dell'Oro Maini in Buenos Aires, Argentina.

OFFICES

CALIFORNIA
425 Market Street, **San Francisco**, CA 94105-2482
Tel: 415 268 7000 **Fax:** 415 268 7522

755 Page Mill Road, **Palo Alto**, CA 94304-1018
Tel: 650 813 5600 **Fax:** 650 494 0792

101 Ygnacio Valley Road, Suite 450, **Walnut Creek**, CA 94596-4095
Tel: 925 295 3300 **Fax:** 925 946 9912

400 Capitol Mall, Suite 2600, **Sacramento**, CA 95814
Tel: 916 448 3200 **Fax:** 916 448 3222

555 West Fifth Street, Suite 3500, **Los Angeles**, CA 90013-1024
Tel: 213 892 5200 **Fax:** 213 892 5454

19900 MacArthur Boulevard, Twelfth Floor, **Irvine**, CA 92612
Tel: 949 251 7500 **Fax:** 949 251 0900

1925 Century Park East, Suite 2200, **Los Angeles**, CA 90067-2701
Tel: 310 203 4000 **Fax:** 310 203 4040

3811 Valley Centre Drive, Suite 500, **San Diego**, CA 92130-2332
Tel: 858 720 5100 **Fax:** 858 720 5125

COLORADO
5200 Republic Plaza, 370 Seventeenth Street, **Denver**, CO 80202-5638
Tel: 303 592 1500 **Fax:** 303 592 1510

DISTRICT OF COLUMBIA
2000 Pennsylvania Avenue, NW, Suite 5500,
Washington, DC 20006-1888
Tel: 202 887 1500 **Fax:** 202 887 0763

NEW YORK
1290 Avenue of the Americas, **New York**, NY 10104-0050
Tel: 212 468 8000 **Fax:** 212 468 7900

VIRGINIA
1650 Tysons Boulevard, Suite 300, **McLean,** VA 22102
Tel: 703 760 7700 **Fax:** 703 760 7777

CONTACTS

Business ....Nicholas J Spiliotes
Labor ....Raymond L Wheeler
Litigation ....Lori A Schechter
Tax ....Paul H Frankel
....Steve L Feldman

MORRISON | FOERSTER

O'MELVENY & MYERS LLP

THE FIRM

Chairman: Arthur B Culvahouse, Jr

Number of partners: 243
Number of other lawyers: 684

Website: www.omm.com

FIRM OVERVIEW: O'Melveny & Myers is a values-driven law firm guided by the principles of excellence, leadership and citizenship. With the breadth, depth and foresight to serve clients competing in a global economy, the firm's attorneys devise innovative approaches to resolve problems and achieve business goals. With more than 900 attorneys in 14 offices around the world, O'Melveny & Myers' capabilities span virtually every area of legal practice, including antitrust/competition; capital markets; corporate finance; entertainment and media; global enforcement and criminal defense; intellectual property and technology; labor and employment; litigation; mergers and acquisitions; private equity; project development and real estate; restructuring and insolvency; securities; tax; and trade and international law.

MAIN AREAS OF PRACTICE

Transactions: With approximately 300 attorneys, the Transactions Department represents a wide variety of corporations, financial institutions, governmental entities, and individuals. The department consists of the following practice areas: mergers and acquisitions/private equity; finance and restructuring; capital markets; business practice; entertainment and media; project development and real estate; and international. **Labor & Employment:** The Labor and Employment Department deals with issues concerning class actions, discrimination, harassment, wage and hour, and employee benefits matters and advises clients regarding workers' compensation, the Employee Retirement Income Security Act (ERISA), occupational safety and health, privacy, and all other types of personnel challenges.

Tax: The Tax Department is in the vanguard of the international and corporate tax fields, offering advanced capability in executive compensation and employee benefits law, and has been instrumental in developing a number of new products in the closely watched tax-exempt financing area. The firm's 40-plus tax attorneys handle all tax matters affecting its domestic and international clients firm wide, as well as a full range of estate planning and probate matters.

Intellectual Property & Technology: The Intellectual Property and Technology Department provides comprehensive and integrated advice on all aspects of the acquisition, exploitation, and enforcement of intellectual property rights. The firm's attorneys include internationally recognized experts in all facets of intellectual property law, including patent, trademark, trade secret, copyright, and internet law. The firm's clients include start-ups, emerging and middle market companies, major international corporations, entertainment leaders, venture capitalists, and financial institutions.

Litigation: The Litigation Department, which was named Litigation Department of the Year by 'The American Lawyer' in January 2004, is comprised of the following practice areas: appellate; environmental; white collar and regulatory defense; class actions; entertainment/sports/media; healthcare; SEC; antitrust and trade regulation; insurance and professional liability; international dispute resolution; telecommunications; securities; transportation/aviation; international trade; and strategic counseling.

US OFFICES

CALIFORNIA
114 Pacifica, Suite 100, **Irvine**, CA 92618
Tel: 949 737 2900   **Fax:** 949 737 2300

1999 Avenue of the Stars, **Los Angeles**, CA 90067
Tel: 310 553 6700   **Fax:** 310 246 6779

400 South Hope Street, **Los Angeles**, CA 90071
Tel: 213 430 6000   **Fax:** 213 430 6407

2765 Sand Hill Road, **Menlo Park**, CA 94025
Tel: 650 437 2600   **Fax:** 650 473 2601

610 Newport Center Drive, **Newport Beach**, CA 92660
Tel: 949 760 9600   **Fax:** 949 823 6994

Embarcadero Center West, 275 Battery Street,
San Francisco, CA 94111
Tel: 415 984 8700   **Fax:** 415 984 8701

DISTRICT OF COLUMBIA
1625 Eye Street, NW, **Washington**, DC 20006
Tel: 202 383 5300   **Fax:** 202 383 5414

NEW YORK
7 Times Square, **New York**, NY 10036
Tel: 212 326 2000   **Fax:** 212 326 2061

INTERNATIONAL OFFICES

The firm also has offices in Beijing, Brussels, Hong Kong, London, Shanghai and Tokyo.

CONTACTS

Transactions	David Krinsky (Newport Beach)
	John Suydam (New York)
Litigation	Mark Wood (Los Angeles)
Intellectual Property & Technology	Mark Samuels (Los Angeles)
Labor & Employment	Robert Siegel (Los Angeles)
Tax	Robert Rizzi (Washington, DC)

INTERNATIONAL WORK:

Asia: The Asia practice covers the full spectrum of business and commercial matters and controversies from establishing joint ventures, to providing advice on complex acquisition, investment, commercial, financial, and capital markets transactions, to international trade matters and other cross border disputes.

London: The London office is strategically positioned to handle the domestic, cross-border and multi-jurisdictional aspects of our clients' legal and business requirements throughout Europe. The London office has key strengths within private equity, corporate finance/M&A, banking, financing and capital markets. The London office offers full transactional service to its clients with resident experts supporting the fund and deal teams in the following areas of legal practice: taxation (including cross-border structuring), real estate, employment, regulatory, IP/IT and arbitration.

Brussels: The Brussels office focus on EU and member country competition and regulatory law, including mergers and acquisitions and joint ventures, anti-competitive agreements and concerted practices, cartel investigations, abuse of monopoly positions and state aid.

ORRICK, HERRINGTON & SUTCLIFFE LLP

THE FIRM

Chairman & Chief Executive Officer: Ralph H Baxter, Jr
Chief Operating Officer: Douglas Benson
Number of partners: 273
Number of other lawyers: 447

AREAS OF PRACTICE:

Corporate	16%
Litigation	15%
Intellectual Property	12%
Private Finance	10%
Public Finance	10%
Structured Finance	10%
Real Estate	7%
Employment Law	6%
Energy & Project Finance	6%
Tax	6%
Compensation & Benefits	2%

FIRM OVERVIEW: Established in 1836, Orrick is a global law firm with 14 offices and approximately 700 lawyers worldwide. The firm provides advice under US, English, French, Italian, German and Japanese law. Orrick's clients include major commercial and investment banks, industrial and financial corporations, technology companies, developers, universities and other public institutions, and governmental entities.

MAIN AREAS OF PRACTICE:

Corporate: Orrick's Corporate Practice covers a wide range of areas, from banking and commercial finance to market regulation, mergers and acquisitions, public and private offerings, emerging companies, and venture capital financings.

Real Estate: Orrick's Real Estate Group represents clients in the US, Asia and Europe on all phases of real estate investment, development, financing and operations, ranging from purchases and sales, leases and financings to sophisticated joint ventures and large portfolio, multi-state, and cross-border transactions.

Compensation & Benefits: Orrick's Compensation and Benefits Group advises clients on all aspects of their employee benefits and compensation arrangements including advice regarding executive compensation, benefit plan investments, mergers and acquisitions, qualified retirement plans and ESOPs, welfare plans, and disputes and litigation.

Tax: Orrick's Tax Practice advises companies of all sizes on all aspects of United States fedral, state, and international tax planning and litigtion. The group also provides tax planning advice to individuals through its private group.

ADVOCACY

Litigation: Orrick's national Litigation Practice encompasses virtually every business-related issue encountered today-intellectual property, securities, antitrust, distribution and trade regulation, product liability, environmental, tax, and white collar criminal defense.

Employment: Many of Orrick's employment lawyers are ranked best in their respective areas. All handle all varieties of employment litigation, wrongful discharge claims, EEO affirmative action compliance, and general employment matters.

Intellectual Property: The firm's national IP Team was ranked second in the US for IP defense. Orrick's attorneys have extensive experience in virtually every aspect of intellectual property law, including patent, copyright, and trademark infringement, unfair competition, and trade secret actions. They also advise clients in licensing, litigation avoidance, due diligence, and other matters across the complete spectrum of intellectual property issues.

FINANCE

Public Finance: The firm's Public Finance Practice is the largest and most diverse in the US. The firm ranks first in the country in the volume of

OFFICES

The Orrick Building, 405 Howard Street, **San Francisco**, CA 94105
Tel: 415 773 5700   **Fax:** 415 773 5759
Email: info@orrick.com

CALIFORNIA
1000 Marsh Road, **Menlo Park**, CA 94025-1021
Tel: 650 614 7400   **Fax:** 650 614 7401

777 South Figueroa Street, Suite 3200, **Los Angeles**, CA 90017-5855
Tel: 213 629 2020   **Fax:** 213 612 2499

400 Capitol Mall, Suite 3000, **Sacramento**, CA 95814-4497
Tel: 916 447 9200   **Fax:** 916 329 4900

4 Park Plaza, Suite 1600, Irvine, **Orange County**, CA 92614-2558
Tel: 949 567 6700   **Fax:** 949 567 6710

DISTRICT OF COLUMBIA
Washington Harbour, 3050 K Street, NW, **Washington,** DC 20007-5135
Tel: 202 339 8400   **Fax:** 202 339 8500

NEW YORK
666 Fifth Avenue, **New York**, NY 10103-0001
Tel: 212 506 5000   **Fax:** 212 506 5151

PACIFIC NORTHWEST
719 Second Avenue, Suite 900, **Seattle**, WA 98104-7097
Tel: 206 839 4300   **Fax:** 206 839 4301

1125 North West Couch Street, Suite 800, **Portland**, OR 97209
Tel: 503 943 4800   **Fax:** 503 943 4801

INTERNATIONAL OFFICES

The firm also has offices in France, Italy, Japan, Taiwan, and the United Kingdom.

financings for which it serves as bond counsel and as underwriters counsel.
Structured Finance: Orrick is a key player in the development of new structures for the asset-securitization market throughout the United States, Asia and Europe, and as counsel to issuers, underwriters, credit enhancers, selllers, servicers, and insitiutional purchasers. Orrick serves the world's leading fincial institutions in securitization transactiobns that add real value to companies and institutions around the world.

Energy, & Project Finance: Orrick's global energy, communications and infrastructure attorneys work collaboratively on projects throughout the world, including power plants, telecommunications facilities, industrial plants, waste disposal and resource recovery facilities, pipelines, toll roads, and other infrastructure projects.

Private Finance: The firm's Private Finance Practice has broad expertise in virtually every area of commercial finance, including secured and unsecured lending, project and infrastructure finance, leasing and asset-based financing, aircraft finance, institutional private placements, letters of credit, swaps and other hedging mechanisms, asset-backed commercial paper financings, workouts, bankruptcy, and bank regulatory issues.

CLIENTS: Orrick's clients include major commercial and investment banks, industrial and financial corporations, technology companies, developers, and public and governmental entities.

INTERNATIONAL WORK: Orrick is one of the world's leading securitization and structured finance firms. Its securitization group has been active in Europe and Asia. The firm's project finance and infrastructure experience in extensive, and boasts projects throughout Latin America, Asia, and Europe. Orrick also has one of the leading emerging market financial sector reform and corporate debate restructuring practices, and is currently increasing its high-profile work in the IT and telecommunications sectors.

PACHULSKI, STANG, ZIEHL, YOUNG, JONES & WEINTRAUB P.C.

THE FIRM

Management Committee: Richard M Pachulski, Dean A Ziehl, Ira D Kharasch, William P Weintraub, Laura Davis Jones, Henry C Kevane

Number of partners: 29
Number of other lawyers: 50

FIRM OVERVIEW: Pachulski, Stang, Ziehl, Young, Jones & Weintraub P.C. was founded in 1983, and has developed into one of the largest insolvency practices in the US. With over 70 attorneys in four offices, the firm's attorneys concentrate on business reorganizations (workouts, restructurings and chapter 11), commercial and real estate transactions, general commercial law and business litigation. Because the core of the firm's practice involves debtor-creditor relations and sophisticated financial restructurings, all of the firm's senior attorneys have broad and deep experience in business reorganization, bankruptcy and insolvency matters.

MAIN AREAS OF PRACTICE:

Business Reorganization & Workouts: The firm has a nationally recognized bankruptcy practice that is one of the largest in the country. The firm represents all of the major constituencies in bankruptcy proceedings and out of court workouts, including debtors, creditors' committees, equity committees, trustees, secured and major unsecured creditors, bondholders, asset purchasers and third-party plan proponents.

Litigation: The firm represents both plaintiffs and defendants in general commercial and business litigation, as well as banking, bankruptcy and insurance litigation. The prosecution and defense of litigation in bankruptcy court is a particular strength and the firm's litigators are well versed in bankruptcy jurisdictional disputes. The firm's national insolvency practice frequently requires client representation in fraudulent conveyance, preference and other bankruptcy-related litigation.

Corporate & Transactional: The firm's transactions practice features expertise over a broad spectrum, including real estate purchase and sales, development and commercial leasing; financing and workouts; sales of companies or their assets. The firm's transactional attorneys are uniquely qualified to handle the problems and issues associated with representing clients in complex bankruptcy transactions.

High Technology/Telecommunications: The firm has considerable experience with the special issues facing high technology/telecommunications debtors and sophisticated acquirers of high technology/telecommunications companies, including Covad Communications Group, Inacom Corp., Northpoint Communications, Peregrine Systems Inc., Tie Communications Inc., UniSil Corporation and Yipes Communications.

Retail & Restaurant Chains: The firm's combination of insolvency, real estate and commercial financial expertise enables members of the firm to represent a wide range of interests arising from the insolvency of large restaurant chains and retail outlets, including B.U.M. International Inc., C&R Clothiers Inc., Fedco Inc., The Boston Store, Sizzler International Inc. and Specialty Restaurants Corporation.

Insurance & Reinsurance: The firm's extensive involvement with restructuring in the insurance industry has given its lawyers recognized expertise in handling insurance and reinsurance disputes. Members of the firm have represented receivers, reinsurers, policyholders and other creditors in some of the largest insurance and reinsurance insolvencies in the world, including First Capital Holdings, Corp., First Executive Corporation (Executive Life Insurance Company), Superior National, Transit, Mission, Fremont and Kwelm.

Entertainment Insolvency: The firm has played prominent roles in some of the nation's largest production and distribution company chapter 11 cases, including United Artists, Loews Cinemas, General Cinemas, Mann Theaters, 21st Century Film Group and Quintex Entertainment, and has been involved in the cases of high-profile entertainers/athletes, including Toni Braxton, Ronald Isley, Johnny Gill and Mike Tyson.

CLIENTS: The firm acts or has acted as bankruptcy counsel to many large public and private corporations, including AgriBioTech Inc., American Rice Inc., AmeriServe Food Distributors Inc., Breed Technologies Inc., F&C Corp., Federal-Mogul Inc., Gencor Inc., Harnischfeger Industries Inc., HomePlace Stores Inc., Imperial Hotels Corporation, LogoAthletics Inc., MVP.com, PG&E Corporation, RBX Corporation, Sunbelt Nursery Group Inc., Trans World Airlines, TreeSweet Juice Company, Tri Valley Growers, Webvan Group (Homegrocer.com), W.R. Grace & Co. and Zenith Electronics. The firm has also served as counsel to court-appointed committees of creditors or other interest groups in the chapter 11 cases of America West Airlines Inc., Cirrus, DirecTV Latin America LLC, Fruit of the Loom, FundAmerica, Guy F. Atkinson Company, Home Fed Corp., Lynx Golf Inc., Orange County, Pannell Kerr Forster, Pioneer Take-Out Corp., and Sun World International Inc. Other clients represented by the firm in litigation, transactions or as creditors or other parties in interest in bankruptcy cases include Chicago Title, DSL Transportation, Farmers Commonwealth Insurance Co., Fuji Photo Film USA Inc., Gilda Marx Incorporated, Heller Financial Inc., Hilton Hotels, Imperial Hotels Inc., National Broadcasting Company Inc., PaineWebber Funding Inc., Peoplesoft Inc., Safeway Corporation, The Hahn Company and Xerox Corporation.

INTERNATIONAL WORK: The firm has substantial expertise in international or cross-border insolvency cases. A member of the firm, Arnold Quittner, is a frequent lecturer and internationally recognized expert in this area. He is joined in this practice by Jeremy Richards, a graduate of both Oxford and Harvard Law School, and a founding member of the British-American Bar Association. Both have published articles on cross-border insolvency issues. Among other matters, Mr Quittner acted as chief counsel in the first and largest concurrent reorganization case in Japan and the United States (Maruko Inc. in the Tokyo District Court and US Bankruptcy Court), and represented Bramalea Inc. in parallel Canadian-American reorganization proceedings. The firm also represents Bell Canada in the dual Canadian-American reorganization proceedings of Teleglobe Inc.

HEAD OFFICE

CALIFORNIA
10100 Santa Monica Boulevard, Suite 1100, **Los Angeles**, CA 90067
Tel: 310 277 6910   **Fax:** 310 201 0760
Email: dziehl@pszyj.com
Website: www.pszyj.com

BRANCH OFFICES

CALIFORNIA
3 Embarcadero, Suite 1020, **San Francisco**, CA 94111
Tel: 415 263 7000   **Fax:** 415 263 7010

DELAWARE
919 North Market Street, Suite 1600, **Wilmington**, DE 19801
Tel: 302 652 4100   **Fax:** 302 652 4400

NEW YORK
780 Third Avenue, 36th Floor, **New York**, NY 10017-2024
Tel: 212 561 7700   **Fax:** 212 561 7777

PAUL, HASTINGS, JANOFSKY & WALKER LLP

THE FIRM

Chair of the Firm: Seth M Zachary
Managing Partner: Greg M Nitzkowski

Number of partners: 242
Number of other lawyers: 723

Email: info@paulhastings.com
Website: www.paulhastings.com

FIRM OVERVIEW: Founded in 1951, Paul Hastings currently conducts its global law practice through an international network of offices that links the world's leading financial centres. The firm has approximately 960 attorneys in 15 offices and is considered one of the top law firms in the world. The firm's position as a leading international law firm is built on its ability to draw upon the resources of its globally integrated practice areas that are organised into five departments: corporate, real estate, tax, litigation and employment law. The firm provides legal advice and services to Fortune 500 and Forbes International 500 companies, as well as smaller and emerging business enterprises.

MAIN AREAS OF PRACTICE:

Corporate: With a mix of US, UK, France, Belgium, Hong Kong, PRC and Japanese qualified lawyers, Paul Hastings provides a full range of advice in international and cross-border corporate transactions. The firm advises on a wide range of transactions under the laws of several jurisdictions and provides in-depth experience in many world markets, including all parts of Europe, Asia and Africa. The firm's attorneys have advised on a range of transactions, including commercial finance transactions, equity and debt offerings, secured financings and international corporate restructurings and workout transactions, venture capital transactions, and project and acquisition finance around the world. The Corporate Department was recently named M&A Law Firm of the Year by Mergers & Acquisitions Advisor.

Employment Law: The firm has counseled its international clients with respect to traditional labor law, equal employment opportunity laws, wrongful discharge, sexual harassment, employee benefits matters and other employment related issues. Recently ranked as the #1 Employment and Labor Law Firm by Chambers USA and named the 'Labor and Employment Litigation Department of the Year' by The American Lawyer, the firm is frequently called upon by many of the nation's leading attorneys and law firms to represent them in their employment law matters. The firm's experience in identifying and understanding cultural differences is invaluable in its representation of international clients in this area.

Litigation: The firm handles litigation and arbitration proceedings as well as government investigations involving entities based abroad, ranging from anti-trust to breach-of-contract cases. The firm has particular expertise in handling international trade and commercial disputes and intellectual property issues. Many of the cases the firm handles are cross-border in nature. The firm's international litigation and arbitration practice brings together practitioners in its US and non-US offices alike, offering clients zealous advocacy in disputes involving a wide variety of subject areas. The firm has extensive experience in handling discovery in an international context, and its attorneys are knowledgeable on the Hague Conventions on Service of Judicial Documents and Evidence Taking, and other conventions and treaties imposing limitations on discovery by foreign countries, as well as other limitations affecting international arbitration and litigation.

US OFFICES

CALIFORNIA
695 Town Center Drive, **Costa Mesa**, CA 92626
Tel: 714 668 6200 **Fax:** 714 979 1921

515 South Flower Street, **Los Angeles**, CA 90071
Tel: 213 683 6000 **Fax:** 213 627 0705

55 Second Street, **San Francisco**, CA 94105
Tel: 415 856 6000 **Fax:** 415 856 7100

3579 Valley Centre Drive, **San Diego**, CA 92130
Tel: 858 720 2500 **Fax:** 858 720 2555

CONNECTICUT
1055 Washington Boulevard, **Stamford**, CT 06901
Tel: 203 961 7400 **Fax:** 203 359 3031

DISTRICT OF COLUMBIA
875 15th St, NW, **Washington**, DC 20005
Tel: 202 551 1700 **Fax:** 202 551 1705

GEORGIA
600 Peachtree Street, NE, **Atlanta**, GA 30308
Tel: 404 815 2400 **Fax:** 404 815 2424

NEW YORK
75 East 55th Street, **New York**, NY 10022
Tel: 212 318 6000 **Fax:** 212 319 4090

INTERNATIONAL OFFICES

The firm also has offices in Beijing, Brussels, Hong Kong, London, Paris Shanghai and Tokyo.

Real Estate: The firm's real estate practice is among the largest and most experienced of any US law firm and is internationally recognized for its excellence, having been named International Real Estate Law Firm of the Year by Chambers Global, The World's Leading Lawyers 2002-03 audited by the British Market Research Bureau. The firm's partners' cumulative experience extends to the lending, acquisition, leasing and investment of real estate assets on a national and international scale. The firm has been at the forefront of the introduction of international standards and practices to the acquisition, financing and workout of non-performing secured and unsecured real estate and corporate loans and assets.

Tax: The firm's international tax practice covers mergers and acquisitions, capital market offerings, investment and joint venture structuring, leasing, structured and project finance, and financial product planning and structuring, as well as tax controversy and tax litigation matters. Matters have included the formation of local and international entities on behalf of Netherlands, British Virgin Islands, Cayman Islands and Panamanian corporations as well as Cayman Islands and Bermuda Trusts and Liechtenstein Anstalts. Paul Hastings recently advised Telkom South Africa on a $487 million IPO, a transaction that was recognised by International Tax Review as the 'Deal of the Year 2003'.

QUINN EMANUEL URQUHART OLIVER & HEDGES, LLP

THE FIRM

Managing Partner: John B Quinn

Number of partners: 71
Number of other lawyers: 160

FIRM OVERVIEW: Quinn Emanuel Urquhart Oliver & Hedges, LLP is a 230+ lawyer business litigation firm - the largest in the United States devoted solely to business litigation. The firm has a very substantial trial practice. At last count the firm's lawyers tried 987 cases and won 92.1%. When representing defendants, the firm's trial experience allows it to achieve better settlements and defense verdicts. When representing plaintiffs, the firm's lawyers have garnered over $3.1 billion in judgments and settlements. The firm obtained one of the 10 largest jury verdicts in the US in 2002 and 2003. Obtained the largest reported settlements in those years as well.

MAIN AREAS OF PRACTICE:

Business Litigation: In the areas of intellectual property (patent, copyright, trademark and trade secrets litigation); international and domestic arbitration; unfair competition, antitrust and trade regulation litigation; employment and employee movement litigation; securities litigation; entertainment litigation; real estate development and construction litigation; banking and financial institution litigation; government contracts litigation and counseling; insurance coverage; healthcare; internet and new media litigation; white collar criminal litigation; corporate governance and internal investigations.

CLIENTS: IBM; Mattel, Inc.; Shell Oil; Time Warner; Genentech; Nike; Seiko Epson Corporation; Electronic Arts; PalmOne; Computer Science Corp.; Oracle; The Zurich Group; American West Homes Incorporated; Delphi Automotive Systems; DirecTV; Electronic Arts; Kaufman and Broad Home Corporation; MP3.com, Inc. Credit Suisse First Boston; TRW Inc.; AIG; Oracle Corporation; Izumi Products Company; The Parsons Corporation; Hughes Electronics Corporation; Jefferies & Company, Inc.; Fox, Inc.; Nextel Communications, Inc.; Union Bank of California, N.A.; The Walt Disney Company; Washington Mutual Bank; Invensys Software Systems; Mirage Animation, Inc.; Idealabs; ING Barings, LLC; PharmaSystem Therapeutics, Inc.; Bancorp Services; GMAC Mortgage Corporation; Academy of Motion Picture Arts and Sciences; Callidus Software, Inc.; United Talent Agency; Borland Software, Inc.; Loral Space and Communications; Computer Sciences Corporation; Vishay Siliconix; Trust Company of the West Lazard Freres & Co. LLC; Marsh & McLellan Companies, Inc.; Tribune Company; Hollywood Entertainment; CBS, Inc.; Home Box Office; Kmart; Avery Dennison Corporation; Leland Stanford University; Newscorp; eBay Inc.; General Motors Corporation; Johnson & Johnson; Lockheed Martin Corporation; The Los Angeles Times; Northrop Grumman Corporation; Sony Electronics; PeopleSoft; Intuit; Hyundai.

INTERNATIONAL WORK: The firm has advised international companies operating within the US, and also advised US companies on their overseas activities. The firm represents Dr Enrico Bondi, the trustee in the bankruptcy of Parmalat. In addition, the firm's lawyers have arbitrated cases under rules of the London Court of International Arbitration, the International Chamber of commerce, and the American Arbitration Association, UNCITRAL, ICSID, and arbitration statutes of various countries, in New York, Los Angeles, London, Paris, Stockholm, Bermuda, Montreal and Lima involving companies from England, Germany, Greece Peru,

Sweden, the United Kingdom, Russia, Venezuela etc. Each year the firm sponsors an international arbitration conference attended by advocates and arbitrators from around the world. The firm's lawyers are familiar with, and in some cases helped draft, international and domestic arbitration codes.

HEAD OFFICE

CALIFORNIA
865 South Figueroa Street, 10th Floor, **Los Angeles**, CA 90017
Tel: 213 443 3000   **Fax:** 213 443 3100
Email: johnquinn@quinnemanuel.com
Website: www.quinnemanuel.com

BRANCH OFFICES

CALIFORNIA
555 Twin Dolphin Drive, Suite 560, **Redwood Shores**, CA 94065
Tel: 650 620 4500   **Fax:** 650 620 4555
Email: claudestern@quinnemanuel.com

50 California Street, 22nd Floor, **San Francisco**, CA 94111
Tel: 415 875 6600   **Fax:** 415 875 6700
Email: charlesverhoeven@quinnemanuel.com

45-025 Manitou Drive, Suite 8, **Indian Wells,** CA 92210
Tel: 760 345 4757   **Fax:** 760 345 2414
Email: halhopp@quinnemanuel.com

4445 Eastgate Mall, Suite 200, **San Diego**, CA 92121
Tel: 858 812 3107   **Fax:** 858 812 3336
Email: michadanzig@quinnemanuel.com

NEW YORK
335 Madison Ave, 17th Floor, **New York**, NY 10017
Tel: 212 702 8100   **Fax:** 212 702 8200
Email: michaelcarlinsky@quinnemanuel.com

CONTACTS

Los Angeles	John B Quinn
	A William Urquhart
	Fred G Bennett
New York	Michael Carlinsky
	Peter E Calamari
San Francisco	Charles K Verhoeven
Silicon Valley	Claude M Stern
San Diego	Mitch Danzig
Palm Springs	Harold W Hopp

quinn emanuel trial lawyers
quinn emanuel urquhart oliver & hedges, llp

STUTMAN, TREISTER & GLATT PROFESSIONAL CORPORATION

THE FIRM

Chairman of the Executive Committee: Robert A Greenfield

Number of partners and senior of counsel: 20
Number of counsel: 9
Number of associates: 7

HEAD OFFICE

CALIFORNIA
1901 Avenue of the Stars, Twelfth Floor, **Los Angeles**, CA 90067
Tel: 310 228 5600 **Fax:** 310 228 5788
Email: info@stutman.com
Website: www.stutman.com

FIRM OVERVIEW: Stutman, Treister & Glatt Professional Corporation is a pre-eminent law firm in the practice of reorganization, bankruptcy, and insolvency law. The firm has long been known as a creative innovator in its field, focusing primarily on creating viable business reorganizations. The firm has successfully concluded some of the most complex and difficult out-of-court restructurings, prepackaged and pre-negotiated chapter 11 plans and chapter 11 reorganizations, and related purchases and sales of assets and businesses.

MAIN AREAS OF PRACTICE: Since 1948, the law firm has focused particularly on the representation of (i) financially troubled business organizations; (ii) creditors' and equity holders' committees; (iii) sellers and buyers of troubled companies; (iv) bondholders and bondholders committees; (v) significant secured and unsecured creditors; and (vi) parties in bankruptcy and insolvency related litigation.

Firm Lawyers: The firm's lawyers are well-known throughout the country for their leadership and contributions to the practice: three lawyers are members of the National Bankruptcy Conference, seven lawyers are members of the American College of Bankruptcy, two lawyers are editors of 'Collier's on Bankruptcy', numerous lawyers are listed on various 'Who's Who' lists, 13 lawyers were listed as California Super Lawyers 2004, and the firm's lawyers routinely publish articles and lecture at professional conferences. Collectively, seven lawyers have more than 30 years experience, an additional 10 lawyers have 20 to 30 years of experience, and an additional nine lawyers have 10 to 20 years of experience.

CLIENTS: ST&G's national practice is highlighted by the cases in which the firm has been actively involved. The firm's debtor representations, both in-court and out-of-court, include Applied Magnetics Corporation, Barney's Inc., Barry's Jewelers, Inc., Broadbandsports.com, Bumble Bee Seafoods, Inc., Carter Hawley Hale Stores, Inc., Clark Retail Enterprises, Inc., County of Orange, Daewoo Motor America, Inc., Diva Systems Corporation, Edwards Theatres Circuit, Inc., El Camino Resources, Ltd., Graham & James LLP, Hawaiian Holdings, Inc., Home Fed Corporation, Huntsman Corporation, Itel Corporation, Kenetech Windpower, Inc., Krause's Furniture, Inc., Lamonts Apparel, Inc., Leasing Solutions, Inc., Lyon & Lyon LLP, Mariner Health Group, Maxicare, MTP Grand Place Tower, a Maguire Company, NBI, Public Service Co. of New Hampshire, The Regent Las Vegas (The Resort at Summerlin), Restaurant Enterprises Group, Inc., Southern California Edison Company, Sirius Satellite Radios, Standard Brands Paint Co., Storage Technology Corporation, Store of Knowledge, Inc., Thrifty Oil Co., Toy Time.com, Inc., Westmoreland Coal Company, and Wickes Companies, Inc. ST&G's present and former creditor, equity and strategic investor clients include Apollo Advisors, LP, Ares Corporate Opportunities Fund LP, The Baupost Group, BP America, Inc., Catholic Healthcare West, Converse, Inc., Davidson Kempner Partners, DDJ Capital, Elliot Advisors, Fantastic Sams, Fidelity Investments, FINOVA, First American Title Insurance Co., General Cinemas, Home Savings of America, Leonard Green and Partners, Leucadia National Corporation, Litton Industries, Metro-Goldwyn-Mayer Studios, Inc., Paramount Pictures Corporation, Pennzoil Co., Pouschine Cook Capital

Management, LLC, RC Aviation LLC, Sony Corporation of America (and its affiliates), Tri-Star Pictures, United Airlines, Inc., U.S. Airways, Inc., and Viacom, Inc. The firm also represents creditors and creditor's committees in chapter 11 cases and out-of-court restructurings, including formal and informal committees; such representations have been in connection with the restructuring of Adelphia, Aladdin Gaming LLC, American Restaurant Group, Bally's Grand, Inc., Charter Medical Corporation, Consolidated Freightways, Inc., Enron Corp., Global Crossing, Globalstar, Golden Ocean Group, Limited, House2Home, Inc., JP Stevens, NRG, Orion Pictures Corporation, Owens-Corning, Papercraft Corporation, PRIMESTAR, Inc., Resorts International, Inc., and WorldCom.

INTERNATIONAL WORK: The firm has represented foreign debtors, or their foreign representatives. These representations have included both chapter 11 cases for a foreign debtor with assets in the United States and ancillary proceeding pursuant to Section 304 of the United States Bankruptcy Code to enjoin the enforcement of remedies against assets located in the United States or the continuation of litigation.

LAW OFFICES

STUTMAN

TREISTER

& GLATT

PROFESSIONAL

CORPORATION

THELEN REID & PRIEST LLP

THE FIRM

Chairman: Thomas J Igoe, Jr
Vice Chairman: Mark P Weitzel
Managing Partner, Administration & Executive Director: Michelle L Johnson
Number of partners: 200
Number of other lawyers: 249

FIRM OVERVIEW: Thelen Reid & Priest LLP is a national law firm with more than 440 attorneys and offices in New York, San Francisco, Washington, DC, Los Angeles, Silicon Valley and Florham Park, NJ. Serving Fortune 500 companies and their privately held counterparts, the firm provides superior legal services with a focus on complex commercial litigation, corporate and capital markets transactions, project and asset finance, construction and government contracts, labor and employment, intellectual property, domestic and international tax, employee benefits, government affairs, and real estate. Thelen Reid is recognized as a leader in the construction, infrastructure, and energy and utilities industries in the United States.

MAIN AREAS OF PRACTICE:

Commercial Litigation: Thelen Reid's Commercial Litigation Team has earned a national reputation for excellence in areas including antitrust, arbitration, banking, bankruptcy, corporate governance, entertainment, environmental, insurance, intellectual property, product liability, real estate, securities, technology, toxic tort and white collar investigations and criminal defense. Thelen Reid has been at the forefront of international arbitration law and practice and has pioneered efforts to develop faster, more economical mechanisms for resolving commercial disputes outside of traditional litigation.

Construction & Government Contracts: Thelen Reid's Construction Practice is the preeminent practice of its kind in the United States. Its lawyers work with clients from the initiation of projects and preparation of contract documents through dispute resolution, including negotiation, mediation, arbitration and trial. The firm's construction attorneys have worked on projects ranging from individual buildings through some of the largest infrastructure projects in the world. In 2003, the firm launched Masons Thelen Reid LLP, a joint venture with Masons of the United Kingdom, creating the largest construction, engineering and infrastructure practice in the world. The firm's attorneys have substantial experience in the broad range of issues involved in, and process of, contracting with the federal, state, and local governments.

Corporate & Capital Markets: The firm's growing Business and Finance Practice provides legal representation and counseling in a wide range of domestic and international corporate and commercial finance transactions. The practice is involved in capital markets transactions, telecommunications, mergers and acquisitions, general corporate representation and cross-border structured finance. The practice also focuses on matters involving federal regulation of utilities, securities law compliance, private equity, general contract matters, partnerships, creditors' rights, and patent, copyright and trademark prosecution and counseling.

Government Affairs: The firm's Government Affairs Team represents key players in today's global economy on complex and sophisticated issues before Congress and the Executive Branch. Thelen Reid government affairs attorneys, representing a group of Nevada dairy farmers, won a 2003 decision before the United States Supreme Court.

Intellectual Property: Thelen Reid's IP Practice reflects its attorneys' broad expertise in the areas of patent, trademark and copyright, trade secret and competition law. The firm provides the comprehensive IP value services and continuity of legal care increasingly required by businesses whose growth depends on effectively managing IP portfolio assets across the three critical stages of IP value growth: acquiring and protecting IP assets, managing and developing the value of IP rights and assets, and enforcing IP rights and access to IP-related markets.

Labor & Employment: With attorneys representing clients on a national

HEAD OFFICES

CALIFORNIA
101 Second Street, Suite 1800, **San Francisco**, CA 94105
Tel: 415.371.1200 **Fax:** 415 371 1211

NEW YORK
875 Third Avenue, 10th Floor, **New York**, NY 10022
Tel: 212 603 2000 **Fax:** 212 603 2001
Website: www.thelenreid.com

CONTACTS

Business & Finance ....David P Graybeal
Commercial Litigation ....Michael S Elkin
Construction & Government Contracts ....Stephen V O'Neal
Government Affairs ....William A Kirk, Jr, Walter L Raheb
Intellectual Property....................Glynna K Christian, Mark Fox Evens
Labor & Employment...Linda S Husar
Project & Asset Finance ....
......................Mark P Weitzel, Richard M Farmer, Thomas B Glascock
Real Estate ....Richard J Kane
Tax & Employee Benefits ....James I Warren

OFFICES

San Francisco Office Managing Partner ....Michael C Hallerud
New York Office Managing Partner ....Jonathan D Siegfried
Washington, DC Office Managing Partner ....Andrew D Ness
Los Angeles Office Managing Partner ....Thomas E Hill
Silicon Valley Office Managing Partner ....Kenneth L Nissly
Morristown, NJ Office Managing Partner ....Marc B Lasky

basis in connection with high-stakes employment litigation, discrimination and wage and hour class actions, and matters involving workplace torts, ADA and traditional labor issues, Thelen Reid's Labor and Employment Department is one of the largest such practices of any full service firm in the nation. The firm has developed long-term partnerships with some of the nation's largest employers, and has helped to create in-house training and compliance programs and audits that help clients manage and remedy problems before potential litigation can begin.

Project & Asset Finance: Thelen Reid's project and asset finance attorneys have represented clients in the development and acquisition of energy and infrastructure projects throughout the US and in more than 60 foreign countries. The firm has been rated in the top group of US project finance law firms by *The American Lawyer, Privatization International* and *Euromoney*, and draws upon the unsurpassed expertise of its construction law and dispute resolution groups.

Tax & Employee Benefits: The firm provides business and individual clients with a full range of tax planning, administrative and litigation services relating to corporate taxation; taxation of financial instruments; federal, state and local taxation; partnerships and limited liability companies; and employee benefits and compensation. The firm also represents foreign corporations from over 40 countries and US-based multinational corporations and institutional investors.

Real Estate: Thelen Reid's Real Estate Practice covers the entire spectrum of real estate and real estate financing, representing domestic and foreign individuals and institutional investors, lenders and investment bankers in connection with the acquisition, sale, financing, development, leasing, management, rehabilitation and construction of all types of commercial and industrial properties.

INTERNATIONAL WORK: Thelen Reid represents clients around the world in their international endeavors. Their attorneys' extensive foreign language capabilities and knowledge of different cultures and legal systems allows them to understand the particular needs of the firm's international clientele, resolve problems and attain critical objectives.

WESTON BENSHOOF ROCHEFORT RUBALCAVA & MacCUISH LLP

THE FIRM

Managing Partner: Edward J Casey
Number of partners: 31
Number of other lawyers: 35

FIRM OVERVIEW: Weston Benshoof is a California-based law firm focused on business counseling, complex commercial litigation, environmental law, and real estate development. The firm provides a range of integrated legal services, maintaining the highest level of responsiveness to help clients achieve their goals.

MAIN AREAS OF PRACTICE:

Business Litigation: Weston Benshoof's Commercial Litigation Practice is distinguished by the substantial court experience of its attorneys, who have successfully handled complex trials of national significance in diverse industries. The firm's experience includes antitrust, unfair competition, consumer class actions, contract disputes, and a variety of other major claims facing large and small businesses.

Construction: The firm provides a full range of construction law services to owners, contractors and construction managers primarily in large public and private infrastructure, industrial and commercial projects. This expertise includes project planning, procurement and contracting; project start-up, counseling and close-out; and litigation of complex construction claims.

Corporate & Business Transactions: Weston Benshoof provides counseling to businesses at all stages of their growth, from inception through public offering. This expertise includes mergers and acquisitions, securities offerings, debt and equity financing, restructurings, corporate governance, licensing agreements, joint ventures, and technology transfer agreements.

Energy: Weston Benshoof's full-service Energy Group assists in positioning clients in California's unique energy market. The group has years of experience in the power industry, integrating the firm's broad capabilities in business counseling, land development, environmental permitting and compliance, public law, construction and litigation.

Environmental Compliance & Litigation: Environmental law has been one of Weston Benshoof's core practice areas since the firm's founding, matching the specific needs of each client for permitting, compliance, counseling, and lobbying. The firm also handles a wide range of environmental litigation matters, including government enforcement, citizen suits, toxic tort, and Proposition 65 actions.

Franchise: Weston Benshoof provides franchise and distribution counseling to oil companies, manufacturers, restaurants, and a variety of goods and service franchisors and franchisees alike. The firm's extensive litigation experience includes enforcing franchise agreements, upholding challenged franchise terminations, and defending nationwide franchise and distribution practices in precedent-setting antitrust cases.

Insurance: The firm represents commercial policyholders in obtaining settlements and judgments from their insurers when first or third party coverage has initially been disputed. This experience includes a range of general liability, environmental, toxic tort, professional liability, employer's liability, construction bond, intellectual property, workers' compensation, and oil and gas issues.

Intellectual Property: Weston Benshoof has extensive experience in intellectual property litigation, with an emphasis in the areas of trade secrets, trademarks and economic espionage, in addition to patents and copyrights. The firm also guides clients through complex licensing agreements, including joint technology development projects with leading universities and other research institutions.

Labor & Employment: The firm has assisted clients with litigation and counseling on all manner of employment-related claims, including wrongful termination, discrimination, harassment, wage and hour issues, OSHA matters, 'whistle blower' cases, union issues, restrictive covenant

disputes, and protection of trade secret matters.

Land Use: Weston Benshoof's Land Use Practice is one of the largest in the region, and has a range and depth of experience unrivaled by any other California law firm. The firm's attorneys have assisted clients with obtaining and defending land use entitlements for all types of development projects, including residential and master planned communities, commercial and retail centers, industrial operations and infrastructure projects.

Real Estate: Weston Benshoof is uniquely situated among California law firms because of its track record of providing premier 'A to Z' counseling and legal services on major commercial real estate projects. The firm has experience in structuring, drafting, negotiating and closing a broad spectrum of real estate deals - including acquisition, disposition, secured finance, and leasehold transactions.

Telecommunications: California has emerged as one of the key centers for telecommunications, and Weston Benshoof represents leading companies in the industry, including major providers of wireless service and infrastructure. A team of attorneys provides a wide range of litigation, transactional, counseling, and governmental advocacy services to meet the unique needs of communications and information technology businesses.

Toxic Torts/Product Liability: The firm is a recognized leader in resolving complex toxic tort and product liability lawsuits on behalf of aerospace, petroleum, chemical, manufacturing, waste disposal, and other companies. The firm's creative defense strategies and case management techniques reflect its substantial technical and legal experience across the spectrum of environmental law and litigation.

Water Resources: Weston Benshoof provides a full range of water-related counseling and legal services to public agencies, private water companies, residential developers, and other clients. This experience includes a broad spectrum of matters involving water rights, water quality, conjunctive use, import and export of water, infrastructure projects, water reclamation and water marketing.

CLIENTS: Weston Benshoof's clients range from Fortune 500 corporations to emerging companies to public agencies at all levels of government.

HEAD OFFICE

CALIFORNIA
333 South Hope Street, 16th Floor, **Los Angeles,** CA 90071
Tel: 213 576 1000 **Fax:** 213 576 1100
Website: www.wbcounsel.com

BRANCH OFFICE

CALIFORNIA
2801 Townsgate Road, Suite 215, **Westlake Village,** CA 91361
Tel: 805 497 9474 **Fax:** 805 497 8804

CONTACTS

Business Litigation & Franchise	Kurt V Osenbaugh
Construction	G. Christian Roux
Corporate & Business Transactions	Jonathan M Gordon
Energy	David S MacCuish
Environmental Compliance	Sharon Rubalcava
Environmental Litigation	Kurt Weissmuller
Insurance	Richard Giller
Intellectual Property	Louis A Karasik
Labor & Employment	Martha S Doty
Land Use	Steven W Weston
Real Estate	Pamela J Privett
Telecommunications	Jesse M Jauregui
Toxic Torts/Product Liability	Samuel C Taylor
Water Resources	Edward J Casey

WILSON SONSINI GOODRICH & ROSATI

THE FIRM

Chairman & CEO: Larry W Sonsini

Number of partners: 161
Number of attorneys: 600

FIRM OVERVIEW: Wilson Sonsini Goodrich & Rosati is the premier legal advisor to technology and growth business enterprises worldwide. The firm's legal expertise serves clients at all stages of development, from venture-backed start-up companies to multi-billion dollar global enterprises. Wilson Sonsini Goodrich & Rosati's broad range of services and legal disciplines are focused on serving the principal challenges faced by management and the board of directors of the business enterprise. The firm's clients are in a variety of industries including information technology, software, life sciences and retail. Wilson Sonsini Goodrich & Rosati is nationally recognized as a leader in corporate governance, public and private offerings of equity and debt securities, mergers and acquisitions, securities class action litigation, intellectual property litigation, joint ventures and strategic alliances, and technology licensing and other intellectual property transactions. Over the past four decades, the firm has established its reputation by having a superior knowledge of its clients' industries, as well as deep and long-standing contacts throughout the technology sector.

MAIN AREAS OF PRACTICE: Wilson Sonsini Goodrich & Rosati's main areas of practice include corporate law and governance; corporate finance – private equity, public equity, and debt finance; mergers and acquisitions; litigation – securities litigation, intellectual property litigation, commercial litigation, white collar crime and internal investigations, and employment law; intellectual property counseling and transactions – technology transactions, intellectual property counseling and patents, trademarks, copyrights and advertising; antitrust counseling; employee benefits and compensation; fund services; real estate and environmental; tax; and wealth management.

CLIENTS: Wilson Sonsini Goodrich & Rosati's client base includes: communications and networking, electronics/computer hardware, financial institutions, information service providers, life sciences, media and entertainment, retail and consumer products and services, semiconductors, software and venture capital.

INTERNATIONAL WORK: Headquartered in Silicon Valley, with offices in six technology hubs throughout the US, Wilson Sonsini Goodrich & Rosati has a national presence with a global reach. Over the past four decades, the firm has developed a wide ranging international practice, with particular strength in Asia and Europe. Wilson Sonsini Goodrich & Rosati represents both US and foreign clients in a variety of international matters including: cross-boder merger and acquisition transactions, joint ventures, foreign investment, branch operations, and intellectual property.

HEAD OFFICE

CALIFORNIA
650 Page Mill Road, **Palo Alto**, CA 94304-1050
Tel: 650 493 9300   **Fax:** 650 493 6811
Email: wsgr@wsgr.com
Website: www.wsgr.com

BRANCH OFFICES

CALIFORNIA
12235 El Camino Real, Suite 200,
San Diego, CA 92130
Tel: 838 350 2300   **Fax:** 858 350 2399

One Market, Spear Tower, Suite 3300,
San Francisco, CA 94105-1126
Tel: 415 947 2000   **Fax:** 415 947 2099

NEW YORK
12 East 49th Street, 30th Floor,
New York, NY10017-8203
Tel: 212 999 5800   **Fax:** 212 999 5899

TEXAS
8911 Capital of Texas Highway North, Westech 360, Suite 3350,
Austin, TX 78759-8497
Tel: 512 338 5400   **Fax:** 512 338 5499

UTAH
2795 East Cottonwood Parkway, Suite 300,
Salt Lake City, UT 84121-6928
Tel: 801 993 6400   **Fax:** 801 993 6499

VIRGINIA
Two Fountain Square, Reston Town Center, 11921 Freedom Drive,
Suite 600, **Reston**, VA 20190-5634
Tel: 703 734 3100   **Fax:** 703 734 3199

WASHINGTON
701 Fifth Avenue, Suite 1500, **Seattle**, WA 98033-7384
Tel: 206 883 2500   **Fax:** 206 883 2699

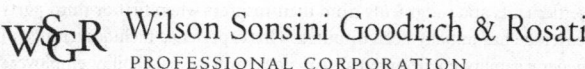

Wilson Sonsini Goodrich & Rosati
PROFESSIONAL CORPORATION

CONTENTS: Corporate/M&A p.303; Employment: p.305; Environment p.307; Intellectual Property p.309; Litigation: p.310; Real Estate p.313; Individuals' Profiles p.316 Firm; Profiles p.324.

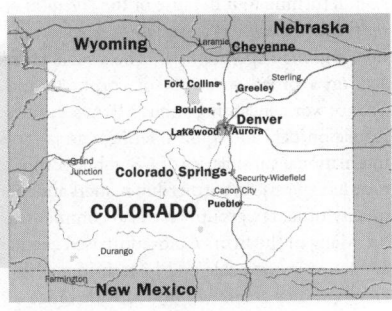

How lawyers are ranked

The opinions we gather from clients — mainly from in-house lawyers but also from other purchasers of legal services — are balanced by opinions from colleagues and competitors. Together, they provide two different perspectives — an all-round view — and biased viewpoints cancel each other out.

CORPORATE/M&A

Colorado
Leading firms (Corporate/M&A)

1. COOLEY GODWARD LLP *Broomfield*
   HOGAN & HARTSON LLP *Denver*
   HOLME ROBERTS & OWEN LLP *Denver*
2. BARTLIT BECK HERMAN PALENCHAR *Denver*
   BROWNSTEIN HYATT & FARBER PC *Denver*
   DAVIS GRAHAM & STUBBS LLP *Denver*
3. FAEGRE & BENSON LLP *Denver*
   HOLLAND & HART LLP *Denver*
   SHERMAN & HOWARD LLC *Denver*

Leading individuals (Corporate/M&A)

1. HILTON Paul *Hogan & Hartson*, Denver
   LEVINE Ronald *Davis Graham*, Denver
   LINFIELD James *Cooley Godward*, Broomfield
   PALENCHAR James *Bartlit Beck*, Denver
   SALTER Dean *Holme Roberts*, Denver
   WHEELER Francis *Cooley Godward*, Broomfield
2. HOLMES Whitney *Hogan & Hartson*, Denver
   JENSEN Garth *Holme Roberts*, Denver
   LEVY Mark *Holland & Hart*, Denver
   PLUMRIDGE Richard *Holme Roberts*, Denver
   SIEGEL Steven *Brownstein Hyatt*, Denver
   WALSH Christopher *Hogan & Hartson*, Denver
   WRIGHT Douglas *Faegre & Benson*, Denver
3. ARKELL Betty *Holland & Hart*, Denver
   BLAIR Andrew *Sherman & Howard*, Denver
   CAMPBELL William *Faegre & Benson*, Denver
   CUDNEY Kevin *Brownstein Hyatt*, Denver
   KNETSCH Jeffrey *Brownstein Hyatt*, Denver
   KRENDL Cathy *Krendl Krendl*, Denver
   MAGUIRE Charles *Holme Roberts*, Denver
   MOYE John *Moye Giles*, Denver
   RUPPERT John *Brownstein Hyatt*, Denver
   RUSSO Richard *Gibson Dunn*, Denver
   STEPHENS Thomas *Bartlit Beck*, Denver
   STOCKS Bruce *Perkins Coie*, Denver
   TROUPE Warren *Morrison & Foerster*, Denver
   VAN WESTRUM Anthony *Denver*

Firms and Individuals are listed alphabetically in each band.

Band 1

Cooley Godward LLP

The Firm: *"Cooley rode the hi-tech boom, enjoying stunning growth"* acknowledge competitors. However, even though the sector has slumped, Cooley Godward remains *"at the top for corporate work"* in Denver. Its success was put down to *"first-rate venture capital connections and good people at the top."* The firm certainly fields a highly capable corporate team, with experience in public company work, securities offerings and complex structured M&A. Its overwhelming strength, however, is in the vencap field, and the team boasts a justifiably fine reputation for advising hi-tech and growth companies. Though this remains a huge part of the practice, the group's recent work has also tended towards high-value refinancings and restructurings, often with an international element.

The Lawyers: *"Bespoke attorney"* **Francis Wheeler** moves up to *Chambers'* top tier this year following enthusiastic praise from interviewees. *"One of the most superb technical attorneys imaginable,"* he is said to be *"so technically good, creative and thoughtful that he gets onto the most complex and exciting deals."* Though he has a slice of private equity work, his main focus is general corporate and securities law. He advises public companies on financing, high yield debt, securities law compliance and some M&A. In contrast, *"king of hi-tech"* **Jim Linfield** has an unmatched reputation for advising venture capital funds on their investments in emerging companies. Interviewees think of him as *"a relationship guy with a good reputation for client care,"* and note his skill as a rainmaker for the firm's impressive venture capital practice.

The Clients: The firm represents a mixture of private and public companies, especially in the hi-tech and telecoms fields. It also serves an impressive roster of venture capital clients.

Hogan & Hartson LLP
See firm details p.484

The Firm: With 17 partners in Denver – eight of them full time on M&A and securities – plus offices in Boulder and Colorado Springs, this is one of the largest practices in the state. The team is acknowledged to be *"at the top for corporate work,"* and is increasingly seen by interviewees as the firm to beat. Competitors noted *"lots of strength and really good people at different levels."* This full-service firm has grown quickly in recent years, but has been operating a strategy of more organic growth of late, helping it to maintain high standards of quality. Recent highlights in the corporate finance arena include closing a new $400 million senior credit facility for Trans-Montaigne.

The Lawyers: *"Outstanding securities lawyer"* **Paul Hilton** (see p.319) is the team's best known name. Rivals acknowledge that he *"has great relationships and is always going to be a strong player."* Another excellent securities lawyer is *"extremely bright"* **Whitney Holmes** (see p.319), who divides his time between M&A and securities/corporate finance. He has been advising a public company client on a proposed $1.4 billion acquisition, and has recently acted on several of the highest value transactions in the state. Interviewees noted his New York background and his considerable self-confidence. *"Talented new arrival,"* **Chris Walsh** (see p.323), was described as a *"younger guy who is developing a substantial practice."* He earned particular praise for his finance work. Walsh led the team that advised Regal Entertainment Group on its $200 million acquisition of Signature Theaters. Another recent arrival at partner level is George Hagerty, previously at Dorsey & Whitney's London office.

Holme Roberts & Owen LLP
See firm details p.326

The Firm: *"If I have to lose to anyone..."* said one rival, the bitter pill is easier to swallow if that someone is Holme Roberts, because of the firm's acknowledged excellence in this area. Clients keep returning to it because of the *"breadth of the firm, the quality of the service and representation, and the responsiveness."* The sizable team acts on a broad spectrum of corporate and finance work, including public M&A, securities regulation, debt and equity offerings and sales of international subsidiaries of US public companies. Its expertise in partnership matters and the quality of its tax group were also commented on. Many of the firm's Colorado-based clients are active in the cable and hi-tech industries, although they are drawn from a wide range of sectors.

The Lawyers: Dean Salter is undoubtedly *"the dean of the Colorado corporate Bar"* according to many interviewees, who added *"he is just a pleasure to work with."* Peers acknowledge that he *"has a first-rate reputation – and it's deserved."* He remains involved in frontline practice, recently advising UnitedGlobalCom on a combined $1 billion rights offering and $600 million debt offering. **Richard Plumridge** was singled out for his *"wealth of experience,"* notably in PIPE deals for hi-tech companies. Recent transactions of this type have raised over $75 million for clients. A new name in the tables is *"practical, but technically excellent"* **Garth Jensen**, described by clients as an *"unflappable but creative"* adviser. Clients were also full of praise for *"the level of trust he has established with the SEC."* Jensen handles a broad range of corporate finance work for public companies, and recently closed a $500 million MTN program for MDC Holdings, one of the largest housebuilders in the USA. **Charlie Maguire** was also recommended to researchers by peers and clients alike. He coordinates the firm's commercial law and securities practice group.

The Clients: An impressive list of public company clients includes UnitedGlobalCom and Newmont Mining.

Band 2

Bartlit Beck Herman Palenchar & Scott

The Firm: Bartlit Beck's compact but influential corporate team has been consistently busy over the past year. This is due in part to its strong foothold in the energy and mining sectors, which have been active despite the recession affecting other parts of Colorado's business community. Here, its share of major transactions includes the $1 billion acquisition of most of the US coal operations of German company, RAG Coal International, by First Reserve and Blackstone Capital Partners. As this also suggests, the group has considerable experience in private equity acquisitions and financing. The firm's ability to pull off big deals with small teams, and its flexibility over fee arrangements, have proved hits with clients.

The Lawyers: According to peers, **James Palenchar** is *"pretty close to the top of the pack."* His *"consistently high quality"* has helped him carve out a *"fantastic reputation"* nationwide. Sources particularly noted his work for First Reserve. During the past year, he advised Alpha Natural Resources on a senior loan note offering and secured revolving credit facility with a combined value of $350 million. Colleague **Tom Stephens** is experienced in M&A and securities work. His recent highlights include representing Sterling Holding Company in a $60 million merger with Stratos Lightwave (a US public company). Post-merger, Stephens continues to provide the merged company with strategic legal advice.

The Clients: Alongside companies like Alpha Natural Resources and Sterling Holding Company, the group has represented well-known private equity firms throughout the USA.

Brownstein Hyatt & Farber PC
See firm details p.324

The Firm: According to clients, this is a team of *"good commercial lawyers – they're very savvy on the business side of things."* Peers, meanwhile, single it out for the *"consistent quality of its partners,"* who they dub *"fantastic negotiators."* Another selling point was said to be its strong political connections (*"If you have a problem with access to politicians, go there."*) A team of around 20 operates throughout the region. It has been relatively unharmed by the slowdown in the region's tech economy, benefiting from a steady stream of midmarket transactions for funds and merchant banks, laced with the occasional megadeal.

The Lawyers: Steven Siegel (see p.322) is the firm's standout name. *"Bright, articulate, business-focused and cost-effective,"* according to clients, he *"protects us from the minutiae and doesn't waste time negotiating pointless stuff."* Siegel represents a number of private equity funds and investment banks. He recently advised Kohlberg & Company on its $100 million acquisition of parts of Coach USA from the UK's Stagecoach Group. **Jeffrey Knetsch** (see p.319) has a broad corporate practice. He was recently involved in the $1.6 billion sale of rural telephone exchanges by Qwest. **John Ruppert** (see p.321) leads the firm's bankruptcy and restructuring group; his highlights of the year include advising the Greenspun Corporation on a $400 million share conversion transaction with Cox Communications. Recently moved from Arnold & Porter LLP, *"seasoned attorney"* **Kevin Cudney** (see p.317) specializes in private equity work. According to clients, he is a talented, practical lawyer who *"looks at the business aspects of a deal, not just the law."* His recent highlights include representing the controlling shareholder in the $85 million sale of Dharmacon to Fisher Scientific.

The Clients: As well as major names like the Greenspun Corporation and Kohlberg, the firm assists a number of other private equity houses, investment banks and local and national manufacturers.

Davis Graham & Stubbs LLP

The Firm: The team has seen a welcome resurgence this year in M&A and private equity activity. The firm was sheltered from the worst of the tech slump because it hadn't committed itself to that sector as deeply as some. However, it is now doing work for some more established technology companies. The practice has also been helped by activity in sectors like energy and mining, where it has traditionally been strong: for example, the firm represents some of the biggest private equity investors in the Colorado mining industry. Asset management has been another growth area during the past year, and the firm has seen an increasing amount of work for hedge funds and mutual funds.

The Lawyers: *"Corporate star"* **Ronald Levine** is linked to many of the largest deals in the region. Long-term clients commend his *"knowledgeable and thorough"* approach, and appreciate his *"familiarity with our business, approach and demands."* He recently represented two international investment banks as underwriters in a $1 billion bond offering on behalf of Anglo-Gold.

The Clients: Coors family trusts; Apex Silver Mines; Cyantech; M2P Capital and Endeavour Capital.

Band 3

Faegre & Benson LLP
See firm details p.1022

The Firm: *"It has grown in Denver; it has grown smartly in Boulder,"* with the 2002 merger with Chrisman, Bynum & Johnson: observers report that the Minneapolis-based firm is *"really making a move in this market."* The firm has noticed a considerable upturn in instructions since the end of 2003, including a couple of IPOs and some cross-border M&A. It has been especially active in the securities market. Highlights include closing a $140 million common stock public offering for StarTek and a $320 million senior notes 144A transaction for Cenveo.

The Lawyers: Doug Wright (see p.323) is thought to be *"someone whose word you can rely on."* A popular M&A and securities lawyer, his work over the past year has included advising RogueWave, a software company, on its $72 million cash and stock sale to Quovadx. Clients *"would not hesitate to recommend"* **Bill Campbell** (see p.317). He provides ongoing counsel to a number of major companies – including ACT Teleconferencing – on international finance and corporate governance requirements.

The Clients: Time Warner Telecom; StarTek; Frontier Airlines; CIBER; CH2M HILL; Colorado Rockies and Displaytech.

Holland & Hart LLP

See firm details p.325

The Firm: This is a *"good solid firm with a cheaper price tag than New York firms,"* according to clients. They especially appreciate its combination of pragmatic business understanding with high-quality lawyering: *"They're responsive and provide sophisticated advice but are mindful of the economics of any given job – they don't over-lawyer the small stuff or under-lawyer the big stuff."* The firm's corporate practice encompasses all types of transactional and finance work, with a particular emphasis on complex structures. The team recently acted for Exabyte Corporation on a combined PIPE offering and share-for-share exchange with a total value of $45 million.

The Lawyers: A *"very strong"* public companies specialist, **Mark Levy** (see p.320) heads the firm's securities practice and co-heads its corporate finance group. Of late, he has been advising a client on the securities and business law aspects of a share transaction with a total value of $1.1 billion. **Betty Arkell** (see p.316) is best known for her venture capital and emerging/growth company work, though her practice is broader and encompasses M&A and finance for public companies. She recently closed a major restructuring of public company Navigant International, combining a new $170 million senior debt facility with $72 million of convertible subordinated debt. According to clients she is *"a very careful thinker who doesn't just jump out of the chute with the first answer,"* and she

also has a talent for *"conveying complex legal ideas in a way that we can understand."*

The Clients: Along with companies like Exabyte Corporation and Navigant International, the firm represents other well-known funds, financial services firms, and public and private companies in a range of sectors.

Sherman & Howard LLC

The Firm: A 40-strong team of attorneys at this venerable Colorado firm handles a variety of corporate and real estate transactional work. The emphasis is firmly on M&A and securities, often involving clients with national and international reach. For example, the international entertainment group, Liberty Media, retained the firm on a recent take-private transaction involving two of its subsidiaries. Other recent successes for the team include arranging a $1.4 billion rolling credit facility for a Japanese communications company.

The Lawyers: *"Accomplished corporate practitioner"* **Andy Blair** was commended by clients for his *"good judgment and common sense,"* as well as the quality of his work. He continues to be active in the securities arena.

The Clients: General Communications, Bubba Gump Shrimp Co and Liberty Media feature in the client list.

Other Notable Practitioners

A new entrant to this year's tables is the *"eminently respected"* **John Moye**, a founding partner of Denver-based Moye, Giles, O'Keefe, Vermeire & Gorrell LLP. Interviewees are enthusiastic in their praise for this *"high-energy, very positive deal-maker."* Moye's clients range from local entrepreneurs to major national corpora-

tions; his work for them generally involves structuring complex transactions and related business counseling. He is currently advising Auto-Chlor on its acquisition of a New Mexico-based competitor. **Richard Russo** (see p.322), of Gibson, Dunn & Crutcher LLP's Denver office, acted recently for Janus on a debt-for-equity swap, following which the company's rating returned to investment grade. Clients, many of which are NYSE-listed companies, depict Russo as *"both technically oriented and hands-on"* – a combination that delighted them. **Bruce Stocks** is a private equity specialist at Perkins Coie LLP. His most visible recent transactions include representing CHB Capital Partners on the sale of its interest in Boulder-based skiwear manufacturer, Spyder Active Sports. **Warren Troupe** (see p.323), the co-chair of Morrison & Foerster LLP's national corporate group, enjoys a high profile in the state. *"He has built up a successful practice,"* according to interviewees, who highlight his *"strong client service and excellent reputation."* A considerable proportion of Troupe's work is in real estate finance and public offerings. His national client base includes United Dominion Realty Trust, an NYSE-traded REIT; he recently advised the trust on an $800 million offering of medium-term notes, and regularly acts for it on smaller debt and equity offerings. **Anthony van Westrum**, a sole practitioner, enters the tables following plaudits for his work for unincorporated bodies and partnerships. Peers at large firms report regularly referring work to him in these areas. Finally, interviewees singled out **Cathy Krendl**'s corporate skills for praise. Krendl, a founding partner in small Denver firm Krendl Krendl Sachnoff & Way PC, specializes in securities and M&A work.

EMPLOYMENT

MAINLY DEFENDANT

Colorado
Leading firms
(Employment: Mainly Defendant)
① HOLLAND & HART LLP *Denver*
SHERMAN & HOWARD LLC *Denver*
② BROWNSTEIN HYATT & FARBER PC *Denver*
③ DAVIS GRAHAM & STUBBS LLP *Denver*
FAEGRE & BENSON LLP *Denver*
HOGAN & HARTSON LLP *Denver*
HOLME ROBERTS & OWEN LLP *Denver*
Firms are listed alphabetically in each band.

Band 1

Holland & Hart LLP

See firm details p.325

The Firm: This *"excellent, large and successful"* team is acknowledged to be *"one of the top*

employment groups in the state," if not the top group. According to clients, it is *"a great sounding board for labor-relations issues,"* with *"no obvious room for improvement."* The Midwest giant operates from five offices in Colorado. Its employment workload has recently been dominated by 'bet-the-company' class actions, notably in the food retail sector. The labor law practice also continues to thrive: recent high-profile union disputes in the airline industry have undoubtedly contributed to a rise in profile of this area of the firm's practice.

The Lawyers: Probably the most experienced labor and employment lawyer in the state, **John Husband** (see p.319) is widely considered *"the most senior member of the Colorado employment Bar."* A *"prominent and competitive lawyer with an excellent practice,"* he is popular with judges and good with juries. His particular forte is felt to be labor law – he counsels UPS on union-related issues – though he also handles some of

the biggest class actions in the state and is admired for his counseling work. Colleague **Gregory Eurich**'s (see p.317) strengths lie in the courtroom, where he is acclaimed as a *"seasoned trial lawyer"* with a softly spoken but devastatingly intelligent approach. His name is especially associated with major discrimination and wrongful dismissal cases. Practice group head, **Brian Mumaugh** (see p.321), enters this year's tables following warm recommendations from clients. *"If you've got a serious personnel problem,"* said one, *"he's almost like a clergyman: he understands the emotional aspects but he can also be firm."*

The Clients: The firm acts for a range of local and national employers, including UPS, AIMCO and United Technologies.

Colorado
Leading individuals
(Employment: Mainly Defendant)

1 EURICH Gregory *Holland & Hart,* Denver
HUSBAND John *Holland & Hart,* Denver
OADE K Preston *Holme Roberts,* Denver
POWELL David *Brownstein Hyatt,* Denver

2 ARO Edwin *Hogan & Hartson,* Denver
DEENY Raymond *Sherman,* Colorado Springs
GALLAGHER Sean *Hogan & Hartson,* Denver

3 LEE Jessica *Gibson Dunn,* Denver
MACDONALD Elizabeth *Faegre & Benson,* Denver
MUMAUGH Brian *Holland & Hart,* Greenwood Village
NEWCOM Charles *Sherman & Howard,* Denver
SATRIANA Daniel *Clisham Satriana,* Denver
SAVAGE Janet *Ducker Montgomery,* Denver
SIEBERT W Bernie *Sherman & Howard,* Denver
STACY David *Elzi Pringle,* Denver
WEESE Charles *Faegre & Benson,* Denver

Individuals are listed alphabetically in each band.

Sherman & Howard LLC

The Firm: In the words of one rival: "*When I think of the competition I think of Sherman & Howard.*" This "*fantastic*" group continues to command a high level of respect in employment law circles. The large and expanding team now numbers around 30 lawyers exclusively serving employers. It enjoys a steady diet of discrimination and wrongful discharge cases, which have increased rapidly in recent years. It also has a sizable practice in the traditional labor arena, including litigation before the NLRB, collective bargaining, union organizing campaigns and protecting employers' rights in labor stoppages.
The Lawyers: The highest profile in the department belongs to **Raymond Deeny**. His "*aggressive, take no prisoners*" approach is popular with a lot of clients, and he has built up a loyal following. He is also admired for his ability to attract and retain work from high-profile employers. Deeny is renowned for his labor law practice, which comprises almost half of his workload, and for his dynamic performance in the courtroom. Veteran lawyer **Bernie Siebert** has practiced traditional labor law for over 30 years, combining it with discrimination and wrongful dismissal claims. Much of his time over the past year has been spent defending class actions: Siebert has been instrumental in formulating a preemptive strategy to defeat class certification. According to some interviewees, **Chuck Newcom** "*prefers to be in the background but is a really smart employment lawyer.*" His work combines defending employers against discrimination and wrongful discharge claims with wage and hour disputes and some health and safety counseling. His current workload includes a number of racial and sexual harassment claims, and a claim for wrongful termination for poor performance.

The Clients: The group represents various well-known national employers, notably in the natural resources and mining sectors. Typical names from its client roster include national employers like Newmont Mining, Cleveland-Cliffs and Kroeger.

Band 2

Brownstein Hyatt & Farber PC

See firm details p.324
The Firm: Brownstein Hyatt is widely considered the up-and-coming firm in Colorado's labor and employment market, especially since David Powell's arrival in 2002. "*A formidable force,*" according to commentators, the compact team has developed a great reputation and serves an impressive client list in, inter alia, the real estate, banking, investment and automotive industries. Its caseload covers the range of employment discrimination, wrongful discharge and noncompete claims. Labor issues represent a smaller part of its practice, although this is a growing field for the team.
The Lawyers: "*Sincere, charming and honest,*" **David Powell** (see p.321) was universally commended for his "*integrity and great ability as a lawyer.*" Clients admire him while competitors consider him a popular choice for referrals. His arrival at the firm almost three years ago has clearly had a highly positive effect on its profile in this area. Powell recently defended an ADA retaliation claim in the Tenth Circuit Court of Appeals. This important case established that the plaintiff was not entitled to compensatory damages – a significant victory for his client.
The Clients: United Airlines; HealthONE; Wellbridge; Fiesta Restaurants; Agilera and Qwest.

Band 3

Davis Graham & Stubbs LLP

The Firm: This smaller but growing team is best known for its strong track record in employment litigation. Here it has extensive experience, both of winning jury trials and resolving problems before they come to court. Its expertise spans a wide variety of discrimination claims, and the practice is seeing an increasing volume of wrongful termination cases. Another growth area for the team is the defense of class actions involving Wage Act claims.
The Lawyers: **Janet Savage** does some labor work and handles her share of counseling, but she is best known as an energetic and aggressive employment litigator. In this field, she recently obtained a summary judgment for her client in a major sexual harassment case. She is defending an increasing number of class actions, notably in the FLSA and wage and hour areas.
The Clients: The firm has assisted local and national employers in connection with a variety

of labor and employment claims, ranging from religion, race and sex discrimination cases to appearances before the NLRB. Clients include local and national corporations, municipalities, hospitals and healthcare systems.

Faegre & Benson LLP

See firm details p.1022
The Firm: Interviewees praised the firm's substantial employment group for its experience and "*excellent client care.*" Its attorneys are "*so responsive,*" said one client: "*If they don't have the answer immediately, there's a lot of depth to the firm so they'll get it for me.*" In the past year, the Denver-based team has defended several household-name clients against gender and age discrimination claims. It has also handled a number of important noncompete disputes.
The Lawyers: It remains too early to say whether Bruce Sattler's forthcoming retirement will have much effect on Faegre's employment practice. Stepping into the breach is **Chuck Weese** (see p.323), who practices primarily as a litigator. Though he has yet to attain Sattler's prominence, clients expressed their pleasure with the "*exceptional job*" he has made of some "*very complex reorganizations.*" Recent highlights include resolving several disputes involving noncompete obligations, including one on behalf of an orthopedic practice in Wyoming. Also popular with clients is **Beth MacDonald** (see p.320). She is said to be good at "*providing us with options and risk assessments and keeping us up to date with changes in the field.*"
The Clients: Mortenson; State Farm; United Agri Products; Colorado Rockies; Koala Corporation; Enterprise Rent-A-Car; Talbot Financial; Exempla Healthcare and Republic Financial Corporation.

Hogan & Hartson LLP

See firm details p.484
The Firm: The Colorado team of this large, international firm continues to act on a steady stream of employment discrimination cases. This has recently included successfully defending a large class action concerning an employers alleged failure to pay overtime to a whole category of employees. Clients were full of praise for the firm: "*I've been really impressed by all the Hogan lawyers I've ever encountered*" said one.
The Lawyers: "*Experienced and practical*" **Edwin Aro** (see p.316) offers expertise in a mixture of employment and general commercial litigation. He spent much of last year advising a major mutual fund on the employment and commercial aspects of a regulatory investigation, which involved both litigation and counseling. According to clients, he is "*great at crystallizing the important issues in a case and talking through what's best for the company, while still allowing us to make the final decision.*" Clients were also full of praise for

Sean Gallagher (see p.318). His *"excellent follow through"* was particularly commended: *"He will always get back quickly, even in the evenings."* Gallagher undertakes both contentious work and counseling, principally in connection with conventional discrimination claims. He is also the principal editor of the Colorado Bar Association's Treatise on Employment Law.

The Clients: The firm assists a range of clients, many of them household names, with employment law issues.

Holme Roberts & Owen LLP
See firm details p.326

The Firm: The firm's sound and solid employment group received a volume of highly positive feedback – *"We hear a lot of good things,"* said one commentator, especially about its labor practice. There was some suspicion, however,

that its reputation is perhaps a little closely bound up with that of its star employment partner. The team handles a range of labor, employment and employee benefits work and is a regular performer in high-profile cases in the appeal courts.

The Lawyers: *"Clearly the dean,"* **Preston Oade**'s name is rarely out of the press, according to commentators, and he boasts an enviable track record of trial success. Interviewees describe him as a *"skillful trial lawyer who really knows his way around a courtroom."*

The Clients: The firm represents a range of local and national employers, including some nationally well-known names.

Other Notable Practitioners

Jessica Lee (see p.320), a partner in Gibson, Dunn & Crutcher LLP's Denver office, was sin-

gled out to researchers as a highly successful younger lawyer. *"Smart, capable and practical,"* she was enthusiastically recommended by clients. Lee has developed the firm's Colorado employment practice from scratch since the mid nineties. She recently represented RemedyTemp in a successful mediation arising from a dispute over noncompete obligations. **Daniel Satriana** recently left Hall & Evans to found his own firm, Clisham, Satriana & Biscan LLC. He enjoys a busy and successful trial practice and, in addition to his litigation work, counsels his clients on various aspects of their employment policies and practices. **Dave Stacy** of Ducker Montgomery, Arnstein & Bess, PC is considered more of a generalist than some in the list, but his *"great skill in the courtroom"* has won him a loyal and appreciative client base.

ENVIRONMENT

Colorado
Leading firms (Environment)

1	DAVIS GRAHAM & STUBBS LLP *Denver*
	FAEGRE & BENSON LLP *Denver, Boulder*
	HOGAN & HARTSON LLP *Denver, Boulder*
	HOLLAND & HART LLP *Denver*
2	GREENBERG TRAURIG LLP *Denver*
	HOLME ROBERTS & OWEN LLP *Denver*
	SHERMAN & HOWARD LLC *Denver*
	TEMKIN WIELGA & HARDT LLP *Denver*

Leading individuals (Environment)

1	LAWRENCE Robert *Davis Graham*, Denver
	PHILLIPS Paul *Holland & Hart*, Denver
	ROCKWOOD Linda *Faegre & Benson*, Denver
	SPAANSTRA James *Faegre & Benson*, Denver
	STRICKLAND Tom *Hogan & Hartson*, Denver
	TEMKIN Elizabeth *Temkin Wielga*, Denver
2	ARFMANN Dennis *Hogan & Harston*, Boulder
	CONNERY Robert *Holland & Hart*, Denver
	DUNN Daniel *Holme Roberts*, Denver
	EDDY Ronald *Sherman & Howard*, Denver
	EID Troy *Greenberg Traurig*, Denver
	FOGNANI John *Fognani Guibord*, Denver
	MILLER Zach *Davis Graham*, Denver
	RAISCH Jerry *Vranesh and Raisch*, Boulder
	REISCH Scott *Hogan & Hartson*, Denver

Firms and individuals are listed alphabetically in each band.

Band 1

Davis Graham & Stubbs LLP

The Firm: Commentators admire this *"large and competent"* environment practice for its *"solid longevity and wealth of Superfund lawyers,"* as well as its *"good share of transaction-*

al work." The group of around 15 full-time attorneys has a wide variety of experience, undertaking hazardous waste, Superfund, compliance, litigation and air and water quality work. It also regularly collaborates with the firm's real estate group on brownfield and development matters.

The Lawyers: Former EPA attorney **Bob Lawrence** is a *"worthy foe and a fine guy,"* according to rivals. He was admired for both the quality of his work, especially his CERCLA/RCRA practice, and his *"excellent clients."* Environmental practice group head **Zach Miller** is thought by some to be *"one of the finest in the state"* for air quality, wetlands and NEPA compliance work. He enjoys a healthy slice of transactional work along with his contentious practice. Miller recently acted for a client in Idaho who was sued under NEPA, in connection with an application for expansion of a mining project, successfully obtaining summary judgment for his client.

Faegre & Benson LLP
See firm details p.1022

The Firm: *"Firmly established at the top"* is how commentators describe Faegre's impressive team. Clients were reassured by the group's stability and consistent quality, noting that *"the whole team is outstanding and you always know who to call."* The group represents a number of large industrial clients and brownfield developers. Recent highlights include advising Continuum Partners on the Belmar shopping center redevelopment project. Faegre partners have also represented federal clients in Superfund proceedings throughout the Midwest.

The Lawyers: *"Respectable senior partner"*

Jim Spaanstra (see p.322) can be relied upon to *"come to reasonable solutions,"* say clients. His practice is primarily noncontentious. It includes work for a number of national waste and environmental remediation companies, advising on the establishment, operation and expansion of hazardous waste facilities throughout the US. Spaanstra has also been involved in the cleanup of former Cold War nuclear weapons facilities, such as Rocky Flats in Colorado. Another element of his practice is brownfield work – he recently advised Kaiser-Hill on the cleanup and development aspects of the $750 million mixed-use Belmar project in Lakewood, Colorado. **Linda Rockwood**'s (see p.321) varied practice includes Superfund, brownfield and redevelopment work, as well as air quality matters. Over the past year, she has been busy with several multiparty Superfund cases. Delighted clients describe her as *"amongst the finest environmental lawyers in Colorado."*

The Clients: As well as Continuum Partners and Kaiser-Hill, the team's client roster contains a number of other impressive names drawn from the energy, utilities, natural resources, pharmaceuticals, and financial and manufacturing sectors.

Hogan & Hartson LLP
See firm details p.484

The Firm: With offices in Denver and Boulder, and close links with strong teams in DC and Los Angeles, Hogan & Hartson *"is making good progress upwards"* according to commentators. The team is active in brownfield and Superfund work, recently advising Kroenke Sports on the development of a new stadium for the Colorado Rapids on a brownfield site. Clients expressed their pleasure with the group's *"expertise, level of service, flexibility and willingness to play any role we need,"* and describe the attorneys as *"invaluable in providing contacts within regulatory agencies."* This role is only likely to be augmented by the recent recruitment of former congressman, Scott McGuinness.

The Lawyers: A notable recent lateral hire from Holme Roberts & Owen, **Dennis Arfmann** (see p.316), was attracted to the firm by its unrivaled presence in DC. He specializes in air quality work, and sits as the only nongovernment figure on the Denver Regional Air Quality Council. He represents a number of energy clients, including ChevronTexaco and Cemex. **Scott Reisch** (see p.321), described by clients as *"very knowledgeable and practical in his approach,"* divides his time between contaminated land and cleanup work, defense of civil and criminal enforcement actions and corporate support. He was recently involved in the multimillion-dollar cleanup of the Miami Airport area. *"Rainmaker"* **Tom Strickland** (see p.322) is thought to be *"adept at bringing in clients."* With his impressive political background and contacts, Strickland's recent arrival provides the group with another level of expertise. His experience includes ski areas and the mining industry.

The Clients: Suncor; Coors Brewing Company; Cemex USA; Williams Energy; The Western Sugar Cooperative; ChevronTexaco and Wolf Creek Ski Area.

Holland & Hart LLP

See firm details p.325

The Firm: A *"well-rounded practice,"* according to rivals, which is competent in all types of environmental representation. The team includes several mining and utilities specialists, and recent work has included the establishment of a joint venture between two gold mining companies in Nevada.

The Lawyers: *"Thoughtful and bright"* **Robert Connery** (see p.317) has *"made a reputation in air quality since the statute was in its infancy,"* according to interviewees. He has practiced in this area for over 35 years and advises a number of Colorado companies, including several mining companies, utilities and electricity generators, on air quality issues amongst other things. Over the past year he has been busy with the permitting of several new coal-fired power plants. According to clients, **Paul Phillips'** (see p.321) great skill is as an *"outstanding negotiator, especially with the regulators."* His practice is focused on environmental compliance work and litigation for large corporate clients, including both CERCLA and toxic tort claims. An unusual recent instruction from a major refin-

ing company involved Phillips in a dispute over hydrocarbon pollution of a creek adjacent to two oil refineries, one owned by his client and the other by a competitor.

The Clients: Major corporate clients include: Bechtel; Duke Energy; Saunders Construction and Valero Energy.

Band 2

Greenberg Traurig LLP

See firm details p.564

The Firm: According to market commentators, this is a *"young, hungry and aggressive"* newcomer to the Denver environmental scene. It has *"put on a lot of talent in the last year"* and won instructions from some important clients. The most notable addition to the team was Troy Eid who joined from the Governor's office. The practice already boasts around 35 attorneys and offers a full-service environment practice. Areas of focus include land use in general, as well as air and water act issues.

The Lawyers: **Troy Eid** (see p.317) leads the team here. A recent recruit with a background in the Colorado Governor's cabinet, he has hit the ground running. Highlights from the past year include acting as lead counsel to Wal-Mart in the widely reported enforcement action brought by the DOJ and EPA alleging violations of the Clean Water Act and Storm Water Act. This was successfully brought to a positive settlement. Eid is also an expert in Indian tribal law, and is currently involved in rights of way negotiations for a proposed pipeline across the Navajo reservation.

The Clients: The firm assists a variety of national corporate clients, such as Wal-Mart and El Paso.

Holme Roberts & Owen LLP

See firm details p.326

The Firm: The group of nearly 20 environmental attorneys is seeing a steady increase in its caseload. On a number of recent occasions, its attorneys have represented Colorado developers and natural resources companies in disputes with various pressure groups. Of late the group has seen an increasing amount of toxic tort litigation and other cases with environmental roots.

The Lawyers: The practice has suffered some recent losses – Dennis Arfmann being the obvious example – but it continues to boast a *"pretty darn good"* name in **Daniel Dunn**. He divides his practice between environmental and toxic tort litigation and has been busy over the past year defending several uranium-mining companies against toxic tort claims. His practice also includes Superfund work: Dunn has advised on one of the largest and most expensive Superfund cleanups to date.

The Clients: The firm acts for a number of Fortune 500 clients, as well as regional developers and companies with natural resources issues.

Sherman & Howard LLC

The Firm: Sherman & Howard's compact environmental group has had to adjust to the temporary departure of *"one of the top environmental lawyers in the state,"* Alan Gilbert, to the Colorado Attorney-General's office. Nonetheless, the firm retains *"a solid practice"* in the opinion of market commentators. The firm is active in the administrative area, obtaining permits and advising in negotiations with the regulator, and defends clients in a range of environmental litigation. It also advises on the environmental aspects of various transactions.

The Lawyers: With Alan Gilbert temporarily out of the picture, **Ronald Eddy** is undoubtedly *"the centerpiece of the practice"* at Sherman & Howard. *"Solid, senior and seasoned,"* he is held in high regard by competitors and clients alike. A litigator by training, Eddy specializes in hazardous substances, air and water quality and asbestos litigation.

Temkin Wielga & Hardt LLP

The Firm: This six-attorney environmental boutique is well known in the market, despite only having been created in 1999. The firm undertakes the full spectrum of contentious and noncontentious environmental work, but is perhaps best known for civil and environmental litigation in the traditional enforcement areas. Its clients are drawn from around the US and range from Fortune 500 companies to individual entrepreneurs.

The Lawyers: Although all three name partners were mentioned, it is *"bright, high-caliber"* **Betsy Temkin** who attracted the most praise. One interviewee even went so far as to say: *"She is not only the best environmental lawyer I've ever worked with, but one of the best lawyers,"* because of her *"ability to focus on the important points and stay in tune with clients' needs."* Temkin's hazardous waste and Superfund work received particular acclaim.

Other Notable Practitioners

According to some commentators, **Jerry Raisch**, a partner at Vranesh and Raisch, LLP is *"head and shoulders above everyone else for water quality work."* **John Fognani**, a former Holland & Hart partner now at his own firm, Fognani Guibord & Homsy, LLP, is known in the market for his CERCLA/RCRA, Clean Air Act and Clean Water Act experience.

308   All quotes in the text are from interviews with clients and competitors.

CHAMBERS USA 2005

INTELLECTUAL PROPERTY

Colorado
Leading firms (Intellectual Property)

1. FAEGRE & BENSON LLP *Denver, Boulder*
   TOWNSEND AND TOWNSEND *Denver*
2. COOLEY GODWARD LLP *Broomfield*
   GIBSON, DUNN & CRUTCHER LLP *Denver*
   HOGAN & HARTSON LLP *Denver*
   HOLLAND & HART LLP *Denver*

Leading individuals
(Intellectual Property)

1. BEATON Glenn *Gibson Dunn, Denver*
   GIBBY Darin *Townsend and Townsend, Denver*
   HANLON-LEH Natalie *Faegre & Benson, Denver*
   MICHAELS Jane *Holland & Hart, Denver*
2. BROGAN James *Cooley Godward, Broomfield*
   HAVLICK Scott *Holland & Hart, Denver*
   HILYARD Chad *Faegre & Benson, Denver*
   JEWETT Steve *Townsend and Townsend, Denver*
   KINSELLA Peter *Faegre & Benson, Denver*
   SIPIORA David *Townsend and Townsend, Denver*

Firms and individuals are listed alphabetically in each band.

Band 1

Faegre & Benson LLP

See firm details p.1022

The Firm: From a starting point of just three attorneys in 2000, Faegre's team in Colorado has now grown to 18 specialists, many of whom have scientific backgrounds. The firm offers a full-service IP practice, comprising patent prosecution, trademark registration, litigation and licensing/transactional support. Clients appreciate the mix of pragmatism and technical expertise. *"What I like,"* said one, *"is that they're very practical – I don't have to worry that I'm going to get a ten-page memo."* At the same time, though, the team *"does a great job of dealing with the paperwork and produces consistently good advice."* The patent litigators are currently busy with two high-profile biotech patent infringement claims: Philips v AWH and Genetic Technologies Limited v Applera Corporation.

The Lawyers: *"Highly driven"* **Natalie Hanlon-Leh** (see p.318) was among the first names to be mentioned by most interviewees. Her *"incredible"* litigation practice includes patent, trademark, copyright and some trade secrets work; she also has a supervisory role in the firm's non-contentious trademark and brand management practice. Hanlon-Leh has been providing ongoing counsel to USA Hockey on the protection of its trademarks, with particular regard to counterfeit products. Younger partner **Peter Kinsella** (see p.319) is considered a solid IP expert by peers, while clients described him as *"highly informative, thorough and knowledgeable."* He handles a large amount of transactional IP work,

with particular regard to trademarks and technology licensing, as well as undertaking a range of litigation. He recently advised the Certified Financial Planner Board of Standards on the trademark aspects of its international reorganization. A notable lateral hire from Townsend and Townsend and Crew, **Chad Hilyard** (see p.319) brings with him an impressive reputation for patent work.

The Clients: Quark; Bad Boy Brands; Meredith Corporation; Level 3 Communications and Genetic Technologies.

Townsend and Townsend and Crew LLP

The Firm: Known to commentators as *"one of the most vibrant practices in the market,"* the Denver office of this renowned national IP specialist continues to attract quality work. Though it has recently lost several lawyers – notably Chad Hilyard – to Faegre & Benson, this was not felt to have seriously undermined its capacity. The team undertakes the full spectrum of IP work, and emphasizes the protection and commercial exploitation of IP rights. It boasts a long tradition of representing inventors, entrepreneurs and smaller companies, which often sees it representing David in David v Goliath battles. However, the firm also advises its share of household names. Much of its work also comes from the West Coast, where companies increasingly appreciate the more competitive rates and flexible arrangements that it can offer.

The Lawyers: **Darin Gibby**, the partner in charge of the Denver office, is known in the market as *"a highly qualified and talented patent prosecutor."* He specializes in representing medical device manufacturers and computer hardware and software developers. **Steve Jewett** is of counsel to the group, and has previously worked in-house at US West (now Qwest) and NCR as a patent counsel. Interviewees describe him as *"a wonderful patent strategist and transactional lawyer."* **David Sipiora** combines a leading litigation practice with transactional work. He was chosen to represent Intergraph in Intergraph v Intel, a high-profile patent infringement and antitrust claim.

The Clients: In addition to a number of small companies and start-ups, the firm also represents Qwest, CoorsTek and First Data.

Band 2

Cooley Godward LLP

The Firm: Cooley Godward's Broomfield office benefits from the influence of its parent office in California for referrals and introductions, and much of its work has a West Coast, or even an international flavor. The firm has made a particular name for itself representing hi-tech and

communications companies. The Colorado team's practice spans a wide range of issues, but leans heavily towards litigation and patent prosecution.

The Lawyers: Commentators singled out **Jim Brogan** for his litigation and prosecution work. He has a background in electrical engineering, and typically represents biomedical equipment and software companies, and semiconductor manufacturers. Over the past year Brogan has acted for a Colorado manufacturer of semiconductors on an ongoing patent infringement claim.

The Clients: Hi-tech clients include: Advanced Energy; Applied Films; eBay and PicoLight.

Gibson, Dunn & Crutcher LLP

See firm details p.285

The Firm: This international full-service firm has a substantial IP practice in the state, with *"enough really top-notch people"* to compete with the boutiques. The emphasis here is on patent work, with nine attorneys practicing full time in this area, though it handles a wide range of IP matters. The focus of the department was felt to lie more in the national than the local market; competitors envy Gibson Dunn's national network, which gives the group access to major clients from across the country.

The Lawyers: *"Well-rounded, hard-working"* **Glenn Beaton** (see p.316) is the star of this team: interviewees acknowledged that he is *"of a national caliber and much of his work is national."* One client described him as *"incredibly good – if there is a patent available, he will get it for you."* He has a background in aerospace engineering, which helps with one aspect of his work on patent infringement. Recent highlights include acting as primary external IP counsel to Aristocrat, an international gaming equipment manufacturer headquartered in Australia. Aristocrat has retained him to pursue several patent infringement claims relating to slot machine patents. Beaton also acts for medical device manufacturers.

The Clients: As well as Aristocrat, the firm assists a number of well-known clients from a variety of sectors beyond technology and communications.

Hogan & Hartson LLP

See firm details p.484

The Firm: Hogan & Hartson is building a considerable reputation in the region, particularly for patent prosecution but also for a range of litigation. In the words of one interviewee: *"The firm has made impressive inroads in this market,"* and serves a notable roster of clients from a variety of sectors, including healthcare and life sciences. Major selling points include the firm's renowned strength in antitrust and regulatory matters, and the strength of its growing international network.

The Lawyers: Bill Kubida is the contact partner here for intellectual property matters.

The Clients: The firm is known to serve some impressive companies in the healthcare and life sciences markets.

Holland & Hart LLP

See firm details p.325

The Firm: "*Always a major player,*" according to market sources, Holland & Hart's IP team is said to be building "*a fine reputation for IP litigation.*"

The team handles a mixture of noncontentious trademark and copyright work, patent prosecution and IP litigation. It is particularly well regarded for trademark work, and has enjoyed a lot of growth recently in advisory work concerning non-traditional trademarks. Other highlights include a major branding project for a large retailer.

The Lawyers: **Jane Michaels** (see p.320) garners equal amounts of respect for her IP and general commercial litigation work. In both fields, her practice leans heavily towards arbitration, both as advocate and arbitrator. Recently

she chaired a panel of three arbitrators at a month-long, multimillion-dollar arbitration relating to computer software. A "*particularly good*" adviser, according to clients, **Scott Havlick** (see p.318) focuses on noncontentious, trademark-related work. He has been busy of late advising a Colorado-based regional airline on methods of protecting the distinctive appearance of the tail portions of their aircraft.

The Clients: The client list includes national names such as Sears Roebuck and Frontier Airlines.

LITIGATION

GENERAL COMMERCIAL

Colorado
Leading firms
(Litigation: General Commercial)
1 BARTLIT BECK HERMAN PALENCHAR *Denver*
DAVIS GRAHAM & STUBBS LLP *Denver*
HOFFMAN REILLY POZNER *Denver*
HOLLAND & HART LLP *Denver*
2 HILL & ROBBINS PC *Denver*
JACOBS, CHASE, FRICK, KLEINKOPF *Denver*
ROTHGERBER JOHNSON & LYONS LLP *Denver*
WHEELER, TRIGG & KENNEDY LLP *Denver*
3 BALLARD SPAHR ANDREWS *Denver*
FAEGRE & BENSON LLP *Denver*
GIBSON, DUNN & CRUTCHER LLP *Denver*
HOLME ROBERTS & OWEN LLP *Denver*

Leading firms (Litigation: White-Collar
Crime & Government Investigations)
1 HADDON, MORGAN, MUELLER, JORDAN *Denver*
2 BALLARD SPAHR ANDREWS *Denver*
HOGAN & HARTSON LLP *Denver, Colorado Springs*
ISAACSON, ROSENBAUM, WOODS & LEVY *Denver*
ROTHGERBER JOHNSON & LYONS LLP *Denver*
Firms are listed alphabetically in each band.

Bartlit Beck Herman Palenchar & Scott

The Firm: Interviewees expressed universal admiration for this firm of trial litigators: "*The firm's name alone is a good enough advertisement,*" said one source. Interviewees agree that it is "*just an absolutely top-level firm,*" because it offers "*the ability and experience to take any case to trial.*" The firm's practice is now so national in scope that it is felt to be more visible outside Colorado than within it. As well as the enormous resources available at the firm, and the experience on offer, Bartlit Beck attorneys are well known for their hi-tech approach to managing litigation, and their trailblazing use of alternative fee structures.

The Lawyers: With his high-profile nationwide practice, "*everyone talks about*" **Fred Bartlit**. He

is held in the highest regard by peers, and is particularly noted for his "*remarkable*" courtroom performances. He has defended clients such as General Motors and Bayer at trial. Bartlit recently defended private equity firm, Forstmann, Little & Co, against a claim brought by the State of Connecticut's pension funds, a case which was followed closely by the national media. "*Very effective litigator*" **Donald Scott** is also known nationally, especially for his successful defense of NL Industries in the widely reported lead paint claims brought in Maryland and Rhode Island.

The Clients: As well as General Motors and Bayer, the team has assisted a number of Fortune 100 companies on a case-by-case basis.

Davis Graham & Stubbs LLP

The Firm: Interviewees agree that Davis Graham & Stubbs remains among the "*top few outstanding firms for traditional civil litigation*" in Colorado. Its expertise is broad, as demonstrated by the praise lavished on its securities, antitrust and "*really strong natural resources litigation practice.*" Securities disputes, in particular, are an area in which the large team is felt to excel, and it has also enjoyed some considerable products liability cases for its impressive national client base.

The Lawyers: Commentators confirmed that **Gale Miller** enjoys "*a strong reputation for antitrust work*" in the market. "*Stellar*" **Dale Harris** is more of a general commercial litigator, although he also undertakes some interesting antitrust cases. A recent example was his work for a small Denver concert promoter (who, unusually for the firm, was the plaintiff) in an antitrust claim against entertainment giant, Clear Channel Communications. The case has since settled on terms favorable to Harris' client.

The Clients: The firm represents clients from around the region and nationally in a variety of industries.

Hoffman Reilly Pozner & Williamson

The Firm: This is "*probably the leading firm of trial lawyers in the state,*" according to a large

number of interviewees. The firm's practice encompasses the spectrum of criminal and civil litigation, and it was recommended for work as diverse as securities litigation, general commercial disputes, and criminal and white-collar criminal defense. Commentators note that the firm is "*not as classically defendant-oriented*" as some of its rivals, which can give it an interesting angle on cases. Sean Connelly is a recent hire at partner level and is expected to bolster its offering in the white-collar area.

The Lawyers: The firm's figurehead, **Daniel Hoffman**, is felt to be taking a more supervisory role these days, and peers report seeing him less often in court, though he does still appear. He remains "*enormously respected in the commercial litigation area,*" and is a vital resource for the firm's clients. "*Highly prominent*" **Daniel Reilly** is said to be "*a first-rate attorney*" who is ensuring the firm's high standards are maintained. Fellow litigators are effusive in their praise for Reilly's courtroom performances, describing him as "*an absolutely fearless, tough, savvy adversary.*" Reilly's highest profile case in recent months has been the widely reported dispute over the ownership of the Denver Broncos franchise.

Holland & Hart LLP

See firm details p.325

The Firm: As one of the largest firms in the Rocky Mountain region, Holland & Hart is universally acknowledged to have "*quite extraordinary capabilities in a wide variety of areas,*" and was felt by some interviewees to be "*the best institutional group of litigators in town.*" A huge group adopts a style described as "*litigation-friendly,*" an attitude reflected in the presence in-house of everything from a jury consultancy to a courtroom graphics department. Clients are delighted with the group's work, noting that "*it's exactly what we want and expect: the reports are timely and the fees are in line with the quality of work.*" In recent months the firm has been busy representing AT&T in the ongoing Qwest litigation.

310   All quotes in the text are from interviews with clients and competitors.

CHAMBERS USA 2005

Colorado
Leading individuals
(Litigation: General Commercial)

Senior Statesman	
HOFFMAN Daniel	*Hoffman Reilly*, Denver
[1] BARTLIT Jr Fred	*Bartlit Beck*, Denver
CHASE Jeffrey	*Jacobs Chase*, Denver
HILL Robert	*Hill & Robbins*, Denver
LYONS James	*Rothgerber Johnson*, Denver
[2] BARKER Scott	*Holland & Hart*, Denver
BLACK Bruce	*Holme Roberts*, Denver
CERIANI Gary	*Davis & Ceriani*, Denver
REILLY Daniel	*Hoffman Reilly*, Denver
THOMASCH Roger	*Ballard Spahr*, Denver
[3] BAUMANN Frederick	*Rothgerber Johnson*, Denver
HARRIS Dale	*Davis Graham*, Denver
SCOTT Donald	*Bartlit Beck*, Denver
WHEELER Malcolm	*Wheeler Trigg*, Denver
[4] CURTIS George	*Gibson Dunn*, Denver
FRICK Ann	*Jacobs Chase*, Denver
GARNSEY Walter	*Kelly Haglund*, Denver
GOLDBERG Charles	*Rothgerber Johnson*, Denver
GOTTSCHALK Hugh	*Wheeler Trigg*, Denver
MCCARTHY Michael	*Faegre & Benson*, Denver
MILLER Gale	*Davis Graham*, Denver

Leading individuals (Antitrust)

[1] BLACK Bruce	*Holme Roberts*, Denver
HARRIS Dale	*Davis Graham*, Denver
HARTLEY James	*Holland & Hart*, Denver
HILL Robert	*Hill & Robbins*, Denver
KANAN Gregory	*Rothgerber Johnson*, Denver
MILLER Gale	*Davis Graham*, Denver
SHIVELY John	*Faegre & Benson*, Denver

Leading individuals (Litigation:
White-Collar Crime &
Government Investigations)

[1] BAUMANN Frederick	*Rothgerber Johnson*, Denver
EVANS Kevin	*Steese & Evans*, Denver
FOREMAN Lee	*Haddon Morgan*, Denver
HADDON Harold	*Haddon Morgan*, Denver
LOZOW Gary	*Isaacson Rosenbaum*, Denver
MACKEY Pamela	*Haddon Morgan*, Denver
RICHILANO John	*Richilano & Ridley*, Denver
SHEA Daniel	*Hogan & Hartson*, Denver
SHEA Kevin	*Ballard Spahr*, Denver
SHOEMAKER Andrew	*Hogan & Hartson*, Denver
WALSH John	*Hill & Robbins*, Denver
ZISSER David	*Isaacson Rosenbaum*, Denver

Individuals are listed alphabetically in each band.

The Lawyers: "*Fine strategic thinker*" **Scott Barker** (see p.316) is currently defending several large gas royalty class actions for BP USA, a long-standing client of the firm. Clients praise him as "*great on his feet in the courtroom*" and "*highly responsive to our requirements.*" Barker's workload encompasses large and complex commercial disputes, often, though far from exclusively, with a natural resources flavor. "*Great* *antitrust lawyer*" **James Hartley** (see p.318) heads the firm's antitrust litigation group, and specializes in advising clients in the healthcare industry. He combines his antitrust practice with some patent litigation.
The Clients: AT&T, BP USA and First Data are among the clients.

Hill & Robbins PC
The Firm: This smaller but highly respected litigation team enjoys a fine reputation for its work in class actions, generally representing plaintiffs. Consumer law and pensions cases have been particularly busy areas for the firm in recent years. "*A strong force, especially in antitrust and securities litigation,*" the team also has its share of work for defendants.
The Lawyers: "*Successful and impressive*" **Robert Hill** has a varied workload, which includes a considerable volume of plaintiff work in the securities arena. Over the past year he has made headlines by successfully defending the town of Black Hawk, CO, in a high-profile antitrust claim brought by a neighboring community. This related to the town's limited-stakes gambling industry. His ongoing work in the IBM pensions class action recently bore fruit in the form of a $320 million partial settlement. "*Amazing attorney,*" **John Walsh**, is best known for his top-notch white-collar crime practice, and is a popular choice for referrals. A candidate for Denver District Attorney in 2004, Walsh was singled out to researchers for his "*excellent instinct*" and "*impressive level of credibility and trust with government.*"
The Clients: The firm's work for the town in the Black Hawk case is well known, as is its work for plaintiffs in consumer and pension class actions.

Jacobs, Chase, Frick, Kleinkopf & Kelley
The Firm: This specialist litigation firm was recommended to researchers as "*extremely strong*" in a number of areas. These include a variety of complex disputes, including securities work and First Amendment cases. The team is dominated by the profile of its standout partner, however it is far from a one-man show, as the ranking this year of Ann Frick demonstrates. The firm commonly represents companies with a Colorado connection in litigation throughout the USA.
The Lawyers: Market commentators agree that the star player at this firm is the "*utterly brilliant*" **Jeff Chase**. Loved by clients and admired by peers, he was universally praised for his "*talented and aggressive*" handling of cases, and is described as "*unbelievable in the courtroom.*" He recently won a multimillion-dollar award in a major stockholder dissenters' rights case in Colorado. He has also represented a class of plaintiffs in a major securities-related class action, and is admired for his success in First Amend-

ment cases. "*Savvy and knowledgeable*" **Ann Frick** has particularly impressed the market with her work as an arbitrator, though she also has a well-regarded general commercial litigation practice.

Rothgerber Johnson & Lyons LLP
The Firm: This sizable team was praised by clients as "*quick on the uptake,*" and good at finding "*the appropriate response,*" whether the situation demands litigation, mediation or arbitration. The firm has seen considerable growth of late in its securities litigation practice, and it is also witnessing a growth of civil litigation with parallel criminal proceedings. Its clients range from small Colorado companies to well-known national and international players.
The Lawyers: "*Extremely talented*" **James Lyons** (see p.320) is a respected trial lawyer who "*can do it all*" according to interviewees. He was also recommended to researchers as an "*influential attorney with lots of political clout and clout in the city.*" Lyons is currently representing a ski resort operator in a $90 million breach of contract claim arising from the purchase of Steamboat Springs ski area. "*Excellent*" up-and-coming partner, **Fred Baumann** (see p.316), continues to assist Lyons in his work for Qwest, and is thought by many to be "*Jim Lyons' skilled protégé.*" He has acted on behalf of Qwest directors on derivative claims, culminating in favorable settlements in three different courts. His general commercial practice includes a substantial element of white-collar litigation and regulatory work. Peers describe **Chuck Goldberg** (see p.318), a former Denver District Court judge, as "*a solid and well-known general litigator.*" Unusually, he is also known for his expertise in religious institutions law, and acts as general counsel to the Archbishop of the diocese of Denver. **Greg Kanan** (see p.319) is well known in the state for his antitrust practice, which includes both plaintiff and defense litigation, and the defense of criminal antitrust charges.
The Clients: The roster includes Qwest, Alpine Partners and Triple Peaks.

Wheeler, Trigg & Kennedy LLP
The Firm: This "*vibrant, top-quality*" litigation specialist, a new entrant to the tables, was set up in 1998 by a group of "*really talented trial lawyers*" and has since "*established an excellent reputation in the state,*" according to peers. The firm focuses on trial work and, though headquartered in Denver, represents major clients at trial throughout the country. The team of around 40 boasts four Fellows of the American College of Trial Lawyers among its partners.
The Lawyers: "*A superb trial lawyer,*" **Hugh Gottschalk** is blessed with an enviable client list and a diverse practice, which encompasses everything from trade secrets to products liability.

He is currently representing star client ConocoPhillips on a number of matters, including a construction dispute and an environmental claim. Formerly with Skadden Arps, **Mal Wheeler** was described as *"a big name"* by interviewees, who comment that *"he's based in Denver but he has a national practice."* His client base includes Fortune 100 companies such as Ford and Pfizer.

The Clients: ConocoPhillips; Duke Energy; FMC and BDO Seidman.

Ballard Spahr Andrews & Ingersoll LLP
See firm details p.1541

The Firm: *"Good trial lawyers"* are to the fore in this well-established, national firm. The team has been bolstered by the recent arrival of Carl Eklund, formerly managing partner of LeBoeuf, Lamb, Greene & MacRae's now-closed Denver office. An expert in bankruptcy litigation, his presence is expected to bolster the team's offering in this field. A team of four attorneys practice solely in the white-collar crime area, and their experience encompasses securities fraud, antitrust, government and SEC investigations, and environmental crime.

The Lawyers: Sources agreed that *"prodigious worker"* **Roger Thomasch** (see p.323) *"does a wonderful job for his clients in really tough cases."* An *"eloquent, articulate"* advocate, his workload over the past year has been dominated by his work as Goodyear's national trial counsel. Thomasch represented Goodyear in a high-profile products liability class action, which recently settled following three jury trials. Commentators characterize white-collar crime expert **Kevin Shea** (see p.322) as *"one of the more thoughtful lawyers practicing in the area."* He was particularly commended for his knack of devising *"creative solutions."* Shea's clients are typically high-level executives in public companies who are under investigation by the SEC.

The Clients: The firm represents a number of major public companies, such as Goodyear and Comcast.

Faegre & Benson LLP
See firm details p.1022

The Firm: The litigation team at this large firm is packed with *"thoroughly skilled lawyers,"* according to our feedback. Its antitrust practice is felt to be particularly strong, though it is also busy in a wide range of other areas, including products liability, general commercial cases, bankruptcy and securities litigation, and IP. The team successfully represented Frontier Airlines in two national class actions brought by classes of travel agents.

The Lawyers: *"Smart, hard-working"* **Michael McCarthy** (see p.320) continues to be busy in defending State Farm in a number of class action law suits involving consumer, insurance

coverage and contract claims. He has also represented the Colorado Rockies in numerous claims. His practice spans contract disputes and consumer law, and he undertakes a volume of securities litigation. **John Shively** (see p.322) is best known as an antitrust litigator, though he also has a broad practice. He recently handled the antitrust elements of a vertical restriction claim against State Farm.

The Clients: Aventis; BFI Waste Systems of America; Colorado Rockies; The Denver Post; DuPont; Frontier Airlines; Novartis; State Farm and Zateca Foods.

Gibson, Dunn & Crutcher LLP
See firm details p.285

The Firm: The litigation group at the Denver office of this huge international firm emphasizes antitrust, securities and regulatory work. Its lawyers won praise from major clients for their *"confident approach to legal issues and business strategy."* This skill was on show recently in a major antitrust claim. The firm prosecuted antitrust monopolization claims and tort claims in federal court in Utah on behalf a nationwide truck stop chain, which led to the client receiving a $49 million settlement and license agreements.

The Lawyers: **George Curtis** (see p.317) specializes in defending corporate clients in securities litigation, and advising them on regulatory compliance. In the opinion of one client, *"for this type of work, George is one of the best in the city."* In addition to an active trial and regulatory practice, an important part of his work over the past year has been the ongoing Boston Chicken insolvency litigation, where claimed damages of over $1 billion are at stake.

The Clients: The client list includes leading names in the financial world, including: Merrill Lynch; Deloitte & Touche; Lehman Brothers and UBS.

Holme Roberts & Owen LLP
See firm details p.326

The Firm: This solid and impressive outfit can be relied upon for a *"top-class service,"* according to clients. Although it has endured some departures to other firms, affecting its visibility, the venerable Denver outfit maintains a prominent profile in the market, especially for complicated securities and antitrust disputes.

The Lawyers: Commentators are full of respect for **Bruce Black**, who is considered by some sources to be *"the smartest, most tenacious lawyer in the securities area"* in Colorado, with a superb track record of large wins. Black's practice also emphasizes large, complex antitrust litigation.

Other Notable Practitioners

"Skilled, experienced trial lawyer," **Gary Ceriani**, at Davis & Ceriani continues to make a fine impression on commentators. Acclaimed by rivals as *"one of the best jury trial lawyers"* in the

state, especially for securities litigation, he is frequently called upon to represent high-profile clients on appeal. Recently he represented a group of bond companies in a massive securities fraud case in Spokane, WA. Previously a partner at Hogan & Hartson, **Kevin Evans** (see p.317) has recently formed his own firm, Steese & Evans PC. An *"aggressive and well-regarded"* attorney, he is praised by peers for his dynamic representation of individual directors and officers in regulatory investigations, and regularly receives referrals from larger firms. **John Richilano** at Richilano & Ridley PC is another recognized figure in the white-collar crime area, and was described by one fellow professional as *"top of the stack."* His white-collar work is part of a wider criminal litigation practice, which has undoubtedly contributed to his high profile in the state. At Kelly Haglund Garnsey + Khan, **Walter Garnsey**'s (see p.318) diverse workload includes both commercial and employment litigation. He was engaged recently as local counsel to advise on major fraud litigation involving three former Qwest executives. He also maintains a niche in advising Indian tribes on contentious land use issues.

Haddon, Morgan, Mueller, Jordan, Mackey & Foreman PC

The Firm: Interviewees had no doubt that this small specialist firm *"would be at the top of everybody's list"* for white-collar criminal work. The team is said to be *"very deep with lots of great lawyers,"* which, together with its considerable track record, helps to keep it at the top. In the more general criminal litigation arena, the group has made headlines recently with its defense of Los Angeles Lakers star, Kobe Bryant, against high-profile sexual assault charges, which have since been dropped.

The Lawyers: Well-known figure **Harold Haddon** is *"the best by far"* in this arena, according to a number of sources. He garners unanimous approval from peers, and is said to have ascended to *"rock star"* status. **Pamela Mackey** is *"great at white-collar crime across the board,"* say interviewees. She also offers a renowned criminal defense practice. **Lee Foreman** is thought of as the firm's *"figurehead"* and senior statesman. He was particularly praised for his *"sensitive and creative approach to making a problem go away to everyone's satisfaction."*

Hogan & Hartson LLP
See firm details p.484

The Firm: Though only four years old, the white-collar crime and securities litigation department in Hogan's Denver office is going from strength to strength. The group counts three former SEC employees among its attorneys, and is eagerly anticipating the imminent arrival of Bob Troyer from the US Attorney's Office. The former leading light of the group, Ty

All quotes in the text are from interviews with clients and competitors.

Cobb, now operates mainly in the firm's DC office, demonstrating the seamless nature of the firm's national litigation and regulatory practice. As clients observe: "*One of the nice things about them is that you really have a team working for you – they all play valuable roles.*"

The Lawyers: "*Dedicated, client-focused*" **Daniel Shea** (see p.322) acted for Amvescap during a recent investigation by the SEC, and has also been involved in the ongoing Qwest litigation. He recently made submissions to the SEC on behalf of a former Qwest executive, as a result of which the SEC has agreed to drop all charges. **Andrew Shoemaker** (see p.322) concentrates on internal investigations and regulatory defense; a recent matter of note was the SEC investigation of Gemstar TV Guide, which has settled favorably following a high level of cooperation between his team and the SEC. Formerly with the SEC, Shoemaker has made a fine impression on clients: "*He is absolutely penetrating in his insights,*" said one, adding that, "*he has flawlessly made the transition from government into private practice.*"

The Clients: Vail Resorts; University of Colorado; Qwest and UBS PayneWebber.

Isaacson, Rosenbaum, Woods & Levy, PC

The Firm: Securities litigation, government investigation and white-collar crime defense represent a significant proportion of this Denver firm's litigation practice.

The Lawyers: **David Zisser** formerly worked at the SEC, and is now "*doing a lot of great securities work*". Zisser leans more towards the civil side of securities litigation. He regularly collaborates with "*star*" **Gary Lozow**, who has a broader criminal defense practice, and is highly recommended for white-collar criminal defense.

REAL ESTATE

Colorado
Leading firms (Real Estate)

1 BROWNSTEIN HYATT & FARBER PC *Denver*
OTTEN, JOHNSON, ROBINSON, NEFF *Denver*

2 BALLARD SPAHR ANDREWS *Denver*
HOLME ROBERTS & OWEN LLP *Denver*
ISAACSON, ROSENBAUM, WOODS & LEVY *Denver*
JACOBS, CHASE, FRICK, KLEINKOPF *Denver*
SHERMAN & HOWARD LLC *Denver*

3 DAVIS GRAHAM & STUBBS LLP *Denver*
FAEGRE & BENSON LLP *Denver*
LOTTNER RUBIN FISHMAN BROWN *Denver*
STEINER, DARLING & HUTCHINSON LLP *Denver*

Leading individuals (Real Estate)

Senior Statesman
CARPENTER Willis *Carpenter & Klatskin, Denver*

1 BARAD Edward *Brownstein Hyatt, Denver*
BROWN Robert *Sherman & Howard, Denver*
RAGONETTI Thomas *Otten Johnson, Denver*
ROBINSON Frank *Otten Johnson, Denver*
STERNBERG John *Otten Johnson, Denver*

2 CULHANE James *Davis Graham, Denver*
FIELDS Leslie *Faegre & Benson, Denver*
JACOBS Paul *Jacobs Chase, Denver*
PERMUT Barry *Isaacson Rosenbaum, Denver*
QUAIL Beverly *Ballard Spahr, Denver*
SENN Mark *Senn Lewis, Denver*

3 BACH Robert *Holme Roberts, Denver*
DONOVAN Lawrence *Isaacson Rosenbaum, Denver*
HOLMES Robert *Holme Roberts, Denver*
LINQUANTI Richard *Ireland Stapleton, Denver*
LOTTNER Alan *Lottner Rubin, Denver*
MCNEIVE Lynda *Brownstein Hyatt, Denver*
SAMUELS JONES Karen *Perkins Coie, Denver*
WESTOVER Michael *Otten Johnson, Denver*

Firms and individuals are listed alphabetically in each band.

Band 1

Brownstein Hyatt & Farber PC

See firm details p.324

The Firm: Known as "*a substantial player in the market,*" interviewees report that the firm is enviably placed to attract clients from outside the state: "*It's well known nationally so it's likely to get national clients first.*" On the local level, commentators report that the firm's size is an advantage in the Colorado real estate market – entrepreneurial clients often prefer mid-sized firms with a genuine real estate focus as opposed to megafirms. As in other practice areas, the firm's political connections are also perceived as an advantage; in the words of one interviewee: "*Where they add extra value is in providing access to certain government resources that other firms can't match.*"

The Lawyers: "*Sophisticated, proactive and smart*" **Ed Barad** (see p.316) heads the group. "*You hear great things, and they are justified,*" admit peers. Barad generally represents developers and is currently involved in the acquisition and redevelopment of an 1800-acre site at Denver International Airport. The project will incorporate a hotel, offices and housing space. Another element of his practice is commercial leasing; he oversees the leasehold management work at the Denver Design Center and The Collection. **Lynda McNeive** (see p.320) enters the tables following recommendations for her "*fabulous*" development practice. She is heavily involved in the ongoing redevelopment of the Denver LoDo area. **Bruce James** (see p.319), the firm's managing partner, is well known for his hotels work. He led a significant recent transaction involving the sale of the San Juan Grand Hotel and Casino in San Juan, Puerto Rico. He also advised on the sale of the Riata at Bel Mar multifamily housing project in Lakewood, which sold for the highest price ever paid for a Colorado multifamily project. **Wayne Forman**'s (see p.318) practice incorporates both land use and environmental representation, and he is well regarded in both arenas.

The Clients: The firm acts for a number of important local developers, as well as developers, lenders, landlords and tenants nationwide.

Otten, Johnson, Robinson, Neff & Ragonetti, PC

The Firm: Market sources acknowledge that this renowned real estate boutique thoroughly deserves its place at the top of Chambers' tables. "*The premier firm in development work, and very strong in other areas,*" it has been busy over the past year advising on aspects of a number of huge housing developments. It has also spearheaded several major resort projects and redevelopments, and transport schemes. The firm is said to boast the largest land use and zoning department in the region.

The Lawyers: Sources lavished praise on **Frank Robinson**, describing him as "*one of the smartest, most experienced, most creative real estate lawyers*" in the state. Others consider him simply "*the best,*" citing his "*hard work and great attention to detail*" as major selling points. **John Sternberg** is praised for his "*ability to grasp the big picture and the minutiae.*" Peers, meanwhile, note his pragmatic, deal-making attitude: "*With Sternberg on the other side, you know you'll get the deal done.*" His unrivaled experience of the construction and commercial development industries was also highlighted. "*Articulate and practical,*" **Tom Ragonetti**'s skills lie in land use and development. Fellow attorneys acknowledge that he is their first port of call "*when we get out of our depth with zoning and land use issues.*" Clients, meanwhile, appreciate that "*he really understands how the city works, as well as the developer angle.*" His practice has recently emphasized developments connected to

Leading individuals
(Real Estate: Zoning/Land Use)

1 **FORMAN Wayne** *Brownstein Hyatt*, Denver
GRIMSHAW Thomas *Grimshaw & Harring*, Denver
KAPLAN Stephen *Kaplan Kirsch*, Denver
MACDONALD Thomas *Otten Johnson*, Denver
RAGONETTI Thomas *Otten Johnson*, Denver
ROCKWELL Sarah *Kaplan Kirsch*, Denver

Leading individuals
(Real Estate:Hotels and Resorts)

1 **CLOWDUS Michael** *Ballard Spahr*, Denver
FISCHER Rebecca *Sherman & Howard*, Denver
KLEINKOPF David *Jacobs Chase*, Denver
STEINER Beat *Steiner Darling*, Denver

2 **CALVIN Charles** *Faegre & Benson*, Denver
JAMES Bruce *Brownstein Hyatt*, Denver
LINQUANTI Richard *Ireland Stapleton*, Denver

Individuals are listed alphabetically in each band.

Denver's expanding light rail network. Ragonetti often collaborates with partner **Tom Macdonald**, who "*works incredibly hard,*" according to sources. Other land use attorneys praised his skills both as a lawyer and as a teacher. On the real estate finance side, commentators point to **Michael Westover** as an attorney who is rapidly gaining in stature in the field.

The Clients: In addition to star client Vail Resorts, the firm acts for a range of Colorado clients, including Denver Tech Center and Oakwood Homes.

Band 2

Ballard Spahr Andrews & Ingersoll LLP

See firm details p.1541

The Firm: This is "*one of the first names that comes to mind*" for real estate work, particularly real estate finance, according to interviewees. Ballard Spahr consistently represents lenders and institutional pension funds on some of the largest deals in the state, and its "*strong practice and national clients*" make it a favorite choice. It also enjoys a good name for hotel and resorts work, and clients were particularly impressed with the depth and quality of the team, right down to associate level.

The Lawyers: "*Rainmaker*" **Beverly Quail** (see p.321) leads the real estate lending practice. She has recently advised a major insurance company in connection with two loans, of $150 million and $99 million, in California and Maryland. She also acts for the Gates Corporation, which recently took a lease of 286,000 sq ft in downtown Denver – an unusually large deal in an otherwise quiet leasing market. "*She has a wonderful energetic demeanor,*" commented delighted clients, who particularly admire "*her ability to create situations in negotiations where both sides win.*" **Mike Clowdus**

(see p.317) is a renowned specialist in hotels and resorts matters. Recent growth areas in his practice include new mixed-use developments within the established ski resorts, and the development and sale of condominium hotels. He also advises on the formation, structuring, financing and regulation of golf clubs and other private membership clubs.

The Clients: TIAA-CREF; Metropolitan Life Insurance Company; The Gates Corporation and Pennsylvania State Employees Retirement System.

Holme Roberts & Owen LLP

See firm details p.326

The Firm: According to loyal clients, this team is "*one of the best in town*" for real estate. It is particularly appreciated for being "*fair and reasonable on fees.*" With its heavy emphasis on finance, the firm represents star client Wells Fargo on all its construction and real estate lending in the Rocky Mountain West. Over the past year it has handled a large number of acquisitions, with much of the activity falling in the multifamily, retail and industrial fields. The firm has been involved in the development of many of Colorado's ski resorts.

The Lawyers: **Robert Bach** divides his practice between real estate finance and development. In recent months his workload has included advising Red Peak Properties on acquisitions and new apartment developments. Clients see him as "*business-oriented, diligent and thorough,*" while competitors acknowledge him as "*young, aggressive and good for his clients.*" Bach also represents Alliance Commercial Partners. **Robert Holmes** also advises on both finance and development work, but with more of an emphasis on workouts and foreclosure. In the words of one interviewee: "*I would turn to him for a second opinion on almost anything, especially foreclosure issues.*"

The Clients: Some of the largest lenders in the West, including Wells Fargo Bank, turn to Holme Roberts for advice.

Isaacson, Rosenbaum, Woods & Levy, PC

The Firm: Well known in the market, this firm is "*one of the first that comes to mind for general real estate work,*" according to interviewees. Its attorneys were praised for their constructive attitude to negotiations and their knowledge of areas like development and leasing. In addition to its general practice, the firm is gaining increasing recognition for land conservation work – still something of a niche area in the region.

The Lawyers: "*Terrific*" **Barry Permut** "*doesn't let his ego get in the way of getting the deal done for the client,*" according to market sources. His work includes a mixture of real estate development, acquisition and financing. **Lonny Donovan** enters *Chambers'* tables this year following

lowing highly positive market feedback. Observers note that he has "*really come into the limelight*" in recent years, and describe him as "*a real team player, who makes everyone around him work better.*" Donovan has a broad-based practice with a focus on commercial retail leasing.

The Clients: The firm is known for serving general real estate and development clients with interests in areas like retail, industrial and multifamily use.

Jacobs, Chase, Frick, Kleinkopf & Kelley

The Firm: The firm is a particularly notable player in the Colorado resorts and hotels arena, due in part to its "*fantastic work*" for star client Intrawest, one of the world's largest resort developers. Its sports development work is also earning the firm a reputation well beyond the state. However, the practice is much broader than this, and includes large acquisition deals for developers and real estate finance for major retailers.

The Lawyers: Experienced attorney **Paul Jacobs** is well regarded in the market, especially for his niche in sports facility development. "*A brilliant guy and a gentleman,*" he has just completed the new, $1 billion ballpark in San Diego, CA. Jacobs has also been busy this year with the urban redevelopment project surrounding the park, and has been retained by the City of San Diego to advise on the development of a new National Football League stadium. **Dave Kleinkopf** enters *Chambers'* tables on the strength of his stellar reputation for hotels and resorts work. According to his peers: "*Dave's work for Intrawest is just great.*"

The Clients: A diverse client list includes names such as Intrawest, City of San Diego and Denver Regional Transportation District.

Sherman & Howard LLC

The Firm: Sherman & Howard benefits from a broad client base, which encompasses lenders, developers, investment funds and general corporate clients. Of late, the team has been handling a large amount of development work in Denver, and some interesting resort work, however it has also been increasingly involved in bankruptcy and foreclosure.

The Lawyers: **Robert Brown** remains extremely well regarded in the market, and "*would be high on anyone's list,*" according to interviewees. Following the successful completion of a $300 million hospital campus, he is currently leading the team on another hospital building project in Denver. His broad practice spans purchases, sales and development, real estate finance, foreclosures, leasing and land use. A more unusual aspect of his recent work has been the sale of several 'trophy ranches', one of which sold for in excess of $20 million. Colleague **Rebecca Fischer** is highly active in the resorts sector, where her practice is described as

All quotes in the text are from interviews with clients and competitors.

CHAMBERS USA 2005

"very high level."

The Clients: The firm provides counsel to substantial lenders, corporate clients and funds.

Band 3

Davis Graham & Stubbs LLP

The Firm: Davis Graham & Stubbs continues to field a good real estate team, with a notable focus on development and student housing work. James Culhane remains the group's big draw, but he has the support of *"a full complement of young people,"* according to commentators. Over the past year, the group has been involved in numerous development projects in the residential, student and healthcare sectors.

The Lawyers: James Culhane is regarded as *"one of the senior statesmen"* of the Colorado real estate Bar. He is still active in the market, with a thriving general real estate and finance practice. In recent months he has advised a major developer of student housing on the disposal of its interests in four different housing projects.

The Clients: The group represents national developers and house builders.

Faegre & Benson LLP

See firm details p.1022

The Firm: Faegre's sizable team is active in all areas of the real estate market, from commercial leasing to development and workouts. *"Nationally high profile,"* the firm's Denver office handles some major leasing for large portfolios, as well as industrial and retail development. The group is particularly well regarded for its eminent domain and condemnation work.

The Lawyers: Commentators agree that **Leslie Fields** (see p.318) is *"absolutely the best in the field"* of condemnation litigation, a niche that makes her a unique name in our list. She was recently involved in high-profile open space condemnation proceedings in Telluride. **Chuck Calvin** (see p.316) is known in the state for advising on the development of planned communities and resort condos, although he also handles some real estate finance. Recent years have seen him increasingly involved in workouts of incomplete resort projects that have run into financial difficulties.

The Clients: Xcel Energy; Buffets; Stewart Title Guaranty Company; DR Horton; INVESCO Realty Advisors; Lincoln Property Company; Club Telluride Owners Association and Beaver Creek Lodge Condominium Association.

Lottner Rubin Fishman Brown & Saul, PC

The Firm: This well-known real estate boutique has managed to attract a number of national clients on the strength of its reputation for real estate finance and construction. Clients appreciate its cost-effective advice as well as the pragmatism and professionalism of the group's attorneys. Typical work is in the range of $5-75 million, however the team has also acted in considerably larger projects.

The Lawyers: Peers admire **Alan Lottner** for his high-end finance practice. He typically advises lenders on construction and mortgage loans, and mezzanine financing for a variety of development projects. He also advises some of the state's larger developers.

The Clients: Bank of America; Wells Fargo; KeyBank and Ohio Savings.

Steiner, Darling & Hutchinson LLP

The Firm: A true real estate boutique, this five-partner firm has an enviable record of acting for major national developers and financiers. The firm is particularly respected for its work in the resorts and leisure area: over the past year the team has advised Wells Fargo on the $25 million financing of Winter Park Resort, and acted as Colorado counsel to KeyBank on the $60 million acquisition financing of Crested Butte Resort. The team also advises on the development of golf clubs, casinos and hotels.

The Lawyers: **Beat Steiner** is *"absolutely charming,"* and also a *"very bright corporate lawyer."* He has a general real estate practice with a considerable resort development emphasis. A recent deal led by Steiner, which attracted considerable media attention, was the sale of Seven Lakes Lodge to golfer Greg Norman. He also maintains a thriving land use practice.

The Clients: KeyBank; Wells Fargo; Shea Homes and Castle Rock Development Company.

Other Notable Practitioners

According to several sources, **Mark Senn** at Senn Lewis & Visciano is *"recognized as one of the country's leading experts in commercial leasing."* **Willis Carpenter** of Carpenter & Klatskin *"is the dean of the real estate Bar: a fount of great information,"* particularly on rural farm and ranch transactions. **Karen Samuels Jones** has recently moved from Gorsuch Kirgis to Perkins Coie LLP, bringing with her a reputation among clients as *"an incredibly thorough, knowledgeable, customer service-oriented"* attorney and an *"excellent team player, who adjusts to us as the client."* She focuses almost exclusively on real estate finance for key institutions, such as First National Bank of Colorado and Allstate. **Stephen Kaplan** and **Sarah Rockwell** are both partners at Kaplan Kirsch & Rockwell LLP, a small Denver firm specializing in land use, environmental and transportation law. Rivals practicing in the area regard both as *"serious competitors for land use work."* **Tom Grimshaw**, a name partner at Grimshaw & Harring PC, also received plaudits for his land use practice, which makes up a considerable proportion of the firm's diet of real estate work. Meanwhile, **Richard Linquanti**, a partner at Ireland Stapleton Pryor & Pascoe PC, is noted for his expertise in condominium and planned unit development matters. He was heavily involved with the development of the Snowmass resort.

Leaders in Colorado

ARFMANN, Dennis
Hogan & Harston LLP, Boulder
720 406 5374
darfmann@hhlaw.com
Recommended in Environment
Practice Areas: Practice focuses on air quality; hazardous waste and water quality, with particular emphasis on resolving notices of violation and citizen suits; legislative and regulatory development issues; environmental litigation; and helping industry negotiate flexible permits. He has tried over 100 cases to the court or to juries.
Prof. Memberships: Chairman, Air Regulatory Committee, Colorado Association of Commerce and Industry; Member, Denver Regional Air Quality Council; Member, American Bar Association SONREEL; Member, Colorado Bar Association; Member, Nebraska Bar Association.
Career: Career as environmental litigator representing refineries, energy companies and manufacturers in high-profile clean air act permitting, enforcement investigation, and litigation matters throughout the Intermountain West.
Publications: Published author and frequent lecturer on environmental topics. Lectures include: 'Regulatory and Air Quality Trends in the Rocky Mountains', Colorado Bar Association (March 2005). Publications include: 'Kyoto Protocol Enters into Force' (16 February 2005); 'Environment and Energy - Climate Change Update', Hogan & Hartson L.L.P. (16 February 2005); 'The Grand Canyon Visibility Transport Commission: Reasonable Progress Toward the National Visibility Goal', Environmental Lawyer (June 1996); 'Logistical Problems of Implementing the Clean Air Act Operating Permit Program at the State Level', Shepard's Clean Air Reporter (1993); 'Air Toxics for 1990's and Beyond', Colorado Bar Journal (1991).
Personal: LLM, Environmental Law, with highest honors, The George Washington University Law School (1991); JD, University of Nebraska - Lincoln College of Law (1979); BA, University of Nebraska - Lincoln (1974).

ARKELL, Betty
Holland & Hart LLP, Denver
303 295 8321
barkell@hollandhart.com
Recommended in Corporate/M&A
Practice Areas: Head of the firm's Corporate Finance Practice Group with 30 years of experience as a corporate and securities lawyer. She specializes in venture capital investments, mergers, acquisitions, leveraged buyouts, acquisition finance, corporate restructurings, and general corporate counseling. She also has experience in the formation of private and public venture capital funds. Her clients include established and emerging growth companies as well as venture capital and other private equity funds. She recently completed a $72 million Rule 144A offering and $170 million senior secured financing for Navigant International, Inc.
Prof. Memberships: Member of the American Bar Association; Colorado Bar Association; and Denver Bar Association. Appointments: Board of Directors, Colorado Software and Internet Association; Leadership Council, Center for Entrepreneurship, University of Colorado at Denver; Board of Advisors, CTEK; Past Chair, Business Law Section, Colorado Bar Association; Past President, Colorado Association of Corporate Counsel.
Career: Admitted to the Colorado Bar (1975). Partner at Holland & Hart since 1994. Previously a Partner in the Denver office of Kirkland & Ellis.
Personal: Received a JD (Order of the Coif) from the University of Colorado (1975), an MA from the University of Colorado (1972) and a BA (with honors) from Northwestern University (1969).

ARO, Edwin
Hogan & Hartson LLP, Denver
303 899 7389
eparo@hhlaw.com
Recommended in Employment
Practice Areas: Litigation Partner, Practice Group Director, Labor and Employment Group, Co-Chair, Colorado Litigation Group. A trial lawyer who represents businesses in intellectual property, commercial and employment matters.
Prof. Memberships: Colorado Bar Association.
Career: Law Clerk to the Hon. Richard P Matsch, U S District Court, District of Colorado. Joined Hogan & Hartson in 1998, after nine years with Holme Roberts & Owen. Adjunct Law Professor at the University of Denver since 1994.
Personal: Born 20 July 1964, in Colorado Springs, Colorado. BA Denver University. JD, magna cum laude, Boston University. Member and Editor, 'Boston University Law Review'.

BACH, Robert
Holme Roberts & Owen LLP, Denver
303 861 7000
Recommended in Real Estate

BARAD, Edward N
Brownstein Hyatt & Farber PC, Denver
303 223 1108
ebarad@bhf-law.com
Recommended in Real Estate
Practice Areas: Shareholder and co-chair of Brownstein Hyatt & Farber's Real Estate Group. Focuses on commercial development and finance. Extensive experience representing developers and lenders in commercial real estate transactions.

Prof. Memberships: Board of Governors, American College of Real Estate Lawyers; Member, Colorado & American Bar Associations; Chairman, Legislative Speaker's Bureau; Supreme Court Grievance Committee; Co-Chairman, Opinion Letter Standards Committee Colorado Bar Real Estate Section; Hearing Examiner Colorado Bar Ethics Committee; Vice-Chairman, Opinion Letter Subcommittee University of Colorado Real Estate Council.
Personal: University of Colorado School of Law (JD, 1973); University of Colorado (BS, 1969).

BARKER, Scott
Holland & Hart LLP, Denver
303 295 8513
sbarker@hollandhart.com
Recommended in Litigation
Practice Areas: Partner practicing in complex civil litigation, with experience in more than 65 trials, one third of which were to juries. Cases tried in Colorado, Utah, Wyoming, Idaho, New Mexico, California and Washington. Extensive experience in complex litigation, including class actions. Mr Barker was voted Best of the Bar for business litigation in 2003 by his peers, which was sponsored by a leading Colorado business publication.
Prof. Memberships: ACTL Fellowship; International Association of Defense Counsel; American Bar Association; Colorado Bar Association; Denver Bar Association; and the American and Colorado Bar Foundations. Appointments: Fellow of the American College of Trial Lawyers.
Career: Admitted to Colorado Bar (1981). Past Chair of Holland & Hart's Management Committee.
Personal: Received a JD from Harvard University (cum laude) 1981, a MPhil from Oxford University (1973) and a BA from the US Air Force Academy (1970). Rhodes Scholar.

BARTLIT, Fred
Bartlit Beck Herman Palenchar & Scott, Denver 303 592 3100
Recommended in Litigation

BAUMANN, Frederick J
Rothgerber Johnson & Lyons LLP, Denver 303 628 9542
fbaumann@rothgerber.com
Recommended in Litigation
Practice Areas: Practice focused on complex corporate and business litigation representing individual and corporate defendants in connection with class actions and claims under federal securities laws. Represents local and national corporate entities in contract, fraud and other business litigation. Extensive experience in federal and state courts, as well as in the arbitration of business disputes.

Prof. Memberships: Fellow, American College of Trial Lawyers; Master Barrister, William E. Doyle American Inn of Court; Member, Committee on Conduct, US District Court, District of Colorado; Chair, Legal Aid Foundation of Colorado (2000-01); American, Colorado, and Denver Bar Associations.
Career: Admitted to practice in Colorado and New York state courts, the US District Court for the Southern and Eastern Districts of New York and the District of Colorado, and the US Court of Appeals for the Second and Tenth Circuits.
Personal: JD, New York University (1979); BA, Williams College (1976).

BEATON, Glenn
Gibson, Dunn & Crutcher LLP, Denver
303 298 5773
gbeaton@gibsondunn.com
Recommended in Intellectual Property
Practice Areas: Co-Chair of the firm's Intellectual Property Practice Group. Advises on intellectual property litigation and appeals, including patents, trademarks, copyrights and trade secrets. Experience includes counseling a number of patent infringement, misappropriation of trade secret cases, Patent Office proceedings, and prosecuting over 200 patent applications to issuance and numerous reexamination, reissuance and interference proceedings.
Career: Appointed a Special Master in the US District Court of Colorado.
Publications: Former adjunct professor and frequent lecturer on intellectual property.
Personal: JD, University of Denver, 1982, Order of St Ives, member of DU Law Review.

BLACK, Bruce
Holme Roberts & Owen LLP, Denver
303 861 7000
Recommended in Antitrust, Litigation

BLAIR, Andrew
Sherman & Howard LLC, Denver
303 297 2900
Recommended in Corporate/M&A

BROGAN, James
Cooley Godward LLP, Broomfield
720 566 4000
Recommended in Intellectual Property

BROWN, Robert
Sherman & Howard LLC, Denver
303 297 2900
Recommended in Real Estate

CALVIN, Charles
Faegre & Benson LLP, Denver
303 607 3677
ccalvin@faegre.com
Recommended in Hotels and Resorts
Practice Areas: Real estate.
Prof. Memberships: Colorado, Denver and American Bar Associations.
Career: Representations include: Own-

ers' association for a 700-member resort condominium; developers of mixed-use condominium projects in Denver; non-profit healthcare organization in acquiring multiple hospitals, clinics and related facilities across Colorado; construction lender for major Denver office building.
Publications: 'Legislative Framework/Common Interest Ownership Act' NBI; 'Owners' Associations: Management and Operations During Declarant Control' NBI; 'Realizing on Multiple Assets Securing the Same Debt: Some Thoughts on Wells Fargo Realty Advisors Funding v. UIOLI' CLE International; 'Participation and Intercreditor Agreements' CLE International.
Personal: BA, Pomona College, cum laude; JD, Yale University.

CAMPBELL, William J
Faegre & Benson LLP, Denver
303 607 3630
wcampbell@faegre.com
Recommended in Corporate/M&A
Practice Areas: Corporate finance, mergers and acquisitions, international business, and corporate governance.
Prof. Memberships: Colorado Bar Association, Business and International Law Sections; First Judicial District Bar Association, Past President; Colorado Association of Corporate Counsel; World Trade Center Denver, Board of Directors; Colorado College, Board of Trustees.
Career: Over 30 years of general corporate practice, with recent emphasis on public companies, corporate governance, and international business.
Personal: BA in Economics, Colorado College (1967), cum laude, Phi Beta Kappa; JD, University of Colorado, Boulder (1971), Law Review; Rotary Foundation Graduate Fellow in Economics, University of Newcastle, New South Wales, 1969.

CARPENTER, Willis
Carpenter & Klatskin, Denver
303 534 6315
Recommended in Real Estate

CERIANI, Gary
Davis & Ceriani, Denver
303 534 9000
Recommended in Litigation

CHASE, Jeffrey
Jacobs, Chase, Frick, Kleinkopf & Kelley, Denver
303 685 4800
Recommended in Litigation

CLOWDUS, Michael W
Ballard Spahr Andrews & Ingersoll LLP, Denver 303 299 7351
clowdus@ballardspahr.com
Recommended in Hotels and Resorts
Practice Areas: Concentrates his practice in resort development. Over the last five years, he has represented developers in the design, documentation, registration, financing (both debt and equity),

construction and marketing and sales of more than twenty high end fractional projects at major resorts throughout the Rocky Mountain West and in Mexico.
Prof. Memberships: He is currently Chair of the Federal Issues Committee and is the past Chair of the State Legislative Committee of the American Resort Development Association (ARDA) and also serves as a member of the Urban, State and Local Government and Real Property Probate and Trust Law sections of the American Bar Association.
Career: Admitted to the Colorado Bar (1975); joined as Partner (1986).
Personal: JD, University of Denver (1975); AB, cum laude, Duke University (1972).

CONNERY, Robert T
Holland & Hart LLP, Denver
303 295 8133
rconnery@hollandhart.com
Recommended in Environment
Practice Areas: Partner practicing environmental law with experience in environmental planning, permitting, and compliance work on major industrial and mining projects and environmental litigation. Represented major natural resource companies in complex litigation over environmental impact statement requirements, EPA regulatory requirements, state regulations and enforcement actions, including cases before US District Courts, Courts of Appeal for the District of Columbia, the Ninth and Tenth Circuits, and the US Supreme Court. Covered regulatory matters such as air and water quality requirements, solid and hazardous waste requirements, reclamation, historic preservation laws, threatened and endangered species laws, and fish and wildlife coordination.
Prof. Memberships: Former Council Member and Past Chairman, Air Quality Committee of the American Bar Association's Natural Resources, Energy and Environment Section, and former Trustee of the Rocky Mountain Mineral Law Foundation.
Career: Admitted to the Colorado (1966) Bar.
Personal: Received a LLB (1966) from Harvard and a BA (1962) from Yale.

CUDNEY, Kevin
Brownstein Hyatt & Farber PC, Denver
303 223 1166
kcudney@BHF-Law.com
Recommended in Corporate/M&A
Practice Areas: Shareholder in Brownstein Hyatt & Farber's Corporate & Securities Group. His practice focuses on mergers and acquisitions, private equity, public and private securities offerings, capital formation and securities advice (including SEC compliance), and complex business transactions. His clients include large and middle-market businesses, private equity funds, investment banking firms, and emerging tech-

nology and biotechnology companies.
Personal: Case Western Reserve University (JD, 1975); Harpur College-State University of New York at Binghamton (BA, 1972).

CULHANE, James
Davis Graham & Stubbs LLP, Denver
303 892 9400
Recommended in Real Estate

CURTIS, George B
Gibson, Dunn & Crutcher LLP, Denver
303 298 5743
gcurtis@gibsondunn.com
Recommended in Litigation
Practice Areas: Counsels on complex corporate, securities and accountancy matters, specifically defending allegations of securities law violations, professional negligence and related causes of action. Has tried cases before judges, juries, self-regulatory organizations, and in federal and state administrative tribunals. Represents clients before the SEC, the Department of Justice, the NYSE and the NASD and in settlement proceedings and procedures conducted by federal and state magistrates.
Publications: Lectures on accounting matters and Sarbanes-Oxley certification requirements.
Personal: JD, University of Chicago, 1976, Russell Sage Foundation Fellowship in law and social science. PhD, MA, American Legal History, University of Virginia.

DEENY, Raymond
Sherman & Howard LLC, Colorado Springs 719 475 2440
Recommended in Employment

DONOVAN, Lawrence
Isaacson, Rosenbaum, Woods & Levy, PC, Denver 303 292 5656
Recommended in Real Estate

DUNN, Daniel
Holme Roberts & Owen LLP, Denver
303 861 7000
Recommended in Environment

EDDY, Ronald
Sherman & Howard LLC, Denver
303 297 2900
Recommended in Environment

EID, Troy A
Greenberg Traurig LLP, Denver
303 572 6500
eidt@gtlaw.com
Recommended in Environment
Practice Areas: Governmental affairs; environmental; land development; energy and natural resources negotiations.
Prof. Memberships: Advisory Board Member, Natural Resources Law Center, University of Colorado School of Law. Co-Chair, Governor's Commission on Civil Service Reform. Member, Governor's Commission on Science and Technology. Chairman, Colorado Board of Ethics. Board Member, Legal Aid Foundation of Colorado
Publications: 'Strategic Democracy-

Building: How States Can Help' (co-authored with Governor Bill Owens), in Alexander T.J. Lennon, editor, Winning Hearts and Minds: Using Soft Power to Undermine Terrorist Networks (Massachusetts Institute of Technology Press, 2003), pp. 130-149. 'The European Union: A Brief Introduction,' The Colorado Lawyer, May 2002.

EURICH, Gregory
Holland & Hart LLP, Denver
303 295 8166
geurich@hollandhart.com
Recommended in Employment
Practice Areas: Partner practicing in labor law, with particular emphasis on litigation of labor disputes. Work has included defending major clients against claims of race, sex, age, disability and national origin discrimination, actions involving collective bargaining agreements, and wrongful discharge claims in lawsuits before state and federal trial and appellate courts in much of the Western United States. Lead trial counsel in nearly 100 trials, a substantial portion of which have been jury trials.
Prof. Memberships: Member of the Colorado Supreme Court Committee on Pattern Jury Instructions; Colorado Trial Lawyers Association; the Association of Trial Lawyers of America; Defense Research Institute; and the Colorado Defense Lawyers Association. Appointments: Co-Chair of the Colorado Pledge to Diversity Law Firm Group.
Career: Admitted to the Colorado and US District Court, District of Colorado (1973), US Court of Appeals, Tenth Circuit (1977) and US Supreme Court.
Personal: Received JD (magna cum laude, Order of the Coif) from the University of Michigan (1973) and a BA (cum laude, Phi Beta Kappa) from the University of Michigan (1970).

EVANS, Kevin D
Steese & Evans PC, Denver
720 200 0613
kdevans@s-elaw.com
Recommended in Litigation
Career: Clients have described Evans as 'tough, tenacious and extremely talented.' His peers note that his work ethic and talent translates into a 'terrific trial lawyer'. Evans represents clients in white collar criminal defense, SEC and complex litigation matters, as well as internal investigations. Most recently, he has represented numerous individuals in SEC proceedings, a large French chemical company in a criminal RCRA case, a large French company in antitrust litigation, several clients in qui tam litigation, the United States Olympic Committee, and several Olympic and professional athletes, as well as the owner of various professional sports teams.

FIELDS, Leslie
Faegre & Benson LLP, Denver
303 607 3622
LFields@faegre.com
Recommended in Real Estate

Practice Areas: Eminent domain; land use; property tax valuations.

Career: Represented governments in major open space acquisitions; private landowners in the condemnation of 15,000 acres of land, mineral and water rights for the new Denver International Airport; private landowners in prosecuting and defending the condemnation of property for private purposes; private landowners in unauthorized urban renewal takings; and a wide assortment of condemnation cases involving waste transfer facilities, churches, athletic facilities, restaurants, high rise office buildings, fast food franchises, gas stations, manufacturing facilities, residential subdivisions, and others.

Personal: BA, University of Denver (1978); JD, Denver College of Law (1981).

FISCHER, Rebecca
Sherman & Howard LLC, Denver
303 297 2900
Recommended in Hotels and Resorts

FOGNANI, John
Fognani Guibord & Homsy LLP, Denver
303 382 6200
Recommended in Environment

FOREMAN, Lee
Haddon, Morgan, Mueller, Jordan, Mackey & Foreman PC, Denver
303 831 7364
Recommended in Litigation

FORMAN, Wayne F
Brownstein Hyatt & Farber PC, Denver
303 223 1120
wforman@bhf-law.com
Recommended in Real Estate

Practice Areas: Shareholder in Brownstein Hyatt & Farber's Water Rights, Public Lands, Real Estate, Environmental Law, Administrative Law, and Litigation Groups. A counsel of record in a number of reported appellate decisions involving water rights matters. Represented private landowners and public entities in a variety of land use and condemnation matters. Extensive experience in the water quality area, including NEPA compliance, Section 404 permitting, and Section 401 state certifications.
Prof. Memberships: American Bar Association; Colorado Bar Association; Denver Bar Association.
Personal: University of Colorado School of Law (JD, 1984); Cornell University (BS, 1980).

FRICK, Ann
Jacobs, Chase, Frick, Kleinkopf & Kelley, Denver 303 685 4800
Recommended in Litigation

GALLAGHER, Sean
Hogan & Hartson LLP, Denver
303 454 2415
srgallagher@hhlaw.com
Recommended in Employment

Practice Areas: Litigation Group Partner. Trial lawyer who represents businesses in employment, commercial and public policy litigation matters. Has tried numerous litigation matters to juries and judges in both state and federal courts.
Prof. Memberships: Member, Employment Rights and Responsibilities Sub-Committee, Labor Law Committee, American Bar Association; Member, Colorado Bar Association.
Publications: One of two managing editors of 'The Practitioner's Guide to Colorado Employment Law', published by the Colorado Bar Association; 'Privacy Versus Freedom of Speech: Telemarketing and Government's Ability to Limit It', The Colorado Lawyer, Colorado Bar Association (1 October 2004).
Personal: JD, University of Denver College of Law (1987); BA, Baylor University (1984).

GARNSEY Jr, Walter W
Kelly Haglund Garnsey + Kahn, Denver
303 296 9412
wgarnsey@khgk.com
Recommended in Litigation

Practice Areas: Complex commercial litigation in federal and state courts, administrative agencies, and arbitration tribunals. Commercial litigation emphasis on law of contracts, business entities, financial institutions, construction, and real estate. Additional emphasis on employment litigation and land use matters under federal Indian law.
Prof. Memberships: Fellow, American College of Trial Lawyers; Member, American, Colorado, and Denver Bar Associations.
Career: Associate, Holland & Hart (Denver, Colorado): 1971-73; Trial Attorney, Denver Regional Litigation Center, Equal Employment Opportunity Commission: 1973-1974; Member, Kelly Haglund Garnsey + Kahn LLC: 1974-present.
Personal: Stanford University Law School, JD 1971; Yale University, BA (cum laude) 1967.

GIBBY, Darin
Townsend and Townsend and Crew LLP, Denver
303 571 4000
Recommended in Intellectual Property

GOLDBERG, Charles
Rothgerber Johnson & Lyons LLP, Denver 303 628 9533
cgoldberg@rothgerber.com
Recommended in Litigation

Practice Areas: Complex civil litigation, religious liberty issues, condemnations, professional and products liability lawsuits, personal injury lawsuits, securities arbitrations and will contests. Rep-

resents religious organizations, colleges, and universities in litigation in Colorado. Represents clients before the Colorado Commission on Judicial Discipline, the Colorado Supreme Court's Grievance Committee, and other administrative bodies. He regularly serves as a mediator and arbitrator.
Prof. Memberships: Fellow, American College of Trial Lawyers (2003-present); Colorado Supreme Court's Committee on Pattern Civil Jury Instructions (1977-97); Colorado Trial Lawyers Association (1964-present); Executive Committee for the National Diocesan Attorneys Association (1992-present); Large Complex Case Panel of Arbitrators, American Arbitration Association; Denver and Colorado Bar Associations (1964-present).
Career: Admitted to Colorado, US District Court, District of Colorado, US Court of Appeals, Tenth Circuit, and US Supreme Court. Appointed by the Colorado Supreme Court as the first chairman of the Board of Trustees of the Colorado Attorneys' Fund for Client Protection. He is a former director of the National Client Protection Organization.
Personal: JD, University of Denver College of Law (1964), Board of Editors, University of Denver Law Journal; BA, University of Colorado (1961).

GOTTSCHALK, Hugh
Wheeler Trigg Kennedy LLP, Denver
303 292 2525
Recommended in Litigation

GRIMSHAW, Thomas
Grimshaw & Harring PC, Denver
303 839 3800
Recommended in Real Estate

HADDON, Harold
Haddon, Morgan, Mueller, Jordan, Mackey & Foreman PC, Denver
303 831 7364
Recommended in Litigation

HANLON-LEH, Natalie
Faegre & Benson LLP, Denver
303 607 3639
Nhanlon-Leh@faegre.com
Recommended in Intellectual Property

Practice Areas: Intellectual property litigation (including patents, copyrights, trademarks, unfair competition, false advertising and trade secrets); trademark, brand management and copyright counseling and licensing
Prof. Memberships: Chair, Colorado Bar Association Intellectual Property Section; Programs Committee, International Trademark Association; Past President, Colorado Women's Bar Association.
Publications: Frequent speaker and author on intellectual property and technology law issues. Adjunct professor, University of Colorado School of Law.
Personal: JD, Harvard University, cum laude; BS, University of Colorado, Boul-

der, cum laude; Judicial Clerk, Judge John Portfilio, 10th Circuit (1989-90).

HARRIS, Dale
Davis Graham & Stubbs LLP, Denver
303 892 9400
Recommended in Antitrust, Litigation

HARTLEY, James E
Holland & Hart LLP, Denver
303 295 8237
jhartley@hollandhart.com
Recommended in Antitrust

Practice Areas: Partner with primary areas of practice in antitrust litigation and counseling, and patent infringement litigation. Represented clients before state and federal criminal grand juries and defended deceptive practice cases brought by the Federal Trade Commission. Advised clients concerning pre-merger notification rules and frequently makes presentations about antitrust compliance procedures. Extensive trial experience in cases dealing with antitrust, patent infringement, trade secrets, trademark and copyright infringement, and unfair competition claims.
Prof. Memberships: Former adjunct professor at the University of Denver School of Law; Member of the American Bar Association section on Antitrust Law.
Career: Admitted to the Colorado Bar (1974).
Personal: Received a JD (1974) and a BA (1971) from the University of California at Berkeley.

HAVLICK, Scott
Holland & Hart LLP, Denver
303 473 2710
shavlick@hollandhart.com
Recommended in Intellectual Property

Practice Areas: Partner heading the Intellectual Property Practice Group with specialization in US and foreign trademark matters. Assists with all phases of trademark management from the selection, searching, investigation and clearance of new brands to the registration and proper use of trademarks that have been selected. Handled a wide range of trademark litigation matters on behalf of both plaintiffs and defendants involving counterfeit goods, gray market importation, passing off, reverse passing off, dilution, and fair use. Tried numerous trademark cases in state and federal courts, and the US Court of Appeals, as well as before the US Trademark Trial and Appeal Board.
Prof. Memberships: Member, International Trademark Association; Member, American Intellectual Property Lawyers Association; Member, Patent, Trademark and Copyright Sections of the American and Colorado Bar Associations; Former co-Chair, Intellectual Property Section, Boulder County Bar Association.
Career: Admitted to the Colorado (1986) Bar and the US District Court,

District of Colorado; (1987) US Court of Appeals, Ninth Circuit; (1991) US Court of Appeals, Tenth Circuit.
Personal: Received a JD (1986) from the University of Utah and a BA (1981) from the University of Colorado.

HILL, Robert
Hill & Robbins PC, Denver
303 296 8100
Recommended in Antitrust, Litigation

HILTON, Paul
Hogan & Hartson LLP, Denver
303 454 2414
philton@hhlaw.com
Recommended in Corporate/M&A
Practice Areas: A Practice Group Director of firm's Corporate, Securities and Finance Group. His practice focuses on securities, mergers and acquisitions, corporate governance, and general corporate matters. He represents public companies, startups and venture-backed companies, investment banking firms, venture capital and private equity firms, and public and private acquirers and targets in acquisition transactions.
Prof. Memberships: Colorado Bar Association.
Career: Began career on Wall Street, was a partner, corporate group leader and executive committee member at a law firm based in Denver, and following that was the Managing Partner of the Colorado office of a San Francisco-based international law firm.
Publications: Co-author, 'Director's Guide to Sarbanes-Oxley Compliance', (Gorham Lamont August 2004); 'SEC Issues New Interpretive Guidance Regarding MD&A', SEC Update, Hogan & Hartson L.L.P. (30 January 2004); 'Disclosure Regarding Director Nomination Process and Security Holder Communications With Boards of Directors', SEC Update, Hogan & Hartson L.L.P. (16 December 2003).
Personal: JD, Cornell University Law School (1977); MA, University of Colorado (1977); BA, with honors, University of Colorado (1972).

HILYARD, Chad S
Faegre & Benson LLP, Denver
303 607 3696
Chilyard@faegre.com
Recommended in Intellectual Property
Practice Areas: Intellectual property and technology law, including patent prosecution, trademark prosecution, intellectual property licensing and litigation, and intellectual property portfolio counseling and management.
Prof. Memberships: American Intellectual Property Law Association; Licensing Executive Society; Past Chair, Colorado Bar Association, Intellectual Property Section.
Publications: Frequent speaker and author on intellectual property and technology law issues.
Personal: JD, Arizona State University, cum laude; BSEE, University of Nebraska, Lincoln, High Distinction.

HOFFMAN, Daniel
Hoffman Reilly Pozner & Williamson, Denver 303 893 6100
Recommended in Litigation

HOLMES, Robert
Holme Roberts & Owen LLP, Denver
303 861 7000
Recommended in Real Estate

HOLMES, Whitney
Hogan & Hartson LLP, Denver
303 454 2420
wholmes@hhlaw.com
Recommended in Corporate/M&A
Practice Areas: Partner specializing in public and private securities and corporate finance, mergers and acquisitions. Represents a broad spectrum of companies in venture capital financings, initial public offerings, secondary offerings, and private placements of equity and debt securities, as wells as all aspects of friendly and hostile acquisitions, asset acquisitions, mergers, leveraged buyouts, joint ventures, and proxy contests. He frequently represents public and private companies in financing transactions, including bank credit financing and public and private placements of debt securities, reporting obligations under federal securities laws and general corporate governance matters.
Prof. Memberships: American Bar Association. Colorado Bar Association. Chairman, Securities Law Subsection of the Business Law Section of the Colorado Bar Association, September 2002 to present.
Career: Practiced for 12 years, including eight for Willkie Farr & Gallagher in New York City, before joining Hogan & Hartson in 1999.
Publications: Frequent speaker on SEC, corporate governance, mergers and acquisitions, and corporate finance issues.
Personal: JD magna cum laude, Cornell University Law School (1987). Served as notes editor of the 'Cornell International Law Journal'. BA, English Literature, Pomona College (1984)

HUSBAND, John
Holland & Hart LLP, Denver
303 295 8228
jhusband@hollandhart.com
Recommended in Employment
Practice Areas: Partner practicing in labor and employment law. Mr Husband was voted Best of the Bar by his peers for labor and employment law which was sponsored by a leading Colorado business publication. He has been involved in hundreds of cases, has tried cases in 20 states and been lead trial counsel in over 300 adversarial proceedings, trials, major arbitrations or administrative actions that have been tried to conclusion. He advises on a range of employment matters, including class action lawsuits, wrongful discharge, equal employment opportunity, trade secrets and covenants not to compete, wage and hour, privacy, disability, occu-

pational safety, affirmative action and the law involving collective action, strikes, unions and collective bargaining.
Prof. Memberships: Appointments: Fellow, College of Labor and Employment Lawyers; American Bar Association, co-Chair, Class Action and Complex Litigation Sub-Committee, Column Editor, 'The Colorado Lawyer'; Editor, the Colorado Employment Law Letter; Director and Officer, Colorado Safety Association; and Board of Governors, University of Toledo, College of Law. Member of the National Labor Relations Board, Practices and Procedures Committee Region 27; Leadership Denver Association.
Career: Admitted to Colorado Bar (1978).
Personal: Received a JD from University of Toledo (1977) and a BS from Ohio State University (1974).

JACOBS, Paul
Jacobs, Chase, Frick, Kleinkopf & Kelley, Denver 303 685 4800
Recommended in Real Estate

JAMES, Bruce A
Brownstein Hyatt & Farber PC, Denver
303 223 1167
bjames@bhf-law.com
Recommended in Hotels and Resorts
Practice Areas: Managing Partner and CEO of Brownstein Hyatt & Farber. Practice involves real estate, corporate finance and real estate development, dispositions, and acquisitions.
Prof. Memberships: Colorado Bar Association; Denver Bar Association; Board Member, Junior Achievement; Littleton Hospital.
Personal: University of Denver College of Law (JD, 1985); University of Michigan (BBA, 1982).

JENSEN, Garth
Holme Roberts & Owen LLP, Denver
303 861 7000
Recommended in Corporate/M&A

JEWETT, Steve
Townsend and Townsend and Crew LLP, Denver 303 571 4000
Recommended in Intellectual Property

KANAN, Gregory B
Rothgerber Johnson & Lyons LLP, Denver 303 628 9530
gkanan@rothgerber.com
Recommended in Antitrust
Practice Areas: General corporate, commercial, securities, and antitrust litigation. Antitrust representation includes plaintiff and defense litigation and defense of criminal antitrust charges. Experience includes cases dealing with price fixing, monopolies, attempts to monopolize, unlawful dealer termination and exclusive dealing, and illegal tying arrangements. Advises hospitals, physicians, and health care practice associations on antitrust issues.
Prof. Memberships: American Board of Trial Advocates; Past Chair and Board

Member, Colorado Lawyers Committee; National Health Lawyers Association; Board of Governors, Denver Bar Association (2003-04); Member, Colorado and American Bar Associations.
Career: Admitted to Colorado, US District Court, District of Colorado, US Court of Appeals, Tenth Circuit, and US Supreme Court.
Personal: JD, University of Colorado School of Law (1975), Order of the Coif, Case Note Editor, 'University of Colorado Law Review'; BA, University of Colorado (1972).

KAPLAN, Stephen
Kaplan Kirsch & Rockwell LLP, Denver
303 825 7000
Recommended in Real Estate

KINSELLA, Peter
Faegre & Benson LLP, Denver
303 607 3500
pkinsella@faegre.com
Recommended in Intellectual Property
Practice Areas: Intellectual property protection and commercialization; international and domestic licensing and distribution; technology related corporate and commercial; transactions; intellectual property litigation and counseling; trademark portfolio and brand management; e-business, computer and internet law; software and product development and distribution; open source licenses.
Personal: BS, North Dakota State University, Dean's List; JD, University of Minnesota, Dean's List.

KLEINKOPF, David
Jacobs, Chase, Frick, Kleinkopf & Kelley, Denver
303 685 4800
Recommended in Hotels and Resorts

KNETSCH, Jeffrey
Brownstein Hyatt & Farber PC, Denver
303 223 1160
jknetsch@bhf-law.com
Recommended in Corporate/M&A
Practice Areas: Shareholder in Brownstein Hyatt & Farber's Corporate & Securities Group. Represents corporations, venture capital firms, and investment banking firms in a wide range of complex corporate transactions, including mergers and acquisitions, public and private securities offerings, corporate restructurings and workouts, exchange offers, tender offers, leveraged buy-out transactions, and bank financings.
Prof. Memberships: American Bar Association; Colorado Bar Association; New York Bar Association.
Personal: University of Southern California (JD, 1982); University of Virginia (BA, 1978).

KRENDL, Cathy
Krendl Krendl Sachnoff & Way PC, Denver 303 629 2600
Recommended in Corporate/M&A

LAWRENCE, Robert
Davis Graham & Stubbs LLP, Denver
303 892 9400
Recommended in Environment

LEE, Jessica
Gibson, Dunn & Crutcher LLP, Denver
303 298 5944
jlee@gibsondunn.com
Recommended in Employment
Practice Areas: Advises clients in a wide array of labor and employment matters, including nationwide class actions, employment discrimination, wrongful termination, retaliation, misappropriation of proprietary information, breach of contract, breach of fiduciary duty, unfair competition, and ERISA before state and federal agencies such as the EEOC and the Colorado Civil Rights Division. Has tried employment cases in jury and non-jury settings and has argued significant matters before state and federal courts of appeals.
Career: Frequent author and speaker on labor and employment issues.
Personal: JD, University of Texas, 1993, Executive Editor, 'Texas Law Review', Order of the Coif.

LEVINE, Ronald
Davis Graham & Stubbs LLP, Denver
303 892 9400
Recommended in Corporate/M&A

LEVY, Mark
Holland & Hart LLP, Denver
303 295 8073
mlevy@hollandhart.com
Recommended in Corporate/M&A
Practice Areas: Has substantial experience with securities laws. Assists public companies with ongoing compliance with securities laws, including periodic reports, proxy statements, corporate governance, press releases, Section 16 matters, Rule 144 sales, fiduciary duties and other matters. Also works on public and private offerings. Substantial experience in the acquisitions and dispositions of a variety of small and large businesses, bank loans and other private financings, the formation and operation of corporations and general business agreements.
Prof. Memberships: Member of the Federal Securities Regulation and Law and Accounting Committees of the Section of Business Law, American Bar Association; and Rockies Venture Club. Appointments: Chairperson (1999-2000), Colorado Bar Association Convention Committee; Member, Colorado Bar Association, Article 8 (Securities Transactions) of the Uniform Commercial Code Committee (1995-96) (review of Article for Colorado); Chairperson (1994-95), Alumni Board of Directors, University of Colorado Law School; and Co-Chairman (1989-91), Colorado Bar Association, Securities Law Review Committee (prepared the Colorado Securities Act enacted in 1990 and

proposed legislation on investment advisers).
Career: Admitted to Colorado Bar (1972).
Personal: Received a JD (1972, Order of the Coif) and a BA (1968) from the University of Colorado.

LINFIELD, James
Cooley Godward LLP, Broomfield
720 566 4000
Recommended in Corporate/M&A

LINQUANTI, Richard
Ireland Stapleton Pryor & Pascoe PC, Denver 303 623 2700
Recommended in Hotels and Resorts, Real Estate

LOTTNER, Alan
Lottner Rubin Fishman Brown & Saul, PC, Denver 303 292 1200
Recommended in Real Estate

LOZOW, Gary
Isaacson, Rosenbaum, Woods & Levy, PC, Denver 303 292 5656
Recommended in Litigation

LYONS, James M
Rothgerber Johnson & Lyons LLP, Denver 303 628 9546
jlyons@rothgerber.com
Recommended in Litigation
Practice Areas: Complex business litigation, mediation, and commercial arbitration, including high technology, intellectual property, corporate, environmental, and securities law. More than 30 years of courtroom and jury trial experience in state and federal courts. Extensive government relations and international trade experience. Recent clients include Anschutz Corporation, Qwest Communications (Board of Directors), Bell Canada Enterprises, City and County of Denver, General Electric, HealthOne, Rocky Mountain Health Care, and Triple Peaks Ski Corporation.
Prof. Memberships: President, Faculty of Federal Advocates of the US District Court, District of Colorado (2003); Fellow, American College of Trial Lawyers; Fellow, International Academy of Trial Lawyers; Master Barrister, Doyle's Inn Chapter of the American Inns of Court; Colorado, Denver, and Illinois Bar Associations.
Career: Admitted to Colorado, Illinois, US District Court, District of Colorado, US District Court, Northern District of Illinois, US Court of Appeals, Seventh and Tenth Circuits and US Supreme Court. Served as an instructor with the University of Denver College of Law, the University of Colorado School of Law, and the National Institute of Trial Advocacy. Served as Special Advisor to the President of the United States and the Secretary of State for Economic Initiatives in Ireland. Prior to this role, President Clinton appointed him as US Observer, International Fund for Ireland (1993-2001). Served as general counsel for the office of President-Elect Bill

Clinton.
Personal: Honorary Doctor of Laws (LLD), University of Ulster, Belfast, Northern Ireland (2002); JD, DePaul University College of Law (1971), associate editor, 'DePaul Law Review'; BA, College of the Holy Cross (1968).

MACDONALD, Elizabeth A
Faegre & Benson LLP, Denver
303 607 3680
EMacDonald@faegre.com
Recommended in Employment
Practice Areas: Age discrimination, alternative dispute resolution, Americans With Disabilities Act, arbitrations, breach of contract, employer counseling, employment law, employment litigation, Family and Medical Leave Act, internal investigations, mediations, race discrimination, sexual harassment, Title VII, trial practice, wrongful discharge.
Prof. Memberships: The American Employment Law Council.
Personal: BA, Middlebury College (1975), magna cum laude, Phi Beta Kappa JD, University of Colorado, Boulder (1982).

MACDONALD, Thomas
Otten, Johnson, Robinson, Neff & Ragonetti, PC, Denver
303 825 8400
Recommended in Real Estate

MACKEY, Pamela
Haddon, Morgan, Mueller, Jordan, Mackey & Foreman PC, Denver
303 831 7364
Recommended in Litigation

MAGUIRE, Charles
Holme Roberts & Owen LLP, Denver
303 861 7000
Recommended in Corporate/M&A

MCCARTHY, Michael S
Faegre & Benson LLP, Denver
303 607 3670
mmccarthy@faegre.com
Recommended in Litigation
Practice Areas: Civil trial practice; class action, corporate, securities, complex commercial, environmental, energy and natural resources, insolvency and bankruptcy litigation.
Prof. Memberships: Fellow, American College of Trial Lawyers; ABA; CBA; DBA; Fellow, Colorado Bar Foundation.
Career: Lead trial counsel for the Colorado Rockies Baseball Club in numerous matters; including successful trial defense of the Club and its owners in a Bankruptcy Court fraudulent transfer claim involving valuation of the Rockies franchise. Lead trial counsel for State Farm Insurance in multiple Colorado class action claims.
Personal: BA, University of Michigan; JD, University of Colorado, Boulder, Law Review.

MCNEIVE, Lynda A
Brownstein Hyatt & Farber PC, Denver
303 223 1129
lmcneive@bhf-law.com
Recommended in Real Estate
Practice Areas: Shareholder in Brownstein Hyatt & Farber's Real Estate Group. Focuses on commercial real estate transactions, representing developers of retail, office, industrial, residential, and mixed-use properties. Counsels clients from the initial due diligence stage through site acquisition, entitlement approvals, construction and permanent financing, construction of improvements, leasing, and sale.
Prof. Memberships: National Association of Industrial and Office Properties; Title Standards Committee of the Colorado Bar Association; American Bar Association; Colorado Bar Association; Denver Bar Association; Colorado Women's Bar Association.
Personal: Stanford Law School (JD, 1980); Marymount College, (BA, 1970).

MICHAELS, Jane
Holland & Hart LLP, Denver
303 295 8162
jmichaels@hollandhart.com
Recommended in Intellectual Property
Practice Areas: Partner specializing in intellectual property and complex commercial litigation, with an emphasis on telecommunications and computer industry cases. Extensive experience in complex jury trials, as well as bench trials, in trademark, trade secrets, patent, copyright, and technology cases. Certified arbitrator and mediator. Has handled numerous arbitrations and mediations, both as an advocate and as the arbitrator or mediator. Has lectured around the country on intellectual property and trial advocacy issues.
Prof. Memberships: Past President, Denver Bar Association; Member, American Intellectual Property Law Association; Member, International Trademark Association; Member, American Bar Association, Intellectual Property Litigation Committee; Member, Patent, Trademark and Copyright Section, Colorado Bar Association; Fellow, American Bar Foundation. Honors: Fellow, American College of Trial Lawyers; Fellow, International Society of Barristers; listed in publication 'Best Lawyers in America'.
Career: Admitted to the Colorado Bar(1973), US District Court, District of Colorado; US Court of Appeals, Tenth Circuit (1974); US Supreme Court (1985); US Court of Appeals for the Federal Circuit (1999); US Court of Appeals, Sixth Circuit (2002); US Court of Appeals, Fourth Circuit and District of Columbia (2003).
Personal: Received JD (1973) from Boston University (cum laude), MAT (1970) from Harvard University (cum laude), and BA (1968) from Wellesley (with distinction).

MILLER, Gale
Davis Graham & Stubbs LLP, Denver
303 892 9400
Recommended in Antitrust, Litigation

MILLER, Zach
Davis Graham & Stubbs LLP, Denver
303 892 9400
Recommended in Environment

MOYE, John
Moye, Giles, O'Keefe, Vermeire & Gorrell LLP, Denver 303 292 2900
Recommended in Corporate/M&A

MUMAUGH, Brian
Holland & Hart LLP, Greenwood Village
303 290 1067
bmumaugh@hollandhart.com
Recommended in Employment
Practice Areas: Partner practicing in labor and employment law. Represents major employers in a broad range of matters including claims of race, sex, age, disability and national origin discrimination, FLSA collective actions, wrongful discharge, breach of contract, public policy discharge, covenants not to compete, and management in union issues. Represented employers as lead counsel in hundreds of proceedings in Federal and State courts and Agencies in the Western US and other parts of the country. Significant experience representing management in labor matters including unfair labor practice proceedings, unit determinations, representation elections, collective bargaining, and major arbitrations.
Prof. Memberships: Member, American Bar Association; Colorado Bar Association; Nebraska Bar Association; Colorado Defense Lawyers Association; and contributor to the 'Colorado Employment Law Letter'. Member, Board of Directors, Executive Committee, The Children's Museum of Denver; Board Member, Rocky Mountain Children's Cancer Foundation.
Career: Admitted to the Nebraska (1983) and Colorado Bar (1989); US District Court, District of Colorado; US District Court, District of Columbia; US District Court, District of Nebraska; US Court of Appeals, Eighth, Ninth and Tenth Circuits.
Personal: Received a JD (1982) from Creighton University and a BA (1979) from the University of Nebraska. Chair, Holland & Hart Labor & Employment Group.

NEWCOM, Charles
Sherman & Howard LLC, Denver
303 297 2900
Recommended in Employment

OADE, Preston
Holme Roberts & Owen LLP, Denver
303 861 7000
Recommended in Employment

PALENCHAR, James
Bartlit Beck Herman Palenchar & Scott, Denver
303 592 3100
Recommended in Corporate/M&A

PERMUT, Barry
Isaacson, Rosenbaum, Woods & Levy, PC, Denver 303 292 5656
Recommended in Real Estate

PHILLIPS, Paul D
Holland & Hart LLP, Denver
303 295 8131
pphillips@hollandhart.com
Recommended in Environment
Practice Areas: Partner practicing in environmental law and litigation. Substantial experience defending companies against citizens' suits and EPA actions brought under Clean Water Act, RCRA, Clean Air Act, other environmental statutes; toxic tort litigation; environmental audits; and preparing detailed 'permit letters' outlining all state and federal environmental laws and regulations applicable to new projects.
Prof. Memberships: Admitted to the Colorado Bar (1977); US Supreme Court, DC and other Circuit Courts of Appeal and various other courts.
Career: Named 'Best of the Bar' in Environmental Law, 2004, Denver Business Journal.
Publications: Mr Phillips has published extensively in both legal and technical periodicals. Founding editor of 'Natural Resources and Environment', the ABA's Natural Resources magazine, and issues editor for 'Environmental Permitting: Negotiating the Maze'.
Personal: Received a JD (1976) from Yale and a BA (1973) from Harvard. Chairman, Holland & Hart Management Committee.

PLUMRIDGE, Richard
Holme Roberts & Owen LLP, Denver
303 861 7000
Recommended in Corporate/M&A

POWELL Jr, David D
Brownstein Hyatt & Farber PC, Denver
303 223 1157
dpowell@bhf-law.com
Recommended in Employment
Practice Areas: Shareholder and co-chair of Brownstein Hyatt & Farber's Employment Group. Specializes in the counsel and defense of employers on a variety of matters arising from the employer-employee relationship, including wrongful discharge, disability and family leave issues, sexual harassment and discrimination based on race, national origin, gender, and age.
Prof. Memberships: American Bar Association; Sam Cary Bar Association; Community Advisory Board, Rocky Mountain Public Broadcasting System; Colorado Bar Association; National Bar Association; Faculty of Federal Advocates; Editor, 'Colorado Employment Law Letter'.

Personal: UCLA Law School (JD, 1983); Univesity of Santa Clara (BA, 1980).

QUAIL, Beverly J
Ballard Spahr Andrews & Ingersoll LLP, Denver 303 299 7305
quail@ballardspahr.com
Recommended in Real Estate
Practice Areas: She concentrates her practice on all aspects of real estate matters with an emphasis on financing and development.
Prof. Memberships: Past Chair of the American Bar Association, Section of Real Property, Probate and Trust. She has been a Governor and Treasurer of the American College of Real Estate Lawyers, and is a Fellow in the American College of Mortgage Attorneys.
Career: Admitted to the Colorado Bar (1974); joined as Partner (1996).
Publications: Authors Colorado Real Estate Forms.
Personal: JD, University of Denver (1974); BA, magna cum laude, University of Southern California (1971).

RAGONETTI, Thomas
Otten, Johnson, Robinson, Neff & Ragonetti, PC, Denver 303 825 8400
Recommended in Real Estate

RAISCH, Jerry
Vranesh and Raisch, LLP, Boulder
303 443 6151
Recommended in Environment

REILLY, Daniel
Hoffman Reilly Pozner & Williamson, Denver 303 893 6100
Recommended in Litigation

REISCH, Scott H
Hogan & Hartson LLP, Denver
303 899 7355
shreisch@HHLAW.com
Recommended in Environment
Practice Areas: Practice includes litigation and counseling on environmental matters with emphasis on Superfund, Brownfields, and voluntary cleanups as well as environmental issues in commercial transactions, environmental laws affecting the food and agriculture industries, and compliance with state and federal laws relating to hazardous and solid wastes. Also represents clients in audits and in developing environmental management programs.
Prof. Memberships: Member, Advisory Council, Environmental Law Section, Colorado Bar Association; Member of Colorado, California and District of Columbia Bars.
Publications: 'Dirty Money: EPA Issues Brownfields Grant Guidelines', co-authored with Catherine M. van Heuven, The Colorado Lawyer (April 2003); 'The Brownfields Amendments: New Opportunities, New Challenges - Parts I and II', The Colorado Lawyer (June 2002 and September 2002); 'EPA's Final TMDL Rule: A Load of Trouble for Agriculture and Industry', co-authored with Catherine M. van Heuven, The

Colorado Lawyer (May 2001); 'Colorado's Not-So-Little Pig Farms Meet the Big Bad Wolf', The Colorado Lawyer (June 1999); 'Yielding "Green" Harvests from "Brownfields": Strategies for Protecting Lenders from Liability at Contaminated Sites', The Colorado Lawyer (January and February 1997).
Personal: JD, Stanford University (1988); BA, with distinction, Stanford University (1985).

RICHILANO, John
Richilano & Ridley PC, Denver
303 893 8000
Recommended in Litigation

ROBINSON, Frank
Otten, Johnson, Robinson, Neff & Ragonetti, PC, Denver
303 825 8400
Recommended in Real Estate

ROCKWELL, Sarah
Kaplan Kirsch & Rockwell LLP, Denver
303 825 7000
Recommended in Real Estate

ROCKWOOD, Linda
Faegre & Benson LLP, Denver
303 607 3642
LRockwood@faegre.com
Recommended in Environment
Practice Areas: Administrative law; air quality; brownfields and voluntary cleanups; environmental audits; environmental law; environmental liability and litigation; environmental aspects of corporate and real estate transactions; environmental permitting, auditing, and compliance; land use/zoning/environmental review; natural resource damages; site remediation; superfund and hazardous waste; toxic substances control act; alternative dispute resolution and asbestos abatement.
Personal: BA, University of Denver, Phi Beta Kappa; JD, University of Texas, Order of the Coif, with honors.

RUPPERT, John L
Brownstein Hyatt & Farber PC, Denver
303 223 1170
jruppert@bhf-law.com
Recommended in Corporate/M&A
Practice Areas: Shareholder in Brownstein Hyatt & Farber's Corporate and Securities, Corporate Finance, Mergers and Acquisitions, and Finance Groups and leads the firm's Bankruptcy and Restructuring Group. He practices in the areas of mergers and acquisitions, corporate and partnership finance, commercial finance, restructurings and workouts, and federal income tax.
Prof. Memberships: American Bar Association; Colorado Bar Association.
Personal: New York University (LLM, 1979); The University of Denver College of Law, (JD, 1978); Northwestern University, (BA, 1975).

RUSSO, Richard
Gibson, Dunn & Crutcher LLP, Denver
303 298 5715
rrusso@gibsondunn.com
Recommended in Corporate/M&A
Practice Areas: Co-Chair of the firm's Corporate Transactions Practice Group. Advises local, national and international clients on the representation of business entities, with emphasis on securities and disclosure matters, public and private debt and equity offerings, mergers and acquisitions, restructurings and corporate governance matters. Counselor for independent directors in connection with acquisitions, spin-offs and leveraged buyouts. Clients include Qwest Communications, CSK Auto, The Williams Companies, Petro Stopping Centers.
Career: Member of the firm's Executive and Management Committees.
Publications: Co-author of Colorado Limited Liability Company, Forms and Practice Manual.
Personal: JD, Yale Law School, 1974, Director, Yale Moot Court of Appeals.

SALTER, Dean
Holme Roberts & Owen LLP, Denver
303 861 7000
Recommended in Corporate/M&A

SAMUELS JONES, Karen
Perkins Coie LLP, Denver
303 291 2322
Recommended in Real Estate

SATRIANA, Daniel
Clisham, Satriana & Biscan LLC, Denver 303 468 5400
Recommended in Employment

SAVAGE, Janet
Davis Graham & Stubbs LLP, Denver
303 892 9400
Recommended in Employment

SCOTT, Donald
Bartlit Beck Herman Palenchar & Scott, Denver 303 592 3100
Recommended in Litigation

SENN, Mark
Senn Lewis & Visciano, Denver
303 298 1122
Recommended in Real Estate

SHEA, Daniel
Hogan & Hartson LLP, Denver
303 454 2475
dfshea@hhlaw.com
Recommended in Litigation
Practice Areas: Practice includes defending white collar criminal and complex civil litigation as well as Securities and Exchange Commission (SEC), New York Stock Exchange (NYSE), and National Association of Securities Dealers (NASD) enforcement proceedings; conducting internal investigations; and providing advice regarding corporate governance and broker-dealer/investment adviser compliance issues.
Prof. Memberships: Member of the Colorado, District of Columbia, and Massachusetts Bars.

Career: Prior positions include serving in an in-house capacity with UBS PaineWebber, Inc. as director of compliance for regulatory affairs, policy, products and trading and as deputy general counsel; director of the central region for the SEC, based in Denver, Colorado; trial attorney for the SEC and the US Departments of Justice and Energy; and in private practice in Washington, DC, defending regulatory enforcement actions and handling civil litigation involving federal securities, energy, and antitrust laws.
Publications: 'How Juries and Judges are Reexamining Directors', Officers' Duties in the Wake of Corporate Scandals', Corporate Counsel Weekly (28 January 2004).
Personal: BA, College of the Holy Cross; MA, The Catholic University of America; JD, The Catholic University of America, Columbus School of Law.

SHEA, Kevin
Ballard Spahr Andrews & Ingersoll LLP, Denver 303 299 7337
shea@ballardspahr.com
Recommended in Litigation
Practice Areas: Practice focuses on complex civil and criminal business, environmental, constitutional, legal malpractice and insurance coverage litigation. Has tried numerous cases to verdict in federal and state courts throughout the Western United States as well as before regulatory and private arbitration panels. Numerous appearances in state and federal appellate courts as well. Likewise has represented numerous corporations and individuals in federal and state grand jury and regulatory investigations throughout the country.
Prof. Memberships: Member of the American Bar Association, Colorado Bar Association, and Denver Bar Association, the National Association of Criminal Defense Lawyers, and the Colorado Criminal Defense Bar Association, and serves on the Board of Trustees for the Legal Aid Foundation of Colorado. Past Chairman of Colorado Bar Association Criminal Law Section; Past Vice-Chair of American Bar Association Environmental Crimes Section.
Career: Admitted to the Colorado Bar (1976); US District Court for the District of Colorado (1976); US Court of Appeals for Tenth Circuit (1976); United States Supreme Court (1983). Deputy District Attorney, Boulder, Colorado 1976-80; Associate/Partner Roath & Brega P.C., Denver, CO 1980-83; Partner Holme, Roberts & Owen LLP Denver, CO 1984-94; Partner Ballard Spahr Andrews & Ingersoll, LLP Denver, CO 1995-Present. Listed in 'Who's Who in America'.
Personal: JD, University of Detroit (1976); BS, University of Colorado (1973).

SHIVELY, John D
Faegre & Benson LLP, Denver
303 607 3616
jshively@faegre.com
Recommended in Antitrust
Practice Areas: Antitrust litigation and counseling; litigation of agribusiness, business torts, complex contract, computer system performance, and insurance coverage and fraud cases; and alternative dispute resolutions and arbitrations.
Personal: AB, Harvard University, cum laude; JD, Harvard University; Judge Advocate and Special Court Martial Judge, US Marine Corps, 1973-77; Staff Attorney, Federal Trade Commission, 1979-81; 'Who's Who in Law', Denver Business Journal, 2003 and 2004.

SHOEMAKER, Andrew
Hogan & Hartson LLP, Denver
303 454 2423
arshoemaker@hhlaw.com
Recommended in Litigation
Practice Areas: Practice includes complex civil litigation and representation in connection with government investigations. He has handled disputes involving securities fraud, corporate governance, shareholder rights, executive compensation and termination, patent infringement, misappropriation of trade secrets, and breach of contract. He regularly represents corporations, board committees, and individual directors and officers in connection with internal and regulatory investigations. He also represents broker-dealers and clearing firms in connection with customer disputes and inquiries by government agencies and self-regulatory organizations.
Prof. Memberships: Member of the Colorado, District of Columbia and Virginia Bars.
Career: Enforcement attorney with the Central Regional Office of the US Securities Exchange Commission (SEC) and as a special assistant United States attorney for the District of Colorado; law clerk for the Honorable Charles R Richey of the US District Court in Washington, DC Awarded the Federal Bar Association's Manuel F Cohen Award (Outstanding young SEC attorney), 1998.
Personal: JD, University of Virginia School of Law, 1992; BA, summa cum laude, Hampden-Sydney College, 1989.

SIEBERT, Bernie
Sherman & Howard LLC, Denver
303 297 2900
Recommended in Employment

SIEGEL, Steven
Brownstein Hyatt & Farber PC, Denver
303 223 1150
sssiegel@bhf-law.com
Recommended in Corporate/M&A
Practice Areas: Shareholder and head of Brownstein Hyatt & Farber's Corporate & Securities Group. Concentrates on mergers and acquisitions, leveraged

buy-outs, public and private securities offerings, senior and subordinated debt financings, restructurings and general corporate advice for both public and private entities, including start-ups.
Prof. Memberships: American Bar Association; New York Bar Association; Colorado Association of Corporate Counsel.
Personal: University of Chicago Law School (JD,1987); Wharton School of the University of Pennsylvania (BS, 1984).

SIPIORA, David
Townsend and Townsend and Crew LLP, Denver 303 571 4000
Recommended in Intellectual Property

SPAANSTRA, James R
Faegre & Benson LLP, Denver
303 607 3629
jspaanstra@faegre.com
Recommended in Environment
Practice Areas: Environmental law; natural resource and energy; land use/zoning/environmental review.
Personal: BS, Grand Valley State University, with highest honors; JD, University of Michigan.

STACY, David
Ducker, Montgomery, Aronstein & Bess, P.C., Denver
303 861 2828
Recommended in Employment

STEINER, Beat
Steiner, Darling & Hutchinson LLP, Denver 303 837 2380
Recommended in Hotels and Resorts

STEPHENS, Thomas
Bartlit Beck Herman Palenchar & Scott, Denver 303 592 3100
Recommended in Corporate/M&A

STERNBERG, John
Otten, Johnson, Robinson, Neff & Ragonetti, PC, Denver 303 825 8400
Recommended in Real Estate

STOCKS, Bruce
Perkins Coie LLP, Denver
303 291 2322
Recommended in Corporate/M&A

STRICKLAND, Tom
Hogan & Hartson LLP, Denver
303 899 7364
tlstrickland@hhlaw.com
Recommended in Environment
Practice Areas: Managing Partner of Denver office. Represents clients in a wide range of industries and business issues, including environmental, natural resources, public lands, transportation, real estate, government relations, and business finance. He also has a significant practice focused on white collar criminal defense, securities enforcement and internal investigations.
Prof. Memberships: Member, Colorado Bar Association.
Career: US attorney for the District of Colorado from 1999 through 2001.

Prior to his appointment as the top Justice Department official for Colorado, he spent 15 years with another major Denver law firm where he was a senior partner in charge of the regulatory, administrative, and public law practice. He also served as director of policy for Colorado Governor Richard D Lamm, chaired the Colorado Transportation Commission, served as legal counsel to the Denver Metro Chamber of Commerce, and was a founder and board member of Great Outdoors Colorado, the lottery-funded endowment for Colorado's public parks system. He served as a law clerk for US District Judge, The Honorable Carl Bue, Jr. from 1977 to 1979.
Personal: JD, with honors, University of Texas School of Law (1977); BA, with honors, Louisiana State University (1974).

TEMKIN, Elizabeth
Temkin Wielga & Hardt LLP, Denver
303 292 4922
Recommended in Environment

THOMASCH, Roger
Ballard Spahr Andrews & Ingersoll LLP, Denver 303 299 7301
thomasch@ballardspahr.com
Recommended in Litigation
Practice Areas: Has concentrated in the trial of business cases for over 35 years. He has appeared before courts throughout the country and has tried to verdict virtually every type of business and commercial case.
Prof. Memberships: Fellow of the American College of Trial Lawyers, Fellow of the American Bar Foundation and the Fellow of the Colorado Bar Foundation.

Career: Chairman of the firm's Litigation Department and Managing Partner of the firm's Denver office. Trial Attorney, United States Department of Justice (1970-73); Visiting Professor of Law, Drake University School of Law (1973-74) (Recipient of LeLand Forest Outstanding Professor Award). Has lectured at trial lawyer seminars in over 30 cities in the United States and Canada. Admitted to the Connecticut Bar (1967); admitted to the Colorado Bar (1974).
Personal: LLB, Duke University (1967); BA, The College of William and Mary (1964).

TROUPE, Warren
Morrison & Foerster LLP, Denver
303 592 2255
wtroupe@mofo.com
Recommended in Corporate/M&A
Practice Areas: Primarily focused on transactional and financing matters, as well as corporate, securities, and mergers and acquisitions. Concluded a large number of mergers and acquisitions for both public and private companies, including tender offers, hostile proxy contests, and negotiated acquisitions. Represented companies in a range of financing and restructurings, including public and private equity offerings, traditional loan structures, debt placements, subordinated debt financings, workouts, recapitalizations, and formation and financing of REITs.
Career: Admitted to practice in Colorado and Florida. Chair of the firm's Denver Corporate Group.
Personal: BA, Colorado State University, 1975; JD, Denver College of the Law, 1978.

VAN WESTRUM, Anthony
Anthony van Westrum LLC, Denver
303 295 1515
Recommended in Corporate/M&A

WALSH, Christopher J
Hogan & Hartson LLP, Denver
303 454 2480
cjwalsh@hhlaw.com
Recommended in Corporate/M&A
Practice Areas: Mergers and acquisitions, public offerings and private placements of equity and debt securities, leveraged buyouts, tender offers, proxy contests and joint ventures. He also counsels public and private companies in all aspects of their business, including compliance and reporting obligations under the federal securities laws and corporate governance matters.
Prof. Memberships: Member, Colorado Bar Association
Career: Joined firm after nine years of practice, including as in-house counsel for a Nasdaq listed company and a privately held technology company.
Personal: JD, University of Wyoming (1991); BS, University of Wyoming (1988).

WALSH, John
Hill & Robbins PC, Denver
303 296 8100
Recommended in Litigation

WEESE, Charles W
Faegre & Benson LLP, Denver
303 607 3663
CWeese@faegre.com
Recommended in Employment
Practice Areas: Labor and employment law.
Personal: BA, Rice University; JD, Boston University, Law Review (Executive Editor), magna cum laude.

WESTOVER, Michael
Otten, Johnson, Robinson, Neff & Ragonetti, PC, Denver
303 825 8400
Recommended in Real Estate

WHEELER, Francis
Cooley Godward LLP, Broomfield
720 566 4000
Recommended in Corporate/M&A

WHEELER, Malcolm
Wheeler Trigg Kennedy LLP, Denver
303 292 2525
Recommended in Litigation

WRIGHT, Douglas R
Faegre & Benson LLP, Denver
303 607 3671
dwright@faegre.com
Recommended in Corporate/M&A
Practice Areas: Corporate counseling; corporate finance and securities; entrepreneurial and emerging companies; initial public offerings; mergers and acquisitions; private debt and equity financings; venture capital financing; distribution agreements; proxy contests; securities regulation.
Career: Representation of several public companies in merger and acquisition and financing transactions, including IPOs and 144A transactions. Negotiation of over $1.5 billion in private equity investments for a state public employees retirement fund. Corporate and securities counseling for a major Denver-based airline.
Personal: BA, Hamilton College; JD, Cornell Law School, Law Review (Research Editor).

ZISSER, David
Isaacson, Rosenbaum, Woods & Levy, PC, Denver 303 292 5656
Recommended in Litigation

BROWNSTEIN HYATT & FARBER

THE FIRM

Founding Shareholders: Norman Brownstein
Steven W Farber
Jack A Hyatt (retired)
Managing Shareholder: Bruce A James

Number of shareholders: 53
Number of other attorneys: 60
Number of policy advisors: 7

FIRM OVERVIEW: Founded in the late 1960s, Brownstein Hyatt & Farber has a national client base, four offices, 120 attorneys and policy advisors, and more than 20 practice and industry groups. The firm is committed to providing top-quality legal counsel that is cost-effective, accessible, and comprehensive. Operating in partnership with their clients, they strive to be a seamless extension of in-house resources, linked by constant interaction and an infrastructure that allows them to bring resources to bear on the full range of business and legal issues.

MAIN AREAS OF PRACTICE:

Corporate & Securities: Brownstein Hyatt & Farber's senior attorneys regularly handle sophisticated finance and securities transactions for companies across the United States. They focus on matters related to mergers and acquisitions, emerging business and technology, corporate finance, public and private transactions, and general corporate representation.

Real Estate: With the largest Real Estate Practice in the Rocky Mountain region, the firm handles all aspects of real estate law including leasing, acquisition, development, disposition, water and mineral rights, finance, lending, taxation, public/private partnerships, municipal financing, zoning, and land use.

Litigation: Representing clients in virtually every industry, Brownstein Hyatt & Farber employs an integrated and cost-effective approach to each case. If the courtroom is the only alternative, the firm's senior litigators draw upon a wealth of trial experience that includes hundreds of jury trials and other major adversarial proceedings.

Employment Law: Specializing in employment-related issues impacting businesses of all sizes, the firm's employment lawyers handle disputes related to age, gender, sexual orientation, religion, race, and national origin.

Government Relations: Comprised of lawyers and policy advisors, the group helps companies, associations, and organizations interpret and integrate federal, state, and local government actions, solve challenges and seize opportunities through interaction with legislative and executive branch officials and private institutions.

Environment & Natural Resources: The firm works closely with corporate clients to create well planned, carefully executed, and proactive environmental strategies. Firm believers in prevention, Brownstein Hyatt & Farber's team of seasoned attorneys perform environmental due diligence and audits. When problems arise, they have the knowledge, know-how, and relationships to help mitigate environmental risk.

Banking & Finance: The firm offers clients comprehensive banking and commercial finance counsel, providing guidance in an array of secured and unsecured loans and credit facilities. Representing leading financial institutions and corporate borrowers, the group has closed more than $4 billion in loans in 40 states in the past five years.

Public Finance: The firm has a multi-faceted finance practice encompassing bond transactions for state and local governments and governmental authorities. They are well-equipped to assist any participant in a municipal bond transaction.

HEAD OFFICE

COLORADO
410 Seventeenth Street, Twenty-Second Floor, **Denver,** CO 80202-4437
Tel: 303 223 1100 **Fax:** 303 223 1111

BRANCH OFFICES

DISTRICT OF COLUMBIA
1350 I Street, N.W., Suite 510, **Washington, DC**, 20005-3344
Tel: 202 296 7353 **Fax:** 202 296 7009

NEW MEXICO
201 Third Street N.W., Suite 1500, **Albuquerque**, NM 87102
Tel: 505 244 0770 **Fax:** 505 244 9266

COLORADO
PO Box 357, 888 Colorado Ave., Suite 306, **Glenwood Springs**, CO 81602-0375
Tel: 970 945 5302 **Fax:** 970 384 2360

Additional Practice Areas: Bankruptcy and restructuring; corporate finance; employee benefits/ERISA; energy law; engineering and construction; family law; housing finance; intellectual property and technology; land use; litigation; mergers and acquisitions; regulatory and administrative law.

CLIENTS: AIG SunAmerica, Inc., City of Albuquerque, New Mexico, Comcast Corporation, Credit Suisse First Boston, Idaho Power Company, KeyBank, National Cable Television Association, Qwest, Lennar Homes, Shea Homes, Trammell Crow Company, US Bank.

Brownstein | Hyatt | Farber

HOLLAND & HART LLP

THE FIRM

Managing Partner: Edward H Flitton III
Senior Partner: Paul D Phillips (Chair, Management Committee)

Number of partners: 147
Number of other lawyers: 149

Email: info@hollandhart.com
Website: www.hollandhart.com

FIRM OVERVIEW: Since its inception in 1947, Holland & Hart has grown to more than 300 lawyers in 12 offices in Colorado, Wyoming, Idaho, Montana, New Mexico, Utah, and the District of Columbia. The firm offers a full range of integrated legal solutions to companies of all sizes, from emerging businesses to *Fortune* 500 corporations located throughout the country and internationally. The firm is focused on the issues facing clients who have business interests in the Mountain West. Holland & Hart is the only law firm based in the Rocky Mountain Region to make a leading American legal publication's list of the top 200 firms in the United States.

MAIN AREAS OF PRACTICE: The firm handles appellate; bankruptcy; broadband transactions; business transactions and litigation; construction and real estate transactions and litigation; corporate finance; credit finance and lending; emerging growth and venture capital; employee benefits; energy; environment and resources; intellectual property protection and litigation; international; labor and employment; mining; oil and gas; project development and finance; taxes and estates; technology transfer; torts and insurance; water.

CLIENTS: Holland & Hart represents business entities of all sizes, including more than 100 of the *Fortune* 500 companies. Holland & Hart serves clients in a wide variety of industries, including aerospace, agriculture, airlines, biotechnology, construction, energy, financial, healthcare, hospitality, manufacturing, mining, oil and gas, real estate, resorts and recreation, retail, services, technology, telecommunications and broadband, and water rights and quality, among others.

INTERNATIONAL WORK: The firm has been involved in a broad range of transactions in most Latin American, Pacific Rim and European countries. These transactions have included mergers, project finance transactions, venture capital investments, mezzanine financings, telecommunications (including telephony, internet services and cable television), power generation and distribution projects, private placements, license or concession acquisitions, privatizations, environmental matters and capital markets transactions.

HEAD OFFICE

COLORADO
Suite 3200, 555 Seventeenth Street, **Denver**, CO 80202
Tel: 303 295 8000   **Fax:** 303 295 8261

BRANCH OFFICES

COLORADO
Suite 104, 600 East Main Street, **Aspen**, CO 81611
Tel: 970 925 3476   **Fax:** 970 925 9367

Suite 300, Boulder Plaza, 1800 Broadway, **Boulder**, CO 80302
Tel: 303 473 2700   **Fax:** 303 473 2720

Suite 1000, 90 South Cascade Avenue, **Colorado Springs**, CO 80903
Tel: 719 475 7730   **Fax:** 719 634 2461

Suite 400, 8390 East Crescent Parkway, **Greenwood Village**, CO 80111
Tel: 303 290 1600   **Fax:** 303 290 1606

DISTRICT OF COLUMBIA
Suite 550, 1200 G Street, NW, **Washington**, DC 20005
Tel: 202 347 9272   **Fax:** 202 347 1684

IDAHO
Suite 1400, 101 South Capitol Blvd, **Boise**, ID 83702
Tel: 208 342 5000   **Fax:** 208 343 8869

MONTANA
Suite 1500, 401 North 31st Street, **Billings**, MT 59101
Tel: 406 252 2166   **Fax:** 406 252 1669

NEW MEXICO
Suite 1, 110 North Guadalupe, **Santa Fe**, NM 87504
Tel: 505 988 4421   **Fax:** 505 983 6043

UTAH
Suite 2000, 60 East South Temple, **Salt Lake City**, UT 84111
Tel: 801 595 7800   **Fax:** 801 364 9124

WYOMING
Suite 450, 2515 Warren Avenue, **Cheyenne**, WY 82001
Tel: 307 778 4200   **Fax:** 307 778 8175

Suite 200, 25 South Willow Street, Box 68 **Jackson Hole**, WY 83001
Tel: 307 739 9741   **Fax:** 307 739 9744

CONTACTS

Appellate	Marcy Glenn
Bankruptcy	Risa Wolf-Smith
Broadband Transactions	Stephen Villano
Business Transactions	Brad Wiskirchen
Coal	Patrick Day
Commercial Litigation	Christopher Toll
Construction & Real Estate Litigation	Daniel Frost
Emerging Growth & Venture Capital	Betty Arkell
Employee Benefits	Jane Francis
Energy	Robert Pomeroy
Environment & Resources	Bradford Berge
Financial	Robert Faucher
Indian Law	Jennifer Harvey
Intellectual Property Litigation	Donald Degnan
Intellectual Property Protection	Scott Havlick
International	Kevin Johnson
Labor & Employment	Brian Mumaugh
Mining	Michael Feldewert
Oil & Gas	Donald Schultz
Project Development & Finance	Mark Safty
Real Estate Transactions	Rebecca Dow
Securities	Mark Levy
Taxes & Estates	John Maxfield
Technology Transfer	Kevin Crandell
Product Insurance & Tort Defense	Joe Teig
Water	Christopher Thorne

HOLME ROBERTS & OWEN LLP

THE FIRM

Managing Director: Kenneth W Lund

Number of Directors: 108
Number of other lawyers: 111

FIRM OVERVIEW: Holme Roberts & Owen LLP (HRO) is an international law firm with more than 200 lawyers and eight offices in Denver, Boulder, Colorado Springs, Salt Lake City, San Francisco, Los Angeles, London and Munich with a focus on corporate law and securities and litigation. The firm also has a variety of support practices that include antitrust, banking, constitutional law, employee benefits, intellectual property, international business transactions, emerging growth, employment, environmental, mergers and acquisitions, real estate, products liability, sports and entertainment and tax.

MAIN AREAS OF PRACTICE:

Commercial Law & Securities: Approximately 75 lawyers spend all or a substantial amount of their time on sophisticated corporate deals both nationally and internationally. HRO participates in the general representation of corporations, partnerships and other business entities, large and small. This practice includes general business planning, mergers and acquisitions, tender offers, joint ventures, public and private securities offerings, venture capital and traditional finance, franchising and corporate reorganizations, bankruptcy and liquidation proceedings.

Litigation: HRO has more than 75 lawyers in its litigation practice which includes former federal and state prosecutors, former Justice Department attorneys and a former member of the United States Solicitor General's office, who have tried cases and have appeared in all of Colorado's state and federal courts and in numerous other courts and tribunals across the United States, including the United States Supreme Court. These cases have covered virtually all areas of civil and criminal litigation, including antitrust, bankruptcy, business torts, securities fraud, shareholder rights, contracts, insurance coverage, intellectual property, products liability, personal injury, professional malpractice, federal criminal defense and civil and criminal appeals. HRO's general litigators have also represented firm clients in a wide range of arbitrations and administrative proceedings, and they have participated in all forms of formal and informal alternative dispute resolution.

CLIENTS: Coors Brewing Company, Johns Manville, Lockheed Martin, Louis Vuitton, Questar, Qwest, Rolex, Skyy Vodka, UnitedGlobalCom, Union Pacific Railroad, Vail Resorts and Wells Fargo.

INTERNATIONAL WORK: HRO's international practice serves a substantial number of US based and foreign clients with multi-national interests. With offices in London and Munich, the firm is involved in substantial international transactions. The group assists clients with international contracts, acquisitions, mergers and financing of foreign companies, international tax, financing and investments, technology transfer issues, export licensing and international dispute resolution.

HEAD OFFICE

COLORADO
1700 Lincoln Street, Suite 4100, **Denver**, CO 80203-4541
Tel: 303 861 7000   **Fax:** 303 866 0200
Email: information@hro.com
Website: www.hro.com

BRANCH OFFICES

COLORADO
1801 13th Street, Third Floor, **Boulder**, CO 80302
Tel: 303 444 5955   **Fax:** 303 444 1063

90 South Cascade Avenue, Suite 1300, **Colorado Springs,**
CO 80903-1615
Tel: 719 473 3800   **Fax:** 719 633 1518

CALIFORNIA
One Maritime Plaza, Suite 2400A, **San Francisco**, CA 94111-3404
Tel: 415 268 2000   **Fax:** 415 268 1999

777 Figueroa, Suite 3650, **Los Angeles**, CA 90017
Tel: 213 892 4925   **Fax:** 213 892 4942

UTAH
299 South Main Street, Suite 1800, **Salt Lake City**, UT 84111-2263
Tel: 801 521 5800   **Fax:** 801 521 9639

INTERNATIONAL OFFICES

The firm also has offices in London and Munich.

CONTACTS

Corporate Law & Securities ....Charles D Maguire Jr
Litigation ....David S Steefel

Holme Roberts & Owen LLP
Attorneys at Law

CONTENTS: Corporate/M&A p.327; Employment p.329; Litigation: p.331; Real Estate p.333; Individuals' Profiles p.336; Firms' Profiles p.339.

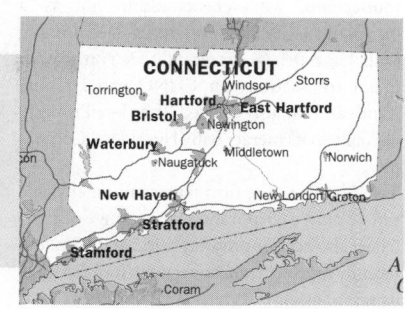

How lawyers are ranked

The opinions we gather from clients — mainly from in-house lawyers but also from other purchasers of legal services — are balanced by opinions from colleagues and competitors. Together, they provide two different perspectives — an all-round view — and biased viewpoints cancel each other out.

CORPORATE/M&A

Connecticut
Leading firms (Corporate/M&A)

1	**FINN DIXON & HERLING LLP** *Stamford*
2	**EDWARDS & ANGELL LLP** *Hartford*
	MURTHA CULLINA LLP *Hartford*
	WIGGIN & DANA LLP *New Haven*
3	**DAY, BERRY & HOWARD LLP** *Hartford*
	ROBINSON & COLE LLP *Hartford*
	SHIPMAN & GOODWIN LLP *Hartford*

Leading individuals (Corporate/M&A)

1	**FINN III** Harold *Finn Dixon, Stamford*
	LOTSTEIN James *Edwards & Angell, Hartford*
2	**ALBIN** David *Finn Dixon & Herling, Stamford*
	DIXON Brett *Finn Dixon & Herling, Stamford*
	DOWNEY III Charles *Finn Dixon & Herling, Stamford*
	FLASCHEN Evan *Bingham McCutchen, Hartford*
	HERLING Michael *Finn Dixon & Herling, Stamford*
	MARCO Frank *Wiggin & Dana, New Haven*
	PINNEY Willard *Murtha Cullina, Hartford*

Up-and-coming individuals

	SMITS Anthony *Bingham McCutchen, Hartford*

Firms and Individuals are listed alphabetically in each band.

Band 1

Finn Dixon & Herling LLP
See firm details p.339

The Firm: There is little doubt about which firm is top of the tree for corporate work in Connecticut. According to clients, the levels of quality and responsiveness at this "*absolutely superb*" corporate boutique are "*often better than New York firms — they also only put as many guys onto your account as you need.*" The "*low-key, collegiate*" group continues to win plaudits for its technical expertise and "*personalized*" service. Its attorneys "*are not out to start wars, just to get the deal done as efficiently as possible,*" say clients. Interviewees also appreciated the amount of contact they can rely on from the "*extraordinarily successful*" senior partners. This is all part and parcel of the service at a firm that is admired for "*bucking the trend to globalization.*" Finn Dixon, clients imply, is not interested in becoming the biggest firm in the market; its focus is on service, quality and value. The firm wins acclaim for its sophisticated M&A and corporate finance practices – both boast nationwide private equity and venture capital firms as clients and frequently work outside the state. Its corporate tax department is also highly regarded, especially for tax controversy and executive compensation work. The firm continues to undertake securities transactions for a number of public corporations and has an established investment management practice, which is particularly noted for its expertise in advising hedge funds.

The Lawyers: Dubbed "*the state's best-known corporate lawyer,*" **Harold Finn** (see p.336) remains a leader for securities law and compliance matters. He is also noted for his work on investment management, where he represents both advisers and private investment companies. Recent work has included some major bond transactions, and an important tender offer. **Brett Dixon** (see p.336) heads the firm's tax practice and is admired for his technical knowledge. Clients described him as "*detail-oriented and permanently available,*" and rate him "*the go-to guy for intricate tax planning.*" According to peers, meanwhile, "*the trust factor that he engenders in clients is extraordinary.*" Dixon has recently worked on a number of transactions for private equity and venture capital funds, including a structured investment for an offshore group of companies. Private equity and venture capital specialist **Michael Herling** (see p.337) is an "*extraordinarily fine lawyer,*" say clients. His business acumen and professionalism were particularly noted, and clients valued his problem-solving skills and "*ability to really focus on what is important.*" "*Smooth operator*" **Charles Downey** (see p.336) was recommended to researchers as a tremendous and "*extremely ethical*" transactional attorney. He handles private equity work for important names and M&A for buyers and sellers. Clients especially appreciate his ability to "*cut through the nonsense in order to get the deal done.*" **David Albin** (see p.336) is considered an "*exceptionally thorough*" attorney with deep knowledge of the M&A arena. His broad expertise also spans private equity and venture capital work, securities law and corporate governance. An "*exceptional resource on asset purchases,*" according to clients there is "*never anything too large or too small for him.*"

The Clients: An impressive client list ranges from major international to midmarket public companies, and leading private equity and venture capital firms. The group has recently handled several major investments for Oak Investment Partners, and is working on the sale of a company valued at more than $100 million for a private equity client. It has also recently completed a public offering of senior notes for a large telecom company.

Band 2

Edwards & Angell, LLP

The Firm: The lawyers here win favor with clients for their outstanding advisory skills and responsive manner. Sources describe them as "*extremely knowledgeable*" about the law, but also note that "*they are business practitioners who behave as counselors.*" The team operates from offices in Hartford and Stanford, which form part of an integrated network that also covers Massachusetts, Florida and New Jersey. The firm boasts sophisticated private equity expertise and a well-respected M&A team that has recently appeared in a number of impressive transactions. For example, it represented CUNO in the $110 million acquisition of WTC Industries, which included obtaining the necessary credit facility from a syndicate of banks to fund the deal. It also advised Dresser-Rand, a business unit of Ingersoll-Rand, in its $1.2 billion purchase by an affiliate of First Reserve.

The Lawyers: **James Lotstein** is universally regarded as one of the two "*preeminent*" corporate lawyers in the state. Peers rate him for *"having a good feel for the business aspects of transactions,"* while clients admire him as *"a meticulous negotiator"* with unmatched drafting skills. His expertise has recently been on show in major transactions for CUNO and Dresser-Rand, and he also assisted Travelers Property Casualty in its merger with The St Paul Companies.

The Clients: The firm represents an enviable raft of public corporations on a range of matters. It also acts for privately held companies and recently represented Connecticut Tool & Mfg in its sale of assets to Whitcraft LLC. Other clients include: Gerber Scientific; Thomson; Bristol Technology and Brynwood Partners.

Murtha Cullina LLP

The Firm: This *"first-class bunch of lawyers"* offers a broad range of corporate and contractual expertise. They act as general counsel for a number of the region's best-known businesses, who appreciate their dedication and commitment. As one source explained to researchers, its attorneys are like *"an extension of my own staff – if I need them to drop everything to get something done, they will."* Their business acumen was also highly prized. Sources laud the team for taking *"a businessman's approach"* to transactions, limiting the unnecessary use of jargon and technical detail. The firm offers expertise in M&A and securities transactions for both public and private companies on a multistate basis. It also acts for a number of governmental bodies, often combining corporate advice with advice on issues such as environmental law.

The Lawyers: *"Absolutely spectacular"* **Willard Pinney** is commended for his outstanding corporate practice and his excellent securities know-how. A *"meticulous, precise and knowledgeable"* attorney, his ability to grasp complex issues quickly is a hit with clients, as are his instinctive business acumen and strong technical expertise.

The Clients: The team continues to serve clients from a number of industry sectors including defense, distribution, construction and insurance. Examples include: Kaman; Specialized Technology Resources; Lydall; UPS and EI DuPont de Nemours.

Wiggin & Dana LLP

The Firm: The firm's business practice group has been substantially bolstered by the absorption in 2004 of a group from Mintz Levin Cohn Ferris Glovsky. According to sources, combining two of Connecticut's strongest teams for venture capital and emerging business advice has established the firm as a dynamic force in the market.

Indeed, the enhanced group is tipped to become a formidable player in national and even international markets, particularly for biotech and hi-tech clients, and already has a national reputation for PIPE securities transactions. Clients also appreciate its *"solid but creative"* advice in a range of other M&A and venture capital deals.

The Lawyers: **Frank Marco** is renowned within the state for his expertise in venture capital and technology transfer work, where he is particularly experienced at aiding clients involved in entrepreneurial technology and biotech work. *"The state's hi-tech startup guy,"* he was praised by clients for coupling *"exceptionally deep"* industry knowledge with a *"methodical"* approach. He recently represented CiDRA Corporation in its $75 million stock repurchase and spin-off of a biotech affiliate.

The Clients: The firm recently advised Cellular Genomics in connection with a $35 million capital raising led by Lilly BioVentures. Other clients include: Pfizer; Saab; United Illuminating; Yale University; UCONN; Biovitrium; Hyperion Software; Axiom Ventures; Genaissance and Meta Group.

Band 3

Day, Berry & Howard LLP

The Firm: This established transactional and counseling department boasts experience in everything from public M&A and securities advice, through private equity and venture capital work, to Sarbanes-Oxley Act compliance and succession planning. Operating from several offices across the state, the corporate team can call upon the support of other well-respected departments, such as IP, tax planning and environment.

The Lawyers: Rob Siegel is the primary contact partner in the New Haven office and a member of the firm's business law and tax groups. He has extensive experience of transactions involving midmarket companies, particularly in the healthcare and biotech sectors. Sabino (Rod) Rodriguez is the contact partner in Stamford, and is particularly experienced in tax-sensitive transactions.

The Clients: The firm undertakes cross-border and international work for a range of large to midsized corporations and venture capital firms.

Robinson & Cole LLP

See firm details p.340

The Firm: The business team here serves an established base of impressive clients and is a regular player in the M&A arena, where it

undertakes a high volume of deals of varying size. The group possesses flair in acquisitions, disposals and securities transactions, and has built a good name for emerging company and private equity work. Particular areas of strength include the pharmaceutical and technology industries.

The Lawyers: Larry Cossain and John Lynch co-chair the M&A group here and are both based in the Hartford office. Cossain represents national clients in a range of transactions, while Lynch specializes in sophisticated business acquisitions.

The Clients: The group advises public and private companies, ranging in size from multinational corporations to startups. The team frequently undertakes cross-border transactions, and is particularly rated by clients in the technology and pharmaceutical sectors.

Shipman & Goodwin LLP

The Firm: This firm offers clients a multifaceted team of advisers who practice under the broad category of commercial law. The group was recommended to researchers for its ability to handle a variety of corporate transactions, and is noted for its sure touch in combining this with financial expertise and dispute resolution know-how. This is exemplified in the sophisticated advisory service that it has built up within its white-collar defense, investigations, and corporate compliance group, which seamlessly combines expertise from the firm's corporate and litigation departments.

The Lawyers: John Kreitler is a contact partner in this area, and has experience in corporate acquisitions and disposals and insurance-related matters.

The Clients: The firm has an established client base of midrange to large corporations, and enjoys a particularly strong showing in the healthcare, insurance and technology sectors.

Other Notable Practitioners

"Diligent and knowledgeable," **Evan Flaschen** of Bingham McCutchen LLP was praised for his results-oriented approach. He is particularly well regarded for his expertise in private placements. At the same firm, **Anthony Smits** was recommended as *"one of the best young bankruptcy lawyers"* in Connecticut. Clients particularly value his negotiating skills and his active involvement in casework – *"he doesn't drop the ball,"* said one.

EMPLOYMENT

MAINLY DEFENDANT

Connecticut
Leading firms
(Employment: Mainly Defendant)

[1] **DAY, BERRY & HOWARD LLP** *Hartford*

[2] **MCCARTER & ENGLISH LLP** *Hartford*
SHIPMAN & GOODWIN LLP *Hartford*
WIGGIN & DANA LLP *New Haven*

[3] **DURANT, NICHOLS, HOUSTON,** *Bridgeport*
JACKSON LEWIS *Stamford*
LEBOEUF, LAMB, GREENE & MACRAE, *Hartford*
MURTHA CULLINA LLP *Hartford*
SIEGEL, O'CONNOR, ZANGARI, *Hartford*
TYLER COOPER & ALCORN, LLP *Hartford*

Leading individuals
(Employment: Mainly Defendant)

[1] **CLOHERTY Thomas** *Murtha Cullina,* Hartford
O'BRIEN George *Tyler Cooper,* New Haven
SPRINGER Felix *Day Berry,* Hartford
ZAKARIAN Albert *Day Berry,* Hartford

[2] **CLEMOW Brian** *Shipman & Goodwin,* Hartford
DURANT E Terry *Durant Nichols,* Bridgeport
LEFEBER Peter *Wiggin & Dana,* New Haven
ZANDY John *Wiggin & Dana,* New Haven

[3] **KEE Conrad** *Jackson Lewis,* Stamford
NOKES Gregory *McCarter & English,* Hartford
ROHBACK Thomas *LeBoeuf Lamb,* Hartford
SCHWARTZ Daniel *Day Berry,* Stamford
VOIGT Richard *McCarter & English,* Hartford
WATERS Barry *Murtha Cullina,* New Haven

Firms and Individuals are listed alphabetically in each band.

Band 1

Day, Berry & Howard LLP

The Firm: There can be little doubt as to which firm is the "*preeminent*" force for employment in Connecticut. With its "*intelligent and experienced*" attorneys, and its extensive trial experience at the state and federal levels, Day, Berry & Howard is respected across New England and enjoys a national footprint. While the practice has a good name for labor issues, what the team really prides itself upon is its outstanding record of employment cases. It won plaudits for keeping on top of current hot topics, such as class actions relating to the FLSA. Whistle-blowing and wage and hour cases increasingly feature as part of a healthy diet of more standard issues, such as age discrimination and sexual harassment cases. However, there is next to nothing that the team cannot handle, from ERISA and ADEA cases, to family and medical leave, ADA and workplace violence. Notwithstanding its impressive trial background, the group was also warmly praised by clients for taking a pragmatic approach to cases – the ones that did not come to court are often said to constitute its greatest successes.

The Lawyers: A seasoned employment law generalist, **Felix Springer** is renowned as "*a tenacious and intellectually strong litigator.*" His experience covers the spectrum of employee claims, including harassment and discrimination class actions and wrongful discharge cases. He is particularly renowned for advising local educational institutions, although he also assists large corporations and nonprofit organizations. Sources admire his impressive trial record, attributing it to a "*smart, creative and straightforward approach.*" With more than 30 years of experience in employment litigation, **Albert Zakarian** is considered the "*guiding force*" of this department. Clients describe him as "*the all around package:*" an attorney who combines "*wisdom, good judgment and keen analytical capabilities.*" "*He goes a step beyond our expectations every time,*" added one. Recent highlights have included defending the Governor of Connecticut in a discrimination class action brought by a number of unions on behalf of 3000 ex-employees. He also represented the Pratt & Whitney division of United Technologies in a race discrimination case. **Daniel Schwartz** was described by clients as "*a wonderful mentor.*" They were particularly impressed with his ability to provide practical advice that "*simplifies employment matters without diluting their legal meaning.*" His practice spans race and gender discrimination, and he is particularly experienced in restrictive covenant cases. Recent work in this area has included representing Guardsmark in the federal court in an effort to enforce restrictive covenants against former employees.

The Clients: Fortune 500 and nonprofit organizations feature in an enviable client list. The firm represents companies from a variety of industry sectors, including insurance, healthcare, technology, energy, manufacturing and retail. For example, attorneys recently defended Gentiva Health Services against employees in connection with alleged trade secrets claims.

Band 2

McCarter & English LLP

See firm details p.1152

The Firm: Any dust produced by the opening of the Hartford office in late 2003, and the subsequent arrival at the Stamford office of a team from Cummings & Lockwood, seems to have settled and, according to market sources, this prominent northeast firm has evolved into one of the state's strongest employment law players. Clients enjoy working with a "*responsive*" team that is "*attentive to our needs,*" and appreciate its "*clear-thinking approach*" to complex disputes. The department is well regarded for advising employers on both contentious and noncontentious matters. This year, in accordance with

national trends, it has experienced an increase in age and disability discrimination cases, along with a range of glass ceiling cases related to race or gender issues. On the traditional labor side, the firm enjoys a good reputation for the efficient handling of collective bargaining negotiations. The group also undertakes substantial levels of trade secrets litigation, and is renowned for its OSHA work.

The Lawyers: **Richard Voigt** (see p.338) has an established reputation in the employment and labor sphere. Clients were impressed by his ability to "*assess thoroughly the legal issues in a situation before coming up with a strategy or approach – and without doing excessive research.*" He has considerable experience in jury trials and is also accomplished in labor arbitration and administrative cases. His expertise in OSHA work was particularly noted. **Gregory Nokes** (see p.337) heads the firm's employment and labor team and was recommended to researchers as a skilled and dedicated attorney "*well versed in both state and federal law.*"

The Clients: The team assists employers from a range of industry sectors, including pharmaceutical, biotech, financial services and manufacturing companies.

Shipman & Goodwin LLP

The Firm: Shipman & Goodwin enjoys an established reputation for handling traditional labor law on behalf of large private companies, which stretches back to the 1960s. Today, it is especially well respected for its experience in a range of labor relations issues. It specializes in resolving complex, high-end cases for the public sector – particularly Connecticut's educational institutions. This includes a steady stream of advice on union organizing, collective bargaining, grievance issues and labor arbitrations. The group also assists clients with a host of employment issues.

The Lawyers: **Brian Clemow** is valued by clients for his advisory skills and for the dedication with which he attempts to keep cases out of court and prevent problems from arising. He advises a number of major public companies, as well as undertaking a considerable amount of work for private companies and nonprofit organizations within the state.

The Clients: The firm represents large and midsized companies from a range of industry sectors including insurance, financial services and healthcare. Its client roster also includes a number of nonprofit organizations and educational institutions.

Wiggin & Dana LLP

The Firm: The labor and employment team here frequently defends the management of prominent US corporations. It boasts considerable expertise in handling collective bargaining, union-organizing campaigns and decertification, as well as labor disputes and arbitrations before various bodies, such as the NLRB. On the employment side, it offers a range of advice to employers, and regularly appears in discrimination cases relating to the primary fields of race, gender, religion and disability, as well as a variety of more unusual cases.

The Lawyers: **John Zandy** is especially well respected for his expertise in union issues. Peers note his pragmatic, sensible approach and ability to make *"the right decisions,"* while clients value the air of calm he brings to labor law negotiations: *"He is very laid back but will be frank when you need him to be."* **Peter Lefeber**, meanwhile, is *"a sharp, competent and confident"* labor attorney who is admired by clients for his *"aggressive style."* Together, sources agree, they make a highly effective team: both are appreciated by clients for fostering strong working relationships and for bringing a sense of humor to their work.

The Clients: The firm's client base ranges from large, multistate corporations to startup companies and nonprofit organizations. Attorneys represent management in a variety of industries, including technology and biotech, manufacturing, healthcare, banking and financial services, construction, retail, publishing and education.

Band 3

Durant, Nichols, Houston, Hodgson & Cortese-Costa, P.C.

The Firm: This employment boutique enjoys a strong local presence, and is particularly recognized in the marketplace for its long track record in traditional labor matters. The firm was admired for its expertise in union avoidance, collective bargaining, and litigation and administrative proceedings before a number of bodies, including the NLRB. However, the team is also well acquainted with more general employment disputes and is building its capacity in a range of civil litigation. It is considered to be a particularly good choice for education institutions and municipalities.

The Lawyers: *"Top-notch, traditional labor lawyer"* **Terry Durant** continues to receive strong client endorsement for his work. Sources particularly value his considerable experience in both the labor and employment spheres, and his long track record of success.

The Clients: City of New Haven and Norwalk Hospital, AIG and Chubb Specialty Insurance.

Jackson Lewis

The Firm: This *"unbelievably competent"* labor and employment team is a popular choice with clients, and is renowned for formulating HR advice for large businesses. Its focus is on preventative strategies and solutions; however the team is more than capable of taking a *"tough-*

line approach," and has cultivated an aggressive reputation for traditional labor and employment disputes. Clients are reassured that, when it comes to navigating complex class actions, the Connecticut team not only enjoys years of experience, but is supported by a *"seamless"* national network. Recent work has included a number of high-level cases involving multimillion-dollar claims by financial executives. The firm also offers expertise in the trade secrets arena and was recommended for its knowledge of employment liabilities insurance.

The Lawyers: **Conrad Kee** is *"good on his feet,"* according to sources, and is also rated for his business acumen. Over the past year, he has handled a number of trade secrets cases, often for major corporations. He is also experienced at trial work and has been involved in a number of ERISA disputes within Connecticut.

The Clients: The team advises corporations of varying scale in a variety of industry sectors, including financial services, pharmaceuticals, healthcare, insurance, oil and technology.

LeBoeuf, Lamb, Greene & MacRae, LLP

See firm details p.1358

The Firm: With LeBoeuf Lamb's dominant reputation in insurance and energy work, and its growing international network, the firm's employment offering can sometimes be overshadowed. However, it boasts a strong and integrated national network assisting employers from a variety of sectors. The Hartford office is an important link in this chain, and impressed clients who were seeking a compact team with national, and if necessary international, reach. The group has a strong litigation focus, and is particularly experienced in discrimination cases. It also offers specialized expertise in employee benefits and executive compensation.

The Lawyers: *"Persuasive, loyal and thorough,"* **Thomas Rohback** (see p.337) is *"a forceful advocate"* who is *"quick-minded in the courtroom."* Clients particularly value the way in which he grasps their business requirements and *"really knows how to hone in on an issue."* He combines a steady stream of employment cases with a more general commercial caseload.

The Clients: The firm acts for local and national employers within a range of industry sectors. Employee benefit clients include plan sponsors, insurers and business associations.

Murtha Cullina LLP

The Firm: According to feedback, this cross-departmental labor and employment group is full of accomplished, practical attorneys handling *"high-quality"* labor relations work. It offers expertise in collective bargaining negotiations, with a special emphasis on M&A-related matters. The team is also regularly involved in substantial arbitrations and litigation – includ-

ing class actions – related to a variety of labor and employment issues. Recent work has ranged from several national labor disputes to advice on loyalty provisions and employee benefit schemes in accordance with recent changes in federal law.

The Lawyers: *"Excellent"* employment lawyer **Thomas Cloherty** was described by sources as a clever and effective negotiator and litigator. He is admired for his ability to be pragmatic while remaining *"tough when necessary,"* and for maintaining a *"strong sense of honor."* **Barry Waters** is also said to be *"an efficient and savvy employment lawyer."* He is experienced in a range of employment matters, and regularly appears in noncompete and trade secrets work.

The Clients: Clients range from national corporations to midsized businesses, as well as municipalities and public sector organizations.

Siegel, O'Connor, Zangari, O'Donnell & Beck PC

The Firm: Market sources continue to endorse the work of this growing boutique firm. It acts for clients – often smaller and midsized businesses – at the state and federal levels and is noted for the national character of much of its work. The team is particularly experienced in handling union-organizing drives and constitutional matters, wage and hour claims and OSHA matters, which makes it a popular choice for a range of public sector organizations.

The Lawyers: Hartford-based Shawn Coyne is a contact partner for the firm's labor and employment group.

The Clients: Clients include the State of Connecticut Judicial Branch and Kimberly-Clark. The firm also advises trade associations, governmental departments and education boards.

Tyler Cooper & Alcorn, LLP

The Firm: This *"outstanding"* labor and employment group has a solid grounding in litigation and is particularly experienced in union-related matters and collective bargaining. It also offers a business counseling service, dispensing *"useful preventative"* advice, which, clients admit, has *"helped us become more adept at dealing with legal matters."* On the employment side, the team has been involved in several major discrimination and wrongful discharge claims of late, and it has also advised on labor and employment issues connected to M&A transactions. Recent work has also touched upon municipal arbitration and town redevelopment matters.

The Lawyers: **George O'Brien** maintains a fine reputation in the state and is a popular senior counsel to a number of prominent businesses. Clients value his ability to *"see through to the heart of a problem with amazing clarity,"* while, according to peers, *"if he is doing a case, he is doing it 100% – his thoroughness knows no bounds."* He is experienced as both an arbitrator

330   All quotes in the text are from interviews with clients and competitors.

CHAMBERS USA 2005

and a litigator, and was commended for handling everything from union strike activity to discrimination claims.

The Clients: Hospitals, banks, municipalities, educational institutions, transport companies and telecom corporations feature in the firm's client roster. The firm also represents retail clients, including several national shopping mall companies.

LITIGATION

Connecticut
Leading firms
(Litigation: General Commercial)

1	**DAY, BERRY & HOWARD LLP** *Hartford*
2	**WIGGIN & DANA LLP** *New Haven*
3	**CARMODY & TORRANCE LLP** *New Haven*
	MURTHA CULLINA LLP *Hartford*
	SHIPMAN & GOODWIN LLP *Hartford*
4	**HURWITZ & SAGARIN LLC** *Milford*
	JACOBS, GRUDBERG, BELT, *New Haven*
	MCCARTER & ENGLISH LLP *Hartford*
	ROBINSON & COLE LLP *Hartford*

Leading individuals
(Litigation: General Commercial)

Senior Statesman

	GROARK Thomas *Day, Berry*, Hartford
	STAPLETON James *Day, Berry*, Hartford
	WADE James *Robinson & Cole*, Hartford
1	**BRADY Francis** *Murtha Cullina*, Hartford
	DUNHAM Edward *Wiggin & Dana*, New Haven
	FITZGERALD Anthony *Carmody*, New Haven
	SULLIVAN Shaun *Wiggin & Dana*, New Haven
2	**BELT David** *Jacobs, Grudberg*, New Haven
	BRIGHT William *McCarter & English*, Hartford
	FOGARTY James *Fogarty, Cohen*, Greenwich
	GREENSPAN Steven *Day, Berry*, Hartford
	ROBERTSON James *Carmody & Torrance*, Waterbury
	SAGARIN Daniel *Hurwitz & Sagarin*, Milford
	SICILIAN James *Day Berry*, Hartford
3	**FITZMAURICE Daniel** *Day, Berry*, Hartford
	MORRISON Francis *Day, Berry*, Hartford
	SANSON Paul *Shipman & Goodwin*, Hartford
	SHEARIN James *Pullman & Comley*, Bridgeport
	SILVESTRI Frank *Levett Rockwood*, Westport
	TAYLOR Allan *Day Berry*, Hartford
	WYLD Robert *Shipman & Goodwin*, Hartford

Up-and-coming individuals

	HARRINGTON Michael *Murtha Cullina*, Hartford
	SIMPSON Robert *Shipman & Goodwin*, Hartford

Firms and Individuals are listed alphabetically in each band.

Band 1

Day, Berry & Howard LLP
The Firm: This "*excellent*" team enjoys an established reputation as "*the state's leading litigation practice.*" With its impressive range of clients and enviable trial record, it has "*substantially more depth and greater breadth through its number of top-line people*" than its competitors. Clients laud the firm for the "*good judgment and high-quality service*" of its lawyers, while peers also praised its senior attorneys for their "*outstanding contribution*" to litigation in Connecticut and beyond. The group handles a large volume of jury trials in areas like antitrust, insurance, IP and products liability. It is still seeing an increased volume of securities work and continued growth in its white-collar crime and governmental investigations practice. Alongside general commercial disputes, the litigation department also assists clients with environmental and regulatory matters. The growing firm has recently opened branches in New Haven and West Haven and, with additional offices in Massachusetts and New York, it is firmly established as one of the region's primary business litigation outfits.

The Lawyers: In recent years **James Stapleton** has been building a particular reputation for his work in mediation and arbitration. His "*extensive experience*" and skill in "*analyzing a situation, then making clear and cogent recommendations*" make him well suited for this approach, though he also remains popular with litigation clients. He recently tried a case on behalf of the Bishop and the Roman Catholic Diocese of Fairfield County, involving efforts by several newspapers to obtain sealed files and court papers from settled cases. "*Tremendous trial lawyer*" **Thomas Groark** is a senior attorney who exudes "*integrity and thoughtfulness.*" Described by clients as "*smart, genial but deadly*" and "*a master at reducing complex matters to simple themes,*" he has recently been focused on insurance and securities work, and cases relating to environmental asbestos claims. His "*knowledge of the local courts*" and his expertise in class action litigation – the development of Connecticut class action law is largely attributed to his efforts – are held to be unsurpassed. "*Phenomenal lawyer*" **Steven Greenspan** is a "*tough*" trial attorney who is renowned for his work in franchise and distributorship litigation. "*Remarkable on his feet in court,*" he also wins client approval for his "*creative*" approach to meeting business requirements. He has recently represented BP Amoco and ExxonMobil in franchise-related matters. **James Sicilian** is a specialist in class action litigation. He recently defended Dell in a law suit brought by Computers Plus Center, and has also been busy defending several universities against Atlantic Coast Conference in a case involving college athletics. He is popular with clients and peers alike. "*Outstanding trial lawyer*" **Francis Morrison** (see p.337) wins plaudits for his products liability work. A "*bright and dedicated*" attorney, he offers expertise in a range of general commercial and IP litigation. "*Knowledgeable*" **Daniel FitzMaurice** is praised as a good all-rounder with outstanding experience of Connecticut's litigation environment. Clients appreciated his "*superb responsiveness and attention to detail.*" "*Excellent appellate lawyer*" **Allan Taylor** regularly assists insurance companies and large business entities. Clients praised his "*top-class analytical abilities and legal writing,*" while his "*impeccable integrity*" and "*genuine interest in the client's perspective*" were also appreciated.

The Clients: The firm serves some well-known companies in the insurance industry, as well as from the aerospace, energy, data communications, computer software and manufacturing sectors. Examples include United Technologies and Advest.

GENERAL COMMERCIAL

Band 2

Wiggin & Dana LLP
The Firm: According to market sources, the "*excellent*" attorneys at this firm rank "*among the best in the country*" for franchise and distribution work. Now visibly reaping the benefits of its 2003 merger with Howe & Addington, the Connecticut office is, according to some of its clients, "*on a par with the top national law firms.*" Peers envy the firm's "*exceptional client base,*" which increasingly includes New York-based outfits. Clients, meanwhile, appreciate the "*outstanding writing ability and quality legal work at all levels,*" and the skill of the team's "*significant trial attorneys*" in front of a jury. Over the past year, the firm has witnessed an increase in white-collar crime and corporate compliance work. Its professional liability expertise also continues to grow, and is often employed on behalf of accountancy firms. Additional areas of expertise include distribution, IP and medical malpractice. The group is particularly known for advising the Subway chain, and has recently been busy handling an antitrust law suit for Doctors Associates.

The Lawyers: An accomplished general litigator and "*fantastic*" trial attorney, **Shaun Sullivan** is well established in local litigation circles. He is particularly renowned for his work in large management cases where he "*leaves no stone unturned.*" Interviewees admired his knowledge and perseverance, as well as his unerring ability to "*tell the difference between what is important and what is not.*" "*Bright and focused*" franchise disputes specialist **Edward Wood Dunham** has developed a national practice with work in a number of states, including Texas. His business acumen was said to help him "*really understand the strengths and weaknesses of a case without spending a lot of time on theoretical issues.*" One client even went so far as to describe him as "*among the best US lawyers I've seen,*" for his "*articulate, intelligent and intensely empathetic*" manner.

The Clients: Yale-New Haven Hospital; Yale Medical School; Yale Psychiatric Institute; US DOJ's Antitrust Division; Banfi Vintners; Cendant and Doctor's Associates (Subway).

Band 3

Carmody & Torrance LLP

The Firm: According to market sources, this "*amenable, responsive and extremely experienced*" midtier firm is a good choice for national and international corporations requiring local business litigation counsel. The team operates from offices in New Haven, Southbury and Waterbury. It is particularly rated for environmental and partnership issues, and also offers expertise in antitrust, products liability, securities and IP litigation. Clients are full of admiration for the firm's attorneys, who they praise for "*never creating extra unnecessary work,*" and for their accessibility. "*There is no hesitation or pause in calling anyone about anything at that firm,*" said one.

The Lawyers: "*Terrific lawyer*" **Anthony Fitzgerald** is well respected both inside and outside Connecticut. According to interviewees. "*He is everything you want in a trial lawyer,*" combining "*great judgment and great reactions.*" Clients value his knowledge and rate him "*a real gentleman; an honor to work with.*" Fitzgerald has recently been occupied with litigation related to public infrastructure matters, as well as malpractice cases and partnership disputes. "*Exceptionally experienced*" **James Robertson** has tried a number of high-profile cases in the state and federal courts. His practice includes IP, products liability and environmental claims, and he is well known for his commitment to alternative dispute resolution and work as a mediator and arbitrator. Sources commend his ability "*to lead a situation and to read judges and juries successfully.*"

The Clients: Connecticut banks, utilities, insurers and governmental bodies feature among this firm's raft of clients.

Murtha Cullina LLP

The Firm: This firm maintains a reputation across New England as "*a responsive litigation outfit that gets the results clients want.*" The team commands a strong stand-alone practice, but

was also praised for the seamlessness of its cross-departmental work. It has carved out a name as a "*top national firm for insurance coverage cases,*" and often represents corporate officials in shareholder disputes. Recent examples include defending the board of directors of a major Connecticut bank in a depositor class action challenge to a demutualization and merger plan. The firm also undertakes a substantial amount of work in the environmental litigation sphere. Clients recommend the group as an "*excellent resource with a range of capabilities and real dedication.*"

The Lawyers: **Francis Brady** is widely acknowledged to be the firm's leading light. An "*excellent tort lawyer*" and a "*wonderful individual,*" he is a specialist in big-ticket insurance coverage litigation, particularly concerning major environmental law suits. However, clients agree that he "*knows the law inside out*" and is "*absolutely terrific for any kind of litigation.*" Up-and-comer **Michael Harrington** is a "*hard-working, committed and bright*" attorney whose great potential has brought him to the attention of market sources.

The Clients: Clients include Kaman Corporation, UPS and DuPont. The group also advises banks, hospitals and nursing homes.

Shipman & Goodwin LLP

The Firm: This well-established firm has noteworthy trial experience, and the recent opening of a fourth office, in Greenwich, is felt to have increased its clout further. The group offers expertise in a range of complex business litigation, and was noted for its expertise in healthcare cases, particularly in the sphere of healthcare fraud. It is active in the growing fields of IP and technology and has been developing its white-collar and investigatory practice, while also boasting experience in franchising, tort, products liability, securities and antitrust work. In addition, the firm operates an ombudsman practice, which advises companies and organizations on a national basis.

The Lawyers: **Robert Wyld** maintains a broad commercial litigation practice. Dubbed "*a smart and engaging guy,*" he has recently been busy in a variety of complex business disputes, many of them settled by arbitration. "*Outstanding trial lawyer*" **Paul Sanson** is well regarded by clients, who describe him as a "*down-to-earth, extremely thorough and tough*" attorney who "*never leaves any point unchecked.*" He frequently acts for ExxonMobil and Shell. **Robert Simpson** continues to show great promise, according to market sources. "*Effective but not arrogant,*" he is said to be "*growing stronger every day.*" His work in class action disputes and products liability was particularly noted.

The Clients: DaimlerChrysler; GE; Lego; Shell; Dunkin' Donuts; Home Depot; American Express; Coca-Cola; Eaton Corporation; Hal-

liburton; National Association of Securities Dealers (NASD) and United Technologies.

Band 4

Hurwitz & Sagarin LLC

The Firm: This Milford-based firm has a strong local reputation for its work in the field of business litigation. With expertise that spans antitrust, securities, trade secrets and corporate stockholder disputes, among other things, the group is familiar with trial work at all levels of the US court system. It is particularly experienced in class actions disputes and is noted for the cross-departmental expertise that allows it to coordinate cases seamlessly.

The Lawyers: "*Savvy practitioner*" **Daniel Sagarin** is the "*talented, creative and experienced*" attorney who is credited with much of the firm's success in business litigation. His "*impressive, exceptionally mixed workload*" covers class action work in antitrust, fraud, securities and ERISA matters. He is also recognized in the marketplace for his work as a plaintiff attorney, a role in which he is acknowledged to be "*a top opponent every time*" by peers who have seen him on the other side.

The Clients: Large public corporations, commercial banks, private companies and individuals are typical clients.

Jacobs, Grudberg, Belt & Dow PC

The Firm: According to clients, this boutique houses "*some of the best commercial litigators in the state.*" With a large volume of business disputes passing through the firm, the group is well practiced in court and boasts an impressive range of trial experience. This makes it a good choice for large and complex matters; as one client observed: "*The bigger and more complicated the ideas, the more you benefit from dealing with this firm.*" Although the team remains best known for its prowess in the criminal and personal injury fields, its commercial expertise includes antitrust, bankruptcy, and trade secrets disputes, and it has a growing IP practice. Recent work has included a class action brought against Big Y Foods and a long-running contract claim against an international aerospace concern.

The Lawyers: **David Belt**'s practice covers a range of business disputes, including unfair trade practices and antitrust cases. Clients praise his "*brilliantly developed intellect,*" noting his combination of lateral thinking with thoroughness: "*He takes time to think through a problem, then always crosses his t's and dots his i's.*" Peers, meanwhile, appreciate the fact that he "*doesn't play cheap shots.*"

The Clients: Memry Corporation; Big Y Foods; United Aluminum and Chelsea GCA Realty.

332   All quotes in the text are from interviews with clients and competitors.

CHAMBERS USA 2005

McCarter & English LLP

See firm details p.1152

The Firm: Observers believe that the absorption of Cummings & Lockwood's Hartford-based practice by New Jersey firm McCarter & English has been a success, although "*there is still potential for further development*." The group of "*wonderful*" lawyers is supported by a network of national offices, which is particularly strong in the Northeast Corridor. Post-merger, the firm has increased its volume of IP cases, including patent infringement and trade secrets-related work, and witnessed considerable growth in products liability cases, particularly within the pharmaceutical industry. It has also been occupied with securities litigation, insurance disputes and toxic torts. Recent work has included trying a distributor termination case for CUNO and a number of commercial arbitrations for the Connecticut Resources Recovery Authority. Its long-running asbestos-related work is also ongoing.

The Lawyers: "*Talented trial attorney*" **William Bright** (see p.336) is this firm's leading light in litigation. He wins plaudits for his "*extremely good understanding of domestic franchise and distributor law*" and, according to clients, is "*great at analytically assessing cases*" in a range of general commercial areas. He was recently co-counsel for Forstmann Little in a $125 million claim brought by the Treasurer of the State of Connecticut, and has also been handling several patent infringement cases.

The Clients: Diamond Shamrock; Bristol-Myers Squibb; MetLife; Eli Lilly; Owens-Illinois; CUNO; GE; GAF and Forstmann Little & Co.

Robinson & Cole LLP

See firm details p.340

The Firm: This "*terrific big firm*" is historically a serious player in the Connecticut marketplace, renowned for its record in land use, healthcare and insurance litigation. Its broad practice also includes experience in securities, bankruptcy, antitrust and products liability cases, and the firm is developing a name for white-collar criminal litigation. Recent highlights have included a civil rights action, an environmental degradation trial, and antitrust work for a major computer company. The team of "*top-notch trial lawyers*" is also increasingly being seen outside of Connecticut.

The Lawyers: **James Wade** (see p.338) was dubbed one of the "*best and brightest generalists*" in the state. "*A tenacious cross-examiner who conducts himself as a perfect gentleman in the courtroom*," Wade's constructive personal manner makes him popular with clients: "*He treats everyone with respect so people want to cooperate with him.*" Rivals, meanwhile, acknowledge his knack of "*finding a crack that opens a door.*"

The Clients: The firm serves a client base composed predominantly of large and midsized Connecticut-based corporations, including Fortune 500 companies, as well as startups and sole proprietors.

Other Notable Practitioners

James Fogarty of Fogarty, Cohen, Selby & Nemiroff LLC was described as a talented litigation attorney who combines "*all of the important intellectual qualities*" with an accomplished trial manner. **James Shearin** (see p.337) of Pullman & Comley LLC was admired for his strategic business insight: "*He figures out what matters and really drives a case forward.*" He recently acted for International Network Solutions in a case against Belgian telephone company Belacom. According to peers, he is "*dependable, thorough and careful,*" while clients note his "*focused, supple mind*" and ease at grasping complex issues. "*Intelligent, organized and conscientious*" **Frank Silvestri** (see p.337) of Levett Rockwood PC is recommended for a range of litigation expertise that includes antitrust and contractual disputes. He is admired for "*getting to the heart of a matter quickly*" and remaining calm throughout: "*He doesn't get excited just because his opponent wants him to!*"

REAL ESTATE

Connecticut	
Leading firms (Real Estate)	
1	ROBINSON & COLE LLP *Hartford*
2	BINGHAM MCCUTCHEN LLP *Hartford*
	BROWN RUDNICK BERLACK ISRAELS *Hartford*
	DECHERT *Hartford*
	SHIPMAN & GOODWIN LLP *Hartford*
	WIGGIN & DANA LLP *New Haven*
3	DAY, BERRY & HOWARD LLP *Stamford*
	KRASOW, GARLICK & HADLEY LLC *Hartford*
	NEUBERT, PEPE & MONTEITH PC *New Haven*
Firms are listed alphabetically in each band.	

Band 1

Robinson & Cole LLP

See firm details p.340

The Firm: With its headquarters in Hartford and an outstanding local reputation, sources agree that this is the state's leading firm, especially for land use. One of the original players in the market, it is widely credited with "*the shaping of today's Connecticut land use law.*" The one-stop shop land law department unites "*nimble*" attorneys in several major disciplines, including environmental law, planning, zoning and construction. A number of engineers, accountants, land planners and environmental specialists are on hand to bolster the team's overall expertise. Beyond this, it is experienced in a wide range of real estate matters, including affordable housing issues, waterfront developments and common interest communities. It also advises clients on public-private ventures and tax-advantaged transactions, picking up plaudits for offering a "*first-rate legal service*" provided by attentive, "*business-savvy*" lawyers.

The Lawyers: Dubbed "*the best land use lawyer in the state,*" **Dwight Merriam** (see p.337) enjoys a strong reputation in national real estate circles. As the firm's "*extremely gifted*" senior land use attorney, he has a deep understanding of zoning and government regulatory issues, which he places at the service of his developer clients. He was recommended for his "*capable, competent, and creative*" method of working, and clients appreciated his skill at "*advising us through all the potential traps that we could fall into.*" "*Extremely knowledgeable*" **Gurdon Buck** (see p.336) is noted for his academic excellence. A specialist in common interest communities within the sphere of condominium work, he has recently advised on several successful luxury flat conversion projects in Connecticut. A "*terrific real estate talent,*" **Frank Baker** (see p.336) was recommended to researchers for possessing excellent business judgment, which allows him to find "*creative, practical solutions to problems.*" According to clients, he is sensitive to the right issues and "*realistic in his counseling.*"

The Clients: Institutional lenders, trade groups, corporate real estate users, state agencies, schools, residential developers, healthcare institutions, hotel chains and manufacturers feature in the firm's client list. The team also acts for several water-based clients including fisheries, high-speed ferries and oyster farms. The group recently acted for TJX Companies on a 1.3 million sq ft distribution facility, which has since led to work for the same corporation in other states.

Band 2

Bingham McCutchen LLP

The Firm: The firm is a natural choice for the largest and most important developments in the state. It underlined this recently with roles on the redevelopments of the Hartford Civic Center and the Hartford Hilton Hotel, two signature projects for the city. It also has a specialty in major financings and restructurings, often for financial institutions. For example, it represented UBS in connection with a $1.2 billion call

Connecticut
Leading individuals (Real Estate)

1
ASMAR Mark *Brown Rudnick*, Hartford
BRYSON Susan *Wiggin & Dana*, New Haven
HAWKINS Barry *Shipman & Goodwin*, Hartford
MERRIAM Dwight *Robinson & Cole*, Hartford

2
APPICELLI Frank *Bingham McCutchen*, Hartford
BAKER III Frank *Robinson & Cole*, Stamford
BERKMAN Jerome *Day, Berry*, Stamford
BUCK Gurdon *Robinson & Cole*, Hartford
DEROSA Franca *Brown Rudnick*, Hartford
GILLIES John *Dechert*, Hartford
HOLLISTER Timothy *Shipman & Goodwin*, Hartford
KRASOW Herbert *Krasow, Garlick*, Hartford
LUBIN Andrew *Neubert, Pepe*, New Haven
OLAND Mark *Bingham McCutchen*, Hartford
SVONKIN Mark *Sole Practitioner*, West Hartford

Individuals are listed alphabetically in each band.

company facility restructuring. The firm offers clients a broad-based commercial real estate practice with depth in national and international markets. It frequently advises institutional owners of real estate across the USA on financing and refinancing, and assists developers in acquisitions and development projects, including handling zoning matters and government regulation.

The Lawyers: Frank Appicelli is widely considered to provide much of the motive force behind the firm's recent successes. According to peers, he has the potential to become one of the state's major players, as he possesses *"similar qualities to the best old guys."* In particular, sources appreciate his *"focused, straightforward"* approach: *"He is there to make the deal happen."* **Mark Oland** is recommended as *"a real go-to person,"* particularly for representing institutions and developers on the borrower side. The arrival of CIGNA's former in-house counsel, Bruce Douglas, with his experience in the insurance field is expected to boost the firm's profile among national institutional clients.

The Clients: The firm serves a client base of financial institutions, including insurance companies and commercial banks, real estate development companies and owners.

Brown Rudnick Berlack Israels

The Firm: The real estate practice at this *"high-end"* firm wins plaudits for its excellent individual practitioners and for the *"political clout"* it wields within the state. Clients were particularly impressed with its level of dedication: *"We are a small business but they treat us as a major client,"* said one. The group works closely with teams in its other offices to advise on a range of important commercial real estate developments. For example, it recently acted in the Trumbull Center scheme, viewed as the first new residential project to be completed in Downtown Hartford in more than 20 years. This includes

substantial car parking, residential and retail space. It has also been busy assisting Hartford Downtown Revival, the owner of the private portion of the former G Fox Building in Hartford, where a $30 million refinancing was recently closed.

The Lawyers: According to clients, **Mark Asmar** combines *"first-class talent"* in the real estate arena with *"unimpeachable"* integrity. *"Supremely intelligent and pragmatic,"* according to interviewees, he wins the respect of clients by *"balancing a knowledge of the law with a practical sense of how to move forward."* He recently acted as lead counsel for the bank group in a $43 million loan for the new Marriott Hotel at Adriaen's Landing in Hartford. Other highlights of the year include advising the borrower in connection with a five- building Connecticut office project, and assisting the developer of 5000 housing units to be rebuilt on air force bases. The *"consistently excellent"* **Franca DeRosa** specializes in environmental law and frequently advises on the environmental aspects of real estate transactions. Sources point to DeRosa's long-standing involvement with municipal planning and zoning boards and the quality of her advice: *"Her work is always 100% solid and she has never had to retract or amend anything,"* said one client.

The Clients: Prominent clients include a raft of pension funds, insurance companies, banks and other financial institutions. Healthcare organizations are also represented, alongside clients in the energy and telecom industries.

Dechert

See firm details p.418

The Firm: The Connecticut office of this prominent international firm plays an important role as part of a network of offices across the USA and beyond. Real estate work and complex financing have long been two of the firm's strongest suits, so it is no surprise to find it offering a specialized real estate financing service to clients with a focus on fund advice and the application of capital markets to real estate projects. Its attorneys boast a full range of commercial real estate skills, which includes advice on debt restructurings, foreclosures and bankruptcies. The team is regularly involved in work of national importance, and recently advised on the construction and permanent financing of the new headquarters for the Department of Transportation in Washington DC.

The Lawyers: John Gillies (see p.336) is credited with generating much of the firm's local success; however his practice is not limited to Connecticut, and he enjoys a good name in New York and Philadelphia. According to sources, he is an *"exceptionally bright guy,"* with an *"acute legal mind,"* and clients particularly appreciate his efforts to *"keep the solutions as much business-oriented as legal."* He is particularly admired for

his expertise in real estate finance, particularly on deals for financial institutions.

The Clients: Pacific Life; Wells Fargo; Freddie Mac; GMAC; Starwood Capital Group; Aetna; Criimi Mae; The Hartford and Citigroup.

Shipman & Goodwin LLP

The Firm: This firm advises clients on the full spectrum of commercial and residential real estate work, and has great expertise in condominium and common interest projects. However, it is probably best known for its excellent work in the field of real estate litigation. Here it regularly appears at the trial and appellate levels, while maintaining a strong reputation for pre-litigation and general advisory work. Its expertise was recently employed for the benefit of the Department of Public Works of the State of Connecticut in proceedings before the Connecticut Claims Commissioner. This concerned the design and construction costs arising out of the conversion of the former G Fox department store in Hartford into the Capital Community College. The group is also busy in transactional work, land use and zoning, and development. In late 2004, it concluded the leasing of a new headquarters facility for Front Point, a privately owned hedge fund that relocated from New York City to Greenwich.

The Lawyers: *"Awesome"* **Barry Hawkins** is renowned for his work with lenders in the real estate sphere. Much of his reputation derives from his skill as *"a genuine litigator"* who is *"quick on his feet"* in the courtroom. Here, he recently represented Eureka V in a case against the Town of Ridgefield, Connecticut, which concerned the condemnation value of 467 acres of land. However, he also wins plaudits for his skill in transactional work, where he is considered a shrewd and efficient negotiator. *"Outstanding"* **Timothy Hollister** represents some of the state's most important developers. He has a well-established name in litigation concerning affordable housing.

The Clients: A raft of local companies, individuals and municipalities, including banks and hospitality companies, form the backbone of this firm's client list. It continues to advise the owners of the two largest office landlords in both Stamford and in Greenwich on management matters and lease administration.

Wiggin & Dana LLP

The Firm: Clients view this as *"one of the best firms in the state,"* and describe its real estate team as *"responsive, professional and tuned into the needs of the Connecticut marketplace."* The active real estate, environment and land use department has a strong reputation for work within the state and beyond. It boasts an established name in residential and commercial work that incorporates the buying, selling and leasing of property. Specialized attorneys also offer

334

All quotes in the text are from interviews with clients and competitors.

CHAMBERS USA 2005

expertise in urban redevelopment and refinancing. The team is currently advising Yale-New Haven Hospital in connection with the development of a state-of-the-art cancer center.

The Lawyers: Susan Bryson is considered by her clients to be "*among the finest real estate lawyers in the USA.*" This impressive judgment is based on her "*extraordinary intelligence*" and "*exceptional level of experience – she knows it all, from transactional law to environmental work.*" Her flair for land use and zoning – in particular "*quirky urban issues*" – is said to set her apart from the herd, as is her knowledge of the complicated financing of Connecticut redevelopment projects. Sources also appreciate her interpersonal skills, particularly when dealing with "*complex and trying*" situations.

The Clients: The group has recently advised the Connecticut Center for Science and Exploration in connection with the development of a Caesar Pelli-designed museum in Hartford, and has also been engaged to represent the Long Wharf Theater. Additional clients include: New London Development; Olin; Mutual Housing Association of Southwestern Connecticut; Broadway Partners; Bayer; Bristol Hospital and Kelda.

Band 3

Day, Berry & Howard LLP
The Firm: This large, well-respected firm is a formidable presence in the Connecticut marketplace with offices in Hartford, Stanford, Greenwich, New Haven and West Hartford. A "*finance-oriented*" real estate department represents lenders, developers and investors in a variety of commercial transactions, such as joint ventures, acquisitions, leasing, workouts and restructurings. It also continues to act for commercial banks and equity participants in the development and management of affordable housing. Recent highlights include assisting with the redevelopment of the General Reinsurance headquarters in Stanford. Clients were full of praise for the "*excellent analytical skills*" that the group brings to bear in complex cases.

The Lawyers: Jerome Berkman specializes in commercial leasing work, where he represents both landlords and tenants. Recent examples of this include advising a major international company on the leasing of a new headquarters in Fairfield County. A "*practical and knowledgeable*" attorney, and "*a gentleman*" to boot, according to interviewees, he also enjoys a busy practice assisting developers, borrowers and investors in lending transactions. Recent highlights include advising a client on the purchase of a major building in Fairfield County, and associated financing.

The Clients: The real estate client base includes banks, multinational insurance companies, municipalities and state agencies. The team also offers advice to clients in the energy sector.

Krasow, Garlick & Hadley LLC
The Firm: This compact team is admired for its ability to combine transactional and development expertise with complex land use and zoning work. This was on show recently when it advised a developer on the construction and zoning of a combination warehouse and distribution facility, as part of a combined office and retail complex. The group also advises on commercial transactions and development projects, handling the contract negotiations, leasing and regulatory work. Examples include acting for developers in several recent projects in and around Hartford, such as a retail store and a residential community.

The Lawyers: "*Guiding light of the firm*" in real estate matters is the "*experienced and knowledgeable*" **Herbert Krasow** (see p.337). He represents banks and commercial finance entities, as well as owners and developers, in a range of commercial transactions, and is valued as a "*deal-doer*" who listens to clients' needs. He was also widely recommended for his land use work.

The Clients: Local banks and businesses in the retail, manufacturing, residential and hospitality sectors feature among the firm's client list. The team regularly advises sellers, purchasers, landlords, tenants and investors on a variety of matters within the state and beyond.

Neubert, Pepe & Monteith PC
The Firm: This is one of the largest firms in New Haven County, and it enjoys a growing reputation within the state. Its "*hungry*" real estate team is said to be full of "*aggressive*" lawyers, who are experienced in both transactional and litigation matters. Alongside its noted financing expertise, the team boasts experience in land use, zoning and permitting. It was particularly recommended for its work with small businesses, and recently advised on the acquisition and development of a 100-unit housing project.

The Lawyers: According to peers, **Andrew Lubin** is "*clearly an excellent transactional lawyer,*" who is tipped to become a major player in the Connecticut market. Clients, meanwhile, praise him as a pragmatic and knowledgeable attorney with "*a great deal of common sense.*" He handles a mixture of acquisitions and sales of land, real estate finance and leasing. According to observers, he has settled into the firm well following his recent move from Susman, Duffy & Segaloff.

The Clients: The team regularly advises businesses and individuals within the planning and construction industries, including developers, builders, architects and engineers. It also represents healthcare clients.

Other Notable Practitioners
"*Intelligent and capable*" **Mark Svonkin**, eponymous head of The Law Office of Mark J. Svonkin PC, was endorsed by clients as an "*excellent, cost-effective choice for the smaller business owner.*" He is considered particularly efficient at day-to-day retail leasing and institutional financing.

Leaders in Connecticut

ALBIN, David I
Finn Dixon & Herling LLP, Stamford
203 325 5000
dalbin@fdh.com
Recommended in Corporate/M&A
Practice Areas: Focus on private equity, mergers and acquisitions and securities law matters. Also has broad experience in venture capital transactions, corporate governance matters and the general representation of public and private business entities.
Prof. Memberships: Admitted to the Bar of the State of Connecticut. Member of the Negotiated Acquisitions Committee of the Business Law Section of the American Bar Association, and reporter for such committee's Model Asset Purchase Agreement. Vice Chairman of the Business Law Section of the Connecticut Bar Association.
Publications: Publications of numerous articles in the areas of mergers and acquisitions, venture capital and business law. Frequent lecturer in areas of mergers and acquisitions and venture capital, including frequent lecturer in the American Bar Association's National Institute's Annual Program on 'Negotiating Business Acquisitions.'
Personal: Received undergraduate degree from Trinity College with honors in political science in 1981 and received law degree from Yale University in 1984.

APPICELLI, Frank
Bingham McCutchen LLP, Hartford
860 240 2700
Recommended in Real Estate

ASMAR, Mark
Brown Rudnick Berlack Israels, Hartford 860 509 6524
Recommended in Real Estate

BAKER III, Frank Lewis
Robinson & Cole LLP, Stamford
203 462 7501
fbaker@rc.com
Recommended in Real Estate
Career: Frank Baker's practice embraces the full range of major real estate project legal management, real estate financing, commercial leasing, joint ventures for real estate development, tax-advantaged transactions, and economic redevelopment projects. Cochair of the firm's Real Estate Group, Mr Baker is also a Counselor of Real Estate (CRE) and has completed numerous transactions in US jurisdictions and abroad. He has lectured on topics of interest to the Bar, including advanced commercial leasing and financing courses. He graduated from Yale University, with honors, and the University of Virginia Law School, where he was a member of the Virginia Law Review.

BELT, David
Jacobs, Grudberg, Belt & Dow PC, New Haven 203 772 3100
Recommended in Litigation

BERKMAN, Jerome
Day, Berry & Howard LLP, Stamford
203 977 7300
Recommended in Real Estate

BRADY, Francis
Murtha Cullina LLP, Hartford
860 240 6000
Recommended in Litigation

BRIGHT Jr, William H
McCarter & English LLP, Hartford
860 275 6767
wbright@mccarter.com
Recommended in Litigation
Practice Areas: Mr Bright represents clients in complex business litigation matters. He appears in state and federal courts both in Connecticut and around the country. He also has represented clients in numerous commercial arbitrations. While Mr Bright has handled a wide variety of business matters, he has particular experience in disputes between manufacturers and their distributors, intellectual property disputes and complex contract matters.

BRYSON, Susan
Wiggin & Dana LLP, New Haven
203 498 4343
Recommended in Real Estate

BUCK, Gurdon
Robinson & Cole LLP, Hartford
860 275 8222
gbuck@rc.com
Recommended in Real Estate
Career: Gurdon Buck practices real estate, zoning, condominium, land development, and financing law. His clients include developers, lenders, and community and homeowner associations nationwide. His residential real estate development practice focuses on common interest communities and new residential communities. He has written the documentation of over 400 common interest communities, authored over a dozen special development district ordinances, and led rezoning teams for new residential and mixed-use communities in more than 20 towns. Mr Buck received his JD from the University of Pennsylvania and his BA from Lehigh University.

CLEMOW, Brian
Shipman & Goodwin LLP, Hartford
860 251 5000
Recommended in Employment

CLOHERTY, Thomas
Murtha Cullina LLP, Hartford
860 240 6000
Recommended in Employment

DEROSA, Franca
Brown Rudnick Berlack Israels, Hartford 860 509 6524
Recommended in Real Estate

DIXON, Brett W
Finn Dixon & Herling LLP, Stamford
203 325 5000
bdixon@fdh.com
Recommended in Corporate/M&A
Practice Areas: Practices primarily in the law relating to federal and state business taxation, including planning for taxable and tax-free acquisitions and dispositions of public and private entities. Represents principals and investors in structuring partnerships and other new business vehicles.
Prof. Memberships: Admitted to the Bars of the State of Connecticut and the United States Tax Court. Member of the Corporate Tax Committee of the Tax Section of the American Bar Association and of the Executive Committee of the Tax Section of the Connecticut Bar Association.
Personal: Graduated magna cum laude from Williams College in 1977. Received law degree, magna cum laude, from Cornell Law School in 1982 and MBA, with distinction, from Johnson School of Management at Cornell University in 1981.

DOWNEY III, Charles J
Finn Dixon & Herling LLP, Stamford
203 325 5000
cdowney@fdh.com
Recommended in Corporate/M&A
Practice Areas: Focus on private equity, mergers and acquisitions and venture capital. Also has broad experience in securities law matters (including PIPE transactions and advising private equity funds, venture capital funds and hedge funds with respect to securities law matters).
Prof. Memberships: Admitted to the bars of the States of Connecticut and New York. Member of the Business Law Section of the American Bar Association and the Business Law Section of the Connecticut Bar Association. Member of the Board of Directors of the Connecticut Venture Group.
Publications: Publications and lectures in the areas of mergers and acquisitions, private equity, venture capital and securities law matters.
Personal: Graduated cum laude from Wharton School of the University of Pennsylvania (BS Economics, Major in Finance) in 1986 and received law degree from New York University School of Law in 1989.

DUNHAM, Edward Wood
Wiggin & Dana LLP, New Haven
203 498 4400
Recommended in Litigation

DURANT, E Terry
Durant, Nichols, Houston, Hodgson & Cortese-Costa, P.C., Bridgeport
203 366 3438
Recommended in Employment

FINN III, Harold B
Finn Dixon & Herling LLP, Stamford
203 325 5000
hfinn@fdh.com
Recommended in Corporate/M&A
Practice Areas: Concentrates practice in the law relating to business organizations and financial transactions, including corporate governance, mergers and acquisitions, the public and private offering of securities, banking and lending, and related litigation. Represents both publicly-held corporations and private companies, including pooled investment vehicles in the form of partnerships, limited liability companies and trusts.
Prof. Memberships: Admitted to the bars of the States of Connecticut and New York. Former Member of the Council of the Business Law Section of the American Bar Association and former Chair of such Section's Banking Law Committee. Chairman of the Securities Advisory Committee to the Banking Commissioner of the State of Connecticut. Past Co-Chair of Task Force on the Revision of the Connecticut Business Corporation Act. Former Chair of the Business Law Section of the Connecticut Bar Association. Elected Member of the American Law Institute.
Personal: Received undergraduate degree from Yale University in 1960 and received law degree, magna cum laude, from Columbia University in 1966, where he was articles editor of the Columbia Law Review. Following law school, he served as a law clerk to the late Chief Justice Earl Warren and the late Associate Justice Stanley F. Reed.

FITZGERALD, Anthony
Carmody & Torrance LLP, New Haven
203 777 5501
Recommended in Litigation

FITZMAURICE, Daniel
Day, Berry & Howard LLP, Hartford
860 275 0100
Recommended in Litigation

FLASCHEN, Evan
Bingham McCutchen LLP, Hartford
860 240 2700
Recommended in Corporate/M&A

FOGARTY, James
Fogarty, Cohen, Selby & Nemiroff LLC, Greenwich 203 661 1000
Recommended in Litigation

GILLIES Jr, John J
Dechert, Hartford
860 524 3938
john.gillies@dechert.com
Recommended in Real Estate

Practice Areas: Mr Gillies is a Partner and Member of the Executive Committee of Dechert's Finance and Real Estate Group. He represents institutional investors and investment advisers in the creation, acquisition, and disposition of investments in real estate.

Prof. Memberships: Member, New Jersey and Connecticut Bars; Member, American College of Real Estate Lawyers; Member, American College of Investment Counsel.

Career: Joined Dechert in 1997. Partner, Hebb & Gitlin, Hartford, Connecticut, 1979-97.

Personal: Georgetown University (AB, 1968); Boston College Law School (JD, 1971).

GREENSPAN, Steven
Day, Berry & Howard LLP, Hartford
860 275 0100
Recommended in Litigation

GROARK Jr, Thomas
Day, Berry & Howard LLP, Hartford
860 275 0100
Recommended in Litigation

HARRINGTON, Michael
Murtha Cullina LLP, Hartford
860 240 6000
Recommended in Litigation

HAWKINS, Barry
Shipman & Goodwin LLP, Hartford
860 251 5000
Recommended in Real Estate

HERLING, Michael J
Finn Dixon & Herling LLP, Stamford
203 325 5000
mherling@fdh.com
Recommended in Corporate/M&A

Practice Areas: Firm practice leader in private equity and venture capital. Has extensive experience in mergers and acquisitions, securities law, corporate finance, and venture capital and private equity. He represents venture capital and private equity funds, publicly held and private corporations and entrepreneurs in connection with acquisition, finance and securities activities, as well as general business matters.

Prof. Memberships: Admitted to the bar of the State of Connecticut. He is a member of the Business Law Section of the Connecticut Bar Association and the Section of Business Law of the American Bar Association, as well as the Venture Capital and Private Equity Committee of the Section of Business Law. He also served as the co-reporter for the Task Force on the Connecticut Business Corporation Act.

Personal: Received undergraduate degree from Colgate University in 1979 and received law degree from Stanford Law School in 1982.

HOLLISTER, Timothy
Shipman & Goodwin LLP, Hartford
860 251 5000
Recommended in Real Estate

KEE, Conrad
Jackson Lewis, Stamford
203 961 0404
Recommended in Employment

KRASOW, Herbert
Krasow, Garlick & Hadley LLC, Hartford
860 549 7100
hkrasow@krasowgarlick.com
Recommended in Real Estate

Practice Areas: Extensive experience in complex commercial real estate transactions, including leasing, all phases of development and financing, and land use.

Prof. Memberships: Admissions to Bar: Pennsylvania; Connecticut. Advisor to the Connecticut Law Revision Commission on: The Connecticut Common Interest Ownership Act; The Uniform Land Security Interest Act; Open-End Mortgages as Security for the Guaranty of an Open-End Loan; Mortgagor Liability; The Connecticut Validating Acts; Revised Article 9 of the Uniform Commercial Code. Member: Hartford County, Connecticut (Executive Committee, Real Property Section), and American Bar Associations; US District Court for the District of Connecticut and the Eastern District of Pennsylvania; US Court of Appeals for the Second Circuit; American College of Real Estate Lawyers; Panel of Arbitrators, American Arbitration Association.

Personal: BA, University of Connecticut; LLB, Temple University School of Law. Associate editor, Temple Law Review.

LEFEBER, Peter
Wiggin & Dana LLP, New Haven
203 498 4400
Recommended in Employment

LOTSTEIN, James
Edwards & Angell, LLP, Hartford
860 525 5065
Recommended in Corporate/M&A

LUBIN, Andrew
Neubert, Pepe & Monteith PC, New Haven 203 821 2000
Recommended in Real Estate

MARCO, Frank
Wiggin & Dana LLP, New Haven
203 498 4343
Recommended in Corporate/M&A

MERRIAM, Dwight
Robinson & Cole LLP, Hartford
860 275 8228
dmerriam@rc.com
Recommended in Real Estate

Career: Dwight Merriam represents developers, municipalities, landowners, and advocacy groups in land use matters. He has published over 180 professional articles on land use law, authored 'The Complete Guide to Zoning', coedited 'Inclusionary Zoning Moves Downtown', and coauthored 'The Takings Issue'. He is a Past President and Fellow of the American Institute of Certified Planners, and member of the American

Planning Association, American College of Real Estate Lawyers and The Counselors of Real Estate. Mr Merriam received his BA, cum laude, from the University of Massachusetts, MRP from the University of North Carolina and JD at Yale Law School.

MORRISON, Francis
Day, Berry & Howard LLP, Hartford
860 275 0100
Recommended in Litigation

NOKES, Gregory
McCarter & English LLP, Hartford
860 275 6712
gnokes@mccarter.com
Recommended in Employment

Practice Areas: Mr Nokes provides strategic advice and counsel to employers regarding the full range of legal issues arising from the workplace. His practice includes all aspects of union-management matters, discrimination, harassment and wrongful termination claims and litigation, and business immigration. He represents management in such matters in mediation and arbitration proceedings, before state and federal agencies, and in trial and appellate courts. He has extensive experience under the Fair Labor Standards Act as well as related state laws which regulate wages and hours of employees.

O'BRIEN, George
Tyler Cooper & Alcorn LLP, New Haven
203 784 8200
Recommended in Employment

OLAND, Mark
Bingham McCutchen LLP, Hartford
860 240 2700
Recommended in Real Estate

PINNEY Jr, Willard
Murtha Cullina LLP, Hartford
860 240 6000
Recommended in Corporate/M&A

ROBERTSON Jr, James
Carmody & Torrance LLP, Waterbury
203 573 1200
Recommended in Litigation

ROHBACK, Thomas
LeBoeuf, Lamb, Greene & MacRae, LLP, Hartford 860 293 3557
trohback@llgm.com
Recommended in Employment

Practice Areas: In addition to employment his practice has involved numerous areas of law, including antitrust, class actions, telecommunications, cable television, insurance and complex commercial litigation. His litigation practice also covers environmental, bankruptcy and construction litigation, including trials and appeals. Of his membership in numerous federal courts, he has tried three cases during one three-month period winning a directed verdict in each of the cases.

Prof. Memberships: New York Bar; Pennsylvania Bar; Connecticut Bar
Career: Joined LeBoeuf in 1978

Personal: Columbia University (JD) 1978; Columbia University (MA) 1975; Union College (BA) 1973

SAGARIN, Daniel
Hurwitz & Sagarin LLC, Milford
203 877 8000
Recommended in Litigation

SANSON, Paul
Shipman & Goodwin LLP, Hartford
860 251 5000
Recommended in Litigation

SCHWARTZ, Daniel
Day, Berry & Howard LLP, Stamford
203 977 7300
Recommended in Employment

SHEARIN, James T
Pullman & Comley LLC, Bridgeport
203 330 2240
jtshearin@pullcom.com
Recommended in Litigation

Practice Areas: Chair of Litigation Department. Has wide-ranging experience in state and federal courts (trial and appellate levels) and before arbitration and mediation boards. Represents clients in areas of commercial, intellectual property, banking, securities, antitrust, civil rights, employment and general civil litigation.

Prof. Memberships: Connecticut Legal Service Corp. (director), University of Connecticut Law School Foundation, Inc. (director), Greater Bridgeport Bar Association (former president), Executive Committees of Federal Practice (co-chair) and Intellectual Property Sections of Connecticut Bar Association, Raymond E. Baldwin Inn of Court, American Red Cross (director).

Career: Joined firm, 1988; became Partner, 1994; Executive Committee member.

Personal: JD, high honors, University of Connecticut School of Law, 1986; BA, summa cum laude, University of Connecticut, 1983.

SICILIAN, James
Day, Berry & Howard LLP, Hartford
860 275 0100
Recommended in Litigation

SILVESTRI Jr, Frank J
Levett Rockwood P.C., Westport
203 222 0885
fsilvestri@levettrockwood.com
Recommended in Litigation

Practice Areas: Commercial litigation, arbitration.

Prof. Memberships: Fellow, American College of Trial Lawyers; ABA (Litigation, Antitrust Sections); Connecticut Bar Assoc. (Co-chair, Federal Practice Section 2004 -; member, Task Force on Confidentiality and Courts 2003 -); American Inns of Court; Federal Bar Council; American Health Lawyers Association.

Career: Member, Levett Rockwood, P.C., 2004 -; Zeldes, Needle & Cooper, P.C., Bridgeport CT 1975-2004; Law

Clerk, US Circuit Judge J. Joseph Smith, 2d Circuit, 1974-75.

Publications: Has spoken on litigation topics for Connecticut Bar Association.

Personal: Yale Law School (JD 1974); Georgetown University (AB 1968, summa cum laude, Phi Beta Kappa); US Navy 1968-71.

SIMPSON, Robert
Shipman & Goodwin LLP, Hartford
860 251 5000
Recommended in Litigation

SMITS, Anthony
Bingham McCutchen LLP, Hartford
860 240 2700
Recommended in Corporate/M&A

SPRINGER, Felix
Day, Berry & Howard LLP, Hartford
860 275 0100
Recommended in Employment

STAPLETON, James F
Day, Berry & Howard LLP, Hartford
860 275 0100
Recommended in Litigation

SULLIVAN, Shaun
Wiggin & Dana LLP, New Haven
203 498 4400
Recommended in Litigation

SVONKIN, Mark
The Law Office of Mark J. Svonkin P.C.,
West Hartford 860 521 2811
Recommended in Real Estate

TAYLOR, Allan
Day, Berry & Howard LLP, Hartford
860 275 0100
Recommended in Litigation

VOIGT, Richard
McCarter & English LLP, Hartford
860 275 6776
rvoigt@mccarter.com
Recommended in Employment

Practice Areas: Mr Voigt represents employers in a wide variety of employment-related matters, including wrongful discharge cases, employment discrimination cases, state and federal court injunction actions, breach of contract cases, trade secret/proprietary information cases, NLRB unfair labor practice proceedings, arbitration matters, OSHA citation cases, and wage-hour claims.

Career: Mr Voigt has been a frequent speaker on labor and employment issues before many industry and trade associations. He was selected for inclusion in 'Best Lawyers in America' 2005-2006 edition in the category of labor and employment law.

WADE, James A
Robinson & Cole LLP, Hartford
860 275 8270
jwade@rc.com
Recommended in Litigation

Career: Jim Wade is a preeminent trial attorney, litigating numerous criminal and civil cases across the United States. Mr Wade served as outside counsel to the Connecticut Democratic Party and has represented the party before the United States Supreme Court. He has represented numerous public officials in Connecticut in litigation involving constitutional election and voting issues and has represented numerous Fortune 500 companies on various compliance issues, including grand jury investigation compliance, securities regulation, banking issues, and environmental concerns. Mr Wade received his BA from Yale University and his LLB from the University of Virginia.

WATERS, Barry
Murtha Cullina LLP, New Haven
203 772 7700
Recommended in Employment

WYLD, Robert
Shipman & Goodwin LLP, Hartford
860 251 5000
Recommended in Litigation

ZAKARIAN, Albert
Day, Berry & Howard LLP, Hartford
860 275 0100
Recommended in Employment

ZANDY, John
Wiggin & Dana LLP, New Haven
203 498 4400
Recommended in Employment

FINN DIXON & HERLING LLP

THE FIRM

Founding Partners: Harold B Finn III
Brett W Dixon (also Managing Partner)
Michael J Herling

Number of partners: 13
Number of other lawyers: 17

FIRM OVERVIEW: With 30 attorneys, Finn Dixon & Herling LLP provides a broad spectrum of legal services to the business and financial community. The firm's clients are located throughout the United States, and many of them have international operations. Since its founding in 1987, Finn Dixon has focused on issues affecting businesses and business transactions. The firm strives to provide the highest level of customer service and practical, solution-oriented advice, grounded on a thorough understanding of each client's business. The firm has developed a litigation capability that supports the firm's core client base and serves other clients involved in commercial litigation matters.

MAIN AREAS OF PRACTICE

BUSINESS: Finn Dixon's business practice is focused on eight key areas:

Mergers & Acquisitions/Private Equity: Represents buyers, sellers and investors in various transactions, including mergers and other business combinations, leveraged buy-outs and recapitalizations, growth capital investments, 'add-on' acquisitions, proxy contests, stock swaps and public company mergers.

Venture Capital/Emerging Companies: Represents venture capital firms in both early-stage and growth capital investments and in the formation, organization and operation of venture capital funds.

Investment Management: Represents domestic and offshore investment partnerships and trusts, common and collective trust funds, investment advisers, commodity trading advisers and commodity pool operators and registered broker-dealers. Investment advisory clients include a number of nationally-renowned firms, as well as smaller state-registered entities. Also represents sources of private equity and money managers in their investments in domestic and offshore funds, including hedge funds and other alternative investment vehicles.

Securities: Advises clients regarding federal and state securities laws that affect public offerings and private placements by both publicly-held companies and privately-owned businesses, annual reports and proxy statements and the organization of, and offerings by, private investment companies.

Banking & Lending: Advises banks and other financial institutions on all aspects of lending and other credit transactions. Also assists such clients on various regulatory issues, including with respect to general compliance as well as acquisitions and dispositions of banks and bank holding companies and the establishment by out of state banks of branch offices or other operations in Connecticut.

Public Finance: Represents issuers, underwriters and trustees in municipal bond issuances, including the state of Connecticut, state agencies and municipalities in general finance or specialized project finance matters.

Tax: Finn Dixon offers tax expertise, including structuring and other advice to its transactional clients as well as advice in connection with federal and state taxation of the ongoing activities of its corporate, partnership and limited liability clients.

General Business Representation: Finn Dixon helps many clients address a wide variety of operational and strategic issues on a continuous basis, including consultation on choice of entity, protection and coordination of the rights of owners, commercial real estate transactions, employment matters, including executive compensation, severance arrangements, stock options and employee benefits, financings, licensing and strategic alliance and joint venture arrangements and compliance with regulatory requirements.

LITIGATION: Finn Dixon's litigation practice encompasses civil litigation in state and federal courts, appellate advocacy, arbitration and other forms of alternative dispute resolution and proceedings before administrative agencies. The firm's practice also includes bankruptcy and workouts and employment law.

CLIENTS: Finn Dixon's clients include a wide array of commercial entities, from substantial private equity and venture capital groups, middle market public and private corporations, and banks and financial institutions to risk-taking entrepreneurs and start-up ventures.

HEAD OFFICE

CONNECTICUT
One Landmark Square, Suite 1400, **Stamford**, CT 06901 2689
Tel: 203 325 5000   **Fax:** 203 348 5777
Website: www.fdh.com

BRANCH OFFICES

CONNECTICUT
31 Whitney Avenue, 2nd Floor, **New Haven**, CT 06510
Tel: 203 848 6488   **Fax:** 203 497 8122

ROBINSON & COLE LLP

THE FIRM

Managing Partner: Eric D Daniels

Number of partners nationwide: 92
Total number of lawyers: 225

FIRM OVERVIEW: For 160 years, Robinson & Cole has served business and governmental clients—regionally, nationally and internationally. Each one of the firm's lawyers and professional staff is committed to quality, innovation and exceptional service. Robinson & Cole's objective is simple: to achieve client goals through innovative, cost-effective and responsive results. The firm aggressively utilizes technology to aid in this mission. The firm is seen as a leader in legal skills for clients in manufacturing, insurance, healthcare, biotech and medical devices, pharmaceutical, high tech, financial/banking, energy (unregulated) and utility, environmental, food and beverage, government/municipal, fuel cells, media and entertainment, nonprofit and education, retail and wholesale, real estate and construction, and transportation.

MAIN AREAS OF PRACTICE

LandLaw: This practice encompasses all areas of law dealing with land related resources and business operations: environmental, land use, real estate, construction, and utilities. Its 60 LandLaw lawyers and professional analysts operate as part of an integrated team delivering an array of cost-effective legal services, on the client's timeline, to achieve defined objectives. Services include due diligence, transactions, risk and responsibility allocation, defense, contracting, permitting and compliance.

Business: The firm regularly works with public and privately held clients on stock and asset acquisitions, joint ventures, securities offerings, and other debt and equity financings. In addition to transactional representation, it provides ongoing corporate, securities and commercial law counseling to a substantial number of US and foreign-based clients in the areas of tax planning, finance, IP, technology, trade regulation and privacy.

Business Litigation: Litigation can impose a serious drain on company finances. The firm counsels clients in minimizing litigation risks, reducing dispute resolution costs, and conserving valuable time and resources. This practice spans everything from claims of contract breach, business torts (fraud, misrepresentation, conversion, interference with contract), unfair and deceptive trade practices, and RICO violations to securities and antitrust violations, intellectual property claims and class actions. The cases it handles are as varied as the entities it represents.

Labor, Employment & Benefits Law: The firm offers the full array of employment legal services—benefits, counseling, immigration, labor relations, litigation and training. Because Robinson & Cole understands the legal implications for all these areas, it can advise clients when issues arise beyond the immediate context of the matter under discussion.

Public Finance: Robinson & Cole has been providing bond counsel services for securities offerings by states, municipalities, public authorities and agencies for more than half a century.

CLIENTS: The firm represents Fortune 100 and Global 500 companies as well as new ventures and nonprofit organizations. Various of the firm's practices represent the following clients, sometimes in a Preferred Provider relationship: United Technologies Corporation, Unilever US, Pfizer, Crompton Corporation, General Electric, Health Net, Pitney Bowes, Metromedia Company, Tyco International (US), The Hartford, VNU, ACNielsen, Phibro, Oxford Health Plans, Raymarine, Bank of America, American International Group, St. Paul Travelers, Stop & Shop and Diageo North America.

HEAD OFFICE

CONNECTICUT
280 Trumbull Street, **Hartford**, CT 06103-3597
Tel: 860 275 8200

Website: www.rc.com

BRANCH OFFICES

CONNECTICUT
Financial Centre, **Stamford**, CT 06904-2305
Tel: 203 462 7500

80 Field Point Road, **Greenwich**, CT 06836-1538
Tel: 203 862 4100

75 Eugene O'Neill Drive, **New London**, CT 06320-6306
Tel: 860 437 5000

FLORIDA
1800 Second Street, Suite 965W, **Sarasota**, FL 34236-5992
Tel: 941 330 0822

MASSACHUSETTS
One Boston Place, **Boston**, MA 02108-4404
Tel: 617 557 5900

NEW YORK
885 Third Avenue, Suite 2800, **New York**, NY 10022-4834
Tel: 212 451 2900

120 Bloomingdale Road, **White Plains**, NY 10605-1522
Tel: 914 761 0055

CONTACTS

Real Estate	Frank Baker
Environmental	Earl Phillips
Land Use	Brian Blaesser, Thomas Cody
Construction	Elizabeth Brennan, Christopher Hug
Business	Jack Kennedy
	Lawrence Coassin, David Garbus
Business Litigation	Craig Raabe
	Joseph Clasen, Bradford Babbitt
International	William Sellay
Immigration	Alice DeTora
Labor & Employment	Jeffrey Hirsch
Benefits	Bruce Barth
Public Finance	Frank D'Ercole

ROBINSON & COLE LLP

CONTENTS: Bankruptcy/Restructuring p.341; Chancery p.343; Corporate/M&A p.346; Employment p.347; Intellectual Property p.348; Real Estate p.349; Individuals' Profiles p.351; Firms' Profiles p.359.

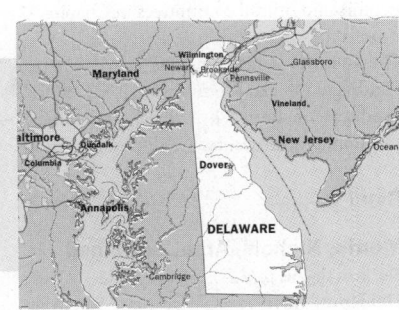

How lawyers are ranked

The opinions we gather from clients — mainly from in-house lawyers but also from other purchasers of legal services — are balanced by opinions from colleagues and competitors. Together, they provide two different perspectives — an all-round view — and biased viewpoints cancel each other out.

BANKRUPTCY/RESTRUCTURING

Delaware
Leading firms
(Bankruptcy/Restructuring)

[1] SKADDEN, ARPS, SLATE, MEAGHER *Wilmington*
YOUNG CONAWAY STARGATT *Wilmington*

[2] MORRIS, NICHOLS, ARSHT & TUNNELL *Wilmington*
RICHARDS LAYTON & FINGER *Wilmington*
SAUL EWING LLP *Wilmington*

[3] PACHULSKI, STANG, ZIEHL, *Wilmington*
PEPPER HAMILTON LLP *Wilmington*
POTTER ANDERSON & CORROON LLP *Wilmington*

[4] ASHBY & GEDDES *Wilmington*
GREENBERG TRAURIG LLP *Wilmington*
LANDIS RATH & COBB LLP *Wilmington*
MORRIS, JAMES, HITCHENS *Wilmington*
THE BAYARD FIRM *Wilmington*

Leading individuals
(Bankruptcy/Restructuring)

[1] GALARDI Gregg *Skadden Arps*, Wilmington
PATTON James *Young Conaway*, Wilmington

[2] BRADY Robert *Young Conaway*, Wilmington
CHEHI Mark *Skadden Arps*, Wilmington
COLLINS Mark *Richards Layton*, Wilmington
DAVIS JONES Laura *Pachulski Stang*, Wilmington
PERNICK Norman *Saul Ewing*, Wilmington
SUDELL William *Morris Nichols*, Wilmington

[3] CLARK Anthony *Skadden Arps*, Wilmington
DEHNEY Robert *Morris Nichols*, Wilmington
FATELL Bonnie *Blank Rome*, Wilmington
LANDIS Adam *Landis Rath*, Wilmington
SELBER SILVERSTEIN Laurie *Potter*, Wilmington
STRATTON David *Pepper Hamilton*, Wilmington

[4] BOWDEN William *Ashby & Geddes*, Wilmington
COUSINS Scott *Greenberg Traurig*, Wilmington
DEFRANCESCHI Daniel *Richards*, Wilmington
FELGER Mark *Cozen O'Connor*, Wilmington
FOURNIER David *Pepper Hamilton*, Wilmington
GWYNNE Kurt *Reed Smith*, Wilmington
KNIGHT John *Richards Layton*, Wilmington
MORGAN Pauline *Young Conaway*, Wilmington
SHANNON Brendan *Young Conaway*, Wilmington

Firms and individuals are listed alphabetically in each band.

Band 1

Skadden, Arps, Slate, Meagher & Flom LLP & Affiliates
See firm details p.1372

The Firm: *"Leading the pack,"* Skadden has developed a national practice in terms of both its depth of resources and the platform on which it represents clients. The vast majority of work is on the debtor side, although the group also has experience counseling creditors and acquirers of assets from troubled companies. Its involvement in countrywide proceedings such as its representation of RCN in its New York-based Chapter 11 action has meant that these attorneys are sometimes less visible in their home state. A further example of such geographic spread is advice to Verizon Capital in the USGen bankruptcy in Maryland. Clients praised the group for its *"competent and efficient manner"* and ability to *"move the case on with tenacity and a sense of purpose."* The specialist bankruptcy attorneys are supported by a respected commercial litigation team and lawyers with tax, banking, corporate and securities expertise.

The Lawyers: The widely respected **Gregg Galardi** (see p.353) is credited as a *"good field general,"* who *"can be aggressive, but is also a great bridge builder."* He has broad experience representing public and privately held companies in out-of-court restructurings and Chapter 11 reorganizations and assisting financial institutions in bankruptcy-related proceedings. **Mark Chehi** (see p.352) has *"really come into his own"* recently. He has been involved in a number of high-profile workout, restructuring and Chapter 11 proceedings and has a *"very effective, persistent but low-key approach to dealing with opposing counsel."* **Anthony Clark** (see p.352) heads the bankruptcy litigation practice in Wilmington. He is one of the best litigators in the state with his *"magnificent manner in court"* and vast experience in high-value cases. His practice is divided between bankruptcy and corporate litigation.

The Clients: The group acted for Hayes Lemmerz International in post-confirmation litigation and Gores Technology in proceedings following the proposed purchase of assets out of the Cable & Wireless bankruptcy. Other clients include RCN and Verizon Capital.

Young Conaway Stargatt & Taylor LLP
See firm details p.365

The Firm: This highly regarded Delaware firm has a large and long-established bankruptcy practice that is *"clearly top of the tree."* Interviewees praised the 33-strong group for its intelligence and ability to offer clients an impressive depth and breadth of expertise. The team principally represents debtors, acting for large clients such as Touch America Holdings, which it advised on its ability to provide services and collect receivables while in bankruptcy. The attorneys also have expertise in mass tort bankruptcy proceedings and in representing creditors and creditors' committees. For example, the group negotiated the first successful asbestos prepackaged bankruptcy, and serves as sole counsel to the Official Committee of Unsecured Creditors in the $3 billion reorganization of Trenwick America.

The Lawyers: Firm chairman **James Patton** (see p.356) has earned himself a fantastic reputation, particularly for his work in large asbestos bankruptcies such as Armstrong World Industries, Kaiser Aluminum and Babcock & Wilcox. He is widely respected for his sensitive handling of complex cases and is *"never fazed in the courtroom, because of this thorough preparation."* **Robert Brady** (see p.351) was widely recommended for his *"ability to build consensus and remain positive"* in contentious cases. He is chair of the bankruptcy and corporate restructuring group and *"has the depth of experience to quickly spot issues and effectively strategize."* **Pauline Morgan** (see p.355) has a *"terrific knowledge of the bankruptcy code"* and is *"very good on her feet."* **Brendan Shannon** (see p.357) has a great amount of experience representing corporate debtors and official committees in Chapter 11 proceedings.

The Clients: Clients include Touch America Holdings, Official Committee of Unsecured Creditors of Trenwick America and Official Committee of Unsecured Creditors of Polaroid.

Band 2

Morris, Nichols, Arsht & Tunnell
See firm details p.364

The Firm: This is a sizable Delaware-based outfit with a depth of bankruptcy experience that attracts national clients such as The Loewen Group, Fruehauf Trailer and USN Communications. The dynamic practice is particularly rated for its litigation prowess, displaying a strong combination of extensive subject matter expertise and sophisticated individual advocates who are both "*knowledgeable and creative.*" It continues to advise debtors' and unsecured creditors' committees and has seen a rise in individual creditor work over the past twelve months. The group continues to act as lead counsel for Orion Refining and has also been representing debtors Rouge Industries and AstroPower. It also undertakes co-counsel roles, a recent example of which was in the bankruptcy of Kentucky-based restaurant chain Gilligans.

The Lawyers: **William Sudell** (see p.358) is a first-rate and popular litigator, who possesses "*a great courtroom presence.*" His practice spans commercial litigation, bankruptcy and creditors' rights and he has represented Arthur Andersen. Another team member with respected bankruptcy and workout expertise is **Robert Dehney** (see p.352). "*He has an uncanny ability to spot issues that he can use to his clients' advantage,*" say sources.

The Clients: On the debtor side, clients include The Loewen Group; Fruehauf Trailer; USN Communications; Orion Refining; Rouge Industries and AstroPower. It has also advised unsecured creditors' committees in proceedings related to United Artists, Level Propane Gases and Steel Heddle.

Richards Layton & Finger

The Firm: This is an accomplished practice that continues to hold its own in this competitive market. Its impressive track record of representations and continued involvement in large cases speaks for itself. The team of 15 is considered "*knowledgeable, approachable and creative*" by market sources. It has one of the strongest local secured creditor practices representing high-profile clients such as JPMorgan Chase, Congress Financial, Bank of America and GE Capital. Attorneys are also experienced on the debtor side, recently having acted as lead counsel to Teleglobe Communications in its Chapter 11 proceedings. In this case, they worked close-

ly with Canadian lawyers on cross-border elements of the plan.

The Lawyers: **Mark Collins** is the head of the firm's restructuring and bankruptcy group. The "*gentlemanly attorney and great trial lawyer*" has a strong practice representing secured lenders. With a slightly more debtor-focused practice, **Daniel DeFranceschi** is a lawyer who "*knows his way around the code and the courtroom.*" He has experience in the telecom, natural resources and healthcare sectors. The "*terrific*" **John Knight** enters *Chambers*' tables this year following market endorsement of his technical expertise and sound judgment. "*He really understands what is best for his client in the long term.*"

The Clients: JPMorgan Chase; Congress Financial; Bank of America; GE Capital; Teleglobe Communications; USG; FINOVA Group and Armstrong World Industries.

Saul Ewing LLP
See firm details p.1561

The Firm: This firm distinguishes itself from others in the market through its diversity of practice and involvement in high-value, national cases. It is also one of the few with significant depth outside its Delaware office and a commitment not to act for national banks or major financial institutions. This pledge bolsters clients' claims that the group is a prime choice for debtor representation. In a keynote case from the past year, the group acted for a leading glass and material systems company in Chapter 11 proceedings that were precipitated by the company's mass tort liabilities. It also won a landmark case establishing the rights of a software licenser vis-à-vis a licensee in Chapter 11.

The Lawyers: **Norman Pernick** (see p.356) is the standout practitioner in this group. He has "*a good sense of what the court will do and how to maneuver in his clients' best interests.*" With specialist expertise as lead counsel to companies in Chapter 11, he has a "*strong sense of integrity, excellent communication skills*" and the ability to "*use his personality as a tool.*"

The Clients: The group represents debtors, secured and unsecured creditors, committees, trustees and landlords in sectors ranging across real estate, healthcare, insurance, retail and telecom.

Band 3

Pachulski, Stang, Ziehl, Young, Jones & Weintraub P.C.
See firm details p.296

The Firm: Although this relatively new group sometimes faces the perception that it is an outsider in this market, Pachulski is a renowned national bankruptcy boutique that fields attorneys who are "*every bit as good as the leading Delaware players.*" It has a busy debtor practice representing high-profile companies going through Chapter 11 and a lower profile but

equally adept creditors' committee offering. Where necessary, the group is able to draw on general commercial, ERISA and insurance litigation expertise from attorneys at the firm.

The Lawyers: **Laura Davis Jones'** (see p.352) sharp-shooting style may not be to everyone's taste, but she is "*one of the strongest debtor lawyers*" and someone "*who will do whatever it takes to protect her clients.*"

The Clients: Clients include Chapter 11 debtors in: Focal Communications; Superior TeleCom; WR Grace; American Tissue; Federal-Mogul Global and RBX. The firm has also represented the creditors' committees in Key3Media, FINOVA Group and Exodus Communications.

Pepper Hamilton LLP
See firm details p.1558

The Firm: "*Bright, effective and well prepared*" was how one interviewee described this national firm. The adroit group in the Delaware office represents debtors in Chapter 11, creditors' committees and parties buying assets out of bankruptcy. Following a successful year on all fronts, clients suggested that this team is "*a measure ahead.*" It remains counsel to Conectiv through the ongoing Enron dispute and advised the creditors' committee in the substantial Chapter 11 filing of a home decor retailer. Other notable representations include guiding the largest borrower through the bankruptcy of a healthcare financing company and a bank through the Cone Mills proceedings.

The Lawyers: The "*top-notch*" **David Stratton** (see p.357) was recommended to researchers for his healthy creditor practice. Peers report that they "*have no qualms about referring clients to him because of his wealth of experience*" and problem-solving skills. **David Fournier** (see p.353) is another "*terrific adviser,*" whose caseload features secured lending transactions, workout counseling and bankruptcy litigation.

The Clients: This group represents debtors, creditors' committees and parties buying assets out of bankruptcy in proceedings in the environmental, transportation, retail, healthcare and real estate sectors.

Potter Anderson & Corroon LLP

The Firm: This "*industrious and tenacious*" group of six focuses on creditor representation. In addition to handling Chapter 11 proceedings, it is well equipped to handle out-of-court restructurings and workouts, foreclosures on mortgages, state law receivership and secured transactions. Where necessary, the "*rational and responsible*" team is able to draw on further expertise from the firm's corporate, tax, ERISA and litigation teams. A keynote case from the past year was its representation of the creditors' committee in the St. Louis-based Aurora Foods reorganization proceedings.

The Lawyers: Laurie Selber Silverstein was praised as an attorney who is "*able to take on matters for creditors that are seemingly impossible, and solve them in a fashion that benefits the client.*"
The Clients: SBC Telecommunications; ConAgra; Fleet National Bank; CIBC; Bechtel Enterprises; Perot Systems and Norfolk Southern.

Band 4

Ashby & Geddes
See firm details p.359
The Firm: This is a "*compact and highly regarded*" regional group that has a diverse litigation and transactional practice representing debtors, official and unofficial creditors' committees and secured creditors and lenders. The team of nine won praise for its "*sheer level of involvement and immersion in the market.*" It advised the Chapter 11 trustee of Napster in the sale of the company's assets and confirmation of the liquidating plan. The firm also acted as co-counsel to the official committee of unsecured creditors in Kaiser Aluminum and to the debtors in Trenwick Group.
The Lawyers: According to market commentators, **William Bowden** is a "*masterly practitioner*" and a consummate professional.
The Clients: This group represents the whole range of clients including debtors, official and unofficial committees, secured creditors and lenders, bidders and purchasers of assets, and other parties in interest.

Greenberg Traurig LLP
See firm details p.564
The Firm: The small size of this Delaware outpost belies the depth of resources that the firm has at its disposal. The six dedicated attorneys provide a "*first-rate*" service to debtors' and creditors' committees in local and national bankruptcy proceedings, drawing on further expertise from the other offices of this global firm where required. Recent highlights include obtaining a structured dismissal for Reno-based MJ Research and counseling Florida Power & Light through bankruptcy proceedings in New York. The group also has cross-border expertise: this year it advised the world's largest steel manufacturer, Ispat Nova Hut, in the Chapter 11 of Kaiser Group.
The Lawyers: Lead partner **Scott Cousins** (see p.352) "*has tip-to-toe talent*" and a broad experience of all forms of workout and bankruptcy related litigation.
The Clients: The team represents multiple corporate debtors in some of the largest Chapter 11 cases in Delaware and elsewhere and acts as restructuring counsel for multiple entities with respect to their out-of-court restructuring efforts.

Landis Rath & Cobb LLP
The Firm: This bankruptcy and commercial litigation boutique is the "*new kid on the block,*" earning a name for itself as a "*dynamic practice.*" The office was opened in July 2003, by three young partners with experience counseling debtors, creditors and creditors' committees, lenders and asset acquirers in a variety of proceedings. The talented group advised the creditors' committees in the Arcadia Energy, AstroPower and Trend Holdings proceedings. It also assisted the lenders in the Just for Feet and Alliance Communications cases and advised major creditors of Coram Healthcare, Cable & Wireless and Budget Group.
The Lawyers: Interviewees recommended the "*very sharp and tenacious*" **Adam Landis** for his ability to guide parties through Chapter 11, particularly on the lender side. He can tailor his approach to the needs of the case and "*can be either aggressive or conciliatory in negotiations.*"
The Clients: Debtor representations include Blackstone Technology Group and Matlack. The group also represents creditors, lenders and other interested parties.

Morris, James, Hitchens & Williams LLP
See firm details p.363
The Firm: This smaller but highly capable group represents creditors, committees, purchasers and investors in bankruptcy proceedings ranging from reorganization and liquidation to out-of-court workouts and debt restructurings. The team of seven won praise from clients because of its local awareness: "*It knows the system, knows the law and knows opposing counsel.*" Attorneys here also have significant experience in preference and fraudulent conveyance actions, recently having represented the defendant in the Primary Health Systems proceedings.
The Lawyers: Chair of the bankruptcy group is Stephen Miller; he is a noticeable player on the Delaware circuit.
The Clients: The group acts on behalf of creditors, debtors, liquidating agents, creditors' committees and trustees.

The Bayard Firm
See firm details p.360
The Firm: This "*proficient, reliable and practical*" group works well as a team and is active in the midmarket. It predominantly advises debtors' and creditors' committees but also has expertise in discrete creditor and trustee representations. Recent debtor clients include Mobile Tool and Woodworkers Warehouse. It also counseled the equity committee in the reorganization proceedings of seismic data company Seitel. Attorneys here have developed niche expertise representing bank groups in asbestos cases and have been involved in large cases such as Owens Corning and WR Grace.
The Lawyers: Neil Glassman is firm chairman and head of the bankruptcy group.
The Clients: The firm has represented debtors such as Mobile Tool, Woodworkers Warehouse and AmeriKing and the committees in the Magnatrax and Exide Technologies proceedings.

Other Notable Practitioners
Bonnie Glantz Fatell (see p.353) at Blank Rome LLP is a knowledgeable attorney who has made a name for herself through her involvement in high-profile cases such as USGen and ANC Rental. She won plaudits from interviewees for her "*astute manner and first-rate problem-solving skills.*" **Mark Felger** at Cozen O'Connor is earning a strong reputation as a creditors' lawyer, who "*skillfully represents his clients' interests.*" At Reed Smith LLP, **Kurt Gwynne** is one of the market's rising stars. "*He is a brilliant courtroom advocate with terrific knowledge of the bankruptcy code,*" say peers.

CHANCERY AND COMMERCIAL LITIGATION

Band 1

Morris, Nichols, Arsht & Tunnell
See firm details p.364
The Firm: This is one of the state's largest chancery specialists with an "*indisputable*" level of success in the courtroom. Its impressive market share in Delaware marries with referrals from leading Wall Street firms to create a strong national client base. According to sources, the "*practical team provides excellent quality and value.*" Of its "*highly competent and reasonable*" attorneys, the majority work primarily within the Court of Chancery, while others routinely appear in the Superior and District Courts. The group offers acclaimed expertise in a range of specialties including breach of fiduciary, appraisal and special litigation committee cases. Recent highlights have included the granting of a summary judgment dismissing the claims of an $800 million derivative suit that alleged insider trading by the CEO and CFO of Oracle.
The Lawyers: Clients recommended **Gilchrist Sparks** (see p.357) for his "*authoritative judgment*" on critical matters – which is "*always absolutely bang-on.*" He adopts a team approach to the running of his cases and manages to draw

Delaware
Leading firms
(Chancery & Commercial Litigation)

[1] **MORRIS, NICHOLS, ARSHT & TUNNELL** *Wilmington*
RICHARDS LAYTON & FINGER *Wilmington*

[2] **POTTER ANDERSON & CORROON LLP** *Wilmington*
SKADDEN, ARPS, SLATE, MEAGHER *Wilmington*
YOUNG CONAWAY STARGATT *Wilmington*

[3] **ASHBY & GEDDES** *Wilmington*
BOUCHARD MARGULES *Wilmington*
GRANT & EISENHOFER PA *Wilmington*
MORRIS, JAMES, HITCHENS *Wilmington*

[4] **DUANE MORRIS LLP** *Wilmington*
GREENBERG TRAURIG LLP *Wilmington*
THE BAYARD FIRM *Wilmington*

Leading individuals
(Chancery & Commercial Litigation)

[1] **FINKELSTEIN Jesse** *Richards Layton, Wilmington*
SPARKS III A Gilchrist *Morris Nichols, Wilmington*

[2] **ALLINGHAM II Thomas** *Skadden Arps, Wilmington*
BALOTTI Franklin *Richards Layton, Wilmington*
MCBRIDE David *Young Conaway, Wilmington*
NACHBAR Kenneth *Morris Nichols, Wilmington*
PAYSON Robert *Potter Anderson, Wilmington*
SELBER SILVERSTEIN Laurie *Potter, Wilmington*
WALSH Jr Peter *Potter Anderson, Wilmington*
WOLFE Jr Donald *Potter Anderson, Wilmington*

[3] **BOUCHARD Andre** *Bouchard Margules, Wilmington*
CLARK Anthony *Skadden Arps, Wilmington*
EISENHOFER Jay *Grant & Eisenhofer, Wilmington*
GOLDMAN Michael *Potter Anderson, Wilmington*
LASTER J Travis *Richards Layton, Wilmington*
SILVERSTEIN Bruce *Young Conaway, Wilmington*
STONE Alan *Morris Nichols, Wilmington*
WILLIAMS Gregory *Richards Layton, Wilmington*

[4] **ABRAMS Kevin** *Richards Layton, Wilmington*
HEYMAN Kurt *The Bayard Firm, Wilmington*
JENKINS Stephen *Ashby & Geddes, Wilmington*
LAFFERTY William *Morris Nichols, Wilmington*
LAZARUS Lewis *Morris James, Wilmington*
MCNALLY Edward *Morris James, Wilmington*
REED John *Duane Morris, Wilmington*
REESE Cathy *Greenberg Traurig, Wilmington*
SAUNDERS Robert *Skadden Arps, Wilmington*
SHANNON Kevin *Potter Anderson, Wilmington*
WELCH Edward *Skadden Arps, Wilmington*

Firms and individuals are listed alphabetically in each band.

out the best from those around him. He is also widely respected for his *"very effective treatment"* of witnesses, both in and out of the courtroom. *"Well prepared and extremely focused,"* **Kenneth Nachbar** (see p.355) scoops plaudits for his teamwork and advocacy skills. According to sources, his style rejects *"histrionic acting"* in favor of *"straightforward communication,"* resulting in an *"excellent mastery of the case."* **Alan Stone** (see p.357) is respected for visibly *"fighting in the trenches."* Specialties include advising on valuation issues and proxy contests

where clients particularly value his negotiation skills. The *"brilliant"* **William Lafferty** (see p.354) was praised for the *"capable and approachable"* manner he employs in complex proceedings.

The Clients: Altria Group; Unocal; Viacom; Ford; Oracle and United Artists.

Richards Layton & Finger

The Firm: This well-established practice enjoys a reputation as one of the state's *"original and best"* legal outfits, with *"real strength from top to bottom."* Alongside its advice to local and regional clients, the team enjoys national recognition for its expertise in a range of litigation, arbitration and mediation matters. It regularly represents clients before the Delaware Supreme Court and has *"substantial experience"* in handling both defense and appellate matters. Its attorneys have served as members and chairpersons of the Court of Chancery and Superior Court Civil Rules Advisory Committees, which ensures that the group has an insight into the mechanics of the courts.

The Lawyers: *"Absolutely brilliant"* **Jesse Finkelstein** is rated by clients as one of the leading chancery specialists in Delaware. Valued as a well-rounded and extremely skilled practitioner, he fosters an *"intellectual point of view,"* which assists his clients in court. Due to his *"wealth of experience,"* **Franklin Balotti** has a deservedly high profile in the chancery arena. He is particularly noted for his ability to *"develop the strategy"* behind major cases. The *"talented"* **Gregory Williams** scooped plaudits as a relatively *"young but polished, smart and capable"* practitioner. *"Intellectual and smart,"* **Travis Laster** is tipped to become a significant player within the state. In particular, sources commended his academic performance and his professional enthusiasm, claiming: *"He just loves the law!"* **Kevin Abrams** is praised for his technical skill, and particularly noted for his ability to delegate work efficiently among his team.

The Clients: Goldman Sachs; Boeing; Lucent Technologies; Texas Instruments; ExxonMobil and Vivendi Universal.

Band 2

Potter Anderson & Corroon LLP

The Firm: This firm wins acclaim for punching above its weight as a relatively compact department with *"high-quality"* lawyers and success in attracting an impressive client list. With two litigation groups, its teams specialize in representing clients in the Court of Chancery and in Delaware's additional courts. Cases relating to corporate governance, fiduciary matters and M&A issues are handled by a specialized chancery group, which is particularly recommended for its work on hostile takeovers. It has recently represented Sony, alongside Dewey Bal-

lantine, in relation to its merger with MGM. It also continues to represent Disney in connection with its recent proxy litigation. Though the firm is typically trial-oriented, it also handles appellate matters.

The Lawyers: The *"outstanding"* **Robert Payson** attracts market acclaim as a talented chancery specialist, especially admired for his courtroom style. **Donald Wolfe** is an extremely able practitioner who has worked on a range of high-profile litigation matters. His *"exquisite advocacy skills"* have won him a following among peers and clients. Although best known for her bankruptcy practice, **Laurie Selber Silverstein** has impressed the market with her chancery skills. *"Deserving of high praise,"* **Peter Walsh** is recognized for his *"practical and reasonable"* approach to his clients' needs. **Michael Goldman** won plaudits for his strong technical knowledge. Market observers singled out **Kevin Shannon** as one of the firm's rising stars. He is commended for his *"excellent judgment"* and, in line with the whole group, adopts a practical and highly commercial approach to his cases.

The Clients: PeopleSoft; Disney; Barnes & Noble; Nextel; Deutsche Bank; CIBC and Butler Manufacturing.

Skadden, Arps, Slate, Meagher & Flom LLP & Affiliates

See firm details p.1372

The Firm: As a global player, this is *"one regional office that transcends the Delaware market,"* but remains committed to fielding chancery law expertise within the state. According to sources, attorneys at this practice command *"incredible respect"* from peers for the depth of their expertise. Clients value their local business knowledge and exposure to international resources. Close links to the New York office ensure a steady flow of cases, including involvement in some of the market's most interesting work. These attorneys also attract a healthy number of cases generated from within Delaware alone. In particular, the group is recommended for its work on federal securities cases alongside complex, contested matters including acquiring assets from troubled companies, and creditor-related litigation.

The Lawyers: The *"bright and articulate,"* **Thomas Allingham** (see p.351) is esteemed for possessing *"the whole package"* with both excellent trial skills and his thoughtful counseling. Sources admire his *"polished presence"* in the courtroom. *"Talented"* **Anthony Clark** (see p.352) utilizes his restructuring knowledge in a litigation capacity. Alongside Chapter 11 work, he specializes in troubled company-related litigation, including securities, class action and commercial contract disputes. **Robert Saunders** (see p.356) is tipped as *"one to watch"* in the commercial litigation field, due to his extensive legal acumen. **Edward Welch** (see p.358) is a widely respected corporate litigator, primarily

344   All quotes in the text are from interviews with clients and competitors.

CHAMBERS USA 2005

valued for his academic contribution to the field of corporate law.

The Clients: RCN; Hayes Lemmerz International; MacAndrews & Forbes Holdings; Tyson Foods; Compaq and Cantor Fitzgerald.

Young Conaway Stargatt & Taylor LLP

See firm details p.365

The Firm: This firm approaches the dispute resolution field with a combined corporate counseling and litigation practice group that places an emphasis on avoiding trials as well as the successful representation of clients in the Delaware courts. The commercial litigation team is well equipped to handle the prosecution and defense of contests for corporate control, going-private transactions and valuation disputes. Market observers commended the team's work on stockholders' and derivative litigation. It has continued to act for Michael Ovitz in litigation brought by stockholders of Disney.

The Lawyers: *"Extremely able"* **David McBride** (see p.355) is popular with clients and peers alike for his extensive chancery experience and ability to communicate complex issues to the layman. According to sources, he is a lawyer *"who you can always count on."* The *"creative and dynamic"* **Bruce Silverstein** (see p.357) is renowned for balancing his chancery expertise with esteemed plaintiff work. According to clients, he is a *"real team player"* who effectively utilizes legal strategy to cover *"every aspect of the case."*

The Clients: Revlon; Time Warner; QVC; Oracle and Omnicare.

Band 3

Ashby & Geddes

See firm details p.359

The Firm: Market sources have been impressed by this relatively small firm's recent performance on high-profile cases for national clients. The growing commercial litigation practice fosters lawyers, who frequently represent clients in the Delaware Court of Chancery, the US District Court for the District of Delaware, and the Bankruptcy Court for the District of Delaware. The group of experienced attorneys is well versed in business law matters across the region. Specialties include derivative and class action litigation, proxy contests, takeover battles and going-private transactions. Environmental matters and insurance coverage claims also form a significant portion of the workload.

The Lawyers: **Stephen Jenkins** utilizes his *"aggressive litigation skills"* to develop a reputation as one of the state's leading institutional stockholder attorneys.

The Clients: Hewlett-Packard; PeopleSoft; AIG and Telxon.

Bouchard Margules & Friedlander PA

The Firm: This *"terrific litigation firm"* has continued to expand its resources in the field of chancery and commercial litigation. Market commentators identified its *"hands-on, intensive"* service to clients, and high level of partner involvement in cases as its distinguishing strength. Key members of the state's *"up-and-coming crowd,"* its attorneys are *"all smart – you can't go wrong, whichever one you work with."* According to clients, the group has *"accomplished great things in a short time"* on large plaintiff settlements, making it a popular choice for conflict and referral work. Alongside class and derivative cases, the firm undertakes traditional defense representation in the Court of Chancery such as equitable claims and large corporate governance cases.

The Lawyers: *"Worthy opponent"* **Andre Bouchard** is recommended as a well-schooled trial lawyer, who wins plaudits for being *"reasonable and practical"* to deal with.

The Clients: Ford; McKesson; Disney and Liberty Mutual.

Grant & Eisenhofer PA

See firm details p.362

The Firm: This *"successful, young and hungry"* complex commercial litigation practice is well regarded for its success in the Court of Chancery. Its newly opened New York office has increased the firm's presence outside of the state and bolstered both the firm's resources and access to new clients. Its work in shareholder actions is particularly well regarded and the group houses *"leading institutional stockholder attorneys"* whose *"aggressive"* litigation skills serve clients well. The group also represents clients in property, employment, corporate and bankruptcy-related claims.

The Lawyers: *"Extremely bright"* **Jay Eisenhofer** (see p.352) is commended for his *"phenomenally successful track record,"* owing to his consistently strong courtroom performances.

The Clients: Florida State Board of Administration; New York City pension funds; California Public Employees' Retirement System (CalPERS); Alaska Permanent Fund; State of Wisconsin Investment Board; Oppenheimer-Funds; Capital Research and Management; Bastion Capital and ING Pilgrim Investments.

Morris, James, Hitchens & Williams LLP

See firm details p.363

The Firm: This firm has built a respected profile in the state, fielding teams dedicated to both business litigation and chancery work. Both groups have a strong focus on trial work, frequently appearing in jury trials at the Chancery, Superior and US District Courts. The caseload

here covers a range of matters, and the group is especially experienced in corporate and fiduciary litigation, and disputes relating to alternative entities. It has recently settled a major class action involving Edison Brothers Stores, and in another highlight, it settled a class action concerning Uni-Mart. It has also advised a major chemical company in a recent joint venture dispute.

The Lawyers: **Lewis Lazarus** (see p.354) is admired for his *"proven expertise"* in the corporate fiduciary field. **Edward McNally** (see p.355) balances his time between corporate advice and business litigation. He wins plaudits for his *"formidable performance"* in the courtroom, say sources.

The Clients: Garden Ridge; Union Financial Group; University of Delaware; DuPont; Uni-Mart and Edison Brothers Stores.

Band 4

Duane Morris LLP

See firm details p.1550

The Firm: This national outfit has continued to develop its litigation practice through a number of strategic hires. While considered *"small but effective,"* interviewees do not fail to recognize the experience and courtroom skills of its litigators. Attorneys here act as lead counsel for a number of prominent businesses within Delaware, as well as acting as local counsel for out-of-state firms. While the group undertakes work in the Court of Chancery, it is also renowned for its corporate litigation expertise. This includes the defense of company directors, and the representation of large stockholders and former chairmen. In a recent highlight, the group represented LNR Property in several consolidated class actions brought to enjoin the sale of LNR to Riley Property Holdings.

The Lawyers: **John Reed** (see p.356) is noted for his *"warm presentation"* and robust litigation style. Clients value his *"strong credentials,"* including experience *"on the other side of the fence"* in his previous work as state prosecutor.

The Clients: Deephaven Capital Management; Merrill Lynch; JPMorgan Chase; Getty Petroleum; Amkor Technology and Tiffany & Co.

Greenberg Traurig LLP

See firm details p.564

The Firm: The *"developing, business-oriented"* Delaware branch of this national firm is rated for the breadth of its litigation practice. Attorneys here frequently act for corporations, directors and shareholders in both the Delaware Court of Chancery and the US District Court. Its areas of expertise include corporate governance and securities disputes, and the group has recently seen an increase in the representation of companies and major shareholders involved in going-private transactions. Of late, the team has been involved in overturning a billion-dollar judgment against clients in the tobacco industry, and also represented the Catholic Church in a case concerning allegations of abuse by priests.

The Lawyers: Interviewees endorsed **Cathy Reese** (see p.356) as a *"well-known face"* in the commercial litigation field and a technically astute and client-focused attorney.

The Clients: P&C Bank; SportsLine.com; Lipton; Wal-Mart; Wilmington Trust and St. Francis Hospital.

The Bayard Firm
See firm details p.360

The Firm: This firm garnered praise for its expertise across a spectrum of commercial issues in the Delaware Court of Chancery. Corporate governance cases, including corporate election disputes, derivative actions and breaches of fiduciary duty are all to be found in the firm's recent portfolio. For example, attorneys recently obtained a dismissal of the claims against Wilmington Trust and Cenlar FSB in an

action alleging that they had negligently released insurance proceeds to a contractor performing reconstruction on a property destroyed by fire. The team is also experienced in federal securities litigation and indemnification cases.

The Lawyers: *"Proactive and always available,"* **Kurt Heyman** (see p.354) is valued for his litigation and transactional experience. In particular, sources appreciate his capacity to *"hold the hand"* of clients in order to guide them through the technical complexities.

CORPORATE/M&A

Delaware
Leading firms (Corporate/M&A)

[1]	**MORRIS, NICHOLS, ARSHT & TUNNELL** *Wilmington*
	RICHARDS LAYTON & FINGER *Wilmington*
[2]	**POTTER ANDERSON & CORROON LLP** *Wilmington*
	SKADDEN, ARPS, SLATE, MEAGHER *Wilmington*
[3]	**MORRIS, JAMES, HITCHENS** *Wilmington*
	PRICKETT, JONES & ELLIOTT PA *Wilmington*
	YOUNG CONAWAY STARGATT *Wilmington*

Leading individuals (Corporate/M&A)

★	**BLACK Lewis** *Morris Nichols, Wilmington*
[1]	**ALEXANDER Frederick** *Morris Nichols, Wilmington*
	BUSSARD Donald *Richards Layton, Wilmington*
[2]	**BALOTTI Franklin** *Richards Layton, Wilmington*
	FINKELSTEIN Jesse *Richards Layton, Wilmington*
	JOHNSTON John *Morris Nichols, Wilmington*
	SPARKS III A Gilchrist *Morris Nichols, Wilmington*
[3]	**ALTMAN Paul** *Richards Layton, Wilmington*
	EASTON Richard *Skadden Arps, Wilmington*
	GENTILE Mark *Richards Layton, Wilmington*
	GOLDMAN Michael *Potter Anderson, Wilmington*
	HERING Louis *Morris Nichols, Wilmington*
	MCBRIDE David *Young Conaway, Wilmington*
	MULLEN Thomas *Prickett Jones, Wilmington*
	O'TOOLE Matthew *Morris James, Wilmington*
	PINCUS Robert *Skadden Arps, Wilmington*
	SMALL John *Prickett Jones, Wilmington*
	SYMONDS Robert *Morris James, Wilmington*
	TUTHILL Walter *Morris Nichols, Wilmington*
	WAXMAN Scott *Potter Anderson, Wilmington*

Firms and individuals are listed alphabetically in each band.

Band 1

Morris, Nichols, Arsht & Tunnell
See firm details p.364

The Firm: This excellent firm comes highly recommended for the top-quality corporate advice provided by a *"well-seasoned"* team that displays the *"personal touch and great client service."* Clients noted a sense of camaraderie within the corporate law group, and endorsed its extensive knowledge of issues relating to Delaware gener-

al corporation law. Close ties to the corporate litigation department have led clients to view this firm as a one-stop shop for both transactional matters and dispute resolution. While the firm is renowned for its expertise in the field of alternative entities, it also specializes in public company M&A work, spin-offs and financings. In addition, clients note the firm's ability to handle private equity and corporate governance issues. Attorneys counsel commercial boards, particularly in relation to takeovers and going-private transactions.

The Lawyers: *"Long-time expert"* **Lewis Black** (see p.351) is esteemed as *"a practical guy with a big presence"* in the state. According to one client: *"If you have him on your side you can't do much better."* *"Extremely practical"* **Frederick Alexander** (see p.351) was praised for his *"expert advice"* in the M&A field. Clients particularly appreciate his speedy responses and attention to their needs. Experienced **Gilchrist Sparks** (see p.357) possesses a *"very deep base of knowledge"* of local corporate issues. With *"excellent contacts in legislature,"* he is admired for his thorough preparation and ability to *"predict likely outcomes in court."* **John Johnston** (see p.354) is a leading adviser for pure corporate matters and those day-to-day issues facing clients with transactions in Delaware. *"Outstanding"* **Louis Hering** (see p.353) is recommended for his work on alternative entities, a field in which **Walter Tuthill** (see p.358) has also cultivated a strong reputation.

The Clients: Colgate-Palmolive; Interactive Corporation; Viacom; Ford and Coca-Cola.

Richards Layton & Finger

The Firm: This well-established firm has a long history within the state. Sources commended the group as *"top class"* both in its ability to attract a volume of mandates and the value and complexity of its transactions, which are often national in scope. A breadth of expertise is on offer here and the team is widely respected for its work in the securities arena. Alongside its deal expertise, the group advises on corporate governance matters relating to the fiduciary duties of directors and shareholders.

The Lawyers: **Donald Bussard**, dubbed one of the best deal-oriented attorneys in the state, adopts a *"reasonable, practical and thorough,"* approach that clients rate highly. They also appreciate his dedication in keeping them informed throughout legal proceedings. *"Excellent adviser"* **Jesse Finkelstein** displays an expertise and technical ability within the corporate field that has won him a following among both clients and peers. **Franklin Balotti**'s practice encompasses both corporate litigation and advisory work, while the *"thoughtful"* **Paul Altman** is a popular port of call for corporate structuring and issues relating to alternative entities due to his broad knowledge. *"Experienced"* **Mark Gentile** enjoys a prominent reputation within the state for his smooth handling of transactions.

The Clients: Toronto-Dominion Bank; Disney; Oracle and Univision Communications.

Band 2

Potter Anderson & Corroon LLP

The Firm: Interviewees identified the growing presence of this group in the market following involvement in some key transactions. The corporate and commercial practice is home to *"excellent and talented"* attorneys, whose range of experience includes M&A, asset sales and recapitalizations. The group also counsels a wide range of corporations within Delaware on issues of corporate governance. Among its recent highlights, the firm has acted for PeopleSoft in its merger with Oracle and advised Sony on its acquisition of MGM.

The Lawyers: **Michael Goldman** practices in both the corporate law and litigation spheres. He is praised for his understanding of issues affecting Delaware business entities. *"Knowledgeable"* **Scott Waxman** is said to be *"a master in his field"* and a *"terrifically hard worker."* Popular among peers and clients, he is rated for his technical accuracy and commitment to client needs.

The Clients: PeopleSoft; Sony; DuPont; Alaris Medical Systems; Charter One; US Oncology; Griffin and Qwest.

Skadden, Arps, Slate, Meagher & Flom LLP & Affiliates
See firm details p.1372
The Firm: This giant of an international law firm is perceived by the market as "*a different animal*" to other players in Delaware, but it maintains an active client base within the state and continues to attract new clients. Its access to global resources is highly prized by Delaware business entities with multijurisdictional legal needs. The Wilmington office works closely with attorneys in New York and is particularly recommended for its expertise in handling alternative entities work.
The Lawyers: "*Savvy and well connected,*" **Richard Easton** (see p.352) is one of the state's leading deal lawyers, and valued by clients for his skill on a range of company formations and transactions. "*Practical*" **Robert Pincus** (see p.356) continues to be commended for his expertise on restructuring and financial services work.
The Clients: Concord EFS; Polaroid; Cendant and Hayes Lemmerz International.

Band 3

Morris, James, Hitchens & Williams LLP
See firm details p.363
The Firm: This firm has secured a highly credible reputation for its work in the corporate sphere, in which a variety of advisory and transactional services are offered to business clients

across the state. Alternative entities work is one of the group's major strengths and it fields one of Delaware's largest dedicated teams in this sector. The experienced group frequently carries out work on structured finance, M&A and joint ventures for clients, who are regional, national and global in nature. It has recently advised a large multinational mortgage lender in a structured lending program.
The Lawyers: "*Creative and responsive,*" **Matthew O'Toole** (see p.356) is a "*problem solver*" who is highly valued for his substantial level of experience in the corporate arena. The market rates **Robert Symonds** (see p.358) as a "*thorough and knowledgeable*" transactional lawyer.
The Clients: The firm's clients include corporations, limited and general partnerships, limited liability companies and statutory trusts.

Prickett, Jones & Elliott PA
The Firm: While this firm continues to be primarily associated with litigation work in Delaware, its transactional expertise is becoming more widely recognized by the market. Many of its esteemed attorneys divide their practice between litigation and corporate work. M&A and corporate governance advice relating to Delaware law are key areas of practice and the team is respected for its activity within the financial investment sphere. Interviewees also admired the group's experience in structured finance, such as securitizations, and insurance-related issues.

The Lawyers: **John Small** possesses a "*broad-based understanding*" of corporate governance matters. A popular port of call for referrals, he is "*one of the few people in Delaware who has real insurance expertise,*" and is also valued by clients for his sound commercial judgment. "*Outstanding, practical adviser*" **Thomas Mullen** is commended for his work in corporate law and issues facing alternative entities.
The Clients: EDS; CSFB; Dell and Computer Associates.

Young Conaway Stargatt & Taylor LLP
See firm details p.365
The Firm: This large commercial firm has had success in attracting a variety of regional, national and international clients. Its corporate counseling and litigation department is well equipped to handle a range of transactions, both public and privately financed as well as assisting on general commercial advisory issues. Some of the department's most prominent work has involved landmark corporate disputes in the Delaware Supreme Court.
The Lawyers: Highly esteemed by market observers, "*superb*" **David McBride** (see p.355) specializes in both litigation and transactional work for a variety of corporate clients across the state and beyond.
The Clients: The client base includes corporations, directors, officers, stockholders and other law firms locally, nationally and internationally.

EMPLOYMENT

MAINLY DEFENDANT

Delaware
Leading firms
(Employment: Mainly Defendant)
[1]	**YOUNG CONAWAY STARGATT** *Wilmington*
[2]	**POTTER ANDERSON & CORROON LLP** *Wilmington*
[3]	**MORRIS, JAMES, HITCHENS** *Wilmington*

Leading individuals
(Employment: Mainly Defendant)
[1]	**SANDLER Sheldon** *Young Conaway, Wilmington*
[2]	**MCDONOUGH Kathleen** *Potter Anderson, Wilmington*
	WILLOUGHBY Barry *Young Conaway, Wilmington*
[3]	**BOWSER William** *Young Conaway, Wilmington*
	WILLIAMS David *Morris James, Wilmington*

Up-and-coming individuals
HOLT Scott *Young Conaway, Wilmington*

Firms and individuals are listed alphabetically in each band.

Band 1

Young Conaway Stargatt & Taylor LLP
See firm details p.365
The Firm: Heralded as the state leader for employment, this firm is home to Delaware's largest employment and labor law practice. The team has expanded to embrace a new discrimination specialist and totals eight full-time attorneys, with an additional support provided by an employee benefits adviser. Clients admire the team approach: "*They all have the same knack for providing practical advice and boiling an issue down to its essence.*" The broad-based practice spans all forms of management-side representation. The trend for class actions is fully represented here, and the group has seen an increase in proceedings before the EEOC, where discrimination issues loom large. The firm's high-quality advisory practice tends to focus on management protocol and also provides training in a wide range of workplace matters. Clients also look to the firm for traditional labor advice,

including union avoidance, collective bargaining and arbitration.
The Lawyers: "*Straightforward, prompt and practical,*" **Sheldon Sandler** (see p.356) is a distinguished lawyer with more than 30 years of experience under his belt. Clients also pointed to his ability to advise on any issue thrown at him. His recent caseload has included defending retail giant Rite Aid in EEOC proceedings. A good people's person, **Barry Willoughby** (see p.358) chairs the employment law department and is adept at "*getting the firm's name into the community.*" He successfully defended his client in the widely reported case of Michele Curay-Cramer v Ursuline Academy, where the plaintiff filed charges tantamount to gender discrimination following her dismissal from a Catholic independent school for signing a pro-choice advertisement. He successfully defended Procter & Gamble against allegations of race discrimination. The "*knowledgeable*" **William Bowser** (see p.351) is another popular choice for employment discrimination, wrongful termination and whistle-blowing suits. He also repre-

sents employers in collective bargaining and administrative proceedings before the NLRB. Newcomer to the list, **Scott Holt** (see p.354) was made partner in 2004. He has impressed market sources with his sensible approach to litigation, and his recent cases include wage and hour suits.

The Clients: High-profile clients include MBNA; Ciba Specialty Chemicals; ING and Procter & Gamble.

Band 2

Potter Anderson & Corroon LLP

The Firm: This full-service firm offers employment counseling and litigation avoidance strategies to a healthy base of national and multinational clients. As a reflection of the struggling economy the firm has built up experience in downsizing, with an emphasis on outsourcing organizational functions for clients. Attorneys also handle high-stakes employment defense litigation: recent successes include a multijurisdictional trade secrets case. Other strengths lie in traditional labor work, where the team represents clients with respect to union issues such as collective bargaining, union grievances, and unfair labor practices. The firm is also equipped to advise on benefits and ERISA-related matters.

The Lawyers: An adviser with a *"keen head for business"* **Kathleen Furey McDonough** is the founder and head of the firm's labor and employment department. Rated by peers as a *"highly knowledgeable"* practitioner, she is skilled in both litigation avoidance and courtroom proceedings.

The Clients: DuPont, Hercules and Bristol-Myers Squibb are all clients of this labor and employment practice.

Band 3

Morris, James, Hitchens & Williams LLP

See firm details p.363

The Firm: This firm is well regarded for its capacity to handle a variety of employment-related litigation. The three-attorney team is experienced in discrimination cases, wrongful discharge, affirmative action and ERISA litigation. Other activities include negotiating collective bargaining agreements, and representing employers in arbitration hearings. The firm also provides on-site training on employment matters for clients. Although the firm typically represents institutional clients, it also acts on behalf of individuals, which some sources feel gives the group an understanding of how to run cases smoothly.

The Lawyers: Winning acclaim for his public sector practice, **David Williams** (see p.358) is identified as one of Delaware's leading employment lawyers. He continues to represent the State of Delaware against a DOJ action relating to cognitive tests given to the police. His practice extends to encompass governmental relations and education.

The Clients: The team represents municipalities and numerous school districts.

INTELLECTUAL PROPERTY

Delaware
Leading firms (Intellectual Property)

1	MORRIS, NICHOLS, ARSHT & TUNNELL *Wilmington*
2	CONNOLLY BOVE LODGE & HUTZ LLP *Wilmington*
	FISH & RICHARDSON *Wilmington*
3	ASHBY & GEDDES *Wilmington*
	POTTER ANDERSON & CORROON LLP *Wilmington*
	RICHARDS LAYTON & FINGER *Wilmington*
	YOUNG CONAWAY STARGATT *Wilmington*

Leading individuals
(Intellectual Property)

1	BLUMENFELD Jack *Morris Nichols*, Wilmington
2	HUTZ Rudolf *Connolly Bove*, Wilmington
	MARSDEN William *Fish & Richardson*, Wilmington
3	CONNOLLY Arthur *Connolly Bove*, Wilmington
	GEIGER Kathleen *Potter Anderson*, Wilmington
	GRAHAM Mary *Morris Nichols*, Wilmington
	HORWITZ Richard *Potter Anderson*, Wilmington
	NOREIKA Maryellen *Morris Nichols*, Wilmington
	SHAW John *Young Conaway*, Wilmington
4	BALICK Steven *Ashby & Geddes*, Wilmington
	COTTRELL III Frederick *Richards Layton*, Wilmington
	INGERSOLL Josy *Young Conaway*, Wilmington
	ROVNER Philip *Potter Anderson*, Wilmington

Up-and-coming individuals

	LOUDEN Karen *Morris Nichols*, Wilmington

Firms and individuals are listed alphabetically in each band.

Band 1

Morris, Nichols, Arsht & Tunnell

See firm details p.364

The Firm: This outstanding full-service firm is widely regarded as the home of the state's preeminent IP practice. Clients speak highly of the team's ability to handle technically complex patent litigation with ease and to *"argue effectively in court."* The group is experienced in representing both patent holders and alleged infringers, acting as both first chair and state counsel. It also represents clients on matters relating to trademarks and trade secrets. Particularly recommended for its expertise in the pharmaceutical and electronics fields, the team has recently acted for Paulcom in a case against Texas Instruments. Its practice crosses state lines, and a recent case has taken the firm to the New Jersey, New York and Pennsylvania courtrooms. In this event, the team represented Pfizer in a series of patent infringement suits against Par Pharmaceutical concerning the use of generic glaucoma medicine.

The Lawyers: *"Superb trial lawyer"* **Jack Blumenfeld** (see p.351) is highly regarded within the state for his *"unique skill set."* According to sources, he is particularly skilled at *"taking complex chemical concepts and making them understandable"* to the court. He is also respected for his *"tremendous work ethic"* and thorough preparation. The *"highly capable and very smart"* **Mary Graham** (see p.353) is recommended for fostering a terrific understanding of the law and for her ability to offer *"exceptionally practical"* advice. *"Talented"* **Maryellen Noreika** (see p.355) is a *"tenacious litigator"* in the IP field, an accolade largely attributed to her *"great grasp of technical matters."* She is highly responsive and, according to both clients and peers, a delight to work with. Up-and-coming **Karen Jacobs Louden** (see p.355) has impressed with her advocacy skills and detailed preparation. She is tipped to *"blossom"* with further experience.

The Clients: Pfizer; AstraZenca; QUALCOMM; Merck and AT&T Wireless.

Band 2

Connolly Bove Lodge & Hutz LLP

See firm details p.361

The Firm: This well-established firm is widely regarded as a major IP player within the state and beyond. Known for the volume of its lead counsel work, the team is also recommended by clients for its *"accomplished"* first-chair role within patent infringement cases. Supported by an additional office in Washington, DC, the IP group offers expertise in both patent litigation and patent prosecution, alongside trademark applications. Additional specialties include copyright, trademark and trade secrets litigation. Its *"bright, capable"* attorneys *"know the intricacies of technology issues"* and understand the needs of their client base extremely well.

The Lawyers: *"Seasoned"* attorney **Rudolf Hutz**

(see p.354) has *probably the most first-chair experience of any Delaware patent lawyer,* sources reported. Clients rate him as a *tough litigator,* who is focused on the representation of his clients' interests. *Gentlemanly attorney* **Arthur Connolly** (see p.352) has cultivated a long track record as an IP litigator within the state and brings to his cases a wealth of experience.
The Clients: Pfizer; IBM; Colgate-Palmolive; Philip Morris; Steelcase and Bayer.

Fish & Richardson
The Firm: The Delaware branch of this firm continues to develop within the state, supported by a well established, national reputation for its IP expertise. With a focus on high-end, hi-tech patent litigation, the team has recently advised Chi Mei Optoelectronics, a Taiwanese manufacturer of LCD screens, on its IP issues. A growing team, which consists of technical experts in physics, chemistry and engineering, enables it to represent clients in patent prosecution as well as litigation. The department also offers general patent counseling and IP-related business advice.
The Lawyers: The *reliable and trusted* **William Marsden** is recommended for his application of common sense to the legal profession. Sources rate his ability as a lead counsel on complex, technical cases.
The Clients: Clients include Chi Mei Optoelectronics, Ciena and Genzyme.

Band 3

Ashby & Geddes
See firm details p.359
The Firm: This well-respected firm is one of Delaware's prominent litigation players and as such is a popular port of call for those clients with IP and patent litigation issues. The group enjoys a good reputation within the state and frequently represents major clients in patent disputes before the US District Court for the Dis-

trict of Delaware. It also offers general IP advice, which includes trademark work, to a range of clients as both local adviser and Delaware counsel.
The Lawyers: **Steven Balick** is the firm's leading patent lawyer. He wins plaudits for his experience as local counsel and for his *great technical understanding* of the intellectual property field.
The Clients: A range of companies, including hi-tech entities, requiring IP advice or representation within the state.

Potter Anderson & Corroon LLP
The Firm: This firm is one of Delaware's prominent commercial litigation players and as a result, its IP litigation team also maintains a strong reputation within the state. Particularly admired for its patent infringement expertise, the group frequently represents major clients in IP disputes within Delaware. It also offers general advice on trademark and copyright matters.
The Lawyers: *Seasoned trial lawyer* **Richard Horwitz** is well respected as a patent litigator who brings *breadth of knowledge* to his practice. He also represents clients on general commercial and chancery matters. **Kathleen Geiger** is well regarded for her expertise as a patent prosecutor with substantial experience of working in the biotech field. *Quintessential trial lawyer* **Philip Rovner** also wins praise for his *excellent brief writing.* He also impresses sources in the courtroom where he is *aggressive on behalf of his clients – he really goes for the jugular!*
The Clients: DuPont, Hercules Chemical and Baxter feature in the firm's client roster.

Richards Layton & Finger
The Firm: This firm has developed an established IP practice, which is especially recommended for its work on complex patent litigation. While primarily associated with defense work, the team also acts for clients on the plaintiff side and is noted for its work within the hi-tech, biotech and pharmaceutical

fields. Additional areas of expertise include trademark and copyright prosecution, alongside general IP-related business advice.
The Lawyers: *Proactive* **Frederick Cottrell** wins plaudits for his local work as leading counsel. According to sources, his significant involvement as the partner leading a case *adds real value.*
The Clients: Clients include Novo Nordisk, St. Clair Intellectual Property Consultants and Safety 1st.

Young Conaway Stargatt & Taylor LLP
See firm details p.365
The Firm: This firm is admired for its trial work and is renowned for its ability to assist law firms outside of the region with IP work within the state. It regularly appears in the Delaware District Court and offers expertise in patent matters, alongside work on trademarks and trade secrets. According to market observers, patent litigation is the group's real forte as its attorneys are *among the best commercial litigators in the state.* The team also interfaces with other departments at the firm, particularly the corporate team, to offer clients general business counseling advice.
The Lawyers: **John Shaw** (see p.357) is *very good on his feet* and *well respected by the judges,* according to observers. He is rated as an attorney who *shows real promise and can take on the market,* especially impressing with his engineering background. Sources particularly value **Josy Ingersoll**'s (see p.354) involvement in patent cases and rate her thoughtful counseling skills.
The Clients: This firm regularly assists out-of-state law firms with its representation of IP clients. Its clients are drawn from a range of industry sectors including telecom, biotech, hardware and software, and pharmaceuticals.

REAL ESTATE

Delaware	
Leading firms (Real Estate)	
1	RICHARDS LAYTON & FINGER *Wilmington*
	YOUNG CONAWAY STARGATT *Wilmington*
2	KLETT ROONEY LIEBER & SCHORLING *Wilmington*
	MORRIS, JAMES, HITCHENS *Wilmington*
	MORRIS, NICHOLS, ARSHT & TUNNELL *Wilmington*
	SAUL EWING LLP *Wilmington*
Firms are listed alphabetically in each band.	

Band 1

Richards Layton & Finger
The Firm: Clients provided favorable reviews of this experienced real estate team, endorsing its *positive approach to the practice of law.* Five attorneys concentrate full time on real estate matters with an emphasis on transactional work. The practice spans a wide range of commercial real estate activities from acquisitions, leasing and sales to land use issues. The firm has successfully attracted a raft of national clients on both residential and commercial development projects, a trend that has been on the rise in the

last year. In the land use sphere, the group is well equipped to handle permitting, zoning and advice related to environmental regulation. A further string to its bow is the representation of lenders and borrowers in real estate financing.
The Lawyers: **Robert Krapf** is widely admired for his experience of high-end matters: *In terms of technical expertise it doesn't get any better than Krapf,* clients say. A *highly professional, efficient and practical lawyer,* he shoulders a broad and varied workload. His highly respected partner **Daniel Kristol** enjoys an equally diverse practice. Described as *the dean of the real estate Bar* he brings years of experience to the table. Chair-

Delaware
Leading individuals (Real Estate)

1. **KRAPF Robert** *Richards Layton*, Wilmington
2. **DIPRINZIO Eugene** *Young Conaway*, Wilmington
   ISKEN Donald *Morris Nichols*, Wilmington
3. **BERGER Benjamin** *Blank Rome*, Wilmington
   GEE William *Saul Ewing*, Wilmington
   KLEIN Daniel *Richards Layton*, Wilmington
   KRISTOL Daniel *Richards Layton*, Wilmington
   LAMB Christopher *Pepper Hamilton*, Wilmington
   LEVINE Richard *Young Conaway*, Wilmington
   LISICKY Joseph *Morris James*, Wilmington

Leading individuals
(Real Estate: Zoning/Land Use)

1. **GOODMAN Lisa** *Young Conaway*, Wilmington
   STABLER Wendie *Saul Ewing*, Wilmington
2. **FORSTEN Richard** *Klett Rooney*, Wilmington
   MANNING William *Klett Rooney*, Wilmington
   PARADEE John *Prickett Jones*, Wilmington
   SCOTT Pamela *Saul Ewing*, Wilmington
   TARABICOS Larry *Young Conaway*, Wilmington

Individuals are listed alphabetically in each band.

man of the real estate group, **Daniel Klein** is an *"imaginative"* adviser, who is skilled in negotiations. Described by clients as a *"detail-oriented practitioner,"* he specializes in complex business transactions and in public-private joint ventures. **The Clients:** Clients are varied and include: landlords; tenants; lenders; borrowers; title insurance companies and developers.

Young Conaway Stargatt & Taylor LLP
See firm details p.365
The Firm: This successful firm is home to the largest number of dedicated real estate attorneys in the state, who win plaudits for their *"down-to-earth"* approach. The department incorporates the firm's banking law practice to provide clients with a full range of services tailored toward real estate acquisition, development, financing and disposition. Its preeminent land use team has also won the respect of the market. Expertise lies in affordable housing projects and local development projects for national clients.
The Lawyers: *"Results-oriented,"* **Eugene DiPrinzio** (see p.352) wins high praise from clients for his *"can-do attitude."* His forte lies in acting for banks and other financial institutions in asset-based lending and commercial mortgage loans. **Richard Levine** (see p.355) has a sophisticated understanding of business transactions and structured finance, which he puts to use in his general real estate practice. Interviewees rave about *"highly accomplished land use lawyer,"* **Lisa Goodman** (see p.353), who advises in the areas of zoning, sewer and traffic capacity, and code compliance. Clients single her out for her technical skill and her ability to *"get the*

job done." **Larry Tarabicos** (see p.358) is similarly well practiced in this area with extensive experience in commercial real estate, zoning and land development.
The Clients: Developers, banks and other financial institutions and insurance companies.

Band 2

Klett Rooney Lieber & Schorling
See firm details p.1555
The Firm: This firm is best known for its expertise in land use matters. The three-attorney team is well equipped to work on large-scale zoning and development projects; it also handles land use litigation. The busy practice extends beyond this to include commercial, residential and financing matters, where acquisitions, dispositions and leasing are high on the agenda. Recent projects include obtaining subdivision approval on behalf of a client for the development of a multiunit golf course community. The firm continues to represent clients involved in the Parkside residential scheme in Middleton, Delaware, and the Brandywine Town Center rezoning project.
The Lawyers: *"Hands-on"* practitioner, **Richard Forsten** is highly thought of in the areas of land use and related litigation. He is a technically minded attorney who is *"extremely well respected for his long experience."* **William Manning** enjoys a reputation as a *"statesman,"* and is a senior shareholder in the firm's Wilmington office. His practice encompasses land use regulation, government affairs and general business transactions.
The Clients: Clients include developers, owners, lenders and other businesses.

Morris, James, Hitchens & Williams LLP
See firm details p.363
The Firm: This well-established firm enjoys a long history in the state for offering real estate expertise across a spectrum of client needs. Representing a host of major developers, investors and builders, the team advises on a range of transactions. Particular specialties include advising lenders and borrowers on real estate financings including construction-related costs as well as acquisition and asset-based financings. The team also advises clients on leasing, zoning, subdivision and other land use matters.
The Lawyers: **Joseph Lisicky** (see p.355) is respected for his real estate transactional work within the state and beyond. He is particularly admired for his work on acquisitions and sales where he promotes a *"calm presence"* and displays strong technical expertise.
The Clients: Clients include The Buccini/Pollin Group and Harvey Development.

Morris, Nichols, Arsht & Tunnell
See firm details p.364
The Firm: This firm represents both institutional and entrepreneurial clients on a range of financing and development work within the state. With a reputation for representing both local and national clients, it has recently represented Shell in its sale of a refinery located in Delaware City. The team works closely with other commercial attorneys at the firm when necessary, and its prominence in land use rests alongside its transactional expertise. It has recently worked on the development of a medical institution, owned by a consortium of doctors specializing in neurological disorders.
The Lawyers: **Donald Isken** (see p.354) is credited as the driving force behind this real estate department. His role as an *"excellent real estate generalist"* within the state is attributed to his broad commercial experience.
The Clients: GE Capital; JPMorgan Chase; Shell; Delaware River & Bay Authority and Port of Wilmington.

Saul Ewing LLP
See firm details p.1561
The Firm: This firm is renowned for its work in the real estate field, with well-regarded expertise on both transactional and development issues. It regularly acts for borrowers and lenders in a range of real estate finance transactions, and has developed particular expertise on commercial leasings and acquisitions. Regular work on development issues includes rezonings and variances. It is also noted for its skill at obtaining approval for development plans.
The Lawyers: *"First-class"* practitioner **Wendie Stabler** (see p.357) is recommended as an attorney whose practice is *"devoted"* to land use and zoning work. She also offers general real estate advice to clients. Recommended by clients and peers alike, **Pamela Scott** (see p.357) is ranked *"among the best in the state"* for land use matters. **William Gee** (see p.353) is a *"sophisticated adviser on real estate developments,"* and is noted as a *"practical, objective and thorough attorney"* who can keep the bigger picture in mind.
The Clients: Conectiv; Wawa; AT&T Wireless; The Welfare Foundation; Wilmington College and AstraZeneca.

Other Notable Practitioners
"Well-seasoned" practitioner **John Paradee** at Prickett, Jones & Elliott PA is commended for his experience in land use law. With a background in commercial law, he combines this specialty with his transactional practice and can often be found handling residential real estate matters. **Benjamin Berger** (see p.351) of Blank Rome LLP typically represents local developers in commercial, residential and recreational projects. The firm acted for Invista in connection with the relocation of the company's headquar-

350   All quotes in the text are from interviews with clients and competitors.

CHAMBERS USA 2005

ters to Delaware. At Pepper Hamilton LLP, **Christopher Lamb** (see p.354) "*has the makings of being one of the best in the state,*" according to interviewees. Clients also appreciate his "*even-handed*" style when it comes to representing financial institutions and commercial real estate developers in their acquisition, finance and development of real estate projects.

Leaders in Delaware

ABRAMS, Kevin
Richards Layton & Finger, Wilmington
302 658 6541
Recommended in Chancery

ALEXANDER, Frederick H
Morris, Nichols, Arsht & Tunnell, Wilmington 302 351 9228
falexander@mnat.com
Recommended in Corporate/M&A
Practice Areas: Corporation Law Counseling Group: providing advice on the Delaware General Corporation Law and related matters; counseling boards of directors and board committees; and providing formal legal opinions on Delaware corporate law issues.
Prof. Memberships: Member, Delaware State Bar Association; Member, Council of the Corporation Law Section of DSBA; Member, Negotiated Acquisitions Committee of ABA Business Law Section and Acquisitions of Public Companies Task Force. Serves on the ABA Business Law Section's Committee on Federal Regulation of Securities, and its Task Force on Shareholder Proposals.
Career: Partner.
Publications: Co-author of 'The Delaware Corporation; Legal Aspects of Organization and Operation', 1-4th C.P.S. (BNA 2004); recent articles: 'Analysis of the 2004 Amendments to the Delaware General Corporation Law' (Aspen Law & Business 2004); 'Delaware Supreme Court Decision On Protection Of The Stockholder Franchise', 35 Sec. Law & Regulation 243 (BNA 2003); 'Delaware Supreme Court Addresses Deal Protection, Enjoins Acquisition In Omnicare, Inc. v. NCS Healthcare, Inc.' 6 Mergers & Acquisitions, 101 (BNA 2003).
Personal: Georgetown Law Center (JD, magna cum laude, 1988); University of Maryland (BA 1985).

ALLINGHAM II, Thomas J
Skadden, Arps, Slate, Meagher & Flom LLP & Affiliates, Wilmington
302 651 3070
tallingh@skadden.com
Recommended in Chancery
Practice Areas: Has experience in a wide range of corporate litigation, including mergers and acquisitions, shareholder and bankruptcy litigation, and statutory appraisal actions. For example, headed the firm's Litigation Team in The Southland Corporation's 1991 Chapter 11 restructuring, represented the Chairman of Avondale Industries, Inc. against insurgent efforts

to unseat the Chairman, and worked on the successful defenses of Walt Disney Productions against Saul Steinberg and Irwin Jacobs, Pogo Producing Co. against Northwest Industries, and Warner Communications against Rupert Murdoch.
Career: JD, University of Pennsylvania, 1977; BA, Williams College, 1974 (cum laude).

ALTMAN, Paul
Richards Layton & Finger, Wilmington
302 658 6541
Recommended in Corporate/M&A

BALICK, Steven
Ashby & Geddes, Wilmington
302 654 1888
Recommended in Intellectual Property

BALOTTI, Franklin
Richards Layton & Finger, Wilmington
302 658 6541
Recommended in Chancery, Corporate/M&A

BERGER, Benjamin
Blank Rome LLP, Wilmington
302 425 6476
berger@BlankRome.com
Recommended in Real Estate
Practice Areas: Represents primarily developers and investors in complex real estate transactions, including acquisitions and financing for commercial development. He has also represented several landlords in major leasing transactions for both office and retail facilities. He is a licensed title insurance agent in Delaware and Pennsylvania, and has been engaged by national title insurance companies to assist in the closing of multi-state transactions, and to represent such companies on complicated title insurance claims.
Prof. Memberships: Admitted in Colorado (1984), Delaware (1989) and Pennsylvania (1989).
Career: He is a frequent lecturer on a variety of real estate topics.
Personal: Born December 13, 1958; JD, University of Denver College of Law, 1984; BA, magna cum laude, Boston University, 1980.

BLACK Jr, Lewis S
Morris, Nichols, Arsht & Tunnell, Wilmington 302 351 9201
lblack@mnat.com
Recommended in Corporate/M&A
Practice Areas: Member of the Corporation Law Counseling Group concen-

trating in the area of corporation and securities law.
Career: DSBA (1964); District of Columbia Bar (1965); New York Bar (1966).
Publications: Author, Drexler, Black and Sparks, Delaware Corporation Law and Practice (2004).
Personal: Yale Law School (LLB, 1963), Princeton University (AB, 1960).

BLUMENFELD, Jack B
Morris, Nichols, Arsht & Tunnell, Wilmington 302 351 9291
JBlumenfeld@MNAT.com
Recommended in Intellectual Property
Practice Areas: Member of the Intellectual Property Litigation Group, concentrating in patent litigation encompassing many different areas of technology.
Prof. Memberships: ABA; DSBA (1979); has served on the Third Circuit Advisory Committee, Advisory Committee to the US District Court for the District of Delaware, the Civil Justice Reform Act Advisory Group and the Intellectual Property Advisory Committee of that Court; and has chaired the Delaware Minority Job Fair Committee of the Delaware State Bar Assocation.
Career: Partner since 1985; Associate, 1979-84; Law Clerk to The Honorable Walter K Stapleton, US District Court for the District of Delaware, 1977-79.
Publications: 'Solving the Mystery of Patentees' "Collective Enthusiasm" for Delaware', Del. Law. Rev. 7:145-162 (2004) (with/D Parsons, M Graham and L Polizoti).
Personal: Yale University (JD, 1977); State University of New York at Albany (BA, 1974); has served on the Board of Trustees of the Jewish Federation of Delaware and the Albert Einstein Academy.

BOUCHARD, Andre
Bouchard Margules & Friedlander PA, Wilmington 302 573 3500
Recommended in Chancery

BOWDEN, William
Ashby & Geddes, Wilmington
302 654 1888
Recommended in Bankruptcy

BOWSER, William W
Young Conaway Stargatt & Taylor LLP, Wilmington 302 571 6601
wbowser@ycst.com
Recommended in Employment
Practice Areas: Advises and represents employers in all areas of labor and employment law, including federal and

state employment discrimination claims, collective bargaining, wrongful discharge litigation, and litigation of claims governed by the NLRB.
Prof. Memberships: Admitted to practice in Delaware (1983). Past Chair, Delaware State Bar Association Section on Labor and Employment Law.
Career: Joined Young Conaway as Partner, 1993. County Attorney, New Castle County, Delaware, 1989-93.
Publications: Editor, Delaware Employment Law Letter.
Personal: JD (cum laude), Villanova University, 1983; BA, University of Delaware, 1979. Governor-Appointed Chair of the Delaware Advisory Council on Cancer Incidence and Mortality.

BRADY, Robert S
Young Conaway Stargatt & Taylor LLP, Wilmington 302 571 6690
rbrady@ycst.com
Recommended in Bankruptcy
Practice Areas: Partner in the Business Reorganization and Restructuring Department. Bankruptcy clients have included, among others, Continental Airlines, Integrated Health Services, Budget Rent-a-Car, Golden Books, Alterra Healthcare and Touch America Corporation.
Prof. Memberships: Member: Delaware State (Member, Sections on: General Corporation Law; Litigation) and American (Member, Sections on: Business Law; Litigation) Bar Associations; American Bankruptcy Institute; Federal Bar Association.
Career: Admitted to Delaware Bar (1990).
Publications: Co-author, 'TWA Evens the Score on the Availability of the 502(d) Claim Preclusion Defense in Delaware (2004); co-author, 'Determining and Preserving the Assets of Dot-Coms' (2003).
Personal: Born Salem, New Jersey, November 20, 1964. Education: Virginia Polytechnic Institute and State University (BS, 1987); Dickinson School of Law (JD, cum laude, 1990). Member, Woolsack Honor Society, a law school honorary society limited to graduates in the top 10% of their class. Member, Dickinson Law Review, 1989/90.

BUSSARD, Donald
Richards Layton & Finger, Wilmington
302 658 6541
Recommended in Corporate/M&A

www.ChambersandPartners.com

All quotes in the text are from interviews with clients and competitors.

351

CHEHI, Mark S
Skadden, Arps, Slate, Meagher & Flom LLP & Affiliates, Wilmington
302 651 3160
mchehi@skadden.com
Recommended in Bankruptcy

Practice Areas: Focuses on negotiated and contested workouts and restructurings, 'prepackaged' bankruptcies and traditional Chapter 11 cases. Has represented public company debtors, creditors, shareholders, lenders, acquirors, creditors' committees, committee members and board special committees in a wide variety of matters, including international and cross-border situations and related litigations. Advises officers and directors on corporate governance and fiduciary duty matters, and he has experience representing companies confronting asbestos and other mass tort liabilities.
Prof. Memberships: Member, Turnaround Management Association; Member, International Federation of Insolvency Practitioners.
Career: JD, The University of Chicago Law School, 1990; BA, Haverford College, 1980.

CLARK, Anthony W
Skadden, Arps, Slate, Meagher & Flom LLP & Affiliates, Wilmington
302 651 3080
tclark@skadden.com
Recommended in Bankruptcy, Chancery

Practice Areas: Heads the Corporate Restructuring and Bankruptcy Litigation Practice in Wilmington. Handles complex corporate, securities and general litigation matters. Has extensive experience representing debtors, creditors and acquirors in major corporate reorganization cases. Significant Chapter 11 debtor representations include Hayes Lemmerz International, Inc., Interstate Bakeries Corporation, Mid-American Waste Systems, Inc., UDC Homes, Wang Laboratories, Inc., and Cardinal Industries Inc.
Prof. Memberships: President (2001-03) and Bencher, Richard S. Rodney Chapter, American Inns of Court; Member, Board of Visitors, Temple University School of Law.
Career: Adjunct professor, University of Pennsylvania Law School; JD, Temple University School of Law, 1979; BA, State University of New York at Cortland, 1973.

COLLINS, Mark
Richards Layton & Finger, Wilmington
302 658 6541
Recommended in Bankruptcy

CONNOLLY Jr, Arthur
Connolly Bove Lodge & Hutz LLP, Wilmington 302 658 9141
aconnollyjr@cblh.com
Recommended in Intellectual Property
Practice Areas: Intellectual property, corporate/commercial litigation. Mr

Connolly is a former President of the Delaware State Bar Association, a Fellow of the American College of Trial Lawyers, and served on the State Public Integrity Commission from 1991-2003, the last two years as Chair.
Prof. Memberships: Delaware State Bar Association, American Bar Association, and the American Bar Foundation.
Career: Partner since 1967. Adjunct professor at Widener Law School (1981-86).
Personal: Georgetown University Law Center (JD, 1962); Georgetown University (BSS, 1959).

COTTRELL III, Frederick
Richards Layton & Finger, Wilmington
302 658 6541
Recommended in Intellectual Property

COUSINS, Scott
Greenberg Traurig LLP, Wilmington
302 661 7000
cousinss@gtlaw.com
Recommended in Bankruptcy

Practice Areas: Reorganization, bankruptcy and restructuring; real estate operations.
Publications: Editor and an administrative Board Member of The Delaware Journal of Corporate Law; author of a chapter on assets dispositions and acquisitions in conjunction with prepackaged plans of reorganization in the treatise, 'Bankruptcy Business Acquisitions'; author, 'Postpetition Financing of Dot-Coms,' The Delaware Journal of Corporate Law, Volume 27, No. 3 2002; author, 'Chapter 11 Asset Sales,' The Delaware Journal of Corporate Law, Volume 27, No. 3 2002.

DAVIS JONES, Laura
Pachulski, Stang, Ziehl, Young, Jones & Weintraub P.C., Wilmington
302 652 4100
ljones@pszyjw.com
Recommended in Bankruptcy

Practice Areas: Laura Davis Jones is a name shareholder and the managing shareholder of the firm's Delaware office. She has represented numerous debtors, creditors' committees, bank groups, acquirers, and other significant constituencies in national Chapter 11 cases and workout proceedings. Her cases include Chapter 11 debtors in Focal Communications, Superior Tele-Com, Redback Networks, ACandS, Trans World Airlines, W.R. Grace & Co., American Tissue, Federal Mogul Global, Harnischfeger Industries, Fleming Companies, Zenith Electronics, Inacom, and RBX Corporation; creditors' committees in Key3Media, Finova Group, Exodus Communications, Duke and Long Distributing Company, and Purina Mills. She lectures at national bankruptcy and litigation seminars, and has authored numerous articles. Ms Jones was named 'Deal Maker of the Year' by The American Lawyer in 2002, and has previously been profiled in The Ameri-

can Lawyer. For numerous years, she has been named by her peers as one of the 'Best Lawyers in America' and as one of the 'Best Lawyers in Delaware.' Ms Jones has been recognized in the K&A Restructuring Register and has been named repeatedly to the International Who's Who of Insolvency and Restructuring Lawyers.
Prof. Memberships: Private Panel of Bankruptcy Trustees, District of Delaware, 1989-; Delaware State Bar Association Bankruptcy Subcommittee; American Bar Association Business Bankruptcy Committee Subcommittee on Chapter 11 Bankruptcies; American Bar Association Business Bankruptcy Committee Subcommittee on Bankruptcy Rules.
Career: Law clerk for former Chief Judge Helen Balick of the United States Bankruptcy Court for the District of Delaware. Admitted to practice in the State of Delaware and the District of Columbia.
Publications: Contributing author, 'Bankruptcy Business Acquisitions,' LexMed Publishing, 1998.
Personal: Dickinson School of Law (JD, 1986); University of Delaware (BSBA, magna cum laude, 1983). Alpha Mu Alpha; Beta Gamma Sigma; Delta Theta Phi (Officer, 1984-85).

DEFRANCESCHI, Daniel
Richards Layton & Finger, Wilmington
302 658 6541
Recommended in Bankruptcy

DEHNEY, Robert J
Morris, Nichols, Arsht & Tunnell, Wilmington 302 351 9353
rdehney@mnat.com
Recommended in Bankruptcy

Practice Areas: Member of the Bankruptcy Group focusing on corporate restructuring and bankruptcy. Currently represents publicly-held (e.g., Oakwood Homes) and privately-held (e.g., Thaxton Group, Inc.) companies in their efforts to restructure; represents official and ad hoc creditors' committees (e.g., Applied Extrusion), and acquirors of assets (e.g., EchoStar in Loral Space Communications & Satellite).
Prof. Memberships: ABA; TMA; ABI; Admissions to Practice: Connecticut (1990); New York (1995); Delaware (1997); Pennsylvania (1997).
Career: Partner; Law Clerk to the Honorable Prudence Beatty, US Bankruptcy Judge, SDNY.
Personal: Pace University (JD, 1990); Dickinson College (BA, 1987); Managing Editor Environmental Law Review.

DIPRINZIO, Eugene A
Young Conaway Stargatt & Taylor LLP, Wilmington 302 571 6664
ediprinzio@ycst.com
Recommended in Real Estate

Practice Areas: Partner; his practice emphasizes the handling of complex commercial real estate transactions and the representation of financial institu-

tions and other lenders involving commercial mortgage loans and asset-based lending. In addition, he has represented numerous property developers and borrowers in connection with their overall activities and has more than 20 years experience in closing real estate transactions on a primary basis. He has been engaged in many substantial leasing transactions on behalf of landlords and tenants and has successfully represented building owners in prosecuting their property tax assessment appeals. He is counsel to title insurers and assists with the closing of multi-state transactions.
Prof. Memberships: He is a member of the American College of Real Estate Lawyers and Fellow and Delaware State Chair of the American College of Mortgage Attorneys and a frequent lecturer on a variety of real estate topics.
Career: Admitted to practice law in both Pennsylvania and Delaware.

EASTON, Richard L
Skadden, Arps, Slate, Meagher & Flom LLP & Affiliates, Wilmington
302 651 3040
reaston@skadden.com
Recommended in Corporate/M&A

Practice Areas: Has a wide-ranging corporate practice, concentrating on mergers and acquisitions, securities and Delaware corporate law matters. Advises other lawyers in the firm and its affiliates on the Delaware law aspects of their transactions and leads the firm's representation in other transactions. Has represented many corporate, investment banking and individual clients in a variety of transactions, including negotiated acquisitions, contested takeovers, proxy contests and going-private, leveraged buyout and restructuring transactions. Has also represented both issuers and underwriters in public offerings of debt and equity securities.
Career: JD, Georgetown University Law Center, 1975; BA, Wesleyan University, 1972 (cum laude).

EISENHOFER, Jay W
Grant & Eisenhofer PA, Wilmington
302 622 7050
jeisenhofer@gelaw.com
Recommended in Chancery

Practice Areas: Represents institutional investors in corporate and securities litigation, and corporate governance actions. Litigation counsel to many public and private institutional investors and is lead counsel in the securities class actions involving Global Crossing and Tyco. Lead counsel in three of the ten largest securities class action recoveries in history including the $300 million settlement from DaimlerChrysler and the $325 million partial settlement involving Global Crossing's officers and directors. Was lead attorney in the seminal case of Carmody v. Toll Brothers, wherein the Delaware Court of Chancery first ruled that so-called 'dead-hand' poison pills violated Delaware law.

Prof. Memberships: Member of the American, Delaware and Pennsylvania Bar Associations and the ABA Business Law and Litigation Sections. Vice-Chairman of the Business Torts Committee of the ABA Business Law Section.

Publications: Has written and lectured widely on securities fraud and insurance coverage litigation, business and employment torts, directors' and officers' liability coverage, and the Delaware law of shareholder rights and directorial responsibilities.

Personal: University of Pittsburgh, 1978; Villanova University School of Law, 1986 (magna cum laude); Order of the Coif. Law clerk to the Honorable Vincent A. Cirillo, President Judge of the Pennsylvania Superior Court.

FATELL, Bonnie Glantz
Blank Rome LLP, Wilmington
302 425 6423
fatell@blankrome.com
Recommended in Bankruptcy

Practice Areas: Chair of the firm's Business Restructuring and Bankruptcy Group and member of the firm's Partner Board. Ms Fatell has extensive experience in major bankruptcy reorganizations, out of court restructurings and other commercial matters in Delaware and nationally, representing secured and unsecured creditors, creditors' committees, debtors, plan of reorganization proponents, asset purchasers, landlords and other parties in interest. Recent representations include representing the debtors in ANC Rental Corporation, USGen New England Corporation and New Global Telecom and the creditors committees in Datatec Systems, InaCom Corporation, Bills Dollar Stores and Merry Go Round Enterprises.

Prof. Memberships: Fellow in American College of Bankruptcy, American Bankruptcy Institute, International Women's Insolvency and Restructuring Confederation, Bencher in Delaware Bankruptcy Inn of Court.

Career: Admitted to practice: Pennsylvania, 1981; Delaware, 1999; United States Supreme Court, 2002.

Publications: Contributing author, 'Collier Bankruptcy Forms Manual' (2005), 'Checklist of Personal Liabilities of Corporate Fiduciaries on the Eve of Bankruptcy', Fourth Annual Business Lawyers' Institute, Pennsylvania Bar Institute (co-author) (1998), 'Debtors Beware: Strict Interpretation of Section 365(d)(4) Bodes Well for Landlords', American Bankruptcy Institute Journal, June (1996).

Personal: Temple University School of Law, JD, 1981; Pennsylvania State University, BS, 1973.

FELGER, Mark
Cozen O'Connor, Wilmington
302 295 2000
Recommended in Bankruptcy

FINKELSTEIN, Jesse
Richards Layton & Finger, Wilmington
302 658 6541
Recommended in Chancery, Corporate/M&A

FORSTEN, Richard
Klett Rooney Lieber & Schorling, Wilmington 302 552 4200
Recommended in Real Estate

FOURNIER, David
Pepper Hamilton LLP, Wilmington
302 777 6565
fournierd@pepperlaw.com
Recommended in Bankruptcy

Practice Areas: Partner, Bankruptcy and Reorganization Group, Wilmington, Delaware. Experienced in: secured lending, workout counseling and bankruptcy litigation. Represents secured and unsecured creditors, official creditors' committees and debtors in various industries including retail, food processing, equipment leasing and financing, communications.

Prof. Memberships: Member, Caesar Rodney Inn of Court. Delaware Bar Association, Chair, International Law Committee.

Career: JD 1989 Villanova University School of Law; BA 1985 Pennsylvania State University.

GALARDI, Gregg M
Skadden, Arps, Slate, Meagher & Flom LLP & Affiliates, Wilmington
302 651 3150
ggalardi@skadden.com
Recommended in Bankruptcy

Practice Areas: Represents major corporations in business reorganizations, restructurings, acquisitions and divestitures. Clients have included debtors, creditors, creditors' committees, bank groups, investors, acquirors and financial advisors in all stages of complex restructuring transactions, from Chapter 11 reorganizations to out-of-court negotiations and workouts.

Career: University of Pennsylvania: JD, 1990 (cum laude; Special Projects Editor, University of Pennsylvania Law Review, 1989-90, Associate Editor 1988-89); PhD, Philosophy, 1990; MA, Economics, 1985; BA, 1979 (cum laude; honors in dual majors).

GEE, William S
Saul Ewing LLP, Wilmington
302 421 6823
wgee@saul.com
Recommended in Real Estate

Practice Areas: Partner in firm's Real Estate Department. Focuses on complex commercial transactions, with emphasis on real estate-related matters. Experience in acquisition and disposition of commercial real estate portfolios. Worked extensively as Delaware opinion counsel in connection with corporate, partnership and limited liability company law.

Prof. Memberships: Admitted in Delaware, Delaware Supreme Court, and US District Court for the District of

Delaware. Member, American and Delaware State Bar Associations.

Career: Acted as lead counsel in billions of dollars worth of multi-state acquisitions, sales, and financings.

Personal: JD (summa cum laude), Washington and Lee University School of Law, BA, Yale University.

GEIGER, Kathleen
Potter Anderson & Corroon LLP, Wilmington 302 984 6000
Recommended in Intellectual Property

GENTILE, Mark
Richards Layton & Finger, Wilmington
302 658 6541
Recommended in Corporate/M&A

GOLDMAN, Michael
Potter Anderson & Corroon LLP, Wilmington 302 984 6000
Recommended in Chancery, Corporate/M&A

GOODMAN, Lisa
Young Conaway Stargatt & Taylor LLP, Wilmington 302 571 6683
lgoodman@ycst.com
Recommended in Real Estate

Practice Areas: Partner practicing land use, zoning, and subdivision law.

Prof. Memberships: Member, Delaware State Bar Association and American Bar Association.

Career: Joined Young Conaway Stargatt & Taylor in 1994, became Partner in 2002. Wolcott Law Clerk, Delaware Supreme Court, 1993-94.

Publications: 'Preserving Urban Estates: A Case Study', Delaware Lawyer, Fall 2000; 'One Aspect of the Land Use Debate: Cellular Transmission Sites', In Re, September 1996.

Personal: JD Widener University School of Law; MA University of Delaware; BA West Chester University.

GRAHAM, Mary B
Morris, Nichols, Arsht & Tunnell, Wilmington 302 351 9254
mgraham@mnat.com
Recommended in Intellectual Property

Practice Areas: Member of Intellectual Property Litigation Group, litigating patent and trade secret cases involving diverse technologies from pharmaceuticals and chemicals to software and medical devices.

Prof. Memberships: ABA; DSBA; Member, District of Delaware Intellectual Property Advisory Committee; Delaware State Board of Education (Member, 1999-present); Delaware Higher Education Commission (Chair, 1993-99); Board on Professional Responsibility (Member 1999-2005); Preliminary Review Committee of Board on Professional Responsibility (Member, 1994-99).

Career: Partner; admission to practice: Delaware, 1983; Law Clerk to The Honorable Walter K Stapleton, United States District Court for the District of Delaware.

Publications: Parsons, Blumenfeld, Graham & Polizoti, 'Solving the Mystery of Patentees' "Collective Enthusiasm" for Delaware,' 7 Del. L. Rev. 145, 145-161 (2004).

Personal: Stanford University (BS in mathematics, with distinction, 1974); Massachusetts Institute of Technology (MS in mathematics, 1978); Yale Law School (JD, 1982).

GWYNNE, Kurt F
Reed Smith LLP, Wilmington
302 778 7550
kgwynne@reedsmith.com
Recommended in Bankruptcy

Practice Areas: Head of Corporate Restructuring & Bankruptcy Group in, and Managing Partner of, the Wilmington office; represents clients in bankruptcy cases and creditors' rights litigation in many jurisdictions.

Prof. Memberships: Business Bankruptcy Committee, ABA; Delaware Bankruptcy Inn of Court; Eastern District of Pennsylvania Bankruptcy Conference.

Career: Law clerk, Honorable Bruce Fox, US Bankruptcy Court, Eastern District of Pennsylvania.

Publications: Co-authored revisions to Chapter 40, Contempt, 'Collier Bankruptcy Practice Guide,' and numerous bankruptcy articles.

Personal: University of Pennsylvania Law School (JD, 1992), senior editor, 'Journal of International Business Law'; University of Central Florida (BA, 1988).

HERING, Louis G
Morris, Nichols, Arsht & Tunnell, Wilmington 302 351 9213
lhering@mnat.com
Recommended in Corporate/M&A

Practice Areas: Commerical law counseling including mergers and acquisitions, organization and structuring of all Delaware alternative entities, secured transactions and opinions on full range of Delaware legal issues.

Prof. Memberships: ABA Business Law Section Committee on Partnerships and Unincorporated Business Associations; DSBA Committees responsibile for updating Delaware limited liability company, partnership and statutory trust acts.

Career: Partner; admissions to practice: Delaware; New York; District of Columbia; Law Clerk to Honorable Carolyn Berger, Delaware Court of Chancery.

Publications: Frequent lecturer and author on alternative entity matters including co-author of BNA Portfolio on LLCs.

Personal: Cornell University (AB 1982); UCLA (JD 1986).

HEYMAN, Kurt M
The Bayard Firm, Wilmington
302 429 4235
kheyman@bayardfirm.com
Recommended in Chancery

Practice Areas: Practice concentrated in corporate governance litigation before the Delaware Court of Chancery, as well as disputes involving limited partnerships and limited liability companies, and claims involving fiduciary duties, consumer fraud, deceptive trade practices and trade secrets. Also advises corporate boards and special and audit committees in negotiations of mergers/transactions and internal investigations.
Prof. Memberships: Member, Delaware State Bar Association, and Secretary (2004-05), Corporate Council. Member, American Bar Association, and Vice-Chair (2004-05), Corporate Counseling & Litigation Subcommittee of Business Law Section. Member, Richard S. Rodney Inn of Court. Member, Editorial Board, Delaware Law Review.
Career: Law Clerk to The Honorable Jack B Jacobs, Delaware Court of Chancery, 1991-92. Director, The Bayard Firm, 1999-present. Serves on the firm's Executive Committee.
Publications: Co-author, 'Recent Developments in Corporate Law: Recent Supreme Court Reversals and the Role of Equity in Corporate Jurisprudence', 6 Del. L. Rev. 451 (2003). Co-author, 'The Disappearing Distinction Between Derivative and Direct Actions', 4 Del. L. Rev. 145 (2001). 'Expedited Proceedings in the Delaware Court of Chancery: Things of the Past?', 23 Del J. Corp. L. 145 (1998).
Personal: Born, Chicago, Illinois, 1966. AB, University of Michigan, 1988 (With High Distinction; Phi Beta Kappa). JD, University of Chicago, 1991.

HOLT, Scott
Young Conaway Stargatt & Taylor LLP, Wilmington 302 571 6623
sholt@ycst.com
Recommended in Employment

Practice Areas: Partner and member of Young Conaway's Employment and Litigation Departments. Area of practice includes laws concerning FMLA, ADEA, Title VII, ADA, NLRA, FLSA, WARN, trade secrets and restrictive covenants, and defense of class actions.
Prof. Memberships: Admitted in Delaware and Third, Fourth and Sixth Circuit Courts of Appeals. Labor & Employment Sections, ABA and DSBA (Past Chairman).
Career: Delaware Supreme Court clerkship; joined Young Conaway Stargatt & Taylor, LLP in 1995.
Publications: Delaware Employment Law Letter, editor; Navigating the WARN Act, ABA Section of Business Law (Spring 2002).
Personal: Temple University (high honors); Widener University, JD (honors).

HORWITZ, Richard
Potter Anderson & Corroon LLP, Wilmington 302 984 6000
Recommended in Intellectual Property

HUTZ, Rudolf E
Connolly Bove Lodge & Hutz LLP, Wilmington 302 658 9141
rhutz@cblh.com
Recommended in Intellectual Property

Practice Areas: Intellectual property law, litigation, patents, trademarks, trade secrets, and antitrust law. Mr Hutz has conducted successful IP trials, ADR proceedings, and appeals before various United States Courts, including the United States Supreme Court in Dawson v. Rohm and Haas, 448 U.S. 176 (1980). His experience extends to such technologies as pharmaceuticals, herbicides, medical devices, genetically engineered plants and biological chemicals.
Prof. Memberships: Delaware State Bar Association, American Intellectual Property Law Association, Philadelphia Intellectual Property Law Association, Federal Bar Association, Federal Circuit Bar Association, American College of Trial Lawyers - Fellow.
Career: Partner since 1967.
Publications: Mr Hutz has written and lectured extensively on a variety of IP matters, and has acted as an arbitrator/special master in resolving intellectual property disputes.
Personal: Georgetown University Law Center (JD, 1963); Princeton University (BA, 1959).

INGERSOLL, Josy W
Young Conaway Stargatt & Taylor LLP, Wilmington 302 571 6672
jingersoll@ycst.com
Recommended in Intellectual Property

Practice Areas: Firm Practice Leader intellectual property, commercial, corporate litigation.
Prof. Memberships: Admitted Delaware (1980). Member, Delaware Board of Bar Examiners (1991-2002); Delaware Intellectual Property Committee; Delaware Bar Association; Governor's Commission on Major Commercial Litigation Reform; ABA; IBA.
Career: Joined firm, 1980; Partner, 1986. Member of firm's Management Committee (main planning and policy group).
Publications: 'Marking the Right Time - Pros and Cons on a Timeline for Scheduling the Markman Hearing' (article); Business Strategy Protection a/k/a 'The White Knight Privilege' (outline); 'Shareholder Rights Bylaws' (article), others.
Personal: JD, Temple University; AB, Douglass College; Phi Beta Kappa, Cum Laude.

ISKEN, Donald N
Morris, Nichols, Arsht & Tunnell, Wilmington 302 351 9222
disken@mnat.com
Recommended in Real Estate

Practice Areas: Member of the Commercial Law Counsel Group with a concentration in real estate law and land use regulation.
Prof. Memberships: ABA; DSBA (1978), (Real Property Committee (Co-Chairman of subcommittee to Revisions to the Delaware Unit Property Act, 1989-92); Member, American College of Real Estate Lawyers; Board of the Directors of the Association of Retarded Citizens.
Career: Partner; admission to practice: Delaware (1978).
Personal: Bucknell University (AB, 1975); University of Miami School of Law (JD, cum laude, 1978).

JENKINS, Stephen
Ashby & Geddes, Wilmington 302 654 1888
Recommended in Chancery

JOHNSTON, John F
Morris, Nichols, Arsht & Tunnell, Wilmington 302 351 9203
jjohnston@mnat.com
Recommended in Corporate/M&A

Practice Areas: Corporation Law Counseling Group: providing advice on the Delaware General Corporation Law and related matters; counseling boards of directors and board committees; and providing formal legal opinions on Delaware corporate law issues.
Prof. Memberships: ABA (Member, Federal Regulation of Securities Committee, Business Law Section); Delaware State Bar Association.
Career: Partner since 1985.
Publications: Has written extensively on corporate governance matters.
Personal: Northwestern University (BA 1968); Duke University (PhD 1972); University of Pennsylvania (JD, cum laude, 1977).

KLEIN, Daniel
Richards Layton & Finger, Wilmington 302 658 6541
Recommended in Real Estate

KNIGHT, John
Richards Layton & Finger, Wilmington 302 658 6541
Recommended in Bankruptcy

KRAPF, Robert
Richards Layton & Finger, Wilmington 302 658 6541
Recommended in Real Estate

KRISTOL, Daniel
Richards Layton & Finger, Wilmington 302 658 6541
Recommended in Real Estate

LAFFERTY, William M
Morris, Nichols, Arsht & Tunnell, Wilmington 302 351 9341
wlafferty@mnat.com
Recommended in Chancery

Practice Areas: Member of Corporate Litigation Group involving corporate and commercial litigation with an emphasis on cases involving mergers and aquisitions, proxy contests and consent solicitations, and shareholder class

and derivative actions; concentrating in the Delaware Court of Chancery and Supreme Court of Delaware.
Prof. Memberships: ABA (Member Business Law Section Committee on Business and Corporate Litigation); DSBA (1989), Member of Corporation Law Section and Committee on Professional Ethics; appointed by Delaware Supreme Court to Board of Bar Examiners (2001-); appointed by the Delaware Supreme Court as Chair of the Delaware Commission on Continuing Legal Education (2004-); Pennsylvania State Bar Association (1990).
Career: Law Clerk to The Honorable Maurice A Hartnett, III, Delaware Court of Chancery (1989-90).
Publications: Has written a number of articles on Delaware law issues and is a contributing editor of two chapters of Contemporary Corporation Forms (Dissenters' Rights and Inspection of Records).
Personal: University of Delaware (BSBA (1985); The Dickinson School of Law (JD 1989), Articles Editor, Dickinson Law Review 1988-89.

LAMB, Christopher J
Pepper Hamilton LLP, Wilmington 302 777 6548
lambc@pepperlaw.com
Recommended in Real Estate

Practice Areas: Partner, Wilmington, Delaware. Experienced in: commercial law in major US corporate venue, including real estate acquisitions, secured financing, leasing and public finance. Litigation experience includes representation of creditors and debtors in workouts, foreclosures, mechanics' lien actions and state court proceedings. Represents financial institutions, developers and investors.
Prof. Memberships: Member, Committee of 100; Delaware Homebuilders; Delaware and American Bar Associations.
Career: JD 1988 Temple University School of Law, BA 1984 La Salle University.

LANDIS, Adam
Landis Rath & Cobb LLP, Wilmington 302 467 4400
Recommended in Bankruptcy

LASTER, J Travis
Richards Layton & Finger, Wilmington 302 658 6541
Recommended in Chancery

LAZARUS, Lewis H
Morris, James, Hitchens & Williams LLP, Wilmington 302 888 6970
llazarus@morrisjames.com
Recommended in Chancery

Practice Areas: Member, Corporate and Commerical Litigation Practice Group.
Prof. Memberships: Admitted to practice in California, Delaware and District of Columbia. Member, Council of Corporation Law Section of the Delaware State Bar Association. Member, Ameri-

can Bar Association Litigation Section's Class Actions and Derivative Suits Committee.

Career: Joined Morris James, 1985; Partner, 1989; Member, Executive Committee.

Publications: Author, 'Standards of Review of Conflict of Interest Transactions: An Examination of Decisions Rendered on Motions to Dismiss,' 26 Del. J. Corp. L. 911 (2001).

Personal: JD, Stanford Law School, 1982; BA (high honors), Swarthmore College, 1978. Member, Phi Beta Kappa. Fluent in Spanish.

LEVINE, Richard A
Young Conaway Stargatt & Taylor LLP, Wilmington 302 571 6640
rlevine@ycst.com
Recommended in Real Estate

Practice Areas: Administrative Partner; practices in the areas of real estate, commercial transactions and banking law. In the real estate area, he has substantial experience representing purchasers and sellers of commercial real estate, including shopping centers, office buildings and industrial properties. His work in this area includes land acquisition and disposition, leasing and financing. He has also represented lenders with respect to construction and permanent financing. His practice outside of real estate includes the representation of banks and financial institutions with respect to Delaware law and the representation of buyers and sellers of business entities, whether structured as equity or asset sales. These transactions have varied from local 'mom and pop' businesses to participation as local counsel in transactions of national scope. In particular, his practice frequently involves rendering opinions of Delaware law with respect to local, national and international business and financial transactions, including the Uniform Commercial Code. He has also assisted in the sale of several entities involved in reorganization proceedings.

LISICKY, Joseph G
Morris, James, Hitchens & Williams LLP, Wilmington 302 888 6834
jlisicky@morrisjames.com
Recommended in Real Estate

Practice Areas: Member of the Real Estate Practice Group. He represents individuals, corporations and other business entitles in a broad range of real estate matters, with an emphasis on acquisitions, sales, financing and leasing.
Prof. Memberships: Admitted to practice in Delaware and Pennsylvania. Member of American, Delaware and Pennsylvania Bar Associations.
Career: Joined Morris James, 1999; became Partner, 1999.
Personal: JD (cum laude), Temple University School of Law, 1988; MRP, University of Massachusetts, 1985; BA, Penn State University, 1983.

LOUDEN, Karen Jacobs
Morris, Nichols, Arsht & Tunnell, Wilmington 302 351 9227
klouden@mnat.com
Recommended in Intellectual Property

Practice Areas: Member of the Intellectual Property Litigation Group focusing primarily on patent litigation. Ms Louden is also involved in a wide variety of other intellectual property and commercial litigation, including copyright, trademark, trade secret and unfair competition litigation, and contract and licensing disputes.
Prof. Memberships: ABA; Delaware State Bar Association (1990); AIPLA; President, Delaware Volunteer Legal Services; Co-Chair, Delaware State Bar Professional Guidance Committee; Women and the Law Section (Former Chair and present Executive Committee Member); Board of Bar Examiners (prior Associate Member).
Career: Partner; Admissions to Practice: Delaware (1990); District of Delaware (1991); US Court of Appeals for the Third Circuit (1991); US Court of Appeals for the Federal Circuit (1998); US Supreme Court (2000).
Publications: Louden and Fonesca, 'Does the Federal Trademark Dilution Act Provide A Right Without A Remedy? The Supreme Court's First Foray Into Trademark Dilution; Moseley v. V Secret Catalogue', 7 Del. L. Rev. 31 (2004); Grimm, Louden and Heaney, 'Trademarks in Cyberspace' (Delaware Lawyer, Vol 18, No. 4, Winter 2000-01).
Personal: University of Pennsylvania (BA, summa cum laude, 1987); Harvard Law School (JD, cum laude 1990); Past Appointments: Committee for Provision of Legal Services to Low Income People; American Civil Liberties Union of Delaware (Past Legislative Chair and Board Member); Gubernatorial appointment to State of Delaware Council on Early Care and Education (2001-03); recipient of Delaware State Bar Association Community Service Award 2003.

MANNING, William
Klett Rooney Lieber & Schorling, Wilmington 302 552 4200
Recommended in Real Estate

MARSDEN Jr, William
Fish & Richardson, Wilmington 302 652 5070
Recommended in Intellectual Property

MCBRIDE, David
Young Conaway Stargatt & Taylor LLP, Wilmington 302 571 6639
dmcbride@ycst.com
Recommended in Chancery, Corporate/M&A

Practice Areas: Practice is concentrated in the area of corporate law and corporate and commercial litigation, including involvement in a plethora of Delaware corporate law cases, particularly in the area of mergers and acquisi-

tions, including Paramount Communications Inc. v. QVC Network, Inc., Paramount Communications Inc. v. Time Inc., Revlon Inc. v. MacAndrews & Forbes Holding Inc., In re First Boston Inc. Shareholders Litig., In re Resorts Int'l. Shareholders Litig., Freedman v. Restaurant Associates Indus., Inc., Robert M. Bass Group, Inc. v. Evans (Macmillan, Inc.), Shamrock Holdings Inc. v. Polaroid Corp., In re RJr Nabisco, Inc. Shareholders Litigation, Henley Group v. Santa Fe Southern Pacific Corp., Pennzoil Co. v. Getty Oil Co., Edelman v. Phillips Petroleum, Omnicare, Inc. v. NCS Healthcare, Inc., and In re Oracle Corporation Derivative Litigation.
Prof. Memberships: Admitted to practice in Delaware (1975). Member of the American Law Institute, Vice-Chairman and Chairman Elect (2004-06) of the Corporate Council of the Corporate Law Section of the Delaware State Bar Association, the Rules Committee of the Delaware Court of Chancery, the Board of Editors of the Delaware Lawyer, a director of the Historical Society for the Court of Chancery.
Career: Partner, Young Conaway. Serves on firm's management committee. Began in private practice in 1975.
Personal: JD, Emory University School of Law, 1975; BSFS, Georgetown University.

MCDONOUGH, Kathleen
Potter Anderson & Corroon LLP, Wilmington 302 984 6000
Recommended in Employment

MCNALLY, Edward M
Morris, James, Hitchens & Williams LLP, Wilmington 302 888 6880
emcnally@morrisjames.com
Recommended in Chancery

Practice Areas: Chair of Litigation Practice Group. Focuses practice on corporate law and business litigation. Has extensive experience in representing stockholders, directors, special committees and corporations in corporate disputes. He has also represented plaintiffs and defendents in jury and bench trials.
Prof. Memberships: Admitted to Delaware Bar, 1972. Member of American and Delaware Bar Associations.
Career: Joined Morris James, 1972; became Partner, 1976. Part Chairman, Supreme Court Lawyers' Fund for Client Protection.
Publications: Author, Delaware Voluntary Mediation Act.
Personal: Born in Wilmington, DE. JD, Columbia University, 1972; BA, Boston College, 1969.

MORGAN, Pauline
Young Conaway Stargatt & Taylor LLP, Wilmington 302 571 6707
pmorgan@ycst.com
Recommended in Bankruptcy

Practice Areas: Partner; specializing in the representation of Chapter 11 debtors-in-possession and official com-

mittees appointed in Chapter 11 corporate reorganizations.
Prof. Memberships: Member: Delaware, Pennsylvania, and New Jersey Bars; American Bankruptcy Institute; District Court Advisory Committee for the US District Court for the District of Delaware.
Personal: Education: University of Pennsylvania Law School (JD, 1987); Duquesne University (BA, cum laude, 1978).

MULLEN, Thomas
Prickett, Jones & Elliott PA, Wilmington 302 888 6500
Recommended in Corporate/M&A

NACHBAR, Kenneth J
Morris, Nichols, Arsht & Tunnell, Wilmington 302 351 9294
knachbar@mnat.com
Recommended in Chancery

Practice Areas: Member of Corporate Litigation Group concentrating in litigation arising from mergers and acquisitions and disputes relating to Delaware corporations, and advice to corporate boards of directors and special committees with respect to transational and litigation issues.
Prof. Memberships: ABA; DSBA (1981); Member, Rules Committee of US District Court for the Distrct of Delaware; Chairman, Delaware Board on Certified Court Reporters.
Career: Partner; Admissions to Practice: Delaware (1981); Member, New York University Review of Law and Social Change (1980-81).
Publications: Contributor, Drexler, Black and Sparks, Delaware Corporation Law and Practice; Contributor, Settlement Agreements in Commercial Disputes (Ed. Richard Rosen, 2000); author, 'Revlon Inc., v. MacAndrews and Forbes, Inc. The Requirements of a Level Playing Field in Contested Mergers, And Its Effect on Lock-Ups and Other Bidding Deterrents,' 12 Del.J.Corp. 473 (1987).
Personal: Haverford College (BA, 1978); New York University School of Law (JD, 1981).

NOREIKA, Maryellen
Morris, Nichols, Arsht & Tunnell, Wilmington 302 351 9278
mnoreika@mnat.com
Recommended in Intellectual Property

Practice Areas: Member of the Intellectual Property Litigation Group concentrating on patent cases in a variety of technical areas, including digital technology, consumer products and pharmaceuticals.
Prof. Memberships: ABA; DSBA; Delaware District Court Advisory Committee; Delaware District Court Local Rules Subcommittee.
Career: Partner (2001-present); Associate (1993-2000).
Personal: Lehigh University (BS, 1988); Columbia University (MS, 1990); Uni-

versity of Pittsburgh (JD, magna cum laude, 1993).

O'TOOLE, Matthew J
Morris, James, Hitchens & Williams LLP, Wilmington 302 888 6875
motoole@morrisjames.com
Recommended in Corporate/M&A

Practice Areas: Focuses on corporate and business transactions, particularly structure and use of Delaware business entities.
Prof. Memberships: Admitted to Delaware Bar in 1994.
Career: Joined Morris James, 1993; became Partner, 2000. Member, Council of Corporation Law Section of Delaware State Bar Association; member of Council's limited liability company/partnership subcommittee.
Publications: Co-author, 'Delaware Limited Liability Company Practice Guide,' State Limited Liability Company & Partnership Laws, published by Aspen Law & Business.
Personal: JD, College of William & Mary, 1992; MA,1988, BA, 1985, Fordham University.

PARADEE, John
Prickett, Jones & Elliott PA, Wilmington 302 888 6500
Recommended in Real Estate

PATTON Jr, James L
Young Conaway Stargatt & Taylor LLP, Wilmington 302 571 6684
jpatton@ycst.com
Recommended in Bankruptcy

Practice Areas: Corporate restructurings and mass tort related insolvencies. Clients have included, among many others, Continental Airlines, Inc., Columbia Gas Systems, Inc., Days Inns of America, Inc., MEI Diversified, Inc., Simmons Upholstered Furniture, Inc., Lomas Financial Corporation, Fuller-Austin Insulation Company; Florida Coast Paper Company, Alterra Healthcare Corporation, the Asbestos Future Claims Representative in connection with The Celotex Corporation, Babcock & Wilcox Company, Owens-Corning, Armstrong World Industries, Inc., Federal-Mogul Global Inc., USG Corporation, Pittsburgh Corning Corporation, Kaiser Group International, Inc., Narco, and Halliburton Company, as well as debtors in over 40 prepackaged bankruptcy cases.
Prof. Memberships: Member, Delaware State Bar Association, Chairman, Bankruptcy Law Subcomittee, Commercial Law Section (1986-); Member, American Bar Association, Business Law Section, Business Bankruptcy Committee, Claims Trading Subcommittee (Vice-Chair, 2002-); Member, Association of Trial Lawyers of America; Member, American Bankruptcy Institute; Member of Board of Contributors, Fletcher Corporate Bankruptcy, Reorganization and Dissolution, Clark, Boardman, Callaghan (1992); Participant on Judge

Scirica's Working Group on Mass Torts in connection with the Report of the Advisory Committee on Civil Rules and the Working Group on Mass Torts to the Chief Justice of the United States and to the Judicial Conference of the United States (1999); Fellow, American College of Bankruptcy.
Career: Chairman,Young Conaway Stargatt & Taylor, LLP; joined firm in 1983 and became Partner in 1989.
Publications: Co-author, 'Effects of Bankruptcy on Director & Officer Liability' and 'Directors & Officer Liability Insurance Presented at Third Circuit Judicial Conference', 2002; co-author, 'Futures Representative's Informational Brief', Mealey's 'Asbestos Bankruptcy Conference', 2001; co-author, 'Dancing with Scylla and Charybdis: the Tough Job of Directors of a Troubled Company', presented at the American Bar Association, Section of Business Law, Spring Meeting, 2000.

PAYSON, Robert
Potter Anderson & Corroon LLP, Wilmington 302 984 6000
Recommended in Chancery

PERNICK, Norman L
Saul Ewing LLP, Wilmington 302 421 6824
npernick@saul.com
Recommended in Bankruptcy

Practice Areas: Chair of Saul Ewing's Bankruptcy and Reorganization Department. Practices in bankruptcy and workouts, representing debtors, creditors' committees, secured and unsecured creditors, and trustees.
Prof. Memberships: Admitted in Delaware, the US District Court for the District of Delaware, and the Third Circuit Court of Appeals.
Career: Currently lead counsel for Owens Corning in its Chapter 11 case. Ranked one of Delaware's Top Business Bankruptcy Lawyers by Delaware Today. Rated 'AV' by Martindale Hubbell.
Publications: Author, Bankruptcy Deadline Checklist.
Personal: JD, The National Law Center, George Washington University, (with honors); BA, Brandeis University, (magna cum laude, with high honors).

PINCUS, Robert B
Skadden, Arps, Slate, Meagher & Flom LLP & Affiliates, Wilmington 302 651 3090
bpincus@skadden.com
Recommended in Corporate/M&A

Practice Areas: Represents and advises clients in a wide variety of corporate matters, including mergers and acquisitions, private equity investments and unsolicited takeovers. Extensive experience in advising clients and other lawyers in the firm on Delaware law aspects of transactions and fiduciary duty and corporate governance matters.
Career: LLM, Securities Regulation, Georgetown University Law Center,

1983; JD, American University, The Washington College of Law, 1980 (magna cum laude); BBA, College of William and Mary, 1977.

REED, John L
Duane Morris LLP, Wilmington 302 657 4943
jlreed@duanemorris.com
Recommended in Chancery

Practice Areas: John L Reed is the Managing Partner of the Wilmington office. Mr Reed is an established trial attorney and maintains a national litigation practice, including trials and appeals, that covers virtually all facets of business law. He concentrates his practice on corporate, securities and partnership matters and has considerable experience in matters before Delaware's Court of Chancery, which includes the representation of all types of business entities and their boards, as well as investors, with regard to breach of fiduciary duty claims, merger-and-acquisition litigation, and all issues involving corporate governance and Delaware law.
Prof. Memberships: American Bar Association; Delaware State Bar Association - Nominating Committee, Corporation Law Section, Litigation Section; American Inns of Court - Master, 2003-present, Barrister, 1992-94, 2001- present; Federal Civil Panel - United States District Court, District of Delaware.
Career: State of Delaware - Deputy Attorney General, 1991-95, General Counsel, Delaware Secretary of Labor, 1991-94, Delaware Secretary of Education, 1994-95; admitted to practice in Delaware, Pennsylvania, United States Court of Appeals for the Third Circuit, United States District Court for the District of Delaware, United States District Court for Eastern District of Pennsylvania.
Personal: Widener University School of Law, JD, 1991.

REESE, Cathy L
Greenberg Traurig LLP, Wilmington 302 661 7389
reesec@gtlaw.com
Recommended in Chancery

Practice Areas: Litigation; corporate and securities; technology, media and telecommunications.
Prof. Memberships: Member, Board of Trustees; Delaware Leadership Foundation (1999-present); Member, Board of Trustees, and Corporate Secretary, Delaware Hospice, Inc. (1995-present); Member, Board of Directors, Wilmington Women in Business (1993-96).
Publications: Author, 'Locked and Loaded: Delaware Supreme Court Takes Aim at Deal Certainty', M&A Lawyer, June 2003; Author, 'Avoiding the Next Enron', Fortune, April 15, 2002; Author, Director and Shareholder Accountability In The Age Of Enron', Corporate Counsel, March 2002; Author, 'Shoring Up Against the Next Wave of Shareholder Suits: Advice for Corporate Counsel', Fulcrum, July 2001.

ROVNER, Philip
Potter Anderson & Corroon LLP, Wilmington 302 984 6000
Recommended in Intellectual Property

SANDLER, Sheldon N
Young Conaway Stargatt & Taylor LLP, Wilmington 302 571 6673
ssandler@ycst.com
Recommended in Employment

Practice Areas: Partner in the Employment Law Department of Young Conaway Stargatt & Taylor, LLP. He also serves on the firm's Management Committee.
Prof. Memberships: Only Delaware Fellow of the College of Labor and Employment Lawyers; Founding Chairman of the Delaware State Bar Association's Labor and Employment Law Section, has chaired the Lawyers' Advisory Committee to the Court of Appeals for the Third Circuit, served as President of the Delaware Chapter of the Federal Bar Association, served on the Delaware Court of Chancery Rules Committee, and has taught Legal Aspects of Human Resource Management in Widener University's MBA program.
Publications: Author of the chapter on employment law in 'The Delaware Supreme Court: The First Fifty Years', a book commissioned by the Delaware Supreme Court in commemoration of its first half-century as Delaware's highest court. In surveys of Delaware lawyers published in Delaware Today Magazine in 1996, 1999 and 2001, he was named one of Delaware's leading labor lawyers.
Personal: He is a graduate of the University of Michigan and the University of Pennsylvania Law School, and holds a degree of Master of Laws in Labor Law from Temple University.

SAUNDERS, Robert S
Skadden, Arps, Slate, Meagher & Flom LLP & Affiliates, Wilmington 302 651 3170
rsaunder@skadden.com
Recommended in Chancery

Practice Areas: Handles litigation in federal and state courts, concentrating on cases involving the governance of business organizations, with emphasis on mergers and acquisitions and limited partnerships. Provides transactional advice on Delaware limited partnership law. Has extensive experience in litigation arising from mergers and acquisitions and in litigation involving Delaware limited partnerships and private equity funds.
Career: JD, University of Virginia School of Law, 1991 ('Virginia Law Review'); AB, Dartmouth College, 1987.

SCOTT, Pamela J
Saul Ewing LLP, Wilmington
302 421 6878
pscott@saul.com
Recommended in Real Estate

Practice Areas: Ms Scott is a Partner in Saul Ewing's Real Estate Department. She handles commercial transactions and land use approvals for large commercial, institutional and residential projects, and site approvals for the telecommunications industry. She works extensively with State and local government boards and agencies.
Prof. Memberships: Admitted to practice in Delaware, New Jersey, and Pennsylvania.
Career: Member, Real Property Section of the Delaware Bar, the Board of Directors of the Committee of 100, the Small Business Legislative Committee of the Delaware State Chamber and TMA Delaware.
Personal: JD, Widener University School of Law, BS, University of Delaware.

SELBER SILVERSTEIN, Laurie
Potter Anderson & Corroon LLP, Wilmington 302 984 6000
Recommended in Bankruptcy, Chancery

SHANNON, Brendan Linehan
Young Conaway Stargatt & Taylor LLP, Wilmington 302 571 6696
bshannon@ycst.com
Recommended in Bankruptcy

Practice Areas: Partner; specializing in the representation of Chapter 11 debtors-in-possession and official committees appointed in Chapter 11 corporate reorganizations.
Prof. Memberships: Member of the Delaware and Pennsylvania Bars, and a Member of the Delaware Chapter of the Federal Bar Association and the American Bankruptcy Institute.
Personal: He is a graduate of Princeton University and Marshall-Wythe School of Law at the College of William and Mary.

SHANNON, Kevin
Potter Anderson & Corroon LLP, Wilmington 302 984 6000
Recommended in Chancery

SHAW, John
Young Conaway Stargatt & Taylor LLP, Wilmington 302 571 6689
jshaw@ycst.com
Recommended in Intellectual Property

Practice Areas: Mr Shaw practices in the intellectual property, commercial litigation, and trial and litigation practice departments of Young Conaway Stargatt & Taylor, LLP. Mr Shaw appears before all state and federal courts in the State of Delaware, and he has extensive experience in a wide variety of intellectual property and commercial disputes pending before the United States District Court for the District of Delaware.

Mr Shaw also devotes a significant portion of his practice to counseling intellectual property owners on trademark, patent, trade secret, and other intellectual property matters.
Prof. Memberships: Admitted to practice in Delaware, Pennsylvania, and the United States Courts of Appeals for the Third and Federal Circuits; registered to practice before the United States Patent & Trademark Office; Co-Chair, Intellectual Property Advisory Committee to the United States District Court for the District of Delaware; Member, Patent Jury Instruction Revision Committee of the Delaware Bar Association.
Career: Law Clerk for the Honorable Murray M. Schwartz, Senior District Judge, United States District Court of Delaware, 1994-95; joined Young Conaway Stargatt & Taylor, LLP in 1995; became Partner, January, 2002.
Personal: JD (magna cum laude), University of Pittsburgh, 1994; BS (with high honors and distinction), Pennsylvania State University, 1989.

SILVERSTEIN, Bruce L
Young Conaway Stargatt & Taylor LLP, Wilmington 302 571 6659
bsilverstein@ycst.com
Recommended in Chancery

Practice Areas: Chairman of firm's Corporate Litigation and Counseling Section. Extensive experience both litigating on behalf of clients and counseling clients in corporate and commercial matters, including significant merger and acquisition transactions. Prosecuted and defended a number of significant corporate and commercial matters before the Delaware Court of Chancery and Delaware Supreme Court. Appointed Master in Chancery Pro Hac Vice and has lectured with members of the Court of Chancery on litigation practice in that Court and substantive legal issues. Advised clients on a number of significant merger and acquisition transactions.
Prof. Memberships: Admitted to practice in Delaware (1986). Member, Corporate Council of the Corporate Law Section, Delaware Bar Association; former associate member of the Delaware Board of Bar Examiners; American Bar Association.
Career: Joined Young Conaway, 1986; became Partner, 1992. Significant cases include: Alabama By-Products Corp. v. Cede & Co., Elliott Assocs, L.P. v. Avatex Corp., In Re Best Lock Corporation Shareholder Litigation, In re Pure Resources, Inc. Shareholders Litigation, In re RJR Nabisco, Inc. Shareholders Litigation, M.G. Bancorporation v. Le Beau, Paramount Communications Inc. v. QVC Network, Inc., Paramount Communications, Inc. v. Time, Inc., Rapid-American Corp. v. Harris, and Robert M. Bass Group, Inc. v. Evans.
Publications: Serves on Editorial Board

of 'Judges & Lawyers Business Valuation Update'; contributed editorial comment and review for 'The Lawyer's Business Valuation Handbook' and 'Valuing a Business: The Analysis and Appraisal of Closely Held Companies'; various law review articles and seminar materials.
Personal: JD, Villanova University (1986; cum laude); BA, Beaver College (1983).

SMALL, John
Prickett, Jones & Elliott PA, Wilmington 302 888 6500
Recommended in Corporate/M&A

SPARKS III, A Gilchrist
Morris, Nichols, Arsht & Tunnell, Wilmington 302 351 9276
asparks@mnat.com
Recommended in Chancery, Corporate/M&A

Practice Areas: Member of the Corporate Litigation Group and works closely with the Corporate Counseling Group, concentrates in litigation and counseling arising from mergers, acquisitions and disputes relating to the governance of Delaware corporations.
Prof. Memberships: ABA; DSBA (1973); Delaware Supreme Court Advisory Committee on Delaware Uniform Rules of Evidence (Co-Chairman); The American Law Institute (Member); ABA Committee on Corporate Laws of Business Law Section (Member); Board of Advisors, University of Pennsylvania Institute for Law and Economics (Member); American Bar Foundation; Delaware Law Review (Executive Editor); Advisory Board, Weinberg Center for Corporate Governance (Co-Chairman).
Career: Partner; admissions to practice: Delaware (1973); Delaware Supreme Court (1973); US District Court of Delaware (1973); Third Circuit Court of Appeals (1982; United States Supreme Court (1984); Second Circuit Court of Appeals (1991).
Publications: Author, Drexler, Black and Sparks, 'Delaware Corporation Law and Practice'; Sparks and Alexander, 'The Delaware Corporation': Legal Aspects of Organization and Operation', 1-4th C.P.S. (BNA).
Personal: Yale University (BA, magna cum laude, 1966); University of Pennsylvania (JD, magna cum laude, 1973); University of Pennsylvia Law Review, Associate Editor (1971-72), Editor (1972-73).

STABLER, Wendie C
Saul Ewing LLP, Wilmington 302 421 6865
wstabler@saul.com
Recommended in Real Estate

Practice Areas: Ms Stabler is a Partner in the firm's Real Estate Department. In her land use and administrative practice, she has worked with State and local governmental boards and departments. Her zoning and land use work has included

successful negotiations and application for rezonings, traffic mitigation agreements, level of service waivers, variances, historic zone overlays and other similar permits/approvals.
Prof. Memberships: Admitted in Delaware and Georgia; Co-Chair, New Castle County Economic Development Council.
Career: Named one of Delaware's Top 75 'Power Lawyers' in Delaware Today Magazine.
Personal: JD, Emory University School of Law, BA (magna cum laude), Tufts University.

STONE, Alan J
Morris, Nichols, Arsht & Tunnell, Wilmington 302 351 9277
astone@mnat.com
Recommended in Chancery

Practice Areas: Member of the Corporate Litigation Group, primarily litigating cases arising out of corporate mergers and acquisitions, proxy contests and consent solicitations, complex valuation disputes and interested party transactions, as well as providing advice to corporate boards of directors and special committees with respect to transactional and litigation issues.
Prof. Memberships: ABA; DSBA; Delaware (1988); New York (1988).
Career: Partner; Law Clerk to The Honorable Andrew GT Moore, II, Delaware Supreme Court.
Personal: Tulane University (BSE, cum laude, 1983); Tulane University (JD, magna cum laude, 1987); Senior Notes and Comments Editor, 1987-86, Tulane Law Review.

STRATTON, David B
Pepper Hamilton LLP, Wilmington 302 777 6566
strattond@pepperlaw.com
Recommended in Bankruptcy

Practice Areas: Partner, Executive Committee Member; Wilmington, Delaware. Experienced in representing debtors, creditors' committees, secured creditors, individual creditors. Lead counsel and co-counsel in bankruptcy courts in Delaware, Maryland and New York in 'a7 304 and Chapter 11 proceedings involving retailers, high-tech companies, entertainment, transportation companies, manufacturing, energy and others. Handles complex bankruptcy litigation. Advises on bankruptcy and litigation strategy, asset sales, restructurings and dispute resolution.
Prof. Memberships: Member, American Bankruptcy Institute; American Bar Association. Board of Directors, Better Business Bureau of Delaware, Inc.
Career: JD 1978 University of Pittsburgh School of Law, AB 1975 Gettysburg College.

SUDELL Jr, William H
Morris, Nichols, Arsht & Tunnell,
Wilmington 302 351 9284
wsudell@mnat.com
Recommended in Bankruptcy

Practice Areas: Member of the Bankruptcy Litigation and General Business Litigation Groups concentrating in the areas of commercial litigation and bankruptcy and creditors' rights. Has represented or is currently representing debtors, creditors' and bondholders' committees, unsecured creditors, secured creditors, DIP lenders, acquirers and other parties in interest in many of the major Chapter 11 cases that have been filed in the District of Delaware since 1990.

Prof. Memberships: ABA; DSBA; Delaware Community Legal Aid Society (Board Member and past president).

Career: Partner; admissions to practice: Delaware (1971); Third Circuit Court of Appeals (1978); Supreme Court of the United States (1990).

Personal: Brown University (BA and BS (Aerospace Engineering), 1966); University of Pennsylvania (JD 1971).

SYMONDS Jr, Robert L
Morris, James, Hitchens & Williams LLP,
Wilmington 302 888 6803
rsymonds@morrisjames.com
Recommended in Corporate/M&A

Practice Areas: Chair of Transactions Group. Focuses practice on corporate and business transactions, particularly the structure and use of Delaware business entities.

Prof. Memberships: Admitted to practice in Delaware, 1986. Member of Delaware State Bar Association and American Bar Association. Member of DSBA drafting committees for Delaware Limited Liability Company Act; Delaware Statutory Trust Act; Delaware Revised Uniform Limited Partnership Act; Delaware Revised Uniform Partnership Act.

Career: Joined Morris James, 1990; became Partner, 1994.

Personal: Born in Danbury, CT. JD, University of Pittsburgh, 1985; BA, Villanova University, 1975.

TARABICOS, Larry J
Young Conaway Stargatt & Taylor LLP,
Wilmington 302 571 6667
ltarabicos@ycst.com
Recommended in Real Estate

Practice Areas: Firm practice leader in real estate. Has extensive experience in commercial real estate, zoning and land development.

Prof. Memberships: Admitted to practice in Delaware (1986). Member, Delaware State Bar Association; American Bar Association.

Career: Joined Young Conaway, 1993; became Partner 1993.

Personal: JD, Emory University; BAAS, University of Delaware. Finalist, Jessup Cup International Law Southeast Regional Moot Court Competition (1985). Frequent lecturer on commercial real estate and land use topics.

TUTHILL, Walter C
Morris, Nichols, Arsht & Tunnell,
Wilmington 302 351 9204
wtuthill@mnat.com
Recommended in Corporate/M&A

Practice Areas: Member of the Commercial Law Counseling Group, concentrating in the fields of partnership, limited liability company and business trust law, as well as bank and insurance regulatory matters, consumer banking law and general merger and aquisition and contract law matters.

Prof. Memberships: ABA Business Law Section Committee on Partnerships and Unincoporated Business Associations; Delaware State Bar Association, Chairman, Partnerships/Limited Liability Company Subcommittee of Corporate Law Section of Delaware Bar.

Career: Partner; admissions to practice: Delaware (1977).

Publications: Co-author of Tuthill, Pulsifer, Hering & Lessner, 'Limited Liability Companies: Legal Aspects of Organization, Operation and Dissolution' (The Bureau of National Affairs, Inc., 1996); contributing author of 'The General Partnership, L.P. and L.L.P.: Formation and Organization; Transactional Lawyer's Desk Book: Advising Business Entities' (West Publishing Co., 2001).

Personal: Northwestern University (MM and JD, cum laude, 1977); Denison Unversity (BA, 1973).

WALSH Jr, Peter
Potter Anderson & Corroon LLP,
Wilmington 302 984 6000
Recommended in Chancery

WAXMAN, Scott
Potter Anderson & Corroon LLP,
Wilmington 302 984 6000
Recommended in Corporate/M&A

WELCH, Edward P
Skadden, Arps, Slate, Meagher & Flom LLP & Affiliates, Wilmington
302 651 3060
ewelch@skadden.com
Recommended in Chancery

Practice Areas: Concentrates on corporate and securities litigation, including the defense of class and derivative actions, with an emphasis on mergers and acquisitions. Frequently represents clients in administrative proceedings, usually in connection with mergers and acquisitions. Provides Delaware General Corporation Law advice with respect to transactional matters.

Prof. Memberships: Member, Board of Directors of the Mary Campbell Center, Inc. (1985-present); Vice-Chair, Delaware Corporation Law Council.

Career: JD, Villanova University School of Law, 1976; BS, Georgetown University, 1972.

WILLIAMS, David H
Morris, James, Hitchens & Williams LLP,
Wilmington 302 888 6900
dwilliams@morrisjames.com
Recommended in Employment

Practice Areas: Member, Government Relations and Employment Law and Education Law Practice Groups. Has extensive experience in preventive counseling concerning employment matters, employment litigation, administrative hearings and collective bargaining negotiations.

Prof. Memberships: Admitted Delaware Bar, 1975. Member of Labor and Employment Law Sections of the Delaware State and American Bar Associations; National School Boards Association Council of School Attorneys; President, Delaware Council of School Board Attorneys.

Career: Joined Morris James, 1975; became Partner 1980. Member, Morris James' Executive Committee; Managing Partner, effective January 1, 2004.

Personal: Born Wilmington, DE. JD, Dickinson School of Law, 1975; BA, Gettysburg College, 1972.

WILLIAMS, Gregory
Richards Layton & Finger, Wilmington
302 658 6541
Recommended in Chancery

WILLOUGHBY, Barry M
Young Conaway Stargatt & Taylor LLP,
Wilmington 302 571 6666
bwilloughby@ycst.com
Recommended in Employment

Practice Areas: Partner; Chair, Employment Law Department of Young Conaway Stargatt & Taylor, LLP. Mr Willoughby's practice is primarily limited to representation of employers in claims of employment discrimination, retaliation, and 'wrongful discharge' under federal and state law, including defense of charges of racial and sexual harassment. He also defends public employers in First Amendment 'whistleblower' cases and other constitutional law allegations such as asserted violations of due process or equal protection. He also represents employers in union related conflicts, including representation in organizing campaigns, unfair labor practice proceedings, and grievance/arbitration hearings. Mr Willoughby has achieved an 'A' rating in Martindale-Hubbell and is listed in a leading legal publication for management labor and employment law attorneys.

Prof. Memberships: Community and civic activities include pro bono service as Counsel and ex-officio Board Member of the United Way of Delaware, Inc. and General Counsel and Corporate Secretary of Junior Achievement of Delaware, Inc.

Publications: In surveys of Delaware lawyers published by Delaware Today magazine, he was named one of Delaware's leading labor lawyers.

Personal: Graduated from the University of Delaware in 1976 with High Honors and with Distinction. In 1979, he graduated cum laude from the Dickinson School of Law where he was a member of the Law Review and Woolsack Society, a law school honor society limited to graduates in the top 10 percent of their class.

WOLFE Jr, Donald
Potter Anderson & Corroon LLP,
Wilmington 302 984 6000
Recommended in Chancery

ASHBY & GEDDES

THE FIRM

Managing Partner: Lawrence C Ashby

Number of partners: 12
Number of other lawyers: 13

AREAS OF PRACTICE:
Bankruptcy 40%
Corporate Litigation & Transactions 30%
Intellectual Property Litigation 12%
Commercial Litigation & Transactions 12%
Personal Injury/Medical Malpractice 5%
Public Utility Law 1%

FIRM OVERVIEW: Ashby & Geddes was founded in 1979 and is best known for its litigation expertise. The firm litigates in all state and federal courts in Delaware, representing clients ranging from Fortune 500 corporations to individuals. In addition to its litigation practice, Ashby & Geddes has a substantial corporate reorganization practice and regularly provides transactional and opinion services to local, national and international clients in connection with matters involving Delaware law. The firm remains committed to its founding principle of painstaking attention to detail and the best possible work product at highly competitive rates.

MAIN AREAS OF PRACTICE:

Bankruptcy: Ashby & Geddes represents a wide variety of nationally based enterprises with diverse interests in most of the larger Chapter 11 reorganization proceedings filed in Delaware. These representations include debtors, creditor committees, secured creditors and lenders, prospective acquirers of assets, and other parties-in-interest. For example, the firm recently achieved confirmation of the plan of liquidation for Napster, Inc. (n/k/a Enco Recovery Corp.) in that company's Chapter 11 case and also represents Trenwick America in its Chapter 11 case. The firm also represents the creditor committees in the Kaiser Aluminum, DeVlieg Bullard II, Inc. and a number of other bankruptcy proceedings.

Corporate Litigation & Transactions: The firm frequently represents corporate clients, directors, and officers in stockholder derivative and class actions challenging a wide variety of corporate matters, including business combinations, hostile takeovers, going-private transactions, and proxy contests. For example, the firm served as Delaware counsel for Walter Hewlett in connection with his proxy contest and court challenge to the Hewlett-Packard merger with Compaq. In addition, the firm serves as counsel to boards of directors and special committees in connection with proposed transactions, internal investigations, and similar matters requiring Delaware law advice and opinions.

Intellectual Property Litigation: The firm's intellectual property lawyers regularly appear in federal court in Delaware where they serve as Delaware counsel to some of the country's largest corporations in prosecuting and defending patent, trademark, and other intellectual property litigation.

HEAD OFFICE

DELAWARE
222 Delaware Avenue, 17th Floor, PO Box 1150,
Wilmington, DE 19899
Tel: 302 654 1888 **Fax:** 302 654 2067
Website: www.ashby-geddes.com
Email: lashby@ashby-geddes.com

CONTACTS

Generally . . . . .Lawrence C Ashby
Bankruptcy . . . . .William P Bowden
Corporate Litigation & Transactions . . . . .Stephen E Jenkins
Intellectual Property Litigation . . . . .Steven J Balick
Commercial Litigation . . . . .Philip (Lee) Trainer
Commercial Transactions . . . . .James McC Geddes
Public Utility Law . . . . .James McC Geddes
Personal Injury/Medical Malpractice . . . . .Randall E Robbins

Commercial Litigation & Transactions: Ashby & Geddes' attorneys represent corporate and banking clients in the litigation of a wide variety of matters, including contract disputes, secured transactions, product liability claims, environmental matters, business torts, and insurance coverage issues. In addition, the firm has experience in the formation of various business entities and advises clients with respect to commercial transactions, including the purchase and sale of businesses and other assets.

Public Utility Law: The firm has specialized expertise in public utility law and rate regulation matters. In addition to advising clients generally about such matters, the firm acts as special counsel to the Governor and the Attorney General in connection with the Delaware Public Service Commission, an agency with exclusive jurisdiction over matters concerning the regulation of investor-owned gas and electric utilities. Most recently, the firm has provided consulting services for a major industrial client with regard to service reliability and rate issues involving an out of state utility.

Personal Injury/Medical Malpractice Litigation: The firm has extensive experience in litigating personal injury matters, importantly including the successful representation of plaintiffs in medical malpractice cases.

CLIENTS: Ashby & Geddes' clients range from large national and multinational businesses (or their directors or officers) in corporate and commercial litigation to local businesses in a wide array of commercial matters to individual clients in personal injury and medical malpractice cases.

THE BAYARD FIRM

THE FIRM

Chairman: Neil B Glassman

Number of partners: 15

Number of other attorneys: 19

HEAD OFFICE

DELAWARE
222 Delaware Avenue, Suite 900, PO Box 25130, **Wilmington**, DE 19899
Tel: 302 655 5000   **Fax:** 302 658 6395
Website: www.bayardfirm.com

FIRM OVERVIEW: The Bayard Firm is one of Delaware's premier law firms. The original members of the firm included former Delaware Supreme Court Chief Justice Daniel L Herrmann and Associate Justice William Duffy as well as Alexis I DuPont Bayard. The firm has a national practice in the areas of commercial bankruptcy, corporate litigation, commercial litigation, corporate law and partnership, business trust and limited liability company law, intellectual property, commercial transactions and insurance law. The firm also offers a full service practice in many other areas, including trial and appellate litigation in state and federal courts; real estate and land use; business transactions; federal and state taxation; estate planning; family law; employment law; regulatory and administrative law; personal injury; products liability and white collar crime. The Bayard Firm is the sole Delaware member of Meritas, the largest worldwide association of national and international business law firms. The firm's subsidiary, The Delaware Corporation Agency, Inc., is a registered agent of the Secretary of State of Delaware, enabling the firm to provide a full range of services relating to formation of new Delaware entities and registered agent services for new and existing Delaware entities.

MAIN AREAS OF PRACTICE:

Bankruptcy and Creditor's Rights: The firm provides services to debtors, creditors, official committees of unsecured creditors and equity holders, bank groups, purchasers, trustees and shareholders in bankruptcy and other insolvency proceedings. The firm's insolvency attorneys are experienced in federal bankruptcy cases, in state corporate receiverships and insurance company rehabilitations and liquidations. The firm has served or continues to serve as counsel to debtors, trustees, creditors' committees and bank groups in many Chapter 11 and Chapter 7 cases. The firm represents business entities in cases across the country, but has focused its practice on cases in the District of Delaware and has participated in virtually every significant bankruptcy case in Delaware in the last decade.

Business Litigation: The firm's Business Litigation Group has broad experience in all types of business litigation matters in Delaware state and federal courts. The firm has a strong expertise in corporate litigation in the Delaware Court of Chancery, the preeminent state court in the nation for the adjudication of corporate matters. Delaware is the forum of choice for incorporations and the creation of alternative business entities such as limited liability companies, business and statutory trusts, and limited partnerships. The firm's litigators have handled numerous types of corporate governance cases, including contests for the control of boards of directors; corporate election disputes; stock appraisal cases; stockholder class and derivative actions alleging breaches of fiduciary duty; proceedings involving the rights of preferred stockholders and debt holders; expedited proceedings for the inspection of corporate records; limited liability company and partnership governance and dissolution proceedings; and litigation against lenders and accounting firms. The firm also handles commercial disputes in state and federal courts in Delaware and other jurisdictions, in both jury and nonjury trials. The firm's experience includes business contract and tort litigation; consumer fraud defense; construction and mechanic's lien litigation; and environmental cases. The Business Litigation Group shares with the Intellectual Property Group the ability to represent clients in trade secrets, unfair competition and deceptive trade practice litigation.

Opinions/Transactions: The firm renders third party legal opinions regarding corporations and all alternative entities (LLCs, general and limited partnerships and statutory trusts), and transactions in which they engage. Its lawyers regularly advise clients in connection with the formation and operation of Delaware entities, including corporations, limited liability companies, general and limited partnerships and statutory trusts. The firm also advises clients regarding purchase/sale of businesses and assets, asset based financing and securitizations. The firm represents corporate trustees in structured finance and securitization transactions, frequently through the use of Delaware statutory trusts involving institutional investors.

Intellectual Property: The firm represents a wide variety of clients on matters concerning intellectual property, both in litigation and in negotiating resolutions prior to litigation (unfair competition, breach of employment or confidentiality agreements, theft or misuse of trade secrets and patent infringement). The firm counsels clients on the selection, protection and enforcement of trademarks as well as securing copyright or trademark protection and drafting technology and software licensing and sales agreements and non-competition arrangements.

Real Estate: The firm has a diverse Real Estate Practice, representing clients engaged in all aspects of the real estate industry throughout Delaware and the surrounding states. The firm's clients include residential and commercial buyers and sellers, owners and developers of apartment complexes, office buildings and residential subdivisions, homebuilders, and real estate lenders. The firm handles all aspects of title insurance business.

Taxation, Estate Planning & Probate: The firm handles both business and personal tax planning, personal estate planning, wills, trusts, guardianships, probate and trust administration. The firm advises clients in the law of income tax, gift and estate tax and taxation of partnerships, corporations, and other business entities.

Family Law: The firm's Family Law Practice includes representation of clients in connection with divorce and separation, child custody and support, and negotiation of prenuptial agreements.

CONNOLLY BOVE LODGE & HUTZ LLP

THE FIRM

Managing Partner: Jeffrey B Bove

Number of partners: 37
Number of other lawyers: 46

FIRM OVERVIEW: Connolly Bove Lodge & Hutz LLP serves international, national and local clients in a wide range of legal disciplines. Founded in 1944, the firm began in Wilmington, Delaware as an intellectual property firm but soon became a full service law firm with a broad range of legal specialties. These practice areas now include not only all phases of intellectual property, but also corporate, commercial, and bankruptcy law, for which the Delaware courts are renowned, as well as taxation, and a range of personal law services. In 2001 the firm established an office in Washington, DC, which gives it a presence close to the United States Patent and Trademark Office and the United States Court of Appeals for the Federal Circuit, the patent appeals court.

MAIN AREAS OF PRACTICE:

Intellectual Property: The firm handles all types of intellectual property matters, many of national and international significance. It has served as lead counsel in trials and appeals in courtrooms throughout the country since the inception of the firm. The firm's patent work has always concerned important inventions of the time, including miniaturized electronics, pharmaceuticals, industrial chemicals, films, herbicides, and freeze-dried coffee. The firm has continued as a major player over the decades, more recently adding biotechnology, crop science, computer and Internet specialties as those technologies developed. They remain at the forefront not only in patent litigation, but also in patent prosecution, trademarks, trade secrets, copyrights and all other facets of intellectual property law. The firm has handled numerous patent cases centering on important issues of first impression.

Corporate, Commercial & Business Law: Connolly Bove Lodge & Hutz's services to commercial clients range from the selection and formation of the proper business structure to all of the contract, tax and other transactional work or litigation necessary to keep the venture within the optimum legal framework.

Bankruptcy: Connolly Bove Lodge & Hutz's Bankruptcy Group represents local, regional, and national clients in some of the largest and most complex reorganization and liquidation bankruptcy cases in the country. Their bankruptcy group represents trustees, creditors, debtors and other interest holders including lenders, government agencies, trade vendors, landlords, equipment lessors, contractors, asset purchasers, insurance companies, bondholders and stockholders. They also represent clients in all types of bankruptcy related litigation, such as actions to recover preferential transfers and fraudulent conveyances.

HEAD OFFICE

DELAWARE
1007 North Orange Street, PO Box 2207, **Wilmington**, DE 19899
Tel: 302 658 9141   **Fax:** 302 658 5614
Email: cblh@cblh.com
Website: www.cblh.com

BRANCH OFFICES

DISTRICT OF COLUMBIA
1990 M Street NW, Suite 800, **Washington**, DC 20036-3425
Tel: 202 331 7111   **Fax:** 202 293 6229

CONTACTS

Intellectual Property ....Rudolf E Hutz
Corporate, Commercial & Business Law ....Henry E Gallagher Jr
....Collins J Seitz Jr
Bankruptcy ....Jeffrey C Wisler
Commercial & Residential Real Estate ....Richard D Levin
Tax & Estates ....Charles J Durante

Commercial & Residential Real Estate: The firm has one of the largest real estate sections of any law firm in Delaware. It conducts numerous closings each year and provide a broad range of other services to owners, tenants and purchasers in zoning, leasing, environmental issues, taxation, mortgages, liens and litigation.

Tax & Estates: The firm provides individuals with a whole spectrum of services including wills, trusts, and estate planning and administration.

CLIENTS: Connolly Bove Lodge & Hutz LLP serves international, national and local clients from multinational, publicly-held corporations to start-up enterprises. Representative clients: Pfizer Inc.; Steelcase Inc; Bayer AG; Bayer Healthcare; Rohm and Haas Company; Colgate-Palmolive, Company; Altria Group, Inc.; Henkel Corporation; Agfa-Gevaert NV; Helena Chemical Company.

CONNOLLY BOVE LODGE & HUTZ LLP
ATTORNEYS AT LAW

GRANT & EISENHOFER, P.A.

THE FIRM

Managing Partners: Jay W Eisenhofer, Stuart M Grant

Number of partners: 9
Number of other lawyers: 23

FIRM OVERVIEW: Grant & Eisenhofer (G&E) is a national litigation boutique that concentrates on federal securities and corporate governance litigation. G&E exclusively represents institutional investors, both public and private, who have been damaged by corporate fraud, greed and mismanagement. After the enactment of the Private Securities Litigation Reform Act of 1995, G&E achieved national recognition in representing institutional investors in federal securities fraud and related litigation. The firm has obtained over two billion dollars in recoveries in cases where the firm served as lead counsel. In fact, G&E has been lead counsel in four of the 12 largest securities class actions in history and was lead counsel in the case with the largest recovery in the history of The Delaware Court of Chancery.

MAIN AREAS OF PRACTICE:

Securities Litigation: G&E has substantial experience in handling a wide variety of complex civil matters in state and federal courts, and represents institutional investors in securities actions and corporate governance matters throughout the country. G&E has distinguished itself from plaintiffs' firms by representing almost exclusively institutional investors with large holdings. The firm does not file securities class actions on behalf of stockholders who do not hold significant blocks of stock, nor does it file a high volume of cases. And unlike the corporate defense bar, G&E does not have issue conflicts that prevent them from taking positions helpful to its institutional investor clients. G&E regularly serves as lead counsel in national securities class actions. Where its clients' losses are sufficient to justify an individual opt-out action, G&E has filed individual actions for those clients and successfully negotiated settlements that are exponentially higher than what the clients would have received in the class action. In both class actions and in litigation on behalf of individual investor clients, G&E has achieved notable results.

Corporate Governance: An acknowledged industry leader in corporate governance, the firm's partners are frequently invited to address industry conferences and have written extensively on corporate governance. Because of Delaware's unique position as the state of incorporation for over 58% of public companies and the national reputation of the Delaware judiciary, G&E frequently is called upon to render advice to institutional investors regarding Delaware corporate law, methods by which institutional investors can influence corporate management, and the validity, or likelihood of success, of particular corporate actions.

Monitoring: The firm monitors all new and potential litigation in the areas of shareholder derivative actions and federal securities litigation including pending cases, as well as financial and business news that may ultimately result in private litigation or claims by federal or state regulators, to offer institutional investor clients an opportunity to become aware at an early stage of any litigation or potential litigation that may impact their investments.

HEAD OFFICE

DELAWARE
Chase Manhattan Centre, 1201 North Market Street,
Wilmington, DE 19801
Tel: 302 622 7000   **Fax:** 302 622 7100
Email: info@gelaw.com
Website: www.gelaw.com

BRANCH OFFICES

NEW YORK
45 Rockefeller Center, 630 Fifth Avenue, 15th Floor
New York, NY 10111
Tel: 212 755 6501   **Fax:** 212 755 6503

CONTACTS

All Areas ....Jay W Eisenhofer
All Areas ....Stuart M Grant

CLIENTS: G&E's clients include some of the world's largest institutional investors including public pension funds, Taft-Hartley funds, private mutual funds, trust companies, fund managers, insurance companies and foreign investment managers.

INTERNATIONAL WORK: The firm represents a number of international and non-US based institutional investors in matters involving both corporations headquartered in US as well as in many other countries.

MORRIS, JAMES, HITCHENS & WILLIAMS LLP

THE FIRM

Managing Partner: David H Williams

Number of partners: 30
Number of other lawyers: 20

FIRM OVERVIEW:

Morris, James, Hitchens & Williams LLP recently celebrated its 70th anniversary. The firm, one of the largest in the state of Delaware, is organized into two major sections: litigation and transactions. The Morris James Litigation Group represents a wide variety of domestic and international clients in corporate/fiduciary litigation, bankruptcy and business litigation. The Transactions Group represents national and international clients as well as regional clients engaged in corporate and alternative entity transactions, commercial real estate transactions and business tax and estate planning. The firm's innovative legal work, creative use of technology and responsiveness to client needs have led to many significant client representations. For example, the DuPont Company selected Morris, James, Hitchens & Williams LLP as a member of its Primary Law Firm Network. The firm is also an ALFA International member.

MAIN AREAS OF PRACTICE:

LITIGATION

Corporate/Fiduciary Litigation: The firm devotes a major portion of its litigation practice to corporate disputes and disputes involving limited liability companies, partnerships, trusts and other entities in which fiduciary duty constitutes an integral part of the parties' relationship. Morris James litigators have significant experience in expedited proceedings before the Delaware Court of Chancery. Members of the litigation group have served as counsel for independent board committees to negotiate transactions in which certain board members may not be disinterested.

Bankruptcy: The firm represents debtors, creditors, creditors' committees, purchasers, investors and other parties in interest before the United States Bankruptcy Court for the District of Delaware. Morris James bankruptcy attorneys also counsel clients in both reorganization and liquidation cases before the Bankruptcy Court and in out-of-court workouts and debt restructurings.

Business Litigation: The firm has a substantial business litigation practice that involves representing clients in contract disputes, tort claims and insurance coverage litigation. This practice includes trials before judges and juries in every trial court in Delaware and appeals to the Delaware Supreme Court. The firm also serves as Delaware counsel in intellectual property litigation.

TRANSACTIONS

Delaware Corporations & Alternative Entities; Structured Finance: The firm provides strategic advice to clients who are establishing, managing, investing in or financing business ventures that take advantage of Delaware's unique corporate, business and tax laws. A substantial portion of the firm's alternative entity practice involves structuring Delaware special purpose entities for use in asset securitizations and other structured finance transactions. Morris James transactions attorneys frequently render legal opinions on matters of Delaware and United States federal law, and regularly participate in the drafting of Delaware's corporate and alternative entity legislation.

Real Estate: The firm represents many of the major developers, investors and builders doing business in the Delaware real estate industry. Morris James real estate attorneys advise lenders and borrowers in a full spectrum of financial transactions, from acquisition and construction financing to permanent financing, working capital, receivables, and other asset-based financings ancillary to real estate as well as conveyancing, leasing, zoning, subdivision, variance and other land use matters.

HEAD OFFICE

DELAWARE
222 Delaware Avenue, 10th Floor, **Wilmington**, DE 19801
Tel: 302 888 6800 **Fax:** 302 571 1750
Email: mjhw@morrisjames.com
Website: www.morrisjames.com

BRANCH OFFICES

DELAWARE
29 North State Street, Suite 100, **Dover**, DE 19901-3832
Tel: 302 678 8815 **Fax:** 302 678 9063
Email: mjhw@morrisjames.com
Website: www.morrisjames.com

16 Polly Drummond Hill Road, **Newark**, DE 19711-5703
Tel: 302 368 4200 **Fax:** 302 368 6259
Email: mjhw@morrisjames.com
Website: www.morrisjames.com

803 North Broom Street, **Wilmington**, DE 19806-4624
Tel: 302 655 2599 **Fax:** 302 655 8831
Email: mjhw@morrisjames.com
Website: www.morrisjames.com

CONTACTS

Corporate/Fiduciary Litigation	Lewis H Lazarus
Bankruptcy	Stephen M Miller
Business Litigation	Edward M McNally
Corporations & Alternative Entities; Structured Finance	Robert L Symonds Jr
Real Estate	Richard P Beck
Business Tax & Estate Planning	Norris P Wright

Business Tax & Estate Planning: The firm assists clients with complex business transactions, including purchase and sale agreements, joint ventures, mergers, consolidations, spin-offs, split-ups, acquisitions and divestitures. Morris James tax attorneys have substantial experience in the formation of tax-exempt organizations and obtaining determination letters for such entities. The firm's estate and trust practice provides advice as to the tax advantages of family giving and charitable gift planning, including the use of various types of trusts to accomplish the tax and non-tax objectives of the firm's clients.

CLIENTS: Morris, James, Hitchens & Williams LLP regularly represents large multi-national corporations, major financial institutions and other law firms, both within and outside of Delaware. The firm's attorneys are frequently consulted on matters of Delaware and United States federal law.

MORRIS, NICHOLS, ARSHT & TUNNELL

THE FIRM

Managing Partner: Walter C Tuthill
Number of partners: 40
Number of other lawyers: 48

FIRM OVERVIEW: Morris, Nichols, Arsht & Tunnell was founded in 1930 by former United States District Judge Hugh M Morris. The firm combines a broad national practice of corporate, intellectual property, bankruptcy and commercial law and litigation with a general business, tax, estate planning and real estate practice within the State of Delaware. The firm is regularly involved as lead counsel or co-counsel in matters of national and international significance, as well as those affecting its immediate community.

MAIN AREAS OF PRACTICE:

Delaware Corporation Law: Given the national preeminence of Delaware corporation law, the firm has long focused much of its practice on transactional and litigation matters involving Delaware corporations, as well as related business entities such as limited partnerships and limited liability companies. The firm's corporate counseling practice often involves representing boards of directors and board committees or advising on such matters as mergers and acquisitions, spin-offs, financings and other complex business transactions. The firm also provides legal opinions on major transactions. The firm's corporate litigation practice focuses on business litigation in the Delaware courts, principally the Court of Chancery and the Delaware Supreme Court. Such litigation often involves derivative suits or class actions in connection with M&A transactions, takeover battles and proxy contests. Both the firm's litigation and transactional attorneys regularly provide counseling on such matters as corporate governance and fiduciary duties, and play an important role in drafting and updating the Delaware General Corporation Law and related statutes.

Bankruptcy Litigation: The firm appears in jurisdictions throughout the US representing debtors and creditors in reorganization proceedings under the Bankruptcy Code. The firm regularly advises national and international clients concerning creditors' and debtors' rights issues and assists clients in negotiating workouts, restructurings and other solutions outside of formal insolvency proceedings. The firm has represented debtors-in-possession, secured and unsecured creditors, official committees of unsecured creditors, bondholders' committees, pre and post-petition lenders, purchasers of assets and other parties in interest, both as lead and local counsel.

Banking & Financial Services: The firm represents lenders, borrowers, issuers, and investors in all forms of financing transactions. The firm provides bank and insurance regulatory counseling and represents clients before the Delaware's Office of the State Bank Commissioner and Department of Insurance.

Commercial Transactional/Alternative Entities: The firm provides a complete range of commercial law services to local, national and international clients. Delaware has the most advanced statutes governing the formation and operation of limited liability companies, general and limited partnerships, and statutory business trusts. The firm provides specialized advice on all types of alternative entity transactions and handles all phases of a variety of complex legal transactions. In addition, because Delaware law is often selected as the governing law for major national and international transactions, the firm works with both in-house and regular outside counsel in the structuring and documenting of such transactions.

General Business/Environmental Litigation: The firm provides a full range of litigation services, including commercial, contract, environmental and employment cases, to national, international and local clients. The firm regularly appears before all Delaware trial and appellate courts, state and federal, local boards and administrative agencies, and before trial and appellate courts nationwide. The firm defends its clients in connection with governmental investigations including negotiations of consent orders or other types of settlements.

OFFICE

DELAWARE
1201 North Market Street, PO Box 1347, **Wilmington**, DE 19899
Tel: 302 658 9200 **Fax:** 302 658 3989
Website: www.mnat.com

CONTACTS

Corporate Litigation	A Gilchrist Sparks, III
Corporate Counseling	Frederick H Alexander
Bankruptcy Litigation	William H Sudell, Robert J Dehney
Commercial Transactional/Alternative Entity	Walter C Tuthill
General Business/Environmental Litigation	Donald E Reid, R Judson Scaggs, Jr
Income Tax/Trust & Estate	Thomas R Pulsifer
Intellectual Property	Jack B Blumenfeld
Real Estate	Donald I Isken
Regulation/Governmental Affairs	Michael Houghton

Income Tax/Trust & Estate: The firm advises individuals and businesses concerning all aspects of Delaware income tax law including the use of Delaware holding companies designed to minimize state income taxation incurred with respect to intangible assets such as trademarks, patents and investment property. In addition, the firm provides federal income, estate, gift and generation-skipping transfer tax advice to individuals, trusts, estates, business enterprises and their owners, and charitable organizations nationwide. The firm also advises on employee benefits matters including ERISA compliance. Delaware is widely regarded as one of the most advantageous jurisdictions in which to settle trusts. The firm acts as trust counsel to wealthy families settling trusts in Delaware and numerous Delaware trust companies and national banks conducting trust business in Delaware as well as large institutional and individual trustees and beneficiaries of trusts in Delaware and other jurisdictions.

Intellectual Property: The firm has been at the forefront of the development of IP law and has the reputation as the premier patent litigation firm in Delaware. As a result, the firm has achieved pre-eminence in IP litigation, in Delaware and nationwide. At the core of the firm's Patent Litigation Practice is the venue of the State of Delaware.

Real Estate: The firm provides legal advice with respect to planning, zoning, subdivision and development of real property, environmental matters and contracts for purchase and sale of residential and commercial property. The firm also represents lenders and borrowers in the financing, acquisition and development of residential, commercial and industrial property, and landlords and tenants in the leasing of property of all types.

Regulation/Governmental Affairs: The firm represents various public entities and agencies, as well as private sector clients, before legislative bodies and city, county, state and federal regulatory agencies and is involved in drafting, advocating and monitoring legislation and regulations that affect clients.

REPRESENTATIVE CLIENTS:

Abbott Laboratories, Advanced Energy, AstraZeneca, AstroPower, Bausch & Lomb, Biogen Idec, BP Amoco, Citicorp, Coca-Cola Company, Ford Motor Company, Honeywell, Invista, JPMorgan Chase, Marsh & McLennan, Medtronic, Merck, New York Life Insurance & Annuity Corporation, Oracle Corporation, Pfizer, Qualcomm, Rambus Inc., Sabre/Travelocity, Unocal Corporation and Viacom Inc. Sample representation of debtors in Chapter 11 cases include Fruehauf Trailer Corporation, The Loewen Group, Net2000 Communications, eToys, CyberCash, Valley Media, Oakwood Homes, Orbcomm Global, L.P., G-Mark, Inc. and USN Communications, Inc.; representative unsecured creditors' committees in bankruptcy cases include Montgomery Ward, Planet Hollywood, Safety-Kleen and United Artists.

YOUNG CONAWAY STARGATT & TAYLOR, LLP

THE FIRM

Chairman: James L Patton, Jr
Administrative Partner: Richard A Levine
Number of partners: 54
Number of other lawyers: 47

AREAS OF PRACTICE:

Bankruptcy & Corporate Restructuring 33%
Corporate Counseling & Litigation 21%
Personal Injury & Workers' Compensation 10%
Employment Law 8%
Commercial Real Estate, Banking & Land Use 8%
Tax/Trusts & Estate & Benefits 6%
Litigation & Trial Practice 5%
Business Planning, Transactions & Restructuring 4%
Intellectual Property Litigation 3%
Environmental Law 2%

FIRM OVERVIEW: Founded in 1959, Young Conaway Stargatt & Taylor, LLP has grown into Delaware's second-largest law firm, with more than 100 attorneys experienced in a wide range of practice areas important for business clientele throughout the state and around the world. Young Conaway attorneys appear frequently before state and federal agencies and actively participate in vital issues pending before its state legislature.

MAIN AREAS OF PRACTICE:

Bankruptcy & Corporate Restructuring: The largest in Delaware, playing a major role in virtually every significant bankruptcy in this district. The group routinely represents debtors, creditor committees, and shareholder groups in this jurisdiction and around the country. It provides a full array of services including out-of-court workouts, debt restructurings and pre-planned bankruptcies. This group is often referred to as Delaware's leading bankruptcy experts by the media.

Corporate Counseling & Litigation: One of the most experienced teams in the country, providing advice to corporations, stockholders and other law firms throughout the world. The practice ranges from structuring corporation transactions to litigating takeover battles and shareholder suits. The team includes members of the Council of the Corporation Law Section of the Delaware State Bar Association, which drafts amendments to the Delaware General Corporation Law.

Personal Injury & Workers' Compensation: The firm's personal injury litigators are recognized as some of the most experienced and skilled trial attorneys in the state. The litigators handle an array of personal injury matters including automobile and construction accident litigation, medical negligence, product liability and premises liability actions, complex tort litigation and workers' compensation, and consistently obtain substantial verdicts and settlements.

Employment Law: The Employment Law Group is the largest in Delaware, providing services to private and public employers in every area of employment law, including discrimination and sexual harassment claims, wrongful discharge lawsuits, union issues, workforce reductions, immigration and restrictive covenant issues.

Commercial Real Estate, Banking & Land Use: The firm offers a full range of services required for commercial development and financing for interstate and intrastate projects, including acquisitions, sales, financing for banks or businesses, leasing, zoning and land use projects such as shopping centers, office buildings, residential developments, and communications towers.

Tax/Trusts & Estate & Benefits: The firm's Taxation Group is engaged in federal and state tax planning for businesses and individuals. The group advises large and small businesses and their owners on matters of equity formations, shareholder, partnership and LLC agreements, business orga-

HEAD OFFICE

DELAWARE
1000 West Street, The Brandywine Building, 17th Floor
Wilmington, DE 19801
Tel: 302 571 6600 **Fax:** 302 571 1253
Website: www.YoungConaway.com

BRANCH OFFICES

DELAWARE
110 West Pine Street, **Georgetown**, DE 19947
Tel: 302 856 3571 **Fax:** 302 856 9338

CONTACTS

Bankruptcy & Corporate Restructuring . . . . .Robert S Brady
Corporate Counseling & Litigation .Bruce L Silverstein
Personal Injury & Workers' Compensation . . . . . .Richard A DiLiberto, Jr
Employment Law . . . . .Barry M Willoughby
Commercial Real Estate, Banking & Land Use . . . . .Larry J Tarabicos
Tax/Trusts & Estate & Benefits . . . . .Jerome K Grossman
Litigation & Trial Practice . . . . .Melanie K Sharp
Business Planning, Transactions & Restructuring . . . . .Craig D Grear
Intellectual Property Litigation . . . . .Josy W Ingersoll
Environmental Law . . . . .Anthony G Flynn

nization, sales and acquisitions, employee benefits, pension plans and more. The estate planning attorneys represent individuals in the creation of trusts and wills for intergenerational asset management and tax and charitable giving planning.

Litigation & Trial Practice: The continued success and growth of the firm's litigation experience, coupled with client needs, led to the formation of one of Delaware's largest litigation teams. The group combines the strongest litigators and trial practitioners from every practice section within the firm, coordinating the depth and experience in all traditional practice areas with extensive litigation and trial experience in both bench and jury trials throughout Delaware and the United States. Representative matters include the handling of complex commercial disputes, contract and fraud claims, and applications for expedited injunctive relief.

Business Planning, Transactions & Restructuring: The section handles matters arising at every stage in the formation, growth and development of corporations, limited liability companies, limited partnerships and other types of entities. The attorneys combine expertise in Delaware corporate law, alternative-entity law, tax, commercial transactions and bankruptcy reorganizations.

Intellectual Property Litigation: The firm's intellectual property attorneys represent national corporate clients and local businesses in the litigation of intellectual property disputes, including issues of trade secrets, trademarks, copyrights, patent infringement and unfair competition.

Environmental Law: The firm provides counsel on regulatory compliance matters and representation in administrative agency proceedings and in public and private party litigation, as well as matters ranging from compliance law to permits to environmental audits.

CLIENTS: Ranging from national and international corporations (some doing business as Delaware business entities), to businesses throughout the Delaware Valley (including state and local governments, school districts, banks, developers, professional practices) and individuals.

CONTENTS: Antitrust p.366; Bankruptcy p.371; Construction p.373; Corporate/Commercial p.376; Employee Benefits p.378; Employment p.379; Energy p.381; Environment p.390; Healthcare p.397; Insurance p.400; Intellectual Property p.403; Investment Management p.405; Litigation p.407; Media & Entertainment p.413; Projects p.415; Real Estate p.417; Tax p.422; Telecom p.425; IT & IT Outsourcing p.430; Individuals' Profiles p.430; Firms' Profiles p.477.

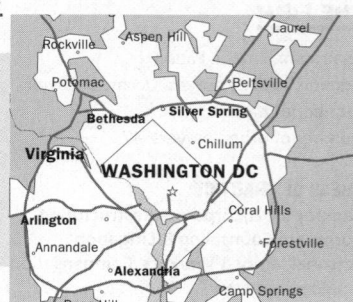

How lawyers are ranked

The opinions we gather from clients — mainly from in-house lawyers but also from other purchasers of legal services — are balanced by opinions from colleagues and competitors. Together, they provide two different perspectives — an all-round view — and biased viewpoints cancel each other out.

ANTITRUST

District of Columbia
Leading firms (Antitrust)

1. **ARNOLD & PORTER LLP** Washington, DC
2. **CLEARY GOTTLIEB STEEN** Washington, DC
   JONES DAY Washington, DC
3. **GIBSON, DUNN & CRUTCHER LLP** Washington, DC
   HOGAN & HARTSON LLP Washington, DC
   HOWREY SIMON ARNOLD & WHITE Washington, DC
   O'MELVENY & MYERS LLP Washington, DC
   WEIL, GOTSHAL & MANGES LLP Washington, DC
   WILMER CUTLER PICKERING HALE Washington, DC
4. **BOIES, SCHILLER & FLEXNER** Washington, DC
   FRESHFIELDS BRUCKHAUS Washington, DC
   FRIED, FRANK, HARRIS, SHRIVER Washington, DC
   KING & SPALDING LLP Washington, DC
   MORGAN, LEWIS & BOCKIUS LLP Washington, DC
   SKADDEN, ARPS, SLATE, MEAGHER Washington, DC
   WHITE & CASE LLP Washington, DC
5. **COVINGTON & BURLING** Washington, DC
   CROWELL & MORING LLP Washington, DC
   KIRKLAND & ELLIS LLP Washington, DC
   MAYER, BROWN, ROWE & MAW LLP Washington, DC
   MCDERMOTT WILL & EMERY Washington, DC
   PAUL, WEISS, RIFKIND, WHARTON Washington, DC
   SHEARMAN & STERLING Washington, DC

Firms are listed alphabetically in each band.

Band 1

Arnold & Porter LLP

See firm details p.478

The Firm: A historical presence, coupled with a "*critical mass*" of 69 attorneys throughout its offices, lends the group legal cachet and "*the talent to shine,*" industry sources said. The team is experienced in litigation, counseling and M&A, including advising GE/NBC in its $13 billion acquisition of Vivendi Universal Entertainment. Clients said they appreciate the firm's ability to balance "*the degree of being candid and cooperative.*" The team also provided SBC Communications and Cingular Wireless with antitrust and telecommunications regulatory assistance in connection with Cingular's $41 billion acquisi-

tion of AT&T Wireless Services. The transaction is reported to be one of the largest all-cash deals in US history. "*They make finely honed, clearly supported arguments,*" authorities said of the firm's antitrust lawyers. In litigation, the group appeared for Hoffmann-La Roche and Roche Vitamins in the Empagran case, which held significant implications for international antitrust law. The Supreme Court proceedings pertained to worldwide price-fixing allegations made by a purported class of foreign vitamin purchasers.
The Lawyers: **Bill Baer**'s (see p.432) "*combination of experience, judgment and ability to make things happen in the government*" make him "*a strong candidate in a lot of different fields,*" commentators said. An "*articulate and personable*" attorney, his broad portfolio of expertise includes M&A, non-merger investigations and litigation such as cartel disputes. He acted for SAP AG and SAP America in relation to Oracle's proposed acquisition of PeopleSoft. **Michael Sohn** (see p.469) earned "*the highest regard*" among peers for his sophisticated judgment calls and credibility before government agencies. He acted for Sanofi-Synthelabo in its $60 billion acquisition of Aventis. **Deborah Feinstein** (see p.442) concentrates on M&A and agency investigations. For example, she co-led for GE Medical Systems in obtaining antitrust clearance for its proposed acquisition of Instrumentarium. **Kenneth Letzler** (see p.452) is known for his litigation bent and is particularly adept in the areas of pharmaceutical, biotech and consumer product distribution. He defended Monsanto in multiple state court class actions alleging price-fixing of genetically modified seed. **Richard Rosen** (see p.465) applies his "*fine analytical mind*" on behalf of a telecom, IT and media clientele, while **Bruce Montgomery** (see p.458) is described as "*one heck of a litigator*" by rivals, who admire his wisdom and judgment. **Douglas Wald**'s (see p.473) profile spans a range of antitrust matters, including significant litigation. He represented Genzyme in connection with its acquisition of Novazyme.

The Clients: ArvinMeritor; Philip Morris; Komatsu; Pfizer; Guardian Industries; SAB Miller; Recording Industry Association of America; Ingram Micro; Kraft; Yamanouchi; Serono; Allergan; Wyeth; Microsoft; Micron Technology; Ocean Spray Cranberries; GlaxoSmithKline; Roche Molecular Systems; State Farm; Visa USA and Pegasus Development Corporation.

Band 2

Cleary Gottlieb Steen & Hamilton LLP

See firm details p.1342

The Firm: "*Globally, you can't beat*" this practice, whose talented DC team is enhanced by a "*strong transatlantic reach,*" analysts said. The heart of the broad-based practice is M&A, including a recent flurry of mergers in the software industry. Clients appreciate the top-to-bottom quality of the organization, adding: "*They are the type of firm that when you retain them, they'll certainly go all out for you.*" The group represented PeopleSoft in connection with the DOJ's challenge to Oracle's $7 billion hostile bid for the company. With respect to appearances before regulatory entities, the team is able to "*move the process forward quickly and understand what the likely outcome will be early on in the process,*" sources said. In litigation, the group acted for Aspen Technology regarding the FTC's challenge of its acquisition of Hyprotech. The team is also a strong contender in cartel defense matters.
The Lawyers: "*Superb and versatile*" **Mark Leddy** (see p.452) instills confidence with his "*careful, and creative*" approach. He effectively wields influence using a combination of "*experience and judgment,*" and the "*ability to make things happen,*" a competitor said. He acted for T-Mobile USA in its acquisition of Cingular Wireless' California and Nevada PCS networks and certain related spectrum. Both he and **George Cary** (see p.437) "*handle matters with a*"

District of Columbia
Leading individuals (Antitrust)

[1] BAER Bill *Arnold & Porter*, Washington, DC
LEDDY Mark *Cleary Gottlieb*, Washington, DC
SIMS Joe *Jones Day*, Washington, DC

[2] CARY George *Cleary Gottlieb*, Washington, DC
MCDAVID Janet *Hogan & Hartson*, Washington, DC
MELAMED Doug *Wilmer Cutler*, Washington, DC
NEWBORN Steve *Weil Gotshal*, Washington, DC
PARKER Richard *O'Melveny & Myers*, Washington, DC
PROGER Phillip *Jones Day*, Washington, DC
RILL James *Howrey Simon*, Washington, DC
RULE Charles *Fried Frank*, Washington, DC
SOHN Michael *Arnold & Porter*, Washington, DC

[3] DENGER Michael *Gibson Dunn*, Washington, DC
FLEXNER Donald *Boies Schiller*, Washington, DC
KATTAN Joseph *Gibson Dunn*, Washington, DC
KLAWITER Donald *Morgan Lewis*, Washington, DC
KOLASKY William *Wilmer Cutler*, Washington, DC
LOFTIS III James *Gibson Dunn*, Washington, DC
NANNES John *Skadden Arps*, Washington, DC
SCHECHTER Mark *Howrey Simon*, Washington, DC
SCHILDKRAUT Marc *Howrey Simon*, Washington, DC
YDE Paul *Freshfields Bruckhaus*, Washington, DC

[4] ANTALICS Michael *O'Melveny & Myers*, Washington, DC
FEINSTEIN Deborah *Arnold & Porter*, Washington, DC
GIDLEY J Mark *White & Case*, Washington, DC
LETZLER Kenneth *Arnold & Porter*, Washington, DC
MALESTER Ann *Weil Gotshal*, Washington, DC
MONTGOMERY Bruce *Arnold & Porter*, Washington, DC
MURIS Timothy *O'Melveny & Myers*, Washington, DC
ROSEN Richard *Arnold & Porter*, Washington, DC
SMITH Randolph *Crowell & Moring*, Washington, DC
SULLIVAN Kevin *King & Spalding*, Washington, DC
SUNSHINE Steven *Cadwalader*, Washington, DC

[5] ATWOOD James *Covington & Burling*, Washington, DC
BELL Robert *Wilmer Cutler*, Washington, DC
BLOCH Robert *Mayer Brown*, Washington, DC
CRISMAN C Benjamin *Skadden Arps*, Washington, DC
DENIS Paul *Dechert*, Washington, DC
EGAN James *Weil Gotshal*, Washington, DC
FAVRETTO Richard *Mayer Brown*, Washington, DC
FENTON Kathryn *Jones Day*, Washington, DC
GALLO Kenneth *Paul Weiss*, Washington, DC
GARZA Deborah *Fried Frank*, Washington, DC
GELFAND David *Cleary Gottlieb*, Washington, DC
HENRY Roxann *Howrey Simon*, Washington, DC
IMUS Neil *Vinson & Elkins*, Washington, DC
JACOBSEN Ray *McDermott Will*, Washington, DC
KRAUSS Joseph *Hogan & Hartson*, Washington, DC
LIPSKY Abbott *Latham & Watkins*, Washington, DC
MOLTENBREY MJ *Freshfields*, Washington, DC
SCHLOSSBERG Bob *Freshfields*, Washington, DC
SIMONS Joseph *Paul Weiss*, Washington, DC
SMITH Tefft *Kirkland & Ellis*, Washington, DC
VARNEY Christine *Hogan & Hartson*, Washington, DC
WALD Douglas *Arnold & Porter*, Washington, DC

Up-and-coming individuals
MCFALLS Michael *Jones Day*, Washington, DC
POPOFSKY Mark *Kaye Scholer*, Washington, DC
TALADAY John *Howrey Simon*, Washington, DC

Individuals are listed alphabetically in each band.

high success rate," with Cary's "vibrancy" impressing sources. Cary is acting for Glaxo-SmithKline in federal litigation concerning allegations of patent misuse related to Augmentin and other prescription drugs. Having returned from a three-year residency in the firm's Brussels office, **David Gelfand** (see p.444) leverages his experience on both sides of the Atlantic to make him "uniquely able to counsel." His "low-key, pragmatic" approach suits complex disputes such as Dow Chemical's complaint against Stolt-Nielsen, Odfjell, Jo Tankers and Tokyo Marine. Allegations include bid rigging, price-fixing, and territorial allocation in marine shipping services.
The Clients: ConocoPhillips; Air Liquide; Time Warner; United Technologies; Alcoa; American Express; UCB; T-Mobile USA; Fred Meyer; Siemens and DSM.

Jones Day
See firm details p.485
The Firm: "As good as it gets," the DC group remains the driving force in the firm's international antitrust practice, which particularly shines when handling contentious matters such as high-profile merger investigations. The group advised RJ Reynolds Tobacco Holdings in the merger of RJ Reynolds Tobacco Company and the US operations of Brown & Williamson Tobacco. The "effective and respected" cadre also was retained to act as global coordinating and trial counsel for UPM-Kymmene and its subsidiary, Raflatac, in multiple class actions alleging price-fixing and market allocation surrounding the sale of pressure-sensitive labelstock. The team's worldwide offices "complement each other extremely well," said clients who stress the increasingly important role of international antitrust law on US mergers.
The Lawyers: Much of the group's eminence in the field radiates from practice chair **Joe Sims** (see p.468), who is described by one prominent client as simply "the best antitrust litigator I've ever met." His forceful advocacy and candor appeal to clients looking for "a powerful adviser in front of the agencies." Sources extol his "judgment, experience and willingness to tell it like it is," and find it difficult to "argue with his success." **Phillip Proger** (see p.463) "can deliver the goods for the client" as an all-rounder. He was among a team that represented Bayer and its affiliates in connection with multiple class actions alleging price-fixing and market allocation of synthetic rubber products, urethanes and urethane chemicals. **Kathryn Fenton** (see p.442) "projects logical arguments," particularly in a counseling capacity involving complex M&A, while "talented" associate **Michael McFalls** (see p.456) impresses with his sophisticated familiarity of antitrust issues involving IP, biotech and pharmaceuticals. He also served as attorney-adviser to former FTC chairman Robert Pitofsky.

The Clients: Abbott Laboratories; Aetna; AOL; Cabot; ChevronTexaco; CIGNA; Clear Channel; Dell; DIRECTV; Eastman Chemical; GenCorp; General Motors; ICANN; Koch Industries; Liberty Media; Nextel; Nokia; Procter & Gamble; SBC California; UPM-Kymmene; Viacom and Yamaha.

Band 3

Gibson, Dunn & Crutcher LLP
See firm details p.285
The Firm: A "deep bench of talent" effectively wields across-the-board expertise, impressing clients with a "thoughtful, analytical and responsive" approach to a steady diet of antitrust matters. Though perhaps stronger in California, the "top shelf" DC team nevertheless consistently demonstrates a "solid understanding of the law" and attracts particular praise in the realm of litigation. It secured a preliminary injunction for Atlantic Coast Airlines, blocking a hostile takeover attempt by Mesa Air Group on antitrust grounds. Its success in litigation led one client to say: "When I use them I'm always confident." Other ongoing matters involve merger, cartel and other government investigations. Practitioners won client confidence for "working well with the fellows at the FTC."
The Lawyers: Clients highlight **Michael Denger** (see p.439) for his "focus on the practical approaches to complicated business and legal challenges." An antitrust generalist described as the team's "quarterback," he represented Transamerica in First American Corporation's acquisition of the tax reporting and flood certification businesses of Transamerica Financial. "Quick study" **Joseph Kattan** (see p.450) is "able to retain a massive amount of information," say clients. An "outstanding analyst," he has a particular profile in antitrust issues related to technology and IP. For example, he advised Sony Corporation of America and Sony Music Entertainment regarding a joint venture combining the recorded music businesses of Sony and Bertelsmann. Along with Denger, **James Loftis** (see p.454) is "one of the two bookends" of the DC practice, sources said. Clients dub him "a great thinker" who quickly "gets to the heart of the issue." In addition to a wealth of experience in civil and criminal litigation, he also has an established specialty in matters relating to the defense industry. Loftis represented Northrop Grumman in its acquisition of XonTech, a science and technology firm specializing in missile defense.
The Clients: Ticketmaster; Unocal; Intel; PeopleSoft; Callaway Golf; Conexant; Cadence Design Systems; First Reserve; New Times; Del Monte Foods; Schlumberger; Daiichi Pharmaceutical and 3D Systems.

Hogan & Hartson LLP

See firm details p.484

The Firm: This *"top-notch"* antitrust practice won client acclaim for its *"effective relationships with policy makers,"* particularly with regards to M&A. Some areas of expertise include healthcare, media and technology. *"The depth of their telecom practice is tremendous,"* commentators said. For example, the team counseled EMI in relation to the DOJ's investigation into the online music industry. Another jewel in its crown concerns Mandalay Resort Group's $7.9 billion merger with MGM Mirage. Clients also endorsed the firm's counseling practice, including advising a number of college football conferences with respect to the Bowl Championship Series. At issue were a national championship game and other post-season games among major college teams in the USA. The firm also effectively handles legislative matters involving antitrust law.

The Lawyers: **Janet McDavid** (see p.456) *"has one of the best reputations at the antitrust Bar,"* clients said. *"In terms of working the agencies, she is terrific."* Much of her time is spent in matters pending before US government agencies or the EC. One of the most prominent highlights involved Anthem Blue Cross and Blue Shield in a $16 billion acquisition of WellPoint Health Networks. *"Consistently excellent,"* **Christine Varney** (see p.472) is *"great at client relationships."* Focused on technology, she has cultivated a considerable profile in antitrust matters related to the online music industry. Formerly at the FTC, **Joseph Krauss** (see p.451) also gained client commendation for his *"strategically sound"* advice and *"strong negotiation skills with the agencies."*

The Clients: Advocate Health Care; American Express; American Hospital Association; Business Roundtable; Carnival Cruise Lines; eBay; Ford; General Dynamics; IBM; News Corporation; PacifiCare Health Systems; Symbol Technologies; Synopsys; Gemstar-TV Guide and Twentieth Century Fox.

Howrey Simon Arnold & White

The Firm: Considered to *"certainly have bench strength,"* the DC arm of this international practice is noted for being *"very attuned to the Washington scene and what's going on in the agencies."* A boost to its profile is the firm's involvement in some of the most significant merger decisions of the year. These include the DOJ v Oracle and FTC v Arch Coal, which involved the successful representation of Arch Coal in litigation surrounding its proposed acquisition of Triton Coal Company. The group also acted for Nestlé in a dispute concerning its proposed merger with Dreyer's. In that case, the FTC attempted to block the deal amid concerns that the merger would reduce market competition and raise prices for superpremium ice cream.

The Lawyers: *"A legend at the antitrust Bar,"* **James Rill** is *"still very much in his game."* His rainmaking skills, teamed with tremendous experience and government background, mean that he remains *"a giant of the antitrust Bar."* His *"solid understanding of the agencies"* helped BMG obtain antitrust clearance for its merger with Sony Music Group, a deal which was reviewed by the FTC and the EC. **Marc Schildkraut** and **Mark Schechter** together make *"a powerful combination,"* commentators said. They continue to win *"fans"* in the antitrust field for their intellectual elegance. In a key victory for Oracle, Schechter helped convince a federal court judge that the company's proposed hostile bid for PeopleSoft would not pose a threat to competition in the corporate software market. *"Terrific"* Roxann Henry (see p.219492) is noted for her strength on both the merger and the cartel fronts. She is considered to be *"doing extremely well in developing a strong practice,"* evidenced by her leading role on the Arch Coal matter. **John Taladay** *"knows how to approach the agencies,"* say sources. He is *"fairly forceful"* when needed, resulting in effective representation in matters such as criminal and civil investigations. He also has been retained on various international matters.

The Clients: Verizon; Intel; BMG; Oracle; Nestlé; Xerox; Rockwell Collins; Arch Coal and Checkpoint Systems.

O'Melveny & Myers LLP

See firm details p.294

The Firm: A *"formidable group"* is now considered to have *"the critical mass that puts them on the map,"* sources said. Clients appreciate the group's *"affable, highly skilled"* cadre of professionals. *"You can't go wrong"* with them, one client said. Backed by a distinctive West Coast presence, the team tackles a variety of work including merger reviews, government investigations and antitrust litigation. One high-profile matter was representing Triton Coal Company in a case involving the FTC, resulting in a significant decision regarding the coordinated effects theory of merger jurisprudence. *"From a value point of view, they are pretty rare considering the size of the firm and the type of work they are doing,"* a client said. *"As far as competence is concerned, the people are all top-flight, experienced lawyers who are not learning on your nickel."*

The Lawyers: Clients are attracted to **Richard Parker**'s *"breadth of expertise and the extent of his contacts."* He has forged a reputation as *"a street-smart lawyer"* whose effective litigation skills have earned *"a great deal of respect and credibility."* Another notable feature of his practice is his understanding of the US regulatory environment. **Michael Antalics** does *"an excellent job"* for clients in such areas as merger and criminal government investigations, while the arrival of the former chairman of the FTC

Timothy Muris is *"making a splash"* in the marketplace. This popular *"ideas man"* and antitrust scholar is expected to bolster the firm's profile, with one peer adding: *"Hats off to O'Melveny for getting him."*

The Clients: Honeywell; Marriott; Fannie Mae; Degussa and Crompton Corporation.

Weil, Gotshal & Manges LLP

See firm details p.1378

The Firm: Following last year's plunder of several Clifford Chance antitrust attorneys, the DC group of this nationally recognized practice has augmented its standing among market sources. Clients cited *"real synergy in the way attorneys work and support each other,"* resulting in fantastic results across a wide swath of antitrust law. On the merger side, the team acted for Vivendi Universal in its $14 billion joint venture with NBC to form NBC Universal, which combines the companies' entertainment assets. Regulatory authorities said the firm's *"frank and direct approach"* – led by Steve Newborn – serves clients well. *"They're fierce advocates for their position - not rollovers."* In litigation, the team represented DaimlerChrysler in class actions alleging that the company conspired with other major automobile manufacturers to prevent the flow of gray market imports of new vehicles from Canada to the USA.

The Lawyers: Co-head of the firm's antitrust practice group, **Steve Newborn** (see p.459) *"gets to the heart of the matter instantly."* Clients rely on his *"tough-skinned"* approach to *"getting results,"* though it is precisely this professional characteristic that has led others to label him *"an acquired taste."* Mergers reviews and investigations are his drawing card, but he also thrives on litigation. A former director of litigation at the FTC's competition bureau, he has defended Johnson & Johnson and several of its subsidiaries in a case alleging the company's bundling policies are anti-competitive. Clients celebrate *"extremely capable litigator"* **James Egan** (see p.440) as *"well prepared, careful and thorough."* He defended Shell in a case relating to employees' salaries, bonuses and benefits. At issue was whether the information was used to illegally set salaries at artificially low prices. Sources hailed **Ann Malester** (see p.455), a recent recruit from the FTC, as *"one of the very best at the government,"* where she served as Deputy Director of the Bureau of Competition. Her expertise in the pharmaceutical and defense industries combined with a *"no-nonsense way"* led one analyst to say: *"She'll knock the lights out."*

The Clients: Citibank; Great Lakes Chemical; Hoffman-La Roche; Johnson & Johnson; Kinder Morgan; Kodak Polychrome Graphics; Olin Corporation; Sherwin-Williams; The Sports Authority; Staples; Sun Chemical and Walgreens.

Wilmer Cutler Pickering Hale and Dorr LLP

See firm details p.497

The Firm: This "*first-rate*" antitrust practice earned client praise for its "*thoughtful and creative analysis.*" The group is "*manifestly dedicated and committed to clients' business objectives,*" and careful not to "*over-lawyer*" a case. It is a top contender "*If you're looking for a firm to handle an agency review of a transaction, Wilmer's ahead of the rest,*" another client said. The merger with Hale and Dorr has deepened the firm's antitrust bench, adding life science, IT and IP expertise. Another area of strength to emerge from the firm's "*big picture mentality*" is cartel enforcement, which is enhanced by recent transfers to the DC office from the Brussels branch.

The Lawyers: "*Careful thinker*" **Doug Melamed** (see p.457) is "*exceptionally bright analytically,*" and he is able to convert his "*intellectual depth*" into "*vibrant*" results. His familiarity of hi-tech, telecom and financial services has attracted a loyal following. In a recent case, he acted for Rambus in an FTC administrative trial alleging the company did not disclose its IP interests to a standard-setting organization before they were incorporated into industry standards. Interviewees said **William Kolasky** (see p.451) is "*among the most thoughtful and insightful practitioners*" at the Bar. His "*effective*" advocacy and understanding of the US regulatory environment have been demonstrated in such cases as Empagran v Hoffman-La Roche. On behalf of one of the principal petitioners, he helped convince the US Supreme Court to reverse a lower court decision concerning jurisdiction over claims for damages suffered outside of the US market. **Robert Bell** (see p.433) "*fits right into the mold of the external counsel who listens carefully and understands the business environment,*" said clients, who value his "*communication skills and interpersonal style.*" A major highlight for him has been successfully representing Eastman Kodak in securing approval for the sale of its remote sensing business to ITT Industries.

The Clients: Avfuel; Educational Testing Service; BAE Systems; Reichhold; Unimin; Regal Entertainment Group; Sony; Verizon Communications; Danaher; Datum; Johns Manville; Pacer International; Sallie Mae; ARAMARK; Odjfell ASA; PwC; Qwest; Philips and The Seattle Times.

Band 4

Boies, Schiller & Flexner

See firm details p.1337

The Firm: A nationally renowned litigation specialist, the firm features some of the most highly recognized trial lawyers in the USA. "*A recent but very significant player*" in the antitrust arena, the group has defended and prosecuted high-stakes litigation. Highlights have included the affirmation of summary judgment in the Eleventh Circuit Court of Appeals, dismissing claims of price-fixing conspiracy in the case of Holiday Wholesale Grocery etc al v Philip Morris USA. Defending Del Monte, the team battled claims by competitors concerning the fruit grower and distributor's 'Gold' pineapple. The cadre of "*clearheaded*" practitioners tends to skew toward antitrust-related federal court litigation although due to the boutique nature of the practice, it also has a thriving plaintiff's practice.

The Lawyers: "*Outstanding trial lawyer and antitrust thinker*" **Donald Flexner** continues to receive approbation for his experience – including litigation, counseling, government investigations and merger reviews.

The Clients: EchoStar; Del Monte Foods; Northwest Airlines and DuPont.

Freshfields Bruckhaus Deringer LLP

The Firm: Rivals deem this "*a strong practice which is getting stronger.*" Established in May 2002, the US arm of the European powerhouse has "*hit the ground running.*" Clients acknowledged the group's commitment "*to get the job accomplished.*" The group represented Wella Group in a second request review by the DOJ concerning Wella's $6 billion acquisition by Procter & Gamble. Agency work forms the bedrock of the practice, which includes a substantial amount of merger defense and analysis in addition to a raft of FTC and DOJ investigations. Acting for Amersham, the team handled the DOJ investigation of its $10 billion acquisition by GE. It also represented Piedmont Health Alliance and individual defendants in litigation brought by the FTC alleging collusive contracting practices.

The Lawyers: Clients dub **Paul Yde** "*a businessman's lawyer,*" alluding to his pragmatism when handling antitrust issues arising from M&A transactions, joint ventures, distribution and IP arrangements. "*His opinion is weighted very strongly.*" He advised Duke Energy regarding the FTC review of its divestiture of Empire Pipeline System. **MJ Moltenbrey** brings her experience at the DOJ to bear for the group. Clients endorse her "*tremendous insight*" and described her as a "*good strategist, particularly on DOJ enforcement actions.*" Her practice is agency-focused, handling civil and criminal investigations, cartel matters and merger defense. "*Particularly client-friendly*" **Bob Schlossberg** joins the team from Morgan, Lewis & Bockius. Interviewees praise his ability to "*focus on the facts of the situation,*" a characteristic that clients value in areas such as merger defense and related counseling.

The Clients: Alcan; AmerisourceBergen; Anheuser-Busch; ArcLight Capital Partners; Continental AG; Continental Airlines; Duke Energy Fields Services; HEB Supermarkets; Infineon Technologies; Lufthansa Cargo; Mannesmannrohren-Werke; Messer Group; Monsanto; The Thompson Corporation and Vitro Corporativo.

Fried, Frank, Harris, Shriver & Jacobson LLP

See firm details p.1349

The Firm: Based in New York and DC, the team delivers "*intelligent, well-reasoned, thoughtful and useful judgments.*" It is active in the regulatory review process of transactions, but also boasts expertise in litigation. Joint ventures, strategic alliances and B2B networks are other areas of focus. The team acted for MGM Mirage in its $7.6 billion acquisition of Mandalay Resort Group. Another highlight involved the Pasha Group in a conditional plea agreement with the DOJ that preserves the company's ability to present its defenses to a federal district court. In other matters, the team is also well versed in unfair competition issues and consumer protection claims.

The Lawyers: "*One of the most renowned antitrust experts in the US,*" **Rick Rule** (see p.466) enjoys national approval for his "*credibility and insight.*" Clients appreciate the "*clear and concise advice*" he provides. **Deborah Garza** (see p.443) "*absolutely stands out,*" clients said. "*Her excellent analytical skills and practical, business-sensitive judgment*" proved valuable in difficult situations, including complex M&A. Her reputation was further cemented by a presidential appointment to chairperson of the Antitrust Modernization Commission in March 2004.

The Clients: The group's representation of Microsoft continues to be a highlight of the practice. Other prominent clients include: ExxonMobil; Goldman Sachs; TradeWeb; US Airways; Wrigley and Canadian Automobile Dealers Association and Merck & Co.

King & Spalding LLP

See firm details p.635

The Firm: This "*preeminent southern law firm*" inspires client confidence for being able to hold its own against top-flight DC players. Sources said they "*can't speak highly enough*" of its broad antitrust offering, which encompasses litigation, cartel matters and transactional expertise. The team represents The Home Depot in litigation against Visa and MasterCard alleging anti-competitive violations. On the transactional side, the group obtained antitrust clearance for Excel's $328 million acquisition of Tibbett & Britten. "*Skilled across the board,*" it also features cross-border advice, particularly those issues involving Canada.

The Lawyers: William Blumenthal was recently appointed general counsel to the FTC. However, the firm still has the highly regarded **Kevin Sullivan** (see p.470). He is commended for his cartel and litigation-oriented practice. For

www.ChambersandPartners.com

All quotes in the text are from interviews with clients and competitors.

369

example, he is acting for Mylan Pharmaceuticals in an opt-out indirect purchaser antitrust action filed by a number of healthcare insurers. The case involves an alleged illegal supply agreement between Mylan and one of its active pharmaceutical ingredient suppliers.

The Clients: Angola LNG; Agrium; BHP Billiton; Brown & Williamson Tobacco; Coca-Cola; GE; GrafTech International; Miller Brewing Company; Milliken & Company; Rock-Tenn Company; Scientific-Atlanta; Sprint; Wolters Kluwer; UCB and UPS.

Morgan, Lewis & Bockius LLP
See firm details p.1556

The Firm: Clients said they "*specially reserve antitrust work for this outstanding team,*" which commands respect in cartel investigations, civil litigation, merger reviews and IP-related competition matters. A significant development in 2004 was the loss of Bob Schlossberg to Freshfields, though clients remain confident they will continue to retain the 30-lawyer group for complex cases. In addition to its considerable presence in the Northeast and West Coast, the firm also boasts European offices to assist on cross-border matters.

The Lawyers: Sources recognize **Donald Klawiter** (see p.450) for his criminal and cartel-based expertise – an area in which he is considered a go-to lawyer in the marketplace.

The Clients: Clients include Degussa AG and Jungbunzlauer. In addition, the firm has also represented a number of US and non-US senior executives embroiled in government investigations.

Skadden, Arps, Slate, Meagher & Flom LLP & Affiliates
See firm details p.1372

The Firm: This international corporate powerhouse naturally receives a steady flow of DC antitrust work, keeping its cadre of "*high-caliber attorneys*" busy on a range of antitrust matters. Particularly on large multinational mergers, the firm is "*able to marshal a team that is unparalleled.*" Clients equally praise the team's litigation prowess and sophisticated global outlook. The group represented News Corporation in connection with its acquisition of a significant interest in Hughes Electronics Corporation, including its DIRECTV subsidiary.

The Lawyers: Clients are attracted to **John Nannes** (see p.459) for his experience in dealing with regulatory agencies. He is distinguished for his intellectual firepower, dividing his practice between M&A, litigation and counseling. A former acting assistant attorney general in charge of the DOJ's antitrust division, he also specializes in airline-related work. He acted for KLM Royal Dutch Airlines in connection with its merger with Air France. "*First-rate*" lawyer **Benjamin Crisman** (see p.438)

impresses clients with his "*judgment, analytical skills and interpersonal relations with government regulators.*" His reputation is primarily cultivated in the transactional arena, particularly with regards to international M&A. He represented Aventis Behring when it was acquired by CSL Ltd.

The Clients: KLM; News Corporation; BHP Billiton and Entergy.

White & Case LLP
See firm details p.1379

The Firm: Clients endorse the team for its "*superior*" work, particularly noting its high level of client services. "*They will take calls in the middle of the night, and drop what they're doing in an emergency,*" one client said. The DC team of this global platform is active in criminal investigations, follow-on civil litigation and transactional matters. The group advised Stolt-Nielsen Transportation Group in a legal challenge to the DOJ's attempt to expel it from its Corporate Leniency Program. The team also defended a consortium of Southeast Asian rubber-thread producers in a case concerning global price-fixing allegations by US-based purchasers.

The Lawyers: **Mark Gidley**'s (see p.444) "*smart, proactive*" approach to M&A expertise has caught the market's attention. Described as "*well-schooled in the industry,*" he is also valued for his ability to turn complex technical points into issues that are "*penetrable*" to the layman.

The Clients: Coca-Cola Enterprises; Comcast; Houghton Mifflin Company; International Iron and Steel Institute; Interland; Ivax; Koninklijke Ahold; Stop & Shop Supermarket; SunGard and Traveler's Express.

Band 5

Covington & Burling
See firm details p.481

The Firm: The team won "*marks across the board*" for its "*sophistication*" in general advisory, regulatory and litigation matters. In addition to its "*effective and practical*" advice, the group also attracts clients with an unrivaled combination of pharmaceuticals and antitrust expertise. The firm represented a group of defendants in the National Resident Matching Program (NRMP) antitrust litigation, and was instrumental in securing legislation affording retroactive antitrust immunity to the disputed system. The 40-attorney DC team also draws upon other areas such as IP, transportation and food industry experience to round out its practice.

The Lawyers: **James Atwood** (see p.431) is deemed "*extraordinarily capable of analysis,*" and is particularly noted for his IP-related proficiency as part of a broader practice. A highlight involved PPL in a series of antitrust-related gov-

ernment investigations and related private lawsuits involving wholesale electricity.

The Clients: AstraZeneca; Bacardi; Bank One; Eli Lilly; ExxonMobil; GlaxoSmithKline; Microsoft; Procter & Gamble; Trane and Union Pacific.

Crowell & Moring LLP
See firm details p.482

The Firm: The "*highly successful*" team continues to win client confidence with its "*adept delivery*" in antitrust matters. Particularly active in the telecom sector, it was involved in the regulatory review of the Cingular Wireless/AT&T Wireless merger, which is considered to be one of the largest cash tender offers in the USA. While M&A has been its forte this year, the team's litigation expertise was also commended, mainly due to such work as the defense of several class actions on behalf of DuPont. The matter involved price-fixing allegations in the synthetic rubber industry. Another area of increased visibility has been international cartel investigations spanning the US and other jurisdictions.

The Lawyers: The group's antitrust profile is attributed to the "*phenomenally well-versed*" practice group leader **Randolph Smith** (see p.469), whose solid understanding of market dynamics impresses clients. He spends the bulk of his time in the M&A arena, though he also has expert knowledge of cartel investigations.

The Clients: SBC Communications; Alcoa; DuPont; United Technologies; Reed Elsevier; CSX Transportation and Georgia-Pacific.

Kirkland & Ellis LLP
See firm details p.770

The Firm: "*First choice for a large piece of complex and difficult litigation,*" this "*outstanding collection*" of trial lawyers is able to draw on antitrust expertise throughout its network of offices in the USA and beyond. Its "*strong team concept*" is also brought to bear in the areas of M&A and joint ventures. Highlights have included advising Barr Laboratories on a nationwide class action involving the alleged wrongful delay of the introduction of a lower-priced generic version of the antibiotic Cipro. The "*highly organized and aggressive approach*" proved successful in battling cases such as the FTC's challenge to the Heinz/Beech-Nut baby food merger. Its "*strategic thinking*" was also illustrated in transactions such as Alpharma's acquisition of the generic oral solid dose pharmaceutical business of FH Faulding & Co.

The Lawyers: Transferred to DC from the Chicago office, **Tefft Smith** (see p.469) maintains a solid foundation from which to launch a "*hands-on*" line of attack. In charge of the firm's antitrust and competition practice group, he is respected for his "*rigorous analytical*" style, which is often parlayed on sensitive merger

370   All quotes in the text are from interviews with clients and competitors.

CHAMBERS USA 2005

clearances, criminal investigations and class action price-fixing cases.

The Clients: BP America; Allstate; Dow Chemical; SC Johnson & Son; Bayer; Chiquita Brands International and Coors Brewing Company.

Mayer, Brown, Rowe & Maw LLP
See firm details p.771

The Firm: This group's penchant for "*always putting the client first*" wins applause from clients, who also approve its ability to "*put the best team together.*" Sources highlighted the firm's strength in both the transactional and litigation arenas. One client said: "*No one compares to the kind of service, knowledge base and results we've had with Mayer Brown.*" Key matters have included advising BellSouth in connection with the sale of its Latin American wireless telephone business, including related antitrust advice spanning several Latin American countries.

The Lawyers: **Robert Bloch** (see p.434) is "*highly sought after in healthcare antitrust,*" while seasoned antitrust lawyer **Richard Favretto** (see p.441) has "*a good sense of the courtroom,*" sources said. Favretto's generalist antitrust practice also includes merger reviews, which he covers with "*a soundness and balance to his judgment.*" He is handling several ongoing state and federal antitrust class actions involving products including synthetic rubber and magazine paper.

The Clients: Cargill; Marconi; Brunswick Corporation; Bertelsmann; VHA Novation; DSM Copolymer; DSM Elastomers Europe and Bowater.

McDermott Will & Emery
See firm details p.773

The Firm: Clients appreciate the team's "*concerted effort to understand us and our products,*" resulting in a "*tailored assessment of risk and legal analysis.*" The group's impressive client base is forged from an established market presence in antitrust law, covering mergers, litigation, distribution issues and IP matters. Highlights have included representing Lockheed Martin in an antitrust and trade secrets dispute against Boe-

ing concerning a multibillion dollar US Air Force launch vehicle.

The Lawyers: **Ray Jacobsen** (see p.448) is pitched as "*the face of the firm*" by many commentators, who also admire his effective leadership of the firm's antitrust and competition practice group.

The Clients: Amgen; Covance; Medtronic; FMC; HMA; Orica; RAG Coal; The Timken Company and Hillenbrand.

Paul, Weiss, Rifkind, Wharton & Garrison
See firm details p.1362

The Firm: This fledgling DC practice complements an already established New York antitrust force, resulting in a "*terrific*" blend of litigation, transactional and investigative expertise. The group successfully represented Automatic Data Processing in its acquisition of Pro Business, which was the subject of a DOJ second request investigation. The team is also representing MasterCard in more than 30 state class actions alleging anti-competitive business practices involving debit and credit cards. Highlights include representing MasterCard in over 30 state class actions involving the alleged tying of debit and credit cards. The group also successfully acted for Time Warner in the DOJ investigation of Movielink, a joint venture of major movie studios relating to Video on Demand.

The Lawyers: Observers are "*keeping an eye*" on **Joseph Simons** (see p.468), the "*talented*" co-chair of the firm's antitrust group who served as director of the FTC's Bureau of Competition from June 2001 to August 2003. Renowned as "*tough on the economic side of the analysis,*" he has the potential of being equally capable in private practice, analysts said. "*Ferocious*" litigator **Ken Gallo** (see p.443) impresses peers and clients alike, some dubbing him one of "*the best litigators I've ever seen in terms of his oral arguments.*"

The Clients: The group's clients include Time Warner, MasterCard and CIT Group.

Shearman & Sterling
See firm details p.1369

The Firm: Its well-defined antitrust muscles won client respect, which is further enhanced by a deep bench of support in New York and elsewhere. The team acts for Syngenta in allegations against Monsanto concerning possible anti-competitive activities in the corn seed business. Other highlights include advising Global Telecom in connection with a criminal investigation concerning the termination of international telephone calls to the Philippines. The case potentially could determine the reach of US laws to alleged cartels operating in foreign countries.

The Clients: BASF; Novartis; De Beers; Anglo American; Viacom; BOC; Linde and Watson Pharmaceuticals.

Other Notable Practitioners

Steven Sunshine, who recently moved to Cadwalader, Wickersham & Taft LLP, has "*a terrific grasp of the law,*" according to clients, who appreciate his "*strategic sense of how to resolve difficult problems.*" He is formerly of Shearman & Sterling. "*Meticulous, thoughtful, and popular with clients,*" **Paul Denis** (see p.439) of Dechert focuses on antitrust issues related to M&A, joint ventures and other business combinations across a range of industries. "*Solid merger lawyer*" **Neil Imus** (see p.448) of Vinson & Elkins LLP is also credited with a "*respectable*" litigation practice, while **Tad Lipsky** (see p.453) of Latham & Watkins LLP is "*brilliant technically.*" Clients often retain him on issues involving regulated industries such as in the airline, communications and financial arenas. He is also valued for his international experience; he was involved in the formation of Spansion LLC and AMD Corporation. Despite his relative youth, "*ferociously smart*" **Mark Popofsky** (see p. 462) at Kaye Scholer LLP is described as a "*scholarly lawyer*" who is also "*commercially pragmatic,*" according to clients. His practice combines regulatory work and litigation matters. One highlight involves helping to secure merger clearance on behalf of RJ Reynolds Tobacco in connection with its proposed merger with Brown & Williamson.

BANKRUPTCY

Band 1

Arnold & Porter LLP
See firm details p.478

The Firm: A weighty practice built around representation of debtors, unsecured creditors' committees and asset purchasers, Arnold & Porter was identified by numerous interviewees as a leader in the DC market. Its attorneys are "*always worthy adversaries,*" one peer noted. The

firm is representing US Airways in its second, highly publicized, Chapter 11 filing. It is also retained by the Office of the People's Counsel, intervener in the Mirant case, and is currently arguing the question of duality of jurisdiction between the bankruptcy courts and FERC.

The Lawyers: The "*top-notch*" **Daniel Lewis** (see p.453) heads this impressive group. His approach is "*professional in every respect*" and promotes the amicable resolution of disputes.

Picked out by numerous sources as deserving recognition for his "*above-average approach, energy and productivity,*" **Michael Bernstein** (see p.434) is a young attorney who has built up a wide-ranging practice in bankruptcy and related litigation. His "*terrific insight and judgment*" won him praise from other attorneys, who indicated that he "*brings a lot of substance to the table.*"

District of Columbia

Leading firms (Bankruptcy)

1 ARNOLD & PORTER LLP
  SWIDLER BERLIN SHEREFF FRIEDMAN LLP
  WILMER CUTLER PICKERING HALE AND DORR
2 AKIN GUMP STRAUSS HAUER & FELD LLP
  COVINGTON & BURLING
  DICKSTEIN SHAPIRO MORIN & OSHINSKY LLP
3 ARENT FOX
  HOGAN & HARTSON LLP
  WHITE & CASE LLP
  ZUCKERMAN SPAEDER LLP

Leading individuals (Bankruptcy)

1 FRANKEL Roger *Swidler Berlin*, Washington, DC
  LEWIS Daniel *Arnold & Porter*, Washington, DC
  PERLSTEIN William *Wilmer Cutler*, Washington, DC
2 BAXTER Michael *Covington & Burling*, Washington, DC
  KUNEY David *Sidley Austin*, Washington, DC
  LITT Daniel *Dickstein Shapiro*, Washington, DC
  SAMORAJCZYK Stanley *Akin Gump*, Washington, DC
3 ALBERTS Sam *White & Case*, Washington, DC
  BERNSTEIN Michael *Arnold & Porter*, Washington, DC
  DOLAN Edward *Hogan & Hartson*, Washington, DC
  GOLDSTEIN Bruce *Zuckerman Spaeder*, Washington, DC
  PLEVIN Mark *Crowell & Moring*, Washington, DC
  WYRON Richard *Swidler Berlin*, Washington, DC

Up-and-coming individuals

  GOLDBLATT Craig *Wilmer Cutler*, Washington, DC

Firms and individuals are listed alphabetically in each band.

The Clients: The firm has undertaken large reorganizations on behalf of clients such as Fannie Mae and American West. Other clients include Chase Manhattan Bank; Owens Corning; Citicorp North America; Hewlett Packard and Toshiba.

Swidler Berlin LLP

See firm details p.495
The Firm: A national practice with substantial expertise in the energy sector, Swidler has carved a niche representing public utility companies in Chapter 11 proceedings, acting on behalf of National Grid in the US Gen reorganization and Pepco in the Mirant bankruptcy. The firm is also heavily involved in asbestos-related cases, where the increasing dominance of pre-packaged bankruptcies keeps the team busy. In addition, it is involved in the second US Airways reorganization, representing a major secured creditor.
The Lawyers: A "*dean of the bankruptcy practice,*" **Roger Frankel** (see p.442) heads the group and can be counted upon to "*play straight and take a problem-solving approach.*" He is currently representing the Future Claims Representative in the WR Grace matter. **Richard Wyron** (see p.476) is an experienced partner within the team. He has cultivated a strong reputation as an imaginative strategist whose forte is reassessing complicated matters.

The Clients: Pepco and US Gen are examples of the firm's clientele, which is made up of debtors, indenture trustees, secured and unsecured creditors and banks and other financial institutions.

Wilmer Cutler Pickering Hale and Dorr LLP

See firm details p.497
The Firm: This firm has "*substantial depth*" augmented by a considerable New York presence and effective "*give and take*" between the two offices. A diverse practice, it represents the whole range of clients, from troubled companies seeking restructuring assistance to large commercial lenders and bondholders, and buyers and sellers of distressed assets. The past 12 months have seen the firm assist KB Toys in the Chapter 11 reorganization of its retail operations, and represent insurance companies in the recent spate of asbestos-related bankruptcies.
The Lawyers: The strength of the overall team drew comment from interviewees, impressed by the prevalence of attorneys who are "*active in taking the lead*" and who bulk to form "*substantial bench strength.*" Firm chairman and head of the bankruptcy practice, **Bill Perlstein** (see p.461) is a "*cerebral attorney, attuned to both the legal and business nuances.*" Known particularly for his debtor work, although his practice is broader than this, Perlstein is an attorney with "*great poise and composure.*" A "*smart young lawyer,*" **Craig Goldblatt** (see p.445) recently represented the debtor in the Integrated Telecom Express case before the Third Circuit Court of Appeals. He is seen as an "*energetic and responsive attorney.*"
The Clients: Verizon; AOL; Fannie Mae; The Washington Post; Iridium LLC and ElderTrust.

Band 2

Akin Gump Strauss Hauer & Feld LLP

See firm details p.477
The Firm: This focused, integrated practice capitalizes on a "*deep national bench.*" It is well regarded for its strength in noncontentious bankruptcy cases, and has developed a niche representing insurance companies in asbestos-related bankruptcies to avoid the immediate payment of future claims. On the creditor representation side, the practice has been defending two Kmart creditors in preference claims. It is also notable for its distinct international expertise. The firm has this year formed an informal creditors committee to negotiate with Iraq on behalf of contractors engaged, but not paid, by Saddam Hussein.
The Lawyers: The leading light at the firm is **Stanley Samorajczyk** (see p.466). Known as a facilitative, consensus-driven attorney and an experienced strategist, the head of the group has

"*undeniable credibility and inherent validity.*"
The Clients: The firm's clientele is made up of creditors in large bankruptcy cases, insurance companies and purchasers of distressed companies or their assets.

Covington & Burling

See firm details p.481
The Firm: A steady stream of creditor work has kept the practice busy this year, as it continues to guide clients through complex bankruptcy proceedings. It is experienced in a variety of industry sectors and over the past year has been representing Gillette in the Women First HealthCare bankruptcy. The group is also fully versed in Chapter 11 reorganizations, having been involved in the Dow Corning and Armstrong World Industries proceedings. A recent highlight was the representation of Rail World in an asset purchase agreement following the Bangor & Aroostook filing.
The Lawyers: Key partner **Michael Baxter** (see p.432) is credited with developing the firm's practice into a truly national one. He has an "*excellent understanding of risk tolerance,*" clients said, and a "*candid, trustworthy manner.*" He takes the lead on the firm's noncontentious practice and is a "*capable, savvy operator.*"
The Clients: The firm acts on behalf of official committees in bankruptcy, debtors, creditors and other interested parties.

Dickstein Shapiro Morin & Oshinsky LLP

See firm details p.483
The Firm: In the main a creditors' practice, competitors concede that this firm is well established in the region, and a significant force for "*one-off, hard-nosed litigation.*" Its work ranges from asset purchases from distressed companies to representation of lenders' interests throughout bankruptcy proceedings. With principal clients of the stature of Allied Capital, it is little wonder that the firm has cultivated a strong reputation. The team also undertakes a small amount of debtor work; highlights here have included the reorganization of a local hospital. Sector focuses include IP and energy.
The Lawyers: Chair of the group, **Daniel Litt** (see p.453) comes to bankruptcy from a litigation background. He is especially adept at predicting the judiciary's reaction to an argument and "*pursuing a strategy that you can get done without wasting time.*"
The Clients: Clients range from lenders such as Allied Capital to creditors' committees and debtors in bankruptcy.

Band 3

Arent Fox PLLC

The Firm: A strong, local practice with a "*growing profile,*" this firm represents a broad portfo-

372   All quotes in the text are from interviews with clients and competitors.

CHAMBERS USA 2005

lio of debtors, creditors, creditors' committees and third parties acquiring assets. Its burgeoning creditors' committee practice operates out of both the DC and New York offices, whilst the creditor and debtor work feeds from both national and local markets. The firm recently acted as co-counsel to the debtor in the Mattress Discounters reorganization, and represents an international paper manufacturer in its US bankruptcy. The firm has niche expertise in the construction sector.

The Lawyers: Particularly known for their skills as business counsel, attorneys in this well-led team were applauded for being "*communicative and able to understand the client's goals.*" At the helm is Mary Joanne Dowd.

The Clients: The firm acts on behalf of creditors' committees, debtors, indenture trustees, bondholders and noteholders in a wide variety of industries including construction, manufacturing and e-commerce.

Hogan & Hartson LLP

See firm details p.484

The Firm: A solid outfit that provides "*excellent service,*" the firm has been involved in most of the major sectors afflicted by bankruptcy over recent years. Most recently it has been involved with Internet and telecom companies and the airline industry. The firm concentrates on representation of secured and unsecured creditors and asset purchasers. It has also developed expertise counseling executory contract coun-

terparties in negotiations to update terms and conditions in line with the maturing of the Bankruptcy Code. A highlight from the past year was its representation of AEP on the acquisition of existing contracts from Enron's international coal team.

The Lawyers: With a background in representing financial institutions, **Edward Dolan** (see p.439) stands out as a "*responsive, knowledgeable attorney who knows how to speak in layman's terms.*"

The Clients: The firm represents secured and unsecured creditors, asset purchasers and executory contract counterparties.

White & Case LLP

See firm details p.1379

The Firm: The recent hire of Sam Alberts from Akin Gump Strauss Hauer & Feld propels this firm into the rankings this year. It focuses on representation of creditors' committees and recently served as counsel to the official committee of unsecured creditors in the bankruptcy of a local hospital. The group also has a mid-Atlantic focus and works closely with other White & Case offices in this regard. For example, it is currently assisting the existing debtors counsel in the Mirant case.

The Lawyers: Drawing great loyalty from clients, **Sam Alberts** (see p.430) is known for his expertise in the healthcare industry. He has a "*strong ability to translate the law and to educate lay people so they function effectively and efficiently.*"

The Clients: Mirant and debtor affiliates; DCHC Liquidating Trust; Grupo IMSA, SA de CV and secured and unsecured creditors' committees.

Zuckerman Spaeder LLP

The Firm: Working closely with its Delaware office, this small practice acts for a range of clients from debtors to secured creditors and creditors' committees, across a variety of industry sectors. Though the firm has a litigation pedigree, commentators noted its focus on company reorganizations and its efforts in guiding clients out of Chapter 11 proceedings.

The Lawyers: **Bruce Goldstein** was lauded for his "*ability to understand problems and how to get to a reasonable solution.*"

Other Notable Practitioners

Widely respected for his abilities as a litigator, Sidley Austin Brown & Wood LLP's **David Kuney** (see p.452) is "*an intellectual leader*" in DC. His practice in complex, cases has seen him heavily involved in the Enron power litigation of late. At Crowell & Moring LLP, **Mark Plevin** (see p.462) is "*one of the most sought-after lawyers around*" for asbestos-related work. He recently took the lead role in the MidValley case and is an "*effective attorney*" and "*very sharp thinker.*" His expertise spans both insurance and bankruptcy.

CONSTRUCTION

District of Columbia
Leading firms (Construction)

1	THELEN REID & PRIEST LLP *Washington, DC*
2	BASTIANELLI, BROWN & KELLEY *Washington, DC*
	DLA PIPER RUDNICK GRAY CARY *Washington, DC*
	MCMANUS SCHOR ASMAR *Washington, DC*
	SPRIGGS & HOLLINGSWORTH *Washington, DC*
3	GIBSON, DUNN & CRUTCHER LLP *Washington, DC*
	HOLLAND & KNIGHT LLP *Washington, DC*
	SEYFARTH SHAW LLP *Washington, DC*
4	ARENT FOX PLLC *Washington, DC*
	ARNOLD & PORTER LLP *Washington, DC*
	BELL, BOYD & LLOYD *Washington, DC*

Firms are listed alphabetically in each band.

Band 1

Thelen Reid & Priest LLP

See firm details p.300

The Firm: One of the largest international construction, engineering and infrastructure practices; the firm's tentacles touch upon some of the most significant projects on the planet. Its history stretches back to the Hoover Dam and is

more recently linked to projects such as the Eurotunnel and the reconstruction of Iraq. "*A significant cadre of competent construction practitioners*" delivers adroit performances on a variety of issues. In DC, the focus has been on construction litigation, government-related projects and various international proceedings. "*Clearly in a class of its own,*" the "*nucleus of good people*" is seemingly ubiquitous, lending crispness to a host of high-profile deals, commentators said. The team helped structure power plants in developing countries, defended contractors in litigation with hundreds of millions of dollars at stake, and marshaled clients through the regulatory web connected to certain projects. "*They're efficient, quick and reasonable,*" a client said, "*reasonable in terms of price as well as the legal positions they take.*" In addition, a 2003 alliance with the UK-based Masons has further enhanced the firm's strong grip on the global market. Also supporting the DC construction team are experts in related areas such as insurance, tax and employment. "*Their skills set is extraordinary,*" sources said.

The Lawyers: **Andrew Ness** is considered "*one of the best practitioners anywhere. People trust him.*" His predominantly litigation practice is shaped by variety rather than specialty, sprinkled with a dose of alternative dispute resolution techniques. He is as comfortable on the domestic stage as in the international arena – handling offshore oil projects in the Middle East, processing facilities in Venezuela and various assignments in Southeast Asia. "*Dogged litigator*" **Michael Jaffe** is often retained to crush the competition in the courtroom. "*Don't use him for the everyday, mundane stuff,*" one client said. "*He's for the threatening cases with potentially catastrophic consequences.*" A generalist with extensive construction law expertise, the renowned litigator is said to be "*an even better strategist,*" able to accurately read the opposition. He has advised foreign-based companies entangled in disputes in the USA. Another hard-nosed operator is **Barbara Werther**, whose focus is closer to home. She thrives on a practice that involves contractors and owners in disputes linked to delays, acceleration and inefficiencies among other similar issues.

District of Columbia
Leading individuals (Construction)

1
BASTIANELLI Adrian *Bastianelli Brown*, Washington, DC
NESS Andrew *Thelen Reid*, Washington, DC
WEST Joseph *Gibson Dunn*, Washington, DC

2
HARRIS Larry *DLA Piper*, Washington, DC
JAFFE Michael *Thelen Reid*, Washington, DC
KEATING Geoffrey *McManus Schor*, Washington, DC
PATIN Douglas *Spriggs & Hollingsworth*, DC
STEPHENSON Andrew *Holland & Knight*, Washington, DC
TAUB Kathy *Arent Fox*, Washington, DC

3
MCMANUS Joseph *McManus Schor*, Washington, DC
PRESTON Richard *Seyfarth Shaw*, Washington, DC
RUBINSTEIN Joel *Bell Boyd*, Washington, DC
SCHOR Laurence *McManus Schor*, Washington, DC
WERTHER Barbara *Thelen Reid*, Washington, DC

Individuals are listed alphabetically in each band.

The Clients: Bechtel; Anheuser-Busch; Fiat; Centex; AMEC and Clark Construction.

Band 2

Bastianelli, Brown & Kelley

The Firm: This ten-attorney specialist firm profits from a construction practice that also straddles related areas such as government contract procurement, admiralty/maritime issues and environmental remediation. Its pool of talent includes a former judge of the Armed Services Board of Contract Appeals and a former attorney with the US Navy's Naval Air Systems Command. According to interviewees, the crux of the team is Adrian Bastianelli, whose market profile is key to the firm's overall success. Its experience encompasses domestic and international heavy construction projects such as rapid transit systems, power generators, wastewater treatment facilities and manufacturing plants. Other high-profile assignments involve extensive road networks and irrigation projects overseas. The team has also been associated with bid protests, regulatory compliance proceedings and other construction-related litigation.

The Lawyers: Though pitched as *"more of an arbitrator than a courtroom trial lawyer,"* **Adrian Bastianelli** *"can do anything,"* sources said. *"But he doesn't do irascible."* His status as *"dean of the Bar"* helped propel his achievements in a raft of construction cases, primarily in the alternative dispute resolution realm. The registered engineer has served as chairman of five dispute resolution boards (DRBs) related to Boston's Central Artery project – dubbed one of the largest and most complex urban transportation projects in the USA.

The Clients: The firm often advises government contractors, subcontractors, engineers, architects, developers and financial institutions among others.

DLA Piper Rudnick Gray Cary US LLP
See firm details p.765

The Firm: Though still in its nascent stages, the alliance between the UK-based DLA and American firms Piper Rudnick and Gray Cary is perceived as one that will further bolster the DC construction team, particularly in its push toward the arbitration realm. In the nation's capital, it is the Piper Rudnick part of the combination that anchors the practice, which is inextricably tied to the firm's real estate and litigation departments. Its high notes are public construction projects, such as a two-tower office complex on behalf of the government in DC. The team is also advising a prominent construction company working in Iraq. Federal procurement inevitably features prominently on the menu, followed by an array of civil work such as condominiums, healthcare facilities and company headquarters.

The Lawyers: *"Marvelous"* **Larry Harris** (see p.447) is credited with much of the firm's prominence in the construction field, winning plaudits for his compelling blend of *"interpersonal skills"* and technical agility. His litigation practice has diversified to include more alternative dispute resolution matters, including a significant project in Boston.

The Clients: International contractors, subcontractors, owners and developers feature in the firm's client list.

McManus Schor Asmar & Darden, L.L.P.

The Firm: Although the practice's prominence is mainly due to its domestic portfolio, it can also claim a host of international projects. It proved particularly adept on United States Agency for International Development (USAID) and military-related matters, having participated in sophisticated engagements across the world – including Saudi Arabia, Russia and Mexico. Nationwide, the 18-lawyer firm has played key roles in contract drafting, project development and related dispute resolution linked to various hotels, hospitals and residential housing establishments. Another specialty involves prison construction, and the group has helped broker important settlements on behalf of contractors, suppliers and others.

The Lawyers: Of Counsel **Geoffrey Keating**'s splendid reputation is forged from more than 30 years of practice, which is slightly tilted toward public works and international infrastructure projects. Head of the government contracts practice, **Laurence Schor** is recognized for his work on behalf of USAID, the government agency that provides economic and humanitarian assistance worldwide. In addition, his litigation skills have been rendered on extensive matters such as claims associated with the historic renovation of Florida's Royal Palm Crowne

Plaza hotel in South Beach. Clients also appreciate the *"clear, direct manner"* of **Joseph McManus**, who *"understands how construction and government contracts work."*

The Clients: The firm takes its cue from owners, contractors, home builders, subcontractors, sureties, construction managers and design professionals in projects such as airports, hospitals, hotels, power generators and public buildings.

Spriggs & Hollingsworth
See firm details p.491

The Firm: Dispute resolution – including cases with a strong insurance twist – is the name of the game at this *"substantive"* firm. Its *"broad base of talent"* supports a variety of clients, many of whom are caught in difficult problems concerning such issues as bid protests, fiduciary duties, government contracts and builders' risks. *"Always on the short list,"* according to one observer, it is often associated with headline litigation such as insurance and claim issues stemming from Boston's Central Artery project, also called the Big Dig. Another highlight is a dispute linked to a prominent hotel resort in Florida. On behalf of contractors, it is handling matters involving luxury hotels and retail space in New Orleans, Louisiana, and a hotel and casino in Las Vegas, Nevada. The firm also commands respect from regulatory officials, a trait favored by many of its customers. *"The people on the power side like them,"* a client said.

The Lawyers: **Douglas Patin**'s (see p.461) knowledge of insurance law attracts a loyal following in the construction sector. Deemed as *"one of the best construction attorneys"* in DC, he delivers excellent results in difficult problems, clients said. *"Everything he has done is great. He follows through, and never misses a deadline."* His involvement in the Central Artery project has earned widespread recognition.

The Clients: The firm has represented Tompkins Builders, Massachusetts Turnpike Authority and John J Kirlin.

Band 3

Gibson, Dunn & Crutcher LLP
See firm details p.285

The Firm: A relatively small but crucial element to the firm's national construction profile, it attracts owners and contractors on complex matters, especially those associated with government contracts. The team proved agile on dispute resolution, succeeding on many groundbreaking cases pertaining to areas such as risk assessment. In DC, the coterie of *"marvelous, enthusiastic"* operators helped prevent a particularly thorny problem before it went to trial, clients said. *"We were impressed with the long-term consideration, including the effects on other parties we might have to deal with in the future."* Indeed, the firm has benefited from its

All quotes in the text are from interviews with clients and competitors.

deliberate cultivation of alternative dispute resolution as a focus point. If the case ends up in court, few are better suited to devote the necessary resources to complex litigation, clients said.

The Lawyers: A registered civil engineer, **Joseph West** (see p.475) thrives from an ability to accurately measure the *"situations and business relationships,"* said clients, one of whom added: *"I never had anyone lay out more clearly the moral, ethical and legal stuff."* His high notes involve dispute resolution, particularly that related to government contracts, followed by his grasp of transactional advice. Formerly of Arnold & Porter, he is conversant in the intricacies of government-related projects.

The Clients: The DC team forges a clientele that is heavily weighted toward aerospace companies. Others relate to government agencies, manufacturers, financial institutions and construction companies.

Holland & Knight LLP

See firm details p.1352

The Firm: Hinged on the firm's real estate profile, the construction and design group cuts a wide swath across the practice area. Its drawing card is the wealth of its expertise to handle the whole length of the project, including litigation when necessary. *"When you have a question, they've got the answer,"* a client said. On offer is international support from places such as Dubai to enhance its national network, which includes former architects on the roster. In DC, a varied diet has involved power plants, hotels and public buildings. The group delivers *"technical, accurate"* advice on matters such as contract negotiation, risk-related counseling and construction delay claims. Related issues pertain to indoor air quality, project finance and employee safety standards.

The Lawyers: **Andrew Stephenson** (see p.470), leader of the firm's construction industry practice group, won respect for his adroit performances on complex litigation as part of a much broader practice. *"He knows the law,"* a client said. *"He's accurate, precise and practical."* His profile is also flavored with various aspects of employment, design and government contracts law.

The Clients: Owners, architect-engineers, general contractors and subcontractors form the base of the firm's clientele.

Seyfarth Shaw LLP

See firm details p.777

The Firm: The DC team is a driving force behind the firm's construction capability. Fuelled by a substantial emphasis on dispute resolution, it has helped clients avert expensive litigation as well as winning their cases in the courtroom. Other expertise pertains to risk management programs as related to assignments such as the design and construction of sports stadiums. A team of *"impressive advocates"* has shepherded construction sites involving wastewater treatment plants, manufacturing facilities, commercial office buildings and residential housing projects among others. The group also boasts cross-border expertise, either assisting foreign companies investing in the USA or advising domestic businesses overseas.

The Lawyers: Benefiting from a more international aura, **Richard Preston**'s drawing card is his established dispute resolution skills. He is especially valued for his arbitration skills, having participated in dozens of proceedings before the AAA, ICC and other organizations.

The Clients: Among the firm's broad clientele are owners, contractors, architects and engineers.

Band 4

Arent Fox PLLC

The Firm: Straddling the firm's litigation and government contracts groups is its construction team, which also works closely with other departments to undertake a smorgasbord of work. Its generalist approach has resulted in acclaim as a *"strong group with the unique ability to apply knowledge with great interpersonal skills and business judgment."* The team has helped orchestrate a number of projects on behalf of Fannie Mae, including prominent facilities in Dallas, Maryland and DC. Its national scope means that the team is able to tackle multiparty cases involving issues such as contract negotiation, inter-party agreements and operating procedures among others. Surety bond claims and related damage issues are also featured.

The Lawyers: **Kathy Taub** balances a clientele comprising contractors and developers, predominantly on transactional matters. She helped structure transactions and negotiated contracts associated with such landmarks as the Padres Ballpark, the new ballpark for the San Diego Padres. Other projects include Miller Park, home to the Milwaukee Brewers baseball team, and the $150 million MCI Center in DC.

The Clients: The firm has represented some of the nation's most prominent general contractors, subcontractors, owners, developers and architects.

Arnold & Porter LLP

See firm details p.478

The Firm: The 2004 defection of Joseph West to Gibson Dunn & Crutcher came as a crushing blow to the firm's construction team, which is relatively small compared to some of its competitors, industry analysts said. Though blessed by its own brand of mental toughness, the firm has continued to weave various core strengths in areas such as litigation, corporate and real estate to deliver consistency to its construction clientele. Also linked to its government contracts arm, the group encompasses regulatory litigation, and fraud and abuse claims. Projects handled include hotels and power stations among others.

The Lawyers: Gary Humes is a key contact partner for the firm. Though his practice is tilted toward real estate, he has also demonstrated proficiency on the construction front.

The Clients: On behalf of contractors and developers, the team has participated on a variety of transactions and disputes, including arbitration cases.

Bell, Boyd & Lloyd

The Firm: The satellite office of this Chicago-based firm integrates attorneys from several key areas – including real estate, corporate and bankruptcy – to prevail on important cases for its clients. Though it offers transactional and litigation expertise, it is the firm's dispute resolution prowess that attracts marketplace attention. Its team of *"brilliant"* practitioners has participated in lawsuits relating to building projects, bidding procedures and mechanics' liens. It has also handled compliance issues relating to construction plans, specifications and professional standards. Moreover, enduring political links have enhanced the firm's construction profile by way of government contracts, observers said.

The Lawyers: **Joel Rubinstein** is portrayed as *"the foundation"* of the firm's construction capability, *"fitting the bill"* on a host of difficult problems involving bid protests, performance claims and subcontract disputes among other issues. The chair of the firm's government contracts and construction law group has appeared before various administrative boards of contract appeals, state and federal courts and arbitration tribunals.

The Clients: The firm often counsels owners, developers, contractors, suppliers, sureties, architects and engineers.

www.ChambersandPartners.com
All quotes in the text are from interviews with clients and competitors.
375

CORPORATE/COMMERCIAL

District of Columbia
Leading firms (Corporate/Commercial)

[1] GIBSON, DUNN & CRUTCHER LLP *Washington, DC*
HOGAN & HARTSON LLP *Washington, DC*
[2] LATHAM & WATKINS LLP *Washington, DC*
[3] ARNOLD & PORTER LLP *Washington, DC*
SHAW PITTMAN *Washington, DC*
[4] COVINGTON & BURLING *Washington, DC*
DICKSTEIN SHAPIRO MORIN *Washington, DC*
KIRKLAND & ELLIS LLP *Washington, DC*
WILMER CUTLER PICKERING HALE *Washington, DC*

Leading individuals
(Corporate/Commercial)

[1] ADLER Howard *Gibson Dunn, Washington, DC*
GLOVER Stephen *Gibson Dunn, Washington, DC*
GORRELL J Warren *Hogan & Hartson, DC*
[2] LENNON Daniel *Latham & Watkins, Washington, DC*
ROBBINS Robert *Shaw Pittman, Washington, DC*
STAMAS George *Kirkland & Ellis, Washington, DC*
[3] JACK Andrew *Covington & Burling, Washington, DC*
KAPLAN Steven *Arnold & Porter, Washington, DC*
MAZO Mark *Hogan & Hartson, Washington, DC*
MUTRYN William *Holland & Knight, Washington, DC*
POLON Ira *Dickstein Shapiro, Washington, DC*

Up-and-coming individuals
CURRAN Denis *Gibson Dunn, Washington, DC*

Leading individuals
(Corporate/Commercial: Securities)

[1] DYE Alan *Hogan & Hartson, Washington, DC*
GROSKAUFMANIS Karl *Fried Frank, Washington, DC*
HUBER John *Latham & Watkins, Washington, DC*
TRAGER Michael *Arnold & Porter, Washington, DC*
WEISS Harry *Wilmer Cutler, Washington, DC*

Firms and individuals are listed alphabetically in each band.

Band 1

Gibson, Dunn & Crutcher LLP
See firm details p.285
The Firm: "*At the top of the pile for corporate work in DC,*" the firm is known for its breadth of experience and ability to adapt to the market. Its robust national and regional reputation draws in household-name clients such as Del Monte, Friedman Billings Ramsey and People-Soft, keen to utilize expertise spanning M&A, IPOs, venture capital and securities compliance. Over the past 12 months the group has represented NLX in its $125 million sale of the company to Rockwell Collins, and has represented the audit committees of a number of local, publicly held companies.
The Lawyers: **Howard Adler** (see p.430) is the relationship partner for Friedman, Billings, Ramsey Group, for whom he has handled numerous IPOs and subsequent offerings. One satisfied client summed up his appeal as an abil-

ity to "*objectively and unemotionally look at situations,*" to "*dissect them down to the root cause and know how to fix and improve them.*" More than this, "*he has brilliant business sense – he won't let legal aspects override business perception.*" His partner **Stephen Glover** (see p.444) is also "*as good as they come.*" His broad-based workload has recently included two acquisitions for United Defense. He is a "*bright, unflappable attorney who's not interested in wasting time*" and "*a pleasure to work with.*" Sources said the younger attorney **Denis Curran** (see p.438) is a quick study, with an ability to "*go right to the heart of issues.*"
The Clients: Friedman, Billings, & Ramsey Group; United Defense; Marriott International; Sallie Mae; Del Monte; GE and Atlantic Coast Airlines

Hogan & Hartson LLP
See firm details p.484
The Firm: This firm is "*particularly active in the big-company M&A arena,*" argued one peer. The broad corporate practice is currently representing Liberty Media in its $700 million acquisition of French cable network, Noos. It has also been pushing capital markets over the past 12 months, and in one week closed two IPOs totalling $500 million and six other public offerings totaling over $1 billion. The firm has a special interest in REIT work, for which it is "*head and shoulders ahead.*" It represents trusts in corporate transactions such as the $1.5 billion acquisition of Cornerstone Realty Income Trust by Colonial Properties Trust. Additionally, a push into life sciences has paid off, with competitors taking note. The group is also active in energy and telecom sectors.
The Lawyers: "*There is no one better*" than **Warren Gorrell** (see p.445). The leader of the team was instrumental in developing the firm's REIT practice, and clients picked him out for his "*superb technical knowledge in combination with a rare business acumen.*" **Mark Mazo** (see p.456) has developed the international side of the practice, and has a particular focus on cross-border M&A with European companies. He is said to have "*a way of getting his arms around a project and pulling it together.*" On securities obligations and restrictions **Alan Dye** (see p.440) is the "*go-to*" partner. Clients say he is "*a wonderful business partner*" with "*incredible depth of experience.*"
The Clients: Colonial Properties Trust; News Corporation; Equity Office Properties Trust; XM Satellite Radio Holdings; GE Commercial Finance; The Anschutz Corporation; Umicore; Webster; CarrAmerica and Host Marriott Corporation.

Band 2

Latham & Watkins LLP
The Firm: Strong on both the traditional transactional work and securities regulatory advice, this team has "*a deep bench that is representing corporate America throughout the country.*" Working in tandem with the firm's New York office, the team has close relationships with the financial community, drawing clients from the ranks of LBO sponsors, private equity firms and venture capital funds. It "*will always give 110%*" and approaches all transactions with "*ferocious energy,*" clients said. On the securities side, the firm easily handles compliance issues for companies and audit committees
The Lawyers: **Daniel Lennon** is recognized as a leading light in the market. As client partner for the Carlyle Group, he has been at the forefront of the corporate finance practice for many years. **John Huber** is a "*revered*" securities specialist who, with both litigation and transactional experience, is the bedrock of the practice. At present, he is acting as outside counsel to two national accountancy firms.
The Clients: New Horizons Venture Capital; United Defense; The Carlyle Group; Gemini Networks and HMC Acquisition Properties.

Band 3

Arnold & Porter LLP
See firm details p.478
The Firm: Clients hail this team as "*equally plugged-in on the government and transactional sides,*" and peers recognized its leading position in the market. In the past year, Arnold & Porter has continued to develop a traditional regulatory practice, whilst also promoting M&A, sovereign finance and securities work. Transactions of note include the highly publicized proposed acquisition of Farm Credit Services of America for Rabobank. On the sovereign finance side, the group was involved in a dozen transactions with an aggregate total close to $10 billion. This period of growth extends to developing the international reach of the practice as the firm draws clients from Brazil and Panama to Israel. Sector focuses include life sciences, government contracting and real estate.
The Lawyers: The "*impressive*" **Steven Kaplan** (see p.449) heads the corporate team. Interviewees confirm that he is a "*confident and practical lawyer who knows how to get a deal done.*" **Michael Trager** (see p.472) is an exceptional SEC practitioner, clients said. His practice focuses on defending governmental investigations and counseling corporations on crisis management, disclosure and governance. A man of many talents, interviewees report that he is "*smart, resourceful, dogged, caring and extremely hard-working.*"

The Clients: The firm has a strong client base in the financial sector acting for clients such as Rabobank, Perseus LLC and M&T Bank. It also acts on behalf of biomedical and medical companies and a variety of industrial companies.

Shaw Pittman

See firm details p.490

The Firm: This "*good, solid shop*" has increasing market presence in DC despite the decline of the technology market with which it was traditionally associated. It continues to represent issuers in REIT transactions, bringing a weight of securities and tax expertise to the table. It also has a successful corporate finance practice, and a major coup this year was its appointment to Schroders' global panel. The firm was commended to researchers as a "*proactive, user-friendly firm that does not put on airs and graces*" and cultivates "*strong relationships between lawyers and clients.*" At time of press the firm announced its merger with Pillsbury Winthrop LLP to form Pillsbury Winthrop Shaw Pittman.

The Lawyers: Chair of the corporate practice, "*frank*" **Bob Robbins** (see p.464) "*has an immense amount of experience and is willing to take the initiative to get the right result.*" He was instrumental in developing the practice beyond the technology sector.

The Clients: The group attracts clients from across the USA and internationally, including Crescent Real Estate Equities Company, GenCorp, Serono, Macquarie Investment Holdings and Schroders.

Band 4

Covington & Burling

See firm details p.481

The Firm: Entering the rankings this year following a successful merger with a New York boutique, Covington is "*a great traditional regulatory firm that is now doing more and more corporate deals.*" The practice is organized into dedicated industry groups covering life sciences, sport, media and communications, energy and technology. In life sciences the firm was involved in significant transactions such as Eisai's acquisition of Zonegran, and the collaboration and licensing deal between AstraZeneca and Abgenix. Peers commented on the firm's "*quality from top to bottom*" and its numerous "*talented lawyers.*"

The Lawyers: Clients picked out **Andrew Jack** (see p.448) as an attorney with a "*thorough understanding of the business factors at issue.*"

Jack acts as outside counsel for two principal clients, JLG Industries and the District of Columbia Sports and Entertainment Commission, which he assisted in its effort to bring the Montreal Expos to the RFK Memorial Stadium.

The Clients: Bacardi; Bank of America; Calpine; ExxonMobil; Freddie Mac; IBM; GlaxoSmithKline; Goodyear; Johnson & Johnson; JPMorgan Chase; Kerr McGee; Medarex; Merck; Microsoft; National Football League; National Hockey League; Owens Corning; Pfizer; Procter & Gamble; Schering-Plough; 3M; UBS and Union Pacific.

Dickstein Shapiro Morin & Oshinsky LLP

See firm details p.483

The Firm: "*The thing that turns me on about Dickstein is that they have very good people who have outstanding knowledge and judgment.*" So said one interviewee of this national practice. The firm has a large team with particular focus on the energy and telecom industries. "*All major issues go to them,*" clients commented. Transactions of note include representing Loews in its $1 billion acquisition of Texas Gas Transmission and advising KeySpan in the acquisition of Gulf Canada assets and the subsequent IPO. The group has a noteworthy international track record, representing clients based in countries across Europe and the Americas.

The Lawyers: Ira Polon (see p.462) has acted as client partner for the Harbour Group for the past 25 years and has led the team on five transactions for them in the past year. He is "*an excellent attorney who knows how to execute a transaction.*"

The Clients: Examples of the firm's clientele include KeySpan, Harbour Group and Loews.

Kirkland & Ellis LLP

See firm details p.770

The Firm: The "*private equity stalwart*" in the DC market, this firm has witnessed a strengthening of the market recently, with activity picking up through all deal stages. In its capacity as primary counsel to New Enterprise Associates (NEA), it is proving itself to be a robust venture capital counselor, although it has also been targeting fund formation, M&A, IPOs and portfolio transactions. Recent noteworthy transactions include the representation of Constellation Energy in its acquisition of the New Energy business from AES. The practice has also been active in the public company arena and boasts expertise across the sports, healthcare and tech-

nology industries.

The Lawyers: George Stamas (see p.469) is widely credited as the active, "*visible*" force in the team, developing the practice and forging close client relationships. He is a "*real character*" who "*radiates knowledge and energy.*"

The Clients: MidOcean Partners; Constellation Energy Group; NEA; Friedman, Billings, Ramsey Group and Legg Mason Wood Walker.

Wilmer Cutler Pickering Hale and Dorr LLP

See firm details p.497

The Firm: The firm warrants its place in the table on the basis of its "*nationally preeminent SEC enforcement practice.*" Although it does have a dedicated corporate transactional practice, its most prominent areas of expertise are defending companies in enforcement proceedings brought by the SEC and DOJ, advising clients during internal investigations and counseling them on the regulatory aspects of transactions. Acting as counsel to various board committees or corporations, the group has been involved in some of the highest profile investigations of late including WorldCom (now MCI), Qwest, Cablevision and Nortel.

The Lawyers: This experienced group of government alumni and securities experts has the deepest bench and largest book of all securities practices in DC. SEC alumnus **Harry Weiss** (see p.474) is a prominent member of the group, counseling clients on disclosure and corporate compliance issues. He is "*an excellent attorney at the cutting edge of the practice.*"

The Clients: The firm represented the Special Investigative Committee of the board of directors of Enron in the internal investigation into the company's collapse. It also counts almost every Wall Street financial services firm as a client for advice on securities issues.

Other Notable Practitioners

William Mutryn (see p.458) at Holland & Knight LLP focuses upon midmarket M&A for a clientele of federal contractors in the IT sector. He is a "*superb negotiator*" who is "*genuinely motivated to find a win-win solution.*" Clients also appreciated the depth and breadth of his commercial knowledge and his creative solutions. **Karl Groskaufmanis** (see p.446) at Fried, Frank, Harris, Shriver & Jacobson LLP is a widely known and well-respected name for SEC enforcement and defense counseling. His practice also covers insider trading and corporate internal investigations.

EMPLOYEE BENEFITS

District of Columbia
Leading firms (Employee Benefits)
[1] **GROOM LAW GROUP** *Washington, DC*
KILPATRICK STOCKTON LLP *Washington, DC*
O'MELVENY & MYERS LLP *Washington, DC*
STEPTOE & JOHNSON LLP *Washington, DC*
[2] **GIBSON, DUNN & CRUTCHER LLP** *Washington, DC*
HOGAN & HARTSON LLP *Washington, DC*
KIRKPATRICK & LOCKHART *Washington, DC*

Leading individuals (Employee Benefits)
[1] **ECCLES Bob** *O'Melveny & Myers*, Washington, DC
GALLAGHER Robert *Groom Law Group*, Washington, DC
NUSSDORF Melanie *Steptoe & Johnson*, Washington, DC
[2] **FORD Gary** *Groom Law Group*, Washington, DC
ONDRASIK Paul *Steptoe & Johnson*, Washington, DC
SACHER Steven *Kilpatrick Stockton*, Washington, DC
SCHMIDT William *Kirkpatrick & Lockhart*, Washington, DC
[3] **BREYFOGLE Jon** *Groom Law Group*, Washington, DC
DAVIS Robert *Mayer Brown*, Washington, DC
FERRERA Tess *Sole Practitioner*, Washington, DC
GIGOT Thomas *Groom Law Group*, Washington, DC
KILBERG William *Gibson Dunn*, Washington, DC
MILLER Evan *Hogan & Hartson*, Washington, DC
MYERS Donald *Reed Smith*, Washington, DC
WINCEK Mark *Kilpatrick Stockton*, Washington, DC

Up-and-coming individuals
TELL Gary *O'Melveny & Myers*, Washington, DC
WAHLE Karen *O'Melveny & Myers*, Washington, DC
Firms and individuals are listed alphabetically in each band.

Band 1

Groom Law Group

The Firm: *"The premier employee benefits boutique in the USA,"* both peers and clients commented it has depth of expertise in ERISA. With more than 50 dedicated lawyers, the practice is able to field specialists in areas such as tax, litigation, fiduciary responsibility and the transactional elements of ERISA. This is of premium value to clients who *"can get a national specialist on any issue."* The firm has particular expertise in advising corporate sponsors of pension plans on regulatory, planning and defense issues and is widely credited for its successful dealings with the Pension Benefit Guaranty Corporation (PBGC). Recent highlights include representing clients subject to government investigations and a string of cases regarding pension plans investing in company stock. This is a firm that can *"provide the whole package in relation to client service."* Clients appreciate that its attorneys deliver *"good financial analysis and practical solutions."* Its *"responsiveness is tremendous"* and the firm *"takes practical business solutions a step further, always assessing the risk."*

The Lawyers: **Robert Gallagher** is *"the greatest thing since sliced bread."* A former Department of Labor (DOL) practitioner he *"has been*

doing ERISA since it was created," and is *"sharp, responsive and always coming up with practical business solutions."* **Gary Ford** was general counsel to the PBGC and focuses on the firm's dealings with the agency, particularly with regard to the treatment of health and pension plans in major corporate transactions. He is a *"tough, knowledgeable and widely respected"* adviser. **Jon Breyfogle** is *"younger, but very knowledgeable on how to deal with the labor department."* A hardworking attorney, his practice focuses on the health aspects of employee benefits law. Another younger practitioner, **Tom Gigot**, is *"certainly one to look out for,"* agreed sources. Primarily a litigator, he *"has an ability to think clearly about the scope of fiduciary liability and how to define and contain it."*

The Clients: A significant corporate client base includes a number of Fortune 100 companies; Watson Wyatt; Central States Pension Fund; American Association of Health Plans and the American Benefits Council.

Kilpatrick Stockton LLP

See firm details p.634

The Firm: The employee benefits group of this full-service firm maintains a *"boutique-like character,"* offering a depth of specialist expertise. Praised by clients as *"well connected and responsive,"* it also has an ability to *"look at issues from a holistic perspective."* Areas of focus include ERISA litigation, executive compensation and health and welfare plans. Fiduciary responsibility has featured highly recently, with the group continuing to defend RJ Reynolds in an ERISA class action. It also represented a Fortune 150 publicly held company in a dispute surrounding investment in the company's 401(k) plan. A niche area of focus for the group is the regulation of mutual funds at its intersection with ERISA. It has recently been advising a client on market-timing issues before the DOL.

The Lawyers: **Steven Sacher** (see p.466) is a *"devoted, sophisticated and approachable"* counselor, who is highly regarded for his legislative expertise and successful dealings with agencies. He is *"intimately familiar with ERISA"* and *"has an enormous reservoir of knowledge of employee benefit plans,"* clients commented. *"The renaissance human resources lawyer,"* **Mark Wincek** (see p.476) won plaudits from clients for his depth of experience and ability to offer practical solutions. He is a *"complete delight to work with"* and a *"wonderful teacher."*

The Clients: The firm acts on behalf of financial institutions, investment advisers, third-party administrators, corporations and ERISA fiduciary committees.

O'Melveny & Myers LLP

See firm details p.294

The Firm: This firm merits its place in the top tier because it is *"one of the best Title I litigation practices in the country."* It was developed in conjunction with offices on the West Coast and the groups continue to work closely together, operating as one national practice. The DC attorneys are best known for their litigation expertise, although they are equally adept in other subspecialties. Recent highlights focus upon fiduciary responsibility. The group is defending US Trust on appeal against allegations of breach of fiduciary duty in Keach v US Trust and arguing more technical fiduciary issues in Dupree v Prudential Insurance. It has put arguments to the US Supreme Court in CIGNA Healthcare of Texas v Calad on the preemption of ERISA over medical malpractice claims.

The Lawyers: **Bob Eccles** is *"the premier ERISA litigator in the USA."* The head of the practice has experience working for both the DOJ and the DOL. He recently argued his first case before the US Supreme Court and is credited with *"superb judgment – he understands ERISA more thoroughly than any other lawyer."* Working with Bob are two standout younger partners. **Gary Tell** is an *"excellent, knowledgeable and responsive"* attorney whose practice leans more toward fiduciary counseling and regulatory advice than the other two. He has *"had a lot of good opportunities, handled a lot of responsibility and done a first-rate job."* The *"extraordinary"* **Karen Wahle** is *"beginning to come into her own, developing an exceptional reputation."* Her area of expertise is ERISA litigation.

The Clients: Spread across different sectors, the firm's clientele ranges from employers through to financial institutions. US Trust; CIGNA; Verizon Communications and Humana count as representative examples.

Steptoe & Johnson LLP

See firm details p.492

The Firm: One of Washington's principal firms in this arena, Steptoe *"pulls ahead due to the depth and breadth of its experience."* The practice covers Titles I and IV of ERISA, litigation, tax, transactions and legislation for plan sponsors, fiduciaries and consultants. Other clients include banks, insurers and investors. The renowned litigation group has been defending members of the administrative committee of the Enron plan and the custodial trustee in the Qwest Savings and Investment Plan ERISA litigation. On the noncontentious side, the firm was successful in obtaining class exemptions for qualified professional asset managers from the DOL. It has also been involved in SEC investigations on behalf of financial institutions.

The Lawyers: On the regulatory side, *"everybody in the world likes"* **Melanie Nussdorf** (see p.460). She is *"outstanding at big-picture systems*

All quotes in the text are from interviews with clients and competitors.

CHAMBERS USA 2005

analysis," and "on the cutting edge of what is going on within the department." An exceptionally bright and very direct attorney, one client commented: "God forbid, if I ever got investigated, I would go to her." Practice head **Paul Ondrasik** (see p.460) leads the litigation group. Recent successes include defending breach of fiduciary duty claims in Albrecht v Committee on Employee Benefits of the Federal Reserve Employee Benefits System. He "gets through to the issues and has an intuitive understanding of what needs to be done."

The Clients: The firm represents a broad ranging clientele drawn from plan sponsors and fiduciaries. It acts for the public employee pension plans of several states, trade associations that focus on ERISA issues, and corporations.

Band 2

Gibson, Dunn & Crutcher LLP
See firm details p.285
The Firm: This "sophisticated group" is involved in some of the country's highest profile ERISA litigation. It is representing Merrill Lynch in proceedings following the WorldCom bankruptcy, defending Merrill's role as directed trustee to the company's 401(k) plan. It is also advising the respondent in Jebian v Hewlett-Packard; a case concerning the appropriate standard of review on appeal of benefits decisions. Offering the whole range of employee benefits expertise, the practice also covers transactional, design and compliance advice for all types of plans. It has "a marvelous sense of how federal government regulates pensions," peers commented.

The Lawyers: An erudite practitioner, **Bill Kilberg** (see p.450) is equally adept at employment and employee benefits work. Formerly with the DOL, he is "politically well connected"

and a "fundamentally fine gentleman."
The Clients: The firm counsels companies of all sizes including Merrill Lynch; Hewlett-Packard; Aetna and Boeing.

Hogan & Hartson LLP
See firm details p.484
The Firm: Previously focused upon the development of health benefits plans, the group has diversified to provide a broader mix of counseling and litigation services. It has launched into the defense of corporations and executives in the current spate of fiduciary liability litigation, and recently counseled Bernie Ebbers in the World-Com ERISA proceedings. It also provided transactional guidance to the DynCorp pension plan and its trustee in the acquisition of DynCorp by Computer Sciences Corp. Clients praised the team for its ability to "quickly grasp the exposure to us, so we could make effective business decisions."
The Lawyers: Among peers, partner **Evan Miller** (see p.457) is cultivating a reputation as an ERISA litigator with excellent substantive knowledge. Clients appreciated the fact that he "sees the issues downstream, proposes solutions and offers alternatives." He is also considered a forthright communicator who "does not hesitate to tell you when he thinks you are heading out of bounds."
The Clients: CNA Trust; Winn-Dixie Stores; Blue Cross Shield of Massachusetts; Blue Cross Shield of Hawaii and Medco Health Services.

Kirkpatrick & Lockhart Nicholson Graham LLP
See firm details p.291
The Firm: With national depth and local prominence, this group leads the market in financial services and products expertise. Primarily recommended for its force in the non-contentious elements of ERISA, it focuses on

counseling, planning the manner in which financial institutions provide services, and assisting plan sponsors in audits and investigations undertaken by federal agencies. The practice is integrated with national focus groups that deal with executive compensation and employee stock ownership plans.
The Lawyers: A renowned member of this group is the "smart and innovative" **William Schmidt** (see p.467). He "knows everything there is to know" about fiduciary and DOL issues and is recognized by clients and competitors alike as a go-to person for matters before the DOL.
The Clients: The clientele of this group is made up of investment managers, advisers and sponsors.

Other Notable Practitioners

The outstanding **Bob Davis** (see p.438) at Mayer, Brown, Rowe & Maw LLP is "an excellent resource" for clients. He has a "great understanding of how the DOL thinks and what their approach is likely to be." Recent focuses include fiduciary responsibility; he defended the trustee of a substantial 401(k) plan during the DOL investigation. Reed Smith LLP's **Donald Myers** (see p.458) is popular with the banking fraternity and highly regarded by peers and clients for his regulatory expertise. In the past year he filed an amicus brief on behalf of the American Bankers Association in the Enron litigation. He is "very knowledgeable about the DOL" and a pleasure to work with agreed both clients and peers. **Tess Ferrera** recently moved from Kilpatrick Stockton LLP to set up her own practice. She concentrates on Title I defense litigation and compliance advice. A former ERISA attorney at the DOL, she has "an ability to analyze issues clearly" and excellent technical knowledge.

EMPLOYMENT

MAINLY DEFENDANT

Band 1

Gibson, Dunn & Crutcher LLP
See firm details p.285
The Firm: "Our first choice for anything of significance across the US," asserted one client among the many who "could not give this firm a high enough recommendation." It has strength in numbers and "everybody there is premier." The firm adds depth to its robust practice with niche focus areas and a successful track record in high-level litigation. Over the past 12 months it has seen increasing numbers of whistle-blower actions under Sarbanes-Oxley; it represented Atlantic Coast Airlines in one of the first such cases to be tried before a judge. It is also experienced in sex and age discrimination cases. A notable action was Cline v General Dynamics, which was heard before the Supreme Court.

The Lawyers: **William Kilberg** (see p.450) practices both labor and employment law and advises on employee benefits. He is considered by clients to have exceptional experience; "He knows everyone and he knows the law," and "from day one he has treated us as though we are his only client." The "absolutely outstanding" **Gene Scalia** (see p.466) was commended for his "creativity and grasp of legal principles" and his "incredible ability to articulate his ideas." He has the capacity to "boil down to the right issues immediately." Scalia recently successfully defended the Parsons Corporation in a negligence dispute. **Baruch Fellner** (see p.442) is the OSHA specialist within the group, and he has "an encyclopedic knowledge of the law." Inspiring incredible client confidence, Coca-Cola and Pepsi recently declared a truce in order to both retain his services in defense of sweeping OSHA citations.

The Clients: Parsons Corporation; King Pharmaceuticals; FLYi; Boeing; Coca-Cola; PepsiCo; Oldcastle; US Chamber of Commerce and UPS.

Jones Day
See firm details p.485
The Firm: This energetic group has "top-flight people capable of handling the most sophisticated disputes," while its breadth of activity ensures clients use it as a "one-stop shop" for all labor and employment matters. Primarily focused on litigation, the firm has seen a dramatic increase in wage and hour and discrimination class actions over the past 12 months. It obtained dismissal of the Johnson v Delphi wage and hour suit and reached settlement in proceedings against Pfizer alleging sexual harassment and negligent supervision. The growing labor practice has represented clients in high-profile negotiations,

www.ChambersandPartners.com
All quotes in the text are from interviews with clients and competitors.
379

District of Columbia
Leading firms
(Employment: Mainly Defendant)

1 GIBSON, DUNN & CRUTCHER LLP *Washington, DC*
  JONES DAY *Washington, DC*

2 AKIN GUMP STRAUSS HAUER *Washington, DC*
  MORGAN, LEWIS & BOCKIUS LLP *Washington, DC*
  PAUL, HASTINGS, JANOFSKY *Washington, DC*

3 DICKSTEIN SHAPIRO MORIN *Washington, DC*
  HOGAN & HARTSON LLP *Washington, DC*
  OGLETREE, DEAKINS, NASH, SMOAK *Washington, DC*
  SEYFARTH SHAW LLP *Washington, DC*

Leading individuals
(Employment: Mainly Defendant)

1 BROWN Barbara *Paul Hastings, Washington, DC*
  GOLDSMITH Willis *Jones Day, Washington, DC*
  KILBERG William *Gibson Dunn, Washington, DC*
  SCALIA Eugene *Gibson Dunn, Washington, DC*

2 CHATILOVICZ Peter *Seyfarth Shaw, Washington, DC*
  FORTNEY David *Fortney & Scott, Washington, DC*
  KRAMER Andrew *Jones Day, Washington, DC*
  LIVINGSTON Donald *Akin Gump, Washington, DC*

3 BASKIN Maurice *Venable, Washington, DC*
  COHEN Charles *Morgan Lewis, Washington, DC*
  COOPER Ronald *Steptoe & Johnson, Washington, DC*
  DAVIS Robert *Mayer Brown, Washington, DC*
  DE BERNARDO Mark *Winston & Strawn, Washington, DC*
  FELLNER Baruch *Gibson Dunn, Washington, DC*
  KELLEY James *Morgan Lewis, Washington, DC*
  KELLY Deborah *Dickstein Shapiro, Washington, DC*
  MARSHALL Alison *Jones Day, Washington, DC*
  MOLLEN Neal *Paul Hastings, Washington, DC*
  SKELLY Paul *Hogan & Hartson, Washington, DC*
  YOHAY Stephen *Arent Fox, Washington, DC*

Up-and-coming individuals

  HOLMES Jacqueline *Jones Day, Washington, DC*
  LIAN Robert *Akin Gump, Washington, DC*

Firms and individuals are listed alphabetically in each band.

including those following the grocery strikes in California. It also supported Verizon Communications through contentious contract negotiations.

The Lawyers: "*You cannot find a better labor lawyer in the US than* **Willis Goldsmith**" (see p.445), claimed one client. The chair of the group "*commands respect from judges and arbitrators.*" His "*affable, easygoing manner*" makes him "*a pleasure to deal with*" although he is nevertheless a tough, effective operator. Another prominent partner is the "*creative and client-focused*" **Andy Kramer** (see p.451). He is recognized in the market for his "*great collective bargaining skills,*" particularly in dealings with the NLRB. **Alison Marshall** (see p.455) is "*simply superb.*" An outstanding litigator with the ability to employ a range of weapons, she is particularly reputed for her expertise in discrimination cases. Senior associate **Jackie Holmes** (see p.447) is recognized as an up and comer this year on the basis

of excellent client feedback. She is an attorney with whom "*you can have good, intellectual, analytical discussions.*"

The Clients: Albertsons; Delphi; Federated Department Stores; Knight Ridder; The Washington Post; Verizon Communications and Verizon Wireless.

Band 2

Akin Gump Strauss Hauer & Feld LLP

See firm details p.477

The Firm: Offering "*one of the best teams in the country,*" Akin Gump is a strong competitor at both local and national levels. Clients praised a "*thorough group,*" which has "*the ability to provide nationwide support.*" A spate of high-profile cases and a client list filled with household names has raised the profile of the group; recent work includes wage and hour and discrimination litigation and labor disputes. The group has been defending Allstate in suits brought by employees claiming workplace discrimination, and it continues its work on cases arising out of 9/11, representing a number of Middle Eastern clients.

The Lawyers: The "*analytical and thoughtful*" **Donald Livingston**'s (see p.453) "*knowledge base is above the norm.*" He "*knows the world of civil rights law inside out*" and has a canny ability to foresee developments. A former general counsel of the EEOC, he is "*still thoroughly familiar with their personnel and practices.*" **Robert Lian** (see p.453) is "*an excellent younger partner.*" He was recommended as a "*bright and capable litigator*" who "*can handle any kind of legal issue.*" Previously ranked, the highly regarded George Salem recently went in-house.

The Clients: The group's clientele spans a wide range of commercial employers across a variety of industry sectors. Representative names include Starbucks Coffee Company; Food Lion; CSX; National Football League and Tyson Foods.

Morgan, Lewis & Bockius LLP

See firm details p.1556

The Firm: Historically a major force in the DC market, Morgan Lewis is recognized for its bench strength and for having the labor market "*sewn up tight.*" The group has seen a steady stream of traditional labor relations matters of late, particularly in the transportation sector. It represented Rolls-Royce in negotiations with the Auto Workers Union and ABX Air in complex NLRB litigation against the Air Line Pilots Association. It continues to work closely with the teams specializing in employee benefits and health and welfare plans.

The Lawyers: Former NLRB member **Charles Cohen** (see p.437) focuses on high-level government negotiations. He is a "*smart, experienced*" attorney whose approach "*leads to the*

solution of problems." Cohen represented IBM in a precedent-setting NLRB case on the comparative rights of union and nonunion employees. **James Kelley** (see p.450) has a broad practice that covers both labor and employment matters. His experience inspires confidence, and he has an outgoing character, "*although that does not mean he is not cerebral,*" commented one client.

The Clients: BellSouth; IBM; ABX Air; Federal Aviation Administration; Pacific Maritime Association; American Airlines and United Space Alliance.

Paul, Hastings, Janofsky & Walker LLP

See firm details p.297

The Firm: "*A cutting-edge practice,*" this office of the nationally strong employment firm has "*all-round strength*" across an excellent range of areas. Of late it has been active at appellate level in a variety of class actions. It represented Boeing in several suits; one concerned alleged sex discrimination at the company's facilities in Puget Sound and also raised a multitude of procedural issues. It also continues to be active in railway and airline labor disputes and executive employment terminations, winning summary judgment for American Red Cross when a former CEO challenged her demotion and termination. The "*talented senior lawyers*" have earned strong reputations as producers of "*stellar work.*" Other areas of expertise include counseling federal contractors and international employment issues, such as global mobility and hiring and termination.

The Lawyers: **Barbara Brown** (see p.436) enjoys a "*wonderful reputation.*" "*She is my idol!*" exclaimed one peer. An experienced attorney noted particularly for her discrimination expertise, clients are impressed by her "*excellent strategic-thinking capabilities and mediation skills.*" Appellate lawyer **Neal Mollen** (see p.458) is a "*sound technical lawyer,*" who is appreciated by clients for his "*ability to thoroughly research and analyze*" issues.

The Clients: The group represents law firms, technology companies, Fortune 50 companies and trade associations. Examples include: Ford; Boeing; American Red Cross and Dow Chemical.

Band 3

Dickstein Shapiro Morin & Oshinsky LLP

See firm details p.483

The Firm: This is an energetic team that is actively building an employment practice offering both noncontentious and litigation expertise. The group recently boosted its profile with the hiring of Tammy McCutchen. The former administrator of the Wage and Hour Division of the DOL is the author of the new overtime regulations and a fantastic resource for related compliance issues. The group has developed a useful Web-based desktop, tailored to each client's policies, that helps multistate companies through the regulatory web of federal and state laws. Litigation triumphs from the past year have arisen particularly in the discrimination arena, although sexual harassment has also featured prominently. The team successfully defended race and national origin discrimination allegations in Bhatia v AT&T.

The Lawyers: Deborah Kelly (see p.450) is "*knowledgeable and comfortable telling a client what they need to hear.*" Also a "*very effective advocate,*" the head of the employment practice won praise for her pleasant and constructive approach: she is a person to "*only focus on the target and not get distracted by baloney of lawyering.*"

The Clients: AT&T; Discovery Communications; Fannie Mae; Greenwich Capital Markets; National Association of Chain Drug Stores; Sears Roebuck and Unilever.

Hogan & Hartson LLP

See firm details p.484

The Firm: Known as a "*sound local employment practice*" by competitors, this DC firm has "*lots of talented attorneys*" who provide "*watertight legal advice and guidance.*" A relatively small team, it punches above its weight, regularly advising Fortune 100 clients on litigation, counseling and labor issues. It recently defended a well-known communications company in sexual harassment and retaliation claims. The well-regarded labor practice advised George Washington University in proceedings before the NLRB during the attempt by a rival union to replace the Service Employees International Union as collective bargaining representative. The attorneys were praised by clients for their ability to "*efficiently work side by side with our counsel.*"

The Lawyers: Head of the group, Paul Skelly (see p.468) is a "*resolute advocate*" who will always "*stick to his guns.*" His broad practice also covers counseling and labor issues. Skelly won plaudits for his "*strong legal acumen*" and "*ability to communicate the law to clients.*"

The Clients: The George Washington University; Virginia Hospital Center; Georgetown University; National Geographic Society; Pepco and EADS North America.

Ogletree, Deakins, Nash, Smoak & Stewart, PC

See firm details p.638

The Firm: Traditional labor kingpin, Ogletree Deakins is still highlighted as "*the go-to firm for union busting work.*" Despite the general slowdown in work in the local labor market, the group continues to act as general counsel for various trade associations and to involve itself in government lobbying. Following the merger with Heenan, Althen & Roles it is also cultivating a reputation for its "*exceptionally good safety practice,*" with niche expertise in the mining industry. It represented the Peabody Coal Company in a case involving a challenge to the Commissioner of Social Security's interpretation of the Coal Industry Retiree Health Benefits Act. The group is said to be "*extremely responsive*" and "*forms great relationships with agencies.*"

The Lawyers: The 14-strong DC-based team has "*some terrific lawyers.*" On the mine safety side, Michael Heenan is a prominent figure.

The Clients: Clients include Fortune 100 companies and trade associations.

Seyfarth Shaw LLP

See firm details p.777

The Firm: Seyfarth Shaw is another deep-rooted DC firm with a national reputation for its labor practice. It is emerging as a prominent player in the hospitality industry, and in particular represented all unionized hotels in the Master Hotel negotiations. The group also regularly advises the Howard University on discrimination issues. Other areas of concentration include wage and hour, employee benefits and executive compensation, international labor law and workplace harassment counseling. It is "*substantively very sound,*" offering "*timely, practical solutions.*"

The Lawyers: Peter Chatilovicz is the high-profile member of the group. Clients recommended him as a good choice for difficult labor situations that require "*a tough, direct approach.*"

The Clients: United Way of America; Goodwill Industries International; Hilton Hotels; Marriott and Howard University.

Other Notable Practitioners

David Fortney of Fortney & Scott, LLC runs a boutique practice that focuses upon compliance issues. He is particularly fêted for his substantive wage and hour experience. "*He really thinks through how the governing statute works and how to apply it in factual circumstances,*" commented one peer. Clients like his "*no-nonsense*" style and the fact that he "*does not beat around the bush.*" At Venable LLP, Maurice Baskin is "*low key, but effective.*" In BE&K Construction he defended a national contractor against unfair labor practice charges before the NLRB. The "*terrific*" Ronald Cooper's (see p.438) practice at Steptoe & Johnson LLP has an international flavor. Described as "*extraordinarily expert,*" he has been involved in litigation in the USA and overseas regarding the termination of employment of employees based outside the USA, and the effect of this on eligibility for stock options. Bob Davis (see p.438), of Mayer, Brown, Rowe & Maw LLP, concentrates on wage and hour compliance and litigation. A former solicitor of the DOL, he is "*damn smart*" and has the ability to "*navigate different paths very nimbly.*" At Winston & Strawn, "*excellent tactician*" Mark de Bernardo (see p.438) is a nationally recognized expert in drug testing and substance abuse in the workplace. He is also in the know on what the government might do legislatively – "*an inside-the-belt person but not a lobbyist.*" "*The top OSHA lawyer in the country for utility matters,*" Steve Yohay is "*excellent on every level.*" This Arent Fox PLLC attorney is "*the person to go to when you want a fight.*"

ENERGY

Band 1

Sidley Austin Brown & Wood LLP

See firm details p.778

The Firm: Most sources consider this "*probably the premier practice in the country for oil pipeline work.*" It is prominent in both the Alaskan market and in the lower 48 states, handling a mix of regulatory issues and litigation. The team has been kept particularly busy in recent years representing ExxonMobil in various cases in Alaska. A highlight here was winning a considerable victory for ExxonMobil Produc-

tion Company. The court ruled that Exxon was entitled to refunds because its oil has been undervalued for years, due to its being intermingled with inferior oil in the Trans Alaska Pipeline. In the other states, the firm tends to represent the oil pipelines themselves. Here it has been busy working on various rate proceedings before FERC. The group also does some gas pipeline work, and has recently been advising Dominion on rate cases, and Tractebel on the proposed pipeline to transport LNG from the Bahamas to Florida.

OIL & GAS

The Lawyers: Eugene Elrod (see p.441) is universally considered to be "*absolutely, positively a first-tier guy.*" He focuses on Alaska issues, where he remains an out-and-out leader in the field. According to interviewees, his purposeful and pragmatic approach lies at the heart of his success: he just "*gets the job done year in year out.*" Frederic Berner (see p.434) specializes in natural gas pipeline work and was lead counsel for the Millennium Pipeline that brings gas from Canada to suburban New York. Peers describe him as "*a smart and effective lawyer.*" Lawrence Miller (see p.458) represents oil pipelines in the

District of Columbia
Leading firms (Energy: Oil & Gas)

1 SIDLEY AUSTIN BROWN & WOOD LLP, *DC*
SKADDEN, ARPS, SLATE, MEAGHER *Washington, DC*
STEPTOE & JOHNSON LLP *Washington, DC*

2 BAKER BOTTS LLP *Washington, DC*
VINSON & ELKINS LLP *Washington, DC*

3 FULBRIGHT & JAWORSKI LLP *Washington, DC*
HOGAN & HARTSON LLP *Washington, DC*
LEBOEUF, LAMB, GREENE *Washington, DC*

4 ANDREWS KURTH LLP *Washington, DC*
BRACEWELL & GIULIANI LLP *Washington, DC*
JONES DAY *Washington, DC*
MORGAN, LEWIS & BOCKIUS LLP *Washington, DC*

5 CROWELL & MORING LLP *Washington, DC*
DEWEY BALLANTINE LLP *Washington, DC*
KIRKLAND & ELLIS LLP *Washington, DC*
TROUTMAN SANDERS LLP *Washington, DC*
VAN NESS FELDMAN PC *Washington, DC*
WRIGHT & TALISMAN PC *Washington, DC*

Leading individuals (Energy: Oil & Gas)

1 BROSE Steven *Steptoe & Johnson*, Washington, DC
ELROD Eugene *Sidley Austin*, Washington, DC
NAEVE Clifford *Skadden Arps*, Washington, DC

2 ACKER Lawrence *LeBoeuf Lamb*, Washington, DC
ANDRIL David *Vinson & Elkins*, Washington, DC
EASTMENT Thomas *Baker Botts*, Washington, DC
O'NEILL Brian *LeBoeuf Lamb*, Washington, DC
SCHERMAN William *Skadden Arps*, Washington, DC
WILLIAMS William *Fulbright & Jaworski*, Washington, DC

3 HASKELL Mark *Morgan Lewis*, Washington, DC
KIELY Bruce *Baker Botts*, Washington, DC
LEGGETTE Poe *Fulbright & Jaworski*, Washington, DC
LIPSON Kevin *Hogan & Hartson*, Washington, DC
REED Steven *Steptoe & Johnson*, Washington, DC

4 AVIL Richard *Jones Day*, Washington, DC
BERNER Frederic *Sidley Austin*, Washington, DC
CROWLEY Lisanne *Troutman Sanders*, Washington, DC
FREMUTH Michael *Andrews Kurth*, Washington, DC
MCMANUS Randolph *Baker Botts*, Washington, DC
NEWMAN Karol *Morgan Lewis*, Washington, DC
SHONEMAN Charles *Bracewell*, Washington, DC
SUNDBACK Mark *Andrews Kurth*, Washington, DC

5 ALEXANDER Lee *Dickstein Shapiro*, Washington, DC
BOWE James *Dewey Ballantine*, Washington, DC
COHEN David *Vinson & Elkins*, Washington, DC
HEFFERNAN Barbara *Schiff Hardin*, Washington, DC
MILLER Lawrence *Sidley Austin*, Washington, DC
RICHARDSON Julia *Van Ness*, Washington, DC
THOMPSON Carolyn *Jones Day*, Washington, DC
THOMPSON Michael *Wright*, Washington, DC
WATERS Jennifer *Crowell & Moring*, Washington, DC

Up-and-coming individuals
NEVINS Patrick *Hogan & Hartson*, Washington, DC
WILSON Anita *Vinson & Elkins*, Washington, DC

Firms and individuals are listed alphabetically in each band.

lower 48 states. A Rhodes Scholar, he is particularly renowned for his mastery of market power cases.

The Clients: Colonial Pipeline; Explorer Pipe Line; Marathon Ashland pipeline; Association of Oil Pipelines; BP; Shell; Sierra Pacific Power Company and Nevada Power Company.

Skadden, Arps, Slate, Meagher & Flom LLP & Affiliates
See firm details p.1372

The Firm: This DC energy team's expertise extends beyond its renowned electricity base to encompass major work in the natural gas sector. Skadden Arps is consistently in the first tier of recommended energy firms and deserves its leading reputation for its "*depth across the board*" and its work on complex deals. Indeed, many sources even view the firm as "*the best for gas work.*" This year it has focused on LNG work, regularly advising clients on the regulatory aspects of shipping contracts and supply contracts, and the financing of the LNG facilities themselves. The group also represents gas companies in the acquisition of additional assets, and advises on combination mergers of gas and electricity assets.

The Lawyers: Mike Naeve (see p.458) is unanimously named as "*the premier energy lawyer*" in DC, and "*the sector's leading light.*" His general FERC expertise covers both power and gas issues. In recent times, he has been concentrating more on policy work rather than being in the trenches every day. **Bill Scherman** (see p.466) also turns his hand to gas issues. He is "*a highly regarded lawyer who occupies a significant place at FERC,*" say market sources, and he was particularly recommended for tough cases because "*he understands the process better than anyone and has deep resources at hand.*"

The Clients: Clients include Sempra Energy, Hunt Oil and Atlantic LNG.

Steptoe & Johnson LLP
See firm details p.492

The Firm: Universally known in the market as "*the preeminent firm for representing oil pipelines,*" Steptoe & Johnson has had a busy year acting for high-profile clients in a number of important FERC proceedings. It is a key player in Alaska, where it represents the Trans Alaska Pipeline, and it recently played an important role in major litigation concerning the setting of rates for movements that stay within the state. Other highlights from the year include appearing for pipelines at FERC in connection with several million dollars of disputed reparations, and advising US pipelines on the acquisition of new lines. The firm is also doing some gas work for Enterprise Products Partners.

The Lawyers: Steven Brose (see p.436) is one of the sector's undisputed leaders. He boasts considerable experience and was recommended for his tenacious approach to negotiations and his creativity. Sources agree that he "*knows the oil pipeline field better than anyone else.*" **Steven**

Reed (see p.464) is also acknowledged to be "*a really good oil pipeline practitioner.*" Interviewees particularly commended him as "*an exceptionally able writer.*"

The Clients: Enbridge (which runs Canada's largest oil pipeline); Frontier Pipeline Company; Santa Fe Pacific Pipeline Partners; TEPCO; Cook Inlet Pipeline Company; Rocky Mountain Pipeline; ConocoPhillips; ExxonMobil; Colonial Pipeline and Enterprise Products Partners.

Band 2

Baker Botts LLP
See firm details p.1708

The Firm: Clients praise the "*flawless service*" provided by this renowned oil and gas firm. It offers broad transactional and regulatory expertise covering oil and natural gas pipeline issues, royalties, and LNG projects. A real highlight of the year was winning lower rates for BP in the seminal SFPP case concerning the regulation and rates for the transportation of oil and refined petroleum products through pipelines. The firm is also a key player in the blossoming LNG sector. Highlights here include representing Hunt Oil as the developer of the Camisea LNG facility in Peru, and advising AES on its proposal for an LNG facility in the Bahamas. On top of this upstream experience, Baker Botts also has expertise in all aspects of developing receiving terminals in the USA.

The Lawyers: Tom Eastment (see p.440) is a regulatory lawyer who concentrates on oil pipelines issues. He is particularly experienced in royalty cases and recently represented ChevronTexaco before the US Department of the Interior in connection with claims for additional royalties. Peers say that he is "*low key but very effective.*" **Bruce Kiely** (see p.450) heads the DC LNG practice and is considered by some to be "*one of the most experienced FERC lawyers in the USA.*" Clients also report that he is "*client-oriented and hands-on.*" **Randy McManus** (see p.456) is another experienced LNG attorney and is leading on the AES Bahamas project. Sources say he is "*a serious, solid, sensible lawyer with a good perspective on issues.*"

The Clients: BP; Shell; ExxonMobil; ConocoPhillips; ChevronTexaco; Hess LNG; Wisconsin Distributor Group; Guardian Pipeline; BTC Pipeline; Fort Chicago Energy Partners; BASF; Weaver's Cove Energy and American Petroleum Institute.

Vinson & Elkins LLP
See firm details p.1724

The Firm: Peers respect this eminent, Texas-headquartered energy firm for "*the breadth, longevity and experience of the practice.*" Clients, meanwhile, appreciate the quality and consistency of expertise, emphasizing that "*the high level of competence holds throughout the firm.*"

The cornerstone of the practice is the representation of gas pipeline companies at FERC, and the group is highly regarded for this type of work. It also has considerable experience in the LNG sector, which has served the firm well of late, given the current burst of activity. It has been representing BG in the development of the LNG facility in Trinidad for years, and is now moving more into LNG import facilities in the USA, including work for BP on the development of a terminal at Galveston.

The Lawyers: The "*aggressive and effective*" **David Andril** (see p.431) has been busy this year advising BG on the Trinidad LNG project. Clients were full of admiration for his expertise, with one even claiming "*he is the most knowledgeable FERC attorney I have come across.*" **David Cohen** (see p.437) is also considered a "*knowledgeable and diligent*" attorney, with clients appreciating his "*versatility.*" **Anita Wilson** (see p.476) is a younger partner who has been doing a lot of work recently for BG. According to impressed sources, she is "*diligent and a delight to work with,*" and clients also alluded to her "*particular skill in negotiations.*"

The Clients: Duke Energy; Tuscarora (a Western pipeline); Enbridge; BG Group; Total; Sierra Pacific; AIG; TransAlta; Shell and NRG Energy.

Band 3

Fulbright & Jaworski LLP
See firm details p.1715

The Firm: The DC branch of this major international energy firm works alongside the Texas offices, providing regulatory support on high-profile oil and gas transactions. The group focuses on natural gas, but also handles some oil and power work. This year, it has been busy advising its gas pipeline clients on the new FERC rules regarding their relationships with their energy affiliates. It also has considerable experience of counseling on compliance procedures, and has been representing National Fuel Gas Supply in a FERC investigation. In a notable recent development, the firm recruited a number of former in house lawyers from El Paso – a coup which will undoubtedly further deepen the team's expertise.

The Lawyers: **Bill Williams** (see p.475) is a renowned natural gas specialist. According to our sources he is "*as quick as can be*" and "*as good as they come for litigation.*" **Poe Leggette** (see p.452) is the industry's expert on royalty matters, and peers commend his "*deep knowledge*" of this subject area.

The Clients: National Fuel Gas Company; El Paso Pipelines; Texas Gas Transmission and Alliance Pipeline.

Hogan & Hartson LLP
See firm details p.484
The Firm: The market recognizes this as "*one*

of the largest and most prominent practices*" in the natural gas area. Its growing size hasn't affected the firm's service mentality though, as clients report: "*You know they're really busy, but when you call them, they treat you like you're their only client.*" The group won a major victory recently for Southern California Edison, when El Paso agreed to pay $1.7 billion to California ratepayers as compensation for its role in the recent energy crisis. This is the largest settlement at the time by any regulated gas company. The firm has also been working on FERC enforcement actions, and advising developers of LNG projects in the USA.

The Lawyers: **Kevin Lipson** (see p.453) is the practice's lead gas attorney. According to clients he is both "*energetic*" and "*extremely responsive.*" One even went so far as to say that he is "*one of the few outside counsel you can always rely on.*" Younger partner, **Pat Nevins** (see p.459), joins him in this year's rankings. Peers and clients alike report that he is "*smart and capable.*"

The Clients: Dominion; Southern California Edison; Nicor Gas and Dominion Cove Point LNG.

LeBoeuf, Lamb, Greene & MacRae, LLP
See firm details p.1358
The Firm: This long-established energy firm has developed a substantial LNG practice, working on both regulatory approvals and procurement agreements. Its highest profile projects from the past year include representing Tractebel in connection with one of the proposed pipelines to connect a Bahamas LNG facility with Florida. It also advised Occidental Petroleum on the development of the Corpus Christi LNG receiving terminal in Texas.

The Lawyers: As well as being a leading electricity lawyer, **Larry Acker** (see p.430) has been heavily involved in the firm's LNG work. Observers say that he is "*in the premier league for FERC litigation,*" and note that "*his sense of humor and dry wit serves him well in the courtroom.*" **Brian O'Neill** (see p.460) is another of the firm's LNG experts. Sources describe him as "*more low key but a skilled lawyer and negotiator nonetheless.*"

The Clients: Anadarko Petroleum; Idaho Power; Tractebel Calypso; Occidental Petroleum; Sempra Energy Global Enterprises; TransCanada; ConocoPhillips; Transwestern Pipeline Company and Colonial Pipeline Company.

Band 4

Andrews Kurth LLP
See firm details p.1707
The Firm: The firm boasts an historic reputation as one of the leaders for representing natural gas pipelines. Although the team lost one of its major clients when the company decided to

do its work in-house, the firm retains its ranking on the strength of its deep industry knowledge and continuing good work for the rest of its clients. It remains active in filings and disputes before FERC, and has been working on rate cases, complaint proceedings, tariff issues and certificate issues.

The Lawyers: **Michael Fremuth** (see p.443) has long been the team's most visible lawyer. Despite the decision of a major client to move its work in-house, he retains his ranking following enthusiastic praise for his talent, experience and long-established position in the field. The "*smart and assertive*" **Mark Sundback** (see p.471) has been active in the past year on behalf of the Northern Border Pipeline Company.

The Clients: Southern Natural Gas Pipeline; Northern Border Pipeline Company; Tennessee Gas Pipeline; Rowan Companies and The Williams Companies.

Bracewell & Giuliani LLP
See firm details p.1710
The Firm: The energy regulatory team here works on both gas and electricity issues, but the market particularly endorses its work for the gas industry. Clients warmly commend its "*responsiveness, value for money and long experience in the sector.*" The group specializes in representing the customers of gas and pipeline companies, and handles a volume of litigation involving rate increases and changes to terms of service. A highlight in the past year involved acting as lead counsel for the customer interest in the rate case initiated by Florida Gas Transmission Company, which was settled on terms favorable to its client. The team has also been heavily involved in the sale of Enron's pipelines following the bankruptcy, representing Citibank in connection with an investigation into a loan made by the bank, and advising the lenders to certain purchasers of Enron pipelines.

The Lawyers: **Charles Shoneman** (see p.467) is the firm's leading gas regulatory lawyer. According to interviewees, he is "*a powerful litigator who brings good judgment and a good sense of humor*" to the table. His success has apparently been built upon "*a knack of knowing when to be aggressive and when to look for compromise, and a talent for understanding his client.*"

The Clients: Shell; Peoples Gas System; Citibank and JPMorgan Chase.

Jones Day
See firm details p.485
The Firm: Jones Day has "*a long history and a good reputation*" in the gas regulatory sector, say clients. It is particularly known for its substantial experience in the development of domestic LNG projects. Here it has recently been advising BP America in connection with the Cove Point LNG terminal in Maryland. Another key characteristic of the DC gas practice is its active case-

load on behalf of CenterPoint Energy's pipeline subsidiaries and natural gas local distribution companies.

The Lawyers: **Richard Avil** (see p.431) has developed a reputation in the market as a *"prominent and capable"* gas lawyer with *"a good understanding of the sector."* The firm also boasts the services of the *"effective"* **Carolyn Thompson** (see p.471). According to interviewees, she is *"a serious, capable and reliable lawyer"* with considerable talent and energy sector experience.

The Clients: ChevronTexaco; CenterPoint Energy; BP America and SCANA Corporation.

Morgan, Lewis & Bockius LLP
See firm details p.1556

The Firm: Morgan Lewis enters the oil and gas table this year following a positive spree of prominent lateral hires. The new additions have placed the practice firmly on the radar screen. It has been developing a broad range of expertise that includes compliance issues and sales and acquisitions for energy marketers, rate-related work for utilities, and advice on LNG projects. The group is also representing Tractebel and BP Energy in connection with the FERC investigation into the California energy crisis.

The Lawyers: **Mark Haskell** (see p.447) has recently joined this growing international outfit from energy boutique, Brunenkant & Haskell, something which, observers agree, *"adds luster"* to the Morgan Lewis practice. He is a *"high-profile and hard-working"* lawyer and sources report that, *"you can trust him completely to do a top-notch job and to be honest and upfront."* **Karol Lyn Newman** (see p.459), formerly of Hogan & Hartson, is another *"huge new name"* for the firm. According to interviewees, she enjoys a reputation as a *"tenacious and bright"* attorney.

The Clients: Anadarko Petroleum; Tractebel; BP Energy; FP&L; Allegheny Energy; Occidental Petroleum; Marathon LNG company and Ameron.

Band 5

Crowell & Moring LLP
See firm details p.482

The Firm: Recognized by observers as a talented and prominent group, the team at Crowell & Moring handles a mix of LNG and oil work. It is the licensing counsel on one of the largest offshore LNG projects in the USA, and has also been advising the owner and operator of an oil pipeline on issues related to tariffs, rates and terms and conditions. The energy practice also has an international dimension, and the team is currently representing an oil and gas exploration company in an international arbitration with a foreign government.

The Lawyers: The *"smart"* **Jennifer Waters** (see p.474) is, says the market, the office's most visible gas attorney. She is the lead attorney for the East Tennessee Group, a group of 26 gas pipeline customers.

The Clients: Clients include East Tennessee Group, Laclede Gas Company and MLGW.

Dewey Ballantine LLP
See firm details p.1347

The Firm: Dewey Ballantine's *"incredibly effective"* energy practice has been busily cornering the market for natural gas storage work. Clients particularly appreciate the team's *"extremely high standards."* It excels at processing applications for authorization to construct natural gas storage facilities, and is currently involved in a major FERC proceeding to allow Sempra Energy Trading to build the Pine Prairie Energy Center. The group is also advising a major international commodities firm on potential acquisitions of natural gas transmission capacity in North America.

The Lawyers: **James Bowe** (see p.435) heads the natural gas practice here. He is highly rated by peers and clients alike.

The Clients: Sempra Energy Trading; SGR Holdings; eCorp; Redlake Gas Storage and Enstor.

Kirkland & Ellis LLP
See firm details p.770

The Firm: According to clients, this sizable international firm has quickly developed a *"strong energy background."* The oil and gas team is especially notable for its recent high-profile work on behalf of premier client, BP. For example, it is lead counsel for the Destin pipeline, BP's main pipeline in the Gulf of Mexico. Over the past four years, the firm has worked on $2.5 billion worth of divestitures of pipelines and refineries for BP. Among these are the $1.1 billion disposal of the Alliance refinery in Louisiana, and the $135 million sale of the Cushing-Chicago pipeline system to Enbridge.

The Lawyers: Neil Levy and Mitch Hertz are the firm's leading gas partners.

The Clients: Clients include BP, CornerStone Propane and DP&L.

Troutman Sanders LLP

The Firm: This *"excellent"* firm has a diverse gas practice, and is involved in day-to-day counseling in a number of different areas. This year, it has been representing an interstate pipeline at FERC in connection with certification and rate issues. Other typical matters include advising natural gas storage clients on regulatory and transactional matters and representing shippers in pipeline rate proceedings.

The Lawyers: **Lisanne Crowley** was recommended to researchers as *"a bright and skilled lawyer who commands immediate respect."* Clients report that they keep going back to her because she is *"always accessible and turns work around in a timely fashion."*

The Clients: Iroquois Gas Transmission System; Saltville Gas Storage; New Jersey Natural Gas and Sempra Energy Trading.

Van Ness Feldman PC

The Firm: As well as boasting a renowned electricity practice, this leading energy boutique is also a major player in the LNG field. A keynote of the past year has been work on reactivating or expanding existing LNG terminals in the USA. For example, it recently handled the successful reactivation of the Cove Point LNG Import Facility, one of the country's four existing terminals. The team also advises clients on the development of new projects, and here its highlights include the development of new terminals at Long Beach, California, and Hackberry, Louisiana.

The Lawyers: **Julia Richardson** coordinates the LNG practice here. According to peers she is *"an exceptional and very sharp lawyer."*

The Clients: The practice works for, among others, LNG project developers and natural gas pipelines.

Wright & Talisman PC

The Firm: This high-class boutique is much better known on the electricity side, however it also boasts an excellent gas pipeline practice. Here the team has been busy in a number of high-profile proceedings, and recently represented Williams Gas Processing in an important case that reined in FERC's jurisdiction on gas gathering. Interviewees expressed their admiration for the group's *"competent and technically-oriented"* lawyers.

The Lawyers: **Michael Thompson** is a well-known natural gas lawyer. According to peers he is *"very talented and extremely competent in technical issues."*

The Clients: The firm represents a number of gas companies, including Williams Gas Processing.

Other Notable Practitioners

Lee Alexander (see p.431) from Dickstein Shapiro Morin & Oshinsky LLP represents natural gas pipelines and storage projects. Market sources consider him to be *"in the premier league for FERC work"* and *"a zealous advocate for his clients."* **Barbara Heffernan** (see p.447) of Schiff Hardin LLP is well known for her work on behalf of Columbia Gulf Transmission Co's gas pipeline. Peers say: *"You can spot her work a mile off because she's a great writer and a big-picture thinker."*

ENERGY

ELECTRICITY

District of Columbia

Leading firms (Energy: Electricity)

1 SKADDEN, ARPS, SLATE, MEAGHER *Washington, DC*

2 STEPTOE & JOHNSON LLP *Washington, DC*

3 DEWEY BALLANTINE LLP *Washington, DC*
   DICKSTEIN SHAPIRO MORIN *Washington, DC*
   LATHAM & WATKINS LLP *Washington, DC*
   LEBOEUF, LAMB, GREENE *Washington, DC*
   SWIDLER BERLIN LLP *Washington, DC*
   WRIGHT & TALISMAN PC *Washington, DC*

4 BAKER BOTTS LLP *Washington, DC*
   CHADBOURNE & PARKE LLP *Washington, DC*
   CROWELL & MORING LLP *Washington, DC*
   HUNTON & WILLIAMS *Washington, DC*
   JONES DAY *Washington, DC*
   MILLER, BALIS & O'NEIL, PC *Washington, DC*
   TROUTMAN SANDERS LLP *Washington, DC*
   VAN NESS FELDMAN PC *Washington, DC*

5 BRUDER GENTILE & MARCOUX LLP *Washington, DC*
   HOGAN & HARTSON LLP *Washington, DC*
   KIRKLAND & ELLIS LLP *Washington, DC*
   MCDERMOTT WILL & EMERY *Washington, DC*
   MORGAN, LEWIS & BOCKIUS LLP *Washington, DC*
   VINSON & ELKINS LLP *Washington, DC*
   WINSTON & STRAWN *Washington, DC*

Firms are listed alphabetically in each band.

Band 1

Skadden, Arps, Slate, Meagher & Flom LLP & Affiliates

See firm details p.1372

The Firm: Universally hailed as "*the top FERC firm*," the team maintains its prominence due to its central involvement in many of the year's highest profile cases. The knowledge base here is undeniably deep, and impressed clients state: "*The lawyers stay completely on top of the latest orders and regulations at FERC*." The quality and style of its lawyers are also first rate. As one client emphasized, Skadden Arps has "*really bright attorneys who can look at matters in an innovative way.*" At present the firm is heavily involved in cutting-edge litigation, which is shaping the development of the electric transmission market throughout the USA. For example, a highlight of the year was its prominent role in a groundbreaking case in which FERC overruled state laws to allow AES to join the PJM Interconnection. Another important part of the practice involves handling the regulatory work generated by the firm's prolific energy M&A practice. Here it is particularly strong on the interface with competition matters. The group is also kept busy representing energy companies in FERC compliance cases. But it is not simply the brilliance of its attorneys and the high-profile nature of Skadden's work that make it the clear standout firm; it also has a breadth of clients that is hard to rival. The team represents all segments of the electric industry, including utilities in every region of the USA, as well as generators and developers.

The Lawyers: **Mike Naeve** (see p.458), a former commissioner at FERC, has an unrivaled status in the sector. Awed clients describe him as "*an absolute powerhouse*" and "*brilliant in public hearings.*" The words of one commentator sum up the market consensus: "*Everyone agrees that he is one of the most talented people at the Bar.*" **Bill Scherman** (see p.466) is a former general counsel at FERC. Clients enthusiastically commend him for "*having his finger on the political pulse of DC,*" and for his "*thorough and thoughtful*" approach to the law. Peers, meanwhile, report that he is "*one of the country's top regulatory lawyers and an absolutely excellent litigator.*" **John Estes** (see p.441) is highly recommended for complex litigation. His clients describe him as "*an excellent strategist*" who "*becomes the central spokesperson in multiparty litigation and ensures a high-profile position for the client – he leaves the back benches for lesser attorneys.*" **John Moot** (see p.458) is another "*effective litigator,*" and clients particularly value the fact that "*he's not just a yes man; he's really straight and candid with you.*" **Lynn Coleman** (see p.437) has a distinguished career in the sector, and was particularly commended for his expertise in matters relating to the Public Utility Holding Company Act (PUHCA).

The Clients: Exelon; Entergy; Mirant; Sithe Energy; Portland General Electric; Dynegy; Florida Power & Light; Synergy Corp; Great Plains Energy; Allegheny Energy and PG&E.

Band 2

Steptoe & Johnson LLP

See firm details p.492

The Firm: Admired by peers as "*the classic utility firm,*" this practice has "*a huge and well-established presence*" in the electricity market. Clients, meanwhile, unanimously describe the team as "*knowledgeable, able and consistent in delivering good results.*" It continues to be actively involved in the regulatory aspects of M&A and in high-profile energy litigation. This year it has focused in particular on market power and competition issues, representing key clients like AEP, Idaho Power, and Duke Energy in this area. It is also a key player in the development of Regional Transmission Organizations (RTO) and Independent System Operators (ISO) throughout the country. For example, it is representing Northwest Utilities in the New England ISO, Southern California Edison in the Western market, and AEP in the Midwest.

The Lawyers: **Lon Bouknight** (see p.435) heads the firm's electric power practice. Peers commend him as "*the model for FERC litigation*"

with a "*relentless and savvy*" approach. Clients, meanwhile, "*really value his insight in crafting workable solutions that help us avoid lengthy litigation.*" **Doug Green** (see p.445) has carved out an impressive reputation as "*a phenomenal litigator*" who is "*as smart as they come on market concentration matters.*" Clients also appreciate his "*close, hands-on relationship with the senior staff of the key agencies.*" **Rick Roberts** (see p.465) enjoys a considerable profile in the sector due to his active involvement in the California litigation. In this context he picked up numerous recommendations as "*a real force and a savvy litigator.*" **David Raskin** (see p.463) is another "*strong and feisty*" lawyer who was particularly noted for his "*superb tactical mind.*" He is the practice's expert on RTO matters.

The Clients: Dominion; El Paso Electric; Con Edison; DuPont and former shareholders of KMR Power Corp.

Band 3

Dewey Ballantine LLP

See firm details p.1347

The Firm: This international energy outfit represents the generator community to an "*A-plus plus*" standard. It has been involved in important market-shaping work, including leading the charge to eliminate pancake charges within regional markets, and advocating the supplier's position on LYCAP pricing in the New England market. However, its wide and varied practice stretches well beyond this established specialty. For example, the regulatory practice is often found working in a commercial context, supporting the firm's New York capital markets practice. It is representing a number of the financial institutions and hedge funds that have started investing in energy trading, including JPMorgan Chase, one of the largest investors in wind energy. The team also acts for the utilities, and has had a leading role in representing PG&E through its bankruptcy proceedings. Clients keep returning to the group because of its "*exacting high standards.*"

The Lawyers: **Earle O'Donnell** (see p.460) is said to be the central cog that makes the firm's electricity practice work so smoothly. A leader in the generating community, he is highly valued by clients for his "*intelligence, good business sense, and instructive analysis of tough problems.*" Sources also recommended **Donna Attanasio** (see p.431) as an "*experienced and knowledgeable lawyer.*"

The Clients: The firm represents a number of generators, including Edison Mission Energy; Midwest Generation and Lake Road. It also acts for utilities, such as PG&E, and financial institutions like JPMorgan Chase and BNP Paribas.

District of Columbia
Leading individuals (Energy: Electricity)

★ NAEVE Clifford *Skadden Arps*, Washington, DC

[1] ACKER Lawrence *LeBoeuf Lamb*, Washington, DC
BOUKNIGHT J A *Steptoe & Johnson*, Washington, DC
DOWNS Clark *Jones Day*, Washington, DC
ESTES III John *Skadden Arps*, Washington, DC
O'DONNELL Earle *Dewey Ballantine*, Washington, DC
SCHERMAN William *Skadden Arps*, Washington, DC

[2] EISENSTAT Larry *Dickstein Shapiro*, Washington, DC
GREEN Doug *Steptoe & Johnson*, Washington, DC
JAFFE Kenneth *Swidler Berlin*, Washington, DC
MCMANUS Randolph *Baker Botts*, Washington, DC
MOOT John *Skadden Arps*, Washington, DC
ROBERTS Richard *Steptoe & Johnson*, Washington, DC
SCHWARTZ David *Latham & Watkins*, Washington, DC

[3] ANGLE Stephen *Vinson & Elkins*, Washington, DC
BALIS Stanley *Miller Balis*, Washington, DC
COLEMAN Lynn *Skadden Arps*, Washington, DC
JORDAN J Phillip *Swidler Berlin*, Washington, DC
MCGRANE John *Morgan Lewis*, Washington, DC
NORDHAUS Robert *Van Ness Feldman*, Washington, DC
NORTON IV Floyd *Morgan Lewis*, Washington, DC
RASKIN David *Steptoe & Johnson*, Washington, DC
SHAPIRO Howard *Van Ness Feldman*, Washington, DC
SMALL Michael *Wright & Talisman*, Washington, DC
SMITH Roger *Troutman Sanders*, Washington, DC
SPECTOR Barry *Wright & Talisman*, Washington, DC

[4] BEHRENDS Samuel *LeBoeuf Lamb*, Washington, DC
BELL Joseph *Hogan & Hartson*, Washington, DC
CONTRATTO Dana *Crowell & Moring*, Washington, DC
GENTILE Carmen *Bruder Gentile*, Washington, DC
GERGEN Michael *Latham & Watkins*, Washington, DC
MOORE Margaret *Van Ness Feldman*, Washington, DC
O'SULLIVAN John *Chadbourne & Parke*, Washington, DC
PERLIS Mark *Dickstein Shapiro*, Washington, DC
QUINT Arnold *Hunton & Williams*, Washington, DC
SHAPIRO Robert *Chadbourne & Parke*, Washington, DC
SIKORA Clifford *Troutman Sanders*, Washington, DC
WENNER Adam *Chadbourne & Parke*, Washington, DC

[5] ATTANASIO Donna *Dewey Ballantine*, Washington, DC
BACHMAN Gary *Van Ness Feldman*, Washington, DC
BLACKBURN Thomas *Bruder Gentile*, Washington, DC
CLARKE Donald *Law Offices of GKRSE*, Washington, DC
DANKNER Donald *Winston & Strawn*, Washington, DC
KIRKWOOD Martin *Jones Day*, Washington, DC
KRAMER Merrill *Chadbourne & Parke*, Washington, DC
MADDEN William *Winston & Strawn*, Washington, DC
RUTKOWSKI Joanne *Baker Botts*, Washington, DC
SMITH Douglas *Van Ness Feldman*, Washington, DC
SULLIVAN Mary *Hogan & Hartson*, Washington, DC
VASILE James *Davis Wright*, Washington, DC
WALSH Linda *Hunton & Williams*, Washington, DC
YUFFEE Michael *McDermott Will*, Washington, DC

Up-and-coming individuals
REED Wendy *Wright & Talisman*, Washington, DC

Individuals are listed alphabetically in each band.

Dickstein Shapiro Morin & Oshinsky LLP
See firm details p.483

The Firm: The team here has carved out a strong market reputation as "*a forceful proponent of the generator perspective.*" It has been busy of late advising clients on sales and acquisitions of generating assets, energy trading compliance, and market restructuring issues. For example, it recently assisted Duke Energy in its involvement in the California ISO. Despite being an established brand name for representing generators, the firm also boasts considerable experience in regulated utility work. Clients value the group because of the "*exceptional client service,*" and because "*you get the quality of legal advice you would expect from a top New York firm but at a much better price.*" Peers, meanwhile, report that its lawyers are "*absolute pit bulls when it comes to litigation.*" This has stood them in good stead in the California energy litigation, where they are representing Duke Energy.

The Lawyers: **Larry Eisenstat** (see p.440) is renowned as an assertive negotiator. As clients comment: "*He knows when to be sweet and when to show his steel – and when he shows his steel the other side had better watch out.*" His other strengths include "*a proactive and strategic business mind*" and his ability to "*master the extracurricular, political side of the game.*" **Mark Perlis** (see p.461) has been representing Duke Energy this year in the California proceedings. His background is in litigation rather than energy law, but he has swiftly become an experienced FERC attorney producing high-quality work.

The Clients: The team's largest clients are Duke Energy and Constellation Energy Group, and it does a wide variety of work for both the regulated and unregulated sides of these companies. Other clients include KeySpan Energy and InterGen.

Latham & Watkins LLP

The Firm: Latham & Watkins is another "*excellent*" firm that has made an art of representing power generators and marketers. It has a particularly strong FERC and PUHCA practice, and has been active this year in a number of qualifying facility challenges, succeeding in maintaining this prized status for its clients. It has also been a primary player in the California litigation concerning long-term contracts with generators. Another branch of the practice is busy representing investors into the competitive power sector. Whichever side they are dealing with, clients express their pleasure at the "*great advice and great results.*"

The Lawyers: "*Rising star*" **David Schwartz** is a younger lawyer who is said to be doing work equal to that of attorneys many years his senior. He is known as "*a nimble litigator*" who "*can focus on the problem and find the appropriate solution.*" **Michael Gergen** has been focusing in

recent months on California matters. He ably brings his economic background to bear on market concentration issues, and is said by sources to be "*a smart regulatory policy attorney.*"

The Clients: Sithe Energy; Michigan Power Limited Partnership; Sempra Energy; Mirant; Citigroup; Goldman Sachs and Société Générale.

LeBoeuf, Lamb, Greene & MacRae, LLP
See firm details p.1358

The Firm: LeBoeuf Lamb has been working in the power sector "*since time immemorial*" and enjoys a long-standing reputation as an outright leader. It has a large regulatory practice, complementing its transactional firepower, and this year it has been particularly highly involved in FERC litigation. The firm is lead counsel for the non-generator companies involved in the West Coast refund litigation, and it is involved in a number of major bankruptcy-related actions on behalf of Enron companies. These include disputes over existing power purchase agreements. According to interviewees, the team's lawyers are "*tough in their approach*" and are renowned for being "*well plugged into the industry.*"

The Lawyers: The "*first-rate*" **Larry Acker** (see p.430) is one of the most established names in the market. Among his many advantages, say interviewees, are his "*good eye for strategy and ability to coordinate large, complex cases.*" Clients also appreciate his "*service-oriented and responsive*" approach, and he is renowned as "*a poised attorney who doesn't overreact.*" **Sam Behrends** (see p.433) was also enthusiastically recommended to researchers, and is considered "*one of the best strategic thinkers on FERC issues.*"

The Clients: Idaho Power; IDACORP; Tractebel Energy Marketing; Energy East; Sempra Energy; Occidental Petroleum; TransCanada; AGL Resources; Colonial Pipeline Company and The LA Department of Water & Power.

Swidler Berlin LLP
See firm details p.495

The Firm: Swidler Berlin has shot up *Chambers'* rankings this year due to its prominence in one of the most active and interesting fields within the power sector. It has been in the thick of things, representing regulated utilities in the development of RTOs and ISOs in the Northeast, Midwest and California. Big-name competitors describe this smaller firm as "*a significant competitor with an outstanding FERC practice.*" Clients, meanwhile, are impressed by the standards of service and satisfied with "*the quick turnaround and the quality of the work first time around.*" Its largest client is the California ISO and it has been busy this year dealing with the fallout from the state's energy crisis. The team also represents key members of other ISOs and has taken an active role in the proposal to

386

All quotes in the text are from interviews with clients and competitors.

CHAMBERS USA 2005

convert the New England ISO into a fully-fledged RTO, through its representation of National Grid.

The Lawyers: Peers dub **Kenneth Jaffe** (see p.448) "*one of the best litigators out there,*" and report that, "*we prepare much more than usual if we're up against him.*" Clients, meanwhile, appreciate his "*quick mind*" and "*thoughtful, level-headed approach.*" **Phillip Jordan** (see p.449) is the principal lawyer for the California ISO and was warmly praised for his "*sound judgment.*" According to market observers, "*he has a diplomat's personality and really understands group dynamics.*"

The Clients: As well as advising the California ISO, the team also represents a subsidiary of First Energy in the PJM RTO, and a subsidiary of National Grid in both the New England and New York ISOs. Other clients include Connecticut Yankee Atomic Company and Potomac Electric Power.

Wright & Talisman PC

The Firm: Despite lacking the size of some of its competitors, this is known as "*one of the best boutiques in the market for regulatory work,*" and is packed with "*really tough and smart operators.*" In particular, it has carved out a reputation as the first port of call for RTO and ISO issues. It has an unrivaled position when it comes to representing the RTOs and ISOs themselves, and the real jewel in its crown is its work for PJM Interconnection. Wright & Talisman represented the client throughout a number of FERC proceedings this year, which have led to it becoming the world's largest grid operator. Additionally, the team excels at advising members of other transmission operating systems.

The Lawyers: **Michael Small** enjoys a great reputation in the market based on the "*top-notch*" work he does for the transmission owners who formed the Midwest ISO. **Barry Spector** is also said to be "*a real leader in the field.*" The lead attorney for PJM Interconnection, he was recommended to researchers as "*a balanced and thoughtful lawyer who is an effective advocate for his client.*" **Wendy Reed**, a younger lawyer, was recommended for the strong work she has been doing with the Midwest ISO and joins the table this year.

The Clients: Among the transmission operating bodies, Wright & Talisman represents PJM Interconnection, the South West Power Pool and the transmission owners that formed the Midwest ISO. It also advises Bangor Hydro Electric Company and Maine Public Service Company as members of the New England RTO.

Band 4

Baker Botts LLP

See firm details p.1708

The Firm: The Baker Botts energy practice is, of course, highly renowned for its oil and gas work, but it also has an "*extremely good*" FERC practice. It advises a number of well-known clients on federal regulatory matters, such as tariff, rates, transmission and new facility certificate proceedings. The practice has probably enjoyed its highest profile in the market of late for representing Reliant in the California proceedings, where "*it is doing nice work.*" It also has a well-established PUHCA practice, and this year represented Exelon in its $2.2 billion acquisition of Illinois Power Company from Dynegy. The team has been dipping its toes recently into renewable energy, and has represented the developer of the Blue Canyon wind farm in Oklahoma. Clients particularly praised "*the good associate talent and cost-conscious approach.*"

The Lawyers: **Randy McManus** (see p.456) is the main power attorney in this team. A "*good and experienced litigator,*" his many virtues, according to interviewees, include "*a good judicious temperament.*" He is joined in the tables this year by **Joanne Rutkowski** (see p.466), who is the firm's PUHCA expert.

The Clients: Reliant Energy; Zilkha Renewable Energy; CenterPoint Energy; Exelon; Madison Gas & Electric Company; Mirant; Texas Pacific Group and AES.

Chadbourne & Parke LLP

See firm details p.1341

The Firm: The lawyers here wrote the book on IPPs, and continue to handle a volume of sales and acquisitions despite the recent slowdown in the sector. The "*high-quality*" team has "*lots of good, experienced lawyers*" and has recently broadened its work to include more of a mix of transactional and regulatory. It advises a number of utilities on interconnection and M&A issues, and represents financial institutions investing in the energy sector. The practice also has an interesting international dimension. Here, it is involved in international dispute resolution regarding an IPP in Mexico, and is working with a major state-owned company in Latin America on developing a bid process for cogeneration units.

The Lawyers: **John O'Sullivan** (see p.461) is a "*sharp*" utility specialist who can turn his hand to practically anything within this sector. He is popular with clients, who report that he is "*able to see all sides of a question and address issues with a broad understanding.*" **Robert Shapiro** (see p.461) is a "*really thorough*" regulatory lawyer and is said to be a top recommendation for complex filings and behind-the-scenes counseling, while **Adam Wenner** (see p.474) is known for his ability to get things done and is recommended as "*a strong implementation person.*"

Merrill Kramer (see p.451) is considered more of a transactional lawyer. He was described to researchers as "*bright, creative and highly experienced.*"

The Clients: Cemex; AES; GE Structured Finance; Ormat; El Paso; GE Energy and Exelon.

Crowell & Moring LLP

See firm details p.482

The Firm: This firm boasts a broad general energy practice that covers regulatory, transactional and litigation advice. Its particular forte is felt to be power purchase and prepayment transactions, in which area it had one of its highlights of the past year, representing Memphis Light Gas & Water in a $1.5 billion prepayment arrangement with the Tennessee Valley Authority. The firm also has a significant international practice, often advising on large power purchase agreements and international arbitrations. A highlight in this latter field was defending the Republic of Bolivia against a claim relating to an electric and water distribution concession.

The Lawyers: **Dana Contratto** (see p.438) handles a considerable amount of international work. Clients particularly value him for his "*encyclopedic knowledge of the electric utility industry.*"

The Clients: As well as the Republic of Bolivia and Memphis Light Gas & Water, the firm has represented a number of well-known utilities and power generators.

Hunton & Williams

See firm details p.1775

The Firm: This impressive regulatory practice is principally known for doing transmission work, in which field it has "*a great and long-standing reputation.*" Most notable is its representation of the New York ISO. The team also spends a considerable amount of time advising the utilities on transmission issues. In recent years, the practice has been broadening, and it now represents the developers of generating facilities, and advises banks on generating facilities that are struggling financially. A recent highlight for the group was its success in negotiating innovative rate treatments from FERC on behalf of American Transmission Company.

The Lawyers: **Arnold Quint** (see p.463) is perhaps best known for his role representing the New York ISO. Peers report that he is well respected in the industry and "*does a great job for his clients,*" while to clients themselves, he is "*hardworking and can do anything and do it well.*" **Linda Walsh** (see p.473) has been leading the American Transmission Company work, and is praised for her exceptional organizational skills.

The Clients: The team has acted for Superior Renewable Energy and Madison Gas & Electric Company.

Jones Day

See firm details p.485

The Firm: Jones Day has a strong federal regulatory practice based in DC and benefits from the support of offices throughout the USA. Clients emphasize the practice's "*expertise and experience*" and also the accessibility of the lawyers. In the past year they have been busy advising the Texas Central Company on $1.8 billion of dispositions. Another real highlight from the past twelve months was the team's success in gaining approval from FERC for Oklahoma Gas & Electric Company's purchase of a generation station from a bankrupt firm at a deeply discounted price.

The Lawyers: **Clark Downs** (see p.439) has enjoyed a long and illustrious career and is widely recognized as "*one of the deans of the regulatory Bar.*" He brings "*a tremendous amount of experience*" to the table, according to his admirers, and is "*great in negotiations.*" Clients particularly appreciate his skill at "*calming a situation and resolving a matter without necessarily having to go to litigation.*" Though Downs is far and away the leading light in this practice, **Martin Kirkwood** (see p.450) also stands out, particularly for his recent work in the California litigation. Clients report that he is a good appellate lawyer who can "*identify the important issues and cut considerably back on the massive volume of paper presented in court.*"

The Clients: AEP; Oklahoma Gas & Electric Company; CenterPoint Energy and Entergy.

Miller, Balis & O'Neil, PC

The Firm: Miller Balis is a boutique firm that specializes in representing the municipal customers of electric and gas companies, and it is widely acknowledged to be a market leader in this niche. Typical work includes drafting the contracts between municipalities and suppliers, and negotiating fair prices and conditions on behalf of its clients. In this, sources say, it is "*a forceful and effective advocate.*"

The Lawyers: **Stanley Balis** is the firm's best-known practitioner. Sources commented: "*If you want an advocate for a municipal interest you can't do better than him,*" and several interviewees reported that his reputation is so strong that his name alone will increase their chances of success. He handles a mix of gas and electric work.

The Clients: Clients include public agencies and associations, consumer-owned electric distribution systems, the owners of electricity generating facilities, wholesale customers of utilities and natural gas distribution systems.

Troutman Sanders LLP

The Firm: Though this sizable firm is less well known in the industry than some of the other firms on the list, it is certainly beginning to make its mark. Clients appreciate its intelligent and pragmatic advice, while even peers acknowledge it as "*a young, eager group that is making real headway in the sector.*" It advises a number of traditional utilities on matters such as mergers, asset sales, compliance, FERC and PUHCA regulations. The team has also been active of late in the extensive litigation in the Western states.

The Lawyers: **Roger Smith** is one of the practice's senior regulatory partners. According to interviewees, he is a "*careful, diligent and knowledgeable*" adviser. The firm also boasts the services of **Cliff Sikora**, who leads the energy group and was described as "*the driving force of the practice.*" According to sources, he has "*a sharp mind and a good nose for business.*"

The Clients: The team mainly works for traditional utilities, and its main client is Southern California Edison.

Van Ness Feldman PC

The Firm: This firm is frequently described as "*the best energy boutique in the country,*" and is renowned for its "*deep bench strength.*" The experienced and well-established team has been busy this year advising electric utilities on a broad range of issues. On top of traditional electricity regulation matters, it has been focusing on clean air, climate and energy technology issues. It also offers renowned litigation and appellate capabilities.

The Lawyers: As a former general counsel at FERC and the DOJ, **Robert Nordhaus** has a distinguished track record of work in government, and brings this considerable weight of experience to bear on his private practice. According to commentators he is a "*wise lawyer with extraordinarily good judgment.*" The "*terrific*" **Howard Shapiro** is best known for his high-quality appellate practice. Interviewees also note his extensive knowledge of all aspects of energy law. **Peg Moore** is another strong attorney, with a particularly good reputation for PUHCA and Public Utility Regulatory Policy Act (PURPA) compliance issues. Joining them in this year's rankings are **Gary Bachman** and **Douglas Smith**. Bachman has made a name for himself in recent months through his involvement in the California litigation. Peers praise him as "*a thorough, solid attorney who does a great job for his clients.*" Smith, meanwhile, is another former general counsel at FERC. He coordinates the firm's energy practice.

The Clients: The diverse client base includes major investor-owned utilities, smaller utilities, trade associations, independent generators and power marketers.

Band 5

Bruder Gentile & Marcoux LLP

The Firm: This is hailed as "*a good boutique firm for regulatory work*" and its lawyers were enthusiastically praised for their "*thorough knowledge of FERC issues.*" Clients were also appreciative of the more manageable size of the practice. As one put it: "*You get to know all the lawyers and feel valued as a customer.*" The team enjoys a diverse caseload, which includes transmission matters, power marketing, acquisitions and divestitures, and disputes over rates.

The Lawyers: **Carmen Gentile** was described by peers as "*a tough lawyer who is difficult to beat.*" Clients, meanwhile, praised his "*great knowledge of FERC proceedings, policies and personnel.*" The team also includes **Thomas Blackburn**, a younger lawyer who is considered to be "*knowledgeable and thorough in whatever he does.*"

The Clients: NStar Electric & Gas; California Power Exchange; Progress Energy; Pepco Holdings; El Paso Electric and Dominion.

Hogan & Hartson LLP

See firm details p.484

The Firm: Hogan & Hartson's "*sharp and well-connected energy team*" has one of the broadest-based practices in the business. Its considerable experience includes a number of enforcement actions, and the team is currently representing Public Service of Mexico in investigations and proceedings concerning liability for refunds, disgorgement of profits and alleged damages associated with the turmoil in California. It is also heavily involved in high-profile transmission work. Here, a highlight of the year was representing Dominion in the transfer of control over its transmission system to PJM. The team is also advising on electricity trading, sales and acquisitions and various disputes.

The Lawyers: **Joe Bell** (see p.433) is the head of the energy department. He works in a variety of areas and is said to be "*unbelievably bright, with good judgment, and the papers he writes hit the mark.*" **Mary Anne Sullivan** (see p.470) is a former general counsel at the Department of Energy and advises companies on long-term trends and policies within the sector. She has recently been representing the California ISO in rate proceedings. Clients report that she has "*a broad knowledge base and is thorough and well prepared.*"

The Clients: American Electric Power; Dominion Resources; Public Service Company of New Mexico; California Independent System Operator; Southern California Edison; Western Electricity Coordinating Council; Edison Mission Energy; Midwest Generation EME; Peabody Energy; Cleco and Bonneville Power Administration.

Kirkland & Ellis LLP

See firm details p.770

The Firm: The firm enters the table this year on the strength of interesting work done by both the regulatory and transactional arms of the energy practice. On the commercial side, the firm has been helping to renegotiate Constellation's $1 billion supply contract with the State of California. This is particularly notable as it is the first successful renegotiation of a California power contract. As a giant in private equity, it is also busy assisting private investors into the electricity sector. For example, the group advised Morgan Stanley in its first venture into this market, namely its acquisition of the Brooklyn Navy Yard cogeneration plant. On the regulatory side, the team is a market leader in counseling independent generators on grid interconnection issues. Additionally, Kirkland & Ellis was debtor's counsel in the high-profile NRG bankruptcy, and the energy team worked on the energy-specific side of this work.

The Lawyers: The practice consists of a team of seven lawyers, headed by Mitch Hertz.

The Clients: Morgan Stanley Capital Partners; Tenaska Energy; Constellation Energy; Calpine; InterGen; Invenergy; NRG Energy; BP; Orion Power Holdings; The Energy Cooperative; AES; Cedar Bay Generating Company; Westinghouse and Reliant Energy.

McDermott Will & Emery
See firm details p.773

The Firm: The energy practice at this international heavyweight enters *Chambers'* rankings this year following enthusiastic recommendations from clients for its invaluable specialist service. It is particularly valued for offering "*a unique combination*" of expertise in both FERC regulations and energy trading. The firm has built its energy regulatory practice around its transactional practice, and hence the team spends the majority of its time on trading commodities. Peers comment that the "*aggressive and savvy*" lawyers are favorites with sophisticated customers like Mirant. They are also increasingly representing the trading affiliates of financial institutions as they seek to enter this market. A highlight deal from the year was acting for Merrill Lynch & Co in its purchase of the Entergy-Koch energy trading business.

The Lawyers: **Michael Yuffee** (see p.476) is the firm's FERC expert.

The Clients: Clients include Morgan Stanley Capital Group, Merril Lynch Commodities and Mirant.

Morgan, Lewis & Bockius LLP
See firm details p.1556

The Firm: This is one of the most well rounded firms in the DC energy market, with a "*solid and competent*" electricity practice complementing a strong oil and gas offering and a market-leading nuclear team. Over the past twelve months, the electricity group has represented clients in a number of FERC investigations, for example, advising Arizona Public Service on compliance issues. Competition, transmission issues and the California litigation have been other areas of focus.

The Lawyers: **John McGrane** (see p.456) stands out from the pack here as "*a particularly smart and capable guy.*" Also enthusiastically recommended was **Mac Norton** (see p.439); his clients describe him as someone who "*never forgets anything and understands the industry inside out.*" Peers were also impressed by his performances – according to one he is "*smart and creative and has been successful in crafting strategies that win for his client.*"

The Clients: Minnesota Power; Entergy; Exelon; Alliant Energy; Black Hills; Cargill Power Markets; Northeast Utilities and Excel Energy.

Vinson & Elkins LLP
See firm details p.1724

The Firm: As a highly visible player in energy sales and acquisitions, Vinson & Elkins' regulatory practice is kept busy ensuring that clients' transactions go to plan. The team is as likely to appear on either side of the table in these deals. For example, it recently advised AIG Financial as the lender in an acquisition of a portfolio of power generating assets; represented Duke

Energy in the sale of eight merchant generation plants in the southeast; and assisted another client in the purchase of assets in Texas. On the dispute resolution side, the group also played a part in the California energy litigation proceedings, and appeared for TransAlta Energy Marketing in a claim against some generator clients for compensation for reactive power charges.

The Lawyers: Peers were full of respect for the work of **Stephen Angle** (see p.431), while clients keep returning to him because he is "*cost conscientious with great foresight and commercial acumen.*"

The Clients: Matlin Patterson; Entergy; Reliant Energy; Reservoir Capital; AIG Financial and Allegheny Energy.

Winston & Strawn
See firm details p.780

The Firm: While the firm is best known for its specialty in nuclear energy, it does have a broader power practice in DC, which encompasses work outside this niche. In particular, it boasts a FERC practice full of "*knowledgeable*" attorneys. They have recently been representing former PG&E subsidiary National Energy Group in bankruptcy proceedings.

The Lawyers: **Donald Dankner** is respected in the industry as "*a strong analytical thinker.*" He leads the firm's FERC practice, and is ably assisted by **William Madden**, who was rated by interviewees as a good choice for anything connected to hydroelectric regulation.

The Clients: The firm has a wide range of clients in the electricity sector.

Other Notable Practitioners
Donald Clarke, from the Law Offices of GKRSE, is a leading hydroelectric specialist and represents, among other clients, the National Hydropower Association. **James Vasile** (see p.472) of Davis Wright Tremaine LLP is another "*highly skilled*" hydroelectric lawyer, and acts for major clients like Calpine.

ENERGY

NUCLEAR

District of Columbia
Leading firms (Energy: Nuclear)

1	MORGAN, LEWIS & BOCKIUS LLP *Washington, DC*
	SHAW PITTMAN *Washington, DC*
	WINSTON & STRAWN *Washington, DC*

Firms and individuals are listed alphabetically in each band.

Band 1

Morgan, Lewis & Bockius LLP
See firm details p.1556

The Firm: This is a full-service law firm for the nuclear industry, and peers dub it "*an excellent practice and a strong and vibrant competitor.*" Clients, meanwhile, report that it is "*well quali-*

fied and does a top-notch job." Over the years, the team has captured an enviable share of the market. There are around 100 nuclear power plants in the country, and this firm provides regulatory advice to half of them, advising Arizona Public Service on the running of the Palo Verde station, the largest nuclear complex in the USA. The group's expertise spans a number of different areas, including defending companies against whistle-blower cases brought by workers, and representing the vendors of advanced reactor designs. It also appears for a number of clients, including Constellation, in suits brought against the government for failure to meet its obligation to take on responsibility for spent fuel. A recent highlight was advising FirstEner-

gy on the high-profile shutdown of the Davis-Besse nuclear plant.

The Lawyers: **George Edgar** (see p.440) is the most senior lawyer in the practice and has had a long and distinguished career in the industry. This experience, combined with his technical background, makes him "*one of the most knowledgeable, well-qualified and technically savvy lawyers in the business.*" **Jay Gutierrez** (see p.446) is another "*effective and aggressive*" lawyer, and is felt to be particularly strong in whistle-blower investigations. Clients say that he is "*knowledgeable and responsive and excels at explaining complicated nuclear issues in simple terms.*" **Steven Frantz** (see p.442) is the firm's expert on the design of advanced reactors.

District of Columbia
Leading individuals (Energy: Nuclear)

1 **EDGAR George** *Morgan Lewis*, Washington, DC
REYNOLDS Nicholas *Winston & Strawn*, Washington, DC
SILBERG Jay *Shaw Pittman*, Washington, DC

2 **CURTISS James** *Winston & Strawn*, Washington, DC
GUTIERREZ Jay *Morgan Lewis*, Washington, DC
LEWIS David *Shaw Pittman*, Washington, DC

3 **FRANTZ Steven** *Morgan Lewis*, Washington, DC
O'NEILL Jr John *Shaw Pittman*, Washington, DC
PETERSON Charles *Shaw Pittman*, Washington, DC
REPKA David *Winston & Strawn*, Washington, DC

Individuals are listed alphabetically in each band.

Clients see him as their *"detailed, on-the-ground individual,"* and appreciate his deep technical knowledge and background.

The Clients: The team's core group of clients are investor-owned utilities that possess nuclear plants throughout the USA. These include: Exelon; FirstEnergy; Constellation; Dominion; Pinnacle West; Southern California Edison; PPL; PSEG; STP and TXU.

Shaw Pittman

See firm details p.490

The Firm: This firm has 15 full-time lawyers covering the gamut of legal requirements for the nuclear industry. Clients value the team for its *"excellent knowledge of the industry, broad depth, and good relationship with the Nuclear Regulatory Commission."* They also report that it *"handles matters expeditiously, and provides conscientious support and good advice."* Over the past year it has been active advising on many of the most important current developments in the industry. It is leading the field in license renewals

for power plants, for example, and has worked on a number of power upgrade proceedings. It is also counsel to the Indian Point power plant and has been kept busy addressing security concerns relating to the threat of a terrorist strike. The firm is well known in the market for its expertise in nuclear waste issues. Here it is taking a lead in pursuing the government to meet its obligation to deal with spent fuel, and is representing a number of companies in pending lawsuits connected to this. The firm also acts for Private Fuel Storage, a controversial project to build a temporary facility to store spent fuel on an Indian reservation in Utah. At time of press the firm announced its merger with Pillsbury Winthrop LLP to form Pillsbury Winthrop Shaw Pittman.

The Lawyers: **Jay Silberg** (see p.467) is the firm's nuclear waste specialist and, according to clients, he has *"more experience with the Nuclear Regulatory Commission than anyone else out there."* He has taken on the leadership role in connection with a number of high-level waste claims against the government. **David Lewis** (see p.453) is felt to be an industry leader when it comes to license renewal work, while **John O'Neill** (see p.460) was recommended as *"a skilled attorney with a good understanding of the Nuclear Regulatory Commission rules."* **Charles Peterson** (see p.462) has a unique practice specializing in advising companies on getting funding from the Department of Energy for new technologies. He is currently working on hydrogen technology and new commercial nuclear reactors.

The Clients: The team represents US utility companies with nuclear power sites. This list includes: AEP; Entergy; Xcel Energy; Duke Ener-

gy; Michigan Power; Florida Power & Light; Omaha Public Power System and Detroit Edison. Other clients include the University of Chicago and the Private Fuel Storage consortium.

Winston & Strawn

See firm details p.780

The Firm: This firm offers *"a large and well-rounded nuclear capability,"* with a considerable depth of resources, and provides a full counseling and legal service to the nuclear industry. Clients consider the team *"a wonderful asset because of its deep knowledge of how the NRC works and its political connections in DC."* Its caseload recently has been a varied one, including certification proceedings for new advanced reactors, early site permit applications for future plants, and license proceedings for a commercial uranium enrichment facility. It has also been advising Yankee Atomic Electric on the decommissioning of its Yankee Row nuclear plant.

The Lawyers: **Nick Reynolds** (see p.464) heads the team and is the department's *"great rainmaker,"* as well as being one of the best-known and most respected attorneys in the nuclear field. **James Curtiss** is a former NRC commissioner and clients report that he is wonderful in front of judges: *"He prepares really well but he can also think on his feet,"* which gives him the ability to *"walk circles around other lawyers and witnesses."* **David Repka** (see p.464) also handles a lot of litigation work, but is particularly renowned for *"his expertise on the technical writing side."*

The Clients: ARRIVA; Entergy; Duke Energy; Louisiana Energy Services; Yankee Atomic Electric; Connecticut Yankee Co; Exelon; AEP and Chemico.

ENVIRONMENT

Band 1

Hunton & Williams

See firm details p.1775

The Firm: This international outfit has earned important market recognition as the firm of choice for the electric utilities. It is an *"excellent practice,"* according to enthusiastic commentators; almost all peers agree that it is *"one of the top-two Clean Air Act firms."* High-profile New Source Review (NSR) cases serve to raise the firm's flag ever higher, and place it solidly at the heart of developments in CAA law. Beyond air issues, it also boasts internationally renowned environmental specialists in fields such as wetlands and international regulation. Attorneys are recommended for issues as diverse as European chemicals regulation and the implications of the Kyoto Treaty.

The Lawyers: **Virginia Albrecht** (see p.430) is acknowledged as *"one of the top-five wetlands experts in the country."* Her *"very active"* practice covers not only the West Coast and Florida, but also includes areas such as New Jersey and Puerto Rico. **William Brownell** (see p.436) is *"exceedingly thoughtful and careful,"* which is precisely the demeanor favored by his clients. He is visible in global-warming issues, *"very strong in air,"* and he provides expertise in CWA and waste issues. Another attorney adjudged to be *"terrific in air"* is **Andrea Field** (see p.442). Selected for praise as *"a fine lawyer,"* she has been a lynchpin for crucial CAA issues. Her foresight is also appreciated on the strategic and policy issues that clients face when trying to map an uncertain regulatory future. **Henry Nickel** (see p.459) is also a top-flight CAA expert who is frequently seen working alongside Field. They are *"virtually joined at the hip and do a good job,"*

according to one client. Peers note that he *"has always been excellent,"* both in CAA issues and beyond. **Turner Smith** (see p.469), once the former managing partner of the firm's Brussels office, now heads the firm's international environmental practice. The market respects his ability to solve problems with an international perspective; as well as extensive European expertise in issues including hazardous waste transportation and developments in the Registration, Evaluation, Authorisation of chemicals (REACH) policy, Smith has growing presence in Latin America. He has also been involved in war crimes litigation before the International Criminal Tribunal for the Former Yugoslavia.

The Clients: The firm acts for a variety of national and international companies, though it is most visible representing major energy utilities, both individual companies and consortia, in rule-making challenges and general litigation.

District of Columbia
Leading firms (Environment)

1. HUNTON & WILLIAMS *Washington, DC*
   LATHAM & WATKINS LLP *Washington, DC*
   SIDLEY AUSTIN BROWN & WOOD LLP *Washington, DC*

2. ARNOLD & PORTER LLP *Washington, DC*
   BEVERIDGE & DIAMOND PC *Washington, DC*
   HOGAN & HARTSON LLP *Washington, DC*
   MORGAN, LEWIS & BOCKIUS LLP *Washington, DC*

3. BAKER BOTTS LLP *Washington, DC*
   COVINGTON & BURLING *Washington, DC*
   GIBSON, DUNN & CRUTCHER LLP *Washington, DC*
   KING & SPALDING LLP *Washington, DC*
   KIRKLAND & ELLIS LLP *Washington, DC*
   SHAW PITTMAN *Washington, DC*
   SWIDLER BERLIN LLP *Washington, DC*
   VENABLE LLP *Washington, DC*

4. DLA PIPER RUDNICK GRAY CARY *Washington, DC*
   FOLEY & LARDNER *Washington, DC*
   GOODWIN PROCTER LLP *Washington, DC*
   JONES DAY *Washington, DC*
   MCKENNA LONG & ALDRIDGE LLP *Washington, DC*
   PILLSBURY WINTHROP LLP *Washington, DC*
   SKADDEN, ARPS, SLATE, MEAGHER *Washington, DC*
   VAN NESS FELDMAN PC *Washington, DC*
   VINSON & ELKINS LLP *Washington, DC*
   WALLACE KING DOMIKE *Washington, DC*
   WEIL, GOTSHAL & MANGES LLP *Washington, DC*
   WILLKIE FARR & GALLAGHER *Washington, DC*
   WILMER CUTLER PICKERING HALE *Washington, DC*

Firms are listed alphabetically in each band.

Latham & Watkins LLP

The Firm: As a multifaceted organization with international reach and excellent presence across the USA, this firm is increasingly seen as one of the most robust environmental practices around. While its recommended attorneys operate in specialisms from CAA to Toxic Substances Control Act (TSCA), proven litigation strength helps to convince the market of Latham & Watkins' status as a rounded environmental practice. A rise in environment-related toxic torts litigation has kept the firm busy, and it has been involved in several natural resources disputes. In one such matter, attorneys represented the Metropolitan Water District of Southern California in a water rights dispute. The scarcity of water in the western states, and large-scale federal ownership of land is set to make such natural resource cases more common in the future. The firm is also acknowledged as a player in clean air issues, and several of its "*very bright folks*" are active in the areas of chemicals and pesticides, most usually through toxic torts litigation or in regulatory issues insofar as these affect a variety of industry sectors, from electronics to agriculture.

The Lawyers: Former Deputy Secretary of the Department of the Interior, **David Hayes** is a premier practitioner who has achieved the highest praise for his work in natural resources disputes. "*One of the most prominent in the field,*" his broad knowledge of governmental issues is all-important for clients seeking excellent first-hand experience of policy-shaping issues. Peers "*think the world of his expertise.*" Former Secretary of the Department of the Interior Bruce Babbitt assists the firm as special counsel. Babbitt is noted for his natural resources experience. **Robert Sussman** is "*creative and innovative*" in his approach to chemicals and clean air issues. His fans proclaim him to be "*absolutely the best,*" and applaud his "*excellent work*" in reaching settlements or assisting clients with strategic advice on pesticides and industrial chemicals. He also has a good profile acting for energy companies. **Julia Hatcher** is "*bright and analytical*" and highly focused on chemicals work, in which she is still one of the few recognized authorities on perfluorooctanoic acid (PFOA). Her knowledge extends to several other persistent chemicals that have been found in the bloodstream. Aside from toxic torts litigation she counsels clients on strategic decisions concerning chemicals usage. Her clients include chemicals manufacturers as well as users, for example, companies in the semiconductor industry. **Ken Weinstein** is one of the most respected pesticides practitioners around and represents some of the largest pesticides manufacturers in the country. His practice has matured to become a first port of call for endangered species issues, the Federal Insecticide, Fungicide and Rodenticide Act (FIFRA), the CWA and CAA. He is visible acting for coalitions and trade associations.

The Clients: American Chemistry Council; 3M; Metropolitan Water District of Southern California; Semiconductor Industry Association; Southern Nevada Water Authority; Bayer and Syngenta.

Sidley Austin Brown & Wood LLP

See firm details p.778

The Firm: Showing the right combination of expertise, market recognition and sheer longevity, this firm still stands out as "*the group to go to.*" Major litigation and leading-edge regulatory advice are to the fore, with clients confirming satisfaction when "*the hardest questions*" have been put to the firm. Attorneys are engaged on matters relating to ozone-destroying gases and CAA interpretation, as well as some of the largest contamination cases in the country. The firm has been engaged on Superfund cleanup following the historical dumping of PCBs in the Hudson River, a practice which ended in 1977 but has involved client GE in litigation ever since. A number of CAA cases have also been noted, and the market is impressed by those of the group's attorneys who specialize in NSR. The firm acts for power utilities such as AEP, as well as companies in, for example, chemical manufacturing and mining. Its robust defense work takes in white-collar crime issues.

The Lawyers: David Buente (see p.436) attracts a crescendo of praise. Market commentators are impressed by his proactive nature, saying, "*he just gets right in there.*" On enforcement defense and Superfund work this "*top environmental litigator*" is second to none; his DOJ experience and, later, his time as a Justice Department attorney at the EPA, is part of the appeal. His visibility has been further enhanced through large toxic torts cases; he is acting on one that involves a phosphate mine, which was last operated by Coronet Industries. The mine is now subject to an action that features 900 plaintiffs and has ramifications for environmental agencies. **Angus Macbeth** (see p.454) is also universally recognized as an expert problem solver. Another DOJ émigré, he is complimented not merely for his immensely broad knowledge, but also the fact that he will "*dig in*" to issues. He was the attorney best recognized for assisting GE on issues relating to PCBs in the Hudson River. Almost all leading practitioners agree that it is a mixture of practical experience and strategic foresight that earns him the plaudit "*outstanding.*"

The Clients: GE; CITGO Petroleum; Honeywell; AEP; ExxonMobil; Cinergy; Coronet Industries and Continental Carbon.

Band 2

Arnold & Porter LLP

See firm details p.478

The Firm: Acting for a broad range of clients, the ten partners at the DC office of this firm are busy in a variety of environmental fields. The view from the market is that the practice is "*obviously very able*" and "*particularly good in litigation.*" In clean air matters the firm has made strides to capture a market share, and its clients include BP and mobile source clients. Elsewhere, the firm is a proven force in toxic substances and pesticides, both in terms of litigation and regulatory issues. Attorneys "*think well strategically,*" which stands them in good stead when tackling meaty litigation.

The Lawyers: Thomas Milch (see p.457) is labeled a contamination guru. He is acknowledged as "*smart*" in resource conservation issues and toxic torts, and acts on some of the major Superfund work which still passes through the hands of the large firms. His clients include Honeywell and BP, and he has recently acted on a spate of contaminated lakes cases in New York, New Jersey and Georgia. **Blake Biles** (see p.434) has built a reputation as a toxic substances and chemicals expert. Perceived as a "*leader in his field,*" he is one of a number of lawyers who can claim expertise on fluoropolymers, which are now seen as persistent chemicals.

The Clients: BP; Altria; Honeywell and Occidental Petroleum.

District of Columbia
Leading individuals (Environment)

Senior Statesman

GARRETT Theodore *Covington & Burling*, Washington, DC
WARREN Edward *Kirkland & Ellis*, Washington, DC

[1] BUENTE David *Sidley Austin*, Washington, DC
HAYES David *Latham & Watkins LLP*, Washington, DC
MACBETH Angus *Sidley Austin*, Washington, DC

[2] ALBRECHT Virginia *Hunton*, Washington, DC
BROWNELL William *Hunton*, Washington, DC
BUCKLEY Christopher *Gibson Dunn*, Washington, DC
FIELD Andrea *Hunton & Williams*, Washington, DC
HAGEN Paul *Beveridge & Diamond*, Washington, DC
KNAUSS Charles *Swidler Berlin*, Washington, DC
LEWIS William *Morgan Lewis*, Washington, DC
MILCH Thomas *Arnold & Porter*, Washington, DC
NICKEL Henry *Hunton & Williams*, Washington, DC
QUARLES John *Morgan Lewis*, Washington, DC
STARR Judson *Venable*, Washington, DC
STEINBERG Michael *Morgan Lewis*, Washington, DC
SUSSMAN Robert *Latham & Watkins*, Washington, DC

[3] BIEKE James *Goodwin Procter*, Washington, DC
BILES Blake *Arnold & Porter*, Washington, DC
BOURDEAU Karl *Beveridge & Diamond*, Washington, DC
BUMPERS William *Baker Botts*, Washington, DC
DINKINS Carol *Vinson & Elkins*, Houston
ELLIOTT E Donald *Willkie Farr & Gallagher*, Washington, DC
GAYNOR Kevin *Vinson & Elkins*, Washington, DC
HATCHER Julia *Latham & Watkins*, Washington, DC
LUDWISZEWSKI Raymond *Gibson Dunn*, Washington, DC
LUXTON Jane *King & Spalding*, Washington, DC
MENOTTI David *Shaw Pittman*, Washington, DC
RAHER Patrick *Hogan & Hartson*, Washington, DC
RHYNE Katherine *King & Spalding*, Washington, DC
RITTS Leslie *Hogan & Hartson*, Washington, DC
SMITH Turner *Hunton & Williams*, Washington, DC
WEINSTEIN Ken *Latham & Watkins*, Washington, DC

[4] BANKS Jim *Hogan & Hartson*, Washington, DC
BERGESON Lynn *Bergeson & Campbell*, Washington, DC
BLOCK Joseph *Venable*, Washington, DC
BUMPERS Heidi *Jones Day*, Washington, DC
CARR Don *Pillsbury Winthrop*, Washington, DC
DOMIKE Julie *Wallace King*, Washington, DC
DRAKE Stuart *Kirkland & Ellis*, Washington, DC
FROST Don *Skadden Arps*, Washington, DC
HOLEWINSKI Kevin *Jones Day*, Washington, DC
JACKSON Thomas *Baker Botts*, Washington, DC
KASTNER Ken *Hogan & Hartson*, Washington, DC
LOHMANN Walter *Kirkland & Ellis*, Washington, DC
O'CONNOR III Charles *McKenna Long*, Washington, DC
PENNA Richard *Van Ness*, Washington, DC
STOLL Richard *Foley & Lardner*, Washington, DC
STRAND Margaret *Venable*, Washington, DC
WEINBERG David *Howrey Simon*, Washington, DC

Individuals are listed alphabetically in each band.

Beveridge & Diamond PC
See firm details p.480

The Firm: This renowned environmental boutique is most highly praised by its clients for offering "*a uniformly great experience.*" "*It is more specialized than the big firms,*" they say. In the past year the firm advised on a spread of domestic and international issues- contentious, transactional and regulatory. The firm has been involved in issues concerning the environmental impact of the Cartagena Protocol on Biodiversity, as well as utilization of the Data Quality Act to challenge decisions and studies made by environmental agencies. Peers acknowledge that the practice is "*strong in hazardous waste*" and RCRA issues on the domestic front, while internationally it is a mine of information for companies operating in China. The firm was involved, on a pro bono basis, with the drafting of Afghanistan's new environmental laws.

The Lawyers: With the market singing his praises, **Paul Hagen** (see p.446) is "*highly quoted*" on international treaty issues. Clients see his "*considerable*" international expertise to be his most attractive feature; his work has involved the negotiation on behalf of industry bodies and subsequent implementation of multilateral environmental agreements. His client base features several large, multinational finance companies, including the IFC, which he advises on the environmental aspects and requirements of major international projects. He also advised an American nonprofit organization on the implications of the global moratorium on commercial whaling. **Karl Bourdeau** (see p.435) focuses on liability arising out of contaminated sites and peers agree that he is one of the lawyers they "*would name first*" for hazardous waste advice. Clients like his practical approach, with one saying: "*I can go to him and get the top RCRA knowledge that I need.*" Bourdeau is an exponent of the use of data quality legislation to aid companies in their defense of litigation.

The Clients: The firm's broad range of clients covers multinational companies and national bodies, as well as nonprofit organizations.

Hogan & Hartson LLP
See firm details p.484

The Firm: "*Another top air group,*" is the general view of this environmental practice, which, as one of the firms attempting CAA rulemaking challenges, mixes with esteemed company. The firm boasts several major mobile source clients and advises them on CAA compliance as well as strategic issues. It has also acted for a cross-industry trade association in CAA issues, including NSR rulemaking challenges. The association includes oil companies, electric utilities, chemical companies, transportation companies and vehicle manufacturers and has had some success in the regulatory arena.

The Lawyers: Patrick Raher (see p.463) "*is recognized in air issues as a leading practitioner,*" according to commentators. He is a member of the EPA's CAA panel and cochairs its NSR committee, which demonstrates the depth of his knowledge in this field. Preventive counseling is one of the central pillars of his practice, and he services clients in both the fixed and mobile source fields. He also advises on international laws and the harmonizing of regulations, especially in relation to Europe. **Leslie Sue Ritts** (see p.464) is "*a real smart air specialist*" and "*deeply involved in CAA amendments.*" Her representations for trade associations have led to widespread praise: to enthusiastic market commentators she is "*absolutely the best.*" **Jim Banks** (see p.432) is the firm's CWA specialist, and he has been active in litigation between Florida and Georgia over water rights. Banks is also heavily involved with agricultural clients such as the National Chicken Council and the National Turkey Federation, and work in this field is set to rise with further water disputes and natural resources shortages looming on the horizon. Peers who have seen Banks in action agree that he is worthy of "*respect.*" **Ken Kastner** (see p.449) has a name in chemicals and hazardous waste transportation. He spends a significant portion of his time providing strategic advice, which can be vital to clients wanting to know which chemicals to use and which to phase out. He is also active on enforcement matters and contamination disputes. The market additionally acknowledges Doug Wheeler, formerly California's Secretary for Resources, for his endangered species expertise and burgeoning natural resources practice.

The Clients: Mercedes-Benz; Procter & Gamble; National Chicken Council; National Corn Growers Association; Cinergy; PSE&G; Rhodia; Verizon; Mitsubishi Motors and Merck.

Morgan, Lewis & Bockius LLP
See firm details p.1556

The Firm: Covering a broad spread of activities, the firm has achieved prominence in its CAA litigation and regulatory work, though it is also "*extremely effective on rulemaking and lobbying issues.*" The multidisciplinary nature of the practice enables litigators to work alongside regulatory lawyers, and clients enthuse about the firm's "*excellent EPA contacts,*" confirming that its good working relationships with the agency and the DOJ inspire confidence. Highlights have included extensive EPA rulemaking challenges, where the firm is a favorite of trade associations, especially in the burgeoning NSR field. Achievements in clean air have led commentators to label this side of the practice as "*outstanding.*" Superfund and hazardous waste are also fields in which the firm's "*very talented*" attorneys are recognized.

The Lawyers: "*One of the experts on New Source*"

392

All quotes in the text are from interviews with clients and competitors.

CHAMBERS USA 2005

District of Columbia
Leading individuals
(Environment: Mainly Transactional)
[1] BERLIN Kenneth *Skadden Arps*, Washington, DC
[2] BERZ David *Weil Gotshal*, Washington, DC
CONNOLLY Annemargaret *Weil Gotshal*, Washington, DC
FROST Don *Skadden Arps*, Washington, DC
LOHMANN Walter *Kirkland & Ellis*, Washington, DC
Individuals are listed alphabetically in each band.

Review" and "*surprisingly accessible*," **William Lewis** (see p.453) is best known for his CAA work. In EPA rulemaking challenges his clients include a coalition of ten major trade associations representing a broad cross-section of industry. Clients say he is "*as practical as anybody, can cut to the issue quicker than most and he writes brilliant briefs.*" He is also acknowledged as a leading name for Title V permits. As one of the most respected environmental leaders, **John Quarles** (see p.463) continues to attract market praise as a no-nonsense lawyer who can "*give you his true read of a situation.*" An ex-EPA administrator, he is viewed as a smart choice for advocacy of policy and admired for his RCRA and Superfund expertise. Clients appreciate the way he blends experience with a practical approach. "*Excellent*" **Michael Steinberg** (see p.470) impresses with his hazardous waste, Superfund and toxic work. A former assistant chief of the Environmental Defense Section at the DOJ, his litigation pedigree is beyond doubt, and clients flock to him for both rulemaking challenges and defense representations.

The Clients: Pfizer; Owens-Illinois; Motiva; Interstate Natural Gas Association of America; Cytec; ConocoPhillips; Ciba Specialty Chemicals and American Chemistry Council.

Band 3

Baker Botts LLP
See firm details p.1708

The Firm: Though many know the firm "*mostly for air work,*" there are signs that the practice group is actively pursuing a lead role in some of the growing international issues – "*they are carving out an international climate practice.*" Clients are attracted by the firm's lobbying abilities, an aspect not to be overlooked in a practice area and a city where Capitol Hill is the constant backdrop.

The Lawyers: The market reserves the lion's share of its praise for **William Bumpers** (see p.437), who has "*a dynamic air practice*" and a client roster including major electric utilities. As "*the settlement guy in several major cases,*" his abilities are understood by clients and peers alike. **Thomas Jackson** (see p.448) is special counsel to the firm and handles both litigation and counseling, particularly in relation to Environmental Impact Statements and endangered

species issues. "*Well known and respected in wetlands and endangered species,*" he has attracted spontaneous praise from those aware of his "*interesting cases.*"

The Clients: The firm acts for a variety of industries and organizations, including the IFC, ChevronTexaco and American Portland Cement Alliance.

Covington & Burling
See firm details p.481

The Firm: The "*well-known*" Covington & Burling attorneys remain the favorites of a variety of big-name clients. Toxic torts and insurance claims have complemented traditional environmental defense work, and outside the contentious arena, the firm is said to be skilled in its compliance advice, servicing clients as diverse as Del Monte Foods, Aerojet and American Chemistry Council. Some clients also rely on the firm's food and drug expertise.

The Lawyers: In the eyes of the market, **Ted Garrett** (see p.443) has earned his title as "*a respected senior statesman.*" Peers agree that he is "*first class,*" both in terms of his experience and the quality of his advice. Currently, he is occupied with Superfund and pesticides work, and he additionally serves as liaison to the ABA Standing Committee on Environmental Law. Extensive writing and speaking engagements serve to show that his commitment to environmental law is stronger than ever.

The Clients: Microsoft; Kansas City Power & Light; Kerr-McGee; Vulcan Materials Company; Nestlé; Solutia; Northrop Grumman; Boeing; American Chemistry Council; Del Monte Foods; Holly Corporation; Aerojet and Itochu.

Gibson, Dunn & Crutcher LLP
See firm details p.285

The Firm: Working within "*a well-regarded generalist firm,*" this practice group does not appear to have captured the attention of rivals, yet the views of clients tell a different story. "*I would recommend them unconditionally,*" remarked one, who appreciated the preparation and strategic strength that he found at the firm. Clients point to the extensive experience within the firm as the "*main attraction,*" confirming capabilities in chemicals litigation, CAA issues (including NSR), CWA, bankruptcy, RCRA and Superfund.

The Lawyers: When clients mention "*seasoned litigator*" **Chris Buckley** (see p.436), they speak with great enthusiasm. He is "*one of the finest civil litigators I have worked with in my 25-year litigation career,*" according to one. Buckley's profile is the strongest of those within the environment and natural resources practice group, which he founded and chairs. Peers call him "*one of the godfathers of environmental law.*" Last year he represented the California Farm Bureau Federation in a judicial review concerning the ambitious CALFED Bay-Delta project.

Raymond Ludwiszewski (see p.454) is visible in a range of litigation. He was formerly acting general counsel of the EPA and he is perceived as a "*CWA expert,*" as well as being active in related toxic torts. Ludwiszewski has further shown his capability in NSR and mobile source CAA issues.

The Clients: The firm assisted the American Farm Bureau and the California Farm Bureau in the Court of Appeals and the US Supreme Court case concerning water usage. The firm also acts for Solutia, the City of Cincinnati and the Atlantic Salmon Federation.

King & Spalding LLP
See firm details p.635

The Firm: This firm received warm feedback highlighting "*good toxic expertise.*" Mixing litigation, compliance advice and strategic thinking, its DC attorneys often work in conjunction with teams in Atlanta and Houston to service large industry groups and influential trade associations. As well as registering concerns, the firm provides extensive lobbying support to such groups. For example, aside from being important in the USA, metals and chemicals regulation is set to be an area of growing prominence elsewhere in the world, especially in the EU. The group acts for the North American Metals Council, which is a broad coalition of 73 trade associations interested in regulatory developments, both domestic and international.

The Lawyers: Metals expert **Jane Luxton** (see p.454) has "*breadth of expertise*" and is active in several major cases on behalf of her coalition clients. She is well known for the work she has done for the Coalition for Mercury Management; indeed, some 80% of her work pertains to the metals industry, including an increasing amount in the lead smelting sector. Beyond metals, she advises on other chemicals and related CWA issues. **Katherine Rhyne**'s (see p.464) practice has increasingly incorporated toxic torts, although she is still primarily viewed as a regulatory lawyer. Her focus on the chemicals and petrochemicals industries has led her to act for trade associations such as the Pine Chemicals Association. Peers applaud her "*deep knowledge of risk assessment.*"

The Clients: North American Metals Council; The Coalition for Mercury Management; The Chlorine Institute; 3M; Bridgestone/Firestone; Coca-Cola and Dow Chemical.

Kirkland & Ellis LLP
See firm details p.770

The Firm: This seven-attorney practice is active in several fields. A "*premier appellate firm,*" say some commentators, while others stressed its representation of mobile source clients in CAA issues. It is one of several DC practices seen to be providing very effective support on corporate transactions where environmental issues and liabilities are of key importance. Bankruptcy is another steady source of work, and in this sphere the group is recommended for its knowhow. In litigation, the firm's representation of automobile industry clients, including GM, is the aspect most commented upon. Finally, the firm has made an impression in rulemaking challenges concerning California's stance on emissions.

The Lawyers: Walter Lohmann (see p.454) is the group's best-known environment transactional expert. Peers enthuse that he is "*pragmatic and congenial,*" adding that "*he understands the real world and what risks can be accepted.*" His approach is viewed as "*zealous in the advocacy of his client's interests, but not unreasonably so.*" Lohmann's practice has come to be regarded by some as one of the top for transactional support outside of New York, though he is also acknowledged for his general environmental counseling. In a recent highlight he acted for Madison Dearborn Partners in its acquisition of the forest products division of Boise Cascade for $3.7 billion. **Edward Warren** (see p.474) is a name that impresses commentators. As one of the "*first generation*" of environment attorneys, he has an "*excellent and extensive appellate record,*" with rulemaking challenges now his "*bread and butter.*" Warren is an adjunct professor at the University of Chicago. **Stuart Drake** (see p.439) is another name frequently mentioned by commentators, in his case as "*one of the best for mobile source CAA knowledge.*" He has the loyalty of major clients in the automobile industry and possesses enviable vehicle and engine expertise as well as an extensive counseling and litigation track record.

The Clients: GM; Madison Dearborn Partners; Sun Capital; Bain Capital; First Atlantic Capital; ICV Capital Partners and JPMorgan Partners.

Shaw Pittman
See firm details p.490

The Firm: Operating as a small team within the firm's public practices group, the five environment attorneys at Shaw Pittman act for an extensive energy clientele. One facet of their work is CAA issues, and in this area the firm is an admired player in enforcement defense as well as rulemaking challenges. Attorneys were commended for their chemicals knowledge, as illustrated by the words of one client who said: "*Frankly, I am very impressed.*" Work in the chemicals sector brings with it cutting-edge biotech issues, and the firm is additionally noted as an active adviser to the agricultural sector. At time of press the firm announced its merger with Pillsbury Winthrop LLP to form Pillsbury Winthrop Shaw Pittman.

The Lawyers: Commentators reserved their highest praise for "*pragmatic and tenacious*" **David Menotti** (see p.457), who is credited with "*a marvelous brain.*" Clients are impressed by his

commitment: "*He will do his damnedest to address your issues.*" CAA, Federal Insecticide, Fungicide, and Rodenticide Act (FIFRA) and Toxic Substances Control Act (TOSCA) are securely within his knowledge base. His EPA experience is said to be an invaluable asset. Highlight work includes representing trade associations in advocacy regarding the National Ambient Air Quality Standards, as well as advising on issues stemming from organophosphate insecticides.

The Clients: American Coke and Coal Chemicals Institute; Hearth, Patio and Barbecue Association; Coke Oven Environmental Task Force; National Oilseed Processors Association; American Iron and Steel Institute; Emerson Electric Company and Asahi Glass.

Swidler Berlin LLP
See firm details p.495

The Firm: "*Excellent, particularly for legislation issues,*" say peers of this firm's profile in rulemaking challenges. Litigation forms the bulk of its environmental activities, much of it being CAA-related; however, attorneys are also known for their counseling and transactional support. Commentators commend them for their NSR knowledge and experience in Title V permits. The practice group is known to be "*strong in both energy and environment,*" though the energy sector is not the only important source of clients and strong relationships have been built with clients in manufacturing and the automobile sector.

The Lawyers: "*The big name at Swidler,*" **Chuck Knauss** (see p.451) is "*excellent*" in NSR issues and Title V permits. He was active in shaping the 1990 CAA amendments so, when peers say he can be "*set apart by the depth of his understanding,*" such comments are all the more credible. His clientele covers manufacturing and the automobile industry (for both stationary and mobile source issues).

The Clients: ExxonMobil; BMW; GE; Georgia-Pacific and Ford.

Venable LLP

The Firm: With the growth in environmental criminal defense requirements, the market fully understands why Venable is "*getting more and more busy.*" Its broad client base is just one reflection of the fact that criminal defense is becoming a ubiquitous aspect of environmental law. Almost 20 attorneys make up a practice group that divides evenly into criminal defense and general environmental advice/civil litigation. "*They don't have any loopholes; they have it all covered,*" said one commentator. Specialist expertise in a variety of niche areas, for example endangered species and wetlands, merely serves to reinforce this idea. In the past year the firm has acted for a manufacturer under investigation in several states for alleged environmental

and OSHA violations, and advised a cruise line in issues involving maritime law in multiple jurisdictions.

The Lawyers: Judson Starr enjoys a stellar reputation as "*the dean of the environmental crimes Bar.*" He heads the practice group and is largely responsible for the firm's focus on the environmental crimes. Most of the firm's major criminal cases benefit from his guidance in some way or other. **Joseph Block** has a similar work profile to Starr and is seen as another "*top name.*" A former DOJ attorney, his future is said to look very bight indeed. This year the market also sang the praises of **Peggy Strand**, who is lauded as "*one of the best wetlands lawyers in the country.*" She is the chairwoman of the ABA's Wetlands Committee and has acted in cases concerning CWA and wetlands issues at a golf course and ski resort.

The Clients: The firm acts for a varied clientele including a cruise line, a wastewater treatment plant, a large construction company, land developers, retail companies and manufacturers.

Band 4

DLA Piper Rudnick Gray Cary US LLP
See firm details p.765

The Firm: This "*robust*" and now expansive international firm has a mature environmental practice located within the core government affairs group. Its "*huge Baltimore presence*" complements the capabilities of lawyers in DC and together the group is active regionally and nationally on everything from RCRA and Superfund, through TOSCA and FIFRA to CAA and CWA. Its lobbying work is widely recognized by the market and clients took time to praise, in particular, its "*excellence in CAA issues.*"

The Lawyers: Though no individual was singled out as the group's leading light, Doug Green and Bill Weissman deserve mention. Weissman practices across the board on regulatory, enforcement defense and administrative matters, while Green has served as joint lead counsel for the Utility Solid Waste Activities Group, a consortium of approximately 80 trade associations and electric utilities.

The Clients: The firm's clients include many manufacturers, power utilities and trade associations.

Foley & Lardner
See firm details p.1828

The Firm: This firm is recommended for services in several environmental areas: in the regulatory and litigation fields it acts for both individual companies and trade associations, for example, a Portland cement industry association and the Cement Kiln Recycling Coalition. Experience in CAA issues is complemented by RCRA and hazardous waste expertise, and the group has been commended for its proactive advice on developing sciences such as nanotech, which may have very significant environmental ramifications. The DC attorneys advise on cross-border hazardous waste issues, often matters emanating from the firm's offices in Tokyo and Brussels.

The Lawyers: Former EPA assistant general counsel **Richard Stoll** (see p.470) "*knows his way around the block.*" Peers credit him with extensive knowledge and experience in RCRA and CAA work. Though he has related expertise in healthcare and drugs, the majority of his practice is still environment-focused, and his time as a deputy general counsel at the Chemical Manufacturers' Association (now the American Chemistry Council) is viewed as an important asset. Stoll is cochair of the rulemaking committee at the ABA's Administrative Law Section.

The Clients: The firm acts for a broad range of clients from nationwide manufacturers to trade associations.

Goodwin Procter LLP
See firm details p.980

The Firm: On October 1, 2004, the 70-attorney firm of Shea & Gardner became a part of the 500-attorney firm of Goodwin Procter. The "*skilled*" environmental attorneys of the smaller firm can now draw upon a larger pool of resources to tackle a national market. Peers are impressed by the work the group does in Superfund and toxic substances issues, such as the cleanup of the Housatonic River in Pittsfield and the Hudson River. These sites were contaminated by PCB toxins and the group's attorneys have for some considerable time acted for GE on complex, big-money negotiations.

The Lawyers: **James Bieke** (see p.434) has been active in the GE hazardous waste cleanup work. "*He knows all the details*" and is regarded as a trusted practitioner who is ideal for such complex cases. Beyond Superfund, he shows a good command of CWA, TOSCA and RCRA issues. Michael Giannotto and Laurence Kirsch were also mentioned by the market.

The Clients: GE; Freeport-McMoRan Copper & Gold; Newmont Mining and Rockwell Automation.

Jones Day
See firm details p.485

The Firm: "*Excellently staffed for environment;*" although the team is compact, the firm's cross-departmental support is wonderfully organized and, consequently, the team is praised for its efficiency. A full service is provided to a trade association and manufacturing client base, with attorneys covering not only litigation and compliance but also transactional support and projects management. The firm's nationwide services to Bridgestone/Firestone, for example, are thought to be comprehensive in scope. A steady stream of work keeps the five DC part-

ners busy, with toxic torts (often hand in hand with hazardous waste and contamination issues) an area of growth.

The Lawyers: Heidi Bumpers (see p.437) has "*superb*" contamination and toxic torts knowledge and her Superfund analysis work is said to be comprehensive. In keeping with the team's style, clients say, "*efficiency is the key factor for her.*" **Kevin Holewinski** (see p.447) heads the environmental practice in DC. He is a knowledgeable and experienced regulatory lawyer and litigator with a background at the DOJ's environmental enforcement section and a focus on enforcement defense. Holewinski's "*strengths lie in his deep knowledge of the regulatory and legal processes behind Superfund.*" He recently acted for manufacturer Eramet on issues of natural resources damages.

The Clients: Bridgestone/Firestone; Brush Wellman; Eastman Chemical Company; IBM; PCS Nitrogen; Textron; Dole Food Company; The Riverside Company; The Sherwin-Williams Company and Yellow Roadway.

McKenna Long & Aldridge LLP
See firm details p.636

The Firm: Clients are "*absolutely comfortable*" in recommending this practice, especially for chemicals work. The firm's clients come from a variety of industries, from manufacturing and hi-tech to chemicals and pharmaceuticals, and it has been noted for its support of specialist trade associations in the chemicals sector. For international work, the firm fields specialists who can advise on chemicals regulation in specific jurisdictions, such as China. The leading attorneys enjoy excellent relationships with regulators, not just the environmental agencies but also at the FDA, reflecting the expansion of the practice to cover food and drugs. This new emphasis is seen by a number of commentators as going "*hand in glove*" with the firm's chemicals and pharmaceuticals expertise, which encompasses a significant portion of pesticides work.

The Lawyers: A "*respected*" leading practitioner in pesticides, **Charles O'Connor**'s (see p.460) practice covers environmental issues such as FIFRA, TOSCA and CAA as well as FDA work. Clients say he is "*one of the best litigators in the area.*" The market also mentioned rainmaker Frederick Anderson, who was the first full-time president of the Environmental Law Institute.

The Clients: DuPont; Hewlett-Packard; Spray Drift Task Force and Consumer Specialty Products Association.

Pillsbury Winthrop LLP
See firm details p.1364

The Firm: The long experience of this "*excellent firm with a strong background*" inspires great confidence in clients. The firm has been quick to embrace natural resources and endangered

species, and its work in these fields cover a wide geographic area. For example, it is an instrumental player in a major project to transform aging oil rigs off the coast of California into artificial reefs. The firm is also involved in entrepreneurial wetlands mitigation, and beyond the USA, it advised Canadian mining company Teck Cominco on its opposition to the EPA's attempts to apply US Superfund law extraterritorially. At time of press the firm announced its merger with Shaw Pittman LLP to form Pillsbury Winthrop Shaw Pittman.

Lawyers: The "*extremely knowledgeable*" **Don Carr** (see p.437) is "*doing a combination of pretty much everything,*" according to peers. A former DOJ attorney, his litigation expertise is beyond question and his transactional analysis is also keenly developed. He ran the wildlife and marine resources section of the DOJ and has 20 years of experience in endangered species and a well-developed wetlands practice.

The Clients: Teck Cominco; ChevronTexaco; Sargent Ranch; The Morgan Crucible Company; Great Dismal Swamp Restoration Bank and Kimberly-Clark.

Skadden, Arps, Slate, Meagher & Flom LLP & Affiliates
See firm details p.1372

The Firm: This firm has attracted attention by choosing to meet the environmental requirements of its transactional work – "*even the gigantic deals*" – from its DC office rather than New York. The lead individuals in this group of "*terrific transactional people*" are as recognized in New York as they are in their home city. The firm is also gaining recognition for litigation, specifically bankruptcy-related environmental cases: it represented United Airlines in issues stemming from its bankruptcy, with the firm's regulatory attorneys and litigators assisting the airline in claims concerning the cleanup of contamination at JFK Airport.

The Lawyers: Don Frost (see p.443) has impressive regulatory knowledge and litigation experience, as well as excellent capabilities in transactional analysis. He was involved in the contamination issues at JFK Airport on behalf of United Airlines and has represented other major clients in Superfund issues. The "*very capable*" **Kenneth Berlin** (see p.433) is the firm's lynchpin for transactions. "*If I had a hard, high-end environmental corporate question I'd put that to him,*" said one rival attorney. Clients like the fact that "*he is knowledgeable, reasonable and cooperative; he's very commercial.*" Berlin travels extensively to provide support on national and international deals and projects.

The Clients: Sealed Air; Kmart; United Airlines; Axel Johnson and Diamond International.

Van Ness Feldman PC

The Firm: A name in the energy sector, Van Ness boasts a plethora of well-known clients. Its *"very experienced team"* of environmental attorneys have earned their fair share of praise too. Aside from the inevitable CAA issues, they concentrate on the areas most relevant to the core client base, including natural resources and Indian law. The firm has a strong reputation for its automobile industry work, where it counsels clients on mobile source emissions. The firm has also developed its knowledge of the intricacies of emissions trading proposals.

The Lawyers: Richard Penna is viewed as the firm's prime contact for mobile source emissions expertise. His work also covers fuel standards and related regulatory issues. Robert Nordhaus is the established contact for the firm's energy clients when seeking environmental advice. A former general counsel of the Federal Energy Regulatory Commission, he advises on CAA regulatory issues and climate change proposals. Commentators remarked on Bill Frick's arrival at the firm, viewing him as a potential rainmaker. A former general counsel of the American Petroleum Institute, he has also served as general counsel to the EPA.

The Clients: The firm's clients include multinational manufacturers, energy utilities, vehicle companies and trade associations.

Vinson & Elkins LLP

See firm details p.1724

The Firm: The firm's CAA and NSR expertise is valuable to its energy sector clientele. Beyond air issues, the firm is a knowledgeable player in Superfund matters and its transactional support is known to be thorough. V&E's other offices aid the practice group's all-round profile, with some of the Houston attorneys spending a significant amount of their time in DC. Peers are of the opinion that the *"excellent people"* at this firm are busy and maintaining an impressive profile in the market. However, it is from client sources that the most rewarding feedback comes. *"They have done a great job,"* said one, while another who had used the firm for an enforcement defense matter confirmed: *"We were able to settle on fair and reasonable terms."*

The Lawyers: Kevin Gaynor (see p.444) stands out at the firm. A former DOJ attorney, he is cochair of the energy, environmental and natural resources section of the ABA. *"He has the substantive knowledge and the relationships,"* according to clients, and peers say he is *"clearly one of the best litigators around."* For example, he recently reached a settlement for the Southern Indiana Gas & Electric Company (SIGECO) in NSR issues. Despite a full and eventful workload, he is still *"very much accessible and generous with his time."* Traditionally seen in Houston, **Carol Dinkins** (see p.439) has also caught the attention of the DC market. Her waste work is extensive

and she is strong in natural resource matters.

The Clients: The firm's clients include utilities companies, such as SIGECO, as well as multinational oil companies.

Wallace King Domike & Branson PLLC

The Firm: *"An impressive boutique"* admired for its dedication and experience, Wallace King acts for some of the highest profile clients in the oil industry (Shell USA and ChevronTexaco, for example) and enjoys an impressive following in many other industries. Leading CAA practitioners are also acting for mobile source clients on a nationwide basis. Boasting 18 specialist attorneys, this firm is geared towards providing a focused service, especially in enforcement litigation and toxic torts. It suffered something of a blow when former name partner Chris Marraro returned to Howrey Simon Arnold & White (a firm he, Richard Wallace and Tony King had left in 1998). Yet it remains renowned for having all the benefits of a large full-service firm's environmental department, while enjoying a compact structure.

The Lawyers: Now a name partner, **Julie Domike** is one of the firm's leading lights. Her expertise lies in CAA issues, and her NSR experience has been deployed in notable settlements. Domike acts for both stationary and mobile source clients, with her automobile clientele including the Volvo companies of North America.

The Clients: Clients include Shell USA, ChevronTexaco and the Volvo companies of North America.

Weil, Gotshal & Manges LLP

See firm details p.1378

The Firm: The combination of environmental law and bankruptcy continues to create an interesting and lucrative workload for the 12 environmental attorneys at this major transactional firm. Clients are delighted by the *"tremendous range of issues"* within the DC practice group's capabilities, though transactional matters still form the bread and butter. It is one of the few firms willing to forego the DC-New York split between regulatory and transactional work to provide a one-stop shop. The firm can claim litigation capability and can point to successes in negotiations over contamination and remediation. The firm took its place in the Parmalat bankruptcy and has acted for Elementis in transactions and disputes.

The Lawyers: The managing partner of the firm's DC office, **David Berz** (see p.434), is *"a big-picture guy"* with a wide range of skills. Now heavily involved in bankruptcy-related matters, in the past he litigated extensively and helped to negotiate the NAFTA trade agreement. His transactional knowledge is warmly praised: *"He knows how deals are done, he understands leverage and he has a tremendous amount of experience."* Products liability litigation is yet another

string to his bow. **Annemargaret Connolly** (see p.438) has a largely transactional practice. She made a noted contribution to the firm's work for Vivendi, inspiring peers to say: *"We love her... she's very sharp, personable and effective – she does a good deal."* Her know-how in successor liability, particularly in asbestos issues and hazardous waste, is one of her main strengths.

The Clients: Viacom; Vivendi Universal; Citibank; Lehman Brothers; GE Capital; Safety-Kleen Systems; Elementis; Parmalat; Pirelli and Enron Corporate Estate.

Willkie Farr & Gallagher LLP

See firm details p.1380

The Firm: This firm continues to produce good work in both the regulatory and transactional spheres. Clients like the fact that it is *"good at quantifying costs and very active in identifying ways of minimizing environmental risk."* The DC office's eight specialist attorneys are busy dispensing regulatory and rulemaking advice, and the firm has plentiful work in hazardous waste and chemicals. Although the New York environmental practice is still nascent, it is expected to complement the deep knowledge already in place in DC. The arrival of Robert Fabricant in New York represents a boost to the firm as a whole; Fabricant was general counsel at the EPA until 2003 and comes equipped with fresh contacts and experience. Clients include multinational manufacturers such as automobile parts maker Federal-Mogul, which the firm advises on issues within and beyond the United States. The firm has also assisted the Commonwealth of Puerto Rico in relation to the cleanup of Vieques, an island previously used by the US Navy as a bombing and live ammunition range and allegedly contaminated by depleted uranium.

The Lawyers: *"Familiar with all the environmental issues which turn up,"* **Donald Elliott** (see p.440) is the department's overall head and a man of many talents. He can lay claim to an academic background, having been a respected professor on environmental risk assessment at Yale. Not content with one past life, he too was an EPA general counsel. As an influential thinker on environmental and toxic risks, Elliott is viewed as *"a top adviser on any aspect of policy,"* yet he has also worked on some of the largest clean air settlements.

The Clients: Federal-Mogul; Commonwealth of Puerto Rico; FirstEnergy; Toyota; Bristol-Myers Squibb; NRG Energy and Dow Chemical.

Wilmer Cutler Pickering Hale and Dorr LLP

See firm details p.497

The Firm: Wilmer Cutler has a broad range of clients seeking assistance on issues ranging from CAA permitting to hazardous waste and pesticides. The firm is keen to draw business from across a variety of sectors; indeed, one client is the Corporate Environmental Enforcement Counsel (CEEC), which is a multi-industry organization comprised of 30 companies. The firm advises CEEC on public policy matters relating to civil and criminal enforcement of environmental law. More generally, topics such as the application of NSR to non-utilities clients are a fertile source of work. Clients applaud attorneys for "*staying on top of issues.*"

The Lawyers: Ken Meade combines a fine CAA reputation with a keen eye for transactional analysis.

The Clients: Clients include trade organizations and Fortune 100 companies.

Other Notable Practitioners

Lynn Bergeson of Bergeson & Campbell PC is "*a pretty prominent lawyer*" in pesticides and chemicals. Peers enthuse that she is "*excellent, pragmatic and effective,*" and features on the board of directors at the Environmental Law Institute. "*A solid force,*" **David Weinberg** chairs the environmental group at Howrey Simon Arnold & White and is "*well regarded*" as a chemicals practitioner with a strong battery industry following. He is also a fine pesticides lawyer. Historically, he is credited with reaching the nation's first Superfund settlement in 1982, and he has lobbied successfully on several legislative issues.

HEALTHCARE

<table>
<tr><td colspan="2">District of Columbia
Leading firms (Healthcare)</td></tr>
<tr><td>1</td><td>EPSTEIN BECKER & GREEN PC Washington, DC
HOGAN & HARTSON LLP Washington, DC
REED SMITH LLP Washington, DC</td></tr>
<tr><td>2</td><td>FULBRIGHT & JAWORSKI LLP Washington, DC
GARDNER CARTON & DOUGLAS Washington, DC
MCDERMOTT WILL & EMERY Washington, DC
SONNENSCHEIN NATH & ROSENTHAL Washington, DC</td></tr>
<tr><td>3</td><td>ARENT FOX PLLC Washington, DC
JONES DAY Washington, DC
LATHAM & WATKINS LLP Washington, DC</td></tr>
</table>

<table>
<tr><td colspan="2">Leading firms
(Healthcare: Pharmaceutical/
Medical Products Regulatory)</td></tr>
<tr><td>1</td><td>ARNOLD & PORTER LLP Washington, DC
COVINGTON & BURLING Washington, DC</td></tr>
<tr><td>2</td><td>HYMAN PHELPS & MCNAMARA Washington, DC
MORGAN, LEWIS & BOCKIUS LLP Washington, DC</td></tr>
</table>

<table>
<tr><td colspan="2">Leading individuals (Healthcare)</td></tr>
<tr><td>1</td><td>BARRY Dennis Vinson & Elkins, Washington, DC
BRENNAN John Crowell & Moring, Washington, DC
CARDER-THOMPSON Elizabeth Reed, Washington, DC
HASTINGS Douglas Epstein Becker, Washington, DC
HUTT Peter Covington & Burling, Washington, DC
LUCE Gregory Jones Day, Washington, DC
MICHAELS Joel McDermott Will, Washington, DC
ROBINSON Frederick Fulbright, Washington, DC
SULLIVAN T J Gardner Carton, Washington, DC
TILLMAN Eugene Reed Smith, Washington, DC
VICKERY Ann Hogan & Hartson, Washington, DC
VODRA William Arnold & Porter, Washington, DC</td></tr>
</table>

Firms and individuals are listed alphabetically in each band.

Epstein Becker & Green PC

The Firm: Clients benefit enormously from a practice of tremendous longevity. This "*boutique to beat all boutiques*" has devoted itself to healthcare for more than 30 years, tirelessly adapting itself to the fluctuations of the market. It has developed "*a profound knowledge of virtually every aspect of the industry.*" Corporate, tax, finance, regulatory and reimbursement matters are all on the menu in DC, one of its two founding offices. The DC office – the hub of operations with more than half of the firm's "*hugely talented health attorneys*" – also handles employment and general government contracts work. Along with the New York branch, it forms a renowned national practice.

The Lawyers: **Doug Hastings** is "*a towering figure on the national stage as well as in Washington circles.*" "*A man whose knowledge one instinctively bows to,*" he is both a transactional and regulatory expert. His practice is heavily flavored with M&A and joint venture transactions for health providers, but is commodious enough to take in reimbursement, fraud and abuse, and tax issues.

The Clients: Hospitals, health systems, long-term care facilities, medical groups and pharmaceutical companies are featured in the firm's roster.

Hogan & Hartson LLP

See firm details p.484

The Firm: All the attendant experience of government departments and agencies cultivated in its 100-year history in DC has turned Hogan & Hartson into one of the foremost regulatory experts in the field. "*Intimately associated with the cogs and wheels of the legislative process,*" it has guided its healthcare clients through this rough regulatory terrain for more than 25 years now. The firm's practice as a whole, though, is much more extensive in its scope, taking as its theme the interface between government and industry. Its lawyers, many of whom have had experience in both spheres, undertake fraud and abuse, Medicare and Medicaid work, transactional matters and IT-related health issues. Clients come from across the spectrum and speak as one in endorsing a "*terrifically responsive and utterly tuned-in practice.*" Among these the Biotechnology Industry Organization uses the team on reimbursement, FDA and nonprofit issues while the American Health Association consults it on all putative class actions challenging the tax-exempt status of hospitals nationwide. On the transactional side, the firm has recently successfully completed a recapitalization and reorganization for a leading national homecare services provider, in excess of $50 million.

The Lawyers: Interviewees marveled at the "*supreme organizational skills*" of health practice director **Ann Morgan Vickery** (see p.473). Flourishing in her leadership role with duties as managing partner of the DC office, she also gained respect for her regulatory knowledge, much of which was gleaned from a number of years' service in the federal government.

The Clients: The firm has represented hospitals, hospices, pharmaceutical manufacturers, biotech companies, physician groups and cancer centers among others.

Reed Smith LLP

See firm details p.1560

The Firm: Over three decades, Reed Smith's DC base has fostered a practice that is now of national as well as regional significance. Starting from a platform rich in reimbursement work, it has flowered sufficiently to now be designated "*a true all-rounder of distinction.*" Fraud and abuse, antikickback issues and Medicaid questions are all fielded by a team whose remit extends to every corner of the market bar malpractice suits. Interviewees were particularly taken with its efforts in long-term care whilst also commending its pharmaceutical practice. These pharmaceutical clients benefit magnificently from a regulatory capability that has been fortified by the arrival of several alumni from the FDA. Their arrival is a boon to a group widely seen as "*expanding wisely and going in the right direction.*"

The Lawyers: **Elizabeth Carder-Thompson** (see p.437) is a key player on the provider side whose practice embraces reimbursement, fraud and abuse, and Medicare/Medicaid issues. "*An enthusiastic type of attorney whose commitment is there for all to see,*" she is part of a team that includes **Eugene Tillman** (see p.471). Tillman recently headed up a group of 20 of the firm's attorneys in representing national pharmacy benefits manager AdvancePCS in its $6 billion sale to a leading prescription benefits manager.

The Clients: The firm represents a full gamut of health providers and drug manufacturers, including GlaxoSmithKline, Inspire Pharmaceuticals and Bristol-Myers Squibb.

Fulbright & Jaworski LLP
See firm details p.1715

The Firm: The Washington offshoot of this renowned Texas outfit does much to uphold the firm's national reputation for excellence. The national practice is a wide-ranging one but the 15-strong DC team is probably best known for its regulatory and litigation prowess. It does tackle some transactional work but is more likely to be seen fighting suits and offering advice to providers and manufacturers around the country. The firm is involved in development and implementation of regulatory compliance plans for several device manufacturers and pharmaceutical companies; it also deals with Medicare and Medicaid reimbursement for hospitals, physicians and hospices. The *"rugged litigation team is capable of withstanding any philippic from the opposition,"* and has appeared in a wave of class action suits against nonprofit hospitals.

The Lawyers: Frederick Robinson (see p.465) is *"a hard as nails litigator"* whose previous experience as a white-collar criminal practitioner helped to forge his steely character. Observers admired his *"forceful but utterly fair"* approach and the manner in which he leads his team. This group successfully acted for the Association of American Medical Colleges and two other bodies who sponsor the National Resident Matching Program in an antitrust claim brought against the scheme.

The Clients: The firm has represented hospitals, physicians, hospices and various healthcare organizations, including the Association of American Medical Colleges.

Gardner Carton & Douglas LLP
See firm details p.767

The Firm: The firm's DC office forms a valuable adjunct to its central engine room in Chicago. The team here may be constructed on more modest lines than at the operation's headquarters but it is well capable of handling a diverse practice that reflects the firm's efforts nationally. It takes on corporate, fraud and abuse, tax, managed care and reimbursement matters while proving particularly strong on issues relating to nonprofit hospitals. The office is also home to the firm's pharmaceutical group, who has advised drug manufacturers on regulatory compliance both at home and abroad. Observers endorsed the firm, as having *"greater history than most and a commensurate level of skill."*

The Lawyers: TJ Sullivan (see p.470) is *"right in the front rank when it comes to healthcare tax issues."* His knowledge, derived in part from his tenure as Special Assistant (Health Care) to the IRS Assistant Commissioner, is such that he possesses *"simply a greater understanding of the arcana of this area than anyone else."* He represents clients on corporate, tax and regulatory matters and acts as general counsel for the Coalition for Nonprofit Health Care.

The Clients: The firm represents all sectors of the health industry – including hospitals, long-term care providers, managed care organizations, physician groups and academic medical centers.

McDermott Will & Emery
See firm details p.773

The Firm: Although perhaps not the most important spoke in the wheel of this firm's much praised national healthcare operation, the DC office plays its part well. Upholding the overall firm's unrivaled reputation in this field, its attorneys tend to concentrate on regulatory and litigation issues. Certainly, the team is seen on the transactional side, but is more often witnessed advising its diverse mix of clients on the latest from Capitol Hill. About ten lawyers counsel on Medicare matters, health plans, Office of Inspector General (OIG) investigations and government probes affecting health insurers. One member also provides expertise on tax-exempt issues for nonprofit systems. Recent matters handled by the firm include a successful legislative lobbying campaign on behalf of a number of hospitals to revise Medicare reclassification regulations. This resulted in an improved Medicare reimbursement to the tune of $4 million per year.

The Lawyers: Joel Michaels (see p.457) was said to be *"as hot as a pistol"* on healthcare insurance matters. Fully conversant with all of the legislation devoted to the healthcare arena, he heads up the department here.

The Clients: The firm acts for the full range of healthcare institutions and also has a number of pharmaceutical clients on its books.

Sonnenschein Nath & Rosenthal
See firm details p.779

The Firm: More of a recent phenomenon in the healthcare field compared to some of its competitors, Sonnenschein is nonetheless *"an increasing force, and is getting better year on year."* Its DC office is one of nine nationally, and it is representative of the firm's efforts countrywide to deliver a multidimensional approach to clients. It takes in most areas, including healthcare financing, reimbursement and managed care issues. Fraud and abuse capability is more concentrated here than elsewhere, and its 23 health attorneys are more likely to appear on compliance and lobbying issues than litigation and M&A transactions.

The Lawyers: The practice has been careful to hire wisely in pursuit of its ambitions in this field. Though none have emerged as a clear marquee name, the firm has nonetheless captured the likes of Bruce Fried, who has 25 years' experience in the business, and Mac Thornton, former chief counsel to the inspector general of the US Department of Health & Human Services. Thornton's presence alongside some of his former colleagues at the HHS ensures Sonnen-

schein's exalted standing when it comes to fraud and abuse matters.

The Clients: The team has advised physician groups, hospitals, academic medical centers, healthcare systems, Internet-related healthcare companies and health plans.

Arent Fox PLLC

The Firm: This firm offers a wide, traditional healthcare practice but was felt by our interviewees to do its best work on the regulatory side. The firm represents clients before the full panoply of federal and state agencies including the HHS, FTC and the Centers for Medicare and Medicaid Services. Much of its work is taken up with advising on participation in Medicare and Medicaid programs and on anti fraud and abuse and reimbursement policies. Its lawyers are often brought in by healthcare bodies to offer a one-stop-shop service on compliance. They can do this largely due to the fact that a healthy proportion of their number has had experience of working in various government health-related bodies. Examples of the firm's work include devising compliance programs for all types of providers and acting for a national care corporation whose practices are under investigation by the HHS and the DOJ.

The Lawyers: Alan Reider heads up the health care practice. He represents providers, manufacturers and individual practitioners on regulatory issues involving federal programs relating to areas such as reimbursement, coverage, and certification. His experience includes acting as lead defense the government investigation into National Medical Care. This was, at the time, the largest healthcare fraud case in history.

The Clients: The firm acts for hospitals, nursing homes, academic medical centers, pharmaceutical companies and other health-related entities.

Jones Day
See firm details p.485

The Firm: The DC office of this national juggernaut won support for its *"sophisticated, self-confident healthcare team."* The practice's main thrust is toward regulatory compliance and litigation. Displaying a noted strength in antitrust law, the team advised Caremark RX in an investigation concerning its $6 billion acquisition of AdvancePCS. As counsel to Lee Memorial Health System, it acted on action brought by an insurance company alleging price-fixing. In other significant matter, it represented MedStar Health and University Hospitals of Cleveland in the Jung v Association of American Medical Colleges litigation, a class action suit challenging the National Resident Matching Program.

The Lawyers: Greg Luce's (see p.454) litigation and regulatory knowledge is such that he can claim to have represented the American Hospital Association, as well as many other health institutions. *"An excellent litigator of*

proven ability," he advises on issues such as Medicare reimbursement, and fraud and abuse.
The Clients: Healthcare providers, insurance companies and technology concerns who service the health industry feature prominently in the firm's clientele.

Latham & Watkins LLP

The Firm: Litigation and transactional work are the twin pillars of the practice here, and the office is part of a respected national network that has a stake in every sector of the healthcare economy. The team of eight partners handles many shades of litigation, from fraud and abuse disputes to white-collar criminal defense and healthcare patent matters. It acts for leading healthcare organizations such as HCA and Teva Pharmaceuticals. The transactional side is at the forefront of an office that has always had an interest in corporate work due to its long association with The Carlyle Group. Some commentators expressed doubt as to whether the team had reached its full potential on regulatory matters, yet the group appears to be thriving in the life sciences sector. Here, it acts for the likes of Boston Scientific.
The Lawyers: Stuart Kurlander is at the helm offering congeries of corporate, regulatory and litigation advice. A former government official, he is also cochairing the firm's global healthcare and life sciences practice.
The Clients: The firm acts for a mix of providers, manufacturers and healthcare organizations.

Arnold & Porter LLP

See firm details p.478
The Firm: "*One of the best in the business at helping clients dodge bullets,*" this team concentrates on the manufacturers of health-related products to an extent few can match. Servicing those who manufacture pharmaceuticals, medical devices, vaccines and blood products, its attorneys take a three-pronged attack; FDA approval advice, reimbursement processes, and fraud and abuse issues form the main props with many of the lawyers enjoying a proficiency in each of these areas. The emphasis is very much on having an integrated team and these lawyers are known for working together in "*a well-drilled, cohesive unit.*" The practice is also very capable of offering IP and antitrust advice and has been involved in some major matters. Its advice to Pfizer over its acquisition of Phar-

macia, for example, was just one high-profile matter undertaken. Other cases have included working with Novartis to counteract Medicare's reluctance to cover some of their products.
The Lawyers: The group's gravitas is partly due to the presence of **Bill Vodra** (see p.473). A former associate chief counsel at the FDA, he is described by some as the "*pharmaceutical king*" for his "*experience and aggression in defending his clients*" before his old employer. He is part of a sizable contingent of the department's attorneys who have worked in the government, including former Health Care Financing Administration (HCFA) man Grant Bagley and the recently hired Dara Corrigan, who was at the HHS.
The Clients: The firm generally acts for the suppliers of healthcare products. Among these are some household names such as Pfizer, AstraZeneca and Wyeth.

Covington & Burling

See firm details p.481
The Firm: The firm's food and drug regulatory capability acts as a splendid ancillary to its "*internationally renowned life sciences practice.*" The practice has a lengthy and distinguished history stretching back to the firm's foundation in 1919, when its team acted for the National Canners Association. Since then it has grown and its present incarnation consists of nine partners, including two former chief counsels to the FDA. They act before the FTC, USDA and FDA itself, and also advise on Medicare and Medicaid matters before the Health Care Financing Administration. Very popular with a star-studded client base encompassing the likes of Pfizer and GlaxoSmithKline, this is "*a firm that many of the biggest pharmaceutical companies in the business have very good cause to thank.*"
The Lawyers: The team houses one of the pioneers of the discipline in senior counsel **Peter Barton Hutt** (see p.448). Peter Safir is also on hand to offer expert advice.
The Clients: The firm represents food, drug, biological product, medical device, and cosmetic manufacturers.

Hyman Phelps & McNamara

The Firm: The foremost of three offices nationwide, the DC branch has been offering a specialist regulatory practice for a quarter of a century. Its remit is to advise and litigate on all laws and regulations relating to food, drugs and medical devices. In pursuing this, its "*thoroughly well-schooled team*" relies upon its extensive experience gained through government service. Many of its attorneys have worked for the FDA or Drug Enforcement Agency (DEA); the experience gained provides an excellent grounding in legal matters pertaining to FDA regulation. As one interviewee said: "*These guys act as a reliable guide through the treacherous rocky outcrops of the FDA landscape.*"
The Lawyers: Name partners Paul Hyman and James Phelps have both worked at the FDA and are well-respected names in the market.
The Clients: The group acts for individuals, small companies and multinational corporations affected by food and drug laws.

Morgan, Lewis & Bockius LLP

See firm details p.1556
The Firm: Centered on the manifest talents of Kathryn Gleason, this FDA and healthcare regulation practice comprises a dozen attorneys in DC. Its work involves all areas of regulatory compliance relating to medical devices, food, and pharmaceutical and biological products. Clients, both domestic and international, responded well to a firm whose repertoire covers every aspect of a product's life from pre-market development to marketing and beyond.
The Lawyers: Kathryn Gleason heads the team.
The Clients: Pharmaceutical, medical device and food companies all benefit from the specialist counsel on offer here.

Other Notable Practitioners

Dennis Barry (see p.432) of Vinson & Elkins LLP is considered a legal expert on Medicare, having advised clients before federal courts, administrative law judges and the Provider Reimbursement Review Board among others. He also demonstrates agility in navigating the False Claims Act. Chair of the firm's healthcare group, **John Brennan** (see p.435) of Crowell & Moring LLP is a seasoned authority on healthcare fraud and abuse matters. The former hospital administrator has advised clients on disputes relating to federal false claims, anti-kickback rules and physician self-referral (Stark law) issues.

District of Columbia
Leading firms (Insurance: Insurer Firms)

1 HOGAN & HARTSON LLP *Washington, DC*
STEPTOE & JOHNSON LLP *Washington, DC*
WILEY REIN & FIELDING LLP *Washington, DC*

2 BAACH ROBINSON & LEWIS PLLC *Washington, DC*
CROWELL & MORING LLP *Washington, DC*

3 CHADBOURNE & PARKE LLP *Washington, DC*
HUNTON & WILLIAMS *McLean, Virginia*
ROSS DIXON & BELL LLP *Washington, DC*

Leading individuals
(Insurance: Insurer Firms)

1 BOWMAN William *Hogan & Hartson*, Washington, DC
FOGGAN Laura *Wiley Rein*, Washington, DC
ROCAP III James *Steptoe & Johnson*, Washington, DC
WARIN Roger *Steptoe & Johnson*, Washington, DC

2 BAACH Martin *Baach Robinson*, Washington, DC
KALISH Paul *Crowell & Moring*, Washington, DC
RAIM David *Chadbourne & Parke*, Washington, DC
SOTTILE James *Zuckerman Spaeder*, Washington, DC
STANDISH Daniel *Wiley Rein*, Washington, DC

3 ANDREWS Walter *Shaw Pittman*, McLean
BRUNNER Thomas *Wiley Rein*, Washington, DC
DIXON Gary *Ross Dixon*, Washington, DC
HENDLER Clifford *Crowell & Moring*, Washington, DC
HENSLER David *Hogan & Hartson*, Washington, DC
HOWARD Theodore *Wiley Rein*, Washington, DC

Up-and-coming individuals
RUGGERI James *Hogan & Hartson*, Washington, DC
YANG John *Wiley Rein*, Washington, DC

Firms and individuals are listed alphabetically in each band.

Band 1

Hogan & Hartson LLP
See firm details p.484

The Firm: This formidable group won market recognition for "*providing first-rate advice over a long period of time.*" It is frequently involved in cases of significant value, such as its representation of Federal Insurance Company in litigation brought by Campbell Soup over a $25 million policy. Peers recognized that the team "*warrants its top billing,*" while clients commended the strong negotiation skills and litigation capabilities that the team brings to the table. The group provides advice in sectors such as asbestos, toxic torts and environment, and has recently branched out to represent an archdiocese regarding the recent spate of sexual misconduct claims. It also has a dedicated professional liability unit that is "*emerging as a serious player.*"
The Lawyers: The "*agile and skilled*" **William Bowman** (see p.435) focuses on insurance litigation, a field in which he excels as a "*smart and shrewd negotiator.*" He is also recommended for his alternative dispute resolution expertise. **David Hensler** (see p.447) combines a "*fabu-*

lous legal mind and a business-like approach.*" An experienced litigator, he is "*sharp, knowledgeable and pragmatic.*" One of the younger members of the team, **James Ruggeri** (see p.466) is a highly effective litigator. He recently led the firm's representation of The Hartford in the asbestos-related litigation, In re Congoleum Corp.
The Clients: The firm has a well-documented relationship with The Hartford. Over the past twelve months it has represented the company in litigation surrounding the property insurance for the World Trade Center and various asbestos claims. Other clients include: St Paul Travelers; Federal Insurance Company; Genesis Professional Liability Underwriters; Executive Liability Underwriters; Chubb Group and XL Professional.

Steptoe & Johnson LLP
See firm details p.492

The Firm: This is a "*uniformly excellent*" coverage firm with expertise in asbestos, directors and officers (D&O) and environmental claims. Clients turn to the group for counseling in complex disputes and praise its "*professional, responsive and timely service.*" In addition, its flair for litigation and arbitration enables it to "*satisfy all our professional needs,*" declared clients. The team is consistently impressive, winning a loyal following as "*thoughtful, insightful lawyers,*" although it will be significantly strengthened by the recent recruitment of James Rocap from Baker Botts. Recent highlights include a major Wellington Agreement arbitration with Celotex and representing AIG in a dispute with Alco Aluminum regarding its cleanup obligations.
The Lawyers: The "*extremely bright*" **James Rocap** (see p.465) has an "*excellent ability to analyse complex coverage issues.*" An effective oral advocate, he has an established relationship with St Paul Travelers and niche expertise in smokeless tobacco claims. **Roger Warin** (see p.474) is "*probably one of the top-ten insurance litigators in the US.*" He was recently named managing partner of the firm and "*has the ability to see issues in a broader context.*" He is "*the kind of lawyer you can trust to give the best advice,*" declared observers.
The Clients: AIG; Allstate; Zurich; Swiss Re; St Paul Travelers; Liberty Mutual and The Hartford.

Wiley Rein & Fielding LLP
See firm details p.496

The Firm: Highly respected by both clients and peers alike, this firm is "*at the top of the pile*" in the DC coverage market. The group has all bases covered with expertise ranging across products liability, real estate and environmental claims. Following the recent spate of corporate scandals, it has placed considerable emphasis on developing its professional liability practice, counseling

clients such as Chubb on a range of issues. The firm also has a niche reinsurance practice involving the continental European markets. It won acclaim from clients for its "*innovative approach, high level of professionalism and outstanding work product.*" Market commentators also picked out the group's penetration at appellate level: "*They are filing amicus briefs all over the US.*"
The Lawyers: Clients picked out **Laura Foggan** as "*one of the most well-rounded attorneys.*" A respected litigator, she acts as counsel for the Complex Insurance Claims Litigation Association (CICLA). "*She is the best! She knows everything, is a great writer and an excellent orator.*" **Dan Standish** heads the professional liability group and won plaudits from clients for his writing, litigation and negotiation skills. He "*can quickly assess issues*" and adopts "*a pragmatic approach*" to matters. Practice founder **Thomas Brunner** (see p.436) has vast experience both in private practice and on the academic circuit. He specializes in emerging insurance issues such as obesity and punitive damages. **Ted Howard** is a "*reasonable and businesslike attorney*" who has "*real diplomacy skills.*" His area of expertise is asbestos. **John Yang** is a "*good point person on strategy for amicus briefings.*" He represents clients in toxic tort and products liability claims and has niche experience representing industry trade associations.
The Clients: Chubb Group; Genesis Professional Liability Underwriters; Excel Insurance Services; Gulf Insurance Associates and CNA.

Band 2

Baach Robinson & Lewis PLLC
The Firm: Enjoying a reputation as the leading authority on the London markets, Baach Robinson & Lewis combines its substantial transactional, regulatory, litigation and ADR experience to tremendous effect. Although this firm's "*specialist expertise is a considerable draw*" for clients, it is also a skillful operator in the asbestos, pollution, and health hazards fields. Increasingly it is becoming involved in reinsurance arbitration and litigation as these issues become more prominent in the market. The firm is also adept at the more common mass tort actions. This past year it was involved in suits concerning pharmaceutical and chemical claims.
The Lawyers: **Martin Baach** is a "*classic wise counselor*" figure. The firm's founding partner, he "*understands that there are two avenues of attack,*" and is a capable negotiator who "*gives well-considered advice.*"
The Clients: The firm plays a substantial role in both domestic and international insurance markets. It represents underwriters at Lloyd's as well as other London market insurance companies.

Crowell & Moring LLP

See firm details p.482

The Firm: Noteworthy for its "*tip-to-toe excellence*," this DC-based firm operates on a national basis, handling coverage litigation across the USA. It is closely linked with the firm's other practice groups, such as litigation, bankruptcy and corporate, enabling clients to use the firm as a "*one-stop shop*" when issues branch out. A particular area of expertise for the group is asbestos liability, principally where it overlaps with bankruptcy. It also serves as counsel for the Coalition for Litigation Justice, a trade group of insurers acting to eliminate possible abuses in the current asbestos and products liability tort litigation scene.

The Lawyers: **Paul Kalish** (see p.449) is an "*excellent, effective and responsive*" attorney. His practice centers on civil litigation and his role as lead counsel for the Coalition for Litigation Justice. The "*intelligent and dogged*" **Clifford Hendler** (see p.447) chairs the insurance litigation practice. He has "*terrific knowledge*" of both the world of insurance and litigation.

The Clients: The group acts for many big names in the insurance world including ACE and the Coalition for Litigation Justice.

Band 3

Chadbourne & Parke LLP

See firm details p.1341

The Firm: This firm was recommended to researchers for the success of its deep bench of devoted attorneys, who are "*willing to put in the necessary time and effort to produce a fantastic result.*" The practice group is involved in reinsurance, general coverage and insolvency-related issues. It is active in environmental, asbestos and other toxic tort suits, as well as professional liability claims. A dedicated litigation group further underscores the depth of expertise. The

group recently acted as lead defense counsel in a suit by Dow Corning seeking coverage for its breast implant liability.

The Lawyers: **David Raim** (see p.463) is the national head of the group and maintains a high profile in the DC market for his "*extraordinary litigation and arbitration skill set.*" He was also recommended for his work in the London markets.

The Clients: Travelers; ITT Hartford; United States Fidelity & Guaranty; Fremont Indemnity Insurance Company and American Republic Insurance Company.

Hunton & Williams

See firm details p.1775

The Firm: The eclectic insurance group at Hunton & Williams is based in McLean, Virginia, but included in our DC chapter this year due to its seeping penetration of this market. This group recently moved to Hunton & Williams from Shaw Pittman in Northern Virginia. It is best known for its role in the property litigation following 9/11 but the team also has expertise in asbestos, mold, construction, business interruption, errors and omissions (E&O) and directors and officers (D&O). Clients rate it as an "*excellent, well-versed and responsive*" group, while peers recognize its "*significant presence on the coverage side.*" Recent litigation successes include summary judgment in gun liability claims in South Carolina and in a hospital business interruption claim following Hurricane Hugo.

The Lawyers: **Walter Andrews** (see p.431) is an "*extremely knowledgeable and savvy operator,*" who has developed a huge book of business.

The Clients: The group has an impressive client base of global insurance carriers.

Ross Dixon & Bell LLP

The Firm: Clients of Ross Dixon & Bell feel that "*the firm is the best in the industry.*" This boutique is "*small but perfectly formed.*" It has national insurance counseling and litigation experience, with particular expertise in the professional liability/D&O arena. Other areas of activity include reinsurance, environment, mass tort and health claims. The group won acclaim as "*consistently pragmatic, extremely professional and enormously responsive.*" It successfully represented a client against claims made by a major tobacco company for coverage of a billion-dollar settlement and the millions spent on a scorched earth litigation strategy.

The Lawyers: One of the founding partners **Gary Dixon**'s greatest asset is his "*tremendous reservoir of knowledge.*" The "*sharp litigator*" is an expert in D&O liability litigation.

The Clients: The firm's clientele is drawn from domestic and international insurance companies active in a wide range of industry sectors. Areas of experience include asbestos and products liability.

Other Notable Practitioners

James Sottile has recently joined Zuckerman Spaeder LLP from Baach Robinson & Lewis. He has extensive experience in the London markets and continues to represent Equitas and the Lloyd's Underwriters it insures following his move. He possesses "*a fine intellect and can speak in plain language,*" clients commented. His practice focuses on arbitration, an area in which he is "*pretty hot,*" and utilizes the litigation expertise of the firm when necessary. In this context, he won praise as someone who "*understands that there are two sides to a problem*" and appreciates the "*commercial goal of driving matters to final resolution*" that runs in tandem with legal rights.

INSURANCE

POLICY HOLDER

District of Columbia
Leading firms (Insurance: Policy Holder)

1	COVINGTON & BURLING *Washington, DC*
2	DICKSTEIN SHAPIRO MORIN *Washington, DC*
	GILBERT HEINTZ & RANDOLPH LLP *Washington, DC*
	HOWREY SIMON ARNOLD & WHITE *Washington, DC*
	SWIDLER BERLIN LLP *Washington, DC*

Firms are listed alphabetically in each band.

Band 1

Covington & Burling

See firm details p.481

The Firm: Unrivaled as the "*number one firm,*" Covington & Burling is very much at the front

of the DC policyholder Bar with many of the market's most prominent attorneys having started their careers here. Sources described its approach to the market as "*sophisticated, aggressive and savvy.*" As with many firms, it has seen a move from domestic litigation to arbitration in the resolution of disputes. It has had recent successes in two separate international arbitrations involving major coverage matters for Fortune 100 clients. Interviewees praised the ability of the group to "*listen and deliver*" and appreciated that "*every lawyer is client-oriented.*" Areas of focus include D&O and ERISA fiduciary disputes, property, and mass tort. It is very active in the asbestos sphere, securing, for example, $500 million in related coverage for a major policy-

holder client. It is also developing niche expertise at the intersection of asbestos insurance and bankruptcy.

The Lawyers: Winning phenomenal respect across the board, **Robert Sayler** (see p.466) has an enormous depth of experience because he "*was there when it all started.*" He has had a fantastic career litigating billion-dollar coverage disputes for policyholders and is "*an absolutely top-flight trial lawyer*" and a wonderful oral advocate. **Mitchell Dolin** (see p.439) is "*one of, if not the, best trial lawyers in this field in the US,*" claim some commentators. He has an excellent track record in high-value litigation and arbitration matters and is "*extremely intelligent and creative*" with a "*strong practical sense of how to*"

---

www.ChambersandPartners.com

All quotes in the text are from interviews with clients and competitors.

401

District of Columbia
Leading individuals
(Insurance: Policy Holder)

1 DOLIN Mitchell *Covington & Burling*, Washington, DC
GILBERT Scott *Gilbert Heintz*, Washington, DC
OSHINSKY Jerold *Dickstein Shapiro*, Washington, DC
SAYLER Robert *Covington & Burling*, Washington, DC

2 BUCHANAN John *Covington & Burling*, Washington, DC
GREANEY William *Covington & Burling*, Washington, DC
HEINTZ John *Gilbert Heintz*, Washington, DC
KELLNER Leon *Dickstein Shapiro*, Washington, DC
PLUMER Mark *Swidler Berlin LLP*, Washington, DC
SHULMAN Robert *Howrey Simon*, Washington, DC
SKINNER William *Covington & Burling*, Washington, DC

3 ENGH Anna *Covington & Burling*, Washington, DC
GOODMAN Saul *Covington & Burling*, Washington, DC
KLEIN David *Swidler Berlin*, Washington, DC
MASTERS Lori *Jenner & Block*, Washington, DC
SMOYER Divonne *Dickstein Shapiro*, Washington, DC

Up-and-coming individuals
LATHROP Alex *Swidler Berlin*, Washington, DC
THOMPSON Gary *Gilbert Heintz*, Washington, DC

Individuals are listed alphabetically in each band.

resolve matters." Another "*exceptionally intelligent and dedicated*" lawyer is **William Skinner** (see p.468). He is particularly knowledgeable on captive insurance, but also has considerable experience in breast implant, asbestos and environmental claims. He is "*loyal to his clients*" and "*highly articulate*." **John Buchanan** (see p.436) has "*always been a tenacious advocate for his clients*," and according to sources, "*no-one knows the subject matter better than him.*" **William Greaney** (see p.445) is a "*walking encyclopedia*" and he has an outgoing personality that helps get deals done. "*He is never overly aggressive, but he gets the message across.*" **Saul Goodman** (see p.445) has spent a lot of time recently on a complicated coverage dispute in the steel sector. As practice coordinator he takes much of the credit for the raft of rising stars such as **Anna Engh** (see p.441). Engh has "*really come into her own of late.*" She has been leading the firm's representation of Owens Corning in the asbestos bankruptcy area and brings her insurance expertise to this field.
The Clients: Cardinal Health; Conrail; Dow Corning; Gillette; Goodrich; Massachusetts Financial Services; McDonald's; National Football League; NCR; Norfolk Southern; Owens Corning; PPL; UBS; Wal-Mart and XM Satellite Radio.

Band 2

Dickstein Shapiro Morin & Oshinsky LLP
See firm details p.483
The Firm: This practice has the sheer numbers to support the amazing range of cases flowing through the office every day. The expertise encompasses such areas as products liability, first party property, asbestos, environmental coverage and goods lost in transit. On the environmental side, it is developing expertise in obtaining coverage through accessing old policies. The team is also increasingly active in D&O and SEC issues. It recently reached a significant settlement with Credit Bancorp on behalf of the receiver, following litigation alleging a scheme to defraud investors. It is widely respected within the market with clients commenting upon the team's robust depth of knowledge.
The Lawyers: For many commentators, **Jerold Oshinsky** (see p.461) is the dean of the policyholder Bar, and "*truly at the center of the growth of the coverage market.*" This "*energetic and creative*" attorney has the "*uncanny ability to size up the strengths and weaknesses of a dispute.*" A former US Attorney in Florida, **Leon Kellner** (see p.450) has the "*rare combination of integrity and practicality*" that, when combined with his "*commitment to finding a way to do the deal,*" ensures him a loyal following among clients and peers. He is "*a good guy to deal with, even if he is on the other side!*" **Divonne Smoyer** (see p.469) is one of the younger members of the group. She leads negotiation and settlement efforts in D&O, asbestos and products liability disputes. The "*wonderfully intelligent*" attorney is also admired for her drafting skills. Richard Fields, respected by insurers and outside counsel alike, recently moved to Dickstein Shapiro in New York where he is a partner in the Litigation & Dispute Resolution Group.
The Clients: Large industrial policyholders, small companies, municipalities, state governments and charities make up the diverse client roster.

Gilbert Heintz & Randolph LLP
The Firm: It is hard to say whether this firm is better known for its stellar performance as policyholder counsel or for the vibrant personality and creative approach of its attorneys. Either way, it is "*an innovative, aggressive boutique*" with a pioneering asbestos practice. The firm takes a robust line on the negotiation of settlements and is currently representing the remaining solvent signatories of the Wellington Agreement in disputes with insurers. It was at the forefront of the development of the pre-pack asbestos bankruptcy and maintains expertise in this field, representing entities in bankruptcy proceedings as special insurance counsel. The "*raft of savvy attorneys*" is also active in first party property insurance, D&O and E&O for professional services.
The Lawyers: **Scott Gilbert** is a "*genius,*" claimed one client. The "*extremely brilliant and quick*" attorney is the "*red suit in a sea of grey.*" An asbestos and bankruptcy specialist, he is a skilled negotiator, who is "*totally in command of the facts*" and "*knows all the players.*" **John Heintz** has a "*marvelous courtroom presence*" and a broad skill set that enables him to undertake a range of insurance-related matters. **Gary Thompson** enters the rankings following endorsement from clients for his growing practice. He is a "*thorough and loyal*" attorney whose level of experience belies his relative youth.
The Clients: AOL; Dana Environmental Services; Dow Corning; The Equal Rights Center; Host Marriott; Millennium Chemicals; Pfizer; Schlumberger; SEPCO and Verizon Communications.

Howrey Simon Arnold & White
The Firm: This is a full-service group with respected market presence and a large, talented team of attorneys. The diverse array of expertise and "*responsive, well-researched*" approach make this a go-to firm on all counts. The proactive team leads forays into some of the most current areas of market concern. It is advising clients concerned about their interests following the Spitzer allegations against Marsh, AIG and ACE. Other areas of experience include D&O and products liability. It has been actively representing International Paper in continuing disputes surrounding the alleged failures of hardboard siding.
The Lawyers: **Robert Shulman** "*has all the skills,*" report market observers. The practice cochair is an excellent attorney who is recommended as a "*fantastic strategic thinker*" with experience in complex disputes.
The Clients: International Paper; Symbol Technologies; LG&E Energy; ConocoPhillips and Amerada Hess.

Swidler Berlin LLP
See firm details p.495
The Firm: More than any other firm – and despite the highly publicized loss of numerous New York partners – Swidler Berlin is emerging as a forward-looking group with a focus upon diversification. "*It has come out shining,*" claimed clients, who also praised the team as "*very professional, capable and successful operators.*" It has been on the cutting edge of recent developments, advising the Asbestos Study Group on the bill to set up a $140 billion trust fund to settle claims and end litigation. This "*super*" firm is also developing D&O, E&O and first party property expertise. It continues to be an active force on environmental coverage as well as in the oil, utilities and mining industries.
The Lawyers: "*I have got better results because* **Mark Plumer** (see p.462) *is on my side,*" asserted one client. The chair of the group "*understands the big picture*" and is "*always one step ahead of the other side.*" **David Klein** (see p.451) has a successful practice recovering proceeds for companies in the energy, gas and electric, mining and financial services sectors. An "*eloquent*"

402   All quotes in the text are from interviews with clients and competitors.

CHAMBERS USA 2005

attorney, he is *"aggressive in the defense of his clients but never goes overboard."* Associate **Alex Lathrop** (see p.452) *"has never been found to be wrong."* He is developing into a highly effective insurance litigator.

The Clients: BP Amoco; 3M; Waste Manage-ment; Wisconsin Electric Power Company and the Asbestos Study Group.

Other Notable Practitioners
Lori Masters (see p.455) at Jenner & Block LLP is a *"rising star."* Her practice covers insurance arbitration, often in London, and litigation involving construction defects, employment liability and toxic torts. She was lead trial counsel for the policyholder in the Ticona arbitration, securing the full policy limit of $75 million for her client.

INTELLECTUAL PROPERTY

District of Columbia
Leading firms (Intellectual Property)

1	FINNEGAN HENDERSON FARABOW *Washington, DC*
2	ARNOLD & PORTER LLP *Washington, DC*
	HOWREY SIMON ARNOLD & WHITE *Washington, DC*
3	BANNER & WITCOFF LTD *Washington, DC*
	FISH & RICHARDSON *Washington, DC*
	KIRKLAND & ELLIS LLP *Washington, DC*
	MAYER, BROWN, ROWE *Washington, DC*
	MCDERMOTT WILL & EMERY *Washington, DC*
	PROSKAUER ROSE *Washington, DC*
	SHAW PITTMAN *Washington, DC*
	SIDLEY AUSTIN BROWN & WOOD *Washington, DC*
	SKADDEN, ARPS, SLATE, MEAGHER *Washington, DC*
	STERNE, KESSLER, GOLDSTEIN *Washington, DC*
	WEIL, GOTSHAL & MANGES LLP *Washington, DC*

Leading individuals (Intellectual Property)

1	DUNNER Donald *Finnegan Henderson*, Washington, DC
2	DAVIS James *Howrey Simon*, Washington, DC
	FARABOW Ford *Finnegan Henderson*, Washington, DC
	FREED Joel *Arnold & Porter*, Washington, DC
	LUPO Raphael *McDermott Will*, Washington, DC
3	ASSAF Eugene *Kirkland & Ellis*, Washington, DC
	BAUMGARTEN Jon *Proskauer Rose*, Washington, DC
	CORDELL Ruffin *Fish & Richardson*, Washington, DC
	GOTTS Lawrence *Shaw Pittman*, Washington, DC
	HADJIS Alex *Weil Gotshal*, Washington, DC
	KAUFMAN Kenneth *Skadden Arps*, Washington, DC
	LIPSEY Charles *Finnegan Henderson*, Washington, DC
	PAULSON Mark *Mayer Brown*, Washington, DC
	POTENZA Joseph *Banner & Witcoff*, Washington, DC
	SHARER Paul *Mayer Brown*, Washington, DC
	STERNE Robert *Sterne Kessler*, Washington, DC
	WILDER Richard *Sidley Austin*, Washington, DC

Firms and individuals are listed alphabetically in each band.

Band 1

Finnegan Henderson Farabow Garrett & Dunner LLP

The Firm: *"In a class of its own,"* one of the largest IP teams in the country consistently dominates the field with a sophisticated full-service practice, advising a diverse client base ranging from Fortune 500 companies to emerging businesses. With more than 300 attorneys in seven branch offices in the USA and abroad, the firm's *"full complement"* of resources garnered client confidence in virtually every business sector. Biotechnology, pharmaceuticals, chemicals and electronics all figure highly on its agenda. In addition, the group boasts expertise in telecom, consumer products and publishing. This *"untouchable"* team is particularly renowned for its handling of complex disputes, including a significant settlement on behalf of Bell Communications Research (now Telcordia Technologies). In another prominent case the firm represented Gateway in a lawsuit against Companion Products regarding an alleged trademark infringement linked to a black and white spotted plush monitor cover.

The Lawyers: The practice is driven by two of the industry's most *"illustrious"* practitioners – **Don Dunner** and **Ford Farabow**. Dunner, the *"don"* of the DC IP Bar, commands terrific respect from clients and peers alike for his imposing litigation practice. The *"real legend"* was involved in a global settlement of a patent dispute between Nikon and ASML, which concluded in a payment of $145 million. Dunner brings *"vast"* technical expertise to bear in the areas of chemical engineering, chemistry, biotechnology and pharmaceuticals. At the *"top of his game"* is Farabow, whose fortitude in the chemical and metallurgical arenas won commendation. His dispute resolution profile also includes domestic and foreign arbitration. **Charles Lipsey** also receives accolades as a prime player in the field. His repertoire emphasizes biotech and pharmaceutical disputes.

The Clients: The firm's clientele is forged from the likes of Gateway, Nikon and Bell Communications Research (now Telcordia Technologies).

Band 2

Arnold & Porter LLP
See firm details p.478
The Firm: Two interdependent teams cover both the transactional and litigious aspects of IP, culminating in *"terrific"* work highlighted by its representation of Microsoft in a prominent case involving patent interpretations. Another focus is the emerging field of Internet-related issues such as advertising copyright law as related to the Web. Working closely with its London office, the firm offers an international perspective on cases and is particularly lauded for its bioscience practice. Non-commercial clients such as universities and federal government agencies help enhance the firm's portfolio.

The Lawyers: Spearheading the technology litigation practice, **Joel Freed** (see p.443) is *"the main man,"* commentators said. Formerly of the Patent and Trademarks Office, he nurtures a *"preeminent"* reputation in litigation and prosecution of IP rights. Freed appeared as lead counsel in the Intergraph v Intel case in addition to representing Microsoft in a variety of patent infringement matters.

The Clients: Microsoft; Intel; Xerox; AOL and Micron Technology.

Howrey Simon Arnold & White

The Firm: A *"go-to"* firm for IP matters, this well-established team provides litigation, prosecution and counseling services to national and international clients. Its *"impressive"* deep bench strength distinguishes the practice, which spans seven major US cities in addition to Europe and Asia. With an excellent cohort of trial lawyers, this firm is *"making waves"* in the market by expanding its international reach. The DC team is handling Zoltek v US, a Court of Federal Claims case concerning a patent infringement suit regarding military hardware. Other successes have included a significant case against Microsoft.

The Lawyers: The *"incredibly humble"* **Jim Davis** anchors the practice. Formerly a judge for the US Court of Claims, he is often credited for the success of the firm's IP practice. The *"top-notch"* practitioner defended a $40 million judgment relating to patent infringement and fraud in the case of Tronzo v Biomet.

The Clients: The firm acts for a wide range of high-profile clients in the pharmaceutical, electronics and manufacturing industries.

Band 3

Banner & Witcoff, Ltd

The Firm: A consistently rigorous analysis of the facts earns this firm tremendous market confidence: *"They really delve to the bottom of things,"* clients said. Actively engaged in the procurement, enforcement and litigation of IP rights globally, the team's *"terrific"* technical expertise is illustrated in such cases as a groundbreaking copyright infringement lawsuit pertaining to the resale of a freelance author's articles to online databases. Also supported by the firm's Chicago headquarters, other features of the practice involve patents, trademarks and computer franchises. For example, the firm advised on a patent infringement case with regards to software downloads from the Internet.

The Lawyers: The insightful **Joseph Potenza** is pitched as a "*wonderful and well-rounded*" attorney whose practice includes patents, copyrights and licensing, clients said. In addition, he has experience on Section 337 investigations at the ITC and often counsels clients in the areas of electronics, e-commerce and business methods.

The Clients: The firm fields a broad client base that includes hi-tech businesses, toy companies and pharmaceutical manufacturers.

Fish & Richardson

The Firm: The stratified practice of this specialist firm more than holds its own against the nation's generalist full-service powerhouses, commentators said. With more than 300 lawyers working in eight offices nationwide, the group balances IP and corporate matters, taking on both transactional and litigation work. The pride of the firm is its patent team, which averages about 4200 patents a year. Its litigation prowess also grabs headlines with a wide range of high-stakes legal battles involving issues such as trademark, prosecution and trade secret disputes. A major victory emerged from a patent infringement suit concerning fiber optic technology; in the US District Court the firm acted for Ciena, a Maryland company providing integrated network solutions.

The Lawyers: Formerly of the US Patent and Trademark Office, **Ruffin Cordell** is described as one of the "*premier*" lawyers for ITC matters in the nation, clients said. "*His responsiveness and client concerns are first class.*" One of Cordell's significant wins is DSC Communications v Pulse communications, a case in which he helped secure an appellate victory. His work also includes Section 337 proceedings before the ITC. An IP generalist, he particularly commands respect in patent law involving digital electronics, display parts and processors, and telecom equipment.

The Clients: The firm advises companies in areas such as computer software, hardware technology, medical devices and the Internet. Examples include Intel and Alcatel.

Kirkland & Ellis LLP
See firm details p.770

The Firm: This litigation supremo wields significant clout in the field of IP dispute resolution, deemed by clients as the destination for crucial, complex problems. More than 200 lawyers firmwide deal with IP-related litigation, transactions and related counseling. Clients said the firm is worth every dollar: "*The lawyers are always extremely hardworking across the board.*"

A significant development in its practice relates to the Internet and e-commerce, advising AOL Time Warner (now Time Warner) in the so-called Browser Wars action against Microsoft. At stake were antitrust issues involving PC operating systems.

The Lawyers: **Eugene Assaf** (see p.431) provides clients with "*a great deal of attention to detail,*" advising not only on patents but also matters involving antitrust, trade secrets and defamation among others. His thorough approach is also suited to technically complex issues concerning customs and securities fraud.

The Clients: Cable & Computer Technology; Brown & Williamson Tobacco; Motorola and Dow Corning.

Mayer, Brown, Rowe & Maw LLP
See firm details p.771

The Firm: The 2004 arrival of several lateral hires to the DC office of this massive international player made waves in the marketplace and bolstered "*demand for the firm,*" clients said. The six former Pillsbury Winthrop lawyers added life sciences capability to the group, indicating the firm's overall strategy to enhance its global capacity in this area. "*You want a one-stop shop so you don't have to go out and recruit a particular contract expert on licensing, for example,*" clients said. "*And the quality of work is excellent.*" Commanding a significant international presence in Europe and Asia, the group delivers "*advice that is comprehensive and in a business dialogue,*" another client said. Its IP litigators further benefit from the support of the firm's appellate practice group.

The Lawyers: With an international clientele stretching as far afield as Europe and Australia, **Mark Paulson** is recognized for his "*comprehensive and businesslike*" ability to bring a global view to the table. Paulson's patent litigation focus often involves federal court cases, while the "*sharp*" **Paul Sharer** (see p.467) commands respect for his transactional skills. He often assists clients with acquisitions, divestitures and financing opportunities relating to IP, patents and other related matters.

The Clients: The firm represents a large number of Fortune 100 companies across a diverse range of industries. Examples include IVAX, DSM Desotech and Uniqema.

McDermott Will & Emery
See firm details p.773

The Firm: Packing a hefty punch with its team of diligent and dynamic lawyers, the DC office remains the engine of the firm's international IP profile. It is commended for attracting practitioners with a range of technological backgrounds and various scientific strengths. Clients emphasize the quality of the firm's technical expertise, particularly DC's six-attorney team that deals exclusively with trademarks, copy-

rights and Internet-related work. Also boasting an impressive ITC practice, this group is regarded by market commentators as a strong contender especially for mid-market advice. Another feature is the team's expertise in the medical devices arena; it was involved in a case involving spinal technology patents.

The Lawyers: The head of DC's IP practice, **Ray Lupo** (see p.454) garners respect for his authority on patent infringement cases. He has appeared before the federal courts and the ITC, with a significant proportion of his work concerning complex issues linked to computer technology.

The Clients: The firm represents clients in the technology, consumer products and manufacturing sectors.

Proskauer Rose
See firm details p.1365

The Firm: Close collaboration with the firm's New York office has bolstered the firm's ability to attract a diverse smorgasbord of work. Transactional expertise is offered, but the firm is particularly commended for its "*great*" copyright abilities. It is involved in cutting-edge issues involving new media and technology in addition to a traditional base of copyright matters. Acting on behalf of the recording and software industries, the firm is battling at the forefront of the Internet's anti-piracy efforts; it has also played a leading role in shaping government policy for the digital world. IP litigation helps round out the practice.

The Lawyers: The "*superbly able*" **Jon Baumgarten** (see p.432), head of the firm's IP team, garnered praise for his technical brilliance in copyright law. Having previously served on a number of government delegations, this publishing expert "*knows everything- all of it,*" sources said. "*He's a real one-off.*"

The Clients: The firm's clientele is generated from the publishing, computer, motion picture, music, communications, arts and Internet sectors.

Shaw Pittman
See firm details p.490

The Firm: The IP team draws from a multidisciplinary deep bench of resources, culminating in "*outstanding*" client services with regard to matters such as copyright, trade secrets and publishing. The cadre provides "*good results*" on a range of issues, including patents, trademarks and IP-related antitrust matters, clients said. "*We send them the most complex patent cases with confidence.*" The firm is also a port of call for issues such as "*difficult data manipulation applications.*" At time of press the firm announced its merger with Pillsbury Winthrop LLP to form Pillsbury Winthrop Shaw Pittman.

The Lawyers: The "*bright and responsive*" **Larry Gotts** (see p.445) is at the center of a "*high quality*" talent pool. Known as a technically brilliant litigator, Gotts has represented clients rang-

404   All quotes in the text are from interviews with clients and competitors.

CHAMBERS USA 2005

ing from emerging small-cap companies to Fortune 100 multinationals *"Regardless of the case, he always produces great results,"* a client said. Another added: *"He has a very good presence in front of the judge and jury."*

The Clients: Cingular Wireless, Waters Corporation and Honeywell Aerospace are examples of the firm's clients.

Sidley Austin Brown & Wood LLP

See firm details p.778

The Firm: This expansive international firm with a reputation for its tremendous well of resources provides a range of litigation, licensing, counseling and prosecution services. With more than 60 IP lawyers nationwide, the DC team benefits from a vast support system to handle some of the industry's most complex cases. Another feather in its cap is the firm's appellate practice, which straddles the IP practice area.

The Lawyers: Boasting a high-profile international and national client base, the *"extremely responsive"* **Richard Wilder** (see p.475) is commended for his dispute resolution skills, particularly as related to e-commerce. Clients appreciate his *"optimistic, upbeat and focused"* attitude and timeliness. *"We set deadlines and he usually beats them."*

The Clients: Clients include Fortune 500 corporations, emerging-growth companies, non-profit organizations and financial institutions.

Skadden, Arps, Slate, Meagher & Flom LLP & Affiliates

See firm details p.1372

The Firm: The *"cream of the crop,"* this firm is recognized for its smooth handling of complex cases especially in the computer, entertainment and communications industries. Offering clients legal services such as IP-related acquisitions, licensing and enforcement, the group has cultivated vast transactional and litigation experience. Technology transfers, outsourcing and strategy analysis also feature as attorneys often work at the cutting edge of IP law.

The Lawyers: Head of the IP group **Ken Kaufman** (see p.450) is described as a *"top-notch"* player whose *"imaginative, thorough and creative"* work has attracted a wide range of clients in the online, entertainment and communications industries. Also lauded for his technical expertise, the *"back-pocket expert"* is dealing with a case involving Internet file sharing.

The Clients: Virgin Mobile USA; Starz Encore Group; Vulcan Northwest; Waters Corporation and Cingular Wireless.

Sterne, Kessler, Goldstein & Fox P.L.L.C.

See firm details p.493

The Firm: The DC IP specialists at this firm have impressed clients with their considerable expertise, particularly in arbitration. This firm has made an impact with its commercially savvy decisions and technological expertise. Clients are also impressed by its *"integrity, commitment and outstanding disposition to interact with a team."* The firm's more specialist nature also means that it is able to be more versatile; for example, a recent development is focusing on nanotechnology. Other experience involves software, biotech, pharmaceuticals, telecom and industrial designs.

The Lawyers: **Rob Sterne** (see p.470) parlays *"superb"* IP transactional skills into *"truly great"* advice, sources said. Particularly on licensing, this *"super sharp shooter"* has *"incredible dynamism."* An expert on software and business method patents, Sterne led the team at IBM in the federal test case that led to the implementation of the USPTO software patent guidelines.

The Clients: Nanosys; Archer Daniels Midland; Biogen IDEC; Human Genome Sciences; Reebok; Hasbro; University of Pennsylvania and Locus Pharma.

Weil, Gotshal & Manges LLP

See firm details p.1378

The Firm: The fledgling practice is already making an impact with clients such as Matsushita, Japan's largest electronics manufacturer. Supported by an extensive international network of IP specialists, its breadth allows for strong transactional links that often crosses over into the firm's eminent corporate profile. The DC office of this international IP practice comprises two partners, who have advised luminaries such as Intel and Cisco Systems. Their experience includes DVD copyright formatting and encryption, complex patent litigation and trade disputes among others.

The Lawyers: Formerly of Fish & Richardson, **Alex Hadjis** (see p.446) has established a notable practice that combines IP and antitrust. He has previous ITC experience, which attracts clients seeking technical proficiency in addition to litigation fortitude. Hadjis has been involved in a number of prominent cases such as a dispute relating to recordable compact discs.

The Clients: Intel; Genesis Microchip; Media Tek; Samsung; Cypress Semiconductor and Atmel.

INVESTMENT MANAGEMENT

District of Columbia Leading firms (Investment Management)
1 DECHERT *Washington, DC* KIRKPATRICK & LOCKHART *Washington, DC* MORGAN, LEWIS & BOCKIUS LLP *Washington, DC* SHEARMAN & STERLING *Washington, DC* WILMER CUTLER PICKERING HALE *Washington, DC*
2 CROWELL & MORING LLP *Washington, DC* MORRISON & FOERSTER LLP *Washington, DC* SUTHERLAND ASBILL & BRENNAN *Washington, DC*
Firms are listed alphabetically in each band.

Band 1

Dechert

See firm details p.1547

The Firm: Dechert has the kind of extensive presence and diversity of practice that draws comment across the board. Its roster of former regulators attracts an outstanding client base, with interviewees praising the ability of attorneys to *"apply experience in a pragmatic way"* and to *"recognize the business implications of their advice."* Although new fund formation has slowed, the group continues to be active in alternative investments. A highlight this year was the $58 million all-stock merger between JPMorgan Chase and Bank One. The group can also draw upon the experience of the firm's financial services securities litigation team when

dealing with hostile regulators and adversarial proceedings.

The Lawyers: Although the firm has adopted a philosophy of teamwork, a number of attorneys have significant individual visibility in the market. The *"terrific"* **Robert Helm** (see p.447) has a unique practice that covers both domestic and international investment management. He has *"an excellent boardroom demeanor"* and is *"insightful, articulate and extremely bright."* His primary strength is his *"prompt responsiveness and ability to coordinate access to other people,"* clients said. **Jeff Puretz** (see p.463) has niche expertise in insurance products, having been involved in three market timing actions in the past year. He *"takes a very practical approach"* and is *"always there for his clients."* With experience at both the Division of Investment

District of Columbia
Leading individuals
(Investment Management)

[1] BARBASH Barry *Shearman & Sterling*, Washington, DC
HELM Robert *Dechert*, Washington, DC
MCGRATH Kathryn *Crowell & Moring*, Washington, DC
SMYTHE Marianne *Wilmer Cutler*, Washington, DC

[2] ADELFIO Marco *Morrison & Foerster*, Washington, DC
AMBLER Diane *Kirkpatrick & Lockhart*, Washington, DC
BECKER Brandon *Wilmer Cutler*, Washington, DC
BROWN Arthur *Kirkpatrick & Lockhart*, Washington, DC
HARMAN Thomas *Morgan Lewis*, Washington, DC
KANTER Jane *Dechert*, Washington, DC
PURETZ Jeffrey *Dechert*, Washington, DC

[3] LYBECKER Martin *Wilmer Cutler*, Washington, DC
MCGUIRE W John *Morgan Lewis*, Washington, DC
MCMILLAN Karen *Shearman & Sterling*, Washington, DC
MONACO Stephanie *Crowell & Moring*, Washington, DC
MURPHY Jack *Dechert*, Washington, DC
ROTH Stephen *Sutherland Asbill*, Washington, DC
STONE Steven *Morgan Lewis*, Washington, DC
TYLE Craig *Shearman & Sterling*, Washington, DC
ZUTZ Robert *Kirkpatrick & Lockhart*, Washington, DC

Up-and-coming individuals
ANDERSON James *Wilmer Cutler*, Washington, DC
BAGNALL Robert *Wilmer Cutler*, Washington, DC
FORD John *Morgan Lewis*, Washington, DC

Individuals are listed alphabetically in each band.

Management and the DOL's Office of the Solicitor, **Jane Kanter** (see p.449) is *"a significant business leader with a very strong following of clients." "She has a good, common-sense approach to issues"* and is *"well versed in all the legal requirements."* Another SEC alumnus, **Jack Murphy** (see p.458), is a fine lawyer with the ability to give *"a balanced viewpoint based on his practical knowledge and sense of what the regulators are up to."* He can *"put himself in the client's skin"* and has *"an encyclopedic knowledge of precedent."*

The Clients: AEGON; American Express; Quellos Capital Management; Pacific Investment Management and its funds; Goldman Sachs Asset Management and Fidelity Investments.

Kirkpatrick & Lockhart Nicholson Graham LLP
See firm details p.291

The Firm: Despite his relocation to San Francisco, market sources argue that this practice group is still as strong as when Dick Phillips held the reins. It has *"a very good bunch of younger lawyers who will do extremely well"* and a solid client base that is *"so impressed with its work that we keep expanding our use of the firm."* The practice focus has evolved to accommodate the current climate of increasing regulation, and now concentrates on governance, compliance and enforcement matters. Interviewees particularly commended the group for its compliance exper-

tise, an area where it has been involved in a number of internal reviews. It has also developed niche expertise on the relationship between funds and distribution channels. Over the past twelve months, it was involved in investigation and enforcement proceedings brought by the SEC that led to the sale of a company and heavy fines.

The Lawyers: Diane Ambler (see p.431) is *"a practical lawyer who gives straightforward business answers."* Her *"broad-based knowledge"* makes her an *"instrumental adviser"* and her even-tempered approach allows her to *"build a good, open relationship"* with a client. **Arthur Brown** (see p.436) has *"an aura that commands respect."* His *"years of experience and excellent judgment"* make him an *"excellent, reliable and steady attorney."* Another name that impresses is **Robert Zutz** (see p.476); he is *"a superb communicator"* who *"always takes a balanced perspective."*

The Clients: An enviable client list includes mutual funds, banks, insurance companies, broker-dealers, investment advisers and trust companies.

Morgan, Lewis & Bockius LLP
See firm details p.1556

The Firm: A *"first-class firm doing high-quality work"* is how a number of interviewees summed up this group. As well as the standard mutual and hedge fund work, it has *"top-notch complementary practices,"* particularly on the broker-dealer and enforcement sides. The group *"partners nicely with clients,"* taking a *"professional, proactive"* approach across a number of specialties. Investment scheme work spans all types of funds; in one recent matter, attorneys obtained favorable relief from the SEC on behalf of First Data. The firm continues to advise on the creation of new products, such as Barclays Global Investors' first exchange-traded fund to invest only in Chinese securities. It has also been undertaking a large amount of compliance work for companies such as Rydex and Hansberger.

The Lawyers: Thomas Harman (see p.446) is a *"strong legal technician"* with a good reputation in the market. A *"reasonable and thoughtful"* attorney, he is also ex-SEC and now primarily works with fund groups. Meanwhile, *"proactive and responsive"* **John McGuire** (see p.456) is heavily involved in the registration and regulation of mutual funds. Commentators say: *"He will never stall business with legal issues."* Managing partner **Steven Stone** (see p.470) is *"probably the leading expert on wrap accounts."* Stone is *"very deep in the brokerage industry"* and *"an excellent business lawyer, who recognizes the need to move forward."* **John Ford** (see p.442) is a younger partner who enters our tables this year on the basis of favorable client feedback; he is *"very familiar, operationally, with how we work,"* confirmed one client. Ford focuses on new products and won plaudits for displaying knowl-

edge and versatility beyond his years. Previously ranked in this section of *Chambers*, Thomas Lemke has now left the firm.

The Clients: ABN AMRO; Goldman Sachs; Vanguard; Fidelity Investments; Schwab Funds; Merrill Lynch and a number of industry associations.

Shearman & Sterling
See firm details p.1369

The Firm: A relatively new player in the market, this firm appears to be full of drive and energy. *"The firm's key practitioner Barry Barbash has done a great job building the practice,"* commented numerous interviewees. *"It is now a significant force both in terms of the attorneys and the work undertaken."* The group has been focusing on enforcement and compliance issues over the past twelve months, having represented numerous companies in various actions before government agencies. Other areas of experience include market timing, brokerage and revenue sharing matters and service provider enforcement procedures. The group is closely linked with attorneys in the New York office and has *"excellent judgment"* and *"a good sense of where the regulators are coming from."*

The Lawyers: *"Shearman & Sterling has moved into the top ranks because of* **Barry Barbash** (see p.432)." This *"fabulous"* lawyer was the director of the division of investment management at the SEC before joining the firm and still has *"good contacts down at the SEC."* He *"knows the peculiarities of the '40 Act better than anyone else."* **Karrie McMillan** (see p.457) *"has got what you want"* – she is *"extremely strong on client service, substance and follow-up."* **Craig Tyle** (see p.472), is *"a real catch"* for the firm. The former general counsel of the Investment Company Institute is a *"top-notch lawyer"* and has *"had the opportunity to be involved in all cutting-edge issues from both a litigation and policy perspective."*

The Clients: Clients include private equity funds, venture capital funds, hedge funds, directors and other institutional investors.

Wilmer Cutler Pickering Hale and Dorr LLP
See firm details p.497

The Firm: Part of *"one of the best investment management firms in the country"* and strongly aligned to its *"preeminent securities group,"* this team is a real force in the DC market. Considered the foremost regulatory firm by some *"because there are so many SEC alumni there,"* it has recently been advising clients on changes to the regulation of trading in securities. It has been focusing more on enforcement and compliance of late, having represented major financial services firms on market timing and transfer agent matters, as well as assisting in their compliance reviews. Wilmer Cutler's merger with Hale and Dorr means the DC operation can

All quotes in the text are from interviews with clients and competitors.

now draw on lawyers with further expertise in the representation of funds and fund advisers. Overall, the firm is viewed as a "*tremendous asset*" to clients, bringing "*great bench strength*" and having "*a true specialty*" in this area.

The Lawyers: **Marianne Smythe** (see p.469) "*ought to be on everyone's shortlist.*" She takes "*a business-oriented approach towards solving legal problems,*" is "*very effective at working with difficult clients or in tricky situations,*" and is recognized as "*one of the smartest lawyers around.*" Co-chair of the securities department **Brandon Becker** (see p.433) is "*extremely knowledgeable*" and has "*a very practical sense of what goes on in the day-to-day world of a broker-dealer.*" The "*brilliant*" **Martin Lybecker** (see p.454) acts as outside counsel to several mutual fund companies. Previously the associate director of the division of investment management, he is "*a real character who is fun to work with.*" Recommended as a great writer as well as a practitioner, **Robert Bagnall** (see p.432) always has "*a detailed knowledge of the legal issues and potential consequences.*" Finally, clients "*really appreciate*" **James Anderson** (see p.431) and his "*common-sense, practical way of addressing issues.*"

The Clients: Citigroup; PIMCO; GM Investment; Merrill Lynch and National Planning Holding.

Band 2

Crowell & Moring LLP
See firm details p.482

The Firm: The distinguishing feature of this budding practice group is its clear focus on compliance work; it has undertaken some of the most complex compliance reviews, helping elaborate funds develop comprehensive and practicable procedures. Acting for investment managers and funds, it has been involved in the recent market timing investigations and advised clients on how to change procedures and protect shareholders. By drawing on the resources of the firm's highly respected securities regulation and enforcement team, the relatively small group also tackles enforcement matters. It additionally has expertise in regulatory and disclosure matters under the '40 Act and ERISA.

The Lawyers: Foremost amongst this team of excellent attorneys is the "*sensational*" **Kathie McGrath** (see p.456). She is a "*multitalented attorney*" who has "*a very good sense of the SEC's attitude*" and the ability to use her talents to "*make her client's case very effectively.*" **Stephanie Monaco** (see p.458) is "*very knowledgeable on adviser issues*" and someone whom competitors would "*turn to for a judgment check.*" As an aside, commentators also informed researchers of her "*really fun personality.*"

The Clients: The firm acts for insurance and investment management companies, broker-dealers, banks. and domestic and offshore hedge funds.

Morrison & Foerster LLP
See firm details p.293

The Firm: This firm has developed a "*substantial practice*" representing registered investment companies. Notably it aligns a successful transactional practice with regulatory and compliance expertise. One of its recent highlights was advising Wells Fargo on the acquisition of assets worth $34 billion from Strong Financial. The team also has an active practice representing commercial banks and other financial institutions on mutual fund and investment adviser issues. It has become "*more prominent as the banks have become more involved,*" competitors said.

The Lawyers: "*Gentlemanly*" **Marco Adelfio** (see p.430) is a "*courteous attorney,*" who is able to steer his clients to "*find practical solutions to complicated problems.*" He won plaudits from clients for a "*proactive approach*" that "*helps events to evolve.*"

The Clients: Clients include investment advisers, venture capital managers and financial institutions.

Sutherland Asbill & Brennan LLP
See firm details p.494

The Firm: Known particularly for its variable insurance product practice, this is a firm that "*clearly deserves to be on the list.*" It gives development and compliance advice regarding all types of insurance product; in this niche area, it is "*incontrovertibly a leader,*" peers said. The group also has specialist expertise advising business development companies; a highlight from the past year was its representation of Apollo Investments in a high-value IPO. It is also supporting a number of clients through SEC inquiries regarding market timing and late trading issues, as well as changes to compliance programs.

The Lawyers: **Steve Roth** (see p.465) is a "*very solid substantive lawyer.*" The chair of the firm's business practices group, he is a "*smart guy*" who is "*respected by the SEC.*"

The Clients: TIAA-CREF; Metropolitan Life; Merrill Lynch; ING; AEGON USA; Lincoln Financial Group and State Farm.

LITIGATION
APPELLATE

District of Columbia
Leading firms (Litigation: Appellate)

1	**FARR & TARANTO** *Washington, DC*
	GIBSON, DUNN & CRUTCHER LLP *Washington, DC*
	JENNER & BLOCK LLP *Washington, DC*
	JONES DAY *Washington, DC*
	MAYER, BROWN, ROWE & MAW LLP *Washington, DC*
	ROBBINS, RUSSELL, ENGLERT *Washington, DC*
	SIDLEY AUSTIN BROWN & WOOD *Washington, DC*
	WILMER CUTLER PICKERING HALE *Washington, DC*

Firms are listed alphabetically in each band.

Band 1

Farr & Taranto

The Firm: Operating on the 'small is beautiful' principle, this specialist team is devoted exclusively to Supreme Court and appellate litigation. Both partners are hugely experienced, having negotiated more than 30 Supreme Court cases between them. Such talents are consistently in demand, with recent appearances that include California Franchise Tax Board v Hyatt.

The Lawyers: **Bartow Farr** is largely responsible for the institution of Supreme Court litigation boutiques in the USA, having been part of one as long ago as 1981. "*Urbane and persuasive in his addresses,*" he is described as "*an advocate who purrs mellifluently into ears of the justices.*" He is complemented by partner **Richard Taranto**, "*one of the most exhaustive and eloquent brief-writers in the business.*"

Gibson, Dunn & Crutcher LLP
See firm details p.285

The Firm: A large group of talented and experienced practitioners is on hand to grapple matters of extreme complexity at short notice. Regarded as having "*a rare intellectual oomph,*" its team shows "*real diversity and a willingness to tackle the most contentious litigation around.*" Thus, it has both acted for George W Bush in the 2000 Bush v Gore election litigation and appeared in Gasparini v The Center for Humanities, a matter which turned on questions of 13th century British law. Its lawyers were also successful in Rice v Cayetano, which resulted in a Supreme Court ruling averring that racial voting restrictions in Hawaii were in violation of the Fifteenth Amendment.

The Lawyers: An already enviable team has been inexorably bolstered by the return to practice of **Ted Olson** (see p.460). "*A smooth, effective orator who understands the justices' minds,*" Olson completed his tenure as Solicitor General of the United States and is expected to pick up where he left off as "*a figure of considerable stature in the Supreme Court.*" He returns to a practice already distinguished by the presence of

District of Columbia
Leading individuals
(Litigation: Appellate)

Senior Statesman
STARR Kenneth *Kirkland & Ellis*, Los Angeles DC

[1] DELLINGER Walter *O'Melveny & Myers*, Washington, DC
ENGLERT Roy *Robbins Russell*, Washington, DC
ESTRADA Miguel *Gibson Dunn*, Washington, DC
FARR Bartow *Farr & Taranto*, Washington, DC
GELLER Kenneth *Mayer Brown*, Washington, DC
MAHONEY Maureen *Latham & Watkins*, Washington, DC
NAGER Glen *Jones Day*, Washington, DC
OLSON Theodore *Gibson Dunn*, Washington, DC
PHILLIPS Carter *Sidley Austin*, Washington, DC
ROBBINS Lawrence *Robbins Russell*, Washington, DC
SMITH Paul *Jenner & Block*, Washington, DC
TARANTO Richard *Farr & Taranto*, Washington, DC
VERRILLI Donald *Jenner & Block*, Washington, DC
WAXMAN Seth *Wilmer Cutler*, Washington, DC

[2] BRINKMANN Beth *Morrison & Foerster*, Washington, DC
CARVIN Michael *Jones Day*, Washington, DC
GARRE Gregory *Hogan & Hartson*, Washington, DC
LAMKEN Jeff *Baker Botts*, Washington, DC
LONG Robert *Covington & Burling*, Washington, DC
TAGER Evan *Mayer Brown*, Washington, DC
UNTEREINER Alan *Robbins Russell*, Washington, DC

Individuals are listed alphabetically in each band.

Miguel Estrada (see p.441). "*An exceptionally smart, high-octane performer,*" he recently appeared in Aetna v Davila Health. Acting for the plaintiff, he successfully argued that federal law preempts state laws that give patients the right to sue managed care organizations.

Jenner & Block LLP
See firm details p.768
The Firm: The well-regimented team continues to do important appellate work across the board, particularly shining in the media sector. It enjoyed a notable success on behalf of NextWave Personal Communications when it persuaded the Supreme Court that the Federal Communications Commission had acted unlawfully in canceling wireless phone spectrum licenses awarded to the company. In addition the team has presented an amicus brief on behalf of the Recording Industry Association of America in Eldred v Ashcroft. To highlight the fact that its influence extends far beyond just the media, it also appeared in Vieth v Jubelirer, a case that examined the limits of partisan gerrymandering in Pennsylvania's congressional redistricting plan.
The Lawyers: Two sophisticated attorneys form the hub of the firm's Supreme Court practice. **Paul Smith** (see p.468) has 11 Supreme Court arguments under his belt; some of them – such as Lawrence v Texas – are considered true causes célèbres. "*Supremely industrious and with a free-flowing and genuine style of delivery,*" he epitomizes the firm's strength in First Amend-

ment law having recently appeared in United States v American Library Association. Fellow partner **Donald Verrilli** (see p.472) is the younger of the two. He "*appears much wiser than his age, promoting a sagacious air that inspires confidence.*" His star performance in the NextWave litigation earned widespread acclaim.

Jones Day
See firm details p.485
The Firm: A consistent performer at all levels, Jones Day can claim to have eight attorneys who have tackled 16 US Supreme Court cases in the last five years. "*Technically proficient and utterly battle-hardened,*" these attorneys are known for their "*strong legal analysis*" and "*durability in the face of the most taxing of cases.*" Matters handled include Lorillard Tobacco v Reilly, an important First Amendment case addressing state regulations relating to the advertisement of tobacco products. The team has also presented amicus briefs in a number of important matters, including the far-reaching case of State Farm Mutual Automobile Insurance v Campbell.
The Lawyers: **Glen Nager** (see p.459) heads the firm's issues and appeals practice. Although best known as an employment specialist, he is wide ranging in his scope and has argued nine Supreme Court cases. His team includes **Mike Carvin** (see p.437), a constitutional expert who has won a following with "*an entertaining but deeply thoughtful style.*" He was one of the lead lawyers before the Florida Supreme Court appearing for George Bush in the election recount litigation.

Mayer, Brown, Rowe & Maw LLP
See firm details p.771
The Firm: Whereas other groups tend to coalesce around one or two big names, Mayer Brown is slightly different in having a large number of appellate experts, many of them with strong independent reputations of their own. No less than four former Deputy Solicitors General are on hand in a firm-wide appellate practice that contains 26 partners, four counsel and 30 associates. Such staffing levels allow the team to tackle all shades of cases, although the focus is largely on issues of primary importance to the business community such as punitive damages and employment matters. Amid a steady diet of top-flight cases, it has recently appeared in F. Hoffman-La Roche v Empagran and the Central Laborers' Pension Fund v Heinz.
The Lawyers: **Kenneth Geller** (see p.444) has been at the forefront of much of the firm's best work in this area for some time. Clients value his "*forceful but never unduly aggressive stance in court*" and particularly admire his "*fulgent mind.*" His colleague **Evan Tager** (see p.471) is comparatively less likely to be seen arguing cases in the Supreme Court, but has provided countless amicus briefs such as that filed on behalf of

the US Chamber of Commerce in State Farm Mutual Automobile Insurance v Campbell. Each time he deploys "*a grasp of language and argument that is a marvel to behold.*"

Robbins, Russell, Englert, Orseck & Untereiner LLP
The Firm: It is less than five years since this estimable team decided to band together as a specialist firm but already theirs is a name that stands for quality. More than half of the team have clerked in federal courts of appeal in addition to others who have worked in the Office of the Solicitor General. Major clients from the business world make the pilgrimage here, confident of "*a matchless specialist service.*" Its record of success also proved attractive: of the 33 arguments presented in the Supreme Court, the team has won 28 and lost only three.
The Lawyers: **Lawrence Robbins**, one of the founding partners of the firm, has obtained some wonderful results in the Supreme Court. Market perception is that he has become more of a trial lawyer of late but continues to offer his "*unparalleled acuity*" in matters such as Dura Pharmaceuticals v Broudo; in that case, he filed an amicus brief on behalf of the American Institute of Certified Public Accountants. His colleagues include **Roy Englert**, "*a performer with the winning touch*" whose latest outings have included advising on City of Rancho Palos Verdes V Abrams. Also recommended is **Alan Untereiner**, "*one of the best of the next generation.*" He advised the US Chamber of Commerce in the matter of Bates v Dow AgroSciences.

Sidley Austin Brown & Wood LLP
See firm details p.778
The Firm: The team here has been at work in the appellate arena with such vigor that its record is approaching 100 Supreme Court cases. It has also handled appeals in every United States Court of Appeal and has tackled matters in most of the state supreme courts. Its lawyers in DC form part of a national practice that undertakes matters touching on almost every important legal business issue, though the group has a particular interest in challenges of a constitutional nature. "*A significant shop involved in a myriad of major cases,*" Sidley Austin's efforts have included representing the totality of the railroad industry in litigation relating to the disposal of mass asbestos claims in West Virginia.
The Lawyers: The firm is fortunate indeed to have one of the superstars of the appellate Bar. **Carter Phillips** (see p.462) has now argued well over 40 cases before the Supreme Court, making him "*an absolute magnet for anyone with a will to win.*" His success is founded on an "*intimate, utterly relaxed and nonconfrontational style.*" He successfully represented the plaintiff in Sosa v Alvarez-Machain, a case relating to the

408   All quotes in the text are from interviews with clients and competitors.

CHAMBERS USA 2005

Alien Tort Claims Act, and separately achieved a unanimous victory in Raytheon v Hernandez, which pertains to the ADA.

Wilmer Cutler Pickering Hale and Dorr LLP

See firm details p.497

The Firm: On current form it is hard to look past this team as one of the best around, with 15 lawyers who have argued more than 100 cases in the Supreme Court between them. This constitutes *"an incredible pool of talent"* that has *"seen more than most"* in a repertoire of unusual breadth. Telecom, securities, trade, tax and death penalty cases are just a few of the matters handled by a team particularly known for its agile maneuvering of cases that hinge on public policy. Examples of this diverse output include representation of the government of Hawaii in Lingle v Chevron and separate appearances in two business cases – Bates v Dow AgroSciences and City of Rancho Palos Verdes v Abrams.

The Lawyers: **Seth Waxman** (see p.474), by dint of his sheer brilliance, tends to outshine colleagues at the firm, many of whom are talented attorneys in their own right. It is not just Waxman's experience – he was President Clinton's Solicitor General and has argued over 40 cases in the Supreme Court – but also his manner that makes him *"legal dynamite in the business world."* He is pitched as *"the most punctilious and dedicated of adherents to the cause,"* and a man *"capable of getting to the kernel of a subject in double-quick time."* These attributes were showcased in his successful representation of Senators McCain and Feingold in McConnell v Federal Election Commission, the case that dealt with the legality of the Bipartisan Campaign Reform Act.

Other Notable Practitioners

Kenneth Starr (see p.470) of Kirkland & Ellis LLP may have been catapulted to global stardom during the Clinton presidency through his work as Independent Counsel on the Whitewater matter, but both before and after that episode he was hailed as an appellate lawyer nonpareil. The veteran of countless Supreme Court matters, his is *"a voice of compelling authority."* His appointment as Dean of Pepperdine Law School in California has resulted in a move to the West Coast, but he is still a big name in the capital and one regularly retained on an 'of counsel' basis to advise on weighty matters. **Walter Dellinger** of O'Melveny & Myers LLP has all the credentials anyone could need to thrive in the rarefied and competitive world of appellate law. An Assistant Attorney General in 1993, he then served as acting US Solicitor General for one term in 1997. Since returning to private practice, he has headed the talented team at O'Melveny with *"grace and leadership,"* continuing to argue cases such as Brown v Legal Foundation of Washington. *"Blessed with an ability to think up angles that would scarcely occur to others,"* he is *"a smart and insightful lawyer with an effectively disarming oral advocacy style."* Leading Latham & Watkins LLP's appellate and constitutional practice, **Maureen Mahoney**, too, has a strong pedigree in government. In between her two periods of service at the firm, she had various government appointments including a stint as United States Deputy Solicitor General. *"A serious player whom the business community views as good for bet-the-company cases,"* she is known for her *"thoroughness and ability to adapt to changing circumstances."* These qualities were on display in Grutter v Bollinger, where she successfully

defended the University of Michigan Law School's affirmative action program. She has also acted for Arthur Andersen in litigation arising out of the Enron saga. **Bob Long** (see p.454) of Covington & Burling is *"one of the unsung heroes of the appellate Bar."* *"An unpretentious figure and a real gentleman,"* he has quietly amassed a reputation for reliability through appearances in such matters as Harris Trust and Savings Bank v Salomon Smith Barney. His *"thoughtful and articulate approach"* is mirrored by **Gregory Garre** (see p.443) of Hogan & Hartson LLP. Garre has only recently returned to private practice from the DOJ but is expected to develop his firm's profile in quick time. **Beth Brinkmann** (see p.436), the head of Morrison & Foerster LLP's appellate practice group, has participated in more than 20 Supreme Court cases. Her portfolio includes both the gay rights case Lawrence v Texas and the University of Michigan affirmation matter. In both instances Brinkmann submitted amicus briefs. *"Superb at building cases from the ground and a ferocious performer when called upon to be so,"* she is widely expected to go from strength to strength. Another with a seemingly rosy future is **Jeff Lamken** (see p.452) of Baker Botts LLP. Now recently ensconced as the leader of his firm's appellate practice, he is the main strut of a practice with ambitions. Commentators believe that his experience in government (where he argued 15 cases before the Supreme Court) allied to his *"limitless drive and undoubted will to win"* makes for a potent combination. He recently appeared in City of Rancho Palos Verdes v Abrams.

LITIGATION

GENERAL COMMERCIAL

District of Columbia

Leading firms

(Litigation: General Commercial)

1	**WILLIAMS & CONNOLLY LLP** *Washington, DC*
2	**ARNOLD & PORTER LLP** *Washington, DC*
	BAKER BOTTS LLP *Washington, DC*
	COVINGTON & BURLING *Washington, DC*
	KIRKLAND & ELLIS LLP *Washington, DC*
	SKADDEN, ARPS, SLATE, MEAGHER *Washington, DC*
	WILMER CUTLER PICKERING HALE *Washington, DC*
3	**GOODWIN PROCTER LLP** *Washington, DC*
	HOGAN & HARTSON LLP *Washington, DC*
	HOWREY SIMON ARNOLD & WHITE *Washington, DC*
	JONES DAY *Washington, DC*
	SIDLEY AUSTIN BROWN *Washington, DC*
	STEPTOE & JOHNSON LLP *Washington, DC*
	VINSON & ELKINS LLP *Washington, DC*

Firms are listed alphabetically in each band.

Band 1

Williams & Connolly LLP

The Firm: Breadth of experience is the watchword for DC's finest. Its *"concentrated team of top-flight performers"* tackles every possible shade of litigation from criminal infractions to hugely convoluted civil matters. Virtually every type of case is handled from IP, securities and banking matters to libel defense and mass torts. The firm has a particularly strong name in white-collar work, advising individuals and corporations who find themselves in troubled waters. Fundamental to the team's success in the round is *"an ability to fight like junkyard dogs and get results."* As one client put it: *"If you want a tough firm to handle a tough case this is the one."* Rivals were keen to point out, however, the intellectual foundations of its deep bench:

"More than just 'put 'em up pugilists,' these guys have wonderful commercial sense and an ability to write fantastic briefs."

The Lawyers: The firm chooses not to compartmentalize; it encourages instead the fostering of robust individuals who can then be sequestered into specific teams as necessary. Although marked by a general reputation for bullishness, these foot soldiers come in many guises. **Brendan Sullivan** is the most celebrated of them all. Known best for defending Oliver North, he is a *"street-savvy performer"* with a broad practice and *"a tremendous grounding in white-collar cases."* He is an *"obvious choice when it comes to fighting a focused issue before a jury."* **Paul Wolff** shares Sullivan's reputation for proficiency in a number of areas. He is *"the classic Williams & Connolly lawyer, mixing spirit and good sense in equal measure."* **John Villa's**

District of Columbia
Leading individuals
(Litigation: General Commercial)

1 HENSLER David *Hogan & Hartson*, Washington, DC
JEFFRESS William *Baker Botts*, Washington, DC
MCLUCAS William *Wilmer Cutler*, Washington, DC
SULLIVAN Brendan *Williams, & Connolly*, Washington, DC
YANNUCCI Thomas *Kirkland & Ellis*, Washington, DC

2 BURCHFIELD Bobby *McDermott Will*, Washington, DC
MCDANIELS William *Williams & Connolly*, Washington, DC
SAYLER Robert *Covington & Burling*, Washington, DC
VARDAMAN John *Williams & Connolly*, Washington, DC

3 ALDOCK John *Goodwin Procter*, Washington, DC
BOWMAN William *Hogan & Hartson*, Washington, DC
BROGAN Stephen *Jones Day*, Washington, DC
GERSCH David *Arnold & Porter*, Washington, DC
GORELICK Jamie *Wilmer Cutler*, Washington, DC
HOLDER Eric *Covington & Burling*, Washington, DC
KENDALL David *Williams & Connolly*, Washington, DC
KLEIN Michael *Wilmer Cutler*, Washington, DC
NIELDS John *Howrey Simon*, Washington, DC
SACKS Stephen *Arnold & Porter*, Washington, DC
VILLA John *Williams & Connolly*, Washington, DC
WOLFF Paul *Williams & Connolly*, Washington, DC

Leading individuals
(Litigation: White-Collar Crime & Government Investigations)

1 BENNETT Robert *Skadden Arps*, Washington, DC
BRAY John *King & Spalding*, Washington, DC
GREEN Thomas *Sidley Austin*, Washington, DC
JEFFRESS William *Baker Botts*, Washington, DC
MCLUCAS William *Wilmer Cutler*, Washington, DC
SILBERT Earl *DLA Piper*, Washington, DC
WEINGARTEN Reid *Steptoe & Johnson*, Washington, DC

2 EGGLESTON W Neil *Howrey Simon*, Washington, DC
MAHONEY Colleen *Skadden Arps*, Washington, DC
NATHAN Irvin *Arnold & Porter*, Washington, DC
RAUH Carl *Skadden Arps*, Washington, DC
ROBERTS Michele *Akin Gump*, Washington, DC
SHAPIRO Howard *Wilmer Cutler*, Washington, DC
TUOHEY Mark *Vinson & Elkins*, Washington, DC
WILKINSON Beth *Latham & Watkins*, Washington, DC

Individuals are listed alphabetically in each band.

practice is narrower, focusing largely on bank fraud and legal malpractice. "*A friend to many a large legal firm that finds itself in difficulties,*" he has represented "*one of the finest in the business.*" **John Vardaman**'s bent lies more toward mass tort claims, an area in which he excels as "*a rigorously schooled and thoroughly pleasant opponent.*" **William McDaniels** enjoys a significant reputation born of 35 years practice. His career has taken in trials for the likes of The Washington Post Company and Twentieth Century Fox as part of a practice that, while wide in scope, has a prominent strain of First Amendment cases. This facility is shared with **David Kendall**, a white-collar crime expert to boot, whose "*intellectualism and discreet approach allied to a*

coolness under fire" wins respect among many commentators.

The Clients: Anheuser-Busch; American Airlines; Marriott International; Waste Management; National Steel; Time Warner and GE.

Band 2

Arnold & Porter LLP
See firm details p.478

The Firm: One of the bigger players in the DC market, Arnold & Porter "*has the bodies, good sense and commercial sense to take on the most sizable and protracted of litigation matters.*" Historically, it structured the practice on the back of a strong showing in antitrust and securities, both of which continue to loom large in its day-to-day business. Increasingly, though, it has succeeded in creating a more extensive practice, now regularly involved in matters of enhanced complexity and variety for a client base of manifest prestige. Another drawing card is its ability to fashion one of the strongest products liability practices in the country, leading to its involvement in such matters as smoking-related litigation concerning Philip Morris. It also represented Atlantic Richfield in the lead pigment litigation and Pfizer in the Rezulin litigation. Commentators suggest that the firm is probably best known for strategy and counseling rather than full-blooded trial work. Nevertheless, it has enjoyed notable success in cases tried to verdict, acting amongst others for Philip Morris, whom it represented in defeating an attempt to block the company's plan to change its name to Altria. Involvement in the Wyeth diet drug litigation has proved another high point for a firm with "*a creativity and dynamism that makes it catnip to some of the largest companies in the country,*" commentators said. Its recent capture of attorneys from both Fulbright & Jaworski and Dorsey & Whitney further enhances the firm's status.

The Lawyers: **Stephen Sacks** (see p.466) seasons a strong securities practice with a significant amount of general commercial litigation. "*One of the grand old men of the Washington legal scene,*" he continues to cut a swath through the opposition, having recently represented Motorola in takeover litigation relating to its cash tender offer of Next Level Communications. Also a distinguished figure in a healthy team is **David Gersch** (see p.444). Probably best known for appellate work that has seen him acting in matters such as the Carl Icahn/TWA pension liability saga, he is a general commercial litigator hailed as "*a thorough professional and a tough nut to crack.*" On the white-collar front **Irvin Nathan** (see p.459) is hailed as "*a lawyer with penetrating insights.*"

The Clients: Philip Morris; Wyeth; Motorola; Inter-American Development Bank; Bank One Delaware and Hoffmann-La Roche.

Baker Botts LLP
See firm details p.1708

The Firm: Baker Botts emphatically came to the fore of the DC litigation market by absorbing the highly respected boutique, Miller Cassidy, at the turn of the millennium. The move afforded the firm true trial capability and ensured its involvement in some of the most enviable cases in the city. Now strong in complex civil litigation both locally and nationally, it has further stretched its influence into international arbitration and white-collar work, representing a former official of Tyco and handling two significant investigations in the insurance industry. "*Confident, well-connected and willing to trade blows with the best in the business,*" the attorneys here have recently obtained a $200 million award for Kia Motors in the ICC. They also continue to handle a host of matters for key client Liberty Media and successfully defended the company against a $1 billion claim for breach of fiduciary duties brought by Gary Klesch of Klesch & Co.

The Lawyers: Former head of the trial department **Bill Jeffress** (see p.448) is "*not a face opponents want to see when peering round the courtroom door.*" Comfortable before juries of whatever composition, he has appeared in nine different states in pursuance of a general practice that is heavy on white-collar crime. A habitué of investigations relating to both corporations and individuals, his is "*a name big business can have complete trust in,*" sources said.

The Clients: The firm's prestigious clientele comprises such heavyweights as Kia Motors and Liberty Media among others.

Covington & Burling
See firm details p.481

The Firm: "*DC's blue-blood firm*" Covington & Burling achieved preeminence in the city long before many others on the list, mainly due to the years of unimpeachable service to its many institutional clients. Reputed as "*a name that stands for reliability and quality,*" it relies on a strategic and analytical approach that sees many of its matters settled before trial. Such a stance has proved profitable across a wide range of disciplines, with the firm appearing to particular effect in antitrust, insurance, white-collar crime and securities law. Recently its team obtained a $52 million jury verdict for Caliper Technologies in IP litigation and separately defended Warner-Lambert in the Brand-Name Prescription Drugs Antitrust litigation. Its lawyers have also appeared for Owens Corning in a series of lawsuits concerning insurance coverage for asbestos liabilities. Another highlight involves Tyco International's special committee of the board of directors.

The Lawyers: The departure of the highly respected Bobby Burchfield to McDermott Will & Emery has left something of a gap in the firm's ranks. Commentators agree, however, that the residual quality of attorney on offer is more than ample to offset this reverse. Leading the ranks is **Bob Sayler** (see p.466), now in his 40th year at the firm. In that time frame, he has carved a practice of exemplary diversity that takes in IP and antitrust litigation in strong measure. Clients speak of him as "*a mast you can lash yourself to in the most stormy of seas,*" praising his "*serenity and worldly wisdom.*" He works alongside **Eric Holder** (see p.447), a deputy attorney general under President Clinton, whose "*proficiency in corporate investigations is beyond cavil.*"

The Clients: Boeing; Dow Corning; 3M; Monsanto; Exxon and National Football League.

Kirkland & Ellis LLP
See firm details p.770

The Firm: An established presence for about 75 years, Kirkland & Ellis' DC office has been a strong contender in litigation, with more than half of its attorneys devoted to the practice area. The team has demonstrated proficiency in securities, environmental, IP, products liability and, above all, antitrust litigation. Its strong team pursues that Kirkland brand of "*staunch resolution and willingness to engage*" that has made the firm such a key litigation force nationwide. The practice operates in high-stakes disputes for prominent national clients and wins admiration for its "*excellence in a number of specialist areas.*" Corporate and regulatory expertise is also on the menu.

The Lawyers: **Thomas Yannucci** (see p.476) is "*one of the hardest working men in the legal community,*" interviewees said. A protean figure, he tackles IP, antitrust and securities matters among others while maintaining an enviable reputation for First Amendment work. Clients hail his "*sympathetic ear and willingness to forcefully assert claims other lawyers might baulk at.*"

The Clients: Honeywell; Morgan Stanley; Time Warner and Siemens.

Skadden, Arps, Slate, Meagher & Flom LLP & Affiliates
See firm details p.1372

The Firm: Skadden generally evokes respect for its formidable transactional practice. Its DC branch, however, has followed the lead of many of its offices nationally in establishing an increasingly potent litigation capability. Its capacity here is built on the twin pillars of securities and white-collar criminal defense, areas where it introduces "*a tough grittiness and singularity of purpose*" that makes it a match for anyone. Clients refer to lawyers "*steeped in their subject and ever ready to take up the call to arms.*"

The Lawyers: Credit for Skadden's enhanced prominence in DC litigation circles rests squarely on the shoulders of **Bob Bennett** (see p.433). An attorney who has represented both former President Clinton in the Paula Jones affair and

Enron in its labyrinthine dealings, he is "*quite simply one heck of a good lawyer.*" His "*powerful force*" and "*imperious command of space and attention*" led one observer to dub him "*a king of the white-collar world in DC.*" In these endeavors, he is assisted by **Carl Rauh** (see p.464), the leader of the firm's government enforcement litigation department. Also present is **Colleen Mahoney** (see p.455), a former deputy director of the enforcement division of the SEC. Her knowledge of the commission and "*ability to assess and represent situations concisely*" make her an invaluable asset to the firm's securities practice.

The Clients: The team has assisted some of the nation's top blue-chip clients, including some that have been embroiled in the recent spate of corporate scandals

Wilmer Cutler Pickering Hale and Dorr LLP
See firm details p.497

The Firm: Wilmer Cutler's name is often associated with the best that DC has to offer in the litigation sphere. It has a tremendous pedigree on the most intractable problems related to bet-the-company cases. Its scope is wide ranging, taking in general commercial matters, products liability, white-collar criminal defense and regulatory litigation, all of which is tackled with "*an uncanny level of intelligence.*" In one area, however, it reigns supreme: "*Hands down, the major firm of choice for securities investigations*" is Wilmer Cutler. Its marquee securities team has defended mutual fund advisers in the market timing litigation and taken a leadership role in the defense of over 300 consolidated securities class actions in the IPO laddering case. The firm's recent absorption of IP supremos Hale and Dorr also suggests that this blooming reputation can only flourish. Recent highlights include securing a jury verdict for IGEN International allowing the termination of a licensing agreement and separately representing Boeing in conducting an internal investigation concerning the US Air Force KC-767 Tanker Program. On behalf of Wyeth, it handled litigation involving polio vaccines.

The Lawyers: If any one name at this firm affords an air of national stature, it is **William McLucas** (see p.456). A former director of enforcement at the SEC, he is "*the securities guru and a big draw when it comes to bringing in business.*" Not only does he have "*tremendous cachet and credibility with the SEC,*" but he also backs this up with "*a work ethic that makes Hercules look like a sluggard.*" No one-man band, the firm has other redoubtable performers in the "*worldly-wise*" securities expert **Michael Klein** (see p.451) and **Jamie Gorelick** (see p.445), a former US Deputy Attorney General whose "*corporate and governmental knowledge is hard to rival.*" **Howard Shapiro** (see p.467) shares Gorelick's

fine reputation on white-collar crime and government investigations, winning plaudits for his "*tenacity and close scrutiny of legal problems.*" He led the team on the IGEN International litigation.

The Clients: Boeing and Wyeth are examples of the firm's distinguished clientele.

Band 3

Goodwin Procter LLP
See firm details p.980

The Firm: In an attempt to secure a firm foothold in the DC litigation market, Boston favorite Goodwin Procter has absorbed the respected litigation specialist Shea & Gardner. This move affords it a team of more than 80 litigators schooled in approaching cases from a partner-heavy standpoint. Now operating from a broader canvas, the team tackles complex commercial litigation, class actions, products liability and mass torts. Insurance, consumer financial services defense and employment litigation all feature prominently. Environmental litigation and white-collar crime expertise is also at hand in a firm that "*has the potential to break the bonds of its Boston branding,*" commentators said. Significant matters include the defense of a ten-company group – including the likes of Union Carbide, Dow Chemical and Dana Corporation – in resisting claims relating to multidistrict litigation mass tort settlement agreements.

The Lawyers: The pith and sinew of Shea & Gardner's practice for many years, **John Aldock** (see p.430) now finds himself the pivotal figure in a new environment. "*A man of great integrity,*" he has forged a fine practice in class actions, products liability and mass tort. He has represented Prudential in nationwide RICO healthcare class actions, Arthur Andersen in several securities class actions and Lefarge North America as national counsel for silica litigation.

The Clients: GE; Prudential; Lafarge North America; Dana Corporation; Rockwell Automation; Countrywide Financial and CertainTeed.

Hogan & Hartson LLP
See firm details p.484

The Firm: This "*powerhouse*" firm handles a prodigious amount of litigation spinning off from a comparatively more focused client base heavy on healthcare and pharmaceutical concerns. Commentators chorused their approval of a practice that is "*multidisciplinary in outlook and always alive to a fresh challenge.*" Internal and government investigations, antitrust, IP, general class actions and insurance litigation all flourish in a firm that busies itself with the best in both remunerated and pro bono actions. Its 120-lawyer team won a significant trial victory for the Fred Hutchinson Cancer Research Center in a case relating to bone marrow clinical tri-

als. It also represented the American Hospital Association in about 50 class action lawsuits filed against nonprofit hospitals. No strangers to cases of public interest, the group also appeared in *Christopher Jackson v State of Texas*, a matter relating to alleged racism and dishonesty in the police force of the small Texas town of Tulia.
The Lawyers: Most interviewees agreed that the firm is still recovering from the departure of the talismanic John Roberts, who went to the US Court of Appeals for the DC circuit in 2003. Nevertheless, all accepted that talent lies in abundance. **David Hensler** (see p.447) is lauded as a "*24-carat commercial litigator whose flair extends across the business world.*" He is a "*truly admirable trial lawyer*" who recently appeared on behalf of Mylan Pharmaceuticals in litigation relating to two anti-anxiety drugs. His wide-ranging practice is similar to that of his colleague, the "*shrewd and dependable*" **William Bowman** (see p.435). His capacity in commercial, antitrust and environmental litigation is set alongside his better-known insurance coverage practice.
The Clients: Hughes Network Systems; Anthem; Mylan Pharmaceuticals; American University and American Hospital Association.

Howrey Simon Arnold & White

The Firm: Not one to trifle on the periphery, Howrey Simon pursues the larger cases around. It has a broad scope that encompasses all forms of civil litigation but the firm really hits the heights in two key areas: Through antitrust work it formed the bedrock of its reputation only to see its standing further improved by the establishment of a premier IP litigation service. Commentators admire its "*ruthless pursuit of its goals*" while further commending its white-collar practice, which is built around "*some of the best attorneys in the business.*"
The Lawyers: **Neil Eggleston** provides the backbone to the firm's white-collar practice. A veteran of countless government investigations, he has recently represented a number of corporations and individuals accused of securities fraud. Clients described him as "*a calm performer who can envision a case three or four steps ahead.*" At time of press, Eggleston announced that he would be joining Debevoise & Plimpton. He cochairs the firm's white-collar defense practice with **John Nields**, a versatile litigator who "*combines intelligence and a meticulous nature with a good demeanor in court.*"
The Clients: The firm's clientele encompasses a variety of blue-chip companies in such areas as manufacturing, telecom, consumer products and energy.

Jones Day

See firm details p.485
The Firm: Although stronger and more visible outside the city, "*Jones Day's appearances on the DC litigation scene are both telling and hugely*

impressive," observers said. Its forays take it into the realms of securities, employment, products liability, contract disputes and antitrust litigation all of which are prosecuted with the firm's trademark "*vigor and unshakeable belief.*" The firm may not have the deepest bench but this matters little when one considers the quality of attorney on offer. As one client puts it: "*It doesn't matter what area of the law it is, this firm is always a good fit and is home to some of the most skilled practitioners in the business.*"
The Lawyers: **Steve Brogan** (see p.436) combines an extensive litigation practice with his responsibilities as managing partner of the firm. "*A tough guy, he is very much in the firm-but-fair mold.*" His many and various activities have included acting for GM in the air bag safety and Cadillac V8-6-4 litigation. He has also represented Northrop Corporation in a grand jury investigation of alleged misconduct.
The Clients: GM; Gillette; Bridgestone/Firestone, First American Corporation and Dart Group.

Sidley Austin Brown & Wood LLP

See firm details p.778
The Firm: This national heavyweight commands attention in DC mainly for its appellate prowess. This shouldn't detract, however, from its "*high-quality and consistent general litigation service.*" Applying all of its renowned skills on behalf of regional, national and international clients, its tentacles extend into antitrust, banking, IP, products liability and environmental litigation. Many other areas are featured, with the firm particularly hitting the heights on white-collar work. "*Always fully prepared and up to scratch on the latest developments,*" the team here is proving a growing force year on year.
The Lawyers: **Thomas Green** (see p.445), who heads the firm's white-collar defense practice, is pitched as "*a real personality who has flat out seen it all. He is a famous old-time Washington table-pounder who can shake the opposition into submission.*" His triumphs include obtaining a defense verdict for Tyson Foods in a criminal case in which the company was charged with participating in a scheme to employ illegal workers in violation of the immigration laws. "*Any corporation under government investigation should turn to Tom Green at the first sign of trouble,*" sources said.
The Clients: The firm has advised a variety of top-flight clients in the banking, IP, healthcare, food and manufacturing sectors among others.

Steptoe & Johnson LLP

See firm details p.492
The Firm: A presence for about 60 years in DC, this firm has grown from humble beginnings into a highly recognizable name in the nation's capital. Its practice has expanded exponentially over time to become one of real diversity, but its lawyers are most readily connected with insur-

ance litigation, toxic torts and white-collar crime. The existence of a contingent of former high-level government officials makes the quality of its participation in the latter arena one of high caliber.
The Lawyers: A glut of talented white-collar practitioners is spread across a number of firms in the capital. Perhaps the hottest of these at the moment is **Reid Weingarten** (see p.474) whose "*reputation for pulling big victories out of the hat*" is well entrenched. He was recently seen defending Mark A. Belnick, chief corporate counsel of Tyco International, against charges of first-degree grand larceny, securities fraud and falsifying business records. Weingarten benefits from "*a relaxed style that masks a ferociously analytical and driven approach.*"
The Clients: The team acts for a clutch of Fortune 500 companies.

Vinson & Elkins LLP

See firm details p.1724
The Firm: The DC arm of this Texas-based player adds a valuable contribution to the firm's overall profile. It operates within a matrix of international offices representing clients on all forms of litigation – including antitrust, securities, and above all white-collar criminal defense. Commentators identified a "*fearlessness when going to trial*" and commended a team that is adept at marshaling the resources available to it. It represented Halliburton and its subsidiary KBR in a grand jury investigation and separately defended Governor McGreevy of New Jersey in an investigation of political corruption.
The Lawyers: **Mark Tuohey** (see p.472) enjoys the full confidence of some of the biggest names in the land. "*A great man who has been effortlessly felling the opposition for years,*" he is part of a team that has represented clients in many prominent investigations. By way of example, it defended a former senior official at a major accountancy firm in a tax shelter investigation and defended several healthcare companies in grand jury investigations.
The Clients: The team's eminent clientele includes top-flight companies in the areas of healthcare, energy, manufacturing and banking among others.

Other Notable Practitioners

The hugely respected **Earl Silbert** (see p.468) of DLA Piper Rudnick Gray Cary can claim a legal history that goes back to service as the first Watergate prosecutor. He is "*something of a legend in the annals of white-collar crime history,*" one source said. "*A true lawyer's lawyer who takes the full burden of a case upon himself, his low-key style is shot through with a confidence born of years of experience.*" Former Enron CEO Kenneth Lay's decision to appoint him as his representative during the investigation of the corporation's financial collapse tells its own

412   All quotes in the text are from interviews with clients and competitors.

CHAMBERS USA 2005

story. **John Bray** (see p.435) of King & Spalding LLP is no less exalted. Active across the USA, his many cases have seen him appearing for corporations in Operation Ill Wind. He also successfully represented the chief defendant from a major chemical manufacturer charged in a pesticide pollution conspiracy case in Virginia. **Beth Wilkinson** is cochair of the white-collar crime group at Latham & Watkins LLP. Famed for her role in the prosecution of the Oklahoma City bombers, she "*has taken up the reins of private practice proving an adept juggler of many important matters.*" Examples include counseling the

Salt Lake Organizing Committee regarding the government's investigation into the bid selection process for the 2002 Winter Olympics and separately representing the board of directors of Ford in the Ford/Firestone investigation. Finally, two of the most respected performers in town have changed their surroundings this year. **Bobby Burchfield** (see p.437) has arrived at McDermott Will & Emery having enjoyed a successful career at Covington & Burling. He is "*a corporate litigator of some distinction*" whose activities on behalf of household-name clients have seen him handle numerous jury trials and

appeals. He has also made an appearance in the Supreme Court on behalf of the Republican National Committee in McConnell V Federal Election Commission. **Michele Roberts** (see p.465), meanwhile, has arrived at Akin Gump Strauss Hauer & Feld LLP from the now defunct Shea & Gardner. "*Capable of singing a siren song to judge or jury,*" she has transferred the skills learned in a celebrated criminal law career to a newly constituted civil and white-collar practice.

MEDIA & ENTERTAINMENT

District of Columbia
Leading firms (Media & Entertainment)

[1]	**LEVINE SULLIVAN KOCH & SCHULZ** *Washington, DC*
	WILLIAMS & CONNOLLY LLP *Washington, DC*
[2]	**DAVIS WRIGHT TREMAINE LLP** *Washington, DC*
	JENNER & BLOCK LLP *Washington, DC*
[3]	**BAKER & HOSTETLER LLP** *Washington, DC*
	HOLLAND & KNIGHT LLP *Washington, DC*
	NIXON PEABODY LLP *Washington, DC*

Leading individuals
(Media & Entertainment:)

[1]	**BAINE Kevin** *Williams & Connolly, Washington, DC*
	CORN-REVERE Robert *Davis Wright, Washington, DC*
	HANDMAN Laura *Davis Wright, Washington, DC*
	LEVINE Lee *Levine Sullivan, Washington, DC*
	SMITH Paul *Jenner & Block, Washington, DC*
	YANNUCCI Thomas *Kirkland & Ellis, Washington, DC*
[2]	**BARNETT Robert** *Williams & Connolly, Washington, DC*
	BERNIUS Robert *Nixon Peabody, Washington, DC*
	KENDALL David *Williams & Connolly, Washington, DC*
	SULLIVAN Michael *Levine Sullivan, Washington, DC*
	TOBIN Charles *Holland & Knight, Washington, DC*
	ZWEIFACH Gerson *Williams & Connolly, Washington, DC*
[3]	**BROWN Jay** *Levine Sullivan, Washington, DC*
	SANFORD Bruce *Baker & Hostetler, Washington, DC*
	SIEGEL Nathan *Levine Sullivan, Washington, DC*

Firms and individuals are listed alphabetically in each band.

Band 1

Levine Sullivan Koch & Schulz LLP
The Firm: Moving up the tables is this "*magnificent player*" in media, attracting clients by delivering "*phenomenal*" results in representing news, entertainment and media organizations in libel, privacy and First Amendment disputes nationwide. It parlays a "*tough but fair*" approach into some of the "*most talked about cases of the year,*" clients note. This has included successfully representing several media organizations – including the Los Angeles Times, the Denver Post, ESPN and CBS – in the high-pro-

file case People v Kobe Bryant. Its involvement in the Plame leak investigation also won peer respect; in that case, the firm successfully represented a journalist subpoenaed in connection to a leak to the press concerning the identity of CIA operative Valerie Plame. In the matter Berry v CBS Broadcasting, the team effectively represented the CBS television network, producers 60 Minutes and correspondent Morley Safer in defamation actions.

The Lawyers: "*Depth and talent*" are qualities attributed to **Lee Levine**, who represented journalists for the Associated Press and the Los Angeles Times in resisting subpoenas issued by nuclear scientist Wen Ho Lee, which sought to compel them to disclose their confidential sources. Clients described him as "*the best thing since sliced bread.*" **Michael Sullivan** and the "*outstandingly smart*" **Jay Brown** defended the Baltimore Sun in a trespass action brought by former congressman Parren Mitchell in a case arising from an interview conducted by two Baltimore Sun reporters in a nursing home. Former ABC in-house counsel **Nathan Siegel** was commended for his "*rock solid knowledge*" of media law. He is representing ESPN in Knievel v ESPN, a defamation action involving motorcycle daredevil Evel Knievel.

The Clients: ABC; ALM; the Chicago Tribune; Court TV; Emmis Communications; Condé Nast Publications; Gannett; The Hartford Courant; Infinity Broadcasting; King World Productions; MTV Networks; National Public Radio; Newsday; New York Press Association; The New York Times Company; The Orange County Register; Ottaway Newspapers; Paramount Pictures; Radio One; Reuters; Science Magazine; Tribune Company; TVG Network; Univision Communications and Viacom.

Williams & Connolly LLP
The Firm: This "*huge, vibrant player is the go-to firm for sophisticated media work,*" clients say. The group has "*embraced new media like a newborn baby*" in addition to maintaining its com-

mand of traditional "*highly complex*" media matters. The team's strength stems from its deep bench and years of solid experience in the field, sources said. A significant number of copyright infringement cases for studios contribute to the group's status as "*a true heavyweight.*" It also assists major corporations in media and entertainment-related litigation, contract negotiations, crisis management, regulatory advice and other similar proceedings.

The Lawyers: Clients consider the "*spectacularly knowledgeable*" **Kevin Baine** among "*the best in the business.*" Also in the running is **David Kendall**, pitched as "*smart as a whip.*" His "*sophisticated and practical*" sensibilities attract a loyal group of clients, who regularly seek his "*top-notch advice every time.*" Entertainment specialist **Bob Barnett** is, according to clients, a "*leader for book publishing.*" He also receives accolades for representing television news producers and correspondents such as Sam Donaldson, Judy Woodruff and Jeff Greenfield. The "*gifted*" **Gerson Zweifach** is "*bright, energetic and responsive*" and respected for "*consistent quality of work*" particularly as regards libel defense.

The Clients: The Washington Post; CNN; Time; The Walt Disney Company; Newsweek; ABC; NBC; CBS; News Corporation; Twentieth Century Fox Film; Time Warner; CNN; Time; Paramount Pictures; MGM Studios; Sony Pictures Entertainment; Tribune Company; The National Enquirer and Simon & Schuster. Individuals include: Christiane Amanpour; Brit Hume; Andrea Mitchell; David Gergen; Ray Suarez and Lisa Myers.

Band 2

Davis Wright Tremaine LLP
See firm details p.1796
The Firm: The "*astonishingly high standards and solid expertise*" at the firm guarantees a clientele that includes prominent media organizations, publishers, broadcasters and producers.

The team's *"consistent, top-quality players"* are often retained on prominent matters such as petitioning Governor George E. Pataki to grant New York's first posthumous pardon to the late comedian Lenny Bruce. Moreover it defended CBS Broadcasting in an FCC investigation alleging indecent broadcasting arising from the brief exposure of Janet Jackson's breast during the controversial 2003 Super Bowl halftime show. In a different matter the group acted for the American Teleservices Association in its judicial challenge to the National Do Not Call registry.

The Lawyers: **Laura Handman** (see p.446) is a *"savvy go-getter"* whose expertise in prepublication counsel and litigation impresses clients. She advises national and international book, magazine, newspaper and electronic publishers and broadcasters on matters such as libel, copyright, privacy and First Amendment rights. *"Sensational"* **Bob Corn-Revere** (see p.438) is *"a leader in the field"* with particular experience in First Amendment law, Internet-associated matters and FCC regulatory concerns. Clients said they *"worship the ground he walks on."* His latest legal battles have involved the Child Online Protection Act, the Communications Decency Act, Internet content filtering in public libraries and public broadcasting regulations.

The Clients: The New York Times; The New Yorker; The Economist; New York Daily News; BBC; Discovery Communications, A&E Television Networks; American Teleservices Association; ANA; Association of Public Television Stations; Black Entertainment Television; Center for Democracy and Technology; Courtroom Television Network; Enigma Software Group; Fox Entertainment Group; Motion Picture Association of America; National Association of Broadcasters and Playboy Enterprises.

Jenner & Block LLP

See firm details p.768

The Firm: This *"wonderful team"* earned plaudits for delivering *"terrific work"* on some of the most *"talked about matters"* nationwide. In one of the most significant entertainment copyright cases of the year, the team advised on Metro-Goldwyn-Mayer Studios et al. v Grokster et al. in a case concerning Internet-based file-sharing of music, movies and other digital media. The group also represented the American Library Association in a case involving its First Amend-

ment challenge to the federal Children's Internet Protection Act.

The Lawyers: Managing partner **Paul Smith** (see p.468) has a *"second to none"* media and First Amendment practice, which is recognized as *"virtually untouchable,"* commentators said. He handled several high-profile cases including Wen Ho Lee v United States DOJ, a case involving reporters' confidential sources.

The Clients: The firm has represented a broad array of clients, including publishers, broadcasters and related industry organizations. It also advises non-media companies on issues such as Internet copyright, video games access and confidentiality.

Band 3

Baker & Hostetler LLP

The Firm: This *"high-level, broad-based group"* represents a range of media clients including publishers, cable operators, and television and radio broadcasters. Its dispute resolution prowess has led to its key involvement in defamation, copyright, privacy and trademark infringement cases. It is also renowned for its success in challenging the government on First Amendment rights. Its effective legal skills have, in more recent years, expanded into the new media arena. In this field, the team's work crosses over into the government policy side and involves issues such as the Internet.

The Lawyers: *"First Amendment connoisseur"* **Bruce Sanford** has been dubbed *"one of the most influential lawyers in the country,"* according to peers. Although best known for his defamation work, the former corporate and securities lawyer served as outside corporate counsel to Pioneer Hi-Bred International, a subsidiary of chemical giant DuPont and one of the world's leading commercial seed producers.

The Clients: ABC; Bertelsmann; Chicago Sun-Times; Denver Rocky Mountain News; The EW Scripps Company; El Dia; FOX Television; The New York Times and The Washington Times.

Holland & Knight LLP

See firm details p.1352

The Firm: This team *"has beefed up"* its resources and now totals 22 attorneys, many of whom are former journalists and in-house media counsel. The *"pool of talented lawyers"*

offer exclusive counsel to publishers and broadcasters. Before the US Court of Appeals for the Fourth Circuit, the team argued a case examining reporters' requests to view affidavits pertaining to search warrants linked to several Muslim nonprofit organizations and residences in Northern Virginia. The case examines reporters' requests to view affidavits requesting search warrants linked to several Muslim nonprofit organizations and residences in northern Virginia. Furthermore the group successfully argued a case challenging more than 100 published articles in Worrell-Payne v Gannett.

The Lawyers: Former newspaper reporter **Chuck Tobin** (see p.472) is a *"crème de la crème"* First Amendment lawyer, according to commentators. He also offers advice to media companies concerning privacy matters and libel.

The Clients: The firm has counseled Gannett, The Times of Northwest Indiana and Cartoon Network.

Nixon Peabody LLP

See firm details p.1361

The Firm: This accomplished team of lawyers advises a gamut of media clients, including newspapers, publishing companies and television stations. It acts on a range of issues including privacy, defamation and access. Further bolstered by a significant copyright profile, the team has been involved in various new media issues such as Internet-related proceedings.

The Lawyers: *"Smart and formidable"* **Bob Bernius** (see p.434) advises corporate clients in litigation such as libel, discrimination, Internet and general commercial matters. He was formerly assistant district attorney in Brooklyn, New York.

The Clients: The team continues to advise established client Gannett and its subsidiaries among others.

Other Notable Practitioners

Generalist **Thomas Yannucci** of Kirkland & Ellis LLP is considered somewhat of a virtuoso litigator with regards to media law, sources said. He has represented companies as plaintiffs in defamation, libel and similar matters, often with devastatingly lethal results to the defense.

414   All quotes in the text are from interviews with clients and competitors.

CHAMBERS USA 2005

PROJECTS

District of Columbia
Leading firms (Projects)

1. **CHADBOURNE & PARKE LLP** *Washington, DC*
   WHITE & CASE LLP *Washington, DC*
2. **LATHAM & WATKINS LLP** *Washington, DC*
   SKADDEN, ARPS, SLATE, MEAGHER *Washington, DC*
3. **CLIFFORD CHANCE US LLP** *Washington, DC*
   MAYER, BROWN, ROWE & MAW LLP *Washington, DC*
   PAUL, HASTINGS, JANOFSKY *Washington, DC*
   VINSON & ELKINS LLP *Washington, DC*
4. **HOGAN & HARTSON LLP** *Washington, DC*
   HUNTON & WILLIAMS *Washington, DC*
   WINSTON & STRAWN *Washington, DC.*

Leading individuals (Projects)

1. **DESANTIS Victor** *White & Case*, Washington, DC
   FITZGERALD Peter *Chadbourne & Parke*, Washington, DC
   SACHS John *Latham & Watkins*, Washington, DC
2. **KLEPPER Martin** *Skadden Arps*, Washington, DC
   MACHLIN Barry *Mayer Brown*, Chicago
   MARTIN Keith *Chadbourne & Parke*, Washington, DC
   MCISAAC Christopher *Winston & Strawn*, Washington, DC
   NEAHER Edward *White & Case*, Washington, DC
   WARD Erica *Skadden Arps*, Washington, DC
3. **BRASHER Lance** *Skadden Arps*, Washington, DC
   HANSEN Kenneth *Chadbourne & Parke*, Washington, DC
   MAIZEL Jonathan *Milbank Tweed*, Washington, DC
   MILES Steven *Baker Botts*, Washington, DC
   MURPHY J Andrew *Hunton & Williams*, Washington, DC
   PENDER Bob *Hogan & Hartson*, Washington, DC
   SCHROEDER Jeffrey *Paul Hastings*, Washington, DC
   SPIVAK Mark *Vinson & Elkins*, Washington, DC

Up-and-coming individuals

HUNT Paul *Latham & Watkins*, Washington, DC
SCHUHMACHER Kenneth *Latham*, Washington, DC
TAYLOR John *Mayer Brown*, Chicago

Firms and individuals are listed alphabetically in each band

Band 1

Chadbourne & Parke LLP

See firm details p.1341

The Firm: Chadbourne & Parke boasts one of the longest established project finance practices in the USA, and it has succeeded in maintaining its status as one of the leading firms in the field. As one client stated: "*Lawyers are only as good as their last deal, and Chadbourne lawyers continue to perform at a high level.*" The team, which is particularly renowned for representing the sponsor companies, offers acknowledged expertise in power infrastructure projects, both in the USA and abroad. For example, the team has been advising El Paso on its disposal of a huge portfolio of electricity projects, and is representing Interconexión Eléctrica ISA Bolivia SA in the financing of its electric transmission lines in Bolivia. The team is also well known for working on behalf of the multilateral agencies, and

has been heavily involved this year in the emerging markets of Africa and Latin America. Recent highlights include acting for the IFC in connection with the financing of the La Higuera hydropower project in Chile.

The Lawyers: Peter Fitzgerald (see p.442) enjoys a national reputation for his expertise in political risk insurance and is active in representing multilateral agencies. Clients value his ability to "*deal with difficult issues in a nonconfrontational way*" and his skill at "*finding solutions rather than problems.*" **Keith Martin** (see p.455) is felt by many to be "*absolutely top*" for the tax side of projects. Sources say "*everyone gravitates towards him because he explains complex tax issues in an understandable way.*" **Kenneth Hansen** (see p.446) has been in-house at both Ex-Im Bank and the Overseas Private Investment Corporation (OPIC) and so is well-placed for his role in representing the multilateral agencies.

The Clients: The firm represented the Inter-American Development Bank on a loan to a Costa Rican financial institution for on-lending to various small infrastructure projects in Latin America. It also acted for Sovereign Risk Insurance regarding a capital markets issuance by the Turkish bank, Finansbank, and assisted Greka Energy in connection with the financing of a coal-bed methane project in China.

White & Case LLP

See firm details p.1379

The Firm: This "*polished and professional*" firm successfully utilizes its global network of offices to help it secure mandates on the international mega-projects. With the firm's strong banking background, it is hardly surprising to find that it has a particular emphasis on representing the lenders. The DC office is a pivotal part of this international practice, and enjoys a fine reputation for assisting lenders and multilateral agencies. It is especially visible in Latin America, where it has been involved in a number of oil and gas, power and toll road schemes. A highlight this year was representing the Inter-American Development Bank and Ambac Assurance as financial guarantors to the Costanera Norte toll road project in Santiago, Chile. With its great lender practice, the strength of the firm's sponsor work is often overlooked, however it does also represent sponsors in some high-profile projects, such as the El Cajon hydroelectric project in Mexico.

The Lawyers: Clients report that all the lawyers here have "*a strong business sense and are really hands-on.*" At the top of the tree, **Victor DeSantis** (see p.439) is "*simply one of the best for representing the multilateral agencies.*" Clients and peers identified a long list of his strengths, but particularly singled him out for his "*outstanding

technical expertise*" and the "*incredible interpersonal skills that give him the ability to find solutions during tricky negotiations.*" **Edward Neaher** (see p.459) is also praised for his negotiation skills, with sources reporting that he is "*diligent, even tempered and concentrates on getting the deal done.*"

The Clients: The firm represented the IFC, Société Générale and Bancomext as lenders in the $250 million Rio Bravo III and IV power projects in Mexico, and also acted for the IFC and Société Générale, along with OPIC, in the $700 million financing of the Macae power plant project in Brazil. The team is also active in Asia and has been representing the sponsors in the West Seno upstream oil and gas project in Indonesia. Other clients include: Deutsche Bank; Ex-Im Bank; Mid-American Holdings and BNP Paribas.

Band 2

Latham & Watkins LLP

The Firm: The "*robust*" DC office of this dynamic firm is renowned for representing sponsor companies. Clients rave about the team, commenting that it is "*responsive and client-driven: you get senior people on the deal, and it has a deep bench at both partner and associate level.*" Displaying its international reach and the expertise in the power practice, the group's largest deal this year was the refinancing of the $700 million Uch power project in Pakistan for the sponsor company. It has also represented the sponsors in a number of wind energy projects this year. The team has been kept busy with a series of M&A transactions, typically representing bidders for portfolios of generating assets, both in the USA and abroad. It also enjoys a strong name for assisting the multilateral agencies, and recently acted for the Inter-American Development Bank on the $458 million financing of a 1200-mile transmission line in Brazil.

The Lawyers: Clients report that **John Sachs** has "*more depth and knowledge in the power sector than anyone else out there.*" They also love the fact that he has "*great international experience, so can bring a fresh perspective to the table.*" **Paul Hunt** is emerging as "*a real rising star,*" according to market sources. He has been focusing of late on representing the Tag 1 and 2 power plants in Mexico during their restructuring. **Ken Schuhmacher** concentrates on international projects and is said to be "*thorough and driven.*"

The Clients: CDC Globeleq; Nord/LB; Government of Jamaica; Dynergy; Pennsylvania Power & Light Global; United Technologies and BTU Power. In the renewable energy sector, the team has been representing Marubeni America Corporation and Catamount Energy.

Skadden, Arps, Slate, Meagher & Flom LLP & Affiliates
See firm details p.1372

The Firm: The DC office of this corporate powerhouse prides itself on the breadth of its projects practice, which this year has represented banks, developers and multilateral agencies in a variety of deals, both domestically and internationally. The firm is known for its "*tough, relentless and thorough*" approach, and its wealth of knowledge and resources. As one representative client said: "*I have not found anyone better than Skadden in terms of knowledge of the market and project finance experience.*" Like many firms, it has been involved this year in a number of acquisitions and disposals in the projects field. For example, it has undertaken a range of transactions for key client ArcLight Capital Partners, including the $244 million acquisition of the West Virginia natural gas operations of Allegheny. In another high-profile transaction, the team represented Enron in the sale of its 50% interest in the Ecoelectrica project in Puerto Rico for $177 million.

The Lawyers: **Martin Klepper** (see p.451) heads the DC projects practice and is worshipped by his clients as "*one of the great gods of project finance.*" Clients particularly rate his skill in supervising complex projects and managing large teams of lawyers. **Erica Ward** (see p.474) focuses on representing the developers of power projects and is another high-profile member of the team. Sources say that "*she spends none of her time posturing and 100% of her time trying to get deals done.*" **Lance Brasher** (see p.435) is a real hands-on member of the team and was praised for "*rolling up his sleeves and getting stuck into projects.*"

The Clients: The firm has represented KBC Bank in a number of transactions, including a $335 million financial restructuring for the AES Wolf Hollow power plant in Texas, and a $300 million financing in Louisiana. It also advised Enron on restructuring its international energy businesses into a newly formed entity, Prisma Energy. The DC team also does work for the multilateral agencies, and this year has represented Ex-Im Bank on a telecom project in India and an entertainment project in Israel

Band 3

Clifford Chance US LLP
See firm details p.1343

The Firm: The global project finance practice of Clifford Chance frequently tops polls for its worldwide involvement in major projects. The DC outpost, consisting of just two full-time partners, is able to punch above its weight due to its access to this massive resource. The team plays to this strength and specializes in working on international projects for the multilateral agencies. It has played a part in a number of high-profile deals this year, including representing the Inter-American Development Bank in the financing of the $800 million Camisea gas pipeline in Peru. The team also regularly represents sponsors in Latin American projects, and has been acting for EDF in the development of the $592 million Rio Bravo III and IV power plants in Mexico.

The Lawyers: The contacts for projects in DC are partners David Evans and Kate McCarthy.

The Clients: The DC team worked closely with the Paris office in representing the IFC and a large group of lenders in a $1.3 billion telecom financing in Turkey. It also represented the IFC in connection with the financing of an $800 million telecom project in Nigeria.

Mayer, Brown, Rowe & Maw LLP
See firm details p.771

The Firm: This major global firm is prominent in the sphere of international projects as it enjoys particular expertise in representing the multilateral agencies. With its strong financing capacity and client list, it also regularly appears for commercial banks in major international projects. For example, the team has been actively involved in the current concentration of projects in the Middle East, and has been representing Ex-Im Bank in the financing of a $550 million ammonia production facility in Egypt. It has been busy this year in the restructuring of projects, and has been working on two large coal-fired power plant developments in Indonesia, again for Ex-Im Bank.

The Lawyers: **Barry Machlin** (see p.454) co-chairs the firm's global project finance practice group. He is popular with his clients because he "*goes above and beyond the call of duty*" and provides "*an exceptional level of client service.*" He works closely with new partner **John Taylor** (see p.471). Sources say that Taylor is "*helpful at getting the deal moving*" and can look forward to a bright future.

The Clients: As well as acting for Ex-Im Bank on the projects mentioned above, the firm has been representing commercial lenders in connection with a $75 million Mexican hydropower project.

Paul, Hastings, Janofsky & Walker LLP
See firm details p.297

The Firm: Paul Hastings enters the table following an acquisitive year of high-profile lateral hires, including a group of lawyers from Hunton & Williams. The "*first-rate*" firm concentrates on representing developers in both domestic and Latin American projects, although in recent months the bulk of its work has been located in the USA. For example, a marquee deal from the past year was representing InterGen in the development and subsequent sale to Southern Edison of a 1000MW gas-fired power plant in California. The team also advised the equity investor in the $940 million construction and lease financing of the Springerville power plant in Arizona. According to clients, it is already excelling in this field: "*It's as good a team as we've ever used for domestic power projects,*" said one.

The Lawyers: Interviewees agreed that "*experienced and thorough*" **Jeffrey Schroeder** (see p.467) is a serious player in the international projects market. Peers report that "*you feel tested when you work opposite him.*" He recently joined the firm from Hunton & Williams.

The Clients: The firm's main clients are InterGen, DTE Energy Services, National Energy & Gas Transmission, GE Energy and John Hancock. The firm represented a consortium including DTE Energy and Goldman Sachs in the $300 million purchase of utility systems at eight DaimlerChrysler plants. Other recent highlights include acting for the sponsor company, Logan Project, in the refinancing of a coal-fired plant in New Jersey.

Vinson & Elkins LLP
See firm details p.1724

The Firm: This quintessential full-service energy firm brings its breadth of energy expertise to bear with good effect on the projects market. The fine DC office is a vital part of the practice, and has taken the lead in many of the firm's most international deals. For example, attorneys from DC were busy advising the lenders, WestLB, in the high-profile $780 million El Cajon hydroelectric power project in Mexico, one of the largest financings in the country to date. The team also regularly represents sponsor companies and has undertaken a considerable amount of work for PSEG Global. This year, this has included a $220 million disposition of its interest in the Meiya Power Company, which owns a series of power projects throughout Asia.

The Lawyers: **Mark Spivak** (see p.469) has been practicing in the energy sector for over 20 years. In addition to enjoying this wealth of experience, he is, peers report, a "*smart*" attorney who "*represents his clients well.*"

The Clients: The firm has been advising AIG in connection with its acquisition of some domestic projects from El Paso, and has been handling some dispositions in Bolivia and Peru on behalf of NRG Energy. As well as WestLB and PSEG Global, it also does some work for AES.

Band 4

Hogan & Hartson LLP
See firm details p.1775

The Firm: This firm has been involved in some prominent domestic projects, but the DC powerhouse is especially noteworthy for its international reach in the projects market. In the past year alone, it has advised on projects in Latin America, Africa, India and the Middle East, typically on behalf of sponsor companies. Particular highlights include advising AES on the restructuring of distressed projects in Latin America, and continuing to advise Petrobras on its Bolivian pipeline project. On the domestic front, the firm's marquee deal was advising Sithe Energy and Reservoir Capital on the largest acquisition of Enron generating assets.

The Lawyers: **Robert Pender** is the director of the firm's projects and international finance group. Sources say that he is "*up there amongst the finest in terms of knowledge and experience.*"
The Clients: In Africa, the firm has been advising Gapco on its $1.5 billion, Guinea-based alumina facility. It represents Jet Airways in India, and Israel Electric in the Middle East, while in Latin America, it has been acting for Pemex. Other clients include: Dominion Power; Florida Power & Light; Global Aluminium and OPIC.

Hunton & Williams

See firm details p.1775
The Firm: Clients report that the firm continues to provide "*an outstanding service*" despite the recent departure of a group of lawyers. The remaining attorneys have kept hold of a broad client base, comprising both developers and financial institutions. They have been busy this year working on the development of new projects and the restructuring of distressed projects. The firm also has a fine reputation in the market for its niche in equipment lease financing,

while the DC office stands out in particular for its expertise in privatization and market development. Recent international highlights include advising the Government of Guam on the privatization of its water industry.

The Lawyers: **Andrew Murphy** (see p.458) heads the projects group and is a key name for the firm in this area. Peers and clients alike noted his "*practical and deal-oriented approach.*"
The Clients: The firm does a lot of work for DTE Energy and DTE Energy Services, recently representing them in the acquisition of a power plant in Alabama. Traditionally the firm has concentrated on representing developers, however it is increasingly gaining financial institutions as clients. Examples include John Hancock Life Insurance and MetLife.

Winston & Strawn

See firm details p.780
The Firm: This firm was named by both clients and peers as one of the leaders when it comes to representing multilateral agencies. Clients particularly like the group because its lawyers are "*very hands-on and really get stuck into projects,*" as well as being "*accomplished at achieving success in negotiations.*" As a brief look at the year's highlight projects will demonstrate, the team has wide experience in many different sectors, from power to telecom to oil and gas, though its energy sector roots are, not surprisingly, to the fore in much of its largest work. For example, it

closed the financing of the Ibiritermo power project in Brazil on behalf of Ex-Im Bank and the Italian export credit agency SACE: this is a rare accomplishment in the troubled Brazilian power sector. In Indonesia, it represented OPIC in the financing of the $1.1 billion West Seno oil and gas project, and advised the same client, alongside KfW, on the financing of the privatization and expansion of Lima's international airport.

The Lawyers: Clients name **Christopher McIsaac** as a "*first choice*" for a range of power projects, due to his "*strong stance in negotiations*" and his "*attention to detail.*"
The Clients: The firm represented AES in connection with the financing of four electric projects in Panama, and acted for Crédit Lyonnais as the lead arranger in the financing of a power project on Long Island, New York.

Other Notable Practitioners

Milbank, Tweed, Hadley & McCloy's high-profile projects practice is mainly run from the New York and California offices, but **Jonathan Maizel** is a well-known projects lawyer based in DC. He worked on the Nigeria NGL project and was admired for his "*practical and no-nonsense*" approach. **Steven Miles** (see p.457) from Baker Botts LLP is held to be "*extremely knowledgeable about the LNG business*" and is becoming increasingly prominent in LNG projects.

REAL ESTATE

District of Columbia
Leading firms (Real Estate)

1	**ARENT FOX PLLC** *Washington, DC*
	DLA PIPER RUDNICK GRAY CARY *Washington, DC*
	HOLLAND & KNIGHT LLP *Washington, DC*
	SHAW PITTMAN *Washington, DC*
2	**ARNOLD & PORTER LLP** *Washington, DC*
	BINGHAM MCCUTCHEN LLP *Washington, DC*
	HOGAN & HARTSON LLP *Washington, DC*
3	**GREENSTEIN DELORME & LUCHS** *Washington, DC*
	GROSSBERG YOCHELSON FOX *Washington, DC*
	MAYER, BROWN, ROWE & MAW LLP *Washington, DC*
4	**AKIN GUMP STRAUSS HAUER** *Washington, DC*
	COVINGTON & BURLING *Washington, DC*
	GOULSTON & STORRS *Washington, DC*
	NIXON PEABODY LLP *Washington, DC*
	VENABLE LLP *Washington, DC*

Firms are listed alphabetically in each band.

Band 1

Arent Fox PLLC
The Firm: Historically one of the pre-eminent real estate firms in DC, the firm not only holds its own but is also strengthening its practice,

industry analysts said. Predicated on a solid, core group of leading attorneys, the team is best known for its development business, often working with established entrepreneurial developers. However, financing is increasingly becoming the keystone of the practice, and public financing in particular. It advises on the funding of government facilities, principally those leased to federal government agencies in addition to the development of these projects. It is also recognized for its niche capabilities on tax-exempt bond financing. Rounding out the practice is the group's prominent expertise in the assisted living and hospitality sectors, advising on a number of tourism-related issues that utilize PPP elements. The department is also respected for its deft handling of multifamily and commercial residential matters in addition to various retail projects.

The Lawyers: Leading competitors view the firm's partners as a "*superstar cast.*" **Joseph Fries** is perceived as "*the dean*" of the area's real estate Bar. Experienced and practical, his legal efficiency led one interviewee to comment: "*If you and I take 500 words to explain something, he'll take 100.*" **David Osnos** has earned "*the respect,*

loyalty and confidence" of a number of important clients in the DC area, commentators said. "*They look to him for wisdom and advice.*" The "*spectacularly gifted lawyer*" is perhaps best known for his dispute resolution expertise. This "*wonderful counselor and great advocate*" employs an "*extremely practical and result-oriented*" method in his work. **Richard Newman** is leading the firm's charge in PPP work, assisting many of DC's large-scale cultural institutions. He is said to have "*successfully carved a niche for himself*" in the area of real estate law that's linked to non-profit organizations, low-income housing and municipal finance. His careful style is also applied to bond financing, so much so that some consider him "*the go-to tax-exempt bond lawyer*" in DC.
The Clients: The practice is handling a public-private venture for the building of a new Frank Gehry-designed museum wing in suburban Maryland. It is assisting a hi-tech vaccine manufacturer on the development of its new site outside of DC. In addition, it also represents private equity funds in their investments, including the acquisition of non-performing and sub-performing loans secured by real estate

District of Columbia
Leading individuals (Real Estate)

1   EPSTIEN Jay *DLA Piper*, Washington, DC
    FRIES Joseph *Arent Fox*, Washington, DC
    KLEIN Frederick *DLA Piper*, Washington, DC
    ROSENTHAL Barry *Bingham McCutchen*, Washington, DC

2   BEYDA Richard *Grossberg Yochelson*, Washington, DC
    GOODWIN Michael *Arnold & Porter*, Washington, DC
    GREENSTEIN Abraham *Greenstein*, Washington, DC
    HUMES Gary *Arnold & Porter*, Washington, DC
    OSNOS David *Arent Fox*, Washington, DC
    PARMLEY Bruce *Hogan & Hartson*, Washington, DC
    SEGAL Earl *Akin Gump*, Washington, DC
    VOLLMANN Alan *Holland & Knight*, Washington, DC
    WEISEL Sheldon *Goulston & Storrs*, Washington, DC
    WILLNER Keith *Mayer Brown*, Washington, DC

3   DWYER Jeffry *Greenberg Traurig*, Washington, DC
    ENGEL John *Shaw Pittman*, Washington, DC
    HENNEBURG Frank *Akin Gump*, Washington, DC
    HOROWITZ Philip *Venable*, Washington, DC
    KAHN David *Holland & Knight*, Washington, DC
    NEWMAN Richard *Arent Fox*, Washington, DC
    PLANNING Anne *Shaw Pittman*, Washington, DC
    PORTER Stephen *Arnold & Porter*, Washington, DC
    SPARTIN Debbie *Shaw Pittman*, Washington, DC
    TUCKER Stefan *Venable*, Washington, DC
    WEISS Erica *Bingham McCutchen*, Washington, DC

4   GAGE Robert *Covington & Burling*, Washington, DC
    KING Carol *Hogan & Hartson*, Washington, DC
    LUCHS Richard *Greenstein Delorme*, Washington, DC
    MILLER Lawrence *Grossberg Yochelson*, Washington, DC
    MOYER Dennis *Goulston & Storrs*, Washington, DC
    ROGERS Ed *Nixon Peabody*, Washington, DC
    ZAX Leonard *Latham & Watkins*, Washington, DC

Leading individuals
(Real Estate: Zoning/Land Use)

1   QUIN Whayne *Holland & Knight*, Washington, DC

2   DWYER Maureen *Shaw Pittman*, Washington, DC
    FEOLA Phil *Shaw Pittman*, Washington, DC
    GLASGOW Norman *Holland & Knight*, Washington, DC
    PRINCE Allison *Shaw Pittman*, Washington, DC

Individuals are listed alphabetically in each band.

assets. The team advised Public Broadcasting Service (PBS) on the relocation of its headquarters, financing the cost of some building improvements with tax-exempt bonds. It also represented the Corporate Executive Board Company on the lease of its new headquarter at the 620,000 sq-ft Waterview project under development in Rosslyn, Virginia.

DLA Piper Rudnick Gray Cary US LLP
See firm details p.765

The Firm: The nationwide real estate practice, which is led from DC, concentrates on leading sophisticated commercial real estate transactions. This work focuses on acquisitions, dispositions, financings and leasings in preference to land use or zoning work. Although the DC office is not the largest in the table, the overall quality is considered one of the best *"when you look at the client base, the level of expertise and work that is carried out."* Its pragmatic attorneys *"know how to get a transaction done"* and frequently link up with individuals from other offices as needed. The practice also assists on investments in the DC market from German and other large pension fund investors. Other features include the purchase and sale of large buildings, related financings and major development projects. The clients' view this firm as *"excellent and deep."*

The Lawyers: **Jay Epstien** (see p.441) is national chair of the firm's robust real estate practice group. Described by peers as *"a lawyers' lawyer,"* he represents the Bureau of National Affairs (BNA) on the evaluation of its corporate headquarters facilities and possible relocation. *"He just does the entire package,"* said commentators, who also portrayed him as *"a talented, honorable, smart and hard-working guy."* His direct approach *"inspires confidence in his clients."* **Frederick Klein** (see p.451) represents both owners and lenders on acquisitions, dispositions and financings. *"First and foremost a bright and technically capable lawyer,"* he advised Boston Properties in the formation of a complicated joint venture with New England Development, Archstone-Smith and May Department Stores to develop a new mixed-use project. Observers also highlighted his legal agility, *"both in terms of knowing what's important and what's not, as well as being able to manage the situation."* Coupled with *"a good sense of humor,"* he *"can navigate and manage all deal situations."*

The Clients: The group represented SEB ImmoInvest in a simultaneous tax-free exchange transaction involving the $292 million acquisition of Two Park Avenue in New York City and also the sale of 1333 New Hampshire Avenue in DC for more than $100 million. It assisted MCI as the owner in bankruptcy of a Virginia office complex in a 540,000 sq ft lease with the Transportation Security Administration (TSA). The practice also advised both sellers Acacia Life and lenders Wells Fargo Bank in the sale of an historic two-building complex with adjacent development rights for $125 million. Other clients include: Bureau of National Affairs; Cisco Systems; Jones Lang LaSalle; New York Life; Prudential and Smith Commercial/Vornado.

Holland & Knight LLP
See firm details p.1352

The Firm: This *"all-encompassing"* department is blessed with one of the largest real estate groups in DC, ably tackling complex issues on a nationwide basis. It has increased the residential component of its work as a result of clients moving into this area in preference to capital markets. In addition, a greater proportion of its practice is now devoted to the execution of multiuse urban retail projects in preference to trophy buildings. For example, it acted for a prominent Wall Street real estate fund on the redevelopment of the Brickyard Mall retail development in Chicago and separately represented Florida Rock Properties in seeking approval for a proposed project covering more than a million sq ft featuring a hotel, residences, offices and retail on the banks of the Anacostia River. The team is said to occupy *"an important space in the market representing people before the DC government"* while remaining best known for its zoning practice.

The Lawyers: *"Just a crackerjack,"* **Alan Vollmann** (see p.473) is considered by some to be one of *"the finest real estate leasing attorneys"* in DC. His expertise led others to acknowledge that he is *"almost a leasing lawyer to other lawyers. If there is ever a complicated situation in a lease, it's Vollmann who pops up."* His success was attributed to *"an extraordinary ability to grasp minute details in a major transaction."* He counsels the John Akridge Companies in the 1.4 million sq ft development above Union Station to provide office, hotel facilities and a new intermodal transportation hub for Amtrak among other services. Former chair of the firm's real estate group, **David Kahn** (see p.449) primarily represents lenders. A strong advocate with a *"toughnosed"* negotiating style, he is respected as a *"talented and extremely smart"* financing practitioner. Named as a *"key go-to person for complicated, litigious zoning matters,"* **Whayne Quin** (see p.463) acts as special counsel to Fannie Mae on continuing zoning and land use matters relating to the Waterside Mall campus. His expertise, bolstered from his past experience as head of the Zoning Commission, is *"massive,"* interviewees said. *"He has zoned just about every main building in DC."* Such knowledge culminates in the necessary contacts and the adroitness to *"figure out a practical, politically effective solution."* **Norman Glasgow** (see p.444) also concentrates on zoning and probably *"understands the District processes better than the District does,"* observers said. His *"smart and effective"* methodology enables him to demonstrate efficiency on such projects as the $100 million transaction to acquire the historic Watergate Hotel and convert it to luxury cooperative apartments; he advised owner/developer Monument Realty, in partnership with Lehman Brothers, on the zoning and land use aspects of the project. His colleague and national real estate chair Chad Tiedemann also played a key role.

The Clients: The group represented Roadside Development and Madison Marquette on the development and leasing of a high-profile retail and residential renovation and new construction project on top of the Tenley Metro Station.

The team also counseled the Government of Sweden on the development and acquisition of a new embassy building on a prominent site near the Potomac River. Other clients include: John Akridge Companies; Cellular Telecommunications & Internet Association; Collier Shannon; CTTWB; CVS; Fannie Mae; Georgetown Renaissance; The Johns Hopkins University; Kodiak Properties; Metropolitan Life Insurance; Monument Realty; NGP Capital Partners; Protestant Episcopal Cathedral Foundation; Shell Hydrogen; Thrivent Financial for Lutherans and Waterfront Associates.

Shaw Pittman
See firm details p.490

The Firm: A jewel in this practice's crown is its involvement in the military housing subsector. It has assisted developers with more than $1 billion worth of US Navy housing privatizations since 2000, including those involving PPPs. It possesses extensive experience in multifamily housing transactions, including acquisitions and dispositions of existing properties, joint ventures and financings, among other deals. Its retail leasing business increased substantially as a result of its experience as principal outside counsel for one of the largest REITs in the USA. This is in addition to one-off leases for commercial enterprises. The practice also represents a number of private, single-asset REITs in the disposition of their properties through the sale of REIT shares. Additionally, it regularly advises landlords in the negotiation of major law firm leases and on financially troubled tenants, lease restructurings and the enforcement of landlord rights as related to bankruptcy proceedings. At time of press the firm announced its merger with Pillsbury Winthrop to form Pillsbury Winthrop Shaw Pittman.

The Lawyers: The team comprises a number of key attorneys ably led by the skilled and pragmatic negotiator **John Engel** (see p.441), who chairs the firm's real estate and bankruptcy practice group. "*Diligent and focused,*" Anne Planning (see p.462) and **Debbie Spartin** (see p.469) gained plaudits for the close attention they devote to their leasing work. Zoning and municipal law specialist **Maureen Dwyer** (see p.440) "*knows her subject matter upside down and backwards.*" Her no-nonsense approach wins respect in the market, and her position is further bolstered by her strong links to the community. "*She is wired into everybody,*" one commentator said. She specializes in advising nonprofit groups, universities and private schools. Her colleague **Phil Feola** (see p.442) also specializes in zoning law, attracting a loyal clientele with his "*get-it-done*" attitude. **Allison Prince** (see p.463) is a new addition to the tables following recommendations for her knowledge of the sector, "*response time and contacts.*"

The Clients: The team represented Lehman Brothers as underwriter's real estate and environmental counsel on the privatization of Pearl Harbor's US Navy housing. It has represented Fannie Mae on more than 1,000 low-income housing tax credit transactions to provide affordable housing nationwide. It worked with two nonprofit entities to develop both a new property for the Shakespeare Theatre and a new headquarters building for the International Union of Bricklayers and Allied Craftworkers. The firm also retains "*a nice stable of Northern Virginia developers*" and local businesses as clients, with technology and outsourcing singled out as important areas for the firm. Other clients include: Boston Properties; Clark Enterprises; Commercial Net Lease Realty; Corporate Office Properties Trust; Crescent Real Estate Equities Company; Federal Realty Investment Trust; The George Washington University; JBG Companies; The Mark Winkler Company; Penzance Properties; Saul Centers; Scottish Widows; T-Rex Capital and Vornado REIT.

Band 2

Arnold & Porter LLP
See firm details p.478

The Firm: This high-profile firm approaches real estate from a public policy perspective, frequently on a national basis. In addition to development projects, the team is one of several to have pursued the nascent but flourishing PPP sector. Key supplemental areas include Tax Increment Financings (TIFs) and large build-to-suit leases. It is involved in a significant number of headline transactions such as advising the JBG Companies on the development, construction and financing of the new 1.35 million sq ft Department of Transportation headquarters. Clients believe that the firm "*distinguishes itself with a well-experienced group and great depth of resources, particularly in extremely large transactions.*" They also praise the firm's abilities in major bond financings and extended lease negotiations involving the government.

The Lawyers: The team of "*talented and bright*" individuals maintains "*extremely consistent quality of work,*" industry sources said. **Michael Goodwin** (see p.445) advises on PPPs and is particularly adept at tax increment finance transactions, having assisted on the drafting of related legislation. He is also recommended for his municipal incentive work and capability on transferable development rights. "*One of the brightest lawyers in the city,*" he is commended for his "*practical and pragmatic*" approach. He worked with the publicly traded real estate investment trust Host Marriott nationwide in connection with many of its hotel acquisitions and dispositions throughout the USA. He also acted for The Kaempfer Company on the redevelopment of the Bowen Building.

Stephen Porter (see p.462) acted for purchaser DGB Enterprises on the acquisition of the Watergate office building and related securitized financing. On behalf of the Washington Baseball Club, he has worked with government officials and major league baseball officials in reviewing and finalizing a final site for its new stadium. He also fulfils a more global role in developing client relationships and delivering strategic advice on leading matters. "*Composed, smart and responsive,*" **Gary Humes** (see p.448) focuses on build-to-suit issues and large leases. "*Thoughtful, deliberate and unflappable,*" he impresses with his ability to "*solve, identify and resolve the big issues for his client.*" He represented the Kimpton Hotel and Restaurant Group in connection with the ground lease and redevelopment of the historic Tariff Building into the 170-room boutique Hotel Monaco.

The Clients: The group represents the District of Columbia on its disposition and redevelopment of the ten-acre Old Convention Center site and separately advises Gallery Place Associates – a joint venture between Western Development Company and the John Akridge Companies – on the development of a mixed-use downtown development. It continues to assist the Shakespeare Theatre in all aspects of the development of its new theatre, and marshaled private developer Gould Property through its effort to develop a 1,500-room convention center and hotel. Other clients include: DGB Enterprises; FFC Capital; Gould Property; Gudelsky Group; The Hillman Company; Horning Brothers; Host Marriott; John Akridge Company; The Kaempfer Company; KanAm; MeriStar Hospitality; National Health Museum; Professional Golf Association of America; Prometheus Real Estate Group; Truland Systems; Union Labor Life Insurance Company; SEC and Wilmer, Cutler & Pickering LLP.

Bingham McCutchen LLP

The Firm: The practice is a popular recommendation among clients for its "*integrity, focus and broad knowledge of transactional matters,*" particularly those with a more regional focus. The team works with lenders, owners and developers on transactions such as financings, acquisitions, joint ventures and leasings, among others. Its DC group is relatively small, but remains at the forefront of some major deals. It is "*integrated with an understanding of business issues,*" which makes its lawyers "*practical and wise counsel,*" interviewees said. Another drawing card is the firm's "*timely, balanced service*" and business focus.

The Lawyers: **Barry Rosenthal**, who is cochair of the group, splits his time between financing, acquisitions and joint ventures. Peers placed him "*on the cutting edge of transactions,*" partly bolstered by his sophisticated combination of business and legal skills. "*Balanced,*" *astute, careful and pragmatic,*" he is particularly suited for complex negotiations that require a "*thoughtful, articulate and calm*" demeanor, clients said. He represented JBG Companies on the purchase of the L'Enfant Plaza Hotel and office complex. **Erica Weiss** won client confidence for her ability to be "*tough as nails*" when required, clients said. She knows "*when to push hard, as well as when to back off.*" Weiss represented a real estate investment fund in connection with a $330 million loan secured by properties located across the country. In addition to the quality of its upper echelon of talent, the firm was also commended for its "*seamless support group,*" which comprises "*a good crop of associates.*"

The Clients: The department represented US Bank as agent on behalf of the lenders for a syndicated loan in relation to a large retail mall. It also advised lenders in connection with loans concerning several DC-area residential condominium conversion projects. Other clients include: Bank of America; The Bernstein Companies; First Washington Realty; GMAC- Residential Funding Corporation; JBG Companies; Paradigm Development; Perseus Realty; TA Associates Realty and Wells Fargo Bank.

Hogan & Hartson LLP

See firm details p.484

The Firm: The firm's large REIT and securities practice ensures regular involvement in a large number of real estate acquisitions. It also plays a prominent role on both sales and purchases in the resurgent hotel and hospitality market. Its "*depth of knowledge of the way the industry works*" often attracts clients, as does its "*prompt*" delivery of transaction advice. Combined with ample business acumen, the department was said by one client to be "*able to understand how we do things and what it is we look for in an investment.*" The group acted for Highland Hospitality Corporation on its complex $227 million acquisition of four hotels from Wyndham Hotel Corporation. The deal involved structuring and negotiation with Hyatt Hotels regarding management and operational agreements for the newly branded Hyatt Regency Wind Watch in Long Island.

The Lawyers: **Bruce Parmley** (see p.461) is well regarded by peers, who described his aptitude at conducting deals with a "*humorous, diligent and extremely pragmatic*" style and "*without one ounce of non-constructive input.*" Clients spoke of someone who "*counsels us as to what's important and possible and what's not,*" but who can also be "*pretty zealous in his arguments.*" He represented Exclusive Resorts on the formation and structuring of a joint venture project for the development of a $300 million private residential resort off Kapalua Bay on the island of Maui,

Hawaii. He also assists local developers and owners. **Carol Weld King** (see p.450) advised the Mohegan Tribal Gaming Authority, owner and operator of the Mohegan Sun Resort in Connecticut, in tender offers for $575 million in senior and subordinated financings, as well as joint venture investments for new casino and resort projects to be developed in Wisconsin and Washington.

The Clients: The team assisted UK-based Centurion Capital on the construction and development of the Mandarin Oriental, Prague, a new five-star hotel and spa located at an historically and archeologically significant site in the Czech capital. Another highlight involved Thayer Lodging Group as the sponsors of a newly formed private equity fund raising more than $200 million and targeting the acquisition of US hospitality assets. It also assisted Yale University on the formation and structuring of a multimillion-dollar hotel investment fund in conjunction with a major hotel operator. Other clients include Exclusive Resorts, Highland Hospitality Corporation and Mohegan Tribal Gaming Authority.

Band 3

Greenstein Delorme & Luchs

The Firm: This DC-based real estate specialist maintains a relatively small practice which is focused on its twin strengths – land use and transactional real estate – and linked to a significant leasing profile. It predominantly advises area owners and developers on such issues as housing and urban development, condominium conversion and regulatory proceedings.

The Lawyers: To many interviewees, **Abraham Greenstein** personifies the practice. He is respected as "*one of the old lions*" of real estate in DC. A "*hard-working, knowledgeable guy,*" he chiefly deals with commercial leasing, though a broader practice also features acquisition, development and financing. He utilizes an approach described as "*assiduous, without being aggressive.*" **Richard Luchs** parlays his real estate and litigation skills into a successful practice in the fair housing sector and in the specialized area of tenants' rights. Other lawyers seek his expertise on multifamily residential transactions.

The Clients: The practice assists commercial and residential real estate developers, construction contractors, property managers and real estate brokers.

Grossberg Yochelson Fox & Beyda

The Firm: This "*mature and sophisticated*" real estate specialist earned kudos for its efficient handling of the more traditional sort of work. It is one of the smallest practices in the table, yet maintains a high level of transactional activities

in areas such as acquisitions, developments, and leases and loans on behalf of borrowers and lenders. Commentators noted that it represents "*almost every developer in the city*" among other types of clients.

The Lawyers: **Richard Beyda** brings a "*wonderful perspective and calm demeanor*" to proceedings. This established practitioner enjoys an extensive roster of entrepreneurial developers and successfully applies a "*genteel, patient and nonconfrontational*" approach to his work. Interviewees underlined the team's "*practical, problem-solving*" skills, illustrated by key players such as **Lawrence Miller**.

The Clients: The group assists borrowers and lenders, building owners and developers, landlords and tenants.

Mayer, Brown, Rowe & Maw LLP

See firm details p.771

The Firm: Considered "*a great firm nationwide*" for real estate, the practice is enthusiastically recommended by commentators as "*good for anything, the whole gamut,*" with corporate real estate and REIT work singled out as its most salient features. While the practice also maintains a strong profile in acquisitions and development projects related to the hospitality industry, it does not appear, according to observers, to have deep bench strength in construction and land use and zoning. The "*high competency level*" of the DC team complements the firm's international network, which often attracts cross-border proceedings.

The Lawyers: **Keith Willner** (see p.475) emerged as the most prominent name in this "*excellent*" group. He acted on behalf of a major private equity fund in the $197 million acquisition and three-tiered financing of a multifamily apartment and condominium project in Alexandria, Virginia. A "*thorough*" adviser, he participated in a number of similar deals for publicly traded REITs, developers and pension funds. He also worked with a national pension fund adviser in a prominent building lease in Howard County, Maryland, to a major defense contractor.

The Clients: The team represented a national office developer on the development, sale and financing of a significant DC mixed-use project. It also acted for a lender in the purchase through bankruptcy auction proceedings of an office building in Tyson's Corner. Examples of its clientele include: Archstone-Smith; Berwind Property Group; Carlyle Realty Group; CarrAmerica Realty; CTF Hotels and Resorts; Fremont Investment & Loan; Kennedy Associates Real Estate Counsel; Kimsouth Realty; MetLife; New York Life; Starwood Capital Group and the State Board of Administration of Florida.

Band 4

Akin Gump Strauss Hauer & Feld LLP

See firm details p.477

The Firm: The practice is constructed around a real estate finance core and noted for its assistance to lenders. A broader range of expertise also includes commercial leasing matters and dispute resolutions. Globally, the firm has recently acquired lateral hires to bolster its cross-border profile, which also reflects its international clientele. Though inevitably linked to other practice areas at the firm, the DC real estate team gained credibility through an established reputation that also includes specialist expertise. For example, one practitioner boasts a niche in buying and selling servicing rights while others offer expertise on tenancy in common (TIC) proceedings.

The Lawyers: The *"talented and practical"* **Earl Segal** (see p.467) garnered respect in acquisitions, developments and financings. *"Bright, hard working and honest,"* he often represents developers, among others, on retail and hotel purchases and sales. He also serves as general counsel to the Greater Washington Board of Trade – the largest business organization in the region – on matters relating to political action committees, including corporate governance and real estate issues. Competitors viewed **Frank Henneburg** (see p.447) as *"an excellent real estate lawyer."* His wide-ranging practice incorporates a variety of real estate finance assistance, including loan restructuring. This *"knowledgeable, meticulous and careful"* operator also offers advice to institutional lenders on equity joint ventures with developers.

The Clients: Investment banks; contractors; hospitals; institutional lenders; domestic and offshore investors; major public and private corporations; developers; insurance groups; pension funds; REITs and REMICs (real estate mortgage investment conduits).

Covington & Burling

See firm details p.481

The Firm: The real estate team is a key component of this firm's overall profile, which remains resolutely a corporate and litigation force. This practice is focusing on PPPs in common with many firms in the DC market, notably development and multifaceted deals involving the public sector. It possesses recognized expertise in the nonprofit sector and tends to represent public entities and organizations rather than developers. The firm was also distinguished for its niche in advising on stadia and related projects.

The Lawyers: Sole partner **Bob Gage** (see p.443) is well known for work on behalf of non-profit organizations, including their real estate concerns. For example, he is principal outside counsel to the Carolina Communities Development Group, a land acquisition and develop-ment company, on a 600-acre project that comprises 2500 residential units, a shopping center and golf course, in Raleigh, North Carolina. He also counsels clients such as the American Trucking Association and the American Council of Life Insurers on the leasing or development of their headquarters facilities.

The Clients: The firm recently handled a $3.3 billion restructuring and secured asset refinancing for Goodyear and separately advised The JBG Companies on a major office lease. In the nonprofit sector, the team counseled the Union Station Redevelopment Corporation, which owns and manages the ground lease on Union Station. The firm is also assisting on a $25 million parking garage project and is advising on the development of air rights over an adjacent railroad yard. Other clients include: American Trucking Associations; Carolina Communities Development Group; GOJO Industries; National Capital Revitalization Corporation and Ourisman's World of Ford.

Goulston & Storrs

The Firm: The Boston-based firm is making inroads into the DC market, mainly through some recent lateral hires that significantly raised the profile of its team. Though somewhat over-shadowed by the prominence of its Massachu-setts team, the DC group is making an impact through its transactional expertise. In that sphere, it has helped orchestrate various acquisitions, developments and financings.

The Lawyers: **Sheldon Weisel** is frequently cited as one of the best leasing lawyers in DC, although his experience covers a wider range of real estate specialties. Noted for his technical ability, he gained client confidence as a capable and respected figure in the market. **Dennis Moyer** is considered an *"exceptional real estate lawyer"* whose practice centers on transactional and leasing work. *"He has all the knowledge and the experience, plus the judgment to go with it,"* interviewees said.

The Clients: Contractors; corporate tenants; financial institutions; hotel operators; insurance companies; owners and developers; real estate managers and brokers.

Nixon Peabody LLP

See firm details p.1361

The Firm: The department boasts a long-established and significant syndication practice, advising on equity investment in real estate. It provides strong, underlying advice to clients on tax credit transactions and the related structuring of such transactions. In addition, it marshals companies through regulatory proceedings and workouts of troubled transactions. The practice also possesses a strong affordable housing practice, advising multifamily housing developers, financial institutions and public housing agencies.

The Lawyers: Regarded as a dealmaker, **Ed Rogers** (see p.465) advises on a spectrum of real estate development and commercial finance work. His focus on the development of large-scale, mixed-use projects also gained distinction.

The Clients: Developers; direct and secondary investors; entertainment and communications companies; hotel and resort operators; major financial institutions; museum operators; national and regional retailers; not-for-profit groups; public agencies; real estate developers; syndicators and trade associations.

Venable LLP

The Firm: The group assists its clients on a full range of real estate requirements, garnering particular applause for its low income tax credit practice. Real estate development provides another leading tranche of work, and sees the firm advising buyers, sellers and financiers of such projects. Its repertoire has included office, hotel, warehouse and multifamily residential developments. Transactional expertise involves pension fund portfolios, joint ventures and stock purchase agreements in addition to a specialty niche in tax-related real estate issues.

The Lawyers: **Philip Horowitz** represented building landlord Louis Dreyfus Property Group on its lease negotiation with Ernst & Young pertaining to a 130,000 sq ft project on New York Avenue in DC. **Stefan Tucker** is particularly well regarded in the market for his tax-related work among a *"broad range of capabilities."* He weds an occasionally adversarial approach with a professorial style as appropriate to the negotiation, a tactic valued by loyal clients.

The Clients: The department acted for MGP Real Estate on its $40 million divestment of the Metroplex office complex in Landover, Maryland. It has also advised anchor client Fannie Mae with numerous purchases of pools of loans secured by multifamily properties; these included a $400 million credit facility for a major operator of manufactured housing communities. Other clients include: The Penrose Group, Louis Dreyfus Property Group and the Worldgate Retail Mall.

Other Notable Practitioners

Jeffry Dwyer (see p.440) of Greenberg Traurig proficiently combines corporate and real estate experience to deliver transactional expertise. He is notably involved in setting up international REITs and conducting large-scale real estate transactions in the DC area. On behalf of New York pension advisory group Sentinel Real Estate Corporation, he helped frame its dual REIT structure involving multifamily apart-ments. **Leonard Zax** of Latham & Watkins heads the firm's DC real estate group and advises REITs, private investment funds and financial institutions on real estate transactions both within DC and further afield.

TAX

District of Columbia
Leading firms (Tax)

1. SKADDEN, ARPS, SLATE, MEAGHER *Washington, DC*
2. CAPLIN & DRYSDALE *Washington, DC*
   MCKEE NELSON LLP *Washington, DC*
3. BAKER & MCKENZIE *Washington, DC*
   IVINS, PHILLIPS & BARKER *Washington, DC*
   MCDERMOTT WILL & EMERY *Washington, DC*
   MILLER & CHEVALIER CHARTERED *Washington, DC*
4. FRIED, FRANK, HARRIS, SHRIVER *Washington, DC*
   KING & SPALDING LLP *Washington, DC*
   STEPTOE & JOHNSON LLP *Washington, DC*
   SUTHERLAND ASBILL & BRENNAN *Washington, DC*
5. DEWEY BALLANTINE LLP *Washington, DC*
   FRESHFIELDS BRUCKHAUS *Washington, DC*
   LATHAM & WATKINS LLP *Washington, DC*
   MORGAN, LEWIS & BOCKIUS LLP *Washington, DC*
   SHEARMAN & STERLING *Washington, DC*
   WILMER CUTLER PICKERING HALE *Washington, DC*

Leading individuals (Tax)

1. GOLDBERG Fred *Skadden Arps*, Washington, DC
   OOSTERHUIS Paul *Skadden Arps*, Washington, DC
   ROSENBLOOM David *Caplin & Drysdale*, Washington, DC
2. GIDEON Kenneth *Skadden Arps*, Washington, DC
   LIBIN Jerome *Sutherland Asbill*, Washington, DC
   MAGEE John *McKee Nelson*, Washington, DC
   MCKEE William *McKee Nelson*, Washington, DC
   NELSON William *McKee Nelson*, Washington, DC
   SCHNEIDER Leslie *Ivins Phillips*, Washington, DC
   SILVERMAN Mark *Steptoe & Johnson*, Washington, DC
   TERR Leonard *Baker & McKenzie*, Washington, DC
3. BELLER Herb *Sutherland Asbill & Brennan*, Washington, DC
   BENNETT Mary *Baker & McKenzie*, Washington, DC
   CULBERTSON Robert *King & Spalding*, Washington, DC
   GRANWELL Alan *Ivins Phillips*, Washington, DC
   MAY Gregory *Freshfields Bruckhaus*, Washington, DC
   MOORE Robert *Miller & Chevalier*, Washington, DC
   OLSON Pamela *Skadden Arps*, Washington, DC
   PARI Joseph *Dewey Ballantine*, Washington, DC
   SWENSON David *Baker & McKenzie*, Washington, DC
   WELLEN Robert *Ivins Phillips*, Washington, DC
   WEST Philip *Steptoe & Johnson*, Washington, DC
   WILCOX Gary *Morgan Lewis*, Philadelphia
   WILLIAMS B John *Shearman & Sterling*, Washington, DC
4. BAUMBUSCH Peter *Gibson Dunn*, Washington, DC
   FARMER Scott *McKee Nelson*, Washington, DC
   GIBBS Lawrence *Miller & Chevalier*, Washington, DC
   HYDE Terrill *Wilmer Cutler*, Washington, DC
   KADEN Alan *Fried Frank*, Washington, DC
   KAFKA Gerald *Latham & Watkins*, Washington, DC
   KLEIN Kenneth *Mayer Brown*, Washington, DC
   MANN Phillip *Miller & Chevalier*, Washington, DC
   RIEDY James *McDermott Will*, Washington, DC
   ROADY Celia *Morgan Lewis*, Washington, DC
   RUDNICK Robert *Shearman & Sterling*, Washington, DC
   WELLS Stephen *McDermott Will*, Washington, DC
   WIACEK Raymond *Jones Day*, Washington, DC

Firms and individuals are listed alphabetically in each band.

Band 1

Skadden, Arps, Slate, Meagher & Flom LLP & Affiliates
See firm details p.1372

The Firm: *"Unquestionably the leader in the field,"* according to interviewees, Skadden Arps is placed at the top of the tax table. Proving to be *"a class-A tax team run by lawyers who know how the market operates,"* sources agreed its practice has *"supremacy in terms of magnitude and quality compared to its competitors,"* particularly when considering international capability. The team of almost 40 tax attorneys has amazed onlookers with its capacity to handle any kind of tax issue; rivals point to the firm's huge corporate client base and the group's ability to deal effectively with transactional and planning matters. Recently more emphasis has been placed on IRS work, and a sizable tax controversy practice is on offer to clients, be they large corporations, individuals or estate trusts. Clients commend the group's well-developed dispute resolution skills, attributing these to both the team's litigation and policy expertise.
The Lawyers: *"True gentleman"* **Fred Goldberg** (see p.444) is, according to clients, a *"wonderful facilitator."* He represents several of the world's largest financial institutions in a variety of governance, administrative and planning matters. *"Good-humored"* **Paul Oosterhuis** (see p.460) *"brings unusual depth of analysis and insight to his interpretation of the most complex international tax matters."* He recently advised Schering-Plough in its collaboration agreements with Bayer in the USA and Japan. Furthermore, he acted for Lockheed Martin in the sale of its interest in Intelsat, and advised Shell in its restructuring. **Kenneth Gideon** (see p.444) has a broad grasp of tax work and *"possesses terrific problem-solving skills,"* clients say. His contemporaries hailed his *"sharp intellect"* and his *"tremendous gift"* on the controversy side. Gideon was involved in the representation of client FedEx in a tax refund action in the Federal District Court – Western District of Tennessee, the first case to address the deductibility of aircraft engine maintenance costs and a major victory for the air carrier industry in general. *"Top-drawer"* **Pamela Olson** (see p.460) *"brings a great deal of depth to the team."* She counsels on a range of matters relating to domestic and international taxation, having also served as assistant secretary for tax policy at the Treasury Department and been the first woman to chair the ABA Section of Taxation.
The Clients: Sample clients include FedEx, Schering Plough, Lockheed Martin and Levi Strauss.

Band 2

Caplin & Drysdale
The Firm: This tax boutique produces *"remarkable"* work, and this, say clients, is due in no small part to its *"legendary attorneys."* Recently the firm branched out into complex commercial litigation, receiving plaudits for its asbestos litigation; for tax litigation it is certainly very highly respected. The group recently advised a US multinational corporation on a series of multiyear controversies concerning, among other things, foreign tax credits, transfer pricing and foreign exchange issues. In another recent matter it advised a client on the correction and revision of the complex and long-neglected structure of a US-owned, Asia-targeted venture capital fund.
The Lawyers: *"Scholarly"* **David Rosenbloom** was hailed by one of his many fans as *"the country's finest international tax lawyer."* Others confirm that his *"extraordinary mind"* enables him to *"put pieces together that the rest of us struggle to keep up with."* This *"extremely loyal and decent"* attorney focuses mainly on international work, but also incorporates a significant amount of controversy, derivatives and financial institutions work into his busy agenda.
The Clients: The team acts for a broad range of financial institutions and large national and international corporations.

McKee Nelson LLP
See firm details p.489

The Firm: Rival firms acknowledge that McKee Nelson has developed *"one of the principal tax practices in the state,"* while the firm's clients applaud the group for its *"terrific efforts"* and its accomplishment in building *"such a prompt, effective and strong practice in such a short period of time."* Among the tax group's success stories is its representation of GlaxoSmithKline Holdings (Americas) on a large transfer-pricing case in the US Tax Court. In another matter it achieved a victory for a subsidiary of GE Capital, where the federal district court in Connecticut ordered the IRS to refund tax deposits of over $62 million. It also successfully represented Dow Chemical in a federal district court case that sustained the company's entitlement to federal income tax benefits arising from its corporate-owned life insurance policies.
The Lawyers: *"Energetic"* **William McKee** (see p.456) is, according to interviewees, *"untouchable in the partnership tax arena."* Clients love his *"flamboyant style"* and say he has *"achieved miracles within his firm."* McKee deals primarily with Fortune 500 companies, often involved in large joint ventures, though he also works closely with his partners in advising clients on the interaction between partnership tax provisions

and the international and corporate provisions of the Internal Revenue Code (IRC). **John Magee** (see p.455) has a reputation as "*one of the best tax controversy players in the country.*" Clients value his careful, "*technical approach*" and the way he "*eliminates the opponent systematically.*" He also deals with international tax issues, including transfer pricing, and has extensive experience in a broad spectrum of income tax planning, IRS administrative proceedings and tax litigation. Former chief counsel for the IRS, **William Nelson** (see p.459) is "*as tough as nails;*" clients insist "*you just can't go wrong with his counsel.*" He has been working on large litigation and enforcement matters during the past year, his most notable recent victory being the TIFD III-E dispute, in which he was involved in the representation of GE in its $62 million dispute with the IRS. "*Exceptional*" **Scott Farmer** (see p.441) is said to have "*wonderful technical skills.*" He is involved in international tax planning for large corporations in a range of industries, and is thought to be equally adept at inbound and outbound transactions, including capital market transactions, structuring joint ventures and foreign tax planning on the disposal of overseas businesses.

The Clients: Dow Chemical, GlaxoSmithKline Holdings (Americas) and GE Capital are among the firm's prestigious clients.

Band 3

Baker & McKenzie
See firm details p.761

The Firm: This worldwide player is well known for its "*bedrock strength in international tax.*" The 25-attorney DC group is additionally known to clients for "*its appetite to always be the best at what they do.*" The team deals with a vast array of issues including tax planning, transfer pricing, and tax dispute resolution and litigation. Clients acknowledge also the "*continuously increasing strength of the team*" in tax treaty work.

The Lawyers: "*Outstanding*" **Len Terr** (see p.471) is considered "*the pick of the crop*" in the international tax arena. Active involvement in controversies, lobbying and tax planning has earned him "*respect and admiration*" from clients and rivals. Above all else clients rate his ability to deal with any issue put before him. Hot on his heels is **Mary Bennett** (see p.433), who "*although a tad more quiet, is amazingly bright and decisively accurate.*" Very different in character is "*live wire*" **David Swenson**, who focuses primarily on transfer pricing, controversy and tax planning. Researchers noted the shower of praise for Swenson from market observers – clients love working with him, rivals want to hire him.

The Clients: The Clorox Company; AOL (now Time Warner); Boeing; Honeywell; Lucent Technologies; Subaru and Transamerica

Ivins, Phillips & Barker
The Firm: This 40-lawyer boutique is a notable feature of the DC tax landscape. Interviewees waxed lyrical about a team, which they say is "*a collection of the crème de la crème,*" with "*a fantastic grasp of the issues at hand.*" Over the past year the firm has devoted a great deal of effort to the area of accounting method changes and the implementation of newly introduced regulations.

The Lawyers: Clients describe **Leslie Schneider** as an "*insightful and creative*" tax lawyer. He particularly shines on the inventory taxation area and dedicates a fair amount of his time to accounting method changes and the implementation of the new INDOPCO regulations. **Robert Wellen** impressed clients with his "*wealth of experience and splendid mind.*" Although he continues to advise on corporate transactions and spin-offs, he now concentrates more on restructurings and controversies. Wellen represented Visa in connection with the US tax planning aspects of the restructuring and spin-off of its European business into a separate company, including the preparation of tax sharing arrangements, obtaining a tax ruling from IRS, and working out the disparities between UK and US law with UK tax counsel. Clients commended former PwC "*star*" **Alan Granwell**, who also dealt with the representation of Visa and has advised several foreign corporations on how to structure their US distribution activities in a business and tax-efficient manner.

The Clients: The group represents several Fortune 500 clients and provides counsel to Grant Thornton, RSM McGladrey, Crowe Chizek & Company, American Express Tax & Business Services, BDO Seidman, BKD LLP and MHM Business Services.

McDermott Will & Emery
See firm details p.773

The Firm: With around 25 lawyers in its DC tax group, the Chicago-headquartered firm offers a "*high-quality*" service. Clients and peers were full of praise for this "*uniformly outstanding player,*" adding that "*its attorneys have the ability to think outside of the box.*" The broad practice deals with a volume of international transactions for major multinational corporations as well as providing expert counsel on domestic M&A, dispositions and lobbying. Away from transactional work, its "*absolutely first-rate litigation expertise seems second to none,*" clients say. The team appears regularly before the IRS and has "*the capacity and talent to deal with the most complex of matters.*"

The Lawyers: "*Rock-solid*" **James Riedy** (see p.464) concentrates his "*highly technical*" practice on international matters. These include a broad range of tax issues for US-based multinationals, be this the tax aspects of structuring and financing acquisitions or the restructuring of

existing businesses. Furthermore, he has impressed sources with his know-how in matters concerning transfer pricing, including tangible and intangible property, cost-sharing agreements and documentary compliance requirements. "*Smart and thoughtful*" **Stephen Wells** (see p.474), partner in charge of the DC tax practice, is "*someone to take seriously.*" He has advised on the taxation aspects of several transactions involving US and foreign corporations, and is adept at all manner of acquisitions, disposals, reorganizations and other restructurings and corporate ventures.

The Clients: Clients include public multinational corporations as well as privately owned companies.

Miller & Chevalier Chartered
The Firm: The group has long been viewed as "*a strong specialist,*" and with over 50 tax attorneys it maintains its position as "*one of the most remarkable players in the field.*" Though the team handles all aspects of corporate tax, tax policy, international tax, tax accounting and financial products, clients were particularly impressed with the group's efforts to "*excel at tax controversy.*" More recently it has made a push to resolve controversies with the IRS.

The Lawyers: Senior figure **Robert Moore** is "*a fine tax litigator*" and widely associated with the fact that "*he's won a lot of big cases.*" He is also closely associated with client Exxon Mobil, for whom he won many of those big cases. More junior colleagues find him to be a valuable mentor. Another very established name is that of **Lawrence Gibbs**, who as a former commissioner of the IRS is steeped in its culture. In private practice he is terrific, interviewees confirmed, pointing to his "*good judgment*" and years of experience. **Phillip Mann**, now no longer chair of the firm, is active in the tax practice on both the advisory and contentious sides. On policy issues he has a wealth of experience, benefiting from having served at the Treasury Department, sat on IRS advisory panels and chaired the ABA Tax Section.

The Clients: Clients include Black & Decker and Global Crossing plus many other big names.

Band 4

Fried, Frank, Harris, Shriver & Jacobson LLP
See firm details p.1349

The Firm: Sources applauded this "*fine global outfit,*" describing it as "*home to some of the best tax experts in the country.*" The team prides itself on being able to draw on resources from its New York office and is felt to offer an energetic New York-style tax practice with a primarily transactional focus. It recently advised BellSouth, parent of Cingular Wireless, in its acquisition of

AT&T Wireless Services for $41 billion. In a different matter it offered counsel to The Rouse Company in its acquisition by General Growth Properties for $12.6 billion.

The Lawyers: Chair **Alan Kaden** (see p.449) has for the most part a transactional background and deals with major public and private corporations and partnerships, supporting both domestic and international transactions. Market sources spoke well of his efficiency and responsiveness, saying he is "*a well-rounded and bright attorney.*" He represents clients in both transactional and litigation scenarios, and acts for names such as El Paso, Cargill and Bell-South. Commentators made a point of celebrating the "*genius*" of Martin Ginsburg, a well-respected professor of law at Georgetown Law Center and of counsel in Fried Frank's tax department.

The Clients: BellSouth; The Rouse Company; Northrop Grumman; WPP Group and Permira.

King & Spalding LLP
See firm details p.635

The Firm: This team maintains its long-standing reputation for "*top-notch*" tax advice. Its DC tax practice is well known for working closely with clients' own in-house tax advisers and staff to resolve complex international tax issues. The group deals with both US and non-US industrial companies and financial institutions on a broad range of matters arising from structural tax planning, cross-border transactions and audits. It has a niche in the US foreign tax credit and anti-deferral rules. The group recently lost "*transfer pricing guru*" Mike Durst, who returned to PwC; however, new lateral hires from the Treasury Department and other firms in private practice have strengthened the group's international and financial products expertise.

The Lawyers: "*Technical*" **Robert Culbertson** (see p.438) is, according to clients, "*a very intelligent, decent and incredibly thorough person.*" He is the former associate chief counsel at the IRS and now focuses on international tax planning and controversy resolution for a variety of clients. He recently advised a Fortune 50 industrial company before the IRS regarding a request for technical advice, and dealt with a further Fortune 50 company concerning tax planning for acquisitions and financing transactions. Additionally, he has dealt with a number of US and foreign banks on cross-border funding transactions.

The Clients: The group advises many Fortune 500 companies, financial institutions and other international and domestic clients.

Steptoe & Johnson LLP
See firm details p.492

The Firm: Peers and clients paid tribute to this "*thoughtful and uniformly balanced practice.*" In recent times the group represented a coalition of financial services companies in order to obtain an interpretive agreement, and advised on tax-advantaged structures involving foreign tax credit planning and double-dip financing. It also offers strategic advice concerning interaction with the IRS and the Treasury Department on a range of international tax matters, as well as on the tax opportunities and traps created by recent tax legislation. Another specialty is advice on tax-efficient structures for foreign investment in US real estate.

The Lawyers: "*Extremely clued-up*" **Mark Silverman** (see p.468) "*thinks hard and plays hard.*" A "*prolific speaker and writer,*" he predominantly works in the areas of audit and controversy, planning and transactional tax. One of his recent matters involved a significant tax controversy relating to the interaction of the foreign tax credit, Controlled Foreign Corporation (CFC) and transfer-pricing rules. **Philip West** (see p.475), former Treasury International Tax Counsel, has "*a brilliant mind.*" This has led to a reputation for "*finding best solution possible.*" He focuses mainly on international tax issues, primarily transactional in nature, and he advises both domestic and foreign clients.

The Clients: The group offers counsel to venture capital groups, tax-exempt organizations and corporations.

Sutherland Asbill & Brennan LLP
See firm details p.494

The Firm: This "*sophisticated*" group is built of "*smart and professional*" attorneys who tackle a broad range of tax matters relating to a variety of industries. It is particularly commended for the solid tax litigation and controversy advice though it also counsels in corporate, international and partnership taxation as well as advising on legislation, accounting and state and local tax.

The Lawyers: **Jerome Libin** (see p.453) has "*earned a place at the very top,*" clients say. In one of the controversies he handled recently for State Farm he secured his client a $57 million refund under the alternative minimum tax rules. "*Brilliant*" **Herb Beller** (see p.433) is, according to competitors, "*a serious thinker who recognizes the issues at hand.*" The former chair of the ABA Tax Section is said to be "*a joy to work with.*" He was recently involved in offering tax advice for the structuring of a complex nine-figure LBO transaction involving a foreign-controlled US company and performed the same role for a multinational company involved in an even larger financing. In a different matter he represented a public company in two tax controversies, each involving nine-figure proposed tax deficiencies.

The Clients: GM; Hershey Foods; Honeywell and Altria Group.

Band 5

Dewey Ballantine LLP
See firm details p.1347

The Firm: Despite the relatively small size of its DC tax practice, Dewey Ballantine maintains a desirable reputation in transactional and planning matters as well as tax controversy. The department provides ongoing advice to Life-Point Hospitals with respect to transactions and tax planning. Attorneys here also act as primary tax litigation counsel to Deutsche Bank and Deutsche Bank Alex Brown, and are representing both entities in tax shelter-related litigations. PG&E turned to the firm on several significant bankruptcy restructuring matters and for assistance in obtaining the first IRS ruling approving a spin-off in a bankruptcy context.

The Lawyers: According to clients, **Joseph Pari** (see p.461) is "*a terrific analytical thinker and takes nothing for granted.*" Rivals confirm he is "*affable and decent but don't be fooled, he is tough and takes no prisoners.*" Pari continues to advise HCA on transactional matters, federal tax planning and tax controversy issues. Recent matters include a like-kind exchange transaction and a significant proposed IRS adjustment involving the consolidated return loss disallowance regulations.

The Clients: LifePoint Hospitals; Deutsche Bank; Deutsche Bank Alex Brown; PG&E; HCA; Triad Hospitals; Burns, Philp & Company; Sumitomo Corporation of America and Omnicare.

Freshfields Bruckhaus Deringer LLP

The Firm: Working on financial products, including derivatives, structured finance, cross-border transactions and private equity, the Freshfields team has made its mark in DC. It advises US research and engineering company Science Applications International on all aspects of US federal income tax, including audits, tax planning and cross-border transactions. For client Amersham it handled tax matters arising from the company's acquisition by GE and GE Investments for $9.5 billion.

The Lawyers: **Gregory May** has been described as "*dignified and ethical.*" He is hailed as "*an extremely smart advocate,*" and clients are enthusiastic about his "*amazing business sense.*"

The Clients: Fox Paine Capital Fund II International; Amersham; Science Applications International; The Carlyle Group and Carlyle Europe Venture Partners.

Latham & Watkins LLP

The Firm: Interviewees commended the firm for having "*some incredibly accomplished players within its group.*" It has become more visible and represents clients such as Ernst & Young with respect to a range of aspects of the IRS investigation of its tax shelter promotion activities, and AT&T Wireless regarding a pending Tax Court case with respect to numerous issues, including depreciation, amortization and tax accounting involving more than $100 million. It is also trial counsel for FedEx with respect to a pending Tax Court case concerning a tax accounting issue involving more than $10 million.

The Lawyers: "*A rock-solid performer,*" **Gerald Kafka** handles a diverse practice. It integrates over 30 years of tax litigation with a more recent focus on controversy work.

The Clients: HCA; Ernst & Young; AECOM Technology and AT&T Wireless Services.

Morgan, Lewis & Bockius LLP
See firm details p.1556

The Firm: Commentators consider this firm to be "*on the up*" and "*a real contender*" in the tax exempt area. Over the past year the tax group has expanded, adding some "*highly respected*" partners including Miriam Fisher, who recently joined from Hogan & Hartson. Attorneys provide strategic tax planning advice and counsel on a range of complex transactions for domestic and foreign corporations, partnerships and individuals. The firm's international tax practice also plays a key role.

The Lawyers: "*Brilliant*" **Gary Wilcox** (see p.475) is a success with clients, who feel "*he does a fine job.*" He advises US and international clients on a broad array of tax-related matters, including M&A, joint ventures, spin-offs and other divestitures. **Celia Roady** (see p.464) offers "*first-rate*" advice to what rivals describe as "*an amazing clientele.*" In particular, wisdom concerning Sarbanes-Oxley is incorporated into advice for developing best governance practices for non-profits. Her expertise concerning the conduct of international charitable programs in compliance with the Patriot Act and advising charitable organizations in IRS audits and investigations is also noted. Roady was involved in the creation of new charitable affiliates such as the Pew Research Center for the Pew Charitable Trusts.

The Clients: Ford Foundation; The Pew Charitable Trusts; The Smithsonian Institution; The National Geographic Society; National Merit Scholarship Corporation and George Washington University.

Shearman & Sterling
See firm details p.1369

The Firm: This group includes several "*admirable tax attorneys,*" who handle a gamut of tax matters ranging from cross-border M&A and spin-offs to debt and equity financings and restructurings. Competitors feel the firm is becoming "*a force to reckon with,*" evidenced by the fact that the team has expanded its controversy capability and has been busier in tax structuring and planning for startup companies, particularly in the area of e-commerce.

The Lawyers: "*Key player*" **John Williams** (see p.475) is "*aggressive but successful,*" clients say. He brings to the table "*a distinctive viewpoint on IRS examinations,*" having been former chief counsel for the IRS. Another "*prominent*" name is that of **Robert Rudnick** (see p.465), who is "*a well-known authority on financial products.*" The bulk of his practice involves the structuring of financial transactions, including securitized funding and acquisition finance.

The Clients: Recent clients have included Corning, BT, Novartis, Thyssen Industrie and Citicorp.

Wilmer Cutler Pickering Hale and Dorr LLP
See firm details p.497

The Firm: For a smaller group, this tax practice elicited a great deal of favorable comment. One very satisfied contact said of his chosen firm: "*They were incredible; they took client service to a level I never knew existed.*" 2004 has been a year of change, with May bringing the merger between Wilmer Cutler Pickering and Hale & Dorr. A long-standing practice in DC represents a multinational group of clients in diverse transactions and hearings.

The Lawyers: "*Sophisticated*" **Terrill Hyde** (see p.448) served as deputy tax legislative counsel for regulatory affairs at the Treasury Department. Sources greatly admire this "*timely and organized, responsive*" attorney. She advises clients on the structuring and restructuring of multinational groups in connection with M&A and spin-offs, bankruptcy and insolvency, and cross-border investments. Furthermore she offers counsel to exempt organizations on issues relating to formation and ongoing activities such as IRS ruling requests.

The Clients: Clients include the Carnegie Institution of Washington, Commonfund Educational Testing Service and The Phillips Collection.

Other Notable Practitioners

"*Outstanding*" **Peter Baumbusch** (see p.432) of Gibson, Dunn & Crutcher LLP concentrates on international and domestic corporate taxation, M&A, restructurings and foreign investment in the USA. He recently advised Investcorp Bank BSC regarding its hedge funds and over a billion dollars of corporate and real estate transactions in the USA and Europe. He has obtained successful results in several IRS rulings, audits and court cases, and advises foreign governments with respect to the US tax system. **Kenneth Klein** (see p.451) of Mayer, Brown, Rowe & Maw LLP is reputed for "*sophisticated*" cross-border tax planning, structuring and restructuring for a number of US and non-US multinationals. He was part of the Mayer Brown team that structured BellSouth's estimated $6 billion sale of its Latin American operations to Spanish company Telefonica. Clients note how he "*effortlessly identifies the issues at hand,*" especially on matters concerning tax controversies and tax policy. **Raymond Wiacek** (see p.475) of Jones Day represented Pfizer in the post-acquisition, global integration of Pharmacia, Upjohn and Searle, and in the disposition of acquired businesses not central to Pfizer's mission, such as Schick-Wilkinson Sword, Chiclets-Dentyne-Halls and Tetra. Furthermore, he acted for Bank of America in a number of large, cross-border, tax-intensive structured financings. He also advised Isuzu Motors in Japan and the US with respect to two significant transfer pricing examinations.

TELECOM, BROADCAST & SATELLITE REGULATORY

Band 1

Kellogg, Huber, Hansen, Todd & Evans PLLC

The Firm: The firm's cadre of "*talented*" attorneys "*sets the standard for quality representation in the communications arena,*" according to interviewees. Some speculate that it is "*the best in town for court work,*" especially in the appellate sphere. Demonstrating flair in litigating against the FCC, the group has been credited with groundbreaking work in the contentious regulatory field. Recent highlights include representing Verizon in relation to the DC Circuit Court's upheaval of the FCC's triennial review order.

The Lawyers: "*A real smart guy*" who "*clearly knows as much as anyone in the field, if not more,*" **Michael Kellogg** won distinction for his "*incredible success record,*" especially as regards to appellate litigation. **Mark Evans** also earned market plaudits for his "*good judgment*" in telecom-related litigation.

The Clients: The firm's diverse clientele has included Verizon and other Bell companies.

Latham & Watkins LLP

The Firm: The practice turns an adroit hand to "*the FCC stuff,*" winning applause in the marketplace in various regulatory negotiations. For example, it is marshaling Leap in seeking

District of Columbia

Leading firms (Telecom, Broadcast & Satellite: Regulatory)

1 KELLOGG, HUBER, HANSEN, TODD *Washington, DC*
LATHAM & WATKINS LLP *Washington, DC*
WILEY REIN & FIELDING LLP *Washington, DC*

2 COVINGTON & BURLING *Washington, DC*
HARRIS, WILTSHIRE & GRANNIS LLP *Washington, DC*
HOGAN & HARTSON LLP *Washington, DC*
LAWLER, METZGER, MILKMAN *Washington, DC*
LEVINE, BLASZAK, BLOCK *Washington, DC*
WILLKIE FARR & GALLAGHER LLP *Washington, DC*
WILMER CUTLER PICKERING HALE *Washington, DC*

3 MINTZ LEVIN COHN FERRIS GLOVSKY *Washington, DC*
MORRISON & FOERSTER LLP *Washington, DC*
PAUL, WEISS, RIFKIND, WHARTON *Washington, DC*
SIDLEY AUSTIN BROWN *Washington, DC*

4 ARNOLD & PORTER LLP *Washington, DC*
DOW, LOHNES & ALBERTSON *Washington, DC*
JENNER & BLOCK LLP *Washington, DC*
KELLEY DRYE & WARREN *Washington, DC*
LEVENTHAL SENTER & LERMAN *Washington, DC*
PRESTON GATES ELLIS & ROUVELAS *Washington, DC*
SKADDEN, ARPS, SLATE, MEAGHER *Washington, DC*
SWIDLER BERLIN LLP *Washington, DC*

Firms are listed alphabetically in each band.

approval before the FCC and the DOJ concerning its reemergence following bankruptcy. The team's "*incredibly broad*" remit also encompasses transactional and litigation expertise; and due to its international network it enjoys "*an impressive global reach.*" In addition, the group has also represented several smaller clients in the spectrum auction area.
The Lawyers: Former FCC bureau chief **Gary Epstein** has made a splash by delivering consistently impressive work to "*a number of decent clients,*" particularly on behalf of BellSouth. He also gained credence for his work "*on the Hill.*" **Jim Barker** has been especially busy in relation to wireless and satellite matters. He has been assisting DIRECTV disposing of various assets, in particular advising on the regulatory aspects of the $4.3 billion takeover of PanAmSat by a group of investors consisting of KKR, The Carlyle Group and Providence Equity Partners.
The Clients: QwestDex; Carlyle Private Equity; Verizon Video; Global Crossing; Spanish Broadcasting System; Cogent Technologies; DIRECTV and Inmarsat.

Wiley Rein & Fielding LLP

See firm details p.496
The Firm: "*One of the highest quality shops in town,*" according to competitors, the firm is especially regarded for its "*Capitol Hill stuff.*" A broader remit covers a gamut of telecom, media and wireless work in the domestic and international arenas. "*They have a lot of people who've come from the FCC,*" observers said, "*so when they have an argument, the FCC tends to listen.*"

In a headline case, the firm represented the Newspaper Association of America in arguing against a challenge to the FCC's rules allowing increased consolidation of media ownerships.
The Lawyers: The market consensus on "*brilliant*" **Dick Wiley** (see p.475) was summed up by one commentator: "*He's been the king of the telecom world for a long time.*" Having "*helped to invent modern telecom law*" as well as being "*well connected as a Republican with a Republican administration in town,*" he has had his fingers in some of the nation's most important cases. In addition to the challenge to FCC rules concerning media ownerships, he is also representing CBS, and its parent company Verizon, in a retransmission consent case against EchoStar. The "*collegial*" **Larry Secrest** heads the firm's media practice, and is said by peers to be "*a steady, unflappable, very careful lawyer.*"
The Clients: Verizon; Motorola; AT&T; CTIA; PCIA; Nokia; ICI; Toshiba America; LZ; Sharp and the Newspaper Association of America.

Band 2

Covington & Burling

See firm details p.481
The Firm: "*Certainly a high quality firm*" in the area of broadcast, the group has represented about 650 "*TV stations affiliated with the networks.*" Recent highlights include advising a group of TV stations in a national dispute against the networks; the case involves the right to substitute local programming in place of network programming where appropriate. In addition, he has been advising Amazon.com and a group of websites in helping ensure broadband telecom systems will not discriminate against independent websites. Another matter has involved a consortium of satellite interests in seeking to reinstate a satellite license that had been revoked by the FCC.
The Lawyers: "*A first-rate broadcast attorney with a first-rate mind,*" **Jonathan Blake** (see p.434) heads the firm's technology, media and communications group. "*One of the leading lawyers for TV stations in the country, if not the leading lawyer,*" he regularly participates in the firm's most complex issues in this arena.
The Clients: The Network Affiliated Stations Alliance; Association For Maximum Service Television; NBC Television Affiliates Board; WDBJ-TV; CBS Television Network Affiliates Board; Public Broadcasting Service; National Geographic; NFL; Radio One; Microsoft; Amazon.com; Qualcomm and Panasonic.

Harris, Wiltshire & Grannis LLP

The Firm: The "*quality boutique*" is noted for its international telecom work, partly due to the firm's managing partner, Scott Blake Harris, who emerged "*from the international side of the FCC.*" A notable clientele is forged from a range

of hi-tech, new carriers and wireless companies in addition to those in the traditional satellite and cable industries. Its work has often involved the FCC and other government entities in regulatory proceedings. In litigation, the team has appeared before state and federal courts; its work here has included significant appellate cases that have helped change the landscape of the industry overall.
The Lawyers: Managing partner **Scott Blake Harris** has "*a strong international pedigree*" from having been the first chief of the international bureau at the FCC. He has advised clients involved in areas such as terrestrial wireless, software and hardware and satellite, among others. A prestigious client roster includes foreign governments, trade associations and prominent investors. "*Responsive, bright and not afraid to roll up his sleeves and get ensconced in the business,*" **John Nakahata** is especially noted for his regulatory work and "*insight into the FCC,*" peers said. Others appreciate his "*good judgment and attention to detail.*" **Bill Wiltshire** advises on a range of issues including transfer-of-control transactions, spectrum allocation, IP and telemarketing among others.
The Clients: Cisco Systems; Microsoft; Dell; DIRECTV; Level 3; Nextel; T-Mobile; AT&T; News Corporation; Discovery Communications; Tyco; North American Submarine Cable Association and The World Bank.

Hogan & Hartson LLP

See firm details p.484
The Firm: The firm is recognized in the telecom field for "*going out there and doing good work for many good clients,*" commentators said. Over the years, this practice has sustained consistency in its regulatory expertise, while also advising its telecom, media and entertainment clients on a range of corporate, litigation and IP issues. One of its anchor clients is DIRECTV, which it represented in an agreement with SkyTerra Communications to acquire 50% of a new entity that will contain the assets of Hughes Network Systems' VSAT business, a transaction valued at approximately $360 million. The team represented the same client along with News Corporation in connection with a series of transactions with Grupo Televisa, Globopar and Liberty Media in Latin America.
The Lawyers: Communications group co-director **Peter Rohrbach** (see p.465) is described by peers as having "*been around quite some time*" in the telecom sector, with his practice focusing on M&A and related regulatory work.
The Clients: Clients include media and entertainment providers, radio and television broadcasters, direct-to-home satellite operators and print media companies. The firm also represents entrepreneurs and emerging companies, mature enterprises, underwriters and private equity firms.

426

All quotes in the text are from interviews with clients and competitors.

CHAMBERS USA 2005

District of Columbia
Leading individuals (Telecom, Broadcast & Satellite: Regulatory)

★ WILEY Richard *Wiley Rein*, Washington, DC

[1] BLAKE Jonathan *Covington & Burling*, Washington, DC
EPSTEIN Gary *Latham & Watkins*, Washington, DC
KELLOGG Michael *Kellogg Huber*, Washington, DC
VERVEER Philip *Willkie Farr*, Washington, DC

[2] HARRIS Scott *Harris Wiltshire*, Washington, DC
LAKE William *Wilmer Cutler*, Washington, DC
METZGER Richard *Lawler Metzger*, Washington, DC
ROHRBACH Peter *Hogan & Hartson*, Washington, DC
SPECTOR Phillip *Paul Weiss*, Washington, DC
TRITT Cheryl *Morrison & Foerster*, Washington, DC

[3] LEVINE Henry *Levine Blaszak*, Washington, DC
LIPMAN Andrew *Swidler Berlin*, Washington, DC
NAKAHATA John *Harris Wiltshire*, Washington, DC
QUALE John *Skadden Arps*, Washington, DC
SYMONS Howard *Mintz Levin*, Washington, DC

[4] BARKER James *Latham & Watkins*, Washington, DC
BLASZAK James *Levine Blaszak*, Washington, DC
BOOTHBY Colleen *Levine Blaszak*, Washington, DC
BRANDS Henk *Paul Weiss*, Washington, DC
COOK BUSH Antoinette *Skadden Arps*, Washington, DC
DESANCTIS Michael *Jenner & Block*, Washington, DC
EVANS Mark *Kellogg Huber*, Washington, DC
FERRIS Charles *Mintz Levin*, Washington, DC
JOHNSTON Mark *Levine Blaszak*, Washington, DC
KEENEY Regina *Lawler Metzger*, Washington, DC
LAWSON David *Sidley Austin*, Washington, DC
LERMAN Steven *Leventhal Senter*, Washington, DC
MILKMAN Ruth *Lawler Metzger*, Washington, DC
NUECHTERLEIN Jonathan *Wilmer Cutler*, Washington, DC
REED Kevin *Dow Lohnes*, Washington, DC
SECREST III Lawrence *Wiley Rein*, Washington, DC
SINEL Norman *Arnold & Porter*, Washington, DC
TOBEY Margaret *Morrison & Foerster*, Washington, DC
VERRILLI Donald *Jenner & Block*, Washington, DC
WADLOW R Clark *Sidley Austin*, Washington, DC
WILTSHIRE William *Harris Wiltshire*, Washington, DC

Individuals are listed alphabetically in each band.

Lawler, Metzger, Milkman & Keeney, LLC

The Firm: This boutique has "*made its business in representing small entrants*" to the telecom sector, though it has also rubbed shoulders with giants in the field. The practice particularly profits from "*bridging the gap over to the wireline field as well as wireless,*" observers said. It has represented clients such as MCI and T-Mobile in various FCC proceedings. In addition, the group provides regulatory advice to various investors and outside consultants.

The Lawyers: Clients credited **Richard Metzger** with having "*both the history in the telecom field and the knowledge of some fairly technical elements.*" Former FCC bureau chief **Gina Keeney** is especially noted for her work on behalf of Nextel. She won acclaim as the "*point person*" on Nextel's recent megahertz acquisition, described as "*one of the most significant and*

most complicated FCC proceedings on the wireless side recently.*" **Ruth Milkman** was noted for her expertise in relation to "*unbundled network element work.*"

The Clients: Nextel, MCI and T-Mobile are among the firm's distinguished clients.

Levine, Blaszak, Block & Boothby LLP
See firm details p.488

The Firm: This "*cost-effective*" boutique often represents "*large buyers of telephone services.*" Dubbed "*the class act in that niche,*" its lawyers "*really speak the language of telecom,*" observers said. "*When you hire them,*" another commentator agreed, "*that's when you're saying you're going to be serious.*"

The Lawyers: **Hank Levine** (see p.452) "*wrote the gospel on telecom negotiation,*" according to clients, who also feel that "*he's more than an attorney – he really knows the technology.*" His specialty is telecom users and providers built on emerging technologies. "*He's highly experienced so he never has to start from scratch – he's always up to speed.*" "*Capable of moving things forward without hand holding,*" **Jim Blaszak** (see p.434) has represented purchasers in relation to AT&T Tariff 12 proposals. He also handles comparable custom network service agreements with AT&T's major competitors and customized agreements in areas such as cellular, frame relay and satellite services. The "*professional*" **Colleen Boothby** (see p.435) has advised on a range of telecom business and regulatory matters, while the "*tenacious*" **Mark Johnston** (see p.449) "*has an easy-going attitude, but hangs tough and wears down the vendors.*"

The Clients: Morgan Stanley; Merrill Lynch; IBM; Visa and WPP.

Willkie Farr & Gallagher LLP
See firm details p.1380

The Firm: This practice hinges on the presence of its leading partner Phil Verveer. "*As long as he is there, they'll get work and be respected,*" one commentator said. Its communications expertise encompasses broadcasting, cable TV and the Internet. Other interests involve satellite and undersea cable, and wireless and wireline communications. Its profile also crosses over into the IP side. The firm has participated in the regulatory aspects of Sprint's merger with Nextel. On behalf of ACNielsen, the team helped steer its introduction of Local People Meters, which is used for market research purposes.

The Lawyers: Another former FCC bureau chief, the "*perennial*" **Phil Verveer** (see p.473) is noted for his work on behalf of Time Warner. "*An extraordinary practitioner in the realm of broadcast litigation,*" he is a favorite destination "*if you want a wise counsel to navigate your way through a difficult problem at the FCC.*" In addition to the Sprint/Nextel combination, he is also

acting for New Skies Satellites in its acquisition by Blackstone.

The Clients: New Skies Satellites; TelMex; ACNielsen and ComCast.

Wilmer Cutler Pickering Hale and Dorr LLP
See firm details p.497

The Firm: The firm makes its mark in the industry through substantial work on behalf of Verizon and Quest of the Bell companies. It has proven particularly adept on the enforcement front, including federal regulatory work. Also on offer are matters pertaining to state regulations, the Internet, e-commerce and privacy. Rounding out the practice is its considerable expertise in litigation. In Verizon v Trinko, the team acted for the US Telecom Association in a Supreme Court case that resulted in a ruling that an antitrust claim cannot be based on a violation of the Telecom Act.

The Lawyers: **Bill Lake** (see p.452) garnered acclaim for his regulatory expertise in the telecom sector, though he also advises in relation to competition, IP and related trade issues. A former FCC deputy general counsel, **John Nuechterlein** (see p.460) focuses on appellate litigation and antitrust, especially in relation to federal telecom laws. He often advises incumbent telephone companies.

The Clients: The practice has represented Verizon Wireless in a settlement involving Nextel. On the Voice over Internet Protocol (VoIP) front, the practice has been advising SBC Communications in relation to FCC proceedings.

Band 3

Mintz Levin Cohn Ferris Glovsky and Popeo PC

The Firm: Especially rated by peers for its cable expertise, the practice includes various regulatory and legislative issues such as those pertaining to emerging broadband, ownership limits and VoIP matters. Other interests involve issues that affect those entering the cable TV market by direct broadcasting satellite and other new alternative delivery facilities.

The Lawyers: "*Still prominent*" is **Howard Symons**, who represents clients including cable, wireless, and telecom companies in various regulatory and legislative matters, including implementation of the Telecommunications Act of 1996. Former FCC chair **Charlie Ferris** is well known for his cable expertise, so much so that one commentator noted: "*Mintz Levin is certainly a name in the field because of Charlie Ferris.*"

The Clients: Clients include large cable multiple-system operators, major cable program networks, and national and state cable industry trade associations. Broadcast stations and networks also feature in its roster.

Morrison & Foerster LLP

See firm details p.293

The Firm: This practice "*shows up on both the wireless and the wireline side,*" and is noted for its work on behalf of Sprint. Clients feel its lawyers are "*responsive*" and have "*good business sense, judgment and knowledge of the subject areas.*" A leaf in its laurel was participating in Cingular's $41 billion acquisition of AT&T Wireless. On behalf of ALLTEL, the team appeared before the FCC in connection with an effort to obtain competitive eligible telecom carrier status in rural areas for its wireless ventures in multiple states. Another matter involved representing a coalition of telecom management consultants in an FCC complaint against AT&T Corporation for alleged violation of consumer disclosure laws.

The Lawyers: A former bureau chief at the FCC, **Cheryl Tritt** (see p.472) is hovering at "*the top of her game for expertise and practical advice*" in both regulatory and transactional work, clients said. Combining "*technical ability with the tactical side of it,*" she is a top choice for pursuing cases immersed in "*a somewhat political environment.*" In addition to the Cingular/AT&T Wireless combination, her recent work includes representing T-Mobile USA in its $2.5 billion purchase of Cingular's California wireless network. **Margaret Tobey** (see p.472) was noted for her broadcast expertise. Her practice extends to the international stage, and also contains a considerable dose of litigation expertise.

The Clients: Clients include T-Mobile USA, ALLTEL and Clearwire.

Paul, Weiss, Rifkind, Wharton & Garrison

See firm details p.1362

The Firm: Described by peers as having "*a strong communications focus,*" the group has received particular accolades with regards to "*satellites and space.*" Its expertise encompasses traditional telecom and media regulatory issues in addition to a healthy diet of transactional work. The group's remit often relates to advanced technologies, convergence and the Internet. A highlight for the practice involved Fox Entertainment Group's long-term, multi-satellite agreement with PanAmSat.

The Lawyers: Head of the firm's communications and technology group, **Phil Spector** was praised for his regulatory expertise, particularly his "*international work for SingTel.*" In addition, he has assisted SES Americom in its acquisition of a substantial portion of the assets of Verestar; the transaction followed the FCC's recent approval of the transfer of Verestar's communications licenses to Americom. "*He's prominent and he's made Paul Weiss prominent in this area.*" **Henk Brands** is noted as "*an emerging talent*" who's "*a good broadcast litigator.*" His work for Time Warner is a particular highlight, along with his expertise on ownership issues.

The Clients: News Corporation; Fox Entertainment Group; SES Americom; Tencent Holdings; TCL Communications and Time Warner.

Sidley Austin Brown & Wood LLP

See firm details p.778

The Firm: Historically noted for its representation of AT&T, many in the market acknowledge that the group is a significant player "*as long as AT&T exists.*" Others however appreciate that with the firm's international reach and excellent clientele, the DC group is bound to benefit from substantive cross-references. Its expertise includes advising clients in the areas of telecom, broadcasting and new technologies in relation to corporate, regulatory, antitrust and appellate litigation matters.

The Lawyers: "*A fine broadcast lawyer,*" **Clark Wadlow** (see p.473) heads the firm's communications group. A notable figure in the industry, he cochairs the annual Practicing Law Institute program on telecommunications policy and regulation with Dick Wiley. **David Lawson** (see p.452) won respect with "*a real profile acting for AT&T.*"

The Clients: Clients include media and broadcast companies, satellite carriers, cable programming networks, wireless and PCS companies, mobile satellite service providers and telecom equipment manufacturers.

Band 4

Arnold & Porter LLP

See firm details p.478

The Firm: "*Preeminent in the niche of cable franchise work,*" according to peers, the practice also advises a number of telecom clients such as local, long-distance and wireless telephone companies in relation to regulatory, transactional and litigation proceedings. The team often demonstrates expertise on IP, antitrust and legislative issues. It has acted before state and federal courts and government agencies such as the FCC among others.

The Lawyers: Practice head **Norman Sinel** (see p.468) attracted commendation as "*a principal part of this practice,*" which has historically handled cable TV licensing issues across the country. In this respect, he has been especially active for Comcast in recent times. On the telecom side, his work has involved the likes of SBC Communications in relation to acquisitions and related regulatory work.

The Clients: SBC Communications; Comcast; Crowley Enterprises and the Recording Industry Association of America.

Dow, Lohnes & Albertson, PLLC

The Firm: "*Famous for its cable work,*" this practice deftly illustrates its wealth of expertise in transactional activity on behalf of media and communications clients. M&A is a particular forte, and in this aspect of its work its close relationship with Cox Communications has proved especially valuable. Its lawyers are familiar with the ever-changing legal landscape that affects telecom issues, handling FCC and state regulatory proceedings. The team is also experienced in legislative matters.

The Lawyers: Head of the firm's communications law practice group, **Kevin Reed**'s practice encompasses transactional work involving the purchase or sale of broadcast stations and other regulated communications companies. Another drawing card is his experience before the FCC.

The Clients: Cox Communications; Paxson Communications; Media General; Insight Communications; Gannett Broadcasting; First Media Television and Simmons Broadcasting.

Jenner & Block LLP

See firm details p.768

The Firm: This practice boasts expertise before the FCC on a variety of regulatory issues – including VoIP, intercarrier compensation, telephone competition and spectrum licensing among others. Its "*deep background*" has attracted work such as advising MCI and other competitive carriers in a major proceeding involving FCC local competition rules. Before the US Supreme Court, the team successfully represented NextWave in a case that established that the Bankruptcy Code prohibited the FCC from reclaiming $5 billion worth of licenses for wireless spectrum.

The Lawyers: Telecom practice chair **Don Verrilli** (see p.472) was commended for his "*top-notch ability to articulate complex matters with insight,*" while **Michael DeSanctis** (see p.439) was described by clients as "*a terrific advocate*" before the FCC, particularly in relation to matters arising under the Telecommunications Act of 1996. Both were also commended for their courtroom experience.

The Clients: The team has represented the National Association of Broadcasters in a challenge to FCC media ownership rules. Other clients include MCI, NextWave, Covad Communications and Cellular Telecommunications and Internet Association (CTIA).

Kelley Drye & Warren

The Firm: "*A New York firm with a large DC office,*" this practice is historically noted for its work in the competitive local exchange carrier market. Clients say that its lawyers are "*sharp*" and have been "*in the business a long time,*" with a number of them having come from Wiley Rein & Fielding. Its expertise includes regulatory, compliance and litigation advice. In addition, it has participated in international telecom contractual, corporate and financing procedures.

The Lawyers: Robert Aamoth chairs the firm's telecom group, and is seen as a key player on related regulatory, antitrust and litigation aspects, often involving common carriers.

The Clients: Clients include competitive local exchange carriers, interexchange carriers, internet service providers, wireless carriers and international carriers.

Leventhal Senter & Lerman PLLC

The Firm: Described as a "*niche broadcast boutique,*" this DC firm is especially noted for its close relationship with Infinity Broadcasting. Its expertise includes regulatory and business matters impacting the traditional broadcast, satellite and common carrier industries.

The Lawyers: **Steve Lerman** is primarily known as a key relationship partner for Infinity as part of a broader practice. On behalf of that client, he advised on various disputes that stemmed from Janet Jackson's 'wardrobe malfunction' during the Super Bowl's halftime show.

The Clients: American Tower; Beasley Broadcast Group; CBS; Entercom Communications; Great Scott Broadcasting; Grupo Televisa; Infinity Broadcasting; Lockheed Martin; Maritime Telecommunications Network; MMG Ventures; Playboy Entertainment Group; Telemundo; TRW and Viacom.

Preston Gates Ellis & Rouvelas Meeds LLP

The Firm: Though best known for "*supremely important client*" Microsoft, the team has expanded its role as advocate to cover a much broader range of clients. The firm consistently delivers quality on commercial technology, corporate finance and related transactions. Its broader repertoire also includes regulatory, public policy and related litigation advice.

The Lawyers: Martin Stern is the firm's global head of telecom and media.

The Clients: Clients include wireline and wireless carriers, backbone providers, Internet service providers, content providers, cable and satellite operators, equipment manufacturers, broadcasters, technology developers, software companies and large users of network services.

Skadden, Arps, Slate, Meagher & Flom LLP & Affiliates

See firm details p.1372

The Firm: This practice remains active for key client News Corporation, which it represented along with Viacom and NBC in the recent FCC media ownership proceedings. Strongly rated for its corporate and transactional expertise in the communications sector, it also advises on regulatory issues in the same sector and expertly handles licensing proceedings before the FCC, US Congress and various government entities. The firm's vast international experience also means that it is often a port of call for foreign governments.

The Lawyers: **John Quale** (see p.463) is pitched as "*an expert in telecom M&A deals,*" whose experience includes proceedings on the regulatory front. Returning to the firm after a three-year stint at a startup company, **Toni Cook Bush** (see p.438) is set to be "*a shot in the arm*" for the practice, especially on the legislative front, commentators said.

The Clients: The firm has also been advising Border Media in relation to acquiring a number of mainly Spanish-language radio stations in the Southwest. Other clients include: Fox Cable; Gemstar-TV; News Corporation; Gray TV and Virgin Mobile.

Swidler Berlin LLP

See firm details p.495

The Firm: Especially noted by peers for its traditional representation of new entrants to the telecom market, this practice features regulatory, transactional and litigation proceedings. It also assists clients in legislative matters and other telecom-related work, such as land use.

The Lawyers: Vice chairman of the firm and the chairman of its telecom, Internet and new technologies practice, **Andy Lipman** (see p.453) won respect for his historical representation of competitive local exchange carriers.

The Clients: Clients include telephone common carriers, Internet, wireless, satellite and competitive video services, telecom equipment manufacturers and hi-tech applications companies.

TELECOM, BROADCAST & SATELLITE

FINANCE

District of Columbia
Leading firms (Telecom, Broadcast & Satellite: Finance)
1 **MILBANK, TWEED, HADLEY** *Washington, DC*

Leading individuals (Telecom, Broadcast & Satellite: Finance)
1 **GERSTELL Glenn** *Milbank Tweed, Washington, DC*
Firms and individuals are listed alphabetically in each band.

Band 1

Milbank, Tweed, Hadley & McCloy

The Firm: This firm remains the predominant firm for telecom finance, both for financial parties and for companies, with continued heavy involvement in the emerging markets of Asia and Latin America. Its clients include the "*large investment banks of the world,*" and its lawyers are described as "*cost-efficient and hard-working.*" "*They understand the business very well.*" A feather in its cap involved Ex-Im Bank and Export Development Canada in connection with a $750 million financing to Reliance Infocomm, which related to the expansion of its fixed-line and wireless networks throughout India.

The Lawyers: Global communications practice head and managing partner of the firm's DC office, the "*confident*" **Glenn Gerstell** demonstrates considerable talent in the field, handling a range of cross-border work. He also participates in M&A and bankruptcy-related matters, earning plaudits as "*the guy with the bright ideas,*" observers said. "*He's brilliant on both the operator and sponsor side.*"

The Clients: The team represented WestLB and ABN AMRO as agents in connection with the restructuring of approximately $350 million of debt for BellSouth Colombia (formerly Celumóvil). In addition, it advised on the $1.75 billion restructuring and $625 million sale of BCP SA, the cellular operator in São Paulo, Brazil, to América Móvil. Other clients include: CANTV; Tele Norte Leste Participações; ABN AMRO; Inter-American Development Bank and Deutsche Bank.

IT & IT OUTSOURCING

District of Columbia
Leading firms (IT & IT Outsourcing)

1. MAYER, BROWN, ROWE & MAW LLP *Washington, DC*
   SHAW PITTMAN *Washington, DC*

Leading individuals (IT & IT Outsourcing)

1. MASUR Daniel *Mayer Brown*, Washington, DC
   ZAHLER Robert *Shaw Pittman*, Washington, DC

Firms and individuals are listed alphabetically in each band.

Band 1

Mayer, Brown, Rowe & Maw LLP

See firm details p.771

The Firm: This DC office retains a *"prominent and first-class"* outsourcing practice, according to interviewees, who note its historical representation of suppliers such as Accenture. A broader remit has included such transactions as Hallmark's outsourcing agreement with IBM to develop, maintain and support a new Hallmark Web site.

The Lawyers: The *"efficient"* **Dan Masur** (see p.455) elicited commendation for his proficiency: *"If you want a deal done quickly, he's the guy to go to,"* a client said. In addition to the Hallmark transaction, he also represented Wachovia in connection with the outsourcing to Accenture of the development and maintenance of a new online banking Web site.

The Clients: Hallmark; Wachovia; Procter & Gamble; Marathon Oil; Valor Telecom; Eastman Kodak and Chubb Group.

Shaw Pittman

See firm details p.490

The Firm: This DC office is noted as *"one of the leading firms around."* It wins plaudits for its *"zealous"* advocacy on behalf of clients, turning intellectual flair to deliver excellent results. Furthermore, the team benefits from *"considerable institutional consulting expertise in-house."* Significant work has included representing Morgan Stanley in a renegotiation of an existing IT arrangement with IBM, which has involved moving data to IBM's new on-demand computer facilities. At time of going to press, the planned merger between Pillsbury Winthop LLP and Shaw Pittman LLP had not yet been finalized.

The Lawyers: The *"sharp"* **Bob Zahler** (see p.476) was described as *"one of the premier outsourcing lawyers around,"* especially on the customer side.

The Clients: The practice has advised Capital One, American Express and GE on a range of technology matters. Other clients include: Morgan Stanley; JPMorgan Chase; Discover Financial Service's; Equifax; US Department of the Treasury Financial Management Service and Solectron.

Leaders in District of Columbia

ACKER, Lawrence G
LeBoeuf, Lamb, Greene & MacRae, LLP, Washington, DC 202 986 8016
lacker@llgm.com
Recommended in Energy
Practice Areas: Litigates major complex cases before administrative agencies and secures regulatory authorizations for substantial energy projects, including those with competing applicants. Advises senior company officials respecting competition matters, contract negotiation and corporate compliance with regulatory requirements. Assists clients in every phase of the administrative process from strategic planning and initiation to document preparation and witness examination through appeals.
Prof. Memberships: Energy Bar Association.
Career: Joined LeBoeuf in 1984; Bracewell & Patterson (1981-84); Federal Energy Regulatory Commission (1978-81); Acker & Mansfield, Arlington, Virginia (1976-78); Arlington Legal Aid Society (1974-76).
Personal: Georgetown University (JD) 1974; Syracuse University (BA) 1971.

ADELFIO, Marco
Morrison & Foerster LLP, Washington, DC 202 887 1530
madelfio@mofo.com
Recommended in Investment Management
Practice Areas: Focuses on investment companies and investment advisers. Clients include open- and closed-end funds, multi-class funds and master-feeder funds. Advises on ongoing SEC regulatory and registration activities. Handles complex acquisition and reorganization transactions for fund companies and consolidations following mergers of advisers. Serves as independent counsel to independent directors of fund companies. Advises private equity funds, exchange funds, and operating companies on structural and 1940 Act matters. Counsels registered investment advisers on regulatory and transactional matters. Advises on fiduciary responsibilities, the provision of investment management services, and compliance matters.
Career: Admitted to practice in District of Columbia and Massachusetts.
Personal: BA, Bucknell University, 1978; JD, magna cum laude, Order of the Coif, Boston College Law School, 1982.

ADLER, Howard B
Gibson, Dunn & Crutcher LLP, Washington, DC 202 955 8589
hadler@gibsondunn.com
Recommended in Corporate/Commercial
Practice Areas: Represents corporations, investment and merchant banks and financial institutions in securities offerings, M&A, joint ventures and venture capital investments. M&A representations: Arlington Capital (NLX, LLC, Secor) Arguss Communications, Inc. in its sale to Dycom Industries, Inc., after staving off proxy challenge for Arguss, Capital One Financial Corp (People-First.com and AmeriFee Corporation). Finance representations: IPO - Friedman, Billings, Ramsey & Co., Inc., American Capital Strategies Ltd., Corporate Executive Board; American Home Mortgage, Inc., Franklin Bank; KMG America, Inc., significant follow-on offerings and major 144A transactions.
Personal: JD, New York University School of Law, Note and Comment Editor, Law Review.

ALBERTS, Sam J
White & Case LLP, Washington, DC 202 626 3600
salberts@whitecase.com
Recommended in Bankruptcy
Practice Areas: Concentrates on financial restructuring, Chapter 11 bankruptcies, healthcare restructurings, crossboarder issues and creditor committees. Recent engagements include Mirant (debtor's counsel) and Doctors Community Heathcare Corp. (committee counsel/trustee). Frequent speaker on insolvancy issues.
Prof. Memberships: American Bankruptcy Institute, INSOL, Walter Chandler Inns of Court, Maryland and Virgina Bankruptcy Bars.
Career: Admitted: District of Columbia, Virginia and Washington (all courts); Maryland (federal only); Courts of Appeal for Fourth and Ninth Circuits.
Personal: JD, George Washington University (1992); BA, New York University (1987).

ALBRECHT, Virginia S
Hunton & Williams, Washington, DC 202 955 1943
valbrecht@hunton.com
Recommended in Environment
Practice Areas: Virginia Albrecht's practice focuses exclusively on environmental law and administrative law - in particular, the Clean Water Act (CWA) wetlands program, the Endangered Species Act (ESA), the National Environmental Policy Act (NEPA) and other federal regulatory programs that affect the use of land. Experience in permit negotiation, litigation of policy issues, lobbying Congress and the Administration, enforcement defense, and compliance counseling. Representative clients include development companies, agricultural and mining companies, state and local agencies, and trade associations. Extensive experience with federal environmental agencies both in Washington and in district and regional offices.

ALDOCK, John
Goodwin Procter LLP, Washington, DC 202 346 4000
jaldock@goodwinprocter.com
Recommended in Litigation
Practice Areas: Mr Aldock specializes in complex litigation, class actions and mass torts. Representative clients for which Mr Aldock has been lead counsel include Prudential Insurance Company of America in numerous state and federal class actions including MDL and other national class actions brought by physicians and healthcare subscribers under RICO, ERISA and state law;

Arthur Andersen LLP in class actions brought under the US securities laws; and Rockwell Automation in multiple toxic tort class actions at the Rocky Flats nuclear weapons plant in Colorado and the Hanford Reservation in Washington State.

Prof. Memberships: CPR Institute; Panel of Distinguished Neutrals: Member; Commercial Arbitration Panel of the American Arbitration Association: Member; US District Court for the District of Columbia: Mediator; Washington Legal Clinic for the Homeless: Member of the Board of Directors; American Bar Foundation: Fellow; American College of Trial Lawyers: Fellow.

Personal: JD, University of Pennsylvania Law School, 1967 (cum laude); BS, Northwestern University, 1964.

ALEXANDER, Lee
Dickstein Shapiro Morin & Oshinsky LLP, Washington, DC 202 775 4731
AlexanderL@dsmo.com
Recommended in Energy

Practice Areas: Practices energy, regulatory, and environmental law. Focuses on federal regulatory and transactional energy issues, including natural gas and oil pipelines, storage facilities, and natural gas producers, as well as marketers and electric generators.

Prof. Memberships: Energy Bar Association.

Career: Partner, Dickstein Shapiro; prior experience in a variety of positions at the Federal Energy Regulatory Commission, including Deputy Chief of Staff to the Chairman, and Interstate Commerce Commission.

Publications: Lectured and written extensively on energy issues.

Personal: Pennsylvania State University (BS, 1973); University of Pittsburgh Law School (JD, 1976).

AMBLER, Diane
Kirkpatrick & Lockhart Nicholson Graham LLP, Washington, DC
202 778 9886
dambler@klng.com
Recommended in Investment Management

Practice Areas: Experience in financial institution regulation under federal securities laws, including USA PATRIOT Act and Sarbanes-Oxley Act; mutual fund governance and compliance activities of mutual funds, private funds and variable insurance product issuers and distributors.

Prof. Memberships: Chair, Executive Council of the FBA Securities Law Committee; Co-Chair, Committee on Developments in Investment Services of the ABA Section of Business Law; Chair, Investment Committee of the Board of Directors of the American Bar Retirement Association.

Publications: Co-Editor, 'Sarbanes-Oxley Planning & Compliance' (2003); 'Fund Director's Guidebook', 2nd ed. (2003).

Personal: Villanova Law School (JD, 1978) University of Rochester (BA, 1971).

ANDERSON, James E
Wilmer Cutler Pickering Hale and Dorr LLP, Washington, DC 202 663 6180
james.anderson@wilmerhale.com
Recommended in Investment Management

Practice Areas: Advises and represents investment advisers, broker-dealers, banks, mutual funds and other investment companies on investment adviser, investment company and broker-dealer regulatory and compliance issues; on related issues pertaining to pension plans and other types of retirement accounts; in investigations and proceedings brought by the Securities and Exchange Commission; and in civil litigation.

Publications: Co-author, 'Investment Advisers: Law & Compliance', a leading treatise on investment adviser regulation; contributing author, 'Mutual Fund Regulation', a treatise on investment company regulation.

Personal: Brigham Young University, J. Reuben Clark Law School (JD 1992); University of Utah (BA 1988).

ANDREWS, Walter J
Hunton & Williams, McLean
703 714 7642
wandrews@hunton.com
Recommended in Insurance

Practice Areas: Contract and insurance coverage litigation and counseling. Represent insurers in coverage and bad faith disputes involving business interruption, construction defect, e-commerce issues, and other emerging claims. Matters involve a variety of insurance contracts, including professional liability, first party property and general liability insurance policies. Represent clients in contract matters, particularly those involving technology disputes. Extensive experience in trial and appellate courts nationwide.

Prof. Memberships: ABA, Section of Litigation; FDCC; DRI; IADC; admitted to practice in Virginia and the District of Columbia and pro hac vice in 38 states.

Career: Hunton & Williams, McLean, VA, Partner 2005 to present; Shaw Pittman, McLean, VA, Partner 1999 to 2005; Wiley, Rein & Fielding, Washington, DC, Partner 1989-99, Associate 1983-89.

Publications: 'Nanotechnology: Tiny Technology, Big Risk?', Andrews Insurance Coverage Litigation, Vol. 15, December 17, 2004; 'Many Faxes: Little Coverage?', Mealey's Emerging Insurance Disputes, Vol. 9, No. 22, November 16, 2004; 'The Vioxx Recall and Its Insurance Implications', Coverage, Vol. 14, No. 4, November 2, 2004; 'Coverage Issues In Products Liability Litigation As Impacted By The Reinstatement (Third) Of Torts', Coverage, Vol. 14, No. 4, July/August 2004; 'Business Interruption

Coverage: What Constitutes 'Necessary Suspension of Operations' in the Wake of a Catastrophic Event?', Mealey's Business Interruption Insurance, Vol. 2, No. 5 (April 2003); 'Is There Insurance Coverage for Lawsuits Against the Firearm Industry?', Nevada Law Journal, Vol. 2, No. 2, (Fall 2002); 'Insurance Coverage Issues Surrounding Anthrax and Other Bio-Attacks and Hoaxes,' Mealey's Litigation Report: Insurance, Vol. 16, No. 4 (November 27, 2001).

Personal: University Of Chicago Law School, JD, 1982. Swarthmore College, BA with honors, 1979. Board of Directors of Swing Fore the Cure, a 501(c)(3) charitable organization dedicated to raising funds to find a cure for breast cancer.

ANDRIL, David T
Vinson & Elkins LLP, Washington, DC
202 639 6542
dandril@velaw.com
Recommended in Energy

Practice Areas: Practice concentrates on natural gas and liquefied natural gas sales and transportation contracting, and regulation of the natural gas industry in the United States and overseas.

Prof. Memberships: Federal Energy Bar Association.

Career: Admitted to District of Columbia Bar in 1980. Came to the firm in 1980 and was admitted to the partnership in January 1989.

ANGLE, Stephen
Vinson & Elkins LLP, Washington, DC
202 639 6565
sangle@velaw.com
Recommended in Energy

Practice Areas: Electric utility ratemaking, restructuring, power markets, regional transmission organizations.

Prof. Memberships: Energy Bar Association; American Bar Association, Section of Public Utilities, Transportation and Communication.

Career: Former Assistant General Counsel for Electric Lititgation, Federal Energy Regulatory Commission.

Publications: Frequent speaker on topics affecting electric industry.

Personal: University of Texas Law School (JD, 1974); Texas Christian University (BA, 1971).

ANTALICS, Michael
O'Melveny & Myers LLP,
Washington, DC 202 383 5300
Recommended in Antitrust

ASSAF, Eugene F
Kirkland & Ellis LLP, Washington, DC
202 879 5196
eassaf@kirkland.com
Recommended in Intellectual Property

Practice Areas: Mr Assaf focuses his practice in complex business litigation and technological disputes in numerous emergency injunctive relief cases, including antitrust, trade secrets and contract claims. As trial counsel, he has appeared in front of federal court

judges, juries and arbitration panels for intellectual property, antitrust, fiduciary duty, customs fraud, securities fraud and contract cases.

Personal: Dickinson College, BA, 1984. University of Essex, MA, 1987. University of Notre Dame Law School, JD, 1989.

ATTANASIO, Donna
Dewey Ballantine LLP, Washington, DC
202 429 2372
dattanasio@deweyballantine.com
Recommended in Energy

Practice Areas: Donna Attanasio practices in the Energy Group, working closely with the project finance, bankruptcy and litigation groups with respect to energy matters. Ms Attanasio's practice consists of counseling and representing developers of independent generation and their lenders and investors; electric utilities; energy marketers; transmission providers; and other integrated and disaggregated utility service providers with respect to matters arising under the Federal Power Act, the Public Utility Regulatory Policies Act, and the Public Utility Holding Company Act.

Career: Partner, Dewey Ballantine LLP.

Personal: Born February 22, 1959. AB, Smith College, 1981. JD, Harvard Law School, 1988.

ATWOOD, James
Covington & Burling, Washington, DC
202 662 5298
jatwood@cov.com
Recommended in Antitrust

Practice Areas: Chair of firm's Antitrust Group. Extensive litigation practice (trial and appellate) in defending class actions, government investigations, and monopolization claims. Broad advisory practice focusing on international transactions.

Career: Senior Deputy Legal Adviser (1979-80) and Deputy Assistant Secretary for Economic and Business Affairs, US Department of State (1978-79); Acting Professor, Stanford Law School (1980); clerk to Chief Justice Warren Burger, US Supreme Court (1970-71), and Judge Shirley Hufstedler, US Court of Appeals (1969-70).

Publications: Antitrust and American Business Abroad (2d ed. 1980); numerous legal articles.

Personal: Stanford University (JD, 1969); Yale University (BA in economics and political science, 1966).

AVIL, Richard
Jones Day, Washington, DC
202 879 5401
rdavil@jonesday.com
Recommended in Energy

Practice Areas: Chairs the firm's Energy Practice for the Government Regulation Group. He represents natural gas, oil, and electric industry clients in counseling activities with respect to energy and public utility law, as well as related fields, and has participated in numerous

adversarial proceedings before administrative agencies and courts. His practice includes advising clients concerning regulatory and other matters relevant to various types of transactions and to the development of energy-related projects. Listed in 'Who's Who in America' and 'Who's Who in American Law.'
Prof. Memberships: Energy Bar Association.

BAACH, Martin
Baach Robinson & Lewis PLLC, Washington, DC 202 833 8900
Recommended in Insurance

BACHMAN, Gary
Van Ness Feldman PC, Washington, DC 202 298 1800
Recommended in Energy

BAER, Bill
Arnold & Porter LLP, Washington, DC 202 942 5936
William.Baer@aporter.com
Recommended in Antitrust
Practice Areas: Heads Arnold & Porter LLP's highly regarded Antitrust Practice.
Career: Currently represents clients in high stakes antitrust litigation and provides antitrust counsel on a wide range of issues, including mergers and joint ventures in the high-tech, pharmaceutical and communications sectors, antitrust and intellectual property and criminal investigations by DOJ's Antitrust Division. From 1995-99, he served as Director of the Federal Trade Commission's Bureau of Competition. Among other matters he oversaw the Commission's successful court challenges to the Staples/Office Depot and drug wholesaler mergers, review of Time Warner's acquisition of Turner Broadcasting System and the Ciba-Geigy/Sandoz merger, as well as challenges to exclusionary tactics of Toys-R-Us, Intel and Mylan Laboratories. Practiced law at Arnold & Porter from 1980-95, where he helped secure the 1994 acquittal of the General Electric Company on criminal price fixing charges. He also served at the Federal Trade Commission from 1975-80, where he held a number of positions, including Attorney Advisor to the Chairman, and Assistant General Counsel and Director of Congressional Relations.
Publications: 'Taking Stock: Recent Trends in U.S. Merger Enforcement'; 'Transatlantic Tension'; 'Competition Leniency'; 'Solving Competition Problems in Merger Control: The Requirements for an Effective Divestiture Remedy'; 'Item 4(c): The Next Step in HSR Reform Education'.
Personal: Mr Baer holds a JD from Stanford Law School (1975) and a BA from Lawrence University (1972).

BAGNALL, Robert G
Wilmer Cutler Pickering Hale and Dorr LLP, Washington, DC
202 663 6974
robert.bagnall@wilmerhale.com
Recommended in Investment Management
Practice Areas: Practice focuses on investment management regulation, concentrating on investment company and investment adviser matters.
Career: Served as Senior Special Counsel in the Office of Chief Counsel of the SEC's Division of Investment Management from 1995 through 1996, supervising no-action letters and special projects and serving as liaison for interpretive questions arising in disclosure review and in inspections of investment companies and investment advisers. Served as Assistant Chief of the Office of Regulatory Policy, which is responsible for rulemaking under the Investment Company Act and other federal securities laws.
Personal: Harvard Law School (JD 1985); Yale College (BA 1977).

BAINE, Kevin
Williams & Connolly LLP, Washington, DC 202 434 5000
Recommended in Media & Entertainment

BALIS, Stanley
Miller, Balis & O'Neil, PC, Washington, DC 202 296 2960
Recommended in Energy

BANKS, Jim
Hogan & Hartson LLP, Washington, DC 202 637 5802
jtbanks@hhlaw.com
Recommended in Environment
Practice Areas: Environmental, including audits and compliance programs, Clean Water Act issues (also wetlands), water resources, fisheries, enforcement and debarment defense, hazardous waste, solid waste and superfund issues.
Career: 1996-present, Hogan & Hartson, Partner; prior to joining Hogan, served for 10 years in the private sector after a decade as a public-interest environmental lawyer; positions included General Counsel of Chemical Waste Management, Inc.; Senior Attorney/Director of Clean Water Project, Natural Resources Defense Council; Staff Attorney, US Marine Mammal Commission.
Personal: University of Michigan Law School (JD, 1975); University of Kansas (BS, CE, 1972).

BARBASH, Barry
Shearman & Sterling, Washington, DC 202 508 8060
BBarbash@shearman.com
Recommended in Investment Management
Practice Areas: Partner at Shearman & Sterling and head of the Asset Management Group. Expertise includes mutual fund operations and regulation, hedge fund formation and regulation, private equity fund structuring and financing, venture capital fund operations and offerings, and asset management merger and acquisition transactions.
Prof. Memberships: Member of the District of Columbia, New York, Massachusetts and American Bar Associations; Presidential Distinguished Rank Award for exceptional achievement as a member of the Senior Executive Service of the United States.
Career: Director of the Securities and Exchange Commission's Division of Investment Management, 1993-98.
Personal: BA, summa cum laude, Bowdoin College (1975); JD, Cornell Law School (1978).

BARKER, James
Latham & Watkins LLP, Washington, DC 202 637 2200
Recommended in Telecom, Broadcast & Satellite

BARNETT, Robert
Williams & Connolly LLP, Washington, DC 202 434 5000
Recommended in Media & Entertainment

BARRY, Dennis
Vinson & Elkins LLP, Washington, DC 202 639 6791
dbarry@velaw.com
Recommended in Healthcare
Practice Areas: Healthcare, Medicare and Medicaid, compliance.
Prof. Memberships: Healthcare Financial Management Association (HFMA), past president of Washington Metro chapter; American Health Lawyers Association (AHLA), Chair, Medicare and Medicaid Institute.
Career: Ohio Wesleyan University, BA in economics, 1972 (Phi Beta Kappa); University of Virginia School of Law, JD, 1975 (Co-editor, 'Virginia Journal of International Law').
Publications: Dennis Barry's Reimbursement Advisor, monthly newsletter published by Aspen Publishers; Cost Reimbursement in (AHLA Health Law Practice Guide), Chpt. 15 (West 2004); Legal Issues Surrounding Hospital and Physician Relationships, in Health Care Fraud and Abuse: Practical Perspectives (ABA & BNA 2003).

BASKIN, Maurice
Venable LLP, Washington, DC 202 962 4800
Recommended in Employment

BASTIANELLI, Adrian
Bastianelli, Brown & Kelley, Washington, DC 202 293 8815
Recommended in Construction

BAUMBUSCH, Peter L
Gibson, Dunn & Crutcher LLP, Washington, DC 202 955 8530
pbaumbusch@gibsondunn.com
Recommended in Tax
Practice Areas: Provided legal and tax advice relating to the acquisition of over $10 billion in US corporate and real estate investments. Provides advice to hedge funds and with respect to multi-jurisdictional option and compensation programs.
Prof. Memberships: Former Chair of the ABA Tax Section Committee on Foreign Activities of US Taxpayers.
Publications: Has lectured on international taxation, tax shelters, transfer pricing and cost sharing. Primary draftsperson of ABA 'White Paper on Section 482 Intercompany Pricing,' and assisted Senator Bill Bradley in developing tax reform proposals.
Personal: JD, Harvard Law School, 1972, 'Harvard Law Review' and Board of Student Advisors.

BAUMGARTEN, Jon
Proskauer Rose, Washington, DC 202 416 6810
jabaumgarten@proskauer.com
Recommended in Intellectual Property
Practice Areas: He is widely recognized as one of the country's leading domestic and international intellectual property lawyers, with particular emphasis in copyright matters. Emphasis on domestic and international copyright, licensing, contract, litigation and related matters pertaining to the publishing, computer, motion picture, music and recording, communications, arts and internet communities.
Prof. Memberships: Serves on several bar association committees on copyright and is past Chair of the Committee on International Copyright of the Section of Patent, Trademark and Copyright Law of the American Bar Association. He is a member of the Editorial Board of the 'Copyright Society's Journal', the Advisory Boards of the 'Patent, Trademark and Copyright Journal', 'World Intellectual Property Report', 'Computer Lawyer' and 'Journal of Proprietary Rights', and was a founding director of the American Copyright Council, the Computer Law Association, the DC Computer Law Forum and Washington Area Lawyers for the Arts.
Publications: Author of numerous articles and a book entitled 'U.S.-U.S.S.R. Copyright Relations Under the Universal Copyright Convention.'
Personal: City College of the City University of New York, BA, 1964. New York University School of Law, LLB, 1967; Research Editor, 'New York University Law Review', 1966-67.

BAXTER, Michael St Patrick
Covington & Burling, Washington, DC 202 662 5164
mbaxter@cov.com
Recommended in Bankruptcy
Practice Areas: Practice includes advising creditors in bankruptcy cases, representing companies in bankruptcy reorganization, advising on the structuring

of transactions involving financially troubled companies, counseling companies in workouts and debt restructurings, representing official committees in bankruptcy cases, and acting as Chapter 11 bankruptcy trustee.

Prof. Memberships: American Law Institute; American College of Bankruptcy; International Insolvency Institute; Vice Chair, ABA Business Bankruptcy Committee; Select Advisory Committee on Business Reorganization; Law Society of Upper Canada.

Career: Covington & Burling, 1983 to present.

Publications: Contributing editor, 'Norton Bankruptcy Law and Practice 2d'. Contributing author, 1999 'Annual Survey of Letter of Credit Law & Practice'. Co-author, 'The Art & Science of Bankruptcy Law'. He has published extensively in the insolvency area and is a frequent speaker at professional programs.

Personal: LLM, Harvard Law School, 1983; LLB, University of Western Ontario, 1979. Law clerk to the Chief Justice of Ontario, 1981-82.

BECKER, Brandon
Wilmer Cutler Pickering Hale and Dorr LLP, Washington, DC 202 663 6979
brandon.becker@wilmerhale.com
Recommended in Investment Management

Practice Areas: Co-Chair of the firm's Securities Department. Practice focuses on advising broker-dealers and other financial market participants regarding various transactional and compliance matters, as well as the development of new financial products and trading systems.

Prof. Memberships: Chair, Subcommittee on Market Regulation, Federal Regulation of Securities Committee, American Bar Association Section of Business Law. Member of Board of Advisers of the Center for the Study of Securities Markets. On editorial advisory boards for International Finance and wallstreetlawyer.com. Has taught various courses regarding corporate law and securities regulation at American University, George Mason University, and Georgetown University.

Career: Lawyer at the US Securities and Exchange Commission, 1978-96. Served as Director of the SEC's Division of Market Regulation. Previously Staff Member, President's Working Group on Financial Markets; Member, Financial Products Advisory Committee of the Commodity Futures Trading Commission; and SEC's representative to Secondary Markets Working Party of the International Organization of Securities Commissions. Joined WCP in 1996.

Personal: Columbia University (LLM, Associate-in-Law, 1979); University of San Diego (JD 1977, magna cum laude); University of Minnesota (BA 1974, summa cum laude).

BEHRENDS IV, Samuel
LeBoeuf, Lamb, Greene & MacRae, LLP, Washington, DC 202 986 8018
sbehrend@llgm.com
Recommended in Energy

Practice Areas: Has represented utilities before the Federal Energy Regulatory Commission, the Nuclear Regulatory Commission, and state commissions in various matters involving traditional rate cases, mergers and acquisitions, transmission both before and after open access, power marketing and code of conduct issues, qualified facilities and independent power producers. His present clients include, among others, power marketers and independent energy producers.

Prof. Memberships: District of Columbia Bar; American Bar Association.

Career: Joined LeBoeuff in 1982; Reid & Priest, Washington, DC 1979-82.

Personal: Wake Forest University (JD) 1979; Harvard University (BA) 1974.

BELL, Joseph C
Hogan & Hartson LLP, Washington, DC 202 637 5780
jcbell@hhlaw.com
Recommended in Energy

Practice Areas: Energy regulation and policy; project and international finance; international transactions (energy and non-energy); recent focus on oil and economic development; special expertise with respect to Poland.

Prof. Memberships: Council on Foreign Relations; Polish American Freedom Foundation (Founding Director); International Senior Lawyers Project (Director); International Bar Association; Energy Bar Association; ABA (International, Administrative and Business Sections).

Career: 1969-70 Cabinet Task Force on Oil Import Control, Attorney; 1970-72 US Department of Justice, Attorney Advisor, Antitrust Division; 1972-74 Duke University Law School and Institute for Public Policy, Assistant Professor; 1974-77 Federal Energy Administration, Assistant General Counsel, International and Special Programs; 1979-89, Citizens Energy Corporation, Outside General Counsel; 1989-90, Special Counsel to Ministry of Finance, Poland; 1977-present Hogan & Hartson, partner; 2003-present, pro bono adviser to Sao Tome and Principe regarding Oil Revenue Management law.

Publications: 'Sao Tome and Principe Enacts Oil Revenue Law, Sets New Governance, Transparency, and Accountability Standards for Industry.' OGEL, Vol. 3 Issue 1, March 2005; 'Systematic Risk Factors in Russian and Eurasia,' Russian-Eurasian Renaissance? (2003); 'Legal Issues in Resource Management Laws.' Escaping the Resource Curse (tent.) (forthcoming).

Personal: Yale Law School (JD, 1968); Harvard University (MA, Economics, 1965); University of Colorado (BA, summa cum laude, 1962).

BELL, Robert B
Wilmer Cutler Pickering Hale and Dorr LLP, Washington, DC 202 663 6533
robert.ell@wilmerhale.com
Recommended in Antitrust

Practice Areas: Has extensive experience in securing antitrust clearance for mergers and acquisitions from both the Department of Justice and the Federal Trade Commission. Practice includes antitrust litigation, both criminal and civil; merger clearance; and antitrust counseling on issues ranging from competitor collaborations to vertical distribution arrangements. Has represented clients from a wide variety of sectors, including imaging, communications, defense, entertainment, manufacturing, mining, chemicals and transportation.

Publications: Articles have appeared in Antitrust, Global Competition Review (March 2003, P.9), Legal Times, and National Law Journal.

Personal: Stanford Law School (JD 1980); Cambridge University (MA 1977); Dartmouth College (BA 1975).

BELLER, Herbert N
Sutherland Asbill & Brennan LLP, Washington, DC 202 383 0120
herb.beller@sablaw.com
Recommended in Tax

Practice Areas: Transactional tax planning, including acquisitions, dispositions, spin-offs and other restructurings involving domestic and foreign entities. IRS National Office and Treasury matters. Tax controversy matters at administrative and judicial levels. Representation of private foundations, public charities and other non-profit entities.

Prof. Memberships: Chair, American Bar Association Section of Taxation (2002-03). Editor-in-Chief, The Tax Lawyer, (1993-96). Co-Chair, National Conference of Lawyers and CPA's (2000-06). Regent, American College of Tax Counsel (2003-06). Trustee, American Tax Policy Institute (2003-05). Fellow, American Bar Foundation.

Personal: JD, cum laude, Northwestern University School of Law, 1967. BSBA, Northwestern University, 1964. Law Clerk to US Tax Court Judge Theodore Tannenwald, Jr. (1967-68). Certified Public Accountant. Listed in Best Lawyers in America, International Who's Who of Corporate Tax Advisers, and International Tax Review's Guide to the World's Leading Tax Advisers.

BENNETT, Mary
Baker & McKenzie, Washington, DC 202 452 7045
mary.c.bennett@bakernet.com
Recommended in Tax

Practice Areas: Specializes in US tax planning and controversies for multinational corporations (eg withholding taxes, cross-border financings, foreign tax credits, controlled foreign corporations, and tax treaties). Deals regularly with IRS to obtain letter rulings, competent authority determinations, and regu-

latory relief, and represents companies on tax policy matters before US Treasury and Congress. Adjunct Professor of Advanced International Tax, Georgetown University Law Center, 2001-04.

Prof. Memberships: International Fiscal Association, ABA Tax Section.

Career: Deputy International Tax Counsel, US Treasury, 1987-90.

Personal: AB, cum laude, Harvard University, 1976; Universite de Paris, 1974-75; JD, Columbia Law School, 1979; LLM, Tax, Boston University, 1985.

BENNETT, Robert S
Skadden, Arps, Slate, Meagher & Flom LLP & Affiliates, Washington, DC 202 371 7180
rbennett@skadden.com
Recommended in Litigation

Practice Areas: Heads Skadden's International Government Enforcement Group. Leads civil and criminal litigation practice in the Washington, DC office. Has tried several high-profile cases. Represents corporations, directors and officers in criminal, civil and SEC enforcement matters. Advises management and boards on preventive and remedial measures. Assists boards and audit committees in conducting internal investigations. Represents corporations and officers and directors in complex civil and criminal matters and qui tam actions. Has extensive experience representing clients before Congressional committees.

Career: LLM, Harvard Law School, 1965; LLB, Georgetown Law Center, 1964; University of Virginia Law School, 1961-62; BA, Georgetown University, 1961.

BERGESON, Lynn
Bergeson & Campbell PC, Washington, DC 202 557 3800
Recommended in Environment

BERLIN, Kenneth
Skadden, Arps, Slate, Meagher & Flom LLP & Affiliates, Washington, DC 202 371 7350
kberlin@skadden.com
Recommended in Environment

Practice Areas: Heads the firm's East Coast and International Environmental Practice. Has extensive background in representing clients analyzing environmental issues in business transactions and in environmental litigation, including representing parties in environmental cleanup, bankruptcy, criminal and civil penalty cases, and arguing cases in federal appeals court. Has significant experience in representing clients in connection with environmental issues at controversial facilities, dealing with environmental and community groups, and preparing complex environmental impact assessments.

Career: JD, Columbia Law School, 1973; BA, University of Pennsylvania, 1969.

BERNER, Frederic
Sidley Austin Brown & Wood LLP,
Washington, DC 202 736 8232
fberner@sidley.com
Recommended in Energy

Practice Areas: Frederic Berner, Partner in Washington, DC, has served as lead counsel for many partnerships and joint ventures of energy companies in the development of major energy projects such as the Millennium Pipeline Project and the Great Plains Coal Gasification Project. He has represented a broad spectrum of clients in the litigation of energy issues before federal and state commissions and courts. Mr Berner has prepared and negotiated hundreds of construction, supply, and transportation agreements.

Career: The George Washington University Law School, JD, 1973; American University, MBA, 1970; Middlebury College, BA, 1965. Bar admission: District of Columbia, 1973.

BERNIUS, Robert
Nixon Peabody LLP, Washington, DC
202 585 8312
rbernius@nixonpeabody.com
Recommended in Media & Entertainment

Practice Areas: Litigation for corporate clients in libel, discrimination, general commercial, and internet-related cases.
Prof. Memberships: Admitted to practice in New York, Maryland, DC, US Supreme Court, US Courts of Appeals (Second, Third, Fourth, Sixth, Ninth, Tenth, Eleventh, DC Circuits), US District Courts (Eastern, Northern, Southern, Western Districts of NY; DC; MD, Colo.). Chair, Professional Standards Committee. Advisory Board, Media Law Reporter. Formerly Managing Partner, Washington, DC, office. Former assistant DA, Brooklyn, New York. Fellow, American College of Trial Lawyers.
Publications: Lectures on First Amendment issues throughout US.
Personal: Yale Law School, JD; Brown University, ScBEE, magna cum laude.

BERNSTEIN, Michael
Arnold & Porter LLP, Washington, DC
202 942 5577
Michael.Bernstein@aporter.com
Recommended in Bankruptcy

Practice Areas: Michael Bernstein represents parties in bankruptcy and work-out matters, and in related litigation throughout the United States.
Prof. Memberships: American Bankruptcy Institute; ABA Business Bankruptcy Committee; Walter Chandler American Inn of Court.
Career: Mr Bernstein has been involved in bankruptcy and insolvency matters in many industries, including telecommunications, energy, real estate, finance, manufacturing, technology, retail, airline, healthcare, and pharmaceuticals. His clients have included America Online, American Capital Strategies,

American Red Cross, Ardent Communications Creditors' Committee, Bear Stearns, Boehringer Ingelheim, Cingular Wireless, CRIIMI Mae Creditors' Committee, Dynex Bondholders Committee, Glaxo, Guinness Import Company, Health Care REIT, Lennar Partners, Major League Baseball, Perseus LLC, Sodexho, Texas Pacific Group and The George Washington University, among others.
Publications: Mr Bernstein is co-author of 'Bankruptcy in Practice,' published by the American Bankruptcy Institute. He is a member of the ABI Journal's editorial board and co-authors a monthly column on Chapter 11 issues. He has also written articles, lectured on bankruptcy law topics, and been interviewed by major newspapers and on television and radio.
Personal: JD, Northwestern University School of Law, 1989; BA, Brandeis University, 1986.

BERZ, David
Weil, Gotshal & Manges LLP,
Washington, DC 202 682 7190
david.berz@weil.com
Recommended in Environment

Practice Areas: Bankruptcy litigation, product liability/mass tort/environmental, litigation/regulatory.
Career: With over 20 years experience representing clients in major US legislative/regulatory developments, Berz heads the firm's Environmental Practice. He serves as lead counsel in civil and criminal environmental matters involving federal and state water, air, and hazardous waste issues, and regularly counsels multinational corporations and their boards of directors in developing environmental compliance programs. Berz is also responsible for evaluation and litigation relating to environmental issues that arise in bankruptcy and merger and acquisition matters.
Personal: George Washington University, BA, JD.

BEYDA, Richard
Grossberg Yochelson Fox & Beyda,
Washington, DC 202 296 9696
Recommended in Real Estate

BIEKE, James
Goodwin Procter LLP, Washington, DC
202 346 4000
jbieke@sheagardner.com
Recommended in Environment

Practice Areas: Mr Bieke specializes in environmental and natural resources law and policy, with a particular emphasis on complex scientific, technical, economic and legal issues. For the past 25 years, Mr Bieke has handled cases in federal and state courts and before federal and state administrative agencies. He provides advice to clients on numerous legal, technical, scientific and policy issues under the Comprehensive Environmental Response, Compensation and Liability Act (CERCLA), the

Resource Conservation and Recovery Act (RCRA), the Toxic Substances Control Act (TSCA), the Clean Air Act, the Clean Water Act, and other federal and state environmental statutes and regulations.
Personal: LLM, New York University Law School, 1971; JD, University of Michigan Law School, 1970 (Order of the Coif); MA, University of Michigan, 1970; BA, Sacred Heart Seminary, 1967.

BILES, Blake A
Arnold & Porter LLP, Washington, DC
202 942 5836
Blake.Biles@aporter.com
Recommended in Environment

Practice Areas: Blake Biles has provided services to business interests concerning the full range of substantive environmental requirements and virtually all types of legal matters - counseling, transactions, rulemakings, compliance audits, and enforcement and appellate litigation. He has particular expertise in the regulation of commercial chemicals and products, including toxic substances legislation, hazard communication and right-to-know standards, biotechnology and life sciences legal frameworks, consumer product safety laws, and related product liability matters. Mr Biles also advises concerning international environmental treaties and laws.
Prof. Memberships: Mr Biles began his career at the US EPA, and served as the first Director of the Agency's new-chemicals notification program. In addition to his work for business interests, Mr Biles has been active in a number of American Bar Association committees and programs, and he regularly represents clients in Arnold & Porter LLP pro bono matters.
Career: Mr Biles served the Environmental Protection Agency, first in the Agency's Office of Water Enforcement, and then in the Office of the General Counsel. Thereafter, he was the first Director of the Premanufacture Review Division in the Office of Toxic Substances.
Personal: JD, University of Kansas School of Law, 1975; BA, University of Kansas, 1968.

BLACKBURN, Thomas
Bruder Gentile & Marcoux LLP,
Washington, DC 202 296 1500
Recommended in Energy

BLAKE, Jonathan D
Covington & Burling, Washington, DC
202 662 5506
jblake@cov.com
Recommended in Telecom, Broadcast & Satellite

Practice Areas: Communications (spectrum issues, television, broadband, cable, wireless, satellite, new technologies), media, education, mergers and other deals, international, legislation, litigation, and corporate governance. Highlights: represented Adelphia Special

Committee of Independent Directors; helped launch digital television; led battle on media ownership rules.
Prof. Memberships: American Bar Association - Chair, 1993-99, International Telecommunications Committee; Federal Communications Bar Association - President, 1984-85.
Career: Former Chair of the firm's Management Committee, 1996-01, Head of firm's Technology, Media and Communications Group; Senior Communications Partner; named one of top 100 most powerful lawyers by leading legal publication, 1997-2002.
Publications: Numerous publications and speeches.
Personal: Yale University (LLB, 1964; BA 1960); Oxford University (MA in Law); Phi Beta Kappa, Rhodes Scholar; Yale Law Journal. Married to Elizabeth Shriver. Five children.

BLASZAK, James S
Levine, Blaszak, Block & Boothby LLP,
Washington, DC 202 857 2541
jblaszak@lb3law.com
Recommended in Telecom, Broadcast & Satellite

Practice Areas: Specialization is evaluating, negotiating and documenting telecommunications service contracts for buyers of such services. He has advised purchasers in connection with scores of those agreements, as well as customized agreements for cellular, frame relay, and satellite services. Among the clients he has assisted are numerous Fortune 100 companies. Also has participated in complex rate and regulatory cases, and has prosecuted applications for radio licenses and operating authority and satellite system authorizations. He has counseled clients on a wide range of matters implicating federal and state telecommunications laws. He is counsel to the Ad Hoc Telecommunications Users Committee, whose members are among the largest purchasers of communications services.
Prof. Memberships: Member of the District of Columbia Bar and the Federal Communications Bar Association.
Career: Partner at Gardner, Carton and Douglas before joining Levine, Blaszak, Block & Boothby as a Partner. Before entering private practice, he served in a variety of positions at the Federal Communications Commission, including Chief of the Domestic Facilities and Satellite Branch and Legal Advisor to the Chief, Common Carrier Bureau. Graduated from the University of Texas School of Law.

BLOCH, Robert E
Mayer, Brown, Rowe & Maw LLP,
Washington, DC 202 263 3203
rbloch@mayerbrownrowe.com
Recommended in Antitrust

Practice Areas: Represents major corporations and officials in criminal and civil investigations before Antitrust

Division and FTC for price fixing, bid rigging, boycotts and mergers; defense of private class action litigation in federal and state courts. Antitrust counsel in major mergers/acquisitions and joint ventures. Recent antitrust class action defenses: Bertelsmann, Inc. (in In re Compact Disc Antitrust Litigation and Compact Disc Minimum-Advertised Price Antitrust Litigation); ETI Explosives Technologies International, Inc. in In re Commercial Explosives Antitrust Litigation and defense of Cargill, Inc. in In re Citric Acid Antitrust Litigation and In re High Fructose Corn Syrup Antitrust Litigation. Antitrust counsel to major healthcare companies and leading academic medical centers.

Career: Mayer, Brown, Rowe & Maw LLP, Washington, DC, 1993-date; Partner, 1993. Antitrust Division, US Department of Justice: Chief Professions and Intellectual Property Section, 1988-93; Assistant Chief, Litigation I, 1985-88; Assistant Chief, Trial Section, 1981-85; Trial Attorney, 1975-81. Assistant Attorney General, Office of the Attorney General of Ohio, Antitrust Section, 1973-75.
Publications: Writes and speaks extensively on antitrust issues.
Personal: JD (honors) George Washington University, 1973. BA, Franklin and Marshall College, 1969. John Marshall Award, 1992. US Department of Justice: The Harold M. Stevens Award for Outstanding Service, 1993.

BLOCK, Joseph
Venable LLP, Washington, DC
202 962 4800
Recommended in Environment

BLUMENTHAL, William
King & Spalding LLP, Washington, DC
202 737 0500
Recommended in Antitrust

BOOTHBY, Colleen
Levine, Blaszak, Block & Boothby LLP,
Washington, DC 202 857 2550
cboothby@lb3law.com
Recommended in Telecom, Broadcast & Satellite
Practice Areas: Represents telecommunications users, IT companies, and associations (including IBM, Microsoft, First Data, the Ad Hoc Telecommunications Users Committee, and the High Tech Broadband Coalition) before the US Federal Communications Commission and courts. Provides strategic counsel on a broad range of subjects, including the regulation of telecommunications, information services, IT products, the internet and public/private intranets; privacy, telemarketing, and proprietary network information; inside wire and building access; and the pricing of local exchange and interexchange services. Frequent speaker before enterprise customer groups.
Prof. Memberships: Federal Communications Bar Association (Co-Chair, Common Carrier Practice Committee,

1998-99). District of Columbia Bar Association (Steering Committee, Administrative Law and Agency Practice Committee, 2000-04).
Career: Admitted to District of Columbia Bar in 1980. Federal Communications Commission (Deputy and Associate Chief, Tariff Division; Legal Assistant to the Bureau Chief, Common Carrier Bureau; Senior Supervising Attorney, International and Tariff Divisions), 1983-93.
Personal: AB, Pomona College, 1977. JD, Boalt Hall School of Law (associate editor, California Law Review), 1980.

BOUKNIGHT, J A
Steptoe & Johnson LLP,
Washington, DC 202 429 6222
jbouknight@steptoe.com
Recommended in Energy
Practice Areas: Partner in the Washington office of Steptoe & Johnson LLP. Primarily represents electric power clients involving regulatory, commercial, and antitrust matters. Practice includes litigation in trial and appellate courts and the conduct of proceedings before federal and state regulatory agencies, including Federal Energy Regulatory Commission (FERC) and Nuclear Regulatory Commission (NRC), as well as representation of clients in the development of both domestic and international power projects and related regulatory and commercial arrangements.
Personal: JD, Duke University, 1968; BA, Wofford College, 1965.

BOURDEAU, Karl S
Beveridge & Diamond PC,
Washington, DC 202 789 6019
kbourdeau@bdlaw.com
Recommended in Environment
Practice Areas: Practices principally in a wide range of litigation, regulatory, transactional and legislative matters involving hazardous substance and hazardous waste issues under the federal Resource Conservation and Recovery Act (RCRA), the Comprehensive Environmental Response, Compensation and Liability Act (CERCLA), and analogous state laws. Also has been active in representing clients on a variety of international environmental and federal Information Quality Act issues.
Prof. Memberships: American Bar Association; District of Columbia Bar Association; Federal Bar Association; Member of the Board of Advisors of the National Brownfields Association.
Career: Admitted to District of Columbia Bar (1978). Director of Beveridge & Diamond, P.C. Frequent lecturer and author on hazardous substance liability issues, and presently serves as a member of the Board of Advisors of the National Brownfields Association.
Publications: Author: 'Energy Conservation in the 94th Congress: A Solution to the Problem or Problems with the Solution?,' 1 Harv. Envtl. L. Rev. 225

(1977); 'Corrective Action Requirements Under the Resource Conservation and Recovery Act,' Environmental Risk Management - A Desk Reference, RTM Communications, Inc. (1991); co-author: 'Investing in the USA: Environmental Compliance and Liability,' Law Business Research, The American Legal Yearbook (1998).
Personal: JD from Harvard University (1978) and BS (summa cum laude) from Muhlenberg College (1975).

BOWE Jr, James F
Dewey Ballantine LLP, Washington, DC
202 429 1444
jbowe@deweyballantine.com
Recommended in Energy
Practice Areas: Energy (including energy project development, energy regulatory matters, energy company M&A). Project finance (US, North America, Latin America). Oil and gas law.
Prof. Memberships: Energy Bar Association. American Bar Association. Member of the Bar of the District of Columbia and the bars of several federal courts.
Career: Admitted to practice 1982, District of Columbia. Private practice since 1982. Partner, Dewey Ballantine LLP, July 1994-present. Adjunct professor, Oil and Gas Law, Georgetown University Law Center, 1990-95.
Personal: BA, Williams College, 1977. JD, Northwestern University School of Law, 1982.

BOWMAN, William
Hogan & Hartson LLP, Washington, DC
202 637 6434
wjbowman@hhlaw.com
Recommended in Insurance, Litigation
Practice Areas: Focuses principally in the area of litigation, including trial and appellate matters involving commercial, insurance coverage, environmental, contract, and product liability litigation. He has practiced actively in federal and state courts throughout the country.
Prof. Memberships: Member, ABA; Member, District of Columbia Bar Association.
Career: Former assistant US attorney for the District of Columbia; former chief counsel to the US Senate Judiciary Committee Subcommittee on Juvenile Justice; Former law clerk for Judge Thomas A. Flannery of the US District Court of the District of Columbia.
Personal: Georgetown University Law Center (JD).

BRANDS, Henk
Paul, Weiss, Rifkind, Wharton & Garrison, Washington, DC 202 223 7300
Recommended in Telecom, Broadcast & Satellite

BRASHER, Lance
Skadden, Arps, Slate, Meagher & Flom LLP & Affiliates, Washington, DC
202 371 7402
lbrasher@skadden.com
Recommended in Projects
Practice Areas: Concentrates in the development, financing, and acquisition of power, LNG and gas pipeline assets, sports facilities and other large energy and infrastructure projects. Handles major transactions involving privatizations and restructurings. Also advises clients on power procurement and renewable energy matters. Represents sponsors, financial institutions, utilities, contractors and fuel suppliers in transactions in the US, Europe, Asia, Australia, South America and the Caribbean. Lecturer at project financing and energy conferences and author.
Career: JD, Harvard Law School, 1990 (cum laude); BS, United States Naval Academy, 1982 (with distinction).

BRAY, John
King & Spalding LLP, Washington, DC
202 626 5618
jbray@kslaw.com
Recommended in Litigation
Practice Areas: Over 35 years experience in civil and criminal litigation in federal district courts including: asbestos liability, federal tax, environmental, defense procurement, insurance coverage, antitrust cases, and cases presenting a host of business, financial and government regulatory issues. Has also been involved in numerous historic criminal conspiracy cases and trials throughout the US dealing with complex issues in: tax, antitrust claims, international investigations, fraudulent conveyances, environmental issues and insurance coverage.
Prof. Memberships: Fellow of the American College of Trial Lawyers.
Personal: Undergraduate degree from St. Louis University and JD degree from St. Louis University School of Law.

BRENNAN Jr, John T
Crowell & Moring LLP, Washington, DC
202 624 2760
jbrennan@crowell.com
Recommended in Healthcare
Practice Areas: John Brennan is Chair of Crowell & Moring's Health Care Group. He focuses on healthcare fraud and abuse matters, especially relating to federal false claims, antikickback, and Stark Law issues. He advises on compliance matters and conducts internal investigations related to potential fraud and abuse issues.
Prof. Memberships: American Health Lawyers Association and American Bar Association's White Collar Crime Health Law Subcommittee; former Chair of the AHLA's Substantive Law Committee on Fraud and Abuse, Self-Referrals and False Claims.
Career: Voted one of the nation's top

healthcare provider attorneys by Nightingales in 2004; former hospital administrator.

BREYFOGLE, Jon
Groom Law Group, Washington, DC
202 857 0620
Recommended in Employee Benefits

BRINKMANN, Beth
Morrison & Foerster LLP,
Washington, DC 202 887 1544
bbrinkmann@mofo.com
Recommended in Litigation
Practice Areas: Focuses on the US Supreme Court and other appellate matters. Consults on complex civil litigation and federal regulatory matters. Has argued 20 cases before the Supreme Court, more than any other women in private practice.
Career: Admitted to practice in California and District of Columbia. From 1993-2001, served as Assistant to the Solicitor General of the United States, arguing on behalf of the United States before the Supreme Court. Served as an Assistant Federal Public Defender from 1991-93. Law clerk, Justice Harry A Blackmun, Supreme Court of the United States, 1986-87. Chair, Appellate Practice Group. Named a top Washington constitutional lawyer by 'The Washingtonian' magazine.
Personal: AB, University of California, Berkeley, 1980; JD, Yale University Law School, 1985.

BROGAN, Stephen J
Jones Day, Washington, DC
202 879 3939
sjbrogan@jonesday.com
Recommended in Litigation
Practice Areas: Jones Day's Managing Partner. Extensive litigation practice, including securities, banking, contests for corporate control, corporate criminal investigations, product liability, independent counsel investigations, and qui tam actions. Matters include representing: J.C. Penney in a grand jury investigation; General Motors in the GM-Toyota joint venture, air bag safety, and Cadillac V8-6-4 litigation; Gillette in a takeover contest; General Electric in a grand jury defense; Bridgestone/Firestone in product liability litigation; the directors of Northrop in a grand jury investigation; Dart Group in a corporate governance dispute; and First American and First American Bankshares in investigations arising from the collapse of BCCI.

BROSE, Steven
Steptoe & Johnson LLP,
Washington, DC 202 429 6250
sbrose@steptoe.com
Recommended in Energy
Practice Areas: Head of the Energy and Natural Resources Department at Steptoe & Johnson LLP and resident in the Washington office. Has more than 30 years of experience in a broad range

of administrative and judicial matters, principally involving the oil and natural gas industries. Counsels numerous pipeline companies with respect to their rates, regulated practices, and business opportunities. Has also represented entities in a variety of sectors on the natural gas industry in matters involving rates, certificates, royalties and abandonments.
Personal: JD, Columbia University, 1972; BA, Pennsylvania State University, 1969.

BROWN, Arthur
Kirkpatrick & Lockhart Nicholson Graham LLP, Washington, DC
202 778 9046
abrown@klng.com
Recommended in Investment Management
Practice Areas: Experience in corporate and federal securities laws. Focus on investment management regulation: investment company, investment adviser and broker-dealer representations; counsel to sponsors of registered investment companies and independent directors of such companies. Experience in compliance and regulatory matters and has been lead attorney in many significant legal matters affecting the industry.
Prof. Memberships: American Bar, Federal Bar, International Bar.
Career: Securities and Exchange Commission 1974-82, Chief of Investment Company Act rulemaking office and special counsel in Division of Investment Management; Partner at K&LNG since 1983.
Personal: New York University (JD, 1973); City College of New York (BS, 1970).

BROWN, Barbara B
Paul, Hastings, Janofsky & Walker LLP, Washington, DC 202 551 1717
barbarabrown@paulhastings.com
Recommended in Employment
Practice Areas: Represents employers in entire range of employment law matters, particularly discrimination class actions, executive and law firm personnel matters, harassment investigations, and selection criteria and compensation self-audits and litigation defense.
Prof. Memberships: Past Co-Chair, EEO Committee of the American Bar Association Labor and Employment Law Section; Section Council Member; Fellow, College of Labor and Employment Lawyers.
Publications: Co-author: 'Equal Employment Law Update' (BNA 7th ed, Fall 1999), and 'The Legal Guide to Human Resources' (West/Thomson, 3d Rev Ed 1996, Supp. 2004).
Personal: BA - Harvard University (magna cum laude, Phi Beta Kappa); JD - Yale Law School.

BROWN, Jay
Levine Sullivan Koch & Schulz LLP, Washington, DC 202 508 1100
Recommended in Media & Entertainment

BROWNELL, William
Hunton & Williams, Washington, DC
202 955 1555
bbrownell@hunton.com
Recommended in Environment
Practice Areas: William Brownell's practice focuses on environmental litigation, regulation and counseling, including clean air regulation, environmental licensing and auditing, waste transportation and management, dangerous substances testing and labeling and water quality regulation. He represents clients in both the United States and Europe. In the United States, his practice involves proceedings before federal and state agencies, courts and Congress; in Europe, it involves advice to multinational corporations on European Community and national environmental law.

BRUNNER, Thomas W
Wiley Rein & Fielding LLP,
Washington, DC 202 719 7225
tbrunner@wrf.com
Recommended in Insurance
Practice Areas: Chairs firm's 40-attorney insurance practice (among the largest and most prominent in the US). Counsels insurance industry clients in major trial and appellate cases; active in coverage litigation for insurers for more than 20 years. Named by Corporate Counsel as one of the 'Best Lawyers in America' for excellence in business litigation.
Prof. Memberships: Member, Mealey Publications, Insurance Advisory Council.
Career: Member, Center for Public Resources Distinguished Panel of Insurance Neutrals; Counsel, Complex Insurance Claims Litigation Association; Counsel, National Health Care Anti-Fraud Association; Counsel, National Insurance Crime Bureau.
Personal: Yale Law School (JD); Columbia University (AB, cum laude).

BUCHANAN, John
Covington & Burling, Washington, DC
202 662 5366
JBuchanan@cov.com
Recommended in Insurance
Practice Areas: Represents policy holders in complex insurance coverage disputes and transactions. Experience covers wide range of property/casualty claims, including environmental, asbestos and other GL claims; media liability, IP- and competition-related claims; D&O, Software E&O, and fidelity claims; product tampering, time-element, marine, satellite in-orbit, and other first-party claims.
Prof. Memberships: American Law Institute; American Bar Association, Lit-

igation Section, Insurance Coverage Litigation Committee (current Subcommittee Co-Chair; past Task Force Co-Chair and Annual Meeting Co-Chair).
Career: Partner since 1986. Firm's first Insurance Practice Group Coordinator, 1987-97. Admitted DC Bar, 1979. Law Clerk, 3d Circuit US Court of Appeals, 1978-79.
Publications: Frequent speaker and writer on insurance topics, including chapters in 'E-Commerce Law & Business' (Aspen 2003); 'Law & Practice of Insurance Coverage Litigation' (West 2000); 'Manual for Complex Insurance Coverage Litigation' (Prentice Hall 1995).
Personal: JD, Harvard, 1978; Honours BA (1st Class), Oxford, 1974; AB (Phi Beta Kappa), Princeton, 1972.

BUCKLEY, Christopher
Gibson, Dunn & Crutcher LLP,
Washington, DC 202 887 3621
cbuckley@gibsondunn.com
Recommended in Environment
Practice Areas: Extensive experience in environmental, natural resource, and toxic tort litigation. Has led the defense of some of the largest and most significant toxic tort cases ever filed. Focus includes complex cases involving design and construction of water and wastewater treatment plants, design and manufacture of fossil fuel and nuclear power plants, operation of nuclear weapons manufacturing facilities, allocation of natural resources, such as Western water and endangered species.
Prof. Memberships: Member, Executive Committee of Board of Directors of Environmental Law Institute.
Publications: Frequent lecturer and author on environmental regulatory programs and environmental litigation.
Personal: JD, Harvard Law School.

BUENTE, David
Sidley Austin Brown & Wood LLP,
Washington, DC 202 736 8000
dbuente@sidley.com
Recommended in Environment
Practice Areas: David Buente represents clients in environmental litigation, legislative and rulemaking matters.
Prof. Memberships: Mr Buente is Vice-Chair of the American Bar Association's Environmental Litigation Committee and the National Association of Criminal Defense Lawyers' Environmental Crimes Committee.
Career: Mr Buente was Chief of the Environmental Enforcement Section, Environment and Natural Resources Division with the Department of Justice, directing all federal, civil and criminal environmental enforcement litigation. He handled federal environmental trial and appellate litigation for the EPA and other federal agencies as a Department of Justice trial attorney. He has extensive experience in agency rulemakings from prior service with the Interior Depart-

ment and the Pennsylvania Attorney General's Office. Admitted to DC Bar.

BUMPERS, Heidi
Jones Day, Washington, DC
202 879 7616
hhbumpers@jonesday.com
Recommended in Environment

Practice Areas: Previously Section Chief in the EPA's Office of Enforcement. Litigated RCRA enforcement cases, Superfund defense and natural resource damage cases, EPCRA, OSHA, and asbestos enforcement actions. Negotiated Superfund voluntary cleanup agreements and private cost recovery settlements. Represented purchasers, lenders, and sellers in corporate acquisitions and real estate deals. Client counseling included setting up an environmental management system for a high-tech manufacturer, coordinating environmental matters and legislative strategy for a tire manufacturer, and advising on compliance audits, records retention, EPCRA filings, pollution prevention, multimedia inspections, and release reporting.

BUMPERS, William
Baker Botts LLP, Washington, DC
202 639 7718
william.bumpers@bakerbotts.com
Recommended in Environment

Practice Areas: Focuses practice on environmental compliance and litigation. Clients represented include petroleum refiners, electric generators, and pharmaceutical and chemical manufacturers. Regarded as a national authority on new source review issues affecting the electric generation and petroleum refinery industries.
Prof. Memberships: Member, District of Columbia Bar; Member, American Bar Association.
Career: Admitted to DC Bar in 1984. Joined Baker Botts in 1996.
Personal: Hendrix College, BA, 1977; Antioch College, MA, 1979; University of Virginia, JD, 1984.

BURCHFIELD, Bobby R
McDermott Will & Emery,
Washington, DC 202 756 8003
bburchfield@mwe.com
Recommended in Litigation

Practice Areas: Co-Chair, firm's Washington, DC office; Head of firm's Complex Litigation Group. Corporate litigation, including jury and bench trials, appeals, and arbitrations for such clients as The Washington Post Company's subsidiary Legi-Slate, Inc., the American Automobile Association, Dow Corning Corporation, the Republican National Committee, and Northrop Grumman Corporation. Constitutional litigation, including arguing McConnell v FEC, 540 US (Dec 10, 2003).
Prof. Memberships: Federalist Society; American Bar Association; George Washington Law School Dean's Advisory Board (2002-present); Board of

Trustees, Wake Forest University (2004-present); President, Wake Forest University Alumni Association (2000-01).
Career: Law Clerk (1979-81) for Judge Ruggero J Aldisert, US Court of Appeals for the Third Circuit; joined Covington & Burling in 1981, became Partner in 1987. General Counsel, Bush-Quayle '92. Named one of 20 top trial lawyers in Washington, DC region by 'Legal Times' (June 16, 2002) and highly rated in two top legal publications.
Publications: Author, 'Enemies of the First Amendment', 'The Weekly Standard' (October 11, 1999), reprinted in 'Political Money: Deregulating American Politics' (A Anderson, editor, 2000).
Personal: Born 23 October 1954. JD (with high honors, George Washington Law School 1979. BA (cum laude) Wake Forest University 1976. Editor in chief, 'George Washington Law Review' (vol. 47, 1978-79).

CARDER-THOMPSON, Elizabeth
Reed Smith LLP, Washington, DC
202 414 9213
ecarder@reedsmith.com
Recommended in Healthcare

Practice Areas: Represents associations and individual providers and suppliers of health services, including hospitals, physicians, hospices, pharmaceutical manufacturers, suppliers and manufacturers of medical equipment, nursing homes. Specific responsibility includes reimbursement, fraud and abuse, and regulatory, legislative, and enforcement issues.
Prof. Memberships: Board of Directors of American Health Lawyers Association, Co-Chair of its annual Healthcare Fraud and Compliance Forum; DC Bar; past Chair, Health Law Forum, Women's Bar Association.
Personal: College of William & Mary (JD, 1978), Notes and Comments Editor of 'William & Mary Law Review'; Brown University (AB, 1975), Phi Beta Kappa.

CARR, Don
Pillsbury Winthrop LLP, Washington, DC
202 775 9877
dcarr@pillsburywinthrop.com
Recommended in Environment

Practice Areas: Mr Carr is a Partner in the Environment Land Use and Natural Resources Group and the local section leader of the Pillsbury Winthrop group. He has extensive experience in environmental and natural resources issues, including those affecting military installations and national security. Mr Carr has also been responsible for a broad range of assignments involving oil, gas and minerals development, fisheries and marine mammal management regimes, law of the sea, wetlands, endangered species, biotechnology, marine pollution and hazardous waste. He has handled significant Superfund matters, white-collar environmental crime cases, and counseled on compliance with Clean Air

Act, RCRA, CWA, CZMA and NEPA. In addition, Mr Carr has worked on major projects involving Native American conservation and development issues.
Career: Admitted to practice: US Supreme Court; US Courts of Appeals for the District of Columbia, and the Second, Fourth, Fifth, Ninth, and Tenth Circuits; US Court of Federal Claims; and the US District Court for the District of Columbia.
Personal: JD, George Washington University, 1974; BA, Cornell University of Washington at Seattle, 1970.

CARVIN, Michael A
Jones Day, Washington, DC
202 879 7643
macarvin@jonesday.com
Recommended in Litigation

Practice Areas: Specializes in constitutional, appellate, civil rights, and civil litigation against the federal government. He has argued numerous cases in the US Supreme Court and in virtually every federal appeals court. These cases include the decisions overturning the federal government's plan to statistically adjust the census, limiting the Justice Department's ability to create 'majority-minority' districts, and preventing the Justice Department from seeking $280 billion against the tobacco industry under RICO. He was one of the lead lawyers, and argued before the Florida Supreme Court, on behalf of now-President George W Bush in the 2000 election Florida recount controversy.

CARY, George S
Cleary Gottlieb Steen & Hamilton LLP,
Washington, DC 202 974 1920
gcary@cgsh.com
Recommended in Antitrust

Practice Areas: Antitrust counseling and litigation, focusing on mergers and acquisitions, FTC and DOJ investigations, antitrust issues in high technology markets, and antitrust and intellectual property issues. Representative clients and transactions: Dow Chemical (Union Carbide), Time Warner (AOL and EMI), SmithKline Beecham (GlaxoWelcome), Cable & Wireless (MCI Internet), Northern Telecom (Bay Networks), Conoco (Phillips Petroleum), AspenTech (Hyprotech), Lafarge (Blue Circle), Broadcom, Toyota.
Prof. Memberships: California and DC Bars. ABA Antitrust Section, (past Chair, Government Antitrust Litigation Committee). California Judicial Nominees Evaluation Commission (Commissioner).
Career: Joined firm as a Partner, 1998. Deputy Director, Bureau of Competition, Federal Trade Commission (1995-98) (responsible for merger enforcement), Partner, Irell & Manella (1984-95). Trial Attorney, FTC Bureau of Competition (1976-84). JD, Boalt Hall School of Law, UC Berkeley (1976), BA, (Economics) UC Santa Cruz (1973).
Publications: 'Mergers in Media Indus-

tries'; 'Government Enforcement Priorities for High Technology Industries'; 'Software Mergers: The Enforcement Record'; 'US View on Refusal to License IP and Antitrust'; 'Patent Settlements and Antitrust'; 'Antitrust Implications of Patent Settlements'; 'Hoechst/Andrx - Anatomy of a Restraint of Trade'.

CHATILOVICZ, Peter
Seyfarth Shaw LLP, Washington, DC
202 463 2400
Recommended in Employment

CLARKE, Donald
Law Offices of GKRSE, Washington, DC
202 408 5400
Recommended in Energy

COHEN, Charles
Morgan, Lewis & Bockius LLP,
Washington, DC 202 739 5710
ccohen@morganlewis.com
Recommended in Employment

Practice Areas: Charles I Cohen is a Partner in the Labor and Employment Law Practice. Mr Cohen represents management in complex labor and employment law matters in the private sector. Mr Cohen has a comprehensive background in collective bargaining issues and all facets of labor and employee relations and litigation. Mr Cohen served as a Member of the National Labor Relations Board (NLRB) from 1994-96.
Prof. Memberships: American Bar Association; US Chamber of Commerce - NLRB Subcommittee; Chair - Fellow, College of Labor and Employment Lawyers; Committees on Practice and Procedure Under the National Labor Relations Act.

COHEN, David
Vinson & Elkins LLP, Washington, DC
202 639 6566
dcohen@velaw.com
Recommended in Energy

Practice Areas: Practice concentrates on mergers and acquisitions, joint ventures and project development.
Career: Admitted to District of Columbia Bar in 1989 and was admitted to the partnership in 1991.

COLEMAN, Lynn R
Skadden, Arps, Slate, Meagher & Flom LLP & Affiliates, Washington, DC
202 371 7600
lcoleman@skadden.com
Recommended in Energy

Practice Areas: Started and led domestic and international energy practice and coordinates the legislative and public policy practice. Handles energy transactions, regulatory proceedings and complex litigation; deals with oil, gas, electric, coal and nuclear energy issues. Represents clients on issues of government policy including legislation in Congress and executive branch initiatives, and has worked extensively on government regulation of energy projects and transactions as well as privatizations; also repre-

sents international energy companies on US and multilateral trade sanctions.
Career: LLB, University of Texas, 1964 (Editor, Texas Law Review; Order of the Coif; Chancellor); BA, Abilene Christian College, 1961.

CONNOLLY, Annemargaret
Weil, Gotshal & Manges LLP, Washington, DC
202 682 7037
annemargaret.connolly@weil.com
Recommended in Environment
Practice Areas: Environmental, transactions, litigation.
Career: Ms Connolly practices environmental, health and safety law, advising on a wide range of environmental concerns, most notably in the context of mergers and acquisitions, real estate transfers and financing transactions. She works with consultants, engineers and environmental professionals to quantify potential liabilities, and drafts/negotiates contract language to allocate the risk of environmental liabilities between parties. Ms Connolly also counsels clients on environmental topics touching on corporate and restructuring issues, including compliance with hazardous waste laws, occupational safety, asbestos and corporate and successor liability.
Personal: George Washington University, JD; Syracuse University, BA, BS.

CONTRATTO, Dana
Crowell & Moring LLP, Washington, DC
202 624 2600
dcontratto@crowell.com
Recommended in Energy
Practice Areas: Dana Contratto is Chair of Crowell & Moring's Energy Group. He focuses on oil, natural gas and electricity regulation, litigation and ADR, legislation, commercial transactions, project development and financing. He handles projects involving oil and gas concessions, electric power generation and transmission, natural gas pipeline and distribution systems, liquid petroleum gas fuels procurement, oil and natural gas purchases and sales, and complex commercial and corporate arrangements. His representations include Memphis Light, Gas and Water Division, Knoxville Utilities Board, and Petroleos Mexicanos.
Personal: Undergraduate degree in marketing from Southern Illinois University; JD from Washington University.

COOK BUSH, Antoinette
Skadden, Arps, Slate, Meagher & Flom LLP & Affiliates, Washington, DC
202 371 7230
abush@skadden.com
Recommended in Telecom, Broadcast & Satellite
Practice Areas: Represents companies in administrative, legislative, and transactional matters involving communications issues as well as other legislative matters. A significant portion of practice is devoted to representing clients before the Federal Communications Commis-

sion. Specifically, clients include entities involved in the broadcast, cable, satellite, telephone and mobile communication business. Also represents a number of not-for-profit communications companies.
Career: JD, Northwestern University School of Law, 1981; BA, Wellesley College, 1978.

COOPER, Ronald
Steptoe & Johnson LLP, Washington, DC 202 429 8075
rcooper@steptoe.com
Recommended in Employment
Practice Areas: Partner, Steptoe & Johnson LLP, Washington, DC. Defended employers in employment discrimination cases under federal and state law. Represented employers in administrative proceedings including 'Glass Ceiling' investigations concerning utilization of women in senior management. Defended and prosecuted cases involving restrictions on post-employment competition. Defended and prosecuted executive compensation cases; successfully represented the employer in Oracle Corp. v Falotti, 319 F.3d 1106 (9th Cir. 2003). Employer Co-Chair of ABA Labor and Employment Section International Labor Law Committee. Managed force reduction involving selection and management of counsel in 20 foreign jurisdictions.
Personal: University of Georgia, JD 1969; AB, 1966.

CORDELL, Ruffin
Fish & Richardson, Washington, DC
202 783 5070
Recommended in Intellectual Property

CORN-REVERE, Robert
Davis Wright Tremaine LLP, Washington, DC 202 508 6625
bobcornrevere@dwt.com
Recommended in Media & Entertainment
Practice Areas: Partner, communications and media law. Advises clients on First Amendment, internet-related issues and FCC regulatory matters. Served as counsel for litigation involving Communications Decency Act, internet content filtering in public libraries, public broadcasting regulations, telemarketing regulation and encryption software matters.
Prof. Memberships: Admitted to District of Columbia Bar and Bar of United States Supreme Court.
Career: Former Partner, Hogan & Hartson LLP. Former chief counsel, FCC.
Publications: Frequent writer/speaker on First Amendment and communications-related issues.
Personal: JD, Columbus School of Law, Catholic University of America, 1983. MA, University of Massachusetts - Amherst, 1980. BA, Eastern Illinois University, 1977.

CRISMAN Jr, C Benjamin
Skadden, Arps, Slate, Meagher & Flom LLP & Affiliates, Washington, DC
202 371 7330
bcrisman@skadden.com
Recommended in Antitrust
Practice Areas: Focuses on antitrust, trade regulation and white collar crime matters. Has obtained Department of Justice and Federal Trade Commission approval for a number of high profile and complex US and international mergers and acquisitions. Specializes in technology, defense sector and natural resources. Regularly counsels clients on sophisticated, cross-border joint ventures and compliance progams. Represents clients in international cartel and antitrust grand jury investigations.
Career: JD, Creighton University, 1975 (senior editor, Creighton Law Review); BA, Syracuse University, 1970.

CROWLEY, Lisanne
Troutman Sanders LLP, Washington, DC 202 274 2950
Recommended in Energy

CULBERTSON, Robert
King & Spalding LLP, Washington, DC
202 626 2642
rculbertson@kslaw.com
Recommended in Tax
Practice Areas: Over 20 years' experience in international taxation, both the public and private sectors, specializing in international tax planning/controversy resolution.
Career: Prior to joining King & Spalding, he was Leader of the Washington international tax services office of PricewaterhouseCoopers. Began his career with the IRS drafting regulations. Joined staff of the Joint Committee on Taxation working on international provisions of the Tax Reform Act of 1986. Rejoined IRS in 1986, then served as Associate Chief Counsel International 1991-95, responsible for international tax regulations, rulings, and litigation policy.
Personal: BA, Yale College and graduate of Harvard Law School.

CURRAN, Denis A
Gibson, Dunn & Crutcher LLP, Washington, DC 202 955 8520
dcurran@gibsondunn.com
Recommended in Corporate/Commercial
Practice Areas: Representation of business organizations regarding corporate securities, corporate finance, M&A and general business and contract matters. Experienced in a wide range of corporate, commercial and financing transactions - including formation of pooled investment funds, private equity financings, structuring and documenting joint venture relationships, and representation of buyers and sellers in connection with mergers, acquisitions and strategic investments. Clients range from start-ups to large, multinational corporations across a diverse cross-section of industries.

Personal: JD, George Washington University Law School, 1997, articles editor of George Washington Law Review and member of Order of the Coif.

CURTISS, James
Winston & Strawn, Washington, DC
202 371 5700
Recommended in Energy

DANKNER, Donald
Winston & Strawn, Washington, DC
202 371 5700
Recommended in Energy

DAVIS, James
Howrey Simon Arnold & White, Washington, DC 202 783 0800
Recommended in Intellectual Property

DAVIS, Robert P
Mayer, Brown, Rowe & Maw LLP, Washington, DC 202 263 3207
rdavis@mayerbrownrowe.com
Recommended in Employee Benefits, Employment
Practice Areas: Represents employers in trial and appellate employment litigation in federal and state courts. Extensive experience in Fair Labor Standards Act and state wage and hour litigation. Trial and appellate ERISA litigation. Advises on Fair Labor Standards Act and state counterpart statutes. ERISA advice on fiduciary issues, prohibited transactions, and other matters under Title I. Advisory opinions and prohibited transaction exemptions. Substantial experience in OSHA regulatory and enforcement matters. Former solicitor of the US Department of Labor under the senior President Bush (1989-91).
Career: Mayer, Brown, Rowe & Maw LLP, Washington, 1991 to date; Partner, 1991. Solicitor of Labor, US Department of Labor, Washington, DC, 1989-91. Chief of Staff to the Secretary of Transportation, US Department of Transportation, Washington, DC, 1983-85. US Department of Justice, Washington, DC: Special Assistant to the Deputy Attorney General, 1978-80; Senior Staff Member, Office of the Attorney General, 1974-78. Senior Staff to the Majority Leader, New York State Senate, 1973-74.
Personal: JD (magna cum laude), Georgetown University,1980; editor, Georgetown Law Journal. MPA, Syracuse, 1973. MA, Boston University, 1972. AB, Brown University, 1971. Chairman, Tripartite Advisory Panel on International Labor Standards, 1989-91. Outstanding performance awards from three US Attorneys General.

DE BERNARDO, Mark
Winston & Strawn, Washington, DC
202 371 5760
mdebernardo@winston.com
Recommended in Employment
Practice Areas: Labor and employment; senior executive employment terminations; employment litigation; drug testing and substance-abuse prevention;

management of employment-related class actions.

Prof. Memberships: District of Columbia Court of Appeals; US Supreme Court; American Bar Association.

Career: Exec. Director, Institute for a Drug-Free Workplace; General Counsel, Council for Employment Law Equity; Director, Labor Law and Special Counsel for Domestic Policy, US Chamber of Commerce; testified more than 40 times to Congress and regulatory agencies; wrote 11 amici curiae briefs to the US Supreme Court.

Publications: Has authored more than 18 publications on labor and employment issues, including on drug testing, plant closings, labor relations, wage-hour, and occupational safety and health issues.

Personal: Georgetown University, JD, 1979; Marquette University, BA in journalism and english literature, cum laude, 1976.

DELLINGER, Walter
O'Melveny & Myers LLP, Washington, DC 202 383 5300
Recommended in Litigation

DENGER, Michael L
Gibson, Dunn & Crutcher LLP, Washington, DC 202 955 8526
mdenger@gibsondunn.com
Recommended in Antitrust

Practice Areas: Partner and Co-Chair of Gibson, Dunn & Crutcher's Antitrust Practice Group. He has over 30 years of experience in civil and criminal antitrust investigations (domestic and international) and litigation, including substantial experience in government enforcement actions, private antitrust litigation, class actions, and corporate takeover litigation.

Prof. Memberships: Chair, ABA Antitrust Section, 1992-93. Served on the five-member Antitrust Section Task Force which prepared a report to the Bush administration on 'Federal Antitrust Enforcement'. Serves on the US Chamber of Commerce Antitrust Council.

Personal: Graduated cum laude from Harvard Law School.

DENIS, Paul T
Dechert, Washington, DC
202 261 3430
paul.denis@dechert.com
Recommended in Antitrust

Practice Areas: Mr Denis is a Partner in Dechert's Antitrust Group. He has over 20 years of experience, including high-level government service, and has acted as lead antitrust counsel in scores of complex transactions across industries such as consumer goods, transportation, and pharmaceuticals. He also handles a wide range of non-merger investigations, litigation, and counseling.

Prof. Memberships: Member, New York and District of Columbia Bars.

Personal: Villanova University (BA,

summa cum laude, 1980); University of Michigan (MA, 1983; JD, cum laude, 1984).

DESANCTIS, Michael
Jenner & Block LLP, Washington, DC
202 637 6323
mdesanctis@jenner.com
Recommended in Telecom, Broadcast & Satellite

Practice Areas: Michael B DeSanctis is a Partner in Jenner & Block's Washington, DC office. He is a member of the firm's Appellate and Supreme Court, Litigation, Products Liability and Mass Tort Defense, Entertainment and New Media, and Telecommunications Practices. Mr DeSanctis represents leading telecommunications companies in the federal courts and before the Federal Communications Commission in all range of matters, and specializes in matters arising under the Telecommunications Act of 1996. Pursuant to the firm's role as national coordinating counsel for MCI Inc.'s litigation under Section 252 of the 1996 Act, Mr DeSanctis has primary responsibility for outside counsel's role in the management of those cases nationwide. His telecommunications practice has extended to the United States Supreme Court, the United States Courts of Appeals for the District of Columbia, Third, Fourth, Sixth, Eight, Ninth and Eleventh Circuits, as well as federal district courts and state courts across the country. In addition, Mr DeSanctis regularly appears as lead counsel for national communications companies in enforcement matters before the Investigations and Hearings Division and the Market Disputes Resolution Division of the FCC's Enforcement Bureau. Mr DeSanctis also has an active complex civil litigation and mass tort practice. His appellate and trial litigation work in these areas has focused on a diverse range of substantive fields including product liability, commercial contract disputes, aviation, banking and copyright.

Personal: New York University School of Law, JD, 1995, cum laude.

DESANTIS, Victor J
White & Case LLP, Washington, DC
202 626 3607
vdesantis@whitecase.com
Recommended in Projects

Practice Areas: Partner in the Corporate Department, concentrating in international, multi-lender project finance, and other cross-border financing and investment transactions. Extensive experience representing sponsors, multilateral and commercial lenders and export credit agencies on enterprises financed on a project basis. Has been involved in financings involving a wide range of sectors, including power, mining, oil and gas, transportation, telecommunications and other industrial projects.

Prof. Memberships: New York State

Bar, 1986; District of Columbia, 1987.

Personal: BA Yale University, 1982; JD Harvard Law School, 1985.

DINKINS, Carol
Vinson & Elkins LLP, Houston
713 758 2528
cdinkins@velaw.com
Recommended in Environment

Practice Areas: Chairs Vinson & Elkins' administrative and environmental law practice. Practice includes client counseling on business transactions and permit matters; civil litigation, mediation, and criminal defense.

Prof. Memberships: Immediate Past Chair: Standing Committee on Federal Judiciary, American Bar Association.

Career: Admitted to practice: Texas, 1971. Joined Vinson & Elkins, 1973; admitted to partnership, 1980. Served as: Assistant Attorney General in charge of the Environment and Natural Resources Division of the Department of Justice, 1981-83; Deputy Attorney General of the United States, 1984-85.

Personal: The University of Texas, BS, 1968; University of Houston, JD, 1971.

DIXON, Gary
Ross Dixon & Bell LLP, Washington, DC
202 662 2000
Recommended in Insurance

DOLAN, Edward
Hogan & Hartson LLP, Washington, DC
202 637 5677
ecdolan@hhlaw.com
Recommended in Bankruptcy

Practice Areas: Edward Dolan practices in the areas of bankruptcy, creditors' rights and complex commercial financing.

Prof. Memberships: Director, past-President, Maryland Bankruptcy Bar Association Master, Chandler Bankruptcy Inn of Court Member, Maryland District and Bankruptcy Courts Liaison Committee Member, past-Chair, Maryland Bankruptcy Court's Local Rules Committee.

Career: He represents secured and unsecured creditors, vendors, investors and asset purchasers in debt restructurings, asset transfers and liquidations, including multinational transactions. Edward has extensive experience in litigating commercial claims and enforcing creditors' rights in state and federal courts.

Personal: Columbia University (BA, 1975); Georgetown University Law Center (JD, 1978).

DOLIN, Mitchell F
Covington & Burling, Washington, DC
202 662 5210
mdolin@cov.com
Recommended in Insurance

Practice Areas: Practice concentrated on the litigation, arbitration, and mediation of complex commercial cases, with particular emphasis on representing corporate policyholders in insurance

disputes concerning asbestos and mass torts, directors and officers, professional liability, first party property, and other large loss situations.

Prof. Memberships: American Arbitration Association (National Roster of Neutrals); American Law Institute (Member); CPR Institute for Dispute Resolution (Regional Panel of Neutrals).

Career: With Covington & Burling since 1982, as a Partner since 1989. Served as law clerk to Chief Judge Charles Clark, US Court of Appeals for the 5th Circuit, from 1981-82.

Publications: Author of book chapters and articles on insurance, civil practice, and arbitration topics; has spoken on these topics at conferences of the ABA, ALI-ABA, CPR, and other organizations.

Personal: Tufts University, BA, 1978; New York University School of Law, JD, 1981.

DOMIKE, Julie
Wallace King Domike & Branson PLLC, Washington, DC 202 204 1000
Recommended in Environment

DOWNS, Clark Evans
Jones Day, Washington, DC
202 879 3883
cedowns@jonesday.com
Recommended in Energy

Practice Areas: His practice is concentrated on North American electricity markets and related areas of state and federal regulation of rates and competition and includes administrative and appellate litigation and counseling. He has especially broad experience in dealing with the federal regulation of mergers and acquisitions and with the full range of traditional utility rate and other regulatory issues. He is listed in numerous publications that recognize the world's leading energy lawyers. He regularly appears before the FERC and state public service commissions.

Prof. Memberships: ABA; Energy Bar Association. Fellow of the American Bar Foundation.

DRAKE, Stuart
Kirkland & Ellis LLP, Washington, DC
202 879 5094
sdrake@kirkland.com
Recommended in Environment

Practice Areas: Mr Drake has represented companies whose products are subject to air pollution control regulation by the US Environmental Protection Agency and various State government agencies. His work includes the defense of enforcement actions in federal and State courts and before the agencies, other litigation involving regulations, and the representation of clients in agency rulemaking processes and in Congressional matters.

Personal: Yale University, BA, 1977. Cambridge University, M Litt, 1981. Yale University, JD, 1981.

DUNNER, Donald
Finnegan Henderson Farabow Garrett & Dunner LLP, Washington, DC
202 408 4000
Recommended in Intellectual Property

DWYER, Jeffry
Greenberg Traurig LLP, Washington, DC
202 331 3100
dwyerj@gtlaw.com
Recommended in Real Estate
Practice Areas: Real estate; corporate and securities.
Prof. Memberships: Former adjunct Professor of Real Estate Planning at Georgetown University Law Center from 1974-80; Member, District of Columbia Bar Association; Member, New York State Bar Association; Member, American College of Real Estate Lawyers; Corporate Secretary and General Counsel, Association of Foreign Investors in US Real Estate, 1988-96.
Publications: Co-authored a major law treatise on real estate financing.
Personal: Georgetown University Law Center (JD, 1970); Georgetown University, Foreign Service (BS, 1967).

DWYER, Maureen
Shaw Pittman LLP, Washington, DC
202 663 8834
maureen.dwyer@shawpittman.com,
maureen.dwyer@pillsburylaw.com
Recommended in Real Estate
Practice Areas: Maureen Dwyer's practice concentrates on zoning and municipal law and she represents clients in the development of new corporate, retail, institutional, office and residential properties. Her knowledge extends from site selection and initial acquisition through land use, historic preservation, environmental, and building code approval process, including litigation and appellate work. Her clients include real estate developers and investors, corporate owners, institutions, foundations and individuals. She has a special emphasis on representing private colleges and universities.
Prof. Memberships: DC Building Industry Association, the Greater Washington Board of Trade, the Urban Land Institute, Lambda Alpha and the DC Chamber of Commerce.
Personal: (At press time, Shaw Pittman LLP had entered into a merger agreement with Pillsbury Winthrop LLP. The merger is expected to close by April 2005. Post closing, the name of the firm will be Pillsbury Winthrop Shaw-Pittman LLP.)

DYE, Alan L
Hogan & Hartson LLP, Washington, DC
202 637 5737
aldye@hhlaw.com
Recommended in Corporate/Commercial
Practice Areas: Alan Dye concentrates his practice on advising public companies and their directors and officers regarding their obligations under the federal securities laws.
Prof. Memberships: Chairman, Securities, Commodities and Exchanges Committee, Administrative Law and Regulatory Practice Section, American Bar Association; Member, Securities Law Committee, American Society of Corporate Secretaries.
Career: SEC, 1982-86; adjunct professor, Georgetown University Law Center, 1991-96; co-author of numerous books and articles on federal securities laws.
Personal: Emory University (BA, with high honors, 1975); University of Georgia (JD, salutatorian and Order of the Coif).

EASTMENT, Thomas
Baker Botts LLP, Washington, DC
202 639 7717
tom.eastment@bakerbotts.com
Recommended in Energy
Practice Areas: Represents producers, refiners and other shippers in oil and gas pipeline transportation and enforcement matters before FERC and federal trial and appellate courts; represents producers regarding royalty matters before the Department of the Interior and in state and federal courts; represents project owners regarding FERC certificate applications for pipeline projects; and represents electric generation and other clients on gas supply and transportation contract matters.
Prof. Memberships: District of Columbia Bar; New York Bar; Energy Bar Association.
Personal: JD from the University of Michigan Law School, 1975; BChE from Manhattan College, 1972.

ECCLES, Bob
O'Melveny & Myers LLP, Washington, DC 202 383 5300
Recommended in Employee Benefits, Litigation

EDGAR, George
Morgan, Lewis & Bockius LLP, Washington, DC 202 739 5459
gedgar@morganlewis.com
Recommended in Energy
Practice Areas: George L Edgar is a Partner in the Energy Practice and the firm's Client Service Partner. Mr Edgar represents nuclear industry clients before the Nuclear Regulatory Commission (NRC) and in related litigation in the federal courts.
Prof. Memberships: Member, Nuclear Energy Institute Lawyers' Committee; Vice Chairman, American Bar Association, Section of Public Utility, Communications and Transportation Law, Atomic Energy Law Committee.
Career: Mr Edgar became a Partner at Morgan Lewis in 1973, remaining until 1983, when he became a Partner at Newman & Holtzinger (later became Newman, Bouknight & Edgar). He rejoined Morgan Lewis in 1994.

EGAN Jr, James C
Weil, Gotshal & Manges LLP, Washington, DC 202 682 7036
jim.egan@weil.com
Recommended in Antitrust
Practice Areas: Antitrust/competition, litigation/regulatory.
Career: Represents corporate clients in complex litigation involving price fixing, mergers, joint ventures, boycotts, and other horizontal/vertical restraints; extensive experience in multidistrict class actions. Formerly Director of Litigation, Assistant Director for General Litigation, and Assistant Director for Mergers and Joint Ventures at FTC's Bureau of Competition; recipient, Brandeis Award for Litigation. Supervised various FTC enforcement programs including horizontal restraints, mergers, healthcare, and International Antitrust; participated in drafting DOJ/FTC Statements of Antitrust Enforcement Policy in Healthcare.
Personal: St. John's University, JD; University of South Florida, BA (economics); Officer, United States Army 1966-69.

EGGLESTON, Neil
Howrey Simon Arnold & White, Washington, DC 202 783 0800
Recommended in Litigation

EISENSTAT, Larry
Dickstein Shapiro Morin & Oshinsky LLP, Washington, DC 202 828 2224
EisenstatL@dsmo.com
Recommended in Energy
Practice Areas: Counsels utilities, independent power producers, marketers and others on market design, generation, transmission, interconnection, trading and compliance issues, and on efforts to build and finance generation and transmission facilities throughout the US and abroad. Lead counsel in a variety of energy-related lawsuits, administrative litigation and rulemakings before federal and state courts and administrative agencies regarding divestitures, restructurings, power procurements, contract disputes, transmission and market access complaints, and market power, bidding and enforcement issues.
Career: Partner, Head of Dickstein Shapiro's Electric Power Practice.
Publications: Lectured and written extensively on energy issues.
Personal: University of Chicago (BA, 1982; JD, 1985).

ELLIOTT, E Donald
Willkie Farr & Gallagher LLP, Washington, DC 202 303 1120
delliott@willkie.com
Recommended in Environment
Practice Areas: Chair of the firm's worldwide Environmental Law Department. Advises companies in both the European Union and the US on environmental aspects of complex corporate and real estate sales and acquisitions, and also represents companies and trade associations on major regulatory policy issues, class action litigation, product liability and legislative matters. Practice includes crisis management involving product and site contamination issues, as well as environmental advocacy and legislative work for companies, trade associations and governments. Also has significant experience in environmental enforcement cases, class actions and complex product liability and toxic tort litigations.
Prof. Memberships: Served as a member of the National Academy of Sciences Board on Environmental Studies and Toxicology, the top group that advises the federal government on environmental issues. Formerly served on the Regulation Committee of the Administrative Conference of the United States, the OTA Committee on Innovative Regulatory Techniques, the Federal Courts Study Committee, the Carnegie Commission on Science, Technology and Government, and Yale's 'Next Generation Project' to reform environmental laws. Also previously served as Sector Chair for the National Environmental Policy Institute and Chair and Vice Chair of the American Bar Association's Administrative Law & SONREEL Committees. A member of the advisory boards of the Center for Clean Policy, the Environment Reporter, the Journal of Industrial Ecology and the Carnegie Mellon University Center for the Study and Improvement of Regulation.
Career: Has over 25 years of experience in all aspects of environmental and product liability law, including serving as General Counsel of the US Environmental Protection Agency (1989-91), where he was the primary legal advisor to EPA Administrator William Reilly. At the EPA, he was responsible for managing 125 attorneys, a $15 million legal budget and a litigation docket of more than 450 cases.
Publications: Author of more than 60 articles in professional journals, and a treatise on environmental regulation of the chemical industry.
Personal: From 1981 through 1993, served as a tenured professor at the Yale Law School, teaching complex litigation, torts, environmental law, toxic torts, administrative law and constitutional law. Continues as an adjunct professor of environmental and administrative law and complex civil litigation at the school. Has lectured to international audiences on international and comparative environmental law and risk management topics in Germany, Italy, Belgium, Spain, Brazil and the United States. Received a JD (1st in class) from Yale Law School in 1974 and a BA from Yale College (Phi Beta Kappa, summa cum laude) in 1970.

ELROD, Eugene R
Sidley Austin Brown & Wood LLP, Washington, DC 202 736 8206
eelrod@sidley.com
Recommended in Energy

Practice Areas: Eugene Elrod focuses on federal and state regulation of the production, transmission and distribution of natural gas, crude oil, petroleum products, and electric energy. He has represented a range of clients, including oil and gas producers, pipelines, local distribution and storage companies; electric utilities; and end-users of natural gas and electric power. He has tried cases at the Federal Energy Regulatory Commission, in state courts and before state regulatory commissions, and has briefed and argued cases in both federal and state appellate courts.
Prof. Memberships: He currently serves on the Advisory Board of the Institute for Energy Law of The Center for American and International Law, served as a Director of the Energy Bar Association and served as the Association's liaison with FERC's Administrative Law Judges.
Career: Mr Elrod was a trial attorney for gas pipeline and electric utility rate matters (1974-76) at the Federal Power Commission and also worked at the Federal Energy Administration (predecessor of DOE) on crude oil pricing and allocation matters. Emory University School of Law, JD, 1974; Dartmouth College, AB, 1971. Bar Admissions: District of Columbia and Georgia.

ENGEL, John
Shaw Pittman LLP, Washington, DC
202 663 8863
john.engel@shawpittman.com,
john.engel@pillsburylaw.com
Recommended in Real Estate

Practice Areas: Mr Engel's practice includes counseling institutional lenders; local, regional, and national developers; international organizations and non-profit institutional clients; and others involved in all aspects of real estate transactions. As Chair of the firm's Real Estate Group, he works with more than 45 lawyers and other real estate specialists who concentrate on the firm's growing and diverse real estate practice, including traditional purchase and sale transactions to complex project finance matters, privatization of military housing, and structuring joint ventures.
Prof. Memberships: American Bar Association, International Council of Shopping Centers, District of Columbia Building Industry Association.
Career: From 1971-75, he worked as an attorney with The Rouse Company, the developer of Faneuill Hall in Boston and Harbor Place in Baltimore.
Personal: Mr Engel is a graduate of Yale University, and received his law degree from Georgetown University Law Center. (At press time, Shaw Pittman LLP had entered into a merger agreement with Pillsbury Winthrop LLP. The merg-

er is expected to close by April 2005. Post closing, the name of the firm will be Pillsbury Winthrop ShawPittman LLP.)

ENGH, Anna
Covington & Burling, Washington, DC
202 662 5221
aengh@cov.com
Recommended in Insurance

Practice Areas: Handles coverage litigation and negotiating insurance recoveries on behalf of corporate policyholders for a variety of claims, including asbestos, breast implants, lead, and other mass tort claims; environmental liability; political risks; and directors and officers and errors and omissions claims. Represents policyholders in bankruptcy proceedings; Currently Special Insurance Counsel for Owens Corning in its Chapter 11 proceeding. Other clients include Textron Inc., Nestle USA, Cytec Industries Inc., Societe Generale, and Dow Corning.
Publications: 'Settlement of Insurance Coverage Disputes,' in Law and Practice of Insurance Coverage Litigation (2000) (co-author); 'Chapter 58, Insurance' in Business and Commercial Litigation in Federal Courts (1998) (co-author).
Personal: William and Mary Law School, (JD, 1989); Davidson College (BA, 1981).

ENGLERT, Roy
Robbins, Russell, Englert, Orseck & Untereiner LLP, Washington, DC
202 775 4500
Recommended in Litigation

EPSTEIN, Gary
Latham & Watkins LLP, Washington, DC 202 637 2200
Recommended in Telecom, Broadcast & Satellite

EPSTIEN, Jay
DLA Piper Rudnick Gray Cary US LLP, Washington, DC
202 861 3850
jay.epstien@dlapiper.com
Recommended in Real Estate

Practice Areas: Real estate.
Career: Represents owners, developers and users in all aspects of real estate transactions involving urban office buildings, shopping centers, and multi-family residential projects. The lead lawyer on many of the largest downtown office leases in Washington, DC. He was named the Top Real Estate Lawyer in DC by the Washington Business Journal and is listed in The Best Lawyers in America, An International Who's Who of Real Estate Lawyers, PLC's Global Counsel Handbook of Corporate Real Estate, and LMG's Guide to the World's Leading Real Estate Lawyers.
Personal: JD, Cornell University; BS, Case Western Reserve University.

ESTES III, John N
Skadden, Arps, Slate, Meagher & Flom LLP & Affiliates, Washington, DC
202 371 7950
jestes@skadden.com
Recommended in Energy

Practice Areas: Focuses on complex litigation involving restructured electric markets. Recent cases have involved the design of the capacity markets in New England, whether FERC should grant exemptions from state laws preventing a utility from joining an ISO, refunds stemming from California electric crisis, and efforts to abrogate long-term contracts in California. Handles a broad variety of other energy regulatory matters, including utility mergers and contractual matters. Spent five years at the Federal Energy Regulatory Commission briefing and arguing cases before the various United States courts of appeals.
Career: JD, Louisiana State University, 1983; BA, Tulane University, 1979.

ESTRADA, Miguel
Gibson, Dunn & Crutcher LLP, Washington, DC 202 955 8257
mestrada@gibsondunn.com
Recommended in Litigation

Practice Areas: Co-Chair of the Appellate Practice. Represented clients in federal and state courts and in international arbitrations. Handled numerous matters before United States Supreme Court, under False Claims Act, bankruptcy law, RICO, and ERISA. Extensive experience includes lead counsel (Prometheus Radio Project v FCC, Aetna v Davila) and part of team (Bush v Gore).
Prof. Memberships: Trustee, Supreme Court Historical Society.
Career: US Supreme Court Law Clerk; Assistant, Solicitor General of US; Assistant, US Attorney and Deputy Chief of Appellate Section, US Attorney's Office, Southern District of New York.
Personal: JD, Harvard Law School, 1986, editor, Harvard Law Review.

EVANS, Mark
Kellogg, Huber, Hansen, Todd & Evans PLLC, Washington, DC 202 326 7900
Recommended in Telecom, Broadcast & Satellite

FARABOW, Ford
Finnegan Henderson Farabow Garrett & Dunner LLP, Washington, DC
202 408 4000
Recommended in Intellectual Property

FARMER, Scott
McKee Nelson LLP, Washington, DC
202 775 8672
sfarmer@mckeenelson.com
Recommended in Tax

Practice Areas: Practice areas: taxation, tax controversy, international taxation. Advises clients on all aspects of international tax planning and controversy with the Internal Revenue Service. Clients include US firms engaged in for-

eign business activities, as well as foreign-based firms operating within the United States.
Career: Prior to joining McKee Nelson in January 2000, was Head of the International Tax Practice at Miller & Chevalier, Chartered, Washington, DC. Is Vice Chair of the US. Council for International Business and a frequent lecturer at the World Trade Institute and the Tax Executives Institute.
Publications: Has written frequently on international tax topics, including 'Branching Out - Reexamining Branch Rules in the Context of Check-the-Box,' 15 Tax Notes International 1951 (December 15, 1997).
Personal: Received LLM in taxation, with highest honors, from the George Washington University Law School in 1983, and JD from the University of North Carolina at Chapel Hill Law School in 1982.

FARR, Bartow
Farr & Taranto, Washington, DC
202 775 0184
Recommended in Litigation

FAVRETTO, Richard J
Mayer, Brown, Rowe & Maw LLP, Washington, DC 202 263 3250
rfavretto@mayerbrown.com
Recommended in Antitrust

Practice Areas: Veteran of both 15 years' service in the Antitrust Division of the US Department of Justice, culminating in service as Deputy Assistant Attorney General and Acting Assistant Attorney General, and two decades of private practice focusing on antitrust law. Experience in government and private practice covers the entire range of US and international antitrust substance and procedure involving mergers and acquisitions, joint ventures, criminal and civil litigation, and appellate litigation, including US Supreme Court argument. Rose to highest position in DOJ Antitrust Division and served successively as a Trial Attorney, Assistant to the Director of Operations, Assistant Chief of the Trial Section, Deputy Director of Operations, Deputy Assistant Attorney General, and Acting Assistant Attorney General in charge of the Antitrust Division.
Career: Mayer, Brown, Rowe & Maw LLP, Washington, DC, 1981 to date; Partner, 1981. Antitrust Division, US Department of Justice: Deputy Assistant Attorney General, 1979-81; Deputy Director of Operations, 1976-79; Assistant Chief, Trial Section, 1973-76; Assistant to the Director of Operations, 1970-73; Trial Attorney, New York Field Office, 1966-70.
Personal: LLB, Catholic University, 1966; Student Material Editor, Law Review. BA (cum laude), Iona College, 1963.

FEINSTEIN, Deborah
Arnold & Porter LLP, Washington, DC
202 942 5015
Deborah.Feinstein@aporter.com
Recommended in Antitrust

Practice Areas: Ms Feinstein has concentrated on antitrust and trade regulation matters since joining the firm. She represented The Kroger Co. in its acquisition of Fred Meyer, the largest grocery store transaction ever completed. She represented Philip Morris and Kraft in connection with their acquisition of Nabisco. She also represents General Electric in transactions involving a variety of its business units, most recently its transactions with Instrumentarium, a competing medical equipment provider, and Vivendi.

Career: From 1989-91, she served as a special assistant to the Director of the Bureau of Competition of the Federal Trade Commission and attorney advisor to Commissioner Dennis Yao.

Publications: 'Merger Enforcement in Innovation Markets: The Latest Chapter - Genzyme/Novazyme'; 'The Antitrust Source', July 2004. 'Taking Stock: Recent Trends in U.S. Merger Enforcement'; 'Antitrust. Volume 18, No 2', Spring 2004. 'Item 4(c): The Next Step in HSR Reform; Clayton Act Newsletter, Vol I, No 2', Spring 2001.

Personal: In July 2004, Ms Feinstein was named in Global Competition Review's international list of 'Top 100 Women in Antitrust,' which profiles 100 women who are at the top of their field from around the world. In addition, she has been named by Chambers & Partners' Global survey of 'The World's Leading Lawyers' as one of the 'top' antitrust attorneys in Washington, DC in each year from 2001-05.

FELLNER, Baruch
Gibson, Dunn & Crutcher LLP,
Washington, DC 202 955 8591
bfellner@gibsondunn.com
Recommended in Employment

Practice Areas: Practice focuses on employment law with special emphasis on occupational safety and health. Extensive experience in litigation, including labor and pension issues. Has argued numerous cases in all the courts of appeals throughout the nation and two major constitutional cases in the Supreme Court of the United States.

Career: Served as Department of Labor Counsel for Appellate and Regional Litigation for Occupational Safety and Health and as Pension Benefit Guaranty Corporation Associate General Counsel for Litigation.

Publications: Frequent speaker on OSHA and ERISA matters.

Personal: JD, Harvard Law School, 1968.

FENTON, Kathryn M
Jones Day, Washington, DC
202 879 3746
kmfenton@jonesday.com
Recommended in Antitrust

Practice Areas: Practices in the antitrust and government regulation areas and has represented clients in a variety of industries (including energy, healthcare, media, and airlines) in mergers and acquisitions and on competitive issues before the DOJ, FTC, DOT, and FCC. She counsels numerous leading corporations on antitrust issues and is a frequent lecturer and author on antitrust and ethics issues.

Prof. Memberships: ABA and the District of Columbia Bar Association. She has served as ABA Antitrust Section Committee Officer, Secretary, Publications Officer, Council Member, and editorial Chair of the 'Antitrust Law Journal'.

FEOLA, Phil
Shaw Pittman LLP, Washington, DC
202 663 8789
phil.feola@shawpittman.com,
phil.feola@pillsburylaw.com
Recommended in Real Estate

Practice Areas: Phil Feola represents clients with matters involving land use, zoning, housing, planned unit developments, historic preservation, urban renewal, environmental law, real estate contracts, condemnation, administrative litigation and governmental licensing. He represents clients before the DC Council, the DC Zoning Commission, the Board of Zoning Adjustment, the Historic Preservation Review Board, the Mayor's Agent for Historic Preservation, the Commission of Fine Arts and other agencies. His civil litigation practice involves zoning, historic preservation, environmental and other local regulatory issues.

Prof. Memberships: Admitted to Practice: District of Columbia, Maryland; US District Court for the District of Columbia; Urban Land Institute; American Bar Association; Maryland Bar Association; American Planning Association; Lambda Alpha International; District of Columbia Bar Association.

Career: Before practicing law he was a senior planner with the City of San Antonio, and was a planner for the City of Paterson, New Jersey. He is currently an adjunct Professor of Law at The George Washington University.

Personal: Catholic University, Columbus School of Law, JD 1979, Florida State University, MS, 1971; University of Notre Dame, BA, 1969.

FERRERA, Tess
The Law Firm of Tess J. Ferrera, LLC,
Washington, DC 202 293 1720
Recommended in Employee Benefits

FERRIS, Charles
Mintz Levin Cohn Ferris Glovsky and Popeo PC, Washington, DC
202 434 7300
Recommended in Telecom, Broadcast & Satellite

FIELD, Andrea Bear
Hunton & Williams, Washington, DC
202 955 1500
afield@hunton.com
Recommended in Environment

Practice Areas: Andrea Bear Field's practice focuses on environmental and administrative law, with emphasis on representation of companies in federal and state enforcement actions brought by EPA under the Clean Air Act and in federal rulemakings and litigation arising under the Clean Air Act. Representative clients include electric utility, paper, coal, oil, chemical, and flexible packaging companies.

FITZGERALD, Peter
Chadbourne & Parke LLP,
Washington, DC 202 974 5600
pfitzgerald@chadbourne.com
Recommended in Projects

Practice Areas: Represents multilateral agencies, lenders and developers in international project financings. Involved in power, telecom, oil and gas, transportation, petrochemical and other projects in emerging markets. Negotiates project financings involving multilateral and/or bilateral agency support. Represents foreign investors, lenders and political risk insurers in investment disputes and political risk matters, including political risk insurance and contract claims.

Prof. Memberships: New York State Bar Association; District of Columbia Bar Association; American Bar Association; International Bar Association.

Career: Previously served as chief counsel for project finance and political risk insurance matters at the Overseas Private Investment Corporation.

FLEXNER, Donald
Boies, Schiller & Flexner,
Washington, DC 202 237 2727
Recommended in Antitrust

FOGGAN, Laura
Wiley Rein & Fielding LLP,
Washington, DC 202 719 7000
Recommended in Insurance

FORD, Gary
Groom Law Group, Washington, DC
202 857 0620
Recommended in Employee Benefits

FORD, John M
Morgan, Lewis & Bockius LLP,
Washington, DC 202 739 5856
jmford@morganlewis.com
Recommended in Investment Management

Practice Areas: John M Ford is a Partner in the Investment Management/Securities Industry Practice at Morgan Lewis. His practice focuses on investment company and investment adviser regulation, and counseling clients on the complex legal and operational issues affecting major financial institutions operating in today's challenging climate. He serves as fund counsel to a broad array of mutual fund complexes, and is experienced in the diverse issues impacting both large-scale fund operations and smaller complexes operating as niche players. Mr Ford routinely counsels fund and adviser clients in mergers, acquisitions and fund reorganizations and adoptions.

FORTNEY, David
Fortney & Scott, LLC, Washington, DC
202 689 1200
Recommended in Employment

FRANKEL, Roger L
Swidler Berlin LLP, Washington, DC
202 424 7500
rfrankel@swidlaw.com
Recommended in Bankruptcy

Practice Areas: Leads Bankruptcy and Creditors' Rights Group. Practice ranges from multi-bank out-of-court workouts to proceedings under state insolvency statutes and Federal Bankruptcy Code. Counsels clients in a variety of industries including healthcare, energy and asbestos.

Prof. Memberships: Admitted to practice in Washington, DC (1971); Maryland (1972). Member, Maryland Merit Selection Panels.

Career: Joined Swidler Berlin in 1992; served as Managing Partner from 1998-2000.

Publications: Co-author, 'Inside the Minds: The Art and Science of Bankruptcy Law', (2003).

Personal: Born 6 April 1946; JD (with Honors), George Washington Law School, 1971; BA, Brandeis University, 1968.

FRANTZ, Steven
Morgan, Lewis & Bockius LLP,
Washington, DC 202 739 5460
sfrantz@morganlewis.com
Recommended in Energy

Practice Areas: Steven P Frantz is a Partner in the Energy Practice. Mr Frantz represents and counsels electric utilities, manufacturers of reactors and materials licensees on the regulation and licensing of nuclear power plants, as well as other facilities regulated by the Nuclear Regulatory Commission (NRC) and the Department of Energy (DOE). Mr Frantz has devoted a substantial part of his practice to assisting utilities in developing strategies for helping nuclear plants obtain permission to resume construction or operation following NRC enforcement action.

Career: Before joining the firm, Mr Frantz was a shareholder at Newman, Bouknight & Edgar.

FREED, Joel

Arnold & Porter LLP, Washington, DC
202 942 6602
Joel.Freed@aporter.com
Recommended in Intellectual Property

Practice Areas: Joel Freed, a Partner in the Washington office, is Head of the firm's Intellectual Property and Technology Litigation Practice and an adjunct professor at Georgetown University Law Center where he has lectured on intellectual property law for over 25 years. A recognized leader of the Patent Bar, Mr Freed's practice covers nearly every aspect of intellectual property law, including trial practice, appellate advocacy, licensing, and practice before the United States Patent and Trademark Office and the International Trade Commission. He has appeared as lead counsel in numerous patent cases, including Intergraph Corp. v Intel Corp., a major pronouncement by the Federal Circuit on the interface between the patent and antitrust laws of the United States. He is also currently representing Microsoft and Dell in a number of separate computer-related patent infringement matters. In addition to his patent litigation experience, Mr Freed has been trial counsel in several high profile trademark litigations and trial counsel in significant trade secret litigation. He also is a former Patent Examiner and since leaving the Patent and Trademark Office has maintained an active patent prosecution practice involving patent applications in the electrical, mechanical, pharmaceutical, and biotechnology fields.

Personal: Mr Freed received his JD from the Georgetown University Law Center, where he was a staff editor of the Georgetown University Law Journal. He holds a BA and a BS in mechanical engineering from Lehigh University.

FREMUTH, Michael

Andrews Kurth LLP, Washington, DC
202 662 2720
mfremuth@andrewskurth.com
Recommended in Energy

Practice Areas: Mike Fremuth practices in the areas of federal regulation and antitrust counseling for energy companies, with particular emphasis in the natural gas and petroleum industries. For over 20 years, he has represented regulated energy companies before federal agencies and non-regulated energy companies seeking to maintain non-regulated status, including one of the largest offshore gathering companies in the Gulf of Mexico. With respect to antitrust counseling for energy companies, Mike has advised oil and gas companies regarding the antitrust-related aspects of their sales, marketing and joint venture activities. He has obtained clearance before the DOJ and FTC for several billion-dollar mergers and acquisitions in the natural gas and oil-drilling services industries.

Prof. Memberships: Federal Energy (Chairman, Antitrust Committee, 1984-85). Bar Associations: State Bar of California, District of Columbia Bar.

Career: Partner in the Energy Section of the Washington, DC office. Has been with Andrews Kurth since 1982 and has been a Partner since 1988.

Personal: Received undergraduate degree summa cum laude and Phi Beta Kappa from Princeton University in 1969 and law degree with honors from Stanford University in 1976. Prior to attending law school, he was a professional pitcher with the Detroit Tigers and Philadelphia Phillies organisations.

FRIES, Joseph

Arent Fox PLLC, Washington, DC
202 857 6000
Recommended in Real Estate

FROST Jr, Don J

Skadden, Arps, Slate, Meagher & Flom LLP & Affiliates, Washington, DC
202 371 7422
dfrost@skadden.com
Recommended in Environment

Practice Areas: Focuses on environmental litigation, including civil and criminal enforcement matters, government cost recovery actions, administrative cleanup and permitting proceedings, private cost recovery and contribution actions, bankruptcy matters, and alternative dispute resolution proceedings. Has substantial experience in environmental transactional matters and compliance counseling.

Career: JD, Duke University School of Law, 1988 (with honors; Articles Editor, 'Alaska Law Review'); MA, Duke University Graduate School, 1988 (Resource Economics and Policy); BA, Carleton College, 1983 (cum laude).

GAGE, Robert

Covington & Burling, Washington, DC
202.662.5636
rgage@cov.com
Recommended in Real Estate

Practice Areas: Firm Practice Leader in commercial real estate, including acquisitions, joint ventures, financings, development, construction, leasing and sales. Significant representation of not-for-profit organizations, including quasi-governmental entities.

Prof. Memberships: (1977) Member, District of Columbia Bar Association, Urban Land Institute, DC. Building Industry Association. Admitted to practice in the District of Columbia.

Career: Joined Covington & Burling, 1977; became Partner, 1985.

Publications: Author of 'Chapters in The Workout Game: Managing Non-Performing Real Estate Assets' (Executive Enterprises Publications, 1987); Co-author of Article on Cost-of-Living increase provisions in commercial leases in 'The Practical Real Estate Lawyer' (ALI-ABA, 1992); co-author of Article on 'Control of Rent Increases' in 'The Washington Lawyer' (DC Bar Association, 1992).

Personal: Born June 9, 1951; JD (cum laude), Harvard Law School, 1977; MPP, Harvard University John F Kennedy School of Government, 1977; BA (summa cum laude), Kent State University, 1973.

GALLAGHER, Robert

Groom Law Group, Washington, DC
202 857 0620
Recommended in Employee Benefits, Litigation

GALLO, Kenneth A

Paul, Weiss, Rifkind, Wharton & Garrison, Washington, DC
202 223 7356
kgallo@paulweiss.com
Recommended in Antitrust

Practice Areas: Represents clients in private and government antitrust disputes including claims related to monopolization, tying, mergers and acquisitions, civil and criminal price fixing, Kodak theories, product distribution and the interplay between the antitrust and intellectual property laws. Litigation partner with substantial trial experience, focusing on antitrust, intellectual property and major commercial disputes. Has tried antitrust, patent, copyright, and breach of contract and fraud cases. Has trial experience involving the banking and payments industries, computer hardware and software products, medical and telecommunications equipment, commercial real estate, and biotech oncology care products. Managing Partner of the Washington, DC office.

GARRE, Gregory G

Hogan & Hartson LLP, Washington, DC
202 637 5665
gggarre@hhlaw.com
Recommended in Litigation

Practice Areas: Head of firm's Supreme Court and Appellate Practice. Argued 11 cases before Supreme Court on commercial, regulatory, and constitutional matters.

Prof. Memberships: Supreme Court Fellows Commission (appointed by Chief Justice); Legal Advisory Council, National Legal Center for Public Interest; Edward Coke Appellate Inn of Court.

Career: Assistant to the Solicitor General, Department of Justice; law clerk to Chief Justice William Rehnquist and Chief Judge Anthony Scirica, Court of Appeals for Third Circuit; adjunct professor, George Washington University Law School.

Personal: George Washington University Law School (JD, Order of the Coif); Dartmouth College (BA, Rufus Choate Scholar).

GARRETT, Theodore

Covington & Burling, Washington, DC
202 662 5398
TGarrett@cov.com
Recommended in Environment

Practice Areas: Mr Garrett is Co-Chair of the firm's Environmental Practice Group. His practice involves major compliance, regulatory and enforcement issues, particularly involving air quality, water quality, hazardous waste and OSHA matters. He has represented clients in numerous Superfund sites including Chem-Dyne, Aceto, Blackbird Mine, Arlington Blending, Stoller, Price Landfill, Holden Mine, and Britannia Mine. The more than 50 reported cases handled by Mr Garrett include Michigan v EPA, 213 F.3d 663 (DC Cir. 2000); Kelley v EPA, 25 F.3d 1100 (DC Cir. 1994); Chemical Mfg. Ass'n v NRDC, 470 US 116 (1985), and Friends of the Earth v Facet Enterprises, 618 F. Supp. 532 (W.D.N.Y. 1984).

Prof. Memberships: Mr Garrett is past Chair of the ABA Section of Environment, Energy and Resources. Mr Garrett is listed prominently in the 2004 'International Who's Who of Environmental Lawyers' as 'the most highly nominated lawyer' not only in the USA but also globally. He was listed in 1994 as one of the 100 most influential lawyers in America by the 'National Law Journal'. Mr Garrett is a Member of the bars of DC, New York, and the US Supreme Court.

Career: Law Clerk to Chief Justice Warren Burger, US Supreme Court. Special Assistant to Assistant Attorney General William Rehnquist, US Department of Justice. Partner in Covington & Burling since 1976.

Publications: Mr Garrett is the editor and principal author of the 'Environmental Guide for Corporate Counsel' (1993), the editor of 'The Environmental Law Manual' (1992), and the 'RCRA Compliance Manual' (2004), is a co-author of the 'Clean Air Deskbook' (1992), and has authored chapters of 'Environmental Litigation' (ABA 1999), and 'The Clean Water Act Handbook' (2003). He has written numerous articles on environmental law topics.

Personal: BA, Yale University; JD, Columbia Law School.

GARZA, Deborah

Fried, Frank, Harris, Shriver & Jacobson LLP, Washington, DC 202 639 7270
Deborah.Garza@friedfrank.com
Recommended in Antitrust

Practice Areas: Antitrust Partner. Focuses practice on full range of antitrust counseling and litigation, with a particular focus on mergers and acquisitions.

Prof. Memberships: Chairperson of US Antitrust Modernization Commission, by appointment of President George W Bush; Member, Antitrust Council to US Chamber of Commerce; Member,

Board of Directors, National Capital Area American Red Cross.

Career: Joined firm as Partner 2001. Partner, Covington & Burling (1989-2001). Chief of Staff and Counselor (1988-89) and Special Assistant (1983-84) to the Assistant Attorney General for Antitrust, US Department of Justice. Editorial Chair, American Bar Association Magazine (2001-04); Team Leader, International Competition Network private sector merger guidelines project (entry barriers). Admitted District of Columbia.

Personal: Born 1956. Received JD from the University of Chicago in 1981 and BS from Northern Illinois University.

GAYNOR, Kevin
Vinson & Elkins LLP, Washington, DC
202 639 6688
kgaynor@velaw.com
Recommended in Environment

Practice Areas: Co-chairs the firm's Environmental Practice.

Prof. Memberships: Co-Chair: Environment, Energy, and Natural Resources Steering Committee, DC Bar. Member: Environment and Litigation Sections, American Bar Association.

Career: Admitted to Connecticut Bar in 1973, District of Columbia Bar in 1978, and Maryland Bar in 1991. Joined the firm as a Partner in 1993.

Publications: Environmental Enforcement Developments in 2003, 'The Environmental Law Reporter', News & Analysis, January 2004. TVA Decision Calls EPA's Unilateral Enforcement Authorities Into Question, 'Environment Reporter', Analysis & Perspective, August 2003.

GELFAND, David I
Cleary Gottlieb Steen & Hamilton LLP, Washington, DC 202 974 1690
dgelfand@cgsh.com
Recommended in Antitrust

Practice Areas: Antitrust and litigation. Represents clients in M&A before DOJ and FTC. Litigates cases in state and federal courts. Matters include: Alcoa/Reynolds merger; Glaxo/SmithKline merger; Conoco/Phillips merger; Siemens' acquisition of Alstom's turbine business; DSM's acquisition of Roche's vitamins business; Alcoa's acquisition of Russian aluminum rolling mills; UCB's sale of its chemicals business, and treble damage actions in various courts. Counsels clients on antitrust aspects of proposed business arrangements including electronic platforms, IP licenses, patent settlements.

Career: Joined firm, 1991, became Partner, 1997. JD, summa cum laude, Georgetown University Law Center (1987); BS, magna cum laude, University of Pennsylvania (1981).

GELLER, Kenneth S
Mayer, Brown, Rowe & Maw LLP, Washington, DC 202 263 3225
kgeller@mayerbrownrowe.com
Recommended in Litigation

Practice Areas: Appellate litigation, specializing in Supreme Court and appellate practice. Wrote or edited some 300 briefs and certiorari petitions in the Supreme Court. Argued some 40 cases in the Supreme Court.

Career: Joined Mayer, Brown, Rowe & Maw LLP as Partner, 1986. Partner in Charge of Washington, DC, office and Member of firm Management Committee. Former Deputy Solicitor General, US Department of Justice, 1979-86; Assistant to the Solicitor General, United States Department of Justice, 1975-79; Assistant Special Prosecutor, Watergate Special Prosecution Force, 1973-75; Nickerson, Kramer, Lowenstein, Nessen and Kamin, New York, 1972-73; Law Clerk to The Honorable Walter R Mansfield, US Court of Appeals for the Second Circuit, 1971-72.

Publications: Co-author: 'Supreme Court Practice', 8th ed, 2002; 7th ed, BNA (1993). Contributing Author: 'Business and Commercial Litigation In Federal Courts', Robert L Haig, ed, West Group & ABA (1998).

Personal: Born 22 September 1947. Harvard University, JD magna cum laude, 1971; editor, 'Law Review'. City College of New York, BA magna cum laude, 1968. Presidential Award for Distinguished Service, 1983.

GENTILE, Carmen
Bruder Gentile & Marcoux LLP, Washington, DC 202 296 1500
Recommended in Energy

GERGEN, Michael
Latham & Watkins LLP, Washington, DC 202 637 2200
Recommended in Energy

GERSCH, David P
Arnold & Porter LLP, Washington, DC
202 942 5125
David.Gersch@aporter.com
Recommended in Litigation

Practice Areas: David Gersch, a Senior Partner of Arnold & Porter LLP, is an experienced trial and appellate lawyer who has appeared as lead counsel in numerous complex commercial and tort actions.

Career: Mr Gersch has a broad litigation practice. In recent years, he has successfully tried jury cases involving diet drugs and transfusion-AIDS. He has also tried significant commercial disputes. He has argued appeals in the United States Courts of Appeal and state appellate courts. He is national counsel in multi-state class actions for a major insurer and represents clients in significant antitrust matters. Other actions handled by Mr Gersch include defense of intellectual property, pension, and toxic tort suits.

Personal: JD, New York University School of Law, 1982; AB, Oberlin College, 1978.

GERSTELL, Glenn
Milbank, Tweed, Hadley & McCloy, Washington, DC 202 835 7500
Recommended in Technology, Telecom, Broadcast & Satellite

GIBBS, Lawrence
Miller & Chevalier Chartered, Washington, DC 202 626 5800
Recommended in Tax

GIDEON, Kenneth W
Skadden, Arps, Slate, Meagher & Flom LLP & Affiliates, Washington, DC
202 371 7540
kgideon@skadden.com
Recommended in Tax

Practice Areas: Focuses on representation of clients before the US Department of the Treasury and the Internal Revenue Service; clients seeking guidance on novel transactions; and issues of federal tax law, tax controversy and tax planning. Advises clients on a wide variety of guidance, controversy (including tax litigation) and planning matters. Advises clients in connection with corporate mergers, acquisitions and restructurings, particularly in situations in which the transaction may require a ruling or informal discussion with the IRS.

Prof. Memberships: Chair, ABA Section of Taxation (2004-05).

Career: JD, Yale University Law School, 1971; BA, Harvard University, 1968.

GIDLEY, J Mark
White & Case LLP, Washington, DC
202 626 3609
mgidley@whitecase.com
Recommended in Antitrust

Practice Areas: Chair, White & Case Global Antitrust Group. Extensive experience representing parties before global competition agencies and in court. Active merger and joint venture practice. Represents defendants in global cartel and class action cases. Strong transnational focus in practice. Recent antitrust trial wins: Stolt-Nielsen v United States, FTC v Schering-Plough, Dee-K v Heveafil, DOJ v SunGard. Worldwide Merger Survey editor.

Prof. Memberships: ABA (Antitrust Section).

Career: Acting Assistant Attorney General, US Department of Justice (DOJ) Antitrust Division, 1992-93; Deputy Assistant Attorney General, Antitrust Division, 1991-92.

Personal: JD, Columbia Law School, 1986; Notes and Comments Editor, 'Columbia Law Review', 1985-86.

GIGOT, Thomas
Groom Law Group, Washington, DC
202 857 0620
Recommended in Employee Benefits

GILBERT, Scott
Gilbert Heintz & Randolph LLP, Washington, DC 202 772 2225
Recommended in Insurance

GLASGOW Jr, Norman
Holland & Knight LLP, Washington, DC
202 955 3000
norman.glasgowjr@hklaw.com
Recommended in Real Estate

Practice Areas: Partner in the firm's Real Estate Section, representing real estate developers in zoning, building code and historic preservation law matters before the Board of Zoning Adjustment, Zoning Commission, State Historic Review Board and Commission of Fine Arts. He has handled numerous cases before the Board of Zoning Adjustment and has participated in many major Zoning Commission cases. He also represents clients in street and alley closings. He is active in civic affairs; addressing the area's affordable housing crisis by working extensively with a number of nonprofit affordable housing providers and community development corporations.

GLOVER, Stephen I
Gibson, Dunn & Crutcher LLP, Washington, DC 202 955 8593
siglover@gibsondunn.com
Recommended in Corporate/Commercial

Practice Areas: Represents public and private companies in M&A, joint ventures, equity and debt offerings and corporate governance matters.

Prof. Memberships: DC Representative, New York Tribar Opinion Committee. Securities Regulation Committee, Negotiated Acquisitions Committee and Venture Capital Committee of ABA's Business Law Section.

Career: Served as Adjunct Professor at Georgetown University Law Center.

Publications: Author/co-author of several books and articles on corporate and securities law issues. Member, Advisory Board of BNA's 'Mergers & Acquisitions Law Report'. Editorial Board, 'The M&A Lawyer'.

Personal: JD, Harvard Law School, 1980; Managing editor, 'Harvard Law Review'. Law clerk, Supreme Court Justice Thurgood Marshall.

GOLDBERG Jr, Fred T
Skadden, Arps, Slate, Meagher & Flom LLP & Affiliates, Washington, DC
202 371 7110
fgoldber@skadden.com
Recommended in Tax

Practice Areas: Focuses on advising clients as special tax counsel on sensitive matters and representing clients on tax controversies, IRS administrative and regulatory proceedings, and tax legislation. Has directed compliance and management reviews on behalf of senior executives and boards of directors of various companies. Represents business, tax-exempt and individual clients during all phases of civil audit, administrative appeals and litigation. Also represents clients involved in IRS collection matters, clients subject to third-party

IRS discovery proceedings and clients involved in IRS criminal investigations.
Career: Former IRS Chief Counsel (1984-86); former IRS Commissioner (1989-91); former Assistant Secretary for Tax Policy (1992); JD, Yale University, 1973; BA, Yale University, 1969.

GOLDBLATT, Craig
Wilmer Cutler Pickering Hale and Dorr LLP, Washington, DC 202 663 6483
craig.goldblatt@wilmerhale.com
Recommended in Bankruptcy
Practice Areas: Practice focuses on complex civil and appellate litigation, with an emphasis on bankruptcy-related litigation and other restructuring matters. Has represented debtors, creditors, secured lenders and asset purchasers in all stages of bankruptcy proceedings. Involved in a range of civil litigation matters outside of bankruptcy, with an emphasis on complex disputes and appellate litigation.
Prof. Memberships: Advisory Committee of the United States District Court for the District of Columbia on Electronic Filing and Electronic Case Management.
Personal: University of Chicago Law School (JD 1993); Georgetown University (BA 1990).

GOLDSMITH, Willis J
Jones Day, Washington, DC
202 879 3920
wgoldsmith@jonesday.com
Recommended in Employment
Practice Areas: Chairs the firm's Labor & Employment Practice. He has appeared before state and federal trial and appellate courts in matters arising under the National Labor Relations Act, the Taft-Hartley Act, ERISA, the Civil Rights Act of 1964, the Occupational Safety and Health Act, and the Bankruptcy Code. Identified as one of the top 36 labor and employment lawyers in the country by 'The National Law Journal.'
Prof. Memberships: Fellow of the College of Labor and Employment Lawyers; Labor Law Advisory Committee of the Chamber of Commerce of the United States; Adviser, American Law Institute (Restatement Third, Employment Law).

GOLDSTEIN, Bruce
Zuckerman Spaeder LLP, Washington, DC 202 778 1800
Recommended in Bankruptcy

GOODMAN, Saul
Covington & Burling, Washington, DC
202 662 5472
sgoodman@cov.com
Recommended in Insurance
Practice Areas: Represents policyholders in complex insurance coverage disputes, transactions and advice. Experience includes coverage for wide range of losses, including asbestos and other mass torts, environmental, D&O, first party property, IP and other major losses. Practice group coordinator for Cov-

ington's 70-member policyholder practice group since 1997.
Career: Joined Covington in 1987; became Partner in 1989. Law Clerk to Judge Carl McGowan, US Court of Appeals for the District of Columbia Circuit (1978-79) and Justice Potter Stewart, US Supreme Court (1979-80).
Publications: Insurance publications include: 'Settlement of Insurance Coverage Disputes', in 'Law and Practice of Insurance Coverage Litigation' (West 2000).
Personal: BA, cum laude, Yale, 1975; JD, Virginia, 1978; Executive Editor, 'Virginia Law Review' (1977-78).

GOODWIN, Michael
Arnold & Porter LLP, Washington, DC
202 942 5558
Michael.Goodwin@aporter.com
Recommended in Real Estate
Practice Areas: Practice encompasses all facets of commercial real estate, with special focus on development, hospitality, financing and public/private partnership transactions. He represents developers in assemblages, debt and equity financing, and sales, and is heavily involved in structuring and negotiating public incentives for real estate development such as TIFs, PILOTs and tax abatement. He also represents hotel owners and operators in the acquisition, development, operation and sale of hospitality properties nationwide, including full service, convention center and resort hotels.
Prof. Memberships: He is a graduate of Harvard Law School, and a Member of the American College of Real Estate Lawyers.

GORELICK, Jamie
Wilmer Cutler Pickering Hale and Dorr LLP, Washington, DC 202 663 6500
jamie.gorelick@wilmerhale.com
Recommended in Litigation
Practice Areas: Represents corporations and individuals on a wide array of problems, particularly in the regulatory and enforcement arenas. Particular experience in corporate governance and compliance, as well as internal corporate investigations.
Career: Vice Chair of Fannie Mae, largest source of housing finance in the US; Deputy Attorney General, US Department of Justice; General Counsel, US Department of Defense. Served on numerous government boards and commissions. Joined WCP in 2003. Consistently listed in a leading legal publication and 'Washingtonian Magazine's '50 Best Lawyers in Washington'. Also listed in Fortune's 'Fifty Most Powerful Women in Business', Working Mother Magazine's 'Twenty-Five Most Influential Working Mothers in America', and Forbes.com's 'Smartest Women with Money'.
Publications: Co-author of leading treatise on the maintenance of corporate documents, 'Destruction of Evidence'

(Wiley 1983).
Personal: Harvard School of Law (JD 1975); Harvard University (BA 1972).

GORRELL Jr, J Warren
Hogan & Hartson LLP, Washington, DC
202 637 8618
jwgorrell@hhlaw.com
Recommended in Corporate/Commercial
Practice Areas: Warren Gorrell is Chairman of Hogan & Hartson and a co-director of the Corporate, Securities and Finance Practice Group. His practice, which is primarily transactional, covers several different areas and involves a diverse array of industries. He represents publicly and privately held companies and real estate investment trusts (REITs) and their controlling shareholders in all aspects of their businesses, including mergers and acquisitions, public offerings and private placements of equity and debt securities, senior and subordinated debt financings, tender offers and exchange offers, restructurings and recapitalizations, joint ventures, and general business matters. Warren also represents a number of major investment banking firms in connection with domestic and international offerings of both equity and debt securities, including initial public offerings, primary and secondary offerings (including 144A placements), and corporate restructurings and reorganizations.
Career: He joined Hogan & Hartson LLP as an associate in 1979 and became a Partner in 1986. He was recognized in 1999 as a Dealmaker of the Year by The American Lawyer.
Personal: Princeton University (AB, magna cum laude, 1976); University of Virginia School of Law (JD, 1979).

GOTTS, Lawrence J
Shaw Pittman LLP, Washington, DC
703 770 7604
lawrence.gotts@shawpittman.com
lawrence.gotts@pillsburylaw.com
Recommended in Intellectual Property
Practice Areas: Intellectual property: patent, trademark, copyright and trade secret litigation and counseling; litigation in federal district courts throughout the United States and the ITC; appeals before the Court of Appeals for the Federal Circuit.
Prof. Memberships: American Intellectual Property Association; American Bar Association; Tau Beta Pi; Pi Tau Sigma.
Career: Awarded 'Washington's Top IP Lawyer', 2004, Washington Business Journal; Chair: Litigation and Intellectual Property Group; Registered to Practice Before USPTO.
Personal: BSME, University of Maryland, 1980, summa cum laude; JD, George Washington, 1985, high honors; married with two children. (At press time, Shaw Pittman LLP had entered into a merger agreement with Pillsbury

Winthrop LLP. The merger is expected to close by April 2005. Post closing, the name of the firm will be Pillsbury Winthrop Shaw Pittman LLP.)

GRANWELL, Alan
Ivins, Phillips & Barker, Washington, DC
202 393 7600
Recommended in Tax

GREANEY, William
Covington & Burling, Washington, DC
202 662 5486
wgreaney@cov.com
Recommended in Insurance
Practice Areas: Represents corporate policyholders in insurance coverage disputes before federal and state courts throughout the country, including disputes over coverage for underlying asbestos, environmental, toxic tort, intellectual property, construction defects, securities and broker-dealer claims. Also has extensive experience representing policyholders in disputes arising under first-party property policies, including coverage for business interruption and contingent business interruption losses under 'all-risk' property policies and disputes arising under crime/fraud and fidelity policies.
Publications: Writes and speaks extensively on insurance coverage topics and has served on several ABA committees addressing environmental, insurance and litigation issues.
Personal: Harvard University (JD 1981, cum laude); University of Maryland (BA 1977, summa cum laude).

GREEN, Doug
Steptoe & Johnson LLP, Washington, DC 202 429 6212
dgreen@steptoe.com
Recommended in Energy
Practice Areas: Partner in Steptoe & Johnson LLP's Washington office. Vice-Chairman of the firm. Practice encompasses electric power, litigation, and antitrust. Represents domestic and international companies in the electric power sector in matters involving competition, mergers and acquisitions, restructuring, commercial transactions, and FERC and SEC regulation. Litigation practice includes toxic and mass torts, commercial disputes, including breach of contract, fraud and money laundering, torts, class actions, and major arbitration and mediation matters. Antitrust practice includes mergers, counseling, treble damages litigation, and handling matters before the federal antitrust enforcement agencies.
Personal: JD, Georgetown University Law Center, 1973; BA, Bowdoin College, 1968.

GREEN, Thomas C
Sidley Austin Brown & Wood LLP, Washington, DC 202 736 8069
tcgreen@sidley.com
Recommended in Litigation
Practice Areas: Tom Green is a nation-

ally known and highly regarded trial lawyer who has tried countless complex criminal and civil cases. He counsels corporate officials in connection with state and federal criminal investigations and conducts internal investigations of alleged corporate wrongdoings and advises on implementation of compliance and anti-fraud programs. Representative matters include: Pickett v Tyson Fresh Meats (M.D.Alabama) in which as lead trial counsel for the class action in which plaintiffs claimed $2 billion in damages, he obtained a successful verdict for Tyson Foods; Coronet Industries (Florida Cir.Ct.) in which he is lead counsel for Coronet in both a class action and a putative joinder involving over 900 plaintiffs; United States v Cinergy (S.D. Indiana) in which he represents Cinergy in 'bet the company' litigation involving the Clean Air Act. His victory for Tyson Foods in a jury trial was named National Law Journal's top defense verdict of the year for 2003 and he was named as one of the top five white collar criminal defense lawyers in 2003 by Corporate Crime Reporter. Mr Green has represented Members of Congress, public officials and individuals in connection with state, federal and Congressional investigations and advised the World Bank on compliance and anti-fraud programs.

Prof. Memberships: Mr Green is a Fellow of the American College of Trial Lawyers, a past president of the Assistant United States Attorneys Association of Washington, DC as well as a member of the National Association of Criminal Defense Lawyers where he served as the initial Chairman of the Committee on Environmental Crime.

Career: Mr Green is a former Assistant US Attorney for the District of Columbia. Yale Law School, LLB, 1965; Dartmouth College, BA, 1962. Admitted to US Supreme Court; DC and Minnesota Bars.

GREENSTEIN, Abraham
Greenstein Delorme & Luchs,
Washington, DC 202 452 1400
Recommended in Real Estate

GROSKAUFMANIS, Karl
Fried, Frank, Harris, Shriver & Jacobson LLP, Washington, DC 202 639 7314
Karl.Groskaufmanis@friedfrank.com
Recommended in Corporate/Commercial

Practice Areas: Corporate and Securities and Enforcement Partner. Practice includes United States Securities and Exchange Commission enforcement actions, civil and criminal insider trading investigations, corporate internal investigations, securities litigation and corporate counseling.

Prof. Memberships: Co-Chairman of the Practising Law Institute's Advanced Securities Workshop; Co-Chair of the Civil Litigation and SEC Enforcement

Subcommittee of the American Bar Association's Committee on Federal Regulation of Securities.

Career: Joined Fried Frank in 1988 and became a Partner in 1995. Admitted to the Bar in the District of Columbia and Massachusetts.

Personal: Born 1961. JD in 1988 from the University of Pennsylvania, his LLB in 1987 from the University of Toronto Law School and his BS, with honors, in 1984 from Cornell University.

GUTIERREZ, Jay
Morgan, Lewis & Bockius LLP,
Washington, DC 202 739 5466
jgutierrez@morganlewis.com
Recommended in Energy

Practice Areas: Jay M Gutierrez is the Energy Practice Group Leader, a group that represents approximately half the utilities in the US. Mr Gutierrez represents companies in a variety of matters before the US Nuclear Regulatory Commission (NRC), including licensing, inspection, investigation, and enforcement issues.

Prof. Memberships: Member, American Bar Association, editor, Rutgers Law Journal.

Publications: Mr Gutierrez authored a text in 1995 on Fundamentals of Nuclear Regulation in the US, and is an active lecturer on the subject before clients and at industry conferences, including at the Institute of Nuclear Power Operations (INPO).

HADJIS, Alex
Weil, Gotshal & Manges LLP,
Washington, DC 202 682 7506
alex.hadjis@weil.com
Recommended in Intellectual Property

Practice Areas: Intellectual property/media, patent litigation, litigation/regulatory.

Career: Alex Hadjis focuses on complex litigation, including cases involving the interface between IP and antitrust and cases involving technology standards. He has served as lead counsel before several federal district courts and the US International Trade Commission on cases involving patent, antitrust and breach of contract issues and semiconductor, optical storage media, liquid crystal display, telecommunications, computer network, software, xerography, chemical and automotive component technologies. Intel, Genesis Microchip, MediaTek, Samsung, Cypress Semiconductor and Atmel are among his clients.

Personal: George Washington University, LLM; University of Pittsburgh, JD; Ohio State University, BA.

HAGEN, Paul
Beveridge & Diamond PC,
Washington, DC 202 789 6022
phagen@bdlaw.com
Recommended in Environment

Practice Areas: As Chair of the firm's International Environmental Practice

Section, he counsels multinational corporations, trade associations and leading non-profit organizations on the negotiation and implementation of regional and global environmental agreements. Works extensively with clients in the chemicals, electronics and pharmaceuticals sectors. His work includes representing clients on a wide range of product stewardship legislation and on issues arising under numerous international agreements, including the Basel Convention, the Biosafety Protocol, the Kyoto Protocol, the Rotterdam Prior Informed Consent Convention, and the Stockholm Convention on Persistent Organic Pollutants. Advises clients on the environmental and social guidelines of the World Bank and IFC and on the environmental aspects of trade and investment agreements, including matters arising under the NAFTA and WTO. His domestic practice includes counseling on environmental compliance and enforcement matters. He has recently assisted several non-profits on efforts to protect whales, albatross and rainforests in Asia.

Prof. Memberships: Currently serves on the Board of Directors of the Environmental Law Institute (ELI) and the American Bird Conservancy. Appointed to the ABA Standing Committee on Environmental Law. Member of the IUCN Commission on Environmental Law.

Career: Admitted to Maryland (1990) and District of Columbia (1992) Bars. Director of Beveridge & Diamond, P.C. Adjunct professor of law, Washington College of Law at American University. He has advised governments in Asia, Africa and the Middle East on the development of environmental and natural resources legislation.

Publications: Author: 'The Green Diplomacy Gap,' The Environmental Forum (August 2000); co-author: 'The Cartagena Protocol on Biosafety: New Rules for International Trade in Living Modified Organisms,' Georgetown International Environmental Law Review (2000); co-author: 'The Convergence of Trade and Environmental Law,' 8 Natural Resources and Envir. 2 (ABA 1993); co-author: 'Courts Examine U.S. Environmental Law's Extraterritorial Reach,' National Law Journal (September 1993); co-author: 'The Application of the United States Hazardous Waste Cleanup Laws in the Canada-U.S. Context,' 18 Can.-U.S. L.J. 137 (1992); co-author, 'Wetlands' in Environmental Law and Practice Guide (Mathew Bender 1992); author: 'The International Community Confronts Plastics Pollution from Ships: MARPOL Annex V and the Problem that Won't Go Away,' 5 Am. U.J. Int'l L. & Pol'y 425 (1990).

Personal: Received BA, Providence College (1986) and JD, Washington College of Law at American University (1990).

HANDMAN, Laura R
Davis Wright Tremaine LLP,
Washington, DC 202 508 6600
laurahandman@dwt.com
Recommended in Media & Entertainment

Practice Areas: Partner, defending media companies and authors in libel, privacy, intellectual property and other First Amendment matters. Clients include: BBC, Discovery Communications, Amazon.com, The Economist, U.S. News & World Report.

Prof. Memberships: Past Chair, Communications/Media Law Committee of Association of the Bar, New York City. Founder/past Chair, Media Law Committee, DC Bar. Past President, Defense Counsel section, Libel Defense Resource Center.

Publications: 'Protection of Confidential Sources: A Moral, Legal and Civic Duty', Notre Dame Journal of Law, Ethics & Public Policy, Spring 2005; NAA/NAB/Media Law Resource Center Biennial Conference, Co-Moderator of opening dinner panel (1995, 1997, 1999, 2002, 2004).

HANSEN, Kenneth
Chadbourne & Parke LLP,
Washington, DC 202 974 5656
khansen@chadbourne.com
Recommended in Projects

Practice Areas: Represents project sponsors, banks, bilateral and multilateral agencies, and political risk insurers in international infrastructure financings, trade financings, and the settlement of political risk insurance claims and investment disputes. Advised both agencies and commercial insurers on the design and implementation of novel financial guaranty products. Sectoral experience includes power generation, transmission and distribution, oil and gas, transport, telecoms, and tourism. Representative clients include OPIC, US Ex-Im Bank, ADB, IIC and EBRD.

Prof. Memberships: Admitted in the District of Columbia and Massachusetts; Washington Foreign Law Society (President, 2004-05).

Career: Formerly General Counsel, US Ex-Im Bank; Associate General Counsel, OPIC.

HARMAN, Thomas
Morgan, Lewis & Bockius LLP,
Washington, DC 202 739 5662
tharman@morganlewis.com
Recommended in Investment Management

Practice Areas: Thomas Harman is a Partner in the Investment Management Practice. Mr Harman's practice focuses on investment management matters involving mutual funds, closed-end funds, private investment companies, ETFs and investment advisers. He also serves as counsel to the board of directors of several fund families.

Career: Mr Harman served as chief

counsel, subsequently associate director (chief counsel), of the Securities and Exchange Commission's Division of Investment Management from 1988-94. From 1987-88, he directed the Division's Office of Disclosure and Adviser Regulation. Mr Harman was an adjunct Professor in the securities law program at Georgetown University Law Center from 1991-2002.

HARRIS, Larry D
DLA Piper Rudnick Gray Cary US LLP, Washington, DC 202 861 6423
larry.harris@dlapiper.com
Recommended in Construction
Practice Areas: Construction; government contracts.
Prof. Memberships: Fellow, American College of Construction Lawyers, Board of Governors.
Career: Experience in government contracts and construction matters including litigation before boards of contract appeals and arbitration tribunals in cases involving changes, cost reimbursement, acceleration, delay, disruption, defective work and termination. Counseled domestic and international contractors, subcontractors, and owners regarding claims and changes under supply, service, aerospace, healthcare, and construction contracts. He has also served as a mediator, arbitrator and dispute review Board Member in construction matters.
Personal: JD, George Washington University; BS, University of Dayton.

HARRIS, Scott
Harris, Wiltshire & Grannis LLP, Washington, DC 202 730 1300
Recommended in Telecom, Broadcast & Satellite

HASKELL, Mark
Morgan, Lewis & Bockius LLP, Washington, DC 202 739 5766
mhaskell@morganlewis.com
Recommended in Energy
Practice Areas: Mark R Haskell is a Partner in the Energy Practice. His practice focuses on Federal Energy Regulatory Commission (F.E.R.C.) matters, including F.E.R.C. investigations, litigation and related court appeals.
Prof. Memberships: Member, American Bar Association- Energy, Environment and Resources Sections (Vice Chair, Committee on Electric and Natural Gas Marketing, 2000-02).
Career: Mr Haskell possesses over 17 years of industry experience in matters relating to federal regulation of natural gas, electric energy and ancillary services, and interstate pipeline safety and infrastructure. He was recognized as a leading gas and electric lawyer in the 2004 edition of Chambers USA.

HASTINGS, Douglas
Epstein Becker & Green PC, Washington, DC 202 861 0900
Recommended in Healthcare

HATCHER, Julia
Latham & Watkins LLP, Washington, DC 202 637 2200
Recommended in Environment

HAYES, David
Latham & Watkins LLP, Washington, DC 202 637 2200
Recommended in Environment

HEFFERNAN, Barbara
Schiff Hardin LLP, Washington, DC 202 778 6440
bheffernan@schiffhardin.com
Recommended in Energy
Practice Areas: Energy, telecommunications, and public utilities.
Prof. Memberships: American Bar Association, Energy Bar Association, Women's Council on Energy and the Environment, American Arbitration Association.
Career: Ms Heffernan is Co-Leader of Schiff Hardin's Energy, Telecommunications, and Public Utilities Group. She has represented numerous clients before the Federal Energy Regulatory Commission and the federal courts for 25 years on a variety of matters concerning the regulation of natural gas and electricity.
Personal: University of Maryland (BA, 1975), Catholic University Law School (JD, 1978).

HEINTZ, John
Gilbert Heintz & Randolph LLP, Washington, DC 202 772 2225
Recommended in Insurance

HELM, Robert W
Dechert, Washington, DC 202 261 3356
robert.helm@dechert.com
Recommended in Investment Management
Practice Areas: Investment companies and funds, alternative investments, investment advisers, insurance companies, broker-dealers, and other financial institutions in regulatory and corporate matters.
Prof. Memberships: Chair, Investment Funds and Trusts Committee, International Bar Association; advisory board, Mutual Fund Directors Forum; editorial board, Villanova Journal of Law and Investment Management; Member, Securities and Commodities Law Committees of American Bar Association and DC Bar Association.
Career: Joined Dechert in 1984.
Publications: Authored articles published in Review of Securities and Commodities Regulation, The Investment Lawyer, Journal of International Banking Law, and other publications.
Personal: Stanford University (AB, distinction, 1979); Stanford Law School (JD, 1982).

HENDLER, Clifford B
Crowell & Moring LLP, Washington, DC 202 624 2928
chendler@crowell.com
Recommended in Insurance

Practice Areas: Cliff Hendler is Chair of Crowell & Moring's Complex Insurance Coverage Litigation Group. He serves as national counsel for ACE USA Insurance Companies (formerly CIGNA Property & Casualty Companies). He has orchestrated the successful negotiation of global resolutions of disputes involving dozens of insurance companies and underlying case policyholder liabilities.
Career: Appointed by the US District Court for the District of Columbia to mediate to resolution a 20-year dispute regarding taped conversations recorded by former President Richard Nixon.
Personal: Undergraduate degree from Yale University with honors, 1975; JD from Stanford Law School, 1978, Order of the Coif Member.

HENNEBURG, Frank H
Akin Gump Strauss Hauer & Feld LLP, Washington, DC
202 887 4333
fhenneburg@akingump.com
Recommended in Real Estate
Practice Areas: Advises owners and lenders in acquisition, construction, leasing, financing and disposition of large commercial projects throughout the United States. Has significant experience in single property financings involving all property types, and has served as lead counsel in portfolio financings involving as many as 50 properties in 20 states. Also advises on complex financing, including participating and convertible debt, as well as mezzanine lending. Has managed numerous consensual restructurings of troubled real estate loans and has considerable experience with foreclosure and bankruptcy proceedings.
Prof. Memberships: Illinois and District of Columbia Bars.
Personal: AB, Georgetown University; JD, University of Chicago.

HENRY, Roxann
Howrey Simon Arnold & White, Washington, DC 202 783 0800
Recommended in Antitrust

HENSLER, David
Hogan & Hartson LLP, Washington, DC 202 637 5630
djhensler@hhlaw.com
Recommended in Insurance, Litigation
Practice Areas: A director of the firm's Litigation Practice. Handles complex commercial litigation with a focus on securities fraud, internal investigations, insurance coverage disputes, aviation and noise impact litigation, government contracts, patent infringement, and other general commercial litigation.
Prof. Memberships: Fellow, American College of Trial Lawyers (ACTL) and Chair of the State Committee for the ACTL, District of Columbia; Member, District of Columbia Bar Association; Member, Litigation Section, ABA; Mem-

ber, Federal Bar Association.
Career: Formerly served in General Counsel's Office of the Securities and Exchange Commission.
Publications: Co-author of several articles on asset valuation in the context of corporate takeovers and divestitures.
Personal: St. Louis University (JD, cum laude).

HOLDER, Eric
Covington & Burling, Washington, DC 202 662 5372
eholder@cov.com
Recommended in Litigation
Practice Areas: Handles complex civil and criminal cases, domestic and international advisory matters, and internal corporate investigations.
Career: Deputy Attorney General of the US (1997-2001); US Attorney for the District of Columbia (1993-97); Associate Judge of the Superior Court of the District of Columbia (1988-93); Department of Justice Public Integrity Section (1976-83). As Deputy Attorney General, supervised all of the DOJ's litigating, enforcement, and administrative components in both civil and criminal matters. Under his guidance, the DOJ developed and issued its guidelines on the criminal prosecution of corporations (the so called 'Holder Memorandum').
Personal: Columbia University (JD, 1976; BS, 1973).

HOLEWINSKI, Kevin
Jones Day, Washington, DC 202 879 3797
kpholewinski@jonesday.com
Recommended in Environment
Practice Areas: Coordinator of the Environmental, Health and Safety Practice in the firm's Washington Office. He has substantial complex civil, environmental, toxic tort, and criminal litigation experience. He has represented clients in civil enforcement actions, criminal investigations, insurance coverage litigation, toxic tort litigation, and private party cost recovery litigation. He has written and lectured on topics including the defense of environmental civil penalty and injunctive claims; the treatment of environmental claims in bankruptcy; environmental criminal enforcement; federal contractor wartime claims against the US; the EPA's compliance with Office of Management and Budget requirements, and the federal Data Quality Act.

HOLMES, Jacqueline M
Jones Day, Washington, DC 202 879 3620
jhomes@jonesday.com
Recommended in Employment
Practice Areas: Represents clients in occupational safety and health, labor, and employment matters. Her experience includes litigating and resolving OSHA matters before administrative law judges and the Occupational Safety and Health Review Commission, and

advising clients in OSHA rulemaking proceedings and compliance issues. Her practice emphasizes ergonomics, lockout/tagout, confined space, chemical process safety management, and industrial hygiene issues. She also represents clients before state and federal administrative agencies and federal and state trial and appellate courts in a variety of labor and employment matters.

Publications: Co-authored articles on workplace safety issues, focusing on ergonomics and General Duty Clause enforcement.

HOROWITZ, Philip
Venable LLP, Washington, DC
202 962 4800
Recommended in Real Estate

HOWARD, Theodore
Wiley Rein & Fielding LLP,
Washington, DC 202 719 7000
Recommended in Insurance

HUBER, John
Latham & Watkins LLP,
Washington, DC 202 637 2200
Recommended in Corporate/Commercial

HUMES, Gary
Arnold & Porter LLP, Washington, DC
202 942 5001
Gary.Humes@aporter.com
Recommended in Real Estate

Practice Areas: Build-to-suit transactions and large-scale office leases, public-private partnerships and other complex transactions involving the Federal Government, and real estate development and financing. Clients include Fortune 500 companies, non-profit organizations, large law firms, hotel owners and operators, and real estate developers. Structures and negotiates ground and space leases, joint ventures, purchase agreements, design and construction contracts, brokerage and development management agreements, and tax-exempt and taxable financings.

Personal: Education: JD from Cornell Law School (1981), SM from the University of Chicago (1974), PhD candidate in Theoretical Physics (1974-76), BA from Wesleyan University (1972).

HUNT, Paul
Latham & Watkins LLP,
Washington, DC 202 637 2200
Recommended in Projects

HUTT, Peter Barton
Covington & Burling, Washington, DC
202 662 5522
phutt@cov.com
Recommended in Healthcare

Practice Areas: Specializes in food and drug regulation, biotechnology, and trade association law.

Prof. Memberships: Member of the Institute of Medicine of the National Academy of Sciences; served on the IOM Executive Committee, and other NAS and IOM committees; currently

serves on the Panel on the Administrative Restructuring of the National Institutes of Health.

Career: Served as Chief Counsel for the Food and Drug Administration (1971 - 75). Teaches a full course on Food and Drug Law during Winter Term at Harvard Law School (1994 - present). Noted by The Washingtonian magazine as one of Washington's 50 best lawyers (out of more than 40,000) and as one of Washington's 100 most influential people; by the National Law Journal as one of the 40 best health care lawyers in the United States; and by European Counsel as the best FDA regulatory specialist in Washington, DC.

Publications: Co-author (with Professor Richard A Merrill of the University of Virginia Law School) of 'Food and Drug Law: Cases and Materials' (Foundation Press, 1st edition 1980, 2nd edition 1991).

Personal: Harvard University (LLB, 1959); New York University (LLM, in Food/Drug Law, 1960); Yale University (BA, 1956, magna cum laude).

HYDE, Terrill
Wilmer Cutler Pickering Hale and Dorr LLP, Washington, DC 202 663 6238
terrill.hyde @wilmerhale.com
Recommended in Tax

Practice Areas: Provides advice on structuring and restructuring of multinational groups in connection with acquisitions; domestic mergers, acquisitions and spin-offs; bankruptcy and insolvency restructurings; and structuring cross-border investments. Advises exempt organizations on issues relating to formation and ongoing activities, including IRS ruling requests, structuring innovative programs and transactions, intermediate sanctions and private foundation provisions.

Prof. Memberships: Former member of the Council of the ABA Section of Taxation; former Council Director for the Corporate Tax and Affiliated and Related Corporations Committees.

Personal: University of Nebraska College of Law (JD 1979); South Dakota State University (MA 1976); Dakota State College (BS 1973).

IMUS, Neil W
Vinson & Elkins LLP, Washington, DC
202 639 6675
nimus@velaw.com
Recommended in Antitrust

Practice Areas: US antitrust including practice before the DOJ and FTC in HSR, merger and acquisitions and other agency investigations and in antitrust litigation.

Prof. Memberships: ABA Antitrust Section - Book & Treatises Co-Chair.

Career: Partner.

Publications: Editor: Premerger Notification Practice Manual, Third Ed.

Personal: Georgetown University Law Center (JD, 1985); George Washington

University (MBA, 1981); Davidson College (BS, 1975).

JACK, Andrew
Covington & Burling, Washington, DC
202 662 5232
ajack@cov.com
Recommended in Corporate/Commercial

Practice Areas: Diverse corporate and securities practice with clients principally in the manufacturing, real estate and sports and entertainment industries. Experience includes mergers and acquisitions, financing activities, venture capital, securities law compliance, and significant corporate governance counseling.

Prof. Memberships: Society of Corporate Secretaries and Governance Professionals.

Career: 19 years with Covington highlighted by serving as lead transactional counsel in: successful effort to return Major League Baseball to Washington DC (2002-05), Cleveland Browns relocation and expansion (1996-99), JLG Industries' acquisitions of Gradall Industries (1999) and OmniQuip (2003).

Personal: George Washington University, (JD, 1986, with highest honors; BA, 1983).

JACKSON, Thomas C
Baker Botts LLP, Washington, DC
202 639 7710
thomas.jackson@bakerbotts.com
Recommended in Environment

Practice Areas: Tom Jackson handles all aspects of environmental law, including client counseling, permitting, trial court and appellate litigation, administrative hearings and arbitrations, and legislative matters. He also helps clients assess proposed rules and other public documents such as Environmental Impact Statements.

Prof. Memberships: District of Columbia Bar, United States Court of Federal Claims, United States Courts of Appeals (for the Third, Fifth, Ninth, Eleventh, Federal, and District of Columbia Circuits), United States District Court for the District of Columbia, United States Supreme Court.

Personal: JD (with honors), Harvard Law School (1984), BA (summa cum laude), Political Science, Amherst College (1981).

JACOBSEN, Ray
McDermott Will & Emery,
Washington, DC 202 756 8026
rayjacobsen@mwe.com
Recommended in Antitrust

Practice Areas: Head of firm's Regulation and Government Affairs Department and its Antitrust and Competition Practice. Focuses on mergers, acquisitions and other antitrust work, with significant experience in the defense, high-tech, consumer product, energy and health care industries. Successfully defended over 100 complex mergers,

acquisitions and joint ventures in the US, Europe and the Far East. Successfully defended civil litigation, including class actions, in over 30 federal and state courts as well as the Federal Trade Commission and US Justice Department investigations involving alleged price-fixing, exclusive distribution arrangements, intellectual property issues, unfair trade and false advertising. One of the first to obtain amnesty for a client under the Justice Department's expanded amnesty program.

Prof. Memberships: Chairman of two American Bar Association Committees.

Career: Listed in Best Lawyers in America (2003-04), An International Who's Who of Competition Lawyers, The World's Leading Competition and Antitrust Lawyers, the Best of the Best 2001 antitrust/competition lawyers and the 2002 outstanding International Business lawyers.

Personal: Earned JD from Georgetown University Law Center in 1975. Earned BA (cum laude) in 1971 from University of Delaware.

JAFFE, Kenneth
Swidler Berlin LLP, Washington, DC
202 424 7500
kgjaffe@swidlaw.com
Recommended in Energy

Practice Areas: Specializes in regulatory matters affecting participants in competitive energy markets. Represents electric untilities and other market participants in wide range of transactions and regulatory proceedings. Particular concentration on matters connected with restructuring of the electiric utility industry and operations of independent systems operators and regional transmission organizations.

Prof. Memberships: Admitted to practice in Washington, DC (1981).

Career: Joined Swidler Berlin LLP in 1985; became Partner, 1990.

Personal: Born 5 June 1957. JD (cum laude), Harvard University; BA (honors) State University of New York at Binghamton, 1978.

JAFFE, Michael
Thelen Reid & Priest LLP,
Washington, DC 202 508 4000
Recommended in Construction

JEFFRESS, William
Baker Botts LLP, Washington, DC
202 639 7751
william.jeffress@bakerbotts.com
Recommended in Litigation

Practice Areas: Has tried 30 complex criminal and civil cases to juries in nine states and Washington DC, plus dozens of nonjury trials before judges and administrative tribunals. Matters include fraud, securities, antitrust, federal procurement, international transactions, newsgathering, public corruption, tax, money laundering, professional liability and others. Deals regularly with Justice Department, Treasury Department, State Department, S.E.C. and other agencies.

Career: Serves on firm's Executive Committee. Former editor-in-chief of 'Yale Law Journal', law clerk to Supreme Court Justice Potter Stewart, fellow of American College of Trial Lawyers, Former Member of ABA Ethics Committee and Chair of Criminal Justice Standards Committee.

JOHNSTON, Mark G
Levine, Blaszak, Block & Boothby LLP, Washington, DC 202 857 2548
mjohnston@lb3law.com
Recommended in Telecom, Broadcast & Satellite

Practice Areas: Specializes in advising on and negotiating communications, network outsourcing, and IT sourcing arrangements for commercial enterprises purchasing products and services. Represents clients in contract disputes with carriers and network services providers. Represents clients in transactions involving the development, licensing, maintenance, and hosting of software applications. Advises clients on carriers' regulatory obligations and the regulatory status of service offerings incorporating communications services. Represents commercial telecommunications customers and IT companies in FCC proceedings.

Prof. Memberships: Member of the New York State and the District of Columbia Bar Associations, American Bar Association, and Federal Communications Bar Association.

Career: Admitted to the Bars of New York and the District of Columbia. Associate and Partner with Levine, Blaszak, Block & Boothby, LLP, since 1997. Prior to joining LB3, practiced EC competition law with Van Bael & Bellis, in Brussels, Belgium, and practiced with the firm of Shiomi & Yamamoto in Osaka, Japan, specializing in the negotiation of international sales, distribution, and licensing transactions.

Personal: BA, magna cum laude and University Honors, University of Illinois, Urbana-Champaign, 1987. JD, cum laude, University of Michigan, 1991.

JORDAN, J Phillip
Swidler Berlin LLP, Washington, DC 202 424 7500
jpjordan@swidlaw.com
Recommended in Energy

Practice Areas: Extensive experience in electric industry. Focus on regulatory, corporate, competitive, transactional issues arising from movement toward deregulation. Represents foreign companies seeking investment in US.

Prof. Memberships: Admitted to practice in Georgia (1974), Washington, DC (1979), Maryland (1984); Energy Bar Association.

Career: Clerk to US Supreme Court Justice Lewis Powell (1975 Term); Special Assistant to US Attorney General

(1977-79); Joined Swidler Berlin, 1987; Managing Partner, 1994-96; Executive Committee, 1992-96.

Personal: Born 19 December 1948. JD (Phi Beta Kappa, Order of the Coif, editor in chief, 'University of Virginia Law Review'), University of Virginia, 1974; AB (magna cum laude), Princeton University 1971.

KADEN, Alan
Fried, Frank, Harris, Shriver & Jacobson LLP, Washington, DC 202 639 7073
Alan.Kaden@friedfrank.com
Recommended in Tax

Practice Areas: Tax Partner. Works closely with all the firm's practice groups, and is an integral member of the firm's Corporate Transactional Practice. Practices in all the principal areas of tax law, with particular emphasis on the structuring and negotiation of taxable and tax-free corporate acquisitions, reorganizations, spinoff transactions and dispositions of ongoing business enterprises, the structuring of investment funds, the development of partnership and other joint-venture arrangements for various business ventures and tax planning for financings and other capital formation transactions. Also active in tax controversy matters.

Prof. Memberships: Included in a leading legal publication in America (2003-04 edition), The Best Lawyers in America (2003-04 edition), The International Who's Who of Corporate Tax Lawyers (3rd edition), and listed in the Euromoney Guide to the Leading US Tax Lawyers (1997). Member of various tax committees and has authored (or co-authored) a number of published articles, including a frequently cited piece analyzing tax-free spinoff transactions. Previously an adjunct professor of law at Georgetown University Law Center, where he taught negotiated mergers and acquisitions and corporate tax II (reorganizations).

Career: Admitted District of Columbia and New York. Joined firm in 1981 and became Partner in 1987.

Personal: Born 1956. Received JD from Columbia University in 1981 and BS from University of Pennsylvania.

KAFKA, Gerald
Latham & Watkins LLP,
Washington, DC 202 637 2200
Recommended in Tax

KAHN, David S
Holland & Knight LLP, Washington, DC 202 955 3000
david.kahn@hklaw.com
Recommended in Real Estate

Practice Areas: Head of the firm's Real Estate Practice Group in Washington, DC. Practices in the areas of commercial real estate development and finance, and commercial leasing. He represents numerous real estate developers, as well as institutional owners, investors and lenders, including domestic and foreign

insurance companies, pension funds and national banks in connection with their real estate development/investment activities nationwide. This representation includes the negotiation and documentation of purchase and sale agreements, development agreements, construction and permanent loan agreements, deeds of trust, ground leases, loan and equity participations, joint venture agreements, construction contracts, and office and retail leases.

KALISH, Paul W
Crowell & Moring LLP, Washington, DC 202 624 2644
pkalish@crowell.com
Recommended in Insurance

Practice Areas: Paul Kalish is Co-Chair of Crowell & Moring's Insurance Group. He serves as national counsel for property and casualty companies regarding asbestos, silica, and other claims. He also serves as counsel for the Coalition for Litigation Justice, a group formed by property and casualty insurers to address abuses in the mass tort litigation environment.

Prof. Memberships: He served as Co-Chair for the American Bar Association Section of Litigation's 2002 Annual Meeting, a member of ABA's Task Force on the State of the Civil Justice System, and a Co-Chair of the Section of Litigation's Pretrial Practice and Discovery Committee.

KANTER, Jane A
Dechert, Washington, DC
202 261 3302
jane.kanter@dechert.com
Recommended in Investment Management

Practice Areas: Ms Kanter focuses on the regulation and counseling of investment advisers, mutual funds, closed-end funds, fund directors, and private investment funds. She also handles insurance companies and investment and insurance product matters.

Career: Attorney, Office of the Solicitor, Plan Benefits Security Division, US Department of Labor (1979-80); special counsel, US Securities and Exchange Commission's Division of Investment Management (1981-84); Vice-President and legal counsel, T. Rowe Price Associates, Inc. (1984 to 1987); private practice for past 18 years.

Personal: Queens College (BA, honors, 1970); Brooklyn Law School (JD, 1973); Washington University School of Law (LLM in Taxation, 1978).

KAPLAN, Steven
Arnold & Porter LLP, Washington, DC 202 942 5998
Steven.Kaplan@aporter.com
Recommended in Corporate/Commercial

Practice Areas: Steven Kaplan is the Responsible Partner for Arnold & Porter LLP's Corporate and Securities Practice Group. He serves as corporate and securities counsel to a wide range of corpo-

rations, including those in financial services, life sciences, transportation, and a variety of other industries, with emphasis on mergers and acquisitions, public and private securities offerings, corporate governance and Securities and Exchange Commission compliance matters.

Prof. Memberships: In October 2004, Mr Kaplan began a three year term as a member of the Municipal Securities Rulemaking Board. He also is a member of the Board of Washington Trustees of the Federal City Council, the Economic Club of Washington and the Japan Commerce Association of Washington. He has addressed Bar, trade, and professional education conferences on corporate and securities law matters, including programs sponsored by the Securities Industry Association, the American Institute of Certified Public Accountants, the Bank Administration Institute, the District of Columbia Bar, the North Carolina Banking Institute, the Strategic Research Institute, Executive Enterprises Inc. and the Israel Securities Authority.

Career: Mr Kaplan has represented clients in scores of business combination and divestiture transactions valued in the tens of billions of dollars, most recently representing CSX Corporation in the $1.15 billion sale of its global port assets to Dubai Ports International, Provident Financial Group in its $2.1 billion merger with National City Corporation and Ruesch International in its sale to a private equity fund sponsored by Welsh Carson Anderson & Stowe.

Publications: He has published articles on legal topics in Legal Times of Washington, The National Law Journal and Banking Expansion Reporter.

KASTNER, Ken
Hogan & Hartson LLP, Washington, DC 202 637 5653
kmkastner@hhlaw.com
Recommended in Environment

Practice Areas: Nationally recognized authority on hazardous waste and hazardous materials transportation. Represents clients in all EPA regions and states on complex compliance and enforcement matters, remediation, litigation, permitting, and regulatory and legislative advocacy.

Career: Private practice, including Partner 2002-present at Hogan & Hartson; 1982-88, Assistant General Counsel for waste and transportation matters at the Chemical Manufacturers Association (currently American Chemistry Council).

Publications: Editorial Board of Hazardous Waste Consultant; frequent author for American Bar Association, Bureau of National Affairs, and American Corporate Counsel Association publications.

Personal: University of Virginia (JD 1978) (BA 1974); London School of Economics, visiting student (1973).

KATTAN, Joseph
Gibson, Dunn & Crutcher LLP,
Washington, DC 202 955 8239
jkattan@gibsondunn.com
Recommended in Antitrust

Practice Areas: Antitrust litigation,
counseling, and advocacy before
enforcement agencies. Areas of concentration include M&A, joint ventures,
intellectual property antitrust, high
technology, and international antitrust.
Major Matters: Shepherded numerous
mergers and acquisitions through the
antitrust review process in the US and
throughout the world. Represent many
of the world's leading technology companies. Litigated leading IP antitrust
cases involving standard-setting, patent
pools, and refusals to license. Represented Intel in litigation against FTC, AMD,
Intergraph, and Via.

Publications: Published numerous articles. Participated by invitation at government hearings on global competition, joint ventures, intellectual property, and mergers.

KAUFMAN, Kenneth M
Skadden, Arps, Slate, Meagher & Flom
LLP & Affiliates, Washington, DC
202 371 7170
kaufman@skadden.com
Recommended in Intellectual Property

Practice Areas: Focuses on intellectual
property, internet, e-commerce law,
entertainment law, content and music
licensing and evolving new technologies
in the computer and entertainment
fields. Represents a wide range of clients
in online, entertainment and communications industries, including television
networks, e-commerce companies,
media businesses and computer and
Internet technology companies.

Prof. Memberships: Chair, Copyright
Society of the USA, Washington, DC
Chapter (2003-present); Washington
Area Lawyers for the Arts, Board of
Directors (1996-present); Washington
Area Music Association, Advisory Board
(1996-present).

Career: JD, Yale Law School, 1972 (Editor, 'Yale Law Journal'); AB, Harvard
College, 1969 (magna cum laude).

KEATING, Geoffrey
McManus Schor Asmar & Darden,
L.L.P., Washington, DC 202 296 9260
Recommended in Construction

KEENEY, Regina
Lawler, Metzger, Milkman & Keeney,
LLC, Washington, DC 202 777 7700
*Recommended in Telecom, Broadcast
& Satellite*

KELLEY, James J
Morgan, Lewis & Bockius LLP,
Washington, DC 202 739 5095
jkelley@morganlewis.com
Recommended in Employment

Practice Areas: James J Kelley, II is a
Partner in the Labor and Employment
Law Practice Group. Mr Kelley is
engaged in the full range of labor and
employment law practice areas, including employment litigation, collective
bargaining, grievance administration
and arbitration, Department of Labor
regulatory compliance, trade secrets and
wage and hour laws. Mr Kelley also
counsels clients on developing Employee Assistance Programs in the workplace. Mr Kelley concentrates in manufacturing, defense, aerospace and downstream oil industries.

Prof. Memberships: American Bar
Association - Employment Law Section,
College of Labor and Employment
Lawyers.

KELLNER, Leon B
Dickstein Shapiro Morin & Oshinsky
LLP, Washington, DC 202 828 2283
KellnerL@dsmo.com
Recommended in Insurance

Practice Areas: General, civil, and
insurance coverage litigation in federal
and state courts. Represents policyholders in complex insurance coverage matters including asbestos, environmental,
first-party losses, directors and officers
insurance, and errors and omissions
policies. Successfully represented clients
in fraud- and employment discrimination-related litigation matters.

Prof. Memberships: ABA.

Career: Partner and Co-Head, Dick-
stein Shapiro's Insurance Coverage Prac-
tice; Partner, Anderson Kill Olick &
Oshinsky, LLP; US Attorney for the
Southern District of Florida, 1985-88;
Civil Division Chief, 1982-84.

Personal: Harvard Law School (JD,
1971); State University of New York at
Buffalo (BA, 1967).

KELLOGG, Michael
Kellogg, Huber, Hansen, Todd & Evans
PLLC, Washington, DC 202 326 7900
*Recommended in Telecom, Broadcast
& Satellite*

KELLY, Deborah
Dickstein Shapiro Morin & Oshinsky
LLP, Washington, DC 202 775 4772
KellyD@dsmo.com
Recommended in Employment

Practice Areas: Employment litigation
and compliance; counsels companies in
restrictive covenants, non-competes and
contracts; conducts training in all
aspects of EEO compliance and HR
issues; drafts employee policy manuals;
defends companies against employment
claims, including jury trial litigation.

Prof. Memberships: ABA; Executive
Committee Member, Council for Court
Excellence.

Career: Head of Dickstein Shapiro
Employment Practice; Deputy General
Counsel. Professor, American Universi-
ty, 1983-88, 1992-93.

Publications: Co-management editor,
ABA Employment Law Update, 2002,
2004; Regular news media appearances,
including CNN and ABC.

Personal: University of Vermont (BS,
1974); Johns Hopkins University (MA,
1977; PhD, 1982) American University
School of Law (JD, 1988).

KENDALL, David
Williams & Connolly LLP,
Washington, DC 202 434 5000
*Recommended in Litigation, Media &
Entertainment*

KIELY, Bruce
Baker Botts LLP, Washington, DC
202 639 7711
bruce.kiely@bakerbotts.com
Recommended in Energy

Practice Areas: Practice involves regulatory, transactional litigation, project
development work for project sponsors,
gas pipelines, local distribution companies, LNG sellers, buyers and terminal
operators. Experience includes LNG
sales and purchase agreements, project
development including permitting of
pipelines and LNG terminals, fuel supply agreements, administrative and
appellate litigation, and advice on
changing regulatory policy.

Prof. Memberships: District of Columbia Bar; Virginia Bar; Federal Energy Bar
Association.

Career: Head of firm-wide LNG prac-
tice and Global Projects Department in
Washington office; Partner in charge of
Washington office.

Personal: JD from The University of
Texas School of Law, 1970; BS from the
University of Colorado, 1967.

KILBERG, William J
Gibson, Dunn & Crutcher LLP,
Washington, DC 202 955 8573
wkilberg@gibsondunn.com
*Recommended in Employee Benefits,
Employment*

Practice Areas: Counsels and represents clients in employee relations, labor
relations, and employee compensa-
tion/benefits. Has argued significant
matters before US Supreme Court and
US Court of Appeals, involving age discrimination, ERISA and the Americans
with Disabilities Act. Has appeared
numerous times in federal/state courts.

Career: Solicitor, US Department of
Labor; Associate Solicitor, Labor for
Labor Relations/Civil Rights; General
Counsel, Federal Mediation and Concil-
iation Service; and White House Fel-
low/Special Assistant, Secretary of Labor
George Shultz.

Publications: Co-author, 'Saga of
Reform: Regulation of Worker Overtime.' Frequent speaker on employment
and employee benefits issues.

Personal: JD, Harvard Law School,
1969.

KING, Carol Weld
Hogan & Hartson LLP, Washington, DC
202 637 5634
cwking@hhlaw.com
Recommended in Real Estate

Practice Areas: Carol Weld King practices principally in commercial real
estate, with emphasis in transaction
structuring, financing, acquisition and
development activities in the hospitality
industry.

Prof. Memberships: Member, ABA.

Career: Carol represents various owners, investors, developers and lenders in
a broad range of transactional work for
hospitality and gaming, office, multi-
family and mixed-use projects. She
serves as principal counsel to several
hotel equity funds and public and private corporations in connection with a
series of hotel acquisitions, financings
and ground up developments throughout the United States.

Personal: University of Virginia (JD,
1986); University of Virginia (BA, with
distinction, 1983).

KIRKWOOD, Martin
Jones Day, Washington, DC
202 879 3439
mvkirkwood@jonesday.com
Recommended in Energy

Practice Areas: Specializes in energy
law and regularly represents electric and
natural gas utilities before the FERC, the
US Department of Energy, state utility
commissions, and the appellate courts.
He has successfully represented applicants in proceedings involving electric
utility mergers, market-based rates,
exempt wholesale generator status, and
major rate cases. He regularly advises
clients of new developments in utility
regulation compliance matters.

Prof. Memberships: Maryland State Bar
Association; District of Columbia Bar
Association; Energy Bar Association.

Publications: Contributing author to
'Energy Law and Transactions.' He has
authored articles analyzing state and
federal regulation of natural gas and
electric utility companies.

KLAWITER, Donald
Morgan, Lewis & Bockius LLP,
Washington, DC 202 739 5222
dklawiter@morganlewis.com
Recommended in Antitrust

Practice Areas: Donald C Klawiter is a
Partner in the Antitrust Practice Group
at Morgan Lewis. His practice focuses
on antitrust civil and criminal investigations and litigation, and corporate
antitrust investigations and compliance.
He has defended corporations from
many countries in major civil treble
damage litigation and he has defended
corporations and their senior executives
in government enforcement matters,
civil and criminal. He has regularly
served as international coordinating
counsel in multi-jurisdictional cartel
investigations. Mr Klawiter previously
held senior positions at the Antitrust
Division, US Department of Justice.

Prof. Memberships: Professional Membership: Chair, Section of Antitrust Law,
American Bar Association (2005-06);
previously, Chair-Elect (2004-05); Vice
Chair (2003-04); Program Officer

(2001-03); Secretary (2000-01); Chair, Criminal Practice and Procedure Committee (1995-97).

KLEIN, David F
Swidler Berlin LLP, Washington, DC
202 424 7500
dfklein@swidlaw.com
Recommended in Insurance

Practice Areas: Spcecializes in insurance recovery for corporate policyholders. Matters include litigation and negotiated settlements involving general liability, environmental, first party and fidelity coverage. Special emphasis on resolving disputes without litigation through presentations to insurers integrating legal, technical and economic analysis.
Prof. Memberships: Admitted to practice in Washington, DC (1990) and New York (1989).
Career: Joined Swidler Berlin LLP in 1996; became Partner, 2000. Law clerk to Hon Julia Cooper Mack, DC Court of Appeals.
Personal: Born February 1963. JD Yale Law School, 1988; BA (summa cum laude, Phi Beta Kappa), Boston University, 1985.

KLEIN, Frederick
DLA Piper Rudnick Gray Cary US LLP, Washington, DC 202 861 6668
frederick.klein@dlapiper.com
Recommended in Real Estate

Practice Areas: Real estate; real estate finance.
Career: He practices in all areas of commercial real estate law, representing construction and permanent lenders, domestic and foreign banks, life insurance companies, local and national developers, and owners and developers of office buildings, multifamily projects, shopping centers and urban and suburban office buildings. Has handled the acquisition, disposition, and financing, of commercial projects in the mid-Atlantic region and elsewhere throughout the United States.
Publications: Co-author, 'American Bar Association's Real Property Tax Deskbook' chapter on District of Columbia real property taxation.
Personal: JD, University of Miami; AB, Duke University.

KLEIN, Kenneth
Mayer, Brown, Rowe & Maw LLP, Washington, DC 202 263 3377
kklein@mayerbrownrowe.com
Recommended in Tax

Practice Areas: International taxation of multinational corporations, including planning, transactions, controversies, and public policy work in numerous industries. Advises on outbound/inbound investments, structuring/restructuring, joint ventures, income bifurcation and amalgamation, controlled foreign corporations, US property investments, offshore intangibles, manufacturing, transportation, and

other areas. Advises on cross-border financings, portfolio interest, conduit financing arrangements, withholding tax, tax treaties, investment funds, swaps, other derivatives, CDOs, and other financing vehicles. Taxation of artists and athletes. International individual tax planning.
Career: Partner, Mayer, Brown, Rowe & Maw LLP, Washington, DC, July 2002 to date. Cadwalader, Wickersham & Taft, 1990-2002. Internal Revenue Service, Associate Chief Counsel (technical), 1988-90. Cadwalader, Wickersham & Taft, 1981-88. Internal Revenue Service, Assistant Branch Chief and Attorney, Legislation & Regulations Division and General Litigation Division, 1977-81. Fellow, American Society of International Law, 1976-77.
Publications: Speaks on international tax issues at numerous tax seminars and writes extensively on international tax issues in numerous publications.
Personal: JD (cum laude), University of Georgia School of Law, 1976; Articles Editor, Georgia Journal of International & Comparative Law. MLT, Georgetown University Law Center, 1980. BA (magna cum laude) University of Delaware, 1973.

KLEIN, Michael
Wilmer Cutler Pickering Hale and Dorr LLP, Washington, DC 202 663 6620
michael.klein@wilmerhale.com
Recommended in Litigation

Practice Areas: Actively involved in taking companies public, taking them private, and representing and counseling them, their executives and/or directors in both postures. Designated 'Special Counsel' to boards of directors and special committees of boards of directors of many public companies in a variety of settings. These engagements have included such subjects as control contests, reviews of internal controls and proper accounting, and inquiries into questioned foreign and domestic conduct.
Prof. Memberships: American Law Institute; Editorial Board, 'Insights', (corporate and securities law journal).
Personal: University of Miami (BBA 1963; JD 1966); Harvard University (LLM 1967).

KLEPPER, Martin
Skadden, Arps, Slate, Meagher & Flom LLP & Affiliates, Washington, DC
202 371 7120
mklepper@skadden.com
Recommended in Projects

Practice Areas: Specializes in the development, financing, acquisition, privitization and restructuring of energy facilities, sports stadiums and other large infrastructure projects throughout the world. He has been the lead lawyer representing owners, lenders, investors, fuel suppliers and contractors in the electric power, gas and LNG industries involving transactions exceeding $10 billion.

Prof. Memberships: Board of Trustees, Legal Aid Society of the District of Columbia.
Career: Adjunct Professor, Georgetown Law School, 2002 - present; JD, Rutgers Law School, 1973 (articles editor, 'Rutgers Law Review'); BS, University of Pennsylvania, Wharton School, 1969.

KNAUSS, Charles
Swidler Berlin LLP, Washington, DC
202 424 7500
chknauss@swidlaw.com
Recommended in Environment

Practice Areas: Nationally recognized authority on Clean Air Act. Extensive experience in complex federal and state environmental compliance counseling, permitting, enforcement, commercial rulemaking, and legislative matters.
Prof. Memberships: District of Columbia Bar (1982); American Bar Association (ABA); Air & Waste Management Association (A&WMA).
Career: Joined firm as Partner, 1990 (current Member, Board of Directors); Counsel, US House of Representatives Committee on Energy and Commerce, 1985-90.
Publications: Authored several books and articles. Regular speaker at ABA and A&WMA conferences.
Personal: Born 3 September 1955. JD, University of Michigan (1981); AB, Brown University (1977).

KOLASKY, William J
Wilmer Cutler Pickering Hale and Dorr LLP, Washington, DC 202 663 6357
william.kolasky@wilmerhale.com
Recommended in Antitrust

Practice Areas: Co-chairs the firm's Antitrust and Competition Department. Practice includes the full range of antitrust representation and counseling. Has secured antitrust clearance from the Federal Trade Commission and Department of Justice for more than 100 mergers and acquisitions, including many Second Request investigations; has coordinated merger reviews in multiple other jurisdictions around the world, including the European Commission. Has represented companies and individuals in numerous criminal and civil antitrust investigations and has represented clients in a broad range of private litigation.
Prof. Memberships: Section on Antitrust Law, American Bar Association. Private sector advisor to International Competition Network merger-working group.
Career: Deputy Assistant Attorney General for International Enforcement, Antitrust Division, US Department of Justice, 2001-02. Taught antitrust law at the Washington College of Law of American University.
Publications: Has published more than 40 articles on antitrust law.
Personal: Dartmouth College (AB 1968); Harvard University (JD 1971).

KRAMER, Andrew
Jones Day, Washington, DC
202 879 4660
akramer@jonesday.com
Recommended in Employment

Practice Areas: Experienced in a wide range of labor and employment law. He has represented employers in state and federal courts and before administrative agencies; negotiated collective bargaining agreements; and provided counseling and advice with respect to the development of employment and labor relations strategies. He has lectured on labor and employment law matters at numerous conferences, including the ABA, the American Newspaper Publishers Association, the Industrial Relations Research Association, and the Practising Law Institute. Identified as one of the country's best employment/labor lawyers by leading business and legal publications.
Prof. Memberships: The College of Labor and Employment Lawyers; ABA.

KRAMER, Merrill
Chadbourne & Parke LLP, Washington, DC 202 974 5660
mkramer@chadbourne.com
Recommended in Energy

Practice Areas: Represents energy industry clients in the US and internationally, including public utilities, power project developers, private equity investors, commercial lenders and commodity energy traders. Broad experience with project finance and structured finance transactions, mergers and acquisitions, derivatives, and regulatory matters before the SEC and Federal Energy Regulatory Commission. Represented many of the most active and innovative players in the deregulating energy industry.
Prof. Memberships: Energy Bar Association; former member of EBA's Board of Directors; former Vice Chair of EBA's International Energy Committee.
Career: Former Head of Cogeneration and Independent Power Task Force; former Senior Trial Attorney, FERC.

KRAUSS, Joseph G
Hogan & Hartson LLP, Washington, DC
202 637 5832
jgkrauss@hhlaw.com
Recommended in Antitrust

Practice Areas: Joseph Krauss' practice is devoted to antitrust and economic regulation, merger and acquisition counseling, regulatory review, and litigation.
Prof. Memberships: Member, Antitrust Law Section, ABA (Chair, Mergers and Acquisitions Committee).
Career: Joe joined Hogan & Hartson in 1999 after serving 11 years at the FTC. During his tenure at the FTC, he served in a variety of capacities, including Assistant Director of the Premerger Notification Office. Joe also was acting Assistant Director and deputy assistant director of the Mergers II Division

where he was responsible for investigations of proposed mergers in a number of industries.

Publications: 'Antitrust Investigations 501: Successfully Managing Your Relationship with Agency Staff and Increasing Your Chances for Approval', ACC Docket, Association of Corporate Counsel (9/1/2004); 'Coordinated Effects Analysis in Mergers', Global Competition Review. (9/1/2003).

Personal: Delaware Law School of Widener University (JD); Member, Delaware and District of Columbia Bars.

KUNEY, David
Sidley Austin Brown & Wood LLP, Washington, DC 202 736 8650
dkuney@sidley.com
Recommended in Bankruptcy

Practice Areas: David Kuney represents both debtors and creditors in complex Chapter 11 cases, including complex partnership cases, retail bankruptcies, real estate bankruptcies and corporate cases. He has extensive litigation experience and served as lead counsel in both jury and non-jury civil matters throughout the United States.

Prof. Memberships: Mr Kuney chairs the American College of Real Estate Lawyers Bankruptcy Committee.

Career: Mr Kuney is an Adjunct Professor of Bankruptcy at Georgetown University Law Center and chairs the annual 'Views from the Bench' symposium. University of Virginia School of Law, JD, 1973; University of Virginia, BA, 1967. Admitted: US Supreme Court; DC, 1976; MD, 1973.

Publications: Mr Kuney has published numerous articles, and is the author of 'Commercial Real Estate Leases in Bankruptcy'.

LAKE, William T
Wilmer Cutler Pickering Hale and Dorr LLP, Washington, DC 202 663 6725
william.lake@wilmerhale.com
Recommended in Telecom, Broadcast & Satellite

Practice Areas: Partner and Member of the firm's Management Committee. Advises companies in the US and international communications industries on regulatory, competition, intellectual property and trade issues.

Prof. Memberships: Federal Communications Bar Association, the American Bar Association, the American Society of International Law and the US Council for International Business.

Career: Law clerk to Justice John M Harlan, US Supreme Court, 1969-70, and to Judge Henry J Friendly, US Court of Appeals for the Second Circuit, 1968-69. Joined firm in 1973 and became Partner in 1977. Served as Principal Deputy Legal Adviser at the US Department of State from 1980-81. Writes and speaks frequently on telecommunications topics.

Personal: Yale University (BA 1965); Stanford University (LLB 1968).

LAMKEN, Jeffrey A
Baker Botts LLP, Washington, DC 202 639 7978
jeff.lamken@bakerbotts.com
Recommended in Litigation

Practice Areas: Mr Lamken is the Head of the Supreme Court and Appellate Practice in the firm's Washington office. Prior to Baker Botts, Mr Lamken served as Assistant to the Solicitor General in the United States Department of Justice. Mr Lamken has argued 16 cases before the United States Supreme Court. His cases have involved administrative law, antitrust, bankruptcy, civil rights, criminal procedure, intellectual property, search/seizure, and telecommunications law.

Prof. Memberships: District of Columbia Bar; California Bar.

Personal: JD, Stanford Law School, 1990 (Order of the Coif, Nathan Abbott Scholar); BA (magna cum laude), political science, Haverford College, 1986.

LATHROP, Alex
Swidler Berlin LLP, Washington, DC 202 424 7500
ajlathrop@swidlaw.com
Recommended in Insurance

Practice Areas: Specializes in assisting corporate policyholders to obtain recovery from their insurers for costs incurred as a result of environmental and other long-tail liabilities. Practice involves mix of ominibus settlements outside of litigation and coverage litigation.

Prof. Memberships: Admitted to practice in Washington, DC (2001); Virginia (1999).

Career: Joined Swidler Berlin LLP in 1999.

Personal: Born 1 September 1968. JD, University of Virginia, 1999; BA (high honors), University of California, 1991.

LAWSON, David
Sidley Austin Brown & Wood LLP, Washington, DC 202 736 8000
dlawson@Sidley.com
Recommended in Telecom, Broadcast & Satellite

Practice Areas: David L Lawson, Co-Chair of the firm's Washington DC Communications Group, represents AT&T Corp. and other communications clients on a wide range of competition-related matters involving state and federal regulation, mergers and acquisitions, constitutional and appellate litigation and federal district court litigation. Mr Lawson also represents energy firms in a variety of matters involving litigation, economic regulation and legislation.

Career: Mr Lawson clerked for the Honorable Stephen F Williams, United States Court of Appeals for the District of Columbia Circuit. Bar Admissions: DC and Texas.

LEDDY, Mark
Cleary Gottlieb Steen & Hamilton LLP, Washington, DC 202 974 1570
mleddy@cgsh.com
Recommended in Antitrust

Practice Areas: US and European antitrust law, including civil and criminal litigation, analysis of competitive issues in mergers and acquisitions, and appearances before antitrust regulatory agencies and courts.

Prof. Memberships: Bars in Massachusetts and the District of Columbia. Admitted to practice before US Supreme Court and US Courts of Appeal.

Career: Joined firm as Partner, 1986. Worked for US Department of Justice (1972-86); named Deputy Assistant Attorney General (1984). Adjunct Professor at Georgetown Law School (1996). JD Boston College Law School (1971), BA Boston College (1968).

LEGGETTE, Poe
Fulbright & Jaworski LLP, Washington, DC 202 662 4646
pleggette@fulbright.com
Recommended in Energy

Practice Areas: Litigation; administrative law.

Prof. Memberships: Mr Leggette is a trustee of the Rocky Mountain Mineral Law Foundation.

Career: Poe Leggette joined the Washington DC office of Fulbright & Jaworski LLP as a Partner in 1998. His practice focuses on judicial and administrative litigation concerning natural resources development on federal and Native American lands. In private practice, Mr Leggette has successfully handled cases at all levels of the federal court system. Prior to private practice, Mr Leggette served as assistant solicitor for the US Department of Interior. While with the Department of Interior, he authored or co-authored virtually all briefs filed in the federal courts on outer continental shelf issues, obtaining, among other things, two Supreme Court reversals of unfavorable Ninth Circuit decisions. A Co-Chairman of the firm's Energy Practice Group, Mr Leggette is a frequent speaker and writer on issues of national energy policy involving energy efficiency, alternative energy sources, and traditional energy sources.

Personal: BA, magna cum laude, Tufts University (1974); JD, University of Virginia (1977).

LENNON, Daniel
Latham & Watkins LLP, Washington, DC 202 637 2200
Recommended in Corporate/Commercial

LERMAN, Steven
Leventhal Senter & Lerman PLLC, Washington, DC 202 429 8970
Recommended in Telecom, Broadcast & Satellite

LETZLER, Kenneth
Arnold & Porter LLP, Washington, DC 202 942 5921
Kenneth.Letzler@aporter.com
Recommended in Antitrust

Practice Areas: Specializes in antitrust and trade regulation with an emphasis on the pharmaceutical business, biotechnology, and similar high tech fields. Served as counsel in private antitrust litigation and in merger matters before the Federal Trade Commission and the Department of Justice, including cases where the principal assets were patent, know-how, and other intellectual property. He clerked for the US Court of Appeals, District of Columbia Circuit. Admitted to the District of Columbia Bar and to practice before the US Supreme Court.

Personal: JD from Harvard Law School, 1968; BA from Columbia University, 1965.

LEVINE, Henry D
Levine, Blaszak, Block & Boothby LLP, Washington, DC 202 857 2550
hlevine@lb3law.com
Recommended in Telecom, Broadcast & Satellite

Practice Areas: Specializing in the representation of large telecommunications users in transactions and disputes with carriers, he has negotiated contracts and resolved disputes on behalf of such Fortune 100 Companies as Merrill Lynch, General Motors, IBM, Marriott, Lockheed Martin, the Securities Industry Association, Honeywell and Visa.

Prof. Memberships: The District of Columbia Bar, the ABA Forum Committee on Communications Law, and the Federal Communications Bar Association.

Career: Admitted to the Bars of New York, the District of Columbia, and Federal courts including the United States Supreme Court. From 1983 through 1992, he was a Partner in the Washington, DC office of Morrison & Foerster , where he founded and chaired the firm's Communications Group. He has been a Partner in Levine, Blaszak, Block & Boothby, LLP since the firm was founded in 1993. In 1996, Network World named him one of the 25 most powerful people in networking, citing his 'unique experience, knowledge and savvy' in 'dealing with the pricing, terms and conditions that shape custom network contracts'.

Personal: BA (magna cum laude) from Yale in 1972; JD (magna cum laude) from Harvard Law School in 1976; Master's Degree in Public Policy from Harvard's Kennedy School of Government in 1976.

LEVINE, Lee
Levine Sullivan Koch & Schulz LLP, Washington, DC 202 508 1100
Recommended in Media & Entertainment

LEWIS, Daniel
Arnold & Porter LLP, Washington, DC
202 942 5661
Daniel.Lewis@aporter.com
Recommended in Bankruptcy
Practice Areas: As Head of the firm's Bankruptcy Practice Group, Mr Lewis has extensive experience in all aspects of Chapter 11 practice. He has particular experience in representing parties in large, complex Chapter 11 reorganizations and has played a significant role in many of the country's most notable Chapter 11 cases. For example, he is representing U.S. Airways, Inc. in its most recent Chapter 11 filing, and has represented Braniff Airways, Inc., Baker Hughes Inc., Owens Corning, Allied Chemical, New York Life, Texas Pacific Group, Fannie Mae, Boehringer Ingelheim, Glaxo Wellcome, Coopers & Lybrand, the Official Committee of Unsecured Creditors of CRIIMI MAE Inc., the Official Committee of Unsecured Creditors of Covanta Energy Corp., Honeywell, the Official Equity Securities Holders Committee in the Global Marine reorganization, the State of Maryland and other parties in major Chapter 11 bankruptcy proceedings throughout the United States.
Career: Mr Lewis, who has served as a panelist and lecturer, has testified before Congress as an independent expert on amendments to the Bankruptcy Code and has authored numerous articles on issues and trends in bankruptcy law.

LEWIS, David
Shaw Pittman LLP, Washington, DC
202 663 8474
David_Lewis@shawpittman.com,
david.lewis@pillsburylaw.com
Recommended in Energy
Practice Areas: National and international regulation of nuclear activities and nuclear business transactions. He has represented companies on nuclear matters of all kind before the NRC, other federal and state agencies, courts and Congress. He has been at the forefront of nuclear plant license renewal and new plant licensing, having represented the lead applicants for license renewal and early site permitting. He has advised domestic and foreign companies on procurement of new nuclear plants, acquisitions of existing plants, imports and exports, and numerous other transactions.
Prof. Memberships: American Nuclear Society; Energy Division of the Bar Association of the District of Columbia; member of numerous working groups of the Nuclear Energy Institute. Admitted to Practice: District of Columbia Court of Appeals; US Courts of Appeals for the Second, Third, Fourth, Fifth, Sixth, Ninth and District of Columbia Circuits; US Supreme Court.
Career: Partner since 1991; Attorney-advisor (honors program) for the Nuclear Regulatory Commission's Atomic Safety and Licensing Board,

1982-83; USMC.
Publications: He has written and lectured extensively on nuclear matters, including license renewal, plant acquisitions, regulation of DOE facilities, and regulation of nuclear waste. He co-authored the chapter on Radioactive Materials in Bender's Environmental Law Practice Guide. He also authored 'The Renewal of Nuclear Power Plant Operating Licenses' for the Committee on Nuclear Technology and Law of the Association of the City of New York, and 'An Industry Perspective on the External Regulation of DOE Facilities'.
Personal: George Washington University Law School, JD, 1982; Massachusetts Institute of Technology, BS, 1979. (At press time, Shaw Pittman LLP had entered into a merger agreement with Pillsbury Winthrop LLP. The merger is expected to close by April 2005. Post closing, the name of the firm will be Pillsbury Winthrop ShawPittman LLP.).

LEWIS, William
Morgan, Lewis & Bockius LLP, Washington, DC 202 739 5145
wlewis@morganlewis.com
Recommended in Environment
Practice Areas: William Lewis is senior counsel in the Litigation Practice. His practice has focused almost exclusively on issues related to implementation of the 1990 Clean Air Act Amendments. He regularly represents corporate clients on clean air issues in district court and appellate litigation, rulemaking proceedings, enforcement actions, new source review and other permitting matters, and compliance counseling.
Prof. Memberships: American Bar Association; District of Columbia Bar Association; State Bar California; EPA's National Clean Air Act Advisory Committee; EPA's National Clean Air Act, Subcommittee for air toxics, permits and enforcement (Co-Chair).

LIAN Jr, Robert G
Akin Gump Strauss Hauer & Feld LLP, Washington, DC 202 887 4358
blian@akingump.com
Recommended in Employment
Practice Areas: Robert G Lian Jr is a Partner in the Labor and Employment Practice of Akin Gump. His practice focuses on labor and employment litigation, workplace safety investigations and regulatory litigation, and representing management in labor controversies.
Personal: BA, Colby College (1990); JD (with distinction), Catholic University of America (1993) (member, Catholic University Law Review).

LIBIN, Jerome
Sutherland Asbill & Brennan LLP, Washington, DC 202 383 0145
jerome.libin@sablaw.com
Recommended in Tax
Practice Areas: Handles domestic and international corporate taxation matters for US and foreign clients. Concentrates

on corporate and financial transactions involving domestic and/or international tax considerations. Works in the tax planning and the tax controversy areas, and successfully litigated many federal tax cases. Handles constitutional challenges to state tax statutes. Experienced in matters involving the participation of the Treasury Department. Has handled legislative matters involving presentations to the Congressional tax-writing Committees. Participated in the development of international tax proposals that became part of the Internal Revenue Code of 1986.
Prof. Memberships: President, (10,000-Member) International Fiscal Association (IFA); a VP of the USA Branch of IFA; former Member, Council of the Tax Section of the ABA and Former Chair of both its Special Committee on Standing to Sue and its Committee on Integration; past Chair of the Taxation Division of the District of Columbia Bar; Fellow of the American College of Tax Counsel; and a Master of the Bench of the J Edgar Murdock American Inn of Court.
Career: Clerked for Associate Justice Charles E Whittaker of the US Supreme Court.
Personal: JD, University of Michigan, 1959, editor in chief, 'Michigan Law Review'; BS, Northwestern University, 1956.

LIPMAN, Andrew D
Swidler Berlin LLP, Washington, DC
202 424 7500
adlipman@swidlaw.com
Recommended in Telecom, Broadcast & Satellite
Practice Areas: Telecommunications Group Chair; extensive national and international experience in telecommunications law and related fields - regulatory, transactional, litigation, legislative, land use.
Prof. Memberships: Admitted to practice in California, 1977; District of Columbia, 1978.
Career: Joined Swidler Berlin, 1988; Vice Chair of firm, 1996 -; Senior Vice President Legal and Regulatory Affairs, MFS Communications.
Publications: 'Critiquing the Review' (2003); 'The Art of Adaptation' (2003); 'The FCC and the New Millennium-Regulating the Internet in an Era of Deregulation' (2001).
Personal: Born 20 October 1951; JD Stanford University (Phi Beta Kappa), 1977; BA (summa cum laude) University of Rochester, 1974.

LIPSEY, Charles
Finnegan Henderson Farabow Garrett & Dunner LLP, Washington, DC
202 408 4000
Recommended in Intellectual Property

LIPSKY, Abbott
Latham & Watkins LLP, Washington, DC 202 637 2200
Recommended in Antitrust

LIPSON, Kevin J
Hogan & Hartson LLP, Washington, DC
202 637 5614
kjlipson@hhlaw.com
Recommended in Energy
Practice Areas: Energy, including natural gas pipeline, local distribution company, regulatory, and commercial issues, generation fuel management, electric generation procurement, and energy commercial and contracting issues; antitrust, competition and consumer protection; infrastructure; environmental; legislative; litigation.
Prof. Memberships: ABA; Energy Bar Association; Woodbine House Publishing Company (Board of Directors); Port Clyde Properties, Inc. (Board of Directors); Anti-Defamation League, B'nai B'rith (Lay Board); Jewish Advocacy Center (President and Co-Founder).
Career: Partner with Hogan & Hartson since 1994; has been in private practice since 1980.
Personal: Washington University (JD, 1980); The George Washington University (BA, 1977).

LITT, Daniel
Dickstein Shapiro Morin & Oshinsky LLP, Washington, DC 202 775 4747
LittD@dsmo.com
Recommended in Bankruptcy
Practice Areas: Represents diverse clients (creditors, debtors, trustees, creditors' committees, equity interest holders) in bankruptcy courts throughout US. Participated in hundreds of bankruptcy cases over the last 25 years involving commercial real estate; airlines; government contracting firms; radio, television, and telecommunications businesses; healthcare; retail; manufacturing and others.
Prof. Memberships: American Bankruptcy Institute; served on Rules Committee for the US Bankruptcy Court for the District of Maryland.
Career: Chairs Dickstein Shapiro's Bankruptcy and Creditors' Rights Practice; bankruptcy practitioner since 1979.
Publications: Quoted in The Washington Post and Washington Business Journal.
Personal: Syracuse University (BS, 1974); Georgetown University (JD, 1978).

LIVINGSTON, Donald R
Akin Gump Strauss Hauer & Feld LLP, Washington, DC 202 887 4242
dlivingston@akingump.com
Recommended in Employment
Practice Areas: Represents large employers in all aspects of civil rights and employment discrimination law, with emphasis on employment litigation. Has served as defense litigation counsel in numerous fair employment class actions.
Prof. Memberships: Elected Member, College of Labor and Employment Lawyers; Chapter Chair, 'Employment

Discrimination Law' (Lindemann & Grossman); Member, Georgia and District of Columbia Bars.
Career: Former General Counsel, US Equal Employment Opportunity Commission.
Personal: AB and JD, University of Georgia.

LOFTIS III, James R
Gibson, Dunn & Crutcher LLP, Washington, DC 202 955 8581
jloftis@gibsondunn.com
Recommended in Antitrust

Practice Areas: Extensive experience in antitrust, competition and consumer protection matters. Provides counseling and litigation advice on civil and criminal antitrust, franchise and consumer protection, including guidance on pricing issues, M&A counseling, joint ventures, teaming, strategic alliances, vertical distribution restraints, and IP.
Career: Trial counsel, United States v NL Industries; involved in defense industry mergers, including Northrop Grumman/TRW, Lockheed Martin/ Northrop Grumman, Raytheon/TI, Northrop Grumman/Westinghouse, Alliant/Olin, and others.
Publications: Frequent lecturer on antitrust and microeconomics. Contributing author for numerous publications.
Personal: JD, George Washington University Law School, 1968, Order of the Coif and editor-in-chief of 'The George Washington Law Review.'

LOHMANN, Walter H
Kirkland & Ellis LLP, Washington, DC 202 879 5923
wlohmann@kirkland.com
Recommended in Environment

Practice Areas: Walter Lohmann leads the firm's Environmental Transactional Practice Group. His practice has focused on managing environmental compliance and liability issues as they arise in the context of corporate and real estate transactions, both in the US and around the world including conducting or coordinating environmental due diligence assessments, retaining and supervising technical experts, counseling clients on deal-related liability and risk allocation issues, drafting and negotiating contract language and pursuing post-closing resolution of issues identified in the course of due diligence.
Personal: Cornell University, AB, 1980; George Washington University Law School, JD, 1983.

LONG Jr, Robert A
Covington & Burling, Washington, DC 202 662 5612
rlong@cov.com
Recommended in Litigation

Practice Areas: Chairs Covington's appellate and Supreme Court litigation group. Experience includes 11 oral arguments before the Supreme Court of the United States and a substantial role in nearly 100 appellate cases, with a focus on administrative law, antitrust, banking, communications law, constitutional law, ERISA, and intellectual property issues.
Prof. Memberships: American Bar Association (Litigation, Administrative Law, and Antitrust Sections); American Academy of Appellate Lawyers; American Law Institute.
Career: Law Clerk to Justice Lewis F Powell, Jr, US Supreme Court, and Judge John Minor Wisdom, US Court of Appeals for the Fifth Circuit. Assistant to the Solicitor General of the United States, 1990-93. Associate and Partner (since 1995), Covington & Burling.
Personal: Yale Law School (JD, 1985, Note Editor, Yale Law Journal); Oxford University (BA/MA 1982, Rhodes Scholar); University of North Carolina at Chapel Hill (BA 1980, Morehead Scholar). Adjunct Professor of Law, Georgetown University; Lecturer in Law, University of Virginia.

LUCE, Gregory
Jones Day, Washington, DC
202 879 4278
gmluce@jonesday.com
Recommended in Healthcare

Practice Areas: A member of the firm's Health Care Practice, his experience includes litigation and regulatory matters for the healthcare industry. He has represented healthcare institutions in litigation involving state and federal fraud and abuse laws and the False Claims Act, Medicare reimbursement, and the design and implementation of compliance programs. He has also written and lectured on healthcare-related issues.
Prof. Memberships: American Health Lawyers Association (Board of Directors, 1995-2001; Fellow, elected 2005); ABA Health Law Section; Virginia State Bar Health Law Section (Chair, 1990-91); Who's Who in American Law; Best Lawyers in America.

LUCHS, Richard
Greenstein Delorme & Luchs, Washington, DC 202 452 1400
Recommended in Real Estate

LUDWISZEWSKI, Raymond
Gibson, Dunn & Crutcher LLP, Washington, DC 202 955 8665
rludwiszewski@gibsondunn.com
Recommended in Environment

Practice Areas: Has handled the defense of numerous significant civil and criminal environmental enforcement actions and the defense of 'contaminated community' toxic tort cases.
Career: Served as General Counsel at US Environmental Protection Agency. Serves as Special Counsel to the Assistant Attorney General for the Environment and Natural Resources Division at the Justice Department. Major environmental enforcement cases include United States v Tyco International, United States v Bethlehem Steel, United States v Raymark, United States v General Motors.
Publications: Frequent speaker/writer on environmental issues.
Personal: JD, Harvard Law School, 1984. Editor, 'Harvard Law Review.'

LUPO, Raphael
McDermott Will & Emery, Washington, DC 202 756 8366
rlupo@mwe.com
Recommended in Intellectual Property

Practice Areas: Partner in the Intellectual Property Department. Focuses on patent, trademark, copyright and trade secrets litigation and counseling. Has extensive experience as lead counsel in federal district courts and before International Trade Commission. Has presented and argued over 100 appeals before Court of Appeals for the Federal Circuit and its predecessor (CCPA). Has represented clients in complex technology areas involving computers and computer-related technologies, including integrated circuit cases involving DRAMs, SRAMs, EPROMs, ASICs, flash memories, microprocessors and other semiconductor configurations. Has also represented clients in other complex areas including medical devices and chemical technologies.
Prof. Memberships: Former President of the Giles S Rich American Inn of Court, 1995.
Career: US patent examiner, 1964-69. Associate Solicitor, US Patent Office, 1969-77 and acting Member, Board of Patent Interferences and Director, Patent Planning Staff. Deputy assistant general counsel for patents, Department of Energy, 1977. Went into private practice in 1980.
Personal: Received BSEE and JD from George Washington University. Admitted to Virginia, District of Columbia, US Supreme Court, the Court of Appeals for the Federal Circuit, the District Court for the District of Columbia, and the District Court for the Eastern District of Virginia.

LUXTON, Jane
King & Spalding LLP, Washington, DC 202 626 2627
jluxton@kslaw.com
Recommended in Environment

Practice Areas: Environmental practice with a focus on environmental regulation of toxic substances, particularly metals, under the full range of federal and state environmental laws, as well as international environmental regulation. Extensive experience in international trade matters and litigation.
Prof. Memberships: American Bar Association; District Court for the District of Columbia; District of Columbia Circuit, 4th, 11th and Federal Circuit; District of Columbia Bar; US Supreme Court.
Personal: AB, cum laude, Harvard University, 1973; JD, Cornell University, 1976.

LYBECKER, Martin E
Wilmer Cutler Pickering Hale and Dorr LLP, Washington, DC 202 663 6240
martin.lybecker@wilmerhale.com
Recommended in Investment Management

Practice Areas: Serves as counsel to investment companies and their independent directors, investment advisers, broker-dealers, depository institutions and their holding companies, insurance companies and several financial services trade associations.
Prof. Memberships: Chair, American Bar Association, Section of Business Law's Committee on Banking Law; American Law Institute; and Editorial Advisory Board of The Investment Lawyer (Aspen Law & Business).
Personal: University of Pennsylvania Law School (LLM 1973); New York University School of Law (LLM 1971); University of Washington (JD 1970); University of Washington (BA 1967).

MACBETH, Angus
Sidley Austin Brown & Wood LLP, Washington, DC 202 736 8000
amacbeth@sidley.com
Recommended in Environment

Practice Areas: Angus Macbeth heads Sidley's environmental law practice. His practice emphasizes matters including contaminated sediments cases under remedial and natural resource damage provisions of Superfund; power plant operation impact on aquatic biota in conjunction with mitigating wetland restoration; and corporate environmental management programs' shaping and direction. He has experience with multi-facility enforcement cases under the Clean Air and Clean Water Acts and with regulatory advocacy and challenges under those statutes. He has dealt repeatedly with State-federal issues under RCRA and the hazardous waste management statutes and those controlling the discharge of pollutants to the environment. He is a member of the firm's Executive Committee.
Career: Mr Macbeth clerked for Judge Harold R Tyler, Jr in the Southern District of New York and was an Assistant US Attorney in the Criminal Division of the Southern District of New York. Mr Macbeth has written and spoken extensively on topics in environmental law. Yale Law School, LLB, 1969; Yale University, BA, 1964. Bar Admissions: DC and New York.

MACHLIN, Barry N
Mayer, Brown, Rowe & Maw LLP, Chicago 312 701 8574
bmachlin@mayerbrownrowe.com
Recommended in Projects

Practice Areas: Partner and Co-Chair of Global Project Finance Practice. Represents international banks and financial institutions and multilateral and bilateral official lending agencies. Transactions include the $226 million San Fernando

gas pipeline project (Mexico), the $440 million Baijio power project (Mexico), the $800 million Quezon power project (Philippines), a CDMA telecom upgrade financing (Mexico), the $2.5 billion Paiton I project (Indonesia), and the Khalda and Qarun oil concession developments (Egypt). Also represents banks and financial institutions in syndicated lending and Eurodollar transactions, sovereigns, state-owned enterprises and investors in privatisation and restructuring matters, and parties in cross-border investment and financial transactions. Widely experienced in representing clients in connection with transactions throughout Europe, Asia and the Middle East.
Career: Joined Mayer, Brown, Rowe & Maw LLP as a Partner, 1997, serving first in Washington, DC, and currently in Chicago. Partner (first associate) with White & Case, Washington, DC, and London, 1985-97.
Publications: Speaking engagements: 'Building Infrastructure Projects in Developing Markets,' Practising Law Institute; 'Project Finance,' 'International Bar Association; 'Venture Capital and Private Equity Investments in Emerging Markets,' Harvard International Development Conference.
Personal: JD, Harvard Law School, 1985; BA, summa cum laude, Brandeis University, 1982; Phi Beta Kappa.

MADDEN, William
Winston & Strawn, Washington, DC
202 371 5700
Recommended in Energy

MAGEE, John B
McKee Nelson LLP, Washington, DC
202 775 8671
jmagee@mckeenelson.com
Recommended in Tax
Practice Areas: Taxation, tax controversy, international tax, transfer pricing. Has extensive experience in all aspects of income tax planning, IRS administrative proceedings and tax litigation.
Career: Joined McKee Nelson in January 2000, after 23 years at the Washington, DC law firm of Miller & Chevalier. Heads the Tax Litigation Group and serves on the executive committee of the firm.
Personal: Received an LLM in Taxation from Georgetown University Law Center in 1977 and a JD in 1972 from the University of Washington School of Law, where he served on the Law Review and received the Order of the Coif distinction.

MAHONEY, Colleen P
Skadden, Arps, Slate, Meagher & Flom LLP & Affiliates, Washington, DC
202 371 7900
cmahoney@skadden.com
Recommended in Litigation
Practice Areas: Heads the firm's Securities Enforcement and Compliance Practice in the Washington, DC office.

Represents corporations and their officers, directors and employees in SEC and other law enforcement investigations, as well as in federal court securities litigation. Assists management and boards of directors performing internal investigations. Advises public companies, financial services firms and financial institutions on preventive and remedial measures before and after securities-related issues arise. Counsels clients on issues in the emerging field of consumer financial regulation.
Career: JD, American University, 1981 (summa cum laude); BA, American University School of Government and Public Administration, 1978 (magna cum laude).

MAHONEY, Maureen
Latham & Watkins LLP,
Washington, DC 202 637 2200
Recommended in Litigation

MAIZEL, Jonathan
Milbank, Tweed, Hadley & McCloy,
Washington, DC 202 835 7500
Recommended in Projects

MALESTER, Ann
Weil, Gotshal & Manges LLP,
Washington, DC 202 682 7500
ann.malester@weil.com
Recommended in Antitrust
Practice Areas: Antitrust/competition; litigation/regulatory.
Career: Prior to joining Weil Gotshal, Ms Malester was Deputy Director of the FTC's Bureau of Competition, where she helped supervise antitrust enforcement activities. During her 12 previous years as an Assistant Director, she headed FTC merger enforcement in a wide range of markets, including the pharmaceutical, biotech, and medical device and equipment industries. She also served for 10 years as the FTC's liaison with the US Department of Defense, and led the FTC's antitrust review of transactions in the defense and aerospace industries. As Assistant Director, Ms Malester led the Mergers I Division in investigating, litigating, and obtaining consent agreements in hundreds of significant mergers, acquisitions, and joint ventures, including many that involved patent and licensing issues. As a senior antitrust litigator, she handled several major cases in federal district court and administrative hearings, including obtaining a preliminary injunction in a defense industry merger. Ms Malester won numerous awards at the FTC, including the Brandeis Award for best litigator. She is fluent in French.
Personal: George Washington University Law School, JD; Bryn Mawr College, BA.

MANN, Phillip
Miller & Chevalier Chartered,
Washington, DC 202 626 5800
Recommended in Tax

MARSHALL, Alison
Jones Day, Washington, DC
202 879 7611
abmarshall@jonesday.com
Recommended in Employment
Practice Areas: An active litigator with extensive experience handling complex employment litigation matters. She counsels employers on wage and hour law developments, ADA compliance, workplace violence, early retirement programs, reductions in force, compensation analyses, employment practice audits, and racial and sexual harassment policies and investigations. She is a frequent speaker on employment and civil rights issues and the author of numerous published articles on EEO issues. She also represents colleges and universities on employment matters, with particular emphasis on issues of gender discrimination in intercollegiate athletics.
Prof. Memberships: ABA; National Association of College and University Attorneys.

MARTIN, Keith
Chadbourne & Parke LLP,
Washington, DC 202 974 5600
kmartin@chadbourne.com
Recommended in Projects
Practice Areas: Provided tax advice last year to 102 companies and worked on transactions in the United States and 11 foreign countries. Frequent speaker at conferences on project and structured finance, particularly in the energy sector. Author of more than 120 articles on tax subjects. Editor of Chadbourne's Project Finance NewsWire and a contributing editor of International Tax Report, Practical US/International Tax Strategies and Natural Gas & Electricity. Also lobbies the US government on policy issues.
Career: Former counsel to Senator Daniel Patrick Moynihan (D-NY) and a legislative assistant to Senator Henry M Jackson (D-Wash). Partner at Chadbourne since 1983.

MASTERS, Lori
Jenner & Block LLP, Washington, DC
202 639 6076
lmasters@jenner.com
Recommended in Insurance
Practice Areas: Lorie S Masters is a Partner in Jenner & Block's Washington, DC office. She is a member of the firm's Insurance Litigation and Counseling, Arbitration: Domestic and International, and Litigation Practices. Since, 1983, Ms Masters has advised and represented companies and individuals seeking to enforce their insurance coverage for tort, environmental, high-tech, and other liabilities under general liability, directors and officers, first-party property, health, and other types of insurance. She also has extensive experience in e-commerce issues and related records-management and electronic-discovery issues. Ms Masters has handled, tried, and settled cases in state and federal trial and appel-

late courts across the country, more recently, in arbitration in the United States and abroad. At issue in these cases typically have been millions of dollars of insurance coverage for asbestos-related personal injury and property damage, environmental liability under the federal Superfund statute and related state statutes, silicone gel breast implant claims, and other types of product liability. Ms Masters served as lead trial counsel for policyholder Hoechst Celanese Corporation in its action enforcing general liability insurance coverage for what the press called the largest property damage class action settlement ever. The National Law Journal called the jury's verdict in Hoechst Celanese's coverage case one of the "most significant jury verdicts of 1997." Most recently, Ms Masters obtained an award of more than $92 million for a major pharmaceutical and chemical manufacturer in an arbitration conducted in London under the English Arbitration Act, 1996.
Personal: Notre Dame Law School, JD, 1981.

MASUR, Daniel A
Mayer, Brown, Rowe & Maw LLP,
Washington, DC 202 263 3226
dmasur@mayerbrownrowe.com
Recommended in Business Process Outsourcing: National, IT Outsourcing
Practice Areas: Partner in the Global Outsourcing Practice. Formerly Vice President and General Counsel of I-NET, a provider of information technology, network and outsourcing services. Represents national and international firms in a broad range of business process and information technology outsourcing transactions. Representative transactions include the onshore, nearshore, and offshore outsourcing of business processes and functions (including finance/accounting, human resources, consumer relations, e-commerce processing and support, billing, and procurement), IT infrastructure services and support, application development and maintenance, telecommunications services, network management and support, and help desk/call center services. Representative clients include established and emerging companies in aerospace, defense contracting, electronic commerce, financial services, pharmaceuticals, insurance, healthcare, banking, life sciences, chemicals, consumer products, apparel, manufacturing, oil/gas, real estate, forestry products, telecommunications, information technology, airline and utility/electrical power industries. Recognized by Chambers for the fifth consecutive year.
Prof. Memberships: Admitted to practice in the District of Columbia (1977).
Career: Joined Mayer, Brown, Rowe & Maw LLP as a Partner in 1997. Prior to that, served as a Partner with Reed, Smith, Shaw & McClay (1977-94), and as Vice President and General Counsel

of I-NET, Inc. (1994-97).

Personal: JD, Georgetown University, 1977; editor, 'Georgetown Law Journal'. BA, Marquette University, 1974.

MAY, Gregory
Freshfields Bruckhaus Deringer LLP, Washington, DC 202 777 4500
Recommended in Tax

MAZO, Mark
Hogan & Hartson LLP, Washington, DC
202 637 5673
memazo@hhlaw.com
Recommended in Corporate/Commercial

Practice Areas: Mark Mazo's practices focuses on cross-border transactions with particular emphasis on strategic and financial investments, joint ventures, and acquisitions for major international investors and European and US companies.
Career: Mark represents major international investors and European and US companies in mergers and acquisitions and strategic investments and alliances in Western Europe and the United States. He also handles equity and debt financings.
Personal: Harvard Law School (JD, cum laude, 1974); Princeton University (AB, magna cum laude, Phi Beta Kappa, US Army Distinguished Military Graduate, 1971).

MCDANIELS, William
Williams & Connolly LLP, Washington, DC 202 434 5000
Recommended in Litigation

MCDAVID, Janet L
Hogan & Hartson LLP, Washington, DC
202 637 8780
jlmcdavid@hhlaw.com
Recommended in Antitrust

Practice Areas: Focuses on antitrust, competition, and trade regulation, with a particular emphasis on government investigations, litigation, and antitrust policy issues.
Prof. Memberships: Former Chair, Section of Antitrust Law, ABA (1999-2000); Chair-Elect (1998-99), Vice-Chair (1997-98), and Program Officer, ABA Antitrust Section (1994-97); Member, Antitrust Section Council (1991-94); and Chair or Vice-Chair, Antitrust Section's Committees on Franchising, Section 2 of the Sherman Act, and Civil Practice and Procedure (1985-97); Member, Antitrust Council of the US Chamber of Commerce and the US Council for International Business.
Career: Advisor to the Transition Team for the Federal Trade Commission (FTC) for the Bush Administration in 2000 and a member of the FTC Transition Team for the Clinton Administration in 1992. Served as Co-Chair of the ABA Antitrust Section's Task Force on Competition Policy, which provided advice on antitrust issues to the Clinton Administration. Served on two US

Department of Defense (DoD) Antitrust Task Forces (1993-94 and 1996-97) appointed by the Secretary and General Counsel of the DoD to advise on antitrust issues involved in defence industry mergers and joint ventures, and on vertical integration and supplier decisions among defence contractors.
Publications: Author/co-author of many books and articles involving antitrust law, including: 'Mergers & Acquisitions', 'The Antitrust Evidence Handbook', 'Antitrust and Health Care', and 'Antitrust & Trade Associations Practice Guide' (all published by the ABA Antitrust Section). She is a frequent speaker on antitrust issues.
Personal: Georgetown University Law Center (JD, editor of the Georgetown Law Journal); Northwestern University (BA, with honors).

MCFALLS, Michael
Jones Day, Washington, DC
202 879 3864
msmcfalls@jonesday.com
Recommended in Antitrust

Practice Areas: Most of his work involves government merger and non-merger investigations; the remainder consists of counseling on antitrust issues involving intellectual property and joint ventures. He has focused on matters in the pharmaceutical, diagnostics, biotechnology, defense, consumer products, mining, broadcast, airline, automotive, financial services, and software industries. He has spoken and written about antitrust issues involving mergers, intellectual property and joint ventures.
Prof. Memberships: Co-Chair of the Intellectual Property Committee of the Antitrust Law Section of the ABA.
Publications: Co-Founder and former editor of 'Antitrust and Intellectual Property.'

MCGRANE, John
Morgan, Lewis & Bockius LLP, Washington, DC 202 739 5621
jmcgrane@morganlewis.com
Recommended in Energy

Practice Areas: John D McGrane is a Partner in the Energy Practice and has more than 25 years of experience representing electric utilities, power marketers and other participants in the electric power industry. Mr McGrane advises clients on market investigations; restructuring; mergers, acquisitions and asset transactions; affiliate issues; power purchase sales and agreements; antitrust; and reliability issues. He has particular experience in transmission related issues and has also been involved in recent investigations by the Federal Energy Regulatory Commission's Office of Market Oversight and Investigations.
Prof. Memberships: Edison Electric Institute (Legal Committee); American Bar Association; Energy Bar Association.

MCGRATH, Kathryn
Crowell & Moring LLP, Washington, DC
202 624 2944
kmcgrath@crowell.com
Recommended in Investment Management

Practice Areas: Kathryn McGrath is a Partner in Crowell & Moring's Securities, Regulation and Enforcement Group, and concentrates on the representation of mutual funds, investment managers, broker-dealers and other financial services providers.
Prof. Memberships: Member of the NASD's Legal Advisory Board.
Career: Director of the Division of Investment Management, US Securities and Exchange Commission, 1983-90. Other positions include associate director of the Division of Market Regulation, where she headed the Office of Self-Regulatory Oversight; and assistant and then associate general counsel to the SEC and assistant director of the Division of Corporate Finance.

MCGUIRE, W John
Morgan, Lewis & Bockius LLP, Washington, DC 202 739 5654
wjmcguire@morganlewis.com
Recommended in Investment Management

Practice Areas: John McGuire is a Partner in the Investment Management/ Securities Industry Practice at Morgan Lewis. His practice focuses on investment company and investment adviser regulation. He counsels clients on a wide variety of regulatory and transactional matters, including development of new products and services. He has extensive experience in the establishment and representation of exchange traded funds, popularly known as 'ETFs', their advisers and listing markets.
Prof. Memberships: American Bar Association; District of Columbia Bar Association; former Chair of the DC Bar's Investment Management Committee.
Career: Securities and Exchange Commission, Division of Investment Management, 1986-90.

MCISAAC, Christopher
Winston & Strawn, Washington, DC
202 371 5700
Recommended in Projects

MCKEE, William
McKee Nelson LLP, Washington, DC
202 775 8580
bmckee@mckeenelson.com
Recommended in Tax

Practice Areas: Taxation. Practice encompasses all areas of federal taxation, with a special emphasis on partnership taxation.
Career: Prior to founding the firm in November 1999, was a Tax Partner in the DC office of King & Spalding. Joined King & Spalding in 1983. Served as Tax Legislative Counsel at the US Treasury Department from 1981-83. Is a member

of the American Law Institute, the American College of Tax Counsel, and the National Institute for Tax Professionals. Was a law professor at the University of Virginia School of Law from 1969-81. Also a visiting professor in the Graduate Tax Programme at the New York University School of Law from 1975-77. Frequent speaker at seminars around the country on the subject of partnership taxation.
Publications: Co-author of the treatise 'Federal Taxation of Partnerships and Partners' (Warren, Gorham & Lamont, 3rd edition, 1997), and also co-authored 'Federal Taxation of Partnerships and Partners: Structuring and Drafting Agreements' (Warren, Gorham & Lamont, 2nd edition, 1993).
Personal: A 1966 cum laude graduate of Yale University, received a JD, magna cum laude, in 1969 from the Harvard Law School, and was an editor of the 'Harvard Law Review'.

MCLUCAS, William
Wilmer Cutler Pickering Hale and Dorr LLP, Washington, DC 202 663 6622
william.mclucas@wilmerhale.com
Recommended in Litigation

Practice Areas: Co-Chair of the firm's Securities Department, with a practice that focuses on securities enforcement, regulation and litigation matters.
Career: Admitted to Pennsylvania (1975), District of Columbia (1998), and New York (1999) Bars. Has been a partner of the firm since joining in 1998. Formerly with the US Securities and Exchange Commission's Division of Enforcement, where he served as Director of Enforcement for eight years. While at the SEC, received the National Public Service Award, the Tom C Clark Outstanding Lawyer Award, and the President's Award for Distinguished Executive Service. Named one of the One Hundred Most Influential Attorneys in America by a leading US law journal.
Personal: Pennsylvania State University (BA 1972); Temple University (JD 1975).

MCMANUS, Randolph
Baker Botts LLP, Washington, DC
202 639 7725
randy.mcmanus@bakerbotts.com
Recommended in Energy

Practice Areas: Practice focuses on energy-related regulatory, litigation and transactional work on behalf of project sponsors, merchant energy companies, utilities, and LNG importers and terminal operators. Experience includes mergers and acquisitions, power and gas sales agreements, transmission issues, interconnection agreements, fuel supply arrangements, permitting of major energy projects and administrative and appellate litigation before federal agencies and courts.
Prof. Memberships: District of Colum-

DISTRICT OF COLUMBIA

bia Bar; State Bar of Texas; Energy Bar Association.

Career: Head of firm-wide Energy Regulatory Practice.

Personal: JD from the University of Houston Law School, 1975 (Order of the Barristers); BA from Williams College, 1972.

MCMANUS, Joseph
McManus Schor Asmar & Darden, L.L.P., Washington, DC 202 296 9260
Recommended in Construction

MCMILLAN, Karen
Shearman & Sterling, Washington, DC 202 508 8160
kmcmillan@shearman.com
Recommended in Investment Management

Practice Areas: Partner in Shearman & Sterling's Asset Management Group. Directed several examinations of major fund complexes; counsels clients on regulatory examinations and enforcement; counsel to alternative investment products managers; provides regulatory advice; participates in numerous international mergers and acquisitions of fund managers.

Prof. Memberships: Member, Texas and District of Columbia Bar Associations.

Career: US Securities and Exchange Commission's Division of Investment Management (1991-98); Adjunct Professor Georgetown University Law Center, 2004.

Publications: 'Don't Ask, Don't Tell: The Proper Scope of Joint Transactions Under Section 17(d)', The Investment Lawyer (June 2001).

Personal: BA, College of William and Mary (1983); JD, University of Virginia School of Law (1987).

MELAMED, Doug
Wilmer Cutler Pickering Hale and Dorr LLP, Washington, DC
202 663 6090
doug.melamed@wilmerhale.com
Recommended in Antitrust

Practice Areas: Co-Chair of the firm's Antitrust and Competition Department. Has secured clearance for major acquisitions in the merger clearance process, argued cases in the United States Supreme Court and other appellate courts, litigated in federal and state trial courts and before the Federal Trade Commission, and counseled numerous firms on a wide range of antitrust matters.

Prof. Memberships: American Bar Association, Antitrust Section; American Law Institute.

Career: Acting Assistant Attorney General, Antitrust Division, US Department of Justice (2000-01) and Principal Deputy Assistant Attorney General, Antitrust Division, US Department of Justice (1996-2000). Distinguished Visitor from Practice (1992-93) and Adjunct Professor (1993-94) at Georgetown University Law Center.

Personal: Harvard Law School (JD 1970); Yale College (BA 1967).

MENOTTI, David E
Shaw Pittman LLP, Washington, DC
202 663 8675
david.menotti@shawpittman.com,
david.menotti@pillsburylaw.com
Recommended in Environment

Practice Areas: David Menotti's practice emphasizes the regulation of hazardous substances under laws such as the Federal Insecticide, Fungicide, and Rodenticide Act; the Toxic Substances Control Act; the Federal Food, Drug, and Cosmetic Act; and the Clean Air Act. He also represents clients with matters arising under related state laws and regulations.

Prof. Memberships: Environmental sections of the American and District of Columbia Bar Associations. Order of the Coif.

Career: Partner at Shaw Pittman since 1994. Between 1974-82 he served in various positions at the Environmental Protection Agency, including Associate General Counsel, Pesticides; Associate General Counsel, Toxic Substances; and Associate General Counsel, Air and Radiation.

Publications: has lectured and written on environmental issues. Visiting professor, University of Virgina Law School (1982).

Personal: Syracuse University (AB, 1964). University of Pennsylvania (JD, Magna Cum Laude, 1967). Editor, University of Pennsylvania Law Review (1966-67). (At press time, Shaw Pittman LLP had entered into a merger agreement with Pillsbury Winthrop LLP. The merger is expected to close by April 2005. Post closing, the name of the firm will be Pillsbury Winthrop Shaw Pittman LLP.)

METZGER, Richard
Lawler, Metzger, Milkman & Keeney, LLC, Washington, DC 202 777 7700
Recommended in Telecom, Broadcast & Satellite

MICHAELS, Joel
McDermott Will & Emery, Washington, DC 202 756 8375
jmichaels@mwe.com
Recommended in Healthcare

Practice Areas: Partner in charge of Washington Health Practice. Has extensive experience in health care insurance and delivery system organization, financing and regulation. Assists in obtaining state and federal licenses, contracts and approvals and developing viable organizational and contractual arrangements. Counsels on federal law issues, including Medicare and Medicaid regulation, False Claims Act, Federal Anti-Kickback Statute, ERISA, Federal Food, Drug and Cosmetic Act, and Health Insurance Portability and Accountability Act (HIPAA). Has worked with health plans in develop-

ment of policies and procedures relating to individual participant rights issues, including ERISA claims review and appeal procedures and privacy rights under HIPAA, and development and management of pharmacy benefits. Works on complex litigation matters in health insurance industry, including payment and claims processing disputes.

Prof. Memberships: Fellow and member of American Health Lawyers Association, served on its Board of Directors and chaired its HMOs and Health Plans Substantive Interest Law Committee. Member of the District of Columbia and Maryland Bars.

Personal: Earned JD in 1975 from American University-Washington College of Law, and BA in 1972 from George Washington University. Currently serves as an adjunct member of the American University, Washington College of Law school faculty.

MILCH, Thomas
Arnold & Porter LLP, Washington, DC
202 942 5030
Thomas.Milch@aporter.com
Recommended in Environment

Practice Areas: A Partner in Washington, DC, he directs the firm's national Environmental Group. His practice principally includes federal enforcement and private party litigation, counseling multinational companies on environmental compliance, and addressing environmental issues that arise in complex corporate transactions. He has served as lead counsel on major Superfund cleanups and in contaminated property litigation for Fortune 100 companies. He has particular expertise in complex environmental disputes involving toxic tort claims, natural resources damages, sediment cleanups and corporate environmental liability, such as parent/subsidiary and successor liability.

Prof. Memberships: He served as a Member of the ABA's Standing Committee on Environmental Law (1996-98), and was Chairman of the ABA's Special Committee on Environmental Litigation Techniques (SONREEL) (1991-94). From 1992-98, he served on the Board of Directors and Executive Committee of the Environmental Law Institute. From 1999 until 2003, he also served on the Board of Wildlife Trust International, an international conservation group. He has served for many years on the Board of RESOLVE, Inc., a nonprofit organization committed to alternative dispute resolution in the environmental field.

Personal: He is a graduate of Yale College summa cum laude and Yale Law School, where he served as an officer of the 'Yale Law Journal.'

MILES, Steven
Baker Botts LLP, Washington, DC
202 639 7951
steven.miles@bakerbotts.com
Recommended in Projects

Practice Areas: Practice focuses on project development and finance, with emphasis on the liquefied natural gas (LNG), natural gas, and electric power industries, both in the United States and internationally.

Prof. Memberships: District of Columbia Bar; American Bar Association, Committee on International Energy and Resources, Vice Chair, 2001; Saudi Arabia Country Coordinator, 1996; Phi Beta Kappa; National US-Arab Chamber of Commerce, General Counsel, 1995-2004.

Career: Manages the Middle East Practice at Baker Botts.

Personal: JD from the Cornell Law School in 1984; MBA from Cornell University in 1984; BA (summa cum laude) from Union College in 1980.

MILKMAN, Ruth
Lawler, Metzger, Milkman & Keeney, LLC, Washington, DC 202 777 7700
Recommended in Telecom, Broadcast & Satellite

MILLER, Evan
Hogan & Hartson LLP, Washington, DC
202 637 5776
emiller@hhlaw.com
Recommended in Employee Benefits

Practice Areas: Fiduciary counseling, ERISA litigation, COBRA, HIPAA, and legislation. Pension and welfare benefit plan issues under Titles I and IV of ERISA. He is routinely involved in obtaining opinion letters and exemptions from the US Department of Labor and Pension Benefit Guaranty Corporation. Handles fiduciary audit and other benefit-related investigations conducted at the regional and national level by the US Department of Labor, and in excise tax matters before the Internal Revenue Service (IRS). Fiduciary breach allegations, challenges to retiree health modifications, withdrawal liability, preemption of law, and single employer plan termination issues.

Prof. Memberships: ABA: Current Co-Chair, Employee Benefits Committee, Labor and Employment Section; Employee Benefits Committee, Tax Section.

Career: Partner since 1994.

Publications: 'COBRA Primer', ABA/JCEB National Institute on ERISA Basics (5/1/2004); 'Update on Class Action Litigation Involving Employer Securities', Continuing Legal Education Institute (1/1/2004); 'Class Action Litigation Under ERISA', ABA/JCEB ERISA Litigation National Institute (11/1/2003); 'Current ERISA Developments', Practicing Law Institute Conference (10/1/2003).

Personal: Georgetown University Law Center (JD, 1981); Columbia University (BA, 1978).

MILLER, Lawrence
Sidley Austin Brown & Wood LLP, Washington, DC 202 736 8209
lmiller@sidley.com
Recommended in Energy

Practice Areas: Lawrence Miller focuses on regulatory, antitrust and other matters pertaining to telecommunication, railroad and pipeline common carriers. He has practiced before the ICC, FERC, state and federal courts. For the last 15 years, Mr Miller's practice has focused primarily on crude oil and petroleum product pipelines with respect to rate, competitive access and discrimination issues.

Career: Yale Law School, JD, 1976; Northwestern University, BA, 1969; Oxford Rhodes Scholar, 1969-73. Bar admissions: Illinois, 1976; District of Columbia, 1992.

MILLER, Lawrence
Grossberg Yochelson Fox & Beyda, Washington, DC 202 296 9696
Recommended in Real Estate

MOLLEN, Neal D
Paul, Hastings, Janofsky & Walker LLP, Washington, DC
202 551 1738
nealmollen@paulhastings.com
Recommended in Employment

Practice Areas: Chair of Washington Office Employment Law Department. Represents employers in employment litigation, with emphasis on class actions and appellate matters; advises employers in bargaining disputes under the NLRA and RLA, and represents management in labor arbitrations and labor-management litigation; particular expertise in the use of experts in employment litigation.

Publications: Chapter co-editor, 'Employment Discrimination Law' (ABA-BNA) (2000, 2002, and 2005 editions); Contributing author, 'Equal Employment Law Update' (ABA-BNA) (through Fall 1999); contributing author, 'Employee Benefits Law' (ABA-BNA 1991).

Personal: JD - University of Richmond, 1985, with honors; Notes and Comments Editor, Law Review.

MOLTENBREY, MJ
Freshfields Bruckhaus Deringer LLP, Washington, DC 202 777 4500
Recommended in Antitrust

MONACO, Stephanie
Crowell & Moring LLP, Washington, DC
202 624 2982
smonaco@crowell.com
Recommended in Investment Management

Practice Areas: Stephanie Monaco is a Partner in the Securities, Regulation and Enforcement Group and focuses on investment company and investment adviser regulation and compliance. She advises registered investment companies; hedge funds; private equity funds; investment advisers; and other entities

seeking either to become registered or to structure their business affairs to avoid registration and regulation.

Career: Worked at Securities and Exchange Commission, Division of Investment Management in the chief counsel's office, 1983-86; Branch Chief in the SEC's Office of Investment Company Regulation, 1988, and was acting Assistant Director from March 1990 until July 1991.

MONTGOMERY, Bruce
Arnold & Porter LLP, Washington, DC
202 942 5679
Bruce.Montgomery@aporter.com
Recommended in Antitrust

Practice Areas: Bruce Montgomery specializes in antitrust and trade regulation law and complex litigation. He has tried private antitrust cases before juries and judges, has taken and defended hundreds of depositions, argued numerous motions in federal trial courts and appeals in federal courts of appeals, and in FTC proceedings. Representing Roche Vitamins Inc., he acted as lead defense liaison counsel in the multiparty Vitamins MDL private antitrust litigation. He also represented Roche in the criminal citric acid and vitamins cases. He has often been responsible for the development of economic testimony by expert witnesses and for the examination of opposing expert witnesses.

Career: Prior to joining Arnold & Porter LLP, he was a Trial Attorney with the Department of Justice.

Personal: LLB, Yale Law School, 1960; BA, Rice University, 1957.

MOORE, Margaret
Van Ness Feldman PC, Washington, DC
202 298 1800
Recommended in Energy

MOORE, Robert
Miller & Chevalier Chartered, Washington, DC 202 626 5800
Recommended in Tax

MOOT, John S
Skadden, Arps, Slate, Meagher & Flom LLP & Affiliates, Washington, DC
202 371 7310
jmoot@skadden.com
Recommended in Energy

Practice Areas: Represents clients in all aspects of electric utility regulation and deregulation, with particular emphasis on mergers, acquisitions and divestitures; regional transmission organizations; retail restructuring; stranded cost recovery; and transmission access and rates. Has acted as lead trial or appellate counsel on such matters before the Federal Energy Regulatory Commission, state Public Utility Commissions, and federal and state courts.

Career: JD, American University, 1988 (cum laude); BA, St. Lawrence University, 1983.

MOYER, Dennis
Goulston & Storrs, Washington, DC
202 721 0011
Recommended in Real Estate

MURIS, Timothy
O'Melveny & Myers LLP, Washington, DC 202 383 5300
Recommended in Antitrust

MURPHY, J Andrew
Hunton & Williams, Washington, DC
202 955 1543
dmurphy@hunton.com
Recommended in Projects

Practice Areas: Drew Murphy is the head of the firm's Project and Energy Finance Team. His practice focuses on the financing of energy and infrastructure assets. He has extensive experience in representing developers, investors and lenders in a wide variety of US and international project and structured financings, including private equity financings, syndicated bank loans, secured lease obligation bonds, private placements of equity and corporate and lease obligation debt, and other structured financings.

MURPHY, Jack W
Dechert, Washington, DC
202 261 3303
jack.murphy@dechert.com
Recommended in Investment Management

Practice Areas: Mr Murphy focuses his practice on investment management matters for mutual funds, fund directors, and fund managers.

Prof. Memberships: Member, District of Columbia and New York Bars.

Career: Division of Investment Management (1985); private practitioner (1988); associate general counsel of PaineWebber/Mitchell Hutchins Asset Management, Inc. (1991-94); Associate Director and Chief Counsel of the Division of Investment Management (1994-97).

Personal: State University of New York at Albany (BA, 1980); Boston College Law School (JD, 1983).

MUTRYN, William
Holland & Knight LLP, Washington, DC
202 955 3000
william.mutryn@hklaw.com
Recommended in Corporate/Commercial

Practice Areas: Co-Leader of the Corporate and M&A Practice Group, his practice emphasizes M&A, securities, corporate governance and corporate finance. Served as lead counsel for middle market M&A transactions in buy-side and sell-side engagements. Mutryn serves as principal outside counsel to regional and national businesses in fields including government IT services, healthcare, defense and aerospace, computer software, telecommunications and satellites, environmental, energy, manufacturing, finance, and staffing. He rep-

resents companies in M&A, debt and equity financing, stock transactions, joint ventures and complex agreements; and parties in securities offerings, private equity and venture capital transactions and acquisitions of subsidiaries or divisions.

MYERS, Donald J
Reed Smith LLP, Washington, DC
202 414 9231
dmyers@reedsmith.com
Recommended in Employee Benefits

Practice Areas: Represents corporations and financial institutions on a variety of benefits issues, specializing in the fiduciary responsibility provisions of ERISA.

Prof. Memberships: Chairman, Prohibited Transactions Subcommittee, ABA Taxation Section Committee on Employee Benefits; Charter Fellow of the American College of Employee Benefits Counsel.

Career: Counsel for ERISA Regulation and Interpretation, Department of Labor; Assistant Chief of the Office of Disclosure Policy, SEC.

Publications: Author of numerous books, chapters, and other publications.

Personal: Cornell Law School (JD); Georgetown University Law Center (LLM); College of the City of New York (BA); Adjunct Professor, Georgetown University Law Center.

NAEVE, Clifford M
Skadden, Arps, Slate, Meagher & Flom LLP & Affiliates, Washington, DC
202 371 7070
mnaeve@skadden.com
Recommended in Energy

Practice Areas: Involved in energy policy and regulatory matters such as the restructuring of the electric power industry, having represented clients in a variety of federal and state regulatory proceedings and restructuring transactions. Has represented numerous utilities before the FERC in merger proceedings and has been involved in several friendly and unsolicited merger transactions. Has worked with a variety of utilities on innovative electric transmission cases, wholesale rate proceedings and retail access experiments. Has represented major oil and gas producers, natural gas pipelines, electric co-operatives and financial institutions in a variety of commercial and regulatory matters.

Prof. Memberships: Member, Electricity Advisory Board to the Secretary of Energy.

Career: JD, George Washington University, 1984 (highest honors; Order of the Coif); MPA, LBJ School of Public Affairs, The University of Texas at Austin, 1972; BS, Mechanical Engineering, The University of Texas at Austin, 1970.

NAGER, Glen
Jones Day, Washington, DC
202 879 5464
gdnager@jonesday.com
Recommended in Litigation

Practice Areas: Chairs the firm's Issues ad Appeals Practice. He has argued 10 cases before the US Supreme Court. He has argued appeals in a wide range of subject areas, including IP, government contracts, and environmental cases. His substantive specialty is employment law, with particular emphasis on age discrimination, civil rights, and employee benefits law. Named one of the top 12 employment lawyers in Washington, DC in 2004.

Prof. Memberships: Member of the Edward Coke Appellate American Inn of Court, the editorial advisory council of the Employee Relations Law Journal, and the Advisory Board of the Washington Legal Foundation.

NAKAHATA, John
Harris, Wiltshire & Grannis LLP, Washington, DC 202 730 1300
Recommended in Telecom, Broadcast & Satellite

NANNES, John M
Skadden, Arps, Slate, Meagher & Flom LLP & Affiliates, Washington, DC
202 371 7500
jnannes@skadden.com
Recommended in Antitrust

Practice Areas: Broad antitrust practice includes mergers and acquisitions reviewed by US and foreign antitrust agencies, civil non-merger governmental investigations, US and foreign cartel investigations and private treble-damage actions. Substantial experience in network industries such as airlines, securities, shipping and energy.

Prof. Memberships: Trustee of the Legal Aid Society of Washington, DC and of the Supreme Court Historical Society.

Career: Acting Assistant Attorney General (2001); Deputy Assistant Attorney General, Antitrust Division, US Department of Justice (1998-2001); Law clerk to Chief Justice William Rehnquist (1974-75); JD (1973) and BBA (1970), University of Michigan.

NATHAN, Irvin
Arnold & Porter LLP, Washington, DC
202 942 5070
Irvin.Nathan@aporter.com
Recommended in Litigation

Practice Areas: A senior litigation Partner who represents corporations, and their officers, directors, and employees, in criminal and complex civil litigations, including antitrust, securities fraud, civil RICO, and corporate compliance matters. He was past Chairman of the DC Bar Legal Ethics Committee. He has tried many jury and bench trials and emergency injunctive hearings in federal and state courts, including civil antitrust trials. He has also successfully represent-

ed corporate and individual targets of federal antitrust grand jury investigations.

Prof. Memberships: He is a Member of American College of Trial Lawyers, American Law Institute, and American Bar Foundation.

Career: In addition to his practice at Arnold & Porter, he has served as Principal Associate Deputy Attorney General at the US Department of Justice (1993-94); Deputy Assistant Attorney General for Enforcement in the Criminal Division (1979-81); Special Minority Counsel to the United States Senate Intelligence Committee (1981); Chairman of the White Collar Crime Committee of the Criminal Justice Section of the American Bar Association (ABA) (1982-84); and has served as a liaison for the ABA's Criminal Justice Section to the ABA's Antitrust Section.

Personal: He received a LLB at Columbia Law School in 1967 and a BA at Johns Hopkins University in 1964.

NEAHER, Edward
White & Case LLP, Washington, DC
202 626 3622
eneaher@whitecase.com
Recommended in Projects

Practice Areas: Corporate transactional lawyer, specializing in domestic and international project finance and international private equity. Represents lenders, developers and other participants in infrastructure projects in a wide variety of sectors, including power, oil and gas, airports, toll roads, telecommunications and other industrial projects. Also represents international private equity investors. Extensive experience in complex project financings involving commercial banks, multilateral and bilateral institutions, bond offerings and monoline insurers. Broad international experience, having been previously based in Hong Kong and London and extensive experience in Latin America, Asia and the Middle East.

Personal: Williams College (BA,1980), Cornell University (JD, 1983).

NELSON, William F
McKee Nelson LLP, Washington, DC
202 775 8582
wnelson@mckeenelson.com
Recommended in Tax

Practice Areas: Taxation, tax controversy. Practice encompasses all areas of federal taxation, with a special emphasis on partnership taxation and controversy matters.

Prof. Memberships: Prior to founding the firm in November 1999, was a Tax Partner in King & Spalding's Atlanta office, joining the firm in 1972. From 1986-88, served as Chief Counsel for the Internal Revenue Service, returning to King & Spalding at the end of his appointment. Received a JD from the University of Virginia School of Law in 1972, where he was editor in chief of the

'Virginia Law Review' and was named to the Order of the Coif.

Publications: Co-author of the treatise 'Federal Taxation of Partnerships and Partners' (Warren, Gorham & Lamont, 3rd edition, 1997), and also co-authored 'Federal Taxation of Partnerships and Partners: Structuring and Drafting Agreements' (Warren, Gorham & Lamont, 2nd edition, 1993). Has written articles on tax law for numerous journals, including 'The Tax Law Review', 'Taxes', and the 'Virginia Law Review'. Frequent lecturer at various tax institutes.

Personal: Received his JD from the University of Virginia School of Law in 1972. Served as Editor-in-Chief of the Virginia Law Review, and was named to the Order of the Coif.

NESS, Andrew
Thelen Reid & Priest LLP, Washington, DC 202 508 4000
Recommended in Construction

NEVINS, Patrick
Hogan & Hartson LLP, Washington, DC
202 637 6441
jpnevins@hhlaw.com
Recommended in Energy

Practice Areas: Represents clients in regulatory, litigation and commercial matters in gas, LNG and oil industries; clients include gas and oil pipelines, major customers on pipelines, an LNG terminal, storage providers, and new entrants acquiring energy assets; practice also focuses on FERC proceedings, project development and FERC-influenced commercial transactions; experience in State regulatory proceedings and judicial appeals of agency decisions.

Prof. Memberships: ABA; Energy Bar Association.

Career: 1994-present, Hogan & Hartson; private practice since 1992.

Personal: Georgetown University Law Center (JD, magna cum laude, Order of the Coif, 1992); University of Virginia (BA, with distinction, 1989).

NEWBORN, Steve A
Weil, Gotshal & Manges LLP, Washington, DC 202 682 7005
steven.newborn@weil.com
Recommended in Antitrust

Practice Areas: Antitrust/competition; litigation/regulatory.

Career: Steven Newborn serves as global Co-Head of Weil Gotshal & Manges' Antitrust Practice. Previously, he was Director of Litigation at the Federal Trade Commission's Bureau of Competition, in charge of its Merger Enforcement Program, and was a major contributor to the 1992 Federal Merger Guidelines. He received the Brandeis Award presented to the Commission's finest litigator. Mr Newborn's clients include many Fortune 100 companies in both high stakes litigation and 'bet the company' mergers. He has been cited by every publication that ranks antitrust

lawyers as a leader in the field.

Personal: St. John's University, JD; Long Island U. Brooklyn, BA.

NEWMAN, Karol Lyn
Morgan, Lewis & Bockius LLP, Washington, DC 202 739 5786
klnewman@morganlewis.com
Recommended in Energy

Practice Areas: Ms Newman is a Partner in the Energy Practice, representing major energy companies on liquefied natural gas (LNG), natural gas storage and transportation projects including representation in related federal agency and court proceedings.

Prof. Memberships: Member, American Bar Association; Member, District of Columbia Bar Association Chair, Federal Energy Bar Association - Legislation and Regulatory Reform Committee.

Career: Recognized as a leading gas lawyer in 2004 Chambers USA, Ms Newman has worked in the industry for over 25 years. She is actively involved in legislative efforts in the industry, including the representation of clients on energy matters in Congress.

NEWMAN, Richard
Arent Fox PLLC, Washington, DC
202 857 6000
Recommended in Real Estate

NICKEL, Henry
Hunton & Williams, Washington, DC
202 955 1561
hnickel@hunton.com
Recommended in Environment

Practice Areas: Henry Nickel's practice focuses on administrative and judicial proceedings arising under the National Environmental Policy Act, the Clean Air Act and the Clean Water Act. He has represented electric utilities in every major Clean Air Act rulemaking and judicial rerview proceeding since 1977. He has defended clients in major Clean Air Act enforcement actions and citizen suits. Over the years he has lobbied Congress on Clean Air Act and regulatory reform legislation. He is Head of the firm's Administrative Law Group.

NIELDS, John
Howrey Simon Arnold & White, Washington, DC 202 783 0800
Recommended in Litigation

NORDHAUS, Robert
Van Ness Feldman PC, Washington, DC
202 298 1800
Recommended in Energy

NORTON IV, Floyd L
Morgan, Lewis & Bockius LLP, Washington, DC 202 739 5620
fnorton@morganlewis.com
Recommended in Energy

Practice Areas: Floyd Norton is a Partner in the Energy Practice. His practice focuses on electric utility issues, with an emphasis on utility responses to competition. Mr Norton has broad and comprehensive experience in electric utility market power issues, utility mergers and acquisitions, the negotiation of power contracts, and wholesale and transmission rates and services. Mr Norton has represented a number of electric utility clients in the areas of market pricing, mergers and industry restructuring, and investigations of electric trading practices.

Prof. Memberships: American Bar Association (Chair, Public Utility Law Section Antitrust Committee).

NUECHTERLEIN, Jonathan
Wilmer Cutler Pickering Hale and Dorr LLP, Washington, DC 202 663 6850
jonathan.nuechterlein@wilmerhale.com
Recommended in Telecom, Broadcast & Satellite

Practice Areas: Practice focuses on appellate litigation and competition issues, particularly those arising under federal telecommunications law. Has represented major telecommunications clients before the FCC in connection with federalism issues, unbundling policy, broadband deployment, and intercarrier compensation. Has also represented clients in the US Supreme Court and the federal courts of appeals on a range of issues arising under the environmental laws, the Sherman Act, and the Telecommunications Act of 1996.

Publications: Author (with Phil Weiser) of Digital Crossroads: American Telecommunications Policy in the Internet Age (MIT Press 2005).

Personal: Yale Law School (JD 1990); Yale College (BA 1986).

NUSSDORF, Melanie
Steptoe & Johnson LLP,
Washington, DC 202 429 3009
mnussdorf@steptoe.com
Recommended in Employee Benefits

Practice Areas: Partner in the Washington office of Steptoe & Johnson LLP. Practice spans the entire range of employee benefits, from tax-based rules for qualified pension plans to fiduciary issues, welfare benefits, and plan termination. Represents numerous financial institutions, including banks, brokerage houses, and insurance companies. Has substantial experience with ERISA issues relating to hedge funds and private equity vehicles, the exemption and advisory opinion process, and related legislation. Significant legislative background with the laws that affect employee benefit plans.

Personal: JD, New York University, 1973; BA, University of Pennsylvania, 1970.

O'CONNOR III, Charles A
McKenna Long & Aldridge LLP,
Washington, DC 202 496 7586
coconnor@mckennalong.com
Recommended in Environment

Practice Areas: Environmental counsel, focusing on chemical and pesticide regulation by federal, state and international agencies. Practice includes regulations affecting the manufacture, market-

ing and use of agricultural, antimicrobial and non-agricultural pesticides, industrial and specialty chemicals and formulated chemical products. Clients include chemical, aerospace and electronics manufacturers facing proceedings before the Environmental Protection Agency, OSHA and the Consumer Product Safety Commission. Has represented registrants in most of the major pesticide cancellation proceedings before the EPA, including those brought by the agency against DDT, heptachlorchlordane, lindane and dicofol, and in the proceeding before the Lindane Review Board appointed by the Canadian Health Minister. Has directed challenges to the federal pesticide effluent guidelines, California's Proposition 65 and its pesticide formulators' exemption and New York's ban of higher-concentration DEET products. Represents over a dozen industry testing joint ventures and coalitions, including the Spray Drift Task Force, the Pyrethrin Joint Venture, and the Residential Exposure Joint Venture. Has served as Counsel to the Consumer Specialty Products Association for 30 years. Principal author, 'TSCA Handbook' and 'Pesticide Regulation Handbook'.

Prof. Memberships: American Bar Association, District of Columbia Bar Association.

Personal: MALS, Georgetown University, 1985; JD, Georgetown University, 1967; AB, cum laude, Harvard University, 1964.

O'DONNELL, Earle
Dewey Ballantine LLP, Washington, DC 202 429 2327
eodonnell@deweyballantine.com
Recommended in Energy

Practice Areas: Energy (including trial and appellate litigation, energy project development, energy company M&A, and compliance).

Prof. Memberships: Member of the United States Supreme Court Bar; Vice-President Foundation of the 'Energy Law Journal'; Member, Board of Directors, Charitable Foundation of the Energy Bar Association (2002-04).

Career: Chair of Energy Practice Group, Dewey Ballantine LLP; private practice since 1975.

Publications: Consulting editor and co-author of 'Global Overview' and United States Chapters, Electricity Regulation 2003, published by Global Competition Review (2003-05).

Personal: JD with honors, George Washington University National Law Center ('Law Review', Order of the Coif), 1975.

OLSON, Pamela F
Skadden, Arps, Slate, Meagher & Flom LLP & Affiliates, Washington, DC 202 371 7240
polson@skadden.com
Recommended in Tax

Practice Areas: Tax policy and tax con-

troversy. Former assistant secretary for tax policy at the US Department of the Treasury, where she had supervisory responsibility for providing policy analysis, advice and recommendations relating to issues of federal taxation, including all legislative proposals, regulatory guidance and tax treaties. Was responsible for official estimates of all government receipts for the president's budget, fiscal policy decisions and Treasury cash management decisions. First woman to chair the ABA Section of Taxation.

Prof. Memberships: Board of Directors, Tax Analysts (2004-present).

Career: University of Minnesota: MBA, 1984; JD, 1980; BA, 1976 (magna cum laude).

OLSON, Theodore
Gibson, Dunn & Crutcher LLP,
Washington, DC 202 955 8668
tolson@gibsondunn.com
Recommended in Litigation

Practice Areas: One of the nation's premier appellate and US Supreme Court advocates, argued 41 cases in the Supreme Court (including Bush v Gore cases). Practice encompasses constitutional law, appellate, federal legislation, media, commercial disputes (involving civil/criminal law, securities, antitrust, 1st/5th/7th/14th Amendments). Handled cases at all levels of state/federal court systems; US/international tribunals.

Prof. Memberships: American College of Trial Lawyers, American Academy of Appellate Lawyers.

Career: Solicitor General of the United States; Assistant US Attorney General Office of Legal Counsel; Private counsel for Presidents Ronald Reagan and George W Bush.

Personal: JD, University of California - Berkeley, 1965.

ONDRASIK, Paul
Steptoe & Johnson LLP,
Washington, DC 202 429 8088
pondrasik@steptoe.com
Recommended in Employee Benefits, Litigation

Practice Areas: Heads Steptoe & Johnson LLP's ERISA Group in the Washington office. National ERISA practice, emphasizing litigation, fiduciary, and government matters. 25 plus years of experience. Lead counsel in numerous ERISA class and other actions. Lead defense role in prominent cases challenging employer stock investments. Handled ERISA cases involving preemption, investments, ESOPs, contingent workers, provider fees, and complex corporate transactions. Key role in Supreme Court decisions on ERISA remedies. Former Law Clerk to Chief Justice Burger, Charter Fellow - American College of Employee Benefit Counsel. Frequent author and speaker.

Personal: JD, University of Virginia, 1975; AB, Princeton University, 1972.

O'NEILL, Brian D
LeBoeuf, Lamb, Greene & MacRae, LLP, Washington, DC 202 986 8012
boneill@llgm.com
Recommended in Energy

Practice Areas: Advises clients on energy projects, privatizations and regulatory matters. Clients include electric utilities, major natural gas and oil pipelines and several LNG companies. He is an experienced litigator in regulatory proceedings involving complex ratemaking issues, multi-million dollar construction projects, transportation and supply contract matters. He is an author and lecturer on energy matters.

Prof. Memberships: American Bar Association; Energy Bar Association; Florida Bar; DC Bar.

Career: Joined LeBoeuf in 1980; Farmer, Shibley, McGuinn & Flood (1975-80); Federal Power Commission, Trial Attorney (1972-75); Military Service: US Air Force (1971-72).

Personal: Florida State University (JD)1971; Florida State University (BA)1968.

O'NEILL Jr, John H
Shaw Pittman LLP, Washington, DC 202 663 8148
john.o'neill@shawpittman.com
Recommended in Energy

Practice Areas: Partner, Chair, Public Practices Group; energy, nuclear energy; commercial energy transactions; energy - energy litigation and alternate dispute resolution; litigation - energy; government contracts; government relations.

Prof. Memberships: Admitted to practice: District of Columbia, Maryland; US Supreme Court; US Courts of Appeals for the Federal and Third Circuits; US District Court for the District of Columbia; Court of Appeals of Maryland; District of Columbia Court of Appeals; International Bar Association; International Nuclear Law Association; US Naval Academy Foundation, Trustee.

Career: Officer, United States Navy serving on nuclear submarines; licensed by the Atomic Energy Commission to supervise the operation and maintenance of naval nuclear propulsion power plants; member of Shaw Pittman's Board of Directors.

Personal: Yale Law School, JD, 1976; US Nuclear Power School, 1969; US Naval Academy, BS, with Distinction, 1968.

OOSTERHUIS, Paul W
Skadden, Arps, Slate, Meagher & Flom LLP & Affiliates, Washington, DC 202 371 7130
poosterh@skadden.com
Recommended in Tax

Practice Areas: Represents clients on a wide range of international and domestic tax matters with experience in international M&A, dispositions and joint venture transactions. Represents US and non-US multinational companies in cross-border financing arrangements and non-transactional international tax planning, and acquisitions. Has represented various clients with respect to the international aspects of public spin-off transactions. Regularly represents clients on international tax planning matters generally, including transfer pricing matters. Represents clients before the US Department of Treasury and the Congress on tax policy matters and technical issues.

Career: JD, Harvard University, 1973 (cum laude); BA, Brown University, 1969 (magna cum laude).

OSHINSKY, Jerold
Dickstein Shapiro Morin & Oshinsky LLP, Washington, DC 202 828 2251
OshinskyJ@dsmo.com
Recommended in Insurance

Practice Areas: Counsels policyholders nationwide on insurance coverage issues. Litigated many of the most significant insurance coverage cases, including matters involving directors and officers, general liability, construction contracts, IP, fidelity bonds, first-party property policies, and environmental liability.

Career: Joined Dickstein Shapiro as a name Partner, 1996; Head of Insurance Practice.

Publications: Principal author and editor of 'Practitioner's Guide to Litigating Insurance Coverage Actions' (Aspen Law & Business, Second Edition 2002), a multi-volume set, updated yearly; includes legal commentary, practical advice, and forms for attorneys involved in insurance coverage litigation.

Personal: Brooklyn College (BA, 1964); Columbia Law School (JD, 1967).

OSNOS, David
Arent Fox PLLC, Washington, DC 202 857 6000
Recommended in Real Estate

O'SULLIVAN, John
Chadbourne & Parke LLP, Washington, DC 202 974 5600
josullivan@chadbourne.com
Recommended in Energy

Practice Areas: Represents independent power producers, off-takers, and lenders, including in FERC and state regulatory proceedings, in negotiations for interconnection, power purchase, and transmission contracts, and in project financing; active in facility or corporate acquisitions (including participation in and conducting RFPs) and in bankruptcy matters; substantial international experience in project development, privatization, and political risk insurance claims.

Prof. Memberships: New York, District of Columbia, US Court of Appeals for the Second, Third and District of Columbia Circuits.

Career: Previously New York City Assistant Corporation Counsel, and FERC Chief Advisory Counsel and Assistant General Counsel for Electric Rates and Corporate Regulation.

PARI, Joseph
Dewey Ballantine LLP, Washington, DC 202 862 4516
jpari@deweyballantine.com
Recommended in Tax

Practice Areas: Tax.

Prof. Memberships: Former Council Director for American Bar Association Tax Section's Corporate Tax Committee, Committee on Affiliated and Related Corporations and Bankruptcy Committee; adjunct faculty Georgetown University Law Center; Advisory Boards of New York University Institute on Federal Taxation, Federal Bar Association, National Foreign Trade Council, Inc.; 'Journal of Corporate Taxation' and 'Corporate Business Taxation Monthly'.

Career: Partner, Dewey Ballantine LLP, since 1996; adjunct faculty member at the Georgetown University Law Center.

Personal: LLM, 1988, Taxation, New York University School of Law; JD, 1987, Boston College Law School (magna cum laude); BS, 1984, Providence College (cum laude).

PARKER, Richard
O'Melveny & Myers LLP, Washington, DC 202 383 5300
Recommended in Antitrust

PARMLEY, Bruce
Hogan & Hartson LLP, Washington, DC 202 637 5644
BEParmley@HHLAW.com
Recommended in Real Estate

Practice Areas: For over 25 years, Bruce Parmley has served as principal counsel in hundreds of transactions involving acquisition, development, investment, financing, leasing, management, portfolio consolidation and securitization of commercial properties, with a major focus on hotels and resorts.

Prof. Memberships: Former Co-Chair, Real Estate Division, DC Bar Member, Real Property Section, ABA.

Career: Bruce's practice is international. He is Co-Director of the firm's Real Estate Practice and its Hospitality Group, and has been elected twice by Hogan & Hartson's partners to the firm's five-member Executive Committee.

Personal: The Catholic University of America (JD, 1976); Ohio University (BSC, 1970).

PATIN, Douglas L
Spriggs & Hollingsworth, Washington, DC 202 898 5841
dpatin@spriggs.com
Recommended in Construction

Practice Areas: Firm Practice Leader in construction. Also one of the firm's practice leaders in government contracts.

Prof. Memberships: Admitted to practice in Virginia, Maryland, and the District of Columbia.

Publications: Author, '2003 Government Contract Decisions of the Federal Circuit', American University Law Review (2004). Co-editor, 'State Public

Construction Law Sourcebook', CCH Incorporated (2002). Co-author, 'Construction Insurance', Chapter 45, Law and Practice of Insurance Coverage Litigation (West 2000). Author, 'U.S.A., Dispute Resolution and Conflict Management in Construction', An International Review (E&FN Spon 1998). Co-author, 'Construction Insurance: Coverages and Disputes' (Michie 1994). Co-author, 'Construction Contracting', George Washington University National Law Center, Government Contracts Program (September 1991). Co-author, 'Surety's Role in Default Terminations', Construction Briefings, No. 90-4, Federal Publications (March 1990). Co-author, 'Liability Insurance', Construction Briefings, No. 89-9, Federal Publications (August 1989).

Personal: Born, 8 August 1954. University of Wisconsin-River Falls (BA, with highest honors, 1976). George Washington University Law Center (JD, 1979).

PAULSON, Mark
Mayer, Brown, Rowe & Maw LLP, Washington, DC 202 263 3310
mpaulson@mayerbrownrowe.com
Recommended in Intellectual Property

Practice Areas: Litigation of intellectual property rights. Experience in all phases of patent, trademark, trade secret and unfair competition litigation (including extensive work before the Federal Circuit). Handles patent interferences, patent reexaminations and reissues before the US Patent and Trademark Office. Works with clients with respect to creation and structuring of IPR to create value. Experience in technical fields involving intellectual property matters encompassing a broad spectrum of areas including telecommunications, electrical, medical devices, pharmaceutical, chemical and biochemical arts. Represents clients in range of activities relating to protecting, creating, enhancing and enforcing intellectual property rights. Mr Paulson has an extensive client base in Europe and Australia as well as the United States. He has extensive experience in IPR protection programs and licensing programs, as well as working on mergers, acquisitions, technology transfer agreement and joint ventures, where technology is the driving force behind the relationship.

Career: Mayer, Brown, Rowe & Maw LLP, Washington, DC, 2004 to date. Pillsbury Winthrop LLP, 1989-2004. Law Clerk to the Honorable Jean Galloway Bissel, US Court of Appeals for the Federal Circuit, 1987-89. Nabisco, Food Scientist, 1977-83; Legal Department, 1983-87.

Personal: JD, Temple University Law School, 1987. BA, Western Connecticut University, 1981.

PENDER, Bob
Hogan & Hartson LLP, Washington, DC 202 637 6814
rbpender@hhlaw.com
Recommended in Projects

Practice Areas: Partner, Practice Group Director, Project & International Finance Group. Focus on infrastructure project finance, with a concentration on power, transportation and energy, including LNG. Represents independent power companies, utilities and investors in the development, financing, restructuring and purchase and sale of energy facilities. Represented AES restructure multiple projects in South America and United States. Represented Sithe Energies in its sale by Exelon to Dynergy.

Career: Worked on over $15 billion in projects throughout the United States, South America, Central America and South Asia.

Personal: Georgetown University Law Center (JD, 1982); Middlebury College (BA, 1976). White House Staff 1978-80.

PENNA, Richard
Van Ness Feldman PC, Washington, DC 202 298 1800
Recommended in Environment

PERLIS, Mark
Dickstein Shapiro Morin & Oshinsky LLP, Washington, DC 202 775 4703
PerlisM@dsmo.com
Recommended in Energy

Practice Areas: Broad federal regulatory and litigation practice on energy and environmental matters with electric utility and industry restructuring emphasis. Represents clients in Federal Energy Regulatory Commission adjudicatory and rulemaking proceedings. Counsels on energy commercial agreements, contract disputes, and tradable environmental allowances.

Prof. Memberships: Emissions Marketing Association (former Board of Directors, Vice-President); ABA.

Career: Partner, Dickstein Shapiro; Partner, Hopkins & Sutter; Tax Legislative Counsel's Office, US Treasury Department.

Publications: Writes extensively on emissions trading, electricity industry restructuring, and emerging energy and telecommunications markets.

Personal: Yale College (BA, 1974); Harvard Law School (JD, 1977).

PERLSTEIN, William J
Wilmer Cutler Pickering Hale and Dorr LLP, Washington, DC 202 663 6274
william.perlstein@wilmerhale.com
Recommended in Bankruptcy

Practice Areas: Co-Chair of the firm's Management Committee and former Head of the firm's Bankruptcy and Commercial Department. Represents creditors' committees, bank groups, debtors, trustees and claims acquirers in bankruptcy and workout cases around the country.

Prof. Memberships: Fellow and Counsel to the American College of Bankruptcy; American Law Institute, American Bar Association Business Bankruptcy Committee.

Publications: At the Intersection of Regulation and Bankruptcy; Minimizing Risks When Acquiring Assets From A Financially Troubled Company.

Personal: Yale Law School (JD 1974); Union College (BA 1971); London School of Economics, 1970.

PETERSON, Charles

Shaw Pittman LLP, Washington, DC
202 663 8083
charles.peterson@shawpittman.com
Recommended in Energy

Practice Areas: Energy: fuel and energy trading, international transactions including Japan, Russia and European countries, advanced nuclear reactors; major commercial transactions and international dispute resolution.

Prof. Memberships: American Bar Association, International Nuclear Lawyers Association, California Bar Association, District of Columbia Bar Association, American Nuclear Society.

Career: Chief Engineer aboard several nuclear submarines, retired from the reserves as a Captain; General Electric, Nuclear Power Division, 1973 and Nuclear Fuel Department, 1975; General Electric Aircraft Equipment Division, Division Counsel, 1979; Cogema, the French Nuclear Fuel Company, Executive Vice President of U/S/ Subsidiary, 1983; Nuexco, President 1987; Shaw Pittman, Partner, 2001.

Personal: Stanford Law School, JD, 1973; Stanford Business School, MBA, 1971; US Naval Academy, BS, 1960; leads pro bono projects related to nuclear nonproliferation and the abolition of nuclear weapons.

PHILLIPS, Carter

Sidley Austin Brown & Wood LLP, Washington, DC 202 736 8270
cphillips@sidley.com
Recommended in Litigation

Practice Areas: Carter Phillips heads the firm's Appellate Practice, routinely representing clients before the United States Supreme Court, state supreme courts, federal courts of appeals and other appellate forums. Mr Phillips is Managing Partner of Sidley's Washington, DC office, and is a member of the firm's Management and Executive Committees. He served as assistant to the Solicitor General for three years, during which time he argued nine cases on behalf of the federal government in the US Supreme Court. To date, he has argued 45 cases before the Supreme Court. In 2004, he argued six Supreme Court cases including: Intel Corp v Advanced Micro Devices, where he represented the European Commission in its first appearance before the Court (in an amicus brief); Norfolk Southern

Railway v Kirby, in which the Court ruled unanimously in favor of Sidley client Norfolk Southern in a case involving contracts of carriage in international trade; and Sosa v Alvarez-Machain, in which the Court issued a unanimous ruling in favor of Sidley client Sosa, limiting the scope of the Alien Tort Statute.

Prof. Memberships: Mr Phillips is a member of the American Law Institute, the American Academy of Appellate Lawyers, and a Fellow in the American College of Trial Lawyers. He is Chairman of the Federal Circuit Advisory Committee and Chairman of the Dean's Advisory Committee of Northwestern University's School of Law. He is on the Publications Committee of the Supreme Court Historical Society, the Amicus Curiae Committee of the Federal Bar Association, and the Board of Directors of the Institute of Judicial Administration at New York University School of Law. He serves on the Advisory Committee of Georgetown University Law Center's Supreme Court Institute and the Editorial Board of the National Law Journal.

Career: Mr Phillips served as a law clerk to both Judge Robert Sprecher on the United States Court of Appeals for the Seventh Circuit and Chief Justice Warren E. Burger on the United States Supreme Court. Northwestern University School of Law, JD, 1977; Northwestern University, MA, 1975; The Ohio State University, BA, 1973. Bar Admissions: US Supreme Court; all US Courts of Appeals; District of Columbia, 1979; Illinois, 1977.

PLANNING, Anne K

Shaw Pittman LLP, Washington, DC
202 663 9164
anne.planning@shawpittman.com,
anne.planning@pillsburylaw.com
Recommended in Real Estate

Practice Areas: Anne Planning has been involved in commercial lease transactions for office and retail space from both the landlord's and tenant's perspective. Ms Planning has represented real estate clients in the purchase and sale of office buildings, shopping centers and unimproved land. She also is experienced in negotiating and drafting loan documentation representing both lenders and borrowers.

Prof. Memberships: National Association of Industrial and Office Parks, International Conference of Shopping Centers, American Bar Association, Virginia Bar Association.

Career: Before entering private practice, Ms Planning served on the staffs of former US Senator David F Durenberger and the Senate Subcommittee on Intergovernmental Relations.

PLEVIN, Mark

Crowell & Moring LLP, Washington, DC
202 624 2801
mplevin@crowell.com
Recommended in Bankruptcy

Practice Areas: Mark Plevin is a Partner in Crowell & Moring's Litigation Group and litigates in the bankruptcy and insurance coverage areas. He has assumed lead counsel role on behalf of insurers in key asbestos bankruptcy cases including Mid-Valley, Combustion Engineering, Congoleum, Federal-Mogul, Harbison-Walker, JT Thorpe, and Owens Corning. He serves as bankruptcy counsel to both the American Insurance Association and the Coalition for Litigation Justice, a group formed by property and casualty insurers to advance awareness about asbestos issues. In insurance coverage, he served as lead counsel representing insurers in cases involving environmental, asbestos, and products liability underlying claims.

PLUMER, Mark J

Swidler Berlin LLP, Washington, DC
202 424 7500
mjplumer@swidlaw.com
Recommended in Insurance

Practice Areas: Insurance Group Chair. Specializes in litigation and innovative settlement of complex insurance coverage disputes on behalf of policyholder corporations. Extensive experience regarding coverage claims involving products (including asbestos and medical devices), environmental, and general business related claims, including errors and omissions, fidelity, directors and officers, intellectual property and first party.

Prof. Memberships: Admitted to practice in Pennsylvania (1987), District of Columbia, (1987); American Bar Association.

Career: Joined Swidler Berlin LLP 1994. Member, Board of Directors.

Personal: Born 20 April 1961; JD (cum laude) George Washington University Law School, 1986; BA (cum laude) Franklin & Marshall College, 1983.

POLON, Ira H

Dickstein Shapiro Morin & Oshinsky LLP, Washington, DC 202 828 2238
PolonI@dsmo.com
*Recommended in
Corporate/Commercial*

Practice Areas: Corporate law practice with substantial experience in mergers, acquisitions, and financing. Personally directed the representation of buyers and sellers in more than 175 transactions, involving a wide variety of industrial companies, government contractors, and other businesses.

Career: Partner and Head of Dickstein Shapiro's Mergers and Acquisitions Section; has practiced with the firm since 1971.

Publications: Lectured and written on mergers and acquisitions extensively; Co-authored 'Asset Sales - Were Causes of Action Transferred?' which appeared in The M & A Lawyer (April 2002).

Personal: Columbia University School

of Law (LLB, 1968); Lehigh University (BA, 1965).

POPOFSKY, Mark

Kaye Scholer LLP, Washington, DC
202 682 3530
mpopofsky@kayescholer.com
Recommended in Antitrust

Practice Areas: Partner and Chair, Technology and Competition Practice Group. Represents clients in antitrust, intellectual property, and commercial litigation, counsels clients concerning a variety of competition-related matters, and represents parties in mergers and other transactions before the US Department of Justice and Federal Trade Commission.

Prof. Memberships: Chair, Section 2 Committee, American Bar Association, Antitrust Section; Past Vice Chair of Internet Committee; Member, US Council for International Business; California Bar Association Antitrust and Trade Regulation Section; District of Columbia Antitrust Trade Regulation and Consumer Affairs Section.

Career: Senior Counsel, Antitrust Division, US Dep't of Justice, 1994-99; Law Clerk to Judge Dorothy W Nelson, US Court of Appeals for the Ninth Circuit; JD (magna cum laude), Harvard Law School, 1993, executive editor, Harvard Law Review; AB (magna cum laude), Brown University, 1990, Phi Beta Kappa.

Publications: Charting Antitrust's New Frontier, 9 Geo. Mason L. Rev. 656 (2001). The New Competition Law Paradigm, Symposium, UWLA L. Rev. (2001). Vertical Restraints in the 1990s, 62 Antitrust L.J. 729 (1994).

PORTER, Stephen

Arnold & Porter LLP, Washington, DC
202 942 5004
Stephen.Porter@aporter.com
Recommended in Real Estate

Practice Areas: Has practiced in the real estate, tax, and corporate areas for more than 35 years. In 1974, he was a founding Partner of Dunnells, Duvall & Porter. His practice principally involves large-scale, complex real estate transactions, corporate and real estate financing, leasing, and general business counseling. He has counseled a number of major corporations, non-profit organizations, and professional firms seeking to relocate their offices, as well as developers of hotels, marinas, and office buildings.

Prof. Memberships: He has also served as a Member of the Advisory Board of the Center for Strategic & International Studies; Chairman of the Board of the Washington Performing Arts Society; Chairman of the Board of the Forum for Psychiatry and the Humanities; and as a Member of the Board of Directors of the Washington School of Psychiatry. He is currently a Member of the Board of Trustees of the Federal City Council and a Member of the Boards of both the

Greater Washington Board of Trade and the District of Columbia Chamber of Commerce and is Chair of the Board of Trade's Public Affairs Committee and is Chair Elect of the District of Columbia Chamber of Commerce. He also serves on the District of Columbia Comprehensive Planning Task Force by appointment of Mayor Williams.

POTENZA, Joseph
Banner & Witcoff, Ltd, Washington, DC
202 508 9100
Recommended in Intellectual Property

PRESTON, Richard
Seyfarth Shaw LLP, Washington, DC
202 463 2400
Recommended in Construction

PRINCE, Allison
Shaw Pittman LLP, Washington, DC
202 663 8853
allison.prince@shawpittman.com, allison.prince@pillsburylaw.com
Recommended in Real Estate

Practice Areas: Real estate; zoning and land development, focusing on education and nonprofit; litigation; litigation for land use, real estate and construction; healthcare; life sciences.
Prof. Memberships: Admitted to practice: District of Columbia, Virginia; Greater Washington Board of Trade; Commercial Real Estate Women; Jubilee Support Alliance Advisory Council; The Real Estate Group.
Career: Partner, Wilkes Artis, Washington, DC; Partner in Shaw Pittman's Real Estate Group.
Personal: Catholic University, Columbus School of Law, JD, 1983; Bucknell University, BA 1980. (At press time, Shaw Pittman LLP had entered into a merger agreement with Pillsbury Winthrop LLP. The merger is expected to close by April 2005. Post-closing, the name of the firm will be Pillsbury Winthrop Shaw Pittman LLP.)

PROGER, Phillip A
Jones Day, Washington, DC
202 879 4668
paproger@jonesday.com
Recommended in Antitrust

Practice Areas: Practices antitrust law with emphasis on matters before US and international enforcement agencies, including mergers and cartel investigations, as well as antitrust litigation. He has testified before Congress, the Federal Trade Commission, and the International Competition Policy Advisory Committee. Regularly writes and speaks on antitrust topics.
Prof. Memberships: Member of the Board of Governors of the American Bar Association. Fellow of the American Bar Foundation. Advisory board member of 'BNA Antitrust & Trade Regulation Report' and 'The M&A Lawyer.'

PURETZ, Jeffrey S
Dechert, Washington, DC
202 261 3358
jeffrey.puretz@dechert.com
Recommended in Investment Management

Practice Areas: Mr Puretz coordinates the Financial Services Group's services for insurance companies. He also concentrates on investment management matters for mutual funds, fund directors, and fund managers.
Prof. Memberships: Member, Advisory Board, Mutual Fund Directors Forum; member, Regulatory Affairs Committee, National Association of Variable Annuities.
Career: Founder and Co-Chair of the Practising Law Institute conference on 'Understanding Securities Products of Insurance Companies'; former staff attorney with the SEC's Division of Investment Management.
Personal: University of Maryland (BA, 1976); The Catholic University of America School of Law (JD, 1981); Georgetown University Law Center (graduate course work in securities law).

QUALE, John C
Skadden, Arps, Slate, Meagher & Flom LLP & Affiliates, Washington, DC
202 371 7200
jquale@skadden.com
Recommended in Telecom, Broadcast & Satellite

Practice Areas: Represents companies on a broad range of communications law issues arising in regulatory, legislative and transactional matters. Clients include broadcast, satellite and wireless companies, venture capital and investment firms and commercial banks. Counsels on structuring transactions and assists in negotiating and documenting purchases and sales of media properties. Advises clients concerning FCC multiple and alien ownership regulations and assists in rule waivers to permit market entry. In connection with these transactions, obtained FCC approval of license transfers in large numbers of contested cases.
Career: JD, Harvard Law School, 1971 (cum laude); AB, Harvard College, 1968 (cum laude).

QUARLES, John
Morgan, Lewis & Bockius LLP, Washington, DC 202 739 5150
jquarles@morganlewis.com
Recommended in Environment

Practice Areas: John Quarles is a Partner in the Litigation Practice. Mr Quarles's practice focuses on a variety of environmental law issues, providing counseling and litigation assistance on Superfund, hazardous waste, and air and water pollution matters. He heads several groups working on Superfund and RCRA implementation and reauthorization issues.
Prof. Memberships: American Bar

Association (Environment, Energy & Resources Section); District of Columbia Bar Association; Environmental Law Institute.
Career: Mr Quarles served as the Environmental Protection Agency's first general counsel from 1970 through 1973, and then served four years as deputy administrator, also serving two periods as Acting Administrator.

QUIN, Whayne
Holland & Knight LLP, Washington, DC
202 955 3000
whayne.quin@hklaw.com
Recommended in Real Estate

Practice Areas: Partner and Practice Group Leader in the Real Estate Section, practicing in the area of municipal law focusing on land use, zoning, urban planning, building and housing codes, historic preservation, environmental, transportation and urban real estate matters. His clients have included builders, developers, educational institutions, nonprofit organizations, financial institutions, chanceries, international and national agencies, and property owners. Nationally, he has been a consultant to the private sector in the fields of land use, historic preservation, housing and building-related matters. As an urban strategist, he has advised clients on the procedures necessary to accomplish residential, commercial and industrial development.

QUINT, Arnold
Hunton & Williams, Washington, DC
202 955 1542
aquint@hunton.com
Recommended in Energy

Practice Areas: Arnold Quint's practice focuses on all aspects of regulation, deregulation and restructuring of the electric utility industry, including electric rates and corporate regulation, long-term power sales agreements, transmission access and pricing, the licensing of hydroelectric projects and competition issues arising in the public utility industry. He represents utility companies, independent system operators and transcos in connection with matters arising under the Federal Power Act and the Public Utility Holding Company Act especially in matters pending before the Federal Energy Regulatory Commission (FERC).

RAHER, Patrick M
Hogan & Hartson LLP, Washington, DC
202 637 5682
pmraher@hhlaw.com
Recommended in Environment

Practice Areas: Environmental, including Clean Air Act Permitting of Stationary Sources, defense of companies in Clean Air Act Enforcement Actions; transportation, including safety regulation of mobile sources and railroad equipment; legislative.
Prof. Memberships: EPA Clean Air Act Advisory Committee; EPA Mobile

Source Advisory Committee; EPA New Source Review Subcommittee (Co-Chairperson); ABA (Co-Chairman, Ad Hoc Committee on Government Attorneys-EPA); District of Columbia Judicial Tenure Commission.
Career: 1973-present, Hogan & Hartson, current Environmental Practice Director; 1992-present, appointed member, Environmental Protection Agency Clean Air Act Advisory Committee.
Publications: 'Lead in Office Building Drinking Water: A Key Environmental Analysis Issue for the 1990's,' Environmental Liability in Commercial Transactions Reporter, February 1991; 'Hidden Pitfalls in Groundwater Cleanup Rules,' Prentiss Hall Environmental Hazards Reporter, May 1990; '"Gualtney" and its Progeny: The Current Status of Citizen's Suits Under the Clean Water Act,' The Environmental Counselor, October 1989; 'Being Aware of 18 U.S.C. 1001 and the EPA Regulatory Thicket,' Corporate Counsel's Guide to Environmental Law, 1989; 'What Might the Supreme Court Say on Officer and Director Liability if US v. Park Applies to Environmental Statutes?' Corporate Counsel, 1989; 'How to Get Things Done At the EPA' The Brief, Winter 1986; 'Economic Internationalism vs. National Parochialism: Barcelona Traction: Journal of Law and Policy in International Business,' Fall 1971.
Personal: Georgetown University Law Center (JD, 1972); University of Notre Dame (BBA, with honors, 1969).

RAIM, David
Chadbourne & Parke LLP, Washington, DC 202 974 5625
draim@chadbourne.com
Recommended in Insurance

Practice Areas: Heads Reinsurance and Insurance Group, experienced in handling arbitrations and litigations, particularly those involving insurance and reinsurance issues. Provides advice to clients in the reinsurance and insurance business on a wide range of subject matters.
Prof. Memberships: Member of the District of Columbia Bar, Chairman 1988-94 and Member of Benefits Committee.

RASKIN, David
Steptoe & Johnson LLP, Washington, DC 202 429 6254
draskin@steptoe.com
Recommended in Energy

Practice Areas: Partner, Steptoe & Johnson LLP, Washington, DC. Represents electric power industry clients in cases involving electric industry restructuring, mergers and acquisitions, wholesale electric and transmission service rates, transmission access, contract disputes, fuel procurement practices, antitrust issues, and stranded investment. Negotiates and structures com-

plex bulk power and transmission service transactions and joint projects to construct and operate transmission lines and generating facilities. Participated in negotiations to establish Regional Transmission Organizations. Experienced with cases before the Nuclear Regulatory Commission concerning the licensing and operation of nuclear power plants.
Personal: JD, Georgetown University Law Center, 1979; BA, University of Pennsylvania, 1976.

RAUH, Carl S
Skadden, Arps, Slate, Meagher & Flom LLP & Affiliates, Washington, DC
202 371 7190
crauh@skadden.com
Recommended in Litigation
Practice Areas: A Leader of the firm's Government Enforcement Litigation Department. Represents corporations, directors, officers and employees in complex litigation, particularly matters involving simultaneous criminal, civil and administrative proceedings. Has defended corporations and their officers in cases involving allegations of procurement fraud, securities and tax violations, environmental crimes, healthcare fraud, bank and insurance fraud, antitrust offenses, food and drug adulteration, bribery and conflicts of interest.
Career: LLM, Georgetown University Law Center, 1968; LLB, University of Pennsylvania Law School, 1965; AB, Columbia University, 1962.

REED, Kevin
Dow, Lohnes & Albertson, PLLC, Washington, DC 202 776 2000
Recommended in Telecom, Broadcast & Satellite

REED, Steven
Steptoe & Johnson LLP, Washington, DC 202 429 6232
sreed@steptoe.com
Recommended in Energy
Practice Areas: Partner in Steptoe & Johnson LLP's Washington office. Focuses on federal and state energy regulation, particularly for oil and gas pipelines. Represents numerous US oil pipeline companies before the FERC, state regulatory agencies, arbitrators, and US Courts of Appeals covering various pipeline issues, such as tariff rates, development of the cost-of-service approach, and pipeline market power. Gas pipeline regulatory experience includes royalty issues, abandonments, and gas pipeline certificates. Frequently assists pipeline clients in structuring proposed transactions to meet regulations and in securing regulatory approvals for innovative rate approaches.
Personal: JD, Harvard Law School, 1979; BA, Harvard College, 1974.

REED, Wendy
Wright & Talisman PC, Washington, DC
202 393 1200
Recommended in Energy

REPKA, David A
Winston & Strawn, Washington, DC
202 371 5726
drepka@winston.com
Recommended in Energy
Practice Areas: Regulation of nuclear power and radiological materials. Extensive experience in administrative hearings; licensing, compliance and enforcement matters; investigations; and federal court appeals.
Prof. Memberships: District of Columbia Bar.
Career: Partner since 1991.
Publications: Co-author 'The Revival of Nuclear Power Plant Licensing,' Natural Resources & Environment, ABA Section of Environment, Energy, and Resources, Vol 19, No 3, Winter 2005; Speaker, 'NRC Licensing Hearings - Uncertainty and Reform,' NEI International Uranium Fuel Seminar, San Diego, California, October 2003.
Personal: Northwestern University, BA, 1978; Georgetown University Law Center, JD, 1981.

REYNOLDS, Nicholas S
Winston & Strawn, Washington, DC
202 282 5717
nreynolds@winston.com
Recommended in Energy
Practice Areas: Electric utilities in connection with industry restructuring, deregulation, and Sarbanes-Oxley, as well as mergers and acquisitions; nuclear power reactor and materials licensees before the US Nuclear Regulatory Commission, the Department of Labor, and the courts.
Personal: Wilkes College, BS, 1968; College of William and Mary School of Law, 1968-70; The George Washington University Law School, JD, with honors, 1971.

RHYNE, Katherine L
King & Spalding LLP, Washington, DC
202 626 3743
krhyne@kslaw.com
Recommended in Environment
Practice Areas: Focuses on chemical risk assessment issues in the context of environmental regulation or tort litigation. Experience includes environmental tort litigation, environmental litigation, scientific programs, environmental regulation, and site-specific risk assessment.
Prof. Memberships: American Bar Association (Member, Environmental and Natural Resources, Toxic Tort Sections); District of Columbia Bar; Virginia State Bar; Women's Bar Association of the District of Columbia.
Personal: University of Virginia, Phi Beta Kappa; University of Virginia Law School, 1980.

RICHARDSON, Julia
Van Ness Feldman PC, Washington, DC
202 298 1800
Recommended in Energy

RIEDY, James
McDermott Will & Emery, Washington, DC 202 756 8314
jriedy@mwe.com
Recommended in Tax
Practice Areas: Partner in Tax Department. Main area of work includes US federal income tax law applicable to cross-border transactions and investments. Practice encompasses both US multinational investments outside the US and non-US, multinational investments in the US. Practice includes consulting on technical tax matters, advising on major corporate acquisitions, corporate internal restructuring and transfer pricing.
Prof. Memberships: Member of Tax Section of the American Bar Association and International Fiscal Association.
Career: Admitted to the Kansas Bar in 1977; District of Columbia, 1981; and US Supreme Court, 1982. Joined the tax division, appellate section of the US Department of Justice in 1977; Lee, Toomey & Kent from 1981-93; McDermott, Will & Emery to the present.
Publications: Frequent commentator and lecturer on US international tax issues.
Personal: Born 25 July 1952; juris doctor degree in 1977 from the University of Kansas; master of laws degree in taxation from Georgetown University in 1981.

RILL, James
Howrey Simon Arnold & White, Washington, DC 202 783 0800
Recommended in Antitrust

RITTS, Leslie Sue
Hogan & Hartson LLP, Washington, DC
202 637 6573
lsritts@hhlaw.com
Recommended in Environment
Practice Areas: Clean Air Act enforcement, compliance and permitting; EU chemical regulation; toxic tort/general environmental litigation; environmental due diligence; and energy.
Prof. Memberships: Federal Clean Air Act Advisory Committee (New Source Review Simplification and Operating Permit Subcommittees); ABA (Section on Environmental Law); Virginia Bar Association (Section on Environmental Law); District of Columbia Bar Association (Section on Environmental Law).
Career: Hogan & Hartson, Partner; 1993-96, Chair, Air & Waste Management Association's Government Affairs Committee.
Publications: 'Clear Skies Legislation and NSR Reform: The Polictics of Clean Air,' 61 PUBL POWER 22 (Jan. 2003); 'Protecting Wastewater Assets After 9/11...Legal Issues At A Time Of Crisis Checklist,' AMSA (2001); 'The Shields Are Failing: An Analysis of the Clean Air Act Permit Shield,' 3 J. ENVIT'L PERMITTING 315 (Summer 1992).
Personal: William and Mary School of

Law (JD, 1980); Princeton University (AB, cum laude, 1977).

ROADY, Celia
Morgan, Lewis & Bockius LLP, Washington, DC
202 739 5279
croady@morganlewis.com
Recommended in Tax
Practice Areas: Ms Roady is a Partner in the Tax Practice. Ms Roady focuses her practice on the representation of tax-exempt organizations, including charities, foundations, colleges and universities, museums, associations and other nonprofit coalitions.
Prof. Memberships: Vice Chair - Communications, American Bar Association Taxation Section; Fellow, American College of Tax Counsel.

ROBBINS, Lawrence
Robbins, Russell, Englert, Orseck & Untereiner LLP, Washington, DC
202 775 4500
Recommended in Litigation

ROBBINS, Robert B
Shaw Pittman LLP, Washington, DC
202 663 8136
robert.robbins@shawpittman.com
Recommended in Corporate/Commercial
Practice Areas: Bob Robbins was Chair of Shaw Pittman's Corporate Securities Practice Group and is Co-Chair of Pillsbury Winthrop Shaw Pittman's Corporate Securities Section. He focuses on the federal securities laws and corporate transactions. His practice has included corporate acquisitions and divestitures; securities offerings and restructuring transactions involving public companies, public and private partnerships and real estate investment trusts; institutional offerings by private investment funds; mergers, restructurings and consolidation of corporations and public and private limited partnerships; proxy contests representing both management and dissident shareholders and limited partners; tender offer defense planning for public corporations and public limited partnerships; public and private securities offerings; and federal regulation of broker-dealers and investment advisers.
Career: Bob graduated from Cornell University in 1972, magna cum laude, and from Harvard Law School in 1975, cum laude. He clerked on the US Court of Appeals for the District of Columbia Circuit for before joining Shaw Pittman in 1976, and was named a Partner of Shaw Pittman in 1982.
Publications: Bob is a frequent lecturer on subjects relating to federal securities laws, and is the author of numerous articles in the field. He has served for many years as Co-Chair of the annual three-day course of study, 'Regulation D Offerings and Private Placements,' jointly sponsored by the American Law Institute-American Bar Association (ALI-

ABA) and the Federal Bar Association. He also has served for many years on the faculty of the twice-yearly ALI-ABA two-day course of study, 'Securities Law for Nonsecurities Lawyers'. He is a former Chair of the steering committee of the DC Bar Section on Corporation Finance and Securities Law. Recent publications include 'Regulation D Offerings and the Internet', Rev. of Secs. and Comm. Reg. (December 31, 2003) and 'The Fiduciary Duties of Directors of Corporate General Partners; Ten Years after USACafes', Rev. of Secs. and Comm. Reg. (March 27, 2002).

ROBERTS, Michele
Akin Gump Strauss Hauer & Feld LLP, Washington, DC 202 887 4306
mroberts@akingump.com
Recommended in Litigation
Practice Areas: Michele Roberts is regarded as one of the "finest pure trial lawyers in Washington - magic with juries, loved by judges, feared by opposing counsel." After beginning her career as a DC Public Defender, where she cut her teeth in more than 40 jury trials, she has built a fearsome reputation as a talented, determined and very persuasive advocate for her clients in complex civil and criminal litigation.

ROBERTS, Richard
Steptoe & Johnson LLP, Washington, DC 202 429 6756
rroberts@steptoe.com
Recommended in Energy
Practice Areas: Partner in the Washington office of Steptoe & Johnson LLP. Practice focuses primarily on energy law, antitrust, and litigation. Represents electric power companies in a variety of regulatory and antitrust proceedings before the FERC, federal courts, and state regulatory commissions focusing on the restructuring of the power industry, including market power litigation, the formation of ISOs and other power pools, and the sale and purchase of power plants. Is a central figure in the on-going clean up of the California power crisis of 2000-01.
Personal: JD, University of Maryland School of Law, 1988; BS, Towson State University, 1984.

ROBINSON, Frederick
Fulbright & Jaworski LLP, Washington, DC 202 662 4534
frobinson@fulbright.com
Recommended in Healthcare
Practice Areas: Health law, criminal law, and litigation.
Prof. Memberships: American Bar Association, Criminal Justice Section, White Collar Crime Committee, Health Care Fraud Subcommittee; American Lawyers Association; District of Columbia Bar Association; Maryland Bar Association; National Association of College and University Attorneys.
Career: Rick Robinson began his legal career in Fulbright's Litigation Group,

where, beginning in 1982, he represented a wide variety of corporations and their officers in government investigations and white-collar criminal cases. Mr Robinson is now the partner-in-charge of the Health Law Practice in Fulbright & Jaworski's Washington, DC, office. His cases cover all phases of trial and appellate practice in both criminal and civil cases, including qui tam and 'whistle blower' lawsuits under the federal False Claims Act. He also advises clients on internal investigations and voluntary disclosure matters.
Personal: BA- Duke University (1979); JD - Duke University (1982).

ROCAP III, James
Steptoe & Johnson LLP, Washington, DC 202 429 8152
jrocap@steptoe.com
Recommended in Insurance
Practice Areas: Complex civil litigation with a current emphasis on large insurance coverage disputes. Experience in a wide range of large-scale civil and white collar criminal matters. Represented numerous companies and individuals in complex business litigation, including claims involving antitrust violations, fraud, tortious interference with contract, and breach of contract. Active in pro bono work. Represented death row inmate for 20+ years, and provides legal services to the homeless.
Career: Serves on firm's ALAS, Client Relations, and Office Space Committees.
Personal: JD, Georgetown University Law Center, 1975; articles/notes editor, 'Georgetown Law Journal'; BA, University of Notre Dame, 1971.

ROGERS, Ed
Nixon Peabody LLP, Washington, DC 202 585 8726
erogers@nixonpeabody.com
Recommended in Real Estate
Practice Areas: Real estate development, commercial finance and related corporate matters, large-scale, mixed-use projects. Projects: shopping centers, office buildings, museums, theatres, hotels, resorts, telecommunications facilities, entertainment/ communications companies, and national/international investors. Currently representing: the District of Columbia (a convention center hotel development); Freedom Forum/Newseum, Inc. (a major mixed-use project that will house a world-class museum, the Freedom Forum's international headquarters, a conference center, residential housing, retail facilities and parking); Waterfront Associates (a mixed-use project near the southeast DC waterfront); and Forest City Washington.
Prof. Memberships: Admitted to practice in DC and NY.
Personal: University of Virginia, JD, BA.

ROHRBACH, Peter
Hogan & Hartson LLP, Washington, DC 202 637 8631
parohrbach@hhlaw.com
Recommended in Telecom, Broadcast & Satellite
Practice Areas: Co-Director of the firm's Communications Group and a leading member of the US Communications Bar. He has extensive experience in the telecommunications area, with particular emphasis on the telephone industry, satellite communications, and information services. He has played a major role in many of the key regulatory developments in these industry segments. His clients have included major national and international carriers, as well as newer companies that have grown in response to opportunities created by the Internet, liberalized opportunities for competition, and related developments.
Prof. Memberships: Member, Federal Communications Bar Association.
Career: Peter has taught a law school seminar in communications law, speaks regularly on telecommunications policy matters, and participates in various industry organizations.
Personal: Stanford University Law School (JD); Yale University (BA, magna cum laude).

ROSEN, Richard L
Arnold & Porter LLP, Washington, DC 202 942 5499
Richard.Rosen@aporter.com
Recommended in Antitrust
Practice Areas: Richard Rosen handles a wide range of antitrust matters, with a focus on clients in the telecommunications, information technology and media industries. His practice includes representation of clients in mergers and acquisitions and civil and criminal enforcement matters before federal antitrust agencies, as well as antitrust counseling and litigation. He has represented SBC Communications and Cingular Wireless in Cingular's $41 billion acquisition of AT&T Wireless; Computer Associates in its acquisitions of Legent Corporation, Platinum Technology International and Sterling Software; and Cisco Systems in its acquisition of the Linksys Group. Mr Rosen has been recognized as a leading competition lawyer by the 'Chambers Global - The World's Leading Lawyers' as 'highly recommended' by Global Counsel's Competition Law Handbook; and in Who's Who Legal - The International Who's Who of Business Lawyers.
Career: Prior to joining Arnold & Porter LLP, Mr Rosen served as Chief of the Communications and Finance Section of the US Department of Justice Antitrust Division, Assistant Director of the Federal Trade Commission's Bureau of Competition, and as Attorney Advisor to the Chairman of the Federal Trade Commission.

ROSENBLOOM, David
Caplin & Drysdale, Washington, DC 202 862 5000
Recommended in Tax

ROSENTHAL, Barry
Bingham McCutchen LLP, Washington, DC 202 778 6150
Recommended in Real Estate

ROTH, Stephen E
Sutherland Asbill & Brennan LLP, Washington, DC 202 383 0158
steve.roth@sablaw.com
Recommended in Investment Management
Practice Areas: Chairs the firm's Business Practices Group and Financial Services Team. Leading authority in the development of new insurance products, including registration of variable life, fixed life and annuity contracts with the Securities and Exchange Commission. Advises in the development, regulation and compliance of mutual funds and other regulated investment companies, as well as securities compliance and regulatory issues affecting broker/dealers and investment advisers. Counsels financial service clients on insurance regulatory and licensing matters as well as on merger, acquisition and reinsurance transactions.
Prof. Memberships: Member, American Bar Association. Member, ABA's Committee on Federal Regulation of Securities. Member, ABA's Subcommittee on Securities Activities of Insurance Companies. Member, Association of Life Insurance Counsel.
Personal: JD, Yale Law School, 1976, editor, Yale Law Journal; AB, summa cum laude, University of Notre Dame, 1973, Phi Beta Kappa.

RUBINSTEIN, Joel
Bell, Boyd & Lloyd, Washington, DC 202 466 6300
Recommended in Construction

RUDNICK, Robert
Shearman & Sterling, Washington, DC 202 508 8100
rrudnick@shearman.com
Recommended in Tax
Practice Areas: Partner in Shearman & Sterling's Tax Group. Represents clients in federal income tax matters, including corporate tax, partnership tax, the taxation of financial products and tax controversy work. Participated in the creation of many novel financial products with tax significance, including the first CMO, the first foreign-targeted CMO, the REMIC legislation, credit card securitization and stripped mortgages.
Prof. Memberships: American Bar Association Tax Section.
Career: Joined Shearman as Partner in 1997; Previously a Partner at Cadwalader, Wickersham & Taft (1981-97).
Personal: BA, Colby College (1969); JD, Cornell University (1972).

RUGGERI, James
Hogan & Hartson LLP, Washington, DC
202 637 5875
jpruggeri@hhlaw.com
Recommended in Insurance

Practice Areas: Focuses principally in the areas of litigation, including trial and appellate involving insurance coverage, general commercial and bankruptcy litigation. He practices actively in federal and state courts around the country.
Prof. Memberships: Member, American Bar Association; Member, New York Bar Association.
Career: Prior to joining Hogan & Hartson, James served as law clerk to the Honorable Rebecca Beach Smith, US District Judge for the US District Court for the Eastern District of Virginia.
Personal: Vanderbilt University (JD).

RULE, Charles F (Rick)
Fried, Frank, Harris, Shriver & Jacobson LLP, Washington, DC 202 639 7300
Rick.Rule@FriedFrank.com
Recommended in Antitrust

Practice Areas: Chair of the firmwide Antitrust Department. Practice is focused on all aspects of US and international antitrust, including regulatory clearance of mergers, structuring of joint ventures and other transactions, intellectual property licensing, civil and criminal investigations by antitrust authorities in the US and other jurisdictions, private and governmental antitrust litigation, appellate litigation, and counseling. Clients include Microsoft, ExxonMobil, MGM Mirage, Northrop Grumman, Dow Jones, Goldman Sachs, Eli Lilly, and Goodyear.
Prof. Memberships: Member, Advisory Board of BNA's Antitrust & Trade Regulation Report; Member, Advisory Board of the Washington Legal Foundation and of the Landmark Legal Foundation. Former Chair, Economics Committee of the American Bar Association Antitrust Section; Former Chair, Corporations, Securities and Antitrust Practice Group of the Federalist Society.
Career: Admitted District of Columbia. Joined firm as a Partner in 2001. Partner, Covington & Burling (1989-2001). Assistant Attorney General, Antitrust Division of the Justice Department (1986-89), Deputy Assistant Attorney (1984-86) and Special Assistant to the Assistant Attorney General (1982-84).
Personal: Born 1955. Received JD from the University of Chicago Law School in 1981 and BA from Vanderbilt University in 1978.

RUTKOWSKI, Joanne
Baker Botts LLP, Washington, DC
202 639 7785
joanne.rutkowski@bakerbotts.com
Recommended in Energy

Practice Areas: Partner in the Washington Office. Has extensive experience in the area of utility law, utility mergers and acquisitions, and Holding Company Act matters. She regularly advises clients regarding utility restructuring, acquisitions, strategic planning, and governmental and regulatory procedures, both federal and state.
Career: Earlier in her career, was a senior attorney at the Securities and Exchange Commission and co-author 1995 study of the Regulation of Public Utility Holding Companies, the first comprehensive review of the Holding Company Act since its enactment.
Personal: JD, Harvard Law School, 1983; BA (magna cum laude), Mathematics, Albright College, 1979.

SACHER, Steven
Kilpatrick Stockton LLP,
Washington, DC 202 508 5800
SSacher@KilpatrickStockton.com
Recommended in Employee Benefits

Practice Areas: Mr Sacher is a Partner in the law firm of Kilpatrick Stockton LLP in Washington, DC. He counsels corporate clients on ERISA/employee benefits matters and represents them in the federal courts and before relevant federal agencies and congressional committees. Before entering private practice in 1981, was intimately involved in the development and drafting of ERISA during 1972-74, in its administration and enforcement during 1975-77, and in the legislative consideration and enactment of the Age Discrimination in Employment Act Amendments of 1978, and the Multiemployer Pension Plan Amendments Act of 1980.
Prof. Memberships: A charter fellow of the American College of Employee Benefits Counsel and a fellow of the College of Labor and Employment Lawyers, Mr Sacher lectures and publishes frequently on ERISA/employee benefits matters. He co-chaired the Senior Editors of Employee Benefits Law (Bureau of National Affairs, 1991, 2000), an annually-supplemented ERISA case law treatise, from its inception in 1991 until 2000.
Career: Mr Sacher is listed in The Best Lawyers in America for Employee Benefits and Labor Law (continuously since 1988); The Top Benefits Lawyers, National Law Journal (1998); The Best Employee Benefits Lawyers, Corporate Counsel magazine (2003); Who's Who (U.S., the East, Law (continuously since 1983); and is top-ranked by Chambers USA (2004). BS, University of Wisconsin, with senior honors, 1964; JD, University of Chicago, 1967.

SACHS, John
Latham & Watkins LLP,
Washington, DC 202 637 2200
Recommended in Projects

SACKS, Stephen
Arnold & Porter LLP, Washington, DC
202 942 5681
Stephen.Sacks@aporter.com
Recommended in Litigation

Practice Areas: Specializes in litigation, with particular emphasis on securities fraud and commercial disputes. He has also represented a number of corporate and accounting firm clients in investigations conducted by the SEC and in class actions alleging securities law violations. Representative clients include Fannie Mae, Motorola, Rhodia, PricewaterhouseCoopers, Deloitte & Touche, the PGA, and Bear Stearns.
Career: Prior to joining Arnold & Porter LLP, Mr Sacks was Assistant to the General Counsel, Department of the Army.
Personal: LLB, Harvard Law School, 1966; BS, Cornell University, 1963.

SAMORAJCZYK, Stanley J
Akin Gump Strauss Hauer & Feld LLP,
Washington, DC 202 887 4002
ssamorajczyk@akingump.com
Recommended in Bankruptcy

Practice Areas: Represents debtors, creditors and other parties in complex national and cross-border restructuring, bankruptcy, insolvency and creditors' rights cases, often leading multidisciplinary teams of professionals in addressing clients' needs. He has lectured nationally and internationally on business reorganization and restructuring and has served as an expert witness on creditors' rights and reorganization.
Prof. Memberships: Fellow, American College of Bankruptcy; Chairman, Mid-Atlantic Institute on Bankruptcy and Reorganization; Member, District of Columbia and Virginia Bars.
Personal: AB, Georgetown University; JD, Catholic University.

SANFORD, Bruce
Baker & Hostetler LLP, Washington, DC
202 861 1621
Recommended in Media & Entertainment

SAYLER, Robert
Covington & Burling, Washington, DC
202 662 6000
RSayler@cov.com
Recommended in Insurance, Litigation

Practice Areas: Partner who has been lead counsel for successful insurance policy holders in billion dollar-plus insurance coverage disputes for asbestos, DES, environmental clean-up, and breast implant liabilities; acting for Armstrong World Industries, Boeing, Pittston, Dow Corning, 3M, Monsanto, Exxon, Procter & Gamble, ITT, National Medical Enterprises and the National Football League.
Prof. Memberships: Chair, Litigation Section, of the American Bar Association; Fellow of the American College of Trial Lawyers and the American Bar Foundation; CPR DC Panel of Distinguished Arbitration Neutrals; and the CPR Commission on the Future of Arbitration.
Career: 1965-present, Covington & Burling.

Publications: Author of dozens of articles and book chapters on insurance coverage issues, ADR, civility, trial strategies and oral advocacy skills.
Personal: Received an LLB from Harvard University and an AB from Stanford University.

SCALIA, Eugene
Gibson, Dunn & Crutcher LLP,
Washington, DC 202 955 8500
escalia@gibsondunn.com
Recommended in Employment

Practice Areas: Co-Chair of the firm's Labor and Employment Practice Group and Chair of the Administrative Law and Regulatory Practice Group. Experienced in a broad range of labor and employment matters (including discrimination law, labor relations, and ERISA) and regulatory matters involving SEC, FCC, Department of Transportation, and other agencies.
Career: 2002-03, Solicitor of Labor: principal legal officer, Department of Labor, responsible for government litigation involving ERISA, OSHA, Family/Medical Leave Act, wage-hour requirements, and Sarbanes-Oxley. 1992-93, Special Assistant, Attorney General of US.
Publications: More than 30 articles and papers.
Personal: JD, University of Chicago, editor-in-chief, 'Law Review'.

SCHECHTER, Mark
Howrey Simon Arnold & White,
Washington, DC 202 783 0800
Recommended in Antitrust

SCHERMAN, William S
Skadden, Arps, Slate, Meagher & Flom LLP & Affiliates, Washington, DC
202 371 7060
wscherma@skadden.com
Recommended in Energy

Practice Areas: Provides strategic, commercial, regulatory, legislative and litigation advice to clients regarding US and international energy markets. At FERC, played a key role in a number of major pro-competitive policy initiatives. For example, helped guide FERC's efforts to foster greater competition in the electric utility industry, contributed to the development of the Energy Policy Act of 1992 and testified before Congress on numerous occasions with regard to legislation and other energy policy-related matters.
Career: JD, University of Louisville School of Law, 1984 (articles editor, 'Law Review'); BA, George Washington University, 1980.

SCHILDKRAUT, Marc
Howrey Simon Arnold & White,
Washington, DC 202 783 0800
Recommended in Antitrust

SCHLOSSBERG, Bob
Freshfields Bruckhaus Deringer LLP,
Washington, DC 202 777 4500
Recommended in Antitrust

SCHMIDT, William
Kirkpatrick & Lockhart Nicholson
Graham LLP, Washington, DC
202 778 9373
william.schmidt@klng.com
Recommended in Employee Benefits
Practice Areas: Employee benefits reg-
ulation, fiduciary responsibility matters
under ERISA, pension plan investment.
Representation before the US DOL and
ERISA litigation.
Prof. Memberships: ABA, FBA, Ameri-
can College of Employee Benefits Coun-
sel (charter fellow).
Career: K&LNG Partner since 2001.
Former counsel for US DOL.
Publications: Writes and speaks on
ERISA issues. Editorial Boards of the
Investment Lawyer, The Benefits Law
Journal and The Journal of Pension
Planning and Compliance. Adjunct Pro-
fessor of Law, Georgetown University
Law Center.
Personal: Georgetown University
(LLM, 1983), University of Virginia (JD,
1973; BA 1970)

SCHNEIDER, Leslie
Ivins, Phillips & Barker, Washington, DC
202 393 7600
Recommended in Tax

SCHOR, Laurence
McManus Schor Asmar & Darden,
L.L.P., Washington, DC 202 296 9260
Recommended in Construction

SCHROEDER, Jeffrey P
Paul, Hastings, Janofsky & Walker LLP,
Washington, DC
202 551 1789
jeffschroeder@paulhastings.com
Recommended in Projects
Practice Areas: Practice focuses on
project development and finance (both
domestic and international), restructur-
ing of financing and commercial
arrangements for projects and stock and
asset acquisitions and dispositions.
Prof. Memberships: Member, District
of Columbia Bar.
Publications: Co-author: 'Regulatory
Considerations for Cross-Border Power
Plant Development' (Project Finance,
September 2001).
Personal: BA, University of Virginia; JD,
Washington and Lee (cum laude).

SCHUHMACHER, Kenneth
Latham & Watkins LLP,
Washington, DC 202 637 2200
Recommended in Projects

SCHWARTZ, David
Latham & Watkins LLP,
Washington, DC 202 637 2200
Recommended in Energy

SECREST, Lawrence
Wiley Rein & Fielding LLP,
Washington, DC 202 719 7000
*Recommended in Telecom, Broadcast
& Satellite*

SEGAL, Earl L
Akin Gump Strauss Hauer & Feld LLP,
Washington, DC 202 887 4160
esegal@akingump.com
Recommended in Real Estate
Practice Areas: Handles acquisition,
sale and development of commercial,
retail, hotel, residential and mixed-use
developments; commercial and retail
leasing; ground leasing; real estate lend-
ing; arbitration of real estate disputes.
Prof. Memberships: General Counsel,
Board Member, Greater Washington
Board of Trade; American College of
Real Estate Lawyers; Board of Directors,
Washington, DC, Golden Triangle Busi-
ness Improvement District.
Career: Outstanding Service Award,
Washington Lawyers' Committee for
Civil Rights and Urban Affairs; Recipi-
ent, Burton Award for Legal Achieve-
ment; contributing editor, 'The Practical
Real Estate Lawyer' and 'The Journal of
Real Estate Finance.'
Personal: BA, Pennsylvania State Uni-
versity; JD, University of Pittsburgh.

SHAPIRO, Howard
Van Ness Feldman PC, Washington, DC
202 298 1800
Recommended in Energy

SHAPIRO, Howard
Wilmer Cutler Pickering Hale and Dorr
LLP, Washington, DC 202 663 6606
howard.shapiro@wilmerhale.com
Recommended in Litigation
Practice Areas: Co-Chair of the firm's
Litigation Department. Practice focuses
largely on white collar criminal defense,
complex civil litigation and internal
investigations. An experienced trial
lawyer who led a trial team in IGEN
International, Inc. v Roche Diagnostics
GmbH that secured a jury verdict for
IGEN that allowed it to terminate its
licensing agreement with Roche, IGEN's
key business objective and awarded $505
million in damages. The United States
Court of Appeals for the Fourth Circuit
sustained the termination right, after
which Roche purchased IGEN in a $1.25
billion deal. The $505 million jury ver-
dict, which the Fourth Circuit reduced,
ranks fourth in the National Law Jour-
nal's top verdicts of 2002.
Career: General Counsel, Federal
Bureau of Investigation, 1993-97; Assis-
tant United States Attorney, Southern
District of New York, 1987-92; Associate
Professor of Law, Cornell Law School,
1993.
Publications: 'America needs more
spies', the Economist, July 2003 (with
others); 'Terrorism in a Democratic
Society', 1 J.Nat.Sec.Law 95 (1997); 'The
FBI in the 21st Century', 28 Cornell Int'l
LJ 219 (1995).
Personal: Yale Law School (JD 1985);
Williams College (AB 1982). Clerk for
Judge Pierre N Leval of the US District
Court for the Southern District of New
York (1985-87).

SHAPIRO, Robert
Chadbourne & Parke LLP,
Washington, DC 202 974 5670
rshapiro@chadbourne.com
Recommended in Energy
Practice Areas: Project finance, utility
and energy law, representing firms and
developers that build, finance, own,
operate, sell and use energy output from
renewable resource, cogeneration, waste
to energy, and conventional power facilities in the US and abroad. Also representation of investors and lenders to these
facilities. Extensive experience in negotiating power purchase agreements,
tolling agreements, other standard hedging agreements, fuel and operating and
maintenance agreements, and the
defense of long-term power contracts
before federal and state regulatory agencies and courts. Worked on numerous
power project developments, financings
and privatizations in Latin America.
Career: FERC, 1977-84.

SHARER, Paul
Mayer, Brown, Rowe & Maw LLP,
Washington, DC 202 263 3340
psharer@mayerbrownrowe.com
Recommended in Intellectual Property
Practice Areas: Extensive intellectual
property counseling expertise in handling a broad range of intellectual property issues in the biotech/pharma/med-
ical device industry. In particular, Mr
Sharer's expertise includes transactions
for example acquisitions and divestitures and financing for the biotech/
pharma/medical device intellectual
property intensive businesses, patent litigation and interferences, patent licenses
and joint development agreements,
developing and strategically managing
large patent estates, and patentability,
validity, non-willfulness, and clearance
opinions.
Career: Mayer, Brown, Rowe & Maw
LLP, Washington, DC, 2004 to date.
Pillsbury Winthrop LLP, Washington,
DC, 1997-2004; Member of the Office
Management Committee, 2001-04;
Managing Partner, DC Office, 2000-01.
Dickinson, Wright, Moon, Van Dusen &
Freeman, Washington, DC, 1995-97. ICI
Americas, Inc., Wilmington, DE, 1991-
95.
Personal: JD, Widener University
School of Law, 1991. B Sc Ch Eng.,
Drexel University, 1985. Mr Sharer is a
frequent lecturer at national/interna-
tional forums such as the GCTBIO
International Conference on Vaccines
and was recently featured in the Busi-
ness Section of the Washington Post.

SHONEMAN, Charles H
Bracewell & Giuliani LLP,
Washington, DC 202 828 5860
charles.shoneman@bracewellgiuliani.com
Recommended in Energy
Practice Areas: Expertise includes federal and state energy regulatory matters
before the Federal Energy Regulatory
Commission, Department of Energy,
Department of Interior, various state
public utility commissions, and appellate courts. Has advised clients with
respect to the regulatory aspects of commercial transactions, mergers and acquisitions, financings and litigation; federal
royalty matters; natural gas and electric
import and export matters; liquefied
natural gas matters; and the restructuring of the gas and electric industries.
Personal: JD, with honors, The George
Washington University Law School,
1972; BA, Duke University, 1969.

SHULMAN, Robert
Howrey Simon Arnold & White,
Washington, DC 202 783 0800
Recommended in Insurance

SIEGEL, Nathan
Levine Sullivan Koch & Schulz LLP,
Washington, DC 202 508 1100
*Recommended in Media &
Entertainment*

SIKORA, Clifford
Troutman Sanders LLP,
Washington, DC 202 274 2950
Recommended in Energy

SILBERG, Jay
Shaw Pittman LLP, Washington, DC
202 663 8063
jay.silberg@pillsburylaw.com
Recommended in Energy
Practice Areas: Energy - litigation;
nuclear energy, litigation representing
clients in the US and abroad on all
aspects of civilian uses of nuclear energy
before federal and state agencies, courts
and legislative bodies; nuclear energy, all
phases of nuclear projects from initial
contracting, through licensing and construction, regulatory counseling and
enforcement, purchases and sales, and
ultimately project decommissioning and
termination; environmental; litigation -
appellate.
Prof. Memberships: Admitted to Practice: District of Columbia, New Jersey;
US Supreme Court; US Courts of
Appeals for the Second, Sixth, Seventh,
Ninth, Tenth, Eleventh, District of
Columbia, and Federal Circuits; US District Courts for the Districts of New Jersey and Columbia; US Court of Federal
Claims; Supreme Court of New Jersey.
Career: 35 years experience before the
US Nuclear Regulatory Commission
(NRC), state agencies and the courts
encompasses the full range of licensing
and regulatory activities including construction permits, operating licenses,
license amendments, enforcement
actions, rulemaking proceedings, license
transfers, and other regulatory actions.
As the lead lawyer for industry activities
on nuclear waste issues, he appears
before the US Department of Energy,
the NRC and the courts.
Publications: Seven Years and Counting:
Presentation for Institute of Nuclear
Materials Management - Spent Fuel

Management Seminar XXII Continuing the Battle on DOE's Acceptance of Spent Fuel: Presentation for Institute of Nuclear Materials Management - Spent Fuel Management Seminar XX Managing Nuclear Waste Disposal: Presentation for Nuclear Power Outlook 2004 - Developing and Financing New Nuclear Projects Spent Fuel Storage and Disposal for U.S. Utilities: Practical Problems and Legal Logjams: Presentation for INLA Nuclear Inter-Jura '99 Conference Continuing Battle on the Acceptance of Spent Fuel: Is There an Appropriate Remedy?: Presentation for INMM Spent Fuel Management Seminar The Private Fuel Storage Facility: Presentation for INMM Spent Fuel Management Seminar XV.
Personal: Harvard Law School, JD, 1966; Amherst College, BA, cum laude, 1963. (At press time, Shaw Pittman LLP had entered into a merger agreement with Pillsbury Winthrop LLP. The merger is expected to close by April 2005. Post closing, the name of the firm will be Pillsbury Winthrop Shaw Pittman LLP.).

SILBERT, Earl
DLA Piper Rudnick Gray Cary US LLP, Washington, DC 202 861 6250
earl.silbert@dlapiper.com
Recommended in Litigation
Practice Areas: Litigation; professional liability and ethics; white collar.
Prof. Memberships: President, American College of Trial Lawyers, 2000-01; Master of Bench, American Inn of Court.
Career: He had a distinguished career in public service before entering private practice, including five years in the US Department of Justice, service as the first Watergate prosecutor, and five years as the US Attorney for the District of Columbia. He has lectured and authored numerous articles on evidence, the attorney-client and work product privileges, RICO and representations in grand jury investigations.
Personal: LLB, Harvard Law School; BA, Harvard University.

SILVERMAN, Mark
Steptoe & Johnson LLP, Washington, DC 202 429 6450
msilverman@steptoe.com
Recommended in Tax
Practice Areas: Head of the Tax Practice and Partner in the Washington office of Steptoe & Johnson LLP. Practice focuses on corporate tax transaction and planning matters. Has extensive experience in structuring acquisitions, mergers, and spin-off transactions for large public corporations as well as closely held businesses. Focuses on the resolution of tax policy and administrative issues before Congress and the Treasury Department. Handles significant audit and controversy matters with the IRS, including resolution of tax shelter matters on behalf of promoters and investors.

Personal: LLM, New York University School of Law, 1971; JD, Suffolk University Law School, 1970

SIMONS, Joseph
Paul, Weiss, Rifkind, Wharton & Garrison, Washington, DC 202 223 7370
jsimons@paulweiss.com
Recommended in Antitrust
Practice Areas: Co-Chair of Antitrust Group. Former Director of Bureau of Competition at the Federal Trade Commission (FTC). Extensive experience representing clients before the FTC, Department of Justice (DOJ), Department of Defense, and Congress in a wide range of antitrust and regulatory matters. Appointed by DOJ and Federal Communications Commission (FCC) as trustee for wireless telephone businesses relating to the GTE/Bell Atlantic/Vodafone and Cingular/AT&T Wireless transactions. Co-Developer of 'Critical Cost Analysis', technique for market definition that has been adopted and used by DOJ, FTC, and the US Court of Appeals. Has published a wide range of articles on antitrust-related topics.

SIMS, Joe
Jones Day, Washington, DC
202 879 3863
jsims@jonesday.com
Recommended in Antitrust
Practice Areas: Chairs the firm's Antitrust and Competition Law Practice. Concentrates on antitrust and related areas of government regulation, including litigation and counseling before state and federal courts and antitrust enforcement agencies. Experienced with mergers and acquisitions and the full range of antitrust issues involving technology, telecommunications, and the electronic media industries. Has been named one of the world's top 10 antitrust lawyers by Global Counsel, one of the 'Dealmakers of the Year' by The American Lawyer magazine, and is regularly recognized by other publications as one of the leading antitrust lawyers in the world.

SINEL, Norman
Arnold & Porter LLP, Washington, DC
202 942 5222
Norman.Sinel@aporter.com
Recommended in Telecom, Broadcast & Satellite
Practice Areas: Norman Sinel has practiced communications law since 1971. Experienced in development and regulation of new technologies, he has counseled communications companies, governmental agencies, and local governments on legislative issues, project development and implementation matters, franchising and licensing needs, and transactional requirements. Mr Sinel also has represented clients on administrative matters before the Federal Communications Commission.
Career: Prior to joining Arnold &

Porter LLP, he served as Senior Vice President and General Counsel of the Public Broadcasting Service.
Publications: PLI Cable Law (Annually).
Personal: LLB, Stanford Law School, 1966; BA, Yale University, 1963.

SKELLY, Paul
Hogan & Hartson LLP, Washington, DC
202 637 8614
pcskelly@hhlaw.com
Recommended in Employment
Practice Areas: Counsels on employment practices and compliance with employment law requirements; Employment litigation; Class action defense; Labor union-management relations; Noncompetition/trade secrets litigation; Union organizing campaigns, collective bargaining, and administrative proceedings before the NLRB; Executive compensation and employment agreements.
Prof. Memberships: ABA; VABA.
Career: Partner since 1988.
Publications: 'Keeping Your Executives Out of Hot Water: Protecting the CEO and Other Senior Officials from Employment Claims', Hogan & Hartson L.L.P. Managing Your People: From Hiring to Firing and Everything in Between, Hogan & Hartson L.L.P. (5/6/2004).
Personal: University of Virginia School of Law (JD, 1979); University of Virginia (BA, 1976).

SKINNER, William P
Covington & Burling, Washington, DC
202 662 5470
wskinner@cov.com
Recommended in Insurance
Practice Areas: Principal areas of practice include insurance coverage litigation, insurance advice, group captive insurers and general litigation. He has extensive experience with general liability, errors and omissions, D&O and first party-property insurance policies written on a wide variety of insurance forms, including US forms, Bermuda forms and London forms. His clients include manufacturers of industrial products, utilities, pharmaceutical companies, banks, mutual funds and other financial services companies. His insurance litigation experience includes the Armstrong Non-Products ADR, the 3M Breast Implant Litigation, the Dow Corning Breast Implant Litigation, the PSE&G environmental coverage case and the Coordinated California Asbestos Coverage Cases.
Publications: Recent publications include 'Non-Products Coverage For Asbestos-Related Bodily Injury Claims' Eurolegal Conference (May, 2002); 'Allocation Between Claims-Made and Occurrence Policies' in Vol. 10, No. 1 Coverage (ABA 2000); and 'The Mother of All Battles - The Quest For Asbestos Insurance Coverage' by Robert N Sayler and William P Skinner, in Vol. 27, No. 1

Litigation (ABA 2000).
Personal: JD, Harvard Law School, 1975, magna cum laude; BA, Harvard College, 1972.

SMALL, Michael
Wright & Talisman PC, Washington, DC
202 393 1200
Recommended in Energy

SMITH, Douglas
Van Ness Feldman PC, Washington, DC
202 298 1800
Recommended in Energy

SMITH, Paul
Jenner & Block LLP, Washington, DC
202 639 6060
psmith@jenner.com
Recommended in Litigation, Media & Entertainment
Practice Areas: Paul M Smith is the Managing Partner of Jenner & Block's Washington, DC office and a member of the firm's Management Committee. Mr Smith is also Co-Chair of the firm's Appellate and Supreme Court, and Media and First Amendment Practices. He has had an active Supreme Court practice for two decades, including oral arguments in 11 Supreme Court cases. These arguments have included, most recently, Norton v Southern Utah Wilderness Alliance, involving the enforcement of affirmative duties to protect potential wilderness areas from impairment by off-road vehicles, Vieth v Jubelirer, a congressional redistricting case, Lawrence v Texas, involving the constitutionality of the Texas sodomy statute, United States v American Library Ass'n, involving a First Amendment challenge to the Children's Internet Protection Act. His first argument was in Celotox Corp. v Catrett in 1986. He represented a group of congressional interveners in Department of Commerce v U.S. House of Representatives, involving the constitutionality of 'sampling' and the census. He also worked extensively on several other First Amendment cases in the Supreme Court, including Rubin v Coors (1995), dealing with restrictions on beer labeling, Reno v ACLU (1997), involving a challenge to content restrictions on the Internet in the Communications Decency Act, and Masson v New Yorker Magazine, Inc. (1991), a significant defamation case. Mr Smith also represents various clients in trial and appellate cases involving commercial and telecommunications issues, the First Amendment, intellectual property, antitrust, and redistricting and voting rights, among other areas.
Personal: Yale Law School, JD, 1979.

SMITH, Roger
Troutman Sanders LLP, Washington, DC 202 274 2950
Recommended in Energy

SMITH, Tefft W
Kirkland & Ellis LLP, Washington, DC
202 879 5212
tsmith@kirkland.com
Recommended in Antitrust

Practice Areas: A Senior Partner with Kirkland & Ellis, Mr Smith leads the firm's 100-person Antitrust and Competition Practice. He has 30 years of civil and criminal antitrust and merger trial experience and has led government criminal, class-action, price fixing and civil antitrust cases for US and international companies. He has managed many sensitive mergers and acquisitions through the clearance process and has expedited numerous multinational transactions, requiring coordination of EU, member-state, and other national filings. Mr Smith has appeared in many courts, including the United States Supreme Court.
Personal: Brown University, BA, 1968. University of Chicago, JD, 1971.

SMITH, Wm Randolph
Crowell & Moring LLP, Washington, DC
202 624 2700
wrsmith@crowell.com
Recommended in Antitrust

Practice Areas: Wm. Randolph Smith is a Senior Partner at Crowell & Moring, a member of the Management Board, and Chair of the firm's Antitrust Group. His practice involves mergers, acquisitions, joint ventures, trade association law, cartel enforcement and the intersection of antitrust laws and intellectual property. Recent matters include advising SBC in its proposed acquisition of AT&T Corp. and SBC/Cingular Wireless in its acquisition of AT&T Wireless. He also served as the antitrust counsel for United Technologies Corp. and its Pratt & Whitney division in the proposed acquisition of Boeing Co.'s Rocketdyne liquid space propulsion and power unit. Other principal clients include Alcoa, CSX Transportation, DuPont, and Georgia-Pacific.
Career: Prior to joining the firm in 1981, he completed six years of service with the Federal Trade Commission, where his positions included serving as executive assistant to the Chairman.

SMITH, Jr, Turner T
Hunton & Williams, Washington, DC
202 955 1692
tsmith@hunton.com
Recommended in Environment

Practice Areas: Turner Smith's international Environmental Law Practice focuses on international environmental and energy law, and involves policy, transactional and litigation work, as well as regulatory reform and US regulatory work. He is the Head of Hunton & Williams' International Environmental Practice and the former Resident Managing Partner of the firm's Brussels office, and has specialized in energy and environmental law for over 25 years.

SMOYER, Divonne
Dickstein Shapiro Morin & Oshinsky LLP, Washington, DC 202 572 2665
SmoyerD@dsmo.com
Recommended in Insurance

Practice Areas: Negotiation and litigation involving complex, multi-party disputes pertaining to asbestos, silicone implants, pharmaceutical products and other mass torts, and in insurance coverage disputes. Successfully represented policyholders in insurance disputes for directors and officers, and errors and omissions liabilities.
Career: Counsel since 2004; previously, an attorney with Kaye Scholer, LLP and Gilbert Heintz & Randolph, LLP, and a mediator with the Bickerman Dispute Resolution Group, PLLC.
Publications: Taught courses on negotiation and alternative dispute resolution at the Georgetown University Law Center and The George Washington University Law School.
Personal: Harvard Law School (JD, 1995); Smith College (BA, 1992).

SMYTHE, Marianne
Wilmer Cutler Pickering Hale and Dorr LLP, Washington, DC 202 663 6711
marianne.smythe@wilmerhale.com
Recommended in Investment Management

Practice Areas: Advises and represents banks, investment banking firms, mutual funds and other investment companies, investment advisers, pension fund administrators and insurance companies on investment company, investment adviser, and broker-dealer regulatory issues, related issues affecting banks and pension funds and other matters involving investment and financial products.
Prof. Memberships: Served as a Council Member of the American Bar Association's Section of Administrative Law and Regulatory Practice; Member, ABA Task Force on Hedge Funds. Served on the NASD Regulation's Investment Companies Committee and on the NASD's Legal Advisory Board; Member, Federal Bar Association's Executive Council and Securities Law Committee.
Career: Joined the firm in May 1993. Director, Division of Investment Management, US Securities and Exchange Commission, 1990-93; Executive Assistant to SEC Chairman Richard C Breeden; Associate Director, Division of Investment Management, 1988-90. Professor, 1981-87, and Assistant Provost, University of North Carolina at Chapel Hill School of Law.
Personal: University of North Carolina at Chapel Hill (JD 1974); Bucknell University (BS 1963).

SOHN, Michael N
Arnold & Porter LLP, Washington, DC
202 942 5000
Michael.Sohn@aporter.com
Recommended in Antitrust

Practice Areas: Mike Sohn, Chairman of Arnold & Porter LLP, maintains a substantial antitrust practice of international scope. A former General Counsel of the Federal Trade Commission, his practice encompasses a broad range of antitrust and consumer protection matters, with particular focus on the antitrust aspects of mergers and acquisitions and treble damage class-actions. He has represented such clients as Wyeth (formerly American Home Products Corporation), Boston Scientific Corporation, Brunswick Corporation, General Electric Company, Hoffmann-La Roche Inc., Homestore.com, Intel Corporation, Merck & Company, Inc., Occidental Petroleum Corporation, PepsiCo, Inc., and Sanofi-Synthelabo in merger investigations and litigations before the FTC and the Justice Department.
Career: During his tenure as General Counsel of the FTC, he was designated a Council Member of the Administrative Conference of the United States and a Member of the Executive Committee of the Regulatory Council of the United States.
Publications: Mr Sohn is a contributing author to 'The Ernst & Young Management Guide to Mergers and Acquisitions.' He has written a variety of articles of interest in the antitrust field including an overview of the Department of Justice's high profile monopolization suit entitled, 'The Microsoft Case' and an article on merger remedies entitled, 'Crown Jewel Provisions in Merger Consent Decrees.'
Personal: He has been listed as a leading lawyer in the field of antitrust by a top legal publication, and 'Chambers & Partners' 2002-03 and 2001-02 editions of 'Chambers Global' named him as one of the five top-ranked antitrust attorneys in Washington, DC. Most recently, he was also listed as a Legal Times 2005 Leading Antitrust Lawyer in Washington, DC.

SOTTILE, James
Zuckerman Spaeder LLP, Washington, DC 202 778 1800
Recommended in Insurance

SPARTIN, Debbie B
Shaw Pittman LLP, Washington, DC
202 663 8526
debbie.spartin@shawpittman.com
Recommended in Real Estate

Practice Areas: Debbie Spartin represents a wide variety of clients with respect to all facets of commercial real estate, including acquisition, disposition, exchange, development, financing, leasing and build-to-suit transactions, involving all types of real estate.
Prof. Memberships: American Bar Association, District of Columbia Building Industry Association, The Real Estate Group of Washington, DC.
Publications: New Code on Old Cabling: Something to Untangle, Washington Business Journal, July 9, 2004.
Personal: Harvard Law School (JD, 1987); University of Virginia (BA, 1984).

SPECTOR, Barry
Wright & Talisman PC, Washington, DC
202 393 1200
Recommended in Energy

SPECTOR, Phillip
Paul, Weiss, Rifkind, Wharton & Garrison, Washington, DC 202 223 7300
Recommended in Telecom, Broadcast & Satellite

SPIVAK, Mark
Vinson & Elkins LLP, Washington, DC
202 639 6664
mspivak@velaw.com
Recommended in Projects

Practice Areas: Development, financing and restructuring of US and overseas infrastructure projects, including energy, telecommunications and other infrastructure and industrial projects. Mergers, acquisitions and dispositions of infrastructure assets, and companies owning infrastructure assets. Advise clients in connection with obtaining political risk insurance from multilateral institutions and private insurers.
Prof. Memberships: District of Columbia Bar.
Career: Partner at V&E since 1994.
Personal: Georgetown University Law Center (JD, 1983); Muhlenberg College (BA, 1980).

STAMAS, George
Kirkland & Ellis LLP, Washington, DC
202 879 5090
gstamas@kirkland.com
Recommended in Corporate/Commercial

Practice Areas: Mr Stamas is a Senior Partner of Kirkland & Ellis LLP, dividing his time between the Washington, DC and New York offices. For the past two decades, Mr Stamas has been the lead legal advisor on numerous public and private corporate transactions, including most recently the $1.6 billion management buyout of DB Capital Partners, the largest private equity secondary, as well as corporate transactions for numerous leading companies and financial institutions such as Constellation Energy Group and NEA.
Personal: University of Pennsylvania, BS, 1973; University of Maryland School of Law, JD, 1976.

STANDISH, Daniel
Wiley Rein & Fielding LLP, Washington, DC 202 719 7000
Recommended in Insurance

STARR, Judson
Venable LLP, Washington, DC
202 962 4800
Recommended in Environment

STARR, Kenneth W
Kirkland & Ellis LLP, Los Angeles
213 680 8440
kstarr@kirkland.com
Recommended in Litigation
Practice Areas: Joined Kirkland & Ellis in February 1993. In August 1994, he was appointed Independent Counsel on the Whitewater matter and served until October 1999. From May 27, 1989 to January 20, 1993, he served as Solicitor General of the United States, where he argued 25 cases before the Supreme Court involving a wide range of governmental regulatory and constitutional issues of commercial importance. Prior to that, he served as a United States Circuit Judge appointed on October 11, 1983.
Personal: Brown University, AM, 1969. George Washington University, AB, 1968. Duke Law School, JD, 1973.

STEINBERG, Michael W
Morgan, Lewis & Bockius LLP, Washington, DC 202 739 5141
msteinberg@morganlewis.com
Recommended in Environment
Practice Areas: Michael Steinberg is senior counsel in the Litigation Practice. His practice focuses exclusively on environmental law matters, with special emphasis on litigation and counseling involving (1) hazardous waste issues under the Resource Conservation and Recovery Act, (2) liability, cleanup, and enforcement issues under the federal Superfund program, and (3) environmental justice issues under federal and state civil rights laws. Mr Steinberg rejoined Morgan Lewis after serving as Assistant Chief of the Environmental Defense Section at the US Department of Justice, where he supervised and handled litigation against EPA under all of the federal environmental statutes.
Prof. Memberships: American Bar Association; District of Columbia Bar Association.
Career: Mr Steinberg was Assistant Chief of the Environmental Defense Section at the US Department of Justice, where he supervised and handled litigation against EPA under all of the federal environmental statutes.

STEPHENSON, Andrew
Holland & Knight LLP, Washington, DC
202 955 3000
andrew.stephenson@hklaw.com
Recommended in Construction
Practice Areas: Partner in charge of the Construction Industry Practice Group, practices in the areas of construction and labor law, representing owners, architect-engineers, general contractors, and construction managers in virtually all phases of the private and public sectors of the industry. Stephenson's construction experience covers the drafting and negotiation of construction contract documents, counsel during project administration, and dispute resolution on a wide-range of both medium size

and large, complex building and infrastructure projects including billion dollar design-build projects. He also has been involved in the construction of numerous power generation facilities, including both nuclear and fossil fuel power plants.

STERNE, Robert
Sterne, Kessler, Goldstein & Fox P.L.L.C., Washington, DC
202 772 8555
rsterne@skgf.com
Recommended in Intellectual Property
Practice Areas: Specializes in intellectual property issues in the electronics and computer arenas as well as the monetization of patents and patent licensing.
Prof. Memberships: Admitted to practice in Maryland (1977); Maryland Court of Appeals (1977); US Court of Claims (1978); US Court of Appeals for the District of Columbia (1980); US District Court for the District of Maryland (1981); US Court of Appeals for the Federal Circuit (1993); US District Court for the District of Columbia (2001); US Supreme Court (2002). Member of American Bar Association (1977); Maryland State Bar Association (1977); Bar Association of Baltimore City (1979); AIPLA (1979); The District of Columbia Bar Association (1980); Licensing Executives Society (2003).
Career: Founding Partner, Director of Sterne, Kessler, Goldstein & Fox P.L.L.C. and its predecessor firms. Internationally recognized as a thought leader and an expert on software and business method patents having been lead attorney for IBM in the Federal Circuit case that led to the USPTO Software Patent Guidelines.
Publications: Most recent publications co-authored include: 'Why directors must take responsibility for intellectual property', Robert Sterne and Trevor Chaplick, Intellectual Asset Management Magazine, February/March 2005 'Business method patents for financial products and services', Robert Greene Sterne, Michael Q. Lee and Richard M. Libman, IP Value 2005 'The 2005 U.S. Patent Landscape For Electronic Companies', Robert Greene Sterne, Michael Q. Lee, Patrick E Garrett, Michael V Messinger and Donald R Banowit, Course Handbook from Computer & Internet Law (25th Annual) program, March 2005.
Personal: Born 15 November 1951. LLM Candidate (course work only) George Washington University Law School (1979-83); JD (with honors) University of Maryland (1977); MS Tufts University (1975); BS Electrical Engineering, Tufts University (1973); FCC Extra Class License-WK3W.

STOLL, Richard G
Foley & Lardner, Washington, DC
202 295 4021
rstoll@foley.com
Recommended in Environment
Career: Richard G Stoll is a Partner in the Washington, DC office of Foley & Lardner and a member of the firm's Regulatory Department. Mr Stoll concentrates his practice on federal administrative and environmental law matters. He counsels corporations and trade associations on environmental issues before the US Environmental Protection Agency (EPA) and state environmental agencies. He also handles a variety of administrative, rulemaking, and judicial review matters in the fields of intellectual property, healthcare, and environmental law. He has frequently litigated in the DC Circuit and other federal courts regarding agency rulemakings and other actions.

STONE, Steven W
Morgan, Lewis & Bockius LLP, Washington, DC 202 739 5453
sstone@morganlewis.com
Recommended in Investment Management
Practice Areas: Steven W Stone leads the Investment Management/Securities Industry Practice at Morgan Lewis and serves as Managing Partner of the Washington office. His practice focuses on broker-dealer and investment manager regulation and enforcement defense and securities markets regulation. He has extensive experience in all aspects of broker-dealer and investment management regulation, representing major investment banks, broker-dealers and investment managers in a broad range of matters. Mr Stone serves as counsel to the private wealth management businesses of several Wall Street firms, and the trading desks of major broker-dealers and investment managers on complex trading issues.

STRAND, Margaret
Venable LLP, Washington, DC
202 962 4800
Recommended in Environment

SULLIVAN, Brendan
Williams & Connolly LLP, Washington, DC 202 434 5000
Recommended in Litigation

SULLIVAN, Kevin
King & Spalding LLP, Washington, DC
202 626 2624
krsullivan@kslaw.com
Recommended in Antitrust
Practice Areas: Defends and prosecutes antitrust civil cases from initiation through trial and appeal, and provides counseling services to clients on antitrust and telecommunications issues. Extensive experience in international antitrust matters and has coordinated merger approvals and responses to foreign government antitrust investigations.

Prof. Memberships: District of Columbia Bar; Pennsylvania Bar; Bar of the United States Supreme Court.
Personal: BA, Gannon University, 1971; JD, Catholic University, 1975.

SULLIVAN, Mary Anne
Hogan & Hartson LLP, Washington, DC
202 637 3695
masullivan@hhlaw.com
Recommended in Energy
Practice Areas: Electricity, alternative energy technologies and climate change, Department of Energy contracts/grants, nuclear issues, and energy class action defense.
Prof. Memberships: District of Columbia Bar Association (Energy and Environment Section); Department of Energy Contractor Attorneys Association (Board of Directors).
Career: 1984-93 and since 2001, Partner, Hogan & Hartson; 1998-2001, general counsel, US Department of Energy; 1994-98, deputy general counsel for Environment & Nuclear Programs, DOE; 2004, Senior Lecturer at Law at Duke University Law School, teaching energy law.
Publications: 'Kyoto Protocol Enters into Force February 16, 2005', Climate Change Update, Hogan & Hartson (2/16/2005); 'The Hard Realities of Energy Policy in an Election Year', Electric Light & Power (9/1/2004); 'Standard Market Design: What Went Wrong? What Next?', The Electricity Journal (7/1/2003).
Personal: Yale Law School (JD, 1976); Fordham University (BA, summa cum laude, 1973).

SULLIVAN, Michael
Levine Sullivan Koch & Schulz LLP, Washington, DC 202 508 1100
Recommended in Media & Entertainment

SULLIVAN, T J
Gardner Carton & Douglas LLP, Washington, DC 202 230 5157
tsullivan@gcd.com
Recommended in Healthcare
Practice Areas: Healthcare, tax Partner; represents clients in corporate, tax, regulatory matters; formerly Special Assistant (Healthcare) to the Internal Revenue Service Assistant Commissioner (Employee Plans and Exempt Organizations), where he concentrated in matters involving tax treatment of hospitals, HMOs, other tax-exempt organizations; coordinated development of Service positions on healthcare matters, advised field agents during examinations, co-chaired Exempt Organizations Health Care/College and University Industry Specialization Program ("ISP") team; served on White House Task Force on Health Reform (1993); Founding Director, General Counsel, Coalition for Nonprofit Health Care.
Prof. Memberships: Board of Directors, American Health Lawyers Association

(1995-2001); Chair, Tax Issues Program Committee, American Health Lawyers Association; Co-Chair, Health Care Subcommittee, Committee on Exempt Organizations, American Bar Association Tax Section; Editorial Advisory Board, BNA's Health Law Reporter; Editorial Advisory Board, The Exempt Organization Tax Review.

Career: Prior to joining IRS, private practitioner in health law; evaluated federal health policies with US General Accounting Office.

Publications: Frequent author, lecturer on tax, healthcare issues.

Personal: George Washington University, JD, 1985, Graduated with Honors; Georgetown University Law Center, LLM, 1991, Graduated with Distinction; West Virginia University, 1979, Masters of Public Administration; Salem College, BA, 1977.

SUNDBACK, Mark
Andrews Kurth LLP, Washington, DC
202 662 2755
msundback@andrewskurth.com
Recommended in Energy

Practice Areas: Representations have focused on the rates, terms and conditions associated with gaining access to regulated energy transmission systems, transactions involving changes in ownership of jurisdictional assets, and unbundling matters. Particularly, Mark's practice includes a wide array of issues under the Federal Power Act, the Natural Gas Act, and related federal and state statutes involving the regulation of energy industry participants.

Prof. Memberships: District of Columbia Bar; Federal Energy Bar Association

Career: Mark is a Partner in the Energy Section of the Washington, DC office. Since 1981 he has been extensively engaged in the representation of energy industry participants before federal and state agencies charged with jurisdiction over energy markets and their participants.

Personal: Mark received his JD from Columbia University in 1981, editor, Columbia Journal of Transnational Law. He received his BA, magna cum laude, from Dickinson College in 1978.

SUNSHINE, Steven
Cadwalader, Wickersham & Taft LLP,
Washington, DC 202 862 2200
Recommended in Antitrust

SUSSMAN, Robert
Latham & Watkins LLP,
Washington, DC 202 637 2200
Recommended in Environment

SWENSON, David
Baker & McKenzie, Washington, DC
202 452 7000
Recommended in Tax

SYMONS, Howard
Mintz Levin Cohn Ferris Glovsky and Popeo PC, Washington, DC
202 434 7300
Recommended in Telecom, Broadcast & Satellite

TAGER, Evan
Mayer, Brown, Rowe & Maw LLP,
Washington, DC 202 263 3240
etager@mayerbrownrowe.com
Recommended in Litigation

Practice Areas: Appellate litigation. Areas of expertise include punitive damages, constitutional and procedural limitations on class actions, limiting expert testimony, enforcement of arbitration provisions, and the dormant Commerce Clause.

Career: Mayer, Brown, Rowe & Maw LLP, Washington, DC., 1988 to present; Partner, 1994. Weil, Gotshal & Manges, Washington, DC, 1986-88. Law Clerk to The Honorable Mary M Schroeder, US Court of Appeals for the Ninth Circuit, Phoenix, Arizona, 1985-86.

Publications: Recent publications: 'The Implications of State Farm v Campbell for the Future of Punitive Damages in Bad Faith Litigation,' Mealey's Litigation Report: Insurance Bad Faith, Apr. 22, 2003, at 28. 'The Constitutional Limitations on Class Actions,' Mealey's Litigation Report: Class Actions, Jan. 2001, at 34. 'Punitive Damages Claims in Environmental Tort Cases: Lessons from Johansen v Combustion Engineering, Inc.,' 29 Environmental Law Reports 10196 (Mar. 2000). 'Tips on Preserving Arguments for Appeal,' Mealey's Insurance Law Weekly, December 1, 1998, at 18. 'Punitive Damages After BMW of North America, Inc. v Gore,' Mealeys Litigation Report: Bad Faith, Sept. 10, 1997, at 14.

Personal: JD, Stanford Law School, 1985; articles editor, Law Review. BA (magna cum laude), Princeton University, 1982.

TALADAY, John
Howrey Simon Arnold & White,
Washington, DC 202 783 0800
Recommended in Antitrust

TARANTO, Richard
Farr & Taranto, Washington, DC
202 775 0184
Recommended in Litigation

TAUB, Kathy
Arent Fox PLLC, Washington, DC
202 857 6000
Recommended in Construction

TAYLOR, John
Mayer, Brown, Rowe & Maw LLP,
Chicago 312 701 7151
jdtaylor@mayerbrown.com
Recommended in Projects

Practice Areas: Represents a variety of financial institutions, including export credit agencies, multilateral institutions and commercial lenders in project finance transactions. Representative transactions include the restructuring of a $2.5 billion financing of a power project (Indonesia), the rescheduling of a $1.7 billion financing of a power project (Indonesia), a $2.2 billion financing of a copper/zinc mining project (Peru), a $400 million financing of a power project (Mexico), a $400 million financing of an ammonia plant (Egypt), a $226 million financing of a natural gas pipeline (Mexico) and a $70 million financing of a hydroelectric project (Mexico).

Prof. Memberships: Illinois, 1994. District of Columbia, 1996.

Career: Mayer, Brown, Rowe & Maw LLP, Chicago, 1998 to date; Partner, 2004. International Finance Corporation, Washington, DC, 1997-98.

Personal: University of Virginia, School of Law, JD, 1994; Articles Review Board, Virginia Journal of International Law. Georgetown University, School of Foreign Service, BSFS cum laude, 1989.

TELL, Gary
O'Melveny & Myers LLP,
Washington, DC 202 383 5300
Recommended in Employee Benefits

TERR, Leonard
Baker & McKenzie, Washington, DC
202 452 7087
leonard.b.terr@bakernet.com
Recommended in Tax

Practice Areas: Mr Terr has over 25 years' experience representing US and foreign based multinationals, foreign governments, international organizations and trade associations in all phases of international tax practice. Mr Terr's practice includes tax planning for multi-country restructurings, mergers and acquisitions, divestitures and tax minimization strategies involving companies in the automotive, aerospace, consumer products, electronics, insurance, natural resources, pharmaceutical, services, telecommunications and other industries; securing Advance Pricing Agreements; providing comments and testimony on pending tax treaties and proposed regulations; and obtaining favorable settlements in Exam, Appeals or Competent Authority of tax controversies involving most European, Asia-Pacific and North American treaty jurisdictions.

Prof. Memberships: Mr Terr is a Member of the International Fiscal Association and was US National Reporter. He sits on the American Bar Association Tax Section's Foreign Activities of US Taxpayers Committee and has served as Chairman of the Section 367 Subcommittee and chaired the Source Subcommittee. Mr Terr serves on the Tax Sections Task Force on Global Tax Policy. He has chaired the Washington International Tax Study Group since 1990.

Career: Mr Terr served as International Tax Counsel of the US Treasury Department from 1987-89. He headed the US delegation in the negotiation of the current US-Germany tax treaty, in addition to over a dozen other US tax treaties and protocols. He directed Treasury's work on international tax legislation and regulations, the transfer pricing White Paper and other US and OECD international tax policy initiatives. He served as Law Clerk to Chief Judge Wilson Cowen of the US Court of Appeals for the Federal Circuit. He is an Adjunct Professor of International Tax Law at the Georgetown University Law Center.

Personal: Mr Terr holds an AB from LaSalle College, an AM and PhD from Brown University and a JD from Cornell University. He served as Law Clerk to Chief Judge Wilson Cowen of the US Court of Appeals for the Federal Circuit.

THOMPSON, Carolyn
Jones Day, Washington, DC
202 879 5426
carolynthompson@jonesday.com
Recommended in Energy

Practice Areas: Represents electric and gas utilities and gas pipelines before the Federal Energy Regulatory Commission. She has participated in numerous ratemaking and rulemaking proceedings on behalf of interstate pipelines, intrastate pipelines, local distribution companies, investor-owned electric utilities, and cogenerators. She has assisted clients with drafting tariffs, precedent agreements, and contracts. She has represented clients in enforcement matters at the FERC and has represented electric utilities at the Department of Energy in securing presidential permits and export authorizations for the export of electricity across international borders. She is articles editor for the 'Energy Law Journal.'

Prof. Memberships: Energy Bar Association.

THOMPSON, Gary
Gilbert Heintz & Randolph LLP,
Washington, DC 202 772 2225
Recommended in Insurance

THOMPSON, Michael
Wright & Talisman PC, Washington, DC
202 393 1200
Recommended in Energy

TILLMAN, Eugene
Reed Smith LLP, Washington, DC
202 414 9244
etillman@reedsmith.com
Recommended in Healthcare

Practice Areas: Counsels hospitals and other institutional and alternate site providers, manufacturers of pharmaceuticals and medical devices, pharmacy benefits, managers, retail drug chains, mail order and other specialty pharmacies, and healthcare professional and trade associations. Concentrates on Medicare and Medicaid payment and coverage issues, acquisitions and provider integration issues, and licensing and regulatory matters.

Prof. Memberships: Past President, American Health Lawyers Association; member of California and DC Bar Associations.
Career: Four years in the Department of Health and Human Services.
Personal: University of California at Los Angeles School of Law (JD, 1976); UCLA (1973).

TOBEY, Margaret
Morrison & Foerster LLP, Washington, DC 202 887 6935
mtobey@mofo.com
Recommended in Telecom, Broadcast & Satellite

Practice Areas: Focuses on domestic and international communications matters, including licensing, regulatory compliance, transactions and litigation involving radio and television stations (both commercial and non-commercial), direct broadcast satellite operators, common carriers, fiber optic network operators, providers of new technology services, equipment manufacturers and lenders to the communications industry.
Prof. Memberships: Former President (2001-02), President-Elect (2000-01), and Secretary (1999-2000), Federal Communications Bar Association (FCBA), leading professional organization for communications attorneys. Previously served an elected three-year term on its Executive Committee and as Chair of FCBA Foundation.
Career: Admitted to practice in District of Columbia.
Personal: BA (1974), MA (1980), University of Iowa; JD, with high distinction, University of Iowa College of Law, 1980, editor-in-chief, Iowa Law Review (1979-80).

TOBIN, Charles D
Holland & Knight LLP, Washington, DC 202 955 3000
charles.tobin@hklaw.com
Recommended in Media & Entertainment

Practice Areas: Partner in the firm's National Media Law Team. A former journalist, Tobin has appeared in state and federal courts around the country at the trial and appellate levels. He also conducts pre-publication review for newsrooms; provides journalists with advice on subpoenas, access, and freedom of information matters; and advises commercial clients on unfair competition claims. Tobin spent eight years as inhouse counsel at Gannett Co., Inc., which publishes 'USA TODAY' and owns newspapers and television stations throughout the country. He is editor-in-chief of the ABA publication 'LITIGATION' and chairs the DC Bar Media Law Committee.

TRAGER, Michael D
Arnold & Porter LLP, Washington, DC 202 942 6976
Michael.Trager@aporter.com
Recommended in Corporate/Commercial

Practice Areas: Partner in the Washington, DC office of Arnold & Porter LLP. Mr Trager heads the firm's Securities Enforcement Practice and represents a wide array of clients, including public companies, broker-dealers, investment advisers, hedge funds, accounting firms, financial institutions, and individuals. Mr Trager's practice, which is international in scope and includes many high profile matters, involves defending investigations conducted by the Securities and Exchange Commission, Department of Justice, other federal agencies, Congress, NASD, NYSE, and state regulators. He also conducts internal investigations, defends securities litigation, and counsels on compliance, crisis management, corporate governance, and disclosure matters.
Prof. Memberships: Mr Trager is a member of several bar associations and committees and has served on Task Forces established by the American Bar Association and District of Columbia Bar.
Career: Mr Trager has two decades of private practice experience devoted exclusively to securities enforcement matters. Prior to entering private practice, he served as an attorney in the SEC's Division of Enforcement in Washington, DC, where he conducted investigations and represented the government in litigation.
Publications: Mr Trager has authored numerous publications and spoken frequently on SEC enforcement issues.

TRITT, Cheryl
Morrison & Foerster LLP, Washington, DC 202 887 1510
ctritt@mofo.com
Recommended in Telecom, Broadcast & Satellite

Practice Areas: Advises a wide range of telecommunications firms, focusing on wireless, satellite, multimedia and international issues. Focuses on advising clients on regulatory implications of emerging technologies and transactional matters, including mergers, acquisitions, stock spin-offs and new business ventures.
Prof. Memberships: Member American Bar Association, Federal Communications Bar Association.
Career: Admitted to practice in District of Columbia and Illinois. Joined the firm in 1993, after serving as Chief of the Common Carrier Bureau, Federal Communications Commission. Co-Head of firm's Communications Practice.
Personal: BS, cum laude, Phi Beta Kappa, University of Nebraska; MS, Journalism, Northwestern University; JD, cum laude, Northwestern University School of Law, 1976.

TUCKER, Stefan
Venable LLP, Washington, DC 202 962 4800
Recommended in Real Estate

TUOHEY, Mark H
Vinson & Elkins LLP, Washington, DC 202 639 6660
mtuohey@velaw.com
Recommended in Litigation

Practice Areas: Complex civil and white collar litigation; internal investigations; representation of corporate corporations and their officers and directors in regulatory investigations and litigation.
Prof. Memberships: DC Bar (President 1993-94); American Bar Association; Fellow, American College of Trial Lawyers.
Career: Admitted to DC Bar, 1973; New York, 1981; former Assistant US Attorney, DC 1973-77; Special Counsel to Attorney General, 1978-79; Principal Deputy Independent Counsel, 1994-95.
Publications: Frequent author and lecturer on trial advocacy, legal ethics and white collar litigation.
Personal: Chair, DC Sports & Entertainment Commission 2003-. Mark and his wife Marty live in Washington, DC.

TYLE, Craig
Shearman & Sterling, Washington, DC 202 508 8100
craig.tyle@shearman.com
Recommended in Investment Management

Practice Areas: Partner in Shearman & Sterling's Asset Management Group.
Prof. Memberships: Member of the American Bar Association, Member of the Association of the Bar of the City of New York, Member of NASDAQ Quality of Markets Committee through the end of 2003 (served as Co-Chairman in 2003).
Career: Investment Company Institute, 1988-2004 (served as General Counsel 1997-2004).
Publications: Co-author, 'Mutual Funds, Investment Advisers and the National Securities Markets Improvement Act', 52 The Business Lawyer 419 (February 1997).
Personal: BA with high honors, Swarthmore College (1982); JD, magna cum laude, Harvard Law School (1985).

UNTEREINER, Alan
Robbins, Russell, Englert, Orseck & Untereiner LLP, Washington, DC 202 775 4500
Recommended in Litigation

VARDAMAN, John
Williams & Connolly LLP, Washington, DC 202 434 5000
Recommended in Litigation

VARNEY, Christine
Hogan & Hartson LLP, Washington, DC 202 637 6823
cvarney@hhlaw.com
Recommended in Antitrust

Practice Areas: Practice provides full service assistance to companies doing business globally, including providing advice on antitrust, privacy, business planning and corporate governance, intellectual property, and general liability issues.
Prof. Memberships: Chair, Committee on Election Law, ABA (1998-2000); ABA, Antitrust Section (1986-present); (District of Columbia Bar Association (1986-present); Secretary/Treasurer, Vice-President's Residence Foundation (1997-2000) National Lawyers' Council (1985-present).
Career: Federal Trade Commissioner (1994-97). Prior to becoming a federal trade commissioner, Christine was an assistant to the president and secretary to the Cabinet. She also served as Chief Counsel to the Clinton/Gore Campaign, general counsel to the 1992 Presidential Inaugural Committee, and general counsel to the Democratic National Committee from 1989-92.
Publications: She regularly contributes to a variety of publications, including Newsweek, Antitrust Magazine, and Wired.
Personal: Georgetown University Law Center (JD); Syracuse University (MPA); State University of New York at Albany (BS).

VASILE, James
Davis Wright Tremaine LLP, Washington, DC 202 508 6662
jamesvasile@dwt.com
Recommended in Energy

Practice Areas: Partner, energy law. Practice emphasizes federal regulation of electric power industry, FERC regulation of independent power producers, hydroelectric project licensing, and SEC regulation of public utility holding company systems. Representative experience includes regulation and development of independent power projects under Federal Power Act, and licensing and regulation of holding company systems under Public Utility Holding Company Act.
Prof. Memberships: Member, District of Columbia Bar and American Bar Association.
Career: Joined firm as Partner, 2001. Former Partner, Steptoe & Johnson LLP. Former Chair, Energy Bar Association, Hydroelectric Regulation Committee.
Personal: JD, Georgetown University, 1974. BA, Physics, Rutgers University, 1966.

VERRILLI, Donald B
Jenner & Block LLP, Washington, DC 202 639 6095
dverrilli@jenner.com
Recommended in Litigation, Telecom, Broadcast & Satellite

Practice Areas: Donald B Verrilli, Jr serves as Chair of the firm's Telecommunications Practice, and Co-Chair of Appellate and Supreme Court Practice. He is a member of the firm's Policy Committee. Mr Verrilli has argued

numerous cases before the United States Supreme Court, including General Dynamics Land Systems v Cline, a case in which the Court ruled that the Age Discrimination in Employment Act does not authorize 'reverse discrimination' suits, FCC v NextWave Personal Communications, a case in which the Court returned to NextWave billions of dollars worth of wireless phone spectrum licenses that the FCC had sought to repossess from NextWave while it was in bankruptcy, and Verizon Communications v FCC, the most recent case arising out of the Telecommunications Act of 1996. On a pro bono basis, he successfully defended the right to effective counsel in Wiggins v Smith. As part of his First Amendment practice, Mr Verrilli successfully represented the National Association of Broadcasters in a case involving a First Amendment challenge to the compulsory copyright provisions of the Satellite Home Viewer Improvement Act. He was counsel to NAB in Turner Broadcasting System v FCC, the landmark case upholding the must-carry provisions of the 1992 Cable Act. He was counsel in Reno v American Civil Liberties Union, the Supreme Court decision establishing the First Amendment rights of internet speakers. Mr Verrilli also represents the Recording Industry Association of America on matters arising out of the Digital Millennium Copyright Act.
Personal: Columbia University School of Law, JD, 1983.

VERVEER, Philip L
Willkie Farr & Gallagher LLP, Washington, DC 202 303 1117
pverveer@willkie.com
Recommended in Telecom, Broadcast & Satellite
Practice Areas: Partner in the Telecommunications Department, specializing in communications, antitrust, and administrative law. Provides counseling and administrative agency representation to a variety of communications clients. An internationally recognized authority in antitrust and communications law. Significant matters in 2004 include serving as regulatory counsel to Sprint Corp. in its $35 billion merger with Nextel Communications Inc.
Prof. Memberships: Admitted to the Bar of the District of Columbia. Member of the Federal Communications Bar Association and the American Bar Association.
Career: From 1969-77, served as a trial attorney in the Department of Justice's Antitrust Division, where he was the first lead counsel in the investigation and prosecution that led to the Bell System divestiture. Also served as a supervisory attorney in the Federal Trade Commission's Bureau of Competition from 1977 to 1978. Between 1978-81, was Chief of the Federal Communication Commission's Cable Television Bureau,

Broadcast Bureau, and Common Carrier Bureau. Served as Chairman of the Federal Public Safety Wireless Advisory Committee and as US Representative to the INTELSAT Panel of Legal Experts. Was a charter member of the US Government Senior Executive Service. In 1980, received the Distinguished Presidential Rank Award, one of the highest awards given to federal government employees. In 1996, received the Cellular Telecommunications Industry Association President's Award.
Personal: Received a JD from the University of Chicago in 1969 and a BSFS from Georgetown University in 1966.

VICKERY, Ann Morgan
Hogan & Hartson LLP, Washington, DC 202 637 8605
amvickery@hhlaw.com
Recommended in Healthcare
Practice Areas: Represents manufacturers, associations, and providers of various healthcare products and services; counsels clients regarding the impact of payment policies on their businesses, with particular emphasis on federal government regulation.
Prof. Memberships: ABA; American Health Lawyers Association; National Hospice Foundation (Trustee).
Career: 1978-present, Hogan & Hartson, currently managing partner of the Washington, DC, office and Health Practice Director; 1975-78, US Secretary of the Treasury staff; 1969-74, White House researcher and staff assistant.
Publications: Speaks and writes on Medicare and Medicaid reimbursement, legislative developments, and trends in healthcare. Publications and presentations include: 'A Washington Lawyer's View of National Health Policy,' Health Policy Institute Lecture Series, University of Pittsburgh (September 17, 2003); 'Reimbursement and Coverage for New Technology,' seminar at Stanford University sponsored by Hogan & Hartson and the California Healthcare Institute (December 8, 1997); 'When Staff Object to Participating in Care' (with Anne M Dellinger), 28 Journal of Health and Hospital Law 269 (1995).
Personal: Georgetown University Law Center (JD, 1978); Mary Baldwin College (AB, 1965); Woman of the Year, National Hospice and Palliative Care Organization, 1986.

VILLA, John
Williams & Connolly LLP, Washington, DC 202 434 5000
Recommended in Litigation

VODRA, William
Arnold & Porter LLP, Washington, DC 202 942 5088
William.Vodra@aporter.com
Recommended in Healthcare
Practice Areas: William Vodra specializes in regulatory issues involving the safety, effectiveness, and marketing of medical products and in crisis manage-

ment. He has led teams defending embattled products and has successfully represented corporations and individuals in white-collar criminal, product liability, and unfair competition cases.
Prof. Memberships: Food and Drug Law Institute; Drug Information Association; American Bar Association.
Career: Prior to joining Arnold & Porter LLP, Mr Vodra served as the Associate Chief Counsel at the Food and Drug Administration and Assistant Chief Counsel at the Drug Enforcement Agency.
Publications: Most recently are: 'Do Users Fees Compromise the Integrity of the FDA?,' Regulatory Affairs J. (Pharma), 2004; 'Anchors Away: FDA's Use of Disgorgement Abandons Legal Moorings,' Food & Drug, 2004; 'Proposal to Revise Drug Safety Reporting Rules Will Increase Manufacturers' Legal Obligations,' Regulatory Affairs J. (Pharma), 2003; 'Being Prepared,' A Practical Guide to Food and Drug Regulation, 2nd Edition, 2002; ''Did He Really Say That?' Survey Evidence in Deceptive Advertising Litigation,' The Trademark Reporter, 2002; 'How to Write Letters to FDA,' How to Work with the FDA, 2000.
Personal: JD, Columbia Law School, 1968; BA, College of Wooster, 1965.

VOLLMANN, Alan
Holland & Knight LLP, Washington, DC 202 955 3000
alan.vollmann@hklaw.com
Recommended in Real Estate
Practice Areas: Mr Vollmann has handled many complex real estate transactions on behalf of foreign and domestic institutional owners and investors, most recently, representation of the bond underwriter for the US Patent and Trademark Office, the Kingdom of Sweden in the development of its new embassy, and Johns Hopkins University in the development of its Montgomery County campus. Vollmann is an adjunct professor of the Berman Real Estate Institute, Johns Hopkins University and has taught Land Transactions at Catholic University Law School. Vollmann is a 1980 graduate of Catholic University Law School, where he was editor-in-chief of the Law Review.

WADLOW, R Clark
Sidley Austin Brown & Wood LLP, Washington, DC 202 736 8215
rwadlow@sidley.com
Recommended in Telecom, Broadcast & Satellite
Practice Areas: Clark Wadlow heads the firm's Communications Group and represents a broad range of communications clients in connection with their corporate, regulatory and industry issues.
Prof. Memberships: He has served on numerous committees of the American Bar Association, including the Governing Committee of the Forum on Com-

munications Law, which he chaired from 1987-89, and the Standing Committee on the Continuing Education of the Bar, which he has chaired from 1993-98. He was a Member-at-Large on the Association's Board of Governors. Mr Wadlow served as President of the Federal Communications Bar Association in 1997-98.
Career: Mr Wadlow served as law clerk to the Honorable George F Boney, Chief Justice of the Supreme Court of Alaska. Harvard Law School, JD, 1971; Dartmouth College, AB, 1968. Admitted: US Supreme Court, 1974; DC and Alaska District Courts, 1971; DC Bar, 1972.
Publications: He is a frequent lecturer and author, focusing on current developments in communications regulation and policy.

WAHLE, Karen
O'Melveny & Myers LLP, Washington, DC 202 383 5300
Recommended in Employee Benefits

WALD, Douglas
Arnold & Porter LLP, Washington, DC 202 942 5112
Douglas.Wald@aporter.com
Recommended in Antitrust
Practice Areas: Specializes in antitrust and trade regulation, and general litigation. Since joining the firm, his experience has involved a broad range of antitrust matters, including counseling, private litigation (including federal class actions), and representation before governmental agencies. He has advised clients on matters involving marketing, pricing, and distribution restrictions (Sherman Act 1), price discrimination (Robinson-Patman Act), monopolization (Sherman Act 2), and joint ventures and acquisitions (Clayton Act 7). He has also represented clients on appellate matters such as 3M Company v Browner, 17 F.3d 1453 (D.C. Cir. 1994) (applicability of federal statute of limitations to agency civil penalty proceedings).
Career: Prior to joining Arnold & Porter LLP in 1980, he clerked for Judge William H Timbers on the US Court of Appeals for the Second Circuit.
Personal: He graduated in 1979 from Harvard Law School (JD), and was an editor of the 'Harvard Law Review.' He received an AB from Harvard College in 1975.

WALSH, Linda
Hunton & Williams, Washington, DC 202 955 1526
lwalsh@hunton.com
Recommended in Energy
Practice Areas: Linda Walsh's practice focuses on regulatory matters affecting electric utilities, particularly in industry restructuring, rates and administrative litigation. FERC counsel to a stand alone transmission company, providing ongoing representation in transmission rate proceedings, negotiating generator interconnection agreements and provid-

ing general regulatory advice on transmission and RTO formation issues; prepared initial FERC filings to establish a transmission tariff and rates for the newly formed transco; obtained FPA Section 204 authorizations for the issuance of debt, prepared Section 203 filings for the acquisition of facilities, and prepared Section 205 filings for approval of incentive rate treatments.

WARD, Erica A
Skadden, Arps, Slate, Meagher & Flom LLP & Affiliates, Washington, DC
202 371 7050
eward@skadden.com
Recommended in Projects
Practice Areas: Advises on development, construction and financing, as well as acquisition and sale, of major industrial facilities throughout the world, with emphasis on electric power projects. Represents utility companies and their unregulated subsidiaries, independent power companies, commercial lenders, investment banks, and equity investors in project finance and utility transactions. Experience includes transactions involving construction and long-term debt instruments, equity/debt syndications, leveraged leases, public and private securities offerings, guarantees, support obligations, municipal bond financings, international agency financings and interest rate swaps.
Career: JD, University of Michigan Law School, 1975 (managing editor, 'Michigan Law Review'); BA, Stanford University, 1972.

WARIN, Roger
Steptoe & Johnson LLP,
Washington, DC 202 429 6280
rwarin@steptoe.com
Recommended in Insurance
Practice Areas: Head of the Litigation Department and Partner in the Washington office of Steptoe & Johnson LLP. Lead counsel in numerous major nationwide insurance coverage disputes involving asbestos, toxic substances, and environmental claims. Recognized as one of the leading legal malpractice defense lawyers. Successfully handled a wide range of complex commercial litigation cases involving securities fraud, the Racketeer Influenced and Corrupt Organizations Act, libel, trademark, products liability, directors' and officers' liability, employment discrimination, attorneys' fees, First Amendment, legal malpractice and other professional liability, negligence, real estate, surety, construction, environmental, toxic tort, and insurance coverage claims. Also a successful appellate advocate, having argued more than 20 cases in various federal circuit courts of appeals and state supreme courts.
Personal: JD, Georgetown University, 1970; AB, Creighton University, 1967.

WARREN, Edward W
Kirkland & Ellis LLP, Washington, DC
202 879 5018
ewarren@kirkland.com
Recommended in Environment
Practice Areas: Mr Warren has extensive litigation experience before federal agencies and courts under a broad range of federal statutes. He also has appellate litigation experience including approximately 50 significant arguments before the US Courts of Appeals, state Supreme Courts and the US Supreme Court.
Personal: Yale College, BA, 1966. University of Chicago Law School, JD, 1969.

WATERS, Jennifer N
Crowell & Moring LLP, Washington, DC
202 624 2715
jwaters@crowell.com
Recommended in Energy
Practice Areas: Jennifer N Waters is a Partner in Crowell & Moring's Energy Group and a member of the firm's Management Board. She focuses on energy law, having participated in the restructurings and transformations of the natural gas and electric industries that have occurred in the last two decades. She represents the Los Angeles Department of Water & Power in developing strategic natural gas and electric projects. She represents the cities of Knoxville, Memphis, and Nashville, which turn to her to manage their relationships with the Tennessee Valley Authority. She also represents a major international oil company and LNG producer.

WAXMAN, Seth
Wilmer Cutler Pickering Hale and Dorr LLP, Washington, DC 202 663 6800
seth.waxman@wilmerhale.com
Recommended in Litigation
Practice Areas: Partner in the firm's Litigation Department, focuses on Supreme Court, appellate, and complex civil and criminal trial litigation; corporate advice on complex litigation and public policy challenges. He has argued over 40 cases in the Supreme Court and has tried and argued dozens of other high profile, complex civil and criminal cases in federal and state courts across the United States.
Prof. Memberships: Fellow, American College of Trial Lawyers, American Academy of Appellate Lawyers, American Law Institute, American Bar Foundation. Director, 'Legal Affairs' magazine, Supreme Court Institute, Supreme Court Historical Society. Admitted, District of Columbia, United States Supreme Court, all federal courts of appeals.
Career: Former Solicitor General of the United States (1997-2001), he also served in a number of other senior positions in the United States Government. In 20 years of private practice he has garnered numerous awards for trial and appellate litigation. He sits on the law faculty at Georgetown University and

previously taught at Harvard University's Kennedy School of Government.
Personal: Yale Law School (JD 1977); Harvard College (AB 1973).

WEINBERG, David
Howrey Simon Arnold & White, Washington, DC
202 783 0800
Recommended in Environment

WEINGARTEN, Reid
Steptoe & Johnson LLP,
Washington, DC 202 429 6238
rweingarten@steptoe.com
Recommended in Litigation
Practice Areas: Partner in Steptoe & Johnson's Washington office. Practice focuses mainly on complex criminal matters in state and federal courts at the pre-trial, trial, and post-trial stages, including cases involving public corruption, the Racketeer Influenced and Corrupt Organizations Act, bank fraud, accounting fraud, bribery, government procurement fraud, antitrust, healthcare fraud, and tax and securities fraud. Nationally recognized for his representation of many high profile individuals including former senior executives of major US corporations, as well as the president of a national labor union and former cabinet-level government officials.
Personal: JD, Dickinson Law School, 1975; BA, Cornell University, 1971.

WEINSTEIN, Ken
Latham & Watkins LLP,
Washington, DC 202 637 2200
Recommended in Environment

WEISEL, Sheldon
Goulston & Storrs, Washington, DC
202 721 0011
Recommended in Real Estate

WEISS, Erica
Bingham McCutchen LLP,
Washington, DC 202 778 6150
Recommended in Real Estate

WEISS, Harry J
Wilmer Cutler Pickering Hale and Dorr LLP, Washington, DC 202 663 6993
harry.weiss@wilmerhale.com
Recommended in Corporate/Commercial
Practice Areas: Represents clients in SEC enforcement matters and counsels corporations and their officers regarding disclosure and corporate compliance issues.
Prof. Memberships: Co-Chair of the Securities Enforcement Subcommittee of the ABA Litigation Section; Boards of the National Society of Compliance Professionals and the Regulatory Data Corporation.
Career: Served on the staff of the Securities and Exchange Commission for 11 years, ultimately as Associate Director of the Division of Enforcement, leading investigations involving insider trading, financial reporting, accounting and dis-

closure problems and broker-dealer and investment adviser violations.
Personal: Boston University School of Law (JD 1976); Johns Hopkins University (AB 1973).

WELLEN, Robert
Ivins, Phillips & Barker, Washington, DC
202 393 7600
Recommended in Tax

WELLS, Stephen E
McDermott Will & Emery,
Washington, DC 202 756 8316
swells@mwe.com
Recommended in Tax
Practice Areas: Partner in charge of Washington Tax Practice. Focuses on taxation of transactions involving US and foreign corporations, including formation of corporate ventures, reorganizations and restructurings, corporate distributions and liquidations, and corporate acquisitions and dispositions, including spinoffs. Has been instrumental in structuring and implementing many of the largest corporate M&As, joint ventures and spinoffs undertaken by various prominent public and private multinational corporations. Has developed and implemented numerous innovative tax strategies of major corporate transactions, and in pursuing or defending against hostile tender offers.
Prof. Memberships: Former Chairman of Corporation Tax Committee of the District of Columbia Bar, and a member of Corporate Tax Committee of the American Bar Association. Currently vice chairman of Institute For Research on the Economics of Taxation, a non-profit organization whose primary goal is to assist the formulation of public economic policies that will contribute to economic growth, efficiency, and competitiveness.
Career: From 1973-78, employed in various capacities in the Reorganization Branch, Corporation Tax Division, of Internal Revenue Service national office, receiving several superior performance awards during his tenure.
Personal: Earned JD in 1975 and LLM in 1977 from Georgetown University Law Center. Earned BS in 1971 from University of Maryland.

WENNER, Adam
Chadbourne & Parke LLP,
Washington, DC 202 974 5600
awenner@chadbourne.com
Recommended in Energy
Practice Areas: More than 25 years experience in the energy industry, representing power generators, electric utilities, transmission projects, and lenders and financial institutions in transactions, regulatory hearings and litigation. Represents energy companies before the Federal Energy Regulatory Commission (FERC) and state commissions and before the SEC in proceedings under the Public Utility Holding Company Act of 1935, and project developers and finan-

cial institutions in the development and sale of power and transmission projects.
Prof. Memberships: DC Bar Association; Florida Bar; Energy Bar Association.
Career: Deputy Assistant General Counsel, FERC.

WERTHER, Barbara
Thelen Reid & Priest LLP,
Washington, DC 202 508 4000
Recommended in Construction

WEST, Joseph D
Gibson, Dunn & Crutcher LLP,
Washington, DC 202 955 8658
jwest@gibsondunn.com
Recommended in Construction, Government Contracts
Practice Areas: Extensive experience with government and construction contracts. Represents contractors, subcontractors and government agencies. Areas of expertise include contract formation counseling, dispute avoidance/resolution, claims analysis, suspension/debarment, and ADR. Has engaged in cases before various United States Courts of Appeals and District Courts, the United States Court of Federal Claims, and Federal Government Boards of Contract Appeals.
Prof. Memberships: Fellow, American College of Construction Lawyers.
Career: Engineer and former officer of the United States Navy Civil Engineer Corps.
Personal: JD, George Washington University, 1977, editor, 'The George Washington Law Review,' Order of the Coif.

WEST, Philip
Steptoe & Johnson LLP,
Washington, DC 202 429 6247
pwest@steptoe.com
Recommended in Tax
Practice Areas: Partner in Steptoe & Johnson LLP's Washington office. 20 years legal tax experience. Focuses on complex international tax matters. Extensive experience with transactions, tax controversies, tax minimization planning, and advocacy before IRS, Treasury, Congress, courts, and attest auditors. Expert on deferral, foreign tax credit, transfer pricing, and treaty matters. Served as the Treasury Department's International Tax Counsel and led US work at OECD. Practical experience with foreign tax systems and good relationships with foreign tax officials and private practitioners. Frequent speaker and author.
Personal: LLM, Georgetown University Law Center, 1987; JD, New York Law School, 1984.

WIACEK, Raymond
Jones Day, Washington, DC
202 879 3908
rjwiacek@jonesday.com
Recommended in Tax
Practice Areas: Coordinator of the firm's Tax Group. His practice involves

the tax and business aspects of corporate and international transactions, including structured and cross-border financings, mergers and acquisitions, restructurings, transfer pricing, and international licensing for intellectual property, as well as disputes with the IRS and foreign governments related to such transactions. Testified on international tax matters and proposed regulations before the House Ways and Means Committee, the Senate Finance Committee, the Senate Foreign Relations Committee, and the IRS. Named a top lawyer in 'The World's Leading Lawyers', 'America's Leading Lawyers for Business', Euromoney's 'International Tax Review', and other publications.

WILCOX, Gary B
Morgan, Lewis & Bockius LLP,
Philadelphia 215 963 5043
gwilcox@morganlewis.com
Recommended in Tax
Practice Areas: Mr Wilcox is Partner in the Tax Practice. Mr Wilcox advises US and international clients on a wide range of tax matters, including tax aspects of mergers and acquisitions, spin-offs, formations of joint ventures and partnerships, and structuring REIT offerings and transactions. He has advised multinational clients in cross-border transactions, including tax-minimization structures and post-acquisition integration planning. Further, Mr Wilcox represents clients in US federal tax controversies and appears before the US Treasury and Internal Revenue Serivce (IRS) to seek published guidance and rulings on behalf of clients.
Career: Formerly the Deputy Chief Counsel for the IRS.

WILDER, Richard
Sidley Austin Brown & Wood LLP,
Washington, DC 202 736 8017
rwilder@sidley.com
Recommended in Intellectual Property
Practice Areas: Richard Wilder counsels US and foreign business, governments and intergovernmental organizations on intellectual property policy and protection and dispute resolution. His practice covers a wide range of technologies, including optics, semiconductor products, fabrication equipment, mechanical devices and biotechnology. Mr Wilder served as Director of the Global Intellectual Property Issues Division of the World Intellectual Property Organization where he was responsible for various WIPO programs dealing with diverse issues, including biotechnology, genetic resources, health care, traditional knowledge, folklore and human rights. Mr Wilder was also responsible for relations between WIPO and the non-governmental organizations and the private sector. Earlier in his career, Mr Wilder served in the Office of Legislative and International Affairs of the US Patent and Trademark Office,

where he participated in a number of bilateral and multilateral negotiations involving international intellectual property obligations including under the TRIPS Agreement. Mr Wilder served as the chief negotiator for the US on what became the Geneva Act of the Hague Agreement for the International Registration of Industrial Designs.
Career: Franklin Pierce Law Center, JD, 1984; University of Washington, BS in Mechanical Engineering, 1979. Bar Admissions: US Patent & Trademark Office, 1985; District of Columbia; New Hampshire, 1985.

WILEY, Richard E
Wiley Rein & Fielding LLP,
Washington, DC 202 719 7010
rwiley@wrf.com
Recommended in Telecom, Broadcast & Satellite
Practice Areas: Head of largest Communications Practice in United States. Former FCC Chairman and widely recognised as the leading communications attorney in the United States. Profiled in The New York Times ('Telecommunications Ubiquitous Man of Influence'), The Los Angeles Times ('The Sixth Commissioner'), The Globe and Mail ('Father of High-Definition Television'), The American Lawyer ('Brand Name of Communications Bar') and the National Law Journal ('An Enduring Influence and one of the nation's 100 Most Influential Lawyers').
Prof. Memberships: Chair, American Bar Association Section on Administrative Law and Regulatory Practice; past President, Federal Bar Association; and Federal Communications Bar Association; Chairman, FCC's Advisory Committee on Digital Television (1987-96).
Career: FCC Chairman, Commissioner and General Counsel; firm's Managing Partner.
Personal: Northwestern University (BS with honors and JD); Georgetown University (LLM).

WILKINSON, Beth
Latham & Watkins LLP,
Washington, DC 202 637 2200
Recommended in Litigation

WILLIAMS, B John
Shearman & Sterling, Washington, DC
202 508 8150
bjwilliams@shearman.com
Recommended in Tax
Practice Areas: Partner in Shearman & Sterling's Tax Group. Represents clients in Internal Revenue Service examinations and appeals and before federal trial and appeals courts in tax litigation.
Prof. Memberships: American College of Tax Counsel, American Law Institute, American Bar Association's Tax Section
Career: Rejoined Shearman after 18 months as Chief Counsel for the IRS. Formerly a Judge of the US Tax Court, Deputy Assistant Attorney General in the Tax Division of the Justice Depart-

ment and Special Assistant to Chief Counsel of the IRS.
Personal: BA with honors, George Washington University (1971); JD with distinction, George Washington University Law School (1974).

WILLIAMS, William
Fulbright & Jaworski LLP,
Washington, DC 202 662 4673
wwilliams@fulbright.com
Recommended in Energy
Practice Areas: He was an attorney for the Federal Energy Regulatory Commission from 1977-80. The majority of his practice deals with the representation of interstate pipelines and other clients before the Federal Energy Regulatory Commission and in related appellate matters. He has also represented clients in state regulatory proceedings. In addition to his regulatory practice, he advises clients involved in litigation or commercial transactions with regulated companies.
Prof. Memberships: Virginia Bar, District of Columbia Bar, Federal Energy Bar Association.
Personal: Lives in Falls Church, Virginia; two children, William and Erin; leisure activitites involve spending time with his children.

WILLNER, Keith
Mayer, Brown, Rowe & Maw LLP,
Washington, DC 202 263 3215
kwillner@mayerbrownrowe.com
Recommended in Real Estate
Practice Areas: Represents institutions in major real estate financing, acquisition, sale, venture, and leasing transactions. Counsels major REITs, pension funds, banks, insurance companies, credit companies, and other investors on their real estate needs. Structures and executes acquisitions and dispositions of major commercial property types. Organizes investment and ownership vehicles to purchase and operate real estate projects. Assists clients in permanent, construction, mezzanine, securitized, and syndicated loans on all types of commercial real estate. Handles complex portfolio and multistate transactions. Serves as national leasing counsel for leading companies across US including major headquarters leases.
Career: Joined Mayer, Brown, Rowe & Maw LLP as Partner, 1996. Formerly with Morrison & Foerster; Lane and Edson, P.C.; Bronson, Bronson & McKinnon. Served on Steering Committee of Real Estate Section of DC Bar Association and as Chair of Commercial Transactions Committee and Commercial Leasing Committee.
Publications: Articles in numerous publications, including 'Mortgage and Real Estate Executives Report', 'CREI Interactive', 'The Corridor Real Estate Journal', and 'Real Estate Rescues'. Frequent speaker and author on real estate topics.

Personal: Born 10 December 1959. University of Virginia School of Law, JD, 1984; 'Virginia Tax Review'. University of Virginia, BA, magna cum laude, 1981; Phi Beta Kappa.

WILSON, Anita
Vinson & Elkins LLP, Washington, DC
202 639 6776
awilson@velaw.com
Recommended in Energy

Practice Areas: Federal and state energy regulation and energy transactions. Represents natural gas pipelines, storage facility operators and shippers in proceedings before the Federal Energy Regulatory Commission. Advises clients in certificate, rate, restructuring and rule-making proceedings, as well as compliant and enforcement matters, related appellate litigation, and due diligence review of pipeline and LNG assets.
Prof. Memberships: American Bar Association; Energy Bar Association.
Career: Partner since 1999.
Personal: University of Virginia (JD 1990) (President of Law School Class); College of William and Mary (BS 1986) (Phi Beta Kappa).

WILTSHIRE, William
Harris, Wiltshire & Grannis LLP, Washington, DC 202 730 1300
Recommended in Telecom, Broadcast & Satellite

WINCEK, Mark D
Kilpatrick Stockton LLP, Washington, DC 202 508 5800
MWincek@KilpatrickStockton.com
Recommended in Employee Benefits
Practice Areas: Employee benefits, with an emphasis on qualified retirement plans, welfare benefits and flexible and executive compensation.
Prof. Memberships: American College of Employee Benefits Counsel; ECFC Flex Advisory Council; American Bar Association, Tax Section (Chairman of the Statutory Welfare Benefits Subcommittee, 1986-90).
Career: Staff of US House Ways and Means Committee (1976-81); former adjunct professor of law at Georgetown University Law Center; Head of the firm's Employee Benefits Group.
Publications: Frequently lectures and writes on employee benefits matters; Editorial Advisory Board, 'Benefits Law Journal' (1988-present).
Personal: BA and JD degrees, cum laude, from Boston College in 1972 and 1976.

WOLFF, Paul
Williams & Connolly LLP, Washington, DC 202 434 5000
Recommended in Litigation

WYRON, Richard H
Swidler Berlin LLP, Washington, DC
202 424 7500
rhwyron@swidlaw.com
Recommended in Bankruptcy
Practice Areas: Represents debtors, creditors, equity holders, contracting

parties, officers, directors and asset purchasers in connection with proceedings under Chapter 11; also in non-judicial workouts, including related transactional and litigation matters. Extensive experience representing debtors, future claimants representatives and others in asbestos-related bankruptcy matters.
Prof. Memberships: Admitted to practice in Washington, DC (1980); Maryland (1987); member, American Bankruptcy Institute.
Career: Law Clerk to Honorable Albert V Bryan, Jr, US District Court for the Eastern District of Virginia, 1979-80; joined Swidler Berlin LLP as Partner, 1992.
Personal: Born 10 September 1954. JD, University of Virginia 1979; BA, University of Virginia 1976.

YANG, John
Wiley Rein & Fielding LLP, Washington, DC 202 719 7000
Recommended in Insurance

YANNUCCI, Thomas D
Kirkland & Ellis LLP, Washington, DC
202 879 5056
tyannucci@kirkland.com
Recommended in Litigation, Media & Entertainment
Practice Areas: Acted as trial and appellate counsel in individual and class action suits involving claims in the following areas: defamation, antitrust, intellectual property, securities, government enforcement and regulatory matters (DOJ, FDA, EPA, FTC, SEC, ITC, FEC, CIA, NLRB), RICO, insurance coverage, ERISA, international trade and white collar crime. Has handled jury and bench trials, and has appeared in state and federal courts as well as in arbitrations. He also has served as an arbitrator for complex commercial cases for the American Arbitration Association.
Personal: University of Notre Dame, AB, 1972. University of Notre Dame Law School, JD, 1976.

YDE, Paul
Freshfields Bruckhaus Deringer LLP, Washington, DC 202 777/969 4500
Recommended in Antitrust

YOHAY, Stephen
Arent Fox PLLC, Washington, DC
202 857 6000
Recommended in Employment

YUFFEE, Michael
McDermott Will & Emery, Washington, DC 202 756 8066
myuffee@mwe.com
Recommended in Energy
Practice Areas: Member of Energy and Derivatives Markets Group. Represents energy clients on various regulatory, litigation and transactional matters. Represents and advises on all facets of the wholesale power market, including various Independent System Operator (ISO) and Regional Transmission Organization (RTO) proceedings, rate and market design proceedings, merger pro-

ceedings, and investigation and litigation matters before Federal Energy Regulatory Commission (FERC), state public utilities commissions, and federal courts. Has advised on structured physical energy transactions and wholesale power transactions. Participated in many FERC proceedings concerning development of ISO and RTO markets. Represented clients in cases before FERC and federal courts seeking refunds and retroactive contract modification arising from western energy crisis of 2000-01.
Career: Formerly an attorney-advisor in FERC's Office of Administrative Law Judges, assisting in all aspects of electricity and natural gas regulatory cases, including adjudication of electric and natural gas rate proceedings, mergers, and utility restructuring proceedings.
Personal: Earned JD in 1994 from Washington University School of Law, and BA cum ladue in 1991 from Boston University. Admitted to practice before Maryland State Bar, District of Columbia Bar, Court of Appeals for the District of Columbia Circuit Bar, and Court of Appeals for the Ninth Circuit Bar.

ZAHLER, Robert
Shaw Pittman LLP, Washington, DC
202 663 8130
robert.zahler@shawpittman.com
Recommended in Business Process Outsourcing: National, IT Outsourcing
Practice Areas: Robert Zahler, a Partner and Founder of Shaw Pittman's Global Sourcing Practice Group and Lead Director of the firm's Management Board, has been practicing law for 30 years. He participates in a wide range of legal and business consulting work, with special emphasis on sourcing, both information technology outsourcing (ITO) and business process outsourcing (BPO). This work includes business process and information technology outsourcing arrangements (both onshore and offshore and covering data center operations, distributed computing, desktop support, and applications development and maintenance), the structuring of telecommunications and managed network services transactions, the development of systems integration and custom system development contracts, the protection of intellectual property rights, the licensing of computer software and, over the last five years, significant business process outsourcing relationships focusing on human resources, finance and accounting, procurement and supply chain management, among others. His work includes cutting-edge transactions across most major industries and in the United States, Canada, Latin and South America, Europe, South Africa and Australia. During the past 20 years, Mr Zahler and his colleagues at Shaw Pittman have represented more than 450 corporations and governmental entities on strategic sourcing initiatives with a total contract value in excess of $350 billion.

Prof. Memberships: Society of Sigma Xi (scientific honorary); admitted to practice: District of Columbia (1975); District of Columbia Court of Appeals; US Supreme Court; US Court of Appeals for the First, Third, Fourth and District of Columbia Circuits; US District Court for the District of Columbia.
Publications: Mr Zahler has written widely on the subjects of outsourcing and procuring complex information technology and business process services. He was a key contributor to the Global Sourcing group's MOSAIC framework and VALUECHAIN methodology. He is a frequent speaker on the subject having appeared at conferences sponsored by CIO, Fortune and Forbes magazines, the Society of Information Management (SIM), the Sourcing Interests Group, the Outsourcing Institute, the Information Technology Association of American (ITAA), Digital Consulting, Inc., and the Yankee Group.
Personal: Harvard Law School, JD, cum laude, 1975; Massachusetts Institute of Technology, SB, Physics, 1972. (At press time, Shaw Pittman LLP had entered into a merger agreement with Pillsbury Winthrop LLP. The merger is expected to close by April 2005. Post closing, the name of the firm will be Pillsbury Winthrop Shaw Pittman LLP.)

ZAX, Leonard
Latham & Watkins LLP, Washington, DC 202 637 2200
Recommended in Real Estate

ZUTZ, Robert
Kirkpatrick & Lockhart Nicholson Graham LLP, Washington, DC
202 778 9059
rzutz@klng.com
Recommended in Investment Management
Practice Areas: Experience in federal securities laws and corporate law matters, with special emphasis on the representation of investment management clients, including broker-dealers, investment advisers, registered investment companies and their independent directors and trustees. Extensive experience in regulatory, compliance, public offering and corporate governance matters.
Prof. Memberships: American Bar Association; District of Columbia Bar.
Career: Law clerk to N.J. Superior Court Judge (1977-78); US Securities and Exchange Commission, Staff Attorney (1978-81) and Legal Counsel to Commissioner John Evans (1981-83).
Personal: New York University School of Law (JD, 1977); Tufts University (BA, 1974).

ZWEIFACH, Gerson
Williams & Connolly LLP, Washington, DC 202 434 5000
Recommended in Media & Entertainment

AKIN GUMP STRAUSS HAUER & FELD LLP

THE FIRM

Chairman: R Bruce McLean

Number of lawyers: 950

FIRM OVERVIEW: Recognized for its sophisticated clients and capabilities as well as its outstanding team of professionals, Akin Gump Strauss Hauer & Feld is one of the world's largest law firms, with 13 offices and over 900 lawyers in more than 50 practice disciplines. Akin Gump's steadfast dedication to providing exemplary client service and its visionary leadership are key factors in this first-generation law firm's swift rise to the top of the profession. A 2004 survey of corporate directors ranked Akin Gump among corporate America's 20 most-admired law firms.

MAIN AREAS OF PRACTICE:

Corporate and Securities: Akin Gump advises on mergers and acquisitions, corporate finance, international transactions, investment fund management and restructuring, and provides sophisticated counsel on US and international tax and governance issues.

Energy: The firm is well-known for its sophisticated, diverse and full-service Energy Law Practice, encompassing both transactional and regulatory matters. The firm's lawyers have represented virtually every major segment of the energy industry on issues ranging from energy policy to tax questions to environmental and land use challenges.

Financial Restructuring: Akin Gump has represented committees of bondholders, noteholders, institutional investors and trade creditors in more than 100 major restructurings since 1999. Among its most significant recent engagements is the representation of the official creditors' committee in the WorldCom reorganization, the largest corporate bankruptcy in history.

Intellectual Property: The firm provides counsel on patent prosecution and litigation, trademark, copyright, trade secret and unfair competition matters to Fortune 500 companies, multinational corporations and entertainment conglomerates, as well as small businesses, universities, research foundations, government agencies and individual inventors.

Labor & Employment: The firm advises management in both traditional matters, such as collective bargaining and discrimination lawsuits, and emerging issues, including class action wage-hour and EEO litigation. A 2004 survey of the Fortune 250 ranked Akin Gump among corporate America's 10 most-frequently relied-upon firms for significant labor and employment matters.

Litigation: Akin Gump represents many of the country's largest Fortune 500 companies, as well as numerous smaller business entities and individuals, in civil and criminal matters in state and federal trial and appellate courts.

Project & Infrastructure Development: The firm provides fully integrated project development counsel in the fields of environment and land use, development, energy, transportation, construction and project finance.

Public Law & Policy: Akin Gump has one of the world's most sophisticated and diverse US and international public law and policy practices, representing corporations, individuals, nonprofits, foreign governments, and coalitions and trade associations.

INTERNATIONAL WORK: The firm is recognized for its Russia/CIS practice, which is comprised of two former ambassadors to the Russian Federation and top-ranking former US government officials with significant experience in the region. The firm also numbers among its members former ambassadors to South Korea, Japan and the United Nations.

HEAD OFFICES

DISTRICT OF COLUMBIA
Robert S Strauss Building, 1333 New Hampshire Avenue, NW, **Washington,** 20036
Tel: 202 887 4000   **Fax:** 202 887 4288
Email: washdcinfo@akingump.com

TEXAS
1700 Pacific Avenue, Suite 4100, **Dallas,** 75201
Tel: 214 969 2800   **Fax:** 214 969 4343
Email: dallasinfo@akingump.com

Website: akingump.com

BRANCH OFFICES

CALIFORNIA
2029 Century Park East, Suite 2400, **Los Angeles,** 90067-3012
Tel: 310 229 1000   **Fax:** 310 229 1001

Three Embarcadero Center, Suite 2800, **San Francisco,** 94111-4066
Tel: 415 765 9500   **Fax:** 415 765 9501

NEW YORK
590 Madison Avenue, **New York,** 10022-2524
Tel: 212 872 1000   **Fax:** 212 872 1002

PENNSYLVANIA
One Commerce Square, 2005 Market Street, Suite 2200, **Philadelphia,** 19103-7013
Tel: 215 965 1200   **Fax:** 215 965 1210

TEXAS
300 West 6th Street, Suite 2100, **Austin,** 78701-2916
Tel: 512 499 6200   **Fax:** 512 499 6290

1111 Louisiana Street, 44th Floor, **Houston,** 77002-5200
Tel: 713 220 5800   **Fax:** 713 236 0822

300 Convent Street, Suite 1500, **San Antonio,** 78205-3732
Tel: 210 281 7000   **Fax:** 210 224 2035

INTERNATIONAL OFFICES:

The firm has offices in Brussels, Riyadh (Affiliate Office), London and Moscow.

AKIN GUMP STRAUSS HAUER & FELD LLP

ARNOLD & PORTER LLP

THE FIRM

Chairman: Michael N Sohn
Managing Partner: James J Sandman

Number of partners worldwide: 250
Number of other lawyers worldwide: 410

FIRM OVERVIEW: Arnold & Porter LLP is an international firm responsive to the needs of clients in a highly competitive and litigious marketplace. With offices in Washington, DC, New York, London, Brussels, Los Angeles, Northern Virginia, and Denver, and over 650 lawyers worldwide, Arnold & Porter has a distinct perspective on the pivotal relationship between government and business. The firm offers clients a unique window on the legal, policy, and political processes affecting almost every aspect of the international economy. Arnold & Porter maintains substantial litigation, transactional, and regulatory practices, as well as those involving many contemporary areas of law.

EXPERIENCE: The firm represents clients in a full range of legal and policy processes affecting both the national and international economy and business. The firm conducts business with companies in many jurisdictions around the globe including North America, Europe, Latin America, and Asia.

MAIN AREAS OF PRACTICE:

Antitrust/Competition & Trade Regulation: The firm has a strong tradition in antitrust/competition policy and trade regulation policy. Lawyers work with clients from a broad range of industries and represent them in matters under federal, state, and European laws governing competition, pricing, distribution, advertising, and intellectual property.

Commercial, Corporate & Securities: The firm's Corporate Practice has particular experience in mergers and acquisitions and corporate control matters involving banks, savings associations, and other financial institutions. The firm also represents issuers, underwriters, security holders, and indenture trustees in a full range of public and private offerings of debt and equity securities.

Employment Benefits: The firm represents employers and employees, pension plans, unions, corporations, and nonprofit organizations in matters ranging from tax qualification requirements to the use of employee stock ownership plans (ESOPs) in buyouts and other takeovers.

Environmental: Arnold & Porter represents corporations, developers, utilities, and public agencies in a wide range of environmental regulatory matters. Litigation is a prominent aspect of the firm's work in this area.

Financial Services: The firm's practice covers every aspect of the legal, business, and regulatory issues encountered by financial institutions, including growth and expansion, regulatory matters, financial products and services, capital markets, and corporate governance.

Government Contracts: The firm works with companies doing substantial business with government agencies. It advises on matters such as white-collar crime, compliance programs, litigation, corporate transactions, privatization, outsourcing, policy, and legislation.

Healthcare: Arnold & Porter attorneys combine insight into the healthcare fraud and abuse enforcement processes, substantive knowledge of the full range of federal and state healthcare laws and regulations, and a clear understanding of the healthcare and pharmaceutical industries.

Intellectual Property & Technology: This group has wide experience in the acquisition, protection, exploitation, and enforcement of intellectual property rights. It is particularly knowledgeable in the areas of computer and information technology, the Internet, pharmaceuticals, and biotechnology.

HEAD OFFICE

DISTRICT OF COLUMBIA
555 Twelfth Street, NW, **Washington,** DC 20004-1206
Tel: 202 942 5000 **Fax:** 202 942 5999
Website: www.arnoldporter.com

BRANCH OFFICES

NEW YORK
399 Park Avenue, **New York,** NY 10022-4690
Tel: 212 715 1000 **Fax:** 212 715 1399

CALIFORNIA
777 South Figueroa Street, 44th Floor, **Los Angeles,** CA 90017-5844
Tel: 213 243 4000 **Fax:** 213 243 4199

COLORADO
370 Seventeenth Street, Suite 4500, **Denver,** CO 80202-1370
Tel: 303 863 1000 **Fax:** 303 832 0428

VIRGINIA
1600 Tysons Boulevard, Suite 900, **McLean,** VA 22102-4865
Tel: 703 720 7000 **Fax:** 703 720 7399

INTERNATIONAL OFFICES

The firm also has offices in London and Brussels.

International Trade: The firm represents domestic and foreign corporations, governments, government agencies, international organizations, trade associations, labor unions, nongovernmental organizations, investors, banks, financial institutions, and individuals in virtually all aspects of international activity.

Life Sciences/Biotech: Arnold & Porter offers an innovative, integrated Life Sciences/Biotech Practice with a global perspective. The depth of the firm's involvement in life sciences places it squarely in the forefront of the development and evolution of the new life science technology drivers or 'toolbox.' The firm is closely attuned to the current state of play and future of genomics, proteomics, bioinformatics, biochips, pharmacogenetics, and the other technological developments of the day.

Litigation: This is a major area of the firm's work, with almost half of its domestic lawyers involved. Product liability, antitrust, and securities have been traditional areas of strength. The firm's work is diverse and includes civil and criminal, regulatory and commercial, and national and international matters.

National Security Law & Policy: The dramatic and ongoing consolidation of the defense, aerospace, communications, and information technology industries, and the increasing trend toward transnational consolidation in these industries, raise numerous legal and policy issues. Proposed mergers, acquisitions, and joint ventures in these industries are frequently subject to close scrutiny by both the Department of Defense and antitrust regulatory agencies, as well as by other Executive Branch agencies involved in national security and by the Congress. Arnold & Porter is able to offer clients sophisticated guidance on the national security decision-making process. The national security group represents clients in their dealings with the US State Department, the US Defense Department, other national security agencies, and the Congress, to make certain that their interests are fully taken into account when key foreign policy and national security decisions are being made.

ARNOLD & PORTER LLP

Pharmaceutical & Medical Devices: When it comes to the pharmaceutical and medical devices industries, Arnold & Porter covers the field in transatlantic litigation, regulatory, and transactional matters. The largest global pharmaceutical companies, as well as the smaller ones, frequently turn to the Arnold & Porter team for product liability and European regulatory counsel.

Privacy: The growing patchwork of privacy laws and regulations presents companies with serious legal and compliance challenges. Companies failing to abide by privacy laws face civil and criminal prosecution, administrative enforcement actions, and private and class action lawsuits by plaintiffs' lawyers. Equally important, reports of privacy violations splashed across the front page of newspapers can result in serious harm to a business's reputation. Arnold & Porter's privacy team provides legal and strategic counsel through its command of key laws and regulations, understanding of emerging technology platforms, and deep experience with key industry sectors to help companies meet their privacy obligations in a demanding and competitive marketplace.

Product Liability: Managing complex product liability litigation requires a coordinated legal strategy that is sensitive not only to demands of the litigation, but also to the regulatory, congressional, and public relations concerns that often arise during a product liability crisis. With more than 100 of its attorneys actively engaged in product liability matters, Arnold & Porter is one of the most experienced firms in defending large and complex mass tort matters, acting both as national counsel and as trial counsel in cases asserting personal injury and property damage claims. The European Product Liability Group has wide experience in handling the defence of all types of product liability claims, from individual cases to major multi-claimant 'group actions', and is a recognized leader in the field in both the UK and Europe. The combined expertise of the US and European product liability groups means that Arnold & Porter is eminently placed to offer clients an integrated product liability service on a transatlantic basis.

Real Estate: The firm's Real Estate Practice mirrors the increasing complexity, sophistication, and international integration of the global economy in the twenty-first century. The firm's attorneys structure and negotiate real estate deals for owners and developers in connection with acquisition, development, construction, federal transactions, financing, leasing, management and sale of office buildings, shopping centers, industrial sites, multifamily projects, single family home developments, condominiums, hotels, resorts, and recreational developments. The firm handles all aspects of inbound investments by foreign funds and individuals who invest in US real estate and provides counsel to its US-based developers when they undertake projects in the UK and Europe, working closely with its tax department to maximize the after-tax returns.

Tax: With approximately 30 attorneys in the firm's Washington and New York offices, the Tax Practice provides representation in all major areas of corporate, partnership, employment, individual, trusts and estates, and gift tax law.

Telecommunications: The firm provides regulatory, administrative, litigation, and legislative advice to corporations, government entities, institutions, and individuals. Governments and enterprises from other countries also seek the firm's advice on the domestic and international implications of existing and emerging technologies and on new regulatory and marketplace structures.

INTERNATIONAL
LONDON OFFICE
Tower 42, 25 Old Broad Street, London EC2N 1HQ, United Kingdom
Lawyers: 29
Office Profile: Arnold & Porter's London office advises on a full range of regulatory, transactional, and litigation matters, and focuses especially on competition, corporate transactions, intellectual property and technology, life sciences, litigation, product liability litigation and regulation, and telecommunications. The firm is committed to strategic growth in London in these and other areas with the same emphasis on quality of service and in-depth expertise as it provides in the United States. Arnold & Porter's London office has grown rapidly to include: the leading team of attorneys for the pharmaceutical and medical technology industries in product liability litigation and regulatory matters; one of the largest groups of intellectual property and technology lawyers of any US firm operating in the UK, including the UK's leading life sciences transactions group; a leading IP/IT transaction group and a major IP litigation capability; one of the leading European regulatory and commercial telecommunications groups; a powerful competition practice combined with its leading US antitrust practice; and a growing corporate and commercial transactional capability.

BRUSSELS OFFICE
11, Rue des Colonies-Koloniënstraat 11, B-1000 Brussels, Belgium
Lawyers: 7
Office Profile: Arnold & Porter opened its Brussels office in 2003 to serve the firm's multinational client base by complementing their top-ranked US antitrust practice, most recently designated the number one antitrust law firm in the US (2004) and in North America (2003) by Chambers & Partners. Arnold & Porter's Brussels team represents clients before the European Commission in regard to a range of competition concerns under EU laws - including allegations of abuse of dominant position or anti-competitive practices. The firm's lawyers also have experience in dealing with major antitrust inquiries, price-fixing issues, distribution and licensing agreements, strategic alliances, and joint ventures. Members of the team undertake and coordinate the work necessary to obtain competition clearances for mergers, acquisitions, and joint ventures from the European Commission and from national authorities in the EU, Central/Eastern Europe and beyond, as well as advising on other aspects of EU law, particularly those relating to the free movement of goods, advertising, and other regulatory laws within the EU.

ARNOLD & PORTER LLP

BEVERIDGE & DIAMOND, P.C.

THE FIRM

Managing Director: Robert Brager
Number of Directors: 33
Number of other lawyers: 45

FIRM OVERVIEW: Since opening in 1974, Beveridge & Diamond, P.C. has focused on environmental law and litigation. In court, in negotiations, and before government agencies, Beveridge & Diamond resolves complex problems and disputes, particularly in the environmental area, keeping in mind its clients' business goals.

MAIN AREAS OF PRACTICE:

Environmental: Beveridge & Diamond's practice encompasses all areas of environmental law, and the firm's long history and experience allow it to successfully handle the most significant and complicated environmental matters. Beveridge & Diamond represents domestic and international clients on environmental issues related to air, surface water and groundwater, solid and hazardous wastes, product use, stewardship and recycling, environmental reporting and disclosure, and compliance with the wide array of federal and state environmental laws and regulations. The firm also represents clients across the country with regard to environmentally contaminated properties, including 'brownfields' projects, and in negotiations with buyers, sellers, developers, and insurers of these properties. In addition, Beveridge & Diamond provides strategic advice to clients with regard to their environmental management systems, and has assisted clients with their environmental due diligence efforts in the United States and across the world.

Environmental Litigation & ADR: The firm's Environmental Litigation and Alternative Dispute Resolution Practice challenges agency actions in administrative, trial and appellate proceedings, defends against government enforcement actions and citizen suits, and represents clients in cases brought under the federal 'Superfund' law, other federal or state statutes, or common law with regard to the extent of remediation necessary to protect the environment and who should pay for the rememdiation. The firm litigates numerous other environmental cases in state and federal courts across the country, including takings and related land use matters.

Civil & White Collar Litigation: Beveridge & Diamond's Civil Litigation Practice is accomplished in defending against toxic tort, product liability, and mass tort claims, and includes a strong commercial litigation component. The firm's appellate practice safeguards clients' rights after trial, and its litigators have pursued or defended against countless appeals in the United States Supreme Court, every federal circuit court of appeals, and state appellate courts around the country. In the white collar criminal area, the firm has extensive experience in assisting its clients in responding to ever increasing criminal enforcement efforts aimed at corporate entities and individual officers, directors, and employees. Its white collar attorneys have a unique environmental criminal practice, combining their experience on criminal matters with the firm's renowned reputation in environmental law to provide comprehensive and effective defenses.

Project Development: Major private project developments in the United States generally require one or more federal, state, or local permits or approvals under statutes protecting endangered species, wetlands, and other environmentally sensitive areas. The firm assists its clients with successful development strategies that are comprehensive, timely, and responsive to project needs and environmental regulatory requirements.

HEAD OFFICE

DISTRICT OF COLUMBIA
Suite 700, 1350 I Street, NW, **Washington**, DC 20005-3311
Tel: 202 789 6000 **Fax:** 202 789 6190
Email: contact.bd@bdlaw.com
Website: www.bdlaw.com

BRANCH OFFICES

CALIFORNIA
Suite 1800, 456 Montgomery Street, **San Francisco**, CA 94104-1251
Tel: 415 262 4000 **Fax:** 415 262 4040

31st Floor, 555 West Fifth Street, **Los Angeles**, CA 90013-1018
Tel: 213 996 8350 **Fax:** 213 996 8304

400 Capitol Mall, Suite 900, **Sacramento**, CA 95814-4407
Tel: 916 449 3946 **Fax:** 916 444 0279

MARYLAND
Suite 2210, 201 North Charles Street, **Baltimore**, MD 21201-4150
Tel: 410 230 3850 **Fax:** 410 230 3868

MASSACHUSETTS
45 William Street, Suite 120, Wellesley, MA 02481-4004
Tel: 781 416 5700 **Fax:** 781 416 5799

NEW JERSEY
Beveridge & Diamond, 26 Franklin Street, **Tenafly**, NJ 07670-2515
Tel: 201 568 2797 **Fax:** 201 568 9570

NEW YORK
15th Floor, 477 Madison Avenue, **New York**, NY 10022-5802
Tel: 212 702 5400 **Fax:** 212 702 5450

CONTACTS

Environmental/Environmental Litigation ....Donald J Patterson, Jr
Litigation ....John N Hanson
Project Development ....Jennifer L Hernandez

CLIENTS: Beveridge & Diamond represents domestic and international resource and energy companies, manufacturers, chemical companies, makers of pesticides, biotechnology companies, producers of raw materials, transportation companies, high-tech component makers, food and consumer products companies, financial institutions, trade associations, and real estate developers.

INTERNATIONAL WORK: As clients pursue international trade and investment opportunities, the firm has continued to expand its International Environmental Practice in order to help companies identify, understand, and comply with the expanding body of international, national, and sub-national environmental law in countries and regions throughout the world. The firm regularly advises clients on a wide range of matters arising under multilateral environmental agreements, the environmental aspects of multilateral trade and investment agreements, and significant environmental regulatory and policy developments across the globe.

COVINGTON & BURLING

THE FIRM

Chair of Management Committee: Stuart C Stock

Number of partners worldwide: 173
Number of other lawyers worldwide: 353

FIRM OVERVIEW: Covington & Burling is one of the world's preeminent law firms, representing leading multinationals on many of their most significant transactional, litigation, regulatory, and public policy matters. Founded in 1919, the firm has long emphasized the strength its corporate and litigation practices derive from the firm's industry expertise acquired through various regulatory practices.

MAIN AREAS OF PRACTICE:

Litigation: Covington & Burling's Litigation Practice in the United States covers virtually every important area of civil and criminal law. Covington prosecutes and defends cases before juries and judges in state and federal courts nationwide, before arbitration panels convened by US and international arbitral organizations, before all major federal agencies, and in the courts of selected foreign jurisdictions. The subject matters of the firm's Civil Litigation and Arbitration Practice cover the range of high-stakes commercial disputes, but focus heavily on antitrust, employment and ERISA, insurance coverage, intellectual property, product liability, and securities litigation. The firm's Criminal Practice covers all areas of white-collar criminal representation, on behalf of both corporate and individual clients, and the related areas of regulatory enforcement, internal investigations, and ethics inquiries.

Corporate, Tax & Benefits: With over 140 lawyers actively practicing in the corporate, securities, finance, bankruptcy, real estate, tax, and employee benefits areas, Covington provides a full range of transactional and advisory services. The firm's corporate and securities lawyers draw on the firm's deep regulatory expertise in areas such as communications, food and drug law, transportation, energy, financial institutions, environmental regulation, antitrust, and international trade. The firm's substantial Intellectual Property and Information Technology Practices provide an important additional resource in handling its clients' multidisciplinary needs efficiently and comprehensively. During the past few years, the firm has advised Calpine Corporation on more than $16.5 billion of capital markets financings. Recent public market transactions include Kerr-McGee's $3.4 billion acquisition of Westport Resources, UBS Warburg's $8 billion acquisition of Enron's natural gas and power trading platform and Computer Associates' $4 billion acquisition of Sterling Software. The firm also advises private equity firms, including GE Equity, and companies in control and significant minority investments.

Technology, Media & Communications: Covington & Burling's Technology Practice covers the full range of issues confronting companies engaged in technology, supported by lawyers who are authorities on such subjects as Internet intellectual property, electronic payment systems, encryption and data privacy. The firm advises clients on all aspects of the technology and software industry, combining experience in Internet intellectual property, telecommunications, and other cutting-edge fields with traditional strength in such important areas as antitrust, securities and finance, and tax. Covington assists companies around the world in the creation, acquisition, protection and exploitation of intellectual property rights. In representing clients such as Microsoft and the Business Software Alliance, the firm has been at the forefront of international efforts to strengthen software copyright protection. The firm's Communications Practice is one of the most comprehensive in Washington. Covington is well known for its experience in broadcasting, mass media, telecommunications, multi-channel video distribution, satellite, PCS/cellular, international, programming, newsgathering and the first amendment.

HEAD OFFICE

DISTRICT OF COLUMBIA
1201 Pennsylvania Avenue NW, **Washington**, DC 20004-2401
Tel: 202 662 6000   **Fax:** 202 662 6291
Website: www.cov.com

OTHER OFFICES

CALIFORNIA
One Front Street, **San Francisco**, CA 94111
Tel: 415 591 6000   **Fax:** 415 591 6091

NEW YORK
1330 Avenue Of The Americas, **New York**, NY10019
Tel: 212 841 1000   **Fax:** 212 841 1010

INTERNATIONAL OFFICES

The firm also has offices in London and Brussels.

CONTACTS

Antitrust & International Trade ....Jim Atwood, Stuart Eizenstat
Corporate, Tax & Benefits ....Scott Smith
Life Sciences ....Richard Kingham
Litigation ....Gregg Levy, Will Phillips, Sonya Winner
Technology, Media & Communications ....Jonathan Blake

Antitrust & International Trade: The firm's practices in antitrust and international trade involve a wide range of transactional, litigation, and regulatory matters. The firm has handled complex civil and criminal antitrust and consumer protection matters, including major treble-damage actions, nationwide class actions, internal investigations, and short fuse preliminary injunction proceedings. The firm's antitrust work in the merger arena includes the ExxonMobil transaction. In the antitrust litigation field, the firm's recent successes include the outright dismissal of a high profile action challenging the National Football League's eligibility rules and a class action lawsuit against leading medical schools and teaching hospitals. The firm's International Trade and Finance Practice ranges from trade policy and regulatory advice to trade disputes and international arbitration - and draws on the resources of all of the firm's offices. The firm appears on behalf of companies and national governments in antidumping, countervailing duty, and other proceedings brought pursuant to the US and European trade laws. To complement and strengthen its international trade and other capabilities, the firm recently formalized a strategic alliance with the international advisory firm, Kissinger McLarty Associates.

INTERNATIONAL WORK: Covington & Burling's offices in London and Brussels, formed respectively in 1988 and 1990, now include about 60 lawyers. The major practice areas in Europe include the top-ranking global life sciences and pharmaceutical regulatory practice, corporate and securities law, intellectual property, communications and technology issues, taxation, litigation and arbitration, competition and trade, and legislative issues.

CROWELL & MORING LLP

THE FIRM

Chairman: John Macleod
Managing Partner: Herbert J Martin

Number of partners: 116

FIRM OVERVIEW: Crowell & Moring is a full-service law firm with more than 300 attorneys practicing in more than 40 diverse practice areas. Over two-thirds of the firm's attorneys regularly litigate disputes on behalf of international corporations, start-up businesses, and individuals. Crowell & Moring's client work ranges from providing tax planning for both US-based and foreign-based multinational manufacturers to extensive work in the nation's leading victims of terrorism practice.

MAIN AREAS OF PRACTICE:

Litigation: The firm's core strength is litigation, and it represents a range of international clients in federal and state trial and appellate courts, administrative tribunals, and before international arbitration panels. The firm has been selected by DuPont as a primary law firm and often represents clients as national coordinating counsel. It is home to a former White House Counsel to President Clinton and former United States Attorney for the District of Columbia.

Antitrust: The firm advises on antitrust and trade regulation; civil litigation and investigations; mergers and acquisitions; criminal grand jury investigations and trials; and on ways to manage antitrust risks in all manner of business transactions. Recent and ongoing work includes providing antitrust counsel for United Technologies Corp. and its Pratt & Whitney division in the proposed acquisition of Boeing Co.'s Rocketdyne liquid space propulsion and power unit, and serving as a lead antitrust counsel for SBC Communications Inc. in its proposed acquisition of AT&T Corp.

Securities Regulation & Enforcement: The firm has extensive experience defending investigations conducted by the Securities and Exchange Commission, the NYSE, the NASD Regulation, Inc., and other securities regulators on behalf of institutional and individual clients. Attorneys include a former Director of the Division of Investment Management, SEC, and other former senior enforcement officials who are at the forefront of defending against ever-changing regulatory priorities and investigative initiatives.

Intellectual Property: The firm advises on the full array of intellectual property legal services, including patent, trademark, unfair competition, copyright, and trade secret matters. The firm's marquee antitrust practice often works closely with the intellectual property practice on corporate matters, including those before the FTC and the Antitrust Division of the US Department of Justice. Attorneys include a former member of the staff of the Antitrust Division of the DOJ and former engineers at Fortune 500 manufacturers.

Government Contracts: The firm's more than 30 government contracts attorneys advise some of the world's largest and most prestigious contractors on pricing issues, bid protests, claims, litigation, and allegations of fraud. Recent representations include successfully defending Foundation Health Services in a series of protests involving billion dollar procurements for managed care health services under the US Department of Defense's TRICARE program; defeating a defective pricing claim of several hundred million dollars brought by the Department of Defense against United Technologies Corporation, Pratt & Whitney; and obtaining dismissals of a series to False Claims Act whistleblower cases brought against clients in the health care, defense, and telecommunications industries.

HEAD OFFICE

DISTRICT OF COLUMBIA
1001 Pennsylvania Ave, NW, **Washington**, DC 20004
Tel: 202 624 2500 **Fax:** 202 628 5116
Website: www.crowell.com

OTHER OFFICES

CALIFORNIA
3 Park Plaza, 20th Floor, **Irvine**, CA 92614-8505
Tel: 949 263 8400 **Fax:** 949 263 8414

INTERNATIONAL OFFICES

The firm also has offices in London and Brussels.

CONTACTS

Litigation	David B Siegel
Antitrust	Wm Randolph Smith
Securities Regulation & Enforcement	Pat S Conti
Intellectual Property	Jeffrey D Sanok
Government Contracts	George D Ruttinger
Corporate	James R Stuart III

Corporate: The firm's active Corporate Group advises directors and senior executives on disclosure, governance and compliance issues. Clients include large public corporations, emerging companies and privately held firms in a wide range of industries, including major defense contractors, aerospace and telecommunications companies, and financial institutions.

INTERNATIONAL WORK: The firm's European offices provide a range of transactional, counseling, regulatory, and litigation capabilities. International work ranges from high-profile antitrust concerns for Fortune 500 companies to strategic counsel through C&M International, the firm's international trade and investment consulting affiliate. The firm's international arbitration work includes assisting clients with informal negotiations, mediations, and arbitrations in the US, Canada, England, France, India and Switzerland.

DICKSTEIN SHAPIRO MORIN & OSHINSKY LLP

THE FIRM

Managing Partner: Michael E Nannes
Managing Partner, New York: Robin L Cohen
Managing Partner, Los Angeles: Linda D Kornfeld
Managing Partner Emeritus: Angelo V Arcadipane

Number of attorneys: 350

FIRM OVERVIEW: Dickstein Shapiro Morin & Oshinsky LLP, founded in 1953, is a multiservice law firm with 325 attorneys in offices in Washington, DC, New York City, and Los Angeles, representing clients in diverse industries with a wide variety of requirements. While Dickstein Shapiro's work generally originates from a client's need for legal representation, the firm is mindful that legal service is but one ingredient in achieving a client's strategic business goals. The firm prides itself on learning and understanding client objectives and partnering with clients to generate genuine business value. Dickstein Shapiro is proud that the diversity of its clients coincides with the diversity of its practice. Clients include more than 100 of the *Fortune* 500 companies, as well as start-up ventures and entrepreneurs, multinational corporations and leading financial institutions, charitable organizations, and government officials in high-profile investigations. Dickstein Shapiro's five core practice groups involve the firm in virtually every major form of counseling, litigation, and advocacy. Dickstein Shapiro provides comprehensive representation to clients through the multiple resources available in its five core groups listed below. Detailed descriptions of each practice and biographies of individual attorneys, are available upon request.

MAIN AREAS OF PRACTICE:

Corporate & Finance Group: Dickstein Shapiro is a leader in providing sophisticated legal services to business entities of all types, including financial institutions and individuals. The firm's Corporate and Finance Group is international in scope and involves representation of some of the world's largest corporations, commercial banks, investment banks, and venture capital firms. The Group's practice ranges from small, traditional transactions to large, highly complex transactions, and provides a full range of corporate, finance, and transactional legal services to its clients. To best meet all the needs and objectives of its clients, the Corporate and Finance Group offers the complete resources of the firm for problem solving and transaction implementation. Regardless of the transaction or the client, Dickstein Shapiro brings to the table its reputation as an innovative, effective, and efficient law firm.

Energy Group: Dickstein Shapiro offers a multiservice, domestic and international energy and natural resources practice, with particular strengths in federal and state energy regulation, and international and domestic energy transactions. The firm's clients are engaged in all aspects of electricity, natural gas, LNG and petroleum production, transmission, and distribution. They include utilities, natural gas and petroleum pipelines, independent power producers, natural gas storage providers, LNG developers, energy marketers, trade groups, financial institutions, energy customers, governmental entities, and others. The firm's work ranges from the acquisition, sale, financing, and structuring of US and international energy companies and energy assets, to the development, construction, operation, and restructuring of generating facilities, natural gas and crude oil pipelines, and gas storage facilities. The firm also represents suppliers and purchasers of water, water treatment services, and desalinized water in connection with the financing, construction of, and permitting of facilities, as well as with respect to contract negotiations and ongoing operational issues.

Intellectual Property Group: Dickstein Shapiro works with companies to develop strategies which capitalize on their intellectual property assets so as to achieve the companies' business objectives. The firm has the experience, skill, and knowledge to solve these and other intellectual property problems successfully for clients striving to succeed in this ever-changing, high-

HEAD OFFICE

DISTRICT OF COLUMBIA
2101 L Street, NW, **Washington**, DC 20037-1526
Tel: 202 785 9700 **Fax:** 202 887 0689
Email: info@dsmo.com
Website: www.DicksteinShapiro.com

BRANCH OFFICES

NEW YORK
1177 Avenue of the Americas, **New York**, NY 10036-2714
Tel: 212 835 1400 **Fax:** 212 997 9880

CALIFORNIA
10866 Wilshire Boulevard, Suite 300, **Los Angeles**, CA 90024-4350
Tel: 310 441 8460 **Fax:** 310 441 8470

CONTACTS

Corporate & Finance Group	Frederick M Lowther
Energy Group	Kenneth M Simon, Larry F Eisenstat
Intellectual Property Group	Gary M Hoffman
Legislative & Regulatory Affairs Group	L Andrew Zausner
Litigation & Dispute Resolution Group	Richard J Leveridge

ly competitive arena. The firm is engaged in all phases of pursuing, licensing, acquiring, and litigating intellectual property rights and rights in all areas of technology, including electronics, telecommunications equipment, pharmaceuticals, biotechnology, polymers and other specialty chemicals, and computer hardware and software. Such litigation includes representation before the US courts, the International Trade Commission, various state courts, and coordination of litigation in foreign countries.

Legislative & Regulatory Affairs Group: The Legislative and Regulatory Affairs Group seeks to advance clients' interests before the legislative and executive branches of government – a practice unique to Washington, DC. Increasingly, this demands a sophisticated combination of political and substantive resources, as well as a close coordination of skills drawn from traditionally separate disciplines, including government representation, regulatory and administrative counseling, and even litigation.

Litigation & Dispute Resolution Group: Dickstein Shapiro provides clients with creative and sophisticated strategies to resolve some of the most complex, multifaceted disputes in the United States and abroad. The firm is widely known for its settlement and litigation capabilities. The Dickstein Shapiro team of more than 160 litigators and negotiators, which includes 17 former federal prosecutors, has a track record of recovering billions of dollars for clients and saving comparable amounts by keeping them out of court. The firm is prepared to – and often does – try cases to conclusion, but only after exploration of alternative solutions that may better serve clients' needs. The firm's premier Insurance Coverage Practice recently expanded the breadth and depth of its services with the addition of the attorneys and staff from the Los Angeles, California-based law firm of Pasich & Kornfeld, LLP.

CLIENTS: The firm is proud of the breadth and depth of its client roster. Dickstein Shapiro represents *Fortune* 500 companies, Global 1000 companies, and small, regionally-based concerns across a variety of industries. They also represent nonprofit and government entities. For more information on their representative clients, please visit www.DicksteinShapiro.com.

Legal Innovators

HOGAN & HARTSON LLP

THE FIRM

Chairman: J Warren Gorrell, Jr

Number of partners: 418
Number of other lawyers: 578

FIRM OVERVIEW: Founded in 1904, Hogan & Hartson is the oldest and the largest major law firm based in Washington, DC. Today, it has over 1000 lawyers serving clients in a practice that cuts across virtually all legal disciplines. In addition to its Washington, DC office, which provides a natural base for the firm's national and international practice, the firm has European offices in Berlin, Munich, Brussels, London, Paris, Budapest, Prague, Warsaw, Moscow; Asian offices in Beijing, Shanghai and Tokyo; and US offices in New York, Baltimore, Northern Virginia, Miami, Los Angeles, Denver, Boulder, and Colorado Springs.

MAIN AREAS OF PRACTICE: More than 40% of Hogan & Hartson's lawyers handle corporate, securities, financial, intellectual property, tax, and other transactions throughout the world. Approximately a quarter litigate commercial and other disputes before state, federal and international tribunals, and engage in domestic and international arbitration. About 30% of the lawyers in the firm practice in areas of government regulation and policy, where decisions made in Washington, Brussels and other world capitals affect the competitive position and strategies of organizations around the globe.

INTERNATIONAL WORK: The firm's Berlin, Munich, Brussels, London, Paris, Budapest, Prague, Warsaw, and Moscow offices provide Hogan & Hartson with a strong presence and capability throughout Europe. The firm works extensively on European business transactions, and on European Union law and regulation, and assists European entities doing business in the United States. In Asia, where the firm has offices in Beijing, Shanghai and Tokyo, Hogan & Hartson has a long history of representing both Asian clients, as well as Western clients doing business throughout the region. In Beijing, the resident lawyers and legal professionals represent local and multinational clients in cross-border mergers and acquisitions, joint ventures and other investments, financings, infrastructure development and company restructurings; government regulatory matters, with a significant focus on international trade; and intellectual property. The firm's practice in Tokyo focuses principally on patent and intellectual property matters, corporate and securities, and legal issues associated with doing business in Japan. In the Middle East and Africa, attorneys in the firm's US and European offices represent clients in a wide range of projects and matters, as well as Middle Eastern and African clients doing business in the United States and Europe. The firm also has extensive experience assisting clients with matters involving Central and South America and the Caribbean, particularly in the areas of project and international finance, mergers and acquisitions, joint ventures and other investments, and international trade.

CLIENTS: Hogan & Hartson's clients range from start-up ventures to large multinational corporations in industries such as information technology; healthcare; biotechnology; pharmaceuticals; medical devices; education; food and agriculture; communications (satellite, common carrier, broadcast, and cable); energy; environmental; government procurement; real estate; media and entertainment; sports organizations; hospitality; insurance; and transportation and infrastructure. In addition, the firm represents private equity, venture capital and investment banking firms, financial institutions, nonprofit associations, quasi-governmental organizations, and foreign governments.

HEAD OFFICE

DISTRICT OF COLUMBIA
555 Thirteenth Street, N.W, **Washington**, DC 20004
Tel: 202 637 5600   **Fax:** 202 637 5910
Website: www.hhlaw.com

BRANCH OFFICES

NEW YORK
875 Third Avenue, **New York**, NY 10022
Tel: 212 918 3000   **Fax:** 212 918 3100

MARYLAND
111 South Calvert Street, **Baltimore**, MD 21202
Tel: 410 659 2700   **Fax:** 410 539 6981

VIRGINIA
8300 Greensboro Drive, **McLean**, VA 22102
Tel: 703 610 6100   **Fax:** 703 610 6200

FLORIDA
Mellon Financial Center, 1111 Brickell Avenue, **Miami**, FL 33131
Tel: 305 459 6500   **Fax:** 305 459 6550

CALIFORNIA
2049 Century Park East, **Los Angeles**, CA 90067
Tel: 310 789 5100   **Fax:** 310 789 5400

Biltmore Tower, 500 South Grand Avenue, **Los Angeles**, CA 90071
Tel: 213 337 6700   **Fax:** 213 337 6701

COLORADO
1470 Walnut Street, **Boulder**, CO 80302
Tel: 720 406 5300   **Fax:** 720 406 5301

Two North Cascade Avenue, **Colorado Springs**, CO 80903
Tel: 719 448 5900   **Fax:** 719 448 5922

One Tabor Center, 1200 Seventeenth Street, **Denver**, CO 80202
Tel: 303 899 7300   **Fax:** 303 899 7333

CONTACTS

Business & Finance ....James J Rosenhauer
Government Regulation ....Richard S Rodin
Intellectual Property ....James J Rosenhauer
Litigation ....Austin S Mittler

HOGAN & HARTSON LLP

JONES DAY

THE FIRM

Managing Partner: Stephen J Brogan
Number of partners worldwide: 616
Number of other lawyers worldwide: 1592
Website: www.jonesday.com

AREAS OF PRACTICE:

Litigation 60%
Business Practice 27%
Tax 8%
Government Regulation 5%

FIRM OVERVIEW: Jones Day encompasses more than 2,200 lawyers resident in 30 locations and ranks among the world's largest and most geographically diverse law firms. Surveys repeatedly list Jones Day as one of the law firms most frequently engaged by US corporations, and many of the firm's lawyers have achieved national recognition in their disciplines. In 2004, Jones Day was ranked number one for client service by BTI Consulting Group; was the second most cited outside counsel in Corporate Counsel's 'Who Represents America's Biggest Companies' survey; and was named Product Liability Litigation Department of the Year by The American Lawyer. The firm consistently ranks number one in M&A for number of deals worldwide; was ranked as one of the top competition practices in the world by Global Counsel in 2004; and was recognized by The American Lawyer as one of 'bankruptcy's big four' in 2003.

CLIENTS: The firm advises more than half of the Fortune 500 companies, as well as a wide variety of other entities, including privately held companies, financial institutions, investment firms, health care providers, retail chains, foundations, educational institutions, and individuals. In addition, Jones Day represents many major companies based in Europe, the Middle East, Asia, and Latin America.

INTERNATIONAL WORK: Jones Day maintains a significant presence in the principal legal and regulatory capitals of the world. In Europe, nearly 400 lawyers are based in Brussels, Frankfurt, London, Madrid, Milan, Moscow, Munich, and Paris. In Asia, approximately 140 lawyers are based in Beijing, Hong Kong, New Delhi, Shanghai, Singapore, Sydney, Taipei, and Tokyo. The firm's international practice focuses primarily on mergers and acquisitions and joint ventures; securities and finance matters; tax, labor, environmental, competition, and other regulatory matters; and international litigation and arbitration.

US OFFICES

IRVINE

3 Park Plaza, Suite 1100, Irvine CA 92614-8505

Office Profile: Jones Day's Irvine office is located in the center of Southern California's Technology Coast. The office provides legal services to both emerging and established companies responding to today's accelerated business environment. These services involve focused legal teams active in litigation and intellectual property.

LOS ANGELES

555 West Fifth Street, Suite 4600, Los Angeles CA 90013-1025

Office Profile: Jones Day's Los Angeles office represents many of California's major corporations, institutions, and emerging companies. The office has a dominating litigation practice and is home to the firm's strong health care practice and a burgeoning technology and intellectual property practice.

US OFFICE CONTACTS

CALIFORNIA
3 Park Plaza, Suite 1100, **Irvine** CA 92614-8505
Tel: 949 851 3939   **Fax:** 949 553 7539
Email: counsel@jonesday.com

555 West Fifth Street, Suite 4600, **Los Angeles** CA 90013-1025
Tel: 213 489 3939   **Fax:** 213 243 2539
Email: counsel@jonesday.com

2882 Sand Hill Road, Suite 240, **Menlo Park** CA 94025
Tel: 650 739 3939   **Fax:** 650 739 3900
Email: counsel@jonesday.com

12750 High Bluff Drive, Suite 300, **San Diego** CA 92103-2083
Tel: 858 314 1200   **Fax:** 858 314 1150
Email: counsel@jonesday.com

555 California Street, 26th Floor, **San Francisco** CA 94104
Tel: 415 626 3939   **Fax:** 415 875 5700
Email: counsel@jonesday.com

DISTRICT OF COLUMBIA
51 Louisiana Avenue, NW, **Washington** DC 20001-2113
Tel: 202 879 3939   **Fax:** 202 626 1700
Email: counsel@jonesday.com

GEORGIA
1420 Peachtree Street, NE, Suite 800, **Atlanta** GA 30309-3053
Tel: 404 521 3939   **Fax:** 404 581 8330
Email: counsel@jonesday.com

ILLINOIS
77 West Wacker, **Chicago** IL 60601-1692
Tel: 312 782 3939   **Fax:** 312 782 8585
Email: counsel@jonesday.com

OHIO
North Point, 901 Lakeside Avenue, **Cleveland** OH 44114-1190
Tel: 216 586 3939   **Fax:** 216 579 0212
Email: counsel@jonesday.com

325 John H McConnell Boulevard, Suite 600, **Columbus** OH 43215-2673
Tel: 614 469 3939   **Fax:** 614 461 4198
Email: counsel@jonesday.com

NEW YORK
222 East 41st Street, **New York** NY 10017-6702
Tel: 212 326 3939   **Fax:** 212 755 7306
Email: counsel@jonesday.com

PENNSYLVANIA
One Mellon Bank Center, 31st Floor, 500 Grant Street,
Pittsburgh PA 15219-2502
Tel: 412 391 3939   **Fax:** 412 394 7959
Email: counsel@jonesday.com

TEXAS
2727 North Harwood Street, **Dallas** TX 75201-1515
Tel: 214 220 3939   **Fax:** 214 969 5100
Email: counsel@jonesday.com

717 Texas, Suite 3300, **Houston** TX 77002-2712
Tel: 832 239 3939   **Fax:** 832 239 3600
Email: counsel@jonesday.com

JONES DAY cont'd

MENLO PARK

2882 Sand Hill Road, Suite 240, Menlo Park CA 94025

Office Profile: The Menlo Park office enables the firm's technology practice to provide high-quality legal services for Silicon Valley entrepreneurial and venture capital clients and also provides localized capacity for new and existing public companies focused on emerging technology.

SAN DIEGO

12750 High Bluff Drive, Suite 300, San Diego CA 92130-2083

Office Profile: Jones Day's San Diego office is located in the center of San Diego's biotechnology industry. The office provides legal services to both emerging and established companies responsible for the significant growth of San Diego's life sciences community. These services are provided by lawyers with advanced technical degrees and experience in the full spectrum of intellectual property issues facing Southern California's technology-driven companies.

SAN FRANCISCO

555 California Street, 26th Floor, San Francisco CA 94104

Office Profile: Opened in May 2003, the San Francisco office extends Jones Day's presence into a region where clients face significant litigation and other legal problems. The 37 lawyers in San Francisco focus primarily on complex civil litigation, including antitrust, employment law, product liability, and securities.

WASHINGTON, DC

51 Louisiana Avenue, NW, Washington DC 20001-2113

Office Profile: Jones Day established its Washington office in 1946. Today, more than 245 lawyers provide a complete range of legal services and are conversant with industry-specific areas such as manufacturing, technology, banking, financial services, real estate, healthcare, energy, consumer products, retail, and telecommunications.

ATLANTA

1402 Peachtree Street, NE, Suite 800, Atlanta GA 30309-3053

Office Profile: Jones Day Atlanta, opened in 1989, is composed of more than 130 lawyers. The diverse business law practice addresses the legal needs of capital users and capital providers under the leadership of experienced corporate and real estate practitioners. The office has substantial litigation, tax, finance, and banking practices.

CHICAGO

77 West Wacker, Chicago IL 60601-1692

Office Profile: Jones Day's Chicago office opened in 1987. With more than 150 lawyers, the office provides a full range of legal services for clients ranging from Fortune 500 companies to privately held and emerging companies and international concerns. Chicago lawyers handle a wide variety of US and international business transactions as well as litigation.

CLEVELAND

North Point, 901 Lakeside Avenue, Cleveland OH 44114-1190

Office Profile: Jones Day Cleveland, the firm's original office, opened in 1893. Today, the Cleveland office encompasses more than 270 lawyers who provide legal services in business transactions, government regulation, litigation, and tax to a diverse group of clients based throughout the United States and around the world.

COLUMBUS

325 John H McConnell Boulevard, Suite 600, Columbus OH 43215-2673

Office Profile: Opened in 1980, Jones Day Columbus today has approximately 90 lawyers and provides a full range of legal services to public and private businesses and individuals located or having legal needs in Central Ohio and around the country.

NEW YORK

222 East 41st Street, New York NY 10017-6702

Office Profile: Opened in 1986, the New York office has grown to more than 270 lawyers, ranking it among the largest New York offices of any non-New York-based national firm. Jones Day New York plays a leading role in the Firm's capital markets and international activities.

PITTSBURGH

One Mellon Bank Center, 31st Floor, 500 Grant Street, Pittsburgh PA 15219-2502

Office Profile: Jones Day opened its Pittsburgh office in January 1989 as the firm's 14th office. It has more than 55 lawyers who provide legal services in five principal areas of practice: business practice and transactions; real estate; environmental; litigation; and labor and employment law.

DALLAS

2727 North Harwood Street, Dallas TX 75201-1515

Office Profile: Jones Day's Dallas office consists of more than 180 lawyers. The office represents a wide variety of corporate clients engaged in the banking, financial services, investment, technology, electronic commerce, software services, oil and gas, energy, healthcare, real estate, construction, manufacturing, consumer products, and retail industries.

HOUSTON

717 Texas, Suite 3300, Houston TX 77002-2712

Office Profile: Opened on January 1, 2001, the Houston office has more than 50 lawyers who provide legal services in three principal areas of practice: business transactions, litigation, and energy regulation. The office is also the worldwide headquarters of the firm's Energy Specialized Industry Practice, which brings the best of the firm's practice resources and extensive industry experience to the representation of energy clients.

KIRKPATRICK & LOCKHART NICHOLSON GRAHAM LLP

THE FIRM

**Chairman of the Management Committee &
Managing Partner:** Peter J Kalis
Number of partners: 323
Number of other lawyers: 627

Website: www.klng.com

FIRM OVERVIEW: Kirkpatrick & Lockhart Nicholson Graham LLP (K&LNG) – the product of one of the largest Anglo-American legal combinations in history on January 1, 2005 – comprises 950 lawyers who practice from offices throughout the US and in London, England. K&LNG represents entrepreneurs, growth and middle-market companies and leading global corporations in every major industry group. The firm practices across all legal disciplines within the corporate, litigation and regulatory fields. K&LNG's extensive knowledge about the business sectors in which our clients operate enables the practice to be at once regional, national and international in scope, cutting edge, complex, and dynamic. K&LNG was the only law firm in the world to receive the CIO Magazine CIO 100 Award for three consecutive years, while the official publication of the Minority Corporate Counsel Association selected K&LNG as one of only four American law firms to feature for their innovative diversity initiatives.

MAIN AREAS OF PRACTICE:

Corporate: K&LNG practices law on an integrated and firm-wide basis. The multi-office, international corporate and transactional practice is one of the most substantial in the profession. The firm closed over 100 M&A transactions last year, and is perennially a leader as issuer's counsel in equities issued by corporate clients, both in terms of number of transactions and proceeds. K&LNG has completed hundreds of public debt and equity offerings over the last decade.

Litigation: K&LNG's litigation engagements including, among other substantive areas, insurance coverage, intellectual property, real estate, white-collar criminal, construction, professional liability, environmental, toxic tort, products liability, franchise, tax, bankruptcy and insolvency, antitrust and competition, employment, benefits, and securities fraud are among the largest and most attractive enjoyed by any law firm. The firm has been rated a leading practice in the representation of corporate policyholders in the insurance coverage area, and as a leading litigation firm for the financial sector. It is active in jurisdictions around the US and in the UK as well as in various international arbitration forums.

Regulatory: K&LNG's Regulatory Practice cuts across the many disciplines that require highly specialized knowledge and experience to address governmental regulation of the private markets. The firm's lawyers regularly represent clients before regulatory bodies in both the US and the UK. Its premier regulatory practice is in the diversified financial services area. K&LNG represents a large majority of the major financial institutions and securities firms in a variety of disciplines, and the investment management practice is a perennial leader. Many of the firm's practice leaders as well as more junior lawyers have governmental experience that enhances their ability to serve K&LNG's clients in regulatory fields, while others have held prominent positions in regulated industries.

Emerging Practices: The firm continuously allocates resources so that its capabilities reach to the forefront of emerging disciplines. K&LNG's Intellectual Property Practice, with approximately 100 practicing lawyers, and its Technology Practice, serving growth companies in disciplines such as biotechnology, internet services, medical devices, and information systems, are examples of how this investment has borne fruit. Most frequently, the firm continues to recruit lateral partners in such disparate fields as structured finance, bankruptcy, real estate, food and drug, ERISA litigation, Small Business Administration financing, telecommunications, project finance, intellectual property, private equity, trademarks, employment and public sector technology to address the evolving needs of its

OFFICES

CALIFORNIA
10100 Santa Monica Boulevard, 7th Floor, **Los Angeles**, CA 90067
Tel: 310 552 5000 **Fax:** 310 552 5001

Four Embarcadero Center, 10th Floor, **San Francisco**, CA 94111
Tel: 415 249 1000 **Fax:** 415 249 1001

DISTRICT OF COLUMBIA
1800 Massachusetts Avenue, NW, 2nd Floor, **Washington**, DC 20036-1221
Tel: 202 778 9000 **Fax:** 202 778 9100

FLORIDA
Miami Center, 201 South Biscayne Boulevard, 20th Floor,
Miami, FL 33131-2399
Tel: 305 539 3300 **Fax:** 305 358 7095

MASSACHUSETTS
75 State Street, **Boston**, MA 02109
Tel: 617 261 3100 **Fax:** 617 261 3175

NEW JERSEY
One Newark Center, 10th Floor, **Newark**, NJ 07102-5252
Tel: 973 848 4000 **Fax:** 973 848 4001

NEW YORK
599 Lexington Avenue, **New York**, NY 10022-6030
Tel: 212 536 3900 **Fax:** 212 536 3901

PENNSYLVANIA
Payne Shoemaker Building, 240 North Third Street, **Harrisburg**, PA 17101-1507
Tel: 717 231 4500 **Fax:** 717 231 4501

Henry W. Oliver Building, 535 Smithfield Street, **Pittsburgh**, PA 15222-2312
Tel: 412 355 6500 **Fax:** 412 355 6501

TEXAS
2828 North Harwood Street, Suite 1800, **Dallas**, TX 75201-6966
Tel: 214 939 4900 **Fax:** 214 939 4949

INTERNATIONAL OFFICES

The firm also has an office in London, UK

clientele. The firm strives to maintain a creative, interdisciplinary approach to the practice, as evidenced by the extraordinary convergence of disciplines that permitted its K&LNG colleague, former US Attorney General Dick Thornburgh, to act as the court appointed Examiner in the WorldCom bankruptcy proceeding – the largest bankruptcy in US history – and the firm itself to act as his counsel.

CLIENTS: K&LNG currently represents or recently has performed projects for over half of the FORTUNE 100; 21 of the 25 largest mutual fund complexes or their investment managers; and 18 of the 20 largest US bank holding companies or their affiliates. Representative clients include Alcoa, Bank of America, DuPont, Fidelity, Halliburton, Mellon, PPG, United Technologies, Wachovia, and World Wrestling Entertainment. The firm is a multiple winner of DuPont's Meeting the Challenge Award for its 'remarkable and extraordinary accomplishments' for that client, and is the only law firm on which PPG Industries has conferred its Excellent Supplier Award.

INTERNATIONAL WORK: With offices throughout the US and in London, K&LNG represents clients across North America and the United Kingdom on matters that span the globe. K&LNG's primary working language is English, but the firm has attorneys fluent in Afrikaans, Chinese (Mandarin), Farsi, French, German, Greek, Hebrew, Hindi, Italian, Japanese, Korean, Polish, Portuguese, Russian and Spanish. Various members of the firm have foreign degrees, which enable them to take into account legal and cultural differences in representing the firm's clients in international transaction and litigation matters worldwide.

LEVINE, BLASZAK, BLOCK & BOOTHBY, LLP

THE FIRM

Senior Partner: Henry D Levine

Number of partners: 14
Number of other lawyers: 3

AREAS OF PRACTICE:
Telecom/IT Procurement 60%
Telecom/IT Workouts & Dispute Resolution 20%
Telecom/IT Regulation 20%

HEAD OFFICE

DISTRICT OF COLUMBIA
2001 L Street NW, Suite 900, **Washington**, DC 20036
Tel: 202 857 2550 **Fax:** 202 223 0833
Website: www.lb3law.com

FIRM OVERVIEW: Founded in 1993, Levine, Blaszak, Block & Boothby, LLP (LB3) specializes in communications and technology law, with particular emphasis on the representation of large users (including approximately 50% of the Fortune 100), information technology companies, and companies built on new technologies. LB3 has unparalleled experience in negotiating custom network service agreements, network outsourcings, and related transactions on behalf of large users. In partnership with its consulting affiliate, TechCaliber, LLP, the firm provides its clients with the legal and financial expertise they need to secure leading edge telecom contracts. The firm is also the principal representative of large end users and IT companies before the FCC and other regulators, and before courts and arbitrators when their relationships with communications providers break down. And LB3 advises clients in connection with e-business and software development, implementation and maintenance agreements, and telecom related acquisitions and securities offerings.

MAIN AREAS OF PRACTICE:

Custom Network Service Agreements: LB3 specializes in the negotiation of custom network service agreements and other complex telecommunications transactions. Such agreements typically involve an array of voice and data services, and may include satellite, VOIP, internet and network management services as well. The purchase/lease of complex equipment and wireless services may be folded in or negotiated separately. LB3 lawyers pioneered these agreements, and today assist clients in the development of telecom procurement strategies; assist in vendor selection; and negotiate the required contracts.

Network Outsourcing/Managed Network Services: Over the past decade, network service arrangements have evolved to encompass sophisticated management services and the purchase of customer equipment, software licenses and the hiring of customer personnel as part of an agreement under which the customer outsources telecommunications operations and/or management to a third party. LB3 has represented the purchaser in many of the largest and most sophisticated telecom outsourcings.

Internet & E-business: The firm develops creative and durable frameworks that minimize risk and scale to meet clients' evolving workforces, network topologies, and application platforms. LB3 lawyers have negotiated agreements for internet access, internet protocol multicasting, Virtual Private Networks (VPNs), and voice-over-internet services to support client business requirements. LB3 attorneys have also structured e-business transactions ranging from web hosting to application hosting, content management, remote application maintenance, streaming media, co-branding and global portal development. In connection with web services, the firm negotiates software agreements covering applicatons development, implementation and maintenance.

Carrier Purchasers & New Entrants: Carriers have turned to the firm for advice on carrier-to-carrier transport and dark fiber agreements. The firm also represents new carriers in negotiating (and arbitrating) interconnection agreements.

Corporate & IPO Support: The firm frequently works with securities counsel on the telecommunications regulatory or industry-specific portions of SEC filings and prospectuses.

Communications Policy & Regulation: LB3 keeps large users informed of regulatory and legal developments that affect their service acquisition strategies, and represents them in policy proceedings before regulatory and legislative bodies. The firm is known for its ability to penetrate the complex issues spawned by changes in the telecom law and regulations; the growth of competition; the emergence of new technologies; the convergence of IT and communications; and the rise of the internet. The policy debates confronting the information technology industry often raise issues for which there is no precedent. In these areas, the firm has helped to write, not just interpret, the law. The issues in which LB3 has been involved include usage-based charges for internet services; efforts to regulate the internet; competitive deployment of broadband services, cable equipment, and wireless internet services; and US digital television standards.

Contract Workouts: Disputes are inevitable, and the firm is a leader in the representation of purchasers in disputes arising out of the terms or termination of their telecom agreements. The firm has been involved in the amicable (or not so amicable) resolution of scores of disputes involving service levels; shortfall penalties; and billing.

FCC Complaints & Litigation: The firm's lawyers have broad and deep expertise with telecom-related claims and complaint proceedings before courts, state regulators and the FCC. The firm's lawyers have also assisted parties and counsel when communications issues arise in areas such as the interpretation of contracts and tariffs; service cost and reliability; and billing disputes, and have served as expert witnesses on such issues in a variety of settings.

CLIENTS: The firm's international clients include General Motors, IBM, DuPont, Merrill Lynch, Pearson, Inc., WPP, Nestlé, and Hyatt International.

INTERNATIONAL WORK: The firm has helped a number of the world's largest multinational corporations negotiate contracts to purchase telecommunications and related services on a regional or global basis with reasonable uniformity of terms, appropriate accountability for performance, and due regard for the special regulatory, technical and business challenges posed by these transactions.

MCKEE NELSON LLP

THE FIRM

Senior Partners: William S McKee, William F Nelson

Number of partners: 35
Number of other lawyers: 75

FIRM OVERVIEW: McKee Nelson LLP is an independent, entrepreneurial law firm specializing in structured finance, tax litigation and tax planning, founded with the common vision to engage only in those practices in which it could be truly excellent. Built by experienced lawyers who were leaders of their former practices and firms, McKee Nelson serves the tax litigation, transactional structuring and capital markets needs of multinational companies. Established in 1999, the firm has grown rapidly to include over 120 lawyers, solidifying its broad experience in its chosen areas and positioning itself to help companies conduct business throughout the world.

MAIN AREAS OF PRACTICE:

Structured Finance & Securitization: Recognized as one of the biggest players nationwide in mortgages, auto loans and collateralized debt obligations (CDOs), McKee Nelson is experienced in all asset classes, including domestic and cross-border offerings and private placements of mortgage-backed and asset-backed securities through US and offshore issuing vehicles. The firm has structured a broad range of transactions, fixed and revolving, including REMICs, FASITs, owner trusts, grantor trusts, master trusts and commercial paper vehicles, using virtually every cash flow structure and form of credit enhancement, as well as a wide array of complex structured products. In addition, the firm's structured finance and securitization attorneys have represented every major Wall Street investment bank, most major federal agency guarantors and sponsors, and numerous other parties in domestic and international structured finance transactions, including CDO offerings. From the establishment of the CDO practice in 2003 through the end of 2004, McKee Nelson has served as counsel in the closing of approximately 50 different CDOs. The firm's lawyers generally serve as transaction counsel, representing both the issuer and the commercial or investment bank, and have also represented numerous asset managers in CDO transactions.

Tax Litigation: Attorneys in McKee Nelson's Tax Litigation Practice represent US and foreign taxpayers in some of the largest and most legally significant federal tax cases. McKee Nelson offers clients the combination of technical tax expertise and tax litigation experience to respond effectively to any federal tax challenge – from IRS audits, appeals and competent authority matters, to the most complex trial and appellate litigation. Attorneys in this practice area are tax lawyers as well as veteran trial and appellate lawyers with considerable insight into government behavior. The group includes a former IRS Chief Counsel, former IRS and US Treasury Department officials, and former IRS and Justice Department tax litigators. They have appeared before the US Tax Court, US Court of Federal Claims, US District Courts and numerous US Courts of Appeals.

Tax Planning: The firm's founding partners, Bill McKee and Will Nelson, co-authored the leading treatises on partnership taxation and the structuring and drafting of partnership agreements. Mr Nelson was Chief

Counsel of the IRS, and Mr. McKee was the Tax Legislative Counsel at the US Treasury Department. Their practice helps businesses strategize and structure complex transactions in ways that minimize their tax burden. Transactions often involve multinationals doing business in multiple jurisdictions, regions and countries, where tax implications can be significant. The key areas of focus include partnerships, joint ventures, asset securitizations, complex financings, mergers, acquisitions and dispositions. Because most deals are economically complex and require significant structuring, the practice makes cross-disciplinary solutions a top priority.

Transfer Pricing: Attorneys in McKee Nelson's Transfer Pricing Practice help large corporations plan transfer pricing strategies to configure their businesses with the greatest efficiency in the most challenging global tax environments. The firm's lawyers have a mastery of complex tax rules, a facility with economic principles, an ability to harness voluminous factual data, and a capacity to navigate worldwide regulatory regimes. McKee Nelson offers clients a unique combination of resources and expertise to handle all phases of complex, global transfer pricing transactions. By integrating transfer pricing planning, documentation and controversy into a unified platform, the firm helps corporations manage their transfer pricing positions.

Corporate/Securities, Finance & Mergers & Acquisitions: This practice handles a diverse range of the most sophisticated public and private transactions. The firm provides sector-specific expertise to corporations from various industries doing business in multiple jurisdictions, regions and countries, and its lawyers are experienced in closing deals that are complex and require significant structuring. They also make cross-disciplinary solutions a top priority by working closely with premier structured finance and tax planning practices to structure and execute innovative transactions.

CLIENTS: McKee Nelson represents some of the world's largest corporations. The firm's clients are generally Fortune 500 companies, including nine of the Fortune 16, from a diverse range of business sectors. Clients include US firms engaged in foreign business activities, as well as foreign-based firms operating within the United States.

HEAD OFFICE

DISTRICT OF COLUMBIA
1919 M Street NW, Suite 800, **Washington**, DC 20036
Tel: 202 775 1880   **Fax:** 202 775 8586
Email: info@mckeenelson.com
Website: www.mckeenelson.com

BRANCH OFFICES

NEW YORK
5 Times Square, 35th Floor, **New York**, NY 10036
Tel: 917 777 4200   **Fax:** 917 777 4299
Email: info@mckeenelson.com

McKee Nelson LLP

SHAW PITTMAN LLP

THE FIRM

Managing Partner: Stephen B Huttler

Number of lawyers: 400

FIRM OVERVIEW: Founded in 1954, Shaw Pittman's nearly 400 attorneys, consultants, and business professionals serve as trusted advisors to clients with complex legal and business issues. Shaw Pittman features multidisciplinary legal teams that provide thorough regulatory, transactional, litigation, and legislative counsel to its clients. The firm's US and international clients include *Fortune 500* firms, established and emerging corporations, governments and government agencies, and public sector organizations. With locations in both the US and abroad, Shaw Pittman delivers comprehensive legal representation to clients on every continent. *At press time, Shaw Pittman LLP had entered into a merger agreement with Pillsbury Winthrop LLP. The merger is expected to close by March 31st 2005. Post-closing, the name of the firm will be Pillsbury Winthrop Shaw Pittman LLP.*

MAIN AREAS OF PRACTICE:

Aviation: Shaw Pittman specializes in aviation law, with one of the premier aviation practices in the nation. The firm represents many of the largest commercial airlines and airports in the world on cutting-edge issues that have transformed the regulatory landscape. The firm's lawyers provide strategic advice to a broad array of clients from every sector in the aviation and aerospace industry, including major US airlines, airport owners and operators, foreign airlines, new entrant airlines, commuter airlines, charter airlines, manufacturers, state and local governments, repair stations, tour operators, trade associations, and financial institutions.

Communications: Shaw Pittman lawyers advise clients on matters concerning communications networks and facilities, mass media and related technology, satellites, and telecommunications. The firm's clients include communications enterprises, satellite operators and vendors, broadcast networks, television and radio stations, cable companies, and internet service providers.

Corporate: Shaw Pittman has represented clients in some of the largest mergers, acquisitions, and initial public offerings (IPOs) in US history. The firm helps clients explore and resolve regulatory and compliance issues, identify and secure venture capital, launch IPOs, and pursue or defend against litigation. Shaw Pittman's clients include start-up companies, established enterprises, banks, investment firms, issuers, and underwriters.

Energy: For more than 50 years Shaw Pittman has been recognized as one of the preeminent energy-related practices in the world. Shaw Pittman advises clients on matters related to electric power, natural gas, coal, petroleum, and nuclear energy. The firm created the country's first nuclear energy practice more than forty years ago.

Financial Institutions: Shaw Pittman serves financial institutions' needs in regulatory and statutory compliance, sales and secured transactions, enforcement proceedings, legislative and lobbying activities, electronic banking, and tax matters. The firm represents more than fifty US and international commercial and savings banks, affiliates, holding companies, and thrifts in 15 countries around the world.

Intellectual Property: Shaw Pittman counsels clients on patents, trademarks and unfair competition, and domain name disputes. The firm also advises clients on matters related to copyrights, information technology, trade secrets, technology transfers, and publishing.

HEAD OFFICE

DISTRICT OF COLUMBIA
2300 N Street, NW, **Washington**, DC 20037
Tel: 202 663 8000   **Fax:** 202 663 8007
Website: www.shawpittman.com

BRANCH OFFICES

CALIFORNIA
1950 University Avenue, Suite 505, **East Palo Alto**, CA 94303
Tel: 650 833 4700   **Fax:** 650 833 4701

NEW YORK
335 Madison Avenue, 26th Floor, **New York City**, NY 10017
Tel: 212 603 6800   **Fax:** 212 603 6801

VIRGINIA
1650 Tysons Boulevard, **McLean**, VA 22102
Tel: 703 770 7900   **Fax:** 703 770 7901

INTERNATIONAL OFFICES

Shaw Pittman also has offices in London and Taipei.

Litigation: Shaw Pittman lawyers have successfully litigated multimillion dollar cases in more than 40 different states. The firm's litigators represent clients in matters involving technology and intellectual property, commercial disputes, and energy and environmental claims. The firm also litigates issues related to employment disputes, defamation, insurance, international trade, government enforcement, and white-collar crime.

Real Estate: Shaw Pittman is home to one of the most highly regarded real estate practices in the US. The firm helps US and international investors, lenders, and borrowers secure financing, buy and sell real estate, and structure REITs. The firm also helps clients respond to regulatory actions, negotiate contracts, qualify for real estate tax credits, and adhere to zoning, land use, and development laws. Shaw Pittman recently closed the largest privatization of military housing in US history.

Tax: The firm helps its clients resolve tax issues by offering tax counseling and strategic planning, conducting transactions, and litigating tax controversies. The firm also responds to and defends tax rulings, reviews tax policy, and performs legislative and regulatory lobbying.

Technology: Shaw Pittman is globally recognized as the world's premier technology practice. The firm pioneered the field of technology outsourcing more than 15 years ago and has successfully completed more outsourcing transactions than any other law firm in the world. Shaw Pittman's 450 technology transactions have a total value in excess of $325 billion. The firm's Global Sourcing Practice includes an integrated group of non-legal consultants who provide a broad range of business, technical, financial and change management skills. The Global Sourcing Practice assists clients throughout all phases of the sourcing lifecycle and has been at the forefront of information technology outsourcing, business process outsourcing (BPO), and offshore outsourcing.

ShawPittman LLP

A Limited Liability Partnership Including Professional Corporations

SPRIGGS & HOLLINGSWORTH

THE FIRM

Managing Partner: William J Spriggs

Number of partners: 34
Number of other lawyers: 36

FIRM OVERVIEW: Founded in 1982, Spriggs & Hollingsworth specializes in complex civil, criminal, and administrative litigation and associated regulatory counseling. The firm works with clients to achieve not only jury and bench trial verdicts, but also pre-trial summary judgments, post-trial appellate decisions, third-party allocations of responsibility, and negotiated settlements. The practice is national, and its expertise extends beyond traditional litigation and counseling into innovative alternative dispute resolution at both international and domestic sites. The firm is proud to represent some of the largest and most competitive companies in a number of major industries, and values its strong relationships with its clients, many of whom the firm has worked with for more than 20 years.

MAIN AREAS OF PRACTICE:

Pharmaceutical Products: The firm represents some of the world's largest pharmaceutical manufacturers in individual cases and serial litigation involving personal injuries alleged to be associated with the use of prescription drugs. The firm handles these matters from the earliest pre-trial proceedings through Daubert hearings, trials and appeals, and often appears as national trial counsel.

Toxic Torts & Products Liability: The firm defends class actions, mass torts and single-site suits arising from alleged chemical exposures and defective products, defense of federal agency proceedings, and associated regulatory representation and counseling.

Financial Institutions: The firm's expertise in banking litigation extends to savings associations and credit unions as well as the holding companies of all types of financial institutions. Their attorneys also represent officers, directors and shareholders of financial institutions in connection with civil, criminal and administrative litigation and investigations of all kinds. They work closely with financial institutions and their regulatory counsel (inside or outside the institutions) to defend the conduct of the institutions and their officials or to pursue damage claims on behalf of injured institutions.

Federal Claims: The firm handles prosecution of federal contract and Fifth Amendment taking and due process cases and related regulatory litigation against federal, state and local governments.

Construction: The firm's attorneys have extensive experience handling all types of construction disputes or claims. They have prepared and defended delay, inefficiency and various direct cost claims. Outside of the traditional construction claim arena, the firm has specialized expertise in bid protests, construction insurance claims, performance and payment bond issues, and fiduciary duty claims.

Government Contracts: The firm's Government Contracts Practice handles all aspects of government procurement, from bid preparation, contract negotiation and bid protests to claim preparation, negotiation and dispute resolution. It counsels clients on all legislative, regulatory and administrative issues arising from government procurement.

Insurance: The firm has pursued insurance recoveries for environmental liabilities, product liabilities, construction, and other claims involving amounts upwards of a billion dollars on behalf of its national and interna-

HEAD OFFICE

DISTRICT OF COLUMBIA
1350 I Street, NW, **Washington**, DC 20005
Tel: 202 898 5800 **Fax:** 202 682 1639
Email: info@spriggs.com
Website: www.spriggs.com

CONTACTS

Pharmaceutical Products	Joe G Hollingsworth
Toxic Tort & Products Liability	Joe G Hollingsworth
Financial Institutions	Jerry Stouck
Federal Claims	Jerry Stouck
Construction	Douglas L Patin
Government Contracts	William J Spriggs, Douglas L Patin
	Jerry Stouck
Insurance	Marc S Mayerson, Douglas L Patin
Environmental	Donald W Fowler
White-Collar Defense	Charles S Leeper, Stephen R Spivack

tional corporate client base. This includes leading pharmaceutical, bioscience, and chemical-manufacturing companies, consumer products companies, manufacturers, holding companies, construction and facilities-management firms, and asbestos defendants (producers, installers, premises owners).

Environmental: The firm's Environmental Practice encompasses the full spectrum of business, regulatory and litigation issues that companies regularly confront. It advises clients on the meaning and impact of state and federal regulatory requirements with respect to all environmental media. The firm evaluates, designs and audits compliance programs and assists its clients in managing environmental aspects of business transactions.

White Collar Defense: The firm represents corporations and individual corporate executives; high-ranking government officials, including White House and Cabinet officials; and other individuals, in a wide range of matters relating to alleged criminal law violations, civil fraud proceedings, administrative enforcement actions, Independent Counsel investigations, and related congressional hearings and proceedings.

STEPTOE & JOHNSON LLP

THE FIRM

Managing Partner: Roger Warin
Vice Chair: Doug Green

Number of partners: 143
Number of other lawyers: 273

FIRM OVERVIEW: With more than 400 attorneys, Steptoe & Johnson LLP provides counsel and representation in a wide range of legal matters. In more than 50 years of practice, the firm has gained a national and international reputation for vigorous representation of clients before governmental agencies, successful advocacy in litigation and arbitration, and creative and practical advice in guiding business transactions. The firm has offices in Washington, New York, Phoenix, Los Angeles, London, and Brussels.

MAIN AREAS OF PRACTICE:

Business Solutions: Whether routine or complex, national or global, this practice group of over 100 attorneys capably advances clients' business interests. Steptoe attorneys have extensive experience in corporate legal services and offer clients general business counseling and transactional services, along with specific support in the areas of tax, employee benefits (ERISA), labor and employment, bankruptcy and creditor rights, and real estate, with a strong focus on clients' bottom line.

Energy, Environment, & Natural Resources: With one of the broadest and most experienced energy practices in the country, Steptoe is well-equipped to find creative solutions to complex energy, environmental, chemical regulatory, and natural resource matters. Steptoe has long had one of the leading electric utility practices in the country, involving federal and state regulation of utilities, approval of utility mergers, and global transactional matters. Clients of the pipeline practice include major oil companies, independent pipelines, and foreign governments. The firm's Energy Transactions Practice serves major energy producers and suppliers, foreign governments, domestic and international pipelines, holding companies, and quasi-governmental corporations. The Chemical Regulatory Practice has extensive international experience in US, EU, and UK regulation of pesticides and other chemicals.

International Trade & Investment: For more than four decades, Steptoe has been consistently involved in complex and high-profile international trade cases. The lawyers in the firm's International Trade and Investment Group have in-depth knowledge and experience in a wide range of areas, including international trade litigation, international trade policy and strategy, World Trade Organization, EU law, export controls and international regulatory compliance, customs, immigration, international arbitration, international business transactions, international aviation, and public international law.

Litigation: When the future of a company hangs in the balance, many of the nation's high-profile executives and corporations choose Steptoe. According to a recent *National Law Journal* survey, Steptoe is among the most often used litigation outside counsel for a number of Fortune 500 companies. The firm's experience includes litigation in such areas as antitrust, ERISA, employment, government contracts, insurance, toxic torts, and surface transportation. The firm also has substantial experience in complex commercial litigation, white-collar criminal defense, and intellectual property dispute resolution. The insurance litigation practice is widely respected, as is the litigation group's skill in handling multi-party, multi-jurisdictional litigation.

HEAD OFFICE

DISTRICT OF COLUMBIA
1330 Connecticut Ave, NW, **Washington**, DC 20036
Tel: 202 429 3000   **Fax:** 202 429 3902
Email: jneidecker@steptoe.com
Website: steptoe.com

BRANCH OFFICES

ARIZONA
Collier Center, 201 East Washington St, Suite 1600, **Phoenix**, AZ 85004
Tel: 602 257 5200   **Fax:** 602 257 5299

CALIFORNIA
633 West 5th Street, Suite 700, **Los Angeles**, CA 90071
Tel: 213 439 9400   **Fax:** 213 439 9599

NEW YORK
750 Seventh Avenue, Suite 1900, **New York**, NY 10019
Tel: 212 506 3900   **Fax:** 212 506 3950

INTERNATIONAL OFFICES

The firm also has offices in London and Brussels.

CONTACTS

Antitrust	Mark Horning
Energy & Natural Resources	Steve Brose
ERISA/Employment	Paul Ondrasik
Insurance	Toni Ianniello
International	Sue Esserman
IP & Telecomm	Alfred Mamlet
Litigation	Roger Warin
Tax	Mark Silverman
Technology	Alfred Mamlet
Transactions	Fil Agusti/Scott Katzman
White-Collar Crime	Mark Hulkower

Technology: This leading national and international practice represents innovative information technology, financial services, intellectual property, e-commerce, telecommunications, and other technology-intensive companies on cutting-edge legal issues. Through a highly integrated service approach, the technology practice unites the firm's regulatory, corporate, and litigation experience with its tax, antitrust, and other capabilities. The firm's significant US and EU regulatory and corporate capabilities offer technology clients experienced representation on both sides of the Atlantic.

STEPTOE & JOHNSON LLP

STERNE, KESSLER, GOLDSTEIN & FOX P.L.L.C

THE FIRM

Managing Director: Jorge A Goldstein, PhD

Number of directors: 21
Number of other lawyers: 50

FIRM OVERVIEW: Sterne, Kessler, Goldstein & Fox P.L.L.C specializes in the creation, protection and transfer of intellectual property. The firm services the high value intellectual property needs of its clients with industry-savvy teams of attorneys who are as scientifically learned as they are legally astute. Founded in 1978 and based in Washington, DC, the law firm has over 100 patent attorneys, agents and technical specialists who have a unique combination of legal and technical skills.

MAIN AREAS OF PRACTICE:

Abbreviated New Drug Application Filings: The firm counsels clients in matters arising at the interface between patent law and the FDA approval process. Its practice includes patent validity and infringement analyses, exclusivity strategies, preparation of patent certifications for ANDA's, ANDA-related litigation and appeals before the Court of Appeals for the Federal Circuit.

Interferences: Sterne, Kessler, Goldstein & Fox's experience runs the gamut from pre-declaration activities to successful appeals to the Federal Circuit. The firm is experienced in all phases of the practice, including the copying of claims, motions, count formation, testimony period, depositions, corroborated proofs, etc, as well as final hearings before the PTO Board of Patent Appeals and Interferences and appeals to the court. It has represented US and foreign clients in two-party and multiparty interferences and has acted on behalf of either junior or senior parties. The firm has successfully represented patentees in defending against post issuance interferences and also have successfully represented applicants against both patentees and other applicants.

Litigation, Trial & Appellate: Sterne, Kessler, Goldstein & Fox's attorneys have experience in all phases of litigation practice. The firm adroitly handles both complex litigation as well as enforcement matters. Its experience litigating patent infringement disputes extends to a variety of technologies including biotechnology, communications, consumer products, electronics, mechanical equipment, pharmaceuticals, robotics, semiconductors and wireless. In addition, it has extensive litigation experience in the fields of trade secret law, contracts, trademarks, and design patents. The firm has experience practicing before numerous Federal District Courts throughout the United States. In addition, the firm's attorneys have successfully appeared before the Court of Appeals for the Federal Circuit and other regional Circuit Courts of Appeal.

Nanotechnology: The firm began serving nanotechnology clients in 1994 and has steadily seen interest grow in this area of its practice since that time. Sterne, Kessler, Goldstein & Fox currently represents nanotechnology clients in areas including semiconductors, nanoelectronics, nanocomputing, quantum dots, biosensors and microfluidics.

Patent Preparation & Prosecution: The firm has extensive experience in preparing and prosecuting patent applications. It prosecutes and enforces utility and design patents for a variety of clients ranging from those with extensive, active patent portfolios, to small, start-up companies that rely on the patent system to obtain funding and to head off competition. The firm's patent professionals have expertise in a broad range of technologies including: biotechnology, bioinformatics, computer hardware and software, communications, consumer products, medical equipment, mechanical devices, microfluidics, nanotechnology and pharmaceuticals.

HEAD OFFICE

DISTRICT OF COLUMBIA
1100 New York Avenue, NW, **Washington**, DC 20005
Tel: 202 371 2600 **Fax:** 202 371 2540

Website: www.skgf.com

CONTACTS

ANDA	Robert C Millonig, Jr, PhD
Appellate	Kenneth C Bass, III
Biotechnology	Jorge A Goldstein, PhD
Interferences	Jorge A Goldstein, PhD
Litigation	David KS Cornwell
Nanotechnology	Donald J Featherstone
Negotiation, Electronics	Robert Greene Sterne
Technology Transfer	Timothy J Shea, Jr
Trademark	Tracy-Gene G Durkin

Technology Transfer: Sterne, Kessler, Goldstein & Fox is committed to working closely with clients' business, legal and scientific personnel to develop contractual relationships that will advance their business objectives through agreements intended to govern alliances instead of adversarial relationships. The firm is adept at working with its clients to develop strategies for exploiting their technologies and for navigating the myriad legal and technological issues that arise in drafting and negotiating agreements involving technology transfer. It has experience in drafting and negotiating all types of technology and tangible asset transfer agreements. The firm's attorneys are well-versed in both intellectual property law and transactional law.

Trademark: Sterne, Kessler, Goldstein & Fox provides counsel to trademark clients in industries that range from consumer products to cutting edge technologies like bio-pharmaceutical products. Among the services it provides are federal, state and foreign trademark clearance, registration, licensing, enforcement and defense, domain name registration and dispute resolution, oppositions and cancellations, protection of non-traditional marks, review of product literature and corporation communications, website audit and trademark valuation.

CLIENTS: Legal pioneers in fields such as the intellectual property of biotechnology, software, bioinformatics, genomics, e-commerce, generic pharmaceuticals, nanotechnology and business methods, the firm represents a broad range of clients, including emerging and established companies, venture capital firms, universities and select individuals.

SUTHERLAND ASBILL & BRENNAN LLP

THE FIRM

Managing Partner: Mark D Wasserman (Atlanta, GA)
Administrative Partner: W Mark Smith (Washington, DC)
Number of partners: 152
Number of associates: 193
Total number of attorneys: 411

FIRM OVERVIEW: Sutherland Asbill & Brennan LLP is a national law firm known for solving challenging business problems and resolving unique legal issues for many of the nation's largest corporations, as well as emerging and smaller, established companies. Sutherland was founded in 1924. Throughout its history, the firm has served clients across America. It has grown to become a firm of more than 400 lawyers handling matters in every part of the world. The firm consistently attracts lawyers who have the skills and perspective to address issues of national significance in virtually every area of practice. Seven major practice areas - corporate, financial services, energy, intellectual property, litigation, real estate and tax - provide the framework that contains an extensive range of specialty areas, allowing its lawyers to serve a diverse client base that includes a number of Fortune 500 companies.

MAIN AREAS OF WORK

Corporate & Financial Services: The firm's Corporate and Financial Services practices encompass the full range of legal services required by corporations and other business entities. The practices include representation of public and private companies in their general commercial affairs, public and private buyers and sellers in acquisitions and dispositions of business, lenders and borrowers in corporate finance transactions, and issuers and underwriters and broker-dealers in securities law matters, including initial and secondary public offerings of debt and equity securities and enforcement matters. In addition, the firm's lawyers have extensive experience working with mutual funds and other investment companies, including insurance company separate accounts and business development companies. The firm counsels investment advisors, including those affiliated with investment companies and those affiliated with non-investment company institutional and individual clients; companies in or facing financial distress; companies undertaking financial restructurings; issuers, underwriters and financial institutions in tax-exempt and taxable bond issues; financial institutions in regulatory and transactional matters; and federal government sponsored enterprises. The firm also represents companies and financial institutions in a variety of structured finance transactions designed to accomplish specific investment, tax, liquidity and balance sheet management goals.

Energy: Sutherland has a highly active Energy Regulatory, Transaction, Finance, and Litigation Practice at the state, federal and international levels. Matters handled by the group embrace virtually all aspects of the natural gas, electric power and petroleum industries. The firm's lawyers have been at the forefront of the developing regulatory issues surrounding the energy industries, both at the policy stage and in the implementation phases. The firm has also developed extensive experience analyzing and assisting clients in taking advantage of business opportunities involving natural gas, electricity, cogeneration and petroleum products.

Intellectual Property: Sutherland has an extensive Intellectual Property Practice. The firm represents a broad mix of clients - emerging technology start-ups, small and mid-sized companies and Fortune 500 and other public companies - in all areas including patents, trademarks, service marks, copyrights, trade secrets and unfair competition. The firm handles intellectual property matters in a number of technical fields including biotechnology, pharmaceuticals, computers, chemical technology, telecommunications, software and minerals. A significant number of Sutherland's intellectual property lawyers hold specialized or advanced degrees in biology, chemical engineering, computer engineering, mechanical engineering, microbiology, immunology, molecular genetics and other scientific disciplines, and many are registered to practice before the United States Patent and Trademark Office.

Litigation: Litigation is a major part of the firm's practice. Approximately one third of its 400 lawyers practice in this area and have tried and/or argued cases in the US Supreme Court, all thirteen circuits of the United States Court of Appeals, the Court of Federal Claims, the Tax Court and many other federal district and state trial and appellate courts. The firm also has extensive experience in arbitrations and mediations as well as in administrative proceedings and hearings before various federal and state agencies. The areas of concentration within the firm's Litigation Group include general commercial and civil litigation; antitrust, trade regulation and consumer protection; construction and procurement litigation; criminal investigations and litigation; education; employment and ERISA; environmental; healthcare; insurance; intellectual property; international trade disputes; motor vehicle franchise law; professional liability litigation; securities litigation; tax litigation; telecommunications; and timber.

Real Estate: The Real Estate Practice is national in scope; handling real estate matters in virtually every state and in all major real estate markets. The broad range of experience of the firm's real estate lawyers enables it to provide this continuity. The lawyers in the Real Estate Group have the ability to manage dispute resolutions, to provide creditors' rights and bankruptcy advice and representation, to advise on regulatory issues, and to identify and resolve tax questions, thus saving the expense and inefficiency of engaging different legal counsel for each of a client's separate business and legal problems. The areas of focus for the firm's Real Estate Practice include acquisition and development; real estate finance and equity formation; pension fund investments; commercial leasing; hospitality industry; international transactions; natural resources; foreclosure; bankruptcy and workouts; mergers and acquisitions; partnerships and partnership taxation; and environmental issues.

Tax: The firm serves as tax counsel to a number of major corporations and medium-sized and small corporations and their shareholders, as well as cooperatives, partnerships, joint ventures, tax-exempt organizations, trusts, estates and individuals. By virtue of the size of the Tax Practice and its varied client base, the firm has an active practice in almost every area of taxation, including corporate taxation, employee benefits and executive compensation, taxation of financial products, timber taxation, international taxation, partnership taxation, state and local tax, tax accounting, tax legislation, federal tax litigation, business and estate planning and tax-exempt organizations.

HEAD OFFICES

GEORGIA
999 Peachtree Street, NE, **Atlanta**, GA 30309-3996
Tel: 404 853 8000   **Fax:** 404 853 8806
Email: info@sablaw.com
Website: www.sablaw.com

DISTRICT OF COLUMBIA
1275 Pennsylvania Avenue, NW, **Washington**, DC 20004-2415
Tel: 202 383 0100   **Fax:** 202 637 3593

Sutherland Asbill & Brennan LLP also has offices in Austin, Houston, New York and Tallahassee. For more details please visit the website.

SWIDLER BERLIN LLP

THE FIRM

Managing Partner: Barry B Direnfeld

Number of partners: 64
Number of other lawyers: 90

FIRM OVERVIEW: With attorneys in offices in Washington, DC and New York City, Swidler Berlin LLP is one of the nation's 200 largest law firms. The firm has premier capabilities in many different practice areas, covering a full range of issues, from arbitrage to venture capital. Swidler has two wholly-owned subsidiaries - The Harbour Group LLC, which develops public relations campaigns, crisis communications tactics, and legislative strategies, and Harbour Consulting, LLC which provides technical and analytical services to support the firm's insurance clients.

MAIN AREAS OF PRACTICE:

Arbitrage: The Risk Arbitrage Group at Swidler Berlin advises a broad-based group of 'Wall Street' clients regarding the legal, regulatory and legislative risks associated with proposed corporate restructurings, proposed legislation and regulatory changes, and corporate litigation.

Bankruptcy & Creditors' Rights: The firm is involved in virtually all aspects of representing clients in connection with insolvency matters. Swidler has represented: borrowers and lenders in multi-party out-of-court restructurings and workouts; debtors, committees, indenture trustees, secured and unsecured creditors, equity holders and other interested parties in complex chapter 11 cases; banks and other financial institutions dealing with borrowers with financial problems in significant matters; and parties seeking to take control of or purchase assets from financially troubled entities, in and out of court.

Corporate: Swidler's Corporate Group advises clients in corporate finance, venture capital, mergers and acquisitions, securities law matters, public and private offerings, e-commerce, non-profit matters, and other commercial issues across a wide variety of industries.

Energy: The Swidler Energy Group has a wide-ranging practice before the Federal Energy Regulatory Commission (FERC), before state commissions, and in connection with energy-related transactions and litigation.

Environmental: Swidler's Environmental Group engages in a broad-based, national environmental practice, representing a variety of clients in federal and state regulatory, administrative, complex litigation, and legislative matters.

Government Affairs: The Government Affairs Group at Swidler represents a diverse group of clients before the Congress, the Executive Branch and independent federal agencies. Ranked among the top 20 law firm lobbying practices in Washington, Swidler has been active in a broad range of issue areas, including antitrust, asbestos, aviation, banking, congressional oversight, environment, energy, finance, health care, Indian affairs, intellectual property, international trade, occupational safety and health, securities, tax, telecommunications, and transportation.

Insurance: The Insurance Group is a multi-disciplinary practice designed to assist corporate policyholders in their efforts to recover on multimillion dollar complex insurance claims presented to the worldwide insurance markets.

Intellectual Property: The Intellectual Property Group of Swidler Berlin handles all aspects of intellectual property law including patent litigation, trademark litigation, copyrights, anti-cybersquatting, patent prosecution, and trademark prosecution.

Litigation: Swidler's Litigation Group represents clients in civil, criminal and investigative matters before the US Supreme Court, state and federal appellate and trial courts, state and federal administrative agencies, and Congressional committees.

OFFICES

DISTRICT OF COLUMBIA
The Washington Harbour, 3000 K Street NW Suite 300,
Washington, DC 20007-5116
Tel: 202 424 7500 **Fax:** 202 424 7643

NEW YORK
The Chrysler Building, 405 Lexington Avenue, **New York**, NY 10174
Tel: 212 973 0111 **Fax:** 212 891 9598

Website: www.swidlaw.com

CONTACTS

Arbitrage	Robert D Jacobs
Bankruptcy & Creditors' Rights	Roger L Frankel
Corporate	John J Klusaritz, Kenneth I Schaner
Energy	Steven J Agresta
Environmental	Robert N Steinwurtzel
Government Affairs	Barry B Direnfeld
Insurance	Mark J Plumer
Intellectual Property	Edward A Pennington
Litigation	Ky E Kirby, Peri N Mahaley
Real Estate/Structured Finance	Kenneth G Lore
Tax	Glenn S Miller
Telecommunications, Media & Technology	Andrew D Lipman

Real Estate/Structured Finance: The Structured Finance Group specializes in securitizations, public finance, project finance, and banking. The Real Estate Group specializes in government related matters, leasing, and land use and zoning.

Tax: Principal practice areas of the Swidler Tax Group include business organizations, financings, acquisitions, dispositions and reorganizations, international tax planning for businesses and institutional investors, domestic and international telecommunications and internet tax issues, public and private investment companies, real estate and structured finance, qualified retirement plans, employee benefits and executive compensation arrangements, tax-exempt organizations, tax planning for businesses and individuals, estate and gift planning, wills, trusts and estate administration, and federal and state tax controversies and litigations.

Telecommunications, Media & Technology: The Telecommunications, Media & Technology Group is one of the country's largest telecommunications legal departments with practices in virtually every aspect of telecommunications law and related fields.

CLIENTS: Swidler's diversified roster of national and international clients includes Fortune 100 companies, smaller business enterprises, families and individuals.

INTERNATIONAL WORK: The firm has international experience in the areas of telecommunications, energy, tax, corporate, real estate/structured finance, intellectual property, litigation, government affairs, bankruptcy, environmental, insurance, and arbitrage.

SWIDLER BERLIN LLP

WILEY REIN & FIELDING LLP

THE FIRM

Managing Partner: Richard E Wiley

Number of partners: 117
Number of other lawyers: 140

FIRM OVERVIEW: Wiley Rein & Fielding LLP attorneys counsel leaders in numerous industries nationwide, conduct business in over 50 countries throughout the world, and practice in more than twenty federal departments and agencies in Washington, DC, as well as in federal and state courts across the country. With offices in Washington, DC and Northern Virginia, the firm has more than 250 attorneys practicing in more than two-dozen specialties of law. Clients range from Fortune 500 corporations and start-up ventures to trade associations and individuals with substantial business interests. The firm is led by Richard E Wiley, former Chairman of the Federal Communications Commission; Bert W Rein, former Deputy Assistant Secretary of State for Economic and Business Affairs; Fred F Fielding, former Counsel to the President of the United States; and Thomas W Brunner, head of the firm's Insurance Law Practice. Many partners have held high federal government posts in the legislative and executive branches and come to the firm with distinguished careers in private law practice as counselors, litigators, negotiators and strategic advisors.

MAIN AREAS OF PRACTICE:

Communications: Wiley Rein & Fielding has the most comprehensive team of communications law specialists in the United States. Led by Richard E Wiley, former Chairman, Commissioner and General Counsel of the Federal Communications Commission (FCC), the group includes more than 75 attorneys, engineers and specialists. WRF represents clients in virtually all aspects of the federal, state and international laws governing the media and telecommunications industry, with particular experience in international and satellite, litigation, media, telephony and wireless services. The group handles the full scope of media transactions - from headline-setting, billion-dollar mergers to the sale of a single radio station - in addition to business disputes and regulatory initiatives.

Government Contracts: WRF's Government Contracts Practice, led by *Leading Lawyer* Rand L Allen, is comprised of more than 25 attorneys and consultants handling every aspect of government contracting, including bid protests, disputes, commercial litigation, terminations, mergers and acquisitions and regulatory issues. Clients rely on WRF's Government Contracts Practice for advice and representation on local and international procurement-related matters. The attorneys regularly appear in every legal forum that addresses government contract issues, including the US Government Accountability Office, US district courts and courts of appeals, the US Court of Federal Claims (COFC), the US Court of Appeals for the Federal Circuit and the numerous agency Board of Contract Appeals.

Insurance: WRF's Insurance Practice is among the largest and most prominent in the United States. Led by Thomas W Brunner, a nationally recognized authority in this field and outside counsel to several insurance industry associations, the practice includes more than 40 attorneys, whose work encompasses counseling and litigation concerning general liability coverage, Directors & Officers and Errors & Omissions coverage, cutting edge property insurance and other first and third party coverage, reinsurance disputes, construction, privacy and other regulatory issues, health insurance and insurance fraud. Many clients seek the firm's expertise in interpreting policies, developing new types of coverage, negotiating innovative settlements and evaluating large claims exposures.

HEAD OFFICE

DISTRICT OF COLUMBIA
1776 K Street NW, **Washington,** DC 20006
Tel: 202 719 7000 **Fax:** 202 719 7049
Website: www.wrf.com

BRANCH OFFICE

VIRGINIA
7925 Jones Branch Drive, Suite 6200, **McLean,** VA 22102
Tel: 703 905 2800 **Fax:** 703 905 2820

International Trade: WRF's 20 member International Trade Group, led by internationally recognized attorney Charles O Verrill Jr, represents clients in domestic and international trade regulation and dispute resolution, including antidumping and countervailing duty investigations, safeguards proceedings, Section 337 actions to protect intellectual property rights, export enforcement proceedings and investor/state arbitration. The firm regularly provides advice on market access issues, the negotiation of trade agreements, customs regulation and privacy requirements of US and European law. Additionally, the attorneys represent foreign and domestic clients in corporate structuring, overseas financial transactions, Treasury Department sanctions and embargoes, licensing and distributorship arrangements, government export financing, export trade certificates of review and the Foreign Corrupt Practices Act.

Litigation: Wiley Rein & Fielding provides clients with unparalleled advocacy in federal and state courts across the country. More than half of the firm's attorneys are seasoned litigators whose combined experience encompasses a wide range of trial, appellate, alternative dispute and agency tribunal matters. Members of the Litigation Team include six former clerks to the Supreme Court of the United States and more than 40 former clerks to courts of appeals and district courts; others have served as federal prosecutors, general counsels of federal agencies and senior government officials. The breadth of the team's experience is matched by a substantive depth of knowledge in numerous specialized areas of law, including communications, criminal/congressional investigations, election law, employment, First Amendment, franchise, government contracts, healthcare, insurance, Internet and intellectual property. The firm's specialized litigation expertise, in tandem with its innovative and creative approaches to complicated legal issues, has resulted in a proven record of success in the courtroom. Recent landmark decisions obtained by WRF for our clients include verdicts that have appeared on the *The National Law Journal's* annual list of 'Top 100 Verdicts.' Many of the cases the firm handles are high-profile matters that garner widespread media attention.

WILMER CUTLER PICKERING HALE AND DORR LLP

THE FIRM

Co-Managing Partners: William F Lee, William J Perlstein
Email: law@wilmerhale.com
Website: www.wilmerhale.com

FIRM OVERVIEW: Wilmer Cutler Pickering Hale and Dorr LLP offers unparalleled legal representation across a comprehensive range of practice areas that are critical to the success of its clients. The firm has over a thousand lawyers operating in five countries and practices at the very top of the legal profession. With a practice unsurpassed in depth and scope by any other major firm, it has the ability to anticipate obstacles, seize opportunities and get the case resolved or the deal done – and the experience and know-how to prevent it from being undone. Wilmer Cutler Pickering Hale and Dorr was formed in May 2004 through the merger of two of the nation's leading law firms, Hale and Dorr LLP and Wilmer Cutler Pickering LLP. The formation of the new firm fused two storied pro bono and public service traditions. This commitment continues to be an integral part of the cultural fabric of the firm.

MAIN AREAS OF PRACTICE:

Antitrust & Competition: With more than 50 years' experience and over 75 competition lawyers in the US and Europe, the firm has secured antitrust clearance for hundreds of complex mergers and joint ventures, helped clients avoid fines and prison terms in many cartel investigations, and won numerous victories for clients in private and government litigation.

Aviation: Regarded as having one of the world's premier commercial aviation practices, the firm advises airlines, airports, associations and governments on aviation-specific legal and policy issues, from certification to licensing to enforcement. It provides strategic counseling on litigation and dispute resolution, aircraft acquisition and finance transactions, joint ventures, and bankruptcy, tax and distribution issues.

Bankruptcy & Commercial: Named by *Business Week* as one of the 'top bankruptcy shops' in the United States, the firm has broad experience representing debtors, creditors and creditors' committees in bankruptcy, insolvency and debt restructuring matters, and in related litigation and commercial transactions.

Communications: Wilmer Hale has played a major role in shaping the rules governing the wireline and wireless telecommunications, e-commerce and mass media industries. When important issues and transactions arise in these fiercely competitive industries, companies turn to them for the highest quality representation and effective problem solving.

Corporate: The firm is widely recognized for its preeminence in the representation of technology and life sciences companies in the US and Europe. Its corporate lawyers are renowned for their work in initial public offerings, venture capital and private equity, mergers and acquisitions, strategic alliances, corporate governance matters and the representation of start-up companies.

Defense, National Security & Government Contracts: With extensive experience serving in senior national security posts in the US government, their lawyers provide regulatory, legislative, transactional and enforcement advice to clients supplying products and services to military, governmental and commercial customers worldwide.

Environmental: Clients rely on the firm to address complex environmental liabilities, permit key operations and understand evolving environmental laws.

FDA: The firm's FDA Practice includes considerable experience before the FDA and other administrative agencies, Congress and the federal courts.

Financial Institutions: Over the past 30 years, the firm has built a practice of extensive breadth and depth in regulatory, transactional and litigation matters for banks and other financial institutions.

Intellectual Property: The Intellectual Property Practice serves as a one-stop solution for clients' intellectual property prosecution, litigation and licensing needs in the US and Europe. In 2004, *The American Lawyer* recognized Wilmer Hale for having one of the top IP litigation departments in the US, and *IP Law and Business* named it one of the top ten US law firms for biotech patent prosecution.

International Trade & Market Access: Recognized as one of the world's leading trade law firms, Wilmer Hale represents clients from the US, EU and more than 30 other countries before administrative, judicial and legislative bodies across the globe, as well as in proceedings under the WTO, NAFTA and the World Customs Organization.

Labor & Employment: With capabilities including comprehensive labor and employment law counseling, employment litigation and custom-designed training programs, the firm offers clients in the US and Europe practical solutions for effectively dealing with employment issues and achieving their business objectives.

Litigation & Arbitration: The firm's preeminent Litigation Practice is widely recognized for its excellence in civil and criminal trial and appellate litigation, as well as in intellectual property and securities litigation. In addition, it has one of the world's leading international arbitration practices. Many of its litigators formerly held senior government positions and have particular expertise in litigation strategies designed to advance clients' objectives in regulatory and political arenas.

Private Client: Attorneys in the Private Client Group advise clients on gift, estate and income taxation, sophisticated gifting and diversification strategies, private philanthropy, trusts and fiduciary investments, and the administration of estates.

Real Estate: The firm has extensive expertise in real estate capital management, institutional and pension fund equity and debt investment, development and permitting, leasing and foreign investment.

Tax: The firm's top-ranked Tax Practice includes lawyers recognized by *Who's Who Legal* as among 'the world's leading tax practitioners.' It handles all aspects of domestic and international tax advice for public and private companies, non-profit organizations and individuals.

OFFICES

DISTRICT OF COLUMBIA
2445 M Street, NW, **Washington**, DC 20037-1420
Tel: 202 663 6000 **Fax:** 202 663 6363

The Willard Office Building, 1455 Pennsylvania Avenue, NW, **Washington**, DC 20004
Tel: 202 942 8400 **Fax:** 202 942 8484

MARYLAND
100 Light Street, **Baltimore**, MD 21202
Tel: 410 986 2800 **Fax:** 410 986 2828

MASSACHUSETTS
60 State Street, **Boston**, MA 02109
Tel: 617 526 6000 **Fax:** 617 526 5000

Hale and Dorr Venture Group, Bay Colony Corporate Center, 1100 Winter Street, **Waltham**, MA 02451
Tel: 781 966 2000 **Fax:** 781 966 2100

NEW YORK
399 Park Avenue, **New York**, NY 10022
Tel: 212 230 8800 **Fax:** 212 230 8888

VIRGINIA
1600 Tysons Boulevard, Suite 1000, **McLean**, VA 22102
Tel: 703 251 9700 **Fax:** 703 251 9797

Reston Town Center, 11951 Freedom Drive, **Reston**, VA 20190
Tel: 703 654 7000 **Fax:** 703 654 7100

INTERNATIONAL OFFICES

The firm has offices in Beijing, Berlin, Brussels, London, Munich and Oxford.

CONTENTS: Antitrust p.498; Banking & Finance p.500; Bankruptcy p.501; Construction p.505; Corporate/M&A p.509; Employment p.511; Environment p.515; Healthcare p.517; Insurance p.519; Litigation: General Commercial p.520; Real Estate: p.525; Tax p.529; Individuals' Profiles p.533; Firms' Profiles p.555.

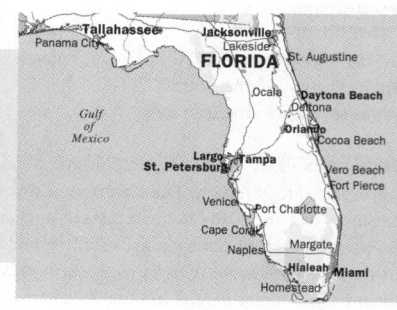

How lawyers are ranked

The opinions we gather from clients — mainly from in-house lawyers but also from other purchasers of legal services — are balanced by opinions from colleagues and competitors. Together, they provide two different perspectives — an all-round view — and biased viewpoints cancel each other out.

ANTITRUST

Florida
Leading firms (Antitrust)

1
AKERMAN SENTERFITT *Orlando*
KENNY NACHWALTER PA *Miami*

2
BOIES, SCHILLER & FLEXNER LLP *Miami*
CARLTON FIELDS, PA *Tampa*
HOLLAND & KNIGHT LLP *Miami*
HUNTON & WILLIAMS *Miami*

3
BERMAN DEVALERIO PEASE *West Palm Beach*
FOLEY & LARDNER *Tallahassee*
GREENBERG TRAURIG LLP *Miami*
NAGIN GALLOP FIGUEREDO PA *Coconut Grove*
TRENAM, KEMKER, SCHARF, O'NEILL *Tampa*
ZUCKERMAN SPAEDER LLP *Miami*

Leading individuals (Antitrust)

1
BLECHMAN Bill *Kenny Nachwalter*, Miami
COUTROULIS Chris *Carlton Fields*, Tampa
PERWIN Scott *Kenny Nachwalter*, Miami
ROUNSAVILLE Keith *Akerman Senterfitt*, Orlando

2
ARNOLD Richard *Kenny Nachwalter*, Miami
HOFFMAN Jerome *Holland & Knight*, Tallahassee
NAGIN Stephen *Nagin Gallop*, Coconut Grove
PALMER Scott *Berman DeValerio*, West Palm Beach
SILVERMAN Lawrence *Akerman Senterfitt*, Miami
SINGER Stuart *Boies Schiller*, Miami

3
DAVIDSON Barry *Hunton & Williams*, Miami
KING Kimberly *Sole Practitioner*, Tallahassee
LANDIS James *Foley & Lardner*, Tampa
LITCHFORD Hal *Litchford & Christopher*, Orlando
RAVIKOFF Ronald *Zuckerman Spaeder*, Miami
STEINBERG Marty *Hunton & Williams*, Miami

Firms and individuals are listed alphabetically in each band.

Band 1

Akerman Senterfitt
See firm details p.555
The Firm: With more than 400 attorneys, this is one of the largest Florida-based law firms with offices throughout the state. The "*worthy*" 15-lawyer antitrust team succeeds in the defense of clients in federal courts in Florida and in sever-al other states in claims under the Sherman Act, the Clayton Act, the Robinson-Patman Act and the Federal Trade Commission Act among other antitrust statutes. The "*high quality*" consistently delivered by this established group attracts a loyal clientele, sources said. On behalf of the Gulfstream Racetrack in Florida, the team advised on several federal antitrust claims. The attorneys here combine "*a wealth of experience*" with a winning streak, ensuring that they will be "*around for a long time.*"
The Lawyers: Head of the antitrust and trade regulation department **Keith Rounsaville** (see p.549) earned acclaim for his tenacity in understanding the facts and legal principles. Clients trust him to know "*how to get to the core of the deal and get the job done.*" For others he is a "*thorough, patient yet passionate*" antitrust attorney whose polished performances include acting for Pasco Beverage Group in a DOJ civil investigation. He also co-led the defense of Gulfstream Racetrack with partner **Lawrence Silverman** (see p.550), whose profile is on the ascendancy partly due to his success in two class actions pertaining to the Florida Deceptive and Unfair Trade Practices Act; he obtained dismissals on behalf of hotel chain Boca Resorts in matters pertaining to service charges. He is certainly "*a great pillar of the firm,*" observers said.
The Clients: Allied Universal; Gulfstream Park Racing Association; Historic Tours of America; Pasco Beverage Group; Samsung Electronics and Transitions Optical.

Kenny Nachwalter P.A.
See firm details p.566
The Firm: This "*top-notch*" antitrust litigation boutique captured attention for its "*impressive scale of cases and great credentials,*" commentators said. With top lawyers operating in three offices in Florida, this group is "*at the forefront prosecuting claims in the antitrust arena.*" Its capability stretches beyond state borders to encompass, for instance, handling several antitrust claims throughout the country involv-ing Goodyear. This "*cream of the crop in the Southeast*" shows remarkable efficiency with regards to carrying out "*premium*" plaintiff litigation and defense work.
The Lawyers: **Bill Blechman** attained the praise of both clients and competitors for his "*cutting-edge*" work, including his key participation in the antitrust claims linked to Goodyear. "*His tenacity sets him apart,*" peers said. Interviewees praise **Scott Perwin** as "*another star*" in the firm. In a recent development, he acted for the US subsidiary of a major jewelry manufacturer in a high-profile antitrust case. He is also encountered on cases involving generic drugs sales. Perwin has "*eyes for every single detail on a case,*" sources said. "*Brilliant tactician*" **Richard Arnold** has tried antitrust cases for both plaintiffs and defendants. Peers see Arnold as "*one of the top five*" antitrust litigators in Florida.
The Clients: The team represents both plaintiffs and defendants, including retailers, consumer products manufacturers and government entities.

Band 2

Boies, Schiller & Flexner LLP
See firm details p.1337
The Firm: This national litigation heavyweight has recently consolidated its presence in Florida to offer "*greater depth on the plaintiff side,*" though the 12-attorney antitrust squad is also an acknowledged force on the defense side, having tackled issues pertaining to the Sherman Act among others. It continues to represent Del Monte in several complex antitrust matters.
The Lawyers: Analysts distinguish **Stuart Singer** as "*a formidable leader*" in the Florida market. An important case for Singer is representing NASCAR in several national lawsuits. This "*brilliant and hard-working*" practitioner also acts for Del Monte in several antitrust proceedings across the country.
The Clients: Del Monte, Philip Morris and NASCAR are featured in the firm's client roster.

Carlton Fields, PA

See firm details p.560

The Firm: The full-service firm impresses with its "*depth*" in the area, fielding about 20 attorneys whose stronghold in the Tampa business community has resulted in significant assignments. Its advocates are blessed with "*precision*," leading them to be "*brilliant at analyzing details*," sources said. The firm acted for the USA Equestrian Trust in a case involving a challenge to certain rules established by a national governing body concerning horse competitions. Another highlight involved a successful settlement linked to Acushnet, a golf equipment company. Commentators see this team as "*the place to go*" in Tampa for antitrust disputes.

The Lawyers: **Chris Coutroulis**, who leads the firm's antitrust & trade regulation practice group, is commended for "*thinking outside of the box*," sources said. The "*even-handed, knowledgeable*" operator is representing VISA USA in an indirect purchaser case and separately handled the Acushnet settlement. One client added: "*Chris sheds a lot of light in the matter at hand – I am very grateful for that. I would retain him again and again.*"

The Clients: Acushnet Company, USA Equestrian Federation and VISA USA are among the firm's significant clients.

Holland & Knight LLP

See firm details p.1352

The Firm: With more than five offices in the state, this multinational law firm guarantees "*strong presence across the board*," providing clients with a one-stop shop offering a range of services regardless of location. Observers singled out the prowess of its Tallahassee office, which is further enhanced by an international network of offices. The antitrust team has a varied and multifaceted experience representing clients in all industries including manufacturing, new media and healthcare.

The Lawyers: "*Bright and able litigator*" **Jerome Hoffman** (see p.542) has stamped his seal in healthcare M&A, according to interviewees. Clients praise his "*diligent*" approach on such matters as defending a major car insurance company in an antitrust class action lawsuit. The firm also houses Robert Feagin, who is often credited as a key player in building the firm's antitrust profile, and served as managing partner from 2001-2003.

The Clients: The firm's clientele comprises companies in the manufacturing, healthcare, food processing, utility and media sectors, and includes Morris Communications.

Hunton & Williams

See firm details p.1775

The Firm: The firm's overall strength in commercial litigation inevitably lends cachet to its antitrust capability, which is highly prized partly due to its "*ability to cherry-pick*" highly skilled attorneys for the job. "*Uniformly balanced across the board,*" the coterie of lawyers succeeded in concluding a drawn-out Hilton Hotels franchise dispute

The Lawyers: "*Smooth*" litigator **Barry Davidson** (see p.538) is often pitched as one of the best lawyers in the state; for example, he successfully represented a major appliance manufacturer under a price-fixing investigation by the Florida Attorney General. He also acted in the Hilton dispute, while **Marty Steinberg** (see p.551) primarily defends Fortune 500 companies in federal investigations.

The Clients: The firm has represented companies in the manufacturing, energy, pharmaceutical, lodging and telecom sectors among others.

Band 3

Berman DeValerio Pease Tabacco Burt & Pucillo

The Firm: Competitors admire this "*well-fortified*" team for the extensive antitrust class actions experience under its belt. The team often parlays its legal authority into successful bids on behalf of plaintiffs in antitrust cases. Its attorneys certainly "*know what they are doing,*" competitors said. In one major recent development, the group helped secured a multimillion-dollar settlement against major contact lens manufacturers.

The Lawyers: "*Well-rounded*" **Scott Palmer** "*knows when to fight over issues*" and when to negotiate for settlements. The "*fabulous*" advocate acted in the antitrust dispute concerning Canadian car imports, which alleged that efforts to block such imports into the US cost consumers more money on each car purchased.

The Clients: The team predominantly represents plaintiffs in multiparty lawsuits.

Foley & Lardner

See firm details p.1828

The Firm: With five of its 19 worldwide offices located in major cities in Florida, this firm has a widely esteemed antitrust team with extensive coverage in the state. The group is fluent in matters ranging from everyday corporate counseling to high-profile antitrust litigation. Its tentacles reach into almost every corner of antitrust law across the state, sources said. In addition, the overall firm's broader scope means that the team is able to handle issues on a national scale.

The Lawyers: "*The firm's best guy in Tampa,*" **James Landis** (see p.544) is highly skilled in representing clients in antitrust litigation. A former attorney with the DOJ's Antitrust Division, he "*knows when and how to fight over issues.*"

The Clients: The firm has counseled manufacturers, wholesalers and suppliers among others.

Greenberg Traurig LLP

See firm details p.564

The Firm: Though a relatively smaller outfit compared to some of its competitors, the three-attorney team in Florida commands "*an excellent reputation everywhere in the state,*" sources said. Its "*capable*" team has advised plaintiffs and defendants in landmark cases concerning monopolization, price-fixing and other antitrust matters.

The Lawyers: Though a generalist by practice, David Ross's inclination toward competition law has attracted market attention.

The Clients: Among others, the firm has been retained by companies in the tobacco, insurance and manufacturing sectors.

Nagin Gallop Figueredo PA

The Firm: This "*innovative*" Miami-based boutique excels in representing business clients on a nationwide basis in matters ranging from patent and trademark infringement to anticompetitive exclusion. Market observers praise its "*highly experienced, solid and well-regarded*" attorneys, who are often seen in some of the region's most important disputes. The team achieved a successful verdict for Magnivision in a patent infringement and unfair competition trial.

The Lawyers: Peers respect **Stephen Nagin** for his "*outstanding analytical skills and profound familiarity with trade regulations.*" Nagin acted for Magnivision and separately advised Niles Audio in an arbitration concerning patented electronic circuitry. Peers see him as a "*consistent practitioner*" who is able to combine patent and trademark law with antitrust expertise.

The Clients: The firm often represents regional businesses in antitrust matters.

Trenam, Kemker, Scharf, Barkin, Frye, O'Neill & Mullis PA

The Firm: With more than 60 attorneys in its Tampa and St. Petersburg offices, this "*exceptional*" Florida firm handles unfair competition, trade regulations and Hart-Scott-Rodino issues as part of a broader scope of practice. This "*highly respected*" group demonstrates "*intellectual fervor*" in some considerable cases, including an antitrust-related litigation involving national regulations linked to equestrian sports.

The Lawyers: Antitrust litigator Edward LaRose was appointed judge in 2004, while founding member Marvin Barkin remains a key contact in this practice area.

The Clients: The firm focuses on solving legal problems for businesses ranging from startup companies to major corporations.

Zuckerman Spaeder LLP

The Firm: Peers pitch the firm as a "*leading choice*" for criminal antitrust issues. Competitors mention that this team draws on "*tons of expertise as one of the key white-collar criminal defense*

boutiques in the state" to excel in this practice area. On the menu is expertise in distribution law and unfair trade practice litigation among other antitrust matters. It is also a favorite destination among clients for antitrust compliance.

The Lawyers: Top business litigator and managing partner of the firm's Miami office, **Ronald Ravikoff** was singled out for "*his profound acquaintance with all the dealings in complex antitrust law.*" A senior competitor added: "*He is*

the guy I would consider if I needed to refer out a case."

The Clients: Retailers, healthcare organizations, and manufacturers in the automotive, shipping, boating, and airline industries are among the firm's clients.

Other Notable Practitioners

Formerly with Pennington, Moore, Wilkinson, Bell & Dunbar, PA, **Kimberly King** now has a

solo practice that incorporates healthcare-related antitrust counseling in Tallahassee. Sources said **Hal Litchford** is a strong contender in Orlando, having built a respected plaintiff antitrust practice. The cofounder of Litchford & Christopher is advising a national publishing firm in a landmark noncompete case. Sources added: "*He knows antitrust inside and out.*"

BANKING & FINANCE

Florida
Leading firms (Banking & Finance)

1	**HOLLAND & KNIGHT LLP** *Miami*
	SHUTTS & BOWEN LLP *Miami*
2	**AKERMAN SENTERFITT** *Orlando*
	WHITE & CASE LLP *Miami*
3	**GREENBERG TRAURIG LLP** *Miami*
	GUNSTER, YOAKLEY & STEWART, PA *Miami*
	HUNTON & WILLIAMS *Miami*

Leading individuals (Banking & Finance)

1	**ALVAREZ Victor** *White & Case, Miami*
	AVILA Alcides *Holland & Knight, Miami*
	BROWN Bowman *Shutts & Bowen, Miami*
	CARDWELL J Thomas *Akerman Senterfitt, Orlando*
	VAZQUEZ-BELLO Clemente *Gunster Yoakley, Miami*
2	**ALVAREZ Pedro** *White & Case, Miami*
	BASILE Michael *Stroock & Stroock, Miami*
	FORNARIS Carl *Greenberg Traurig, Miami*
	GREELEY Jack *Smith Mackinnon, Orlando*
	JONES Rod *Shutts & Bowen, Orlando*
	LOUMIET Carlos *Hunton & Williams, Miami*
	STUTTS Charles *Holland & Knight, Tampa*

Firms and individuals are listed alphabetically in each band.

Band 1

Holland & Knight LLP

See firm details p.1352

The Firm: This national giant offers clients the "*full panoply of banking and financial services law.*" As one of the largest law firms in the state, it is recognized not only for its core work, but also "*specialties in various fields not always related to day-to-day banking.*" One of the strongest areas of the practice is the representation of international banks, among them Banco Popular Español, Caja de Ahorros del Mediterraneo and Caja Galicia, in their foundation or expansion in the USA. Latin American institutions are well covered, helped by the fact that every member of the group is bi-lingual. Alongside foreign finance matters, attorneys handle bank and broker-dealer securities, banking sector M&A, real estate finance and public finance. The firm also maintains an eminent regulatory practice to

cope with recent magnified attention on compliance and the Patriot Act. Key jurisdictions for the firm include South Florida for international banking, Washington, New York, Boston and Chicago.

The Lawyers: Alcides Avila (see p.533) leads the firm's banking and finance group nationally and is well known for his thorough, knowledgeable approach to work: "*He tends to have a pragmatic, low-key approach.*" One client applauded the way Avila "*takes a proactive role in making us aware of matters.*" **Charles Stutts** (see p.552) possesses the key requisite of "*a strong understanding of the regulatory framework,*" thanks in part to his prior role as general counsel to the Florida Comptroller's Office and the Department of Banking and Finance. He impresses many with his attitude: "*He cares about solving business problems.*"

The Clients: Caja de Madrid; Banco de Credito del Peru; Banco Popular Espanol; Wachovia; Bank of America; NetBank; SouthTrust Bank and Prudential.

Shutts & Bowen LLP

See firm details p.573

The Firm: This firm excels in the Latin America-oriented market in Miami, where competitors agree it deserves its reputation and ranking. The practice has a strong international flavor, and has historically represented out-of-state domestic banks and foreign banks with a presence in the area. Of particular importance was its representation of Citibank in connection with the organization's Latin American activities. Attorneys undertake general regulatory work for trust companies and other financial services providers, as well as a degree of licensing work for private banks. Increased activity in the real estate market has provided additional opportunities to work with commercial and residential mortgage lenders.

The Lawyers: "*Standout*" **Bowman Brown** (see p.535) is described as "*a dean of the bank regulatory world – if you want to set up in Florida, he's your guy.*" He enjoys a diverse workload and also excels in international matters. **Rod Jones** (see p.543) represents a number of community

banks around the state, seeing them through growth, evolution and merger transactions. In addition, he has recently worked on the Southern Community Bank transaction, where the firm increased its assets to more than $1 billion with the acquisition of the Community Bank.

The Clients: Citibank; Banco Santander; JPMorgan Chase; American Express; Banco de Chile; Merrill Lynch; Ocean Bank and Royal Bank of Canada.

Band 2

Akerman Senterfitt

See firm details p.555

The Firm: This proficient nine-office Florida firm has its main office in Orlando, where it takes part in sophisticated deals and represents the general and domestic interests of many companies in the financial services industry in the state. Clients who use the large body of lawyers term them "*proficient, prompt and strong.*" The firm is heavily involved in regulatory matters due to its representation of the Florida Bankers Association for whom it does a lot of lobbying work. Attorneys have fostered good relationships with clients over almost eight decades of the firm's existence; said one client: "*We've always had a close and cordial relationship with them, built on years of mutual trust and respect.*"

The Lawyers: The "*outstanding*" **Thomas Cardwell** (see p.536) "*knows and understands the banking business and is well connected.*" Cardwell's long-standing relationship with Florida Bankers Association is reflective of his prominence in the banking regulatory sphere at state and federal level. Always active in public policy decisions, clients find him "*extremely capable and multitalented.*"

The Clients: BankAtlantic; Citicorp; SunTrust Bank; Bank of America; Wachovia; Colonial Bank; Florida Bankers Association and SouthTrust Bank.

500   All quotes in the text are from interviews with clients and competitors.

CHAMBERS USA 2005

White & Case LLP

See firm details p.1379

The Firm: What really distinguishes this well-regarded *"powerhouse"* firm is its focus on cross-border financing and securitization, and the Latin American markets. The firm's Miami office has represented clients in transactions in Argentina, Brazil, Colombia and Mexico lately, and it continues to bolster its presence as an adviser to European financial institutions lending in these areas. The lawyers are *"well versed in the different legal aspects pertaining to other countries"* and *"very accessible at partner level."* This is a diversified practice, which is also known for its activities in syndicated lending to structured finance and equity capital markets. In a recent matter, the firm advised BellSouth Columbia in its $650 million refinancing and restructuring proceedings, involving intercreditor arrangements and support agreements.

The Lawyers: Victor Alvarez's (see p.533) continued preeminence in a competitive field earns him the highest plaudits from competitors. *"Clear and concise in communication,"* he enjoys a reputation for being *"incredibly prompt and always reachable; he has a good demeanor and keeps everything level and professional."* Sources note that although his focus is Latin America, his knowledge base extends across a number of different products and markets. Pedro Alvarez (see p.533) was described as *"confident"* by one client, who added: *"He told me what could and what could not be done – he mastered the art of this. When push came to shove he was strong."* Pedro Alvarez advised ICE, an autonomous entity owned by the Republic of Costa Rica, as issuer in a series of significant deals totaling $200 million.

The Clients: BellSouth International; Banco Santander; ING Barings; Wachovia; BBVA Securities and Corporación Durango.

Band 3

Greenberg Traurig LLP

See firm details p.564

The Firm: The Florida giant is a new addition to the banking and finance tables this year thanks to its growing presence in the market. The firm acts on bank regulatory and compliance matters plus lending, finance and securitization. The group is experienced in foreign business and has represented financial institutions and borrowers in Latin American transactions of all types. Clients turn to lawyers for complex litigation relating to banking, broker-dealer compliance and syndicated loan and borrower work. Group members collaborate across practice areas, as well as geographic areas, to serve the needs of financial institutions, their subsidiaries and affiliates in the USA as well as Latin America, Europe and Asia.

The Lawyers: Younger figure **Carl Fornaris** (see p.540) has attracted clients to the firm with his *"outstanding work on transactions"* and inside working knowledge of the industry. One satisfied client commended him in several ways, saying: *"He has a flexible viewpoint and attitude to resolving problems, and I like this. He has good judgment and is an excellent listener with terrific communication skills. Also, he won't sit on a job for weeks; he is service-oriented."*

The Clients: The client base includes numerous multinational banks, financial groups and institutions, mortgage lenders and trust companies.

Gunster, Yoakley & Stewart, PA

The Firm: The financial services division of this firm is a multidisciplinary team that is more than able to tackle regulatory compliance, M&A, securities and international banking. The group works out of six offices across Florida and is mostly known and respected in the south Florida environs. Rivals commended its *"pragmatic approach to deal-making"* and its insight and advice on structures, terms and strategy.

The Lawyers: Eminent practitioner and *"anti-money laundering specialist"* **Clemente Vazquez-Bello** has been with the firm for more

than 30 years. He has considerable experience dealing with US banking and governmental authorities as well as the Florida International Bankers Association, and is recognized as a leading light in relation to Patriot Act and other compliance issues.

The Clients: The firm acts for Capital City Bank Group, Atlantic States Bank and First Peoples Bank among others.

Hunton & Williams

See firm details p.1775

The Firm: This finance stalwart fields a team of nine banking and finance attorneys from its Miami office and represents foreign, particularly Latin American, and domestic banks, private lenders, borrowers, underwriters and insurance companies. The firm represented Banco Santander in connection with its acquisition of the US operations of Coutts & Co for $375 million, and has played a critical role in the development of investment banking products for a number of financial institutions.

The Lawyers: The impression in the market of **Carlos Loumiet** (see p.545) is of a smart and respected lawyer working over a range of regulatory, corporate, lending and securities work. He represented Banco Santander Hispano in connection with various private lending transactions in excess of $300 million. He also acted for SunTrust Bank in connection with innovative capital markets transactions and timeshare projects.

The Clients: Leading international banks, domestic entities and private equity groups are among the group's clients.

Other Notable Practitioners

Michael Basile of Stroock & Stroock & Lavan LLP is highly respected for his advice on compliance with federal and state regulations. His firm represents more than 400 investment companies and private funds. At Smith Mackinnon PA, **Jack Greeley** is a key name for community and smaller banks; he has an excellent reputation for his work in new bank formations.

BANKRUPTCY

Band 1

Berger Singerman

See firm details p.558

The Firm: This top-tier law firm *"always does an incredible job"* and is regarded by many as the *"top debtors' counsel in the state."* The business reorganization team fields a bank of experienced lawyers from four offices who are involved in significant corporate restructurings both in and

out of court. It boasts specific expertise in industries such as telecom, transportation, restaurant and food service, and general and commercial aviation. For example, the team served as Florida co-counsel to Atlas Air in the high-profile Atlas Air Chapter 11 reorganization plan. Its prolific representation of debtors, creditors' committees, trustees and private equity firms prompts commentators to note: *"If those guys aren't busy, then no one is busy."*

The Lawyers: *"Preeminent bankruptcy lawyer"* **Paul Singerman** (see p.550) draws universal praise from the industry for his enduring practice and the effectiveness of his work. He represents both debtors and creditors and is lauded as *"very knowledgeable with tremendous business acumen."* Singerman succeeds in balancing the talent of *"an aggressive business-getter"* with his reputation as a *"consummate gentleman"* who is *"extraordinarily adept at reaching compromises*

All quotes in the text are from interviews with clients and competitors.

Florida
Leading firms (Bankruptcy)

1 BERGER SINGERMAN *Fort Lauderdale, Miami*
   GREENBERG TRAURIG LLP *Miami, Fort Lauderdale*
   KOZYAK TROPIN & THROCKMORTON *Miami*
   STICHTER, RIEDEL, BLAIN & PROSSER PA *Tampa*
2 AKERMAN SENTERFITT *Orlando, Fort Lauderdale*
   BILZIN SUMBERG BAENA PRICE, *Miami*
   GENOVESE JOBLOVE & BATTISTA, PA *Miami*
   HUNTON & WILLIAMS *Miami*
   KLUGER, PERETZ, KAPLAN & BERLIN PL *Miami*
   SMITH HULSEY & BUSEY *Jacksonville*
   TRENAM, KEMKER, SCHARF, BARKIN *Tampa*
3 CARLTON FIELDS, PA *Tampa, West Palm*
   FERRELL SCHULTZ CARTER & FERTEL PA *Miami*
   FOLEY & LARDNER *Tampa*
   GLENN RASMUSSEN FOGARTY & HOOKER *Tampa*
   GRONEK & LATHAM *Orlando*
   HOLLAND & KNIGHT LLP *Orlando*
   MELAND RUSSIN HELLINGER & BUDWICK *Miami*
   RICE PUGATCH ROBINSON, *Miami, Fort Lauderdale*
   STEARNS WEAVER MILLER *Miami, Tampa*
   WHITE & CASE LLP *Miami*

Firms are listed alphabetically in each band.

when they can be reached." Competitors credit "*skillful and polished lawyer*" **Jordi Guso** (see p.541) with the ability to "*think through a problem and reason his way to a solution while being aware of people's needs.*" Before joining Berger Singerman **Arthur Spector** (see p.551) was a chief bankruptcy judge in the Eastern District of Michigan for 18 years. "*An exceedingly bright and capable lawyer,*" he works from the Fort Lauderdale office and has a focus on matters with international ramifications.

The Clients: AT&T; Florida Department of Transport; Espirito Santo Bank; BellSouth Telecommunications and Renaissance Cruises.

Greenberg Traurig LLP
See firm details p.564
The Firm: This influential law firm possesses an excellent reputation and is acknowledged by certain competitors to have "*the broadest scope*" and "*the most depth in the state.*" The group is growing a strong national practice and has an integrated cross-country network of experienced practitioners to call upon. It recently worked on the Atlas Air Worldwide Holdings case and represented the purchaser Perry Ellis in the Tropical Sportswear Chapter 11 petition. Other significant corporate representations include Textron Financial and Sequa, in which the firm was praised for its "*responsive, capable work.*"

The Lawyers: **Mark Bloom** (see p.535) is "*as smart as they come,*" and for this he earns the highest plaudits from his peers. With over 20 years' experience in the market, he has expertise spanning all areas of financial restructuring, acquisition and bankruptcy, although he is most

commonly involved in reorganizations. Market sources note his high energy and the thorough, articulate manner with which he makes presentations in court. **Brian Gart** (see p.540) has substantial experience in complex bankruptcy matters, including an increased focus on M&A transactions with respect to distressed business entities and their assets. He is admired for his representation of Perry Ellis on the Tropical Sportswear case and is termed "*an effective litigator; very demanding when fighting for his client.*"

The Clients: Imperium Bank; Sequa; Southeast Banking; Perry Ellis and Hyatt Hotels.

Kozyak Tropin & Throckmorton
See firm details p.568
The Firm: Size matters less than reputation for this natural leader in the Florida market. One client reported: "*This is one of the best firms I have ever dealt with, regardless of subject matter.*" The group undertakes "*sophisticated work on complex matters*" for clients of all sizes, who recognize the efficiency and quality of its "*go-to*" partners and associates. The patronage of a number of blue-chip clients, including Marriott International, Ritz-Carlton and CSFB, underscores the group's reputation for having achieved "*a level of accomplishment that leaves many firms behind.*"

The Lawyers: **John Kozyak** (see p.544) is "*a superb strategist,*" possessed of great skill and flexibility in the management of successful client relationships. "*Relentless but reasonable,*" he was co-counsel for the creditors' committee in the reorganization of Piccadilly Cafeterias and continues to take on substantial work for Lennar Partners and Ritz-Carlton. The "*superlative*" **Charles Throckmorton** (see p.552) is a bankruptcy litigation specialist who represents high net-worth individuals and financial institutions. Sources agree he is "*thorough, tenacious and smart – I would want him on my team.*" The verdict on **Laurel Isicoff** (see p.543) is also unanimously positive. With over 20 years of practice behind her, she handles complicated transactions effectively and is "*one of the people everyone goes to when they want to buy an asset out of bankruptcy.*" An "*incredibly accomplished negotiator*" with a "*terrific demeanor in court,*" she is focused and controlled with even the most demanding of clients. "*Fine lawyer*" **Corali Lopez-Castro** (see p.545) enters the tables this year with a string of favorable recommendations to her credit. She continues to develop a sterling reputation in trustee work and bankruptcy litigation and has "*taken the lead*" in some prominent cases.

The Clients: CSFB; Mellon United National Bank; Marriott International; Ritz-Carlton and Lennar Partners.

Stichter, Riedel, Blain & Prosser PA
See firm details p.576
The Firm: Observers agree that this is a "*premier debtors' firm handling a number of large cases.*" Many were effusive about the quality of the lawyers at the Tampa firm, where a team of "*solid, aggressive*" attorneys is also said to have earned widespread respect from judges. A specialized insolvency practice with 12 attorneys, it is a popular choice for referrals on complex cases and impresses competitors with its ethical outlook and manner. In a recent notable case, the firm represented the debtors in the Linc.net and US Plastic Lumber Chapter 11s. Clients range from small companies to large, publicly owned corporations.

The Lawyers: Without hesitation, peers named **Harley Riedel** "*the preeminent debtors' counsel in Florida.*" A gentleman as well as a scholarly lawyer, "*he's a delight to be around, even when he is beating you,*" according to one competitor. Sources note that he is bright, thoughtful and creative, and engenders "*a tremendous amount of deference because of his professional manner.*" **Russell Blain** has a "*wealth of experience*" in handling Chapter 11 reorganizations. Competitors believe he is a "*persistent, hardworking lawyer – a creative person who develops consensus.*" Sources also acknowledge the skill with which **Don Stichter** has built up this successful boutique firm during his distinguished career in the field.

The Clients: The firm advised affiliated companies in the Linc.net and US Plastic Lumber bankruptcy cases and continues to represent a range of creditors and trustees.

Band 2

Akerman Senterfitt
See firm details p.555
The Firm: The insolvency and creditors' rights group of this full-service law firm, one of the largest in Florida, represents clients in every major market area, though banks and financial institutions have featured large lately. Known as "*the best creditor group in the state,*" Akerman Senterfitt can draw upon talent from offices across the country. The firm has also gained kudos for picking up the debtor representation for Tropical Sportswear in Chapter 11 bankruptcy protection. Clients acknowledge that the "*quality of the work is first class*" and the attorneys are "*responsive and professional.*"

The Lawyers: "*Outstanding*" **Jules Cohen** (see p.537) concentrates on representing secured creditors in Chapter 11 proceedings. With his "*broad-based knowledge,*" he is recognized by clients as a "*wonderful resource*" and the "*kind of person you would go to with a serious ethical issue.*" **Michael Goldberg** (see p.540) "*stands above the crowd*" as a professional, talented lawyer. He recently represented HIG Capital in

Florida
Leading individuals (Bankruptcy)

Senior Statesman
CARTER Francis *Ferrell Schultz*, Miami
STICHTER Don *Stichter Riedel*, Tampa

★ RIEDEL Harley *Stichter Riedel*, Tampa
SINGERMAN Paul *Berger Singerman*, Fort Lauderdale

[1] BAENA Scott *Bilzin Sumberg*, Miami
BATTISTA Paul *Genovese Joblove*, Miami
BLOOM Mark *Greenberg Traurig*, Miami
BUSEY Stephen *Smith Hulsey*, Jacksonville
COLTON Roberta *Trenam Kemker*, Tampa
KOZYAK John *Kozyak Tropin*, Miami
THROCKMORTON Charles *Kozyak Tropin*, Miami

[2] BERLIN Howard *Kluger Peretz*, Miami
BLAIN Russell *Stichter Riedel*, Tampa
COHEN Jules *Akerman Senterfitt*, Orlando
GART Brian *Greenberg Traurig*, Fort Lauderdale
GENOVESE John *Genovese Joblove*, Miami
GILBERT Leonard *Holland & Knight*, Tampa
GLENN Robert *Glenn Rasmussen*, Tampa
GOLDBERG Michael *Akerman*, Fort Lauderdale
GUSO Jordi *Berger Singerman*, Miami
ISICOFF Laurel *Kozyak Tropin*, Miami
MOOREFIELD Harold *Stearns Weaver*, Miami
MORA Mindy *Bilzin Sumberg*, Miami
RASILE Craig *Hunton & Williams*, Miami
REDMOND Patricia *Stearns Weaver*, Miami
SORIANO Robert *Carlton Fields*, Tampa
WOLFSON Mark *Foley & Lardner*, Tampa

[3] BUDWICK Michael *Meland Russin*, Miami
CHARBONNEAU Robert *Kluger Peretz*, Miami
EMMANUEL John *Fowler White*, Tampa
GILBERT Robert *Carlton Fields*, West Palm Beach
KOBERT Roy *Broad and Cassel*, Orlando
LAURIA Thomas *White & Case*, Miami
OLSON John *Stearns Weaver*, Tampa
RUSSIN Peter *Meland Russin*, Miami
SCHILLER Lisa *Rice Pugatch*, Miami
SHUKER R Scott *Gronek & Latham*, Orlando
SPECTOR Arthur *Berger Singerman*, Fort Lauderdale
ZEWADSKI William *Trenam Kemker*, Tampa

Up-and-coming individuals
LOPEZ-CASTRO Corali *Kozyak Tropin*, Miami

Individuals are listed alphabetically in each band.

the acquisition of Supra Telecom for $30 million pursuant to a plan of reorganization. Clients appreciate his "*intelligence and his manner of getting the problem solved.*"

The Clients: SunTrust Banks; CRIIMI MAE; Banco Popular; CHEP International and Choice Hotels.

Bilzin Sumberg Baena Price & Axelrod LLP

See firm details p.559

The Firm: This elite law firm operates a statewide practice from its office in Miami, where its reputation inspires loyalty in clients. The group excelled on the Atlas Air case, the quickest and largest reorganization of 2004: it served as counsel both to the ad hoc committee of noteholders in pre-petition negotiations with debtors and to the official committee of unsecured creditors. Attorneys also acted for the secured creditor in the SunCruz case, and the "*solid, capable*" group has continued its representation of the committee of bondholders in the Southeast Bank matter, litigating in Chapter 7 bankruptcy case.

The Lawyers: The two partners who appear in Chambers' tables work effectively together, their styles complementing each other. **Scott Baena** (see p.534) is lauded as a "*first-rate lawyer*" with a dominant personality and an "*exceptionally good national reputation.*" Baena "*brings a tremendous amount of practical experience to the table*" in his work on large bankruptcy litigation and asbestos-related Chapter 11 cases around the country (he has completed arbitrations of more than 600 contested property damage claims). "*Hard-working and industrious*" **Mindy Mora** (see p.546) is also known to be a great strategic thinker. She worked on the Viasource proceedings, where she represented the creditors' committee in restructuring, then initiated a directors, and officers' liability insurance claim, the sale of the company's corporate shell and various preference actions.

The Clients: Foothill Capital; WR Grace; All American Semiconductor; Celotex; Mulholland Capital; Heilig-Meyers; KBC Bank and Douglas Publications.

Genovese Joblove & Battista, PA

See firm details p.563

The Firm: This quality boutique covers all areas of creditors' rights and insolvency matters and routinely represents Chapter 11 and Chapter 7 trustees, debtors in possession, creditors' committees and receivers. Acknowledged to be adept in national representations and cross-border transactions, it is noted by competitors for its involvement in large cases.

The Lawyers: Market sources have the highest regard for **Paul Battista**. A strong all-rounder, he "*understands the bigger picture and combines intellectual, courtroom and people skills*" with a professional demeanor. **John Genovese** is widely respected for his complex bankruptcy litigation work. This "*tenacious fighter*" does a fantastic job of attracting business to the firm. **The Clients:** Clients include a number of high-profile companies and individuals.

Hunton & Williams

See firm details p.1775

The Firm: Recent partner additions to this firm have proved beneficial, enabling "*a growing practice in Miami*" to match an already substantial presence across the state. A multifaceted group gets involved in bankruptcy restructuring and insolvency work for a wide array of clients including debtors, trustees, creditors' committees, equity committees and financial institutions. It represented Bank of New York in two large Chapter 11s and maintains substantial representation in airline bankruptcy, including work for owners on the Atlas Air case.

The Lawyers: The "*energetic and hard-working*" **Craig Rasile** (see p.548) has cemented his position in the firm and is widely regarded by clients and peers to be a "*good thinker, able to sort out issues and wrestle with them on a very fast timetable.*"

The Clients: Bank of New York; HSBC; CIT Business Credit and Philip Morris Capital.

Kluger, Peretz, Kaplan & Berlin PL

See firm details p.567

The Firm: A popular choice for referrals, this firm is recommend by clients as a "*one-stop shop*" with quality across the board. Its 10-lawyer team represented the creditors in the Supra Telecom and the Linc.net cases and was retained as debtor's counsel by Pan American Hospital, a nonprofit organization in Dade County. The "*good practice and solid supporting cast*" has come to the attention of competitors, who also praise its preparedness and specialty litigation work.

The Lawyers: Founding partner **Howard Berlin** (see p.535) is known for his committee work and liquidating trust activities. Sources praise his focus, "*good people skills*" and "*practical approach to problems.*" One client had seen him "*get the judge to understand as if he had visual aids in front of him.*" **Robert Charbonneau** (see p.536) is making his mark in the bankruptcy arena, acting as lead counsel on the Supra case, one of the largest recoveries in unsecured creditors in the history of telecoms.

The Clients: Clients include Pan American Hospital.

Smith Hulsey & Busey

See firm details p.574

The Firm: The bankruptcy lawyers at this Jacksonville firm represent a first-class lineup of debtors, creditors, committees and trustees in businesses at all stages of growth. The high-energy, hard-working lawyers have substantial experience in bankruptcy litigation and have undertaken a variety of Chapter 11 reorganizations.

The Lawyers: **Stephen Busey** (see p.536) is quite simply "*as good as there is in the state,*" according to senior market sources. Continually excellent, he is described as "*inexorable and indefatigable,*" and plugged into many of the major deals in the state because of his willingness and ability to take on difficult and controversial assignments. As well as being a skillful litigator, Busey is "*a persuasive and energetic speaker.*"

The Clients: Clients include financial institutions, healthcare providers, investors and venture capitalists.

Trenam, Kemker, Scharf, Barkin, Frye, O'Neill & Mullis PA

The Firm: A creditor-focused Tampa firm, it's clients are drawn from state and national financial institutions, landlords, and Chapter 7 and Chapter 11 trustees and examiners. A team of *"very good lawyers with a lot of experience"* produces a *"standout"* bankruptcy practice that is widely acknowledged by the market.

The Lawyers: *"Excellent"* **Roberta Colton** garners widespread praise from peers and clients for her *"terrific manner and highly positive attitude – she is unflappable and well prepared."* She takes the lead in the firm for creditor and creditors' committee representation as well as bankruptcy trustee representation, and is deemed by competitors to be a *"creative and hard-working"* lawyer who will fight hard in a professional manner. **William Zewadski** has been involved in all aspects of bankruptcy and workouts since his arrival more than 30 years ago. *"A fine lawyer,"* he is more than qualified to take on a variety of complex cases.

Band 3

Carlton Fields, PA

See firm details p.560

The Firm: Carlton Fields has been a significant player in the Florida market for over 50 years. Frequently recommended by clients, the firm deals with an assortment of banks, lenders and insurance companies in bankruptcy proceedings, litigation and workouts.

The Lawyers: **Robert Soriano** stands out for his deep experience and *"ability to eliminate unnecessary steps and get right to the heart of the matter."* Known for being *"practical and focused on the result,"* he recently made an impression representing a critical vendor in the Tropical Sportswear case. He is *"levelheaded and a good negotiator,"* which explains his success in litigation. Clients appreciate the manner in which **Robert Gilbert** *"presents strategic alternatives in a clear way."* He devotes a large proportion of his time to creditors' committee and secured creditor work.

The Clients: Clients include Wachovia Bank, Fortress Investment Group and Anchor Glass.

Ferrell Schultz Carter & Fertel PA

The Firm: This Miami-based group has affiliations with major firms across South and Central America. These are profitable relationships that have produced a stream of cross-border cases and transactions. The three attorneys in the bankruptcy group take on creditor and debtor cases and draw on the resources of a larger litigation department. The firm recently represented secured creditors in the Atlas Air proceedings.

The Lawyers: Esteemed attorney **Francis Carter** prompts the highest recommendations from interviewees, who admire what he has achieved in his career. One competitor noted how he is *"tremendously knowledgeable, practical and resourceful – the best deal-maker we have down here."* *"An engaging guy both in and out of court,"* Carter knows how to negotiate and reach consensus.

The Clients: Clients include HSBC, Goldman Sachs and UBS Investment Bank.

Foley & Lardner

See firm details p.1828

The Firm: Most of the work taken on by this *"terrific"* firm concerns creditors' committees, secured creditor representation and the buying of assets out of bankruptcy. The firm also takes on some debtor cases, for example the case of Apache Products, a manufacturer of building and roofing products. It also worked on the Jet1 Center case being litigated between the airport authority and the debtor.

The Lawyers: Energetic and diligent **Mark Wolfson** (see p.554) is enthusiastic about his work and impresses interviewees by being active and hands-on. *"He is not afraid to go out on a limb for his clients,"* who describe him as *"focused, bright and effective in getting to practical solutions."*

The Clients: Taylor Woodrow Communities; Bank of America; RMC Property Group; Ocwen and Apache Products.

Glenn Rasmussen Fogarty & Hooker

The Firm: The firm is well versed in complex bankruptcy, foreclosure, receivership and credit workout matters, and is principally associated with the representation of creditors and committees. The boutique nature of the firm appeals to clients who appreciate close working relationships between the team of four attorneys and the fact that few conflicts are generated by this approach to the practice.

The Lawyers: **Robert Glenn** is well regarded around the country and well connected in the state of Florida. One client singled him out as the *"leading credit attorney in Tampa,"* not least because he is *"very thorough, with years of experience in analyzing conflict and credit agreements."*

The Clients: The group has represented many creditors' committees and indentured trustees in Chapter 11 proceedings.

Gronek & Latham

The Firm: Hailed as *"the leading bankruptcy firm in Orlando,"* Gronek & Latham fields a team whose principal concern is debtor matters. It also works on Ponzi scheme cases and has achieved renown through its representation of the Chapter 11 trustee in the Evergreen Security case, a $200 million case that settled in 2004. The firm has recently recruited Elizabeth Green (who has 20 years' experience) to replace Rod-ney May, who went to the bench.

The Lawyers: *"Driving force"* **Scott Shuker** is known to represent most of the major companies that file large Chapter 11s in Orlando. He is described as *"intelligent, creative and skilful in his litigation and negotiation,"* with a reputation for dealing with leading players in the tourism industry.

The Clients: Clients have included Evergreen Security and debtors for the Planet Hollywood International and Transit Group Chapter 11 reorganization cases.

Holland & Knight LLP

See firm details p.1352

The Firm: The Orlando office is an integral part of a nationwide network of departments and attorneys serving a wide spectrum of clients. As such it is experienced in all areas of bankruptcy practice and has an excellent track record for both creditors and debtors in cross-border and international workouts and bankruptcies. The firm has recently recruited bankruptcy partners from the firm Akerman Senterfitt.

The Lawyers: **Leonard Gilbert** (see p.540) is *"the main guy in the Tampa office."* Despite taking a lesser role in 2004, he enjoys a strong, enduring reputation and has represented numerous secured and unsecured creditors' committees, financial institutions and public bodies.

Meland Russin Hellinger & Budwick

The Firm: The boutique firm has practiced bankruptcy law since its foundation in 1993, and competitors note that it has notched up real success in recent years. It has extensive experience with complex reorganizations and readily considers alternative conflict resolution where appropriate. A number of the bankruptcy specialists are seen to be *"coming into their own,"* and although still relatively young, possess admirable experience. A broad spectrum of clients use the firm for all areas of insolvency, including plans of reorganization, prepackaged plans, litigation and bankruptcy appeals, and all types of debtor and creditor claims.

The Lawyers: **Michael Budwick** has completed a significant Chapter 11 representation in the Supra proceedings, with some competitors viewing the case as his coming of age. Top-rated **Peter Russin** is a cofounder of the firm and has built up a healthy practice; competitors acknowledge the hard work that has gone into this.

The Clients: The firm has represented corporate and institutional clients, trustees, receivers and Fortune 500 companies.

504   All quotes in the text are from interviews with clients and competitors.

CHAMBERS USA 2005

Rice Pugatch Robinson & Schiller

The Firm: Based in Miami and Fort Lauderdale, this bankruptcy specialist offers a multifaceted insolvency practice including workouts and bankruptcies under Chapter 11 and Chapter 7. Set up in 1980, the firm has a client base of creditors, debtors, trustees and receivers. In Chapter 11 filings, the group represented the debtor Southeast Offset, a Miami printing company, in its successful plan of reorganization. The firm was co-counsel for the debtor Linc.net and its subsidiaries, a diversified group of companies providing construction, engineering and implementation services. On the creditor side, the group acted for a major entity in the bankruptcy of Far & Wide Travel and for the venture capital fund Apple Tree Partners.

The Lawyers: The active and well-regarded name partners of this firm work on all areas of bankruptcy and litigation. "*Effective*" **Lisa Schiller** has an unusually strong arsenal of expertise and a tenacious, professional manner. She works with a particular emphasis on business reorganizations and bankruptcy litigation.

Stearns Weaver Miller Weissler Alhadeff & Sitterson, PA

The Firm: "*Some fine lawyers*" at this firm assist a number of creditors, particularly secured creditors in foreclosure proceedings. The group represents large national and regional companies in Chapter 11 reorganizations and is viewed as a good choice for air transportation-related cases, which have, of course, increased in prevalence in recent years. "*A good group of people*" work on matters both in Florida and across the country, and have found themselves increasingly involved in litigation in the bankruptcy courts, including the representation of St Paul Travelers in the Linc.net proceedings. Real estate bankruptcies also account for a substantial slice of the business.

The Lawyers: **Patricia Redmond** commonly acts for those that are acquiring assets out of bankruptcy. Competitors recognize her aptitude for "*bringing opposing sides together and getting speedy resolutions*." **Hal Moorefield** spends time on high-end bankruptcy litigation and has covered all areas from the traditional to the unconventional. Competitors say he is "*good at consensus building, ethical and well respected.*" The effectiveness of **John Olson** is also recognized by peers. He has spent much time completing trustee work for US and foreign banks and other institutional creditors.

The Clients: Clients include airlines and manufacturing and retail concerns, as well as Bank of America, Wachovia Bank and IVAX.

White & Case LLP

See firm details p.1379

The Firm: A "*first-class team*" of 20 Miami insolvency lawyers maintains a thriving national and international practice. They represent clients in all aspects of restructuring and bankruptcy, handling debtors, creditors, equity owners and distressed buyers of assets and companies. Many of the firm's recent deals have been among the largest and most complex in the USA: the firm acted as principal bankruptcy counsel for Mirant, one of the largest producers, generators and marketers of electricity in the world, and is acting for participants in the Adelphia Communications case, one of the most detailed ever brought in the Southern District of New York. The Asia market is particularly important to the group, reflected by its representation of Asia Pulp & Paper in connection with the restructuring of over $12 billion worth of financial indebtedness. In another paper and wood products matter, White & Case filed concurrent Mexican and US proceedings for Corporacion Durango.

The Lawyers: "*Brilliant bankruptcy lawyer*" **Thomas Lauria** (see p.544) is cochairman of the firm's financial restructuring and insolvency department. Taking on a variety of Chapter 11 debtor representations and creditor matters, he is admired for his work on tough cases. According to clients, his greatest strength is his conviction; he is an "*extremely persuasive litigator and negotiator.*"

The Clients: Mirant; The Williams Companies; United Pan-Europe Communications; Corporacion Durango and Bank of America.

Other Notable Practitioners

John Emmanuel of Fowler White Boggs Banker in Tampa primarily represents creditors and creditors' committees. He has represented the major creditor in the reorganization of Pan American Hospital and also handles numerous cases involving resorts and hotels. Peers note he is "*extremely solid*" and shows "*a complete understanding of the bankruptcy market.*" **Roy Kobert** from the Orlando office of Broad and Cassel is "*diligent and impressive, and knows how to get things done.*" He acts for individual creditors, creditors' committees and commercial debtors around the country.

CONSTRUCTION

Band 1

Boose Casey Ciklin Lubitz Martens McBane & O'Connell

The Firm: Market opinion confirmed this litigation-focused firm as "*absolutely the top guys in the West Palm Beach area.*" A team of eight specialists advises on all aspects of construction law throughout Southeast Florida. The attorneys' experience is such that they are comfortable advising on everything from small residential developments to $100 million high-rise structures. Other areas of focus include complex litigation on subjects such as toxic mold and construction delay.

The Lawyers: **Bruce Alexander** has forged an enviable reputation following Lou McBane's retirement. Peers acclaim his "*remarkable knowledge of construction law at the highest level,*" which places him firmly "*at the cutting edge of the law.*" Rivals also appreciate his "*sophisticated demeanor*" in the courtroom: "*He doesn't try to bash heads together.*" Alexander divides his time between litigation and noncontentious advice. He led the team advising Suffolk Construction on the development of the high-rise Las Olas River House in Fort Lauderdale.

The Clients: A diverse client base includes significant private developers and public sector bodies such as the City of Fort Myers Beach.

Carlton Fields, PA

See firm details p.560

The Firm: A huge team of 28 attorneys at this renowned Florida firm provides "*very tough competition*" for its rivals. Interviewees were in no doubt that "*it's one of the most prominent firms in Florida – they're right at the front doing a lot of great things.*" The size and depth of the group makes Carlton Fields the natural choice for many of the largest projects in the state. At present, it is advising a joint venture vehicle on the $600 million expansion of the Orange County Convention Center. Much of the firm's workload is contentious, and its attorneys have experience of such diverse areas as designer malpractice, bad site conditions and mechanics' liens. Attorneys are currently defending a surety client against a construction defects claim relating to a desalination plant.

The Lawyers: Unusually for a construction lawyer, **George Meyer** runs an entirely transactional practice, which has earned him a reputation as "*probably the leading transactional lawyer in the state.*" By contrast, **Mike Nuechterlein** combines contentious and noncontentious work. In the last year, he has represented the City of Sanibel in a defective materials claim relating to a bridge and advised the City of Panama City Beach on its ambitious Front Beach Road redevelopment project. Fellow attorneys like his litigation style, saying: "*He's knowledgeable and mature, and doesn't fight over unnecessary*

| **Florida** |
| **Leading firms** (Construction) |
| [1] **BOOSE CASEY CIKLIN LUBITZ** West Palm Beach |
| **CARLTON FIELDS, PA** Miami, Orlando, Tampa |
| **GREENBERG TRAURIG LLP** Orlando |
| **HOLLAND & KNIGHT LLP** Orlando |
| **MOYE, O'BRIEN, O'ROURKE, PICKERT** Maitland |
| **PECKAR & ABRAMSON** Miami |
| **SIEGFRIED, RIVERA, LERNER,** Miami |
| [2] **BECKER & POLIAKOFF PA** Fort Lauderdale |
| **FERENCIK, LIBANOFF, BRANDT** Fort Lauderdale |
| **LEIBY STEARNS LINKHORST,** Fort Lauderdale |
| **VEZINA LAWRENCE & PISCITELLI** Fort Lauderdale |
| **WELBAUM, GUERNSEY, HINGSTON,** Miami |
| [3] **AKERMAN SENTERFITT** Orlando |
| **BROAD AND CASSEL** Orlando |
| **BROWN CLARK DEMAY & FROMAN PA** Sarasota |
| **DANIELS, KASHTAN, DOWNS** Miami |
| **FOLEY & LARDNER** Orlando |
| **FORIZS AND DOGALI PL** Tampa |
| **GRAY ROBINSON PA** Orlando |
| **KIRWIN NORRIS PA** Winter Park |
| **WRIGHT, FULFORD, MOORHEAD** Orlando |
| Firms are listed alphabetically in each band. |

things." Nuechterlein is also well known as a mediator and arbitrator. **Charles Cacciabeve** is felt to be growing in stature and "*definitely moving towards the top tier*." Primarily a litigator, he recently obtained summary judgment for a public sector client in a road construction claim and successfully defended a private contractor against a construction defects claim relating to a new shopping center. "*Courteous, knowledgeable and professional*" **Bruce King** is a specialist in construction surety law and earns favorable comment from peers in this regard.
The Clients: In addition to the cities of Sanibel and Panama City Beach, the firm acts for private sector clients such as Turnberry Villas, Fairfield Resorts and Hillsborough County Aviation Authority.

Greenberg Traurig LLP
See firm details p.564
The Firm: One of Florida's largest firms, Greenberg Traurig is home to a team of 15 construction attorneys who concentrate on representing large private developer-owners and contractors in both litigation and transactional work. Competitors point to Leslie O'Neal-Coble's arrival from Holland & Knight as a positive influence on the firm's profile, suggesting that the team now "*has the depth and experience to handle really major projects*." Recent highlights include advising private developers on several new city center mixed-use developments of about $500 million and playing a significant role in airport expansion throughout the state.
The Lawyers: **Michael Hornreich** (see p.542) frequently handles water intrusion claims and was recently the lead attorney in a $10 million

dollar claim for water intrusion in a newly constructed REIT-owned apartment community. The successful resolution of this case, which also involved O'Neal-Coble, demonstrated the full extent of the team's technical expertise. Commentators acknowledge his "*broad range of substantive knowledge*." Hailed as "*tremendously talented*," **Leslie O'Neal-Coble** (see p.547) is particularly experienced in toxic mold litigation, which often has a significant overlap with construction defect claims. She recently settled a substantial claim relating to toxic mold and water intrusion problems in a luxury private home. On the transactional side, she often represents developers of condominiums and resorts, and has seen a resurgence in instructions from high-end luxury homebuilders. Interviewees agreed, "*Her name would come up in any discussion of top lawyers.*"
The Clients: The firm acts for Florida and national construction companies, and public bodies such as the Florida Department of Transportation.

Holland & Knight LLP
See firm details p.1352
The Firm: The construction practice group at Holland & Knight is based mainly in the Orlando and Tampa offices. A varied practice includes the representation of power industry clients in the construction of new generating facilities in the state. The team also maintains a substantial litigation caseload. Though its profile in the field of toxic mold has inevitably diminished following the departure of Leslie O'Neal-Coble, the recent hurricanes have resulted in a glut of water penetration claims and the group has been engaged by various general contractors to defend claims by owners of recently constructed condominiums.
The Lawyers: **Christopher Weiss** (see p.553) was singled out for praise by commentators, who believe his background in the construction industry has endowed him with the ability to "*understand very technical issues within the industry – a proficiency not shared by many other lawyers.*" He predominantly represents general contractors in contract drafting, litigation and related issues. Of late, he has been counseling the Kennedy Space Center on claims for delay and disruption brought about post-9/11. He has also advised a general contractor on a massive defective construction claim based on the use of fly ash as structural foundation. Younger lawyer **Ben Subin** (see p.552) represents clients in the power industry and recently settled a construction claim regarding a $550 million power generating facility. Interviewees agreed that "*while he's not at the top just yet, he certainly will be.*"
The Clients: The team represents general contractors and power generating companies.

Moye, O'Brien, O'Rourke, Pickert & Martin, LLP
See firm details p.570
The Firm: This Lakeland-based boutique enjoys an enviable reputation for its "*recognized high quality*" in construction law. The firm has successfully established a nationwide civil engineering practice.
The Lawyers: Managing partner **James Moye**'s (see p.546) name has been linked to significant construction and civil engineering projects throughout the USA. Recent highlights, reflecting Moye's "*first-tier status*," include the Northeast Corridor high-speed rail project and the construction of new terminals at Miami International Airport. He has also advised on the construction of a large bridge in Connecticut. **Stephen Pickert** (see p.547) is a tenacious litigator with an emphasis on construction defect cases relating to new developments. Fellow professionals revealed him to be a popular choice for referrals. One said: "*I'd call him if I ever needed some extra firepower.*" **Gregory Martin**'s (see p.545) practice is essentially non-contentious; he represents general contractors from contract stage to completion. Much of his work is in the public infrastructure field, and in the past year he has acted on road and bridge construction projects with an aggregate value of more than $100 million.
The Clients: The list includes national and international investors, builders, designers and subcontractors.

Peckar & Abramson
See firm details p.1363
The Firm: A renowned national construction law specialist with offices in Miami and Fort Lauderdale, Peckar & Abramson continues to grow in stature. In the words of one leading competitor, "*If they don't deserve to be in the top tier, nobody does.*" Much of the firm's caseload has been composed of construction defect claims arising from hurricane damage, and the team benefits from the presence of several engineers and construction managers who act as consultants to the practice. The firm has used its Florida presence as a springboard to enter the Caribbean and Latin American markets.
The Lawyers: **Stephen Reisman** (see p.548) is acknowledged by peers as "*one of the top construction lawyers*" in the state. The past year has seen him involved in several huge redevelopment projects, including the $120 million Village of Merrick Park retail development in Coral Gables. The project, which is intended to anchor the regeneration of the city, was completed to an extremely demanding timetable.
The Clients: Peckar & Abramson concentrates on representing construction managers and general contractors.

Florida
Leading individuals (Construction)

Senior Statesman

GRANDOFF J Bert *Allen Dell*, Tampa

WELBAUM Earl *Welbaum Guernsey*, Miami

[1]

ALEXANDER Bruce *Boose Casey*, West Palm Beach

DOWNS Joe *Daniels Kashtan*, Miami

HORNREICH Michael *Greenberg Traurig*, Orlando

LEIBY Larry *Leiby Stearns*, Fort Lauderdale

MEYER George *Carlton Fields*, Tampa

MOYE James *Moye O'Brien*, Maitland

NUECHTERLEIN Mike *Carlton Fields*, Tampa

O'NEAL-COBLE Leslie *Greenberg Traurig*, Orlando

REISMAN Stephen *Peckar & Abramson*, Miami

SIEGFRIED Steven *Siegfried Rivera*, Miami

WEISS Christopher *Holland & Knight*, Orlando

[2]

ASHBY Kimberly *Akerman Senterfitt*, Orlando

BRANDT A Peter *Ferencik Libanoff*, Fort Lauderdale

CACCIABEVE Charles *Carlton Fields*, Orlando

FERENCIK Robert *Ferencik Libanoff*, Fort Lauderdale

KING Bruce *Carlton Fields*, Miami

LESSER Steven *Becker & Poliakoff*, Fort Lauderdale

RAKUSIN Steve *Stephen Rakusin*, Fort Lauderdale

VEZINA Rob *Vezina Lawrence*, Tallahassee

WEINTRAUB Lee *Becker & Poliakoff*, Fort Lauderdale

WILSON Michael *Broad and Cassel*, Orlando

[3]

BAXA Edmund *Foley & Lardner*, West Palm Beach

BROWN Daryl *Brown Clark*, Sarasota

CAREY Michael *Carey O'Malley*, Tampa

CUNNINGHAM Malcolm *Cunningham*, West Palm Beach

DOGALI Andy *Forizs and Dogali*, Tampa

DURKIN Denis *Baker & Hostetler*, Orlando

GURLEY David *Gurley Dramis*, Sarasota

ICARD Thomas *Icard Merrill*, Sarasota

KEINER Jeffrey *Gray Robinson*, Orlando

KIRWIN Brian *Kirwin Norris*, Winter Park

LANE Joe *Lowndes Drosdick*, Orlando

LIBANOFF Ira *Ferencik Libanoff*, Fort Lauderdale

LYON Fred *The Lyon Firm*, Winter Park

MARTIN Gregory *Moye O'Brien*, Maitland

PHALIN Lawrence *Mateer & Harbert*, Orlando

PICKERT Stephen *Moye O'Brien*, Maitland

PISCITELLI Michael *Vezina Lawrence*, Fort Lauderdale

SUBIN Ben *Holland & Knight*, Orlando

Individuals are listed alphabetically in each band.

Siegfried, Rivera, Lerner, De La Torre & Sobel, PA

The Firm: This small Coral Gables firm places a strong emphasis on construction and real estate law. Its team of attorneys represents a broad spectrum of clients, including lenders, developers, suppliers and contractors, in contract negotiations, litigation and arbitration.

The Lawyers: **Steven Siegfried** is recognized as "*a pretty big presence in the South Florida market.*" He handles a variety of construction litigation and arbitration matters, including delay and defect claims. A published author, Siegfried is also an adjunct professor at the University of Miami School of Law.

Band 2

Becker & Poliakoff PA

The Firm: A medium-sized, full-service firm with offices throughout the state, Becker & Poliakoff is noted in the market for its "*committed expertise in construction and litigation.*" More particularly, it is well known for advising on condominium developments.

The Lawyers: **Lee Weintraub**, a self-confessed generalist, has litigated disputes of all kinds, from defects to delays. He has also recently advised a substantial commercial property investor on the contractual and insurance implications of its first venture into condominium development. Rivals view Weintraub as "*a top younger lawyer who certainly knows his stuff.*" **Steven Lesser** also received his fair share of compliments; market commentators describe him as "*a really talented player in the niche area of condo development.*"

Ferencik, Libanoff, Brandt, Bustamante & Williams

The Firm: A seven-partner construction boutique based in Fort Lauderdale, this firm moves up the rankings following a great deal of positive feedback for its attorneys. Its clientele includes a raft of contractors as well as design professionals, materials suppliers, owners and surety providers.

The Lawyers: **Robert Ferencik** was acclaimed for his courtroom prowess. "*I was very impressed to be up against him in trial; he has a great presentation style,*" said one past opponent. Both Ferencik and fellow name partner **Ira Libanoff** spend much of their time in the courtroom, while a third name partner, **Peter Brandt**, makes his first appearance in Chambers' tables on the strength of his reputation as "*one of the best surety lawyers.*"

The Clients: ANECO; ANF Group; Astaldi Construction; Ballast Nedam Construction; Casino Drywall; Charter Builders; Concreform; Current Builders of Florida; Florida Department of Transportation; GLF Construction; Jennings Construction; Lanzo Construction and Pavarini Construction.

Leiby Stearns Linkhorst & Roberts, PA

See firm details p.569

The Firm: This compact Fort Lauderdale boutique is reputed to be "*one of the movers and shakers*" in the market. As a commercial construction specialist, the firm represents contractors, surety providers, subcontractors, construction owners, material suppliers, and design professionals in relation to contract negotiation, liens, bonds, litigation and arbitration.

The Lawyers: It is said of **Larry Leiby** (see p.544) that "*he was practicing in the area long before it became fashionable.*" Other attorneys

reveal they "*refer constantly to his treatises.*" He is certified as a circuit court mediator for construction disputes, and also regularly acts as an arbitrator.

Vezina Lawrence & Piscitelli

The Firm: This well-regarded construction and administrative law boutique divides its attorneys between offices in Tallahassee and Fort Lauderdale. Most of the firm's work is within the state, though the team is notably involved in the development of, and disputes arising from, the DART light rail system in Dallas.

The Lawyers: **Rob Vezina** advises contractors on large public procurements for infrastructure projects, as well as contract claims arising from them. Recent examples include an $80 million road bridge in North Carolina and, within Florida, the $100 million Hathaway Bridge replacement project. Partner **Michael Piscitelli** is a prominent litigator, with a special interest in surety law.

Welbaum, Guernsey, Hingston, Greenleaf & Gregory LLP

The Firm: Best known as a specialist in the contract surety field, this firm has branched out into general construction, real estate and insurance law. Eight attorneys make up the well-respected team.

The Lawyers: While commentators agreed that **Earl Welbaum** was a senior statesman of the construction bar, they were quick to emphasize that "*he certainly still practices full time.*" He is especially rated for his surety law know-how – several interviewees described him as "*the grandfather of surety law*" – and counts many payment and performance bond sureties among his clients.

The Clients: Andrade Gutierrez Construction; Atlantic Interiors; Bovis Lend Lease; CIGNA Companies; Coastal Construction; Copeland Steel Erectors; JJW Construction; Rovel Construction; Western Surety and Wesley Construction.

Band 3

Akerman Senterfitt

See firm details p.555

The Firm: Well known as one of the state's largest full-service firms, Akerman Senterfitt boasts an active construction department spread throughout its network of Florida offices. The practice group has been busy on both litigation and transactional work of late. The former is largely a result of the recent hurricane damage, which has triggered an abundance of construction defect claims; the latter, however, is evidence of a more positive trend toward new resort construction in central Florida. Another element of the litigation practice that has seen rapid growth is indoor air quality, which encompasses personal injury and property damage caused by pollutants such as toxic mold and asbestos. The

www.ChambersandPartners.com
All quotes in the text are from interviews with clients and competitors.
507

prevailing market opinion of the group is that "*they have real potential – they're hiring good-quality people and carving out a niche for themselves.*"
The Lawyers: **Kimberly Ashby** (see p.533) has spent the last year advising on some of the largest developments in the state. Two of her recent highlights were seeing the early completion of the $520 million Grande Lakes Resort in Orlando and acting on the complete renovation of the famous Gulfstream Race Track in Hallandale.
The Clients: Clients include developers, contractors and hotel and resort chains.

Broad and Cassel

The Firm: Broad and Cassel, a full-service firm with eight Florida offices, sustains a small team of construction attorneys. In recent times the group's client focus has shifted toward representing owner-developers, in order to provide a better fit with the firm's real estate client base.
The Lawyers: Interviewees point to **Michael Wilson** as the leading light, saying: "*He's as talented as anyone around.*" Wilson is credited by many with the continuing growth of this area of the firm's practice. Primarily a litigator, he has represented developer clients in a variety of contract disputes, including significant claims for delay and construction defects.

Brown Clark DeMay & Froman PA

The Firm: Sources confirm the position of this smaller outfit as "*the best construction firm in Sarasota.*" Eight attorneys advise on contract negotiations, litigation, arbitration and adjudication at the West Coast firm. Its reputation in the field of construction law is closely tied to that of partner **Daryl Brown**.

Daniels, Kashtan, Downs, Robertson & Magathan

The Firm: Market commentators were in no doubt about this group's status as "*the best in the business for design professionals.*" Clients include architects and engineers, and the firm is praised for bringing specialist expertise in this area to the deal table.
The Lawyers: **Joe Downs** received compliments for his "*creative thinking,*" with many of his peers praising the length of his experience and his "*ability to deal with the crux of a case rather than the peripheries.*"

Foley & Lardner

See firm details p.1828
The Firm: As a major player in the Florida market, Foley & Lardner's construction team has access to a national network of offices and clients. While some interviewees felt that Foley's construction practice had been stronger in the past, most agreed that its "*statewide presence*" was a considerable advantage. The team primarily acts for contractors and owners, generally in the commercial, industrial and healthcare sectors.

The Lawyers: "*Bright and honorable*" **Edmund Baxa**'s (see p.534) litigation caseload has recently included a construction defects claim against a subcontractor, relating to defective carpentry in a theme park resort hotel in Orlando. He is also representing a road maintenance contractor in a bid protest.

Forizs and Dogali PL

The Firm: This mid-sized Tampa establishment boasts a construction department that belies its four-attorney size. Clients are drawn from all corners of the construction world, and include owners, architects, engineers and contractors.
The Lawyers: In addition to handling a number of smaller, hurricane-related claims, managing partner **Andy Dogali** successfully represented the architect of the new Orlando Airport terminal in a construction-related claim. Fellow attorneys depict Dogali as "*honest and hard-working.*"

Gray Robinson PA

The Firm: Commentators characterized the construction department of this large Florida firm as "*particularly experienced on the engineering and design professional side.*" This is borne out by its recent caseload, which includes the defense of designers and architects against water intrusion claims arising from hurricane damage.
The Lawyers: "*A formidable adversary and an honest, straight shooter,*" **Jeffrey Keiner** is a general commercial litigator who is placing an increasing emphasis on construction litigation. About half his workload is now construction related, generally from the perspective of architect or engineer clients. He recently defended six such clients against accessibility claims under the Federal Fair Housing Act.

Kirwin Norris PA

The Firm: A new entry to *Chambers'* tables, this construction and commercial litigation specialist was described by competitors as "*a great firm with really terrific lawyers.*" It is particularly well regarded for its dispute resolution prowess and each of the nine attorneys has some prior experience of the construction industry.
The Lawyers: **Brian Kirwin** was warmly recommended by peers, who were "*very impressed by his abilities*" and convinced "*he will be a big player in the future.*" The majority of Kirwin's clients are public sector bodies such as school boards, water districts and municipalities. Typical disputes include payment and performance bond claims, design and plan errors, delay, disruption and lost labor productivity claims.

Wright, Fulford, Moorhead and Brown PA

The Firm: Wright Fulford's 12-strong team of litigators handles construction disputes nationwide. Rivals had no hesitation in endorsing the

firm as "*the go-to people for a case involving a design professional – they're real heavy hitters on a national level.*"
The Lawyers: Don Wright is the main contact partner for this work.
The Clients: An impressive list of engineering clients includes: Professional Service Industries; Parsons Brinckerhoff; URS Corporation; XL Environmental and Tetra Tech.

Other Notable Practitioners

Steve Rakusin of Stephen Rakusin PA is a household name in the sector, largely because of his status as a published author. One lawyer said, "*I refer to his treatises all the time – he has published a five-volume book. He has a fine reputation.*" An acclaimed expert on lien law, Rakusin also has his own thriving litigation practice in Fort Lauderdale. **Michael Carey** of Carey, O'Malley, Whitaker & Manson PA in Tampa has a high profile in the state and is portrayed as "*a tenacious but professional litigator.*" **Malcolm Cunningham** practices with two assistants as Cunningham Law Firm in West Palm Beach, and is highly regarded for his work for public sector clients. "*Skilled, outstanding*" **Denis Durkin** is a partner at national firm Baker & Hostetler's Orlando office. He maintains an unusual practice, which focuses on heavy construction projects for federal government; he advises general contractors in their bids for this work, and assists them with bid protests where necessary. **David Gurley** practices in three-partner Sarasota construction boutique Gurley Dramis, and is highly recommended by his peers, while **Thomas Icard** is also a Sarasota-based lawyer. Formerly of Carlton Fields and now at Icard, Merrill, Cullis, Timm, Furen & Ginsburg PA, Icard focuses on trial practice in his construction work. **Joe Lane** of Orlando firm Lowndes Drosdick Doster Kantor & Reed PA is described as "*hardworking, knowledgeable and easy to deal with.*" He is an experienced construction attorney with a particular focus on disputes concerning construction defects and design errors or omissions. **Fred Lyon** is a sole practitioner at the Lyon Firm PA who was singled out for his representation of municipalities and public bodies; he is particularly active in the energy and utilities sectors and operates out of Winter Park. **Lawrence Phalin** is popular with fellow professionals for his "*fair and balanced view. He takes a painstaking approach which is more likely to help clients resolve a problem.*" Phalin is a partner at Mateer & Harbert P.A., a full-service firm with offices in Orlando and Ocala. Meanwhile, the Tampa firm of Allen Dell is home to **Bert Grandoff**, who is "*extremely distinguished and well known nationally.*" He is acting as lead trial counsel in a complex ongoing construction dispute. A founding fellow of the American College of Construction Lawyers, he is also its current president.

508   All quotes in the text are from interviews with clients and competitors.

CHAMBERS USA 2005

CORPORATE/M&A

Florida
Leading firms (Corporate/M&A)

1 AKERMAN SENTERFITT *Miami*
GREENBERG TRAURIG LLP *Miami*
HOLLAND & KNIGHT LLP *Jacksonville*

2 CARLTON FIELDS, PA *Tampa*
FOLEY & LARDNER *Jacksonville*
STEEL HECTOR & DAVIS LLP *Miami*
TRENAM, KEMKER, SCHARF, BARKIN *Tampa*
WHITE & CASE LLP *Miami*

3 GLENN RASMUSSEN FOGARTY *Tampa*
HILL, WARD & HENDERSON, PA *Tampa*
KIRSCHNER & LEGLER *Jacksonville*
SHUMAKER LOOP & KENDRICK LLP *Tampa*
SHUTTS & BOWEN LLP *Miami*
STEARNS WEAVER MILLER WEISSLER *Miami*

Leading individuals (Corporate/M&A)

Senior Statesman
CANNON Kinder *Holland & Knight, Jacksonville*

1 EPSTEIN Gary *Greenberg Traurig, Miami*
GRAMMIG Robert *Holland & Knight, Tampa*
MCGUIGAN Thomas *Steel Hector & Davis, Miami*
RODDENBERRY Stephen *Akerman Senterfitt, Miami*

2 ALVAREZ-FARRÉ Emilio *White & Case, Miami*
ARONSON Daniel *Greenberg Traurig, Fort Lauderdale*
AWNER Jonathan *Akerman Senterfitt, Miami*
DOLINER Nathaniel *Carlton Fields, Tampa*
KLINGHOFFER Teddy *Akerman Senterfitt, Miami*
LEGLER Mitchell *Kirschner & Legler, Jacksonville*
RASMUSSEN Robert *Glenn Rasmussen, Tampa*
SONBERG Steven *Holland & Knight, Miami*
TEBLUM Gary *Trenam Kemker, Tampa*

3 AMES Stuart *Stearns Weaver, Miami*
BELL Rodney *Holland & Knight, Miami*
DAVIS Gardner *Foley & Lardner, Jacksonville*
DE ARMAS Luis *Shutts & Bowen, Miami*
FELMAN David *Hill Ward, Tampa*
KELSO Linda *Foley & Lardner, Jacksonville*
KIRSCHNER Kenneth *Kirschner & Legler, Jacksonville*
LEISNER Richard *Trenam Kemker, Tampa*
PEREZ Luis *Akerman Senterfitt, Miami*
YADLEY Gregory *Shumaker Loop, Tampa*

Firms and individuals are listed alphabetically in each band.

Band 1

Akerman Senterfitt
See firm details p.555

The Firm: At the *"top of the market"* in corporate law statewide, this set of *"brilliant, tremendous players"* recently acted for a major private prison management operator in two refinancing issues and a buyout. Peers praise the *"sizable practice"* of the Miami office, which succeeds in securities and M&A. This *"stellar lineup"* represents domestic and foreign private companies, in addition to prominent individuals such as tycoon Wayne Huizenga in private and public

deals. Another highlight involved Spanish-speaking television station operator Bela Broadcasting and its subsidiaries in a multimillion-dollar equity financing. Commentators commend the firm's Latin American capabilities. The international scope of the team includes a nine-figure cash tender offer of a Chilean company listed on both the Santiago and New York stock exchanges.

The Lawyers: The *"impressive track record"* of **Stephen Roddenberry** (see p.549) attracted acclaim, with one commentator adding: *"He's extremely capable, knowledgeable and deal-savvy"* for both competitors and clients. Head of the corporate department **Jonathan Awner** (see p.534) benefits from *"a sophisticated practice with impressive deals,"* including a $400 million note offering for a client in the telecom sector. The *"top-notch attorney"* has also guided clients through SEC-led investigations. *"First-class attorney"* **Teddy Klinghoffer** (see p.544) is pitched as *"the gentleman of the table"* in M&A negotiations. His continued representation of IVAX in a diverse range of corporate transactions has attracted kudos. In addition, he helped close a deal for client CarePlus Health Plan in a takeover by Humana. Competitors also noted the *"wide span"* of the international corporate practice of **Luis Perez** (see p.547), who plays a significant role in the firm's success in Latin America. In a considerable setback for the firm, five corporate lawyers recently departed to join Greenberg Traurig.

The Clients: The firm has attracted corporate clients such as CarePlus Health Plan, IVAX and Boca Resorts. Individual representation involved high-flyers, for example Wayne Huizenga who helped launch enterprises such as Blockbuster, AutoNation and Waste Management.

Greenberg Traurig LLP
See firm details p.564

The Firm: The prowess and strength of this *"preeminent"* law firm *"has more depth"* than some of its competitors, attracting clients who are lured by its combination of national presence and broad understanding of the legal intricacies regionally. A *"stellar constellation of lawyers, cherry-picked from the best around,"* forms the basis for the practice, which is prized by clients for its *"law as business"* approach. This gives the firm an edge over the competition, said market observers, who also credited its boldness to the firm's success. The Fort Lauderdale office recently scored a coup when it recruited five corporate lawyers from rival Akerman Senterfitt. A broad swath in the corporate realm includes expertise in M&A, bankruptcy, private equity and venture capital among other areas. The team won client confidence by consistently delivering *"New York-style approach and expertise."*

The Lawyers: Peers respect the *"elite"* **Gary Epstein** (see p.539) for his bankruptcy practice and overall corporate experience, including several financing transactions on behalf of Rail-America. He takes a *"methodical"* approach, and wins respect for his thorough representation. Formerly of New York's Wachtell Lipton Rosen & Katz, **Daniel Aronson** (see p.533) is credited for *"thinking on his feet in a fight,"* according to peers. His adroit representation in private equity, venture capital financing and corporate M&A has attracted praise, with one analyst adding: *"Dan is the man I would refer people to, as I have confidence that he'll do a good job."*

The Clients: Among the firm's clients are Rail-America, CNL Hospitality Properties and Equity One. A flurry of emerging companies also feature on the roster.

Holland & Knight LLP
See firm details p.1352

The Firm: This *"outstanding stable of corporate lawyers"* has achieved a strong presence throughout Florida and the rest of the country, according to interviewees. Peers acknowledge the vigor of the Tampa office in the corporate arena: They're *"number one for sure."* On behalf of NASDAQ-listed Kos Pharmaceuticals, the team participated in the acquisition of a new respiratory product. Market sources are also impressed by its array of high-flying deals, signifying that its role as a contender in corporate law has been cemented in South Florida.

The Lawyers: **Robert Grammig** (see p.541) *"makes things happen."* A force to be reckoned with in Tampa, he recently handled the acquisition of a major American IT consulting firm for a significant Canadian client. Sources admire his capacity to get what he wants at the negotiating table, without having to resort to philippic behavior. He is also a *"securities lawyer of choice."* **Steven Sonberg** (see p.551), who chairs the firm's 325-lawyer business law section, has a *"number-one reputation"* in corporate transactional work. In one recent highlight, he represented healthcare provider ProxyMed in its acquisition of PlanVista. Together with Sonberg, **Rodney Bell** (see p.534) acted in various transactions for Kos Pharmaceuticals. Peers say Bell *"is a rising star of the operation,"* while **Kinder Cannon** (see p.536) earned distinction for his *"excellent business mind."* The *"excellent mentor"* offers established expertise in public and private offerings involving equity and debt securities as part of a broader repertoire.

The Clients: Kos Pharmaceuticals, Mayor's Jewelers and ProxyMed are featured in the firm's clientele.

Band 2

Carlton Fields, PA

See firm details p.560

The Firm: Clients find this firm *"exceptionally professional, knowledgeable and always ready to take the task on board."* Described as *"one of the top five (corporate practices) in Florida"* for its presence and experience, the group's remit includes M&A, private equity and tax-related matters. One highlight was the team's participation in the sale of BREED Technologies. Another drawing card for the firm is its emphasis on helping emerging companies through various stages of growth. Sources praised the *"outstanding resourcefulness, responsiveness and sophistication"* of the business group.

The Lawyers: One of the *"best acquisition attorneys,"* according to clients and competitors, **Nathaniel Doliner** chairs the firm's corporate, securities, taxation, and asset-based financing practice group. Doliner recently acted in the combination of two major telecom companies. Clients admire his ability to get *"all the corners covered"* at the negotiating table. His *"incisive"* approach means that he is *"good at seeing all sides of the deal."*

The Clients: BREED Technologies; Walter Industries; Coast Financial Holdings; Eagle Supply Group; Northeast Bancorp; Allen Systems Group and Whitney Information Networks.

Foley & Lardner

See firm details p.1828

The Firm: The seven-attorney corporate team *"has a strong presence and well-deserved reputation."* Based in Jacksonville, the group's flourishing reputation in the midmarket arena has impressed observers, who often come across the firm in various M&A, public and private offerings, and other related issues. One of its more notable accomplishments is a $342.8 million offering for NYSE-listed Regency Centers.

The Lawyers: Peers single out **Gardner Davis** (see p.538) as one of the *"finest corporate attorneys in Jacksonville."* He made a name for himself as lead counsel in major M&A in the food processing and distribution industry. *"Clients love him,"* said interviewees. Together with partner **Linda Kelso** (see p.543), he recently acted for Fidelity National Financial, a Fortune 300 Jacksonville company, in a $305 million acquisition. Kelso won applause as *"frankly, one of the most impressive securities lawyers I have ever worked with,"* one observer said. She also scooped plaudits for her real estate investment trusts, securities and corporate compliance work.

The Clients: Fidelity National Financial and Regency Centers feature, among others, on the client list.

Steel Hector & Davis LLP

See firm details p.575

The Firm: The firm's *"overall excellence"* consistently attracts a bevy of well-respected clients. The 50-attorney Florida team specializes in corporate, securities and tax matters among other related issues. Its workload is highlighted by equity and debt financing in private placements totaling more than $500 million. In addition, the group counseled the seller of minority interests in a major private telecom company.

The Lawyers: *"Outstanding"* **Thomas McGuigan** (see p.546) recently led for the purchaser of a leading minerals and fuels business in a deal valued at more than $120 million. The *"highly respected"* operator is valued for telling clients *"exactly like it is."* His *"direct"* advice is on offer on a range of corporate and securities issues.

The Clients: The firm also acts for clients that range from NASDAQ-listed retailers to privately held emerging telecom and defense contractors.

Trenam, Kemker, Scharf, Barkin, Frye, O'Neill & Mullis PA

The Firm: This full-service, 80-attorney law firm has two offices in Florida, dispensing *"skilled"* performances on a range of transactions. Its *"highly active"* team continues to act for key client Chico's, a retail clothing chain. Another alluring key strength is its deft capability in real estate and commercial litigation, which helps to sustain the firm's distinguished corporate profile.

The Lawyers: **Gary Teblum** cochairs the corporate and business transactions practice group. Sources identify him as one of *"the best-known and talented"* transactional attorneys who also offers proficient tax advice. **Richard Leisner** won praise for his securities work. Leisner has acted for professional investors and venture capitalists in connection to matters involving several technology companies.

The Clients: Womenswear retailer Chico's and business process outsourcer AcclarisSM are included in this firm's client roster.

White & Case LLP

See firm details p.1379

The Firm: Competitors praise the *"significant expertise in the Spanish-speaking world"* that helped bolster the strength of the Miami office. This global firm benefits from Florida's role as a gateway to Latin America, embracing cross-border financing and M&A transactions. It has advised Corporación Durango in a multimillion-dollar finance restructuring proceeding.

The Lawyers: Dubbed a *"legend in Latin American deals,"* **Emilio Alvarez-Farré** (see p.533) recently counseled the Government of Argentina in several privatization matters. He also led negotiations for Corporación Durango and separately negotiated on a raft of other Latin American transactions. The *"remarkable expert"* has also advised underwriters with a Latin American connection.

The Clients: Latin American corporate heavyweights and governments, and US-based multinationals with cross-border Latin American interests are among the clients.

Band 3

Glenn Rasmussen Fogarty & Hooker

The Firm: Though its corporate practice covers a range of expertise, it is seen more often than not in deals that involve some aspects of financing or refinancing. In this capacity, *"the team does big firm work with small firm economy."* The corporate finance group was retained as a special Florida counsel for a UK-based manufacturer in a multimillion-dollar line-of-credit and buyout transaction involving a private equity firm. On behalf of a national bank, it also participated in the renewal and modification of an $85 million floorplan credit facility from two banks.

The Lawyers: **Robert Rasmussen** has continued to excel in private financing transactions, including representation of financial institutions in significant credit transactions and private placements for emerging companies. His *"tenacious"* advocacy and *"eye for detail"* help attract important work such as a multimillion-dollar wholesale warehouse mortgage credit facility on behalf of a considerable US bank.

The Clients: The select clientele includes NYSE-listed manufacturers and Florida top banks.

Hill, Ward & Henderson, PA

The Firm: The ten-attorney corporate and business group of this Tampa firm is recognized for its excellence in venture capital and M&A work. The team recently represented Intellitec Products in its acquisition of Intellitec, a division of General Dynamics. Clients state that *"this firm is very strong technically and the lawyers know what they're talking about."* The team continues to represent clients in transactions involving automobile franchises across the USA. Sources also admire its *"integral and client-focused"* service.

The Lawyers: *"Straight shooter"* **David Felman** thrives in a practice that covers venture capital and lending work. An *"extremely bright, elite"* securities lawyer, he acted for Stonehenge Capital in connection with its multimillion-dollar acquisition of a Jacksonville-based transport company.

The Clients: Asbury Automotive Group, Ballast Point Venture Partners and Stonehenge Capital are examples of the firm's clientele.

Kirschner & Legler

The Firm: This two-attorney transactional boutique makes up for what it lacks in size with *"wide legal knowledge, deep business understanding, practicality and strategic thinking."* The team was recently involved in obtaining a credit facility in excess of $600 million for a Fortune 200 company. This *"go-to firm in North Florida"* not only advises companies but also interfaces between clients and other law firms.

The Lawyers: *"Extremely knowledgeable"* **Kenneth Kirschner** is *"highly practical and results-oriented."* His extensive and varied corporate and M&A practice is highlighted by a $100 million financing for client Winn-Dixie. *"Top-notch"* **Mitchell Legler** is *"a lawyers' lawyer,"* commentators said, referring to his depth of knowledge in business and real estate law. He was lead counsel in a $150 million secured facility for Stein Mart.

The Clients: This firm also counsels other Florida private companies and publicly traded multinationals.

Shumaker Loop & Kendrick LLP

The Firm: The stability, efficiency and prowess of this 150-attorney regional firm have not gone unnoticed in Florida, where the team caters to a sophisticated clientele that includes midmarket companies. The group recently engineered a particularly difficult merger for a NASDAQ-listed client and involves another healthcare firm. The transaction involved wide-ranging SEC reviews, accounting and profitability issues, and a complex shareholder base.

The Lawyers: At the helm of the corporate practice group is **Gregory Yadley**, who handles substantial M&A, securities and corporate governance work. Clients view Yadley *"as someone who gets things done in every environment and sector."* He recently negotiated the sale of a multibillion-dollar Florida bank group to a supra-regional bank holding company.

The Clients: Banks and healthcare providers are among the clientele.

Shutts & Bowen LLP

See firm details p.573

The Firm: Competitors say this firm *"has carved an important niche in banking"* to enhance its overall capability in corporate law. Its team of *"clients' lawyers"* delivers expertise in such prominent dealings as the purchase of all the Colombian operations of Chiquita Brands International. The 12-attorney corporate group acted for NYSE-listed World Fuel Services in the purchase of London-based Tramp Holdings, one of the largest independent resellers of marine fuel in the world; the transaction is valued at about $83 million.

The Lawyers: Chair of the corporate transactions practice group, **Luis de Armas** (see p.538) continues to ladle out *"tremendous experience and capacity of zeroing in on key issues."* In addition to representing companies in worldwide transactions, he is also advising the buyer Invesmar in the Chiquita transaction.

The Clients: Invesmar and World Fuel Services are among the team's clients.

Stearns Weaver Miller Weissler Alhadeff & Sitterson, P.A.

The Firm: This full-service commercial law firm has about 100 attorneys in Miami, Ft. Lauderdale and Tampa, offering *"finance technicalities"* as related to M&A, securities offerings and other related proceedings. The group has also appeared before the SEC, FTC and other government agencies concerning the regulatory aspects of business transactions, and securities offerings and filings.

The Lawyers: **Stuart Ames** is *"one of the leading corporate lawyers in Florida."* Ames leads the firm's commercial and asset-based finance practice, and has proven to be particularly adept in representing lenders and borrowers.

The Clients: Publicly-held Fortune 500 companies, financial institutions, real estate developers and airlines figure in this firm's client roster.

EMPLOYMENT

MAINLY DEFENDANT

Florida
Leading firms
(Employment: Mainly Defendant)
1 FORD & HARRISON LLP *Orlando, Tampa*
MORGAN, LEWIS & BOCKIUS LLP *Miami*
ZINOBER & McCREA, PA *Tampa*
2 COFFMAN, COLEMAN, ANDREWS, *Jacksonville*
FISHER & PHILLIPS *Fort Lauderdale, Orlando, Tampa*
JACKSON LEWIS *Miami, Orlando*
3 AKERMAN *Fort Lauderdale, Miami, Orlando*
CONSTANGY, BROOKS *Jacksonville, Lakeland, Tampa*
FOLEY & LARDNER *Jacksonville, Orlando*
FOWLER WHITE BOGGS BANKER *Tampa*
HOLLAND & KNIGHT LLP *Jacksonville, Miami, Tampa*
STEARNS WEAVER MILLER *Miami*
THOMPSON, SIZEMORE & GONZALEZ *Tampa*
4 BAKER & HOSTETLER LLP *Orlando*
CARLTON FIELDS, PA *Tampa*
EPSTEIN BECKER & GREEN PC *Miami*
GREENBERG TRAURIG LLP *Miami*
STEEL HECTOR & DAVIS *Miami, West Palm Beach*
Firms are listed alphabetically in each band.

Band 1

Ford & Harrison LLP

See firm details p.631

The Firm: *"They're fine competitors, particularly the Orlando office,"* commented several attorneys. This national labor and employment boutique, with four offices in the state, has seen a dramatic revival in its traditional labor practice. Clients in the healthcare and hospitality industries are flocking to the firm for advice on handling organization campaigns. The employment litigation side is equally busy as a result of the general trend towards collective actions.

The Lawyers: **John-Edward Alley** (see p.533) is thought to be one of the leading lights of traditional labor law in Florida. A busy year for *"talented go-getter"* Alley has included collective bargaining on behalf of a Chicago-based client with Florida operations, which successfully defeated an attempt by the Teamsters to unionize the client's Florida workforce. **Thomas Garwood** (see p.540) was frequently described as *"one of the best all-round employment lawyers – a great guy with a terrific practice."* He now manages all four Florida offices, and has seen a considerable shift in his workload towards the labor side. He has advised clients, including Life Care Centers of America, on collective bargaining and negotiation, as well as counseling them on contingency planning in this area. He has also undertaken a heavy employment caseload, and has frequently been involved in mediations. In addition to having a diverse employment litigation practice, which includes defending a substantial number of wage and hour claims, **James Brown** (see p.536) is also a certified mediator. He handles a caseload of some 50 labor and employment mediations each year. The third element of his practice is traditional labor law, an area that has been resurgent in Florida in recent times.

The Clients: In addition to Life Care Centers of America, the firm also represents national corporate clients such as American Airlines; FedEx; Gate Gourmet International; Lockheed Martin and Nike.

Morgan, Lewis & Bockius LLP

See firm details p.1556

The Firm: This national giant maintains a *"very professional"* labor and employment practice in Florida. A sole office in Miami houses 15 attorneys, several of whom are among the most highly regarded of the management-side bar. Long-term clients were in no doubt that *"the* quality runs right through the firm – you don't get to work for that group unless you're producing a very high standard of work." Improved integration across the firm's network of international offices has led to several notable internal referrals.

The Lawyers: **Russell Hamilton** (see p.542) continues to enjoy a "top-notch" reputation. He combines a busy employment practice, which emphasizes litigation, with niche employee benefits work. The latter involves representing clients in ERISA, COBRA and OWBPA compliance as well as employee benefits litigation – increasingly the focus of this side of his practice. "He works so hard to understand a company's culture and has a detailed knowledge of our business," say delighted clients. Hamilton recently reached a noteworthy settlement with the EEOC on behalf of an important corporate client. **Terry Connor**'s (see p.537) name is linked to many of the highest profile discrimination claims. Recent highlights include successfully obtaining summary judgment in the widely reported pregnancy discrimination case of Waltham v Ortho-McNeil et al., where the court affirmed that his client's actions had been entirely appropriate. He is also well known for representing airlines and railroad operators and has significant experience of the Railway Labor Act.

The Clients: Major national corporations such as Northrop Grumman turn to Morgan Lewis for employment and labor advice in Florida.

Zinober & McCrea, PA

The Firm: Market opinion of this boutique was overwhelmingly favorable: "There's no question in my mind – that firm is absolutely at the top. If I had to hire a lawyer to defend me or my firm that's where I'd go." Sixteen attorneys cover the full gamut of employment counseling and litigation and labor relations. Building on its unrivalled reputation, the firm has capitalized on recent beauty contests to tempt several blue-chip clients away from competitors.

The Lawyers: **Peter Zinober** received acclaim from lawyers and clients, and was described on several occasions as "probably the best employment lawyer in the state." He is particularly renowned for his market-leading labor practice, though he is also very active in the courtroom. "I really can't praise him highly enough," commented one senior attorney, while clients and lawyers recognize that "he's one of the few who's genuinely risen to the top of the profession." His partner **Rich McCrea** also received compliments from interviewees. A "classy and polished" attorney, he is known for his expertise in the growing area of noncompete and trade secrets litigation. **Frank Brown** is building upon a fine reputation and "getting really well known in the community." A former Assistant Attorney General, Brown derives clear advantage from his government background when advising the firm's public sector clients.

The Clients: The firm's lengthy client list includes many household name public companies, along with Florida private companies, universities and other public sector clients.

Band 2

Coffman, Coleman, Andrews & Grogan

The Firm: "Clearly the premier firm in Jacksonville," this boutique practices exclusively labor, employment and immigration law. The latter area is gaining in reputation under the stewardship of Robert Devine, while the firm is also noted for representing clients in OSHA proceedings. Rivals confirmed the firm's position as "one of the largest and best practices in the north of the state."

The Lawyers: **Patrick Coleman** is "undeniably the dean" in the opinion of the Florida labor and employment bar. Though he is now reported to be taking more of a supervisory role, his profile remains extremely high in the market. "Super bright younger lawyer" **Eric Holshouser** has spent much of the past year in federal court, defending various discrimination claims and wage and hour class actions. He is also active in labor representation, and recently completed collective bargaining on behalf of the Jacksonville Port Authority. He is well known among senior members of the bar, who describe him as "a fine trial lawyer and a great tactician." **Michael Grogan** remains "one of the big names" in the opinion of his peers, who think of him as "particularly well versed in public law," while **William Andrews** was endorsed as "accomplished for traditional labor law matters."

The Clients: In addition to private sector clients such as American Home Products, Anheuser-Busch, Dillard's, Kmart and Winn-Dixie, the firm represents public bodies such as the City of Jacksonville Beach and Jacksonville Housing Authority.

Fisher & Phillips LLP

See firm details p.630

The Firm: This renowned national labor and employment boutique currently operates two Florida offices, in Fort Lauderdale and Orlando. The firm has been expanding aggressively of late, and plans to open an office in Tampa in the near future. Rivals acknowledge the group as "strong competitors."

The Lawyers: **Charles Caulkins** (see p.536) has a general practice with a litigation bias. Approximately three-quarters of his time is spent on employment litigation and counseling, with the remainder devoted to traditional labor law. He recently advised a fast-growing client on the acquisition of a heavily unionized company, which involved negotiation with two separate unions. **Theresa Gallion** (see p.540) is the leading light of the firm's trial practice: "She's

extremely articulate, and has a great presence and a superb manner with her clients." Highlights of the past year include winning an age discrimination claim on behalf of Hyatt Hotels in the US District Court in Cincinnati. Gallion is soon to take charge of the firm's new Tampa office. "Eloquent, hands-on" **Carlos Burruezo**'s (see p.536) workload has been dominated by significant multiparty litigation, including the defense of a restaurant chain against a race discrimination claim by seven plaintiffs. He remains managing partner of the Orlando office. Clients appreciate his calm demeanor: "While other lawyers are fighting and butting heads, he listens carefully and figures out where is the best place to apply pressure."

The Clients: Clients include both national and Florida-based employers.

Jackson Lewis

The Firm: This "dignified" labor and employment boutique is highly thought of by competitors: "Their reputation goes before them." The two offices, in Miami and Orlando, can call upon the firm's considerable resources across the USA. In addition to the mainstream areas, the team's expertise encompasses such niche areas as workplace violence, pension and benefit administration, OSHA, substance abuse and drug testing, employee privacy, immigration and affirmative action.

The Lawyers: "Highly effective" **Susan McKenna** defends corporate clients against all manner of discrimination claims. Her practice also involves a significant element of counseling and workplace training. She advises both senior management and workforces generally. In the past year she has obtained a favorable settlement in a substantial class action, and also handled an increasing number of mediations – a notable trend in the employment sphere. Clients welcome her close attention: "She's always in the middle of the action. We value her so much that we've followed her between firms for over 20 years." **David Block**, who manages the firm's Miami office, has spent most of the past year defending FLSA claims. In addition, he is engaged in several high-value claims alleging breach of contract by senior executives. In the opinion of interviewees: "He's doing a very good job developing the Miami office."

Band 3

Akerman Senterfitt

See firm details p.555

The Firm: Following last year's merger with boutique Muller Mintz, Akerman now boasts the largest labor and employment group in the state. The firm's expansion has not gone unnoticed by the market: "It's been making much more of an impact in the past year and growing at a rate of knots." The much reported recent departure of Kevin Shaughnessy's labor team to Baker and

512   All quotes in the text are from interviews with clients and competitors.

CHAMBERS USA 2005

Florida
Leading individuals
(Employment: Mainly Defendant)

Senior Statesman

COLEMAN Patrick *Coffman Coleman*, Jacksonville

★ ZINOBER Peter *Zinober & McCrea*, Tampa

[1] CASEY Michael *Epstein Becker*, Miami

DICKINSON John *Constangy Brooks*, Jacksonville

FARMER Guy *Holland & Knight*, Jacksonville

GARWOOD Thomas *Ford & Harrison*, Orlando

HAMILTON Russell *Morgan Lewis*, Miami

MCCREA Richard *Zinober & McCrea*, Tampa

ROBINSON John *Fowler White*, Tampa

TURK Robert *Stearns Weaver*, Miami

[2] ALLEY John-Edward *Ford & Harrison*, Tampa

CONNOR Terence *Morgan Lewis*, Miami

DEMEZA Willliam *Holland & Knight*, Tampa

FLEMING Joseph *Greenberg Traurig*, Miami

GALLION Theresa *Fisher & Phillips*, Tampa

GONZALEZ Thomas *Thompson Sizemore*, Tampa

GROGAN Michael *Coffman Coleman*, Jacksonville

HOLSHOUSER Eric *Coffman Coleman*, Jacksonville

HYDE Kevin *Foley & Lardner*, Jacksonville

MCKENNA Susan *Jackson Lewis*, Orlando

SHAUGHNESSY Kevin *Baker & Hostetler*, Orlando

[3] ANDREWS William *Coffman Coleman*, Jacksonville

BARFORD George *Carlton Fields*, Tampa

BRAMNICK James *Akerman Senterfitt*, Miami

CAULKINS Charles *Fisher & Phillips*, Fort Lauderdale

EISENBERG Susan *Akerman Senterfitt*, Miami

KOFMAN Robert *Stearns Weaver*, Miami

KORNREICH David *Akerman Senterfitt*, Orlando

KUNKEL Daniel *Kunkel Miller*, Tampa

[4] BLOCK David *Jackson Lewis*, Miami

BROWN Frank *Zinober & McCrea*, Tampa

BROWN James *Ford & Harrison*, Orlando

BURRUEZO Carlos *Fisher & Phillips*, Orlando

HOLIFIELD Marilyn *Holland & Knight*, Miami

LOWRY Patricia *Steel Hector*, West Palm Beach

PETERSON Ralph *Beggs & Lane*, Pensacola

STAGE Jon *Stearns Weaver*, Fort Lauderdale

Up-and-coming individuals

BEVERIDGE Cathy *Fowler White*, Tampa

JOHNSON Carmen *Akerman Senterfitt*, Miami

Leading individuals
(Employment: Mainly Defendant ERISA)

[1] HAMILTON Russell *Morgan Lewis*, Miami

Individuals are listed alphabetically in each band.

Hostetler suggests that challenges may lie ahead for the combined firm. Nonetheless, there is little doubt among interviewees that the firm remains a force to be reckoned with in this market, particularly in the south of the state.

The Lawyers: "*Notable*" **James Bramnick** (see p.535) divides his workload between labor and employment, with the emphasis on the latter. In the past year he has triumphed for a major Florida client in a sensitive labor arbitration, and has also defended a number of discrimination and FLSA claims. Additionally, he has seen an increased demand from clients for general counseling on avoiding wage and hour claims. "*His customer service deserves the highest ranking I could give,*" enthused one client. **Susan Eisenberg** (see p.539) focuses primarily on litigation. Recent highlights of her practice include winning defense verdicts at two federal court jury trials involving allegations of age and disability discrimination. She is also known for her FLSA expertise, and an increasing proportion of her caseload concerns wage and hour issues. **David Kornreich** (see p.544) has developed an unusual niche of advising the firm's corporate clients on the labor law implications of M&A transactions involving one or more unionized entities. He is currently advising on two significant deals involving parties in the power and pharmaceutical industries and a major private provider of custodial services. **Carmen Johnson** (see p.543) makes her first appearance in the rankings following warm approval from clients: "*She's been a tremendous asset to the company, and genuinely feels like a part of our management team.*" Her practice is litigation oriented, though she also conducts training sessions on FLSA and FMLA compliance.

The Clients: American Automobile Association; Banco Popular; CHEP USA; Domino's Pizza; Landstar Homes; Marriott International; Ocean Spray Cranberries; PETsMART and Sprint.

Constangy, Brooks & Smith, LLC

The Firm: A nationwide labor and employment specialist, with Florida offices in Tampa, Jacksonville and Lakeland. The firm is thus particularly noted in the north of the state. In addition to possessing competence in mainstream employment litigation and labor relations, the team is competent in the more esoteric areas of affirmative action, business-related immigration law and OSHA.

The Lawyers: The firm's reputation is closely allied with the status of **John Dickinson**, managing partner of the Jacksonville office. He enjoys a stellar reputation among his peers, who depict him as "*a gifted scholar with a great personality.*" Of late, much of Dickinson's time has been occupied with defending wage and hour collective actions and race discrimination lawsuits. In addition to engaging in litigation, he counsels clients on wage and hour compliance.

The Clients: BellSouth; Boeing; Duke Energy; FedEx; HCA; Kmart; RadioShack and University of South Florida.

Foley & Lardner
See firm details p.1828

The Firm: A nationwide firm with a focus on Florida, Foley & Lardner maintains five offices in the state. "*A good solid labor and employment group*" undertakes a substantial amount of litigation and sustains a traditional labor practice. The group counsels business clients on trade secrets and noncompete obligations, implementing diversity policies, avoiding discrimination and harassment, ADA and FMLA compliance and reductions in force. The firm makes notable use of technology to conduct remote e-learning seminars for clients.

The Lawyers: Fellow professionals describe **Kevin Hyde** (see p.543) as "*just outstanding. You'd have to work for the next ten years to find anyone who'd say anything against him.*" His practice includes labor and employment, the former making up approximately one-fifth of his workload. In the past year, he has defended key clients against several wage and hour collective actions, together with two Sarbanes-Oxley antiretaliation claims. His former partner Richard DuRose has now retired.

Fowler White Boggs Banker

The Firm: A compact but growing team of 12 attorneys practice employment law at this renowned Florida firm's ten offices. High-profile cases successfully handled by the team include a multimillion-dollar sexual harassment suit brought by the EEOC.

The Lawyers: "*A superstar*" who is "*absolutely on top of his game,*" **John Robinson** received plaudits from many interviewees. His litigation practice encompasses the full spectrum of discrimination and sexual harassment claims, combined with union-related and employee benefits/ERISA disputes. Of late, he has seen a dramatic increase in the number of ADA cases brought against clients, particularly those in the hospitality business. Rising star **Cathy Beveridge** has been occupied with a variety of whistleblower and retaliation claims. Her sizeable caseload includes counseling employers on leave entitlements arising from FMLA and ADA.

The Clients: Leading names include: the New York Yankees; FedEx; Nielsen Media Research; Taylor Woodrow; John Hancock and Raymond James.

Holland & Knight LLP
See firm details p.1352

The Firm: As Florida's largest firm, Holland & Knight boasts a national group of 65 labor and employment lawyers. Thought to be "*a first-class firm*" by clients, the team is strong in both traditional labor representation and employment litigation. Clients also had praise for the team's consistent ability, right down to junior associate level.

The Lawyers: **Guy Farmer** (see p.539) sustains a strong traditional labor practice, and is noted for representing key client Albertson's in labor relations matters. Rayonier, another long-term client of the firm, has recently called upon Farmer's expertise to defend an ERISA claim in federal court; in addition, he has handled several labor arbitrations for this client. "*I rate his labor expertise extremely highly,*" said one delighted client. **Bill deMeza**'s (see p.538) workload has lately been dominated by class actions, some with potential classes of thousands. The majority of these are wage and hour claims brought under FLSA – a trend repeatedly cited by interviewees. His thorough and detailed approach to litigation has won him the admiration of clients: "*He leaves no stone unturned in his preparation for a case, and never cuts corners.*" **Marilyn Holifield** (see p.542) is a "*very impressive*" litigator. A considerable proportion of her caseload involves trade secrets and noncompete covenants, and she is also noted for handling class actions. She leads the firm's Caribbean initiative, which concentrates on advising US businesses operating in the Caribbean, as well as Caribbean-based business and government clients.

The Clients: As befits a firm of this stature, the roster includes major national corporates such as Albertson's, UPS and Marriott International.

Stearns Weaver Miller Weissler Alhadeff & Sitterson, PA

The Firm: This "*highly professional*" team of 17 labor and employment attorneys continues to grow in reputation, and is now mentioned in the same breath as the state's leading boutiques. The firm has seen particular recent success in defending discrimination claims, and the group also has expertise in traditional labor representation. The firm also boasts a distinct employee benefits practice group.

The Lawyers: Sources concurred that "*charming and bright*" **Bob Turk** is the secret of the group's success. Dividing his time equally between counseling and litigation, he has recently tried a diverse array of cases, including racial and sexual discrimination claims, Equal Pay Act and FLSA claims and an unusual lawsuit arising out of a client's affirmative action policy. Clients are delighted with his style: "*He knows the law inside out, but he's also very practical – he's not afraid to put the business filter on.*" Turk's "*just fantastic*" partner **Robert Kofman** also received his share of compliments, with commentators highlighting his close relationship with the government. **Jon Stage** recently joined the firm from Akerman Senterfitt. Primarily an employment discrimination litigator, he also counsels clients on workplace safety matters arising under OSHA.

The Clients: The firm acts for local and national employers, including: AutoNation; CompUSA; Hilton Hotels; Publix Super Markets; Bank of America; ANC Rental Corporation and Denny's.

Thompson, Sizemore & Gonzalez
See firm details p.577

The Firm: This boutique remains high in the estimation of many commentators. Since the previous edition, William Sizemore has sadly and unexpectedly died, which (given his prominence as a name partner) may have a substantial impact on the firm's profile. Nonetheless, much larger rivals affirmed their respect for this group of specialists.

The Lawyers: In the opinion of market commentators, **Thomas Gonzalez** is "*one of the leaders, who deserves to be ranked highly.*" Whistleblower claims make up the bulk of his current caseload, though he is also experienced in defending all types of discrimination cases.

Band 4

Baker & Hostetler LLP

The Firm: While Baker & Hostetler enjoys a top-tier reputation for labor and employment law in its home state of Ohio, the Orlando office had no real presence in the sector until the end of 2004. However, Kevin Shaughnessy's arrival from Akerman Senterfitt, together with partner Patrick Muldowney and a sizable team of associates, looks likely to create an enviable profile for the firm in this market. In the words of one competitor, echoing the opinions of many others, "*There's no doubt that's a pretty significant move.*"

The Lawyers: Clients are "*absolutely delighted*" with **Kevin Shaughnessy** – "*he's a great communicator who makes you feel like his only client.*" He has handled a significant number of wage and hour and ADA claims in the recent past, culminating in the widely reported case of Booker Perry v Orange County. This decision marked a turning point in the courts' attitude to frivolous discrimination claims, and resulted in an unprecedented award of costs in favor of the defendant.

The Clients: The firm's international reach provides the Orlando office with access to a collection of household name clients. Examples include: Sprint; Wachovia; CHEP USA; Darden Restaurants; Wuesthoff Hospital; Novartis Pharmaceuticals; Oak Street Mortgage; Winn-Dixie and Bernard Egan & Co.

Carlton Fields, PA
See firm details p.560

The Firm: Carlton Fields' employment group continues to expand, and now boasts lawyers in each of the firm's six Florida offices. The team is particularly experienced in litigation, and over the past year has successfully defended age discrimination, ADA, FLSA and race discrimination claims in federal and state court.

The Lawyers: **George Barford** has been occupied with a large number of whistleblower retaliation claims in the past year; he also handled a

race and national origin discrimination claim in federal and state courts. He combines his trial prowess with a thriving labor law practice; the past year saw him represent a significant client in collective bargaining. In the opinion of his clients, "*his temperament and approach are ideal*" for the frequently delicate nature of this type of work. In addition, he advises clients on compliance with the ADA and Immigration Control and Reform Act.

The Clients: AIG; Hospital Corporation of America; Walgreen Co; Progressive Casualty Insurance Company; Citibank; NuVox; Exxon Corporation and The Mahaffey Apartment Company.

Epstein Becker & Green PC

The Firm: Epstein Becker & Green is a national firm with a heavy emphasis on labor and employment. The firm is a recent arrival in Florida – the Miami office was opened at the beginning of 2004 – but is rapidly establishing a significant name for itself in the state. In addition to representing employers based in Florida and the Southeast, the office acts as a gateway for companies with a presence in Central and South America. As an indication of its rapid growth, the group has established a specialist ADA Title III practice group – still something of a niche area, but one of great concern to many of the firm's clients.

The Lawyers: Peers showered praise on **Michael Casey**, the founding partner of the Florida office and "*a big name*" in the state. Casey is predominantly a litigator who retains a small amount of traditional labor work. He is currently handling a substantial trade secrets claim, based in Atlanta, in collaboration with the firm's New York office. Recent work has also included successfully challenging a union organizing campaign at a large Florida hospital.

The Clients: A diverse client base includes many of the largest names in the banking and financial services industries, including UBS PaineWebber, Deutsche Bank and CSFB. Other clients are active in the manufacturing and healthcare industries.

Greenberg Traurig LLP
See firm details p.564

The Firm: This well-known Florida-based firm continues to expand its employment practice, both within the state and nationwide. "*It's clearly one of the preeminent firms in the state,*" in the opinion of clients. While the team in Florida is small, attorneys can call upon the resources of an impressive national network of offices.

The Lawyers: **Joseph Fleming** (see p.539) is lauded for his cross-discipline expertise. He combines employment law with environmental law – a blend that has come into its own with the trend towards whistleblower retaliation claims. He is also uniquely placed to advise on OSHA issues, which often combine the two disciplines. Clients are clearly impressed with his eclectic approach: "*It's a joy to watch him in court – I've never seen another attorney who can move from citing relevant case law to quoting Andy Warhol without missing a beat.*"

The Clients: The firm serves clients in a wide variety of industries, including insurance, healthcare, entertainment, financial services, construction, retailing and professional services.

Steel Hector & Davis
See firm details p.575

The Firm: This large full-service firm makes its debut in *Chambers'* employment rankings following highly positive client feedback. "*They skillfully guided us through major litigation,*" said one, "*and since then have been a great help with ongoing counseling.*" A sizable practice group includes employee benefits and labor teams.

The Lawyers: Pat Lowry (see p.545) was recommended to researchers for her employment litigation practice, which she combines with product liability litigation. "*I'd never hesitate to refer to her,*" said one senior competitor.

Other Notable Practitioners

Daniel Kunkel makes his debut in *Chambers'* tables on the strength of positive market feedback: "*He's very bright and should definitely be on your list,*" reported other attorneys. Name partner in an eight-strong boutique, Kunkel Miller & Hament, he serves a range of Florida-based corporate clients. Peers revealed that **Ralph Peterson** (see p.542), a partner at Pensacola-based Beggs & Lane, was a popular choice for referrals. He preserves a thriving trial practice.

ENVIRONMENT

Florida
Leading firms (Environment)

[1]	HOPPING GREEN & SAMS, P.A. *Tallahassee*
[2]	HOLLAND & KNIGHT LLP *Orlando*
	LANDERS & PARSONS *Tallahassee*
	LEWIS, LONGMAN & WALKER *West Palm Beach*
[3]	CARLTON FIELDS, PA *Tampa*
	GREENBERG TRAURIG LLP *Miami*
	GUNSTER, YOAKLEY & STEWART *West Palm Beach*
	OERTEL, FERNANDEZ, COLE, *Tallahassee*
	RUDEN MCCLOSKY SC *Tallahassee*
	SHOOK, HARDY & BACON LLP *Miami*
	WHITE & CASE LLP *Miami*

Firms are listed alphabetically in each band.

Band 1

Hopping Green & Sams, P.A.
See firm details p.565

The Firm: Once again, this environmental and land use specialist leads the pack, with one prominent competitor enthusing: "*They deserve to have their name up at the top...they truly live up to their reputation.*" A large group of attorneys covers the practice area comprehensively, to the extent that "*they've made it hard for others to compete.*" The firm has been very active in policy-making in the past year, lobbying the state government for regulatory reform and the downlisting of the manatee's endangered species status. "*Accomplished and formidable*" land use specialists have been equally busy, securing local government approval for development on behalf of a number of major industrial clients. A new infrastructure-funding group has recently been established to raise finance for community development districts.

The Lawyers: Wade Hopping (see p.542) is the figurehead of the firm and widely acknowledged as its key rainmaker. "*An exceptional lawyer of great strength,*" his practice has recently become more specialized as he takes on a greater management responsibility. **Bill Green** (see p.541) is the firm's primary representative on Everglades restoration matters, representing agricultural interests in litigation and permit review before the EPA. Fellow attorneys are full of admiration for Green's experience: "*He's one of the most intelligent men I've ever met – he combines a doctorate in physical chemistry with legal experience to produce a highly competent package.*" **Frank Matthews** (see p.546) specializes in land use matters involving wetlands areas. "*He has a remarkable ability to look at problems from every possible viewpoint and bring all the aspects together to achieve a successful resolution.*" In addition to his work for private clients, he acts as counsel and lobbyist for the Florida Electric Power Coordinating Group, Florida Chamber of Commerce and Florida Home Builders Association. "*Bright, forceful advocate*" **Gary Sams'** (see p.549) practice incorporates both environmental and land use issues, and he is best known for representing industrial and development clients in environmental permitting, also handling litigation on their behalf. **Peter Cunningham** (see p.537), an air quality specialist, has developed a niche acting for utility clients, including Florida Power & Light, on the permitting and development of new power generation facilities. His connections in government make him a valuable lobbying resource. Finally, **Ralph DeMeo** (see p.538) has a hazardous waste practice and recent litigation experience in the rapidly developing toxic mold area. "*A stickler for details,*" he is characterized as a highly persuasive advocate.

The Clients: Air Products and Chemicals; CF Industries; EBSCO Industries; DuPont; Exxon Mobil Corporation; Fina Oil & Chemical; Florida Electric Power Coordinating Group; Florida Power & Light; Gulfstream Natural Gas System; MCI Telecommunications; Progress Energy Florida; Seminole Electric Cooperative; Sugar Cane Growers Cooperative of Florida; Sunniland Pipe Line and The Williams Companies.

Band 2

Holland & Knight LLP
See firm details p.1352

The Firm: National clients turn to this firm for help with Florida environmental issues because "*their rapport with the regulators is great for building trust and getting things done.*" While this huge Florida firm has environmental lawyers operating throughout the state, interviewees singled out the Tampa and Tallahassee offices as particularly praiseworthy.

The Lawyers: Lawrence Sellers (see p.550) is a senior member of the environmental bar. "*He's been around since the early days of environmental law, and is one of the top lawyers in the state,*" say peers. Sellers advises on permitting and enforcement matters, and is experienced in representing clients' interests before the state legislature. **Roger Sims** (see p.550) offers expertise in water resources, and is renowned for his connections to the phosphate industry, where "*his reputation precedes him.*" His chosen specialty sees him dealing on a regular basis with the state's Water Management Districts, as well as federal agencies such as the EPA and US Fish and Wildlife Service. **Lawrence Curtin** (see p.538) also works with the phosphate industry; as counsel to the Florida Phosphate Council, he is particularly active in lobbying at state legislature level. He advises a number of large industrial clients on the permitting and expansion of power-generating facilities in the state.

The Clients: An impressive client roster includes Rinker Materials, National Stone, Sand and Gravel Association and National Association of Home Builders.

Landers & Parsons

The Firm: This "*terrific regulatory boutique*" received numerous plaudits from market commentators. A team of eight undertakes all manner of environmental work, and is especially noted for its representation of sugar growers.

Florida
Leading individuals (Environment)

Senior Statesman
HOPPING Wade *Hopping Green*, Tallahassee

[1] GREEN William *Hopping Green*, Tallahassee
HALSEY Douglas *White & Case*, Miami
LEWIS Terry *Lewis Longman*, West Palm Beach
MATTHEWS Frank *Hopping Green*, Tallahassee
PARSONS Philip *Landers & Parsons*, Tallahassee
PRESTON William *William D Preston*, Tallahassee
SELLERS Lawrence *Holland & Knight*, Tallahassee
SMALLWOOD Mary *Ruden McClosky*, Tallahassee

[2] BARKETT John *Shook Hardy*, Miami
COLE Terry *Oertel Fernandez*, Tallahassee
CURTIN Lawrence *Holland & Knight*, Tallahassee
DEE David *Landers & Parsons*, Tallahassee
MALEFATTO Alfred *Greenberg Traurig*, West Palm Beach
SAMS Gary *Hopping Green*, Tallahassee
SIMS Roger *Holland & Knight*, Orlando
WALKER Steve *Lewis Longman*, West Palm Beach

[3] BURGESS Rick *Gunster Yoakley*, Fort Lauderdale
COGLIANESE Matthew *Bilzin Sumberg*, Miami
CUNNINGHAM Peter *Hopping Green*, Tallahassee
DEMEO Ralph *Hopping Green*, Tallahassee
LEWIS Steve *Lewis Longman*, West Palm Beach
LOCKETT Laurel *Carlton Fields*, Tampa
NOBLE Ron *Fowler White*, Tampa
RILLSTONE Douglas *Broad and Cassel*, Tallahassee
SLEETH Tim *Smith Hulsey*, Jacksonville
WORSHAM Lee *Ruden McClosky*, West Palm Beach

Individuals are listed alphabetically in each band.

The Lawyers: Philip Parsons' workload is composed almost exclusively of Everglades-related matters, a field in which he is renowned among competitors. It is said that "*his understanding of the Everglades ecosystem and regulatory issues is second to none.*" **David Dee**'s varied practice includes solid and hazardous waste, land use and water law, with commentators confirming his strengths in each of these areas.

Lewis, Longman & Walker PA
The Firm: This "*top-class boutique*" is regarded by many as "*the obvious place to go if you want an environmental lawyer.*" The firm's greatest strengths are to be found in water law, endangered species and Everglades litigation.
The Lawyers: Terry Lewis is a senior lawyer with CWA expertise. "*He's very calm and deliberate, which makes him an excellent negotiator,*" according to fellow professionals. In addition to private clients, Lewis advises a variety of local governments on CWA, National Pollutant Discharge Elimination System and Endangered Species Act concerns. **Steve Walker**'s practice focuses on Everglades litigation, where interviewees acknowledge him as "*in the highest echelon.*" He is well known for his representation of the Seminole Tribe, and advises it on Everglades issues and water rights. Finally, he acts as general counsel to the South Florida Water Manage-

ment District. **Steve Lewis** has built up a loyal following for his knowledge of the niche areas of sovereign submerged lands and endangered species. "*He's in a class of his own for those specialties.*"
The Clients: In addition to the Seminole Tribe, the firm represents a range of public and private sector clients, including South Florida Water Management District, Sugar Cane Growers Cooperative of Florida and Palm Beach County.

Band 3

Carlton Fields, PA
See firm details p.560
The Firm: A household name in the Florida legal market, the practice makes its first appearance in the environmental rankings on the strength of positive feedback. The firm's offices in Tampa and Tallahassee are thought to be particularly strong for environmental work. Emphasis is placed on brownfield and Superfund-related advice.
The Lawyers: Laurel Lockett's forte is hazardous waste. Her typical workload includes permitting and regulation, and negotiation of consent orders and remediation plans with local, state, and federal environmental agencies. Lockett is also in great demand among the firm's corporate attorneys, and she frequently undertakes environmental due diligence for corporate and real estate transactions.
The Clients: The firm acts for local government entities, trade associations, manufacturers and companies in heavy industry.

Greenberg Traurig LLP
See firm details p.564
The Firm: This Florida giant is said to be "*historically very strong in land use*" – for some it is "*the dominant player*" – while its environmental practice also received its share of compliments. A substantial proportion of the group's work draws on both areas of expertise; for example, attorneys regularly advise on brownfield redevelopment, which encompasses regulatory consent, land use and water law. The team additionally advises clients on asbestos contamination in older buildings.
The Lawyers: With a background as an environmental lawyer who is particularly known for his "*outstanding*" water law expertise, **Alfred Malefatto**'s (see p.545) practice has recently moved more into land use. Malefatto represents many of Florida's major home builders, assisting them in obtaining development consent and permits, and negotiating with the various water management districts.
The Clients: A diverse group of clients includes: The Ginn Company; Centex Homes; Kolter Property; GL Homes; On Top of the World Communities; Flagstone Property Group; Lubert-Adler; Maefield Development; Diplomat Properties and Miami-Dade County.

Gunster, Yoakley & Stewart PA
The Firm: A compact team of five attorneys practice environmental and land use law at this well-regarded, full-service firm. Their land use work is thought to be "*excellent – the firm's real forte.*" The team provides specialist support on M&A transactions, and maintains a thriving stand-alone practice, which includes Superfund and brownfield matters.
The Lawyers: Rick Burgess was singled out for most praise. Much of his time recently has been spent on Everglades-related work; he is heavily involved with the newly announced accelerated remediation program and has represented the interests of a number of agricultural clients. Another developing area of his practice is urban redevelopment, which involves elements of both real estate and environmental law. Specifically, he is advising developers on the environmental and zoning aspects of the conversion of former commercial marinas into luxury apartments.
The Clients: Corporate clients include Republic Services and AutoNation, while the firm also counsels numerous agricultural interests on Everglades matters

Oertel, Fernandez, Cole & Bryant, PA
The Firm: This small Tallahassee firm places a heavy emphasis on environmental, regulatory and healthcare law. Typically, matters for the environmental team concern water resources, water and air quality, wetlands permitting, mining, submerged lands and growth management.
The Lawyers: Before entering private practice, **Terry Cole** was assistant secretary and general counsel at the Florida Department of Environmental Regulation. He retains enviable connections with the state government, and is more than familiar with issues of water quality and National Pollutant Discharge Elimination Systems. Clients, many of them in the forestry industry, and peers "*think very highly of him.*"
The Clients: The firm acts for many of the state's trade associations as well as big names in food production and forestry.

Ruden McClosky SC
The Firm: This is a sizable full-service firm with ten offices in the state. Commentators concur that the firm's environmental practice group owes its prominence to the presence of Mary Smallwood. Said one: "*When I think Ruden, I think Mary.*" The group's greatest strength is to be found in the regulatory field.
The Lawyers: Mary Smallwood's background in the Florida Department of Environmental Regulation enables her to "*see the whole playing field*" and makes her a popular choice for regulatory representation. A recent arrival at the firm, she is "*able to parachute in at short notice and deal with a problem area.*" **Lee Worsham,**

based in West Palm Beach, focuses on water law, with particular regard to drainage, wetlands and the permitting aspects of urban and agricultural development.

Shook, Hardy & Bacon LLP
See firm details p.1067

The Firm: This renowned international firm operates two Florida offices, in Miami and Tampa, and is known for its abilities in environmental litigation, particularly Superfund matters.
The Lawyers: "*Star*" **John Barkett** (see p.534) is best known for his role as an arbitrator and mediator in many of the state's highest-profile environmental disputes. Peers lavish praise on his expertise as a Superfund mediator: "*He's so good at it, he could be a judge.*" He continues to act as Special Master overseeing the Everglades remediation program, and is also an acknowledged authority on hazardous waste.

White & Case LLP
See firm details p.1379

The Firm: The practice's office in Miami houses a core team of three environmental attorneys who are assisted by the firm's general litigators. It won a notable victory when it obtained summary judgment in a toxic tort test case, allowing 50 other similar claims based on the same facts to be dismissed.
The Lawyers: "*Terrific, top-tier*" **Doug Halsey** (see p.542) is primarily a litigator, but also has

regular input on environmental due diligence and maintains a small regulatory practice. Everglades-related litigation inevitably forms a significant part of his caseload; he has, for example, represented an association of aggregate producers in a dispute relating to the working of limestone quarries in the Everglades. Interviewees concur that Halsey is "*very knowledgeable and great on his feet.*"
The Clients: A varied roster includes Clear Channel, Tarmac America and the Miccosukee Tribe.

Other Notable Practitioners
Viewed as "*the dean*" by many, **William Preston** (see p.547) practices as a sole practitioner. His clientele is made up of notable Florida corporates and, to a lesser extent, public sector bodies. In the past year contaminated land has proved the focus of his workload, with real estate lawyers often seeking out his specialist knowledge in this area, particularly regarding groundwater contamination. Recent work has involved the remediation of two disused industrial sites. Preston's network of contacts in the regulatory agencies also makes him a popular choice for negotiating permits and consents. **Matthew Coglianese** (see p.536) of Bilzin Sumberg Baena Price & Axelrod LLP is primarily a litigator with a special interest in toxic tort claims (including toxic mold, a notable growth area). Clients involved in these complex disputes value his sci-

entific background. The other substantial element of his practice is Superfund and brownfield redevelopment; the past year has seen him negotiate a resolution to a seven-year-long Superfund cleanup involving a number of prominent oil companies. Recognizing his achievements in this area, competitors depict him as "*very competent and thorough.*" **Ron Noble** is a partner at the Tampa office of venerable Florida firm Fowler White Boggs Banker. Described as "*all-around excellent*" by commentators, Noble has an unusual niche practice advising owners and operators of petroleum storage systems and underground storage tanks on permitting and cleanup operations. He also has experience in the related area of waste water treatment enforcement and permitting. **Douglas Rillstone**, a partner in the Tallahassee office of Broad and Cassel, is a regulatory lawyer with a special interest in endangered species. He generally represents landowners wishing to develop or make use of land inhabited by protected species. He is also influential in lobbying, and represents the interests of industry on the Fish and Wildlife Conservation Commission. Finally, **Tim Sleeth** makes his first appearance in *Chambers'* tables. A litigator at Jacksonville-based Smith Hulsey & Busey, with particular experience in Superfund cost allocation, Sleeth's caseload also includes toxic tort claims.

HEALTHCARE

Florida	
Leading firms (Healthcare)	
[1]	MCDERMOTT WILL & EMERY *Miami*
[2]	AKERMAN SENTERFITT *Tampa*
	BROAD AND CASSEL *Miami, Fort Lauderdale*
	CARLTON FIELDS *Miami*
	FOWLER WHITE BOGGS BANKER *Tampa*
	GREENBERG TRAURIG LLP *Miami*
	HOLLAND & KNIGHT LLP *Miami, Tampa, Tallahassee*
	RUDEN MCCLOSKY SC *Miami*

Firms are listed alphabetically in each band.

Band 1

McDermott Will & Emery
See firm details p.773

The Firm: Interviewees were unanimous in their praise for this international giant's Florida healthcare practice. Operating from a sole office in Miami, the "*high-gear*" group of 12 is reputed to be highly visible on transactions. Market commentators agree that this is the only group in the state with enough depth to cover the full range of regulatory, commercial and con-

tentious representation for providers and payers: "*We have the highest respect in the world for Gary Davis and his crew.*" Clients were delighted with the firm's ability to put together a team of specialists at short notice: "*They give you access to superior intelligence throughout the firm, and no matter who's working on the deal, it always seems like they're your personal attorney.*"
The Lawyers: Fellow professionals have "*the highest respect in the world*" for "*incredibly well-known*" **Gary Scott Davis** (see p.538), whose primary focus is in the managed care sector. A significant proportion of his workload involves restructuring and unwinding complex joint ventures between physicians which have run into financial difficulties. **Ira Coleman** (see p.54633) also represents providers, insurers and HMOs, but the standout element of his practice is advising private equity firms on investments in healthcare companies. A recent highlight was the establishment, financing and NASDAQ listing of NationsHealth, a national supplier of medical supplies and specialty pharmaceuticals and one of the largest sponsors of discount drug cards. Clients draw attention to Coleman's leg-

endary client care: "*He constantly introduces us to possible business opportunities, but never from a selfish perspective. He genuinely cares for his clients and their businesses.*"
The Clients: Pediatrix Medical Group; Symbion Healthcare; Mount Sinai Health Systems; University Community Health and Mayo Clinic.

Band 2

Akerman Senterfitt
See firm details p.555

The Firm: A sizable and experienced team of 25 is active in all sectors of the healthcare world. The team's recent successes include acting for a Belgian manufacturer of proton beam therapy accelerator equipment in a $100 million deal to supply, install and maintain the equipment in Florida's hospitals. The group is equally active on the litigation side, and has seen a surge in disputes with physicians over noncompete obligations. Healthcare clients were impressed with the firm's depth of expertise and attention to detail: "*They're a one-stop shop for all types of legal services, but they handle each practice area*

Florida
Leading individuals (Healthcare)

[1]
COLEMAN Ira *McDermott Will*, Miami
DAVIS Gary *McDermott Will*, Miami
DAVIS Kirk *Akerman Senterfitt*, Tampa
HOPKINS Edward *Broad and Cassel*, West Palm Beach
IMPERATO Gabriel *Broad and Cassel*, Fort Lauderdale
MILLER Morris *Holland & Knight*, Tallahassee
SCHMIDT Don *Carlton Fields*, Tampa

[2]
BARCLAY James *Ruden McClosky*, Tallahassee
CURRIER Maria *Hunton & Williams*, Miami
GEARY Jr Francis *Fowler White*, West Palm Beach
KENNEDY III James *Buchanan Ingersoll*, Tampa
REZNICSEK Rick *Reznicsek & Fraser*, Ponte Vedra Beach
RUGG Joseph *Akerman Senterfitt*, Tampa
SEGAL Mike *Broad and Cassel*, Miami
SIEGEL Stephen *Ruden McClosky*, Miami
WALLER Jr Edward *Fowler White*, Tampa

Individuals are listed alphabetically in each band.

with the same attention to detail as a boutique."
The Lawyers: **Kirk Davis** (see p.538) is a litigator who represents providers in a broad range of claims, from antitrust to clinical negligence. He is also particularly well regarded for peer review work. Clients describe Davis as "*knowledgeable, responsive, creative and dedicated,*" while fellow attorneys appreciate his "*straightforward and above-board*" manner. **Joe Rugg** (see p.549), the managing partner of the firm's Tampa office, practices on the corporate side of healthcare law. He advises providers and health systems on the corporate and tax aspects of M&A. Clients appreciate his "*ability to be practical as well as predict the legal issues.*"

Broad and Cassel
The Firm: Rivals point to this outfit as one of the small number of full-service firms with a significant presence in the sector. Twenty-seven attorneys counsel healthcare systems and physician groups on contentious, compliance and transactional issues, and also advise on fraud and abuse investigations.
The Lawyers: **Edward Hopkins** is renowned for his technical excellence and broad experience: "*If I had any kind of conflict, that's where I'd go.*" He generally advises healthcare providers on M&A transactions, Health Insurance Portability and Accountability Act (HIPAA) and regulatory compliance and internal investigations, and is also involved in litigation. "*One of the true good guys,*" he is held in the highest regard by other professionals. **Gabe Imperato** "*is right up there*" for litigation. He represents healthcare clients in criminal and civil healthcare fraud, abuse and antitrust claims. "*Gabe is the real deal for fraud cases,*" agreed several interviewees. **Mike Segal** has a transactional tax background; he advises on the structuring and regulatory aspects of physician joint ventures.
The Clients: Caremark; Podiatry Insurance

Company of America; Cancer Treatment Holdings; Mease Hospitals; Morton Plant Hospital; Fonar Corporation; Health Management Corporation of America; Adventist Health and Prison Health Services.

Carlton Fields
See firm details p.560
The Firm: A 12-strong team of attorneys handles a variety of work for healthcare clients, including licensing, joint ventures, certificates of public need, corporate reorganization and lobbying. On the litigation side, the group conducts malpractice defense and health insurance litigation, and has a significant involvement in peer review.
The Lawyers: **Don Schmidt** undertakes complex business litigation with a strong healthcare flavor. He typically advises on disputes between healthcare systems and physicians arising from employment relationships. Schmidt also represents hospitals in peer review hearings, and has a niche expertise in advising hospitals on antitrust matters. Clients "*recommend him highly, especially for peer review. His thorough attention to detail is the reason for his consistent success.*"
The Clients: In addition to headline client HCA, the firm represents an impressive list of clients, including: Johnson & Johnson; Pfizer; AvMed Health Plans and Aztec Medical Systems.

Fowler White Boggs Banker
The Firm: This long-established Florida firm maintains a sizable healthcare group. A team composed of both of specialist healthcare attorneys and experienced lawyers drawn from other practice areas offers healthcare clients the full spectrum of representation.
The Lawyers: Interviewees enthusiastically placed **Edward Waller** at the "*top of the list*" for healthcare referrals. As practice group leader for the healthcare group, he oversees a team of approximately 16 attorneys. Waller's focus is litigation, including class actions. Also a litigator, **Francis Geary** handles disputes ranging from antikickback and regulatory compliance to malpractice defense on behalf of physician, nursing and healthcare medical practices and medical professionals. Long-term clients commend Geary as "*a highly impressive attorney.*"

Greenberg Traurig LLP
See firm details p.564
The Firm: This large firm's healthcare team concentrates primarily on deal support, although the Tallahassee office also advises long-term clients on pertinent regulatory issues. The group has advised star client Mayo Clinic on its establishment and expansion in Jacksonville, and also benefits from referrals from the firm's nationwide network of offices.
The Lawyers: Mike Cherniga, in the firm's Tallahassee office, is the contact partner.

The Clients: The firm represents the Mayo Clinic as well as other specialty hospitals, clinical laboratories and managed-care organizations.

Holland & Knight LLP
See firm details p.1352
The Firm: This Florida giant draws attorneys from several practice areas to compose a healthcare team of over 50 lawyers nationwide. The team's work for healthcare clients often has a corporate and finance emphasis, reflecting the firm's preeminence in the business sector.
The Lawyers: **Morris Miller** (see p.546) practices on the transactional side, where many of his deals involve a significant real estate finance element. His clients are typically providers and senior housing developers. "*He's so responsive,*" said satisfied clients, "*even at nights and weekends.*" He recently advised a senior housing investment fund on the $110 million acquisition and $75 million ongoing financing of three continuing care communities. Interviewees describe him as "*professional, personable and low key.*"
The Clients: The group's clients include senior housing investment funds and hospital systems.

Ruden McClosky SC
The Firm: Fourteen attorneys practice healthcare law across several offices within the state at this sizable firm. A rapidly expanding team counsels physicians on the establishment and development of group practices and joint ventures, and undertakes both criminal and civil defense in kickback, false billing and other disputes.
The Lawyers: "*Top senior guy*" **Chet Barclay**'s practice combines regulatory representation with counseling on HIPAA compliance. His clients are providers and statewide healthcare associations. Other attorneys regard Barclay as "*the wise sage of Tallahassee*" and frequently turn to him for a second opinion. **Stephen Siegel**'s workload has more of a corporate slant. He advises providers and physicians on joint ventures, and mergers and acquisitions.

Other Notable Practitioners
Maria Currier (see p.538), a partner in the Miami office of national firm Hunton & Williams LLP, is particularly recommended for her "*very fine*" managed care work; she advises major managed care providers and payers on the corporate and regulatory implications of their businesses. She led a team on the establishment of a new HMO, which involved financing, structuring, regulatory clearance and Medicare/Medicaid licensing. **Rick Reznicsek**, formerly of Akerman Senterfitt, is the founding partner of a healthcare and technology boutique, Reznicsek & Fraser PA. He enjoys a solid reputation in the state; fellow lawyers describe his legal analysis as "*spot on.*" A corporate lawyer by

training, Reznicsek advises physicians on combinations, disposals and acquisitions of practices and joint ventures. Interviewees concurred that

James Kennedy (see p.543) in the Tampa office of Pennsylvanian firm Buchanan Ingersoll PC merited attention for his healthcare work. He is

particularly recognized for his high-profile representation of Tampa General Hospital.

INSURANCE

Florida
Leading firms (Insurance)

1. **AKERMAN SENTERFITT** *Tallahassee*
   CARLTON FIELDS *Miami*
   FOWLER WHITE BOGGS BANKER *Tampa*
2. **FOLEY & LARDNER** *Orlando*
   HOLLAND & KNIGHT LLP *Jacksonville*
   PENNINGTON, MOORE, WILKINSON *Tallahassee*
   RADEY, THOMAS, YON & CLARK *Tallahassee*
3. **BUTLER PAPPAS WEIHMULLER KATZ** *Miami*

Leading individuals (Insurance)

1. **BROWN** Daniel *Carlton Fields*, Tallahassee
   KATZ Allan *Akerman Senterfitt*, Tallahassee
2. **ALDRICH** Marcy *Akerman Senterfitt*, Miami
   COX W Donald *Fowler White*, Tampa
   CULPEPPER Bruce *Akerman Senterfitt*, Tallahassee
   DELEGAL Mark *Pennington Moore*, Tallahassee
   JONES Thomas *Holland & Knight*, Tallahassee
   MAIDA Thomas *Foley & Lardner*, Tallahassee
   THOMAS Harry *Radey Thomas*, Tallahassee
   WACHTER Charles *Fowler White*, Tampa
   YON David *Radey Thomas*, Tallahassee

Firms and individuals are listed alphabetically in each band.

Band 1

Akerman Senterfitt
See firm details p.555

The Firm: Akerman made the headlines in 2004 through its merger with Katz, Kutter, Haigler, Alderman, Bryant & Yon, one of the insurance market's most respected players. The merger adds a highly acclaimed regulatory practice to Akerman's existing specialist insurance litigation group, and sends the combined firm straight into the top tier of the rankings. Unrivaled for size in the Sunshine State, there is little doubt that the team will now set the pace in the Florida insurance law market, with clients reporting a *"comfort level"* yet to be matched by other firms. The Miami office specializes in insurance litigation, whilst the expanded regulatory practice remains based in Tallahassee.

The Lawyers: *"Hugely knowledgeable"* **Allan Katz** (see p.543) has taken charge of the enlarged regulatory practice in Tallahassee. Well known throughout the state for his rapport with the regulatory authorities, Katz is also involved in the development of the firm's government relations practice group. **Bruce Culpepper** (see p.537) also practices on the regulatory side – an

area that will undoubtedly grow in stature following the merger – and has been heavily involved in the integration of Katz Kutter into the Tallahassee office. **Marcy Levine Aldrich** (see p.533) continues to attract praise for her complex insurance litigation practice: *"She's a truly impressive partner, and her team is great too."* Class actions are an increasing feature of her practice – she regularly juggles a caseload of over 50 such claims. In the past year, she succeeded in achieving the dismissal of two major class actions relating to motor insurance; the dismissals were upheld on appeal to the Second District Court of Appeals.

The Clients: The group has a long history of advising Humana on both regulatory and merger activity. Other notable clients include Aetna and Liberty Mutual.

Carlton Fields
See firm details p.560

The Firm: *"A strong, traditional player in the market and always one of our major competitors,"* agreed rivals. Approximately 20 attorneys make up the insurance team, which covers both high-end litigation and regulatory advice. Clients are delighted with the firm's considerable abilities and *"willingness to develop competitive fee arrangements."*

The Lawyers: **Daniel Brown** represents major carriers before the Office of Insurance Regulation, and advises clients in litigation both before the regulatory bodies and with contracting parties. In recent times, he has also handled some class action defense, generally on behalf of property insurers. Attorneys agree that Brown is *"absolutely top for litigation;"* while clients describe him as *"one of the best trial attorneys we've ever worked with – he's thorough, smart and always anticipates what the other side's going to do."*

The Clients: Carlton Fields represents major national carriers such as AIG, Prudential Insurance Company of America and State Farm.

Fowler White Boggs Banker
The Firm: Clients describe the insurance group at this ubiquitous Florida firm as *"standing head and shoulders above other firms – they exemplify what we look for in external counsel."* The whole team is cohesive and of a high caliber: *"Where appropriate, partners delegate to associates without any loss in quality."* The recent opening of a Jacksonville office has bolstered the firm's exper-

tise in this area; the team here now includes four lateral hires from LeBoeuf, Lamb, Greene & MacRae.

The Lawyers: **Donald Cox** is a *"first-rate litigation partner,"* according to clients. Cox's practice has grown out of a general litigation caseload, and he has dedicated the vast majority of his time to the representation of insurers, who report that they are *"extremely pleased with his work and style."* Of late, he has defended national clients against class actions brought under the Florida no-fault statute. He has also continued to advise property carriers on the implications of toxic mold. *"Great strategist"* **Charles Wachter** was commended by clients for his constructive approach to handling complex litigation – *"you know you're in safe hands with Charles."* He also represents insurers in mediation.

The Clients: John Hancock, AIG and MetLife are among this firm's major insurance clients.

Band 2

Foley & Lardner
See firm details p.1828

The Firm: The insurance practice at this colossal national firm is spread across both regulatory and litigation disciplines. Its attorneys also provide specialist support for corporate transactions. The Florida team is housed in the firm's Tallahassee office, and accordingly is best known for its regulatory representation.

The Lawyers: **Thomas Maida** (see p.545) is the managing partner of the Tallahassee office, and maintains a thriving regulatory and litigation practice. Clients highlight his considerable abilities in both areas: *"I've seen him in court and before the regulators, and it's very unusual for one attorney to be so skilled in both."* Maida is also said to be *"a terrific attorney to have on the other side of a case"* for his reasonable stance and thorough knowledge of the law.

The Clients: The firm has attracted a varied client base including health insurance companies, broker-dealers and mutual funds.

Holland & Knight LLP
See firm details p.1352

The Firm: Commentators endorsed the litigation skills possessed by attorneys in this major national firm. The group certainly has expertise in this area, but is also active in the regulatory sphere. The department draws upon a range of specialists in Florida, New York and Washington, DC. It has also acted as outside counsel to several state regulators.

The Lawyers: While **Thomas Jones**' (see p.543) practice combines litigation and transactional work, it is the latter that now comprises the majority of his workload. He deals with the regulatory aspects of the formation, acquisition and disposal of regulated entities, and accordingly is often called upon as the firm's insurance expert to assist the M&A transaction team. He is currently advising on the creation of a new HMO, which is expected to become active in mid-2005. He is also active in the continuing care sector – a niche area requiring knowledge of both insurance and healthcare law.

The Clients: The firm advises the range of insurers, brokers, agents and adjusters.

Pennington, Moore, Wilkinson, Bell & Dunbar, PA

The Firm: Insurance work is the cornerstone of this *"well-positioned firm,"* which has a particular focus on lobbying and regulatory advice. The team is highly experienced in representing carriers before the Florida Department of Financial Services and the Office of Insurance Regulation. Market commentators endorsed its *"very strong*

connections within the regulatory authorities."

The Lawyers: Interviewees describe **Mark Delegal** as *"very influential in the regulatory sphere."* He regularly represents property and casualty insurers before state agencies and the Florida legislature. His regulatory expertise also encompasses healthcare and government affairs.

The Clients: The firm has attracted a broad clientele of insurance companies, reinsurance brokers and insurance trade associations.

Radey, Thomas, Yon & Clark

The Firm: This group split from Katz, Kutter, Haigler, Alderman, Bryant & Yon some time before that firm's merger with Akerman Senterfitt. Concentrating predominantly on insurance work, with the emphasis on regulatory representation, this steadily expanding firm was tipped by observers as *"the one to watch."* The team also undertakes complex litigation, including class actions and coverage claims.

The Lawyers: **David Yon** is acknowledged to be an influential figure in the Florida market due to his highly esteemed regulatory practice. In the words of one prominent competitor: *"If I had to refer anything with a political angle, I'd go straight to David."* In addition to his regulatory work, Yon has a thriving transactional practice;

in this respect, he is a popular choice for insurers wishing to establish a presence in the state. For litigation, peers revealed that **Harry Thomas** was a top choice for referrals. Of late, his workload has been dominated by a number of substantial class actions.

Band 3

Butler Pappas Weihmuller Katz Craig LLP

The Firm: Butler Pappas is a dedicated insurance litigation defense firm with three offices in the state. Though not as prominent in high-end technical litigation as some of its rivals, the firm is thought to be *"really knowledgeable and good at the fundamentals of insurance law."* A substantial team defends a lengthy list of clients in all types of coverage, liability, subrogation and extracontractual claims.

The Lawyers: John Pappas is a key contact in the insurance group.

The Clients: The firm has provided defense counsel to many of the best-known names in the insurance world, including: Aetna; Allianz; First Floridian Auto and Home Insurance Company; General Accident; John Hancock; Liberty Mutual; Royal & SunAlliance and St. Paul Travelers.

LITIGATION

GENERAL COMMERCIAL

Florida
Leading firms
(Litigation: General Commercial)

1	**GREENBERG TRAURIG LLP** *Miami*
	KENNY NACHWALTER PA *Miami*
	PODHURST ORSECK, PA *Miami*
2	**AKERMAN SENTERFITT** *Orlando*
	BEDELL, DITTMAR, DEVAULT *Jacksonville*
	COLSON HICKS EIDSON *Coral Gables*
	HILL, WARD & HENDERSON, PA *Tampa*
	HUNTON & WILLIAMS *Miami*
	KOZYAK TROPIN & THROCKMORTON *Coral Gables*
3	**HOGAN & HARTSON LLP** *Miami*
	KING, BLACKWELL & DOWNS PA *Orlando*
	RICHMAN GREER WEIL BRUMBAUGH *Miami*
	STEARNS WEAVER MILLER WEISSLER *Miami*
	ZUCKERMAN SPAEDER LLP *Miami*
4	**CARLTON FIELDS** *Miami*
	DEAN, MEAD, EGERTON, BLOODWORTH *Orlando*
	HOLLAND & KNIGHT LLP *Tallahassee*
	JONES, FOSTER, JOHNSTON *West Palm Beach*
	SHOOK, HARDY & BACON LLP *Miami*
	STEEL HECTOR & DAVIS LLP *Miami*

Firms are listed alphabetically in each band.

Greenberg Traurig LLP
See firm details p.564

The Firm: This *"extraordinary talent pool"* is perceived as a real force in dispute resolution, often succeeding by having *"an edge over the competition,"* commentators said. The *"pioneering platform"* of their national group practice *"does very well at coordinating both trial and appellate work."* Analysts appreciate its *"crucial communicative approach"* and ability to parlay the *"highest caliber skills"* into legal victories. For example, the appellate team, described as having *"real force,"* successfully reverted a 12-figure judgment. Peers recognize its *"firepower"* nationwide, and acknowledge the *"unsurpassed premium"* team in such specialist areas as white-collar crime and real estate litigation.

The Lawyers: *"Top appellate lawyer"* **Barry Richard** (see p.548) has advised luminaries such as established client Governor Jeb Bush in a case involving constitutional issues. He also recently settled a multimillion-dollar suit against client ConocoPhillips. **David Ross** (see p.549) led in the defense of Lorillard Tobacco, and separately represented Ernst & Young in a class action in Florida. *"A superb lawyer,"* **Arthur England** (see p.539) is considered in many legal circles to be *"a legend."* The chair of the appellate department, England acted on the Lorillard Tobacco

Company case along with **Elliot Scherker** (see p.549), a *"commanding, Hemingway-like figure in court."* Scherker is valued for his propensity *"to ensure all the Is are dotted and the Ts are crossed."* The *"bright"* **Charles Auslander** (see p.533) also focuses on appellate law, while **Hilarie Bass** (see p.534) is pitched as *"a star in her own style."* The head of the national litigation practice group is a *"particularly sharp but very personable"* operator. She has successfully acted as co-counsel for Microsoft in a national class action. As business litigator and cochair of the white-collar crime group, **Mark Schnapp** (see p.550) *"stands out"* for his involvement in significant disputes such as defending PolyMedica in an alleged healthcare fraud case. *"Extremely thorough"* **Holly Skolnick** (see p.550) was highlighted as a star white-collar litigator whose practice also crosses over into the securities arena. The group has recently received a significant boost by the addition of **Jacqueline Becerra** (see p.534), former special counsel to the United States Attorney for the Southern District of Florida. This year Greenberg Traurig mourned the death of the esteemed Henry Latimer, a former judge with *"established credibility with the bench and the bar."* He impressed his peers with his wealth of experience in commercial litigation and arbitration.

Florida
Leading individuals
(Litigation: General Commercial)

1 DEVAULT John *Bedell, Dittmar, DeVault,* Jacksonville
HILL III Benjamin *Hill Ward,* Tampa
JOSEFSBERG Robert *Podhurst Orseck,* Miami
NACHWALTER Michael *Kenny Nachwalter,* Miami
TROPIN Harley *Kozyak Tropin,* Miami

2 CRITCHLOW Richard *Kenny Nachwalter,* Miami
FROST II John *Frost Tamayo,* Bartow
GONZALEZ Ervin *Colson Hicks,* Coral Gables
GREER Alan *Richman Greer,* Miami
KING David *King Blackwell & Downs PA,* Orlando
MARTINEZ Roberto *Colson Hicks,* Coral Gables
PODHURST Aaron *Podhurst Orseck,* Miami
RICHARD Barry *Greenberg Traurig,* Tallahassee
STEARNS Eugene *Stearns Weaver,* Miami
STEINBERG Marty *Hunton & Williams,* Miami
WAKSHLAG Stanley *Akerman Senterfitt,* Miami

3 BASS Hilarie *Greenberg Traurig,* Miami
BLOODWORTH Darryl *Dean Mead,* Orlando
BRUMBAUGH John *Richman Greer,* Miami
COLSON Dean *Colson Hicks,* Coral Gables
DAVIDSON Barry *Hunton & Williams,* Miami
DAVIS Alvin *Steel Hector,* Miami
DIAZ Victor *Podhurst Orseck,* Miami
LICKO Carol *Hogan & Hartson,* Miami
LILES Rutledge *Liles Gavin,* Jacksonville
MATTHEWS Joseph *Colson Hicks,* Coral Gables
MEEKS Thomas *Zuckerman Spaeder,* Miami
MOSS Edward *Shook Hardy,* Miami
NICHOLS Tracy *Holland & Knight,* Miami
PILLANS III Charles *Bedell Dittmar,* Jacksonville
REID Benjamine *Carlton Fields,* Miami
REILLY Kenneth *Shook Hardy,* Kansas City
RICHMAN Gerald *Richman Greer,* Miami
ROSS David *Greenberg Traurig,* Miami
SOTO Edward *Weil Gotshal,* Miami
SPECTOR Brian *Kenny Nachwalter,* Miami
STUBBS Sidney *Jones Foster,* West Palm Beach
THOMSON Parker *Hogan & Hartson,* Miami

Up-and-coming individuals
BECERRA Jacqueline *Greenberg Traurig,* Miami
MILLER Brian *Akerman Senterfitt,* Miami

Individuals are listed alphabetically in each band.

The Clients: Lorillard Tobacco Company; Florida Department of Agriculture & Consumer Services; Four Seasons Hotels & Resorts; Microsoft and Governor of Florida Jeb Bush.

Kenny Nachwalter PA
See firm details p.566
The Firm: Counterparts portray this 20-attorney litigation specialist as *"one of the most pre-eminent teams in Florida."* This *"well-connected set of lawyers"* deftly handles complex business litigation, benefiting from a range of expertise that includes securities, IP, employment and white-collar crime among others. Another drawing card is *"a niche in plaintiff antitrust litigation nationwide,"* though the firm also acts on the defense side.
The Lawyers: Recognized as a leading litigator statewide, **Mike Nachwalter** is well respected by peers as *"a fighter off to climb into the ring"* when litigating. His profile centers on antitrust as part of a broader practice. Peers portray **Richard Critchlow** as an effective all-rounder whose repertoire has included a considerable number of securities cases, while **Brian Spector** is both *"pleasant and fabulous."* Commentators also said he is a *"demon with rules,"* referring to his grasp for details.
The Clients: The team has represented companies from an array of industries, including airline, automobile, food, insurance, real estate, pharmaceutical and telecom. It has also represented individuals such as attorneys, accountants, officers and directors.

Podhurst Orseck, PA
The Firm: This strong 12-lawyer boutique thrives in complex litigation, in addition to being distinguished as one of a few law firms in Florida with established *"civil and criminal capacity,"* sources said. Commercial disputes comprise over half of its practice, and the group is inevitably *"at the top of everybody's list."* The team successfully represented international design firm Perry Ellis in a trademark and contract dispute. Living up to its excellent reputation in mass tort, the firm acted for about 750,000 doctors nationwide in a class action against most of the major US medical insurance carriers. The case involves a challenge to their payment and reimbursement policies.
The Lawyers: *"Dean of the Miami Bar,"* **Bob Josefsberg** stands out for his knack of establishing a rapport with juries, rivals said. *"Mr Ethics,"* as one interviewee dubbed him, is so highly respected that other law firms often retain him to represent them in litigation such as malpractice suits. *"Superbly skilled"* **Aaron Podhurst** has been a key player in the firm's success, described as a *"go-to guy"* for complex legal battles. **Victor Diaz** continues to boost his profile through prominent work, while the *"outstanding"* appellate lawyer **Joel Eaton** gained plaudits for his *"polished practice."* Joel Perwin has left the firm to concentrate on his solo appellate practice.
The Clients: Perry Ellis International; Ryder System; United National Bank; Lennar Corporation and Florida East Coast Properties.

Akerman Senterfitt
See firm details p.555
The Firm: Observers noted that this significant player has enhanced its strength as one of Florida's largest law firms by expanding to Washington DC, offering clients broader scope to tackle complex issues. With more than 400 attorneys in eight offices throughout Florida's main metropolitan areas, this *"wonderful group"* is particularly recognized for its securities litigation strength. It was lead counsel for Rolls-Royce in Royal Caribbean Cruises v Rolls-Royce.
The Lawyers: Peers described *"highly articulate"* **Stanley Wakshlag** (see p.553) as having a wonderful courtroom presence and being *"one of the best in Florida"* in complex commercial litigation. Commentators noted his exceptional stance at dealing with an increase in litigation arising from Sarbanes-Oxley, SEC and corporate governance litigation matters. **Brian Miller** (see p.546) was also endorsed for his ascending profile in securities disputes.
The Clients: Tropical Sportswear; Aerosonic Corporation; CRYO-CELL International; Rolls-Royce and Cross Country Healthcare.

Bedell, Dittmar, DeVault, Pillans & Coxe
The Firm: Peers hail this boutique as an *"operationally efficient"* team that is equally comfortable immersed in a complex cross-border dispute as a regional legal battle. The 15-lawyer team continues to take on civil and criminal litigation, including alternative dispute resolution. In one of the firm's highlight cases, it successfully defended Comerica Bank as trustee for the heirs of a General Motors founder in a lawsuit seeking millions of dollars in compensatory and punitive damages.
The Lawyers: Clients and competitors recognize **John DeVault** as the *"finest of the league."* Renowned as a specialist in complex commercial litigation and legal malpractice defense, he *"clearly stands out as a superb trial lawyer of the highest caliber."* DeVault effectively led the representation of Comerica and separately defended another lawyer accused of breaching standards of care. He was commended for *"a great ability to cope with unanticipated developments."* A pillar of the firm, **Charles Pillans** concentrates on complex litigation involving financial transactions, legal malpractice defense and some white-collar criminal defense. Pillans successfully completed an arbitration involving several hundred thousand dollars on behalf of an individual investor against a major security firm. **Hank Coxe** plays a key role in the team's criminal defense profile. A *"star in court,"* according to peers, his portfolio includes a major case involving worker compensation fraud.
The Clients: Clients are predominantly Florida-based public companies, small businesses and individuals such as law professionals and others.

Colson Hicks Eidson
See firm details p.561
The Firm: Interviewees refer to this group as *"one of the best law firms in the country: period."* The 18-attorney litigation specialist is highly respected by clients and peers for its expertise in products liability. The group's capability also

Florida
Leading firms (Litigation: White-Collar Crime & Government Investigations)

1
GREENBERG TRAURIG LLP *Miami*
MOSCOWITZ, MOSCOWITZ & MAGOLNICK *Miami*
RASKIN & RASKIN PA *Miami*
ZUCKERMAN SPAEDER LLP *Miami*

2
BEDELL, DITTMAR, DEVAULT *Jacksonville*
BLACK, SREBNICK, KORNSPAN *Miami*
COLSON HICKS EIDSON *Coral Gables*
GEORGE & TITUS PA *Tampa*
HOLLAND & KNIGHT LLP *Miami*
LEVENTHAL & SLAUGHTER PA *Orlando*
PODHURST ORSECK, P.A. *Miami*
RUDEN MCCLOSKY SC *Fort Lauderdale*
SALE & KUEHNE PA *Miami*
SHOOK, HARDY & BACON LLP *Miami*

Leading individuals
(Litigation: White-Collar Crime & Government Investigations)

1
BLACK Roy *Black Srebnick*, Miami
GAY Faith *White & Case*, Miami
HOGAN John *Holland & Knight*, Miami
JOSEFSBERG Robert *Podhurst Orseck*, Miami
MARTINEZ Roberto *Colson Hicks*, Coral Gables
MOSCOWITZ Jane *Moscowitz Moscowitz*, Miami
MOSCOWITZ Norman *Moscowitz Moscowitz*, Miami
PASANO Michael *Zuckerman Spaeder*, Miami
RASKIN Jane *Raskin & Raskin*, Miami
RASKIN Martin *Raskin & Raskin*, Miami
SCHNAPP Mark *Greenberg Traurig*, Miami
SKOLNICK Holly *Greenberg Traurig*, Miami
ZIMET Bruce *Sole Practitioner*, Fort Lauderdale

2
AARON William *William Aaron*, Miami
BRONIS Stephen *Zuckerman Spaeder*, Miami
BROWN Christopher *Shook Hardy*, Miami
CACCIATORE Ronald *Ronald K Cacciatore*, Tampa
CHAYKIN Steven *Zuckerman Spaeder*, Miami
COXE Henry *Bedell Dittmar*, Jacksonville
GEORGE Peter *George & Titus*, Tampa
JUNG William *Jung & Sisco*, Tampa
KUEHNE Benedict *Sale & Kuehne*, Miami
LEVENTHAL Robert *Leventhal & Slaughter*, Orlando
MANDEL David *Mandel & Cale*, Miami
MASON J Cheney *Sole Practitioner*, Orlando
QUIÑON Jose *Sole Practitioner*, Miami
SALE Jon *Sale & Kuehne*, Miami
SHEPPARD William *Sheppard White*, Jacksonville
SHOHAT Edward *Bierman Shohat*, Miami
SLAUGHTER Harrison *Leventhal*, Orlando
SREBNICK Howard *Black Srebnick*, Miami
TARBE Susan *Colson Hicks*, Coral Gables
TROMBLEY Gary *Trombley & Hanes*, Tampa
UDOLF Bruce *Ruden McClosky*, Fort Lauderdale
WEINBERG Jr Morris *Zuckerman Spaeder*, Tampa

Up-and-coming individuals
TEIN Michael *Shook Hardy*, Miami

Firms and individuals are listed alphabetically in each band.

includes commercial litigation, professional malpractice, white-collar crime and appellate law. Some figures in the team have been lead counsel on widely publicized matters such as personal injury and wrongful death cases arising out of the Ford/Firestone multidistrict litigation. Another matter involved class actions stemming from the gravesite desecrations at the Menorah Gardens in Fort Lauderdale.

The Lawyers: "*Extraordinarily capable across the board,*" managing partner **Dean Colson** (see p.537) is an unassailable figure who gets involved in major cases. Broadly known for his personal injury work, Colson is "*one of the finest trial litigators in Miami.*" Others admire **Roberto Martinez** (see p.545) as "*the ultimate role model,*" while **Ervin Gonzalez** (see p.541) was pitched as the "*hottest trial lawyer in the state.*" He effectively dealt with the Menorah Gardens case. The "*academically strong*" **Joseph Matthews** (see p.546) successfully acted for a Venezuelan real estate developer in a series of multicourt lawsuits and arbitration proceedings against a Canadian hotel chain. Observers said that the "*even-tempered*" operator is "*very adept with the jury.*" **Marc Cooper** (see p.537), who is commended for his appellate work, co-counseled a high-profile receivership case with Martinez. "*Tenacious*" **Susan Tarbe** (see p.552) does an "*impressive*" job in her white-collar crime practice. New arrival Curtis Miner impresses with a "*superb CV,*" which includes a stint as a former Assistant US Attorney in the Southern District of Florida.

Hill, Ward & Henderson, PA

The Firm: Observers distinguish this "*go-to in Tampa*" general practice as "*technically strong*" in all areas. Clients don't hesitate to recommend this "*talented set of lawyers*" for the combination of cost-effectiveness, excellent client service and integrity. Among other prominent matters, the team is representing Honeywell in litigation involving possible fraud.

The Lawyers: Interviewees described top-ranked litigator **Ben Hill** as a "*doyen of the field.*" The firm's president has a broad caseload that includes professional liability, products liability, and other general commercial matters. In addition to some work on behalf of Honeywell, he has also been retained to represent a law firm accused of legal malpractice and allegedly breaching fiduciary duties. Peers said he is "*an excellent communicator who is always prepared, judicious and highly effective in the courtroom.*"

The Clients: DaimlerChrysler, Honeywell and Asbury Automotive Group are among the firm's clients.

Hunton & Williams
See firm details p.1775

The Firm: Competitors admire the expanded Florida presence of this "*well-respected*" international firm, which is able to advise on "*substantial*" commercial and civil litigation supported by a range of other expertise. Peers hailed the broad-based expertise here to be among the best for complex cases. For example, the group acted for a healthcare insurer in a multimillion-dollar national lawsuit in the District Court. Another highlight involved Hilton Hotels in a franchise dispute.

The Lawyers: With significant knowledge of antitrust matters, **Marty Steinberg** (see p.551) has also built a "*fantastic, well-deserved reputation*" as a commercial litigator. A "*bulldog*" in court who "*knows when to be intellectual,*" Steinberg has represented Exxon and Bacardi in several national class actions. Peers noted he also acted for Eli Lilly after the company was sued for its marketing practices related to Prozac Weekly. Peers commend the "*excellent courtroom style*" of **Barry Davidson** (see p.538), who is "*low key but direct, factual and ethical.*" He recently argued a case involving one of the largest funeral services companies in the country. Another matter involved the estate of Pablo Picasso concerning misappropriation of the Picasso name.

The Clients: ExxonMobil; Bacardi; Eli Lilly; Diageo; American Airlines and Hilton Hotels.

Kozyak Tropin & Throckmorton
See firm details p.568

The Firm: Market observers commend this 20-attorney litigation boutique as among the best of its kind statewide for its "*unique approach to litigation both in plaintiff and defendant sides.*" This "*well-respected*" group's key practice areas are bankruptcy, complex securities litigation, professional malpractice, and class actions. Its "*leading*" expertise in commercial proceedings has led to such national cases as a multimillion-dollar class action against major health insurers.

The Lawyers: Peers agree that "*star of the firm*" **Harley Tropin** (see p.553) is a tenacious fighter who "*gets the jobs done.*" He is co-counsel for the doctors and medical associations suing health insurers Humana, UnitedHealthcare, PacifiCare, Prudential and WellPoint.

Hogan & Hartson LLP
See firm details p.484

The Firm: This international firm is nurturing its "*tremendous force*" in Florida by adding to the existing Miami office a new presence in West Palm Beach. The Florida group recently assisted world-renowned nonprofit biomedical organization The Scripps Research Institute. This eight-partner litigation team effectively covers complex commercial matters that include some substantial constitutional cases. For example, it recently acted for the City of Miami in a contentious matter involving First Amendment issues.

The Lawyers: Miami managing partner and constitutional law specialist **Parker Thomson** (see p.552) is often pitched as among the top ten best lawyers in Florida, winning loyalty through some of the most groundbreaking legal conflicts. For example, he is representing the State of Florida in one of the longest running multistate water rights litigation in the country. "*Strong litigator*" **Carol Licko** (see p.545) has built a well-known commercial practice typified by constitutional issues. Observers singled out her representation of The Scripps Research Institute before the state legislature. She also prevailed on the defense of the Florida Department of Highway Safety in a lawsuit that involved a host of constitutional issues.

The Clients: City of Miami, Florida Department of Highway Safety and The Scripps Research Institute are among the clients.

King, Blackwell & Downs PA

The Firm: Recommended for its consistent quality, this "*small but very strong*" litigation specialist boasts a six-attorney team. It has earned "*very well-deserved respect in the Orlando and Tampa areas*" for undertaking complex litigation proceedings, including a billion-dollar trade secret case for Boeing.

The Lawyers: "*Particularly respected litigator*" and practice leader **David King** acted in a major dispute over the control of a Daytona Beach newspaper and separately successfully defended CNL Hotels and Resorts in a class action. He was described as "*an action lawyer.*" King continues to act for Boeing in the trade secret case in addition to handling legal malpractice cases.

The Clients: The firm has represented a variety of corporations such as Boeing, and CNL Hotels and Resorts.

Richman Greer Weil Brumbaugh Mirabito & Christensen

See firm details p.571

The Firm: This is a 22-lawyer commercial litigation operation with "*the reputation of a big player.*" Commentators refer to "*the substantial weight*" of the firm when dealing with the current increase in major national class action work. In addition, it has also been recommended in such areas as appellate, real estate and corporate issues.

The Lawyers: Interviewees singled out **Alan Greer** (see p.541) for his vast experience and "*sharp legal mind.*" Greer acted for a leading provider of outsourced customer care drawn into a multimillion-dollar fraudulent merger. He is "*sought after as local counsel*" by other law firms. **Gerald Richman** (see p.548) served as chairman of the legal counseling team for the Kerry-Edwards 2004 US presidential campaign. Richman, president of the firm, has successfully

handled many plaintiff cases, including a $5 million real estate dispute. "*Aggressive litigator*" **John Brumbaugh** (see p.536), described as "*a star lawyer,*" has represented 3M in litigation.

The Clients: Equifax; 3M; Precision Response and Merrill Lynch.

Stearns Weaver Miller Weissler Alhadeff & Sitterson, PA

The Firm: The high-octane litigation group is pitched as a port of call for "*difficult cases,*" commentators said. In a highly publicized case, the team won a $1 billion verdict against Exxon on behalf of direct-service dealers. Its team of "*super*" attorneys regularly advises Fortune 500 clients who are embroiled in complex litigation. Comprising more than 100 attorneys in Florida, its developed practice also includes an increase in labor and employment-related matters, including immigration issues.

The Lawyers: Competitors concur that **Eugene Stearns**, president of the firm and chairman of the litigation department, is "*superbly aggressive.*" Stearns acted in the case against Exxon. He has strong client relationships with such luminaries as Bank of America.

The Clients: BankAtlantic; Bank of America; IVAX and Miami HEAT.

Zuckerman Spaeder LLP

The Firm: This team is "*very well put together*" and thrives as a premier litigation specialist. Its "*star stable of lawyers*" has a wealth of experience in white-collar crime and various complex business disputes. In a landmark case against Citigroup, the team argued the right of a company to seek redress for false analyst reports; the case involved Jack Grubman, former telecom analyst for Salomon Smith Barney, a unit of Citigroup. Clients commended the "*personalized professionalism* " of the team, which also handled a highly publicized dispute concerning the estate of the late tycoon Victor Posner.

The Lawyers: **Michael Pasano** is "*one of the most cerebral lawyers*" whose "*rigorous and thoughtful*" approach is highly prized by clients. Pasano acted for a top executive of a company dealing in Viaticals. "*Super-talented trial attorney* " **Steven Chaykin** has a workload of complex criminal litigation cases, including matters associated with fraud. Competitors commended Chaykin's "*good timing*" with juries. **Stephen Bronis** is an "*excellent tactician and a fighter in court.*" He fronts a lot of healthcare-related criminal cases. **Morris Weinberg** successfully defended a DC-based law firm sued by a media conglomerate for alleged malpractice, while **Thomas Meeks** is recognized for his keen interest in technical issues and the intricacies of major business litigation. Meeks is an expert in business torts, and he has acted in high-profile breach of contract disputes and music copyright cases. One of his recent cases involved a major

securities-related dispute on behalf of clients against Citigroup.

Carlton Fields

See firm details p.560

The Firm: Clients admire this "*world-class litigation firm*" for its depth and dedication. The competence of this team is consistently illustrated in business litigation, particularly with regards to appellate law. The group recently obtained a complete defense verdict on behalf of client AIG Claims in a case against Ford.

The Lawyers: Peers lauded **Benjamine Reid** for his defense of RJ Reynolds along with other prominent clients. His "*down-to-earth*" style has helped to win clients such as the South Florida Water Management District. Leader of the firm's appellate practice group, **Sylvia Walbolt** is pitched as "*one of the greatest appellate lawyers in the state*" by competitors. Walbolt obtained the reversal of a multimillion-dollar judgment against GM.

The Clients: GM; Southwest Airlines; Manor Care of Florida and Verizon.

Dean, Mead, Egerton, Bloodworth, Capouano & Bozarth PA

The Firm: This firm is widely respected for its successful representation of small to medium-sized clients in litigation. The variety of legal services includes corporate litigation, white-collar crime and legal malpractice. This team acted for a major law firm sued for professional misconduct and separately advised an individual entangled in a contentious case between Boeing and Lockheed Martin.

The Lawyers: **Darryl Bloodworth** is a respected corporate litigator recognized for his involvement in prominent commercial disputes, probate litigation and eminent domain cases. He has represented the individual in the case involving Boeing and Lockheed Martin.

Holland & Knight LLP

See firm details p.1352

The Firm: This "*excellent Miami firm*" continues to enhance its reputation for commitment and responsiveness, further benefiting from a network of practice areas in various parts of the country. This helps ensure that clients get the "*right man with the right experience,*" commentators said. The team acted for a major ICT player in an eight-year long dispute.

The Lawyers: Observers point towards the experience of **Tracy Nichols** (see p.547) as a key component of the firm's success. The leader of the securities litigation group acted for Sykes Enterprises in a securities class action. "*Terrific appellate attorney*" **Rodolfo Sorondo** (see p.551) advised a group of Lloyd's Underwriters in major litigation, bringing "*a tremendous amount of legal knowledge to the task.*" **John Hogan** (see p.542) chairs the firm's litigation practice in south Florida. For rivals, Hogan "*inspires respect and has tremendous gravitas.*" Bringing his previous experience in the DOJ to the fore, Hogan delivers "*top-notch*" advice particularly in white-collar criminal defense proceedings.

The Clients: The firm has represented Fortune 500 companies, small businesses and nonprofit organizations.

Jones, Foster, Johnston & Stubbs, PA

The Firm: This "*West Palm Beach star*" of a firm cuts a wide swath on the litigation front, delivering legal victories through the "*integrity and resourcefulness*" of its 17 litigators. This "*excellent and experienced*" set of attorneys recently defended a major law firm in a multimillion-dollar malpractice case.

The Lawyers: "*Lawyer of choice in West Palm Beach,*" **Sidney Stubbs** (see p.551) has won client confidence for approaching dispute resolution – including mediations and arbitrations – with ample good judgment. According to competitors, Stubbs is a "*worthy, very experienced litigator who handles hot issues.*"

The Clients: Abbott Laboratories, Dow Chemical and Mercedes-Benz are examples of the firm's clientele

Shook, Hardy & Bacon LLP

See firm details p.1067

The Firm: This well-established international law firm benefits from an extensive network of 11 offices worldwide, culminating in a well-established reputation for litigation. The "*highly experienced*" group of litigators, who are based in offices in Tampa and Miami, includes former US Attorney for the Southern District of Florida, Guy Lewis, who joined the firm in 2004. "*They can try any case with their vast experience,*" commentators said.

The Lawyers: "*Wonderful cross-examiner*" **Edward Moss** (see p.546) made a splash with his involvement in the tobacco litigation, effectively delivering a "*Perry Mason-style*" approach to obtain success. He is also handling a massive multidistrict litigation against a national pharmaceutical client. He works closely with **Kenneth Reilly** (see p.548), managing partner of the firm's Miami office. "*One of the finest trial lawyers in the state,*" Reilly often defends public companies in products liability suits. **Michael Tein** (see p.552) and **Christopher Brown** (see p.535) also won acclaim for their work in complex litigation.

The Clients: The firm has advised an array of Fortune 500 companies including Philip Morris and Lorillard Tobacco.

Steel Hector & Davis LLP

See firm details p.575

The Firm: Competitors agree that managing partner Alvin Davis is "*the talent behind*" the excellent reputation of this team. With offices in key metropolitan areas in Florida, Latin America and the UK, this firm has the dexterity to act in highly complex proceedings for both Fortune 500 companies and individuals. Observers also highlighted its continuing representation of Florida Power & Light.

The Lawyers: "*Raconteur*" **Alvin Davis** (see p.538) received admiration for his "*ample experience*" in complex litigation, further bolstered by the fact that he is, "*by and large, well regarded by judges.*"

The Clients: The firm has advised prominent clients such as Florida Power & Light among other public companies.

Moscowitz, Moscowitz & Magolnick PA

The Firm: Clients are impressed by the "*excellent representation throughout – outside and inside the court.*" The "*enviable combination of talents*" of the husband-and-wife team is particularly impressive in white-collar criminal matters.

The Lawyers: "*Tough, smart and highly effective,*" **Jane Moscowitz** uses her vast experience of federal cases to focus on the defense of highly prominent clients. She won the landmark acquittal of Greenpeace in a federal case. **Norman Moscowitz** continues to represent Norwegian Cruise Line in negotiating a favorable settlement of an environmental case. Peers said the assiduous litigator is prized for his "*ability to simplify things so the jury understands the line of his defense.*" Norman recently settled a case involving alleged caviar smuggling.

The Clients: Among the firm's clientele are public companies such as Norwegian Cruise Line, nonprofit organizations and smaller businesses.

Raskin & Raskin PA

The Firm: The criminal boutique is recommended for its high-profile defense of clients indicted for federal crimes. Competitors agree: "*They are a good team to get you out of trouble.*" The firm has represented an Internet pharmacy operation in a federal grand jury investigation concerning nationwide distribution of controlled substances.

The Lawyers: The husband-and-wife duo **Jane Raskin** and **Martin Raskin** gained plaudits for their white-collar crime expertise. Observers admire their effectiveness in federal trials, particularly those involving corruption issues. On behalf of a law firm, they successfully forced the return of thousands of pages of privileged client documents seized by the government for investigation.

Black, Srebnick, Kornspan & Stumpf PA

The Firm: Interviewees hail this 11-attorney firm for the "*extraordinarily hard work*" it regularly delivers to clients nationwide. The team's focus on criminal defense and related civil litigation has paid dividends. For example, the "*highly skilled*" set of litigators represented a top executive of a bank that went into receivership. The team has also been retained to counsel major corporate clients in government-related compliance proceedings.

The Lawyers: One of the "*most recognizable faces in litigation*" statewide, **Roy Black** led the defense of a former top executive of collapsed communication giant WorldCom. Commentators said his "*stellar*" performance won applause, as did "*his superb trial skills, jury-friendliness and wonderful presence in court.*" **Howard Srebnick** is also "*terrific*" in criminal matters. He has represented a former top officer of a collapsed Florida bank.

George & Titus PA

The Firm: This Tampa specialist is described as a leader for white-collar crime, government investigations and related litigation. The "*three-man band*" benefits from an established reputation in an increasingly dynamic area of law, representing both companies and individuals. The team has handled a variety of criminal matters, including those involving environmental, tax and healthcare law.

The Lawyers: "*Bulldog*" **Peter George** is well experienced and very respected, according to competitors. He is one of the best trial lawyers in the area, handling varied cases in white-collar criminal defense.

Leventhal & Slaughter PA

The Firm: This "*excellent Orlando firm*" impresses commentators with its track record covering all areas of criminal corporate defense. Established in 1988, this three-attorney boutique is commended for its adroit criminal defense expertise, often representing clients before federal and state courts.

The Lawyers: Partners **Robert Leventhal** and **Harrison Slaughter** are "*creative, responsive, well regarded by the court and easy to work with,*" in the eyes of peers.

Ruden McClosky SC

The Firm: The ten-lawyer white-collar practice of this full-service firm offers preemptive counsel to clients in the reviews of internal policies and procedures to spot potential problems. Commentators acknowledge the team's tireless efforts to help clients navigate through various investigations among other proceedings. The firm's prowess was further boosted with the addition of an office in Orlando, housing attorneys who are "*well versed*" in corporate criminal litigation.

Florida
Leading individuals
(Litigation: Appellate)

[1]
AUSLANDER Charles *Greenberg Traurig*, Miami
PERWIN Joel *Sole Practitioner*, Miami
RICHARD Barry *Greenberg Traurig*, Tallahassee
ROSS Lauri *Sole Practitioner*, Miami
SCHERKER Elliot *Greenberg Traurig*, Miami
SORONDO Rodolfo *Holland & Knight*, Miami
STRAFER Richard *Sole Practitioner*, Miami
WALBOLT Sylvia *Carlton Fields*, St Petersburg

[2]
BERANEK John *Ausley & McMullen*, Tallahassee
COOPER Marc *Colson Hicks*, Coral Gables
EATON Joel *Podhurst Orseck*, Miami
ENGLAND Arthur *Greenberg Traurig*, Miami
GLAZIER Robert *Sole Practitioner*, Miami
KREUSLER-WALSH Jane West Palm Beach
LAWRENCE Adam *Lawrence & Daniels*, Miami
LEVY Jay *Sole Practitioner*, Miami
ROGOW Bruce *Sole Practitioner*, Fort Lauderdale

Individuals are listed alphabetically in each band.

The Lawyers: Peers said partner **Bruce Udolf** *"goes the extra mile"* in the defense of clients in white-collar criminal cases. He *"puts 150% of his heart on the case and does a bang-up job,"* acting for corporate entities or individuals.

Sale & Kuehne PA
The Firm: This *"aggressive, pioneering, and top-quality"* three-attorney firm excels in federal and state corporate criminal defense matters that include securities fraud, and defense contracts and procurement. It has also played key roles in various internal investigations and money laundering disputes. In a recent development, the team is involved in a significant case concerning a Hispanic voter registration group in Florida.
The Lawyers: Peers value the achievements of *"politically connected and articulate"* attorney **Ben Kuehne** in corporate criminal cases. Both Kuehne and partner **Jon Sale** receive admiration as *"extremely smart and experienced"* operators on highly complicated cases, particularly those with corruption issues.

Other Notable Practitioners
Interviewees describe **Faith Elizabeth Gay** (see p.540) as a *"sharp legal mind."* Gay is defending a major French engineering conglomerate with respect to multinational securities fraud and Foreign Corrupt Practices Act allegations. This *"bright, articulate and exceptional trial lawyer"* leads the white-collar practice for White & Case LLP out of the Miami and New York offices. **Bruce Zimet** is *"the best trial lawyer for my money in South Florida,"* according to one commentator. He also proves valuable for his *"first-rate courtroom presence and trial skills."* **Joel Perwin** is also a sole practitioner who *"is still as excellent as ever."* He currently co-counsels in an action against mass marketers in violation of federal statutes. Peers say he is a *"well-rounded star analyst who's fabulous with complex issues."* Competitors commend sole appellate practitioner **Lauri Ross** for her star performances on behalf of plaintiffs and defendants. A recent highlight involved an appellate case concerning a major tire manufacturer. Peers see sole practitioner **Richard Strafer** as *"a premier appellate lawyer in South Florida."* Strafer acted in a prominent trial involving the former head of the Medellín cartel. Commentators praise him for being *"courageous in the causes he pursues."* Tallahassee firm Ausley & McMullen is home to former judge **John Beranek**, who impresses peers with his elegant legal insights. Clients see sole practitioner **William Aaron** as *"very substantial"* in the courtroom. *"His presentation is prepared like a good novel to get the judges' attention,"* said one source. Aaron represented a restaurant chain regarding an alleged multimillion-dollar cash skimming operation. Competitors recommend him as a top-flight negotiator. Sole practitioner **Ronald Cacciatore** has an enviable reputation in handling corporate trial and appellate matters, while **William Jung** is *"smart as a whip."* Managing partner of Tampa firm Jung & Sisco, Jung is *"very understated but has well-deserved respect"* for his practice. *"Brilliant trial attorney"* **John Frost** (see p.540) of Frost Tamayo Sessums & Aranda PA *"deserves top marks."* Frost is well known for his medical malpractice specialty. Market observers said **David Mandel** (see p.545), head of Miami law firm Mandel & Cale LLP, is *"genuinely great."* Also described as someone who *"puts a lot of energy into his cases,"* Mandel has built a prominent profile in criminal defense. Sole practitioner **Cheney Mason** also holds a leading position in white-collar crime, while Miami-based sole practitioner **Jose Quiñon** impresses interviewees with *"his aggressive fight for his clients."* Observers recommend **William Sheppard** of Jacksonville firm Sheppard, White & Thomas PA as *"top notch"* for his white-collar crime defense practice. Miami's Bierman, Shohat, Loewy & Klein PA is home to **Edward Shohat**, whose aggressive approach won client confidence. He is *"quick on his feet in court and battles tooth and nail for his clients."* At Trombley & Hanes **Gary Trombley** is portrayed as a *"go-to"* litigator in Tampa. This *"real pro"* is also a former prosecutor. Competitors think very highly of Miami-based sole practitioner **Robert Glazier** (see p.540), a *"scholarly and talented"* operator. Sole practitioner **Jane Kreusler-Walsh** received admiration for her *"excellence and competence"* as an appellate attorney, operating from a West Palm Beach office. Miami litigator **Adam Lawrence** of Lawrence & Daniels garnered praise for his immense experience, while sole practitioner **Jay Levy** is pitched as a top choice for appellate law. *"A great contender with terrific court skills,"* **Bruce Rogow** runs *"a star appellate practice"* in Fort Lauderdale. **Rutledge Liles** – the managing partner of Jacksonville law firm Liles, Gavin, Costantino & Murphy – is considered *"one of the finest plaintiff lawyers in Florida."* He boasts terrific experience in handling professional malpractice cases. **Edward Soto** (see p.551) of Weil, Gotshal & Manges LLP defended a major healthcare provider in a large multidistrict litigation.

REAL ESTATE

Bilzin Sumberg Baena Price & Axelrod LLP
See firm details p.559
The Firm: A full-service Miami firm, Bilzin Sumberg has developed a broad-based real estate group staffed by *"sophisticated attorneys."* Pointing to *"a very high concentration of major clients,"* market commentators are well aware of the group's involvement in various fields of activity, both within and beyond state lines. Operating a series of practice area-specific subgroups, the firm is felt to have two particularly strong suits – real estate finance and development – though attorneys are also said to be *"top notch"* for land use and resorts work. A strong stable of home builder clients keeps attorneys busy, with recent work including the representation of key client Lennar Homes on the development and financing of ten national home-building projects.
The Lawyers: *"Bright, creative and experienced"* **Brian Bilzin** (see p.535) combines a class-leading real estate finance practice with more general corporate finance advice, and is accordingly a popular choice among lender clients for securitization and structured finance. **John Sumberg**'s (see p.552) practice emphasizes development, and his name is frequently linked to the largest deals. In the past year, he advised a developer client on the $90 million Whitney condominium development in Palm Beach, and acted for a French construction client on the $200 million conversion of an apartment block into a condominium complex. **Stanley Price** (see p.547), head of the firm's land use practice group, was also involved in the zoning aspects of

www.ChambersandPartners.com
All quotes in the text are from interviews with clients and competitors.
525

Florida
Leading firms (Real Estate)

1. BILZIN SUMBERG BAENA PRICE, *Miami*
   GREENBERG TRAURIG LLP *Miami*
2. AKERMAN SENTERFITT *Orlando*
   LOWNDES DROSDICK DOSTER KANTOR *Orlando*
   RUDEN MCCLOSKY SC *Fort Lauderdale*
   STEARNS WEAVER MILLER WEISSLER *Miami*
3. BROAD AND CASSEL *Orlando*
   CARLTON FIELDS, PA *Tampa*
   DEAN, MEAD, EGERTON, BLOODWORTH *Orlando*
   HOLLAND & KNIGHT LLP *Miami*
   ROGERS, TOWERS, BAILEY, JONES *Jacksonville*
   TEW CARDENAS LLP *Miami*
   TRENAM, KEMKER, SCHARF, BARKIN *Tampa*
   WHITE & CASE LLP *Miami*
4. FOLEY & LARDNER *Tampa*
   GRAY ROBINSON PA *Orlando*
   GUNSTER, YOAKLEY & STEWART *Fort Lauderdale*
   HILL, WARD & HENDERSON, PA *Tampa*
   LEBOEUF, LAMB, GREENE & MACRAE *Jacksonville*
   SHUTTS & BOWEN LLP *Miami*
   SMITH HULSEY & BUSEY *Jacksonville*
   SMITH, GAMBRELL & RUSSELL, LLP *Jacksonville*
   SQUIRE, SANDERS & DEMPSEY LLP *Tampa*

Leading individuals (Real Estate)

1. ALHADEFF Richard *Stearns Weaver, Miami*
   BILZIN Brian *Bilzin Sumberg, Miami*
   BOZARTH Stephen *Dean Mead, Orlando*
   GORSON Matthew *Greenberg Traurig, Miami*
   RYAN Michael *Lowndes Drosdick, Orlando*
   SOMERSTEIN Barry *Ruden, Fort Lauderdale*
   TAGUE Brian *Tew Cardenas, Miami*
   WALKER William *White & Case, Miami*
2. BROWN II C David *Broad and Cassel, Orlando*
   HANSON Karl *LeBoeuf Lamb, Jacksonville*
   HENDERSON Thomas *Hill Ward, Tampa*
   KINSOLVING Ruth *Carlton Fields, Tampa*
   MITCHELL Stephen *Squire Sanders, Tampa*
   SAUL Gary *Greenberg Traurig, Miami*
   SEAY James *Holland & Knight, Orlando*
   SMULIAN Andrew *Akerman Senterfitt, Miami*
3. COMMANDER III Charles *Foley, Jacksonville*
   COWAN Kevin *Shutts & Bowen, Miami*
   RIDLEY Fred *Foley & Lardner, Tampa*
   SCHEU William *Rogers Towers, Jacksonville*
   SLATER James *Broad and Cassel, Orlando*
   SOLLNER Richard *Trenam Kemker, Tampa*
   STANFORD Douglas *Smith Gambrell, Jacksonville*
   SUMBERG John *Bilzin Sumberg, Miami*
   WILSON III Harry *Smith Hulsey, Jacksonville*

Leading individuals (Hotels and Resorts)

1. FILDES Richard *Lowndes Drosdick, Orlando*
   GENET Chava *Stearns Weaver, Miami*
   POPE Nicholas *Lowndes Drosdick, Orlando*
   ROBINS Andrew *Gunster Yoakley, Fort Lauderdale*
   SMITH Robert *Holland & Knight, Miami*
   SULLIVAN Michael *Greenberg Traurig, Orlando*
   WEISSLER Robert *Stearns Weaver, Miami*

Firms and individuals are listed alphabetically in each band.

this transaction. Peers admire Price for his *"aggressive but diplomatic style; he knows the players and the politics."*

The Clients: In addition to Lennar Homes, the firm acts for many national developers and hotel chains as welll as Florida-based investors and developers.

Greenberg Traurig LLP
See firm details p.564

The Firm: Market commentators rated this large Florida firm for both real estate and land use work. The practice group is exceptionally large (with about 100 lawyers across the firm's five Florida offices) and, consequently, involved in every aspect of the real estate market. Recent highlights include advising a private REIT on the $210 million acquisition of 26 medical office buildings, and acting on the development of several $100 million high-rise apartment blocks in South Florida. The firm's land use attorneys have lately acted on several conversions of disused waterside commercial properties into apartment complexes. Work takes place both locally and nationally.

The Lawyers: In the Miami office, *"smart"* transactional lawyer **Matthew Gorson** (see p.541) maintains his top-tier status. Peers say he *"catches on quickly"* and rate his negotiation style highly. His involvement with major lenders and developers is commonly on a multistate basis. **Gary Saul** (see p.549) is renowned for his *"terrific experience in condominium law,"* a field in which *"his knowledge is second to none."* He represents the developers of new projects and is heavily involved in the growth area of converting existing apartment buildings into new condominiums. **Clifford Schulman** (see p.550) is a land use lawyer who is *"absolutely at the top of his game,"* according to peers. His practice straddles the boundary between real estate and environmental law; illustrating this point, he is currently acting on the cleanup of a brownfield site and the subsequent construction of a $1.5 billion, 6000-unit residential complex. **Debbie Orshefsky** (see p.547), chair of the firm's national land development practice group, is noted for her expertise in the niche area of developments of regional impact, where she is acknowledged as the state's leading light. **Julie Kendig-Schrader** (see p.543) handles environmental permitting issues attached to large new developments, especially in wetlands areas. As a result, she boasts considerable experience in endangered species law, and interviewees were in no doubt that *"she has a bright future ahead of her."* **Lucia Dougherty**'s (see p.539) land use practice concentrates on top-end development, where she advises major commercial developers on all aspects of permitting. She also counsels historic preservation developers seeking Certificate of Appropriateness for restoration and demolition. Fellow professionals confirmed founding partner **Robert Traurig**'s (see p.552) status as *"the*

dean of land use." These days he combines his land use and governmental relations practice with an increasing amount of community and charitable involvement. Michael Sullivan sustains a high-profile hospitality-oriented practice, focusing on the acquisition and sale of major hotel portfolios and negotiation of related management contracts. Sullivan numbers many of the large US hotel chains among his clients and recently advised on all aspects of the establishment of a 1280-room hotel in Orlando.

The Clients: The Related Group of Florida; Swire Pacific Holdings; Michael Swerdlow Companies; Trump Group; Mellon United National Bank; Lowell Homes and Wachovia National Bank.

Akerman Senterfitt
See firm details p.555

The Firm: This ubiquitous full-service firm received plaudits for its *"excellent geographical coverage"* and *"great client list,"* with one commentator concluding that the firm was *"a household name in every city."* The real estate team is particularly strong in zoning and land use, though its coverage of a broad range of work types is beyond doubt. Akerman Senterfitt attorneys represented Ryder System in the leasing of its new 250,000-sq-ft world headquarters in Miami and the related sale of its existing headquarters for $39 million.

The Lawyers: Admired for his intelligence, **Andrew Smulian** (see p.551) heads the practice group. His recent work has been heavily oriented towards real estate finance; for example, he advised Minto Communities on the negotiation and closing of a $62.5 million development and construction loan facility. **Dwight Saathoff** (see p.549) is acknowledged as the rising star of the firm's land use group: *"He's developing his practice and has great potential,"* say rivals. **Cecilia Bonifay** (see p.535) is depicted as *"well positioned"* to provide land use advice on major projects; her other areas of expertise include indoor air quality and local government law. **Ted Brown** (see p.536) has considerable experience in wetlands and endangered species protection, and often advises on these and other environmental aspects of proposed mixed-use developments. He represents clients in negotiations with the state regulatory bodies and the US Fish and Wildlife service.

The Clients: America's Capital Partners; Bayrock Group; Fisher Island Holdings; Westbrook Partners; Codina Group; Parmenter Realty Partners; Bluegreen; Boca Resorts; IBM; TIAA; Lowe's Home Centers and Four Seasons.

Lowndes Drosdick Doster Kantor & Reed, PA

The Firm: *"A high-powered group geared to real estate representation,"* this firm maintains a heavy emphasis on real estate and land use work. Many of the firm's clients are drawn from the hospitality sector, and recent substantial financings in this area include a $1.5 billion loan facility for the development of five high-class resorts. The same client also turned to the firm for advice on the $400 million acquisition of a San Diego hotel.

The Lawyers: Commentators point to **Michael Ryan** as the firm's leading real estate lawyer, while **Hal Kantor** was described as "*really excellent*" for land use. Kantor's practice emphasizes the transactional support elements of land use, whilst **Miranda Fitzgerald** is involved in land use litigation. She also enjoys a prominent reputation for development of regional impact work: in the words of other attorneys, "*The depth of her experience is really impressive.*" **Richard Fildes** and **Nicholas Pope** lead the charge for the firm in the hotels and resorts sector. In the past twelve months, they have facilitated the creation of new resorts in Miami, Hawaii, California and Arizona, many at a cost of over $1 billion. Rivals note with approval that the team is "*able to stay on top of huge hotel transactions.*"

Ruden McClosky SC

The Firm: This full-service outfit is known for its "*substantial presence in South Florida,*" with commentators highlighting the team's "*excellent political relationships in Broward County.*" The real estate group includes attorneys with experience in acquisition and development, real estate litigation, finance, title examination, land use and zoning.

The Lawyers: "*Hard-working, creative and experienced*" **Barry Somerstein** is a transactional real estate attorney with a focus on finance and workouts. The land use team counts name partner **Donald McClosky** among its members. Undoubtedly the firm's figurehead, McClosky "*has his finger on the pulse,*" according to peers. **Dennis Mele** was also strongly recommended for land use. Interviewees pointed to his background with the South Florida Regional Planning Council as a significant advantage when dealing with state planning bodies, saying: "*Not only is he an articulate advocate, but he has good personal relationships with the authorities.*"

Stearns Weaver Miller Weissler Alhadeff & Sitterson, PA

The Firm: Commended as "*the best real estate firm in Tampa,*" Stearns Weaver also operates from offices in Miami and Fort Lauderdale. It is acknowledged as a significant presence in every corner of the market; in addition to its mainstream real estate attorneys, the firm boasts a considerable number of finance and hospitality specialists.

The Lawyers: Sources showered praise on **Richard Alhadeff**'s transactional prowess, happy that "*he understands what a deal needs,*

doesn't waste time on nonsense and always gets it done." Meanwhile, "*dynamic, articulate and creative*" **Ronald Weaver** was recommended as a land use specialist who, in addition to operating a thriving practice, is a regular contributor to academic publications. **Robert Weissler** is a transactional attorney who specializes in high-value sales and acquisitions of hotels, golf clubs and casinos. He also advises clients in the hospitality industry on real estate finance, and recently closed a $350 million securitized financing on behalf of a consortium of hotel operators. **Chava Genet** counsels hotel and resort operators on the acquisition, development and day-to-day operation of their businesses. She additionally has experience in construction law, and drafts and negotiates construction contracts for new developments.

Broad and Cassel

The Firm: This sizable Florida practice is particularly well regarded for its "*strong political connections.*" The team recently acted for both lenders and developers on several conversions of apartments into condominium complexes, the largest of which was valued at $90 million. Other finance-related instructions include a multimillion-dollar refinancing of an office property portfolio.

The Lawyers: Much of the firm's reputation can be attributed to the stature of its chairman **David Brown**. "*A political figure with close connections to the governor,*" he is considered a significant draw for clients. "*Splendid attorney*" **James Slater** concentrates on the representation of developers, advising them on all aspects of development from land acquisition and permitting to construction and sale. In the past year, he advised a major developer client on the $53 million sale of a high-rise apartment block for redevelopment as a condominium.

The Clients: In addition to private sector lenders and developers, the firm represents a number of local authorities and government agencies.

Carlton Fields, P.A.

See firm details p.560

The Firm: Carlton Fields boasts offices spread throughout the state. However, its strongest is felt to be Tampa, where "*it has a real presence.*" The substantial statewide team undertakes commercial leasing, acquisition, development and financing, and though traditionally a Florida firm, practice is not limited by state boundaries. For example, in the past year Carlton Fields attorneys have advised contractor clients on the $900 million expansion of the McCormick Center in Chicago and the construction of the new $350 million NFL stadium in Phoenix.

The Lawyers: Interviewees agreed that **Ruth Kinsolving** "*is a significant presence in the sector.*" She advises commercial landlords and

investors, including overseas investors, on acquisition, leasehold management and new development, with an emphasis on retail and resort property.

Dean, Mead, Egerton, Bloodworth, Capouano & Bozarth PA

The Firm: Known throughout the state for its tax practice, this medium-sized firm also houses a significant real estate team. The group's "*splendid*" reputation belies its size – the firm is mentioned in the same breath as many of its larger competitors.

The Lawyers: In the opinion of his peers, **Stephen Bozarth** is "*at the top – excellent, conscientious, capable and efficient.*" His general real estate practice encompasses development, sales and purchases, leasing and secured and unsecured lending.

Holland & Knight LLP

See firm details p.1352

The Firm: Florida's largest firm boasts over 100 real estate attorneys. The group is active across the board and advises some of the largest national home builders on their acquisition of development land. The team has also benefited from the trend among home builders to enter into joint ventures for development and has built up considerable expertise in this growing area.

The Lawyers: **James Seay** (see p.550) acts almost exclusively for commercial investors and developers. In particular, he represents equity investors wishing to participate in new-build or refurbishment projects and assists them with exit strategies. He recently advised Pizzuti on the $120 million sale of part of its Florida office property portfolio. Peers described **Susan Delegal** (see p.538) as "*very knowledgeable about the zoning process.*" The bulk of her practice involves obtaining planning approvals for major developers; she recently advised a national homebuilder on the conversion of a disused school site into a sizable housing complex. Delegal also serves as general counsel to the Clerk of Courts for Broward County. "*Capable*" **Robert Smith** (see p.551) is known as a hospitality specialist, though his expertise extends to complex finance and general commercial leasing. Two of Akerman Senterfitt's real estate team recently moved to join the firm. **Joseph Goldstein** (see p.540) has a broad land use practice, as demonstrated by his representation of the Scripps Research Institute in the development of regional impact and zoning aspects of the expedited permitting of the Palm Beach County Biotechnological Research Park. **Juan Mayol**'s (see p.546) practice encompasses the public funding aspects of zoning and development; he recently obtained school board approval of the first educational facilities benefit district in Miami-Dade County.

The Clients: In addition to Pizzuti, the firm acts for developers such as Lennar Homes.

Florida
Leading firms
(Real Estate: Zoning/Land Use)

[1] **AKERMAN SENTERFITT** *Orlando*
BILZIN SUMBERG BAENA PRICE *Miami*
GREENBERG TRAURIG LLP *Miami*
HOPPING GREEN & SAMS, PA *Tallahassee*
LOWNDES DROSDICK DOSTER KANTOR *Orlando*
PAPPAS METCALF JENKS *Jacksonville*

[2] **BERCOW & RADELL PA** *Miami*
FOWLER WHITE BOGGS BANKER *Tampa*
GUNSTER, YOAKLEY *Fort Lauderdale*
HOLLAND & KNIGHT LLP *Miami*
RUDEN MCCLOSKY SC *Fort Lauderdale*
STEARNS WEAVER MILLER WEISSLER *Miami*

[3] **BRICKLEMYER SMOLKER & BOLVES PA** *Miami*
FOLEY & LARDNER *Tampa*
GRAY ROBINSON PA *Orlando*
ROGERS, TOWERS, BAILEY *Jacksonville*
SHUBIN & BASS *Miami*
SHUTTS & BOWEN LLP *Miami, Orlando*

Leading individuals
(Real Estate: Zoning/Land Use)

Senior Statesman
HOPPING Wade *Hopping Green*, Tallahassee
MCCLOSKY Donald *Ruden McClosky*, Fort Lauderdale
SIEMON Charles *Sole Practitioner*, Boca Raton
TRAURIG Robert *Greenberg Traurig*, Miami

[1] **FITZGERALD Miranda** *Lowndes Drosdick*, Orlando
KANTOR Hal *Lowndes Drosdick*, Orlando
PAPPAS Lynn *Pappas Metcalf*, Jacksonville
PRICE Stanley *Bilzin Sumberg*, Miami
SCHULMAN Clifford *Greenberg Traurig*, Miami

[2] **DELEGAL Susan** *Holland & Knight*, Fort Lauderdale
HALL Donald *Gunster Yoakley*, Fort Lauderdale
LAW Rhea *Fowler White*, Tampa
MELE Dennis *Ruden McClosky*, Fort Lauderdale
ORSHEFSKY Debbie *Greenberg*, Fort Lauderdale
PELHAM Thomas *Fowler White*, Tallahassee
SAATHOFF Dwight *Akerman Senterfitt*, Orlando
WEAVER Ronald *Stearns Weaver*, Tampa
WOODSON R Duke *Foley & Lardner*, Tallahassee

[3] **BERCOW Jeffrey** *Bercow & Radell*, Miami
BONIFAY Cecilia *Akerman Senterfitt*, Orlando
BRICKLEMYER Keith *Bricklemyer Smolker*, Miami
BRINDELL James *Gunster Yoakley*, West Palm Beach
BROWN Ted *Akerman Senterfitt*, Orlando
DOUGHERTY Lucia *Greenberg Traurig*, Miami
GOLDSTEIN Joseph *Holland & Knight*, Miami
GOREN Samuel *Goren Cherof*, Fort Lauderdale
GRINDSTAFF Michael *Shutts & Bowen*, Orlando
HAINLINE Jr Theodore *Rogers Towers*, Jacksonville
KENDIG-SCHRADER Julie *Greenberg Traurig*, Orlando
LEONHARDT Frederick *Gray Robinson*, Orlando
MAYOL Juan *Holland & Knight*, Miami
SHUBIN John *Shubin & Bass*, Miami

Firms and individuals are listed alphabetically in each band.

Rogers, Towers, Bailey, Jones & Gay, PA

The Firm: This sizeable group is widely acknowledged to be *"one of the best firms in Jacksonville."* Competitors praised the firm's team of *"reasonable, intelligent deal-makers,"* highlighting the land use group's *"impeccable reputation."*
The Lawyers: **William Scheu**'s real estate practice focuses on the acquisition, development and leasing of shopping centers and office buildings. He numbers several REITs and institutional investors among his clients, and also acts for national retailers in their leasehold negotiations. **Theodore Hainline** is the firm's leading land use attorney, and has sat on numerous land use and development committees, including the Jacksonville mayor's Growth Management Task Force.

Tew Cardenas LLP

The Firm: A medium-sized establishment with offices in Miami and Tallahassee, Tew Cardenas boasts ten real estate attorneys. The Miami office is thought to be the firm's center of gravity.
The Lawyers: The market clearly pointed to *"enormously creative"* **Brian Tague** (see p.552) as the firm's star player. Renowned for his deal-making skills, Tague concentrates on major acquisitions and disposals, real estate and project finance, and related debt workouts.

Trenam, Kemker, Scharf, Barkin, Frye, O'Neill & Mullis PA

The Firm: A noted presence in the Tampa market, this firm has grown dramatically in recent years. A *"very solid group"* of ten real estate attorneys has built up an impressive list of clients, and advises on acquisitions, disposals, leasing and financing.
The Lawyers: **Richard Sollner** was recommended by his peers for his strong real estate finance background. His practice includes an unusual public finance element, involving advice to public bodies on the issue of housing bonds.

White & Case LLP

See firm details p.1379
The Firm: The Miami office of this international giant boasts a small but influential real estate team. By contrast with many of its lender-oriented competitors, this team concentrates on representing developers and landlords. In a recent high-profile matter, the group advised one of the world's largest resort hotel companies on a strategic alliance in the timeshare business.
The Lawyers: **William Walker** (see p.553) is a senior figure at the Florida bar. He is particularly active in the development and leasehold management of shopping centers and planned residential communities. He led the team advising Lexin Capital on the $21.1 million acquisition of the Downtown Celebration complex in Disney's Celebration project, and also acted on

the sale of the SunTrust International Center for $75.2 million.
The Clients: Arvida Corporation; JMB Realty; Crocker and Company; Hannover Ruckversicherungs; Disney; AMFAC Property; Codina Development and Temple Development.

Foley & Lardner

See firm details p.1828
The Firm: A major national firm with a significant presence in the state, Foley & Lardner has a compact Florida real estate group. The firm was particularly praised for its land use proficiency.
The Lawyers: **Fred Ridley** (see p.548) is highly rated by competitors. Partner-in-charge of the real estate group in Tampa, he stands out for his expertise in the financing and development of golf courses and resorts. **Charles Commander** (see p.537) was also singled out for his *"great reputation,"* and is also a member of the golf and resort services industry team. For land use, rivals hailed **Duke Woodson** (see p.554) as a popular choice for referrals. Head of the firm's Florida environmental practice, his focus is on water law and its relationship to real estate transactions. He also advises private clients on the sale of environmentally sensitive lands to government, which involves both transactional skills and careful negotiation with water management districts.
The Clients: The firm represents resort developers and lenders, including: Meadowbrook Golf Group; Pacific Life Insurance; OakRidge Investments and Textron Financial.

Gray Robinson PA

The Firm: This sizable Florida firm makes its debut in *Chambers'* tables following positive market feedback. "They've grown aggressively of late, and positioned themselves well in the market," concluded one commentator. The firm's unusual internal structure places real estate and land use attorneys in the government law practice group, allowing cross-pollination from environmental and administrative lawyers. The team is presently advising on 55 West, a $250 million mixed-use infill project in downtown Orlando, which will have a significant impact on the regeneration of the locale.
The Lawyers: Sources point to **Frederick Leonhardt** as the firm's rainmaker. Many rivals envy his political contacts – a significant advantage when lobbying government authorities on behalf of developer clients. Much of his current workload consists of obtaining permits for brownfield or infill development in urban areas.

Gunster, Yoakley & Stewart, PA

The Firm: *"Strong in South Florida,"* this full-service firm is regarded most highly for its land use practice. Gunster Yoakley attorneys have been involved in a number of condominium developments, including the first entirely new development in Palm Beach for 25 years.

The Lawyers: *"Politically shrewd"* **Donald Hall** is *"highly effective before local governments,"* according to rivals. He represents exclusively developers at all stages of the permitting process. **James Brindell**, an attorney with a background in environmental law, now concentrates on land use and zoning; his experience makes him an obvious choice for real estate transactions with a significant environmental element. Commended by fellow hospitality specialists, **Andrew Robins** is director of the firm's leisure and resorts group.

Hill, Ward & Henderson, PA

The Firm: In addition to winning a stellar reputation for litigation, this Tampa firm maintains a small but active real estate team. Its client base encompasses both developers and lenders.

The Lawyers: Name partner **Thomas Henderson** heads the group. His specialty is real estate finance, and he counsels the firm's impressive roster of lender clients on loan negotiations, loan renewals and workouts.

LeBoeuf, Lamb, Greene & MacRae, LLP

See firm details p.1358

The Firm: This major international firm operates a single Florida office in Jacksonville. The real estate team serves predominantly major developers and institutional investors, and is developing a real estate finance practice. Much of the group's work is Florida based, such as the $60 million sale of the Enterprise Center in Jacksonville.

The Lawyers: **Karl Hanson** (see p.542) is the standout partner. He undertakes a good deal of

work for LeBoeuf's star client Fidelity Investments. For example, he is providing ongoing counsel regarding the establishment and expansion of the company's corporate campus in Jacksonville.

The Clients: In addition to Fidelity Investments, the firm acts for investors such as Ever-Bank and Synovus Bank.

Shutts & Bowen LLP

See firm details p.573

The Firm: About 30 attorneys practice real estate law at this long-established Florida firm. Real estate finance, zoning and land use are perceived to be the group's strongest suits.

The Lawyers: **Kevin Cowan** (see p.537) is chair of the real estate group. His practice is twofold: representing developers and institutional investors in development, acquisitions and disposals, and leading the commercial leasing team. **Michael Grindstaff** (see p.541) enters the rankings following praise from competitors. It is said that *"he knows how to cut to the chase and organize information in a way that is most useful to the client."* A land use and zoning expert, he has a workload that comprises both transactional support and real estate litigation.

Smith Hulsey & Busey

See firm details p.574

The Firm: Smith Hulsey's real estate group is a significant player in the Jacksonville market. While the practice group covers all the traditional areas, it is perhaps best known for transactional and finance advice, notably for key client Wachovia Bank.

The Lawyers: **Harry Wilson**'s peers commended his negotiating style by praising the fact that he *"always tries to make the deal rather than*

break it." As chairman of the real estate team, he has built up an impressive finance practice and is recognized as *"certainly one of the top real estate lawyers in Jacksonville."*

Smith, Gambrell & Russell, LLP

The Firm: Headquartered in Atlanta, this large full-service firm also has a well-respected office in Jacksonville. A team of five advises on acquisitions and disposals, development, leasing and finance. The firm acts for a varied clientele, including corporate users, commercial banks, investment banks, institutional investors, public and private companies, landlords and tenants, and the developers of office and industrial buildings, apartment and condominium communities, golf courses, hotels, shopping centers, resorts and multiuse developments.

The Lawyers: **Douglas Stanford** has a great name in the construction, financing and leasing of large office complexes and big-box stores.

Squire, Sanders & Dempsey LLP

The Firm: International firm Squire Sanders operates two small Florida offices in Miami and Tampa. Sources confirmed that the firm's real strength in the state lies in the public finance arena; indeed, the Tampa office focuses almost exclusively on this area. Squire Sanders has advised the state government and other public bodies on more Florida municipal bond issues than any other firm.

The Lawyers: **Stephen Mitchell** was strongly recommended by peers. His practice encompasses both development and finance, and he has a particular interest in the hospitality industry, being well known for his representation of Marriott Hotels.

TAX

Band 1

Greenberg Traurig LLP

See firm details p.564

The Firm: Esteemed *"one of the best tax groups in central and south Florida,"* the Miami and Orlando offices of this massive firm remain among the most highly rated in the market. As a whole, the firm is thought to be particularly strong in international tax work, where its size and well-developed national network are considered distinct advantages.

The Lawyers: While interviewees emphasized that the whole team is *"very deep in terms of talent,"* several pointed to **Joel Maser** (see p.546) as particularly worthy of recognition. Much of his work is linked with the real estate development industry. *"I see him all the time on transactions and think very highly of him,"* said a peer at a

rival firm. A renowned transactional tax attorney, Maser recently advised INVESCO in connection with various investments in condominium developments. **Skip Stiver** (see p.551) also concentrates on transactional tax. Matters handled include corporate reorganizations, partially and fully taxable acquisitions, tender offers, spin-offs and poison pills. Peers hail Stiver as *"a worthy competitor"* with notable experience in multinational corporate affairs. **Steve Lapidus** (see p.544), a tax lawyer by training, specializes in executive compensation and employee benefits. His expertise is much in demand among clients undertaking M&A. In addition to corporate support, his practice encompasses the negotiation and drafting of executive employment agreements and equity compensation plans, together with counseling employers on 401(k) and pension plans.

The Clients: INVESCO; Hilton Hotels; The Related Group of Florida and Swire Properties.

Holland & Knight LLP

See firm details p.1352

The Firm: Clients were delighted with their experience of this huge firm's tax group: *"We demand results of a high caliber, and they've been so exceptional that we've stayed with them for 15 years,"* enthused one. Rival attorneys acknowledged that the team *"has talent everywhere."* With more than 70 lawyers in its firmwide tax practice, the group offers planning and advice on federal, state and local and international taxation. It also handles a wide spectrum of litigation and controversy and transaction structuring issues. The firm maintains a distinct practice for tax-exempt entities.

Florida
Leading firms (Tax)

1 GREENBERG TRAURIG LLP *Miami*
HOLLAND & KNIGHT LLP *Lakeland*

2 AKERMAN SENTERFITT *Miami*
BAKER & MCKENZIE *Miami*
BILZIN SUMBERG BAENA PRICE *Miami*
DEAN, MEAD, EGERTON, BLOODWORTH *Orlando*
STEEL HECTOR & DAVIS LLP *Miami*
TESCHER GUTTER CHAVES JOSEPHER *Boca Raton*
WHITE & CASE LLP *Miami*

3 AUGUST, KULUNAS *West Palm Beach*
CARLTON FIELDS, P.A. *Tampa*
FOWLER WHITE BOGGS BANKER *Tampa*
HOPPING GREEN & SAMS, P.A. *Tallahassee*
PACKMAN, NEUWAHL *Coral Gables*
VICKERS MADSEN & GOLDMAN *Tallahassee*

4 AUSLEY & MCMULLEN *Tallahassee*
BARNETT, BOLT, KIRKWOOD, LONG *Tampa*
BROAD AND CASSEL *Miami*
BRONSTEIN, CARLSON, GLEIM *St Petersburg*
COMITER, SINGER & BASEMAN *Palm Beach Gardens*
GUNSTER, YOAKLEY & STEWART, P.A. *Miami*
JOHNSON, POPE, BOKOR, RUPPEL *Clearwater*
KARP & GENAUER PA *Coral Gables*

Firms are listed alphabetically in each band.

The Lawyers: "*Very sharp*" transactional tax lawyer **Bernie Barton** (see p.534) is known in Florida for his state and local practice. He recently devised a tax-efficient structure for a $130 million real estate secured loan, which saved his client $455,000 in Florida taxes. "*An exceptional lawyer of high ethical standards,*" he is "*great at bringing closure to a matter.*" Most impressively, say clients, Barton "*can actually get the Department of Revenue to see our point of view.*" Highly visible writing and speaking on tax shelters and professional ethics, **Andrew Weinstein** (see p.553) also maintains a busy international private client practice, often advising clients in the shipping industry on US and international financial planning and wealth management. "*Extremely practical and client friendly,*" Weinstein "*has the drive to see things through to a successful conclusion,*" report interviewees. His contribution to the profession was recognized by his recent election to the American College of Trust and Estates Counsel. One of the team's most senior attorneys, **Jim Ervin** (see p.539) is considered the leading light at the practice for tax controversy and litigation. In the opinion of fellow litigators, he "*handles cutting-edge issues for an excellent stable of clients.*" **Mark Holcomb** (see p.542) also focuses on contentious tax matters and is frequently seen representing major corporations in disputes with the Florida Department of Revenue. Clients appreciate Holcomb's "*down-to-earth, but tough*" attitude and his commitment to their interests: "*I think of him as more than just legal counsel – we have formed a business relationship,*

and I know I can count on him," one said.
The Clients: The firm acts for a raft of corporate clients, including: Buchanan Automotive Group; BellSouth; Nationwide Mutual Insurance Company and Wyeth.

Band 2

Akerman Senterfitt
See firm details p.555
The Firm: This Florida giant enjoys a fine reputation in the state for tax advice. A team of attorneys, divided between five offices, covers a diverse range of tax issues. The firm received particular acclaim for its state and local practice, but also maintains a busy workload of international structuring and transactional matters.
The Lawyers: "*The top person for tax-exempt organizations,*" **Hank Raattama** (see p.548) garners respect in the field for his representation of charitable and nonprofit organizations. Raattama is currently guiding a leading university through a major IRS audit. He also advises private clients and closely held companies. **Don Duffy** (see p.539) continues to win plaudits from competitors for M&A and deal structuring: "*I think of him as one of the leaders in south Florida,*" one said. **Russell Hale** (see p.542) enters *Chambers'* tables this year following a raft of positive feedback from peers. He heads up the firm's small but highly active state and local practice, which advises major corporate clients on the tax implications of their Florida business activities. He is also known for lobbying the state legislature and Florida Department of Revenue on state and local tax issues. Sources acknowledged younger attorney **Frank Cordero**'s (see p.537) "*definite quality.*" His practice includes complex tax planning at both international and domestic levels.
The Clients: The firm serves a wide range of clients, including: Darden Restaurants; Mears Transportation Group; Florida Bankers Association and Florida Bankers Insurance Trust.

Baker & McKenzie
See firm details p.761
The Firm: Thanks to the firm's status as one of the largest in the world, Baker & McKenzie's Miami office enjoys access to a remarkable roster of clients. The group maintains a reputation for quality in international tax matters. "*I'd never hesitate to refer to them,*" say rival attorneys.
The Lawyers: A perennial favorite for referrals, **Robert Hudson** (see p.542) is "*on everybody's list*" for international tax advice. Hudson frequently undertakes restructuring and global tax planning for foreign-controlled businesses with US interests. He also advises a select few high net-worth individuals, often non-US nationals seeking to invest in Florida. Known as "*a formidable force*" in the state, Hudson enjoys a stature such that "*any aspiring competitor had better pay attention to him – he is simply the dominant play-

er.*" "*Fine young lawyer*" **Ozzie Schindler** (see p.549) continues to gain in prominence. The focus of his practice has shifted somewhat toward advising wealthy private clients on investing or relocating in Florida, though he still represents multinationals and US public companies. He has also seen a notable increase in clients seeking advice on inbound real estate investment.

Bilzin Sumberg Baena Price & Axelrod LLP
See firm details p.559
The Firm: This full-service Miami firm made the headlines at the beginning of 2005 with its recruitment of William Townsend, Samuel Ullman and Rex Ware from Steel Hector & Davis. The arrival of this high-powered triumvirate places Bilzin Sumberg firmly at the top end of the market.
The Lawyers: **William Townsend** (see p.552) practices exclusively in state and local tax. He advises large corporate clients from all over the USA on the tax implications of doing business in Florida. "*One heck of a lawyer,*" according to his peers, Townsend is also well known for managing the firm's relationships with its major tax clients. One such client declared, "*He has the most complete understanding of Florida tax – and he has connections everywhere.*" Fellow attorneys "*think the world of*" **Samuel Ullman** (see p.552), who is widely perceived to be "*the dean.*" "*Technically knowledgeable*" in the fields of federal and state and local work, he is enthusiastically described as "*one of the leaders in the profession.*" He practices as a transactional tax lawyer, combining business structuring and tax planning with a smaller amount of controversy and corporate support. In the words of one client, "*Sam is the only tax lawyer I use, and there's a reason for that – he's absolutely brilliant.*" **Rex Ware** (see p.552), the third lateral hire from Steel Hector & Davis, practices in the Florida state arena. Best known as a litigator, he has a background in the Florida Department of Revenue.

Dean, Mead, Egerton, Bloodworth, Capouano & Bozarth PA
The Firm: This medium-sized firm with three offices in the state enjoys a peerless reputation for its tax practice. With 16 attorneys practicing exclusively in this area, the group is able to offer the entire spectrum of representation from tax planning to litigation. The team serves both corporate and tax-exempt organizations.
The Lawyers: **Charles Egerton**, a popular attorney known as "*one of the characters of the tax bar,*" is highly regarded by interviewees for his work with partnerships and tax-exempt entities. Egerton's practice has recently swung heavily towards tax planning, with an emphasis on advising real estate investment and development clients.

Florida
Leading individuals (Tax)

Senior Statesman
BOGGS Jack *Fowler White*, Tampa
KARP Joel *Karp & Genauer*, Coral Gables
SIMMONS Sherwin *Buchanan Ingersoll*, Miami

[1] **GRAGG Lawrence** *White & Case*, Miami
HUDSON Robert *Baker & McKenzie*, Miami
LEDERMAN Alan *Broad and Cassel*, Miami
TOWNSEND William *Bilzin Sumberg*, Miami
ULLMAN Samuel *Bilzin Sumberg*, Tallahassee
WEBER Victoria *Hopping Green*, Tallahassee

[2] **AUGUST Jerald** *August Kulunas*, West Palm Beach
BARTON Bernard *Holland & Knight*, Tampa
EGERTON Charles *Dean Mead*, Orlando
GUTTER Marvin *Tescher Gutter*, Boca Raton
HOLCOMB Mark *Holland & Knight*, Tallahassee
MASER Joel *Greenberg Traurig*, Orlando
PANOFF Robert *Sole Practitioner*, Miami
RAATTAMA Henry *Akerman Senterfitt*, Miami
VICKERS Cass *Vickers Madsen*, Tallahassee
WEINSTEIN Andrew *Holland & Knight*, Miami

[3] **BOKOR Bruce** *Johnson Pope*, Clearwater
BRONSTEIN Joel *Bronstein Carlson*, St Petersburg
BURKE David *Carlton Fields*, Tampa
COMITER Richard *Comiter, Singer*, Palm Beach Gardens
DUFFY Don *Akerman Senterfitt*, Miami
ERVIN James *Holland & Knight*, Tallahassee
GINSBURG Dennis *Packman Neuwahl*, Coral Gables
GOLDMAN Robert *Vickers Madsen*, Tallahassee
HALE Russell *Akerman Senterfitt*, Orlando
HOROWITZ Mitchell *Fowler White*, Tampa
JOSEPHER Richard *Tescher Gutter*, Boca Raton
PIERCE Robert *Ausley & McMullen*, Tallahassee
ROSENBERG Michael *Packman*, Coral Gables
SAWYER Ed *White & Case*, Miami
TESCHER Donald *Tescher Gutter*, Boca Raton

[4] **DOLINER Nathaniel** *Carlton Fields*, Tampa
KIRKWOOD Peter *Barnett Bolt*, Tampa
PRESS Martin *Gunster Yoakley*, Fort Lauderdale
STIVER Charles *Greenberg Traurig*, Miami
WARE Rex *Bilzin Sumberg*, Miami
WARNER Jonathan *Sole Practitioner*, Miami
WINSTON Richard *Steel Hector*, Miami

Up-and-coming individuals
CORDERO Frank *Akerman Senterfitt*, Miami
KASNER Stewart *Karp & Genauer*, Coral Gables
SCHINDLER Ozzie *Baker & McKenzie*, Miami

Leading individuals
(Tax: Employee Benefits)
[1] **DIXON Sharon** *Stearns Weaver*, Miami
LAPIDUS Steve *Greenberg Traurig*, Miami

Individuals are listed alphabetically in each band.

Steel Hector & Davis LLP
See firm details p.575
The Firm: "*The Rolls-Royce of law firms*," said one client, "*the quality runs right through the team*." Other lawyers in the state also note the firm's robust reputation for both federal and state and local tax matters. Recent departures to Bilzin Sumberg have thinned the ranks slightly, but these are balanced by the promotion of highly regarded Richard Winston to partner.
The Lawyers: "*Brilliant man and brilliant tax strategist*" **Richard Winston** (see p.554) is a new entry to *Chambers'* tables following an abundance of highly positive client feedback. Of counsel to the group, he specializes in advising corporate clients on structuring cross-border transactions, including the $190 million acquisition by the Oxbow of a division of a publicly traded corporation. The target division had subsidiaries in 15 jurisdictions.

Tescher Gutter Chaves Josepher Rubin Ruffin & Forman PA
The Firm: This tax boutique remains popular with rivals, who commend the firm as "*very good indeed*" for estate planning, international and controversy work. The firm combines a respected controversy practice with Florida-based tax and estate planning activity. Typical clients are high net-worth individuals and closely held companies; the team is currently handling two of the largest probate estates in Florida.
The Lawyers: Peers had no hesitation in endorsing **Marvin Gutter** as "*a good, solid all-rounder*." His "*excellent technique in dealing with government and the IRS*" was singled out for praise. Interviewers were told that **Donald Tescher** "*should definitely be on the list*" as a well-respected estate planning specialist. **Richard Josepher** is a "*really bright*" attorney with a high profile in the state for partnership taxation.

White & Case LLP
See firm details p.1379
The Firm: This international powerhouse maintains a thriving tax practice out of its Miami office. The firm is undoubtedly best known for international work, but sources were quick to point out that, "*It also has a strong practice at state level, which is unusual for an international firm.*"
The Lawyers: "*Very bright attorney*" **Lawrence Gragg**'s (see p.541) forte is advising major real estate players on tax structuring. He recently represented a community development district on the issue of special assessment revenue tax-exempt bonds with an aggregate value of over $200 million, in order to finance one of the state's largest public utility districts. **Ed Sawyer** (see p.549) enjoys a broad corporate tax practice, encompassing the tax and non-tax aspects of joint ventures, limited partnerships, limited liability partnerships, limited liability companies, corporations, trusts and estates. One competitor described him as someone who "*really stands out from the rest*."
The Clients: Berkley Group; Codina Group; Crocker & Company; CRT Properties; Gulf Bay Group; Kelly Tractor; PhyAmerica Physician Group; Stiles and Westgate Resorts.

Band 3

August, Kulunas & Dawson, PA
The Firm: One of the state's best-known boutiques, this five-partner firm undertakes the full range of tax counseling and litigation but is particularly renowned for advising on the taxation of S corporations.
The Lawyers: Several interviewees held up **Jerald August** as "*one of the preeminent S corporation guys in the country*." He is also recognized in the state for his expertise in tax planning for closely held businesses.

Carlton Fields, P.A.
See firm details p.560
The Firm: "*One of the two top Tampa firms*," the firm handles a range of tax matters from its six Florida offices. A 12-strong group of attorneys undertakes international, federal and state and local work for corporate clients. Market observers note with approval, "*The team is really growing the practice.*"
The Lawyers: "*Leading state tax guy*" **David Burke** advises corporate clients on tax planning and controversy. While he is particularly well known for his input on major M&A deals, at least half of his time is spent representing clients before the tax authorities. In the past year he has advised on the federal, state and local tax elements of several major M&A deals in a variety of industries. **Nathaniel Doliner** is primarily a corporate lawyer, but is well respected in the market for his tax expertise. He is a popular choice for advising on complex M&A deal structures.
The Clients: Amalie Oil; Healthcare Parking Systems; Progress Telecom; Navistar and Key Safety Systems.

Fowler White Boggs Banker
The Firm: A substantial firm with nine offices within the state, the firm is seen to be growing in prominence in the tax arena. The Tampa office in particular is regarded "*among the leading firms in the city*" and is highly regarded for tax controversy work.
The Lawyers: Chairman of the firm **Jack Boggs** remains at the pinnacle of the Florida tax bar. His professional standing is undiminished among fellow tax attorneys, who recognize his long-standing experience in the field. Younger partner **Mitchell Horowitz** has already established an impressive reputation for controversy work. Many commentators pointed to his presence in Tampa as the basis of the office's good standing.

Hopping Green & Sams, PA

See firm details p.565

The Firm: While this Tallahassee firm is nationally renowned for environmental representation, the presence of Victoria Weber ensures that the firm is also consistently recommended for state and local tax.

The Lawyers: Interviewees had nothing but the highest praise for **Victoria Weber** (see p.553). "*She's right at the top,*" said clients, "*and has had very varied experience both with the legislature and in private practice.*" Peers also endorsed Weber as the leading light in the state and local arena. In addition to providing ongoing counsel to a raft of blue-chip clients, she is active in lobbying the state government on tax proposals put forward under the citizen initiative process.

The Clients: The firm offers tax advice to many Fortune 500 companies such as Disney, GM, Florida Power and Light and ExxonMobil.

Packman, Neuwahl & Rosenberg

The Firm: Endorsed by fellow professionals as "*superb for international asset protection,*" this "*terrific*" Miami boutique undertakes the full range of tax planning and controversy work for high net-worth individuals.

The Lawyers: Name partner **Michael Rosenberg** enjoys a distinguished reputation in the state for international estate planning and immigration advice. "*A first-class attorney who is committed to the profession,*" he is described by his contemporaries as "*absolutely honest and fair with his clients.*" **Dennis Ginsburg**'s practice complements Rosenberg's: he recently handled the structuring of a pre-immigration tax plan for a wealthy Latin American private client seeking to relocate to the USA. He also advises US-based clients on tax-efficient outbound investment. Fellow attorneys describe Ginsburg as "*a gentleman with whom you can collaborate without fear of one-upmanship,*" and were full of praise for his skill at explaining complex tax concepts to inexperienced clients: "*Like Michael, Dennis is great at dealing with clients who need a lot of hand-holding.*"

Vickers Madsen & Goldman

The Firm: "*A fine boutique that does nothing but state and local,*" this three-partner Tallahassee firm is well known in the Sunshine State as a significant niche player.

The Lawyers: **Cass Vickers** and **Robert Goldman** were praised by interviewees for their state and local expertise. Vickers is "*highly recommended*" for general state and local advice. Goldman's practice has a focus on the tax treatment of telecommunications, where he has "*more expertise than anyone else in the state.*"

Band 4

Ausley & McMullen

The Firm: Though compact, the firm's two-partner tax team has a solid reputation for state and local advice. Attorneys also advise on tax planning and structuring for limited partnerships, joint ventures and limited liability companies.

The Lawyers: "*One of the top guys for state and local,*" **Robert Pierce** is a former general counsel of the Florida Department of Revenue. His connections with the state government, combined with the firm's location in Tallahassee, contribute to an excellent reputation for lobbying at state level.

Barnett, Bolt, Kirkwood, Long & McBride

The Firm: "*An outstanding boutique,*" in the opinion of several rivals. While it is not exclusively a tax practice, eight attorneys out of the firm's 18 devote all their time to tax matters. Rivals single out the group's gift and estate tax work as particularly noteworthy.

The Lawyers: **Peter Kirkwood** undertakes both planning and controversy work. His client list includes both companies and high net-worth individuals. Kirkwood has lately been occupied with several large estate tax audits.

The Clients: The firm maintains a client roster of closely held private companies and high net-worth individuals.

Broad and Cassel

The Firm: This small department is dominated by the substantial reputation of its leading practitioner Alan Lederman. The practice accepts referrals at its eight Florida offices, and is particularly visible in the field of affordable housing tax credits.

The Lawyers: Peers agreed that "*exceedingly smart and technically excellent*" **Alan Lederman** is "*a tax lawyer's tax lawyer.*" He is universally admired by other attorneys for the depth of his knowledge: "*Call Alan with a difficult tax question and he'll recite you chapter and verse without pausing for breath.*" Particularly active in the real estate sector, Lederman is also well known for publishing regular articles in academic journals.

Bronstein, Carlson, Gleim & Smith, PA

The Firm: Five attorneys advise on taxation, general corporate law, estate planning and healthcare law. The boutique enjoys a loyal following among local high net worth individuals.

The Lawyers: **Joel Bronstein** was noted for his representation of some of Florida's most wealthy private clients on complicated tax arrangements. Competitors call him "*a leader in this area.*"

Comiter, Singer & Baseman LLP

The Firm: This Palm Beach Gardens boutique has eight attorneys dealing exclusively with the full spectrum of tax reputation. Interviewees noted the group's thoroughness and well-rounded expertise.

The Lawyers: **Richard Comiter** counsels small companies and private investors on deal structures, joint ventures and partnership agreements. He also maintains a niche in advising businesses on tax-efficient structuring of executive compensation packages. "*A diligent, thorough lawyer who works incredibly hard,*" Comiter was last year's chair of the Florida bar's tax section.

Gunster, Yoakley & Stewart, PA

The Firm: Gunster Yoakley is a substantial full-service firm with six offices in the state. A team of three attorneys handles both international and domestic taxation matters for companies, partnerships and private clients.

The Lawyers: **Martin Press** undertakes a varied workload, which includes estate planning, and inbound and outbound international advice for private clients in both the USA and the UK. He also retains a high profile in tax controversy matters.

Johnson, Pope, Bokor, Ruppel & Burns, PA

The Firm: This medium-sized commercial firm has offices in Clearwater and Tampa. Observers suggest that the firm's "*very fine*" tax group owes its prominence to the widespread reputation of name partner Bruce Bokor.

The Lawyers: "*They don't come any better than*" **Bruce Bokor**, who heads up the tax department. His focus is tax planning for business sales and purchases. Bokor also advises charitable organizations on tax planning and tax-efficient charitable giving.

Karp & Genauer PA

The Firm: This Miami boutique of four tax specialists boasts one of the state's most senior tax attorneys, Joel Karp, and is praised by rivals for taking on new talent.

The Lawyers: Senior partner **Joel Karp** has a reputation as a "*trusted senior statesman*" among fellow international tax practitioners. "*Sharp young lawyer*" **Stewart Kasner** has also made an impression on fellow international tax practitioners, who commend him for his "*thorough and cautious*" manner.

Other Notable Practitioners

Sherwin Simmons recently moved from Steel Hector & Davis LLP to Buchanan Ingersoll PC. One of the best known figures of the tax bar, he maintains a remarkable roster of professional and academic activities. Interviewees nominated sole practitioner **Jason Warner** as an impressive competitor with a "*practical approach to finding solutions.*" Many rivals named him as favorite choice of co-counsel on matters that require "*a

532   All quotes in the text are from interviews with clients and competitors.

CHAMBERS USA 2005

real expert." **Robert Panoff**, also a sole practitioner, is one of the best-known civil and criminal tax litigation attorneys in the state. Regularly mentioned as a leader in this area, Panoff is a popular choice among larger firms for referrals of cases with a criminal aspect. **Sharon Quinn Dixon**, a partner at Stearns Weaver Miller Weissler Alhadeff & Sitterson, PA in Miami, is thought to be "*extremely knowledgable*" in the employee benefits field. She advises corporate clients on the establishment and maintenance of ESOPs, 401(k) plans, and retirement, disability and medical plans, and also undertakes due diligence in connection with acquisitions.

Leaders in Florida

AARON, William
William Aaron, Miami
305 371 5800
Recommended in Litigation

ALDRICH, Marcy Levine
Akerman Senterfitt, Miami
305 374 5600
marcy.aldrich@akerman.com
Recommended in Insurance
Career: Marcy Levine Aldrich is a shareholder and focuses her practice on class actions, complex insurance litigation and securities litigation. In particular, she represents automobile, property and life insurance companies in the defense of major class action litigation and other complex litigation in both state and federal courts. Ms Aldrich also represents securities industry firms in class action cases, as well as disputes before the Nasdaq and New York Stock Exchanges. She is a Member of the American Bar Association and has written for the Defense Research Institute and American Bar Association publications on the subject of class action litigation.

ALEXANDER, Bruce
Boose Casey Ciklin Lubitz Martens McBane & O'Connell, West Palm Beach
561 832 5900
Recommended in Construction

ALHADEFF, Richard
Stearns Weaver Miller Weissler Alhadeff & Sitterson, P.A., Miami
305 789 3200
Recommended in Real Estate

ALLEY, John-Edward
Ford & Harrison LLP, Tampa
813 261 7801
jalley@fordharrison.com
Recommended in Employment
Practice Areas: Having practiced in traditional labor and employment law for more than 30 years, John-Edward Alley has represented employers in hundreds of union election cases, including the decertification of incumbent unions. He has negotiated union contracts and handled trials of representation cases and unfair labor practice charges. In addition, he has successfully represented employers in hundreds of discrimination charges and lawsuits, including employment class actions. He earned his undergraduate and law degrees (with honors) from the University of Florida and his LLM (Labor Law) from New York University.

ALVAREZ, Pedro A
White & Case LLP, Miami
305 995 5246
palvarez@whitecase.com
Recommended in Banking & Finance
Practice Areas: Mr Alvarez's practice involves a broad range of corporate and corporate finance matters with an emphasis on transactions related to Latin America. He regularly counsels private and public companies in all aspects of general corporate matters including mergers and acquisitions. His practice also involves the representation of issuers, underwriters and lenders in a wide variety of corporate finance transactions. Mr Alvarez has also participated extensively in the formation and restructuring of significant transnational joint ventures in the financial, telecommunications, mining and other sectors.
Prof. Memberships: Florida Bar Association.

ALVAREZ, Victor M
White & Case LLP, Miami
305 995 5223
valvarez@whitecase.com
Recommended in Banking & Finance
Practice Areas: Mr Alvarez is engaged primarily in the representation of financial institutions in corporate and structured finance transactions, particularly in Latin America. He represented Bell-South Corporation in connection with US$750 million of acquisition financing related to its Colombia wireless operations (Celumóvil S.A. and Cocelco S.A.), and has extensive experience in the representation of issuers, underwriters and other financial intermediaries in all aspects of international and Latin American capital markets transactions.
Prof. Memberships: American Bar Association; Florida Bar Association.

ALVAREZ-FARRÉ, Emilio
White & Case LLP, Miami
305 995 5219
ealvarez@whitecase.com
Recommended in Corporate/M&A
Practice Areas: Mr Alvarez-Farré concentrates in cross-border mergers and acquisitions, including privatizations, and international financial transactions. Most recently, he has represented Corporacion Durango S.A. de C.V., the largest paper company in Latin America, in numerous acquisitions, dispositions and financings. He has represented Banco Santander Central Hispano and Deutsche Bank in financings involving Latin American issuers and borrowers. He has also represented the governments of Argentina, Chile, Venezuela and Panama in numerous privatizations.
Prof. Memberships: The Florida Bar.

AMES, Stuart
Stearns Weaver Miller Weissler Alhadeff & Sitterson, PA, Miami
305 789 3200
Recommended in Corporate/M&A

ANDREWS, William
Coffman, Coleman, Andrews & Grogan, Jacksonville 904 389 5161
Recommended in Employment

ARNOLD, Richard
Kenny Nachwalter P.A., Miami
305 373 1000
Recommended in Antitrust

ARONSON, Daniel H
Greenberg Traurig LLP, Fort Lauderdale
954 768 8201
aronsond@gtlaw.com
Recommended in Corporate/M&A
Practice Areas: Corporate and securities, mergers and acquisitions.
Prof. Memberships: Florida Venture Forum - Florida Venture Capital Conference, Executive Committee (1998-present). Member, State of Florida, Capital Development Board and Capital Development Advisory Committee (appointed by governor) (1997-present) Member, Executive Advisory Board, Council for Entrepreneurship and Innovation (University of Florida, Warrington College of Business Administration).
Publications: Author, 'Raising Capital for the Emerging Business: A Primer for Entrepreneurs', Donnelley (4th Edition - 2001); author, 'Venture Capital Transactions: Current Themes, Key Objectives and Structural Attributes' (Federal Securities Institute, Glasser LegalWorks, Feb. 2001).

ASHBY, Kimberly
Akerman Senterfitt, Orlando
407 843 7860
kim.ashby@akerman.com
Recommended in Construction
Career: Kimberly Ashby, a shareholder Board Certified in appellate law, focuses her practice on commercial litigation, construction litigation, and appellate law. She was named one of the 'Top 5 Women in Construction Litigation in 1998' and a 'Top 40 under 40' by the Orlando Business Journal, and as an Appellate Specialist in Florida Trend's Legal Elite 2005. She is Chair of The Florida Bar Construction Certification Committee, Co-Chair of the ABA Construction Litigation Committee, and a member of The Florida Bar Appellate Court Rules Committee. She is General Counsel for Central Florida Builders Exchange.

AUGUST, Jerald
August, Kulunas & Dawson, PA, West Palm Beach 561 835 9600
Recommended in Tax

AUSLANDER, Charles
Greenberg Traurig LLP, Miami
305 579 0500
auslanderc@gtlaw.com
Recommended in Litigation
Practice Areas: Appellate law; litigation.
Career: 2002 Champions for Children, Chairman's Recognition Award, Children's Services Council; 2002 Child Professional of the Year Award, Department of Children and Families, State of Florida; Alliance for Human Services of Miami-Dade County, Recognition Award for commitment to Children, Youth and Families, November 2002; Kathleen Wright Award, October 21 2000, presented by Family Central, Inc.; 'Put Something Back, Child Advocacy' pro bono award, Dade County Bar Association, April 1994.

AVILA, Alcides
Holland & Knight LLP, Miami
305 374 8500
alcides.avila@hklaw.com
Recommended in Banking & Finance
Practice Areas: Partner in the firm's Business Law Section, focusing on international and domestic banking law and commercial transactions. A significant portion of his practice involves the representation of state and national banks, bank holding companies, Edge Act corporations, international bank agencies and representative offices. Specific areas of experience include counseling foreign banks, bank holding companies, and foreign investors on establishing banking operations in the United States; licensing, de novo charters, and regulatory compliance matters; complex bank holding company formations; bank acquisitions; and the general representation of banking clients before all state and federal regulatory agencies.

AWNER, Jonathan L
Akerman Senterfitt, Miami
305 374 5600
jonathan.awner@akerman.com
Recommended in Corporate/M&A
Career: Jonathan Awner is the Chair of the firm's Corporate Practice Group. He has broad experience in public and private securities transactions, mergers and acquisitions, private equity investments, and corporate governance issues. He has served as lead issuer's counsel in underwritten public equity and debt offerings that have raised over $4 billion, including several IPO transactions. He also has represented buyers, sellers, boards of directors and other stakeholders in over 300 mergers and acquisitions with an aggregate transaction value exceeding $10 billion. His clients include AutoNation Inc., Jacuzzi Brands Inc., Republic Services Inc., Spherion Corporation, and several private equity funds.

BAENA, Scott L
Bilzin Sumberg Baena Price & Axelrod LLP, Miami 305 350 2403
sbaena@bilzin.com
Recommended in Bankruptcy
Career: Chair of firm's Restructuring and Bankruptcy Department with a personal focus on bankruptcy, restructurings and commercial loan transactions. Active in the development of Florida's commercial laws, having co-sponsored the 1980 revisions to Article 9 of Florida's Uniform Commercial Code. Frequent lecturer and author on subjects within his specialty areas. Has counseled high-visibility clients in many major bankruptcy proceedings, nationally, as well as in Florida. Listed as one of America's Top 100 in the 2003 and 2004 editions of the 'K&A Restructuring Register' and in 'Best Lawyers in America' since 1988.

BARCLAY, James
Ruden McClosky SC, Tallahassee
850 412 2000
Recommended in Healthcare

BARFORD, George
Carlton Fields PA, Tampa
813 223 7000
Recommended in Employment

BARKETT, John
Shook, Hardy & Bacon LLP, Miami
305 358 5171
jbarkett@shb.com
Recommended in Environment
Practice Areas: Environmental law, commercial litigation, labor law and antitrust litigation. Over the years, has been a commercial litigator, independent investigator, environmental litigator, environmental counselor and, for the past several years, a peacemaker and problem solver, serving as an arbitrator, mediator, facilitator or allocator in a variety of substantive contexts.
Prof. Memberships: Admitted to practice in Florida and before the US Court

of Appeals for the Eleventh Circuit. Member of American Bar Association and The Florida Bar. serves on the CPR Institute for Dispute Resolution's 'Panel of Distinguished Neutrals.' Is a member of the Chartered Institute of Arbitrators and was a guest lecturer in the International Commercial Arbitration class at Yale Law School.
Career: Joined Shook, Hardy & Bacon, 2000 (as Partner).
Publications: Is the author of numerous publications and speeches.
Personal: JD, Yale University School of Law, 1975; BA, summa cum laude, University of Notre Dame, 1972.

BARTON, Bernard
Holland & Knight LLP, Tampa
813 227 8500
bernie.barton@hklaw.com
Recommended in Tax

Practice Areas: Partner in the Business Law Section, practices federal, state and local taxation, emphasizing tax planning relating to entity and business transaction structuring. Has substantial experience in administrative and litigated tax disputes. Primary client focus is the representation of entrepreneurs, but also represents public companies and regulated industries in tax related matters. Barton has supervised and handled financing related matters, including leveraged leases, sale/leasebacks, synthetic leases and tax aspects of tax-exempt financing. Substantive areas of his state tax experience include sales and use taxes, corporate income tax, documentary stamp tax, intangible tax, ad valorem tax and various excise tax.

BASILE, Michael
Stroock & Stroock & Lavan LLP, Miami
305 358 9900
Recommended in Banking & Finance

BASS, Hilarie
Greenberg Traurig LLP, Miami
305 579 0745
bassh@gtlaw.com
Recommended in Litigation
Practice Areas: Litigation.
Prof. Memberships: American Bar Association - American Bar Association Member, Commission on Women in the Profession (2002-), Chair, Admissions and Credentials Committee, House of Delegates (2002-),Member, House of Delegates (1988-95; 2000-), Member, Litigation Section Council (2002-). President, The Florida Bar Foundation Chair, Administration of Justice IOTA Grant Committee (1991-93). The Florida Bar Member, Rules of Civil Procedure Committee. Dade County Bar Association, Board of Directors. President, Young Lawyers Section, Dade County Bar Association. United Way of Dade County. Chair, Board of Directors (1997-99). Chair, Success by Six Program (1999-).

BATTISTA, Paul
Genovese Joblove & Battista, P.A., Miami 305 349 2300
Recommended in Bankruptcy

BAXA Jr, Edmund T
Foley & Lardner, West Palm Beach
407 244 3268
ebaxa@foley.com
Recommended in Construction
Career: Ed Baxa is a member of Foley & Lardner's Management Committee and is the Managing Partner of the firm's Orlando and West Palm Beach offices. He is a member of the Litigation Department and the Construction Practice Group. Mr Baxa maintains a complex commercial litigation practice focusing on construction law. This specialty includes representation of owners, general contractors, design professionals, subcontractors, and suppliers in contract drafting and negotiation, bid protests, workouts, claims litigation, and arbitration proceedings. Mr Baxa is a graduate of the University of Virginia (BA, 1975) and its School of Law (JD, 1978).

BECERRA, Jacqueline
Greenberg Traurig LLP, Miami
305 579 0534
becerraj@gtlaw.com
Recommended in Litigation
Practice Areas: Litigation.
Prof. Memberships: Second Vice President, Federal Bar Association, South Florida Chapter Member, Big Brothers and Big Sisters of Miami-Dade County.
Career: Federal Bar Association's Young Federal Lawyers Award, 2000. Director's Award for Superior Performance, Executive Office for the United States Attorneys, 2001 Tim Evans Memorial Award for Outstanding Performance as an Assistant United States Attorney, 2001.
Personal: JD, Yale Law School, 1994. BA, cum laude, University of Miami, 1991.

BELL, Rodney H
Holland & Knight LLP, Miami
305 374 8500
rodney.bell@hklaw.com
Recommended in Corporate/M&A
Practice Areas: Partner in the Business Law Section, practicing in the areas of securities, mergers and acquisitions, venture capital and corporate governance. He regularly represents public and private companies in financing and acquisition transactions. Bell assists pharmaceutical, software and other technology companies with licensing, development, product acquisition and other arrangements. In addition, he advises public companies, boards of directors and their audit committees on disclosure and compliance matters arising out of Securities and Exchange Commission rules. Bell is a frequent speaker and writer on topics involving securities regulations, corporate governance and venture capital.

BERANEK, John
Ausley & McMullen, Tallahassee
850 224 9115
Recommended in Litigation

BERCOW, Jeffrey
Bercow & Radell PA, Miami
305 374 5300
jbercow@brzoninglaw.com
Recommended in Real Estate
Practice Areas: Has represented developers, landowners, institutional clients, lenders and other property owners and purchasers for over 20 years. His practice covers all aspects of local, state and federal real estate permitting and licensing, including zoning approvals, amendments of local government comprehensive plans, developments of regional impacts (DRIs), due diligence reviews, growth management, concurrency and environmental matters.
Prof. Memberships: Member of the Environmental Law and Land Use Section of the Florida Bar; served on the Regulation of Land Use Committee of the American Bar Association's Section on Real Property, Probate and Trust Law; served as the reporter for the Eleventh Circuit for the Committee's national newsletter on land use law; Vice-Chairman of the Board of Directors of the Downtown Development Authority, where he serves on the DDA's Executive Committee and presently chairs its Downtown Development of Regional Impact Committee; and former Chairman of the Expressway Authority Committee of the Greater Miami Chamber of Commerce's Transportation Group. An active member of the Builders Association of South Florida, during 2004 Mr Bercow served as the Association's representative on Miami-Dade County's Working Group on Public Schools Overcrowding Relief. Chaired the Metropolitan Dade County Transportation, Infrastructure and Concurrency Task Force from 1991-93, advising the Board of County Commissioners on transportation, mass transit, and other infrastructure matters. Member of the Miami Beach Zoning Board of Adjustment from 1992-97, and is a Board Member and Secretary of the Downtown Miami Community Development Corporation. In 1998 and 1999, he served as a member of the State of Florida's Transportation and Land Use Study Committee, created by the 1998 Legislature, as an appointee of the Secretary of the Department of Community Affairs.
Career: Shareholder of Bercow & Radell, PA He was previously a Partner and practiced land use and zoning law with the Miami office of Stroock & Stroock & Lavan and prior to that, with Steel Hector & Davis. He has practiced land use and zoning law for over 20 years, and also has practiced in the fields of real estate law and litigation.

Publications: Author: 'The Need for a Development Plan Under Chapter 380,' The Florida Bar Journal, (June, 1985); 'Modifying Approved Developments of Regional Impact,' The Florida Bar Journal (October, 1987).
Personal: Admitted to Bar, 1979, Florida. BA (cum laude), Yale University, 1975; JD (cum laude), Boston College, 1978.

BERLIN, Howard
Kluger, Peretz, Kaplan & Berlin P.L., Miami 305 379 9000
hberlin@kpkb.com
Recommended in Bankruptcy
Practice Areas: Co-Chair of the Bankruptcy and Creditors' Rights Group. Has more than 20 years experience representing corporate debtors, secured lenders, creditors' committees and individual creditors in federal, bankruptcy and state court insolvency proceedings, as well as out of court workouts, debt restructuring negotiations and business reorganization proceedings. Has successfully reorganized a variety of business enterprises and serves as the Trustee for Piper Aircraft Corporation Irrevocable Trust, a large, lengthy and complex trusteeship which has generated payment of 100% of eligble claims.
Prof. Memberships: Member of the American Bar Association, Dade County Bar Association, previously served as Chairman of the Florida Bar Business Law Section as well as the Bankruptcy UCC Committee. Completed the American Arbitration Association's 40-hour Circuit Court Mediation Training Program.
Career: Admitted to the Florida Bar (1979), the US District Court, Southern and Middle Districts of Florida (1979), and to the US Court of Appeals, Eleventh Circuit (1981). A founder and managing member of Kluger, Peretz, Kaplan & Berlin PL Served as an adjunct faculty member of the Nova University Banking Institute, the Freidt School of Business and Entrepreneurship.
Publications: Co-author of the 1987 revisions to Chapter 727 of the Florida Statutes' Assignments for the Benefit of Creditors.
Personal: Earned a JD from the University of Miami School of Law (1979) and a BA from George Washington University in Washington DC (1976). Served as Mayor of the City of Bal Harbour, Florida and currently serves as City Councilman.

BEVERIDGE, Cathy
Fowler White Boggs Banker, Tampa 813 228 7411
Recommended in Employment

BILZIN, Brian L
Bilzin Sumberg Baena Price & Axelrod LLP, Miami 305 350 2363
bbilzin@bilzin.com
Recommended in Real Estate
Career: Founding Partner of firm and

serves as counsel to several of South Floridas foremost public and private companies. Leads the practice in its commitment to provide able and expert representation in a broad spectrum of legal areas including the full range of complex commercial real estate and corporate transactions. His own practice includes all major real estate matters, from sales, purchases, and leases to financing, workouts, and reorganizations. In the area of general corporate law, handles mergers and acquisitions, joint ventures, and lending matters, including structured financings. Director of LNR Property Corporation (NYSE:LNR).

BLACK, Roy
Black, Srebnick, Kornspan & Stumpf PA, Miami 305 371 6421
Recommended in Litigation

BLAIN, Russell
Stichter, Riedel, Blain & Prosser PA, Tampa 813 229 0144
Recommended in Bankruptcy

BLECHMAN, Bill
Kenny Nachwalter P.A., Miami 305 373 1000
Recommended in Antitrust

BLOCK, David
Jackson Lewis, Miami 305 577 7600
Recommended in Employment

BLOODWORTH, Darryl
Dean, Mead, Egerton, Bloodworth, Capouano & Bozarth PA, Orlando 407 841 1200
Recommended in Litigation

BLOOM, Mark D
Greenberg Traurig LLP, Miami 305 579 0537
bloomm@gtlaw.com
Recommended in Bankruptcy
Practice Areas: Reorganization, Bankruptcy and Restructuring Practice. Retail Industry Group.
Prof. Memberships: Past President, Bankruptcy Bar Association of the Southern District of Florida. Section of Litigation Leadership, American Bar Association. United Way of Miami-Dade County. Past Director, Zoological Society of Florida. Founding Chair and Master of Ceremonies, Leukemia Society of America Annual Barristers' Bash Cystic Fibrosis Foundation.
Publications: Contributing Author, Norton Bankruptcy Law Treatise. Co-author, 'Businesses Should Brace for Change,' Miami Daily Business Review, August 2001. Co-author, 'Saybrook Manufacturing: The Death of Cross Collateralization and the Mootness Doctrine,' Norton Bankruptcy Law Adviser, September 1992.

BOGGS, Jack
Fowler White Boggs Banker, Tampa 813 228 7411
Recommended in Tax

BOKOR, Bruce
Johnson, Pope, Bokor, Ruppel & Burns, PA, Clearwater 727 461 1818
Recommended in Tax

BONIFAY, Cecelia
Akerman Senterfitt, Orlando 407 843 7860
cecelia.bonifay@akerman.com
Recommended in Real Estate
Career: Cecelia Bonifay is a shareholder focusing her practice on land use, zoning, environmental permitting, real property and administrative law. She has held positions with the Tallahassee Department of Community Affairs as assistant to the secretary and as the agency's lobbyist; and the Department of Administration, as liaison to the state's eleven regional planning councils. She has represented the City of Mount Dora, the Lake County School Board and large Central Florida land owners and developers. She is featured as one of the 'Top 5 Rainmakers in the State' by a local publication and is listed in Florida Trend's Legal Elite.

BOZARTH, Stephen
Dean, Mead, Egerton, Bloodworth, Capouano & Bozarth PA, Orlando 407 841 1200
Recommended in Real Estate

BRAMNICK, James
Akerman Senterfitt, Miami 305 374 5600
james.bramnick@akerman.com
Recommended in Employment
Career: James Bramnick is a shareholder and Board Certified by The Florida Bar in labor and employment law. He has 30 years of experience in exclusively representing employers in labor and employment law matters including labor relations, human resources advice, and employment litigation. Mr Bramnick represents clients from various industries including automotive, banking and financial institutions, public utilities, healthcare, and leisure and hospitality. He is a former Chairman of the Labor and Employment Law Section of The Florida Bar.

BRANDT, Peter
Ferencik, Libanoff, Brandt, Bustamante & Williams, Fort Lauderdale 305 949 8003
Recommended in Construction

BRICKLEMYER, Keith
Bricklemyer Smolker & Bolves PA, Miami 813 223 3888
Recommended in Real Estate

BRINDELL, James
Gunster, Yoakley & Stewart PA, West Palm Beach 561 655 1980
Recommended in Real Estate

BRONIS, Stephen
Zuckerman Spaeder LLP, Miami 305 358 5000
Recommended in Litigation

BRONSTEIN, Joel
Bronstein, Carlson, Gleim & Smith, PA, St Petersburg 727 898 6688
Recommended in Tax

BROWN, Bowman
Shutts & Bowen LLP, Miami 305 379 9107
bbrown@shutts-law.com
Recommended in Banking & Finance
Practice Areas: Chairman Executive Committee, Financial Services Industry Practice Group.
Prof. Memberships: Florida, New York, District of Columbia.
Career: Member of Executive Committee and Chairman of Regulatory and Legislative Affairs Committee of Florida International Bankers Association; formerly University of Miami Adjunct Professor of Banking Law, Chairman of Florida Bar Banking Law and Credit Regulation Committee, Trustee of Pan American Development Foundation.
Publications: Editor - 'International Banking Centres' published by Euromoney, London, 1982; 'Private Banking and the Law' published by LatinFinance, 1992; Member of Editorial Advisory Board of Banking and Financial Services Policy Report.
Personal: MBA, JD Cornell University.

BROWN, Christopher
Shook, Hardy & Bacon LLP, Miami 305 960 6951
cdbrown@shb.com
Recommended in Litigation
Practice Areas: Tort, aviation, employment and commercial litigation. Is a former Adjunct Professor of international law at Florida International University and speaks French, Russian and Spanish. Has tried numerous cases in both state and federal courts and has argued before the Supreme Court of Florida.
Prof. Memberships: Admitted to practice in Florida. Member of The Florida Bar, American Bar Association and Dade League of Prosecutors.
Personal: JD, University of Miami School of Law, 1994; MALD, Fletcher School of Law and Diplomacy, 1995; Diplôme d'Etudes Supérieures, University of Geneva, 1994; BA, Dartmouth College (Russian Language), 1986.

BROWN, Daniel
Carlton Fields, Tallahassee 850 224 1585
Recommended in Insurance

BROWN, Daryl
Brown Clark DeMay & Froman PA, Sarasota 941 957 3800
Recommended in Construction

BROWN, Frank
Zinober & McCrea, P.A., Tampa 813 224 9004
Recommended in Employment

BROWN, James
Ford & Harrison LLP, Orlando
407 418 4342
jbrown@fordharrison.com
Recommended in Employment
Practice Areas: Jim Brown concentrates his practice on labor and employment law, representing employers before the National Labor Relations Board and the State of Florida Public Employees Relations Commission, and the Department of Labor. He also defends employers in federal and state courts in civil rights litigation involving race, sex, national origin, discrimination, sexual harassment, disability and age discrimination. Jim earned his JD from the University of North Carolina at Chapel Hill where he was on the Holderness Moot Court.

BROWN, Ted
Akerman Senterfitt, Orlando
407 843 7860
ted.brown@akerman.com
Recommended in Real Estate
Career: Ted Brown is a shareholder representing developers and owners active in land acquisition and development. He has been involved in the acquisition of over one billion dollars worth of real estate and has extensive experience in land use and development activities with special emphasis in wetlands and habitat conservation planning in the context of land development. He is a full Member of the Urban land Institute and was a gubernatorial appointee to the Private Property Rights Study Commission II. Prior to joining the firm he served as VP/General Counsel to Arvida Company.

BROWN II, C David
Broad and Cassel, Orlando
407 839 4200
Recommended in Real Estate

BRUMBAUGH, John M
Richman Greer Weil Brumbaugh Mirabito & Christensen, Miami
305 373 4015
jmb@richmangreer.com
Recommended in Litigation
Practice Areas: Federal and state civil litigation matters, including commercial and complex litigation, officer and director representation, employment law litigation and ADR/mediation/arbitration.
Prof. Memberships: A Fellow of The American College of Trial Lawyers, the International Society of Barristers, and the American Bar Foundation, Mr Brumbaugh is admitted to The Florida Bar, the Bars of The Middle and Southern Districts of Florida, the Circuit Courts of Appeal for Fifth and Eleventh Circuits and the US Supreme Court.
Career: Law Clerk to US District Judge C Clyde Atkins 1970-72; Shareholder since 1976; Managing Shareholder since 1990; Board Certified Civil Trial Lawyer (Fla. Bar); Former Chair of the Florida

Board of Legal Specialization and Education; Former Chair of the ABA Standing Committee on Specialization.
Publications: Certification from a National Perspective 'Florida Bar Journal' April 2003.
Personal: Wabash College (BA 1967); University of Florida (JD 1970).

BUDWICK, Michael
Meland Russin Hellinger & Budwick, Miami 305 358 6363
Recommended in Bankruptcy

BURGESS, Rick
Gunster, Yoakley & Stewart, P.A., Fort Lauderdale 954 462 2000
Recommended in Environment

BURKE, David
Carlton Fields PA, Tampa
813 223 7000
Recommended in Tax

BURRUEZO, Carlos
Fisher & Phillips LLP, Orlando
407 541 0888
cburruezo@laborlawyers.com
Recommended in Employment
Practice Areas: Carlos Burruezo is Managing Partner of the Orlando office of the national law firm of Fisher & Phillips LLP, practicing exclusively in labor and employment law representing management. An experienced trial lawyer, his practice includes proceedings before federal and state administrative agencies and federal and state trial and appellate courts. Carlos also conducts management and other preventive training on workplace issues. He is the Chairman of the firm's Hispanic Business Practice Group, which provides Spanish-language labor and litigation support services to clients with Spanish-speaking employees. He received his JD from Cornell Law School in New York in 1989.

BUSEY, Stephen D
Smith Hulsey & Busey, Jacksonville
904 359 7777
busey@smithhulsey.com
Recommended in Bankruptcy
Practice Areas: Complex commercial litigation and insolvencies.
Prof. Memberships: Chair; Business Law Section, The Florida Bar (1998-99); President, Jacksonville Bar Association (1981-82); Chair, Local Rules Advisory Committee, United States District Court, Middle District of Florida (1993-95); Chair, The Florida Bar's Special Study Commission on the Rules of Professional Conduct; Chair, Judicial Nominating Commission for Florida's Fourth Judicial Circuit and Master of the Bench, Chester Bedell, Inn of Court.
Personal: Born, Chicago, Illinois, October 29, 1944; Stetson University, BBA 1966; Stetson University, JD 1969.

CACCIABEVE, Charles
Carlton Fields, Orlando
407 849 0300
Recommended in Construction

CACCIATORE, Ronald
Ronald K Cacciatore PA, Tampa
813 223 4831
Recommended in Litigation

CANNON, Kinder
Holland & Knight LLP, Jacksonville
904 353 2000
kinder.cannon@hklaw.com
Recommended in Corporate/M&A
Practice Areas: Partner in the firm's Jacksonville office, serves as Holland & Knight's general counsel. He is a business lawyer and has concentrated his practice in the areas of corporate finance, securities, mergers and acquisitions, venture capital, and franchising law, including corporate finance services to technology start-up and emerging companies. He has extensive experience in venture capital financings, corporate credit facilities, leveraged buy-outs, joint ventures and other capital transactions. He has represented a broad range of businesses in public and private offerings of equity and debt securities, in business acquisitions and in the development, marketing and expansion of franchise programs.

CARDWELL, J Thomas
Akerman Senterfitt, Orlando
407 843 7860
tom.cardwell@akerman.com
Recommended in Banking & Finance
Career: J Thomas Cardwell is a Fellow of the American College of Trial Lawyers. He has extensive experience representing clients in litigation, administrative, and regulatory matters. Mr Cardwell has served as General Counsel for The Florida Bankers Association since 1982. He is currently Chairman and CEO of the firm.

CAREY, Michael
Carey, O'Malley, Whitaker & Manson PA, Tampa 813 250 0577
Recommended in Construction

CARTER, Francis
Ferrell Schultz Carter & Fertel PA, Miami 305 371 8585
Recommended in Bankruptcy

CASEY, Michael
Epstein Becker & Green PC, Miami
305 373 4088
Recommended in Employment

CAULKINS, Charles
Fisher & Phillips LLP, Fort Lauderdale
954 525 4800
ccaulkins@laborlawyers.com
Recommended in Employment
Practice Areas: Since 1977, Charles Caulkins has represented employers nationally in labor and employment law matters. This includes advising employers on the development and implementation of preventive labor relations programs to avoid charges and lawsuits, protection of trade secrets, and resolution of disputes. He regularly counsels employers during union representation

elections, decertifications, corporate campaigns, collective bargaining negotiations, strikes, and lockouts. He handles employment related litigation and arbitrations before state and federal courts and administrative agencies involving claims of discrimination, wrongful discharge, contract breach, OSHA and other statutory claims. Mr Caulkins is currently President of the Academy of Florida Management Attorneys.

CHARBONNEAU, Robert
Kluger, Peretz, Kaplan & Berlin P.L., Miami 305 379 9000
rcharbonneau@kpkb.com
Recommended in Bankruptcy
Practice Areas: Co-Chair of the Bankruptcy and Creditors' Group. Represents corporate debtors, secured lenders, creditors' committees, panel bankruptcy trustees, and individual creditors in Federal Court, Bankruptcy Court, and state court insolvency proceedings. Handles out-of-court workouts and debt restructuring negotiations.
Prof. Memberships: President of the Bankruptcy Bar Association of the Southern District of Florida; member of the Dade County Bar Association; member and former Chair of the Commerical Law Section of the Broward County Bar Association; Vice-Chair of the Florida Bar Grievance Committee.
Career: Admitted to the Florida Bar and the US District Court, Southern District of Florida in 1992. Admitted to the US District Court, Middle District of Florida and the United States Court of Appeals, Eleventh Circuit. Board certified in business bankruptcy by the American Board of Certification.
Personal: JD, Boston College, Boston, Massachusetts; BA University of Florida, Gainsville, Florida. Recognized by peers as one of the 'Best of the Bar' in the area of Bankruptcy and Creditors' Rights by the South Florida Business Journal in 2004. Honored by the Florida legal community for the past three years having been selected as one of Florida's 'Legal Elite' in a survey conducted by 'Florida Trend magazine.'

CHAYKIN, Steven
Zuckerman Spaeder LLP, Miami
305 358 5000
Recommended in Litigation

COGLIANESE, Matthew
Bilzin Sumberg Baena Price & Axelrod LLP, Miami 305 350 2404
mcoglianese@bilzin.com
Recommended in Environment
Career: Practices in the area of litigation and environmental law, emphasizing toxic torts, construction defect and mold litigation, CERCLA, RCRA, brownfields redevelopment, and state and local environmental matters. Practice also includes environmental and corporate counseling, permitting and corporate due diligence. Has authored articles and presented numerous courses relating to envi-

ronmental law. Previously served as Assistant Regional Counsel with the United States EPA in Atlanta, Georgia, where he handled enforcement of federal water and air pollution laws. Also served as senior attorney with a major petroleum company based in Los Angeles.

COHEN, Jules
Akerman Senterfitt, Orlando
407 843 7860
jules.cohen@akeman.com
Recommended in Bankruptcy
Career: Jules Cohen is a shareholder with extensive experience in bankruptcy, representing secured creditors, landlords, lessors and buyers of businesses from bankruptcies and defending preference suits. He is certified in business bankruptcy law by the American Board of Bankruptcy Certification. He is past Chair of the Business Law Section and Bankruptcy Committee of The Florida Bar, Board Member Emeritus, Southeastern Bankruptcy Law Institute and Fellow of the American College of Bankruptcy. He is a frequent author and lecturer on bankruptcy for The Florida Bar, the National Business Institute, Attorneys Title Insurance Fund and many other organizations.

COLE, Terry
Oertel, Fernandez, Cole & Bryant, P.A., Tallahassee 850 521 0700
Recommended in Environment

COLEMAN, Ira
McDermott Will & Emery, Miami
305 347 6556
icoleman@mwe.com
Recommended in Healthcare
Practice Areas: Partner-in-charge of Miami office and Head of Miami Health Practice. Concentrates on significant healthcare M&As, and private equity deals. Has also served as counsel in connection with the development and operation of numerous corporate governance programs for clients.
Prof. Memberships: Serves as Chairman for Florida Bar Health Law Section Educational Division, Florida Hospital Associations program on Physician Integration. Served as Vice-Chairman of American Health Lawyers Association Merger and Acquisition Institute. Elected to Florida Bar Health Law Section Executive Council. Serves on Board of the South Florida Hospital & Healthcare Association. Serves on the Board of Nova Southeastern University Law School. Member of Florida Bar, American Bar Association, American Health Lawyers Association, Florida Academy of Healthcare Attorneys and American College of Healthcare Executives.
Personal: Earned JD in 1986 from Nova Southeastern University, Law School, and LLM (tax)in 1987 from University of Miami School of Law. Earned BA in 1983 from State University of New York-Albany. Board-certified in health law by the Florida Bar.

COLEMAN, Patrick
Coffman, Coleman, Andrews & Grogan, Jacksonville
904 389 5161
Recommended in Employment

COLSON, Dean
Colson Hicks Eidson, Coral Gables
305 476 7400
dean@colson.com
Recommended in Litigation
Practice Areas: Personal injury; medical malpractice; aviation; product liability; class actions.
Career: Mr Colson graduated magna cum laude from the University of Miami School of Law in 1977; he served as a law clerk for Justice William H Rehnquist; he joined Colson Hicks Eidson in 1981. Mr Colson's practice has varied from the handling of many multi-million dollar malpractice, aviation and product liability cases for injured plaintiffs to being trial counsel for the class of investors defrauded in the Premium Sales case which settled after the start of trial for $170,000,000.

COLTON, Roberta
Trenam, Kemker, Scharf, Barkin, Frye, O'Neill & Mullis PA, Tampa
813 223 7474
Recommended in Bankruptcy

COMITER, Richard
Comiter, Singer & Baseman, LLP, Palm Beach Gardens 561 626 4742
Recommended in Tax

COMMANDER III, Charles E
Foley & Lardner, Jacksonville
904 359 8702
ccommander@foley.com
Recommended in Real Estate
Career: Charles E Commander III is a Partner in the Jacksonville office of Foley & Lardner. He is a member of the firm's Business Law Department, its Finance and Real Estate Practice Groups, and Golf and Resort Industry Team. He advises and counsels corporate, financial institution and real estate clients in all aspects of their business and is recognized for practice excellence in real estate law by a leading legal publication. Mr Commander received his law degree from the University of Florida (JD, 1965). He is a member of The Florida Bar and the Jacksonville and American Bar Associations.

CONNOR, Terence
Morgan, Lewis & Bockius LLP, Miami
305 415 3316
tconnor@morganlewis.com
Recommended in Employment
Practice Areas: Terence Connor is a Partner in the Labor and Employment Law Practice Group. Mr Connor focuses on federal and state employment and employment discrimination litigation, and state and federal employment law compliance counseling. He has extensive experience in several industries with specialties in the airline, transportation,

biotechnology and pharmaceutical industries. Before joining Morgan Lewis, Mr Connor was a trial attorney with the US Department of Justice and served as Labor Counsel to National Airlines in Florida.
Prof. Memberships: The National Conference for Community and Justice; Florida Bar; College of Labor and Employment Lawyers; Academy of Florida Management Attorneys.

COOPER, Marc
Colson Hicks Eidson, Coral Gables
305 476 7400
marc@colson.com
Recommended in Litigation
Practice Areas: Appellate.
Career: After graduating from Yale University, Mr Cooper attended the University of Miami School of Law as a Reid Scholar and graduated magna cum laude. Following graduation, he served as a law clerk for the Honorable David W Dyer, United States Court of Appeals, Fifth Circuit. For almost 25 years, Mr Cooper has handled appeals of all types in all the appellate courts of Florida, as well as in the Fifth Circuit, Eleventh Circuit and other federal circuits. Hundreds of appellate decisions, both reported and unreported, bear his name.

CORDERO, Frank
Akerman Senterfitt, Miami
305 374 5600
frank.cordero@akerman.com
Recommended in Tax
Career: Frank Cordero is a shareholder and focuses his practice in the area of tax law. He advises clients with respect to complex domestic and international tax planning issues, including issues relating to the structuring of domestic and international business operations, investments and transactions, public and private offerings of equity and debt securities, domestic and international mergers, acquisitions and reorganizations involving public and private companies, domestic and international partnerships and joint ventures, the formation and operation of limited liability companies and other business entities, and executive compensation. Mr Cordero is a Certified Public Accountant and is fluent in Spanish.

COUTROULIS, Chris
Carlton Fields PA, Tampa
813 223 7000
Recommended in Antitrust

COWAN, Kevin
Shutts & Bowen LLP, Miami
305 379 9110
kcowan@shutts-law.com
Recommended in Real Estate
Practice Areas: Co-Chairman of Miami Real Estate Department; involved in corporate and commercial real estate practice, including development, financing, sale and acquisition, foreclosure and work-outs, and leases;

real estate practice focuses on representing developers and institutions in purchase and sale of properties, financing, development, land use, work-outs, and negotiating leases; corporate practice focuses on individuals and medium-sized practices in corporate, partnership and joint venture arrangements.
Prof. Memberships: Florida.
Career: Began career with Paul, Hastings, Janofsky & Walker in California; joined Shutts & Bowen in 1983, elected Partner in 1987.
Personal: BA Ohio State University 1977; JD Emory Law School.

COX, Donald
Fowler White Boggs Banker, Tampa
813 228 7411
Recommended in Insurance

COXE, Henry
Bedell, Dittmar, DeVault, Pillans & Coxe, Jacksonville 904 353 0211
Recommended in Litigation

CRITCHLOW, Richard
Kenny Nachwalter P.A., Miami
305 373 1000
Recommended in Litigation

CULPEPPER, Bruce
Akerman Senterfitt, Tallahassee
850 224 9634
bruce.culpepper@akerman.com
Recommended in Insurance
Career: Bruce Culpepper is a shareholder and former Managing Partner of the firm's Tallahassee office. He has over 40 years of experience representing clients in civil litigation and appellate matters in state, federal and administrative forums. He focuses his practice in the areas of insurance, healthcare, complex commercial litigation and administrative law. Mr Culpepper is a former city commissioner of the City of Tallahassee, serves on The Florida Bar Foundation Board of Directors, and is a frequent lecturer on business litigation and procedure.

CUNNINGHAM, Malcolm
Cunningham Law Firm, West Palm Beach 561 833 6400
Recommended in Construction

CUNNINGHAM, Peter C
Hopping Green & Sams, P.A., Tallahassee 850 222 7500
peterc@hgslaw.com
Recommended in Environment
Practice Areas: Environmental law; emphasis on air quality, power plant licensing and energy policy.
Prof. Memberships: Admitted: Florida, US District Court for Northern Florida and Eleventh US Circuit Court of Appeals. Member National and Florida Small Business Compliance Advisory Panels.
Career: Has represented clients on air quality regulatory issues including legislation, rulemaking, permitting and enforcement for 25 years. Lead counsel

in successful licensing of more than 6,000 megawatts of new electric generating capacity. Represented Florida's electric utilities before Governor's Energy 2020 Study Commission.
Personal: Born March 22, 1952; BA Harvard College, 1975; JD University of Michigan Law School, 1979.

CURRIER, Maria
Hunton & Williams, Miami
305 810 2568
mcurrier@hunton.com
Recommended in Healthcare

Practice Areas: Maria Currier is a Florida Bar Board Certified healthcare law specialist. She has served as counsel to hospitals, nursing homes, home health agencies, HMOs, provider sponsored plans, physician groups, preferred provider organizations, physician-hospital organizations, physician management companies, employer self-insured plans and prepaid health plans. Her practice focuses on state and federal fraud and abuse laws, privacy, Medicare health plan regulation, physician self referral laws, and formation of complex integrated healthcare systems.

CURTIN, Lawrence
Holland & Knight LLP, Tallahassee
850 224 7000
larry.curtin@hklaw.com
Recommended in Environment

Practice Areas: Executive Partner, Tallahassee office. Partner in Public Policy and Regulation Practice Group in the Government Law Section, practicing administrative and governmental law, focusing on environmental matters. Regularly provides advice on permitting and enforcement matters involving federal, state, and local administrative agencies. Has substantial experience in administrative law, including adjudicatory hearings and rulemaking activities. Has extensive experience in permitting major industrial facilities in Florida, including siting of electrical power plants, transmission lines, and natural gas pipelines. He has represented clients before the Florida Legislature for more than 20 years, primarily involving environmental, land use, and administrative law matters.

DAVIDSON, Barry
Hunton & Williams, Miami
305 810 2539
bdavidson@hunton.com
Recommended in Antitrust, Litigation

Practice Areas: Mr Davidson's practice focuses in the area of civil litigation throughout the state of Florida, with an emphasis on complex and class action business litigation, intellectual property, antitrust and products litigation. He also represents airlines and hotel companies and does eminent domain work.

DAVIS, Alvin B
Steel Hector & Davis LLP, Miami
305 577 2835
adavis@steelhector.com
Recommended in Litigation

Practice Areas: Mr Davis is the firm's Managing Partner. He has extensive experience as lead counsel in complex, multidistrict litigation at trial and appellate levels involving securities laws, products liability, intellectual property and utility rate making. Argued successful appeal in reversal of a $146 billion judgment against the tobacco industry.
Prof. Memberships: Admitted to practice in Florida, District of Columbia, and New York. Member of the American Bar Association, the Dade County Bar Association, and the Bar Association of the District of Columbia.
Career: Joined Steel Hector & Davis LLP in 1976.
Personal: LLB Yale University, AB Syracuse University.

DAVIS, Gardner F
Foley & Lardner, Jacksonville
904 359 8726
gdavis@foley.com
Recommended in Corporate/M&A

Career: Gardner Davis is a Partner in Foley & Lardner's Jacksonville office, where he is a member of the Transactional and Securities, Finance, and Business Reorganizations Practice Groups. He is particularly knowledgeable in regard to buying, selling, and recapitalizing companies, restructuring financially distressed enterprises, and counseling officers and directors in corporate governance and control situations. Mr Davis frequently represents buyers and sellers in mergers and acquisition transactions, from management buy-outs to combinations of large public companies. He advises boards of directors and special committees on fiduciary duty issues in various contexts. Mr Davis received his JD degree from Duke University.

DAVIS, Gary Scott
McDermott Will & Emery, Miami
305 347 6520
gsdavis@mwe.com
Recommended in Healthcare

Practice Areas: Board Certified Health Law Attorney as recognized by The Florida Bar Board of Legal Specialization and Education. Concentrates on managed care, emerging health benefit plans, strategic acquisitions, divestitures, restructurings and reorganizations, joint ventures arrangements and related transactional, regulatory and reimbursement issues. Has lectured at more than 130 seminars sponsored by healthcare and legal trade, educational and professional organizations.
Prof. Memberships: Member, American Health Lawyers Association ('AHLA'), American Bar Association, Health Law Section; Florida Bar, Health

Law Section; and Florida Academy of Healthcare Attorneys. Past member AHLA Board of Directors (1994-2000), AHLA Executive Committee and Chairman Membership Committee (1995-99). Recipient of AHLA's prestigious David J Greenburg Service Award (2000) and the Healthcare Financial Management Association's Follmer Bronze Merit Award for Outstanding Service (1993).
Personal: Earned JD in 1982 from The National Law Center, George Washington University (Honors), and BA in 1979 from State University of New York at Binghamton (Honors, Phi Beta Kappa). Member, Board of Directors, Make-A-Wish Foundation of Southern Florida, Inc. [1993-2002; Chairman (1999-2000); Executive Committee (1994-2002)]. Chairman, Wish Friends of Southern Florida, an endowment supporting the Make A Wish Foundation.

DAVIS, Kirk S
Akerman Senterfitt, Tampa
813 223 7333
kirk.davis@akerman.com
Recommended in Healthcare

Career: Kirk Davis, a shareholder and Board Certified Health Law attorney, focuses his practice in the areas of healthcare and civil litigation. His practice includes representation of hospitals and other healthcare providers in general healthcare matters, primarily civil and administrative trial matters. He has extensive experience in the medical-legal aspects of the healthcare practice and in all aspects of medical staff matters from both the physician and hospital perspectives, including hospital based physician contracting. He is an inaugural member of The Florida Bar Health Law Certification Committee and on the Board of Directors of the Florida Academy of Healthcare Attorneys.

DE ARMAS, Luis
Shutts & Bowen LLP, Miami
305 379 9114
ldearmas@shutts-law.com
Recommended in Corporate/M&A

Practice Areas: Chairman of Corporate Transactions Practice Group; focus is banking, corporate and securities, real estate finance and transactions; structuring and negotiating mergers and acquisitions, including acquisitions of financial institutions, leveraged and international transactions; securities offerings and transactions, such as partnership offerings, public offerings and offshore offerings; represents foreign institutions in their US investments and operations.
Prof. Memberships: Florida.
Career: With Shutts & Bowen since 1977; Partner since 1983; served on the firm's Executive Committee from 1988-2000 and as Managing Partner from 1989-94.

Personal: JD Duke University 1977; BS Economics University of Pennsylvania Wharton School of Business; Spanish fluency.

DEE, David
Landers & Parsons, Tallahassee
850 681 0311
Recommended in Environment

DELEGAL, Mark
Pennington, Moore, Wilkinson, Bell & Dunbar, PA, Tallahassee
850 222 3533
Recommended in Insurance

DELEGAL, Susan
Holland & Knight LLP, Fort Lauderdale
954 525 1000
susan.delegal@hklaw.com
Recommended in Real Estate

Practice Areas: Partner in the firm's Real Estate Section, represents clients before agencies of local and state government, administrative agencies, and the federal and state courts. Delegal's practice focuses on zoning and land use approval and permitting, ad valorem tax work, litigation involving governmental entities, and telecommunications issues. Prior to joining Holland & Knight LLP, she served as the County Attorney for Broward County for five years, representing the Board of County Commissioners, County Administrator, and all other Departments, Divisions and Boards of County government in the legal matters affecting the County.

DEMEO, Ralph
Hopping Green & Sams, P.A., Tallahassee 850 222 7500
ralphd@hgslaw.com
Recommended in Environment

Practice Areas: Environmental and land use law; toxic torts litigation; construction defects litigation; general civil and administration law and litigation.
Prof. Memberships: The Florida Bar.
Career: BA, MA, English, Stetson University; JD, FSU; Former College English Professor; Professor of Legal Studies; over 20 years representing private individuals, corporations, and local governments.
Publications: Over 25 articles in publications such as Florida Bar Journal, FSU Journal of Land Use & Environmental Law; Stetson Law Review; the Florida Bar Treatise of Environmental & Land Use Law, and others.
Personal: Frequent lecturer on environmental, land use, and governmental law, and civil litigation.

DEMEZA, Willliam
Holland & Knight LLP, Tampa
813 227 8500
bill.demeza@hklaw.com
Recommended in Employment

Practice Areas: Partner in the firm's Litigation Section, a significant segment of his practice focuses on employee safety and health issues. Clients have included restaurants, manufacturers, financial institutions, department stores, hospitals, physicians' professional associations, employee leasing companies, government contractors, insurance companies, shipyards, and mining companies. DeMeza has served as employers' counsel in race, sex, sexual harassment, age, religion, national origin, and handicap (disability) employment discrimination charges filed with the United States Equal Employment Opportunity Commission, the Florida Commission on Human Relations, and local EEO agencies.

DEVAULT, John
Bedell, Dittmar, DeVault, Pillans & Coxe, Jacksonville 904 353 0211
Recommended in Litigation

DIAZ Jr, Victor
Podhurst Orseck, P.A., Miami
305 358 2800
Recommended in Litigation

DICKINSON, John
Constangy, Brooks & Smith, LLC, Jacksonville 904 356 8900
Recommended in Employment

DIXON, Sharon
Stearns Weaver Miller Weissler Alhadeff & Sitterson, P.A., Miami
305 789 3200
Recommended in Tax

DOGALI, Andy
Forizs and Dogali PL, Tampa
813 289 0700
Recommended in Construction

DOLINER, Nathaniel
Carlton Fields PA, Tampa
813 223 7000
Recommended in Corporate/M&A, Tax

DOUGHERTY, Lucia
Greenberg Traurig LLP, Miami
305 579 0603
doughertyl@gtlaw.com
Recommended in Real Estate
Practice Areas: Environmental and land use.
Prof. Memberships: Chairperson, Archbishop's Charities and Development Drive for Miami-Dade County. Chairperson, Miami Beach Chamber of Commerce Vice-Chairperson, Eminent Domain Committee of The Florida Bar, Adjunct Professor of Law, Nova Southeastern University School of Law. Member, International Women's Forum, Member, Greater Miami and Beaches Hotel Association, Legal Counsel, Greater Miami Convention and Visitors Bureau, City Commission appointment to the Model City Trust.
Publications: Co-authored the Spring 1995 Stetson Law Review Article entitled 'Rights, Remedies and Ratiocination; Toward a Cohesive Approach to Appellate Review of Land Use Orders after Board of County Commissioners v. Snyder'.

DOWNS, Joe
Daniels, Kashtan, Downs, Robertson & Magathan, Miami 305 448 7988
Recommended in Construction

DUFFY, Don
Akerman Senterfitt, Miami
305 374 5600
don.duffy@akerman.com
Recommended in Tax
Career: Donald Duffy is a shareholder and focuses his practice in the area of tax law advising business entities and individuals with respect to transactions relating to international, corporate and partnership tax law. He also represents clients who have tax controversies with the IRS. He served as an attorney in the former Legislation and Regulations Division of the IRS Office of Chief Counsel drafting regulations on international and corporate tax matters and worked with the Treasury Department in the development and enactment of tax legislation. He also served as an Adjunct Professor of tax law at Georgetown University Law Center.

DURKIN, Denis
Baker & Hostetler LLP, Orlando
407 649 4000
Recommended in Construction

EATON, Joel
Podhurst Orseck, P.A., Miami
305 358 2800
Recommended in Litigation

EGERTON, Charles
Dean, Mead, Egerton, Bloodworth, Capouano & Bozarth PA, Orlando
407 841 1200
Recommended in Tax

EISENBERG, Susan
Akerman Senterfitt, Miami
305 374 5600
susan.eisenberg@akerman.com
Recommended in Employment
Career: Susan Eisenberg is a shareholder and Board Certified by The Florida Bar in labor and employment law. She has extensive experience representing local, national and international companies in civil actions involving employment discrimination, labor relations, and civil rights issues. She has extensive litigation experience, including jury trials and appeals in state and federal courts. She is a certified mediator and an arbitrator with the American Arbitration Association. She is the associate editor of the book The Fair Labor Standards Act, and a frequent lecturer for The Florida Bar and American Bar Association on employment issues.

EMMANUEL, John
Fowler White Boggs Banker, Tampa
813 228 7411
Recommended in Bankruptcy

ENGLAND, Arthur J
Greenberg Traurig LLP, Miami
305 579 0605
englanda@gtlaw.com
Recommended in Litigation
Practice Areas: Appellate and litigation.
Publications: Co-author, 'Florida Appellate Practice Manual', 'Practical Guide to the Appellate Courts of Florida', and 'Florida Administrative Practice Manual'; Co-author of the often-referenced article 'Quantity Discounts in Appellate Justice', 60 Judicature 442 (1977); Author, seminal articles on the jurisdiction of the Florida Supreme Court; Author, 'Florida Corporate Income Tax Law' (1971), 'Deceptive and Unfair Trade Practices Act' (1973), and 'Florida Administrative Procedures Act' (1974).
Personal: University of Miami School of Law (LLM, 1972); University of Pennsylvania Law School (LLB, 1961); Wharton School of Finance and Commerce, University of Pennsylvania (BS, 1955).

EPSTEIN, Gary
Greenberg Traurig LLP, Miami
305 579 0894
epsteing@gtlaw.com
Recommended in Corporate/M&A
Practice Areas: Corporate and securities; mergers and acquisitions; public offerings; corporate planning; financing transactions.
Prof. Memberships: Chairman of the Board, American Israel Chamber of Commerce, Florida; President, Miami Beach Jewish Community Center.
Career: Listed, 2004 Legal Elite, Florida Trend Magazine, listing of Florida's top attorneys as selected by their peers; Listed as one of 'South Florida's Top Lawyers' by the South Florida Legal Guide, 2002; Listed in 'The Best Lawyers in America' each year since 1985.
Personal: Harvard University Law School (JD, 1980); New York University (MA, 1970); Yeshiva University (BA, 1969).

ERVIN, James M
Holland & Knight LLP, Tallahassee
850 224 7000
jim.ervin@hklaw.com
Recommended in Tax
Practice Areas: Partner in the Business Law Section, has a multi-forum state tax practice that covers the legislative, administrative and judicial areas. Handles assessment negotiations with auditors and the preparing, filing and resolving of protests against assessments. Through his longstanding relationships with the Department of Revenue, he assists clients in tax inquiries to facilitate tax planning and to resolve any questions concerning potential tax liability. His practice also involves a wide array of state taxes, particularly sales tax, corporate income tax, communications services tax, insurance premiums tax, gross

receipts tax, documentary stamp tax, intangibles tax, pollutants taxes, and severance tax.

FARMER, Guy
Holland & Knight LLP, Jacksonville
904 353 2000
guy.farmer@hklaw.com
Recommended in Employment
Practice Areas: Partner in the Labor and Employment Group, represents employers locally, regionally and nationally in the full range of employment-related issues. Has defended employers in more than 1,000 cases nationwide involving allegations of employment discrimination and other employment and labor-related matters. His litigation and appellate practice has included the defense of employers in cases involving individual claims, claims by federal and state governments and significant class actions. He also counsels and represents employers in connection with labor union issues, including resisting union organizing efforts, defending against unfair labor practice charges, appearing in labor arbitrations and negotiating collective bargaining agreements.

FELMAN, David
Hill, Ward & Henderson, PA, Tampa
813 221 3900
Recommended in Corporate/M&A

FERENCIK, Robert
Ferencik, Libanoff, Brandt, Bustamante & Williams, Fort Lauderdale
305 949 8003
Recommended in Construction

FILDES, Richard
Lowndes Drosdick Doster Kantor & Reed, PA, Orlando
407 843 4600
Recommended in Hotels and Resorts

FITZGERALD, Miranda
Lowndes Drosdick Doster Kantor & Reed, PA, Orlando
407 843 4600
Recommended in Real Estate

FLEMING, Joseph
Greenberg Traurig LLP, Miami
305 579 0517
flemingj@gtlaw.com
Recommended in Employment
Practice Areas: Labor and employment; litigation; environmental; land development; ADA, Accessibility, Building and Life Safety Codes; technology, media and telecommunications.
Prof. Memberships: American Law Institute American Bar Association (ALI-ABA); Member, Advisory Group on Labor Law for the Committee on Continuing Professional Education; Chair, ALI-ABA's Courses on 'The Law of the Workplace Environment and 'Airline and Railroad Labor and Employment Law'; Co-Chair, Historic Preservation on Historic Preservation Law program; Member, America Arbitration Association's Miami Employment Advi-

sory Council and the AAA's Arbitrators Panel.

Publications: Lecturer at seminars and author of articles and published chapters in books on labor, employment and environmental law.

FORNARIS, Carl A
Greenberg Traurig LLP, Miami
305 579 0626
fornarisc@gtlaw.com
Recommended in Banking & Finance
Practice Areas: National financial institutions; international; corporate and securities.
Prof. Memberships: Member, Planning Committee, 2004 Financial Markets Association Securities Compliance Seminar.
Publications: Lecture, 'The Law: Risk and Liability,' Offshore Alert's 3rd Annual Due Diligence and Asset Recovery Symposium, Coral Gables, Florida (2004); Lecture, 'New Threat of Russian Mob's Money Laundering,' ACAMS (2004); Lecture, 'Offshore Banking' session of 3rd Annual Bear Stearns Central American/Caribbean Conference, Key Biscayne, Florida (2003); Lecture, USA PATRIOT Act Update, before International Bank Operations Association (2003).
Personal: The Catholic University of America Columbus School of Law (JD, 1993); University of Miami (BS, 1990).

FROST II, John W
Frost Tamayo Sessums & Aranda PA, Bartow 863 533 0314
jfrost1985@aol.com
Recommended in Litigation
Practice Areas: Board Certified in Civil Trial Practice and Business Litigation by The Florida Bar. His practice deals with banking litigation, construction litigation, eminent domain, personal injury, medical malpractice, aviation, product liability and class actions. He also practices routinely before the District Courts of Appeal and the Supreme Court of Florida, representing both appellants and appellees.
Prof. Memberships: Past President of The Florida Bar; American Board of Trial Advocates; Academy of Florida Trial Lawyers; Association of Trial Lawyers of America; The College of Master Advocates and Barristers, Senior Counsel.
Career: Admitted to The Florida Bar (1969); Began his legal career with Holland & Knight law firm in 1969, becoming a Partner in 1974. Left Holland & Knight in 1981 to establish his present firm which will celebrate its 25th anniversary in 2006. Frost's practice has varied from his handling numerous multi-million dollar negligence, malpractice, aviation and product liability suits to his handling numerous multi-million dollar construction and commercial cases.
Personal: JD from Florida State University with high honors (1969); and BS in

Advertising, University of Florida (1964).

GALLION, Theresa M
Fisher & Phillips LLP, Tampa
813 769 7500
tgallion@laborlawyers.com
Recommended in Employment
Practice Areas: Theresa Gallion is the Managing Partner in the Tampa office of the national law firm of Fisher & Phillips LLP, practicing exclusively in labor and employment law representing management. She represents clients in a variety of industries and has extensive bench and jury trial experience in employment matters. She has special expertise in defending matters arising under Title VII of the Civil Rights Act of 1964, the Age Discrimination in Employment Act, the Americans with Disabilities Act, the Family and Medical Leave Act, and the Equal Pay Act. Theresa received her BA and JD from Louisiana State University.

GART, Brian
Greenberg Traurig LLP, Fort Lauderdale
954 768 8212
gartb@gtlaw.com
Recommended in Bankruptcy
Practice Areas: Reorganization, bankruptcy and restructuring.
Prof. Memberships: Executive Council of the Business Law Section, The Florida Bar, 1996-2002; Committee, Business Law Section, The Florida Bar, 1999-2002; Member, Business Bankruptcy Committee, American Bar Association Section of Business Law; Member, Bankruptcy Bar Association, Southern District of Florida.
Publications: Contributing author, 2001-02 Bankruptcy Law Update, Aspen Publishers; author 'Brace Yourself for the Surge of Health Maintenance Organization Failures', Florida Bar, March 1999; author 'Security Interests in Post-Petition Rents and Hotel Revenues' Florida Bar in 1996.

GARWOOD, Thomas
Ford & Harrison LLP, Orlando
407 418 2315
tgarwood@fordharrison.com
Recommended in Employment
Practice Areas: Tom Garwood concentrates his practice in the area of advising, counseling and representing management and business enterprises in all facets of labor and employment law. He is board certified as a specialist in labor and employment law by the Florida Bar and is admitted to practice before the US Supreme Court, various circuit courts of appeals and all courts in the State of Florida. Tom graduated from Florida State University (BA, with Honors, 1965), and from Stetson University School of Law (JD, 1971).

GAY, Faith Elizabeth
White & Case LLP, Miami
305 995 5218
fgay@whitecase.com
Recommended in Litigation
Practice Areas: Ms Gay concentrates in white collar criminal defense and commercial trial and appellate work. She also represents corporate clients at every stage of civil, criminal and administrative proceedings, from newly filed complaints, corporate internal investigations and grand jury proceedings through discovery, trial, sentencing and appeal.
Prof. Memberships: US Supreme Court; US Court of Appeals for the Second Circuit, Sixth Circuit, Seventh Circuit, Eighth Circuit, and Eleventh Circuit; US District Court, SD New York and ED New York; US District Court, SD Florida; New York State Bar; Florida State Bar; Illinois State Bar; Texas State Bar.

GEARY Jr, Francis
Fowler White Boggs Banker, West Palm Beach 561 655 1100
Recommended in Healthcare

GENET, Chava
Stearns Weaver Miller Weissler Alhadeff & Sitterson, P.A., Miami
305 789 3200
Recommended in Hotels and Resorts

GENOVESE, John
Genovese Joblove & Battista, P.A., Miami 305 349 2300
Recommended in Bankruptcy

GEORGE, Peter
George & Titus PA, Tampa
813 273 0355
Recommended in Litigation

GILBERT, Leonard
Holland & Knight LLP, Tampa
813 227 8500
leonard.gilbert@hklaw.com
Recommended in Bankruptcy
Practice Areas: Partner in the Business Law Section, practicing in the areas of commercial finance, insolvency, and commercial litigation and maintaining an active transactional practice. His emphasis has been in the representation of financial institutions and other institutional lenders. In his bankruptcy practice, he has represented numerous state, national and international banks, and other financial institutions and public bodies, secured and unsecured creditors' committees and equity and has been involved in restructuring LBO transactions. He is past President of The Florida Bar and is active in the Business Law Section of the American Bar Association and the International Insolvency Institute.

GILBERT, Robert
Carlton Fields, West Palm Beach
561 659 7070
Recommended in Bankruptcy

GINSBURG, Dennis
Packman, Neuwahl & Rosenberg, Coral Gables 305 665 3311
Recommended in Tax

GLAZIER, Robert
Robert Glazier - Sole Practitioner, Miami 305 372 5900
glazier@fla-law.com
Recommended in Litigation
Practice Areas: Appeals and trial consultation. Important recent decisions include Tananta v. Cruise Ships Catering and Services, 30 Fla. L. Weekly D18 (Fla. 3d DCA Dec. 22, 2004)(en banc); Chuck v. City of Homestead, 888 So. 2d 736 (Fla. 3d DCA 2004)(en banc); Miami-Dade County v. Omnipoint Holdings, 863 So. 2d 195 (Fla. 2003) (amicus brief); Durruthy v. Pastor, 351 F.3d 1080 (11th Cir. 2003).
Publications: Co-author of 'Handbook of Florida Evidence' (2d ed., with Michael H Graham). Articles published in the Florida Bar Journal, Nova Law Review, Trial Magazine, and other publications. Lectures for Florida Bar and ABA. Former Adjunct Professor, University of Miami School of Law.
Personal: Law clerk to Honorable Gerald B Cope and Honorable Daniel S Pearson, Third District Court of Appeal of Florida. Nova Law School (JD, 1987); New College of Florida (BA, 1981). Executive Editor, Nova Law Review.

GLENN, Robert
Glenn Rasmussen Fogarty & Hooker, Tampa 813 229 3333
Recommended in Bankruptcy

GOLDBERG, Michael
Akerman Senterfitt, Fort Lauderdale
954 463 2700
michael.goldberg@akerman.com
Recommended in Bankruptcy
Career: Michael Goldberg is a shareholder and concentrates his practice on bankruptcy and creditors' rights. He regularly represents creditors, debtors and trustees in bankruptcy proceedings and pre-bankruptcy workouts. He has a masters in business administration in finance and is routinely appointed to serve as receiver of distressed corporations. He has been appointed receiver in numerous high profile cases including the Cyprus Fund, a $90 million Ponzi Scheme; AB Financing and Investments, Inc., a $50 million Ponzi Scheme; the Discovery Capital Group, a defunct broker-dealer; and Loans4Military, a corporation with debts exceeding $30 million.

GOLDMAN, Robert
Vickers Madsen & Goldman, Tallahassee 850 523 0400
Recommended in Tax

GOLDSTEIN, Joseph
Holland & Knight LLP, Miami
305 374 8500
joseph.goldstein@hklaw.com
Recommended in Real Estate
Practice Areas: Partner in Holland &

Knight's Real Estate Section, practices land use and environmental law. Goldstein has significant experience representing developers and private property owners in their efforts to protect their property rights or entitlements and in seeking complex development or other governmental approvals and permits. He has extensive experience in obtaining approvals of developments of regional impact (DRI), zoning and comprehensive plan amendments. Goldstein has represented dozens of the most significant and recognizable development projects in the South Florida region from conception to completion during his approximately 18 years of practicing land use and environmental law.

GONZALEZ, Ervin
Colson Hicks Eidson, Coral Gables
305 476 7400
Ervin@colson.com
Recommended in Litigation
Practice Areas: Product liability; medical malpractice; aviation; class actions; personal injury; toxic torts.
Career: Mr Gonzalez is board certified as a specialist in civil trial law by the Florida Bar and the National Board of Trial Advocacy; board certified in business litigation law by the Florida Bar; graduated from the University of Miami School of Law, Cum Laude in 1985.

GONZALEZ, Thomas M
Thompson, Sizemore & Gonzalez, Tampa 813 273 0050
Recommended in Employment

GOREN, Samuel
Goren Cherof Doody & Ezrol PA, Fort Lauderdale 954 771 4500
Recommended in Real Estate

GORSON, Matthew
Greenberg Traurig LLP, Miami
305 579 0777
gorsonm@gtlaw.com
Recommended in Real Estate
Practice Areas: Real estate, commercial lending and governmental negotiations.
Prof. Memberships: Chairman, Downtown Miami Charter School; Board Member, City of Miami Downtown Development Authority; Board Member, Tulane University President's Council; Board Member, Mt Sinai Hospital.
Career: Listed in 'The Best Lawyers in America', every edition. Listed, 2004 Legal Elite, 'Florida Trend Magazine', listing of Florida's top attorneys as selected by their peers. Named among South Florida's Heavy Hitters in 'Real Estate by the Business Journal', 2004.
Personal: University of Chicago (JD, 1973); Tulane University (BS, 1970).

GRAGG, Lawrence
White & Case LLP, Miami
305 995 5209
lgragg@whitecase.com
Recommended in Tax
Practice Areas: A board certified tax lawyer, Mr Gragg has a transactional

domestic and international practice, a significant portion of which is devoted to general business counseling, including business formations, acquisitions and dispositions. He also has an active federal and state tax practice. Mr Gragg has extensive experience in structuring and negotiating complex joint venture business arrangements, with a particular focus in the real estate area.
Prof. Memberships: Florida Bar; United States Tax Court; United States District Court for the Southern District of Florida; United States Courts of Appeals for the Fifth and Eleventh Circuits.

GRAMMIG, Robert
Holland & Knight LLP, Tampa
813 227 8500
robert.grammig@hklaw.com
Recommended in Corporate/M&A
Practice Areas: Partner in the Business Law Section, practicing in the areas of corporate finance, securities law, general corporate law and international business transactions. His practice currently includes a wide range of corporate, securities and commercial law matters, including: both public offerings and private placements registered under the federal and state securities laws; mergers and acquisitions; periodic reporting and compliance matters under the Securities Exchange Act of 1934; corporate governance matters; contests for corporate control; and other commercial law matters. He has devoted a significant part of his practice to international business transactions, representing both United States and foreign entities.

GRANDOFF, Bert
Allen Dell, Tampa 813 223 5351
Recommended in Construction

GREELEY, Jack
Smith Mackinnon PA, Orlando
407 843 7300
Recommended in Banking & Finance

GREEN, William
Hopping Green & Sams, P.A., Tallahassee 850 222 7500
billg@hgslaw.com
Recommended in Environment
Practice Areas: Environmental law: special emphasis on scientific issues.
Prof. Memberships: Florida State and Federal courts, Federal 11th Circuit Court of Appeals, US Supreme Court, American Bar Association, and Florida Bar; Fellow, Royal Astronomical Society.
Career: 1967-74: Research in Spectroscopy and Lasers, US Naval Research Laboratory; 1974-79: Associate/Partner, Mahoney, Hadlow, Chambers & Adams, P.A.; 1979 to date: Shareholder, Hopping Green & Sams, P.A.
Publications: 25 publications in Physical Chemistry and Astrophysics; two law review articles.
Personal: BS/PhD (Chemistry), University of South Carolina, 1963/1967; JD, Georgetown University, 1973; Visiting

Scholar, University of Cambridge, 1987; Visiting Scientist, Lawrence Berkeley National Laboratory, 1998.

GREER, Alan
Richman Greer Weil Brumbaugh Mirabito & Christensen, Miami
305 373 4010
agreer@richmangreer.com
Recommended in Litigation
Practice Areas: Alan G Greer, who concentrates in civil commercial litigation, is certified by the Florida Bar in both business litigation and in civil trial practice. His other areas of emphasis are: civil appeals, civil litigation, commercial and complex litigation, intellectual property litigation, officer and director representation, and professional malpractice.
Prof. Memberships: A Fellow of the American College of Trial Lawyers (and Chair of its Professionalism Committee), the International Society of Barristers, and the American Bar Foundation), Mr Greer serves as a faculty member and lecturer for the National Institute of Trial Advocacy, teaching continuing legal education courses. Mr Greer is admitted to the Florida Bar, the New York Bar, the Bar of the District of Columbia, the Federal Bars for several District Courts and Circuit Courts of Appeal, the US Tax Court, the US Court of Claims and the US Supreme Court.
Career: After serving six years of active duty in the US Navy Mr Greer began his legal career with his current law firm in 1969 becoming a Shareholder in 1971.
Publications: Mr Greer has authored a number of articles on issues relating to professionalism which have appeared in over 25 Bar journals and other publications.
Personal: US Naval Academy (BS 1961); University of Florida College of Law (JD 1969).

GRINDSTAFF, Michael J
Shutts & Bowen, Orlando
407 835 6927
mgrindstaff@shutts-law.com
Recommended in Real Estate
Practice Areas: Chairman, Orlando Real Estate Practice Group; handles transactions involving acquisition, zoning, permitting, development and sale of retail shopping centers, mixed use developments, multi-family apartment complexes and office buildings; single family residential communities and condominium projects, real estate related litigation, ad valorem taxation disputes, zoning and land use litigation.
Prof. Memberships: Florida, Georgia.
Career: Past Chairman Orange County Planning & Zoning Commission; Director/Chairman of Real Estate Committee and Member of Executive Committee of Univeristy of Central Florida Foundation.
Personal: JD, cum laude, Mercer University 1982; BSBA University of Central Florida.

GROGAN, Michael
Coffman, Coleman, Andrews & Grogan, Jacksonville 904 389 5161
Recommended in Employment

GURLEY, David
Gurley Dramis, Sarasota
941 365 4501
Recommended in Construction

GUSO, Jordi
Berger Singerman, Miami
305 714 4375
jguso@bergersingerman.com
Recommended in Bankruptcy
Practice Areas: Partner in firm's Business Reorganization Team. Frequently represents corporate debtors, secured lenders and committees in reorganization cases and restructurings.
Prof. Memberships: American Bankruptcy Institute; Business Law Section of The Florida Bar; Bankruptcy Bar Association for the Southern District of Florida (Treasurer, 2000-01; Secretary, 2001-02); and Cuban-American Bar Association.
Career: Admitted to the Florida Bar (1990); US District Courts, Southern and Middle Districts (1992), Northern District of Florida (1998), Eleventh Circuit Court of Appeals (1992). Notable recent cases include the representation of: Piccadilly Cafeterias; the Atlas Air debtors, as co-counsel; Aloha Airlines as special transactional counsel; and Lake Worth Generation, LLC.
Publications: Co-author, Fundamentals of Bankruptcy Law & Procedure in Florida, National Business Institute (1994); Co-author, Enforcing Commercial Loans in Florida, Lorman Education Services (2001); co-author, Retention Agreements: How To Get Paid When Your Client Is In Trouble, American Bar Association Section on Business Law, Business Bankruptcy Committee (76th Annual National Conference of Bankruptcy Judges (2002)).
Personal: JD, University of Miami (1990); BS, Political Science, Pi Sigma Alpha, Spring Hill College (1987). Former law clerk to then-Chief United States Bankruptcy Judge Sidney M Weaver, United States Bankruptcy Court, Southern District of Florida (1990-92). Fluent in Spanish.

GUTTER, Marvin
Tescher Gutter Chaves Josepher Rubin Ruffin & Forman PA, Boca Ratón
561 998 7847
Recommended in Tax

HAINLINE Jr, Theodore
Rogers, Towers, Bailey, Jones & Gay, PA, Jacksonville 904 398 3911
Recommended in Real Estate

HALE, Russell
Akerman Senterfitt, Orlando
407 843 7860
russ.hale@akerman.com
Recommended in Tax

Career: Russell Hale is a shareholder and section administrator of the Orlando office's Corporate Department. He is Board Certified in Taxation Law by The Florida Bar and practices primarily in the fields of business planning, taxation and transactions. He has extensive experience in issues of Florida state and local taxation including controversy resolution, administrative compliance and legislative support. He is a registered lobbyist with the legislative and executive branches of the Florida State Government and works on policy issues relating to state taxation, trusts and estates. He is a former Municipal Court Judge and is admitted to Florida and Oregon.

HALL, Donald
Gunster, Yoakley & Stewart, P.A.,
Fort Lauderdale 954 462 2000
Recommended in Real Estate

HALSEY, Douglas
White & Case LLP, Miami
305 995 5268
dhalsey@whitecase.com
Recommended in Environment

Practice Areas: Mr Halsey's practice covers all aspects of environmental law, litigation, transactional advice, and regulatory matters before government agencies. During the last twenty-five years, Mr Halsey tried numerous environmental cases in state and federal court with emphasis on cost recovery claims and land use disputes. He has represented manufacturers, developers, and property owners in complex litigation and defended enforcement actions brought by the EPA, Florida Department of Environmental Protection and local government agencies.
Prof. Memberships: The Florida Bar; United States District Court for the Southern District of Florida; United States Courts of Appeals for the Fifth and Eleventh Circuits.

HAMILTON, Russell
Morgan, Lewis & Bockius LLP, Miami
305 415 3440
rhamilton@morganlewis.com
Recommended in Employment

Practice Areas: W Russell Hamilton III is a Partner in the Labor and Employment Practice. Mr Hamilton's practice focuses on labor, employment and employee benefits matters, representing exclusively employers, employer associations, and employee benefit plans and fiduciaries. Mr Hamilton has represented clients in employee benefits laws; employee benefits and fiduciary litigation; equal employment opportunity and affirmative action matters; and arbitration of all types of emplyment issues.
Prof. Memberships: American Bar Association (Labor and Employment Law Section); Florida Bar Association (Labor and Employment Law Section); Georgia Bar Association (Labor and Employment Law Section); North Carolina Bar Association; Dade County Bar Association.

HANSON Jr, Karl B
LeBoeuf, Lamb, Greene & MacRae, LLP,
Jacksonville 904 630 5330
kbhanson@llgm.com
Recommended in Real Estate

Practice Areas: An experienced commercial real estate attorney concentrating in acquisitions, dispositions, development, financing, leasing and management of real property. He represents clients in all facets of ownership in the real estate area. He has served as counsel to mortgage banking companies in regard to their operations and financing. He is also an experienced real property title insurance attorney, representing several major national title insurance companies in insuring large real estate transactions.
Prof. Memberships: Florida Bar; American Bar Association; Jacksonville Bar Association.
Career: Joined LeBoeuf in 1988.
Personal: University of North Carolina (BA) 1968; University of Florida (JD) 1971.

HENDERSON, Thomas
Hill, Ward & Henderson, PA, Tampa
813 221 3900
Recommended in Real Estate

HILL III, Benjamin
Hill, Ward & Henderson, PA, Tampa
813 221 3900
Recommended in Litigation

HOFFMAN, Jerome
Holland & Knight LLP, Tallahassee
850 224 7000
jerome.hoffman@hklaw.com
Recommended in Antitrust

Practice Areas: Partner in the Litigation Section, practicing primarily in the areas of antitrust, consumer fraud, RICO, and Medicaid and Medicare fraud and other healthcare regulatory matters. Served as General Counsel for the Agency for Health Care Administration, where he supervised 40 attorneys responsible for prosecuting Medicaid overpayments; regulating hospitals, nursing homes, assisted living facilities and home health agencies and prosecuting disciplinary cases before the Board of Medicine. He also served as chief of the Antitrust Section of the Florida Attorney General's Office, handling cases involving bid rigging, price fixing, monopolization and other restraints of trade, and merger reviews.

HOGAN, John M
Holland & Knight LLP, Miami
305 374 8500
john.hogan@hklaw.com
Recommended in Litigation

Practice Areas: Partner in the Litigation Section, his experience includes both civil and criminal litigation in the areas of securities fraud, environmental crimes, bank fraud, money-laundering, and foreign Corrupt Practice Act issues. He has extensive experience assisting corporations with internal investigations and compliance issues. Hogan is the former Chief of Staff to the Attorney General of the United States and has served as Chief Assistant State Attorney for Miami-Dade County, Florida, where he successfully tried a number of significant cases. He also served as the first Statewide Prosecutor of Florida, supervising all consumer protection matters for the State of Florida.

HOLCOMB, Mark E
Holland & Knight LLP, Tallahassee
850 224 7000
mark.holcomb@hklaw.com
Recommended in Tax

Practice Areas: Partner in the firm's Business Law Section, practices in the area of state and local taxation law. He is experienced in representing clients before the Florida Department of Revenue and in litigating state tax cases at the trial and appellate levels. Holcomb represents and advises taxpayers in a broad range of state and local taxes. His experience includes representing manufacturers, retailers, financial institutions, service companies, utilities, equipment leasing companies, alcoholic beverage distributors, insurance companies, trade associations and hotel management companies in tax controversy work and planning opportunities.

HOLIFIELD, Marilyn
Holland & Knight LLP, Miami
305 374 8500
marilyn.holifield@hklaw.com
Recommended in Employment

Practice Areas: Partner in the Litigation Section, represents management and corporate clients in employment matters. Her practice includes business litigation, trade secrets, covenants-not-to-compete and class action litigation. She regularly defends employers in litigation involving wrongful termination cases brought as intentional torts, breach of contract, whistleblower and civil rights discrimination actions. She also counsels and represents employers before local, state and federal agencies in cases involving the Age Discrimination in Employment Act, Americans with Disabilities Act, Title VII and other local, state and federal employment statutes. She was recently named by Black Enterprise Magazine as one of America's top employment lawyers.

HOLSHOUSER, Eric
Coffman, Coleman, Andrews & Grogan,
Jacksonville 904 389 5161
Recommended in Employment

HOPKINS, Edward
Broad and Cassel, West Palm Beach
561 832 3300
Recommended in Healthcare

HOPPING, Wade
Hopping Green & Sams, P.A.,
Tallahassee 850 222 7500
whopping@hgslaw.com
Recommended in Environment, Real Estate

Practice Areas: Lobbying business issues; land use.
Prof. Memberships: The Florida Bar; The Tallahassee Bar; Board of Trustees Pacific Legal Foundation; Board of Directors Florida Chamber of Commerce.
Career: 1968-69: Justice of Florida Supreme Court; President Florida Chamber of Commerce; 1979 to date: Senior Partner, Hopping Green & Sams, P.A.

HORNREICH, Michael
Greenberg Traurig LLP, Orlando
407 418 2397
hornreichm@gtlaw.com
Recommended in Construction

Practice Areas: Litigation; construction law.
Prof. Memberships: Active Member, Associated General Contractors of America (AGC); Member, Board of Directors, Central Florida Chapter of the AGC; Member, AGC's Legislative, Membership, and Safety Committees; Member, AGC National Water Resources Committee, which promoted the development of a national water policy to accommodate growth into the 21st century (1992-94).
Personal: University of Florida Levin College of Law (JD, 1983); University of Florida (BS, 1978).

HOROWITZ, Mitchell
Fowler White Boggs Banker, Tampa
813 228 7411
Recommended in Tax

HUDSON, Robert
Baker & McKenzie, Miami
305 789 8906
bob.hudson@bakernet.com
Recommended in Tax

Practice Areas: Tax planning and tax controversy work, particularly for international private banks and high-net worth clients, foreign client structuring into US real estate and businesses, preimmigration US tax planning and US mutinational outbound planning.
Prof. Memberships: American Bar Association, New York State Bar, Florida Bar (Tax Sections); International Fiscal Association; International Tax Planning Association; American College of Tax Counsels; Society of Trust and Estate Planners.
Career: International Partner, Baker & McKenzie, Miami (1986 to date); Partner, Stearns, Weaver, Miller et al, Miami (1977-86); Associate, Wender, Murase &

White, New York (1973-77); law clerk, Hon Don N Laramore, US Circuit Court of Appeals for Federal Circuit (1972-73).

Publications: 'Federal Tax Considerations of Foreign Investment in the US Real Estate' BNA Portfolio; published over 50 articles to date on a wide range of international tax topics for TMIJ, Tax Notes International, ALI/ABA, PLI, Business Entities Journal, International Tax Journal, etc.

Personal: Active within South Florida civic and cultural community, serving as Board Member (and Vice-Chairman) of the Performing Arts Center Foundation, Concert Association of Florida, Florida International Bankers Association, Camillus House and formerly the Greater Miami Chamber of Commerce, World Trade Center, Rotary Club of Miami and the Japan Society of South Florida.

HYDE, Kevin E
Foley & Lardner, Jacksonville
904 359 8786
khyde@foley.com
Recommended in Employment
Career: Kevin E Hyde is a Partner in the Jacksonville office of Foley & Lardner. He is a member of the firm's Litigation Department and is leader of the Labor & Employment Practice Group for the Southeast Region. Mr Hyde represents employers in a variety of human resources matters. His practice focuses on day-to-day employment counseling, and he regularly advises employers on creating appropriate compensation systems. He has represented employers in numerous charges of discrimination, employment-discrimination cases, wage-hour and management-union matters. Mr Hyde is a graduate of the University of Florida College of Law (JD, with honors, 1988).

ICARD, Thomas
Icard, Merrill, Cullis, Timm, Furen & Ginsburg PA, Sarasota
941 366 8100
Recommended in Construction

IMPERATO, Gabriel
Broad and Cassel, Fort Lauderdale
954 764 7060
Recommended in Healthcare

ISICOFF, Laurel M
Kozyak Tropin & Throckmorton, Miami
305 372 1800
lmi@kttlaw.com
Recommended in Bankruptcy
Practice Areas: Bankruptcy Practice Partner.
Prof. Memberships: Florida Bar; ABA; Bankruptcy Bar, Southern District Florida (President, 1999-2000; current Chair, Pro Bono Task Force); Iron Arrow (2002, University of Miami's highest honor); University of Miami Board, Center for Ethics/Public Policy; FIU, Dean's Advisory Council.

Career: Specializes in commercial bankruptcy, foreclosure, workout matters. Registered Bankruptcy Mediator, US Bankruptcy Court, Southern District Florida. Kozyak Tropin (1992-); Squire Sanders & Dempsey, Miami (1984-91); 'Best Lawyers in America'; Top Lawyers (South Florida Legal Guide; Florida Trend).
Personal: Born NY, NY. Barnard College (BA, 1978, cum laude); University of Miami School of Law (JD, 1982, cum laude).

JOHNSON, Carmen
Akerman Senterfitt, Miami
305 374 5600
carmen.johnson@akerman.com
Recommended in Employment
Career: Carmen Johnson is a shareholder. She is Board Certified in Labor and Employment Law by The Florida Bar. She has 18 years of experience exclusively representing employers in labor and employment law matters including labor relations, human resources advice, and employment litigation. She is former member of the Executive Council of the Labor and Employment Law Section of The Florida Bar, and served as Chair of the Equal Employment Opportunity Committee and Co-Chair of the Individual Employment Rights Committee in the same section. She frequently lectures clients and professional associations on all areas of labor and employment law.

JONES, Rod
Shutts & Bowen, Orlando
407 835 6909
rjones@shutts-law.com
Recommended in Banking & Finance
Practice Areas: Partner, Financial Services Industry Practice Group; formerly Director of Division of Banking of Florida Department of Banking and Finance, responsibilities included licensing and supervising 500+ state chartered financial institutions.
Prof. Memberships: Florida.
Career: Was staff counsel and banking analyst for Florida House of Representatives Committee on Commerce; drafted major revisions to Florida Financial Institutions Codes, including legislation authorizing cross-industry mergers, conversions and acquisitions of Florida financial institutions and Regional Reciprocal Banking Act of 1984; taught at Florida School of Banking and Banking Law Institute.
Personal: JD, with honors, Florida State University; Florida School of Banking, University of Florida.

JONES, Thomas J
Holland & Knight LLP, Tallahassee
850 224 7000
tom.jones@hklaw.com
Recommended in Insurance
Practice Areas: Partner in the firm's Government Section, practices in the area of insurance regulatory law and

commercial litigation. His practice routinely brings him into contact with insurance regulators who have authority over insurance companies and their operations and over specialty insurers such as health maintenance organizations, life care retirement communities and prepaid benefit plans. He represents clients' interests on a broad spectrum of issues before regulatory agencies, in proceedings before administrative law judges, and in state and federal courts.

JOSEFSBERG, Robert
Podhurst Orseck, P.A., Miami
305 358 2800
Recommended in Litigation

JOSEPHER, Richard
Tescher Gutter Chaves Josepher Rubin Ruffin & Forman PA, Boca Ratón
561 998 7847
Recommended in Tax

JUNG, William
Jung & Sisco, Tampa
813 225 1988
Recommended in Litigation

KANTOR, Hal
Lowndes Drosdick Doster Kantor & Reed, PA, Orlando 407 843 4600
Recommended in Real Estate

KARP, Joel
Karp & Genauer PA, Coral Gables
305 445 3545
Recommended in Tax

KASNER, Stewart
Karp & Genauer PA, Coral Gables
305 445 3545
Recommended in Tax

KATZ, Allan J
Akerman Senterfitt, Tallahassee
850 224 9634
allan.katz@akerman.com
Recommended in Insurance
Career: Allan Katz, Managing Shareholder of the Tallahassee office, concentrates his practice on legislative and governmental affairs, local government, public finance and banking, administrative, healthcare and insurance law. He has been a member of the City of Tallahassee City Commission since May of 2002 and is currently Mayor Pro Tem. Prior to entering private practice, he was Assistant Insurance Commissioner and General Counsel for the State of Florida Department of Insurance, General Counsel for the US House of Representatives Commission on Administrative Review, Legislative Director for Congressman David Obey and Legislative Assistant to Congressman Bill Gunter.

KEINER, Jeffrey
Gray Robinson PA, Orlando
407 843 8880
Recommended in Construction

KELSO, Linda Y
Foley & Lardner, Jacksonville
904 359 8713
lkelso@foley.com
Recommended in Corporate/M&A
Career: Linda Kelso is a Partner in the Jacksonville office of Foley & Lardner. A member of the firm's Business Law Department and its Transactional and Securities Practice Group, she counsels business clients in corporate and partnership organization, finance, and securities. Ms Kelso has worked on numerous public and private offerings, represented public companies in connection with their periodic reporting to the Securities and Exchange Commission, formed 'hedge funds' that invest in securities, and handled business combinations for public and private entities. She received her law degree from the University of Florida College of Law (JD, with high honors, 1979).

KENDIG-SCHRADER, Julie
Greenberg Traurig LLP, Orlando
407 418 2417
kendig@gtlaw.com
Recommended in Real Estate
Practice Areas: Real estate; environmental/land use.
Prof. Memberships: Member, Seminole County Development Advisory Board Member, Land Use and Environmental Law Section of Florida Bar; Member, Volusia County Association for Responsible Development.
Publications: Special Editor, Florida Environmental and Land Use Law Treatise - Environmental and Land Use Section of Florida Bar and Regulation files; authored, 'Florida's Private Property Rights Act', Environmental and Land Use Law Section Reporter.
Personal: JD, University of Florida Levin College of Law, 1992; MA, Political Science/Public Administration, University of Florida, 1991; BA, Political Science, University of Florida, 1989.

KENNEDY III, James J
Buchanan Ingersoll PC, Tampa
813 222 8185
kennedyjj@bipc.com
Recommended in Healthcare
Practice Areas: Jim's practice is devoted primarily to the representation of hospitals and other healthcare providers. He is board certified as a Health Law Specialist by The Florida Bar, a distinction earned by fewer than one percent of lawyers in the state. Jim regularly counsels clients on subjects related to healthcare business transactions, joint ventures, corporate compliance, physician contracting, HIPAA, reimbursement, managed care contracting, risk management, and fraud and abuse analysis and prevention.
Prof. Memberships: American Health Lawyer's Association; 'Best Lawyers in America' 2003-04 and 2005-06; Jim is licensed in Florida and Illinois.

Personal: JD DePaul University, 1982; BS Florida State University, 1979.

KING, Bruce
Carlton Fields, Miami 305 530 0050
Recommended in Construction

KING, David
King, Blackwell & Downs PA, Orlando
407 422 2472
Recommended in Litigation

KING, Kimberly
Kimberly L King PA, Tallahassee
850 205 4500
Recommended in Antitrust

KINSOLVING, Ruth
Carlton Fields PA, Tampa
813 223 7000
Recommended in Real Estate

KIRKWOOD, Peter
Barnett, Bolt, Kirkwood, Long & McBride, Tampa 813 253 2020
Recommended in Tax

KIRSCHNER, Kenneth
Kirschner & Legler, Jacksonville
904 346 3200
Recommended in Corporate/M&A

KIRWIN, Brian
Kirwin Norris PA, Winter Park
407 740 6600
Recommended in Construction

KLINGHOFFER, Teddy D
Akerman Senterfitt, Miami
305 374 5600
teddy.klinghoffer@akerman.com
Recommended in Corporate/M&A
Career: Teddy Klinghoffer is a shareholder in the Corporate Practice Group and is a member of the firm's Board of Directors. He focuses his practice in the areas of corporate law, mergers and acquisitions, private equity and venture capital. His principal clients include a number of significant private equity funds, privately-held and public companies and high net worth individuals and entrepreneurs. Mr Klinghoffer's representative clients include Brockway Moran & Partners, CitiGroup Private Bank, IVAX Corporation, MapleWood Partners and MBFX Capital Partners.

KOBERT, Roy
Broad and Cassel, Orlando
407 839 4200
Recommended in Bankruptcy

KOFMAN, Robert
Stearns Weaver Miller Weissler Alhadeff & Sitterson, P.A., Miami
305 789 3200
Recommended in Employment

KORNREICH, David
Akerman Senterfitt, Orlando
407 843 7860
david.kornreich@akerman.com
Recommended in Employment
Career: David V Kornreich is a shareholder and is Board Certified by The Florida Bar in labor and employment

law. He has extensive experience representing employers in all types of labor and employment matters, including administrative proceedings, jury and non-jury trials, and appeals. Prior to entering private practice, Mr Kornreich served with the United States Department of Labor and the National Labor Relations Board. Mr Kornreich is a Fellow of the College of Labor and Employment Lawyers.

KOZYAK, John W
Kozyak Tropin & Throckmorton, Miami
305 372 1800
jk@kttlaw.com
Recommended in Bankruptcy
Practice Areas: Senior Bankruptcy Practice Partner.
Prof. Memberships: Fellow, American College of Bankruptcy (1992-); ABA Business Bankruptcy Committee (CLE Chair; Vice Chair 1997-2002); Fellow, American Academy of Trial Lawyers (2005-); President, Bankruptcy Bar, Southern District Florida (1986).
Career: Former Managing Partner, Chair Litigation Department of major firm. Co-founder KT&T (1982). Represents secured/unsecured creditors, equity, management, committees, trustees in major Florida bankruptcies. National counsel for nation's largest special servicer of securitized commercial mortgages. Listed in 'Best Lawyers in America' (1987 -).
Personal: Born Champaign, Illinois, 1948. University of Illinois (BS Marketing, 1970); Washington University School of Law (JD, 1975).

KREUSLER-WALSH, Jane
Jane Kreusler-Walsh PA, West Palm Beach 561 659 5455
Recommended in Litigation

KUEHNE, Benedict
Sale & Kuehne PA, Miami
305 789 5989
Recommended in Litigation

KUNKEL, Daniel
Kunkel Miller & Hament, Tampa
813 969 3639
Recommended in Employment

LANDIS, James M
Foley & Lardner, Tampa
813 225 4115
jlandis@foley.com
Recommended in Antitrust
Career: James M Landis is a Partner in Foley & Lardner's Tampa office. A member of the Litigation Department and the Antitrust Practice Group, he represents business clients in several states in all forms of commercial litigation, including litigation arising from claims of antitrust and securities violations and unfair competition, as well as copyright, trademark, service mark, franchising, and trade secret challenges and protection. He has counseled and litigated antitrust cases, including price discrimi-

nation cases under the Robinson-Patman Act, securities cases, straight breach of contract claims, UCC cases, fraud claims, franchise cases, and lender liability claims.

LANE, Joe
Lowndes Drosdick Doster Kantor & Reed, PA, Orlando 407 843 4600
Recommended in Construction

LAPIDUS, Steve
Greenberg Traurig LLP, Miami
305 579 0509
lapiduss@gtlaw.com
Recommended in Tax
Practice Areas: Tax, trusts and estates.
Prof. Memberships: Chairman, Greenberg Traurig's Executive Compensation and Employee Benefits Group; Member, Professional Advisory Committee, Foundation of Jewish Philanthropies; Member, Board of Directors, Mercy Hospital Foundation; Former President, South Florida Employee Benefits Council.
Personal: New York University School of Law (LLM, 1977); New York University School of Law (JD, 1973); Wharton School of the University of Pennsylvania (BS, 1969).

LAURIA, Thomas
White & Case LLP, Miami
305 995 5282
tlauria@whitecase.com
Recommended in Bankruptcy
Practice Areas: Mr Lauria serves as Co-Chairman of the Firm's Financial Restructuring and Insolvency Department. He regularly represents bondholders, bank groups, strategic and financial investors, miscellaneous creditor constituencies, soverigns and debtors in connection with bankruptcy and restructuring matters in a variety of industry and market sectors.
Prof. Memberships: The Florida Bar; Texas State Bar; US District Courts for the Southern, Middle and Northern Districts of Florida; US District Courts for the Northern and Southern Districts of Texas; US Court of Appeals for the Fifth and Eleventh Circuits.

LAW, Rhea
Fowler White Boggs Banker, Tampa
813 228 7411
Recommended in Real Estate

LAWRENCE, Adam
Lawrence & Daniels, Miami
305 358 3371
Recommended in Litigation

LEDERMAN, Alan
Broad and Cassel, Miami
305 373 9435
Recommended in Tax

LEGLER, Mitchell
Kirschner & Legler, Jacksonville
904 346 3200
Recommended in Corporate/M&A

LEIBY, Larry R
Leiby Stearns Linkhorst & Roberts, PA, Fort Lauderdale
954 382 9199
lrl@leibylaw.com
Recommended in Construction
Practice Areas: Board certified in construction law.
Prof. Memberships: American Bar Association (Forum Committee on Construction Industry); Florida Bar (1976, Founder and first Chairman of Construction Law Committee; Member of Construction Law Certification Committee, 2004-); Associated Builders and Contractors (Director of East Florida Chapter); Associated General Contractors; Florida Surety Association.
Career: Representative Appellate cases: Rossmoor Corp. v Tri-County Concrete Products, Inc., 375 So.2d 896 (Fla. 4th DCA 1979). Coordinated Constructors, Inc. v Florida Fill, Inc., 387 So.2d 1006 (Fla.3d DCA 1980). Champagne-Webber, Inc. v City of Ft. Lauderdale, 519 So.2d 696 (Fla. 4th DCA 1988). Levitz Electric, Inc. v George Hyman Construction Co., (In re Levitz Electric, Inc.), 100 B.R. 602 (S.D. Fla. 1989). Mursten Construction Co. v C.E.S. Industries, Inc., 588 So.2d 1061 (Fla. 3d DCA 1991). Alexdex Corp. v Nachon Enterprises, Inc., 641 So.2d 858 (Fla. 1994). Hollub Construction Company v Narula, 704 So.2d 689 (Fla. 3d DCA 1997). Fischer-McGann, Inc. v Gene B. Glick Co., Inc., 715 So.2d 994 (Fla. 4th DCA 1998). Hewett-Kier Construction, Inc. v Lemuel Ramos & Associates, Inc., 775 So.2d 373 (Fla. 4th DCA 2000). Bill Stroop Roofing, Inc. v Metropolitan Dade County, 788 So.2d 365 (Fla. 3d DCA, 2001). Rewards Hotel Management, Inc. v Elite General Contractors, Inc., 860 So.2d 1011 (Fla. 3rd DCA 2003).
Publications: 'Florida Construction Law Manual', Shepard's/McGraw-Hill, 1981, seventh edition (2005) published by The West Group. 'Florida Construction Lien and Payment Bond Primer', 1999, 2003. Contributing author 'Licensing for Construction: A Legal Mechanism of Control', Comparative Studies in Construction Law: The Sweet Lectures, published by The Construction Law Press, London, UK (1996); 'Changes to the Florida Construction Lien', Florida Bar Journal, September, 1999; 'Florida Construction Liens and Payment Bonds', 'Contractual Indemnity in Construction for Your Negligence, What Year Is It?' The Florida Bar Journal, July/August, 2003.

LEISNER, Richard
Trenam, Kemker, Scharf, Barkin, Frye, O'Neill & Mullis PA, Tampa
813 223 7474
Recommended in Corporate/M&A

LEONHARDT, Frederick
Gray Robinson PA, Orlando
407 843 8880
Recommended in Real Estate

LESSER, Steven
Becker & Poliakoff PA, Fort Lauderdale
954 987 7550
Recommended in Construction

LEVENTHAL, Robert
Leventhal & Slaughter PA, Orlando
407 849 6161
Recommended in Litigation

LEVY, Jay
Jay M Levy PA, Miami
305 670 8100
Recommended in Litigation

LEWIS, Steve
Lewis, Longman & Walker PA, West
Palm Beach 561 640 0820
Recommended in Environment

LEWIS, Terry
Lewis, Longman & Walker PA, West
Palm Beach 561 640 0820
Recommended in Environment

LIBANOFF, Ira
Ferencik, Libanoff, Brandt, Bustamante & Williams, Fort Lauderdale
305 949 8003
Recommended in Construction

LICKO, Carol A
Hogan & Hartson LLP, Miami
305 459 6612
calicko@hhlaw.com
Recommended in Litigation
Practice Areas: Practice focuses primarily on complex corporate and commercial litigation at all levels from trials
through appeals, with extensive experience in class action litigation, business,
securities and contract litigation.
Emphasis on complex problem-solving,
with experience in corporate law, health
and educational law, and constitutional
law. Represents state and local governments, municipalities, universities and
community colleges, hospitals, television stations and a major science
research institute.
Prof. Memberships: Commissioner,
Florida State Ethics Commission (2000-
04); Chair, Judicial Nominating Procedures Committee, Florida Bar (2003);
Member, ABA.
Career: Former General Counsel to
Governor Jeb Bush.
Personal: University of Miami School
of Law (JD).

LILES, Rutledge
Liles, Gavin, Constantino & Murphy,
Jacksonville 904 634 1100
Recommended in Litigation

LITCHFORD, Hal
Litchford & Christopher, Orlando
407 841 0325
Recommended in Antitrust

LOCKETT, Laurel
Carlton Fields PA, Tampa
813 223 7000
Recommended in Environment

LOPEZ-CASTRO, Corali
Kozyak Tropin & Throckmorton, Miami
305 372 1800
clc@kttlaw.com
Recommended in Bankruptcy
Practice Areas: Bankruptcy Practice
Partner.
Prof. Memberships: Cuban-American
Bar Association (Director, 1998-2001;
2003-04; current President-Elect); Panel
of Bankruptcy Trustees, Southern Dis-
trict Florida (1998-2002); Appointed to
Judicial Campaign Practices Commis-
sion, which considers complaints filed by
candidates during judicial elections in
Miami-Dade County; ABA; Bankruptcy
Bar, Southern District Florida.
Career: Specializes in representation of
creditors and debtors in Chapter 11
bankruptcy cases, Chapter 11 committees, and Trustees in Chapter 7. Kozyak
Tropin (1990-95 & 1997-); Hahn Loeser
& Parks (Cleveland, Ohio, 1995-97).
Personal: Born San Juan, Puerto Rico.
Brown University (AB, 1987); University
of Miami School of Law (JD, 1990, cum
laude).

LOUMIET, Carlos
Hunton & Williams, Miami
305 810 2575
cloumiet@hunton.com
Recommended in Banking & Finance
Practice Areas: Carlos Loumiet has
advised clients in the international business and banking fields in the United
States and overseas for more than 27
years. He has dealt with many different
types of business entities and transactions, at times on a 'cradle to grave' basis.
He has been involved in numerous
mergers and acquisitions, securities
offerings, venture capital deals, financings, infrastructure projects and other
commercial transactions, often across
borders. He has dealt with regulators
and other governmental authorities in
many different countries and in a wide
variety of contexts. Mr Loumiet is also
very active with emerging US Latino
companies.

LOWRY, Patricia E
Steel Hector & Davis, West Palm Beach
561 650 7214
plowry@steelhector.com
Recommended in Employment
Practice Areas: Chairs Products Liability, Labor and Employment and West
Palm Beach Litigation Groups. Extensive experience in both product liability
litigation and employment litigation,
including defense of employment discrimination and harassment claims,
employment agreements, whistleblower
claims, wage and hour claims, appellate
practice, and employment and labor
counseling.
Prof. Memberships: Academy of Florida Management Attorneys, Federal Bar
Association, International Association of
Defense Counsel, Society of Human
Resources Management, Human

Resource Association of Palm Beach
County. Admitted to practice in Florida
and the District of Columbia. Admitted
in all federal trial and appellate courts in
Florida and the Supreme Court of the
United States.
Career: Joined Steel Hector & Davis
LLP in 1984.
Personal: JD, George Washington Uni-
versity, 1981 (highest honors), BA, Uni-
versity of Kentucky, 1978.

LYON, Fred
The Lyon Firm PA, Winter Park
407 647 8900
Recommended in Construction

MAIDA, Thomas J
Foley & Lardner, Tallahassee
850 513 3377
tmaida@foley.com
Recommended in Insurance
Career: Thomas J Maida is the Managing Partner of Foley & Lardner's Tallahassee office. A member of the firm's
Insurance Industry and Public Affairs
Practice Groups, his clients include
some of the world's largest insurance
companies, as well as many leading
regional insurers. He has developed legal
strategies for a number of complex business transactions, including the formation of insurance companies, group
funds, and health maintenance organizations; mergers and acquisitions of
insurance companies; and the demutualization of insurers. He represents
clients in legislative matters before the
Florida Legislature and is a graduate of
the Florida State University College of
Law.

MALEFATTO, Alfred J
Greenberg Traurig LLP, West Palm
Beach 561 650 7908
malefattoa@gtlaw.com
Recommended in Environment
Practice Areas: Environmental; land
use; public infrastructure; public utility;
administrative and governmental law.
Prof. Memberships: Member, Executive
Council, Environmental and Land Use
Law Section of The Florida Bar from
1985-93; served as Section Chairman
from 1991-92; Gubernatorial Appointee
to Board of Treasure Coast Regional
Planning Council, 1984-86; Secretary,
The Forum Club of the Palm Beaches;
Board Member and Vice President,
Friends of the Academy of Environmental Science and Technology, Inc; Board
Member, Grassy Waters Preserve.
Publications: Lectures extensively on
environmental law issues at programs
sponsored by The Florida Bar, the Florida Chamber of Commerce and other
organizations.

MANDEL, David S
Mandel & Cale LLP, Miami
305 374 7771
dmandel@mandel-law.com
Recommended in Litigation
Practice Areas: Currently handles an

array of complex commercial disputes
and white collar criminal defense matters.
Prof. Memberships: Member of the
Bars of Florida, New York, Illinois and
Washington, DC. Member of the Feder-
al Bar Association, the American Bar
Association and former Chair of the
Federal Court Committee of the Dade
County Bar Association. Member of the
Wilson Council at the Woodrow Wilson
International Center for Scholars, Wash-
ington, DC. Also formerly served as the
President of Foster Care Review, an orga-
nization devoted to assisting the judicial
administration of foster children.
Career: Former Assistant United States
Attorney for the Southern District of
Florida, 1989-95.
Personal: Born 23 January 1959. JD
Cornell Law School, 1986; AB (magna
cum laude) Brown University, 1982.

MARTIN, Gregory S
Moye, O'Brien, O'Rourke, Pickert &
Martin, LLP, Maitland
407 622 5250
gmartin@moopm.com
Recommended in Construction
Practice Areas: Construction and
commercial litigation. Has extensive
experience representing US and international owners, contractors and engineer-
ing firms in the USA and the Caribbean
basin in multi-million dollar contracts
and claims.
Prof. Memberships: The Florida Bar;
American Bar Association (Member,
Litigation Section and Forum on the
Construction Industry); Court of Federal Claims Bar Association.
Career: Admitted to Florida Bar (1990);
Partner of Moye, O'Brien, O'Rourke,
Pickert & Martin, LLP (with affiliated
offices in Chicago, Illinois); admitted to
the US District Court, Middle and
Southern Districts of Florida; US Court
of Appeals, Eleventh Circuit; US Court
of Federal Claims.
Personal: Received Bachelor of Building
Construction from the University of
Florida (1987) and a JD from the University of Florida (1990); past President
of Sigma Lambda Chi (School of Building Construction Honor Society); Contractor (Residential/inactive).

MARTINEZ, Roberto
Colson Hicks Eidson, Coral Gables
305 476 7400
bob@colson.com
Recommended in Litigation
Practice Areas: Commercial litigation
and white collar criminal defense
Career: Mr Martinez was United States
Attorney for the Southern District of
Florida where he served as the chief federal law enforcement officer in a district
that extends from Key West to Ft Pierce,
Florida; was responsible for representing
the United States in all criminal and civil
matters in the district; served on the
Attorney General's Advisory Committee
of United States Attorneys; received his

JD degree from the Georgetown University Law Center where he was on the Dean's List; holds a MS in Accounting and a BS in Economics from the University of Pennsylvania, Wharton School of Business.

MASER, Joel
Greenberg Traurig LLP, Orlando
407 418 2389
maserj@gtlaw.com
Recommended in Tax
Practice Areas: Tax; public infrastructure; public utility.
Prof. Memberships: Active member, Executive Council, The Florida Bar Tax Section and has served as Chairperson of several committees within the Tax Section. Member, Tax Section's Long Range Planning Committee and is serving as the Tax Section's workshop director. Director, Tax Section's State Tax Advisory Division (1991-95).
Personal: JD, magna cum laude, University of Miami School of Law, 1984. Articles and Comments Editor, University of Miami Law Review. BS, with honors, University of Florida, 1981.

MASON, Cheney
J Cheney Mason PA, Orlando
407 843 5785
Recommended in Litigation

MATTHEWS, Frank
Hopping Green & Sams, PA, Tallahassee
850 222 7500
frankm@hgslaw.com
Recommended in Environment
Practice Areas: Extensive federal and state environmental practice specializing in wetland and water use permitting; lobbying with the Florida Legislature on behalf of a variety of utility, mining and development issues and has been engaged in the passage of all significant environmental legislation in Florida for the last 20 years.

MATTHEWS, Joseph M
Colson Hicks Eidson, Coral Gables
305 476 7400
joseph@colson.com
Recommended in Litigation
Practice Areas: Commercial law; intellectual property law; insurance law; construction law; arbitration; alternative dispute resolution; class actions.
Career: In 1989, Mr Matthews served as Special Counsel to United States Senator Bob Graham, joining Colson Hicks Eidson later that year; specializes in commercial, intellectual property, fraud, defamation and other business torts, insurance, construction and professional liability litigation; is a member of the American Arbitration Association and the London Court of International Arbitration, as well as the AAA's panel of arbitrators for Large and Complex Cases.

MAYOL, Juan
Holland & Knight LLP, Miami
305 374 8500
juan.mayol@hklaw.com
Recommended in Real Estate
Practice Areas: Mr Mayol is a Partner in Holland & Knight's Real Estate Section practicing in the areas of land use and zoning. He represents builders and developers in all aspects of land use law through the entire development process, from zoning approvals to subdivision and building permit issues. In addition, Mr Mayol handles environmental matters as they relate to the development process. Mr Mayol is a Member of The Florida Bar and is fluent in Spanish.

MCCLOSKY, Donald
Ruden McClosky SC, Fort Lauderdale
954 764 6660
Recommended in Real Estate

MCCREA, Richard
Zinober & McCrea, PA, Tampa
813 224 9004
Recommended in Employment

MCGUIGAN, Thomas R
Steel Hector & Davis, West Palm Beach
561 650 7278
tmcguigan@steelhector.com
Recommended in Corporate/M&A
Practice Areas: Chairman, Commercial Division. Corporate, securities, and financial matters for public and privately held organizations in various stages of development. Public and private offerings of stock, debt and hybrid securities, venture capital, and other financings. Mergers, acquisitions and other business combinations and reorganizations. Corporate governance; takeover and anti-takeover, and executive compensation advice and planning.
Prof. Memberships: Florida Bar; American Bar Association, Business Law Section, Committee on Negotiated Acquisitions.
Career: Joined Steel Hector & Davis in 1974.
Personal: JD with highest honors from University of Miami School of Law. BA with highest honors, LaSalle University.

MCKENNA, Susan
Jackson Lewis, Orlando
407 246 8440
Recommended in Employment

MEEKS, Thomas
Zuckerman Spaeder LLP, Miami
305 358 5000
Recommended in Litigation

MELE, Dennis
Ruden McClosky SC, Fort Lauderdale
954 764 6660
Recommended in Real Estate

MEYER, George
Carlton Fields PA, Tampa
813 223 7000
Recommended in Construction

MILLER, Brian P
Akerman Senterfitt, Miami
305 374 5600
brian.miller@akerman.com
Recommended in Litigation
Career: Brian Miller is a shareholder and focuses his practice on corporate litigation and securities. He has extensive experience representing publicly traded companies, officers and directors, and accounting firms in defense of class actions, SEC enforcement matters, and internal investigations. Before joining the firm, he worked for the US Securities and Exchange Commission as Special Counsel to Commissioner Steven M H Wallman, and with the Washington, DC law firm Covington & Burling. He is former Co-Chair of the Dade County Bar Association Committee on Securities Litigation and is admitted to practice in Florida and District of Columbia.

MILLER, Morris
Holland & Knight LLP, Tallahassee
850 224 7000
morris.miller@hklaw.com
Recommended in Healthcare
Practice Areas: Mr Miller, Partner in the Business Law Section, is experienced in transactional and regulatory matters within the healthcare and senior living industries. Represents owners, developers, and operators of healthcare and senior living facilities and has structured, negotiated, and documented numerous acquisitions, dispositions, financings, and other business arrangements involving such facilities. He also represents healthcare entities in matters involving federal and state 'anti-kick-back' and patient self-referral laws; Medicare and Medicaid reimbursement issues; health facility licensure and other healthcare regulatory issues; and various kinds of contracts for healthcare facilities, senior living facilities, and medical practices.

MITCHELL, Stephen
Squire, Sanders & Dempsey LLP, Tampa 813 202 1300
Recommended in Real Estate

MOOREFIELD Jr, Harold
Stearns Weaver Miller Weissler Alhadeff & Sitterson, P.A., Miami
305 789 3200
Recommended in Bankruptcy

MORA, Mindy A
Bilzin Sumberg Baena Price & Axelrod LLP, Miami 305 350 2414
mmora@bilzin.com
Recommended in Bankruptcy
Prof. Memberships: Association of Commercial Finance Attorneys, Executive Board (1993 - present); The Florida Bar, Bankruptcy and UCC Committee; International Women's Insolvency and Restructuring Confederation, South Florida Chapter, Vice-President (2003-04).
Career: Partner whose practice focuses

on insolvency and workouts, corporate restructuring, commercial finance and asset-based lending. Has counseled high-visibility clients in many major bankruptcy proceedings, both nationally and in Florida. Active in the development of Florida's commercial laws, having co-sponsored the 1997 revisions to Article 8 and 1999 revisions to Article 9 Uniform Commercial Code (chapters 678 and 679, Florida Statutes). Frequent lecturer and author on insolvency and restructuring topics.

MOSCOWITZ, Jane
Moscowitz, Moscowitz & Magolnick PA, Miami 305 379 8300
Recommended in Litigation

MOSCOWITZ, Norman
Moscowitz, Moscowitz & Magolnick PA, Miami 305 379 8300
Recommended in Litigation

MOSS, Edward
Shook, Hardy & Bacon LLP, Miami
305 358 5171
emoss@shb.com
Recommended in Litigation
Practice Areas: Focuses his practice on the handling and trial of product liability matters, as well as complex commercial cases and securities litigation and defense of class actions. Is listed in 'The Best Lawyers in America' and has been selected as one of the top 10 litigators in Florida.
Prof. Memberships: Admitted to practice in Florida and before the US Court of Appeals for the First, Fifth and Eleventh Circuits and the US Supreme Court.
Career: Joined Shook, Hardy & Bacon, 1998 (as Partner).
Personal: JD, cum laude, University of Miami School of Law, 1961; BA, cum laude, University of Florida, 1958.

MOYE, James E
Moye, O'Brien, O'Rourke, Pickert & Martin, LLP, Maitland 407 622 5250
jmoye@moopm.com
Recommended in Construction
Practice Areas: Construction, commercial litigation, management labor relations law, employment relations law. Has extensive experience representing US and international contractors and engineering firms in the USA, the Caribbean basin, Central America and Canada in multi-million dollar claims.
Prof. Memberships: State Bar of Georgia; The Florida Bar; American Bar Association (Member, Sections on Labor and Employment Law, Forum on the Construction Industry); Court of Federal Claims Bar Association.
Career: Admitted to Georgia Bar (1982), Florida (1989); senior partner of Moye, O'Brien, O'Rourke, Pickert & Martin, LLP (with affiliate offices in Chicago, Illinois); admitted to US District Court, Middle and Southern Districts of Florida; US Court of Appeals,

Fifth, Eleventh and DC Circuits; US Supreme Court.

Personal: Received a BSE (cum laude) from University of Central Florida in 1978 and a JD from University of Florida in 1981; inducted into Eta Kappa Nu (Electrical Engineering National Honor Society), Tau Beta Pi (Engineering National Honor Society) and Omicron Delta Kappa; member of the President's Leadership Council and the 'University of Florida Law Review' from 1980-81.

NACHWALTER, Michael
Kenny Nachwalter P.A., Miami
305 373 1000
Recommended in Litigation

NAGIN, Stephen
Nagin Gallop Figueredo PA,
Coconut Grove 305 854 5353
Recommended in Antitrust

NICHOLS, Tracy A
Holland & Knight LLP, Miami
305 374 8500
tracy.nichols@hklaw.com
Recommended in Litigation

Practice Areas: Partner in the firm's Litigation Section, her practice has an emphasis in securities shareholder litigation, complex commercial litigation and class actions. She is the firm's National Practice Group Leader for the Securities Litigation Group and a lifetime fellow of the American Bar Foundation. Appointed by the Chief Judge of the United States District Court for the Southern District of Florida, she serves as the reporter for the Civil Justice Advisory Group, which assists in reducing costs and delays in federal civil litigation.

NOBLE, Ron
Fowler White Boggs Banker, Tampa
813 228 7411
Recommended in Environment

NUECHTERLEIN, Mike
Carlton Fields PA, Tampa
813 223 7000
Recommended in Construction

OLSON, John
Stearns Weaver Miller Weissler Alhadeff & Sitterson, P.A., Tampa
813 223 4800
Recommended in Bankruptcy

O'NEAL-COBLE, Leslie
Greenberg Traurig LLP, Orlando
407 425 8500
loneal@hklaw.com
Recommended in Construction

Practice Areas: Litigation; construction litigation.
Prof. Memberships: Member, West Publishing Construction Group Advisory Board, 2003-present. Fellow, ABA Foundation. Fellow, The Florida Bar Foundation. Member, American Board of Trial Advocates, 2003-present
Career: Best Business Lawyers in Florida, Chambers, 2004. Orange County Bar Legal Aid Society Award of Excellence, 2004. Listed, 2004 Legal Elite, Florida

Trend Magazine. Listed 'Best Lawyers in America,' 2005-06 Edition.
Publications: Author, 'An Overview of 'Toxic' Mold Litigation in Florida', (chapter in 50 State Survey of Mold Litigation).
Personal: JD, University of Florida Levin College of Law, 1977. BA, with honors, University of Florida, 1974.

ORSHEFSKY, Debbie
Greenberg Traurig LLP, Fort Lauderdale
954 768 8234
orshefskyd@gtlaw.com
Recommended in Real Estate

Practice Areas: Environmental and land use.
Prof. Memberships: Member, Urban Land Institute and serves on the Executive Committee of the ULI Southeast/Caribbean Council (2002-present); Co-Chair, Broward General Medical Center, Community Advisory Board of the Comprehensive Cancer Center (2002-present); Chair, Downtown Fort Lauderdale Transportation Management Association from (1992-94).
Publications: Co-Author, 'Developing within a CRA; Signs of a healthy CRA should be the focus of a prudent developer,' Urban Land, October 2003; Co-author: 'Local Government Comprehensive Planning', Florida Environmental and Land Use Law Manual, 1990, 1993 and 1996 Updates.

PALMER, Scott
Berman DeValerio Pease Tabacco Burt & Pucillo, West Palm Beach
561 835 9400
Recommended in Antitrust

PANOFF, Robert
Robert E Panoff PA, Miami
305 670 6547
Recommended in Tax

PAPPAS, Lynn
Pappas Metcalf Jenks and Miller, Jacksonville 904 353 1980
Recommended in Real Estate

PARSONS, Philip
Landers & Parsons, Tallahassee
850 681 0311
Recommended in Environment

PASANO, Michael
Zuckerman Spaeder LLP, Miami
305 358 5000
Recommended in Litigation

PELHAM, Thomas
Fowler White Boggs Banker, Tallahassee 850 681 0411
Recommended in Real Estate

PEREZ, Luis
Akerman Senterfitt, Miami
305 374 5600
luis.perez@akerman.com
Recommended in Corporate/M&A

Career: Luis Perez is a shareholder in the Corporate and International Practice Groups with an emphasis on mergers and acquisitions, corporate, banking

and international law. He has served as principal counsel in hundreds of acquisitions throughout the United States and Latin America. Mr Perez is a member of The Florida Bar and the American Bar Association. He is the Co-Chair of the firm's International Practice Group and is fluent in Spanish and French.

PERWIN, Joel
Joel S. Perwin, P.A., Miami
305 779 6090
Recommended in Litigation

PERWIN, Scott
Kenny Nachwalter P.A., Miami
305 373 1000
Recommended in Antitrust

PETERSON, Ralph
Beggs & Lane, Pensacola
850 432 2451
Recommended in Employment

PHALIN, Lawrence J
Mateer & Harbert P.A., Orlando
407 425 9044
Recommended in Construction

PICKERT, Stephen W
Moye, O'Brien, O'Rourke, Pickert & Martin, LLP, Maitland
407 622 5250
spickert@moopm.com
Recommended in Construction

Practice Areas: Construction litigation in state and federal courts and ADR, involving contracts, construction defects, bonds, liens, delay claims, business torts and statutory claims for public, private, commercial and residential projects and representing owners, developers, general contractors, subcontractors, material suppliers and design professionals.
Prof. Memberships: The Florida Bar, The American Bar Association, Associated Builders and Contractors, The Associated General Contractors of America, Associated Owners & Developers, and member of the Construction Law Committee for the Real Property, Probate and Trust Section of The Florida Bar.
Career: Admitted to The Florida Bar in 1981; Senior Partner with the law firm of Moye, O'Brien, O'Rourke, Pickert & Martin, LLP since 1990; admitted in the United States District Court for the Southern and Middle Districts of Florida and the United States Court of Appeals for the Fifth, Ninth and Eleventh Circuits, as well as the United States Supreme Court.
Publications: Author: 'Civil Theft A Reemerging Weapon in Everyday Commercial Disputes', The Florida Bar Journal; lectured primarily with The Associated General Contractors of America to provide continuing education units for those in the construction industry.
Personal: Received Bachelor of Science in Banking and Finance in 1978 from The University of Florida with high honors and graduated in 1981 from The

University of Florida Law School with honors and as a member of The Law Review; married with three sons.

PIERCE, Robert
Ausley & McMullen, Tallahassee
850 224 9115
Recommended in Tax

PILLANS III, Charles
Bedell, Dittmar, DeVault, Pillans & Coxe, Jacksonville
904 353 0211
Recommended in Litigation

PISCITELLI, Michael
Vezina Lawrence & Piscitelli, Fort Lauderdale 954 728 1270
Recommended in Construction

PODHURST, Aaron
Podhurst Orseck, P.A., Miami
305 358 2800
Recommended in Litigation

POPE, Nicholas
Lowndes Drosdick Doster Kantor & Reed, PA, Orlando 407 843 4600
Recommended in Hotels and Resorts

PRESS, Martin
Gunster, Yoakley & Stewart, P.A., Fort Lauderdale 954 462 2000
Recommended in Tax

PRESTON, William D
William D Preston PA, Tallahassee
850 668 4986
bill@wprestonpa.com
Recommended in Environment

Practice Areas: 25+ years experience in Florida environmental law.
Prof. Memberships: Admitted to practice in Florida (1976). Member of Environmental and Land Use Law Section; 'Best Lawyers of America'; Leadership Florida.
Career: Staff Director, Florida Senate Natural Resources Committee, 1978-79; joined Hopping Boyd Green & Sams, 1979; shareholder 1983-2001; founded William D Preston, P.A., 2001.
Publications: Co-author, 'The Water Quality Assurance Act of 1983–Florida's Great Leap Forward into Groundwater Protection and Hazardous Waste Management,' Florida State University Law Review, 1983; 'The 1993 Amendments to Florida's Solid Waste Management Act: The Continuing Search for Solutions,' Florida State University Law Review, 1993.
Personal: Born 7 August 1947. JD, Florida State University, 1975; BS (Biological Sciences), Rochester Institute of Technology, 1969.

PRICE, Stanley B
Bilzin Sumberg Baena Price & Axelrod LLP, Miami 305 350 2374
sprice@bilzin.com
Recommended in Real Estate

Career: Has worked in the forefront of Florida land use law and has been the principal draftsman of important land use legislation, as well as a frequently consulted expert on the subjects of owners' and developers' rights and complex zoning and permitting issues. Served as special land use counsel to several Florida municipalities and as the special magistrate in land use litigation for Dade and Orange County Circuit Courts. Selected to lecture on the appellate review of land use cases to Dade County Circuit Court, Appellate Division. Adjunct professor of land use law at University of Miami School of Law.

QUIÑON, Jose
Jose M Quiñon - Sole Practitioner, Miami 305 858 5700
Recommended in Litigation

RAATTAMA, Henry
Akerman Senterfitt, Miami
305 374 5600
henry.raattama@akerman.com
Recommended in Tax
Career: Henry Raattama is a shareholder whose practice areas include charitable and tax-exempt organizations, estate planning and business planning. He is a recipient of the Gerald T Hart Outstanding Tax Attorney for 1998-99, and has chaired the Tax Section of The Florida Bar and The Florida Bar Tax Certification Committee. He is also the recipient of the Outstanding Professional Advisor for 2002. Mr Raattama is a member of the American College of Tax Counsel and frequently lectures on tax matters and has taught in the University of Miami Graduate Tax Program.

RAKUSIN, Steve
Stephen Rakusin PA, Fort Lauderdale
954 356 0496
Recommended in Construction

RASILE, Craig
Hunton & Williams, Miami
305 810 2579
crasile@hunton.com
Recommended in Bankruptcy
Practice Areas: Mr Rasile's practice focuses in the insolvency area, emphasizing bankruptcy, corporate restructuring, creditors' rights, workouts, and commercial litigation in several industries, including retail, healthcare, transportation, franchising, REIT's and financial institutions. He typically represents corporate and partnership debtors, trustees, committees and financial institutions in bankruptcy cases and workouts. Recent engagements include: receiver for the Lancer Group, three hedge funds with $1.2B under management, in their receivership and bankruptcy proceedings; several lessors of 747 aircraft in Atlas Air; and the Official Committee in Far & Wide Travel Corp. Mr Rasile is Co-Chair of the firm's Bankruptcy and Financial Restructuring Department.

RASKIN, Jane
Raskin & Raskin PA, Miami
305 444 3400
Recommended in Litigation

RASKIN, Martin
Raskin & Raskin PA, Miami
305 444 3400
Recommended in Litigation

RASMUSSEN, Robert
Glenn Rasmussen Fogarty & Hooker, Tampa 813 229 3333
Recommended in Corporate/M&A

RAVIKOFF, Ronald
Zuckerman Spaeder LLP, Miami
305 358 5000
Recommended in Antitrust

REDMOND, Patricia
Stearns Weaver Miller Weissler Alhadeff & Sitterson, P.A., Miami
305 789 3200
Recommended in Bankruptcy

REID, Benjamine
Carlton Fields, Miami 305 530 0050
Recommended in Litigation

REILLY, Kenneth J
Shook, Hardy & Bacon LLP, Kansas City
305 358 5171
kreilly@shb.com
Recommended in Litigation
Practice Areas: Is nationally known for serving as lead litigation counsel for Fortune 500 corporations. In the last three years, his defense verdicts for high-profile cases have been noted within 'The National Law Journal's Top 10 Verdicts' for each year. Is a frequent lecturer on product liability and professional liability matters as well as trial techniques.
Prof. Memberships: Admitted to practice in Colorado, Florida, Kansas and Missouri. Frequent lecturer to state and local bar associations on trial techniques and civil procedure.
Career: Joined Shook, Hardy & Bacon, 1995; became Partner, 1997. Managing Partner, Shook Hardy & Bacon's Miami, Florida office.
Personal: JD, University of Texas School of Law, 1973; BA, Trinity University, 1970.

REISMAN, Stephen H
Peckar & Abramson, Miami
305 358 2600
sreisman@pecklaw.com
Recommended in Construction
Practice Areas: Managing Partner of Peckar & Abramson's Florida Offices. His primary area of practice is construction law and includes the representation of construction managers, general contractors, subcontractors and owners in the negotiation and preparation of construction documents, and the negotiation, mediation, arbitration and litigation of construction contract claims, construction and design defect claims, insurance claims, and related matters. His construction law practice also includes project administration assistance for the early identification and resolution of potential conflicts and disputes.
Prof. Memberships: He serves on the Construction Advisory Council and Panel of Arbitrators for the American

Arbitration Association. He is a Member of the American Bar Association (Construction Industry Forum and Litigation Section), the Academy of Florida Trial Lawyers, the Florida Bar (Litigation and Business Law Sections) and the Construction Association of South Florida.
Career: He is admitted to practice law before the United States Supreme Court, the United States Court of Appeals for the Fifth and Eleventh Circuits, the United States District Court for the Southern and Middle Districts of Florida, the United States Bankruptcy Court for the Southern District of Florida as well as all courts of the State of Florida. He is the Managing Partner of Peckar & Abramson's Florida offices and formerly a Partner of Rosenberg, Reisman & Stein, which merged with Peckar & Abramson in 2000.
Publications: He has authored several articles and conducted seminars on various construction law topics for The Florida Bar, National Business Institute, Construction Specifications Institute, Construction Association of South Florida, 'Southeast Construction,' and Lorman Educational Services.
Personal: He is a graduate of Emory University (1973) and the University of Miami School of Law (1976).

REZNICSEK, Rick
Reznicsek & Fraser PA, Ponte Vedra Beach 904 567 1060
Recommended in Healthcare

RICHARD, Barry
Greenberg Traurig LLP, Tallahassee
850 425 8503
richardb@gtlaw.com
Recommended in Litigation
Practice Areas: Complex commercial litigation; state and federal constitutional law; government and election law; appellate practice.
Prof. Memberships: Charter member, American Academy of Appellate Lawyers; Member, Florida Legislature (1974-78); Former Deputy Attorney General for the State of Florida.
Publications: Author, 'Arbitration Clause Risks,' The National Law Journal, June 14, 2004; Author, 'Mock Jury Exercises,' The National Law Journal, March 1, 2004; Author, 'Rule 11 Sanctions: Risks to Non-lead Counsel,' The National Law Journal, September 2001; Author, 'Defending Mega-Suits,' The National Law Journal, April 16, 2001; Chapter author, 'Technology,' Successful Partnering Between Inside and Outside Counsel, West Publishing Company.

RICHMAN, Gerald
Richman Greer Weil Brumbaugh Mirabito & Christensen, West Palm Beach 561 803 3500
grichman@richmangreer.com
Recommended in Litigation
Practice Areas: Gerald F Richman is board certified by The Florida Bar as both a civil trial lawyer and business liti-

gation lawyer concentrating in trial and appellate practice, and complex commercial litigation with emphasis on antitrust, securities, contract, construction, federal agency, corporate, banking, civil RICO, professional liability, consumer, employment, civil rights and probate litigation and class action issues, representing both plaintiffs and defendants. He also has extensive experience in real estate litigation, including mortgage foreclosures, condominiums, zoning and land use, brokerage disputes and governmental matters.
Prof. Memberships: Fellow of the American College of Trial Lawyers, and former member of the Board of Governors of the International Society of Barristers. Charter Member of both the Miami Chapter of the American Board of Trial Advocates and the National Association of Consumer Advocates. He is a former President of the Florida Bar, former President of the Dade County Bar Association, and past Chair of the Florida Commission on Human Relations. He is currently a member of the Board of Directors of the Economic Council of Palm Beach County.
Career: After his service in the Army's Judge Advocate General Corps, where he earned the Presidential Service Badge for Honorable service at the White House, Mr Richman joined the firm in 1969 and became a Shareholder in 1971.
Personal: Mr Richman earned a degree in Building Construction, with honors, at the University of Florida, earned his Juris Doctor at the University of Florida College of Law and studied at Georgetown University's Graduate Law School.

RIDLEY, Fred S
Foley & Lardner, Tampa
813 225 4183
fridley@foley.com
Recommended in Real Estate
Career: Fred S Ridley is the Partner in charge of Foley & Lardner's Tampa-based Real Estate Practice Group and chairs the firm's national Golf and Resort Industry Team. His practice is focused in the areas of commercial and residential real estate development and finance, golf and recreational amenity and resort development, and multifamily/condominium developments. Mr Ridley has over 20 years of experience in representing developers of high-end, single-family and multifamily real estate projects and has been lead counsel to several of the most recognized waterfront condominium developments in Florida.

RIEDEL, Harley
Stichter, Riedel, Blain & Prosser PA, Tampa 813 229 0144
Recommended in Bankruptcy

RILLSTONE, Douglas
Broad and Cassel, Tallahassee
850 681 6810
Recommended in Environment

ROBINS, Andrew
Gunster, Yoakley & Stewart, P.A., Fort Lauderdale 954 462 2000
Recommended in Hotels and Resorts

ROBINSON, John
Fowler White Boggs Banker, Tampa 813 228 7411
Recommended in Employment

RODDENBERRY, Stephen
Akerman Senterfitt, Miami
305 374 5600
stephen.roddenberry@akerman.com
Recommended in Corporate/M&A
Career: Stephen K Roddenberry is a shareholder in the Corporate Practice Group where he focuses his practice in the areas of securities, mergers and acquisitions, private equity and venture capital, international and public finance. He has additional industry experience as counsel in aviation, entertainment and sports and banking and financial institutions. He is a member of the American Bar Association, Sports Lawyers Association and the Florida Bar Foundation. Mr Roddenberry's representative clients include Boca Resorts, Inc., Miami Dolphins, Huizenga Holdings, Inc. and Embraer Aircraft Holding, Inc.

ROGOW, Bruce
Bruce S. Rogow, P.A., Fort Lauderdale 954 767 8909
Recommended in Litigation

ROSENBERG, Michael
Packman, Neuwahl & Rosenberg, Coral Gables 305 665 3311
Recommended in Tax

ROSS, David L
Greenberg Traurig LLP, Miami
305 579 0523
rossd@gtlaw.com
Recommended in Litigation
Practice Areas: Litigation; antitrust.
Prof. Memberships: Member, American Bar Association's Litigation Section; Past Chairman, Business Law Section, The Florida Bar; Past Chairman, Business Litigation Committee, The Florida Bar; Member, Board of Trustees, Coconut Grove Playhouse (1991-95); Member, Actor's Playhouse Citizen's Board (1998-99).
Publications: Frequent lecturer for The Florida Bar's Continuing Legal Education Program, on such topics as Trial Techniques, Antitrust Law and Restrictive Covenants; Co-author, 'The Florida Antitrust Act of 1980', The Florida Bar Journal; Author, 'Local Governments and the Antitrust Laws After City of Eau Claire: Is the Fire Finally Out?', Stetson Law Review.

ROSS, Lauri
Lauri Waldman Ross - Sole Practitioner, Miami 305 670 8010
Recommended in Litigation

ROUNSAVILLE, Keith
Akerman Senterfitt, Orlando
407 843 7860
keith.rounsaville@akerman.com
Recommended in Antitrust
Career: Keith Rounsaville is a shareholder, Chair of the firm's Antitrust and Trade Regulation Practice, and Board Certified by the Florida Bar in Antitrust and Trade Regulation. He has served as lead trial counsel and appellate counsel in civil and criminal antitrust actions throughout the United States, including Florida, Georgia, Colorado, Indiana, Texas, Maryland and Virginia. His industry experience in antitrust matters includes pharmaceuticals, electronics, optical lenses, building products, petroleum products, industrial chemicals, automotive products, agricultural products and thoroughbred horseracing. His practice also includes RICO, environmental and intellectual property litigation. He is a Member of the American Law Institute.

RUGG, Joseph W
Akerman Senterfitt, Tampa
813 223 7333
joseph.rugg@akerman.com
Recommended in Healthcare
Career: Joseph Rugg is the Office Managing Shareholder of Akerman Senterfitt's Tampa office. His practice focuses on healthcare and business law, including the purchase and sale agreements with physicians and other healthcare providers, ambulatory surgery centers, employment agreements, provider networks, managed care contracting, and Stark and Fraud and Abuse. Previously, he served as the Director, Center for Quality in Healthcare Law, Stetson College of Law. He writes and lectures on healthcare law topics and is a member of the American Health Lawyers Association and the Sections of Health Law of the American Bar Association and The Florida Bar.

RUSSIN, Peter
Meland Russin Hellinger & Budwick, Miami 305 358 6363
Recommended in Bankruptcy

RYAN, Michael
Lowndes Drosdick Doster Kantor & Reed, PA, Orlando 407 843 4600
Recommended in Real Estate

SAATHOFF, Dwight
Akerman Senterfitt, Orlando
407 843 7860
dwight.saathoff@akerman.com
Recommended in Real Estate
Career: Dwight Saathoff is a shareholder and focuses his practice on land use, zoning and real property law. He represents many of the largest development companies doing business in Florida. As part of his work in winning development entitlements for new projects, Mr Saathoff has structured numerous public/private joint ventures formed for the purpose of financing the construction of major public works projects such as schools, parking garages and regional road networks. He is a frequent lecturer on current development topics, particularly solving the problem of school overcrowding in high growth areas.

SALE, Jon
Sale & Kuehne PA, Miami
305 789 5989
Recommended in Litigation

SAMS, Gary
Hopping Green & Sams, P.A., Tallahassee 850 222 7500
gsams@hgslaw.com
Recommended in Environment
Practice Areas: Environmental and land use strategic counseling and litigation with emphasis on cases before Florida Division of Administrative Hearings.
Prof. Memberships: Admitted to practice in Florida and before all US District Courts in Florida, 11th US Circuit Court of Appeals, and US Supreme Court.
Career: For over three decades has represented throughout Florida: investor-owned, municipal, and independent electric power producers in licensing electrical power plants; land owners and developers; water and wastewater utilities, pipeline and petroleum products companies; mining companies, agricultural interests and natural resource users; and governmental entities in both regulatory and proprietary activities.

SAUL, Gary
Greenberg Traurig LLP, Miami
305 579 0846
saulg@gtlaw.com
Recommended in Real Estate
Practice Areas: Real estate.
Prof. Memberships: Member, The Florida Bar's Condominium and Planned Development Committee; Former Board Member of, and lecturer for, the Dade County Chapter of the Community Association Institute.
Personal: University of Pennsylvania (JD, 1984); Pennsylvania State University (BA, 1981).

SAWYER, Ed
White & Case LLP, Miami
305 995 5213
esawyer@whitecase.com
Recommended in Tax
Practice Areas: Mr Sawyer represents a broad range of clients, including institutional healthcare providers, real estate development companies, sales and marketing companies, health insurance providers and managed care companies in merger and acquisition, financing, regulatory, general corporate and tax matters. Mr Sawyer's practice also includes representation of clients engaged in software development, medical device manufacturing and shipping and transportation. He has substantial experience with both the tax and non-tax aspects of joint ventures, limited partnerships, limited liability partnerships, limited liability companies, corporations, trusts and estates.
Prof. Memberships: The Florida Bar; United States Tax Court.

SCHERKER, Elliot
Greenberg Traurig LLP, Miami
305 579 0500
scherkere@gtlaw.com
Recommended in Litigation
Practice Areas: Appellate practice; litigation.
Prof. Memberships: Member, American Academy of Appellate Lawyers; Listed, South Florida Legal Guide, 'Top 250 Lawyers' (2002-04).
Publications: Ongoing Co-author, Florida Bar's Florida Appellate Practice (1977-2000); Co-author, 'Rights, Remedies and Ratiocination: Toward a Cohesive Approach to Appellate Review of Land Use Orders After Board of County Commissioners of Brevard County v. Snyder', published in the 1995 Stetson University Law Review Land Use Symposium.

SCHEU, William
Rogers, Towers, Bailey, Jones & Gay, PA, Jacksonville 904 398 3911
Recommended in Real Estate

SCHILLER, Lisa
Rice Pugatch Robinson & Schiller, Miami 305 379 3121
Recommended in Bankruptcy

SCHINDLER, Ozzie
Baker & McKenzie, Miami
305 789 8926
ozzie.schindler@bakernet.com
Recommended in Tax
Practice Areas: Tax planning and controversies for multinational companies, particularly international taxation and mergers and acquisitions; foreign client structuring into US real estate and businesses; tax planning for high-net worth clients; international taxation of e-commerce.
Prof. Memberships: Florida Bar (Co-Chair of International Tax Committee); New York State Bar, International Fiscal Association.
Career: Partner, Baker & McKenzie, Miami (2000 to date); Associate, (1997 to 2000); Coopers & Lybrand, Houston (1995-97); Valdes-Fauli, Cobb, Bischoff, Kriss & Mandler, P.A., Miami (1994); Yuval Levy & Co., Tel Aviv (Fall 1993); Legal Intern, Hon Harvey E Schlesinger, US District Court, Middle District of Florida (1991).
Publications: CCH portfolio on § 367; RIA Tax Advisor Planning Series - 'U.S. Corporations Doing Business Abroad'; co-author BNA Portfolio - Passive Foreign Investment Companies; 'Another Step Towards Uniformity - Relative Consensus of the OECD TAG on Income Characterization on E-Commerce Transactions', 30 Tax Mgmt. Int'l

J. 6 (2001); 'Mostly Old, Something New: Final 'a7 367 Regulations on Outbound Transfers of Stock and Securities and Foreign Corporations and Indirect Stock Transfers', 39 Tax Mgmt. Mem. S-235 (spec. ed. 1998); Chapter on international taxation of e-commerce for the UNCTD Manual.
Personal: Fluent Hebrew; conversational Spanish; Black Belt in Tang Soo Do.

SCHMIDT, Don
Carlton Fields PA, Tampa
813 223 7000
Recommended in Healthcare

SCHNAPP, Mark
Greenberg Traurig LLP, Miami
305 579 0541
schnappm@gtlaw.com
Recommended in Litigation

Practice Areas: Litigation; international.
Prof. Memberships: Former President, Assistant United States Attorneys Association; Chairman, Security and Fraud Prevention Committee, Florida International Bankers Association; Member, Board of Directors, B'nai Brith Bench and Bar; Member, Eugene Spellman Inn of Court; Member, Appointed by Chief Judge Zloch to Ad Hoc Committee on Attorney Admissions, Peer Review and Attorney Grievance, S.D. Fla.
Publications: Lectured on money laundering, criminal tax investigations, corporate investigations, and the sentencing guidelines; Instructor to several law enforcement agencies on money laundering and fraud investigations.
Personal: Hofstra University School of Law (JD, 1976); New York University (BS, 1972).

SCHULMAN, Clifford
Greenberg Traurig LLP, Miami
305 579 0613
schulmanc@gtlaw.com
Recommended in Real Estate

Practice Areas: Environmental regulation and permitting; coastal regulation and permitting; FEMA regulatory issues; solid waste; resource recovery; utilities; zoning, land use and comprehensive planning.
Prof. Memberships: Member, Executive Council and Chairman of the Environmental and Land Use Law Section of The Florida Bar; Chairman of the Board, Executive Committee, Aventura Marketing Council.
Publications: Co-editor of The Florida Bar Environmental Law Section newsletter in 1979 and 1980 and editor-in-chief of the continuing legal education manual Environmental Regulation and Litigation in Florida (1981 edition); Co-authored the chapter entitled 'Inverse Condemnation' in Volume 2 of that manual.

SEAY, James
Holland & Knight LLP, Orlando
407 425 8500
james.seay@hklaw.com
Recommended in Real Estate

Practice Areas: Partner in the firm's Real Estate Section, practices in the area of commercial real estate law, with an emphasis on the representation of developers of commercial, mixed-use and residential projects, and acquisition and disposition of income-producing properties. He is experienced in multistate financings of real estate projects, tax deferred exchanges, sale and purchase of agricultural property, acquisition, financings, and sale of restaurants; and acquisition, financings, and sale of office and industrial properties, residential subdivisions, apartment complexes, and shopping centers. He is a graduate of Leadership Orlando and a member of the National Association of Office and Industrial Parks.

SEGAL, Mike
Broad and Cassel, Miami
305 373 9435
Recommended in Healthcare

SELLERS, Lawrence
Holland & Knight LLP, Tallahassee
850 224 7000
larry.sellers@hklaw.com
Recommended in Environment

Practice Areas: Partner in the firm's Government Section, practicing administrative and governmental law focusing on environmental matters. He regularly provides advice on permitting and enforcement matters involving a variety of federal, state, regional and local administrative agencies. He has substantial experience in administrative law, including adjudicatory hearings and rulemaking. For more than 20 years, he has represented clients before the Florida Legislature, primarily on various environmental, land use and administrative law issues. He is a member of the Florida Bar's Board of Governors and a past-Chair of the Environmental and Land Use Law Section of The Florida Bar.

SHAUGHNESSY, Kevin
Baker & Hostetler LLP, Orlando
407 649 4000
Recommended in Employment

SHEPPARD, William
Sheppard, White & Thomas PA, Jacksonville 904 356 9661
Recommended in Litigation

SHOHAT, Edward
Bierman, Shohat, Loewy & Klein PA, Miami 305 358 7000
Recommended in Litigation

SHUBIN, John
Shubin & Bass, Miami
305 381 6060
Recommended in Real Estate

SHUKER, Scott
Gronek & Latham, Orlando
407 481 5800
Recommended in Bankruptcy

SIEGEL, Stephen
Ruden McClosky SC, Miami
305 789 2700
Recommended in Healthcare

SIEGFRIED, Steven
Siegfried, Rivera, Lerner, De La Torre & Sobel, PA, Miami
305 442 3334
Recommended in Construction

SIEMON, Charles L
Charles L Siemon - Sole Practitioner, Boca Raton 561 368 3808
Recommended in Real Estate

SILVERMAN, Lawrence
Akerman Senterfitt, Miami
305 374 5600
lawrence.silverman@akerman.com
Recommended in Antitrust

Career: Lawrence D Silverman is a shareholder who is Board Certified in Antitrust and Trade Regulation. He has significant experience in antitrust and trade regulation, commercial litigation and class actions. Mr Silverman was named the 2001 Pro Bono Attorney of the Year by the Dade County Bar Association. Mr Silverman is a former member of the Council of the ABA Antitrust Section. He is an Adjunct Professor in Law and Economics at the Nova Southeastern University, Shepard Broad School of Law.

SIMMONS, Sherwin
Buchanan Ingersoll PC, Miami
305 347 4060
spstax@bipc.com
Recommended in Tax

Practice Areas: Chair, Florida Tax Practice. Experienced in business transactions including: mergers, acquisitions, reorganizations and partnerships; exempt organizations; healthcare tax issues; international taxation; pension and welfare benefit plans; executive and deferred compensation and fringe benefits; estate planning; civil and criminal tax controversies; tax trials; pension controversies; and legislative and regulatory developments. Expert witness in tax and ERISA matters.
Prof. Memberships: Board Certified in Tax Law, Florida Bar Board of Legal Specialization and Education. Admitted in Florida, Tennessee, US Supreme Court, US Tax Court, Court of Federal Claims.
Personal: Columbia University AB and JD.

SIMS, Roger
Holland & Knight LLP, Orlando
407 425 8500
roger.sims@hklaw.com
Recommended in Environment

Practice Areas: Partner in the firm's Government Law Section, practicing in the areas of water law and environmental and land use law. He is experienced in groundwater, surface water, wetlands, solid waste and hazardous waste issues. He deals with many agencies on a regular basis, including the Department of Environmental Protection, Department of Community Affairs, Southwest Florida and St Johns Water Management Districts. He has particular experience in the permitting of large projects, including developments of regional impact. He served on the American Bar Association Standing Committee on Environmental Law from 2000-03.

SINGER, Stuart
Boies, Schiller & Flexner LLP, Miami
305 539 8400
Recommended in Antitrust

SINGERMAN, Paul
Berger Singerman, Fort Lauderdale
305 714 4343
singerman@bergersingerman.com
Recommended in Bankruptcy

Practice Areas: Bankruptcy, business reorganization. Concentrates in troubled loan workouts, insolvency matters and commercial transactions.
Prof. Memberships: Admitted to practice in Florida (1983). Fellow of the American College of Bankruptcy. Member of The American Law Institute, American Bankruptcy Institute, Commercial Law League of America and The Spellman-Hoeveler American Inn of Court. President of The Bankruptcy Bar Foundation of the Southern District of Florida. Former Chair of the Business Law Section of The Forida Bar (approximately 3,600 members); former Chair of the Bankruptcy/UCC Committee of the Business Law Section of The Florida Bar.
Career: Co-CEO of Berger Singerman, resident in the Miami office.
Publications: Substantial. See engagement materials on firm website at www.bergersingerman.com.

SKOLNICK, Holly
Greenberg Traurig LLP, Miami
305 579 0860
skolnickh@gtlaw.com
Recommended in Litigation

Practice Areas: Litigation.
Prof. Memberships: Chair, Greenberg Traurig Pro Bono Program; President and Founder of the Greenberg Traurig Fellowship Foundation; Member, Board of Directors, Florida Immigrant Advocacy Center; Member, Board of Advisors, University of Miami Law School, Center for Ethics and Public Service; Member, Board of Directors, Equal Justice Works (formerly National Association for Public Interest Law); Former member, Board of Trustees, Planned Parenthood of Greater Miami.
Publications: Co-author of a major article on the use of the RICO statute in civil litigation, 'Civil RICO in the Public Interest: 'Everybody's Darling', 19 American Criminal Law Review, 655 (1982).

SLATER, James
Broad and Cassel, Orlando
407 839 4200
Recommended in Real Estate

SLAUGHTER Jr, Harrison
Leventhal & Slaughter PA, Orlando
407 849 6161
Recommended in Litigation

SLEETH, Tim
Smith Hulsey & Busey, Jacksonville
904 359 7700
Recommended in Environment

SMALLWOOD, Mary
Ruden McClosky SC, Tallahassee
850 412 2000
Recommended in Environment

SMITH, Robert H
Holland & Knight LLP, Miami
305 374 8500
robert.smith@hklaw.com
Recommended in Hotels and Resorts
Practice Areas: A Partner in the firm's Real Estate Department, his practice encompasses most facets of real estate, with special emphasis in the representation of both landlords and tenants in commercial office and retail leases and the representation of institutional lenders in connection with acquisition, construction, and permanent financing transactions. Mr Smith lectures in commercial leasing and serves as an Adjunct Professor in the LLM Real Estate Program at the University of Miami School of Law, teaching commercial leasing. Mr Smith is on the Board of Directors of TreeMendous Miami, Inc., and the City of Miami Committee on Beautification.

SMULIAN, Andrew
Akerman Senterfitt, Miami
305 374 5600
andrew.smulian@akerman.com
Recommended in Real Estate
Career: Andrew Smulian is a shareholder and the Chair of the firm's Real Estate Practice Group. His extensive practice includes the counseling of major developers, lenders and investors in complex real estate and financing transactions. His clients include financial institutions, foreign investors, real estate investment trusts, pension funds and investment advisors. Mr Smulian has structured and negotiated the purchase, sale and ground leasing of industrial, commercial and multi-family residential properties, complex construction and development contracts, joint ventures, financing facilities and loan restructurings.

SOLLNER, Richard
Trenam, Kemker, Scharf, Barkin, Frye, O'Neill & Mullis PA, Tampa
813 223 7474
Recommended in Real Estate

SOMERSTEIN, Barry
Ruden McClosky SC, Fort Lauderdale
954 764 6660
Recommended in Real Estate

SONBERG, Steven
Holland & Knight LLP, Miami
305 374 8500
steven.sonberg@hklaw.com
Recommended in Corporate/M&A
Practice Areas: Chair of the firm's Business Law Section, Sonberg practices in the areas of mergers and acquisitions, securities and corporate law. His broad transactional securities practice involves public and private debt and equity securities offerings, recapitalizations and restructurings of public and closely-held business enterprises, and public company reporting matters. His extensive M&A experience includes the representation of public and private domestic and international businesses in purchases, sales, divestitures and tender offers in a wide range of industries, including pharmaceutical, real estate, healthcare, finance and communications.

SORIANO, Robert
Carlton Fields PA, Tampa
813 223 7000
Recommended in Bankruptcy

SORONDO, Rodolfo
Holland & Knight LLP, Miami
305 374 8500
rodolfo.sorondo@hklaw.com
Recommended in Litigation
Practice Areas: Mr Sorondo is a Partner and heads South Florida's Appellate Practice Group. He began his career at the Dade County State Attorney's Office, then went into private practice specializing in criminal defense. From 1992-2002, he served with distinction as both a trial judge (1992-97), and then as an appellate judge (1997-2002) on Florida's Third District Court of Appeal. In 1998, he was awarded the Justice Gerald Kogan Judicial Distinction Award by the Miami Chapter of the National Association of Criminal Defense Lawyers and in 2004, the Justice Award by the League of Prosecutors.

SOTO, Edward
Weil, Gotshal & Manges LLP, Miami
305 577 3177
edward.soto@weil.com
Recommended in Litigation
Practice Areas: Complex commercial civil litigation.
Career: During 25 years of trial practice, Mr Soto has garnered substantial litigation experience in cases involving: antitrust, business torts, class actions, contracts, employment, fraud, insurance coverage, lender liability, products liability, professional liability and securities litigation. He has handled numerous internal investigations in these areas and has represented clients in matters before the Federal Trade Commission, the Securities and Exchange Commission, and the Federal Communications Commission. He is the Head of the Litigation Practice in the Miami office.
Personal: Columbia University School of Law (JD, 1978); Florida State University (BA, magna cum laude, 1974).

SPECTOR, Arthur
Berger Singerman, Fort Lauderdale
954 713 7511
aspector@bergersingerman.com
Recommended in Bankruptcy
Practice Areas: Partner and Team Manager of Business Reorganization Team. Before taking the bench, engaged in the general practice of law in Bay City, Michigan, emphasizing bankruptcy and litigation.
Prof. Memberships: State Bar of Michigan; The Florida Bar; National Conference of Bankruptcy Judges (Sixth Circuit Governor, 2000-02); American Bankruptcy Institute.
Career: US Bankruptcy Judge, Eastern District of Michigan (1984 -2002, chief judge 1999-2002); private practice of law 1976-83; assistant district attorney, New York County, New York (1974-76). Admitted 1975, New York; US District Court, Southern, Eastern Districts of New York; US Court of Appeals, Second Circuit; 1976, Michigan; US District Court, Eastern District of Michigan; 1979, US Supreme Court; 1981, US Court of Appeals, Sixth Circuit; 2002, Florida; 2003, US District Court, Northern, Southern Districts of Florida; 2004, US Court of Appeals, Eleventh Circuit; 2005, US District Court, Middle District of Florida.
Publications: Contributing editor Norton Bankruptcy Law & Practice II. Authored numerous law review articles, monographs, and 170 published judicial opinions, including 25 in the Dow Corning case alone.
Personal: JD, cum laude, Boston University School of Law (1974); Bachelor of Arts, City College of New York (1971). Adjunct Professor of Law, Thomas M Cooley Law School (1995).

SPECTOR, Brian
Kenny Nachwalter PA, Miami
305 373 1000
Recommended in Litigation

SREBNICK, Howard
Black, Srebnick, Kornspan & Stumpf PA, Miami 305 371 6421
Recommended in Litigation

STAGE, Jon
Stearns Weaver Miller Weissler Alhadeff & Sitterson, P.A., Fort Lauderdale
954 462 9500
Recommended in Employment

STANFORD, Douglas
Smith, Gambrell & Russell, LLP, Jacksonville 904 598 6100
Recommended in Real Estate

STEARNS, Eugene
Stearns Weaver Miller Weissler Alhadeff & Sitterson, P.A., Miami
305 789 3200
Recommended in Litigation

STEINBERG, Marty
Hunton & Williams, Miami
305 810 2505
msteinberg@hunton.com
Recommended in Antitrust, Litigation
Practice Areas: Mr Steinberg's practice focuses on class actions and complex commercial litigation, including contract disputes, business torts, securities litigation, intellectual property, antitrust and product liability. He is a former US Senate Chief Counsel and federal prosecutor with substantial trial experience in a variety of matters. He also has substantial experience representing companies in Grand Jury and Senate inquiries. Mr Steinberg is the Miami Office Managing Partner and a Fellow of the American College of Trial Lawyers.

STICHTER, Don
Stichter, Riedel, Blain & Prosser PA, Tampa 813 229 0144
Recommended in Bankruptcy

STIVER, Charles
Greenberg Traurig LLP, Miami
305 579 0760
stiverc@gtlaw.com
Recommended in Tax
Practice Areas: Tax; structured finance.
Prof. Memberships: Adjunct Professor, University of Miami Law School, course on international tax; Listed, 'Best Lawyers in America,' (2005-06).
Personal: New York University School of Law (LLM, 1975); Stanford Law School (JD, 1974); Stanford University (BA, 1971).

STRAFER, Richard
G Richard Strafer PA, Miami
305 857 9090
Recommended in Litigation

STUBBS, Sidney
Jones, Foster, Johnston & Stubbs, P.A., West Palm Beach 561 659 3000
sstubbs@jones-foster.com
Recommended in Litigation
Practice Areas: Commercial litigation with focus on law firm litigation ranging from firm dissolutions to charges of malpractice; corporate merger and acquisition disputes; and eminent domain cases including some of the largest and most complex in Florida history.
Prof. Memberships: Fellow, American College of Trial Lawyers; Life Fellow, American Bar Foundation; and Certified Civil Trial Advocate, National Board of Trial Advocacy. Has served as a member of The Florida Bar Board of Governors and President of The Palm Beach County Bar Association.
Career: Florida Bar, admitted 1966; Special Counsel to The Honorable Bob Graham, Governor, State of Florida 1983; current President of the firm.
Personal: JD University of Florida College of Law with honors (1965), executive editor of the 'University of Florida Law Review'; BS, History, Florida State University.

STUTTS, Charles
Holland & Knight LLP, Tampa
813 227 8500
charles.stutts@hklaw.com
Recommended in Banking & Finance
Practice Areas: Partner in the firm's
Business Law Department, with an
emphasis on securities and banking law.
As former general counsel to the Florida
Comptroller's Office and the Department of Banking and Finance, he helped
develop the agency's policies on banking, mortgage lending and securities
regulation. He directed the agency's
securities enforcement efforts and coordinated prosecutions under Florida's
antifraud provisions with its federal
counterparts including the US Securities
and Exchange Commission and Commodity Futures Trading Commission.
He devotes a substantial portion of his
practice to federal and state supervision
and regulation of banks, trust companies, securities broker-dealers and
investment advisers.

SUBIN, Ben
Holland & Knight LLP, Orlando
407 425 8500
ben.subin@hklaw.com
Recommended in Construction
Practice Areas: Mr Subin is a Partner
in the firm's Construction Practice
Group. He has handled matters involving complex construction litigation
regarding defects, delay damages, acceleration claims, changed conditions,
default terminations and bid protests.
He also has extensive experience representing clients in power plant construction. He assists clients in construction
contract preparation and review as well
as surety claims and defense.

SULLIVAN, Michael
Greenberg Traurig LLP, Orlando
407 418 2376
sullivanm@gtlaw.com
Recommended in Hotels and Resorts
Practice Areas: Real estate; hotels and
resorts.
Prof. Memberships: Member, Interna-
tional Drive Community Redevelop-
ment Agency; Member, Board of Direc-
tors, Kissimmee/Osceola County Cham-
ber of Commerce; Co-Chair, Yale Col-
lege Alumni Schools Committee of Cen-
tral Florida Member, Board of Directors,
Central Florida Yale Club.
Career: Listed, 2004 Legal Elite, Florida
Trend Magazine. Listed, 'Best Lawyers in
America,' 2005-06.
Publications: 'Remedying Athlete Agent
Abuse: A Securities Law Approach', Vol.
2, No. 1 Fall 1984, Entertainment &
Sports Law Journal, University of Miami
School of Law.
Personal: JD, with honors, University of
Connecticut School of Law, 1984. BA,
Yale University, 1980.

SUMBERG, John C
Bilzin Sumberg Baena Price & Axelrod
LLP, Miami 305 350 2364
jsumberg@bilzin.com
Recommended in Real Estate
Practice Areas: Co-Chair of Real Estate
Group. Mr Sumberg has extensive experience in all aspects of real estate acquisition and disposition, development,
financing, joint ventures, workouts and
restructurings. He represents owners,
investors and lenders in connection with
commercial, retail, mixed-use and residential real estate projects, including
condominiums, condo/hotels, apartments and planned community projects.
Career: Author of various articles on
real estate matters, including urban infill
revitalization, sale leasebacks and commercial leasing. Listed in Best Lawyers of
America and Florida Trend's Legal Elite.
Personal: JD Yale Law School, editor,
Yale Law Journal; BA magna cum laude,
Yale College.

TAGUE, Brian
Tew Cardenas LLP, Miami
305 536 8480
BT@tewlaw.com
Recommended in Real Estate
Practice Areas: Real estate development; real estate finance; joint ventures
and partnerships, commercial leasing;
general commercial law; represents
developers, investors, lenders, landlords
and tenants in all types of real estate and
commercial transactions.
Prof. Memberships: Urban Land Institute.
Career: Listed in 'Best Lawyers in America'; Listed In 'Best Lawyers in Florida';
University of Florida Law School (JD
1972 with Honors); University of Florida (BA with High Honors); Member,
Order of the Coif; Member, Phi Beta
Kappa.
Personal: Married to wife Mary; two
daughters: Megan (age 16); Alison (age
15); member, Board of Trustees Carroll-
ton Sacred Heart School; former Board
Member Miami City Club.

TARBE, Susan J
Colson Hicks Eidson, Coral Gables
305 476 7400
susan@colson.com
Recommended in Litigation
Practice Areas: Commercial law; white
collar criminal defense; class actions.
Career: Ms Tarbe has over 15 years of
experience in commercial litigation and
white-collar criminal defense, specializing in civil and criminal healthcare
fraud, SEC enforcement and internal
corporate investigations; has more than
11 years of federal trial and grand jury
practice as an Assistant United States
Attorney with the United States Attorney's Office where she was Chief of the
Economic Crimes Division; graduated
cum laude from the University of Miami
School of Law; clerked for the Honorable William M Hoeveler, United States

District Court for the Southern District
of Florida.

TEBLUM, Gary
Trenam, Kemker, Scharf, Barkin, Frye,
O'Neill & Mullis PA, Tampa
813 223 7474
Recommended in Corporate/M&A

TEIN, Michael
Shook, Hardy & Bacon LLP, Miami
305 960 6953
mtein@shb.com
Recommended in Litigation
Practice Areas: Specializes in litigation
and trial of complex commercial and
white-collar cases. Represents numerous
high profile corporate and individual
clients in both civil and criminal matters, in state and federal court, as well as
before state and federal administrative
agencies. Has first-chaired more than
two dozen jury trials to verdict in federal
court, filed over forty appellate briefs
and personally argued fifteen cases to
the US Court of Appeals.
Prof. Memberships: Admitted to practice in Florida and Massachusetts and
before the US Court of Appeals for the
Eleventh Circuit. Named as one of
South Florida's 'Up and Coming Attorneys' for the past three years by the
'South Florida Legal Guide.'
Career: Joined Shook, Hardy & Bacon,
2000; became Partner 2003. Appointment: Receiver by the US District Court
for the Southern District of Florida in
two separate enforcement actions.
Serves in a pro-bono capacity as general
counsel to a prominent non-profit
breast-cancer-advocacy organization.
Publications: Devaluation of Non-
White Community in Remedies for
Subsidized Housing Discrimination,
140 U. Pa. L. Rev. 1463 (1992).
Personal: JD, cum laude, University of
Pennsylvania Law School, 1992; BA,
summa cum laude, Yale University.

TESCHER, Donald
Tescher Gutter Chaves Josepher Rubin
Ruffin & Forman PA, Boca Ratón
561 998 7847
Recommended in Tax

THOMAS, Harry
Radey, Thomas, Yon & Clark,
Tallahassee 850 425 6654
Recommended in Insurance

THOMSON, Parker
Hogan & Hartson LLP, Miami
305 459 6613
pdthomson@hhlaw.com
Recommended in Litigation
Practice Areas: Managing Partner of
the Miami office. Focuses primarily on
complex, constitutional and commercial
litigation; including class actions and
multi-state litigation; corporate law,
communications and media law, appellate litigation, environmental law, and
federal and state constitutional issues.
His commitment to public service has
earned him numerous awards for signif-

icant pro bono contributions, for volunteer legal assistance to impoverished
persons and persons with disabilities
and other civic efforts.
Prof. Memberships: Chairman or President, Miami-Dade Performing Arts
Center Trust, 1988-present; President,
Appleseed Center for Law & Justice, Inc.,
1996-present; Chairman, Dade County
Fair Campaign Practices Committee,
1985-91; Chairman, Florida's Advocacy
Center for Persons with Disabilities,
1979-97.
Personal: Harvard Law School (JD,
magna cum laude).

THROCKMORTON, Charles
Kozyak Tropin & Throckmorton, Miami
305 377 0655
cwt@kttlaw.com
Recommended in Bankruptcy
Practice Areas: Bankruptcy; debtors'
and creditors' rights; workouts; com-
mercial litigation.
Prof. Memberships: American Bar
Association; American Bankruptcy
Institute; Bankruptcy Bar Association
for the Southern District of Florida;
Association of Commercial Finance
Attorneys.
Personal: University of Virginia School
of Law, JD 1979; Duke University, BA
(magna cum laude), 1976.

TOWNSEND, William D
Bilzin Sumberg Baena Price & Axelrod
LLP, Tallahassee 850-425-3019
wtownsend@bilzin.com
Recommended in Tax
Prof. Memberships: Florida Bar, Chair
Tax Section 2003-04.
Career: Practicing in the areas of state,
local, and multistate taxation. Represents clients on legislative tax matters,
including telecommunications and
computer services taxes, corporate
income tax issues, sales tax exemption
matters, and tax controversy matters for
corporate, sales, intangibles and
telecommunications taxes. Represents
clients before the Florida Department of
Revenue and revenue departments of
several other states. Consults with major
corporations in state tax planning activities. Author of the BNA portfolio on
Florida Corporate Income Tax. Former
General Counsel, Florida Department of
Revenue. Former Assistant Attorney
General, Florida.

TRAURIG, Robert
Greenberg Traurig LLP, Miami
305 579 0500
traurigr@gtlaw.com
Recommended in Real Estate
Practice Areas: Real estate; environ-
mental; land development.
Prof. Memberships: Member, Citizen's
Board of the University of Miami.
Director, Greater Miami Jewish Federa-
tion; Member, Board of Trustees, Beth
David Congregation; Past Chairman,
Greater Miami Chamber of Commerce;
Immediate past Chairman, Miami

Region of the National Conference; Co-Chairman, Columbus Discovery Commemorative Fund; Past President and currently Chairman Emeritus, Greater Miami Opera Association; Former Member, Board of Directors, New World Symphony; Member, Executive Committee of Partners for Progress; Member, Board of Directors, Inner City Children's Dance Co.
Personal: University of Miami School of Law (JD, 1950); University of Miami (BBA, 1947).

TROMBLEY, Gary
Trombley & Hanes, Tampa
813 229 7918
Recommended in Litigation

TROPIN, Harley S
Kozyak Tropin & Throckmorton, Miami
305 372 1800
hst@kttlaw.com
Recommended in Litigation
Practice Areas: Senior Litigation Practice Partner.
Prof. Memberships: Florida Bar (current Chair, Federal Courts Committee); Eleventh Circuit Judicial Nominating Commission (member, 1986-90; Chair 1989); Eleventh Circuit Judicial Conference (Southern District Delegate, 1994-97); Professor of Trial Advocacy, University of Miami School of Law; Iron Arrow (2003, highest honor attainable at University of Miami).
Career: Specializes in complex commercial litigation and class actions. Co-founder Kozyak Tropin (1982). Valdes-Fauli, Cobb & Petrey, Miami, (Partner, 1981-82). Recognized in 'Best Lawyers in America' (1996-).
Personal: Born Bayside, New York. The George Washington University (BA, 1974); University of Miami School of Law (JD, 1977, cum laude).

TURK, Robert
Stearns Weaver Miller Weissler Alhadeff & Sitterson, P.A., Miami
305 789 3200
Recommended in Employment

UDOLF, Bruce
Ruden McClosky SC, Fort Lauderdale
954 764 6660
Recommended in Litigation

ULLMAN, Samuel C
Bilzin Sumberg Baena Price & Axelrod LLP, Miami 305 350 7300
sullman@bilzin.com
Recommended in Tax
Prof. Memberships: The Florida Bar: former Chairman, Tax Section; Former Chairman, Tax Law Certification Committee. Fellow, American College of Tax Counsel; Fellow, American Law Institute.
Career: Florida Bar Board Certified Tax Attorney since 1983. Business and transactional tax matters, federal tax controversies, state and local tax, tax-exempt organizations. Counsels clients on federal and state tax matters, mergers, acquisitions, business combinations, business

law, and taxation of healthcare related matters. Represents clients in matters before the IRS and state tax authorities. Served as special counsel to the Florida Department of Revenue. Recipient Florida Bar Tax Section Outstanding Attorney Award, 1993-94.

VAZQUEZ-BELLO, Clemente
Gunster, Yoakley & Stewart, P.A., Miami
305 376 6000
Recommended in Banking & Finance

VEZINA, Rob
Vezina Lawrence & Piscitelli PA, Tallahassee 850 224 6205
Recommended in Construction

VICKERS, Cass
Vickers Madsen & Goldman, Tallahassee 850 523 0400
Recommended in Tax

WACHTER, Charles
Fowler White Boggs Banker, Tampa
813 228 7411
Recommended in Insurance

WAKSHLAG, Stanley
Akerman Senterfitt, Miami
305 374 5600
stanley.wakshlag@akerman.com
Recommended in Litigation
Career: Stanley H Wakshlag, a former Managing Partner of the Miami office, is a shareholder who focuses his practice in the areas of securities litigation and regulatory proceedings, complex commercial litigation, antitrust and class actions. Mr Wakshlag's litigation experience includes the representation of major institutional clients in the area of complex commercial litigation including securities, lender liability, banking, foreclosure, antitrust, ERISA, trademark, entertainment, partnership and corporate litigation. He also specializes in internal corporate, audit and special committee investigations. His experience has resulted in numerous favorable published judicial opinions.

WALBOLT, Sylvia
Carlton Fields, St Petersburg
727 822 7000
Recommended in Litigation

WALKER, Steve
Lewis, Longman & Walker PA, West Palm Beach 561 640 0820
Recommended in Environment

WALKER, Jr, H William
White & Case LLP, Miami
305 995 5205
wwalker@whitecase.com
Recommended in Real Estate
Practice Areas: Mr Walker's areas of practice include all aspects of real estate acquisition and disposition, ownership, use, development and finance, and general corporate matters. He has participated in and represented owners of, investors in and lenders to numerous complex commercial, residential, retail, industrial, hospitality and mixed-use

real estate projects, including those of major domestic and international developers. Mr Walker has also participated in the planning, development, financing and sale of a variety of planned communities, including primary housing, resort housing, hospitality and mixed-use properties.
Prof. Memberships: The Florida Bar.

WALLER Jr, Edward
Fowler White Boggs Banker, Tampa
813 228 7411
Recommended in Healthcare

WARE, Rex D
Bilzin Sumberg Baena Price & Axelrod LLP, Tallahassee 850 425 3029
rware@bilzin.com
Recommended in Tax
Prof. Memberships: Assistant Director, State Tax Division, Tax Section of The Florida Bar. Member, ABA Tax Section.
Career: Over 20 years of experience counseling clients on state and local tax issues; representation of clients before the Florida Department of Revenue and local government taxing authorities; litigation of state and local tax controversies in courts and administrative tribunals; legislative and regulatory matters; government contract litigation. He regularly makes presentations to industry, professional and other organizations, focusing on state and local tax litigation. Previously, Deputy General Counsel of the Florida Department of Revenue and has 12 years of private litigation practice.

WARNER, Jonathan
Law Offices of Jonathan H. (Jason) Warner, PA, Miami 305 670 0007
Recommended in Tax

WEAVER, Ronald
Stearns Weaver Miller Weissler Alhadeff & Sitterson, P.A., Tampa
813 223 4800
Recommended in Real Estate

WEBER, Victoria
Hopping Green & Sams, P.A., Tallahassee 850 222 7500
vweber@hgslaw.com
Recommended in Tax
Practice Areas: State and local tax planning and controversy work; economic development incentives; and legislative relations.
Prof. Memberships: The Florida Bar, past Chair, State Tax Division; ABA State and Local Tax Committee; Florida Chamber of Commerce, Past Chair of both Tax Committee and Legislative Affairs Committee.
Career: 26 years in state and local tax, including service as General Counsel to Florida Department of Revenue, Tax Counsel to Florida House of Representatives, and 15 years in private practice representing Florida, national and international businesses, and Florida trade associations.
Personal: JD with honors, and BS, Florida State University.

WEINBERG Jr, Morris
Zuckerman Spaeder LLP, Tampa
813 221 1010
Recommended in Litigation

WEINSTEIN, Andrew
Holland & Knight LLP, Miami
305 374 8500
andrew.weinstein@hklaw.com
Recommended in Tax
Practice Areas: Partner in the firm's Private Wealth Services Group. His practice involves domestic and international tax, trust and estate planning for high net worth clients. Served as lead counsel for multi-billion dollar estates and trusts. Extensive experience in federal tax disputes, especially involving tax shelter compliance. Member of ABA Tax Section of Administrative Practice, Fellow of American College of Tax Counsel and American College of Trusts and Estates Counsel.

WEINTRAUB, Lee
Becker & Poliakoff PA, Fort Lauderdale
954 987 7550
Recommended in Construction

WEISS, Christopher
Holland & Knight LLP, Orlando
407 425 8500
christopher.weiss@hklaw.com
Recommended in Construction
Practice Areas: Partner in the Litigation Section, practicing in the area of commercial litigation with particular emphasis on construction law, defects in construction, design claims, delay, disruption and acceleration claims, lien foreclosures, and arbitration on behalf of contractors, subcontractors, materialmen, developers and public bodies. He is a frequent lecturer and author of many articles in the areas of commercial litigation and construction law for bar and trade association publications. He is an active member and panelist of the American Arbitration Association, Associated Builders and Contractors, the Construction Financial Management Association, Associated General Contractors of America and the American Subcontractors Association.

WEISSLER, Robert
Stearns Weaver Miller Weissler Alhadeff & Sitterson, P.A., Miami
305 789 3200
Recommended in Hotels and Resorts

WELBAUM, Earl
Welbaum, Guernsey, Hingston, Greenleaf & Gregory LLP, Miami
305 441 8900
Recommended in Construction

WILSON, Michael
Broad and Cassel, Orlando
407 839 4200
Recommended in Construction

WILSON III, Harry
Smith Hulsey & Busey, Jacksonville
904 359 7700
Recommended in Real Estate

WINSTON, Richard L
Steel Hector & Davis LLP, Miami
305 577 7025
rwinston@steelhector.com
Recommended in Tax

Practice Areas: Mr Winston focuses on structuring and analyzing domestic and cross-border transactions for US and foreign multinationals. He has experience planning for acquisitions, dispositions, reorganizations, joint ventures, and finance company arrangements. His clients regularly engage him to assist with foreign tax credit planning, tax deferral techniques, 'choice of entity' decisions, repatriation planning, transfer pricing issues, intellectual property development, and 'Subpart F' issues.
Prof. Memberships: International Fiscal Association, USA Branch; American Bar Association (Tax Section).
Publications: Lexis-Nexis Butterworths Tolly (U.K.) International Tax and Investment Service, U.S. Chapter.
Personal: JD, University of Virginia, 1994, (Editor, 'Virginia Law Review' and 'Virginia Tax Review'); BA, University of Virginia, 1990 (High Distinction); LLM (taxation), New York University, 1995.

WOLFSON, Mark J
Foley & Lardner, Tampa
813 225 4119
mwolfson@foley.com
Recommended in Bankruptcy

Career: Mark J Wolfson is Chair of Foley & Lardner's Litigation Department in Tampa, and the leader of the firm's Business Reorganizations Practice Group for the Southeast region. Mr Wolfson has extensive experience in bankruptcy cases, primarily representing secured creditors, creditors committees, buyers of assets in chapter 11, shareholders, and parties to contracts, such as landlords and franchisers. He has experience in both state and US bankruptcy courts litigating fraudulent transfer and preference actions and has been involved in state assignment for the benefit of creditor proceedings. Mr Wolfson received his law degree from the University of Florida.

WOODSON, R Duke
Foley & Lardner, Tallahassee
407 244 3247
dwoodson@foley.com
Recommended in Real Estate

Career: Duke Woodson, Partner in Foley & Lardner's Orlando office, heads the firm's Environmental Law Practice in Florida. A Member of the Regulatory Department, he represents business and governmental clients throughout the state in environmental compliance and permitting matters. He is also a member of the Golf and Resort Services Team. Mr Woodson's extensive experience is in environmental law with emphasis on real estate development. Mr Woodson has been practicing law in Florida since receiving his JD degree from the University of Florida in 1975. He holds undergraduate and master's degrees in civil engineering from Auburn University.

WORSHAM, Lee
Ruden McClosky SC, West Palm Beach
561 838 4500
Recommended in Environment

YADLEY, Gregory
Shumaker Loop & Kendrick LLP, Tampa
813 229 7600
Recommended in Corporate/M&A

YON, David
Radey, Thomas, Yon & Clark, Tallahassee
850 425 6654
Recommended in Insurance

ZEWADSKI, William
Trenam, Kemker, Scharf, Barkin, Frye, O'Neill & Mullis PA, Tampa
813 223 7474
Recommended in Bankruptcy

ZIMET, Bruce
Bruce A Zimet PA, Fort Lauderdale
954 764 7081
Recommended in Litigation

ZINOBER, Peter
Zinober & McCrea, P.A., Tampa
813 224 9004
Recommended in Employment

AKERMAN SENTERFITT

THE FIRM

Chairman & CEO: J Thomas Cardwell

FIRM OVERVIEW: With more than 400 attorneys in eight offices, Akerman Senterfitt is one of the largest law firms in the State of Florida. This presence allows the firm's attorneys to represent the interests of their in-state, national and international clients anywhere in Florida and Washington, DC.

MAIN AREAS OF PRACTICE:

Corporate: Akerman Senterfitt has the largest corporate practice in Florida with more than 100 attorneys. In the past several years the firm has managed billions of dollars worth of transactions. The firm regularly represents domestic and foreign public companies, including nearly half of the largest public companies in Florida. Akerman Senterfitt also represents financial institutions, private equity and venture capital funds, and the companies in which they invest, as well as individual entrepreneurs. Its primary areas of focus are mergers and acquisitions, securities, taxation, public finance, banking and lending and employee benefits.

Environmental: Representing both the private and public sectors, Akerman Senterfitt's environmental attorneys have substantial experience in representing a wide variety of businesses, governmental entities, and other organizations. The firm handles such matters as federal, state, and local regulatory compliance and permitting, managing environmental risks and conducting due diligence investigations, managing the assessment and remediation of contaminated property, defending enforcement actions, and prosecuting or defending civil actions to recover cleanup costs or environmental damages to property.

Government: Few facets of life are not touched by the institutions of government and the people who constitute its bodies. The firm's clients, by virtue of their size or the broad public impact of the projects they undertake, are no exception. In order to represent their interests, Akerman Senterfitt has built a large and effective government practice. The firm has points of entry into almost every governmental or quasi-governmental body in Florida, and into many agencies in Washington as well. The firm is as effective in its lobbying and dialog with these agencies as it is in its administrative proceedings or litigation against them.

Intellectual Property: Akerman Senterfitt's intellectual property practice is the largest and most broadly experienced in Florida. The firm's IP lawyers are engineers and scientists from many rapidly developing fields of industry such as fuel cells, biomedical devices, semiconductor materials and software. This knowledge base helps the firm's lawyers to create broader patents, draft better contracts, develop more profitable licenses, and litigate more effectively. The firm represents clients across the globe including many Fortune 500 firms and major research universities.

International: As Florida's role in international trade and finance expands, Akerman Senterfitt has developed a multilingual, multicultural, cross-disciplinary international practice. The firm's goal is to assist US clients to grow their international business activities and to assist foreign clients to establish businesses and flourish in the United States. The international practice group includes attorneys from all the firm's offices and from every major practice group, including corporate and securities, banking, tax, immigration, admiralty, aviation, intellectual property, real estate, and litigation.

Litigation: The firm has the largest litigation department in Florida, which is chaired by the former Chief Judge of the United States District Court for the Southern District of Florida, Edward B Davis. The former Chief Judge of the United States Court of Appeals for the Eleventh Circuit, Joseph Hatchett, heads the Appellate Practice Group. The experience of the firm's litigators ranges from small disputes to complex lawsuits such as securities, class action, antitrust, trademark and copyright litigation.

US OFFICES

DISTRICT OF COLUMBIA
801 Pennsylvania Avenue NW, Suite 750, **Washington**, DC 20004
Tel: 202 393 6222 **Fax:** 202 393 5959

FLORIDA
Las Olas Centre II, 350 East Las Olas Boulevard, Suite 1600,
Fort Lauderdale, FL 33301-2229
Tel: 954 463 2700 **Fax:** 954 463 2224

50 North Laura Street, Suite 2500
Jacksonville, FL 32202-3646
Tel: 904 798 3700 **Fax:** 904 798 3730

One Southeast Third Avenue, 28th Floor, **Miami**, FL 33131-1714
Tel: 305 374 5600 **Fax:** 305 374 5095

Citrus Center, 17th Floor, 255 South Orange Avenue,
Orlando, FL 32801-3483
Tel: 407 843 7860 **Fax:** 407 843 6610

106 East College Avenue, Suite 1200, **Tallahassee**, FL 32301
Tel: 850 224 9634 **Fax:** 850 222 0103

Wachovia Center, 100 South Ashley Drive, Suite 1500,
Tampa, FL 33602-5311
Tel: 813 223 7333 **Fax:** 813 223 2837

Esperante Building, 222 Lakeview Avenue, Suite 400,
West Palm Beach, FL 33401-6183
Tel: 561 653 5000 **Fax:** 561 659 6313

Real Estate: Akerman Senterfitt has more than 60 lawyers who focus on the needs of clients in the real estate industry. This represents one of the largest full service real estate practices in Florida. The firm provides comprehensive representation through changing business cycles at all levels of activity. The firm manages the legal aspects of large land deals and construction projects, assists developers in meeting tough environmental regulations, and advises on all aspects of transactional work, including workouts and restructurings. The firm's focus areas include land use and entitlements, debt and equity finance, income property, and the acquisition and development of projects within all real estate asset classes.

Trusts, Estates & Family Law: Akerman Senterfitt has carefully built a broadly experienced and highly respected trusts, estates, and family law practice. Not only does the firm administer and litigate personal legal matters, it has crafted some of the laws that govern these affairs. The firm's statewide presence allows it to manage the legal issues of families and their businesses regardless of venue. And while some firms segregate the attorneys in this area into separate groups, the firm believes in the cross-pollination of ideas that results from maintaining one cohesive practice. The firm's planners understand litigation and can design agreements that minimize the possibility of future legal actions.

CLIENTS: Akerman Senterfitt provides a full range of legal services, with experienced attorneys in each area to serve its diverse client base. The firm has served its clients since 1920 and now represents a high percentage of the largest public companies in Florida, as well as private companies, government entities, educational establishments and high net worth individuals.

ASTIGARRAGA DAVIS

THE FIRM

Contact: José I Astigarraga

AREAS OF PRACTICE:
Litigation & Arbitration 100%

FIRM OVERVIEW: Astigarraga Davis is a litigation and arbitration firm. With a broad range of experience, its lawyers prosecute and defend a wide variety of commercial litigation and business tort cases. Serving primarily multinational corporate clients, the firm's principal areas of practice are international litigation and arbitration; financial services litigation including bankruptcy; prosecution of commercial fraud including asset recovery; defense of consumer class actions; and intellectual property litigation.

MAIN AREAS OF PRACTICE:

Litigation & Arbitration: Representing primarily North American and European multinational companies, Astigarraga Davis both prosecutes and defends cases in federal and state courts involving international business disputes. Using its extensive international experience, multilingual capabilities, multicultural background, and broad network of contacts in the region, the firm also oversees and directs substantial business litigation pending in Latin American courts.

The firm has a leading International Arbitration Practice handling cases before the major international arbitral institutions. The firm's lawyers are active in arbitration and litigation initiatives. José Astigarraga, for example, was one of eight delegates appointed by the United States Government to advise the NAFTA Commission on international arbitration and dispute resolution. He is a member of the American Arbitration Association's International Rules Advisory Committee, serves on the London Court of International Arbitration, and has lectured extensively on international litigation and arbitration including to the negotiators of the Free Trade Agreement of the Americas. Astigarraga Davis represents companies in investment disputes with foreign states, including before the International Centre for Investment Disputes (ICSID).

Financial Services Litigation, including Bankruptcy: Astigarraga Davis has extensive litigation experience representing lenders, creditors, banks and other financial institutions in disputes in the United States and abroad. The firm represents financial institutions in state and federal court litigation in investor disputes, securities issues, and loan enforcement. The firm's lawyers handle much creditors' rights litigation including such pre-judgment creditors' remedies as replevin, garnishment, attachment and injunctions.

As well, the firm represents lenders and creditors domestically in bankruptcy courts in Florida and other states, and internationally in Latin America, including in multijurisdictional insolvencies. Founding shareholder Greg Grossman has extensive bankruptcy experience, having handled cases in a number of domestic bankruptcy courts in a diverse array of cases and has lectured on a variety of insolvency related topics. José Astigarraga has served as consultant to the World Bank on Latin American insolvency law issues and has handled international insolvency cases for both bank and non-bank clients.

HEAD OFFICE

FLORIDA
701 Brickell Avenue, 16th Floor, **Miami** FL 33131
Tel: 305 372 8282   **Fax:** 305 372 8202
Email: jia@astidavis.com
Website: www.astidavis.com

Commercial Fraud & Asset Recovery: The firm's work includes a strong practice in fraud prosecution and asset recovery. Working with its network of lawyers and contacts, the firm has pursued fraudsters in a variety of jurisdictions to recover fraudulently obtained assets. The firm also devises fraud prevention and contingency response plans for corporate clients and advises audit committees on such issues. Name partner Edward H Davis, Jr. is a Certified Fraud Examiners and has lectured extensively on fraud prosecution and international asset recovery.

Defense of Consumer Class Actions: Astigarraga Davis has experienced class action litigators, including founding shareholder Edward Mullins who has defended numerous class actions in state and federal courts. He has defended financial institutions and insurance companies in claims involving the Truth-in-Lending Act, the Florida Unfair Trade Practices Act, Florida's usury statute, and claims derived from various consumer insurance statutes. The firm's expertise in arbitration has benefited the class action defense practice, including in litigation over whether arbitration clauses in consumer contracts are unconscionable and unenforceable.

Intellectual Property: The firm has extensive experience in intellectual property, with capabilities including trademark, trade secret, internet, e-commerce, and media law disputes. Founding shareholder Edward Mullins, a former chair of the Florida Bar Media and Communications Law Committee, has represented newspapers, magazines, radio and television stations, and television networks in numerous lawsuits involving libel, slander, invasion of privacy, outrage, tortious interference with advantageous relationships, trademark infringement, copyright infringement and other publication disputes. The firm's deep knowledge allows it to represent its corporate clients in domain name disputes, intellectual property infringement claims based on the internet, and similar publication claims.

CLIENTS: Astigarraga Davis' clients include multinational companies, global banks, Fortune 500 corporations and government entities.

ASTIGARRAGA DAVIS

BERCOW & RADELL, PA

THE FIRM

Managing Partner: Michael Radell
Senior Partner: Jeffrey Bercow

Number of partners: 4
Number of other lawyers: 2

AREAS OF PRACTICE:

Land Use 25%
Zoning 25%
Growth Management 25%
Environmental 25%

FIRM OVERVIEW: Bercow & Radell, PA commenced its law practice in 1996. The firm's attorneys include Jeffrey Bercow and Michael Radell, its co-founding shareholders, as well as partners Ben Fernandez and Michael Larkin, and Graham Penn and Melissa Tapanes Llahues, who are associates with the firm. The firm specializes in land use, zoning, growth management and environmental matters. It represents the interests of landowners and developers seeking approvals from governmental boards and agencies at the local, state and federal levels. The firm handles a range of matters that concern the use of real estate including zoning approvals, amendments of local government comprehensive plans, developments of regional impact (DRIs), due diligence reviews, growth management, impact fees, concurrency issues and environmental matters. The attorneys of Bercow & Radell, PA have represented clients before such local governments as: Miami-Dade County, Miami, Coral Gables, Miami Springs, Aventura, Pinecrest, Miami Beach, Doral, Miami Lakes, Miami Gardens, Medley, North Miami Beach, North Miami, Key Biscayne, Opa-Locka, South Miami, Hialeah, Pembroke Pines, Greenacres, Plantation, Homestead, Collier County, Orange County, Marion County and the City of Ocala. Members of the firm appear frequently before the South Florida Regional Planning Council, Miami-Dade County's Board of County Commissioners, Community Councils/Zoning Appeals Boards, Planning Advisory Board, and the Environmental Quality Control Board; the City of Miami Beach City Commission, Zoning Board of Adjustment, Design Review Board/Historic Preservation Board, and Planning Board; City of Miami City Commission, Zoning Board, and Planning Advisory Board; the South Florida Water Management District; the St. John's Water Management District, and other local governmental bodies, and also frequently lobby staff of the Florida Department of Community Affairs. In addition, the firm often represents its clients in appellate litigation involving the administrative matters it has handled.

HEAD OFFICE

FLORIDA
200 South Biscayne Boulevard, Suite 850, **Miami**, FL 33131
Tel: 305 374 5300   **Fax:** 305 377 6222
Email: Jbercow@brzoninglaw.com

CLIENTS: The firm represents developers, landowners, lenders and others with property interests affected by the laws and regulations that govern the use of real estate in various countries and cities within South Florida. Clients include Florida Rock industries, Home Depot USA, Turnberry Associates, Walgreen Company, Lennar Homes, Gulfside-Dadeland, BMS Management Company, Target Stores, Johnson & Wales University, United Homes, Weitzer Development, City Furniture, R.L. Homes, Pinnacle Housing, Lucky Start, Cornerstone Group, General Real Estate Corporation, Sterling Centrecorp, Century Five, International Place Associates, Marriott International, Miami Beach Vacation Resorts, Peebles Atlantic Development Corporation, Aventura Marina, Trafalgar Associates, Williamson Cadillac Company, Terranova, La Gorce Country Club, BP Amoco, The Doran Jason Group, Landstar Homes, Pelican Bay Development, Ocwen Federal Bank, Maefield Development, Lowell Dunn Company, and Arden Savoy Partners.

BERCOW & RADELL
ZONING, LAND USE AND ENVIRONMENTAL LAW

BERGER SINGERMAN

THE FIRM

Chairman: Mitchell W Berger
Co-Chief Executive Officer: James L Berger
Co-Chief Executive Officer: Paul Steven Singerman

Number of partners: 26
Number of other lawyers: 19

FIRM OVERVIEW: Berger Singerman is a Florida based business law firm with 45 lawyers practicing out of offices in Boca Raton, Ft. Lauderdale, Miami, and Tallahassee. Attorney team members are organized into four practice teams: the Administrative Law Team, the Business Reorganization Team, the Dispute Resolution Team, and the Transaction Team. Since its founding in 1985, Berger Singerman has distinguished itself by the quality of its lawyers and practice, and by its passionate commitment to client service.

MAIN AREAS OF PRACTICE:

Administrative Law: Berger Singerman's Administrative Law Team represents a variety of private and public sector clients in regulatory matters before federal, state, regional and local agencies. The members of the team have had meaningful involvement in shaping the landscape of environmental and land use law in Florida during their long and distinguished careers. In addition, the members are recognized as leaders in the fields of healthcare regulation, waste management, governmental procurement, and white collar crime prevention.

Business Reorganization: The size, depth and national reputation of its Business Reorganization Team distinguish Berger Singerman. Berger Singerman has one of the largest business reorganization practice groups in the region and its members are consistently involved in the most significant business bankruptcy cases and out of court workouts in the region. The team represents business debtors, creditors' committees, trade creditors, institutional and non-institutional secured creditors and lessors, court appointed trustees, receivers and assignees for the benefit of creditors. The team also represents strategic and financial investors in a variety of insolvency related merger and acquisition engagements, including acquisition of distressed businesses, divisions, assets and intellectual property of such businesses.

Dispute Resolution: The Dispute Resolution Team handles a wide variety of complex commercial disputes in federal and state courts and alternative dispute resolution fora throughout the Florida region and across the United States. The team has handled multimillion dollar class action disputes and lender liability cases. The team represents regional, national and international clients ranging from Fortune 500 companies to entrepreneurs. The team regularly represents household names in the equipment leasing industry headquartered throughout the United States. The Dispute Resolution Team regularly litigates a wide range of corporate disputes, such as fights over ownership and control, securities fraud and shareholder derivative claims. Team members bring specialized expertise in business torts such as fraud, breach of fiduciary duty, theft of trade secrets, and tortuous interference with business relationships and contracts, to support more aggressive theories and recoveries in this area. The team also features specialized expertise in employment law and non-compete cases and regularly handles employment termination cases, non-compete and other covenant enforcement actions, and various other claims employees assert. In the intellectual property realm, the team represents companies, investors, franchisors, franchisees and individuals seeking to enforce (or challenge and invalidate) patents, trademarks, copyrights and trade secrets. The Dispute Resolution Team's clients in disputes relating to real estate include developers, governmental agencies, contractors, buyers, sellers, brokers, title companies and lenders.

Transactional Law: Berger Singerman's Transaction Team represents corporate and individual clients in sophisticated international, domestic and foreign transactions. The firm's Transaction Team possesses expertise in corporate, securities, real estate, financing, technology, intellectual property, aviation and tax matters. The Transaction Team attorneys bring multi-disciplinary legal expertise to structure, negotiate, document and close complex business transactions. Most of the Transaction Team's attorneys practice across the traditional legal boundaries of corporate, securities, mergers and acquisitions, commercial real estate, financing and tax. The team utilizes a cross-disciplinary approach - tax partners often structure, negotiate, and handle an entire business deal, rather than merely the 'tax portion' of a transaction – the real estate attorneys have significant experience with complex corporate structuring and transactions, employment agreements and other business agreements – and most of the Transaction Team's lawyers are experienced in transactions which are implemented within a bankruptcy case. By using all the expertise of attorneys familiar with many legal disciplines, the Transaction Team delivers more effective legal representation in a cost effective manner.

REPRESENTATIVE CLIENTS: Stiles Corporation; Atlas Air, Inc.; Polar Air Cargo, Inc.; Regions Bank, an Alabama banking corporation; Banco Espirito Santo International, Ltd., Esb Finance, Ltd. and Banco Espirito Santo S.A. (Nassau Branch); The Piper Aircraft Corporation Irrevocable Trust; AT & Latin American Corporation; HBO Latin America Media Services, Inc.

BILZIN SUMBERG BAENA PRICE & AXELROD LLP

THE FIRM

Managing Partner: John C Sumberg
Number of partners: 45
Number of other lawyers: 50

FIRM OVERVIEW: Bilzin Sumberg is a full service commercial law firm with offices in Miami and Tallahassee. The firm's attorneys work as a cohesive team, combining legal expertise with business insight and innovative solutions to assist clients in achieving their objectives. They view each of their clients and the matters in which it represents them as unique and of paramount importance. Whether in the courtroom or in the boardroom, they shoulder every client's problem as if it were their own.

MAIN AREAS OF PRACTICE:

Capital Markets: Bilzin Sumberg represents the country's largest special servicer of commercial mortgage-backed loans, currently servicing in excess of 140 securitized loan pools totaling more than $100 billion in principal and encumbering real property in all fifty states. They also handle the acquisition of certificated interests in securitized loan pools, B participations and whole and participated mezzanine interests, as well as represent borrowers in significant debt transactions.

Corporate & Securities: The attorneys in the Corporate and Securities Group assist public and private companies and entrepreneurs in every phase of businesses, from start up, through growth and strategic operations, to the ultimate disposition. The group regularly represents clients in complex transactions related to the structuring of joint ventures and strategic relationships, corporate governance matters, public and private offerings, mergers and acquisitions, employment and non-competition arrangements, executive compensation and licensing. They also have substantial venture capital and debt financing experience, including lines of credit, asset-based and cash-flow financing, subordinate and mezzanine financing, securitizations, repurchase, swap and hedging arrangements and equipment lease financing.

Environmental: Bilzin Sumberg represents and counsels clients in a wide range of environmental issues, including all aspects of regulatory permitting (including water, hazardous waste, air and coastal); business transactions and due diligence; compliance counseling; environmental, health and safety audits; defense of regulatory enforcement actions at all governmental levels; environmental, mold, takings and insurance coverage litigation; Superfund common counsel work and litigation; brownfields redevelopment; landfill permitting and regulation; toxic tort counseling and defense; and administrative rule development and challenges. The firm's attorneys were substantially involved in the revision and adoption of the State Uniform Wetland Mitigation Methodology and have lectured extensively on numerous environmental topics.

Insolvency: The Restructuring and Bankruptcy Group has extensive experience with complex in-court and out-of-court restructurings, workouts, assignments for the benefit of creditors and bankruptcy litigation. The firm represents all constituencies in chapter 7 and 11 cases. They currently serve as counsel to Heilig-Meyers, the asbestos committees of W.R. Grace and U.S. Gypsum, the liquidating trustees of Lernout & Hauspie Speech Products, Crown Vantage, ContiFinancial and Southern Pacific Financial, the Celotex Asbestos Property Damage Claims Facility, subordinate noteholders in Southeast Banking Corp., the official committee of Loral Technology and the secured lender of SunCruz Casinos.

Land Use & Government Relations: Bilzin Sumberg represents both public and private clients on matters involving Florida land use law and government relations. Their lawyers have extensive experience in all aspects of land use and environmental law, from planning through permitting. Their government relations experience encompasses state and local taxation, public procurement, public-private partnerships for the development of real property, transportation, finance, telecommunications and aviation. The

OFFICES

FLORIDA
200 South Biscayne Boulevard, Suite 2500, **Miami**, Florida, 33131
Tel: 305 374 7580   **Fax:** 305 374 7593
Email: info@bilzin.com   **Website:** www.bilzin.com

324 West College Avenue, Suite 100, **Tallahassee**, Florida, 32301
Tel: 850 425 3007   **Fax:** 850 425 3013
Email: info@bilzin.com

CONTACTS

Real Estate	John C Sumberg
Corporate & Securities	Alan D Axelrod
Insolvency	Scott L Baena
Land Use	Stanley B Price
Litigation	Alvin D Lodish
Tax & Estate Planning	Richard M Goldstein

firm's attorneys have represented public and private clients in administrative proceedings, trial and appellate litigation and general advisory capacities, including service as special counsel to several Florida governmental entities.

Litigation: The Litigation Group has vast experience trying complex cases before all federal and state trial and appellate courts, as well as federal and state administrative bodies. The group's experience includes class actions, construction, business torts, real estate disputes, bankruptcy, intellectual property, eminent domain, securities, probate, employment, insurance and products liability litigation. Recent representations include: the prosecution and settlement of a fraudulent conveyance action in the W.R. Grace bankruptcy for $1 billion; the defeat of class certification on behalf of a major developer in a large homeowner class action; and a $20 million settlement of an inverse condemnation claim against the South Florida Water Management District.

Real Estate: The Real Estate Group provides legal counsel in all facets of commercial real estate transactions for all types of property, including hotels, hotel/condos and mixed use properties, as well as marinas, retail, office, industrial, residential, entertainment facilities and raw land. Their representation spans development and redevelopment of real estate projects, the purchase and sale of commercial real estate assets, financing (including mortgage and mezzanine), leasing, condominium law, and related governmental and regulatory issues. The firm's attorneys work closely with the Land Use Group and other departments in the firm to provide full service counsel to real estate developers in every step of their projects, from site selection through development, stabilization and the ultimate disposition of the property.

Tax & Estate Planning: The Tax Group provides both domestic and foreign nationals with sophisticated tax counseling and representation, including traditional tax planning; representation in tax litigation; estate planning; and state and local tax issues, such as corporate income taxes, intangible taxes, sales and use taxes, transfer taxes, and internet and electronic commerce taxes. The firm's attorneys provide tax analysis and advice in the structuring of real estate, corporate and other commercial transactions, as well as in bankruptcy cases, litigation matters and settlements.

Technology & Telecommunications: Bilzin Sumberg has a sophisticated practice representing public and private technology, telecommunications and cable television companies; real estate developers; enterprise users of technology and telecommunications; and local governments in all aspects of technology; telecommunications; and voice, video and data law. By combining corporate, tax, real estate and technology disciplines, the firm maximizes the opportunities for success that are available to its clients.

CLIENTS: The firm's clients span a broad array of industries, including aviation, construction, development, financial, entertainment and hospitality, retail, not-for-profit, manufacturing, distribution and sales, software and e-commerce, real estate and luxury hotels and resorts.

CARLTON FIELDS, P.A.

THE FIRM

President & CEO: Thomas A Snow
Number of shareholders: 135
Number of other lawyers: 85

FIRM OVERVIEW: Located in major business centers in Florida and the Southeast, Carlton Fields offers a full range of legal services in more than 30 areas of law. With more than 200 lawyers and government consultants, the firm serves a broad variety of national and local corporations, state and local public entities, and individuals. The firm has represented two-thirds of the nation's Fortune 100 companies.

MAIN AREAS OF PRACTICE:

Antitrust & Trade Regulation: The firm handles civil and criminal antitrust cases and has extensive experience in class action defense and environmental matters. The firm advises clients on a variety of antitrust issues, including advertising, prospective mergers and acquisitions, government filings, pricing and marketing practices, and franchising and licensing agreements.

Appellate Practice & Trial Support: The firm offers a range of appellate-related services in addition to the traditional steps of briefing and arguing cases, including trial support, *Amicus Curiae* briefs, and specialized consulting services. The firm handles appeals on diverse issues such as bad faith claims against insurers, application of the Americans with Disabilities Act to commercial websites, and damages awards in tobacco class actions.

Bankruptcy & Creditors' Rights: The firm has extensive creditors' rights, insolvency, reorganization, and workout experience. The firm represents commercial lenders, creditors' committees, Chapter 11 and Chapter 7 trustees, equity holders, and indenture trustees, among others.

Construction: The firm provides legal services concerning all phases of construction projects, including pre-bid considerations, contract drafting and letting, construction administration, liens, bonds, insurance, and dispute resolution, in projects such as office buildings, power plants, airports, highways, stadiums, and convention centers.

Corporate, Securities, Taxation & Asset-Based Financing: The firm handles mergers and acquisitions and assists in selling and buying businesses, provides comprehensive international, federal, and state tax services, and handles securities transactions including initial and secondary public offerings.

Government Law & Consulting: The firm handles clients' legislative, administrative, procedural, and political issues, and coordinates public relations and grass-roots efforts in all government arenas. The firm provides governmental affairs counseling in areas of lobbying, and regulatory and administrative law.

Healthcare: The firm handles legal services to healthcare clients such as hospitals, DME companies, nursing homes, physician practice groups, physicians, nurses, allied health professionals and health insurance companies.

Intellectual Property: The firm works with clients in acquiring, perfecting and transferring rights to intellectual property of all kinds and represents clients in claims involving infringement and unfair competition. The firm participates in technology issues relating to commerce on the Internet, computer law, licensing, software publishing and copyright protection.

Labor & Employment: The firm represents employers in litigation, including the defense of Equal Employment Opportunity claims, Florida Civil Rights Act claims, Fair Labor Standards Act claims, as well as sex, age, disability, race, national origin discrimination, and sexual harassment claims.

Litigation & Dispute Resolution: The firm defends corporations in national products litigation in automotive and toxic tort cases, defense of class actions involving consumer fraud, antitrust, securities, and environmental claims, as well as telecom and technology, energy, insurance, business torts, personal injury, and employment cases.

Products & Toxic Tort Liability: The firm's defense experience in products liability covers a variety of products, including sporting goods and recre-

HEAD OFFICE

FLORIDA
Corporate Center Three at International Plaza, 4221 West Boy Scout Boulevard, **Tampa**, FL 33607
Tel: 813 223 7000 **Fax:** 813 229 4133
Email: info@carltonfields.com **Website:** www.carltonfields.com

BRANCH OFFICES

FLORIDA
4000 International Place, 100 SE Second Street, **Miami**, FL 33131-9101
Tel: 305 530 0050 **Fax:** 305 530 0055

CNL Center at City Commons, 450 S Orange Avenue, Suite 500, **Orlando**, FL 32801-3336
Tel: 407 849 0300 **Fax:** 407 648 9099

One Progress Plaza, 200 Central Avenue, Suite 2300, **St Petersburg,** FL 33701-4352
Tel: 727 821 7000 **Fax:** 727 822 3768

215 S Monroe Street, Suite 500, **Tallahassee,** FL 32301-1866
Tel: 850 224 1585 **Fax:** 850 222 0398

Esperante, 222 Lakeview Avenue, Suite 1400, **West Palm Beach,** FL 33401-6149
Tel: 561 659 7070 **Fax:** 561 659 7368

GEORGIA
One Atlantic Center, 1201 W. Peachtree Street, Suite 3000, **Atlanta**, GA 30309
Tel: 404 815 3400 **Fax:** 404 815 3415

CONTACTS

Antitrust & Trade Regulation	Chris Coutroulis (Tampa)
Appellate Practice & Trial Support	Sylvia Walbolt (Tampa)
Bankruptcy & Creditors Rights	Rob Soriano (Tampa)
Construction	Mike Nuechterlein (Tampa)
Corporate, Securities, Taxation & Asset Based Financing	Nat Doliner (Tampa)
Government Law & Consulting	Nancy Linnan (Tallahassee)
Healthcare	Don Schmidt (Tampa)
Intellectual Property	Doug McDonald (Tampa)
Labor, Employment	George Barford (Tampa)
Litigation & Dispute Resolution	Gary Sasso (Tampa)
Products & Toxic Tort Liability	Gregory Cesarano (Miami)
Real Estate & Mortgage Financing	Ed Lester (Tampa)

ational products, electrical equipment, chemical and pharmaceutical products, power equipment, tobacco, automobiles and auto parts, medical devices, security systems, and others.

Real Estate & Mortgage Financing: The firm represents clients in all aspects of real property acquisition, development, investment, regulation, title insurance, financing, leasing, ownership, and use and transfer.

CLIENTS: Firm clients represent a diverse group of industries that includes banking and finance, transportation, government, insurance, energy, healthcare, manufacturing, pharmaceutical, technology, telecommunications, environmental, construction, real estate, tax, and securities, among others.

INTERNATIONAL WORK: The firm represents American clients forming corporations, establishing subsidiaries, and participating in joint ventures abroad, and assists foreign companies in establishing a presence in the United States. The firm supports foreign and domestic clients in international business matters including sales, construction, manufacturing, development, and financing.

CARLTON FIELDS
ATTORNEYS AT LAW

COLSON HICKS EIDSON

THE FIRM

Managing Director: Dean Colson
Number of partners: 12

FIRM OVERVIEW: Colson Hicks Eidson, one of Miami's oldest and most accomplished law firms, is considered among the top, full-service trial firms in the United States, having won hundreds of multi-million dollar verdicts and settlements for its clients. With decades of experience in personal injury, commercial, securities, business torts, insurance, professional liability litigation and white collar criminal defense, as well as domestic and international arbitration, the firm enjoys a long history of landmark decisions that have resulted in national and international recognition.

MAIN AREAS OF PRACTICE:

Product Liability: Colson Hicks Eidson has litigated cases involving the design and manufacture of airplanes, motor vehicles, boats, tires, medical devices, and children's toys. Long considered one of the innovators in the field of product liability law, Mike Eidson, a founding partner of the firm, serves as the national co-lead counsel in the multi-district Fort/Firestone litigation for all personal injury claims.

Commercial & Business Litigation: Colson Hicks Eidson handles cases involving complex insurance, construction, intellectual property, and other commercial matters as well as fraud and other business torts. The firm members litigate business lawsuits to judges, juries and arbitration panels. The firm has prosecuted and defended bad faith claims involving major insurance companies. A member of the firm has served as a receiver appointed by the United States District Court in actions brought by the Federal Trade Commission, and the firm's partners have served on plaintiffs' committees in some of the most complex, multi-party class action securities fraud and RICO cases in South Florida. Members of the firm have represented owners, contractors, developers, design professional, lenders, and insurers in construction disputes. The firm has obtained numerous multi-million dollar verdicts, judgments, arbitration awards and settlements on behalf of small and large business enterprises, individual entrepreneurs, and in class action cases involving real estate, lender liability, professional malpractice and other business disputes.

White Collar Criminal Defense: With the addition of the former United States Attorney for the Southern District of Florida, Roberto Martínez, former Chief of the Economics Crime Section for that office, Susan Tarbe, and former Assistant United States Attorney Curtis Miner, the firm now offers extensive experience and expertise in federal criminal litigation. These experienced federal litigators have represented businesses and their officers in connection with investigations and trails in matters including securities, money laundering, foreign corrupt practices, asset foreiture, tax; healthcare, bank fraud, environmental, antitrust, obstruction of justice, export, RICO and extortion. In addition to representing business clients in investigations and trials, Colson Hicks Eidson attorneys have provided legal counseling to banks and other financial institutions to ensure compliance with the federal money laundering and currency reporting laws.

Personal Injury & Wrongful Death: Colson Hicks Eidson has decades of experience in prosecuting personal injury actions on behalf of its clients. The firm has handled hundreds of multi-million dollar cases arising from wrongful death, traumatic brain injuries, spinal cord injuries and burn cases.

Professional Malpractice: Colson Hicks Eidson has handled dozens of medical malpractice cases that have resulted in verdicts and settlements in excess of one million dollars since the firm won the first million-dollar medical malpractice verdict in the United States. The firm has also handled significant legal malpractice cases for both plaintiffs and defendants. Colson Hicks Eidson has been selected to defend several national and regional law firms when they have been accused of professional negligence. In the personal injury and construction fields, the firm has

HEAD OFFICE

FLORIDA
255 Aragon Avenue, Second Floor, **Coral Gables** FL 33134
Tel: 305 476 7400   **Fax:** 305 476 7444
Website: www.colson.com

successfully prosecuted and defended claims for professional negligence involving architects, engineers, and other design professionals. The firm was involved in evaluating and prosecuting over $100 million of claims involving engineering, architectural and construction negligence arising out of the destruction caused during Hurricane Andrew.

Aviation: Colson Hicks Eidson has represented many clients in litigation arising out of the crashes of commercial and private aircraft over the past two decades. The firm often works in conjunction with local counsel in other states and countries. In several mass death cases, the firm has represented a majority of the passengers in the plane. The firm also has handled individual claims in private aviation crashes relating to failed component parts, faulty design and manufacture and inadequate warnings.

Recent Cases of Note: In 2003, the firm announced a settlement of $100 million in a grave desecration case against Service Corporation International, the world's largest cemetery and funeral company, to settle the individual and class action claims of victims with loved ones buried at Menorah Gardens funeral homes in Florida. In 2002 the firm obtained a $19 million judgment in federal court in Miami against the Government of Aruba on behalf of racecar promoter Ralph Sanchez in connection with the failed efforts to build a racetrack in Aruba. In 2002 the firm obtained a $10 million settlement for the wrongful death caused by the faulty design and installation of a security gate system at a condominium. In 2001 the firm obtained a federal court judgment in the amount of $16 million confirming an arbitration award against the Miccosukee Tribe of Indians arising out of a breach of contract regarding the management of the Indian's gambling operations. A member of the firm was co-lead counsel in the litigation against the Cuban Air Force and the Cuban Government over the murders of their clients who were shot down by the Cuban Air Force while flying a humanitarian mission for Brothers to the Rescue, resulting in a judgment of $188,000,000.00 against the Cuban Air Force and Cuban government. Two of the firm's partners served as co-lead trial counsel on behalf of the Plaintiff class in The Premium Sales case, the largest mass fraud case in South Florida history. The case was settled after the start of trial for $170,000,000. The firm served as co-counsel for nearly two-thirds of the family members of the passengers aboard AeroPeru flight 603, which originated in Miami and crashed off the coast of Peru on October 2nd, 1996. The firm helped the families receive one of the largest cash awards stemming from an airplane crash outside the United States aboard a non-US carrier. The firm represented a Canadian telecommunications company in a complex commercial litigation case involving breach of contract, fraud and intentional interference of a business relationship. Firm members won a jury verdict of $31.2 million for their client, SIRIT Technologies Inc., against Able Telcom-whose largest shareholder is MCI WorldCom, Inc. Two of the firm's partners obtained a $30.7 million jury verdict against the Ford Motor Company for the improper installation of the air valve on the right-rear tire of a 1999 Ford Econoline 15-passenger van that caused the van to crash and roll over on top of a nine-year-old girl.

Colson
Hicks
Eidson

FROST TAMAYO SESSUMS & ARANDA P.A.

THE FIRM

Managing Partner: John W Frost, II

Number of partners: 5
Number of other lawyers: 4

HEAD OFFICE

FLORIDA
395 South Central Avenue, PO Box 2188, **Bartow,** FL 33830
Tel: 863 533 0314   **Fax:** 863 533 8985

FIRM OVERVIEW: This nine lawyer litigation boutique firm is about to celebrate its 25th anniversary. The firm handles complex commercial litigation in both the state and federal courts, statewide and in other states. It's commitments to its clients and their needs has been the hallmark of this firm. Because it is ideally situated in the heart of Florida, the firm can offer its clients the benefit of local representation in the vast judicial circuits in Florida. Since its inception in 1981, the firm has been committed to both excellence and the pursuit of the most effective, expeditious and cost-effective course of action for its clients. The firm's attorneys consider it their responsibility to provide not only the highest level of service and expertise to its clients, but to provide service and leadership to the profession and the community as well. The firms lawyers: John W Frost, II, is Board Certified in Business Litigation. He is recognized by clients as 'highly skilled and honorable' and who 'can take on anything'. Frost specializes in the trial and appeal of complex commercial litigation. Robert J Aranda, is fluent in Spanish and concentrates his civil litigation practice in the areas of employment law. A Brent Geohagan's practice areas include business torts, contract litigation, agricultural litigation, business and commercial litigation. John Marc Tamayo focuses his practice on commercial and general civil litigation, and eminent domain. He is fluent in Spanish. Mark A Sessums is Board Certified in Family and Matrimonial Law and a Fellow in the American Academy of Matrimonial Lawyers. Peter W van den Boom, is fluent in Dutch and German. His practice focuses on general commercial litigation. Kimble C Bouchillon specializes in the areas of trucking law and commercial litigation. Richard E Dantzler is a former Florida State Senator and handles business mediations. He provides the firm with unparalleled knowledge of the inner workings of Florida government and the issues facing the nation's fastest developing state. Rafael J Nobo, III practices in the commercial litigation area and is fluent in Spanish.

MAIN AREAS OF PRACTICE:

Business & Corporate Litigation: The firm's litigation practices encompass civil litigation in state and federal courts, appellate advocacy, arbitration and other forms of alternative dispute resolution and proceedings before administrative agencies. Through the years, the firm has provided complete and efficient legal services to THE Bank for which it serves as general counsel, small local businesses as well as numerous large state and national corporations involved in a variety of commercial activities.

Discrimination Litigation: The firm has an active practice in representing individuals and businesses with employment issues.

Appellate Practice: The firm handles all aspects of appeals in both the state and federal courts.

Real Property Litigation: Since its inception, the firm has represented developers, title insurance companies, lenders, and individual sellers and buyers in real estate litigation.

Land Use Litigation: The firm provides legal services for cases that deal with eminent domain and inverse condemnation.

Banking Law: The firm serves as general counsel to a local financial institution. The practice includes traditional banking representation in such areas as collection matters, commercial loan transactions, foreclosures and lender liability.

CLIENTS: The firm's clients include a bank, small and large corporations and other business entities, professionals, including accountants and attorneys.

Law Offices
Frost
Tamayo
Sessums &
Aranda, P.A.

GENOVESE JOBLOVE & BATTISTA, P.A.

THE FIRM

Managing Partners: John H Genovese, Michael D Joblove

Number of partners: 12
Number of other lawyers: 13

FIRM OVERVIEW: Genovese Joblove & Battista P.A. (GJB), with one of the largest insolvency practices in Florida, is a 25 lawyer litigation and bankruptcy boutique. Its lawyers are heavily involved in complex reorganizations and insolvency litigations in Florida and throughout the US. The firm has a nationally recognized franchise practice and represents franchisors, nationally, in workouts, litigation and Chapter 11s of multiple unit franchises. The firm is also recognized for its expertise and experience in litigation involving directors and officers' liability and in complex business litigation matters.

MAIN AREAS OF PRACTICE

Commercial Litigation: GJB handles sophisticated business litigation matters, at the trial and appellate levels in all federal and state courts, as well as in arbitration and other alternative dispute resolution forums. The firm represents businesses and individuals, as plaintiffs and defendants, in all types of commercial litigation matters.

Insolvency, Bankruptcy & Creditors' Rights: GJB's Insolvency, Bankruptcy and Creditors' Rights Practice is one of the largest in Florida and the firm's lawyers regularly appear in both federal and state courts throughout the country representing major players in creditor litigation, out of court workouts and restructures and insolvency proceedings, bankruptcy or non-bankruptcy, and all related litigation. In addition to roles in Florida Chapter 11 matters such as AT&T Latin America and Far & Wide Travel, GJB has a significant role in the Enron Chapter 11 in New York and the Delaware Chapter 11s of Ameriservice and Safety-Kleen.

Franchise Litigation: The firm has Florida's premier franchise litigation practice. GJB represents Miami based Burger King Corporation throughout the nation, and has handled matters in South Florida for a variety of franchise systems including BP Amoco, Brinker International (franchisor of the Chili's® and Romano's Macaroni Grill® concepts), Carlsons Restaurants Worldwide (for its TGI Friday's® concept), Jamba Juice, Metromedia, Inc. (for its Bennigans® and Steak & Ale® concepts), Schlotzky's, Inc. and Taco Bell Corp.

Real Estate Litigation: GJB has one of Florida's leading real estate litigation practices. The firm's attorneys have represented developers, general contractors, subcontractors and professionals for nearly 20 years, including Minto Communities, Inc., one of South Florida's largest developers. Other prominent real estate clients have included Bendersen Development, Capital Realty Services, Zuckerman Homes, and Affiniti Architects.

Governmental Affairs Consulting: GJB provides consulting and lobbying services for clients seeking strategic representation before various local, state and federal government departments and agencies.

Securities Litigation: The firm represents numerous small and large investors in individual and class action suits and arbitration proceedings before the NASD, NYSE, and other exchanges. Members of the firm include a former assistant general counsel to a major securities brokerage firm. Firm attorneys have experience with various securities law issues, including issues arising under the Private Securities Litigation Reform Act of 1995, the Securities and Exchange Acts of 1933 and 1934, state securities law and common law. GJB has been successful in aiding investors recoup millions of dollars lost to unscrupulous brokers and corporate officials as a result of their financial wrongdoing.

HEAD OFFICE

FLORIDA
Bank of America Tower, 100 Southeast Second Street, 36th Floor,
Miami, FL 33131
Tel: 305 349 2300   **Fax:** 305 349 2310
Email: plawson@gjb-law.com
Website: www.gjb-law.com

CONTACTS

Commercial Litigation	Michael D Joblove
Insolvency, Bankruptcy & Creditors' Rights	John H Genovese
	Paul J Battista
Franchise Litigation	Michael D Joblove
	Jonathan E Perlman
Real Estate Litigation	Michael D Joblove
Governmental Affairs Consulting	Al Maloof
	John H Genovese
Securities Litigation	Jonathan E Perlman
	Melanie S Cherdack
Employment Litigation	Michael D Joblove
	Jonathan E Perlman
Class Action Litigation	Jonathan E Perlman

Employment Litigation: GJB maintains an active practice in the growing area of employment law. The firm counsels its clients on various types of employment policies and prepare and update manuals containing policies that protect the rights of both employer and employee in complying with the various applicable laws in effect.

Class Action Litigation: The firm enjoys a reputation for successful litigation of significant, complex class action cases. Opposing counsel are generally the largest, most powerful law firms in the country. GJB has won settlements or judgments for class members of millions of dollars.

INTERNATIONAL WORK: GJB's professionals have substantial experience in assisting clients in the negotiation and documentation of international transactions involving project financing, investment and import/export. One of the firm's senior partners has practiced in these areas throughout his career including as general counsel of a national bank which financed a variety of businesses throughout Latin American and the Caribbean.

GENOVESE JOBLOVE & BATTISTA P.A.
Attorneys at Law

GREENBERG TRAURIG, LLP

THE FIRM

Chief Executive Officer: Cesar L Alvarez
Number of partners: 553
Number of other lawyers: 706

FIRM OVERVIEW: Greenberg Traurig, LLP is an international business law firm with more than 1200 attorneys and governmental professionals working in 24 offices across the United States and Europe. Greenberg Traurig is the only major law firm in the United States with a Latin CEO and a team of senior lawyers that includes the former Chief Justice of the Appellate body of the World Trade Organization. As a full-service business law firm, Greenberg Traurig is uniquely able to provide its clients integrated, multi-disciplinary cross-border solutions to their problems.

MAIN AREAS OF PRACTICE:

Corporate & Securities: Greenberg Traurig helps its clients with the legal and business aspects of organizing, operating, financing and expanding their businesses. The firm routinely handles complex mergers, acquisitions and business combinations, divestitures, corporate restructurings and bankruptcy reorganizations, private equity and venture capital financings, leveraged buyouts, IPOs and underwritten securities offerings, project financings, securitizations, going-private transactions, credit enhancement transactions, broker-dealer and investment company advisory matters, derivatives transactions and syndicated lending transactions.

Litigation: Greenberg Traurig has been at the center of some of the most pivotal cases of recent times, from tobacco and securities class actions to the landmark George W Bush for President trial court proceedings and appeal. With more than 300 seasoned lawyers, the firm has extensive experience in cases involving class actions, products liability, securities regulation, insurance coverage disputes, commercial and construction contracts, government contracts, partnership disputes, white collar criminal defense and intellectual property issues.

Real Estate: Greenberg Traurig's representation and counsel spans the entire range of local, national and international real estate transactions affecting commercial, residential, retail and industrial properties, including: acquisitions; traditional and securitized financing; planning and development; hotels; condominium and cooperative offerings; leasing; sale/leaseback transactions; tax free exchanges; and foreclosures, litigation and restructurings.

Tax, Trusts & Estates: Greenberg Traurig's tax attorneys help clients develop and implement tax strategies to maximize returns and minimize taxes anywhere in the world. The firm's wealth preservation attorneys assist high net worth individuals, families and closely held businesses grow family assets through planning. It has developed tax saving techniques and designed innovative wealth preservation programs to facilitate the transfer of family wealth to future generations at significant tax savings.

Intellectual Property: Multinational companies know that patents, trademarks, copyrights and trade secrets are among their most valuable assets. The firm's Intellectual Property Department offers full-service protection for the intellectual property of clients in all technologies, from biotechnology, pharmaceuticals, medical devices and chemistry to mechanical, electronics and computer software and e-commerce.

Government: Greenberg Traurig has a team of preeminent and politically connected professionals who represent corporations and governmental entities before the legislative and executive branches in federal, state and local governments. The firm's team includes former elected officials, top aides and policy officials for members of the US House and Senate and various state legislatures and local government bodies.

International Trade Regulation & Trade Disputes: The team is headed by the former Chief Justice of the Appellate body of the World Trade Organization. The firm advises clients on international trade agreements, trade legislation and lobbying, anti-trust and Foreign Corrupt Practices Act counseling, US Foreign Military Sales Program, US anti-boycott and embargo regulations, identification of complex export control for high tech, defense and aerospace companies, defense of corporations in export-related criminal investigations and unfair trade cases.

Reorganization, Bankruptcy & Restructuring: Greenberg Traurig's practice is one of the largest and most active in the nation. As part of an integrated national network of professionals who focus their practice on all aspects of reorganizations, bankruptcies, restructurings, workouts and buyouts, the firm's attorneys are able to respond quickly to complex troubled situations arising anywhere and in any industry.

Employment: The firm is aware that companies today require labor and employment attorneys who will provide advice and counseling on all aspects of the employment relationship; handle matters involving union avoidance and organizational work; formulate strategies to anticipate problems; keep them informed of new developments in the law; assist in drafting policies and procedures; and defend the company against discrimination charges at the agency level and in court. Greenberg Traurig delivers these services at all levels of the administrative and litigation process.

Entertainment: With offices in the center of the entertainment industry, Greenberg Traurig has a preeminent, full-service entertainment practice. The team focuses on the music, motion picture, television, live stage and cable industries, including the convergence of new technologies, digital delivery systems and the role of advertising and sponsor-driven financing models. The firm has access to key players in the entertainment industry and provide clients with the pragmatic counsel needed in today's multi-disciplined, multimedia entertainment marketplace.

Corporate Governance & Foreign Private Issuers: Greenberg Traurig coordinates different interrelated specialty areas and thereby provides clients with highly efficient legal services. The firm's experience is focused on matters of corporate governance and shareholders initiatives, including issues affecting corporate strategy, executive contracts, compensations and benefit plans, and innovative corporate structures. The firm has worked with corporate clients from almost every jurisdiction and is accustomed to coordinating with counsel.

Immigration: Members of the US Immigration Law Department are experienced in all aspects of corporate immigration law, particularly multinational non-immigrant visa and permanent residency work. The attorneys understand the immigration process in all its complexity. They represent clients in such industries as finance, tourism, insurance, electronics, healthcare, shipping and pharmaceuticals with their immigration needs.

Public Finance: Members of Greenberg Traurig's Public Finance Department have extensive experience in serving the needs of state and local issuers and underwriters in all areas of public finance. The firm has broad experience in all forms of tax-exempt financing. For the past several years, the firm has been among the top bond counsel firms in the US, according to the ranking criteria developed by Securities Data Co. and The Bond Buyer, a municipal finance publication.

CLIENTS: The firm represents a diverse client base, including public/private companies, financial institutions, governmental entities and entrepreneurs.

US OFFICES

The firm has offices in Albany, Atlanta, Boca Raton, Boston, Chicago, Dallas, Denver, Fort Lauderdale, Los Angeles, Miami, New Jersey, New York, Orange County, Orlando, Philadelphia, Phoenix, Silicon Valley, Tallahassee, Tysons Corner, Washington, DC, West Palm Beach, Wilmington

INTERNATIONAL OFFICES

The firm also has offices in Zurich in Switzerland and Amsterdam in The Netherlands. For further details of all offices please see firm's website: www.gtlaw.com

HOPPING GREEN & SAMS

THE FIRM

Chairman, Management Committee: Peter C Cunningham
Number of shareholders: 21
Number of other lawyers: 16

FIRM OVERVIEW: Hopping Green & Sams, P.A., has a specialty practice in administrative and governmental law, legislative representation, litigation, and appellate practice. Within these areas there is emphasis on environmental and land use law, public lands, state and local government taxation, special districts, utility regulation and governmental contracts. The firm represents both private and public sector clients with interests affected by government.

MAIN AREAS OF PRACTICE:

ENVIRONMENTAL LAW

Air Quality: Firm lawyers have been continuously involved on behalf of industrial clients in Florida's implementation of the federal Clean Air Act and related state statutes, in legislation and rulemaking at the state level, and in federal and state air facility permitting and enforcement.

Coastal Permitting: The firm counsels coastal developers on coastal zone management and regulatory issues, and guides coastal developments through the complex state and federal coastal regulatory process.

Endangered & Threatened Species Protection: The firm evaluates federal and state endangered and threatened species laws and regulations and assists clients when related issues arise that might affect their projects.

Everglades Restoration: Federal and state authorities are refocusing on the remaining Everglades ecosystem to improve its ecological health in a litigious and costly process. The firm has been at the forefront of these matters through representation of growers adjacent to the Everglades.

Groundwater Regulation/Real Property Contamination: The firm represents clients in all types of matters pertaining to groundwater regulation and real property contamination, including 'due diligence' for real property acquisition.

Solid & Hazardous Waste: The firm handles solid and hazardous waste and pollutant permitting, regulation, enforcement and litigation, under federal, state and local laws.

Water Resources: Firm lawyers practice in all areas of water resource regulation, from standard-setting to the permitting of consumptive uses.

LAND USE LAW

Planning & Entitlements: Firm lawyers represent landowners and developers in seeking changes to local government land use plans and in obtaining entitlements for residential, commercial, industrial, resort and mixed-use projects. The representation includes appearing before state, regional and local agencies throughout the state.

Submerged Lands: Firm lawyers have experience in determining when proprietary consent for use of state lands submerged beneath navigable waters is required, and in negotiating needed approvals for public and private users.

Oil & Gas: The firm has extensive experience in licensing on-shore and off-shore oil and gas projects, including exploration, production, storage and transportation.

LEGISLATIVE LOBBYING

Firm legislative attorneys have been involved in the drafting and passage of most of Florida's landmark environmental and land use legislation for 25 years. As a large lobbying organization, the firm has the experience and relationships to effectively represent clients before the Florida Legislature.

SPECIAL DISTRICTS

Florida government requires new development to provide infrastructure to accommodate growth, putting pressure on developers to finance, provide and maintain various types of facilities. Firm lawyers have established and serve as counsel to more than 30 community development districts which levy taxes and assessment and issue bonds to provide infrastructure for new communities.

HEAD OFFICE

FLORIDA
123 South Calhoun Street, **Tallahassee**, FL 32301
Tel: 850 222 7500   **Fax:** 850 224 8551
Website: www.hgslaw.com

STATE & LOCAL TAXATION

The firm represents Florida, national and international businesses with state and local tax issues. Areas covered include: State and local tax planning and advice; legislative representation on tax and fee bills; participation in Department of Revenue rulemaking and policy development; representation before the Department, administrative tribunals and the courts in tax controversy matters of all types; and assistance securing economic development incentives.

UTILITY REGULATION

Energy Facilities Licensing: The firm provides assistance in all types of matters concerning new and expanded electrical power plants, electric transmission lines, and fuel pipelines to public and private electric utilities, natural gas companies, and oil companies.

Telecommunications Regulation: The firm represents telecommunications clients before the Florida Public Service Commission, the Florida Legislature, and the courts.

Water & Wastewater Utility Regulation: Providing water to meet rapidly growing needs continues to consume the attention of state regulators and utilities. The firm represents water utilities before the Public Service Commission and local economic regulators in this area.

LITIGATION

Administrative & Civil Litigation: Firm lawyers represent Florida's development, industrial, and commercial communities as well as public entities in litigation on many highly technical disputes. The firm's lawyers are experienced in using expert witnesses to develop clear, cogent testimony on complex scientific and technical subjects.

Bid Protests: Firm lawyers have extensive experience representing contractors in matters involving government contracts, reviewing bid specifications for a contractor to determine whether to challenge the fairness of the bid process, and representing contractors in challenging or defending a bid award by an agency.

APPELLATE PRACTICE

The firm represents clients on issues at the cutting edge of law and public policy. That representation occasionally requires appeals of administrative agency or lower court decisions to federal or state appellate courts. The firm includes attorneys with special skills and qualifications to handle appellate issues.

Hopping Green & Sams
Attorneys and Counselors

KENNY NACHWALTER P.A.

THE FIRM

HEAD OFFICE

FLORIDA
1100 Miami Center, 201 South Biscayne Blvd., **Miami**, FL 33131
Tel: 305 373 1000   **Fax:** 305 372 1861
Email: admin@knsacs.com
Website: www.knsacs.com

FIRM OVERVIEW: Kenny Nachwalter, P.A., was founded in 1978 and has since grown from three to 20 attorneys. The firm's practice is devoted to complex business litigation, including antitrust, securities, professional liability and intellectual property litigation, common law business torts and defending white collar criminal prosecutions, concentrating its efforts on a small number of relatively large cases. The firm is frequently retained in cases involving complicated economic and factual issues, multiple counsel, multiple parties, multiple interrelated cases, competing claims to limited resources, intense discovery and discovery problems, and substantive issues requiring superior legal scholarship and forensic skills. It devotes most of its time to dispute resolution, and as such regularly litigates in federal and state courts, and in various arbitration tribunals. They represent clients before federal administrative bodies and in white collar criminal investigations. Many of the firm's cases originate through referrals from other law firms in the South Florida area and throughout the United States. The firm has a team-oriented approach to staffing cases. Typically, two or more attorneys will work together on a complex case to increase attorney availability, to provide a basis for consultation, and to furnish legal services in a cost efficient and professional manner through allocation of assignments. In situations involving particularly complicated or difficult issues, however, firm lawyers not generally involved in the representation may contribute their particular experience.

MAIN AREAS OF PRACTICE:

Antitrust: Includes both plaintiff and defense work in cases in federal and state courts nationwide, in which the firm has represented large public and private corporations, privately held companies, individual entrepreneurs, and government entities. On behalf of plaintiffs, these have included conspiracy cases involving domestic and international cartels, and monopolization cases. The firm also represents antitrust defendants in proceedings-including both civil and criminal investigations-arising under the Sherman Act and related federal and state statutes.

Complex Business Litigation: These disputes, litigated in state and federal courts as well as argued before administrative bodies and arbitration tribunals, cover the gamut of business and legal matters-trade secrets, RICO, class and derivative actions, director and officer liability, lender liability, False Claims Act and qui tam, construction, commercial lease disputes and other real estate related matters, trade libel, tortious interference, franchise and business opportunities, employment and discrimination matters, contracts, fraud and other common law and statutory business torts.

Intellectual Property Litigation: The firm's Intellectual Property Practice area helps clients protect their rights. The firm has done so for the makers of computer software, clothing, automobiles, handbags, jewelry and accessories, and the satellite broadcaster of network television signals. Often the firm investigates and prosecute civil injunctive and damage actions against individuals and companies infringing upon, counterfeiting, or diluting the trademarks and copyrights of the legitimate owners of those trademarks and copyrights.

Professional Liability: The issue of the responsibilities of professionals has increasingly become a focus of regulatory bodies and agencies. Because of the expertise this firm has acquired in the area of professional liability, they are often called upon to counsel lawyers and other professionals about issues of ethical behavior and professional responsibilities. They also represent licensees before their state disciplinary bodies, and have represented professionals sued by the FDIC and RTC, as well as architects sued for professional malpractice. In doing so, the firm has defended claims covering malpractice, breach of fiduciary duty, RICO and securities law violations, and fraudulent conveyances under state law and the Bankruptcy Code.

Securities: The firm's Securities Practice involves arbitrations against, and the defense of, brokerage firms and registered representatives before the New York Stock Exchange and the National Association of Securities Dealers. These arbitrations have included allegations of churning, selling away, fraud, breach of fiduciary duty, suitability, breach of contract, negligence, civil theft, conversion, and other violations of state and federal securities laws. The firm also represents brokerage firms and their employees, securities issuers and their managements and directors, and accountants in SEC, NYSE and NASD investigations, as well as brokers in federal criminal prosecutions. The firm is not, however, involved in private offerings or public registrations of securities.

White Collar Criminal Practice: The firm has represented, during investigation and after indictment, doctors; accountants, lawyers; bankers; corporate managers; healthcare providers; public officials, securities brokers and others accused of wrongdoing-price-fixing and bid-rigging; bribery and related offenses; mail, wire and securities fraud; embezzlement; Medicare fraud; money laundering; and economic crimes. Since the reach of the law extends beyond national borders, the firm represents individuals and organizations that were the subject of requests for international extradition, and arguing such issues before federal and state courts of appeal.

KLUGER, PERETZ, KAPLAN & BERLIN P.L.

THE FIRM

Managing Director: Howard Berlin
Administrative Director: Stuart Silver

Number of lawyers: 55

FIRM OVERVIEW: Kluger, Peretz, Kaplan and Berlin P.L. (KPKB) is a Miami multi-cultural boutique that is known as 'The Lawyers' Law Firm' because it receives the majority of its work from quality, referring law firms throughout the United Sates and Latin America. The firm purposely limits its practices to four areas where it is among the very best in the market: litigation and dispute resolution, bankruptcy and creditors rights, commercial and real estate transactions, and intellectual property. For clients needing expertise beyond these four areas, the firm utilizes its vast, worldwide network of quality law firms, accounting firms, and investment banking firms. The firm is best known for effective and efficient handling of complex business matters where the stakes are very high for the clients of KPKB.

MAIN AREAS OF PRACTICE:

Litigation & Dispute Resolution: KPKB's Litigation and Dispute Resolution Practice is broad based, focusing on developing creative solutions to the unique and varied problems faced by the business community. While its lawyers are capable of handling any commercial dispute, the firm has developed some unique concentrations, where it can often assist other counsel and their clients. Some of the firm's specialties include: accounting malpractice, construction claims, director and officer liability issues, merger and acquisition disputes, product liability claims, real estate disputes, bankruptcy litigation and sports management issues.

Bankruptcy & Creditors' Rights: KPKB's Bankruptcy and Creditors' Rights Practice encompasses every aspect of companies, or high profile individuals, experiencing financial distress. From workouts to bankruptcy proceedings, the firm provides aggressive counsel to its clients on how to protect their position. KPKB is a key participant in both local and national cases in a wide array of industries. The firm represents debtors in both out-of-court workouts and in bankruptcy proceedings, creditor committees in Chapter 11 proceedings in Florida and elsewhere, and acquirers of distressed or bankrupt companies. Members of the firm both serve as and represent receivers and trustees in State, Federal and Bankruptcy Court.

Business & Real Estate Transactions: KPKB's Business and Real Estate Transaction Practice encompasses representation of buyers or sellers in the purchase of businesses, commercial real estate, or other assets. The firm is also extensively involved with the formation of corporations, partnerships, and joint ventures designed to carry out a wide array of business purposes, both domestically and internationally. One of the strengths of the practice is that the group includes lawyers who are serving, or have served, as General Counsel or Associate General Counsel of large companies headquartered in South Florida.

Intellectual Property: KPKB's Intellectual Property Practice advises clients regarding the protection and/or commercialization of a broad range of intellectual property, both domestically and internationally. Some of the firm's more common representations include preparation of trademark and copyright registrations, trademark, copyright, patent, and trade secret litigation, intellectual property audits and portfolio management; advising with respect to intellectual property licensing, and preparation of nondisclosure and trade secret agreements in connection with corporate acquisitions, joint-venture relationships, and employment agreements.

HEAD OFFICE

FLORIDA
Miami Center, 201 South Biscayne Blvd.,17th Floor, **Miami**, FL 33131
Tel: 305 379 9000   **Fax:** 305 379 3428
Website: www.kpkb.com

CONTACTS

Litigation & Dispute Resolution	Abbey Kaplan
	Andrew Gold
Bankruptcy & Creditors' Rights	Howard Berlin
	Robert Charbonneau
Business & Real Estate Transactions	Eliot Abbott
Intellectual Property	Steve Peretz
Latin American Gateway	Jorge Espinosa
	Mike Ehrenstein
Equity Fund Group	Jason Oletsky
Real Estate Industry Group	Jon Chassen
Contractors Industry Group	Mike Ehrenstein
Retail Industry Group	Stuart Silver

CLIENTS: KPKB serves a diverse group of domestic and international clients. Although the firm serves Fortune 500 companies, it is most often used by entrepreneurs and equity funds who appreciate the entrepreneurial spirit which resulted in KPKB being selected as the '2003 Best Professional Service Firm' by the South Florida Business Journal. KPKB serves clients in a wide variety of industries, but the firm is best known for its work serving real estate entrepreneurs, contractors, retailers, sports and entertainment professionals, and equity funds. The firm has Industry Groups for these five industries which are very important to the economy of South Florida.

INTERNATIONAL WORK: Operating through an active network of quality firms throughout Latin America, KPKB is heavily involved with both inbound and outbound legal work for clients who appreciate the business insights of a multi-cultural firm of lawyers. Lawyers, in each of the firm's practice areas and industry groups, are fluent in languages that are important to the South Florida market.

KLUGER, PERETZ, KAPLAN & BERLIN

KOZYAK TROPIN & THROCKMORTON, P.A.

THE FIRM

Founding Shareholders: John W Kozyak
Harley S Tropin
Charles W Throckmorton

Managing Shareholder: Gail A McQuilkin

Number of shareholders: 12
Number of other attorneys: 8

FIRM OVERVIEW: Founded over 20 years ago in Miami, Kozyak Tropin & Throckmorton, P.A. is an AV rated law firm, which specializes in complex commercial litigation and bankruptcy.

MAIN AREAS OF PRACTICE:

Complex Commercial Litigation: Kozyak Tropin focuses its Litigation Practice in the areas of complex commercial contract and tort litigation and securities fraud. Kozyak Tropin also serves as special counsel for a number of local corporations, banks, and prominent individuals. In addition, the firm's attorneys represent clients in matters involving professional malpractice, lender liability, foreclosure, and intellectual property/unfair competition.

Class Actions: The firm represents various classes of individuals in multimillion dollar class action matters involving claims including fraud, breach of contract, misrepresentation, and other causes of action. Kozyak Tropin has served as co-lead counsel in many high profile class action cases including *In Re: Humana, Inc.,* and *In Re: US Oil & Gas.*

Commercial Bankruptcy: In its Bankruptcy Practice, Kozyak Tropin has broad experience in representing the full array of client constituencies—including debtors, creditors, statutory and liquidating trustees, creditors' committees, equity holders, and asset purchasers--in business bankruptcy cases and high net-worth individual cases. The firm also represents some of the largest companies and lending institutions in the country when they are involved in workouts and bankruptcy matters in Florida and other jurisdictions.

CLIENTS: Kozyak Tropin's Representative Clients include: American Cyanamid Company; Bank of America, N.A.; Bayer Corporation; Bombardier Capital; Carnival Cruise Lines, Inc.; Canadian Imperial Bank; The CIT Group/Industrial Financing, Inc.; DBT Online, Inc.; Development Specialists, Inc.; Dole Food Co.; Dole Fresh Flowers, Inc.; Dollar Bank; Ferrari Spa; Greenwich Capital Markets, Inc.; Harch Capital Management, Inc.; Host-Marriott, Inc.; Knight-Ridder, Inc.; Lady Burd Cosmetics; Lennar Partners, Inc.; Marriott International, Inc., MasterCard International; Mellon United National Bank; Miami-Dade County, Mpower Communications; Novartis Animal Health, US, Inc.; The Ritz-Carlton Hotel Company, LLC.; The Rouse Company; Salt Creek, Inc.; SEQUA, Corp.; Siemens Dematic Corporation; Skechers USA, Inc.; Swiss Watch International; Time, Inc.; Total Bank; and Visa International, Inc.

HEAD OFFICE

FLORIDA
2525 Ponce de Leon, 9th Floor, **Miami**, FL 33134
Tel: 305 372 1800   **Fax:** 305 372 3508
Website: www.kttlaw.com

INTERNATIONAL WORK: With its office located in Miami, the gateway to Latin America, Kozyak Tropin represents various Central and South American clients. The firm also serves as co-lead counsel in several class action lawsuits brought in the US on behalf of Latin American citizens. Additionally, Kozyak Tropin attorneys handle many intellectual property matters for multinational corporations such as Dole, Novartis, and Swiss Watch.

KOZYAK · TROPIN
THROCKMORTON
ATTORNEYS AT LAW

LEIBY STEARNS LINKHORST & ROBERTS, P.A.

THE FIRM

Founding Partner: Larry R Leiby
Partners: Michael E Stearns
Adam C Linkhorst
Douglas J Roberts

Number of other lawyers: 6

FIRM OVERVIEW: The firm limits its practice to the area of construction law. The firm represents contractors, sureties, construction owners, subcontractors, suppliers, and design professionals. The firm suggests preventive representation in preference to remedial as being in the economic best interest of the client. The firm is AV rated by, and a member of the Preeminent Attorneys Register (in construction law) of, Martindale-Hubbell, Inc.

MAIN AREAS OF PRACTICE:

Bidding: Preparation of invitation-to-bid and bid forms. Counseling on the law of bidding. Interpretation of statutory and contract requirements. Administrative and judicial bid protests. Debarment issues.
Contracts: Preparation and review. Training of clients for review and understanding of construction contract clauses, purchase orders, design contracts, design-build contracts, construction management contracts, and subcontracts.
Payment & Performance Bond Drafting & Review: Florida statutory and common law bonds.
Construction Arbitration: Serving as advocate in construction arbitration. Serving as arbitrator in construction arbitration.
Construction Litigation: Advocate in trials and appeals in state and federal courts in Florida.
Payment Bond & Performance Bond Claims & Defense: Contractor, owner, subcontractor, and surety analysis upon claimed default. Enforcement and defense of payment bond claims. Enforcement and defense of performance bond claims. Counseling, review, and advice on takeover and liquidating agreements. Indemnity claims - prosecution and defense.
Construction Contract Administration: Training, counseling, and correspondence/document drafting and review. Counseling on the consequences and documentation of facts as they develop to maximize the opportunity for success in disputes.
Contract Claims: Counseling and advice in preparation of claims for extra work, delay, interference, acceleration, lost productivity, defects, and non-performance. Counseling and assistance in defense of such claims.
Construction Liens: Counseling and advice in connection with preparing and enforcing liens. Counseling and advice in preparing to avoid and defend liens. Advice and document preparation in connection with payment procedures. Lien enforcement actions and defense.
Construction Insurance: Advice and review of insurance requirements, coverage issues, insurance certificates. Claims enforcement and defense.
Construction Mediation: Serving as advocate in construction mediations. Serving as mediator in construction mediations.
Defect Claims & Defense: Counsel and representation in connection with claims for building defects, including mold.
Training: Seminars and classes for continuing education and/or skills development in construction legal issues.

HEAD OFFICE

FLORIDA
1390 North University Drive, **Fort Lauderdale**, FL 33322
Tel: 954 382 9199 **Fax:** 954 382 9063
Email: (Initials)@leibylaw.com
Website: www.leibylaw.com

REPRESENTATIVE REPORTED CASES: Rossmoor Corp. v Tri-County Concrete Products, Inc., 375 So.2d 896 (Fla. 4th DCA 1979); Coordinated Constructors, Inc. v Florida Fill, Inc., 387 So.2d 1006 (Fla.3d DCA 1980); Acadia Development Corp. v Rinker Materials Corp., 419 So.2d 1142 (Fla. 3d DCA 1982); Vincent J. Fasano, Inc. v School Board of Palm Beach County, 436 So.2d 201 (Fla. 4th DCA 1983); Coral 97 Associates, Ltd. v Chino Electric, Inc., 501 So.2d 69 (Fla. 3d DCA 1987); Builders Glass & Metal, Inc. v M.E.T. Construction, Inc., 528 So.2d 988 (Fla. 3d DCA 1988); Champagne-Webber, Inc. v City of Ft. Lauder-dale, 519 So.2d 696 (Fla. 4th DCA 1988); Fidelity and Deposit Company of Maryland v Delta Painting Corp., 529 So.2d 781 (Fla. 4th DCA 1988); Levitz Electric, Inc. v George Hyman Construction Co., et al (In re Levitz Electric, Inc.), 100 B.R. 602 (S.D. Fla. 1989); Mursten Construction Co. v C.E.S. Industries, Inc., 588 So.2d 1061 (Fla. 3d DCA 1991); In re: Simco Mechanical, Inc., 151 B.R. 978 (S.D. Fla. 1993); Alexdex Corp. v Nachon Enterprises, Inc., 641 So.2d 858 (Fla. 1994); Williams Hatfield & Stoner, Inc. v Malcolm, 687 So. 2d 295 (Fla. 4th DCA 1997); Hollub Construction Company v Narula, 704 So.2d 689 (Fla. 3d DCA 1997); Fischer-McGann, Inc. v Gene B. Glick Co., Inc., 715 So.2d 994 (Fla. 4th DCA 1998); Continental Concrete, Inc. v Lakes at La Paz III Ltd. Ptnrshp., 758 So.2d 1214 (Fla. 4th DCA 2000); Grimsley v Inverrary Resort Hotel, Ltd., 770 So.2d 708 (Fla. 4th DCA 2000); Hewett-Kier Construction, Inc. v Lemuel Ramos & Associates, Inc., 775 So.2d 373 (Fla. 4th DCA 2000), cert denied 791 So.2d 1098 (2001); Bill Stroop Roofing, Inc. v Metropolitan Dade County, 788 So.2d 365 (Fla. 3d DCA, 2001); H. W. Gay Enterprises, Inc. v John Hall Electrical Contracting, Inc., 792 So.2d 580 (Fla. 4th DCA 2001); Miller and Solomon Gen. Contractors, Inc. v Brennan's Glass Co., 837 So.2d 1182 (Fla. 4th DCA 2003); Rewards Hotel Management Co, LLC. v Elite General Contractors, Inc., 860 So.2d 1011 (Fla. 3rd DCA 2003).

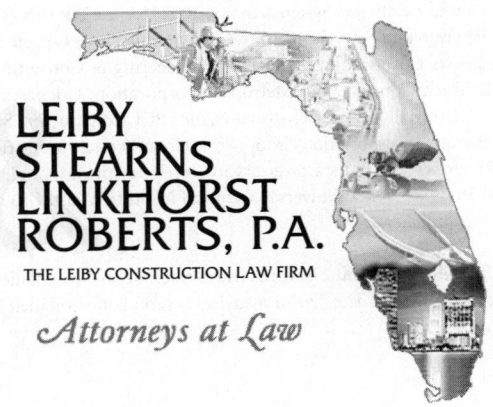

LEIBY STEARNS LINKHORST ROBERTS, P.A.
THE LEIBY CONSTRUCTION LAW FIRM

Attorneys at Law

MOYE, O'BRIEN, O'ROURKE, PICKERT & MARTIN, LLP

THE FIRM

Managing Partner: James E Moye
Senior Partners: James E Moye
Stephen W Pickert
Gregory S Martin

Number of partners: 5
Number of other lawyers: 11

AREAS OF PRACTICE:

Construction Litigation 85%
Labor & Employment 10%
Commercial Litigation..................................... 5%

FIRM OVERVIEW: Established in 1989, Moye, O'Brien, O'Rourke, Pickert & Martin, LLP dedicates its practice to the representation of national and international clients within the construction industry. The firm has dedicated itself to the prompt, efficient, and economic delivery of such legal services. The firm's philosophy is to provide aggressive, high quality legal services at a fair rate, while always striving to extricate its clients from unavoidable controversies at the earliest practicable, most economical and beneficial juncture.

MAIN AREAS OF PRACTICE

Construction Litigation: The firm represents clients, including national and multinational general contractors, owners, design professionals and other construction-related entities, from contract preparation, review and negotiation through ultimate dispute resolution including litigation, arbitration and other alternative resolution procedures.
Labor & Employment: The firm has a wide range of experience in representing clients in all phases of labor and employment law, including union and trade dealings and employment practices and disputes.
Commercial Litigation: The firm represents clients in a variety of contract and tort disputes between corporate entities.

CLIENTS: The firm has represented clients throughout the United States of America, the Caribbean basin, Central America, and Canada. A representative listing of clients includes: Archer-Western Contractors, Ltd.; Arden Villas University, Ltd.; Balfour Beatty, Inc.; Balfour Beatty Construction, Inc.; Balfour Beatty Rail Systems, Inc.; Centex Homes; The City of Hollywood; Hazen and Sawyer, P.C.; Peter Kiewit Sons', Inc.; Leggett & Platt, Inc.; Loews Corporation; MACTEC Engineering & Consulting, Inc.; Marta Track Constructors; Metroplex Corporation; Odebrecht Construction, Inc.; PCL Civil Constructors, Inc.; PCL Construction Services, Inc.; Parsons Transportation Group; Professional Services Industries, Inc.; QORE Property Sciences; Universal City Development Partners, Ltd; Universal Studios Florida; Universal Technical Institute; Walsh Group, Inc.; ZOM Companies.

INTERNATIONAL WORK: The firm advises international companies operating within the US. The firm also advises US companies on their foreign activities.

HEAD OFFICE

FLORIDA
800 South Orlando Avenue, **Maitland**, FL 32751
Tel: 407 622 5250   **Fax:** 407 622 5440
Email: moopm@earthlink.net

AFFILIATE OFFICE

ILLINOIS
O'Rourke, Hogan, Fowler & Dwyer
10 South LaSalle Street, Suite 2900, **Chicago**, IL 60603
Tel: 312 739 3500   **Fax:** 312 739 3535

RICHMAN GREER WEIL BRUMBAUGH MIRABITO & CHRISTENSEN P.A.

THE FIRM

Managing Partner: John Brumbaugh
Number of partners: 15
Number of other lawyers: 7

FIRM OVERVIEW: Richman Greer Weil Brumbaugh Mirabito & Christensen, P.A., has developed an international reputation for successfully handling complex business litigation in state and federal courts. The firm, founded in 1961, is best known for its tenacious and effective courtroom presence. This trial capability allows the firm to negotiate favorable results for clients not involved in litigation, in areas ranging from corporate transactions and real estate to estate planning, family law and employment matters. The firm industry expertise reflects the New Economy (i.e. telecommunications, media and entertainment) highly regulated businesses (i.e. financial services, energy and manufacturing) and the traditional economy of South Florida: real estate and construction, agriculture, tourism and transportation. The firm also represents high profile individuals, units of state and local government and non-profits.

MAIN AREAS OF PRACTICE

Complex Commercial Litigation: The firm has a long history in all types of business litigation, including commercial class action lawsuits, First Amendment cases and securities fraud matters. Richman Greer acts as counsel to Fortune 500 corporations facing litigation in Florida and is regularly retained on litigation steering committees by the world's largest law firms. Richman Greer lawyers have served on American Arbitration Association panels and have been appointed to serve as mediators for federal and state litigation. Many firm attorneys are board certified by the Florida Bar in civil trial law, and/or business litigation. In addition, members of the firm have been named as fellows of the American College of Trial Lawyers, the International Society of Barristers, the American Board of Trial Advocacy and the International Academy of Trial Lawyers. The firm's alumni include a senior United States Court of Appeals judge, a United States District judge and several state court trial judges.

Condominium Litigation: The firm had a major role in the first Florida Supreme Court decision regarding condominium law and has successfully defended a critical case brought by the Federal Trade Commission in its investigation of condominium sales practices. The firm remains a leader in condominium law development, representing both developers, and condominium associations.

Corporate/Business Services: Richman Greer provides general business representation, such as assisting in corporate formations or other transactions, and representing parties in business sales and acquisitions.

Employment Litigation: Richman Greer represents employers in matters of racial, ethnic, sexual, age and disability discrimination, as well as sexual harassment and fair employment practices. The firm also represents employers in Equal Employment Opportunity Commission proceedings at the administrative level.

Environmental Law: The firm handles disputes regarding land use, environmental compliance, water quality, contamination and has litigated environmental contamination cases.

Estate Planning, Probate & Trusts: Richman Greer represents clients in probate court litigation, including will contests and estate administration disputes, and provides estate planning services and trust administration. The partner heading this area of practice is board certified by the Florida Bar in wills, trusts and estates.

Family Law: Richman Greer has a substantial practice in family law including dissolution of marriage and child custody matters, with particular expertise in representing business executives, sports and entertainments figures and spouses of such individuals. The partner heading this area of practice is board certified by the Florida Bar in marital and family law.

OFFICES

FLORIDA
Miami Center, Suite 1000, 201 So. Biscayne Boulevard,
Miami, FL 33131-4325
Tel: 305 373 4000   **Fax:** 305 373 4099
Website: www.richmangreer.com

One Clearlake Centre, Suite 1504, 250 Australian Avenue South
West Palm Beach, FL 33401-5016
Tel: 561 803 3500   **Fax:** 561 820 1608

CONTACTS

Miami ....John Brumbaugh, Alan Greer
West Palm Beach ....Gerald Richman

Insurance Defense: The firm represents insurance carriers, claims administrators and self-insured entities in the defense of tort claims.

Intellectual Property, Communications & Technology: The firm has litigated major trademark, copyright and patent litigation cases in federal court, successfully defending the rights of international corporate clients.

Manufacturer/Product Liability: The firm represents numerous manufacturers, distributors and self-insured entities in the defense of product liability claims.

Officer/Director Representation: The firm has defended officers and directors of several public companies, including failed financial institutions.

Real Estate/Construction: The firm represents major institutional lenders, developers, buyers, sellers and managers of commercial and residential property in real estate development, financing and litigation. This includes significant construction litigation matters, such as failure to fulfill contractual obligations, allegations of defects, and disagreements over financial responsibility.

Securities Litigation: The firm has been actively involved in significant antitrust and securities litigation, including shareholder's lawsuits and alleged violations of securities law.

CLIENTS: Representative clients of the firm include Minnesota Mining and Manufacturing Co.; the Republic of Panama; Arthur Anderson (World Wide); Hallmark; DirecTV; Solutia, Merrill Lynch; Precision Response Corporation; City National Bank; First International Bank; Landmark Education Corporation; Best Buy; Banque Artesia, S.A.; Goldman Sachs & Co.; Hughes Electronic Corporation; Mt. Sinai Medical Center; Purity Wholesale Grocers; Blood Diagnostics, Inc. and Genstar.

INTERNATIONAL WORK: With language capabilities in English, Spanish and Gaelic and membership in Meritas, a leading worldwide association of business law firm, Richman Greer regularly serves overseas clients, having represented foreign governments, banks, airlines, television stations, investment and insurance interests and individuals.

SHUBIN & BASS, P.A.

THE FIRM

Contact: John K Shubin

AREAS OF PRACTICE:

Land Use, Administrative & Municipal Litigation	35%
Business Litigation & Dispute Resolution	35%
Strategic Regulatory Analysis & Governmental Affairs	15%
Appellate Practice	15%

FIRM OVERVIEW: Established in 1992, Shubin & Bass continues to define itself as a small law firm which handles mission critical matters for a select number of public and private institutional clients, local governments, and large law firms who place a premium on our ability to handle the most complex litigation and administrative matters. They are not a large law firm, and do not aspire to be a large law firm, and they do not measure their success by the number of lawyers they employ or the number of new files open. The firm instead measure its success purely by the results obtained for its clients and the level of trust they place in their abilities.

MAIN AREAS OF PRACTICE:

Land Use, Administrative, & Municipal Litigation: Throughout the State of Florida, the firm has represented the interests of property owners, governmental bodies, and affected individuals and advocacy groups in all types of litigation and administrative proceedings addressing the proposed development of land and government's regulation of land This representation includes matters relating to eminent domain and the prosecution and defense of claims for inverse condemnation.

Business Litigation & Dispute Resolution: The firm has extensive experience in the litigation of complex business and real estate disputes throughout the State of Florida. The firm is highly selective with respect to the litigation it undertakes on behalf of clients, and limits its caseload to those cases which present unique issues of law or which would benefit from the firm's experience in having litigated and tried many complex cases involving its core practice areas. The firm is also regularly called upon to serve as local counsel to numerous national law firms with respect to litigation in the state and federal courts in Florida, and prides itself in its ability to identify, negotiate, and consummate the settlement of extremely contentious matters.

Strategic Regulatory Analysis & Governmental Affairs: The firm possesses lawyers with an academic background in economics and public policy analysis, particularly in the context of regulated industries, and combines this academic perspective with years of litigation and public advocacy experience at all levels of municipal, state, and federal government. This balance of theoretical and practical experience enables the firm to offer counsel to clients whose businesses or investments are directly affected by governmental regulation policies. Although most of this representation involves analysis of the regulation of land, it has also offered counsel with respect to water rights, timber rights, and the regulation of various extractive industries, particularly limerock mining.

Appellate Practice: The firm has considerable experience in representing its clients before state and federal appellate courts, particularly with respect to complex or novel legal issues presented in the land use, municipal law, and commercial litigation contexts. Many of the published opinions arising out of the firm's representation of its clients before these appellate tribunals are well recognized as definitive caselaw in these respective practice areas.

HEAD OFFICE

FLORIDA
46 S.W. First Street Third Floor **Miami**, FL 33130
Tel: 305 381 6060   **Fax:** 305 381 9457
Email: jshubin@shubinbass.com
Website: www.shubinbass.com

CLIENTS: The firm's clients include: Atlantic Civil Engineering, Inc.; Brickell Equities Corporation; Citadel Investment Group; City of Aventura; City of Coral Gables; City of North Miami; City of Vero Beach; Codina Group, Inc.; Core Communities; Crescent Real Estate Equities, L.L.C.; Cuban American Bar Association; Fairfield Residential, L.L.C.; Finger Companies; Flagstone Property Group; Florida Association for Women Lawyers Miami-Dade Chapter; Florida Rock & Sand Company; Gator Investments; GB/JT Hotel Partners; GFS Corporation; Grovenor House; Hellmann Worldwide Logistics; Hispanic National Bar Association; Indian River County; Intervest Properties; Montenay Power Corporation; 9000 Centre Associates; Performing Arts Center Foundation; Premier Developers; Properties of Hamilton; Related Group of Florida; Residential Funding Corporation; Rouse Companies; Stranahan House; Sunny Development, LLC; Swerdlow Development Group; State of Florida, Florida Department of State; Town of Golden Beach, University of Miami; Village of Key Biscayne; and White Rock Quarries.

SHUTTS & BOWEN LLP

THE FIRM

FIRM OVERVIEW: Shutts & Bowen is a leading Florida law firm, with more than 160 attorneys in offices located in Miami, Fort Lauderdale, West Palm Beach, Orlando, Tallahassee, Amsterdam and London.

MAIN AREAS OF PRACTICE

Financial Services: The Financial Services Practice Group represents foreign banks with a Florida presence, out-of-state banks which have a presence in the state or are attempting to establish one, and local banks and savings and loan associations, and local and national investment banking firms and investment advisors. Unlike other law firms which primarily represent local banks, the firm's practice is largely centered on the representation of foreign and out-of-state banks.

Corporate: The Corporate Group provides a wide range of corporate and business services, including structuring and negotiating new business ventures, mergers and acquisitions and advising on traditional corporate, partnership and commercial law issues. In the securities area, we counsel clients in private and public securities offerings in the United States and abroad, as well as assist in preparing corporate and insider filings required by the Securities and Exchange Commission and the stock exchanges.

Real Estate: The Real Estate Department represents a broad range of domestic and foreign entrepreneurs, developers, investors and lenders, with emphasis on institutional clients such as national and multi-national corporations, insurance companies and banks. The firm advises its clients in all aspects of their real estate transactions, including acquisitions, sales, development, land use, zoning, environmental, financing, leasing and construction. It also assists the corporate and international departments in structuring the real estate aspects of large corporate and international transactions.

Litigation: The Commercial Litigation Department has vigorously represented clients at all levels of federal and state court systems and before numerous state and federal agencies, commissions, boards, and other regulatory and administrative authorities. The firm handles all aspects of the litigation process, from counseling and alternative-dispute-resolution mechanisms, through the prosecution or defense of discovery, pretrial, and trial proceedings in lawsuits, to post trial remedies and review in appellate courts. The Litigation Department's practice includes a wide variety of administrative, trial, and appellate cases.

International/Tax: The International/Tax Department advises US clients, multi-national corporations, investors in foreign countries and foreign clients investing in the US. The firm counsels its clients in a broad range of tax problems, including foreign tax, partnerships, corporate and individual tax, tax exempt organizations, qualified plans and local taxation, particularly as it relates to banks and private placement tax opinions. The department handles appeals before the IRS and tax court litigation.

Estate Planning: The Estate Planning Group assists clients in distributing their assets, while minimizing the payment of estate taxes, through estate planning and estate administration. The firm's services include counseling clients to assure the orderly and efficient transfer of property to their beneficiaries with a minimum of estate, gift, generation-skipping and income tax costs.

OFFICES

FLORIDA
1500 Miami Center, 201 South Biscayne Boulevard, **Miami,** FL 33131
Tel: 305 358 6300 **Fax:** 305 381 9982
Website: www.shutts-law.com

200 East Broward Boulevard, Suite 2100, **Fort Lauderdale,** FL 33301
Tel: 954 524 5505 **Fax:** 954 524 5506

One Clearlake Centre, 250 Australian Avenue South, Suite 500,
West Palm Beach, FL 33401
Tel: 561 835 8500 **Fax:** 561 650 8530

300 South Orange Avenue, Suite 1000, **Orlando,** FL 32801
Tel: 407 423 3200 **Fax:** 407 425 8316

215 South Monroe Street, Suite 804, **Tallahassee,** FL 32301
Tel: 850 521 0600 **Fax:** 850 521 0604

CONTACTS

Miami	Bowman Brown
Fort Lauderdale	Allan Rubin, George Platt
West Palm Beach	Arthur J Menor
Orlando	James G Willard
Tallahassee	Eric Thorn

CLIENTS: Shutts & Bowen offers its clients, whether local, state, national or international, a diverse and complete range of high quality and responsive legal services. The firm represents major industrial corporations and life insurance companies, utilities companies, securities brokerage firms, transportation concerns, national and international financial institutions, local banking firms, major foreign companies, healthcare organizations, local municipalities, local corporations, and individuals and smaller enterprises of every nature.

SMITH HULSEY & BUSEY

THE FIRM

Chairman: Stephen D Busey
Managing Partner: William E Kuntz

FIRM OVERVIEW: Smith Hulsey & Busey is a full service Florida business law firm which began as Lamson & Smith in 1936. The firm has a proven track record of sound counsel, innovative problem solving and successful dispute resolution. Clients with national and international operations provide the firm regular experience in major transactions and dispute resolution throughout the world. The firm offers the very best legal services with an efficiency not typical in larger firms.

MAIN AREAS OF PRACTICE

Business & Finance: The firm advises clients in mergers and acquisitions; venture capital investments; initial public offerings; public offerings, periodic reporting and SEC compliance for publicly held companies; regulation of broker-dealers, investment advisors, and mutual funds; and partnership and other syndication transactions. In addition, the firm's Public Finance Group has extensive experience representing clients in every aspect of tax-exempt public financing transactions, including bond counsel, disclosure counsel, underwriter's counsel, bank counsel, trustee's counsel and borrower's counsel.

Environmental: Florida has a strong commitment to the protection of the natural environment. As a result, the firm has developed a comprehensive Environmental Law Practice, assisting its clients with compliance, permitting and clean up issues as well as development of business plans to economically manage environmental obligations. The firm has special expertise in identifying and enforcing insurance coverage rights for environmental problems. The Environmental Group also assists the firm's Real Estate and Land Use Group with environmental problems of real property owners and managers.

Healthcare: The firm has one of the largest and most diverse healthcare practice groups in Florida. The firm represents hospitals and health systems, academic medical centers, continuing care retirement communities, home healthcare providers, skilled nursing facilities, clinical laboratories, medical technology companies, managed care companies, IDOs, PHOs, physician group practices and individual physicians throughout Florida. The firm's Healthcare Practice includes formation of healthcare entities, strategic alliances of healthcare providers, mergers and acquisitions, joint ventures, reimbursement, Medicare, Medicaid, regulatory matters, fraud and abuse, licensing, certificates of need, risk management, and labor relations. Attorneys in the Healthcare Group have expertise in the many areas that affect health industry clients, including antitrust, insurance regulation, tax exemption, and financing. Additionally, members of the Healthcare Group work closely with legislators and other officials from the State of Florida, as well as the Agency for Healthcare Administration, to help shape state healthcare legislation, rules and regulations.

Insolvency: The firm has represented debtors, creditors, committees, trustees and examiners in major business reorganizations throughout the United States. The firm has represented a number of New York Stock Exchange companies as debtors in successful reorganization proceedings in Florida. The firm counsels financially troubled companies outside of bankruptcy proceedings regarding their restructuring alternatives, and fiduciary and governance issues. The firm has special expertise in healthcare insolvencies. The firm also is experienced in assignments for the benefit of creditors and bankruptcy liquidations.

HEAD OFFICE

FLORIDA
225 Water Street, Suite 1800, **Jacksonville** FL 32202
Tel: 904 359 7700   **Fax:** 904 359 7708
Website: www.smithhulsey.com

CONTACTS

Business & Finance	M Richard Lewis Jr
Environmental	Tim E Sleeth
Healthcare	M Richard Lewis Jr
Litigation & Insolvency	Stephen D Busey
Real Estate & Land Use	Harry M Wilson III

Litigation: The firm's lawyers try complex commercial disputes, class actions, mass torts and catastrophic injury cases before juries in state and federal courts throughout Florida. The firm tries high exposure cases on a regular basis. Although the firm is experienced and successful in taking complex litigation through trial, the firm's goal is to resolve disputes short of the risk or expense of trial. The firm's reputation for trying cases, and the results it has achieved, help facilitate early resolution of disputes.

Real Estate & Land Use: The firm's real estate and land use attorneys represent developers, investors, lenders, and business users in the acquisition, development, financing, sale, and leasing of real estate throughout the Southeast. The firm is experienced in planning the structure of and negotiating complex real estate transactions, as well as the legal analysis and documentation. The firm's expertise includes condominium and time-sharing forms of ownership, real estate syndication, taxation of real estate, zoning, and the regulation of land use.

Other Practices: For further practice area detail, including the firm's tax, intellectual property, labor, estate planning and governmental affairs practices, and information regarding the firm's lawyers, please refer to their website: www.smithhulsey.com.

STEEL HECTOR & DAVIS LLP

THE FIRM

Managing Partner: Alvin B Davis
Number of partners: 83
Number of other lawyers: 92

FIRM OVERVIEW: Founded in 1925, Steel Hector & Davis LLP is one of Florida's largest and oldest law firms. The firm has a well-established domestic practice with offices in Miami, West Palm Beach, Key West, and Tallahassee. From the Fortune 500 company requiring help in handling complex commercial litigation and transactions, to the individual who needs assistance with immigration matters, the firm has lawyers working in more than 50 practice areas in Florida, Latin America, Tel Aviv, and London, who provide clients with comprehensive and cutting-edge legal representation.

MAIN AREAS OF PRACTICE: The firm serves a broad range of public and private clients from such diverse industries as banking and financial services, airlines, insurance, public utilities, pharmaceuticals, and real estate. The firm's core practice groups include the following:

Corporate, Securities & Finance: The firm handles multifaceted corporate, securities and finance matters domestically and globally. The firm counsels clients in the United States, Latin America, Tel Aviv, London, and the Caribbean on complex corporate matters. It represents publicly traded and privately owned large corporations, as well as small businesses. This has allowed the firm to develop and maintain a substantial and sophisticated finance and securities practice that includes work in the following areas: Antitrust and trade regulation, banking, bankruptcy and creditors, corporate governance, energy, financial services, franchising and distribution, hospitality and travel, immigration, intellectual property, mergers and acquisitions, private placements, project finance, technology, telecommunications, and venture capital.

Government & Regulatory: The firm's Government and Regulatory Practice consists of a core group of experienced attorneys and consultants who regularly deal with policy makers and regulators on a wide variety of issues such as those relating to environmental regulations and permitting, labor laws, insurance, industrial development statutes, land use, utilities, contracts, and procurement. The firm helps US and foreign companies comply with, and operate competitively under, the laws, regulations and policies applicable to their jurisdiction. The firm also has extensive experience assisting clients in connection with government investigations and in defending against alleged violations of laws, ethics, and regulations.

Labor & Employment: The firm's Labor and Employment Practice has been at the forefront of today's most critical employment and labor issues, locally, nationally, and internationally. The firm represents employers in federal and state litigation involving allegations of discrimination and harassment, breach of contract, wage and hour violations, non-competition and non-solicitation, etc. The firm represents myriad clients in administrative proceedings before local, state and federal administrative agencies and assists them in handling investigations by government agencies. The firm also provides diversity training to Fortune 100 companies.

Litigation: More than half of the firm's lawyers are dedicated to litigation, particularly complex litigation. For decades, the firm's Litigation Department has enjoyed a nationwide and international scope of practice. The firm's litigators work daily alongside leaders of major industries, helping them to contend with the complex legal challenges and issues that invariably arise as companies pursue their business plans. The firm's multilingual litigators represent companies facing all types of legal challenges in a broad array of industries throughout Florida, the US, and Latin America. The firm's White Collar Criminal Defense and Corporate Compliance Practice defends complex domestic and international criminal cases and conducts internal investigations for private and public corporations. They advise clients who are subject to investigations, often preventing indict-

HEAD OFFICE

FLORIDA
200 South Biscayne Boulevard, 41st Floor, **Miami** FL 33131-2398
Tel: 305 577 7000   **Fax:** 305 577 7001
Website: www.steelhector.com

BRANCH OFFICES

FLORIDA
309 Whitehead Street, **Key West** FL 33040
Tel: 305 292 7272   **Fax:** 305 292 7271

215 South Monroe Street, Suite 601, **Tallahassee** FL 32301-1804
Tel: 850 222 2300   **Fax:** 850 222 8410

199 Phillips Point West, 777 South Flagler Drive,
West Palm Beach FL 33401-6198
Tel: 561 650 7200   **Fax:** 561 655 1509

ment or minimizing the impact of criminal charges.

Private Client: The firm offers assistance in trust and estate planning, immigration, probate administration, and litigation. The firm's lawyers provide a wide range of services to clients who require and demand privacy and immediate results. The firm has a strong record of successful management of individuals' significant legal portfolios.

Real Estate: The firm handles the acquisition and sale of real property, land use and development, condominium and multi-residential planning and documentation, as well as mortgage lending and commercial leasing. The firm's clients include Fortune 500 corporations, money center banks, life insurance companies, and national developers. The firm has one of the preeminent construction law practices in the United States and Latin America. The firm counsels US, foreign, and multinational corporations, project owners, developers, contractors, government-controlled entities, financial institutions, and individuals in a vast array of domestic and international construction-related matters.

Tax: The firm has a large and diverse federal, state, and local tax practice, perhaps the largest and most diverse of any firm in Florida. The firm's Domestic Tax Practice is complemented by the wide and divergent practice in its foreign offices. The firm's domestic federal practice handles a broad spectrum of federal taxation matters, including: transactional planning for domestic and international businesses and individuals; advising on employee benefits, pensions and executive compensation; formation and representation of tax-exempt entities; and advising on charitable giving and estate and private wealth planning. In addition, the firm handles civil and criminal audits, administrative hearings, trials and appellate proceedings, as well as legislative and regulatory advocacy. The firm's Tax Controversy Practice includes tax audits, criminal investigations and grand jury inquiries. Civil trials before the United States Tax Court, the Court of Federal Claims, and civil and criminal trials in the district courts, as well as appellate/mediation/arbitration proceedings are part of the firm's extensive tax practice.

INTERNATIONAL WORK: With Miami's unique position as the gateway to Latin America, the firm serves as a critical link connecting Florida with the business and economic centers of South and Central America, as well as Europe. Steel Hector & Davis' offices in Caracas, São Paulo, Rio de Janeiro, Santo Domingo, Buenos Aires, Tel Aviv, and London, enable the firm to provide its international clients with a superior level of sophisticated legal services both in country and across borders. The firm has a substantial cross-border transactional practice and international arbitration practice that spans Europe, Latin America and the United States. In addition to English, Steel Hector & Davis lawyers offer legal services in Spanish, Portuguese, German, French, Hebrew, Italian, Russian, and Japanese.

STICHTER, RIEDEL, BLAIN & PROSSER, PA

THE FIRM

Founding Partners: Don M Stichter
Harley E Riedel

Number of partners: 9
Number of other lawyers: 3

FIRM OVERVIEW: Stichter, Riedel, Blain & Prosser, PA is a 12-lawyer firm specializing in the representation of parties in bankruptcy cases, insolvency matters, out-of-court workout arrangements, and related civil litigation. The firm was described in Chambers USA: America's Leading Business Lawyers (2003-2004 ed), as 'undoubtedly the first port of call for debtor's work in Florida,' and was rated as one of only three 'tier one' insolvency firms in the entire state of Florida. Since its inception in 1974, the firm has been rated AV by Martindale-Hubbell. All of the name partners have served as presidents and chairs of the Tampa Bay Bankruptcy Bar Association. Don M Stichter and Harley E Riedel are Fellows of the American College of Bankruptcy. Mr Stichter was named the Outstanding Lawyer in Hillsborough Country, Florida in 2003 and was the first recipient of the Lifetime Achievement Award by the Tampa Bay Bankruptcy Bar Association in 2004.

MAIN AREAS OF PRACTICE: Stichter, Riedel, Blain & Prosser, PA, advises clients faced with insolvency or bankruptcy issues. It regularly represents parties in cases pending in all of the bankruptcy courts in Florida, as well as in other states. As a 'boutique' insolvency firm, Stichter Riedel begins many of its engagements as a result of referrals from other professionals who have a long-standing attorney-client or accountant-client relationship with the client.

CLIENTS: The firm has represented numerous debtors in Chapter 11 cases as well as substantial creditors, purchasers, defendants, committees, trustees, or other parties in interest in a number of significant Chapter 11 and Chapter 7 cases. The largest segment of its practice consists of the representation of corporate debtors in Chapter 11 cases. The firm's practice is geographically centered in the state of Florida with clients ranging from small companies to large publicly-owned corporations. Most cases involve companies with assets, liabilities, or annual revenues in excess of $5 million, ranging in size to companies with assets and liabilities of more than $3 billion. Lawyers with Stichter, Riedel, Blain & Prosser, PA have been involved in more than 300 reported decisions including matters in the Circuit Courts of Appeals, the US District Courts, and the US Bankruptcy Courts.

HEAD OFFICE

FLORIDA
110 E. Madison Street, Suite 200, **Tampa**, FL 33602
Tel: 813 229 0144   **Fax:** 813 229 1811
Website: www.srbp.com

THOMPSON, SIZEMORE & GONZALEZ

THE FIRM

Managing Partner: Gregory A Hearing
Senior Partner: Thomas M Gonzalez

Number of partners: 4
Number of other lawyers: 11

AREAS OF PRACTICE:
Labor & Employment Defense 100%

FIRM OVERVIEW: Since 1983 Thompson, Sizemore & Gonzalez has been recognized as a leader in the labor and employment arena representing owners and managers of business and governmental entities. The firm takes great pride in the representation of its clients and aggressively utilizes every available business tool in its representation to ensure a successful result for its clients.

MAIN AREAS OF PRACTICE:

Labor & Employment: The firm is equipped to provide legal advice on all matters affecting the relationship between an employer and its employees. In the past 50 years a myriad of federal and state laws have been enacted to restrict an employer's free choice in dealing with employees. The setting in which our firm can aid management in retaining as much freedom as the law permits includes: Defense of employment discrimination charges/suits, employment torts, defeating union organizational campaigns, collective bargaining (contract administration and labor arbitration), problems under The Wage and Hour Laws, family and medical leave, occupational safety and health, drug testing and employee screening, general employment problems and human resource and personnel policy development.

CLIENTS: The firm represents clients in the following industries: healthcare, construction, transportation, manufacturing, media, public sector (including school boards, municipalities and counties), retail/commercial, authorized insurance defense counsel, utilities, education, professional organizations, automobile dealerships, telecommunications and numerous non-profit organizations.

HEAD OFFICE

FLORIDA
501 East Kennedy Blvd, Suite 1400 **Tampa**, FL 33602
Tel: 813 273 0050   **Fax:** 813 273 0072
Website: www.tsg-law.com
Email: tgonzalez@tsg-law.com

CONTENTS: Antitrust p.578; Banking & Finance p.580; Bankruptcy p.582; Construction p.584; Corporate/M&A p.586; Employment: p.589; Energy & Natural Resources p.591; Environment p.592; Healthcare p.594; Intellectual Property p.595; Litigation: p.598; Real Estate p.601; Tax p.603; Individuals' Profiles p.604; Firms' Profiles p.626.

How lawyers are ranked

The opinions we gather from clients — mainly from in-house lawyers but also from other purchasers of legal services — are balanced by opinions from colleagues and competitors. Together, they provide two different perspectives — an all-round view — and biased viewpoints cancel each other out.

ANTITRUST

Georgia
Leading firms (Antitrust)

1 **ALSTON & BIRD LLP** *Atlanta*
BONDURANT, MIXSON & ELMORE *Atlanta*
KING & SPALDING LLP *Atlanta*

2 **ROGERS & HARDIN** *Atlanta*
VAUGHAN & MURPHY *Atlanta*

3 **JONES DAY** *Atlanta*
KILPATRICK STOCKTON LLP *Atlanta*
PAUL, HASTINGS, JANOFSKY *Atlanta*
POWELL GOLDSTEIN LLP *Atlanta*
SMITH GAMBRELL & RUSSELL LLP *Atlanta*
TROUTMAN SANDERS LLP *Atlanta*

Leading individuals (Antitrust)

1 **BONDURANT Emmet** *Bondurant Mixson*, Atlanta
GRADY Kevin *Alston & Bird*, Atlanta
POWERS Tony *Rogers & Hardin*, Atlanta

2 **ALLEN Randall** *Alston & Bird*, Atlanta
CASHDAN Jeffrey *King & Spalding*, Atlanta
HARRIS H Stephen *Alston & Bird*, Atlanta
MURPHY Charles *Vaughan & Murphy*, Atlanta
NEWTON Trammell *Jones Day*, Atlanta
RHODES Thomas *Smith Gambrell*, Atlanta
SAUNTRY June *Troutman Sanders*, Atlanta

3 **ASBILL Rick** *Paul Hastings*, Atlanta
MARSHALL John *Powell Goldstein*, Atlanta
MULLIS Carl *Paul Hastings*, Atlanta
ROGERS CB *Rogers & Hardin*, Atlanta
RUSS Michael *King & Spalding*, Atlanta
VAUGHAN C David *Vaughan & Murphy*, Atlanta

Firms and individuals are listed alphabetically in each band.

Band 1

Alston & Bird LLP
See firm details p.626
The Firm: The group is renowned as one of the top antitrust practices in the state. "*Solid and seasoned,*" it is seen by clients as "*a one-stop store for every antitrust need.*" Its diverse client base leads to a wide range of work, with attorneys acting in matters across the insurance, banking, agriculture, sports and communications sectors. Adept at both litigation and corporate matters, the firm has acted on several large M&A transactions recently and is currently involved in a major residential fiberglass litigation. Although best known for its defense work, the group handled a high-profile matter for plaintiff Jes Properties in Florida Middle District Court. The case concerned a claim that horse show promoters were organizing in such a way as to prevent new entrants coming into the market.
The Lawyers: "*Expert*" **Kevin Grady** (see p.613) was recommended by clients as "*one of the guys you go to where you need nothing less than solid gold advice.*" He has just finished a year-long stint as the chair of the ABA antitrust section, which, as one pundit put it, "*doesn't necessarily mean you're a top-flight antitrust lawyer...but he genuinely is.*" Well known for his healthcare work, he recently acted in a highly publicized DOJ investigation into joint ventures between two hospitals in West Virginia. **Steve Harris** (see p.613) is the firm's practice group leader and is widely admired as "*a sensible and straightforward lawyer with an in-depth knowledge of the nuances of antitrust law.*" He has particular expertise in federal and international antitrust litigations. The "*standout*" **Randall Allen** (see p.605) is hailed as a "*highly personable*" practitioner who "*puts clients at ease.*" He conducts a large amount of merger counseling and frequently represents public bodies before the DOJ and FTC.
The Clients: Mohawk Industries; Sabre; Borden Chemical; Boral Industries; Nokia and Imerys.

Bondurant, Mixson & Elmore, LLP
See firm details p.629
The Firm: This boutique litigation firm is felt by market commentators to have "*undeniable strength in antitrust matters.*" The firm "*belies its size to provide a top-quality, high-level service*" and is "*definitely the antitrust practice which other antitrust lawyers turn to.*" Attorneys have acted in a number of civil and criminal antitrust matters, including class actions, multidistrict proceedings and federal and state criminal grand jury investigations. The firm boasts a fantastic client base in healthcare, airlines, motor sports and manufacturing.
The Lawyers: For some, **Emmet Bondurant** (see p.607) is "*the dean of the Atlanta antitrust Bar.*" He brings a huge amount of experience to the table and is "*the solid base their very good antitrust practice is built upon.*" Bondurant is known for his superb courtroom presence and is undeniably an asset to any party in a trial.
The Clients: Delta Air Lines; Michelin; International Dairy Queen; Blue Circle Cement; Athens Regional Hospital and Penske Motorsports.

King & Spalding LLP
See firm details p.635
The Firm: This "*superb*" practice is viewed by clients as "*a sharp, practical and business-orientated group,*" which according to market commentators is building up; it boasts an "*undeniably heavyweight client base*" and a close working relationship with the firm's regulatory team in Washington, DC. Though the group is skilled in both litigation and transactional matters, two of the past year's highlights fall into the former category. Attorneys represented Scientific-Atlanta in a series of suits involving infringement against Gemstar concerning interactive TV program guides. The cases have been consolidated as a multidistrict litigation in Atlanta. Attorneys also represented Michelin in a federal court action in Atlanta, alleging price discrimination and conspiracy in the sale of tires to retailers.
The Lawyers: The team is felt by clients to be "*as talented as the New York firms but without the price tag.*" "*Prominent*" **Jeffrey Cashdan** (see p.608) was endorsed as "*a thoroughly resourceful attorney with a great client manner.*" He recently represented Home Depot in a Sherman Act violation action against Visa and MasterCard, and

has handled three different criminal grand jury matters for companies under investigation. **Michael Russ** (see p.622) is said to offer "*the full range of antitrust skills,*" with clients remarking on his "*great ability to keep a dozen balls in the air at once.*" Russ recently handled a Section 4c restraint of trade matter brought by BellSouth to stop a former vice chair from moving to a competitor.

The Clients: Agrium; Brown & Williamson Tobacco; Coca-Cola; GE; Milliken & Company; Scientific-Atlanta and UPS.

Band 2

Rogers & Hardin
See firm details p.639

The Firm: Offering "*a personal touch,*" this highly regarded firm is, for some, "*a cool drink of water*" compared with its larger competitors. Workwise, it covers the whole waterfront from regulatory advice through to litigation in both state and federal court. In the past year it has handled a number of cases in the textile, carpet and motor sports industries.

The Lawyers: The "*small, diligent*" team includes "*heavy hitter*" **Tony Powers** (see p.621), "*a sharp and informed lawyer who'll offer you a fresh viewpoint in complex matters.*" Powers has earned a reputation as one of the state's leading practitioners, and has lately represented Covad Communications in its ongoing antitrust litigation against BellSouth. The case, a monopolization claim concerning high-speed Internet access, was heard by the Supreme Court. Veteran attorney **CB Rogers** (see p.622) is recommended as "*a skilled litigator with an in-depth knowledge of the antitrust market.*"

The Clients: The group has a strong Georgia client base and represents clients in the textile and carpet industries, as well as in transport, healthcare, chemical, distribution and construction.

Vaughan & Murphy

The Firm: This boutique firm is singled out for its antitrust litigation prowess and earns special praise for its handling of criminal prosecutions. An experienced team, it has worked on numerous large litigations across the region, representing both plaintiffs and defendants. The group continues to have an international dimension to its practice, and has recently been involved in a case concerning the overseas application of federal antitrust laws.

The Lawyers: **Charles Murphy** is recommended as "*a thoughtful attorney*" with a particular niche in the representation of individuals in antitrust matters. One competitor noted: "*If you have a weak argument in court it can be torture to be against him.*" **David Vaughan** is admired for "*combining a rich antitrust knowledge with a large slice of common sense.*"

The Clients: The group represents clients in the real estate, construction, soft drink, chemical and computer industries.

Band 3

Jones Day
See firm details p.485

The Firm: The firm enters the rankings this year on the back of client endorsements. It recently represented paper manufacturer UPM-Kymmene in multiple federal and state cases concerning alleged price-fixing, and was involved in issues arising out of the merger of two hospitals. The Atlanta attorneys have strong links with the firm's highly rated Washington office and are involved in cases filed around the country.

The Lawyers: "*Diligent*" **Trammell Newton** (see p.619) is said to be "*a direct attorney, who doesn't beat around the bush.*" He is recommended for both his experience and his versatility. Newton recently represented Air Canada in a nationwide case brought by travel agents, which challenged the elimination of the base commissions paid by the airlines.

The Clients: The group has been particularly active in recent times in pharmaceuticals and a number of large vitamin cases. It boasts a client base of large international corporates and regional bodies.

Kilpatrick Stockton LLP
See firm details p.634

The Firm: The team continues to enjoy endorsements from across the marketplace, with commentators picking out its knowledge and professionalism. It handles the full range of transactional and litigation work, including state, federal and grand jury investigations. In the past year, it was involved in a major investigation into an Atlanta-based construction company. It also acted on a DOJ matter for a major North American bank. It has undertaken some substantial M&A work, including representing Seattle's Best Coffee in its merger with Starbucks.

The Lawyers: Stephens Clay and Stan Gorinson are the best-known members of the Atlanta team.

The Clients: The group represents major national and international corporates.

Paul, Hastings, Janofsky & Walker LLP
See firm details p.297

The Firm: This "*friendly, professional*" team was described as "*a business-focused group with great client empathy.*" It handles antitrust litigation and counseling for mid to large-capital companies, and has a special interest in aspects of franchising and distribution. Last year it advised on the merger between two telecom companies, a deal worth $41 million.

The Lawyers: Clients recommend **Rick Asbill** (see p.605) as "*a truly balanced lawyer, who does-*"

n't get caught up in the inconsequential issues and keeps his eye on the big picture." He has particular experience in hospitality and healthcare matters. His practice encompasses both corporate and franchising issues. **Carl Mullis** (see p.619) is selected for his litigation skills; clients say he is "*a smart, diligent and dedicated attorney.*" He recently represented a major tire manufacturer in a substantial price-fixing case within the state.

The Clients: The group represents regional and international companies.

Powell Goldstein LLP

The Firm: This group maintains a reputation as a strong performer with good experience. It has recently been involved in corporate governance matters and has witnessed a growing trend in special investigations, initiated either by the government or companies themselves. It has also been involved in consumer class actions, in most cases for defendants.

The Lawyers: **John Marshall** retains a good reputation among peers and clients, and has been in demand as a mediator in recent times.

The Clients: The group represents large corporates and banks.

Smith Gambrell & Russell LLP

The Firm: This small team is best known for its litigation work and has handled a number of large cases in Atlanta and the Southeast in recent times. It also earns praise for its regulatory work, which is often conducted in conjunction with attorneys in the firm's Washington DC office. Clients consider it "*equal to some much bigger firms.*"

The Lawyers: **Thomas Rhodes** is "*an astute, direct, value-for-money attorney,*" who is excellent in a courtroom setting. He recently defended a leading sporting goods manufacturer in a class action concerning price-fixing and a major airline in a large antitrust litigation brought by travel agents.

The Clients: The team represents regional and national companies, including several involved in manufacturing and transportation.

Troutman Sanders LLP

The Firm: Another smaller team that has earned its stripes is that at Troutman Sanders. "*Undeniably focused and offering a top-rate service,*" it handles a combination of civil and criminal antitrust litigation, counseling and M&A support. It is particularly active in the healthcare sector and also attracts energy-related work from Washington DC. The team recently advised a professional association in an investigation by the state attorney's office.

The Lawyers: **June Ann Sauntry** is "*a fantastic litigator with a great knowledge of antitrust law, so she can answer any question off the top of her head.*" She also has a "*great resource of contacts in government.*" Sauntry recently represented a company in a lawsuit against the AMA and the American Neurological Association over claims that the two bodies had campaigned against a new medical treatment.

The Clients: YKK; Southeastern Electric Exchange; AGCO; Bill Harbert International Construction; Komatsu Forklift USA; Southern Company and Impact Medical Consulting.

BANKING & FINANCE

Georgia
Leading firms (Banking & Finance)

1. **KING & SPALDING LLP** Atlanta
   PAUL, HASTINGS, JANOFSKY Atlanta
2. **ALSTON & BIRD LLP** Atlanta
   JONES DAY Atlanta
   KILPATRICK STOCKTON LLP Atlanta
   PARKER, HUDSON, RAINER & DOBBS Atlanta
3. **HUNTON & WILLIAMS** Atlanta
   POWELL GOLDSTEIN LLP Atlanta
   TROUTMAN SANDERS LLP Atlanta

Leading individuals (Banking & Finance)

1. **CARSON Christopher** Jones Day, Atlanta
   CONRAD Albert King & Spalding, Atlanta
   DOBBS C Edward Parker Hudson, Atlanta
   MOLEN Chris Paul Hastings, Atlanta
2. **ACORD Bobbi** Parker Hudson, Atlanta
   GRICE Richard Alston & Bird, Atlanta
   HILL B Harvey Alston & Bird, Atlanta
   JORDAN Hilary Kilpatrick Stockton, Atlanta
3. **ALFORD Carolyn** King & Spalding, Atlanta
   AUSTIN Jesse Paul Hastings, Atlanta
   CUSHING Paul Alston & Bird, Atlanta
   DEMPSTER Hazen Troutman Sanders, Atlanta
   MOORHEAD Bruce Hunton & Williams, Atlanta
   STRAUSS Robert Troutman Sanders, Atlanta

Up-and-coming individuals
   BLUMEN Rick Alston & Bird, Atlanta
   LAFIANDRA Aldo Alston & Bird, Atlanta
   LEVEILLE Michael Parker Hudson, Atlanta

Firms and individuals are listed alphabetically in each band.

Band 1

King & Spalding LLP
See firm details p.635

The Firm: As the "*undisputed big gun*" on the transactional side, this firm is especially renowned for its established relationship with SunTrust Banks. The work handled by the team of attorneys is varied, encompassing syndicated and single lender senior credit facilities, mezzanine finance, third party sponsored loan programs and private debt financing.

The Lawyers: **Albert Conrad** (see p.609) is a "*first-rate lawyer and a nice guy to boot.*" He maintains his elevated position in the rankings due to a combination of impressive client feedback and high-market visibility. Conrad has been involved in major work for Bank One and

various receivables financing facilities. **Carolyn Alford** (see p.605) is described as "*very thorough and knowledgeable*" by peers, who were also quick to commend the increasingly sophisticated nature of her work. Alford has represented groups of noteholders, and closed an Inner City Broadcasting deal, in connection with Goldman Sachs, for $185 million.

The Clients: UPS Capital; GE Capital; Bank One; ING Capital; Coca-Cola Financial; Prudential; Wachovia Bank. New clients include CapitalSource Finance.

Paul, Hastings, Janofsky & Walker LLP
See firm details p.297

The Firm: Commentators concur that this firm's asset-based lending practice is "*second to none.*" With a client list containing major international financial institutions, national banks and other lenders, much of the group's attention is on M&A funding, asset-based and cash-flow lending, and structured finance. Attorneys have been involved in a $750 million cross-border syndicated loan transaction, acting for the Dutch lender Rabobank.

The Lawyers: Interviewees identified **Chris Molen** (see p.618) as a "*big-time player*" who "*brings huge credibility to every deal.*" The fact that one client "*would trust him with his life*" underlines his ability to inspire confidence. Much of Molen's work involves representing senior lenders on single bank transactions. **Jesse Austin** (see p.605) enters the rankings on the back of impressive peer feedback.

The Clients: Bank of America; Citigroup; CIBC World Markets; Toronto-Dominion Bank; Wachovia Bank; SunTrust Bank; Foothill Capital; GE Capital; Congress Financial; Wells Fargo Retail Finance and CIT Group.

Band 2

Alston & Bird LLP
See firm details p.626

The Firm: With genuine strength on both the transactional and regulatory sides, this "*sophisticated team*" continues to impress. Clients were unanimous in their praise of "*an excellent group of banking lawyers who know exactly how to get deals done.*" The firm has represented SunTrust Bank and SunTrust Robinson Humphrey on a $500 million credit facility to Equifax.

The Lawyers: **Richard Grice** (see p.613) leads the structured lending practice group and is viewed by peers as a syndicated loan specialist. Grice represented Gold Kist in connection with restructuring issues resulting from the company's conversion from a Georgia cooperative to a Delaware corporation. According to peers, **Harvey Hill** (see p.614) is "*a true expert*" and "*ready to climb mountains for his clients if needs be.*" Hill's client portfolio includes an impressive number of insurance sector companies. "*Mr Dependability*" **Paul Cushing** (see p.610) has made a "*big splash*" in the sector over the past year. Acting as counsel to Wachovia Bank in its capacity as agent on a $550 million unsecured credit facility to an equity real estate investment trust has enhanced his market profile. Head of the firm's financial services practice **John Douglas** (see p.611) "*has the midas touch,*" and is doing "*sterling work,*" according to clients. His "*absolute comprehension of all the technical details*" leads to his continued presence at the top of the rankings. **Chip MacDonald** (see p.617) garnered positive feedback for his varied work on both the transactional and regulatory sides of the practice, while up-and-comer **Rick Blumen** (see p.606) impressed interviewees with his industry and the "*refreshing approach*" he brings to transactions. Tipped as one for the future, **Aldo Lafiandra** (see p.617) is particularly respected for his ability to analyze complex structured finance transactions.

The Clients: Wachovia Bank; BNP Paribas; Bank of America; UnumProvident; Regions and Union Planters.

Jones Day
See firm details p.485

The Firm: This highly regarded asset-based lending practice has achieved prominence in the market through its involvement in significant international financings. Competitors note the benefits of the firm's national network of finance lawyers, conceding that "*it can give them an edge in certain situations.*" Major recent work includes assisting KeyBank with regard to a $750 million syndicated, secured revolving and term loan facility to a major contact lens manufacturer. The team also advised Wachovia Bank in connection with a $450 million syndicated, secured asset-based revolving loan to a leading participant in the petroleum and coal products industry.

Georgia
Leading firms
(Banking & Finance: Mainly Regulatory)

1 ALSTON & BIRD LLP *Atlanta*

POWELL GOLDSTEIN LLP *Atlanta*

2 KILPATRICK STOCKTON LLP *Atlanta*

TROUTMAN SANDERS LLP *Atlanta*

3 MILLER HAMILTON SNIDER & ODOM *Atlanta*

SMITH GAMBRELL & RUSSELL LLP *Atlanta*

WOMBLE CARLYLE SANDRIDGE & RICE *Atlanta*

Leading individuals
(Banking & Finance: Mainly Regulatory)

1 DOUGLAS John *Alston & Bird, Atlanta*

MOELING Walter *Powell Goldstein, Atlanta*

2 CHEATHAM Richard *Kilpatrick Stockton, Atlanta*

KNUDSON Kathryn *Powell Goldstein, Atlanta*

POWELL Thomas *Troutman Sanders, Atlanta*

3 DUNLEVIE Steven *Womble Carlyle, Atlanta*

MACDONALD III Ralph *Alston & Bird, Atlanta*

PANNELL H Gary *Miller Hamilton, Atlanta*

SCHWARTZ Robert *Smith Gambrell, Atlanta*

Firms and individuals are listed alphabetically in each band.

The Lawyers: "*Star player*" **Christopher Carson** (see p.608) is highly respected by peers and "*always makes things happen.*" His practice is divided between finance and bankruptcy matters. Recently, he has assisted Wachovia in connection with a $35 million syndicated, asset-based secured revolving credit and letter of credit financing to a frozen foods distributor in the Southeast. Edgar Snow has now left the firm.

The Clients: Wachovia; Citigroup; Société Générale; CIT Group; James River Coal Company and commercial banks and other commercial lenders.

Kilpatrick Stockton LLP
See firm details p.634

The Firm: Renowned for its strength in the fields of syndicated lending and structured finance, this team of "*bright and knowledgeable lawyers*" has an established client following. Recent highlights have included acting for community banks throughout the Southeast, in addition to national finance institutions and credit unions.

The Lawyers: Clients were impressed by **Hilary Jordan**'s (see p.615) passion for "*getting the job done properly.*" Jordan is considered a "*very sound lawyer*" by market commentators, and is noted for his expertise in syndicated lending. On the regulatory side the "*cerebral*" **Richard Cheatham** (see p.608) was "*still top dog*" for a number of those interviewed.

The Clients: The firm's finance arm has undertaken corporate finance matters for Wachovia Bank, SunTrust Bank and BNP Paribas Bank.

Parker, Hudson, Rainer & Dobbs LLP

The Firm: This "*innovative*" boutique impressed commentators and clients alike with its ability to "*think outside the box.*" The market consensus is that the firm handles a sophisticated level of work on the lending side, offering representation to banks and other institutions in new business loans. It also assists in the provision of syndicated credit facilities for private and public sector entities.

The Lawyers: "*Prince of the profession,*" **Edward Dobbs** is "*a real go-getter*" in the view of clients, and this is reflected in his rise to the second tier of the rankings. Said by commentators to "*live and breathe the law,*" Dobbs has represented hedge funds and undertaken significant work on syndicated lending matters. The market considers **Bobbi Acord** to be "*an integral part of the firm's recent success.*" She has impressed clients with the quality of her work and her steadfast commitment to "*always ensuring that the problem is solved.*" Up-and-comer **Michael Leveille** is "*very accomplished*" and considered by many to have "*star quality written all over him.*"

The Clients: Bank of America; Wachovia Bank; Congress Financial; Wells Fargo; P&C Bank; SunTrust Bank; Regions Bank and BBNT.

Band 3

Hunton & Williams
See firm details p.1775

The Firm: This firm enters the rankings for its achievements in an impressive range of financing matters, including leveraged finance transactions, asset-based lending and acquisition finance for private equity deals. Peers predicted a bright future for the banking team, describing them as "*a force to be reckoned with.*"

The Lawyers: **Bruce Moorhead** (see p.619) has joined the firm from Smith, Gambrell & Russell and is considered to bring "*real gravitas*" to every transaction he takes on. Moorhead's arrival has resulted in a significant boost to the firm's client portfolio.

The Clients: Bank of America; GE Capital; CIT Business Credit and Wachovia Bank.

Powell Goldstein LLP

The Firm: The community banking practice of this firm continues to be well regarded by the market. In addition to straight lending, "*robust and pragmatic*" advice is offered to clients in areas such as M&A financing, regulation and compliance, securities and capital management, Internet banking, de novo banking, holding companies, wealth management and insurance. Significant work over the past year has included acting for major clients, Georgian Bank and Riverside Holdings.

The Lawyers: **Walter Moeling** is said to possess "*immense knowledge,*" and maintains his place at the top of the regulatory rankings. A "*great small bank lawyer,*" Moeling is "*very impressive*" when explaining concepts to clients. The teamwork between Moeling and **Kathryn Knudson** is said to be seamless in nature, with Knudson seen as a "*steady, effective, solid performer*" who "*isn't afraid to stir things up a bit when necessary.*"

The Clients: Habersham Bank; Gwinnett Commercial Group; Synovus Financial and FLAG Financial.

Troutman Sanders LLP

The Firm: Perceived expertise on the regulatory and transactional sides lead to rankings in both banking tables for this firm. The team's work on M&A and capital formation transactions for community banks and thrifts has turned heads in the market, with one prominent source commenting: "*If there's a better place to go in Georgia for capital formation transactions, I don't know about it.*" The straight financing arm of the practice was also singled out for praise.

The Lawyers: For many, **Hazen Dempster** remains a "*top-notch performer.*" Also respected as a lecturer, his pragmatic approach to matters was valued by clients who emphasized that "*he doesn't mess around with small details, he just gets on with it.*" **Bo Strauss** enters the rankings on the back of market recognition for his niche practice in the area of equipment leasing, while **Thomas Powell**'s knowledge on the regulatory side also attracted plaudits. Powell is outside counsel for Cotton States Insurance Group and Georgia Theatre Company-II.

The Clients: Federal Home Loan Bank of Atlanta; CNB Holdings; Cotton States Insurance Group; Southeastern Banking and First Community Bancorp.

Miller Hamilton Snider & Odom LLC

The Firm: The Atlanta office of this Alabama-based firm is emerging as a noteworthy player. Commentators noted how the regulatory expertise of the team "*seems to increase year by year.*"

The Lawyers: The "*very well-versed*" **Gary Pannell** is considered "*a true great*" in the regulatory arena, and is thought to draw well upon his experience as the former district counsel for the Southeastern district of the Office of the Comptroller of the Currency. Several former Wachovia in-house counsel further bolster the team's expertise.

The Clients: Wachovia Bank, Colonial Bank and a number of community banks are clients.

Smith Gambrell & Russell LLP

The Firm: The departure of a number of the firm's transactional lawyers to Hunton & Williams has meant that it is principally the firm's regulatory practice that stands out for interviewees. A commitment to new bank formations and also banking sector M&A were noted by the market, with one source com-

www.ChambersandPartners.com

All quotes in the text are from interviews with clients and competitors.

581

menting on the firm's *"new sense of direction"* in these areas.

The Lawyers: Regulatory specialist **Robert Schwartz** is a member of the firm's corporate department, but has significant involvement in the banking sector. He is described as *"a great character"* who *"brings verve to every transaction."*

The Clients: First National Bankshares of Georgia; Thomasville Bancshares; Fifth Third Bank and other financial institutions.

Womble Carlyle Sandridge & Rice PLLC
See firm details p.1402

The Firm: Although it is generally perceived that the firm's main power base lies in its North Carolina offices, the Atlanta branch can also take credit for Womble Carlyle's market presence in the Southeast with regard to banking sector M&A and regulatory matters.

The Lawyers: Interviewees agree that **Steven Dunlevie** (see p.611) *"packs a real punch"* in regulatory matters, with a practice centered on acting for a number of community banks and coordinating significant M&As.

The Clients: BPP Corporation; Main Street Banks; United Community Banks and Mid Country Financial Corp.

BANKRUPTCY

Georgia
Leading firms (Bankruptcy)

1 ALSTON & BIRD LLP *Atlanta*
KING & SPALDING LLP *Atlanta*

2 KILPATRICK STOCKTON LLP *Atlanta*
MCKENNA LONG & ALDRIDGE *Atlanta*
PARKER, HUDSON, RAINER & DOBBS *Atlanta*

3 GREENBERG TRAURIG LLP *Atlanta*
LAMBERTH, CIFELLI, STOKES & STOUT *Atlanta*
PAUL, HASTINGS, JANOFSKY & WALKER *Atlanta*
POWELL GOLDSTEIN LLP *Atlanta*
TROUTMAN SANDERS LLP *Atlanta*

Leading individuals (Bankruptcy)

1 AUSTIN Jesse *Paul Hastings, Atlanta*
BATSON R Neal *Alston & Bird, Atlanta*
BORDERS Sarah *King & Spalding, Atlanta*
COHEN Ezra *Troutman Sanders, Atlanta*
CONNOLLY Dennis *Alston & Bird, Atlanta*
DOBBS C Edward *Parker Hudson, Atlanta*
PARDO James *King & Spalding, Atlanta*
STEIN Grant *Alston & Bird, Atlanta*

2 CAMPBELL Charles *McKenna Long, Atlanta*
CIFELLI James *Lamberth Cifelli, Atlanta*
DORSEY Rufus *Parker Hudson, Atlanta*
FERDINANDS Paul *King & Spalding, Atlanta*
KAUFMAN Mark *McKenna Long, Atlanta*
LUREY Alfred *Kilpatrick Stockton, Atlanta*
MEIR Dennis *Kilpatrick Stockton, Atlanta*

3 ELLMAN Jeffrey *Jones Day, Atlanta*
KELLEY Jeffrey *Troutman Sanders, Atlanta*
KURZWEIL David *Greenberg Traurig, Atlanta*
LEVIN Matthew *Alston & Bird, Atlanta*
MARSH Gary *McKenna Long, Atlanta*
MEYERS Todd *Kilpatrick Stockton, Atlanta*
NICHOLSON Penn *Powell Goldstein, Atlanta*
ROSENBLATT Paul *Kilpatrick Stockton, Atlanta*
WILLIAMSON Robert *Scroggins & Williamson, Atlanta*

Up-and-coming individuals

WALSH Brian *King & Spalding, Atlanta*
WING Michael *Greenberg Traurig, Atlanta*

Firms and individuals are listed alphabetically in each band.

Band 1

Alston & Bird LLP
See firm details p.626

The Firm: This firm possesses *"the best lawyers, the best skill set and the best slices of work,"* according to the market. This commercial bankruptcy practice focuses largely on debtor work and Chapter 11, with a smaller interest in creditors' committee matters. It is known for its extensive client base, having handled matters for corporates across the country. Attorneys were heavily occupied by work arising out of the Enron collapse, which, although now receding, has boosted the team's profile and *"given everyone a taste of exactly what they can do."*

The Lawyers: Splitting his time between Georgia and Colorado, **Neal Batson** (see p.606) remains one of the group's prime assets. He is regarded as *"a dynamite lawyer who never lets a point go easily,"* and is best known for his work on the Enron bankruptcy. *"Expert"* **Dennis Connolly** (see p.609) has *"wonderful courtroom presence."* He recently acted as co-counsel to the committee of 100-year-old textile company Dan River in its reorganization and deleveraging. The practice group is headed by the *"insightful"* **Grant Stein** (see p.623), who is adept at *"getting to the heart of issues quickly."* He, too, was involved in matters arising from Enron. **Matthew Levin** (see p.617) is hailed as *"a professional and responsive attorney, who is superb on technical points."* Levin usually works on the debtor side and, of late, has counseled on matters in the textile, tourism and health sectors.

The Clients: The group represents public and private companies, including Prudential, LaRoche Industries and Gayley & Lord.

King & Spalding LLP
See firm details p.635

The Firm: Rising up to share the top spot in the bankruptcy table this year, King & Spalding is hailed by clients as *"extremely sharp on legal matters, understanding and precise on business issues, and offering quality from top to bottom."* The firm's practice group acts for debtors, lenders and creditors' committees and is well known for its capabilities in distressed lender transactions and bankruptcy litigations. One of the group's major matters from the past year was the representation of Sprint in its assertion of approximately $300 million in claims against MCI, and its defense of approximately $40 million in counterclaims.

The Lawyers: **Sarah Borders** (see p.607) is deemed *"outstanding."* Clients endorsed her lofty position in the table, referring to her *"tremendous knowledge of bankruptcy law, especially in credit banking issues."* She is also said to be *"amazing in a courtroom setting."* Borders recently completed the Centennial HealthCare reorganization, which, in a heavily regulated field, dealt with 89 nursing homes across 19 states – a purchase price of $160 million was finally agreed. **James Pardo** (see p.620) has *"a phenomenal knowledge"* of bankruptcy law and is *"highly adept at cutting through legal knots."* He and Borders have been working on the multi-million-dollar Dan River bankruptcy. **Paul Ferdinands** (see p.612) is *"a smart, sophisticated"* lawyer who earns respect for his debtor work and mastery of transactions involving financially distressed companies. He recently advised private equity firm Crescent Capital Investments in its $190 million purchase of Tender Loving Care Health Care Services. New to the guide is **Brian Walsh** (see p.625), whose restructuring experience is increasingly sought after. *"He is definitely one to watch – he offers clients help eight days a week."*

The Clients: Centennial HealthCare; Crescent Capital Investments; Dan River; GE Capital; Russell; Sprint and SunTrust Banks.

Band 2

Kilpatrick Stockton LLP
See firm details p.634

The Firm: Kilpatrick Stockton's *"smart, efficient"* financial restructuring team earns client approval for its *"great strength in depth."* The team handles debtor and creditors' committee matters as well as providing individual creditor representation. It enjoys a particularly good reputation in the communications sector, representing, for example, BellSouth in a multimillion-dollar claim against VarTech. Although based in Atlanta, the group is seen to have a presence on the national stage.

The Lawyers: The *"thoroughly experienced and knowledgeable"* **Alfred Lurey** (see p.617) has *"a great knack of making the difficult seem easy."* He is known specifically for his work on complex transactions and, more generally, for the range of his legal expertise. Lurey recently acted in the bankruptcy of a large airline. **Dennis Meir** (see p.618) is regarded as *"an excellent committee lawyer"* and *"a sensible attorney, who has seen it all."* He is particularly renowned for his litigation prowess. *"Sharp"* **Paul Rosenblatt** (see p.622) received plaudits for both his transactional and litigation endeavors. Though seen as the communications expert within the group, he is versatile and is currently representing a large furniture company in a bankruptcy litigation. **Todd Meyers** (see p.618) continues to draw praise, especially for his workout skills.

The Clients: The group represents GE Capital, Nextel International and BellSouth among others.

McKenna Long & Aldridge
See firm details p.636

The Firm: This *"tenacious team of expert attorneys"* is best known for litigation and represents debtors, committees and secured creditors. It has recently represented a number of litigation trustees in their pursuit of claims. Recently it was working on the bankruptcy of a financial company, which involved claims against the company's auditors. The firm is currently advising another law firm, which was counsel for a now bankrupt financial company and is presently being sued by creditors.

The Lawyers: Litigator **Charles Campbell** (see p.608) is regarded by clients as *"a talented, quick-thinking attorney, who you'd want on your side in a courtroom."* He recently handled a litigation arising from the bankruptcy of diaper manufacturer Paragon Trade Brands. This drawn-out case involved claims against numerous parties, including former owners of the group. Particularly well known for his work for secured creditors and committees, **Mark Kaufman** (see p.616) is *"a busy lawyer who talks a lot of sense."* His advocacy skills came in for warm praise. *"Astute"* **Gary Marsh** (see p.618), meanwhile, was picked out for his work for utilities. He is said to *"construct great arguments."*

The Clients: The firm's clients include banks, financial companies and energy entities. It also has a particular following in the realm of convenience stores.

Parker, Hudson, Rainer & Dobbs LLP

The Firm: This boutique firm is deemed *"more than capable of taking on the big guys."* It has enjoyed a busy year, handling a large number of small to medium-sized bankruptcies, as well as a variety of liquidation cases. Its primary focus is the representation of financial institutions as creditors or lessors, though it also represents debtors, creditors' committees and bankruptcy trustees, when called upon. The firm has recently been involved in the bankruptcy of Gayley & Lord, acting for a creditor owed $160 million. Its Georgia location has not prevented the firm from being active across the East Coast.

The Lawyers: **Edward Dobbs** was recommended as *"a strong attorney and a strong presence; he's the firm's magnet for good quality work."* A forthright litigator, Dobbs recently represented HSBC Bank USA in issues arising out of the Bush Industries bankruptcy in Buffalo, New York. **Rufus Dorsey** is hailed as a *"quick-witted and nimble"* litigator and praised for his secured creditor work. He has recently been appointed examiner in the New Power bankruptcy.

The Clients: Bank of America; Branch Banking & Trust; CapitalSource; CIT Business Credit; Congress Financial; GE Capital; PNC Bank; Regions Financial; Textron Financial; Wachovia and Wells Fargo.

Band 3

Greenberg Traurig LLP
See firm details p.564

The Firm: The deal, according to clients, is *"high-quality work at a reasonable price."* As part of a nationwide network, Greenberg Traurig's Atlanta office is acknowledged to have superb support and an international flavor to its work. Healthcare providers feature prominently in the client list and the firm has recently handled a number of private workouts.

The Lawyers: **David Kurzweil** (see p.617) was recommended by one client as *"the best negotiator I have ever worked with."* He has *"an excellent grasp of all the facts, their implications and the possible consequences. He not only advises on law, but on business issues."* Kurzweil recently acted for the creditors' committee in the Centennial HealthCare case, the assets of which were valued at around $450 million. New to the guide is up-and-comer **Michael Wing** (see p.625), *"a smart guy who does a good job."*

The Clients: The group represents clients in healthcare, retail, real estate, manufacturing and textiles.

Lamberth, Cifelli, Stokes & Stout, P.A.

The Firm: This is a focused bankruptcy group, seen by the market as *"the first stop in debtor work."* It has experience in Chapter 11, reorganizations, workouts, creditors' rights and litigation. The firm is also recommended for its input into the sale and purchase of distressed companies.

The Lawyers: Within the team, **James Cifelli** has the highest profile. He is *"a superb litigator with a great knowledge of the workings of a bankruptcy case."*

The Clients: The group's clients include airlines, agricultural companies, healthcare providers and hi-tech ventures.

Paul, Hastings, Janofsky & Walker LLP
See firm details p.297

The Firm: Felt to be a *"go-to"* team, particularly on lending work, this group of attorneys primarily represents banks and financiers and senior secured individual lenders. It has handled large national cases, as well as cross-border transactions and several matters relating to the UK. In the past year it acted for NorthWestern Corporation in its reorganization and recapitalization, and on the DIP financing of U-Haul.

The Lawyers: *"Responsive"* **Jesse Austin** (see p.605) is said by clients to be *"easy to work with – he has a thorough grip of the issues and doesn't dazzle you with science."* Austin is particularly known for his secured debt activity.

The Clients: The firm represents construction, energy, financial services, healthcare, real estate and transport companies.

Powell Goldstein LLP

The Firm: Despite earning most plaudits for its debtor and creditors' committee work, this small team is active in the full range of bankruptcy matters and has high-level experience in both litigation and transactions. Key clients are to be found in healthcare, retail and the media.

The Lawyers: **Penn Nicholson**, who leads the team, is acknowledged for his transactional expertise, with one source commenting: *"You know the boat won't be rocked too much with him on board."* He is also known for his sure touch in general business litigation.

The Clients: Clients are from manufacturing, real estate, telecom and institutional lending sectors.

Troutman Sanders LLP

The Firm: The firm is felt to have taken a hit with the departure of one of its top-ranked lawyers, Mary Grace Diehl, to the bench. Nonetheless, it still boasts a knowledgeable team with *"an enviable client base."* Primarily oriented toward litigation, the group represents secured and unsecured creditors and debtors, leaving colleagues in other departments to look after transactional matters. It recently represented a major airline in its bankruptcy, a matter that was national in scope.

The Lawyers: Former bankruptcy judge **Ezra Cohen** is recommended as *"one of the grand old men of the Atlanta bankruptcy Bar. What he doesn't know is not worth knowing."* Recently Cohen acted for the Southern Company in

litigation arising from the bankruptcy of former parent company Merritt. **Jeff Kelley** is the big hitter brought in to replace Diehl, and although he has not been at the firm particularly long, he is seen to be *"making progress."*
The Clients: Southern Company; Nationwide Furniture; New Power Holdings and Wachovia.

Other Notable Practitioners

Robert Williamson of Scroggins & Williamson is recommended as *"a switched-on lawyer with a great understanding of debtor work."* He represents small to medium-sized companies and has recently acted to stabilize a large trucking and mining concern in Chapter 11. Jones Day lawyer **Jeffrey Ellman** (see p.611), who is new to the guide, is described by clients as *"extremely responsive, intelligent and diligent."* He focuses on debtor work and recently acted for a bank in the settlement of a claim worth $200 million.

CONSTRUCTION

Georgia
Leading firms (Construction)

1. **GRIFFIN COCHRANE & MARSHALL** *Atlanta*
   KILPATRICK STOCKTON LLP *Atlanta*
   SMITH, CURRIE & HANCOCK LLP *Atlanta*
2. **ALSTON & BIRD LLP** *Atlanta*
   HENDRICK, PHILLIPS, SALZMAN *Atlanta*
   KING & SPALDING LLP *Atlanta*
   SMITH GAMBRELL & RUSSELL LLP *Atlanta*
3. **SEYFARTH SHAW LLP** *Atlanta*
   SHAPIRO FUSSELL *Atlanta*
   WEINBERG, WHEELER, HUDGINS, GUNN *Atlanta*

Leading individuals (Construction)

1. **ASSELIN Thomas** *Smith Gambrell, Atlanta*
   BECK Philip *Smith Currie, Atlanta*
   DORRIS William *Kilpatrick Stockton, Atlanta*
   FLETCHER Jennifer *Griffin Cochrane, Atlanta*
   HENDRICK David *Hendrick Phillips, Atlanta*
   HINCHEY John *King & Spalding, Atlanta*
   KELLEHER Thomas *Smith Currie, Atlanta*
   SHAPIRO J Ben *Shapiro Fussell, Atlanta*
   SPANGLER III John *Alston & Bird, Atlanta*
2. **ABERNATHY Thomas** *Smith Currie, Atlanta*
   BUTLER James *Smith Currie, Atlanta*
   CHAMBERS Robert *Smith Currie, Atlanta*
   COLEMAN Aubrey *Smith Currie, Atlanta*
   CORGAN Brian *Kilpatrick Stockton, Atlanta*
   CREWDSON Robert *Alston & Bird, Atlanta*
   DAVIS Lee *Griffin Cochrane, Atlanta*
   DIAL David *Weinberg Wheeler, Atlanta*
   GENBERG Ira *Smith Gambrell, Atlanta*
   GREER Scott *King & Spalding, Atlanta*
   HAFER Randall *Kilpatrick Stockton, Atlanta*
   HUGHES William *Alston & Bird, Atlanta*
   MCCABE F Barry *Griffin Cochrane, Atlanta*
   MOLAVI Kamyar *Seyfarth Shaw, Atlanta*
   PATRICK Elizabeth *Kilpatrick Stockton, Atlanta*
   PHILLIPS Stephen *Hendrick Phillips, Atlanta*
   ROBERTS Lee *Weinberg Wheeler, Atlanta*
   SALZMAN Martin *Hendrick Phillips, Atlanta*
   SMITH George *Kilpatrick Stockton, Atlanta*
   STAIR Kent *Carlock Copeland, Atlanta*
   SWEENEY Neal *Kilpatrick Stockton, Atlanta*

Firms and individuals are listed alphabetically in each band.

Band 1

Griffin Cochrane & Marshall
See firm details p.632

The Firm: In a year that brings the 25th anniversary of this leading boutique firm, there was little doubt among commentators that it continues to hold its own in the market. Offering a full range of services to clients – bid protests, negotiation and preparation of contracts, advice and counsel during contract performance, dispute avoidance, claims preparation and analysis, and various forms of dispute resolution – the group has real presence both nationally and internationally.
The Lawyers: **Jennifer Fletcher** (see p.612) has extensive jury trial experience. Described by peers as *"an incredibly effective trial lawyer,"* she has served as lead counsel in numerous trials, arbitrations, mediations and appellate arguments. Fêted for his *"cool, calm, composed approach,"* **Barry McCabe** (see p.618) represents clients in a plethora of disputes, including stadium, hotel, casino, industrial, pharmaceutical and courthouse projects. He has prosecuted and defended claims for delay, acceleration, inefficiency, defective construction and fraud among other things. **Lee Davis** (see p.610) enters the rankings due to widespread praise for his project work. For some, Davis is *"the epitome of how an attorney should be: articulate, intelligent and persuasive."* His practice incorporates issues relating to power plants, industrial facilities, wastewater treatment plants, the hospitality and healthcare sectors, and residential, commercial and retail properties.
The Clients: Poole & Kent; Black & Veatch; LK Comstock; Lafarge Industries; Whiting-Turner Contracting and Blue Circle.

Kilpatrick Stockton LLP
See firm details p.634

The Firm: The construction practice at this multiservice firm continues to evolve as a result of an expansive recruitment strategy that has seen the size of the team increase from 16 to 26 attorneys in the past year alone. This growth in size and stature has not passed unnoticed by commentators, who were quick to acknowledge that the firm is *"increasingly a dominant force"* in the Georgia marketplace. The team's client base tends toward general contractors and construction managers, for whom it is equally adept in an advisory capacity or providing representation in litigation or alternative dispute resolution. The firm recently represented the authorities of a Dallas suburb on more than $30 million worth of claims against the designers and contractors who worked on a failed advanced wastewater treatment facility. Internationally it has represented the turnkey operator on the $1 billion light rail mass transit system for San Juan, Puerto Rico.
The Lawyers: **William Dorris** (see p.611) was described to researchers as *"a very smart attorney who is consistently ahead of the game."* Though much of his practice is now geared toward mediation and other alternative dispute resolution methods, he has extensive experience of trials, arbitrations and administrative proceedings, including a nine-month hearing before the Armed Services Board of Contract Appeals. **Neal Sweeney** (see p.624) focuses on federal, state and local contracting and bid protests across the country. His practice includes both private and public projects involving office buildings, hotels, hospitals, airports, schools and wastewater treatment plants. Head of the firm's construction and public contracts group, **Randy Hafer** (see p.613) has represented many of the major participants in the construction industry on a wide variety of construction and engineering projects. He impresses clients with his ability to *"get to the heart of the matter in seconds."* **Brian Corgan** (see p.609), meanwhile, handles construction disputes involving nuclear and coal-fired power plants, international airport runways, cogeneration (power, cement and lime) plants, wastewater treatment plants, steel mills, oil refineries and hospitals. Corgan has a broad client base, ranging from owners to engineering and materials testing firms, general contractors, subcontractors, suppliers, sureties, and design professionals. This year the tables include two additional names from the Kilpatrick Stockton bench. **Elizabeth Patrick** (see p.620) joined the team from Troutman Sanders' Atlanta office; clients consider her to be *"a top-drawer attorney, who is intelligent and personable."* She has considerable experience in assisting owners, devel-

opers, construction companies and others with planning and managing complex development and construction projects, design and construction contract preparation and negotiation, risk management, dispute resolution and litigation. Ex-Sutherland Asbill & Brennan attorney **Tony Smith** (see p.623) is also widely respected by peers. Smith has substantial experience as lead trial attorney in large, complex, multiparty construction disputes. His clients include general and subcontractors, owners, professionals, sureties and insurers.

The Clients: Siemens Transportation Systems; Massachusetts Water Resources Authority; Milwaukee Metropolitan Sewerage District and LG&E Energy.

Smith, Currie & Hancock LLP

The Firm: Even though this firm is very much steeped in all the history and tradition one would expect from one of the country's original construction law specialists, interviewees nonetheless praised the *"forward-thinking dynamism"* of its attorneys. Construction clients from across the USA and the rest of the world are represented on a wide range of matters; the services offered include delivery systems and project documentation, in addition to traditional litigation and arbitration of disputes. A large team of 40 attorneys supports the contention by one commentator that *"they have the manpower to handle anything."*

The Lawyers: Market sources agreed that **Philip Beck** *"brings kudos to everything he works on."* He has tried construction cases before federal Boards of Contract Appeals, numerous state and local administrative bodies as well as various state and federal courts, and has represented clients in arbitrations and mediations conducted throughout the country. With extensive government and construction contract experience, **Thomas Kelleher** is able to advise on a spectrum of issues involving bidding, changes, differing site conditions, delays and terminations. He has represented clients on hospital projects, airport facilities, research laboratories, convention facilities, prisons, courthouses and resort hotels, and has appeared before various federal Boards of Contract Appeals, as well as federal and state courts. **Thomas Abernathy** represents owners, general contractors, subcontractors, and sureties on issues involving bid and award protests and performance problems related to changes, changed conditions, delays, suspensions of work and termination of contracts. Described by peers as *"impressively sharp,"* he has been involved in construction projects ranging from federal offices, courthouses and high-rise buildings to bridges and highways, power plants and industrial construction projects. **James Butler**'s practice is concentrated in the negotiation, arbitration and litigation of construction contracts and environmental issues.

With a vast array of project experience under his belt, Butler has continued to catch the eye of commentators, who remarked on how he *"remains calm and professional in the most pressurized of situations."* **Robert Chambers** is heavily involved in environmental matters within the construction field, including water issues and CERCLA/Superfund liability and site remediation/cleanup. Chambers won plaudits for his *"perfect blend of intelligence and pragmatism,"* which makes him *"a pleasure to work with."* Finally, peers consider the *"cerebral"* **Aubrey Coleman** to be *"a true authority"* on construction and government contracts.

The Clients: Turner Construction; Caddell Construction; Endress+Hauser System & Gauging; Golder Associates; Birmingham Steel; Williams Group International; Allen & O'Hara Construction; Caddell Construction; Chapman Corporation; McCarl's; RPC Mechanical; Simpson Bridge; The Saxon Group and Whitehead Electric.

Band 2

Alston & Bird LLP

See firm details p.626

The Firm: This team of 12 attorneys focuses exclusively on construction and government contracts law, offering a host of services to a broad mix of both contractors and owners. The market applauds its *"energetic, professional approach to getting things done."* The firm's largest client on the contractor side is Skanska USA Building, which it has represented in disputes arising out of the construction of improvements at JFK International Airport, airport terminals in Boston and Tampa, a performing arts center in Columbus, Georgia, and a criminal investigative laboratory for the US Army Corps of Engineers. The group has also been engaged on a national basis in the past year by prominent owner clients such as Archstone-Smith, The Rouse Company, Lowe's and Federal Realty Investment Trust.

The Lawyers: Chair of the firm's construction group, **John Spangler** (see p.623), rises in the rankings following impressive market feedback. Sources were enthusiastic in their praise of an attorney who *"seems to know everything."* Spangler advises on joint ventures, the negotiation of design-build, construction and construction management contracts, and the drafting of program management and development agreements. Fêted for a birth-to-death practice that focuses on drafting and negotiating design and construction contracts, **William Hughes** (see p.615) maintains his market position. He frequently works with companies in the energy and industrial sectors to structure, negotiate and draft multiparty agreements for large energy and privatized public works projects. **Robert Crewdson** (see p.610) enters the rankings this

year. His practice is both transactional and dispute based, with his clients including owners and contractors. Crewdson is seen as a *"no-nonsense attorney who is prepared to bust a gut for his clients."*

The Clients: Manhattan Construction; Barton Mallow; Brasfield & Gorrie; Whiting-Turner Contracting; AG Spanos Development; Emory University; TIC (The Industrial Company); Industrial Developments International; Municipal Electric Association of Georgia; Beazer Homes; Mirant; Koch Industries and Lurgi AG.

Hendrick, Phillips, Salzman & Flatt PC

See firm details p.633

The Firm: This boutique firm with a truly national reach won acclaim due to its attorneys' ability to utilize their extensive experience to the full benefit of clients. An impressive client base of subcontractors, contractors and owners bears testimony to the overriding market feeling that this firm is *"a quality outfit that specializes in keeping clients happy."* Considerable emphasis is placed on corporate structuring, contracting and project organizing.

The Lawyers: Across the board, interviewees judged **David Hendrick** (see p.614) as *"a first-rate lawyer who deserves all the credit he gets."* His practice is comprised of an impressive range of contract negotiation, formation and project structuring work. Hendrick also has substantial experience in dealing with dispute avoidance and dispute resolution. Commentators were also impressed with **Martin Salzman**'s (see p.622) attention to detail: *"He has an incredible capacity for accurate, in-depth analysis."* Salzman's practice covers all types of construction disputes and general litigation in federal and state judicial, administrative and arbitration proceedings. **Stephen Phillips** (see p.620) is very active in the roofing industry and serves as counsel to the National Roofing Contractors Association and the National Roofing Legal Resource Center.

The Clients: Centex Construction; Siemens Energy & Automation; Keene Construction; ARCADIS Geraghty & Miller International and John W Rooker & Associates.

King & Spalding LLP

See firm details p.635

The Firm: Maintaining its market position after positive client feedback for the construction and procurement group's *"efficient and intelligent outlook,"* this firm continues to show considerable strength in both litigation and transactional work. Recent highlights include the representation of BHP Billiton in the drafting and negotiation of engineering, procurement and construction management agreements for a copper mining facility in the Chilean Andes. The team also represented Turner Broadcasting

www.ChambersandPartners.com

All quotes in the text are from interviews with clients and competitors.

585

companies in the negotiation and drafting of construction agreements for major projects in New York and Atlanta.

The Lawyers: The *"very well-versed"* **John Hinchey** (see p.614) leads the practice group and drew comment about the quality and accuracy of his advice. *"He doesn't just solve the problem, he makes sure it won't happen the next time,"* reported one client. Hinchey represents large-cap companies, consulting firms, universities, state, city and county governments, public authorities, medical institutions, public utilities, private developers and owners, design professionals and contractors. Former engineer **Scott Greer** (see p.613) is a new addition to the rankings. A *"star in the making"* in the eyes of the market, he also impressed clients with his work on construction agreements and operations contracts.

The Clients: American Arbitration Association; Ambac Assurance; BHP Billiton; CEMEX; Coca-Cola; El Paso/Southern Natural Gas; Freeport LNG (ConocoPhillips); Financial Guaranty Insurance; GE Real Estate; Holcim (US); Norfolk Southern; Turner Broadcasting System and UPS.

Smith Gambrell & Russell LLP

The Firm: Clients extolled the virtues of the construction group at this multiservice firm, describing its attorneys as *"honest, hard-working and good value."* Peers were equally convinced of the firm's credentials, noting with approval its involvement in major projects. Representation is provided to architects, engineers, suppliers and property owners, nationally and internationally.

The Lawyers: The *"exceptionally well-connected"* **Ira Genberg** *"has a practice to die for"* in both the national and international arenas. Genberg is popular with clients, who approve of his *"powerful and charming demeanor."* Recently he won a precedent-setting victory, which established a new law throughout the European Community; and as counsel for a group of industrial contractors in another landmark case, he proved the existence of a nationwide price-fixing conspiracy, the damage and injunctive relief amounting to nearly $500 million. The group's other *"big star"* is **Thomas Asselin**, who is deemed *"incredibly knowledgeable and easy to deal with."* Asselin has arbitrated and litigated on many projects, among them those relating to conference centers, banks, prisons, airports, public utilities and a number of governmental and military facilities.

The Clients: Foster Wheeler Group; Kerzner International; Tyco International; Winn-Dixie; Home Depot; Shimizu; Sierra Aluminum; HKL Cladding and BHN Corp.

Band 3

Seyfarth Shaw LLP
See firm details p.777

The Firm: *"A class act from top to bottom"* was the market verdict on this firm, which assists clients on the negotiation, drafting and performance of construction and related contracts. Close links with professional bodies have led to significant expertise in developing standard form agreements for architects, general contractors and suppliers.

The Lawyers: One source described **Kamyar Molavi** as *"one hell of a smart lawyer;"* indeed, interviewees were unanimous in their admiration of the breadth and quality of his advice. Molavi's client base is predominantly composed of design professionals, owners and bonding companies, for whom he acts on a variety of alternative dispute resolution and contract matters.

The Clients: Clear Channel Outdoor; Earth-Link; Unisource Worldwide; Siemens Building Technologies and Home Depot.

Shapiro Fussell

The Firm: Fielding 25 attorneys, this group has acquired a national practice providing corporate services and contract drafting, evaluation and negotiation for general contractors, subcontractors, developers, trade organizations and insurance carriers. The group also provides a comprehensive dispute service.

The Lawyers: **Ben Shapiro** maintains his market profile as a *"diligent and effective litigator."* He represents owners, general contractors, subcontractors, suppliers and design professionals in all manner of construction claims in state and federal courts as well as arbitrations and mediations.

Weinberg, Wheeler, Hudgins, Gunn & Dial, LLC

The Firm: Although principally known for its insurance defense focus, this firm has, in the eyes of the market, *"made grand strides"* in recent years. It has developed project expertise in the construction and renovation of federal, state and local facilities and has substantial experience in alternative dispute resolution and litigation.

The Lawyers: **David Dial** was described as *"a big-name lawyer who is perfect for the big-name cases."* His litigation and arbitration skills were roundly applauded by interviewees, who also noted his alternative dispute resolution skills. *"Respected"* **Lee Roberts** was singled out for his industrious nature; in fact, one humorous commentator described him as *"more committed than a lunatic in an asylum."* He handles a mixed caseload of construction, commercial litigation, and labor and employment law.

The Clients: Affiliated Building Services; Bagwell Construction; EllisDon Construction; KMI Contracting and Walton Construction.

Other Notable Practitioners

Kent Stair of Carlock Copeland Semler & Stair, LLP won market recognition for his representation of design professionals, general contractors, subcontractors and owners in a full range of disputes and transactions.

CORPORATE/M&A

Band 1

Alston & Bird LLP
See firm details p.626

The Firm: *"The team is such a top-quality outfit for acquisitions and transactional work,"* was the verdict of one market expert of the Alston & Bird offering. *"Genuinely a national player,"* it earns plaudits for its work on a range of complex corporate transactions for a *"truly impressive client base"* of public and private companies. The experience of the firm's Atlanta attorneys is not limited to US deals, as is evidenced by the international work featuring in the past year's deal tally. In a recent highlight, the firm acted in the third largest IPO on record – Wells Real Estate Investment Trust's $7.7 billion offering.

The Lawyers: Transactional expert **Sidney Nurkin** (see p.619) is rated as *"an absolute genius M&A lawyer. He has an attuned sense of the nuance of contract and negotiation."* Nurkin is recommended for his in-depth work for mutual funds, and is known for his representation of CGW Southeast Partners. The *"highly experienced"* **Hill Jeffries** (see p.615) has *"a superb understanding of the links between law and business."* He is described as *"one of the leading securities attorneys in the state"* and recently acted for Morgan Stanley in three public offerings by AGCO. These deals had a combined value of $715 million, with one set to finance the acquisition of the business of Valtra, a global tractor and off-road engine manufacturer based in Finland. **Vaughan Curtis** (see p.610) is skilled in public company work and well known for his expertise in healthcare matters. He is endorsed as *"a smart, hard-working attorney who it's always a pleasure to deal with."* Although he does not yet have quite the profile of some of his colleagues, **Nils Okeson** (see p.619) is recommended as *"an impressive young lawyer who is diligent and precise."* He works extensively in

Georgia
Leading firms (Corporate/M&A)

1 ALSTON & BIRD LLP *Atlanta*
KING & SPALDING LLP *Atlanta*

2 ROGERS & HARDIN *Atlanta*
SUTHERLAND ASBILL & BRENNAN *Atlanta*
TROUTMAN SANDERS LLP *Atlanta*

3 ARNALL GOLDEN GREGORY LLP *Atlanta*
KILPATRICK STOCKTON LLP *Atlanta*
PAUL, HASTINGS, JANOFSKY *Atlanta*

4 JONES DAY *Atlanta*
MCKENNA LONG & ALDRIDGE *Atlanta*
PARKER, HUDSON, RAINER & DOBBS *Atlanta*
POWELL GOLDSTEIN LLP *Atlanta*

Leading individuals (Corporate/M&A)

1 EGAN Michael *King & Spalding*, Atlanta
NURKIN Sidney *Alston & Bird*, Atlanta

2 BAXLEY C William *King & Spalding*, Atlanta
HARDIN Edward *Rogers & Hardin*, Atlanta
JEFFRIES M Hill *Alston & Bird*, Atlanta
LONG Clay *McKenna Long*, Atlanta
RICHARDS Russell *King & Spalding*, Atlanta

3 CAPERS John *King & Spalding*, Atlanta
GOLDEN Jonathan *Arnall Golden*, Atlanta
JOSPIN Walter *Paul Hastings*, Atlanta
SPALDING William *King & Spalding*, Atlanta
STEIN Jeffrey *King & Spalding*, Atlanta

4 BRADLEY Wayne *Paul Hastings*, Atlanta
CURTIS J Vaughan *Alston & Bird*, Atlanta
FOX Steven *Rogers & Hardin*, Atlanta
GROUT Robert *Troutman Sanders*, Atlanta
HUDSON Paul *Parker Hudson*, Atlanta
KAUFMAN Mark *Sutherland Asbill*, Atlanta
KELLEY John *King & Spalding*, Atlanta
LAYSON Frank *Paul Hastings*, Atlanta
MILLER Rick *Powell Goldstein*, Atlanta
PASCUAL Rey *Kilpatrick Stockton*, Atlanta
PRINCE Alan *King & Spalding*, Atlanta
SMITH James *Troutman Sanders*, Atlanta
STOCKTON David *Kilpatrick Stockton*, Atlanta
THOMAS Lizanne *Jones Day*, Atlanta

Up-and-coming individuals
OKESON Nils *Alston & Bird*, Atlanta

Firms and individuals are listed alphabetically in each band.

both technology and healthcare matters.
The Clients: Assurant; Bertelsmann; CGW Southeast & Affiliates; Cingular Wireless; Denny's; Mohawk Industries; Regions Financial; Sabre Holdings and Wachovia.

King & Spalding LLP
See firm details p.635
The Firm: Hailed by some market sources as *"the best firm in the state,"* King & Spalding has a corporate group that handles the full gamut of transactional work, including M&A, securities and project finance. It represents *"an enviable client base"* of prestigious Fortune 500 companies, multinationals and, increasingly, banks and financial institutions, with some client relationships stretching back more than 100 years. The firm has national reach and is recommended by clients for its international capability. The past year saw the group act for UPS on a $1 billion joint venture with Ford, concerning the delivery of finished vehicles to Ford dealers.
The Lawyers: **Mike Egan** (see p.611) earns great feedback as *"an absolutely expert deal-maker."* He is praised as *"a top-dollar attorney with great communication skills and superb client ability."* Egan gets involved in a range of transactions and is particularly noted for cross-border deals. He boasts a niche in the representation of sports clients, recently acting for Atlanta Spirit in its acquisition of the Atlanta Hawks, Atlanta Thrashers and the Philips Arena. **Bill Baxley** (see p.606) wins client endorsement as *"an intelligent, practical, efficient problem solver. He has a photographic memory and a gentlemanly approach, so you always feel confident with him at your side in negotiations."* Recently he acted for SunTrust Banks in its acquisition of National Commerce Financial, a deal valued at $7 billion. The *"pragmatic"* **Russ Richards** (see p.621) was said by clients to have *"great judgment and a highly impressive work ethic."* He is also described as *"a man of easy temperament and great negotiating skills."* Although he draws client support across many industries, Richards is known for technology work and acted for information company ChoicePoint in the acquisition of Superior Information Services. *"Precise"* **Jack Capers** (see p.608) *"loves complex transactions."* He *"always stays calm in the hectic-paced and panicked mode that deals sometimes find themselves in."* Capers acted for UPS in its $2.7 billion acquisition of Celltech. **Jeffrey Stein** (see p.623) is recommended as *"a smart to-the-point lawyer with a great practice"* in financial and securities transactions. He has ample experience of offshore offerings and institutional private offerings. **William Spalding** (see p.623) heads up the firm's private equity and investment funds practice group and is endorsed as *"a steady hand; a guy who gets a deal done with no drama or fuss."* Meanwhile, **John Kelley** (see p.616) is head of the firm's corporate finance group and is viewed as *"a positive lawyer with a wide skill set."* Finally, **Alan Prince** (see p.621) earns his fair share of market respect. He recently acted in a multimillion-dollar IPO for Great Wolf Resorts.
The Clients: UPS; Coca-Cola; GE; SunTrust Robinson Humphrey; Crescent Capital Investments and Citigroup.

Band 2

Rogers & Hardin
See firm details p.639
The Firm: This smaller firm has been operating in Atlanta for almost 30 years. Its corporate team has a reputation as *"a dynamic transactional practice, which combines experience with energy and enthusiasm."* It is frequently recommended by larger firms in conflict of interest situations and admired by smaller firms for *"occupying the place we'd like to."* The group earns particular praise for its corporate governance and investigations advice.
The Lawyers: The best-known member of the team is *"knowledgeable, smart and direct"* **Edward Hardin** (see p.613). Clients appreciate the range and depth of his expertise, calling him *"a business-savvy lawyer who doesn't just see the legal side of an issue."* **Steve Fox** (see p.612) was portrayed by commentators as *"patient and cool in the face of any problem."* He excels in both transactions and the minutiae of corporate governance.
The Clients: The group's clients are medium to large-sized public and private companies. It is active in a number of industry sectors, but has a strong following in manufacturing.

Sutherland Asbill & Brennan LLP
See firm details p.494
The Firm: Although not felt to have the breadth of the two firms in the top band, this group is *"a fine collection of top-quality lawyers with a superb client base."* Lawyers work closely with colleagues in the highly rated tax team – a factor which gives it an edge on transactional matters. Recently the firm represented the Rayovac Corporation in its acquisition of Remington Products, a deal worth $165 million. It also represented the company in its purchase of Brazil's largest battery company, Microlite S.A.
The Lawyers: *"Impressive"* lawyer **Mark Kaufman** (see p.616) handles corporate and securities transactions. He represented ING in the sale of its subsidiary Life Assurance Company of Georgia, a deal worth $250 million.
The Clients: ING; Nextec Applications; Six Continents and USFilter.

Troutman Sanders LLP
The Firm: Troutman Sanders, which rises in the table, is commended by clients as *"one of the prime firms in the state – superb in corporate transactions and in straightforward corporate advice."* The corporate group is said to boast a good bench of *"reliable and responsive attorneys"* who are particularly admired for their work in financings. The group recently represented a large healthcare company on a major refinancing of its subordinate public debt, and it is well known for its work in the energy sector, having handled large matters for a number of local and regional power companies.

www.ChambersandPartners.com

All quotes in the text are from interviews with clients and competitors.

587

The Lawyers: James Smith has "*a strong corporate presence; he brings knowledge and gravitas to a deal.*" Smith is experienced in public offerings and securities matters, and recently acted for a private real estate company on a $100 million rollout transaction. New to the guide is **Bob Grout**. One client confirmed that he gave "*an absolute commitment to making sure we have what we need. He is a great business person.*" Grout impresses most on tax and healthcare-related issues.

The Clients: The firm is particularly known for its clients in the healthcare, energy, real estate and insurance sectors.

Band 3

Arnall Golden Gregory LLP

See firm details p.627

The Firm: This midsized firm has a strong technology base and a growing presence in the healthcare sector. Despite flourishing in hi-tech matters, its reputation is still that of "*an experienced and versatile team.*" In the past year it acted on the $525 million private equity buyout of a technology company and advised a large retail operation, which was sold for $300 million.

The Lawyers: "*Well-respected*" **Jonathan Golden** (see p.613) "*brings bags of experience to the table. It's almost impossible to surprise him in a corporate deal.*" He is known for his work for SYSCO, but boasts a wide range of clients and recently sold a number of businesses involved in power plant maintenance.

The Clients: SYSCO; Cryolife; Costco; Georgia Baptist Healthcare System and Profit Recovery Group.

Kilpatrick Stockton LLP

See firm details p.634

The Firm: The "*committed, responsive and hard-working team*" is rated for its transactional work, in particular securities and financing matters. It acts across the region, representing mid to large-cap companies, both public and private.

The Lawyers: While the group was praised collectively, **David Stockton** (see p.624) was the attorney who stood out most. He is known to be "*a creative, persistent lawyer with outstanding judgment and common sense.*" Stockton recently acted for James River Coal in its public offering, estimated at $300 million. He has also been involved in a good many corporate internal investigations, either as part of a special committee or the auditing committee of the board. **Rey Pascual** (see p.620) was also warmly endorsed; his work involves both US and Latin American matters.

The Clients: INVESCO; DVT; Miller Industries; National Vision; BellSouth; Krispy Kreme; Allied Capital and Turbochef Technologies.

Paul, Hastings, Janofsky & Walker LLP

See firm details p.297

The Firm: This firm is deemed to be making good progress in the state. Its corporate group is said to be "*efficient, business-minded and professional,*" with its attorneys "*a font of new ideas.*" The group works predominantly for large national and international clients; for example, it recently represented GE in its purchase of AstroPower and in a number of other transactions.

The Lawyers: The "*brilliant*" **Walter Jospin** (see p.615) was hailed by clients as "*a really great lawyer and a superb deal-maker.*" He boasts a full set of corporate skills, which he puts to good effect in some headlining transactions, such as a recent pipeline deal for Cross-Country Energy worth $800 million. **Frank Layson** (see p.617) is "*technically terrific*" and "*excellent on the cultural aspects of multinational deals.*" He joined the firm from McKenna Long & Aldridge in March 2004, and has since then acted on the restructuring of a major telecom company, which involved a $175 million bond offering. New to the guide is aviation and aerospace expert **Wayne Bradley** (see p.607), who earned respect as "*a ceaselessly committed lawyer who never gives less than 100%.*" The group is also commended for its strength in depth at associate level.

The Clients: The firm acts for several large national and multinational conglomerates, including GE, GE Power Systems and Delta Airlines.

Band 4

Jones Day

See firm details p.485

The Firm: A new entrant to the table, Jones Day's Atlanta office was recommended to researchers as "*an efficient, reliable team.*" While, of course, benefiting from access to a large international network of offices, the Atlanta offering has a particular reputation for private equity work. The food, chemical and media industries have been a focus of late; lawyers recently acted in a series of transactions leading to the acquisition of 33 radio stations across seven states with a combined value of $160 million.

The Lawyers: **Lizanne Thomas** (see p.624) heads the business practice group and is rated by clients for her "*diplomacy skills*" and "*decisive and commercially sound judgments.*" A highlight was her representation of Flowers Foods in the $240 million sale of Mrs. Smith's Bakeries frozen dessert business to The Schwan Food Company.

The Clients: Eastman Chemical; Flowers Foods; Cumulus Media; Georgia Gulf; Integrity Media and Hagemeyer North America.

McKenna Long & Aldridge

See firm details p.636

The Firm: The Atlanta office is a sizable part of this eight-office firm and it fields a healthy corporate group that is known for its transactional work, corporate governance advice and general counseling. It can claim niche expertise in sports, entertainment and technology-related matters.

The Lawyers: **Clay Long** (see p.617) is recommended as "*an absolutely superb corporate lawyer – he always talks a lot of common sense.*" Though most commentators are familiar with his transactional work, he also focuses on environmental and conservation work.

The Clients: The group represents financiers, travel companies and a range of other corporate clients.

Parker, Hudson, Rainer & Dobbs LLP

The Firm: A smaller Georgia and Florida firm that will celebrate its 25th anniversary next year, Parker Hudson has a "*solid*" corporate practice that does especially well in financing. It has undeniable strength in the healthcare sector and frequently represents major hospitals and medical teaching institutions.

The Lawyers: M&A expert **Paul Hudson** remains the best-known member of the group. He is proficient at advising clients' governing bodies on various governance issues and fiduciary obligations.

The Clients: The firm's client roster includes private, public and multinational corporations and nonprofit and charitable organizations.

Powell Goldstein LLP

The Firm: Powell Goldstein is an old-line Atlanta firm with a Washington DC office and a proud history. Lawyers in the broad-based corporate group are recognized for their handling of financings, acquisitions and restructurings. The group has a following in the healthcare sector and is currently helping to restructure a major healthcare provider with 300 facilities across the country. It also recently handled the restructuring of an airline.

The Lawyers: Strong as a group, Powell Goldstein's corporate practice benefits enormously from the presence of "*insightful*" **Rick Miller**. Clients report that he is "*a business-focused lawyer of great integrity.*" He co-heads the practice group and, beyond transactional matters, has experience of business disputes and proxy contests for corporate control.

The Clients: The firm has a number of clients in healthcare and healthcare finance, as well as technology and manufacturing.

EMPLOYMENT

MAINLY DEFENDANT

Georgia
Leading firms
(Employment: Mainly Defendant)

1 ALSTON & BIRD LLP *Atlanta*
KILPATRICK STOCKTON LLP *Atlanta*
KING & SPALDING LLP *Atlanta*
PAUL, HASTINGS, JANOFSKY *Atlanta*

2 ASHE, RAFUSE & HILL, LLP *Atlanta*
ELARBEE, THOMPSON, SAPP *Atlanta*
FISHER & PHILLIPS LLP *Atlanta*
FORD & HARRISON LLP *Atlanta*
OGLETREE, DEAKINS, NASH, SMOAK *Atlanta*
ROGERS & HARDIN *Atlanta*
TROUTMAN SANDERS LLP *Atlanta*

3 CONSTANGY, BROOKS & SMITH, LLC *Atlanta*
HOLLAND & KNIGHT LLP *Atlanta*
HUNTON & WILLIAMS *Atlanta*
JACKSON LEWIS *Atlanta*

Leading individuals
(Employment: Mainly Defendant)

1 ASHE Lawrence *Ashe Rafuse, Atlanta*
HUGHES III Hunter *Rogers & Hardin, Atlanta*
WYMER John *King & Spalding, Atlanta*

2 BOICE William *Kilpatrick Stockton, Atlanta*
BOISSEAU Richard *Kilpatrick Stockton, Atlanta*
BUCKLER Robert *Troutman Sanders, Atlanta*
DEAKINS Homer *Ogletree Deakins, Atlanta*
JOHNSTON Mike *King & Spalding, Atlanta*
WEIRICH Geoff *Paul Hastings, Atlanta*

3 COIL James *Kilpatrick Stockton, Atlanta*
ENSOR R Steve *Alston & Bird, Atlanta*
GERAKITIS Richard *Troutman Sanders, Atlanta*
JOHNSON Weyman *Paul Hastings, Atlanta*
OAKLEY Mary *Holland & Knight, Atlanta*
WILSON Stanford *Elarbee Thompson, Atlanta*

4 CAMPBELL Margaret *Ogletree Deakins, Atlanta*
CLINEBURG William *King & Spalding, Atlanta*
DENT Leslie *Paul Hastings, Atlanta*
KASSIN Thomas *Ford & Harrison, Atlanta*
KILPATRICK J Thomas *Alston & Bird, Atlanta*
MATCHETT Sam *King & Spalding, Atlanta*
PITTMAN Alisa *Elarbee Thompson, Atlanta*
POWELL Kurt *Hunton & Williams, Atlanta*
RAFUSE Nancy *Ashe Rafuse, Atlanta*
RIDDELL Stephen *Troutman Sanders, Atlanta*
WILSON Brent *Elarbee Thompson, Atlanta*

Up-and-coming individuals
CLELAND Craig *Ogletree Deakins, Atlanta*

Firms and individuals are listed alphabetically in each band.

Band 1

Alston & Bird LLP
See firm details p.626
The Firm: The employment practice group maintains its top-tier ranking due to significant market approval of the "*strong sense of direction*" emanating from the firm. One prominent com-

mentator noted that: "*The lawyers know where they're going and they sure as hell don't need a map to get there.*" Clients were equally impressed with the team; a picture was painted of "*a reassuringly smooth outfit,*" which excels when confronted with complex interpretative issues. Specializations in disability discrimination and OSHA matters, among other things, set the team apart from most of its rivals, and strength is also undoubtedly present on the litigation side.
The Lawyers: "*The team's golden boy*" **Steve Ensor** (see p.611) "*has the whole package*" according to peers who commended him for the "*drive and dynamism he brings to every piece of work he takes on.*" In the past year Ensor has been advising Aflac on various labor-related matters and has continued to provide counsel to UPS on national policy issues. **Tom Kilpatrick** (see p.616) is viewed as a "*terrific competitor*" who "*does sterling work for his clients.*" Commended particularly for his litigation skills, Kilpatrick has been involved in defending cases at all levels for a predominantly financial institution client base.
The Clients: UPS; Alcoa; Wachovia; SunTrust Bank and Fortis.

Kilpatrick Stockton LLP
See firm details p.634
The Firm: This firm is notable among the top-tier firms for its success in maintaining a strong traditional labor law practice while also concentrating resources on newer employment areas. The group attracted market praise for its ability to provide counsel to employers on union disputes, collective bargaining and arbitrations, so much so that one prominent source remarked that it appears to have access to a "*bottomless well of knowledge on union-related issues.*" Equal opportunities work also features heavily in the team's portfolio, with wage and hour cases a third area in which valuable expertise is proffered.
The Lawyers: Lauded by commentators as "*a hugely influential figure*" at the Georgia employment Bar, **William Boice** (see p.607) sustains his impressive position in the rankings. Boice has a broad practice and continues to be active in high-profile ERISA litigation on behalf of long-standing client Delta Air Lines, as well as appearing in a number of important summary judgment hearings. **Richard Boisseau** (see p.607) is renowned for his work on wage and hour matters. "*He inspires confidence in clients by fighting hard for them,*" was the verdict of one interviewee. **James Coil**'s (see p.609) practice focuses on discrimination and he is described by peers as a "*safe pair of hands for tough cases.*"
The Clients: The Pepsi Bottling Group; Nestlé Waters; Sara Lee; Georgia-Pacific; INVESCO; Krispy Kreme and Boeing.

King & Spalding LLP
See firm details p.635
The Firm: The market was quick to bestow praise on the employment practice of this major full-service firm. The group secured a top-band ranking on the back of considerable market approval for the depth and quality of the personnel at clients' disposal: "*They have the manpower to handle anything that crops up.*" Litigation is a particular strength, though general policy advice is provided to a client base that includes numerous top-flight institutions.
The Lawyers: The "*vastly accomplished*" **John Wymer** (see p.625) "*is truly at home in the courtroom*" and was identified by interviewees as "*the first guy in the state to call if you want a matter litigated sensibly and effectively.*" Wymer has continued to represent major client Home Depot in ADA cases, while expanding his arbitration practice for clients such as Oracle and Xerox. **Mike Johnston** (see p.615) is a "*hugely capable attorney*" who has been involved as primary external counsel to Coca-Cola on various cases. Johnston's "*no-frills*" approach in the courtroom won him plaudits from clients and peers alike. Commentators were agreed that **Bill Clineburg** (see p.609) has "*fantastic presentation skills,*" which he employs to considerable effect in defending class actions for a number of major companies in the automotive, tobacco and retail industries. For many, **Sam Matchett** (see p.618) is the future of the firm's employment practice. Matchett has built up a strong reputation in the field, having won summary judgments for a large carpet manufacturer in cases involving disability discrimination.
The Clients: Home Depot; Coca-Cola; Mass-Mutual; Belk; GlaxoSmithKline; Winn-Dixie; Zale Corporation; Lodgian; Oracle and Weyerhaeuser.

Paul, Hastings, Janofsky & Walker LLP
See firm details p.297
The Firm: Praised by the market for possessing a "*huge work ethic,*" it is little surprise that the employment group at this national firm's Atlanta office maintains its place in the top tier. With a top-notch client roster and a "*seriously impressive group of attorneys*" to match, the work covered by the group tends to be both high profile and complex. Expertise is provided in areas such as discrimination, wage and hour claims, immigration and traditional labor matters, and a specialization in defending class actions continues to grow. Interviewees are of the opinion that the national reach of the firm ensures the group has the resources to deal satisfactorily with every issue.
The Lawyers: **Weyman Johnson** (see p.615) commands respect at the Georgia employment

Bar due to the depth of his expertise in defending class actions. In the past year Johnson has successfully argued for a denial of certification on behalf of a major retail employer as well as dealing with significant matters resulting from OSHA and FLSA. **Geoff Weirich** (see p.625) is also considered "*a master technician for class actions*" and has attracted plaudits on the back of his work for Boeing. Clients welcomed the fact that **Leslie Dent** (see p.611) "*thinks from a business standpoint*" and is not "*wedded to legalese.*" Dent is considered to be particularly strong on wage and hour matters.

The Clients: UPS; Cracker Barrel Old Country Store; Wal-Mart; Publix Super Markets; Turner Broadcasting System; CNN and American Airlines.

Band 2

Ashe, Rafuse & Hill, LLP
See firm details p.628

The Firm: "*Indisputably on the rise*" is the market view of this relatively recently formed boutique, which continues to expand through a combination of organic growth and lateral hires. It is considered to be highly influential in the sphere of equal opportunities.

The Lawyers: "*The class-action king*" **Lawrence Ashe** (see p.605) is promoted to the first tier of the rankings following significant market respect for the truly national reach of his litigation practice. One interviewee was not alone in expressing the sentiment that although Ashe "*might ruffle some feathers no one can doubt his end product.*" Ashe was a key player in the resolution of litigation involving Cracker Barrel and arising out of the FLSA. "*Steely competitor*" **Nancy Rafuse** (see p.621) is the firm's other leading light and she garnered considerable praise for her work defending Waffle House in a series of class actions.

The Clients: Cracker Barrel Old Country Store; Lockheed Martin; Coca-Cola; Educational Testing Service; Equitable Life Assurance Society; Home Depot and Marsh.

Elarbee, Thompson, Sapp & Wilson, LLP

The Firm: This large boutique practice commands respect for the depth of experience and breadth of expertise of its attorneys. Equally adept in acting for both public and private sector clients in a wide range of matters, the firm attracted especial praise for its case preparation: "*These guys leave no stone unturned before a trial.*" The work handled by the firm includes discrimination, union avoidance and wage and hour compliance.

The Lawyers: Described by peers as an "*exceptionally shrewd character,*" **Stanford Wilson** has elevated his position in the table by virtue of his involvement in a number of significant cases. He

recently acted for a major paper manufacturer in a multiplaintiff age discrimination action and is also considered an authority on cases arising from restrictive covenants. **Brent Wilson** was lauded for his "*truly innovative approach*" and has been involved in a number of prominent reverse race discrimination cases in DeKalb County. "*Dogged competitor*" **Alisa Pittman** enters the rankings as an up-and-comer following market approval of her defense of major sex discrimination cases.

The Clients: Engelhard; Florida Power & Light; ChoicePoint; Citibank; Lockheed Martin; Pirelli and Goodyear.

Fisher & Phillips LLP
See firm details p.630

The Firm: With a network of 13 offices across the USA, this national firm has built a strong reputation for dispensing accurate advice in a variety of employment disputes. The Atlanta office houses a number of well-respected attorneys with expertise ranging across the whole employment spectrum, including litigation and counseling on preventative measures and compliance issues. Interviewees singled out the group's responsiveness and ability to identify the key issues quickly as particular strengths.

The Lawyers: Tex McIver is a senior partner in the Atlanta group.

The Clients: The firm acts for a varied client base that features large multinationals as well as smaller entrepreneurs. Its clients are active in the manufacturing, financial, construction, insurance and healthcare sectors.

Ford & Harrison LLP
See firm details p.631

The Firm: In the eyes of the market, which was quick to note the highly specialized nature of the firm's practice, Ford & Harrison boasts "*a fine group of attorneys.*" Though the firm acts for a broad spread of clients, it is its work for the airline sector that particularly stands out; attorneys are considered to have specific abilities in handling labor law matters and concessionary bargaining with unions.

The Lawyers: **Thomas Kassin** (see p.615) was singled out for praise by clients who admired his "*common-sense approach to problem solving.*" A former naval aviator, much of Kassin's work centers on airline labor and employment, with particular strengths in collective bargaining and arbitration.

The Clients: The client roster features national and multinational entities, including air carriers, manufacturers, hospitals, retailers and restaurants.

Ogletree, Deakins, Nash, Smoak & Stewart, PC
See firm details p.638

The Firm: An ever-expanding national labor

and employment practice provides support to the firm's Atlanta office, which continues to be a major player in the Georgia market. Considered by commentators to be at the top end of the second tier, this "*quality outfit*" won widespread plaudits for its focus on continuing legal education. As a result, its attorneys are renowned for their "*irresistible combination of knowledge and drive.*" Union-based matters are at the heart of the firm's practice; nevertheless, praise was also reserved for litigation successes, particularly with regard to whistle-blower retaliation suits.

The Lawyers: Although **Homer Deakins** (see p.610) splits his time between the Carolina and Atlanta offices, he is still considered a "*true heavyweight figure*" in Georgia. He is admired for the way he remains "*sharp and attentive to his clients' needs*" and "*can hit big when necessary.*" **Margaret Campbell** (see p.608) is a new addition to the table and has cultivated a reputation as an effective litigator. Much of her work involves collective actions arising from the FLSA. Up-and-comer **Craig Cleland** (see p.609) caught the attention of interviewees due to the quality of his class action work. Cleland has done significant work for Home Depot and GE of late. Finally, the market was saddened by the death of Martha Perrin in the past year.

The Clients: The firm provides counsel to multinational companies from the energy, manufacturing, automobile, healthcare, service and banking industries.

Rogers & Hardin
See firm details p.639

The Firm: This highly respected firm maintains its ranking due to the quality of advice provided to the management of big-name clients with regards to discrimination claims. Expertise is also provided on a variety of employment-related torts, including interference with contractual relations, intentional infliction of emotional distress and defamation. The market noted the litigation capabilities of the attorneys and was quick to praise the "*sense of professionalism that runs throughout the firm.*"

The Lawyers: Such is the extent of **Hunter Hughes**' (see p.615) national profile as a mediator that comments such as "*extraordinarily good*" and "*peerless*" were regularly encountered by researchers in any discussion of this stellar attorney's practice. Hughes has "*the full respect of the plaintiff Bar*" and is "*still at the top of his game*" when it comes to class actions. He continues to be heavily involved in mediation matters for major clients such as Boeing and Wal-Mart.

The Clients: The group represents a number of blue-chip companies, including major airlines, as well as midsized public and private companies.

Troutman Sanders LLP

The Firm: This highly respected full-service firm attracted market praise for its *"results-based approach"* and continues to offer a valuable standalone labor and employment practice. The services provided by the attorneys at this firm are *"not cheap but definitely worth it,"* was the view of one satisfied client. Much of the group's work is generated from the firm's close relationship with Georgia Power and Georgia-Pacific, and the past year has seen the firm successfully defend these clients in race discrimination cases. **The Lawyers:** The market considers **Robert Buckler** to be a *"true fireball"* who utilizes his wide experience in employment litigation to consistently *"pull rabbits out of hats for clients."* Buckler is an expert in litigating claims arising out of Title VII, FLSA, ADEA and ADA, and has been working on overtime payment cases in the past year. The *"effortlessly dynamic"* **Richard Gerakitis** *"never pulls a punch"* and won favor with clients for his accessibility and responsiveness. He is renowned for his work on noncompetition covenants and employee breach of fiduciary duty claims. **Stephen Riddell** was applauded by peers for his class action work and is considered to be adept at explaining highly technical concepts to clients in accessible language. **The Clients:** UPS; AT&T; Turner Broadcasting System; Mirant; Randstad; Temporary Services; AGCO and Allied Holdings.

Band 3

Constangy, Brooks & Smith, LLC

The Firm: Interviewees were quick to point out the firm's greatest strength lies in traditional union-related advice; nonetheless, specialist employment litigators do operate in areas such as race, sex and age discrimination as well as wage and hour matters. The Atlanta office has also succeeded in building up an extensive OSHA practice. **The Lawyers:** Ed Katze is the Atlanta office's managing partner. **The Clients:** Hertz, Sara Lee and Watkins Motor Lines figure prominently in the firm's client list.

Holland & Knight LLP

See firm details p.1352

The Firm: Although it was conceded that the Atlanta branch of this nationwide firm does not have the same market presence as that of its offices in Florida, interviewees felt the firm warranted inclusion in the Georgia rankings due to the quality of its litigation of a number of employment matters. Its attorneys were commended for their *"foresight and attention to detail."* **The Lawyers:** **Mary Ann Oakley** (see p.619) is the leading light in the office and is respected by peers as a *"feisty yet effective litigator, who will always put up a good fight for her clients."* **The Clients:** Marriott International, US South and Cardinal Health figure prominently among the firm's clientele.

Hunton & Williams

See firm details p.1775

The Firm: A new addition to this year's rankings, this national full-service firm's inclusion results from positive client feedback for the Atlanta employment group. Clients welcomed the way the team is able to *"innovate and remain reassuring"* when providing advice on a number of different types of employment dispute. Specialist areas include arbitration and litigation on claims resulting out of ADA, FLSA and AEDA. **The Lawyers:** Atlanta managing partner **Kurt Powell** (see p.621) was singled out for especial praise by clients who described him as *"absolutely superb at getting to the heart of the matter."* Powell is considered particularly adept in defending class actions. **The Clients:** The client list is peppered with an array of companies from industries including transportation, natural gas distribution, electronics, paper, coal, construction, and wholesale food distribution, as well as a number of hospitals and healthcare facilities.

Jackson Lewis

The Firm: The Atlanta office of this national labor and employment firm continues to garner respect from peers for the depth of its resources and the breadth of its practice. The full package of labor and employment issues are covered by the group with discrimination claims and union-related matters considered particular areas of strength. **The Lawyers:** The group is led by Stuart Newman. **The Clients:** The team acts for a client base of leading national and international companies.

ENERGY & NATURAL RESOURCES

Georgia
Leading firms
(Energy & Natural Resources)

1	**SUTHERLAND ASBILL & BRENNAN** *Atlanta*
	TROUTMAN SANDERS LLP *Atlanta*
2	**ALSTON & BIRD LLP** *Atlanta*
	MCKENNA LONG & ALDRIDGE *Atlanta*
3	**KING & SPALDING LLP** *Atlanta*

Firms are listed alphabetically in each band.

Band 1

Sutherland Asbill & Brennan LLP

See firm details p.494

The Firm: *"No one else can get near them for across-the-board energy expertise,"* enthused one market source of this wide-ranging practice, which covers energy trading, regulatory compliance, project financing and energy litigation. The team is, as one client put it, *"well equipped*

to deal with whatever is thrown at them."* Energy sector public offerings have featured significantly in the past year, with attorneys representing Goldman Sachs and JPMorgan as underwriters for two electric cooperatives. **The Lawyers:** It is said that **Cada Kilgore** (see p.616) will *"walk on water for his clients;"* his energy finance work is certainly held in high esteem by the entire market. Significant work from the past year has included the restructuring of the generation, transmission and system operations relationships among the electric cooperatives within Georgia. Kilgore also worked with a national bank to structure two potential financings for the acquisition of an interest in a two-unit nuclear generating facility. **Herbert Short** (see p.622) enters the rankings on the back of impressive client feedback. Short is renowned for his expertise in the electric utility industry and his strong interpersonal skills. Michael Bradley has left the firm for a new role

with NewSouth Energy. **The Clients:** Oglethorpe Power; JPMorgan Chase; Goldman Sachs; Great River Energy and CoBank.

Troutman Sanders LLP

The Firm: *"These guys hit the right note every time,"* marveled clients. The group's close association with Georgia Power (Southern Company) has aided the development of an energy practice that is the envy of many firms in the state. Clients are represented in regulatory matters, power contract negotiations, synthetic lease financings of power plants and revising fuel supply strategies among other things. Strong links with the firm's Washington office ensure that the group is active at a national level. **The Lawyers:** Fêted by peers for his cross-examination skills, **Kevin Greene** was pinpointed as one of Georgia's premier regulatory lawyers. This attorney is *"totally unflappable"*

Georgia
Leading individuals
(Energy & Natural Resources)

[1] **FORRY Robert** *Troutman Sanders, Atlanta*
GREENE Kevin *Troutman Sanders, Atlanta*
KILGORE III Cada *Sutherland Asbill, Atlanta*

[2] **DEGNAN Peter** *Alston & Bird, Atlanta*
DOWDY L Craig *McKenna Long, Atlanta*
MERCER John *Troutman Sanders, Atlanta*
SHORT Herbert *Sutherland Asbill, Atlanta*
SWENSON Erik *King & Spalding, Atlanta*
WELLS Della *Alston & Bird, Atlanta*

Up-and-coming individuals
CAEN Melissa *Troutman Sanders, Atlanta*

Individuals are listed alphabetically in each band.

and, apparently, *"never afraid to innovate if he thinks it will help his clients."* Greene has taken the role of lead trial counsel before the Georgia Public Service Commission for a number of clients. Described by fellow professionals as *"breathtakingly good,"* **Robert Forry** is elevated to the top tier of the tables following market recognition of the quality of his legislative work. Meanwhile, projects practice group leader **John Mercer** makes an appearance in the rankings by virtue of his *"enormous knowledge in the electricity sphere."* Finally, commentators predicted a bright future for **Melissa Caen**; one source was particularly impressed with her ability to be both *"incisive and insightful."* Caen is heavily involved in projects.

The Clients: Georgia Power, Kansas City Southern and other major utility companies and independent power producers in the Southeast feature on the client list.

Band 2

Alston & Bird LLP
See firm details p.626

The Firm: This group, which *"can hit big when it needs to,"* won approval from the market for the strength of its municipal practice. A client list that includes authorities for Mississippi and Georgia bears testimony to this. Regulatory expertise is provided in territorial matters, rate cases, pipeline safety and purchase power agreements, and the team is equally active in governmental lobbying and corporate energy work.

The Lawyers: Della Wager Wells (see p.625) has a successful energy financing practice and is considered an expert on bond matters. She worked with the Municipal Gas Authority of Georgia in pioneering a transaction for the prepayment for long-term natural gas supplies from the proceeds of tax-exempt bonds. **Peter Degnan** (see p.610) is an active litigator and is viewed by peers as *"a solid attorney who puts across his points well."*

The Clients: Municipal Gas Authority of Mississippi; Orlando Utilities Commission; Verizon Select Services; Verizon South; MEAG Power and Tennessee Energy Acquisition.

McKenna Long & Aldridge
See firm details p.636

The Firm: This firm maintains its position in the tables due to considerable peer approval of its regulatory practice. To an array of clients from the electricity and natural gas industries, the practice group offers a service that is judged to be *"absolutely top-rate."* Its litigation capabilities are also held in high regard by interviewees, who welcomed the team's no-nonsense

approach: *"Their lawyers don't waste time; they get straight to the matter in hand."*

The Lawyers: With a focus on state and federal regulatory representation for energy companies, **Craig Dowdy** (see p.611) is the group's leading figure. According to peers, he *"comes into his own when dealing with complex matters"* and is a specialist on pipeline replacement issues and rates cases, both areas in which he has been particularly active in the past year.

The Clients: Atlanta Gas Light; Chattanooga Gas; Virginia Natural Gas; Cleco and Public Service Company of New Mexico.

Band 3

King & Spalding LLP
See firm details p.635

The Firm: Profiting from being a part of this firm's highly respected national energy practice, the Atlanta office of the firm stands out for the quality of its corporate and financial restructuring work. A clientele of major industrial and commercial energy consumers ensures that the team is active in a number of significant transactions.

The Lawyers: **Erik Swenson** (see p.624) remains a key player in the Georgia energy transactional sphere despite the fact that he splits his time between the firm's Atlanta and Houston offices. Swenson recently helped a major electricity consumer obtain a competitive supply contract.

The Clients: The group's client base features a mixture of retailers, developers and energy generating companies.

ENVIRONMENT

Georgia
Leading firms (Environment)

[1] **ALSTON & BIRD LLP** *Atlanta*
KING & SPALDING LLP *Atlanta*
TROUTMAN SANDERS LLP *Atlanta*

[2] **HUNTON & WILLIAMS** *Atlanta*
KILPATRICK STOCKTON LLP *Atlanta*
MCKENNA LONG & ALDRIDGE *Atlanta*

[3] **HUNTER, MACLEAN, EXLEY & DUNN** *Savannah*
MORRIS, MANNING & MARTIN, LLP *Atlanta*
SMITH GAMBRELL & RUSSELL LLP *Atlanta*

Firms are listed alphabetically in each band.

Band 1

Alston & Bird LLP
See firm details p.626

The Firm: A *"great team that pulls out all the stops for its clients"* was the market appraisal of

this firm's environmental practice. With a particular emphasis on air pollution work, the group has cemented its position as a market leader in the sector. While the firm is active in prominent litigation, it is the advisory side of the practice that attracted most praise from clients. Expertise is proffered in regulatory matters and corporate compliance, in addition to a significant niche in the transportation of hazardous materials and dangerous goods.

The Lawyers: Head of the firm's combined environmental and land use group, **Lee DeHihns** (see p.11) was praised for his negotiation skills and retains his position at the top of the rankings. DeHihns' regulatory experience means he is *"very well connected"* in the eyes of clients, who were quick to extol the *"dynamic, energetic"* outlook he brings to every deal. The market was impressed with **James Stokes**'s (see p.624) work on the regulatory side. *"He grasps the key issues

in a matter of seconds,"* noted one commentator. **Nill Toulme** (see p.624) is viewed by peers principally as a technology specialist, though he has also earned plaudits for his knowledge of hazardous and toxic substances. **Robert Mowrey** (see p.619) enters this year's rankings on the back of positive peer feedback for his litigation work, being described as a *"real go-getter"* who *"gives his all for his clients."*

The Clients: Dalton Utilities; Dow Chemical; Union Carbide; Printpack; Genuine Parts Company; Electrolux North America; Home Depot; Weyerhaeuser; Wal-Mart; Bank Of America and UPS.

King & Spalding LLP
See firm details p.635

The Firm: For many of those interviewed, this firm was quite simply *"the home of environmental litigation in Georgia."* The high-profile nature

Leading individuals (Environment)		
1	**BARMEYER Patricia** *King & Spalding*, Atlanta	
	DEHIHNS III Lee *Alston & Bird*, Atlanta	
	HORDER Richard *Kilpatrick Stockton*, Atlanta	
	JOHNSON Jr John *Troutman Sanders*, Atlanta	
2	**ERNST Andrew** *Hunter Maclean*, Savannah	
	HOGFOSS Robert *Hunton & Williams*, Atlanta	
	KAZMAREK Edward *McKenna Long*, Atlanta	
	O'DAY Stephen *Smith Gambrell*, Atlanta	
	STOKES James *Alston & Bird*, Atlanta	
	TISDALE Jr Charles *King & Spalding*, Atlanta	
3	**DOMBY Arthur** *Troutman Sanders*, Atlanta	
	GALLO Barbara *Epstein Becker*, Atlanta	
	LITTLE Catherine *Hunton & Williams*, Atlanta	
	MOWREY Robert *Alston & Bird*, Atlanta	
	OAKES Leslie *King & Spalding*, Atlanta	
	PERRY Charles *Jones Day*, Atlanta	
	POPE David *Carr Tabb*, Atlanta	
	POUNCEY Gerald *Morris Manning*, Atlanta	
	SILLIMAN R Todd *McKenna Long*, Atlanta	
	TOULME Nill *Alston & Bird*, Atlanta	

Up-and-coming individuals	
HENDERSON Douglas *Troutman Sanders*, Atlanta	
LASETER Scott *McKenna Long*, Atlanta	
RICHARDSON Susan *Kilpatrick Stockton*, Atlanta	

Individuals are listed alphabetically in each band.

of the work undertaken in the past year adds weight to this contention and serves to maintain the firm's lofty position in the rankings. Notably, the group acted for National Service Industries in the successful defense of a CERCLA case asserting liability for contamination at a landfill site. Representation has also been provided to the State of Georgia in connection with federal reformulated gas issues, as well as to parties involved in state and federal Superfund sites.

The Lawyers: Peers consider **Patricia Barmeyer** (see p.606) to be a *"grade-A litigator"* and note how she is a *"tough but fair opponent"* in the courtroom. Described as *"a client magnet,"* Barmeyer is one of the group's leading figures and has acted for GE in negotiations and administrative actions with Georgia EPD and US EPA concerning corrective action at GE's facility in Rome, Georgia. **Charles Tisdale** (see p.624) *"knows the law backwards"* on Superfund matters and represented 143 parties in the Arivec State Superfund Site in Douglasville. Tisdale also acted for Honeywell in negotiating one of the first agreements to conduct a cooperative assessment of the natural resource damage issues at LCP Chemical's site. **Leslie Oakes** (see p.619) is considered to be *"absolutely awesome"* on regulatory matters and utilizes his experience as a former environmental engineer to impressive effect.

The Clients: Honeywell; Brown & Williamson Tobacco; Inland Paperboard and Packaging; Coca-Cola; Duracell; Eaton; Timken and Magna.

Troutman Sanders LLP

The Firm: Elevated into the top tier following overwhelming market support for the varied nature of its work, Troutman Sanders' environmental practice can rightly claim to be a leading player. Much of the group's work stems from flagship client Southern Company, although representation has also been provided to the Georgia Department of Transportation and the City of Covington in litigation concerning alleged violations of the NEPA arising from an airport expansion plan. The group has counseled a major financial institution in remediating and obtaining a limitation of liability on property in the first cleanup project completed under the Georgia EPD's newly established Brownfields Program. The firm is considered to have *"expertise at every level"* and was praised by clients for its quick response times.

The Lawyers: **John Johnson** heads up the firm's environmental and natural resources group. Clients picked out Johnson's meticulous approach to transactions as a real advantage. His close relationships with regulatory agencies were also considered to stand him in good stead; the comment that *"he seems to have all the answers at his fingertips"* was indicative of the prevailing mood in the market. **Arthur Domby** enters the rankings on the back of peer approval for his environmental compliance work. **Douglas Henderson** is a further addition to the table, having garnered considerable praise for his litigation skills. Henderson, a former environmental scientist, is considered an *"exceptional technician."*

The Clients: Delta Air Lines; Wal-Mart; Omaha Public Power Direct; Kerr-McGee and Public Service Company of New Mexico.

Band 2

Hunton & Williams

See firm details p.1775

The Firm: Benefiting hugely from the breadth of resources available through the firm's prominent national practice, the Atlanta office houses a number of highly respected attorneys for national and state environmental matters. Traditional expertise in the oil pipeline sector has been supplemented by increased activity in other areas, with the past year seeing the group undertake significant work arising out of the CAA, with wetlands also featuring heavily in its portfolio.

The Lawyers: Commentators were of the opinion that **Robert Hogfoss** (see p.614) brings *"huge kudos to every deal he works on"* and this is reflected in his rise up the rankings. Seen principally as a pipeline specialist, regulatory work is another area in which Hogfoss is particularly well known. **Catherine Little** (see p.617) makes a first appearance in the tables following positive endorsements for her strong regulatory compliance practice.

The Clients: Oil pipeline companies and national corporations figure largely in the group's client base.

Kilpatrick Stockton LLP

See firm details p.634

The Firm: This firm maintains its healthy position in the market due to expertise in compliance and permitting matters. Litigation is the area in which it truly excels; enforcement actions and contamination claims are regularly defended on behalf of big-name clients.

The Lawyers: According to peers **Richard Horder** (see p.614) possesses *"tremendous business acumen,"* which comes in part from ten years' in-house experience in a large, multinational forest product corporation. Horder *"knows what his clients are looking for and makes sure he delivers."* In the past year he has been particularly involved in wetland work, with a focus on habitat conservation. **Susan Richardson** (see p.621) enters the rankings on the back of market recognition of her involvement in infrastructure problem solving.

The Clients: Sun Chemical; Georgia-Pacific; BellSouth and Aronov Realty.

McKenna Long & Aldridge

See firm details p.636

The Firm: Best known for its work on behalf of the State of Georgia, this firm is considered a genuine player in the environmental arena. Peers were effusive in their praise of how the group links up well with the firm's strong governmental practice, noting that there seems to be *"expertise in all areas"* within the firm. It has niche specialties in pesticide and chemical registration.

The Lawyers: **Edward 'Skip' Kazmarek** (see p.616) is an *"extraordinarily effective negotiator,"* and is seen by the market as the firm's leading figure. A strong litigator, Kazmarek has particular expertise in the field of toxic torts and has acted in a number of contamination matters over the past year. The *"very accomplished"* **Todd Silliman** (see p.623) enters the rankings on the back of praise for his *"bright and creative"* approach and established water practice. Up-and-comer **Scott Laseter** (see p.617) is considered *"destined for big things"* and specializes in manufactured gas plant issues.

The Clients: Hood Industries, Transco Products and various utilities corporations.

Band 3

Hunter, Maclean, Exley & Dunn, PC

The Firm: This Savannah-based practice has the monopoly on coastal environmental work in the state. While permitting is an area of especial expertise, the interpretative talents of the group with regards to new regulations was also considered a significant strength. The past year has brought work on the creation of Liberty Ridge MidCoast Business Center and various planning permit applications for a major redevelopment project in Savannah.

The Lawyers: Andrew Ernst leads the group and has built up a highly respected niche practice in the coastal development field.

The Clients: Large resort developers and golf course constructors are on the firm's books.

Morris, Manning & Martin, LLP

See firm details p.637

The Firm: This firm has been propelled into the spotlight through its involvement in the EPA award-winning Atlantic Station Project. Commentators were agreed that the project represented a *"coming of age"* for the firm, noting in particular its capabilities in brownfield work.

The Lawyers: *"Environmental project guru"* **Gerald Pouncey** (see p.620) attracted considerable praise for his ability to marshal projects successfully. Pouncey leads the team and is viewed as an expert on redeveloping environmentally impacted properties.

The Clients: Work is mainly undertaken for financial institutions and real estate companies.

Smith Gambrell & Russell LLP

The Firm: With notable strength on both the litigation and transactional sides, this firm has real presence in Georgia. According to the market, the litigators *"ooze class"* at both state and federal levels. Much of the noncontentious work comes from the manufacturing and real estate sectors.

The Lawyers: Lead practitioner **Stephen O'Day** is considered unique in that he represents both the business and the environmental community. A really *"smart and thoughtful individual"* is the view of clients, who were also quick to point out his ability to explain complicated technical concepts in simple terms.

The Clients: Arch Chemicals; Arch Wood Protection; Plantation Pipeline and MACTEC Engineering and Consulting.

Other Notable Practitioners

Barbara Gallo of Epstein Becker & Green was applauded by peers for her waste practice, one prominent source commenting *"there's nobody else in the state who can match her knowledge in that area."* Gallo has been undertaking transactional support work for clients such as Michelin, Centex Destination Properties and Transco. The arrival of **Charles Perry** (see p.620) from Hunton & Williams ensures that the market now speaks of his new firm, Jones Day, as *"one to watch"* in environmental matters. He is considered an authority on toxic tort cases and defending enforcement actions. Commentators rate the litigation skills of **David Pope** of Carr, Tabb, Pope & Freeman LLP and describe him as *"the sort of guy you want fighting on your side."* Pope is the only individual in the firm who specializes in environmental work, which means he has built up considerable experience in different areas. In the past year he has represented a national waste hauling company in a case involving problems at a waste transfer station.

HEALTHCARE

Georgia
Leading firms (Healthcare)

1	ALSTON & BIRD LLP *Atlanta*
	KING & SPALDING LLP *Atlanta*
2	KILPATRICK STOCKTON LLP *Atlanta*
	PARKER, HUDSON, RAINER & DOBBS *Atlanta*
	POWELL GOLDSTEIN LLP *Atlanta*

Leading individuals (Healthcare)

1	HUGHES Randall *Powell Goldstein, Atlanta*
	PARKER John *Parker Hudson, Atlanta*
	REED Glen *King & Spalding, Atlanta*
	SCHRODER Jack *Alston & Bird, Atlanta*
	SHACKELFORD Richard *King & Spalding, Atlanta*
2	BERGESON Donna *Alston & Bird, Atlanta*
	HUDSON Paul *Parker Hudson, Atlanta*
	ROEDER Kim *Powell Goldstein, Atlanta*
	STREET Phillip *Kilpatrick Stockton, Atlanta*

Up-and-coming individuals

	KEENAN Robert *King & Spalding, Atlanta*

Firms and individuals are listed alphabetically in each band.

Band 1

Alston & Bird LLP

See firm details p.626

The Firm: *"Leading the way in healthcare law"* was the verdict of the market. Equally at home when dealing with corporate, regulatory or litigation matters, this firm's practice group is noted for its representation of large academic facilities and pharmaceutical companies. Clients were quick to extol the virtues of a team that is

"everything you'd want from a law firm – responsive, dedicated and, best of all, accurate." In recent years, the firm has been particularly active in advising on the development and implementation of national healthcare policies.

The Lawyers: Jack Schroder (see p.622) is *"a big-time player in the sector."* *"He has unrivalled knowledge"* of credentialing and peer review matters, having served as general counsel to the Georgia Hospital Association for the past 30 years. Chair of the firm's healthcare regulatory group, **Donna Bergeson** (see p.606) has impressed commentators with her work on academic medical center legal issues, healthcare contracting and regulatory compliance. Bergeson's clients like her *"practical and dedicated approach."*

The Clients: Emory University; Emory Healthcare; ALTERNA; Guidant and Ardent Health Services.

King & Spalding LLP

See firm details p.635

The Firm: Boasting one of the Southeast's largest healthcare groups, this multiservice firm has the resources to justify its top-tier ranking. Clients and commentators alike spoke of *"a truly outstanding practice,"* which is *"unwavering in its commitment to getting the job done properly."* Attorneys have extensive experience counseling healthcare industry clients on a wide range of regulatory and corporate issues as well as defending both class and individual actions against healthcare providers and professionals.

The Lawyers: Glen Reed (see p.621) is described as a *"damned fine lawyer"* with *"immense knowledge in the transactional sphere."* He is noted for his work for providers, concerning their contractual relationships with payors. Reed serves as general counsel to the American Association of Homes and Services for the Aging. **Rick Shackelford**'s (see p.622) *"fantastic interpersonal skills"* have proved a big hit with clients: *"He knows exactly what sort of service we want and delivers it."* Shackelford is the Atlanta office's premier healthcare litigator and regularly represents clients in the defense of False Claims Act actions and government investigations. New partner **Robert Keenan** (see p.616) won plaudits from clients for his *"enthusiastic demeanor,"* while peers commented that he was *"clearly ready for the big time."* Keenan has spent a great deal of time providing comprehensive Health Insurance Portability and Accountability Act (HIPAA) compliance support for health sector clients.

The Clients: Piedmont Medical Center; Central Georgia Health Systems; Memorial Medical Center, Savannah; St Mary's Hospital, Athens; Humana and WellCare HMO.

Band 2

Kilpatrick Stockton LLP

See firm details p.634

The Firm: Offering the full range of regulatory, commercial and contentious representation to a client list including hospitals, academic

594 All quotes in the text are from interviews with clients and competitors.

CHAMBERS USA 2005

medical centers, managed care providers and rehabilitation facilities, the healthcare group at this firm has achieved prominence in the market. Commentators spoke glowingly of a *"team of seriously smart lawyers,"* while clients endorsed the firm's cost-effective approach: *"They don't waste time, they aim to bring closure to every issue."*

The Lawyers: Phillip Street's (see p.624) dual role as chair of both the firm's healthcare group and its health and life sciences group indicates the breadth of his expertise in the sector. Described by clients as an *"exceptional human being"* who is *"very well connected,"* Street's *"impressive depth of knowledge"* was noted by peers who were quick to endorse his work in the formation and structuring of single and multi-specialty physician groups.

Parker, Hudson, Rainer & Dobbs LLP

The Firm: With a focus on regulatory and corporate healthcare matters, this firm of 60 attorneys has turned heads due to the quality of its work for community hospitals. Areas of particular expertise include Medicare/Medicaid reimbursement and compliance, involving Stark Bill and Anti-Kickback Statute compliance, Emergency Medical Treatment and Active Labor Act (EMTALA) compliance, licensure and medical staff issues.

The Lawyers: John Parker is *"a true master in the healthcare regulatory sector."* Commentators singled out certificates of need issues as an area in which he excels. Although **Paul Hudson** spends much of his time on pure corporate matters, he has developed a niche in the representation of healthcare institutions in strategic affiliations and M&A activity. Hudson *"clearly knows the path from the trees"* and drew admiration from peers for his attention to detail.

Powell Goldstein LLP

The Firm: An enviable workload that involves transactions, reimbursement issues and litigation leaves little room for doubt that this firm merits its place in the rankings. Advice is also proffered on regulatory compliance involving governmental payors, government contracts, tax-exempt entities, HIPAA issues, privacy and confidentiality.

The Lawyers: The *"highly respected"* **Randall Hughes** *"brings a degree of class to absolutely everything he works on."* Hughes is the Atlanta office's practice group leader and has particular expertise in healthcare reimbursement and regulatory compliance investigations. Market sources applauded the way **Kim Roeder** *"seems to know everything about the industry."* She represents public and private healthcare facilities, suppliers, physician practice groups and managed care organizations.

INTELLECTUAL PROPERTY

Georgia
Leading firms (Intellectual Property)

1	**KILPATRICK STOCKTON** *Atlanta*
	NEEDLE & ROSENBERG, PC *Atlanta*
2	**ALSTON & BIRD LLP** *Atlanta*
	KING & SPALDING LLP *Atlanta*
3	**FINNEGAN HENDERSON FARABOW** *Atlanta*
	HUNTON & WILLIAMS *Atlanta*
	JONES DAY *Atlanta*
	SMITH GAMBRELL & RUSSELL LLP *Atlanta*
	SUTHERLAND ASBILL & BRENNAN LLP *Atlanta*
	THOMAS KAYDEN HORSTEMEYER *Atlanta*
	TROUTMAN SANDERS LLP *Atlanta*

Firms are listed alphabetically in each band.

Band 1

Kilpatrick Stockton LLP

See firm details p.634

The Firm: Widely regarded as a top firm in the state, Kilpatrick Stockton has *"an outstanding practice with a great bunch of lawyers from top to bottom."* The group handles the full range of IP disciplines for *"a great raft of clients,"* and is adept in patent prosecutions, trademark disputes, licensing issues and general transactional support. It is especially well known for its biotech expertise, and its national – and indeed international – reach is felt to make it a first port of call for a range of top multinational clients. The final ingredient in this winning formula is the *"great attitude"* of the attorneys.

The Lawyers: *"The best-known trademark lawyer in the state"* is how commentators described **Miles Alexander** (see p.605), adding: *"He has extraordinary judgment and knowledge.*

That's great, as it means he can literally handle anything." Alexander acts for a number of large companies with their own sophisticated in-house legal teams, evidence perhaps of the value he adds to his clients' ventures. He is increasingly busy in mediation and arbitration. **Tony Askew** (see p.605) is portrayed as *"an intelligent, highly experienced attorney who represents superb value for money."* Lately he has been active in a major dispute within the pharmaceutical industry, and has also handled an international patent infringement case concerning latex gloves. Peers rate him as *"one of the deans of the patent Bar."* Copyright expert **Joseph Beck** (see p.606) was hailed by one client as *"a magnificent attorney whose knowledge of the law and the market has been crucial to the development of our company."* He recently defeated an attempt to block the release of a major Hollywood film. The *"immensely practical"* **Jim Ewing** (see p.612) is *"a formidable opponent; terrifically experienced with a steady hand."* This former engineer draws plaudits for his skills in telecom and software technologies. The *"standout"* **Jerre Swann** (see p.624) impresses as *"a technically brilliant lawyer with an in-depth knowledge of the copyright market."* He represented Outkast and its record label in a dispute with civil rights leader Rosa Parks over the use of her name in one of their song titles. The firm's managing partner, **William Brewster** (see p.607) has a presence that is felt in the market. He is praised for his *"strong commitment and substantive knowledge"* and is particularly admired for his work in copyright, trademarks and restrictive covenants. Technology expert **James Johnson** (see p.615) is *"the heavy gun you bring out on biotech matters."* He

is recommended for his skill at negotiation and his ability as a litigator. *"Tenacious and dedicated attorney"* **John Pratt** (see p.621) heads the practice group and is a patent specialist. He recently settled an action between Milliken and his client Interface concerning a carpet tile design patent.

The Clients: Collegiate Licensing; Georgia-Pacific; Interface; Morgan Crucible; Vanderbilt University; Bioniche Life Sciences; Smith & Nephew; Delta Air Lines; Sony and Blue Cross and Blue Shield Association.

Needle & Rosenberg, PC

The Firm: This firm retains its position in the top band because of the *"sheer expertise and experience"* of its attorneys. It remains a highly successful boutique with the capability to cover the IP waterfront. The team earns top marks for its litigation prowess and is especially commended for its patent prosecution practice, which accounts for the lion's share of activities. The firm has a giant following, certainly across the South, in the biotech, pharmaceutical and chemical industries, with growing support in the areas of mechanical and software development and manufacturing. Although the group has its biggest concentration of clients in the South, it does also represent entities elsewhere in the USA, including Alaska and the West Coast. A number of peers confirmed this to be the firm to which they most often referred clients.

The Lawyers: Founder member **Bill Needle** is rated as *"one of the most talented patent lawyers in the state."* He is recommended as *"truly skilled and experienced; a font of knowledge and*

Georgia

Leading individuals

(Intellectual Property)

1 ALEXANDER Miles *Kilpatrick Stockton*, Atlanta
ASKEW Anthony *Kilpatrick Stockton*, Atlanta
NEEDLE William *Needle & Rosenberg*, Atlanta

2 BABER Bruce *King & Spalding*, Atlanta
BANKOFF Joseph *King & Spalding*, Atlanta
BECK Joseph *Kilpatrick Stockton*, Atlanta
BLACKSTOCK Jerry *Hunton & Williams*, Atlanta
EWING Jim *Kilpatrick Stockton*, Atlanta
FLINN Patrick *Alston & Bird*, Atlanta
NODINE Larry *Needle & Rosenberg*, Atlanta

3 ELGISON Martin *Alston & Bird*, Atlanta
HAWKINS Holmes *King & Spalding*, Atlanta
LUNSFORD III Rodgers *Smith Gambrell*, Atlanta
RAGLAND William *Hunton & Williams*, Atlanta
SWANN Jerre *Kilpatrick Stockton*, Atlanta

4 BREWSTER William *Kilpatrick Stockton*, Atlanta
JOHNSON James *Kilpatrick Stockton*, Atlanta
KUESTER Jeffrey *Thomas Kayden*, Atlanta
LISCHER Dale *Smith Gambrell*, Atlanta
MCGRATH Robin *Alston & Bird*, Atlanta
NORTH John *Sutherland Asbill*, Atlanta
PRATT John *Kilpatrick Stockton*, Atlanta
ROSENBERG Sumner *Needle & Rosenberg*, Atlanta
ROSENBLOUM Robert *Greenberg Traurig*, Atlanta
SALYERS Douglas *Troutman Sanders*, Atlanta
SETTY Nagendra *Jones Day*, Atlanta
SMITH III Frank *Alston & Bird*, Atlanta
TAYLOR Roger *Finnegan Henderson*, Atlanta
YOUNG Jeffrey *Alston & Bird*, Atlanta

Individuals are listed alphabetically in each band.

precedent." This veteran litigator has been involved in a number of mediations in the past year as mediator. **Larry Nodine** is also hailed for his advocacy skills and comes recommended by clients as "*a smart, sharp lawyer who makes the effort to learn and understand our needs.*" He is particularly praised for his skills in media work. He has recently been involved in optical-fiber litigation, which has a large international element. Computer issues expert **Sumner Rosenberg** is endorsed as "*a courtroom specialist with a great knowledge of the industry.*" He once worked for MIT programming the guidance computers in the early moon missions, and his technological background is felt to give him the edge.

The Clients: Panasonic, Lexmark and Yale University feature on the client list.

Band 2

Alston & Bird LLP

See firm details p.626

The Firm: Clients refer to Alston & Bird as "*a firm with truly broad experience and expertise.*" Proficient in litigation, transactional support and general counseling, it is praised as "*a business-focused firm that is a cut above the rest.*" Happy that the attorneys have the clout to pro-tect their interests, clients were also impressed that they were "*very responsive, very thorough and very personable.*" The capability of the Atlanta office is undoubtedly strengthened by its close working relationship with the "*highly professional*" patent specialists (both lawyers and patent agents) in North Carolina, where the firm has offices in the Research Triangle and Charlotte.

The Lawyers: The "*energetic and enthusiastic*" **Patrick Flinn** (see p.612) is "*an excellent litigator and a superb strategic thinker.*" He is rated for his technology work, having run important litigations concerning electronics, computer software and telecom. Peers say he is "*a lawyer who can control the courtroom.*" Another skilled litigator, **Martin Elgison** (see p.611) in fact leads the IP transactional group, handling the negotiation and structuring of deals involving IP assets, technology and software agreements, media and sponsorship agreements, as well as matters concerning the Internet. One client said of Elgison: "*I'm always glad he is on my side.*" **Jeffrey Young** (see p.625) is recommended for his expert knowledge of the computer and technology industries and, even more so for his niche work in mechanical patents. He is outside counsel for UPS's worldwide patent program. Peers reveal him to be "*a good person to speak to if you have an awkward little problem; he can generally see a way through.*" Expert patent litigator **Frank Smith** (see p.623) is "*a sensible guy to deal with. He doesn't charge into a dispute swinging a sledge hammer.*" He successfully represented one of the two defendants in the Milliken & Company v Mohawk Industries, et al, carpet tile patent infringement case. The "*impressive*" **Robin McGrath** (see p.618) earns plaudits for her courtroom expertise. Last year she tried two cases: a trademark infringement and breach of contract case, Go Medical Industries and Alexander O'Neil v Rusch and Alpine Medical, in which she secured a verdict for the plaintiff; and the Milliken & Company patent infringement.

The Clients: Bank Of America; Fortis; Georgia-Pacific; Lowe's; Intergraph; Reebok International; Springs Industries; Wachovia and World Wildlife Fund.

King & Spalding LLP

See firm details p.635

The Firm: This 130-year-old Atlanta firm has an IP practice that is a growing force in Georgia. As one commentator put it: "*They've invested well and are building up a very good shop.*" It is recommended for its litigation skills, and also known for its transactional work and expertise in strategic patent protection. The group continues to have an international dimension to its work: it liaises with colleagues in other US cities and London and represents major multinational corporations. It is currently acting for Coca-Cola against PepsiCo in a patent case involving a mechanical fountain dispensing agreement, and for Avaya against BellSouth in a dispute over telephone answering technology.

The Lawyers: Litigator **Joseph Bankoff** (see p.606) has "*a superb courtroom presence, so that you know your case is in good hands the moment he shows up.*" Having come from a background in general commercial litigation, Bankoff now earns his highest acclaim for patent cases, particularly those emanating from the technology sector. He recently acted for Scientific-Atlanta against Gemstar TV Guide over a cable, digital and interactive TV guide. **Bruce Baber** (see p.605) has "*expertise, lots of experience and a winning record,*" and according to clients: "*He has tremendous instincts.*" He is admired for his advocacy skills and recently acted for a major international sporting body in patent issues across the USA. Though experienced in a variety of different types of case, **Holmes Hawkins** (see p.614) is particularly well regarded for new media patent disputes and is described as "*a go-to guy with an encyclopedic knowledge of the market.*"

The Clients: The group's client base includes many large local and regional concerns, as well as national and international conglomerates.

Band 3

Finnegan Henderson Farabow Garrett & Dunner LLP

The Firm: This substantial IP boutique has developed a fantastic name in the 40 years since its creation in 1965. The Georgia practice is hailed by clients as "*a focused, smart team that understands the small issues but has a nationwide reach.*" It advises on corporate transactions as well as developing strategies for the growth and protection of brands. Attorneys are especially rated for their litigation expertise, and handle large and complex patent, trademark and copyright disputes. The firm's caseload is split between teams in Atlanta, Washington DC, Cambridge, MA, Reston, VA, and Palo Alto, with international matters handled in conjunction with its global offices in Brussels, Taipei and Tokyo. Its lengthy roster of blue-chip clients is a fitting testament to the caliber of attorneys and the firm's standing in the marketplace.

The Lawyers: The "*accessible and responsive*" Atlanta managing partner **Roger Taylor** is praised by peers as "*a high-quality lawyer who we always welcome on the other side of a case. He's professional and understands what it means to find a resolution.*" Taylor has been representing MeadWestvaco in a patent dispute relating to beverage containers, is working on a trade secrets case relating to microprocessors for Hewlett-Packard in Delaware, and is dealing with a patent infringement case for Mitsubishi Heavy Industries relating to printing presses in Dallas.

596   All quotes in the text are from interviews with clients and competitors.

CHAMBERS USA 2005

The Clients: Hewlett-Packard; Gateway; Wentworth Industries; BMW and Fuji Xerox.

Hunton & Williams
See firm details p.1775

The Firm: *"Responsive and creative"* is how commentators described this litigation and business practice. The group is praised for its skills in patent matters, particularly complex patent litigation. The firm's international reach is a major attraction to larger clients, and is felt to give the group an edge in the pursuit of high-value, cross-border work. It is currently involved, for example, in a patent infringement matter for the American subsidiary of a German corporate. Another client, Vanderlande Industries of the Netherlands, brought a patent infringement case in Washington DC with a parallel civil claim in Atlanta. The company succeeded in gaining a bar order preventing the material listed in the patent from being imported into the country, and recently achieved a very large settlement on its damages claim in Atlanta.

The Lawyers: **Jerry Blackstock** (see p.606) is a highly rated litigator with a winning combination of *"guile, skill and experience."* His work on technology matters was noted across the marketplace, and in the past year he successfully concluded a major patent infringement action for a subsidiary of Siemens. **William Ragland** (see p.621) is *"a busy, energetic lawyer,"* also recommended for his expertise in technology matters. He represents technology, computer and biotech companies and is well known for his representation of AudioFAX. His practice is split between IP litigation and licensing; in the latter area he has handled licenses for NEC, MCI, LogicaCMG and AccessLine Communications.

The Clients: MeadWestvaco; Siemens Dematic; Quest International and ExxonMobil.

Jones Day
See firm details p.485

The Firm: New to this year's guide, Jones Day is commended as *"an excellent litigation firm, which has won a lot of admirers."* It has worked well in the area of new technology patents, particularly on transfers and licensing arrangements. The past year has seen the group represent individual and corporate defendants in a software trade secrets case. It also represented CipherTrust in the enforcement of its Iron-Mail trademark, which protects a leading security and antispam product.

The Lawyers: **Nick Setty**'s (see p.622) experience of complex litigation and interest in the technology and biotech industries are his unique selling points. As one client said: *"Most people in the IP space are either superb litigators and don't understand the science, or they know the science and don't understand the strategic cost. He is superb at bringing both together."*

The Clients: Witness Systems; CipherTrust; Velant; Acuity Brands and Scientific Games.

Smith Gambrell & Russell LLP

The Firm: This sizable team is applauded for its good-quality lawyers, varied skill set and wealth of experience. It represents a number of high-profile companies in trademark, copyright and patent disputes and enforcements. Although best known for its litigation work, the team is also more than capable in M&A-related support and IP transfers and licensing. The group boasts a strong scientific/biotech following, and has handled matters pertaining to chemical engineering, computer software, e-commerce, electrical engineering, electronics, mechanical engineering and pharmaceuticals.

The Lawyers: *"Dynamite IP litigator"* **Rodgers Lunsford** is rated as one of the most sage lawyers in this field. He takes on much of the group's international litigation caseload and is also much in demand for mediations. New to the tables is **Dale Lischer**, who is recommended for his patent prosecution and litigation. Lischer has handled matters in the energy, telecom and leisure industries.

Sutherland Asbill & Brennan LLP
See firm details p.494

The Firm: This technology-focused team is renowned for its litigation strength and for fielding lawyers who *"not only understand the law, but truly grasp the science."* It handles the full range of IP issues for a variety of large companies, as well as boasting niche expertise in electrical engineering, computer software and Internet issues. Although the group is based in the South, it frequently litigates right across the country; among recent cases were a number of matters for Teva Pharmaceutical and the well-known Gemstar interactive TV guide litigation.

The Lawyers: **John North** (see p.619) chairs the IP group. He is seen as being particularly strong on trademark issues, in which he has appeared at federal and state courts. He recently represented Coca-Cola and First Data in the prosecution of patent infringement claims.

The Clients: BASF; BresaGen; Coca-Cola; Gemstar TV Guide; GE; GMP Companies; Jordan Outdoor Enterprises; Lanier Worldwide; Rinker Materials and Western Union.

Thomas Kayden Horstemeyer & Risley LLP

The Firm: This boutique firm of some 25 specialists receives plaudits for its *"excellent patent prosecution work."* Clients admire the *"consistency of quality at associate level"* and the national reach the firm has achieved. Several clients come from the software and telecom sectors, and in the past year the firm has represented BellSouth on a number of matters.

The Lawyers: Within a group that is deemed *"superb on customer service,"* perhaps because the majority have scientific or technical as well as legal qualifications, the standout name is *"attentive"* **Jeffrey Kuester**, who has a background in electrical engineering. This *"smart, responsive lawyer"* is *"never flustered by hard work"* and proves an excellent team manager.

The Clients: BellSouth; Hewlett-Packard; Georgia Tech and Emery University.

Troutman Sanders LLP

The Firm: A well-regarded group that is recommended by clients for *"being as close to an in-house counsel as an external firm can be,"* or put another way, its lawyers are *"business people who just happen to be lawyers."* The firm wins praise for its patent litigation, prosecution and procurement work, though it also counsels on licensing, marketing and distribution issues. A network of offices in southeast USA, London and Hong Kong assists the Atlanta hub.

The Lawyers: Heading the practice group is **Doug Salyers**, who is recommended as *"a smart, trustworthy lawyer with great communication skills."* His work is primarily patent based, and he handles litigation and advisory work.

The Clients: The group's diverse client base includes manufacturers, software companies, utilities and sporting goods companies.

Other Notable Practitioners
Highly rated trademark lawyer **Robert Rosenbloum** (see p.622) of Greenberg Traurig LLP boasts a strong IP/media practice. He represents recording artists, producers and songwriters, as well as Fortune 100 companies. Rosenbloum has recently worked on strategic issues for the Recording Academy, protecting the Grammy logo.

Georgia
Leading firms
(Litigation: General Commercial)

[1] **ALSTON & BIRD LLP** *Atlanta*
    KING & SPALDING LLP *Atlanta*

[2] **BONDURANT, MIXSON & ELMORE, LLP** *Atlanta*
    KILPATRICK STOCKTON LLP *Atlanta*
    ROGERS & HARDIN *Atlanta*
    SUTHERLAND ASBILL & BRENNAN LLP *Atlanta*

[3] **HOLLAND & KNIGHT LLP** *Atlanta*
    JONES DAY *Atlanta*
    POWELL GOLDSTEIN LLP *Atlanta*
    TROUTMAN SANDERS LLP *Atlanta*

[4] **DOFFERMYRE, SHIELDS, CANFIELD** *Atlanta*
    HUNTON & WILLIAMS *Atlanta*
    MORRIS, MANNING & MARTIN, LLP *Atlanta*
    PAUL, HASTINGS, JANOFSKY & WALKER *Atlanta*
    SMITH GAMBRELL & RUSSELL LLP *Atlanta*

Leading individuals
(Litigation: General Commercial)

[1] **BONDURANT Emmet** *Bondurant Mixson, Atlanta*
    CHANDLER John *Sutherland Asbill, Atlanta*
    DALTON John *Troutman Sanders, Atlanta*
    GRAVES Judson *Alston & Bird, Atlanta*
    ROGERS CB *Rogers & Hardin, Atlanta*
    SINKFIELD Richard *Rogers & Hardin, Atlanta*
    VARNER Chilton *King & Spalding, Atlanta*

[2] **BASSETT Peter** *Alston & Bird, Atlanta*
    BOICE William *Kilpatrick Stockton, Atlanta*
    FLEMING John *Sutherland Asbill, Atlanta*
    MARSHALL John *Powell Goldstein, Atlanta*
    MIXSON H Lamar *Bondurant Mixson, Atlanta*
    PERSONS Oscar *Alston & Bird, Atlanta*
    RUSS Michael *King & Spalding, Atlanta*

[3] **BLACKSTOCK Jerry** *Hunton & Williams, Atlanta*
    BRAMLETT Jeffrey *Bondurant Mixson, Atlanta*
    BUTLER James *Butler Wooten, Columbus*
    CAHOON Susan *Kilpatrick Stockton, Atlanta*
    CLAY Stephens *Kilpatrick Stockton, Atlanta*
    DANIEL Harold *Holland & Knight, Atlanta*
    DANIEL Laurie *Holland & Knight, Atlanta*
    DAVID Todd *Alston & Bird, Atlanta*
    FLOYD John *Bondurant Mixson, Atlanta*
    FORTE Stephen *Smith Gambrell, Atlanta*
    GARRETT G Lee *Jones Day, Atlanta*
    HAYNES Joseph *King & Spalding, Atlanta*
    LOVELAND Joseph *King & Spalding, Atlanta*
    MURPHY Paul *King & Spalding, Atlanta*
    PERSONS Ray *King & Spalding, Atlanta*
    REINHARDT Daniel *Troutman Sanders, Atlanta*
    REMAR Robert *Rogers & Hardin, Atlanta*
    SMITH Gordon *King & Spalding, Atlanta*

Firms and individuals are listed alphabetically in each band.

Band 1

Alston & Bird LLP
See firm details p.626

The Firm: "*One of the biggest and best litigation groups,*" according to commentators, the team earns plaudits as "*a top-quality creative team, which is assertive enough for litigation, but not so aggressive that that's the only option.*" Particularly recommended for its securities expertise, the group impresses in the areas of medical negligence, products liability, construction and general commercial litigation. Its geographical reach appeals to clients: the group works in conjunction with colleagues in four other US offices and has handled both national and international matters. It recently represented an energy company in allegations regarding the price-fixing of the California energy market and has received a number of key rulings in securities disputes relating to a global technology company.

The Lawyers: Jud Graves (see p.613) has "*a dynamic courtroom presence*" and "*a great track record; he has an almost sixth sense of what a judge wants to hear.*" Graves focuses on products liability, mass torts and medical negligence, and has a long-standing relationship with MAG Mutual Insurance, a Georgia-based group that offers insurance to physicians. "*First-rate*" Oscar Persons (see p.620) has "*an outstanding reputation that is thoroughly deserved.*" Highly experienced, he is an expert on securities class actions and restrictive covenants. Peter Bassett (see p.606) is also rated for his securities work. According to clients, this "*smart and experienced lawyer understands how to get us through cases unscathed, even when they're dauntingly large and complex.*" New to this year's table is Todd David (see p.610), whose practice includes securities and products liability as well as government investigations. He is praised as "*a standout lawyer, who is incredibly knowledgeable and good on his feet.*" David recently achieved the dismissal of a securities claim against Georgia disease management company Matria Healthcare. White-collar crime and government investigation specialist Mitch Mitchelson (see p.618) continues to be widely endorsed across the marketplace. Described by one client as "*an incredibly good lawyer who I've never seen fazed,*" he advises both companies and executives and recently acted for a major energy client in an investigation into its accounting practices.

The Clients: Bank of America; Georgia-Pacific; Genuine Parts Company; Delta Air Lines; HealthSouth; UPS; Verizon and Vulcan Materials.

King & Spalding LLP
See firm details p.635

The Firm: "*Outstanding,*" "*attentive,*" "*committed,*" "*sensible and intelligent*" are just some of the adjectives interviewees used to describe this large litigation team. It won garlands for its work on products liability, securities, antitrust matters, white-collar crime, export control and general commercial disputes. "*Frankly,*" said one client, "*if you have a high value, complex case you make King & Spalding your first call.*" Among a clientele of national and international corporates as well as large southeastern companies is GlaxoSmithKline, which attorneys are in the process of defending in a large class action relating to the alleged side effects of one of its products.

The Lawyers: The "*truly outstanding*" Chilton Varner (see p.625) is "*a terrific litigator and a dynamite courtroom presence.*" Clients warn: "*When you have a dispute you have to try your damnedest to get her before the other side does.*" Varner leads the firm's products liability group and is currently acting as national counsel for OxyCotton in a large class action with more than 500 claims filed around the country. Michael Russ (see p.622) is another "*top-quality litigator*" and "*a great communicator who can get to the essence of the situation quickly.*" To an extent, his practice leans toward securities and antitrust litigation, but it is varied and takes in a range of complex commercial litigation. Feedback for experienced Gordon Smith (see p.623) indicates that he is "*a great to work with, solution-driven attorney.*" He is strong on products liability and represents large tobacco, automotive, pharmaceutical and heavy equipment manufacturers. Paul Murphy (see p.619), who is viewed as "*a great moderator with very seasoned judgment,*" is known for his defense of tort claims in the pharmaceutical and chemical industries. Joseph Haynes (see p.614), meanwhile, continues to earn kudos for his broad-based civil litigation work. Joseph Loveland (see p.617) joins the tables this year. "*Superb on his feet and adept at seeing his way through the most complex issues,*" he recently defended Coca-Cola over allegations of financial and accounting impropriety. Ray Persons (see p.620) is also new to the tables; he is rated as "*a thoughtful gentleman whose easygoing manner means he's excellent in front of a jury.*" Persons served as counsel to GM in a toxic tort case that followed an alleged release of polychlorinated biphenyls. The "*smart and skilled*" Stephen Cowen (see p.609) continues to impress in his white-collar crime representations of corporate and individual clients. He recently acted in a criminal fraud case for the former executive of a large communications company, and has handled matters connected with Enron.

The Clients: 3M; Brown & Williamson Tobacco; ChevronTexaco; Coca-Cola; Ernst & Young; ExxonMobil; GE; GM; Georgia-Pacific and Honeywell.

598   All quotes in the text are from interviews with clients and competitors.

CHAMBERS USA 2005

Georgia
Leading individuals
(Litigation: White-Collar Crime &
Government Investigations)

1   **ABBOTT Michael** *Sole Practitioner*, Atlanta
     COWEN Stephen *King & Spalding*, Atlanta
     DEANE Richard *Jones Day*, Atlanta
     GILLEN Craig *Gillen Parker*, Atlanta
     MALOY Bruce *Maloy & Jenkins*, Atlanta
     MITCHELSON Jr William *Alston & Bird*, Atlanta

Individuals are listed alphabetically in each band.

Band 2

Bondurant, Mixson & Elmore, LLP
See firm details p.629

The Firm: This litigation boutique boasts one of the best names in the Georgia marketplace and is hailed as *"a spectacular firm with experience of every type of dispute."* It stands out from many other Atlanta firms in that it represents plaintiffs as well as defendants. It also receives a great many referrals from other law firms. Securities, antitrust, white-collar crime, patent and employment disputes are all on the agenda alongside more general commercial matters.

The Lawyers: *"The dean of the Georgia litigation bar,"* **Emmet Bondurant** (see p.607) retains his crown for another year. He is *"a fantastically experienced attorney who is genuinely at home in the courtroom."* In an impressive career, Bondurant has taken on securities cases, business litigation, products liability and white-collar crime; he remains particularly recommended for antitrust cases. **Micky Mixson** (see p.618) also earns praise as *"a top-class litigator who can handle anything – he is the go-to guy on difficult, complex matters."* Researchers found, however, that he was particularly highly regarded for his securities work. The *"superb"* **Jeffrey Bramlett** (see p.607) is yet another attorney who boasts a truly wide practice; in his case, it is one that ranges from professional liability and insurance issues to personal injury and murder cases. **John Floyd**'s (see p.612) practice leans predominantly to RICO and healthcare matters. He is rated as *"an incredibly fine lawyer."*

The Clients: Avon Products; Bed, Bath & Beyond; Brinks Home Security; Conoco; Delta Air Lines; Fina Oil & Chemical; Lincare; Primerica Financial Services and the State of Georgia.

Kilpatrick Stockton LLP
See firm details p.634

The Firm: This *"top-notch team"* is picked out for its commercial and IP litigation and offers *"quality attorneys from top to bottom."* A number of sources pointed to the firm's global reach, with one client saying: *"We don't just use them for local issues, but also for anything international."* Involvement in high-profile class actions from the past year has meant representations for Xerox and Delta Air Lines.

The Lawyers: **William Boice** (see p.607) is *"a superb litigator – he's a definite presence in the courtroom and a man who really understands how to win over a jury."* His commercial litigation practice includes patent and trade secrets matters. For example, he successfully defended Interface against a patent infringement claim brought by Milliken. **Susan Cahoon** (see p.607) is rated for her *"amazing ability to handle complex matters and see them through completely."* She chairs the litigation practice group and splits her time between litigation and IP. She is currently conducting a large commercial dispute. Finally, clients recommend **Stephens Clay** (see p.608) as *"a highly impressive and energetic lawyer."*

The Clients: Lockheed Martin; Delta Air Lines; Xerox; Interface; BellSouth; Equifax; RJ Reynolds; Krispy Kreme and Sara Lee.

Rogers & Hardin
See firm details p.639

The Firm: While this firm is recommended for a range of commercial litigation work, it is particularly known for its expertise in securities litigation. According to clients, *"it has some of the top SEC lawyers in the state,"* while one lawyer added: *"I would certainly go to them in a dispute, or even if there was an obscure point of securities law I wasn't sure of."* The midsized group has a practice that extends beyond its southeast home and is genuinely national in scope.

The Lawyers: Founder partner **CB Rogers** (see p.622) is regarded as *"without a doubt one of the most experienced litigators in Georgia."* He is recommended for his knowledge of securities and corporate governance, and is said to *"have the wonderful ability to see down the line so that nothing that happens is truly a surprise."* *"First-class trial lawyer"* **Richard Sinkfield** (see p.623) is for many *"one of the best securities lawyers in the USA."* This top-tier attorney recently defended a large pharmaceutical company on a products liability case concerning diet pills. **Robert Remar** (see p.621) is hailed as *"a great mediator as well as litigator."* He focuses on complex litigation and has a niche practice in constitutional matters.

The Clients: The group is active in the banking, healthcare, technology, insurance, computers, real estate, textiles and entertainment industries.

Sutherland Asbill & Brennan LLP
See firm details p.494

The Firm: Clients regard this group as *"a thorough, professional, sensible litigation department, which understands business as well as law."* It is recommended for its securities work, but also draws plaudits for its achievements in medical negligence, products liability, accounting malpractice and complex contract disputes. The group's network of offices ensures a healthy East Coast client following. It also represents clients from other parts of the USA and the world. In the past year it has acted for Ford in a class action brought by Ford heavy truck dealers following the sale of the business to FreightLiner and successfully defended PwC in a case that alleged faulty accounting practices.

The Lawyers: **John Chandler** (see p.608) is *"a tough, no-nonsense litigator with good client skills."* The *"thoroughly experienced"* attorney is praised for his securities work and is rated as *"one of the sharpest commercial lawyers in Atlanta."* *"Outstanding"* **John Fleming** (see p.612) is, for his clients, *"a lawyer of good standing who gives true value for money."* He is the firm-wide chair of the litigation group and his practice incorporates complex commercial disputes, including tax and limited liability matters. He also has a niche in school funding litigation.

The Clients: Ford; Merrill Lynch; State of Missouri; Procter & Gamble; Rinker Materials; KPMG; Ernst & Young and City of Atlanta.

Band 3

Holland & Knight LLP
See firm details p.1352

The Firm: Holland & Knight's litigation group joins the tables this year following enthusiastic client endorsement. *"We'd recommend it without qualification,"* they said; *"it is an impressive, easy-to-use, responsive, value-for-money team."* The group is thought to have hired well and developed a great bench of attorneys who *"always give their full attention."*

The Lawyers: *"Superb trial lawyer"* **Harold Daniel** (see p.610) is deemed to be *"skilled in arbitration, on appeals and in front of difficult juries."* His practice encompasses securities, tort issues and RICO cases. He recently acted for Arrow Electronics against E.ON in a case involving environmental damages and reimbursement of taxes following the acquisition of two manufacturing plants. **Laurie Webb Daniel** (see p.610) chairs the group's appellate practice team and is *"great on complex contractual problems."* She stands her ground in class actions and environmental issues, and is applauded as *"a fantastic lawyer, a brilliant writer and a great issue spotter."* She is currently representing the Kingdom of Spain against ABS (the ship classification society, which sets standards for oil tankers) in its claim to recover a sum in excess of $1 billion.

The Clients: Arrow Electronics; Komatsu Dresser; Ingersoll-Rand; Pfizer; Gard and Bridgestone Americas Holding.

Jones Day
See firm details p.485

The Firm: *"A cutting-edge team at the top of its game"* was how one commentator described the Atlanta office of this worldwide firm. It is felt to have made great inroads into the Georgia market, to have hired well and to now be a definite force. The group is acknowledged for its work in products liability, securities, class actions, corporate governance and complex commercial disputes. It has a strong client base in the tobacco industry and recently represented RJ Reynolds in a high-profile smoking and health case in Florida.

The Lawyers: **Lee Garrett** (see p.613), who heads the litigation practice in Atlanta, was viewed by one of his clients as "*a great, results-driven attorney who greatly improved our situation.*" He is further recommended as "*a great motivator of the younger lawyers; he is a real mentor with an inspiring attitude.*" Garrett is known for his construction cases as well as complex commercial and civil litigation. A former assistant US attorney, "*smart*" **Richard Deane** (see p.610) continues to earn praise in the field of white-collar crime. He has handled various fraud and SEC matters in the past year.

The Clients: The international nature of the firm means the team represents a number of large multinationals. It is also seen to be building up a substantial southeastern client base.

Powell Goldstein LLP

The Firm: Comprising "*a sharp litigation team,*" which continues to impress the market with its versatility and depth, Powell Goldstein's attorneys earn kudos for their banking, securities, products liability, healthcare and consumer class actions as well as their white-collar crime work. The Atlanta group is thought to combine well with the Washington DC group on larger cases.

The Lawyers: Highly rated **John Marshall** "*is so experienced he has done everything it is possible to do at the Bar.*" Although of late he has been in demand as a mediator and arbitrator, Marshall has been active in various corporate special investigations and class actions.

The Clients: Clients include regional and national corporates, and the firm has a following in the banking sector.

Troutman Sanders LLP

The Firm: "*Perennial player*" Troutman Sanders continues to win endorsements for its special investigations and securities, products liability and media and entertainment work. It also earns glowing praise for its involvement in technology and telecom matters. The sizable team is felt to offer consistency of quality and guile in the handling of large disputes.

The Lawyers: "*Hugely experienced*" **Jack Dalton** is "*one hell of a litigator; someone to be impressed with.*" Beyond his general commercial caseload lies niche work in media disputes and the representation of utilities. **Daniel Reinhardt**

is the other "*outstanding litigator*" singled out for praise. He is "*great at getting along with adversaries, which makes him a wonderful negotiator.*" Reinhardt is said to be as experienced as anyone at the Georgia Bar, especially in the area of products liability.

The Clients: The group's clients are both national and international names and include large corporations and broadcasters.

Band 4

Doffermyre, Shields, Canfield, Knowles & Devine

The Firm: This litigation boutique is best known for its products liability representation, notably for plaintiffs in high-profile cases. It does, however, retain a strong b2b litigation team, again primarily representing plaintiffs. The group has recently handled matters relating to antitrust, RICO, trademarks, breach of contract and fraud.

The Lawyers: Name partner Everette Doffermyre is the key figure for business litigation.

The Clients: The group represents businesses ranging from smaller family concerns to large corporations.

Hunton & Williams
See firm details p.1775

The Firm: Of the litigation group at Hunton & Williams, clients say: "*If it's a large case, it has the skills and manpower to throw at it.*" The firm covers the full range of commercial litigation and represents a variety of national and international clients. Its network of US and overseas offices is felt to give it the geographical reach that some other Atlanta firms lack.

The Lawyers: **Jerry Blackstock** (see p.606) chairs the litigation group and is particularly recommended for his knowledge and experience of the technology sector. He has recently acted on a number of patent matters, as well as representing an ICI subsidiary in issues relating to the withdrawal of a soft drink in Japan. Clients confirm that Blackstock is "*very responsive and focused on the job at hand.*"

The Clients: The group's clients include large multinationals as well as regional companies.

Morris, Manning & Martin, LLP
See firm details p.637

The Firm: This well-respected and growing team earns market respect for its "*top-notch lawyers, who are skilled and experienced across the board.*" The group is recognized for its strengths in IP (especially patents), trade secrets and securities. It recently defended a Fortune 100 company in several securities cases arising out of claims of improper accounting at a subsidiary.

The Lawyers: Joseph Manning heads the litigation team in Atlanta.

The Clients: McKesson; Bank of America; Louisiana-Pacific; Georgia Gulf and Michelin.

Paul, Hastings, Janofsky & Walker LLP
See firm details p.297

The Firm: Researchers learnt that the firm continues to make inroads into the Georgia market and boasts "*a practical and forthright team.*" Securities litigation remains one of the group's success stories, though it also enjoys recognition for its IP, employment and products liability work. Attorneys have recently represented Delta Air Lines in a dispute with Gate Gourmet, which produces in-flight meals.

The Lawyers: John Parker leads the litigation department in the Atlanta office.

The Clients: GE; GE Capital; Bovis Lend Lease; AIG; Delta Air Lines and State Street Bank.

Smith Gambrell & Russell LLP

The Firm: Although to an extent overshadowed by its highly regarded antitrust group, the firm's commercial litigation contingent continues to draw praise. It does well in the areas of financial litigation, construction litigation and disputes within the aircraft industry. The team recently acted in a large real estate dispute involving a real estate public trust that imploded. It has also handled a large arbitration against an Australian company.

The Lawyers: **Stephen Forte** is "*a dynamic trial attorney.*" He has been active in a number of construction disputes in the past twelve months, including cases brought in Italy and Spain.

The Clients: Wachovia, AirTran Airways and PwC feature on the client list.

Other Notable Practitioners

James Butler of Butler, Wooten, Fryhofer, Daughtery & Sullivan LLP is recommended as "*terrific with people, which makes him great before juries.*" He earns endorsements for his skills in business litigation and construction disputes. Sole practitioner **Michael Abbott** continues to earn praise for his white-collar crime practice. This "*fine lawyer*" is "*definitely great for criminal litigation*" and represents both companies and individuals. He has continued to represent a corporation in dispute with the government. **Bruce Maloy** of Maloy & Jenkins is described as "*a tremendous attorney*" and is particularly renowned for his work for corporate executives. New to this year's table is **Craig Gillen** of Gillen Parker & Withers LLC, who is included for his highly commendable representation of individuals in white-collar cases.

600   All quotes in the text are from interviews with clients and competitors.

CHAMBERS USA 2005

REAL ESTATE

Georgia
Leading firms (Real Estate)

1. **KING & SPALDING LLP** *Atlanta*
2. **ALSTON & BIRD LLP** *Atlanta*
   KILPATRICK STOCKTON LLP *Atlanta*
   SUTHERLAND ASBILL & BRENNAN *Atlanta*
   TROUTMAN SANDERS LLP *Atlanta*
3. **MCKENNA LONG & ALDRIDGE** *Atlanta*
   MORRIS, MANNING & MARTIN, LLP *Atlanta*
   PAUL, HASTINGS, JANOFSKY *Atlanta*
   POWELL GOLDSTEIN LLP *Atlanta*
   SHELEY & HALL *Atlanta*

Leading individuals (Real Estate)

1. **ADAMS Alfred** *Sutherland Asbill, Atlanta*
   STEPHENSON Mason *King & Spalding, Atlanta*
2. **ARNOLD Scott** *King & Spalding, Atlanta*
   BRANNON Jeanna *Morris Manning, Atlanta*
   CARSSOW Tim *Kilpatrick Stockton, Atlanta*
   GRIFFIN John *Troutman Sanders, Atlanta*
   JORDAN James *Sutherland Asbill, Atlanta*
   RUSCHE Mark *Alston & Bird, Atlanta*
3. **ALDRIDGE John** *McKenna Long, Atlanta*
   BENDER Albert *Alston & Bird, Atlanta*
   FARRIS James *Alston & Bird, Atlanta*
   FRYER William *King & Spalding, Atlanta*
   KAUSS Andrew *Kilpatrick Stockton, Atlanta*
   LEVIN Jay *Powell Goldstein, Atlanta*
   PAKENHAM Timothy *Alston & Bird, Atlanta*
   PARKS John *Powell Goldstein, Atlanta*
   SHARBAUGH Charles *Paul Hastings, Atlanta*
   SHELEY Raymond *Sheley & Hall, Atlanta*
   STEVENS William *McKenna Long, Atlanta*
   WALKER Homer *Alston & Bird, Atlanta*

Firms and individuals are listed alphabetically in each band.

Band 1

King & Spalding LLP

See firm details p.635

The Firm: This full-service firm continues to set the standard for real estate work in Georgia. Recognized by commentators as "*the only place to go for the really big transactions,*" the team has an impressive knowledge of investment and development issues. Particular areas of expertise are found in fund formation and equity investment. Clients attested to receiving a premium service from the firm's lawyers, noting that although "*they are expensive, there's no one else in town that gets near them for quality and depth of analysis.*" Highlights of the past year include the formation of the $750 million Macquarie Global Property fund for investments in Asia and Europe. The group also represented ING Clarion in connection with the $440 million purchase of MD Hodges from The Blackstone Group.

The Lawyers: The group's head, **Mason Stephenson** (see p.624), is an "*accomplished big hitter*" who "*handles the large deals with assurance.*" His position in the top band was fully endorsed by peers, who described him as "*unfailingly impressive with the complex stuff.*" Stephenson has been working on a variety of joint venture projects for GE Real Estate in the past year. **Scott Arnold** (see p.605) rises into the second tier due, in part, to market recognition of his considerable experience representing non-US investors with inbound investment. Arnold is considered "*incisive and insightful*" and has "*bucket loads of business acumen.*" He has represented The Brookdale Group in connection with the formation of a $460 million real estate investment fund comprised of major university endowments and private foundations. Clients welcomed the way in which "*charismatic*" **William Fryer** (see p.612) is always "*full of fresh ideas.*" He is particularly renowned for his work with developers and banks.

The Clients: GE Real Estate; The Brookdale Group; Edens & Avant; Hines; InTown Suites Management; Kuwait Finance House; Morgan Stanley Real Estate; Paladin Realty Partners; Post Apartment Homes; VEF Advisors and West-Wind Capital Partners.

Band 2

Alston & Bird LLP

See firm details p.626

The Firm: Reports of "*a highly responsive team*" that is "*willing to dig deep where necessary*" come from a clientele who is undoubtedly convinced of the firm's real estate credentials. Rivals were almost as complimentary about the firm, with particular praise reserved for the "*impressive depth of practice.*" A team of 30 attorneys handles a wide range of issues, with a focus on office leasing and landlord and tenant matters, as well as the usual array of portfolio acquisitions, joint ventures, refinancing and fund formation work.

The Lawyers: Practice group leader **Mark Rusche** (see p.622) is "*never hurried because he's on top of every single detail.*" His laid-back manner appeals to clients, who note how "*he puts you completely at ease with his obvious ability.*" Rusche is active in office leasing, but also has considerable expertise in investment acquisitions and joint venture projects. **Bert Bender** (see p.606) won plaudits from peers who considered him to be "*always flexible and responsive to his clients' needs.*" He is an authority on mezzanine loan enforcement issues and equity participation mortgages. The "*charismatic and effective*" **Tim Pakenham** (see p.620) is singled out for his knowledge of the hotel industry. He is also engaged as counsel to the developer of one of the world's largest and most technologically advanced aquariums. Clients appreciate the fact that **Lee Walker** (see p.625) "*will always go the extra mile in order to get the deal done;*" while peers were equally quick to praise "*an outstanding technician who cuts no corners.*" Walker has achieved prominence through his representation of the owner of the Tower Place mixed-use development, on which a range of complicated real estate issues have arisen. **Jay Farris** (see p.612) enters the rankings on the back of market recognition of his work for industrial distribution facility developers.

The Clients: Wachovia; GMAC; Apollo Investments; KPMG; Lend Lease; Pacific Life Insurance; Prudential Real Estate Investors; Six Continents Hotels and UPS.

Kilpatrick Stockton LLP

See firm details p.634

The Firm: "*Controlled aggression personified*" was the market verdict on this firm's real estate group. Clients certainly concur with this view, attesting to a service that is "*dynamic and effective.*" The group's work includes development, office leasing and the formation of investment vehicles. One of its recent highlights has been the representation of Orlando-based Avanti Properties in a large volume of real estate acquisitions.

The Lawyers: **Tim Carssow** (see p.608) is respected by peers for the sophisticated nature of his distressed loan practice. Carssow's pragmatic approach supports one commentator's view that "*he takes no prisoners and always achieves great results for his clients.*" He has further expertise in development and land use matters. Clients extolled the virtues of **Andrew Kauss**'s (see p.616) "*bullish yet innovative*" methodology. "*He comes up with the right answers at the right time,*" enthused one prominent source. Kauss is chair of the firm's real estate group and is considered highly proficient in representing clients in the organization of ownership structures for real estate assets.

The Clients: Wachovia; Avanti Properties Group; ING; GMAC; BellSouth; Cingular Wireless and Pope & Land Enterprises.

Sutherland Asbill & Brennan LLP

See firm details p.494

The Firm: This team of lawyers who "*don't do things by halves*" impresses competitors with the "*positive ethos*" that runs throughout the firm. The group acts for clients in the retail, hospitality and leisure fields, and has specialist knowledge in securitized finance. The firm is cultivating a niche in the representation of pension funds in the timber industry.

The Lawyers: According to commentators, **Al Adams** (see p.604) is "*reassuringly professional,*" and is winning clients over by "*always being able to see the bigger picture.*" Said to possess tremendous judgment and strong analytical skills, Adams rockets up the rankings on the back of his high-profile work for sellers and institutional investors. Peers were united in their approval of the *"extremely personable"* **Jim Jordan** (see p.615), who *"knows how to get a deal done and does it in style."* His focus lies in development and leasing, and he regularly represents clients engaged in buying, selling, developing and leasing retail, office and industrial properties.

The Clients: Home Depot; Sembler Retail; Ben Carter Properties; Holder Properties; Six Continents Hotels; GMAC; UBS and Florida State Board of Administration.

Troutman Sanders LLP

The Firm: Rising to the second tier on the back of strong market feedback, this team of *"impressive individuals"* has achieved prominence due in part to its major disposition work for Cousins Properties. Expertise is proffered in an array of areas, including project development, real estate lending and commercial leasing.

The Lawyers: The group's leading light, **John Griffin**, is *"a practical, composed solution finder"* who is *"not afraid to stick his neck out for his clients."* Fêted for his vast knowledge of the real estate world, Griffin has particular expertise in the acquisition, development and financing of office and retail space and the formation of joint ventures for such projects.

The Clients: Portman Properties; Bank of America; Cousins Properties; Chick-fil-A and Wells Capital.

Band 3

McKenna Long & Aldridge
See firm details p.636

The Firm: Although the real estate practice at this firm mainly concentrates on representing entrepreneurs and developers, significant work on the lending side is carried out for banks, pension funds, insurance companies and risk capital investors. Commentators noted the quality of the real estate work emanating from the firm's governmental affairs group, describing the team as *"a stronghold for fresh ideas."*

The Lawyers: *"Seasoned campaigner"* **John Aldridge** (see p.604) retains his high profile in the market and continues to represent US

lenders all over the world in distressed debt matters. In the past year Aldridge has been involved in complex restructurings in Poland and Germany. Clients consider him *"hugely reassuring."* **William Stevens** (see p.624) makes an appearance in the tables by virtue of his extensive work on joint venture transactions and the quality of his advice on mortgage lending conduits.

The Clients: Column Financial; GMAC Commercial Mortgage; JPMorgan; KSL Recreation; Bank Of America; KeyBank; Lehman Brothers; Lennar; Midland Loan and Morgan Stanley Real Estate Funds.

Morris, Manning & Martin, LLP
See firm details p.637

The Firm: Commentators were enthusiastic about this firm's ability to *"walk the walk and talk the talk"* on real estate matters. Thrust into the spotlight after its appointment to the Atlantic Station project, the group has gone from *"strength to strength"* in the eyes of peers, who noted significant activity in the golf course development sphere.

The Lawyers: **Jeanna Brannon** (see p.607) continues to augment her reputation as a new urbanism specialist with her role as the outside general counsel for the Atlantic Station project. Brannon garnered praise from all quarters for her *"tremendously thorough approach."*

The Clients: The group represents many of the most active developers and investors in the Southeast.

Paul, Hastings, Janofsky & Walker LLP
See firm details p.297

The Firm: Syndicated loan work forms much of the real estate practice at this national firm. An impressive client base is composed mainly of large developers and institutional lenders. Market sources were quick to praise the *"finesse and composure"* exhibited by the firm's attorneys on major transactions.

The Lawyers: **Charles Sharbaugh** (see p.622) is the firm's leading real estate figure and is seen by peers as a *"true intellectual heavyweight who can trade blows with the best of them."* Sharbaugh has been doing extensive work on condominium conversion projects in the past year.

The Clients: GE Real Estate; Merrill Lynch; Morgan Stanley; Citigroup; Bank of America; KeyBank; Lehman Brothers and Beazer Homes.

Powell Goldstein LLP

The Firm: Close links with the firm's DC office mean that the real estate group can call on the services of approximately 50 attorneys. Areas in which the team excels are development and financing with regard to affordable housing, hospitality and public transport. Clients spoke glowingly of the services provided by this firm, referring to a *"group of lawyers who are unflinching in their dedication to getting the job done properly."*

The Lawyers: **John Parks** was commended by peers as *"a smooth operator"* and possesses expertise in an impressively wide variety of real estate matters. His efficiency and responsiveness were noted by clients who described him as *"truly professional; he'll never let you down."* **Jay Levin** is considered more of a specialist – much of his practice centers on the field of new urbanism. Lauded by the market for his *"complete grasp of what clients need,"* Levin continues to represent government agencies such as the Metropolitan Atlanta Rapid Transit Authority (MARTA), Georgia World Congress Center Authority and Atlanta Public Schools in a range of matters pertaining to the financing, development, construction, sale, purchase and leasing of real estate.

The Clients: Pulte Homes; ING; Bank of America; Compass Bank; Bank of North Georgia; AIMCO and Trammel Crow Residential.

Sheley & Hall

The Firm: This respected boutique practice was formed in 2003 by three former King & Spalding attorneys. Commentators predicted *"a rosy future"* for the firm, noting that its niche expertise rendered it peerless in the office-leasing sector.

The Lawyers: **Raymond Sheley** was selected for inclusion in the tables by a number of interviewees who were aware of his burgeoning office leasing practice. They described Sheley as *"a niche operator of the highest quality."*

602   All quotes in the text are from interviews with clients and competitors.

CHAMBERS USA 2005

TAX

Georgia
Leading firms (Tax)

1 ALSTON & BIRD LLP *Atlanta*
KING & SPALDING LLP *Atlanta*
SUTHERLAND ASBILL & BRENNAN *Atlanta*

2 CHAMBERLAIN HRDLICKA WHITE *Atlanta*
KILPATRICK STOCKTON LLP *Atlanta*
MORRIS, MANNING & MARTIN, LLP *Atlanta*
PAUL, HASTINGS, JANOFSKY *Atlanta*
POWELL GOLDSTEIN LLP *Atlanta*

Leading individuals (Tax)

1 BLOOM Herschel *King & Spalding*, Atlanta
COALSON Jr John *Alston & Bird*, Atlanta
COHEN Jerold *Sutherland Asbill*, Atlanta
WOODWARD Robert *King & Spalding*, Atlanta

2 ALLEN Pinney *Alston & Bird*, Atlanta
AUGHTRY David *Chamberlain Hrdlicka*, Atlanta
COOK Philip *Alston & Bird*, Atlanta

3 BEAUDROT Charles *Morris Manning*, Atlanta
CRISAFI Frank *Powell Goldstein*, Atlanta
FEESE Suzanne *King & Spalding*, Atlanta
LOKEY James *King & Spalding*, Atlanta
PETRIK Michael *Alston & Bird*, Atlanta
WHITE Benjamin *Alston & Bird*, Atlanta

4 CLARK Reginald *Sutherland Asbill*, Atlanta
GENZ Peter *King & Spalding*, Atlanta
HARRIS Morton *Hatcher Stubbs*, Columbus
HASSON Jr James *Sutherland Asbill*, Atlanta
HENSEL Donald *King & Spalding*, Atlanta
HISHON Robert *The Hishon Firm*, Atlanta
KAYWOOD Sam *Alston & Bird*, Atlanta
MARZETTI Phil *Paul Hastings*, Atlanta
SMITH Jerry *Kilpatrick Stockton*, Atlanta
THROWER Randolph *Sutherland Asbill*, Atlanta
WASSERMAN Michael *Holt Ney*, Atlanta

Up-and-coming individuals
HODGES Charles *Chamberlain Hrdlicka*, Atlanta

Firms and individuals are listed alphabetically in each band.

Band 1

Alston & Bird LLP
See firm details p.626

The Firm: This firm's "*unique*" state and local tax practice is considered by many to be "*streets ahead*" of its competitors, and so deserving of its top-tier ranking. With a large team of specialist attorneys, who "*bring authority to every transaction*," the expertise on show is varied, ranging from international cross-border work to the proffering of advice on real estate investment trusts and internal corporate organization projects. In the past year the group has been litigating a number of tax shelter cases.

The Lawyers: **John Coalson** (see p.609) was singled out as a strong practitioner who "*knows the ropes and is not afraid to throw them down to those below him.*" His expertise on federal mat-

ters attracted particular praise from the market. **Pinney Allen**'s (see p.605) ability to comprehensively organize a deal drew plaudits. She is considered to be instrumental in "*keeping the whole practice running smoothly,*" and has expertise in the structuring of complex business transactions. **Philip Cook**'s (see p.609) practice tends towards federal tax and ERISA controversies. As the firm's deputy managing partner, his time is divided between Atlanta and Washington. Chair of the state and local tax practice **Michael Petrik** (see p.620) is "*a big name who commands instant respect.*" Petrik's major focus is on multistate tax planning for businesses. **Benjamin White** (see p.625) carries "*buckets of kudos*" and garnered praise for the quality of his tax planning advice for exempt organizations. Finally, **Sam Kaywood** (see p.616) enters the rankings on the back of positive peer feedback for his international practice.

The Clients: Delta Air Lines; UPS; Home Depot; Bank of America; Panasonic USA; Bose; CNN; Turner Broadcasting System and Komatsu.

King & Spalding LLP
See firm details p.635

The Firm: The huge global reach of this firm, which has offices in New York, DC and London, leaves clients with the overriding impression that "*no stone is left unturned on tax matters.*" The sheer breadth of the firm's international tax work distinguishes it from the other market leaders, and the team's willingness to "*always go the extra mile for the client*" is noted by the market. Equally, interviewees are aware of the high level of technical expertise found within the group; indeed, several of the attorneys are former US Treasury and IRS officials.

The Lawyers: **Herschel Bloom** (see p.606) was praised for his "*excellent tax mind,*" with clients perceiving him as being "*one of the few attorneys who can successfully integrate business with tax issues.*" Bloom earned further plaudits for the wide-ranging nature of his expertise; he additionally advises on corporate, partnership and real estate issues. **Robert Woodward** (see p.625) received acclaim from clients for his industrious approach to difficult issues, and maintains his top-tier ranking accordingly. Considered to be an exceptional analyst ("*he only takes risks that are well thought out*"), Woodward's tax specializations relate to M&A, restructuring and financing. Peers enjoy working with **Suzanne Feese** (see p.612) due to her "*sensible and effective approach.*" Considered "*calm, assured and totally unflappable*" by clients, she is especially renowned for her tax controversy and litigation work. The "*understated*" **James Lokey** (see p.617) "*always does a fine job for his client,*" and earns market standing through his expertise on partnership matters.

Interviewees considered Lokey's previous experience as Associate Tax Legislative Counsel in the Treasury Department to be a distinct advantage. For many, younger partner **Donald Hensel** (see p.614) is "*still on an upward curve,*" with clients considering his work to be "*first rate.*" **Peter Genz** (see p.613) enters this year's tables on the back of strong market approval for his work relating to the structuring of inbound investment.

The Clients: Sprint; UPS; SunTrust Bank; International Paper; Jefferson-Pilot and Post Properties.

Sutherland Asbill & Brennan LLP
See firm details p.494

The Firm: Unrivaled for its strength on tax controversy matters, this firm continues to be a major force in the Georgia market. By virtue of its long-standing commitment to tax advice, the firm has assembled an impressive array of experts into a "*truly top-notch team.*" Clients welcomed the fact that these attorneys "*know how to fight the fight when necessary.*" The firm appears more than comfortable in a number of spheres, including corporate, international, partnership, and state and local taxation.

The Lawyers: **Jerold Cohen** (see p.609) has earned considerable respect in the field and is seen by many as the state's premier controversy lawyer. A number of interviewees picked out his negotiation skills as a particular strength, while also noting that close links with the IRS mean that he "*brings huge kudos to every case he works on.*" **Reginald Clark**'s (see p.608) practice tends to focus on corporate taxation and planning corporate acquisitions and restructurings. **James Hasson** (see p.614) attained strong market feedback for his work on behalf of nonprofit organizations, and additionally boasts considerable expertise in the healthcare sector. Elder statesman **Randolph Thrower** (see p.624) makes good use of "*a wise head,*" and is considered to provide invaluable advice on federal tax matters.

The Clients: Nortel Networks; Coca-Cola Enterprises; Procter & Gamble; Philip Morris and Forest Capital Partners.

Band 2

Chamberlain Hrdlicka White Williams & Martin

The Firm: According to commentators, this firm's name has "*huge gravitas*" in the tax controversy sphere. While a significant amount of the attorneys' time is spent defending civil tax fraud cases and tax-motivated transactions, considerable praise was also bestowed on their tax planning capabilities.

The Lawyers: For many of those interviewed

David Aughtry is a *"big-time player"* who *"brings depth and know-how to every case he works on."* He is renowned for his contentious work on tax shelter cases. Up-and-comer **Chuck Hodges** (see p.614) has increased visibility in the market, and is considered particularly adept at linking the planning and litigation elements of his tax practice.
The Clients: The firm advises public companies, privately owned businesses, trusts, estates and tax-exempt organizations.

Kilpatrick Stockton LLP
See firm details p.634
The Firm: *"An enviably broad practice"* was the verdict of one prominent commentator on the group at this firm. The full spectrum of tax work is covered, though there are particular specializations in M&A, joint ventures and the tax aspects of bond transactions and financial instruments.
The Lawyers: Ex-KPMG partner **Jerry Smith** (see p.623) is viewed as the leading light of the tax group now that Harold Abrams has stepped back from practice in this area. Federal transactional work and international tax advice form the mainstay of Smith's practice, but he is also highly regarded for his corporate state and local tax practice.
The Clients: Bell South; Southern Company; Equifax and Certegy.

Morris, Manning & Martin, LLP
See firm details p.637
The Firm: The firm's place in this year's rankings can be attributed to the complexity and quality of work taken on by the tax group. It continues to represent the Behringer Harvard Headquarters in Dallas with regards to REITs

and publicly offered limited partnerships. It is also heavily involved in designing tax-efficient compensation systems for real estate-based companies.
The Lawyers: **Charles Beaudrot** (see p.606) works mainly on the corporate side and is fêted for his ability to *"make even the most complex tax transactions comprehensible for the layman."* Said to *"always hit the right note,"* Beaudrot excels in conjuring up creative solutions for clients. He has particular expertise in flow-through entities in Georgia, having participated in the drafting process for Georgia's LLC and LLP legislation.
The Clients: Clients include Hartman Real Estate Trust and Cole Capital Partners in Phoenix.

Paul, Hastings, Janofsky & Walker LLP
See firm details p.297
The Firm: Consistently recognized by the market for its work on tax-structured real estate transactions, the Atlanta office of this big national player has *"come on leaps and bounds"* in the past few years. An impressive portfolio of complex tax work for local and midmarket companies offers a compelling reason for its inclusion in the rankings.
The Lawyers: Interviewees applauded **Phil Marzetti**'s (see p.618) pragmatism, the consensus being that *"he always comes up with the goods."* In addition to mainstream corporate tax advice, Marzetti has developed a niche practice in representing developers and institutional investors in connection with affordable housing projects that qualify for tax credits.
The Clients: GE Capital; UPS; Qatar Petroleum and Korean Telecom.

Powell Goldstein LLP
The Firm: Market sources were in no doubt that this firm merited its place in the rankings. Positive feedback confirmed the tax group's noncontentious capabilities, with interviewees especially commending the team's work for tax-exempt organizations.
The Lawyers: **Frank Crisafi** (see p.610) was identified as the firm's leading tax practitioner, having impressed peers with his doggedness (*"he just keeps working away at a problem until he gets the answer"*) and drawn client praise for being *"extremely proactive and responsive."* International tax planning and corporate M&As form the majority of his workload, but he is equally adept at the establishment and financing of domestic corporations' foreign subsidiaries.
The Clients: Clients include Mariner and Omega, as well as household goods suppliers and companies from the technology and aerospace sectors.

Other Notable Practitioners
Michael Wasserman of Holt Ney Zatcoff & Wasserman LLP is recognized for his real estate tax practice, the majority of his client base being various tax-exempt organizations; for example, The University Financing Foundation. **Morton Harris** of Hatcher, Stubbs, Land, Hollis & Rothschild LLP generates a lot of respect in the sector and is considered to be one of the leading tax lawyers in Columbus. Sole practitioner **Robert Hishon** of The Hishon Firm LLC is a *"top-drawer"* trial attorney, who *"takes no prisoners at all"* and provides representation in both criminal and civil tax suits.

Leaders in Georgia

ABBOTT, Michael
C Michael Abbott PC, Atlanta
404 885 1994
Recommended in Litigation

ABERNATHY, Thomas
Smith, Currie & Hancock LLP, Atlanta
404 521 3800
Recommended in Construction

ACORD, Bobbi
Parker, Hudson, Rainer & Dobbs LLP,
Atlanta 404 523 5300
Recommended in Banking & Finance

ADAMS Jr, Alfred G
Sutherland Asbill & Brennan LLP,
Atlanta 404 853 8014
al.adams@sablaw.com
Recommended in Real Estate
Practice Areas: Chairs Sutherland's Real Estate Group. Focuses primarily on real estate and creditors' rights, repre-

senting foreign and US investors, lenders and developers on varying projects. Works in the acquisition and development area and on mortgage and joint venture financing of commercial projects. Experienced in real estate workouts, foreclosures and bankruptcy reorganizations. Speaks often at CLE seminars. Serves on the editorial advisory board of the 'Retail Law Strategist'.
Prof. Memberships: Former Chair, Real Property Section of the State Bar of Georgia; co-chaired the State Bar of Georgia's Committee on Legal Opinions in Real Estate Transactions; Fellow in the American College of Mortgage Attorneys; Member, State Bar of Georgia; Member, International Council of Shopping Centers; Member, National Association of Industrial and Office Parks; and Member, Board of Visitors of Duke Law School.

Publications: 'Springing Exclusive - Another Technique to Resolve Exclusive Use Issues', 'Retail Law Strategist', (2002); 'Developing a Shopping Center on a Ground Lease', 'Retail Law Strategist', (2001); 'The Mortgagee's Guide to Single Asset Bankruptcy Reorganizations', 98 'Commercial Law Journal' 351(1993).
Personal: JD with distinction, Duke University School of Law, 1974, Order of the Coif, Administrative Law Editor, 'Duke Law Journal'; AB, Duke University, 1970.

ALDRIDGE Sr, John G
McKenna Long & Aldridge, Atlanta
404 527 4030
jaldridge@mckennalong.com
Recommended in Real Estate
Practice Areas: Restructuring advisor and legal counsel for US investment banks, financial institutions and

investors. Assisted in purchase, restructure and liquidation of more than $25 billion in performing and non-performing commercial loans and assets in the United States, Europe and South America. Develops strategic planning programs for senior management and special loan divisions of US financial institutions to address distressed debt portfolios and high-risk, high-yield lending. Trains loan officers and asset managers in analyzing, managing and resolving under- and non-performing loans. Co-founder of Long Aldridge & Norman, predecessor firm of McKenna Long & Aldridge.
Prof. Memberships: American Bar Association; Atlanta Bar Association; District of Columbia Bar Association; Georgia Bar Association; American College of Real Estate Lawyers; Central

604   All quotes in the text are from interviews with clients and competitors.

CHAMBERS USA 2005

Atlanta Progress, Board of Directors (Past); Columbia Theological Seminary, Board of Trustees; Commerce Club, Board of Directors, President; Leadership Atlanta; Leadership Georgia; Presbyterian PLSE, Chair of the Board; Samaritan Center, Chairman of the Board of Directors (Past); Georgia Council on Child Abuse, Inc., Board of Directors (Past); Presbyterian College, Board of Visitors (Past); Homeward, Inc., Board of Directors (Past).
Personal: JD, University of North Carolina School of Law, with honors, 1968. BA, Duke University, 1965.

ALEXANDER, Miles
Kilpatrick Stockton LLP, Atlanta
404 815 6410
MAlexander@KilpatrickStockton.com
Recommended in Intellectual Property
Practice Areas: Nationally known intellectual property and ADR lawyer who has served as lead counsel for numerous Fortune 500 companies in major trademark disputes.
Prof. Memberships: ABA; DC/Georgia Bar; International Trademark Association (past legal counsel, member of Board of Directors, editor in chief, 'The Trademark Reporter'); American College of Trial Lawyers.
Career: Taught at Harvard Law School; served two years as a USAF Judge Advocate; Partner since 1963; Chair/Co-Chair of firm since 1996.
Publications: Written a number of articles in the trademark and unfair competition fields.
Personal: BA, Emory University, Phi Beta Kappa, 1952; JD, Harvard Law School, cum laude, 1955.

ALFORD, Carolyn Zander
King & Spalding LLP, Atlanta
404 572 3551
czalford@kslaw.com
Recommended in Banking & Finance
Practice Areas: Represents lenders and borrowers in debt financings, including syndicated and single lender senior credit facilities (for both leveraged and investment grade credits), asset based loans, mezzanine financing and third-party sponsored loan programs.
Prof. Memberships: Atlanta Bar Association; Women's Finance Exchange; State Bar of Georgia, Chair of the Legal Opinion Committee of the Business Law Section; Fellow of the American College of Investment Counsel.
Personal: BA, Duke University, magna cum laude, 1989, Phi Beta Kappa; JD Harvard Law School, cum laude, editor of 'Harvard Journal on Legislation'.

ALLEN, Pinney L
Alston & Bird LLP, Atlanta
404 881 7485
pallen@alston.com
Recommended in Tax
Practice Areas: Concentrates on the structuring and effecting of complex business transactions, including part-

nership and corporate tax planning and litigation.
Prof. Memberships: Former trustee and former Chair of the Atlanta Tax Forum, a past Chair of the Tax Sections of the State Bar of Georgia and Atlanta Bar Association and a member of the American Bar Association Tax Section.
Career: Recently completed a four year term on the firm's Partners' Committee and chaired the committee in 2002. Co-Chair of Tax Section.
Publications: Frequent author and speaker on corporate, partnership, and real estate income tax problems.
Personal: AB (1976), JD (1979) - Harvard University.

ALLEN, Randall L
Alston & Bird LLP, Atlanta
404 881 7196
rallen@alston.com
Recommended in Antitrust
Practice Areas: Concentrates on complex commercial litigation with a focus on antitrust litigation and counseling.
Prof. Memberships: Former Vice-Chair of the Section 1 Committee of the Antitrust Section of the ABA and Chairman of the Antitrust Section of the Georgia State Bar; member of Georgia State University, College of Law; Board of Visitors and Vice-Chairman and general counsel for Ronald McDonald Children's Charities.
Career: Leads the firm's antitrust merger counseling effort and frequently appears before the Department of Justice and Federal Trade Commission on behalf of large public clients.
Personal: BA (1982), JD (1986) - Georgia State University.

ARNOLD, Scott
King & Spalding LLP, Atlanta
404 572 4908
sarnold@kslaw.com
Recommended in Real Estate
Practice Areas: Represents investors (both foreign and domestic) in large commercial properties throughout the US in commercial real estate transactions. Represents real estate investment funds and developers in consolidating within the commercial real estate industry. Assists domestic investors in acquiring and divesting properties.
Prof. Memberships: American College of Real Estate Lawyers; American Bar Association; Atlanta Bar Association; State Bar of Georgia.
Personal: BA, Economics, University of Missouri, Phi Beta Kappa, 1972; JD, magna cum laude, University of Michigan Law School, 1975.

ASBILL, Rick
Paul, Hastings, Janofsky & Walker LLP, Atlanta 404 815 2236
rickasbill@paulhastings.com
Recommended in Antitrust
Practice Areas: Business and commercial law, domestic and international franchising, licensing, intellectual prop-

erty, antitrust counseling, mergers and acquisitions.
Prof. Memberships: American and International Bar Associations, past Chair IBA International Franchising Committee and ABA Forum on Franchising.
Career: Partner, Atlanta office; Co-Chair of firm's Franchise and Distribution Group; Chair, Atlanta Office Corporate Department.
Publications: Co-author and editor, 'Fundamentals of International Franchising' (ABA Press, 2001); co-author, 'Franchising Law: Practice and Forms' (Specialty Technical Publishers, Inc., ed 2004); frequently writes and lectures on franchising and distribution at legal and business seminars.
Personal: AB Politics, Princeton University, 1965; JD, University of North Carolina, 1968.

ASHE, Lawrence
Ashe, Rafuse & Hill, LLP, Atlanta
404 253 6001
lawrenceashe@asherafuse.com
Recommended in Employment
Practice Areas: Concentrates practice in employment law, civil rights and litigation matters. Is nationally recognized for his class-action experience and employee selection expertise, and is the second career employment law attorney inducted as a Fellow of the American College of Trial Lawyers.
Prof. Memberships: Member, State Bar of Georgia; Member, Bar of District of Columbia; Fellow, The College of Labor and Employment Lawyers; Past Chair - AELC; Past Management Chair - ABA EEO Committee of Labor and Employment Law Section; Representative for Northern District of Georgia, Eleventh Circuit Court of Appeals' Committee on Lawyer Qualifications and Conduct (2001-06).
Career: Founding Partner of Ashe, Rafuse & Hill, LLP. Founder of Atlanta office of 800 attorney international law firm where he served for 10 years as the Chair of Atlanta office and then as Chair of the firm's East Coast employment law and labor practices.
Personal: AB degree, High Honors - Princeton University (1962); LLB degree, Honors - Harvard Law School (1967).

ASKEW, Anthony
Kilpatrick Stockton LLP, Atlanta
404 745 2401
TAskew@KilpatrickStockton.com
Recommended in Intellectual Property
Practice Areas: Patent, trademark and copyright law and litigation.
Prof. Memberships: State Bar of Georgia (Board of Governors and Disciplinary Board); US District Court Bar Council (Chair of the Disciplinary Committee); UGA Law School's Advisory Board for the 'Journal of Intellectual Property Law'.

Career: Former patent attorney for Eastman Kodak Company; Special Assistant Attorney General for the State of Georgia for intellectual property matters since 1983; adjunct faculty member at Emory Law School.
Publications: US Trademark Association's 'The Trademark Reporter' (former editorial board); 'Wiley Intellectual Property Law Update' (former co-editor).
Personal: BA Chemistry, Vanderbilt University, 1962; JD, Emory University, 1965.

ASSELIN, Thomas
Smith Gambrell & Russell LLP, Atlanta
404 815 3500
Recommended in Construction

AUGHTRY, David
Chamberlain Hrdlicka White Williams & Martin, Atlanta 404 659 1410
Recommended in Tax

AUSTIN, Jesse
Paul, Hastings, Janofsky & Walker LLP, Atlanta 404 815 2208
jesseaustin@paulhastings.com
Recommended in Banking & Finance, Bankruptcy
Practice Areas: Concentrates practice in bankruptcy law, particularly Chapter 11 reorganization cases and large commercial workouts. A principal focus of his workout and insolvency practice is the representation of institutional senior secured lenders in syndicated credit facilities, with particular experience in debtor-in-possession lending and in the healthcare, communications, energy and retail. Also closes senior credit facilities and assists other financial services lawyers in structuring senior credit facilities and negotiating subordination provisions of subordinated debt issues.
Personal: BS, Business Administration, Phi Beta Kappa, University of North Carolina (1976). JD, with distinction and MBA from Emory University (1980).

BABER, Bruce
King & Spalding LLP, Atlanta
404 572 4826
bbaber@kslaw.com
Recommended in Intellectual Property
Practice Areas: Intellectual property and technology law with focus in patent, trademark, trademark counterfeiting, false advertising and copyright infringement cases before the International Trade Commission and the United States Patent and Trademark Office. Substantial experience in the protection of trademarks, copyrights and other forms of intellectual property, including registration applications prosecution and implementation of worldwide protection strategies.
Prof. Memberships: American Bar Association; Atlanta Bar Association; State Bar of Georgia.

Personal: BA, with distinction, Princeton University, 1976; JD, cum laude, Duke University, Order of the Coif, 1979.

BANKOFF, Joseph
King & Spalding LLP, Atlanta
404 572 4796
jbankoff@kslaw.com
Recommended in Intellectual Property
Practice Areas: Technology, communication disputes and contracts relating to software, copyrights, trade secrets, distribution channels and traditional/new media organizations. Experienced trial lawyer in patent, copyright, trade secret, media and technology-related matters.
Prof. Memberships: American Bar Association; American Law Institute; Atlanta Bar Association; Georgia Center for Advanced Telecommunications Technology (Board); Illinois State Bar; National Institute for Trial Advocacy (Board of Trustees); State Bar of Georgia.
Personal: BS, Purdue University, 1967; JD, University of Illinois, Omicron Delta Kappa, Order of the Coif, 1971.

BARMEYER, Patricia
King & Spalding LLP, Atlanta
404 572 3563
pbarmeyer@kslaw.com
Recommended in Environment
Practice Areas: Regulatory compliance and environmental litigation in the areas of water, waste, air and environmental tort issues. Former assistant attorney general for the State of Georgia. Expertise combines detailed knowledge of environmental law with courtroom experience in environmental cases.
Prof. Memberships: American Bar Association (member, Section on Natural Resources, Energy and Environmental Law); American Bar Foundation; Atlanta Bar Association; Fellow, Atlanta Volunteer Lawyers Foundation (past President); State Bar of Georgia.
Personal: BA, Hollins College, 1968; JD, cum laude, Harvard University, 1971.

BASSETT, Peter Q
Alston & Bird LLP, Atlanta
404 881 7343
pbassett@alston.com
Recommended in Litigation
Practice Areas: Focuses on litigation and trial work covering a broad spectrum of securities class actions, claims, and investigations.
Prof. Memberships: Member of the AIG National Union Nation Panel counsel for the defense of securities class actions and D&O claims, member of the State Bar of Georgia and the Atlanta Bar Association.
Career: Listed in two leading US legal publications for business litigation. Frequent author and speaker on topics relating to securities claims, class actions and D&O insurance.
Personal: AB, Princeton University (1971); JD, George Washington University (1975).

BATSON, R Neal
Alston & Bird LLP, Atlanta
404 881 7267
nbatson@alston.com
Recommended in Bankruptcy
Practice Areas: Concentrates practice in Chapter 11 corporate reorganizations and out-of-court debt restructurings, as well as commercial litigation, corporate investigations, arbitration and mediation.
Prof. Memberships: Former Chair of the American College of Bankruptcy (2001-03), member of the American College of Trial Lawyers, former president of the Atlanta Bar Association, conferee of the National Bankruptcy Conference, former member of the Advisory Committee on Bankruptcy Rules by appointment of Chief Justice Rehnquist.
Career: Former court appointed Examiner for Southmark Corporation and Enron Corp. Listed in several leading US legal publications.
Personal: BA (1963), JD (1966) - Vanderbilt University.

BAXLEY, C William
King & Spalding LLP, Atlanta
404 572 3580
bbaxley@kslaw.com
Recommended in Corporate/M&A
Practice Areas: Domestic and international mergers and acquisitions and joint ventures in the consumer products, telecom, banking, insurance, transportation, retail and restaurants industries, involving public company mergers, private company acquisitions and dispositions, joint ventures, strategic investments, going private transactions, special committee representations, tender offers and proxy contests.
Prof. Memberships: American Bar Association; State Bar of Georgia.
Personal: BS, summa cum laude, University of Alabama, 1986; JD, magna cum laude, Harvard University, 1989. Named one of the top 15 young Atlanta lawyers by 'The Fulton County Daily Report' in 2002.

BEAUDROT Jr, Charles R
Morris, Manning & Martin, LLP, Atlanta
404 504 7753
cbeaudrot@mmmlaw.com
Recommended in Tax
Practice Areas: General corporate, international, mergers and acquisitions, real estate capital markets, taxation, wealth planning.
Prof. Memberships: Atlanta Bar Association (Taxation), American Bar Association (Taxation), State Bar of Georgia.
Career: Chuck is a Senior Partner in the firm's taxation and real estate capital markets groups. He advises clients with respect to tax issues involving real estate partnerships, real estate investment trusts and their related umbrella partnerships.
Personal: Member of the American Society of Composers and Publishers, the National Academy of Recording Arts

& Sciences, the Association of Anglican Musicians, and the Choir of the Cathedral of St. Philip in Atlanta.

BECK, Joseph
Kilpatrick Stockton LLP, Atlanta
404 815 6406
JBeck@KilpatrickStockton.com
Recommended in Intellectual Property
Practice Areas: Copyright, first amendment, entertainment law. Lead Counsel in SunTrust Bank v Houghton Mifflin; Estate of Martin Luther King, Jr., Inc. v CBS, Inc.; Rosa Parks v LaFace Records; Cooper v Sony Music Entertainment; Fantasy v LaFace Records; D.C. Comics, Inc. v Unlimited Monkey Business, Inc. and numerous other intellectual property cases.
Prof. Memberships: Copyright Society of the USA (former trustee); Georgia First Amendment Foundation (Board of Directors).
Career: Adjunct professor (IP and First Amendment) at Emory University; frequent lecturer at law schools across the United States and abroad.
Personal: BA Emory University; JD Harvard University.

BECK, Philip
Smith, Currie & Hancock LLP, Atlanta
404 521 3800
Recommended in Construction

BENDER Jr, Albert E
Alston & Bird LLP, Atlanta
404 881 7385
bbender@alston.com
Recommended in Real Estate
Practice Areas: Commercial real estate investment, development and financing, especially complex, multi-state and portfolio joint ventures, financings, purchases, sales and workouts.
Prof. Memberships: ICSC, MBA, NAIOP, ABA.
Career: Alston & Bird Real Estate Practice Quality Coordinator; Counsel Coordinator; New Business Acceptance Committee; Legal Education Task Force.
Publications: Seminar presentations include mezzanine loan enforcement issues, 'Mixing Bowl' joint venture transactions, equity participation mortgages, construction loans and workouts, alternative legal fee systems.
Personal: AB (Urban Affairs), St. Louis University (1980), Phi Beta Kappa; JD, Northwestern University School of Law (1983).

BERGESON, Donna
Alston & Bird LLP, Atlanta
404 881 7278
dbergeson@alston.com
Recommended in Healthcare
Practice Areas: Academic medical center legal issues, healthcare contracting, regulatory compliance.
Prof. Memberships: Member, State Bar of Georgia; Georgia Academy of Health Care Attorneys; American Health Lawyers.

Career: Former Chair, Alston & Bird Health Care Regulatory Group. Past General Counsel of the Emory Clinic. Frequent author and speaker on compliance and life sciences-related legal issues. Certified as a professional coder by the American Academy of Professional Coders.
Personal: BA, University of South Carolina (1981); JD, University of South Carolina (1984).

BLACKSTOCK, Jerry
Hunton & Williams, Atlanta
404 888 4298
jblackstock@hunton.com
Recommended in Intellectual Property, Litigation
Practice Areas: Jerry Blackstock's areas of trial experience after over 35 years of practice and over 200 trials include intellectual property rights involving patents, trademarks and copyrights, trade dress and trade secret issues, diverse business problems such as financing, false advertising, tax disputes, unfair competition claims, contract and lease disputes, corporation-shareholder problems, partnership disputes and employer-employee relationships including employment agreement litigation. He is also experienced in litigation involving real estate issues and insurance coverage issues. He has tried cases in state and federal courts in Georgia, and other states, and he has handled arbitration trials all over the country.

BLOOM, Herschel
King & Spalding LLP, Atlanta
404 572 4929
hbloom@kslaw.com
Recommended in Tax
Practice Areas: Corporate, partnership and real estate tax matters, particularly real estate investment trusts, life insurance companies and state tax issues and controversies.
Prof. Memberships: American Bar Association; American College of Tax Counsel; American Law Institute; State Bar of Georgia (former Chairman, Tax Section).
Personal: AB, magna cum laude, Vanderbilt University, 1965; JD, cum laude, Harvard University Law School, Phi Beta Kappa; Omicron Delta Kappa, 1968. Former Associate Professor of Law at University of Mississippi Law School. Frequent speaker on corporate and partnership tax subjects.

BLUMEN, Rick D
Alston & Bird LLP, Atlanta
404 881 7895
rblumen@alston.com
Recommended in Banking & Finance
Practice Areas: Debt finance, secured and unsecured syndicated credit facilities, structured finance, private placements, high-yield debt offerings, trust preferred securities offerings, mezzanine finance, acquisition finance.
Prof. Memberships: Member, State Bar of Georgia.

Career: Served as counsel to several of the largest US commercial banks and insurance companies. Former judicial intern with The Honorable Lawrence S Margolis, US Court of Federal Claims. Former intern with President Jimmy Carter.
Publications: Published in 'Georgia State University Law Review.'
Personal: BA, Emory University (1986); JD, George Washington University (1990).

BOICE, William
Kilpatrick Stockton LLP, Atlanta
404 815 6464
BBoice@KilpatrickStockton.com
Recommended in Employment, Litigation
Practice Areas: Has substantial trial experience representing significant corporate clients in a wide variety of cases. Trial practice focused on complex litigation including patent and trade secret litigation, class actions, business torts, securities and other business litigation.
Prof. Memberships: Litigation Section of the Atlanta Bar Association and the State Bar of Georgia; Bleckley Inn of Court; Lawyers Club of Atlanta.
Career: United States Navy officer (1968-70); Partner since 1980; Litigation Practice Group Chairman (1997-2001).
Personal: BA Economics, Emory University, 1968; JD, University of Virginia School of Law, 1974.

BOISSEAU, Richard
Kilpatrick Stockton LLP, Atlanta
404 815 6317
RBoisseau@KilpatrickStockton.com
Recommended in Employment
Practice Areas: Employment relations law with a primary focus in traditional labor relations matters under the National Labor Relations Act.
Prof. Memberships: Board of Directors of the Visiting Nurse Health System of Metropolitan Atlanta, Inc. (past President); ABA's Committee on Labor Arbitration and the Law of Collective Bargaining Agreements.
Career: Has lectured and written on employment-related topics; contributing author to the sixth edition of 'How Arbitration Works,' Elkouri & Elkouri, the most widely used manual on labor arbitration.
Personal: Undergraduate degree, Drexel University, cum laude, 1968; JD, Temple University, cum laude, 1974.

BONDURANT, Emmet J
Bondurant, Mixson & Elmore, LLP, Atlanta 404 881 4126
bondurant@bmelaw.com
Recommended in Antitrust, Litigation
Practice Areas: Antitrust and unfair competition, appellate, business torts, constitutional, dispute resolution, franchise, professional liability, securities, and white collar criminal defense litigation.
Prof. Memberships: Served as Chairman, Atlanta Charter Commission;

President, Atlanta Legal Aid Society; President, University of Georgia Law School Association. Fellow, American Bar Foundation. Member: Atlanta Bar Association (Member: Executive Committee and Litigation Section; Chair, Fulton Indigent Defense Commission); State Bar of Georgia (Antitrust Section); American Bar Association (Member: Antitrust, Business, Litigation, and Individual Rights and Responsibilities Sections); American Law Institute; American College of Trial Lawyers; American Academy of Appellate Lawyers; American Inns of Court (Member, Executive Committee, Bleckley and Lumpkin Inns); Member, University of Georgia Board of Visitors; Chairman, Board of Directors of the Georgia Appellate Practice and Education Resource Center; Chairman, Board of Directors of Common Cause/Georgia; Chairman, Georgia Public Defender Standards Council; Chairman, Fulton County Criminal Justice Blue Ribbon Commission.
Career: Has represented clients in nearly every forum available for a legal dispute, from rural trial courts through the United States Supreme Court (Hishon v King & Spalding, 467 US 69 (1984), Toombs v Fortson, 379 US 809 (1965), Westberry v. Sanders, 376 US 1 (1964)). During the course of his career he has earned a reputation as an independent and implacable adversary who does not shy away from controversial cases, and combines innovative legal theories with sheer determination. In 2001, he was recognized as one of the top 10 trial lawyers in the United States by the National Law Journal.
Personal: University of Georgia (AB, cum laude, 1958; LLB, magna cum laude, 1960); Harvard University (LLM, 1962); Law Clerk to the late Honorable Judge Clement F Haynsworth, Jr, United States Court of Appeals for the Fourth Circuit, 1960-61.

BORDERS, Sarah
King & Spalding LLP, Atlanta
404 572 3596
sborders@kslaw.com
Recommended in Bankruptcy
Practice Areas: Insolvency law issues, extensive experience representing creditors and debtors in large workouts, restructurings and bankruptcy cases in the retail, textile, real estate and healthcare industries.
Prof. Memberships: American Bar Association; American Bankruptcy Institute; American Law Institute (former President); Atlanta Bar Association; State Bar of Georgia.
Personal: BS, Louisiana State University, 1984; JD, University of Virginia, 1988. Frequent speaker on restructuring issues.

BRADLEY, Wayne N
Paul, Hastings, Janofsky & Walker LLP, Atlanta 404 815 2202
waynebradley@paulhastings.com
Recommended in Corporate/M&A
Practice Areas: Strategic matters including mergers, acquisitions and joint ventures; private equity and venture capital; internal investigations; representation of non-US companies in connection with US matters. Chief outside counsel for a number of firm clients.
Prof. Memberships: Corporate Code Committee (State Bar of Georgia); Board Member, Atlanta Bar Association Business and Finance Section; Association for Corporate Growth; Board Member, Thione International, Inc.
Career: Russ Berrie & Co. (NYSE:RUS) (1983-87); Clerk, Hon. Emmett Cox, US Court of Appeals for Eleventh Circuit (1990-91); McKenna Long & Aldridge (1991-2004; Chair, Corporate Department 2001-04).
Personal: Emory Law School (editor in chief, Emory Law Journal); Rutgers College.

BRAMLETT, Jeffrey
Bondurant, Mixson & Elmore, LLP, Atlanta 404 881 4192
bramlett@bmelaw.com
Recommended in Litigation
Practice Areas: Trial lawyer with extensive experience representing both plaintiffs and defendants in business disputes, especially class actions. Repeatedly certified by courts as lead counsel in class actions. Frequently called upon to represent lawyers and their law firms. Experienced in appellate advocacy, arbitration, mediation, and the resolution of cross-border disputes.
Prof. Memberships: Served as President of the Atlanta Bar Association and chaired its Section on Litigation. Represents Atlanta on the State Bar of Georgia's Board of Governors. Master Bencher, Lamar American Inn of Court.
Personal: JD, University of Texas School of Law; Editor, Texas Law Review; Law Clerk to Hon. Jerre S Williams, United States Court of Appeals for the Fifth Circuit; Legislative Aide to Hon Bob Eckhardt, Member of Congress (Texas); BA, University or Maryland.

BRANNON, Jeanna
Morris, Manning & Martin, LLP, Atlanta 404 504 7717
jbrannon@mmmlaw.com
Recommended in Real Estate
Practice Areas: Real estate capital markets, real estate development and finance.
Prof. Memberships: State Bar of Georgia, (Real Property Section), International Council of Shopping Centers.
Career: Jeanna is a Partner in MMM's real estate development and finance, and real estate capital markets groups. Her primary area of practice is real estate

development, with a concentration in mixed-use developments, shopping center development, and resort development. She has extensive experience in air rights development and residential resort developments in the Carribean.

BREWSTER, William
Kilpatrick Stockton LLP, Atlanta
404 815 6549
BBrewster@KilpatrickStockton.com
Recommended in Intellectual Property
Practice Areas: Client counseling and litigation in trademark, copyright, false advertising, unfair competition, trade secrets, and restrictive covenants.
Prof. Memberships: INTA (Brand Names Education Foundation Committee; former Publications and US Legislation Committees); AIPLA (Chair of the Trademark Litigation Committee); ACLA; NCLA; State Bar of Georgia (Antitrust, Intellectual Property and Sports & Entertainment Sections).
Career: Managing Partner; adjunct professor at the Emory University School of Law; lectures on trademark dilution, trade dress, trade secret, and restrictive covenant issues.
Personal: BA, Political Science and Economics, Emory University, with honors, 1984; MA Political Science, Emory University; JD, University of Virginia, 1987.

BUCKLER, Robert
Troutman Sanders LLP, Atlanta
404 885 3000
Recommended in Employment

BUTLER, James
Butler, Wooten, Fryhofer, Daughtery & Sullivan, LLP, Columbus
706 322 1990
Recommended in Litigation

BUTLER, James
Smith, Currie & Hancock LLP, Atlanta
404 521 3800
Recommended in Construction

CAEN, Melissa
Troutman Sanders LLP, Atlanta
404 885 3000
Recommended in Energy

CAHOON, Susan
Kilpatrick Stockton LLP, Atlanta
404 815 6325
SCahoon@KilpatrickStockton.com
Recommended in Litigation
Practice Areas: Patent infringement and trade secrets litigation and complex commercial litigation. Trained as a mediator and an arbitrator.
Prof. Memberships: ABA (Former Chair of committees in the TIPS and Litigation Sections and associate editor, 'Litigation'); American Arbitration Association (Georgia-Alabama Complex Case Panel); CPR Institute for Dispute Resolution (Panelist); American College of Trial Lawyers; American Law Institute; Lumpkin Inn of Court.
Career: Serves as firm General Counsel and ex officio member of the Executive

Committee; Partner since 1977.
Personal: BA History and Economics, Emory University, summa cum laude, 1968; JD, Harvard University, cum laude, 1971.

CAMPBELL, Charles E
McKenna Long & Aldridge, Atlanta
404 527 4590
ccampbell@mckennalong.com
Recommended in Bankruptcy
Practice Areas: Concentrates in bankruptcy, business litigation and public utilities law. Represents trustees, debtors and creditors and has served as a court-appointed trustee in bankruptcy reorganization proceedings. Served as lead counsel in the Pinegate bankruptcy litigation. Handles jury and non-jury cases involving securities, contracts, fraud, lender liability, trade secrets, computer software, professional malpractice and defamation. Founding member and managing director of Hicks, Maloof & Campbell, which merged with Long Aldridge & Norman, a predecessor firm to McKenna Long & Aldridge.
Prof. Memberships: American College of Bankruptcy; American College of Trial Lawyers; Richard B Russell Foundation, Chairman.
Publications: Co-editor, 'Bankruptcy Forms and Faculty' for seminars on bankruptcy law and rules for 'Norton Institutes on Bankruptcy Law'.
Personal: JD, Georgetown University Law Center, 1971. MA and BA, University of Georgia, 1964.

CAMPBELL, Margaret H
Ogletree, Deakins, Nash, Smoak & Stewart, PC, Atlanta 404 881 1300
meg.campbell@ogletreedeakins.com
Recommended in Employment
Practice Areas: Employment, class and collective action, whistleblower, and employment contract litigation, employment and labor law.
Prof. Memberships: American, Georgia, and Atlanta Bar Associations, Virginia State Bar, Georgia Association of Women Lawyers.
Career: Admitted: Georgia, Virginia, US Supreme Court, US Courts of Appeals (Fourth, Sixth, and Eleventh Circuits). Fellow, College of Labor and Employment Lawyers. Member, Ogletree Deakins' Board of Directors.
Publications: 17 Georgia Jurisprudence, 'Liability for Intentional Acts Committed in the Employment Setting', Lawyers Cooperative Publishing 1995.
Personal: Goucher College (AB, with Honors in Economics, 1978), Washington & Lee University School of Law (JD, 1981).

CAPERS, John
King & Spalding LLP, Atlanta
404 572 4658
jcapers@kslaw.com
Recommended in Corporate/M&A
Practice Areas: Corporate transactions, including domestic and international mergers, acquisitions, securities offerings, joint ventures and governmental and quasi-governmental borrowings. Extensive experience in public offerings of corporate finance and merger, acquisition and joint venture transactions involving different industry groups, including telecommunications, technology, and retail companies. M&A experience includes representing public and private companies, boards of directors and special committees, and financial advisors to companies involved in M&A transactions.
Prof. Memberships: American Bar Association; Atlanta Bar Association; State Bar of Georgia.
Personal: Vanderbilt University, high honors,1975; JD, high honors, University of Georgia School of Law, Order of Coif, 1978.

CARSON, Christopher L
Jones Day, Atlanta
404 581 8035
clcarson@jonesday.com
Recommended in Banking & Finance
Practice Areas: Chairs the firm's Financial Institutions Practice Committee. Has extensive experience in lending transactions, including secured and unsecured commercial loans, commercial finance, real estate loans, leasing transactions (including leveraged and synthetic leases), and letters of credit, as well as in Chapter 11 cases and workouts, primarily representing creditors, especially commercial banks and commercial finance companies. Recognized as a leading lawyer in numerous publications.
Prof. Memberships: American College of Commercial Finance Lawyers; State Bar of Georgia; Atlanta Bar Association; Southeastern Bankruptcy Law Institute; Georgia Financial Lawyers Conference.
Publications: Author and frequent lecturer on banking, bank lending, and bankruptcy matters.

CARSSOW, Tim
Kilpatrick Stockton LLP, Atlanta
404 815 6610
TCarssow@KilpatrickStockton.com
Recommended in Real Estate
Practice Areas: Commercial real estate including development and land use issues, limited liability companies and partnerships, and troubled real estate projects.
Prof. Memberships: American College of Real Estate Lawyers; Fernbank Museum and Freedom Park Conservancy (trustee); Midtown Alliance (Board of Directors); Paideia School (trustee); NAIOP; American Bar Association; Atlanta Bar Association; Georgia State Bar (former Chairman of the Real Property Law Section).
Career: Partner since 1976; Managing Partner of the firm (1996-2001).
Personal: BA, Trinity University, 1967; JD, University of Texas School of Law, 1970.

CASHDAN, Jeffrey
King & Spalding LLP, Atlanta
404 572 4818
jcashdan@kslaw.com
Recommended in Antitrust
Practice Areas: Antitrust, merger and acquisition and complex business litigation counseling, including securities, purported class actions and appellate matters.
Prof. Memberships: American Bar Association (Vice-Chair, Sherman Act Section 2, Antitrust and Litigation Sections); Editorial Board for the 2000 Annual Review of Antitrust Law Developments; 'Antitrust Law Journal' (former Editor); Atlanta Bar Association; Illinois State Bar; State Bar of Georgia (Chair, Antitrust Section).
Personal: BA, cum laude, Claremont McKenna College, 1987; London School of Economics and Political Science; JD, University of Chicago, 1990.

CHAMBERS, Robert
Smith, Currie & Hancock LLP, Atlanta
404 521 3800
Recommended in Construction

CHANDLER, John A
Sutherland Asbill & Brennan LLP, Atlanta 404 853 8029
john.chandler@sablaw.com
Recommended in Litigation
Practice Areas: Tries business cases. Has represented clients in numerous complex professional liability, securities, insurance and RICO cases. Has represented all of the Big Four accounting firms, several local accounting firms, several law firms, insurance companies, individuals and partnerships.
Prof. Memberships: Served as President of the Atlanta Bar Association, the Atlanta Council of Younger Lawyers, the Atlanta Legal Aid Society, the Atlanta Volunteer Lawyers Foundation, Travelers Aid of Metropolitan Atlanta. Chair of the Fulton County Ethics Board and Chair of the City of Atlanta Board of Ethics. Member of the Board of Governors of the State Bar of Georgia. Member of the International Association of Defense Counsel, Past President of the Bleckley American Inn of Court, a Master of the Lumpkin American Inn of Court, member of the Board of Visitors of the University of Tennessee College of Arts and Sciences, a Fellow of the American Bar Foundation and a Fellow of the American College of Trial Lawyers.
Personal: JD, Vanderbilt University School of Law, 1972, Order of Coif, Managing Editor, 'Vanderbilt Law Review'; BS, University of Tennessee, 1966.

CHEATHAM, Richard R
Kilpatrick Stockton LLP, Atlanta
404 815 6570
RCheatham@KilpatrickStockton.com
Recommended in Administrative & Public Law, Banking & Finance
Practice Areas: Financial institution representation, including bank regulatory matters and corporate and securities law applicable to financial institutions and their holding companies and other affiliates.
Prof. Memberships: American Bar Association; State Bar of Georgia.
Career: Partner since 1975.
Publications: Regularly speaks at seminars on the financial institutions industry.
Personal: BS, Commerce, University of Virginia, with Distinction, 1965; LLB, Harvard University, cum laude, 1968.

CIFELLI, James
Lamberth, Cifelli, Stokes & Stout, P.A., Atlanta 404 262 7373
Recommended in Bankruptcy

CLARK, Reginald J
Sutherland Asbill & Brennan LLP, Atlanta 404 853 8032
reggie.clark@sablaw.com
Recommended in Tax
Practice Areas: A tax practitioner with particular experience in corporate taxation and in planning corporate acquisitions, restructurings and other transactions. Practice includes advising a number of cooperative organizations, both tax-exempt and taxable. Also experienced in handling tax controversies and representing clients before the National Office of the Internal Revenue Service in connection with requests for rulings or technical advice.
Prof. Memberships: Former adjunct professor of law in the Emory University School of Law's Graduate Tax Program. Presently Chair-Elect of the Corporate Tax Committee of the American Bar Association's Tax Section, and has spoken at a number of tax seminars and bar programs. Member of the Board of Trustees of the Southern Federal Tax Institute and the Georgia Federal Tax Conference, and member of the American Law Institute.
Personal: JD, with distinction, Duke University School of Law, 1978, Notes and Comments Editor, 'Duke Law Journal'; AB, Duke University, 1975 Phi Beta Kappa.

CLAY, Stephens
Kilpatrick Stockton LLP, Atlanta
404 815 6514
SClay@KilpatrickStockton.com
Recommended in Litigation
Practice Areas: Trial and appellate experience in a broad range of business litigation matters, including contract disputes, products liability and business tort actions, and intellectual property disputes. Extensive experience in international arbitration disputes in Europe, the United States and Latin America, frequently serving as an advocate and as an arbitrator.
Prof. Memberships: American Bar Association Antitrust Section; Georgia, Pennsylvania and District of Columbia Bar Associations; Chartered Institute of Arbitrators.

Career: Certified mediator; former adjunct professor, University of Virginia. **Personal:** BA, Yale University, 1964; JD, University of Virginia School of Law, 'Virginia Law Review,' 1967.

CLELAND, A Craig
Ogletree, Deakins, Nash, Smoak & Stewart, PC, Atlanta
404 881 1300
craig.cleland@ogletreedeakins.com
Recommended in Employment
Practice Areas: Employment law, class action defense, litigation.
Prof. Memberships: ABA. Georgia and Atlanta Bar Associations.
Career: Partner since 2003.
Publications: Contributor, Lindemann/Grossman, Employment Discrimination Law (4th ed). Co-editor, Lindemann/Grossman, Employment Discrimination Law (3d ed).
Personal: Georgia 'Legal Elite' Labor & Employment Lawyer, Georgia Trend magazine (2003 & 2004). Law Clerk, The Hon Marvin H. Shoob (N.D. Ga.). Editor in chief, Georgia State University Law Review. Georgia State University (JD, cum laude 1992). Yale University (STM, honors 1983). Vanderbilt University (M Div, honors 1981/Folkerth Scholar). Valdosta State University (BA, cum laude 1978).

CLINEBURG, William
King & Spalding LLP, Atlanta
404 572 4701
bclineburg@kslaw.com
Recommended in Employment
Practice Areas: Employment litigation, representing Fortune 100 automotive, chemical, tobacco, computer, oil, textile and retail companies. Also represents hospitals and colleges in state and federal courts throughout the country.
Prof. Memberships: American Bar Association (Member, EEO Subcommittee, Labor and Employment Law Section); Atlanta Bar Association; fellow, College of Labor and Employment Lawyers; State Bar of Georgia.
Publications: 'Employment Discrimination,' 35 Mercer Law Review 1169 (1984).
Personal: BA, Brown University, 1965; JD, cum laude, University of Georgia School of Law, 1970.

COALSON Jr, John L
Alston & Bird LLP, Atlanta
404 881 7482
jcoalson@alston.com
Recommended in Tax
Practice Areas: Focuses on counseling/planning as well as dispute and litigation work in the state and local tax area, and unclaimed property.
Prof. Memberships: Trustee and member of the Advisory Board of the Paul Hartman Memorial Institute on State and Local Taxation and Editorial Board of the Journal of Multistate Taxation.
Publications: Authored or co-authored over a dozen law review articles that

have appeared in the 'Tax Lawyer', 'Journal of State Taxation', 'Georgia Law Review', 'Mercer Law Review', and 'The Georgia Bar Journal', as well as the 'BNA Portfolio on Unclaimed Property'.
Personal: BBA, Emory University (1974); JD, University of Georgia (1977).

COHEN, Ezra
Troutman Sanders LLP, Atlanta
404 885 3000
Recommended in Bankruptcy

COHEN, Jerold
Sutherland Asbill & Brennan LLP, Atlanta 404 853 8038
jerry.cohen@sablaw.com
Recommended in Tax
Practice Areas: Represents clients in domestic and international tax planning and controversy matters. Has planned and structured corporate acquisitions and dispositions, successfully litigated federal tax cases, handled matters before the IRS and Treasury Department, and handled legislative matters for clients. Has testified before Congressional tax writing committees and worked with the Joint Committee on Taxation.
Prof. Memberships: Former Chair, IRS Advisory Council; Chair, American College of Tax Counsel; Past Chair, Tax Section of the ABA; Member, Board of Advisors, Virginia Tax Review; Past Member, Little Brown and Commerce Clearing House Tax Advisory Boards; Vice Chair, American College of Tax Counsel; Former Member, Board of Advisors, IRS's Continuing Professional Education Program; Former Member, Advisory Group to the Staff of the Senate Finance Committee on its Subchapter C Revision Act; Member, American Law Institute and its Tax Advisory Board.
Publications: Published in 'The Journal of Taxation', 'The Tax Lawyer', Practicing Law Institute publications, 'The Journal of the American Bar Association' publications and the N.Y.U Tax Institutes, and has spoken at numerous tax institutes. Adjunct professor of law, Emory University (1967-76).
Personal: LLB, magna cum laude, Harvard Law School, 1961, Book Review Editor, 'Harvard Law Review'; BBA, Tulane University, 1957, Beta Gamma Sigma.

COIL, James
Kilpatrick Stockton LLP, Atlanta
404 815 6348
JCoil@KilpatrickStockton.com
Recommended in Employment
Practice Areas: Represents management in all phases of employment matters. Numerous successful jury verdicts and summary judgments, and favorable settlements in many other cases. Successfully defended multi-plaintiff and class action claims alleging wage/hour; race, sex, and age discrimination; and ERISA violations.

Prof. Memberships: Atlanta Bar Association.
Career: Captain, Judge Advocate, US Marine Corps.
Publications: Frequent speaker and author or co-author of more than 50 articles, including 'The New Supervisorís EEO Handbook,' a guide to help front-line managers become familiar with federal antidiscrimination laws
Personal: BA, Duke University, 1967; JD, Harvard Law School, 1970; Atlanta Symphony Orchestra (Board of Directors).

COLEMAN, Aubrey
Smith, Currie & Hancock LLP, Atlanta
404 521 3800
Recommended in Construction

CONNOLLY, Dennis J
Alston & Bird LLP, Atlanta
404 881 7269
dconnolly@alston.com
Recommended in Bankruptcy
Practice Areas: Commercial bankruptcy.
Prof. Memberships: Chair, Bankruptcy Section of the Atlanta Bar Association and member of State Bar of Georgia and American Bankruptcy Institute; Fellow, American College of Bankruptcy.
Career: Recent engagements include representing Chapter 11 debtors, LaRoche Industries and Galey & Lord, and creditors' committees for Einstein Noah Bagel and Dan River. Represented the Enron Corp. Examiner in the Enron Corp. bankruptcy.
Publications: Published widely in 'Legal Times', the 'Bankruptcy Strategist', and the 'Norton Annual Survey of Bankruptcy Law'.
Personal: BA, University of Michigan (1982); JD, cum laude, University of South Carolina (1986).

CONRAD, Albert H
King & Spalding LLP, Atlanta
404 572 4807
cconrad@kslaw.com
Recommended in Banking & Finance
Practice Areas: Representing banks and lending institutions in private debt financings and major financing transactions. Serves as the principal outside lawyer for a number of the firm's corporate and REIT clients.
Prof. Memberships: American Bar Association (Banking Law Section); American College of Commercial Finance Lawyers (former Chair, Uniform Commercial Code Committee); Atlanta Bar Association; State Bar of Georgia (Chair, Corporate and Banking Law Section).
Personal: BS, with highest honors, University of Tennessee, 1972; JD, University of Virginia, Omicron Delta Kappa; Phi Kappa Phi; Order of the Coif, 1975. Frequent speaker on lending-related topics.

COOK, Philip C
Alston & Bird LLP, Atlanta
404 881 7491
pcook@alston.com
Recommended in Tax
Practice Areas: Concentrates practice on federal tax and ERISA controversies.
Prof. Memberships: Member of the Board of Editors of the Journal of Taxation of Financial Institutions (formerly the Journal of Bank Taxation). Has also served as Chair of the Committee on Banks and Savings Institutions of the ABA Tax Section.
Career: Deputy Managing Partner of the firm. Frequent speaker at national Bank Tax Conferences and other seminars and institutes. Listed in two leading legal publications.
Personal: BS, with honors, Georgia Institute of Technology (1968); JD, cum laude, Harvard University (1971).

CORGAN, Brian
Kilpatrick Stockton LLP, Atlanta
404 815 6217
BCorgan@KilpatrickStockton.com
Recommended in Construction
Practice Areas: Construction contracts, litigation, and alternative disputes resolution. Has handled construction disputes involving nuclear and coal-fired power plants, international airport runway construction, cogeneration (power, cement and lime) plants, wastewater treatment plants, steel mills, oil refineries, hospitals, and other projects.
Prof. Memberships: Georgia and Louisiana Bar Associations; American Arbitration Association's National Panel of Arbitrators.
Publications: Writes and lectures extensively throughout the US on the subjects of avoiding litigation on large and complex construction projects, alternative disputes resolution procedures and processes, and effective construction litigation.
Personal: BA, Tulane University, 1976; JD, Tulane University, summa cum laude, 1979.

COWEN, Stephen
King & Spalding LLP, Atlanta
404 572 4688
scowen@kslaw.com
Recommended in Litigation
Practice Areas: Special matters focusing on white collar criminal defense of corporations, individuals, and civil fraud matters, including healthcare, government procurement, securities, tax, antitrust, foreign payments and campaign finance investigations. Representations have included defense of government and Congressional inquiries and litigation of civil fraud and misrepresentation actions. Extensive government experience as a prosecutor and civil litigator. Frequent lecturer on corporate investigations.
Prof. Memberships: State Bar of Georgia, Florida and the District of Columbia.

Personal: Emory University, 1969; JD, Harvard Law School, 1972.

CREWDSON, Robert
Alston & Bird LLP, Atlanta
404 881 7291
rcrewdson@alston.com
Recommended in Construction
Practice Areas: Construction contracts; mediation and arbitration of construction claims.
Prof. Memberships: Member, International Council of Shopping Centers, American College of Healthcare Executives, American Health Lawyers Association, State Bar of Georgia, Atlanta Bar Association (former Chair, Construction Law Section).
Career: National transactional and litigation practice. Listed in 2005-06 edition of 'The Best Lawyers in America.'
Publications: Lectures and publishes frequently regarding a broad range of construction matters. Current guest lecturer, Georgia Institute of Technology.
Personal: BA, magna cum laude, University of the South (1983); MA, College of William & Mary (1987); JD, University of Virginia (1987).

CRISAFI, Frank
Powell Goldstein LLP, Atlanta
404 572 6600
Recommended in Tax

CURTIS, J Vaughan
Alston & Bird LLP, Atlanta
404 881 7397
vcurtis@alston.com
Recommended in Corporate/M&A
Practice Areas: Represents both public and private companies in merger and acquisition transactions, including advising boards and outside board members on matters of corporate governance, change of control issues, and anti-takeover strategies. Also represents issuers and underwriters in securities offerings.
Career: Co-Head of the firm's Transactional Practices. Former member of firm's Executive Committee. Listed in two leading legal publications in both corporate finance and healthcare. Prior to joining Alston & Bird in 1978, worked at The White House during the Ford Administration.
Personal: BA (1973), MA (1975), JD (1978) - University of Kentucky.

CUSHING, Paul M
Alston & Bird LLP, Atlanta
404 881 7578
pcushing@alston.com
Recommended in Banking & Finance
Practice Areas: Focuses his practice on representing both financial institutions and companies in a wide variety of corporate finance transactions, including syndicated financings, secured financings, acquisition financings, asset-based loans, securitizations, structured financings, leveraged and synthetic leases and private placements. Much of his practice

centers on the representation of financial institutions and their capital markets groups in the financing of real estate companies.
Prof. Memberships: Member of the Business Law Section of the American Bar Association and has served as the Chairman of UCC Subcommittee of the Business Law Section of the Georgia State Bar.
Career: Member of the firm's Leveraged Capital Group.
Personal: BA, magna cum laude, (1984), JD (1987) - Vanderbilt University School of Law.

DALTON, John
Troutman Sanders LLP, Atlanta
404 885 3000
Recommended in Litigation

DANIEL, Harold T
Holland & Knight LLP, Atlanta
404 817 8500
harold.daniel@hklaw.com
Recommended in Litigation
Practice Areas: Partner in the firm's Litigation Section, maintains a firm-wide commercial litigation practice. He has handled many lengthy jury trials and routinely deals with complex factual and legal issues involving antitrust, securities, business torts and commercial law. Daniel represented the Eleventh Circuit on the Standing Committee of the Federal Judiciary of the American Bar Association from 2000-03. He is a fellow of the American College of Trial Lawyers, a former president of the State Bar of Georgia, and received the Distinguished Service Award of the State Bar of Georgia in 2001.

DANIEL, Laurie Webb
Holland & Knight LLP, Atlanta
404 817 8500
laurie.daniel@hklaw.com
Recommended in Litigation
Practice Areas: Partner in the firm's Litigation Section, she chairs the Appellate Practice Team at Holland & Knight LLP. Her appellate work frequently addresses business, competition, and medical liability issues, among others. Daniel's active motions practice includes class action and other types of complex litigation. She has substantial experience in the trial courts and has argued before the United States Supreme Court. Daniel has served as a commentator for CNN on Supreme Court arguments and on the faculty of many continuing legal education programs.

DAVID, Todd R
Alston & Bird LLP, Atlanta
404 881 7357
tdavid@alston.com
Recommended in Litigation
Practice Areas: D&O litigation, securities litigation, internal investigations and corporate governance, professional liability litigation, complex commercial litigation.

Prof. Memberships: State Bar of Georgia.
Career: Co-Chair, Alston & Bird Litigation Area; member, firm Management Committee; Former Chair, Alston & Bird Securities Litigation Group. Served as lead counsel in numerous class actions, trials, arbitrations, and mediations; served as law clerk for Honorable Marvin H Shoob, United State District Judge.
Publications: Numerous authorships in such publications as 'Securities Regulation Law Journal,' 'The National Law Journal,' 'The Journal of Investment Compliance,' 'Directors Monthly,' 'The Trial Lawyer,' National Association of Corporate Directors,' and 'Legal Times.'
Personal: BA, Queens College (1982); JD, Northeastern University (1985).

DAVIS, Lee
Griffin Cochrane & Marshall, Atlanta
404 523 2000
lcdavis@gcm-atty.com
Recommended in Construction
Practice Areas: Construction law.
Prof. Memberships: American (Litigation and Public Contracts Sections, Forum on Construction Industry) and Atlanta (Alternative Dispute Resolution, Construction, and Litigation Sections) Bar Associations; State Bar of Georgia.
Career: President and Shareholder, Griffin Cochrane & Marshall; Martindale Hubbell AV rated; listed in 'The Best Lawyers in America' (2005-06); selected by peers as 'Georgia Super-lawyer' in construction (2004, 2005 by Atlanta Magazine). Lead counsel in complex cases in court (trials before both judges and juries), arbitration, negotiation, and mediation, throughout the nation and internationally in disputes relating to power plants, industrial facilities, wastewater treatment plants, hotels, resorts, condominiums, shopping centers, hospitals, office buildings, and apartments.
Publications: Co-author: 'Construction Law for Builders, Owners and Designers' (1999); 'Design-Build Strategies' (1999); 'Environmental Problems of the Georgia Jobsite' (1992). Lecturer: 'Design-Build Construction,' Centers for Disease Control and Prevention, Atlanta, GA (2004); 'Fundamentals of Construction Law,' Sterling Education Services (2004); 'Practical Construction Law,' Federal Publications (1989-91; 2000-04); 'Construction Contracts Year in Review Conference,' Thomson-West (2003); 'Masters Institute in Construction Contracting,' Federal Publications (2000-03); 'Construction Management,' American Institute for Professional Training and Development (2000); 'Design-Build Strategies,' American Institute for Professional Training (1999-2000); 'Construction Claims,' American Institute for Professional Training (1997-99); 'Environ-

mental Problems on the Georgia Jobsite,' Federal Publications (1992); 'Construction Law,' The American Law Center in Moscow, Russia (1992); 'Architect/Engineer Liability under Georgia Law' (1988); 'Construction Law' Colorado State University (1983).
Personal: Emory University (JD, 1982); Williams College (BA, magna cum laude, 1978). Commercial pilot and flight instructor.

DEAKINS Jr, Homer L
Ogletree, Deakins, Nash, Smoak & Stewart, PC, Atlanta 404 881 1300
homer.deakins@ogletreedeakins.com
Recommended in Employment
Practice Areas: Labor and employment law, employment litigation.
Prof. Memberships: Bar Associations of: GA, DC, NY, SC, TN, TX, American Bar Association.
Career: Admitted Georgia, South Carolina, Tennessee, Texas, DC, New York, US Supreme Court, US Court of Appeals (Second, Fourth, Fifth, Sixth, Eleventh Circuits, DC), US District Courts (South Carolina; Northern, Middle, Southern Georgia; Eastern and Middle Tennessee; DC; Southern and Eastern Texas; Southern Alabama). Listed in The Best Lawyers in America; fellow, College of Labor and Employment Lawyers.
Personal: Southern Methodist University (BA, 1957), University of Texas School of Law (LLB, cum laude, 1960).

DEANE, Richard
Jones Day, Atlanta
404 581 8502
rhdeane@jonesday.com
Recommended in Litigation
Practice Areas: Concentrates on corporate criminal investigations and general litigation. He has extensive experience in conducting grand jury investigations and acquired a wide range of unique litigation experience while serving as a US magistrate judge. Appointed by President Clinton as US attorney for the Northern District of Georgia in 1998. During his term, Attorney General Janet Reno appointed him to serve on the Attorney General's Advisory Committee. In March 2001, he was named by Time Magazine to the 'Time 100 List of Innovators' for his creativity and determination in the application of the RICO Statute.

DEGNAN, Peter
Alston & Bird LLP, Atlanta
404 881 7743
pdegnan@alston.com
Recommended in Energy
Practice Areas: Focuses practice on energy law, legal issues impacting secondary educational institutions and environmental litigation.
Prof. Memberships: Member of the State Bar of Georgia, Atlanta Bar Association.
Personal: BS, US Naval Academy (1968); JD, Syracuse University (1976).

DEHIHNS III, Lee A
Alston & Bird LLP, Atlanta
404 881 7151
ldehihns@alston.com
Recommended in Environment
Practice Areas: Concentrates on regulatory, environmental and environment defense litigation matters, including corporate audits, compliance program development, debarment, white collar criminal defense, hazardous waste, air quality, water quality and wetlands matters.
Prof. Memberships: Member of the Council of the American Bar Association's Section of Environment, Energy and Resources, Chair of Strategic Planning Committee, previous Chair of Water Quality and Wetlands Committee.
Career: Frequent speaker and author on water quality and quantity, corporate environmental responsibility, and citizen suits. Listed in a leading US legal publication.
Personal: BS, University of Scranton (1967); JD, Catholic University of America (1974).

DEMPSTER, Hazen
Troutman Sanders LLP, Atlanta
404 885 3000
Recommended in Banking & Finance

DENT, Leslie
Paul, Hastings, Janofsky & Walker LLP, Atlanta 404 815 2233
lesliedent@paulhastings.com
Recommended in Employment
Practice Areas: Practice involves all aspects of employment litigation and counseling for private employers. Has tried nearly 25 cases, most of which were individual employment discrimination cases. Also represents employers in class action litigation and multiple plaintiff cases.
Prof. Memberships: American Bar Association Labor and Employment Law Section, State Bar of Georgia, Atlanta Bar Association.
Career: Partner at Paul, Hastings, Janofsky & Walker LLP.
Personal: Received her BA degree, magna cum laude with honors, in 1980 from Vanderbilt University, and JD degree in 1983 from Northwestern University School of Law.

DIAL, David
Weinberg, Wheeler, Hudgins, Gunn & Dial, LLC, Atlanta 404 876 2700
Recommended in Construction

DOBBS, Edward
Parker, Hudson, Rainer & Dobbs LLP, Atlanta 404 523 5300
Recommended in Banking & Finance, Bankruptcy

DOMBY, Arthur
Troutman Sanders LLP, Atlanta
404 885 3000
Recommended in Environment

DORRIS, William
Kilpatrick Stockton LLP, Atlanta
404 815 6104
BDorris@KilpatrickStockton.com
Recommended in Construction
Practice Areas: Though much of his practice is focused on assisting clients in avoiding construction disputes or resolving them through mediation or other alternative dispute resolution methods, he has been extensively involved in trials, arbitrations, and administrative proceedings.
Prof. Memberships: State Bar of Georgia; Kentucky Bar Association; American Bar Association.
Publications: Has written a number of articles on construction law, and co-authored the two volume book, 'Construction Disputes: Practice Guide with Forms'.
Personal: BA, University of Kentucky, high Distinction, Phi Beta Kappa, 1976; JD, University of Kentucky, high Distinction, Order of the Coif, 1979.

DORSEY, Rufus
Parker, Hudson, Rainer & Dobbs LLP, Atlanta 404 523 5300
Recommended in Bankruptcy

DOUGLAS, John L
Alston & Bird LLP, Atlanta
404 881 7880
jdouglas@alston.com
Recommended in Administrative & Public Law, Banking & Finance
Practice Areas: Regulation of financial institutions, mergers, acquisitions and other transactions.
Prof. Memberships: Steering Committee, Financial Services Volunteer Corps.; member, State Bar of Georgia and Bar of Washington DC; member, Executive Committee, Banking Law Section, Federal Bar Association.
Career: General Counsel, Federal Deposit Insurance Corporation (1987-89); listed in four leading legal publications with regards to banking law.
Publications: Chairman, Editorial Board, Electronic Banking Law and Commerce Report.
Personal: BA, cum laude, Davidson College (1972); JD, magna cum laude, University of Georgia (1977).

DOWDY, L Craig
McKenna Long & Aldridge, Atlanta
404 527 4180
cdowdy@mckennalong.com
Recommended in Energy
Practice Areas: Focuses on state and federal public utility law, energy, telecommunications and campaign and election law. Work includes strategic counseling and commercial and regulatory litigation for corporate clients. Practice also includes commercial litigation and public policy representation. Previously served as manager of business and product planning responsible for strategic planning, product development and marketing communications

when he left Westinghouse Power Systems to practice law.
Prof. Memberships: 2000 George W Bush for President Campaign, Cobb County Co-Chairman, Georgia Steering Committee, and Finance Committee; 2000 George W Bush Recount Team - West Palm Beach, Florida; Barr for Congress Campaign Chairman, Treasurer, and Counsel; Saxby Chambliss for Senate Leadership Council; Governor-Elect Sonny Perdue Inaugural Committee; Cobb County Republican Party, General Counsel; Coverdell Leadership Institute; Georgia Republican Foundation; Georgia Republican Lawyers Foundation; Georgia Republican Party, State Committee; Georgia State Bar; National Moot Court Committee (Past Chairman); Federalist Society.
Personal: JD, Georgia State University College of Law, 1988. BS, Electrical Engineering, Auburn University, 1979. Listed as one of the Best Lawyers in Atlanta in 'Atlanta Magazine'. He is the Endowment Board Chairman and Administrative Committee Chairman of St. Peter St. Paul Episcopal Church.

DUNLEVIE, Steven S
Womble Carlyle Sandridge & Rice PLLC, Atlanta 404 888 7401
sdunlevie@wcsr.com
Recommended in Administrative & Public Law, Banking & Finance
Practice Areas: Mr Dunlevie has advised 250+ financial services companies as special counsel on regulatory compliance, corporate governance, capital formation, mergers/acquisitions, de novo bank organization and problem asset resolution.
Prof. Memberships: State Bar of Georgia; Atlanta and American Bar Associations; Board of Directors, Georgia and Metro Atlanta Chambers of Commerce; Board of Visitors, University of North Carolina.
Career: Leader, Bank Regulatory Team of Capital Markets Practice Group; Managing Member, Atlanta; member, firm Management Committee. Founding Partner, Parker, Johnson, Cook & Dunlevie, which merged with Womble Carlyle in 1996.
Personal: JD, 1973, Emory University; AB, 1970, University of North Carolina.

EGAN, Michael
King & Spalding LLP, Atlanta
404 572 4753
megan@kslaw.com
Recommended in Corporate/M&A
Practice Areas: Mergers and acquisitions, joint ventures and strategic alliances. Substantial experience representing international companies in cross-border transactions. Serves as counsel for the Atlanta Falcons NFL franchise. Served as European Transactions Counsel to The Coca-Cola Company.
Prof. Memberships: American Bar

Association; International Bar Association; State Bar of Georgia.
Personal: BA, University of North Carolina, 1978; JD, cum laude, Harvard University, Phi Beta Kappa, 1982; Morehead Scholar, University of North Carolina.

ELGISON, Martin J
Alston & Bird LLP, Atlanta
404 881 7167
melgison@alston.com
Recommended in Intellectual Property
Practice Areas: Founder and Co-Coordinator of the firm's intellectual property practice groups and the leader of the Intellectual Property-Transactional Group. Practices in all facets of intellectual property law with a focus on sports, media, technology, and electronic commerce.
Career: Listed in a leading US legal publication since 1991-92.
Publications: Spoken and written frequently on intellectual property matters, including copyright protection for computer screen displays, the use of metatags and hyperlinks, the Digital Millenium Copyright Act, and intellectual property litigation.
Personal: BA, University of South Florida (1972); JD, cum laude, University of Miami, (1981).

ELLMAN, Jeffrey B
Jones Day, Atlanta
404 581 8309
jbellman@jonesday.com
Recommended in Bankruptcy
Practice Areas: Coordinator of the Business Restructuring and Reorganization Practice in Jones Day's Atlanta office. Practices primarily on corporate bankruptcy, restructuring, and bankruptcy litigation matters. He has provided insolvency-related advice to clients in litigation and transactional contexts and has participated in out-of-court restructurings. He counsels clients on fraudulent conveyance, illegal dividend, preferential transfer, fiduciary duty, and corporate formalities issues. Named as one of the 'Outstanding Young Bankruptcy Lawyers' in the United States in Turnarounds & Workouts in 2001.
Prof. Memberships: American Bankruptcy Institute; Turnaround Management Association; Bankruptcy Section of the Atlanta Bar Association.

ENSOR, R Steve
Alston & Bird LLP, Atlanta
404 881 7448
sensor@alston.com
Recommended in Employment
Practice Areas: Represented management for over 19 years in all areas of labor and employment law, including employment litigation, traditional labor union relations and affirmative action planning.
Prof. Memberships: Member of the State Bar of Georgia, the Georgia Bar Association and the American Bar Association.

Publications: Lectured and written extensively in all areas of labor and employment law. Frequent speaker and panelist for the American Management Association and the Institute for Applied Management and Law.
Personal: BA, Duke University (1982); JD, Wake Forest University (1985).

ERNST, Andrew
Hunter, Maclean, Exley & Dunn, PC, Savannah 912 236 0261
Recommended in Environment

EWING, Jim
Kilpatrick Stockton LLP, Atlanta
404 815 6494
JEwing@KilpatrickStockton.com
Recommended in Intellectual Property
Practice Areas: Intellectual property strategy, patent litigation and patent portfolio prosecution and management.
Prof. Memberships: Patent Bar of the United States; American Intellectual Property Law Association; American Bar Association; State Bar of Georgia; Atlanta Bar Association; Practicing Law Institute Annual Program on Patent Litigation (Co-Chair); Federalist Society's IP Committee (Chair).
Career: Partner since 1989.
Publications: Writing and speaking credits include American Law Media's Patent Strategist (Board of Editors); authored 'Patent Litigation: Strategic Planning' chapter in Aspen Publishing Company's new book on patent litigation.
Personal: BS, Aerospace Engineering, United States Naval Academy, 1973; JD, University of Virginia Law School, 1981.

FARRIS Jr, James G
Alston & Bird LLP, Atlanta
404 881 7896
jfarris@alston.com
Recommended in Real Estate
Practice Areas: Real estate; commercial real estate investment; development and leasing.
Prof. Memberships: Pension Real Estate Association (PREA); Association of Foreign Investors in US Real Estate (AFIRE); State Bar of Georgia; Atlanta Bar Association.
Career: Extensive experience representing and counseling pension funds and their advisors, other institutional investors, as well as developers, in various aspects of real estate law. 'Cradle to grave' practice including land acquisition, development, joint ventures, redevelopment, protective covenants, financing, acquisitions, leasing, and sales.
Publications: Frequent speaker and writer on commercial real estate issues.
Personal: BA, Wesleyan University (1984); JD, University of North Carolina (1989).

FEESE, Suzanne
King & Spalding LLP, Atlanta
404 572 4600
sfeese@kslaw.com
Recommended in Tax
Practice Areas: Represents clients in all

stages of the IRS administrative process and in tax litigation. Extensive experience in a wide range of business/transactional tax areas, with particular emphasis on the taxation of partnerships, taxation of foreign persons with US activities, and the representation of clients in complex partnership and structured financing transactions
Prof. Memberships: State Bar of Georgia; American Bar Association (Member, Tax Section).
Personal: BA, Agnes Scott College, 1984, valedictorian; JD Yale University, 1987.

FERDINANDS, Paul
King & Spalding LLP, Atlanta
404 572 3450
pferdinands@kslaw.com
Recommended in Bankruptcy
Practice Areas: Bankruptcy and commercial matters, focusing on representing parties in connection with transactions occurring in Chapter 11 cases, debtors in connection with business bankruptcy cases and with the bankruptcy aspects of structured finance transactions. Represents Chapter 11 debtors in a variety of industries, creditors' committees, parties in connection with the purchase and sale of secured and unsecured claims, institutional lenders extending debtor-in-possession financings, and companies in out-of-court debt restructurings.
Prof. Memberships: American Bar Association; Atlanta Bar Association (Member, Section on Banking and Bankruptcy); State Bar of Georgia.
Personal: BA, magna cum laude, University of Virginia, 1983; JD, Stanford University, 1986.

FLEMING, John H
Sutherland Asbill & Brennan LLP, Atlanta 404 853 8065
john.fleming@sablaw.com
Recommended in Litigation
Practice Areas: Chaired Sutherland's Litigation Group (1999-2004). Experienced in complex business litigation, including franchise, professional liability, intellectual property, tax and securities. Experienced as an attorney and arbitrator in alternative dispute resolution mechanisms. Serves as Eastern Regional Counsel for dealer and general litigation for an automobile manufacturer. Trial victories for both owners of intellectual property and alleged infringers, favorable jury verdicts in state and federal court in Georgia and elsewhere, successful defense of RICO class action claims in consumer litigation and an arbitration award for an insurance company in excess of $55,000,000. Handled an appointed death penalty case, from 1980 through 1992, in which he had the death penalty reversed once by the United States Supreme Court and twice by the Georgia Supreme Court, and finally won before a jury. Served as an adjunct professor at Emory Law

School.
Career: Clerked in Dallas with Judge Irving Goldberg of the US Court of Appeals for the Fifth Circuit.
Personal: JD, magna cum laude, Harvard Law School, 1975, Senior Editor, 'Harvard Law Review'; MA, Florida State University, 1972; BA, Emory University, 1970, Phi Beta Kappa.

FLETCHER, Jennifer
Griffin Cochrane & Marshall, Atlanta
404 523 2000
jwfletcher@gcm-atty.com
Recommended in Construction
Practice Areas: Construction industry issues exclusively.
Prof. Memberships: American College of Construction Lawyers (Fellow); Lumpkin Inn of Court (Master); American Arbitration Association (Construction Arbitrator); ABA (Forum on the Construction Industry; Public Contracts, Litigation Sections); Atlanta Bar Association (Construction, Litigation Sections); State Bar of Georgia; The Florida Bar.
Career: Shareholder since 1988.
Publications: Has lectured extensively on construction industry matters, including Managing Complex Construction Cases (ABA), Construction Contracts Year in Review and Practical Construction Law (Federal Publications), Design-Build Strategies, and at Georgia Tech.
Personal: University of Georgia School of Law (JD cum laude, 1981); University of Florida (BA high honors, 1978).

FLINN, Patrick J
Alston & Bird LLP, Atlanta
404 881 7920
pflinn@alston.com
Recommended in Intellectual Property
Practice Areas: Focuses practice on the resolution of technology-based disputes, particularly patent, trade secret, and copyright litigation.
Prof. Memberships: Chair of National Law Alumni Board of Georgetown University Law Center.
Career: Listed in a leading US legal publication.
Publications: Writer and lecturer on subjects of law and technology. Author of the 'Handbook of Intellectual Property Claims and Remedies'. Speaks regularly in national CLE presentations on Patent Law, Computer Law and other technology subjects.
Personal: AB, Stanford University (1978); JD, Georgetown University (1982).

FLOYD, John
Bondurant, Mixson & Elmore, LLP, Atlanta 404 881 4159
floyd@bmelaw.com
Recommended in Litigation
Practice Areas: Extensive experience in business torts litigation, particularly civil litigation under federal and state Racketeer Influenced and Corrupt Organiza-

tions (RICO) statutes. Has also worked as a special prosecutor in two of the state of Georgia's largest RICO prosecutions. Also experienced in litigation under the Federal False Claims Act and the conduct of corporate internal investigations.
Prof. Memberships: Member: American Bar Association (Chair: Antitrust Section Civil RICO Committee, 1997-2001); State Bar of Georgia; Atlanta Bar Association; Special Assistant Attorney General, State of Georgia, 1997-2000; Special Assistant District Attorney, Augusta, 1997-2000, and Stone Mountain Judicial Districts; Member: Fulton County Board of Ethics, 1998-2004; Faculty Member: National College of District Attorneys, White Collar Crime Course, 2002-05.
Publications: 'RICO State by State: A Guide to Litigation Under the State Racketeering Statutes' (American Bar Association, Section of Antitrust Law, 1998); 'The Right Against Self-Incrimination in Civil Litigation' (American Bar Association, Section of Antitrust Law, 2001)(editor and chapter author).
Personal: AB degree, with honors, Brown University, 1980; JD degree, Emory University, 1983.

FORRY, Robert
Troutman Sanders LLP, Atlanta
404 885 3000
Recommended in Energy

FORTE, Stephen
Smith Gambrell & Russell LLP, Atlanta
404 815 3500
Recommended in Litigation

FOX, Steven F
Rogers & Hardin, Atlanta
404 522 4700
SEF@rh-law.com
Recommended in Corporate/M&A
Practice Areas: Corporate finance; mergers and acquisitions; corporate governance.
Prof. Memberships: American Bar Association; Federal Regulation of Securities Committee; State Bar of Georgia: Committee on Securities Law; Former Chairman, Business Law Section, State Bar of Georgia.
Career: Founding Partner.
Publications: Frequent author and speaker on topics of corporate and securities law.
Personal: University of Michigan (JD, 1973); University of North Carolina (BA, 1968).

FRYER, William
King & Spalding LLP, Atlanta
404 572 4911
bfryer@kslaw.com
Recommended in Real Estate
Practice Areas: Mergers, acquisitions, funds formation and project developments with emphasis on real estate securitizations.
Prof. Memberships: American Bar Association; Atlanta Bar Association; State Bar of Georgia; University of Vir-

ginia School of Law (Alumni Council).
Personal: BA, University of Virginia,
1971; JD, University of Virginia, Phi Beta
Kappa, Omicron Delta Kappa, Order of
the Coif, 1974.

GALLO, Barbara
Epstein Becker & Green PC, Atlanta
404 923 9000
Recommended in Environment

GARRETT, G Lee
Jones Day, Atlanta
404 581 8013
ggarrett@jonesday.com
Recommended in Litigation
Practice Areas: Heads the Litigation
Group of the Atlanta office. His practice
emphasizes complex litigation and has
involved First Amendment, product liability, construction, contract, and envi-
ronmental-related issues; First Amendment litigation, libel, slander, defamation, and causes of action arising under
the Fair Credit Reporting Act; and environmental litigation. He has argued
cases before various US District Courts,
US Courts of Appeal, the United States
Supreme Court, the United States Government Board of Contract Appeals, the
Environmental Protection Agency, and
various state and local courts.
Prof. Memberships: American Board of
Trial Advocates.
Publications: Has written and lectured
extensively.

GENBERG, Ira
Smith Gambrell & Russell LLP, Atlanta
404 815 3500
Recommended in Construction

GENZ, Peter
King & Spalding LLP, Atlanta
404 572 4935
pgenz@kslaw.com
Recommended in Tax
Practice Areas: Tax lawyer concentrating on corporate, partnership, and real
estate tax matters, and also tax controversies. Particularly qualified in matters
relating to structuring inbound foreign
investment, real estate investment trusts
and troubled company workouts.
Prof. Memberships: American Bar
Association; State Bar of Georgia; The
Florida Bar.
Personal: MLT, Georgetown University,
1982; JD, University of Florida, 1980;
BSBA, University of Florida, 1975.

GERAKITIS, Richard
Troutman Sanders LLP, Atlanta
404 885 3000
Recommended in Employment

GILLEN, Craig
Gillen Parker & Withers LLC, Atlanta
404 842 9700
Recommended in Litigation

GOLDEN, Jonathan
Arnall Golden Gregory LLP, Atlanta
404 873 8700
jonathan.golden@agg.com
Recommended in Corporate/M&A
Practice Areas: Mr Golden practices
primarily in the areas of corporate and
mergers and acquisitions. He is listed in
The Best Lawyers in America and is
Chairman of the firm.
Prof. Memberships: Adjunct professor,
Emory Law School (Securities and Cor-
porate Finance, 1974-79; Mergers &
Acquisitions, 1988-89); American Bar
Association; State Bar of Georgia.
Career: Director, The Profit Recovery
Group International, Inc. (NASDAQ),
1996 - present; Director, Sysco Corpora-
tion (NYSE) 1983-present; Director,
Intermedics, Inc. (NYSE) 1983-88*;
Director, Automatic Service Company
(AMEX) 1970-76*; Director, Butler
Shoe Corp. (NYSE) 1965-68*; Director,
Rich Products Corporation; Chairman,
The Livingston Foundation; Trustee,
The Southern Center for International
Studies; Member, Board of Counselors,
The Carter Center (*Company acquired
at last date).
Personal: Harvard Law School (LLB,
1962); Princeton University (AB, 1959).

GRADY, Kevin E
Alston & Bird LLP, Atlanta
404 881 7164
kgrady@alston.com
Recommended in Antitrust
Practice Areas: Competition and trade
regulation matters: litigation and coun-
seling.
Prof. Memberships: Immediate Past
Chair of the ABA Section of Antitrust
Law, 2004-05; Elected Member of Amer-
ican Law Institute.
Career: Member of US Delegation to
International Competition Network,
Merida, Mexico, 2003. Listed in three
leading legal publications.
Publications: Co-editor, 'Georgia Hos-
pital Law Manual' (4th ed. 1997); author
of Georgia Chapter in 'State Antitrust
Practice and Statutes' (3rd ed. 2004);
author of 'A Framework for Antitrust
Analysis of Health Care Joint Ventures',
61 'Antitrust Law Journal' 765.
Personal: AB, Vanderbilt University
(1969); JD, Harvard Law School (1974).

GRAVES, Judson
Alston & Bird LLP, Atlanta
404 881 7279
jgraves@alston.com
Recommended in Litigation
Practice Areas: Concentrates practice
in jury trial work with emphasis on
products liability, medical malpractice
and intellectual property.
Prof. Memberships: Member of State
Bar of Georgia, Florida Bar, Atlanta Bar
Association, American Bar Association,
and Lawyers Club of Atlanta.
Career: Fellow of the American College
of Trial Lawyers; profiled in the 14
August 2000 'National Law Journal' fea-

turing 10 of the top litigators in the
United States.
Publications: Published in 'Journal of
the Medical Association of Georgia',
'Journal of College and University Law'
and 'Georgia State Bar Journal'.
Personal: BA, Dartmouth College
(1969); JD, with distinction, Emory University School of Law (1975).

GREENE, Kevin
Troutman Sanders LLP, Atlanta
404 885 3000
Recommended in Energy

GREER, Scott
King & Spalding LLP, Atlanta
404 572 2755
sgreer@kslaw.com
Recommended in Construction
Practice Areas: Focuses on practice of
construction law and construction litigation. Represents clients in all aspects of
a construction project, including structuring, drafting, modifying and negotiating of construction, engineering, architectural and development agreements,
and negotiating, mediating, arbitrating
and litigating claims on construction
defects, delay, design deficiencies, wrongful termination, non-payment and surety bonds. Focuses on the representation
of owners and developers. Extensive
experience in LNG matters.
Prof. Memberships: American Bar
Association; American Concrete Institute; Atlanta Bar Association; State Bar
of Georgia.
Personal: BS, Oklahoma State University, 1987; MS, University of Illinois,
Champaign-Urbana, 1988; JD, Emory
University, 1995.

GRICE, Richard
Alston & Bird LLP, Atlanta
404 881 7576
rgrice@alston.com
Recommended in Banking & Finance
Practice Areas: Emphasizes representation of domestic and foreign commercial banks, underwriters and debt issuers
in a variety of financings including
recapitalizations, leveraged buyouts and
other acquisition financings, public debt
issues, private placements, cross-border
financings and various asset-based
financings. He also represents creditors
and debtors in pre-bankruptcy restructurings and Chapter 11 proceedings.
Career: Voted among the best lawyers in
a leading US legal publication for the
years 1998-2005. Named as a 'Super
Lawyer' in the State of Georgia in 2003
and 2005.
Publications: Written and lectured on
numerous topics of interest to commercial lenders and borrowers.
Personal: BA, University of Wisconsin
(1981); JD, Cornell University (1984)

GRIFFIN, John
Troutman Sanders LLP, Atlanta
404 885 3000
Recommended in Real Estate

GROUT, Robert
Troutman Sanders LLP, Atlanta
404 885 3000
Recommended in Corporate/M&A

HAFER, Randall F
Kilpatrick Stockton LLP, Atlanta
404 815 6289
RHafer@KilpatrickStockton.com
Recommended in Construction
Practice Areas: Focuses primarily on
the representation of owners on a wide
variety of construction projects, including mass transit systems, power plants,
waste water treatment plants, bridges and
highways, hospitals, office buildings,
sports arenas, schools, resorts, manufacturing and processing plants and tunnels.
Prof. Memberships: American Underground Construction Association.
Career: Head of the firm's Construction
and Public Contracts Group; member of
firm's Executive Committee.
Publications: Has lectured and written
extensively on a variety of construction
industry topics.
Personal: BS, Georgia State University,
cum laude, 1975; JD, with high honors,
University of Tennessee, 1983.

HARDIN, Edward J
Rogers & Hardin, Atlanta
404 522 4700
EJH@rh-law.com
Recommended in Corporate/M&A
Practice Areas: Mergers and acquisi-
tions, corporate law.
Prof. Memberships: Council on For-
eign Relations; American Law Institute;
International Bar Association; State Bar
of Georgia: Chairman (1982-83), Secre-
tary (1981-82), Section on Business &
Banking Law, Chairman (1981-82),
Committee on Securities Law; Associa-
tion of the Bar of the City of New York:
Secretary (1970-71), Committee on Pro-
fessional & Judicial Ethics; Inter-Ameri-
can Bar Association; American Bar
Association.
Career: Founding Partner.
Publications: Editor, Corporate Vol-
ume, Southeast Litigation Guide
(Matthew Bender 1983); editor in chief,
Vanderbilt Law Review, (1967-68).
Personal: Vanderbilt University (JD,
Founder's Medalist, 1968); Wesleyan
University (BA, 1965); Order of the
Coif.

HARRIS, Morton
Hatcher, Stubbs, Land, Hollis & Rothschild, LLP, Columbus
706 324 0201
Recommended in Tax

HARRIS Jr, H Stephen
Alston & Bird LLP, Atlanta
404 881 7197
sharris@alston.com
Recommended in Antitrust
Practice Areas: Concentrates practice
on US and transnational antitrust litigation, as well as other complex commercial litigation and arbitration.
Prof. Memberships: Member of the

Council of the ABA Antitrust Section.
Career: Listed in a leading legal publication. Selected as a leading competition lawyer in another recent legal publication.
Publications: Editor in chief and author of the Overview chapter of the two-volume ABA treatise, Competition Laws Outside the United States.
Personal: AB, magna cum laude, Cornell University (1977); JD, Columbia University School of Law (1982). Certified with Honors by the Parker Program in International and Foreign Law, Columbia University (1982).

HASSON Jr, James K
Sutherland Asbill & Brennan LLP,
Atlanta 404 853 8083
jim.hasson@sablaw.com
Recommended in Tax
Practice Areas: Practices in the areas of tax, healthcare and finance. Regularly represents closely-held businesses, family offices, universities, private foundations, hospitals and other organizations. Advises clients and resolves conflicts with the IRS and other federal and state governmental agencies. Focuses on the design and negotiation of acquisition or affiliation contracts, financing arrangements, organizational structures and tax planning for business continuity. Has published numerous articles and speaks at various conferences nationwide. Served as a member of the Exempt Organization Advisory Group to the Commissioner of the IRS, and as an Adjunct Professor of Law at Emory University School of Law.
Prof. Memberships: Member of the American and Atlanta Bar Associations; Former Division Coordinator, ABA's Tax Section to the Tax Exempt and Governmental Entities Division of the IRS; Former Chair, the Exempt Organizations Committee of the Tax Section of the ABA; Fellow, the American College of Tax Counsel; member of the National Association of College and University Attorneys and the American Health Lawyers Association.
Personal: JD, Duke University School of Law, 1970, Order of the Coif, Comment and Project Editor, 'Duke Law Journal'; BA, Duke University, 1967.

HAWKINS, Holmes
King & Spalding LLP, Atlanta
404 572 2443
hhawkins@kslaw.com
Recommended in Intellectual Property
Practice Areas: Intellectual property law, focusing on patent litigation, including patent infringement lawsuits involving computer systems and software, internet-related technologies, telecommunications and electronics systems, financial service models, consumer products, medical devices, patents, trademarks, copyrights and licensing matters.
Prof. Memberships: American Bar Association; Atlanta Bar Association;

American Intellectual Property Law Association; Georgia Institute of Technology, Atlanta (Visiting Professor); State Bar of Georgia (Intellectual Property Section).
Personal: BEE, high honors, Georgia Institute of Technology, 1990; JD, cum laude, University of Georgia, 1993. National Institute of Trial Advocacy, National Trial Skills program, Colorado.

HAYNES, Joseph B
King & Spalding LLP, Atlanta
404 572 4792
bhaynes@kslaw.com
Recommended in Litigation
Practice Areas: Civil and commercial litigation, representing accounting firms in malpractice, securities litigation and professional liability matters, including antitrust, commercial contract litigation, franchisor franchisee relationships, internal corporate investigations, class action lawsuits, derivative shareholder suits, civil RICO claims, banking litigation, construction contract suits, corporate espionage and competitive intelligence.
Prof. Memberships: American Bar Association; American College of Trial Lawyers; Atlanta Cancer Society; State Bar of Georgia; State Bar of New York; Atlanta Chamber of Commerce (Public Affairs Committee).
Personal: BA, University of the South, 1962; LLB, New York University, Phi Beta Kappa, Omicron Delta Kappa, 1965.

HENDERSON, Douglas
Troutman Sanders LLP, Atlanta
404 885 3000
Recommended in Environment

HENDRICK Esq, David R
Hendrick, Phillips, Salzman & Flatt P.C.,
Atlanta 404 522 1410
drh@hpsf-law.com
Recommended in Construction
Practice Areas: Construction law, construction contract counseling and construction dispute and claim resolution, including negotiation, mediation, arbitration, administrative processes, and judicial litigation. Also, represents local, state, and national construction industry trade associations.
Prof. Memberships: American College of Construction Lawyers, fellow and past President; American Bar Association, Forum on Construction, Member and past Chair of two Division Steering Committees; Atlanta Bar Association, Construction Law Section, Member and past Chairman; American Arbitration Association, Large, Complex Case National Arbitrator Panel Member and previously served as Member of the AAA Large Case Dispute Resolution Committee; Georgia Bar Association, Member; District of Columbia Bar Association, Member; Atlanta Bar Association, served as Member Board of Directors; Atlanta Council of Younger

Lawyers, Board of Directors and President 1980-81.
Career: Mr Hendrick has been recognized and listed in 'Best Lawyers in America' in Georgia regarding 'Construction Law'. He has also been recognized as a 'Georgia Super Lawyer' in the construction law field (recognized by peers as being in the top five percent of all practitioners) and as one of the 'top one hundred' lawyers in the state of Georgia as listed in Atlanta Magazine (2004).
Personal: BS (Chem Eng), Tufts University, 1968; JD University of Virginia, 1973; Law Clerk to Honorable Albert J Henderson, Judge, United States District Court, ND Ga 1973-75.

HENSEL, Donald
King & Spalding LLP, Atlanta
404 572 4644
dhensel@kslaw.com
Recommended in Tax
Practice Areas: Corporate, partnership, real estate, and international tax matters, with a particular emphasis on corporate mergers, acquisitions and restructuring transactions.
Prof. Memberships: Corporate Tax Committee of the Tax Section of the American Bar Association; State Bar of Georgia.
Personal: BA, Rollins College, summa cum laude, 1992; JD, magna cum laude, Harvard Law School, 1995, editor of the 'Harvard Law Review'.

HILL Jr, B Harvey
Alston & Bird LLP, Atlanta
404 881 7446
hhill@alston.com
Recommended in Banking & Finance
Practice Areas: Concentrates on mergers and acquisitions, joint ventures, and business matters for companies generally and for insurance companies specifically.
Prof. Memberships: American Bar Association, State Bar of Georgia, Atlanta Bar Association.
Career: Listed in two leading legal publications for his corporate law expertise.
Personal: BA, cum laude, Yale University (1961); LLB, Member of the Order of the Coif and the Virginia Law Review editorial board, University of Virginia Law School (1964).

HINCHEY, John
King & Spalding LLP, Atlanta
404 572 4922
jhinchey@kslaw.com
Recommended in Construction
Practice Areas: Construction and commercial contracting matters, including large capital companies; consulting firms; private and public schools and universities; state, city and county governments; public authorities; medical institutions; public utilities; private developers and owners; and design professionals.
Prof. Memberships: American Arbitra-

tion Association; American Bar Association; American College of Construction Lawyers; Atlanta Bar Association; Chartered Institute of Arbitrators; International Bar Association; London Court of International Arbitration; State Bar of Georgia.
Personal: AB, Emory University, 1964; LLB, Emory University, 1965; M Litt, Oxford University, 1980; LLM, Harvard University, 1966.

HISHON, Robert
The Hishon Firm, LLC, Atlanta
404 817 7791
Recommended in Tax

HODGES, Charles
Chamberlain Hrdlicka White Williams & Martin, Atlanta 404 658 5439
charles.hodges@chamberlainlaw.com
Recommended in Tax
Practice Areas: Represents businesses, individuals, and estates in various areas of tax law, including federal tax disputes and tax planning. Handled matters at all administrative levels within the IRS. Litigated in US Tax Court, US District Courts, Court of Federal Claims, Court of Appeals for the Fifth and Eleventh Circuits.
Prof. Memberships: American Bar Association (Tax Section), State Bar of Georgia (Tax Section - Chair-Elect).
Career: Partner since 2001.
Publications: Columnist for 'Journal of Taxation'. Authored numerous tax articles for 'Journal of Taxation', 'Taxation of Exempts', and 'Estate Planning'.
Personal: University of Florida College of Law (LLM, Taxation); Mercer University (JD); Clemson University, (BS, Finance).

HOGFOSS, Robert
Hunton & Williams, Atlanta
404 888 4042
rhogfoss@hunton.com
Recommended in Environment
Practice Areas: Robert Hogfoss' practice focuses exclusively on environmental and administrative law, with emphasis on Pipeline Safety Act, Clean Water Act, Oil Pollution Act, RCRA, CERCLA and TSCA issues. Experience in compliance advice, enforcement defense, administrative adjudication and environmental litigation. Representative clients include oil and natural gas pipelines, chemical manufacturers and the pulp and paper industry. Recognized by Chambers 'Clients' Guide to Leading US Business Lawyers' as a leading lawyer in the environmental practice, and as one of the top Georgia Environmental/Land Use lawyers, selected by Georgia attorneys and published in Atlanta Magazine and Georgia Super Lawyers Magazine, March 2005.

HORDER, Richard
Kilpatrick Stockton LLP, Atlanta
404 815 6538
RHorder@KilpatrickStockton.com
Recommended in Environment

Practice Areas: Experienced in all areas of environmental law, from negotiating permits through litigating environmental cases, particularly water, wetlands, waste, and endangered species matters.
Prof. Memberships: State Bar of Georgia; The Florida Bar; American Bar Association.
Career: Assistant United States Attorney, Northern District of Georgia (Civil Division) (1974-77); Associate General Counsel, Georgia-Pacific Corporation (1978-89).
Publications: Authored numerous papers on environmental law, toxic tort litigation, and litigation management, and a frequent seminar lecturer on these subjects.
Personal: BA, University of Florida, 1968; JD, University of Florida, 1971; LLM, London School of Economics and Political Science, 1974; MBA, Georgia State University, 1977.

HUDSON, Paul
Parker, Hudson, Rainer & Dobbs LLP, Atlanta 404 523 5300
Recommended in Corporate/M&A, Healthcare

HUGHES, Randall
Powell Goldstein LLP, Atlanta
404 572 6600
Recommended in Healthcare

HUGHES III, Hunter R
Rogers & Hardin, Atlanta
404 522 4700
HRH@rh-law.com
Recommended in Employment
Practice Areas: Labor and employment law, litigation, and alternative dispute resolution.
Prof. Memberships: Fellow, The College of Labor and Employment Lawyers; Fellow, American College of Civil Trial Mediators; American Employment Law Council Chair (2000-01); College of Labor & Employment Lawyers (1997 - present); National Employment Law Institute; American Bar Association; Atlanta Bar Association; State Bar of Georgia; Georgia Arbitrators Forum (2003 - present); American Arbitration Association Commercial Panel (2001).
Career: Partner since 1978.
Publications: Published widely in the area of labor and employment law.
Personal: University of Virginia (JD, with honors, 1970); University of Virginia (BA, 1965).

HUGHES Jr, William H
Alston & Bird LLP, Atlanta
404 881 7273
bhughes@alston.com
Recommended in Construction
Practice Areas: 'Birth to earth' construction law practice includes drafting and negotiating design, construction and joint venture contracts, for large energy, infrastructure, commercial, hospitality, healthcare, and multi-family housing projects; counseling project participants during construction; and

mediating, arbitrating, and litigating disputes after project completion.
Career: Practice is national in scope, including projects in 38 states and Mexico. Over the past eight years, has negotiated contracts for over $1.8 billion in construction work, and litigated or arbitrated over $100 million in claims.
Personal: BA, University of North Carolina (1980); JD, University of Virginia (1983).

JEFFRIES, M Hill
Alston & Bird LLP, Atlanta
404 881 7823
hjeffries@alston.com
Recommended in Corporate/M&A
Practice Areas: Practice focuses on securities and corporate finance, including public offerings and the ongoing securities and corporate representation of public companies, as well as mergers, acquisitions and dispositions of both public and private companies.
Prof. Memberships: A founding director of the Business and Finance Law Section of the Atlanta Bar Association and a member of the Securities Committee of the Business Law Section of the State Bar of Georgia.
Career: Heads the firm's Capital Markets Group and co-heads the firm's Transactional Practice Groups. Listed in two leading legal publications.
Publications: Authored numerous articles on securities and M&A topics.
Personal: BA, with high distinction (1977), JD (1980) - University of Virginia.

JOHNSON, James
Kilpatrick Stockton LLP, Atlanta
404 745 2455
JJohnson@KilpatrickStockton.com
Recommended in Intellectual Property
Practice Areas: Chemical and biotechnology patent prosecution and licensing of chemical technology and biotechnology.
Career: Former professor at Emory University School of Medicine in the Departments of Biochemistry and Medicine; former adjunct member in the Biology Department at Georgia State University; former senior research scientist at the Veterans Administration Hospital Research Laboratories.
Personal: BA Chemistry, University of the South; PhD Biochemistry Post Doctoral Fellowship, Emory University School of Medicine, Scripps Institute of Oceanography; JD, Emory University, with honors, 1984.

JOHNSON, Weyman
Paul, Hastings, Janofsky & Walker LLP, Atlanta 404 815 2209
weymanjohnson@paulhastings.com
Recommended in Employment
Practice Areas: Practices exclusively in labor and employment law, representing management.
Prof. Memberships: Immediate past Chair, Labor and Employment Law Section, State Bar of Georgia; Fellow, College of Labor and Employment Lawyers;

adjunct professor, University of Georgia School of Law.
Career: Frequent speaker on legal, and community affairs, and a contributing editor to various publications.
Publications: Co-editor, 'Negligence in Employment Law', BNA (2001); co-author, WARN Act Handbook, BNA (1989).
Personal: AB degree, Mercer University, cum laude, (1973); JD degree, University of Georgia School of Law (1979). Decisions editor,' Georgia Law Review'.

JOHNSON Jr, John
Troutman Sanders LLP, Atlanta
404 885 3000
Recommended in Environment

JOHNSTON, Mike
King & Spalding LLP, Atlanta
404 572 3581
mjohnston@kslaw.com
Recommended in Employment
Practice Areas: Labor, ERISA and employment law matters, representing clients in pharmaceutical, grocery, food service and distribution, soft drinks, manufacturing, technology, entertainment and healthcare industries.
Prof. Memberships: American Bar Association; Atlanta Bar Association; the Florida Bar; State Bar of Georgia.
Personal: BS, with academic distinction, US Air Force Academy, 1975; LLM, Georgetown University, 1986; JD, with high honors, University of Florida, Order of the Coif, 1980.

JORDAN, Hilary P
Kilpatrick Stockton LLP, Atlanta
404 815 6362
HJordan@KilpatrickStockton.com
Recommended in Banking & Finance
Practice Areas: Syndicated lending, asset-based lending, and asset securitizations.
Prof. Memberships: State Bar of Georgia's Business Section (Chair, 1998-99; Member of Executive Committee, 1996-2000); State Bar of Georgia's Uniform Commercial Code Committee (Chair, 1996-97); American Bar Association.
Career: Partner since 1984; Chair of the firm's Finance, Real Estate and Restructuring Department.
Publications: Co-author of 'Georgia Jurisprudence: Uniform Commercial Code' (Lawyers Cooperative, 1995); lectures on various commercial lending topics.
Personal: BA Political Science, University of Arizona, high distinction, 1974; JD, Harvard University, cum laude, 1977.

JORDAN, James B
Sutherland Asbill & Brennan LLP, Atlanta 404 853 8101
jim.jordan@sablaw.com
Recommended in Real Estate
Practice Areas: Chairs the firm's Retail Practice. Devotes substantial time to retail development and leasing matters. Represents developers and retailers regarding all retail product types, from freestanding facilities, to neighborhood and power center developments, to

enclosed regional malls. Represents landlords and tenants in office and industrial development matters and leasing transactions. Clients include one of the largest, most prominent retailers in the United States, as well as other national and regional retail and office developers. Regularly contributes to local and national CLE seminars.
Prof. Memberships: Member, American College of Real Estate Lawyers; Member, International Council of Shopping Centers; past Chair, Real Property Law Section of the State Bar of Georgia and past Chair of the Legislative and Legal Opinion Committees of this section; co-author of the Report on Legal Opinions to Third Parties in Georgia Real Estate Secured Transactions (October 15, 1997), establishing a model opinion for Georgia secured loan transactions.
Personal: JD, magna cum laude, University of Michigan, 1980, Order of the Coif, Phi Beta Kappa; BBA, with highest honors, University of Michigan, 1977.

JOSPIN, Walter
Paul, Hastings, Janofsky & Walker LLP, Atlanta 404 815 2203
walterjospin@paulhastings.com
Recommended in Corporate/M&A
Practice Areas: Mergers and acquisitions, corporate finance, securities, private equity and general corporate practice; SEC and SRO enforcement matters; internal investigations.
Prof. Memberships: Georgia Bar (Chair, Securities Committee, 2000 -); American Bar Association; International Bar Association (Vice-Chair, publications subcommittee, Securities Committee (Committee Q) 2004 -).
Career: Prosecutor, Division of Enforcement, US Securities & Exchange Commission (1980-83).
Publications: 'Georgia Corporations, Other Business Organizations & Securities Regulation', Lawyers Cooperative Publishing, 1995; 'Representing a Witness in an SEC Investigation', 22 Georgia Bar Journal 122 (1985).
Personal: BS Economics, Wharton School, University of Pennsylvania, 1974; JD Emory Law School, 1979.

KASSIN, Thomas
Ford & Harrison LLP, Atlanta
404 888 3839
tkassin@fordharrison.com
Recommended in Employment
Practice Areas: Tom Kassin focuses his practice on airline labor and employment. He counsels clients on all types of personnel and labor relations matters that arise under the Railway Labor Act. Tom has extensive experience in handling a wide range of airline arbitration cases, having successfully represented clients in more than 300 cases. He spends a substantial portion of his practice in collective bargaining and Railway Labor Act litigation. Prior to joining

Ford & Harrison, Tom was a Senior Attorney with Delta Air Lines. He graduated from University of Virginia School of Law.

KAUFMAN, Mark D
Sutherland Asbill & Brennan LLP, Atlanta 404 853 8107
mark.kaufman@sablaw.com
Recommended in Corporate/M&A
Practice Areas: Co-chairs the firm's Corporate Teams. Practices in the areas of corporate and securities law. Practice focuses on the general representation of corporations. Has extensive experience in the representation of public corporations, including all aspects of SEC reporting, and in acquisitions and sales of businesses, having worked on more than 50 in the last several years. In addition, has been significantly involved in public and private offerings of securities and has represented underwriters in public offerings of securities. Has extensive experience with fast-growth companies, including their start-up, financing and public offering and sale. In addition, represents companies in a wide variety of businesses, including consumer products, finance, fulfillment, healthcare, hospitality, insurance, internet banking, manufacturing, quick service restaurants and textiles, among many others. Experienced in acquiring businesses in Europe and Latin America.
Prof. Memberships: Served for 20 years as Legal Counsel to the Atlanta Bar Association and the Atlanta Bar Foundation. Listed in the 'Best Lawyers in America.'
Personal: JD, with distinction, Duke University School of Law, 1974, Order of the Coif, Note and Comment Editor, 'Duke Law Journal'; BA, Northwestern University, 1971.

KAUFMAN, Mark S
McKenna Long & Aldridge, Atlanta 404 527 4120
mkaufman@mckennalong.com
Recommended in Bankruptcy
Practice Areas: Senior Partner in the firm's Restructuring and Bankruptcy Department. Practice devoted to Chapter 11 and out-of-court financial restructurings. Has extensive litigation background and a substantial focus of his practice utilizes those skills and his understanding of financial and accounting principles. Practice includes the representation of secured creditors and creditors committees, though he has also handled significant debtor Chapter 11 cases. Has appeared in bankruptcy and district courts through the country and argued before four courts of appeal.
Prof. Memberships: Past President Atlanta Bar Association Bankruptcy Section; Chairperson Georgia Bench and Bar Bankruptcy Conference; Director, Southeastern Bankruptcy Law Institute.
Personal: BS Cornell University, 1969, with High Distinction; Phi Kappa Phi, Alpern Memorial Scholar; JD Harvard

University, 1973, cum laude; frequent lecturer on bankruptcy and related litigation.

KAUSS, Andrew
Kilpatrick Stockton LLP, Atlanta 404 815 6620
AKauss@KilpatrickStockton.com
Recommended in Real Estate
Practice Areas: Advises on a broad range of sophisticated real estate transactions, including development, leasing and acquisitions and sales, with a specialization in representing clients in the organization of ownership structures for real estate assets, and the formation of institutional capital for investment in real estate.
Prof. Memberships: American College of Real Estate Lawyers.
Career: Chair of the firm's Real Estate Section.
Personal: BA, History and International and Comparative Studies, Boston University, summa cum laude, with distinction, Phi Beta Kappa, 1974; JD, University of California at Los Angeles, Order of the Coif, 1977, 'UCLA Law Review' (Special Articles Editor).

KAYWOOD, Sam K
Alston & Bird LLP, Atlanta 404 881 7481
skaywood@alston.com
Recommended in Tax
Practice Areas: Federal income tax, international tax, cross border M&A, joint ventures.
Prof. Memberships: Former Chair, ABA Tax Section Committee on US Affairs of Foreigners and Tax Treaties; member, International Fiscal Association; member, State Bar of Georgia.
Career: Chair, Alston & Bird Federal Income Tax Group. Experience with most forms of cross-border investment, particularly in Canada, Europe, and Latin America.
Publications: Frequent author and lecturer on a variety of international tax topics. Has presented to such organizations as the International Bar Association, the American Bar Association, and Tax Executives Institute.
Personal: BS, Babson College (1979); JD, Emory University (1986).

KAZMAREK, Edward 'Skip'
McKenna Long & Aldridge, Atlanta 404 527 4160
skazmarek@mckennalong.com
Recommended in Environment
Practice Areas: Partner in the firm's Environmental Practice. Concentrates practice in environmental litigation, including toxic tort defense, cost recovery actions and the defense and prosecution of statutory claims.
Prof. Memberships: American Bar Association, State Bar of Georgia, American Chemical Society.
Personal: JD, University of Southern California, 1983. AB, University of California, Los Angeles, 1977. While in grad-

uate school, Skip performed research in air pollution control and was involved in the testing of the first automobile in the US powered by liquid hydrogen. He was also a teaching assistant and taught undergraduate-level courses in systems engineering principles. After graduate school in Environmental Engineering Systems, he worked in the environmental engineering section of a large, national forestry corporation where he was responsible for the company's compliance with laws regulating chemical substances.

KEENAN, Robert
King & Spalding LLP, Atlanta 404 572 3591
RKeenan@kslaw.com
Recommended in Healthcare
Practice Areas: Mergers and acquisitions focusing on health systems, hospitals, pharmaceutical and medical device companies, pharmacy benefit management companies, physicians and physician organizations, and managed care organizations on a wide variety of federal and state regulatory matters, including health information privacy, fraud and abuse, certificate of need, reimbursement, licensure and managed care/insurance issues.
Prof. Memberships: Georgia Academy of Healthcare Attorneys; American Health Lawyers Association; Health Law Section of the American Bar Association; State Bar of Georgia.
Personal: BS, University of Illinois, 1985; JD, University of Georgia, 1988.

KELLEHER, Thomas
Smith, Currie & Hancock LLP, Atlanta 404 521 3800
Recommended in Construction

KELLEY, Jeffrey
Troutman Sanders LLP, Atlanta 404 885 3000
Recommended in Bankruptcy

KELLEY, John
King & Spalding LLP, Atlanta 404 572 3401
jkelley@kslaw.com
Recommended in Corporate/M&A
Practice Areas: Corporate finance transactions and securities matters in Rule 144 and Regulation S public offerings and private placements in the technology, real estate, healthcare and manufacturing industries. Advises corporations regarding SEC reporting and disclosure requirements, securities transactions and compliance matters. Merger and acquisition transactions, including tender offers, leveraged buy-outs, going private transactions, stock and asset sales and partnership and joint venture transactions.
Prof. Memberships: American Bar Association; Atlanta Bar Association; the Florida Bar; State Bar of Georgia.
Personal: AB, cum laude, Hamilton College, 1982; JD University of Virginia, Phi Beta Kappa, 1985.

KILGORE III, Cada T
Sutherland Asbill & Brennan LLP, Atlanta 404 853 8196
cada.kilgore@sablaw.com
Recommended in Energy
Practice Areas: Practice includes the representation of lenders, underwriters, utilities and other electric industry participants in financings, mergers and acquisitions, power project and corporate transactions and power supply matters. Experience includes publicly-issued and privately-placed bond financings, a variety of secured and unsecured loan arrangements, leasing transactions, corporate restructurings, mergers and acquisitions and government-guaranteed financings. Practice has included construction and permanent financings for electric power plants, mortgage bond financings for electric generation, transmission and distribution systems, power supply arrangements, retail competition, stranded cost recovery and other aspects of industry restructuring.
Prof. Memberships: Member of the Business Law Section, the Section of Public Utility, Communications and Transportation and the Section of Environment, Energy and Resource Law of the American Bar Association; Director, Electric Cooperative Bar Association; Member, G&T Lawyers' Association and the G&T TAC Subcommittee.
Personal: MBA, University of Georgia, 1979; JD, magna cum laude, University of Georgia School of Law, 1979, Order of the Coif, Notes Editor, 'Georgia Law Review'; BBA, magna cum laude, Georgia College, 1975, Phi Kappa Phi.

KILPATRICK, J Thomas
Alston & Bird LLP, Atlanta 404 881 7819
tkilpatrick@alston.com
Recommended in Employment
Practice Areas: Focuses his practice on complex and class action employment litigation and traditional labor law.
Prof. Memberships: Member of the Board of Directors of the Georgia Chamber of Commerce and serves as Counsel to the Chamber for labor and employment matters.
Career: Senior member of the firm's Labor and Employment Law Group. Member of the Bars of Georgia and Tennessee, the United States Supreme Court and various federal trial and appellate courts nationwide.
Publications: Lectures frequently throughout the country on labor management matters.
Personal: BS (1965), JD (1968) - University of Tennessee.

KNUDSON, Kathryn
Powell Goldstein LLP, Atlanta 404 572 6600
Recommended in Administrative & Public Law, Banking & Finance

KUESTER, Jeffrey
Thomas Kayden Horstemeyer & Risley LLP, Atlanta 770 933 9500
Recommended in Intellectual Property

KURZWEIL, David
Greenberg Traurig LLP, Atlanta
678 553 2680
kurzweild@gtlaw.com
Recommended in Bankruptcy
Practice Areas: Reorganization, bankruptcy and restructuring and financial institutions.
Prof. Memberships: Member, State Bar of Georgia, Bankruptcy Law and Creditors' Rights Sections; Member, Atlanta Bar Association, Bankruptcy Law Section; Member, Turn-Around Management Association; Member, American Bankruptcy Institute.
Publications: Speaker, 'Transactions with Financial Troubled Companies,' Law Seminars International Conference, Atlanta, Georgia, February 2001 Speaker, 'Deals with Financial Troubled Technology,' Law Seminars International Conference, Atlanta, Georgia, March 2001.
Personal: JD, Emory University School of Law, 1987. BS, Cornell University, 1984.

LAFIANDRA, Aldo L
Alston & Bird LLP, Atlanta
404 881 7890
alafiandra@alston.com
Recommended in Banking & Finance
Practice Areas: Has represented borrowers and lenders in various types of secured and unsecured credit arrangements, typically in syndicated loan transactions. Has advised creditors and publicly and privately held companies and their boards of directors in connection with complex out-of-court workouts, debt restructurings, and Chapter 11 bankruptcy cases.
Prof. Memberships: Director and President, Turnaround Management Association (Atlanta Chapter); Director, National Association of Certified Turnaround Directors (ACTD).
Career: Member of the firm's Leveraged Capital and Bankruptcy Reorganization and Workout Groups.
Publications: Written and lectured on numerous topics of interest.
Personal: BA, St. John's University (1986); JD, University of Virginia (1989).

LASETER, Scott
McKenna Long & Aldridge, Atlanta
404 527 4370
slaseter@mckennalong.com
Recommended in Environment
Practice Areas: Practice includes litigation, regulatory and transactional aspects of environmental law. For the last dozen years, has devoted a substantial portion of practice to manufactured gas plant issues ranging from investigation and remediation oversight to lost recovery, insurance coverage and common law lit-

igation. Has also devoted a substantial portion of practice to representing publicly traded real estate companies, parties to CMBS transactions, financial institutions, REITs, developers and private investors in connection with environmental problems arising out of buying, selling, owning and financing real estate.
Prof. Memberships: American Bar Association, State Bar of Georgia, Past Chair of Environmental and Toxic Tort Section of Atlanta Bar Association. Chairman of GA Justice Project.
Personal: Mercer University (JD, 1990); University of the South (BA, 1984).

LAYSON, Frank
Paul, Hastings, Janofsky & Walker LLP, Atlanta 404 815 2206
franklayson@paulhastings.com
Recommended in Corporate/M&A
Practice Areas: Concentrates in domestic and international mergers, acquisitions and joint ventures for both public and private companies.
Prof. Memberships: American Bar Association; State Bar of Georgia (Corporate Code Revision Committee); Atlanta Bar Association (M&A Forum).
Personal: BA, Emory University, 1988, Phi Beta Kappa; JD, magna cum laude, University of Georgia, 1991, Order of the Coif, Woodruff Scholar.

LEVEILLE, Michael
Parker, Hudson, Rainer & Dobbs LLP, Atlanta 404 523 5300
Recommended in Banking & Finance

LEVIN, Jay
Powell Goldstein LLP, Atlanta
404 572 6600
Recommended in Real Estate

LEVIN, Matthew W
Alston & Bird LLP, Atlanta
404 881 7940
mlevin@alston.com
Recommended in Bankruptcy
Practice Areas: Concentrates his practice on corporate restructurings, bankruptcy litigation and commercial litigation.
Prof. Memberships: Member of the Bankruptcy Sections of both the Atlanta Bar Association and the State Bar of Georgia.
Career: Member of the firm's Bankruptcy Group.
Publications: Spoken and written on bankruptcy issues both in Georgia and nationally.
Personal: BA (1988), JD (1991) - University of Virginia.

LISCHER, Dale
Smith Gambrell & Russell LLP, Atlanta
404 815 3500
Recommended in Intellectual Property

LITTLE, Catherine
Hunton & Williams, Atlanta
404 888 4047
clittle@hunton.com
Recommended in Environment
Practice Areas: Practice focuses exclu-

sively on energy-related, environmental and administrative law at the federal, state and local levels. Emphasis on regulatory compliance, enforcement defense and administrative adjudication under the Pipeline Safety Act, Clean Water Act, including wetlands, the Oil Pollution Act and CERCLA. Experience also includes natural resource damage assessment claims, endangered species issues, hazardous waste issues and issues arising under TSCA. Representative clients include oil and natural gas pipelines and chemical manufacturers.

LOKEY Jr, James
King & Spalding LLP, Atlanta
404 572 4927
jlokey@kslaw.com
Recommended in Tax
Practice Areas: Real estate and private equity investment fund formation, private equity investment structures, real estate transactions (representing both developers and financial institutions in connection with new investments as well as 'workouts'), corporate joint ventures, acquisitions and reorganizations, investments by non-US persons (including foreign governments) in the United States, and tax problems of tax-exempt organizations.
Prof. Memberships: American Bar Association (Member, Taxation Section); Atlanta Bar Association; State Bar of Georgia.
Personal: BS, David Lipscomb University, magna cum laude, 1974; JD, Vanderbilt University, Founder's Medal for First Honors, Order of the Coif.

LONG, Clay C
McKenna Long & Aldridge, Atlanta
404 527 4050
clong@mckennalong.com
Recommended in Corporate/M&A
Practice Areas: Focuses on general business and corporate matters with a concentration on corporate counseling and on the purchase and sale of businesses. Represents such companies as food and beverage, communications, agribusiness, merchant banks and venture capital firms. Prior to the merger with McKenna & Cuneo, was a founding Partner and Chairman of Long Aldridge & Norman. Has been listed for several years as one of the Most Influential Georgians and was selected as one of Georgia's Legal Elite in 2003 and 2004 in a survey of lawyers conducted by Georgia Trend magazine.
Prof. Memberships: Atlanta Bar Association; State Bar of Georgia; American Bar Association; Georgia Bar Foundation; American Law Institute.
Personal: LLB, Harvard Law School, magna cum laude, 1962. AB, Birmingham-Southern College, summa cum laude, 1958.

LOVELAND, Joseph
King & Spalding LLP, Atlanta
404 572 4783
jloveland@kslaw.com
Recommended in Litigation
Practice Areas: Focuses on complex business litigation and class actions. Extensive trial experience in toxic tort, trademark infringement, breach of contract, fraud, misappropriation of trade secrets, corporate alter ego and fraudulent conveyance claims, antitrust violations, and RICO.
Prof. Memberships: American Bar Association; Atlanta Bar Association; International Association of Defense Counsel; State Bar of Georgia; Texas State Bar.
Personal: BA, University of North Carolina, 1973; JD, Harvard, 1976.

LUNSFORD, Rodgers
Smith Gambrell & Russell LLP, Atlanta
404 815 3500
Recommended in Intellectual Property

LUREY, Alfred
Kilpatrick Stockton LLP, Atlanta
404 815 6360
ALurey@KilpatrickStockton.com
Recommended in Bankruptcy
Practice Areas: Bankruptcy and insolvency matters.
Prof. Memberships: The Southeastern Bankruptcy Law Institute, Inc. (former President and Chairman of the Board of Directors); State Bar of Georgia, UCC Committee of the Corporate and Banking Law Section (former chairman); American College of Bankruptcy; American Bar Association.
Career: Former adjunct professor at Emory Law School.
Publications: Wrote the chapters on Insider Litigation and Preferences in the 'Prentice Hall Law & Business Bankruptcy Litigation Manual' (Michael L Cook ed); lectures at seminars on bankruptcy, creditors' rights, and secured lending.
Personal: AB, Duke University, summa cum laude, 1964; LLB, Harvard University, cum laude, 1967.

MACDONALD III, Ralph F
Alston & Bird LLP, Atlanta
404 881 7582
cmacdonald@alston.com
Recommended in Administrative & Public Law, Banking & Finance
Practice Areas: Practice emphasizes securities, mergers and acquisitions, financial institutions, Bank Holding Company Act and corporate governance matters.
Prof. Memberships: The American Bar Association; Alabama State Bar (chairman, Banking, Business, and Corporation Law Section, 1986-87); Financial Markets Association; Associate Member, ESOP Association; and American Bar Association Subcommittee on Corporate Governance and Banking Law.
Career: Named in two leading legal

publications. Frequent speaker and author on various matters related to financial institutions.

Personal: BS, Washington And Lee University (1975); MBA, JD, University of Virginia (1979).

MALOY, Bruce
Maloy & Jenkins, Atlanta
404 875 2700
Recommended in Litigation

MARSH, Gary W
McKenna Long & Aldridge, Atlanta
404 527 4150
gmarsh@mckennalong.com
Recommended in Bankruptcy

Practice Areas: Represents creditors and debtors in Chapter 11 reorganization proceedings, out of court restructurings and debtor/creditor litigation. Board Certified Business Bankruptcy and Creditors' Rights attorney who has extensive experience representing creditors in and out of bankruptcy court. Analyzes and defends against preference and fraudulent conveyance actions, represents buyers of assets out of bankruptcy and represents landlords and other parties who have leases or contracts with debtors.

Prof. Memberships: American Bar Association; Georgia Bar Association; Atlanta Bar Association; American Bankruptcy Institute; Emory University, Lamar Inn of Court.

Publications: Fellow in the American College of Bankruptcy; Named by 'Georgia Trend' as one of Georgia's 2003 Legal Elite and by 'Atlanta Magazine' as one of Georgia's Super Lawyers for 2004.

Personal: JD, Emory University School of Law, 1985. BA, American University, cum laude, 1982.

MARSHALL, John
Powell Goldstein LLP, Atlanta
404 572 6600
Recommended in Antitrust, Litigation

MARZETTI, Phil
Paul, Hastings, Janofsky & Walker LLP, Atlanta 404 815 2258
philmarzetti@paulhastings.com
Recommended in Tax

Practice Areas: US federal and state tax matters encompassing most areas of corporate, partnership and individual income taxation, including the tax aspects of mergers and acquisitions, the structuring of partnerships and joint ventures, and international taxation.

Prof. Memberships: ABA, Georgia Federal Tax Conference (Trustee), Atlanta Tax Forum, International Fiscal Association.

Career: Partner at Paul Hastings since 1992. Associate and Partner at Atlanta-based firm from 1975-92.

Publications: Pre-Sale Tailoring - Charitable Giving and Charitable Remainder Trusts (USC Tax Inst); co-author of prior Tax Management Portfolios regarding S Corporations.

Personal: Harvard Law School (JD, 1975); Boston College (BA, 1972).

MATCHETT, Sam
King & Spalding LLP, Atlanta
404 572 2414
smatchett@kslaw.com
Recommended in Employment

Practice Areas: Employment relationship matters, emphasis in labor and employment litigation in state and federal courts, governmental agencies and arbitration tribunals, including employment discrimination matters. Advice on avoidance of employee-related problems, presenting seminars concerning all aspects of employment law. Litigation involving Civil Rights Acts of 1866 and 1964, Age Discrimination in Employment Act and Americans with Disabilities Act.

Prof. Memberships: Appeals Court of Georgia; Georgia State Bar; Institute of Applied Management and Law (IAML) (faculty member).

Personal: BA, magna cum laude, Morehouse College, 1981; JD, University of Georgia, 1984.

MCCABE, F Barry
Griffin Cochrane & Marshall, Atlanta
404 523 2000
fbmccabe@gcm-atty.com
Recommended in Construction

Practice Areas: Construction law; commercial litigation.

Prof. Memberships: State Bar of Georgia (Litigation section); State Bar of New Mexico.

Career: Shareholder since 2002; Martindale-Hubbell AV-rated; selected by peers as one of best business litigation attorneys in Georgia ('Legal Elite,' 2004, by Georgia Trend magazine); selected by peers as 'Georgia Superlawyer' in construction (2004, 2005 by Atlanta Magazine).

Personal: Emory University School of Law (JD with distinction, 1994); New Mexico State University (BS, 1991); London School of Economics and Political Science (General Course Diploma, 1990).

MCGRATH, Robin L
Alston & Bird LLP, Atlanta
404 881 7923
rmcgrath@alson.com
Recommended in Intellectual Property

Practice Areas: Focuses her practice on patent, internet, trademark and copyright litigation and counseling.

Career: Has extensive experience with all facets of patent litigation and domain name and Internet dispute issues, representing numerous companies in domain name disputes and action under the Federal Anticybersquatting Consumer Protection Act and ICANN's Uniform Domain Name Dispute Resolution Policy.

Publications: Has authored a number of articles in the trademark and internet area.

Personal: BBA, magna cum laude, University of Texas (1989); JD, with high honors, University of Florida College of Law (1995).

MEIR, Dennis
Kilpatrick Stockton LLP, Atlanta
404 815 6364
DMeir@KilpatrickStockton.com
Recommended in Bankruptcy

Practice Areas: Bankruptcy and insolvency matters, with significant involvement in representation of debtors, secured and unsecured creditors, creditorsí committees, and trustees.

Prof. Memberships: Georgia State Bar, Bankruptcy section, (former Chairman); American Bar Association, Business Law section; Atlanta Bar Association, Bankruptcy section.

Career: Partner since 1978.

Publications: Has lectured and written extensively on bankruptcy issues.

Personal: Undergraduate degree, Amherst College, cum laude, 1967; JD, Harvard University, cum laude, 1972.

MERCER, John
Troutman Sanders LLP, Atlanta
404 885 3000
Recommended in Energy

MEYERS, Todd
Kilpatrick Stockton LLP, Atlanta
404 815 6482
TMeyers@KilpatrickStockton.com
Recommended in Bankruptcy

Practice Areas: Bankruptcy and insolvency matters, including representation of committees, individual creditors, secured lenders and debtors in both workouts and bankruptcy proceedings. Significant experience in healthcare and telecommunications bankruptcy proceedings.

Prof. Memberships: State Bar of Georgia, Bankruptcy Section; American Bankruptcy Institute; Atlanta Bar Association, Bankruptcy Section.

Publications: Co-authored the chapter on secured transactions under Article 9 of the Georgia Uniform Commercial Code for the treatise Georgia Jurisprudence.

Personal: BS Accounting, Indiana University, 1988; JD, Emory University, with honors, 1991.

MILLER, Rick
Powell Goldstein LLP, Atlanta
404 572 6600
Recommended in Corporate/M&A

MITCHELSON Jr, William (Mitch) R
Alston & Bird LLP, Atlanta
404 881 7661
mmitchelson@alston.com
Recommended in Litigation

Practice Areas: Concentrates on defense of government investigations, internal corporate investigations, and corporate legal compliance.

Career: Leader of firm's Government Investigations and Compliance Team and chair of False Claims Act Working Group. Designated Georgia Legal Contact for the Health Care Compliance Association. Former Assistant US Attorney for the Middle District of Florida, Criminal Division.

Publications: Authored articles on voluntary disclosures to the government, conducting plea negotiations with government prosecutors, development of corporate compliance plans, and incorporating sentencing guidelines considerations into criminal trial strategies.

Personal: AB, Duke University (1982); JD, University of Chicago (1985).

MIXSON, H Lamar
Bondurant, Mixson & Elmore, LLP, Atlanta 404 881 4171
mixson@bmelaw.com
Recommended in Litigation

Practice Areas: Business torts, corporate governance, partnership and fiduciary disputes, insurance coverage and bad faith litigation, attorney and accountant liability, RICO, tender offer, proxy and securities litigation.

Career: A Fellow of the American College of Trial Lawyers. Has represented individuals and corporations involved in a wide variety of business disputes for more than 25 years. Has successfully presented complex commercial disputes to juries, arbitration panels, and judges. Was co-counsel for the plaintiffs in a breach of fiduciary duty case which resulted in a $454,000,000 jury verdict, the largest verdict ever awarded in Georgia (a verdict which was affirmed on appeal and paid in full). Represented the plaintiff class in Abdallah v Coca-Cola Co., which settled for $192.5 million, the largest class action racial discrimination settlement in history. Selected as a finalist for the Trial Lawyer of the Year Award by the Trial Lawyers for Public Justice for the Abdallah case. Also has an excellent record on the defense side, having obtained summary judgments, dismissals, and defense verdicts of major claims.

Personal: BA degree, magna cum laude, honors with exceptional distinction in English, Washington & Lee University, 1970; JD degree, cum laude, Harvard University, 1974. Editor, Harvard Law Review, 1972-73.

MOELING, Walter
Powell Goldstein LLP, Atlanta
404 572 6600
Recommended in Administrative & Public Law, Banking & Finance

MOLAVI, Kamyar
Seyfarth Shaw LLP, Atlanta
404 892 6412
Recommended in Construction

MOLEN, Chris D
Paul, Hastings, Janofsky & Walker LLP, Atlanta 404 815 2210
chrismolen@paulhastings.com
Recommended in Banking & Finance

Practice Areas: Complex commercial and banking transactions, debt restructurings and workouts, asset-based and cash flow financings, and healthcare and communications industry lending practices.

Prof. Memberships: Georgia Bar Association, Atlanta Bar Association, Association for Corporate Growth (Director and Past President of Atlanta Chapter), and Georgia Finance Lawyers.

Career: Over 25 years of experience representing banks and finance companies in loan transactions ranging from $5 million to $3 billion.

Personal: Graduated first in class from Indiana University School of Business in 1974 with BS degree in Accounting, and from Indiana University School of Law in 1977 with a JD degree, cum laude.

MOORHEAD, Bruce W
Hunton & Williams, Atlanta
404 888 4090
bmoorhead@hunton.com
Recommended in Banking & Finance

Practice Areas: Co-Head of Lending Services Team. Practice is concentrated in corporate and commercial finance on behalf of banks and other financial institutions, with a primary focus on syndicated and leveraged lending. Extensive experience representing financial institutions and intermediaries in connection with the resolution of problem loans, as well as DIP and exit financing.

Prof. Memberships: Member, State Bar of Georgia; Founding Member and Director, Georgia Financial Lawyers Conference; Member, Standards Committee, Association for the Certification of Turnaround Professionals; Member, Turnaround Management Association; Chairman Emeritus of the Board, The Bridge.

MOWREY, Robert
Alston & Bird LLP, Atlanta
404 881 7242
bmowrey@alston.com
Recommended in Environment

Practice Areas: Environmental law, toxic tort litigation, hazardous waste, Clean Water Act, corporate compliance.

Prof. Memberships: State Bar of Georgia (former Chair, Environmental Section).

Career: Extensive nationwide experience handling hazardous waste and clean water enforcement and litigation matters. Experienced in the defense of citizens' suits, cost recovery actions, and enforcement actions. Adjunct professor, Emory University School of Law.

Publications: Publishes regularly on environmental issues, most recently in the 'ABA Section on Environment, Energy and Resources Journal.'

Personal: BA, summa cum laude, Wittenberg University (1985); JD, cum laude, University of Chicago (1988).

MULLIS, Carl W
Paul, Hastings, Janofsky & Walker LLP, Atlanta 404 815 2225
carlmullis@paulhastings.com
Recommended in Antitrust

Practice Areas: Antitrust litigation and counseling. Complex business and securities litigation.

Prof. Memberships: Chairman of Antitrust Section of State Bar of Georgia, 1992-94; Board of Trustees of Georgia ICLE, 1993-94.

Career: Of Counsel, Paul Hastings, 2001- present. Partner and Head of Antitrust Team at Long & Aldridge, 1986-2001. Senior Trial Attorney, Antitrust Division, United States Department of Justice, 1975-86.

Publications: Authored numerous articles and contributed to several ABA antitrust treatises.

Personal: Emory Law School Council; Board of Directors, Georgia Museum of Art; BA in Economics, Yale University, 1975; JD with Distinction, Emory Law School, 1975; Law Review; Best Brief Award.

MURPHY, Paul B
King & Spalding LLP, Atlanta
404 572 4730
pbmurphy@kslaw.com
Recommended in Litigation

Practice Areas: Special matters and governmental investigations focusing on white collar criminal defense, internal corporate investigations, complex civil litigation, and corporate compliance and governance matters.

Prof. Memberships: State Bar of Georgia.

Personal: BA, Vanderbilt University, 1985; JD, University of Georgia School of Law, 1988.

MURPHY Jr, Charles
Vaughan & Murphy, Atlanta
404 577 6550
Recommended in Antitrust

NEEDLE, William
Needle & Rosenberg, P.C, Atlanta
678 420 9300
Recommended in Intellectual Property

NEWTON, Trammell
Jones Day, Atlanta
404 581 8308
tnewton@jonesday.com
Recommended in Antitrust

Practice Areas: Has extensive antitrust and trade regulation experience, including dealing with the FTC, the Antitrust Division of the US Department of Justice, and state attorneys general on regulatory matters. He has represented clients in state and federal trial and appellate courts, including the US Supreme Court. He also counsels clients on structuring arrangements so as to minimize antitrust and related regulatory risk.

Prof. Memberships: ABA; State Bar of Georgia; and the bars of the US District Court for the Northern District of Georgia, the US Court of Appeals for the Eleventh Circuit, and the US Supreme Court.

NICHOLSON, Penn
Powell Goldstein LLP, Atlanta
404 572 6600
Recommended in Bankruptcy

NODINE, Larry
Needle & Rosenberg, P.C, Atlanta
678 420 9300
Recommended in Intellectual Property

NORTH, John L
Sutherland Asbill & Brennan LLP,
Atlanta 404 853 8358
john.north@sablaw.com
Recommended in Intellectual Property

Practice Areas: Extensive experience in controversies involving patent infringement, trade secret misappropriation and related unfair competition and antitrust controversies. Has tried cases in state and federal court, and has arbitrated and mediated a number of disputes.

Prof. Memberships: Member of the American Intellectual Property Law Association, and Intellectual Property Law, Science & Technology and Litigation Sections of the American Bar Association. Currently editor in chief of the SciTech Lawyer. Served as council member of the Science & Technology Section, Vice Chair of the Standing Committee on Scientific Evidence, Section Liaison of the ABA's Standing Committee of Publishing Oversight, and editor of the Scientific Evidence Review. Past President of the Atlanta Chapter of the Federal Bar Association.

Personal: JD, cum laude, Emory University School of Law, 1987, notes and comments editor, 'Emory Law Journal'; BA, magna cum laude, Duke University, 1984. Recognized in Chambers USA as one of America's Leading Business Lawyers, 2004-05. Named 2005 Georgia Super Lawyer by Atlanta Magazine.

NURKIN, Sidney J
Alston & Bird LLP, Atlanta
404 881 7260
snurkin@alston.com
Recommended in Corporate/M&A

Practice Areas: Concentrates practice on mergers and acquisitions, leveraged buyouts, corporate finance and corporate governance matters.

Prof. Memberships: Membership in the Atlanta and American Bar Associations and the State Bar of Georgia. Co-Chair of the Committee of the Corporate and Banking Law Section that developed the Report on Legal Opinion to Third Parties in Corporate Transactions and the accompanying Interpretive Standards. Served as a member of the ABA Committee on Corporate laws, and currently serves as a member of the Corporate Code Revision Committee of the Corporate and Banking Law Section of the State Bar of Georgia.

Career: Serves as the financial Partner of the firm and as a member of the firm's Partners Committee. Frequent author and speaker on topics of corporate governance, director and officer lia-

bility, negotiated acquisitions and legal opinions. Listed in three leading legal publications.

Personal: BS (1963), LLB (1966) - Duke University.

OAKES, Leslie
King & Spalding LLP, Atlanta
404 572 3314
loakes@kslaw.com
Recommended in Environment

Practice Areas: Experienced in permitting and enforcement actions, air and water pollution and hazardous waste. Environmental due diligence in a number of complex transactions involving industrial facilities and properties. Over 11 years as environmental engineer with the Environmental Protection Division, Georgia Department of Natural Resources.

Prof. Memberships: American Bar Association; State Bar of Georgia.

Personal: BME, Georgia Institute of Technology, 1974; MS, Georgia State University, 1981; JD, Georgia State University, 1986.

OAKLEY, Mary Ann
Holland & Knight LLP, Atlanta
404 817 8500
maryann.oakley@hklaw.com
Recommended in Employment

Practice Areas: Partner in the firm's Litigation Section, practicing for more than 30 years in the area of labor and employment law, appeals and alternative dispute resolution. She has substantial experience in administrative proceedings, trials, and appellate practice in all aspects of labor and employment law and is a trained mediator and arbitrator. She has advised numerous clients about personnel, human resources, and employment practices including drafting contracts, policies and procedures. She has experience training employers in a wide variety of employment matters including discrimination, harassment, retaliation, Fair Labor Standards Act and Americans with Disabilities Act Title III issues.

O'DAY, Stephen
Smith Gambrell & Russell LLP, Atlanta
404 815 3500
Recommended in Environment

OKESON, Nils
Alston & Bird LLP, Atlanta
404 881 7889
nokeson@alston.com
Recommended in Corporate/M&A

Practice Areas: Securities regulation, mergers and acquisitions and corporate governance.

Prof. Memberships: Member, Advisory Board, Weinberg Center for Corporate Governance at the University of Delaware; former member, Board of Directors, Business & Finance Section, Atlanta Bar Association; Member, American Bar Association, State Bar of Georgia and Atlanta Bar Association.

Career: Co-chairs the firm's Corporate Governance Practice Quality Team and a Partner in the firm's Corporate Health Care and Technology Groups.
Personal: BA, with distinction, (1987), JD (1990) - University of Virginia.

PAKENHAM, Timothy J
Alston & Bird LLP, Atlanta
404 881 7755
tpakenham@alston.com
Recommended in Real Estate

Practice Areas: Focuses his practice on the development and financing of commercial real estate. Also has extensive experience in large multi-party credit facilities and in the acquisition, development and financing of hotel properties.
Prof. Memberships: Member of the American College of Real Estate Lawyers, the Urban Land Institute, the Pension Real Estate Association and CoreNet, the Real Property Section of the State Bar of Georgia and the Atlanta Bar Association.
Career: One of the 10 members of the firm's Partners' Committee. Listed for commercial real estate in a leading US legal publication.
Publications: Written or spoken on a variety of real estate matters, particularly in the real estate finance area.
Personal: BA, University of Notre Dame (1978); JD (1983), MBA (1983) - Duke University.

PANNELL, Gary
Miller Hamilton Snider & Odom LLC, Atlanta 404 602 3700
Recommended in Administrative & Public Law, Banking & Finance

PARDO Jr, James
King & Spalding LLP, Atlanta
404 572 4794
jpardo@kslaw.com
Recommended in Bankruptcy

Practice Areas: Financial restructuring transactions, focusing on representation of secured and unsecured creditors in both bankruptcy cases and out of court debt restructurings.
Prof. Memberships: American Bankruptcy Institute; fellow, American College of Bankruptcy; State Bar of Georgia (past Chairman, Bankruptcy Section); 'Collier on Bankruptcy' and 'Collier Bankruptcy Manual' (former contributing Editor); Southeastern Bankruptcy Law Institute (Director).
Personal: BA, with honors, University of Virginia, Phi Beta Kappa, 1979; JD, University of Virginia, Order of the Coif, 1979. Frequent lecturer on bankruptcy and commercial litigation.

PARKER, John
Parker, Hudson, Rainer & Dobbs LLP, Atlanta 404 523 5300
Recommended in Healthcare

PARKS, John
Powell Goldstein LLP, Atlanta
404 572 6600
Recommended in Real Estate

PASCUAL, Rey
Kilpatrick Stockton LLP, Atlanta
404 815 6132
RPascual@KilpatrickStockton.com
Recommended in Corporate/M&A

Practice Areas: Securities offerings, mergers and acquisitions, private equity, investment management, general securities and corporate law. Regularly represents middle market public companies in transactional and other strategic matters. Recent transactions include: $102 million TurboChef Technologies Public Offering; $500 million sale of PracticeWorks to Kodak; and $51 million acquisition of Trophy Radiologie in Paris, France.
Prof. Memberships: ABA (Business Law Section and Member Latin American Legal Initiatives Council); Georgia Bar (Business/Banking Section).
Career: Member of firm's Executive Committee. Founder and Director, United Americas Bank, N.A.
Personal: AB, Syracuse University; JD, Creighton University, both with honors. Fluent in Spanish.

PATRICK, Elizabeth
Kilpatrick Stockton LLP, Atlanta
404 815 6573
LPatrick@KilpatrickStockton.com
Recommended in Construction

Practice Areas: Represents owners, developers, construction companies and others with planning and managing complex development and construction projects, design and construction contract preparation and negotiation, risk management, dispute resolution and litigation.
Prof. Memberships: Atlanta Bar Association, Construction Law Section (Past Chair); American Bar Association's Forum on the Construction Industry (Owner's and Lender's Division Chair); Georgia Chamber of Commerce (Board of Directors); Construction Owners Association of American (Member).
Publications: Writes and lectures extensively on construction issues.
Personal: BA, University of Georgia, 1985; JD, Tulane University School of Law, magna cum laude, 1988; Special Olympics Georgia (Honorary Board); Leadership Atlanta 2002 Graduate.

PERRY, Charles
Jones Day, Atlanta
404 581 8236
caperry@jonesday.com
Recommended in Environment

Practice Areas: Practice focuses on a wide range of environmental matters, including defense of administrative enforcement actions, litigation (including toxic tort cases), and advisory services related to business transactions. He was a co-founder of an insurance company offering one of the first environmental transactional products in the early 1990s. He lectures regularly before various organizations, including the

State Bar of Georgia Environmental Section.
Career: Former Assistant US Attorney representing the US EPA and the Army Corps of Engineers, and served as Regional Counsel for the US EPA Region IV.

PERSONS, Oscar N
Alston & Bird LLP, Atlanta
404 881 7249
opersons@alston.com
Recommended in Litigation

Practice Areas: Extensive trial and appellate experience. Concentrates practice on complex litigation, with emphasis on securities class action and mergers and acquisitions matters. e.g., Bryant v Avado Brands, 187 F.3d 1271.
Prof. Memberships: Member of the State Bar of Georgia and the Atlanta Bar Association.
Career: Has been a lecturer in numerous seminars on trial practice, appellate advocacy, securities litigation, restrictive covenants/trade secrets, corporate litigation, and discovery.
Publications: 'Forward-Looking Statements under the Reform Act,' Alston & Bird, LLP, Securities Litigation Forms and Analysis (West Publishing Co. 2003).

PERSONS, Ray
King & Spalding LLP, Atlanta
404 572 2494
rpersons@kslaw.com
Recommended in Litigation

Practice Areas: Focuses on complex litigation, including class actions and mass torts. Regularly appears before the state and federal courts and has been lead counsel in more than 50 jury trials. Has written numerous articles and conducted lectures across the country on strategies for defending complex cases.
Prof. Memberships: American Board of Trial Advocates; American College of Trial Lawyers; Atlanta Bar Association; Federation of Insurance and Corporate Counsel; International Society of Barristers; State Bar of Georgia.
Personal: BS, Armstrong State University, 1975; JD, Ohio State University, 1978.

PETRIK, Michael T
Alston & Bird LLP, Atlanta
404 881 7479
mpetrik@alston.com
Recommended in Tax

Practice Areas: Concentrates his practice on multistate tax planning for businesses, including income tax, franchise tax, sales/use tax, and other state and local taxes.
Prof. Memberships: Serves on the boards of the United Way of Metropolitan Atlanta, Leadership Atlanta, Lawyers Committee for Civil Rights Under Law, and the Vasser Woolley Foundation.
Career: Chair of the firm's State and Local Tax group.
Publications: Frequent author and speaker on state tax topics, including

constitutional questions involving the due process and commerce clauses.
Personal: BS (1979), BA (1979) - Eastern Illinois University; JD, Duke University (1983).

PHILLIPS, Stephen
Hendrick, Phillips, Salzman & Flatt P.C., Atlanta 404 522 1410
smp@hpsf-law.com
Recommended in Construction

Practice Areas: Construction law; commercial roofing.
Prof. Memberships: Fellow, American College of Construction Lawyers. Counsel, National Roofing Contractors Association; National Roofing Legal Resource Center
Career: 1976-81 Stokes & Shapiro, 1981 - present Hendrick, Phillips, Salzman & Flatt, Atlanta, GA.
Publications: 'Construction Technology for Lawyers: Roofing Systems'; 'Liabilities of Parties Engaged in Re-roofing'; 'Avoiding Problems With Defective Materials'; 'Roofing Contractors' Guide to Mold'; 'Building Codes and Contractor Liability'; 'Pollution Exclusions'; 'Roofing Warranties'; 'Avoiding OSHA Liability Resulting from Employee Misconduct'; 'Indemnification Agreements; How To Combat Proprietary Specifications'.
Personal: Born: December 9, 1949, Philadelphia, PA; George Washington University, BA 1971; Emory University, JD 1976.

PITTMAN, Alisa
Elarbee, Thompson, Sapp & Wilson, LLP, Atlanta 404 659 6700
Recommended in Employment

POPE, David
Carr, Tabb, Pope & Freeman, LLP, Atlanta 404 442 9000
Recommended in Environment

POUNCEY, Gerald
Morris, Manning & Martin, LLP, Atlanta
404 504 7738
gpouncey@mmmlaw.com
Recommended in Environment

Career: Gerald L Pouncey, Jr heads the environmental law and land use section of Morris, Manning & Martin, LLP. His primary focus is the redevelopment of and litigation concerning environmentally impacted properties (including state and federal superfund sites), as well as corporate mergers/acquisitions involving such properties, and he lectures nationally on these topics. He has led efforts in the acquisition and redevelopment of numerous industrial properties throughout the country, including the nation's largest brownfield redevelopment. He has also served as lead negotiator for industry (both foreign and domestic) considering locating in Georgia. He has written numerous articles on redevelopment of environmentally impacted properties and is a contributing author to the American

Bar Association publication Brownfields, A Comprehensive Guide to Redeveloping Contaminated Property. Mr Pouncey is a past Board Member and Chair of the Environmental and Toxic Tort Section of the Atlanta Bar Association. He serves on the National Environmental Subcommittee for the International Council of Shopping Centers, the Board of Directors and Executive Committee for the Council for Quality Growth and the Environmental Committee for the Atlanta Chapter of the Urban Land Institute. He also served as a legislative appointee to the Committee formed to review reauthorization of Georgia's Hazardous Waste Trust Fund and during his service on this legislative committee Mr Pouncey was the principal author of Georgia's new brownfield legislation. He has also been voted as one of Georgia's Super Lawyers by Atlanta Magazine, and as Who's Who in the Law by Atlanta Business Chronicle.

POWELL, Kurt
Hunton & Williams, Atlanta
404 888 4015
kpowell@hunton.com
Recommended in Employment
Practice Areas: Mr Powell's practice focuses exclusively on representing management in labor and employment law matters, including employment litigation, trade secret and non-compete litigation, union avoidance, collective bargaining, and preventive employee relations counseling. He has extensive experience in civil rights litigation, defending class actions and 'mass' actions involving employment discrimination, consumer discrimination, and ERISA claims. He has received recognition in Who's Who in Law and Accounting, as published in Atlanta Business Chronicle, November 2003 and 2004, and named an Employment Litigation Super Lawyer, as published in Atlanta Magazine and Georgia Super Lawyers magazine, March 2004 and March 2005.

POWELL, Thomas
Troutman Sanders LLP, Atlanta
404 885 3000
Recommended in Administrative & Public Law, Banking & Finance

POWERS, Tony
Rogers & Hardin, Atlanta
404 420 4632
TGP@rh-law.com
Recommended in Antitrust
Practice Areas: Antitrust, securities, complex business litigation, governmental investigations.
Prof. Memberships: American Bar Association; State Bars of Georgia and Texas; President, Lamar Inn of Court, Emory University School of Law (2000-01), Member, executive committee (1998-2004); Practising Law Institute.
Career: Partner since 1991. Associate professor of law, University of Miami Law School, 1983-86. Adjunct professor

of law, litigation, Georgia State University, 1987-88.
Publications: Extensive seminars, papers and presentations in antitrust and securities.
Personal: Yale University (JD, 1979); University of Tennessee (MA, 1975); University of Tennessee (BA, with highest honors, 1974), Phi Beta Kappa, Phi Kappa Phi.

PRATT, John
Kilpatrick Stockton LLP, Atlanta
404 815 6367
JPratt@KilpatrickStockton.com
Recommended in Intellectual Property
Practice Areas: Patent portfolio development and management, litigation and licensing.
Prof. Memberships: AIPLA, LES.
Career: Founded and led the firm's Atlanta patent prosecution practice; chairs the firm's intellectual property practice; appointed by the Federal court as a special master to handle patent infringement cases. Served from 1999 through 2001 as general counsel to the Internet consulting firm Enterpulse.
Publications: Was involved in drafting the Georgia Trade Secrets Act of 1990; regularly lecturers at continuing education seminars, particularly on patent law, licensing, trade secret protection and restrictive covenants.
Personal: BS Electrical Engineering, Clemson University, 1974; JD, Harvard University, 1977.

PRINCE, Alan
King & Spalding LLP, Atlanta
404 572 3595
aprince@kslaw.com
Recommended in Corporate/M&A
Practice Areas: Corporate finance transactions and securities matters, representing issuers and underwriters in connection with initial and secondary public offerings, 'shelf' offerings, Rule 144A offerings and other private placement transactions. Extensive experience in public offerings of equity securities, including initial public offerings, SEC reporting and disclosure requirements and corporate governance issues. Private merger and acquisition transactions, including mergers, tender offers and stock and asset transactions.
Prof. Memberships: American Bar Association; Atlanta Bar Association; State Bar of Georgia.
Personal: BA, cum laude, Wake Forest University, 1986; JD, cum laude, University of Georgia, 1989.

RAFUSE, Nancy
Ashe, Rafuse & Hill, LLP, Atlanta
404 253 6002
nancyrafuse@asherafuse.com
Recommended in Employment
Practice Areas: Concentrates practice in employment law, litigation, civil rights matters and defense of class actions. Named as one of the top employment lawyers in Georgia by

'Georgia Trend Magazine' (December 2004) and as one of Georgia's top employment lawyers and top women lawyers for 2005 by 'Law & Politics Magazine' and 'Atlanta Magazine' ('Georgia Super Lawyers 2005').
Prof. Memberships: Member, Northern District of Georigia's Bar Council and Disciplinary Committee; Board of Directors, Atlanta Urban League; Board of Directors, Atlanta Zoo; Member, ABA and Georgia Bar.
Career: Founding Partner of Ashe, Rafuse & Hill, LLP, largest employment firm in Georgia with a female name partner. Former Partner of 800 attorney international law firm where she served as Chair of the Employment Law Department of the Atlanta office.
Personal: BBA, cum laude, University of Georgia (1988); JD, magna cum laude, University of Georgia (1991), Order of the Coif, Notes Editor of the 'Georgia Law Review'.

RAGLAND Jr, William M
Hunton & Williams, Atlanta
404 888 4182
wragland@hunton.com
Recommended in Intellectual Property
Practice Areas: Bill Ragland's practice focuses on intellectual property litigation and licensing. He has extensive experience in litigating disputes involving patents, copyrights, trademarks, trade secrets and non-competition agreements. A leading technology lawyer, Ragland also provides strategic advice on the structure, negotiation and implementation of IP enforcement and licensing programs. His clients include computer, software, telecommunications, chemical, paper products and manufacturing companies. He has been featured in 'Corporate Counsel' magazine and 'IP Law & Business' magazine, regarding leaders in innovative intellectual property enforcement and licensing programs.

REED, Glen
King & Spalding LLP, Atlanta
404 572 3393
gareed@gslaw.com
Recommended in Healthcare
Practice Areas: Focuses on general representation of healthcare systems; specialized regulatory support to healthcare technology, pharmaceutical and device companies; and specialized projects involving compliance planning, healthcare industry restructuring, reimbursement, fraud and abuse, antitrust, managed care, healthcare policy and new service development.
Prof. Memberships: American Bar Association; American Health Lawyers Association Fellow; Georgia Academy of Hospital Attorneys; State Bar of Georgia.
Personal: BA, University of Tennessee, 1972; JD, Yale, 1976.

REINHARDT, Daniel
Troutman Sanders LLP, Atlanta
404 885 3000
Recommended in Litigation

REMAR, Robert
Rogers & Hardin, Atlanta
404 522 4700
RBR@rh-law.com
Recommended in Litigation
Practice Areas: Complex litigation.
Prof. Memberships: American College of Trial Lawyers; Federal Bar Association; Lawyers Club of Atlanta; American Bar Association; Atlanta Bar Association; Bencher, Lamar Inn of Court; The Best Lawyers in America.
Career: Adjunct professor of law, Georgia State University College of Law, 1984-96. Bar Council, US District Court, Northern District of Georgia, 1996-99. Board of Directors, Federal Defender Program. Hearing Officer, Georgia Public Service Commission, 1984-97. American Civil Liberties Union Board of Directors since 1986 (Executive Committee since 1981). City of Atlanta Board of Ethics.
Personal: Boston College (JD, 1974); University of Massachusetts (BA, 1970).

RHODES, Thomas
Smith Gambrell & Russell LLP, Atlanta
404 815 3500
Recommended in Antitrust

RICHARDS, Russell
King & Spalding LLP, Atlanta
404 572 4695
rrichards@kslaw.com
Recommended in Corporate/M&A
Practice Areas: Representing clients in connection with the acquisition and sale of publicly-held and privately-owned companies and establishing domestic and international joint ventures in the United States and in Canada, Mexico, South America, the United Kingdom and Continental Europe.
Prof. Memberships: American Bar Association; Atlanta Bar Association; BTI Consulting Group, Inc.'s 2002 Client Service All-Star Team; State Bar of Georgia.
Personal: BS, high honors, University of Tennessee, 1971; JD, high honors, Duke University, 1974.

RICHARDSON, Susan
Kilpatrick Stockton LLP, Atlanta
404 815 6330
SuRichardson@KilpatrickStockton.com
Recommended in Environment
Practice Areas: Environmental law, including regulatory and compliance counseling, due diligence for real estate and corporate transactions, permitting, enforcement and hazardous site remediation. Represents municipal governments with regard to wastewater collection and treatment issues, including permitting and enforcement issues.
Prof. Memberships: Georgia Bar Association, Environmental Law Section (Chair).

Career: Partner since 1998.
Publications: Co-authored a chapter in the '2003 Construction Law Update' published by Aspen Publishers, Inc.; Lectures frequently on environmental regulation, particularly with respect to water and wastewater issues.
Personal: BS Biology, University of Tulsa, cum laude, 1988; JD, Tulane University, magna cum laude, 1991.

RIDDELL, Stephen
Troutman Sanders LLP, Atlanta
404 885 3000
Recommended in Employment

ROBERTS, Lee
Weinberg, Wheeler, Hudgins, Gunn & Dial, LLC, Atlanta
404 876 2700
Recommended in Construction

ROEDER, Kim
Powell Goldstein LLP, Atlanta
404 572 6600
Recommended in Healthcare

ROGERS, CB
Rogers & Hardin, Atlanta
404 522 4700
CBR@rh-law.com
Recommended in Antitrust, Litigation
Practice Areas: Corporate and commercial law and litigation.
Prof. Memberships: American College of Trial Lawyers, state Chairman 1991-92; Lawyers Advisory Committee to the Eleventh Circuit Judicial Conference; Bencher and Executive Court Member of the Lumpkin, Bleckley and Lamar American Inns of Court; American Law Institute; Atlanta Bar Association; State Bar of Georgia.
Career: Founding Partner.
Personal: Emory University School of Law (LLB, 1953); Emory University (BA, 1951).

ROSENBERG, Sumner
Needle & Rosenberg, P.C., Atlanta
678 420 9300
Recommended in Intellectual Property

ROSENBLATT, Paul M
Kilpatrick Stockton LLP, Atlanta
404 815 6321
PRosenblatt@KilpatrickStockton.com
Recommended in Bankruptcy
Practice Areas: General bankruptcy with a focus on bankruptcy and related litigation including fraud, fraudulent conveyances, preferences and telecom issues. Bankruptcy transactional issues including asset sales and auctions. Has represented Fortune 100 companies as creditors and purchasers in major bankruptcy cases.
Prof. Memberships: American Bankruptcy Institute.
Career: Partner since 2003.
Publications: Frequently lectures on the interplay of bankruptcy and telecom issues.
Personal: BBA Accounting, Emory University, 1991; JD, Emory University, 1994.

ROSENBLOUM, Robert
Greenberg Traurig LLP, Atlanta
678 553 2250
rosenbloumb@gtlaw.com
Recommended in Intellectual Property
Practice Areas: Entertainment, intellectual property, technology, media and telecommunications.
Prof. Memberships: Chairman, Southeastern Chapter of the Copyright Society of the USA, Governing Committee Member, ABA Forum on the Entertainment & Sports Industries
Publications: 'The Publishing Problem and The Call for a New Compulsory License', American Bar Association October, 2002; 'The Collision of Music, Television and the Net - An Analysis of the DMCA Section 104 Report as it Pertains to the Music Industry', American Bar Association, October 2001; 'Sorting Through the Confusion endash Interpreting Standard Recording Agreement Provisions in the Digital Era', Talent in the New Millennium, MIDEM 2001.

RUSCHE, Mark C
Alston & Bird LLP, Atlanta
404 881 7281
mrusche@alston.com
Recommended in Real Estate
Practice Areas: Practice focuses on commercial office leasing, acquisitions and dispositions, joint venture work and senior housing transactions.
Career: Practice group leader for the firm's Real Estate Group. Represents landlords and tenants across the country in major office leasing transactions. On the Board of Editors of Commercial Leasing Law & Strategy, a nationally circulated monthly newsletter. Handled over $600 million in senior housing transactions in the past five years. Frequent writer and speaker on commercial leasing and other real estate topics.
Personal: BA, Furman University (1981); JD, cum laude, Order of the Coif, University of South Carolina (1985).

RUSS, Michael
King & Spalding LLP, Atlanta
404 572 4774
mruss@kslaw.com
Recommended in Antitrust, Litigation
Practice Areas: Corporate and securities litigation, SEC and tax investigations, as well as general commercial disputes. Specializes in representation of corporate clients in securities and antitrust class actions and internal corporate investigations.
Prof. Memberships: American Bar Association; American College of Trial Lawyers; The District of Columbia Bar; State Bar of Georgia.
Personal: AB, Duke University, 1966; JD, Duke University, Order of the Coif, 1969.

SALYERS, Douglas
Troutman Sanders LLP, Atlanta
404 885 3000
Recommended in Intellectual Property

SALZMAN, Martin
Hendrick, Phillips, Salzman & Flatt P.C., Atlanta 404 522 1410
mrs@hpsf-law.com
Recommended in Construction
Practice Areas: Construction litigation and advise; Government Contract Law.
Prof. Memberships: Member of Georgia, Kentucky and New Jersey Bar Associations; Member of American Bar Association and Forum Committee on the Construction Industry.
Publications: Co-author: 'Formal and Informal Discovery Procedures and their Enforcement in Arbitration', Alternative Dispute Resolutions in the Construction Industry, Wiley Law Publication, 1991.
Personal: BS in Business Administration, Boston University, summa cum laude, 1976; JD, Emory University, with distinction, 1979.

SAUNTRY, June
Troutman Sanders LLP, Atlanta
404 885 3000
Recommended in Antitrust

SCHRODER, Jack
Alston & Bird LLP, Atlanta
404 881 7685
jschroder@alston.com
Recommended in Healthcare
Practice Areas: Healthcare, regulatory compliance, peer review, certificate of need, legislative advocacy.
Prof. Memberships: State Bar of Georgia; Georgia Academy of Healthcare Attorneys (former President); Atlanta Bar Association (former President); Atlanta Bar Foundation (former President); American Health Lawyers Association (former member, Board of Directors).
Career: Frequent lecturer on programs sponsored by the American Health Lawyers Association, the American Bar Association, and the Georgia Hospital Association. Listed in three leading legal publications for healthcare expertise.
Publications: Author, 'Credentialing Strategies for a Changing Environment,' BNA's Health Law & Business Series.
Personal: AB, Emory University (1970); JD, University of Georgia (1973).

SCHWARTZ, Robert
Smith Gambrell & Russell LLP, Atlanta
404 815 3500
Recommended in Administrative & Public Law, Banking & Finance

SETTY, Nagendra
Jones Day, Atlanta
404 581 8560
nsetty@jonesday.com
Recommended in Intellectual Property
Practice Areas: His practice covers all aspects of intellectual property counseling and litigation, including patent, trade secret, trademark, and copyright matters, with particular emphasis on complex patent litigation. He has been lead counsel in patent litigation proceedings covering a wide range of industries and technologies, including soft-

ware, telecommunications, electronics arts, chemical, pharmaceutical, and mechanical technologies. He is a frequent author and lecturer.
Prof. Memberships: ABA Intellectual Property Law Section (co-editor of the section's quarterly newsletter, 2002-present; Co-Chair of Committee 903, 2002-present); Asian Patent Attorneys Association; Atlanta Bar Association; State Bar of Georgia; International Trademark Association.

SHACKELFORD, Richard L
King & Spalding LLP, Atlanta
404 572 4995
rshackelford@kslaw.com
Recommended in Healthcare
Practice Areas: Healthcare Practice and Business Litigation focusing on health systems, hospitals, home health agencies, long term care facilities, physician organizations, pharmaceutical and medical device companies, and managed care organizations in a wide variety of litigation and regulatory matters.
Prof. Memberships: American Bar Association; American Health Lawyers Association; Atlanta Bar Association; State Bar of Georgia.
Personal: BA, University of Georgia, 1976; JD, University of Georgia, 1979.

SHAPIRO, Ben
Shapiro Fussell, Atlanta
404 870 2200
Recommended in Construction

SHARBAUGH, Charles
Paul, Hastings, Janofsky & Walker LLP, Atlanta 404 815 2213
charliesharbaugh@paulhastings.com
Recommended in Real Estate
Practice Areas: Real estate.
Prof. Memberships: American Bar Association, Georgia Bar Association, Atlanta Bar Association.
Career: Partner, Paul, Hastings, Janofsky & Walker LLP.

SHELEY, Raymond
Sheley & Hall, Atlanta
404 880 1350
Recommended in Real Estate

SHORT Jr, Herbert J
Sutherland Asbill & Brennan LLP, Atlanta 404 853 8491
herbert.short@sablaw.com
Recommended in Energy
Practice Areas: Represents electric utilities and underwriters in financing and corporate transactions, including public bond offerings, leveraged leasing, tax-exempt bond offerings, revolving lines of credit, government-guaranteed financing, commercial paper offerings and mergers and acquisitions.
Prof. Memberships: Chairman, Business Law Section of the State Bar of Georgia (1996-97). Member, Corporation, Banking and Business Law Section. Member, Public Utility Law Section. Member, Electric Cooperative Bar Association of the American Bar Association.

Member, Business and Finance Section of the Atlanta Bar Association. Member, Board of Directors of the Georgia Chamber of Commerce.

Personal: JD, magna cum laude, University of Georgia School of Law, 1985, Phi Kappa Phi, Order of the Coif; BBA, summa cum laude, University of Georgia, 1982, First Honor Graduate.

SILLIMAN, R Todd
McKenna Long & Aldridge, Atlanta
404 527 4914
tsilliman@mckennalong.com
Recommended in Environment

Practice Areas: Concentrates on advising and representing clients in regulatory matters, environmental litigation and transactions involving commercial real estate. Assists clients in obtaining water supply, industrial wastewater discharge, wetlands dredge and fill, and air pollution control permits and defends clients in regulatory enforcement actions. Is a member of the legal team representing the State of Georgia in interstate water allocation negotiations with the States of Alabama and Florida and in related litigation in Atlanta, Alabama, and Washington, DC against the US Army Corps of Engineers concerning operation of federal reservoirs in Georgia. Has significant experience in cost recovery actions associated with contaminated sites throughout the country. Advises local governments and developers on issues related to privatization of water and wastewater treatment systems.

Prof. Memberships: State Bar of Georgia, Environmental Section (Chair 2001); Institute for Georgia Environmental Leadership.

Personal: University of Virginia School of Law (JD, 1993); University of North Carolina (BA, with Honors and Highest Distinction, 1990).

SINKFIELD, Richard H
Rogers & Hardin, Atlanta
404 522 4700
RHS@rh-law.com
Recommended in Litigation

Practice Areas: Complex business litigation.

Prof. Memberships: Fellow, American College of Trial Lawyers; Fellow, International Academy of Trial Lawyers; American Bar Association; National Bar Association; State Bar of Georgia; Atlanta Bar Association; Gate City Bar Association. Professional Listings: The Best Lawyers in America - Business Litigation; Atlanta Magazine's Top 100 Georgia Super Lawyers for 2005 and one of the 10 Top Lawyers in Georgia.

Career: Founding Partner.

Personal: Vanderbilt University School of Law (JD, 1971); Tennessee State University (BS, 1968).

SMITH, George Anthony
Kilpatrick Stockton LLP, Atlanta
404 815 6070
TSmith@KilpatrickStockton.com
Recommended in Construction

Practice Areas: Construction contract negotiation, arbitration, litigation, and International dispute resolution, focusing on power, water and wastewater, transportation and other major infrastructure projects.

Prof. Memberships: International, American, Georgia, and Kentucky Bar Associations; American College of Construction Lawyers; Centre for International Legal Studies; Chartered Institute of Arbitrators; London Court of International Arbitration; Construction Panel Advisory Committee of the CPR Institute for Dispute Resolution (Chair).

Publications: Has lectured and written extensively on many topics of interest to the construction industry and the international arbitration community.

Personal: BA, with Distinction, University of Kentucky, 1970; JD, with High Distinction, University of Kentucky, 1973.

SMITH, Gordon
King & Spalding LLP, Atlanta
404 572 4777
gsmith@kslaw.com
Recommended in Litigation

Practice Areas: Defense of high profile products liability cases across the US. Served as lead trial and appellate counsel for a number of the country's largest tobacco, automotive, pharmaceutical and heavy equipment manufacturers. Successfully coordinated defense of hundreds of product liability cases on behalf of several manufacturers as regional and national counsel.

Prof. Memberships: American Bar Association; American College of Trial Lawyers; Atlanta Bar Association; State Bar of Georgia.

Personal: ABJ, magna cum laude, University of Georgia, 1975; JD, University of Georgia, 1978, Order of the Barrister, Chairman of the Moot Court Board.

SMITH, James
Troutman Sanders LLP, Atlanta
404 885 3000
Recommended in Corporate/M&A

SMITH, Jerry
Kilpatrick Stockton LLP, Atlanta
404 815 6529
JnSmith@KilpatrickStockton.com
Recommended in Tax

Practice Areas: US federal and state tax matters, including advice regarding merger, acquisition structuring; federal and state tax credits; and optimal ownership of intellectual property. Has advised corporations regarding inbound and outbound investments. Has represented corporations and partnerships related to controversy matters before the IRS and state departments of revenue.

Prof. Memberships: American Institute of Certified Public Accountants; American Bar Association.

Career: Spent 20 years with KPMG as a tax partner. Tax Partner at Kilpatrick Stockton since 2004.

Personal: BS Accounting, University of North Carolina, Chapel Hill, 1979; JD, Vanderbilt Law School, 1985, Associate Editor, Vanderbilt Law Review.

SMITH III, Frank G
Alston & Bird LLP, Atlanta
404 881 7240
fsmith@alston.com
Recommended in Intellectual Property

Practice Areas: Intellectual property litigation, including patents and copyrights; antitrust; white collar crime.

Prof. Memberships: State Bar of Georgia.

Career: Co-Chair, Alston & Bird IP-Litigation Group. Former member of firm's Partners' Committee. Litigated complex matters in federal courts in Alabama, California, Florida, Georgia, Louisiana, Mississippi, North Carolina, South Carolina, Massachusetts, Michigan, and Virginia.

Publications: Authored numerous articles on intellectual property issues and litigation generally.

Personal: BA, Davidson College (1974); JD, Stanford University (1977).

SPALDING, William
King & Spalding LLP, Atlanta
404 572 3385
bspalding@kslaw.com
Recommended in Corporate/M&A

Practice Areas: Private equity and investment funds, representing strategic funds and companies in connection with a variety of private equity transactions ranging from non-control investments in technology and biotech companies to control investments and sales of established operating companies. Representing publicly-held corporations in corporate governance and SEC compliance and reporting matters.

Prof. Memberships: American Bar Association; Atlanta Bar Association; State Bar of Georgia.

Personal: AB, with honors, Dartmouth College, 1981; JD, summa cum laude, Washington & Lee University, 1984.

SPANGLER III, John I
Alston & Bird LLP, Atlanta
404 881 7146
jspangler@alston.com
Recommended in Construction

Practice Areas: 25 years' experience with construction disputes and transactions, including design-build, construction management, general construction, design and program management. Experienced in project finance transactions and in prosecuting and defending delay, interference, acceleration, extended overhead and defective construction and design claims.

Prof. Memberships: Atlanta Bar Association Construction Law Section, Past Chair (1994-95); American Bar Association (Construction Industry Forum and Litigation Sections); Forum Governing Committee (2004-07); former Chair Forum Division Two (Contract Documents); and State Bar of Georgia (Litigation Section).

Career: Chairs the firm's Construction and Government Contracts Group.

Publications: Authored numerous articles on construction law issues, including 'The Evolving Liabilities of Construction Managers,' The Construction Lawyer, January 1999 and 'Battling for the Bucks: The Great Contingency Payment Clause Debate,' The Construction Lawyer, July 1996; co-editor of 'The Construction Contracts Book' (ABA 2004).

Personal: AB, University of Illinois (1977); JD, Washington University (1980). Named Georgia's Top 100 Super Lawyers (2004-05); 'The Best Lawyers in America' 2004-05 edition.

STAIR, Kent
Carlock Copeland Semler & Stair, LLP, Atlanta 404 522 8220
Recommended in Construction

STEIN, Grant T
Alston & Bird LLP, Atlanta
404 881 7285
gstein@alston.com
Recommended in Bankruptcy

Practice Areas: Practice includes regular representation of debtors, secured and unsecured creditors, creditors' committees, and fiduciaries in complex out-of-court workouts, debt restructurings, and bankruptcy cases, and in bankruptcy related litigation.

Prof. Memberships: Fellow, American College of Bankruptcy; Director, Southeastern Bankruptcy Law Institute, Director and Vice President, Association of Insolvency and Restructuring Advisors (AIRA).

Career: Heads Alston & Bird's Bankruptcy, Reorganization and Workouts Group. Listed in leading legal publications.

Publications: Written numerous articles on bankruptcy and workout issues, and regularly lectures around the country.

Personal: BBA, cum laude, Emory University (1978); JD, cum laude, University of Georgia (1981).

STEIN, Jeffrey
King & Spalding LLP, Atlanta
404 572 4729
jstein@kslaw.com
Recommended in Corporate/M&A

Practice Areas: Corporate finance transactions and securities matters, focusing on public offerings, representing corporate issuers and underwriters in shelf registrations of investment-grade debt securities, medium-term note programs, high-yield securities offerings and initial public offerings of common stock. Advice regarding SEC reporting and disclosure requirements, securities transactions and corporate governance and compliance matters.

Prof. Memberships: American Bar Association (Legal Opinions Committees); New York State Bar Association; New York City, County and State Bar Associations (Tri-Bar Legal Opinion

Committee); State Bar of Georgia.
Personal: BA, summa cum laude, Yeshiva University, 1977; JD, Harvard University, 1980.

STEPHENSON, Mason W
King & Spalding LLP, Atlanta
404 572 4945
mstephenson@kslaw.com
Recommended in Real Estate
Practice Areas: Commercial real estate law, representing banks, credit companies, life insurance companies, pension funds and institutional investors in secured financings and equity investments in income properties, including office buildings, hotels, apartments and industrial properties. Extensive experience in workout, restructure and foreclosure of real estate investments.
Prof. Memberships: American College of Real Estate Lawyers; Atlanta Bar Association (former Chairman, Real Estate Section); State Bar of Georgia (former Member, Executive Committee, Real Estate Section).
Personal: AB, cum laude, Phi Beta Kappa, Davidson College, 1968; JD, University of Chicago, 1971. Frequent lecturer on commercial real estate and ethics topics.

STEVENS, William
McKenna Long & Aldridge, Atlanta
404 527 8510
wstevens@mckennalong.com
Recommended in Real Estate
Practice Areas: Head of the Real Estate Practice Group and works primarily in the area of advising and representing the interests of clients lending money secured by real estate projects and of clients purchasing completed projects, whether entirely for their own account or through joint ventures with others. Also advises clients on creating mortgage lending conduits and preparing standard form lending and securitization documents for use by such lending operations.
Prof. Memberships: Member of Duke Law School Board of Visitors; Chair of the Board of Trustees of The Galloway School.
Personal: Duke University School of Law (JD, 1970); University of North Carolina (BS, 1967).

STOCKTON, David
Kilpatrick Stockton LLP, Atlanta
404 815 6444
DStockton@KilpatrickStockton.com
Recommended in Corporate/M&A
Practice Areas: Advises businesses in all aspects of corporate finance, including initial, secondary and follow-on public offerings, private placements, securities regulations, and mergers and acquisitions. Advises special committees, management groups and issuers in structuring, negotiating and documenting going private transactions.
Prof. Memberships: State Bar of Georgia (chair-elect of the Business Law Sec-

tion, former chairman of its Securities Committee); Atlanta Bar Association (past chair- Business Practice Section).
Publications: 'Going Private: The Best Option?' National Law Journal (June 2003).
Personal: BA, Emory University; JD, University of North Carolina at Chapel Hill School of Law (Order of the Coif).

STOKES, James S
Alston & Bird LLP, Atlanta
404 881 7294
jstokes@alston.com
Recommended in Environment
Practice Areas: Over 30 years environmental legal experience, including wetlands, water quality, air quality, federal and state Superfund, and solid waste matters.
Prof. Memberships: Former Chair/charter member, Georgia Governor's Environmental Advisory Council; former Chair, Water Resources Committee, Metro Atlanta Chamber of Commerce; former chair, Georgia Bar Environmental Law Section.
Career: Negotiated innovative risk-based cleanup for downtown Atlanta Atlantic Steel site, one of most important brownfield sites in US. Successfully defended Georgia county in nationally-publicized lawsuits by residents of subdivision built over historic landfill.
Personal: AB, Davidson College (1966); LLB, Yale Law School (1969).

STRAUSS, Robert
Troutman Sanders LLP, Atlanta
404 885 3000
Recommended in Banking & Finance

STREET, Phillip
Kilpatrick Stockton LLP, Atlanta
404 815 6455
PStreet@KilpatrickStockton.com
Recommended in Healthcare
Practice Areas: Healthcare and life sciences transactions, including business mergers, acquisitions and joint ventures and the commercialization of life sciences research. Serves as legal advisor to life sciences companies, medical research organizations, medical device and pharmaceutical companies, hospitals and other healthcare and life sciences related companies.
Prof. Memberships: Grady Health System Board of Visitors; State Bar of Alabama; State Bar of Georgia; American Health Lawyers Association; Atlanta Tax Forum.
Career: Chairs the firm's Healthcare and Life Sciences Groups.
Personal: BA, Economics, Vanderbilt University, 1982; JD, Vanderbilt University School of Law, 1986; LLM, in Taxation, New York University, 1989.

SWANN, Jerre
Kilpatrick Stockton LLP, Atlanta
404 815 6540
JSwann@KilpatrickStockton.com
Recommended in Intellectual Property

Practice Areas: Trademark/unfair competition litigation, survey/expert witness issues.
Prof. Memberships: INTA (Director, member of the Special Committee with respect to the FTDA).
Career: Partner since 1972; recipient 2000 Ladas Memorial Award and 2002 INTA Volunteer Service Award for the Advancement of Trademark Law.
Publications: Has authored more than 25 law review articles in the trademark field; has spoken at more than 25 national or regional seminars; former editor in chief of 'The Trademark Reporter.'
Personal: BA, Williams College, Phi Beta Kappa, National Merit Scholar, 1961; University of St. Andrews, Scotland, Rotary Foundation Fellow, 1962; JD, Harvard Law School, 1965.

SWEENEY, Neal
Kilpatrick Stockton LLP, Atlanta
404 815 6616
NSweeney@KilpatrickStockton.com
Recommended in Construction
Practice Areas: Construction law and litigation on major public works and federal projects, including dams, highways, hotels, hospitals, airports, schools, and waste water treatment plants.
Prof. Memberships: State Bar of Georgia; American Bar Association (Forum Committee on the Construction Industry and the Public Contract Law Section); American Arbitration Association's National Panel of Arbitrators; Design - Build Institute of America (lecturer and VP, Southeast Chapter).
Publications: Has written and lectured extensively on construction law and design-build, including editing or co-authoring more than 20 books.
Personal: Rutgers University, with high honors, 1979; JD, George Washington University, with honors, 1982.

SWENSON, Erik
King & Spalding LLP, Atlanta
404 572 3540
eswenson@kslaw.com
Recommended in Energy
Practice Areas: Nationwide representation of energy project participants, including developers, equity investors and lenders and industrial companies in energy matters, including the purchase and sale of electricity and energy regulation matters.
Prof. Memberships: District of Columbia Bar; New York State Bar.
Personal: BA, cum laude, Columbia College; JD, Columbia University School of Law, 1982. Lectures before energy industry leaders on project development and energy regulation. Regular contributor to energy industry publications.

TAYLOR, Roger
Finnegan Henderson Farabow Garrett & Dunner LLP, Atlanta
404 653 6400
Recommended in Intellectual Property

THOMAS, Lizanne
Jones Day, Atlanta
404 581 8411
lthomas@jonesday.com
Recommended in Corporate/M&A
Practice Areas: Serves as firmwide Administrative Partner, with responsibility for overseeing administrative functions across Jones Day's 30 locations worldwide. She is experienced in mergers and acquisitions, corporate finance, defensive planning, and actively involved in general corporate counseling and board advice, including special committee representations. Frequent speaker on corporate governance, director liability and indemnification, and securities law issues.
Prof. Memberships: State Bar of Georgia; World Trade Club-Atlanta; The Salvation Army of Metro Atlanta; Friends of Music of Emory University; Arbor Montessori School; Board of Directors Network; Georgia Chamber of Commerce.

THROWER, Randolph W
Sutherland Asbill & Brennan LLP, Atlanta 404 853 8149
randolph.thrower@sablaw.com
Recommended in Tax
Career: Served as trustee on the boards of several universities and colleges and served as Chair of the Ethics Committee of the City of Atlanta from 1980 until 1992. Joined Sutherland in 1936 and has practiced in both the Washington and Atlanta offices.
Personal: Honorary LLD, Emory University, 1984; JD, first honors, Emory University School of Law, 1936; BPh, Emory University, 1934.

TISDALE Jr, Charles H
King & Spalding LLP, Atlanta
404 572 4820
ctisdale@kslaw.com
Recommended in Environment
Practice Areas: 30 years experience in environmental law, representing clients on air, water, and superfund and hazardous waste issues before state and federal agencies and in litigation.
Prof. Memberships: American Bar Association; Chemical Waste Litigation Reporter (Board); State Bar of Georgia (former Chairman, Environmental Law Section).
Personal: BA, cum laude, Vanderbilt University, 1969; JD, with distinction, Emory University, Order of the Coif; Omicron Delta Kappa, 1972.

TOULME, Nill V
Alston & Bird LLP, Atlanta
404 881 7143
ntoulme@alston.com
Recommended in Environment
Practice Areas: Focused on litigation and counseling regarding environmental, science and toxic tort issues and environmental aspects of mergers and acquisitions and real estate, financial, and fiduciary transactions.

Prof. Memberships: Chairs the Technology Committee of international law firm consortium, Lex Mundi. Founder and past Chairman, Environmental & Toxic Tort Section of the Atlanta Bar Association; past Chairman, State Bar of Georgia Environmental Law Section.
Personal: BA, magna cum laude, Duke University (1974); JD, University of Virginia School of Law (1978).

VARNER, Chilton
King & Spalding LLP, Atlanta
404 572 4789
cvarner@kslaw.com
Recommended in Litigation
Practice Areas: 25 years of courtroom experience defending corporations in product liability, commercial and civil disputes. Trial and appellate counsel for large automotive, pharmaceutical and medical device manufacturers in mass tort litigation, class actions and MDL litigation, including attorney-client privilege and Daubert issues.
Prof. Memberships: American Bar Association; American College of Trial Lawyers; Atlanta Bar Association; Emory University (Trustee); Product Liability Advisory Council (member); State Bar of Georgia.
Personal: AB, with distinction, Phi Beta Kappa, Smith College, 1965; JD, with distinction, Emory University, Order of the Coif, 1976. Distinguished Alumni Award, Emory University Law School.

VAUGHAN, David
Vaughan & Murphy, Atlanta
404 577 6550
Recommended in Antitrust

WALKER, Homer Lee
Alston & Bird LLP, Atlanta
404 881 7338
lwalker@alston.com
Recommended in Real Estate
Practice Areas: Mixed-use and multi-use, retail, hotel, residential and office projects from a developer's perspective. Experienced in joint venture and project finance transactions, as well as complex easement and restrictive covenant agreements related to these types of development projects.
Prof. Memberships: Member of the Real Estate Section of the State Bar of Georgia, the International Council of Shopping Centers, Urban Land Institute, and the Real Estate Group of Atlanta.
Career: Partner in the firm's Real Estate Group. Frequent speaker on developer oriented topics related to commercial real estate assets.
Personal: BA, University of Georgia (1983); JD, Emory University (1986).

WALSH, Brian C
King & Spalding LLP, Atlanta
404 572 2705
bwalsh@kslaw.com
Recommended in Bankruptcy
Practice Areas: Financial restructuring with focus on a range of bankruptcy,

receivership and litigation matters in federal and state courts. Experience representing amici in several significant appeals, including Bank of America v. 203 North LaSalle Street Partnership, Bousley v. United States in the Supreme Court of the United States and In re Welzel in the United States Court of Appeals for the Eleventh Circuit.
Prof. Memberships: State Bar of Georgia, the American Bar Association, the American Bankruptcy Institute and the Atlanta Bar Association.
Personal: BA, Duke University, 1993; JD, Harvard University, 1996.

WASSERMAN, Michael
Holt Ney Zatcoff & Wasserman, LLP, Atlanta 770 956 9600
Recommended in Tax

WEIRICH, Geoff
Paul, Hastings, Janofsky & Walker LLP, Atlanta 404 815 2221
geoffweirich@paulhastings.com
Recommended in Employment
Practice Areas: Exclusively advises and represents employers regarding a wide range of employment law issues. Particularly known for defending complex employment discrimination claims. Has handled approximately three dozen employment class actions.
Prof. Memberships: ABA Labor and Employment Law Section (Publications Chair, Equal Employment Opportunity Committee).
Publications: Editor in chief (Fourth Edition (in progress) and 2002 Third Cumulative Supplement to Third Edition) to the Lindemann & Grossman treatise, 'Employment Discrimination Law.'
Personal: MA, Labor and Industrial Relations and BA, Economics (Michigan State University). JD (Duke University School of Law) (Order of the Coif, executive editor of 'Duke Law Journal').

WELLS, Della Wager
Alston & Bird LLP, Atlanta
404 881 7891
dwells@alston.com
Recommended in Energy
Practice Areas: Concentrates on municipal bond law and authority representation and related corporate, tax and securities matters involving taxable and tax-exempt financings for electric and gas facilities and commodities, water and sewerage facilities and other public projects on behalf of governmental entities.
Prof. Memberships: Member of the National Association of Bond Lawyers and has served two terms on the Executive Committee of the Atlanta Contemporary Art Center.
Personal: BA, magna cum laude, University of Georgia (1980); MA, University of Virginia (1983); JD, with distinction, Emory University (1986).

WHITE, Benjamin T
Alston & Bird LLP, Atlanta
404 881 7488
bwhite@alston.com
Recommended in Tax
Practice Areas: Practice emphasizes exempt organizations as well as estate and tax planning.
Prof. Memberships: Fellow of the American College of Trust and Estate Counsel, founding member of the faculty of the American Institute for Philanthropic Studies, and has served as Chairman of the Fiduciary Law Section of the State Bar of Georgia and as President of the Harvard Law School Association of Georgia. Member of the Section of Real Property, Probate and Trust Law of the American Bar Association and also serves as a Member of the Exempt Organizations Committee of the American Bar Association Tax Section.
Career: Chair of the firm's Exempt Organizations Group and Co-Chair of the firm's Wealth Planning Group. Profiled in a leading legal publication.
Publications: Co-author of a two-volume text, Georgia Estate Planning, Will Drafting and Estate Administration Forms - Practice. Author of Foundation Desk Reference: A Compendium of Private Foundation Rules.
Personal: AB, University of North Carolina (1969); JD, Harvard University (1973).

WILLIAMSON, Robert
Scroggins & Williamson, Atlanta
404 893 3880
Recommended in Bankruptcy

WILSON, Brent
Elarbee, Thompson, Sapp & Wilson, LLP, Atlanta 404 659 6700
Recommended in Employment

WILSON, Stanford
Elarbee, Thompson, Sapp & Wilson, LLP, Atlanta 404 659 6700
Recommended in Employment

WING, Michael R
Greenberg Traurig LLP, Atlanta
678 553 2675
wingm@gtlaw.com
Recommended in Bankruptcy
Practice Areas: Reorganization, bankruptcy and restructuring.
Prof. Memberships: Member, State Bar of Georgia, Real Property Law Section. Member, Atlanta Bar Association.
Publications: Author, 'Extradition Treaties-International Law - The US Supreme Court Approves Extraterritorial Abduction of Foreign Criminals - United States v. Alvarez-Machain,' 23 Ga. J. Intl. & Comp. L. 435.
Personal: JD, University of Georgia School of Law, 1994. Editor in chief, Georgia Journal of International and Comparative Law. BA, University of North Carolina at Chapel Hill, 1990.

WOODWARD, Robert
King & Spalding LLP, Atlanta
404 572 3353
bwoodward@kslaw.com
Recommended in Tax
Practice Areas: Business tax issues, focusing on corporate mergers, acquisitions, restructurings and financings. Experience in tax, business and estate planning issues relating to corporate executives and closely held businesses and owners in tax controversies.
Prof. Memberships: American Bar Association (Chair, Subcommittee on Tax-Free Acquisitions); Atlanta Tax Forum (Former President and Trustee); Georgia Federal Tax Conference (Trustee); State Bar of Georgia.
Personal: BA, magna cum laude, Washington & Lee University, 1971; JD, Yale University, 1975.

WYMER, John
King & Spalding LLP, Atlanta
404 572 2413
jwymer@kslaw.com
Recommended in Employment
Practice Areas: Representing employers (private and public) in labor and employment-related disputes, class action litigation, employment discrimination cases, sexual harassment claims, National Labor Relations Board matters, arbitrations, wage/hour disputes and labor negotiations.
Prof. Memberships: Alabama State Bar; The College of Labor and Employment Lawyers Fellow; Management Labor and Employment Law Roundtable.
Personal: BA, University of Alabama, 1971; JD, University of Virginia, 1974.

YOUNG, Jeffrey E
Alston & Bird LLP, Atlanta
404 881 7857
jyoung@alston.com
Recommended in Intellectual Property
Practice Areas: Patent acquisition, opinions, and licensing; represents clients with extensive worldwide patent programs.
Prof. Memberships: Past Chair of the Intellectual Property Section of the State Bar of Georgia; Georgia Lawyers for the Arts; Board of the Atlanta Young Singers of Callanwolde.
Career: Speaks on intellectual property topics to business organizations and legal groups, and clients' employees.
Publications: Articles for legal and industry publications such as the Licensing Journal, Mealey's Litigation Report, Best's Review, Georgia State Bar Journal.
Personal: BS in Physics, cum laude, The Ohio State University (1972); JD with distinction, Emory University School of Law (1976).

ALSTON & BIRD LLP

THE FIRM

Managing Partner: Ben F Johnson III
Deputy Managing Partner: Philip C Cook
Number of partners: 281
Number of other lawyers: 423

FIRM OVERVIEW: Alston & Bird is a major US law firm, with 700 attorneys located in offices in Atlanta, Charlotte, New York, the Research Triangle and Washington, DC, offering services in virtually every practice area from antitrust to wealth planning. An important factor that differentiates Alston & Bird is its culture. In *Fortune*® magazine's 2004 list of the 'The 100 Best Companies to Work For'™ the firm ranks 2nd and is the first and only law firm ever named to the top five.

MAIN AREAS OF PRACTICE:

Bankruptcy: Alston & Bird's Bankruptcy, Workouts & Reorganization Group has represented secured and unsecured creditors, creditors' committees, debtors, trustees, examiners, shareholders, indenture trustees, franchisors and purchasers of assets in bankruptcy cases. The firm has skilled negotiators and seasoned litigators. The group also has excellent transactional skills; if you need to negotiate and document a deal from the financial side, Alston & Bird has lawyers in the group who are highly skilled in that area. Partner Neal Batson served as the court-appointed Examiner in the Enron Corp. Chapter 11 bankruptcy.

Capital Markets/Mergers & Acquisitions: The firm's attorneys have extensive experience with complex mergers and acquisitions, spin-offs, going private transactions, joint ventures and similar transactions for clients in a broad range of industries. Alston & Bird attorneys work on deals ranging from high-profile public transactions to acquisitions for closely-held businesses. The firm represents bidders, target companies, stockholders, boards of directors and financial advisors. Alston & Bird lawyers have been involved in all aspects of leveraged buyouts and distressed sales and can handle the acquisition and financing of public and non-public companies of any size.

Financial Services: Alston & Bird's Financial Services Group addresses the issues that occupy the time and attention of its clients' chief executive officers, chief financial officers, and general counsels. Whether the issue at hand is a strategic merger, complex regulatory issue, capital markets transaction or significant business alliance, the firm's attorneys work side-by-side with clients to solve the most critical challenges facing financial institutions today.

Healthcare: Alston & Bird has a national healthcare practice with more than 60 attorneys dedicated to the health care industry, the largest healthcare practice in the region and one of the largest in the country. The signature strength of this area of practice is Alston & Bird's ability to master complex representations that draw on the coordinated expertise of the firm's regulatory, transactional, biotechnology, and litigation groups. Tom Scully, former Administrator of the Centers for Medicare & Medicaid Services (CMS) from 2001- 03 is a member of this practice focusing on healthcare regulatory and legislative matters, as well as on advising clients on health policy and strategies for health care delivery.

Intellectual Property: Numbering more than 130 lawyers, including 90 legal professionals registered to practice before the US Patent and Trademark office, Alston & Bird's Intellectual Property Group is the largest in the Southeastern United States and one of the largest in any general practice firm in the country. The group provides a full-range of intellectual property services including: patentability and prosecution both in the United States and worldwide; appeals; oppositions; patent maintenance; counseling regarding infringement avoidance; and validity and infringement studies and opinions. The firm's IP practice also includes a highly specialized team which is a leader in the field of electronic entertainment, counseling developers, publishers and game-console manufacturers from content development through retail sale.

OFFICES

GEORGIA
One Atlantic Center, 1201 West Peachtree Street, **Atlanta**, GA 30309-3424
Tel: 404 881 7000 **Fax:** 404 881 7777
Email: info@alston.com **Website:** www.alston.com

DISTRICT OF COLUMBIA
601 Pennsylvania Avenue, N.W., 10th Floor, North Building
Washington, DC 20004-2601
Tel: 202 756 3300 **Fax:** 202 756 3333

NEW YORK
90 Park Avenue, **New York,** NY 10016-1387
Tel: 212 210 9400 **Fax:** 212 210 9444

NORTH CAROLINA
Bank of America Plaza, 101 South Tryon Street, Suite 4000
Charlotte, NC 28280-4000
Tel: 704 444 1000 **Fax:** 704 444 1111

3201 Beechleaf Court, Suite 600, **Raleigh**, NC 27604-1062
Tel: 919 862 2200 **Fax:** 919 862 2260

Legislative & Public Policy: Alston & Bird's Legislative & Public Policy Group has unique experience with how policy is made with the people who make it. The firm represents clients before Congress, the executive branch, and regulatory agencies. It prepares and delivers testimony before congressional committees on behalf of clients, and works directly with staff and members to help craft legislative and regulatory language. As Special Counsel, Senator Bob Dole's enormous reservoir of knowledge and expertise has proven to be invaluable to the firm's clients who have turned to him and the firm for representation in the nation's capital.

Litigation: Alston & Bird's more than 280 litigators have litigated in every state in the country and in international disputes in virtually every major industrialized jurisdiction, including Latin America, Europe and Asia. The firm's litigation practice groups include antitrust, bankruptcy, construction, environmental and land use, ERISA, international, international trade and regulatory, labor and employment, products liability and securities.

Tax: With nearly 70 tax lawyers, Alston & Bird has one of the largest law firm tax practices in the United States. Divided into six main practice groups – Federal, International, State & Local, Employee Benefits and Executive Compensation, Wealth Planning and Exempt Organizations – Alston & Bird is broadly experienced in serving the tax planning, dispute resolution, and tax legislative and regulatory needs of both US and foreign businesses and their owners.

CLIENTS: AFLAC, Assurant Inc., BellSouth Corporation, The Boeing Company, Delta Air Lines, Inc., The Dow Chemical Company, Genuine Parts Company, IMERYS, Mohawk Industries, Inc., NASCAR, Nokia, The Prudential Insurance Company of America, Regions Financial Corporation, Sabre, Skanska USA Building Inc., UnumProvident Corporation, UPS, Verizon Communications Corporation, and Wachovia.

INTERNATIONAL WORK: Alston & Bird's International Group is a multi-disciplinary team of business investment, intellectual property, tax, finance, regulatory, immigration, customs, and litigation experts. The group has structured deals and handled disputes around the globe - from Latin America and Europe to Asia and the Middle East. Alston & Bird's international practice has extensive experience in planning, structuring and implementing business deals in virtually every major commercial jurisdiction in the world. The firm can find and help you select the best local counsel, as well as help you determine the optimal structure for your business transaction abroad, whether it involves an acquisition, joint venture, licensing arrangement, technology transfer, manufacturing contract, distribution agreement or other arrangement.

ALSTON+BIRD LLP

ARNALL GOLDEN GREGORY LLP

THE FIRM

Chairman: Jonathan Golden
Managing Partner: William H Kitchens
Total number of attorneys: 138

FIRM OVERVIEW: Arnall Golden Gregory LLP is an Atlanta firm that serves the business transaction needs of growing public and private companies. Through mergers and acquisitions, capital markets financing, strategic alliances, joint ventures, litigation and other business-related guidance, the firm helps clients across a broad range of industries turn legal challenges into business opportunities.

MAIN AREAS OF PRACTICE:

Mergers & Acquisitions: AGG's Mergers and Acquisitions Practice covers a range of acquisition-related legal services, including tax, securities, technology and intellectual property, environmental, healthcare, employee benefits, and food and drug law. The firm's clients include companies from a variety of industries and business types, with transaction size typically ranging from $10m to $1b. The firm represents both purchasers and sellers, many of which are public companies and non-US companies engaged in US and non-US transactions.

Real Estate: Attorneys in the Real Estate Practice help domestic and international real estate owners, developers, and investors navigate the diverse business and legal issues that impact commercial real estate transactions. They also have a great deal of experience with foreign investors in US real estate. AGG represents companies in affordable housing, retail and office leasing and development, regional/super regional malls, real estate-based lending, and portfolio investment.

Litigation/Bankruptcy: The firm's Litigation Practice handles matters at the trial and appellate court levels and before administrative agencies. General business, intellectual property, and employment law litigation are key areas of focus. AGG's Bankruptcy Practice concentrates on commercial debt restructuring, settlements, bankruptcy trusteeships, and creditors' rights litigation.

Securities & Corporate Governance: AGG counsels public and private companies, as well as officers, directors, investors, and underwriters, in matters regarding securities transactions, compliance and corporate governance. Clients include entrepreneurial private companies, as well as large companies listed on the NYSE, NASDAQ, AMEX and OTC Bulletin Board.

Healthcare: AGG has a nationally-recognized Healthcare Practice that serves a range of healthcare providers, including hospitals, nursing homes, assisted living facilities, outpatient clinics, home health agencies, and clinical laboratories. Acquisition, financing and reorganization of healthcare facilities, Medicare/Medicaid reimbursement advice and litigation, fraud and abuse compliance, investigations and defense, and HIPAA compliance are all areas in which the firm's healthcare attorneys provide counsel.

Life Sciences: The firm's Life Sciences attorneys help emerging and established medical device, biologics and pharmaceutical companies turn scientific innovation into commercial viability. The firm's attorneys address legal problems and offer counseling at every stage of product development and organizational growth, including FDA compliance and product approval, clinical investigations and bioresearch, acquisitions and strategic alliances, intellectual property protection, and licensing.

HEAD OFFICE

GEORGIA
171 17th Street, Suite 2100, **Atlanta** GA 30363
Tel: 404 873 8500 **Fax:** 404 873 8501
Email: info@agg.com
Website: www.agg.com

BRANCH OFFICES

GEORGIA
201 Second Street, Suite 1000, **Macon** GA 31201
Tel: 478 745 3344 **Fax:** 478 743 0239

CONTACTS

Mergers & Acquisitions	Jeffrey B Stewart
Real Estate	Steven A Pepper
Litigation/Bankruptcy	Stephen M Dorvee, Darryl S Laddin
Securities & Corporate Governance	T Clark Fitzgerald III
Healthcare	Glenn P Hendrix
Life Sciences	Thomas O Duvall, Jr
Growth Companies/Private Equities	Clinton D Richardson
Private Wealth Planning	Bertram L Levy

Growth Companies/Private Equities: The Growth Companies/Private Equities Practice works with growing public and private companies and the financial institutions, venture capital firms, private equity providers, investment banks and individuals that fund their growth. Clients include businesses in the technology, life sciences, information, distribution, manufacturing and service industries. The firm helped found the Southeast's oldest venture capital trade association and plays an active role in the regional venture and entrepreneurial communities.

Private Wealth Planning: The firm's Private Wealth Planning Practice focuses on representing high net worth families in sophisticated wealth transfer matters, as well as fiduciaries in multi-faceted issues occurring during the estate administration process.

INTERNATIONAL WORK: AGG's foreign clients include businesses from over 40 countries whose activities in the United States range from a two person sales office, to a 1,000 employee manufacturing plant, to the Atlanta and New York offices of the world's largest banks. The firm's international attorneys conduct business in the Chinese, German, Spanish and French languages.

ASHE, RAFUSE & HILL, LLP

THE FIRM

Managing Partner: Nancy E Rafuse
Chair: R Lawrence Ashe, Jr

Number of Partners: 6
Number of other lawyers: 16

HEAD OFFICE

GEORGIA
1355 Peachtree Street, N.E., Suite 500, South Tower,
Atlanta, GA 30309-3232
Tel: 404 253 6000   **Fax:** 404 253 6060
Email: nancyrafuse@asherafuse.com
Website: www.asherafuse.com

FIRM OVERVIEW: Ashe, Rafuse & Hill, LLP, has as its three name partners, Lawrence Ashe, Nancy Rafuse and William Hill who are each recognized as some of the "Leading Lawyers" in Georgia, *Georgia Trend Magazine* (Dec 2004) and some of "the Best Attorneys in Atlanta" in *Law & Politics*, as published by *Atlanta Magazine* (March 2004). Ashe, Rafuse & Hill, LLP is a recently formed and rapidly growing law firm based in Atlanta, Georgia, with a focus on employment, civil rights, and commercial litigation. Ashe, Rafuse & Hill, LLP prides itself on providing outstanding legal services more efficiently and at more reasonable rates than are typically associated with national firms. Indeed, the six partners of Ashe, Rafuse & Hill, LLP and many of its 16 other attorneys left a large international law firm of approximately 800 attorneys fueled by the desire to practice law in an environment where the focus is on quality client service at a reasonable price.

MAIN AREAS OF PRACTICE:

Employment & Civil Rights: Ashe, Rafuse & Hill, LLP represents and advises clients on virtually every aspect of employment law, including by way of illustration, representation of employers in response to claims asserted under every non-discrimination statute (e.g., Title VII, ADEA, ADA), traditional labor laws, as well as other employment-related statutes (e.g., WARN, FMLA, OSHA, FLSA) and related state statutes and causes of action. The breadth of Ashe, Rafuse & Hill, LLP's employment practice has resulted in the expansion of its expertise into other areas of civil rights litigation, including Title II, Section 1981, and ADA customer accommodation claims. Recently, Nancy Rafuse and William Hill successfully tried a Title II public accomodation case to a complete zero defense verdict on behalf of a national restaurant chain.

Class & Collective Actions: The partners at Ashe, Rafuse & Hill, LLP have tried to a conclusion more discrimination class actions than any other management employment firm in the country and have defeated class certification in numerous cases. Lawrence Ashe has been recognized by the *National Law Journal* as the "dean of the management class action bar" and is one of only two career employment lawyers selected for membership into the American College of Trial Lawyers. Lawrence Ashe and Nancy Rafuse represented the State of California against a challenge to the use of the State's teacher licensing examination, which is believed to be the largest employment class action ever to be tried to a successful defense result. Ashe, Rafuse & Hill, LLP is frequently retained as co-counsel to many companies' regular outside counsel because of its lawyers' unique experience and expertise in employment and civil rights class and collective actions. The firm also represents employers in FLSA 'opt-in' matters, recently defeating certification of an alleged nationwide challenge to use of the exemption for store managers of a national retail chain.

Commercial Litigation: Ashe, Rafuse & Hill, LLP litigators have litigated complex commercial cases including products liability, trademark infringement, false advertising, theft of trade secrets, breach of fiduciary duties of officers and directors, professional malpractice, breach of restrictive covenants, securities fraud, as well as breach of contract and fraud claims under a variety of different state laws. William Hill, a former trial court judge and the Chair of the litigation section, represented a defendant in a products liability case which was recognized by the *National Law Journal* as one of the top 20 defense verdicts in 2000. In addition to their experience litigating conventional commercial disputes, the lawyers of the commercial litigation section have extensive experience litgating a variety of matters consolidated before the Judicial Panel on Multidistrict Litigation, including by the way of example, products liability, insurance fraud and internet gambling cases.

Reported Cases: *AMAE, et al. v. The State of California, et al.,* 937 F. Supp. 1397 (N.D. Cal. 1996), *affirmed en banc,* 231 F.3d 572 (9th Cir. 2000); *Reid, et al. v. Lockheed Martin Aeronautics Company,* 205 F.R.D. 655 (N.D. Ga. 2001); *Yarbrough, et al. v. Lockheed Martin Aeronautics Company,* 205 F.R.D. 655 (N.D. Ga. 2001); *Rhodes, et al. v. Cracker Barrel Old Country Store, Inc.,* 213 F.R.D. 619 (N.D. Ga. March 7, 2003). *Yaali, Ltd., et al. v. Barns & Noble, Inc., et al.,* 269 Ga. 695, 506 S.E.2d 116 (1998).

BONDURANT, MIXSON & ELMORE, LLP

THE FIRM

Managing Partner: H Lamar Mixson
Senior Partner: Emmet J Bondurant

Number of partners: 11
Number of other lawyers: 16

HEAD OFFICE

GEORGIA
1201 W Peachtree Street, NW, One Atlantic Center, Suite 3900,
Atlanta, GA 30309
Tel: 404 881 4100 **Fax:** 404 881 4111

Website: www.bmelaw.com

FIRM OVERVIEW: The law firm of Bondurant, Mixson & Elmore represents plaintiffs and defendants in a wide variety of disputes, including complex business lawsuits, class actions, multi-party and multi-district cases.

MAIN AREAS OF PRACTICE:

Antitrust: Since the firm's inception, antitrust has been an integral part of its practice. During the last 20 years, it has handled complex civil and criminal antitrust matters arising in a variety of different industries and commercial contexts, including the airline industry, hospital and healthcare, carpet products, dredging, dairy products, poultry products, motorsports, cement and aggregate products, key manufacturing, electrical generation, franchising and distributorship agreements, and others.

Appellate: The firm has extensive experience representing clients in the state and federal appellate courts. Its appellate practice is in part an extension of its trial practice, devoted to representing clients that the firm also represented at the trial level. A significant portion of the firm's appellate practice, however, consists of handling appeals where it was not counsel of record in the trial court. In those cases, the firm typically works closely with trial counsel to ensure the effective representation of its clients in the appellate court.

Business Torts: The firm routinely prosecutes and defends suits arising out of business torts. Over the last several years, the firm has seen substantial growth in the number of such suits as plaintiffs have come to realize that significant verdicts, including punitive damages, may be available to the successful claimant. Recently, the firm was co-counsel to the plaintiffs in the Six Flags v Time Warner case, which resulted in a verdict of $454,000,000, which was affirmed entirely on appeal and which was the largest jury verdict in the history of the State of Georgia.

Contracts: The firm has prosecuted and defended a wide variety of cases involving contract disputes. A complete list of the types of contract disputes Bondurant, Mixson & Elmore has handled would be too lengthy for this publication. However, the following partial list gives an indication of the types of contract disputes the firm has handled: construction disputes, employee/employer relationships, partnership disputes, indemnification disputes, insurance coverage disputes, franchisor/franchisee relationships, shareholder agreements, and covenants not to compete.

Corporate Governance: Bondurant, Mixson & Elmore is one of the preeminent practitioners of corporate governance litigation in the Southeastern region. The firm has represented parties involved in all sides of corporate governance disputes, including minority and majority shareholders, limited and general partners, receivers, and corporate and partnership officers, directors and managers. The firm has also participated in corporate control disputes including hostile tender offers and proxy litigation involving public companies.

Employment & Civil Rights: The firm's attorneys have extensive experience in handling employment and civil rights litigation. This tradition began in 1964, when Emmet Bondurant successfully argued Wesberry v

Sanders in front of the United States Supreme Court, affirming the one-person, one-vote principle. 376 US 1 (1964). In 1984, Bondurant again prevailed in the United States Supreme Court, successfully representing a female attorney who had been denied partnership in a major Atlanta law firm. Hishon v King & Spalding, 467 US 69 (1984). In 2000, the firm served as lead plaintiffs' counsel in the class action race discrimination case against The Coca-Cola Company, Abdallah v The Coca-Cola Company, 133 F.Supp.2d 1364 (ND Ga. 2001). In that case, the firm obtained a $192.5 million settlement - the largest settlement ever achieved in a private race discrimination class action.

Environmental Litigation: Bondurant, Mixson & Elmore has handled cases under CERCLA, RCRA, FIFRA, HSRA and other environmental statutes and regulatory schemes. It has extensive experience handling environmental cases asserting claims under state common law theories (trespass, nuisance, negligence, negligence per se). The firm's environmental cases have included toxic tort (personal injury) claims as well as claims for property damage, response costs and injunctive relief. Bondurant, Mixson & Elmore also has experience handling insurance coverage litigation in the environmental field.

RICO: Bondurant, Mixson & Elmore has extensive experience with the difficult issues presented by litigation under the federal Racketeer Influenced and Corrupt Organizations Act and its numerous state law counterparts. It has represented both plaintiffs and defendants at the trial and appellate levels in federal and state RICO cases.

Professional Liability: The firm has broad and deep experience representing both plaintiffs and defendants in the resolution of high-stakes professional liability disputes. The firm's experience extends to disputes in the fields of accounting, architecture and engineering, but its professional liability practice focuses on the professional duties and liabilities of attorneys, corporate directors and officers, and public officials.

Intellectual Property & Trade Secrets: Bondurant, Mixson & Elmore is dedicated to excellence in litigation on the cutting edge of the law involving the protection of intellectual property. The firm's attorneys have a wealth of experience in the full spectrum of intellectual property litigation including patents, trademarks and unfair competition, copyrights, and trade secrets.

White Collar Crime: The firm has wide experience in the business crimes field particularly in the area of antitrust.

CLIENTS: Avon Products, Inc.; Brinks Home Security Systems, Inc.; Conoco, Inc.; Delta Air Lines, Inc.; Fina Oil and Chemical Company; Lincare, Inc.; Michelin North America, Inc.; Primerica Financial Services, Inc.

FISHER & PHILLIPS LLP

THE FIRM

Chairman: Roger K Quillen
Number of partners: 85
Number of senior counsel : 6
Number of counsel: 19
Number of associates: 72

FIRM OVERVIEW: Fisher & Phillips LLP is one of the oldest and largest firms in the United States which represents management in the areas of labor, employment, civil rights, employee benefits and immigration law. The firm's expertise and continuing focus on employment-related matters provides clients with reduced start-up times, greater cost efficiencies, and better outcomes. The firm's businesslike approach to workplace issues enables it to bring an efficient and practical perspective to today's labor and employment law problems.

MAIN AREAS OF PRACTICE:

Affirmative Action Plans: Fisher & Phillips drafts affirmative action plans and policies and represents clients in enforcement proceedings before the Office of Federal Contract Compliance Programs (OFCCP).

Business Immigration Services: Fisher & Phillips assists businesses in obtaining visas for alien employees, advises employers on compliance with federal employment verification requirements, represents clients in verification audits and defends immigration discrimination claims.

Employee Benefits: The firm handles pension and benefit matters under the Employee Retirement Income Security Act (ERISA), continuation of insurance coverage issues under COBRA, and compliance issues under the Health Insurance Portability and Accountability Act (HIPAA). Attorneys prepare qualified employee benefit plans, executive compensation programs and health and welfare benefit plans.

Employment Discrimination & Harassment: On a daily basis, the firm handles dozens of EEOC and state human rights commission charges, as well as federal and state lawsuits alleging discrimination and harassment on the basis of race, sex, age, national origin, religion and disability. The firm also assists employers in developing effective policies against discrimination and harassment, and in investigating complaints of discrimination and harassment.

Labor Relations: The firm assists its non-union clients in remaining union free and represents its unionized clients in collective bargaining, arbitration and unfair labor practice cases.

Mergers, Acquisitions & Divestitures: Fisher & Phillips advises clients on the labor, employment and benefits aspects of buying or selling a business, including union representation issues, benefit plan mergers and terminations, severance plans, executive employment agreements, and withdrawal liability issues.

Occupational Safety & Health: The firm works with clients to prevent health and safety problems and to achieve practical compliance with applicable requirements. Attorneys also represent employers during safety and health inspections and enforcement proceedings by federal OSHA and state agencies.

Trade Secrets & Unfair Competition: The firm prepares non-competition, non-solicitation, non-disclosure, non-recruitment and confidentiality agreements (where permitted by law) to protect clients' business interests and counsels clients on strategies designed to prevent misappropriation of trade secrets and proprietary information.

Wage & Hour Laws: Fisher & Phillips attorneys emphasize practical, cost-saving approaches to compliance. The firm performs audits of compliance status, preparation for and representation of clients during government wage-hour investigations, defense of wage-hour lawsuits, review and design of pay plans, and advice on exempt/non-exempt classifications.

Workplace Violence: The firm assists clients in developing and enforcing effective policies, responding to threats and violence in the workplace and securing restraining orders where appropriate.

HEAD OFFICE

GEORGIA
1500 Resurgens Plaza, 945 East Paces Ferry Road, **Atlanta**, GA 30326
Tel: 404 231 1400   **Fax:** 404 240 4249
Email: fp@laborlawyers.com
Website: www.laborlawyers.com

BRANCH OFFICES

CALIFORNIA
Suite 400, 18400 Von Karman Avenue, **Irvine,** CA 92612
Tel: 949 851 2424   **Fax:** 949 851 0152

Suite 950, 4225 Executive Square, **La Jolla,** CA 92037
Tel: 858 597 9600   **Fax:** 858 597 9601

Suite 200, City Center, 501 Fourteenth Street, **Oakland,** CA 94612
Tel: 510 763 4411   **Fax:** 510 763 4418

FLORIDA
Suite 800, 450 East Las Olas Boulevard, **Fort Lauderdale,** FL 33301
Tel: 954 525 4800   **Fax:** 954 525 8739

1250 Lincoln Plaza, 300 South Orange Avenue, **Orlando,** FL 32801
Tel: 407 541 0888   **Fax:** 407 541 0887

2525 SunTrust Financial Centre, 401 E Jackson Street, **Tampa,** FL 33602
Tel: 813 769 7500   **Fax:** 813 769 7501

ILLINOIS
1000 Marquette Building, 140 South Dearborn Street, **Chicago,** IL 60603
Tel: 312 346 8061   **Fax:** 312 346 3179

LOUISIANA
Suite 3710, 201 St Charles Avenue, **New Orleans,** LA 70170
Tel: 504 522 3303   **Fax:** 504 529 3850

MISSOURI
Suite 400, 104 West 9th Street, **Kansas City**, MO 64105
Tel: 816 842 8770   **Fax:** 816 842 8767

NORTH CAROLINA
Suite 1400, 201 S College Street, **Charlotte,** NC 28244
Tel: 704 334 4565   **Fax:** 704 334 9774

NEVADA
Suite 650, 3993 Howard Hughes Parkway, **Las Vegas,** NV 89109
Tel: 702 252 3131   **Fax:** 702 252 7411

OREGON
Suite 1600, 1001 SW Fifth Avenue, **Portland,** OR 97204
Tel: 503 242 4262   **Fax:** 503 242 4263

SOUTH CAROLINA
Suite 1400, 1901 Main Street, **Columbia,** SC 29201
Tel: 803 255 0000   **Fax:** 803 255 0202

CLIENTS: The firm has a broad and diverse client base, representing a wide range of public and private employers. Some clients are large multinational corporations with thousands of employees; others are smaller entrepreneurial businesses. Clients include employers in a variety of industries: agriculture, automobile dealerships, banking, broadcasting, casinos and gaming, construction, education, financial services, health care, hospitality, insurance, legal and professional services, manufacturing, mining, real estate, retail, state and local government entities, technology, transportation, and wholesale and distribution industries.

FISHER & PHILLIPS LLP
ATTORNEYS AT LAW

Solutions at Work®

FORD & HARRISON LLP

THE FIRM

Managing Partner: C Lash Harrison

Number of partners: 62
Number of other lawyers: 74

FIRM OVERVIEW: Founded in 1978, Ford & Harrison has evolved into one of the premier national labor and employment law firms with 13 offices in key US markets. The firm provides labor and employment legal advice and services to employers, in areas including employment litigation, discrimination, harassment, class action litigation, affirmative action, wrongful termination, wage and hour law, ADA/FMLA, airline labor law, labor union organizing, collective bargaining, arbitration, layoffs and plant closings, mergers and acquisitions, employment contracts, alternative dispute resolution, business immigration, employee benefits, workplace safety and environmental law.

MAIN AREAS OF PRACTICE:

Employment: Ford & Harrison advises clients on all matters affecting the employment relationship, from recruiting and retention to termination issues. The firm's attorneys design policies and practices that minimize the risk of successful claims of discrimination, equal pay violations, breaches of employment contract and wrongful or retaliatory discharges. Ford & Harrison attorneys counsel clients on the changes in federal and state wage and hour laws, Family Medical Leave Act (FMLA), the Americans With Disabilities Act (ADA) and Health Insurance Portability and Accountability Act (HIPAA). The firm's attorneys and consultants evaluate employment vulnerabilities through personnel audits, reviews of personnel policies or handbooks, and management training. In addition, Ford & Harrison attorneys develop and assist in implementing affirmative action plans. The firm advises clients on health and safety issues, including the establishment of workable safety programs, compliance with the Occupational Safety and Health Act (OSHA) and compliance with employee 'right to know' statutes.

Labor Law: Collective bargaining and union organizing drives can be handled successfully if management teams are given the knowledge and insight necessary to deal with these issues. Ford & Harrison attorneys represent and advise employers in all phases of labor relations matters as they arise under the NLRA and RLA.

Litigation: The proliferation of state and federal laws creating employee rights has prompted an increasing number of lawsuits that make their way into court. Ford & Harrison recognizes that clients expect and deserve quality litigation services, which are delivered efficiently and cost effectively. In addition to representation of management in employment disputes, the firm also represent clients in all types of business litigation. Ford & Harrison attorneys litigate such matters as employment contracts, trade secrets, unfair competition and covenants not to compete and also have significant experience in class action litigation. The firm has successfully opposed class certification in all cases where it has been lead counsel. This experience has given the firm special knowledge about the process in defending class action lawsuits that translates into cost savings for employer clients. Preventing protracted litigation is always a key goal and Ford & Harrison attorneys are leaders in achieving results through preventative strategies.

Employee Benefits: Ford & Harrison's employee benefits group has experience in assisting numerous public and private employers with their compensation and benefit plans. Some of the issues that the firm advises employers on are related to pension plans, profit sharing plans, trusts, welfare benefit plans, leave policies and Department of Labor investigations.

Immigration: The firm's attorneys provide immigration advice to clients who hire or transfer foreign employees. In compliance with the Immigration Reform and Control Act, Ford & Harrison assists clients in obtaining temporary visas and permanent resident status ('Green Cards') in the United States, obtain necessary labor certification and temporary work permits, and counsel employers on hiring and transferring foreign employees.

CLIENTS: The firm's clients, located throughout the United States, include air carriers, manufacturers, print and broadcast media, building and defense contractors, hospitals, medical clinics, automobile dealerships, supermarket and restaurant chains, retailers, and many other small, medium and large employers.

HEAD OFFICE

GEORGIA
1275 Peachtree Street, NE, Suite 600, **Atlanta** GA 30309
Tel: 404 888 3800   **Fax:** 404 888 3863
Website: www.fordharrison.com

BRANCH OFFICES

ALABAMA
2100 Third Avenue North, Suite 400, **Birmingham** AL 35203
Tel: 205 254 9480   **Fax:** 205 254 9848

CALIFORNIA
350 South Grand Avenue, Suite 2300, **Los Angeles** CA 90071
Tel: 213 237 2400   **Fax:** 213 237 2401

COLORADO
1675 Broadway, Suite 2150, **Denver** CO 80202
Tel: 303 592 8860   **Fax:** 303 592 8861

DISTRICT OF COLUMBIA
1300 19th Street NW, Suite 700, **Washington** DC 20036
Tel: 202 719 2000   **Fax:** 202 719 2077

FLORIDA
225 Water Street, Suite 710, **Jacksonville** FL 32202
Tel: 904 357 2000   **Fax:** 904 357 2001

100 SE 2nd Street, Suite 4500, **Miami** FL 33131
Tel: 305 808 2100   **Fax:** 305 808 2101

300 South Orange Avenue, Suite 1300, **Orlando** FL 32801
Tel: 407 418 2300   **Fax:** 407 418 2327

101 East Kennedy Boulevard, Suite 900, **Tampa** FL 33602-5133
Tel: 813 261 7800   **Fax:** 813 261 7899

NEW YORK
100 Park Avenue, Suite 2500, **New York** NY 10017
Tel: 212 453 5900   **Fax:** 212 453 5959

SOUTH CAROLINA
Suite 400, 101 North Pine Street, PO Box 5398
Spartanburg SC 29302-5398
Tel: 864 699 1100   **Fax:** 864 699 1101

TENNESSEE
6750 Poplar Avenue, Suite 600, **Memphis** TN 38138
Tel: 901 291 1500   **Fax:** 901 291 1501

TEXAS
1601 Elm Street, Suite 4450, **Dallas**, TX 75201
Tel: 214 256 4700   **Fax:** 214 256 4701

FORD & HARRISON LLP
Creative Workplace Solutions

GRIFFIN COCHRANE & MARSHALL

A PROFESSIONAL CORPORATION

THE FIRM

Shareholders: Lee C Davis, Jennifer W Fletcher, W Henry Parkman
J Dean Marshall, Jr, F Barry McCabe

Number of other lawyers: 10

FIRM OVERVIEW: Griffin Cochrane & Marshall celebrates its 25th Anniversary this year. Since its founding in 1980, GCM has devoted its practice to providing legal services to the construction industry nation-wide. GCM enjoys the reputation of a specialty practice firm offering equal sophistication and quality to the multi-national mega firms. GCM and its lawyers have achieved the first-tier rating for 'Leading Firms in Georgia (Construction)' by Chambers & Partners; the AV rating by Mar-tindale-Hubbell; and recognition of its partners as 'Georgia SuperLawyers' by Law & Politics. GCM's five shareholders each bring unique talents to the firm's client service, and have resolved successfully many multi-mil-lion dollar disputes for construction contractors, owners, suppliers, and specialty contractors. The four senior shareholders have practiced togeth-er at Griffin Cochrane & Marshall for more than 20 years, and uphold the tradition of service and quality established by firm founder, Harry 'Buck' Griffin, who maintains an office notwithstanding his retirement several years ago. The firm offers state-of-the-art construction counsel, including project planning, dispute avoidance, and dispute resolution. GCM has long been a leader in using mediation and alternative methods to resolve construction disputes. In addition, its lawyers have litigated many large cases to successful resolution, including lead roles in some of the largest and most complex jury trials involving construction issues. GCM's attor-neys are uniquely qualified to draft contracts, provide advice, conduct negotiations, handle bid protests, and to present claims or defenses in arbitration or in court. The firm is committed to achieving excellent results for clients. Whether prosecuting or defending claims, or guiding a client through day-to-day decisions, the firm's goal is to add value to the business efforts of construction industry clients.

MAIN AREAS OF PRACTICE: Construction industry disputes and avoid-ance nationwide.

CLIENTS: GCM represents some of the nation's largest contractors, pub-lic entities, and private owners, including several Fortune 100 corpora-tions, and numerous privately-held construction industry participants. The projects GCM has been involved with include every variety of con-struction work, including infrastructure, commercial, industrial, process, retail, hotel and resort, residential, and public works facilities. The diver-sity of client base and the types of construction matters handled by the firm enables GCM to approach problem-solving from a broad base of knowledge and experience. GCM is committed to understanding its clients and their objectives. The firm prides itself on high level commit-ment and personal attention to each client's needs. GCM maintains its focus on achieving the client's objectives through the most cost-effective and innovative legal and business solutions.

HEAD OFFICE

GEORGIA
127 Peachtree Street, 14th Floor **Atlanta**, GA 30303-1810
Tel: 404 523 2000   **Fax:** 404 523 9655
Website: www.gcm-atty.com

REPORTED CASES:

Federal Appellate Decisions: Venetian Casino Resort, L.L.C. v Lehrer McGovern Bovis, Inc., 92 Fed. Appx. 402, 2004 WL 42384 (9th Cir. Jan. 7, 2004); Eng. Contractors Assoc. of South Florida, Inc. v Metropolitan Dade County, 122 F.3d 895 (11th Cir. 1997), cert. denied, 118 S.Ct. 1186 (1998); Davidson & Jones Dev. Co. v Elmore Dev. Co., 921 F.2d 1343 (6th Cir. 1991); S.J. Groves & Sons Co. v Fulton County, 920 F.2d 752 (11th Cir.), cert. denied, 500 US 959 (1991); Pinnacle Port Community Assn., Inc. v Orenstein, 872 F.2d 1536 (11th Cir. 1989); Weyher/Livsey Con-structors, Inc. v International Chem. Co., 864 F.2d 130 (11th Cir. 1989); Pathman Constr. Co. v United States, 817 F.2d 1573 (Fed. Cir. 1987); T.S.I., Inc. v Metric Constructors, Inc., 817 F.2d 94 (11th Cir. 1987).

Federal District Decisions: Pitt-Des Moines, Inc. v Metropolitan Pier & Exposition Authority, 1999 WL 162786 (N.D. Ill. Mar. 16, 1999); JWP/Hyre Electric Co. v Mentor Village School District, 968 F. Supp. 356 (N.D. Ohio 1996); L.K. Comstock & Co. v Becon Constr. Co., 932 F. Supp. 948 (E.D. Ky 1994), aff'd, 73 F.3d 362 (6th Cir. 1995); USF&G v Ernest Constr. Co., 854 F. Supp. 1545 (M.D. Fla. 1994); Robert Lamb Hart Plan-ners and Architects v Evergreen, Ltd., 787 F. Supp. 753 (S.D. Ohio 1992); Blue Circle Atlantic, Inc. v Falcon Materials, Inc., 760 F. Supp. 516 (D. Md. 1991), aff'd, 960 F.2d 145 (4th Cir. 1992); W.L. Jorden & Co. v Blythe Indus. Inc., 702 F. Supp. 282 (N.D. Ga. 1988); Pinkerton and Laws Co. v Roadway Express, Inc., 650 F. Supp. 1138 (N.D. Ga. 1986); G.D. Searle & Co. v Metric Constructors, Inc., 572 F. Supp. 836 (N.D. Ga. 1983); Robert E. McKee, Inc. v City of Atlanta, 431 F. Supp. 1198 (N.D. Ga. 1977).

State Appellate Decisions: Amprite Elec. Co. v Tenn. Stadium Group, LLP., No. M2002-00892-COA-R3-CV, 2003 WL 22171556 (Tenn. Ct. App. Sept. 22, 2003); J. Kinson Cook, Inc. v Weaver, 252 Ga. App. 868, 556 S.E.2d 831 (2001); Republic Contracting Corp. v S.C. Dept. of Transp., 332 S.C. 197, 503 S.E.2d 761 (1998); R.J. Griffin & Co. v Continental Ins. Co., 230 Ga. App. 822, 497 S.E.2d 586 (1998); Ga. Dept. of Transp. v Dal-ton Paving & Constr. Inc., 227 Ga. App. 207, 489 S.E.2d 329 (1997); Collins v Lunda Constr. Co., 214 Ga. App. 512, 448 S.E.2d 236 (1994); J. Lee Gre-gory, Inc. v Scandinavian House, L.P., 209 Ga. App. 285, 433 S.E.2d 687 (1993); C.B.I. Na-Con Inc. v Macon Bibb County Water & Sewerage Auth., 205 Ga. App. 82, 421 S.E.2d 111 (1992); Lunda Constr. Co. v Clay-ton County, 201 Ga. App. 106, 410 S.E. 2d 446 (1991); Robert & Co. Assocs. v Rhodes-Haverty Partnership, 250 Ga. 680, 300 S.E.2d 503 (1983); Hilton Constr. Co. v Martin Mechanical Contractors, Inc., 251 Ga. 701, 308 S.E.2d 830 (1983); Space Leasing Assoc. v Atlantic Bldg. Sys. Inc., 144 Ga. App. 320, 241 S.E.2d 438 (1977).

Decisions from Federal Claims Court and Board of Contract Appeals: Appeal of J. Slotnik Co., VABCA No. 3254, 94-3 BCA ¶27,012 (1994) (14 consolidated cases); Appeal of Murray Walter, Inc., VABCA No. 1848, 87-2 BCA ¶19,947 (1987); Hoel-Steffen Constr. Co. v United States, 684 F.2d 843 (Ct. Cl. 1982).

HENDRICK, PHILLIPS, SALZMAN & FLATT, P.C.

THE FIRM

Managing Partner: William D Flatt, Esq
Senior Partner: David R Hendrick, Esq

Number of partners: 5
Number of other lawyers: 7

FIRM OVERVIEW: Hendrick, Phillips, Salzman & Flatt has earned a national reputation for providing sophisticated legal services and counseling to businesses involved in the construction industry for over 20 years. Its practice concentrates on the unique and specialized legal needs of such businesses spanning all phases of construction law and construction related legal transactions and involving public, private and 'privatized' construction projects. Additionally, Hendrick, Phillips, Salzman & Flatt offers the full range of legal and business planning services necessary for the successful formation, operation and guidance of construction and related businesses. The firm is dedicated to providing legal services on the basis of a complete understanding of each client's objectives and operations in order to provide efficient, experienced, and personalized service. The firm stresses proper advance counseling with our clients to avoid or minimize their legal and business risks. Its emphasis is on counseling and pursuit of preventive measures and dispute avoidance techniques, seeking to avoid disruptive and costly disputes and to resolve those disputes which do arise in a 'business' rather than 'litigation' context. However, attorneys of the firm are thoroughly familiar with and experienced in all forms of dispute resolution including administrative and judicial litigation in federal and state forums at all levels, as well as alternative dispute resolution procedures such as mediation and arbitration. The firm's attorneys are regularly involved in the prosecution or defense of client interests in large, complex construction disputes in many different jurisdictions and they have tried many cases before national arbitration and administrative panels and courts at all levels and in many different jurisdictions.

MAIN AREAS OF PRACTICE: The principal area of practice is construction law.

CLIENTS: The firm's commitment to and recognition by the construction industry is demonstrated by the broad diversified client base that it maintains throughout the United States. Firm clients include national, regional and local contractors, construction managers, subcontractors, and vendors, as well as public and private owners, developers, design professionals, insurance and surety companies, and international, national and regional trade associations serving the construction industry. The firm has established professional relationships with clients of all sizes and

HEAD OFFICE

GEORGIA
230 Peachtree Street, N.W. Suite 2500 **Atlanta**, GA 30303
Tel: 404 522 1410   **Fax:** 404 522 9545
Email: drh@hpsf-law.com
Website: www.hpsslaw.com

CONTACTS

Construction..David R Hendrick

descriptions. Most of its clients are associated with the construction and development business and include public and private owners, developers, contractors, design professionals, manufacturers and suppliers. The firm is counsel to the National Roofing Contractors Association and the National Roofing Legal Resource Center, has served as counsel to American Subcontractors Association, and is counsel to various state and local contractor and specialty contractor trade associations, including the Associated Builders & Contractors of Georgia, Inc.; Georgia Mechanical Contractors Association, Georgia Lathing and Plastering Contractors Association, Inc., Georgia Concrete and Products Association, Mechanical Industries Council, Roofing & Sheet Metal Contractors Association of Georgia, Montana Roofing Contractors Association and Master Roofing Contractors Association of Atlanta. The following is a representative listing of some of the companies the firm has recently represented or currently represents in construction matters: RMC Allied Readymix Inc.; Arcadis Geraghty & Miller; Archer Western Contractors, Ltd.; Anne Arundel County Public Schools; Bechtel Corporation; Beers/Skanska Construction Company, Inc.; Centex Construction Company; Dudley Barrett Construction Company; E.I. Dupont de Nemours & Co.; Ellis Don Construction Ltd.; ESI Companies Inc.; Fairgreen Capital, Inc./Northside Realty; Fischbach and Moore, Inc.; Grinnell Fire Protection Systems Company; Heery International; InfraSource, Inc.; J.A. Jones Construction Co., Inc.; Juneau Construction Company, LLC; Keene Construction of Central Florida, Inc.; Kemron Environmental Services, Inc.; Lockwood Greene Engineers, Inc.; Mirant Corporation; Morris-Shea Bridge Company, Inc.; Noble-Storemont Investments; Nissan Motor Manufacturing Corporation; RMC Industries Corporation; John W. Rooker Construction Company, Inc.; Samsung Electronics; Siemens Energy and Automation, Inc.; St. Paul Insurance Co.; L.E. Schwartz & Sons, Inc.; Techta America Corporation; United States Fidelity & Guaranty Company; and Yokogawa Corporation of America.

KILPATRICK STOCKTON LLP

THE FIRM

Managing Partner: William H Brewster
Firm Co-Chairs: Miles Alexander, A Stephens Clay, J Robert Elster
Number of partners: 237
Number of other lawyers: 241
Email: webmaster@kilpatrickstockton.com
Website: www.kilpatrickstockton.com

FIRM OVERVIEW: Kilpatrick Stockton LLP is a full-service law firm with over 470 attorneys in nine offices across the eastern United States and in Europe. To suppport the increasing significance of international markets and global business transaction to their clients, Kilpatrick Stockton maintains offices in London and Stockholm. As a result, the firm serves international and multinational clients including those in Europe, Latin Amercia, Asia and Australia. It is one of the world's 100 largest and most successful law firms, and the firm delivers innovative business solutions and results-oriented counsel for corporations at all stages of the growth cycle. Kilpatrick Stockton's core values towards community services resulted in the dedication of almost 26,000 hours of pro bono work, a $7 million value, in 2004.

MAIN AREAS OF PRACTICE:

Corporate: Kilpatrick Stockton's more than 100 corporate attorneys offer valuable counsel through a wide range of general corporate, corporate finance, securities, cross-border transactions, technology licensing and outsourcing, tax, mergers, acquisitions, and transactional services to clients at every end of the business spectrum, from Fortune 500 companies to promising start-ups. On nearly every continent, the firm advises companies in market sectors as diverse as communications, financial, manufacturing, retail and technology. In the US, the firm counseled clients on more than 300 venture capital transactions since the start of the new century.
Intellectual Property: With a force of over 95 dedicated intellectual property attorneys specializing in patent, trademark, and copyright law, Kilpatrick Stockton is unique among general practice firms. In the area of patent law, 40 attorneys registered to practice before the United States Patent and Trademark Office offer experience in well over 100 areas. In an independent worldwide survey taken among in-house and private practitioners, 'Managing Intellectual Property' rated the firm chairman as one of the top two practicing trademark lawyers in the world, and the firm is consistently ranked among the top IP practices in the country.
Litigation: Over 100 lawyers in the Litigation Practice have the depth to aggressively defend the most complex commercial case and the flexibility to represent clients in the routine business disputes that require efficient resolution. The firm appears on behalf of clients in state and federal courts throughout the US and before arbitration tribunals around the world. Kilpatrick Stockton's lawyers have received recognition in numerous national and trade publications for being some of the most experienced litigation attorneys in the world.
Labor, Employment & Employee Benefits: Kilpatrick Stockton's attorneys have advised clients ranging from Fortune 10 to startups in every aspect of labor, employment, and employee benefits law. The firm's attorneys represent employers during union organizational and de-certification attempts, arbitrations, collective bargaining negotiations, unfair labor practice proceedings, and ERISA litigation. Remaining at the forefront of critical developments in the field, the firm helps clients comply with ever-changing affirmative action requirements, occupational safety and health law, benefit plan design, and fiduciary responsibility, as well as reporting and disclosure obligations and executive compensation law.
Finance: Kilpatrick Stockton's Finance Practice Group provides counsel to both large financial institutions and corporate borrowers in a wide variety of corporate and commercial finance transactions, commercial mortgage-

US OFFICES

GEORGIA
Suite 2800, 1100 Peachtree Street, **Atlanta**, GA 30309-4530
Tel: 404 815 6500   **Fax:** 404 815 6555

Suite 1400, Wachovia Bank Building, 699 Broad Street,
Augusta, GA 30901-1453
Tel: 706 724 2622   **Fax:** 706 722 0219

DISTRICT OF COLUMBIA
Suite 900, 607 14th Street NW, **Washington**, DC 20005-2018
Tel: 202 508 5800   **Fax:** 202 508 5858

NORTH CAROLINA
Suite 2500, 214 North Tryon Street, **Charlotte**, NC 28202-2381
Tel: 704 338 5000   **Fax:** 704 338 5125

Suite 400 3737 Glenwood Avenue, **Raleigh**, NC 27612
Tel: 919 420 1700   **Fax:** 919 420 1800

1001 West Fourth Street, **Winston-Salem**, NC 27101-2400
Tel: 336 607 7300   **Fax:** 336 607 7500

NEW YORK
805 Third Avenue, 20th Floor, **New York**, NY 10022
Tel: 212 912 3527   **Fax:** 212 912 3530

International Offices in London and Stockholm

backed securities transactions, and public finance transactions. The firm's attorneys serve as bond issuer and underwriter's counsel with respect to all types of state, county and local obligations.
Real Estate: Kilpatrick Stockton's real estate attorneys annually advise clients on transactions worth billions of dollars and hundreds of millions of square feet. The firm represents large commercial developers, leading lenders, Fortune 500 corporations, and major metropolitan governments in matters including taxation, banking and other private finance, public finance, securities regulation, creditor's rights and debtor's reorganization proceedings, zoning and land use regulation, and foreign investment.
Environmental: Kilpatrick Stockton has one of the largest and most diverse environmental regulatory and litigation practices in the United States. The firm's attorneys assist public- and private-sector clients in avoiding environmental liability and regulatory conflicts through preventive counseling and management of environmental permit processes.
Construction: Kilpatrick Stockton's construction and public contracts attorneys have assisted clients with construction matters in all 50 states and over 25 countries. The firm represents clients from project inception through project completion and beyond.
Government Relations: Kilpatrick Stockton's Government Relations Group represents clients before Congress and federal agencies on a broad range of issues, including healthcare, employee benefits, energy, tax, trade, telecommunication and intellectual property matters. The group is made up of accomplished professionals with extensive Capitol Hill, federal agency and political experience.

CLIENTS: Aaron Rents, Inc., BellSouth Corporation, Certegy, Inc., DaimlerChrysler Corporation, Delta Air Lines, Inc., Equifax, Inc., IMAX Corporation, Interface, Inc., Miller Industries, Inc., Nestle Waters of North America, Office Depot, PepsiCo, Inc.

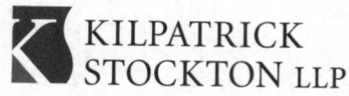

KILPATRICK
STOCKTON LLP
Attorneys at Law

KING & SPALDING LLP

THE FIRM

Chairman: Walter W Driver, Jr
Managing Partner, Atlanta: Mason W Stephenson
Managing Partner, Houston: Randolph C Coley
Managing Partner, London: George S Branch
Managing Partner, New York: Michael J O'Brien
Managing Partner, Washington: J Sedwick Sollers

Number of partners: 240
Number of other lawyers: 560

FIRM OVERVIEW: King & Spalding LLP is an international law firm with more than 800 lawyers in Atlanta, Houston, London, New York, and Washington, DC. The firm represents more than 250 public companies, including over half of the *Fortune* 100.

MAIN AREAS OF PRACTICE:

Antitrust: King & Spalding's antitrust lawyers are trial lawyers who know how to litigate in 'bet the company' situations. The firm has been counsel for clients in numerous antitrust litigation settings, ranging from class actions and multi-district litigation to disputes between particular suppliers and their customers or competitors.

Financial Transactions: The practice group provides legal services for domestic and non-US banks and other financial institutions. It handles all aspects of credit-facilities and financial products.

Construction: Today, the Construction and Procurement Practice Group represents some of the world's largest organizations involved in global construction projects. King & Spalding was one of the first large, general practice firms in the nation to establish a practice devoted to construction and procurement law.

Corporate/M&A: Consistently ranks among the leading M&A practices in the United States in terms of aggregate deal value and total number of transactions handled.

Corporate Finance: The firm represents issuers, underwriters, investors, and other corporate finance participants, as well as providing continuing corporate advice to public and private companies.

Employment & Labor Law: The firm defends *Fortune* 500 corporate defendants against complex claims of unlawful employment policies and conduct involving allegations of discrimination under federal and state non-discrimination statutes.

Energy: The firm's energy attorneys have been involved in transactions throughout the world related to energy and natural resources. King & Spalding's experience includes developing project structures as well as the drafting and negotiating of project agreements, contracts and documentation. Additionally, King & Spalding lawyers have been active advisors to the Liquefied Natural Gas (LNG) marketplace for the last 30 years. As pioneers on this legal scene, the internationally recognized group of lawyers have been key participants in LNG export, transport, and import projects of the 70s, 80s and 90s. Today, King & Spalding's team is sought after by LNG players worldwide owing the depth of experience, knowledge, skill, and determination.

Environment: King & Spalding is recognized as one of the leading environmental firms and combines substantive expertise, technical knowledge and litigation experience on numerous environmental issues.

Insolvency/Corporate Recovery: The Financial Restructuring Group at King & Spalding provides valuable knowledge and experience in the areas of corporate reorganizations, commercial debt restructuring, workouts, bankruptcy, and insolvency litigation.

Intellectual Property: The firm's IP lawyers concentrate on acquiring, creating, licensing, protecting, and litigating intellectual property rights, both domestically and internationally.

HEAD OFFICE

GEORGIA
191 Peachtree Street, **Atlanta**, GA 30303-1763
Tel: 404 572 4600 **Fax:** 404 572 5100
Email: kingspalding@kslaw.com
Website: www.kslaw.com

BRANCH OFFICES

NEW YORK
1185 Avenue of the Americas, **New York**, NY 10036-4003
Tel: 212 556 2100 **Fax:** 212 556 2222
Email: kingspalding@kslaw.com

TEXAS
1100 Louisiana, Suite 4000, **Houston**, TX 77002-5213
Tel: 713 751 3200 **Fax:** 713 751 3290
Email: kingspalding@kslaw.com

DISTRICT OF COLUMBIA
1700 Pennsylvania Avenue, N.W., **Washington,** DC 200006-4706
Tel: 202 737 0500 **Fax:** 202 626 3737
Email: kingspalding@kslaw.com

INTERNATIONAL OFFICES

King & Spalding International LLP, London.

Litigation & Arbitration: The firm provides litigation services in the areas of antitrust, appellate, class action, commercial disputes, product liability, shareholder and securities litigation, trade and customs, and toxic tort. The firm also has a substantial international arbitration practice.

Real Estate: The firm's real estate practice includes acquisition, development, financing and leasing of commercial real estate primarily for nationally recognized developers, and non-US institutional and private investors.

Tax: The firm works with clients on the planning and execution of business transactions of all sizes and types arising in domestic and cross border settings, including acquisitions, disposition, joint ventures, and financing transactions.

CLIENTS: 3M, Brown & Williamson Tobacco Corporation, ChevronTexaco Corporation, The Coca-Cola Company, Credit Suisse First Boston LLC, The Dow Chemical Company, Ernst & Young LLP, ExxonMobil Corporation, General Electric Company, General Motors Corporation, Georgia-Pacific Corporation, GlaxoSmithKline, Goldman Sachs & Company, The Home Depot, Inc., Honeywell International Inc., KPMG LLP, Lehman Brothers Inc., Lockheed Martin Corporation, Merrill Lynch & Co., Inc., Microsoft Corporation, Morgan Stanley Capital Group, Inc., Purdue Pharma L.P., Scientific-Atlanta, Inc., Shell Oil Company, Sprint Corporation, SunTrust Banks Inc., Turner Broadcasting System, Inc., UCB Inc., UPS.

KING & SPALDING LLP

MCKENNA LONG & ALDRIDGE LLP

THE FIRM

Co-Chairpersons: Clay C Long, James J Gallagher

FIRM OVERVIEW: McKenna Long & Aldridge LLP is an international law firm comprised of approximately 350 lawyers and public policy advisors with offices in Atlanta, Brussels, Denver, Los Angeles, Philadelphia, San Diego, San Francisco and Washington, DC. The firm's range of services fall into three broad categories: transactional, litigation and government/regulatory. Within these categories, the firm has extensive experience in over 90 practice area specializations including services in: corporate, environmental, government contracts, intellectual property, international, litigation, public policy and regulatory affairs, real estate finance and development, and restructuring and bankruptcy.

MAIN AREAS OF PRACTICE:

Corporate: The Corporate Practice predominately handles transactions involving public and private corporate finance, mergers and acquisitions and tax planning. Its lawyers focus on helping clients meet their business objectives, while minimizing legal costs and complications.

Real Estate Finance & Development: The Real Estate Finance and Development Practice represents developers, entrepreneurs, institutional lenders and investors.

Restructuring & Bankruptcy: The Restructuring and Bankruptcy Practice helps clients structure and consummate workouts of all types, including traditional economic restructurings, collateral recovery/liquidation workouts, and prepackaged bankruptcy plans. The firm's restructuring lawyers have resolved in excess of $10 billion in problem loans.

Litigation: The Litigation Practice offers experience, depth and high degrees of specialization. Areas of specialization include: product liability and toxic tort litigation, white collar crime, and complex business litigation. The firm's litigation expertise derives from its strong background in corporate and regulatory law. Its depth of experience means that the firm handles everything from routine commercial disputes in local courts to high profile cases in the highest state and federal appellate courts.

Toxic Torts & Product Liability: The Toxic Torts and Product Liability Practice has successfully defended numerous product liability and environmental tort actions such as chlorinated solvents, pesticides, PCBs, mercury and other materials released from or used at facilities, as well as pesticides, pharmaceuticals and consumer products released into the stream of commerce.

Government Relations: The government relations specialists provide extensive legislative and regulatory counsel on behalf of clients who have issues with local, state and federal governments.

Government Contracts: The firm's Government Contracts Practice is the first of its kind and continues as the leading practice in this field in the country. Its lawyers focus on clients who provide the government with highly technical, sophisticated and complex products and systems.

Intellectual Property & Technology: The intellectual property lawyers have extensive experience in representing domestic and international clients in all aspects of intellectual property protection and licensing both in the US and abroad.

Environmental Practice: The Environmental Practice handles all traditional areas of environmental law, structuring its client services in light of a single, guiding principle: environmental solutions must reflect a sound business perspective. With more than 25 lawyers practicing in the environmental field, the firm helps its clients shape the law through litigation, legislative and administrative action.

US OFFICES

CALIFORNIA
444 South Flower Street, 8th Floor, **Los Angeles**, CA 90071
Tel: 213 688 1000   **Fax:** 213 243 6330
Website: www.mckennalong.com

Suite 3300, Symphony Towers, 750 B Street, **San Diego**, CA 92101
Tel: 619 595 5400   **Fax:** 619 595 5450

Spear Tower, Suite 3500, One Market, **San Francisco**, CA 94105
Tel: 415 267 4000   **Fax:** 415 267 4198

COLORADO
Suite 200, 1875 Lawrence Street, **Denver**, CO 80202
Tel: 303 634 4000   **Fax:** 303 634 4400

DISTRICT OF COLUMBIA
1900 K Street, NW, **Washington**, DC 20006
Tel: 202 496 7500   **Fax:** 202 496 7756

GEORGIA
Suite 5300, 303 Peachtree Street, NE, **Atlanta**, GA 30308
Tel: 404 527 4000   **Fax:** 404 527 4198

PHILADELPHIA
28 South Waterloo Road, Suite 101, **Devon**, PA 19333
Tel: 610 687 9750   **Fax:** 610 687 9755

INTERNATIONAL OFFICES

The firm also has an office in Brussels, Belgium.

International: The International Practice assists clients in all aspects of moving goods, services, capital and technology across national boundaries as well as in all aspects of their global enterprises. Developing, licensing, protecting and enforcing intellectual property rights continue to be key services supporting clients' global business strategies.

Homeland Security: The Homeland Security Practice works with clients to shape the regulations for the Department of Homeland Security and policies affecting homeland security. These policies impact businesses, state and local governments, universities and other research institutions in the US.

Compliance & Investigations: The Compliance and Investigations Practice assists clients in identifying and engaging independent fact finders to conduct special or independent investigations. It also handles internal investigations of alleged improprieties and assists clients in making voluntary disclosure.

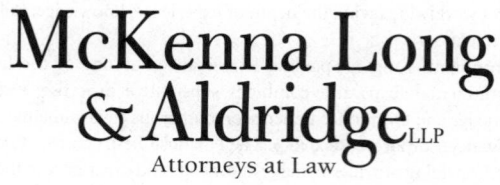

McKenna Long & Aldridge LLP
Attorneys at Law

MORRIS, MANNING & MARTIN, LLP

THE FIRM

Managing Partner: Robert E Saudek

Number of partners: 73
Number of other lawyers: 93

FIRM OVERVIEW: Morris, Manning & Martin, LLP, is a commercial law firm with offices in Atlanta, Washington, DC, Charlotte, Raleigh-Durham, and Princeton representing clients throughout the US. From handling more IPOs than any other law firm in the Southeast, to defending Fortune 50 companies in nationwide class action litigation, to spearheading the most important real estate transaction in Atlanta in the last 50 years - MMM's attorneys have earned a national reputation for commitment to excellence.

MAIN AREAS OF PRACTICE

Corporate Finance & Securities: The firm addresses the needs of both high-growth and established companies raising capital in the public and private markets. Since 1999, it has acted as counsel in initial public offerings that have raised over $7 billion, representing the most significant IPO Practice in the Southeast.

Environmental: This group concentrates on resolution of environmental issues such as liability for releases of hazardous materials to issues ranging from preservation of greenspace to historical resources. The firm addresses environmental issues associated with every type of property, including steel mills, shopping centers, landfills, office complexes, and residential developments.

Hospitality: MMM's hospitality group represents developers, owners, managers and investors in the industry. The firm's attorneys draw from commercial real estate, commercial lending, securities, M&A, employment, and litigation experience to serve their clients' needs.

Insurance: In this nationally recognized practice the firm represents insurers, reinsurers, financial institutions and agencies. MMM's attorneys have industry knowledge of accounting, regulatory, tax, investment, and corporate issues.

International: The firm's international attorneys provide international tax planning, global licensing and distribution, inbound and outbound investment planning, and worldwide protection of intellectual property rights.

Litigation: Products Liability: MMM represents manufacturers and retailers of building materials, chemicals, industrial equipment, automobiles and component parts, and appliances. The firm combines litigation experience with an in-depth understanding of product design, mass exposure, health risk assessment, and environmental science issues.

Litigation: Tech/IP: The firm's attorneys address the full range of disputes that arise in the life of technology businesses, including software IP infringement, misappropriation of trade secrets, and breach of confidentiality agreements.

Mergers & Acquisitions: The firm's M&A attorneys become integral members of their clients' M&A team, working efficiently, effectively, and tirelessly to complete the transaction. The firm handles all forms of mergers and acquisitions ranging in size to billions of dollars.

Real Estate Development & Finance: This group represents developers and investors in all aspects of the acquisition, development, ownership, leasing, financing, and sale of commercial real estate throughout the US.

Real Estate Capital Markets: The firm routinely structures, negotiates, documents and executes private and public equity offerings, REITs, strategic joint ventures, debt funds, tax credit funds, bond financings and UPREIT transactions. In the last 24 months the firm has served as counsel in over $2 billion in registered equity offerings and $500 million in private placements.

Taxation: MMM's unusual combination of tax experience in both corporate and partnership tax gives their clients a significant advantage in effective tax planning for investment funds, complex corporate alliances, and joint ventures. The tax group attorneys serve in major policy-making roles in legislative efforts affecting flow-through entities.

Technology/IP: The firm's IP attorneys are integral members of their clients' technology, marketing, and product development teams, and work with their clients to obtain and protect valuable intellectual property rights and achieve critical business goals.

HEAD OFFICE

GEORGIA
1600 Atlanta Financial Center, 3343 Peachtree Road, NE,
Atlanta, GA 30326
Tel: 404 233 7000 **Fax:** 404 365 9532
Website: www.mmmlaw.com

OFFICES

DISTRICT OF COLUMBIA
City Center Building, 1401 H Street, NW, Suite 760,
Washington, DC 20005
Tel: 202 408 5153 **Fax:** 202 408 5146

NEW JERSEY
601 Ewing Street, Suite C-11, **Princeton**, NJ 08540
Tel: 609 430 1414 **Fax:** 609 430 1411

NORTH CAROLINA
201 S. College Street, Suite 2300, **Charlotte**, NC 28244
Tel: 704 554 7070 **Fax:** 704 554 5050

1000 Park Forty Plaza, Research Triangle Park,
Raleigh-Durham, NC 27713
Tel: 919 806 2969 **Fax:** 919 806 2057

OGLETREE, DEAKINS, NASH, SMOAK & STEWART, P.C.

THE FIRM

Managing Shareholder: L Gray Geddie, Jr
Number of partners: 141

Website: www.ogletreedeakins.com

FIRM OVERVIEW: Ogletree, Deakins, Nash, Smoak & Stewart, P.C. ("Ogletree Deakins") is one of the nation's largest labor and employment law firms, specializing exclusively in the representation of management in all types of employment-related legal matters. The firm has approximately 250 labor and employment lawyers located in 21 offices and has thriving practices focusing on business immigration, employee benefits, and workplace safety and health law. The firm represents a diverse range of clients, including more than half of the Fortune 50 corporations in the United States. Ogletree Deakins is proud to have more lawyers who are Fellows in the College of Labor and Employment Lawyers and listed in Best Lawyers in America than any other labor and employment specialty firm in the United States. Ogletree Deakins' primary focus is client service, a message which is emphasized in the firm's tagline: "Employers and Lawyers, Working Together." Lawyers remain on call 24 hours a day/seven days a week to provide prompt and, most importantly, effective legal advice over the phone, through a computer, or in the field. They regularly conduct comprehensive employment audits with their clients to expose problem areas before they become legal nightmares and conduct management training seminars to equip supervisors to handle tough workplace issues. Often, firm attorneys are called upon to prepare and review employment policies and procedures manuals to ensure compliance with federal and state laws. This combination of educating supervisors on employment issues and giving employees notice of company expectations results in very real cost savings, as well as intangible personnel benefits.

MAIN AREAS OF PRACTICE

Labor & Employment: Ogletree Deakins' dedicated focus on the practice of labor and employment law enables the firm to maintain both "bench strength" and depth of expertise in all areas of the practice, including counseling, training, preventive and proactive workplace strategies, litigation, and diversity management. Because the firm's lawyers are focused on, and prepared to deliver, this full range of labor and employment representation, Ogletree Deakins provides the "continuity of care" that ensures knowledgeable and client-centered solutions and consistent attorney–client relationships. Ogletree Deakins has years of experience with and regularly practice before both the federal and state agencies that regulate the workplace. In fact, some of the firm's attorneys have held high-level positions within several governmental agencies, providing them with the type of access few firms possess. Ogletree Deakins regularly files amicus curiae briefs with the United States Supreme Court on behalf of the US Chamber of Commerce and other organizations on important labor and employment matters. The firm's attorneys are asked by Congress, as well as by state legislatures, to testify on matters in which Ogletree Deakins concentrates its practice.

OFFICES

ALABAMA
1819 5th Avenue North, Suite 1000, **Birmingham**, AL 35203-2118
Tel: 205 328 1900 **Fax:** 205 328 6000

CALIFORNIA
633 West Fifth Street, Suite 5300, **Los Angeles**, CA 90071
Tel: 213 239 9800 **Fax:** 213 239 9045

FLORIDA
80 SW 8th Street, Suite 1830, **Miami**, FL 33130
Tel: 305 374 0506 **Fax:** 305 374 0456

600 N Westshore Boulevard, Suite 200 **Tampa**, FL 33609-1117
Tel: 813 289 1247 **Fax:** 813 289 6530

GEORGIA
600 Peachtree Street, NE, Suite 2100, **Atlanta**, GA 30308
Tel: 404 881 1300 **Fax:** 404 870 1732

ILLINOIS
20 South Clark Street, 25th Floor, **Chicago,** IL 60603
Fax: 312 558 1220 **Fax:** 312 807 3619

INDIANA
One Indiana Square, Suite 2300, **Indianapolis**, IN 46204
Tel: 317 916 1300 **Fax:** 317 916 9076

NEW JERSEY
10 Madison Avenue, Suite 402, **Morristown**, NJ 07960
Tel: 973 656 1600 **Fax:** 973 656 1611

NORTH CAROLINA
400 West Trade Street, **Charlotte**, NC 28202-1627
Tel: 704 342 2588 **Fax:** 704 342 4379

2725 Horse Pen Creek Road, Suite 101, **Greensboro**, NC 27410-8392
Tel: 336 375 9737 **Fax:** 336 375 4430

2301 Sugar Bush Road, Suite 600, **Raleigh**, NC 27612
Tel: 919 787 9700 **Fax:** 919 783 9412

SOUTH CAROLINA
134 Meeting Street, Suite 160, **Charleston,** SC 29401
Tel: 843 853 1300 **Fax:** 843 853 9992

1501 Main Street, Suite 600, **Columbia,** SC 29201
Tel: 803 252 1300 **Fax:** 803 254 6517

300 North Main Street, **Greenville,** SC 29601
Tel: 864 271 1300 **Fax:** 864 235 8806

TENNESSEE
424 Church Street, Suite 800, **Nashville,** TN 37219
Tel: 615 254 1900 **Fax:** 615 254 1908

TEXAS
301 Congress Avenue, Suite 1250, **Austin**, TX 78701
Tel: 512 344 4700 **Fax:** 512 344 4701

8117 Preston Road, 700 Preston Commons, **Dallas**, TX 75225
Tel: 214 987 3800 **Fax:** 214 987 3927

500 Dallas Street, Suite 3000, **Houston,** TX 77002-4709
Tel: 713 655 0855 **Fax:** 713 655 0020

112 East Pecan St, 2600 Weston Centre, **San Antonio,** TX 78205
Tel: 210 354 1300 **Fax:** 210 277 2702

DISTRICT OF COLUMBIA
2400 N Street, NW, Fifth Floor, **Washington,** DC 20037
Tel: 202 887 0855 **Fax:** 202 887 0866

INTERNATIONAL OFFICES

The firm also has an office in the Virgin Islands.

Ogletree
Deakins

Employers & Lawyers, Working Together

ROGERS & HARDIN LLP

THE FIRM

Management Committee: Steven E Fox, Edward J Hardin, Dan F Laney III

Number of partners: 24
Number of other lawyers: 27

FIRM OVERVIEW: Rogers & Hardin LLP maintains the flexibility of a smaller firm, while providing a level of sophistication usually associated with much larger firms. The quality of the firm's attorneys is evidenced by numerous accomplishments and recognitions the firm and its lawyers have received nationally and locally. In addition to published recognitions, the firm's lawyers are frequently asked to speak to business and lawyer groups at regional and national conferences, seminars, and law school courses. The firm has also represented many major law firms in various matters, gaining a reputation as "lawyers' lawyers".

MAIN AREAS OF PRACTICE:

Antitrust: Rogers & Hardin LLP has extensive experience in antitrust matters, including general antitrust litigation, defense of class actions, and representation in government investigations. The firm's attorneys regularly provide antitrust advice under federal and state antitrust laws to a variety of clients, including firms in industrial, transportation, construction, distribution, healthcare and service markets, as well as trade associations.

Broker-Dealer Litigation & Enforcement: Rogers & Hardin LLP has exceptional depth and experience in defending broker-dealers, investment advisors, managers, brokers, and other securities professionals. For almost 30 years, the firm has regularly defended clients against claims by customers before the NASD, the NYSE, and AAA, as well as enforcement proceedings and investigations brought by the SEC, the SROs, and state securities commissions. In addition to litigation, the firm's lawyers regularly counsel brokerage firm clients on internal procedures, compliance with securities laws and regulations, and other issues affecting the securities industry.

Commercial Real Estate/Finance: Rogers & Hardin LLP represents developers, investors, owners, syndicated groups and lenders concerning all aspects of commercial real estate, including acquisitions and dispositions of projects, recapitalization and restructuring of properties and entities, sale/leaseback transactions, and other asset-based financial transactions. The firm also has extensive expertise representing both landlords and tenants in commercial leases.

Complex Litigation: Rogers & Hardin LLP has vast experience in handling a wide variety of complex business litigation matters, and has developed a national reputation for effectively representing clients' interests in cases with complex factual and logistical problems, class actions, and matters involving injunctive or other extraordinary relief.

Corporate Control Contests: Rogers & Hardin LLP has significant experience assisting clients in change of control contests. The firm's attorneys have represented both bidders and target companies as well as financial advisers in change of control transactions, including unsolicited tender offers and proxy fights. In addition, the firm has often been retained as special counsel to advise a company's board of directors or an independent special committee in connection with corporate control contests.

Employment Law: Rogers & Hardin LLP has a nationally recognized employment law practice involving a broad spectrum of claims involving such issues as wrongful discharge, non-compete/restrictive covenant, defamation, interference with contractual relations, intentional infliction of emotional distress and fraud. The firm has established expertise in class actions involving hiring, assignment, promotion, test validation, training, termination and other issues. The firm's attorneys regularly advise employers in connection with employment policies and practices, including strategies for dealing with reductions in force, employee complaints of discrimination, disability laws, and compliance with government regulations.

Mergers & Acquisitions: Rogers & Hardin LLP regularly advises bidders, target companies, stockholders, boards of directors and special committees of boards of directors regarding complex mergers, acquisitions, dispositions, auctions, tender offers, spin-offs, going-private transactions, joint ventures, restructurings and other creative corporate financing techniques in a broad range of industries.

Securities Transactions: Rogers & Hardin LLP represents clients in the areas of securities transactions and securities compliance and disclosure. The firm serves as counsel to issuers, underwriters and selling security holders in public and private offerings of corporate equity and debt securities, in municipal industrial revenue bond financings, exchange offers, tender offers and issuer self-tenders, including Dutch auctions and going-private transactions.

Toxic Torts & Products Liability: The firm has a practice in products liability matters, including defense of toxic tort claims. Rogers & Hardin LLP represents a number of major domestic and international chemical companies in claims filed against them in Georgia and the Southeast region, and has handled cases involving both consumer product liability claims as well as workplace exposure allegations.

CLIENTS: The firm's client base is primarily comprised of large multinational firms and mid-sized public and private companies. The firm also represents promising start-up and development-stage companies, as well as individuals and entrepreneurs.

INTERNATIONAL WORK: As Atlanta's significance as an international commercial center has increased, so has the firm's involvement in international transactions. Rogers & Hardin LLP represents companies in Taiwan, Japan, the British Virgin Islands, and Bermuda as well as individuals who have business interests in the Americas and abroad. Rogers & Hardin LLP is also a member of Interlaw, an exclusive network of premier firms located in some 120 cities worldwide. The Interlaw network provides clients with more than 5,000 lawyers globally who deliver consistently reliable legal services seamlessly across jurisdictional lines.

HEAD OFFICE

GEORGIA
2700 International Tower, 229 Peachtree St NE, **Atlanta**, GA 30303-1601
Tel: 404 522 4700 **Fax:** 404 525 2224
Website: www.rh-law.com

CONTACTS

Antitrust	Tony G Powers
Corporate	Edward J Hardin
Employment	Hunter R Hughes III
Litigation	Richard H Sinkfield

CONTENTS: Bankruptcy p.640; Corporate/M&A p.641; Employment: p.642; Land Use p.643; Litigation: p.644; Real Estate p.646; Individuals' Profiles p.648; Firms' Profiles p.651.

How lawyers are ranked

The opinions we gather from clients — mainly from in-house lawyers but also from other purchasers of legal services — are balanced by opinions from colleagues and competitors. Together, they provide two different perspectives — an all-round view — and biased viewpoints cancel each other out.

BANKRUPTCY

Hawaii
Leading firms (Bankruptcy)

1. **CADES SCHUTTE** *Honolulu*
   CASE BIGELOW & LOMBARDI *Honolulu*
   GELBER, GELBER, INGERSOLL *Honolulu*
   RUSH MOORE CRAVEN SUTTON MORRY *Honolulu*
   WAGNER CHOI EVERS *Honolulu*

Leading individuals (Bankruptcy)

1. **DREHER** Nicholas *Cades Schutte, Honolulu*
   GELBER Don *Gelber Gelber, Honolulu*
   PETTIT Ted *Case Bigelow, Honolulu*
   TIUS Susan *Rush Moore, Honolulu*
   WAGNER James *Wagner Choi, Honolulu*

Up-and-coming individuals
   MUZZI Christopher *Case Bigelow, Honolulu*

Firms and individuals are listed alphabetically in each band.

Cades Schutte

The Firm: This firm's strong ties with many of the state's preeminent financial institutions contribute to the high profile of its bankruptcy practice. Devoted to creditor rights, its attorneys are renowned for enforcement of security interests and creditor remedies, restructurings, workouts and foreclosures. The group is supported by sterling litigation talent with strong expertise in the defense of lender liability claims. It represents local, national and international financial entities in both federal and state courts, and although predominantly acting for creditors, lawyers also represent debtors in Chapter 7 and Chapter 11 bankruptcies.

The Lawyers: According to market sources, **Nicholas Dreher** (see p.648) has "*superb knowledge and is very cost effective*" for clients on bankruptcy issues. His practice also encompasses real estate and corporate finance.

The Clients: The firm acts for creditors and debtors from a variety of industries, including real estate, financial services and tourism.

Case Bigelow & Lombardi, A Law Corporation

See firm details p.652

The Firm: The market recognizes this major business law player for having a broad bankruptcy practice, covering all facets of creditor-debtor relationships. It attracts praise for its experience in foreclosures, receiverships and collection and enforcement of judgments in state and federal courts. Attorneys represent debtors and both secured and unsecured creditors in liquidation proceedings, and are also adept at negotiating workouts and restructurings outside of the bankruptcy courts.

The Lawyers: Interviewees agree that the practice's center of gravity is corporate restructuring specialist **Ted Pettit** (see p.649). He is labeled "*a leading bankruptcy and insolvency lawyer in the state,*" and clients distinguish him as "*absolutely first class in problem solving, innovation and understanding the personalities involved in a transaction.*" He represented GE Capital Hawaii on the $12 million judicial foreclosure, as well as the subsequent acquisition and sale of the Pearl Kai Shopping and Westridge shopping centers. He served as counsel to the official committees of unsecured creditors in the Chapter 11 bankruptcies of H&W Foods and Palama Meat, the largest food distribution and meat processing companies in Hawaii. A newcomer to the tables and former deputy attorney general for the state of Hawaii, **Christopher Muzzi** (see p.649) is viewed by clients as "*on the ball and team oriented.*" His practice revolves around bankruptcy, litigation and tax controversy resolution.

Gelber, Gelber, Ingersoll & Klevansky, A Law Corporation

The Firm: Within what is "*clearly a top-notch corporate and commercial practice in Hawaii,*" attorneys offer depth of advice to clients on business bankruptcy matters. They act for trustees, debtors and creditors such as financial institutions and pension funds, as well as developers and investors in reorganizations. Strong corporate, tax and litigation expertise comple-

ment the practice. The firm has notably worked on two of the state's most important Chapter 11 bankruptcy cases, involving H&W Foods and Palama Meat.

The Lawyers: Sources applauded **Don Gelber**'s commitment to high-quality work in bankruptcy and business reorganization matters. His practice also incorporates civil litigation and real estate work.

Rush Moore Craven Sutton Morry & Beh

The Firm: This 26-attorney firm has offices across the islands in Honolulu, Wailuku and Kailua-Kona. Its bankruptcy group handles a wide variety of matters for both creditors and debtors, and acts for a significant number of institutional lenders in complex real estate and asset-based financings. Alongside workouts, creditor rights and enforcement litigation also play a prominent role in its activities.

The Lawyers: Industry commentators were full of praise for "*quality performer*" **Susan Tius**. She specializes in creditor rights and commercial collections, and has long-standing experience in acting for bankruptcy trustees in commercial cases.

Wagner Choi Evers

The Firm: The firm's involvement in some of Hawaii's highest profile cases makes it a potent force, agreed market sources. Historically, it acts on behalf of creditors, albeit with some debtor representation, on business reorganizations and workouts. Bankruptcy litigation, foreclosures, receiverships and collections are also pillars of the practice. Recent highlights include representing creditors committees in the Chapter 11 cases of Hawaiian Airlines, Liberty House and Crazy Shirts. In other key Chapter 11 matters, it acted for the debtor in the Aloha Tower and the trustee in the Hamakua Sugar bankruptcies.

The Lawyers: **James Wagner** was singled out for his "*distinguished record in creditor-debtor bankruptcy work.*"

CORPORATE/M&A

Hawaii
Leading firms (Corporate/M&A)

1 CADES SCHUTTE *Honolulu*

CARLSMITH BALL LLP *Honolulu*

CASE BIGELOW & LOMBARDI *Honolulu*

GOODSILL ANDERSON QUINN & STIFEL *Honolulu*

2 CHUN, KERR, DODD, BEAMAN & WONG *Honolulu*

GELBER, GELBER, INGERSOLL *Honolulu*

MCCORRISTON MILLER MUKAI *Honolulu*

Leading individuals (Corporate/M&A)

Senior Statesman

CASE Daniel *Case Bigelow*, Honolulu

CASE James *Carlsmith Ball*, Honolulu

1 KIM Gregory *Vantage Counsel*, Honolulu

PRESSMAN Stewart *McCorriston Miller*, Honolulu

REBER David *Goodsill Anderson*, Honolulu

SCHULL E Gunner *Cades Schutte*, Honolulu

2 CRIBLEY James *Case Bigelow*, Honolulu

GELBER Stephen *Gelber Gelber*, Honolulu

INGERSOLL Richard *Gelber Gelber*, Honolulu

KAMIKAWA Ray *Chun Kerr*, Honolulu

SWEET Charles *Carlsmith Ball*, Honolulu

VAN WINKLE J Thomas *Carlsmith Ball*, Honolulu

Leading individuals (Tax)

1 EPSTEIN Roger *Cades Schutte*, Honolulu

GELBER Stephen *Gelber Gelber*, Honolulu

HELLER Ron *Torkildson Katz*, Honolulu

INGERSOLL Richard *Gelber Gelber*, Honolulu

KAMIKAWA Ray *Chun Kerr*, Honolulu

OKUMURA Miki *Goodsill Anderson*, Honolulu

WONG David *Carlsmith Ball*, Honolulu

Up-and-coming individuals

PIPER Jeffrey *Schlack Ito*, Honolulu

Firms and individuals are listed alphabetically in each band.

Band 1

Cades Schutte

The Firm: This well-established team has a proven track record in M&A and general commercial advice. Its blue-chip client base and prominence in tax and real estate contributes to its stellar reputation in the transactional arena.

The Lawyers: Much of the firm's success is attributable to **Gunner Schull**. Franchising and joint ventures are his main strengths, and he has a wealth of experience in handling dealership groups and property-related finance. He also comes with noted experience in leveraged buyouts, spin-offs and corporate formations. Clients hail "*brilliant*" **Roger Epstein** as "*a creative and talented*" tax attorney. One large international company viewed his strategic thinking and documentation skills as "*innovative and cutting edge*," putting him well ahead of the competition. Epstein advises on corporate, partnership and real estate tax-related issues,

and has substantial experience in fiscal matters. **The Clients:** The firm has traditionally acted for some of Hawaii's most well-known corporations as well as small to medium-sized companies. These include: Alexander & Baldwin; Aloha Petroleum; First Hawaiian Bank and Outrigger Hotels & Resorts.

Carlsmith Ball LLP

The Firm: The market recognizes this firm as a leading name in the Pacific region for corporate and commercial work. The transactional team advises on the full gamut of public offerings, M&As and asset-backed securities. It serves an enviable client base of local, national and international investors through an elaborate network of offices in Hawaii (Honolulu, Kapolei, Maui, Hilo and Kona), Guam and Saipan, and is the only firm in the state with a mainland office, in Los Angeles.

The Lawyers: **James Case** has 50 years of experience in corporate law and is regarded by clients and peers as "*an influential force in business.*" He serves as counsel to companies in tourism, financial services and real estate, including Outrigger Hotels, which he assisted in its acquisitions, and American Financial Services of Hawaii in its international offerings. **Charles Sweet** is acknowledged as "*Mr Securities Law in Hawaii.*" He has represented e-commerce, biotech and telecom companies in their NASDAQ listings and other public offerings. At time of press he announced his intention to move to McKee Nelson LLP in Washington, DC. **Thomas Van Winkle** continues to earn kudos for his banking and real estate-related finance work. His practice additionally includes antitrust advice and estate planning. **David Wong** achieved excellent market feedback for his "*premier fiscal expertise.*" He focuses on advising businesses on the federal income tax aspects of commercial transactions.

The Clients: Bank of Hawaii; The Estate of James Campbell; Maui Land & Pineapple; Inter-Island Resorts; Outrigger Hotels & Resorts; American Financial Services of Hawaii and Citizens Utilities Company.

Case Bigelow & Lombardi, A Law Corporation

See firm details p.652

The Firm: This major corporate player maintains an impressive practice in multiple fields. Its attorneys assist businesses, banks and trusts in everything from the creation of companies, partnerships and profit-sharing schemes to M&A, asset purchase and finance transactions, estate planning, tax and UCC matters. One specialty is the creation of corporate structures for real estate transactions.

The Lawyers: Clients and peers bill senior director of the firm **Daniel Case** (see p.648) as

"*an illustrious member of the business community in Hawaii.*" One client praised him for being "*very astute and sensitive to client needs.*" **James Cribley** (see p.648) continues to garner support from clients for his "*superb corporate law expertise.*" Cribley notably acted for Kahala Senior Living Community in the issuance of $182 million of special purpose revenue and taxable bonds.

The Clients: Kahala Senior Living Community; Chevron USA; Amfac and Bank of Hawaii.

Goodsill Anderson Quinn & Stifel

The Firm: This firm earned enthusiastic praise from commentators, who recognized its considerable strength in transactional work. This sterling group acts for local, national and emerging growth companies in M&A, securities law and corporate governance. Attorneys also assist small to large companies in public and private offerings.

The Lawyers: **David Reber** is renowned in Hawaii for his corporate work, especially M&A and securities matters for regulated industries clients. He advised Hawaiian Electric Industries on the refinancing of its $200 million trust preferred securities. In other significant highlights, he was also involved in the purchase by US Marine Repair of Honolulu Shipyard's operations at Pearl Harbor for the repairs of its navy vessels, and advised on the sale of a large automobile parts distributor. **Miki Okumura**, the firm's managing partner, has a fine reputation for tax work. She advises state and mainland businesses on planning and compliance under Hawaii state laws, and defends commercial developers in tax controversy litigation.

The Clients: Bank of Hawaii; Hawaiian Electric Industries; Hawaiian Electric Company; Hawaii Biotech; Hoana Medical; Firetide; AssistGuide; Hawaii Superferry; Cellular Bioengineering; Worldwide Energy Group and Broadband iTV.

Band 2

Chun, Kerr, Dodd, Beaman & Wong

The Firm: This firm provides a full range of legal services to its business clients. The practice has developed into a prominent player, acting for small businesses and large corporations in key local, national and international transactions. While tax and litigation are prominent areas for the firm, it also offers advice on acquisitions, reorganizations and workouts, and real estate finance.

The Lawyers: **Ray Kamikawa** is widely reputed for his business acumen and boasts an impressive Japanese investor client base. His practice centers on business law and tax planning for companies and nonprofits, and federal and state controversies. He previously served as the director of the Department of Taxation for the State of Hawaii.

The Clients: Gannett Pacific; Hawaiian Island Development; Outrigger Hotels and Resorts; Shinsei Bank; The Sanwa Bank; Maui Land & Pineapple and Kaahumanu Center Associates.

Gelber, Gelber, Ingersoll & Klevansky, A Law Corporation

The Firm: This growing corporate and commercial team is emerging into a potent force in Hawaii. Market observers particularly singled out its tax, general business and real estate financing capabilities. Although small in size, when compared to some competitors, it is achieving notable results for clients.

The Lawyers: At the forefront of the practice stand **Stephen Gelber** and **Richard Ingersoll**. Both were endorsed by peers for their acuity in general business and tax law matters.

The Clients: Casden Properties; The CIT Group/Equipment Financing; Hotel Corporation of the Pacific; MacFarms of Hawaii; National Partnership Investments Corp; Trans-Pacific Textiles; Yoshida Kogyo Co and Kamehameha Schools.

McCorriston Miller Mukai MacKinnon LLP

See firm details p.654

The Firm: Sources consider this new entrant to the table not only as "*a first-class practice for real estate finance work*," but also a firm with a burgeoning profile in corporate matters. The team advises on M&A, investment vehicles and state and local government agencies' bond financings. Insurance restructuring, workouts and international transactions involving Asia and the Pacific Rim are also features of the practice.

The Lawyers: Clients and peers regard "*really excellent*" **Stewart Pressman** (see p.649) as a fine transactional specialist. He specializes in M&A and securities law, with notable experience in real estate and public finance issues.

The Clients: The firm counsels local, national and international businesses including AIG Hawaii Insurance, Central Pacific Financial and Seven-Eleven Hawaii.

Other Notable Practitioners

Ronald Heller, from the firm of Torkildson, Katz, Fonseca, Jaffe, Moore & Hetherington Attorneys at Law, A Law Corporation, won high praise from

peers for his tax litigation talents. He is also a CPA, and has litigated tax cases at county, state and national level. At the end of 2004 **Gregory Kim** set up a new firm, Vantage Counsel LLC, together with other former Goodsill Anderson Quinn & Stifel lawyers. Kim is known to be "*very much on the ball*," a trait that should stand him in good stead in this new venture. He is in his element counseling venture capitalists and start ups. The work he had undertaken in recent years was driven by M&A, financings and intellectual property. In the past year he acted for several hi-tech, life sciences and other emerging companies on offerings of convertible preferred stock and bridge notes, as well as advising on the formation of joint ventures for Starbucks Hawaii and Puerto Rico, and Jamba Juice Hawaii and Florida. Another attorney to have left Goodsill is **Jeffrey Piper**, now with Schlack Ito Lockwood Piper & Elkind, LLC. This firm, too, is comprised of a number of ex-Goodsill attorneys. Piper is well known for his great experience with exempt organizations and non profit entities on corporate and fiscal issues.

EMPLOYMENT

MAINLY DEFENDANT

Hawaii
Leading firms
(Employment: Mainly Defendant)

1	**MARR HIPP JONES & WANG** *Honolulu*
	TORKILDSON, KATZ, FONSECA, JAFFE *Honolulu*
2	**ALSTON HUNT FLOYD & ING** *Honolulu*
	CADES SCHUTTE *Honolulu*
	GOODSILL ANDERSON QUINN & STIFEL *Honolulu*
	WATANABE ING KAWASHIMA *Honolulu*

Leading individuals
(Employment: Mainly Defendant)

1	**HIPP Ken** *Marr Hipp*, Honolulu
	KATZ Robert *Torkildson Katz*, Honolulu
	MARR Barry *Marr Hipp*, Honolulu
2	**BANKS David** *Cades Schutte*, Honolulu
	ELENTO-SNEED Anna *Alston Hunt*, Honolulu
	KNOREK John *Torkildson Katz*, Honolulu
	LEONG Ronald *Watanabe Ing*, Honolulu
	NAKASHIMA Steve *Marr Hipp*, Honolulu
	PETRUS Barbara *Goodsill Anderson*, Honolulu
	RAND Richard *Torkildson Katz*, Honolulu
	WANG Sarah *Marr Hipp*, Honolulu

Firms and individuals are listed alphabetically in each band.

Band 1

Marr Hipp Jones & Wang

The Firm: Clients and peers unanimously praise this labor and employment law boutique

as "*outstanding*" and "*very responsive*." Clients value its "*constructive, useful*" advice on general employment and labor relations issues, and point to a raft of excellent lawyers in the firm. It has been involved in some of Hawaii's best-publicized employment cases, recently defending the University of Hawaii and its Board of Regents against claims by Evan Dobelle following the termination of his presidency. In another significant representation, the firm was labor and employment counsel to Hawaiian Airlines during its bankruptcy proceedings. It also acts for Norwegian Cruise Line in complying with federal and state wage and hour laws, union representation and antidiscrimination laws.

The Lawyers: Clients describe employment litigation specialist, **Barry Marr** as "*highly skilled, extremely professional and very thoughtful in his counsel*." His practice focuses on employment discrimination and wrongful termination issues. Clients distinguish **Ken Hipp**, a former attorney at the NLRB, for his "*collective bargaining negotiation abilities and fantastic employment litigation experience*." Management clients also admire **Steve Nakashima** and **Sarah Wang** for their exemplary client service, each displaying "*integrity and professionalism*" in handling a wide spectrum of labor and employment issues.

The Clients: ABC Sports; Bank of Hawaii; Delta Air Lines; Dole Food Company; The General Contractors' Association of Hawaii; Hawaii Employers Council; Norwegian Cruise Line;

University of Hawaii; Safeway; Servco Pacific and United Air Lines.

Torkildson, Katz, Fonseca, Jaffe, Moore & Hetherington Attorneys At Law, A Law Corporation

The Firm: This well-established practice enjoys market accolades for its labor and employment expertise. With offices in Honolulu, Hilo and Maui, it acts for the management of local, mainland and Asia-Pacific Rim clients on trials, dispute resolution, collective bargaining negotiations and investigations of discrimination claims.

The Lawyers: Former cochair of the ABA's employment law section on antitrust and labor relations, the "*preeminent*" **Robert Katz** is acknowledged to be "*a top-line individual at a top-line firm*." A "*solid and dependable*" attorney, **Richard Rand** has extensive experience in litigation, appellate work and preventative advice to management. Newcomer to the tables **John Knorek** has a client following for his advice to management on affirmative action, policy guidance and union elections.

The Clients: The firm represents a broad base of clients ranging from large multinational corporations to national and local companies and partnerships.

Band 2

Alston Hunt Floyd & Ing Attorneys At Law, A Law Corporation
See firm details p.651

The Firm: This talented team has a quality reputation in labor and employment law, and government contract-related affirmative action plans. The group represents management on collective bargaining negotiations, unfair labor practice proceedings and wrongful terminations, employee benefits and health and safety issues.

The Lawyers: **Anna Elento-Sneed** (see p.648) represents clients across the full spectrum of labor and employment issues, having noted experience in advice to employers on litigation and the labor and employment aspects of business transactions.

The Clients: Clients come from regulated industries and the hospitality, property development, health and insurance sectors.

Cades Schutte
The Firm: This prominent corporate and commercial player in Hawaii has a growing reputation in labor and employment law. It benefits from a blue-chip corporate management client base, and advises on employment compliance and the drafting of employment contracts, manuals, policies and procedures.

The Lawyers: **David Banks** heads the labor and employment group. He provides clients with a wealth of experience on issues such as the FLSA, FMLA and Hawaii's wage and hour laws.

The Clients: The firm acts for local, national and international companies.

Goodsill Anderson Quinn & Stifel
The Firm: Clients acclaim this well-respected firm as a growing force in employment law in the state. It defends management clients in employment litigation in state and federal courts, and assists them with staff training in drafting employment policies and procedures and training schemes.

The Lawyers: Corporate clients reported how well **Barbara Petrus** applies her knowledge and expertise to their employment problems. She also has a niche in advising educational institutions on ADA issues, professorial misconduct and campus security requirements.

The Clients: The firm represents a range of employers from sole proprietors and nonprofit organizations to large Hawaii and international companies.

Watanabe Ing Kawashima & Komeiji
The Firm: The firm has ample experience and recognition for its advice on traditional labor law issues and in protecting employers' interests on wrongful discharge, ADA and sexual harassment claims.

The Lawyers: **Ronald Leong** chairs the firm's labor and employment team. Peers admire him as *"a very capable litigator,"* noting that he is dedicated to labor matters.

The Clients: The firm acts for local, national and international companies.

LAND USE

Hawaii
Leading firms (Land Use)

1   **BELLES GRAHAM PROUDFOOT AND WILSON** *Lihue*
  CADES SCHUTTE *Honolulu*
  IMANAKA KUDO & FUJIMOTO *Honolulu*
  TSUKAZAKI YEH & MOORE *Honolulu*
  WATANABE ING KAWASHIMA & KOMEIJI *Honolulu*

Leading individuals (Land Use)

1   **BELLES Michael** *Belles Graham, Lihue*
  GRAHAM Max *Belles Graham, Lihue*
  ING J Douglas *Watanabe Ing, Honolulu*
  KUDO Benjamin *Imanaka Kudo, Honolulu*
  LEONG Donna *Cades Schutte, Honolulu*
  MANCINI Paul *Mancini Welch, Kahului*
  MUNGER Lisa Woods *Goodsill Anderson, Honolulu*
  TSUKAZAKI Ben *Tsukazaki Yeh, Honolulu*

Firms and individuals are listed alphabetically in each band.

Band 1

Belles Graham Proudfoot and Wilson
The Firm: Market sources agree that this six-attorney firm is *"a very prominent name in Kauai for land use."* Advising clients on administrative law, real estate development, zoning and land use matters, it benefits from the resources of a full-service practice with expertise in litigation, corporate and employment law, as well as tax, antitrust and IP.

The Lawyers: Much of the firm's reputation in land use is attributable to partners **Max Graham** and **Michael Belles**. Both are well-known land use specialists, with a statewide reputation for excellence in acting for commercial developers.

The Clients: First Hawaiian Bank; Bank of Hawaii; Grove Farm Co and subsidiaries; Gay & Robinson; Marriott Ownership Resorts; Aetna; Travelers; General Star Insurance and BHP Petroleum Americas Refining.

Cades Schutte
The Firm: This large, full-service firm fields an impressive real estate team that is also singled out by market sources for land use, condemnation and water rights issues. It has established a top-notch reputation in acting for resort hotel developers on shoreline and coastal zone management laws requiring permits from national, local and state land use and zoning commissions.

The Lawyers: *"A-list"* real estate specialist **Donna Leong** wins widespread market praise for her work acting for hotels and resorts on land use issues.

The Clients: Clients include several international, national and local hotels and resorts.

Imanaka Kudo & Fujimoto
The Firm: The market describes this 11-lawyer firm as *"a leading player"* on land use planning and zoning. Founded in 2001, it is building a growing reputation for offering quality service to clients. The team specializes in water and native Hawaiian rights, as well as in the procedures associated with environmental permits, certifications and appeals.

The Lawyers: **Benjamin Kudo** is head of the firm's land use, administrative and environmental law department. He is renowned for representing significant commercial and residential developers on projects in Hawaii.

The Clients: The firm acts for foreign and domestic developers, with an important clientele from the Asia-Pacific region.

Tsukazaki Yeh & Moore
The Firm: Interviewees regard this firm as successfully establishing a presence in land use law. It represents developers on hearings in front of state land and natural resource commissions. In a recent highlight, it has acted for Kamehameha Investment Corp, the for-profit development company of Kamehameha Schools, in a public hearing regarding its 488-acre residential and golf development proposal.

The Lawyers: **Ben Tsukazaki** leads the firm in trailblazing a statewide reputation for excellence in land use law. He notably represented the Hawaii Island Economic Development Board in the University of Hawaii's proposal to build up to six more small telescopes surrounding the two vast telescopes on Mauna Kea.

The Clients: Hawaii Island Economic Development Board, Kamehameha Investment Corp and many other developers are clients.

Watanabe Ing Kawashima & Komeiji
The Firm: This practice places special emphasis on government and regulatory law, and litigation in front of state and federal agencies and

courts. The firm acts for several of Hawaii's major developers on commercial and residential land use projects, as well as natural resource and environmental administrative and litigation proceedings.

The Lawyers: Leading the practice is former gubernatorial appointee member of the Board of Land and Natural Resources for the State of Hawaii, **Douglas Ing**. Peers expressed great admiration for his land use litigation work.

The Clients: Clients include local, national and international developers.

Other Notable Practitioners

Market observers acclaim **Paul Mancini** from the law firm of Mancini Welch & Geiger LLP as a notable land use specialist in Hawaii. His practice also covers municipal, zoning, condemnation and real property advice. Litigation top dog, **Lisa Woods Munger** of Goodsill Anderson Quinn & Stifel is praised for her environmental and land use expertise. She represented the University of Hawaii on the telescopes projects on Mauna Kea.

LITIGATION

GENERAL COMMERCIAL

Hawaii
Leading firms
(Litigation: General Commercial)

1 GOODSILL ANDERSON QUINN & STIFEL *Honolulu*
MCCORRISTON MILLER MUKAI *Honolulu*

2 ALSTON HUNT FLOYD & ING *Honolulu*
CADES SCHUTTE *Honolulu*
CARLSMITH BALL LLP *Honolulu*
KOBAYASHI, SUGITA & GODA *Honolulu*

3 BAYS DEAVER LUNG ROSE BABA *Honolulu*
CASE BIGELOW & LOMBARDI *Honolulu*
CRONIN, FRIED, SEKIYA, KEKINA *Honolulu*
GELBER, GELBER, INGERSOLL *Honolulu*
PAUL, JOHNSON, PARK & NILES *Honolulu*
WATANABE ING KAWASHIMA & KOMEIJI *Honolulu*

Leading individuals
(Litigation: General Commercial)

★ MCCORRISTON William *McCorriston Miller, Honolulu*

1 ALSTON Paul *Alston Hunt, Honolulu*
CHANG Corlis *Goodsill Anderson, Honolulu*
PORTNOY Jeffrey *Cades Schutte, Honolulu*

2 HEIHRE Michael *Cades Schutte, Honolulu*
KAWASHIMA James *Watanabe Ing, Honolulu*
KOBAYASHI Bert *Kobayashi Sugita, Honolulu*
KOMEIJI John *Watanabe Ing, Honolulu*
LAMON Bruce *Goodsill Anderson, Honolulu*
MUNGER Lisa *Goodsill Anderson, Honolulu*
ROSE Crystal *Bays Deaver, Honolulu*

3 EARLE Jacqueline *Goodsill Anderson, Honolulu*
GRIMMER Gary *Carlsmith Ball, Honolulu*
HUNT William *Alston Hunt, Honolulu*
KLEVANSKY Simon *Gelber Gelber, Honolulu*
LACY John *Goodsill Anderson, Honolulu*
NISHIMOTO John *Ayabe Chong, Honolulu*
PAUL James *Paul Johnson, Honolulu*

Firms and individuals are listed alphabetically in each band.

Band 1

Goodsill Anderson Quinn & Stifel

The Firm: The firm has a strong tradition of excellence in litigation and houses a number of Hawaii's top trial specialists. The phalanx of leading litigators is adept at handling business disputes involving financial services, insurance and real estate and construction matters. A diverse caseload also reflects tort claims including aviation, maritime, and products and professional liability matters. Prevention counseling, risk-avoidance audits and negotiated early settlements are other features of the practice, say appreciative clients.

The Lawyers: **Corlis Chang** achieved market recognition as an attorney who is "*ultra capable and excellent for any type of litigation.*" Her diverse practice encompasses the defense of manufacturers of medical devices and pharmaceutical products, and representation of insurance companies in first party claims. In a recent highlight, she successfully represented the owner of a golf course on change order claims of more than $5 million brought by a general contractor. Clients value **Bruce Lamon** as "*a terrific asset*" on complex litigation. He centers his practice in the areas of real estate claims, condemnation and products liability, recently acting for a Fortune 500 company in a major fungicide-related jury trial. "*Fantastic all-rounder*" **Lisa Woods Munger** is particularly noted for work in the areas of environmental, antitrust and land use. She defends companies and landowners on environmental matters involving air, water and wastes, and hazardous substances. **Jacqueline Earle** attracted praise for her representation of clients from the pharmaceuticals industry on products liability cases. She also successfully acted for the State of Hawaii in a litigation involving the telecom system for the University of Hawaii. Further experience lies in professional liability, healthcare and construction disputes. The "*talented*" **John Lacy** rounds off the group of ranked attorneys. Peers point to his success in handling admiralty and aviation litigation. Lacy acts for major shipping companies, cruise lines, foreign underwriters and commercial airlines in Hawaii and the Pacific region.

McCorriston Miller Mukai MacKinnon LLP

See firm details p.654

The Firm: Client sources praise this firm's "*incredible litigation talent,*" describing the team as "*absolutely superb in a courtroom, even when they are acting against us.*" This diverse practice focuses on technology, products and professional liability, corporate disputes and white-collar crime. The team is involved in many of the significant cases in the state, such as the Bishop Estate dispute, the Hawaii antitrust suit against major energy companies, and the defense of the Mayor of the City and County of Honolulu in a case concerning his eligibility for the office of state governor. In conjunction with the employment boutique, Marr Hipp Jones & Wang, it also co-counseled the University of Hawaii and its Board of Regents in the case concerning Evan Dobelle's termination as president.

The Lawyers: "*Leaps above the rest and a larger-than-life presence,*" **William McCorriston** (see p.649) is, according to market sources, "*the supremo name clients turn to for tough trials.*" He is chairman of the firm's litigation department and handles a wide variety of complex and multidistrict litigations. He also focuses on government and insurance-related matters.

The Clients: The practice acts for local, national and international clients.

Band 2

Alston Hunt Floyd & Ing Attorneys At Law, A Law Corporation

See firm details p.651

The Firm: A first-rate commercial practice in Hawaii, this firm has a litigation group that earned high marks from interviewees. It handles a steady stream of disputes from real estate to business torts and contract claims. Banking, construction and class actions are additional strings to the group's bow.

The Lawyers: The group's standout personality is **Paul Alston** (see p.648). Clients praise his "*reliability*" and rivals place him in the "*all-star leagues of trial attorneys.*" His practice focuses on antitrust, banking and lending liability, and creditors' rights. An "*unshakable litigator,*" **William Hunt** (see p.648) received excellent market feedback for his work on commercial, construction and medical malpractice litigation. He also works in the field of arbitration and mediation.

The Clients: Chevron USA; Eaton Corporation; Georgia-Pacific; Keene Corporation and Pittsburgh Corning.

All quotes in the text are from interviews with clients and competitors.

Cades Schutte

The Firm: This firm wins unequivocal market approval for its litigation prowess. Its attorneys have extensive trial experience in the areas of insurance, employment, construction, real estate and mass torts. Professional negligence litigation involving medical, legal and architectural malpractice is another strong suit.

The Lawyers: Clients appreciate **Jeffrey Portnoy**'s "*superlative talent*" in litigation matters. His diverse practice covers employment, media and insurance defense, and he has notably acted for a number of clients in the cruise line, telecom and financial services industries. Interviewees praise **Michael Heihre** as "*a preeminent litigator.*" He focuses on the trial and arbitration of business and real estate disputes and a recent highlight includes acting for a large public company in a series of state class actions centered on the sale and distribution of food products.

The Clients: Norwegian Cruise Lines; SCI Management; Merrill Lynch and Verizon.

Carlsmith Ball LLP

The Firm: The market recognizes this practice as "*a prominent player*" in multijurisdictional antitrust, commercial and environmental litigation matters. Its office in Los Angeles and network of offices throughout the Hawaiian Islands provide the practice with extraordinary reach and a diverse caseload. Commercial leasing, products liability, employment and construction are also key areas of growth for the practice.

The Lawyers: **Gary Grimmer** elicits praise from interviewees, with one billing him as "*the cat's pajamas*" for commercial litigation. His practice focuses on antitrust, business dispute resolution, products liability defense and insurance litigation.

The Clients: The firm acts for local, national and international clients.

Kobayashi, Sugita & Goda

See firm details p.653

The Firm: Interviewees endorse this practice as "*top notch*" for litigation. The firm represents leading companies and institutions in Hawaii on contracts, environmental, public utilities and IP disputes. Attorneys regularly undertake assignments on construction, employment and antitrust matters, with the team also advising on litigation avoidance, negotiating and drafting settlements.

The Lawyers: Leading the team is **Bert Kobayashi**. Market sources say he is "*smart, thorough and talks you through the issues.*" One of the firm's founders, Kobayashi has a wealth of experience in commercial and construction litigation.

The Clients: The University of Hawaii at Manoa, the State of Hawaii and the City and County of Honolulu are among the firm's clients.

Band 3

Bays Deaver Lung Rose Baba

The Firm: A number of the State of Hawaii's landowners and developers praise this firm for its "*leading construction and real estate litigation talent.*" The litigation group acts on behalf of realtors, lenders, buyers, sellers and tenants on a wide variety of contract disputes, fraud and misrepresentation, and land use and zoning violations.

The Lawyers: **Crystal Rose** is the firm's frontrunner for real estate-driven litigation. She acts for clients on construction and management disputes, and trusts and estates counseling. She notably worked on the high-profile case between Kamehameha Schools and Bishop Estate.

The Clients: The firm's clients include a wealth of names in real estate, construction and allied sectors.

Case Bigelow & Lombardi, A Law Corporation

See firm details p.652

The Firm: Commentators expressed a healthy respect for this firm's litigation and dispute resolution capability. Attorneys regularly represent businesses in federal and state courts on real estate, construction, tort and commercial litigation matters. The group is also committed to using mediation, arbitration and negotiated settlement in settling disputes. Roger Moseley is its chair.

The Clients: Liberty House; Crazy Shirts; Amfac Hawaii and Oahu Construction.

Cronin, Fried, Sekiya, Kekina & Fairbanks Attorneys At Law

The Firm: Established in 1973, this 16-lawyer firm concentrates mainly on litigation, applicable to personal injury, medical malpractice, products liability, aviation and admiralty law. It has long-standing experience in handling workplace, automobile and aviation accidents, and is active in toxic substances and defective product-related litigation. Paul Cronin is one of the lead partners.

The Clients: The practice acts for local, national and international clients.

Gelber, Gelber, Ingersoll & Klevansky, A Law Corporation

The Firm: This firm attracts consistent praise for its solid business law practice. Its market reputation rides high on a successful bankruptcy practice, though the firm has a groundswell of support among clients for its impressive trial results. Interviewees distinguish its commercial and real estate litigation expertise as "*first class.*"

The Lawyers: The practice is embodied in **Simon Klevansky**, whose focus lies in commercial litigation and international trade. Clients were impressed with his considered approach to trial work.

The Clients: There is a local, national and international client base.

Paul, Johnson, Park & Niles, Attorneys At Law, A Law Corporation

The Firm: This bijou firm with offices in Honolulu and Maui has market visibility in business litigation, mediation and arbitration. Attorneys have a client following in construction, real estate and title insurance litigation, and the Maui office notably handles a steady diet of work from Hawaii's commercial boating community, for which it secures and protects mooring rights and commercial operating permits.

The Lawyers: **James Paul** is credited with putting the firm on the map in litigation. He represents clients in real estate, construction and investment finance matters.

The Clients: There is a local, national and international clientele.

Watanabe Ing Kawashima & Komeiji

The Firm: This commercial practice is viewed as a "*quality outfit*" with involvement in a wide variety of litigation proceedings. Particular expertise is to be found in the areas of commercial, real estate and insurance defense work.

The Lawyers: **James Kawashima** earns kudos for his insurance defense and commercial litigation experience, while interviewees also pick out **John Komeiji** as "*a superb commercial litigator.*"

The Clients: The practice acts for local, national and international clients.

Other Notable Practitioners

According to industry sources, **John Nishimoto**, from the firm of Ayabe, Chong, Nishimoto, Sia & Nakamura, is a well-respected litigator who specializes in medical and legal malpractice cases.

REAL ESTATE

Hawaii
Leading firms (Real Estate)

1. **CADES SCHUTTE** *Honolulu*
   GOODSILL ANDERSON QUINN *Honolulu*
   MCCORRISTON MILLER MUKAI *Honolulu*

2. **CARLSMITH BALL LLP** *Honolulu*
   CASE BIGELOW & LOMBARDI *Honolulu*
   MANCINI WELCH & GEIGER LLP *Kahului*
   OSHIMA, CHUN, FONG & CHUNG *Honolulu*

3. **ASHFORD & WRISTON** *Honolulu*
   BAYS DEAVER LUNG ROSE BABA *Honolulu*
   IMANAKA KUDO & FUJIMOTO *Honolulu*
   RUSH MOORE CRAVEN SUTTON *Honolulu*
   SCHNEIDER TANAKA RADOVICH *Honolulu*

Leading individuals (Real Estate)

1. **CHUN Deborah** *Oshima Chun*, Honolulu
   EWART Lani *Goodsill Anderson*, Honolulu
   GRAHAM Bruce *Ashford & Wriston*, Honolulu
   HAZLETT Mark *Cades Schutte*, Honolulu
   LEONG Donna *Cades Schutte*, Honolulu
   LOMBARDI Dennis *Case Bigelow*, Honolulu
   MACKINNON D Scott *McCorriston Miller*, Honolulu
   MILLER Clifford *McCorriston Miller*, Honolulu
   PEAR Charles *McCorriston Miller*, Honolulu
   STEVERSON Randall *Goodsill Anderson*, Honolulu

2. **CRIBLEY James** *Case Bigelow*, Honolulu
   DEVLIN Patricia *Carlsmith Ball*, Honolulu
   GABRIO Gino *Cades Schutte*, Honolulu
   IWAMOTO Raymond *Goodsill Anderson*, Honolulu
   LITTMAN Bernice *Cades Schutte*, Honolulu
   MANCINI Paul *Mancini Welch*, Kahului
   RADOVICH Scott *Schneider Tanaka*, Honolulu
   SAKUMOTO Randall *McCorriston Miller*, Honolulu
   SCHLACK Carl *Schlack Ito*, Honolulu
   SCHNEIDER Robert *Schneider Tanaka*, Honolulu
   STRAND Robert *Carlsmith Ball*, Honolulu
   WELCH Thomas *Mancini Welch*, Kahului
   WONG Danton *Chun Kerr*, Honolulu
   YOUNGREN Nancy *Case Bigelow*, Honolulu
   YUEN Leighton *Goodsill Anderson*, Honolulu

Firms and individuals are listed alphabetically in each band.

Band 1

Cades Schutte

The Firm: Clients and peers regard this firm as having "*one of the top real estate practices in Hawaii.*" Its work covers real estate transactions, development and zoning, and real property taxes. Attorneys act for a large number of developers and financial institutions on lending and for both commercial and residential projects. The firm has a notable interest in the hospitality industry, counseling on issues pertaining to hotels, resort condominiums, land use and water rights. It has had an active involvement in representing hotel purchasers from Europe and the mainland with transactions totaling $300 million in the past year.

The Lawyers: Clients recognize **Mark Hazlett** as "*a very experienced and knowledgeable real estate attorney.*" His diverse practice includes real estate finance, acting for lenders. **Donna Leong** wins market approval as "*a leading light*" in Hawaii on both real estate finance and in acting for developers on land use and property tax issues. **Gino Gabrio** commands client and peer respect as an "*experienced and knowledgeable*" attorney on real estate finance and water rights. He is also well versed in federal and Hawaii real estate regulations involving consumer credit and commercial leasing. Interviewees acknowledge **Bernice Littman** as "*part of the club of elite real estate attorneys in Hawaii.*" Her work revolves around the financing and leasing of commercial properties as well as counseling clients on fair housing and ADA issues.

The Clients: Avalon Development, Outrigger Enterprises and A&B Properties are among some of the prominent names on this firm's client roster.

Goodsill Anderson Quinn & Stifel

The Firm: Clients find this firm's real estate group to have "*broadly talented people covering a wide spectrum of services.*" Attorneys represent developers in negotiating and drafting sales and leases, providing expertise on regulatory requirements. One enthusiastic developer referred to the department as "*striking the perfect balance between sound business dealings and legal solutions, realistically tailored to meet the needs of the client.*" It also handles real estate-driven transactions, litigation and land title issues. A key strength is the group's ability to work cross-departmentally with the firm's tax, corporate, labor and environmental groups.

The Lawyers: The "*long-standing real estate expertise*" of **Randall Steverson** is much appreciated by clients and peers alike. His work is centered on commercial and residential development and financing. Notable highlights include his involvement in Shinwa Golf Group's sale of Renaissance Wailea Beach Hotel, and the sale of two other resorts and five golf courses. He also acts for a number of US and foreign lenders and borrowers in negotiating construction and commercial loans. Clients say **Lani Ewart** is "*brilliantly efficient, superbly calm and ultra dependable*" when advising lenders and borrowers on real estate holdings and loan documentation issues. Her practice is particularly geared toward secured lending matters, including credit facilities, loan workouts, leased fees and construction finance.

Sources view "*terrific*" **Raymond Iwamoto** as "*one of the best legal experts in the Hawaiian real estate industry.*" Speaking of his lending practice, one financier described him as "*a businessman who knows how to close a deal.*" His work on sales and leasing transactions revolve around hotels,

shopping centers and office buildings. Clients recognize "*service-oriented*" **Leighton Yuen** as "*the next generation of rising real estate talent in Hawaii.*" He frequently assists in loan documentation matters for Bank of Hawaii and acts for buyers, developers and sellers on resort and shopping center development projects. Yuen acted for Waikoloa Land Company in the development of Waikoloa Beach Resort and Waikoloa Village.

The Clients: Automatic Data Processing; Central Pacific Bank; ConocoPhillips; Bank of Hawaii; Costco Wholesale Center; Financial Plaza of the Pacific; Grosvenor Center; Kukai Grove Shopping Center; Lanai Resorts; Maui Marketplace; Maui Marriott Resort and The Hyatt Regency.

McCorriston Miller Mukai MacKinnon LLP
See firm details p.654

The Firm: This firm's real estate practice is particularly prized for its timeshare and condominium expertise. Attorneys represent landowners, developers and banks on development finance, loan restructurings, acquisitions and disposals, and commercial leasing. The firm represented the Mitsubishi Bank in relation to the agreed sale of the Hyatt Regency Waikoloa, and the Long-Term Credit Bank of Japan on real estate loans in both the state of Hawaii and Guam. In another key transaction, the team was involved in a $113.5 million loan facility, acting for one of the state's leading commercial property and residential condominium developers.

The Lawyers: According to clients, **Clifford Miller** (see p.649) "*practically rewrote the book on condo law.*" He is the firm's business and real estate department chairman and concentrates on acting for hotel developers, owners and equity investors on finance issues and management agreements. In Hawaii, he has advised on such well-known hotels as the Kahala Hilton and Hyatt Regency. Clients consider **Scott MacKinnon** (see p.649) "*utterly reliable at finding creative solutions to real estate transactions.*" Sources also consider him "*a real expert on condo law*" with a broad generalist real estate practice encompassing finance and leasing issues as well as land use and workouts. He has worked on some of the state's leading real estate transactions, including the Nauru and Hawaiki towers and the Kiahuna Plantation. Interviewees distinguish **Charles Pear** (see p.649) as "*one of the leading timeshare experts in the country.*" His extensive knowledge of this topic has led to work on several projects both in and out of state, and overseas. He notably advises the states of Hawaii and California, and Interval International, one of the world's two leading timeshare exchange companies. Clients regard **Randall Sakumoto** (see p.650) as "*one of the better, younger, real estate*

attorneys coming up the ranks." He takes on a variety of real estate acquisitions and development work.

The Clients: Starwood Vacation Ownership; Central Pacific Financial; The Mitsubishi Bank; The Long-Term Credit Bank of Japan and Interval International.

Band 2

Carlsmith Ball LLP
The Firm: This firm has a long-established reputation for excellence in real estate matters. The department acts for developers and major landowners in a broad range of projects, including resort, commercial, residential and industrial. As well as the acquisition, sale, development and leasing of land, attorneys advise on construction and hotel management contracts, tax-deferred exchanges and land use and water rights issues.
The Lawyers: **Patricia Devlin** chairs the department and focuses on finance, development and land use issues. She regularly advises hotel companies, lenders and landowners on commercial and residential matters. **Robert Strand** has long been a part of the state's real estate glitterati. His diverse workload extends to transactions, equipment leasing and public utilities matters. Highlights include acting for the Ala Moana Shopping Center on lease negotiations and representing a major foreign investor in the acquisition of the 4,600 acre Kaluakoi Resort on the island of Molokai. In another matter, he represented the Campbell Estate in the development of the Kapolei Civic Center, and he regularly acts for Hawaii hotel operators on hotel and condominium acquisitions in Waikiki.
The Clients: Ala Moana Shopping Center and Campbell Estate as well as local, national and international clients.

Case Bigelow & Lombardi, A Law Corporation
See firm details p.652
The Firm: Clients speak of this firm's "*efficient and proficient*" real estate team as possessing "*sophistication.*" Representing landowners, purchasers, investors and lenders in the acquisition, sale and financing of all types of commercial and residential developments, the nine-attorney team also undertakes land use, zoning and entitlement matters. It is too early to comment on the full effects of the recent departures of partners Scott Radovich and Robert Schneider but it has not, so far, diminished the firm's profile in the market.
The Lawyers: Clients and peers endorse **Dennis Lombardi** as a lead real estate lawyer with "*a wonderful knack for grasping the issues and coming up with resolutions.*" He served as counsel to Schuler Homes in its $1.6 billion merger with DR Horton, and co-counseled Marriott International in its $128 million acqui-

sition of the Waikiki Beach Marriott Resort. Interviewees recommend **James Cribley** as "*an excellent real estate transactions specialist.*" He has advised various clients on a multitude of complex hotel purchases and sales. Clients also appreciate **Nancy Youngren**, saying she is "*very responsive and able to look at the big picture*" when advising on development projects. She notably acts for Waipouli Beach Resort in the development of a $100 million, 190-unit luxury condominium resort on the island of Kauai.
The Clients: Bank of Hawaii; Textron Financial; Kahala Senior Living Community; Waipouli Beach Resort and Marriott International.

Mancini Welch & Geiger LLP
The Firm: This small real estate boutique wins high market praise in Hawaii, and particularly in Maui, as "*a premier outfit*" for land use issues. Lawyers advise clients on commercial and residential developments as well as matters relating to condominiums, municipal permits and zoning.
The Lawyers: Leading land use specialist, **Paul Mancini** elicits praise, particularly for condemnation cases. Peers acknowledge **Thomas Welch** as "*a top guy*" for general real estate, trusts and estate planning.
The Clients: The practice represents local and statewide clients.

Oshima, Chun, Fong & Chung
The Firm: This small practice is widely viewed as a "*superlative player*" in real estate finance, with attorneys advising developers, lenders and borrowers.
The Lawyers: Much of the firm's standing in the market is attributable to **Deborah Chun**, whom clients and peers alike see as "*one of the leading real estate attorneys in the state for borrower and lender work.*"
The Clients: Attorneys represent international, mainland and local clients.

Band 3

Ashford & Wriston
The Firm: The firm represents financial institutions, developers and mortgage companies on loan documentation and workouts, and handles the whole gamut of commercial and residential developments, condominium projects and leasing, and significant real estate litigation.
The Lawyers: **Bruce Graham** is "*very sound*" on title matters, real estate transactions, commercial leasing and trust administration, notably counseling Hilton Hotels on leasing and contract issues.
The Clients: Sample clients include Hilton Hotels, Roman Catholic Church and Kamehameha Schools Bernice Pauahi Bishop Estate. The firm also acts for numerous landowners and title companies.

Bays Deaver Lung Rose Baba
The Firm: This practice's greatest strength lies in representing developers and investors on real estate disputes, including land use litigation, and statutory and zoning violations. On the transactions front, led by Crystal Rose the team advises business clients with real estate acquisitions and lease agreements.

Imanaka Kudo & Fujimoto
The Firm: The focal points of this firm's real estate activities are finance and land use, though this work is to be found within a full-service real estate practice where attorneys offer assistance with commercial and residential developments, hotel and resort acquisitions, and timeshare finance and regulatory compliance. Mitchell Imanaka is the partner to contact.

Rush Moore Craven Sutton Morry & Beh
The Firm: The firm's real estate practice is achieving a growing profile in Hawaii. Attorneys undertake commercial and residential work in subdivision and condominium development and sales, leasing and mortgage finance work, as well as zoning and land use matters. Walter Beh and Irene Anzai are the key contacts.

Schneider Tanaka Radovich Andrew & Tanaka, LLLC
The Firm: This firm is well respected for its real estate sales and acquisitions, and has recently benefited from the arrival of property finance specialists Scott Radovich and Robert Schneider from Case Bigelow & Lombardi. Industry sources were most impressed with the firm's effectiveness when handling a wide variety of real estate matters, including condominiums, timeshares and various development projects.
The Lawyers: Clients consider **Scott Radovich** an excellent communicator. He particularly specializes in the financing aspects of real estate development projects. **Robert Schneider** is also renowned for his real estate finance and property development expertise.
The Clients: The practice represents local and national clients.

Other Notable Practitioners
Clients identify **Carl Schlack** from the firm of Schlack Ito & Lockwood Piper & Eikind LLC as "*very knowledgeable, thorough and very quick at finding solutions.*" Again, clients are most impressed with **Danton Wong** of Chun, Kerr, Dodd, Beaman & Wong. He is said to "*know his stuff in real estate transactions, and never scores points for the sake of it.*" He continues to act for major developers in Hawaii, including Outrigger Enterprises.

Leaders in Hawaii

ALSTON, Paul
Alston Hunt Floyd & Ing Attorneys At Law, A Law Corporation, Honolulu
808 524 1888
palston@ahfi.com
Recommended in Litigation
Practice Areas: State and federal litigation and ADR, including disputes involving class actions, RICO, securities, real estate, construction defects and contracts, insurance coverage, civil rights, professional malpractice, first amendment rights, and complex business disputes. Mr Alston represents both plaintiffs and defendants.
Prof. Memberships: ABA, Hawaii State Bar Association, American Association of Appellate Attorneys, ABF.
Career: Legal Aid Society of Hawaii 1972-77; Private Practice 1977-present. Special Deputy Attorney General for State of Hawaii in selected federal matters.
Personal: University of So. California JD 1971; 'Best Lawyers in America' 1995-2005 (Business Litigation and First Amendment Law).

BANKS, David
Cades Schutte, Honolulu
808 521 9200
Recommended in Employment

BELLES, Michael
Belles Graham Proudfoot and Wilson, Lihue 808 245 4705
Recommended in Land Use

CASE, Daniel H
Case Bigelow & Lombardi, A Law Corporation, Honolulu 808 547 5400
dcase@casebigelow.com
Recommended in Corporate/M&A
Practice Areas: Practices in the areas of corporate, business, estate planning and trust law. Senior Director of the firm.
Prof. Memberships: Affiliate of the American College of Trust and Estate Counsel. American Bar Association. Hawaii State Bar Association.
Career: Bar Admission: Hawaii State, United States District Court for the District of Hawaii. President, Hawaii State Bar Association, 1978.
Personal: LLB, University of Denver, 1952. AB, Williams College and University of Denver, 1948.

CASE, James
Carlsmith Ball LLP, Honolulu
808 523 2500
Recommended in Corporate/M&A

CHANG, Corlis
Goodsill Anderson Quinn & Stifel, Honolulu 808 547 5600
Recommended in Litigation

CHUN, Deborah
Oshima, Chun, Fong & Chung, Honolulu 808 528 4200
Recommended in Real Estate

CRIBLEY, James M
Case Bigelow & Lombardi, A Law Corporation, Honolulu 808 547 5400
jcribley@casebigelow.com
Recommended in Corporate/M&A, Real Estate
Practice Areas: Director and Head of the firm's Business Group. He advises clients in the areas of general corporate and business law, corporate finance, business acquisitions and real estate law. His clientele includes domestic as well as foreign owners of businesses and properties.
Prof. Memberships: Hawaii State Bar Association.
Personal: JD, University of Michigan, 1969. BA, Miami University, 1963.

DEVLIN, Patricia
Carlsmith Ball LLP, Honolulu
808 523 2500
Recommended in Real Estate

DREHER, Nicholas
Cades Schutte, Honolulu
808 521 9200
Recommended in Bankruptcy

EARLE, Jacqueline
Goodsill Anderson Quinn & Stifel, Honolulu 808 547 5600
Recommended in Litigation

ELENTO-SNEED, Anna
Alston Hunt Floyd & Ing Attorneys At Law, A Law Corporation, Honolulu
808 441 6228
aes@ahfi.com
Recommended in Employment
Practice Areas: Wrongful termination, employment discrimination, labor unions and collective bargaining, wage and hour law, government contracting, benefits, business transactions, personnel management and training, strategic HR planning, safety and health, proprietary rights, workplace privacy.
Prof. Memberships: ABA, Hawaii State Bar Association, Society for Human Resource Management (Pacific-West Region, Hawaii State Director).
Career: Shareholder/Director of the firm. Frequently lectures for universities, business groups, and individual employers.
Publications: Written extensively, including articles in 'The Practical Lawyer,' the 'Hawaii Bar Journal,' and 'The Pacific Employer.'
Personal: Boalt Hall School of Law, UC Berkeley (JD 1983).

EPSTEIN, Roger
Cades Schutte, Honolulu
808 521 9200
Recommended in Tax

EWART, Lani
Goodsill Anderson Quinn & Stifel, Honolulu 808 547 5600
Recommended in Real Estate

GABRIO, Gino
Cades Schutte, Honolulu
808 521 9200
Recommended in Real Estate

GELBER, Don
Gelber, Gelber, Ingersoll & Klevansky, A Law Corporation, Honolulu
808 524 0155
Recommended in Bankruptcy

GELBER, Stephen
Gelber, Gelber, Ingersoll & Klevansky, A Law Corporation, Honolulu
808 524 0155
Recommended in Corporate/M&A, Tax

GRAHAM, Bruce
Ashford & Wriston, Honolulu
808 539 0400
Recommended in Real Estate

GRAHAM, Max
Belles Graham Proudfoot and Wilson, Lihue 808 2454705
Recommended in Land Use

GRIMMER, Gary
Carlsmith Ball LLP, Honolulu
808 523 2500
Recommended in Litigation

HAZLETT, Mark
Cades Schutte, Honolulu
808 521 9200
Recommended in Real Estate

HEIHRE, Michael
Cades Schutte, Honolulu
808 521 9200
Recommended in Litigation

HELLER, Ron
Torkildson, Katz, Fonseca, Jaffe, Moore & Hetherington Attorneys At Law, A Law Corporation, Honolulu
808 523 6000
Recommended in Tax

HIPP, Ken
Marr Hipp Jones & Wang, Honolulu
808 536 4900
Recommended in Employment

HUNT, William S
Alston Hunt Floyd & Ing Attorneys At Law, A Law Corporation, Honolulu
808 524 1800
whunt@ahfi.com
Recommended in Litigation
Practice Areas: Trials in state, federal courts and arbitrations in medical malpractice and personal injury defense, commercial and construction litigation. Clients include ChevronTexaco; Georgia Pacific; Kaiser Permanente; United Technologies.
Prof. Memberships: Hawaii State and Federal Courts/9th Cir. 1973; US Supreme Court 1980; ABA Tort and Insurance Section; Hawaii Bar Association; Defense Research Institute.
Career: Hart Leavitt Hall & Hunt 1973-80; Paul Johnson Alston & Hunt 1980-91; Alston Hunt Floyd & Ing 1991-;

Adjunct Professor, Univ. Hawaii Law School 1976-77.
Publications: 'The Best Lawyers in America' personal injury litigation.
Personal: Colgate University, BA 1968; Columbia University School of Law, JD 1972.

ING, Douglas
Watanabe Ing Kawashima & Komeiji, Honolulu 808 544 8300
Recommended in Land Use

INGERSOLL, Richard
Gelber, Gelber, Ingersoll & Klevansky, A Law Corporation, Honolulu
808 524 0155
Recommended in Corporate/M&A, Tax

IWAMOTO, Raymond
Goodsill Anderson Quinn & Stifel, Honolulu 808 547 5600
Recommended in Real Estate

KAMIKAWA, Ray
Chun, Kerr, Dodd, Beaman & Wong, Honolulu 808 528 8200
Recommended in Corporate/M&A, Tax

KATZ, Robert
Torkildson, Katz, Fonseca, Jaffe, Moore & Hetherington Attorneys At Law, A Law Corporation, Honolulu
808 523 6000
Recommended in Employment

KAWASHIMA, James
Watanabe Ing Kawashima & Komeiji, Honolulu 808 544 8300
Recommended in Litigation

KIM, Gregory
Vantage Counsel LLC, Honolulu
808 780 2495
Recommended in Corporate/M&A

KLEVANSKY, Simon
Gelber, Gelber, Ingersoll & Klevansky, A Law Corporation, Honolulu
808 524 0155
Recommended in Litigation

KNOREK, John
Torkildson, Katz, Fonseca, Jaffe, Moore & Hetherington Attorneys At Law, A Law Corporation, Honolulu 808 523 6000
Recommended in Employment

KOBAYASHI Jr, Bert
Kobayashi, Sugita & Goda, Honolulu
808 539 8700
Recommended in Litigation

KOMEIJI, John
Watanabe Ing Kawashima & Komeiji, Honolulu 808 544 8300
Recommended in Litigation

KUDO, Benjamin
Imanaka Kudo & Fujimoto, Honolulu
808 521 9500
Recommended in Land Use

LACY, John
Goodsill Anderson Quinn & Stifel, Honolulu 808 547 5600
Recommended in Litigation

LAMON, Bruce
Goodsill Anderson Quinn & Stifel,
Honolulu 808 547 5600
Recommended in Litigation

LEONG, Donna
Cades Schutte, Honolulu
808 521 9200
Recommended in Land Use, Real Estate

LEONG, Ronald
Watanabe Ing Kawashima & Komeiji,
Honolulu 808 544 8300
Recommended in Employment

LITTMAN, Bernice
Cades Schutte, Honolulu
808 521 9200
Recommended in Real Estate

LOMBARDI, Dennis
Case Bigelow & Lombardi, A Law
Corporation, Honolulu
808 547 5446
dlombardi@casebigelow.com
Recommended in Real Estate
Practice Areas: Real estate, concentrating in land use and development. Extensive experience in acquisition, permitting, development, financing and sales
of master planned residential, resort and
commercial communities, centers and
projects. He represents not only individuals and firms that are active in the real
estate industry but also institutions with
real estate business needs such as the
purchase or development of headquarters, office building, shopping center,
operation site or hotel properties. He is
President of the firm and a member of
its Executive Committee.
Prof. Memberships: Hawaii State Bar
Association, California State Bar Association.
Career: Bar Admission: Hawaii State,
California State, District of Columbia,
United States District Court for the District of Hawaii.
Personal: JD (summa cum laude), University of Santa Clara, 1977. BA, University of Hawaii at Manoa, 1974.

MACKINNON, D Scott
McCorriston Miller Mukai MacKinnon
LLP, Honolulu 808 529 7300
mackinnon@m4law.com
Recommended in Real Estate
Practice Areas: Real estate, including
finance, leasing, and arbitration; condo-
miniums; eminent domain; land use;
commercial loans/workouts.
Prof. Memberships: Admitted to prac-
tice in California (1973), Hawaii (1974),
US Court of Appeals, Ninth Circuit
(1981). Member of Hawaii State Bar
Association, Section on Real Property
and Financial Services; American Bar
Association, Sections on Business Law,
Real Property, and Probate and Trust
Law; State Bar of California.
Publications: Editor, 'Hawaii Conveyance Manual II', 1988.
Personal: Born 10 April 1948. JD, Uni-
versity of California at Davis, 1973; BA,

University of California at Santa Barbara, 1970. Hawaii's Top Lawyers (Honolulu Magazine).

MANCINI, Paul
Mancini Welch & Geiger LLP, Kahului
808 871 8351
Recommended in Land Use, Real Estate

MARR, Barry
Marr Hipp Jones & Wang, Honolulu
808 536 4900
Recommended in Employment

MCCORRISTON, William C
McCorriston Miller Mukai MacKinnon
LLP, Honolulu 808 529 7300
mccorriston@m4law.com
Recommended in Litigation
Practice Areas: Complex and multi-
district litigation; professional malpractice; insurance; white collar criminal
defense; antitrust; civil rights; constitutional; construction litigation; contracts;
environmental law; government; products liability.
Prof. Memberships: American College
of Trial Lawyers; American Board of
Trial Advocates; State Bar of California;
District of Columbia Bar; Hawaii State
Bar Association (President, 1988); ABA.
Career: Staff Attorney, US Department
of Justice, Civil Division, 1970-73. Assistant US Attorney, 1973-75. Hawaii
Board of Examiners, 1974-85.
Personal: LLM, The National Law Cen-
ter, George Washington University,
1974; JD, University of Oregon, 1970;
BS, University of Oregon, 1967. Hawaii's
Top Lawyers (Honolulu Magazine).

MILLER, Clifford
McCorriston Miller Mukai MacKinnon
LLP, Honolulu 808 529 7300
miller@m4law.com
Recommended in Real Estate
Practice Areas: Real estate; real estate
development; finance; business organi-
zation; international business law; mul-
timedia.
Prof. Memberships: Admitted to prac-
tice in California (1973), and Hawaii
(1974). Member of State Bar of Califor-
nia; Hawaii State Bar Association, Sec-
tions on Real Property and Financial
Services, and Business Law; American
Bar Association, Sections on Business
Law, Real Property, Probate and Trust
Law, International Law and Practice,
and Law Practice Management; American College of Real Estate Lawyers; and
Urban Land Institute.
Personal: Born 31 October 1947. JD,
Pepperdine University, 1973; BA, University of California at Irvine, 1969.
Hawaii's Top Lawyers (Honolulu Maga-
zine).

MUNGER, Lisa Woods
Goodsill Anderson Quinn & Stifel,
Honolulu 808 547 5600
Recommended in Land Use, Litigation

MUZZI, Christopher
Case Bigelow & Lombardi, A Law Cor-
poration, Honolulu
808 547 5400
cmuzzi@casebigelow.com
Recommended in Bankruptcy
Practice Areas: Bankruptcy, litigation,
state tax controversy resolution.
Prof. Memberships: Hawaii State Bar
Association, Sections on Taxation and
Bankruptcy (Director and Secretary).
Personal: JD, Dickinson School of Law,
1997; BS, University of Delaware, 1994.

NAKASHIMA, Steve
Marr Hipp Jones & Wang, Honolulu
808 536 4900
Recommended in Employment

NISHIMOTO, John
Ayabe, Chong, Nishimoto, Sia &
Nakamura, Honolulu 808 537 6119
Recommended in Litigation

OKUMURA, Miki
Goodsill Anderson Quinn & Stifel,
Honolulu 808 547 5600
Recommended in Tax

PAUL, James
Paul, Johnson, Park & Niles, Attorneys
At Law, A Law Corporation, Honolulu
808 524 1212
Recommended in Litigation

PEAR, Charles
McCorriston Miller Mukai MacKinnon
LLP, Honolulu 808 529 7300
pear@m4law.com
Recommended in Real Estate
Practice Areas: Condominium and
vacation ownership development; real
estate development; real property.
Prof. Memberships: Admitted to prac-
tice in Hawaii (1976), Florida (1977) and
Colorado (1994). Member and past
Chair, Real Property and Financial Ser-
vices Section, Hawaii State Bar Associa-
tion; American Bar Association; and
American Resort Development Associa-
tion.
Publications: Contributing author:
'Time Share Registration', 'Hawaii Real
Estate Manual', 1997. Editor, 'Hawaii
Commercial Real Estate Manual', 1988.
Editor, 'Hawaii Conveyance Manual',
1987.
Personal: Born 18 June 1950. JD, Boalt
Hall School of Law, University of Cali-
fornia at Berkeley, 1975; BA, University
of Hawaii, 1972.

PETRUS, Barbara
Goodsill Anderson Quinn & Stifel,
Honolulu 808 547 5600
Recommended in Employment

PETTIT, Ted N
Case Bigelow & Lombardi, A Law Corporation, Honolulu 808 547 5400
tpettit@casebigelow.com
Recommended in Bankruptcy
Practice Areas: Business transactions,
business reorganization, creditor workouts, debt restructuring, commercial

foreclosure actions, commercial litigation. Extensive experience in large bankruptcy cases.
Prof. Memberships: American Bar
Association; Hawaii State Bar Association (President, Bankruptcy Law Sec-
tion, 2001); Federal Bar Association; The
Association of Trial Lawyers; American
Jurisprudence Society; American Bankruptcy Institute.
Publications: Hawaii Collection Law
Manual, 2002; 'Esquire and Discrimination in the Legal Profession', 2 Haw. B.J.
22 (1998); frequent lecturer on commercial real estate financing and bankruptcy.
Personal: JD, Richardson School of
Law, University of Hawaii, 1986 (Execu-
tive Editor, Hawaii Law Review); PhD
(Medical Physiology), University of
Hawaii, 1980; MS (Veterinary Physiolo-
gy), University of Missouri, 1977.

PIPER, Jeffrey
Schlack Ito & Lockwood Piper & Elkind,
LLC, Honolulu 808 523 6040
Recommended in Tax

PORTNOY, Jeffrey
Cades Schutte, Honolulu
808 521 9200
Recommended in Litigation

PRESSMAN, Stewart
McCorriston Miller Mukai MacKinnon
LLP, Honolulu 808 529 7300
pressman@m4law.com
Recommended in Corporate/M&A
Practice Areas: Corporate, mergers
and acquisitions, and securities.
Prof. Memberships: Hawaii State Bar
Association (Business Law Section);
State Bar of California; ABA (Business
Law and Intellectual Property Law Sec-
tions).
Career: Partner since 2000.
Publications: First place award winner
in the American Society of Composers
and Authors (ASCAP) essay contest for
the article entitled 'A Foreign Model for
Performance Royalties in Sound
Recordings'.
Personal: JD, Loyola Law School (cum
laude), 1989 ; BS, University of Southern
California, 1985.

RADOVICH, Scott D
Schneider Tanaka Radovich Andrew &
Tanaka, LLLC, Honolulu
808 792 4200
sradovich@stratlaw.com
Recommended in Real Estate
Practice Areas: Real estate acquisitions,
development and sales, including land
use entitlements and regulatory compliance. Extensive experience with bulk
land sales and acquisitions; residential,
commercial and resort acquisitions,
development and sales; retail land sales;
condominium development and conversions; master planned community
development and associations; time
share development and registration;
general real estate and commercial
transactions. Clients include large land

owners, real estate developers, time share operators, community associations.

Prof. Memberships: Hawaii State Bar Association.
Personal: JD, UCLA, 1984; MBA, University of Colorado, 1981; BS, University of Santa Clara, 1978 (magna cum laude).

RAND, Richard
Torkildson, Katz, Fonseca, Jaffe, Moore & Hetherington Attorneys At Law, A Law Corporation, Honolulu 808 523 6000
Recommended in Employment

REBER, David
Goodsill Anderson Quinn & Stifel, Honolulu 808 547 5600
Recommended in Corporate/M&A

ROSE, Crystal
Bays Deaver Lung Rose Baba, Honolulu 808 523 9000
Recommended in Litigation

SAKUMOTO, Randall
McCorriston Miller Mukai MacKinnon LLP, Honolulu 808 529 7300
sakumoto@m4law.com
Recommended in Real Estate
Practice Areas: Real estate acquisition, development, financing, and leasing.
Prof. Memberships: State of Hawaii Land Use Commission (Vice Chair, July 2004-present); American Land Title Association; Hawaii Developers' Council (Board Member and Secretary, 2000-02); Hawaii State Bar Association; ABA.
Career: Partner since 1996.
Publications: Co-author: 'Hawaii District Court Landlord-Tenant Manual'

(1992). Co-drafter: 'City and County of Honolulu Zoning Code, Land Use Ordinance', Chapter 21, 'Revised Ordinances of Honolulu', 1999.
Personal: JD, Hastings College of the Law, University of California, 1988. BA, University of California, Los Angeles, 1984.

SCHLACK, Carl
Schlack Ito & Lockwood Piper & Elkind, LLC, Honolulu 808 523 6040
Recommended in Real Estate

SCHNEIDER, Robert F
Schneider Tanaka Radovich Andrew & Tanaka, LLLC, Honolulu 808 792 4200
rfs@stratlaw.com
Recommended in Real Estate
Practice Areas: Real estate development and real estate finance. His practice is transactional, with an emphasis on the acquisition, financing, development and sale of undeveloped lands, residential projects, commercial buildings, shopping centers and resort properties. His work also involves commercial leasing and title analysis. His clients include land owners, developers, investors and lending institutions.
Prof. Memberships: Hawaii State Bar Association.
Publications: Co-author of the Hawaii Real Estate Financing Manual (1990) and Hawaii Real Estate Law Manual (1997).
Personal: JD, McGeorge School of Law, University of the Pacific, 1976. BA, Williams College, with honors, 1973.

SCHULL, Gunner
Cades Schutte, Honolulu
808 521 9200
Recommended in Corporate/M&A

STEVERSON, Randall
Goodsill Anderson Quinn & Stifel, Honolulu 808 547 5600
Recommended in Real Estate

STRAND, Robert
Carlsmith Ball LLP, Honolulu
808 523 2500
Recommended in Real Estate

SWEET, Charles
Carlsmith Ball LLP, Honolulu
808 523 2500
Recommended in Corporate/M&A

TIUS, Susan
Rush Moore LLP, Honolulu
808 521 0400
Recommended in Bankruptcy

TSUKAZAKI, Ben
Tsukazaki Yeh & Moore, Honolulu
808 961 0055
Recommended in Land Use

VAN WINKLE, Thomas
Carlsmith Ball LLP, Honolulu
808 523 2500
Recommended in Corporate/M&A

WAGNER, James
Wagner Choi Evers, Honolulu
808 533 1877
Recommended in Bankruptcy

WANG, Sarah
Marr Hipp Jones & Wang, Honolulu
808 536 4900
Recommended in Employment

WELCH, Thomas
Mancini Welch & Geiger LLP, Kahului
808 871 8351
Recommended in Real Estate

WONG, Danton
Chun, Kerr, Dodd, Beaman & Wong, Honolulu 808 528 8200
Recommended in Real Estate

WONG, David
Carlsmith Ball LLP, Honolulu
808 523 2500
Recommended in Tax

YOUNGREN, Nancy
Case Bigelow & Lombardi, A Law Corporation, Honolulu 808 547 5400
nyoungren@casebigelow.com
Recommended in Real Estate
Personal: JD, William S Richardson School of Law, University of Hawaii at Manoa, 1996; MLIS, University of Hawaii at Manoa, 1987; BA, University of Tennessee, 1974.

YUEN, Leighton
Goodsill Anderson Quinn & Stifel, Honolulu 808 547 5600
Recommended in Real Estate

ALSTON HUNT FLOYD & ING

THE FIRM

President: Paul Alston
Managing Director: William Hunt

Number of director-shareholders: 16

AREAS OF PRACTICE:

Business & Personal Injury Litigation 35%
Real Property & Business Transactions 15%
Healthcare 15%
Labor & Employment 13%
Title & Escrow 7%
Banking & Finance 7%
Environmental & Cultural Resources 3%
Government Affairs & Public Interest 2%
Government Procurement & Grant Compliance 2%
Education 1%

FIRM OVERVIEW: Alston Hunt Floyd & Ing (AHFI) is a Hawaii-based firm servicing clients throughout the Pacific Region. The firm is known for high quality, fast, creative and cost-effective service. AHFI is very active in community, business and government organizations. These activities give AHFI attorneys a broader perspective on issues, which enables them to better assist clients in achieving their goals.

MAIN AREAS OF PRACTICE:

Business & Personal Injury Litigation: AHFI represents individual and corporate clients in mediation, arbitration, administrative proceedings, litigation and appeals in federal and state courts. The firm has experience in admiralty and maritime law, the Americans with Disabilities Act, antitrust and trade regulation, business torts, communications and media law, construction law, derivative litigation and shareholder disputes, insurance defense and insurance coverage, non-compete and intellectual property disputes, personal injury defense, real property disputes, RICO, and securities litigation.

Real Property & Business Transactions: The firm assists individual and corporate clients on acquisition and disposition of real property, real estate financing, real estate development and construction, real estate leasing, landlord-tenant issues, formation of business entities, mergers and acquisitions, and partner disputes. Attorneys also advise on intellectual property, venture capital financing, licensing and strategic ventures, and e-commerce transactions.

Healthcare: The firm represents hospitals, health plans, physicians and other health care providers with healthcare litigation, regulatory compliance, and dispute resolution proceedings. Attorneys also advise clients on risk management.

Labor & Employment: AHFI provides advice, counseling and litigation representation to employers in matters involving wrongful termination, equal employment opportunity, labor law and collective bargaining, wage and hour law, government contracting compliance, employee benefits, Taft-Hartley trust funds, business transactions, personnel management, safety and health, immigration, proprietary rights, and workplace privacy. The firm also provides management training and strategic planning assistance.

Title & Escrow: The firm represents title insurance companies and their insureds in policy coverage issues, quiet title actions, defense of adverse title claims, and defense of bad faith claims. AHFI also assists clients with disputes involving easements, boundaries, access claims, surveyors' errors, forged deeds and mortgages.

Banking & Finance: The firm provides advice, counseling and litigation representation in regulatory compliance, lender issues, collections, foreclosures, and bankruptcy to banks, savings and loans, governmental entities, trustees, and judgment creditors.

HEAD OFFICE

HAWAII
1001 Bishop Street, American Savings Bank Tower, Suite 1800
Honolulu, HI 96813
Tel: 808 524 1800   **Fax:** 808 524 4591
Email: info@ahfi.com
Website: www.ahfi.com

BRANCH OFFICES

HAWAII
65-1230 Mamalahoa Hwy., Carter Professional Center, Suite C-21
Kamuela, HI 96743
Tel: 808 885 6762
Email: sfloyd@ahfi.com

CONTACTS

Business & Personal Injury Litigation ....Paul Alston (Honolulu)
Real Property & Business Transactions ..Bruce Noborikawa (Honolulu)
Healthcare ....Ellen Carson (Honolulu)
Labor & Employment ....Anna Elento-Sneed (Honolulu)
Title & Escrow ....Jade Ching (Honolulu)
Banking & Finance ....Louise Ing (Honolulu)
Environmental & Cultural Resources ....Lea Hong (Honolulu)
Government Affairs & Public Interest ......Melissa Pavlicek (Honolulu)
Government Procurement & Grant Compliance Terry Thomason (Honolulu)
Education ....Shelby Anne Floyd (Waimea)

Environmental & Cultural Resources: AHFI provides advice, counseling and litigation representation to public and private sector clients on land use and development, endangered species, environmental impact statements and assessments, preservation of historic sites, Native Hawaiian cultural issues, air and water pollution, solid and hazardous waste management, water rights, and insurance coverage issues.

Government Affairs & Public Interest: The firm provides advice on government and public affairs and represents clients before the state Legislature, county councils and federal, state and local government agencies. This includes bill tracking and monitoring, development of legislative and government relations strategies, drafting of legislation and lobbying.

Government Procurement & Grant Compliance: AHFI provides advice, counseling and litigation representation to contracting agencies, contractors and subcontractors involved in federal, state and county government contracts. These services include privatization issues, solicitation analysis and bid preparation, protests against solicitations and awards, contract interpretation and administration, defense of contract terminations, debarment actions, dispute litigation and resolution, and qui tam actions. AHFI also advises clients with federal grants.

Education: AHFI provides general business counseling for private schools. The firm also advises on First Amendment, privacy, special education and disability rights with respect to public school systems.

INTERNATIONAL WORK: Because of its central location in Hawaii, AHFI represents clients from the US, Europe and Asia who are doing business in the Pacific Region. The firm has language capabilities in English, Japanese, Taiwanese, Spanish and conversational Mandarin.

ALSTON
HUNT
FLOYD
& ING
LAWYERS

CASE BIGELOW & LOMBARDI

THE FIRM

Executive Committee: Dennis M Lombardi, Michael R Marsh, Ted N Pettit
Managing Director: Michael R Marsh
Senior Director: Daniel H Case

Number of Directors: 16
Number of other lawyers: 8

FIRM OVERVIEW: Case Bigelow & Lombardi, A Law Corporation, is a prominent law firm in Hawaii with a diverse civil practice. The firm's attorneys, legal assistants and support staff are committed to client service and quality representation that is efficient and cost-effective. The firm is located in the Pacific Guardian Center in Honolulu on the island of Oahu. Tracing its roots back to 1888, Case Bigelow & Lombardi has a history of providing quality legal services throughout Hawaii. To assure the highest quality of service to its clients, the firm's attorneys, legal assistants and support staff are organized into client service groups. The firm presently has three client service groups, which are: business, estate planning, probate and taxation; litigation, bankruptcy and dispute resolution; and real estate.

MAIN AREAS OF PRACTICE:

Business, Estate Planning, Probate & Taxation: Business attorneys in this practice group assist clients in the formation and operation of corporations, limited partnerships and limited liability partnerships; prepare profit-sharing, pension and other employee benefit plans; assist clients in addressing the opportunities and challenges faced by an ongoing business; and provide advice regarding transactions governed by the Uniform Commercial Code; mergers, acquisitions, dissolutions, asset purchases and financings. In addition to these matters, the firm's corporate attorneys frequently work together with its real estate attorneys with structuring, drafting and closing real estate transactions which are structured as corporate mergers or stock transfers. The estate planning, probate and taxation attorneys represent a broad spectrum of clients, from small businesses, families and individuals to banks and trust companies. Drawing upon its experience in the laws of income, gift, estate, partnerships, corporations, and other business entities, the goal of the practice group is to design and implement comprehensive business and estate plans and analyze and structure a variety of sophisticated transactions that are designed to fit the client's particular circumstances and concerns. While its work is tax-motivated, the firm also works to ensure that the business and estate plans it creates are flexible and adaptable to provide for and respond to shifting and unforeseen situations.

Real Estate: The firm enjoys a sophisticated and diverse real estate practice. Areas of expertise include the structuring of real estate acquisitions and sales; commercial financing, including complex construction and syndicated loans; loan restructuring; real estate sales and administration; office and retail leasing; condominium and vacation ownership development and licensing; community association formation and administration; residential financing; and land use, zoning and entitlement matters. The firm represents landowners, purchasers, investors and lenders in the acquisition, sale and financing of all types of real estate, including undeveloped land, hotels, shopping centers, office buildings and residential developments. The firm's attorneys in the Real Estate Group take pride in assisting in the consummation of real estate transactions as well as providing creative and cost-effective solutions to the needs of its clients.

Litigation, Bankruptcy & Dispute Resolution: The firm's Litigation, Bankruptcy and Dispute Resolution Practice Group is led by a team of skillful, experienced and successful litigators and trial lawyers. Attorneys who practice in the litigation and dispute resolution areas are creative and conscientious in their representation of clients in real estate, business, construction, tort, and commercial litigation matters. The attorneys regularly appear in all federal and state courts in Hawaii, both at the trial and appellate levels, and before administrative officers and regulatory agencies. Lawyers in the Litigation, Bankruptcy and Dispute Resolution Practice Group are committed to efficient dispute resolution through mediation, arbitration, negotiated settlement, and, if necessary, the use of adversary court proceedings. The firm's Bankruptcy Practice covers all aspects of creditor-debtor relationships ranging from foreclosure, receivership, collection and enforcement of judgments in state and federal court to reorganization and liquidation in bankruptcy court. The firm also represents secured creditors, unsecured creditor committees and landlords in all aspects of bankruptcy proceedings. The firm has a team of creditor counsel experienced in negotiating workouts and restructurings outside of bankruptcy court.

CLIENTS: The firm's clientele is varied. They include large international, national and local corporations and businesses, financial institutions, trusts and non-profit organizations, real estate developers, sole proprietors and individuals.

INTERNATIONAL WORK: Case Bigelow & Lombardi is counsel to Asian and Pacific Rim based corporations and entities. The firm assists these clients with their transnational real estate sales, acquisitions and development; corporate formations and business transactions. Case Bigelow & Lombardi is the exclusive member firm for Hawaii of Lex Mundi, the world's leading association of independent law firms. With more than 15,000 lawyers in 560 offices, Lex Mundi firms are present in more than 160 countries, states and provinces covering virtually every business market worldwide. The firm's membership in Lex Mundi provides it with global reach and access to premiere legal resources that enhance its ability to serve its clients' needs around the world. The firm's attorneys and staff are reflective of Hawaii's ethnic diversity and multi-racial culture and are fluent in Japanese, Chinese, French, and Spanish.

HEAD OFFICE

HAWAII
Pacific Guardian Center, Mauka Tower, 737 Bishop Street, Suite 2600, **Honolulu,** HI 96813
Tel: 808 547 5400 **Fax:** 808 523 1888
Email: info@casebigelow.com
Website: www.casebigelow.com

CONTACTS

Business, Estate Planning, Probate & Taxation ....James M Cribley
Litigation ....Roger S Mosley
Real Estate ....Dennis Lombardi

MEMBER

LEX MUNDI

THE WORLD'S LEADING ASSOCIATION
OF INDEPENDENT LAW FIRMS

KOBAYASHI, SUGITA & GODA

THE FIRM

Managing Partner: Kenneth Y Sugita

Number of partners: 22
Number of other lawyers: 12

HEAD OFFICE

HAWAII
999 Bishop Street, 26th Floor, **Honolulu,** HI 96813
Tel: 808 539 8700   **Fax:** 808 539 8799
Email: ksg@ksglaw.com
Website: www.ksglaw.com

FIRM OVERVIEW: The firm specializes in complex litigation and corporate business relations with an emphasis in commercial and construction issues, representation in finance, transactions, banking, general corporate, regulatory, land use, labor management, wrongful termination, immigration, and associated fields. The firm provides critical expertise necessary to ensure present and future clientele with the continuity and quality of representation needed to address legal problems in Hawaii, the Far East, the Pacific Rim, and the continental United States.

MAIN AREAS OF PRACTICE:

General Corporate: The firm's General Corporate Practice includes business formation, corporate governance and structure, contract review, mergers, stock and asset acquisitions (including, but not limited to: due diligence review, negotiation, documentation and closing), corporate reorganizations (involving both foreign and domestic companies), corporate regulatory matters, business development matters, commercial management matters, bankruptcy and antitrust matters, and other legal matters relating to insurance, transportation, estates, trusts, public utilities and telecommunications, and intellectual property.

General Real Estate: The firm's Real Estate Practice involves the representation of local, national and multinational landowners, developers, banks, public agencies, landlords and tenants, title insurers, property managers, and other development parties to facilitate purchase, sales, financing and leasing transactions, including land use and entitlement matters, and legal services relating to commercial property, real property conveyancing, and commercial leasing.

Financial Institutions: The firm provides general and specialized legal services to financial institution and mortgage brokerage clients. Services include corporate compliance, bank regulatory compliance, advise regarding proper procedures and protocols for securing necessary approvals from the State Commissioner of Financial Institutions, the Federal Deposit Insurance Corporation or the Board of Governors' Federal Reserve System, issues relating to the sale of insurance by financial institutions, and other related matters. The firm also provides a full range of loan documentation services, ranging from large development and construction commercial loans to residential loans.

Creditors' Remedies: The firm handles all aspects of complex commercial loan workouts including the comprehensive negotiation and documentation of refinancing, repayment and/or liquidation of collateral by agreement or through foreclosure or bankruptcy.

Liquor Licenses & Administrative Proceedings: The firm assists a broad range of clients in preparing and obtaining new liquor licenses or the transfer of existing licenses under the liquor laws of the State of Hawaii, including representing licensees at public hearings before each county's respective Liquor Commission for liquor license applications or violations.

Environmental: The firm advises owners, developers, contractors and lenders with respect to environmental compliance, liability and exposure, covering a broad spectrum of environmental litigation, consultation and regulatory matters, such as violations of Clean Water Act, cost recovery matters under CERCLA, releases from underground storage tanks, closure of underground storage tanks, due diligence investigations of properties for environmental contamination, and toxic tort cases, and assisting clients with entry into the State of Hawaii Voluntary Response Program.

Commercial Litigation: The firm works in all aspects of commercial litigation in the areas of contracts, environmental issues, intellectual property, employment, antitrust, public utilities, real estate and development, and other related fields.

Construction Litigation: The firm handles complex litigation, arbitration, and mediation matters relating to construction contracts or construction issues involving owners, architects, engineers, consultants and contractors including cases involving breach of contract, cost overruns, problem change orders, mechanic's and materialman's liens, performance and payment bonds, and vendor and subcontractor problems.

Construction Contract Drafting: The firm provides specialized legal counsel on both transactional and litigation matters, handling all stages of the development and construction process, including designing the contracting structure to developing financial and risk management strategies, assuring legal compliance, drafting and administering of contracts, and preventing and ultimately resolving any claims that may arise.

Antitrust: The firm has experience litigating a broad spectrum of antitrust issues, including cases arising under the Sherman Act, Clayton Act, Hawaii Unfair and Deceptive Practices Act, and other state and federal antitrust laws.

Public Utilities: The firm handles a full spectrum of regulatory issues arising before the Hawaii Public Utilities Commission, and has experience with the protocols and procedures that apply to proceedings and dockets arising before the Commission.

Labor & Employment: The firm handles a broad range of labor and employment matters including grievances under collective bargaining agreements, arbitration and civil litigation concerning employment disputes and unfair labor practices in both state and federal courts. The firm is also experienced in common law employment claims arising from 'employment-at-will' including such claims as wrongful discharge in violation of public policy, defamation, emotional distress, invasion of privacy and breach of the duty of loyalty.

Tort Defense & Prosecution: The firm has defended and prosecuted numerous personal injury actions for automobile, premises liability and product liability related accidents, including death and permanent disability claims.

Immigration & Nationality: The firm provides international and domestic clients with a full range of immigration law services and has been recognized for its extensive experience in business immigration and consular processing, visa and custom matters, preparation of complex petitions and applications for visas that allow employment in the United States.

Tax, Estate & Retirement Planning: The firm is involved in all aspects of estate planning, including formulation of lifetime and estate transfer strategies, compiling federal estate gift and generation-skipping tax returns, and drafting wills and all forms of trusts and other estate planning documentation. The firm also advises corporate and individual trustees on their legal and fiduciary obligations, and works in all aspects of tax planning for individual, domestic and foreign corporate clients.

CLIENTS: The firm's clients include: BancWest Corporation; First Hawaiian Bank; Meiji Mutual Life Insurance Co.; Pacific Guardian Life Insurance Co.; AIG Hawaii Insurance Company, Inc., R.J. Reynolds Tobacco Co.; Shell Oil Company; Kiewit Pacific Co.; Seibu Railway Co., Ltd., Insurance Commissioner, Department of Commerce and Consumer Affairs of the State of Hawaii; City and County of Honolulu.

MCCORRISTON MILLER MUKAI MACKINNON LLP

THE FIRM

Managing Partner: D Scott MacKinnon

Number of partners: 33
Number of other lawyers: 9

HEAD OFFICE

HAWAII
Five Waterfront Plaza, 4th Floor, 500 Ala Moana Boulevard
Honolulu, HI 96813
Tel: 808 529 7300   **Fax:** 808 524 8293
Website: www.m4law.com

FIRM OVERVIEW: McCorriston Miller Mukai MacKinnon LLP (M4) was formed in 1989 by several experienced lawyers who were partners with established Hawaii law firms but saw a need for a firm which would provide a specialized expertise in real estate and business transactions and expert counsel in a wide range of litigation matters to both domestic and international clients. Through its commitment to excellence, dedication, hard work, and creative and cost efficient legal representation to its many clients, M4 has become one of Hawaii's largest and most respected law firms, with a reputation spreading throughout the Pacific Basin in a very short period of time.

MAIN AREAS OF PRACTICE:

Real Estate: M4 is well recognized for its work involving real estate development and construction of condominiums and resort properties, commercial and construction financing, loan restructurings and workouts, acquisitions and dispositions of real property, commercial leasing, and equity investments. M4 also has extensive experience in timesharing, including work on numerous projects across the US and in other countries. Timeshare expertise extends to property acquisition, product design and structuring, registrations in various jurisdictions, marketing, management, interim financing, and receivables financing.

Litigation: M4 has a diverse litigation practice. M4 has handled to a successful conclusion numerous disputes involving complex commercial transactions, technological issues, products liability, environmental matters, corporate disputes, professional liability, defense of persons accused of white collar crime, insurance, and other civil litigation. Many major cases in the State of Hawaii in the past decade have involved members of the firm's Litigation Team, including the Bishop Estate litigation, the state antitrust case against the nation's major energy companies, and defense of the Mayor of the City and County of Honolulu.

Hospitality: M4 represents hotel developers and owners, equity investors, ground lessors and lessees, operators, and others involved in the State of Hawaii's principal industry - tourism. Representative transactions include the acquisition, financing and/or development of such well-known hotels as the Kahala Hilton Hotel, Hyatt Regency Hotels - Kaanapali and Waikiki, Ala Moana Hotel, Waikiki Beachcomber, Kona Village Resort, Westin Maui, Kapalua Bay Hotel, Maui Marriott, Kaanapali Embassy Suites Hotel, and Outrigger Prince Kuhio Hotel. M4 also advises clients and has litigated matters concerning hotel management agreements.

Corporate: M4 is accomplished in the formation of corporations, limited liability companies, and limited partnerships for its clients. M4 also provides counsel in mergers and acquisitions, corporate finance, financial services, insurance, investment vehicles, and corporate and insurance restructuring and work-outs. Much of this work is in international transactions involving US and foreign companies doing business in Asia and the Pacific Rim.

Finance: M4 has extensive experience in handling tax-exempt and taxable bond financing transactions for a wide variety of facilities and projects. The firm's lawyers have served as bond counsel, special counsel to state and local bond issuers, underwriter's counsel, counsel to bond trustees, counsel to nonprofit organizations and private developers of bond-financed facilities, and counsel to credit enhancement or liquidity support providers for bond issues. The firm has recognized expertise in the development of financing plans and structures, compliance with federal and state tax and securities laws, negotiation and preparation of financing and security documents, and preparation of official statements and other bond offering circulars used in the marketing of bond issues.

Insurance: M4 represents several major insurers. It has developed a specialty practice in the defense of actions against insurance companies for bad faith and extra-contractual damages. It routinely handles cases involving personal injury, property damage, contracts, products liability, construction issues, employment discrimination, and professional, directors' and fiduciary liability. A considerable part of the practice in this area is devoted to insurance coverage issues, primarily on behalf of insurers. Additionally, M4 has represented the State of Hawaii in the highly specialized field of rehabilitating and/or liquidating insolvent insurance companies.

Employment: M4's lawyers have significant experience and expertise in advising employers in connection with employment-related litigation. The firm also regularly provides advice to clients on matters relating to employee handbooks, personnel policies, personnel action and procedures, wage and hour questions, health and safety issues, and a broad range of other subject areas. Such advice is geared toward assisting clients in avoiding litigation where possible.

Environmental: M4's lawyers are experts in the handling environmental matters, including preparation of environmental impact statements, permitting, and litigation. M4 represents a diverse mix of clients in environmental matters, including landowners, lessees, financial institutions, construction and design professionals, as well as large and small quantity hazardous waste generators.

Healthcare: M4's health care attorneys represent a diverse mix of healthcare clients, including hospitals, healthcare systems, individual doctors, dentists, and other medical practitioners, healthcare payors and insurance companies, pharmaceutical companies, and other participants in the healthcare industry. Each representation is tailored to the client's particular needs and circumstances to ensure that quality service is provided in a timely, responsive, and cost-effective manner.

CLIENTS: M4's clients include architects, construction contractors, landowners, developers, banks, major energy companies, property management companies, insurance companies, governmental entities and officials, healthcare organizations, hotel owners and operators, and timeshare operators.

INTERNATIONAL WORK: M4 represents many international companies doing business in the United States. The firm is recognized in Hawaii as a leader in representing Japan-based organizations. M4's attorneys are also experienced in doing business in the People's Republic of China and Taiwan. The firm has been involved in a number of joint ventures and other investments in the PRC, including real estate and infrastructure development, telecommunications, and other commercial and industrial projects.

CONTENTS: Corporate/M&A p.655; Employment: p.656; Litigation: p.657; Real Estate p.658; Individuals' Profiles p.659.

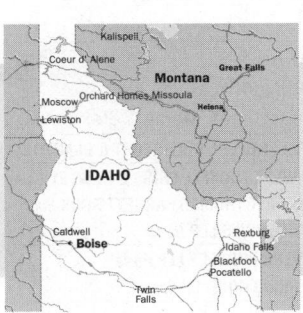

How lawyers are ranked

The opinions we gather from clients — mainly from in-house lawyers but also from other purchasers of legal services — are balanced by opinions from colleagues and competitors. Together, they provide two different perspectives — an all-round view — and biased viewpoints cancel each other out.

CORPORATE/M&A

Idaho
Leading firms (Corporate/M&A)
1. HAWLEY TROXELL ENNIS & HAWLEY *Boise*
2. HOLLAND & HART LLP *Boise*
   STOEL RIVES LLP *Boise*

Leading individuals (Corporate/M&A)
1. BOYD Paul *Stoel Rives*, Boise
   MILLER Nicholas *Hawley Troxell*, Boise
2. MACK J Frederick *Holland & Hart*, Boise
   PRINCE Larry *Holland & Hart*, Boise
3. DRAKE Stephen *Stoel Rives*, Boise
   HARDESTY Stephen *Hawley Troxell*, Boise
   ORMSETH Kris *Stoel Rives*, Boise
   RILEY Richard *Hawley Troxell*, Boise

Firms and individuals are listed alphabetically in each band.

Band 1

Hawley Troxell Ennis & Hawley LLP

The Firm: A classic Idaho law firm, its esteemed corporate group houses strong lawyers and attracts important clients. Noted for its "*overall breadth*" and the "*excellent skill sets of individual lawyers,*" the team has recently been working on a transaction related to the Boise Cascade and Office Max merger. This "*superior*" team has established an outstanding reputation for its corporate finance, M&A and securities work.

The Lawyers: Chair of the business and finance practice, **Nicholas Miller** is tipped as a "*top bond lawyer in Idaho.*" Public entities, such as hospitals and school districts, benefit from his prowess in this field. Praise is further directed at his general corporate, finance and securities practice, which involves public and private companies. The market also commends **Richard Riley** for his broad-based commercial practice. Described as an "*excellent technical draftsman,*" he has particular strengths in the areas of M&A, business planning and secured lending. **Steve Hardesty** is respected for his "*ability to drive transactions.*"

The Clients: The group acts for a number of important clients and institutions, including Boise State University.

Band 2

Holland & Hart LLP

See firm details p.325

The Firm: Clients praise this 12-attorney corporate group for providing "*bang for the buck*" in its full range of corporate representation. They further value the "*great results*" generated by the group's heady combination of "*smart people with good experience.*" Among its strong general practice, a particular highlight is its work with emerging and technology companies.

The Lawyers: **Frederick Mack** (see p.660) holds a prominent position in this market, described as a generalist and "*rainmaker.*" He recently advised on five M&A deals valued between $1-10 million each. The "*phenomenal*" **Larry Prince** (see p.660) is also a nationally known creditors' rights attorney. Described as "*knowledgeable, bright and practical,*" he serves as lead counsel to WinCo and separately represents a range of major financial institutions such as Wells Fargo.

The Clients: WinCo; Wells Fargo; SBC Global Technologies and Banner Bank.

Stoel Rives LLP

The Firm: The "*superb*" local arm of this firm has a sophisticated and broad-ranging corporate practice. Nationally known for its work in the renewable energy field, the corporate team advises Fortune 500 companies and fields a strong emerging company practice. Clients appreciate its high-level expertise and professional approach, deemed to be "*perfect for Boise, Idaho's business climate.*"

The Lawyers: Clients admire **Kris Ormseth**'s "*remarkable ability*" to turn complex strategies into reality. They further describe him as a "*levelheaded and patient*" attorney with "*incredible talent.*" He has worked on several asset purchases for Capital One. **Paul Boyd**'s practice has a heavy emphasis on M&A and general business counsel. Clients are "*extremely committed*" to him as a direct result of his "*great experience*" and "*pragmatic, efficient*" style. Clients feel they're "*well protected*" under his guard. Seen as an important figure in the community, he is the co-founder of the Chamber of Commerce's Venture Capital Committee. **Stephen Drake** demonstrates proclivity toward biotech and life sciences. His clients view him as "*business-savvy,*" "*fast on his feet*" and in possession of "*impressive common sense that is hard to match.*" In addition to the general counsel he provides, he is a highly respected securities lawyer with international reach.

The Clients: American Ecology; ProClarity; Medical Discoveries; DBSI and JR Simplot.

EMPLOYMENT

Idaho
Leading firms
(Employment: Mainly Defendant)
[1] HALL, FARLEY, OBERRECHT & BLANTON *Boise*
[2] HAWLEY TROXELL ENNIS & HAWLEY *Boise*
MOFFATT THOMAS BARRETT ROCK *Boise*
STOEL RIVES LLP *Boise*
[3] GIVENS PURSLEY LLP *Boise*
PERKINS COIE LLP *Boise*

Leading individuals
(Employment: Mainly Defendant)
[1] BERENTER Steven *Hawley Troxell*, Boise
CHANDLER Harry *Stoel Rives*, Boise
DALE Candy *Hall Farley*, Boise
DALE James *Moffatt Thomas*, Boise
[2] DOCKSTADER Kim *Stoel Rives*, Boise
MUNTHER Merrily *Penland Munther*, Boise
WHITE Robert *Givens Pursley*, Boise
Firms and individuals are listed alphabetically in each band.

Band 1

Hall, Farley, Oberrecht & Blanton, PA

The Firm: This firm's five-attorney group is applauded for the *"tremendous quality"* of its employment-related policy reviews, appeals and associated dispute resolution. Clients are particularly impressed by its skillful defense of harassment, discrimination and wrongful discharge claims. In addition, it also demonstrates proficiency in the areas of civil rights, unemployment, and wage and hour litigation. Equally experienced at providing training advice and other forms of preventive measures, the group's *"professional yet personal"* approach is wholly welcomed by clients.

The Lawyers: **Candy Dale** is considered a shining star in the employment world, partly due to her *"fabulous"* performances in employment litigation. Clients highlighted her distinct skills as *"an incredible speaker"* and a *"meticulous writer."* Equipped with a *"good handle on all the legal issues,"* she proves to be *"very persuasive in front of a jury."*

The Clients: Amalgamated Sugar; Idaho Power; Blue Cross of Idaho; LandAmerica and Trinity House.

Band 2

Hawley Troxell Ennis & Hawley LLP

The Firm: This firm's strong labor and employment group focuses on representing management in dispute resolution before state and federal courts. Interviewees report that its *"depth, expertise and experience"* set the group apart, attracting work in a variety of areas such as discrimination, wrongful discharge and breach of contract claims.

The group's *"very well-respected folks"* also offer preventive measures to reduce potential liabilities, often conducting reviews on employment contracts, handbooks and application forms.

The Lawyers: The market holds **Steven Berenter** in the highest regard for his employment counseling and litigation prowess. A *"prince of an attorney,"* he has recently defended a wrongful discharge claim.

The Clients: The firm has acted for clients in the healthcare, technology and manufacturing sectors, among others.

Moffatt Thomas Barrett Rock & Fields

The Firm: With its four offices located in Boise, Twin Falls, Pocatello and Idaho Falls, this long-standing team fields an impressive array of talent. Clients said its interdepartmental approach ensures that *"regardless of the legal issue, there is always a specialist on hand."* The five-partner group expertly defends employment-related claims before state and federal courts; OSHA, discrimination, unemployment civil rights, and wage and hour disputes are among its legal smorgasbord. Training, counseling and traditional labor capabilities round out its highly regarded practice.

The Lawyers: **Jim Dale** has a distinguished reputation in discrimination, OSHA and wage-hour claims in addition to his traditional strength in labor law. Aside from his abilities as an *"outstanding communicator,"* he is *"knowledgeable about the current status of the law"* and always *"keeps the interests of his clients at heart."*

The Clients: Independent Foresters, NORCO and Northwest Nazarene University are among the firm's diverse clientele.

Stoel Rives LLP

The Firm: According to clients, this firm enjoys a deservedly strong reputation for the *"outstanding quality"* of its employment attorneys and legal advice. The Idaho office concentrates on general advisory counseling and employment litigation, mostly involving discrimination, and wage and hour claims. However, it also boasts a respected profile in traditional labor law. The group is further enhanced by the firm's regional strength, and benefits from cross-references from other offices in California, Washington and Utah.

The Lawyers: **Harry Chandler** is respected for his *"unique blend"* of *"legal expertise, business savvy and good understanding of how legal advice translates at a local level."* Encompassing affirmative action, traditional labor law and employment litigation, his practice is cloaked in *"the added value of his tremendous personality."* **Kim Dockstader** focuses on wage and hour, and discrimination claims. Market observers view him as *"especially strong in hi-tech and multistate*

issues." Having spent time as an in-house counsel at Micron – where he was in charge of labor and employment issues throughout the country – he has a *"really good knowledge of how corporations work on the inside."*

The Clients: Among others, the firm has advised St. Luke's Regional Medical Center, Interland and MPC Computers.

Band 3

Givens Pursley LLP

The Firm: This firm's employment practice continues to flourish in Boise. It houses a group of highly experienced attorneys, focused on preventive counseling and training, post-employment counsel and related employment litigation. Interviewees commend its *"technical expertise and business sense"* on such matters as wage disputes, discrimination claims and wrong discharge lawsuits. The team has appeared before state and federal courts, in addition to government agencies such as the Idaho Human Rights Commission, the EEOC and the Department of Labor. Employment tort claims, non-competition covenants and trade secrets litigation also feature in its caseload.

The Lawyers: The market endorses **Bob White** as an *"excellent speaker"* who *"makes it easy for non-lawyers to understand"* the intricacies of employment law. Aside from undertaking employment training and counseling, he is also a highly experienced employment litigator.

The Clients: The team has represented clients in the healthcare, manufacturing, food production, hi-tech, utilities and construction sectors.

Perkins Coie LLP

The Firm: This firm's relatively small group of Boise-based employment lawyers has benefited from the resources and reach of its extensive network of nationwide and international offices. It takes the approach that comprehensive preventive counsel and training is of paramount importance in preventing drawn-out courtroom battles. As such, the Washington-based firm fields experience in training, counseling and dispute resolution in a wide array of employment-related issues.

The Lawyers: Shelly Cozakos is the contact attorney in the labor and employment practice in the Boise office.

The Clients: The firm represents a range of private and public businesses, including construction companies.

Other Notable Practitioners

Merrily Munther of Penland Munther Goodrum garnered acclaim as a *"capable and experienced"* operator whose labor and employment practice also straddles construction and real estate law.

All quotes in the text are from interviews with clients and competitors.

LITIGATION

GENERAL COMMERCIAL

Idaho
Leading firms
(Litigation: General Commercial)

1. **ELAM & BURKE PA** Boise
   HAWLEY TROXELL ENNIS & HAWLEY Boise
   HOLLAND & HART LLP Boise
2. **GREENER BANDUCCI SHOEMAKER** Boise
   MOFFATT THOMAS BARRETT ROCK Boise
   STOEL RIVES LLP Boise
3. **COSHO, HUMPHREY, GREENER** Boise
   EBERLE, BERLIN, KADING, TURNBOW Boise
   PERKINS COIE LLP Boise

Leading individuals
(Litigation: General Commercial)

Senior Statesman
BURKE Carl *Elam & Burke, Boise*

1. BITHELL Walter *Holland & Hart, Boise*
   DINGEL Allyn *Elam & Burke, Boise*
   GREENER Richard *Greener Banducci, Boise*
   MEADOWS Craig *Hawley Troxell, Boise*
2. ANDERSEN Steven *Holland & Hart, Boise*
   BANDUCCI Thomas *Greener Banducci, Boise*
   BOARDMAN Richard *Perkins Coie, Boise*
   CLARK Merlyn *Hawley Troxell, Boise*
   DRYDEN William *Elam & Burke, Boise*
   LARUE James *Elam & Burke, Boise*
   SINCLAIR J Walter *Stoel Rives, Boise*
   SQUYRES Newal *Holland & Hart, Boise*

Firms and individuals are listed alphabetically in each band.

Band 1

Elam & Burke PA

The Firm: This long-standing firm has a "*brilliantly multifaceted*" litigation practice, incorporating products liability and personal injury defense in addition to a steady diet of commercial, environmental and bankruptcy disputes. With its extensive experience and depth of expertise, sources single this firm out as a "*superb*" attribute of the Idaho legal landscape. The 14-attorney litigation team is also "*certainly a leader*" in the field of insurance defense.

The Lawyers: Hailed as "*one of Idaho's finest litigators,*" **Allyn Dingel** is an established authority on insurance coverage. His practice is further concentrated on governmental, contractual, personal injury and products liability litigation. Clients added that he's an "*excellent communicator and top-tier attorney.*" An "*exceptional and thorough attorney,*" **Bill Dryden** defends products liability and personal injury cases with great dexterity. Also heavily involved in commercial and environmental litigation, he is often retained for his "*excellent case strategy skills,*" admirers said. "*Nothing rattles him.*" Prominent on the legal radar screen is **Jim LaRue**, singled out for his combination of "*honesty and integri-*

ty*" and prowess in insurance litigation. **Carl Burke** is a "*firm ambassador,*" an indisputable "*leading light*" whose "*tremendous amount of experience*" has been parlayed into "*truly formidable*" litigation skills.

The Clients: Farmers Insurance; State Farm; DaimlerChrysler; Les Schwab Tire Centers of Idaho; Bogus Basin Recreational Association and Jerome Urban Renewal Agency.

Hawley Troxell Ennis & Hawley LLP

The Firm: As the largest firm in the state, its substantial litigation group houses "*class lawyers*" equipped with a diverse and comprehensive skills set. This ensures expertise in a broad spectrum of litigation matters, including medical malpractice, construction and aviation among other areas. The depth of resources available through its network of offices, coupled with its strong corporate capabilities, further entrenches its deep litigation bench.

The Lawyers: As head of the firm's commercial litigation practice, **Craig Meadows** commands enormous respect in the Boise market. Described as "*a personable and astute attorney,*" he delivers broad-ranging knowledge that includes products liability, legal malpractice and aviation litigation. **Merlyn Clark** is lauded as a "*big, successful mediator,*" setting the state's "*gold standard*" in this field. With his "*fluent knowledge of the rules at state and federal level,*" he often succeeds on behalf of his clients due to a "*smart, adept and professional*" approach. "*Everyone clamors for him,*" sources said.

The Clients: JR Simplot; Washington Group International; Blue Cross of Idaho; Wells Fargo and Albertson's.

Holland & Hart LLP

See firm details p.325

The Firm: This proficient cadre of litigators wields "*a lot of muscle*" in this marketplace, excelling at professional liability, banking, construction and finance litigation among other areas. Within the commercial sphere, it ably litigates on behalf of both defendants and plaintiffs. Further strengths can be discerned in the areas of IP, technology and products liability. The firm's state-of-the-art technology, which enables in-court evidence presentation, receives further applause from its clients.

The Lawyers: Peers applaud **Walter Bithell** (see p.659) as an "*outstanding*" attorney; he is equipped with the remarkable ability to "*beat almost any kind of case.*" Such kudos can be attributed to his abundant skills on behalf of an individual or in a class action. His expertise also extends to products liability, professional liability, insurance and securities litigation. His "*great character*" serves to bolster his impeccable trial skills and steadfastly secures his position as a

leading lawyer. "*Bright and well-organized*" **Steven Andersen** (see p.659) exhibits "*great courtroom presence*" on bad faith and general business disputes. He also fields a strong IP litigation practice. In this regard, he has been involved in many copyright, patent and technology transfer disputes. **Newal Squyres** (see p.660) is applauded for his "*level of integrity and quality of practice.*" Over the course of his practice, he "*has distinguished himself with his cases and clients,*" observers said.

The Clients: The firm acts for a number of important corporations, including ones in the banking, energy, biotech, technology, communications, construction and real estate sectors.

Band 2

Greener Banducci Shoemaker

The Firm: This nascent firm brings together some of Idaho's most eminent litigators. The result is a powerful and promising new Boise addition, which is already equipped with an enviable client base. It has served as a national counsel for a Fortune 100 company.

The Lawyers: As "*one of the best litigators in the state,*" **Richard Greener** is a shining star in Boise. His expertise encompasses malpractice, environmental and insurance matters among others. His clients – a mix of individual plaintiffs and commercial entities – value his "*erudite, quietly aggressive*" approach. **Thomas Banducci** is described as a "*heavy-hitting products liability litigator*" who is distinguished for his "*sharp intelligence.*"

The Clients: The firm has attracted a strong client base that includes Fortune 100 companies.

Moffatt Thomas Barrett Rock & Fields

The Firm: Interviewees observe that this firm's long-standing litigation practice has "*real firepower.*" Its four Idaho offices also benefit from a diverse group of clients, who praise the team's "*high quality*" of work. Its expertise spans products liability, IP, antitrust, environment and aviation.

The Lawyers: Stephen Thomas is a key contact partner in the firm's litigation department.

The Clients: The firm acts for a number of household names, including Chubb Group, Micron and GM.

Stoel Rives LLP

The Firm: The litigation department of this expanding, regional firm is gaining increasing strength in the Idaho market. Interviewees praise its "*well-rounded*" practice, which embraces a comprehensive catalog of litigation capabilities. In acknowledgment of its "*awesome*" regional breadth, many top-flight corporate clients call on its services to assist with pertinent business disputes.

The Lawyers: Peers have the "*utmost respect*" for **Walt Sinclair**'s "*great ability and integrity*." His broad practice covers products liability, mass tort, aviation and real estate disputes. Other interests include agriculture, contract and insurance.

The Clients: This firm has represented prominent companies such as Fred Meyer and GlaxoSmithKline.

Band 3

Cosho, Humphrey, Greener & Welsh, PA

The Firm: Peers and clients praise this firm's litigation group for its "*classy lawyers and unequivocal preparation*." It is involved in many of the state's most important cases, often concerning products liability, aviation and insurance. Also on offer are its skills in malpractice and securities. This long-standing firm also won respect for its superb services on behalf of its clientele, which comprises plaintiffs and defendants.

The Lawyers: Christopher Burke is considered a key player in the litigation team. In a significant departure, Richard Greener left to join a new law firm called Greener Banducci Shoemaker.

The Clients: Clients include Boise Cascade, Regence BlueShield and JR Simplot.

Eberle, Berlin, Kading, Turnbow & McKlveen, Chartered

The Firm: The market reports that this prominent and long-standing firm houses "*many excellent trial lawyers*." As a reflection of this, the group's extensive practice is frequently exercised in some of the state's most interesting cases. Areas of focus include construction, real estate, insurance, products liability, aviation and tax litigation.

The Lawyers: RB Kading is a leading partner of the firm's civil litigation practice.

The Clients: John Hancock Mutual Life Insurance; Regence BlueShield of Idaho; Wells Fargo and Phillips Petroleum.

Perkins Coie LLP

The Firm: This firm has four litigators based in Boise, yet its expanse of regional offices ensures an underlying resource of more than 300 lawyers who can lend support. In addition, it also offers international capability, which helps attract Fortune 500 companies. The group is perceived as a "*steady and growing presence*" in the state, market sources said.

The Lawyers: Peers describe managing partner **Richard Boardman** as "*simply outstanding*." He has a diverse array of skills involving such areas as products liability, construction and IP. Environmental, insurance and civil rights defense have also featured in his repertoire.

The Clients: The firm serves an impressive client roster, which includes Fortune 500 companies from a variety of different industries.

REAL ESTATE

Idaho
Leading firms (Real Estate)

1	GIVENS PURSLEY LLP *Boise*
	HAWLEY TROXELL ENNIS & HAWLEY *Boise*
2	MEULEMAN MILLER LLP *Boise*
	SPINK BUTLER, LLP *Boise*
	STOEL RIVES LLP *Boise*
3	MOFFATT THOMAS BARRETT ROCK *Boise*
	WILLIAMS BRADBURY, ATTORNEYS *Boise*

Idaho
Leading individuals (Real Estate)

	Senior Statesman
	HIGER Dale *Stoel Rives*, Boise
	KNICKREHM Donald *Hawley Troxell*, Boise
	MILLER Robert *Meuleman Miller*, Boise
1	BEESON Christopher *Givens Pursley*, Boise
2	BALLARD Brian *Hawley Troxell*, Boise
	KNIPE Quentin *Stoel Rives*, Boise
	SPINK Michael *Spink Butler*, Boise
3	GOWLAND Kimbal *Meuleman Miller*, Boise
	MILLER L Edward *Givens Pursley*, Boise
	MOLLERUP Richard *Meuleman Miller*, Boise

Leading individuals
(Real Estate: Zoning/Land Use)

1	BUTLER JoAnn *Spink Butler*, Boise
2	BRADBURY Steve *Williams Bradbury*, Boise
	WARDLE Geoffrey *Hawley Troxell*, Boise

Firms and individuals are listed alphabetically in each band.

Band 1

Givens Pursley LLP

The Firm: This firm's real estate group is renowned for its depth of expertise and impressive client roster. The team is particularly knowledgeable on shopping center developments, yet is also superbly qualified to act on warehouse, residential and other retail projects. Owing to the capabilities of its esteemed environmental law practice, the group is able to provide robust advice on related environmental issues. Its "*well-rounded and customer-focused*" practice attracts assignments on complex acquisitions, leasing transactions, disposals and real estate financing proceedings. Land use and zoning are added features of the firm.

The Lawyers: **Chris Beeson** receives praise for his "*tremendously smart and practical*" brand of legal advice. He has a "*strong background*" in a wide variety of real estate transactions, though he also exhibits a certain proclivity toward shopping center developments. A "*good hard-nosed negotiator*," he's "*the man you want working for you*," sources said. **Ed Miller** is commended for his excellent handling of real estate issues, particularly as they relate to healthcare. In that capacity, he also advises on land use procedures.

The Clients: The team is often retained by investment companies, developers, title insurance companies, manufacturers and financial institutions among others.

Hawley Troxell Ennis & Hawley LLP

The Firm: This firm's real estate team is so established in the local landscape that sources consider it an "*integral part of Boise*." It represents developers of office, retail and master-planned residential projects in a range of matters – from acquisitions to financing and sales. Attorneys are also able to advise authoritatively on land use and entitlement proceedings. "*Diversified enough to handle everything you need*," the firm's strong range of expertise ensures that the real estate practice is "*well versed in everything*."

The Lawyers: **Brian Ballard** is viewed as an "*outstanding*" real estate attorney who has "*good business sense*" and proves "*helpful beyond just responding to requests*," commentators said. A prominent figure in the community, he is "*well connected*" and is a great negotiator who can "*distill matters to their key issues*." Invariably trusted for his advice, he has recently been working on the prospective 2005 public infrastructure improvements legislation. **Donald Knickrehm** has carved out an excellent reputation for his title, development and land use work, while **Geoffrey Wardle** earned his spurs with regards to commercial and residential real estate transactions, particularly the land use and entitlement aspects. One client added: "*He's personable, concise and understands the nature of our business.*"

The Clients: Suncore Industries; Albertson's; WGI Heavy Minerals; JR Simplot; Boise Cascade and 5B Investments.

Band 2

Meuleman Miller LLP

The Firm: This firm has a strong reputation in the fields of construction, real estate and general business law. Its highly recommended real estate group concentrates on the acquisition, development and financing of considerable properties on behalf of a range of clients. Its "*excellent knowledge and expertise*" is also rendered on leasing and dispositions.

The Lawyers: A lawyer with a "*great technical understanding*," **Kimbal Gowland** is commended for his thorough yet practical style. He provides skilled advice on the acquisition, sale, leasing and exchange of properties. **Bob Miller** has garnered a "*wealth of experience*" over the years. A "*respected expert in his field*," he is particularly known for his acquisition and sales prowess. His practice also extends to financing, leasing and development-related work. **Richard Mollerup** has developed a respected real estate practice based on his previous experience in title insurance. He has participated in numerous sales, purchases, leases and tax-deferred exchanges among others.

The Clients: Retailers, developers, investors, landlords and title insurance companies feature in the firm's clientele.

Spink Butler, LLP

The Firm: Interviewees report that this niche firm provides "*excellent value for money*" through its cadre of experienced transactional and litigation attorneys. Its reputation is especially strong in land use, with JoAnn Butler – one of the luminaries in that field – at the helm. The practice group cuts a broad swathe in the real estate market, advising on acquisitions and dispositions, leasing, financing, development and litigation.

The Lawyers: JoAnn Butler "*drives the land use engine*" at this firm. Sources said that this is an area in which she has "*carved out an excellent reputation*" for herself, and deservedly so. **Mike Spink** has a broad real estate practice that comprises development and sales; though he particularly excels as an "*excellent real estate litigator*," observers said.

The Clients: In addition to developers, the firm also represents borrowers, lenders, investors, builders and landlords among others.

Stoel Rives LLP

The Firm: This regional firm is conversant in a wide range of real estate matters, and also encompasses specialties in land use and construction. Its "*fine attorneys*" in Boise can also draw on the abundant resources available in its other regional offices. As a full-service firm, it is also enhanced by its strong environmental, corporate and insurance defense capabilities.

The Lawyers: Chair of the Idaho District Council of the Urban Land Institute, **Quentin Knipe** is a respected figure in Boise's real estate circle. He has recently been assisting the Simplot family, which is recognized for agriculture, with various real estate transactions, including acquisitions and financings. **Dale Higer** is viewed as an "*exceptional*" attorney and "*the dean of real estate financing and foreclosure*." Over the past year, he has worked on a large condominium conversion and assisted lenders with real estate-secured financings.

The Clients: Idaho's Simplot family and Eddie Bauer are among the firm's prominent clientele.

Band 3

Moffatt Thomas Barrett Rock & Fields

The Firm: This team advises a client base that ranges from individuals to large developers and significant landowners. It boasts particular experience in the areas of acquisitions and sales, land use and entitlement. In the litigation sphere, the team has battled claims concerning construction defects, zoning and land use, title and escrow services, and a breach of contract.

The Lawyers: Robert Burns is a key player in the firm's real estate profile. He is a former president of the Los Angeles/Ventura division of the Baldwin Company, a homebuilder in California.

The Clients: The firm often advises regional residential and commercial developers, and corporate landowners.

Williams Bradbury, Attorneys at Law

The Firm: This relatively new two-partner outfit is known for its strong land use capabilities. It also provides robust advice to residential developers and established clients. Its expertise in real estate is also linked to the telecom and energy sectors.

The Lawyers: Sources recommend **Steve Bradbury** as an experienced and masterful land use attorney.

The Clients: The firm's roster includes public and private companies, and is dominated by businesses with a more regional flavor.

Leaders in Idaho

ANDERSEN, Steven
Holland & Hart LLP, Boise
280 342 5000
sandersen@hollandhart.com
Recommended in Litigation

Practice Areas: Partner practicing in tort and commercial litigation including products liability, professional negligence, and personal injury. Has tried cases involving insurance disputes, partnership dissolution claims by and against banks, patent and intellectual property claims, as well as automobile, medical malpractice and product defects. Has also tried cases involving governmental liability, aviation, agriculture, farming, and construction.

Prof. Memberships: American Bar Association (Litigation and Business Sections), Idaho State Bar (Continuing Legal Education Committee, Professional Conduct Board).

Career: Admitted to the Idaho Bar (1980), US Court of Appeals, Ninth Circuit (1985). Mr Andersen has been in private practice since 1982 and a Partner with Holland & Hart since 1987. He has lectured statewide on topics of trial preparation and advocacy and has published materials and articles on legal ethics, discovery techniques, and trials.

Publications: Author, 'How to Prepare For, Take and Use a Deposition' (James Publishing).

Personal: Received a JD (with honors) from Brigham Young University in 1981 and a BA (summa cum laude) from Brigham Young University in 1977.

BALLARD, Brian
Hawley Troxell Ennis & Hawley LLP, Boise 208 344 6000
Recommended in Real Estate

BANDUCCI, Thomas
Greener Banducci Shoemaker, Boise
208 319 2600
Recommended in Litigation

BEESON, Christopher
Givens Pursley LLP, Boise
208 388 1200
Recommended in Real Estate

BERENTER, Steven
Hawley Troxell Ennis & Hawley LLP, Boise 208 344 6000
Recommended in Employment

BITHELL, Walter
Holland & Hart LLP, Boise
208 342 5000
wbithell@hollandhart.com
Recommended in Litigation

Practice Areas: Partner with practice emphasis on individual and class action tort litigation, including business and commercial, personal injury, products liability, professional liability, commercial, insurance, securities, and general litigation.

Prof. Memberships: Fellow of the American College of Trial Lawyers, American Inns of Court No. 130 (Master of the Bench), American Trial Lawyers Association (Board of Governors), Idaho Trial Lawyers Association (past President), Idaho State Bar (past President), University of Idaho Foundation (Board of Directors), The American Society of Writers on Legal Subjects

(SCRIBES).

Career: Admitted to Idaho Bar (1968), Admitted to Idaho State and Federal District Courts (1968), US Court of Federal Claims (1991), US Court of Appeals, Ninth Circuit (1992), US Supreme Court (1995). Former Idaho Deputy Attorney General, General Counsel for the Idaho State Department of Insurance and General Counsel for the Idaho State Tax Commission.
Personal: Received JD from University of Idaho (1968) and a BS from the University of Idaho (1965).

BOARDMAN, Richard
Perkins Coie LLP, Boise
208 343 3434
Recommended in Litigation

BOYD, Paul
Stoel Rives LLP, Boise 208 389 9000
Recommended in Corporate/M&A

BRADBURY, Steve
Williams Bradbury, Attorneys at Law, Boise 208 344 6633
Recommended in Real Estate

BURKE, Carl
Elam & Burke PA, Boise
208 343 5454
Recommended in Litigation

BUTLER, JoAnn
Spink Butler, LLP, Boise
208 388 1000
Recommended in Real Estate

CHANDLER, Harry
Stoel Rives LLP, Boise
208 389 9000
Recommended in Employment

CLARK, Merlyn
Hawley Troxell Ennis & Hawley LLP, Boise 208 344 6000
Recommended in Litigation

DALE, Candy
Hall, Farley, Oberrecht & Blanton, PA, Boise 208 395 8500
Recommended in Employment

DALE, James
Moffatt Thomas Barrett Rock & Fields, Boise 208 345 2000
Recommended in Employment

DINGEL, Allyn
Elam & Burke PA, Boise
208 343 5454
Recommended in Litigation

DOCKSTADER, Kim
Stoel Rives LLP, Boise
208 389 9000
Recommended in Employment

DRAKE, Stephen
Stoel Rives LLP, Boise
208 389 9000
Recommended in Corporate/M&A

DRYDEN, William
Elam & Burke PA, Boise
208 343 5454
Recommended in Litigation

GOWLAND, Kimbal
Meuleman Miller LLP, Boise
208 342 6066
Recommended in Real Estate

GREENER, Richard
Greener Banducci Shoemaker, Boise
208 319 2600
Recommended in Litigation

HARDESTY, Stephen
Hawley Troxell Ennis & Hawley LLP, Boise 208 344 6000
Recommended in Corporate/M&A

HIGER, Dale
Stoel Rives LLP, Boise
208 389 9000
Recommended in Real Estate

KNICKREHM, Donald
Hawley Troxell Ennis & Hawley LLP, Boise 208 344 6000
Recommended in Real Estate

KNIPE, Quentin
Stoel Rives LLP, Boise
208 389 9000
Recommended in Real Estate

LARUE, James D
Elam & Burke PA, Boise
208 343 5454
Recommended in Litigation

MACK, J Frederick
Holland & Hart LLP, Boise
208 342 5000
fmack@hollandhart.com
Recommended in Corporate/M&A

Practice Areas: Mr Mack has extensive experience in all aspects of law relating to business transactions and regularly consults business clients on such matters. He represents some of Idaho's largest publicly - and privately - held companies and regularly advises clients in contract negotiations and on the formation and development of start-up companies (including corporations, partnerships, limited partnerships, limited liability partnerships, and limited liability companies), mergers, acquisitions, divestitures, share exchanges, raising capital, and protecting proprietary interests. Mr Mack also has 25 years of experience in complex wealth planning. Among other things, he has prepared both simple and complex wills, trusts and other wealth planning vehicles.
Prof. Memberships: Member of the American Bar Association; Idaho State Bar Association, Section on Business and Corporate Law; and the American Bar Association, Section of Business Law.
Career: Admitted to the Idaho Bar (1973).
Personal: Received a JD (1972) and a BA (1969) from the University of Idaho.

MEADOWS, Craig
Hawley Troxell Ennis & Hawley LLP, Boise 208 344 6000
Recommended in Litigation

MILLER, Edward
Givens Pursley LLP, Boise
208 388 1200
Recommended in Real Estate

MILLER, Nicholas
Hawley Troxell Ennis & Hawley LLP, Boise 208 344 6000
Recommended in Corporate/M&A

MILLER, Robert
Meuleman Miller LLP, Boise
208 342 6066
Recommended in Real Estate

MOLLERUP, Richard
Meuleman Miller LLP, Boise
208 342 6066
Recommended in Real Estate

MUNTHER, Merrily
Penland Munther Goodrum, Boise
208 344 4566
Recommended in Employment

ORMSETH, Kris
Stoel Rives LLP, Boise
208 389 9000
Recommended in Corporate/M&A

PRINCE, Larry E
Holland & Hart LLP, Boise
208 342 5000
lprince@hollandhart.com
Recommended in Corporate/M&A

Practice Areas: Mr Prince specializes in bankruptcy, commercial litigation, and commercial transactions. He has extensive experience in representing secured creditors and debtors in bankruptcy proceedings and in complex credit transactions. He has represented lenders and borrowers in secured and unsecured credit facilities, ESOP transactions, workout and restructuring of problem loans and leases, multi-bank participations and syndications. His work in real estate law includes real estate acquisition and development and construction and suretyship litigation. His commercial litigation practice includes creditors' rights, contract, construction, Uniform Commercial Code, and real estate litigation.
Prof. Memberships: Member of the Idaho State Bar Association, Sections on Commercial Law and Bankruptcy, and Business and Corporate Law; Local Rules Committee, United States Bankruptcy Court for the District of Idaho; American Bankruptcy Institute; and Washington State Bar Association. Appointments: Fellow in the American College of Bankruptcy; 'The Best Lawyers in America.'
Publications: Mr Prince has published articles and is a lecturer on topics of bankruptcy and commercial law. He

also served as a visiting professor at the University of Idaho School of Law.
Personal: Received a JD from the University of California, Hastings College of the Law (1975) and a BA (magna cum laude) from Boise State College (1972).

RILEY, Richard
Hawley Troxell Ennis & Hawley LLP, Boise 208 344 6000
Recommended in Corporate/M&A

SINCLAIR, Walter
Stoel Rives LLP, Boise
208 389 9000
Recommended in Litigation

SPINK, Michael
Spink Butler, LLP, Boise
208 388 1000
Recommended in Real Estate

SQUYRES, Newal
Holland & Hart LLP, Boise
208 342 5000
nsquyres@hollandhart.com
Recommended in Litigation

Practice Areas: Senior litigation Partner practicing in a wide variety of complex civil litigation, including False Claims Act, products liability, construction, insurance coverage and bad faith, employment, aviation, personal injury and commercial. Handled and tried cases before state courts in Idaho and Federal Courts in Idaho, Washington, California, and Pennsylvania.
Prof. Memberships: Member of the American Bar Association (litigation section), and Idaho State Bar (founding member of ADR section).
Career: Admitted to the Texas (1972) and Idaho (1974) Bars; the U. S. District Court, District of Idaho (1974); US Court of Appeals, Fifth (1972) and Ninth Circuits (1980); Law Clerk, US Court of Appeals, 5th Circuit (1972-74); personal staff of US. Attorney General Griffin Bell (1977-79); Faculty, University of Idaho Law School, Trial Advocacy Clinic. Mr Squyres is a frequent speaker on trial preparation and technique and is the Managing Partner of the Boise office of Holland & Hart LLP.
Personal: Received a JD (with honors) in 1972 and a BA in 1968 from Texas Tech University.

WARDLE, Geoffrey
Hawley Troxell Ennis & Hawley LLP, Boise 208 344 6000
Recommended in Real Estate

WHITE, Robert
Givens Pursley LLP, Boise
208 388 1200
Recommended in Employment

CONTENTS: Antitrust p.661; Banking & Finance p.664; Bankruptcy p.668; Construction p.672; Corporate/M&A & Private Equity p.674; Employment p.679; Energy & Natural Resources p.685; Environment p.686; Healthcare p.690; Insurance p.692; Intellectual Property p.695; Litigation p.699; Media & Entertainment p.702; Real Estate p.705; Tax p.709; Technology & IT Outsourcing p.712; Telecom p.714; Individuals' Profiles p.716. Firm Profiles p.760

How lawyers are ranked

The opinions we gather from clients — mainly from in-house lawyers but also from other purchasers of legal services — are balanced by opinions from colleagues and competitors. Together, they provide two different perspectives — an all-round view — and biased viewpoints cancel each other out.

ANTITRUST

Illinois
Leading firms (Antitrust)

1 KIRKLAND & ELLIS LLP *Chicago*
  MAYER, BROWN, ROWE & MAW LLP *Chicago*
  SIDLEY AUSTIN BROWN & WOOD LLP *Chicago*

2 EIMER STAHL KLEVORN & SOLBERG *Chicago*
  FREEMAN, FREEMAN & SALZMAN *Chicago*
  WINSTON & STRAWN LLP *Chicago*

3 BELL, BOYD & LLOYD LLC *Chicago*
  HOWREY SIMON ARNOLD & WHITE *Chicago*
  KATTEN MUCHIN ZAVIS ROSENMAN *Chicago*
  MCDERMOTT WILL & EMERY *Chicago*
  MUCH SHELIST FREED DENENBERG *Chicago*
  SONNENSCHEIN NATH & ROSENTHAL LLP *Chicago*

4 FREEBORN & PETERS *Chicago*
  GARDNER CARTON & DOUGLAS LLP *Chicago*
  JENNER & BLOCK LLP *Chicago*
  SCHOPF & WEISS *Chicago*
  SPERLING & SLATER *Chicago*
  THE WEXLER FIRM *Chicago*

Firms are listed alphabetically in each band.

Band 1

Kirkland & Ellis LLP
See firm details p.770

The Firm: Active in antitrust work since the 1960s, this giant has a pedigree to be proud of. Its *"very effective"* senior partners and batch of younger attorneys combine to create a broad band of specialists who drive the firm's current high profile in this area. Adopting a *"strong litigation mentality"* and with *"tremendous trial experience,"* the firm has a recognized strength in high-stakes international price-fixing litigation and, in keeping with prevailing trends, attorneys are increasingly undertaking criminal defense work. On the advisory and transactional side, the firm's private equity caseload generates business in a steady flow of merger-related work.

The Lawyers: Clients rated the *"very competent and personable"* **James Mutchnik** (see p.743), formerly with the Department of Justice

antitrust criminal prosecution team. This *"good listener, who is open to suggestions,"* now spends a significant amount of time working on criminal antitrust defense, class action defense and merger clearance advice for big corporation. He represented Concord EFS in its $7 billion merger with First Data and served as lead defense counsel for Infineon Technologies in a grand jury investigation of alleged price fixing in the DRAM industry. The *"talented, smart and cordial"* **Andrew Langan** (see p.736) is admired as an efficient generalist practitioner, whose caseload includes merger investigations, high-profile drug prescription litigation, as well as products liability and water rights. He has been acting for BP in a case involving claims concerning the trading of Alaska North Slope crude oil and its alleged effects on California gas prices. The team was significantly boosted by the return of **Robert Robertson** (see p.747), who had been working as senior litigation counsel for the Bureau of Competition at the FTC. With substantial experience in competition matters involving the cruise line, pharmaceutical, and software industries, he has also acted as lead trial counsel in the matter of Chicago Bridge & Iron, the first post-closing merger challenge tried at the FTC in over a decade. With almost 40 years at the firm, the well-respected **Frank Cicero** (see p.722) is considered the elder statesman of the practice. Antitrust litigation is just one string to his bow.

The Clients: Infineon Technologies; Concord EFS; Health Care Service Corporation; Dow AgroSciences; BP; General Motors; Kraft; 3M and Polaris Industries.

Mayer, Brown, Rowe & Maw LLP
See firm details p.771

The Firm: The Chicago office of this international powerhouse has 13 lawyers with antitrust expertise; all are able to tap into a wider pool of resources and many have considerable experience of working with the relevant authorities. The firm's European presence has a noticeable

advantage in a market where antitrust issues commonly demand a global perspective. This reassuringly *"self-confident, creative and competent"* group handles all aspects of antitrust litigation, offers counseling services and is renowned for its abilities in obtaining merger approval from regulators. It has earned praise for its good judgment on pricing and distribution issues, sophisticated pre-trial analysis and a highly impressive trial and appellate capability.

The Lawyers: *"Incredibly smart and a terrific negotiator"* is the client's verdict on **Lee Abrams** (see p.716). They say he is *"a true gent and a skilled adviser,"* noting his experience in a wide variety of antitrust and trade regulation issues as well as franchise relationships. This well-established practitioner remains the lead trial lawyer for Ford in the ChoiceParts antitrust litigation, and he has also acted in the arbitration between Dairy Queen Operators Association and International Dairy Queen relating to a significant breach of agreement claim. International cartel defense and high-stakes commercial litigation make up the bulk of the practice of the *"articulate and persuasive"* **Andrew Marovitz** (see p.739). Managing to split his time between Chicago and DC, Marovitz excels in price-fixing, monopolies, market allocation and conspiracy cases. He has been involved in the vitamin antitrust litigation, acted for BASF Corporation and BASF AG in a massive price-fixing case, and represented DSM Copolymer and DSM Elastomers Europe in a price-fixing conspiracy claim in the synthetic rubber market. Like others of his esteemed colleagues, **Mark McLaughlin**'s (see p.741) practice includes litigation-avoidance advice on distribution issues. Interviewees say he is someone who *"drives the work"* and agree that he is *"good in the courtroom."* The *"smart and savvy"* **Robert Finke** (see p.727) offers M&A counseling as well as representation in antitrust class action litigation. *"Unafraid to call it how he sees it,"* he has been spending much of his time lately on allegations of a price-fixing cartel in the linen industry and

Illinois
Leading individuals (Antitrust)

1
- **ABRAMS** Lee *Mayer Brown*, Chicago
- **EIMER** Nathan *Eimer Stahl*, Chicago
- **FREEMAN Jr** Lee *Freeman Freeman*, Chicago

2
- **BUSEY** Roxane *Gardner Carton*, Chicago
- **CHEFITZ** Joel *Howrey Simon*, Chicago
- **DOUGLAS** Charles *Sidley Austin*, Chicago
- **FREED** Michael *Much Shelist*, Chicago
- **LANGAN** Andrew *Kirkland & Ellis*, Chicago
- **MAROVITZ** Andrew *Mayer Brown*, Chicago
- **MARX** David *McDermott Will*, Chicago
- **MCCAREINS** Mark *Winston & Strawn*, Chicago
- **MCLAUGHLIN** Mark *Mayer Brown*, Chicago
- **MUTCHNIK** James *Kirkland & Ellis*, Chicago
- **ROBERTSON** Robert *Kirkland & Ellis*, Chicago
- **RYAN** Thomas *Sidley Austin*, Chicago
- **SILBERMAN** Alan *Sonnenschein Nath*, Chicago
- **TREECE** John *Sidley Austin*, Chicago

3
- **BIERIG** Jack *Sidley Austin*, Chicago
- **CAMPBELL** Thomas *Gardner Carton*, Chicago
- **CICERO** Frank *Kirkland & Ellis*, Chicago
- **FINKE** Robert *Mayer Brown*, Chicago
- **HACK** Randall *Lord Bissell & Brook*, Chicago
- **JOSEPH** Robert *Sonnenschein Nath*, Chicago
- **KLEVORN** Andrew *Eimer Stahl*, Chicago
- **PASTROFF** Sanford *Sonnenschein Nath*, Chicago
- **SCHOPF** Willam *Schopf & Weiss*, Chicago
- **SENNETT** Michael *Bell Boyd*, Chicago
- **SLATER** Paul *Sperling & Slater*, Chicago
- **WEXLER** Kenneth *The Wexler Firm*, Chicago
- **ZELEK** Eugene *Freeborn & Peters*, Chicago

Individuals are listed alphabetically in each band.

planned US acquisitions and joint ventures for an international steel company.

The Clients: Ford; United States Golf Association; CompUSA; Angus Chemical; News Corporation and Ryerson Tull.

Sidley Austin Brown & Wood LLP
See firm details p.778

The Firm: As well as notable expertise in counseling, Sidley Austin has a much-admired antitrust litigation practice, especially in the areas of price fixing, M&A disputes and monopolization. Interviewees considered the team to be *"practical and efficiently staffed"* and a hot property for gaining merger approval. It recently aided the merger between IMC Global and the Crop Nutrition division of Cargill. Approved by the DOJ, the merged company, one of the world's leading producers of concentrated phosphate and potash crop nutrients, now trades as the Mosaic Company. In the past year, the team also tried a case for Iowa Beef Processors in Alabama.

The Lawyers: Co-chairing the practice development committee is the excellent **Thomas Ryan** (see p.749), who is possessed of *"great judgment and trustworthiness."* A familiar name in the insurance sector, his stable of clients includes BP and he also acted for Amoco in Henson v Amoco

Oil Company, a multimillion-dollar antitrust and breach of contract case involving the pricing of retail gasoline. The *"intellectually and analytically strong"* **John Treece** (see p.756) drew compliments for being a *"great brief writer"* and *"a tremendous, dedicated workhorse."* His practice includes antitrust and intellectual property litigation, a twinning which has brought him success in antitrust disputes affecting the pharmaceuticals industry. He is well known for his representation of GD Searle & Co, acquired by Pfizer, in the long-running Brand Name Prescription Drugs Antitrust Litigation. The firm's managing partner, **Chuck Douglas** (see p.724), earned widespread plaudits. His diverse experience covers antitrust, securities and other commercial litigation. Among his recent cases is a major antitrust class action alleging price-fixing, brought by US retail pharmacists against all of the country's pharmaceutical manufacturers. The *"long-standing and very smart"* **Jack Bierig** (see p.719) enters the tables as an *"excellent regulatory lawyer,"* whose practice also includes antitrust and association law. He advises many associations and healthcare providers in government antitrust and health fraud investigations.

The Clients: AT&T; GlaxoSmithKline; Pfizer (previously Searle & Co); Brunswick Corporation; Aon; Johnson & Johnson; BP; IMC Global and Brother International.

Band 2

Eimer Stahl Klevorn & Solberg
See firm details p.766

The Firm: Eimer Stahl is a four-year-old, *"nice and medium-sized"* boutique firm that came into being as a spin-off from Sidley Austin. The *"effectiveness and flexibility"* of the 13-lawyer antitrust team has found the spotlight, with attorneys collecting praise from many quarters for its merger counseling, antitrust litigation and regulatory advice. The team undoubtedly received a boost from the addition of massive global drug wholesaler AmerisourceBergen to its already healthy client roster.

The Lawyers: Having been *"around the legal block,"* the first-rate **Nate Eimer** drives the firm's broad antitrust practice. On the one hand, *"a boardroom lawyer,"* on the other, *"particularly strong on his feet in court,"* he acts for plaintiffs and defendants and boasts *"an easy manner with colleagues, clients and judges."* His *"trustworthiness and no-nonsense approach"* is clearly valued. With grand jury and price-fixing experience under his belt, he was a natural choice for Union Carbide in a global pricing-fixing case alleging resale price maintenance, known as MM Global. Eimer counsels the same client in lawsuits against several marine shipping companies alleging participation in a worldwide price-fixing cartel, and successfully resolved an alleged national price-fixing case brought against Land O' Lakes. The *"terrific"*

Andrew Klevorn has a commercial litigation practice, which includes a focus on antitrust matters. Leaning more towards merger advice than Eimer, he has been acting for RR Donnelley in its successful defense of a government suit seeking to enjoin the company from acquiring its leading competitor.

The Clients: Dow Chemical; CITGO Petroleum; Land O' Lakes; Corn Products International; AmerisourceBergen and Union Carbide.

Freeman, Freeman & Salzman

The Firm: Clients describe attorneys at this *"very fine litigation boutique"* as *"expert and at the top of their game."* Historically, class action and antitrust plaintiff work has been identified as the firm's bread and butter; however, more recently there has been greater focus on the representation of defendants. To illustrate, Clear Channel Communications turned to the firm for a lawsuit alleging a monopoly in the market for supercross motorcycle racing.

The Lawyers: Considered by some to be following in his father's very large footsteps, the *"honorable and engaging"* **Lee Freeman** attracted much client praise for antitrust and general complex litigation and appellate work. Blessed with a disarming *"laid-back Columbo style,"* Freeman *"invariably gets the job done efficiently and quickly."* He has been acting for major manufacturers, as plaintiffs, in the bulk vitamins, sorbates and carbon dioxide antitrust cases. He has also recently acted, with great success, in high-value employment-related litigation.

The Clients: Central Vermont Power Supply Company; Chicago Mercantile Exchange; Clear Channel; Kraft; Boeing; BP/Amoco; Dean Foods and McKee Foods.

Winston & Strawn LLP
See firm details p.780

The Firm: Clients appreciate the strength of Winston & Strawn's antitrust offering; its attorneys have *"a quick ability to master substantive areas."* Though the firm's profile in this area has long been associated closely with Dan Webb, there is a well-respected team devoted to both civil and criminal cases. Webb is now acknowledged as a 'star lawyer' in the general commercial litigation section. Dealership termination, monopoly and price-fixing cases have all featured recently in the practice's work.

The Lawyers: *"Creative, hard-working and innovative in approach"* were the words used by one client of their chosen attorney, **Mark McCareins** (see p.740). Practicing in both antitrust and intellectual property law, he has acted in key price-fixing antitrust suits. He represented Smurfit-Stone Container in charges filed by a class of purchasers of linerboard, and has also been involved in the sulfuric acid litigation, defending Marsulex in a multidefendant class action against allegations of a price-fixing conspiracy.

The Clients: Abbott Laboratories; Central Glass Co; Smurfit-Stone Container; Sellars Absorbent Materials; Marsulex; The Metals Service Center Institute; The Marmon Group and Summation Legal Technologies.

Band 3

Bell, Boyd & Lloyd LLC

The Firm: This mid-sized firm earned praise for its Chicago antitrust base. There are ten partners in this 22-strong team, which climbs the ranking tables on the back of widespread respect for its general counseling, litigation and complex M&A transactional work. The firm has been active on global distribution and cross-border joint venture issues and impresses with its criminal antitrust practice.

The Lawyers: Good judgment and efficiency were among the reasons cited by observers for choosing *"well-rounded and well-known"* **Michael Sennett**, who chairs the firm's antitrust and trade regulation group. *"He has been and continues to be the firm's leading light,"* indicated one peer. The chair of the white-collar criminal defense group, Steven Kowal, drew plaudits for his defense of civil enforcement proceedings relating to antitrust, the FDA and the FTC.

The Clients: Cardinal Health; Fortune Brands; Great Lakes Chemical; North American Stainless; Deere & Company and California Dental Association.

Howrey Simon Arnold & White

The Firm: Awash with experienced trial lawyers, Howrey Simon is more than capable in the antitrust arena. Alongside its litigation personnel there is an expansive antitrust practice of over 200 lawyers worldwide. Backed by such resources, much of them in DC, the smaller but nonetheless *"highly competent"* Chicago practice offers the full range of merger defense, government civil and criminal investigations, private antitrust litigation and counseling.

The Lawyers: *"Bringing superb advocacy skills to the table"* is the Chicago managing partner, **Joel Chefitz**, who defends all manner of business and antitrust litigation, including high-profile class action cases. *"With a bold and smart style before the FTC and SEC,"* this *"trustworthy market leader"* has been defending multiple securities class actions and fiduciary duty litigation brought against former directors and officers of marchFIRST and Divine. He is also acting for American Medical Security in ongoing antitrust counseling and business litigation.

The Clients: marchFIRST; Zebra Technologies; Chicago Board Options Exchange; American Medical Security; Caterpillar; Rockwell Automation; Chicago Bulls; Divine; Fortune Brands; Koch Industries; Verizon Wireless and Waste Management

Katten Muchin Zavis Rosenman

See firm details p.769

The Firm: Both peers and clients acknowledged the firm's focus and strong track record in healthcare antitrust. Its performance has been highlighted by the successful defense of Vista Health in an intensive investigation by the FTC into the joint venture between Provena Health and Victory Health Services in 2000. The firm has suffered some departures to Howrey Simon, notably Joel Chefitz, but continues to impress, especially in mid-market matters.

The Lawyers: Laura Martin, who is acknowledged as a key player in the team, was recently appointed the chairperson of the Chicago Bar Association antitrust law committee.

The Clients: Technology and new media start-up companies, multinational corporations and healthcare companies feature on the client roster.

McDermott Will & Emery

See firm details p.773

The Firm: Staffing larger matters jointly with other offices, this smaller team of half a dozen antitrust attorneys earned special regional and national commendations in healthcare-related antitrust work. It acted, for example, for West Tennessee Healthcare in dismissing complaints of federal and state antitrust violations.

The Lawyers: Leading the Chicago practice is the *"highly practical, thoughtful and responsive"* **David Marx** (see p.739), whose *"understanding of how the other side thinks"* stems from his experience as a former senior trial attorney with the antitrust division of the DOJ and the FTC. While considered *"one of the best"* for healthcare antitrust, he also acts for other types of client, such as Stora Enso North America and Stora Enso Oyj with regard to an investigation based on allegations of price-fixing by manufacturers and marketers of magazine paper.

The Clients: West Tennessee Healthcare; Stora Enso North America; Mountain View Hospital; Albertsons and Provena Health.

Much Shelist Freed Denenberg Ament & Rubenstein, P.C.

The Firm: *"One of the strongest reputations"* in class action contingency and plaintiff work consolidates this firm's position in the rankings. Having been involved in price fixing class actions involving brand name prescription drugs, the vitamin industry, infant formula and carbon dioxide manufacturing, the group has recently tried the long-standing fructose antitrust litigation.

The Lawyers: Class action and complex antitrust cases are a key part of the practice of *"straight shooter"* **Michael Freed**, who leads the team. Deemed *"very successful in the narrower plaintiff class action field,"* he has been acting for Pharmacy Freedom Fund in a number of antitrust class actions brought by retail pharmacies against manufacturers and wholesalers of prescription drugs and benefit managers. He has also acted for key physicians in a class action antitrust case brought against teaching hospitals and medical associations by medical residents.

The Clients: Pharmacy Freedom Fund; Belvue Drugs; Euromarket Designs; Glabman-Paramount Furniture; Vita Foods; Barry's Drugs and Endler's Pharmacy.

Sonnenschein Nath & Rosenthal LLP

See firm details p.779

The Firm: This is a firm interviewees admired for its *"seamless organization of resources,"* and the razor sharpness of senior practitioners and their commitment to grooming the next generation. Interviewees also praised the group's long-held reputation in antitrust counseling and litigation, both on the defense and plaintiff sides. The firm acted for Sun Microsystems in the long-running private antitrust and monopoly suit against Microsoft, which led to one of the biggest private party settlements. Among other requirements, it called for cash payments to Sun totaling nearly $2 billion.

The Lawyers: A team headed by veteran group chair **Alan Silberman** (see p.752) features the *"skilled, thoughtful and user-friendly"* **Bob Joseph** (see p.734), whose broad practice has a strong distribution focus and a growing emphasis on developing compliance programs for clients. **Robert Joseph** (see p.734) was commended for his fluency in franchising and distribution on behalf of household names such as McDonald's. He's also an authority on price-fixing disputes. The *"practical"* **Sanford Pastroff** (see p.745) is considered by clients to be *"a very valued partner in antitrust counseling,"* particularly on the review of business models and proposals. Litigation, and jury and corporate investigations also contribute to his diverse practice.

The Clients: McDonald's; Sara Lee; Prudential Real Estate; Allstate; Chicago Tribune; Sun Microsystems; Aventis Pasteur; ChoiceParts and Boeing.

Band 4

Freeborn & Peters

The Firm: According to observers, the antitrust and trade regulation practice, one of the firm's largest, merits its place in the rankings on the back of solid expertise in counseling and litigation. The firm recently advised on the complete restructuring of the pricing system used by an international manufacturer, and the drafting and implementation of a new distributor agreement. It has been active in antitrust litigation, often plaintiff work, serving as counsel to the plaintiff in Information Resources v Dun & Bradstreet, a monopolization and attempted monopolization case filed in New York concerning the marketing data industry.

The Lawyers: Clients value the *"wonderfully practical and businesslike mind"* of group chair **Eugene Zelek**, the firm's leading antitrust attorney. In addition to counseling on pricing and distribution issues, he teaches pricing and marketing channels at the Kellogg School of Management, though sources made it clear he is *"considered way more than a scholar."*

The Clients: Noranda; McKinsey & Company; Holley Performance Products; Burlington Northern and Santa Fe Railway Company.

Gardner Carton & Douglas LLP

See firm details p.767

The Firm: One commentator described this *"good old-fashioned practice"* of eight partners and a similar number of associates as *"the first port of call"* for antitrust healthcare expertise. The team represented Oxford Health Plans, a massive New York health insurance plan, in the review by state and federal antitrust enforcement authorities of its acquisition by United-Health Group. Yet it is prevalent not only in the increasingly robust healthcare sector; observers additionally spoke of attorneys' talents in general corporate matters and intellectual property.

The Lawyers: Mostly recognized for her counseling and agency work, **Roxane Busey** (see p.721) is *"an excellent lawyer, who really knows her stuff."* Often the first name to trip off the tongue for healthcare counseling, her practice is broader than this niche. In April 2004, Busey was elected to serve as the chair of the ABA antitrust section's taskforce on modernization commission. Thirty years' experience in antitrust and business disputes drive **Thomas Campbell** (see p.721) into the rankings. Chairing the firm's antitrust and competition group, he is known for trying many of the firm's antitrust cases, among them prominent cases affecting the healthcare industry.

The Clients: Dyson; BC Partners; Enbridge Energy Company; HA International; Hewitt Associates; Hobbico; Illinois Tool Works; INX International; Merchandise Mart Properties; The National Resident Matching Program and Northwestern Memorial Hospital.

Jenner & Block LLP

See firm details p.768

The Firm: Entering the tables this year, this respected old-line firm boasts a clutch of antitrust lawyers who cut their teeth on the opening up of the telecom market. The group represented MCI in the high-profile MCI v AT&T antitrust litigation. As well as heavy-duty civil and criminal litigation, antitrust counseling features large in the workload of the firm, which acts for many European and Japanese clients.

The Lawyers: Norman Hirsch replaced Barbara Steiner as cochair of the antitrust group in January 2005. Donald Harris is the other cochair.

The Clients: American Maize Products Company; Mitsubishi Paper Mills; Nippon Denkyoku; Chicago Board of Trade and GE.

Schopf & Weiss

The Firm: Handling a steady diet of antitrust cases since its formation in 1987, this *"small, specialized litigation boutique"* fields four attorneys in antitrust litigation and has defended clients in price-fixing, market allocation, monopolization and price discrimination cases. The firm attained a favorable summary judgment in the Beef Industry Antitrust Litigation for Tyson Fresh Meats (formerly IBP).

The Lawyers: The firm's founding partner, the *"knowledgeable and efficient"* **William Schopf** (see p.750), has defended an industrial gas manufacturer in large-scale, multidistrict litigation involving the liquid carbon dioxide industry. In a Federal Court in Iowa, he recently obtained a $32 million jury verdict and judgment for Goss International against Japanese company TKS

under the federal Antidumping Act of 1916.

The Clients: Goss International, Crawford Supply and Exide feature in the firm's clientele.

Sperling & Slater

The Firm: With less than 20 lawyers, this almost 30-year-old Chicago outfit offers clients antitrust services under the umbrella of its complex litigation and appellate practice.

The Lawyers: It was the firm's *"energetic and committed"* joint founder, **Paul Slater**, who scooped plaudits from interviewees. This *"smart, good thinker"* is viewed as a *"safe referral"* and boasts a broad complex litigation practice, which includes a large slice of antitrust work.

The Clients: Acting for both defendants and plaintiffs, the firm's clients include public corporations, medium-sized businesses and sole proprietors.

The Wexler Firm

The Firm: This compact four-year-old firm manages antitrust matters from its Chicago office, alongside prescription pricing abuses, civil rights violations, consumer fraud, professional malpractice and shareholder rights.

The Lawyers: Firm founder **Ken Wexler** drew admiring comments as *"a top plaintiff lawyer"* with *"good substantive knowledge"* applied to significant plaintiff antitrust class actions. He is praised for being *"easy to deal with and straightforward."*

The Clients: The firm acts for a range of consumers, employees, special interest groups and shareholders in various civil disputes.

Other Notable Practitioners

Randy Hack of Lord Bissell & Brook earned compliments for his experience in the prosecution and defense of antitrust cases as well as class action defense.

BANKING & FINANCE

Mayer, Brown, Rowe & Maw LLP

See firm details p.771

The Firm: A *"significant diversification in its practice,"* *"strong client relationships"* (such as that with Bank of America) and a *"well-organized team model"* are among the reasons cited for this international giant's lead in the table. There are others: its *"great sense of the market,"* its involvement in *"megadeals"* and its expertise in project finance and emerging markets, especially Latin America. Last year, for example, the team represented Homex, a Mexican builder of affordable homes, on its IPO, which was the first

Mexican IPO on the NYSE in five years. The firm's size and culture has enabled it to adapt well to changes in the Chicago-based banking market and the increasing specialization in the securitization markets. Secured and unsecured lending remains a core strength.

The Lawyers: **Bob Baptista** (see p.718) earned recognition for his general finance practice, which includes the creation of secured and unsecured commercial loans as well as syndicated transactions for corporation and large banks. He is described as *"a knowledgeable and solution-oriented gent"* and *"an extremely practical deal maker."* Baptista recently represented Bank of America in a $300 million credit facility for the

recapitalization of National Bedding Company. **Doug Doetsch**'s (see p.724) intelligence and his experience of emerging market financings make him *"a force to be reckoned with."* Not only did he work on the flotation of Homex and the debt restructuring of Corporacion Durango, Mexico's largest pulp and paper company, but he proved instrumental in advising the steering committee of creditors on the restructuring of $1.4 billion of debt for Banco de Galicia, Argentina's largest private bank. An *"excellent understanding of where businessmen are coming from"* and *"a problem-solving attitude"* give **Paul Forrester** (see p.727) a *"critical perspective,"* instilling in clients *"a high degree of confidence"*

Illinois
Leading firms (Banking & Finance)

[1] MAYER, BROWN, ROWE & MAW LLP *Chicago*
SIDLEY AUSTIN BROWN & WOOD LLP *Chicago*

[2] LATHAM & WATKINS LLP *Chicago*
WINSTON & STRAWN LLP *Chicago*

[3] CHAPMAN AND CUTLER LLP *Chicago*
GOLDBERG, KOHN, BELL, BLACK, *Chicago*
KATTEN MUCHIN ZAVIS ROSENMAN *Chicago*
KIRKLAND & ELLIS LLP *Chicago*
MCDERMOTT WILL & EMERY *Chicago*
SKADDEN, ARPS, SLATE, MEAGHER *Chicago*

[4] BAKER & MCKENZIE *Chicago*
DUANE MORRIS LLP *Chicago*
NEAL, GERBER & EISENBERG LLP *Chicago*
SCHIFF HARDIN LLP *Chicago*
SCHWARTZ, COOPER, GREENBERGER *Chicago*
VEDDER, PRICE, KAUFMAN & KAMMHOLZ *Chicago*

Leading individuals (Banking & Finance)

[1] BAPTISTA Robert *Mayer Brown*, Chicago
BERNSTEIN Bruce *Sidley Austin*, Chicago
CLARK James *Sidley Austin*, Chicago
CRUMBAUGH David *Latham & Watkins*, Chicago
MURRAY Gregory *Winston & Strawn*, Chicago

[2] DOETSCH Douglas *Mayer Brown*, Chicago
DORAN James *Latham & Watkins*, Chicago
FORRESTER J Paul *Mayer Brown*, Chicago
GOLD Michael *Sidley Austin*, Chicago
KOHN Richard *Goldberg Kohn*, Chicago
MASON David *Goldberg Kohn*, Chicago
MCMENAMIN J Robert *McDermott Will*, Chicago
ROKOSZ Ronald *Chapman and Cutler LLP*, Chicago
SCHWARTZ Donald *Latham & Watkins*, Chicago
SHULRUFF Stuart *Katten Muchin*, Chicago
WILLIAMS Douglas *Sidley Austin*, Chicago

[3] BARROW Peter *Neal Gerber*, Chicago
BOEHRER Charles *Winston & Strawn*, Chicago
DRANOFF David *Goldberg Kohn*, Chicago
FRANSON Marc *Chapman and Cutler*, Chicago
GERBER Dean *Vedder Price*, Chicago
JACOBSON Ronald *Winston & Strawn*, Chicago
KAUFMAN Andrew *Kirkland & Ellis*, Chicago
LATIMER Kenneth *Duane Morris*, Chicago
LOOMAN James *Sidley Austin*, Chicago
MCENROE John *Vedder Price*, Chicago
MELAND Creighton *Baker & McKenzie*, Chicago
PERZEK Philip *Latham & Watkins*, Chicago
PICKENS Scott *Schiff Hardin*, Chicago
RADEMAKER Randall *Skadden Arps*, Chicago

Up-and-coming individuals
JACOBSON Michael *Katten Muchin*, Chicago

Firms and individuals are listed alphabetically in each band.

in him. In a practice focusing on structured and project finance, Forrester boasts expertise in the financing of power plants and pipelines. In the Alaska North Slope pipeline project, he and the team represent one of the major participants in the proposed 3000-mile pipeline from the Alaskan North Slope to the lower 48 states at an estimated cost of around $20 billion. He also recently worked on a baseball transaction, representing Bank of America's sports finance advisory and private placement teams in connection with a $300 million project finance and securitization hybrid financing for a new ballpark for the St. Louis Cardinals.

The Clients: Bank of America; Citigroup; CSFB; Wachovia; Homex; Bank of Montréal; Merrill Lynch; ABN AMRO; Textron Financial; Winmark Equipment Finance; Cohen Bros & Company and Gulf Stream Asset Management.

Sidley Austin Brown & Wood LLP
See firm details p.778

The Firm: Peers indicated they had nothing but respect and admiration for this *"exceptional outfit,"* calling it *"a tough competitor"* with *"excellent bench strength"* and *"a strong background."* A significant team of *"nonconfrontational, business and solution-oriented lawyers"* excels in a range of complex transactions, especially syndicated loans. It carries out complex multiparty syndicated financings, including secured, unsecured and asset-based loans for a variety of banks and financial institutions such as JPMorgan Chase, Citibank, ABN AMRO and Bank of America. The Chicago team undoubtedly benefits from close association with the New York office, and has developed a name because of the *"reach and preeminence"* of its securitization practice.

The Lawyers: Enjoying both management responsibilities and a hands-on transactional role, **Bruce Bernstein** (see p.718) earned commendations for his broad-ranging work. He is active in secured transactions, restructurings for banks and asset-based lenders, capital loans, complex securities transactions and lender liability advice. According to peers and clients, the *"practical and pragmatic"* **James Clark** (see p.722) brings *"a good attitude and a nice, Midwestern demeanor"* to the table and *"never misses a point."* He acts in significant transactions for JPMorgan Chase. In one, the client was agent on a $540 million multicurrency letter of credit agreement for Coca-Cola Enterprises; in another it had the same role on a $1.1 billion credit agreement for a multicurrency revolving credit facility for Harley-Davidson Funding. The borrowers' English and Canadian subsidiaries were also involved in each case. **Douglas Williams** (see p.758) has extensive lending and revolving credit facility expertise. He acted for Bank One and Banc One Capital Markets in connection with a $250 million revolving credit facility for Actuant. He also represented JPMorgan Chase and JPMorgan Securities in a $500 million revolving credit facility for Yellow Roadway. Another *"quality syndicated lending lawyer"* is **Michael Gold** (see p.730), who is especially strong in asset-based deals and also handles commercial finance and debt restructurings for banks and other lenders. He worked for Bank of America and Banc of America Securities in connection with a $300 million and Euro-denominated revolving credit facility for Watts Water Technologies. Gold also represented GE Capital in a $205 million bankruptcy emergence revolving and term credit facility for Choice One Communications. Bringing *"significant market and deal experience"* is **James Looman** (see p.737), whose mostly lending practice involves the creation of large syndicated and secured credit facilities on behalf of banks and lenders. He acted for Citibank, as administrative agent, and Citigroup Global Markets as lead arranger, on a $2.5 billion multicurrency revolving credit facility. Looman also represents corporate borrowers, acting for Dean Foods as borrower on a $3 billion credit facility, agented by Wachovia Bank, National Association and co-arranged by Wachovia Capital Markets and JPMorgan Securities.

The Clients: JPMorgan Chase; Bank of America; Citibank; Wachovia; GE Capital; Caterpillar; Dean Foods Company; Merrill Lynch and Barclays Bank.

Band 2

Latham & Watkins LLP

The Firm: Having bulked up its finance and bankruptcy practice to around 30 attorneys, the *"very competent"* Chicago office of this international firm is clearly much admired in the marketplace. One of the firm's drawing cards is its *"excellent international capability,"* especially in the UK, France and Germany; however, domestically, what comes through strongest is the lawyers' expertise in complex structures and debtor and possession financing. Interviewees also noted the *"high visibility"* gained through the firm's representation of a range of lenders, including second-term and mezzanine lenders in highly leveraged secured loan transactions. The firm additionally earned praise for its strong bankruptcy and restructuring practice.

The Lawyers: **David Crumbaugh** cochairs the firm's banking practice group and the Chicago office's finance department. This *"top-class and very knowledgeable"* attorney – a former Winston & Strawn star – performs *"very effectively"* for a *"wonderful clientele."* He is admired for his midmarket, asset-based transactions and has recognized expertise in commercial finance, cross-border transactions, insolvency and troubled companies. Crumbaugh acted for GE Capital as agent for syndicated loans to Playtex Products. Many interviewees noted that *"the gray hair of the group"* **Don Schwartz** enjoys a broad banking practice, which includes municipal finance, lease financing, and structured, project and corporate finance. He is described a *"extraordinarily capable"* in complex foreign transactions. Schwartz has acted in a number of deals with UBS, including a $260 million secured revolving credit facility for General

Cable and a $140 million revolving credit facility for Massey Energy. Another former Winston & Strawn lawyer, **James Doran** impresses with his *"pragmatic approach."* He has been building on the firm's relationship with Merrill Lynch Capital, for whom he acted on a $90 million aggregate senior secured second lien term loan and senior subordinated credit facilities to a manufacturing company. Entering the rankings this year is **Philip Perzek**, considered *"terrific in midmarket, asset-based lending transactions."* His practice includes the representation of lenders in mezzanine and second lien lending transactions and secured and unsecured revolving and term loan facilities.

The Clients: Antares Corporation; Merrill Lynch Capital; GE Capital; ABN AMRO; LaSalle Bank; Foothill Capital; Wells Fargo Bank; Royal Bank of Canada; Crédit Lyonnais and Deutsche Bank.

Winston & Strawn LLP

See firm details p.780

The Firm: Underpinned by a traditionally strong lender reputation, this firm has a presence in midmarket deals in Chicago. The team here was described by one commentator as *"a raft of competent, tough and determined attorneys,"* who have adopted *"a broad-based and solution-oriented approach."* Clients (many acting as agents and lead lenders on all levels of finance transaction) said the team possesses *"a good understanding of what will make a deal work."* Interviewees also referred to attorneys' work on the acquisition of debt portfolios and bankruptcy.

The Lawyers: The *"extremely knowledgeable, committed and diligent"* **Greg Murray** (see p.743) represents banks and financial institutions such as Bank of America, Commerzbank and ABN AMRO in all manner of commercial loans. Viewed as a *"go-to person in the insurance area,"* he advised the agents in letter of credit facilities for Swiss Re aggregating $6 billion. He also acted for JPMorgan Chase Bank as agent in a $1.9 billion letter of credit facility for ING America Insurance Holding. With an emphasis on syndicated and leveraged finance, **Charles Boehrer** (see p.719) acts on behalf of both lenders and borrowers in a range of senior and subordinated credit facilities and other structured finance transactions. He acted for Bank of America in connection with a $600 million credit facility for IDEX, and for Harley-Davidson in connection with its $1.1 billion credit facility with JPMorgan Chase as administrative agent. Clients admired the *"competitive and energetic"* **Ron Jacobson** (see p.733) for his client loyalty and *"never-give-up attitude;"* these qualities, they said, make Jacobson *"the kind of attorney you want."* Acting for clients such as Antares Capital and LaSalle Bank, his practice comprises corporate and cash flow lending,

leveraged and mezzanine financings and debt portfolio acquisitions.

The Clients: Antares Capital; CapitalSource Finance; CIT Group/Business Credit; LaSalle Bank; Madison Capital Funding; Wells Fargo Retail Finance; Deutsche Bank; Bank of America; Harley-Davidson and Lear.

Band 3

Chapman and Cutler LLP

See firm details p.763

The Firm: In conjunction with its two other offices in San Francisco and Salt Lake City, Chapman and Cutler has successfully forged a national reputation for its bond work and public finance. The finance group is comprised of more than 35 *"finely skilled lawyers,"* mostly acting principally as bond or underwriters' counsel in bond issues throughout the USA. There was also consistent praise for the firm's core banking work, the clients of which include Harris Bank, ABN AMRO and Fifth Third Bank. Its performance in securities and corporate finance is admirable, and the recent recruitment of Cynthia Baker from Mayer Brown is intended to drive the firm forward into the field of sports-related financial transactions.

The Lawyers: The *"smart, efficient and practical"* **Ron Rokosz** (see p.748) is considered *"a deal-maker, who lacks a deal-breaking ego."* His practice is split between ABN AMRO, for whom he acts regularly, in particular with their national wholesale client services group and diamond and jewelry group. He acted, for example, for ABN AMRO as agent in a syndicated $60 million secured working capital financing for a significant international jewelry company. In another matter he represented key client Fifth Third Bank as agent under a $75 million syndicated revolving credit facility to a major US pharmaceutical company. Highly visible on the consumer products and retail side of banking, **Marc Franson** (see p.728) is also a well-respected bank M&A lawyer. He and his team acted for Bank of Montréal and its US subsidiary, Harris Bankcorp, in three bank acquisitions, and advised a major foreign bank and its US subsidiaries with reference to the acquisition of a $2 billion credit card portfolio from a regional bank.

The Clients: Bank of New York; Allstate Bank; LaSalle National Bank; Bank of Montréal; ABN AMRO; Fifth Third Bank and Harris Bank.

Goldberg, Kohn, Bell, Black, Rosenbloom & Moritz, Ltd

The Firm: One of Chicago's finest, this well-respected firm boasts a smaller, but *"steady and hard-working,"* group of 19 *"quality and practical"* attorneys. It was considered by one admiring peer to be *"one of the best firms nationally for midmarket secured transactions."* Traditionally

acting for senior lenders, the team has nevertheless noted an increase in the representation of smaller mezzanine second lien lenders. Attorneys were considered *"truly impressive"* for cash flow and asset-based lending in its niche area of smaller to midmarket deals.

The Lawyers: The *"creativity and the ability to bring all parties together"* shown by **David Mason** permeates the entire team. He also garnered praise for his *"terrific organizational skills"* and *"ability to keep the process moving and complete the deal in a timely fashion."* In 2004, workouts and restructurings featured in his workload, alongside midmarket cash flow lending and mezzanine finance. Mason represented Merrill Lynch Capital as agent for the senior lending syndicate in the pre-bankruptcy and bankruptcy financing of Wickes Lumber. The long-standing chair of the commercial finance group **Richard Kohn** is still considered the first port of call by some observers. This *"very talented and knowledgeable"* attorney earned plaudits for his *"attention to detail"* and important role in the development of the group's international loan and contract expertise, most notably in relation to the Far East, Europe and South America. Not only has he spent significant time as co-general counsel to the Commercial Finance Association, the national trade association of commercial finance lenders, he was also involved in the drafting of the legislative guide on secured transactions at the UN. Over 20 years' experience and a broad commercial finance practice lead senior partner **David Dranoff** to his place in the rankings. Observers underlined his *"attention to detail,"* which serves him well in his chosen areas of asset-based secured loans and cash flow transactions.

The Clients: LaSalle Bank; GE Capital; Merrill Lynch; Congress Financial and Bank of America.

Katten Muchin Zavis Rosenman

See firm details p.769

The Firm: This established firm with seven US offices has a *"steady, goal-driven and entrepreneurial"* finance team of over 20 attorneys in Chicago. It acts for lenders at the upper end of the midmarket on deals, mostly between $25-250 million. In one of its top-end deals, it represented Merrill Lynch Capital as administrative agent, joint lead arranger and collateral agent in connection with first and second lien senior secured credit facilities in the aggregate amount of $265 million to TransFirst Holdings. Its expanding relationship with Merrill Lynch was highlighted by another separate deal, in which the team acted for the financial management giant as administrative agent and joint lead arranger for the lenders under first lien and second lien senior secured revolving credit and term loan facilities aggregating $185 million extended to subsidiaries and affiliates of Comsys Holding.

All quotes in the text are from interviews with clients and competitors.

The Lawyers: Stuart Shulruff (see p.752) ensures satisfaction for many clients with his *"pragmatic, encouraging and hands-on"* approach. He is admired for his *"outstanding"* talent and *"ability to communicate the clients' needs to the other side while avoiding transactional pitfalls."* Shulruff, who is head of the structured finance group, represents respected agent banks on syndicated credit facilities and midmarket, cash flow lending transactions. He and the group acted for Antares Capital on first lien and second lien senior secured credit facilities to FFR Acquisition. Entering the rankings as an up-and-coming commercial finance and reorganization partner is **Michael Jacobson** (see p.733), with whom clients felt *"increasingly very comfortable."* Peers, too, acknowledged his growing experience, *"pragmatic and even-keeled approach"* and *"knowledge of the process."*

The Clients: Antares Capital; CapitalSource Finance; GE Capital; LaSalle Bank National Association; Merrill Lynch Capital and Prairie Capital.

Kirkland & Ellis LLP
See firm details p.770

The Firm: Universally acknowledged for an *"excellent corporate practice,"* much of this legal juggernaut's reputation stems from *"its untouchable position"* representing borrowers in a wide array of matters including LBOs and refinancings. The significant experience of recent recruit Michael Wright from Sidley Austin's Chicago office is likely to boost the group's lender capability. Interviewees continue to wax lyrical about the dominance of the firm's private equity practice in Chicago, considered to *"dwarf all other major firms for private equity sponsor work."* Researchers learned of the group's great success with startup companies and clients in bankruptcy.

The Lawyers: At the forefront of the finance group is **Andrew Kaufman** (see p.734), whose nominations for inclusion in the table derive from his *"high intellect, substantive knowledge and long experience."* Considered *"a great borrowers' counsel,"* he has a broad practice, which comprises financing, secured transactions and general corporate work. For client Exide Technologies he carried out the pre-petition financing, debtor-in-possession financing and exit financing connected with its bankruptcy. He also undertook the senior bank financing work for Madison Dearborn Partners in the $3.7 billion acquisition of Boise Cascade's paper, forest products and timberland assets.

The Clients: GM; Dean Foods; Bank One; World Omni; Exide Technologies; Madison Dearborn Partners and NRG Energy.

McDermott Will & Emery
See firm details p.773

The Firm: The finance and banking group in the Chicago office of this well-respected international firm numbers ten attorneys and has *"strong midmarket bench strength."* The *"lean, mean and effective"* team acted for a major food processor/supplier to McDonald's in connection with an $885 million global financing led by Bank of America. The group also acted for Kellwood Company in connection with a $400 million syndicated facility led by Bank of America, and represented Dairy Farmers of America in connection with $400 million of syndicated facilities led by Wachovia Bank. The corporate finance expertise of the group has grown with the addition of two lateral hires from Jones Day and Chapman and Cutler.

The Lawyers: The team's success is closely tied to that of its *"superb"* senior partner **Bob McMenamin** (see p.741), who has over 30 years of experience in practice. Viewed as *"a sounding board for tricky issues,"* he has an active practice in syndicated loans, borrower and issuer work. McMenamin has recently represented Bank of America in connection with a $250 million syndicated facility with DeVry, a $100 million agented facility with Fellowes and an $80 million agented facility with Liquid Container.

The Clients: The Northwestern Mutual Life Insurance Company; The Heico Companies; LaSalle Business Credit and Actuant.

Skadden, Arps, Slate, Meagher & Flom LLP & Affiliates
See firm details p.1372

The Firm: Ubiquitous in the securitization market in New York, Skadden Arps fields a smaller banking and institutional investing team in Chicago, which unquestionably benefits greatly from being able to tap into the giant firm's *"wealth of experience"* in the US financial capital. The group is defined by its significant expertise in refinancing, restructuring and acquisition financing and its strong bankruptcy practice. Praise was consistently directed towards the team's borrower work (both nationally and internationally); however, attorneys do also represent several leading banks and lending institutions.

The Lawyers: Head of the Chicago group, **Randall Rademaker** (see p.747) has a complete understanding of the *"changing cycles"* of the lending market. His practice includes asset-backed and acquisition financing and asset-securitization transactions. He has acted for Bank One, CSFB and BNP Paribas as lenders' counsel and for Ball Corporation, Koch Industries, Sara Lee and Solo Cup Company in connection with secured loans, acquisition financings and securitizations.

The Clients: Sara Lee; Solo Cup; Ball Corporation; Koch Industries; JPMorgan Chase; Bank of America and BNP Paribas.

Band 4

Baker & McKenzie
See firm details p.761

The Firm: Renowned for its national and international work, this firm is making a concerted effort to develop its local presence, with around 25 banking and finance attorneys in Chicago. This office, together with Houston, represented CasaBlanca Resorts and its parent shareholder, a casino and resort group which owns and operates three Nevada casinos, as both New York and federal tax counsel in connection with a $206 million bank and debt capital markets financing.

The Lawyers: There was a *"solid feel"* for the *"competent and hard-working"* **Creighton Meland** (see p.741), who enjoys a general banking and finance practice. He represented Hungary-based steering group banks in a $95 million cross-border debt restructuring for North American Bus Industries and its Hungarian parent, NABI Rt.

The Clients: Alion Science and Technology, PaR Systems and CasaBlanca Resorts feature in an expansive client roster.

Duane Morris LLP
See firm details p.1550

The Firm: A tiny Chicago team of *"low-key but solid"* banking and financial services attorneys joins the rankings this year. Tapping into the resources of this 600-lawyer firm, the group is renowned for real estate finance and secured and unsecured lender work.

The Lawyers: Observers noted that **Ken Latimer** (see p.736) always *"knows his way through the deal."* He advises banks and commercial finance companies on secured and unsecured loans, M&A and regulatory issues and recently completed a $53 million revolving credit facility (acting for the lead lender and agent) for the construction of a new condominium development in Chicago. For Wells Fargo Foothill, he recently completed a $25 million revolving asset-based loan and also a $35 million revolving credit asset-based loan, which included mezzanine financing.

The Clients: Wells Fargo Foothill; Fifth Third Bank; New Century Bank and Lake Forest Bank & Trust.

Neal, Gerber & Eisenberg LLP

The Firm: This Chicago firm's seven-lawyer finance team earned recommendations for a full range of finance transactions, from working capital lines to acquisition financings, to LBOs and structured secured deals. Renowned for its sophisticated work, the group acts for large borrower clients and, according to one client, has *"tentacles that spread throughout the US."* The *"small but practical"* group additionally has a midmarket lender practice, representing the Chicago offices of a number of banks, such as Wells Fargo, Bank of America and National City Bank. The team has recently gained further mezzanine finance and asset-based lending expertise following the arrival of two former Jenkens & Gilchrist attorneys.

The Lawyers: Former assistant general counsel of Bank of America, the *"creative and flexible"* **Peter Barrow** continues to act for not only Bank of America but also JPMorgan Chase and LaSalle Bank. He recently advised LaSalle on the provision of senior debt for a leveraged buyout of a pet food company in the Midwest. His practice also incorporates the representation of borrowers and third parties in the negotiation and documentation of a range of lending and finance transactions.

The Clients: General Growth Properties; National City Bank; LaSalle Bank; Bank of America and First Bank.

Schiff Hardin LLP
See firm details p.775

The Firm: Almost as old as the city of Chicago itself and boasting a finance group that now numbers almost 20 lawyers, Schiff Hardin has a long history in this field. The group has been enhanced by the return of Peter Rossiter, for-

merly executive vice president of Northern Trust Corporation and the potency of its real estate and construction lending expertise has received a boost through additional recruitment. While increased activity in mezzanine lending transactions has raised the firm's visibility, the team has also been advising insurance companies in the private placement market.

The Lawyers: The firm's managing partner in Chicago, **Scott Pickens** (see p.746), represents a range of lenders such as LaSalle Bank, Fifth Third Bank and Allied Irish Bank in a variety of transactions, including syndicated, asset-based and cash flow loans, mezzanine finance, aviation finance and leveraged leasing.

The Clients: First Source Financial; Residual Based Finance Corporation; Midwest Mezzanine Funds; One Mezzanine; Prudential Capital; Bank of America; Fifth Third Bank and LaSalle Bank.

Schwartz, Cooper, Greenberger & Krauss, Chartered
See firm details p.776

The Firm: The bread-and-butter work of this steady 15-lawyer team is its counsel to the range of Midwestern financial institutions that make commercial loans to midmarket businesses. The group carries out a variety of secured, unsecured, asset-based and real estate lending transactions.

The Lawyers: Martin Salzman is one of the

key partners in the firm's banking department.

The Clients: LaSalle Bank; Oak Brook Bank; RBC Builder Finance and Washington Mutual Bank.

Vedder, Price, Kaufman & Kammholz

The Firm: Peers and clients pointed to the niche expertise of this robust player, whose abilities in aircraft, rail and equipment finance are described as *"almost unmatched anywhere."* The group advises financiers, lenders, venture capital funds, private equity and leveraged buyout funds in a range of transactions. Executive compensation, labor law and mutual fund work are other strengths of this respected legal outfit.

The Lawyers: Interviewees pointed to the *"knowledge, efficiency and negotiation skills"* of **John McEnroe**, who performs a *"magnificent job"* for clients. His practice incorporates vast amounts of midmarket, asset-based and cash flow financings, commercial loans and leveraged buyouts. Peers chose also to emphasize the *"excellent reputation"* of **Dean Gerber** in aircraft finance deals and private placement transactions. He is dually qualified as an attorney and a CPA.

The Clients: Export Development Canada; CIT Group; Lehman Global Finance and GMAC Commercial Finance.

BANKRUPTCY

Illinois
Leading firms (Bankruptcy)

1	**KIRKLAND & ELLIS LLP** *Chicago*
	LATHAM & WATKINS LLP *Chicago*
	SKADDEN, ARPS, SLATE, MEAGHER *Chicago*
2	**GOLDBERG, KOHN, BELL, BLACK,** *Chicago*
	SIDLEY AUSTIN BROWN & WOOD LLP *Chicago*
3	**ADELMAN & GETTLEMAN LTD** *Chicago*
	DLA PIPER RUDNICK GRAY CARY US LLP *Chicago*
	FOLEY & LARDNER LLP *Chicago*
	GREENBERG TRAURIG LLP *Chicago*
	JENNER & BLOCK LLP *Chicago*
	JONES DAY *Chicago*
	KAYE SCHOLER LLP *Chicago*
	MAYER, BROWN, ROWE & MAW LLP *Chicago*
	SHAW GUSSIS FISHMAN GLANTZ *Chicago*
	SONNENSCHEIN NATH & ROSENTHAL *Chicago*
	VEDDER, PRICE, KAUFMAN & KAMMHOLZ *Chicago*
	WINSTON & STRAWN LLP *Chicago*

Firms are listed alphabetically in each band.

Band 1

Kirkland & Ellis LLP
See firm details p.770

The Firm: Renowned as a national debtors' practice, this *"outstanding firm"* employs almost 100 restructuring and bankruptcy lawyers from its Chicago headquarters. With access to further resources in its New York, London and LA offices, this *"top class"* bankruptcy team is able to handle *"the biggest and ugliest cases around."* It won plaudits for its management of the Chapter 11 reorganization of Conseco, the third largest filing in history at the time. Other major recent cases include the representation of UAL (United Airlines) in its massive reorganization and advice to NRG Energy in the restructuring of more than $11 billion in debt. The group is also well versed in the representation of creditors.

The Lawyers: The *"technically and commercially sound"* **James Sprayregen** (see p.754) is a great clients' lawyer, admired for his *"unflustered ways."* He offers expertise in distressed companies and M&A as well as corporate governance and advice to boards of directors in bankruptcy situations. Sprayregen acted for UAL in its ongoing restructuring matters, expected to run into

2005, and advised on the Chapter 11 reorganization of Conseco. Clients described him as *"probably the best restructuring lawyer in the world."* The *"incredibly smart"* **Marc Kieselstein** (see p.735) served as counsel in the out-of-court sale of J&L Specialty Steel to Allegheny Steel and a resulting out-of-court composition of creditors. Representing the debtor, he has acted for UAL, TWA and Indesco International. **Anup Sathy** (see p.750) is a *"very promising up-and-comer"* and one of Sprayregen's right-hand men in the Conseco case. He also represented the debtor in the prearranged Chapter 11 restructuring of Chiquita Brands International. **James Stempel** (see p.754) remains admired as a solution-oriented lawyer. He represented National Equipment Services, one of the nation's largest equipment rental companies, and its affiliates in its successful reorganization before the US Bankruptcy Court.

The Clients: UAL; Conseco; Polymer Group; Archibald Candy and National Equipment Services.

Latham & Watkins LLP
The Firm: This international firm possesses a *"depth of resources and the geographical footprint"* to secure a top-flight reputation in the field. A

and Communication Dynamics.

The Clients: DVI; LaSalle Bank; Foothill Capital; Congress Financial; Bank One; Bank of America; Citicorp and GE Capital.

Skadden, Arps, Slate, Meagher & Flom LLP & Affiliates
See firm details p.1372

The Firm: A decline in the market's *"mega-bankruptcies"* and an increase in out of court restructurings have not prevented this *"global and premier debtor"* firm from retaining pole position in the market. Admired for its *"top to bottom strength,"* its transactional focus and its *"speedy get in and get out strategy"* for clients in bankruptcy and Chapter 11 proceedings, around a third of the practice group's 120 attorneys operate from Chicago. Much admired for its company representation, the group also acts for creditors and creditor committees.

The Lawyers: The *"exceptional and as good as it gets"* Jack Butler (see p.721) combines *"great business sense"* and the *"creativity to craft legal solutions"* on behalf of mostly large debtors in Chapter 11 proceedings. This *"very bright and out-of-the-box thinker"* co-leads Skadden's global corporate restructuring practice and has acted in the restructuring in Chapter 11 cases of Haynes International, Kmart and Xerox. Sources appreciated George Panagakis (see p.745) as *"a good point of contact and a great sounding board"* for a range of clients in reorganizations, restructurings and bankruptcy matters. He acted for Comdisco and County Seat Stores in their respective Chapter 11 reorganizations. Acting for a client range, including debtors and secured lenders, the *"very creative and pleasant to work with"* Tim Pohl (see p.746) has worked as lead Chapter 11 counsel for National Steel and IGC Communications, and advised on significant out-of-court restructurings, such as Rural Cellular Communications. The *"senior and highly experienced"* Eric Ivester (see p.733) is lead debtor counsel for Interstate Bakeries in its high-profile Chapter 11 case. He has also acted as lead counsel in the Chapter 11 case and successful reorganization of Hayes Lemmerz International, a leading supplier of automotive wheels.

The Clients: Kmart; Hayes Lemmerz International; Interstate Bakeries; Haynes International; Xerox; The Warnaco Group; Rural Cellular Communications; HealthSouth Corporation and America West Airlines feature among the firm's representations.

Band 2

Goldberg, Kohn, Bell, Black, Rosenbloom & Moritz, Ltd
The Firm: *"Commitment and collegiality"* were considered the hallmarks of this *"smart"* ten-lawyer group. Its *"smart and well-known"* attorneys provide competition for the representation

of senior lenders. The litigation and corporate finance expertise at the 85-lawyer firm also lends further weight to the bankruptcy group, which also serves as counsel to secured creditors, committees, debtors and other participants in complex bankruptcy proceedings.

The Lawyers: Praise continues to pour in for *"scholarly gent"* Gerry Munitz, a senior statesman and key lenders' lawyer whose 44 years' experience is highly regarded. A *"tremendous depth of knowledge"* ensured Munitz the title *"dean of the Bankruptcy Bar,"* and he maintains a high profile for having brought *"integrity and professionalism"* to the community. Former bankruptcy judge Ron Barliant is a highly knowledgeable attorney who has made a successful transition into private practice and is now *"a popular choice for referrals – I'd call him in a heartbeat,"* agreed sources. He has represented the indenture trustee with respect to most of the aircraft operated by United Airlines, and assisted the debtor in a Delaware Chapter 11 case involving significant environmental liabilities. Alan Solow has more than 25 years' experience and an impressive track record. Chair of the Bankruptcy & Creditors' Rights Group, he is a *"very aggressive and hard-hitting"* litigator who acts for secured and unsecured creditors. According to interviewees, Randy Klein is *"one of the best up-and-coming secured creditors' lawyers around."* He acted for Wells Fargo Foothill on behalf of two hedge funds as holders of $135 million senior secured indebtedness.

The Clients: ABN AMRO; Bank of America; BNP Paribas; Citadel Investment Group; Congress Financial; Fleet Capital; Foothill Group; GE Capital; LaSalle Bank and Merrill Lynch Capital.

Sidley Austin Brown & Wood LLP
See firm details p.778

The Firm: Historically viewed as a strong creditor and senior lender practice, this increasingly balanced firm is fast developing a reputation for key debtor work. The restructuring team fields 60 bankruptcy lawyers across four offices, who *"know how to adapt to the client's needs and close out a case."* High-profile representations falling under the spotlight are Federal-Mogul. Skilled litigators, they also advise on significant cross-border Chapter 11 proceedings arising out of the UK, Europe and South America. Interviewees underlined the group's expertise in handling issues of bankruptcy driven by mass tort litigation.

The Lawyers: The driving force behind this respected practice is the leadership of the *"very smart, collaborative and out-of-the-box thinker"* Larry Nyhan (see p.744), who chairs the group. *"A fantastically hard-working lawyer,"* he makes recommendations based on good business judgment and is considered *"respectful and pro-*

Leading individuals (Bankruptcy)

Senior Statesman
MUNITZ Gerald *Goldberg Kohn, Chicago*

[1] BUTLER Jr John *Skadden Arps, Chicago*
SPRAYREGEN James *Kirkland & Ellis, Chicago*

[2] BARLIANT Ronald *Goldberg Kohn, Chicago*
HELLER David *Latham & Watkins, Chicago*
JACOBSON Fruman *Sonnenschein Nath, Chicago*
MILLNER Robert *Sonnenschein Nath, Chicago*
MISSNER David *DLA Piper Rudnick, Chicago*
NYHAN Lawrence *Sidley Austin, Chicago*
SOLOW Michael *Kaye Scholer, Chicago*
TOWBIN Steven *Shaw Gussis, Chicago*

[3] ADELMAN Howard *Adelman & Gettleman, Chicago*
BACON Douglas *Latham & Watkins, Chicago*
BERKOFF Mark *DLA Piper Rudnick, Chicago*
BOTICA Matthew *Winston & Strawn, Chicago*
CONLAN James *Sidley Austin, Chicago*
HARNER Paul *Jones Day, Chicago*
IVESTER Eric *Skadden Arps, Chicago*
KIESELSTEIN Marc *Kirkland & Ellis, Chicago*
KIRIAKOS Thomas *Mayer Brown, Chicago*
LIPKE Doug *Vedder Price, Chicago*
MITCHELL Nancy *Greenberg Traurig, Chicago*
PANAGAKIS George *Skadden Arps, Chicago*
PETERSON Ronald *Jenner & Block, Chicago*
POHL Timothy *Skadden Arps, Chicago*
SHAPIRO Keith *Greenberg Traurig, Chicago*
SOLOW Alan *Goldberg Kohn, Chicago*
STEMPEL James *Kirkland & Ellis, Chicago*
ZAZOVE Daniel *Perkins Coie, Chicago*

Up-and-coming individuals
KLEIN Randall *Goldberg Kohn, Chicago*
SATHY Anup *Kirkland & Ellis, Chicago*

Individuals are listed alphabetically in each band.

growing Chicago team of around 20 attorneys handles numerous creditor representations in the largest cases. For example, the team acted for Bank of America in the Chapter 11 cases of Owens Corning and WR Grace; and Bank One in the UAL Chapter 11.

The Lawyers: The *"excellent and conciliatory"* David Heller cochairs the firm's Insolvency and Restructuring group. Clients appreciated his skill in *"keeping the process moving quickly,"* and the *"vast knowledge he can leverage."* His 25 years' experience and the *"ability to provide guidance to both parties"* give him huge credibility. He acted for Black Diamond in its capacity as debtor-in-possession lender in a hotly contested $40 million loan. He has also been involved in a series of restructurings for GE Capital and represented DVI in a recently confirmed case, where debts exceeded $1 billion. Many liked the *"street-smart, accomplished and appropriately aggressive style"* of Douglas Bacon, whose increasing prominence in representing creditors' committees, lenders and debtors was recognized by sources. His cases include American Sports Products, Trussway

fessional," agree sources. His practice features a substantial number of workouts and restructurings, and his work for debtors includes the representation of Budget Rent A Car and Pegasus Satellite Communications, which has more than $1 billion debt. The Group's Vice Chair, **James Conlan** (see p.723), earned admiration as a _"go-getting rainmaker"_ and a _"well-respected and intelligent partner"_ active in large debtor cases, such as work for Federal-Mogul and T&N.

The Clients: Budget Rent A Car; El Paso Electric; Federal-Mogul; Horizon PCS; Northwestern Steel; Pacific Trail; The Warnaco Group and Zenith Industries

Band 3

Adelman & Gettleman Ltd
See firm details p.760

The Firm: Despite its smaller size when compared to some rivals, this _"highly competent"_ ten-lawyer group has attracted plaudits from a range of commentators. Many underlined the 22-year-old firm as the _"fantastic master of Chapter 11 cases,"_ and praised the technical skill of its attorneys. The team's workload of late has included asbestos-related Chapter 11 cases filed in Delaware. Bank One is a regular client for the team, providing a steady flow of cases, often midmarket workouts.

The Lawyers: The _"smart, talented and aggressive"_ **Howard Adelman** is an experienced partner in the group. With both debtor and secured creditor representations under his belt, he has _"a tremendous knowledge"_ of how to run a case. He also serves on the US Advisory Committee to the Supreme Court on bankruptcy rules.

The Clients: The firm advises debtors, creditors, boards of directors, insurance companies and management.

DLA Piper Rudnick Gray Cary US LLP
See firm details p.765

The Firm: A group of 20 _"talented and seasoned business"_ lawyers at this mammoth international firm has developed a sound regional practice. The experience of its attorneys runs the full gamut of bankruptcy work. Recent examples have included the representation of significant debtors, creditor committees, financial institutions and also directors and officers in insurance-related litigation.

The Lawyers: Chairman of the Chicago group and national cochair of the bankruptcy and business reorganization practice group, **Mark Berkoff** (see p.718) has handled some of the field's most complex cases. Interviewees admired his _"practicality and good courtroom presence."_ The _"extraordinary judgment and great connections"_ of **David Missner** (see p.742) stand him in good stead. He is an intelligent and expe-

rienced attorney, who possesses an _"ability to weave smoothly through a deal and find economic solutions."_

The Clients: NBD Bank, LaSalle National Bank and Cole Taylor Bank feature in the firm's client list.

Foley & Lardner LLP
See firm details p.1828

The Firm: Interviewees highlight the _"bright and exceptional lawyers"_ fielded by the Chicago bankruptcy group of this sizable national firm. With a growing expertise in healthcare-related bankruptcies, the team also handles a broad range of Chapter 11 reorganizations and workouts. The team recently acted for the official creditors committee in the Chapter 11 case for Horizon Natural Resources pending in Lexington, Kentucky. The debtor is the fourth-largest coal producer in the United States.

The Lawyers: Managing partner of the Chicago office is Mark Prager, a former chair of the national business reorganizations practice Group, which is presently led by Michael Small.

The Clients: Creditor committees, secured creditors, debtors and indenture trustees feature among the clientele.

Greenberg Traurig LLP
See firm details p.564

The Firm: The Chicago core of this international firm's bankruptcy group comprises ten lawyers, who act on major cases in the Chicago market. Able to tap into the deep resources of its many offices, the group represents debtors, secured and unsecured creditors, boards of directors and other parties in reorganizations and bankruptcies. The team acted for Mestek in the Chapter 11 case of its wholly owned subsidiary, Met-Coil Systems.

The Lawyers: Clients described **Keith Shapiro** (see p.751) as a _"great strategic thinker,"_ admired for his _"responsiveness, practical approach and strong network of contacts."_ He cochairs the national reorganization, bankruptcy and restructuring practice. Key representations include acting as counsel to the unsecured creditors committee in the Conseco Chapter 11 cases. He also acted for Mesirow Financial's national insolvency practice in its acquisition of KPMG's US corporate recovery practice. The _"hardworking and impressive negotiator"_ **Nancy Mitchell** (see p.742) also figures strongly in the team.

The Clients: Conseco; Mesirow Financial; Mestek; Centennial Healthcare Corporation and City of Chicago.

Jenner & Block LLP
See firm details p.768

The Firm: Observers recognized that this group of 22 bankruptcy lawyers is _"making strides to get into the national league"_ and continues to grow through the addition of a small number of asso-

ciates. With a strong litigation background, the team earned plaudits for the representation of debtors and secured creditors in bankruptcy litigation. It acted for Commercial Financial Services, the largest purchaser of delinquent credit card accounts receivable, in its Chapter 11 bankruptcy proceedings in Oklahoma. The team also acted for Covanta Energy in its Chapter 11 reorganization proceeding in New York.

The Lawyers: A _"seasoned and colorful-in-court"_ **Ron Peterson** (see p.746) won tremendous respect for his insolvency litigation experience, his contribution to the Chicago bankruptcy community and his _"litigate hard, settle hard"_ style. From a traditionally debtor-heavy practice, the practice cochair's caseload saw an increase in bankruptcy litigation and creditor committee representation. He acted for the creditors' committees in the Chapter 11 cases of Keystone Consolidated, Handy Andy Home Centers and Payless Cashways. He is also active in transactional matters, counseling the commercial paper holders in an out-of-court restructuring of Mercury Finance.

The Clients: GE Capital; LaSalle Bank; Commercial Financial Services; McDermott International; Jays Foods; World Access; Gingiss Formalwear and Covanta Energy.

Jones Day
See firm details p.485

The Firm: This national firm is a relatively new entrant to the Chicago bankruptcy market. Continued growth has seen the practice increase from three to 12 lawyers over the last few years. The group can also call upon the resources of respected teams in Ohio and New York. Attorneys here represent a range of debtors, creditors, and others in complex restructurings, out-of-court workouts and Chapter 11 cases. The team is distinguished as a _"powerhouse of a litigation practice."_

The Lawyers: Heading the business restructuring and reorganization group is **Paul Harner** (see p.731), described as a _"terrific debtors lawyer,"_ although his practice also features creditor representations. He acted for National Century Financial Enterprises and its affiliates in the Chapter 11 cases, which involved the largest US healthcare provider of accounts receivable financing. His track record has included the representation of Slater Steel and affiliates in Chapter 11 cases concerning the manufacture and marketing of stainless steels.

The Clients: USG; Slater Steel; National Century Financial Enterprises; Xcel Energy; Burlington Industries and Laidlaw.

Kaye Scholer LLP
See firm details p.1354

The Firm: A group of around ten bankruptcy lawyers are backed up by a _"good bench"_ of around 40 attorneys, who are able to offer advice on the financial and tax aspects of bankruptcy, and a strong litigation team. Observers remarked upon the development of the practice, particularly with its strong creditor caseload, since it is regularly consulted for complex insolvency issues.

The Lawyers: Clients endorsed **Michael Solow** (see p.753) for his *"extensive experience and knowledge of the process"* and a practicality that combines the *"legal issues with the business realities."* He was instrumental in the Formica and the Aladdin Hotel & Casino reorganizations. He also acted for the unsecured creditors in the PG&E National Energy Group bankruptcy. Dividing his time between New York and Chicago, Solow also negotiates the purchases and sales of contracts out of bankruptcy.

The Clients: Bank of America; Citibank; Foothill Capital and Fleet Capital.

Mayer, Brown, Rowe & Maw LLP
See firm details p.771

The Firm: Bank of America remains a flagship client of this respected practice, providing a steady flow of creditors' work. A dedicated 14-strong team in Chicago earns most of its plaudits for its ability to combine technical understanding with a commercial approach to the deal table, particularly in regard to its work with the acquirers of distressed assets. The firm's additional national and international resources also proved to be an attractive draw card for clients.

The Lawyers: An *"ability to see the entire picture and focus on the essentials"* lies at the core of **Thomas Kiriakos**'s (see p.735) practice. A *"smart and tough"* attorney, he acts for commercial banks and a range of creditors in bankruptcies across many industries. He advised on the Chapter 11 of Conseco and was pivotal in the representation of Bank of Montréal, one of the largest unsecured creditors in the bankruptcy cases of DVI and its affiliates in Delaware.

The Clients: Bank of America; CIBC; Bank of Montreal; Union Bank of California and Tennessee Farmers Insurance.

Shaw Gussis Fishman Glantz Wolfson & Towbin LLC

The Firm: Market commentators recognized this firm's strong leaning towards bankruptcy and the associated litigation. Approximately 15 of the 20 lawyers are devoted to this field, earn-

ing credit for its representation of medium-sized debtors in a substantial number of Chapter 11 reorganizations. Clients appreciate that the firm offers *"big firm expertise at competitive prices."*

The Lawyers: A wealth of experience under his belt gives accomplished litigator **Steven Towbin** *"expert judgment and a high degree of analytical ability."* He has the *"ability to size things up quickly"* and effectively negotiate for his clients. He successfully represented Capital Factors in its appeal of an authorization order to pay key vendors in the Kmart bankruptcy.

The Clients: The team acts for parties in complex bankruptcy and reorganization cases, as well as receivership and out-of-court workouts.

Sonnenschein Nath & Rosenthal LLP
See firm details p.779

The Firm: A group of ten bankruptcy lawyers in Chicago can draw upon the resources and additional expertise of its New York office. Although renowned for a mix of debtor and commercial creditor work, the firm continues to build on the *"greater visibility"* and high profile gained through the representation of the creditor committee in the United Airlines proceedings. Other bankruptcy and workout engagements have included the representation of Chapter 11 debtors, secured creditors and insurance companies across the healthcare, technology, energy and retail sectors.

The Lawyers: Interviewees admired **Fruman Jacobson** (see p.733), leader of the National workout, reorganization and bankruptcy practice, for his *"very sharp and bright intellect and strong analytical skills."* He co-heads the representation of the United Airlines official committee of unsecured creditors. Observers endorsed the strong litigation background of **Robert Millner** (see p.742). A highly professional attorney, his *"academic and conceptual creativity"* and responsiveness drive his practice. He acts for financial institutions and insurance companies in significant bankruptcy litigation and represents the official committee of unsecured creditors in the Federal-Mogul bankruptcy in Delaware.

The Clients: A range of debtors, creditors, landlords, officers and directors, trustees and workout consultants.

Vedder, Price, Kaufman & Kammholz

The Firm: This Chicago-based general full-service commercial firm is recognized by sources for its *"sound reputation and experience"* in representing secured creditors in Chicago. Nine of the 13 lawyers operate from Chicago and earn admiration for their representation of secured lenders and equipment lessors in Chapter 11 cases. Observers identified the firm's particular niche in aircraft and equipment finance insolvency matters.

The Lawyers: The *"smart and personable"* **Doug Lipke** chairs the corporate reorganization, bankruptcy and insolvency group. Like the firm, he displays expertise in domestic and international equipment and aircraft leasing and equipment financing, where he acts for financial institutions in structuring, workouts and foreclosures.

The Clients: In bankruptcy and insolvency litigation, the team acts for institutional lenders, investment banks and mutual funds in a variety of industries, such as aircraft, steel, retail and automotive.

Winston & Strawn LLP
See firm details p.780

The Firm: Since its merger with San Francisco bankruptcy boutique Murphy, Sheneman Julian & Rogers, this firm has continued to consolidate its presence in the bankruptcy market. With approaching 20 lawyers, the practice's reputation lies with lender and creditor representation.

The Lawyers: The *"smart and hardworking"* **Matthew Botica** (see p.720) has earned market commendations for his general bankruptcy and reorganization practice, especially for his role as counsel to secured creditors, banks and other lenders.

The Clients: GE Capital; Deutsche Bank; LaSalle Bank and Wells Fargo Bank.

Other Notable Practitioners

Dan Zazove is a talented debtors lawyer with more than 30 years' experience in bankruptcy proceedings. At time of press, he moved from Kaye Scholer to Perkins Coie.

CONSTRUCTION

Illinois
Leading firms (Construction)

1 SCHIFF HARDIN LLP *Chicago*
  STEIN, RAY & HARRIS LLP *Chicago*

2 BELL, BOYD & LLOYD LLC *Chicago*
  CONWAY & MROWIEC *Chicago*
  DLA PIPER RUDNICK GRAY CARY US LLP *Chicago*

3 BEDRAVA & LYMAN *Oak Brook*
  MUCH SHELIST FREED DENENBERG *Chicago*
  OGLETREE, DEAKINS, NASH, SMOAK *Chicago*
  SABO & ZAHN *Chicago*
  SACHNOFF & WEAVER LTD *Chicago*

Leading individuals (Construction)

1 FRIEDLANDER Mark *Schiff Hardin*, Chicago
  LURIE Paul *Schiff Hardin*, Chicago
  LYMAN Bill *Bedrava & Lyman*, Oak Brook
  STEIN Steven *Stein Ray*, Chicago

2 KIKOLER Stephen *Much Shelist*, Chicago
  LAURIE Ty *DLA Piper Rudnick*, Chicago
  SKLAR Stanley *Bell Boyd*, Chicago

3 ALTMAN Ross *DLA Piper Rudnick*, Chicago
  BERG Eric *DLA Piper Rudnick*, Chicago
  BRENNAN Daniel *DLA Piper Rudnick*, Chicago
  COLE Alexandra *Perkins Coie*, Chicago
  CONWAY Timothy *Conway & Mrowiec*, Chicago
  DASH James *Much Shelist*, Chicago
  HARRIS Robert *Stein Ray*, Chicago
  LEWIS Charles *Jenkens & Gilchrist*, Chicago
  MROWIEC John *Conway & Mrowiec*, Chicago
  NEWMAN Margery *Ogletree Deakins*, Chicago
  RAY Stephen *Stein Ray*, Chicago
  ROBERTS Kenneth *Schiff Hardin*, Chicago
  RUFF Randolph *Ogletree Deakins*, Chicago
  SHAPIRO Clifford *Sachnoff & Weaver*, Chicago
  SINGER Eric *Wildman Harrold*, Chicago

Firms and individuals are listed alphabetically in each band.

Band 1

Schiff Hardin LLP

See firm details p.775

The Firm: The deep expertise of this truly national construction practice impresses both clients and peers. Housed in one of Chicago's most established firms, the team of nine offers specialist advice at all stages of the process having expanded from its original design professional roots. The team displays particular strength in energy construction issues. The mid-2004 departures of Ty Laurie and Dan Brennan to Piper Rudnick have been counterbalanced by the arrival of Robert Appel to the New York office, providing a boost to the group's representation of high-profile architects.

The Lawyers: Observers described **Mark Friedlander** (see p.728), co-leader of the construction group, as a *"thoughtful adviser with a sharp legal mind."* Clients also underlined his *"commercial approach, tremendous knowledge of the law"* and experience in the representation of engineers and architects. He has successfully defended the City of Springfield, Illinois in a multimillion-dollar claim by the German multinational company Lurgi Lentjes Bischoff concerning the construction of a sulfur dioxide scrubber system. The *"smart, creative and well-connected"* **Paul Lurie** (see p.738) is a key member of a team that is noted for its strong belief in alternative dispute resolution. His practice encompasses project planning, dispute avoidance and mediation. Both he and Friedlander have advised on the Rush program, a ten-year $500 million expansion/renovation program for one of Chicago's leading medical centers involving numerous buildings over several city blocks. The *"bright and knowledgeable"* **Ken Roberts** (see p.747) (cochair of the group with Friedlander) enters the rankings following client endorsement for his vast experience in the utilities sector. Roberts was engaged by a large Canadian utility to advise on the first phase of a multibillion-dollar project at one of its key nuclear power plants.

The Clients: City of Springfield, Illinois; Ontario Power Generation; Constellation Generation Group; Raymond Professional Group; Midwest Generation; Chicago Transit Authority; VOA Architects; Perkins and Will Architects; Rush Medical Center; NiSource; Province of Ontario and LR Development.

Stein, Ray & Harris LLP

The Firm: This 24-strong team is a key player in the construction market due to its wealth of resources and its commitment to *"fight to the finish for its clients."* One of the largest construction groups in Chicago, it enjoys a national and international practice, acting for engineering, procurement & construction (EPC) companies; design-builders; owners and developers. Clients highlighted the group's *"impressive handling of complex and technical legal issues"* and sophisticated advice in relation to construction and power plant projects, while peers respected its broad skill base.

The Lawyers: The *"highly intelligent and extremely talented"* **Steven Stein** continues to impress as a clear leader in the field for both the trial and arbitration of construction and design disputes. **Stephen Ray**'s thorough preparation and deep legal knowledge has been on display in many types of construction dispute, including defects, delays and mechanics' lien claims. He has defended a publicly traded engineering client in a $40 million claim alleging project delays. **Robert Harris**' practice encompasses commercial litigation as well as a wealth of experience in construction disputes. He has successfully litigated claims concerning building defects, delay claims and environmental issues.

The Clients: University of Chicago; The Art Institute of Chicago; Pizza Hut; Duke Energy; Hunt Construction Group; Bechtel and Earth Tech.

Band 2

Bell, Boyd & Lloyd LLC

The Firm: Two-thirds of this 15-strong highly respected construction group carry out all manner of construction litigation, with the remainder focusing their energies on the contracts and transactional side for every participant in the construction field. The team is acting as special counsel in the Capital Development Board for the State of Illinois in the creation of the Lincoln library and theater.

The Lawyers: Having proudly received the Cornerstone Award from the ABA Forum on the Construction Industry for services to construction, the *"highly recognized marquis player"* **Stan Sklar** continues to elicit praise among interviewees as a *"real heavyweight in the industry."* Almost 30 years' experience and a *"tremendous knowledge of the law"* drive a national practice and his current presidency of the Society of Illinois Construction Attorneys. Historically known as a subcontractor lawyer, he has acted for all parties in all phases of the construction process. Lately, he has been acting for a subcontractor in litigation surrounding the City's high-profile Millennium Project. His workload also comprises a significant and increasing arbitration, mediation and consultation component.

The Clients: The team acts for owners, developers, contractors, subcontractors, design professionals and trade organizations in private and government contracting.

Conway & Mrowiec

See firm details p.764

The Firm: Founded by former Stein, Ray & Harris attorneys, three partners and three associates at this boutique enjoy a very solid local market reputation as an *"excellent up-and-coming firm, that knows how to efficiently try cases."* *"They really understand construction through the eyes of contractors,"* noted one observer, and the team, which added Mark Becker from Schiff Hardin, boasts strength in construction disputes, including mechanics' lien and delay claims. The firm's success for telecom giants in significant mechanics' liens cases has been replaced more recently with cases on behalf of power plants.

The Lawyers: The *"very bright and talented"* **Tim Conway** (see p.723) earned praise for a *"personable and collegiate"* approach to litigation. He has recently prosecuted a priority claim on

All quotes in the text are from interviews with clients and competitors.

behalf of an international EPC contractor and is prosecuting a multimillion claim for a trade contractor on a concert pavilion. The flip side of this partnership coin was the *"equally talented and intelligent"* **John Mrowiec** (see p.743), who successfully resolved, in favor of an international EPC contractor, an eight-figure mechanics' lien priority dispute with a project lender; and a similar amount claimed by the mechanical subcontractor on a power plant project.

The Clients: In addition to the group's reputation acting for contractors, clients include EPC contractors, design-builders, construction managers, trade contractors, architects, owners and sureties.

DLA Piper Rudnick Gray Cary US LLP
See firm details p.765

The Firm: Having grown up in real estate and licensing work, the construction team has been developing critical mass and peers acknowledged its *"increasing commitment to construction."* Now enjoying a greater national and international standing and supporting arguably the largest real estate practice in the entire country, the ten-lawyer Chicago group includes partners Dan Brennan and Ty Laurie, who arrived from Schiff Hardin in July 2004.

The Lawyers: Having returned from five years in-house, the *"well-regarded"* **Ross Altman** (see p.716) enjoys a predominantly transactional practice, although he has been involved in alternative dispute resolution methods. Business counseling, pre-development issues, incentive agreements and project delivery form a significant part of his workload. Well-known and highly active in the ABA Construction Forum, **Dan Brennan** (see p.720) earned many compliments for being a *"good match and partner for the excellent"* **Ty Laurie** (see p.736); and both were highlighted for *"spotting and avoiding the red flags."* *"Excellent at owner representation,"* Laurie is a *"terrific boost"* to the firm's construction litigation practice. The *"sharpness and integrity"* of **Eric Berg** (see p.718) drives him into the ranking tables, lauded by market commentators for a combined transactional and litigation practice and a *"quality service to his clients."*

The Clients: Developers and owners as well as builders, contractors and design professionals form a large slice of the team's clientele.

Band 3

Bedrava & Lyman
The Firm: Although this firm was not considered to rub shoulders with national construction players, interviewees strongly admired this three-lawyer construction team for a sophisticated niche practice in the Chicago suburbs. With a *"get-in and get-out"* approach to litigation, the team represents smaller subcontractors

and owners in private construction transactions and litigation. Recent highlights have included settling an insurance-related construction dispute, a growing area for the firm.

The Lawyers: Considered to be the *"dean of subcontracting law"* **Bill Lyman** boasts *"an excellent academic understanding,"* *"personal industry knowledge"* and a *"practical approach, which does not leave you chasing your tail."* He enjoys a practice, which in addition to a staple diet of negotiations, mediations, arbitrations and litigation, also includes insurance coverage disputes. Jennifer Nielson concentrates on public and private construction-related transactions and litigation, primarily for subcontractors and owners, with strength in mechanics' lien and surety bond litigation.

The Clients: Engineering companies, project owners, and developers form part of the firm's clientele. The group also acts for Dunnet Bay Construction; Air Dynamics; Thorne Associates and Luhr Bros.

Much Shelist Freed Denenberg Ament & Rubenstein, PC
The Firm: This well-recognized firm filters a small but respected strong construction group through a sound commercial litigation funnel. The team of four lawyers earned widespread recognition for its representation of owners and lenders. In addition to substantial mechanics' lien, foreclosure and construction defect cases, the group also *"inspired confidence"* for niche expertise in title insurance defense, acting for a title insurer in a key insurance coverage case. The team also defended a general contractor and its surety against a claim on a federal construction project involving a bond posted under the Miller Act.

The Lawyers: The transactional practice is largely the preserve of the *"particularly sharp and experienced"* **Stephen Kikoler**, whose *"overwhelming rainmaking and business generation skills"* greatly boost the firm's standing. The *"efficient, bright and conscientious"* Kikoler represents the National Demolition Association. **Jim Dash** earned plaudits for an *"in the trenches"* practice that consisted of real estate-related litigation, with an emphasis on construction. This included mechanic's lien claims, as well as title insurance defense work.

The Clients: Brandenburg Industrial Service; DiPaulo Construction; Osman Construction; Tires 'N Tracks; Commonwealth Land Title Insurance; Lawyers Title Insurance and Ticor Title Insurance.

Ogletree, Deakins, Nash, Smoak & Stewart, PC
See firm details p.638

The Firm: Although the firm's merger with Haynsworth Baldwin enhanced this firm's national profile in labor and employment, the construction expertise of the Chicago office's

"highly qualified lawyers" was not to be overlooked. The firm's natural expertise and vast resources boost its construction labor specialists, while the team also earned top marks for its litigation and construction claims practice.

The Lawyers: Considered *"very much in that next generation,"* **Randy Ruff** (see p.749) acts for general contractors and some owners and he has been involved in litigation surrounding the failure of a power generator in Pittsburgh, the failure of roof trusses at a public school, concrete failures at a roof-top parking structure, and a number of delay and disruption events. Observers believed the group to have been strengthened by the arrival of **Margery Newman** (see p.744) from Bell Boyd & Lloyd. The former corporate counsel to the Federation of Women Contractors represents clients in litigation and arbitration relating to the construction industry.

The Clients: Pepper Construction; McShane Construction; Boller Construction; Novak Construction; Capitol Construction; Graycor and Nationwide Fixture Installations.

Sabo & Zahn
The Firm: Bringing the experience of licensed architects to the table, this *"much smaller but smart"* boutique earned market commendation for a practice representing architects, owners and a number of contractors. Considered a *"definite referral for specific construction matters,"* the three-lawyer team boasted a niche within a niche representing owners and architects in copyright disputes over drawings and plans. Despite their size limitations, they offer *"high-quality work"* to design professionals.

The Lawyers: Interviewees recognize the experience of licensed architects and attorneys Werner Sabo and James Zahn, the firm's key players, who focus on litigation and transactions and have been working on a copyright infringement case for an architect in the British Virgin Islands.

The Clients: Architects, owners, contractors, construction managers, engineers and consultants to the construction industry are part of the group's clientele.

Sachnoff & Weaver LTD
The Firm: This small solid team of construction experts enters the tables this year. It is admired by market commentators for its understanding and resolution of litigation, including construction claims, defects, delay, mold and indoor air quality. The team also addressed insurance coverage issues on behalf of insurance policy holders in the construction industry.

The Lawyers: Group chair **Cliff Shapiro** enters the tables, and is considered *"very much a player"* as well as a real force in the niche area of construction insurance coverage litigation. He has defended owners sued for $6 million by a

general contractor for delay and other claims arising out of the construction and conversion of several structures.

The Clients: Owners, developers and contractors form a large part of the team's clientele.

Other Notable Practitioners

Perkins Coie's LLP highly regarded **Alexandra Cole** joins the rankings, acknowledged as a *"very fine and smart transactional lawyer"* in both real estate and construction. The former head of real

estate at Altheimer & Gray joined in 2003 and now chairs the real estate and land use practice. In addition to the *"holistic and broad"* construction advice offered to clients, such as significant design build firms, she also represents hotel owners in the acquisition, sale and refinancing of their properties as well as corporate real estate. Wildman Harrolds Allen & Dixon **Eric Singer** joins the tables, admired by commentators for being a *"top-flight construction lawyer,"* representing a range of parties, particularly

architects, contractors and subcontractors. The chair of the construction group at Jenkens & Gilchrist, **Charlie Lewis** was admired for his experience, skill set and workload, including national and international construction and alternative dispute resolution. He represents general contractors, construction managers, owners, architects and engineers, design builders, subcontractors, and material suppliers in transactional and litigation matters.

CORPORATE/M&A & PRIVATE EQUITY

Illinois
Leading firms
(Corporate/M&A & Private Equity)

1	**KIRKLAND & ELLIS LLP** *Chicago*
	MAYER, BROWN, ROWE & MAW LLP *Chicago*
	SIDLEY AUSTIN BROWN & WOOD LLP *Chicago*
	SKADDEN, ARPS, SLATE, MEAGHER *Chicago*
2	**KATTEN MUCHIN ZAVIS ROSENMAN** *Chicago*
	LATHAM & WATKINS LLP *Chicago*
	WINSTON & STRAWN LLP *Chicago*
3	**JENNER & BLOCK LLP** *Chicago*
	MCDERMOTT WILL & EMERY *Chicago*
	SONNENSCHEIN NATH & ROSENTHAL *Chicago*
4	**BAKER & MCKENZIE** *Chicago*
	JONES DAY *Chicago*
	SCHIFF HARDIN LLP *Chicago*
5	**BELL, BOYD & LLOYD LLC** *Chicago*
	GARDNER CARTON & DOUGLAS LLP *Chicago*
	SACHNOFF & WEAVER LTD *Chicago*

Firms are listed alphabetically in each band.

Band 1

Kirkland & Ellis LLP

See firm details p.770

The Firm: While the Chicago office reigns supreme for a private equity practice unanimously recognized as *"second to none,"* strength in corporate finance, M&A and public company matters is also in evidence. Clients told researchers the attorneys *"give high-quality advice and high-quality service across the board."* Housing approximately 500 lawyers, Chicago remains the largest of the firm's offices. However, the firm is not one to rest on its laurels; 2003 saw the opening of a 40-attorney office in San Francisco.

The Lawyers: According to clients, the firm is *"full of stellar lawyers."* **Jack Levin** (see p.737) remains *"a legend in his own time."* Known far and wide as the practice's *"guru,"* Levin is revered among interviewees as *"the godfather of venture capital in the Midwest."* He acted in First Data's acquisition of Concord EFS and recently worked on numerous acquisitions and fund formations

for Madison Dearborn, Willis Stein, Code Hennessy & Simmons, GTCR Golder Rauner and other private equity funds. **Kevin Evanich** (see p.726) attracts admiration from rivals who hold him up to be *"at the top of his game."* Private equity work forms most of his practice. Evanich represented Code Hennessy & Simmons in its acquisition of AMF Bowling Worldwide and in the going-private transaction of Gundle, a manufacturer of landfill liners. He also represented AMF Bowling Worldwide in the sale of its UK bowling business. *"Responsive, practical and extraordinarily knowledgeable"* **Carter Emerson**'s (see p.726) corporate practice goes from strength to strength. He continues to represent Exide on corporate matters following its exit from bankruptcy and is advising Terra Industries on corporate and M&A matters related to its acquisition from bankruptcy of Mississippi Chemical. As a founding partner of the San Francisco office and *"a strong advocate for negotiating deals,"* **Jeffrey Hammes** (see p.731) divides his time between Illinois and California, catering to a client list that spans the East and West coasts. Sample work includes acting for Golden Gate Capital on its LBO of Leiner Health Products for $650 million. He also advised Bain Capital on its acquisition of $200 million of WorldCom bonds in connection with the restructuring of WorldCom (now called MCI). *"Exceptional"* **Scott Falk**'s (see p.726) *"experience is considerable for someone at his point in his career,"* according to clients. He has made his mark as *"someone who is more than a technical analyst because his business skills are very well developed."* Falk has recently been involved in the closing of the Concord EFS merger with First Data and in settling antitrust litigation brought by the DOJ. He also handled various asset divestitures and securities transactions for United Airlines. *"The iron fist in the velvet glove,"* **Sandy Perl** (see p.745) is a *"great negotiator who knows how to make transactions happen."* Recurring feedback from clients was that Perl *"truly cares about the whole transaction and the client's interests rather than just the outcome."* He advised American Capital Strategies on its purchase of the Kester division from

Northrop Grumman, and also on its purchase of nSpired Natural Foods. Perl also acted for Liberte Investors (now known as First Acceptance) in its acquisition of USAuto Holdings, a deal which was financed in part through a public rights offering. Widely respected as *"one of the premier private equity lawyers for fund formation,"* **Bruce Ettelson** (see p.726) has *"extraordinary technical competency"* and *"really understands the market."* He advises a glittering array of clients including Vestar Capital Partners, Madison Dearborn Partners and Swander Pace Capital. Representative work includes acting for Madison Dearborn Partners in Fund V, which is likely to be targeting over $4 billion. He has also acted for the management team of Soros on its private equity spinout, likely to close in the first quarter of 2005. William Kirsch has left the firm to become president and CEO of Conseco.

The Clients: The firm has attracted such new clients as Paul Capital Partners and Parthenon Capital. Other clients include: Concord EFS; Madison Dearborn Partners; GTCR; Adams Street Partners; Pfingsten Partners; Goense Bounds; Thoma Cressey Equity Partners; Exide; New Zealand Telecom; William Blair & Company; American Capital Strategies; Kraft; BainCapital and Thayer Capital.

Mayer, Brown, Rowe & Maw LLP

See firm details p.771

The Firm: This is *"one of the premier law firms in the USA"* according to clients, who told researchers that *"the big attraction of the Chicago office is that you get a similar product to that of a New York office at lesser cost."* This, coupled with *"strength across the board – you get partners who are at the top of their field and then a broad and deep team of associates to back it up,"* makes for a *"very fine firm."* The firm benefits from an extensive international reach and counsels a stellar client list which includes such giants as Abbott Laboratories, Dow Chemical, ACE and TransCanada.

The Lawyers: **Robert Helman** (see p.732) continues to attract accolades as *"hugely prominent – he has always been a business generator*

Illinois
Leading individuals (Corporate/M&A)

Senior Statesman

HELMAN Robert *Mayer Brown*, Chicago
LEVIN Jack *Kirkland & Ellis*, Chicago

[1] COLE Thomas *Sidley Austin*, Chicago
LOWINGER Frederick *Sidley Austin*, Chicago
MULANEY Jr Charles *Skadden Arps*, Chicago
WALL Robert *Winston & Strawn*, Chicago
WANDER Herbert *Katten Muchin*, Chicago

[2] DAVIS Scott *Mayer Brown*, Chicago
EVANICH Kevin *Kirkland & Ellis*, Chicago
GERSTEIN Mark *Latham & Watkins*, Chicago
KUNKEL William *Skadden Arps*, Chicago
LUBIN Donald *Sonnenschein Nath*, Chicago
SHEPRO Richard *Mayer Brown*, Chicago
THOMAS Frederick *Mayer Brown*, Chicago

[3] CULLEN Gary *Skadden Arps*, Chicago
EMERSON Carter *Kirkland & Ellis*, Chicago
FALK R Scott *Kirkland & Ellis*, Chicago
JUNEWICZ James *Mayer Brown*, Chicago
OSBORNE Robert *Jenner & Block*, Chicago
QASIM Imad *Sidley Austin*, Chicago
SCHREIBER Rodd *Skadden Arps*, Chicago

[4] AIZENSTEIN Neal *Sonnenschein Nath*, Chicago
BEST Edward *Mayer Brown*, Chicago
CHOI Paul *Sidley Austin*, Chicago
FRIEDLI Helen *McDermott Will*, Chicago
FROY Michael *Sonnenschein Nath*, Chicago
GOODMAN Stuart *Schiff Hardin*, Chicago
HAHN Arthur *Katten Muchin*, Chicago
HAMMES Jeffrey *Kirkland & Ellis*, Chicago
KITSLAAR Libby *Jones Day*, Chicago
MACCARTHY John *Winston & Strawn*, Chicago
MEADOWS Stanley *McDermott Will*, Chicago
NAPOLITANO Steven *Katten Muchin*, Chicago
SCHNEIDMAN Edward *Mayer Brown*, Chicago
THEISS Paul *Mayer Brown*, Chicago
TOTH Bruce *Winston & Strawn*, Chicago

Up-and-coming individuals

GROMACKI Joseph *Jenner & Block*, Chicago
GUPTA Shilpi *Skadden Arps*, Chicago

Individuals are listed alphabetically in each band.

edge and a common-sense approach to getting the deal done," say clients. Much of his work has international components, where, observers note, Shepro displays "*keen cross-cultural understanding.*" He acted for Molex on its two-year negotiation to acquire Connecteurs Cinch from SNECMA, a large French company partly owned by the French government. The transaction involved electrical supply and connector businesses based in France, Germany, India, Portugal, China and Brazil and closed in April 2004. Shepro has also been active in advising banks and international insurance and reinsurance companies and their boards of directors on major transactions and industry-specific issues. "*A real gentleman,*" **Frederick Thomas** (see p.755) garnered enthusiastic praise from clients, who benefit from his "*seasoned, well-balanced and business-savvy advice.*" Interviewees told researchers, "*He listens to your concerns and always has your best interests at heart.*" He represented Capital One Financial in its recently announced $191 million acquisition of Onyx Acceptance, a public company in the auto loan business. He also acted for ONDEO Nalco and Suez in the sale of Ondeo Nalco to the Blackstone Group, Apollo Management and GS Capital Partners for $4.2 billion. In addition to his corporate work, **James Junewicz** (see p.734) has lately been involved in several financings, in particular high-yield securities and IPOs. Several years' experience at the SEC gives him an "*intimate knowledge of the SEC process.*" Indeed, one client told researchers, "*I don't know a better SEC lawyer than James – he is a great lawyer who helps you achieve your goals.*" Sample matters include representing Wachovia Capital Markets in an offering of $120 million of high-yield debt securities by Coleman Cable. Singled out for his expertise in corporate matters in the real estate sector, **Edward Schneidman** (see p.750) earns praise from interviewees as a "*client-focused*" attorney who "*brings both a legal and a business perspective to problem solving.*" **Paul Theiss**'s (see p.755) practice spans corporate and securities. He has notable industry expertise in such areas as telecommunications and gaming and represented Isle of Capri Casinos in connection with its winning bid of $518 million in the auction for Emerald Casino, owner of the tenth Illinois gaming license. The deal is still pending. Elsewhere he advised Dobson Cellular Systems in connection with its offering and sale of $825 million of high-yield debt securities. **Edward Best**'s (see p.718) "*extremely quick mind*" makes him a popular figure among lawyers and clients alike. "*He is never stumped by a question,*" researchers were told. His practice has an emphasis on financial institutions and is approximately two-thirds capital markets oriented and one-third M&A. He represented Assured Guaranty, a Bermuda-based financial guaranty company, in its $880 million IPO. Best

also advised Merrill Lynch on several acquisitions of futures and options businesses. **Herbert Krueger**'s (see p.736) practice encompasses specialties in such areas as pension plan investments, executive compensation, ERISA and employee benefit plans. Clients value his "*thorough and balanced advice*" and extol his "*considerable expertise*" in relation to real estate fund transactions. He often represents fund sponsors and large investors in institutional private investment funds. A "*smart, technically proficient lawyer,*" **John Noell** (see p.744) "*knows the ins and outs of the corporate world.*" He advised Lowe Hospitality Investment Partners on a $250 million fund formed to make hotel investments and RLJ Capital Partners on a $220 million plus hotel investment fund.

The Clients: Abbott Laboratories; Dow Chemical; TransCanada; Molex; GATX; REFCO Group; Marconi; Devon Energy; George Weston; ACE; Illinois Tool Works; The Northern Trust Company; Mesirow Financial; Everest Re Group; Molex; JC Robinson Seeds; Capital One Financial; Accenture; Hubbard One; Yum! Brands; Burlington North Santa Fe; Isle of Capri Casinos; Sherritt International; Ameritrade Holding and ProLogis.

Sidley Austin Brown & Wood LLP
See firm details p.778

The Firm: Praise flooded in for this US giant: It is "*a firm with a great reputation and bench depth – its resources are fantastic.*" Interviewees consistently praised the team's "*top-quality work*" and range of expertise. The past year has seen the Chicago lawyers acting in an impressive array of multibillion-dollar deals. These include First Data's $6.9 billion merger with Concord EFS and GE Commercial Finance's $5.4 billion acquisition of Transamerica's commercial finance business and assumption of $3.4 billion of debt. Private equity has also been a source of significant work with the team attracting work from big names such as Madison Dearborn Partners.

The Lawyers: "*A true scholar of corporate and securities law,*" **Thomas Cole** (see p.722) is admired far and wide for his experience and depth of knowledge. A growing part of his practice involves advising boards and their committees on corporate governance matters, mostly in times of crisis. Rivals told researchers "*boards love him – he is highly logical and explains things well,*" while clients extolled his "*responsiveness*" and "*calm, excellent judgment in a crisis.*" He maintains a significant practice alongside the management responsibilities connected with his position as chairman of the firm's executive committee. Cole's recent work includes advising IMC Global in its acquisition of Cargill's fertilizer business (with resulting change in control of IMC Global) and counseling RR Donnelley & Sons on its $2.8 billion acquisition of Moore

and is extremely well respected in the legal and business community." He advised Abbott Laboratories in connection with the spin-off of its core hospital products business into Hospira. He also counsels such names as ACE and GATX. Clients were also quick to praise "*intellectual*" **Scott Davis** (see p.724) for an "*outstanding depth of knowledge in securities and corporate law.*" His "*ability to get everybody back on track*" in deal negotiations was also noted by interviewees. As well as acting for Abbott Laboratories in the aforementioned spin-off, he represented JC Robinson Seeds, the largest of the Golden Harvest Seeds companies, in the sale of a 90% interest in those companies to Syngenta Crop Protection for approximately $180 million. "*Bright and quick on his feet,*" **Richard Shepro** (see p.751) has an "*outstanding depth of knowl-*

Illinois
Leading individuals (Private Equity)

Senior Statesman

LEVIN Jack *Kirkland & Ellis*, Chicago

[1] EVANICH Kevin *Kirkland & Ellis*, Chicago

[2] BALLIS Jon *Sidley Austin*, Chicago

BRADLEY Craig *Katten Muchin*, Chicago

GOLDBLATT Stanford *Winston & Strawn*, Chicago

HAMMES Jeffrey *Kirkland & Ellis*, Chicago

KRUPP Peter *Skadden Arps*, Chicago

NAPOLITANO Steven *Katten Muchin*, Chicago

PERL Sanford *Kirkland & Ellis*, Chicago

[3] BALLANTINE Frank *Sachnoff & Weaver*, Chicago

BRYANT Timothy *McDermott Will*, Chicago

DEBEERS Kimberly *Skadden Arps*, Chicago

GERSTEIN Mark *Latham & Watkins*, Chicago

KRUEGER Herbert *Mayer Brown*, Chicago

MILLER Kenneth *Katten Muchin*, Chicago

NOELL John *Mayer Brown*, Chicago

PECK S Michael *Schiff Hardin*, Chicago

ROSENTHAL Michael *Sonnenschein Nath*, Chicago

WEAVER William *Sachnoff & Weaver*, Chicago

WEINBERG Walter *Katten Muchin*, Chicago

Leading individuals
(Private Equity: Fund Formation)

[1] ETTELSON Bruce *Kirkland & Ellis*, Chicago

Individuals are listed alphabetically in each band.

Wallace. "*Brilliant, precise and practical*" **Frederick Lowinger** (see p.738) is "*extremely creative in coming up with solutions.*" He acted in First Data's acquisition of Concord EFS and in the merger of RR Donnelley & Sons with Moore Wallace. Clients were quick to praise **Imad Qasim**'s (see p.747) "*great business judgment and practical approach to problem solving.*" Sample matters include representing Tellabs in its pending acquisition of Advanced Fibre Communications. "*Smart and levelheaded,*" Qasim acted for Equity Group Investments in a complex equity investment in Danielson Holding, a public company, which used the proceeds in connection with acquiring Covanta Energy, another public company, out of bankruptcy. "*A smart, careful and effective negotiator,*" **Paul Choi** (see p.722) elicited further commendation from clients for his "*ability to apply a very complicated area of law to obtain a client-friendly and legally compliant resolution.*" As well as acting in the First Data/Concord EFS merger, he also completed an IPO for Ardent Health Services. "*All-star*" **Jon Ballis** (see p.717) received resounding praise from peers and clients alike. Rivals predict a rosy future for his practice, telling researchers "*he is fabulous. We will hear more and more about him; he is very bright and has a lot of class.*" Private equity forms the bulk of his practice and sample work includes representing Svoboda, Collins in two recent LBOs, one for Coffee Bean International and the other for Cigars International. He also acted for The Pritzker Group as

equity sponsor in the LBO of AmSafe and its sister company Bridport.

The Clients: Aon; First Data; GE; Exelon; Rewards Network; Kimberly-Clark; Tellabs; Brunswick; Kraft Foods; Alberto-Culver; Smith & Nephew; Telephone & Data Systems; RR Donnelley & Sons; Sara Lee; IMC Global; Maytag; Baxter; CDW; ServiceMaster; Tribune Company; Starwoods; Pritzker Group; BWAY and Looking Glass Networks.

Skadden, Arps, Slate, Meagher & Flom LLP & Affiliates
See firm details p.1372

The Firm: The firm "*stands out from the others across the country, and not least in Chicago,*" clients told researchers. The Illinois team of this "*household name*" firm earns plaudits as a "*creative, responsive and practical*" group which combines "*business sense and top-level legal expertise.*" Market commentators regularly highlighted the practice's presence in top deals and reputation for "*quality work, especially in the public company realm.*" Clients also praised the firm's "*seamless network*" which promotes cooperation between the firm's many US and global offices on big-ticket corporate transactions.

The Lawyers: "*One of the best M&A lawyers around,*" **Charles Mulaney** (see p.743) draws accolades from clients and peers alike. "*Tough, smart and cordial,*" he is often to be seen on major deals such as his recent representation of Abbott Laboratories in its acquisition of TheraSense, reportedly valued at $1.2 billion. Mulaney also acted for Wisconsin Energy in the sale of its WICOR Industries unit to Pentair. Clients admire **William Kunkel**'s (see p.736) "*ability to grasp and achieve corporate goals,*" a talent that enables him to "*quickly gain the confidence of clients and board members.*" He advised American Equity in connection with its IPO of common stock and trust preferred offerings. Another highlight was his representation of Wm. Wrigley Jr. in its acquisition for approximately $260 million of Joyco Group confectionary businesses from Agrolimen, a privately held Spanish conglomerate. Noted for his "*confident client management,*" **Gary Cullen** (see p.724) earns praise for his pragmatic, straightforward advice. "*He gives it to you straight,*" say clients. Active on a range of M&A, offerings and corporate governance matters, Cullen recently advised Russian company SeverStal Group on the $286 million purchase of assets of Michigan-based Rural Cellular out of Chapter 11. He has also acted for Rural Cellular in its issuance of $510 million of high-yield bonds. "*Personable*" **Rodd Schreiber** (see p.751) is said to be both "*practical and innovative*" in deal-making. "*He understands the culture of our company,*" clients told researchers. He advised Playboy Enterprises on a $115 million senior secured note offering and acted for Chicago Mercantile Exchange

Holdings in connection with the restructuring of its holding company, IPO and follow-on offerings. "*Technically excellent*" **Peter Krupp** (see p.736) commands respect for his "*calm, non-adversarial approach.*" Much of his workload is in private equity. Recent transactions include acting for Lake Capital in its acquisitions of Storecast Merchandising and the Dutko Group. Krupp also advised Danielson Holding on the purchase of Covanta Energy. Newly appointed partner **Kimberly deBeers** (see p.724) leapt on to the ranking tables following enthusiastic endorsement of her "*determined*" negotiating style. "*She constantly searches for compromises in difficult situations,*" researchers heard. She represented Solo Cup in connection with Vestar Capital Partners' $240 million equity investment in the company. She also advised Lake Capital on the acquisition of various portfolio companies. "*Forward-thinking*" associate **Shilpi Gupta** (see p.731) also joined this year's table after clients singled him out as "*very, very hard-working – he will bend over backwards to help you achieve your goals.*"

The Clients: Wm. Wrigley Jr.; Packaging Dynamics; Abbott Laboratories; Solo Cup; OXO International; SeverStal Group; American Equity; Wisconsin Energy; Sears Roebuck; Huron Consulting Group; Safety-Kleen; Chicago Mercantile Exchange Holdings; Danielson Holding; Merrill Lynch; Dynal Biotech; Playboy Enterprises and Lake Capital.

Band 2

Katten Muchin Zavis Rosenman
See firm details p.769

The Firm: Market commentators say this is "*a quality practice with energy and dynamism.*" While peers highlighted the group's strength in private equity and venture capital, clients commended attorneys' competence across a variety of corporate matters. "*The quality of people, their work and their ability to get the deal done are all excellent,*" explained one. Twenty-eight partners in Chicago offer expertise in such areas as securities, M&A and related senior and subordinated financing. The group advises private equity funds at all stages of investment from early-stage fund formation to LBOs. Hedge fund matters have been an area of increasing significance for the firm. Chicago-based attorneys work with the firm's New York office in helping structure innovative hedge fund products for various banks and Wall Street brokerage firms.

The Lawyers: "*An extremely well-versed counselor who sees the big picture,*" **Herb Wander** (see p.757) was applauded by clients as "*one of the most respected people around for securities; if you want any answers in securities, Herb is your guy.*" Also highly esteemed for his knowledge of corporate governance, Wander recently represented a number of audit committees carrying out intensive investigations. In M&A, he acted for Butler Manufacturing in its $250 million cash sale to Australian steel company, BlueScope Steel. He also advised Cuno on the acquisition of WTC Industries. Peers singled out chairman of the firm's national financial services practice **Arthur Hahn** (see p.731) as *"a fine lawyer with specialized knowledge of the financial services sector."* Recent work includes counseling LIFFE Exchange on a contract allowing the Chicago Board of Trade to use the LIFFE system for its electronic trading. He also acted for LCH.Clearnet in obtaining a license to be a US derivatives clearing organization. Clients describe **Craig Bradley** (see p.720) as *"exceptionally good in board meetings – CEOs tend to be very comfortable with him".* Bradley represents a number of technology and emerging growth companies, as well as venture capital firms investing in these industries. He recently advised Mobitrac in connection with venture capital funding from USVP and Frazier Technology Ventures. National cochair of the private equity practice group **Steven Napolitano** (see p.743) was lauded as a *"terrific negotiator"* who *"immerses himself in the transaction."* He has advised Wind Point Partners on several transactions, including the sale of Ames True Temper and its affiliates to an entity formed by New York-based private equity firm Castle Harlan. As well as handling private equity, Napolitano handles traditional corporate matters. He recently acted for NewBiotics in its merger with Celmed BioSciences. His fellow national cochair of the firm's private equity practice group, **Kenneth Miller** (see p.742), represents both companies and funds. Rivals praised him as *"steady and easy to deal with,"* while clients deemed him a *"skilled market technician."* Recent months have seen him active on three private equity restructurings, acting on behalf of both portfolio companies and investors. Miller also counseled Liberty Group Publishing on a newspaper exchange with Lee Enterprises. Chairman of the Chicago corporate group **Walter Weinberg** (see p.758) *"knows the ins and outs of"* private equity and venture capital transactions. *"He can close a deal like no one I've ever seen,"* said one client.

The Clients: Butler Manufacturing; Lazy Days RV Center; Ovation Pharmaceuticals; William Blair & Company; Wind Point Partners; Arbor Private Investment; Sterling Partners; Frontenac; Madison Capital Partners; Concentric Equity Partners; Mobitrac; Liberty Group; CUNO; LIFFE Exchange and LCH.Clearnet.

Latham & Watkins LLP

The Firm: This *"energetic and user-friendly"* team *"inspires confidence"* among clients and peers alike. Approximately 35 *"technically savvy"* attorneys work within the Chicago office's corporate department, handling an extensive range of work. A highly successful equities and high-

yield practice sits alongside top-notch public and private M&A capabilities. Recent work includes acting for William Blair & Company as underwriters to Standard Parking in the latter's IPO of $5 million shares of common stock. The team also represented Safeco in the $1.35 billion sale of its life and investments operations to a group of investors led by White Mountains Insurance Group and Berkshire Hathaway. The firm is often to be seen in technology transactions, representing such clients as Orbitz and CMGI. A well-integrated US and global network further enhances its reach.

The Lawyers: M&A global cochair **Mark Gerstein** attracted widespread recommendation among interviewees as a *"personable and engaging"* attorney who *"knows what he's doing."* Clients told researchers, *"He holds his own, no matter who is across the table. You will never get 'outlawyered' with Mark on your side."* Gerstein represented online travel agency Orbitz in its $1.2 billion acquisition by Cendant and also advised First Health Group on its acquisition by Coventry Healthcare.

The Clients: First Health Group; Orbitz; Koch Industries; Safeco; Hyatt; CMGI; Nicor; Bass Pro; Glencoe Capital; William Blair & Company; Deutsche Bank Securities and CSFB.

Winston & Strawn LLP

See firm details p.780

The Firm: Headquartered in Chicago, this *"top-notch"* firm houses an impressive corporate practice visible *"in most of the deals taking place in Illinois."* Historically strong in traditional M&A and securities, the practice has recently increased its focus on private equity transactions. A sizable number of partners advise sponsors and junior capital providers on matters such as fund formation and private placements. The firm also continues to build on its presence on the East and West coasts and in Europe.

The Lawyers: Clients express confidence in **Robert Wall**'s (see p.757) depth of experience in corporate and securities law: *"Very little arises that he hasn't dealt with."* Wall *"doesn't sit on the fence; he always gives you an answer."* He advised the special committee of Orbitz in connection with its $1.25 billion cash merger with Cendant and completed a $450 million restructuring for AirGate PCS involving an exchange of debt for equity. A new entrant to this year's tables, **John MacCarthy** (see p.739) drew positive feedback from peers as a *"seasoned transactional lawyer"* and a *"tough but fair negotiator."* Clients were similarly enthusiastic, praising his *"hands-on, creative"* approach. *"He's absolutely up there with a New York lawyer,"* said one client. MacCarthy regularly counsels Lear on M&A and securities matters, most recently on a $400 million 144A offering of senior notes. He also represented Fortune Brands in its purchase of Therma-Tru. As chairman of the corporate department, he

divides his time between fee-earning and management. **Bruce Toth** specializes in securities and M&A and acted for Heritage Propane in its merger with Energy Transfer. He also counseled Northland in the sale of its gas distribution subsidiary to management. **Stanford Goldblatt** garnered accolades as a *"highly skilled, business-savvy attorney,"* particularly valued for his *"calming influence"* in transactions. Even rivals acknowledge him to be *"one of the deans of the practice."* His practice focuses on private equity transactions. Goldblatt has handled multiple acquisitions for a Chicago area manufacturing company.

The Clients: Lear; Fortune Brands; AirGate PCS; Morgan Stanley; Heritage Propane; Stark Investments; Booth Creek; Keystone Capital and Deutsche Bank.

Band 3

Jenner & Block LLP

See firm details p.768

The Firm: The team is seen to be *"making headway"* in the market following several lateral hires to the firm's corporate department in recent years. Seventeen corporate partners in Illinois handle a range of matters, predominantly M&A, securities and finance. The past few years have also seen a growth in the group's private equity workload. A varied client list includes Fortune 500, midmarket and emerging companies and private equity and venture capital houses as well as financial institutions. The group is well known for its representation of GM.

The Lawyers: Clients warmly recommended **Robert Osborne** (see p.745) as a *"capable and effective negotiator,"* expressing confidence in his ability to *"put a great team together."* Rivals described him as *"unflappable."* He advised General Dynamics on its $1.5 billion acquisition of publicly traded Veridian and represented Sears Roebuck in its $600 million asset acquisition from Kmart. **Joseph Gromacki** (see p.731) was also commended by clients. The past year has seen him counseling GM in its sale of $911 million of News Corporation-preferred American depositary shares in an underwritten public offering.

The Clients: General Dynamics; Chicago Board of Trade; GM and Sears Roebuck.

McDermott Will & Emery

See firm details p.773

The Firm: Noted strength in tax and benefits law complements the firm's broad-based corporate capabilities, making this an attractive one-stop-shop for clients. A well-integrated network of offices in the USA and Europe enhances the team's reach. While traditional corporate and M&A instructions form the bulk of the practice's workload, private equity and cross-border matters have proved areas of growth. Sample work includes advising JW Childs Equity Partners III in its acquisition of the Sunny Delight and Punica beverage businesses' operations in Europe and the USA from Procter & Gamble. The legal team included lawyers from some of the firm's international offices, such as Dusseldorf and London. A Chicago-based team of about 20 private equity lawyers caters to a national client base, featuring both companies and funds.

The Lawyers: Commended for her "*grasp of details and transaction structures,*" **Helen Friedli** (see p.728) "*finds ways to get deals done to the benefit of both parties,*" clients told researchers. She represented the Heico Companies in the purchase of the businesses of Ivaco Rolling Mills and Ifastgroupe and Company. Rivals singled out **Stanley Meadows** (see p.741) as someone who "*really understands business and risk,*" while clients spoke highly of his "*smart, tough*" negotiating style. His wide-ranging practice has recently had him acting on several deals for companies investing in China either through direct purchases or joint ventures. A "*terrific people person,*" **Timothy Bryant** (see p.721) earns high marks from rival lawyers as a "*client-responsive*" attorney. Clients add, "*He fights your corner for you.*" Active on a full range of private equity and venture capital matters, Bryant recently advised Dixon Midland in the sale of Tech Lighting to the Harbour Group. He also represented the investment banking firm Robert W. Baird & Co. in the IPO of common stock of Hudson Highland Group.

The Clients: Heico Companies; Tootsie Roll Industries; Actuant; MK Capital; First Analysis; Signature Capital; Dixon Midland; JW Childs Equity Partners III; Glencoe Capital and Robert W. Baird & Co.

Sonnenschein Nath & Rosenthal LLP
See firm details p.779

The Firm: The firm boasts an impressive client roster, for which it handles a full range of corporate work. In addition to handling a recent surge in M&A and financing work, this "*excellent*" team of lawyers has seen significant growth in outsourcing matters. The practice has a continuing emphasis on venture capital and private equity, where it represents both funds and portfolio companies. The group also advises funds and limited partners on fund formation. Sample work includes representing ABN AMRO Asset Management in acquisitions and dispositions and advising C-SAM on a variety of capital-raising activities.

The Lawyers: Highly respected in the field, **Donald Lubin** (see p.738) maintains a loyal client following for his considerable transactional experience. He has advised Experian Holdings in various corporate matters and in the acquisition of private companies with spe-

cialized marketing technology platforms. **Neal Aizenstein** (see p.716) is also regarded as a key member of the team. He acted for Salton in the refinancing of its $270 million credit facility. **Michael Froy** (see p.728), chair of the firm's corporate and securities practice, brings a "*balanced business and legal approach*" to transactions, say clients. "*He doesn't get bogged down with minutiae.*" His practice covers a wide range of corporate, commercial and securities matters. His extensive list of clients includes Molex and Juno Lighting. He represented William Blair & Company as financial adviser to JM Smucker in its $840 million acquisition of International Multifoods. "*Smart and insightful*" **Michael Rosenthal** (see p.749) impresses rivals with his ability to "*see 360 degrees*" in matters involving private equity and venture capital. He acted for William Blair Capital Partners in the recapitalization of Clear Communications and represented an investor group led by ARCH Development Partners in its investment in Mobitrac.

The Clients: Goldman Sachs; Molex; Sara Lee; McDonald's; Willis Stein & Partners; William Blair Capital Partners; ARCH Development Partners; ABN AMRO Asset Management; Duchossois Technology Partners; White Pines Ventures and C-SAM.

Band 4

Baker & McKenzie
See firm details p.761

The Firm: Interviewees repeatedly cited the firm's international reach as a major draw for clients. "*I have confidence that no matter where I am in the world, if I need top-notch corporate legal advice, Baker & McKenzie will provide it,*" said one. The Chicago team was specifically praised for its "*outstanding*" work for US and multinational businesses. The corporate group provides a full service in such areas as cross-border and domestic M&A and joint ventures, securities and compliance matters. The team also represents private equity funds, venture capital funds and venture-backed technology companies in acquisitions, dispositions and portfolio company issues. Representative matters include acting for Cash America International on the sale of two European subsidiaries to the Rutland Fund.

The Lawyers: Mark Swords coordinates the firm's Chicago corporate and securities practice group, while Bruce Zivian is the coordinator of the global and North American venture capital and private equity practice groups. The team advised CommScope on the international aspects of its acquisition of Connectivity Solutions from Avaya, a deal involving 40 jurisdictions. It also counseled Abbott Laboratories and Hospira in connection with all non-US matters related to the spin-off of Abbott Laboratories' core hospital products division. The Chicago private equity group recently advised PaR Sys-

tems on the sale of 81% of its capital stock to Westinghouse Electric.

The Clients: Abbott Laboratories; CommScope; Gardner Denver; Eaton; Ashland; Sterling Capital Partners; One Equity Partners; EQT and Allianz.

Jones Day
See firm details p.485

The Firm: A team of "*smart, experienced*" lawyers works closely with the firm's highly respected network of national and international offices. Clients commend it as an "*outstanding, full-service law firm.*" The 16-partner Chicago corporate department maintains a broad practice; members are often seen acting in distressed M&A and bankruptcy-related buyouts as well as energy and public utility M&A. A varied client list numbers some new arrivals among its ranks, including Stanley Works, Ryder System and Freescale Semiconductor. The team recently advised the JM Smucker Company on the acquisition of International Multifoods. It also represented Great Lakes REIT in its acquisition by Aslan Realty Partners II, an affiliate of Transwestern Investment.

The Lawyers: Clients appreciate "*experienced*" **Libby Kitslaar**'s (see p.735) "*realistic approach*" to legal matters. Her "*wisdom and judgment on corporate issues*" were widely applauded. She represented Stanley Works on the purchase of Chicago Steel Tape and certain related assets and affiliated companies, known collectively as CST Berger. Her cross-border work includes advising Stanley Works on the acquisition of Frisco Bay Industries in a negotiated tender offer.

The Clients: Abbott Laboratories; Entergy; JM Smucker; Xcel Energy; Johnson Diversey; DaimlerChrysler; Bridgestone Firestone; OGE Energy; Ryder System; Stanley Works; Freescale Semiconductor and Duchossois Industries.

Schiff Hardin LLP
See firm details p.775

The Firm: This "*excellent team*" enjoys a solid reputation in the market. While the firm is predominantly known for its representation of midmarket companies, a glance at its client and transactions lists also indicates a range of high-quality work for blue-chip public companies. The firm has represented long-standing client Northern Trust in numerous acquisitions of banks, bank holding companies and non-banking businesses, and most recently in its acquisition of Legacy South. Similarly, the firm has a 35-year relationship with Newell Rubbermaid, and recently advised the company on its dispositions of Anchor Glass, and Burnes' picture frames, Mirro's cookware and Little Tykes' commercial playground businesses. Securities exchanges also feature on the client list: the team acted on the Chicago Board Options Exchange joint venture with the Chicago Mercantile

Exchange. The firm is also seen to be making its mark in private equity and venture capital following its 2003 acquisition of practitioners from the former Altheimer & Gray.

The Lawyers: Stuart Goodman (see p.730) is a popular figure in the market. Head of the firm's corporate and securities practice area, he has been the principal outside counsel for Newell Rubbermaid for over 35 years. In private equity, **Sy Peck** (see p.745) was applauded as a *"client-friendly"* lawyer who *"really relishes his relationships with clients."* He advised Code, Hennessy & Simmons and Kranson Holding IV on the sale of the latter to AEA Investors. His team also handled the public offering of Beacon Roofing Supply, formerly a portfolio company of Code, Hennessy & Simmons III.

The Clients: Newell Rubbermaid; NiSource; Kraft Foods North America; Northern Trust; Laidlaw; Dorel Industries; Allied Irish Bank; Code, Hennessy & Simmons; Wintrust Financial; Prism Opportunity Fund; Thompson Street Capital; Prospect Partners; AMSTED Industries; Chicago Board Options Exchange; Chicago Bears Football Club and Chicago Stock Exchange.

Band 5

Bell, Boyd & Lloyd LLC
The Firm: This well-established firm with offices in Chicago and Washington DC was highlighted by interviewees predominantly for its work for Chicago-based and midmarket companies. The practice offers expertise in such areas as corporate and securities, venture capital

and private equity investments and fund formation. The past year has seen the team acting for Boise Cascade (now known as OfficeMax) in the disposition of its forest and paper products businesses and its timberland assets to affiliates of Madison Dearborn Partners.

The Lawyers: Mark McMillan chairs the corporate department.

The Clients: The client list includes Fortune 500 and 100 companies, national and international corporations, midmarket businesses, and private equity and venture funds.

Gardner Carton & Douglas LLP
See firm details p.767
The Firm: This *"attentive and responsive"* team impresses clients with its *"valuable commercial as well as legal input."* The securities and corporate law practice caters to a diverse client list which ranges from local businesses to multinational corporations to Native American tribal governments. Sample work has included acting for SPX in several matters, including the acquisition of the assets of Tiros and purchase of Bill-Jay Machine Tool. While recent months have shown substantial activity for the private placement practice, hedge fund project finance has also been an area of increased emphasis for the group. In addition to experiencing significant growth in 2004 in its Washington DC office, the firm has opened new offices in Milwaukee and Albany.

The Lawyers: David Kay OBE is chairman of the corporate department. In addition to holding US qualifications, Kay is qualified as an English barrister and a member of Hogarth

Chambers in London. Corporate governance is a major part of the practice and the team often represents special independent director committees. Partners Troy Calkins and George McKann have been retained as counsel to the corporate governance committee of the board of directors of Starwood Hotels.

The Clients: SPX; Kendro Laboratory Products; Perrigo and Sola International.

Sachnoff & Weaver LTD
The Firm: The Chicago-based firm numbers some 130 lawyers and was highlighted by market sources for its private equity and venture capital work. Clients range from startup companies to those worth several billion dollars. The team is often seen representing developmental companies and their investors.

The Lawyers: Frank Ballantine attracted praise for his business-counseling skills. *"He understands what it takes to form, structure and grow a venture capital-backed company and investments,"* researchers were told. He also regularly advises on M&A and represents borrowers and lenders in finance transactions. *"Experienced and extremely hard-working,"* William Weaver was warmly recommended by interviewees for his thriving corporate and private equity practice. His varied client list features creative software and information technology companies as well as issuers and underwriters.

The Clients: Clients include private equity and venture capital firms, *"angel"* investors, investment banking houses and corporations.

EMPLOYMENT

Band 1

Seyfarth Shaw LLP
See firm details p.777
The Firm: The view of the labor and employment market in Illinois may be summed up in one phrase: *"There is no one better than Seyfarth Shaw."* The firm's impressive national reach and its *"fabulous spectrum and depth"* were raised again and again during interviews, with clients telling researchers, *"We are impressed with the way they assign lawyers to become subject matter experts; this makes the work quick, complete and cost-effective."* Some 275 labor and employment lawyers are based across the firm's US offices well over 100 of them in Chicago. This massive group handles the full spectrum of labor and employment matters and is well known for its expertise in complex litigation. As one interviewee noted, *"If there is a huge class action lawsuit*

to be defended you can expect that Seyfarth Shaw will be handling it." Competitors acknowledged the firm's formidable presence and proactive approach, observing that *"if the going gets tough, there are excellent lawyers there who can handle tough cases."* The firm's lawyers can advise on any aspect of traditional labor law, but are also at the forefront of cutting-edge employment counseling and litigation. A team of approximately 25 lawyers specializes in employee benefits and executive compensation, advising an outstanding client list that includes such international giants as Motorola and Dow Chemical. The office also boasts a separate group of ERISA litigators, which serves as further evidence of the firm's commitment to the area. It is also much appreciated by clients. As one commented, *"If you can find an attorney who understands ERISA and is also a litigator then you have struck a gold-mine – Seyfarth Shaw has this strength."*

MAINLY DEFENDANT

The Lawyers: Michael Warner was universally acknowledged to be *"one of the top people in employment discrimination litigation,"* with a fantastic reputation for achieving *"great results for great clients."* His vast experience in complex class actions is said to make him, in the words of one client, *"a superstar."* Charles Jackson's profile continues to grow, with interviewees reporting his involvement in *"excellent cases."* He focuses on labor law and employment litigation, and is often involved in class actions and collective actions. He also has considerable experience in employee benefits litigation. Recent cases include Perillo et al v AT&T et al. *"Extremely intelligent and creative"* Joel Kaplan also wins the respect of the market for *"representing clients in big matters."* *"A smart and aggressive litigator,"* he specializes in traditional labor-relations law, and is also known for handling complex employment litigation. Clients spoke highly of

Illinois
Leading firms
(Employment: Mainly Defendant)

1. **SEYFARTH SHAW LLP** *Chicago*
2. **FRANCZEK SULLIVAN** *Chicago*
   LANER, MUCHIN, DOMBROW, BECKER *Chicago*
   VEDDER, PRICE, KAUFMAN & KAMMHOLZ *Chicago*
3. **LITTLER MENDELSON** *Chicago*
   MATKOV SALZMAN MADOFF & GUNN *Chicago*
   MECKLER, BULGER & TILSON *Chicago*
   SCHIFF HARDIN LLP *Chicago*
   WINSTON & STRAWN LLP *Chicago*
4. **BRYAN CAVE LLP** *Chicago*
   JENNER & BLOCK LLP *Chicago*
   JONES DAY *Chicago*
   MAYER, BROWN, ROWE & MAW LLP *Chicago*
   MCDERMOTT WILL & EMERY *Chicago*
   MCGUIREWOODS *Chicago*
   MORGAN, LEWIS & BOCKIUS LLP *Chicago*
   NEAL, GERBER & EISENBERG LLP *Chicago*
   SIDLEY AUSTIN BROWN & WOOD LLP *Chicago*

Leading firms (Employee Benefits & Executive Compensation)

1. **MAYER, BROWN, ROWE & MAW LLP** *Chicago*
   MCDERMOTT WILL & EMERY *Chicago*
   SONNENSCHEIN NATH & ROSENTHAL LLP *Chicago*
2. **GARDNER CARTON & DOUGLAS LLP** *Chicago*
   KIRKLAND & ELLIS LLP *Chicago*
   MCGUIREWOODS LLP *Chicago*
   SEYFARTH SHAW LLP *Chicago*
   SIDLEY AUSTIN BROWN & WOOD LLP *Chicago*
   VEDDER, PRICE, KAUFMAN & KAMMHOLZ *Chicago*

Firms are listed alphabetically in each band.

Philip Miscimarra. As one told researchers, "*He is pragmatic and will seek resolutions that are economically favorable to the company.*" Rivals, meanwhile, applauded him as "*an intellectual who knows the law inside and out.*" His broad labor and employment practice spans employment litigation, collective bargaining, labor arbitrations and administrative proceedings. He also cochairs the firm's business restructuring and transactional employment group. Applauded for his "*good judgment,*" **Thomas Piskorski** was described by commentators as "*a bright and dedicated lawyer who has tremendous respect for his clients and puts their needs first.*" His practice covers the range of labor, employment and employee benefits advice, with recent cases including Gresham v Lumbermens Casualty Insurance Company. Here, summary judgment was awarded in a severance pay claim, in which the plaintiff had sought a six-figure payment under an employment security agreement. Commentators were also quick to praise **Kenneth Dolin** for his expertise in labor-related matters, while **Ellen McLaughlin**'s "*high intellect*" and "*tremendous common sense*" make her popular with sources of all kinds. Clients told

researchers, "*Her advice is practical, easy to understand and always right.*" She counsels on a full range of employment law matters. **Camille Olson** is "*a national expert in all areas of labor and employment law, particularly wage and hour.*" Clients put their faith in her, and rely on her "*phenomenal knowledge and practical application of the law to business needs.*" They also said that she projects "*a deep sense of caring about her clients.*" The national chair of the firm's labor and employment group, she often acts in major class action litigation and is a force in jury trials. For example, she recently acted as lead defense counsel for a subsidiary of Dial in a class action alleging Title VII violations in its pre-employment testing practices as applied to female applicants. **John Powers** was also recommended to researchers as a key member of the team. He handles a variety of labor and employment law matters and is outside counsel to a range of employers across the USA.

The Clients: Dial; Belo; Dow Chemical; Motorola; Caterpillar; PACTIV; Abbott Laboratories; Comcast Cable Communications; UAL; Merck & Co; City of New York; Federal-Mogul; Lucent and Beaulieu.

Sonnenschein Nath & Rosenthal LLP
See firm details p.779

The Firm: For most interviewees, this was among the first names to come to mind when asked for the most prominent employee benefits and executive compensation lawyers in Illinois. Five partners handle a wide range of matters including stock options, executive golden parachutes, ESOP and investment fiduciary duties. Typical work includes bankruptcy-related advice for major organizations. For example, the team has been advising the creditors' committee on pension and executive compensation issues connected to the United Airlines bankruptcy. Although the group serves other departments of the firm, such is its reputation that most of its work is stand-alone.

The Lawyers: **Roger Siske** (see p.752) chairs the firm's employee benefits and executive compensation practice, and attracted applause from commentators because "*he brings strong analytical skills to the table, and is a tough negotiator and a smart, knowledgeable lawyer.*" He deals with all areas of employee benefits and executive compensation for public and private companies, and nonprofit entities, as well as advising CEOs in negotiations over benefits, employment contracts and severance contracts. He also acts as special counsel to a number of boards of directors on compensation matters. Recent work includes advising the creditors' committee of Federal-Mogul, currently in bankruptcy, on executive compensation issues, and counseling Monsanto on refinancing its ESOP loans. "*Easy to work with and thoughtful,*" **Pamela Baker** (see

p.717) offers "*extensive knowledge about benefits and executive compensation.*" Peers were also full of praise for her "*tireless contribution to the ABA.*" She advises such names as Exelon, EDS and Principal Financial.

The Clients: McDonald's; Prudential Insurance; Allstate Insurance; Principal Financial; EDS; Lincoln National; Northwestern Memorial HealthCare; Evanston Northwestern Healthcare and Exelon.

Band 2

Franczek Sullivan

The Firm: This firm, which numbers over 40 attorneys skilled in labor and employment, attracted enthusiastic plaudits from both clients and peers. One client said, "*We like everything about the firm,*" before going on to highlight "*the integrity of its lawyers, and the way they are always there for us.*" Also a hit with clients are its "*good bench strength and valuable approach to the law – they can advise on both the strict interpretation of the law and on the practical applications.*" Peers, meanwhile, noted the team's "*superb*" reputation for work in the public sector, where it represents municipalities, large public bodies and educational institutions. It also assists a range of private employers, including the likes of Midwest Generation and Northern Trust.

The Lawyers: "*An excellent strategist,*" **James Franczek** "*is able to handle difficult and delicate situations in a manner that builds confidence.*" Clients were particularly impressed by his pragmatic and personable manner, coupled with profound knowledge and intelligence, which together give him the ability to "*work towards successful resolutions of the most difficult problems.*" He represents a range of public and private sector employers including the City of Chicago, Chicago Public Schools and Roadway Express. **William Sullivan** was praised by interviewees for his "*intelligence, judgment and high degree of professionalism.*" An experienced trial lawyer, he has argued cases before the US Supreme Court and various appellate courts. Peers spoke of **Anthony Crement**'s "*great litigation skills,*" telling researchers that "*He has a knack for getting along with the attorneys on the other side whilst being a good advocate for his client and the position they are taking.*" Clients were also quick to praise him, with one saying, "*I've worked with many different lawyers at top law firms and he has been the most responsive.*" He acts for private employers, with litigation, arbitration and collective bargaining making up the bulk of his practice.

The Clients: City of Chicago; Chicago Public Schools; McCormick Place; Chicago Park District; Roadway Express; Midwest Generation; Northern Trust; Square D; Dentsply International; Safeway; SBC and Oberweis Dairy.

Illinois
Leading individuals
(Employment: Mainly Defendant)

Senior Statesman

MATKOV George *Matkov Salzman*, Chicago
WARNER Michael *Seyfarth Shaw*, Chicago

[1] BERNSTEIN Howard *Neal Gerber*, Chicago
BRITTAIN Max *Schiff Hardin*, Chicago
FRANCZEK James *Franczek Sullivan*, Chicago
GANGEMI Columbus *Winston & Strawn*, Chicago
HARTSTEIN Barry *Morgan Lewis*, Chicago
JEPSON Edward *Vedder Price*, Chicago
LIEBERMAN Richard *McGuireWoods*, Chicago
STILLMAN Nina *Morgan Lewis*, Chicago
SULLIVAN William *Franczek Sullivan*, Chicago
YASTROW Joseph *Laner Muchin*, Chicago

[2] BULGER Brian *Meckler Bulger*, Chicago
CREMENT Anthony *Franczek Sullivan*, Chicago
GAGLIARDO Joseph *Laner Muchin*, Chicago
GOLDEN Gerald *Neal Gerber*, Chicago
JACKSON Charles *Seyfarth Shaw*, Chicago
KAPLAN Joel *Seyfarth Shaw*, Chicago
LOPATKA Kenneth *Perkins Coie*, Chicago
MISCIMARRA Philip *Seyfarth Shaw*, Chicago
MORRIS Ralph *Schiff Hardin*, Chicago
PISKORSKI Thomas *Seyfarth Shaw*, Chicago
SCHNADIG Richard *Vedder Price*, Chicago
SLOVAK Patricia Costello *Schiff Hardin*, Chicago
TILSON Joseph *Meckler Bulger*, Chicago

[3] ADELSTEIN Harvey *Neal Gerber*, Chicago
CRYSTAL Jules *Bryan Cave*, Chicago
DOLIN Kenneth *Seyfarth Shaw*, Chicago
ERF Stephen *McDermott Will*, Chicago
GOLD Brian *Sidley Austin*, Chicago
KLENK Timothy *Bryan Cave*, Chicago
MCLAUGHLIN Ellen *Seyfarth Shaw*, Chicago
MURDOCK Grady *Morgan Lewis*, Chicago
OLSON Camille *Seyfarth Shaw*, Chicago
PARSONS David *Littler Mendelson*, Chicago
POWERS John *Seyfarth Shaw*, Chicago
TORRES Joseph *Winston & Strawn*, Chicago

Leading individuals (Employee Benefits & Executive Compensation)

[1] BAKER Pamela *Sonnenschein Nath*, Chicago
KAPLAN Jared *McDermott Will*, Chicago
KRUEGER Herbert *Mayer Brown*, Chicago
LUEPKER Wayne *Mayer Brown*, Chicago
MENSON Richard *McGuireWoods*, Chicago
RYAN Priscilla *Sidley Austin*, Chicago
SISKE Roger *Sonnenschein Nath*, Chicago

[2] BOIES Bill *McDermott Will*, Chicago
HOOD Vicki *Kirkland & Ellis*, Chicago
ROSENBAUM Michael *Gardner Carton*, Chicago
ROSS Nancy *McDermott Will*, Chicago
STUCKER Robert *Vedder Price*, Chicago
WEISBERG Mark *Winston & Strawn*, Chicago
WOLF Charles *Vedder Price*, Chicago
WOLFE David *Gardner Carton*, Chicago

Individuals are listed alphabetically in each band.

Laner, Muchin, Dombrow, Becker, Levin, Tominberg

The Firm: Clients were full of praise for this *"phenomenal"* 41-lawyer boutique firm, telling researchers that *"labor and employment is all it does and it does it extraordinarily well."* The lawyers' high level of responsiveness was repeatedly highlighted by clients, as was their *"practical view of how to resolve cases – they are creative and flexible when it comes to avoiding litigation."* Interviewees also raved about the premier skills on offer here at every level: the team boasts *"expertise in all matters"* and has experience of representing management from virtually every industry group as well as the public sector.

The Lawyers: Peers described **Joseph Yastrow** (see p.759) as *"a wonderful gentleman – clients really seem to like him and he is very much appreciated on both sides of the aisle."* Clients themselves particularly value his *"no-nonsense, hands-on approach to resolving any complications."* In addition to being praised for his admired labor and employment practice, he is recognized for his expertise in employment liability insurance. He often works for insurance carriers defending their insured in employment matters. Rivals spoke warmly of **Joseph Gagliardo** (see p.728) as *"bright, thorough and hard-working – he engenders confidence in his clients and opposing parties."* Clients, meanwhile, appreciated his *"creative way of dealing with cases,"* and commented enthusiastically on *"the incredible amount of contacts he has in Chicago on the government side."* Known for his strong litigation skills, he has recently been involved in several cases relating to union organizing in the public sector.

The Clients: State of Illinois; University of Illinois; The Chicago Bulls; The Chicago White Sox; Harpo Productions; YMCA; United States Tennis Association; United States Cellular; American Trans Air; Catholic Charities and the Chicago Zoological Society.

Vedder, Price, Kaufman & Kammholz

The Firm: Clients have great confidence in this firm because *"the lawyers do whatever it takes to assist, even if it means working over weekends or overnight."* Despite this enthusiastic approach, *"they are always practical and never over-lawyer."* The firm was established in 1952 and has years of experience in the labor and employment arena, both in Illinois and nationally. However it is clearly not resting on its laurels and continues to nurture the new generation, prompting clients to praise the *"good bench strength and strong associates."* A full gamut of traditional labor law and employment advice is on offer, and is complemented by strength in employee benefits and executive compensation.

The Lawyers: *"Brilliant litigator"* **Edward Jepson** was highly recommended by market sources. *"Extremely smart, but down to earth with it,"* he was described by interviewees as *"phenomenal"* and *"fabulous."* He has extensive experience in class actions and is considered masterful in front of a jury, but also handles a stream of advisory work touching on all types of labor and employment matters. Recent successes include obtaining a jury verdict in Higbee v Sentry Insurance, which concerned allegations of sexual harassment and age discrimination. Clients value **Richard Schnadig**'s *"personable and refreshing approach,"* which is founded upon *"an amazing ability to come up with practical solutions, and a willingness to tell it like it is."* He is widely respected for his skill in major class actions of all kinds, but especially ones concerning alleged employment discrimination. Recent successes include getting an ERISA class action lawsuit dismissed by the federal district court in Chicago, on behalf of Amsted Industries. **Robert Stucker** is the president of the firm and chair of its executive compensation group. *"An excellent negotiator,"* he counsels companies on such matters as executive compensation arrangements in M&A and advises both corporations and executives on hiring and employment arrangements for CEOs. **Charles Wolf** is said to be *"bright with great judgment and a lot of common sense."* He has recognized strength in employee benefits litigation and in the labor aspects of benefits law, including multiemployer and collective bargaining plans. He acted in the Amsted litigation.

The Clients: Novartis; Syngenta; Ciba Specialty Chemicals; Diageo; RR Donnelley & Sons; Avon Products; Rockwell International; Sentry Insurance; Burger King; MEBA Benefit Plans and Amsted Industries.

Gardner Carton & Douglas LLP
See firm details p.767

The Firm: The firm enjoys a strong reputation for benefits and executive compensation, counseling on such matters as ESOPs and ERISA litigation. It is especially well known for providing employee benefits advice to tax-exempt and nonprofit organizations. The team's work for the healthcare industry was the subject of particular commendation. Indeed, some of the largest health systems in the USA feature on the firm's client list, along with Fortune 500 companies and higher education establishments. Recent highlights include representing the retirement plan fiduciary committee of a large for-profit employer in reviewing the committee's fiduciary responsibilities and recommending changes to the plan to reduce exposure under ERISA.

The Lawyers: **Michael Rosenbaum** (see p.748) is *"a great guy whose strength is in the health and welfare context,"* according to peers. The chair of the firm's human resources law department, he focuses on advising tax-exempt

www.ChambersandPartners.com

All quotes in the text are from interviews with clients and competitors.

681

organizations and Fortune 500 corporations on a variety of employee benefit, executive compensation and health and welfare issues. Recent examples include working with a large national health system to review and modify its executive compensation arrangements. **David Wolfe** (see p.758) was also recommended to researchers as a valuable member of the team, not least for his executive compensation and retirement plan work.

The Clients: BP; Walgreens; Children's Hospital of Philadelphia; Providence Health System and Banner Health.

Kirkland & Ellis LLP
See firm details p.770

The Firm: With its preeminence in such areas as private equity and bankruptcy, it is fitting that Kirkland & Ellis was also hailed as *"an incredibly sophisticated practice"* for employee benefits and executive compensation. The five-partner group works closely with the firm's corporate lawyers, providing support on important transactions and advising on matters connected to its highly active fund formation practice. The team's recent bankruptcy and restructuring-related work includes counseling United Airlines and Fleming on the employee benefits and executive compensation aspects of their respective restructurings.

The Lawyers: According to rivals, **Vicki Hood** (see p.733), the head of the firm's employee benefits group, has *"a top-notch reputation for representing major companies."* She advised Hyatt recently on the employee benefits aspects of its purchase of AmeriSuites Hotels, and assisted Forstmann Little in its acquisition of IMG. She also counsels the National Hockey League Players' Association on employment and benefits issues and advises GM Pension Fund on private market investments.

The Clients: The impressive client list includes: Hyatt; Forstmann Little; GM Pension Fund and National Hockey League Players' Association.

Band 3

Littler Mendelson
The Firm: Numbering 20 lawyers, the relatively small size of the Chicago office is deceptive, as the team can draw upon the enormous resources of one of the US's best known national labor and employment firms. This amounts to approximately 400 hundred lawyers based throughout the country, who provide a full service on all matters relating to labor, employment and employee benefits. Leaders in practically every industry can be found in the firm's client roster, and it serves a wide variety of companies ranging from Fortune 500 corporations to small and medium-sized entities.

The Lawyers: **David Parsons** received considerable market commendation and was described as *"an extremely competent lawyer who handles a lot of major cases."* His practice centers on employment discrimination and other employment litigation. As well as conducting cases in federal and state trial and appellate courts, he acts in arbitrations and appears before administrative agencies.

The Clients: Clients are drawn from a variety of industry sectors, including manufacturing, advertising, financial and legal services, the media, construction and real estate.

Matkov Salzman Madoff & Gunn
The Firm: Sources rated this 19-attorney firm as *"particularly strong in traditional labor work."* However, some commentators did express doubt as to whether the firm could hold its position following some recent departures, including that of Kenneth Lopatka to Perkins Coie. Nonetheless, the group still offers a quality service in employment, labor and employee benefits. Typical matters include employment counseling, union negotiation and organizing campaigns, and labor and employment litigation and arbitration before all courts and tribunals.

The Lawyers: Interviewees described **George Matkov** as *"the driving force behind the firm"* and applauded him as *"an excellent litigator and business man with good legal judgment and a well-rounded intellect."* His long-standing experience of counseling companies on labor and industrial relations was the subject of considerable praise.

The Clients: The team represents companies of all sizes and descriptions, ranging from household name multinationals to small, local businesses. They are drawn from such sectors as retailing, insurance, banking, the media, healthcare, construction and manufacturing.

Meckler, Bulger & Tilson
The Firm: Although only founded in 1994, the firm has quickly demonstrated *"an extremely high level of sophistication,"* according to the market. Indeed, some sources consider it to have already established itself as *"one of the strongest boutique firms in Chicago."* Twenty attorneys are active in a comprehensive range of labor and employment matters, often handling major class actions for Fortune 500 companies. In addition to employment discrimination cases, wage and hour class actions have featured high on the recent agenda. Traditional labor law expertise includes collective bargaining, arbitrations and union management relations.

The Lawyers: Rivals were full of admiration for **Joseph Tilson** and his practice, telling researchers, *"He is a strong lawyer; his clients are extraordinarily loyal to him, which says a lot."* His expertise is broad, covering negotiation, counseling, litigation and arbitration in both labor and employment arenas. **Brian Bulger** also

attracted praise as a *"low-key and level-headed attorney; he doesn't get ruffled."* Market sources appreciate the way that *"he is always willing to listen to other people's opinions"* and highlighted his experience of work in the healthcare sector.

The Clients: Archer Daniels Midland; University of Chicago; Cargill; Chicago Board of Trade and Loyola University.

Schiff Hardin LLP
See firm details p.775

The Firm: Interviewees spoke of a *"compact but broad labor and employment practice in a good corporate firm."* *"The two practices feed well off each other,"* say peers. However, a department of about 16 lawyers also attracts plenty of its own clients as well as handling referrals from within the firm. The team handles the full gamut of labor and employment matters and, in addition to state and federal litigation expertise, boasts a strong practice acting for management on traditional labor law issues. Noncompete litigation has featured highly in the caseload in recent months.

The Lawyers: *"Strategic and creative"* **Max Brittain** (see p.720) enjoys an excellent reputation for employment litigation. He acted recently in a first Federal Court of Appeals hearing to deny the right to a jury trial in an ADA retaliation case, and was successful in the Seventh Circuit. Possessed of *"tremendously sound judgment,"* according to interviewees, **Ralph Morris** (see p.743) *"looks at the whole picture and has a feel for the best resolution, both long term and short term."* His practice is divided between traditional labor negotiations and litigation, and June 2004 saw him certified as an employment mediator. Recent highlights include advising the Steppenwolf Theatre on an organizational campaign. Applauded as *"a true contributor to the profession,"* **Patricia Costello Slovak** (see p.723) was also recommended to researchers. She advises management on all aspects of dealing with unions and employees.

The Clients: Hamilton Sundstrand; Bank of America; Federal Signal; Delta Air Lines; Dean Foods; NiSource; Owens-Illinois; Circuit City Stores and Fred Meyer.

Winston & Strawn LLP
See firm details p.780

The Firm: This team was described by clients as *"absolutely first-rate."* Indeed, one client told researchers, *"I work with firms all over the country and they are as good as you get."* The firm's international reach was commented on favorably, as was its *"diversity of staffing: it has people at all levels of experience and ages, so we have confidence in their continuity."* About 30 lawyers handle labor and employment matters in Chicago, and while litigation is the primary focus, other areas of strength include employment counseling and negotiation. The team also has a solid reputation in employee benefits litigation, while a separate employee benefits group specializes in counseling.

The Lawyers: "*Creative*" and gifted with "*a knack for strategy,*" **Columbus Gangemi** (see p.729) is valued highly by clients. In particular, they appreciate his "*outstanding courtroom manner*" and the fact that "*he is capable of speaking to members of the executive office and to individuals less knowledgeable about the law – he can articulate a concept to different levels of audience.*" The national head of the firm's labor and employment relations practice, he handles all manner of labor, employment and employee benefits litigation. Recent highlights include acting for Caterpillar in Caterpillar v Lyons et al, in which an Illinois law restricting the use of temporary workers during a strike was declared unconstitutional. **Joseph Torres** (see p.756) is admired by clients for his "*collaborative, well-versed and disciplined*" approach. He also acted for Caterpillar in the matter above, and was successful in getting a case dismissed prior to trial on behalf of American Airlines. **Mark Weisberg** (see p.758) attracted market recommendation for his employee benefits and executive compensation practice. According to rivals, "*He is a terrific lawyer who makes a complicated area of law understandable to clients.*"

The Clients: Caterpillar; Sun Chemical; American Airlines; Anheuser-Busch and Abbott Laboratories.

Band 4

Bryan Cave LLP

The Firm: Following the firm's opening of an Illinois office in 2001, the two-lawyer labor and employment team was given a boost in 2004 when six attorneys joined from McGuireWoods. The group appears to have settled in well, and clients listed a number of reasons why they appreciate its work: "*The lawyers are efficient and communicate well, they are in tune with the approach we take,*" and "*they suggest strategies to deal with matters without going to trial.*" The department provides a full service, advising on all aspects of labor and employment law.

The Lawyers: **Jules Crystal** inspires the confidence of clients with "*his competency and his sincerity; plus he is diligent and conscientious.*" His practice centers mainly on traditional labor law, both counseling and dispute resolution. "*Wise*" **Timothy Klenk** has also gained the utmost respect of clients. Of counsel at the firm, he offers many years of experience representing companies in employment and commercial litigation.

The Clients: The team represents several Fortune 500 companies as well as smaller and mid-size employers. Clients include Kraft Foods Global, Fifth Third Bank and WDJT-TV.

Jenner & Block LLP
See firm details p.768

The Firm: High-quality work is in evidence here and clients spoke of a team that has "*gotten great results.*" The group is known for representing employers in a broad variety of matters, ranging from traditional union management issues, to preventive advice, to administrative proceedings and litigation before all courts. As well as counseling on specific problems, the firm offers training programs. The ratio of contentious to noncontentious work is approximately 50/50. Lawyers also advise on executive compensation and contractual matters, acting either for the employer or for the employee.

The Lawyers: David Haase cochairs the firm's labor and employment group. Carla Rozycki is also active in this area.

The Clients: The extensive client list includes large corporations and public entities, alongside small and medium-sized businesses and non-profit associations. Representative clients include: Interpublic Group; Sara Lee Coffee & Tea; University of Illinois and General Board of Pension and Health Benefits of the United Methodist Church.

Jones Day
See firm details p.485

The Firm: According to clients, this is "*a hands-on and responsive team.*" They were particularly impressed by the quality and consistency of the offering: as one put it, "*Their work has been impeccable and the results predictably good.*" A total of 15 attorneys in the Chicago office boast expertise in employment litigation and labor relations, including NLRB arbitrations and union decertification. The practice is national in scope and the team has witnessed a tremendous growth of late in class action litigation, particularly in the wage and hour field. In one such recent case, Carnevale et al v GE, its lawyers obtained a favorable settlement to a nationwide FLSA/state wage-hour law class action challenging the exempt status of most of the workforce.

The Lawyers: Steven Catlett and Lawrence DiNardo are key members of the team.

The Clients: An outstanding array of national and multinational corporations, including a number of the Fortune 500, appear in the firm's client list.

Mayer, Brown, Rowe & Maw LLP
See firm details p.771

The Firm: The national reach of the firm's labor and employment practice allows it to handle wage and hour class actions and employment discrimination class actions of national scope. Its "*pragmatic, personable and intelligent*" lawyers have recently handled several Sarbanes-Oxley retaliation cases, attracting particular praise from clients for "*staying one step ahead in terms of the current legislation – we can rely on*

them when it comes to best practice." Counseling and advice form a significant part of the practice, while the employee benefits and executive compensation team was the subject of particular accolades from the market. According to one client, the firm "*has the smartest lawyers in the country – they have great business sense and provide a really terrific package.*" Another told researchers, "*They come up with solutions that are in no way obvious; they just roll up their sleeves and get on with it.*" In addition to executive compensation and employment, the team's expertise spans pension and welfare plans and pension investments.

The Lawyers: "*Although he is in demand, he still gives you the time you need,*" said clients of the "*preeminent*" **Herbert Krueger** (see p.736). A large part of his practice relates to institutional investment, where he advises large trust companies and fund sponsors. He also regularly counsels trust companies and pension funds on ERISA-related fiduciary issues. His expertise in executive compensation impressed clients, who dubbed him "*skilled in sorting through sticky-wicket problems.*" **Wayne Luepker** (see p.738) leads the firm's compensation and benefits practice. A specialist in executive compensation and executive employment, he is "*always at the cutting edge and has a creative and flexible approach.*"

The Clients: Northern Trust; Compensation Committee of the CMGI Board of Directors; Compensation Committee of the USEC Board of Directors; OCE-USA; Ernst & Young; TIAA-CREF; Kraft Foods; University of Chicago; City of Chicago and Abbott Laboratories.

McDermott Will & Emery
See firm details p.773

The Firm: "*This firm goes further than simple client care – working with them is a real pleasure,*" the firm's clients told researchers. The employee benefits litigation group came in for the lion's share of praise, with clients particularly commending its aggressive approach to cases: "*The lawyers are not gun-shy when it comes to taking on controversial litigation.*" The team is often seen acting for employers, as well as individual and corporate fiduciaries and service providers. The noncontentious side of the employee benefits and executive compensation practice also garnered praise, as did the Chicago office's labor and employment group. Its lawyers were particularly valued by clients for being "*well up on the law – they offer viable alternatives and go an extra step to provide them.*"

The Lawyers: **Jared Kaplan**'s (see p.734) ESOP skills are held in high esteem by commentators, who held him up as quite simply "*one of the very top practitioners*" in the field. **Bill Boies** (see p.719) is also appreciated by clients, who rely on his "*level-headed and steady*" manner. His practice encompasses business and trust litigation, and he often acts for benefit plan sponsors and fiduciaries in ERISA class action disputes. **Nancy Ross** (see p.749) focuses on employee benefits class action litigation and counseling under ERISA. Her recent successes include a complex ERISA class action, Keach v US Trust et al. On the labor and employment side, **Stephen Erf** (see p.726) is said by clients to "*quickly identify a strategy and execute it efficiently.*" His practice includes employment counseling and litigation, as well as traditional labor matters.

The Clients: Littlefuse; Computer Sciences; Stora Enso North America; UPM-Kymmene; ChemCentral; Bowe Bell & Howell; FMC; Condell Health Network; Methodist Medical Center of Illinois; Square D; AXA Equitable and BP Amoco.

McGuireWoods

The Firm: This team of approximately 20 labor and employment specialists in Chicago forms part of a large national group spread throughout a considerable network of offices. It offers considerable strength in employment litigation and traditional labor negotiations, and also handles a volume of employment counseling. Market sources also applauded the firm as "*fabulous*" for employee benefits and executive compensation. Here, it advises on retirement plans, health and welfare benefits, fiduciary matters and ERISA litigation.

The Lawyers: **Richard Lieberman** continues to impress clients by being "*innovative, creative and receptive to our enquiries or wishes.*" He focuses on both employment and traditional labor matters, and boasts experience in large, complex litigation, including class actions. He recently obtained a successful result for a large bank, which held that consulting with lawyers and making an employment decision are privileged. Executive compensation and employee benefits specialist **Richard Menson** was highlighted to researchers as "*very much on top of the area; smart and client-oriented.*"

The Clients: The firm acts for publicly and privately held corporations, banks, insurance companies and trusts. Sample names include: Manpower; LaSalle National Bank; Siemens and Amgen.

Morgan, Lewis & Bockius LLP

See firm details p.1556

The Firm: There are already clear signs that the national firm is successfully stamping its mark on Chicago's labor and employment market following the high-profile arrival of Barry Hartstein and Nina Stillman from Vedder, Price, Kaufman & Kammholz in July 2004. Its presence was boosted further by the arrival in September 2004 of a "*to-the-point and responsive*" six-strong group from Jenkens & Gilchrist. Clients spoke of "*exceptional lawyers who really know the law – they have some state-of-the-art*

ideas and approaches and are diligent and professional in their dealings." Complex class action litigation forms one of the mainstays of the practice, and the team complements this with deep skill in counseling and traditional labor law matters. It also offers expertise in employee benefits and executive compensation.

The Lawyers: **Barry Hartstein** (see p.732) was commended by peers for the "*deep intellectual knowledge of the area that he uses very effectively for his clients.*" Clients themselves, meanwhile, simply extolled him as "*a superman.*" He chairs the Chicago labor practice and acts for such clients as Hooters Management, Cancer Treatment Centers of America and Bally Total Fitness. According to sources "*terrific employment litigator*" **Nina Stillman** (see p.754) is so well known that "*she is one of those people you call by one name, like Cher or Madonna.*" She specializes in equal employment opportunities and OSHA, and is well known for her success in complex litigation. Clients hold her up as "*one of the best employment lawyers in the country – she knows the law and knows how to use it to her client's advantage.*" One added, "*She is also a fighter and will fight hard for you.*" Recent highlights include acting for Ingersoll-Rand in an age discrimination class action, which was favorably settled. The team was recently joined by **Grady Murdock** (see p.745), previously with Neal, Murdock & Leroy, LLC. He was praised to researchers as "*a widely known and respected lawyer with a well-rounded background in labor and employment law.*"

The Clients: McCain Foods USA; GATX; Bally Total Fitness; Federal Reserve Bank of Chicago; Cancer Treatment Centers of America; RR Donnelley & Sons; Hooters Management and Chicago Stock Exchange.

Neal, Gerber & Eisenberg LLP

The Firm: Clients applauded this as "*an excellent firm with a good focus on business.*" A team of about 17 attorneys specializes in traditional labor work, as well as handling a steady stream of employment advice and litigation. Its broad focus has proved a hit with the market, and sources spoke of "*an impressive practice with a good reputation – it keeps its name out there and does great work for its clients.*" This work cuts across all areas of labor and employment, from union negotiations and arbitrations to class action defense. However, sources highlighted "*a very sophisticated litigation practice.*" A team of five attorneys handles employee benefits and executive compensation matters.

The Lawyers: Clients applauded **Howard Bernstein** as "*an exceptional labor lawyer.*" His work encompasses counseling, negotiations and litigation, with recent examples including advice to the Illinois Association of Health Care Facilities in negotiations with the Service Employees International Union. According to peers, **Gerald**

Golden "*is a good and intelligent advocate, and is always firm in his position for his client.*" Sources were also impressed with his "*ability to see the bigger picture – he looks closely at how the situation impacts on the employer.*" His practice includes both employment litigation and traditional labor work, and he was recently successful on behalf of a publicly traded company in a major labor dispute involving the reorganization of the company and the transfer of employees between divisions. **Harvey Adelstein**'s skill in dealing with unions was also commended by interviewees, who praised him as "*thoughtful and strategic in everything he does.*"

The Clients: Clients include Illinois Association of Health Care Facilities, Tyson Foods and National Gypsum.

Sidley Austin Brown & Wood LLP

See firm details p.778

The Firm: Clients spoke highly of this team. According to one, "*They have been excellent – professional and very successful – and have offered us solid advice and counsel.*" Over 40 lawyers in the Chicago office assist with a full range of matters, including employee benefits and executive compensation, as well as litigation and counseling in both the employment and labor arenas. As part of an international powerhouse, the practice has a large reach and caters for an outstanding client list, which includes a number of multinational corporations.

The Lawyers: **Brian Gold** (see p.730) heads the firm's labor and employment group and inspires the confidence of clients with his combination of "*knowledge and ability to think through all the options.*" He has had several recent successes in labor arbitrations for Exelon, and recently helped the same client to defeat class certification in an attempted employee benefits class action. Other highlights include defending EMC in an employment discrimination arbitration. **Priscilla Ryan** (see p.749) is known throughout the market for her "*excellent judgment on how to handle things.*" She specializes in employee benefits and executive compensation, including fiduciary issues arising under ERISA. Her work with the ABA was also the subject of praise from peers.

The Clients: Exelon; American Medical Association; Norfolk Southern; CSX; KPMG; Northwestern University; University of Chicago; Brunswick; Bombardier; Aon; Sara Lee and EMC.

Other Notable Practitioners

In May 2004, **Ken Lopatka** moved from Matkov Salzman Madoff & Gunn to Perkins Coie LLP, to help build the latter's labor and employment practice group in Chicago. He acts on both traditional labor and employment disputes and enjoys a strong reputation for his skill in the courtroom.

ENERGY & NATURAL RESOURCES

Illinois
Leading firms
(Energy & Natural Resources)

1 FOLEY & LARDNER *Chicago*
  SIDLEY AUSTIN BROWN & WOOD LLP *Chicago*
2 JONES DAY *Chicago*
  MAYER, BROWN, ROWE & MAW LLP *Chicago*
3 DLA PIPER RUDNICK GRAY CARY US LLP *Chicago*
  LUEDERS, ROBERTSON & KONZEN *Granite City*
  SCHIFF HARDIN LLP *Chicago*
  SONNENSCHEIN NATH & ROSENTHAL LLP *Chicago*

Leading individuals
(Energy & Natural Resources)

Senior Statesman
HANZLIK Paul *Foley & Lardner, Chicago*
READ Sarah *Sidley Austin, Chicago*
RUXIN Paul *Jones Day, Chicago*
1 RIPPIE E Glenn *Foley & Lardner, Chicago*
2 FLYNN Christopher *Jones Day, Chicago*
  MACBRIDE Owen *Schiff Hardin, Chicago*
  ROBERTSON Eric *Lueders Robertson, Granite City*
3 ASTLE Richard *Sidley Austin, Chicago*
  ROGERS III John *Foley & Lardner, Chicago*
  ROONEY John *Sonnenschein Nath, Chicago*
  STAHL David *Eimer Stahl, Chicago*
  THOMAS Dale *Sidley Austin, Chicago*
  TOWNSEND Christopher *DLA Piper Rudnick, Chicago*

Firms and individuals are listed alphabetically in each band.

Band 1

Foley & Lardner
See firm details p.1828

The Firm: This energy team has successfully expanded its national business over the past year. Its workload includes transactional and regulatory work, such as rate work for Nicor, and there has been a flurry of activity for Buckeye Pipe Line Company in its acquisition of assets from Shell. The staple diet is the acquisition of generation assets as well as energy companies through public and private sales. Lawyers also undertake bank and private equity financing work, often entailing highly complex structures. Renewables also feature prominently, and the firm, particularly out of Wisconsin, is a US leader in the tax-efficient financing and development of wind farms. Despite impressive new client wins, among them Florida Power & Light, the jewel in the Chicago crown is still the team's role as principal outside regulatory counsel to the largest utility in the state, Commonwealth Edison.

The Lawyers: The team concentrates in one place "*some of the most extraordinary energy lawyers in the country,*" say observers. Clients appreciate that it is "*big enough to be strong across the US,*" praising lawyers' "*good hands-on*

approach and sound understanding of the sector.*" With over 30 years' experience, "*seriously high-powered*" **Paul Hanzlik** (see p.731) commands enormous respect and has been elevated to the rank of senior statesman this year. He is currently representing Commonwealth Edison on the delicate transition from the rate freeze to a market free-for-all. The practice is seen to be transitioning to the stewardship of "*brilliant attorney*" **Glenn Rippie** (see p.747), increasingly the face whom clients see. He is universally admired for his "*deep understanding of electricity business issues and hard graft at the sharp end.*" Observers describe him as "*deceptively easy going, but one of the best cross-examiners ever.*" Peers and clients both extol the virtues of "*first-class litigator*" **John Rogers** (see p.748), whose "*calm and steady*" control of a case is invaluable on appellate matters.

The Clients: Nicor; WPS Resources; Exelon; Bank One Capital; Invenergy; Corporación EHN; Airtricity; NAC International; Commonwealth Edison; Buckeye Pipe Line Company; Florida Power & Light and The American Transmission Company.

Sidley Austin Brown & Wood LLP
See firm details p.778

The Firm: This "*extremely capable*" national and international player offers transactional and regulatory advice in some of the most exciting deals in the sector. Even competitors rate it "*possibly the most complete practice in the state, and unsurpassed for electricity work.*" Lawyers handle complex and creative transactions that draw on the firm's deep resources. A "*versatile*" team acts principally for utilities or their holding companies, and also some large industrial consumers. Its best-known client is Exelon/Commonwealth Edison. In the words of one commentator, the team has "*handled some huge litigations, and avoided some even bigger ones.*"

The Lawyers: Commentators praised the firm's "*intelligent and knowledgeable*" lawyers, drawing particular attention to their integrity. "*Extraordinarily efficient and creative*" **Sarah Read** (see p.747) focuses on regulatory matters, litigation and dispute resolution, and is known for her involvement in legislation, drafting and strategy at the highest levels. Her experience is such that she is duly seen as something of a grande dame of the industry. "*Brilliant and result-focused*" **Dick Astle** (see p.717) is the key partner for Exelon, and is rated as one of the finest transactional lawyers in the country. Clients declare him "*absolutely phenomenal,*" stating that he is "*the best energy-focused corporate lawyer I've ever come across,*" and "*prepared for absolutely anything you can throw at him.*" **Dale Thomas** (see p.755) handles a broad range of commercial work for key client Common-

wealth Edison, including litigation, competition matters, rate cases and FERC representations. He is also involved in negotiating with power suppliers in the newly competitive environment of IPPs. On a more national platform, Thomas has a name for telecom work, too. Lawyers acted recently for Exelon in two appeals, one relating to a previously obtained competitive services agreement.

Band 2

Jones Day
See firm details p.485

The Firm: The Chicago office fields "*a strong bench*" and is plugged firmly into a global leviathan that handles the full range of regulatory and transactional work for major electric utilities, natural gas pipelines and distribution companies, as well as oil and gas companies throughout the USA. The team can handle state and federal work for just about any client in any state, working in conjunction with lawyers based in Washington DC. Its profile in Illinois has been "*substantially bolstered*" by key client Ameren's acquisition of Illinois Power and generally aggressive recent activity.

The Lawyers: **Paul Ruxin** (see p.749) achieves statesman status in virtue of his long experience and "*colossal stature on the US stage,*" but peers report that he rarely interacts with them on a routine basis. "*Seasoned*" attorney **Christopher Flynn** (see p.727) has "*moved to the forefront*" on the Ameren brief, and is widely seen as "*the man on the ground*" in Chicago. The team advised FirstEnergy and its Ohio electric operating utilities in a variety of matters, including the ongoing deregulation and restructuring proceedings before the Public Utilities Commission of Ohio. As part of its acquisition of the Illinois Power Company, lawyers represented Ameren before the Illinois Commerce Commission.

The Clients: Ameren; AEP; BP America; CenterPoint Energy; The Dayton Power and Light Company; Dominion East Ohio; FirstEnergy; OGE Energy; SCANA Corporation and Xcel Energy.

Mayer, Brown, Rowe & Maw LLP
See firm details p.771

The Firm: This team is active on a national platform and beyond, and renowned for its transactional focus and involvement in gas and petrochemicals. Clients use the team on a wide range of commercial work, often where real estate and lobbying are involved. According to one energy client, this outfit is "*the best law firm I've ever used,*" and even competitors acknowledge "*a gold-plated practice.*" The firm's profile in Illinois hinges on the team's close relationship with Northern Illinois Gas company and ties with Nicor, both of which lawyers have represented before the Illinois Commerce Commission.

The Lawyers: A number of different individuals were championed by clients. Lawyers acted recently for TransCanada PipeLines in its $1.7 billion acquisition of Gas Transmission Northwest from National Energy & Gas Transmission, and its $505 million acquisition of hydroelectric generation assets from US Gen. The team was also involved for PSEG Power in the development of gas-fired power plants in Indiana and Ohio.

The Clients: The main Illinois client is Northern Illinois Gas Company, and the team is also closely identified with Nicor.

Band 3

DLA Piper Rudnick Gray Cary US LLP

See firm details p.765

The Firm: With Piper Rudnick's merger plans progressing both at home and in the USA and Europe, the Illinois team has continued to grow its practice representing competitive energy suppliers and industrial customers, typically in coalitions, before the Illinois Commerce Commission and other regulatory bodies. Much of the practice involves lobbying, all the way up to the federal level. Clients praise the "*highest quality and responsiveness*" of the technically expert team.

The Lawyers: Clients comment effusively on "*extremely helpful*" **Christopher Townsend** (see p.756), highlighting his "*always up-to-date*" knowledge of gas and electric issues, locally and nationally. They say his "*commanding presence*" is a real asset in negotiations. His team successfully represented a coalition of electric suppliers that included Ameren Energy Marketing Company, Constellation NewEnergy, MidAmerican Energy and Peoples Energy Services in FERC proceedings and diverse negotiations. This arose out of Commonwealth Edison's handover of operational control of its transmission wires to the PJM Interconnection RTO. The practice also acted for multiple competitive electric and gas suppliers in Illinois Commerce Commission and FERC proceedings, in litigation and settle-

ment negotiations arising out of Ameren's acquisition of the Illinois Power Company.

The Clients: A. Finkl & Sons; Algonquin Power Income Fund; Ameren Energy Marketing Company; CITGO; Constellation NewEnergy; Direct Energy Marketing; Entergy-Koch Trading; Interstate Gas Supply; MidAmerican Energy Company; NRG Energy; Peoples Energy Services; Perdue Farms; Shell Energy Services; T. Rowe Price and US Energy Savings Corporation.

Lueders, Robertson & Konzen

The Firm: Situated in Granite City, this "*professional and notable*" group operates in a heavily industrialized part of Illinois and traditionally represents the interests of large industrial consumer clients. It also lobbies for these clients at the legislative level. The team has long experience in testing rate cases and handling filings with the full array of relevant authorities.

The Lawyers: "*One of the best advocates in the state,*" **Eric Robertson** is the great draw here, driving forward an enviable practice built by his highly respected father, Randall, who still crops up occasionally at key meetings. Robertson "*knows this industry backwards and forwards*" and peers happily refer clients to him. He recently acted for a group of consumers to reach settlement in a case involving Commonwealth Edison.

Schiff Hardin LLP

See firm details p.775

The Firm: The three main areas of activity of this "*capable and competent*" outfit are: state regulatory advice (focused mainly on Illinois and Indiana) for electric and gas utility clients; federal regulatory advice (handled mostly out of Washington DC) on FERC matters for electric utility clients; and a thriving transactional base, acting for regular utility clients as well as for lenders and guarantors investing into energy businesses. Years of association with Illinois Power have generated a fine and visible profile in the state, though this is bound to evolve now that Ameren has snapped up this key client.

The Lawyers: The "*talented*" **Owen MacBride** (see p.738) is "*always prepared and practical,*" and it is on his shoulders that the team's reputa-

tion principally rests. A man of "*great experience and deep integrity,*" he is expert in regulatory and accounting details. MacBride was primary outside counsel to Illinois Power for years, during which time he has been integral to the redrafting and deregulation of the industry framework. He led the team acting for several competitive local exchange carriers in a rate case filed by SBC Illinois at the Illinois Commerce Commission to set new wholesale rates for SBC's unbundled network elements. He also represented Dynegy and Illinois Power Company on regulatory issues in unconsummated negotiations for the acquisition by Exelon of IPC's assets.

The Clients: AT&T Communications of Illinois; Consolidated Communications and Illinois Consolidated Telephone Company and affiliates; Dynegy and Dynegy Holdings; Illinois Power Company; McLeodUSA Telecommunications Services; RCN Telecom Services of Illinois and TDS Metrocom.

Sonnenschein Nath & Rosenthal LLP

See firm details p.779

The Firm: The heart and soul of this team lie in utility regulatory work at state and federal levels for utilities, gas distributors and industrial consumers. The Chicago team has "*considerable depth and experience,*" and is frequently engaged in legislative representation and advice. This energy practice has a discernible overlap with the firm's telecoms practice, so ensuring plenty of prior experience in the restructuring of an industry sector.

The Lawyers: "*Smart*" **John Rooney** (see p.748) is the key figure here, according to clients who regard him as "*our guy, and the best in the business.*" He also has extensive regulatory experience in telecoms.

Other Notable Practitioners

Eimer Stahl Klevorn & Solberg's **David Stahl** receives high praise from clients who regard him as "*an extraordinary lawyer and a fantastic litigator.*" He has excellent antitrust experience and is outside counsel to some of the industry's most potent players.

ENVIRONMENT

Band 1

Mayer, Brown, Rowe & Maw LLP

See firm details p.771

The Firm: This "*well-resourced, thorough and substantial*" litigation-driven team is a powerful player in the state. It offers full regulatory and transactional support, in addition to its superb

record defending clients against agency action at state and federal levels. The practice is at its best when defending clients such as Nicor against claims by individuals and groups, and minimizing clients' liabilities with respect to ancient coal gas facilities. The client base is rock solid, and a volume of work for Commonwealth Edison keeps the engine running nicely.

The Lawyers: Admiring peers especially rate the firm's appellate work, observing that there are "*a good number of great attorneys, any one of whom can take a leadership role.*" The "*legendary*" **Percy Angelo** (see p.717) is one of the most senior and experienced stalwarts of the Illinois Bar. A "*formidable*" attorney, she is "*super smart, meticulous and tenacious*" and can cause

Illinois
Leading firms (Environment)

[1] **MAYER, BROWN, ROWE & MAW LLP** *Chicago*
   SIDLEY AUSTIN BROWN & WOOD LLP *Chicago*

[2] **JENNER & BLOCK LLP** *Chicago*
   SONNENSCHEIN NATH & ROSENTHAL LLP *Chicago*

[3] **KARAGANIS, WHITE & MAGEL** *Chicago*
   SCHIFF HARDIN LLP *Chicago*
   SEYFARTH SHAW LLP *Chicago*
   WINSTON & STRAWN LLP *Chicago*

[4] **GARDNER CARTON & DOUGLAS LLP** *Chicago*
   HODGE DWYER ZEMAN *Springfield*
   KIRKLAND & ELLIS LLP *Chicago*
   MCGUIREWOODS *Chicago*

Leading individuals (Environment)

Senior Statesman
ANGELO Percy *Mayer Brown, Chicago*
KISSEL Richard *Gardner Carton, Chicago*

[1] **FORT** Jeffrey *Sonnenschein Nath, Chicago*
   ZABEL Sheldon *Schiff Hardin, Chicago*

[2] **BISHOP** Timothy *Mayer Brown, Chicago*
   EGGERT Russell *Mayer Brown, Chicago*
   FRANZETTI Susan *Franzetti Law Firm, Chicago*
   OLIAN Robert *Sidley Austin, Chicago*

[3] **BERGHOFF** John *Mayer Brown, Chicago*
   FORCADE Bill *Jenner & Block, Chicago*
   GRAYSON E Lynn *Jenner & Block, Chicago*
   HARRINGTON James *McGuireWoods, Chicago*
   KARAGANIS Joseph *Karaganis White, Chicago*
   NIJMAN Jennifer *Winston & Strawn, Chicago*
   PERELLIS Andrew *Seyfarth Shaw, Chicago*
   SCHLICKMAN J Andrew *Sidley Austin, Chicago*
   VROMAN James *Jenner & Block, Chicago*
   WHITE Bruce *Karaganis White, Chicago*

[4] **BOYD** Eric *Seyfarth Shaw, Chicago*
   CAHAN James *Sidley Austin, Chicago*
   GADE Mary *Sonnenschein Nath, Chicago*
   HODGE Katherine *Hodge Dwyer, Springfield*
   LYONS Francis *Gardner Carton, Chicago*
   PRILLAMAN Fred *Mohan Alewelt, Springfield*
   RUNNING Andrew *Kirkland & Ellis, Chicago*
   RUSSELL James *Winston & Strawn, Chicago*
   SELMAN Russell *Katten Muchin, Chicago*
   TER MOLEN Mark *Mayer Brown, Chicago*
   VIDMAR Jacqueline *Sonnenschein Nath, Chicago*

Firms and individuals are listed alphabetically in each band.

considerable trepidation in opponents. She heads the team that acts for Aventine Renewable Energy in a raft of environmental matters. Though still pivotal to the practice in her role as senior counsel, she spends less time in Chicago these days and more at her home in Florida. **Timothy Bishop**'s (see p.719) *"gold-standard reputation"* in the appellate arena is second to none, and he has *"accomplished great things"* before the Supreme Court. He successfully represented the South Florida Water Management District against the Miccosukee Tribe, petitioning for writ of certiorari and overturning an adverse Court of Appeals judgment. *"Active and impressive"* **Russell Eggert** (see p.725) is admired as *"a real class act"* and a strong litigator, particularly at the state level, and with Percy Angelo heads the team that was recently named national environmental counsel to Caterpillar. Described as *"a classic litigator and well balanced,"* **John Berghoff** (see p.718) is deeply experienced in environmental matters and boasts a national reputation for handling *"nasty litigation"* involving site cleanups and toxic torts. He leads the team that represents Burlington Northern Santa Fe in defense of cleanup and natural resources damages claims throughout the western USA. **Mark Ter Molen** (see p.755) is a *"bright and energetic"* litigator who gains the approbation of clients for his *"detailed approach and professionalism."* With John Berghoff he acts for Nicor in litigation over former manufactured gas plants.

The Clients: Caterpillar; Burlington Northern Sante Fe; Philips Electronics North America; Nicor; Premcor; Illinois Tool Works; Tyson Foods; The Alliance of Automobile Manufacturers; The American Farm Bureau Federation; The Carlyle Group and ProLogis.

Sidley Austin Brown & Wood LLP
See firm details p.778

The Firm: While the bulk of this *"time and cost-efficient"* team's work is litigation, its *"super-strong"* regulatory compliance offering cannot be ignored and it also offers transactional and management systems advice. Clients declare the team *"tops for knowledge, and always up with the latest and best interpretations."* Lawyers help clients to devise audit programs and arrange permitting, as well as clarifying their liabilities on deals. On the litigation side a *"tremendous"* team largely defends natural resources damages and tort cases. Attorneys successfully defended Kraft in an arbitration concerning contractual indemnification claims by the purchaser of a can manufacturing plant sold by the company. *"Extremely competent personnel"* impress clients by being *"totally reliable"* and showing *"impressive range"* running all the way up to the appellate arena. Of particular note is the practice's ability to attract *"seriously talented"* young lawyers and retain them until ready to flourish as partners.

The Lawyers: The retirement of the hugely influential Thomas McMahon is greeted with a kind of nostalgic regret in the marketplace, though he remains involved with legacy matters. Taking up the mantle is *"bright and articulate"* **Robert Olian** (see p.744), renowned for his litigation prowess and ability to *"negotiate a consensus without brandishing the sword all the time."* Peers relate that he is *"a real trenches guy"* with great courtroom war stories to tell. He heads the team representing BP in litigation brought by residents living near refineries formerly operated by the company, on claims that operations led to groundwater contamination. Another name acknowledged in cleanup litigation circles is that of **Andrew Schlickman** (see p.750), who elicits praise for his thoroughness and reasonableness. **James Cahan**'s (see p.721) clients appreciate his strategic advice, declaring him *"heads above anyone else for his understanding of the subtle implications in major issues."* He is recommended for high-level air work and auditing.

The Clients: BP; GE; NCR; Northwestern University; ServiceMaster; Appleton Paper; Sara Lee; Kraft; Exelon and CITGO.

Band 2

Jenner & Block LLP
See firm details p.768

The Firm: This *"timely, responsive and practical"* group has a diverse practice that covers the full spectrum of work and has a significant overlap with commercial services in fields like IP and employment. It boasts a troupe of strong ex-regulator practitioners with national reputations and national clients. The team handles everything from air, OSHA and CERCLA work, as well as natural resource damage and endangered species matters. It is known in the market for its regulatory depth and skilled litigators. Lawyers *"know how to handle themselves"* and are sought after for white-collar criminal defense.

The Lawyers: Clients praise a raft of quality associates as well as high-profile partners, such as air pollution and enforcement mastermind **Bill Forcade** (see p.727), whose *"responsive and authoritative"* manner goes down well. They extol his *"meticulous"* work and value his excellent contacts and judgment. *"Fine negotiator"* and group cochair **James Vroman** (see p.757) is a big-picture litigator who started his environmental practice handling Superfund cases. **Lynn Grayson**'s (see p.730) patience is not lost on clients, and nor are her *"diligence"* and *"extraordinary capabilities."* Observers declare her to be *"so good that many of her clients won't work with anybody else."* Commentators united to acknowledge her *"amazing professionalism and real leadership,"* one even expressing the desire that she be cloned. She successfully defended General Dynamics in a CERCLA cost recovery action that significantly reduced the client's liability.

The Clients: General Dynamics Ordnance and Tactical Systems; General Dynamics; Neighbor-Space and the Community Economic Development Law Project.

Sonnenschein Nath & Rosenthal LLP
See firm details p.779

The Firm: Clients commend the *"full and impressive range"* of environmental expertise here, from internal investigations and compliance auditing to permitting and litigation in state and federal courts. Commentators draw special attention to strengths in CAA and transactional counseling, as well as the setting up of environmental management systems. Lawyers adopt "*a targeted approach that marries the client's needs with legal practicalities,*" and clients declare them "*always cutting edge and responsive.*" There is a good interface with the firm's vigorous real estate practice, and the team has expertise in a variety of niche sectors. Recently it represented a technology client in contested environmental rulemaking proceedings and, in an ongoing matter for Orix Real Estate Equities, it obtained noteworthy summary judgment and dismissal for a defendant in a contribution action.

The Lawyers: Susan Franzetti's decision to leave the firm to plow her own furrow is greeted with either sadness or relief, depending on the commentator and whether they regard the firm as friend or rival. Yet a strong core of gifted, high-profile lawyers remain, not least among them "*sharp-as-anything*" **Jeffrey Fort** (see p.727), in whose hands clients find great safety. As the engine of the practice, his "*innovative and lucid*" style pleases clients, who flag up his "*terrific attention to detail*" and "*deep insight.*" Fort has a formidable reputation for CAA work and a strong workflow in compliance auditing, a niche in which he pretty much wrote the book. He led the team that carried out an internal compliance investigation in the course of due diligence work for an acquirer client, obtaining a no-penalty termination from the EPA. Clients hail "*practical, insightful and high-energy*" **Mary Gade** (see p.728) as both politically prominent and renowned for her work in air quality matters and permitting. They say she has "*the pulse of the national scene.*" As the ex-director of the Illinois EPA, with long experience at the US EPA before that, she has a commanding pedigree and impeccable credentials, as well as "*the right Rolodex!*" Clients insist that "*it is important to stress just how creative and innovative she is*" when maneuvering within complex regulatory problems. She recently led the negotiations for WE Energies in a major multi-pollutant air settlement with the US EPA, and provided strategic advice on an award-winning brownfield redevelopment in the Chicago area. **Jacqueline Vidmar**'s (see p.756) ability to take the most complex Superfund matters and whittle them down to a simple and optimal solution for her clients is one of her greatest strengths. Peers describe her as "*committed to this area*" and she has, by all accounts, made great strides over the last few years.

The Clients: Sun Chemical; Cargill; McCain Foods; 3M and Wal-Mart.

Band 3

Karaganis, White & Magel

The Firm: The clients of this admired, "*cost-effective and high-quality*" environmental boutique range from Fortune 100 colossi to 'mom-and-pop' enterprises and include a substantial number of municipalities and waste and reclamation companies. The work varies from airport expansion issues to land use, but the major focus is on the brokering of mutually agreeable remedies in Superfund cases, facing both potentially responsible parties and the agencies. There is also considerable experience of recycling issues from fluids to aluminum, and the team earns kudos for its slightly unusual stance in also taking on plaintiff work.

The Lawyers: Quite simply, lawyers here "*perform great.*" All cut their teeth as litigators before specializing in various aspects of environmental law. A steady flow of Superfund/real estate work from Lockheed Martin is part of the daily fare, as is resolving liability surprises for the acquisitive Kraft Foods. "*Landmark*" lawyer **Joseph Karaganis** is widely seen as the force behind the practice. He is something of a noise expert and, like other colleagues, benefits from experience in plaintiff work. "*Deal-maker*" **Bruce White**'s "*first-rate expertise*" in Superfund is the principal peg on which a sterling reputation hangs. He is known for "*zealous advocacy*" and peers declare him "*a fun and worthy opponent.*"

The Clients: The broad client base includes state and local governments, real estate developers, investment funds, insurance companies and private landowners.

Schiff Hardin LLP

See firm details p.775

The Firm: This "*expert, versatile and practical*" team is active in all environmental fields. A particularly fine reputation in air pollution work, say clients, ought not to overshadow "*great coverage*" in water and land also. The team possesses "*real depth of talent,*" and offers services in litigation – "*they kick into another gear*" if matters do end up in the courts – and in counseling, advising a raft of large industrial clients. Electrical utilities matters make up a big chunk of the workload: the team gives compliance, permitting and transactional advice, and has specialist knowledge in coal gas cleanups. As often as not, rich experience before the various agencies helps to keep matters out of the courts but, if needs must, significant appellate experience at state and federal levels stands clients in good stead.

The Lawyers: Clients speak of "*unstuffy and approachable*" attorneys, and point in particular to "*competitive and flexible*" rates. The key figure, and the face that is best known about town, is the "*seriously good*" **Sheldon Zabel** (see p.759), who has long been a mainstay of the local bar. Peers declare him "*right up there, premier,*" and

he is especially well respected for air work and litigation. Clients praise him for "*getting to the crux of the problem quickly, and explaining and managing matters extremely well.*" Such clients are principally old-line utilities; they rate him as "*technically outstanding.*"

The Clients: Newell Rubbermaid; Dynegy Midwest Generation; NiSource; Ford and Northern Indiana Public Service Company.

Seyfarth Shaw LLP

See firm details p.777

The Firm: Though the bulk of the "*remarkably practical*" environmental group at this firm is in Chicago, it boasts offices around the country, including Washington DC. The emphasis is placed on toxic tort work, though commentators also point out a strong regulatory practice and good overlap with the flagship labor practice. Clients seeking safety advice are mostly drawn from the manufacturing sector and include chemical, refinery and energy companies. There are also a good number of waste and landfill clients, and the team additionally offers due diligence services to real estate companies and is national counsel to a major DIY retailer.

The Lawyers: These "*balanced*" lawyers have "*genuine strength*" in environmental law, say clients, who also praise their commercial focus. "*Innovative*" **Andrew Perellis** boasts a "*huge range*" of skills and is singled out for his regulatory and litigation work. **Eric Boyd** is recommended as an "*extremely bright attorney and excellent speaker*" who is best known for his air pollution work. The team acted for a joint venture that included a large public pension fund in the acquisition, development, and subsequent sale of a highly contaminated former defense plant. It also advised a chemical manufacturing client on its response to a US EPA request for information to determine whether past modifications to the plant triggered the CAA's new source review/prevention of significant deterioration requirements.

The Clients: Clients include waste-management companies and manufacturers from various industries, including steel, chemicals, cement and paint.

Winston & Strawn LLP

See firm details p.780

The Firm: This multi-faceted team offers a good range of "*premier-quality*" services, with an emphasis on litigation and enforcement issues. Much of the firm's activities take place outside Illinois, where it utilizes a strong national and overseas network; however, there is enough in the state to keep the "*responsive and accessible*" team busy locally. Clients span the market from small, local companies to global entities, mostly in the manufacturing and financial sectors, resulting in a thriving toxic tort and Superfund

All quotes in the text are from interviews with clients and competitors.

practice. Clients report that the team "*excels in responsiveness and skill.*"

The Lawyers: Lawyers are versatile and experienced in litigation, regulatory and transactional matters. Respondents describe them as "*simply a brighter, sharper bunch.*" **Jennifer Nijman** (see p.744) heads the group and handles all kinds of work, especially Superfund and toxic tort defenses. She is "*always impressive,*" according to clients who praise her "*creative and knowledgeable*" advocacy and understanding of agency employees and methods. "*Business-savvy*" **James Russell**'s (see p.749) clients are bowled over by his responsiveness, honesty and toughness. He successfully defended Clear Channel Entertainment in enforcement litigation threatened by the Illinois Attorney General and Illinois EPA for alleged environmental violations at the Tweeter Center outdoor concert theater. For Eaton Corporation he continues to serve a Nebraska facility in RCRA enforcement litigation brought by the US EPA in 1999, together with private toxic tort litigation prevention.

The Clients: Amsted Industries; Clear Channel Entertainment; Liberty Mutual Group; Zebra Technologies Corporation; Eaton Corporation and Fortune Brands.

Band 4

Gardner Carton & Douglas LLP
See firm details p.767

The Firm: This practice was set up in the 1970s by Richard Kissel, to whom it largely owes its enviable brand recognition in environmental circles. Though the firm itself is a general corporate outfit with useful branches in DC, Milwaukee and New York, in research interviews some impressive clients championed the team for defense of state enforcement proceedings and water issues.

The Lawyers: **Francis Lyons** (see p.738) is experienced in the ways of government, having been at the Department of Justice and former head of US EPA Region 5. Clients turn to him "*to fill in the gaps*" on regulatory questions. **Richard Kissel** (see p.735) is very much a 'father of the house' figure, honored throughout the state and beyond as a sort of chairman emeritus. He still undertakes some choice matters on a part-time basis and, perhaps most importantly, he remains an integral part of the team's client relations function.

The Clients: The diverse client base includes municipalities, private individuals, financial institutions and commercial/industrial operations from such sectors as manufacturing, energy, chemicals, real estate development, and finance.

Hodge Dwyer Zeman
The Firm: Often overshadowed by the luminaries of Chicago is this "*smart Springfield boutique,*" a downstate outfit devoted to environmental law. Lawyers provide expert advice across the board, including on CERCLA, Superfund and water. Peers declare the team to be "*a strong competitor by any standards.*"

The Lawyers: Co-founder **Katherine Hodge** (see p.732) acts for major facilities in the state and on all matters for the Illinois Environmental Regulatory Group. Commentators praise her excellent administrative practice, attributing her success to her "*finesse*" and "*incredible connections.*"

The Clients: Clients are drawn from the local regulated community, and include industrial entities, agricultural cooperatives, municipalities, individuals and business associations.

Kirkland & Ellis LLP
See firm details p.770

The Firm: This well-known "*force in Chicago's legal market*" has ample capability on the environmental side, offering an impressive clientele services in litigation and arbitration as well as regulatory advice. Commentators most often think of them in connection with major asbestos cases where a bankruptcy element is involved.

The Lawyers: The greatest reputation here belongs to **Andrew Running** (see p.749), whose skills in environmental and insurance litigation and arbitration ensure a steady stream of high-value work. He recently successfully established at trial his client's right to $111 million of insurance coverage in pending tort class actions.

McGuireWoods
The Firm: The environmental team here is part of a national network that acts for a diverse mix of manufacturing, energy and natural resources companies throughout the USA and overseas. Lawyers advise on compliance with various regulatory regimes, and are experienced in toxic tort cases and other kinds of litigation.

The Lawyers: **James Harrington** (see p.732) is widely seen as a senior regulatory attorney to the steel industry, and is also admitted to practice in Indiana.

The Clients: Lawyers serve a range of industry clients, traditionally steel, oil, chemicals, plastics, foundries, waste-to-energy, utility and manufacturing entities.

Other Notable Practitioners
"*Terrific and totally reliable*" **Susan Franzetti** is "*organized, efficient and a darned good lawyer.*" Her early training on Richard Kissel's team ensured both caliber and profile; her recent decision to leave Sonnenschein Nath & Rosenthal to go solo with her own Franzetti Law Firm PC is the talk of the town, not least because of the disappointment in so many quarters that she could not be tempted to go and work for them. Her primary areas of activity are in CWA matters and hazardous and non-hazardous waste, site remediation and litigation. She acts for a stream of clients who agree that they "*would stick by Susan and follow her wherever.*" Clients from banks to large laboratories and small companies value her "*commitment to optimal costs and quality.*" Such clients include Abbott Laboratories, First Midwest Bank, Illinois Tool Works, Midwest Generation EME and Safety-Kleen. She is lead counsel for two Superfund sites, and acts for an electrical utility in CWA use classification administrative proceedings. With a long and honored history in the field, **Fred Prillaman** still heads up the environmental team at Mohan, Alewelt, Prillaman & Adami and is known for "*terrific local assistance.*" He handles cases before both administrative and court authorities, particularly the Pollution Control Board. Commentators report that they see more of him on construction matters for suppliers and contractors in real estate developments that run into Superfund issues. "*Eminently capable*" **Russell Selman** (see p.751) is the focus of Katten Muchin Zavis Rosenman's environmental group. He specializes in real estate-related compliance and litigation advice. Peers recommend him for his expertise in Superfund/land pollution cases. He led the team that represented the park district of Oak Park on contamination matters arising from a turn of the century manufacturing gas plant.

HEALTHCARE

Illinois
Leading firms (Healthcare)

[1] **MCDERMOTT WILL & EMERY** *Chicago*
[2] **GARDNER CARTON & DOUGLAS** *Chicago*
[3] **BELL, BOYD & LLOYD LLC** *Chicago*
   KATTEN MUCHIN ZAVIS ROSENMAN *Chicago*
   MCGUIREWOODS *Chicago*
[4] **HOGAN MARREN** *Chicago*
   UNGARETTI & HARRIS *Chicago*

Leading individuals (Healthcare)

[1] **ANTHONY Michael** *McDermott Will, Chicago*
   BRYANT L Edward *Gardner Carton, Chicago*
   DUBE Monte *McDermott Will, Chicago*
   PEREGRINE Michael *McDermott Will, Chicago*
[2] **BECKER Scott** *McGuireWoods, Chicago*
   BROCCOLO Bernadette *McDermott Will, Chicago*
   CALLAHAN Michael *Katten Muchin, Chicago*
   FAHEY Thomas *Ungaretti & Harris, Chicago*
   LADD Jeffrey *Bell Boyd, Chicago*
   MCCAHILL Jane *Bell Boyd, Chicago*
[3] **GLASER D Louis** *Gardner Carton, Chicago*
   MARREN John *Hogan Marren, Chicago*
   MARTIN Laura *Katten Muchin, Chicago*
   RILEY James *McGuireWoods, Chicago*
   ROACH William *McDermott Will, Chicago*
   SKINNER Honey *Sidley Austin, Chicago*
   TECSON Andrew *Chuhak & Tecson, Chicago*

Firms and individuals are listed alphabetically in each band.

Band 1

McDermott Will & Emery

See firm details p.773

The Firm: This is the healthcare market's leading player, with interviewees describing it as both "*the 500lb gorilla in Chicago*" and a national pioneer. Not only is it able to serve clients with an "*enormous number of extraordinary lawyers,*" it also offers a depth and level of expertise that few can match. The practice covers a wide spectrum of healthcare-related issues, including transactional, regulatory and contentious matters. It boosts its service to clients through the support provided by ancillary departments such as the tax and antitrust groups. Its portfolio of recent deals includes acting for Carle Foundation Hospital and separately advising Memorial Medical Center of Springfield, Illinois, on exempt bond issues. It has also assisted Provena Health on various governance and transactional matters. The group's work also includes advising healthcare entities throughout the USA on their captive insurance arrangements and advising clients such as Resurrection Health Care on a number of physician-related activities and commercial disputes.

The Lawyers: This team, comprising around 25 lawyers, was boosted in 2004 by the arrival of

several high-profile individuals from rival firm, Gardner Carton & Douglas. Foremost among them is **Michael Peregrine** (see p.745), who clients characterized as a "*nationally recognized, leading healthcare figure.*" His practice includes a range of business transactions and governance issues. He is also a frequent speaker on the legal questions facing tax-exempt and nonprofit organizations. Sources described **Michael Anthony** (see p.717) as "*one of the best lawyers for understanding the full range of healthcare issues.*" Clients also emphasized that he is extremely easy to work with and praised his skill as a big-picture strategist. **Bernadette Broccolo** (see p.720) is a leading authority on the taxation of exempt organizations. She also advises on health industry joint ventures and Health Insurance Portability and Accountability Act (HIPAA) compliance. Clients reported that, "*She gives you her heart as well as her good brain*" and praised her for her high ethical standards and excellent written skills. **Monte Dube** (see p.725) is a high-profile partner who leads the firm's health department. He stands out for his expertise in transactional matters; he is "*skilled in putting the deals together.*" **Bill Roach** (see p.747) also attracted commendation for his excellent strategic and technical outlook. His varied workload includes advising on the formation of regional and national hospital systems, health industry M&A and joint ventures and corporate compliance programs.

The Clients: Resurrection Health Care; Provena Health; Hillcrest HealthCare System; Middletown Regional Health System; ProMedica Health System; Omnicare; Carle Foundation Hospital; Northwestern Memorial Hospital; Consorta; PeaceHealth; Adventist Health System; Methodist Medical Center of Illinois; Memorial Medical Center of Springfield and William Beaumont Hospitals.

Band 2

Gardner Carton & Douglas LLP

See firm details p.767

The Firm: This group has a long history in the healthcare arena but was dealt a blow in 2004 when several of its high-profile partners left to join McDermott Will & Emery. However, since that time the group has also recruited several individuals to its ranks and continues to be regarded as an important player in the market. The team's work spans the full range of healthcare law and of late has included advising on a flurry of transactions. This has included acting for a hospital in its purchase of a large physician clinic's facilities and on the construction of new, on-campus facilities. It also advised a multihospital system in Illinois in forming several joint ventures with physician groups. The team is also

active in litigation where its work includes defending clients against allegations of price-fixing and Medicare fraud. Attorneys also assist hospitals on physician corrective action cases under medical staff bylaws and win special praise from clients for their employee benefits expertise. Other facets of the workload include negotiating and drafting physician employment agreements, managed care agreements and patent and trademark applications.

The Lawyers: The loss of several Illinois-based partners has been countered by the arrival of other lawyers across the firm's four domestic offices. In Chicago, the undoubted star of the practice is **Ed Bryant** (see p.720). Interviewees crowned him "*one of the deans of healthcare law.*" They admire him for the breadth of his healthcare expertise and believe that he is strongest in the transactional field where he displays "*an excellent understanding of the business considerations.*" Although Bryant is seen as the dominant figure here, there are also a number of younger lawyers making a name for themselves. Sources highlighted **Louis Glaser** (see p.729) as an "*articulate, reasonable and very bright attorney.*" He advises a diverse client base on M&A transactions and tax issues, together with regulatory compliance including Medicare and Medicaid antifraud and abuse.

The Clients: Northwestern Memorial Hospital; Rehabilitation Institute of Chicago; Children's Memorial Medical Center; Healthcare Research & Development Institute, Florida; BroMenn Health System; American Health Information Management Association, Chicago; University of Illinois Hospitals and Clinics; University of Pittsburgh Medical Center; Decatur Memorial Hospital and National Center of Healthcare Leadership.

Band 3

Bell, Boyd & Lloyd LLC

The Firm: This is a strong regional firm that provides its clients with a wide-ranging coverage of health law. Much of its time is spent advising clients on corporate issues such as regulatory compliance, reorganizations and joint operating agreements. Finance assignments are another feature of the workload with lawyers advising on tax-exempt bonds and private placements. The group also has expertise in real estate law and has a strong practice assisting clients in construction and expansion projects. For example, it recently secured a certificate of need for one client, allowing it to build the first new hospital in Illinois for 20 years. Clients also call on the group for assistance in litigation and investigations before state and federal courts and agencies, including the Department of Health.

The Lawyers: **Jeff Ladd** is a well-known figure

690   All quotes in the text are from interviews with clients and competitors.

CHAMBERS USA 2005

in the healthcare community. Interviewees were especially impressed with his work before the Illinois Health Facilities Planning Board, although he is also an authority on tax-exempt municipal bonds. **Jane McCahill** is well versed on Medicare and Medicaid coverage and payment issues although clients also value her for her broad overview of corporate and regulatory healthcare law.

The Clients: The group's clients include: hospitals; ambulatory surgical treatment centers; health insurance companies; managed care entities; physicians and nursing homes.

Katten Muchin Zavis Rosenman
See firm details p.769

The Firm: Clients view this as a "*large and successful*" practice that provides them with an array of healthcare-related services. It frequently advises clients on their corporate and transactional matters but can also provide wider services, including expertise on related areas such as tax and antitrust. For example, the group recently defended Vista Health in an antitrust investigation, which was part of the FTC's national hospital merger retrospective. Lawyers also get involved in a wider variety of investigations and litigation. Working in conjunction with the Illinois Hospital Association and the Metropolitan Chicago Healthcare Council, the team represented 24 hospitals in a proceeding brought by the Department of Health and Office of Inspector General regarding false claims allegations and the 72-hour rule. The group's portfolio of work also includes counseling hospital clients on medical staff credentialing and disciplinary actions.

The Lawyers: Michael Callahan (see p.721) was a popular choice among our interviewees. Competitors warmly described him as a people-oriented attorney and "*a great counselor*," while clients rate him as "*extraordinarily good on medical staff matters*." Although **Laura Martin** (see p.739) covers a spectrum of healthcare law matters, interviewees especially value the antitrust slant that she brings to her practice. One client reported: "*She's one of the smartest people I've worked with.*"

The Clients: Central DuPage Health System; Northwestern Memorial Hospital; Riverside Medical Center and Resurrection Health Care.

McGuireWoods

The Firm: Market sources identified the group's work on behalf of ancillary service providers as its defining strength. Its clients include surgical centers, dialysis and freestanding diagnostic facilities, medical laboratories and multispecial-

ty clinics. The workload includes advising such entities on sales and acquisitions, joint ventures and the drafting and negotiating of various contracts. Regulatory counseling is also central to the service on offer here. Its lawyers provide guidance on federal and state antikickback, fraud and abuse laws, the False Claims Act and the development of compliance programs. Clients also call on the team for assistance in a spectrum of litigation, including cases concerning medical devices as well as antitrust law and white-collar crime.

The Lawyers: Scott Becker is one of the cochairs of the firm's healthcare practice and a key individual in the Chicago office. Interviewees commended him as a leading figure in the world of ambulatory surgical centers, where he advises on a range of operational issues. **Jim Riley** is a long-standing player in the healthcare field and joint head of the department. He counsels clients on corporate and transactional healthcare matters as well as issues such as certificates of need and reimbursement.

The Clients: A varied client base includes: hospitals and hospital systems; surgical centers; dialysis and freestanding diagnostic facilities; medical laboratories; multispecialty clinics; nursing homes; health insurers and physicians.

Band 4

Hogan Marren

The Firm: Interviewees described this niche player as a "*smaller but highly capable*" team that enjoys a respectable standing in the market. One of its key areas of strength lies in the managed care sector. Here, clients particularly praised the team for its skill in negotiating complex contracts and for assisting them in hospital-physician joint ventures. The group's work also includes advising clients on fraud and abuse compliance and on issues surrounding reimbursement. Although the group does not match some of its competitors in terms of size, interviewees were quick to point out that it has the scope to manage large projects and that it has attracted a loyal following of clients.

The Lawyers: Sources identified **John Marren** as the driving force of this practice. He is well known among competitors for his ability to handle sophisticated assignments on behalf of clients and won praise for his ability to "*think outside the box*." He is best known for his work in the managed care arena, although he also devotes time to advising providers on their relationships with physicians and hospitals.

The Clients: The team acts for hospitals, physician groups and other nonprofit entities.

Ungaretti & Harris

The Firm: This smaller group won plaudits from clients for its "*wonderful*" healthcare practice. It received most recognition for its public financing expertise where it acts for a range of clients on tax-exempt healthcare financings. Attorneys also frequently advise underwriters and healthcare providers on the issuance of tax-exempt bonds. The group's wider transactional expertise includes advising healthcare providers, hospitals, managed care facilities and nursing homes on acquisitions, divestitures and joint ventures. The team also assists clients in proceedings before the Illinois Health Facilities Planning Board and its attorneys are well versed in the full array of healthcare regulatory and compliance issues. Interviewees noted that the group has forged excellent relationships with federal and state regulators, agencies and governments and that it is well placed to advise clients on effective federal legislative strategy.

The Lawyers: Clients and competitors nominated managing partner **Tom Fahey** as the leading light of this group. They view him as a "*thoroughbred*" lawyer in the healthcare sphere and particularly emphasized his expertise in public finance law. An "*honorable fellow,*" he won plaudits for his efforts in building up the firm's profile in this area. His team, comprising around seven lawyers, works closely with attorneys from other departments, such as IP and litigation, all of who have experience in the healthcare sector.

The Clients: The team acts as counsel to a variety of clients including hospitals, healthcare associations, clinical laboratories, managed care facilities, medical device manufacturers and health insurance carriers.

Other Notable Practitioners

Sources recommended **Honey Skinner** (see p.752) of Sidley Austin Brown & Wood LLP for her representation of healthcare providers before various governmental agencies. They believe that her excellent circle of contacts makes her an ideal individual for assistance in certificate of need applications. Interviewees also highlighted **Andrew Tecson** of Chuhak & Tecson PC as another talented healthcare attorney. His portfolio of work includes assisting clients on corporate financings and bond issues, together with counseling them on aspects of administrative law unique to the healthcare arena.

INSURANCE

Illinois
Leading firms
(Insurance: Transactional & Regulatory)

1 LORD, BISSELL & BROOK *Chicago*
SIDLEY AUSTIN BROWN & WOOD LLP *Chicago*

2 DLA PIPER RUDNICK GRAY CARY US LLP *Chicago*
FOLEY & LARDNER *Chicago*
MAYER, BROWN, ROWE & MAW LLP *Chicago*

Leading individuals
(Insurance: Transactional & Regulatory)

1 GOODMAN Mark *Lord Bissell, Chicago*
SCHWAB Stephen *DLA Piper Rudnick, Chicago*
STINSON James *Sidley Austin, Chicago*
WYLIE Kenneth *Sidley Austin, Chicago*

2 BIASETTI Jon *Lord Bissell, Chicago*
GAVIN John *Foley & Lardner, Chicago*
GOLDMAN Michael *Sidley Austin, Chicago*
MENDELSOHN David *DLA Piper Rudnick, Chicago*
SHEPRO Richard *Mayer Brown, Chicago*
WATERS Paige *Sonnenschein Nath, Chicago*

Firms and individuals are listed alphabetically in each band.

Lord, Bissell & Brook

The Firm: Clients view this as "*a major go-to firm*" for "*top-flight insurance and reinsurance expertise.*" Few can match its years of experience in the sector, and it continues to sustain a national profile. It is recognized internationally, too, particularly for having secured a healthy stream of work from the London market. With some 50 "*quality lawyers*" in Chicago, this is a sizable group. Even clients from the opposite side of the table spoke warmly of the attorneys: "*They were pragmatic and honorable, and you could have a conversation with them.*" The firm covers transactional, regulatory and litigious matters. It is, for example, a leading destination for insurance M&A, where the input of attorneys is said to be "*extremely insightful and helpful.*" It also advises on the purchase of books of business and a large number of reinsurance-related deals. In a recent matter, it advised Hartford Life Insurance on its acquisition of the annuity, life and investment business of Fortis Financial Group for $1.1 billion. Attorneys are also active in regulatory counseling, especially in the light of Eliot Spitzer's current focus on the insurance industry. And finally, clients are drawn by the group's impressive track record in litigation – both coverage litigation (life and health insurance claims, as well as those arising from tobacco, asbestos and environmental liabilities) and reinsurance disputes – and international arbitration proceedings.

The Lawyers: On the direct insurance side, the highly respected and experienced **John Haarlow** emerged as the group's preeminent practitioner. He leads the international insur-

ance and litigation department and is most closely associated with his London market work. **Leisa Hamm** is another esteemed member of the team, and someone who is "*really gaining in stature.*" She counsels US and overseas insurers and underwriters on emerging claims, while also handling commutations and coverage litigation. **Nick DiGiovanni** won overwhelming support for his performance in reinsurance litigation. Clients say, "*He's an extremely effective trial lawyer,*" who has "*tremendous presence in court.*" They also champion him as someone who is "*helpful, articulate and responsive.*" On the transactional side, **Mark Goodman** stood out as "*a superb attorney*" with excellent industry connections. Clients characterize him as a responsive lawyer who is especially skilled at unraveling complex regulations. He also acts for banks and financial institutions in insurance underwriting and captive insurer matters. Goodman additionally has experience of insolvency proceedings. **Jon Biasetti** is one of the group's emerging talents; he is a "*realistic and reasonable*" force in negotiations and has wide-ranging experience. He counsels clients on market conduct and investment compliance and represents them in reinsurance transactions.

The Clients: The team acts for an impressive stable of clients, including banks and other financial institutions and some of the market's largest insurers and reinsurers. Examples include: Amerisure; Genworth Financial; Hartford Financial Services; ING America Insurance Holdings; Markel; Swiss Re Life & Health America and Union Fidelity Life Insurance Company.

Sidley Austin Brown & Wood LLP
See firm details p.778

The Firm: The market nominated this group as one of the top destinations in the state for reinsurance law; it is said to be ideal for "*heavy lifting*" and the largest and most complex disputes. Many of its most important cases have been arbitrations involving London market personal accident businesses. In one key matter it prevailed at a summary judgment hearing for client CNA Insurance Companies in a case that construed the scope of a commutation agreement between a cedent and an insurer. The team is also a potent force in insurance transactions, and has developed a reputation in the niche field of insurance securitizations. It is active in the crossover areas of insurance, banking and derivatives, where its activities touch on esoteric areas such as the structure and regulation of alternative risk financing mechanisms. On the transactional side, it acted recently for AIG on its acquisition of two Japanese insurance businesses from Royal & SunAlliance. Although the group's profile dips slightly in relation to direct

coverage litigation, it nonetheless offers its services in this area. It is particularly active in class action defense for insurance companies. Clients praised the group for its depth of talent and pointed to its success in cultivating a raft of promising younger lawyers to assist the more established names.

The Lawyers: Interviewees report that head of the reinsurance and insurance insolvency groups **Jim Stinson** (see p.754) is "*as good as anybody in the industry.*" Clients recommended him for his "*tremendous insights on how we should position ourselves in liquidations,*" and characterized him as an extremely experienced practitioner who provides added value in negotiations. His clients include receivers, reinsurers, ceding insurers and creditors. **Ken Wylie** (see p.759) is known for his insights into the nuances of insurance regulations and transactions. In particular, interviewees cited his knowledge of alternative risk transfer vehicles. Wylie has also met with success in reinsurance arbitrations. **Michael Goldman** (see p.730) is well known for his sophisticated transactional work and acts for a glittering client roster that includes the likes of AIG. He advises on a variety of deals including M&A transactions, demutualizations and securitizations. Researchers were impressed with the level of support garnered by **Bill Sneed** (see p.753). This "*intellectually powerful*" individual is "*an incredible worker and quick as a whip.*" His practice is focused on reinsurers and ceding companies in domestic and international reinsurance litigation and arbitration. **Susan Stone** (see p.754) can be "*tough, without being abrasive.*" Clients call on her for assistance in reinsurance disputes, although she also has experience in insurance insolvencies and environmental coverage litigation.

The Clients: AIG; CNA Insurance Companies; The Hartford; Aon; Kemper Insurance; Berkshire Hathaway; JPMorgan Chase; Morgan Stanley; Bear Stearns; Merrill Lynch and Zurich.

DLA Piper Rudnick Gray Cary US LLP
See firm details p.765

The Firm: Interviewees were impressed by this "*aggressive and innovative*" group, which delivers a "*practical, efficient and responsive*" service. Its performance in reinsurance disputes attracted most praise: it is a frequent participant in litigated and arbitrated proceedings regarding 9/11-related losses, film finance, marine losses and environmental liability. Of attorneys, clients say, "*They come with the advantage that they really know the subject area we bring to them.*" Litigators also represent clients in a range of insurance coverage disputes. On the transactional front, M&A and restructurings comprise

All quotes in the text are from interviews with clients and competitors.

Illinois
Leading firms
(Insurance: Reinsurance Litigation)

1 DLA PIPER RUDNICK GRAY CARY US LLP *Chicago*
LORD, BISSELL & BROOK *Chicago*
SIDLEY AUSTIN BROWN & WOOD LLP *Chicago*

2 BUTLER RUBIN SALTARELLI & BOYD *Chicago*
LOVELLS *Chicago*

3 BATES & CAREY *Chicago*
SCHIFF HARDIN LLP *Chicago*

Leading individuals
(Insurance: Reinsurance Litigation)

1 DIGIOVANNI Nick *Lord Bissell, Chicago*
RUBIN James *Butler Rubin, Chicago*
SCHWAB Stephen *DLA Piper Rudnick, Chicago*
SPECTOR David *Schiff Hardin, Chicago*
STINSON James *Sidley Austin, Chicago*

2 MCCULLOUGH Joe *Lovells, Chicago*
SNEED William *Sidley Austin, Chicago*
STONE Susan *Sidley Austin, Chicago*
WYLIE Kenneth *Sidley Austin, Chicago*

3 BATES Jr Robert *Bates & Carey, Chicago*
BURT Antony *Schiff Hardin, Chicago*
GOERING Gail *Lovells, Chicago*
HAAB Eric *Lovells, Chicago*
HERMES Robert *Butler Rubin, Chicago*

Firms and individuals are listed alphabetically in each band.

a significant element of the workload, and the group plays an additional advisory role to industry clients on matters such as the outsourcing of back office functions. Representing a further draw card for clients, the group boasts deep knowledge of industry regulations. Having long advised clients on a national basis, thanks to its spread of domestic offices, following its combination with the UK's DLA, the firm can now genuinely claim to have international capacity.
The Lawyers: The best-known individual here is insurance group chair **Stephen Schwab** (see p.751). Rivals view him as *"a top-tier lawyer"* in both reinsurance litigation and transactional matters, and he has particular experience of insurance insolvency, an area he knows *"as well as anyone."* Clients reveal him to be *"creative – he thinks things through and has resources behind him."* Another esteemed member of the team is **David Mendelsohn** (see p.741), who stands out for his transactional and regulatory expertise. He focuses on M&A, compliance issues and Errors & Omissions risk management.
The Clients: The group acts for major brokers, insurers, reinsurers and trade associations.

Foley & Lardner
See firm details p.1828
The Firm: This team is becoming increasingly visible in the market, with peers viewing it as a particularly strong contender in the corporate insurance arena. Its portfolio of recent work

includes M&A transactions and the purchase and sale of books of business. Lawyers have experience of insurance company formations and licensing matters, and are called on to advise on alternative risk mechanisms. Clients approach the group for its expertise in unraveling regulatory problems and for representation before legislative bodies. Attorneys also provide ancillary services, such as advice on the antitrust aspects of transactions and insurance taxation.
The Lawyers: Researchers were impressed with the support that **John Gavin** (see p.729) has won from various corners of the market. This talented corporate insurance lawyer is described as *"amazingly versatile and well informed."* His Chicago-based team works closely with colleagues in the firm's Milwaukee office.
The Clients: Clients include life, health and property/casualty insurance companies, HMOs, Blue Cross organizations, captive insurance companies, broker-dealers and mutual funds.

Mayer, Brown, Rowe & Maw LLP
See firm details p.771
The Firm: This group is favored by policyholders looking for high-quality service in insurance coverage disputes. While the firm has well-documented strength in litigation, satisfied clients also report that attorneys *"know the policies as well as anyone."* They act for clients in a variety of litigated proceedings at the state, federal and appeal levels, as well as in arbitrations. Recent examples include cases filed on behalf of Union Carbide in New York and West Virginia against 50 insurers for coverage for asbestos liabilities. Reinsurance is another, if less well-known, facet of the practice; in one recent case the firm represented a ceding company in arbitration against its London market reinsurers. Transactional work also accounts for part of the group's time. As well as dealing with the standard diet of M&A and regulatory compliance issues, lawyers have developed expertise in esoteric areas such as insurance securitization and derivatives transactions.
The Lawyers: Clients value the strong personal relationships that they have built up with the attorneys here and believe that they *"do an excellent job in putting the right team together."* **Steven Gilford** (see p.729) is the standout name of the group. One client remarked, *"He's one of the finest insurance coverage lawyers I've had the pleasure to work with."* Others described him as an exceptional negotiator who *"digs deep down to really understand the policies."* Much of his recent work has involved acting for a number of clients in asbestos-related claims against their insurers. Clients told us that **John Vishneski** (see p.757) goes into negotiations with *"a non-threatening demeanor but he shows that we'll move forward and litigate if we have to."* He represented one of his clients in a case concerning insurance coverage for numerous underlying

asbestos suits and environmental matters. **Richard Shepro** (see p.751) is one of the group's leading transactional lawyers. He is *"methodical and professional and pays great attention to detail."* His recent portfolio includes advising Everest Re Group on a succession of public offerings, most recently a $975 million shelf registration and a $320 million offering of trust preferred securities.
The Clients: Bank of America; BASF; Burlington Northern Santa Fe Railway; Caterpillar; Deutsche Financial Services; Illinois Tool Works; Whirlpool; Union Carbide; Abbott Laboratories; UBS PaineWebber and CIBC.

Butler Rubin Saltarelli & Boyd
The Firm: Although a relatively small practice group, Butler Rubin is *"a big player"* in the reinsurance market, interviewees insist. Clients confirm that the team provides *"high-quality advice"* and has a knack for producing excellent results. Much of its work is contentious and it frequently acts for clients in a range of underwriting and claims-related issues. Recent highlights include its successfully representation of Sphere Drake in two matters against All American that went to the Seventh Circuit Court of Appeals. It is also lead counsel for Hartford Insurance in its London market litigation concerning the company's casualty program and various asbestos and environmental claims. Attorneys also advise clients on confidential arbitrations regarding both traditional and financial reinsurance. Away from contentious matters the group counsels clients on various industry-specific and general corporate problems.
The Lawyers: The standout figure here is undoubtedly **Jim Rubin**. One client recommended him as *"one of the best lawyers I've worked with. He's insightful, knowledgeable, thorough and very responsive to clients."* Rubin is particularly strong in arbitrations, where he is *"relentless"* in pursuit of his clients' interests yet also has an ability to *"present a case very persuasively and in a manner that clients understand."* His compact team includes **Robert Hermes**, whose lengthy career has seen him act in a variety of reinsurance litigations and arbitrations.
The Clients: CNA Insurance Companies; Fairfax; Sphere Drake; TIG; Hartford Insurance Group; Liberty; WR Berkley and Zenith.

Lovells
The Firm: Lovells is popular among clients looking for assistance on an international basis, yet its popularity also stems from good old-fashioned *"promptness and reliability."* Interviewees rated the team as one of the strongest in the reinsurance field, a judgment that reflects its practice focus. It has a reputation for handling *"very complex reinsurance litigation and arbitration at the highest level."* One of its largest recent cases saw it acting for Aioi and Carolina Re on a

Illinois
Leading firms
(Insurance: Coverage Litigation)

1 **LORD, BISSELL & BROOK** *Chicago*

2 **JENNER & BLOCK LLP** *Chicago*
KIRKLAND & ELLIS LLP *Chicago*
MAYER, BROWN, ROWE & MAW LLP *Chicago*

3 **BATES & CAREY** *Chicago*
DLA PIPER RUDNICK GRAY CARY US LLP *Chicago*
MORGAN, LEWIS & BOCKIUS LLP *Chicago*
SCHIFF HARDIN LLP *Chicago*
SIDLEY AUSTIN BROWN & WOOD LLP *Chicago*

Leading individuals
(Insurance: Coverage Litigation)

1 **FORADAS Michael** *Kirkland & Ellis*, Chicago
GILFORD Steven *Mayer Brown*, Chicago
HAARLOW John *Lord Bissell*, Chicago

2 **HAMM Leisa** *Lord Bissell*, Chicago
MATHIAS John *Jenner & Block*, Chicago
SHUGRUE John *Morgan Lewis*, Chicago

3 **BATES Jr Robert** *Bates & Carey*, Chicago
BERKELEY Jill *Schiff Hardin*, Chicago
DICKINSON Christopher *Jenner & Block*, Chicago
MARRINSON Thomas *Morgan Lewis*, Chicago
VISHNESKI John *Mayer Brown*, Chicago

Firms and individuals are listed alphabetically in each band.

$2 billion action against Deloitte & Touche regarding the audits of Fortress Re. International involvement came with the representation of RGA Reinsurance in an ICSID arbitration against the Republic of Argentina.

The Lawyers: The team in Chicago operates closely with colleagues in New York and is also supported by the highly esteemed London office. **Joe McCullough** leads the firm's US reinsurance practice and regularly acts for insurers and reinsurers in arbitrations and court proceedings in the USA, Bermuda and Europe. Clients hailed **Gail Goering** as a "*crackerjack lawyer.*" She combines excellent negotiation skills with robust knowledge of both the law and its commercial implications to great effect. Goering advises on life and health insurance as well as reinsurance contracts and environmental and asbestos claims. The group includes Chicago managing partner **Eric Haab**.

The Clients: SCOR; Manulife; London Life; RGA; European Speciality Group; Max Re; Tokyo Marine; NipponKoa; Equitas and ING.

Bates & Carey

The Firm: Bates & Carey is becoming increasingly visible in the market and its work is now well recognized in the insurance coverage litigation and reinsurance arenas. On coverage, the firm defends a range of insurers in environmental and mass tort disputes – one client described it as "*dollar for dollar, the best coverage firm that I'm aware of.*" This aside, the loudest cheers are

reserved for the firm's reinsurance work. Attorneys have been busy acting for Gerling in a case against Travelers concerning the follow-the-fortunes doctrine. They also successfully represented a reinsurer in Michigan federal court in a case where the court ruled that a reinsured is not permitted to annualize the limits of a multiyear reinsurance contract.

The Lawyers: **Robert Bates** has the highest profile in the team. Clients rate him for his business sense and technical ability, confirming that he has a commanding presence in court. He acts for clients in a variety of litigated proceedings, but is increasingly identified with reinsurance arbitrations.

The Clients: American Re; General Re; Swiss Re; Gerling; AIG; XL and Allstate.

Schiff Hardin LLP
See firm details p.775

The Firm: Best recognized for the reinsurance element of its practice, this team caters for a wide variety of insurance company needs. It acts for clients in litigation and arbitration and has a portfolio of cases that includes property/casualty, life and health disputes. The lawyers also have experience of insurance insolvencies. On the direct insurance side, the clients are mainly insurance companies defending actions brought by policyholders. The team is also working hard to build up its transactional and advisory practice, having been especially busy of late advising clients on regulatory issues following Eliot Spitzer's developing interest in the industry.

The Lawyers: **David Spector** (see p.753) is a "*big-name*" reinsurance litigator who "*belongs on the A list.*" Clients view him as ideal for serious reinsurance matters and report that "*he doesn't have any trouble merging his intellect with his practical trial capability.*" Interviewees also had "*great confidence*" in **Antony Burt**'s (see p.721) skills as a litigator. Though he handles a variety of commercial cases, his focus is on reinsurance disputes. **Jill Berkeley** (see p.718) leads the firm's insurance group. Her competitors admire her for the caliber of her work on behalf of both insureds and insurers in coverage litigation.

The Clients: Allstate; Bank of America; Catholic Mutual Group; Gerber Life Insurance; Munich Re; Penn Mutual Life Insurance; Robert Plan; State Farm; Tokyo Marine & Fire Insurance; Transamerica Occidental Life Insurance; Trustmark Insurance; Hartford Insurance; Farmers Insurance; GMAC Insurance; USAA; Liberty Mutual; American United Life Insurance; Attorneys' Liability Assurance Society and St. Paul Travelers.

Jenner & Block LLP
See firm details p.768

The Firm: "*This is one of the best firms on the policyholder side – they're aggressive and know how to do things.*" The firm's success in general

commercial litigation is carried over into its insurance practice, where it provides "*realistic guidance to the client and frank and clear advice.*" Interviewees praised the breadth of the group's expertise, which extends to directors and officers' liability, professional liability and disaster coverage. Some of the group's most prominent work has been on behalf of CSX Transportation, including the successful conclusion of an environmental insurance coverage case and a case regarding bodily injury claims brought by employees. Although reinsurance work is a lesser-known facet of the practice, the firm is active in this field. For example, it acted for one client in a reinsurance arbitration concerning 9/11 death and injury claims.

The Lawyers: Clients admire the team for its litigation prowess and up-to-date knowledge of how industry developments will affect them. They rate **John Mathias** (see p.740) as a highly effective trial lawyer who "*relates well to juries and judges, and has a good, moderate tone.*" He represents policyholders in dispute with their insurers, but also maintains a broader commercial caseload. **Christopher Dickinson** (see p.724) was recommended as "*the go-to guy on a day-to-day basis.*" Clients say, "*He's responsive, well prepared and doesn't overwork a file.*" Dickinson represents financial institutions and other corporate policyholders in insurance recovery claims.

The Clients: The group acts exclusively for policyholders and counts a host of heavyweight domestic and international companies as clients.

Kirkland & Ellis LLP
See firm details p.770

The Firm: True to the firm's overall reputation, this is a litigation-focused practice group, dedicated to the representation of policyholders. Many of those it represents are drawn from the firm's broader client base; however, the group also attracts new clients thanks to its renowned trial capabilities. The view from the market is that the firm "*has the capability to litigate an insurance claim to a successful conclusion, and the insurance carriers know this.*" The market further applauded the team for its practical approach and meticulous preparation of cases. Environmental contamination, toxic torts and products liability appear on the firm's resume, alongside directors and officers' liability and business interruption claims.

The Lawyers: Clients say this group offers them "*a slew of talented individuals*" from which to choose. The key individual is **Michael Foradas** (see p.727), whose common sense and aggressive approach have been successfully imported from his commercial litigation practice. One client explained Foradas' appeal: "*He digs deeply into the issues, understands them very well and prepares heavily for hearings and conferences.*" In the past year he steered a large business interruption case for Republic Engineered Products and continued providing advice to Dow Chemical and Union Carbide on a variety of insurance and non-insurance matters.

The Clients: Alcon Laboratories; BP; Dow Chemical; Dow Corning; Motorola; NL Industries; Gaylord Container; Honeywell; Union Carbide; Raytheon; Siemens and Republic Engineered Products.

Morgan, Lewis & Bockius LLP

See firm details p.1556

The Firm: This firm is a prominent player in policyholder representations, acting for a host of top-flight companies drawn from a range of industries in their claims against their insurers. Recent highlights include securing a summary judgment in favor of client Nicor Gas in an

action regarding its coverage for third-party liability. Lawyers also reached a settlement for Kraft Foods Global in an environmental coverage case in Indiana. Asbestos matters and issues of broker liability have also been high on the agenda. The group's other activities include advice on procuring insurance and establishing captives, as well as giving guidance on the insurance aspects of corporate transactions.

The Lawyers: John Shugrue (see p.752) is a firm favorite with clients; they value his "*encyclopedic knowledge*" and his accessible and non-legalistic approach, adding that he is "*a real partner with his clients.*" While Shugrue clearly dominates the practice, interviewees also pointed to the solid team over which he presides. Research revealed **Tom Marrinson** (see p.739)

to be "*a terrific insurance coverage lawyer.*" He is a new arrival to the team, having previously practiced at Scandaglia Marrinson Ryan.

The Clients: Mobil; Kraft; Sunoco; ConocoPhillips; Nicor Gas and JPMorgan Chase.

Other Notable Practitioners

Paige Waters (see p.757) is a "*knowledgeable, smart and very capable*" young partner at Sonnenschein Nath & Rosenthal LLP, who can draw on experiences representing the Illinois Director of Insurance during her time as senior counsel of the Office of the Special Deputy Receiver. Her practice encompasses all aspects of insurance and reinsurance transactions, as well as regulatory issues and insurance insolvencies.

INTELLECTUAL PROPERTY

Illinois
Leading firms (Intellectual Property)

1	**BRINKS HOFER GILSON & LIONE** Chicago
	KIRKLAND & ELLIS LLP Chicago
	LEYDIG, VOIT & MAYER, LTD Chicago
	MCANDREWS, HELD & MALLOY, LTD Chicago
2	**BANNER & WITCOFF LTD** Chicago
	JONES DAY Chicago
	MAYER, BROWN, ROWE & MAW LLP Chicago
	MCDONNELL BOEHNEN HULBERT Chicago
	NIRO, SCAVONE, HALLER & NIRO Chicago
	PATTISHALL, MCAULIFFE, NEWBURY Chicago
	SIDLEY AUSTIN BROWN & WOOD LLP Chicago
3	**HOWREY SIMON ARNOLD & WHITE** Chicago
	JENNER & BLOCK LLP Chicago
	KATTEN MUCHIN ZAVIS ROSENMAN Chicago
	MARSHALL, GERSTEIN & BORUN Chicago
	MCDERMOTT WILL & EMERY Chicago
	WELSH & KATZ, LTD Chicago

Firms are listed alphabetically in each band.

Band 1

Brinks Hofer Gilson & Lione

See firm details p.762

The Firm: Among the largest IP boutiques in the state, this 150-attorney outfit is "*the old-line, blue-blood firm in town.*" Peers respect its quality across the board, particularly emphasizing strengths in patent litigation as well as trademark and copyright work. The team won a jury verdict of patent and trademark infringement for Aero Products International, resulting in injunctive relief, patent damages of $5.9 million and trademark damages of $1 million. It also successfully represented RJ Reynolds in a trademark case. The jury found that the defendant, which sold gray-market cigarettes bearing the Camel, Win-

ston or Salem trademarks, committed trademark infringement and willful trademark dilution.

The Lawyers: Patent expert **Roy Hofer** (see p.733) has been the firm's "*mainstay in litigation*" for many years and remains "*a top trial lawyer*" according to commentators. He often acts as mediator and arbitrator in patent disputes. Interviewees singled out the "*excellent*" **Gary Ropski** (see p.748) for his adept handling of client relationships and for being a "*confident litigator.*" He was recently appointed the firm's president elect. "*Preeminent*" **Jerome Gilson** (see p.729) remains "*a big name*" in the trademark field. Of late he sustained a high profile, representing the National Association of Realtors® (NAR) before the US Trademark Trial and Appeal Board. The case confirmed that Realtor® and Realtors® function as valid collective service marks belonging to NAR, and are not generic terms referring to all real estate agents. Skilled litigator and president of the firm **Jerold Jacover** (see p.733) primarily focuses on patents. **Laura Miller** (see p.742) impresses sources with her ability to "*play well in crowds.*" Her "*excellent judgment, diplomacy and tact*" make her a "*promising*" attorney. **Ralph Gabric** (see p.728) continues to build a profile.

The Clients: Further successes include acting on behalf of Swanson Tool in persuading the US District Court Chicago to order the seizure of counterfeit tools from a number of importers and retailers. Other clients: BorgWarner; Manitowoc; Herman Miller; Chicago Mercantile Exchange; United Airlines; US Steel; Wrigley; Visteon; Accenture; City of Chicago; Tyco; Goodrich; Amway; Minolta; DoCoMo; Seven Towns; DST Systems; Ferag; Zila and Stericycle.

Kirkland & Ellis LLP

See firm details p.770

The Firm: Amid rivalry between boutiques and general practice firms, the Chicago operation of this national powerhouse manages to win fans on both sides of the divide. One of the original groups to branch into IP, rivals view its now "*substantial team*" as "*real competition.*" It combines understanding of IP law, depth of experience, manpower and an impressive skill set. The firm thereby "*does a great job of institutionalizing clients*" and is ideally placed to handle complicated cases, particularly in the patent area. It offers considerable strengths in biotech, computer software architecture, semiconductor and circuitry, and medical device arenas. The team also has significant experience of acting for gaming machine manufacturers. Highlights have included bringing an action on behalf of Jays Foods to prevent Frito-Lay's campaign in which they claimed that "*Chicago prefers the taste of Lay's 'classic' chips over Jay's 'unflavored' chips,*" allegedly based on consumer taste tests. The team obtained a temporary restraining order, requiring Frito-Lay to remove and stop all advertising relating to this claim, and the case eventually settled. The team also acted for Avid Identification Systems in a patent infringement and false advertising case. Following a summary judgment victory where the defendants were found to have infringed, a settlement was reached.

The Lawyers: Patent litigator **William Streff** (see p.754) is a long-standing presence in the marketplace, with special expertise pertaining to internal combustion engines. His other focus areas include representing technology companies and litigation related to semiconductor processing and circuitry patents. Fellow statesman

Illinois
Leading individuals
(Intellectual Property)

1
HOFER Roy *Brinks Hofer*, Chicago
MALLOY Timothy *McAndrews Held*, Chicago
MCANDREWS George *McAndrews Held*, Chicago
NIRO Raymond *Niro Scavone*, Chicago
ROPSKI Gary *Brinks Hofer*, Chicago
WARNECKE Michael *Mayer Brown*, Chicago

2
AMEND James *Kirkland & Ellis*, Chicago
BOEHNEN Daniel *McDonnell Boehnen*, Chicago
CEDEROTH Richard *Sidley Austin*, Chicago
GILSON Jerome *Brinks Hofer*, Chicago
HARTMANN H Michael *Leydig Voit*, Chicago
HILLIARD David *Pattishall McAuliffe*, Chicago
KOZAK John *Leydig Voit*, Chicago
MCDONNELL John *McDonnell Boehnen*, Chicago
STREFF Jr William *Kirkland & Ellis*, Chicago
WITCOFF David *Jones Day*, Chicago

3
BANNER Mark *Banner & Witcoff*, Chicago
BORUN Michael *Marshall Gerstein*, Chicago
DUNCAN Margaret *McDermott Will*, Chicago
GABRIC Ralph *Brinks Hofer*, Chicago
JACOVER Jerold *Brinks Hofer*, Chicago
MANDELL Floyd *Katten Muchin*, Chicago
MILLER Laura *Brinks Hofer*, Chicago
PRITIKIN David *Sidley Austin*, Chicago
ROPER Harry *Jenner & Block*, Chicago
VEZEAU Timothy *Katten Muchin*, Chicago

Individuals are listed alphabetically in each band.

of the IP bar and rainmaker **James Amend** (see p.716) is an *"extraordinarily intelligent lawyer,"* researchers were told.

The Clients: 3M; Agere Systems; Apple; Boston Scientific; Infineon Technologies; International Game Technologies; Kubota Tractor; Lucent Technologies; Motorola; International Truck and Engine; Siemens and Whirlpool.

Leydig, Voit & Mayer, Ltd

The Firm: A venerable boutique of *"first-class litigators,"* this established outfit ranks alongside the state's top IP firms, peers said. While litigation is a mainstay of the practice the group also offers counseling services to clients. It boasts experience in patent, trademark, copyright and unfair competition cases, in addition to involvement in patent prosecution, copyright and trademark registration, licensing, franchising and trade secrets protection.

The Lawyers: Sources consider **Michael Hartmann** the firm's top litigator in nonpharmaceutical cases. With trial experience encompassing a variety of technology-related areas, his expertise in computer-related matters also drew commendation. **John Kozak** was praised as *"a talented and practical trial lawyer"* skilled in issues relating to heavy industry, although his practice has straddled an array of industry sectors.

The Clients: A *"great client base"* continues to attract the attention of interviewees. It includes

organizations in the biotech, chemistry, chemical engineering, pharmaceutical, electrical, computer and software engineering, and mechanical engineering fields. Universities, start-ups, corporations and the National Institutes of Health all feature as clients.

McAndrews, Held & Malloy, Ltd
See firm details p.772

The Firm: This *"consistently first-rate"* boutique is long established in the patent field. The team's expertise also encompasses trademarks, copyright and unfair competition. As a spin-off from the group's IP practice, the firm's attorneys juggle a caseload of complex technology, antitrust and civil racketeering matters. Significant litigation on behalf of Guidant relating to medical implants was a recent highlight.

The Lawyers: **Timothy Malloy** (see p.739) is widely acknowledged as an established talent when it comes to medical implants. In the past year he was active on behalf of Cardinal. Market opinion indicated **George McAndrews** as *"a fine opponent"* who maintains a *"first-rate"* practice. Recently he focused mainly on software litigation as well as advising on substantial antitrust matters in the healthcare sector.

The Clients: Bausch & Lomb; Stryker; Genlyte; GE; CSP; Broadcom and Rockwood Industries.

Band 2

Banner & Witcoff Ltd

The Firm: The IP bar holds this boutique in high regard. Competitors note the firm's thriving DC practice as adding to the already considerable firepower on offer in Chicago. Further offices are located in Boston and Portland. A major work highlight was the firm's representation of Applied Concepts at an appeal concerning a patent covering a police radar gun. The plaintiff appealed for the original noninfringement ruling to be thrown out, but the Federal Court affirmed the ruling, and dismissed an attempt to reactivate litigation.

The Lawyers: Interviewees endorsed **Mark Banner** as having sustained his profile in the field. His practice takes in patent, trademark and copyright litigation, with an emphasis on jury trials in patent cases. He was active on behalf of Nike in a trade secrets and related claims case. The plaintiff alleged that Nike used his alleged trade secrets in footwear cushioning technology in basketball, running and cross-training shoes. The judge granted summary judgment in favor of the defendants, concluding that the plaintiff had failed to present evidence confirming he had taken reasonable steps to protect the secrecy of the design.

The Clients: In the past year, the team's clients have included Peaceable Planet, CheckFree and Toshiba International.

Jones Day
See firm details p.485

The Firm: The Chicago office is credited with a solid, full-service IP practice, aided by the firm's nationwide presence in the field and a stable of long-standing clients providing a steady stream of work. This ranges from patent litigation to trademark and trade secrets cases, and also includes patent and trademark prosecution. The electronics, hardware, software and e-commerce industries are recent sources of instructions. Successes have included representing Motorola and its semiconductor spin-off Freescale Semiconductor in three patent infringement cases involving more than 20 semiconductor product and process patents. Additional highlights include acting for IBM in several patent infringement cases. These concerned the processing of electronic information in Internet purchases, as well as hardware and software for displaying and manipulating graphics.

The Lawyers: *"Low-key"* practice head **David Witcoff** (see p.758) is believed to have *"the aggression and drive"* to cement his rising profile as *"an excellent lawyer."* His caseload encompasses a variety of hi-tech matters in a range of technologies, most often in the areas of semiconductors, computer hardware and software and Internet-related commerce.

The Clients: Texas Instruments; Kodak; Abbott Laboratories; MOSAID Technologies and HNI Corporation.

Mayer, Brown, Rowe & Maw LLP
See firm details p.771

The Firm: Clients enthused about this *"spectacular group,"* arguing its *"international scope"* and *"depth of expertise"* make for *"an A-class IP group."* The 28-member Chicago group is complemented by a 70-strong nationwide practice. It offers patent litigation, trademark, trade secrets, copyright, breach of contract and licensing expertise. Biotech sector involvement constitutes a recent growth area for the team, in addition to continued focus on pharmaceutical matters. The group represented TriStrata Technology (TTI) in obtaining a jury verdict supporting seven claims that two patents were valid and willfully infringed by Valeant Pharmaceuticals International, formerly ICN Pharmaceuticals. The patents related to TTI's alpha hydroxyacid skincare technology. The team also successfully defended German manufacturer Krauss-Maffei and several of its customers in a series of patent lawsuits, achieving summary judgment backing the team's arguments of noninfringement, a decision upheld at appeal.

The Lawyers: **Michael Warnecke** (see p.757) is *"the life and spirit of the practice"* according to market experts. A *"talented"* patent litigator, recently he concentrated largely on chemical and computer technology industries. Warnecke

acted for Mitsubishi, successfully resolving one of three long-running lawsuits brought against it by Rotec Industries. The cases concerned the provision of tower crane equipment for the Three Gorges Dam project on the Yangtze River. Following the award of a contract to Mitsubishi for two crane units, Rotec brought claims of patent infringement and misappropriation of trade secrets, but the court dismissed the case.
The Clients: Illinois Tool Works; Getty Images; Solvay Pharmaceuticals; Abbott Laboratories; Formica and Diners Club.

McDonnell Boehnen Hulbert & Berghoff LLP
See firm details p.774
The Firm: Clients spoke effusively of this IP boutiques' *"fresh spirit,"* and *"solid and rigorous advice."* Its attorneys' ability to *"connect with people"* means they can *"be firm and authoritative without being condescending."* The team is experienced in biotech, healthcare, telecom and pharmaceutical-related matters, primarily in the patent field. However the firm offers a full service in IP matters. Highlights included acting for startup Corning in a case against SRU Biosystems involving resonant waveguide gratings that are expected to revolutionize high throughput screening of drug candidates by the pharmaceutical industry. The group also defended Roche Diagnostics in a case involving a product widely used by diabetics. Clients claim that the team's *"easy-to-like style makes business so much easier."*
The Lawyers: Clients appreciate **Daniel Boehnen**'s (see p.719) strategic ability, while also commending his patent knowledge and knack of being *"persuasive."* He has been heavily involved on behalf of biotech companies, developing expertise in matters pertaining to RNA Interference. Recently he also acted for Whirlpool in its suit to prevent LG Electronics from infringing patents in the area of washers and dryers. **John McDonnell** (see p.740) is well respected for his work in the pharmaceutical and biotech areas, where his advice and input is highly valued by clients.
The Clients: Pfizer; Serono; Symantec; Sirna Therapeutics; Emerson Electric; Eli Lilly; Aventis; Honeywell; Sprint; 3Com and UTStarcom.

Niro, Scavone, Haller & Niro
The Firm: Rivals relish the opportunity to lock horns with this *"doggone good firm."* Clients deem them a *"terrific team of talented, aggressive and trustworthy"* trial lawyers. They act largely for plaintiff and contingency clients. Recent highlights included filing a case concerning the use of a client's research in the development of a drug for macular degeneration. The group also acted for a client claiming to be the true inventor of Disney's patented Fast Pass system used at its theme parks.

The Lawyers: The cornerstone of this group, **Raymond Niro** is *"a very powerful guy,"* according to commentators. A *"consummate plaintiff lawyer at the patent bar,"* his *"top-notch"* trial work and talent for thinking on his feet have ensured Niro a lasting reputation as one of the state's leading IP attorneys.
The Clients: In addition to individuals and small companies, the group acts for Simmons Mattresses; Black & Decker; ITW; United Technologies and IP Innovations.

Pattishall, McAuliffe, Newbury, Hilliard & Geraldson
The Firm: This team is widely perceived as a market leader for trademark work in Chicago and perceived by some as *"among the leading trademark law firms in the country."* Matters relating to copyright, Internet, e-commerce, advertising, trade secrets and unfair trade practices law are all covered by the practice. A recent success included acting for Deutsche Wurlitzer in an appeal before the Seventh Circuit Court of Appeals. Deutsche Wurlitzer, a spin-off from The Wurlitzer Company, had a license allowing it to use the Wurlitzer trademark in connection with its products. This was terminated by The Wurlitzer Company, on the basis that it was able to do so at will, but the court found that the trademark was terminable for material breach only.
The Lawyers: Trial lawyer **David Hilliard** is *"a true gentleman and scholar"* according to interviewees, who admire his *"stellar reputation"* in the trademark arena.
The Clients: The group's client base encompasses small, medium and large companies, business associations and nonprofit organizations, as well as sole proprietors in a variety of manufacturing and service industries.

Sidley Austin Brown & Wood LLP
See firm details p.778
The Firm: This solid practice benefits from the firm's growing reputation as an *"IP powerhouse."* Patent litigation, principally relating to computer software, medical device and pharmaceutical industries, lies at the core of its practice. The team is also active in trade secrets matters. Meanwhile clients praise its *"excellent patent prosecution operation."* Other focus areas include the contact lens, anesthetic, software, and cellular industries.
The Lawyers: *"Diligent and hard-working"* **Richard Cederoth** (see p.722) continues to impress with his patent litigation-centered practice. Computer and software-related matters account for a major portion of his workload. Practice chair **David Pritikin** (see p.746) is acknowledged for his *"good judgment"* and sound patent litigation skills.
The Clients: Microsoft; Johnson & Johnson; Pfizer; GlaxoSmithKline and AT&T.

Band 3

Howrey Simon Arnold & White
The Firm: This group of *"good, solid trial lawyers"* is noted for its experience in biotech and pharmaceutical industries. Patent litigation, prosecution and opinion work all contribute to the workload. The Chicago team is further bolstered by the firm's national prominence in IP matters, market sources added. Highlights have involved issues relating to, inter alia, recombinant technologies, protein chemistry and plant science. In the pharmaceuticals arena, the caseload incorporated matters relating to hormonal drugs for treating anemia, human growth deficiency and infectious diseases, as well as drugs for testicular and prostate cancer.
The Lawyers: Edward O'Toole is the group's key figure.
The Clients: Amgen; Pharmacia; Boehringer Ingelheim; SC Johnson; ICOS and Lifecodes.

Jenner & Block LLP
See firm details p.768
The Firm: The addition of boutique Roper & Quigg's lawyers has further underlined this firm's reputation as a growing IP practice. Already boasting a premier litigation presence in the state, clients appreciate its *"phenomenal"* IP litigators, who concentrate on patent and trade secrets cases. The team is also experienced in handling trademark, copyright and licensing issues. Highlights included advising General Dynamics on IP and IT issues surrounding the company's $1 billion acquisition of GM's government defense business. The team successfully represented inventor Ole K Nilssen in a one-week arbitration concerning a patent infringement claim, resulting in a substantial award in his favor.
The Lawyers: Patent dispute resolution specialist **Harry Roper** (see p.748) is a hit with clients, who approve of his talent for *"taking difficult concepts and explaining them to juries in understandable terms."* This has brought him an impressive degree of success.
The Clients: The group's client base comprises Japanese companies in the electronic and software business, an area where the group places particular emphasis, especially in the field of educational software. The consumer goods, electronics and pharmaceutical industries are also fruitful sources of instructions for the group.

Katten Muchin Zavis Rosenman
See firm details p.769
The Firm: Clients choose this firm for *"sophisticated, challenging litigation matters,"* in the field of trademark, copyright, trade secrets, unfair competition and advertising, and patent matters. The group is active in a variety of industries, including the pharmaceutical, healthcare,

entertainment, financial services and business process fields. A *"client-friendly"* and *"service-oriented"* approach wins accolades from sources. It negotiated a favorable settlement agreement for Miller Brewing in a patent infringement claim made by patent licensing company Solaia Technologies. The patent concerned a particular use of programmable logic controllers. As a result Miller could continue its operations without re-engineering or making mechanical changes to its equipment. On the trademark side, team members acted for Atkins Nutritionals, against claims made by Jays Foods. The plaintiff company claimed ownership of the trademark Krunchers! for potato chips, and sought injunctive relief and monetary damages following Atkins' use of ATKINS Crunchers for a food product. The litigation was dismissed.

The Lawyers: *"Level-headed"* **Floyd Mandell** (see p.739) *"can really calm down the situation purely by giving insight and knowledge."* His *"extraordinary"* responsiveness and pragmatic understanding of business objectives have made him a client favorite for trademark litigation. He is currently defending Universal Studios and Universal Music Group in a suit arising from 'How High', a movie produced by Universal Studios. Universal Music produced the soundtrack. The plaintiff, the owner of the hip hop clothing trademark FUBU, claims that its right were infringed by the use of BUFU clothing, worn by the main characters. IP litigator **Timothy Vezeau** (see p.756) *"always has in the back of his mind the interest of the client,"* claimed interviewees. He focuses on technology matters, and acted for Lyndex in a patent infringement case against Heartech Precision, Pioneer Trading and Doosung Precision. The defendants sold, offered for sale and/or imported milling chucks into the USA, in acts of infringement, and the litigation was favorably resolved by settlement.

The Clients: AIG; Bausch & Lomb; Cambridge Antibody; Fortune Brands; Intel; Microsoft; NBC Universal; Recording Industry of America (RIAA); Sears Roebuck; Technology Licensing; Biovail; Harris and Euronext.

Marshall, Gerstein & Borun

The Firm: This IP boutique specializes in the acquisition, protection and challenge of patents, trademarks, copyrights and trade secrets. It is specially renowned for advising clients in transactional settings. Sources singled out the team for its biotech expertise, a field in which it is thought to have a *"tremendous presence,"* enhanced by *"bright attorneys who think quickly on their feet."* The firm successfully represented Golden Voice Technology & Training in a patent infringement case concerning telephone center technology against Rockwell Electronic Commerce.

The Lawyers: *"The leading light at the firm,"* **Michael Borun** is a prominent figure in the biotech arena, researchers heard. Involved in both litigation and patent prosecution, he impresses as a *"highly specialized and competent"* attorney.

The Clients: The group is active in the defense/aerospace, chemical engineering, mechanical, nanotechnology, pharmaceuticals, biotech, electrical, computer software and Internet industries.

McDermott Will & Emery

See firm details p.773

The Firm: Research indicated that clients *"absolutely love working with the firm."* Features of the practice that attracted particular praise include its members' lack of ego and ability to *"work collaboratively"* with in-house teams. Highlights include successfully acting in a trademark infringement case on behalf of Menard against Sears Roebuck.

The Lawyers: Head of the Chicago IP practice, **Margaret Duncan** (see p.725) is *"composed and articulate"* in the courtroom, according to clients, who also value her collaborative approach to matters. She practices in all aspects of IP law.

The Clients: Hitachi; Sunny Delight; Ikea; Aladdin Knowledge Systems and WTTW.

Welsh & Katz, Ltd

The Firm: This *"good collection of people"* is known for its *"take no prisoners approach"* to IP work. A dedicated IP firm, its remit includes disputes relating to patent, copyright and trademark infringement, as well as theft of trade secrets, license negotiation, and patent protection matters.

The Lawyers: Firm principal Sidney Katz is the key contact for many matters, especially when it comes to IP mediation.

The Clients: Industry sectors in which the group has considerable experience include biotech, computers, electronics, chemical and entertainment. It acts on behalf of corporations, universities and individuals.

698   All quotes in the text are from interviews with clients and competitors.

CHAMBERS USA 2005

LITIGATION

GENERAL COMMERCIAL

Illinois
Leading firms
(Litigation: General Commercial)

1 KIRKLAND & ELLIS LLP *Chicago*

2 MAYER, BROWN, ROWE & MAW LLP *Chicago*
WINSTON & STRAWN LLP *Chicago*

3 BARTLIT BECK HERMAN PALENCHAR *Chicago*
JENNER & BLOCK LLP *Chicago*
JONES DAY *Chicago*
SIDLEY AUSTIN BROWN & WOOD LLP *Chicago*

4 BAKER & MCKENZIE *Chicago*
KATTEN MUCHIN ZAVIS ROSENMAN *Chicago*
MCDERMOTT WILL & EMERY *Chicago*
SKADDEN, ARPS, SLATE, MEAGHER *Chicago*

5 COTSIRILOS TIGHE & STREICKER LTD *Chicago*
FREEBORN & PETERS *Chicago*
STETLER & DUFFY LTD *Chicago*

Firms are listed alphabetically in each band.

Band 1

Kirkland & Ellis LLP
See firm details p.770
The Firm: With "*great bench strength and depth across the board,*" the litigation juggernaut is a nationwide magnet for high-stakes, bet-the-company litigation. Though considered somewhat expensive by clients, its "*ability to strategize from the start*" and "*superb understanding of the facts of a case*" is worth every penny, commentators said. The team of about 150 "*experienced advocates and courtroom players*" lends "*crispness*" to legal battles, whether it is in IP, products liability, environmental or various commercial cases.
The Lawyers: The "*extremely talented*" **David Bernick** (see p.718) is considered "*excellent in class actions*" and a star performer "*in front of a jury.*" His drawing card is in products liability and mass torts, for example, representing WR Grace in significant asbestos liability litigation. As national trial counsel for Brown & Williamson Tobacco in the "*mother of all trials,*" he is defending the company against charges in the United States involving a possible conspiracy to defraud the American public about the health risks of tobacco; the case also involves other major tobacco companies. The "*smart and hard-working*" **Rick Godfrey** (see p.730) merits his ranking on account of an "*excellent and successful track record.*" Observers acknowledged class actions as a forte. He has been acting for BP America in a nationwide class action alleging breach of contract regarding the operation of oil and gas wells nationally. He has also been representing Allstate in a number of large putative class actions alleging age discrimination in the company's reorganization. **Frank Cicero** (see p.722) scooped compliments as one of the "*firm's best trial lawyers,*" while **John Hickey** (see p.732) is respected as an intellectual heavyweight

who is often called upon during the difficult stages of a trial. His trial experience often pertains to environmental and patent disputes, a slew of which he has handled for 3M. He has also been acting as lead counsel for GM in a prominent personal injury case involving the roof structures in all 1992-99 Chevrolet Suburbans. He has also defended GMAC in a nationwide class action pertaining to the Equal Credit Opportunity Act. The long-standing and experienced **Garrett Johnson** (see p.734) earned admiration for a diverse practice, which includes antitrust, securities and environmental litigation. For example, he secured a defense jury verdict for Motorola in the Arizona groundwater contamination class action. The "*fabulously skilled and diverse*" **Emily Nicklin** (see p.744) obtained a victory for Arthur Andersen in a case against Frederick's of Hollywood concerning the accounting firm's auditing practices. Her practice also drew admiration for high-profile employment litigation and professional liability disputes, usually involving consultants and accountants. **Stephen Patton** (see p.745), whose commercial litigation practice continues to flourish, has been acting for Deloitte & Touche in a $10 billion lawsuit brought by Parmalat's Italian bankruptcy trustee. He has additionally served as lead counsel for Concord EFS in a DOJ attempt to block a $7 billion merger with First Data.
The Clients: Allstate; GM; ExxonMobil; BMW of North America; Walgreen Co; Morgan Stanley; 3M; Aon; Motorola; Honeywell; Brown & Williamson Tobacco; WR Grace; Dow Corning; Ford; BP America; Citicorp and Vodafone.

Band 2

Mayer, Brown, Rowe & Maw LLP
See firm details p.771
The Firm: Clients considered this "*multifaceted*" international firm to be an excellent choice on cutting-edge litigation, employing a large cluster of lawyers across a wide array of substantive areas to obtain favorable solutions. With a phalanx of litigators who "*know when to be aggressive and when to compromise,*" it has dazzled the market on securities class actions and antitrust litigation. Other interests include asbestos, tobacco and mass torts. The "*ability to combine a strong appellate and litigation section*" has also helped bolster its capabilities, commentators said. This is aptly linked with "*top-class oral advocacy and second-to-none written work.*"
The Lawyers: "*Superb judgment*" and previous experience at the US Attorney's Office helped **Vincent Connelly** (see p.723) maintain a place at the top of the tree. Clients said he's as "*smart as a whip,*" and often seek his advice on a wide range of litigation, especially when it has a white-collar criminal defense or SEC element.

He has been defending UBS in an Enron-related dispute. Considered "*an excellent manager of client relationships,*" veteran litigator **Alan Salpeter** (see p.750) carries significant weight in the securities fraud and accounting malpractice areas. He acts for Ernst & Young in litigation brought by Cendant in a case concerning accounting irregularities. He also acts for Oracle and its founder Larry Ellison in securities and derivative litigation. **Stephen Shapiro** (see p.751), whose profile is perceived to be on the ascendancy, exhibits "*superb analytical skills*" and "*a rapid recollection of the facts of a case.*" Clients considered the founder of the firm's supreme court and appellate litigation practice group a "*huge draw.*" He has been acting for BASF in a Supreme Court case that was described by many as one of the most vital antitrust cases in recent years. In spite of management responsibilities, the global cochair of litigation **Herbert Zarov** (see p.759) drew praise for his expertise on mass torts and securities fraud cases. He is lead counsel for Dow Chemical in the breast implant litigation and separately advised Union Carbide in the asbestos litigation. Armed with a "*brilliant mind*" and "*terrific trial skills,*" the former US District Attorney **Thomas Durkin** (see p.725) was deemed "*very much the real deal,*" mixing commercial, products liability, securities and patent knowledge in his broad practice. According to observers, the "*convincing and highly trusted*" **Michele Odorizzi** is "*central to the firm's appellate practice.*" Blessed with a "*deep encyclopedic knowledge,*" her diverse caseload has, of late, leaned toward securities fraud and consumer fraud class actions. On behalf of Deloitte & Touche, she assisted on the litigation arising from the Parmalat bankruptcy. The "*straightforward, competent and experienced*" **Sheila Finnegan** (see p.727) enters the rankings, giving clients "*an extra level of comfort*" on various disputes such as securities class actions, consumer fraud litigation and product defect cases. The "*phenomenal*" **James Ferguson** (see p.726) earned his spurs as a "*high energy*" operator whose practice includes IP and white-collar criminal defense.
The Clients: BASF; Merrill Lynch; SBC; BellSouth; Qwest; Kroger; GM; Ernst & Young and Deloitte & Touche.

Winston & Strawn LLP
See firm details p.780
The Firm: Securities and white-collar litigation earned particular top marks for this blossoming national practice. Commentators recognized "*a set of consistently experienced generalist trial attorneys*" offering "*wonderful*" service across the board. Its claim to fame is demonstrated through such prominent cases as the tobacco litigation on behalf of Philip Morris. In addition,

Illinois
Leading individuals
(Litigation: General Commercial)

Senior Statesman
SULLIVAN Thomas *Jenner & Block*, Chicago
★ WEBB Dan *Winston & Strawn*, Chicago

1 BECK Philip *Bartlit Beck*, Chicago
BERNICK David *Kirkland & Ellis*, Chicago
CONNELLY Vincent *Mayer Brown*, Chicago

2 BARTLIT Fred *Bartlit Beck*, Denver
GODFREY Richard *Kirkland & Ellis*, Chicago
REIDY Daniel *Jones Day*, Chicago
SALPETER Alan *Mayer Brown*, Chicago
VALUKAS Anton *Jenner & Block*, Chicago

3 CICERO Frank *Kirkland & Ellis*, Chicago
CONLON William *Sidley Austin*, Chicago
DOUGLAS Charles *Sidley Austin*, Chicago
HICKEY John *Kirkland & Ellis*, Chicago
LASSAR Scott *Sidley Austin*, Chicago
LINKLATER William *Baker & McKenzie*, Chicago
MOLO Steven *Shearman & Sterling*, New York
SHAPIRO Stephen *Mayer Brown*, Chicago
SOLOVY Jerold *Jenner & Block*, Chicago
SPERLING Robert *Winston & Strawn*, Chicago
STONE Jeffrey *McDermott Will*, Chicago
TARUN Robert *Latham & Watkins*, Chicago

4 ANDERSON Kimball *Winston & Strawn*, Chicago
CARLSON Walter *Sidley Austin*, Chicago
DURKIN Thomas *Mayer Brown*, Chicago
FERGUSON James *Mayer Brown*, Chicago
FINNEGAN Sheila *Mayer Brown*, Chicago
GALLO John *Sidley Austin*, Chicago
HERALD J Patrick *Baker & McKenzie*, Chicago
HOEFLICH Adam *Bartlit Beck*, Chicago
JOHNSON Garrett *Kirkland & Ellis*, Chicago
LERMAN Bradley *Winston & Strawn*, Chicago
MENDELOFF Scott *Sidley Austin*, Chicago
NICKLIN Emily *Kirkland & Ellis*, Chicago
ODORIZZI Michele *Mayer Brown*, Chicago
PATTON Stephen *Kirkland & Ellis*, Chicago
POPE Michael *McDermott Will*, Chicago
ROSENBLOOM David *McDermott Will*, Chicago
RYAN Thomas *Sidley Austin*, Chicago
SKLARSKY Charles *Jenner & Block*, Chicago
STREICKER James *Cotsirilos Tighe*, Chicago
SULLIVAN Barry *Jenner & Block*, Chicago
ZAROV Herbert *Mayer Brown*, Chicago

Individuals are listed alphabetically in each band.

the team's intent to strengthen its appellate practice group was firmly illustrated by the 2004 arrival of Linda Coberly, former law clerk to Stephen G. Breyer – associate justice of the US Supreme Court.
The Lawyers: The firm's litigation practice owes much of its success to **Dan Webb** (see p.758), a former US Attorney in Chicago who is considered in *"a different zone"* and way ahead of the chasing pack. Renowned internationally for his prosecution of retired Admiral John Poindexter in the Iran-Contra affair, his practice

displays a distinct white-collar flavor. His *"gold standard"* is stamped on a flurry of disputes that carry national importance, such as the tobacco litigation. This *"super lawyer"* is *"incredibly in demand,"* leading some clients to surmise that just about his only drawback is the difficulty in retaining him in the first place. The *"savvy litigator"* **Bob Sperling** (see p.753) enters the table on the back of about 30 years' experience handling a range of work for an impressive clientele. Securities class actions form a significant part of his practice; for example, he is representing Bank One in a national consolidated shareholders' class action relating to the First Chicago NBD/Bank One merger. A *"no-nonsense approach"* puts **Bradley Lerman** (see p.737) on the ranking table, further bolstered by his expertise in white-collar, securities and products liability litigation. He acts for clients before the SEC and other government agencies regarding securities, mutual funds and accounting matters. He is also advising McDonald's in the high-profile national obesity class action litigation and separately counseling Morgan Stanley in the SEC investigation regarding market timing and late trading in mutual funds. Terry Grimm earned respect for brokering a settlement for AE Staley Manufacturing – Tate & Lyle's main operating subsidiary in the USA – pertaining to the high fructose corn syrup antitrust litigation. A new entry in the rankings, the *"fantastic"* **Kimball Anderson** (see p.717) caught the public eye for his *"extreme thoroughness."* He is pitched as a talented litigator who can *"think in six different dimensions,"* placing him in a good position to handle complex products liability and IP litigation among other matters. Acting for Lear Corporation, Anderson is handling various IP disputes. He is also serving as arbitrator in a large patent dispute between two prominent telecom manufacturers.
The Clients: Philip Morris; Microsoft; Abbott Laboratories; Accenture; McDonald's; Bank One; CSFB; Goldman Sachs; Merrill Lynch and Morgan Stanley.

Band 3

Bartlit Beck Herman Palenchar & Scott

The Firm: The firm's brand of litigation has been likened to *"well-aimed nukes in a conflict situation,"* commentators said. One of the most successful litigation specialists nationwide, its concentrated focus on complex courtroom battles draws distinction. With offices in Denver and Chicago, about 35 partners with *"unparalleled experience of going to trial"* participate in some of the most important cases around.
The Lawyers: Superb **Philip Beck** *"can blow anyone away,"* observers said. He successfully acted for Residential Funding Corporation in a breach of contract dispute with DeGeorge

Financial Corporation; the case resulted in a $96 million jury verdict in favor of the firm's client. Having created a *"spectacular reputation,"* **Fred Bartlit** is viewed as a *"trial attorney extraordinaire"* whose expertise successfully combines technical mastery with courtroom finesse. Known as counsel to George Bush in the 2000 presidential election, he has participated in disputes involving patents, products liability, white-collar crime and securities among others. New to the rankings is the *"excellent and hard-working"* **Adam Hoeflich**, who has defended Bayer in litigation emanating from the withdrawal of Baycol, a cholesterol-lowering drug.
The Clients: 3M; Bayer; Brunswick Corporation; GM; Hewlett-Packard; Nicor; Reebok; Sears Roebuck; University of Chicago and Verizon.

Jenner & Block LLP
See firm details p.768
The Firm: Gaining praise as *"a long-standing firm with pockets of considerable expertise,"* this outfit boasts *"very good trial attorneys "* with a *"solid track record in trying cases."* A jewel in its crown is the representation of CSX Transportation in insurance coverage litigation. Clients are also attracted to its vast experience in white-collar criminal defense and a burgeoning profile in IP. In this area, the group has been further bolstered by the 2004 arrival of about a dozen lawyers from IP litigation boutique Roper & Quigg.
The Lawyers: **Thomas Sullivan** (see p.755) earned top marks for his legal sagacity. The former US attorney cochaired Illinois Governor George Ryan's commission on capital punishment. The market's emphasis on corporate self-policing leaves the *"well-prepared and excellent"* former US attorney **Anton Valukas** (see p.756) advising boards of directors on investigations and white-collar defense. He *"knows how to try a case,"* commentators said, referring to his expert handling of class actions among other disputes. He acted for PepsiCo in connection with the use of saccharin in fountain drinks. His expertise in libel and defamation is also underlined by his representation of Sara Lee in alleged violations of Title VII and defamation issues. Firm chairman **Jerold Solovy** (see p.753) drew praise for a practice that includes class actions and appellate law among other complex issues. He represented the Boston-based Kennedy family in a lawsuit brought by MetLife for a prepayment penalty dispute over the sale of Chicago's Merchandise Mart. He also acted for Hitachi in several patent infringement cases. The cochair of the firm's white-collar defense and counseling practice, **Charles Sklarsky** (see p.752) drew admiration for a practice that includes a niche in riverboat gambling regulatory practice. He also served as lead counsel for Chicago-based Exelon in matters arising from the sale of its 50% stake in PECO TelCove, a Pennsylvania telecom company. A new entry to the rankings,

700   All quotes in the text are from interviews with clients and competitors.

CHAMBERS USA 2005

Barry Sullivan (see p.755) is cochair of the firm's appellate and Supreme Court practice. He earns respect for a high-profile practice that involves prominent clients such as Covanta Energy.

The Clients: Sara Lee; PepsiCo; MCI; Honeywell; GE Capital; Kellogg; Hitachi; CSX Transportation; Ticona; Steelcase; Canada Life Assurance Company and Century Development Group.

Jones Day
See firm details p.485

The Firm: This "*excellent national firm,*" which boasts around 75 lawyers in its litigation team, derives many of its plaudits from the excellent reputation of former US attorney Dan Reidy. Its products liability expertise is among the best nationwide, as illustrated in such cases as Bridgestone/Firestone's class action litigation stemming from alleged defects in certain Firestone ATX, ATXII and Wilderness AT tires.

The Lawyers: White-collar and general commercial litigation feature prominently in **Dan Reidy**'s (see p.747) practice. Considered "*highly skilled, tenacious and tremendously intellectual,*" Reidy also benefits from "*excellent presence in court.*" His practice has included patent, partnership and securities disputes. Other considerations involve securities, ERISA violations and healthcare. He represented TAP Pharmaceutical in federal and state class actions pertaining to drug pricing, and separately defended another client embroiled in a DOJ investigation linked to municipal bond offerings.

The Clients: Motorola; TAP Pharmaceutical Products; Duchossois Industries; Simon Properties and Abbott Laboratories.

Sidley Austin Brown & Wood LLP
See firm details p.778

The Firm: A key contender for litigation, it particularly excels in complex white-collar criminal defense and corporate governance litigation, partly due to the experience of a considerable number of former US attorneys at the firm. The large pool of "*professionals*" won acclaim for its involvement in complex commercial disputes, such as those involving securities and ERISA. Enhanced by the additional securities enforcement litigation experience in the New York office, the Chicago team is often retained to advise prominent company executives in securities fraud actions.

The Lawyers: Heading the antitrust, commercial and regulatory group, **Charles Douglas** (see p.724) scooped plaudits for his "*tireless energy,*" successfully combining management duties with a busy litigation practice. He acts for AT&T in major securities class actions and separately counseled Microsoft in antitrust litigation. Formerly an assistant US attorney in Chicago, **Bill Conlon** (see p.723) continues to elicit praise for "*an ability to try any case.*" His experience has

included civil class actions as well as white-collar criminal investigations. Another former US attorney for the Northern District of Illinois is the "*very strong*" **Scott Lassar** (see p.736) who is deemed "*a lion at the Chicago Bar.*" With significant federal court experience, his caseload includes white-collar defense, securities fraud and corporate investigations. He successfully acted for Charles Conaway, the former CEO of Kmart, in a bankruptcy-related class action securities fraud action. **Walter Carlson** (see p.722) was recommended for his knowledge of securities law and corporate governance matters. On behalf of regional and national clients, he has advised on SEC investigations and derivative lawsuits. The "*tremendous*" **Thomas Ryan** (see p.749) retained market praise for being "*savvy and results-oriented,*" further boosted by his "*client-friendly*" approach. His workload comprises antitrust and commercial litigation, highlighted by the Henson v Amoco Oil multi-million-dollar antitrust and breach of contract case concerning the pricing of retail gasoline. Another former assistant US attorney in Chicago, **Scott Mendeloff** (see p.741) initially captured attention as one of the government's lead prosecutors in the Oklahoma bombing case. In private practice, his caseload is weighted toward white-collar defense and related investigations. For example, he represented a senior executive at TAP Pharmaceutical in a federal grand jury investigation. The "*bright*" **John Gallo** (see p.728) was complimented for a "*conscientious attitude.*" He has been increasingly involved in corporate internal investigations. He also acted for the CEO of Laidlaw in connection with a securities lawsuit.

The Clients: GE; AT&T; Microsoft; Bayer; Citigroup; Tyson Fresh Meats; Fahey Bank; Dexia Crédit Local; Brunswick Corporation; BP and Aon.

Band 4

Baker & McKenzie
See firm details p.761

The Firm: This international giant has been making a concerted effort to strengthen its global dispute resolution group, a campaign that has had some positive repercussions in the Chicago office. Split into four global regions, the Chicago lawyers are nestled in its North American group. The team earned admiration for products liability, mass tort defense, IP litigation and international arbitration – all expertise that further benefits from the firm's global network.

The Lawyers: The "*smart cookie and gifted negotiator*" **Joe Linklater** (see p.737) stands out as a "*go-to lawyer*" for sophisticated corporate governance matters. The "*smart and well-prepared*" **Patrick Herald** (see p.732) was complimented for his involvement in environment, tax, securities and IP litigation. One important case involves an internal investigation concerning the

collapse of Parmalat.

The Clients: Crompton Corporation; Archer Daniels Midland; Borders Group; Kidde; Meztech and TurtleWax.

Katten Muchin Zavis Rosenman
See firm details p.769

The Firm: A sizable litigation team with recognized expertise in securities litigation, this national firm won plaudits for its particular forte in complex financial fraud and financial restatement cases. Another drawing card is its experience in representing officers and directors in shareholder class actions, having defended Boeing's board of directors and Kmart's officers in securities class action suits. The firm's white-collar team was also selected by the US Trustee's Office to conduct an internal investigation into the bankrupt United Airlines' pension funds.

The Lawyers: The national litigation departmental chair David Kistenbroker also heads the securities litigation department, while Sheldon Zenner fronts the white-collar criminal and civil litigation group.

The Clients: Kmart; Boeing; Cerner; Century Business Services; State Farm and Bridgestone/Firestone.

McDermott Will & Emery
See firm details p.773

The Firm: This respected litigation group earned significant plaudits for a strong reputation in white-collar defense, banking-related disputes and securities litigation. It earned its spurs in a series of government investigations and private litigation arising from SEC audits on behalf of Arthur Andersen. The team has continued to sustain its prominent profile with cases such as a security dispute involving McDonald's. The group's IP litigation expertise is to the fore in a case involving Nike.

The Lawyers: Credited with strengthening the firm's litigation group, "*phenomenal rainmaker*" **Jeffrey Stone** (see p.754) is often placed "*close to the top of anyone's list.*" A former assistant US attorney, he chairs the firm's white-collar criminal defense practice. He continues to represent the tobacco industry in connection with litigation surrounding fee payments to plaintiff lawyers involved in the 1998 master settlement with various states. Leading the firm's international products liability group, **Michael Pope** (see p.746) represents State Farm in class action litigation. He is also advising Blue Cross Blue Shield in an HMO-related class action in Florida. Whistle-blower litigation, healthcare fraud actions and white-collar defense form a core part of **David Rosenbloom**'s (see p.748) practice. A new entry to the table, he has represented nonprofit hospital systems – including Resurrection Health Care and William Beaumont Hospitals – in class actions brought by uninsured patients.

www.ChambersandPartners.com

All quotes in the text are from interviews with clients and competitors.

701

The Clients: Nike; McDonald's; State Farm; ExxonMobil; Arthur Andersen; Trinity Health; ProMedica Health System; DaVita; Philip Morris; Northern Trust and Allianz.

Skadden, Arps, Slate, Meagher & Flom LLP & Affiliates
See firm details p.1372

The Firm: The international corporate powerhouse is making inroads into the Chicago litigation market, emerging as a strong contender in bankruptcy, mass tort and securities litigation. The team's acknowledged strength in post-acquisition disputes also feeds into the Chicago office. With such an eminent international clientele, it enjoys a steady flow of work from inter-office referrals. Clients also benefit from such a widespread network of expertise, though they also pointed to the "*lean and keen*" approach to staffing.

The Lawyers: Tina Tchen is considered a key player in the Chicago office, which comprises nine partners. Tchen's workload has involved shareholder, takeover, securities, employment and IP litigation.

The Clients: Baxter; Exelon; Intel; GlaxoSmithKline; General Mills; Wisconsin Energy and American Express.

Band 5

Cotsirilos Tighe & Streicker Ltd
The Firm: This six-lawyer litigation specialist is recognized for its distinct capabilities in white-collar criminal defense. Although perhaps lacking the national support compared to some of its larger competitors, the group nevertheless earned kudos for its adroit performances on behalf of witnesses and individuals. Due to its high-quality services, it also obtains its fair share of referrals from larger firms.

The Lawyers: Backed by over 20 years' experience in federal criminal litigation and corporate investigations, the "*impressive*" **James Streicker** has successfully defended clients before state and federal courts.

The Clients: The firm often represents individuals embroiled in white-collar criminal disputes.

Freeborn & Peters
The Firm: This Illinois firm has recruited heavily, particularly at the associate level, indicative of its concerted effort to boost the litigation team – which has surpassed the 70-attorney mark. On offer is a range of expertise in such areas as railroad law, IP, products liability and antitrust. The team acted for a client in the linen and uniform sector in an antitrust price-fixing case and separately advised on two public nuisance and negligent entrustment cases involving firearms manufacturers, distributors and retailers.

The Lawyers: Michael Kelly, the firm's managing partner, is a main contact for the litigation team.

The Clients: AEGON USA; BP; Canadian National; Illinois Central Railroad; Citigroup; ExxonMobil; McDonald's; T-Mobile and Boeing.

Stetler & Duffy Ltd
The Firm: Peers consider this eight-lawyer litigation boutique to be "*a terrific outlet.*" It is often a port of call for referrals from larger firms, particularly with regards to white-collar criminal defense. In spite of its relatively smaller size, these experienced, "*go-to*" trial attorneys "*don't miss a beat,*" commentators said.

The Lawyers: Among the talented lawyers at the firm are David Stetler and Joseph Duffy, recognized for their involvement in white-collar investigations among other matters.

The Clients: The firm has acted for company directors and officers at public and private companies.

Other Notable Practitioners
Having joined Shearman & Sterling LLP from Winston & Strawn in 2004, "*smart trial lawyer*" **Steven Molo** (see p.742) gained market commendations for his "*close attention to the details.*" Splitting his time between New York and Chicago, he is representing Viacom's chairman Sumner Redstone in a suit regarding his controlling interest in Midway Games. Molo is also acting for Deutsche Bank and UBS in two separate appeals in the Illinois Supreme Court. "*Sensitive to the clients' needs,*" Latham & Watkins LLP's **Bob Tarun** garnered praise for his white-collar criminal defense practice, which is part of a broader general commercial litigation caseload. The former Winston & Strawn attorney represented Deloitte & Touche in the Parmalat bankruptcy litigation. He has also advised boards of directors in internal investigations and SEC enforcement proceedings.

MEDIA & ENTERTAINMENT

LITIGATION

Illinois
Leading firms
(Media & Entertainment: Litigation)
[1] **JENNER & BLOCK LLP** *Chicago*
SONNENSCHEIN NATH & ROSENTHAL LLP *Chicago*
[2] **FOLEY & LARDNER** *Chicago*
SIDLEY AUSTIN BROWN & WOOD LLP *Chicago*
Firms are listed alphabetically in each band.

Band 1

Jenner & Block LLP
See firm details p.768

The Firm: Clients admire this group of "*top-flight lawyers*" for its "*history of experience in this area.*" The firm's media lawyers represent news and media organizations against claims of libel, defamation and invasion of privacy. They also advise on such issues as access to information and Freedom of Information requests, and guard against attempts to restrict the content of clients' communications, using the First Amendment. The team was recently successful on behalf of Disney in a lawsuit seeking to enjoin its distribution of a movie under the trademark laws. The group also defended three libel cases for television stations owned by client ABC, bringing each action to a successful outcome.

The Lawyers: **David Sanders** (see p.750) cochairs the firm's media and First Amendment group. "*One of the most creative, innovative and strategic minds you'll find in this field,*" he is admired by clients for his "*sage advice*" and "*companionable*" style. His key case this year has been the ongoing representation of the defendants in the case of Global Relief Foundation v The New York Times, et al. This libel action against six separate news organizations concerned reports that the plaintiff, an Islamic charity, was the subject of a federal investigation. The appeal ruling affirmed the dismissal of the suit against all the parties.

The Clients: The team's clients include Crain Communications and Golfweek Magazine.

Sonnenschein Nath & Rosenthal LLP
See firm details p.779

The Firm: "*You're in great hands*" with this dynamic group, according to clients, who are impressed with its "*great institutional memory of how we work and what we do.*" In fact, one went so far as to claim that it could "*do anything it wants in media and entertainment.*" The team's "*broad expertise*" takes in libel, privacy litigation and counseling for print and broadcast clients. It has seen a substantial amount of litigation in recent years related to public information, and is developing strategies to restore the privilege reporters had in federal court to avoid responding to subpoenas. In the wake of 9/11 the courts

All quotes in the text are from interviews with clients and competitors.

have increasingly enforced subpoenas against journalists to reveal confidential sources. Recent highlights include representing Vivendi Universal Games' Davidson & Associates and its Blizzard Entertainment unit, after the defendants in *Davidson & Associates v Internet Gateway* created a program allowing gamers to play pirated copies of Blizzard games online. The first ruling found that the defendants circumvented Vivendi's security measures and trafficked in the circumvention code. An appeal is pending.

The Lawyers: **Sam Fifer** (see p.726) is *"the kind of practical lawyer who can bring you advice on the spot,"* and has the capacity to *"grasp what clients are trying to accomplish with a minimum of effort."* His ability to listen and *"think outside the box"* makes him a terrific asset, according to his clients. His work mirrors that of the wider team, with additional emphasis on trademark and copyright matters. **James Klenk** (see p.735) is another *"experienced and knowledgeable"* media lawyer, whose involvement spans defamation, reporters' privilege issues, and prepublication review of articles. He successfully defended James Cramer, of CNBC's 'Kudlow & Cramer', in a defamation claim against him and his employer, for remarks he made about Jonathan Hoenig in his column.

The Clients: NBC; Chicago Tribune; Chicago Magazine; Chicago Cubs and Home Shopping Network.

Band 2

Foley & Lardner
See firm details p.1828

The Firm: This group is among *"the top echelon"* of Chicago firms when it comes to libel and defamation defense work, and assisting large media organizations in obtaining access to documents that have been shielded from public scrutiny. The team recently won an appeal in the libel suit brought by the Global Relief Foundation, which claimed that it had been unjustly linked to terrorism in a number of news reports. The US Seventh Circuit Court of Appeals found that the firm's clients, The New York Times, the Boston Globe and New York Daily News, had not alleged that the charity had ties to terrorism, but had only printed the truthful assertion that it was being investigated by the government.

The Lawyers: **Michael Conway**'s (see p.723) *"knowledge of local practice"* is valued by clients, who also appreciate his ability *"to think like a litigator."* He represented The New York Times in its successful bid for access to sealed court records concerning Central States, Southeast and Southwest Areas Pension Fund, which is obliged to pay benefits to nearly 500,000 retired Teamsters members.

The Clients: ABC; The Small Newspaper Group; The Wall Street Journal and the Chicago Tribune.

Sidley Austin Brown & Wood LLP
See firm details p.778

The Firm: This group's media expertise includes experience with Freedom of Information Act and news gathering issues, and it is renowned for its skill in the intersection between entertainment, trademark, defamation and First Amendment issues. It has been involved in a variety of important cases, including one of the year's highlights, the defense of Chicago Tribune Company, publisher of the Chicago Tribune. Steve Zucker, a prominent Chicago talent agent, sued the company and its reporter Ellen Warren, for defamation and false light invasion of privacy. The allegations followed the publication of a story that Zucker was seen trying to enter the memorial service of prominent sports broadcaster and former Zucker client Tim Weigel, with whom he had had a publicly acrimonious relationship. The appellate court affirmed the dismissal of the defamation claim, and held that dismissal of the false light claim was also warranted.

The Lawyers: Much of the responsibility for the group's success rests upon the shoulders of **Richard O'Brien** (see p.744), who *"belongs on anyone's list"* as far as rivals are concerned. Clients appreciate not only his ability to *"take care of the law,"* but also his knack of *"taking on our perspective and working around our ideas."* With a background in defamation, O'Brien is also skilled in trademark, copyright and trade secrets issues.

The Clients: The group's principal client is the Chicago Tribune Company.

Other Notable Practitioners

Sole practitioner **Patricia Felch** impresses competitors with her expert knowledge of the field.

MEDIA & ENTERTAINMENT

TRANSACTIONAL

Band 1

Freeborn & Peters

The Firm: The media group at Freeborn & Peters is an established force in the advertising, promotional and marketing field. It gets involved in a wide variety of work, though this year it has been particularly involved in merchandise licensing. Other typical work includes sponsorship matters and agreements, developing cable concepts and programming, and coordinating events. The team's attorneys have also been increasingly involved in documentary film financing.

The Lawyers: Antitrust and trade regulation chair **Eugene Zelek** is a talent in the area of TV and merchandising licensing. Here he has been acting of late for a major educational toy company, and he also advises Nintendo with regard to merchandising issues. IP expert **Andrew Goldstein** is another *"highly respected"* player in the advertising law area. His hard work and intelligence win him plaudits from peers, as does an impressive client base, which includes the likes of RealNetworks.

The Clients: The firm serves the Pritzker Military Library, Nintendo of America and RealNetworks, among other important clients.

Holland & Knight LLP
See firm details p.1352

The Firm: This *"fabulous"* team was credited by a number of clients with being *"crucial to the success of our business."* It brings its considerable experience to bear on the creation, structuring, financing and distribution of film and TV programs and projects, including a considerable volume of work for independent and documentary filmmakers. The group has also been involved in structuring business deals in the music industry. A highlight from the year has been advising Stetson Kennedy, author of 'The Klan Unmasked', in rights negotiations surrounding a potential feature film. The team also

Illinois

Leading individuals

(Media & Entertainment: Transactional)

1. DURCHSLAG Stephen *Winston & Strawn*, Chicago
   HODES Scott *Bryan Cave*, Chicago
   KELLEY Timothy *Sole Practitioner*, Chicago
   LABATE Robert *Holland & Knight*, Chicago
   MENSCH Linda *Sole Practitioner*, Chicago
   REED Mary Hutchings *Winston & Strawn*, Chicago
   SALTIEL David *Bell Boyd*, Chicago
   STRAND Peter *Holland & Knight*, Chicago

2. BROWN Jeffrey *Seyfarth Shaw*, Chicago
   GOLDSTEIN Andrew *Freeborn & Peters*, Chicago
   O'REILLY Peter *Lea + O'Reilly*, Chicago
   ZELEK Eugene *Freeborn & Peters*, Chicago

Up-and-coming individuals

DEMARTE Luke *Seyfarth Shaw*, Chicago
HEIDELBERGER Brian *Winston & Strawn*, Chicago

Individuals are listed alphabetically in each band.

represented producer Robro LLC in the formation, financing and production of the feature film 'Hidden Treasures'.

The Lawyers: **Robert Labate** (see p.736) has a *"wonderful ability to speak the right language"* to clients. His knowledge and support for the Chicago entertainment market won him enthusiastic recommendations from a variety of interviewees. An expert on film and TV production, he recently advised the producer of 'The Apprentice' on a coauthor agreement. The matter is currently awaiting approval. Labate also handles a volume of litigation, and was recently successful on behalf of Aria Model and Talent Management in a sexual harassment and discrimination case. **Peter Strand** (see p.754) *"knows a helluva lot about music,"* according to clients, who place him among *"the crème de la crème"* of the Chicago entertainment Bar. His practice spans all aspects of music and film-related entertainment law, and he recently assisted JHR Records in the preparation and negotiation of a recording agreement.

The Clients: The group has acted for Kartemquin Educational Films, TeamWorks Media and Bunim/Murray Productions, as well as a stable of documentary and independent film producers, aspiring and emerging artists, and independent record companies.

Seyfarth Shaw LLP

See firm details p.777

The Firm: The Chicago IP group of this national operation has a niche in entertainment matters, straddling the music, theater, and publishing arenas. Over the past year it has seen an upsurge in transactions related to cell phone ring tones. Highlights include negotiating an agreement for pop-punk group Allister to appear in MGM's coming-of-age teen movie 'Sleepover'. The team also arranged for the use of four songs on the soundtrack, and the use of recordings in and out of context, including in trailers and advertisements. It negotiated and drafted the terms of a deal with Slim Jim for endorsement and personal appearances on Warped Tour, as well as a ring tone deal. It also negotiated the terms of a starring appearance in an Electronic Arts video game on behalf of a junior lightweight boxing champion.

The Lawyers: *"Practical and no-nonsense"* **Jeffrey Brown** was recommended to researchers as a *"talented and conscientious"* entertainment attorney. Music and theater work form the bedrock of his practice, although he is experienced in a range of other entertainment issues. He acted recently for a tour producer in connection with a 20-city, major-arena concert tour by well-known pop artists. This involved negotiating and drafting sound, lighting, staging, trucking and transport deals. *"Results-oriented"* **Luke DeMarte** *"listens to what his clients say, and doesn't try to take over a deal,"* researchers were told. His practice involves a substantial portion of rap music-related work. A key matter for the year was negotiating a settlement between a record label accused of copyright infringement and a famous music publisher.

The Clients: Other clients include Black Ensemble Theater and Barton Brands.

Winston & Strawn LLP

See firm details p.780

The Firm: This firm is considered to be among *"the best in the business"* for advertising and promotional matters. The sizable group handles work surrounding the marketing of products and services, including counseling on related IP issues, such as copyright, trademark and false advertising claims. Talent agreements, music licensing, sponsorship and tie-in promotional agreements form the bulk of the team's transactional deal flow, while insurance litigation also forms a substantial portion of the workload. The group is currently acting for PepsiCo and advertising agency BBDO in connection with claims by a musical group that a song was used without permission. On the transactional side, the team advised PepsiCo on product placement in 'The Apprentice'.

The Lawyers: Sponsorship specialist **Mary Hutchings Reed** (see p.733) is *"an unparalleled lawyer"* who *"can do anything she sets herself to do,"* according to peers. She is active in marketing, advertising, trademark, copyright, and entertainment matters. *"Brilliant"* **Stephen Durchslag** (see p.725) *"is good at sizing up a legal issue and providing a quick business solution,"* say clients. He handles sponsorship and advertising advice and litigation. Also recommended to researchers was **Brian Heidelberger** (see p.732), a *"well-rounded and practical attorney."*

The Clients: Hoover; Kodak; PepsiCo; BBDO; Office Depot; DDB Chicago; Gage Marketing Group; Carlson Marketing Group; Burrell Communications Group and Wrigley.

Other Notable Practitioners

Scott Hodes of Bryan Cave LLP is *"a demigod locally,"* thanks to his unique practice in the visual arts area. *"The dean of art lawyers,"* with a genuinely national practice, he was said to possess *"a natural connection"* to the Chicago arts scene. Following his departure from McGuire-Woods Ross & Hardies, he founded the Chicago office of Bryan Cave. Hodes' year has been occupied with work for visual and performance artists and playwrights; and his client list includes performance artist Tania Bruguera and Expressions of Culture, the sponsor of the annual SOFA art exhibitions in New York and Chicago. He has also been assisting the McCormick Tribune Foundation with the legal work for an international competition to select a marquee work of art for a new museum in Chicago. A *"smart and dedicated lawyer,"* Sole Practitioner **Timothy Kelley** is most visible for his music-related practice; while sole practitioner **Linda Mensch** (*"one of the pillars of entertainment law in Chicago"*) is also well known for her expertise in music publishing. Her label contacts were particularly noted. *"Straightforward"* **David Saltiel** of Bell, Boyd & Lloyd LLC *"clearly has his clients' interests at heart,"* say peers. He recently advised Twentieth Century Fox and other film and television production companies on the acquisition and disposal of Illinois production services tax credits for projects produced in Illinois. Other highlights have included the organization and syndication of an $8 million theatrical venture created to develop multiple Broadway productions. An expert in sweepstake law, **Peter O'Reilly** of Lea + O'Reilly focuses on promotions, contests and other work connected to consumer offers. His clients include American Hole In One, Fortune Brands, Yahoo! and Publicis.

REAL ESTATE

Illinois
Leading firms (Real Estate)

1 DLA PIPER RUDNICK GRAY CARY US LLP *Chicago*
  KATTEN MUCHIN ZAVIS ROSENMAN *Chicago*
  MAYER, BROWN, ROWE & MAW LLP *Chicago*

2 BARACK FERRAZZANO KIRSCHBAUM *Chicago*
  SIDLEY AUSTIN BROWN & WOOD LLP *Chicago*
  SONNENSCHEIN NATH & ROSENTHAL LLP *Chicago*

3 BELL, BOYD & LLOYD LLC *Chicago*
  GOLDBERG, KOHN, BELL, BLACK *Chicago*
  JENNER & BLOCK LLP *Chicago*
  JONES DAY *Chicago*
  KIRKLAND & ELLIS LLP *Chicago*
  NEAL, GERBER & EISENBERG LLP *Chicago*
  SCHWARTZ, COOPER, GREENBERGER *Chicago*
  SEYFARTH SHAW LLP *Chicago*
  WEINBERG RICHMOND LLP *Chicago*
  WINSTON & STRAWN LLP *Chicago*

4 FOLEY & LARDNER *Chicago*
  GREENBERG TRAURIG LLP *Chicago*
  SHEFSKY & FROELICH *Chicago*

Firms are listed alphabetically in each band.

Band 1

DLA Piper Rudnick Gray Cary US LLP

See firm details p.765

The Firm: Boasting what is arguably the largest real estate capability across the USA, Piper Rudnick has its eye on still bigger things through its alliance with European firm DLA. The 85-strong Chicago group of "*result-oriented, transactional real estate lawyers*" seems to be "*on everyone's list*" this year. A "*very good developer practice*" has strengthened its muscle in the development of stadiums, arenas and sports facilities as well as the redevelopment of military bases. An appendage to the development practice, there is an effective land use department with around ten dedicated attorneys.

The Lawyers: Armed with a great reputation, **David Glickstein** (see p.730) drew compliments as a very fine practitioner for a wide range of transactional matters, including complex secured lending and more conventional construction loans. He has been working for the developer on the joint venture and financing aspects of a project in Scottsdale, Arizona, and for a developer on the acquisition, financing and institutional equity of a two-tower, $200 million high-rise residential project in Chicago. New president of ACREL, the "*tough, strategic and knowledgeable*" **Portia Morrison** (see p.743) handles an array of large and sophisticated transactions, especially those relating to office buildings. She was appointed chief legal counsel to Baldwin Park Development, the master developer for Baldwin Park, a mixed-use redevelopment of the Orlando Naval Training Center,

entitled for over 2000 residential units and over three million sq ft of office space. She is also handling the disposition of the Centergate Residential, an apartment portfolio, involving the sale of approximately $1 billion worth of assets. **Mark Yura** (see p.759) is a name familiar to those involved in the redevelopment of historic buildings in Chicago. This "*practical and reasonable*" attorney has earned praise for both federal income tax-driven work and multifamily housing work. Yura acted for the Laramar Group in the acquisition of a 600-unit apartment complex in suburban Chicago, a deal that involved tax-exempt bond financing and the sale of federal low income housing tax credits. Thirty years of experience and an all-encompassing commercial real estate practice greatly assist the reputation of the firm's cochairman **Lee Miller** (see p.742), who continues to keep his hand in and is considered "*excellent at managing the firm's client relationships.*" Having renounced the chairmanship of the firm in mid-2004, **Harold Pomerantz** (see p.746) now has more time to carry out transactional work for a large corporate clientele, including names such as Siemens, BP, Sara Lee and Spiegel. He also represents Bank of America in branch rollouts in Chicago. **David Sickle** (see p.752) joins the rankings following ample market comment on a practice that includes the representation of REITs, lenders, developers and end users. This "*bright talent*" is deemed "*smart and practical*" and boasts particular knowledge of shopping center financings. Senior statesman **Charles Edwards** (see p.725) is, for many clients, a "*sounding board*" and "*first port of call*" for thorny issues in a wide range of real estate matters, not least finance. Of **Ted Novak** (see p.744), a number of commentators agreed they would "*hire him in a minute*" for land use and zoning issues. He is a "*fountain of knowledge,*" who enjoys a significant workload: he has worked on Trump Tower Chicago (residential and hotel condominium) and numerous residential high-rise buildings with values in excess of $100 million. "*Still waters run deep*" commented observers on the "*unassuming*" **James Beard** (see p.718). Undoubtedly, a "*practical approach*" has helped his growing reputation in many aspects of real estate, including restructurings and workouts.

The Clients: In a client base full of major developers, REITs and retailers, the firm boasts names such as: LaSalle Bank; Bank of America; Club Monaco; Sara Lee; BP; Jones Lang LaSalle and Prudential Financial.

Katten Muchin Zavis Rosenman

See firm details p.769

The Firm: The "*depth of resources*" and "*great breadth of substantive areas*" on offer at this national firm drew consistent praise from commentators. Clients admire the caliber of this "*energetic and diverse*" 40-plus-strong group in development, structured finance, real estate fund formation and related litigation. Viewing issues through "*a practical, real-world prism,*" the team represents owners and investors generally in acquisitions, operations, restructurings and disposals, whilst also excelling in the niche areas of hotel, resort and recreational properties as well as sports complexes. Clients further pointed to a strong institutional investor practice, which profits from "*a high degree of expertise in the financial markets.*"

The Lawyers: With her time split between New York and Chicago, national real estate head **Nina Matis** (see p.740) received widespread compliments from peers and clients alike. This "*commercial powerhouse*" is vastly experienced and "*wonderful to work with,*" not least because of her "*superb negotiating skills*" and ability to make business and legal decisions simultaneously. In addition to acting as general counsel for iStar Financial, she has been utilizing her considerable expertise in structured finance, asset management and joint venture agreements. Matis has also been pouring her knowledge of the hospitality and retail markets into significant structured financings for major hotels. Clients admire the "*senior-level expertise*" of **Ken Jacobson** (see p.733) equally as much as his "*intimate involvement*" in their transactions. Jacobs was involved in the financing of a luxury offshore resort and golf course, and the mezzanine financing of a multifamily residential real estate portfolio. With a national practice, the "*terrific and logical*" **Mark Simon** (see p.752) is known for his "*ability to strike a compromise*" and vast knowledge of the hospitality sector and real estate finance. He has been heavily involved in financing the construction of new or expanding shopping malls. To illustrate, he represented Eurohypo as administrative agent and lead arranger on a $350 million secured revolving credit line to a publicly traded mall REIT. In another matter, he acted for Corus Bank as construction lender in connection with a 60-story condominium building in Miami. The "*extraordinarily skilled and charming*" **Andrew Small** (see p.752) was described as a "*top-notch young partner, who increasingly comes to clients' minds*" for REITs, finance, development and joint venture acquisitions. Assisting Matis in the running of the department is newly ranked "*can-do lawyer*" **David Bryant** (see p.720), who enjoys a strong private real estate opportunity funds practice. Fund and venture formation also feature in the practice of another "*positive*" newcomer to the tables, **Daniel Perlman** (see p.746). He acts for Morgan Stanley, key CMBS conduit lender, as well as for funds for LaSalle

Illinois
Leading individuals (Real Estate)

Senior Statesman
EDWARDS Charles *DLA Piper Rudnick*, Chicago

[1] GEAREN John *Mayer Brown*, Chicago
MATIS Nina *Katten Muchin*, Chicago
MORAN Patrick *Sonnenschein Nath*, Chicago

[2] ARONSON Virginia *Sidley Austin*, Chicago
FERRAZZANO Dennis *Barack Ferrazzano*, Chicago
KATZ Alvin *Mayer Brown*, Chicago
MORRISON Portia *DLA Piper Rudnick*, Chicago
RANDALL Benjamin *Randall & Kenig*, Chicago
RUBIN Joel *Seyfarth Shaw*, Chicago
SCHILLER Eric *Sonnenschein Nath*, Chicago

[3] BEARD James *DLA Piper Rudnick*, Chicago
BELL Stephen *Goldberg Kohn*, Chicago
GLICKSTEIN David *DLA Piper Rudnick*, Chicago
HOMBURGER Thomas *Bell Boyd*, Chicago
JACOBSON Kenneth *Katten Muchin*, Chicago
KIRSCHBAUM Howard *Barack Ferrazzano*, Chicago
KURTZON Michael *Schwartz Cooper*, Chicago
LEE Robert *Jones Day*, Chicago
MEHLMAN Mark *Sonnenschein Nath*, Chicago
MURTAUGH Christopher *Winston & Strawn*, Chicago
NAGELBERG Howard *Barack Ferrazzano*, Chicago
ROSENBLOOM James *Goldberg Kohn*, Chicago
SCHRANK Charles *Sidley Austin*, Chicago
SIMON Mark *Katten Muchin*, Chicago
SMALL Andrew *Katten Muchin*, Chicago
SMOLEN Lee *Sidley Austin*, Chicago
TOMLINSON Stephen *Kirkland & Ellis*, Chicago
YURA Mark *DLA Piper Rudnick*, Chicago

[4] AIELLO Anthony *Sidley Austin*, Chicago
BESSETTE-SMITH Suzanne *Barack*, Chicago
BLACKMAN Jana *Sonnenschein Nath*, Chicago
BRYANT David *Katten Muchin*, Chicago
BUDNY Terrence *Bell Boyd*, Chicago
FEINSTEIN Fred *McDermott Will*, Chicago
HAGY James *Jones Day*, Chicago
HENNING Mark *Winston & Strawn*, Chicago
MILLER Lee *DLA Piper Rudnick*, Chicago
MORITZ Louis *Mayer Brown*, Chicago
PERLMAN Daniel *Katten Muchin*, Chicago
POMERANTZ Harold *DLA Piper Rudnick*, Chicago
RESNICK Donald *Jenner & Block*, Chicago
SARASEK Peter *Quarles & Brady*, Chicago
SICKLE David *DLA Piper Rudnick*, Chicago
SULLIVAN Marcia *Katten Muchin*, Chicago

Up-and-coming individuals
FISHMAN Michael *Greenberg Traurig*, Chicago

Leading individuals
(Real Estate: Zoning/Land Use)

[1] GUTHMAN Jack *Shefsky & Froelich*, Chicago
NOVAK Theodore *DLA Piper Rudnick*, Chicago

[2] KANE Ivan *Mayer Brown*, Chicago

Individuals are listed alphabetically in each band.

Investment Management. Perlman additionally undertakes securitized and mezzanine financing and general development work. Both Perlman

and Bryant are considered by many to be "*the next generation*" at the firm. "*She's very smart, with bags of experience*" noted one interviewee of **Marcia Sullivan** (see p.755), whose real estate finance expertise garnered particular praise. She worked on the $80 million acquisition and redevelopment financing of Market Center in San Francisco, and on three substantial CMBS securitizations for JPMorgan.

The Clients: Among an impressive clientele of leading developers and financial institutions are: Jones Lang LaSalle; JPMorgan; Blackacre Capital Management; iStar Financial; Starwood Capital Group; Bank One; Bank of America and Corus Bank.

Mayer, Brown, Rowe & Maw LLP
See firm details p.771

The Firm: This "*large real estate practice with great coverage*" was considered by market observers to be a "*vital asset*" for the giant international firm. Around 40 lawyers stock a flourishing and multitalented Chicago real estate team, boasting know-how across the entire gamut of real estate and so justifying widespread praise from clients for their ability to "*cover all real estate bases.*" As well as experience in leasing, funds, development and a well-recognized land use and zoning practice, the firm also features prominently in advice to the top REIT debt issuers.

The Lawyers: "*A first-class lawyers' lawyer*" and "*dean of the old guard,*" **John Gearen** (see p.729) inspired the description of "*pragmatic, thoughtful and scholarly.*" Enjoying a strong reputation in funds, debt financing and equity work, he has devoted time to bringing in German investment and acted for major institutions in fund formation. **Alvin Katz** (see p.734) focuses on the higher value joint venture elements of real estate transactions, and represents private equity firms such as the Carlyle Group and a subsidiary of CalPERS, the California Public Employees' Retirement System. He represented Carlyle's affiliate Carlyle Realty in the acquisition and conversion of residential apartment projects into condominiums in Virginia, DC, Florida and California. For California Urban Investment Partners he worked on the development and financing of Time Warner Center, a mixed-use condominium development in New York City. **Louis Moritz** (see p.742) earned market praise for his "*business skills and sound understanding.*" His has a well-respected, complex leasing practice: in addition to acting for JPMorgan Chase, Charlesbank Capital Partners and the Chicago Symphony Orchestra, he represented the interests of his own firm in connection with the 500,000 square foot lease of new Chicago premises. Entering the land use and zoning tables is the "*down-to-earth and approachable*" **Ivan Kane** (see p.734). Well known in Chicago, Kane is described as "*a terrific fit with clients, based on his zoning knowledge and accessibility.*"

He is said to "*understand the bigger picture and the mindset of government officials.*" He acted for the master developer, a joint venture between BP and Jones Lang LaSalle in the securing of master plan zoning entitlements and the execution of all land sales on the Cantera project. Cantera is a business park and mixed-use development on 640 acres in Warrenville, Illinois.

The Clients: AMLI Residential Properties Trust; Takeda Pharmaceuticals North America; Lehman Brothers; Prudential Investment Management; Carlyle Group; California Public Employees' Retirement System and ORIX Real Estate Equities.

Band 2

Barack Ferrazzano Kirschbaum Perlman & Nagelberg

The Firm: Commentators reported a "*uniformity of service*" and a "*hands-on approach*" for this mid-sized firm with "*a high real estate profile.*" The team, which has expanded to around 25 lawyers, conducts work on complex transactions and financings. With a practice well beyond the state's boundaries, the team places strong emphasis on public entities and REITs and counts Ventas, one of the country's largest healthcare REITs, as a client.

The Lawyers: Peers and clients admire "*experienced real estate veteran*" **Dennis Ferrazzano** for being an "*excellent adviser*" who can "*manage difficult adversaries in a powerful way.*" He continues to act for LVMH in the acquisition and development of office buildings in New York. "*Judgment, intellectual ability and speed*" bring **Howard Kirschbaum** many recommendations for a "*versatile and skilled practice,*" especially in lending work. He acted for a publicly traded NYSE entity in connection with a $450 million secured revolving credit facility, and has represented a large developer/owner in connection with a joint venture to acquire and develop an office complex worth $150 million. **Howard Nagelberg** is something of a master of REITs and corporatized real estate work generally. Also admired for her real estate finance practice and expertise in publicly traded REITs is the "*smart, effective and determined*" **Suzanne Bessette-Smith**. She represented a REIT client involved in a joint venture with an Islamic partner acquiring single tenant, triple net leased properties nationally.

The Clients: Bank of America; First Bank; First Industry Realty Trust; Wells Fargo; US Bank; Shell; LVMH; Ventas and Keystone Properties.

Sidley Austin Brown & Wood LLP
See firm details p.778

The Firm: This 40-strong Chicago team has "*a very sound view of real estate lending,*" and enjoys easy access to a much-admired national pool of Sidley Austin real estate lawyers. Commentators noted "*a superb corporate finance practice*," a national reputation in CMBS and an overall excellence in lending and construction loans. A strong corporate client base lends extra weight in the industrial, telecom and hotel sectors, where the firm acts in the development of hotel chains, railroads, steel plants and cellular towers. **The Lawyers:** The "*sharp, realistic and driven*" **Virginia Aronson** (see p.717) won praise for a broad practice, which includes significant REIT transactions, securitizations, construction and permanent mortgage financing. She recently worked on the sale of a large property portfolio to a Chicago REIT, as well as a large mezzanine finance deal for a New York-based property. Aronson recently stepped aside as practice group head, to be replaced by **Lee Smolen** (see p.753), a man described as "*easy to deal with and incredibly conscientious.*" Smolen earned many recommendations for his general real estate finance practice; interviewees like his "*straightforward approach to lending decisions*" and note that he has been managing the firm's relationship with Wells Fargo Bank. **Charles Schrank** (see p.751) also garnered praise for his "*sound judgment in lending transactions.*" He numbers Citigroup among his well-respected clientele. The team boasts "*a highly capable traditional real estate lawyer*" in **Anthony Aiello** (see p.716), whose "*attention to the details of the deal*" is unsurpassed. He has significant experience in the acquisition and disposal of office and hotel buildings and counts BP as a client. **The Clients:** Starwood Hotels & Resorts; Wyndham Hotels & Resorts; BP; Wells Fargo; Corus Bank; Fillmore Capital Partners; Washington Mutual and Bank One.

Sonnenschein Nath & Rosenthal LLP

See firm details p.779

The Firm: Traditionally known for its longstanding relationships with institutional lenders, banks and insurance companies, this sizable Chicago team will celebrate its centenary in 2005. These days it boasts a more diversified real estate practice and the group prides itself on a well-recognized national niche in low-income housing tax credit transactions, a subsection of affordable housing. Lateral hires from Piper Rudnick and the now-defunct Altheimer & Gray are thought to have further strengthened the development and lending practices. **The Lawyers:** "*Talented, versatile and unflappable*" are words used to describe **Pat Moran** (see p.742). There was widespread praise for the "*good perspective and sound judgment,*" which he applies to a practice comprising downtown office developments and other development initiatives. He has been working for a Goldman Sachs subsidiary on a retail development and

undertaken financings for KeyBank and JPMorgan Chase. **Eric Schiller** (see p.750) is "*a great lending lawyer and rainmaker*" with a successful, national, institutional lender practice. He has also acted for McDonald's, the owner of the joint venture retail complex 730 North Michigan Avenue in its sale, and for US Bank in a number of transactions, including the construction loan for a shopping mall in California. With enormous knowledge and creativity, observers tagged **Mark Mehlman** (see p.741) "*a practical and bright lawyer.*" He represents many equity investors and undertakes significant lending and joint venture work. Blessed with "*a strong understanding of a tough market,*" the national practice group chair, **Jana Cohen Blackman** (see p.719), has developed the firm's expertise in tax-advantaged investment and high-value and volume tax credits. She has been acting for Morgan Stanley in the creation and expansion of their tax credit program. **The Clients:** JPMorgan Chase; US Bank; Morgan Stanley; Bank of America; Goldman Sachs; Union Bank of California; Citibank; Wells Fargo Bank and McDonald's.

Band 3

Bell, Boyd & Lloyd LLC

The Firm: The "*competent and collegiate*" real estate lawyers at this 23-lawyer Chicago practice earn high-market praise for their work on a variety of transactions, including many financings and condominium developments, for a range of institutional and developer clients. In August 2004, they welcomed the arrival of Graham Grady, formerly at Mayer Brown, who brought even greater strength to the firm's zoning, land use and government relations practice. The practice has been working on the Palmolive large condominium project on Michigan Avenue. **The Lawyers:** With almost 40 years of experience, **Thomas Homburger** is well known in the market. His practice is broad based, although mezzanine finance has become a growth area and he has been working on REIT formation. The "*bright and perceptive*" chair of the real estate practice, **Terry Budny**, also enters the rankings following commendations for his financing, development and investment practice. **The Clients:** In a client list that features owners, developers, and domestic and foreign banks, the firm also acts for the National Safety Council and Lieberman Management.

Goldberg, Kohn, Bell, Black, Rosenbloom & Moritz, Ltd

The Firm: Smaller than many of its rivals, "*stability and reliability*" are considered the hallmarks of this firm. It has around a dozen real estate attorneys carrying out a mix of local and

national work, and although they do act for borrowers, they are best known for their lending expertise. A subspecialty is to be found in healthcare lending. **The Lawyers:** "*A good draftsman, versatile lawyer and talented negotiator,*" is how one commentator described real estate chair **Stephen Bell**. Bell runs an active finance practice, with a specialty in hotel franchise and healthcare financing. He acts for Mesirow Realty Sale-Leaseback and CB Richard Ellis Investors, and represented Unocal in the breakup of a longstanding joint venture in the Chicago area. The "*well-educated, extremely bright and experienced*" **Jim Rosenbloom** boasts some 30 years' experience. This "*good leasing lawyer*" is deemed to be "*thoughtful about transactions*" and is also adept in real estate bankruptcies. In recent times he has worked on healthcare packages for GE Capital and Merrill Lynch. **The Clients:** Atrium Realty; Chicago Mercantile Exchange; CB Richard Ellis Investors; Focus Development Group; GE Capital Real Estate; Holiday Group; Unocal and Ventas.

Jenner & Block LLP

See firm details p.768

The Firm: This group of 12 attorneys impressed observers with its "*ambition and team-oriented approach*" to handling a wide range of large transactions. As an example, the team acted for LaSalle Bank in connection with a $200 million secured revolving credit facility to GREIT, a property REIT, for multiple office property acquisitions. Locally, it represented Millennium Park, the fund-raising entity for the New Millennium Park project on Lake Michigan, and negotiated a $100 million grant agreement with the City of Chicago, an architects' agreement with Frank Gehry and other development agreements. **The Lawyers:** Observers admire practice chair **Don Resnick** (see p.747). They know him as the "*terrific, well-educated and bright*" marquis player who acted for Sears Roebuck in its acquisition of 50 separate retail stores from Kmart, for around $600 million. He and other team members have also carried out all legal work for Prime Group Realty Trust's development of Bank One Center, a new 1.5 million square foot mixed use/office building in downtown Chicago. The transaction also required advice on construction contracts, architects agreement, and mezzanine and permanent financing. **The Clients:** Sara Lee; General Dynamics; LaSalle Bank; The John Buck Company; Jmb Realty Company; Jupiter Realty and City of Chicago.

Jones Day
See firm details p.485

The Firm: Around a dozen lawyers at the Chicago office of this global firm make up an "*integrated and consistent*" real estate team that features prominently in real estate M&A. The firm handles sophisticated, higher end real estate transactions, acting for funds, Fortune 500 corporate end users and financial institutions in complex lending transactions.

The Lawyers: "*Exceptional personal skills*" and "*a great ability to evaluate complex issues*" were the key traits identified for the "*disciplined and practical*" **Robert Lee** (see p.737). A key player in real estate funds, he advised LaSalle Investment Management and a consortium of institutional investors in the $300 million acquisition and financing of a portfolio of 53 industrial, warehouse and office properties across Mexico. He also advised Highcross Group in the formation of Highcross Regional UK Partners, a £150 million real estate private equity fund investing in UK properties outside of central London. Entering the rankings this year is **Jim Hagy** (see p.731), a man who has been instrumental in the development of the corporate real estate practice in Chicago. Hagy is an active, experienced and highly respected veteran in the field.

The Clients: LaSalle Investment Management; Highcross Group; Orion Capital Management; Great Lakes REIT; CB Richard Ellis Investors; JPMorgan Chase Bank; Washington Mutual and Westbrook Real Estate Funds.

Kirkland & Ellis LLP
See firm details p.770

The Firm: Local commentators expect to see more of this growing and enthusiastic 30-lawyer Chicago team, which inspired the label "*the kings of private equity real estate work.*" A "*tremendous corporate team*" overlaps with this young real estate team, something appreciated by institutional clients putting together development joint ventures and real estate funds. The firm also boasts a robust hospitality sector practice.

The Lawyers: Splitting his time between New York and Chicago, the "*business-oriented and pragmatic*" real estate head **Steve Tomlinson** (see p.756) divides his attention between hospitality-related transactions, national and cross-border fund formation and real estate private equity. He represented LaSalle Investment Management in the formation of LaSalle Japan Logistics Funds I and II, with total commitments of $400 million. He also acted for General Motors Asset Management in the formation of a $2 billion joint venture with The Mills Corporation, to own and operate a portfolio of nine super-regional shopping centers.

The Clients: Starwood Hotels & Resorts; Lazard Freres Real Estate Investors; LaSalle Investment Management; CenterPoint Properties; General Motors Investment Management;

The Lionstone Group; Kimpton Group and Hyatt.

Neal, Gerber & Eisenberg LLP
The Firm: Backed by some very good clients, this smaller outfit enjoys "*a respected profile in the real estate area*" and undertakes a lot of work for shopping center REITs. The team handles the acquisition, financing, development, management, leasing and disposition of hotels, offices and retail, commercial, industrial and residential properties. It acted for a shopping center REIT in a structured acquisition totaling $1.85 billion, involving 26 regional malls and ten community centers throughout the USA.

The Lawyers: Steve Berger leads the real estate team in Chicago.

The Clients: One of the largest publicly held regional shopping center REITs features in a client roster, which also includes local and national corporations, financial institutions and developers.

Schwartz, Cooper, Greenberger & Krauss, Chartered
See firm details p.776

The Firm: "*Timely and efficient*" remarked one commentator of this 20-strong team, whose expertise encompasses complex lending, leasing and a wide range of commercial, residential, shopping and office developments. The group has represented a publicly traded REIT in the sale of more than 50 apartment projects in ten states in recent years, as well as an Illinois-based developer in the acquisition and finance of apartment projects in three states during the past 18 months.

The Lawyers: Recognized for a national practice in real estate finance as well as residential development, the "*bright and practical*" **Michael Kurtzon** was considered to be a "*terrific referral*" in a conflict situation. He acted for a major national bank in a $120 million syndicated apartment building acquisition and renovation project in downtown Chicago, as well as for a Canadian Opportunity Fund in a $65 million office park acquisition in Indiana.

The Clients: LaSalle Bank National Association; Kaiser Development; Wachovia Bank; The Habitat Company; Equity Residential Properties Trust; Freestone Realty Advisors; ING Realty Partners; Mesirow Stein; Pacific Security Capital and Trotter Kent.

Seyfarth Shaw LLP
See firm details p.777

The Firm: Performing well across the gamut of real estate services, this Chicago firm boasts 30 lawyers who practice in leasing, finance, development and construction. In addition to a substantial national investment practice, pension fund work continues to grow. The size and scope of the firm has grown since the October

2003 merger between D'Ancona & Pflaum and Seyfarth Shaw, one of the largest mergers between Chicago-based law firms in recent years.

The Lawyers: The market heaped praise on the former chairman of D'Ancona & Pflaum, **Joel Rubin**. As well as being an active practitioner, he is a "*tremendous rainmaker*" and key client relations manager. Much of his time is spent assisting clients in the acquisition and disposal of office and retail property portfolios around the country. For example, he acted for DB Australia and two publicly traded Australian property trusts in the acquisition of a super-majority partnership interest in a nationwide billion-dollar industrial portfolio. He also acted for a REIT in the acquisition of six retail centers, valued at close to $300 million.

The Clients: Prudential Real Estate; Merrill Lynch; RREEF America; Home Depot; DB Australia; Colorado PERA; Hamilton Partners; LaSalle Bank and Los Angeles County Employees' Retirement Association.

Weinberg Richmond LLP
The Firm: Known until January 2004 as Katz Randall Weinberg & Richmond, this firm has strengthened its real estate bench following the arrival of Timothy Ramsey from Piper Rudnick and Samuel Orticelli from The Inland Group. Peers consider the firm to have "*a strong local practice,*" carrying out acquisitions, sales, finance, development and construction, leasing and lending. In 2004 the firm recorded the departure of Ben Randall, who left to set up his own practice.

The Lawyers: Mark Richmond is a key figure in the group, which has been lead real estate counsel for the CenterPoint Intermodel Center, developed by CenterPoint Properties Trust in Elwood, Illinois.

The Clients: CenterPoint Properties Trust; Darwin Realty & Development; The Inland Real Estate Group of Companies; ORIX Real Estate Equities and Residential Homes of America.

Winston & Strawn LLP
See firm details p.780

The Firm: Much admired for its litigation prowess, this large general practice firm also fields a "*solid and flexible*" group of 16 real estate lawyers in Chicago. Considered by sources to be a valuable adjunct to its corporate practice, the group drew admiration for its transactional emphasis. The firm maintains a sound lending, investment and development reputation and is known for its institutional clientele.

The Lawyers: Observers focused on the long experience and "*no-nonsense approach*" of **Christopher Murtaugh** (see p.743), whose practice includes the representation of developers and institutional clients, such as Alere Property Group, Ashley Capital and GE Asset

Management, in the acquisition and development of city and suburban properties. Clients championed **Mark Henning**, who joins this year's tables in recognition of his "*ability to cut through the legalese*" and "*excellent response time.*" Recent transactional work has included financings for Grand Plaza, a $250 million mixed-use project, and the disposal of a shopping center and related litigation.

The Clients: Alere Property Group; Ashley Capital; Bayer; CIBC World Markets; GE Asset Management; The McShane Companies; ML Realty Partners and State Farm.

Band 4

Foley & Lardner
See firm details p.1828

The Firm: This Milwaukee firm has a presence in Chicago and employs around 16 real estate lawyers whose "*collegiate approach*" and "*smooth integration with the firm's other offices*" drive their reputation. In addition to carrying out complex real estate finance, securitized lending and urban redevelopment, there is expertise in joint venture partnerships for real estate investments. For example, the group represented a German open and closed-end fund on their investment in a trophy building in Chicago.

The Lawyers: Elizabeth Corey heads the Chicago team, which has been involved providing brownfield development and retail leasing services for the expansion of the University of Illinois.

The Clients: The team acts for a range of developers, secured lenders, higher educational institutions and institutional investors.

Greenberg Traurig LLP
See firm details p.564

The Firm: Observers see this powerful national firm as "*one to watch in the coming years*," noting that it has been making a concerted effort to increase its real estate presence in the state. Lateral recruits from the now-defunct Altheimer & Gray are expected to aid this rise in prominence. The firm has acted for Kimco Realty in the development of shopping centers in Mexico and for Archon Group in the development of a 750,000 sq ft shopping center in Michigan.

The Lawyers: In December 2004, **Michael Fishman** (see p.727) joined the group from Mayer, Brown, Rowe & Maw. He has been identified as an "*ambitious and personable*" attorney, who enjoys a cross-border practice acting for US investors in Latin America. He has acted for Corus Bank in the extension of a construction loan for the development of 400 unit luxury hotel and condominium project in California.

The Clients: Archon Group; Kimco Realty; Bally Total Fitness; Saks and Schottenstein Stores.

Shefsky & Froelich

The Firm: With approximately half of its 17 real estate lawyers undertaking land use and zoning work, this smaller Chicago firm enters this year's tables. Driven by an outstanding reputation, the firm further boosted this with the August 2004 arrival of Edward Kus, considered to be a major and much-sought after force in the land use and regulatory area. The team also carries out complex transactions on behalf of retailers and is known for its leasing knowledge.

The Lawyers: Reputed for taking on complex land use and zoning cases in the city of Chicago, **Jack Guthman** earns praise as the firm's trump card with more than 30 years involvement in the real estate and civic community. High-rise and townhouse residential development work has featured prominently and work has included a 240-unit and a 64-story tower on the north side of Chicago as well as the expansion of the Chicago Children's Museum.

The Clients: Capstone Equity; The Prime Group; The Rose Group; First Bank & Trust Company of Illinois; LaSalle National Bank; Senior Lifestyles and Griffin Real Estate Funds.

Other Notable Practitioners
Fred Feinstein (see p.726) of McDermott Will & Emery remains in the rankings, admired for development, zoning and environmental matters in a broader real estate practice. "*Careful*" **Peter Sarasek** of Quarles & Brady LLP enters the tables. Considered by peers as "*a must on the list*," and well respected as a "*high-quality attorney*," Sarasek has a transactional practice with office leasing deemed to be a forte. Having left Katz Randall Weinberg & Richmond at the end of 2003, **Ben Randall** at Randall & Kenig LLP drew admiration for his transactional real estate practice, which includes complex leasing, acquisition, financing and construction. For one of a cadre of clients, he has carried out the mezzanine financing for a downtown office in Chicago

TAX

Illinois Leading firms (Tax)
[1] **KIRKLAND & ELLIS LLP** *Chicago* **MAYER, BROWN, ROWE & MAW LLP** *Chicago*
[2] **MCDERMOTT WILL & EMERY** *Chicago* **SIDLEY AUSTIN BROWN & WOOD LLP** *Chicago* **SKADDEN, ARPS, SLATE, MEAGHER** *Chicago*
[3] **BAKER & MCKENZIE** *Chicago* **LATHAM & WATKINS LLP** *Chicago* **WINSTON & STRAWN LLP** *Chicago*
[4] **JENNER & BLOCK LLP** *Chicago* **KATTEN MUCHIN ZAVIS ROSENMAN** *Chicago*
Firms are listed alphabetically in each band.

Band 1

Kirkland & Ellis LLP
See firm details p.770

The Firm: This firm's Chicago office is "*a high-energy and extremely motivated place, where people give 110%*," according to clients. They add that "*the pace and caliber of the work sees Kirkland & Ellis attract the best talent.*" The firm is renowned for its expertise in the private equity and venture capital arena, a reputation that is complemented by its broader deal record for large companies, both public and private. Bankruptcy matters are also handled with consummate ease. All this provides ample opportunity for the firm's tax attorneys to flex their muscle. The tax controversy and litigation practice also attracts major clients.

The Lawyers: Interviewees were quick to extol **Jack Levin** (see p.737) as "*a shining star without any question*," speaking of his tax expertise in the same breath as his universally admired private equity and corporate skills. In addition to working on numerous acquisitions and fund formations for Madison Dearborn Partners and Willis Stein, he advised Concord EFS in its acquisition by First Data. "*Tremendous*," "*first-rate*" and "*excellent*" are a few of the superlatives that flooded in for **Jeffrey Sheffield** (see p.751). He

acted for Bain Capital in its buyout of chemical distribution company Brenntag and steel trader Interfer from Deutsche Bahn. He also advised GM in its sale of Hughes (now known as DIRECTV) to News Corporation. "*Problem solver*" **Donald Rocap** (see p.748) attracted the accolade "*tax guru. He is always coming up with great ways to structure deals.*" He recently worked on Code Hennessy & Simmons' acquisitions of AMF Bowling Worldwide and The Hillman Companies, as well as the investment by Oaktree Partners in Spirit Airlines. Rocap has numerous fund formations to his name, including Code Hennessy & Simmons Fund V and Gryphon Partners III. Clients applauded "*outstanding*" **William Welke** (see p.758) as "*creative and very skilled at structuring.*" Peers reiterated this praise in their admiration of his "*understanding of how to integrate structure with the goals a client is trying to achieve.*" He advised Madison Dearborn Partners in its acquisition of Boise Cascade's paper, forest products and timberland assets and

Illinois

Leading individuals (Tax)

Senior Statesman

LEVIN Jack *Kirkland & Ellis*, Chicago

[1] **BOWEN Stephen** *Latham & Watkins*, Chicago
FREEMAN Louis *Skadden Arps*, Chicago
SHEFFIELD Jeffrey *Kirkland & Ellis*, Chicago
WILLIAMSON Joel *Mayer Brown*, Chicago

[2] **BANOFF Sheldon** *Katten Muchin*, Chicago
LEMEIN Gregg *Baker & McKenzie*, Chicago
LEVY William *Mayer Brown*, Chicago
LIPTON Richard *Baker & McKenzie*, Chicago
LYNCH James *Winston & Strawn*, Chicago
ROCAP Donald *Kirkland & Ellis*, Chicago
SHERCK Timothy *Mayer Brown*, Chicago
WOOTTON Robert *Sidley Austin*, Chicago
YODER Lowell *McDermott Will*, Chicago
ZIMBLER Jay *Sidley Austin*, Chicago

[3] **BORDERS Thomas** *McDermott Will*, Chicago
CRAVEN George *Mayer Brown*, Chicago
JONES Roger *Mayer Brown*, Chicago
KIMBALL Christian *Jenner & Block*, Chicago
LEDUC André *Skadden Arps*, Chicago
LUCAS Roger *Winston & Strawn*, Chicago
LUSCOMBE II George *Mayer Brown*, Chicago
MANDEL Reid *Katten Muchin*, Chicago
MAYNES Todd *Kirkland & Ellis*, Chicago
SORENSEN Sharp *Sidley Austin*, Chicago
STEPHENS Thomas *Sonnenschein Nath*, Chicago
WEBER III Louis *Winston & Strawn*, Chicago
WELKE William *Kirkland & Ellis*, Chicago

Up-and-coming individuals

GELMAN Bruce *Mayer Brown*, Chicago

Individuals are listed alphabetically in each band.

GTCR in the setting up of its Fund VIII. "*Careful and analytical*" **Todd Maynes** (see p.740) was also felt to be a key member of the team. His practice is increasingly focused on tax litigation and the tax aspects of bankruptcy. The list of high-profile names seeking his counsel includes United Airlines, Alcoa and Conseco. On behalf of the latter company he achieved a successful closing agreement with the IRS in September 2004, regarding the tax treatment of the loss on its investment in Conseco Finance. George Javaras is much mourned following his death in 2004. He was widely admired as one of the US's leading tax lawyers.

The Clients: Madison Dearborn Partners; GTCR Golder Rauner; Goense Bounds; Summit Partners; Parthenon Capital; Bain Capital; Chip-PAC; Concord EFS; GM; United Airlines; Conseco; Alcoa; Northwest Airlines; American Capital Strategies; Code, Hennessy & Simmons; Vestar Capital and Willis Stein.

Mayer, Brown, Rowe & Maw LLP
See firm details p.771
The Firm: One of the reasons why clients entrust themselves to this superb team is that attorneys produce "*work of a very high quality – in fact, extraordinarily high.*" The tax controversy group came in for an enormous amount of praise during recent research. A separate group to that of the firm's noncontentious tax practice, its lawyers are dedicated to tax controversy and litigation and cater to an international client base. Indeed, it has a great deal of involvement in international work including transfer pricing, competent authority and advance pricing agreements. One client told researchers: "*If we have a dicey issue that really matters, then they are the ones to go for. If the issues need fact-finding and are bare-knuckle, then they are the firm to deal with it. They are our pit bull.*" The transactional team has a broad practice encompassing transactional support and direct tax advice. Clients spoke highly of its "*reliability and excellent across-the-board approach. The lawyers have the ability to identify and research difficult issues and solve them.*" In conjunction with a number of the firm's other offices, the team advised BellSouth in the sale of ten Latin American operations to Telefónica Móviles, the wireless affiliate of Telefónica.

The Lawyers: Possessed of "*enormous presence and stature,*" **Joel Williamson** (see p.758) "*is very quick, great at conceptualizing and has excellent communication skills.*" Prior to joining the firm, he was with the Chief Counsel's Office at the US Department of the Treasury and, in 1978, was appointed one of 20 Special Trial Attorneys located throughout the USA. One competitor was of the opinion that "*he probably has more experience in litigating cases than any lawyer in the USA.*" Similarly, a client told researchers: "*He has such a long history with transfer pricing litigation that he has a very good perspective of what matters in the long run and of what really matters in the courtroom.*" Recent cases include The Tribune Company v Commissioner of Internal Revenue. "*Technically strong*" **Timothy Sherck** (see p.752) was commended by rivals as "*one of the most distinguished and thoughtful lawyers in town.*" He has an extensive corporate tax practice and also advises lenders, investors, and debtors on tax issues in financial restructurings and bankruptcy reorganizations. "*A real expert on securitization,*" **William Levy** (see p.737) has also impressed clients: "*He is always successful in coming up with a solution that will work for everyone.*" Levy focuses on the federal income tax aspects of structured financing transactions and has extensive experience in corporate restructurings and planning. He acted for GE Capital in its first public asset-backed offering and in several Rule 144A asset-backed offerings, as well as in a number of bank-sponsored commercial paper conduit financings. Clients admire the way **George Craven** (see p.723) "*is willing to venture out and try new things.*" He garnered respect for his insurance and financial products tax expertise and was deemed "*very knowledgeable, especially in US and European tax matters.*" Recent work includes advising a major public accounting firm and a major law firm on setting up captive insurance companies. He has also advised a large European reinsurance company on setting up a D&O liability insurance company to be owned by, and to issue policies to, blue-chip US and European corporations. The "*excellent*" **George Luscombe** (see p.738) was warmly recommended by market sources. He advises on federal and state taxation and has recently been active in structuring several corporate acquisitions and divestitures, as well as vehicles for making investments qualifying for New Markets Tax Credits and real estate investment vehicles. **Roger Jones** (see p.734) maintains a well-respected practice and has had significant success in tax case appeals at appellate court level. Among the cases to feature on his resume is The Tribune Company v Commissioner of Internal Revenue. Held up by clients to be "*an exceptional real estate tax attorney,*" **Bruce Gelman** (see p.729) is "*innovative, thinks outside the square and is great at working his way round obstacles.*" He often represents fund sponsors and investors in connection with the organization, structuring, and documentation of different types of real estate investment funds and joint ventures. He advised Developers Diversified Realty in the formation of a joint venture with Macquarie Bank to own and operate a portfolio of community shopping centers in the USA. Gelman has also acted as US tax counsel to Australian-listed property trust Macquarie DDR Trust since its formation.

The Clients: BellSouth; Refco Group; The Tribune Company; GE Capital; Strategic Hotel Capital; Developers Diversified Realty; Macquarie DDR Trust; ProLogis; Principal America Office Trust; Lehman Brothers; Principal Real Estate Investors; Intel; Goodrich; UPS; Boeing and Nestlé.

Band 2

McDermott Will & Emery
See firm details p.773
The Firm: With 41 tax lawyers in Chicago, the expertise on offer spans the full gamut of transactional, litigation and controversy work. High on the agenda are matters involving international tax, general corporate and partnership tax, and state income tax. Representative work includes advice to Alliant Energy concerning an IRS ruling request relating to a multimillion-dollar transaction and potential litigation. The team has also been representing the Cincinnati Bengals before the IRS regarding issues relating to stadium financing. A thriving employee benefits and executive compensation practice also came in for praise during recent research.

The Lawyers: Lowell Yoder (see p.759) strikes the market as *"a rising star,"* in particular for his international tax work. He advised TXU on US tax law aspects of the sale of its Australian group of companies. **Thomas Borders'** (see p.720) litigation and tax controversy skills were also much admired by peers, who praised him as *"a very respected lawyer with a lot of integrity."* Sample work includes advising Jenkens & Gilchrist in several battles with the IRS, including one over the scope of attorney-client privilege and the IRS's efforts to obtain law firm records.

The Clients: Caterpillar; Procter & Gamble; TXU; Rockwell Collins; Office Depot; Heidrick & Struggles; Jenkens & Gilchrist; Alliant Energy and Cincinnati Bengals.

Sidley Austin Brown & Wood LLP
See firm details p.778

The Firm: Despite the Chicago tax department's relatively small size – eight partners – this *"professional and capable"* team maintains a highly respected profile. Market sources spoke well of its corporate and M&A expertise and highlighted notable strength in securitizations. Financial transactions and products are handled with ease, and advice in such areas as pooled investment vehicles, venture capital and private equity funds are also prominent in the team's workload. A tax controversy practice, both at IRS level and in the courts, successfully complements the transactional expertise on offer.

The Lawyers: Rivals were quick to praise **Robert Wootton**'s (see p.759) *"ability to bring a steady hand to everything he does; he always manages to steer a sensible course and is able to satisfy competing concerns."* Wootton focuses on federal tax matters and is often to be seen advising on M&A, financing and structuring matters. **Jay Zimbler** (see p.759) was highlighted to researchers as a key member of the team with a practice encompassing international tax planning as well as controversy work. He has recently seen the resolution of two leading cases, one concerning deferred compensation of hedge fund managers and the other involving residual interests in Real Estate Mortgage Investment Conduits (REMICs). **Sharp Sorensen** (see p.753) was also commended during recent research. He works principally on M&A and related transactions, as well as securitizations and securities. Sorenson advised Exelon on its merger agreement with Public Service Enterprise Group to create Exelon Electric & Gas, and First Data in its merger with Concord EFS.

The Clients: An outstanding list of clients includes: Exelon; Tellabs; First Data and RR Donnelley.

Skadden, Arps, Slate, Meagher & Flom LLP & Affiliates
See firm details p.1372

The Firm: This team is famous among competitors for producing *"high-quality work"* and is popular with clients for its *"consistency throughout."* Its fine reputation is attributed to *"a high knowledge base and excellent intellectual capacity."* M&A and corporate work make up a large part of the workload, although the team also has a leading REIT practice. Meanwhile, maintaining the firm's preeminent reputation for bankruptcy are advisers skilled in the tax aspects of bankruptcy and restructuring. Tax controversy work adds a further string to the Chicago office's bow.

The Lawyers: Clients appreciate the way **Louis Freeman** (see p.728) *"attacks issues in creative ways and looks for solutions that deal with the issues."* They also told researchers that *"he stands out for his client service – we feel free to call him anytime."* Experienced in all aspects of federal tax planning and disputes, he is regularly seen in M&A and joint ventures and counsels such names as FMR, The Trump Group and Chicago Mercantile Exchange. **André LeDuc** (see p.737) was identified by peers as *"a very intelligent and thoughtful man."* The majority of his practice is dedicated to restructuring work, of which recent examples include the Hayes Lemmerz International bankruptcy and the Interstate Bakeries restructuring.

The Clients: The Trump Group; Harvest Partners; GE Capital; Fortress Investment Group; Brera Capital Partners; RCN; Unitrin; Van Kampen Funds; Chicago Mercantile Exchange; BlackRock; Insight Venture Partners; Level 3 Communications; Edison Mission Energy and Westfield Holdings.

Band 3

Baker & McKenzie
See firm details p.761

The Firm: According to competitors, this is a team with *"a particularly fine reputation in the international and multinational arena, for both transactional and controversy matters."* Indeed, together with its domestic and international tax planning expertise, the team is widely respected for its controversy work and international tax litigation, most notably in the field of transfer pricing. Clients feel safe in the lawyers' hands, describing them as *"practical, knowledgeable, responsive and frank."* The partnerships and real estate tax practices also garnered plaudits during recent research.

The Lawyers: The combination of **Gregg Lemein**'s (see p.737) *"strong technical and practical skills"* and his *"thorough and collected"* approach has proved a winning formula with clients who spoke of his *"user-friendly advice on complicated issues."* Universally commended by

interviewees for international matters, he has a broad practice ranging from planning through to tax controversies and litigation. Lemein has been representing Square D for several years in a case before the US Tax Court. **Richard Lipton** (see p.737) is *"extremely productive and knowledgeable in real estate, partnership and investment vehicles."* In addition to structuring complex partnership transactions for corporations and high net-worth individuals, he does a lot of work on like-kind exchanges. Recent matters include acting in the IPOs of two publicly traded REITs.

The Clients: Cisco Systems; Microsoft; Seagate; Shorenstein; Square D; Northwestern Mutual and May Department Stores.

Latham & Watkins LLP

The Firm: Market sources acknowledged the firm's national strength in corporate and M&A, and were fully aware that the Chicago tax team's predominantly transactional workload includes matters generated by colleagues both in the Chicago office and beyond. Illustrating this point is a deal in which Harrah's acquired Caesars, with the Chicago tax team working alongside the firm's West Coast corporate lawyers. Lawyers within the team also counsel on tax controversies.

The Lawyers: *"Great mind, great guy"* and *"an extraordinarily talented attorney"* are just two of many accolades that came **Stephen Bowen**'s way. Rivals held the managing partner of the Chicago office up to be *"one of the most highly regarded corporate and M&A lawyers in terms of tax in the USA,"* observing that *"he has clients all over the country and the world."* Bowen advises mainly on taxable and tax-free M&A as well as corporate tax planning. He advised Hyatt in a spin-off of Hyatt Hotels US from a large conglomerate, and then formed a combination of Hyatt Hotels and Hyatt International. Other work includes representing First Health in its acquisition by Coventry Health Care, a transaction consisting of approximately 50% Coventry stock and 50% cash.

The Clients: Hyatt; First Health; Classic Residence; Pritzker Organization; Harrah's and Koch Industries.

Winston & Strawn LLP
See firm details p.780

The Firm: This well-recognized practice sits within *"a fine firm,"* according to market sources who spoke well of the lawyers' transactional and controversy expertise. The group prides itself on offering a high-quality service, ranging from planning right the way through to audit and litigation. It is experienced in US and cross-border structured finance transactions and has a solid reputation for tax controversy and litigation matters, both at state and federal level.

The Lawyers: *"Thoughtful"* **James Lynch**

attracted attention as much for his transactional expertise as for his skills in the tax controversy arena. Clients were quick to praise **Roger Lucas** (see p.738) as *"creative, practical and helpful;"* he has much transactional expertise and advises on M&A, business formations and financings. **Louis Weber** was also singled out by rivals who admired his *"careful and accurate"* approach. In addition to advising public and privately held corporations in tax controversy cases, he counsels on the tax aspects of M&A and issues related to public offerings.

The Clients: The client list includes: Abbott Laboratories; Sears Roebuck; Philip Morris Capital; Motorola; Kellogg; Caremark International and Sara Lee.

Band 4

Jenner & Block LLP

See firm details p.768

The Firm: *"Jenner & Block is a name to watch,"* interviewees recently told researchers, and *"they offer an excellent service and are very responsible."* This Chicago tax group handles many things from tax controversy and income tax, to M&A, financial products, real estate private placements, partnerships and private equity transactions. It recently advised three real estate management companies with respect to their tax-free merger into Inland Retail Real Estate Trust (IRRETI), a publicly owned REIT. In the tax controversy and litigation arena, attorneys have been acting for General Dynamics in federal tax refund litigation with more than $100 million at stake and involving the validity and

applicability of loss disallowance regulations, proper accounting treatment of long lead material contracts and proper accounting treatment for terminated contracts.

The Lawyers: Rivals spoke warmly of **Christian Kimball** (see p.735), calling him *"extremely talented."* They also felt that his previous experience, both in-house and teaching, had served him well. Kimball is cochair of the firm's tax practice and deals with federal income tax matters.

The Clients: The firm's tax clients are drawn from a wide range of market sectors including manufacturing, retail, aerospace, defense and financial services. They include privately and publicly held companies and tax-exempt organizations.

Katten Muchin Zavis Rosenman

See firm details p.769

The Firm: In this firm, clients recognize *"a very responsive and knowledgeable team,"* and appreciate the way *"someone is always available."* Their praise was not limited to the top partners: *"Throughout the firm they have achieved consistency of quality."* Strength is demonstrated in such areas as financial services and financial planning, as well as private equity and venture capital. Lawyers also specialize in tax planning for the real estate industry, covering areas such as real estate investment, ownership, planning and securitization, with hedge fund work becoming ever more prominent.

The Lawyers: *"Intellectual and energetic"* **Sheldon Banoff** (see p.717) stands out for his partnership work in particular. Peers view him

as *"someone who thinks hard about tax law and is very interested in it; he will pursue an issue to the ground, and then some."* Banoff specializes in real estate tax planning and investments using limited liability companies and partnerships. He represented a joint venture between Lehman Brothers and Capstone Partners for developments of residential properties in the western United States with capital investments in excess of $100 million. He also assisted the CIM Group in investing more than $75 million in mezzanine equity and debt in commercial and residential real estate with national developers. **Reid Mandel** (see p.739) was identified as another key member of the team. He spends much of his time on asset-backed securities transactions and works with clients setting up funds, often real estate related. Mandel advised Denali Capital on a $400 million offering of asset-backed securities, closing in August 2004. He also worked on Household Mortgage Loan Trust 2004 HCL, a public offering of securities backed by $750 million in residential mortgage loans.

The Clients: Denali Capital; Sterling Capital Partners; LaSalle Investment Management; LaSalle Bank National Association; Atlantic Premium Brands; Greenfield Partners; Household Finance; iStar Financial and Trizec Properties.

Other Notable Practitioners

Thomas Stephens (see p.754) of Sonnenschein Nath & Rosenthal emerges as *"a very fair lawyer who is reasonable to deal with."* One of two tax partners in the firm's Chicago office, his work takes in corporate and real estate transactions as well as tax credit investing.

TECHNOLOGY & IT OUTSOURCING

Illinois
Leading firms
(Technology & IT Outsourcing)

1	**BAKER & McKENZIE** *Chicago*
	MAYER, BROWN, ROWE & MAW LLP *Chicago*
2	**KIRKLAND & ELLIS LLP** *Chicago*
	SONNENSCHEIN NATH & ROSENTHAL LLP *Chicago*
3	**DLA PIPER RUDNICK GRAY CARY US LLP** *Chicago*
	GARDNER CARTON & DOUGLAS LLP *Chicago*
	GORDON & GLICKSON *Chicago*
	LATHAM & WATKINS LLP *Chicago*

Firms are listed alphabetically in each band.

Band 1

Baker & McKenzie

See firm details p.761

The Firm: Now numbering eight *"responsive and client-oriented"* attorneys, Baker & McKenzie's Chicago technology group was originally built from a solid IP base, rather than as an

adjunct to the corporate department. The volume of feedback received for the firm makes apparent its huge impact on the market – it offers *"breadth, depth"* and, crucially, *"global coverage."* Peers say the Chicago team is *"anchored on the international practice,"* while client after client cited the firm's international capability as the *"compelling component"* in their choice of advisers. Recently, the firm acted for ESPN on an MVNO (mobile virtual network operator) deal with major technology and outsourcing issues. MVNOs are relatively rare in the USA, and Baker & McKenzie possessed the relevant European experience to handle the matter with confidence. The firm's tremendous reach has also assisted the Chicago group in outsourcing projects, both domestic and offshore; it is, for example, chief outside counsel for Hewlett-Packard on outsourcing and technology matters. As well as riding the outsourcing wave, the group demonstrates capability on issues vital to the future of e-commerce, such as data protec-

tion and online security. Of its leading attorneys, one client said: *"They are the only ones approaching issues in a forward-looking way – not just dealing with problems when they arise…I trust Baker & McKenzie not to make errors."*

The Lawyers: The respect accorded to *"erudite"* **Michael Mensik** (see p.741) is testament to his deep focus in this practice area. A *"spearhead,"* he *"clearly understands"* all the issues of the sector, and has proven a worthy leader of the Chicago team, steering it from a standing start to its current leading position. Mensik's IP background provides him with useful tools for technology practice. **Ruth Hill Bro** (see p.720) is a major force in data protection issues. Respect for her work is evident, with peers saying she *"stands out and stays on top of issues."* She is supported by associate Brian Hengesbaugh, formerly of the US Department of Commerce. These two attorneys are known for their work on the US-EU Safe Harbor arrangement on data protection. **Thomas Smedinghoff** (see p.753) is

Illinois

Leading individuals

(Technology & IT Outsourcing)

① KIRCHHOEFER Gregg *Kirkland & Ellis*, Chicago
MENSIK Michael *Baker & McKenzie*, Chicago
PETERSON Brad *Mayer Brown*, Chicago
ROY Paul *Mayer Brown*, Chicago

② BRO Ruth *Baker & McKenzie*, Chicago
DOCKSEY Ross *Sonnenschein Nath*, Chicago
EISNER Rebecca *Mayer Brown*, Chicago
GORDON Mark *Gordon & Glickson*, Chicago
SMEDINGHOFF Thomas *Baker & McKenzie*, Chicago
WEINBERGER Seth *Mayer Brown*, Chicago

③ GEORGE Peter *Baker & McKenzie*, Chicago
HALPERN Marcelo *Latham & Watkins*, Chicago
KRAMER Samuel *Baker & McKenzie*, Chicago
MCKENZIE Diana *Neal Gerber*, Chicago
SANCHEZ Vincent *DLA Piper Rudnick*, Chicago
STETSON Jim *Baker & McKenzie*, Chicago
WALTER Priscilla *Gardner Carton*, Chicago

Up-and-coming individuals

O'CONNOR Karen *DLA Piper Rudnick*, Chicago

Individuals are listed alphabetically in each band.

"*very much a commentator and expert in the digital security market.*" His expertise makes him highly sought after for cutting-edge e-commerce issues, and his client base includes major institutions. He has also represented the US government in negotiations on the proposed UNCITRAL e-contracting convention. **Peter George** (see p.729) is "*technically excellent and practical,*" according to clients. Recently made a partner, this strong outsourcing lawyer with a keen interest in technology has been involved in several major outsourcing deals for hi-tech clients. **Samuel Kramer** (see p.736) exhibits "*tremendous business savvy*" and the motivation to extend his practice into new areas such as MVNO agreements. He has also worked on contracts for PayPal, which will have significance in online transactions. "*High-quality*" attorney, **Jim Stetson** (see p.754) is a consistently good performer and shows great dedication to a deal. IT outsourcing has been the core of his practice lately, although he is also involved in more traditional IT work.

The Clients: CSG; Bank of America; Exxceed; ESPN; Robert Half; Orbitz; MetLife; Kanbay; Hewlett-Packard; Global Logistics Technologies and G2 Switchworks.

Mayer, Brown, Rowe & Maw LLP

See firm details p.771

The Firm: This firm has really made outsourcing its focus, something market commentators are only too aware of when they say the firm is "*phenomenal*" and "*a big name on the customer side.*" Its client base includes some of the largest multinational technology purchasers, and for such major clients its extensive resources are a vital factor in their decision to use the firm. Cer-

tain commentators indicate the firm negotiates aggressively to protect clients' interests; appreciative clients, meanwhile, say that once a deal is negotiated, "*the detail really shows.*" In the past year, attorneys continued to work on the major Star Alliance airline IT and outsourcing project. Again, research indicates that "*experience and international connectivity*" are essential for band one status in this table, and this firm is credited with both.

The Lawyers: "*Extremely bright fellow*" **Brad Peterson** (see p.746) is known for his flexibility: "*He doesn't come with a one-way mentality.*" Undoubtedly a "*first-class*" practitioner, he has been advising Sears Roebuck in the negotiation of a $1.6 billion IT infrastructure outsourcing with Computer Sciences Corporation, and Dow Chemical in the negotiation of a $1.4 billion network services outsourcing agreement with IBM. **Paul Roy** (see p.749) is also praised for his "*world-class*" technology outsourcing practice. Described as "*a very, very strong*" attorney, one client declared he was "*one of the best external counsel we have worked with.*" He worked alongside Peterson on the Dow Chemical outsourcing, and assisted Motorola on the renegotiation of a $1.6 billion global outsourcing transaction. **Rebecca Eisner** (see p.725) was held out to be "*absolutely tremendous*" in her guidance to clients on complex outsourcing and major IT procurement and implementation issues. Satisfied clients marveled at her "*total recall, even on two-year-old contracts.*" She was crucial on the Motorola deal, both in its original incarnation and its subsequent modification. **Seth Weinberger** (see p.758) has been a leading light on the Star Alliance project, which involves various transactions and outsourcing deals in order to create a common platform for services. "*A true counselor and advocate,*" he is praised for his ability to "*not get his ego involved,*" yet still "*fight tenaciously*" for his clients' interests. According to one client, "*the other side were sorry they couldn't use him.*"

The Clients: Motorola; Star Alliance; Dow Chemical; Aon; McDonald's; CNA Financial; TELUS; TXU; Kemper Insurance Companies; Yum! Brands; Marconi; Pepsi Bottling Group and United Airlines.

Band 2

Kirkland & Ellis LLP

See firm details p.770

The Firm: This firm has a well-earned reputation for efficiency and "*good turnaround*" in the provision of technology-related services. IT outsourcing is currently the most prominent area of activity for Kirkland & Ellis technology lawyers, but it boasts experience beyond this lucrative field. The firm's background in joint ventures and technology-led strategic alliances helps to raise market awareness of its ability to

tackle a variety of difficult technology issues. A solid client base is built of Fortune 500 companies in industries ranging from construction to nanotech and RFID (radio frequency identification tags).

The Lawyers: The market is in awe of **Gregg Kirchhoefer** (see p.735), an "*extraordinary attorney*" who "*happens to be an IT expert.*" His expansive practice covers a panoply of transactional and general advisory work for both technology companies and technology buyers. Clients agree that "*his thinking and presentation are elegant.*" Kirchhoefer's reputation as an expert on state-of-the-art technology and transaction structures lead overseas clients to seek him out. In one example, a Canadian company used him on a global alliance, even though the deal did not rely on US law.

The Clients: USG; WW Grainger; Accenture; Morgan Stanley; Allstate; GM and Hitachi.

Sonnenschein Nath & Rosenthal LLP

See firm details p.779

The Firm: This firm has blended a leading outsourcing practice with a wider focus on technology. The "*proactive*" technology and outsourcing group consists of three partners and five associates, and although the current focus is on outsourcing transactions, the group still retains its reputation for technology projects and joint ventures. Working alongside two other discrete practice groups – information security and pure IP – it acts for a broad base of clients, including technology vendors and purchasers as well as companies requiring in-depth advice on issues such as technology licensing. On outsourcing, clients say it is ideal for "*total, end-to-end outsourcing.*"

The Lawyers: **Ross Docksey**'s (see p.724) experience and "*business acumen*" allow him to "*hone in on the important aspects*" of transactions. Peers see him as a "*smart, good guy,*" with a roster of clients on both the vendor side and the buyer side. His outsourcing expertise shows "*a broad business perspective.*" In one recent matter Docksey advised a cable modem transmission device developer on its joint venture with French and German partners, and on systems development and global distribution agreements.

The Clients: ACS; Aon Consulting; Accenture and Daubert Industries.

Band 3

DLA Piper Rudnick Gray Cary US LLP

See firm details p.765

The Firm: This firm has attracted the attention of the market, particularly as commentators agree that it is "*now so global.*" Since the alliance of DLA and Piper Rudnick Gray Cary late in 2004, the resultant practice has emerged as a potent force for transactions in the technology sector. The breadth of the firm's client base is testimony to its expertise and reach; it acts, for example, for financial institutions, pharmaceutical companies, manufacturers and hoteliers on issues from outsourcing to technology licensing. Attorneys work closely with colleagues in the firm's e-commerce and privacy group and its communications group. Clients say their chosen advisers are "*very helpful*" and "*understand what the respective parties want from a transaction.*"

The Lawyers: **Vincent Sanchez**'s (see p.750) "*practical*" approach earns him respect from peers and clients. Starting his career as a Judge Advocate General Corps lawyer, this younger attorney is hot property and has progressed steadily to his current position of admired expert and cochair of the technology transactions practice group. Sanchez works on joint ventures and strategic alliances, as well as licensing and IP matters plus outsourcing. He acts for both technology buyers as well as major providers. According to one client, "*Vinnie has a grasp not just of the legal aspects but also the business aspects.*" Listed as an up-and-comer this year, **Karen O'Connor** (see p.744) is "*prominent for healthcare technology;*" she is a "*tough negotiator*" who impresses clients with her legal skills and presentation style.

The Clients: The firm acts for Accenture and others on both the provider and purchaser sides.

Gardner Carton & Douglas LLP

See firm details p.767

The Firm: With offices covering the Midwestern states and the East Coast, this technology group works in conjunction with colleagues outside Chicago. Clients span the spectrum from startups to multinationals. Maintaining a "*good regional reputation,*" this "*absolutely respectable firm*" has been keen to embrace the potential of sustainable Internet-based commerce, and to nurture promising clients in this field. Many commentators remarked that the firm came to their attention through its work in the healthcare technology field.

The Lawyers: **Pam Walter**'s (see p.757) steady hand is at the helm of the practice group. For more than 20 years she has worked on technology matters, more latterly on cyberlaw and e-business, software protection and licensing, and information security. Clients speak of her "*good resume*" and "*consistent advice.*"

The Clients: Metropolitan Pier and Exposition Authority; Northern Trust; InStranet; Allscripts Healthcare Solutions; Unitech Systems and Pepper Construction Company.

Gordon & Glickson

The Firm: When it comes to recommending a technology boutique in Illinois, the market recalls this firm. "*If you don't want a mega-sized firm, this is the place to go,*" say commentators. The firm has nurtured some of the finest and most diverse technology attorneys in the state; even after the departure of prominent partner Diana McKenzie, it has maintained a good market standing. Celebrating 25 years of devotion to IT matters, this 19-attorney practice offers assistance in everything from financing to litigation, and is highly visible with startups and strategic support. Quick to praise attorneys' efficiency, clients continue to be impressed by the "*substantial expertise*" on offer.

The Lawyers: The eponymous **Mark Gordon** is the fulcrum around which the fortunes of his firm revolve. "*Amongst the best*" for strategic thinking, he is viewed as "*the heart and soul*" of the practice and the reason for its ongoing dedication to technology. For clients, he is "*a valued and trusted adviser,*" while peers note his "*phenomenal*" gift for marketing and practice development.

The Clients: United Technologies; DiamondCluster; Nextel and the University of Illinois.

Latham & Watkins LLP

The Firm: A combination of global influence and attorneys handpicked from leading positions in the technology sector ensures Latham & Watkins position as a strong contender in the market. It is a particularly attractive proposition for clients wishing to take advantage of the firm's international dimension. The Chicago team has a compact core of four attorneys who specialize in transactional matters, particularly insofar as they relate to software for the financial services and healthcare sectors, and data protection for international distributors. A recent highlight for the team was the sale of a major online travel retailer client, Orbitz, to Cendant. The transaction was valued at $1.25 billion.

The Lawyers: The market singles out **Marcelo Halpern**, who has invested a lot of time working with industry groups, particularly on cutting-edge software and technology development issues. Until recently he was on the board of the MPEG-4 Industry Forum. Peers agree that he is "*a straight shooter;*" clients say: "*He gets it – you don't have to constantly remind him of what's important.*"

The Clients: Northern Trust; First Health Group; Koch Industries; Orbitz and INVISTA.

Other Notable Practitioners

Diana McKenzie's departure from Gordon & Glickson and arrival at Neal, Gerber & Eisenberg LLP was an interesting development. Her profile has grown over the last 20 years from her early days in healthcare technology to the stage now where her work encompasses all kinds of complex technology-related transactions. With notable clients following her, peers are interested in how she will bring her new firm to prominence. Clients speak of her "*polish*" and "*judgment,*" confirming that "*she is not overly aggressive; she is firm and polite, and has a certain decorum.*"

TELECOM, BROADCAST & SATELLITE: REGULATORY

Band 1

Mayer, Brown, Rowe & Maw LLP

See firm details p.771

The Firm: Leading the table, this firm continues to impress with its nationwide telecom expertise. The secret to its success may lie in the raft of uniformly "*top-drawer*" attorneys, who in terms of their clients' wider strategies "*know how all the pieces fit in.*" The practice is synonymous with all the major litigation entered into by SBC in the Midwest and beyond. Recently, attorneys assisted SBC in arbitrations with Level 3 Communications, and the fact that these occurred over a broad, national canvas allowed the firm to demonstrate its flexibility and reach. Within the SBC Midwest five-state footprint, the firm represents an effective, total legal solution and its domination of the market from the state commission to the federal level is nothing short of inspiring. Attorneys are also retained by BellSouth for rights of way issues.

The Lawyers: "*Professional and cordial*" **Theodore Livingston** (see p.737) has quite overwhelmed the market with his abilities. Having led the Mayer Brown team from strength to strength since the introduction of the 1996 Telecommunications Act, he is respected nationally as an "*excellent*" lead attorney and "*first-class oral advocate.*" Commentators say he has "*gone above and beyond in providing excellent service and a fantastic work product.*" In the past year Livingston has litigated at all levels and witnessed a blossoming of work beyond the SBC Midwest footprint. **Christian Binnig** (see p.719) is another of the firm's most experienced telecom attorneys, having practiced in this field for over a decade. Clients praise his "*broad insights,*" borne out of his experiences across regulated industries. Litigator **Dennis Friedman** (see p.728) is "*focused and good on his feet.*" He is one of the firm's foremost arbitration specialists

Illinois

Leading firms (Telecom, Broadcast & Satellite: Regulatory)

[1] MAYER, BROWN, ROWE & MAW LLP *Chicago*

[2] JENNER & BLOCK LLP *Chicago*
    SIDLEY AUSTIN BROWN & WOOD LLP *Chicago*

[3] FOLEY & LARDNER *Chicago*
    KELLEY DRYE & WARREN *Chicago*
    MEYER CAPEL, PC *Champaign*
    SCHIFF HARDIN LLP *Chicago*

Leading individuals (Telecom, Broadcast & Satellite: Regulatory)

[1] CARPENTER David *Sidley Austin, Chicago*
    LIVINGSTON Theodore *Mayer Brown, Chicago*

[2] BINNIG Christian *Mayer Brown, Chicago*
    DOW Robert *Mayer Brown, Chicago*
    FRIEDMAN Dennis *Mayer Brown, Chicago*
    HAMILL John *Jenner & Block, Chicago*
    HARRINGTON John *Jenner & Block, Chicago*
    KELLY Henry *Kelley Drye, Chicago*
    MACBRIDE Owen *Schiff Hardin, Chicago*
    MUNCY Dennis *Meyer Capel, Champaign*
    MURPHY Joseph *Meyer Capel, Champaign*

[3] COVEY Tyson *Mayer Brown, Chicago*
    MASCHERIN Terri *Jenner & Block, Chicago*
    METROPOULOS Demetrios *Mayer Brown, Chicago*
    MUENCH John *Mayer Brown, Chicago*
    PASULKA-BROWN Kathleen *Foley & Lardner, Chicago*
    ROONEY John *Sonnenschein Nath, Chicago*

Up-and-coming individuals

DONOVAN Joseph *Kelley Drye, Chicago*
GERMANN Hans *Mayer Brown, Chicago*

Firms and individuals are listed alphabetically in each band.

and, with the glut of interconnection agreement arbitrations his profile is currently running sky high. Peers say "*he does his darnedest to find middle ground,*" but "*he can dominate when he wants to.*" Clients have also used him effectively on proceedings arising from the Triennial Review Order. Young partner **Robert Dow** (see p.725) is an expert on preemption issues, particularly when there are jurisdictional questions; for example, how state commissions interface with the federal courts. Peers agree that he is "*an intellectual powerhouse.*" **Tyson Covey** (see p.723) is another partner with extensive experience in this sector. An "*excellent writer,*" his renown stretches states from the Midwest to California. Clients say he is "*so damned fast*" in his turnaround time, yet the quality of his work is consistently excellent. **John Muench** (see p.743) is "*very good on thinking through strategy.*" He is also an expert on preemption and jurisdictional questions, and as such has extensive appellate experience. Alongside Robert Dow, he has acted for BellSouth nationally on rights of way issues. **Jim Metropoulos** (see p.742) is "*very diligent*" and "*excellent on his feet.*" Whether he is writing briefs or appearing on Triennial Review Order

proceedings, those who have come across his work agree that he does "*a real nice job.*" Crucially, he earns plaudits for being "*a good advocate and easy to work with.*" Finally, "*rising star*" **Hans Germann** (see p.729) impresses with his quick uptake and dedication. "*He appears to work 24 hours a day,*" according to one commentator. Although still an associate, the market predicts that he will go far.

The Clients: The firm's clients include SBC Communications and BellSouth.

Band 2

Jenner & Block LLP

See firm details p.768

The Firm: Jenner & Block litigators have attained distinction for their broad representation of clients in the telecommunications sector. MCI is by far and away the practice group's most prominent client, and the firm provides it with considerable support at the appellate level. "*They have a certain tenaciousness about their approach,*" say market commentators of the group. One leading industry source called the attorneys an "*absolute class act – they always take the high road.*" Interconnection issues, reciprocal compensation and unbundling litigation have kept attorneys on their toes; indeed, interviewees agreed that the firm's Chicago and Washington DC offices see a "*lot of action.*" The firm also acts for data center operators and data providers among others.

The Lawyers: "*Calm, relaxed, articulate and knowledgeable,*" **John Hamill** (see p.731) incorporates telecommunications matters into his broader general, complex litigation caseload. Clients say he has "*great oral advocacy skills – he's always prepared and has a good way of making discrete points.*" Two common sources of litigation – reciprocal compensation for calls to ISPs and high-speed services – have kept him busy of late. "*Knowledgeable, attentive and hard-working*" **John Harrington** (see p.732) also takes on a large share of prominent litigation, delivering a work product that is "*comprehensive and thorough.*" Perhaps "*the most knowledgeable regulatory lawyer in Chicago,*" according to some, he has had notable appellate victories. For his main client MCI, he handles appeals coming out of ten Midwest states, both in state and federal courts. Telecommunication matters are just one element of the general litigation and arbitration caseload of the "*extremely intelligent and very well-organized*" **Terri Mascherin** (see p.740). She, too, works for MCI, in addition to other clients in the industry. For EXDS, for example, she has advised on bankruptcy-related issues and arbitrations.

The Clients: Clients include MCI, McLeodUSA and EXDS.

Sidley Austin Brown & Wood LLP

See firm details p.778

The Firm: "*Coming up all the time,*" this practice is developing an enviable reputation. It has a long-standing relationship with AT&T, for whom it acts on a nationwide scale in conjuncton with the firm's Washington DC office. AT&T's work is the cornerstone of the practice – state and federal appellate litigation, including FCC issues, have kept it busy and in the limelight for some time. Several of the Chicago specialists act for clients other than AT&T, including some cellular companies, and peers agree that, whoever the client, the attorneys are "*worthy adversaries.*"

The Lawyers: **David Carpenter** (see p.722) is "*exceptionally bright, truly methodical and precise.*" He liaises closely with his colleagues in Washington DC to provide AT&T with a top-to-bottom service. Peers are impressed: "*If you know he's on the other side you can expect a good brief with no mistakes.*"

The Clients: The firm acts for AT&T, TDS Telecom and US Cellular.

Band 3

Foley & Lardner

See firm details p.1828

The Firm: Foley & Lardner's lawyers have made inroads into the telecom sector, and are particularly known for their Illinois Commerce Commission representations. They have lately embarked on a relationship with MCI having already built up experience with a number of smaller CLEC (competitive local exchange carrier) and wireless clients. The firm has been representing MCI in an arbitration with local incumbent SBC Communications.

The Lawyers: **Kathy Pasulka-Brown** (see p.745) has now made several appearances at the Illinois Commerce Commission for MCI, although her experience started long before this. A very competent wireless attorney, she is also strong in insurance coverage litigation. Market contacts agree that "*she is doing a good job.*" The firm can also call on John McCaffrey, who has significant experience for wireless clients in licensing and spectrum issues.

The Clients: Clients include MCI, US Cellular and T-Mobile.

Kelley Drye & Warren

The Firm: When it comes to comprehensive representation of CLEC, the firm has this down to an art; the lead attorneys at this practice are "*all CLEC players,*" say market commentators. The firm tackles a range of issues including interconnection disputes and arbitration. In one case it represented Level 3 Communications in multistate arbitrations. The firm was also called in to represent Kentucky Payphone Association in a successful public service commission decision, which was upheld on appeal.

The Lawyers: Peers acknowledge that **Henry Kelly** has "*successfully turned an Illinois-specific practice into a national practice.*" As well as steering a steady course for the group, this "*bright*" attorney excels in a courtroom setting. **Joseph Donovan** has significant telecommunications experience, having spent a part of his career providing policy advice to the Illinois Commerce Commission. Peers confirm that he never fails to rise to a challenge.

The Clients: Z-Tel Communications; Kentucky Payphone Association; Talk America and Level 3 Communications.

Meyer Capel, PC
The Firm: This Champaign firm represents local exchange carriers in their inter-carrier relations as well as wireless companies. "*They are great,*" say clients, "*they know which buttons to push.*" An efficient approach impresses commentators, particularly as this firm has cornered the market for rural ILEC (incumbent local exchange carriers) in need of concise, day-to-day

advice. The firm successfully argued before the Illinois Supreme Court for a broad application of the Universal Service Fund, thereby greatly assisting many of the firm's rural carrier clients.

The Lawyers: "*Good guy,*" **Joseph Murphy** is visible on a range of work, including wireless issues and inter-carrier relations. Of **Dennis Muncy** commentators say: "*He brings a wealth of experience, a meticulous and thoughtful approach to the issues and he's very candid.*"

The Clients: Clients include Associated Network Partners, Cingular Wireless and SBC Advanced Solutions.

Schiff Hardin LLP
See firm details p.775

The Firm: Schiff Hardin is widely respected for regulated utilities work of various types, and the telecommunication sector is no exception. When it comes to representing CLEC, it has a strong grasp of all the major issues facing clients, especially within the orbit of the Illinois Commerce Commission.

The Lawyers: The spearhead of the practice is undoubtedly **Owen MacBride** (see p.738). A "*respected and formidable opponent,*" he can nevertheless "*work to a sensible outcome.*" He has extensive experience at the Illinois Commerce Commission, not just in telecom but energy as well. "*Diligent and impressive,*" he is the choice of many mid-sized CLEC.

The Clients: The firm acts for a range of CLEC, ISP and wireless carriers.

Other Notable Practitioners
John Rooney (see p.748) of Sonnenschein Nath & Rosenthal LLP is a frequent visitor to the Illinois Commerce Commission. He has proven himself to be "*effective and pragmatic*" in his work and "*congenial*" with his peers. Rooney has a long history with Illinois CC, including one-time tenure as Chief Administrative Law Judge. He is active in work for Verizon North and Verizon South on legislative issues and rule implementations.

Leaders in Illinois

ABRAMS, Lee N
Mayer, Brown, Rowe & Maw LLP, Chicago 312 701 7083
labrams@mayerbrownrowe.com
Recommended in Antitrust
Practice Areas: Leading attorney in antitrust and franchising litigation. Has represented numerous Fortune 500 corporations, including General Motors, Ford, Eastman Kodak, Citicorp, Sears, NewsCorp, Capital One, and Pitney-Bowes, PPG, International Paper, CompUSA, and the United States Golf Association. Has frequently litigated intellectual property issues.
Prof. Memberships: American Bar Association: Chair, Franchising Forum, 1982-85; Section of Antitrust Law: Vice Chair, 1991-92; Financial Officer and Council Member, 1977-81; Section of Business Law: Chair, Antitrust Committee, 1995-99; Fellow, American College of Trial Lawyers; Member, CPR Panel of Distinguished Neutrals; Admitted to practice in Illinois (1957), US Supreme Court (1961).
Career: Joined Mayer, Brown, Rowe & Maw LLP in 1957; became Partner 1967.
Publications: Author of numerous articles and speeches on antitrust, trade regulation, litigation, and franchising topics.
Personal: Born 28 February 1935. Earned JD with highest distinction from University of Michigan Law School, 1957; served on Law Review Board of Editors. Holds AB from University of Michigan, 1955; elected to Phi Beta

Kappa in his junior year. Winner, Elijah Watt Sells Award for achieving the highest grade in the United States on the Uniform CPA Examination.

ADELMAN, Howard
Adelman & Gettleman Ltd, Chicago 312 435 1050
Recommended in Bankruptcy

ADELSTEIN, Harvey
Neal, Gerber & Eisenberg LLP, Chicago 312 269 8000
Recommended in Employment

AIELLO, Anthony
Sidley Austin Brown & Wood LLP, Chicago 312 853 7128
aaiello@sidley.com
Recommended in Real Estate
Practice Areas: Anthony J Aiello is a Partner in the Chicago office and practices in the Real Estate Group. His experience includes land acquisition, development and sale (office, retail and industrial); office and retail leasing; real estate loan transactions; and a variety of real estate transactions for heavy industrial and utility companies
Career: DePaul University College of Law, JD, 1986; University of Notre Dame, BBA, 1983. Bar Admission: Illinois, 1986.

AIZENSTEIN, Neal
Sonnenschein Nath & Rosenthal LLP, Chicago 312 876 8938
naizenstein@sonnenschein.com
Recommended in Corporate/M&A

Practice Areas: Partner with extensive experience in public and private financings, acquisitions and dispositions, restructurings, joint ventures and partnerships, securities regulations, venture capital transactions and general corporate and securities counselling. Has represented purchasers, sellers and investors in acquisitions and dispositions; issuers and underwriters in public and private financings; borrowers and lenders in financings such as asset-based loans and private placements.
Prof. Memberships: American Bar Association, Chicago Bar Association.
Personal: Northwestern University School of Law, JD, cum laude, Dean's List; University of Illinois, Champaign, Urbana, BS, Accounting, member, Bronze Tablet, CPA, Lowden-Wigmore Prize recipient.

ALTMAN, Ross
DLA Piper Rudnick Gray Cary US LLP, Chicago 312 368 3442
ross.altman@dlapiper.com
Recommended in Construction
Practice Areas: Construction; real estate.
Career: Represents clients in drafting and negotiation of contracts, and in resolution of disputes and claims. Served as general counsel for two companies going through Chapter 11 reorganization, including a global EPC contractor. Well versed in alternate forms of project delivery, such as BOT, EPC, CM, D/B and multiple prime arrangements. Has

handled commercial and industrial projects domestically and overseas. Experienced in distribution, licensing, warranties, performance guarantees, insurance and bonds. Fellow, American College of Construction Lawyers. Adjunct Law Professor at the University of Miami.
Personal: JD, George Washington University; BS (Architecture), University of Michigan.

AMEND, James M
Kirkland & Ellis LLP, Chicago 312 861 2154
jamend@kirkland.com
Recommended in Intellectual Property
Practice Areas: Has significant litigation and counseling experience in the following technology-related fields: electronics, computers, automotive, chemistry, manufacturing and packaging. He has tried many patent infringement cases to judge and jury and has counseled clients on patent infringement and validity questions and licensing. He also has extensive experience in litigating and counseling in trademark, unfair competition, advertising and copyright fields for major US and foreign companies.
Personal: University of Michigan, BS, 1964; University of Michigan, JD, 1967, editor 'Law Review', Order of the Coif; London School of Economics, Fulbright Scholar,1967-68. Consulting Professor-Stanford Law School, 1996-97, Patents and Intellectual Property.

ANDERSON, Kimball
Winston & Strawn LLP, Chicago
Recommended in Litigation

Practice Areas: Federal and state court trial practice concentrating in professional liability, product liability, insurance coverage, patent infringement, consumer class actions, arbitrations and mediations.

Prof. Memberships: Fellow, American College of Trial Lawyers; American Bar Association, Illinois State Bar Association, and Chicago Bar Association; Member, Federal Circuit Bar Association; Seventh Circuit Bar Association.

Career: Mr Anderson attended the University of Illinois College of Law where he served as Editor of the 'Law Review' and graduated first in his class in 1977. He then joined Winston & Strawn LLP as an associate in 1977 and was elected Partner in 1984. He presently serves as a member of the firm's Executive Committee and as General Counsel of the firm. Mr Anderson has tried numerous cases to verdict around the country. His trials include the representation of large corporations in jury trials lasting four weeks or longer. In addition to many trials in state and federal courts around the country, Mr Anderson has considerable experience as an appellate advocate. He has argued before the United States Supreme Court (two cases), Illinois Supreme Court (two cases), New Jersey Supreme Court (two cases), New Mexico Supreme Court, the Court of Appeals for the Federal Circuit, the Seventh Circuit Court of Appeals (many cases), and the Illinois Appellate Court (many cases). Mr Anderson has received national attention for his representation of former Governor George H Ryan, for his representation of the Illinois Council of Long-Term Health Care, Inc. before the United States Supreme Court, for his representation of a major pharmaceutical client regarding transfusions and associated HIV cases, and for other major commercial litigation.

Publications: See a list of Mr Anderson's publications at www.winston.com.

ANGELO, Percy
Mayer, Brown, Rowe & Maw LLP, Chicago 312 701 7330
pangelo@mayerbrown.com
Recommended in Environment

ANTHONY, Michael F
McDermott Will & Emery, Chicago
312 984 7635
manthony@mwe.com
Recommended in Healthcare

Practice Areas: Served as counsel in connection with provider affiliations, integrated delivery system development, formation of HMOs and PPOs, healthcare mergers, acquisitions and affiliations, various joint ventures, joint operating arrangements, reimbursement systems, medical staff matters, Catholic/non-Catholic transactions, medical

group representation and other legal and policy issues. Served as transaction counsel on behalf of St. David's Health System in its combination with local Columbia/HCA facilities in a complex and court tested partnership arrangement. Assisted four religious congregations in formation of a health maintenance organization and preferred provider organization arrangement to serve the Midwest. Assisted in creation of several joint operating entities, including Alegent Health in Omaha, Nebraska.

Career: Served as department Head of firm's national Health Department for 10 years. Former Senior Vice President for Legal Affairs at American Hospital Association. Worked in various administrative capacities at The Johns Hopkins Hospital, including as administrator for Henry Phipps Psychiatric Clinic.

Personal: Earned JD in 1978 from University of Baltimore School of Law. Earned MHA in 1974 and BS in 1972 from Xavier University. Fellow and past President of the American Health Lawyers Association. Fellow in the American College of Healthcare Executives.

ARONSON, Virginia
Sidley Austin Brown & Wood LLP, Chicago 312 853 7741
varonson@sidley.com
Recommended in Real Estate

Practice Areas: Virginia L Aronson is the global head of the firm's Real Estate Practice and is a member of the firm's Executive and Management Committees. Her experience includes securitizations; bank portfolio sales; real estate investment trusts; construction and permanent mortgage financing, including hotels, office buildings and shopping centers; debt restructuring and workouts; acquisition and sale of office buildings, shopping centers, industrial sites and hotels; negotiation of joint venture agreements, and three-dimensional conveyancing.

Prof. Memberships: Member of the American College of Real Estate Lawyers, the Chicago and American Bar Associations, the Chicago Mortgage Attorney's Association, the Chicago Finance Exchange, The Chicago Network and CREW. She is on the Board of Directors of the Chicago Central Area Committee; the Advisory Board of the University of Chicago Law Review, the Leadership Council of the Chicago Public Education Fund and a member of Northwestern University Associates.

Career: The University of Chicago Law School, JD, 1975; University of Chicago, MA, 1973; University of Chicago, BA, 1969. Bar Admission: Illinois, 1975

ASTLE, Richard W
Sidley Austin Brown & Wood LLP, Chicago 312 853 7270
rastle@sidley.com
Recommended in Energy

Practice Areas: Richard W Astle's practice focuses on general corporate and securities work for closely held and public companies, not-for-profit and tax-exempt entities, and governmental bodies. Mr Astle advises on various corporate matters and procedures; contract review; venture-capital financing; acquisitions and dispositions of assets and businesses; joint ventures; and private and public offerings of securities. His representative matters include the preparation and negotiation of corporate governance documents in connection with investments in closely held entities and mergers of not-for-profit entities; limited liability company agreements and partnership agreements in connection with the formation of joint ventures and new business entities; and agreements relating to the purchase and sale of various businesses and assets. Mr Astle's clients have included public utilities, a manufacturer of fluid transport systems, a tax-exempt product testing laboratory, several national associations, manufacturers, healthcare providers and numerous governmental entities.

Career: Georgetown University Law Center, JD, 1980; University of Pennsylvania, MAcc., 1977; University of Pennsylvania, BS, 1977. Illinois, 1980.

BACON, Douglas
Latham & Watkins LLP, Chicago
312 876 7700
Recommended in Bankruptcy

BAKER, Pamela
Sonnenschein Nath & Rosenthal LLP, Chicago 312 876 8989
pbaker@sonnenschein.com
Recommended in Employee Benefits

Practice Areas: Vice Chair and Partner of Employee Benefits and Executive Compensation Group. Focuses on non-qualified deferred compensation, executive equity incentive arrangements for private and public entities and their treatment in corporate transactions. Represents employers and high-level executives in employment agreements, severance arrangements and golden parachute plans; employers in design, implementation and administration of tax-qualified retirement plans; institutional fiduciaries and financial institutions concerning ERISA issues arising in pension fund investing.

Prof. Memberships: American Bar Association; American College of Employee Benefits Counsel.

Personal: University of Wisconsin Law School, JD, managing editor, 'Wisconsin Law Review'; Smith College, AB, with honors.

BALLANTINE, Frank
Sachnoff & Weaver LTD, Chicago
312 207 1000
Recommended in Private Equity

BALLIS, Jon A
Sidley Austin Brown & Wood LLP, Chicago 312 853 2031
jballis@sidley.com
Recommended in Private Equity

Practice Areas: Jon Ballis regularly represents corporations and private equity funds in public and private mergers and acquisitions and related transactions. Mr Ballis also has extensive experience in the areas of initial public offerings and venture capital. His experience includes over 100 M&A transactions including management buy-outs, leveraged acquisitions, public company mergers, divestitures, joint ventures and private equity investments. His significant M&A clients include True North Communications, Tribune Company, Stone Container Corporation, Brunswick Corporation, H.J. Heinz & Company, FTD.com, BWAY Corporation, Looking Glass Networks, CCH Incorporated, Eagle Point Software Corporation, Svoboda Collins & Company and The Pritzker Group. Mr Ballis also has represented clients in significant joint ventures, including Archipelago's electronic stock exchange with Goldman Sachs and E*Trade Group, and Stone Container's paper bag joint venture with Gaylord Container. In addition, Mr Ballis has represented underwriters and issuers in over 20 initial public offerings and follow-on offerings.

Prof. Memberships: Member of Lehigh University Board of Trustee's Visiting Committee and a Director of Harvard Law Society.

Career: Harvard Law School, JD, 1994; Lehigh University, BA, 1991. Bar Admission: Illinois, 1994.

BANNER, Mark
Banner & Witcoff Ltd, Chicago
312 463 5000
Recommended in Intellectual Property

BANOFF, Sheldon I
Katten Muchin Zavis Rosenman, Chicago 312 902 5256
sheldon.banoff@kmzr.com
Recommended in Tax

Practice Areas: Partner, Chicago. Has concentrated in the area of federal income taxation for over 30 years, with particular concentration in investment, real estate, partnership and limited liability company taxation matters. Practice includes the representation of taxable and tax-exempt investors, ventures and professional service firms.

Prof. Memberships: A past Chairman of the Chicago Bar Association's Federal Taxation and Large Law Firm Committees. Frequent American Bar Association program speaker on tax planning, partnership, limited liability company, executive compensation, and professional firm matters.

Career: Nationally and internationally known author and lecturer. Former Lecturer in Law at the University of Chicago

Law School. Co-author of the 'Journal of Taxation's' monthly Shop Talk column since 1985, he has also written over 100 leading articles in the tax area. Has annually been selected by a national poll of lawyers as one of the best lawyers in America and is profiled in several top legal publications, including 'Chambers Global' directory. Elected a Fellow of the American College of Tax Counsel.
Personal: Graduated with high honors from the University of Illinois at Chicago (Accounting) and received his law degree in 1974 from the University of Chicago Law School, where he was associate editor of the 'Law Review'.

BAPTISTA Jr, Robert C
Mayer, Brown, Rowe & Maw LLP, Chicago 312 701 7101
rbaptista@mayerbrown.com
Recommended in Banking & Finance
Practice Areas: Negotiates and documents secured and unsecured lending agreements, debt restructurings, and other financing transactions. Advises in corporate matters such as borrowing transactions, sale agreements, and long-term production and licensing arrangements.
Prof. Memberships: Admitted to practice in Illinois, 1982.
Career: Served as Judicial Clerk to The Honorable R Lanier Anderson III, US Court of Appeals for the Eleventh Circuit, 1982-83. Joined Mayer, Brown Rowe & Maw LLP in 1983 and became a Partner in 1989.
Publications: Author of 'Bank Credit as Value in Article 4 of the Uniform Commercial Code', U. Ill. L. Rev. 395, 1981; 'Prior Party Set-Off as a Defense Under U.C.C. Section 3-306', U. Ill. L. Rev. 869, 1981; 'Peoria Savings & Loan Association v Jefferson Trust & Savings Bank', 70 Ill. B.J. 191, 1981.
Personal: Born 14 September 1948. Earned JD, summa cum laude, at the University of Illinois in 1982, where was editor-in-chief of the 'Law Review'. Received MA, also summa cum laude, from Northern Illinois University in 1976 and BA from Wheaton College in 1970.

BARLIANT, Ronald
Goldberg, Kohn, Bell, Black, Rosenbloom & Moritz, Ltd, Chicago
312 201 4000
Recommended in Bankruptcy

BARROW, Peter
Neal, Gerber & Eisenberg LLP, Chicago
312 269 8000
Recommended in Banking & Finance

BARTLIT Jr, Fred
Bartlit Beck Herman Palenchar & Scott, Denver 303 592 3100
Recommended in Litigation

BATES Jr, Robert
Bates & Carey, Chicago
312 762 3100
Recommended in Insurance

BEARD, James
DLA Piper Rudnick Gray Cary US LLP, Chicago 312 368 2169
james.beard@dlapiper.com
Recommended in Real Estate
Practice Areas: Real estate, real estate finance, construction, sports facilities development.
Career: He concentrates his practice in commercial real estate law and has represented clients in a wide range of commercial real estate transactions, including acquisitions and dispositions, financing, joint venture formation, construction contract negotiation, lease preparation, and government procurement and contracting. He also represents developers and institutional lenders in restructuring and workout of troubled real estate projects.
Personal: JD, Chicago-Kent College of Law, Illinois Institute of Technology; BS, University of Illinois at Urbana-Champaign.

BECK, Philip
Bartlit Beck Herman Palenchar & Scott, Chicago 312 494 4400
Recommended in Litigation

BECKER, Scott
McGuireWoods LLP, Chicago
312 849 8100
Recommended in Healthcare

BELL, Stephen
Goldberg, Kohn, Bell, Black, Rosenbloom & Moritz, Ltd, Chicago
312 201 4000
Recommended in Real Estate

BERG, Eric
DLA Piper Rudnick Gray Cary US LLP, Chicago 312 368 3448
eric.berg@dlapiper.com
Recommended in Construction
Practice Areas: Construction; litigation; lodging and timeshare.
Career: His practice focuses on construction law in both litigation and transactional work. He has represented owners, contractors, subcontractors, architects, engineers, and lenders. He also has extensive experience in other areas of commercial litigation and alternative dispute resolution. He is well-versed in all facets of the Americans with Disabilities Act and the Fair Housing Act. He has provided counsel on interpretation of and compliance with the ADA, the FHA, and other federal, state and local accessibility statutes.
Personal: JD, Northwestern University; BA, Yale University.

BERGHOFF Jr, John C
Mayer, Brown, Rowe & Maw LLP, Chicago 312 701 7315
jberghoff@mayerbrownrowe.com
Recommended in Environment
Practice Areas: Environmental Practice Leader. Litigates in complex environmental trials and appeals before federal and state courts. Provides counselling and response to environmental 'crisis' situations.

Prof. Memberships: Adjunct Professor, Northwestern University School of Law, 1996 to date. Lecturer on litigation and legal ethics.
Career: Joined Mayer, Brown, Rowe & Maw LLP as Partner, 1986.
Personal: Earned JD, Northwestern University School of Law; Wigmore Key. Holds BA, with honors, from Northwestern University. Board of Trustees, Northwestern University, 1988-94. Chairman, Board of Alumni Regents, Northwestern University, 1998 to date. Vice Chairman, Board of Trustees, Ravinia Festival, 1996 to present.

BERKELEY, Jill B
Schiff Hardin LLP, Chicago
312 258 5598
jberkeley@schiffhardin.com
Recommended in Insurance
Practice Areas: Insurance.
Prof. Memberships: American Bar Association - Tort Trial and Insurance Practice Section, Illinois State Bar Association, Illinois Academy of Laureates, National Risk Retention Association, Illinois Captive and Alternative Risk Funding Insurance Association, Illinois Association of Defense Trial Counsel, Association of Professional Insurance Women, Defense Research Institute.
Career: Ms Berkeley leads Schiff Hardin's Insurance Group. She has extensive experience representing insurers and insureds in coverage litigation.
Publications: More than 50 publications and presentations.
Personal: University of Michigan (BA, magna cum laude, Phi Beta Kappa, 1972), Northwestern University School of Law (JD, 1975).

BERKOFF, Mark
DLA Piper Rudnick Gray Cary US LLP, Chicago 312 368 7090
mark.berkoff@dlapiper.com
Recommended in Bankruptcy
Practice Areas: Bankruptcy and business reorganization.
Career: His practice concentrates on bankruptcy and creditors' rights. He represents debtors, creditors' committees and secured lenders in complex Chapter 11 cases in diverse industries and has experience in many aspects of this area of law. He acts as special litigation counsel to bankruptcy trustees and prosecutes and defends involuntary petitions in bankruptcy.
Personal: JD, University of Chicago; BA, University of Wisconsin-Madison.

BERNICK, David M
Kirkland & Ellis LLP, Chicago
312 861 2248
dbernick@kirkland.com
Recommended in Litigation
Practice Areas: National trial counsel in mass tort litigation in the areas of pharmaceutical litigation, asbestos litigation, including the development of a Chapter 11 strategy for companies with

asbestos liabilities, tobacco cost recovery, holocaust labor, breast implants and radiation exposure in state and federal courts. He has also served as trial counsel in securities fraud, product liability, leveraged-buyout, trade secret misappropriation, breach of contract, RICO, securities and monopoly cases. Currently serves on the Judicial Conference Committee on the Rules of Practice and Procedure.
Personal: University of Chicago, BA, 1974. Yale University, MA, 1975. University of Chicago, JD, 1978.

BERNSTEIN, Bruce
Sidley Austin Brown & Wood LLP, Chicago 312 853 7635
bbernstein@sidley.com
Recommended in Banking & Finance
Practice Areas: Member of the firm's Executive Committee; Group Head Banking/Financial Transactions. Concentrates his practice in secured transactions, commerical finance and restructurings on behalf of commercial banks and asset-based lenders. 1995 to 2001: General Counsel, Commercial Finance Association.
Prof. Memberships: Chicago, Illinois and American Bar Associations. Fellow: American College of Bankruptcy, American College of Commercial Finance Lawyers. Member: National Bankruptcy Conference.
Career: Cornell University, BA, 1965; Harvard Law School, JD, 1968. Bar Admission: Illinois, 1968.
Publications: Frequent lecturer on secured lending and bankruptcy topics and has written numerous articles on the Uniform Commercial Code and Bankruptcy Code.

BERNSTEIN, Howard
Neal, Gerber & Eisenberg LLP, Chicago
312 269 8000
Recommended in Employment

BESSETTE-SMITH, Suzanne
Barack Ferrazzano Kirschbaum Perlman & Nagelberg, Chicago
312 984 3100
Recommended in Real Estate

BEST, Edward S
Mayer, Brown, Rowe & Maw LLP, Chicago 312 701 7100
EBest@mayerbrown.com
Recommended in Corporate/M&A
Practice Areas: Represents issuers, underwriters and selling stockholders in connection with: public offerings of equity in the United States; debt securities in the United States; medium-term note programs; 3(a)(3) and 4(2) commercial paper programs; private and Rule 144A offerings of debt securities; private offerings of equity securities; Eurobond offerings; Euro-MTN and Euro-commercial programs. Represents buyers, sellers and financial intermediaries in connection with public and private: acquisitions; joint ventures;

divestitures; mergers; tender offers; exchange offers; proxy contests; consent solicitations. Represents companies in connection with: Securities Act compliance; Exchange Act compliance; Exchange Act reporting; NYSE or NASDAQ compliance; exchange offers; consent solicitations; stock repurchases and self-tenders; corporate governance; defensive measures (including shareholders' rights plans).

Career: Mayer, Brown, Rowe & Maw LLP, Chicago, 1986 to date; Partner, 1995.

Publications: Co-author: 'Acquisition Structuring in the Aftermath of Epstein v MCA, Inc.,' Insights, Vol. 9, No. 7, July 1995. Speaker: 'Overview of the Williams Act,' Doing Deals, Practicing Law Institute 1995-97.

Personal: JD (cum laude), Loyola University of Chicago School of Law, 1986; research editor, Law Journal. AB, University of Illinois - Urbana, 1983. Adjunct Professor of Law, Illinois Institute of Technology - Chicago Kent School of Law (1996 and 1997).

BIASETTI, Jon
Lord Bissell & Brook, Chicago
312 443 0700
Recommended in Insurance

BIERIG, Jack R
Sidley Austin Brown & Wood LLP, Chicago 312 853 7614
jbierig@sidley.com
Recommended in Antitrust

Practice Areas: Jack R Bierig's practice focuses on litigation challenging government action affecting healthcare providers, copyright and trademark cases, and FDA matters. He represents associations and healthcare providers in government antitrust and health fraud investigations, in actions brought by the Department of Justice and the Federal Trade Commission, and in private antitrust cases. He also counsels clients on a wide variety of antitrust, association law, and regulatory issues. Clients include the American Medical Association, American Dental Association, College of American Pathologists and the American Association of Realtors®.

Prof. Memberships: He is a past President of the Illinois Association of Healthcare Attorneys.

Career: Harvard Law School, JD, 1972; Brandeis University, AB, 1968. Bar Admission: llinois, 1972.

Publications: Frequent author and speaker on antitrust and healthcare litigation topics.

BINNIG, Christian F
Mayer, Brown, Rowe & Maw LLP, Chicago 312 701 0700
cbinnig@mayerbrown.com
Recommended in Telecom, Broadcast & Satellite

Practice Areas: Litigator specializing in telecommunications and regulated industries, particularly gas and electricity. Experienced in antitrust, mergers and acquisitions, emergency litigation, appellate work, professional malpractice, telecommunications and communications network contract negotiations.

Prof. Memberships: American Bar Association, Litigation Section and Public Utilities, Communications and Transportation Law Section; Illinois, 1986. US District Court for the Northern District of Illinois, 1986. Various other US District Courts and Courts of Appeal.

Career: Joined Mayer, Brown, Rowe & Maw LLP, 1986; became Partner, 1994. Formerly with Troutman, Sanders, Lockerman & Ashmore, Atlanta, 1985-86.

Publications: 'Federal and State Supply Issues Separating LDCs from Complete Open-Access Common Carrier Status' (presented as 'Gas Supply Planning and Management as the LDCs Unbundle', Institute of Gas Technology, 1997).

Personal: Born 10 November 1961. University of Michigan Law School, JD, cum laude, 1985. University of Virginia, BA with high distinction, 1982; Phi Beta Kappa.

BISHOP, Timothy S
Mayer, Brown, Rowe & Maw LLP, Chicago 312 701 7829
tbishop@mayerbrownrowe.com
Recommended in Environment

Practice Areas: Responsible for arguing four cases and briefing nearly 50 before the US Supreme Court, handling dozens of appeals in federal and state appellate courts, and briefing dispositive dismissal and summary judgment, motions in federal and state trial courts. Experience in Clean Water Act, Endangered Species Act, land use, property rights, and constitutional appeals and litigation, representing property owners, state and local government bodies, and other regulated entities.

Career: Joined Mayer, Brown, Rowe & Maw LLP, 1991; Partner, 1995. Law Clerk to Justice William J Brennan, Jr, US Supreme Court, 1988-89; Judge James L Oakes, US Court of Appeals for the Second Circuit, 1986-87; Staff Counsel and Skadden Fellow, American Civil Liberties Union, Chicago, 1989-91. Adjunct Professor, University of Chicago Law School, 1990-91; 'Northwestern University School of Law,' 1981-83, 1993-96; IIT-Chicago Kent Law School, 1989-91.

Publications: Recent writings: 'Do Federal Environmental Laws Regulate Commerce?' 17 Natural Resources & Environment 7 (Summer 2002). 'Smart Growth or Dumb Bureaucracy?' 32 Environmental Law Reporter 10822 (July 2002).

Personal: Northwestern University School of Law, JD magna cum laude, 1985; Articles Editor, Northwestern University Law Review. Oxford University, England, Corpus Christi College, BA in Law - First Class Honours, 1979; MA 1983.

BLACKMAN, Jana Cohen
Sonnenschein Nath & Rosenthal LLP, Chicago 312 876 7967
jblackman@sonnenschein.com
Recommended in Real Estate

Practice Areas: Real Estate Practice Chair; Tax-Advantaged Investments Practice Chair. Tax-advantaged investments, particularly, low-income housing tax credits, and historic and new market tax credits expert. Transactions include guaranteed investments, fund investments and direct investments in low-income housing tax credit projects; low-income housing developments financed in, eg, traditional debt/equity, HOPE VI, taxable/tax-exempt bonds and by US Department of Housing and Urban Development (HUD). Collaborates with HUD and Justice Department on affordable or special needs housing issues and federal fair housing claims.

Prof. Memberships: Chicago Bar Association, ABA.

Personal: University of Chicago Law School, JD; Northwestern University, BA, with Honors, Art History.

BOEHNEN, Daniel A
McDonnell Boehnen Hulbert & Berghoff LLP, Chicago
312 913 2130
boehnen@mbhb.com
Recommended in Intellectual Property

Career: Daniel A Boehnen is a Founding Partner of MBHB. His litigation experience covers numerous high-technology industries in all federal courts, including district courts, appeals courts, International Trade Commission actions, and the Court of Claims. His practice focuses on successful strategies to achieve success in disputed matters, including trials, appeals, oppositions, and ADR proceedings, and he has been involved in numerous notable and precedent-setting cases. Mr Boehnen is valued by clients for his clear thinking, insightful explanations, and creative solutions, which are the same factors behind his great success in litigation. In 2003, Mr Boehnen was recognized by the Leading Lawyers Network as one of the leading intellectual property lawyers in Illinois based upon peer recommendations. He has a BS in chemical engineering from the University of Notre Dame and a JD from Cornell University Law School. He is a registered patent attorney with extensive experience in national and international patent litigation, and has been admitted to practice before the US Supreme Court. Mr Boehnen was a governor for the Federal Circuit Bar Association, a founder and an officer of the Association of Patent Law Firms, and former Chair of the Cornell Law Alumni Association of Greater Chicago.

BOEHRER, Charles
Winston & Strawn LLP, Chicago
312 558 5600
cboehrer@winston.com
Recommended in Banking & Finance

Practice Areas: Finance, securities, merger and acquistions.

Career: Mr Boehrer attended the University of Michigan where he served as editor of the 'Law Review.' He then joined Winston & Strawn as an associate in 1985 and was elected Partner in 1993. Mr Boehrer is a Partner in the Corporate Department. His extensive experience includes acting as bank counsel for the structuring of senior and senior second lien credit facilities, including leveraged and investment grade transactions, complex international lending transactions, acquisition and going-private transactions, refinancing and repricings, as well as restructuring and workout transactions. In the last year, he has represented leading financial institutions and borrowers on over $10 billion of senior debt including his representation of Deutsche Bank on the $1.3 billion credit facility to Huntman International; Bank of America on the $600 million credit facility for IDEX Corporation; Harley-Davidson Financial Services, Inc. in connection with its $1.1 billion credit facility; and Lear Corporation in connection with its $1.7 billion senior credit facility. Mr Boehrer served as Chairman of the Financial Institutions Committee of the Chicago Bar Assocation in 1990.

BOIES, Bill
McDermott Will & Emery, Chicago
312 984 7686
bboies@mwe.com
Recommended in Employee Benefits

Practice Areas: Concentrates his practice on business disputes counseling and business litigation throughout the country, including benefits litigation, securities litigation, financial disputes, class actions, alternative dispute resolution, trials and appeals. Regularly represents benefit plan sponsors and fiduciaries in ERISA class action litigation concerning pension plan administration, fiduciary duty, responsibility for asset losses, and changes in welfare benefits. Several of the health benefits class actions he has won resulted in court-approved savings to employers valued at more than $100 million. Currently defending plan sponsors, company officers and corporate fiduciaries in several class actions concerning declines in value of employer stock held in 401(k) plans and ESOPs.

Prof. Memberships: Member, American Bar Association and Chicago Bar Association class litigation committees; Lawyers Club of Chicago; Director, Chicago Bar Foundation; and fellow, American Bar Foundation.

Publications: Co-authored 'The Struggle Over Retiree Medical Benefits: Who's On Top' for the 'Employee Relations Law Journal' and '401(k) Litigation Over Company Stock Fund Performance: It's Only Just Begun' for the 'Benefits Law

Journal.'

Personal: BA from Brown University in 1965 and JD from the University of Chicago Law School in 1968.

BORDERS, Thomas
McDermott Will & Emery, Chicago
312 984 7552
tborders@mwe.com
Recommended in Tax

Practice Areas: Partner in Tax Department, main practice areas include federal tax controversies involving audits, administrative appeals, litigation and defending companies and individuals in fraud and criminal investigations related to tax and securities matters. Worked on numerous US and international tax cases involving corporate tax matters, valuation, finance and accounting issues.
Prof. Memberships: Member of Chicago Bar Association; American Bar Association (Federal Taxation and Litigation Committees).
Career: Admitted to the Indiana Bar in 1974, Illinois, 1979. Also qualified for the US District Court for the Northern District of Illinois, the US Tax Court, various Circuits of the US Court of Appeals, and the US Court of Federal Claims. Prior to joining McDermott in 1986, worked as a trial attorney for the Office of Chief Counsel with the Internal Revenue Service (1975-85), also held position as Adjunct Professor in the graduate tax program at IIT Chicago-Kent College of Law (1987-93). Member of Advisory Board and author for Journal of Taxation of Corporate Transactions and frequent speaker on tax topics.
Personal: Born April 22, 1948. Received BA in 1970 from St. Louis University, JD from Georgtown University Law Centre in 1974, and MBA from Northwestern University in 1984.

BORUN, Michael
Marshall, Gerstein & Borun, Chicago
312 474 6300
Recommended in Intellectual Property

BOTICA, Matthew J
Winston & Strawn LLP, Chicago
312 558 8095
mbotica@winston.com
Recommended in Bankruptcy

Practice Areas: Partner, Corporate Department, Chicago office. Practice concentration in insolvency, bankruptcy, and business reorganization. Co-Chair of the Financial Restructuring Group at Winston & Strawn. More than 25 years' experience representing banks, institutional lenders, creditors' committees, trustees, governmental agencies, and other creditors in the bankruptcy, reorganization, and claims trading areas.
Prof. Memberships: American College of Bankruptcy.
Publications: Author of a chapter on chapter 7 'Business Liquidations' in the Illinois Institute for Continuing Legal Education (IICLE) 'Bankruptcy Practice

Handbook'.

Personal: Boston College, 1972, summa cum laude, Phi Beta Kappa. Harvard Law School, 1975.

BOWEN, Stephen
Latham & Watkins LLP, Chicago
312 876 7700
Recommended in Tax

BOYD, Eric
Seyfarth Shaw LLP, Chicago
312 346 8000
Recommended in Environment

BRADLEY, Craig C
Katten Muchin Zavis Rosenman, Chicago 312 902 5353
craig.bradley@kmzr.com
Recommended in Private Equity

Practice Areas: Partner in the Corporate Department concentrating on the representation of management led leveraged buyouts and private equity backed emerging software, life sciences, internet, communications and other technology companies in obtaining angel and venture capital financing and in connection with initial public offerings, compensation arrangements, and mergers and acquisitions. Also represents venture capital firms and private equity funds.
Prof. Memberships: Member, Board of Directors, Chicago Software Association; Member, Board of Directors, BioAngels; Adjunct Assistant Professor, Northwestern University Kellogg Graduate School of Business.
Personal: JD, cum laude, Indiana University, member, Indiana Law Journal; BS, Finance, summa cum laude, Elmhurst College.

BRENNAN, Daniel
DLA Piper Rudnick Gray Cary US LLP, Chicago 312 368 4085
daniel.brennan@dlapiper.com
Recommended in Construction

Practice Areas: Construction; litigation.
Career: He concentrates his practice in advising owners, designers, and contractors on risk management in the construction process; prosecuting and defending construction claims including professional negligence, personal injury, and delay claims; drafting construction and design contracts for architects, engineers and owners; and advising clients with respect to design and construction of accessible facilities under Title III of the Americans with Disabilities Act and the Fair Housing Act.
Personal: JD, Georgetown University Law Center; BA, University of Notre Dame.

BRITTAIN, Max
Schiff Hardin LLP, Chicago
312 258 5544
mbrittain@schiffhardin.com
Recommended in Employment

Practice Areas: Labor and employment.

Prof. Memberships: American Bar Association; College of Labor and Employment Lawyers.
Career: Mr Brittain leads Schiff Hardin's Labor and Employment Group. He has extensive experience representing management clients in proceedings before the National Labor Relations Board and Equal Employment Opportunity Commission, state and federal courts, and various local, state, and federal agencies.
Personal: Bradley University (BS, 1969), Loyola University Chicago School of Law (JD, cum laude, 1976), Managing Editor, 'Loyola University Chicago Law Review.'

BRO, Ruth Hill
Baker & McKenzie, Chicago
312 861 7985
bro@bakernet.com
Recommended in Technology

Practice Areas: Privacy, security, e-workplace, e-business. Privacy strategy development/implementation; website, HR, customer, and e-marketing policies/procedures; multi-jurisdictional/cross-border issues; privacy crisis management/prevention. Featured speaker: in-house training, conferences. Views noted in WSJ, NY Times, BNA Privacy & Security Law Report, Bloomberg Radio, CNBC.
Prof. Memberships: Co-Chair, ABA E-Privacy Law Committee. Council Member, ABA Section of Science & Technology Law. Editorial Board, 'SciTech Lawyer.' Baker & McKenzie: Global Privacy Steering Committee; North America Editor, 'Privacy Newsletter.'
Career: Admitted in Illinois (1994).
Publications: Editor, 'The E-Business Legal Arsenal' (ABA, 2004); co-author, 'Online Law' (Addison-Wesley, 1996); numerous privacy and e-business articles.
Personal: JD, University of Chicago.

BROCCOLO, Bernadette
McDermott Will & Emery, Chicago
312 984 6911
bbroccolo@mwe.com
Recommended in Healthcare

Practice Areas: Has been advising health industry organizations for 25 years on legal and regulatory compliance matters, information technology acquisition and health information privacy. General health practice includes federal taxation of exempt organizations; health industry joint ventures; corporate governance and restructurings; hospital-physician relationships; clinical research compliance counseling; and internal legal compliance program development and implementation. Health information technology practice includes drafting and negotiating agreements for the development and acquisition of healthcare information and telecommunication systems. Advises health clients in a variety of contexts on complex legal considerations involved in

electronic exchange, and other uses and disclosures of health information, including the requirements imposed by HIPAA and other federal and state privacy and confidentiality laws. Frequent speaker and author in all health industry subspecialties.
Prof. Memberships: Serves leadership positions for organizations serving health industry and legal profession, including American Health Lawyers Association, Illinois Association of Hospital Attorneys and American Bar Association. Currently serves as a member of Governing Council of American Bar Association's Health Law Section and is immediate past Chair of the Health Law Section's Tax & Accounting Interest Group.
Personal: Earned JD in 1980 from University of Notre Dame Law School, and BA in 1977 from Boston College.

BROWN, Jeffrey
Seyfarth Shaw LLP, Chicago
312 346 8000
Recommended in Media & Entertainment

BRYANT, David
Katten Muchin Zavis Rosenman, Chicago 312 902 5380
david.bryant@kmzr.com
Recommended in Real Estate

Practice Areas: David J Bryant concentrates his efforts in commercial real estate law. He has substantial experience in acquisitions, dispositions and investments in real estate assets, real estate development, real estate finance (including mezzanine financing), joint venture and partnership formation and financing. In addition, Mr Bryant has substantial experience in representing sponsors of real estate funds and in establishing joint ventures and other companies to own, operate, finance and develop real estate.
Prof. Memberships: Active member of the Pension Real Estate Association (PREA) and the Urban Land Institute (ULI).
Career: Co-Chair of National Real Estate Practice.
Personal: Mr Bryant received his Bachelor's degree from the University of Illinois in 1984 and his Juris Doctor degree from Northwestern University in 1987.

BRYANT, L Edward
Gardner Carton & Douglas LLP, Chicago 312 569 1259
ebryant@gcd.com
Recommended in Healthcare

Practice Areas: Ed Bryant founded the firm's Health Law Department in 1979, and since then has participated in more than 230 health industry corporate restructurings, in more than 125 hospital mergers or acquisitions and in hundreds of healthcare joint ventures. Other practice areas include integrated delivery systems, hospital closures, managed care arrangements, medical groups and physician contracts, special risk audits (eg Medicare fraud, governance and inurement), canon law compliance through use of civil law, patient care issues, medical staff privileges, academic affiliations, corporate governance trends, federal taxation of exempt and related organizations, and strategizing on implementation of organizational design change through postmerger reorganizations.

Prof. Memberships: Board Member; American Board of Medical Specialties.
Career: He has been a faculty member of Kellogg Graduate School of Management of Northwestern University and Loyola University School of Law. Named one of The Best Lawyers in America for the past 12 years; selected to Best Lawyers in Illinois and Leading Lawyers Network of Illinois. Recipient, James H Douglas, Jr. Award for exemplary participation in public and charitable activities.
Publications: He speaks and publishes widely within the health industry.
Personal: Northwestern University, BA, 1963; JD, 1967.

BRYANT, Timothy
McDermott Will & Emery, Chicago
312 984 2066
tbryant@mwe.com
Recommended in Private Equity

Practice Areas: Corporate Partner and one of the leaders of the firm's Private Equity Group. His practice covers the entire spectrum of corporate finance and securities law. Represents public and private companies, as well as the investment banks, private equity funds, and other financial institutions that support them. Practice involves mergers and acquisitions, negotiated and unsolicited tender offers, private equity and venture capital financings, public offerings, joint ventures, the formation of and investment in private equity funds, and the general representation of public and private companies. Has represented clients in closing over one hundred transactions, ranging from the venture financing of start-up companies and the representation of executives in their equity and compensation arrangements to the $1.7 billion acquisition of a European engine manufacturer and a $150 million equity investment in a public telecom company.
Personal: Graduated from Northwestern University (BA, 1986) and Northwestern University School of Law (JD, 1989). Served as Articles Editor of the 'Northwestern University Law Review'. Served as a Law Clerk for the Honorable James B Zagel of the US District Court for the Northern District of Illinois.

BUDNY, Terrence
Bell, Boyd & Lloyd LLC, Chicago
312 372 1121
Recommended in Real Estate

BULGER, Brian
Meckler, Bulger & Tilson, Chicago
312 474 7900
Recommended in Employment

BURT, Antony
Schiff Hardin LLP, Chicago
312 258 5762
aburt@schiffhardin.com
Recommended in Insurance

Practice Areas: Litigation, reinsurance.
Prof. Memberships: American Bar Association.
Career: Mr Burt focuses in commercial litigation, with a particular concentration in the areas of reinsurance, professional liability, civil fraud investigations, bankruptcy, and antitrust litigation. He has been involved in all aspects of complex civil litigation, including trials, injunctions, appeals, and arbitrations.
Personal: Duke University (AB, 1978), Northwestern University School of Law (JD, 1982), Member, Northwestern Law Review.

BUSEY, Roxane C
Gardner Carton & Douglas LLP, Chicago 312.569.1354
rbusey@gcd.com
Recommended in Antitrust

Practice Areas: Partner, Senior Member of Antitrust Practice Group; former Chair of American Bar Association (ABA) Section of Antitrust Law (2001-02); 30 years' experience in antitrust counseling and litigation; practices before Federal Trade Commission and Department of Justice; substantial experience in antitrust compliance issues and mergers and acquisitions.
Prof. Memberships: Currently, Chair, ABA Antitrust Section Task Force on Modernization (2004-), Co-Chair, Practicing Law Institute Annual Antitrust Institute (Chicago) (2002-); Previously, ABA Antitrust Section, Chair (2001-02); Officer, Council Member (1992-2003); Health Care Committee Chair (1989-92); Member, Special Task Force on Competition Policy to Clinton Transition Team (1992), (ex officio) Special Task Force to Bush Transition Team (2000); Chair, Antitrust Committee, Chicago Bar Association (1990); Chair, Illinois State Bar Association Antitrust Council (1984).
Career: Joined GCD in 1995 as Partner; previously associate and Partner at Hopkins & Sutter (1975-95).
Publications: Frequent author, lecturer on antitrust issues. Recent lecturer at ABA Antitrust Section Masters Program (2004), PLI Annual Antitrust Institute (Chicago) (2005). Testimony before FTC on Health Care (2003); Intellectual Property (2002); Joint Ventures (1997); Global Competition (1995).
Personal: Northwestern University, JD (1975); Northwestern University, MAT (1971); Miami University (Ohio), BA, cum laude, Phi Beta Kappa (1970).

BUTLER Jr, John Wm (Jack)
Skadden, Arps, Slate, Meagher & Flom LLP & Affiliates, Chicago
312 407 0730
jbutler@skadden.com
Recommended in Bankruptcy

Practice Areas: Co-Practice Leader, Worldwide Corporate Restructuring Practice. Specializes in troubled company M&A, financing and restructuring situations, including cross-border transactions and advising officers and directors of public companies involved in debt restructuring on matters relating to corporate governance and fiduciary duty. Representative company matters include the restructuring of Kmart Corporation, Per-Se Technologies, Inc., Rite Aid Corporation, Singer N.V., US Airways Group, Inc. and Xerox Corporation and special counsel representations of 360/networks, inc., Enron Corporation and The Warnaco Group, Inc. Also represented Air Transport International LLC, Comdisco, Inc., Eagle Food Centers, Inc., FPA Medical Management, Inc., Peter J. Schmitt Co., Inc., Service Merchandise Company, Inc. and USN Communications, Inc. in transactions that provided for the disposition of their assets and operating businesses to third parties as part of Chapter 11 cases. Listed in every annual edition of the K&A Restructuring Register, the peer group listing of the top restructuring attorneys and financial advisors in the United States. Six times named by 'Turnarounds & Workouts' in its annual list of the top dozen restructuring lawyers in America. Named as one of the top ten worldwide restructuring lawyers in 2002 by 'Global Counsel Magazine'. Recipient of first-ever Chairman's Award from the Turnaround Management Association in 2001 for his contributions to and standing in the corporate renewal industry.
Prof. Memberships: Fellow, American College of Bankruptcy and International Insolvency Institute.
Career: JD, University of Michigan Law School, 1980; AB, Princeton University, 1977 (magna cum laude).

CAHAN, James N
Sidley Austin Brown & Wood LLP, Chicago 312 853 7750
jcahan@sidley.com
Recommended in Environment

Practice Areas: Jim Cahan focuses his practice in the areas of air pollution, environmental aspects of bankruptcies and transactions, and environmental management. He has extensive experience in working with debtors, creditors, banks and other interested parties regarding strategies, negotiations and resolution of a variety of environmental claims and other bankruptcy issues, and also assists corporations with policies and programs for managing their environmental, health and safety problems. He is well versed in the full range of hazardous waste and Superfund issues;

asbestos and project management, and has extensive experience dealing with the environmental aspects of corporate acquisitions and real estate transactions.
Career: Served in office of the General Counsel, air division, of the Environmental Protection Agency. Washington University School of Law, JD, 1976; Washington University, BA, 1973. Bar Admissions: District of Columbia, 1980 and Illinois, 1976.

CALLAHAN, Michael R
Katten Muchin Zavis Rosenman, Chicago 312 902 5634
michael.callahan@kmzr.com
Recommended in Healthcare

Practice Areas: Concentrates practice in healthcare, assisting hospital, healthcare system and physician clients on a variety of healthcare legal issues including healthcare antitrust, HIPAA, regulatory compliance, medical staff credentialing, hospital/medical staff relations, and mergers and acquisitions. Leads HIPAA and Regulatory Compliance Practice.
Prof. Memberships: American Bar Association; American Health Lawyers Association; Illinois Association of Healthcare Attorneys; Chicago Bar Association.
Career: Served as Law Clerk to Justice Daniel P Ward on the Illinois Supreme Court; recipient of Illinois Association Medical Staff Services Leadership Award; Chair, Health Law Committee and Chicago Bar Association; served on various committees of American Health Lawyers Association.
Publications: Speaks at industry organizations on a variety of topics including, integrated delivery systems, hospital/physician joint ventures, physician recruitment and retention, medical staff matters, Medicare fraud and abuse and HIPAA; Adjunct Professor, DePaul University Masters in Health Law Program.
Personal: DePaul University College of Law (JD 1979); Northern Illinois University (BA 1975); Board Member, Northlight Theater and Center for Craniofacial Anomalies.

CAMPBELL, Thomas
Gardner Carton & Douglas LLP, Chicago 312 569 1356
tcampbell@gcd.com
Recommended in Antitrust

Practice Areas: Chairs Antitrust and Competition Law Practice Group; focuses on trial of antitrust actions, business disputes, including defending pipeline company accused of monopolizing natural gas transportation by manipulating gas purchase contracts; defending manufacturer of concert pianos accused of monopolizing grand pianos' sale; defending baking company accused of monopolization by predatory pricing with below-cost bread; winning side in seven of eight antitrust cases tried to verdict/decision.
Prof. Memberships: Co-Chair, Trial

Practice Committee, ABA Section on Antitrust Law; Member, Board of Governors, Seventh Circuit Bar Association; past Chair, Antitrust Law Committee, Chicago Bar Association.

Career: Recognized for having tried series of cases that contributed to development of application of antitrust law to healthcare industry; a lead attorney defending antitrust action filed by medical residents claiming National Resident Matching Program, among others, conspired to impose scheme of restraints that have effect of fixing, artificially depressing and stabilizing resident physician compensation and other employment terms; adjunct faculty member, Northwestern University; named in 'The Best Lawyers in America' and 'Best Lawyers' (Corporate Counsel). **Publications:** Frequent speaker, author on antitrust issues; co-author, 'Arbitrating Antitrust Cases - The Road Less Traveled,' Fall 2004 Antitrust magazine. **Personal:** Cornell University, JD,1968; Dartmouth College, BA, 1965.

CARLSON, Walter
Sidley Austin Brown & Wood LLP, Chicago 312 853 7734
wcarlson@sidley.com
Recommended in Litigation

Practice Areas: Walter Carlson leads the firm's Securities Litigation Practice and has represented numerous clients in a variety of types of specialized and general commercial litigation. Mr Carlson has served as lead counsel in numerous federal securities fraud lawsuits. He has handled a large number of cases in state and federal courts involving corporate governance and fiduciary duty issues. He also has frequently represented corporations and individual directors in SEC investigations and in derivative lawsuits and officers' and directors' liability claims, and in related directors' and officers' liability insurance issues. Mr Carlson is a member of the firm's Executive Committee.

Career: Harvard Law School, JD, 1978; Yale University, BA, 1975. Bar Admission: Illinois, 1978.

CARPENTER, David
Sidley Austin Brown & Wood LLP, Chicago 312 853 7237
dcarpenter@sidley.com
Recommended in Telecom, Broadcast & Satellite

Practice Areas: David W Carpenter has long been AT&T's principal appellate attorney on antitrust and regulatory matters. He has also worked extensively on antitrust and related matters for other clients. Mr Carpenter has argued five cases in the US Supreme Court and has briefed over 20 additional cases that the Supreme Court decided on the merits. He also has argued over 50 cases in federal courts of appeals and state appellate courts, and briefed numerous other cases on appeal. He has briefed and

argued many dispositive motions in federal district courts and state trial courts. Mr Carpenter was also named to BTI Consulting's All Star Team for Client Service.

Career: Boston University School of Law, JD, 1975; Yale University, BA, 1972; Served as law clerk to Associate Justice William J Brennan, Jr. and to Judge Frank M Coffin of the US Court of Appeals for the First Circuit. Bar Admission: District of Columbia, 1980 Illinois, 1979 Massachusetts, 1975.

CEDEROTH, Richard A
Sidley Austin Brown & Wood LLP, Chicago 312 853 7026
rcederoth@sidley.com
Recommended in Intellectual Property

Practice Areas: Richard A Cederoth is a highly experienced Partner in all aspects of Intellectual Property Practice, with a focus on litigated patent matters, primarily in the software, computer and semiconductor fields, and related counseling.

Prof. Memberships: Mr Cederoth is a member of the Intellectual Property Section of the American Bar Association and the American Intellectual Property Law Association. He is also a Member of the Bradley University Electrical Engineering Alumni Advisory Board.

Career: Mr Cederoth is admitted in several federal courts and registered to practice before the US Patent and Trademark Office and US District Court, N.D. of Illinois - General, 1984. He has lectured about patent protection for computer software and intellectual property from the practicing engineer's perspective. University of Illinois College of Law (JD, 1983). Bradley University (BS in Electrical Engineering, 1980). Bar Admission: Illinois, 1983.

CHEFITZ, Joel
Howrey Simon Arnold & White, Chicago 312 595 1239
Recommended in Antitrust

CHOI, Paul
Sidley Austin Brown & Wood LLP, Chicago 312 853 2145
pchoi@sidley.com
Recommended in Corporate/M&A

Practice Areas: Paul Choi's practice focuses on mergers and acquisitions, dispositions, spin-offs and joint ventures, and he counsels clients on takeover defense and proxy contests. He advised First Data Corporation on its $7 billion acquisition of Concord EFS, Inc., advised Barrett Resources in its response to a hostile takeover attempt and in its agreement to merge with The Williams Companies for $2.8 billion, led the representation of KPMG LLP's spin-off of its management and consulting business and represented Conseco, Inc. in its $7.6 billion acquisition of Green Tree Financial Corporation. Mr Choi represents issuers and underwriters on private and public offerings, including IPO's, and

subsidiary or 'carve-out' offerings. He represented BearingPoint in its $2.3 billion IPO, and handles private equity and debt offerings, Rule 144A transactions, and high yield debt, equity derivative and hybrid securities offerings.

Prof. Memberships: Board of Directors of the Harvard Club of Chicago, the Chicago Committee of the Chicago Council on Foreign Relations, the American Bar Association, the Illinois Bar Association and the Chicago Bar Association.

Career: Served as a Law Clerk to the Honorable Laurence H Silberman on the United States Court of Appeals for the DC Circuit from 1989-90. Harvard Law School (JD, 1989). Harvard University (AB, 1986). Bar Admission: Illinois, 1989.

CICERO Jr, Frank
Kirkland & Ellis LLP, Chicago 312 861 2216
fcicero@kirkland.com
Recommended in Antitrust, Litigation

Practice Areas: Extensive experience in a wide variety of litigation matters. Areas of practice include professional malpractice, admiralty and maritime, antitrust and trade regulation, criminal and civil fraud and securities law, trademark and patent claims, commercial contracts, construction litigation, libel, slander, and First Amendment cases, tax disputes, trade secrets, unfair competition, employment contracts, pollution and toxic substance cases, international arbitrations and litigation, dealer and franchise relationships and terminations, trust, estates and ERISA disputes, divorce and domestic relations law, product liability and warranty claims.

Personal: Amherst College, 1953-54. Wheaton College, AB, 1957. Princeton University, MPA, 1962. University of Chicago, JD, 1965.

CLARK, James
Sidley Austin Brown & Wood LLP, Chicago 312 853 7776
jclark@sidley.com
Recommended in Banking & Finance

Practice Areas: James Clark's practice focuses on commercial and banking law and he represents clients in a broad range of financing and lending transactions. He is a Co-Chair of the firm's Professional Responsibility Committee.

Prof. Memberships: Mr Clark is a member of the American, Chicago and Illinois State Bar Associations and a former Chairman of the Acquisition Financing Subcommittee of the Commercial Financial Services Committee of the American Bar Association Business Law Section.

Career: Educated at University of Chicago (JD, 1976); Brown University (AB, 1970).

Publications: Mr Clark is a Member of the Board of Editors of 'The Bankruptcy Strategist'; co-author of 'Legal Develop-

ments in Secured Financing' (1978-94).

COLE, Alexandra
Perkins Coie LLP, Chicago 312 324 8400
Recommended in Construction

COLE, Thomas A
Sidley Austin Brown & Wood LLP, Chicago 312 853 7473
tcole@sidley.com
Recommended in Corporate/M&A

Practice Areas: Thomas A Cole serves as Chairman of the firm's Executive Committee and is a member of the Management Committee. He has been involved in dozens of public company mergers, including the following, each valued at more than $1 billion: Exelon/PSEG (currently the largest utility merger); Tellabs/AFC; IMC/Cargill; Williams/Barrett (including the successful defense against Shell); Kimberly-Clark/Scott Paper; Monsanto/DeKalb Genetics; Jefferson Smurfit/Stone Container; Interpublic Group/True North; Wolters Kluwer/CCH; Fred Meyer/QFC; Aon/Alexander & Alexander; IMC Global/Vigoro; Tribune/Renaissance Communications; and LBOs of Northwest Industries and Ohio Mattress. Other significant public company merger transactions include Lyphomed/Fujisawa, Unilever/Helene Curtis, Mercantile/Mark Twain, True North/Bozell (including the successful defense against Publicis), Humana/Emphesys, GE Medical/Marquette and Berisford/Scotsman. Corporate governance assignments have included acting as special counsel to the Boards of Prudential Insurance, Zenith Electronics and other public companies, as well as frequent assignments for audit committees and special committees.

Prof. Memberships: Member of The American Law Institute; The Economic Club of Chicago; The Commercial Club of Chicago; the Board of The University of Chicago; the Legal Advisory Committee to the Board of the New York Stock Exchange and is a Fellow of the American Bar Foundation.

Career: Served on the faculty of the Kellogg Corporate Governance Conference of Northwestern University, the Director's College of The University of Chicago's Graduate School of Business and the KPMG Audit Committee Institute, and taught corporate governance at the University of Chicago Law School. University of Chicago Law School (JD, 1975). Johns Hopkins University (AB, 1970). Bar Admission: Illinois, 1975.

COLLINS, Joseph P
Mayer, Brown, Rowe & Maw LLP, Chicago 212 506 2657
jcollins@mayerbrownrowe.com
Recommended in Capital Markets

Practice Areas: Practice Leader, Futures, Securities, and Derivatives Law Practice. Represents brokerage firms, investment management clients, trading and investment advisors, hedge fund operators, investment companies, banks, and pension plans. Practice encompasses securities, futures, forwards, swaps, options, and hybrid securities. Lead attorney in Refco Group's acquisitions of RB&H, Lind-Waldock, LFG, and Main Street Trading Company; Ameritrade's acquisition of Datek, Brokerage America, and Bidwell; and Merrill Lynch's acquisition of Bear Stearn's ISE operations and ABN's securities clearing businesses.

Prof. Memberships: Member, ABA, past Chair, Committee on Regulation of Futures and Derivatives Instruments; Association of the Bar of the City of New York, Futures Regulation Committee; Faculty, IIT-Kent College of Law's Financial Services Law Graduate Program.

Career: Joined Mayer, Brown, Rowe & Maw LLP as Partner in 1994 following 19 years with Schiff Hardin & Waite.

Publications: Participant at ABA Committee on Regulation of Futures and Derivatives Instruments Conferences, SIA and FIA Law and Compliance Conferences, Kent Financial Services Law Conferences, and various other panels and workshops regarding derivative instruments and securities.

Personal: JD, New York University School of Law, 1975; Root-Tilden Scholar. AB (magna cum laude), College of the Holy Cross, 1972. Circuit Secretary, NYU School of Law Root-Tilden Scholarship Program.

CONLAN, James F
Sidley Austin Brown & Wood LLP, Chicago 312 853 6890
jconlan@sidley.com
Recommended in Bankruptcy

Practice Areas: James F Conlan is the Co-Head of the firm's global Corporate Reorganization and Bankruptcy Group. Representative engagements include In re: Federal-Mogul Corporation and T&N (client, Debtors and Administrators); In re: Dow Corning Corporation (client, Baxter International Inc.); General Wireless and Pocket Communications (client, Federal Communications Commission); In re: Columbia Gas Transmission Corporation (client, Unsecured Creditors Committee); In re: One Financial Place Partnership (client, Debtor); In re: Florida Coast Paper (client, parent and purchaser, Smurfit-Stone Container).

Career: University of Iowa College of Law (JD, 1988). University of Iowa (BS, 1985). Bar Admission: Illinois, 1988.

Publications: Co-author, 'U.S. Implications for U.K. Solvent Schemes of Arrangement and More,' the Insurance Receiver, 1998 and numerous articles on insolvency and global restructuring. Frequent lecturer at client and industry meetings on reorganization issues.

CONLON, William
Sidley Austin Brown & Wood LLP, Chicago 312 853 7384

wconlon@sidley.com
Recommended in Litigation

Practice Areas: William F Conlon is a member of the firm's Executive Committee, and serves as the General Counsel of the firm. He has extensive trial experience in commercial, financial, intellectual property, antitrust, and regulatory matters (including SEC and federal criminal). Mr Conlon's trial and appellate experience includes jury and bench trials as well as administrative proceedings in state and federal courts throughout the country. Representative cases have included antitrust, ERISA, securities laws, banking and bank regulatory issues, telecommunications, product liability, insurance and insurance regulatory issues, utilities law, and a variety of complex commercial individual and class action cases. As Assistant United States Attorney in Chicago, prior to joining Sidley, Mr Conlon handled criminal investigations and prosecutions as well as the trial and appeal of a wide variety of civil cases, including class actions. Mr Conlon also served as Chief of the Civil Division of the United States Attorney's Office.

Prof. Memberships: Mr Conlon was a member and Chairman of the Illinois State Board of Ethics from 1982-88, served as Chairman of the Illinois Judicial Inquiry Board 1992-97 and is a Fellow of the American College of Trial Lawyers.

Career: University of Illinois College of Law (JD, 1970). Indiana University (AB, 1967). Bar Admissions: Illinois, 1970; Iowa, 1970.

Publications: Mr Conlon has served as Adjunct Professor at Northwestern University Law School since 1991 and has been a co-author of several articles. He also was a member of the University of Illinois Law Review.

CONNELLY, Vincent J
Mayer, Brown, Rowe & Maw LLP, Chicago 312 701 7912
vconnelly@mayerbrownrowe.com
Recommended in Litigation

Practice Areas: Specializes in securities, antitrust, government contract and program cases, RICO, commercial and financial fraud, and public corruption litigation. Primary trial responsibility in over 70 federal cases, with more than 60 jury trials. Civil litigation representations have included major corporations, corporate directors, and individuals in federal and state court trials, and corporate internal investigations.

Prof. Memberships: Member, American College of Trial Lawyers; Blue Ribbon Committee appointed by the Illinois Supreme Court to review the Attorney Registration and Disciplinary Commission; President, Chicago Inn of Court. Lecturer at Chicago Association of Commerce and Industry; Chicago Bar Association; Department of Justice

Trial Advocacy Institute; FBI Training Academy; State Bar Antitrust Seminar.

Career: Joined Mayer, Brown, Rowe & Maw LLP, Chicago, 1987; became Partner, 1987. Formerly US Attorney's Office, Northern District of Illinois, 1975-87: Chief, Special Prosecutions Division, 1985-87; Chief, Criminal Division, 1983-85.

Publications: 'A Dozen Stops on the Grand Jury Road', Litigation. 'Undercover Work at the Exchanges', Chicago Tribune. 'Unconventional Strategies in White-Collar Criminal Investigations', Litigation.

Personal: Born June 25, 1950. University of Chicago Law School, JD, 1975. University of Notre Dame, BA, summa cum laude, 1972.

CONWAY, Michael M
Foley & Lardner, Chicago
312 832 4351
mconway@foley.com
Recommended in Media & Entertainment

Career: Michael Conway is a Foley & Lardner Partner, Chair of the Chicago office Litigation Department, a member of the firm's General Commercial Litigation; Appellate; and Tax, Valuation and Fiduciary Practice Groups; and the Entertainment and Media Team. He focuses on media, commercial, corporate and federal tax litigation with a particular emphasis on emergency injunctive cases. Mr Conway has been principal trial attorney in a wide variety of media cases. More than 150 reported decisions in the federal and state court system have involved civil cases in which he had primary litigation responsibility at the trial court or on appeal.

CONWAY, Timothy R
Conway & Mrowiec, Chicago
312 658 1100
trc@cmcontractors.com
Recommended in Construction

Practice Areas: Construction law.

Prof. Memberships: Chicago and American (Member, Fidelity and Surety Law Committee) Bar Associations; Builders Association of Greater Chicago; Fox Valley General Contractors Association; Society of Illinois Construction Lawyers; Leading Lawyers Network.

Publications: Author, 'Mechanics Liens and Surety Bonds,' Illinois Construction Law, Aspen, 2003. Co-author, 'Requirements for the Original Contractor's Lien on Private Projects,' Illinois Institute of Continuing Education, 1994, 2000, 2004 eds.

COSTELLO SLOVAK, Patricia
Schiff Hardin LLP, Chicago
312 258 5665
pslovak@schiffhardin.com
Recommended in Employment

Practice Areas: Labor and employment.

Prof. Memberships: National Retail Federation, American Bar Association

(Vice Chair, Labor and Employment Law Section), Chicago Bar Association, College of Labor and Employment Lawyers, American Bar Foundation.

Career: Ms Slovak concentrates in labor and employment law for management. She has extensive experience representing management in all facets of labor and employment relationships.

Publications: Frequent author and lecturer on various employment law issues, and she is an editor of 'The Developing Labor Law.'

Personal: St. Louis University (BA, 1973), University of Chicago (JD, 1977).

COVEY, Tyson J
Mayer, Brown, Rowe & Maw LLP, Chicago 312 701 8600
jcovey@mayerbrownrowe.com
Recommended in Telecom, Broadcast & Satellite

Practice Areas: Specializes in regulated industries litigation and appeals on behalf of telecommunications companies in matters before regulatory agencies and courts. Recent experience includes unbundling disputes, UNE pricing cases, arbitrations, merger approvals, injunction proceedings, and state and federal appeals in several states throughout the country.

Prof. Memberships: Admitted in Illinois, 1991; US District Court for the Northern District of Illinois, 1992; US Court of Appeals for the Seventh Circuit, 1992; US Court of Appeals for the Sixth Circuit, 2000.

Career: Joined Mayer, Brown, Rowe & Maw LLP 1996; became Partner 2000. Formerly with Sidley & Austin, Chicago, 1993-96. US Court of Appeals for the Seventh Circuit, Staff Attorney, 1991-93.

Personal: Born 1965. University of Illinois College of Law, JD, magna cum laude, 1991; Order of the Coif; Administrative Editor, 'University of Illinois Law Review.' Augustana College, BA, magna cum laude, 1987; Phi Beta Kappa.

CRAVEN, George W
Mayer, Brown, Rowe & Maw LLP, Chicago 312 701 7231
gcraven@mayerbrown.com
Recommended in Tax

Practice Areas: Leading authority on tax aspects of financial transactions, cross-border tax arbitrage, offshore insurance arrangements, and deductibility of alternative risk transfer payments. Advises on acquisitions and dispositions of businesses, including structured financings as well as tax aspects of new financial products such as 'Section 483 Notes', and 'Liquid Yield Option Notes'. International tax planning expertise includes Subpart F issues, transactions designed to accelerate or create foreign source income, and redomestication of US insurance companies to foreign jurisdiction.

Prof. Memberships: Admitted to practice in Illinois, 1976, and US Tax Court,

1976. Member of the American Bar Association, Section of Taxation; Financial Transactions Committee.

Career: Joined Mayer, Brown, Rowe & Maw, LLP Chicago, in 1981 and became a Partner in 1983. Prior to that, had worked for Sidley & Austin, Chicago (1976-80) and Ogden, Robertson & Marshall, Louisville (1980-81).

Publications: Lectures widely on tax issues.

Personal: Born 11 March 1951. Earned JD, cum laude, from Harvard Law School in 1976 and BA summa cum laude, from the University of Notre Dame in 1973. Also studied at Sophia University, Tokyo (1970-71).

CREMENT, Anthony
Franczek Sullivan, Chicago
312 986 0300
Recommended in Employment

CRUMBAUGH, David
Latham & Watkins LLP, Chicago
312 876 7700
Recommended in Banking & Finance

CRYSTAL, Jules
Bryan Cave LLP, Chicago
312 602 5000
Recommended in Employment

CULLEN, Gary P
Skadden, Arps, Slate, Meagher & Flom LLP & Affiliates, Chicago
312 407 0680
gcullen@skadden.com
Recommended in Corporate/M&A

Practice Areas: Represents Fortune 500, middle market and emerging companies, as well as investment banking and other financial institutions, in a variety of M&A and corporate finance transactions. Has worked on behalf of buyers and sellers in auctions involving public companies, other stock and asset acquisitions and dispositions, negotiated and contested takeovers, proxy contests and joint ventures. Also represents issuers and investment banking institutions in initial and other public offerings, private placements of securities, and high-yield debt transactions. Advises on corporate governance and disclosure issues.

Career: JD, Columbia University School of Law, 1985; BA, University of Illinois, 1982.

DASH, James
Much Shelist Freed Denenberg Ament & Rubenstein, P.C., Chicago
312 521 2000
Recommended in Construction

DAVIS, Scott J
Mayer, Brown, Rowe & Maw LLP, Chicago 312 701 7311
sdavis@mayerbrownrowe.com
Recommended in Corporate/M&A

Practice Areas: Firm Practice Leader of the Corporate and Securities Group. Extensive experience in mergers and acquisitions and problems arising from real or perceived conflict of interest between corporate officers and shareholders. Representative deals: representation of Crompton in the pending merger in which Great Lakes Chemical is to become a subsidiary of Crompton (approximate value $1.8 billion as of the date of announcement), representation of Devon Energy in the merger in which Ocean Energy became Devon's subsidiary (approximate value US$3.1 billion as of date of announcement), Devon in acquisition of Mitchell Energy and Development (approximate value US$3 billion as of date of announcement), Devon in its acquisition of Anderson Exploration (approximate value US$3.5 billion). Also advises in litigation matters involving derivative, takeover, and securities fraud litigation.

Prof. Memberships: Vice President, Chicago Police Board.

Career: Mayer, Brown, Rowe & Maw LLP, 1977-present; Partner, 1983.

Publications: Author, 'Liability Under Sections 10, 18 and 20 of the Securities Exchange Act of 1934', printed in Understanding the Securities Laws 2000, PLI Corp. Law & Practice Handbook Series, No. B-1198, 2000.

Personal: JD, cum laude, Harvard University, 1976; Member of the Board of Editors, Harvard Law Review. BA, cum laude, Yale University, 1972.

DEBEERS, Kimberly A
Skadden, Arps, Slate, Meagher & Flom LLP & Affiliates, Chicago
312 407 0982
kdebeers@skadden.com
Recommended in Private Equity

Career: JD, DePaul University College of Law, 1995; BS, University of Illinois, 1990.

DEMARTE, Luke
Seyfarth Shaw LLP, Chicago
312 346 8000
Recommended in Media & Entertainment

DICKINSON, Christopher C
Jenner & Block LLP, Chicago
312 923 2858
cdickinson@jenner.com
Recommended in Insurance

Practice Areas: Christopher C Dickinson is a Partner in Jenner & Block's Chicago office. He is a member of the firm's Insurance Litigation and Counseling, Appellate and Supreme Court, and Litigation Practices. Mr Dickinson represents financial institutions and other corporate policyholders pursuing insurance recovery for high-stakes claims in such areas as professional liability, competitive injury, consumer fraud, directors' and officers' liability, intellectual property, fidelity and financial fraud, employment practices liability, fiduciary liability, catastrophic bodily injury, product liability and environmental damage. Through litigation, arbitration or negotiation he has recovered hundreds of millions of dollars for his clients from virtually all of the major insurers in the domestic, London and Bermuda markets. Mr Dickinson also counsels corporate policyholders on claims review and management, insurance program design, crafting policy language, and insurer insolvencies. Mr Dickinson serves on the Board of Directors of the Aids Legal Council of Chicago.

Personal: Mr Dickinson graduated with distinction from the University of Wisconsin - Madison in 1982, and received his law degree cum laude from the University of Wisconsin in 1988. He is admitted to practice in Illinois and Wisconsin, and in several federal trial and appellate courts, including the Trial Bar of the federal district court in Chicago.

DIGIOVANNI, Nick
Lord Bissell & Brook, Chicago
312 443 0700
Recommended in Insurance

DOCKSEY, Ross
Sonnenschein Nath & Rosenthal LLP, Chicago 312 876 8171
jdocksey@sonnenschein.com
Recommended in Business Process Outsourcing: National, Technology

Practice Areas: Partner focusing on domestic, cross-border and global outsourcing of business functions, including finance and administration, human resources, supply chain management, learning and education, information technology and services; technology contracting; joint ventures and alliances; and mergers and acquisitions.

Prof. Memberships: Speaks at legal and outsourcing conferences, including those by Sourcing Interests Group, Conference Board, Bureau of National Affairs, Practicing Law Institute, Mealey's Seminars and Michael Corbett & Associates. Human Resources Outsourcing Association member. Listed by 'HRO Today' and 'FAO Today' as a top five US outsourcing lawyer.

Personal: University of Minnesota JD cum laude. US Military Academy BS.

DOETSCH, Douglas A
Mayer, Brown, Rowe & Maw LLP, Chicago 312 701 7973
ddoetsch@mayerbrownrowe.com
Recommended in Banking & Finance

Practice Areas: Chicago Office Practice Leader in banking and finance. Partner in International Corporate and Finance Practice. Advises on lending for leveraged buyouts, workouts and project financings, particularly in cross-border transactions. Represents clients in cross-border securitization transactions, particularly future cash flow securitizations, debt restructuring and debt exchange offers. Counsels on asset and stock acquisitions and contract negotiations; joint ventures emphasising cross-border ventures in Latin America; Euro-securities offerings, particularly for emerging market companies, and US equity offerings of foreign issuers.

Prof. Memberships: Director, Chicago Council on Foreign Relations; Director, Mid-America Chapter of US-Mexico Chamber of Commerce.

Career: Joined Mayer, Brown, Rowe & Maw LLP in 1988 and became a Partner in 1995. Prior to that, worked for Cleary, Gottlieb, Steen & Hamilton, New York (1986-88) and, before that, worked as a Consultant for Data Resources, Inc. (1979-82).

Publications: Frequently writes and speaks on securitizations by emerging market issuers, debt restructuring, international joint ventures, and issuances of debt securities in the Euro-markets.

Personal: JD, Columbia University, 1986; editor-in-chief, 'Columbia Journal of Transnational Law.' Rotary Graduate Fellow at Université de Dakar, Dakar, Senegal (1982-83). BA, magna cum laude, Kalamazoo College (1979); Phi Beta Kappa. Fluent in French and Spanish.

DOLIN, Kenneth
Seyfarth Shaw LLP, Chicago
312 346 8000
Recommended in Employment

DONOVAN, Joseph
Kelley Drye & Warren, Chicago
312 857 7070
Recommended in Telecom, Broadcast & Satellite

DORAN, James
Latham & Watkins LLP, Chicago
312 876 7700
Recommended in Banking & Finance

DOUGLAS, Charles W
Sidley Austin Brown & Wood LLP, Chicago 312 853 7706
cdouglas@sidley.com
Recommended in Antitrust, Litigation

Practice Areas: Charles Douglas is Chairman of the firm's Management Committee and is a member of the firm's Executive Committee. Mr Douglas has extensive litigation experience in major antitrust, trade regulation, securities, product liability and commercial litigation, and is Head of the firm's global Antitrust, Commercial and Regulatory Litigation Practice. He currently represents Microsoft Corporation in private antitrust litigation, AT&T Corp. in major securities class actions and the accounting firm of Deloitte & Touche, LLP in commercial litigation. He led the successful defense of G.D. Searle & Co. in an antitrust class action seeking billions of dollars in damages and he successfully defended AT&T in two major trials. His trial work for AT&T has spanned two decades, dating back to the representation of AT&T and the Regional Bell Operating Companies in various antitrust actions. Mr Douglas has been trial counsel for several of the firm's clients in a wide range of cases. He successfully tried a major case for IBP, Inc. involving a novel application of the

Packers & Stockyards Act, tried a major antitrust case for Zenith Electronics in Oklahoma and led the successful defense of General Electric in litigation brought across the country following the crash of a United Airlines DC-10 with GE engines.
Career: Harvard Law School (JD, 1974); Northwestern University (BA, 1970). Bar Admission: Illinois, 1974.

DOW Jr, Robert M

Mayer, Brown, Rowe & Maw LLP, Chicago 312 701 8441
rdow@mayerbrownrowe.com
Recommended in Telecom, Broadcast & Satellite
Practice Areas: General and appellate litigation specializing in telecommunications, constitutional law, civil procedure, and mass tort law.
Prof. Memberships: Admitted in Illinois (1993); US Supreme Court; US Courts of Appeals for the Fourth, Fifth, Sixth, Seventh, Ninth, and Eleventh Circuits, Northern District of Illinois. Seventh Circuit Bar Association; Appellate Lawyers Association of Illinois (Director, 2000-02, Treasurer, 2002-03, Secretary, 2003-04, VP, 2004-05).
Career: Joined Mayer, Brown, Rowe & Maw LLP, Chicago, 1995; became Partner, 2002. Law Clerk, Honorable Joel M Flaum, US Court of Appeals for the Seventh Circuit, 1993-94. Teaching Fellow, Harvard College, 1992. Recipient, Derek Bok Center Certificate of Excellence in Undergraduate Teaching, 1992.
Publications: 'Invalidation of Ohio Tort Reform Legislation', 2000 'International Journal of Insurance Law' 85-88 (January 2000) (with John E Muench); 'Arguing for Changes in the Law', 25(2) Litigation 37 (1999) (with James C Schroeder); 'Linking Trade Policy to Free Emigration: The Jackson-Vanik Amendment', 4 'Harvard Human Rights Journal' 128-138 (1991).
Personal: Harvard Law School, JD, cum laude, 1993; University of Oxford, Rhodes Scholar, D Phil in International Relations, 1997, M Phil in International Relations, 1990; Yale University, BA (History and Political Science), summa cum laude with distinction in both majors, 1987; Phi Beta Kappa.

DRANOFF, David

Goldberg, Kohn, Bell, Black, Rosenbloom & Moritz, Ltd, Chicago
312 201 4000
Recommended in Banking & Finance

DUBE, Monte I

McDermott Will & Emery, Chicago
312 984 7549
mdube@mwe.com
Recommended in Healthcare
Practice Areas: Head of firm's Health Department. Represents hospitals and health systems nationwide and has served as counsel in the sale, merger, affiliation and acquisition of hundreds of hospitals and academic medical cen-

ters, hospital restructurings, public hospital privatizations, joint ventures, certificate of need and reimbursement litigation, and hospital and medical staff operational legal issues of all types. Regularly advises boards on the proper exercise of their fiduciary duties.
Prof. Memberships: Member of American Health Lawyers Association, and American, Illinois and Chicago bar associations.
Career: Was a Bigelow Teaching Fellow and Lecturer in Law at the University of Chicago School of Law in 1981 and 1982. Regularly lectures and publishes on hospital-physician relations, hospital merger and affiliation transactions, fiduciary duties of not-for-profit trustees, and rural healthcare issues.
Personal: Earned JD in 1981 from Benjamin N. Cardozo School of Law, and AB in 1977 from Boston University. Admitted to practice before the Illinois Supreme Court, the US District Court for the Northern District of Illinois and the US Court of Appeals for the Third Circuit.

DUNCAN, Margaret M

McDermott Will & Emery, Chicago
312 984 6476
mduncan@mwe.com
Recommended in Intellectual Property
Practice Areas: Head of Chicago Intellectual Property Practice. Focuses on IP litigation, prosecution, counseling and transactions. Litigation experience includes patent, trademark, copyright, unfair competition, right of publicity, domain names and trade secret cases. Experience also includes work as an in-house senior IP counsel for Amoco Corporation and Abbott Laboratories.
Prof. Memberships: Member of Bar of the State of Illinois and is admitted to practice before the US District Court for the Northern District of Illinois, the US Court of Appeals for the Seventh Circuit, the US Court of Appeals for the Federal Circuit and the US Patent and Trademark Office. Admitted to the Trial Bar of the Northern District of Illinois.
Career: While in law school won first place in Giles Sutherland Rich Moot Court Competition, Midwest Region, and was first runner-up in the national competition.
Personal: Earned JD in 1981 from Loyola University of Chicago School of Law. Earned BS of chemistry/biology in 1976 from Xavier University.

DURCHSLAG, Stephen

Winston & Strawn LLP, Chicago
312 558 5288
sdurchslag@winston.com
Recommended in Media & Entertainment
Practice Areas: Intellectual property, trademark, copyright, advertising, entertainment, and promotion.
Prof. Memberships: Board of Directors, Off the Street Club; Board of Directors,

Chicago Advertising Federation; Board of Directors, Anshe Emet Synagogue; Trustee, Nathan Cummings Foundation.
Career: Head, Intellectual Property Department. Joined firm as Partner, 1989.
Personal: University of Wisconsin, BS, 1962; Hebrew University Jerusalem, 1962-63; Harvard Law School, LLB, 1966, Felix Frankfurter Scholarship.

DURKIN, Thomas M

Mayer, Brown, Rowe & Maw LLP, Chicago 312 701 7997
tdurkin@mayerbrownrowe.com
Recommended in Litigation
Practice Areas: Specializes in complex civil litigation (including product liability and patent matters) and criminal defense. Tried approximately 50 federal jury trials to verdict.
Prof. Memberships: Fellow, American College of Trial Lawyers. DePaul Law School, Adjunct Professor, Advanced Criminal Procedure, 1996; 1998. Chicago Bar Association Judicial Evaluation Committee, 1993-95. Merit Selection Panel for US Magistrate, Northern District of Illinois, 1994. Assisted Special Counsel Nicholas Bua, Inslaw Investigation, 1991-92. John Marshall Law School, Adjunct Professor, Trial Advocacy, 1988-91.
Career: Joined Mayer, Brown, Rowe & Maw LLP as Partner, 1993. Former Assistant US Attorney, Northern District of Illinois, 1980-93. First Assistant US Attorney, 1990-93. Law Clerk to The Honorable Stanley J Roszkowski, Northern District of Illinois, 1979-80.
Publications: 'Doing the Right Thing' (Foreign Corrupt Practices Act), Infrastructure Finance, September 1996. Speaker at seminars on Foreign Corrupt Practices Act. Lecturer, Department of Justice Trial Advocacy Institute and FBI Training Academy in Quantico, Virginia.
Personal: DePaul University College of Law, JD with honors, 1978; Illinois Law Issue Editor, Law Review. University of Illinois, BS with honors, 1975. Certified Public Accountant, Illinois, 1975. Excellence in Law Enforcement Award, Chicagoland Chamber of Commerce, 1993. Attorney General's John Marshall Award by US Attorney General Thornburgh, 1991.

EDWARDS, Charles L

DLA Piper Rudnick Gray Cary US LLP, Chicago 312 368 4010
charles.edwards@dlapiper.com
Recommended in Real Estate
Practice Areas: Real estate; real estate finance.
Prof. Memberships: Past Chair Chicago Bar Association Real Property Law Committee and its Real Property Finance Subcommittee, Member of American College of Real Estate Lawyers and American College of Mortgage Attorneys.
Career: Practice concentrated exclusive-

ly in complex commercial real estate transactions, including purchase and sale; mortgage financing; leasing; joint ventures and partnerships; condominiums and cooperatives; general development and all other aspects of commercial real estate practice. He is also an adjunct professor and frequently lectures on real estate finance and leasing subjects.
Personal: JD, University of Chicago; BBA, University of Wisconsin.

EGGERT, Russell R

Mayer, Brown, Rowe & Maw LLP, Chicago 312 701 7350
reggert@mayerbrownrowe.com
Recommended in Environment
Practice Areas: Specializes in trials and appeals of complex regulatory and environmental tort litigation, and counseling on environmental compliance. Experienced in responding to environmental crisis or emergency situations and counseling and strategic management of environmental issues. Tried over 50 environmental cases and argued over 40 appeals in state and federal courts and administrative agencies.
Prof. Memberships: American Bar Association, sections on Natural Resources Law and Litigation.
Career: Joined Mayer, Brown, Rowe & Maw LLP, Chicago, 1987; became Partner 1987. Former Chief (1983-87) and Deputy Chief (1974-79), Environmental Division and Legal Counsel to the Attorney General of Illinois, Chicago. O'Conor, Karaganis & Gail Ltd., Chicago, 1979-83. Graduate Research Associate in Environmental Law, University of Illinois College of Law, 1973-74.
Personal: Born 28 July 1948. University of Illinois, JD, 1973; University of Illinois, AB, 1970.

EIMER, Nathan

Eimer Stahl Klevorn & Solberg, Chicago
312 660 7600
Recommended in Antitrust

EISNER, Rebecca

Mayer, Brown, Rowe & Maw LLP, Chicago 312 701 8577
reisner@mayerbrownrowe.com
Recommended in Business Process Outsourcing: National, Technology
Practice Areas: Specializes in complex global and offshore technology and business process outsourcing transactions, including IT infrastructure, applications development and maintenance, back office processing, ERP implementations, finance and accounting, payroll processing, call center, HR, technology development, system integration and hosting. Also advises clients in services agreements, strategic alliances, joint ventures, licensing, development and telecommunications agreements, and internet and e-commerce law issues, including data transfer and privacy issues and electronic contracting and signatures.

Career: Joined Mayer, Brown, Rowe & Maw LLP, 1989-92; returned, 1996; Partner, 2000. Former Associate Group Counsel and Assistant Vice President, Equifax, Inc., Atlanta, 1993-95. Public Relations and Government Affairs Specialist, The Dow Chemical Company, Midland, Michigan, 1984-86.
Publications: Offshore BPO Conference NYC: 'Privacy Issues in BPO'. 'Avoiding Gotchas in Outsourcing', Illinois Institute of Continuing Legal Education, September 2002. 'Making a Good Match: Strategic Alliances In Technology and E-Commerce', i-Street, May 2002. 'Focus on Legal: Smoothing Over the Privacy Potholes in BPO Outsourcing', 'BPO Outsourcing Journal', March 2002. 'Ignorance Isn't Bliss: What You Need To Know About EU Data Privacy Law', 'CIO Magazine', February 2002.
Personal: University of Michigan Law School, JD cum laude, 1989; 'Michigan Journal of Law Reform'. Ohio State University, BA, cum laude, 1984.

EMERSON, Carter W
Kirkland & Ellis LLP, Chicago
312 861 2052
cemerson@kirkland.com
Recommended in Corporate/M&A
Practice Areas: Carter Emerson has extensive experience in counseling public and private corporations on a wide variety of subjects including corporate and SEC disclosure matters, securities filings and executive compensation. He also has public offering experience, including 12 initial public offerings (IPOs) for issuers and three for underwriters and many Rule 144A debt offerings. His other principal aspects of practice are corporate transactions such as mergers and acquisitions (including leveraged buyouts), public offerings, debt placements and loans, and venture capital investments.
Personal: Miami University (Ohio), BS 1969. Northwestern University, JD, 1972.

ERF, Stephen
McDermott Will & Emery, Chicago
312 984 7637
serf@mwe.com
Recommended in Employment
Practice Areas: Partner in Labor and Employment Group. Concentrates on civil rights and labor/employment counseling and litigation, union organizing, collective bargaining, arbitration, employment discrimination, wrongful discharge, wage and hour and public accommodations. Has worked with clients in a wide range of industries, including healthcare, education, construction, manufacturing, distribution, service, food, social service, chemical and transportation.
Prof. Memberships: Member of the Bar of the State of Illinois, US District Courts for the Northern (Trial Bar), Central and Southern Districts of Illinois, the Eastern and Western Districts

of Wisconsin, the Middle District of Florida, and the US Court of Appeals for the Seventh, Eighth, Eleventh and DC Circuits. Member of the American Bar Association, Illinois State Bar Association and Chicago Bar Association.
Publications: Co-author of a book on labor and employment issues arising in the healthcare field. Has also contributed articles on such matters as disability discrimination and no fault insurance to various publications, including the Loyola Law Journal.
Personal: Earned JD (cum laude) in 1978 from Loyola University of Chicago School of Law, and BA in 1975 from University of Illinois.

ETTELSON, Bruce
Kirkland & Ellis LLP, Chicago
312 861 2326
bettelson@kirkland.com
Recommended in Private Equity
Practice Areas: Mr Ettelson's practice focuses primarily in structuring and forming premier private equity funds and their management companies. He has worked on the formation of over 100 funds. Mr Ettelson represents investors in making and monitoring investments in private equity funds and also private equity clients in private equity and venture capital investments, leveraged buyouts, recapitalizations, mergers and acquisitions and general corporate counseling. He also structures and forms private equity funds associated with commercial and investment banks.
Personal: Wharton School of the University of Pennsylvania, BS, 1986. University of Chicago, JD, 1989.

EVANICH, Kevin R
Kirkland & Ellis LLP, Chicago
312 861 2076
kevanich@kirkland.com
Recommended in Corporate/M&A, Private Equity
Practice Areas: Corporate practice concentrating in mergers and acquisitions, leveraged buyouts and private equity fund formations. Responsible for structuring, supervising and closing a wide variety of leveraged acquisitions and venture capital and other financings and numerous buyout, venture capital and mezzanine funds. Represents general partners and other fund sponsors in fund formations and gatekeepers and other major investors in fund investments. Lead counsel in representation of numerous portfolio companies of private equity funds. Member of firm management committee.
Personal: University of Wisconsin - Milwaukee, BA, 1976; Northwestern University School of Law, JD, 1980.

FAHEY, Thomas
Ungaretti & Harris, Chicago
312 977 4400
Recommended in Healthcare

FALK, R Scott
Kirkland & Ellis LLP, Chicago
312 861 2340
sfalk@kirkland.com
Recommended in Corporate/M&A
Practice Areas: Scott Falk focuses primarily on mergers and acquisitions and securities offerings for public company clients. His broad base of experience includes negotiated mergers, tender and exchange offers, acquisitions and divestitures of subsidiaries and divisions of public companies, private placements and public offerings of securities and securities law counseling. Mr Falk has also structured and negotiated numerous cross-border investments and acquisitions, both in-bound and out-bound.
Prof. Memberships: Member, American Bar Association Section of Business Law.
Personal: Harvard University, AB, 1985; Harvard Law School, JD, 1989.

FEINSTEIN, Fred I
McDermott Will & Emery, Chicago
312 984 7665
ffeinstein@mwe.com
Recommended in Real Estate
Practice Areas: Practice includes general transactional and litigation practice with particular emphasis in real estate development, annexation, zoning and environmental matters. Practice includes governmental relations; purchases, sales, exchanges, and leases of industrial, commercial, retail and farm properties; construction; financing of real estate acquisitions and developments on behalf of both borrowers and lenders; HUD financing; consumer credit; loan pools, REITS and portfolio lending matters; mortgage foreclosures and mechanics' lien matters; loan participation agreements; right of way easements; condemnation litigation; bankruptcy and chancery litigation; real estate taxation matters; condominiums; legal aspects of real estate financing, syndicating and joint venturing for real estate development and multiparcel acquisition; healthcare, retirement housing, and related development.
Prof. Memberships: Member of the American College of Real Estate Lawyers, Illinois State Bar Association, Real Property Section, 1977-83 (Vice Chairman, 1980-81; Chairman, 1981-82) and Legislative Committee, 1984 to present; Lambda Alpha, Beta Gamma Sigma, Chicago Mortgage Attorneys Association; International Association of Attorneys in Corporate Real Estate; Associate Member, American Land Title Association, and the Urban Land Institute.
Career: Admitted to practice in Illinois and before the US Supreme Court.
Personal: Received BSC in 1967 and JD in 1970 from DePaul University.

FELCH, Patricia
Patricia A Felch - Attorney at Law, Evanston 847 475 8085
Recommended in Media &

Entertainment

FERGUSON, James
Mayer, Brown, Rowe & Maw LLP, Chicago 312 701 7282
jferguson@mayerbrownrowe.com
Recommended in Litigation
Practice Areas: Lead counsel for major corporations in: all phases of patent, trademark, trade secret and related litigation in the pharmaceutical, medical, diagnostic, healthcare, financial, electronic, textile and food industries; broad range of commercial and white-collar criminal litigation, including healthcare, antitrust, securities, environmental, employment, insurance, tax, civil fraud, RICO, real estate, franchise and breach of contract cases. Tried more than 30 jury trials to verdict; argued more than 35 appeals; conducted numerous corporate internal investigations; developed comprehensive compliance and corporate integrity programs.
Career: Mayer, Brown, Rowe & Maw LLP, Chicago, 2002 to present. Sonnenschein Nath & Rosenthal, 1989-2002. Assistant US Attorney, Northern District of Illinois, 1979-89. Law Clerk to The Honorable William J Bauer in the US Court of Appeals, Seventh Circuit, 1977-79.
Publications: 'Clinical Trials As Inside Information,' New York Times (Oct. 19, 1997). 'Biomedical Research and Insider Trading,' New England Journal of Medicine (Aug. 28, 1997). 'Biological Weapons and U.S. Law,' Journal of the American Medical Ass'n (Aug. 6, 1997).
Personal: JD, Northwestern University School of Law, 1976; articles editor, Law Review. BA, MA, Indiana University, 1972; Phi Beta Kappa. Recipient, Director's Award for Superior Performance, US Department of Justice, 1988.

FERRAZZANO, Dennis
Barack Ferrazzano Kirschbaum Perlman & Nagelberg, Chicago
312 984 3100
Recommended in Real Estate

FIFER, Sam
Sonnenschein Nath & Rosenthal LLP, Chicago 312 876 8000
sfifer@sonnenschein.com
Recommended in Media & Entertainment
Practice Areas: Intellectual Property and Technology (IP&T) Group Chair. Experience in obtaining licensing and transferring rights in IP&T, entertainment production and distribution, music, publishing, talent agreements, advertising and promotion law; precedent-setting litigation in defamation, privacy and publicity rights, court access, reporters' rights and subpoena defense.
Prof. Memberships: Forum Committee on Communications Law - ABA; INTA; Copyright Society of the United States; Chicago and Illinois Bar Associations; Media Law Resource Center - Defense Counsel Section; Co-Chair, Pre-Publication Committee; Adjunct Professor,

Northwestern University Law School.
Personal: DePaul University, JD cum laude; Northwestern University, BS Speech.

FINKE, Robert F
Mayer, Brown, Rowe & Maw LLP,
Chicago 312 701 7110
rfinke@mayerbrown.com
Recommended in Antitrust
Practice Areas: Specializes in civil, criminal, and antitrust litigation. Represents automotive, chemical, and manufacturing companies in toxic tort, mass disaster, or product liability litigation. Represents financing and financial institutions in general commercial contract and business litigation. Experienced in complex litigation, the proper use of outside counsel and alternative dispute resolution. Counsels on antitrust aspects of acquisitions and mergers, workouts and restructures, distribution, pricing, employee confidentiality, trade secret, and non-competition agreements.
Prof. Memberships: American Bar Association, Vice-Chairman, 1976, Council, 1971-75, Section of Legal Education and Admissions to the Bar, Member, Sections of Business, Antitrust, and Litigation; Committee on Corporate Counsel, Economic Club of Chicago, Lawyers Club of Chicago, University Club of Chicago.
Career: Joined Mayer, Brown, Rowe & Maw LLP, 1967; became Partner, 1973. Law Clerk to The Honorable Richard B Austin, United States District Court for the Northern District of Illinois, 1966-67.
Publications: 'Using Expert Testimony in Lender Liability Litigation', 'The Practical Lawyer', July 1990.
Personal: Born 11 March 1941. Harvard University, JD, 1966. University of Michigan, AB with distinction and high honors, 1963. Trustee, Rush University Medical Center, President, Lyric Opera Guild Board, Member, Lyric Opera of Chicago Board, ex officio. Director, Chicago Botanic Garden.

FINNEGAN, Sheila
Mayer, Brown, Rowe & Maw LLP,
Chicago 312 701 8943
sfinnegan@mayerbrown.com
Recommended in Litigation
Practice Areas: Former federal prosecutor. Extensive trial experience, including over 30 jury trials in federal and state courts. Has conducted numerous corporate internal investigations, and represented corporations and individuals before the SEC, Department of Justice, and State Law Enforcement Agencies in connection with civil and criminal allegations of securities fraud, healthcare fraud, and other wrongdoing. She also has represented major corporations in complex civil litigation, including class actions alleging product defects, securities fraud, and consumer fraud.
Career: Mayer, Brown, Rowe & Maw LLP, Chicago, 2000 to date; US Attorney's Office for the Northern District of Illinois, 1987-2000; Chief, Criminal Division, 1999-2000; Health Care Fraud Coordinator and Deputy Chief, Special Prosecutions, 1996-99. Law Clerk to The Honorable Milton I Shadur, US District Court for the Northern District of Illinois, 1986-87.
Publications: 'The Federal Law Enforcement Perspective on Health Care Fraud,' (May 1999) (Illinois State Bar Association, Health Care Section Council). 'Prosecution of Health Care Fraud and Abuse Cases,' (July 2001) (HCFA Benefit Integrity Conference).
Personal: JD, University of Chicago, 1986. Order of the Coif, Member, Law Review, BSFS, Georgetown University, School of Foreign Service, 1982, Adjunct Professor of Trial Advocacy at Northwestern University Law School.

FISHMAN, Michael T
Greenberg Traurig LLP, Chicago
312 476 5075
fishanm@gtlaw.com
Recommended in Real Estate
Practice Areas: Real estate.
Prof. Memberships: Member, Urban Land Institute.
Publications: Frequent Lecturer at Urban Land Institute Conferences on Mexican Real Estate.
Personal: JD, Cleveland-Marshall College of Law at Cleveland State University, 1995, BA, The Ohio State University, 1991.

FLYNN, Christopher
Jones Day, Chicago
312 269 4156
cwflynn@jonesday.com
Recommended in Energy
Practice Areas: Represents electric and gas utilities before federal and state regulatory agencies and courts in commercial transactions and other ventures. Has represented energy companies in mergers, restructurings, transmission unbundling, transmission open access tariff development, wholesale and retail power supply contracts, commercial dispute resolution, and utility rate proceedings. Current practice involves the development of competitive retail markets, including retail access tariffs, stranded cost recovery mechanisms, independent power projects, and wholesale marketing initiatives and international energy projects. Experienced with energy privatization projects and other commercial projects in Mexico and has spoken before the Spanish National Electricity Commission regarding transmission access issues.

FORADAS, Michael P
Kirkland & Ellis LLP, Chicago
312 861 2308
mforadas@kirkland.com
Recommended in Insurance
Practice Areas: Partner in Litigation Group. Extensive experience in commercial, insurance coverage, business torts, mass tort and product liability, trade secret/intellectual property, securities, and antitrust matters. Particular emphasis in representing policy holders in complex insurance coverage litigation, including general and product liability, directors and officers, and business interruption claims. Clients include Dow Chemical, Motorola, ServiceMaster, Brunswick, and other Fortune 500 companies.
Personal: AB, College of William & Mary, 1978, (Phi Beta Kappa), JD, Northwestern University School of Law, 1981, (Editor-in-chief, Northwestern Law Review, Order of Coif, cum laude). Member, Board of Editors, Insurance Coverage Law Bulletin.

FORCADE, Bill S
Jenner & Block LLP, Chicago
312 923 2964
bforcade@jenner.com
Recommended in Environment
Practice Areas: Bill S Forcade is a partner in Jenner & Block's Chicago office. He is a member of the firm's Environmental, Energy and Natural Resources Law, Trade Secrets and Unfair Competition, Defense & Aerospace, and Association Practices. He has a wide range of experience in environmental law from the perspective of a scientist, a government regulator, an environmental law judge and as an attorney in private practice. He practices in the area of environmental law, with a focus on air pollution, regulatory and permit compliance, and administrative and judicial enforcement matters. Mr Forcade serves on the Illinois Environmental Regulatory Review Commission, which reviews environmental laws in Illinois and makes recommendations to update those laws. He is Chairman of the Groundwater Subcommittee. He has been actively involved in courtroom litigation, client counseling and lobbying. Mr Forcade has represented chemical companies, pulp and paper mills, heavy equipment manufacturers, foundries, smelters, oil and gas production, petroleum refineries, printing and coating companies, natural gas utilities, electric utilities, waste disposal and recycling companies and a wide variety of industrial manufacturing companies. This representation includes lobbying the legislative and executive branches of state and federal governments on environmental matters, participation in formal and notice and comment rule making at the federal and state level, review of permit applications and negotiations with permitting agencies over the terms and conditions of those permits, client counseling over compliance matters and negotiation and litigation regarding enforcement at the administrative and judicial level.
Personal: John Marshall Law School, JD, 1976.

FORRESTER, J Paul
Mayer, Brown, Rowe & Maw LLP,
Chicago 312 701 7366
jforrester@mayerbrownrowe.com
Recommended in Banking & Finance
Practice Areas: Partner in Corporate Finance Practice. Specializes in structured credit products (including credit derivatives, collateralized debt, fund and swap obligations, and structured investment vehicles) and project financings in oil and gas, energy, transportation, refinery and pipeline industries. Also represents clients in mezzanine financings, high-yield debt financings, structured financings, equity and commodity-linked securities transactions, venture capital investments, interest rate, currency, and commodity swap transactions, restructurings, reorganizations, and workouts.
Career: Associate (1980) and Partner (since 1987) with Mayer, Brown, Rowe & Maw LLP, except for one year (1986) as Director of Bildakit Homes Australia. Served variously in Chicago, New York, and London offices. Associate with Allen & Hemsley, Sydney, 1977-80.
Publications: 'Is My SPE a VIE Under FIN46 and, If So, So What?' Journal of Structured and Project Finance, Fall 2003, 'CDOs: Process Not Product,' Euromoney's ABS Yearbook 2002, 'Project Finance CDOs: What? Why? Now?' Independent Power Project Finance Yearbook 2001-02, 'Wanted: A New Financing Model (and Acronym?) for Merchant Power Projects,' Power Economist, February 1997.
Personal: JD, Illinois Institute of Technology, Chicago-Kent College of Law, 1985, LLB, University of Sydney, 1976. Admitted in Illinois, 1988, New York, 1984, and New South Wales, Australia, 1978.

FORT, Jeffrey
Sonnenschein Nath & Rosenthal LLP,
Chicago 312 876 8000
jfort@sonnenschein.com
Recommended in Environment
Practice Areas: Environmental Group Chair. Works with all environmental media, state and federal agencies. Practice includes internal compliance investigations and conducting litigations and defending compliance programs. Experienced in complex air regulatory and permitting matters and evaluating potential risks associated with chemical exposure in remediation and toxic tort claims. Has successfully litigated before state and federal courts and negotiated with state and federal agencies.
Prof. Memberships: Past Chairman Environmental Law Committee - Chicago Bar Association; past Chairman Lake Michigan States Section - Air & Waste Management Association.
Personal: Northwestern University School of Law, JD, cum laude; Monmouth College, BA, Economics.

FRANCZEK, James
Franczek Sullivan, Chicago
312 986 0300
Recommended in Employment

FRANSON, Marc
Chapman and Cutler LLP, Chicago
312 845 2888
franson@chapman.com
Recommended in Banking & Finance
Practice Areas: Consumer credit, credit cards, bank regulation, payment processing systems. Transaction highlights:
sale of US$2.5 billion credit card portfolio
by joint venture entity to major regional
bank; agent bank credit card agreements
with major US banks; purchase of $2
billion credit card portfolio, sale and
alliance agreement for major US bank in
credit card acquiring business; $525 mil-
lion purchase of credit card/ATM
processor, assisted two Canadian financial institutions in joint venture of credit
card merchant acquiring business for
US and Canadian business; assisted
another Canadian business in sale of its
credit card business. Bank regulatory
approvals for five bank acquisitions in
2004 totalling over $2 billion. Sale of
international payment business of
major regional bank.
Prof. Memberships: American Financial Services Association; Chicago Bar
Association; National Home Equity
Mortgage Association; Conference on
Consumer Finance Law.
Career: 1991-present, Chapman and
Cutler; 1983-91, Household International (General Counsel-Credit Card
Services).
Publications/speaker: Conference on
Consumer Finance Law
Programs; Illinois Bankers Association;
Thomson Financial; Chicago Bar Asso-
ciation; Financial Institutions and Con-
sumer Credit Committee.
Personal: BSBA, MBA, JD - Drake Uni-
versity. Married to Marilyn with one
daughter, Elizabeth. Hobbies: gardening,
music, religious and charitable activities.

FRANZETTI, Susan
Franzeck Law Firm PC, Chicago
312 251 5590
Recommended in Environment

FREED, Michael
Much Shelist Freed Denenberg Ament
& Rubenstein, P.C., Chicago
312 521 2000
Recommended in Antitrust

FREEMAN, Louis S
Skadden, Arps, Slate, Meagher & Flom
LLP & Affiliates, Chicago
312 407 0650
lfreeman@skadden.com
Recommended in Tax
Practice Areas: Has extensive experience in all aspects of federal tax planning and dispute work, particularly in
corporate acquisitions and dispositions,
spin-offs, consolidated groups, financings, joint ventures and partnerships.

FREEMAN, Lee
Freeman, Freeman & Salzman,
Chicago 312 222 5100
Recommended in Antitrust

FRIEDLANDER, Mark C
Schiff Hardin LLP, Chicago
312 258 5546
mfriedlander@schiffhardin.com
Recommended in Construction
Practice Areas: Construction
Prof. Memberships: American Bar Association, Illinois State Bar Association,
Chicago Bar Association, American Arbitration Association, Design Build Institute of America, American Consulting
Engineers Council, National Academy of
Science and Engineering, Society of Illinois Construction Attorneys, and American College of Construction Lawyers.
Career: Leads Schiff Hardin's Construction Group. Clients include virtually all
participants in the construction industry. Developed a business structure for
design-build projects - the design professional leads the design-build team
with a general contractor as subcontractor for construction.
Publications: More than 200 publications and speeches.
Personal: University of Michigan (BA,
1978), Harvard Law School (JD, 1981).

FRIEDL, Helen R
McDermott Will & Emery, Chicago
312 984 7563
hfriedl@mwe.com
Recommended in Corporate/M&A
Practice Areas: Partner in Corporate
and Securities Department and a member of the firm's Management and Executive Committees. Practice focuses on
acquisitions, dispositions and joint ventures (including contested takeovers and
proxy contests), public and private equity and debt financings, and corporate
and securities counseling. Recent transactions include acquisitions and financings of businesses engaged in industrial
manufacturing, beverage distribution,
consulting services and professional
sports. Also serves as advisor to boards
of directors of public companies.
Prof. Memberships: Member of the Illinois State Bar, American Bar Association and Chicago Finance Exchange.
Career: Admitted to the Illinois Bar in
1980. Received Industrial Management
degree in 1977. In 1980, received JD, and
joined McDermott Will & Emery.

FRIEDMAN, Dennis G
Mayer, Brown, Rowe & Maw LLP,
Chicago 312 701 7319
dfriedman@mayerbrown.com
*Recommended in Telecom, Broadcast
& Satellite*
Practice Areas: Commercial litigation.
Litigator specializing in telecommunica-
tions. Experienced in complex litigation
and appellate work.
Prof. Memberships: Admitted in Illi-
nois, 1982.
Career: Joined Mayer, Brown, Rowe &
Maw LLP 1982; became a Partner, 1988.
Law Clerk to The Honorable Gerald
Bard T/bfat, United States Court of
Appeals for the Eleventh Circuit, 1981-82.
Personal: Duke University, JD, 1981;
graduated first in class, Amherst College,
BA, cum laude, 1969.

FROY, Michael M
Sonnenschein Nath & Rosenthal LLP,
Chicago 312 876 8222
mfroy@sonnenschein.com
Recommended in Corporate/M&A
Practice Areas: Corporate and securities
Chair who identifies, understands and
meets clients business objectives. Experience includes governance, corporate con-
trol/takeover defense, securities regulation
and representing purchasers, sellers and
investors in M&A transactions valued at
$1M to $1B+, involving individuals, public and private companies and global
assets across industries, private companies
and institutional and corporate investors
in private equity and strategic investments, and issuers and underwriters in
public and private financings.
Prof. Memberships: Illinois Bar, Chairman, Lex Mundi's Cross-Border Transactions Group; Board Member, Chicago
Council on Foreign Relations.
Personal: University of Michigan, AB,
with honors and High Distinction; University of Chicago, JD.

GABRIC, Ralph J
Brinks Hofer Gilson & Lione, Chicago
312 321 4253
rgabric@usebrinks.com
Recommended in Intellectual Property
Practice Areas: Patent, trade secrets,
copyright, trademark and unfair com-
petition litigation, counseling and pros-
ecution.
Prof. Memberships: Illinois Supreme
Court; Court of Appeals, Federal Cir-
cuit; Federal District Court, Northern
District of Illinois; Federal District
Court, Western District of Michigan;
Registered Attorney before United States
Patent and Trademark Office; AIPLA,
ABA; FCBA; Chicago Inn of Court; The
Lawyers Club of Chicago.
Publications: Author, Chapter 2, Trade
Dress and Product Configuration Law',
Protecting Trade Dress (2nd ed 1999),
published by Aspen Law & Business.
Personal: Education: BS, Chemistry,
Boston College (1985); JD, DePaul Univer-
sity (1988), Member DePaul Law Review.

GADE, Mary A
Sonnenschein Nath & Rosenthal LLP,
Chicago 312 876 8934
mgade@sonnenschein.com
Recommended in Environment
Practice Areas: Has 20-plus years of
experience in regulation and enforce-
ment. As Illinois Environmental Protection Agency (EPA) Director, advised
governor on state environmental issues.
Served as Deputy Assistant Administra-
tor, US EPA, and Office of Solid Waste &
Emergency Response and Deputy
Director, Waste Management Division,
US EPA.
Prof. Memberships: Environmental
Council of States, National Environmental Policy Institute, National Academy of Public Administration, presidential appointment to Mickey Leland
Urban Air Toxics Research Center, Trade
and Environmental Policy Advisory Committee, Environmental Research Institute of the States.
Personal: Washington University
School of Law JD, University of Wiscon-
sin, BA, Phi Beta Kappa.

GAGLIARDO, Joseph M
Laner, Muchin, Dombrow, Becker,
Levin, Tominberg, Chicago
312 467 9800
jgagliardo@lanermuchin.com
Recommended in Employment
Practice Areas: Mr Gagliardo has over
25 years' experience in providing counseling and representation to employers
in labor and employment matters,
including complex litigation. He also
actively practices in the area of alternative dispute resolution, and serves as an
arbitrator in employment and commercial disputes. Mr Gagliardo is the Managing Partner of Laner, Muchin, and is
the Chair of the firm's Litigation
Department. Mr Gagliardo previously
served as First Deputy Corporation
Counsel for the City of Chicago.
Prof. Memberships: Mr Gagliardo is
active in many professional organizations and is a past President of the
Chicago Chapter of the Federal Bar
Association and the Justinian Society of
Lawyers. He has also served as Chairperson of the Illinois State Bar Association's
Labor-Law Section Council.

GALLO, John N
Sidley Austin Brown & Wood LLP,
Chicago 312 853 7494
jgallo@sidley.com
Recommended in Litigation
Practice Areas: John Gallo's practice
includes conducting internal investigations for institutions, representing criminal defendants and grand-jury targets,
and representing parties in complex civil
litigation. He has led internal investigations on behalf of institutional clients in
the insurance brokerage, airline, university, healthcare, environmental, accounting, regulated-industry, law, and high-
technology areas. Mr Gallo has repre-

sented a series of clients in grand jury investigations and/or pending criminal matters, and he routinely prosecutes civil cases on behalf of institutional clients seeking redress for having been victimized by fraud. Mr Gallo also has an extensive pro bono practice.

Career: Previously served as Assistant US Attorney in Northern District of Illinois, and as Deputy Chief of the Criminal Division. Currently serves as adjunct professor at Notre Dame Law School, and lectures on federal criminal practice. Harvard Law School, JD, 1986; University of Notre Dame, BA, 1983. Bar Admission: Illinois, 1986.

GANGEMI, Columbus
Winston & Strawn LLP, Chicago
312 558 5811
cgangemi@winston.com
Recommended in Employment

Practice Areas: National Head, Labor and Employment Practice. Concentrates in all areas of labor and employment relations counseling and litigation, representing clients before federal agencies and courts, US Supreme Court, US Congress.

Prof. Memberships: National Labor Relations Board Practice Committee, American Bar Association, 1976-present; Fellow, College of Labor & Employment Lawyers, 1998-present.

Career: Joined firm as associate, 1973. Partner, 1979. Member, Executive Committee. Managing Partner, Chicago Office.

Publications: 'Labor Disputes Planning Workbook, Labor Policy Association, 1999'; 'The Bargaining Order and Related Remedies Under the NLRA', 'The Labor Law Handbook, IICLE, 1998' (with D Barella); 'The Lockout as an Alternative to Union In-Plant Campaign Tactics', 'NLRB Watch, LPA', January 1999 ; 'Retiree Health Plans: Look Back Before Going Ahead With Changes' Benefits Law Journal, 1990/91; 'The Importance of Common Values in Employment Law', Inside the Minds of Leading Labor Lawyers, Aspatore Books, 2002.

Personal: Villanova University, AB, 1969; Temple University, Doctoral Fellow-Philosophy, 1970; Villanova University School of Law, JD, 1973, case and comments editor, 'Villanova Law Review'.

GAVIN, John N
Foley & Lardner, Chicago
312 832 4544
jgavin@foley.com
Recommended in Insurance

Career: John Gavin is a Partner in the Chicago office of Foley & Lardner. A member of the firm's Regulatory Department and the Insurance Industry Group, Mr Gavin has practiced extensively in the insurance and managed care areas. His principal activity is the representation of insurers, managed

healthcare entities, and other parties in corporate and transactional matters. This representation extends to such matters as financings (debt and equity), acquisitions, reorganizations, reinsurance, preparation and review of insurance policies, management agreements, letters of credit, and the formation of captive insurance companies. Mr Gavin received his law degree from Harvard University (1975).

GEAREN, John J
Mayer, Brown, Rowe & Maw LLP,
Chicago 312 701 7278
jgearen@mayerbrownrowe.com
Recommended in Real Estate

Practice Areas: Real estate transactions, representing commercial banks, national insurance companies, and pension funds in negotiating acquisition, construction, and permanent financing for real estate projects and in negotiating workouts. Represents developers of real estate projects in obtaining governmental approvals, financing arrangements, and architectural and construction contracts to develop hotels, offices, residential apartments, and single family residential developments. Represents tenants and landlords in office, commercial, and industrial leases.

Prof. Memberships: American College of Real Estate Lawyers. Chicago Bar Association. Chicago Council of Lawyers.

Career: Joined Mayer, Brown, Rowe & Maw LLP, 1971; Partner, 1978. Law Clerk to The Honorable Spotswood W Robinson, US Court of Appeals, Washington, DC 1970-71.

Publications: Frequent speaker and panelist on real estate issues, including panel on lenders' issues at the annual Law Conference of the International Council of Shopping Centers.

Personal: Born 1 September 1943. Yale University, JD, 1970; Managing Editor, 'Yale Law Journal'. Oxford University, MA, 1967; Rhodes Scholar. Notre Dame, BA, summa cum laude, 1965. Peer selection to several legal publications. Chairman of the Board, Director, Institute for the International Education of Students.

GELMAN, Bruce L
Mayer, Brown, Rowe & Maw LLP,
Chicago 312 701 7288
bgelman@mayerbrownrowe.com
Recommended in Tax

Practice Areas: Tax Partner with extensive experience advising fund sponsors and investors (taxable and tax-exempt, domestic and non-US) in the organization and structuring of real-estate investment funds and joint ventures, including partnerships, limited liability companies, REITs and insurance company separate accounts. Maintains a broad tax planning practice representing REITs and other investors in real estate. Regularly structures investment vehicles for non-US investors.

Prof. Memberships: Illinois, 1993. US Court of Appeals for the Seventh Circuit, 1993. US Tax Court, 1993.

Career: Mayer, Brown, Rowe & Maw LLP, Chicago, 1993 to date; Partner, 2001.

Publications: 'The Insurance Company or the Insured: Where Does Defense Counsel's Loyalty Really Lie?' 70 U. Det. Mercy L. Rev 215, 1992. 'Edmonson v Leesville Concrete Co.' 69 U. Det. Mercy L. Rev. 323, 1992.

Personal: JD (summa cum laude) University of Detroit School of Law, 1992; Editor, Law Review. BA, Boston College, 1990.

GEORGE, Peter
Baker & McKenzie, Chicago
312 861 6587
peter.r.george@bakernet.com
Recommended in Technology

Practice Areas: Outsourcing; information technology law; complex licensing; intellectual property; cross border transactions.

Prof. Memberships: Illinois Bar Association. Adjunct professor, Northwestern University School of Law.

Career: Admitted in Illinois 1997.

Publications: Changing Landscape: New Legal Issues in Outsourcing; Advisory Board, Northwestern Law School Journal of Technology and Intellectual Property Law.

Personal: JD, Northwestern University School of Law.

GERBER, Dean
Vedder, Price, Kaufman & Kammholz,
Chicago 312 609 7500
Recommended in Aviation, Banking & Finance

GERMANN, Hans
Mayer, Brown, Rowe & Maw LLP,
Chicago 312 7018792
hgermann@mayerbrownrowe.com
Recommended in Telecom, Broadcast & Satellite

Practice Areas: Litigator specializing in regulated industries, particularly telecommunications. Experienced in administrative proceedings and appellate matters.

Prof. Memberships: Illinois, 2001.

Career: Mayer, Brown, Rowe & Maw LLP, Chicago, 2001 to date.

Personal: JD, Tulane Law School 2001; Order of the Coif; Member, Tulane Law Review. University of Illinois, 1998. Carleton College, 1995.

GERSTEIN, Mark
Latham & Watkins LLP, Chicago
312 876 7700
Recommended in Corporate/M&A, Private Equity

GILFORD, Steven R
Mayer, Brown, Rowe & Maw LLP,
Chicago 312 701 7909
sgilford@mayerbrownrowe.com
Recommended in Insurance

Practice Areas: Commercial litigation.

International insurance and reinsurance. Coverage disputes. Insurance fraud, regulation and insolvencies. RICO, attorneys' fee and class action litigation. Insurance defense and coordination. Restrictive covenant disputes.

Career: Joined Mayer, Brown, Rowe & Maw LLP as Partner, 1987. Formerly with Isham, Lincoln & Beale.

Publications: Co-author: 'After [?] Goes Away', Best's Review (December 2004); author: 'Insurance Coverage Actions: Who, Where, and When to Sue', The Brief, Fall 1996, Vol. 26, No. 1, ABA Tort & Insurance Practice Section. 'Prior Attention to Arbitration Clauses Help Ensure Fairness', Legal Update, The Review Worldwide Reinsurance, March 1995. 'Alternatives to Insurance Liquidation: A US Perspective', 7th International Reinsurance Congress, October 1993. 'The Responsibilities and Liabilities of Accountants and Actuaries to Life Insurers and in Life Insurance Insolvencies', ABA National Institute on Life Insurer Insolvency, June 1993.

Personal: Born 2 December 1952. Duke University, JD, 1978; Order of the Coif; administrative law editor and Member of the Editorial Board, 'Law Journal'. Duke University, MA, 1978. Dartmouth College, AB, summa cum laude, 1974. Member, Board of Education, Evanston Township High School. Director, Metropolitan Family Services.

GILSON, Jerome
Brinks Hofer Gilson & Lione, Chicago
312 321 4205
jgilson@usebrinks.com
Recommended in Intellectual Property

Practice Areas: Jerome Gilson is a Senior Partner who has specialized in trademark and unfair competition law for more than 40 years.

Prof. Memberships: INTA; AIPLA; ABA; IPLAC. Admitted to practice law in US Supreme Court and eight US Courts of Appeals.

Publications: Co-author with Anne Gilson LaLonde, 'Trademark Protection and Practice' (standard treatise, supplemented twice annually) and articles in numerous publications. Speaker before ABA, INTA, AIPLA and CBA.

Personal: Education: AB, University of Missouri-Columbia (1952); JD, Northwestern University School of Law (1958); Member, Board of Editors, 'Northwestern Law Review'.

GLASER, D Louis
Gardner Carton & Douglas LLP,
Chicago 312 569 1262
lglaser@gcd.com
Recommended in Healthcare

Practice Areas: Lou Glaser is a Partner in the Chicago office of Gardner Carton & Douglas LLP, a member of the firm's Management Committee and Chair of the firm's Health Law Department. His practice includes representation of hospitals and diversified healthcare systems, physicians, pharmaceutical and medical device companies, and other healthcare entities; concentrates in health industry joint ventures; mergers and acquisitions; hospital-physician relations; integrated delivery systems; federal taxation of exempt organizations; Medicare and Medicaid anti-fraud and abuse and other regulatory compliance; managed care; and other general corporate issues. He also is a trained healthcare mediator.

Prof. Memberships: American Health Lawyers' Association; Illinois Association of Healthcare Attorneys.

Career: Selected as one of 40 Under 40 Illinois Attorneys to Watch, 2001 (Law Bulletin Publishing Company); named among The Best Lawyers in America - Health (2003-05) (Corporate Counsel); selected by Nightingale's Healthcare News as one of the nation's Outstanding Hospital Attorneys (2003) and Outstanding Transaction Lawyers (2004).

Publications: Frequent speaker and author of topics pertaining to legal issues in healthcare.

Personal: Loyola University of Chicago, JD, cum laude, 1989; DePauw University, BA, 1984; Ohio State University, MHA, 1986.

GLICKSTEIN, David
DLA Piper Rudnick Gray Cary US LLP, Chicago 312 368 7270
david.glickstein@piperrudnick.com
Recommended in Real Estate

Practice Areas: Real estate; real estate finance.

Career: He has extensive experience in a broad range of real estate transactions including acquisitions and dispositions, financing, development, joint ventures and leasing. He represents owners and developers on local, national and international projects and has significant experience representing lenders and borrowers on complex financing transactions and workouts. He is a member of the American College of Real Estate Lawyers and has been listed for many years in a leading legal publication.

Personal: JD, Northwestern University; BBA, University of Wisconsin.

GODFREY, Richard C
Kirkland & Ellis LLP, Chicago
312 861 2391
rgodfrey@kirkland.com
Recommended in Litigation

Practice Areas: Senior litigation partner and member of the firm's Management Committee. He specializes in complex litigation, including jury and bench trials, arbitration, and appellate work in various fields, including class actions, antitrust, environmental contamination claims, franchise and distribution litigation, and business torts and contract disputes.

Prof. Memberships: Member, Board of Visitors, Boston University School of Law. Member, Board of Trustees, Augustana College. Member, Lawyers' Com-

mittee, National Center for State Courts. Member, American, Illinois, Chicago, Fifth and Seventh Circuit Bar Associations. Member, Board of Governors, The Mid-America Club.

Personal: Augustana College, BA, 1976. Boston University School of Law, JD, 1979.

GOERING, Gail
Lovells, Chicago 312 832 4400
Recommended in Insurance

GOLD, Brian J
Sidley Austin Brown & Wood LLP, Chicago 312 853 2064
bgold@sidley.com
Recommended in Employment

Practice Areas: Brian J Gold is Head of the firm's Employment and Labor Group, and counsels and litigates on a wide range of labor and employment matters. On behalf of Fortune 500 employers as well as mid-size manufacturing and service companies, Mr Gold handles industrial labor litigation, arbitrations, unfair labor practice charges, collective bargaining, alternative dispute resolution, and employment discrimination litigation. He advises clients in connection with corporate acquisitions and has successfully litigated union challenges related to such transactions in the courts and before the NLRB and arbitrators. Mr Gold handles labor issues arising from corporate restructurings and business transactions and has successfully represented corporate clients in emergency litigation brought by unions. He represents global companies with operations in the United States and counsels clients in initiating alternative dispute resolution programs in non-union settings.

Prof. Memberships: Member of the American Bar Association's Dispute Resolution and the Federal Labor Standards Committees and the ABA's Committee on ADR in Labor and Employment Law, and the Fellows Board of Leadership Greater Chicago.

Career: Served as Chairman of the State of Illinois Board of Ethics; Georgetown University Law Center, JD, 1982; Miami University - Oxford, AB, 1979. Bar Admission: Illinois, 1982.

GOLD, Michael
Sidley Austin Brown & Wood LLP, Chicago 312 853 7148
mgold@sidley.com
Recommended in Banking & Finance

Practice Areas: Mr Gold is a Partner in the Chicago office whose area of practice is commercial finance and debt restructurings for banks and commercial finance companies. He focuses on secured and unsecured syndicated financings, including acquisition financings, work-outs and restructurings, and debtor-in-possession financings. Mr Gold also advises investors and companies with respect to acquisition and other financings.

Prof. Memberships: Member of Ameri-

can and Illinois Bar Associations.

Career: John Marshall Law School, JD, 1984; University of Illinois, BS, 1981. Bar Admission: Illinois, 1984.

GOLDBLATT, Stanford
Winston & Strawn LLP, Chicago
312 558 5600
Recommended in Private Equity

GOLDEN, Gerald
Neal, Gerber & Eisenberg LLP, Chicago
312 269 8000
Recommended in Employment

GOLDMAN, Michael P
Sidley Austin Brown & Wood LLP, Chicago 312 853 4665
mgoldman@sidley.com
Recommended in Insurance

Practice Areas: Michael P Goldman's practice focuses on the corporate representation of insurance companies and other insurance entities, with a focus on acquisitions, divestitures and corporate reorganizations (including demutualization and mutual holding company conversions); the formation, capitalization and corporate financing of insurance companies and related ventures; the regulation of insurance holding company systems; the regulation of insurance company investment practices, including the use of derivative instruments and strategies; the structure and regulation of alternative risk financing mechanisms and complex reinsurance arrangements, including insurance securitization and derivatives, loss portfolio transfers and commutations; the structure of unique marketing and insurance distribution systems; and captive insurance companies, risk retention groups and other alternative market mechanisms. He represents investment and commercial banks, private equity funds, investment advisors and derivatives dealers with respect to insurance company relationships and transactions.

Prof. Memberships: Chicago Bar Association's Insurance and Corporate Law Committees and the American Bar Association's (ABA) Tort and Insurance Practice and Business Law Sections.

Career: Loyola University Chicago School of Law (JD, 1985). University of Illinois (BS, 1982) Admissions: Illinois, 1985; US District Court, ND of Illinois.

GOLDSTEIN, Andrew
Freeborn & Peters, Chicago
312 360 6000
Recommended in Media & Entertainment

GOODMAN, Mark
Lord Bissell & Brook, Chicago
312 443 0700
Recommended in Insurance

GOODMAN, Stuart
Schiff Hardin LLP, Chicago
312 258 5711
sgoodman@schiffhardin.com
Recommended in Corporate/M&A

Practice Areas: Corporate and securities.

Prof. Memberships: Chicago Bar Association, American Bar Association, Garrett Corporate and Securities Law Institute.

Career: Concentrates in corporate, securities, and mergers and acquisitions, and heads the firm's practice group that includes these areas. Has broad experience in all aspects of representing both privately and publicly owned corporations.

Personal: University of Illinois at Urbana-Champaign (BA, with highest honors and with distinction, Phi Beta Kappa, 1960), Harvard Law School (JD, magna cum laude, 1963), Member, Harvard Law Review.

GORDON, Mark
Gordon & Glickson, Chicago
312 321 7660
Recommended in Technology

GRAYSON, E Lynn
Jenner & Block LLP, Chicago
312 923 2756
lgrayson@jenner.com
Recommended in Environment

Practice Areas: E Lynn Grayson is a Partner in Jenner & Block's Chicago office. She is a member of the firm's Environmental, Energy and Natural Resources Law and Defense & Aerospace Practices. Ms Grayson has an extensive environmental law background including both private practice and government service experience. Prior to joining the firm, Ms Grayson was the chief legal counsel for the Illinois Emergency Services and Disaster Agency and the State Emergency Response Commission. She has prosecuted federal and state civil and criminal environmental cases including as an Assistant Attorney General for the State of Illinois. Ms Grayson's experience includes advising clients on critical regulatory concerns, performing environmental due diligence for real estate and corporate transactions and conducting environmental audits at manufacturing operations. She also has significant experience negotiating agreements to redevelop brownfields sites throughout the United States. She is an authority on federal and state release reporting obligations. Ms Grayson's recent work includes defending a Fortune 200 company against natural resource damage claims, developing an audit program for a Fortune 50 company with multiple US sites, counseling a client on complex TSCA regulatory matters and conducting environmental due diligence relating to six significant transactions in 2002-03. Ms Grayson is the past Chairperson for the Environmental, Natural Resources and Energy Law Committee of the American Bar Association, Business Law Section, the Lake Michigan States Section of the Air and Waste Management Association and the Illinois State Bar Association's

Environmental Council.

Personal: Indiana University School of Law, JD, 1986, With Distinction.

GROMACKI, Joseph P
Jenner & Block LLP, Chicago
312 923 2637
jgromacki@jenner.com
Recommended in Corporate/M&A

Practice Areas: Joseph P Gromacki is a partner in Jenner & Block's Chicago office. He is a member of the firm's Corporate Practice. Mr Gromacki has experience structuring, negotiating and managing public and private mergers, acquisitions, divestitures, public equity offerings and other highly complex corporate finance transactions. He regularly counsels clients on corporate governance, disclosure and Delaware corporation law matters. Mr Gromacki has represented General Motors Corporation in connection with many important strategic transactions over the course of his career, including the 2003 split-off of Hughes Electronics from GM and the subsequent acquisition by News Corporation of 34% of Hughes for $6.6 billion as part of transactions valued at over $17 billion and GM's 2004 sale of $911 million of News Corporation Preferred ADSs in an underwritten public offering. He also represented GM in several of the world's largest public offerings of equity securities, including the $9 billion exchange offer of GM's Class H common stock for $1-2/3 par value common stock in 2000 and the 2001 proposal to split off Hughes Electronics and merge it with EchoStar Communications Corporation (which was subsequently abandoned). Additionally, Mr Gromacki has represented BP in connection with certain significant transactions, including the 2000 and 2001 divestitures of its Alliance refinery and related assets in transactions valued at over $1.2 billion. He also represents the Chicago Board of Trade on a variety of corporate matters, including its proposed restructuring and demutualization into a for-profit company.

Personal: University of Virginia School of Law, JD, 1992.

GUPTA, Shilpi
Skadden, Arps, Slate, Meagher & Flom LLP & Affiliates, Chicago
312 407 0738
sgupta@skadden.com
Recommended in Corporate/M&A

Practice Areas: Advises Fortune 500, middle market and emerging companies and investment banking and other financial institutions in a variety of M&A and corporate finance transactions and other corporate and securities matters. Represents companies acting as acquirors or sellers, as well as investment banking clients, in mergers, stock and asset acquisitions and divestitures, takeovers (negotiated and contested),

venture capital transactions, restructurings, joint ventures and other strategic alliances. Also represents issuers and investment banking institutions in initial and other public offerings, private placement of securities and high-yield debt transactions.

Career: JD, Georgetown University Law Center, 1994; BS, Columbia University, 1991.

GUTHMAN, Jack
Shefsky & Froelich, Chicago
312 527 4000
Recommended in Real Estate

HAAB, Eric
Lovells, Chicago
312 832 4400
Recommended in Insurance

HAARLOW, John
Lord Bissell & Brook, Chicago
312 443 0700
Recommended in Insurance

HACK, Randall
Lord Bissell & Brook, Chicago
312 443 0700
Recommended in Antitrust

HAGY, James C
Jones Day, Chicago
312 269 4152
jchagy@jonesday.com
Recommended in Real Estate

Practice Areas: Co-chairs Jones Day's Real Estate Practice worldwide and leads the global Corporate Real Estate Services Practice. Has a broad range of real estate law experience, including significant projects in Europe and Asia and in transactions involving multinational participants. Named one of the World's Leading Real Estate Lawyers (Euromoney).

Prof. Memberships: Faculty member of CoreNet Learning; founding member of the editorial board of the Journal of Corporate Real Estate; member of the American College of Real Estate Lawyers.

Publications: His articles appear regularly in journals serving the corporate real estate industry.

HAHN, Arthur
Katten Muchin Zavis Rosenman, Chicago 312 902 5241
arthur.hahn@kmzr.com
Recommended in Corporate/M&A

Practice Areas: Chairman of Katten Muchin Zavis Rosenman's Financial Services Group. His practice includes: representation of major international banks and brokerage firms in connection with their cash and derivatives products, including interfacing with exchanges, regulatory compliance, principal trading and sales practices issues, litigation and enforcement matters; representation of international equity and commodity exchanges and clearing houses in connection with their business structuring, trading rules, technology

initiatives, cross-border Securities Exchange Commission and Commodities Futures Trading Commission licenses and international insolvency issues; representation of technology companies in connection with business strategies, capital formation and mergers and acquisitions.

Prof. Memberships: Currently serves on the Executive Committee of the Institute for Financial Markets, is Chairman of the Illinois Council on Economic Education, and was the founding Faculty Chairman of the Chicago Kent Illinois Institute of Technology Graduate School of Financial Services Law (serving from 1988 through 1999). He is also a Trustee of the Ravinia Festival and a member of the Chicago Advisory Board of Teach for America.

Career: Served on the legislative staff of US Senator Paul H Douglas and clerked on the Federal District Court for the Northern District of Illinois. Member of KMZ Rosenman's Executive Committee.

Personal: Attended the London School of Economics and Political Science. Received his JD degree from Northwestern University School of Law.

HALPERN, Marcelo
Latham & Watkins LLP, Chicago
312 876 7700
Recommended in Technology

HAMILL, John J
Jenner & Block LLP, Chicago
312 923 2684
jhamill@jenner.com
Recommended in Telecom, Broadcast & Satellite

Practice Areas: John J Hamill is a Partner in Jenner & Block's Chicago office. He is a member of the firm's Litigation, Healthcare Law, Appellate and Supreme Court, Telecommunications, and Antitrust and Trade Regulation Practices. Mr Hamill represents and counsels clients in a wide range of complex commercial matters, including appellate, telecommunications, antitrust, unfair competition, intellectual property litigation and other matters. Mr Hamill has been extensively involved in complex telecommunications litigation and counseling since his admission to the bar, including appellate, local competition, antitrust, regulatory and class action matters. With colleagues at the firm, he has been at the forefront of representing carriers in local competition litigation since the adoption of the Telecommunications Act of 1996. Representative cases include Mathias v WorldCom Techs., 121 S. Ct. 1224 (2001), and Bell Atlantic Tel. Cos. v FCC, 206 F.3d 1 (D.C. Cir. 2000), and Illinois Bell Tel. Co. v WorldCom Techs., 179 F.3d 566 (7th Cir. 1999). Mr Hamill also has regularly represented clients in a wide range of antitrust and unfair competition matters, including federal and state court antitrust lawsuits. He rou-

tinely counsels clients on complex antitrust issues. Mr Hamill drafted an amicus curiae brief on behalf of WorldCom in Goldwasser v Ameritech Corp., 222 F.3d 390 (7th Cir. 2000), a case concerning the interplay between the antitrust laws and the Telecommunications Act of 1996.

Personal: Harvard Law School, JD, 1993, cum laude.

HAMM, Leisa
Lord Bissell & Brook, Chicago
312 443 0700
Recommended in Insurance

HAMMES, Jeffrey C
Kirkland & Ellis LLP, Chicago
312 861 2476
jhammes@kirkland.com
Recommended in Corporate/M&A, Private Equity

Practice Areas: He has concentrated his practice on structuring and negotiating complex business transactions including domestic and international mergers, acquisitions, leveraged buyouts and recapitalizations, going private transactions, spinoffs, formation of private equity funds, venture capital investments, debt and equity financings and restructurings and workouts and executive compensation, handling transactions which range in size from several million dollars to over $1 billion.

Personal: University of Wisconsin, BBA, 1980; Northwestern University School of Law, JD, 1985.

HANZLIK, Paul F
Foley & Lardner, Chicago
312 832 4901
phanzlik@foley.com
Recommended in Energy

Career: Paul F Hanzlik, Partner and Member of Foley & Lardner's Management Committee, chairs the Energy Regulation Group. Mr Hanzlik concentrates his practice on energy matters and represents clients before state regulatory agencies and in the courts. His experience includes the restructuring of electric operations, establishing retail rates for bundled utility services and delivery services, construction of new transmission facilities, evaluation of long-term fuel contracts, generating station operations, litigating construction costs for generating facilities, and demonstrating the reliability of system operations and management prudence before administrative agencies and in the courts. Mr Hanzlik received his law degree from Columbia University.

HARNER, Paul E
Jones Day, Chicago
312 269 1528
peharner@jonesday.com
Recommended in Bankruptcy

Practice Areas: Co-chairs Jones Day's firmwide Business Restructuring and Reorganization practice and also coordinates that practice in the Chicago office.

Practice focuses on corporate bankruptcy, restructuring, and other insolvency-related matters. Has been lead counsel in several of the nation's largest corporate restructurings. Has extensive experience representing bank groups, institutional investors, secured lenders, and other parties in bankruptcy cases, out-of-court workouts, and related litigation. In 2003, was named one of the 'Outstanding Bankruptcy Lawyers' in the US by 'Turnarounds & Workouts.'
Prof. Memberships: American Bankruptcy Institute; ABA; Illinois State Bar Association; Ohio State Bar Association.

HARRINGTON, James
McGuireWoods, Chicago
312 558 1000
Recommended in Environment

HARRINGTON, John R
Jenner & Block LLP, Chicago
312 923 2791
jharrington@jenner.com
Recommended in Telecom, Broadcast & Satellite
Practice Areas: John R Harrington is a Partner in Jenner & Block's Chicago office. He is a member of the firm's Telecommunications, Appellate and Supreme Court, and Litigation Practices. Mr Harrington represents competitive local exchange carriers in federal and state courts in a variety of litigation matters, including matters arising under the Telecommunications Act of 1996. He notably has represented MCI and its subsidiaries in litigation concerning 'reciprocal compensation' under the Telecommunications Act for the exchange of calls to internet service providers. He has represented those companies in the United States Supreme Court, several United States Courts of Appeals, as well as in federal district courts, state appellate courts, and state regulatory commissions across the country. Mr Harrington also has represented clients in a variety of other litigation matters in trial and appellate courts around the country, including class actions, copyright matters and commercial litigation matters. From 1995-96, Mr Harrington served as a Law Clerk to the Honorable Patrick D Sullivan of the Indiana Court of Appeals, and from 1996-97 he served as a law clerk to the Honorable John L Coffey of the United States Court of Appeals for the Seventh Circuit. Mr Harrington is a member of the Illinois Bar, as well as the bars of the United States Supreme Court, numerous federal circuit courts, and several federal district courts. He is also a member of the Federal Communications Bar Association.
Personal: Indiana University School of Law, JD, 1995, magna cum laude; Order of the Coif.

HARRIS, Robert
Stein, Ray & Harris LLP, Chicago
312 641 3700
Recommended in Construction

HARRISON, Joseph H
Sidley Austin Brown & Wood LLP, Chicago 312 853 7043
jharrison@sidley.com
Recommended in Capital Markets
Practice Areas: Joseph Harrison advises and represents clients in futures-related regulatory and litigation matters and with respect to alternative investment funds. He has advised the Ministry of International Trade and Industry of Japan, the government of the People's Republic of China and the government of Indonesia. He has extensive experience in structuring and documenting complex investment funds both in the United States and offshore and was involved in the first futures funds sold in Japan, and the first multi-asset alternative strategy funds sold on a retail basis in Japan.
Prof. Memberships: Founding Vice President, Secretary and General Counsel of National Futures Association, 1982-1987; former Director of the Futures Industry Association and member of its Executive Committee; a former Executive Council Member of the American Bar Association Futures Regulation Committee and former Chairman of the Chicago Bar Association, Futures Regulation Committee.
Career: Northwestern University School of Law, JD, 1979; Northwestern University, MA, 1976; Princeton University, AB, 1973; Bar Admission: Illinois, 1979.

HARTMANN, Michael
Leydig, Voit & Mayer, Ltd, Chicago
312 616 5600
Recommended in Intellectual Property

HARTSTEIN, Barry
Morgan, Lewis & Bockius LLP, Chicago
312 324 1140
bhartstein@morganlewis.com
Recommended in Employment
Practice Areas: Mr Hartstein has over 25 years of experience in counseling and representing employers in a broad range of employment law matters. Mr Hartstein's practice also focuses on employment litigation in federal and state court, before various administrative agencies and labor arbitration. He has defended employers around the country in both individual and class action claims.
Prof. Memberships: Mr Hartstein is a founding Member of the Employment Law Alliance, an affiliation of leading labor and employment firms throughout the United States and around the world. He serves as Management Chair of the EEO Committee of the ABA.

HEIDELBERGER, Brian L
Winston & Strawn LLP, Chicago
312 558 5897
bheidelberger@winston.com
Recommended in Media & Entertainment
Practice Areas: Counsels corporations, commerce companies and advertising/

promotion agencies on advertising, marketing, and promotional issues, considering copyright, trademark, right of publicity, false advertising, sweepstakes/contest issues, television network guidelines, and the Screen Actors Guild Commercials Contract. Has expertise in talent, music and sponsorship negotiations, and also web development, software licensing, and other related technology agreements.
Prof. Memberships: Board of Directors, Kaboom, Inc.
Publications: 'Current Issues Facing The Sale and Issuance of Gift Certificates/Gift Cards', Promotion Marketing Association of America (December, 2003).
Personal: BS Marketing, Indiana University (1991). JD Chicago Kent College of Law (1994): 'Law Review', Kent Legal Scholar.

HELLER, David
Latham & Watkins LLP, Chicago
312 876 7700
Recommended in Bankruptcy

HELMAN, Robert A
Mayer, Brown, Rowe & Maw LLP, Chicago 312 701 7020
rhelman@mayerbrownrowe.com
Recommended in Corporate/M&A
Practice Areas: Senior Partner and former Chairman of Mayer, Brown, Rowe & Maw LLP. Expertise in tender offers, mergers and acquisitions, corporate restructurings, and corporate governance issues. Lecturer, University of Chicago Law School.
Career: Joined Mayer, Brown, Rowe & Maw LLP, Chicago, as a Partner in 1967; Chairman, Management Committee, 1984-98. Isham, Lincoln & Beale, Chicago, 1956-66.
Publications: Co-author, 'Commentaries on the Illinois Constitution of 1970'; various articles on corporate and public utility matters.
Personal: BSL (1954) and LLB (1956), Northwestern University; Order of the Coif; Associate Editor, 'Northwestern University Law Review'. Directorships: Northern Trust Corporation, 1986-present; Dreyer's Grand Ice Cream, Inc., 1998-2003; TC PipeLines GP, Inc., 1999-2004; Chicago Stock Exchange, 1993-2000; Zenith Electronics Corporation, 1995-99; The Horsham Corporation, 1990-96; Alberta Natural Gas Company, 1993-96; Southern Pacific Transportation Co., 1987-88; The Brookings Institution, Emeritus Trustee; Council on Foreign Relations; Museum of Contemporary Art, Trustee, 1996-2003; Aspen Institute, Trustee, 1986-92; Citizens Committee on the Juvenile Court of Cook County, Chairman, 1968-83; The Learned Hand Human Relations Award of the American Jewish Committee, Recipient; 1989; Justice John Paul Stevens Award of the Chicago Bar Association, Recipient, 2001; Legal Assistance

Foundation of Chicago, President, 1973-75.

HENNING, Mark
Winston & Strawn LLP, Chicago
312 558 5600
Recommended in Real Estate

HERALD, J Patrick
Baker & McKenzie, Chicago
312 861 2830
j.patrick.herald@bakernet.com
Recommended in Litigation
Practice Areas: Complex commercial litigation trial practice, including but not limited to class actions (consumer, shareholder and derivative claims), internal investigations, unfair competition and intellectual property matters, SEC and other regulatory agency investigations.
Prof. Memberships: The International Academy of Trial Lawyers (Fellow); American College of Trial Lawyers (Fellow); Society of Trial Lawyers; Trial Lawyers Club of Chicago; American Bar Association; Illinois State Bar Association; The Chicago Bar Association; Seventh Circuit Bar Association; International Association of Defense Counsel; and the Defense Research Institute.
Career: Illinois (1972), the Federal Trial Bar, Seventh Circuit Court of Appeals and the United States Supreme Court.

HERMES, Robert
Butler Rubin Saltarelli & Boyd, Chicago
312 444 9660
Recommended in Insurance

HICKEY Jr, John T
Kirkland & Ellis LLP, Chicago
312 861 2348
jhickey@kirkland.com
Recommended in Litigation
Practice Areas: Member of firm's Executive Committee. Lead trial counsel in commercial, intellectual property, environmental, product liability, consumer fraud, securities, shareholder derivative, antitrust, and contract litigation in state and federal courts, arbitrations and administrative proceedings throughout the US. Fellow, American College of Trial Lawyers; Leading Lawyers Network Advisory Board (top 1% of IL lawyers).
Personal: Georgetown University, AB, 1974 magna cum laude, Phi Beta Kappa; University of Chicago, JD, 1977.

HILLIARD, David
Pattishall, McAuliffe, Newbury, Hilliard & Geraldson, Chicago
312 554 8000
Recommended in Intellectual Property

HODES, Scott
Bryan Cave LLP, Chicago
312 602 5000
Recommended in Media & Entertainment

HODGE, Katherine
Hodge Dwyer Zeman, Springfield
217 523 4900
Recommended in Environment

HOEFLICH, Adam
Bartlit Beck Herman Palenchar & Scott, Chicago 312 494 4400
Recommended in Litigation

HOFER, Roy
Brinks Hofer Gilson & Lione, Chicago
312 321 4204
rhofer@usebrinks.com
Recommended in Intellectual Property
Practice Areas: Roy Hofer is a trial lawyer specializing in patent, trade secret and related antitrust and contract matters.
Prof. Memberships: AIPLA; ABA (Litigation, Intellectual Property, Antitrust Sections); FCBA (Board, 1989-95, President, 1993-1994); Seventh Circuit Bar Association; IICLE (Board, 1986-88); IPLAC (Board, 1974-76); CBA (President, 1988-89); Law Club of Chicago; Center for Public Resources' Intellectual Property Panel of Distinguished Neutrals; Center for Conflict Resolution (President, 1991-97).
Personal: Education: BS, Chemical Engineering, Purdue University (1957); JD, Georgetown University (1961); Member, Board of Editors, 'Georgetown Law Journal'.

HOMBURGER, Thomas
Bell, Boyd & Lloyd LLC, Chicago
312 372 1121
Recommended in Real Estate

HOOD, Vicki V
Kirkland & Ellis LLP, Chicago
312 861 2092
vhood@kirkland.com
Recommended in Employee Benefits
Practice Areas: Vicki Hood is the Head of Kirkland's Employee Benefits Group. Her practice focuses on employee/employee benefits aspects of corporate transactions, bankruptcy and workout situations. She has experience in advising venture capital, real estate and leveraged buyout funds regarding the Department of Labor plan asset rules, advising investment managers regarding ERISA fiduciary rules with respect to incentive compensation, prohibited transactions and other compliance issues, and counseling internal employee benefits committees on ERISA fiduciary duties and responsibilities.
Personal: Northwestern University, BA, 1974. Northwestern University Kellogg School of Management, MM, 1977. Northwestern University School of Law, JD, 1977.

HUTCHINGS REED, Mary
Winston & Strawn LLP, Chicago
312 558 5721
mreed@winston.com
Recommended in Media & Entertainment
Practice Areas: Advertising, trademark, copyright, arts and entertainment.
Prof. Memberships: ABA, Chicago Bar Association, Lawyers for the Creative Arts.

Career: Sidley & Austin, Associate, 1976-83; Partner, 1983-89; Winston & Strawn, Partner, 1989-93; Of Counsel, 1994 to present.
Publications: 'The IEG Legal Guide to Sponsorship', (International Events Group, 1990); 'Sponsorship Contracts on Disk', (IEG, 1996); 'The Legal Guide to Cause Marketing' (IEG, 2001); 'The Copyright Primer for Librarians and Educators' (ALA/NEA, 1987); 'Business Torts', contributing editor and author of Chapters, 'Privacy and Publicity' and 'Trademarks' (Matthew Bender, 1989).
Personal: BA Brown University, 1973; MA (Economics) Brown University, 1973; JD Yale Law School 1976.

IVESTER, Eric
Skadden, Arps, Slate, Meagher & Flom LLP & Affiliates, Chicago
312 407 0920
eivester@skadden.com
Recommended in Bankruptcy
Practice Areas: Represents clients in business reorganizations, acquisitions and divestitures. Has represented debtors, creditors, investors, sellers, purchasers and other financial advisors in all stages of complex restructuring transactions, from Chapter 11 reorganizations to out-of-court negotiations, workouts and divestitures.
Career: JD, University of Oklahoma, 1985 (highest honors; Order of the Coif); BA, University of Oklahoma, 1982.

JACKSON, Charles
Seyfarth Shaw LLP, Chicago
312 346 8000
Recommended in Employment

JACOBSON, Fruman
Sonnenschein Nath & Rosenthal LLP, Chicago 312 876 8123
fjacobson@sonnenschein.com
Recommended in Bankruptcy
Practice Areas: Workout, reorganisation and bankruptcy Chair. Represents public/private creditors, debtors, auditors' committees, workout consultants/crisis managers and others with troubled loans/credits. Handles related business issues and litigation in state and federal courts. Represents financial institutions and other lenders; supervises loan/asset reviews; and represents clients in out-of-court workouts or court proceedings. Creditors committee's lead attorney in United Airlines' and Wickes' bankruptcies.
Prof. Memberships: Member, ABA's Business Bankruptcy Committee; Faculty, National Institute of Trial Advocacy; Editorial Board, The Bankruptcy Strategist.
Personal: BA, University of Illinois, with Highest Honors; Phi Kappa Phi. James Scholar; Northwestern University School of Law, JD, cum laude.

JACOBSON, Kenneth M
Katten Muchin Zavis Rosenman, Chicago 312 902 5445
Kenneth.Jacobson@kmzr.com
Recommended in Real Estate
Practice Areas: Partner, Chicago. Concentrates on commercial real estate finance and investment in real estate and real estate-related companies (including, multi-family, office, retail, hotel, resort and mixed-use facilities) for real estate investment trusts, real estate opportunity funds, commercial banks, insurance companies, finance companies and other lenders, as well as developers and other borrowers. Has been involved in complex financings, including mezzanine financing, multi-asset portfolio financing, permanent and line of credit financing, rated and structured financing and other financing and investment activities in a variety of projects such as shopping centers, hotels, resort facilities, office buildings, build-to-suit distribution facilities and multifamily assets. Represents lenders, loan participants, loan purchasers and sellers, investors and borrowers in unsecured and secured lines of credit, construction and permanent financing, mezzanine financing, portfolio financing, workouts, loan dispositions and acquisitions, distressed property transactions and joint ventures. Regularly represents clients in commercial real estate acquisitions and divestitures.
Prof. Memberships: Member of the American College of Real Estate Lawyers, American Bar Foundation and the Chicago Mortgage Attorneys Association. Past President of the Chicago Mortgage Attorneys Association. Served as Vice Chairman of the Legal Opinions in Real Estate Transactions Committee of the Real Property, Probate and Trust Section of the American Bar Association. Chair of Investment Entities Committee of American College of Real Estate Lawyers.
Career: Frequent speaker, panelist and author on a variety of topics, including, limited liability companies and partnerships, mortgage finance, attorneys' opinions, portfolio transactions, deeds in lieu of foreclosure and restrictions and easement agreements.
Publications: Co-author of 'Illinois Limited Liability Company Forms and Practice Manual'.
Personal: Graduated, Phi Beta Kappa, from the University of Illinois in 1976 and received his Juris Doctor degree from Stanford Law School in 1979.

JACOBSON, Michael A
Katten Muchin Zavis Rosenman, Chicago 312 902 5443
michael.jacobson@kmzr.com
Recommended in Banking & Finance
Practice Areas: Partner, Chicago. Michael A Jacobson focuses his practice in a wide variety of areas of corporate finance, including both senior and mezzanine financing. His experience

includes borrower, senior lender and mezzanine investor representation, cash flow and asset-based transactions, leveraged buyouts and build-ups, restructurings and workouts, addressing and negotiating intercreditor and subordination related issues, equity co-investments and healthcare finance transactions for a wide range of clients in a variety of industries.
Personal: Mr Jacobson received his Bachelor of Business Administration degree in finance from the University of Iowa and graduated with honors from DePaul University College of Law.

JACOBSON, Ronald H
Winston & Strawn LLP, Chicago
312 558 5832
rjacobson@winston.com
Recommended in Banking & Finance
Practice Areas: Partner, Corporate Department, Chicago office. Practice concentrated in leveraged finance, structured investment product, private equity, and debt portfolio purchase matters.
Prof. Memberships: Member, American Bar Association Business Law Section, Commercial Finance Association's Education Foundation Founders Leadership Council, Loan Syndications and Trading Association, Inc., and Boy Scouts of America Executive Fund Raising Committee.
Career: Admitted to Illinois Bar, 1988. Joined Winston & Strawn, 1990; Partner, 1997. Annual Presenter, Winston & Strawn Corporate Associate Training Program. Member, Winston & Strawn Income Partner Compensation Committee, Associate Evaluation Committee, Billing and Collection Committee, and Corporate Associate Mentoring Program.
Personal: Born July 23, 1963. Received BA, 1985, with honors, University of Illinois at Urbana-Champaign. Received JD, 1988, with honors, Loyola University Chicago School of Law; managing editor of Loyola Law Journal. Received MBA, 1990, with honors, JL Kellogg Graduate School of Management, Northwestern University, majors in accounting and finance.

JACOVER, Jerold A
Brinks Hofer Gilson & Lione, Chicago
312 321 4214
jjacover@usebrinks.com
Recommended in Intellectual Property
Practice Areas: Jerold A Jacover's practice includes much experience in patent, copyright and unfair competition, including litigation and trials. He is the current President of his firm.
Prof. Memberships: President: IPLAC (2000-01); IPLAC Educational Foundation (1993-94). Board of Directors: NCIPLA (2000-01); National Inventors Hall of Fame (2001-02); AIPLA (1994-98). Member: AIPLA; IPLAC; Decalogue Society of Lawyers.
Publications: Author, articles in 'CBA

Record', 'Chicago Lawyer', and 'AIPLA Bulletin'. Speaker, ABA and other Bar associations.
Personal: Education: BS, Electrical Engineering, University of Wisconsin (1967); JD, Georgetown University (1971); Editor, 'Georgetown Law Journal'.

JEPSON, Edward
Vedder, Price, Kaufman & Kammholz, Chicago 312 609 7500
Recommended in Employment

JOHNSON, Garrett B
Kirkland & Ellis LLP, Chicago
312 861 2268
gjohnson@kirkland.com
Recommended in Litigation
Practice Areas: His practice focuses on the preparation and trial of cases involving a broad range of business-oriented substantive law issues, including securities and futures (fraud, market manipulation, insider trading), antitrust (monopolization, mergers, price-fixing), environmental tort, products liability, fiduciary responsibilities, breach of contract, defamation and lender liability. He counsels clients on corporate and securities issues such as takeover defense, major corporate transactions, public disclosure obligations, government regulatory matters including futures and securities trading practices, antitrust issues including marketing practices, distribution arrangements, mergers, acquisitions and joint ventures.
Personal: Princeton University, AB, 1968; University of Michigan Law School, JD, 1971.

JONES, Roger J
Mayer, Brown, Rowe & Maw LLP, Chicago 312 701 7195
rjones@mayerbrownrowe.com
Recommended in Tax
Practice Areas: Specializes in representing taxpayers in controversies before the IRS and various state taxing authorities; in the US Tax Court; and at all levels of the federal court system and all levels of New York and Illinois courts. Also has extensive experience in the areas of tax planning, compliance and transactional work relating to both state and Federal tax law.
Prof. Memberships: Admitted: Illinois; New York; US Supreme Court; US Court of Appeals - Second, Sixth, Seventh, Eighth, Ninth, Tenth, Eleventh Circuits; US District Court for the Northern District of Illinois; US Court of Federal Claims; US Tax Court.
Career: Joined Mayer, Brown, Rowe & Maw LLP, Chicago, 1987; Partner, 1991. Phillips, Lytle, Hitchcock, Blaine & Huber, Buffalo, NY, 1984-86 (Associate).
Publications: Editor, 'International Trade and Business Law Annual', 1999 to date. 'Intercompany Pricing: Getting It Right and What Happens If You Don't', Taxes, December 1994. 'Staying Out of the Lion's Den,' European Lawyer, September 2003.

Personal: JD (magna cum laude), State University of New York at Buffalo, 1984. PhD, SUNY-Buffalo, 1979. MA, SUNY-Buffalo, 1975. BA (cum laude), SUNY-Buffalo, 1973; Phi Beta Kappa.

JOSEPH, Robert
Sonnenschein Nath & Rosenthal LLP, Chicago 312 876 8165
rjoseph@sonnenschein.com
Recommended in Antitrust
Practice Areas: Has 34 years of experience in antitrust and trade regulation litigation and counseling. Handles issues covering substantive law and procedural litigation. Represents franchisors and suppliers in antitrust disputes, including class actions, and counsels on legal implications of distribution strategies and such issues as tying, resale price maintenance and price discrimination.
Prof. Memberships: Served as Chair, ABA Section of Antitrust Law, Chair-Elect, Vice-Chair, Committee Officer, Member, Chair of Franchise and Dealership Committee and Publications Committee.
Personal: University of Michigan, JD, cum laude. Member - Michigan Law Review, Alpha Sigma Nu, National Honor Society; Xavier University, AB magna cum laude.

JUNEWICZ, James J
Mayer, Brown, Rowe & Maw LLP, Chicago 312 701 7032
jjunewicz@mayerbrownrowe.com
Recommended in Corporate/M&A
Practice Areas: Represents corporations and investment banks in debt and equity financings, including IPOs, high-yield securities, US offerings by foreign issuers and underwritten calls. Major M&A transactions, corporate restructurings and private equity transactions. Advises boards of directors and executive management teams on the requirements of Delaware law; federal securities laws, particularly regarding the disclosure requirements of the Securities Exchange Act of 1934; corporate governance, including Sarbanes Oxley. Particular industry expertise in telecommunications, consumer products, transportation and natural resources.
Career: Joined Mayer, Brown, Rowe & Maw LLP, Chicago, 1984; Partner, 1987. Office of the General Counsel, US Securities and Exchange Commission, Washington, DC, 1979-84; Assistant General Counsel, 1982-84. Law Clerk to The Honorable Gerald J Weber, US District Court for the Western District of Pennsylvania, 1977-79.
Publications: 'The SEC's Recent Enforcement Actions Under Regulation FD', Securities & Commodities Regulation, March 2003; 'The SEC Raises the Stakes in Issuer-Analyst Communications', Securities & Commodities Regulation, November 2000.
Personal: New York University, LLM, corporation law, 1978. Duquesne Uni-

versity, JD, 1976. Georgetown University, BSFS, 1972. Manuel F Cohen Award, given annually to the SEC attorney making an outstanding contribution to the work of the SEC, 1983. Board of Trustees, Chicago Shakespeare Theatre.

KANE, Ivan P
Mayer, Brown, Rowe & Maw LLP, Chicago 312 701 7167
ikane@mayerbrownrowe.com
Recommended in Real Estate
Practice Areas: Practice concentrates in real estate development and a variety of real estate transactions. Development activity includes representing parties in annexation, zoning and governmental and private agreements related to property development. Development clients include real estate companies and corporate users as well as institutional clients such as universities and hospitals. Experience includes a number of corporate headquarters projects. Transactional work includes both acquisitions and dispositions of a wide variety of property types for both real estate companies and corporate and institutional clients. Financing experience includes representing both lenders and borrowers in a variety of construction, long-term, line of credit, mezzanine and other financing structures, as well as assistance in resolving distressed debt situations.
Prof. Memberships: American Bar Association. National Association of Real Estate Investment Trusts. Urban Land Institute.
Career: Mayer, Brown, Rowe & Maw LLP, Chicago, 1981 to date; Partner, 1988.
Personal: Born 19 August, 1956. JD, University of Chicago, 1981; Law Week Award, Casper Platt Award, BA, (highest honors) University of Chicago, 1978; Phi Beta Kappa. 2005 BTI Client Service All-Star Team, honoring attorneys identified by their Fortune 1000 clients for outstanding client service.

KAPLAN, Jared
McDermott Will & Emery, Chicago 312 984 6955
jkaplan@mwe.com
Recommended in Employee Benefits
Practice Areas: Focuses on employee benefits, ERISA, federal tax matters, corporate finance and employee stock ownership plans (ESOPs).
Prof. Memberships: Currently serves on ESOP Association's Valuation Advisory Committee. Former chairman of the State of Illinois Advisory Task Force on Ownership Succession, and has served on the state's Employee-Owned Enterprise Advisory Council. Served as chairman of Legislative and Regulatory Advisory Committee of the ESOP Association from 1985 -90. Past Chairman of Administrative Practice Committee of the American Bar Association's Tax Section. Member of American, Illinois State and Chicago Bar Associations, and

Lawyers' Club of Chicago.
Career: In 1999, completed a three-year term on Board of Directors of Family Firm Institute, and in 2003 was named its general counsel. In 2004, elected a fellow of American College of Employee Benefit Counsel.
Publications: Co-author of Tax Portfolio on Employee Stock Ownership Plans (ESOPs), and Corporate Portfolio on ESOPs in Corporate Transactions, both published by the Bureau of National Affairs. Editor of The Best of Law, published by the Family Firm Institute.
Personal: Earned LLB in 1963 from Harvard Law School, and AB in 1960 from University of California-Los Angeles.

KAPLAN, Joel
Seyfarth Shaw LLP, Chicago
312 346 8000
Recommended in Employment

KARAGANIS, Joseph
Karaganis, White & Magel, Chicago
312 836 1177
Recommended in Environment

KATZ, Alvin Charles
Mayer, Brown, Rowe & Maw LLP, Chicago 312 701 8285
akatz@mayerbrown.com
Recommended in Real Estate
Practice Areas: Extensive experience in complex commercial real estate transactions, including partnerships and joint ventures, acquisitions and dispositions, real estate development, finance, management and leasing. He has a widely diversified practice, representing real estate investors and developers in a broad range of transactions across the United States. His clients include private equity funds, public and private pension funds, investment advisors, developers and real estate investment trusts.
Prof. Memberships: American Bar Association. The Economic Club of Chicago. Lambda Alpha International. Pension Real Estate Association. Urban Land Institute. National Association of Real Estate Investment Trusts.
Career: Joined Mayer, Brown, Rowe & Maw LLP, Chicago as Partner, 1990. Formerly with Neal Gerber & Eisenberg, Chicago, 1984-90; Levy and Erens, Chicago, 1977-84.
Publications: Frequent speaker and panelist at real estate industry and professional conferences, including Information Management Network and Practicing Law Institute programs.
Personal: JD, Stanford University Law School, 1977. BA (with high distinction and honors in economics), University of Michigan,1974.

KAUFMAN, Andrew M
Kirkland & Ellis LLP, Chicago
312 861 2313
akaufman@kirkland.com
Recommended in Banking & Finance
Practice Areas: Mr Kaufman's practice focuses principally in the areas of

financing and secured transactions, structured and project financings, leasing, workouts and reorganizations, and general corporate practice. He heads the firm's Financing & Secured Transactions Practice. His clients include major private equity firms (as both lenders and borrowers); major national lending institutions; technology, telecom, energy, manufacturing, transportation, and banking companies and institutions.
Personal: Yale University, BA, 1971. Vanderbilt University, JD, 1974.

KELLEY, Timothy
Timothy S Kelley - Sole Practitioner, Chicago 312 641 3560
Recommended in Media & Entertainment

KELLY, Henry
Kelley Drye & Warren, Chicago
312 857 7070
Recommended in Telecom, Broadcast & Satellite

KIESELSTEIN, Marc
Kirkland & Ellis LLP, Chicago
312 861 3029
mkieselstein@kirkland.com
Recommended in Bankruptcy
Practice Areas: Mr Kieselstein's practice is focused on debtor/creditor restructurings and workouts, both in Chapter 11 and outside of bankruptcy court. His practice includes debtor and creditor representations, acquisitions of assets out of bankruptcy, debtor-in-possession loan facilities, creditor committee representations, distressed debt trading, cross-border insolvency issues, defense of consumer class actions, and environmental aspects of bankruptcy.
Personal: Queens College of the City University of New York, BA, 1985; University of Chicago, JD, 1988.

KIKOLER, Stephen
Much Shelist Freed Denenberg Ament & Rubenstein, P.C., Chicago
312 521 2000
Recommended in Construction

KIMBALL, Christian
Jenner & Block LLP, Chicago
312 923 2662
ckimball@jenner.com
Recommended in Tax
Practice Areas: Christian E Kimball is a Partner in Jenner & Block's Chicago office, and Co-Chair of the firm's Tax Practice. Mr Kimball has extensive experience with all aspects of the federal income tax, especially in the context of buying and selling businesses, purchasing and issuing financial instruments, and forming, investing in and doing business through corporations, partnerships, limited liability companies and S corporations. From 1998 through 2002, as Chief legal Officer for Bcom3 Group and the Leo Burnett Company, he managed a merger with The MacManus Group to form Bcom3, a $500 million private equity placement with Dentsu,

Inc., a Japanese company, and the $3 billion merger in which Bcom3 Group was acquired by Publicis Group S.A., a French public company. During the same period he managed more than 50 transactions per year - acquisitions, investments and joint ventures - throughout the world, in which Bcom3 invested its own capital. Between 1993-98, Mr Kimball was an Associate Professor at Boston University School of Law where he taught federal income tax, partnership tax, tax policy and the taxation of financial instruments. He is currently an Adjunct Professor in the Chicago-Kent College of Law LLM program, teaching a course on the taxation of financial instruments. Mr Kimball has co-authored a book on the tax aspects of forming a corporation, published articles on the tax treatment of convertible debt and options, and has spoken on numerous subjects related to federal income tax.
Personal: University of Chicago Law School, JD, 1983, with Honors.

KIRCHHOEFER, Gregg
Kirkland & Ellis LLP, Chicago
312 861 2177
gkirchhoefer@kirkland.com
Recommended in Business Process Outsourcing: National, Technology
Practice Areas: Outsourcing (IT, BPO and ASP); telecommunications (including voice, data, video and network management); internet, e-commerce and EDI; strategic alliance, joint venture, consortium and teaming arrangements; system development, software licensing and other computer-related agreements; biotechnology, biogenetics, pharmaceutical and medical device; technology transfer, R&D and licensing agreements; facilities management; entertainment, publishing and new media; bankruptcy-remote and tax-driven intellectual property holding entity mechanisms; intellectual asset-management programs; protection of technology and product development, manufacturing, franchising and distribution arrangements, across a broad spectrum of businesses, technologies and intellectual property rights.
Personal: Saint Louis University, BSC, 1972. Saint Louis University, cum laude, JD, 1982.

KIRIAKOS, Thomas S
Mayer, Brown, Rowe & Maw LLP, Chicago 312 701 7275
tkiriakos@mayerbrownrowe.com
Recommended in Bankruptcy
Practice Areas: Negotiates and documents loan and corporate restructurings and other workout-related matters, primarily as counsel to senior lenders. Represents acquirors or sellers of assets or businesses of financially distressed companies; corporate banks, commercial banks and other clients in bankruptcy cases, including in appeals of bankrupt-

cy-related lower court decisions and in connection with post-petition financing facilities or securitization transactions; corporations and other business entities in acquiring assets in bankruptcy sales; creditors' committees. Implements public and private disposition of personal and real property collateral, including through sales of financially distressed businesses as going concerns. Represents lenders in litigation matters, including in connection with UCC issues, possible lender liability claims, or possible borrower fraud; insurance and reinsurance companies in litigation with regulators over insolvency and rehabilitation issues.
Career: Joined Mayer, Brown, Rowe & Maw LLP, Chicago,1982; Partner, 1989. Law Clerk to The Honorable William W Thinnes (deceased), US Bankruptcy Judge, Northern District of Iowa, 1981-82.
Publications: Co-author: 'Chapter 5: Bankruptcy', of J Kravitt, Securitization of Financial Assets, Aspen Law & Bus. (2nd ed1996). 'Has David Bowie Started a New Era of Celebrity Securitization?', The Financier (December, 1997).
Personal: University of Iowa, JD with distinction, 1981. Grinnell College, BA, 1978.

KIRSCHBAUM, Howard
Barack Ferrazzano Kirschbaum Perlman & Nagelberg, Chicago
312 984 3100
Recommended in Real Estate

KISSEL, Richard J
Gardner Carton & Douglas LLP, Chicago 312 569 1442
rkissel@gcd.com
Recommended in Environment
Practice Areas: Counsel, Environmental Department, Chairman of department from its inception until 1996; has represented municipal and industrial clients in all aspects of Environmental Law, including air, water, solid waste, Superfund; extensive litigation and counseling experience in environmental field.
Prof. Memberships: Illinois State, Chicago, Lake County Bar Associations; Fellow, International Society of Barristers; Member, Board of Advisors, Northwestern University Law School.
Career: Co-drafter of original Illinois Environmental Protection Act, appointed by the late Gov. Richard Ogilvie to first Illinois Pollution Control Board (1970); Private practice in Environmental Law since 1973; adjunct professor at Chicago-Kent College of Law, University of Illinois School of Public Health; recipient, Illinois Award from Illinois Association of Wastewater Agencies.
Publications: Frequent writer, lecturer on Environmental Law issues; author, contributor to Illinois Continuing Legal Education series on Environmental Law.
Personal: Northwestern University, JD, 1961; Northwestern University, BA, 1958

KITSLAAR, Libby
Jones Day, Chicago
312 269 4114
ekitslaar@jonesday.com
Recommended in Corporate/M&A
Practice Areas: Coordinator of the Chicago office Mergers and Acquisitions Practice. Represents companies in public and private mergers and acquisitions, complex financings and restructurings, and securities law matters. Has been the principal lawyer in a variety of US and cross-border M&A, joint venture, and corporate finance transactions and serves as outside securities counsel to numerous publicly held companies. Also advises clients on corporate governance matters, including Sarbanes-Oxley, Board of Directors, fiduciary duty, takeover preparedness, disclosure policy, and related issues.
Personal: Mount Holyoke College (BA cum laude 1979); Case Western Reserve University (Law Review; Order of the Coif; JD 1982).

KLEIN, Randall
Goldberg, Kohn, Bell, Black, Rosenbloom & Moritz, Ltd, Chicago
312 201 4000
Recommended in Bankruptcy

KLENK, James
Sonnenschein Nath & Rosenthal LLP, Chicago 312 876 8000
jklenk@sonnenschein.com
Recommended in Media & Entertainment
Practice Areas: Litigation, intellectual property and technology Partner. Tries in state and federal courts patent, copyright and trademark cases before juries, judges and US Patent and Trademark Office. Litigated novel claims regarding data transmissions over broadcaster television signals; mechanical and electrical patents; companies' damage and valuation claims, tangible and intangible assets; royalties and lost profits for IP intangibles. In antitrust and franchising, has helped companies restructure systems to deliver products/services. Handles libel and privacy matters.
Prof. Memberships: Member, Sonnenschein Management Committee.
Personal: University of Wisconsin, JD, Order of the Coif, articles editor- 'Wisconsin Law Review'; Beloit College, BA, Phi Beta Kappa.

KLENK, Timothy
Bryan Cave LLP, Chicago
312 602 5000
Recommended in Employment

KLEVORN, Andrew
Eimer Stahl Klevorn & Solberg, Chicago
312 660 7600
Recommended in Antitrust

KOHN, Richard
Goldberg, Kohn, Bell, Black, Rosenbloom & Moritz, Ltd, Chicago
312 201 4000
Recommended in Banking & Finance

KOZAK, John
Leydig, Voit & Mayer, Ltd, Chicago
312 616 5600
Recommended in Intellectual Property

KRAMER, Samuel
Baker & McKenzie, Chicago
312 861 7960
samuel.g.kramer@bakernet.com
Recommended in Technology
Practice Areas: Partner, Information
Technology/Commercial Practice
Group. Represents companies on
domestic and international technology
transactions, including outsourcing,
complex licensing, and commercial
matters.
Prof. Memberships: Adjunct faculty
member, The John Marshall Law
School, Information Technology LLM
Program.
Career: DeFrees & Fiske 1991-95. Baker
& Mckenzie since 1995 (elected Partner
1999). Selected one of '40 Attorneys
under 40 in Illinois to Watch' in 2004.

KRUEGER, Herbert W
Mayer, Brown, Rowe & Maw LLP,
Chicago 312 701 7194
hkrueger@mayerbrownrowe.com
*Recommended in Employee Benefits,
Private Equity*
Practice Areas: Advises on the structuring of real estate, private equity and
other investment funds, particularly
with respect to investments in such
funds by ERISA and governmental pension plans and other institutional
investors. Advises banks, trust companies, insurance companies, investment
managers and plan sponsors with
respect to the application of ERISA fiduciary and prohibited transaction rules
and the tax treatment of pension plans
and other institutional investors. Represents senior executives, compensation
committees and corporations with
respect to executive compensation, stock
incentive programs, employment agreements, change in control matters and
severance agreements. Advises on the
establishment and operation of pension
and 401k plans and other tax-qualified
and non-qualified employee benefit
arrangements.
Prof. Memberships: Pension Real Estate
Association Chairman, Governmental
Affairs Committee (1995-97). National
Advisory Board, NYU Real Estate Institute Pension Fund Investment in Real
Estate (1992-95).
Career: Mayer, Brown, Rowe & Maw
LLP, Chicago, 1975-present; Partner,
1981; Management Committee, 1989-
present.
Personal: University of Chicago, JD,
1974; Instructor of Law - University of
Miami School of Law, 1974-75; Mayer,
Brown, Rowe & Maw LLP, Chicago,
1975, Management Committee, 1989-
present.

KRUPP, Peter C
Skadden, Arps, Slate, Meagher & Flom
LLP & Affiliates, Chicago
312 407 0855
pkrupp@skadden.com
Recommended in Private Equity
Practice Areas: Has an active mergers
and acquisitions, private equity and corporate and securities law practice. Regularly represents private equity firms as
well as several of the firm's corporate
and investment banking clients on a
wide variety of acquisition transactions,
leveraged buyouts, private equity and
venture capital transactions, corporate
restructurings and recapitalizations,
joint ventures and other financing transactions. Has substantial transactional
experience in the healthcare and
telecommunications industries.
Career: JD, University of Michigan Law
School, 1986 (cum laude); BA, Albion
College, 1983.

KUNKEL, William R
Skadden, Arps, Slate, Meagher & Flom
LLP & Affiliates, Chicago
312 407 0820
wkunkel@skadden.com
Recommended in Corporate/M&A
Practice Areas: Advises companies in
mergers and acquisitions, corporate
finance, and other corporate and securities matters. Represents companies acting as acquirors or sellers, as well as
investment and merchant banking
clients, in mergers, stock and asset
acquisitions and divestitures, takeovers
(negotiated and contested), leveraged
buyouts, venture capital transactions,
restructurings, joint ventures and other
strategic alliances. Involved in numerous
debt and equity underwritings and private placements, representing companies issuing securities and investment
banking firms acting as underwriters or
placement agents.
Career: JD, Harvard Law School, 1981
(cum laude; editor in chief, Harvard
Environmental Law Review); BS,
Creighton University, 1978.

KURTZON, Michael S
Schwartz, Cooper, Greenberger &
Krauss, Chartered, Chicago
312 346 1300
Recommended in Real Estate

LABATE, Robert
Holland & Knight LLP, Chicago
312 263 3600
robert.labate@hklaw.com
*Recommended in Media &
Entertainment*
Practice Areas: Mr Labate concentrates
his practice in the areas of corporate
restructuring and in developing, financing and distributing feature film and
television programming. He represents
entertainment companies, including
producers of nationally distributed feature and documentary films, screenwriters, best selling authors and actors in a
broad spectrum of contract, financing,

distribution, copyright and right of
publicity issues. Labate is an adjunct
professor at Marquette University
School of Law teaching entertainment
law. He is a trial attorney in the US District Court for the Northern District of
Illinois, where he successfully argued a
two-week federal jury trial in September
2004.

LADD, Jeffrey
Bell, Boyd & Lloyd LLC, Chicago
312 372 1121
Recommended in Healthcare

LANGAN, J Andrew
Kirkland & Ellis LLP, Chicago
312 861 2064
alangan@kirkland.com
Recommended in Antitrust
Practice Areas: Experience as litigation
and trial counsel in commercial,
antitrust, and products liability cases
including class actions. He has been
principal counsel to major corporate
clients in high-stakes class actions alleging violations of the antitrust laws, as
well as class actions alleging products
liability, mass tort and breach of warranty. Has also been principal counsel in
high-profile merger investigations and
related litigation. He has tried, as lead
counsel, seven jury trials, and has been
involved in numerous other contested
proceedings and appeals.
Personal: University of Illinois at
Urbana-Champaign, AB, 1979; Harvard
Law School, JD, 1982.

LASSAR, Scott R
Sidley Austin Brown & Wood LLP,
Chicago 312 853 7668
slassar@sidley.com
Recommended in Litigation
Practice Areas: Scott Lassar's practice
includes white-collar criminal defense,
representation before the SEC, and class
action securities litigation. Mr Lassar has
tried over 35 cases in federal court as a
prosecutor and in private practice,
including trials involving securities and
commodity trading, accountant's liability, trade secrets, and federal criminal
violations. He often conducts investigations for committees of Boards of Directors. Mr Lassar was the United States
Attorney for the Northern District of
Illinois in Chicago, where he managed a
staff of 250 people who handled civil litigation and criminal investigations and
prosecutions involving white-collar
fraud, public corruption, narcotics traf-
ficking and violent crime. While serving
as US Attorney, Mr Lassar personally
tried several cases, including the ADM
price-fixing case, for which he received
the Department of Justice's highest
award.
Prof. Memberships: Mr Lassar is a fellow of the American College of Trial
Lawyers.
Career: Northwestern University School
of Law, JD, 1975; Oberlin College, BA,
1972. Bar Admission: Illinois, 1975.

LATIMER, Kenneth A
Duane Morris LLP, Chicago
312 499 6730
kalatimer@duanemorris.com
Recommended in Banking & Finance
Practice Areas: Represented secured
and unsecured lenders in financing
transactions including asset based lending, credit enhancements with letters of
credit, and real estate and lease financing
for more than 30 years. He also has
assisted lenders in workout proceedings;
represented public and privately held
companies in documenting their financial obligations; and has assisted financial institutions in mergers and acquisitions and other regulatory issues.
Prof. Memberships: American Bar
Association - Business Law Section,
Banking Law Committee, Commercial
Financial Services Committee; Illinois
State Bar Association - former Chair,
Committee on Banking; Association of
Commercial Finance Attorneys; Commercial Finance Association Education
Foundation - Founding Member, Governing Board; American College of
Commercial Finance Attorneys; Fellow,
American Bar Foundation. He has
served as author and lecturer for the Illi-
nois Institute of Continuing Legal Edu-
cation and has spoken on a number of
topics relating to secured lending, letter
of credit and various aspects of the Uni-
form Commercial Code.
Career: Admitted to practice in the District of Columbia and Illinois. Duane
Morris LLP, Partner, 1999-present;
Holleb & Coff, Chicago, Illinois, Partner,
1986-99; Berger, Newark & Fenchel,
Chicago, Illinois, Partner, 1975-86.
Personal: The National Law Center of
The George Washington University, JD,
1969.

LAURIE, Ty D
DLA Piper Rudnick Gray Cary US LLP,
Chicago 312 368 2140
ty.laurie@dlapiper.com
Recommended in Construction
Practice Areas: Construction.
Prof. Memberships: Fellow of the
American College of Construction
Lawyers; Chair of the ABA Forum on
Construction Industry (2005-06).
Career: His representative matters
include reconstruction of sports stadiums; capital improvement, replacement
of hospitals; construction of high-rises
and multiuse complexes. Served as construction counsel for national retailer;
chaired zoning appeals board; belonged
to governor's commission on Americans
with Disabilities Act. Counsels on project delivery methods, negotiates contracts emphasizing dispute avoidance/
resolution, ensures ADA compliance, litigates in state and federal courts, and is a
certified mediator/arbitrator.
Personal: JD, University of Michigan Law
School; BA, Northwestern University.

LEDUC, André
Skadden, Arps, Slate, Meagher & Flom LLP & Affiliates, Chicago
312 407 0770
aleduc@skadden.com
Recommended in Tax
Practice Areas: Has a broad-based federal tax practice. Advises with respect to the federal income taxation of bankruptcy and financial restructurings and tax-advantaged financial products, particularly cross-border transactions. Representative clients: Comdisco Holding Co., Edison Mission Energy, Polaroid Corporation, PSEG Resources, Safety-Kleen Corp.
Prof. Memberships: American Law Institute Federal Income Tax Advisory Group, 1987-95; Adjunct Professor of Law, University of Miami, 1993-95; Adjunct Professor of Law, Graduate Tax Program, Chicago-Kent College of Law, 1985-90; 1998-present.
Career: Counsel, US Senate Committee on Finance, 1981-83. JD, Harvard Law School, 1978 (cum laude); AB, Princeton University, 1975 (summa cum laude).

LEE, Robert C
Jones Day, Chicago 312 269 4173
rclee@jonesday.com
Recommended in Real Estate
Practice Areas: Leader of Jones Day's Real Estate Funds Practice, representing sponsors and investors in the formation of global and geographically focused opportunity funds, value added funds, and core funds using a variety of collective investment vehicles, including domestic and off-shore structures. He also has extensive experience in creating joint ventures, in complex real estate M&A and portfolio transactions, and in subscription and property-based financings in the US, Europe, and Latin America. Named as one of the World's Leading Real Estate Lawyers (Euromoney). He is a frequent speaker on real estate private equity, cross-border investment, and fund structuring-related topics.

LEMEIN, Gregg D
Baker & McKenzie, Chicago
312 861 8013
gregg.d.lemein@bakernet.com
Recommended in Tax
Practice Areas: US federal income taxation of corporations, with emphasis on international tax issues. Extensive experience in international tax planning, transfer pricing and tax controversies before the IRS and in court.
Prof. Memberships: American Bar Association Tax Section.
Career: Joined Baker & McKenzie in 1976 and became a Partner in 1983.
Publications: Numerous published articles.
Personal: Northwestern University Law School, JD, magna cum laude, Order of the Coif; Kellogg Graduate School of Management, Northwestern University, MM, with distinction; and University of Illinois, BS, with high honors.

LERMAN, Bradley
Winston & Strawn LLP, Chicago
312 558 7492
blerman@winston.com
Recommended in Litigation
Practice Areas: Complex commercial litigation, financial and corporate investigations, products liability, white collar criminal defense.
Career: Joined firm as Partner, 1998. Representative clients: Philip Morris, McDonald's, Abbott, Morgan Stanley. Prior experience: Associate Independent Counsel, Madison Guaranty S&L Investigation, Whitewater Investigation, 1994-96; Assistant US Attorney, Northern District of Illinois, 1986-94.
Personal: Yale University, BA in Economics, summa cum laude, 1978, Phi Beta Kappa; Harvard Law School, JD, cum laude, 1981.

LEVIN, Jack S
Kirkland & Ellis LLP, Chicago
312 861 2004
jlevin@kirkland.com
Recommended in Corporate/M&A, Private Equity, Tax
Practice Areas: Practice concentrates on complex business transactions, including mergers, acquisitions, buyouts, private equity/venture capital investing, private equity fund formations, debt and equity restructurings, and executive compensation, emphasizing on tax, corporate, SEC, and structuring aspects, handling transactions ranging in size from several million dollars to over $1 billion.
Personal: Northwestern University School of Business, BS, 1958; Harvard Law School, LLB, 1961 (ranking 1st in class of 500 and serving as officer of 'Harvard Law Review'). CPA and winner of Illinois gold medal. Teaches at Harvard and University of Chicago Law Schools. Author of five books on M&A and private equity.

LEVY, William A
Mayer, Brown, Rowe & Maw LLP, Chicago 312 701 7999
wlevy@mayerbrownrowe.com
Recommended in Tax
Practice Areas: Specializes in tax-related matters emphasizing structured finance, leveraged leasing, partnership taxation, real estate and real estate investment trusts, and multi-jurisdictional corporate tax planning. Extensive experience in all aspects of mortgage and asset-backed securitization and complex real estate partnerships.
Career: Joined Mayer, Brown, Rowe & Maw LLP, Chicago, 1988; Partner, 1997.
Publications: Co-author 'The Securitization of Financial Assets', ch. 10 'Tax Issues', Prentice Hall Law & Business, 1994 edition and 'Equipment Leasing-Leveraged Leasing', ch. 30 'Securitization of Equipment and Auto Leases', Practising Law Institute, 2002 edition.
Personal: University of Chicago Law

School, JD, 1988; associate editor, 'Law Review'. University of Pennsylvania, BA magna cum laude, 1984.

LEWIS, Charles
Jenkens & Gilchrist, Chicago
312 425 3900
Recommended in Construction

LIEBERMAN, Richard
McGuireWoods, Chicago
312 558 1000
Recommended in Employment

LINKLATER, William J (Joe)
Baker & McKenzie, Chicago
312 861 2794
wjl@bakernet.com
Recommended in Litigation
Practice Areas: Practice involves criminal and complex civil litigation.
Prof. Memberships: American College of Trial Lawyers, Fellow; American Board of Criminal Lawyers, Fellow; American Bar Association, White Collar Crime Committee, Criminal Justice Section; Chicago Bar Association (President 2000-01); Illinois, California, Colorado, Seventh Circuit and Federal Bar Associations; National Association of Criminal Defense Lawyers; The Chicago Inn of Court, Master; The Wong Sun Society of San Francisco, International Proctor; World's Leading White Collar Crime Lawyers (Euromoney).
Career: Admitted in Illinois, California, Colorado and various federal District Courts and Court of Appeals.

LIPKE, Doug
Vedder, Price, Kaufman & Kammholz, Chicago 312 609 7500
Recommended in Bankruptcy

LIPTON, Richard
Baker & McKenzie, Chicago
312 861 7590
richard.m.lipton@bakernet.com
Recommended in Tax
Practice Areas: Advises on partnerships, LLCs, other pass-through entities, and real estate transactions for multinational corporations and major owners and investors in real estate.
Prof. Memberships: Member of Chicago Bar Association (Federal Taxation Committee, Chair, 1991-92) and American Bar Association (section of taxation: Chair, 2001-02); Fellow Regent and Officer, American College of Tax Counsel.
Career: Admitted to Illinois Bar and US Tax Court in 1977.
Publications: Contributor and editor to the 'Journal of Taxation'; 'Journal of Pass-Through Entities'; 'Journal of Real Estate Taxation'. Co-author of two treatises. Author of 100+ articles on partnership and real estate taxation.

LIVINGSTON, Theodore A
Mayer, Brown, Rowe & Maw LLP, Chicago 312 701 7180
tlivingston@mayerbrown.com
Recommended in Telecom, Broadcast & Satellite

Practice Areas: Specializes in telecommunications and commercial litigation. Lead outside counsel (1) for SBC Midwest in regulatory and antitrust litigation under the Telecommunications Act of 1996 and (2) for SBC nationally in various telecom-related regulatory litigation. Represents BellSouth in antitrust litigation under the 1996 Act. Has tried and argued cases in state and federal courts throughout the US.
Prof. Memberships: American Bar Association: Administrative Law and Regulatory Practice Section; Antitrust Law Section; Business Law Section; Communications Law Forum; Dispute Resolution Section; Litigation Section; Business Torts Committee of Litigation Section; Public Utilities, Communications and Transportation Law Section; US District Court for the Northern District of Illinois, 1973; US Supreme Court; US Court of Appeals for the Seventh Circuit, 1975; Various other US courts of appeals and district courts.
Career: Joined Mayer, Brown, Rowe & Maw LLP, 1973; became Partner, 1980.
Personal: Born 21 July 1946. University of Kansas, JD, 1973; Order of the Coif; 'Law Review'. McPherson College, BA, summa cum laude, 1969.

LOOMAN, James
Sidley Austin Brown & Wood LLP, Chicago 312 853 7133
jlooman@sidley.com
Recommended in Banking & Finance
Practice Areas: James R Looman's practice covers a broad variety of corporate and commercial finance transactions, including the representation of banks and finance companies in lending transactions, securitization, and equipment leasing. Mr Looman represents banks and commercial finance companies in lending transactions, as well as corporate borrowers. His practice ranges from the representation of bank groups in large syndicated credit facilities, to the representation of lenders in secured credit facilities. In equipment leasing, Mr Looman has represented debt participants, equity sources and lessees in leveraged lease transactions involving railcars, locomotives, aircraft and other equipment. Mr Looman also represents bank-sponsored conduits in the securitization of a variety of financial assets, including auto loans, auto leases, and bank loans.
Prof. Memberships: Mr Looman is a member of the Bar of Illinois and the American and Chicago Bar Associations and a Fellow of American College of Commercial Finance Lawyers. He was Chairman of Commercial and Financial Transactions Committee of the Chicago Bar Association, 1996-97.
Career: University of Chicago, JD, 1978; Valparaiso University, BA, 1974. Bar Admission: Illinois, 1978.

LOPATKA, Kenneth
Perkins Coie LLP, Chicago
312 324 8400
Recommended in Employment

LOWINGER, Frederick C
Sidley Austin Brown & Wood LLP,
Chicago 312 853 7238
flowinger@sidley.com
Recommended in Corporate/M&A
Practice Areas: Mr Lowinger is a
member of the firm's Executive Com-
mittee and Co-Head of the Corporate
Practice Group. He has played a major
role in numerous corporate transac-
tions, including: in R.R. Donnelley &
Sons Company's merger with Moore
Wallace Incorporated; First Data Corporation's acquisitions of Concord EFS,
Inc. and First Financial Management
Corporation; Stone Container Corporation's merger-of-equals with Jefferson
Smurfit Corporation; and Aon Corporation's acquistions. He has represented
special committees, including those of
Wausau Paper Mills Company, of Stauf-
fer Communications, and of Pittway
Corporation. His principal areas of practice includes mergers and acquisitions
and corporate finance, public company
transactions advising boards of directors
and financial advisors, and in hostile or
contested takeover situations.
Prof. Memberships: Mr Lowinger is a
member of the American and Chicago
Bar Associations; the Chicago Committee of the Council on Foreign Relations;
the Lawyers Club of Chicago.
Career: Mr Lowinger served as Law
Clerk to US Supreme Court Justice
William J Brennan Jr. (1981-82) and to
Judge Skelly Wright of the DC Circuit
Court of Appeals; Certified public
accountant. University of Chicago (JD
1980). Bar Admission: Illinois, 1982.
Publications: Is a member of the Planning Committee of Northwestern University's Garrett Corporate and Securities Law Institute.

LUBIN, Donald G
Sonnenschein Nath & Rosenthal LLP,
Chicago 312 876 8007
dlubin@sonnenschein.com
Recommended in Corporate/M&A
Practice Areas: Counsels private and
public companies' boards and manage-
ment on restructurings, takeover
defense, joint ventures, governance and
M&A. Also represents independent
directors or committees. Clients include:
Sears, Molex, Exide.
Prof. Memberships: Lawyer's Club,
Commercial Club (Executive Commit-
tee), Civic Committee (Steering Com-
mittee), Fellow-American Bar Founda-
tion. McDonald's: Senior Director,
chaired Nominating and Corporate
Governance Committee. Molex: Board
member, chaired Audit Committee.
Chairman, Chicago Metropolis 2020;
Chairman, New Schools for Chicago;
Trustee, Rush University Medical Cen-

ter; former Director, Smithsonian Insti-
tution, National Museum of American
History.
Personal: University of Pennsylvania,
BS; Harvard Law School, LLB.

LUCAS, Roger S
Winston & Strawn LLP, Chicago
312 558 5225
rlucas@winston.com
Recommended in Tax
Practice Areas: Tax issues related to
business formations, mergers and acquisitions, divestures, joint ventures, executive compensation, and financings.

LUEPKER, Wayne R
Mayer, Brown, Rowe & Maw LLP,
Chicago 312 701 7197
wluepker@mayerbrownrowe.com
Recommended in Employee Benefits
Practice Areas: Executive compensation and employment: executive
employment agreements and separation
agreements; retention contracts, including golden handcuffs and stay bonuses;
confidentiality and noncompetition
agreements and other restrictive
covenants; nonqualified deferred compensation arrangements; executive
incentive compensation, including
stock-based compensation (stock incentive arrangements, such as stock options
and restricted stock), and related insider
trading (section 16) issues; executive
compensation aspects of corporate
transactions; change in control agreements (including rabbi trusts and gold-
en parachute penalty tax matters); $1
million cap on deductible compensation; expatriate and cross-border compensation for executives. Employee benefits: pension plans; profit sharing plans;
employee stock ownership plans; welfare benefit plans.
Career: Mayer, Brown, Rowe & Maw
LLP, Chicago, 1980 to date; Partner,
1986. Peterson, Ross, Schloerb & Seidel,
Chicago, 1979-80.
Publications: 'Executive Severance
Agreements', Executive Compensation
(2002). 'Applying the Property-Services
Distinction in Corporate Transactions:
The New Economy Tests the Limits,' 29
Taxes 3 (March 2001). Speaker at semi-
nars for the American Bar Association,
Chicago Bar Association, National Asso-
ciation of Stock Plan Professionals,
Practising Law Institute, Profit Sharing
Council of America, Southern Employ-
ee Benefits Conference, Tax Executive
Institute and clients.
Personal: University of Chicago, JD,
1979. Grinnell College, BA, 1971.

LURIE, Paul
Schiff Hardin LLP, Chicago
312 258 5660
plurie@schiffhardin.com
Recommended in Construction
Practice Areas: Construction.
Prof. Memberships: American Arbitration Association, CPR Institute for Dispute Resolution, International Academy

of Mediators, College of Commercial
Arbitrators, American College of Construction Lawyers.
Career: Business/legal counsel for United States and international development
and design firms for more than 35 years,
advising on project planning, contracting, and dispute avoidance and resolution. His knowledge of design and construction firms has made him a valuable
advisor on issues of ownership structure, transition, mergers and acquisitions.
Publications: Co-author - 'Ownership
Transition Options and Strategies';
numerous other publications.
Personal: University of Michigan (BA,
1962), University of Michigan Law
School (JD, 1965).

LUSCOMBE II, George A
Mayer, Brown, Rowe & Maw LLP,
Chicago 312 701 7099
gluscombe@mayerbrownrowe.com
Recommended in Tax
Practice Areas: Partner in Corporate
Taxation Practice in Chicago. Structures
acquisitions and divestitures, taxable
and tax-free, business joint ventures,
leveraged buyouts, and leasing transactions; partnership, joint venture, and
limited liability company vehicles for
real estate, natural resources, and new
technologies; investment vehicles and
companies in various industries. Represents corporations, partnerships, and
limited liability companies in matters
related to general corporate, partnership, real estate and natural resources
taxation.
Prof. Memberships: Admitted to practice in the District of Columbia, 1972,
and Illinois, 1969. Adjunct Professor of
Taxation, Illinois Institute of Technolo-
gy/Chicago-Kent College of Law, 1987-
93. Member of American Bar Association, Section of Taxation; former Chairman, Committee on Capital Recovery
and Leasing; former editor, Tax Notes
column, 'American Bar Association
Journal'.
Career: Office of Chief Counsel, IRS,
Legislation and Regulations Division,
Washington, DC, 1969-73. Mayer,
Brown, Rowe & Maw LLP, 1973-present;
Partner, 1976.
Publications: Author of presentations
for Illinois Institute for Continuing
Legal Education, American Bar Associa-
tion, University of Chicago Tax Institute,
Tulane Tax Institute, and Canadian
Petroleum Tax Society and Canadian
Property Forum.
Personal: LLM, George Washington
University,1972. JD, University of Illi-
nois,1969; Order of the Coif. BS (hon-
ors) University of Illinois, 1966. CPA,
Illinois, 1966.

LYMAN, Bill
Bedrava & Lyman, Oak Brook
630 575 0020
Recommended in Construction

LYNCH, James
Winston & Strawn LLP, Chicago
312 558 5600
Recommended in Tax

LYONS, Francis X
Gardner Carton & Douglas LLP,
Chicago 312-569-1444 ph
flyons@gcd.com
Recommended in Environment
Practice Areas: Mr Lyons, a Partner at
Gardner Carton & Douglas LLP, provides counsel to commercial and indus-
trial concerns on wide-ranging environmental issues, including regulatory
compliance, permit negotiations and
appeals, corporate environmental audits
and due diligence, brownfields redevelopment, and administrative and judicial
enforcement defense and litigation.
Prof. Memberships: ABA; ISBA; CBA;
Board of Directors, Chicago's Environmental Fund; Board of Directors, Lake
Michigan Federation.
Career: Prior to joining Gardner Carton
& Douglas, Mr Lyons was appointed by
President Clinton as Regional Administrator, US Environmental Protection
Agency, Region V, from 1999 until 2001,
where he was responsible for overseeing
all US EPA policy and enforcement initiatives in Illinois, Indiana, Michigan,
Minnesota, Ohio, and Wisconsin,
including the Agency's national and
international policies on the Great
Lakes. Previously, he served as a trial
attorney in both the Environmental
Enforcement Section of the US Department of Justice in Washington DC, and
the Environmental Control and General
Law Divisions of the Illinois Attorney
General's Office in Chicago. Mr Lyons is
the recipient of numerous government
service commendation awards.
Publications: 'Sarbanes-Oxley and the
changing face of environmental liability
disclosure obligations', ABA Trends
(Nov/Dec 2003).
Personal: US Army Reserve Field
Artillery, Discharged as Captain; Loyola
University of Chicago School of Law, JD,
1988.

MACBRIDE, Owen
Schiff Hardin LLP, Chicago
312 258 5680
omacbride@schiffhardin.com
*Recommended in Energy, Telecom,
Broadcast & Satellite*
Practice Areas: Energy, telecommunications, and public utilities.
Career: Mr MacBride focuses in regulation, legislation, and transactions affecting suppliers and consumers of electricity, gas, and water. He represents public
utilities and other entities before the Illinois Commerce Commission in various
matters including rate and tariff proceedings, certifications, complaint cases
and investigations, and rulemakings. He
also represents clients in administrative
proceedings and litigation involving
state and local taxes applicable to utili-

ties and similar businesses, as well as in numerous appeals to the courts from administrative agency decisions.

Personal: University of Michigan (BA, Economics, 1971), Yale Law School (JD, 1975).

MACCARTHY, John L
Winston & Strawn LLP, Chicago
Recommended in Corporate/M&A

Practice Areas: Mergers and acquisitions, securities and corporate governance.

Career: Chairman of the Corporate Department.

Personal: Stanford Law School, JD, Order of the Coif; Williams College, BA, magna cum laude, Phi Beta Kappa.

MALLOY, Timothy J
McAndrews, Held & Malloy, Ltd, Chicago 312 775 8000
tmalloy@mhmlaw.com
Recommended in Intellectual Property

Practice Areas: Litigation and trial of high technology matters, including jury and bench cases, arbitrations, and mediations involving patent and other intellectual property law matters throughout the United States.

Prof. Memberships: Admitted to practice in Illinois and is a member of the bars of many US district and appellate courts, and the US Supreme Court, and registered to practice before the US Patent and Trademark Office.

Career: As a lead trial counsel, Mr Malloy has obtained numerous multi-million dollar verdicts, awards, and settlements for his clients, including $166 million in Advanced Cardiovascular Systems, Inc. v Medtronic, Inc., Civil Action No. 99-05393. (Top ten IP Damage Awards For All Time, Intellectual Property Today, March 2003, p. 43). He prepared and argued before the Supreme Court the case of Eli Lilly and Company v Medtronic, Inc., 496 U.S. 661 (1990) involving patent protection for medical devices. For defendants, he has obtained numerous verdicts and judgments of invalidity and noninfringement.

Personal: Mr Malloy holds BSEE and JD degrees from the University of Notre Dame; elected to the National Register of Who's Who, Chamber's USA - America's Leading Lawyers, and Strathmore's Who's Who.

MANDEL, Reid A
Katten Muchin Zavis Rosenman, Chicago 312 902 5246
reid.mandel@kmzr.com
Recommended in Tax

Practice Areas: Concentrates practice on asset securitization and income taxation. Represents sellers, issuers, investors, investment bankers, collateral managers, trustees and credit enhancers in offerings of interests in pools of bonds, loans and other receivables. Represents clients concerning the structur-

ing of investment vehicles such as REITs, REMICs, CDOs and CLOs; creating investments for qualified retirement plans, foundations and other tax-exempt organizations; and tax planning for real estate and mortgage loan funds.

Prof. Memberships: Chicago and American Bar Associations.

Career: Served as Law Clerk to Justice John Simonett of the Supreme Court of Minnesota. Adjunct professor in the Real Estate Law LLM Program at John Marshall Law School. Past Chair of the Chicago Lawyers' Committee for Civil Rights Under Law.

Personal: Graduated from Yale University. Law degree from New York University School of Law.

MANDELL, Floyd A
Katten Muchin Zavis Rosenman, Chicago 312 902 5235
floyd.mandell@kmzr.com
Recommended in Intellectual Property

Practice Areas: Partner, serves as National Co-Chair of the Intellectual Property group. Practices in the areas of intellectual property counseling and litigation. Areas of concentration include trademarks, trade dress, unfair competition, trade secrets, copyrights, high tech disputes, e-commerce/internet disputes, and false advertising. Represents leading companies in trademark litigation including Bausch & Lomb, Intel, Motorola, Fortune Brands, Home Box Office (HBO). Also represents the Recording Industry Association of America, Inc. (RIAA) and leading record companies, in copyrights litigation and the Motion Picture Association of America (MPAA) in cases involving anti-piracy. Has been involved in over 40 published decisions, many of which have involved 'cutting-edge' issues concerning emerging internet law, and several cases received national exposure. Participated in negotiating statutory language dealing with recent amendments to the Lanham Act involving internet 'cybersquatters'.

Prof. Memberships: International Trademark Association (INTA), American Bar Association Litigation and Intellectual Property Sections, Chicago Bar Association, Intellectual Property Law Association of Chicago, Patent Law Association of Chicago, International Anticounterfeiting Coalition, Inc. Member of several panels as an arbitrator/mediator.

Career: Joined Katten Muchin Zavis Rosenman in November 1976; Partner, 1980; Equity Partner, 1983; Chairman of 75+ attorney Litigation Department 1988-91; Member of firm's Board of Directors.

Publications: Authored a chapter in the treatise, 'Successful Partnering Between Inside And Outside Counsel', published in 2001 by West Group, under the auspices of American Corporate Counsel

Association (ACCA); former faculty Member Chicago-Kent College of Law and Illinois Institute for Continuing Legal Education.

Personal: University of Illinois (JD 1973); Northern Illinois University (BA 1970).

MAROVITZ, Andrew
Mayer, Brown, Rowe & Maw LLP, Chicago 312 701 7116
amarovitz@mayerbrownrowe.com
Recommended in Antitrust

Practice Areas: Chicago Litigation Practice Co-Leader. Specializes in antitrust litigation and high-stakes commercial litigation. Represents national and multinational corporations in monopolization, attempted monopolization, price fixing, market allocation and conspiracy cases. Counsels on general antitrust issues.

Prof. Memberships: Admitted: Illinois, 1989. US District Court for the Northern District of Illinois, 1989. US District Court for the Central District of Illinois, 1995. US Court of Appeals for the Fourth Circuit, 1994. US Court of Appeals for the Seventh Circuit, 1990. US Court of Appeals for the Eighth Circuit, 1998. US Court of Appeals for the DC Circuit, 2000. US Supreme Court, 2004.

Career: Joined Mayer, Brown, Rowe & Maw LLP, Chicago, 1990; Partner, 1998. Law Clerk to The Honorable Richard D Cudahy, US Court of Appeals for the Seventh Circuit, 1989-90.

Publications: 'Empagran and the Globalization of the Sherman Act', Business Law Int'l 197 (Sept 2003); 'Snapshots After Kodak', Of Interest (March 1993) (co-authored with Mark McLaughlin); 'Casting a Meaningful Ballot', 98 Yale L.J. 1193 (1989).

Personal: Yale Law School, JD, 1989; Potter Stewart Prize, Best Team in Moot Court Competition; notes editor, 'The Yale Law Journal'. Amherst College, BA with honors, 1986; Phi Beta Kappa; Harry S Truman Scholar.

MARREN, John
Hogan Marren, Chicago
312 946 1800
Recommended in Healthcare

MARRINSON, Thomas A
Morgan, Lewis & Bockius LLP, Chicago 312 324 1120
tmarrinson@morganlewis.com
Recommended in Insurance

Practice Areas: Thomas A Marrinson is a Partner in the Chicago office of Morgan, Lewis & Bockius LLP. His practice focuses on both commercial litigation and insurance coverage counseling and litigation. His insurance experience spans a broad range of matters, including environmental clean-up, asbestos and other mass tort claims, as well as professional liability and first-party property insurance coverage. He frequently counsels Fortune 500 compa-

nies on insurance-related matters and has significant experience in bankruptcy-related insurance issues. Mr Marrinson is active in the leadership of the American Bar Association's Section of Litigation and writes and lectures frequently on insurance coverage issues.

MARTIN, Laura Keidan
Katten Muchin Zavis Rosenman, Chicago 312 902 5487
laura.martin@kmzr.com
Recommended in Healthcare

Practice Areas: Specializing in healthcare law and antitrust. Healthcare law practice includes mergers and acquisitions, physician integration strategies, provider joint ventures and regulatory compliance, with particular expertise in Stark/fraud and abuse compliance. Clients include hospitals, outpatient facilities, medical supply vendors, therapy management companies, managed care entities and venture capital firms. Antitrust practice includes HSR issues, merger investigations, counseling and compliance plan development for clients in high tech, healthcare, financial services and manufacturing industries.

Prof. Memberships: Illinois Association of Healthcare Attorneys, Board Member and President-Elect; Chair, Antitrust Law Committee, Chicago Bar Association; American Bar Association; American Health Lawyers Association.

Career: Named one of '40 Under Forty Attorneys to Watch' in 2004 by Law Bulletin Publishing.

Publications: 'OIG Special Advisory Bulletin Attacks Certain Contractual Joint Ventures', Hospitals & Health Systems (Summer 2003) (co-author); 'Not so fast, it's regulated', Business Law Today, (September/October 2000); 'Antitrust Guidelines Impact CPA Firm Alliances', CPA Administrator's and Manager's Report, (September-September 2000) (co-author); 'Antitrust Guidelines for Competitor Collaborations', Outside Counsel, (Summer, 2000) (co-author); Past articles editor, ABA Antitrust Law Section's Antitrust Health Care Chronicle.

Personal: Harvard University (JD cum laude 1989); University of Michigan (BA with high distinction 1986).

MARX, David
McDermott Will & Emery, Chicago 312 984 7668
dmarx@mwe.com
Recommended in Antitrust

Practice Areas: Partner in Litigation Department. Concentrates practice in civil and criminal antitrust litigation and counseling, and trade regulation matters. Responsible for Chicago antitrust practice. Serves corporate and healthcare industry clients, and individuals who are the subjects or targets of investigations or enforcement proceedings initiated by federal or state antitrust agencies, and in private civil litigation.

Prof. Memberships: Member of the American Bar Association, including its antitrust and litigation sections and a past chair of the Antitrust Committee of the Chicago Bar Association and the former Chair of the Antitrust Law Committee of the American Health Lawyers Association.
Career: Admitted to the Illinois and New York Bars, the Supreme Court of the United States, the US Court of Appeals for the District of Columbia Circuit, and the 3rd, 6th, 7th and 8th Circuit Courts of Appeals. A Partner of McDermott, Will & Emery since joining the firm in 1987, after serving as trial attorney at the FTC and Antitrust Division of the DOJ. Adjunct professor at Loyola University Chicago School of Law (teaching antitrust in the healthcare field).
Personal: Received JD from Syracuse University College of Law in 1975 and BA (cum laude) from Amherst College in 1972.

MASCHERIN, Terri
Jenner & Block LLP, Chicago
312 923 2799
tmascherin@jenner.com
Recommended in Telecom, Broadcast & Satellite

Practice Areas: Terri L Mascherin is a Partner in Jenner & Block's Chicago office. She is a member of the firm's Telecommunications, Litigation, Arbitration: Domestic and International, Bankruptcy, Workout and Corporate Reorganization, Intellectual Property, and Trade Secrets and Unfair Competition Practices. Ms Mascherin represents clients in trials, appeals and regulatory appeals in state and federal courts throughout the United States. She has first-chaired jury and bench trials and argued appeals in both state and federal court. Ms Mascherin's recent commercial cases have included a jury trial over infringement of a patent for a battery-charging device used in uninterruptible power supplies, an international arbitration over infringement of three patents used in gas-electric hybrid vehicles, a $75 million partnership dispute against a Wall Street investment banking firm, and the defense of a $120 million suit claiming mold contamination. As part of her telecommunications practice, Ms Mascherin acts as lead counsel for WorldCom in several actions under the Telecommunications Act of 1996, and counsels telecommunications providers in matters involving compliance with the FCC's detariffing orders, including compliance with state consumer protection legislation. Ms Mascherin also counsels employers and employees in matters involving restrictive covenants and trade secrets. Ms Mascherin has an active pro bono practice, which has included successfully challenging death sentences imposed on two men on Illinois' death row and defending challenges to the clemency orders issued by former Illinois Governor George Ryan.
Personal: Northwestern University School of Law, JD, 1984, cum laude, Order of the Coif.

MASON, David
Goldberg, Kohn, Bell, Black, Rosenbloom & Moritz, Ltd, Chicago
312 201 4000
Recommended in Banking & Finance

MATHIAS Jr, John H
Jenner & Block LLP, Chicago
312 923 2917
jmathias@jenner.com
Recommended in Insurance

Practice Areas: John H Mathias, Jr is a Partner in Jenner & Block's Chicago office. He is both Chair of the firm's nationally prominent Insurance Litigation and Counseling Practice, and Co-Chair of its Professional Liability Litigation Group. He is also a member of the Class Action Litigation, Arbitration: Domestic and International, and Reinsurance Practices. Mr Mathias is a veteran trial lawyer concentrating on business litigation with particular emphasis upon insurance coverage litigation, class actions, directors and officers litigation, professional liability litigation, and intellectual property litigation. Among cases in which he served as lead counsel are CSX Insurance Company v Certain Underwriters at Lloyd's, London (international reinsurance arbitration in London before Tribunal of Lord Neill of Bladen, QC, Hon. Abner J. Mikva (Ret.) and the Rt Hon. Lord Mustill) (February 2003); Professional Sports Marketing, Inc. v Green Bay Packers, Inc. (commercial arbitration re stadium advertising rights in Lambeau Field) (June 2003); and Sunbeam Corporation v National Union Fire Ins. Co. of Pittsburgh, PA, et al., No. 99-8288-Civ-Middlebrooks, S.D. Fla. (Directors and Officers Insurance Coverage). Mr Mathias has co-authored over 20 legal publications. He is a frequent lecturer on insurance coverage litigation topics. Mr Mathias has been an active member of the American Bar Association's Section of Litigation, where he has served on the Section's Leadership Council. He also has Co-Chaired various Section committees, including the Insurance Coverage Litigation Committee and its bipartisan Task Force on Environmental Insurance Coverage.
Personal: Harvard Law School, JD, 1972.

MATIS, Nina
Katten Muchin Zavis Rosenman, Chicago 312 902 5560
Nina.Matis@kmzr.com
Recommended in Real Estate

Practice Areas: Chair of Real Estate Practice. Concentrates heavily in all areas of commercial real estate development and acquisition (including residential, office, retail, hotel and mixed use developments), financing (including rated and structured financing) and partnership law. Extensive experience in the organization and investment activities of debt and equity funds comprised of pension funds and of domestic and foreign investors and in investment and organizational matters relating to REITs.
Prof. Memberships: Member of the American College of Real Estate Lawyers, Ely Chapter of Lambda Alpha International, Chicago Finance Exchange, Urban Land Institute, REFF, Chicago Real Estate Executive Women, The Chicago Network and The Economic Club of Chicago.
Career: Member of the firm's Executive Committee and the Board of Directors. Served as Adjunct Professor at Northwestern University School of Law teaching Real Estate Transactions. In addition, she is General Counsel and Executive Vice President to iStar Financial Inc. and a Member of the Board of Directors of New Plan.
Personal: Graduated from Smith College, Northampton, Massachusetts with a BA (Honors) in Political Science and holds a law degree from New York University School of Law (1972). Listed in leading publications including Sterling's 'Who's Who'.

MATKOV, George
Matkov Salzman Madoff & Gunn, Chicago 312 332 0777
Recommended in Employment

MAYNES, Todd F
Kirkland & Ellis LLP, Chicago
312 861 2485
tmaynes@kirkland.com
Recommended in Tax

Practice Areas: Todd Maynes focuses his practice in the areas of tax litigation, the tax aspects of bankruptcy and the tax aspects of securitization. His practice involves the handling of federal and state contested tax matters for corporations and individuals. He has represented clients before the United States Supreme Court, the United States Courts of Appeals, the United States Tax Court, federal district court and various state courts. He is an adjunct faculty Member of IIT/Chicago-Kent College of Law.
Personal: Brigham Young University, BA, 1984; Brigham Young University, J Reuben Clark Law School, JD, 1987.

MCANDREWS, George
McAndrews, Held & Malloy, Ltd, Chicago 312 775 8000
Recommended in Intellectual Property

MCCAHILL, Jane
Bell, Boyd & Lloyd LLC, Chicago
312 372 1121
Recommended in Healthcare

MCCAREINS, Mark
Winston & Strawn LLP, Chicago
312 558 5902
rmccareins@winston.com
Recommended in Antitrust

Practice Areas: Antitrust, trade regulation, intellectual property litigation.
Prof. Memberships: American Bar Association; American Inns of Court; American Bar Foundation Fellow.
Career: Joined firm as associate, 1981. Partner, 1988. Litigation Department Advisory Committee.
Publications: Senior editor, 'Antitrust Discovery Handbook', American Bar Association, Antitrust Section, 2003; Vice-Chair, ABA Antitrust Section Civil Practice and Procedure Committee; Co-Author: 'Report of the Task Force on Civil Ligitation', American Bar Association, Section on Antitrust Law, September 2001; adjunct professor of Antitrust, Northwestern University Kellogg Graduate School of Management.
Personal: Northwestern University, BA, with honors, 1978; Washington University, JD, 1981, editor-in-chief, 'Washington University Law Quarterly'.

MCCULLOUGH, Joe
Lovells, Chicago
312 832 4400
Recommended in Insurance

MCDONNELL, John J
McDonnell Boehnen Hulbert & Berghoff LLP, Chicago 312 913 2110
McDonnell@mbhb.com
Recommended in Intellectual Property

Career: John J McDonnell is a Founding Partner of MBHB. His patent practice primarily involves biotechnology, pharmaceuticals, diagnostics, and related healthcare matters, with a particular focus on advising emerging high-technology companies and groups investing in such companies. He is noted for his creative strategies and alternative approaches to intellectual property business objectives, and he has extensive experience in complex lawsuits involving major biotechnology products. Dr McDonnell has more than 30 years of experience in pharmaceutical and diagnostic patent matters. He was formerly chief patent and trademark counsel at G. D. Searle and Company, where he secured a five-year extension of the Aspartame patent and directed the brand ingredient strategy for NutraSweet. He was also Head of the diagnostic patent operations at Abbott Laboratories for five years. Dr McDonnell has a PhD in organic chemistry from Iowa State University and a JD from IIT Kent School of Law. He is a member of the American Intellectual Property Law Association and the Association of Corporate Patent Counsels, and he has spoken widely on many aspects of biotechnology related to intellectual property issues in the United States and abroad.

MCENROE, John
Vedder, Price, Kaufman & Kammholz, Chicago 312 609 7500
Recommended in Banking & Finance

MCKENZIE, Diana
Neal, Gerber & Eisenberg LLP, Chicago
312 269 8000
Recommended in Technology

MCLAUGHLIN, Ellen
Seyfarth Shaw LLP, Chicago
312 346 8000
Recommended in Employment

MCLAUGHLIN, Mark
Mayer, Brown, Rowe & Maw LLP,
Chicago 312 701 7066
mmclaughlin@mayerbrownrowe.com
Recommended in Antitrust
Practice Areas: Litigation and counseling on antitrust and other distribution matters. Has litigated substantial antitrust cases involving a variety of industries and issues, including monopolization claims, challenges to acquisitions, and group boycott, exclusive dealing, sham litigation and price discrimination claims, and claims involving practices in foreign commerce.
Prof. Memberships: Part-time Faculty, Loyola University of Chicago School of Law (antitrust courses), 1983, 1986, 1988-90. Governing Committee, ABA Forum on Franchising, 1992-95. ABA Section of Antitrust Law, Chair, Membership Committee, 1993-96. American Bar Association, Section of Antitrust Law, Forum on Franchising. Chicago Bar Association. Commercial Arbitration Panel. American Arbitration Association. Illinois, 1978. US District Court for the Northern District of Illinois and Trial Bar, 1978. US Court of Appeals for the Seventh and Eleventh Circuits, 1982; Eighth Circuit, 1998; Tenth Circuit, 2004. US District Court for the Central District of Illinois, 1992. US District Court for the Eastern District of Wisconsin, 1992.
Career: Mayer, Brown, Rowe & Maw LLP, 1978-present; Partner, 1985.
Personal: Born 20 April 1953. University of Notre Dame, JD, magna cum laude, 1978; Law Review. University of Notre Dame, BA, summa cum laude, 1975. Board of Directors, American Diabetes Association, Northern Illinois Affiliate, Inc., 1985-94; Chairman, 1990-92.

MCMENAMIN, J Robert
McDermott Will & Emery, Chicago
312 984 3618
rmcmenamin@mwe.com
Recommended in Banking & Finance
Practice Areas: Partner in the Corporate Department of McDermott, Will & Emery's Chicago office. Has 32 years' experience in banking, finance, commercial and corporate law. Experience includes syndicated loans, project financing, leveraged acquisition financing, capital financing, asset-based lending, subordinated debt and mezzanine financing, ESOP lending, securitization, credit enhancement, workouts and restructurings, both in the private and public markets.

Prof. Memberships: American Bar Association; The Lawyers Club of Chicago; and The Economic Club of Chicago. Past President of The Lawyers Club of Chicago. Past Chairman of the Advisory Board of Holy Trinity High School. Director of St. Scholastica Academy.
Career: Received bachelor's degree from the University of Notre Dame in 1968 and graduated from Notre Dame Law School in 1971. Clerked in the US Court of Appeals for the 7th Circuit during 1971-72. Thereafter, practiced law at Mayer, Brown, Rowe & Maw (f/k/a Mayer, Brown & Platt) until 1989, when joined McDermott Will & Emery.

MEADOWS, Stanley
McDermott Will & Emery, Chicago
312 984 7570
smeadows@mwe.com
Recommended in Corporate/M&A
Practice Areas: Practice focused on acquisitions and dispositions of businesses, public and private financings and business counselling. Clients include companies whose securities are publicly traded, buy out funds, entrepeneurs and other buyers of financially distressed companies. Recent matters include acquisitions and financings of businesses engaged in telecommunications, software development, sports and entertainment, restaurant management, phamaceutical distribution, manufacturing, insurance and real estate activities. A number of these transactions involved purchases of assets and restructuring of debt through Chapter 11 proceedings in the US and similar proceeding in Europe and Canada. He has counselled a number of purchasers of professional sports franchises, including financing of the purchase and development of new sports venues. Has represented a number of clients in establishing manufacturing, technology and trading ventures in Asia and Latin America.
Prof. Memberships: Member of the Illinois State Bar and the Florida State Bar.
Personal: Admitted to the Illinois Bar in 1970. Received undergraduate degree from the University of Illinois in 1966 and JD from the University of Chicago Law School in 1970.

MEHLMAN, Mark
Sonnenschein Nath & Rosenthal LLP,
Chicago 312 876 8023
mmehlman@sonnenschein.com
Recommended in Real Estate
Practice Areas: Experience includes financing (including conduit lending), troubled loan workouts, acquisitions and dispositions and partnerships and joint ventures.
Prof. Memberships: Secretary, ABA's Executive Committee of the Real Property, Probate and Trust Section; Member and Treasurer of the Executive Committee, American College of Real Estate

Lawyers; Member, Anglo-American Real Property Institute; Honorary Life Member, Anti-Defamation League; Vice Chairman, Board of Trustees, Spertus Institute of Jewish Studies; Member, Sonnenschein Policy and Planning Committee.
Personal: University of Michigan, LLB; administrative editor, 'University of Michigan Journal of Law Reform'; University of Illinois, BA.

MELAND, Creighton
Baker & McKenzie, Chicago
312 861 2990
creighton.r.meland.jr@bakernet.com
Recommended in Banking & Finance
Practice Areas: Mr Meland concentrates his practice in corporate finance and lending for senior and subordinated debt, including bank debt and private placements; cross-border lending and multi-currency denominated credits; credit enhancements; debt restructurings and workouts.
Personal: He is a graduate of the University of Michigan Law School, magna cum laude, where he was an Articles Editor on the 'Michigan Law Review'. He received his Bachelor of Science degree with a major in Finance from The University of Pennsylvania's Wharton School, cum laude. He is admitted to practice in Illinois and New York.

MENDELOFF, Scott T
Sidley Austin Brown & Wood LLP,
Chicago 312 853 7362
smendeloff@sidley.com
Recommended in Litigation
Practice Areas: Scott Mendeloff's practice includes civil and criminal trial litigation and internal corporate investigations. Mr Mendeloff's civil and criminal practice has ranged from representation of Fortune 100 companies to individuals. He served as primary trial counsel in a series of commercial disputes focussing upon allegations of healthcare fraud and abuse, accounting fraud, contract interpretation, and civil RICO. He has handled numerous substantial internal corporate investigations for the nation's largest corporations, major academic institutions and local charities. Mr Mendeloff served as one of the primary trial lawyers in the government's prosecution of Timothy McVeigh for the Oklahoma City bombing and orchestrated the prosecution's response to the defense case. The United States Justice Department awarded Mr Mendeloff one of its highest honors, the Attorney General's Award. Mr Mendeloff served as assistant US Attorney in Chicago and supervised that office's Criminal and Special Prosecutions Divisions.
Prof. Memberships: Mr Mendeloff serves on the Board of Directors of the Federal Bar Association; Executive Board of Directors of the Chicago Crime Commission; and as Co-Chairman, Criminal Committee of the Chica-

go Counsel of Lawyers.
Career: Georgetown University Law Center, JD, 1983; Georgetown University, MS, 1986; University of Wisconsin Madison, BA, 1979. Bar Admission: Illinois, 1983

MENDELSOHN, David
DLA Piper Rudnick Gray Cary US LLP,
Chicago 312 368 7272
david.mendelsohn@dlapiper.com
Recommended in Insurance
Practice Areas: Insurance and reinsurance.
Prof. Memberships: Associate of Fellows and Legal Scholars of the Center for International Legal Studies.
Career: Handles insurance and reinsurance, and structured finance and alternative risk, transactions and regulatory matters, as well as mediations and arbitrations. He also conducts internal investigations and compliance reviews, and counsels clients on compliance, E&O risk management, ethics, IT and e-commerce, and information management matters, such as records management and retention, contracts management, money laundering, and data privacy and security.
Personal: JD, Chicago-Kent College of Law, Illinois Institute of Technology; Lancaster Gate School of Law; LLB, University College of London.

MENSCH, Linda
Linda S Mensch PC - Sole Practitioner,
Chicago 312 922 2910
Recommended in Media & Entertainment

MENSIK, Michael S
Baker & McKenzie, Chicago
312 861 8941
michael.s.mensik@bakernet.com
Recommended in Business Process Outsourcing: National, Technology
Practice Areas: Focus: outsourcing; information technology; e-commerce. Advises companies on doing business in global environment, physically and electronically, particularly intellectual property protection. He counsels multinationals on how to structure their outsourcing arrangements, from ITO to BPO, and creating background to vendor-to-vendor strategic alliances that support such customer offerings.
Prof. Memberships: Global Co-Coordinator Baker & McKenzie IT/Communications Practice; Editor, 'Global e-Law Alert'.
Career: Admitted in Illinois (1980).
Publications: 'Outsourcing, Offshoring and Employee Privacy Rights' Privacy Litigation Reporter (September 2003); 'Outsourcing Journal' (6 articles, 2002, 2004); 'International Software Licensing', 'Software Localization' (Computer Lawyer 1997, 1991).

MENSON, Richard
McGuireWoods, Chicago
312 558 1000
Recommended in Employee Benefits

METROPOULOS, Demetrios
Mayer, Brown, Rowe & Maw LLP,
Chicago 312 701 8479
demetro@mayerbrown.com
*Recommended in Telecom, Broadcast
& Satellite*

Practice Areas: Commercial litigation.
Representation in: telecommunications
and regulated industries; insurance coverage disputes; products liability; insurance company liquidation; design and
construction disputes; civil RICO;
antitrust.
Career: Mayer, Brown, Rowe & Maw
LLP, Chicago, 1994 to date; Partner,
2002. Law Clerk to The Honorable
Joseph T Sneed, US Court of Appeals for
the Ninth Circuit, 1993-94. Coopers &
Lybrand, Certified Public Accountants,
Detroit, 1985-90.
Publications: 'Constitutional Dimensions of the North American Free Trade
Agreement,' 27 Cornell Int'l L.J. 141,
1994. Note, 'Human Rights, Incorporat-
ed: The European Community's New
Line of Business,' 29 Stan. J. Int'l L. 131,
1993. Note, 'Son of COBRA: The Evolu-
tion of a Federal Malpractice Law,' 45
Stan. L. Rev. 263, 1993. Co-author:
'Putting Attorneys on the Witness Stand
and Their Advice at Issue: The Perils of
Selective Waiver of Privilege,' The Attor-
ney-Client Privilege in Civil Litigation,
Vincent S. Walkowiak, ed., American
Bar Association, 1997.
Personal: JD, Stanford Law School,
1993; Order of the Coif; senior editor,
Stanford Law Review. BBA, University of
Michigan, 1985; Phi Beta Kappa.

MILLER, Kenneth W
Katten Muchin Zavis Rosenman,
Chicago 312 902 5261
ken.miller@kmzr.com
Recommended in Private Equity

Practice Areas: Partner, serves as Co-
Chairman of National Private Equity
Practice. Practice focuses on representing private equity firms and other private investors in equity and debt financings, leveraged buyouts and other acquisitions, dispositions and recapitalizations. Advises portfolio companies of
private equity firms in financings, acquisitions, sales and other transactions. Also
advises executives in compensation and
equity related matters. Has represented
private equity funds in numerous
investments and acquisitions, including
investments in technology, healthcare
and services companies; leveraged buyouts of retailers, distributors, manufacturers and service businesses; and the
formation, financings, acquisitions and
sales of emerging growth companies.

MILLER, Laura B
Brinks Hofer Gilson & Lione, Chicago
312 321 4715
lmiller@usebrinks.com
Recommended in Intellectual Property
Practice Areas: Laura Beth Miller has
litigation experience involving a variety

Internet related issues, as well as in tradi-
tional areas of intellectual property
including patent, trademark, unfair com-
petition, trade secret and copyright law.
Prof. Memberships: Illinois Supreme
Court; United States Supreme Court;
Court of Appeals, Federal Circuit and
the Seventh Circuit; Federal District
Court: Northern District of Illinois,
Southern District of Indiana, Western
District of Michigan, Eastern District of
Wisconsin. Registered Attorney before
the United States Patent and Trademark
Office.
Publications: 'Enforcing and Defending
Against Patent Rights Through Litiga-
tion,' Intellectual Property Law, ICLE
2005. 'Copyright Law in the Digital Age,'
Business, Law and the Internet: Essential
Guidance For You, Your Clients and
Your Firm, ICLE 2002. 'IP: Trade-
marks/Unfair Trade Practices,' Business
Law and the Internet: Essential Guid-
ance For You, Your Clients and Your
Firm, ICLE 2002.
Personal: Education: BA, History, tech-
nical background Chemistry, University
of Virginia (1982); JD, College of
William and Mary (1985).

MILLER, Lee I
DLA Piper Rudnick Gray Cary US LLP,
Chicago 312 368 4029
lee.miller@dlapiper.com
Recommended in Real Estate
Practice Areas: Real estate.
Prof. Memberships: American College
of Real Estate Lawyers.
Career: Joint CEO of the firm and concentrates his practice in commercial real
estate and has represented clients in a
wide range of commercial real estate
transactions, including acquisitions and
dispositions of portfolios, individual
properties and loans, complex financing, joint venture formation, syndications, construction contract negotiations, lease preparation, restructuring
and workout of troubled real estate projects and real estate securitization and
fund investment. Has lectured extensively before bar, trade and professional
associations on a variety of topics.
Personal: JD, Georgetown University Law
Center; BSBA, Georgetown University.

MILLNER, Robert
Sonnenschein Nath & Rosenthal LLP,
Chicago 312 876 7994
rmillner@sonnenschein.com
Recommended in Bankruptcy
Practice Areas: Practices bankruptcy
and commercial litigation. Represents
financial institutions and insurance companies in bankruptcy litigation and
lenders, other creditors and debtors in
complex reorganization real estate matters. Has handled significant cross-border
matters for both debtors and creditors.
Prof. Memberships: Fellow, American
College of Bankruptcy; past Co-Chair,
Bankruptcy and Insolvency Committee,
Litigation Section of the American Bar

Association; Honorary Overseas Member, Commercial Bar Association (London); past Trustee, Anshe Emet Synagogue; Vice President, American Jewish
Congress (Midwest).
Personal: University of Chicago, JD,
University of Chicago Law Review; Wesleyan University, BA magna cum laude,
Phi Beta Kappa.

MISCIMARRA, Philip
Seyfarth Shaw LLP, Chicago
312 346 8000
Recommended in Employment

MISSNER, David
DLA Piper Rudnick Gray Cary US LLP,
Chicago 312 368 2170
david.missner@dlapiper.com
Recommended in Bankruptcy
Practice Areas: Bankruptcy reorganization, commercial transactions and
banking law.
Prof. Memberships: American Bar
Association; Illinois State Bar Associa-
tion; Chicago Bar Association.
Career: He is a frequent lecturer on
banking and bankruptcy-related topics
for the Chicago Bar Association, Illinois
Institute for Continuing Legal Educa-
tion and other professional and trade
organizations.
Publications: 'Chapter 11', 'Representing the Debtor and Representing the
Creditor with a Secured Claim', both
published by Illinois Institute for a Continuing Legal Education.
Personal: BA degree, Miami University,
Oxford, Ohio; JD Degree, Northwestern
University School of Law. Interests
include tennis, hiking and rafting.

MITCHELL, Nancy
Greenberg Traurig LLP, Chicago
312 456 5107
mitchelln@gtlaw.com
Recommended in Bankruptcy
Practice Areas: Reorganization, bank-
ruptcy and restructuring, public finance,
corporate and securities, energy and
natural resources.
Career: Executive Director, CIBC World
Market Corp., 1999-2001.
Personal: JD, cum laude, University of
Michigan Law School, 1987. Contribut-
ing Editor, 'The Michigan Law Review'.
BA, with honors, English and History,
Indiana University Bloomington, 1984.

MOLO, Steven
Shearman & Sterling LLP, New York
212 848 7456
smolo@shearman.com
Recommended in Litigation
Practice Areas: Partner in Shearman &
Sterling's Litigation Group. Active trial
and appellate practice in complex business litigation, regulatory matters and
white-collar criminal matters, including
corporate internal investigations,
throughout the United States and
abroad.
Prof. Memberships: Member, Illinois
Supreme Court Rules Committee; Pro-

grams and Membership Chair, Seventh
Circuit Bar Association; Fellow, Ameri-
can Academy of Appellate Lawyers
Career: Assistant Attorney General,
Chicago (1982-86); Associate, Partner,
Winston & Strawn (1986-2004).
Publications: Co-author of 'Corporate
Internal Investigations' (1989, updated
semi-annually) and 'Your Witness:
Lessons on Cross-examination from
Great Chicago Trial Lawyers' (forthcom-
ing).
Personal: BS (1979) and JD (1982),
University of Illinois.

MORAN, Patrick G
Sonnenschein Nath & Rosenthal LLP,
Chicago 312 876 8132
pmoran@sonnenschein.com
Recommended in Real Estate
Practice Areas: Handles various commercial real estate and related financing
matters, emphasizing development,
leasing and financing. Works with major
office landlords and tenants in developing and leasing more than 10 million
square feet of office space. Financing
practice focuses on multistate secured
and unsecured revolving credit loans to
REITs and other real estate companies
and traditional project loans secured by
office buildings, apartment projects,
shopping centers, golf courses, hotels
and mixed-use projects.
Prof. Memberships: American College
of Real Estate Lawyers; ABA Committee
on Commercial Leasing.
Personal: Georgetown University, JD;
Harvard College, BA.

MORITZ, Louis P
Mayer, Brown, Rowe & Maw LLP,
Chicago 312 701 7255
Lmoritz@mayerbrownrowe.com
Recommended in Real Estate
Practice Areas: Commercial real estate
transactions, with particular emphasis
in serving corporate, institutional and
financial services clients. Concentration
in complex headquarters leasing; office
and industrial build-to-suits; acquisi-
tions/dispositions; and project development. Extensive experience and interest
in counseling clients in complex negotiations and dispute resolution. Additional expertise counseling international
clients in US legal issues and business
practices.
Prof. Memberships: Admitted: Illinois,
1990; Florida, 1996;
Career: Joined Mayer, Brown, Rowe &
Maw LLP, Chicago, 1990; Equity Partner,
1999. Law Clerk to The Honorable Jesse
E Eschbach, United States Court of
Appeals for the Seventh Circuit, 1989-90.
Publications: Lecturer at The University
of Chicago Law School negotiation seminar and speaker on real estate law and
negotiation.
Personal: University of Chicago Law
School, JD with honors, 1989. University
of Chicago, AB, 1986. Conversationally
fluent in French.

MORRIS, Ralph A
Schiff Hardin LLP, Chicago
312 258 5553
rmorris@schiffhardin.com
Recommended in Employment
Practice Areas: Labor and employment.
Prof. Memberships: American Bar Association, Chicago Bar Association, College of Labor and Employment Lawyers.
Career: Mr Morris represents management in both traditional labor matters and employment disputes. He provides presentations on harassment issues and measures employers can take to prevent employment-related litigation, and he has acted as an independent investigator on harassment complaints. He also serves as a mediator on employment issues.
Personal: Valparaiso University (BA, 1967), University of Michigan (JD, magna cum laude, Order of the Coif, 1970), Associate Editor, Michigan Law Review.

MORRISON, Portia Owen
DLA Piper Rudnick Gray Cary US LLP, Chicago 312 368 4013
portia.morrison@dlapiper.com
Recommended in Real Estate
Practice Areas: Real estate; lodging and timeshare; real estate finance.
Prof. Memberships: American College of Real Estate Lawyers.
Career: She represents investors, developers and lenders in multi-family, office, retail, hotel and industrial development and redevelopment projects; construction of infrastructure and buildings; sales and leasing activities; and construction and permanent financing. She has an extensive practice in real estate investment and finance, representing lenders, investors and borrowers, in structuring financing through traditional mortgage loans, joint venture formations, structured debt placements, mezzanine loans and other financing and investment mechanisms.
Personal: JD, University of Chicago; MA, University of Wisconsin; BA, Agnes Scott College.

MROWIEC, John S
Conway & Mrowiec, Chicago
312 658 1100
jsm@cmcontractors.com
Recommended in Construction
Practice Areas: Construction law.
Prof. Memberships: Chicago (Mechanics Lien Subcommittee) and American (Construction Industry Forum, Public Contracts and Litigation Sections) Bar Associations; Builders Association of Greater Chicago; Associated General Contractors; American Institute of Architects; Society of Illinois Construction Lawyers.
Publications: Law Columnist, Midwest Construction News (McGraw-Hill), May, 2000 to present; instructor and

author: 'Construction Law & Contracts,' The Real Estate Center at DePaul University (Mar. 2005, Mar. 2004, Mar. 2003, Dec. 2002); author: 'Mechanics Lien Rights in Illinois, A Practical Guide to Enforcement.' Co-author: 'Requirements for the Original Contractor's Lien on Private Projects,' in Illinois Mechanics Liens, IICLE (1994, 2000, 2004 eds.); author and speaker, 'AIA Documents' (Sept. 2004); 'Public Construction Contracting' (Oct. 2004, Mar. 2002, Aug. 2001, Mar. 2001); 'Fundamentals of Construction Contracts: Understanding the Issues,' (Mar. 2005, Mar. 2004, Oct. 2002, May 2002, Mar. 2002, Feb. 2002, Feb. 2001, 2000); 'Construction Management & Design-Build: Contracting & Claims Avoidance,' (Apr. 2005, Nov. 2004, Apr. 2004, Apr. 2003, Apr. 2002, Mar. 2002, Nov. 2001, Nov. 2000); 'Construction Delay Claims' (May 2005, June 2004, Aug. 2002, Sept. 2000); Construction Law, Associated General Contractor Superintendent Certification (1999).

MUENCH, John E
Mayer, Brown, Rowe & Maw LLP, Chicago 312 701 7059
jmuench@mayerbrown.com
Recommended in Telecom, Broadcast & Satellite
Practice Areas: General and appellate litigation specializing in telecommunications, constitutional law, civil procedure, antitrust, and tort law.
Prof. Memberships: Admitted in Illinois, 1976. US District Court for the Northern District of Illinois, 1976; US Supreme Court, US Courts of Appeals for the Fourth, Fifth, Sixth, Seventh, Ninth, Eleventh, and District of Columbia Circuits.
Career: Joined Mayer, Brown, Rowe & Maw LLP, 1983; became Partner, 1985. Assistant Professor of Law, University of Illinois College of Law, Champaign, 1978-83. Law Clerk to The Honorable John Paul Stevens, Associate Justice, Supreme Court of the United States, Washington, DC, 1977-78. Law Clerk to The Honorable Robert A Sprecher, US Court of Appeals for the Seventh Circuit, 1976-77.
Personal: Born 21 July 1948. Northwestern University School of law, JD, magna cum laude, 1976; Order of the Coif; editor-in-chief, 'Northwestern Law Review'. College of the Holy Cross, AB, magna cum laude, 1970.

MULANEY Jr, Charles W
Skadden, Arps, Slate, Meagher & Flom LLP & Affiliates, Chicago
312 407 0500
cmulaney@skadden.com
Recommended in Corporate/M&A
Practice Areas: Concentrates on mergers and acquisitions (both friendly and hostile), joint ventures, divestitures and spin-offs, corporate financings, restructurings and general corporate governance. Counsels on a range of securities,

corporate and business related matters, including disclosure issues, directors' quote duties and responsibilities, corporate governance and internal investigations.
Prof. Memberships: Lecturer, Corporate Counsel Institute sponsored by Northwestern University School of Law. Member, executive committee, Ray Garrett, Jr. Corporate and Securities Law Institute.
Career: JD, Yale Law School, 1974 (Editor, Yale Law Journal); AB, Georgetown University, 1971 (summa cum laude).

MUNCY, Dennis
Meyer Capel, PC, Champaign
217 352 1800
Recommended in Telecom, Broadcast & Satellite

MUNITZ, Gerald
Goldberg, Kohn, Bell, Black, Rosenbloom & Moritz, Ltd, Chicago
312 201 4000
Recommended in Bankruptcy

MURDOCK Jr, Grady
Morgan, Lewis & Bockius LLP, Chicago
312 324 1105
gmurdock@morganlewis.com
Recommended in Employment
Practice Areas: Grady B Murdock, Jr is a Partner in the Labor and Employment Law Practice with over 30 years of experience. His practice focuses on management representation in nationwide and other class actions, collective actions, pattern and practice actions and individual actions from various federal and state employment laws. Mr Murdock practices traditional labor law leading numerous labor arbitrations. Mr Murdock formerly served as chief labor counsel for a large fast food chain.
Prof. Memberships: National Bar Association, American Bar Association, National Employment Law Council, EEOC Liaison Committee - Chicago Bar Association, Federal Bar Association, American Employment Law Council.

MURPHY, Joseph
Meyer Capel, PC, Champaign
217 352 1800
Recommended in Telecom, Broadcast & Satellite

MURRAY, Gregory
Winston & Strawn LLP, Chicago
312 558 5669
gmurray@winston.com
Recommended in Banking & Finance
Practice Areas: Partner in the Corporate Department. Concentration in syndicated leveraged finance representing numerous prominent US and foreign lending institutions in a variety of senior and subordinated credit facilities, cross-border facilities and structured finance transactions. Extensive experience in structuring multi-tiered acquisition and tender facilities. In recent years has represented agent bank in financings aggregating in excess of US$50 billion.

Career: Joined Winston & Strawn as an associate in 1974. Elected as Partner in 1980.

MURTAUGH, Christopher D
Winston & Strawn LLP, Chicago
312 558 5798
cmurtaugh@winston.com
Recommended in Real Estate
Practice Areas: Chairman of Real Estate Department. More than 30 years' experience focusing on commercial property acquisition and disposition, real estate development, and lending activities.
Prof. Memberships: Member of the American College of Real Estate Lawyers, Order of the Coif, Chicago, Illinois, Florida, and American Bar Associations. Member of the International Council of Shopping Centers.
Career: Joined as associate, 1974. Partner, 1979. Member of the Partner Compensation Committee, Insurance Committee, and the Billing and Collections Committee.
Personal: University of Illinois, 1967. JD, University of Illinois College of Law, 1970.

MUTCHNIK, James
Kirkland & Ellis LLP, Chicago
312 861 2350
jmutchnik@kirkland.com
Recommended in Antitrust
Practice Areas: Represents corporate and individual clients in antitrust, white collar crime, commercial, bankruptcy, and patent litigation in federal and state courts throughout the United States and before a variety of federal and state investigative agencies. In the antitrust area, litigates various matters, from alleged price fixing to price discrimination, and representing clients in dealing with the antitrust aspects of mergers, acquisitions and joint ventures. Counsels a wide range of small and large companies in diverse industries on pricing, marketing, distribution and dealer termination issues.
Personal: University of Pennsylvania, BS, May 1986. Northwestern University School of Law, JD, May 1989.

NAGELBERG, Howard
Barack Ferrazzano Kirschbaum Perlman & Nagelberg, Chicago
312 984 3100
Recommended in Real Estate

NAPOLITANO, Steven
Katten Muchin Zavis Rosenman, Chicago 312 902 5615
steven.napolitano@kmzr.com
Recommended in Corporate/M&A, Private Equity
Practice Areas: Partner and Co-Chair of Private Equity and Emerging Growth Companies Practice. National practice focused on representing private equity funds and emerging growth companies in connection with mergers, acquisitions, leveraged buyouts, venture capital

financings, industry consolidations and corporate restructurings. Substantial experience with private equity transactions involving both private and public targets, including complex management sponsored 'going private' transactions and PIPE financings. Frequently represents equity funds, emerging-growth companies and senior management teams in connection with complex incentive compensation arrangements. Significant experience with private equity, M&A and venture capital transactions in the healthcare sector.

Prof. Memberships: American Bar Association, Association for Corporate Growth and The Executives' Club of Chicago, where he serves as a Member of the Technology Committee. Serves on the Board of Directors of NovaMed Eyecare, Inc. (Nasdaq: NOVA) and is a Member of the Limited Partner Advisory Board of Psilos Group Partners, II, a New York-based venture capital fund specializing in healthcare and new media investing. Serves on the Boards of Directors of the Malignant Hyperthermia Association of the United States (MHAUS) and United Cerebral Palsy of Chicago.

Career: Member of the KMZ Rosenman Board of Directors, Executive and Operating Committee, and Strategic Marketing Committee.

Personal: Received BA degree in Economics from the University of Notre Dame in 1981, where he was elected to the Omicron Epsilon Delta national economics society, and completed graduate work in Monetary Theory at the London School of Economics. He earned his JD degree from the Boston University School of Law in 1985, where he was a G Joseph Tauro Scholar, American Jurisprudence Award recipient and an editor of the 'American Journal of Law and Medicine'.

NEWMAN, Margery
Ogletree, Deakins, Nash, Smoak & Stewart, PC, Chicago 312 558 1258
margery.newman@ogletreedeakins.com
Recommended in Construction

Practice Areas: Construction law, business litigation.

Prof. Memberships: Chicago Bar Association, Illinois State Bar Association, American Bar Association (Forum on Construction), Women Construction Owners & Executives.

Career: Admitted to practice in Illinois, Northern District of Illinois, US Court of Appeals (Seventh Circuit). Served as corporate counsel to the Federation of Women Contractors. Chairperson of Chicago Bar Association Subcommittee on Mechanics Liens. Professional Councils (ASA, LCCA, UCA).

Publications: Has lectured and written extensively on mechanic's liens and construction disputes.

Personal: Brooklyn College (BA, 1969), Roosevelt University (MA, 1973), John

Marshall Law School (JD with high distinction, 1983).

NICKLIN, Emily
Kirkland & Ellis LLP, Chicago
312 861 2387
enicklin@kirkland.com
Recommended in Litigation

Practice Areas: Has been lead trial counsel in cases (both individual and class action) in a number of areas including: professional liability for accountants and consultants, securities, contract, tort (including product liability and personal injury), employment discrimination, constitutional law and municipal law. Has been lead trial counsel in both jury and bench trials, as well as arbitrations, in various state and federal venues including Arkansas, California, Idaho, Illinois, Iowa, Michigan, Missouri, Nebraska, Nevada, New York, Pennsylvania, Texas, and Washington, DC.

Personal: University of Chicago, BA, 1975. University of Chicago, JD, 1977.

NIJMAN, Jennifer
Winston & Strawn LLP, Chicago
312 558 5771
jnijman@winston.com
Recommended in Environment

Practice Areas: Enforcement, including toxic tort, private cost recovery, and Superfund; permitting and siting, compliance issues, and transactions.

Prof. Memberships: President, Chicago Bar Association (2002-03); American Bar Association; Illinois State Bar Association; Public Interest Law Initiative (Board), Center for Conflict Resolution (Board President).

Career: Joined 1994; Practice Group Chair; Diversity Committee; Hiring Committee.

Publications: 'Environmental Law', Illinois Institute of Continuing Legal Education, April 2005; 'Coordination of a Large Environmental Permitting Effort', Natural Resources & Environment, Spring 2001 (winner of 2002 Burton Award).

Personal: University of Illinois, 1984; University of Chicago Law School, JD, 1987, The Legal Forum.

NIRO, Raymond
Niro, Scavone, Haller & Niro, Chicago
312 236 0733
Recommended in Intellectual Property

NOELL Jr, John W
Mayer, Brown, Rowe & Maw LLP, Chicago 312 701 7179
jnoell@mayerbrownrowe.com
Recommended in Private Equity

Practice Areas: Works with issuers that sponsor real estate and other types of investment funds for tax-exempt institutional investors. Active joint venture practice, representing buyers and sellers of professional service companies, investment management firms and other companies. Experienced in initial public offerings and debt and common

stock offerings.

Career: Joined Mayer, Brown, Rowe & Maw LLP, Chicago, 1985-90; 1997 to date; Partner, 1997. General Counsel, JMB Institutional Realty Corporation, 1990-94. Heitman Capital Management Corporation, 1994-97.

Publications: Contributing author: 'Mineral Law: Illinois and Federal Securities Regulation', I.I.C.L.E., 1986.

Personal: Loyola University of Chicago, JD cum laude, 1985; editor-in-chief, 'Law Journal'. University of Notre Dame, BBA cum laude, 1978.

NOVAK, Theodore
DLA Piper Rudnick Gray Cary US LLP, Chicago 312 368 4037
theodore.novak@dlapiper.com
Recommended in Real Estate

Practice Areas: Real estate; governmental affairs, zoning, land use, public incentives and eminent domain.

Prof. Memberships: Member, American College of Real Estate Lawyers (ACREL).

Career: He has been instrumental in the acquisition, disposition, public financing, condemnation, rezoning and development of all types of property. He has extensive litigation experience in trial and appellate courts. He is a lecturer at the University of Chicago Law School and is an Adjunct Professor at Northwestern University School of Law, teaching a course on land use, zoning and condemnation.

Personal: JD, Chicago-Kent College of Law, Illinois Institute of Technology; BS, University of Illinois.

NYHAN, Lawrence
Sidley Austin Brown & Wood LLP, Chicago 312 858 7710
lnyhan@sidley.com
Recommended in Bankruptcy

Practice Areas: Larry Nyhan is Co-Chair of the firm's Corporate Reorganization and Bankruptcy Group and member of the firm's Executive Committee. Representative (public) engagements include: AmeriServe Food Distribution, Inc. (Chapter 11; client, Tricon Global Restaurants, Inc.); Bethlehem Steel Company (Chapter 11; client, postpetition senior lender syndicate); Boston Chicken, Inc. (Chapter 11; client, senior debt syndicate); Budget Group, Inc. (Budget Rent-A-Car) (Chapter 11 and UK Administration; client, debtors and administrator); Columbia Gas Transmission Corporation (Chapter 11; client, unsecured creditors' committee); Devon Convenience Stores, Inc. (Chapter 11; client, debtors); Dow Corning Corporation (Chapter 11; client, Baxter International Inc.); Einstein/Noah Bagel Corp. (Chapter 11; client, senior debt syndicate); Fairchild Aircraft Corporation (Chapter 11; client, senior debt syndicate); Federal Mogul Corporation (Chapter 11 and UK administrations; client, debtors and administrators);

London Fog Industries, Inc. (Chapter 11; client, debtors); Lone Star Steel Company (Chapter 11; client, Lone Star Technologies, Parent); Outboard Marine Corporation (Chapter 11; client, senior debt syndicate); Zenith Electronics, Inc. (pre-packaged Chapter 11; client, Special Committee of Independent Directors).

Career: Extern to The Honorable Robert Eisen, United States Bankruptcy Judge, Northern District of Illinois, 1979-80. Loyola University Chicago School of Law (JD, 1980) University of Chicago (BA, 1977) Bar Admission: Illinois, 1980.

O'BRIEN, Richard
Sidley Austin Brown & Wood LLP, Chicago 312 853 7283
robrien@sidley.com
Recommended in Media & Entertainment

Practice Areas: Richard J O'Brien has a diverse intellectual property and media law practice. Mr O'Brien has handled matters involving copyright, trademark, misappropriation of ideas, false advertising, defamation, invasion of privacy, and trade secrets. Mr O'Brien has been lead trial lawyer for cases in federal and state courts in Chicago and around the country. Many of his cases have involved injunction or other emergency proceedings.

Career: Georgetown University Law Center JD, 1979; St. Louis University BA, 1976; Bar Admission: Illinois, 1979.

O'CONNOR, Karen
DLA Piper Rudnick Gray Cary US LLP, Chicago 312 368 3434
karen.o'connor@dlapiper.com
Recommended in Technology

Practice Areas: Information technology; outsourcing; mergers and acquisitions.

Career: She represents organizations in a variety of industries in large, complex technology-related transactions, including deals involving domestic and off-shore business process and information technology outsourcing, strategic partnering relationships, software licensing and support, software development and equipment acquisitions. She is a frequent speaker and author on technology-related topics.

Personal: JD, Northwestern University; BB, Western Illinois University.

ODORIZZI, Michele
Mayer, Brown, Rowe & Maw LLP, Chicago 312 782 0600
Recommended in Litigation

OLIAN, Robert
Sidley Austin Brown & Wood LLP, Chicago 312 853 7208
rolian@sidley.com
Recommended in Environment

Practice Areas: Robert M Olian is the Co-Head of the firm's national Environmental Practice. Mr Olian works pri-

marily on contested matters involving compliance and civil or criminal enforcement proceedings. He has experience in managing complex legal projects, including environmental impact statement proceedings and the siting of new waste disposal facilities. He served as the Steering Committee Chair for over 300 PRPs at the Fisher Calo site through the signing of a judicial consent decree and as a member of a committee completing the transfer of the remaining remediation at the site. He is now serving as one of three trustees monitoring the consultants' implementation of the cleanup. He has represented: a refinery in federal class action and state court jury trial alleging property value diminution resulting from underground contaminant migration; a waste disposal company in class action jury trial alleging health impacts (including cancer), fear of cancer, and property value diminution (settlement prior to verdict being rendered); an electric utility in connection with an attempt to impose successor liability for the cleanup of a manufactured gas plant, which resulted in verdict of no liability for our client; a major waste disposal company in connection with a criminal investigation of the company's recycled drum transportation procedures, the case was dropped by the US Attorney's office without an indictment being handed up.
Career: Harvard Law School, JD, 1977; Harvard University, MPP, 1977; Harvard University, AB, 1973. Bar Admission: Illinois, 1997.

OLSON, Camille
Seyfarth Shaw LLP, Chicago
312 346 8000
Recommended in Employment

O'REILLY, Peter
Lea + O'Reilly, Chicago
312 755 9127
Recommended in Media & Entertainment

OSBORNE, Robert Stephen
Jenner & Block LLP, Chicago
312 923 2690
rosborne@jenner.com
Recommended in Corporate/M&A
Practice Areas: Robert S Osborne is a partner in Jenner & Block's Chicago office. He is Chair of the Corporate Department and a member of the firm's Management Committee. Mr Osborne has a broad-based practice encompassing most of the department's practice groups, with a particular focus on representing public companies in M&A and securities transactions as well as counseling clients on corporate governance and disclosure matters. Mr Osborne has represented General Motors in many strategic transactions, including the disposition of Hughes Electronics (DirecTV) in 2003, previous spin-offs of EDS, Hughes Defense and Delphi Automotive Systems, and the sale of National

Car Rental and other operating units. He has also represented General Motors in public offerings of common stock, straight and convertible preferred stock, and straight and convertible debt securities that in each case were among the largest securities transactions of their kind. Mr Osborne has represented an investment management subsidiary of GM in a variety of private equity transactions involving fund participations and direct investments. Mr Osborne served in an outside capacity as General Counsel of Lands' End from its initial public offering in 1986 until 1995, and continued to serve as special counsel to its Board of Directors through the sale of the company to Sears in 2002. He has also represented numerous other public companies in M&A and securities matters, and has frequently represented committees of independent directors, including audit, compensation, special investigative, litigation and going private committees.
Personal: Harvard Law School, JD, 1979, magna cum laude.

PANAGAKIS, George N
Skadden, Arps, Slate, Meagher & Flom LLP & Affiliates, Chicago
312 407 0638
gpanagak@skadden.com
Recommended in Bankruptcy
Practice Areas: Represents clients in complex business reorganizations, debt restructurings and insolvency matters. Advises debtors, creditors, investors, sellers, purchasers and other parties in all stages of restructuring transactions, from Chapter 11 reorganizations to out-of-court negotiations, workouts and divestitures.
Career: JD, Northwestern University School of Law, 1990; BA, Northwestern University, 1987.

PARSONS, David
Littler Mendelson, Chicago
312 372 5520
Recommended in Employment

PASTROFF, Sanford
Sonnenschein Nath & Rosenthal LLP, Chicago 312 876 3170
spastroff@sonnenschein.com
Recommended in Antitrust
Practice Areas: Focuses on antitrust and trade regulation counseling and litigation, including class actions. Experience with criminal, government merger and state antitrust and consumer protection authorities' investigations; and foreign antitrust authorities. Antitrust work includes significant healthcare and pharmaceutical industry matters. Commercial litigation includes tort, fraud, securities, real estate, contract and lending.
Prof. Memberships: Member, ABA Section of Antitrust Law; leadership positions included: Chair, Robinson-Patman Act Committee; Vice-Chair, Insurance Industry Committee; Member, Public Service Task Force.

Personal: Northwestern University School of Law, JD, cum laude, Journal of Criminal Law and Criminology, Moot Court Board; University of Michigan, BBA with High Distinction.

PASULKA-BROWN, Kathleen
Foley & Lardner, Chicago
312 832 5164
kpasulka-brown@foley.com
Recommended in Telecom, Broadcast & Satellite
Career: Kathleen Pasulka-Brown, a partner Foley & Lardner's Chicago office, is a member of the firm's Litigation Department and the Insurance Dispute Resolution and Energy Regulation Practice Groups. Her practice focuses on insurance coverage, telecommunications, and energy, and she is involved in litigation and regulatory proceedings. In the telecommunications area, she has represented both wireline and wireless telecommunications carriers in regulatory proceedings, including the arbitration of an interconnection agreement, an expedited complaint proceeding involving issues of service quality and a rulemaking proceeding also involving service quality issues. Ms Pasulka-Brown is a graduate of Harvard Law School (JD, 1986).

PATTON, Stephen
Kirkland & Ellis LLP, Chicago
312 861 2406
spatton@kirkland.com
Recommended in Litigation
Practice Areas: Mr Patton has practiced with Kirkland & Ellis since 1978 and has been a Partner since 1984. He currently serves as Chairman of Kirkland's firmwide Litigation Management Committee. Mr Patton has extensive trial experience in a wide variety of complex commercial litigation, including contract, antitrust, and product liability cases. In addition to his active trial practice, Mr Patton has served as an advisor to senior management in connection with a number of 'bet the company' exposures.
Personal: Indiana University, BA, 1975; Georgetown University Law Center, JD, 1978.

PECK, S Michael
Schiff Hardin LLP, Chicago
312 258 5811
speck@schiffhardin.com
Recommended in Private Equity
Practice Areas: Private equity and venture capital, corporate and securities.
Career: Mr Peck concentrates in leveraged buyouts and other merger and acquisition transactions, as well as general corporate, investment, and financing matters. He principally represents private equity funds in their merger and acquisition activity, as well as the representation of the portfolio companies they acquire with respect to acquisitions, divestitures, public offerings, restructurings, recapitalizations, and general cor-

porate activities. He has handled transactions in a wide variety of industries.
Personal: University of Chicago (BA, 1969), University of Michigan Law School (JD, cum laude, 1972).

PEREGRINE, Michael W
McDermott Will & Emery, Chicago
312 984 6933
mperegrine@mwe.com
Recommended in Healthcare
Practice Areas: Represents nonprofit healthcare facilities and systems and other charitable organizations, with focus on corporate, fiduciary duty, tax and charitable trust issues facing such organizations. Experience includes representation of nonprofits in connection with the organization and operation of healthcare systems, including related governance issues and parent/subsidiary relationships. Has experience with complex business transactions such as mergers, consolidations and acquisitions and corporate and charitable trust law issues associated therewith.
Publications: Frequent author and speaker on legal topics affecting tax exempt, nonprofit corporations. Faculty member of The Governance Institute. Member of editorial boards of BNA's Health Law Reporter and Exempt Organization Tax Review. Has authored over 100 articles on healthcare, tax exempt organization and governance. Most recently co-authored the educational pamphlets, 'An Integrated Approach to Corporate Compliance: A Resource for Health Care Boards of Directors and Corporate Responsibility' and 'Corporate Compliance: A Resource For Health Care Boards of Directors', published by Office of Inspector General, US Department of Health and Human Services and American Health Lawyers Association.
Personal: Earned JD in 1980 from Northwestern University School of Law, and BA in 1977 from Texas Christian University.

PERELLIS, Andrew
Seyfarth Shaw LLP, Chicago
312 346 8000
Recommended in Environment

PERL, Sanford E
Kirkland & Ellis LLP, Chicago
312 861 2291
sperl@kirkland.com
Recommended in Private Equity
Practice Areas: Mr Perl concentrates his practice in the corporate, securities and tax aspects of complex business transactions, including leveraged buyouts of public and private companies; strategic mergers, acquisitions, investments and joint ventures; venture capital, consolidation, and minority equity investments; divestitures; initial public offerings; private equity fund formations; executive compensation; and debt and equity restructurings and workouts. Mr Perl has led transactions in a wide

variety of industries, including healthcare, manufacturing, distribution, internet, biotechnology and media.
Personal: University of Illinois, BS, 1987; University of Michigan Law School, JD, 1990.

PERLMAN, Daniel J
Katten Muchin Zavis Rosenman, Chicago 312 902 5532
daniel.perlman@kmzr.com
Recommended in Real Estate
Practice Areas: Concentrates his practice in real estate, primarily in the area of fund and venture formation, conventional, securitized and mezzanine financing, commercial development and commercial acquisitions and dispositions. Client types include pension funds and their advisors, foreign institutions, national developers and retailers, public and private real estate investment trusts, investment banks, securitized lenders, insurance companies and national banking associations. Mr Perlman has extensive experience in representing sponsors of real estate investment funds and structuring tax efficient investment vehicles and addressing the sponsor's and investors' ERISA concerns. Mr Perlman has been lead counsel on some of the nation's highest profile retail developments. His extensive development experience includes municipal and state incentive financings, joint venture equity investments and construction financings. Mr Perlman also represents several 'Wall Street' securitized lenders and has an in-depth knowledge of the CMBS industry.
Prof. Memberships: Chairman of the American Cancer Society Greater Chicago Downtown Board, Member of the Law Committee of the International Council of Shopping Centers.
Career: Member of the firm's Board of Directors.
Publications: Frequent lecturer and author of articles on issues ranging from REITs' portfolio transactions to joint venture strategies.
Personal: Graduated from the University of Michigan with a Bachelor of Arts degree in Political Science and earned his law degree in 1985 from Northwestern University School of Law.

PERZEK, Philip
Latham & Watkins LLP, Chicago
312 876 7700
Recommended in Banking & Finance

PETERSON, Brad L
Mayer, Brown, Rowe & Maw LLP, Chicago 312 701 8568
bpeterson@mayerbrownrowe.com
Recommended in Business Process Outsourcing: National, Technology
Practice Areas: Outsourcing. Information technology transactions. Joint ventures and strategic alliances. Corporate and securities transactions. E-commerce.
Prof. Memberships: Admitted in Illi-

nois, 1988.
Career: Joined Mayer, Brown, Rowe & Maw LLP, 1995; became Partner, 1998. Formerly at Wildman, Harrold, Allen & Dixon, Chicago, 1992-95; Kirkland & Ellis, Chicago, 1988-92. International Business Machines Corporation, Marketing Representative, Chicago, 1982-85.
Publications: 'The Smart Way to Buy Information Technology: How to Maximize Value and Avoid Costly Pitfalls' (AMACOM Books, New York, 1998, 250 pages). Author of many articles on outsourcing, alliances, and technology transactions.
Personal: Born May 29, 1959. Harvard Law School, JD with honors, 1988; managing editor, 'Harvard Journal of Law and Public Policy'. University of Chicago Graduate School of Business, MBA, cum laude, 1982; Beta Gamma Sigma. Northwestern University, Computer Studies, 1977-80; Phi Beta Kappa.

PETERSON, Ronald R
Jenner & Block LLP, Chicago
312 923 2981
rpeterson@jenner.com
Recommended in Bankruptcy
Practice Areas: Ronald R. Peterson is a Partner in Jenner & Block's Chicago office. He is a member of the firm's Bankruptcy, Workout and Corporate Reorganization, Construction Law, and Defense & Aerospace Practices. Mr Peterson has concentrated his practice in the areas of commercial, insolvency and bankruptcy law, focusing primarily on representing debtors, trustees, creditors' committees, landlords and secured lenders in Chapter 11 cases. Mr Peterson represents the creditors' committees in the bankruptcies of Anicom Inc., Access Air Inc. and Charter Behavioral Health Systems Inc. Mr Peterson was counsel to the creditors' committees in the Chapter 11 cases of Keystone Consolidated, a steel mill and wire plant, Handy Andy Home Centers, a chain of 88 hardware stores, and Payless Cashways Inc., a chain of 100 hardware stores. He was the attorney for the debtor in the bankruptcy cases of Harrah's Jazz Company, The Rath Packing Company and Armstrong's, Inc. In addition to his insolvency litigation practice, Mr Peterson counsels clients on a variety of transactional issues. He represented the commercial paper holders in an out-of-court restructuring of Mercury Finance, a substandard lender of automobile loans, and was involved in the restructuring of the law firms of Keck, Mahin & Cate and Spicer & Oppenheim. Mr Peterson has been a member of the panel of Chapter 7 trustees for the Northern District of Illinois, Eastern Division, since 1987. He presides over approximately 100 consumer bankruptcy cases per month.
Personal: University of Chicago Law School, JD, 1973.

PICKENS, Scott E
Schiff Hardin LLP, Chicago
312 258 5515
spickens@schiffhardin.com
Recommended in Banking & Finance
Practice Areas: Finance, corporate and securities.
Career: Mr Pickens concentrates in the areas of corporate, securities, and commercial law, especially in the representation of creditors in financing transactions. He represents major insurance companies, commercial banks, asset-based lenders, and virtually every other type of participant in the finance markets in a variety of financing transactions and workouts.
Personal: University of Illinois at Urbana-Champaign (BS, 1972), University of Chicago (MBA, 1976), Loyola University Chicago School of Law (JD, cum laude, 1978).

PISKORSKI, Thomas
Seyfarth Shaw LLP, Chicago
312 346 8000
Recommended in Employment

POHL, Timothy R
Skadden, Arps, Slate, Meagher & Flom LLP & Affiliates, Chicago
312 407 0772
tpohl@skadden.com
Recommended in Bankruptcy
Practice Areas: Represents a variety of clients in complex business reorganizations, debt restructurings and distressed mergers and acquisitions. Advises companies in both Chapter 11 and out-of-court restructurings. Also advises lenders to, creditors of and purchasers of or investors in distressed companies.
Career: JD, University of Chicago, 1991; BA, Amherst College, 1988 (magna cum laude).

POMERANTZ, Harold B
DLA Piper Rudnick Gray Cary US LLP, Chicago 312 368 4036
Harold.pomerantz@dlapiper.com
Recommended in Real Estate
Practice Areas: Real estate.
Prof. Memberships: Active Member of the International Council of Shopping Centers.
Career: Concentrates his practice in the area of complex commercial real estate transactions, including acquisitions and dispositions of various types of real estate assets; commercial financing; syndications; partnership and joint ventures; development, operations and management; and commercial leasing transactions. He lectures frequently on commercial real estate issues to both bar associations and real estate industry trade groups.
Personal: JD, Washington University, MBA, Washington University, BA, Washington University.

POPE, Michael
McDermott Will & Emery, Chicago
312 984 7780
mpope@mwe.com
Recommended in Litigation
Practice Areas: Partner in the Trial Department and heads international Product Liability Practice, including complex class action lawsuits. Currently represents the nation's largest automobile insurer in two national class actions challenging the company's claims policies and 17 Blue Cross/Blue Shield plans on the HMO litigation. Has extensive experience handling reinsurance disputes, in the interpretation of excess and umbrella liability insurance policies, and in professional liability and complex business litigation. Active in ADR, both as an advocate and as an arbitrator.
Prof. Memberships: Seventh Circuit Bar Association (President 2003-04), past Chair of the National Judicial College and of the Illinois Equal Justice Foundation. Past president of the International Association of Defense Counsel, Lawyers for Civil Justice and the American Board of Professional Liability Attorneys. Fellow, American College of Trial Lawyers, International Society of Barristers and the International Academy of Trial Lawyers (Board of Directors, 2000-03). Member, American Law Institute; Member, Chicago Bar Association (Board of Managers, 1987-90), Illinois State Bar Association (Chair, Special Committee on Discovery Reform, 1994-95), American Bar Association, Defense Research Institute; and Product Liability Advisory Council.
Personal: Received BS from Loyola University of Chicago and JD from Northwestern University School of Law, cum laude.

POWERS, John
Seyfarth Shaw LLP, Chicago
312 346 8000
Recommended in Employment

PRILLAMAN, Fred
Mohan, Alewelt, Prillaman & Adami, Springfield 217 528 2517
Recommended in Environment

PRITIKIN, David T
Sidley Austin Brown & Wood LLP, Chicago 312 853 7359
dpritikin@sidley.com
Recommended in Intellectual Property
Practice Areas: David Pritikin chairs the firm's national Intellectual Property Practice and has an active trial practice concentrated in that field. Mr Pritikin has represented companies in major patent cases in a range of industries. He has handled cases in the federal district courts and in the International Trade Commission as well as appeals before the Court of Appeals for the Federal Circuit. Mr Pritikin also maintains a civil litigation practice involving antitrust and other commercial cases. He has served as lead counsel in a number of

high profile cases tried before judges and juries. In 2004, Mr Pritikin was inducted into the American College of Trial Lawyers. He is a member of the firm's Executive Committee.
Career: Harvard Law School (JD, 1974) Cornell University (AB, 1971).

QASIM, Imad
Sidley Austin Brown & Wood LLP, Chicago 312 853 7094
iqasim@sidley.com
Recommended in Corporate/M&A
Practice Areas: Imad Qasim focuses on mergers and acquisitions, corporate finance, corporate governance, securities law compliance, public and private securities offerings including high yield, joint ventures and cross-border transactions. He played a major role in a number of public company mergers, including the acquisition of True North Communications by Interpublic Group, Tellabs's proposed merger with CIENA Corporation, Tellabs' acquisition of Advanced Fibre Communications, Quality Food Centers' acquisition by Fred Meyer, Mark Twain Bancshares' acquisition by Mercantile Bancorporation, Kimberly Clark's acquisition of Tecnol Medical Products, Jacor Communications' acquisition by Clear Channel Communications, Concord EFS's acquisitions of Star Systems and Electronic Payment Services, and the acquisition of The Cherry Corporation by the Cherry family. He represented Concord EFS, Inc. in two public offerings in excess of one billion dollars in proceeds. He represents private equity and strategic investors, advises public companies and their Boards of Directors on corporate governance matters.
Prof. Memberships: Member of the securities law section of American Bar Association.
Career: Georgetown University, JD, 1982; Hamilton College, AB, 1979. Bar Admissions: Illinois, 1987; New York, 1983.

RADEMAKER, Randall J
Skadden, Arps, Slate, Meagher & Flom LLP & Affiliates, Chicago
312 407 0930
rrademak@skadden.com
Recommended in Banking & Finance
Practice Areas: Concentrates in banking and financing transactions, including asset-backed financings and asset-securitization transactions, acquisition financings, structured products, financial restructurings and debtor-in-possession financings. Active in acquisition financings involving cross-border and multi-currency borrowings. In 2005, represented equity sponsor group in connection with the US$4 billion financing for the acquisition of MGM. Led the financial restructuring of many companies on both the lender and the borrower side.
Career: JD, University of Chicago, 1982;

BA, Knox College, 1979 (summa cum laude).

RANDALL, Benjamin
Randall & Kenig LLP, Chicago
312 845 2510
Recommended in Real Estate

RAY, Stephen
Stein, Ray & Harris LLP, Chicago
312 641 3700
Recommended in Construction

READ, Sarah
Sidley Austin Brown & Wood LLP, Chicago 312 853 2171
sread@Sidley.com
Recommended in Energy
Practice Areas: Sarah J Read works with the firm's Commercial and Regulatory Litigation Practice Group and its Alternative Dispute Resolution resource group. Ms Read has advised electric and telecommunications companies on a wide variety of regulatory, legislative and strategic planning issues. Ms Read has tried cases before the Illinois, Missouri, Nevada and Ohio public utility commissions and argued appeals in the Illinois State courts. Ms Read also advises clients on a variety of ADR issues.
Career: University of Wisconsin Law School, JD, 1981; Yale University, BA, 1978. Bar Admission: Missouri, 1999.

REIDY, Daniel
Jones Day, Chicago
312 269 4140
dereidy@jonesday.com
Recommended in Litigation
Practice Areas: Litigation Group coordinator in the Chicago office and Chair of the firm's Corporate Criminal Investigations Practice. Divides his time evenly between civil and criminal litigation. He has extensive trial and appellate experience as lead counsel in civil and criminal matters in state and federal court. He has handled numerous 'high-profile' cases of corruption and was extensively involved in complex financial crime prosecutions. He has taught trial practice and has spoken on criminal defense and civil litigation issues at various seminars.
Prof. Memberships: Fellow, American College of Trial Lawyers and International Academy of Trial Lawyers.

RESNICK, Donald I
Jenner & Block LLP, Chicago
312 923 2656
dresnick@jenner.com
Recommended in Real Estate
Practice Areas: Donald I Resnick is a Partner in Jenner & Block's Chicago office. He is Chair of the firm's Real Estate Practice and a member of the firm's Management Committee. Mr Resnick's practice focuses on commercial real estate with significant experience in real estate transactions, financing, development and construction and corporate real estate services. His practice also encompasses real estate related

loan and equity restructuring and workouts and the hospitality, gaming and entertainment industry. Mr Resnick represents clients in connection with all types of real estate transactions, including acquisitions and dispositions, leasing, joint ventures and like-kind exchanges involving office buildings, multi-family apartment projects, retail projects, hotels and industrial facilities. He counsels clients on all facets of real estate transactions, including contract and financing issues, due diligence, lease negotiations, operational and management issues, ownership and equity structures and tax issues. Mr Resnick also represents national banks, REITs and other institutions in connection with all aspects of real estate financing, including both secured and unsecured credit facilities and construction and permanent financing. He also has significant expertise in Tax Increment Financing (TIF) and in advising clients with respect to tax exempt bond financing. Mr Resnick counsels both lenders and borrowers in connection with all aspects and types of real estate and commercial credit facilities including mezzanine loans, participating and other joint venture structured facilities, credit enhancement, revolving lines of credit, loans collateralized by TIF proceeds, securitized lending facilities and multi-lender credit facilities.
Personal: Harvard Law School, JD, 1975.

RILEY Jr, James
McGuireWoods LLP, Chicago
312 849 8100
Recommended in Healthcare

RIPPIE, E Glenn
Foley & Lardner, Chicago
312 832 4910
grippie@foley.com
Recommended in Energy
Career: E Glenn Rippie is a Chicago-based Partner in Foley & Lardner's Regulatory Department and Energy Regulation Practice Group. He advises clients on gas and electric issues and represents industry clients before regulatory agencies including state public utility commissions and the Federal Energy Regulatory Commission, and state and federal courts. He has served as counsel to Illinois' largest energy utility in open access and its first two general unbundled rate proceedings. Mr Rippie's practice focuses on complex strategic, restructuring, operations, and rate matters, and includes both counseling and litigation.

ROACH Jr, William H
McDermott Will & Emery, Chicago
312 984 6941
wroach@mwe.com
Recommended in Healthcare
Practice Areas: Experience includes the formation of regional and national hospital systems, mergers, acquisitions, affiliations and dispositions of health-

care facilities and systems, joint sponsorship of faith-based healthcare facilities and systems, corporate reorganizations, hospital/physician integration arrangements, health industry joint ventures, creation and implementation of corporate compliance plans, focused compliance reviews, tax-exempt organizations, health information privacy and regulation, and medical staff organization, credentialing and contracts. Has represented institutions of higher education in matters relating to governance, student records, joint ventures and faculty organization.
Prof. Memberships: Former President and Founding Director of Illinois Association of Hospital Attorneys and Member of American Health Lawyers Association, and Illinois, Chicago and American Bar Associations.
Career: Before joining McDermott, was a Partner of a major national law firm for 24 years. Prior to his work there, was senior staff counsel at Michael Reese Hospital and Medical Center for two years and vice president for legal affairs at Rush University Medical Center for four years, both large teaching institutions in Chicago.
Personal: Earned JD in 1972 from Vanderbilt University; MS in 1974 from University of Pittsburgh; and BA in 1966 from Columbia University. Licensed as an Illinois Emergency Medical Technician (2002).

ROBERTS, Kenneth M
Schiff Hardin LLP, Chicago
312 258 5704
kroberts@schiffhardin.com
Recommended in Construction
Practice Areas: Construction.
Prof. Memberships: Society of Illinois Construction Attorneys, Society of American Military Engineers, American Bar Association.
Career: Mr Roberts represents owners and contractors in complex multi-project delay claims/loss of efficiency claims; breach of contract claims involving performance and payment clauses; as well as numerous arbitrations involving construction disputes. He works extensively with forensic engineers in determining the causes of structural failures, and he prepares and reviews contracts on behalf of owners, design professionals, and contractors.
Personal: University of Iowa (BGS, with honors, 1982), University of Iowa (JD, with distinction, 1985).

ROBERTSON, Eric
Lueders, Robertson & Konzen, Granite City 618 876 8500
Recommended in Energy

ROBERTSON, Robert
Kirkland & Ellis LLP, Chicago
312 861 2225
rrobertson@kirkland.com
Recommended in Antitrust
Practice Areas: Mr Robertson is a liti-

gation Partner with over 20 commercial or antitrust trials before federal and state courts, administrative agencies, and arbitration panels. From July 2002 through January 2004, Mr Robertson served as the Senior Litigation Counsel for the Bureau of Competition at the Federal Trade Commission in Washington, DC.

Personal: Virginia Military Institute, BA, 1977. University of Chicago Law School, JD, 1990.

ROCAP, Donald
Kirkland & Ellis LLP, Chicago
312 861 2266
drocap@kirkland.com
Recommended in Tax

Practice Areas: His practice focuses on the tax aspects of complex business transactions, including mergers, acquisitions, leveraged buyouts, formation of private equity funds, and debt and equity restructurings and workouts. Is a lecturer at the University of Chicago Law School and is a Volume co-author of 'Mergers, Acquisitions, and Buyouts,' by Martin Ginsburg and Jack Levin, and a Special Editor of 'Structuring Venture Capital, Private Equity, and Entrepreneurial Transactions,' by Jack Levin.

Personal: Duke University, BA, 1977. University of Virginia School of Law, JD, 1980.

ROGERS III, John L
Foley & Lardner, Chicago
312 832 4915
jrogers@foley.com
Recommended in Energy

Career: John L Rogers is a Partner with Foley & Lardner, where he is a member of the Energy Regulation and Securities Litigation, Enforcement and Regulatory Practice Groups. He focuses on representation of clients in SEC enforcement proceedings, as well as clients in the fields of energy and financial services. In his energy practice, Mr Rogers has represented a major Illinois electric utility in a wide variety of matters, including proceedings to recover the costs of decommissioning nuclear power plants; to defend the prudence of nuclear operations; and to establish delivery service charges for commercial and industrial customers.

ROKOSZ, Ronald
Chapman and Cutler LLP, Chicago
312 845 3827
rokosz@chapman.com
Recommended in Banking & Finance

Practice Areas: Senior Partner, Banking Department. Syndicated lending, highly-leveraged transactions, asset securitizations, US Eximbank financings and other cross-border political-risk insurance transactions, trade finance, synthetic lease, aircraft finance and gold consignment financing.

Prof. Memberships: Illinois Bar Association. Member of Illinois Bar and US Federal District Bar of Northern Illinois.

Career: Joined Chapman and Cutler in 1969, became Partner in 1977. Graduate of Northwestern University Law School, Order of Coif, Law Review 1969, Loyola University of Chicago BS 1966 magna cum laude; Member, firm Practicing Standards Committee.

Personal: Born 1944. Well-travelled - Holland and Japan. Plays jazz guitar. Married to Kathleen who works with the deaf community. Has one son, Christopher. Lives in Barrington, Illinois.

ROONEY, John E
Sonnenschein Nath & Rosenthal LLP, Chicago 312 876 8925
jrooney@sonnenschein.com
Recommended in Energy, Telecom, Broadcast & Satellite

Practice Areas: Mr Rooney is a Partner in the Energy and Telecommunications Practice. He works on regulatory and related legislative issues. He has successfully represented clients involved in litigation before the Illinois Commerce Commission on complex issues, including rate cases, regulatory rulemakings and matters concerning competitive marketplace development for energy and telecommunications service providers. He has worked on governance and electric regional reliability council oversight matters and the acquisition and sale of electric generating and transmission assets.

Prof. Memberships: Chicago Bar Association; past Chairman, Public Utilities Law Committee.

Personal: The John Marshall Law School, JD, 'Law Review'; Loyola University, BBA.

ROPER, Harry J
Jenner & Block LLP, Chicago
312 923 8303
hroper@jenner.com
Recommended in Intellectual Property

Practice Areas: Harry J Roper is a Partner in Jenner & Block's Chicago office. He is Chair of the firm's Intellectual Property Practice. Mr Roper is nationally recognized as one of the foremost trial lawyers in the intellectual property field and has extensive trial experience with complex patent litigation cases. Mr Roper has tried numerous patent infringement jury trials on behalf of national and international companies, including The Dow Chemical Company, Johnson & Johnson, Medtronic and Phillips Petroleum Company. He was recently lead trial counsel for Union Carbide Corporation in a patent infringement case in which Union Carbide obtained $152 million jury verdict against Shell Oil Company. Mr Roper has also represented clients in substantial computer-related litigation such as in the field of word processing software used by Microsoft Word and other leading manufacturers. He has also tried a wide variety of cases involving biotech-

nology, medical devices, intraocular lenses and pharmaceuticals. In 2002, he defended a major anti-cancer drug developed by Johnson & Johnson's biotechnology subsidiary, Alza, against a charge of infringement. Mr Roper has written and lectured extensively concerning patent infringement, trade secrets and antitrust litigation matters. He is a member of the American Bar Association; American Intellectual Property Law Association; Federal Circuit Bar Association and its Committee on Jury Instructions; Seventh Circuit Bar Association; Intellectual Property Law Association of Chicago; Chicago Bar Association; Chicago Council of Lawyers; and Barristers of the Patent Law.

Personal: New York University School of Law, LLB, 1966.

ROPSKI, Gary
Brinks Hofer Gilson & Lione, Chicago
312 321 4216
gropski@usebrinks.com
Recommended in Intellectual Property

Practice Areas: Gary Ropski's practice includes litigation in patents, trademarks, trade dress, copyright, trade secrets, right of publicity, and related unfair competition and antitrust matters in federal and state courts.

Prof. Memberships: AIPLA; International (Chair, Patent Subcommittee 1993-96), American, and Chicago Bar Associations; INTA; IPO; LES; IPLAC (Chair, Antitrust Committee 1995-97). Adjunct Professor, Northwestern University School of Law (1981-97).

Publications: Editor, Butterworths 'Patent Litigation: Enforcing A Global Patent Portfolio'.

Personal: Education: BS, Physics, Carnegie-Mellon University (1972); JD (cum laude), Northwestern University School of Law (1976); Executive Editor, 'Journal of Criminal Law & Criminology' (1975-76).

ROSENBAUM, Michael D
Gardner Carton & Douglas LLP, Chicago 312 569 1308
mrosenbaum@gcd.com
Recommended in Employee Benefits

Practice Areas: Partner, Chairman, HR Law Department; practice includes employee benefit, executive/physician compensation matters; extensive experience: designing, implementing tax-qualified retirement plans; designing, implementing, funding executive compensation plans; addressing health and welfare plan design, compliance, operational issues; advising on workers' classification; advising on employee benefit arrangements for executives, physicians of tax-exempt organizations.

Career: Mr Rosenbaum has been with Gardner Carton & Douglas since 1987, is Chairman of the firm's HR Law Department (which includes the Employee Benefit Practice) and is a

member of the firm's Operating Committee.

Publications: Co-author, Employee Benefit Plan Review Journal's Regulatory Update column; articles published in Journal of Accountancy, Employment Relations Today, Medical Practice Management Journal, CCH Tax Transactions healthcare industry book, Callaghan's legal checklist, Illinois Institute for Continuing Legal Education manual. Frequent speaker on employee benefits, executive/physician compensation issues to national conferences of such organizations as Profit-Sharing Council of America, Enrolled Actuaries, American Institute of Certified Public Accountants, American Bar Association, American Medical Association, Chicago Bar Association, Michigan, Illinois CPA Societies, Strategic Research Institute, Institute for International Research, Employers Summit on Healthcare.

Personal: University of Wisconsin, JD, 1987, cum laude; University of Wisconsin, 1985, CPA Illinois; Michigan State University, BA, 1984.

ROSENBLOOM, David
McDermott Will & Emery, Chicago
312 984 7759
drosenbloom@mwe.com
Recommended in Litigation

Practice Areas: Head of the firm's White-Collar Criminal Defense Practice. Practices white collar criminal defense, qui tam litigation, healthcare fraud and abuse compliance, internal investigations, and class actions and other complex commercial litigation. Has represented numerous corporations and individuals in connection with civil and criminal allegations of fraud or wrongdoing. Has extensive experience in representing healthcare providers and manufacturers. Has represented clients in various industries, including securities, insurance, manufacturing and energy, both in response to specific allegations of misconduct and as part of preventive compliance programs. Has represented clients with respect to foreign and US aspects of criminal investigations.

Prof. Memberships: Member of state bars of Illinois, California and Colorado, as well as various United States District Courts and United States Courts of Appeals.

Career: Prior to joining McDermott, served in the US Attorney's Office for the Northern District of Illinois for eight years. Served as a Law Clerk to Judge William G Young of the US District Court for the District of Massachusetts (1985-86).

Personal: Earned JD (magna cum laude) in 1985 from Harvard Law School, and BA (magna cum laude) in 1982 from Colorado College. Has lectured in trial advocacy at Northwestern Law School and Harvard Law School.

ROSENBLOOM, James
Goldberg, Kohn, Bell, Black, Rosenbloom & Moritz, Ltd, Chicago
312 201 4000
Recommended in Real Estate

ROSENTHAL, Michael D
Sonnenschein Nath & Rosenthal LLP, Chicago 312 876 3180
mrosenthal@sonnenschein.com
Recommended in Private Equity
Practice Areas: Corporate and securities Partner. Represents private equity and venture capital funds, and target companies in investments from seed to late stage and in buy-outs, leveraged recapitalizations and workouts; M&A; joint ventures; securities; general corporate counseling. Represents funds in hedge, venture and private equity fund formation and investment structuring and limited partners in fund investments.
Prof. Memberships: Venture Capital and Private Equity Committee, ABA's Business Section; Planning Committee of Illinois Business & Investor Forum.
Personal: University of Michigan Law School, JD magna cum laude, Law Review, Order of the Coif; Washington University, AB magna cum laude, Phi Beta Kappa.

ROSS, Nancy
McDermott Will & Emery, Chicago
312 984 7743
nross@mwe.com
Recommended in Employee Benefits, Litigation
Practice Areas: Partner in the Litigation Department, practices primarily in the area of employee benefits class action litigation and counseling under the Employee Retirement Income Security Act of 1974 (ERISA). Has extensive experience in counseling and representing employers, plan fiduciaries and trustees concerning pension and welfare benefit plans. Experience includes representation of pension plans, ESOPs, trustees and employers in litigation concerning their administration of plan assets and fiduciary responsibilities. Frequently represents directors and officers who are named as defendants in ERISA litigation over 401(k) plans and other employee benefit plans.
Prof. Memberships: Chair, Fiduciary Responsibility Committee of the ABA Employee Benefits Committee in the ABA's Labor and Employment Section.
Publications: Has published articles on employee benefits litigation, including articles surveying the status of retiree medical litigation nationwide published in 'Employee Relations Law Journal', articles published in the 'Benefits Law Journal' addressing 401(k) litigation in the wake of Enron, employers' fiduciary obligations, articles analyzing significant US Supreme Court decisions in Knudson v Great West Life Annuity Insurance Company and Howe, et al v Varity Cor-

poration.
Personal: Received JD from Loyola University of Chicago School of Law in 1985. Received BA with honors from University of Colorado in 1978.

ROY, Paul JN
Mayer, Brown, Rowe & Maw LLP, Chicago 312 701 7370
proy@mayerbrownrowe.com
Recommended in Business Process Outsourcing: National, Technology
Practice Areas: Partner in Corporate, Information Technology, Telecommunications and Outsourcing Practices. Represents corporate clients in a broad range of information technology, telecommunications and outsourcing transactions, including the outsourcing of data and voice networks, data centers, personal computers, help desks, applications development and maintenance, call centers, finance and accounting functions, logistics, human resources and other business process functions. Representative transactions also include software and systems development and implementation, systems integration, strategic alliances and joint ventures. Clients include domestic and international corporations of various sizes, and in a variety of industries, including chemicals, telecommunications, software and computer equipment manufacturing, pharmaceutical, life sciences, banking and finance, securities trading, insurance, professional associations, auditing, consulting, consumer products, and distribution.
Prof. Memberships: Admitted to practice in Illinois. Member of the American Bar Association.
Career: Joined Mayer, Brown, Rowe Maw LLP, 1985. Formerly with The Associates Commercial Corporation, Chicago, manager - personal computer software development, business systems analyst, 1982-85. Borg Warner Corporation, Automotive Parts Division, warehouse department manager, financial analyst, 1979-82.
Personal: Born 15 April 1955. Loyola University of Chicago, JD, 1985. Northwestern University, MBA, 1982. Colby College, BA, 1978.

RUBIN, James
Butler Rubin Saltarelli & Boyd, Chicago
312 444 9660
Recommended in Insurance

RUBIN, Joel
Seyfarth Shaw LLP, Chicago
312 346 8000
Recommended in Real Estate

RUFF, Randolph E
Ogletree, Deakins, Nash, Smoak & Stewart, PC, Chicago
312 558 1220
randolph.ruff@ogletreedeakins.com
Recommended in Construction
Practice Areas: Litigation, construction law.

Prof. Memberships: Chicago Bar Association, American Bar Association.
Career: Admitted to practice in Illinois, US Court of Appeals (Seventh Circuit), US District Court for the Northern District of Illinois, and Federal Trial Bar.
Personal: University of Colorado (BA, 1981), Valparaiso University (JD, 1986).

RUNNING, Andrew R
Kirkland & Ellis LLP, Chicago
312-861-2412
arunning@kirkland.com
Recommended in Environment
Practice Areas: Extensive experience in bankruptcy, environmental, insurance, toxic tort and general commercial litigation. He has tried numerous environmental lawsuits involving claims of property damage and alleged regulatory violations, as well as litigation over the allocation of responsibility for the cleanup of hazardous waste sites. He has successfully defended product liability actions involving allegations of hazardous substance contamination. His arbitration experience includes the trial of cases involving commercial breach of contract claims, disputes between international joint venture partners, non-compete clause disputes, biotechnology licensing disputes and reinsurance and insurance fraud claims.
Personal: University of Chicago, AB, 1979. Yale University JD, 1982.

RUSSELL, James
Winston & Strawn LLP, Chicago
312 558 6084
jrussell@winston.com
Recommended in Environment
Practice Areas: Environmental law and environmental litigation: administrative, civil, and criminal environmental enforcement litigation and cost recovery litigation before state and federal courts and agencies; rulemakings before state agencies and USEPA; permit appeals, permit negotiations, and regulatory counseling; all environmental aspects of corporate transactions, corporate successor liability and lender liability.
Career: Joined as Partner, 1986.
Personal: Ohio Wesleyan University, BA, 1965; The Ohio State University Moritz College of Law, JD, 1969.

RUXIN, Paul
Jones Day, Chicago
312 269 1546
paultruxin@jonesday.com
Recommended in Energy
Practice Areas: Represents natural gas, pipeline, electric, and telephone public utilities before state and federal regulatory bodies and in the courts. He is involved in the development, acquisition, and sale of energy resources and independent power and energy-related projects, the structure and restructuring of public utility and other energy businesses, the impact of antitrust laws on regulated utilities, and the general litigation and commercial problems of ener-

gy and public utility industries. He is a frequent speaker at utility industry meetings and seminars.
Prof. Memberships: ABA; Energy Bar Association; Cleveland Bar Association; The Chicago Bar Association.

RYAN, Priscilla E
Sidley Austin Brown & Wood LLP, Chicago 312 853 7072
pryan@sidley.com
Recommended in Employee Benefits
Practice Areas: Priscilla E Ryan concentrates her practice in employee benefits matters, including fiduciary issues that arise under ERISA and executive compensation, and she provides litigation support in ERISA class action lawsuits. She represents clients on a variety of matters before the Treasury Department, the Internal Revenue Service, the Department of Labor and the Pension Benefit Guaranty Corporation. Ms Ryan is Co-Chair of the firm's Insurance Committee, which is responsible for the administration of all the firm's insurance policies (other than malpractice insurance).
Prof. Memberships: Ms Ryan is a member of the Section of Taxation of the American Bar Association and serves as the Chair of its Employee Benefits Committee. She is a member of the ABA Joint Committee on Employee Benefits, the IRS Great Lakes Area Tax Exempt and Government Entities Council and a Fellow of the American College of Employee Benefits Counsel.
Career: She served as an attorney-advisor in the Office of Tax Policy of the US Treasury Department, advising the Assistant Secretary of Tax Policy. Loyola University Chicago School of Law, JD, 1982; Marquette University, AB, 1969. Bar Admission: Illinois, 1982.
Publications: Ms Ryan has lectured and written many articles on tax and employee benefit issues.

RYAN, Thomas F
Sidley Austin Brown & Wood LLP, Chicago 312 853 7497
tryan@sidley.com
Recommended in Antitrust, Litigation
Practice Areas: Thomas F Ryan serves on the firm's Executive and Finance Committees. He focuses on antitrust and business counseling, arbitration and alternative dispute resolution, and trials before State and Federal Courts. Mr Ryan engages in litigation in several areas including antitrust, class actions, commercial, environmental and securities and was named to the BTI Consulting All Star Team for Client Service.
Prof. Memberships: Mr Ryan has served as a member of the Advisory Committee on Circuit Rules for the Seventh Federal Circuit Court of Appeals and as President of the Seventh Circuit Bar Association.
Career: Wayne State University Law School, JD, 1971; Ferris State University, BS, 1965. Bar Admission: Illinois, 1972.

SALPETER, Alan N
Mayer, Brown, Rowe & Maw LLP,
Chicago 312 701 7051
asalpeter@mayerbrownrowe.com
Recommended in Litigation
Practice Areas: Senior litigator with
approximately 70 bench and jury trials
and 20 appeals. Commercial litigation
cases focusing on alleged malpractice
suits against lawyers, accountants and
consultants; alleged securities fraud;
multiple kinds of class actions; disputes
over information technology; contested
mergers or acquisitions; business torts;
corporate governance and fiduciary
duties; consumer class actions.
Career: Joined Mayer, Brown, Rowe &
Maw LLP, Chicago, 1972; became Partner, 1979. Co-Head Litigation Department, 1994-2000.
Publications: Co-author of a number of
articles and chapters in books on a range
of legal issues. Swiss Reinsurance New
Markets - Conference for Global Accounting Firms: Risk Management Challenges -
Defending Accountants Against Litigation
in the US; Numerous Presentations: The
Inside Story of Lexecon v Milberg Weiss;
Guest Lecturer, Boalt Hall School of Law
(University of California at Berkeley). Lorman Education Services.
Personal: Born 7 October 1947. Villanova University, JD, 1972; managing
editor, 'Villanova Law Review'. The
American University, BS with highest
honors, 1969.

SALTIEL, David
Bell, Boyd & Lloyd LLC, Chicago
312 372 1121
*Recommended in Media &
Entertainment*

SALZMAN, Jerrold
Freeman, Freeman & Salzman,
Chicago 312 222 5100
Recommended in Capital Markets

SANCHEZ, Vincent
DLA Piper Rudnick Gray Cary US LLP,
Chicago 312 368 3420
vincent.sanchez@dlapiper.com
Recommended in Technology
Practice Areas: Technology transactions; outsourcing, electronic commerce
and privacy.
Career: Co-Chair of the firm's Technology Transactions Practice, where he represents companies in acquisitions,
divestitures, joint ventures, strategic
alliances, equity investments and licensing arrangements involving some form
of technology or intellectual property.
His practice also includes representing
companies in the outsourcing of business processes and operations and
advising companies with respect to the
legal and regulatory issues and risks
regarding the use and security of data
and other information as well as transacting business through the internet or
in other networked environments.
Personal: MBA, Northwestern University; JD, University of Notre Dame.

SANDERS, David P
Jenner & Block LLP, Chicago
312 923 2963
dsanders@jenner.com
*Recommended in Media &
Entertainment*
Practice Areas: David P Sanders is a
Partner in Jenner & Block's Chicago
office. Mr Sanders is Co-Chair of the
firm's Media and First Amendment
Practice, and a member of the firm's Litigation Practice. Mr Sanders has served
as regular outside counsel to several
media clients, including ABC Inc., Crain
Communications Inc, Chicago Magazine and Golfweek, and has represented
numerous other publishers, broadcasters, and others in the news and entertainment businesses. Mr Sanders provides litigation and counseling services
to his clients on a wide range of media
and First Amendment law issues. He has
successfully defended numerous libel
and privacy cases on behalf of media
clients. Recently, he successfully defended Forbes in a libel and false light invasion of privacy case brought by a business executive. Other cases have included the defense of a series of libel lawsuits
arising out of an award-winning,
nationally-televised investigative news
report; the trial of a libel claim brought
by the CEO of a corporation against a
newspaper; and the appeal of $9.2 mil-
lion libel judgment - then the largest
damage award in the history of American libel law - against the Alton Telegraph. Mr Sanders regularly handles
other types of litigated matters involving
First Amendment and press issues for
his media clients, and he also counsels
media and non-media clients on a
broad range of problems involving
defamation, privacy, newsgathering,
Freedom of Information Act, copyright,
advertising, promotion, media insurance and related business and legal
issues.
Personal: Georgetown University Law
Center, JD, 1974.

SARASEK, Peter
Quarles & Brady LLP, Chicago
312 715 5000
Recommended in Real Estate

SATHY, Anup
Kirkland & Ellis LLP, Chicago
312 861 2046
asathy@kirkland.com
Recommended in Bankruptcy
Practice Areas: Anup Sathy concentrates his practice in matters relating to
corporate restructurings, workouts and
Chapter 11 reorganizations. He has substantial experience representing companies, buyers and lenders in all aspects of
distressed situations.
Personal: University of Illinois at
Urbana-Champaign, BS, Finance, 1992,
Highest Honors. Northwestern University School of Law, JD, 1995, cum laude.

SAWYIER, David R
Sidley Austin Brown & Wood LLP,
Chicago 312 853 7261
dsawyier@sidley.com
Recommended in Capital Markets
Practice Areas: Partner in the Commodities and Financial Litigation Practice
in Chicago. Advises and represents clients
in investment advisory, hedge fund and
futures-related corporate and regulatory
matters, including the organisation and
offering of interests in commodity pools
and hedge funds and investments in advisory and trading firms.
Career: Educated at Cambridge University, England, 1979; Oxford University,
England, MA, 1974; Harvard College,
AB, 1972; Harvard University, JD, 1977.
Bar Admissions: District of Columbia,
1978 and Illinois, 1977.

SCHILLER, Eric M
Sonnenschein Nath & Rosenthal LLP,
Chicago 312 876 8015
eschiller@sonnenschein.com
Recommended in Real Estate
Practice Areas: Real estate and finance
Partner with 25+ years representing corporate and institutional clients nationwide in real estate and commercial
finance matters. Specializes in financing,
joint ventures, commercial leases, real
estate acquisition and sales and workouts. Matters include multi-state, multi-
asset real estate and commercial transactions involving office buildings, industrial buildings, shopping centers, hotels
and apartment complexes. Counsels
lenders in syndication groups in loans,
as agent and co-lender.
Prof. Memberships: Elected to American College of Real Estate Lawyers;
Member, Chicago and American Bar
associations.
Personal: Northwestern University
School of Law, JD, Editorial Board, Law
Review; Indiana University, BA with
honors.

SCHLICKMAN, J Andrew
Sidley Austin Brown & Wood LLP,
Chicago 312 853 7404
jaschlickman@sidley.com
Recommended in Environment
Practice Areas: J Andrew Schlickman's
practice involves complex environmental enforcement and litigation matters,
including emphasis on contaminated
river and sediment cases, natural
resource damages cases, disputes
between buyers and sellers of contaminated properties, diminution in property value cases, and defense of governmental enforcement actions. He has
tried complex environmental cases, handled appeals of such cases, negotiated a
wide variety of consent decrees and settlements, and participated in hearings
on the fairness of settlements. Named to
BTI Consulting's All Star Team for
Client Service.
Prof. Memberships: Member: American Bar Association, section of Environ-

ment and Natural Resources and the
Chicago Bar Association.
Career: The University of Chicago Law
School (JD, 1978). Georgetown Univer-
sity (BA, 1974). Bar Admission: Illinois,
1978.

SCHNADIG, Richard
Vedder, Price, Kaufman & Kammholz,
Chicago 312 609 7500
Recommended in Employment

SCHNEIDMAN, Edward J
Mayer, Brown, Rowe & Maw LLP,
Chicago 312 701 7348
eschneidman@mayerbrownrowe.com
Recommended in Corporate/M&A
Practice Areas: Mergers of publicly
and privately held corporations, partnerships, limited liability companies and
other entities. Stock and asset acquisitions and divestitures. Corporate and
partnership liquidations and reorganizations. General corporate governance
and compliance. Public and private
offerings. Real estate investment trusts
and other public and private real estate-
related entities. Limited partnerships,
mortgage pools and institutional funds,
including group trusts, separate
accounts, and tax-exempt title-holding
corporations. Federal and state securities law compliance.
Prof. Memberships: Illinois, 1980. US
District Court for the Northern District
of Illinois, 1980.
Career: Joined Mayer, Brown, Rowe &
Maw LLP, Chicago, 1980; became Partner 1987. Corporate Practice Area
Administrator since 1996-2002.
Publications: Illinois Continuing Legal
Education Seminars, Partnership Law
and Aspects of Oil and Gas Law. American Association of Equipment Lessors
Lawyer Forum.
Personal: Born 20 September 1955.
Duke University School of Law, JD with
honors, 1980. University of Pennsylva-
nia, BSE magna cum laude, 1977.

SCHOPF, Willam G
Schopf & Weiss, Chicago
312 701 9300   schopf@sw.com
Recommended in Antitrust
Practice Areas: Over 30 years of successful verdicts and settlements, including lead trial counsel role in numerous
jury trials involving issues such as inter-
national trade, civil RICO, legal mal-
practice, price-fixing, deceptive prac-
tices, breach of contract, fraud, product
liability, toxic torts and negligence. Rec-
ognized in 2004 by the National Law
Journal as one of the top 10 'Winning
Trial Lawyers' in the United States.
Prof. Memberships: American Bar
Association; Chicago Bar Association;
Union Internationale des Avocats.
Career: Founded Schopf & Weiss, 1987;
Partner: Isham, Lincoln & Beale; Reuben
& Proctor 1979-87.
Publications: See www.sw.com.
Personal: Cornell Law School (JD,
1973); Princeton University (AB, 1970).

SCHRANK, Charles E
Sidley Austin Brown & Wood LLP, Chicago 312 853 4140
cschrank@sidley.com
Recommended in Real Estate
Practice Areas: Charles E Schrank is a partner in the Chicago Real Estate Group and represents institutional investors, lenders, insurers, developers, retailers, corporations and multi-investor ventures in connection with sales and acquisitions, equity investments, joint ventures, construction and permanent loans, mezzanine loans, preferred equity investments, mortgage origination for commercial mortgage-backed securitization programs, restructurings and work-outs, sale-leasebacks, and commercial and industrial leasing and development.
Career: University of Wisconsin Law School (JD, 1986). University of Wisconsin - Madison (BBA, 1983). Bar Admissions: Illinois, 1990; Minnesota, 1986; Wisconsin, 1986.

SCHREIBER, Rodd M
Skadden, Arps, Slate, Meagher & Flom LLP & Affiliates, Chicago
312 407 0531
rschreib@skadden.com
Recommended in Corporate/M&A
Practice Areas: Concentrating in mergers and acquisitions, corporate financings and other corporate and securities matters. Has represented corporate clients and financial advisors in a wide variety of domestic and international transactions, including public and private acquisitions and divestitures, negotiated and contested takeovers, leveraged buyouts, spin-offs, joint ventures and other strategic alliances and public and private debt and equity financings. Provides continuing counseling to a number of corporate clients regarding general corporate and securities matters, including governance, securities law compliance and disclosure issues.
Career: JD, University of Michigan, Ann Arbor, 1987 (cum laude); BA, University of Michigan, 1984 (with distinction).

SCHWAB, Stephen W
DLA Piper Rudnick Gray Cary US LLP, Chicago 312 368 2150
stephen.schwab@dlapiper.com
Recommended in Insurance
Practice Areas: International commerce and litigation; insurance and reinsurance.
Career: He is a commercial litigator who concentrates his practice in the areas of insurance and reinsurance, litigation, arbitration and mediation, transactions and regulation. He has published and addressed audiences throughout the world on topics analyzed in an extensive list of book chapters, law review articles and pieces for trade publications on insurance and reinsurance-related subjects.

Personal: JD, The Dickinson School of Law of The Pennsylvania State University; BA, Northwestern University.

SCHWARTZ, Donald
Latham & Watkins LLP, Chicago
312 876 7700
Recommended in Banking & Finance

SELMAN, Russell
Katten Muchin Zavis Rosenman, Chicago 312 902 5390
russell.selman@kmzr.com
Recommended in Environment
Practice Areas: Department Chair. Practices in corporate, real estate, electric and gas utilities environmental compliance and litigation matters. Represents leading parties seeking cost recovery at several sites with remedial costs exceeding $100 million in Illinois, Massachusetts and Minnesota. Defense of a multi-million dollar wetland penalty case in Chicago. Defends toxic tort cases associated with manufactured gas plants and releases of solvents in Chicago. Counsels on matters involving hazardous waste control (Superfund), chemical regulation, worker protection and federal wetlands law. Prepares RCRA compliance plans, Clean Air Act permits, and overall environmental permitting plans for power plant operations. Successful negotiation and litigation with the US Environmental Protection Agency (EPA) for the cleanup of the largest PCB disposal site in the nation. Clients include KeySpan (New York), Boston Gas, SEMCO, ONEOK, PCB Treatment, Inc. Steering Committee, AIG Environmental, Simon Property Group and Park District of Oak Park, IL.
Prof. Memberships: American Bar Association, American Gas Association, Chicago Bar Association, Midwest Gas Association.
Career: Joined Katten in 1993. Served as Special Assistant to the General Counsel (Superfund) and Acting Assistant Enforcement Counsel for the US Environmental Protection Agency, Washington, DC. Developed legal and enforcement policies for EPA environmental programs and worked on the reauthorization of the Superfund statute. Received the EPA's 'Special Achievement' award for litigation. Member of the Bar in Illinois, Missouri and Washington, DC.
Publications: Restaurant critique columnist for Chicago Lawyer.
Personal: Washington University (JD 1979); Syracuse University, Maxwell School (MPA 1978); New College, Sarasota, Florida (BA 1975).

SENNETT, Michael
Bell, Boyd & Lloyd LLC, Chicago
312 372 1121
Recommended in Antitrust

SHAPIRO, Clifford
Sachnoff & Weaver LTD, Chicago
312 207 1000
Recommended in Construction

SHAPIRO, Keith
Greenberg Traurig LLP, Chicago
312 456 8405
shapirok@gtlaw.com
Recommended in Bankruptcy
Practice Areas: National Reorganization, Bankruptcy and Restructuring Practice.
Prof. Memberships: Member, Board of Directors of INSOL International. Member, American Bankruptcy Institute (ABI). Chair, Chicago Bar Association Bankruptcy & Reorganization Committee, 1999-2000. Fellow, American College of Bankruptcy Member, R3 (London). Founder and First Chairman of the Board of Directors, American Bankruptcy Board of Certification, 1992-1995.
Publications: Co-editor-in-chief, Wiley's annual Bankruptcy Law Update. Contributing author, West's Norton Bankruptcy Law and Practice treatise and Wiley's Advanced Chapter 11 Bankruptcy Practice treatise. Authored two editions of the book Guide to Core vs. Noncore Jurisdiction Under the Bankruptcy Code.

SHAPIRO, Stephen R
Mayer, Brown, Rowe & Maw LLP, Chicago 312 701 7327
sshapiro@mayerbrownrowe.com
Recommended in Litigation
Practice Areas: Founder and Senior Member, firm's Supreme Court and Appellate Litigation Practice Group, the largest in the country. Has argued 24 cases in the US Supreme Court and large number of appeals in federal and state courts nationwide. Co-Head of firm's Telecommunications Practice Group. Served on firm's Management Committee. Clients represented on appeal include General Motors, SBC Corp., BASF Corp., Merrill Lynch, ChevronTexaco, ITT Hartford, and the National Association of Manufacturers.
Prof. Memberships: Board of Directors, New York University Law School, Institute of Judicial Administration. Member, American Law Institute, American Academy of Appellate Lawyers. Former trustee of Product Liability Advisory Foundation.
Career: Mayer, Brown, Rowe & Maw LLP, Chicago, 1972-78; 1983-date; Partner, 1978. Deputy Solicitor General, US Department of Justice, 1981-83. Assistant to the Solicitor General, DOJ, 1978-80. Law Clerk to The Honorable Charles M Merrill, US Court of Appeals, Ninth Circuit, 1971.
Publications: Prolific writer. Numerous publications include standard treatise on litigation before US Supreme Court, R Stern, E Gressman, S Shapiro and K Geller, 'Supreme Court Practice' (2002).
Personal: Yale Law School, JD, 1971; Board of Editors, 'Yale Law Journal'. Yale College, BA magna cum laude, 1968; Honors with Exceptional Distinction; Phi Beta Kappa.

SHEFFIELD, Jeffrey
Kirkland & Ellis LLP, Chicago
312 861 2454
jsheffield@kirkland.com
Recommended in Tax
Practice Areas: Concentrates his practice in the areas of business planning; mergers, acquisitions and venture capital investing; tax planning for public and closely-held entities; and executive compensation.
Publications: He has authored or co-authored several articles, including 'How VC/PE Funds Can Deliver Special LTCG Tax Benefits to Individual LPs and GPs'.
Personal: University of Chicago, BA, 1976, Phi Beta Kappa; Harvard Law School, JD, 1979. Former Lecturer at Law, University of Chicago Law School (teaching business planning). Former Adjunct Professor, IIT-Kent Graduate Tax Program (teaching tax-free reorganizations, corporate income tax, advanced income tax).

SHEPRO, Richard Warren
Mayer, Brown, Rowe & Maw LLP, Chicago 312 701 7007
rshepro@mayerbrownrowe.com
Recommended in Corporate/M&A, Insurance
Practice Areas: Chicago Office Practice Leader for Corporate and Securities law. Represents and counsels on acquisitions, restructurings, and securities law; negotiation/planning for acquisitions; offshore corporations; international investment; insurance and reinsurance companies; venture capital, private equity fund work; proxy, consent solicitations; public, private offerings; broker-dealer, investment advisor regulation.
Career: Served as Law Clerk to The Honorable Judge James R Browning, Chief Judge, US Court of Appeals for the Ninth Circuit, 1979-81. Joined Mayer, Brown, Rowe & Maw LLP in 1981 and became Partner in 1986. Lecturer, University of Chicago Law School. Former Visiting Professor, Northwestern University School of Law. Lectured at the London Business School, Ecole des Hautes Etudes Commerciales, and at professional associations. Taught at Harvard University.
Publications: Co-author, 'Bidders & Targets: Mergers and Acquisitions in the US' (1990). Articles on mergers, corporate law, and securities law for such publications as 'Financial Times', 'Harvard Business Review', and 'Business Lawyer'.
Personal: JD (cum laude), Harvard University, 1979; Supreme Court note editor, 'Law Review'. MSc (1976), The London School of Economics; AB magna cum laude (1975), Harvard University. Special Assistant Attorney General of the State of Illinois, 1981-82. Staff Member, US Senate Judiciary Committee, 1978-79. Speaks French and Russian.

SHERCK, Timothy C
Mayer, Brown, Rowe & Maw LLP,
Chicago 312 701 7148
tsherck@mayerbrownrowe.com
Recommended in Tax

Practice Areas: Represents and counsels on all tax aspects of acquisitions and dispositions of business, including consolidated return, carryforward, spinoff and asset basis issues; tax-free reorganizations; corporate joint ventures; tax aspects of business financial restructurings, workouts, and bankruptcy, including debt exchanges and modification, cancellation of indebtedness income, loss carryforwards, and related matters such as tax liens and tax-related aspects of bankruptcy law; acquisitions of financially troubled business; and preparation and handling of requests for private letter rulings before the IRS National Office.
Career: Served as Law Clerk to The Honorable Walter R Mansfield, US Court of Appeals for the Second Circuit, New York, 1974-75. Joined Mayer, Brown, Rowe & Maw LLP in 1975 and became Partner in 1981.
Publications: Author of 'Treatment of Options in Applying Stock Ownership Tests in the Corporate World', 66 Taxes 935 (1988); 'Restructuring Today's Financially Troubled Corporation', 68 Taxes 881 (1990); 'Applying the Property- Services Distinction in Corporate Transactions: The New Economy Tests the Limits', 68 Taxes 120 (2001) (co-author).
Personal: JD, cum laude, from Harvard Law School, 1974; Comment Editor, 'Law Review'. BA, cum laude (1971), Northwestern University.

SHUGRUE, John
Morgan, Lewis & Bockius LLP, Chicago
312 324 2535
jshugrue@morganlewis.com
Recommended in Insurance

Practice Areas: John Shugrue is a Partner in the Litigation Practice, with a focus on insurance recovery. He is experienced in all aspects of litigation, mediation, and arbitration with Lloyd's of London, London and Bermuda market insurers, and all major domestic insurers. He has substantial experience in handling complex litigation and insurance coverage matters involving Commercial General Liability (CGL), Directors & Officers (D&O), Errors & Omissions (E&O), First Party Property and Fidelity policies. He is co-author of the treatise 'Insurance Coverage Disputes' and is past Co-Chair of the ABA Litigation Section's Insurance Coverage Litigation Committee.
Prof. Memberships: American Bar Association.

SHULRUFF, Stuart P
Katten Muchin Zavis Rosenman,
Chicago 312 902 5694
stuart.shulruff@kmzr.com

Recommended in Banking & Finance
Practice Areas: Partner, Chicago; Chair of Commercial Finance Practice. Concentrates practice in all aspects of corporate finance (senior financing, second lien/term B financing, mezzanine financing, equity co-investments) for a variety of institutional and entrepreneurial clients such as Ableco Finance LLC, Antares Capital Corporation, CapitalSource Finance LLC, Dymas Capital Management Company LLC, LaSalle Bank National Association, Prairie Capital, Madison Capital Funding LLC, Merrill Lynch Capital, and Midwest Mezzanine Fund.
Prof. Memberships: Illinois Bar Association, Chicago Bar Association.
Personal: BS, Accountancy (High Honors) from the University of Illinois at Urbana-Champaign, 1981. CPA, 1981. JD (cum laude) from Loyola University School of Law,1984.

SICKLE, David B
DLA Piper Rudnick Gray Cary US LLP,
Chicago 312 368 4081
david.sickle@dlapiper.com
Recommended in Real Estate

Practice Areas: Real estate; landlord leasing.
Career: His practice concentrates in transactional real estate and finance. He represents a wide variety of REITs, banks, and developer and institutional clients and has particular experience in shopping center finance, acquisition, development, leasing, and dispositions. He has recently written and published on the topic of loan workouts and deeds in lieu of foreclosures.
Personal: JD, University of Michigan; BS, University of Pennsylvania.

SILBERMAN, Alan
Sonnenschein Nath & Rosenthal LLP,
Chicago 312 876 8103
asilberman@sonnenschein.com
Recommended in Antitrust

Practice Areas: Antitrust, Marketing Practices, Franchising and Distribution Chair with 40 years of experience in antitrust, franchising and general commercial litigation, counseling and related transactions. Represents franchisors in negotiated, litigated and arbitrated disputes with franchisees and third parties and domestic and international activities. Acts for McDonald's Corporation as outside counsel.
Prof. Memberships: Illinois Franchise Advisory Board; Co-Chair, Practising Law Institute's Annual Antitrust Law Institute; former Chair, ABA's Section of Antitrust Law, ABA House of Delegates member; Illinois, US Supreme Court and various US Courts of Appeal and District Court Bars.
Personal: Yale University, LLB; Northwestern University, BA, with Distinction.

SIMON, Mark C
Katten Muchin Zavis Rosenman,
Chicago 312 902 5301
Mark.Simon@kmzr.com
Recommended in Real Estate

Practice Areas: Partner, Chicago. Represents banks, insurance companies and pension fund advisors making loans and other real estate investments. Frequently acts as agent's counsel on syndicated REIT credit facilities and construction loans in excess of $100 million. Substantial experience documenting mezzanine loans and joint venture investments. Has handled a considerable number of workouts for both lending institutions and developers, including restructuring the indebtedness of entire real estate companies.
Prof. Memberships: Past Chair of the Chicago Bar Association real estate finance subcommittee. Represents not for profit organizations redeveloping urban sites on a pro bono basis.
Personal: Graduated magna cum laude from Carleton College in 1976 and with honors from the University of Michigan Law School in 1979.

SINGER, Eric
Wildman, Harrold, Allen & Dixon,
Chicago 312 201 2000
Recommended in Construction

SISKE, Roger C
Sonnenschein Nath & Rosenthal LLP,
Chicago 312 876 8018
rsiske@sonnenschein.com
Recommended in Employee Benefits

Practice Areas: Employee benefits and executive compensation Chair.
Prof. Memberships: ABA Employee Benefits Committee of the Tax Section; ABA Employee Benefits and Executive Compensation Committee of the Section on Corporation Banking and Business Law; ISBA Section Council of the Employee Benefits Section; ABA Joint Committee on Employee Benefits; CBA Employee Benefits Committee; Advisory Board, Employee Benefits Counselor; Advisory Board, Employment Law Counselor; Advisory Board, ERISA and Benefits Law Journal.
Personal: University of Michigan, JD magna cum laude, Order of the Coif, associate Editor-Law Review; Ohio State University, BS Finance with Honors.

SKINNER, Honey J
Sidley Austin Brown & Wood LLP,
Chicago 312 853 7577
mskinner@sidley.com
Recommended in Healthcare

Practice Areas: Honey Jacobs Skinner represents healthcare providers before government agencies both in Illinois and Washington, DC She assists hospitals, health systems and physician practices in gaining government approval for the expansion of their services and in their efforts to achieve equitable Medicaid reimbursement.
Prof. Memberships: Ms. Skinner is

actively involved in numerous civic endeavors, and serves as a Director of the Chicago Area Foundation for Legal Services and a Director of the Northern Funds.
Career: Northwestern University School of Law, JD, 1981; Harvard University, BA, 1978. Bar Admissions: District of Columbia, 1990 Illinois, 1981.

SKLAR, Stanley
Bell, Boyd & Lloyd LLC, Chicago
312 372 1121
Recommended in Construction

SKLARSKY, Charles
Jenner & Block LLP, Chicago
312 923 2904
csklarsky@jenner.com
Recommended in Litigation

Practice Areas: Charles B Sklarsky is a partner in Jenner & Block's Chicago office. He is Co-Chair of the firm's White Collar Criminal Defense and Counseling Practice, a member of the firm's Litigation Department, Class Action Litigation and Healthcare Law Practices. Mr Sklarsky counsels individuals and companies on a wide range of issues involving litigation or potential litigation, including healthcare fraud and abuse, government contractor fraud and abuse, corporate fraud and abuse, conflicts of interest, public corruption, criminal tax matters, antitrust, theft of trade secrets, securities fraud and regulatory matters. He also has substantial experience in litigating disputes between sellers and purchasers of wholesale electric power. Mr Sklarsky counsels individuals and companies involved in the gaming industry in Illinois and elsewhere and represents clients before the Illinois Gaming Board. Mr Sklarsky counsels companies on compliance issues, conducts compliance audits and assists companies in the drafting and implementation of codes of conduct and compliance programs. Mr Sklarsky joined the firm after serving as an Assistant United States Attorney for the Northern District of Illinois and as an Assistant State's Attorney of Cook County, Illinois. At the United States Attorney's Office, he held the positions of Deputy Chief of Criminal Litigation and later Chief of Criminal Receiving and Appeals. He was one of the architects of Operation Greylord, an unprecedented undercover probe of corruption in the Cook County Judiciary.
Personal: University of Wisconsin Law School, JD, 1973.

SLATER, Paul
Sperling & Slater, Chicago
312 641 3200
Recommended in Antitrust

SMALL, Andrew
Katten Muchin Zavis Rosenman,
Chicago 312 902 5489
Andrew.small@kmzr.com
Recommended in Real Estate

Practice Areas: Partner, Chicago. Concentrates on real estate primarily in the areas of commercial development, structured finance, joint ventures and acquisitions and dispositions. Development practice is focused primarily on ground up development, redevelopment, capital raising, venture formation and financing of retail, hotel, golf course and urban mixed use (office, hotel and residential) projects. Lending practice includes conventional, mezzanine and securitized financing matters, construction loans and preferred equity matters. Has substantial experience representing lenders and borrowers in connection with loan modifications and workouts, public and private developers, public and private REITs, golf course owners and operators, institutional lenders, opportunity funds, insurance companies and securitized lenders. A significant portion of practice relates to the acquisition, disposition, financing and development of golf course projects throughout the country.
Prof. Memberships: Member of the International Council of Shopping Centers where he is a frequent lecturer and contributor.
Career: Co-Hiring Partner for Katten Muchin Zavis Rosenman.
Personal: Graduated from the University of Michigan with a Bachelor's Degree in Business Administration and obtained his law degree in 1989 from the University of Chicago Law School. Completed the Certified Public Accountant's examination in 1987.

SMEDINGHOFF, Thomas J
Baker & McKenzie, Chicago
312 861 8670
smedinghoff@bakernet.com
Recommended in Technology
Practice Areas: E-business; information security; digital signatures and PKI; privacy; information technology. Acts as e-business counsel for clients worldwide; internationally recognized for leadership in addressing legislative and public policy issues relating to information security and electronic signatures.
Prof. Memberships: Member, US Delegation to United Nations Commission on International Trade Law (UNCITRAL); Chair, ABA Section of Science & Technology Law (1999-2000); Chair, ABA E-Commerce Law Division (1995-2003); Chair, Illinois Commission on Electronic Commerce (1996-98).
Career: Admitted Illinois (1978).
Publications: Editor and primary author, 'Online Law' (Addison-Wesley, 1996); numerous e-transaction, security, and IT articles.
Personal: JD University of Michigan Law School (1978).

SMOLEN, Lee M
Sidley Austin Brown & Wood LLP,
Chicago 312 853 7823
lsmolen@sidley.com
Recommended in Real Estate
Practice Areas: Lee M Smolen chairs the Chicago Real Estate Practice and co-chairs the firm's Practice Development Committee. He represents lenders, borrowers, purchasers, sellers and developers of commercial real estate. Mr Smolen's practice focuses on CMBS, various types of financing and structured finance transactions and loan workouts. He represents financial institutions in connection with financing transactions, including senior and junior mortgage financings, construction loans, mezzanine lending transactions, loans to REITs and loans involving a participation or contingent interest feature.
Career: The University of Chicago Law School, JD, 1985; University of Illinois, BS, 1982. Bar Admission: Illinois, 1985.

SNEED, William M
Sidley Austin Brown & Wood LLP,
Chicago 312 853 7899
wsneed@sidley.com
Recommended in Insurance
Practice Areas: William Sneed has extensive experience arbitrating and litigating international and domestic reinsurance disputes on behalf of ceding companies, reinsurers, and receivers. His practice encompasses the property and casualty and life and health areas. He has arbitrated dozens of reinsurance disputes, addressing such issues as allocation of loss payments, aggregation of claims, late notice, ECO/XPL coverage, follow the fortunes, pre-hearing security, cessions of declaratory judgment expenses, and retention warranties. He has tried jury and non-jury cases in state and federal courts, including civil rights, tort, tax, and commercial disputes.
Career: Northwestern University School of Law, JD, 1987; Northwestern University, MM, 1987; Stanford University, AB, 1983. Bar Admission: Illinois, 1987.

SOLOVY, Jerold S
Jenner & Block LLP, Chicago
312 923 2671
jsolovy@jenner.com
Recommended in Litigation
Practice Areas: Chairman Jerold S Solovy is widely regarded as one of the preeminent appellate and trial lawyers in the country. Since 1991, he has been regularly cited in the 'National Law Journal' as one of the 100 most influential lawyers in America. He focuses on litigating complex business matters and insurance coverage issues. In addition, he has handled many high-profile intellectual property and securities cases and has a national reputation in defending national class actions. Most recently, he successfully represented the Illinois Attorney General in reducing the fees

paid to law firms that had represented the State in the nationwide Tobacco Industry litigation from the requested $780 million to a total of $67.5 million. In addition, he successfully re-argued a closely-watched eminent domain case before the State's Supreme Court, in which a state-created body was not allowed to condemn private property in an economically distressed area and to immediately transfer it to another on the premise that the land would be used in a more profitable manner. Mr Solovy successfully represented the Boston-based Kennedy Family by obtaining a declaratory judgment against the mortgage-holding insurance company's claim that $53 million in prepayment penalties were owed to it in connection with the sale of Chicago's Merchandise Mart. He also won a $161 million jury verdict against DirecTV, Hughes Electronics and General Motors Corp. in a breach of contract lawsuit brought on behalf of General Electric Capital Corp.
Personal: Harvard Law School, LLB, 1955, cum laude; American College of Trial Lawyers, Fellow.

SOLOW, Alan
Goldberg, Kohn, Bell, Black, Rosenbloom & Moritz, Ltd, Chicago
312 201 4000
Recommended in Bankruptcy

SOLOW, Michael
Kaye Scholer LLP, Chicago
312 583 2310
msolow@kayescholer.com
Recommended in Bankruptcy
Practice Areas: Partner, Co-Chair, Business Reorganization and Creditors' Rights Group. Michael Solow, a member of the firm's Executive Committee, is a Partner in the firm's Chicago office and Co-Chair of the Business Reorganization and Creditors' Rights Department. He has over 20 years' experience representing creditors, trustees and governmental agencies and other parties in the bankruptcy and insolvency area.
Prof. Memberships: Admissions: Illinois; New York; Northern District of Illinois (Trial Bar); Southern District of New York; District of Arizona; Northern District of Texas; Western District of Michigan; 4th, 6th, 7th, and 8th Circuit Courts of Appeals; US Supreme Court.
Career: JD, Harvard Law School, 1984; BA (summa cum laude), University of Illinois, 1981, Phi Beta Kappa; Bronze Tablet.
Publications: 'Sarbanes-Oxley and the US Bankruptcy Code', INSOL 2005 World Congress (co-author); 'Lease Terminations and Mortgage Foreclosures as Fraudulent Conveyance'; 'Buying Assets in Bankruptcy: A Guide to Purchasers' (co-author); 'Considerations in Dealing with the Federal Savings & Loan Insurance Corporation in Chapter 11' (co-author); 'Lender Liability and Equitable Subordination in the Illinois Institute

for Continuing Legal Education's Secured Transactions 2001' (co-author).
Personal: Married, two children. Active in Chicago District Golf Association Charitable Foundation and March of Dimes.

SORENSEN, Sharp
Sidley Austin Brown & Wood LLP,
Chicago 312 853 7151
ssorensen@sidley.com
Recommended in Tax
Practice Areas: Sharp Sorensen concentrates on federal tax matters. His practice is focused on representing domestic and foreign corporations involved in a wide variety of transactions, including corporate mergers and acquisitions, spin-offs and other divisive transactions, asset securitizations, partnerships and joint ventures, foreign and domestic securities offerings, leveraged leasing and regulated investment companies.
Career: Northwestern University School of Law, JD, 1985; University of Utah, BS, 1982. Bar Admissions: Illinois, 1992; New York, 1986.

SPECTOR, David
Schiff Hardin LLP, Chicago
312 258 5552
dspector@schiffhardin.com
Recommended in Insurance
Practice Areas: Reinsurance litigation.
Prof. Memberships: American Bar Association.
Career: For more than 25 years, Mr Spector has ranked among the preeminent American practitioners in the insurance field. His expertise encompasses a variety of complex matters, including reinsurance litigation and arbitration, insurance company insolvencies, business counseling, and coverage litigation.
Publications: Numerous articles and speeches.
Personal: Northwestern University (BA, 1968), University of Michigan Law School (JD, magna cum laude, Order of the Coif, 1971), notes editor, 'Michigan Law Review'.

SPERLING, Robert
Winston & Strawn LLP, Chicago
312 558 7941
rsperling@winston.com
Recommended in Litigation
Practice Areas: Complex litigation with an emphasis on securities litigation and commercial litigation, including class actions.
Prof. Memberships: American Bar Association, Illinois State Bar Association, Chicago Bar Association.
Career: Has extensive experience representing financial services clients in securities actions, including class actions. Has represented the directors of various companies in derivative shareholders actions and ERISA actions that related to securities claims filed against those companies. Has extensive experience in

national class actions that involved alleged violations of various federal consumer protection statutes.

Personal: DePaul University School of Law, JD, DePaul Law Review, University of Illinois, AB in History.

SPRAYREGEN, James HM
Kirkland & Ellis LLP, Chicago
312 861 2481
jsprayregen@kirkland.com
Recommended in Bankruptcy

Practice Areas: Experience includes the representation of significant companies as debtors in bankruptcy proceedings or in non-bankruptcy fora and large creditors in bankruptcy and insolvency proceedings. On behalf of his clients, has handled a wide variety of matters involving such issues as deleveraging, fraudulent conveyances, equitable subordination, substantive consolidation, preferences, and successor liability. In addition, he has extensive experience in representing boards of directors in troubled situations, the acquisition of companies and assets of companies out of bankruptcy proceedings or from insolvent debtors.

Personal: University of Michigan, BA, 1982; University of Illinois College of Law, JD, 1985.

STAHL, David
Eimer Stahl Klevorn & Solberg, Chicago
312 660 7600
Recommended in Energy

STEIN, Steven
Stein, Ray & Harris LLP, Chicago
312 641 3700
Recommended in Construction

STEMPEL, James
Kirkland & Ellis LLP, Chicago
312 861 2440
jstempel@kirkland.com
Recommended in Bankruptcy

Practice Areas: James Stempel concentrates his practice in counseling debtors in all aspects of Chapter 11 cases, purchasers of distressed companies inside and outside of bankruptcy, investors in distressed debt and claims market, companies and boards of directors in out-of-court workouts and restructurings, secured and unsecured lenders to bankrupt companies. Mr Stempel was named as one of the Outstanding Young Bankruptcy Lawyers of 2002 by 'Turnarounds & Workouts Magazine'.

Personal: University of Michigan, BGS, 1985; IIT/Chicago-Kent College of Law, JD, 1989.

STEPHENS, Thomas M
Sonnenschein Nath & Rosenthal LLP, Chicago 312 876 7485
tstephens@sonnenschein.com
Recommended in Tax

Practice Areas: Nationally recognized in partnership taxation; Head of tax in Affordable Housing Investment Practice. Focuses on tax planning and transaction structuring for partnerships, lim-

ited liability companies, corporations and individuals. Advises for M&A, spin-offs, other restructurings, joint ventures, alliances, organizational structuring, compensation, real estate ventures, investments and workouts, including low-income housing tax credits, developments, offerings, venture capital investments and issuance and holding of financial instruments.

Prof. Memberships: ABA; Subcommittee chair, Partnership Committee of the Tax Section; Advisory Board, Journal of Passthrough Entities.

Personal: New York University, LLM in Taxation; Catholic University School of Law, JD, 1982; University of Connecticut, BA.

STETSON, Jim
Baker & McKenzie, Chicago
312 861 8865
james.l.stetson@bakernet.com
Recommended in Technology

Practice Areas: Information technology/e-commerce. International/domestic ITO and BPO outsourcing; e-commerce infrastructure transactions, complex licensing and distribution agreements; off-shoring transactions; IT/e-commerce strategic alliances/joint ventures.

Prof. Memberships: Chicago Software Association; founder of Entrepreneur's Round Table. Wisconsin Bar Association.

Career: Joined Baker & McKenzie in 1993; became a Partner in 1997. Pro Bono Committee.

Personal: Born in Minneapolis, MN in 1957. Graduate of University of Wisconsin Law School (JD 1982); received Bachelor of Arts degree from the University of Wisconsin, Eau Claire in 1979. Admitted to practice law in Wisconsin and Illinois in 1982.

STILLMAN, Nina G
Morgan, Lewis & Bockius LLP, Chicago
312 324 1150
nstillman@morganlewis.com
Recommended in Employment

Practice Areas: Ms Stillman focuses on labor and employment, equal employment opportunity, and occupational safety and health law matters. She has successfully represented corporations and institutions in large employment class actions, individual employment, health and safety-related cases. Ms Stillman counsels employers nationwide on cross-border workplace issues and counsels international clients on US employment and workplace safety and health law.

STINSON, James R
Sidley Austin Brown & Wood LLP, Chicago 312 853 7203
jstinson@sidley.com
Recommended in Insurance

Practice Areas: James R Stinson leads the firm's Reinsurance and Insurance Insolvency Practices and represents ceding insurers and reinsurers in reinsur-

ance disputes and handles all manner of domestic and non-US insurer insolvency matters, representing receivers, reinsurers, ceding insurers and creditors. He has served as an administrative hearing officer, and as an arbitrator, umpire and mediator in reinsurance and insurance arbitrations.

Prof. Memberships: Reinsurance Association of America, ARIAS-U.S., the American Bar Association, IAIR, Mealey's and the NAIC.

Career: University of Illinois College of Law, JD, 1977; Indiana University, AB, 1973. Admissions: US Court of Appeals, 7th Circuit, 1978; US Court of Appeals, 10th Circuit, 1982; US District Court, ND of Illinois - General, 1977; US District Court, ND of Illinois - Trial Bar; Illinois, 1977.

Publications: He is a past Director of the International Association of Insurance Receivers (IAIR) and edits the Legal Chapter of the National Association of Insurance Commissioner's (NAIC) 'Handbook for Insurance Company Insolvencies'. He also assisted in drafting the Interstate Insurance Receivership Compact and chaired the Compact Commission's Receivership Law Advisory Committee, which drafted the Uniform Receivership Law.

STONE, Jeffrey
McDermott Will & Emery, Chicago
312 984 2064
jstone@mwe.com
Recommended in Litigation

Practice Areas: Head of the firm's Trial Department. Concentrates on white-collar criminal defense, complex commercial litigation, internal investigations and RICO. Represents individuals and corporations in criminal prosecutions and complex commercial litigation.

Prof. Memberships: Fellow of the American College of Trial Lawyers. Member, American Bar Association and the Chicago Council of Lawyers. Member of the board of directors, Harvard Law Society of Illinois; national chairman, Stanford Fund, and Vice Chair, Stanford's Campaign for Undergraduate Education.

Career: Admitted to practice before the Illinois Bar, the US District Court for the Northern District of Illinois (Trial Bar), the US Court of Appeals for the Seventh Circuit and the Supreme Court of the United States. Prior to joining McDermott, Will & Emery, served in the United States Attorney's Office in Chicago, most recently as Deputy Chief of the Criminal Receiving and Appellate Division. As Assistant US Attorney, tried federal jury trials in the area of white-collar crime, focusing on complex financial crime, fraud, public corruption and tax prosecutions.

Personal: Received BA with honors and distinction from Stanford University and JD cum laude from Harvard Law School.

STONE, Susan
Sidley Austin Brown & Wood LLP,
Chicago 312 853 2177
sstone@sidley.com
Recommended in Insurance

Practice Areas: Susan A Stone is a litigation Partner focusing on commercial and financial litigation matters. She has significant trial experience in both state and federal courts, and practices in the areas of insurance insolvency, reinsurance disputes, environmental coverage litigation, white-collar criminal defense and sensitive investigations. Prior to joining the firm, Ms Stone was an Assistant United States Attorney in Los Angeles. She serves as a Co-Chair of the firm's Practice Development Committee.

Career: Harvard Law School, JD, 1987; Yale University, BA, 1983. Served as an Adjunct Professor teaching Trial Practice at DePaul University College of Law. Law Clerk for District Court Judge William J Orrick of the Northern District of California. Bar Admissions: Illinois and California.

Publications: Ms Stone was named by the Chicago Lawyer as one of the '40 Attorneys Under 40'.

STRAND, Peter
Holland & Knight LLP, Chicago
312 263 3600
peter.strand@hklaw.com
Recommended in Media & Entertainment

Practice Areas: Sr Counsel in the firm's Litigation Section, focusing on the entertainment and intellectual property practice areas. He represents artists, managers, songwriters, recording artists, musicians, television and film writers, independent record labels, publishing companies, production companies and writers in litigation and transactional matters. He assists clients in protecting and enforcing copyrights and trademarks and licensing or exploiting their creative works.

STREFF Jr, William A
Kirkland & Ellis LLP, Chicago
312 861 2126
wstreff@kirkland.com
Recommended in Intellectual Property

Practice Areas: William A Streff, Jr has been practicing intellectual property law for almost 30 years, concentrating in intellectual property litigation, including jury trials, and transactions, including international strategic alliances, involving computer hardware, firmware, software and systems; semiconductor processing technology and circuitry, including DRAMs, CCDs and MPUs; optical networks; satellite and cable communications systems; avionics; high definition and satellite television systems; and digitally-controlled fuel systems. He is one of the leaders of the firm's 175-member Intellectual Property Department and is a member of the firm Management Committee.

Personal: Northwestern University, BSME, 1971. Northwestern University School of Law, JD, 1974.

STREICKER, James
Cotsirilos Tighe & Streicker Ltd, Chicago 312 263 0345
Recommended in Litigation

STUCKER, Robert
Vedder, Price, Kaufman & Kammholz, Chicago 312 609 7500
Recommended in Employee Benefits

SULLIVAN, Barry
Jenner & Block LLP, Chicago
312 923 2652
bsullivan@jenner.com
Recommended in Litigation
Practice Areas: Barry Sullivan is a Partner in Jenner & Block's Chicago office. He is Co-Chair of the firm's Appellate and Supreme Court Practice and a member of the Litigation Practice. Mr Sullivan has briefed and argued cases in the United States Supreme Court and in state and federal appellate courts throughout the United States. His cases have included labor and employment cases, bankruptcies and business restructurings, corporate and securities law cases, constitutional and administrative law cases, school and university law and local government law cases, professional licensing and privileges cases, commercial law and arbitration cases and criminal cases. Mr Sullivan has had a varied legal career. In addition to private practice, he has worked in the government and has been involved in university teaching and administration. During 1980 and 1981, Mr Sullivan served as an assistant to the solicitor general of the United States, in which capacity he argued several cases in the United States Supreme Court. Beginning in 1994, Mr Sullivan served for five years as dean of the Washington and Lee University School of Law. In 1998-99, he also served as Vice President of the university. Mr Sullivan has been a visiting professor of law at Northwestern University School of Law, a Fulbright professor of law at the University of Warsaw and a visiting law fellow of the University of London. Most recently, he has taught part-time at the University of Warsaw and at the University of Chicago.
Personal: University of Chicago Law School, JD, 1974.

SULLIVAN, Marcia W
Katten Muchin Zavis Rosenman, Chicago 312 902 5535
Marcia.Sullivan@kmzr.com
Recommended in Real Estate
Practice Areas: Partner, Chicago. Concentrates on commercial real estate finance and structured finance for commercial banks, insurance companies, finance companies and other lenders. Has been involved in complex financing for a variety of projects across the nation - shopping centers, hotels, office build-

ings, build-to-suit, apartments and for-sale residential. Has represented lenders and investors in unsecured and secured lines of credit, permanent financing, workouts and foreclosures. Has also represented lenders, investors, servicers, trustees and borrowers in loan securitizations, as well as in portfolio transactions and structured finance. In conjunction with real estate financing, represents lenders in loan participations, co-lender arrangements and interest rate risk protection products. Regularly represents developers and investors in real estate acquisitions and divestitures, development, leasing and financing.
Prof. Memberships: Served as President and Member of Chicago Real Estate Executive Women and Chicago Real Estate Education Initiative, co-chaired the 13th National Forum for Women Corporate Counsel.
Personal: Graduated, Phi Beta Kappa, from DePauw University in 1972 and received her Juris Doctor degree from the Indiana University School of Law, where she was an associate editor of the 'Indiana Law Review'.

SULLIVAN, Thomas
Jenner & Block LLP, Chicago
312 923 2928
tsullivan@jenner.com
Recommended in Litigation
Practice Areas: Thomas P Sullivan is a Partner in Jenner & Block's Chicago office. With the exception of an almost four year period (July 1977 to April 1981) when he served as the United States Attorney for the Northern District of Illinois, Mr Sullivan has practiced law at Jenner & Block since 1954. At the firm, Mr Sullivan has established himself as one of the nation's most outstanding civil and criminal trial lawyers. He has been called upon to represent some of the most prominent corporations, governmental entities and individuals in Illinois and across the nation. He has tried scores of major cases, both civil and criminal, and has established himself as a premier counselor to clients from every point on the economic spectrum. As the United States Attorney in Chicago from 1977-81, Mr Sullivan was known for his fairness, his devotion to the pursuit of justice and for his initiation of Operation Greylord, the single most wide-ranging investigation of judicial corruption in the nation's history. He served as Co-Chair of Governor George Ryan's Commission on Capital Punishment. The Commission issued its widely-acclaimed report with 85 significant recommendations for reform of the death penalty process in Illinois. As a result of all of his efforts, he received the prestigious 2003 American Bar Association's John Minor Wisdom Award, and in December 2004 was selected as Chicago Lawyer magazine's Person of the Year for 2004.

Personal: Loyola University Chicago School of Law, LLB, 1952, cum laude, Alpha Sigma Nu, Delta Theta Phi.

SULLIVAN, William
Franczek Sullivan, Chicago
312 986 0300
Recommended in Employment

TARUN, Robert
Latham & Watkins LLP, Chicago
312 876 7700
Recommended in Litigation

TECSON, Andrew
Chuhak & Tecson PC, Chicago
312 444 9300
Recommended in Healthcare

TER MOLEN, Mark R
Mayer, Brown, Rowe & Maw LLP, Chicago 312 701 7307
mtermolen@mayerbrownrowe.com
Recommended in Environment
Practice Areas: Toxic tort trials and appeals in state and federal courts. National counsel for corporations facing significant asbestos liabilities. Complex environmental litigation. Environmental regulatory hearings and appeals before state and federal agencies. General corporate counseling on environmental compliance issues and environmental concerns in the context of corporate transactions. Supervising environmental remediations pursuant to various state and/or federal requirements. Condemnation and property valuation actions. Defended and prosecuted trials and appeals in state and federal courts, including lead counsel in People v Jimerson, established innocence of man on death row for 11 years, and Jimerson v Capelli, et al, resulting in a $36 million settlement from Cook County for malicious prosecution.
Career: Mayer, Brown, Rowe & Maw LLP, Chicago, 1988 to date; Partner, 1997. Law Clerk to The Honorable Charles Levin, Michigan Supreme Court, Southfield, Michigan, 1987-88.
Publications: 'Environmental Law for Transactional Attorneys', Illinois Institute of Continuing Legal Education.
Personal: JD, University of Chicago Law School, 1987. AB (magna cum laude), Cornell University, 1984. Illinois State Bar Association John C McAndrews Pro Bono Service Award, 1996.

THEISS, Paul W
Mayer, Brown, Rowe & Maw LLP, Chicago 312 701 7359
ptheiss@mayerbrownrowe.com
Recommended in Corporate/M&A
Practice Areas: Chicago Office Practice Leader for Corporate and Securities Group. Emphasizes mergers and acquisitions, securities offerings, and corporate governance matters. Mergers and acquisitions work has included both public and private transactions, including in the telecommunications, industrial and gaming sectors. Regularly represents both issuers and underwriters in

public debt and equity offerings and Rule 144A private placements, with recent emphasis on equity and high-yield debt issuances. Other specialties include private equity, outsourcing transactions and domestic and international joint ventures.
Prof. Memberships: Admitted in Illinois, 1985.
Career: Joined Mayer, Brown, Rowe & Maw LLP, Chicago, 1985, and became Partner in 1993.
Personal: Born 11 April 1960. Earned JD at University of Chicago, 1985, and BA at Amherst College, 1982.

THOMAS, Dale E
Sidley Austin Brown & Wood LLP, Chicago 312 853 7787
dthomas@sidley.com
Recommended in Energy
Practice Areas: Dale E Thomas advises electric utilities, internet/telecommunications providers, and AT&T on a wide variety of matters, and represents them in state and federal administrative and court proceedings and appeals. Mr Thomas has represented a major utility client in a range of matters, including: rate case and prudence proceedings; a $1.2 billion settlement of five interrelated legal actions involving the utility's rates; the decision to retire a nuclear generating plant; the transfer of cutting edge technology to an unregulated subsidiary for further development and commercialization. Mr Thomas has represented internet/telecommunications providers on FCC and related matters, including: requirements to obtain broadband spectrum licenses from the FCC; obtaining certification to provide telecommunications services at state and federal levels; and adopting corporate structures to limit potential regulatory and tax burdens. He has extensive experience in telecommunications antitrust litigation and in follow-on litigation concerning the interpretation and application of the AT&T Consent Decree. He has represented AT&T in connection with contract negotiations under, and FCC litigation concerning, the Telecommunications Act of 1996.
Career: Yale Law School, JD, 1974; Yale Divinity School, M Div, 1973; Princeton University, AB, 1969. Mr Thomas clerked for Judge Robert P Anderson of the US Court of Appeals, Second Circuit.

THOMAS, Frederick B
Mayer, Brown, Rowe & Maw LLP, Chicago 312 701 7035
fthomas@mayerbrownrowe.com
Recommended in Corporate/M&A
Practice Areas: Partner in Corporate Practice in Chicago. Advises clients on stock acquisitions, asset acquisitions, mergers, joint ventures, financings, tender offers, shareholder disputes, and a variety of other matters involving US, foreign and multinational businesses.

Provides advice to boards of directors and management regarding corporate governance and securities matters. Extensive representation of clients in technology businesses. Represents large US corporations, other US clients of various types and foreign corporations.
Career: Served as Law Clerk to The Honorable John C Godbold, US Court of Appeals for the Fifth Circuit, Montgomery, AL, from 1974-75. Joined Mayer, Brown, Rowe & Maw LLP, Chicago, in 1975. Served in London office from 1978-81 and became Partner in 1981. Serves on Management Committee of Mayer, Brown, Rowe & Maw LLP.
Personal: JD, University of Chicago, 1974; Joseph Henry Beale Prize; Comment Editor, 'University of Chicago Law Review'. AB, magna cum laude, Dartmouth College, 1971; Phi Beta Kappa. Board of Managers of the YMCA of Metropolitan Chicago; Board of Trustees of LaRabida Children's Hospital; Vice-Chair, Planning Committee of Ray Garrett, Jr., Corporate and Securities Law Institute. Adjunct Professor of Law (teaching corporations) at the University of Notre Dame, London Law Center, 1980-81.

TILSON, Joseph
Meckler, Bulger & Tilson, Chicago
312 474 7900
Recommended in Employment

TOMLINSON PC, Stephen G
Kirkland & Ellis LLP, Chicago
312 861 2386
stomlinson@kirkland.com
Recommended in Real Estate
Practice Areas: Stephen G Tomlinson, PC is a Senior Partner in Kirkland & Ellis' Real Estate Practice Group. Mr Tomlinson's practice focuses on complex business transactions in the hospitality and real estate industries for real estate private equity sponsors, institutional investors, real estate investment trusts (REITs) and real estate operating companies engaged in acquisitions and dispositions, operating company investments and formations, and multi-investor fund formations and investments.
Personal: University of Michigan, AB, 1981; University of Michigan, JD, 1984.

TORRES, Joseph J
Winston & Strawn LLP, Chicago
312 558 7334
jtorres@winston.com
Recommended in Employment
Practice Areas: Labor, employment and employee benefits litigation before trial and appellate courts; collective bargaining and labor disputes; labor and employment aspects of corporate mergers, acquisitions, divestitures, and reductions-in-force.
Prof. Memberships: Member, American Bar Association, Labor and Employment Section; Member, Hispanic Lawyers Association of Illinois; Chair-

man, Hispanic Lawyers Scholarship Fund.
Career: Joined firm in 1990; became Partner, 1998; Co-Chair of firm Diversity Committee; Member of Hiring Committee.
Publications: Associate editor, 'The Developing Labor Law' (Bureau of National Affairs); Contributing Editor, 'Employment Discrimination Law' (BNA).
Personal: University of Chicago, 1985; University of Illinois College of Law, 1990.

TOTH, Bruce
Winston & Strawn LLP, Chicago
312 558 5600
Recommended in Corporate/M&A

TOWBIN, Steven
Shaw Gussis Fishman Glantz Wolfson & Towbin LLC, Chicago
312 541 0151
Recommended in Bankruptcy

TOWNSEND, Christopher
DLA Piper Rudnick Gray Cary US LLP, Chicago 312 368 4039
christopher.townsend@dlapiper.com
Recommended in Energy
Practice Areas: Energy; environmental.
Career: He has experience in all aspects of energy, public utility, communications, and environmental law and regulation and regularly counsels clients, including independent power producers, competitive suppliers and customers, in strategic analyses and structuring transactions to conform to legal and regulatory requirements. He has been involved in a wide variety of regulatory proceedings and related appeals, emphasizing matters related to restructuring in the electric and natural gas industries. He frequently assists consumers in negotiating natural gas, electric, on-site generation, chilled water supply, and cable and telecommunications contracts.
Personal: JD, University of Iowa; BA, Augustana College.

TREECE, John
Sidley Austin Brown & Wood LLP, Chicago 312 853 2937
jtreece@sidley.com
Recommended in Antitrust
Practice Areas: John Treece is one of the leaders of the firm's Antitrust Practice. He has substantial experience in multi-district class actions alleging horizontal price-fixing as well as vertical price-fixing and price discrimination cases. He coordinated the successful defense of G.D. Searle & Co. in In Re Brand Name Prescription Drugs Antitrust Litigation, a class action price-fixing trial in which plaintiffs sought $1.1 billion in damages from Searle. After 10 weeks of trial, the court directed a verdict for the defense. He also represented Kimberly-Clark in In re Commercial Tissue Paper Antitrust Litiga-

tion, a multi-district price-fixing action settled in 2000 for less than the plaintiffs' attorneys' fees, and the only defendant to obtain summary judgment in In re Cement and Concrete Antitrust Litigation in the early 1980s. Currently, he represents Searle in numerous 'opt-out' Sherman Act cases, Citibank in In re Currency Conversion Fee Antitrust Litigation, Microsoft in In re Microsoft Corporation Antitrust Litigation, and a Japanese producer in an industrial products price-fixing case. Mr Treece has been closely involved in many state 'indirect purchaser' actions and is experienced with the relevant class certification issues. He is active in healthcare antitrust cases, including the first to consider the antitrust implications of preferred provider organizations. He counsels clients on merger matters (for example, AT&T/NCR, Kimberly-Clark/Scott, and Maytag/Amana) and on Robinson-Patman price discrimination issues.
Prof. Memberships: Member: American and Chicago Bar Associations.
Career: Columbia University School of Law, JD, 1978; Harvard University, BA, 1975. Admission: Illinois.

VALUKAS, Anton
Jenner & Block LLP, Chicago
312 923 2903
avalukas@jenner.com
Recommended in Litigation
Practice Areas: Anton R Valukas is a Partner in Jenner & Block's Chicago office. A former United States Attorney, he specializes in major civil and white collar criminal litigation, representing individuals and leading corporations in contested proceedings throughout the nation. He is Chair of the firm's White Collar Criminal Defense and Counseling Practice and serves on the firm's Policy Committee. He is a Fellow of the American College of Trial Lawyers and is listed in a leading US legal publication for business litigation and criminal law. Mr Valukas has been lead counsel in a variety of matters relating to government contracts and issues of fraud and compliance. He represents many Fortune 500 companies and public entities with conflict of interest, ethics violations and internal corporate investigations. He counsels clients on matters pending before such regulatory bodies as the grand jury, SEC, CFTC, FDA and others. He has successfully defended several media companies, broadcast and print, in cases of libel and defamation, invasion of privacy, and violation of federal eavesdropping laws. Mr Valukas has a wide range of experience in the healthcare area. He has assisted many corporations in developing corporate compliance policies, and conducted internal investigations for matters ranging from sale of products to embargoed countries to misrepresentations in new drug applications. He has successfully

resolved many matters prior to the filing of charges, has handled many qui tam actions regarding Medicare/Medicaid and PATH fraud allegations, and resulting shareholders derivative suits.
Personal: Northwestern University School of Law, JD, 1968.

VEZEAU, Timothy
Katten Muchin Zavis Rosenman, Chicago 312 902 5516
timothy.vezeau@kmzr.com
Recommended in Intellectual Property
Practice Areas: Founder and Manager of the firm's Patent Practice, concentrating in intellectual property litigation, licensing and counseling, particularly handling high-tech patent disputes for clients. Represents individuals, small corporations and large corporations in patent, trademark and copyright infringement matters; unfair competition, unfair trade, and trade secret issues; and employer-employee disputes.
Prof. Memberships: American Bar Association, Chicago Bar Association, Illinois State Bar Association.
Career: 1967, engineer at the McDonnell Douglas Corporation; 1968-70, patent examiner in 1968 in the United States Patent and Trademark Office; 1970-71, patent advisor to the United States Navy; 1971-present, private national IP law practice; 1999, joined Katten Muchin Zavis Rosenman as equity Partner; Member of Board of Directors.
Publications: 'Unreasonable Delay In Pursuing Claims Puts US Patents at Risk', February 2004; 'Intellectual Property and the New Economy', 2 November 2000; 'Trademarks, Patents and the Internet', 29 September 2000.
Personal: Georgetown University Law Center (JD 1971); Saint Louis University (BSEE 1966).

VIDMAR, Jacqueline M
Sonnenschein Nath & Rosenthal LLP, Chicago 312 876 7436
jvidmar@sonnenschein.com
Recommended in Environment
Practice Areas: Environmental Practice Vice Chair, advising on environmental law, from regulatory compliance and enforcement defense to remediation and redevelopment of contaminated properties. Appears before state and federal courts and administrative bodies. Counsels on permitting strategies; compliance requirements; disclosure obligations; governmental approvals; indoor air quality standards; asbestos handling and lead-based paint abatement. Also advises real estate and corporate clients on hazardous waste liability.
Prof. Memberships: ABA Section on Natural Resources and Environmental Law; Treasurer, Board Member, Chicago Committee on Minorities in Large Law Firms; Board Member, Asian American Bar Association for Greater Chicago.

VISHNESKI, John S
Mayer, Brown, Rowe & Maw LLP,
Chicago 312 701 7210
jvishneski@mayerbrownrowe.com
Recommended in Insurance

Practice Areas: Represents policyholders in complex insurance coverage litigation. Special emphasis on environmental and intellectual property insurance coverage disputes, having represented clients before numerous courts in many jurisdictions, including the Supreme Court of Illinois and the Supreme Court of Connecticut. Has represented policyholders in insurance coverage disputes involving diverse types of insurance, including First Party Property policies, General Liability policies, Directors & Officers Liability policies and Employment Practices Liability policies. Practice is nationwide and has also involved Lloyds and the London Market.
Career: Mayer, Brown, Rowe & Maw LLP, Chicago, 2001 to date; Partner, 2001. Neal, Gerber & Eisenberg, Chicago.
Publications: Representative aricles/presentations: 'The Plain Meaning Of 'Wrongful Entry or Eviction or Other Invasion of the Right of Private Occupancy': Why Standard-Form Personal Injury Insurance Coverage Applies to Pollution Claim', Environmental Claims Journal (Winter 1999). 'Insurance Coverage for Internet Liabilities,' A Presentation To Members of the Chicago Bar Association (June 23, 1998). 'The Illinois Estoppel Doctrine: Illinois Courts Make It Costly For Insurers To Breach Their Duty To Defend', Environmental Claims Journal (Autumn 1995).
Personal: JD, University of Virginia, 1988. University of Virginia, BA magna cum laude, 1985; Phi Beta Kappa.

VROMAN, James A
Jenner & Block LLP, Chicago
312 923 2836
jvroman@jenner.com
Recommended in Environment

Practice Areas: James A Vroman is a Partner in Jenner & Block's Chicago office. He is Co-Chair of the firm's Environmental, Energy and Natural Resources Practice. Mr Vroman has extensive experience in a wide variety of environmental and toxic tort matters. He has represented litigation clients in CERCLA cost-recovery actions, both as plaintiffs and defendants. In these matters he has encountered issues ranging from environmental "stigma" to technical impracticability to human health and environmental exposure risks. He has defended clients in RCRA, Clean Water Act and TSCA enforcement actions and in Superfund proceedings initiated by the EPA under 106, 107 and 122 of CERCLA. Mr Vroman negotiated on behalf of a major client of the firm, a ground-breaking CERCLA administrative order on consent which governed the remediation of 38 PCB-contaminated sites located in five EPA regions and

nine states. He has also represented and advised a major client who remediated a former Manufactured Gas Plant site under the Illinois Site Remediation Program. The remediation of this MGP site has become the largest cleanup project under the voluntary Illinois remediation program. Mr Vroman has represented clients in dispute resolution proceedings involving allocation issues before mediators and arbitrators. He has counseled transactional clients on environmental considerations in corporate and real estate matters and has supervised environmental due diligence efforts for significant acquisitions and divestitures. He also has extensive experience in counseling clients remediating or marketing 'brownfield' properties.
Personal: University of Illinois College of Law, JD, 1977, magna cum laude.

WALL, Robert
Winston & Strawn LLP, Chicago
312 558 5699
rwall@winston.com
Recommended in Corporate/M&A

Practice Areas: Senior Partner in Corporate Department. Concentration in mergers and acquisitions and corporate finance for public companies. Represented clients in these areas since 1977. Recently, represented Keebler Foods Company in sale to Kellogg Company; represented Airgate PCS, Inc. in connection with merger involving Alamosa Holdings, Inc.; represented special committee of Board of Directors of Orbitz, Inc. in connection with Cendent Corporation's acquisition of Orbitz; and represented Reyes Holdings, Inc. in connection with its acquisition of Reinhart FoodService, Inc.; represented Morgan Stanley in secondary stock offering of CDW Corporation. Frequent speaker at seminars and member of various securities and merger and acquisition organisations.
Prof. Memberships: Member, Editorial Board, Mergers and Acquisitions and Corporate Control Law Reporter; Chair, Northwestern University's Ray Garrett Securities Institute.
Career: Joined firm as associate, 1977. Partner, 1984.
Personal: University of Virginia, 1970; Northwestern University, BA, with distinction, 1973; Santa Clara University, JD, summa cum laude, 1977, comments editor, 'Santa Clara Law Review'.

WALTER, Priscilla A (Pam)
Gardner Carton & Douglas LLP,
Chicago 312 569 1475
pwalter@gcd.com
Recommended in Technology

Practice Areas: Ms Walter focuses her practice on information technology and e-business, including assisting clients in the development or acquisition of complex information systems and in the protection and distribution of software, databases and multimedia products. Ms

Walter also negotiates technology-focused joint venture and strategic partnering relationships and counsels clients on issues such as website development, privacy and security. Her clients include major banks and other financial institutions, governmental entities, equipment manufacturers and early-stage e-commerce ventures.
Prof. Memberships: Computer Law Association; American Bar Foundation; Society for Information Management; Information Integrity Coalition; Chairman, Chicago Shakespeare Theater; Board of Trustees and Executive Committee, Illinois Institute of Technology; Board of Overseers, Chicago-Kent School of Law; Board of Governors and Executive Committee, Metropolitan Planning Council; The Chicago Network.
Career: Founded firm's Cyberlaw and Intellectual Property Practice, which is part of Technology Department; served for six years on firm's Management Committee.
Publications: Frequent author, lecturer in cyberlaw, technology area.
Personal: Northwestern University, JD, 1978, magna cum laude; London School of Economics, MSc., 1967; Wellesley College, BA, 1965. Law Clerk to Judge Walter J Cummings, Seventh Circuit Court of Appeal, 1978-79.

WANDER, Herbert S
Katten Muchin Zavis Rosenman,
Chicago 312 902 5267
hwander@kmzr.com
Recommended in Corporate/M&A

Practice Areas: Partner, Chicago. Concentrates on all aspects of business law, especially corporate governance, securities law and M&A transactions. Has been the chief legal architect for many major M&A transactions, both negotiated and hostile. The SEC Chairman appointed him to Co-Chair the SEC's Advisory Committee on Smaller Public Companies. The SEC also selected him to be one of two securities lawyers to make a presentation at the SEC's April 2001 Regulation FD Roundtable.
Prof. Memberships: Served as Chair of the ABA's 53,000 member Business Law Section. Appointed by the President of the American Bar Association to serve on the Commission on Multidisciplinary Practice and the Task Force on Attorney Client Privilege. Past-President of the Jewish Federation of Metropolitan Chicago and the Jewish United Fund; Trustee and Vice-Chair of the Michael Reese Health Trust; Director of Telephone & Data Systems Inc., a $5 billion market cap telecommunications company. He is serving his second term as a member of the Legal Advisory Committee to the New York Stock Exchange Board of Governors. In 2002, he was nominated by his peers as one of the world's leading practitioners in the

field of corporate governance and is listed in The International Who's Who of Corporate Governance Lawyers.
Publications: Has authored numerous articles and book reviews in various publications including the Yale Law Journal, the Business Lawyer, the Northwestern University Law Review, and INSIGHTS. He was the first editor of the Business Law Section's magazine, Business Law Today and was the editor of Volume 49 (1993-94) of The Business Lawyer. Frequently speaks at institutes and programs of various business and legal organizations.
Personal: BA degree from the University of Michigan and a law degree from Yale Law School, where he was on the board of editors of the Yale Law Journal.

WARNECKE, Michael O
Mayer, Brown, Rowe & Maw LLP,
Chicago 312 701 8602
mwarnecke@mayerbrownrowe.com
Recommended in Intellectual Property

Practice Areas: First Chair in numerous major patent litigation cases. Experienced in international patent, technology licensing, and other IP matters. Frequent expert witness, arbitrator, and mediator.
Prof. Memberships: Fellow, American College of Trial Lawyers. American Bar Association.
Career: Joined Mayer, Brown, Rowe & Maw LLP, Chicago, 1996; became Partner 1996. Formerly with Keck, Mahin & Cate, Chicago, 1991-96; Neuman, Williams, Anderson & Olson, Chicago, 1967-91; US Patent and Trademark Office, US Patent Examiner, Group 350, Washington, DC, 1963-67.
Publications: Frequent lecturer. Selected by the People's Republic of China trade delegation to host two-day seminar for American automotive and aftermarket companies and the Chinese delegation on the legal aspects of doing business in China. Frequent lecturer and speaker, nationally and internationally, on intellectual property law, including Federal Court of Australia, IP Colloquium II, Melbourne, Australia, March 2001; Presentation to Federal Bench on United States litigation on how to determine issues to litigate and the conducting of Markman hearings on claim construction.
Personal: Born 28 June 1941. George Washington University, JD, 1967. Purdue University, BS, 1963.

WARNER, Michael
Seyfarth Shaw LLP, Chicago
312 346 8000
Recommended in Employment

WATERS, Paige D
Sonnenschein Nath & Rosenthal LLP,
Chicago 312 876 2545
pwaters@sonnenschein.com
Recommended in Insurance

Practice Areas: Insurance regulatory and public law and policy Partner. Han-

dles transactional, regulatory, litigation and insolvency matters involving national and international insurance, HMO, reinsurance and healthcare clients. Conducts internal corporate reviews of insurers and advises on broker and agent relationships, including contingent commission, bid rigging and tying issues. Assists international and domestic assuming and ceding insurers in mergers and acquisitions, entity formations and reinsurance transactions.
Prof. Memberships: Chicago Bar Association; International Association of Insurance Receivers; NCOIL-Industry Education Council; NAIC Insolvency Working Groups.
Personal: IIT Chicago-Kent College of Law, JD; Miami University, BA.

WEAVER, William
Sachnoff & Weaver LTD, Chicago
312 207 1000
Recommended in Private Equity

WEBB, Dan
Winston & Strawn LLP, Chicago
312 558 5856
dwebb@winston.com
Recommended in Litigation
Practice Areas: National trial practice in the areas of major commercial, civil, regulatory, and white-collar criminal cases.
Prof. Memberships: Fellow, American College of Trial Lawyers.
Career: Joined Winston & Strawn as Partner, 1985. Head, Litigation Department; Member, Executive Committee.
Publications: Co-author, 'Corporate Internal Investigations' (Law Journal Seminars Press).
Personal: Western Illinois University, 1967; Loyola University School of Law, JD 1970. Iran-Contra Special Trial Counsel; US Attorney, Northern District of Illinois, 1981-85; Illinois Department of Law Enforcement, 1979-80; Assistant US Attorney, 1970-76.

WEBER, Louis
Winston & Strawn LLP, Chicago
312 558 5600
Recommended in Tax

WEINBERG, Walter S
Katten Muchin Zavis Rosenman,
Chicago 312 902 5405
walter.weinberg@kmzr.com
Recommended in Private Equity
Practice Areas: Partner. Private equity and venture capital (including portfolio equity and mezzanine debt investments and recapitalizations, management representation, portfolio company representation, and fund formation; early stage to leveraged buy-outs); mergers and acquisitions; general corporate counseling.
Prof. Memberships: American Bar Association; Chicago Bar Association.
Publications: Speaker at ABA's Venture Capital and Private Equity Committee meetings and Chicago Bar Association

seminars; Guest Lecturer at Northwestern University Kellogg School of Business.
Personal: University of Chicago, BA (General Honors) - Economics (Phi Beta Kappa); Northwestern University, JD, cum laude (Order of the Coif).

WEINBERGER, Seth J
Mayer, Brown, Rowe & Maw LLP,
Chicago 312 701 7257
sweinberger@mayerbrownrowe.com
Recommended in Technology
Practice Areas: Advises both vendor and customer clients on IT and outsourcing transactions, including information technology development and maintenance, call center, telecommunications and network management transactions. Represents global industry IT joint ventures, including in the aviation, chemical and steel industries. Represents venture capital firms and companies seeking private equity or venture capital funding in various industries, including information technology, telecommunications and biotechnology. Represents Fortune 500 companies in e-business joint ventures and investments with e-business companies. Advises on tender offers, stock and asset purchases, leveraged buy-outs, management buy-outs and joint ventures.
Career: Mayer, Brown, Rowe & Maw LLP, Chicago, 1982 to date; Partner, 1986. Pitney, Hardin, Kipp & Szuch, Morristown, NJ, 1980-82.
Personal: University of Michigan Law School, JD cum laude, 1979. University of Michigan, BA with high honors, 1977. Founder of Innovations for Learning, a not-for-profit corporation that develops software for teaching reading to economically disadvantaged children. Founding director of Evanston First Night and the Cherry Preschool.

WEISBERG, Mark S
Winston & Strawn LLP, Chicago
312 558 8070
mweisberg@winston.com
Recommended in Employee Benefits
Practice Areas: Design, establishment and administration of retirement benefit, welfare benefit, and non-qualified deferred compensation plans. Negotiation and drafting of executive employment and equity compensation plans and agreements on behalf of companies and their compensation committees, individual executives and management teams. ERISA litigation.
Prof. Memberships: American Bar Association; National Association of Stock Plan Professionals.
Career: Previous Partner and Co-Chair of ERISA Group, KMZ Rosenman; to Winston as Partner, 2004.
Publications: Co-author of numerous articles in the 'Benefits Law Journal'; frequent speaker on noteworthy topics.
Personal: University of Pennsylvania, 1985; University of Pennsylvania Law

School, 1988; Trustee, Evanston Police Pension Fund.

WELKE, William R
Kirkland & Ellis LLP, Chicago
312 861 2143
wwelke@kirkland.com
Recommended in Tax
Practice Areas: Mr Welke focuses his practice on the tax aspects of complex business transactions and entities, including: mergers, acquisitions, and leveraged buyouts; venture capital and other private equity investments; formation of private equity funds; joint ventures and partnerships; debt and equity restructurings; and executive compensation.
Personal: Massachusetts Institute of Technology, SB, 1980. University of Michigan Law School, JD, 1983.

WEXLER, Kenneth
The Wexler Firm, Chicago
312 346 2222
Recommended in Antitrust

WHITE, Bruce
Karaganis, White & Magel, Chicago
312 836 1177
Recommended in Environment

WILLIAMS, Douglas H
Sidley Austin Brown & Wood LLP,
Chicago 312 853 7667
dwilliams@sidley.com
Recommended in Banking & Finance
Practice Areas: Partner in the Chicago office. Co-author of 'Legal Developments in Secured Lending (1978-94)'. Advisor to the National Conference of Commissioners on Uniform State Laws Drafting Committee to Revise UCC Article 6.
Prof. Memberships: American and Chicago Bar Associations.
Career: University of Chicago, JD, 1977; MBA, 1977; University of Michigan, BA, 1970. Bar Admission: Illinois, 1977.

WILLIAMSON, Joel V
Mayer, Brown, Rowe & Maw LLP,
Chicago 312 701 7229
jwilliamson@mayerbrownrowe.com
Recommended in Tax
Practice Areas: Firm Practice Leader, Tax Controversy. Has tried 50+ tax cases. Represented clients in six major international transfer pricing cases; financial products cases; captive insurance; Subpart F issues; constructive triangular dividends; R&D moratorium; Brazilian foreign tax credits; Iranian losses and foreign tax credits; tax accounting: sale and leaseback transactions; foreign source income on export sales; IRC Section 338 liquidations; trademark valuation, sale of assets for preferred stock, reorganization versus taxable sale treatment, and proper role of IRS trial counsel in audit examination process and summons enforcement; R&D allocation to DISC.
Career: Mayer, Brown, Rowe & Maw LLP as Partner, 1986-present. Special

Trial Attorney, Chief Counsel's Office, US Department of Treasury, 1972-85.
Publications: 'The Corporate Tax Director: Responsibilities in the New Era of Increased Corporate Accountability,' Taxes, March 2005. 'Litigating Transfer Pricing Cases' and 'Tax-Advantaged Transactions', co-author, Practicing Law Institute, 2001, 2002; 'Mrs. Gregory's Great-Grandchildren: The Lost Generation', 'Journal of Taxation of Global Transactions' (Summer 2002) (with Thomas C Durham and Stuart E Thiel).
Personal: JD, University of Kentucky, 1970; Order of the Coif; Law Review; Moot Court Board; National Moot Court Team. BA (1967), Davidson College. Officer, US Army, Ft. Bragg, NC; Republic of South Vietnam, 1970-72.

WITCOFF, David L
Jones Day, Chicago
312 269 4259
dwitcoff@jonesday.com
Recommended in Intellectual Property
Practice Areas: Specializes in litigating and resolving complex patent and other intellectual property disputes, with a particular emphasis in high-technology matters. He also actively counsels on all aspects of intellectual property and has handled matters across a broad spectrum of technologies, including semiconductor products and processing, Internet and World Wide Web systems and protocols, computer hardware and software, electronic commerce systems, cellular telephones, paging control systems, pharmaceuticals, medical devices, and diagnostic equipment, among others. He is admitted to practice before various US District Courts, the US Court of Appeals for the Federal Circuit, and the US Patent and Trademark Office.

WOLF, Charles
Vedder, Price, Kaufman & Kammholz,
Chicago 312 609 7500
Recommended in Employee Benefits, Litigation

WOLFE, David L
Gardner Carton & Douglas LLP,
Chicago 312 569 1313
dwolfe@gcd.com
Recommended in Employee Benefits
Practice Areas: Partner, HR Law Department; practice covers tax-qualified plans, health and welfare arrangements, executive compensation; benefits issues in corporate acquisitions and divestitures, benefits issues for tax-exempt clients, US benefits for international clients, ERISA fiduciary issues and litigation, cash balance and other hybrid pension arrangements, legal compliance reviews and non-qualified deferred compensation arrangements.
Prof. Memberships: Named in 'The Best Lawyers in America' (1993-2004).
Career: Member, firm Management Committee; frequent lecturer, including before ABA, ISBA, CBA, IICLE.

Publications: Contributor, DePaul Law Review, Akron Law Review, CCH Financial and Estate Planning Reporter, The Practical Lawyer, Legal Checklists, Chicago Bar Record, IICLE Handbooks (on S Corporations and Employee Benefits Law), IICLE, ISBA and ABA outlines, ISBA Employee Benefits Section Newsletter; Contributor, 'Health Care Industry,' CCH Tax Transactions Library; co-author, 'Securing Benefits in an Insecure Time,' Employee Benefits Journal, September 2002; co-author, 'Forewarned and Forearmed: Cash balance plans revisited,' Plan Sponsor, November 2002; co-author, 'Era of Corporate Governance,' Employee Benefit Plan Review, November 2002; co-author, 'Compensation in 2003,' Employee Benefit Plan Review, January 2003; co-author, 'Expensing Stock Options: Ten Predictions for 2003 and Beyond,' Employee Benefit Plan Review, March 2003;

Personal: JD cum laude, University of Michigan, 1976, BS, University of Illinois, 1973; CPA (IL-1993).

WOOTTON, Robert R
Sidley Austin Brown & Wood LLP, Chicago 312 853 7257
rwootton@sidley.com
Recommended in Tax

Practice Areas: Robert Wootton focuses on federal tax matters, with emphasis on the representation of US and Canadian corporations, public and private, in mergers and acquisitions, spin-offs and other restructuring transactions. He has considerable experience in the design and implementation of financial products and in the resolution of disputes with the Internal Revenue Service regarding the tax treatment of such products. Mr Wootton served for two years as the Tax Legislative Counsel of the US Treasury Department and was a principal advisor to the Assistant Secretary for Tax Policy on domestic tax matters.

Career: Yale Law School, JD, 1979; Yale University, BA Economics, 1974; Oxford University, B Philosophy, 1976. Bar Admission: Illinois, 1979.

WYLIE, Kenneth R
Sidley Austin Brown & Wood LLP, Chicago 312 853 7157
kwylie@sidley.com
Recommended in Insurance

Practice Areas: Kenneth R Wylie concentrates his practice in insurance law with emphasis on insurance regulatory matters that affect insurance companies, agents and brokers, and other insurance entities. Mr Wylie has provided legal and counseling services on corporate, commercial and regulatory matters for insurance industry organizations, including the organization and acquisition of insurance companies, the evaluation of captives and alternative risk transfer vehicles, and insurance risk securitizations.

He has extensive experience representing insurance guaranty funds, insureds, reinsurers, reinsureds, claimants and other parties involved in insurance company insolvencies. Mr Wylie handles reinsurance arbitrations, including disputes involving reinsurance pools.

Prof. Memberships: Member: Federation of Regulatory Counsel, AIDA Reinsurance and Insurance Arbitration Society (US), and the Chicago and American Bar Associations, including the respective insurance committees of these two associations.

Career: The University of Michigan Law School (JD, 1977) Michigan State University (BS in Mechanical Engineering, 1973, high honors) Admissions: US District Court, N.D. of Illinois - General, 1977; Illinois, 1977.

YASTROW, Joseph
Laner, Muchin, Dombrow, Becker, Levin, Tominberg, Chicago
312 467 9800
jyastrow@lanermuchin.com
Recommended in Employment

Practice Areas: Management side labor and employment law.

Prof. Memberships: Member; former Chair Chicago Bar Association Labor and Employment Law Committee. Member; Sub-Committee Chair, American Bar Association. Multiple selections to Chambers Guide to America's Leading Business Lawyers and as one of Illinois' Leading Labor and Employment Attorneys.

Career: Mr Yastrow has exclusively represented employers in labor and employment law matters since 1978 primarily with Laner, Muchin where he is a Partner and an Executive Committee member.

Personal: SMU School of Law (JD 1978). Law Review Editor. Member, The Barristers. Dartmouth College (AB 1975). Rufus Choate Scholar. Intercollegiate Rugby 1971-75. Married, two children.

YODER, Lowell D
McDermott Will & Emery, Chicago
312 984 7523
lyoder@mwe.com
Recommended in Tax

Practice Areas: Partner in Tax Department and Co-Chair of International Tax Practice. Focuses on international tax planning for multinationals. Advises on cross-border acquisitions, mergers, financings, restructurings and repatriation. Advises on foreign tax credits, expense allocations, sourcing of income, Subpart F and passive foreign investment companies.

Prof. Memberships: Member of the Illinois Bar Association; American Bar Association; American College of Tax Counsel; International Fiscal Association.

Career: Admitted to the Illinois Bar in 1982. Federal Clerkship, 1982-83, Hon-

orable James M Sprouse, US Circuit Court of Appeals for the Fourth Circuit. Joined McDermott, Will & Emery in 1983. Editor-in-chief of 'Journal of Taxation of Global Transactions' and board member of 'Journal of International Taxation' and 'Tax Management International Journal'. Frequent speaker for Practising Law Institute, Tax Executives Institute and International Fiscal Association. Adjunct Professor of International Tax Law.

Publications: Author of three treatises on Subpart F (rules that apply to foreign operations of US multinationals); author of numerous articles on international tax topics including classification of foreign entities, affect of foreign losses on the use of foreign tax credits, and the treatment of foreign partnerships.

Personal: Attended University of Illinois College of Law 1979 to 1982 (JD, magna cum laude).

YURA, Mark
DLA Piper Rudnick Gray Cary US LLP, Chicago 312 368 4084
mark.yura@dlapiper.com
Recommended in Real Estate

Practice Areas: Real estate.

Career: Concentrates his practice in real estate transaction matters and his clients include lenders, investors and developers. He is a frequent speaker before trade and professional groups on matters of state and federal legislation, multi-family housing financing and commercial real estate lending topics and has taught real estate finance law at the University of Michigan Law School and in the LLM Program in Real Estate Law at The John Marshall Law School.

Personal: JD, University of Michigan, cum laude; BA, University of Michigan, with high honors.

ZABEL, Sheldon
Schiff Hardin LLP, Chicago
312 258 5540
szabel@schiffhardin.com
Recommended in Environment

Practice Areas: Environmental.

Prof. Memberships: American Bar Association.

Career: Mr Zabel concentrates in environmental, natural resources and public utility law. He has principal responsibility for environmental matters for several public utilities. He has participated in significant environmental matters on behalf of operating units of numerous power companies and automobile manufacturers. He also has principal representation of the Steering Committee at the Rose Chemical Site, Holden, Missouri, one of the largest PCB CERCLA sites in the United States.

Personal: Princeton University (AB, Economics, cum laude, 1963), Northwestern University Law School (JD, cum laude, 1966).

ZAROV, Herbert
Mayer, Brown, Rowe & Maw LLP, Chicago 312 701 7317
hzarov@mayerbrownrowe.com
Recommended in Litigation

Practice Areas: Senior litigator and firm Practice Leader in litigation. Extensive experience in mass torts, federal securities law class actions, and complex commercial litigation. Served as national counsel for The Dow Chemical Company in multi-district breast implant litigation and currently national co-counsel for Union Carbide Corporation in asbestos litigation. Also experienced in securities, appellate, and tax litigation.

Prof. Memberships: Admitted in Illinois, 1979; US Supreme Court, 1996; US District Court for the Northern District of Illinois, 1979; US Court of Appeals for the Third Circuit, 1992; US Court of Appeals for the Sixth Circuit, 1995; US Court of Appeals for the Seventh Circuit, 1981; US Court of Appeals for the Ninth Circuit, 1991; US Tax Court, 1984; US Court of Claims, 1985.

Career: Joined Mayer, Brown, Rowe & Maw LLP, 1986; became Partner in 1987. Member of Management Committee and is Co-Chairman of the Litigation Group. Prior firm: Friedman & Koven, Chicago, 1977-86. Taught English and American Studies at Smith College from 1973-76. Also taught at Washington University of St. Louis, University of Missouri, Roosevelt University, Wilson Junior College (now Kennedy-King), pre-1973.

Personal: JD, University of Chicago,1979. MA, University of Chicago, 1968. BA, Columbia University, 1967.

ZAZOVE, Daniel
Perkins Coie, Chicago
312 324 8400
Recommended in Bankruptcy

ZELEK, Eugene
Freeborn & Peters, Chicago
312 360 6000
Recommended in Antitrust, Media & Entertainment

ZIMBLER, Jay
Sidley Austin Brown & Wood LLP, Chicago 312 853 2232
jzimbler@sidley.com
Recommended in Tax

Practice Areas: Practice focused on federal income taxation. Experienced in the taxation of foreign related transactions, mergers and acquisitions, and contested tax matters. Has handled complex appellate cases for a variety of multinational corporations nationwide.

Prof. Memberships: American Bar Association; American College of Tax Counsel Fellow.

Career: Harvard Law School, JD, 1975; University of Michigan, BA, 1972. Certified Public Accountant. Bar Admission: Illinois, 1975.

ADELMAN & GETTLEMAN, LTD.

THE FIRM

Firm Size: 10

Website: www.ag-ltd.com

HEAD OFFICE

ILLINOIS
53 West Jackson Blvd., Suite 1050, **Chicago**, IL 60604
Tel: 312 435 1050   **Fax:** 312 435 1059

FIRM OVERVIEW: Adelman & Gettleman Ltd was founded in March 1983 by Howard L Adelman and Chad H Gettleman, both of whom have devoted their entire professional career to the areas of bankruptcy, corporate reorganization and insolvency, and commercial litigation. The firm presently has six (6) principals including: Howard L Adelman, Chad H Gettleman, Henry B Merens, Brad A Berish, Mark A Carter and Adam P Silverman, all of whom have devoted their entire professional careers to the foregoing areas of concentration. The firm is the only Chicago Bankruptcy boutique firm having its lawyers recognized in Illinois Leading Lawyers Network, Best Lawyers in America, Woodward/White, World's Leading Lawyers by Chambers and Partners, Legal Publishers 2002-2003, and America's Leading Lawyers for Business, Chambers & Partners, Legal Publishers 2004. Two of its attorneys, Chad H Gettleman and Brad A Berish are also non-practicing Certified Public Accountants. In October of 1999, Chief Justice William Rehnquist appointed Howard L Adelman to serve as a member of the Judicial Conference Advisory Committee on the Federal Rules of Bankruptcy Procedure. Mr Adelman is also a Fellow of the American College of Bankruptcy, as part of its Twelfth Class.

AREAS OF PRACTICE: Insolvency, bankruptcy and reorganization law, general civil and trial practice, corporation, commercial, and real estate. In addition to commercial litigation in the State and Federal Courts, the firm has participated in many major bankruptcy and reorganization cases, representing debtors, trustees, secured creditors and committees. Approximately 75% of the firm's matters consist of litigation in the Bankruptcy Courts. The firm has an extensive internal continuing legal education program. Members of the firm participate as speakers in seminars and commercial litigation programs, and offer articles on areas of their concentration. Its bankruptcy and commercial litigation practice is highly regarded and respected in bankruptcy courts throughout Illinois, Indiana, and Wisconsin. They seek innovative approaches and solutions in the workout context, but stand prepared to draw upon our substantial litigation experience in complex bankruptcy litigation when necessary. They are experienced in resolving the business and legal problems that arise when commercial transactions, credit agreements, business plans, and mortgages fail to proceed as intended.

Its bankruptcy attorneys routinely handle the following matters for its clients: advising management, boards of directors, and committees of directors of troubled companies before and during Chapter 11 proceedings, including counselling financially distressed companies of viable alternatives to commencing a bankruptcy case; identifying problems and solutions which may or will arise in bankruptcy cases and structuring the potential resolution of same prior to their emergence; handling cash collateral negotiations and debtor-in-possession financing arrangements; structuring and implementing the purchase and sale of businesses and assets from Chapter 11 debtors; handling complex Chapter 11 plan negotiations and the litigation of contested plan confirmation issues; prosecuting and defending preference litigation and fraudulent conveyance litigation; enforcing the rights of secured creditors; handling single asset real estate partnership cases; providing corporate restructuring advice.

BAKER & MCKENZIE

THE FIRM

Chairman of the Executive Committee: John J Conroy
NA Managing Partner: David P Hackett

Number of North American partners: 170
Number of other lawyers in North America: 415
Number of partners worldwide: 1080
Number of other lawyers worldwide: 2137

Email: info@bakernet.com
Website: www.bakernet.com

FIRM OVERVIEW: For more than 50 years, Baker & McKenzie has provided sophisticated legal advice and services to many of the world's most dynamic global organizations. Helping clients understand and thrive in diverse legal, political, social and economic systems made Baker & McKenzie one of the world's largest law firms and the first to be truly global. With a network of more than 3,000 locally qualified, internationally experienced lawyers in 38 countries, the firm has the knowledge and resources to deliver the broad scope of quality legal services required to respond effectively to both international and local needs – consistently, confidently and with sensitivity for cultural, social and legal practice differences. The 8,400 professionals of Baker & McKenzie share common values of integrity, personal responsibility and tenacity in an enthusiastic client-service culture. The firm is still guided by the entrepreneurial spirit and demanding standards of its founders, and since its earliest days, it has worked to forge close personal relationships among its professionals in order to foster the responsiveness and accountability clients rightfully expect. The firm has a diverse and welcoming culture with a global mindset. The lawyers and other professionals in its network are citizens of more than 60 countries, are admitted to practice in nearly 250 jurisdictions and have been educated at more than 1,200 institutions, including nearly all of the world's leading law schools. More than 60 languages are spoken, with English being the firm's common language. The firm's teams are supported by advanced technologies and sophisticated management systems. These include a single, shared global technology platform, including client intake, financial and billing systems, e-mail, intranet and client extranets as well as global practice standards, a quality audit program and a worldwide conflicts policy based on the standards of the American Bar Association.

MAIN AREAS OF PRACTICE:

Global areas of practice include: Antitrust and trade; banking and finance; corporate, including mergers and acquisitions, private equity and securities; dispute resolution; labor, employment and employee benefits; insurance; intellectual property; international/commercial; information technology and communications; major projects and project finance; real estate; construction; environment; tourism and tax.

CLIENTS: Baker & McKenzie provides exceptional service to domestic and international clients in a wide variety of industries and sectors by forming multi-disciplinary teams that share the clients' interests. The firm's extensive client list includes multinational and domestic entities, a great many of which engage the firm on a multi-jurisdictional basis. Clients include major corporations, financial institutions and other business entities, as well as governments and other organizations. Baker & McKenzie is widely recognized as a pre-eminent provider of legal services by leading publications, professional organizations and research institutions.

INTERNATIONAL WORK: Baker & McKenzie provides legal services to most of the world's largest corporations as well as a broad spectrum of regional and local organizations. The firm is widely recognized as a pre-eminent

US OFFICES

CALIFORNIA
660 Hansen Way, **Palo Alto**, CA 94304
Tel: 650 856 2400   **Fax:** 650 856 9299
Email: peter.j.engstrom@bakernet.com

101 West Broadway, 12th Floor, **San Diego**, CA 92101
Tel: 619 236 1441   **Fax:** 619 236 0429
Email: charles.h.dick@bakernet.com

Two Embarcadero Center, 24th Floor, **San Francisco**, CA 94111
Tel: 415 576 3000   **Fax:** 415 576 3099
Email: peter.j.engstrom@bakernet.com

DISTRICT OF COLUMBIA
815 Connecticut Avenue, NW, **Washington**, DC 20006
Tel: 202 452 7000   **Fax:** 202 452 7074
Email: thomas.j.egan@bakernet.com

FLORIDA
Mellon Financial Center, 1111 Brickell Avenue, Suite 1700, **Miami**, FL 33131
Tel: 305 789 8900   **Fax:** 305 789 8953
Email: roy.larson@bakernet.com

ILLINOIS
One Prudential Plaza, 130 East Randolph Dr, **Chicago**, IL 60601
Tel: 312 861 8000   **Fax:** 312 861 2899
Email: chicago.information@bakernet.com

NEW YORK
805 Third Avenue, **New York**, NY 10022
Tel: 212 751 5700   **Fax:** 212 759 9133
Email: gerald.j.hayes@bakernet.com

TEXAS
2300 Trammell Crow Center, 2001 Ross Avenue, **Dallas**, TX 75201
Tel: 214 978 3000   **Fax:** 214 978 3099
Email: brian.j.hurst@bakernet.com

Pennzoil Place, South Tower 711 Louisiana, Suite 3400, **Houston**, TX 77002
Tel: 713 427 5000   **Fax:** 713 427 5099
Email: graham.k.blair@bakernet.com

INTERNATIONAL OFFICES

Baker & McKenzie has over 50 offices in more than 35 countries outside of the United States.

provider of legal services by leading publications, professional organizations and research institutions. Among its honors: Corporate Board Member magazine rates them among the 10 most admired corporate law firms in the United States. PLC Global Counsel Law Firm Awards has chosen them as 'International Law Firm of the Year' and 'Asia Pacific Law Firm of the Year'. The firm was honored as the 'Latin America Banking and Finance Team of the Year' in the Chambers Global awards. The firm has also been honored for the 'Best Global Use of IT' in awards presented by Legal IT.

BAKER & MCKENZIE

Baker & McKenzie LLP is a member firm of Baker & McKenzie International, a Swiss Verein with member law firms around the world. In accordance with the common terminology used in professional service organizations, reference to a "partner" means a person who is a partner, or equivalent, in such a law firm. Similarly, reference to an "office" means an office of any such law firm.

BRINKS HOFER GILSON & LIONE

THE FIRM

President: Jerold A Jacover

Number of partners: 60
Number of other lawyers: 90

FIRM OVERVIEW: Founded in 1917, Brinks Hofer Gilson & Lione has more than 150 attorneys and is one of the largest intellectual property law firms in the United States. The firm's attorneys specialize in intellectual property litigation and all aspects of patent, trademark, copyright, trade secret and internet work, unfair competition, and technology and licensing agreements. The firm has repeatedly ranked as the leading IP firm in Chicago and the Midwest and is ranked 4th among law firms representing the IP needs of the most companies in the Global 100.

MAIN AREAS OF PRACTICE:

Patents: Brinks patent lawyers have experience prosecuting patents in every major technical field and help clients obtain and license patents, enforce them against infringers, and defend against charges of infringement. *Managing Intellectual Property* magazine ranked the firm 6th among the top 10 law firms for patent litigation in the United States.
Trademarks: The Trademark Group at Brinks performs the full range of trademark-related services in the United States and abroad, including registering, enforcing, opposing, and defending trademark rights. *Managing Intellectual Property* magazine ranked the firm among the top 15 firms in the US for both contentious and non-contentious trademark work.
Trade Secrets: Brinks lawyers regularly advise clients on the application of individual state trade secret laws and regularly represent plaintiffs and defendants in a wide variety of trade secret disputes.
Copyrights: Brinks attorneys assist both artists and businesses prepare and file domestic and foreign applications to register copyrights in many fields, including book, magazine and music publishing; photocopying; sound recordings; the visual arts; television and motion pictures; theater and dance; compilations and databases; computer software; video games; multimedia, virtual reality and the internet; and international treaties.
Unfair Competition: The Unfair Competition Group at Brinks represents victims and alleged infringers in the resolution of unfair competition disputes in multiple areas including trade-dress infringement, counterfeit products, dilution, unfair trade practices and right of publicity.

CLIENTS: Brinks represents a wide range of major US and international corporations.

HEAD OFFICE

ILLINOIS
NBC Tower, Suite 3600, 455 N. Cityfront Plaza Drive, **Chicago**, IL 60611-5599
Tel: 312 321 4200 **Fax:** 312 321 4299
Website: www.usebrinks.com

BRANCH OFFICES

INDIANA
One Indiana Square, Suite 1600, **Indianapolis**, IN 46204-2033
Tel: 317 636 0886 **Fax:** 317 634 6701

MICHIGAN
524 S. Main, Suite 200, **Ann Arbor**, MI 48104
Tel: 734 302 6000 **Fax:** 734 994 6331

VIRGINIA
Crystal Plaza One, Suite 208, 2001 Jefferson Davis Highway, **Arlington**, VA 22202-3603
Tel: 703 415 0303 **Fax:** 703 415 0304

BRINKS

HOFER

GILSON

& LIONE ®

**Intellectual Property
Law Worldwide**

CHAPMAN AND CUTLER LLP

THE FIRM

Chief Executive Partner: Richard A Cosgrove
Chief Operating Partner: Steven L Clark
Number of partners: 115
Number of other lawyers: 83

FIRM OVERVIEW: Founded in 1913, the firm has focused on finance. The firm is one of the country's preeminent law firms in banking, bankruptcy and financial litigation, corporate finance and securities, public finance and tax. This focus enables the firm to consistently develop innovative and practical legal solutions for complex financial transactions. To complement that focus, the firm maintains a substantial corporate practice representing business entities in administrative and regulatory matters, commercial litigation, divestitures, employee benefits, intellectual property, joint ventures, and mergers and acquisitions. The firm also provides sophisticated trust and estate planning services for high net worth individuals.

MAIN AREAS OF PRACTICE:

Asset Securitization: The firm represents clients in domestic and cross-border asset-backed and mortgage-backed securities, tax-exempt and CDO transactions. Asset classes financed include traditional trade receivables, student loans, tobacco settlements, meal credits, timeshares, leases, and 12b-1 fees.

Banking, Bank Regulatory & Consumer Financial Services: The firm has a comprehensive banking practice, with emphasis on syndicated bank credits, asset-based lending transactions, bank mergers and acquisitions, real estate finance, lease finance (including synthetic leases), credit enhancement, swaps and derivatives, consumer financial services, bank regulatory compliance and examination activities, cash management, payment systems and technology and securitization of receivables as well as other traditional commercial bank lending activities.

Bankruptcy, Workouts & Commercial Litigation: The firm is nationally recognized as one of the leading creditors' counsel in bankruptcy, restructuring and workouts and has been involved in many of the largest bankruptcies in the United States, including major airline, utilities, retail and manufacturing cases. In addition, the firm maintains a strong commercial, financial and consumer finance litigation and dispute resolution practice.

Corporate Counseling, Employee Benefits & Intellectual Property: The firm provides general corporate counseling to a variety of domestic and international corporate clients.

Corporate Finance & Securities: The firm represents financial institutions and issuers in connection with public and private offerings of debt and equity securities, including domestic and cross-border private placements and Rule 144A offerings, public offerings, private equity, mezzanine and project finance. The firm also counsels issuers with respect to disclosure requirements, stock exchange rules and compliance with the requirements of the Sarbanes-Oxley Act.

Investment Companies & Investment Partnerships: The firm serves as counsel to investment companies, sponsors and advisors to investment companies, and the independent members of investment company boards of directors.

Lease Finance: The firm is a market leader in representing a wide range of lessees, lessors, capital providers and underwriters in lease finance transactions with extensive experience with all types of lease finance structures. The firm also represents leasing companies in portfolio management, financing and joint venture transactions.

Public Finance: The firm has been one of the country's preeminent law firms in state and municipal finance and has consistently served as bond counsel on more municipal bond issues each year than any other law firm in the country.

Tax: The firm is nationally recognized for its advice on tax issues involved in corporate and municipal finance transactions, with particular emphasis on

HEAD OFFICE

ILLINOIS
111 West Monroe Street, **Chicago**, IL 60603
Tel: 312 845 3000 **Fax:** 312 701 2361
Website: www.chapman.com

BRANCH OFFICES

CALIFORNIA
595 Market Street, **San Francisco**, CA 94105
Tel: 415 541 0500 **Fax:** 415 541 0506

UTAH
50 South Main Street, **Salt Lake City**, UT 84144
Tel: 801 533 0066 **Fax:** 801 533 9595

CONTACTS

Head Office Contacts ....Ronald E Rokosz, Marc P Franson

the representation of state and local governments and financial institutions.
Trust Counsel & Estate Planning: The firm represents the corporate and personal trust departments of financial institutions and provides estate and gift planning and probate services.

CLIENTS: US commercial banks, many of the world's largest foreign banks, insurance companies, investment banks, corporate and governmental issuers, investors and credit providers including: ABN AMRO, Allstate Bank, American General Finance, Bank of America, Bank of Montreal, Bank of New York, Bank of Tokyo-Mitsubishi, Bank One, Bayerische Landesbank, Citizens Financial Group, Dredsner, BNP Paribas, First Midwest Bank, Fifth Third Bank, GE Capital, Harris Bank, HypoVereinsbank, Landesbank Hessen Thuringen, LaSalle Bank, Metris Companies, Mizuho Bank, Moneris Solutions, National Australia Bank, National City Bank, Provident Bank, Rabobank, Royal Bank of Scotland, SunTrust, State Street, Toronto Dominion, Wachovia, Washington Mutual, Westdeutsche Landesbank, US Bancorp and Wells Fargo.

INTERNATIONAL WORK: Due to the international operations of many of the firm's clients, the firm has extensive experience in structuring cross-border financial transactions. This experience includes acting as agent bank and lead investor counsel in structuring LIBOR-based and other multi-currency financings involving foreign obligors and collateral to structuring Eximbank and other financings backed by other export credit agencies or private insurers, letters of credit or bank guarantees. Further, the firm participates in cross-border institutional private placement transactions involving issuers and guarantors domiciled in numerous foreign jurisdictions, including England, Canada, Australia, New Zealand, Ireland, Finland, Sweden, Bermuda, the Cayman Islands, the Netherlands, Germany, Norway, Finland, Switzerland, Malta and Luxembourg. The firm represented institutional investors in the first Rule 144A styled private placement debt transaction and has acted as designated special investor's counsel in numerous additional Rule 144A and like private placement transactions. The firm acted as special issuer's counsel to the first Irish, German and Finnish corporations to close US private placements, as well as counsel to one of the largest corporations in Norway and many corporations listed on the Financial Times FT-SE 100 Index.

CONWAY & MROWIEC

THE FIRM

Partners: Timothy R Conway
John S Mrowiec
Edward B Keidan

Number of other lawyers: 4

AREAS OF PRACTICE:
**Construction Litigation, Contract
Negotiation & Consultation** 100%

HEAD OFFICE

ILLINOIS
20 South Clark, Suite 750, **Chicago**, IL 60603
Tel: 312 658 1100 **Fax:** 312 658 1201
Website: www.cmcontractors.com

FIRM OVERVIEW: Conway & Mrowiec concentrates its practice in construction and public contracts law and litigation. Conway & Mrowiec has broad experience in achieving successful, cost-effective results for contractors, construction managers, design/builders, trade contractors, architects, engineers, owners and sureties, in litigation, arbitration, contract drafting, bidding, and performance issues through claim prosecution or defense. Conway & Mrowiec's goal is to build long-standing relationships with its clients. In that spirit, Conway & Mrowiec employs its extensive mediation, litigation and arbitration experience to provide its clients with special insight in contract drafting, project administration assistance, and project personnel education, as well as in claims prosecution and resolution.

MAIN AREAS OF PRACTICE: Examples of recent issues litigated:
Delay Claims - Gasoline Refinery: Successfully defended design-builder of gasoline refinery from multi-million dollar claims of piping subcontractor for alleged delays, reduced labor productivity and changes at jury trial. The dispute involved a fixed price subcontract based on schematic design with detailed change methodology once the design was completed, the effect of numerous signed change orders thereafter and fraudulently overstated lien clam.
Mechanics Lien Claims - Lien Drafting & Enforcement: Conway & Mrowiec has drafted hundreds and litigated over 100 mechanics lien claims on public and private projects in Illinois and throughout the United States in the last five years. Among the complex issues addressed include the lienability of various services, multiple contracts, fraudulent overstatement, 'last day of work', the allocation of amounts due and completion dates on complex multi-owner projects such as mixed use condominiums, tower, hotel, retail, office buildings.
Bidding Disputes: Obtain favourable judgment after trial on tortious interference and other claims brought by contractor against competing contractor.
Differing Site Condition - Bridge: Represented foundation contractor in successful recovery of claims of unpaid lump sum payments and Type II differing site condition and defended against defense and counterclaim of alleged overpayment of unit prices and delay on highway bridge construction project.
Cost Plus with GMP Contracts - Retail/Hotel Complex: Litigated and successfully mediated on behalf of owners' dispute with contractor under GMP contract for construction of an upscale retail/hotel complex. Issues involve alleged acceleration, disputes regarding scope of the GMP and owner direct payment to subcontractors.
Public Contract Bid Protest - Hospital: Successfully protested award of contract to apparent low bidder on competitively bid public hospital project.

Bankruptcies - Construction: For EPC contractor of power plant, recovered on $16 million dollars plus lien claim after litigating priority over lender and disputes with subcontractors to agreed judgment of foreclosure and allowed secured claim and preparing detailed written bid in bankruptcy court auction sale. For design-builder of telecommunictions facilities, recovered on mechanics liens filed in 11 different states despite bankruptcy of customer.
Design Errors & Omissions - Hotel: Mediated, on behalf of architectural and engineering firm, hotel owner's delay and defective design claims.
Insurance Claims - Crane Collapse: Represented concrete contractor on tender of defense and indemnity to Owner-Controlled Insurance Program's liability insurer, contractor's comprehensive general liability insurer and property insurer including prosecution of coverage action against property insurer for claims by crane supplier to contractor of destruction and rent, prosecution of contractor's acceleration and payment claim and litigating with OCIP builder's risk carrier regarding delayed and inadequate payment after crane collapse and suspension of work by governing authorities on mixed-use highrises.
Reported Cases: Builders Association of Greater Chicago v City of Chicago, 298 F. Supp.2d 725 (N.D. Ill. 2004); Builders Association of Greater Chicago v County of Cook, 256 F.3d 642 (7th Cir. 2001); Mellon Stuart Construction, Inc. v Metropolitan Water Reclamation District, 1995 US Dist. LEXIS 5376 (N.D.Ill. 1995); Builders Association of Greater Chicago v County of Cook, 2000 US Dist. LEXIS 144 (N.D.Ill. 2000); 1998 US Dist. LEXIS 2991 (N.D.Ill. 1998); 1996 US Dist. LEXIS 13142 (N.D.Ill. 1996); Amalgamated Trust & Savings Bank v Silha, 460 N.E.2d 372 (1984); Prisco Serena Sturm Architects, Ltd. v Liberty Mutual Insurance Co., 1995 US Dist. LEXIS 9904 (N.D.Ill. 1995); 1996 US Dist. LEXIS 7278 (N.D.Ill. 1996); US Dist. LEXIS 4350, 3021, 2216 (N.D.Ill. 1996); Downey, Inc. v Bradley Center Corp., 524 N.W.2d 915 (Wis.Ct.App. 1994); Mellon Stuart Construction, Inc. v MWRDGC, 1995 US Dist. LEXIS 3493 (N.D.Ill. 1995); Southwest Financial Bank & Trust Co. v George Hyman Construction Co., 940 F.Supp. 1331 (N.D.Ill. 1996); United States f/u/b DJM Construction, Inc. v Rust Engineering Co., 1996 WL 204318 (N.D.Ill. 1996); Mellon Stuart Construction, Inc. v MWRDGC, 1990 US Dist. LEXIS 7669 (N.D.Ill. 1990); Acme Metals, Inc. v Raytheon Engineers & Constructors, Inc. (In re Acme Metals, Inc.), 257 B.R. 714 (Bankr. Ct. D. Del.2000); Delaney v DeTella, 123 F.Supp.2d 429 (N.D.Ill. 2000); Chase Commercial Corp. v Brandt, 1999 US Dist. LEXIS 16441 (N.D.Ill. 1999).

Conway & Mrowiec
ATTORNEYS

DLA PIPER RUDNICK GRAY CARY US LLP

THE FIRM

Chairman: Senator George J Mitchell
Joint Chief Executive Officers: Francis B Burch Jr, Nigel Knowles
Lee I Miller
Executive Director: Stephen R Colgate
Number of partners worldwide: 1028
Number of other lawyers worldwide: 2861

FIRM OVERVIEW: Relationship-driven lawyers meeting the ongoing legal needs of its clients wherever they choose to do business. Operating across the US, Europe and Asia, they offer 2,700 lawyers in 49 cities in 18 countries. The firm acts for enterprises across the full spectrum of business, including local, national and multinational companies in a wide range of business sectors. Its clients range from single-owner startups to household name companies known worldwide. The firm commits to being a long-term partner with its clients on a day-to-day basis, year after year, and is there for the important everyday business issues that its clients face, as well as 'bet the company' transactions and lawsuits that might come just once in a business lifetime. As an organization, DLA Piper Rudnick Gray Cary US LLP places the highest value on building close working relationships with its clients. To accomplish that, they offer lawyers who are culturally attuned to the business demands and legal requirements of their countries, who have excellent legal skills, and who are totally committed to its client service ethic. Its clients say that this commitment is what really sets them apart.

MAIN AREAS OF PRACTICE: The firm's practice is focused on:
Corporate & Finance: On the corporate and finance side, the firm operates significant transactional based practices and serve not only some of the world's largest companies but numerous middle and upper-mid market clients. The firm is on the panels of a number of major banks and financial institutions and has a substantial bankruptcy and restructuring practice.
Litigation: The group brings together more than 800 top litigators in the US, Europe and Asia and offers lawyers experienced in patent, class action, securities, antitrust, banking and finance, technology, telecommunications and insurance disputes.
Real Estate: With over 200 real estate lawyers in both the US and the UK, its real estate practice is one of the most highly ranked in the world, serving the needs of developers, corporations, retailers and investors.
Legislative & Regulatory: At the federal and state level in the US, and in the individual countries of Europe as well as the EU, its people understand the legislative and regulatory process. To the strengths of its team, which includes chairman, Senator George J Mitchell, adding the firm's alliance with The Cohen Group, the international business consulting firm.
Human Resources: With more than 200 lawyers located in key jurisdictions around the world, its human resources and labor lawyers are equipped to handle both local employment issues and complex cross-border transactions.
Commercial: The group will be a market leader in European Public Private Partnerships (PPPs) and the provision of infrastructure and project finance services to sponsors and funders internationally. The group has lawyers who are particularly experienced in energy, sports, water, defense, healthcare and transportation, and is also recognized worldwide for its top-ranked franchise and distribution practice.
Technology, Media & Communication (TMC): This global practice represents a combination of market-leading teams in information technology/outsourcing, telecommunications, patent, trademark, copyright, media, e-business, sport, data protection and privacy. With over 420 lawyers globally it wil be one of the leading global TMC/TMT practices.

HEAD OFFICE

ILLINOIS
Chicago   **Tel:** 312 368 4000   **Fax:** 312 236 7516
Email: info@dlapiper.com
Website: www.dlapiper.com

BRANCH OFFICES

CALIFORNIA
Los Angeles (Century City)   **Tel:** 310 595 3000   **Fax:** 310 595 3300
Los Angeles (Downtown)   **Tel:** 213 330 7700   **Fax:** 213 835 6001
Sacramento   **Tel:** 916 930 3200   **Fax:** 916 930 3201
San Diego (Golden Triangle) **Tel:** 858 677 1400   **Fax:** 858 677 1401
San Diego (Downtown)   **Tel:** 619 699 2700   **Fax:** 619 699 2701
La Jolla   **Tel:** 858 638 6806   **Fax:** 858 456 3654
San Francisco (Townsend St) **Tel:** 415 836 2500   **Fax:** 415 836 2501
San Francisco (Market St)   **Tel:** 415 659 7000   **Fax:** 415 659 7300
East Palo Alto (Silicon Valley) **Tel:** 650 833 2000 **Fax:** 650 833 2001

DISTRICT OF COLUMBIA
Washington   **Tel:** 202 861 3900   **Fax:** 202 223 2085

FLORIDA
Tampa   **Tel:** 813 229 2111   **Fax:** 813 229 1447

MARYLAND
Annapolis   **Tel:** 443 482 3830   **Fax:** 443 482 3848
Baltimore (Mt Washington)   **Tel:** 410 580 3000   **Fax:** 410 580 3001
Baltimore (Downtown)   **Tel:** 410 580 3000   **Fax:** 410 580 3665

MASSACHUSETTS
Boston   **Tel:** 617 406 6000   **Fax:** 617 406 6100

NEVADA
Las Vegas   **Tel:** 702 737 3433   **Fax:** 702 737 1612

NEW JERSEY
A New Jersey Limited Liability Partnership
(Robert A Assuncao, Managing Partner)
Edison   **Tel:** 732 590 1850   **Fax:** 732 590 1860

NEW YORK
New York   **Tel:** 212 835 6000   **Fax:** 212 835 6001

PENNYSYVANIA
Philadelphia   **Tel:** 215 656 3300   **Fax:** 215 656 3301

TEXAS
Dallas   **Tel:** 214 743 4500   **Fax:** 214 743 4545
Austin   **Tel:** 512 457 7000   **Fax:** 512 457 7001

VIRGINIA
Reston   **Tel:** 703 773 4000   **Fax:** 703 773 5000

WASHINGTON
Seattle   **Tel:** 206 839 4800   **Fax:** 206 839 4801

EIMER STAHL KLEVORN & SOLBERG

THE FIRM

Managing Partner: Nathan P Eimer

Number of partners: 6
Number of other attorneys: 18

FIRM OVERVIEW: Founded in July 2000, Eimer Stahl Klevorn & Solberg engages in complex litigation throughout the United States. It also has substantial experience with respect to the antitrust aspects of proposed transactions. The firm is dedicated to providing top quality legal services in a cost-effective manner. With a commitment to client service and advanced technology, the firm partners with clients to obtain creative solutions to complex legal problems. The firm is proud to serve as trial counsel to some of the country's foremost corporations.

MAIN AREAS OF PRACTICE: The firm concentrates on complex litigation across a variety of subject areas, including antitrust, environmental, commercial, securities, energy, unfair competition, product liability, toxic torts, construction, and regulatory affairs. The firm has particular expertise relating to the defense of class action lawsuits, as well as claims brought under the Sarbanes-Oxley Act. Some of the leading matters on which the firm has recently worked include government investigations and private suits relating to energy prices, defense of class action claims alleging injuries arising from the use of fuel additives, multimillion dollar breach of contract claims in the paper and cement industries, and defense of price-fixing claims in the chemical, dairy and paper industries. The firm also advises clients with respect to obtaining government clearance of proposed mergers and acquisitions. This involves working with antitrust agencies and competition authorities regarding assessment of the competitive effects of contemplated transactions. Members of the firm have provided advice regarding these matters across a wide variety of industries, including consumer goods, paper, chemicals, commercial printing, cosmetics, telecommunications, crop nutrients and fertilizers, foodstuffs, and automotive parts.

CLIENTS: The firm serves clients across a wide array of industries, including CITGO Petroleum, Kimberly-Clark, Dow Chemical, Exelon, Land O' Lakes Dairy, Corn Products International, Praxair, The Williams Companies, and Holcim Inc. Superior client service is a hallmark of the firm's operating philosophy and principles.

HEAD OFFICE

ILLINOIS
224 S. Michigan Avenue, Suite 1100, **Chicago**, IL 60604
Tel: 312 660 7600   **Fax:** 312 692 1718
Website: www.eimerstahl.com

CONTACTS

Antitrust/Commercial Litigation ..Nathan P Eimer, Andrew G Klevorn
Energy/Commercial Litigation ....David M Stahl

EimerStahl

Eimer Stahl Klevorn & Solberg LLP

GARDNER CARTON & DOUGLAS LLP

THE FIRM

Chairman: Harold L Kaplan

Number of partners worldwide: 138
Number of other lawyers worldwide: 113

FIRM OVERVIEW: Founded nearly 100 years ago, Gardner Carton & Douglas LLP (GCD) is a leading national law firm with offices in Chicago; Washington, DC; Milwaukee; and Albany. The firm has more than 250 lawyers and advisors practicing in corporate law, corporate restructuring, government relations, health law, HR Law (employee benefits and employment), intellectual property, litigation and dispute resolution, real estate and environmental law, and wealth planning and philanthropy.

MAIN AREAS OF PRACTICE:

Corporate Law: GCD's Corporate Law Group offers legal counsel in financial and investment services; business transactions, including M&A; securities; and tax law, representing clients ranging from multinational corporations, local businesses and money center banks to privately held companies. The group includes one of the country's most active Hedge Fund practices, which advises commodity pool operators and management companies that act as investment advisors or operate offshore investment funds. The Indian Tribal Governments Practice represents tribes and tribal organizations in every region of the United States.

Corporate Restructuring: GCD's Corporate Restructuring Group represents clients in large-scale, complex restructurings; insolvencies; workouts and bankruptcies, including creditors and indenture trustees with more than $10 billion in defaulted corporate debt. The group also represents numerous creditors' committees in bankruptcy proceedings. Clients include a wide range of industries - from claims trading, manufacturing, transportation, securities and financial services, to oil and gas, retail, hospitality, telecommunications, and healthcare.

Government Relations: GCD's Government Relations Group provides advocacy advice and assistance to a wide array of clients, including healthcare providers, corporations, academic institutions, trade associations, nonprofits, telehealth networks, governmental entities and coalitions.

Health Law: The Health Law Group represents academic medical centers; faculty practice plans; foundations; hospital and licensed professional associations; hospital systems and integrated health systems; long term care providers; managed care and disease management organizations; medical schools and university healthcare programs; the pharmaceutical industry; physician practice groups; and public and private hospitals. The firm also represents clients in industries closely tied to the healthcare industry, such as healthcare venture capital funds, financial services companies that lend to healthcare organizations, technology companies, insurance companies, and healthcare REITs, as well as tax-exempt organizations in their compliance with tax laws, fiduciary laws, and other laws relating to their tax exempt status. In 2004, GCD launched Innovative Health Strategies LLC, a subsidiary that advises hospitals, health systems and academic medical centers on matters of procurement and outsourcing strategies.

HR Law/Wealth Planning & Philanthropy: GCD's HR Law Practice covers employee benefits, executive compensation, ESOPs and stock based compensation plans, ERISA counseling and litigation, retirement plans, international benefits, labor and employment counseling, litigation, and wealth and estate planning and philanthropy.

Intellectual Property: GCD's IP Practice helps clients identify, protect and exploit their full range of intellectual capital and helps them enhance their competitive position in the marketplace, using intellectual property as a tool, not an end in itself. Whether counseling regarding patents, brands,

information technology, unfair competition, copyrights, trade secrets or other proprietary rights, GCD's attorneys understand their clients' business, not only their assets. With experience in a wide range of industries and scientific disciplines, the firm's practitioners are litigators, transactional specialists, registered patent attorneys and counselors. The firm's IP litigators have long represented clients in complex intellectual property disputes, navigating toward successful outcomes, whether by winning in court or by leveraging viable business resolutions. GCD's transactional attorneys concentrate in complex outsourcing, information technology, research and development, technology transfer and in-bound and out-bound licensing arrangements. Their counselors also guide clients through the complex world of new media, branding, technology and advertising.

Litigation & Dispute Resolution: GCD's Litigation Practice includes complex commercial litigation, antitrust and IP work, class action securities, products liability defense, healthcare litigation, and international and domestic arbitrations. Within this practice, the Financial Markets/Insurance and Reinsurance Litigation Group represents brokers, investment advisors, specialists and broker dealers in federal and state courts, and industry arbitration forums, including SEC, NASD, CFTC, and other regulatory organizations.

Real Estate & Environmental: GCD's real estate and environmental attorneys work with developers, lenders, and investors whose primary business is real estate, in addition to corporate, governmental entities and nonprofits for which real estate is an important asset. The group focuses on development, land use and zoning; real estate investment and finance; leasing and property management; nonprofit institutions; business services; and environmental matters. Its environmental lawyers have counseled corporate, municipal and individual clients through the development and implementation of every major federal and state environmental regulatory initiative for more than 30 years. The scope of its environmental legal services includes all aspects of compliance counseling, transaction counseling and litigation.

GCD
Gardner Carton & Douglas

JENNER & BLOCK LLP

THE FIRM

Managing Partner: Gregory S Gallopoulos
Chairman: Jerold S Solovy

Number of partners: 191
Number of other lawyers: 242

FIRM OVERVIEW: Jenner & Block LLP is a national law firm with offices in Chicago, Dallas and Washington, DC. Founded in 1914, the firm has over 400 lawyers who are experienced in virtually every area of the law. Jenner & Block's clients range from large, international conglomerates to small, family-owned businesses and include industrial, commercial, telecommunications, research and development, technology, entertainment, and utility companies, as well as financial and service enterprises. In the public sector, the firm represents a variety of state and local governmental entities. Jenner & Block's reputation as one of the country's most effective law firms has been established by consistently delivering excellent business advice and counsel and by securing victories for its clients from the trial level through the United States Supreme Court. In September Jenner & Block was named to *The American Lawyer's* "A-List" which identifies the 20 law firms in the country that are 'true leaders of the profession.' The magazine's influential rankings were built by analyzing metrics collected on the nation's top law firms' 'core professional values' – client satisfaction, associate satisfaction, diversity and pro bono representation. For the second consecutive year, Jenner & Block is the only Chicago-based law firm to make the magazine's 'A-List.' Jenner & Block is an Illinois Limited Liability Partnership including professional corporations. For more information, please visit www.jenner.com.

MAIN AREAS OF PRACTICE:

Business Transaction: Jenner & Block has a substantial Business Transaction Practice, with experienced groups focusing on corporate and commercial transactions including mergers and acquisitions, corporate governance, securities, corporate and commercial finance, tax, real estate, environmental, insurance, commercial law, technology and intellectual property, bankruptcy and reorganization, benefits, employment, labor and executive compensation, government, healthcare and associations. The firm's lawyers have authored books and treatises in many of these areas, most recently on such topics as director and officer liability, securities, environmental law, insurance coverage, intellectual property and the Uniform Commercial Code. Jenner & Block handles transactional work for a wide range of large public corporations as well as privately held businesses, financial institutions, prominent trade associations, nonprofit organizations, new ventures, and individuals. The firm's lawyers represent many international and domestic clients in connection with mergers and acquisitions, joint ventures, strategic alliances and dispositions of businesses, and regularly advise clients in connection with public and private securities offerings and financings. Jenner & Block was ranked by Global Securities Information, Inc. (GSI) as one of the top 20 law firms in the US in total value of 2003 merger & acquisition transactions.

HEAD OFFICE

ILLINOIS
One IBM Plaza, **Chicago**, IL 60611
Tel: 312 222 9350   **Fax:** 312 527 0484
Website: www.jenner.com

BRANCH OFFICES

DISTRICT OF COLUMBIA
601 Thirteenth Street, NW, Suite 1200 South, **Washington**, DC 20005
Tel: 202 639 6000   **Fax:** 202 639 6066

TEXAS
1717 Main Street, Suite 3150 **Dallas**, TX 75201
Tel: 214 746 5700   **Fax:** 214 746 5757

Litigation: Jenner & Block has one of the most prominent and successful litigation practices in the country. The firm's more than 250 litigators have won impressive victories in a broad range of complex and challenging civil and criminal cases before federal, state and administrative courts. Jenner & Block regularly represents clients before the United States Supreme Court, in all of the 13 United States Circuit Courts of Appeals, and in federal district courts and state courts nationwide. The quality and competence of the firm's trial lawyers is well known. Among them are two partners who are former United States Attorneys, many former Assistant US Attorneys, two former Chairs of the ABA Litigation Section, and numerous leaders of national, state and local bar associations. Currently, 11 partners in the firm are Fellows of the American College of Trial Lawyers, the country's most prestigious trial group. Many of the firm's trial lawyers clerked for judges in the federal and state systems, including eight who clerked for one or more United States Supreme Court Justices. In addition, several former partners now serve as federal judges, maintaining a remarkable history of judicial service by members of the firm.

Public Service: Public service is part of the fabric of Jenner & Block. Throughout its history, the firm has served as a national leader in pro bono advocacy and continues to run one of the strongest and largest public service programs in the nation. The firm's lawyers contribute more than 5% of their billable hours annually to pro bono work. Last year its attorneys logged more than 46,000 pro bono hours firm wide, with an average of nearly 90 hours per lawyer. Of the nation's largest law firms, Jenner & Block is continually ranked among the very top in pro bono work by *The American Lawyer* magazine. The firm received *The National Law Journal's* 2002 'Pro Bono Award' for its remarkable representation of clients in capital punishment cases. And in 2004 Jenner & Block was awarded the Illinois State Bar Association's prestigious John C McAndrews Pro Bono Award.

JENNER&BLOCK

KATTEN MUCHIN ZAVIS ROSENMAN

THE FIRM

Managing Partner: Vincent AF Sergi
Number of partners: +250
Number of other lawyers: +350

FIRM OVERVIEW: Katten Muchin Zavis Rosenman is a Global 100, full-service law firm with offices in the nation's largest centers of business, government, finance and technology. With over 600 attorneys in more than 50 practice areas, the firm provides timely and cost-effective counsel to clients in a broad range of industries. They are business advisors and advocates for a wide array of public and private companies - from global Fortune 100 corporations to emerging growth companies - as well as government entities, major universities, museums and other charitable and cultural organizations. To meet the needs of its increasingly global clientele, the firm also maintains affiliations with leading international law firms. In addition to the firm's practice areas that are profiled below, the firm maintains full service practices in a number of highly focused areas, including the following: antitrust, customs and international trade, employee benefits and executive compensation, healthcare, labor and employment, life sciences, and public finance.

MAIN AREAS OF PRACTICE:

Litigation: The firm's trial lawyers handle cases ranging from contract disputes and regulatory matters to securities class action lawsuits, antitrust matters and other complex commercial litigation. The firm's Securities Litigation Group is nationally recognized for successfully representing corporations and their officers and directors in shareholder class actions, derivative actions, SEC investigations and federal and state criminal investigations. They also represent clients in corporate control disputes and mergers and acquisitions litigation. The firm's White Collar Criminal and Civil Litigation Practice is led by highly respected former federal prosecutors and law enforcement officers with broad investigative, trial and appellate experience. The litigators in the Intellectual Property Group defend and prosecute claims, many involving cutting-edge issues of intellectual property law, in federal and state courts throughout the United States, as well as before the International Trade Commission and the United States Patent and Trademark Office. The firm's Environmental Practice handles some of the largest and most complex environmental litigation in the country involving soil contamination and hazardous waste and substances.

Corporate: The firm's Corporate Department provides sophisticated transactional and corporate counseling representation on a national basis across a broad range of concentrations. Their Mergers and Acquisitions Group is involved in all aspects of public and private mergers, acquisitions and divestitures, representing both targets and bidders in negotiated and hostile takeovers. The firm's nationally recognized Private Equity Group is known for the diversity of its practice, representing leveraged buyout funds, mezzanine debt funds and venture capital funds in a wide variety of acquisitions, divestitures and financing transactions, as well as general partners and institutional limited partners in all aspects of private equity fund formation. Attorneys in the firm's Securities Group assist clients with public and private offerings of equity and debt securities, tender offers, proxy contests and going private transactions. They also provide a full range of Corporate Governance counseling to public and private companies, boards of directors and board committees. Attorneys in the firm's Entertainment and Media Group provide transactional, general corporate, and litigation representation to the entertainment and media industry.

Real Estate: The firm's Real Estate Group, widely recognized as a national leader, has built one of the largest and broadest practices in the country and serves clients in virtually every aspect of real estate law, including acquisitions, dispositions, developments and financings, along with establishment of joint ventures, real estate investment trusts, real estate opportunity funds

HEAD OFFICE

ILLINOIS
525 West Monroe Street, **Chicago**, IL 60661-3693
Tel: 312 902 5200 **Fax:** 312 902 1061
Website: www.kmzr.com

BRANCH OFFICES

CALIFORNIA
2029 Century Park East, Suite 2600, **Los Angeles**, CA 90067-3012
Tel: 310 788 4400 **Fax:** 310 788 4471

260 Sheridan Avenue, Suite 450, **Palo Alto**, CA 94306-2047
Tel: 650 330 3652 **Fax:** 650 321 4746

DISTRICT OF COLUMBIA
1025 Thomas Jefferson St., N.W., East Lobby, Suite 700,
Washington, DC 20007-5201
Tel: 202 625 3500 **Fax:** 202 298 7570

NEW YORK
575 Madison Avenue, **New York**, NY 10022-2585
Tel: 212 940 8800 **Fax:** 212 940 8776

NORTH CAROLINA
401 South Tryon Street, Suite 2600, **Charlotte**, NC 28202-1935
Tel: 704 444 2000 Fax: 704 444 2050

TEXAS
5215 North O'Connor Boulevard, Suite 200, **Irving**, TX 75039-3732
Tel: 972 868 9058 **Fax:** 972 868 9068

and other real estate investment vehicles. Property types include office, retail, hotel, multi-family, industrial and mixed-use and resorts.

Financial Services: Attorneys in the firm's Financial Services Group provide regulatory, transactional and litigation counsel to participants in the financial services arena. The group is experienced in the area of structured products and derivatives and with investment vehicles such as hedge funds, mutual funds, commodity pools, venture capital funds and securitizations of financial assets.

Commercial Finance & Reorganization: Their Commercial Finance and Reorganization Group represents bank and non-bank financial institutions in all aspects of corporate finance, including senior financing, mezzanine financing, equity co-investments, bankruptcy and creditors' rights and workouts. The practice is also adept at structuring commercial paper vehicles, REMICs and other types of securitizations.

Intellectual Property: The firm's Intellectual Property Team secures, protects and enforces patents, trademarks and copyrights. They institute programs to prevent the loss of trade secrets; investigate and defend against infringement; and, in tandem with their corporate technology lawyers, exploit intellectual property rights through licensing, joint venture and technology transfer agreements.

Tax: The firm's Tax Group handles US and international tax planning and advises clients on the tax aspects of mergers and acquisitions, recapitalizations, reorganizations, spin-offs, venture capital and LBO transactions and financings, investment fund formation, securitizations of debt, equipment leasing, public and private partnerships, limited liability companies, and closely held and multinational corporations.

Trusts & Estates: Attorneys in the firm's Trusts and Estates Practice develop sophisticated estate, tax and charitable planning on the state, federal and international levels. They handle all aspects of the administration of estates and trusts, as well as probate, accounting, tax and other litigation on behalf of both fiduciaries and beneficiaries of complex estates and trusts.

KIRKLAND & ELLIS LLP

THE FIRM

Number of partners: 390
Number of other lawyers: 527

FIRM OVERVIEW: Founded nearly 100 years ago, Kirkland & Ellis, one of America's premier law firms, has handled complicated transactional, tax, restructuring, workout and bankruptcy, intellectual property, litigation and counselling matters for major US and international clients. Today, Kirkland & Ellis continues to work with a base of long-standing clients engaged in varied industries such as manufacturing, transportation, telecommunications, private equity capital, pharmaceutical, technology, energy, healthcare, real estate, chemicals, food products, finance, insurance, e-commerce, advertising, and accounting.

MAIN AREAS OF PRACTICE:

Transactional: On the transactional side, Kirkland is known for its ability to negotiate and close highly sophisticated transactions, representing venture capital investors and public and private companies in merger and acquisition, securities, spin-off and split-off, private equity, and real estate transactions. The firm has a premier private equity practice, having represented private investment funds, the private equity groups at several major money center banks and other participants in this industry for over 25 years. In 2002 and 2003, Chambers & Partners chose Kirkland as the Private Equity Law Firm of the Year. The prestigiousness of this award signifies the strength and scope of the firm's Private Equity Practice.

Tax: The firm's practice provides its clients with the most creative tax planning available in a responsive and cost-efficient manner. The firm's tax practice has developed a strong international reputation for providing sophisticated tax counseling on both US, foreign and state tax issues, and effectively representing its clients in tax disputes worldwide. Kirkland's tax practice can be divided broadly into two areas: (1) tax planning in connection with mergers, acquisitions, buyouts, restructurings, financings, executive compensation plans, and other sophisticated transactions; and (2) contested tax matters in connection with challenges by the Internal Revenue Service and by foreign and state tax authorities. Kirkland's goal in both types of matters is the same: to achieve the best possible tax results in the most efficient manner.

Restructuring: The firm's restructuring, insolvency, workout and bankruptcy group provides a broad range of business advisory and crisis management skills with extensive experience in US and international insolvency matters to navigate clients through the turmoil of situations involving financially troubled companies. The group has earned a distinguished national and international reputation for providing outstanding legal advice and judgment to all constituencies in situations where companies face impending insolvency. The firm acts for a varied range of national and international clients: debtors; financial institutions; secured creditors; lessors; unsecured creditors; investors and committees in complex corporate restructuring, workout and bankruptcy planning, negotiation and litigation.

Intellectual Property: Kirkland & Ellis represents some of the world's leading technology companies and brings its expertise to all areas of intellectual property, including biotechnology, semiconductor processing, telecommunications, and internet and e-commerce technology. With a dedicated practice dating from 1925, the firm has been at the forefront of IP developments throughout the 20th century. Kirkland & Ellis has adopted and adapted to the internet and e-commerce, and its approximately 200 intellectual property lawyers understand fully the intricacies, implications, legal issues and arguments surrounding today's and tomorrow's communication and emerging technologies.

Litigation & Arbitration: Kirkland has earned a stellar reputation as trial lawyers (not just 'litigators') by successfully defending companies with business-threatening lawsuits and class actions in diverse legal areas such as commercial, intellectual property, product liability, insurance coverage, environmental, employment, securities law, mass torts, and antitrust issues, handling the trial, appellate, and US Supreme Court phases. This trial-ready reputation has been the impetus for favorable and prompt results for clients through settlements as well as through the various Alternative Dispute Resolution mechanisms (ADRs) employed whenever practicable and desired by the client. In 2004, Kirkland was named by Chambers & Partners as the USA Litigation Law Firm of the Year. The firm was recognized for its ability to run large, complex litigation efficiently and responsibly.

INTERNATIONAL WORK: The European Practice Group consists of approximately 35 lawyers practicing English, German and international law, with several lawyers expert in the international application of US law as well. During the last five years, Kirkland's private equity practice has represented over 50 different clients in hundreds of leveraged acquisitions and other types of transactions and has been principal counsel in over US$70 billion in fund formations. In the M&A and securities area, Kirkland has recently represented clients ranging from some of the world's largest corporations to major banks and investment banks in some of the world's largest and most complex M&A transactions and securities offerings. Lawyers at Kirkland & Ellis are fluent in English, Chinese, French, German, Greek, Hebrew, Hindi, Italian, Japanese, Korean, Russian and Spanish.

BRANCH OFFICES

ILLINOIS
Aon Center, 200 East Randolph Drive, **Chicago** IL 60601-6636
Tel: 312 861 2000   **Fax:** 312 861 2200
Email: dbernick@kirkland.com

CALIFORNIA
777 S. Figueroa Street, **Los Angeles** CA 90017-5800
Tel: 213 680 8400   **Fax:** 213 680 8500
Email: jdavidson@kirkland.com

555 California Street, **San Francisco** CA 94104
Tel: 415 439 1400   **Fax:** 415 439 1500
Email: jhammes@kirkland.com

DISTRICT OF COLUMBIA
655 Fifteenth Street NW, **Washington** DC 20005-5793
Tel: 202 879 5000   **Fax:** 202 879 5200
Email: tyannucci@kirkland.com

NEW YORK
Citigroup Center, 153 East 53rd Street, **New York** NY 10022-4611
Tel: 212 446 4800   **Fax:** 212 446 4900
Email: kradke@kirkland.com

MAYER, BROWN, ROWE & MAW LLP

THE FIRM

Chairman: Tyrone C Fahner
Managing Partner: Debora de Hoyos
Number of partners in US offices: 390
Number of other lawyers in US offices: 584

Website: www.mayerbrownrowe.com
Email: info@mayerbrownrowe.com

AREAS OF PRACTICE:

Litigation & Arbitration	32%
Corporate & Securities	22%
Finance, Banking & Insurance	22%
Tax	9%
Oil, Gas & Real Estate	8%
Antitrust	7%
Other	1%

FIRM OVERVIEW: Mayer, Brown, Rowe & Maw LLP is the sixth largest law firm in the United States and among the 10 largest law practices in the world. The practice has more than 1,300 lawyers in seven US cities and six European cities. Mayer, Brown, Rowe & Maw is a combination of two limited liability partnerships, each named Mayer, Brown, Rowe & Maw LLP, one established in Illinois, USA, and one incorporated in England. A full-service law firm, Mayer, Brown, Rowe & Maw is renowned in the US for its appellate, corporate, banking and finance, litigation, ERISA, outsourcing, and tax practices.

MAIN AREAS OF PRACTICE: The practice handles appellate and litigation, finance, structured bank finance, corporate and M&A, outsourcing, asset securitizations, capital markets and securities, fund management and financial services regulation, commodities and derivatives, international arbitration, global trade.

CLIENTS: Mayer, Brown, Rowe & Maw serves 65 of the Fortune 100 companies, one out of every three US banks, and ranks ninth in both the Financial Times Stock Exchange 100 Index principal advisors survey and its most-used law firm survey. Clients include Abbott Laboratories, Banc One, Bank of America, BASF, Bertelsmann, Brunswick Corporation, Deutsche Bank, Dow Chemical, EMI, General Electric, ICI, Morgan Stanley, Nestlé, Pfizer, Starwood Hotels & Resorts, State Farm Insurance Companies, Unilever, and United Air Lines.

INTERNATIONAL WORK:

Latin American Telecom: Advised BellSouth Corp. in an agreement with Telefonica Móviles to sell its interests in its 10 Latin American operations.
Appellate Strength: Argued nine cases before the US Supreme Court in two latest terms.
Privatized US Toll Bridge: Acted as principal counsel for the City of Chicago on the a $1.83 billion privatization of the Chicago Skyway Toll bridge - the first such deal in the United States.
Outsourcing: Advised TXU Corp.in a $3.5 billion outsourcing deal with CapGemini-believed to be largest reported deal in the energy industry.
International Price-Fixing: Won 8-0 US Supreme Court decision in F. *Hoffmann-LaRoche Ltd. v Empagram, SA*, involving international claims in a multibillion-dollar vitamins case.
Spin-Off: Represented Abbott Laboratories in its $2.5 billion spin-off of Global Hospital Products Company.
Oracle Case: Won summary judgment in favor of Oracle's chairman and CEO and CFO in a derivative action alleging insider trading.
Acquisition: Advised ProLogis in connection with its partnership's $1.6 billion acquisition of Keystone Property Trust.

OFFICES

CALIFORNIA
350 South Grand Avenue, 25th Floor, **Los Angeles**, CA 90071-1503
Tel: 213 229 9500 **Fax:** 213 625 0248

555 College Avenue, **Palo Alto**, CA 94306-1433
Tel: 650 331 2000 **Fax:** 650 331 2060

DISTRICT OF COLUMBIA
1909 K Street, N.W., **Washington**, DC 20006-1157
Tel: 202 263 3000 **Fax:** 202 263 3300

ILLINOIS
190 South LaSalle Street, **Chicago**, IL 60603-3441
Tel: 312 782 0600 **Fax:** 312 701 7711

NEW YORK
1675 Broadway, **New York**, NY 10019-5820
Tel: 212 506 2500 **Fax:** 212 262 1910

NORTH CAROLINA
214 North Tryon Street, Suite 3800, **Charlotte**, NC 28202-2137
Tel: 704 444 3500 **Fax:** 704 377 2033

TEXAS
700 Louisiana Street, Suite 3600, **Houston**, TX 77002-2730
Tel: 713 221 1651 **Fax:** 713 224 6410

INTERNATIONAL OFFICES

Mayer, Brown, Rowe & Maw LLP has offices in Belgium, France, Germany and the United Kingdom. The firm also has two associated offices in China (MBP Consulting Limited LLC) and an independent correspondent firm, Jáuregui, Navarrete, Nader y Rojas, in Mexico.

Pharma Case: Won summary judgment on behalf of Novartis AG in multi-district products-liability litigation concerning products containing phenylpropanolamine.
Maritime Acquisition: Advised TAL International Group, Inc., in connection with its $1.2 billion acquisition of Transamerica Maritime Containers from AEGON N.V.
Ryerson: Represented Ryerson Tull, Inc. in its purchase of Integris Metals, Inc., a joint venture between Alcoa Inc. and BHP Billiton.
London Real Estate: Advised longstanding client, Unilever, on its sale of Unilever House to Sloane Blackfriars Limited - one of the most significant London real estate transactions of 2004.
Hydroelectric: Advised TransCanada in connection with its purchase of USGen New England's hydroelectric assets for $505 million.
Agribusiness: Advised Monsanto Company and its subsidiaries on the disposal to RAGT Génétique S.A. of its European wheat and barley seed business.
Natural Gas: Advised Devon Energy Corporation in stock-for-stock merger (enterprise value $5.3 billion at signing) with Ocean Energy, Inc., making Devon one of the largest independent oil and natural-gas producers in the United States.
Food: Advised Nestlé S.A. in its $2.6 billion acquisition of Chef America.
Suez: Advised Suez on the $4.2 billion sale of its US industrial water treatment services subsidiary to a consortium of private equity sponsors - The Blackstone Group, Apollo Management and Goldman Sachs Capital Partners.

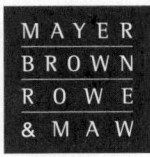

MCANDREWS, HELD & MALLOY, LTD.

THE FIRM

Founding Partners: George P McAndrews, John J Held, Timothy J Malloy, Lawrence M Jarvis, Gregory J Vogler

Senior Partner: George P McAndrews

Number of lawyers: 83

HEAD OFFICE

ILLINOIS
500 West Madison Street, **Chicago**, IL 60661
Tel: 312 775 8000   **Fax:** 312 775 8100
Website: www.mhmlaw.com

FIRM OVERVIEW: McAndrews, Held & Malloy is one of the nation's pre-eminent legal resources for intellectual property and technology matters. The firm's attorneys serve as counsel of choice for companies and institutions ranging from major multinationals and start-ups to world-class colleges and universities. The firm's reputation, founded upon an unparalleled record of litigation successes before juries, as well as in bench trials and ADR proceedings, encompasses a full range of legal services. The firm's attorneys are known for their clear and effective communication skills, expertise and training in engineering and science, their passion for technology law, their command of winning business strategy and their tenaciousness – both inside and outside of the courtroom.

MAIN AREAS OF PRACTICE:

Litigation (Patent, Trademark, Copyright, Antitrust, Trade Secret, Unfair Competition & Other Technology): Includes the firm's primary practice in all areas of intellectual property and complex technology litigation, including jury and bench trials, appeals, practice before the International Trade Commission, as well as ADR proceedings. The firm is strategically located so that its nationwide litigation practice measures up with its coast to coast clientele.

Patent & Trademark Procurement & Portfolio Management: Includes the prosecution of patents (ranging from simple mechanical devices to complex electrical systems) and trademarks, obtaining and maintaining intellectual property assets, and management of overall corporate or institutional holdings.

Patent Interferences: Includes all aspects of these complex, highly specialized proceedings, including pre-interference investigation and patent prosecution.

Trademark Oppositions & Cancellations: Includes all contested administrative proceedings before the Trademark Trial and Appeal Board.

International Practice: Includes all aspects of international intellectual property litigation, foreign prosecution, global transactions, licensing, appeals of patents and trademarks in other jurisdictions, and all issues related to foreign patents.

Intellectual Property/Technology Opinions & Investigations: Includes highly specialized strategic investigations, counsel and opinion analysis.

Due Diligence & M&A Support: Includes merger and acquisition counsel and support involving due diligence processes, investigations regarding asset quality and potential infringements.

Technology Licensing & Joint Ventures: Includes counsel regarding a wide variety of revenue-generating opportunities related to intellectual property holdings.

Technology Transfers & Donations: Includes the donation of intellectual property assets as charitable gifts.

CLIENTS: The firm's clients represent a diverse group of domestic and international clients covering a broad range of technology and proprietary rights. Clients include many leading companies in such diverse industrial and commercial fields as chemical, mechanical, and electrical manufacture, processing and use; such as, cell biology, angioplasty catheters, kidney dialysis equipment, medical imaging, pharmaceuticals, petrochemicals, digital cellular telephony, electronic games, computer memories and other hardware, software, satellite communications, fuel cells, power sources, industrial equipment (from paving equipment through mining equipment through papermaking machinery), printing equipment, sporting goods equipment (such as basketballs, softballs, golf balls and golf clubs), giftware, heating and air-conditioning, measurement instruments, appliances, furniture, aviation, avionics, transportation, confections and foodstuffs, and financial instruments.

MCDERMOTT WILL & EMERY

THE FIRM

Managing Partner: Harvey W Freishtat
Number of partners: 584
Number of other lawyers: 431

FIRM OVERVIEW: McDermott Will & Emery is an international law firm with more than 1,000 lawyers in six European and nine US offices. The firm represents a wide range of industrial, financial and commercial enterprises, both publicly and privately held.

INTERNATIONAL EXPERIENCE: Firm lawyers have been involved in cross-border matters on every continent and in virtually every sector of business. International matters include cross-border mergers and acquisitions; joint ventures; financings; corporate restructuring and reorganizations; the structuring of distributorship, licensing and agency arrangements; the negotiation of commercial contracts; compliance with investment laws; privatization; cross-border tax planning; international litigation and dispute resolution; public law; enviromental; real estate; banking; anti-competition; e-business and intellectual property, acquisitions, dispositions and financings. The firm has represented clients from more than 60 countries.

MAIN AREAS OF PRACTICE: Agribusiness, alcohol beverages and products, antitrust and competition, biotech and life sciences, bankruptcy, construction, corporate, responsibility, e-business, employee benefits and pensions, energy, environmental, executive compensation, finance and banking, financial products, food and beverage, health, hospitality, insurance, intellectual property, international, labour and employment, legislative and government relations, mergers and acquisitions, OSHA, pharmaceutical, private clients, products liability and regulation, real estate, securities, sports and entertainment, taxation, technology, telecommunications, transportation, trial, utilities, venture capital/private equity, white collar crime.

Antitrust & Competition: The practice is comprised of approximately 60 lawyers, many of whom have prior government experience with the European Commission, Federal Trade Commission, the Antitrust Division of the Department of Justice or the office of a State Attorney General.

Finance & Banking: The firm has an integrated finance and banking team of more than 70 lawyers, with recognised experience in all areas of US, UK and international corporate finance.

Bankruptcy: The firm represents debtors, trustees, and various creditor and equality constituencies on a regular basis, including banks, bond-holders, trade creditors, credit corporations and acquirers.

Employee Benefits & Pensions: There are approximately 50 lawyers who practice exclusively in employee benefits and compensation, providing counsel in the international planning, implementation and administration of a wide range of compensation and benefit plans and programs. The employee benefits lawyers advise corporations, partnerships and organizations from all business sectors, including insurance; manufacturing; retailing; technology; media; service industries (such as airlines and hotels); healthcare providers, legal and accounting firms; banks and other financial institutions; telecommunications; and the printing, publishing and paper industries.

Labour, Employment & OSHA: The practice has considerable experience in all employment-related matters, both contentious and non-contentious. Its lawyers advise on wrongful and unfair dismissal, executive severance, confidentiality and restrictive covenants, breaches of fiduciary duty, fraud by employees, sex/race/disability discrimination, early retirement programmes, development of employee manuals, wage-hour compliance, workers' compensation, substance abuse programs, drug testing, equal pay, Working Time Regulations, union recognition and works councils, industrial disputes, EU employment law, TUPE, employment aspects of acquisitions and OSHA.

HEAD OFFICE

ILLINOIS
227 West Monroe Street, **Chicago** IL 60606-5096, USA
Tel: 312 372 2000   **Fax:** 312 984 7700
Website: www.mwe.com

BRANCH OFFICES

CALIFORNIA
18191 Von Karman Avenue, Suite 1100, **Irvine** CA 92612-0187
Tel: 949 851 0633   **Fax:** 949 851 9348

4370 La Jolla Village Drive, **San Diego** CA 92122
Tel: 858 535 9001   **Fax:** 858 597 1585

2049 Century Park East, 34th Floor, **Los Angeles** CA 90067-3208
Tel: 310 277 4110   **Fax:** 310 277 4730

3150 Porter Drive, **Palo Alto** CA 94304-1212
Tel: 650 813 5000   **Fax:** 650 813 5100

DISTRICT OF COLUMBIA
600 13th Street NW, **Washington** DC 20005-3096
Tel: 202 756 8000   **Fax:** 202 756 8087

FLORIDA
201 South Biscayne Boulevard, **Miami** FL 33131-4336
Tel: 305 358 3500   **Fax:** 305 347 6500

MASSACHUSSETTS
28 State Street, **Boston** MA 02109-1775
Tel: 617 535 4000   **Fax:** 617 535 3800

NEW YORK
50 Rockefeller Plaza, **New York** NY 10020-1605
Tel: 212 547 5400   **Fax:** 212 547 5444

INTERNATIONAL OFFICES

The firm also has offices in Düsseldorf, London, Milan, Munich, Rome and Brussels.

Intellectual Property: The firm's IP lawyers hold degrees in a wide variety of technical and scientific fields and are uniquely capable of handling intellectual property matters in virtually every technical or scientific discipline. The firm offers comprehensive legal services in every aspect of intellectual property law. Among these services, the firm's IP Practice is renowned for its trial and appellate experience. The IP Practice includes client counselling, procurement, and licensing in the patent, trademark, trade dress, copyright, trade secret, entertainment and computer law areas. The firm's IP lawyers undertake all forms of IP litigation, and have assisted clients with oppositions in the European Patent Office and the Community Trade Mark Office. The firm's lawyers acted in UK's first trade mark case under the 1994 Trade Marks Act to go to the House of Lords (Supreme Court).

M&A: The firm's lawyers have extensive experience and advise on the purchase, sale and merger of businesses. The firm handles take-overs, acquisitions and disposals, MBOs and MBIs, LBOs and LBIs, and reorganisations and restructurings.

Tax: The firm advises clients on all tax-related areas, including corporate, employee benefits, private clients, state and local taxation, and international matters. The core of the tax practice deals with thousands of statutory tax requirements imposed at international, federal, state and local levels. The firm represents more than half of the Fortune 100 companies in tax matters on a regular basis.

Trial: The trial lawyers are regularly engaged in all aspects of civil, regulatory and white-collar criminal defense litigation in US and international forums. Experience includes handling emergency situations such as temporary restraining orders and preliminary injunctions, bench and jury trials, arbitrations and alternative dispute resolution, including mediations and summary jury trials.

McDONNELL BOEHNEN HULBERT & BERGHOFF LLP

THE FIRM

FIRM OVERVIEW: McDonnell Boehnen Hulbert & Berghoff LLP (MBHB) is an entrepreneurial, mid-size law firm focusing on the intellectual property law needs of technology-driven companies. The firm's clients range from Fortune 100 companies to small start-ups and educational institutions, and encompass industries such as biotechnology, nanotechnology, pharmaceuticals, chemicals, and diagnostics as well as electronics, computer peripherals, software, telecommunications, and traditional manufacturing and engineering. The firm's 67 professionals have strong experience in enforcement, defense, procurement, and licensing of patents, trademarks, copyrights, trade secrets and unfair competition. All of the firm's attorneys are registered patent agents, and more than half of the firm's professionals have a PhD or other advanced technical degree. All MBHB professionals are recognized in their fields as having outstanding technical and legal expertise as well as exceptional interpersonal and communication skills.

MAIN AREAS OF PRACTICE:

Litigation: The firm's work includes extensive litigation and appellate work, as well as prosecution and counseling on behalf of its clients. MBHB attorneys represent clients aggressively, effectively, and efficiently in all types of intellectual property matters before all forums, e.g., the federal courts, the International Trade Commission, the Patent and Trademark Office, and private mediations. The firm's attorneys have also counseled clients on foreign patent prosecution, opposition proceedings and litigation - both plaintiff and defense positions - throughout Europe, Japan, South America, and many developing countries throughout the world.

Patent Practice: MBHB's significant work in multiple cutting-edge areas in all phases of patent practice has built the great reputation the firm enjoys today. MBHB attorneys are known for creative solutions that help clients protect their intellectual property assets and their business. MBHB prides itself on quality, intelligence, and teamwork, helping clients accomplish their goals.

Biotechnology: MBHB's Biotechnology Practice is one of the firm's founding strengths. MBHB attorneys have the combination of technical expertise and legal experience that enables us to represent our clients in the most sophisticated arenas of this rapidly advancing area, including recombinant genes, nucleic acids, proteins, and monoclonal antibodies. The firm has successfully represented clients in numerous cutting-edge sub-specialties, such as the production and use of RNAi, antisense, ribozymes, gene-gun application, and pharmaceutical products for disease treatment and diagnosis, as well as apparatus and techniques for isolating, labeling, and detecting molecules of biological importance. Drawing on its strengths in biomedical and chemical matters, MBHB has prosecuted, licensed, and litigated a wide variety of patents in the pharmaceutical and diagnostics fields, including such technologies as target discovery, high-throughput screening, combinatorial chemistry, drug-delivery systems, therapeutic small molecules, and drug and antibody assay devices, methods, and reagents.

HEAD OFFICE

ILLINOIS
300 South Wacker Drive, **Chicago**, IL 60606-6709
Tel: 312 913 0001   **Fax:** 312 913 0002
Website: www.mbhb.com

Computing, Telecommunications & E-Commerce: Innovations in the field of electrical devices and systems are closely related to developments in computing, telecommunications, and e-commerce. MBHB has applied their expertise in cases involving signaling formats, semiconductors, power regulation systems, high-definition television, biomedical instrumentation, optics and imaging devices, digital video compression, optical and magnetic storage devices, circuit board, chip manufacturing, and online business systems. MBHB represents a broad range of clients in the burgeoning area of telecommunications. They have extensive experience handling patent matters in both analog and digital communications, including digital signal processing, modulation and coding techniques, real-time media transmissions, internet communications, wireless intelligent networks, policy-based networking, and satellite communications.

SCHIFF HARDIN LLP

THE FIRM

Managing Partner: Ronald S Safer

Number of partners worldwide: 169
Number of other lawyers worldwide: 161

FIRM OVERVIEW: Schiff Hardin LLP, founded in 1864, is a general practice firm with local, regional, national, and international clients.

MAIN AREAS OF PRACTICE:

General Litigation: The firm is especially active in the trial of complex matters before state and federal courts, as well as administrative agencies, nationwide and abroad. Schiff Hardin's general litigation practice includes product liability, class actions, construction, labor and employment, antitrust and trade regulation, environmental, bankruptcy and creditors' rights, franchising, and white collar crime.

Intellectual Property: Schiff Hardin provides litigation, counseling, and transactional services involving patents, trademarks, trade dress, trade secrets, copyrights, software, computers, internet, electronic commerce, technology transfers, joint ventures, strategic alliances, technology protection programs, international technology applications, and federal and state regulations.

Reinsurance: Schiff Hardin attorneys have decades of experience in reinsurance litigation. This includes scores of reinsurance arbitrations and lawsuits involving practically the entire scope of the insurance industry.

Corporate & Securities: Schiff Hardin represents a broad range of business organizations and individuals engaged in national, international, regional, and local business. Services involve corporate transactions of every variety, mergers and acquisitions, reorganizations, public and private offerings, venture capital, corporate governance, government contracts, and international business activities. Schiff Hardin's corporate practice also includes securities and futures market regulation, public law and public finance, financial institutions, taxation, employee benefits and executive compensation, telecommunications, energy, healthcare, and sports and entertainment.

Finance: The firm represents lenders, institutional investors, placement agents, borrowers, and lessors/lessees in various commercial and corporate debt financing contexts.

Estate Planning & Administration: The firm has one of the most prominent estate planning and administration practices in the US. Schiff Hardin's practice also includes trust and fiduciary litigation.

Real Estate: Schiff Hardin represents clients in the purchase, sale, leaseback, exchange, and leasing of commercial, office, retail, industrial, residential properties, and vacant land, as well as community investment and development. The firm also assists clients with construction, permanent, asset-based, and other complex types of financing.

INTERNATIONAL WORK: The firm serves international clients in all of its practice disciplines. Main areas of international practice include general litigation, intellectual property, reinsurance, corporate and securities, mergers and acquisitions, finance, and financial institutions. It is a member of two referral networks – TerraLex and the US Law Firm Group.

HEAD OFFICE

ILLINOIS
6600 Sears Tower, **Chicago** IL 60606
Tel: 312 258 5500 **Fax:** 312 258 5600
Website: www.schiffhardin.com

BRANCH OFFICES

GEORGIA
1230 Peachtree Street, 18th Floor, **Atlanta**, GA 30309
Tel: 404 806 3800 **Fax:** 404 806 3801

ILLINOIS
One Westminster Place, **Lake Forest**, IL 60045
Tel: 847 295 9200 **Fax:** 847 295 7810

NEW YORK
623 Fifth Avenue, 28th Floor, **New York**, NY 10022
Tel: 212 753 5000 **Fax:** 212 753 5044

DISTRICT OF COLUMBIA
1101 Connecticut Avenue, NW, Suite 600, **Washington**, DC 20036
Tel: 202 778 6400 **Fax:** 202 778 6460

INTERNATIONAL

The firm also has an office in Dublin, Ireland.

CONTACTS

General Litigation	Roger Pascal (Chicago)
Intellectual Property	Richard J Hoskins (Chicago)
Product Liability	Robert H Riley (Chicago)
Class Actions	Marci A Eisenstein (Chicago)
Construction	Mark C Friedlander (Chicago)
Labor & Employment	Max G Brittain, Jr (Chicago)
Environmental	Sheldon A Zabel (Chicago)
Insurance	Jill B Berkeley (Chicago)
Reinsurance	David M Spector (Chicago)
Antitrust & Trade Regulation	William M Hannay (Chicago)
Bankruptcy & Workouts	J Mark Fisher (Chicago)
White Collar	Ronald S Safer (Chicago)
Corporate & Securities	Stuart L Goodman (Chicago)
Securities & Futures Regulation	Andrew M Klein (Washington)
	Michael L Meyer (Chicago)
Finance	Mark A Sternberg (Chicago),
	Mark C Zaander (Chicago)
Public Law & Public Finance	James M Kane (Chicago)
Financial Institutions	Christopher J Zinski (Chicago)
Taxation	Robert R Pluth, Jr (Chicago)
Employee Benefits	David H Williams (Atlanta)
	Edward Spacapan, Jr (Chicago)
Healthcare	Matthew J Murer (Chicago)
Energy/Telecommunications	Barbara K Heffernan (Washington)
	Patricia Dondanville (Chicago)
Sports	Gary L Mowder (Chicago)
Government Contracts	Garry S Grossman (Washington)
Estate Planning & Administration	David R Hodgman (Chicago)
Real Estate	David A Grossberg (Chicago)
International	William M Hannay (Chicago)

SCHWARTZ COOPER GREENBERGER & KRAUSS

THE FIRM

Managing Principals: Ronald B Grais, Robert Dunn Glick

Number of principals: 45
Number of other lawyers: 27

FIRM OVERVIEW: Schwartz Cooper Greenberger & Krauss is a leading Chicago-based law firm providing services across a range of legal disciplines and industries. The firm's attorneys maintain long-term relationships with clients as a result of the firm's emphasis on listening to and consistently communicating with clients, fast response time and follow-up, and on providing practical business advice that is solution-driven.

MAIN AREAS OF PRACTICE:

Banking & Finance: For more than 80 years, Schwartz Cooper has provided a wide range of legal services to its finance clients, including regulatory compliance, cash flow lending and mezzanine finance, asset-based lending, workouts and loan restructuring, and every imaginable form of debt and equity financing. The firm also represents bank clients in the merger, acquisition and sale of banks and bank holding companies.

Business & Private Wealth Services: The firm assists individuals, families and businesses in handling matters such as estate planning and trust and estate administration, succession planning, tax planning, guardianship and adoption matters, charitable and tax-exempt organizations, and elder law issues.

Creditors' Rights & Bankruptcy: The firm's nationally recognized Bankruptcy Practice includes representation of businesses experiencing financial difficulty, secured and unsecured creditors, creditors' committees, purchasers of insolvent companies, trustees and assignees for the benefit of creditors.

Corporate & Business Law: Schwartz, Cooper provides business law services to middle-market companies and to the banks, private equity funds and other institutions that lend to and invest in them. The firm provides counsel on mergers and acquisitions, corporate and partnership taxation, futures and securities law and regulation, private equity and venture capital, corporate and partnership taxation, employment law and ERISA, environmental law and regulation, and franchise and distribution. The firm also serves the day-to-day legal needs of numerous financial institutions and businesses that are family-owned and -managed.

Litigation: Schwartz Cooper handles litigation matters in Illinois and throughout the country, at the trial and appellate levels involving areas such as antitrust, business torts, construction law, contracts, corporate governance, employment issues, environmental law, financial services, fraud and RICO, intellectual property, international asset recovery, professional liability, real estate, tax issues, technology and trust and probate.

Real Estate: The firm's National Real Estate Practice encompasses real estate financing, leasing, development, acquisitions and dispositions, arbitration and dispute resolution and related litigation.

Technology & Intellectual Property: The firm advises clients on technology transfer and licensing, acquisitions, dispositions and financing, and on trademarks, copyrights and trade secrets.

HEAD OFFICE

ILLINOIS
180 North LaSalle Street Suite 2700, **Chicago**, IL 60601
Tel: 312 346 1300 **Fax:** 312 782 8416
Website: www.schwartzcooper.com

CONTACTS:

Banking & Finance...Martin W Salzman
Business & Private Wealth Services.....................Nancy R Livingston
Creditors' Rights & Bankruptcy...........................Richard M Bendix Jr
Corporate & Business Law ....Andrew H Connor
Litigation ....Stephen H Gistenson
Real Estate ....Robert C Linton
Technology & Intellectual Property ....Dina Ross

CLIENTS: The firm's clients include local and national banking institutions, commercial real estate lenders, investment funds, and small and mid-size public and private entities in industries ranging from manufacturing to technology to retail.

INTERNATIONAL WORK: The firm's International Asset Recovery Group has significant experience and substantial international resources in discovery, seizure and recovery of assets in foreign countries and in enforcing foreign claims domestically. Attorneys in the firm are fluent in several dialects of Chinese, Korean, Spanish and Russian.

SEYFARTH SHAW LLP

THE FIRM

Managing Partner: J Stephen Poor

Number of partners: 301
Number of other lawyers: 324

FIRM OVERVIEW: Founded in 1945, Seyfarth Shaw LLP is a full service firm with more than 600 lawyers practicing in Atlanta, Boston, Chicago, Houston, Los Angeles, New York, Sacramento, San Francisco, Washington, DC and in Brussels, Belgium. Its practice areas include labor and employment law, bankruptcy, workouts and business reorganization; business immigration; commercial litigation; construction; corporate law; employee benefits; environmental, safety and health; intellectual property; and real estate. The firm's practice groups and its attorneys reflect the diversity of the country's business and social fabric. Representing clients throughout the United States and in virtually every industry of the global economy, they are prepared to coordinate legal resources and provide effective solutions wherever and whenever its clients do business. From the beginning, the firm has held that client goals can best be achieved through creative, unique solutions delivered with its ongoing commitment to its core values of innovation, teamwork, client service commitment to excellence. Since then, the firms attorneys have been at the forefront of legal and business knowledge, anticipating developments and delivering coordinated, cross-disciplinary and cost-effective legal advice and business training that meets its clients' immediate needs while preparing them for challenges down the road.

CLIENTS: The firm's clients include national and international companies in banking, finance, government, healthcare, hospitality, insurance, manufacturing, printing and publishing, professional services, retail, technology, and telecommunications.

HEAD OFFICE

ILLINOIS
55 East Monroe Street, **Chicago** IL 60603
Tel: 312 346 8000   **Fax:** 312 269 8869
Website: www.seyfarth.com

BRANCH OFFICES

CALIFORNIA
One Century Plaza, 2029 Century Park East, Suite 3300
Los Angeles, CA 90067-3063
Tel: 310 277 7200   **Fax:** 301 201 5291

400 Capitol Mall Suite 2350 **Sacramento**, CA 95814 4428
Tel: 916 48 0159   **Fax:** 916 558 4839

560 Mission Street, Suite 3100 **San Francisco**, CA 94105
Tel: 415 397 2823   **Fax:** 415 397 8549

DISTRICT OF COLUMBIA
815 Connecticut Avenue, NW Suite 500,
Washington, DC 20006-4004
Tel: 202 463 2400   **Fax:** 202 828 5393

GEORGIA
One Peachtree Pointe 1545 Peachtree Street, NE Suite 700
Atlanta, GA 30309-2401
Tel: 404 885 7500   **Fax:** 404 892 7056

MASSACHUSETTS
Two Seaport Lane, Suite 300, **Boston**, MA 02210-2028
Tel: 617 946 4800   **Fax:** 617 946 4801

NEW YORK
1270 Avenue of the Americas, Suite 2500,
New York, NY 10020-1801
Tel: 212 218 5500   **Fax:** 212 218 5526

TEXAS
700 Louisiana Street, Suite 3700, **Houston**, TX 77002-2797
Tel: 212 218 5500   **Fax:** 212 218 5526

SIDLEY AUSTIN BROWN & WOOD LLP

THE FIRM

Chairman of Executive Committee: Thomas A Cole
Chairman of the Management Committee: Charles W Douglas
Vice-Chairman of Management Committee: Theodore N Miller

Number of partners: 577
Number of other lawyers: 969

AREAS OF PRACTICE:

Commercial/Business Litigation	25%
Securitization & Banking	22%
Corporate Transactions/Contracts	16%
Intellectual Property	6%
Real Estate	6%
Taxation/International	4%
Funds	3%
Insurance & Financial Services	3%
Employment/Labor/Benefits	3%
Product/Professional Liability	2%
Environmental/Energy/Natural Resources	2%
International Trade & Dispute Resolution	2%
Public Finance	2%
Other	4%

FIRM OVERVIEW: Sidley Austin Brown & Wood LLP is one of the world's largest full service law firms. With more than 1,500 lawyers practicing on three continents (North America, Europe and Asia), the firm provides a broad range of integrated services to meet the needs of both large and small businesses as well as governments, institutions, associations, foundations, professional firms and individuals. The firm was named the 'Number One law firm in the US' for overall client service in 2002 and 2004 by *BTI Consulting* in its annual survey of how large corporate law departments rate their outside law firms. According to *BTI*, general counsel from *Fortune* 1000 companies interviewed recognized excellence in 'every aspect of Sidley Austin's client service and delivery, specifically noting the firm's dedication to helping clients and to understanding clients' business-specific issues and goals'.

MAIN AREAS OF PRACTICE: Sidley Austin Brown & Wood LLP has a major corporate and financial transactions practice with significant activity in all areas, including mergers and acquisitions, spin-offs, capital markets, divestitures and joint ventures as well as all types of financings, including public offerings, project financings, asset securitizations and bank lending transactions.

CLIENTS: The firm's clients include individuals, entrepreneurs and executives, industrial and service corporations; venture capital/private equity firms; partnerships; investment banks; commercial banks; public utilities; non-profit organizations; mutual funds; insurance and other financial services companies; and government agencies.

INTERNATIONAL WORK: The firm handles work in Arabic, Bahasa Malaysia, Chinese (Cantonese, Mandarin, Shanghainese), Danish, Dutch, Efik, Finnish, Flemish, French, German, Greek, Hebrew, Hindi, Hungarian, Italian, Japanese, Latvian, Lithuanian, Norwegian, Portuguese, Russian, Sanskrit, Serbian, Spanish, Swedish, Tagalog, Taiwanese, Tamil, Telugu, and Yoruba.

US OFFICES

CALIFORNIA
555 West Fifth Street, **Los Angeles**, CA 90013
Tel: 213 896 6000 **Fax:** 213 896 6600

555 California Street, Suite 5000, **San Francisco**, CA 94104-1715
Tel: 415 772 1200 **Fax:** 415 772 7400

DISTRICT OF COLUMBIA
1501 K Street, NW, **Washington**, DC 20005
Tel: 202 736 8000 **Fax:** 202 736 8711

ILLINOIS
Bank One Plaza, 10 South Dearborn Street, **Chicago**, IL 60603
Tel: 312 853 7000 **Fax:** 312 853 7036

NEW YORK
787 Seventh Avenue, **New York**, NY 10019
Tel: 212 839 5300 **Fax:** 212 839 5599

TEXAS
717 N Harwood, Suite 3400, **Dallas**, TX 75201
Tel: 214 981 3300 **Fax:** 214 981 3400

INTERNATIONAL OFFICES

The firm also has offices in Beijing, Belgium, Hong Kong, Shanghai, Singapore, Switzerland, Tokyo and the United Kingdom.

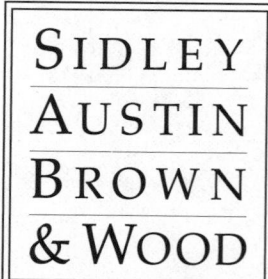

SIDLEY AUSTIN BROWN & WOOD

SONNENSCHEIN NATH & ROSENTHAL LLP

THE FIRM

Chairman: Duane C Quaini
Number of partners: 347
Number of other lawyers: 339
Email: akatz@sonnenschein.com
Website: www.sonnenschein.com

FIRM OVERVIEW: With some 700 attorneys and other professionals in nine US offices and a global reach, Sonnenschein serves many of the world's largest and best-known businesses, nonprofits and individuals.

MAIN AREAS OF PRACTICE:

Antitrust, Marketing Practices, Franchising/Distribution: Counsels and litigates on antitrust, distribution, licensing, franchise and dealer law, marketing, franchisee relations, supplier arrangements.

Bankruptcy & Restructuring: Represents official unsecured creditor, equity committees, Chapter 11 debtors/debtors-in-possession, insurers, indenture trustees, asset acquirers, secured creditors.

Biotech/Life Sciences: Counsels in scientific environment; backgrounds: genetics, organic chemistry, biochemistry, molecular, cellular biology.

Comminications & Media: Advises on federal and state regulation, procurement and outsourcing of telecom/IT services; general counsel to public cable and broadcast TV companies; represents media, publishing, entertainment and sports firms and talent in IP litigation, securities and commercial matters, First Amendment cases, labor and employment.

Corporate & Securities: Advises on mergers, acquisitions; joint ventures, strategic alliances; technology investment, licensing; outsourcing; securities offerings and compliance; private equity transactions; commercial financing; corporate control, takeover defense; corporate governance.

Corporate Diversity Counseling: Develops diversity action plans addressing issues of concern to senior management; advises on best practices.

Employee Benefits & Executive Compensation: Negotiates executive agreements, strategies for change-in-control compensation, equity plans. Counsels in developing, managing tax-qualified retirement plans, deferred compensation, welfare plans, HIPAA; class action defense of ERISA fiduciary, benefit claims.

Environmental/Energy: Counsels on avoiding/minimizing liability; litigates government, private party suits; negotiates alternative agreements; develops plans for managing liability, facilitating new projects, product development, structuring, supporting management programs; develops energy policy, legislation; counsels energy clients.

Government Regulation & Enforcement: Counsels through government contracts process and regulatory bodies, especially in health care and before such federal agencies as the Consumer Product Safety Commission, Food and Drug Administration and the Federal Trade Commission.

Healthcare: Extensive experience in all aspects of healthcare law, including joint ventures, mergers, acquisitions, e-health, managed care transactions, healthcare financing, Medicare/Medicaid reimbursement.

Information Security & Internet Enforcement: Advises on safeguarding information, investigates and seeks redress for computer-based misconduct including intellectual property piracy, unsolicited commercial email and theft of proprietary information; provides immediate legal response to unlawful internet-based conduct.

Insurance: Counsels in crisis management, complex commercial litigation; provides legal solutions, including in major class actions, constitutional cases, coverage disputes, employment, regulatory, compliance matters.

Intellectual Property & Technology: Counsels, litigates on development, use, and protection of intellectual property; including in electronics, computers, telecommunications, aerospace, mechanical design, engineering arts, chemistry, pharmaceutical science, biotech; represents in applications for and protections of patent and trademark rights.

International Trade & Import/Export Regulation: Counsels on laws governing movement of goods, technology across borders. Advises on trade policy, customs regulation, export controls, enforcement, penalties, boycotts, sanctions, embargoes, import relief investigations, including antidumping, countervailing duty scope determinations, unfair trade practices; develops export, import management systems, internal controls.

Labor & Employment: Counsels on compliance issues, including training, internal investigations; representation in all forums, including single employee litigation, arbitrations, administrative investigations, class actions, corporate transactions including mergers, acquisitions, downsizings.

Litigation & Business Regulation: Provides services encompassing class action defense, insurance, white collar crime, product liability, intellectual property, technology, real estate, construction, financial transactions, securities, antitrust, franchising, distribution, government contracts.

Public Law & Policy Strategies: Focuses on issues and strategies before Congress, Executive Branch, national policymakers, state legislators and regulators; assists in direct advocacy, budget, appropriations, grassroots communications and marketing, crisis management, coalition and partnership development, international government relations.

Real Estate: Advises in complex multi-state purchases, dispositions; constructions; financing; equity investment; commercial, multifamily development; leasing; affordable housing; hotels, hospitality.

Taxation: Structures, advises on corporate acquisitions, dispositions involving US and non-US entities, financing techniques, US and non-US planning for USMNCs, partnerships, other joint ventures, real estate, foreign transactions; exempt organizations, tax litigation controversies.

Trusts & Estates: Counsels wealthy on tax, estate planning and related litigation; administers estates, trusts, fiduciary accountings.

Venture Technology: Represents emerging growth clients; counsels management and boards on industry practices, governance, stock option and executive compensation, employment and intellectual property protection.

US OFFICES

CALIFORNIA
601 South Figueroa Street, Suite 1500, **Los Angeles** CA 90017
Tel: 213 623 9300 **Fax:** 213 623 9924

685 Market Street, 6th Floor, **San Francisco** CA 94105
Tel: 415 882 5000 **Fax:** 415 543 5472

DISTRICT OF COLUMBIA
1301 K Street NW, Suite 600, East Tower, **Washington** DC 20005
Tel: 202 408 6400 **Fax:** 202 408 6399

FLORIDA
Phillips Point, East Tower, 777 South Flagler Drive, Suite 600,
West Palm Beach FL 33401
Tel: 561 833 2410 **Fax:** 561 833 8387

ILLINOIS
8000 Sears Tower, 233 South Wacker Drive, **Chicago** IL 60606
Tel: 312 876 8000 **Fax:** 312 876 7934

MISSOURI
4520 Main Street, Suite 1100, **Kansas City** MO 64111
Tel: 816 460 2400 **Fax:** 816 531 7545

One Metropolitan Square, Suite 3000, **St Louis** MO 63102
Tel: 314 241 1800 **Fax:** 314 259 5959

NEW JERSEY
101 JFK Parkway, **Short Hills** NJ 07078
Tel: 973 912 7100 **Fax:** 973 912 9199

NEW YORK
1221 Avenue of the Americas, **New York** NY 10020
Tel: 212 768 6700 **Fax:** 212 768 6800

WINSTON & STRAWN LLP

THE FIRM

Managing Partner: James M Neis
Senior Partner: James R Thompson (Chairman)
Paul Hensel (Administrative Partner)

Number of partners in US: 362
Number of other lawyers in US: 448
Number of lawyers worldwide: 861

FIRM OVERVIEW: Founded in 1853. One of the oldest and largest US law firms with more than 850 attorneys in Chicago; New York; Washington, DC; Los Angeles; San Francisco; Paris, France; London, England; and Geneva, Switzerland.

MAIN AREAS OF PRACTICE:

Litigation: Winston & Strawn's litigators are consistently entrusted with some of corporate America's highest stakes litigation. They have tried major jury trials in virtually every federal district in the United States, and have appeared before the United States Supreme Court and the US Courts of Appeals. Their work involves antitrust; construction, technology, and other contractual disputes; corporate internal investigations and white collar criminal defense; product liability; patent/trademark/copyright infringement; securities; international litigation and arbitration; environmental; employment and ERISA; professional liability; tax controversy; and unfair competition and trade regulation.

Corporate & Financial: The Corporate and Financial Practice Group provides a range of transaction-related legal services to enterprises of all types and sizes. Corporate attorneys advise on mergers and acquisitions, securities transactions and regulation, corporate governance, commercial lending, private equity, information technology, leasing, asset securitization, project finance, public finance, financial services regulatory, and bankruptcy, workout, and financial restructuring.

Labor & Employment Relations: The firm counsels major employers and a variety of closely held business enterprises on labor and employment relations programs and policies, as well as employment, labor, and ERISA litigation in state and federal courts throughout the country. It also represents clients before federal, state, and local administrative agencies, including the EEOC and the NLRB.

Real Estate: Real estate attorneys counsel all types of sophisticated real estate market participants in the acquisition, financing, sale, development, and leasing of commercial, industrial, and multifamily properties.

Intellectual Property: IP lawyers provide general IP counseling; litigation throughout the United States and before the US Patent and Trademark Office and the Federal Circuit Court of Appeals; management of trademark, patent, and copyright portfolios; and patent, trademark, and copyright prosecution and licensing.

Tax: The Tax Practice assists in virtually every area of corporate tax law, from planning through audit as well as appeals and litigation. Its transactional attorneys are known for innovation in domestic and cross-border structured finance transactions, particularly in leasing and asset securitization. Tax controversy attorneys represent clients in judicial and administrative proceedings at both the state and federal levels.

Governmental Relations & Regulatory Affairs: Led by former four-term Illinois governor James R Thompson, this group includes attorneys and advisors who have held major positions with national trade associations, congressional committees, and congressional leaders. Work includes legislative and regulatory representation, counseling and bill analysis, congressional lobbying, executive branch advocacy on policy questions, legislative drafting, and preparation and presentation of congressional testimony.

HEAD OFFICE

ILLINOIS
35 West Wacker Drive, **Chicago** IL 60601
Tel: 312 558 5600 **Fax:** 312 558 5700
Email: info@winston.com
Website: www.winston.com

OTHER OFFICES

CALIFORNIA
333 South Grand Avenue, **Los Angeles** CA 90071
Tel: 213 615 1700 **Fax:** 213 615 1750

101 California Street, **San Francisco** CA 94111
Tel: 415 591 1000 **Fax:** 415 591 1400

DISTRICT OF COLUMBIA
1700 K Street, N.W., **Washington**, DC 20006
Tel: 202 371 5700 **Fax:** 202 371 5950

NEW YORK
200 Park Avenue, **New York** NY 10166
Tel: 212 294 6700 **Fax:** 212 294 4700

CONTACTS

Litigation	Dan K Webb
Corporate & Financial	John L MacCarthy
Labor & Employment Relations	Columbus R Gangemi, Jr
Real Estate	Christopher D Murtaugh
Intellectual Property	Stephen P Durchslag, Virginia R Richard
Tax	Robert F Denvir
Governmental Relations & Regulatory Affairs	James R Thompson
Energy	Nicholas S Reynolds
Environmental	Jennifer T Nijman, William N Hall
Employee Benefits & Executive Compensation	Michael S Melbinger
Healthcare/Maritime & Admiralty	Thomas L Mills
Trusts & Estates	Christine A Albright

Energy: This practice ranks among the largest in the nation, representing entities engaged in all aspects of the energy industry, including production, transmission, and distribution of electricity and natural gas.

Environmental: This practice encompasses all aspects of environmental law, including litigation matters, corporate transactions, and regulatory issues. The Paris practice includes regulatory, transactional, and litigation aspects of environmental law of the European Community.

Employee Benefits & Executive Compensation: The firm advises on issues regarding compensation of employees and the planning and administration of employee benefits. It also assists in the design and drafting of all forms of executive compensation plans.

CLIENTS: Significant relationships with companies including Abbott Laboratories, American Airlines, AON Corporation, Barr Laboratories, Deutsche Bank AG, Exelon Corporation, J.P. Morgan Chase, Lear Corporation, McDonald's Corporation, Microsoft Corporation, Morgan Stanley, Motorola, Inc., PPG Industries, Philip Morris USA Inc., Salomon Smith Barney, and Smurfit-Stone Container.

INTERNATIONAL WORK: Clients include ALSTOM S.A., Altadis, S.A., Bank Audi Group, Cap Gemini S.A., Credit Suisse First Boston, EuroDisney, S.C.A., Export-Import Bank of the United States, Formosa Plastics Group, Iberdola S.A., Luxottica Group S.p.A., Maritech, Ltd., Overseas Private Investment Corporation, PPG Industries, Inc., Rhodia, Rolaco Group, Telefónica, S.A., Terra Networks, S.A., and Vivendi S.A.

CONTENTS: Corporate/M&A p.781; Employment: p.783; Litigation: p.785; Real Estate p.787; Individuals' Profiles p.790; Firms' Profiles p.796.

How lawyers are ranked

The opinions we gather from clients — mainly from in-house lawyers but also from other purchasers of legal services — are balanced by opinions from colleagues and competitors. Together, they provide two different perspectives — an all-round view — and biased viewpoints cancel each other out.

CORPORATE/M&A

Indiana
Leading firms (Corporate/M&A)

1 BAKER & DANIELS *Indianapolis*
ICE MILLER *Indianapolis*

2 BARNES & THORNBURG *Indianapolis*
SOMMER BARNARD ATTORNEYS PC *Indianapolis*

3 BOSE MCKINNEY & EVANS LLP *Indianapolis*

4 HENDERSON DAILY WITHROW *Indianapolis*
KRIEG DEVAULT LLP *Indianapolis*

Leading individuals (Corporate/M&A)

1 ASCHLEMAN James *Baker & Daniels, Indianapolis*
HUMKE Steven *Ice Miller, Indianapolis*
STRAIN James *Sommer Barnard, Indianapolis*

2 BOEGLIN Daniel *Baker & Daniels, Indianapolis*
BRIDGE Catherine *Barnes & Thornburg, Indianapolis*
BROWN J Jeffrey *Baker & Daniels, Indianapolis*
HICKS Robert *Sommer Barnard, Indianapolis*
SWHIER Claudia *Barnes & Thornburg, Indianapolis*
THORNBURGH John *Ice Miller, Indianapolis*
THRAPP Richard *Ice Miller, Indianapolis*
WORRELL David *Baker & Daniels, Indianapolis*

3 BUTCHER David *Bose McKinney, Indianapolis*
CROSS Patrick *Baker & Daniels, Indianapolis*
DENSBORN Donald *Sommer Barnard, Indianapolis*
GREISING Robert *Krieg DeVault, Indianapolis*
HACKMAN Stephen *Ice Miller, Indianapolis*
INVEISS Roberts *Henderson Daily, Indianapolis*
MILLARD David *Barnes & Thornburg, Indianapolis*
WILDMAN Robert *Henderson Daily, Indianapolis*

Up-and-coming individuals
HUPFER Kyle *Ice Miller, Indianapolis*
SHARROW Regina *Sommer Barnard, Indianapolis*

Firms and Individuals are listed alphabetically in each band.

Band 1

Baker & Daniels
See firm details p.796
The Firm: This large firm, with five offices in Indiana alone, continues to lead the field for corporate work. The reasons for its market dominance are threefold: first, its practice is "*broad in scope;*" second, clients appreciate the firm's ability to "*align resources with our needs,*" further commenting on its ability to gain "*a good overview*" of their "*strategic objectives;*" and third, Baker & Daniels has "*technically smart attorneys, who forge great relationships with their clients.*" Particularly recommended for fund formation and securities work, the firm's recent highlights include significant financing transactions for Simon Property Group, including the issue of $900 million in senior notes in a 144A offering. The firm boasts a profile in the life sciences sector, having represented BioCrossroads in the formation of the Indiana Centers for Applied Protein Sciences and the Indiana Health Information Exchange. It also developed the structure and then coordinated the group that formed the Indiana Future Fund I, a $72.6 million institutional investor fund of funds seeking top-quartile returns through early-stage life sciences venture investments.

The Lawyers: Chair of the corporate finance group and "*first-rate corporate attorney*" **Jim Aschleman** (see p.790) impressed clients with his "*knack of getting to the issue quickly without wasting time.*" His practice centers on public company work, including public offerings of debt and equity securities, corporate governance and M&A. In the past year, Aschleman has been representing Anthem in its acquisition of Well-Point Health Networks, which has a transaction value of approximately $17 billion and will, upon completion, form the largest health benefits company in the nation. The "*practical and formidable attorney*" **Dan Boeglin** (see p.791) is praised by clients for his "*good legal advice in the context of our business objectives*" and "*no-nonsense, methodical approach.*" An expert in strategic alliances and joint ventures, Boeglin is particularly active on new product development. In the life sciences sector, he has been working on two joint ventures involving proteomics (the study of proteins in the human body) and was the lead attorney representing BioCrossroads in the formation of the Indiana

Centers for Applied Protein Sciences. A lawyer of "*quality,*" **Jeff Brown** (see p.791) heads the firm's private capital and venture group and was lead attorney on the Indiana Future Fund deal. Though much of Brown's work is venture capital financing, he also handles M&As. **David Worrell** (see p.795) is "*well versed and extremely dependable,*" and continues to impress clients and peers alike, with one client confirming they had "*relied on him heavily in recent times and he always delivered.*" Described as "*a lawyers' lawyer who is particularly strong on securities,*" Worrell also represents banks and financial institutions. He worked on the formation of a new bank in Indianapolis and continues to represent Simon Property Group in 144A offerings. **Pat Cross** (see p.791) makes his debut in the tables this year, having impressed clients for "*the excellent job he does on transactional matters.*" Cross's practice includes healthcare and corporate law and during the year he was pivotal in the corporate representation of one of the largest healthcare providers in the USA.

The Clients: Zimmer; Anthem; ITT Educational Services; Shoe Carnival; Priority Healthcare Corporation; BioCrossroads; Great Lakes Chemical Corporation; Circle K Stores; Integra Bank; Clarian Health Partners; Kimball International and Eli Lilly.

Ice Miller
See firm details p.797
The Firm: Clients refer to the "*responsiveness*" and "*excellent representation*" of this well-respected corporate group and comment on the breadth of issues covered. "*Clearly a top corporate firm,*" Ice Miller has the "*firepower*" to represent some of the most significant clients on some of the most complex deals in the state. One highlight from the past year was the sale of Maxon Corporation (a worldwide leader for industrial combustion equipment with facilities in both the USA and Europe) to an Indiana-based private equity fund that partnered with the company's management. Another was the

firm's work on the largest private gift ever donated to Ball State University – nearly $17.2 million from the estate of Wallace T Miller after it obtained the proceeds of the sale of stock in his company. This project entailed changing the name of the College of Business to the Miller School of Business and transforming the college's offerings for students and faculties.

The Lawyers: *"An upstanding person and a fine lawyer,"* **Steven Humke** (see p.792) continues to impress clients and peers. Clients refer to his *"commitment to delivering on time"* and *"ability to meet the targets set."* Humke mostly represents private companies, devoting the bulk of his time to advising on corporate governance, strategic planning, raising capital and growth through acquisitions. *"Very active in the private arena,"* **John Thornburgh** (see p.794) cochairs the firm's strategic advisers group and is chair of its sports and entertainment group. He focuses on M&A, venture finance and the representation of businesses in the sports and entertainment industries. His style is one that *"clients can really relate to."* **Richard Thrapp** (see p.794) is chair of the firm's business section and continues to garner praise for a thriving general business and M&A practice. He worked on the Maxon Corporation and Wallace Miller estate transactions and has also been heavily involved in the provision of corporate governance advice to the second largest foundation in Indiana, the Lumina Foundation for Education. Commentators consistently referred to his *"ability to get straight to the point, yet also think ahead to what is best for his clients in the long run."* **Stephen Hackman** (see p.792) is another quality attorney who has confirmed his place in the tables. As well as having *"a good reputation in the community,"* he exhibits a *"good business mind and an all-round personable nature."* Hackman's practice encompasses securities, M&A and structured finance, and in the past year he has spent time exploring strategic and financial alternatives for a notable public company. Jack Snyder has now retired; however, commentators agree that there are *"many quality attorneys coming up through the ranks"*. One such attorney is *"extraordinary M&A lawyer"* **Kyle Hupfer**, who is described as being *"able to handle very complex transactions"* because of his *"intuitive grasp of how M&A deals work."*

The Clients: Lumina Foundation for Education; Citizens Gas & Coke Utility; Cardinal Ventures; Standard Life Investments (USA); Dan Slattery; Wal-Mart; Celadon Group; The Indiana Rail Road Company and Morgan Foods.

Band 2

Barnes & Thornburg

The Firm: Seen by the market as *"one of the leading corporate firms in Indiana,"* Barnes & Thornburg is one of the largest in the state. The firm's business, tax and real estate group has deep involvement and an excellent reputation with utilities, large public companies and middle-market businesses, commonly representing them on *"make-or-break"* transactions. The firm represented Tomkins in the sale of Mayfran International to a US private equity fund as part of the group's strategic disposal of noncore businesses. Mayfran, which manufactures a range of equipment used in the metalworking and automotive industries, had annual sales of $61.8 million. Market sources made particular reference to the SEC, banking and IP-related work of the firm, as well as its ability to provide prompt, high-quality advice on corporate governance issues arising out of the Sarbanes-Oxley legislation.

The Lawyers: **Cathy Bridge** chairs the business, tax and real estate department and is said to be *"a good technician who rarely gets caught out."* Her practice is focused on securities, M&A and insurance regulatory matters and she is well known for her strong utilities clientele. Recently, she advised on a complicated merger transaction for a Kansas-based insurance company, was involved in the Tomkins deal and gave corporate governance advice to Vectren. *"Excellent banking practitioner"* **Claudia Swhier** works out of the firm's financial institutions practice group and is respected for her all-round knowledge and experience of the sector, as well as her significant securities and corporate law experience. Highlights from the past year include the $37.7 million acquisition by Lincoln Bancorp of First Shares Bancorp, and her representation of Oak Street Financial Services in a $150 million IPO. Swhier also undertakes Sarbanes-Oxley Act compliance work for her public company clients. **David Millard** is recognized as *"one of the most prominent corporate lawyers in the market,"* and is *"particularly good on entrepreneurial matters."* Millard is the chair of the firm's entrepreneurial services practice group and advises middle-market and high-growth businesses on all types of issue, including sales and acquisitions.

The Clients: Notable clients include Vectren, Dow Agro Sciences and Tomkins.

Sommer Barnard Attorneys PC
See firm details p.799

The Firm: Following the departure of the Ackerson Group after a two-year sojourn at the firm, this organization is now known as Sommer Barnard Attorneys; however, the market does not believe the Ackerson departures will affect the corporate group to any noticeable extent. The firm has 25 corporate lawyers and, although smaller than some of the other firms listed, it is acknowledged to be active on *"some top-end work."* It is particularly noted for its activities in healthcare, IP and government affairs, with clients commending the *"business acumen"* of the attorneys involved in these areas.

Feedback from the market this year suggests this firm is hot on the heels of some of the top firms.

The Lawyers: Chairman of the business law practice group **Jim Strain** (see p.794) is said to have been *"a driving force in the corporate market for a long time."* To his clients, he is *"the corporate attorney of choice for all our large transactions and top-end stuff;"* they praise *"his confidence, good sense of humor and ability to explain even the most complex area of law to the layperson."* Clients also commend him for *"his advice to the board in terms of fiduciary duties, shareholders' rights agreements and presentations on corporate governance issues."* Strain recently represented the public company Quality Dining when it went private, valued at $120 million. Moving up the tables this year is *"one of the best in town,"* **Bob Hicks** (see p.792). Enjoying the loyalty of *"a good client base,"* Hicks is *"very client service-focused, and really does say what he thinks, which is good for both the deal and his client."* His proficiency extends to complex transactions, general business counseling and tax and estate planning. **Donald Densborn** (see p.791) has confirmed his position in the tables following market approval for his *"expertise and strong banking and commercial lending practice."* Able in both public and private corporate finance, his practice is centered on middle-market and emerging growth companies. Clients remain quick to endorse *"good, substantive lawyer"* **Regina Sharrow** (see p.794) for her *"client skills and hard work."* Peers confirm that *"she really has got what it takes to get the deal done."*

The Clients: The firm's client roster includes major corporation in an array of areas. Representative clients include Quality Dining and Vectren.

Band 3

Bose McKinney & Evans LLP

The Firm: This full-service firm has gone from strength to strength in the past year, and is widely recognized as *"a very strong corporate player."* Clients and other attorneys who have worked with the firm readily report that this *"respectable practice"* is *"quick to respond, and has it covered in most areas."* The firm is recommended for general corporate advice, acquisitions and dispositions, and advice in relation to the establishment of stock option plans.

The Lawyers: Interviewees agree that **David Butcher** is rightly considered a fine corporate attorney and *"a sure-fire leader in terms of banking work."* He chairs the firm's business services and financial institutions practice groups.

The Clients: Duke Realty; Steel Dynamics; Emmis Communications and First Indiana Bank.

Band 4

Henderson Daily Withrow & DeVoe
The Firm: This full-service law firm holds a respected place in the market, with onlookers referring to the *"careful, thorough and practical nature of the advice given."* Covering a plethora of business areas, including finance, securities and tax, the firm earns special praise for its venture capital and entrepreneurial services practice group.
The Lawyers: **Bob Wildman**, who is of counsel, continues to garner positive feedback for his transactional practice, where he consistently displays *"a good sense for deals."* Clients single him out for his *"smartness and activity in notable financial transactions."* Wildman is seen as a good choice for both small, entrepreneurial

clients and large companies, and can hold his own on securities matters, franchise law and real estate finance. The *"well-respected"* **Roberts Inveiss** also picked up a fair amount of market endorsement for his transactional practice and debuts in the table as a result. Commentators stressed the fact that he is *"easy to work with."*
The Clients: American United Life Insurance Company, Verizon Wireless and Morgan Stanley are three of the firm's best-known clients.

Krieg DeVault LLP
The Firm: Historically noted for being *"particularly strong in their representation of banks and financial institutions,"* this four-office firm is developing a reputation for its advice to corporate clients. Transactions, securities, real estate development and employee stock option plan-

ning are all areas of growth. Lately, it represented Metrobancorp in its acquisition by First Indiana Corporation, and Old National Bancorp in its acquisition of Insurance & Risk Management.
The Lawyers: *"A very careful lawyer and an extremely capable practitioner in the corporate field,"* **Bob Greising** continues to impress clients and peers alike; he is said to be *"good at getting a deal done with the minimum of fuss."* Greising handles general corporate and secured lending transactions, and is additionally known for advising startup businesses. William Neale chairs the firm's business practice group.
The Clients: First Indiana Bank; Metrobancorp; Old National Bancorp; First Merchants Bank and Fifth Third Bank.

EMPLOYMENT   MAINLY DEFENDANT

Indiana
Leading firms
(Employment: Mainly Defendant)

[1]	**BAKER & DANIELS** *Indianapolis*
	BARNES & THORNBURG *Indianapolis*
	ICE MILLER *Indianapolis*
	OGLETREE, DEAKINS, NASH, SMOAK *Indianapolis*
[2]	**BOSE MCKINNEY & EVANS LLP** *Indianapolis*

Leading individuals
(Employment: Mainly Defendant)

[1]	**BORN II Samuel** *Ice Miller*, Indianapolis
	EBERT Kim *Ogletree Deakins*, Indianapolis
	MILLER David *Baker & Daniels*, Indianapolis
	YERKES Kenneth *Barnes & Thornburg*, Indianapolis
[2]	**BOLDT Michael** *Ice Miller*, Indianapolis
	NEIGHBOURS John *Baker & Daniels*, Indianapolis
	SWIDER David *Bose McKinney*, Indianapolis
	UTKEN Gregory *Baker & Daniels*, Indianapolis
[3]	**BALDWIN Charles** *Ogletree Deakins*, Indianapolis
	BOSHKOFF Ellen *Baker & Daniels*, Indianapolis
	EMERSON Daniel *Bose McKinney*, Indianapolis
	HECKLER Douglas *Barnes & Thornburg*, Indianapolis
	KLAPER Martin *Ice Miller*, Indianapolis
	MCDERMOTT Brian *Ogletree Deakins*, Indianapolis
	NIERMAN Todd *Baker & Daniels*, Indianapolis

Firms and individuals are listed alphabetically in each band.

Band 1

Baker & Daniels
See firm details p.796
The Firm: The firm tops the tables for another year due to the depth of its labor and employment law bench, and to its involvement in much of the highest profile work in the state. Indeed, for many sources this is the first among equals. A huge team is studded with great lawyers at all

levels of seniority, providing technically excellent advice tailored to the needs of individual companies. As one client noted, its lawyers *"listen carefully to what we want to do before doing their level best to try and meet that for us."* The team provides *"practical, prompt and concrete advice"* and *"looks at cases from a businessman's perspective."* It offers a potent mix of employee benefits advice, employment litigation and traditional labor law. Highlights of the year include representing one of the nation's largest long-term healthcare providers in successfully opposing a union-organizing campaign by Service Employees International Union at 50 facilities. It also won a State Supreme Court decision for the largest public school system in the country in a case concerning discovery issues.
The Lawyers: For a number of sources, **David Miller** (see p.793) is *"far and away the best labor and employment lawyer in the state."* He concentrates on traditional labor law, though he also handles employment discrimination work, and devotes about half of his practice to the healthcare field. Highlights of his year include advising on a number of union-organizing efforts in healthcare. The firm is also national counsel to the Child Care Association and Miller is heavily involved in the provision of seminars for them and other nonprofits. The *"increasingly visible"* **John Neighbours** (see p.793) attracted unanimous applause for his activity with trade groups. He concentrates on union avoidance and collective bargaining, as well as having a hand in employment discrimination work. A highlight of his year was defeating a union-organizing attempt at the local facility of a national manufacturer. *"Strategic and creative thinker"* **Greg Utken** (see p.795) moves up the tables this year. The chair of the firm's labor and employment team, he is heavily involved in tra-

ditional labor law. Interviewees described him as *"a real talented lawyer, efficient and practical with a national presence,"* and drew particular attention to his *"great presentation skills before the courts."* This year his workload has included petitioning for certiorari in the US Supreme Court on the issue of employer First Amendment rights in union-organizing campaigns.
Todd Nierman (see p.793) is a *"highly committed"* younger partner. He enjoys a large traditional labor law caseload, handling several important union election campaigns this year for a variety of clients. He also boasts considerable employment law expertise, notably in age discrimination. He is joined in this year's tables by *"real good litigator"* **Ellen Boshkoff** (see p.791). She splits her time between employment litigation and commercial disputes, and brings her wealth of experience to many of the group's highest profile disputes.
The Clients: ArvinMeritor; Borg-Warner Automotive; City of Indianapolis; Eagle Picher Automotive; Eli Lilly; Emmis Communications; Extendicare; Great Dane Trailers; Guidant; hhgregg; Indiana University; Learjet/Bombardier Service Corp; MasterBrand Cabinets; Ryder Logistics; Spectrum Healthcare; Superior/Essex Wire; Tenneco Automotive and Zimmer.

Barnes & Thornburg
The Firm: Everyone agrees that this regional giant is *"clearly capturing a good portion of the market,"* and some would go so far as to say that it *"hosts the most talent."* The team is certainly going from strength to strength, having expanded considerably over the past two years, and handles a wide variety of matters. Clients were particularly impressed by the depth of the regulatory practice, the quality of its work in litigation and its success in lobbying activities. A

feature of the past year has been an increase in the size and quality of the team's employment litigation, and it is also noticing an upturn in collective bargaining. For example, the team represented Hillenbrand Industries in collective bargaining negotiations with five different unions. It is also continuing to work as a structural adviser to the US Chamber of Commerce on the EEOC-issued guidelines on the ADA.

The Lawyers: Ken Yerkes was described to researchers as "*one of the leading employment law attorneys, not just in the state, but on a national basis.*" The chair of the firm's labor and employment group, he is, say sources, "*bright, sharp, hard-working and armed with a knowledge of the whole range of issues.*" His practice spans both employment defense and traditional labor law, and he was involved this year in important national work for Finish Line concerning arbitration agreements. **Doug Heckler** has a "*tremendous labor practice,*" say peers, and boasts considerable experience of representing management in all labor-related issues. He is an advisory board member and instructor for the NLRB.

The Clients: Georgia-Pacific; Wal-Mart; Dennison Parking; Johnson & Johnson; Finish Line; Roche Diagnostics; Columbia House Company and Anthem.

Ice Miller
See firm details p.797
The Firm: For a number of sources, this is "*clearly the number one law firm in Indiana for quality, knowledge and efficiency.*" Its clients in particular regard it as "*the firm of choice for traditional labor as well as employee benefits issues.*" The team assists clients from both the public and private sectors and from a diverse range of industries in some of the most high-profile work in the state. Most notable of all, however, has probably been acting for the State of Indiana in all its collective bargaining negotiations during the year. The group has also cemented its relationship with the US Chamber of Commerce. Age and race discrimination and sexual harassment are other strong areas of practice for the team, and a separate employee benefit plan services group is on hand to advise on all types of employee benefit plans.

The Lawyers: Lawyers in this practice group are held in high regard for "*their expertise and breadth of practice.*" Chief among them is the "*extraordinarily solid, knowledgeable and congenial*" **Chic Born** (see p.791), who remains "*a major force with a phenomenal impact on the market.*" A traditional labor lawyer and certified mediator, he represents management in labor relations issues, union organizing, collective bargaining negotiations, and litigation and admin-

istrative proceedings before various agencies and courts. Another "*first-class labor lawyer*" is **Michael Boldt** (see p.791) He represents management from a number of industries in collective bargaining negotiations, union-organizing campaigns and other traditional labor issues. However, he is best known for his national practice handling labor matters in the construction arena. **Martin Klaper** (see p.793) completes a trio of superb labor lawyers in the team. He stands out, according to the market, because of "*his creativity in designing win-win solutions and his tireless work ethic.*" Heavily involved in labor contract administration and negotiation, Klaper represented the State of Indiana in all its union collective bargaining, which involved over 35,000 employees.

The Clients: Ryley Industries; Oakstreet Mortgages; Great Lakes Chemical; American Steel Foundries; York International; Visteon Systems and Eli Lilly.

Ogletree, Deakins, Nash, Smoak & Stewart, PC
See firm details p.638
The Firm: This highly regarded labor and employment group operates on a national level. It continues to impress sources in the Indiana market by both increasing its size and capacity, and by appearing ever more regularly in much of the best work around. Commentators agree that the merger with Haynsworth Baldwin Johnson & Greaves "*can only give the firm a tactical advantage, and has certainly added strength and experience on the labor side,*" which should filter through to its Indiana offices, adding as it does approximately 50 further attorneys on a national basis. Clients were full of praise for the well-organized, 22-strong team, and appreciated the responsiveness and business acumen of the "*core group of real talented attorneys.*"

The Lawyers: **Kim Ebert** (see p.791) is "*an absolute first-rate lawyer,*" according to his peers. He enjoys "*a stellar reputation in the field*" based on his talent, principles and track record in major cases. As one source noted, he's "*an exceptionally well-regarded stand-up guy who is involved in some of the most significant cases in the state.*" Peers believe that his forte lies in labor law, while clients agree that he is "*the best-known teamsters' union negotiator in the area.*" This has recently seen him handle negotiations surrounding no fewer than six union-organizing campaigns. Clients were also quick to endorse **Chuck Baldwin** (see p.790). Described as having "*a particular forte in workers' compensation and benefits,*" he is also respected for both employment litigation and traditional labor work. With an impressive national client roster,

he is heavily involved in the food industry. Following a recent reduction in the workforce of a major international client, he will be handling an increased volume of litigation over the coming twelve months. Moving up the tables this year is the "*increasingly visible*" **Brian McDermott** (see p.793). "*A young and talented attorney,*" his employment litigation practice is burgeoning, and he recently celebrated obtaining a $600,000 defense judgment.

The Clients: The team was recently retained to handle all the employment work for Hillenbrand Industries, a large multinational company with its headquarters in Indiana. Other clients include: Clarion Health Partners; SBC; Cingular and Kroger.

Band 2

Bose McKinney & Evans LLP
The Firm: Clients were quick to endorse "*the complete employment package this firm has to offer.*" Particular praise was reserved, however, for the team's ability to handle wage and hour cases and trade secrets disputes. Its experience in the sports and entertainment industries was also noted. The team, which boasts both a private sector and a public sector group, also enjoys a good reputation for defending management against discrimination and sexual harassment claims. Issues surrounding executive termination and full-scale audits are also considered specialties.

The Lawyers: The "*practical and business-oriented*" **David Swider** chairs the labor and employment group here. He is admired for both his flourishing litigation practice and his advice on problem avoidance. The principal author of the employee handbook for the Indiana Chamber of Commerce, he was recently involved in the complete wage and hour audit for Eli Lilly, a huge project that completed this year. **Dan Emerson** was highlighted to researchers for his broad labor and employment practice, and in particular his expertise in trade secrets, non-compete agreements and problem avoidance. Described as "*an aggressive litigator,*" he is especially active in the sports and entertainment industries, and is general counsel to the Indianapolis Colts. His recent successes include leading the defense in Product Action International v Carl Mero, a diversity action concerning a former employee's covenant not to compete with a former employer.

The Clients: Eli Lilly; Anthem; Thomson; UPS; Pfizer; Coca-Cola; National City Bank and the Indianapolis Colts.

784   All quotes in the text are from interviews with clients and competitors.

CHAMBERS USA 2005

LITIGATION

GENERAL COMMERCIAL

Indiana
Leading firms
(Litigation: General Commercial)

1 BAKER & DANIELS *Indianapolis*
BARNES & THORNBURG *Indianapolis*

2 BINGHAM MCHALE LLP *Indianapolis*
ICE MILLER *Indianapolis*
SOMMER BARNARD ATTORNEYS PC *Indianapolis*

3 BOSE MCKINNEY & EVANS LLP *Indianapolis*
LOCKE REYNOLDS LLP *Indianapolis*
MCTURNAN & TURNER *Indianapolis*

4 KRIEG DEVAULT LLP *Indianapolis*

Leading individuals
(Litigation: General Commercial)

★ FICKLE Stanley *Barnes & Thornburg, Indianapolis*

1 CAMPBELL David *Bingham McHale, Indianapolis*
MCTURNAN Lee *McTurnan & Turner, Indianapolis*
PENCE Linda *Sommer Barnard, Indianapolis*
SCANLON Chris *Baker & Daniels, Indianapolis*
WHISTLER Philip *Ice Miller, Indianapolis*
YEAGER Jay *Baker & Daniels, Indianapolis*

2 BROWN Alan *Locke Reynolds, Indianapolis*
DEPREZ Anne *Barnes & Thornburg, Indianapolis*
ELBERGER Ronald *Bose McKinney, Indianapolis*
MACGILL Robert *Barnes & Thornburg, Indianapolis*
SHOCKLEY Steven *Sommer Barnard, Indianapolis*
STANLEY Robert *Baker & Daniels, Indianapolis*
TITTLE David *Bingham McHale, Indianapolis*
TURNER Wayne *McTurnan & Turner, Indianapolis*

3 BENNETT Jackie *Sommer Barnard, Indianapolis*
DETHERAGE Andrew *Barnes & Thornburg, Indianapolis*
GELINAS Julia *Locke Reynolds LLP, Indianapolis*
HARRIS Edward *Sommer Barnard, Indianapolis*
HERZOG David *Baker & Daniels, Indianapolis*
HOKANSON Jeffrey *Ice Miller, Indianapolis*
KASPER David *Locke Reynolds, Indianapolis*
MITCHELL Marvin *Mitchell Hurst, Indianapolis*
WELCH Brian *Bingham McHale, Indianapolis*
WILKINS Michael *Ice Miller, Indianapolis*

Leading individuals (Litigation: IP)

1 KNEBEL Donald *Barnes & Thornburg, Indianapolis*

2 IRMSCHER David *Baker & Daniels, Fort Wayne*
TINSLEY Nancy *Baker & Daniels, Indianapolis*

Firms and individuals are listed alphabetically in each band.

Band 1

Baker & Daniels

See firm details p.796

The Firm: "*Overall, this firm is probably the best in the state, top to bottom,*" say impressed sources. This is put down to the quality of its lawyers at all levels: "*The team consists of highly effective, responsive advocates for both transactional and litigious matters.*" Topping the tables for another year, the large regional firm operates from five offices in Indiana. It has the depth and resources to handle the more complex litigation. For example, it recently acted as trial and appellate counsel for Rolls-Royce and General Motors who were seeking recovery from a contractor for cost overruns incurred in the production of an exhaust liner designed to protect the Stealth Fighter from the effects of 4000-degree heat. The action resulted in a judgment in excess of $80 million in favor of the plaintiffs. Large-scale business litigation, complex commercial actions, and high-profile products liability litigation are seen as particular strengths of the group. It has also considerably enhanced its IP arm, recruiting heavily in recent years, and boasts one of the most flourishing practices in the state.

The Lawyers: Clients regard department head **Chris Scanlon** (see p.794) as "*a good strategic thinker*" who is "*particularly strong on complex, nationwide issues.*" "*An excellent insurance coverage lawyer,*" he concentrates on large-scale business litigation, and has been involved in a considerable volume of state and federal class actions and securities litigation. Recent successes include a suit concerning the operation of the Indiana Medicaid reimbursement system and claims processors. Clients also singled out "*aggressive and bright go-getter*" **Jay Yeager** (see p.795). He has "*really distinguished himself in securities and insurance-related litigation,*" they say, where he has become "*a household name.*" His recent highlights include the huge, $80 million Rolls-Royce judgment cited above. "*Class act*" **Bob Stanley** (see p.794) continues to impress clients with his "*deep-rooted expertise in business litigation.*" In recent years he has broadened his practice to include antitrust and probate cases; successes include advising the publicly owned CART open-wheel series on a $7.5 million contractual claim, arising when one of the last races of the season was canceled due to wildfires. Joining them in the tables this year is "*real distinguished practitioner*" **David Herzog** (see p.792). Described by clients as "*a first-rate litigator,*" he returned last year after a stint as executive vice president and general counsel of Conseco – an appointment that commentators agree gives him an added edge. He concentrates on business and commercial litigation and has recently handled a large securities case. Former Eli Lilly research chemist and "*talented IP specialist*" **Nancy Tinsley** (see p.794) also makes her debut in table. Noted for her experience in patent litigation, she has tried cases in fields ranging from medical devices to software. Last year she was involved in two considerable patent disputes, in one of which she obtained summary judgment of no infringement of two patents. **David Irmscher** (see p.792) also appears in the IP table this year. He has been involved in two cases at the Federal Circuit of Appeals, and was enthusiastically supported by clients for his national practice and "*exemplary performance and counsel.*"

The Clients: Allison Engine Company; Cinergy Corp; CSX Transportation; Eli Lilly and Company; Ford; ITT Educational Services; Johnson Controls and Zimmer.

Barnes & Thornburg

The Firm: One of the largest firms in the state, with four offices in Indiana, Barnes & Thornburg represents an impressive national client base and has the depth to handle complex, high-profile national disputes. Over 140 of its 400 attorneys are devoted to litigation, making the firm "*a serious force to contend with.*" Its clients hail the team as "*the market leader for business litigation*" and value its "*particular strength in employment and IP.*" A major coup for the team during the year was its work on Williams v Dow Chemical, a nationwide class action concerning physical and property injuries allegedly caused by Dursban, a non-agricultural pesticide. Cases like this are seen as indicative not just of the high profile of much of the group's litigation, but also its national reach. Clients applaud the quality of the technical support on offer, specifically its jury research and advocacy analysis service, ThemeVision.

The Lawyers: The largest litigation department in the state is home to many talented attorneys. But none of the stars shines brighter than the "*world-class*" **Stan Fickle**. "*The number one appellate lawyer in Indiana; he really is one of the best appellate lawyers you will ever see*" according to sources who have witnessed him in action. A member of the American Academy of Appellate Lawyers, Fickle has many strings to his bow, but is principally involved in appellate advocacy. Here clients highlight his superb presentation skills and a far-reaching intelligence that enables him to effortlessly handle the most complex cases. **Rob MacGill** is the chair of the firm's litigation department and a "*top-notch attorney.*" Interviewees described him as "*a charming man with a smooth and effective way of talking to a jury,*" and he was particularly praised for his experience in complex products liability and trade secrets cases. "*Remarkable securities lawyer*" **Anne DePrez** also attracts plaudits from clients for her unsurpassed experience in securities class actions and business litigation. **Andrew Detherage** has continued to impress clients and peers alike and is considered to be "*a real safe pair of hands.*" Noted for his experience in asbestos and products liability litigation, which he brings to the aid of some impressive national clients, Detherage has been defending 3M this year against an asbestos-related claim involving thousands of plaintiffs. Following overwhelming market applause, "*tremendous IP litigator*" **Don Knebel** enters the rankings this

www.ChambersandPartners.com

All quotes in the text are from interviews with clients and competitors.

785

year at the head of the new IP table. Described to researchers as *"the best in Indiana for patent litigation,"* he is widely respected for his knowledge and experience in patent law and cochairs the firm's IP and business and technology groups.

The Clients: Dow AgraSciences; Simon Property Group; Valspar; Beazer Homes; DePuy Orthopaedics; Georgia-Pacific; Dow Chemical; Mitsubishi; 3M; Whirlpool; Anthem and Eli Lilly.

Band 2

Bingham McHale LLP

The Firm: According to its clients, this team can compete with the best in the market and effectively handle the most complex commercial litigation. The result of a successful merger, the firm now ranks among the largest in Indiana, with over 120 lawyers in three offices across the state, over half of whom are devoted to litigation. The group was praised for its *"exceptional insurance defense practice,"* and clients were also quick to appreciate the *"horsepower and technical support on offer."* The young and dynamic team covers a wide range of disputes from IP to business litigation. It also has experience of handling a variety of different types of class action, from products liability to securities.

The Lawyers: **David Campbell** is a *"distinguished, thoughtful and constantly well-prepared"* attorney. He is noted by sources for *"his great insurance defense practice,"* and clients also appreciate his *"friendly, down-to-earth approach."* Campbell concentrates primarily on business litigation, but has also been heavily involved in IP cases this year. *"Top-notch"* adviser **David Tittle** was warmly recommended by clients. Described as *"a great litigator who really listens to his clients before acting,"* he has been busy of late working on a complex product warranty class action for Thomson and general litigation for National City Bank. **Brian Welch** is an *"extraordinarily able lawyer"* who focuses on general business disputes, but also has experience in the labor and employment field. He has served as state counsel to many national entities in major disputes, and recently took part in an important arbitration for Ernst & Young.

The Clients: Saint-Gobain; Thomson; Aero Corporation; National City Bank of Indiana; Gatorade Trust; Indiana Horse Racing Commission; Xerox; Hart Financial and Odessa.

Ice Miller

See firm details p.797

The Firm: This *"mega full-service law firm"* has both the resources and technical expertise to handle the largest, most complex litigation in Indiana. Historically associated with large insurance defense work, the firm has developed and now handles everything from antitrust to prod-

ucts liability class actions. Clients were particularly impressed with the team's strength in pharmaceutical products liability and contractual disputes. Clients also value the team's *"superb communication skills,"* noting in particular its ability to *"effectively communicate with the other law firms involved in the case, as well as with us."* The team has been heavily involved in arbitrations in the year, including work for Merrill Lynch in over 100 different customer disputes. It also successfully defended Indiana University in a breach of contract suit brought by its basketball coach, Bobby Knight, and acted for DIRECTV in a case alleging the theft of satellite signals. This was the first such case to go to trial and produced one of the largest recoveries to date for DIRECTV.

The Lawyers: *"There are people in this group with a wide variety of expertise who can handle most things,"* say sources. One of these is the cochair of the business litigation group **Philip Whistler** (see p.795). He was described by clients as *"a smart attorney, an excellent writer and very clever in the way he makes a presentation."* His *"well-organized and thoughtful approach"* makes him a favorite with clients for complex commercial disputes, and he is working on an NASD arbitration for Merrill Lynch. **Jeffrey Hokanson** (see p.792) was singled out by clients for *"the excellent bankruptcy side to his practice,"* and continues to be held in the highest regard for his work in relation to creditors' rights. **Michael Wilkins** (see p.795) was described to researchers as *"an exceptional attorney"* who is *"very active in appellate law."* He commands respect for his knowledge of defamation and First Amendment issues, and tried the cases for DIRECTV mentioned above.

The Clients: St Jude Medical Corporation; Emerson Electric Company; DuPont Nemours; DIRECTV; Merrill Lynch Pierce Fenner and Smith; Hoffmann-LaRoche; Indianapolis Motor Speedway and Eli Lilly. The team also successfully represented U-Haul International against SBC Publishing for breach of contract involving yellow page advertising.

Sommer Barnard Attorneys PC

See firm details p.799

The Firm: Following the recent departure of the Ackerson Group, the firm is now known as Sommer Barnard Attorneys. Although this was felt to have had some impact on the group, the firm still fields a wealth of experienced lawyers, and the recent addition of new blood adds further strength. The *"top-flight"* team boasts a tradition of involvement in the more notable pieces of Indiana's commercial litigation, and can draw on a wide range of experience in different fields. It represents both plaintiffs and defendants, and attracted particular recommendation for its work in antitrust and securities disputes, often with national importance.

The Lawyers: **Linda Pence** (see p.793) continues to enjoy a fine reputation in the market. She was described by observers as *"good on her feet, with an uncanny knack of knowing how to work a courtroom to her advantage."* She concentrates on complex civil litigation and federal white-collar criminal defense, and is held in high regard by clients and peers, not least for her success in assembling a high-quality team around her. Of these, *"lawyers' lawyer"* **Steve Shockley** (see p.794) stands out for *"the wonderful job he does for his clients, his skill in figuring out how to win and his fine advocacy."* Shockley heads the appellate practice group, and is a registered Indiana lobbyist. *"First-rate commercial litigator"* **Jackie Bennett** (see p.791) moved to the firm this year from McTurnan & Turner. He is described as *"a high-energy go-getter with a real forte in commercial litigation,"* and is *"a real force to contend with"* for business litigation and white-collar criminal defense. Clients routinely commented on his time at the Justice Department, when he served as senior adviser to Judge Starr in a number of high-profile investigations, including the impeachment referral of William Jefferson Clinton. Another new addition to this year's tables is **Edward Harris** (see p.792). He enjoys a *"fantastic reputation for real sophisticated antitrust and class action work,"* say sources, and represents both plaintiffs and defendants in a wide range of business disputes, typically in the federal court.

The Clients: The team represents a mixture of plaintiffs and defendants. Clients are drawn from major corporations and other bodies operating at both the local and national levels.

Band 3

Bose McKinney & Evans LLP

The Firm: With four offices in Indiana, this full-service law firm doesn't lack the resources to handle the state's more complex and high-profile litigation. It is particularly renowned for representing schools, municipalities and other public sector bodies. However, it handles a wide variety of litigation for a mixture of clients. Of particular importance is its skill in general business and commercial disputes, and related securities and antitrust litigation. Environmental, IP and real estate litigation are also considered strengths of the group, along with professional responsibility and disciplinary law.

The Lawyers: The *"complete, full-spectrum attorney,"* **Ron Elberger** continues to impress. Considered by some to be *"a one-off"* with a *"really creative approach to cases,"* he is acknowledged to be *"a force of nature who always brings a lot to the table."* Elberger's broad practice ranges from constitutional through to entertainment and professional disciplinary law. This year he has continued to assist mountain climber Aron Ralston in promoting his book

'Between a Rock and a Hard Place'. He also represented the Chief Justice of the Indiana Supreme Court, in his ex-officio capacity as a member of the Lake County Judicial Nominating Commission, over a voting right act challenge to Indiana's methods of appointing and retaining judges.

The Clients: Emmis Communications; Emmis Publishing; Chip Ganassi Racing Teams; SABCO Racing and Aron Ralston.

Locke Reynolds LLP

The Firm: Sources consider this *"knowledgeable, responsive and efficient"* team to be on the ascendant at present. Arguably the firm of choice for midsized commercial disputes, Locke Reynolds is felt to be *"particularly strong on commercial contract disputes, construction and insurance defense."* Fielding a raft of talented attorneys, the litigation group recently enjoyed success in obtaining a defense verdict for Graco Children's Products in the Tober v Graco product liability case. This six-day jury trial concerned alleged defects in the harness of a child swing. The department is divided into appellate, business and tort groups, with dedicated specialists on hand in each.

The Lawyers: *"Strong and active business litigator"* **Alan Brown** was widely recommended for his skill in a range of litigation. He chairs the firm's business litigation group and concentrates on complex business and contractual disputes and counseling. **David Kasper** is another new addition to the table. Clients agree that *"he is a top-notch litigator with a strong reputation."* He chairs the firm's tort and insurance litigation team and, as well as general litigation, focuses on professional malpractice and insurance defense. Also picking up her share of market recommendation is *"knowledgeable and efficient appellate lawyer"* **Julia Gelinas**. She focuses on appellate work, and also handles a volume of construction and fidelity and surety cases.

The Clients: As well as acting for Fortune 500 companies, the firm also represents private companies and individuals. Examples include: Citi-

zens Insurance Company America, Phoenix Aviation and Utica National Insurance Group.

McTurnan & Turner

See firm details p.798

The Firm: *"Smaller than some other firms but 100% quality"* is the market's verdict on this *"strong litigation boutique."* Based in downtown Indianapolis, the firm is best known for handling midsized but complex business litigation, and is home to a wealth of experienced practitioners. The team defends class actions in areas ranging from securities law to employment, and gets involved in business litigation related to corporate governance and torts. A highlight from the year was getting an injunction affirmed, which forced a number of companies who had claimed not to meet the criteria for assessment to contribute approximately $8 million to Indiana's high-risk health pool. This avoided interrupting the health coverage of more than 10,000 Indiana residents.

The Lawyers: Both of the name partners here are considered to be *"exceptional attorneys."* **Lee McTurnan** (see p.793) was described to researchers as *"a strong performer with a well-deserved reputation as a top-notch lawyer."* Clients particularly admire the way that he is *"consistently well prepared and never misses anything."* He is especially well known for representing professionals in malpractice cases, but has a broad practice encompassing a variety of complex business disputes. For example, he is acting in a case involving PwC arising out of the bankruptcy of Paul Harris Stores. He is also representing Earlham College in high-profile litigation concerning an endowment established by Colonel Eli Lilly for Earlham and the maintenance of the Conner Prairie Living History Museum in Indianapolis. *"Exceptional attorney"* **Wayne Turner** (see p.795) advises on most facets of business litigation, but his name is particularly associated with securities fraud, antitrust and corporate governance issues. Recent highlights include acting as defense counsel for DIRECTV in a nationwide class

action claim for alleged violation of the Telephone Consumer Privacy Act, the appeal for which is pending.

The Clients: SBC Communications; PwC; Salomon Smith Barney; Citifinancial; ProLiance Energy; General Motors; Onkyo Corporation; Wachovia; Earlham College; DIRECTV and McGraw-Hill Broadcasting (WRTV-6).

Band 4

Krieg DeVault LLP

The Firm: This impressive midsized firm, with four offices in Indiana, continues to be held in particularly high regard for its banking practice. Clients also note the presence of a solid commercial litigation group, boasting considerable experience and the ability to *"really effectively handle contractual disputes."* The team acts for national and regional clients, and its size leaves it well placed to efficiently take on both sophisticated litigation and more straightforward cases. Corporate litigation arising out of mergers or initiated by shareholders is seen as a particular forte of the group.

The Lawyers: **Mark Merkle** heads this *"strong litigation team,"* which comprises over 30 dedicated lawyers. The team offers experience in both the state and federal courts, and has knowledge of appellate practice and procedure. The group also boasts several trained mediators and arbitrators.

The Clients: The team represents both privately owned and publicly traded companies in a range of litigation.

Other Notable Practitioners

Marvin Mitchell of Mitchell Hurst Jacobs & Dick is best known for plaintiff personal injury work, and described by peers as *"a worthy adversary."* He also has a commercial workload, and recently represented Babybacks International against Coca-Cola Enterprises in a case in the Indiana Supreme Court.

REAL ESTATE

Band 1

Barnes & Thornburg

The Firm: The real estate department of this large, full-service firm was declared to be *"marginally above the other law firms in this area."* It has four offices statewide and a stack of talented attorneys, who between them cover the full gamut of real estate matters and act for lenders, developers and users. According to clients, it is *"exceptional on long-term, complex projects that require a delicate touch,"* and is particularly sin-

gled out for its expertise in real estate finance. As well as sustaining its flourishing practice, this *"great relationship firm"* also came in for praise on zoning, land use and overall project development.

The Lawyers: Barnes & Thornburg is home to *"a uniformly impressive group of talented attorneys,"* one of whom is the *"damned good"* **David Warshauer**, who is portrayed as *"a serious lawyer; very studious, bright and quick to react to things."* Warshauer represents a number of developers and home builders in both zoning

and finance matters. He continues to work for Brenwick Development Company, having previously been executive vice president of the same, on the proposal for an extension to a 680-acre project including 400 housing units and the relocation of commercial space in the village of West Clay. *"One of the premier bank attorneys in the state"* and *"icon in the real estate area"* is **Richard Johnson**. Together with **Dennis Johnson**, who also has a flourishing financial institution and development practice, he is seen as being among *"the best real estate lending practitioners in the*

Indiana
Leading firms (Real Estate)

1 BARNES & THORNBURG *Indianapolis*
ICE MILLER *Indianapolis*

2 BAKER & DANIELS *Indianapolis*
BOSE MCKINNEY & EVANS LLP *Indianapolis*
WALLACK SOMERS & HAAS PC *Indianapolis*

3 BINGHAM MCHALE LLP *Indianapolis*
DANN PECAR NEWMAN & KLEIMAN, PC *Indianapolis*

4 KRIEG DEVAULT LLP *Indianapolis*
SOMMER BARNARD ATTORNEYS PC *Indianapolis*
WOODEN & MCLAUGHLIN LLP *Indianapolis*

Leading individuals (Real Estate)

1 BAYT Phillip *Ice Miller,* Indianapolis
HAAS Karl *Wallack Somers,* Indianapolis
SCIMIA Joseph *Baker & Daniels,* Indianapolis
SOMERS George *Wallack Somers,* Indianapolis
WALLACK Barry *Wallack Somers,* Indianapolis
WARSHAUER David *Barnes & Thornburg,* Indianapolis
WEISS Zeff *Ice Miller,* Indianapolis

2 ABRAMS Jeffrey *Dann Pecar,* Indianapolis
CARLINO James *Bose McKinney,* Indianapolis
JOHNSON Richard *Barnes & Thornburg,* Indianapolis
LISHER Mary *Baker & Daniels,* Indianapolis
NICELY Philip *Bose McKinney,* Indianapolis
O'BRYAN Rory *Harrison & Moberly,* Indianapolis
SOLADA Mary *Bingham McHale,* Indianapolis

3 DINWIDDIE Thomas *Wooden & McLaughlin,* Indianapolis
HAMILTON John *Wooden & McLaughlin,* Indianapolis
JOHNSON Dennis *Barnes & Thornburg,* Indianapolis
LAWSON Jack *Beckman Lawson,* Fort Wayne
LEE Stephen *Barnes & Thornburg,* Indianapolis
PONADER Erick *Sommer Barnard,* Indianapolis
SCHWARZ James *Dann Pecar,* Indianapolis
WOLENTY Barbara *Robinson Wolenty,* Indianapolis

Up-and-coming individuals

BIRGE Taggart *Bose McKinney,* Indianapolis
HARDIN Steven *Bingham McHale,* Indianapolis
HIRSCHMAN John *Baker & Daniels,* Indianapolis
TEMPEL Angela *Ice Miller,* Indianapolis

Firms and individuals are listed alphabetically in each band.

state." Dennis Johnson acts for lenders, developers and builders alongside the national Zeta Tau Alpha Fraternity Housing Corporation, which runs 80 chapters across the USA and is headquartered in Indianapolis. **Stephen Lee** earns market recommendation as a real estate generalist. He is admired for his work for one of the Midwest's largest developers of multifamily properties, Flaherty & Collins Properties.

The Clients: Fifth Third Bank, Indiana; Brenwick Development Company; KeyBank National Association; John Hancock Life Insurance; Connecticut General Life Insurance; Zeta Tau Alpha Fraternity Housing Corporation; National City Bank; Flaherty & Collins Properties; Edward Rose Properties; Martin Marietta Materials; Huntington National Bank; Eli Lilly; Georgia-Pacific and Whirlpool.

Ice Miller

See firm details p.797

The Firm: Clients agree that this, *"the most politically well-connected real estate group in Indianapolis,"* not only *"has a very large group capable of tackling the biggest projects,"* but is also home to *"a wealth of multitalented attorneys."* With peers agreeing that this firm is *"a main player"* and clients delighting at the *"responsiveness and timeliness"* of the advice provided, Ice Miller remains in *Chambers'* top tier. The firm is recommended for its experience with developers and retailers, and is also tipped for zoning and contested developments as well as real estate finance. Attorneys have proven their ability to handle the unique issues surrounding the construction and financing of stadiums, arenas and real estate projects in the gaming and motor sports industries. Multitower condominiums, the development of landmark projects, such as the Market Square Arena site (the largest local urban renewal project in the state), and casino gaming on riverboats are just three examples of the diverse work of the team.

The Lawyers: A *"practical, straightforward and especially good attorney,"* **Zeff Weiss** (see p.795) continues to impress others with *"the way he protects his clients while still understanding the importance of completing the transaction in hand."* Weiss, who chairs the firm's real estate group, is a *"prominent land use and zoning, and eminent domain attorney"* with a firm grasp of all the issues involved in real estate development, finance and taxation. **Phillip Bayt** (see p.790) is described as *"a very capable and exceedingly smart attorney, one of the best around and right up there in the 'A' category."* His practice is developer-oriented and he routinely acts on the financial as well as acquisition and construction aspects of his clients' projects. Bayt was lead counsel for the developer on the Conrad Hotel Indianapolis, the city's first five-star offering. Exceeding $100 million in value and consisting of 243 rooms, including four floors of condominiums, this is just one example of the ground-breaking work of the team. Bayt also chairs a new partnership entitled Fostering Core Urban Strategies (FOCUS), the goal of which is to encourage commercial development in certain Indianapolis neighborhoods. New to the tables this year is the *"incredibly hard-working and bright up-and-comer"* **Angela Tempel**. With clients commenting on *"her ability to relate complex issues in an easy-to-understand fashion,"* and peers commending her ability, Tempel is one to watch.

The Clients: Wal-Mart; Whiteco Industries; Buckingham Companies; Simon Property Group; Zimmer Holdings; Integra Bank and City of Indianapolis.

Band 2

Baker & Daniels

See firm details p.796

The Firm: This real estate and land use team is *"hot on the heels"* of the leading two firms. Home to roughly 20 dedicated attorneys in five regional offices, between them they have *"an impressive skill set, are efficient in their representation and deliver a good-quality service."* Clients note the relative strengths of the individual offices, reserving most praise for those in Indianapolis and Fort Wayne. The firm has represented Hearthview Residential in the acquisition and development of condominium sites with a combined total approaching 200 units. It has also advised the Sterling Group on its acquisition and development of Arbors in Terre Haute, Columbus and South Bend, providing a combined total of over 300 multifamily housing units. Another significant transaction was Browning Investments' lease of 500,000 sq ft to Logisco in Air Tech Park, Plainfield.

The Lawyers: Chairman of the real estate and land use team is *"business-minded attorney"* **Joe Scimia** (see p.794). Clients were quick to comment on *"his ability to think like a developer as well as a lawyer"* and *"his way of getting to the point quickly."* Also deemed *"good at thinking on his feet,"* he does *"a good job negotiating and bringing things together."* Scimia's areas of expertise include the construction and permanent financing of developments as well as the acquisition, disposition and leasing of a variety of properties. **Mary Lisher** (see p.793) was also warmly recommended for her *"timely, professional, legal analysis, excellent negotiation and drafting skills and the support she provides to further the business goals of her clients."* Her fans say she combines *"a focus on the details with an understanding of the bigger picture."* Lisher is a general real estate lawyer and covers everything but zoning work. Servicing an impressive client base, she acted for Clarian Health Partners in the sale of the Meridian Corporate Plaza in Carmel to Lauth Property Group for a sale price in excess of $6 million. Another client, Eli Lilly, used her in their acquisition of numerous small parcels of land across the USA. Featuring in the up-and-coming category of the table this year is real estate generalist **John Hirschman** (see p.792). Clients credit him with *"knowing more about what we want than we do,"* and praise his *"sharpness and ability to get to the point quickly and with the minimum of fuss."*

The Clients: Browning Investments; Hearthview Residential; Equity Investment Group; The Sterling Group; Zimmer; Clarian Health Partners; Eli Lilly; Conseco Services; Paragon Properties; Andy Mohr Automotive Companies; UBS Realty Investors and the City of Indianapolis.

788   All quotes in the text are from interviews with clients and competitors.

CHAMBERS USA 2005

Bose McKinney & Evans LLP

The Firm: This firm has four offices in Indiana and *"12 top-flight attorneys"* on hand to deal with a litany of real estate matters. The steadily developing practice moves up the table this year, having been active in assisting regional and national clients on a wide range of real estate matters from zoning and land use, purchases and sales to eminent domain and condominium conversions. Clients referred to the *"strong developer practice"* and made specific reference to the retail and zoning work of the group. The firm continues to advise some of the key names in the sector, including Simon Property Group and Duke Realty, having worked in the past year on a 600-acre mixed-use development for Duke Realty in Boone County.

The Lawyers: Chair of the real estate group and *"one of the real estate icons of the area"* is **Phil Nicely**. *"Extremely practical, pragmatic and experienced,"* Nicely *"really knows his stuff."* He is a frequent lecturer on all issues surrounding zoning and land use, has been involved in many acquisitions and disposals and also represents borrowers on the financial aspects of transactions. **Jim Carlino** is another major player; he combines transactional real estate work with secured lending, construction and environmental law, and represents a variety of developers and institutional property owners. Carlino represented the City of Indianapolis in connection with negotiations with Simon Property Group over the new Simon headquarters, a development that will *"reshape the face of downtown Indianapolis."* The *"very active"* **Tag Birge** confirms his place in the table for another year and has recently been made a partner of the firm. Birge's developing practice concentrates on zoning, leasing and transactional work and he has recently picked up CVS Pharmacy as a client and now undertakes all their acquisition work in the Midwest. He has also represented Sterling America on the leasing of the landmark College Park 'Pyramids' on the north side of Indianapolis.

The Clients: Duke Realty; Prime Care Properties; Gibraltar Properties; Republic Bank; City of Carmel; Scannell Properties; Centex Homes; The Skinner & Broadbent Company; New Boston Fund; Marfield Development; Hills Communities; The Precedent Companies; Eli Lilly; Marathon Ashland Petroleum; CVS Pharmacy; Sterling America; Agricultural Real Estate Partners; BP Pipelines North America and Lauth Property Group.

Wallack Somers & Haas PC

See firm details p.800

The Firm: Clients describe this seven-lawyer boutique as *"an efficient and experienced firm with a very specific real estate focus."* Formerly with Baker & Daniels, the name partners continue to excel and were repeatedly singled out by interviewees for their individual strengths and expertise. The firm garnered praise for its commercial real estate transaction work and was highlighted for its *"canny ability to effectively represent buyers, sellers, landlords, tenants, lenders and local municipalities in all matters of commercial real estate."* Clients referred to the fact that *"as all members in the practice are experienced real estate specialists, there are definite time and cost-efficiency bonuses to be considered too."* As already indicated, the firm is deeply involved in the representation of private developers, but also acts for banks, publicly traded companies and municipalities in urban redevelopment work.

The Lawyers: Karl Haas continues to impress. He is described as *"an exceptional real estate attorney, who is extremely gifted at being able to understand and tackle very complicated and contentious transactions."* He has recently represented the City of Carmel in the negotiation and financing of an expansive redevelopment project designed to revitalize the city. The project includes a performing arts complex and residential, retail, hotel and office buildings. Other recent highlights include projects in West Lafayette, Hammond and Bloomington. *"True deal-maker"* **George Somers** (see p.794) represents developers and insurance companies, REITs and lenders on a local and national basis. Clients refer to his *"efficient, creative approach to dealing with obstacles that hold up a transaction"* and his ability *"to focus on the key terms of a deal, not wasting time on the minutiae."* Peers agree that they happily refer work to him when conflicted. Last year Somers assisted clients in the development and leasing of over one million sq ft of primarily retail space as well as the acquisition of land in preparation for another million sq ft of development. *"Top-notch real estate lawyer"* **Barry Wallack** (see p.795) has also turned heads with *"his conscientious, crisp and responsive advice."* Wallack has represented lenders on numerous real estate and commercial loan transactions, as well as borrowers looking to refinance major office buildings in Cincinnati and Indianapolis. He was involved in the sale of an apartment complex in Indianapolis for a record per unit price.

The Clients: Republic Services; City of Carmel, Indiana; Fifth Third Bank; Kite Realty Group Trust and REI Investments.

Band 3

Bingham McHale LLP

The Firm: Universally considered by both clients and peers to have had a good year, this midsized firm moves up the table. While some commentators pointed to its *"specific expertise in terms of land use and zoning,"* the group covers the full spectrum of real estate activity, from the construction and development of a project to the financing and any litigious aspects. With seven dedicated real estate lawyers acting out of three offices in the state, this firm appears to possess the depth of resources and specialist expertise required to handle some of the more complex projects around.

The Lawyers: Onlookers agree that the fine reputation of the group is largely attributable to the *"exceptional attorney"* **Mary Solada**. Chair of the firm's real estate practice group, Solada is widely revered for her land use and zoning expertise. She represents a variety of clients in this regard, ranging from private sector to government entities. Entering the tables as an up-and-comer this year is another *"fine lawyer,"* **Steve Hardin**. Though his zoning, planning and land use work is combined with acquisitions and disposals, researchers noted he came in for specific recommendation for *"the good job he does on cases involving land use."*

The Clients: Bremner & Wiley; Capital Improvement Board of Managers of Marion County; Davies Homes; First Industrial Realty Trust; Sun Development & Management and Thomson Consumer Electronics.

Dann Pecar Newman & Kleiman, PC

The Firm: Highlighted by clients for its *"sizable"* real estate practice, this *"quality firm with many personable attorneys"* boasts eight dedicated specialists in its Indianapolis office. The firm is well known for its relationship with one of the nation's largest publicly traded real estate companies, Simon Property Group, for whom it works on major construction and securitization financings. The firm handled the substantial negotiations for the construction of the new Simon headquarters in Indianapolis, and recently it acted as borrower's counsel in connection with a $125 million construction loan for the St. Johns Town Center, which was developed by Simon Property Group in Duval County, Florida. The firm is additionally well known for drafting leases for major department stores, big box tenants and out-lot tenants at shopping centers across the USA.

The Lawyers: The *"very professional and conscientious"* **Jeff Abrams** continues to *"really listen to what a client wants to achieve out of a project and go on and get the job done."* He is held in particularly high regard for his commercial lending practice, and represents banks and lending institutions, developers, builders, contractors and owners on all issues from start to finish of major projects. Clients portrayed **Jim Schwarz** as *"responsive, businesslike, cooperative and smart"* and were left asking *"what more could you need in a lawyer?"* A speaker for the International Council of Shopping Center Law Conferences, he combines this specialism with more general involvement for real estate developers and is noted for his contribution in large-scale financing and construction projects for Simon Property Group. He is particularly known for his shopping center work.

The Clients: Street Corner Group; First Indiana Bank; Muncie Housing Authority; Emmis Communications; Sunbeam Development Corporation; Equicor Realty; Meridian Development Asset Management; Colliers Turley Martin Tucker and OB Development.

Band 4

Krieg DeVault LLP

The Firm: Historically known for the strength of its general corporate lending practice, this firm has subsequently built an enviable reputation for real estate finance. It also provides a full service to its real estate client base, advising on everything from development and construction to zoning and condemnation. Interviewees identified the firm's work on multifamily/low-income housing development as a standout feature, and the practice group additionally offers a wide range of environmental services from assisting in due diligence and audits to defending toxic tort or natural resource damages claims.

The Lawyers: Andrew Buroker chairs the 25-strong real estate and environmental law practice group.

The Clients: Well-known clients include Fifth Third Bank and Bank One Indiana.

Sommer Barnard Attorneys PC

See firm details p.799

The Firm: Although its offering is smaller in size than some of the other real estate groups listed, this firm is still *"home to some super real estate lawyers"* and enjoys a reputation as a group that is growing in stature. With six dedicated lawyers operating out of Indianapolis, the firm is recommended for its experience of zoning, planning and land use and its representation of local

government and local developers. The practice group also works closely with the firm's environmental law group on such matters as the drafting of ordinances and land applications, say, for the expansion of landfills. As well as serving local clients, the group also undertakes shopping center and other developments on a regional and national basis.

The Lawyers: *"Fine attorney"* **Erick Ponader** (see p.794) is seen by market sources to have been *"passed the torch"* by Dan Sterner. They say he is *"keeping it burning bright through involvement in notable work for major clients."* Ponader represents clients at all stages of a project, from acquisition through to leasing and sale, and has recently represented clients on the development and leasing of over 2,000,000 sq ft of retail shopping center space.

The Clients: The Skinner & Broadbent Company, Gateway Shoppes and Cook Group are clients of the firm.

Wooden & McLaughlin LLP

See firm details p.801

The Firm: With approximately 30 lawyers operating out of this Indiana firm and nine attorneys concentrating on real estate, Wooden & McLaughlin is seen as an evolving real estate practice that is starting to have involvement in some of the more notable projects in the state. Highlighted by sources for its real estate lending work, it was recommended, too, for its representation of local and regional developers. Financial institutions, construction contractors, brokerage firms and trade associations also feature heavily on the client roster.

The Lawyers: The *"highly respected and very well qualified"* **Tom Dinwiddie** caters to an impressive range of clients from lenders to developers such as the Lauth Property Group.

Dinwiddie has a particular forte in single-family and multifamily mortgage banking, and is considered preeminent in mortgage-backed securities and structured lending. Staking his claim in the tables for another year is **John Hamilton**, said to be *"very knowledgeable and a good man to work with."* He advises institutional investors and private developers on a wide range of real estate issues.

The Clients: The Skinner & Broadbent Company; Kite Properties; Indiana University; Indianapolis Neighborhood Housing Partnership and Lauth Property Group.

Other Notable Practitioners

Rory O'Bryan is the *"extraordinarily intelligent"* former chairman of the real estate group at Baker & Daniels. He now practices with the boutique firm Harrison & Moberly LLP. Said to have *"a unique practice mixing transactional work with a strong academic interest,"* O'Bryan is an adjunct professor at the Indiana School of Law, as well as having *"a national reputation as one of the number one real estate lawyers in Indiana."* He handles all forms of transactional work, including partnerships, LLPs and tax-deferred exchanges. **Jack Lawson** of the Fort Wayne firm Beckman Lawson, LLP was universally acclaimed *"the go-to guy in Fort Wayne,"* particularly for his planning and zoning expertise. Finally, following overwhelming market support, **Barbara Wolenty** of Robinson Wolenty & Young, LLP in Indianapolis debuts in the table this year. Utilizing her *"ability to focus on the important issues for her clients and her tremendous amount of experience and knowledge,"* Wolenty does *"a real good job"* for a variety of clients, large and small.

Leaders in Indiana

ABRAMS, Jeffrey
Dann Pecar Newman & Kleiman, PC, Indianapolis 317 632 3232
Recommended in Real Estate

ASCHLEMAN, James A
Baker & Daniels, Indianapolis
317 237 1131
jim.aschleman@bakerd.com
Recommended in Corporate/M&A
Practice Areas: Represents corporations and other entities in public offerings of debt and equity securities, including IPOs. Extensive experience in corporate governance matters, securities laws aspects of demutualizations of insurance companies, mergers and acquisitions, and stock or asset sales for public and private companies.
Prof. Memberships: Indianapolis, Indiana State, and American Bar Associa-

tions. Fellow, Indiana Bar Foundation.
Personal: Manchester College, BA, summa cum laude, 1966; Harvard University, JD, 1969. Recognized in Chambers USA 2003 and 2004 editions, Corporate/M&A; named Member of The BTI Client Service All-Star Team for Law Firms, 2005; Voted one of 'Top 50 Indiana SuperLawyers', 2004 and 2005; Voted best corporate and best securities lawyer in Indianapolis, 1993.

BALDWIN, Charles B
Ogletree, Deakins, Nash, Smoak & Stewart, PC, Indianapolis
317 916 1300
charles.baldwin@ogletreedeakins.com
Recommended in Employment
Practice Areas: Employment law, labor law, litigation.
Prof. Memberships: Board of Directors,

Indiana Chamber of Commerce; US Chamber of Commerce Labor Relations Committee; Member of various national and local Bar Associations.
Career: Admitted in Indiana; Ohio; various US District Courts and US Courts of Appeals. Selected as Counsel for Amici Curiae 7th Circuit Court of Appeals concerning case of 1st impression under ADA.
Publications: Contributing author, ABA's Model Jury Instructions-Employment Litigation; Seventh Circuit Editor, ABA's Employment & Labor Relations Litigation Newsletter; co-author, Indiana Guide to Preventing Workplace Harassment.
Personal: Valparaiso University (BS, 1980), University of Dayton (JD, 1983).

BAYT, Phillip
Ice Miller, Indianapolis
317 236 2396
phillip.bayt@icemiller.com
Recommended in Real Estate
Practice Areas: Phillip L Bayt is a Managing Partner with a primary practice concentration in real estate law. Mr Bayt assists clients in finance, development, real estate taxes, workouts and foreclosures, mineral law, construction law, leasing and gaming. Mr Bayt is a Member of the Board of Directors for the Indianapolis Children's Museum, the Greater Indianapolis Chamber of Commerce, the Indy Partnership and the Greater Indianapolis Progress Committee.
Prof. Memberships: Member of the American College of Real Estate Lawyers, the Indianapolis Bar Associa-

tion, the Indiana State Bar Association, and past Chairman of the Board of the Near North Development Corporation.

BENNETT, Jackie
Sommer Barnard Attorneys PC, Indianapolis 317 713 3500
jbennett@sommerbarnard.com
Recommended in Litigation
Practice Areas: Member of Sommer Barnard's Litigation Department. Represents corporate and individual clients in grand jury and regulatory investigations, criminal trials, internal investigations, and civil litigation in state and federal courts.
Prof. Memberships: Indianapolis, Indiana State, American and Seventh Circuit Bar Associations; Indianapolis Law Club.
Career: Admitted to Indiana Bar (1983). Served as Assistant US Attorney for the Southern District of Indiana from 1985-88. From 1988-95, was Trial Attorney and Senior Trial Attorney in the Public Integrity Section of the Justice Department's Criminal Division in Washington, DC. Served from 1995 to 1999 as Associate Counsel and principal Deputy to Independent Counsel Kenneth W Starr in the Whitewater Investigation. Recipient of the Attorney General's John Marshall Award 'For Outstanding Legal Achievement' in 1994.
Personal: Received a BA from Hanover College (1980) and JD from Indiana University School of Law (1983). Was Note and Development Editor of the 'Indiana Law Review', 1982-83.

BIRGE, Taggart
Bose McKinney & Evans LLP, Indianapolis 317 684 5000
Recommended in Real Estate

BOEGLIN, Daniel L
Baker & Daniels, Indianapolis
317 569 4644
dan.boeglin@bakerd.com
Recommended in Corporate/M&A
Practice Areas: Chair of firm's Business Department. Represents companies in joint ventures and strategic alliances, including research and development collaborations in the pharmaceutical and medical device industries. Has been lead counsel in the formation of multiparty joint ventures to develop products and services in the fields of information technology and biotechnology, including several public-private partnerships arising out of Indiana's BioCrossroads life sciences initiative. Also represents companies in business acquisitions and financing transactions.
Personal: Indiana University, BS in Accounting, with highest distinction, 1982; University of Virginia, JD, 1985. Recognized in three leading legal publications, including 'America's Leading Business Lawyers' and 'The Best Lawyers in America'.

BOLDT, Michael
Ice Miller, Indianapolis
317 236 2327
michael.boldt@icemiller.com
Recommended in Employment
Practice Areas: Representing employers regarding employment issues generally, with extensive experience concerning collective bargaining, arbitration, union organizing drives, construction labor law, and equal employment opportunity law.
Prof. Memberships: Member: Indianapolis, Indiana and American Bar Associations. Member, board of directors of: Brooke's Place for Grieving Young People, Inc.; Highland Golf & Country Club. Recognized in 'Who's Who in American Law' and 'The Best Lawyers in America'.
Publications: Author of numerous employment related articles/books on collective bargaining and construction labor law. Faculty member for numerous labor-management and collective bargaining seminars for national organizations.
Personal: Wayne State University (BA), University of Michigan (JD).

BORN II, Samuel
Ice Miller, Indianapolis
317 236 2305
born@icemiller.com
Recommended in Employment
Practice Areas: Represents management in labor relations matters including labor litigation, arbitration, negotiations, and administrative proceedings before local, state and federal agencies such as NLRB, EEOC and the Indiana Civil Rights Commission. He is a certified mediator.
Prof. Memberships: Past President of the Indiana State Bar Association (1997-98) and the Indianapolis Bar Association (1988). Member: the American Bar Association House of Delegates (1988-98); US Chamber of Commerce employer labor relations and OSHA committees, Indiana Chamber of Commerce; Associated General Contractors of Indiana; Indiana Manufacturers' Association. Recognized, 'The Best Lawyers in America'.
Publications: Author of Indiana OSHA Guidebook For Employers (5th ed., 2004).

BOSHKOFF, Ellen
Baker & Daniels, Indianapolis
317 237 1266
ellen.boshkoff@bakerd.com
Recommended in Employment
Practice Areas: Leader of the firm's Employment Litigation Practice Group. Represents public and private employers in employment-related disputes at the administrative, state and federal level. Handles complex commercial litigation, including wage and hour class actions and collective actions under the Fair Labor Standards Act.

Prof. Memberships: Indianapolis, Indiana State, and American Bar Associations.
Publications: Co-author, Survey of Employment Law Developments for Indiana Practitioners, 35 Ind.L.Rev. 1369 (2002); co-author, Survey of Employment Law Developments for Indiana Practitioners, 36 Ind.L.Rev. 1035 (2003); Note, Resolving Retroactivity After Teague v. Lane, 65 Ind.L.J. 651 (1990), reprinted in 13 Crim.L.Rev. 589 (1991).
Personal: Swarthmore College, BA, with high honors, 1983; Indiana University School of Law, JD, summa cum laude, 1990.

BRIDGE, Catherine
Barnes & Thornburg, Indianapolis
317 236 1313
Recommended in Corporate/M&A

BROWN, Alan
Locke Reynolds LLP, Indianapolis
317 237 3800
Recommended in Litigation

BROWN, J Jeffrey
Baker & Daniels, Indianapolis
317 569 4613
jeff.brown@bakerd.com
Recommended in Corporate/M&A
Practice Areas: Leads the Private Capital Practice Group and represents corporate issuers with securities offerings, acquisitions and corporate governance matters. Represents financial investors and management participants in venture capital transactions, leveraged buyouts, recapitalizations and other complex transactions. Represents investment advisers, broker-dealers and other financial institutions with structuring and offering of investment vehicles, and represents investment banks with their own legal needs and as counsel to underwriters and financial advisors. Jeff also represents private companies with business law needs.
Personal: Indiana University, BA, 1982; Georgetown University, MBA, 1984; University of Virginia, JD, 1987.

BUTCHER, David
Bose McKinney & Evans LLP, Indianapolis 317 684 5000
Recommended in Corporate/M&A

CAMPBELL, David
Bingham McHale LLP, Indianapolis
317 635 8900
Recommended in Litigation

CARLINO, James
Bose McKinney & Evans LLP, Indianapolis 317 684 5000
Recommended in Real Estate

CROSS, Patrick
Baker & Daniels, Indianapolis
317 569 4844
patrick.cross@bakerd.com
Recommended in Corporate/M&A
Practice Areas: Leads the firm's Strategic Alliances and Joint Ventures Practice. Represents and counsels life sciences

and technology clients, including pharmaceutical and medical device companies, on formation and restructuring of business organizations, mergers, acquisitions, joint ventures, strategic affiliations, research and development collaborations, licensing and manufacturing agreements and corporate governance matters. Advises healthcare and life sciences clients on legal, regulatory, compliance and strategic planning matters.
Prof. Memberships: Indianapolis and Indiana Bar Associations; American Health Lawyers Association; IBA Bar Review lecturer.
Personal: Indiana University, BA, 1987; Indiana University School of Law, JD, magna cum laude, 1993; editor in chief, 'Indiana Law Journal'; Indiana Governor's Fellow; listed in 'The Best Lawyers in America'.

DENSBORN, Donald
Sommer Barnard Attorneys PC, Indianapolis 317 844 4744
ddensborn@sommerbarnard.com
Recommended in Corporate/M&A
Practice Areas: Partner focusing on corporate law, mergers and acquisitions law, venture capital, and real estate.
Prof. Memberships: Admitted to Indiana, (1976). Commissioner, National Conference of Commissioners on Uniform State Laws (Drafting Committee, Uniform Limited Liability Company Act); Indianapolis, Indiana State and American Bar Associations.
Career: Named 'Who's Who in Law and Finance' in Indianapolis Business Journal.
Publications: Numerous articles on topics including business financing techniques, letters of intent, negotiating venture capital funding, and lender liability.
Personal: JD (magna cum laude), Indiana University (Indianapolis), 1976; BS, (magna cum laude), Indiana University, 1973. Beta Gamma Sigma Academic Honorary Fraternity.

DEPREZ, Anne
Barnes & Thornburg, Indianapolis
317 236 1313
Recommended in Litigation

DETHERAGE, Andrew
Barnes & Thornburg, Indianapolis
317 236 1313
Recommended in Litigation

DINWIDDIE, Thomas
Wooden & McLaughlin LLP, Indianapolis 317 639 6151
Recommended in Real Estate

EBERT, Kim F
Ogletree, Deakins, Nash, Smoak & Stewart, PC, Indianapolis
317 916 1300
kim.ebert@ogletreedeakins.com
Recommended in Employment
Practice Areas: Represents employers in the full range of labor and employment matters, including litigation,

administrative proceedings, collective bargaining, union contract administration, and union avoidance.

Prof. Memberships: ABA (past Chair, Employer-Employee Relations Committee, TTIPS), Indiana Chamber of Commerce, Indiana Manufacturers Association. **Career:** Listed in 'The Best Lawyers in America' since 1995. Fellow in The College of Labor and Employment Lawyers. **Publications:** Has lectured and written extensively on labor and employment subjects at local, regional and national programs. Co-author of 'Indiana Employer's Guide to the ADA and FMLA'. **Personal:** Wabash College (BA cum laude, 1972), Indiana University (JD cum laude, 1976).

ELBERGER, Ronald
Bose McKinney & Evans LLP,
Indianapolis 317 684 5000
Recommended in Litigation

EMERSON, Daniel
Bose McKinney & Evans LLP,
Indianapolis 317 684 5000
Recommended in Employment

FICKLE, Stanley
Barnes & Thornburg, Indianapolis
317 236 1313
Recommended in Litigation

GELINAS, Julia
Locke Reynolds LLP, Indianapolis
317 237 3800
Recommended in Litigation

GREISING, Robert
Krieg DeVault LLP, Indianapolis
317 636 4341
Recommended in Corporate/M&A

HAAS, Karl
Wallack Somers & Haas PC,
Indianapolis 317 231 9000
Recommended in Real Estate

HACKMAN, Stephen
Ice Miller, Indianapolis
317 236 2289
stephen.hackman@icemiller.com
Recommended in Corporate/M&A

Practice Areas: Stephen Hackman is Chairman of Ice Miller's Corporate Practice Group. His practice focuses on federal and state securities law, mergers/acquisitions, structured finance, commercial lending and general corporate matters. He regularly provides sound, practical advice to public and large private companies in connection with strategic acquisitions and dispositions, public/private financings, securities law disclosure and compliance issues and corporate governance matters. His clients are involved in a variety of industries, including medical devices, chemical manufacturing, healthcare, finance, contract research and automobile redistribution. **Prof. Memberships:** Member: Indianapolis, American Bar Associations; Indianapolis Lawyers Club; past Chair,

Indianapolis Bar Association's Business Section.

HAMILTON, John
Wooden & McLaughlin LLP,
Indianapolis 317 639 6151
Recommended in Real Estate

HARDIN, Steven
Bingham McHale LLP, Indianapolis
317 635 8900
Recommended in Real Estate

HARRIS, Edward W
Sommer Barnard Attorneys PC,
Indianapolis
317 713 3500
eharris@sommerbarnard.com
Recommended in Litigation

Practice Areas: Chair of the firm's Litigation Department and represents clients in a wide range of business disputes, practicing mostly in federal court. He is particularly experienced in antitrust and class action disputes, representing both plaintiffs and defendants in cases in federal trial and appellate courts throughout the United States. **Prof. Memberships:** Indianapolis, Indiana State, American and Seventh Circuit Bar Associations. **Career:** Admitted to Indiana Bar (1968). **Personal:** BA from Amherst College in 1964 and JD from University of Michigan University in 1967. Note, Comment and Recent Developments Editor, 'Michigan Law Review', 1966-67. Teaching Fellow, Stanford Law School, 1967-68.

HECKLER, Douglas
Barnes & Thornburg, Indianapolis
317 236 1313
Recommended in Employment

HERZOG, David K
Baker & Daniels, Indianapolis
317 237 1240
David.Herzog@bakerd.com
Recommended in Litigation

Practice Areas: Concentrates in business and commercial litigation. Extensive experience in securities, banking, business-tort, and shareholder derivative litigation and has represented defendants in numerous class actions involving claims under the securities laws, the Truth in Lending Act, and various consumer contracts. Has also represented defendants in a number of cases involving mass torts, including cases arising out of natural gas and chemical explosions. **Prof. Memberships:** Indianapolis, Indiana State, Seventh Circuit, and American Bar Associations. **Career:** Partner since 1987; Executive Vice-President, General Counsel and Secretary of Conseco, Inc., September 2000-February 2003. **Personal:** Wabash College, AB, summa cum laude, 1977; Vanderbilt University, JD, 1980.

HICKS, Robert J
Sommer Barnard Attorneys PC,
Indianapolis 317 713 3500
bhicks@sommerbarnard.com
Recommended in Corporate/M&A

Practice Areas: Firm Director focusing practice on complex business and commercial transactions, private equity and venture capital transactions, business advisory services, and tax and estate planning matters. Lead Counsel to sellers and buyers in numerous merger and acquisition transactions and in several private equity and joint venture transactions. **Prof. Memberships:** Indianapolis, Indiana State, and American Bar Associations. Indiana Certified Public Accountant Society. **Career:** Admitted to Indiana Bar (1987); Certified Public Accountant. **Personal:** BS, (Highest Honors) Butler University, 1984; JD, Marshall-Wythe School of Law; College of William & Mary, 1986. Order of the Coif, William & Mary Law Review, 1985-86.

HIRSCHMAN, John
Baker & Daniels, Indianapolis
317 569 4677
john.hirschman@bakerd.com
Recommended in Real Estate

Practice Areas: Represents developers, financial institutions and real estate companies in debt and equity financing transactions, leasing transactions and acquisition and disposition transactions involving office, retail, industrial, multi-family and residential real estate assets throughout the United States. **Prof. Memberships:** Indiana and American Bar Associations. **Publications:** Co-author, 'Current Partnership Issues in Real Estate Equity Investment Transactions'. **Personal:** DePauw University, BA, cum laude, 1991; The University of Alabama, MA, 1994; New York University School of Law, JD, cum laude, 1997.

HOKANSON, Jeffrey
Ice Miller, Indianapolis
317 236 2185
jeff.hokanson@icemiller.com
Recommended in Litigation

Practice Areas: Jeff focuses on bankruptcy and commercial litigation. He assists clients facing economic challenges and those whose businesses are interrupted by others' insolvency. He represents and protects creditor-clients generally. He assists parties with leases and other contracts involved in bankruptcy proceedings, sought the appointment of receivers and trustees, and advised corporate management on matters related to the duties and obligations to businesses facing threatened or mounting insolvency. **Prof. Memberships:** Indianapolis and Indiana State Bar Associations; American Bankruptcy Institute, Indiana Association for Corporate Renewal.

HUMKE, Steven
Ice Miller, Indianapolis
317 236 2394
steven.humke@icemiller.com
Recommended in Corporate/M&A

Practice Areas: Founding Partner of Ice Miller's Strategic Advisors Group. Practice concentration in capital raising strategies, mergers and acquisitions and general corporate matters. Serves as general counsel to many clients. During 2004 represented HHGregg and former shareholders in recapitalization transaction financed by Freeman Spogli; represented ExactTarget, Inc., in venture investment led by Insight Ventures; served as counsel to Monument Capital Partners, in its investments in Hetsco, Inc. and IDC, Inc. **Prof. Memberships:** Director: The Villages; Indiana Humanities Council; TechPoint Foundation. Secretary, Association for Corporate Growth, Alumni of Stanley K. Lacy Executive Leadership Series. **Career:** Formerly practicing Certified Public Accountant.

HUPFER, Kyle
Ice Miller, Indianapolis
317 236 2100
Recommended in Corporate/M&A

INVEISS, Roberts
Henderson Daily Withrow & DeVoe,
Indianapolis 317 639 4121
Recommended in Corporate/M&A

IRMSCHER, David
Baker & Daniels, Fort Wayne
260 460 1602
david.irmscher@bakerd.com
Recommended in Litigation

Practice Areas: Concentrates practice in intellectual property litigation. Has acted as lead counsel in patent litigation, trademark and trade dress matters, including jury trials and appeals in the Federal Circuit. Also has extensive experience with ADR, including commercial arbitrations. Has litigated numerous matters involving orthopedic implants, implanted defibrillators, retractable syringes, electric motors, gas engines, and various types of building and recreational vehicle products. **Prof. Memberships:** Allen County, Indiana State, and American Bar Associations; American Intellectual Property Law Association. **Personal:** Dartmouth College, AB, cum laude, 1979; University of Michigan Law School, JD, 1982. Recognized in 'Indiana Super Lawyers' 2004 and 2005.

JOHNSON, Dennis
Barnes & Thornburg, Indianapolis
317 236 1313
Recommended in Real Estate

JOHNSON, Richard
Barnes & Thornburg, Indianapolis
317 236 1313
Recommended in Real Estate

KASPER, David
Locke Reynolds LLP, Indianapolis
317 237 3800
Recommended in Litigation

KLAPER, Martin
Ice Miller, Indianapolis
317 236 2322
martin.klaper@icemiller.com
Recommended in Employment

Practice Areas: Martin Klaper's practice concentration is in labor contract administration and negotiation; arbitration and NLRB matters; administrative and civil court discrimination matters; OFCCP matters; and union-free maintenance programs. He is also a certified mediator.

Prof. Memberships: Member of: the Bar of the Supreme Court of the United States; the College of Labor and Employment Lawyers (Labor Relations Committee); National Labor Relations Board and Equal Employment Opportunity Sub-committees of the United States Chamber of Commerce; Indiana and American Bar Associations. Recognized in: '2004 Super Lawyers', 'Who's Who in America', 'Who's Who in American Law' and 'The Best Lawyers in America'.

KNEBEL, Donald
Barnes & Thornburg, Indianapolis
317 236 1313
Recommended in Litigation

LAWSON, Jack
Beckman Lawson, LLP, Fort Wayne
219 422 0800
Recommended in Real Estate

LEE, Stephen
Barnes & Thornburg, Indianapolis
317 236 1313
Recommended in Real Estate

LISHER, Mary
Baker & Daniels, Indianapolis
317 237 1081
mary.lisher@bakerd.com
Recommended in Real Estate

Practice Areas: Counsels clients in real estate sales and purchases, ground leases, leases of improved retail, commercial and industrial properties, preparation of easements and other development, construction, and property management agreements and financing transactions.

Prof. Memberships: American (Real Property, Probate and Trust Law Section) and Indianapolis (Business Law Section) Bar Associations; IndyCREW (Indianapolis Commercial Real Estate Women).

Personal: Vanderbilt University, BA, cum laude, 1972; Indiana University, JD, summa cum laude, 1975. Named one of the Influential Women in Indianapolis by the Indianapolis Business Journal in 1999; Voted Top 50 Indiana Super Lawyer (2004) and Top 25 Female Indiana Super Lawyer (2004, 2005); Recognized in Chambers USA, Real Estate practice (2003, 2004); Member, Board of Directors, Lilly Endowment, Inc.

MACGILL, Robert
Barnes & Thornburg, Indianapolis
317 236 1313
Recommended in Litigation

MCDERMOTT, Brian L
Ogletree, Deakins, Nash, Smoak & Stewart, PC, Indianapolis
317 916 2170
brian.mcdermott@ogletreedeakins.com
Recommended in Employment

Practice Areas: Employment law, employment litigation, management labor law, ERISA litigation.

Prof. Memberships: Indiana Bar Association (Member Chair, Labor and Employment Section 2003-04), Indianapolis Bar Association (Member Chair, Labor and Employment Section 2004-05).

Career: Admitted to practice in Indiana, Iowa. Named as an Indiana Super Lawyer in 2005. Faculty Member, Annual Seminar on Labor-Management Relations of the Indiana School of Law-Indianapolis and Region 25 of the National Labor Relations Board.

Publications: Co-author of The Indiana Chamber of Commerce's publication 'The Indiana Employer's Guide to the ADA and FMLA'.

Personal: University of Iowa (JD, 1991), with Distinction.

MCTURNAN, Lee B
McTurnan & Turner, Indianapolis
317 464 8181
lmcturnan@mtlitig.com
Recommended in Litigation

Practice Areas: Business litigation in state and federal trial and appellate courts. For example, corporate securities and corporate governance disputes and breaches of fiduciary duties by directors, officers or employees; defending class actions involving securities, employment discrimination and various fraud claims; other employment matters; defending accountants, lawyers and securities broker-dealers; utility regulation litigation; restraint of trade and antitrust litigation; a wide variety of contract and business tort disputes; First Amendment media issues.

Prof. Memberships: Indianapolis, Chicago (Member, Board of Managers, 1977-78), Indiana State, Illinois State, Seventh Circuit and American Bar Associations; Indianapolis American Inn of Court (Master); Indianapolis Law Club (President, 1988-90); Local Rules Advisory Committee for Southern District of Indiana (1995-2000).

Career: Admitted to practice in Illinois in 1965 and Indiana in 1978. Law Clerk to Justice Goldberg, US Supreme Court, 1963-64. Practiced business litigation with: Sidley & Austin, Chicago, Illinois, as an associate from 1964-69 and as a Partner from 1970-78; and with Smith Morgan & Ryan (later Hackman McClarnon & McTurnan), Indianapolis, Indiana, as a Partner from 1978-88. Co-

Founder of McTurnan & Turner 1989.

Personal: Reared in Bloomington, Illinois. Received AB magna cum laude in 1959 from Harvard University; Diploma in Law from Oxford University (Lincoln College) in 1961; JD, cum laude from University of Chicago Law School in 1963. Was Phi Beta Kappa; editor-in-chief of the 'University of Chicago Law Review' from 1962-63; Order of the Coif.

MILLARD, David
Barnes & Thornburg, Indianapolis
317 236 1313
Recommended in Corporate/M&A

MILLER, David W
Baker & Daniels, Indianapolis
317 237 1316
david.miller@bakerd.com
Recommended in Employment

Practice Areas: Represents management clients in employment matters including union avoidance, charges before Federal/State Fair Employment Practice Agencies and the NLRB, and discrimination suits. Negotiates and administrates collective bargaining agreements, including arbitration of grievances. Counsels on compliance with wage and hour laws, hiring, disciplining, and terminating employees.

Prof. Memberships: Admitted: Indiana; US Court of Appeals for the Fourth, Fifth, Sixth, Seventh and Tenth Circuits.

Publications: 'It's the Law' Federal employment law training modules (2003), National Child Care Association; Co-author, 'The Indiana Guide to Hiring & Firing' (2001 & 1997), Indiana State Chamber of Commerce.

Personal: Indiana University, AB, 1971; JD, summa cum laude, 1976. Listed in Chambers USA 2003 and 2004 editions, Employment. Recognized in 'The Best Lawyers in America' for 10 years.

MITCHELL, Marvin
Mitchell Hurst Jacobs & Dick, Indianapolis 317 633 7680
Recommended in Litigation

NEIGHBOURS, John T
Baker & Daniels, Indianapolis
317 237 1325
john.neighbours@bakerd.com
Recommended in Employment

Practice Areas: Counsels employers in labor and employment law matters, including collective bargaining, employment litigation, maintaining union free workplaces, employment discrimination issues, and day-to-day administration of employee relations.

Prof. Memberships: Member of College of Labor and Employment Law Lawyers; Member, American Bar Association (Council Member, Section on Labor and Employment Law; Chair, Developments Under the National Labor Relations Act Committee, 1997-2000; editor, 4th edition, 1997-2000, assistant editor, 1990-96, and contributing editor, 1985-89, 'Developing Labor Law').

Publications: Editor, 'Indiana Employment Law Letter', M Lee Smith, publisher (1992-present).

Personal: DePauw University, BA, 1971; Indiana University, JD, 1974. Recognized in: Chambers USA 2003 and 2004 editions; 'The Best Lawyers in America' (listed for past 10 years); 'The International Who's Who of Business Lawyers', 'Labor and Employment'; and Euromoney's 'Best Labor and Employment Lawyers in the World'.

NICELY, Philip
Bose McKinney & Evans LLP, Indianapolis 317 684 5000
Recommended in Real Estate

NIERMAN, Todd
Baker & Daniels, Indianapolis
317 237 1312
todd.nierman@bakerd.com
Recommended in Employment

Practice Areas: Counsels employers on the National Labor Relations Act, Fair Labor Standards Act, EEO legislation, union organizing efforts, NLRB representation elections/proceedings, collective bargaining negotiations, wage/hour compliance and employment discrimination. Represents clients before the Indiana Supreme Court, Indiana Court of Appeals, Indiana trial courts, Seventh and Sixth Circuit Courts of Appeals, Federal District Court in Indiana, Ohio, Illinois and Texas, the NLRB, the EEO Commission, the US and Indiana Departments of Labor, and the Indiana Civil Rights Commission.

Personal: University of Michigan, BBA, with distinction, 1983; Vanderbilt University, JD, 1986. Certified Public Accountant, Illinois, 1983. Recognized in Chambers USA 2004 edition - Employment.

O'BRYAN, Rory
Harrison & Moberly LLP, Indianapolis
317 639 4511
Recommended in Real Estate

PENCE, Linda L
Sommer Barnard Attorneys PC, Indianapolis 317 713 3500
lpence@sommerbarnard.com
Recommended in Litigation

Practice Areas: Co-Chairs Litigation Department and Head of the White Collar Criminal Practice. Concentrates practice on federal white collar criminal defense and complex civil litigation, including government procurement contract fraud, tax fraud, violations of securities laws, antitrust violations, and other related matters.

Prof. Memberships: National Association of Criminal Defense Lawyers; American and Indiana State Bar Associations.

Career: Admitted to Indiana Bar (1974); District of Columbia Bar (1982). Nine years with US Department of Justice as Chief, Special Projects Branch; Deputy Chief, Government Fraud Section, Criminal Division; and Trial Attorney, Civil Division.

Personal: BA and JD, Indiana University, 1971 and 1974.

PONADER, Erick
Sommer Barnard Attorneys PC,
Indianapolis 317 713 3500
eponader@sommerbarnard.com
Recommended in Real Estate

Practice Areas: Chairman of the firm's Real Estate Group. Represents clients in commercial law and real estate development, acquisition, sale, leasing and financing. Extensive experience in the sale and purchase of businesses, intellectual property licensing, construction law, aviation law, and medical device and pharmaceutical law.

Prof. Memberships: Indianapolis (Executive Committee-Business Law Section), Indiana State and American Bar Associations.

Career: Admitted to Indiana Bar, 1989 and Illinois Bar, 1985.

Personal: JD, Indiana University (Bloomington), 1985; AB, (Chemistry and Biology), Indiana University, 1982.

SCANLON, Chris
Baker & Daniels, Indianapolis
317 237 1253
chris.scanlon@bakerd.com
Recommended in Litigation

Practice Areas: Business/commercial and securities litigation; class actions; insurance coverage disputes (product liability, environmental, and large loss liabilities).

Prof. Memberships: Indianapolis, Indiana State, Seventh Circuit and American Bar Associations. Local Rules Committee, US District Court, Southern District of Indiana; Indiana IOLTA Advisory Committee, 1997-99.

Personal: Indiana University, BS, 1977; Indiana University, JD, cum laude, 1980. Recipient, 1996 Pro Bono Publico Award, and Distinguished Fellow, Indiana Bar Foundation. Recognized in: Chambers USA 2003 and 2004 - Litigation; 'The Best Lawyers in America' (since 1987); and 'Indiana Super Lawyers' (Top 10), 2004 and 2005.

SCHWARZ, James
Dann Pecar Newman & Kleiman, PC,
Indianapolis 317 632 3232
Recommended in Real Estate

SCIMIA, Joseph
Baker & Daniels, Indianapolis
317 569 4680
joseph.scimia@bakerd.com
Recommended in Real Estate

Practice Areas: Represents developers, contractors, lenders, landlords, tenants and property owners in real estate transactions. Expertise includes construction and permanent financing of commercial, industrial and residential developments; and acquisition, development, leasing and disposition of office, retail, commercial, industrial and residential

properties. Secures land use approvals from local units of government for commercial, industrial, residential and mixed use projects. Leader of the firm's Real Estate and Land Use Practice Group.

Prof. Memberships: Indiana State and Arizona State Bar Associations.

Personal: Indiana University, BS, with high distinction, 1982; Indiana University, JD, magna cum laude, 1985. Recognized in 'The Best Lawyers in America' and Chambers USA 2003 and 2004 editions, Real Estate.

SHARROW, Regina
Sommer Barnard Attorneys PC,
Indianapolis
317 713 3500
rsharrow@sommerbarnard.com
Recommended in Corporate/M&A

Practice Areas: Practices in areas of general corporate law, mergers and acquisitions, securities law and executive compensation, including equity-based plans and packages for executives.

Prof. Memberships: Indianapolis, Indiana State (ISBA) and American Bar Associations; past Chair, ISBA Business Section.

Career: Admitted to California Bar, 1991, Admitted to Indiana Bar, 1996; joined Sommer Barnard; Lecturer: Golden Gate University School of Law, San Francisco, Executive Compensation and ERISA Basics Classes; Speaker: Intermediate Securities Law, Federal, State and EDGAR II for Indiana Paralegal Association and others.

Personal: JD, University of Berkeley, 1991; BS, University of Michigan, 1987.

SHOCKLEY, Steven C
Sommer Barnard Attorneys PC,
Indianapolis 317 713 3500
sshockley@sommerbarnard.com
Recommended in Litigation

Practice Areas: Member of the Litigation, Appellate Practice (Chair) and Governmental Affairs Departments. Represented Indiana State Bar Association in original actions in Indiana Supreme Court to enjoin unauthorized practice of law. Represented state circuit court in original actions in the Indiana Supreme Court seeking jurisdictional writ.

Prof. Memberships: Indianapolis Bar Association, Indiana State Bar Association.

Career: Admitted to Indiana Bar (1984) and Florida Bar (1986) (inactive). Associate with Holland & Knight from 1986-88. Law Clerk to Hon Stanley B Miller, Indiana Court of Appeals (1984-86). 'Indiana Law Review', 1983-84.

Personal: Indiana University (BA, 1978, JD, 1984, magna cum laude).

SOLADA, Mary
Bingham McHale LLP, Indianapolis
317 635 8900
Recommended in Real Estate

SOMERS, George W
Wallack Somers & Haas PC,
Indianapolis 317 231 9000
gws@wshlaw.com
Recommended in Real Estate

Practice Areas: Partner at Wallack, Somers & Haas, concentrating in all types of real estate development. He has provided counsel to local, regional and national developers regarding the acquisition, construction, leasing, financing and disposition of retail, office and mixed-use developments.

Career: Indiana State Bar admission 1979; Baker & Daniels (associate 1979; Partner 1985-99), Wallack Somers & Haas PC (1999-present).

Personal: Graduated St Olaf College (BA, magna cum laude, 1969); Harvard University (MTS, cum laude, 1971); Duke University (MA, 1974); University of Chicago (JD, 1979).

STANLEY, Robert K
Baker & Daniels, Indianapolis
317 237 1254
Robert.Stanley@bakerd.com
Recommended in Litigation

Practice Areas: Federal and state court litigation (including appeals) with particular focus on antitrust and trade cases, estate and trust disputes, bankruptcy litigation, and contract disputes. Leader of firm's Business Litigation Practice Group.

Prof. Memberships: Admitted to practice in all courts of the State of Indiana, US Supreme Court, and US Courts of Appeals for Sixth, Seventh and Eighth Circuits; Member, American and Indiana State Bar Associations.

Personal: Ball State University, AB, summa cum laude, 1978; Indiana University School of Law (Bloomington), JD, summa cum laude, 1981. Recognized in 'The Best Lawyers in America' and Chambers USA 2004, Litigation.

STRAIN, James A
Sommer Barnard Attorneys PC,
Indianapolis 317 713 3500
strain@sommerbarnard.com
Recommended in Corporate/M&A

Practice Areas: Member Executive Committee/Director and Chairman, Business Law Practice Group with extensive experience in mergers and acquisitions matters.

Prof. Memberships: The American Bar Association, Seventh Circuit Bar Association (President, 1995-96 term), Indiana State Bar Association.

Career: Admitted to practice in Indiana (1969). Law Clerk to Judge John S Hastings, US Court of Appeals for Seventh Circuit, 1970-71 and to then Associate Justice William H Rehnquist, US Supreme Court, October Term 1972. A Partner of Sommer Barnard Attorneys, PC since joining the firm in 1996.

Personal: JD (cum laude), Indiana University School of Law, 1969 and AB, Indiana University, 1966.

SWHIER, Claudia
Barnes & Thornburg, Indianapolis
317 236 1313
Recommended in Corporate/M&A

SWIDER, David
Bose McKinney & Evans LLP,
Indianapolis 317 684 5000
Recommended in Employment

TEMPEL, Angela
Ice Miller, Indianapolis
317 236 2100
Recommended in Real Estate

THORNBURGH, John
Ice Miller, Indianapolis
317 236 2405
john.thornburgh@icemiller.com
Recommended in Corporate/M&A

Practice Areas: Co-Chairman of Ice Miller's Strategic Advisors Group and Chairman of the Sports and Entertainment Group, John focuses on general corporate matters, mergers and acquisitions, private equity fund formation, and venture finance transactions. John also represents businesses and individuals in the sports and entertainment industries.

Prof. Memberships: Board of Directors, Indianapolis Symphony Orchestra; Chairman of the Board of Directors, IM Sports Services, LLC; Board of Advisors: CID Equity Partners, Inc.; Major Tool and Machine, Inc.; and Western Reserve Partners, LLC.

Personal: BA, DePauw University; JD, University of Illinois, Champaign.

THRAPP, Richard
Ice Miller, Indianapolis
317 236 2442
richard.thrapp@icemiller.com
Recommended in Corporate/M&A

Practice Areas: Chair of Ice Miller's Business Section, his primary practice areas are in general business, mergers and acquisitions, corporate finance, corporate and commercial law, nonprofit organizations, and shareholder rights.

Prof. Memberships: Member: Indiana Corporate Law Survey Commission; Board of Managers, Indianapolis Bar Association; Indiana State and American Bar Associations; Board of Directors, Indianapolis Bar Foundation. Distinguished Fellow, Indianapolis Bar Foundation; Served on the task force for Limited Liability Companies and on the drafting committee for the Indiana Nonprofit Corporation Act. Member: Board of Governors, Child Advocates, Inc.; Board of Directors, Indianapolis Zoological Society; Board of Directors, Geist Christian Church.

TINSLEY, Nancy
Baker & Daniels, Indianapolis
317 237 1245
nancy.tinsley@bakerd.com
Recommended in Litigation

Practice Areas: Nancy Tinsley concentrates her practice in intellectual property litigation, particularly patent litigation. She has litigated patent cases in a variety of technological areas including medical devices, chemicals, fluid handling, and software. Nancy also counsels clients on licensing matters. She is an inventor with three US patents and is registered to practice before the Patent and Trademark Office.

Prof. Memberships: Indianapolis (Member, Women in the Law Executive Committee, 1998-99); Indiana State (Member, Women in the Law Committee, 1997-present); Seventh Circuit and American Bar Associations. American Intellectual Property Lawyers Association.

Career: Prior to becoming an attorney, Nancy worked at a major pharmaceutical company as a research chemist.

Personal: Purdue University, BS in Chemistry, 1982; Indiana University School of Law, JD, cum laude, 1990. Recognized in 'The Best Lawyers in America,' 2005-06 edition; 'Indiana Super Lawyers,' (Law & Politics) 2004 and 2005.

TITTLE, David
Bingham McHale LLP, Indianapolis
317 635 8900
Recommended in Litigation

TURNER, Wayne C
McTurnan & Turner, Indianapolis
317 464 8181
wturner@mtlitig.com
Recommended in Litigation

Practice Areas: Business litigation in state and federal trial and appellate courts. For example, corporate securities and corporate governance disputes and breaches of fiduciary duties by directors, officers or employees; defending class actions involving securities, employment discrimination and various fraud claims; other employment matters; defending accountants, lawyers and securities broker-dealers; utility regulation litigation; restraint of trade and antitrust litigation; a wide variety of contract and business tort disputes; First Amendment media issues.

Prof. Memberships: Indianapolis, Indiana State, Seventh Circuit and American Bar Associations; Indianapolis Law Club; Defense Research Institute; Indianapolis Bar Foundation (Distinguished Fellow).

Career: Admitted to practice in Indiana in 1985. Associate at Smith Morgan & Ryan (later Hackman McClarnon & McTurnan), Indianapolis, Indiana, from 1985-88. Co-Founder of McTurnan & Turner in 1989.

Personal: Reared in Rising Sun, Indiana. Received BS in Economics, with highest distinction, in 1982 from Purdue University (GA Ross Outstanding Graduate); JD, magna cum laude, in 1985 from Indiana University. Was Note and Development Editor of the 'Indiana Law Review,' 1984-85. Order of Barristers.

UTKEN, Gregory
Baker & Daniels, Indianapolis
317 237 1327
greg.utken@bakerd.com
Recommended in Employment

Practice Areas: Chair of firm's Advocacy Department. Has represented management exclusively in labor and employment law matters and litigation throughout the US for over 30 years, including maintaining non-union status; facility consolidation, work relocation and reduction in force issues; matters before the NLRB; collective bargaining; labor arbitrations; employment discrimination, affirmative action, diversity and wrongful discharge.

Prof. Memberships: Indiana State, Michigan State, and American Bar (Labor and Employment Law Section) Associations; past-President, Indiana University School of Law Indianapolis Alumni Association.

Personal: Indiana University, AB, 1971; JD, magna cum laude, 1974. Recognized in 'The Best Lawyers in America,' Chambers USA 2003 & 2004 editions, and 'Indiana Super Lawyers,' 2004 and 2005 (Law & Politics).

WALLACK, Barry Z
Wallack Somers & Haas PC, Indianapolis 317 231 9000
bzw@wshlaw.com
Recommended in Real Estate

Practice Areas: Partner at Wallack, Somers & Haas, concentrating in leasing, lending, borrowing, development, operation and syndication. He has represented clients in $300 million public debt offerings, sales and purchases of real estate projects of all sizes, development of numerous apartment projects, leasing of office buildings and shopping centers, and lender representation in all types of mortgage loans.

Career: Indiana State Bar admission 1965; Baker & Daniels (associate 1965-69); Klineman Rose Wolf & Wallack (Partner 1969-93; Managing Partner 1986-93); Wallack & Wallack (Partner 1994-99).

Personal: Graduated University of Wisconsin (BS, 1962; JD, 1965). Board Member St. Vincent Hospital Foundation (2000-05).

WARSHAUER, David
Barnes & Thornburg, Indianapolis
317 236 1313
Recommended in Real Estate

WEISS, Zeff
Ice Miller, Indianapolis
317 236 2319
zeff.weiss@icemiller.com
Recommended in Real Estate

Practice Areas: Chairman of Ice Miller's Real Estate section, Zeff's practice concentration is in real estate development, finance and taxation. He is also involved in complex equity and debt structuring, and complex tax and work out matters.

Prof. Memberships: Recognized in: 'Best Lawyers in America'; 'International Who's Who of Real Estate Lawyers'; Indianapolis Business Journal's 'Who's Who in Commercial and Residential Real Estate'. Member of: American College of Real Estate Lawyers; Indianapolis and Indiana State Bar Associations. Executive Committee Member, Board of Directors, The Jewish Federation of Greater Indianapolis, Inc.; past President and Member, Board of Directors, Park Regency.

WELCH, Brian
Bingham McHale LLP, Indianapolis
317 635 8900
Recommended in Litigation

WHISTLER, Philip
Ice Miller, Indianapolis
317 236 2349
philip.whistler@icemiller.com
Recommended in Litigation

Practice Areas: Primary practice concentration in antitrust, trade regulation, securities, product distribution, and franchising, class actions, and complex civil litigation. Over 25 years of trial experience, numerous jury and non-jury trials in state and federal courts, and arbitrations before NASD and AAA.

Prof. Memberships: Recognized in 'Best Lawyers in America'. Member of the Indianapolis, Indiana State, and American Bar Associations. Member of the ABA: Forum Committee on Franchising; Antitrust Committee; and Litigation Section. Local Rules Advisory Committee for the US District Court, Southern District of Indiana.

Personal: Stanford University (BA), Harvard (JD, cum laude).

WILDMAN, Robert
Henderson Daily Withrow & DeVoe, Indianapolis 317 639 4121
Recommended in Corporate/M&A

WILKINS, Michael
Ice Miller, Indianapolis
317 236 2395
mike.wilkins@icemiller.com
Recommended in Litigation

Practice Areas: Mr Wilkins practices in all areas of litigation, focusing on appellate advocacy, media law, and adoption law. Co-Chair of the firm's Appellate Practice Group, he spends the majority of his time representing clients in state and federal appellate courts. He also represents media clients on a variety of issues, from pre-publication review, to access issues, to defense of defamation and other related suits. He devotes significant time to representing families in the adoption process and in all other aspects of family law.

Prof. Memberships: Member, Indianapolis and Indiana State Bar Associations. Advisory Council, St. Elizabeth's/Coleman Pregnancy Services.

WOLENTY, Barbara
Robinson Wolenty & Young, LLP, Indianapolis 317 587 7820
Recommended in Real Estate

WORRELL, David
Baker & Daniels, Indianapolis
317 237 1110
david.worrell@bakerd.com
Recommended in Corporate/M&A

Practice Areas: Represents issuers and underwriters on IPOs, private placements, and hedge fund and other venture capital transactions. Advises public companies on compliance with Sarbanes-Oxley Act, corporate governance requirements, reporting obligations, proxy solicitations and tender offer requirements. Counsels financial institutions (formations, acquisitions, holding companies, regulatory compliance and securities offerings) and directors on fiduciary duties and regulatory responsibilities. Counsels companies on mergers, acquisitions or sales of assets or securities, restructurings and defensive measures on takeover offers.

Prof. Memberships: American Bar Association.

Personal: Wabash College, AB, summa cum laude, 1973; University of Chicago, JD, 1976. Recognized in 'The Best Lawyers in America'; Chambers USA 2004 edition, Corporate/M&A; and 'Indiana Super Lawyers' 2004 and 2005 editions (Law & Politics).

YEAGER, Jay
Baker & Daniels, Indianapolis
317 237 1278
jay.yeager@bakerd.com
Recommended in Litigation

Practice Areas: Business torts and contracts, aviation, shareholder disputes, and class actions. Numerous bench and jury trials and appeals in state and federal courts.

Prof. Memberships: Indianapolis (former Litigation Section Chair), Indiana State and Seventh Circuit Bar Associations; Member, ISBA House of Delegates; Indiana Co-Chair, Seventh Circuit Committee on Administration and Justice; Member, Indiana Continuing Legal Education Commission.

Personal: Harvard University, BA, cum laude, 1979; Indiana University, JD, cum laude, 1983. Recognized in 'The Best Lawyers in America'; Chambers USA 2003 and 2004 editions, Litigation; and 'Indiana Super Lawyers' 2004 and 2005 editions (Law & Politics).

YERKES, Kenneth
Barnes & Thornburg, Indianapolis
317 236 1313
Recommended in Employment

BAKER & DANIELS

THE FIRM

CEO/Chair: Brian K Burke

Number of partners: 143
Number of other lawyers: 164

FIRM OVERVIEW: Since 1863, Baker & Daniels has served clients across the country and around the world. With more than 370 professionals in eight offices in Indiana, Washington, DC and China, Baker & Daniels offers integrated business and legal counsel through legal personnel and the firm's affiliated companies, B&D Sagamore (federal government affairs), B&D Quorum (innovative advocacy and communications), B&D Navigator (human resource consulting/training) and Aventor (medical technology consulting).

MAIN AREAS OF PRACTICE:

Business & Finance: Baker & Daniels represents business enterprises, from start-ups to large multinational companies on issues including business planning; tax planning; raising capital; employee incentives; contract negotiations and dispute resolution; joint ventures; governmental incentives and public/private venture; purchase or sale of business; licensing, franchise, development and distribution agreements; succession planning; buy-sell and service agreements.

Healthcare/Medical Technology: The firm represents hospitals, national and multi-state healthcare systems, nursing and retirement homes, community mental health centers, ambulatory surgery centers, HMOs, PPOs, physicians and other health professionals and trade associations. It also represents medical device and drug companies with intellectual property, FDA, reimbursement, compliance/marketing, liability, clinical trials management and other issues.

Intellectual Property: With 35 attorneys, including 27 registered patent attorneys, Baker & Daniels represents clients around the world in the creation of commercial property rights, as well as the protection and leverage of rights in the patent, trademark, copyright and trade secret area. Professionals have technical and legal expertise in the applied sciences, including electronic and mechanical technologies, chemistry, and computer science.

Labor/Employment & Benefits: Baker & Daniels' labor, employment and employee benefits practice is national in scope. Members of these practice groups have represented employers in 48 of the 50 states. While the firm provides services in every aspect of labor, employment and benefits law, it is best known for its traditional labor law practice and employment litigation defense.

Life Sciences: With experience, expertise, and industry knowledge to advise businesses shaping the future of life sciences, the firm helps new ventures find resources, market leaders stay ahead of the competition, and research universities move new technologies. They help state and local governments create environments that foster targeted growth, and structure and support the complex alliances among industry, academia, government and non-profits that are at the heart of much of the industry's growth. In addition, Baker & Daniels conceived, organized, and structured the Indiana Future Fund, one of the most innovative funding mechanisms in the life sciences industry. This $73 million fund-of-funds resulted from unprecedented collaboration and has invested in regional and national venture capital funds, thereby attracting capital to emerging Indiana life sciences companies.

Litigation: More than 60 litigators and paralegals represent clients in state and federal cases in Indiana and throughout the United States, and serve as national counsel to clients in complex multistate litigation. Product liability team members represent international, national and local manufacturers and distributors in a diverse range of industries, including the medical device, automotive and industrial equipment industries.

Real Estate: The firm represents a diverse group of clients on all aspects of real estate, zoning and land use law. Real estate members plan and devel-

HEAD OFFICE

INDIANA
300 N Meridian Street, Suite 2700, **Indianapolis,** IN 46204
Tel: 317 237 0300   **Fax:** 317 237 1000

Website: www.bakerdaniels.com

BRANCH OFFICES

INDIANA
317 West Franklin Street, **Elkhart**, IN 46515
Tel: 574 296 6000   **Fax:** 574 296 6001

111 East Wayne Street, Suite 800, **Fort Wayne,** IN 46802
Tel: 260 424 8000   **Fax:** 260 460 1700

600 E 96th Street, Suite 600, **Indianapolis,** IN 46240
Tel: 317 569 9600   **Fax:** 317 569 4800

First Bank Building, 205 West Jefferson Boulevard, Suite 250,
South Bend, IN 46601
Tel: 574 234 4149   **Fax:** 574 239 1900

DISTRICT OF COLUMBIA
805 15th Street, NW, Suite 700, **Washington,** DC 20005
Tel: 202 312 7440   **Fax:** 202 312 7441

INTERNATIONAL OFFICES

The firm also has law offices in Beijing and Qingdao, PR China, and a representative office in Shanghai, PR China.

op strategies, negotiate and structure essential terms of a transaction, draft or review agreements and instruments, develop zoning regulations, and obtain zoning approvals.

Tax: Baker & Daniels represents individuals, corporations, partnerships, tax-exempt organizations, financial institutions, trusts/estates, and specialized entities such as real estate investment trusts, with federal, state and local taxation issues.

CLIENTS: Representative clients include Eli Lilly and Co; Zimmer, Inc; Anthem Insurance Companies; Bank One; Wabash National Corporation; Swiss Re; ArvinMeritor; Ispat Inland; Mac's Convenience Stores; Guidant Corporation, Roche Diagnostics Corporation , Kimball International, Cinergy Corporation and American Commercial Lines.

INTERNATIONAL WORK: The international team represents clients around the world regarding all business and legal issues. The firm provides business and legal counsel regarding joint ventures; wholly foreign owned enterprises; international arbitration/litigation; trade disputes; distribution and licensing agreements; protection of intellectual property rights; identification of business partners; foreign governments; negotiations; immigration and emigration; international trade tax issues; government affairs; and venture capital and IPOs. China practice professionals in Beijing, Shanghai and Qingdao provide American, Chinese and international clients with comprehensive service including the identification of business partners, manufacturing sources, key personnel and plant site locations. Baker & Daniels is one of only 40 US law firms licensed to practice in China. Networks: Exclusive Indiana member of Lex Mundi and participating member of TAGLaw.

BAKER & DANIELS
We know the territory

ICE MILLER

THE FIRM

Managing Partners: Philip Bayt, David Mattingly, Melissa Proffitt Reese

FIRM OVERVIEW: Founded in 1910, Ice Miller is one of the largest law firms in Indianapolis with a nationally recognized reputation in many of its practice areas. With additional offices in Chicago and Washington DC, the firm has over 225 lawyers, 40 paraprofessionals and 250 support staff members. Ice Miller is a full-service firm with the resources it needs to counsel its clients and deliver quality legal and business advice.

MAIN AREAS OF PRACTICE:

Private Equity/Venture Finance: Ice Miller is known throughout the United States as a significant player in the private equity fund and venture finance arena. For more than 20 years, the firm's attorneys have represented private equity funds and provided fund formation, structuring and operation services to funds that focus on equity and debt investments in private companies, including seed, venture, mezzanine, buy-out, "cross-over" investment and broad-based private equity funds.

College & University: Public and private colleges and universities can be confronted by unique legal issues. Ice Miller utilizes a multi-disciplinary team that understands how an institution's legal and strategic needs can differ from those in the world of business and corporations. To fully understand and address an institution's needs, Ice Miller attorneys serve as directors and trustees of colleges and universities as well as teach as adjunct faculty at area law schools. The firm also participates in organizations such as the National Association of College and University Attorneys (NACUA) to gain further insight. Ice Miller is well-positioned to react quickly and effectively, offering institutions creative solutions.

HEALTH SERVICES

Healthcare: Ice Miller has substantial experience in the business and regulatory aspects of healthcare. The firm's clients can be found in all branches of the health care industry, including hospitals, multi-specialty physician clinics, physician groups, individual physicians, health maintenance organizations, retirement centers, medical research organizations, and suppliers of medication and medical equipment. Ice Miller provides advice in solving technical as well as practical problems, and, when necessary, thorough representation in litigation, business transactions and municipal finance transactions.

Drug, Device & Chemical Exposure Litigation: Ice Miller has decades of experience in drug, device and chemical exposure claims and litigation. Ice Miller attorneys have served as national, regional, and local counsel in drug, device and chemical exposure litigation where they regularly address scientific, epidemiologic and complex medical issues in multi-jurisdictional litigation. The firm also conducts audits of pharmaceutical products both before and after product launch, and provides counseling on preventative measures and risk management.

EMPLOYMENT SERVICES

Labor: In choosing labor and employment counselors to meet business needs, the client first needs to know what the firm believes and what they stand for. Ice Miller believes that all employers, public and private alike, will be better able to achieve their goals if they are free to use their human resources in the manner they deem productive and efficient, with minimal interference from government regulations and other outside sources. The firm believes such ends can be reached by means that are legal, practical, and consistent with the best interests of the clients' employees. Whether in a union or non-union environment, Ice Miller's chief goal is to assist its employer clients in creating a work force that is world-class in all respects.

HEAD OFFICE

INDIANA
One American Square, Box 82001, **Indianapolis,** IN 46282-0200
Tel: 317 236 2100   **Fax:** 317 236 2219
Email: info@icemiller.com
Website: www.icemiller.com

BRANCH OFFICES

ILLINOIS
500 W Monroe, Suite 1818, **Chicago,** IL 60661
Tel: 312 726 1567   **Fax:** 312 726 7102

DISTRICT OF COLUMBIA
1090 Vermont Ave. NW, Ste. 920, **Washington,** DC
Tel: 202 824 8600   **Fax:** 202 824 8601

Benefits: Current economic pressures and the aging of the work force have made employee benefits a focal point for employers and employees in the public and private sector. Lawyers and consultants in the Ice Miller Employee Benefits Group advise businesses, governments, churches, and plan trustees on how to handle retirement plans, health plans, compensation packages, and other fringe benefits. Nationally recognized in a number of areas (including governmental and church benefit plans), the Benefits Group has an extraordinary breadth and depth of knowledge and experience in representing and advising clients nationally on all aspects of employee benefits.

Nationally Recognized Practice Areas: Ice Miller is recognized nationally for services provided to the gaming industry, the firm's work with public employment retirement funds, NCAA compliance and infractions, and municipal finance.

CLIENTS: Biomet, Inc., Celadon, Inc., CID Equity Partners, Community Hospitals of Indiana, Inc., Eli Lilly & Co., Handy & Harman, Haynes International Inc., Howard Regional Health System, Indiana University, Indianapolis Airport Authority, Indianapolis Motor Speedway, Johnson & Johnson, Pfizer Inc., Remy International, Inc.

INTERNATIONAL WORK: Ice Miller's International Group addresses the business and legal needs of clients around the world including export consultation and licensing, foreign investment in the United States, immigration and international employees, international agreements and antitrust issues, tax and export/import matters. Ice Miller has personnel fluent in: Japanese, Chinese, Spanish, French, Russian, German, Korean, Arabic, Persian and Greek.

McTURNAN & TURNER

THE FIRM

Managing Partners: Lee B McTurnan, Wayne C Turner

Number of partners: 4
Number of other lawyers: 11

AREAS OF PRACTICE:
Business Litigation 100%

HEAD OFFICE

INDIANA
2400 Market Tower, 10 West Market Street, **Indianapolis**, IN 46204
Tel: 317 464 8181   **Fax:** 317 464 8131
Website: www.mtlitig.com

FIRM OVERVIEW: McTurnan & Turner concentrates in relatively complex business litigation. The firm's goal is to provide the high quality of representation expected from the largest firms with the responsive and efficient services that distinguish the best small firms. The firm has assembled a group of unusually talented lawyers who work closely with the client or corporate counsel to plan and implement strategies throughout pre-trial and trial proceedings.

MAIN AREAS OF PRACTICE: The firm's lawyers have litigated issues concerning:

Corporate Securities/Governance: Fraud or misstatements in sales of securities or financial statements; shareholder derivative claims; breaches of fiduciary duties of directors, officers and employees and of corporate governance provisions; tender offers/takeover.

Class Actions: Representing defendants in alleged class actions related to securities laws, equal employment opportunity laws (race, sex and age), consumer fraud, product liability, and federal and state taxation.

Employment/Discrimination Matters: Race, sex and age discrimination; employment contracts; covenants not to compete.

Professional Responsibility: Defending professionals such as accountants, lawyers and securities broker-dealers against claims of negligence or misconduct.

Competition/Regulation: Restraints of trade, antitrust; regulation of utilities (telephone, electric, natural gas).

Contracts: Sales of goods, equipment, or services; insurance; franchises; commissions; guarantees; leases; construction.

Business Torts: Product liability; consumer fraud; lender liability; trade secrets; unfair competition; environmental liability; tortious interference.

First Amendment: Defamation; protection of free speech and press; third-party discovery from media; newsgatherers' rights and privileges; access to public records and proceedings.

Reported Cases: Some reported cases handled by the firm include: Gold Seal Termite And Pest Control Co., et al., on behalf of themselves and others similarly situated, v PrimeTV, LLC and DIRECTV, Inc., Marion Superior Court (defense counsel for DIRECTV in pending nationwide class action settlement of multi-billion dollar claims for alleged violation of the Telephone Consumer Protection Act with respect to unsolicited fax advertisements); M-Plan, Inc., et al. v Indiana Comprehensive Health Insurance Association and Sally McCarty, 809 N.E. 2d 834 (Ind.2004) (requiring exhaustion of administrative remedies for claims against Indiana Insurance Commissioner and involuntary association created by statute); Polinsky and Sutker v Violi, 803 N.E. 2d 684 (Ind. Ct. App. 2004) (addressing issue of first impression concerning mandatory arbitration for claims against controlling shareholders in privity with corporation that entered agreement to arbitrate); Indiana Comprehensive Health Insurance Association, et al. v Avemco Insurance Company, et al., 812 N.E. 2d 108 (Ind. Ct. App. 2004) (affirming injunction forcing approximately $8 million in funding for Indiana's high risk health pool, by companies claiming not to meet the statutory criteria for assessment); Midwest Gas Services, Inc., et al. v Indiana Gas Co., Inc. and ProLiance Energy, LLC, 317 F.3d 703 (7th Cir. 2003) (affirming dismissal of multiple Sherman Act claims); United States Gypsum Inc. v Indiana Gas Co., Inc., ProLiance Energy LLC, et al., 735 N.E.2d 790 (Ind. 2000) (opinion affirming ruling by the Indiana Utility Regulatory Commission that client ProLiance Energy LLC, a natural gas marketer, is not a public utility subject to state regulation); Indianapolis Newspapers v Indiana State Lottery Comm'n and James F. Maguire, 739 N.E.2d 144 (Ind.Ct.App. 2000) (reversing trial court's decision that would have eliminated client Indianapolis Newspapers' statutory right to recover attorneys' fees if it substantially prevails on the merits of its claim for public access to Lottery sales records); Adams v Indiana Bell Telephone Co., Inc. and Ameritech Services, Inc., 2 F. Supp. 2d 1077- 1134 (S.D. Ind. 1998) (summary judgment in favor of client Ameritech Services, Inc. against class and individual claims of age and pension discrimination in downsizing; affirmed as to pension claims and reversed as to age claims, 231 F.3d 414 (7th Cir. 2000)); Indiana Wholesale Wine & Liquor Co., Inc. v State of Indiana ex rel. Indiana Alcoholic Beverage Commission, 695 N.E.2d 99-108 (Ind. 1998) (opinion upholding client Indiana Wholesale's liquor distribution permits on statutory ground; Court of Appeals had ruled for Indiana Wholesale on U.S. constitutional Commerce Clause and 21st Amendment bases, 662 N.E.2d 950-970 (Ind.App. 1996)); In re WTHR-TV and McGraw-Hill Broadcasting Company, Inc. d/b/a WRTV-6; State of Indiana v Krista M. Cline, 693 N.E.2d 1-16 (Ind. 1998) (Indiana Supreme Court's opinion of first impression on Indiana third-party discovery and access to television out-takes); IPALCO Enterprises, Inc. v PSI Resources, Inc., 148 F.R.D. 604-608 (S.D. Ind. 1993) (discovery/privilege issues in merger/tender-offer dispute).

CLIENTS: The firm's corporate clients include SBC Communications, Inc.; PricewaterhouseCoopers LLP; Wachovia Corporation; ProLiance Energy LLC; CitiFinancial; General Motors Corporation; Salomon Smith Barney, Inc.; Western Newspaper Publishing Co.; Earlham College; Redcats USA, LP; and McGraw-Hill Broadcasting Co., Inc. (WRTV-6). The firm is regularly employed by corporate counsel or through other law firms to represent corporate or individual clients in substantial, non-recurring litigation matters.

INTERNATIONAL WORK: The firm has represented a number of non-US clients in litigation within the United States. These clients include: Onkyo Japan; Shell International BV; Langen Packaging, Inc.; Molins PLC; Autoliv; Euribrid, Inc.; Sleeman Breweries, Inc; and Tagsys Q.

SOMMER BARNARD ATTORNEYS, PC

THE FIRM

Number of partners: 49
Number of other lawyers: 44

FIRM OVERVIEW: Sommer Barnard offers a wide array of legal services throughout the Midwest and in Washington, DC. The firm currently has approximately 93 attorneys and 21 practice groups, with its primary concentrations in litigation, business law, bankruptcy law and business workouts, environmental, government services, health and life sciences, intellectual property, labor and employment law, public finance, real estate, and tax and estate planning.

MAIN AREAS OF PRACTICE:

Bankruptcy Law & Business Workouts: The firm has extensive experience representing businesses in Chapter 11 bankruptcy. The firm also has one of the largest practice groups in Indiana dedicated to assisting businesses in their reorganization activities outside Chapter 11. It also represents creditors in the bankruptcy and reorganization process.

Business Law: The firm assists clients in the pursuit of business strategies, including their acquisition, disposition, financing and licensing activities. Members of its business group have guided companies through some of the largest public company mergers and initial public offerings within in the state, routinely serve middle market companies, and have assisted in the start-up and growth of numerous emerging companies, including high-tech ventures.

Environmental Law: The firm's experience includes all areas of environmental law. The firm represents clients in environmental litigation before state and federal courts and in administrative proceedings throughout the United States.

Government Services: The firm's practice involves a wide range of legislative and regulatory activities at the local, state and federal levels, representing business, trade associations and governmental entities.

Health & Life Sciences: The firm's practice group includes a diverse legal team representing health industry clients across the state and beyond. The firm advises clients on rapidly changing legal, regulatory and business developments in the healthcare field.

Intellectual Property: The firm's IP Practice Group provides full intellectual property services in the areas of patent, trademark, copyright and trade secret law, and counsel for new technology transactions, advertising, privacy and e-commerce.

Labor & Employment Law: The firm is well experienced in representing both employers and employees in employment litigation, counseling in traditional labor law areas, and advising employers on various issues concerning their employee benefits.

Litigation: The firm represents plaintiffs and defendants in its nationwide commercial and class action litigation practice for more than 30 years. The practice encompasses complex cases involving antitrust, securities, environmental, real estate and other commercial issues, as well as white-collar criminal litigation.

Public Finance: The firm provides legal services to state and local governments and agencies in the issuance of bonds and other debt instruments, handling all aspects of public financings, including municipal law, securities law, and federal income taxation, as well as providing advice to issuers in connection with continuing legal compliance related to bond issues.

US OFFICES

INDIANA

One Indiana Square, Suite 3500, **Indianapolis** IN 46204
Tel: 317 713 3500   **Fax:** 317 713 3699
Email: info@sommerbarnard.com
Website: www.sommerbarnard.com

8888 Keystone Crossing, Suite 1400, **Indianapolis** IN 46240
Tel: 317 844 4744   **Fax:** 317 844 4780

112 N. 7th Street, PO Box 139, **Vincennes** IN 47591
Tel: 812 886 9970   **Fax:** 812 886 0776

DISTRICT OF COLUMBIA

1666 K Street, NW, Suite 1010, **Washington** DC 20006-1217
Tel: 202 416 4150   **Fax:** 202 416 4151

Real Estate: The firm's real estate attorneys have experience in all aspects of complicated real estate transactions, as well as business transactions involving real estate, including representation of developers in the acquisition, zoning, financing and development of real estate in both local and multi-state transactions. The firm's Real Estate Group often acts as special counsel for the purpose of rendering opinions for borrowers and lenders in connection with complex financing transactions.

Tax & Estate Planning: The firm provides a wide range of tax services for individual clients and businesses and represents taxpayers in administrative and judicial proceedings. The firm counsels individuals and families on estate planning needs, assists fiduciaries in the administration of estates and trusts, counsels on many business succession planning issues, and assists clients in charitable planning.

SOMMER BARNARD
ATTORNEYS, PC

WALLACK SOMERS & HAAS P.C.

THE FIRM

Senior Partners: Barry Z Wallack
George W Somers
Karl P Haas

Number of partners: 5
Number of other lawyers: 2

AREAS OF PRACTICE:

Commercial Real Estate Development 40%
Municipal Redevelopment 25%
Commercial Leasing 15%
Commercial Real Estate Lending 15%
Commercial Real Estate Litigation 5%

FIRM OVERVIEW: Wallack Somers & Haas, P.C. is an Indianapolis, Indiana-based boutique law firm concentrating its practice in all aspects of commercial real estate development, leasing, and financing. Comprised of experienced and innovative attorneys, the firm provides legal advice to local, regional and national clients.

MAIN AREAS OF PRACTICE:

Commercial Real Estate Development: The firm's attorneys have extensive experience in assisting commercial real estate developers in achieving their goals, including the development and redevelopment of shopping malls, retail centers, business campuses, industrial facilities, hotels, sports centers, office buildings and multi-family housing.
Municipal Redevelopment: The firm has an established municipal redevelopment practice, focusing on the unique requirements of urban and suburban mixed, public/private redevelopment projects.
Commercial Leasing: The firm represents both landlords and tenants in office, retail and industrial leasing.
Commercial Real Estate Lending: The firm represents local and national borrowers and lenders for construction and permanent lending, tax credit transactions, mezzanine financing, syndications and securitized lending.
Commercial Real Estate Litigation: The firm acts as counsel to clients in a limited array of commercial real estate disputes, including landlord-tenant disputes and mechanic's liens.

CLIENTS: The firm's clients include a publicly-traded REIT, commercial banks, insurance and other financial institutions, developers, landlords, tenants, non-profit organizations, municipal entities and individual entrepreneurs and investors.

HEAD OFFICE

INDIANA
One Indiana Square, Suite 1500, **Indianapolis**, IN 46204
Tel: 317 231 9000 **Fax:** 317 231 9900
Website: www.wshlaw.com

CONTACTS

Commercial Real Estate Development ....George W Somers
Municipal Redevelopment...Karl P Haas
Commercial Leasing ....Barry Z Wallack
Commercial Real Estate Lending ....Barry Z Wallack
Commercial Real Estate Litigation ....Michael S Wallack

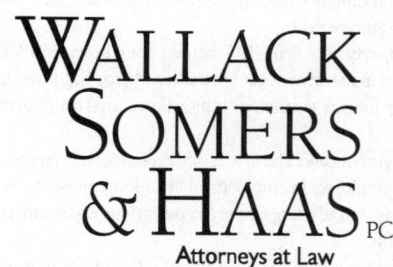

WALLACK
SOMERS
& HAAS PC
Attorneys at Law

WOODEN & MCLAUGHLIN, LLP

THE FIRM

Management Committee: Tom Dinwiddie
Dale Eikenberry
Tom Hanahan

Number of partners: 17
Number of other attorneys: 16

FIRM OVERVIEW: Founded in Indianapolis in 1970, Wooden & McLaughlin offers its clients a high level of experience, knowledge, and accessibility. It is a law firm that strives to exceed the commonly accepted standards of professionalism and client service. The phrase 'raising the bar' is used to describe this philosophy. The phrase 'raising the bar' embodies the philosophy that guides and motivates the lawyers at Wooden & McLaughlin. It is not about the firm's image, but about its identity. It is not a slogan, but a pledge. Most importantly, it is the clients' assurance that when they call Wooden & McLaughlin, they will receive legal representation that is thoughtful, professional, efficient, and, above all, effective.

MAIN AREAS OF PRACTICE:

Commercial Litigation: The firm's trial and litigation attorneys regularly handle all types of commercial litigation including: antitrust, business torts such as trade secrets, interference with business relations and fraud cases, contract disputes, employment matters, eminent domain, insurance matters, intellectual property, lease and mortgage matters, and professional liabilty.

Complex Environmental, Product Liability & Tort Litigation: A significant part of the firm's Litigation Practice includes matters in this area such as: aviation cases, environmental litigation, medical device cases and a wide variety of product liability cases.

Mass Tort Defense Litigation: A number of the firm's trial and litigation attorneys are known for their extensive involvement in defending mass tort claims including: asbestos, latex glove, and silica.

Corporate: Entity selection and formation, along with all possible operational advice needs; mergers and acquisitions; and tax.

Lender Finance: Documentation and negotiation of all types of real estate secured financings, including acquisition, construction, land development and permanent mortgage loans; documentation and negotiation of all types of commercial and asset-based financings; advise on current methods and alternatives in real estate financing and assisting in the structuring and documentation of real estate mortgages and other financing transactions.

Real Estate: Includes representing clients in development, construction, syndication, taxation, financing, leasing, condemnation, litigation, and zoning. Clients include local and regional retail, residential, commercial, and industrial real estate developers; state, regional and national financial institutions; real estate trade associations; architectural firms; general construction contractors; not-for-profit low income housing lenders; and real estate brokerage firms.

HEAD OFFICE

INDIANA
One Indiana Square, Suite 1800, **Indianapolis**, IN 46204
Tel: 317 639 6151   **Fax:** 317 639 6444

Website: www.woodmaclaw.com

CONTACTS

Commercial Litigation	John D Nell
Complex Environmental, Product Liability & Tort Litigation	Daniel D Trachtman
Mass Tort Defense Litigation	Douglas B King
Corporate	Kent M Broach
	Ronald G Salatich
Lender Finance	John W Hamilton
	Thomas M Hanahan
Real Estate	Thomas W Dinwiddie
	E Joseph Kremp

CLIENTS: AIG Aviation, Inc., American State Bank, Apartment Association of Indiana, Inc., AT&T, Barrett & Stokely, Inc., Bechtel Corporation, BP Products North America, Inc., CB Richard Ellis, CNA Insurance Companies, Comerica Bank, Cranfill & Company, CVS Pharmacy, Delphi Corporation, Delta Airlines, Inc., FCCI Insurance Group, Fifth Third Bank, Fleet Mortgage Corp., HP Products Corp., Hughes Group Incorporated, Huntington National Bank, Indiana Beer & Wine Distributors, Inc., Indiana Land Title Association, Indiana Mortgage Bankers, Inc., Indiana Soc. of Prof. Land Surveyors, Indiana University, Indianapolis Neighborhood Housing Partnership, Irwin Mortgage Corp., Irwin Union Corporation, J.C. Hart Company, Inc., Lauth Properties, Lucent Technologies, MED-MARC, Inc., Metropolitan Life Insurance Company, National Bank of Indianapolis, National City Trust, NiSource, Northrop Corporation, Olympia Partners Ltd., P/R Mortgage & Investment Corporation, Peabody Coal Co., Shiel Sexton Co., Inc., Terre Haute Regional Hospital, The May Department Stores Company, The Skinner & Broadbent Company, Trustcorp Mortgage Company, U.S. Aviation Insurance Group, U.S. Bank, United States Aviation Underwriters.

W&M

W O O D E N & M c L A U G H L I N LLP

Attorneys At Law

RAISING THE BAR ᔆᴹ

CONTENTS: Corporate/M&A p.802; Employment: p.804; Litigation: p.806; Real Estate p.809; Individuals' Profiles p.812; Firms' Profiles p.815.

How lawyers are ranked

The opinions we gather from clients — mainly from in-house lawyers but also from other purchasers of legal services — are balanced by opinions from colleagues and competitors. Together, they provide two different perspectives — an all-round view — and biased viewpoints cancel each other out.

CORPORATE/M&A

Iowa
Leading firms (Corporate/M&A)

1   **BELIN LAMSON MCCORMICK** *Des Moines*
    DAVIS, BROWN, KOEHN, SHORS *Des Moines*
    NYEMASTER, GOODE, VOIGTS *Des Moines*

2   **LANE & WATERMAN LLP** *Davenport*
    SHUTTLEWORTH & INGERSOLL PLC *Cedar Rapids*

3   **AHLERS & COONEY, PC** *Des Moines*
    BRADLEY & RILEY, PC *Cedar Rapids*
    BRADSHAW, FOWLER, PROCTOR *Des Moines*
    BROWN, WINICK, GRAVES, GROSS *Des Moines*
    MOYER & BERGMAN, PLC *Cedar Rapids*

Leading individuals (Corporate/M&A)

1   **HANSELL Edgar** *Nyemaster Goode*, Des Moines
    ZUMBACH Steven *Belin Lamson*, Des Moines

2   **CARROLL Frank** *Davis Brown*, Des Moines
    KRAMBECK James *Belin Lamson*, Des Moines
    NEUMANN Gordon *Nyemaster Goode*, Des Moines
    REASONER Carroll *Shuttleworth*, Cedar Rapids
    STREIT Gary *Shuttleworth & Ingersoll*, Cedar Rapids
    WATERMAN III Dana *Lane & Waterman*, Davenport

3   **ADAMS Garth** *Belin Lamson*, Des Moines
    BROWN Donald *Davis Brown*, Des Moines
    CORTESIO John *Bradshaw Fowler*, Des Moines
    DICKINSON Mark *Nyemaster Goode*, Des Moines
    SHORS John *Davis Brown*, Des Moines

4   **BERENSTEIN Marvin** *Berenstein Moore*, Sioux City
    BOYKEN Quentin *Belin Lamson*, Des Moines
    BROWN William *Brown Winick*, Des Moines
    GROSS Doug *Brown Winick*, Des Moines
    HINTZE John *Ahlers & Cooney*, Des Moines
    LAMSON Jeffrey *Belin Lamson*, Des Moines
    RILEY Byron *Bradley & Riley*, Cedar Rapids

Firms and individuals are listed alphabetically in each band.

Band 1

Belin Lamson McCormick Zumbach Flynn, PC

The Firm: With clients claiming that you "*cannot get better advice anywhere*" and that the firm "*exceeded high expectations*" to provide "*a sophistication you would expect from a much larger firm in a much larger city,*" this team again rises to the top of the market's estimation. With a client base encompassing local entrepreneurs, national operators and international corporations, an interdisciplinary approach (there are six CPAs in the corporate practice) has earned the firm involvement in several major transactions. Clients were particularly impressed with how the degree of connectivity of different departments maximized their expertise. Peers and clients further noted this "*top-notch*" firm's policy of recruiting only the "*best of the best.*"

The Lawyers: "*Top-league*" **Steven Zumbach**'s ability to "*see the bigger picture and get deals done*" was prized to such an extent that certain clients "*couldn't imagine doing a deal without him.*" Peers appreciated his combination of legal and financial expertise to provide "*the complete package*" of business advice. Zumbach and fellow partner **Garth Adams** acted for the seller on two major sales of Iowa businesses: Medicap Pharmacies, with 179 drugstores in 33 states, was acquired by Medicine Shoppe International while Color Converting Industries was sold to Siegwerk Group of Cologne, Germany. Adams won praise for his "*detail-focused nature.*" A vital part in the firm's "*well-oiled machine,*" his experience in the venture capital area marked him out as being "*on his way to the top.*" **Jim Krambeck** acted for Ruan Leasing, the truckleasing arm of Ruan Transportation Management Systems, in its sale to Ryder Systems. Peers singled out his advisory skills and noted that "*he brings a lot of experience to the table.*" "*Methodical*" **Quentin Boyken**, who also acted in the Ruan deal, enters the tables following commendation on his negotiation and organizational skills. Praised for being "*very practical in getting solutions worked out,*" **Jeffrey Lamson** completes the firm's roll call in the tables.

The Clients: National Travelers Life; Mid-America Group; R&R Realty Group; Meredith Corporation; EMCO Enterprises; AmerUs Life; Color Converting Industries and WestWind Partners.

Davis, Brown, Koehn, Shors & Roberts, PC

The Firm: This 28-strong group has a "*longstanding history of representing startup businesses*" and a knack for integrating its corporate practice with other areas of expertise including employment, real estate, IP and immigration. As a result, clients value a firm that "*brings all matters fully to our attention.*" The firm is a player on the national scene as well as representing a large number of Iowa-based entities in their general corporate business.

The Lawyers: **Frank Carroll** was praised by peers for his "*pioneering*" approach and for "*expanding the practice into developing areas of law.*" Clients noted his "*diligent, thorough*" nature, which enables him to "*assess all possible options.*" In the past year Carroll has represented Warren Frozen Foods in connection with the sale of its assets to a large public food company, and Metabolic Technology in the sale and licensing of certain of its technology to a large pharmaceutical company. He continues to work with venture capital fund tecTerra Food Capital Fund I on its investments and acquisitions. Carroll and colleague **Don Brown** have together been working on a $75 million debenture issue for FBL Financial Group. The "*intuitive*" Brown has also been involved in the $80 million sale of a retirement community in Florida, while continuing to represent families with respect to intergenerational transfers of wealth under the US estate and gift tax provisions. Peers noted that **John Shors** operates "*in the upper echelon*" of the business community, primarily in corporate tax and healthcare, although he has a strong presence in capital formation areas. He has been involved in tax matters and regulatory health work for Mercy Medical Center; he represents biologics companies; and also acted for the Iowa Capital Investment Corporation, which was awarded $100 million worth of state tax credits to invest in organizations intent on opening businesses in Iowa.

The Clients: Mercy Medical Center; Iowa Orthopaedic Center; Edge Technologies; Iowa Capital Investment Corporation; Warren Frozen Foods and tecTerra Food Capital Fund I.

Nyemaster, Goode, Voigts, West, Hansell & O'Brien, PC

The Firm: "*Strong top to bottom,*" this group of 28 attorneys continues to pick up top work. Assisted by a further nine attorneys in the tax practice, the firm has an impressive strength and depth of resources. It was further noted that the practice is "*well managed,*" allowing the "*vastly experienced and varied*" group to provide clients with advice in all corporate fields.

The Lawyers: "*Meticulous*" **Ed Hansell** has a wealth of experience, "*always knows what he is talking about*" and provides "*crisp advice.*" This "*encourages trust*" among both peers and clients and allows him to rise "*head and shoulders above the rest.*" Hansell both represents and is responsible for coordinating the firm's services for Wellmark. He also numbers other insurers and healthcare entities among his clients. "*Well-connected*" **Rick Neumann** attracted peers' attention for his involvement in the Iowa Capital Investment Board, while his own venture capital practice was described as "*influential.*" His expertise in the healthcare, insurance and construction industries, among others, is well recognized. **Mark Dickinson** is "*really starting to come through.*" His involvement in a number of complicated matters in the past twelve months, including an IPO raising about $90 million and the acquisition of World Insurance by his client American Republic Insurance, has impressed peers.

The Clients: Wellmark Blue Cross and Blue Shield; Meredith; American Republic Insurance; EMC Insurance Group; The Iowa Clinic; Hubbell Realty; The Waldinger Corporation; MidAmerican Energy Company; Alliant Energy and ING Groep.

Band 2

Lane & Waterman LLP

The Firm: Described as the "*go-to firm in the quad cities area*" and the "*dominant firm in Eastern Iowa,*" Lane & Waterman celebrates its 150th year of continuous partnership. Combining a traditional strength in advising startup businesses with an expanding biosciences practice, the firm's 25 business attorneys draw upon the "*deep resources*" of the rest of the firm in representing a strong base of local, regional and national clients.

The Lawyers: Clients praised "*problem solver*" **Dana Waterman** for his ability to "*put transactions together.*" Waterman represented Lee Enterprises on a number of matters, including compliance issues, small acquisitions and exchanges of property on a national basis. He also acts for Sears Manufacturing in its expan-

sion of production and distribution capacities in the Far East, and continues to represent a number of clients on business tax and succession planning. The past twelve months have seen Waterman involve himself in a number of nonprofit ventures in the local area, among them new museum projects.

The Clients: The firm is principal outside IP/IT counsel for Deere & Company. Other clients include: Ryan Companies US; Genesis Health System; Von Maur and Lee Enterprises.

Shuttleworth & Ingersoll PLC

The Firm: Plaudits for this "*long-established*" team include a widespread sentiment that they are the "*best firm in Cedar Rapids.*" The team undertakes the full range of corporate services, from business formation to aiding growth through financing, secured transactions and venture capital. Alongside this comes extensive experience in estate planning and the healthcare industry to provide a "*sophisticated*" package for a clientele that includes public and private companies, both local and statewide.

The Lawyers: **Carroll Reasoner**, the first and still the only female president of the Iowa Bar Association, was identified for her skills in the healthcare sector and in regard to the Uniform Commercial Code. Her enthusiasm for "*educating herself in new areas of law*" assists her practice of secured transactions for a number of banking institutions, including an $80 million financing for a consortium of banks. "*Deal-maker*" **Gary Streit** received enthusiastic acclaim for his estate planning work and was branded as "*the man for real estate.*" He is said to "*understand the full magnitude of any problem.*" His financial background assists in this, allowing an appreciation of both business and tax issues. Further recognition followed for his work on employee benefits.

The Clients: US Bank; McLeodUSA; Iowa Health System; Gazette Communications; The Quaker Oats Company; Federated Mutual Insurance; Fireman's Fund and PMX Industries.

Band 3

Ahlers & Cooney, PC

The Firm: Clients noted this team's history of bond work and "*fabulous reputation on municipal finance.*" A broad approach to public finance features the representation of cities, local councils and school boards, while state regulatory matters form another large part of the firm's workload.

The Lawyers: **John Hintze** is "*one of the pre-eminent corporate lawyers in Iowa*" according to clients, who regard his experience as general counsel of Pioneer Hi-Bred International from 1989 to 1994 as engendering Hintze with a client-focused mindset.

The Clients: State of Iowa Board of Regents;

Iowa Association of School Business Officials and Iowa Public Agency Investment Trust are among the clients.

Bradley & Riley, PC

The Firm: Although almost 25 years old, this firm is regarded as relatively youthful in the Iowa market, and is consequently viewed as a "*fast-emerging*" player on the corporate scene. From its offices in Cedar Rapids and Iowa City the firm provides advice to entrepreneurs, start-up entities and established businesses. Expertise is also offered in both the debt and equity markets, while the team is equally adept in the representation of lending institutions and venture capital funds.

The Lawyers: **Buck Riley** was identified as the leader of a strong team that is "*enjoyable to work with.*" Riley, "*a solid business counselor,*" is also noted for estate planning, probate and taxation work. Pat Courtney earned praise for possessing a "*very sharp mind,*" applied to his general business practice.

The Clients: Alliant Energy; Mount Mercy College; Heartland Inn; Merit Construction and MidAmerica Housing Partnership.

Bradshaw, Fowler, Proctor & Fairgrave, PC

The Firm: The 12 practitioners in the firm's business and corporate group are surrounded by expertise in everything from bankruptcy to real estate, not to mention the firm's renowned operations in the insurance defense field. As a result the team is well placed to provide advice on almost all aspects of transactional work.

The Lawyers: "*First-class*" **John Cortesio** is revered by the profession as a "*business lawyer par excellence.*" He is well known for his representation of physician groups in their corporate matters; however, he also nurtures a practice that includes the litigation of complex matters alongside trade regulation and transactional issues.

The Clients: The firm advises clients across the spectrum of healthcare entities and has a strong presence in the insurance market.

Brown, Winick, Graves, Gross, Baskerville and Schoenebaum PLC

See firm details p.815

The Firm: This increasingly "*well-connected*" firm possesses "*good breadth*" and advisory skills across a range of areas. With a foundation in tax law and grounding in raising capital for businesses, the firm has now branched out into emerging areas of law, notably including the representation of ethanol projects in the Midwest. Yet the basics are not neglected; over the past twelve months the practice has acted for a number of startup businesses and Fortune 500 companies, and was local counsel for national companies on a number of acquisitions and securities issues.

The Lawyers: As well as excelling in taxation issues, **Bill Brown** (see p.812) has a practice that rests on the planning of business transition to maintain key employees and arrangements, and a number of financing and refinancing deals. His involvement in Lisle's acquisition of all the capital stock of a medical equipment manufacturer extended to ensuring a successful transition and the resolution of cross-state tax issues. He represents a number of group foster care providers in a major audit dispute with the State of Iowa. The firm's managing partner, **Doug Gross** (see p.813), joins the tables. Competitors made it plain that Gross is a well-connected figure in the commercial world, particularly among financial institutions. He practices in a diverse array of matters from startups to general commercial transactions, and has gained a reputation for guiding technology companies through the early years of their existence.

The Clients: Lisle; EZ Way; Hagie Manufacturing; Stellar Industries; United Equipment Accessories; Coalition for Family and Children Services in Iowa; Iowa Small Business Coalition; Union Planters Bank; Iowa Capital Investment Board; Bailey Roofing Contractors; Visionary Systems; Clarinda Academy; Woodward Academy; Normative Services; Whitmore and Page County State Bank.

Moyer & Bergman, PLC

The Firm: Commanding respect across the state, this Cedar Rapids-based group of eight attorneys has experience in acting for all types of corporate entity, including partnerships and professional associations. The firm prides itself on offering an interwoven corporate service, which also includes advice on securities, tax and IP matters.

The Clients: American Family Insurance; CRST International; Ag Services of America; State Farm; TrueNorth Companies; Westfield Group and Great America Leasing.

Other Notable Practitioners

"*First-rate*" **Marvin Berenstein** of Berenstein, Moore, Berenstein, Heffernan & Moeller is "*the top guy in Western Iowa.*" A former president of the Iowa State Bar Association, he brings a wealth of experience to each instruction and acts for a number of high-profile local clients, from riverboats to school boards and healthcare institutions to the dairy industry. His encyclopedic knowledge of tax matters was felt to give him the edge.

EMPLOYMENT

MAINLY DEFENDANT

Iowa
Leading firms
(Employment: Mainly Defendant)
[1] **AHLERS & COONEY, PC** *Des Moines*
DICKINSON, MACKAMAN, TYLER *Des Moines*
NYEMASTER, GOODE, VOIGTS, WEST *Des Moines*
[2] **BELIN LAMSON MCCORMICK** *Des Moines*
BRADLEY & RILEY, PC *Cedar Rapids*
DAVIS, BROWN, KOEHN, SHORS *Des Moines*
SHUTTLEWORTH & INGERSOLL PLC *Cedar Rapids*
WHITFIELD & EDDY, PLC *Des Moines*
[3] **BRADSHAW, FOWLER, PROCTOR** *Des Moines*
SIMMONS PERRINE ALBRIGHT *Cedar Rapids*
Firms are listed alphabetically in each band.

Band 1

Ahlers & Cooney, PC

The Firm: This "*standout*" firm won praise for its "*practical*" approach to dealing with clients from both the private and public sectors. Eleven lawyers litigate virtually any kind of employment matter, drawing on the resources of the firm's equally exceptional litigation practice where necessary. Another crucial component of the service, however, is the provision of prevention programs, assistance in drafting disciplinary procedures and aid in internal investigations designed to avoid litigation entirely. Commentators were keen to remark upon the work the firm does for school districts. **The Lawyers:** Clients lavished praise on the "*no-nonsense, persistent*" **Elizabeth Kennedy**. Like peers, they seemed unable to find fault in her work, and were moved to describe her as

"*clearly the best*" and "*in the top echelon of employment law,*" with her "*crisp analysis*" and attention to detail marking her out. Kennedy divides her time between litigating wage and hour, harassment and other matters, and counseling clients on troublesome employment issues. Market observers also noted her experience in employment mediation. "*Quick study*" **Nathan Overberg** joins the tables as a man who's "*going to be a big player.*" Peers lauded his determination and presentation skills. Overberg spends the majority of his time litigating the full gamut of employment issues, and has enjoyed "*great success,*" particularly in the federal court. **The Clients:** Clients include both public and private sector employers.

Dickinson, Mackaman, Tyler & Hagen, P.C.

The Firm: The eight "*top-notch*" attorneys at this firm attract a broad base of work from the manufacturing, banking and medical sectors among others. Ample FMLA experience and recent involvement in difficulties raised by the returning military are coupled with a thriving traditional labor practice that represents a number of Iowa associations. **The Lawyers:** **Helen Adams**, armed with "*an outstanding base of knowledge,*" gained the respect of clients through her ability to "*reduce legal jargon to layman's terms.*" In turn she is felt by peers to be "*very well respected by the federal judiciary.*" Her time is divided between litigation and preventive advice; in the latter sphere, her ability to "*keep up to speed*" makes her a "*valuable resource*" in drafting contracts and manuals

as well as training management. Adams' knowledge of the FMLA and drug testing litigation received particular acknowledgement. "*Savvy*" **Russell Samson** was endorsed for his labor practice, where his collective bargaining skills make him a "*go-to specialist.*" His ability to relate with clients was seen as a distinguishing feature by interviewees. **The Clients:** Clients include trade industry associations and companies, predominantly in manufacturing, banking and the health sector.

Nyemaster, Goode, Voigts, West, Hansell & O'Brien, PC

The Firm: Recognized as Iowa's largest employment practice, this "*sophisticated*" team has "*phenomenal strength in depth*" and represents "*high-quality clientele*" in the public and private sectors. All areas of labor and employment law are handled: union-organizing campaigns, labor negotiations, hearings and employment litigation including unfair labor practices, discrimination and wrongful discharge. Ominously for competitors, the practice continues to grow in size.

The Lawyers: The "*seasoned*" and "*street smart*" **Frank Harty** "*knows what makes people tick, and knows what makes for an effective argument in front of a judge and jury,*" claimed clients. His "*focused*" legal advice puts him "*among the best in Iowa.*" Harty has a large amount of courtroom experience and has been involved in several jury trials involving harassment and discrimination claims in the past twelve months. He is also prominent in the legislative arena and takes on collective bargaining

Iowa
Leading individuals
(Employment: Mainly Defendant)
[1] ADAMS Helen *Dickinson Mackaman*, Des Moines
BAIER Kelly *Bradley & Riley*, Cedar Rapids
HARTY Frank *Nyemaster Goode*, Des Moines
KENNEDY Elizabeth *Ahlers & Cooney*, Des Moines
SWANGER James *Belin Lamson*, Des Moines
ZAIGER Mark *Shuttleworth & Ingersoll*, Cedar Rapids
[2] FOLEY Thomas *Nyemaster Goode*, Des Moines
LA SUER Gene *Davis Brown*, Des Moines
MUCHMORE Iris *Simmons Perrine*, Cedar Rapids
SAMSON Russell *Dickinson Mackaman*, Des Moines
SAMUELSON Jaki *Whitfield & Eddy*, Des Moines
THARNISH Deborah *Davis Brown*, Des Moines
[3] CUNNINGHAM Thomas *Nyemaster*, Des Moines
FISCHER Gordon *Bradshaw Fowler*, Des Moines
MALHEIRO Sharon *Davis Brown*, Des Moines
NAYLER Greg *Whitfield & Eddy*, Des Moines
RECK Michael *Belin Lamson*, Des Moines
Up-and-coming individuals
ARMENTRAUD Randall *Nyemaster*, Des Moines
OVERBERG Nathan *Ahlers & Cooney*, Des Moines
Individuals are listed alphabetically in each band.

work. **Tom Foley**'s "*ability to make good judgments*" in a complex practice that focuses on workplace-related trade secret and unfair competition litigation enhances his reputation. **Tom Cunningham** joined the firm early in 2004 and acts for a number of entities across the north-central part of the USA. Recently he has worked for the construction industry and other employers with occupational safety concerns. "*Hard-working*" **Randall Armentraud** joins the tables following comment that he is "*coming up strong*" in his extensive practice.

The Clients: The firm acts for local and national companies, including Deere & Company and Chubb Group, as well as healthcare and public sector organizations.

Band 2

Belin Lamson McCormick Zumbach Flynn, PC
The Firm: Work continues to flow for this "*dynamite*" firm because it has "*a passion for clients that is projected in their work.*" A strong labor law practice dealing with unfair labor practice representation cases, strike support and the negotiation of collective bargaining agreements, is matched by an employment expertise covering all aspects of litigation and a strategic approach to minimizing litigation through employee handbooks, seminars and other counseling. Among those attracted by this winning package are local companies as well as national and international employers with Iowa business interests.

The Lawyers: Among the "*excellent*" attorneys

here, clients praised the "*good cop, bad cop*" routine of **Jim Swanger** and new-to-the-tables **Michael Reck**. Swanger "*gets straight to the point*" in his traditional labor practice, where peers and clients appreciate his knowledge, patience and responsiveness. In addition to advising clients on the impact of the new FLSA overtime regulations, Swanger has negotiated two five-year collective bargaining agreements involving over 1000 employees, and successfully defeated union-organizing campaigns for his clients. "*Real tough advocate*" Reck "*is better prepared than any other attorney with whom I have been involved,*" claimed an excited client; another praised him for "*making you feel like the only person he is working with.*" The "*inspiring*" Reck litigates on the full spectrum of employment issues, and last year went before the Supreme Court in connection with a wrongful discharge, defamation and fraudulent misrepresentation claim against his client, which he successfully defended.

The Clients: The team represents clients from an array of industries.

Bradley & Riley, PC
The Firm: In the light of increased consciousness of rights law, the team of "*intelligent, hard-working*" individuals at this Iowa City and Cedar Rapids practice continues to grow. It acts primarily for management in traditional labor law matters, including a significant amount of collective bargaining, while maintaining a "*terrific*" reputation for all forms of employment litigation.

The Lawyers: "*Top-notch*" **Kelly Baier** emerged from interviewees' reports as a man of vast knowledge and experience with great "*people and trial skills.*" He is "*professional*" and "*credible*" and, crucially, "*prevails in significant cases.*" Baier undertakes a broad range of work, dividing his time equally between employment and collective bargaining. In the former he is a "*top-level*" litigator and assists in planning for businesses in transition. In the latter he is "*well prepared*" and involves himself directly and, if need be, on a day-to-day basis with clients.

The Clients: Woodward Communications; Alliant Energy; Kirkwood Community College and Chubb Group.

Davis, Brown, Koehn, Shors & Roberts, PC
The Firm: With a "*good grasp of the issues*" and "*the ability to come up with every last possibility,*" this firm is "*broad enough to deal with everything a client might need.*" The nine attorneys in the employment practice were highly regarded for their experience and broad client base, which allows them to deal with every conceivable employment issue. The group acts primarily for management in a vast array of industries, recently including a number of manufacturers at both factory and supervisory level.

The Lawyers: "*Well-respected*" **Gene La Suer** was said by clients to always be "*on top of things.*" La Suer defeated a union certification at a turkey processing plant with 750 workers, and avoided a potential ERISA claim of $20 million. In the past year he has been more heavily involved in wage and hour class actions. **Deborah Tharnish**'s "*good instincts*" and "*ability to reassure*" impressed clients. Tharnish splits her time equally between employment and general commercial litigation. She was involved in two Federal Court wrongful termination cases in the past year and acted on an ERISA case that involved complicated issues as to what changes may be made to deferred compensation plans. Peers respect her for "*focusing on the relevant issues.*" **Sharon Malheiro** adopts a 'prevention is better than cure' approach to her representation of clients, spending half her time training in the areas of harassment and diversity in the workplace. The remainder of her time is spent litigating, mainly in the discrimination area, where peers said that she "*knows when to try and when to settle.*"

Shuttleworth & Ingersoll PLC
The Firm: Peers judged this Cedar Rapids practice as being "*really plugged into the eastern Iowa community*" and stated that its lawyers "*bring good litigation to an area of law that they know all about.*" Predominantly, the practice acts for employers in the defense of work-related claims asserted by employees, including age and sex discrimination charges, sexual harassment claims, claims for employee benefits, breach of contract claims, and claims involving alleged violations of noncompete and trade secret covenants. The firm also represents employees seeking to protect their rights.

The Lawyers: "*Client-oriented*" **Mark Zaiger** is "*the guy to call in Cedar Rapids.*" His experience in the Supreme Court, particularly in the proprietary rights/noncompete area allowed him to "*earn his stripes.*" This is a lawyer who is not afraid to tell clients "*what they need as well as what they want to hear.*" Zaiger's trial skills at both hearings and appellate level have earned the respect of his peers.

The Clients: Clients include AEGON USA and Amana Society, alongside local and national businesses.

Whitfield & Eddy, PLC
The Firm: This broad-based litigation practice offers several attorneys with experience in the employment arena and has benefited from lateral hires in the past year.

The Lawyers: A "*business-minded,*" "*articulate advocate,*" **Jaki Samuelson** was identified by peers for her ability to work towards a resolution "*rather than getting bogged down in detail.*" Her practice in the past year has included traditional discrimination cases, ERISA litigation, and employment law issues in the entertainment and retail sectors. **Greg Nayler**, who joined from Pingel & Templer, was rated by competitors as "*a very good trainer and educator in the employment area.*" His work concentrates on labor union work, and peers noted his collective bargaining expertise.

The Clients: Wells Fargo Bank; Iowa NA; American Equity Investment Life Insurance and Midwest Heritage Bank.

Band 3

Bradshaw, Fowler, Proctor & Fairgrave, PC

The Firm: The employment and labor practice group of this acclaimed litigation firm provides legal advice for employers on a number of concerns, including wrongful discharge, employment discrimination and labor law.

The Lawyers: Gordon Fischer was praised by colleagues for striking a balance between his knowledge of the law and his trial experience. His speaking and writing also earned kudos among his peer group.

Simmons Perrine Albright & Ellwood PLC

The Firm: This Iowa City and Cedar Rapids-based practice undertakes an extensive labor law practice in both private and public sectors. This includes the negotiation and administration of collective bargaining agreements, arbitration of contract disputes, representation of clients in administrative and judicial proceedings involving claims of unlawful discrimination, unemployment compensation, occupational safety and health complaints, unfair labor practice charges, wrongful discharge claims and a variety of related personnel matters.

The Lawyers: "*Forthright*" **Iris Muchmore** is commended for her "*versatility*" and "*good judgment.*" She acts for both unions and management.

LITIGATION

GENERAL COMMERCIAL

Iowa
Leading firms
(Litigation: General Commercial)

1	**AHLERS & COONEY, PC** *Des Moines*
	LANE & WATERMAN LLP *Davenport*
2	**BELIN LAMSON MCCORMICK** *Des Moines*
	NYEMASTER, GOODE, VOIGTS, WEST *Des Moines*
3	**BRADSHAW, FOWLER, PROCTOR** *Des Moines*
	FINLEY, ALT, SMITH, SCHARNBERG *Des Moines*
	SHUTTLEWORTH & INGERSOLL PLC *Cedar Rapids*
	WHITFIELD & EDDY, PLC *Des Moines*
4	**BRADLEY & RILEY, PC** *Cedar Rapids*
	BROWN, WINICK, GRAVES, GROSS *Des Moines*
	DAVIS, BROWN, KOEHN, SHORS *Des Moines*
	DICKINSON, MACKAMAN, TYLER *Des Moines*
	DUTTON, BRAUN, STAACK *Waterloo*
	ELDERKIN & PIRNIE PLC *Cedar Rapids*
	HANSEN, MCCLINTOCK & RILEY *Des Moines*
	SIMMONS PERRINE ALBRIGHT *Cedar Rapids*

Firms are listed alphabetically in each band.

Band 1

Ahlers & Cooney, PC

The Firm: Commentators praised this "*top-flight*" firm for its ability to "*cover all bases well*" and "*serve clients aggressively but professionally.*" This has led to a "*great track record in the courtroom.*" Reports of the large breadth and depth of the practice are borne out by the firm's involvement in disputes ranging from antitrust and trade regulation, bankruptcy and debtor/creditor matters, business law, contract interpretation and enforcement to corporate law and finance matters. This extensive general litigation practice is well supplemented by the firm's highly rated employment team.

The Lawyers: Rick Santi, a fellow of the American College of Trial Lawyers, was endorsed for his ability to "*make smart courtroom decisions*" through "*sound practical judgment.*" His overall breadth of experience most impressed interviewees, with one commenting that he "*knows everybody and everything.*" He was particularly applauded for his "*high-class*" work in the insurance and products liability fields. **Ed Remsburg**'s practice in the past year has included construction contract and antitrust disputes as well as employment litigation. He is admired for "*zealously representing his client without making the litigation unpleasant.*" His work for school districts was also noted by peers, who commended his particular desire to "*work towards a resolution.*" The "*courageous*" **Randall Stefani** has earned respect for his willingness to take "*cases which require effort*" and for his "*good people and jury skills,*" particularly in the PI field. "*Quietly effective*" **Wade Hauser** and **David Swinton** join the tables on the back of praise from both clients and peers. "*Methodical*" Swinton was noted for his ability to "*separate what is important from what is not important*" and for his "*polished*" advocacy. "*Versatile*" Hauser has a strong presence in banking litigation and noncompete work, and was hailed for being "*quick on his feet*" and for "*always getting a good grasp of the problem.*"

The Clients: The firm acts for local, national and international corporate clients.

Lane & Waterman LLP

The Firm: Branded "*the class of the quad cities area,*" this firm has a "*generations-long reputation for good quality.*" Time and again interviewees referred to the large talent pool of 20 litigation lawyers, which is backed by "*great support staff.*" The practice covers the full range of commercial litigation, representing, among others, the healthcare industry, hospital systems and Catholic dioceses. Peers claim that, whatever the sector, there is a huge resource of experience in handling big or complex litigation.

The Lawyers: "*Smart and confident*" **Bob Waterman** continues his "*standout*" medical malpractice work, including the representation of Genesis HealthCare System. His ability to "*marshal evidence*" and experience in the courtroom made an impression on peers. His reputation as "*a safe pair of hands*" was underlined by his retention by the Iowa Bar Association to counsel Iowa lawyers concerned about professional malpractice claims. Both he and the "*analytical*" **Thomas Waterman** were retained by Abbott Laboratories as state attorneys in the OxyContin painkiller litigation. In the past twelve months, Thomas Waterman has acted in trademark cases and PI litigation relating to lead paint hazards, and successfully defended an alderman of Davenport accused of slander, achieving both a summary dismissal and a subsequent affirmation of that dismissal at the Iowa Court of Appeals. Clients praised him for "*getting results.*" His activity in class action disputes and employment cases was also noted by interviewees.

The Clients: The practice advises a number of major media companies, railroads, manufacturers, retailers, financial institutions, utilities and contractors.

Band 2

Belin Lamson McCormick Zumbach Flynn, PC

The Firm: Pitched by one client as "*one of the highest quality firms we do business with, regardless of location; one of the best in the USA,*" the all-

All quotes in the text are from interviews with clients and competitors.

Iowa
Leading individuals
(Litigation: General Commercial)

Senior Statesman
ELDERKIN David *Elderkin & Pirnie*, Cedar Rapids
JAMES Dwight *The James Law Firm*, Des Moines
MCCLINTOCK John *Hansen McClintock*, Des Moines

[1] DUTTON David *Dutton Braun*, Waterloo
ROBY Patrick *Elderkin & Pirnie*, Cedar Rapids
SANTI Richard *Ahlers & Cooney*, Des Moines
SAPP Richard *Nyemaster Goode*, Des Moines
WATERMAN Thomas *Lane & Waterman*, Davenport
WATERMAN Robert *Lane & Waterman*, Davenport

[2] BROWN David *Hansen McClintock*, Des Moines
COLLINS Kevin *Shuttleworth*, Cedar Rapids
FANTER Robert *Whitfield & Eddy*, Des Moines
FIGENSHAW Michael *Bradshaw Fowler*, Des Moines
FINLEY Thomas *Finley Alt Smith*, Des Moines
HAYES James *Hayes Lorenzen*, Iowa City
HOUGHTON Robert *Shuttleworth*, Cedar Rapids
LEDERER Gregory *Simmons Perrine*, Cedar Rapids
MCCORMICK Mark *Belin Lamson*, Des Moines
PHIPPS David *Whitfield & Eddy*, Des Moines
REMSBURG Edward *Ahlers & Cooney*, Des Moines
STEFANI Randall *Ahlers & Cooney*, Des Moines

[3] APPEL Brent *Dickinson Mackaman*, Des Moines
BICKEL John *Shuttleworth & Ingersoll*, Cedar Rapids
COOK Guy *Grefe & Sidney*, Des Moines
CRITELLI Nicholas *Law Chambers*, Des Moines
DRAPER Hayward *Nyemaster Goode*, Des Moines
GAFFNEY Todd *Finley Alt Smith*, Des Moines
GUNDERSON Joseph *Gunderson Sharpe*, Des Moines
HAUSER III Wade *Ahlers & Cooney*, Des Moines
HILMES Jack *Finley Alt Smith*, Des Moines
MANSFIELD Edward *Belin Lamson*, Des Moines
SWINTON David *Ahlers & Cooney*, Des Moines
TANK David *Davis Brown*, Des Moines
THARNISH Deborah *Davis Brown*, Des Moines
THOMSON Don *Bradley & Riley*, Cedar Rapids
TRIPP Mark *Bradshaw Fowler*, Des Moines
WEINHARDT Mark *Belin Lamson*, Des Moines

Individuals are listed alphabetically in each band.

round pedigree of the firm only serves to enhance the position of its litigation practice. Peers readily acknowledge its "*strength in handling complex business litigation*." A team of 30 attorneys represents clients drawn by its dominant corporate practice and its particular strength in appellate matters. Without exception, interviewees across the state noted the tragic loss of Roger Stetson, who was ranked in the top band last year. **The Lawyers: Mark McCormick**, a former Supreme Court judge, is viewed by some as "*the foremost appellate practitioner in the state*." He appears before the Iowa Supreme Court on a monthly basis, and his work allowed one peer to claim that he is "*the smartest person who happens to be a lawyer that I've ever been around*." In the past year McCormick obtained a favorable rul-

ing from the Supreme Court in an equal protection challenge to the taxation of gambling entities in a case with more than $100 million at issue. He is also defending significant class actions, including one for Toyota USA and a multimillion-dollar dispute arising from the demutualization of the Principal Financial Group. The "*cerebral*" **Edward Mansfield**, "*capable of complex analysis at speed*" and retained by "*some of the most satisfied clients in the USA*," debuts in the table. Clients noted that he is an "*excellent advocate at hearings, trial and appellate level*" and were "*astonished*" at his preparation and quick-wittedness. With expertise in antitrust litigation, insurance/reinsurance and much more, Mansfield argued and won an insurance coverage dispute before the Iowa Supreme Court. He is awaiting a US Court of Appeals decision in an IP dispute in which the firm obtained a $38 million verdict for its client. **Mark Weinhardt** is applauded for being "*sensitive to clients' needs*," and according to those clients he is "*creative, responsive and understands what a client's long-term objectives are better than most*." Competitors say he "*keeps his eye on the ball and picks his fight carefully*." Weinhardt, who also has a notable white-collar crime practice, successfully defended Maytag against a claim of $14 million by a trademark licensee. He currently represents a major international investment bank in two lawsuits (each seeking damages in excess of $100 million) brought against multiple investment banks arising from the sale of Enron securities.
The Clients: Midwest Oilseeds; Mediacom; MidAmerican Energy Company; Unisys and Maytag.

Nyemaster, Goode, Voigts, West, Hansell & O'Brien, PC
The Firm: Accounting for almost half of Iowa's largest law firm, the litigation practice of 35 attorneys impressed interviewees with both its size and quality. A complement of "*good lawyers*" back up "*standout leaders*." Peers also commented on the regularity of the firm's involvement in "*top-rate*" litigation, across the full spectrum of contentious matters, although expertise in pharmaceutical, banking, trade secrets litigation and products liability were felt to be especially worthy of note.
The Lawyers: Richard Sapp "*knows the game*," and was described by clients as being "*astute on the issues and tremendously helpful in dissecting them to provide advice*." Known for his great expertise in the products liability area, Sapp is one of only two Iowa lawyers to have been elected to the national Product Liability Advisory Council. He represents many Fortune 500 companies in major products liability, commercial and intellectual property disputes in Iowa, including Deere & Company and Glaxo-SmithKline. Peers applaud Sapp for a "*superb*

job" in successfully challenging the constitutionality of the Governor of Iowa's line-item veto of a major economic bill in the Supreme Court. In the past year, he has also been involved in major pharmaceutical litigation for Aventis concerning hemophilia medication, which reached a successful conclusion before the Eight Circuit Court of Appeals. **Hayward Draper** joins the tables this year. Clients viewed him as "*a disciplined, persistent technician on the law*" who excels at "*translating complicated situations into comprehensible language*." His victories in complex banking litigation and representation of healthcare entities have not gone unnoticed by competitors.
The Clients: Clients include Fortune 500 companies, other large corporations and small local businesses.

Band 3

Bradshaw, Fowler, Proctor & Fairgrave, PC
The Firm: You can "*always count on a quality product*," claimed competitors of this well-established, 30-strong, "*mainstream*" practice. Primarily recommended for its insurance defense work, the firm concentrates heavily on litigation and is active in medical malpractice, products liability, environmental torts and asbestos litigation.
The Lawyers: Michael Figenshaw, characterized as "*one of the top names in the state*" for medical malpractice defense, has been involved in several trials representing both medical practitioners and hospitals in the past year. His trial skills and "*articulacy*" came in for particular praise from interviewees. **Mark Tripp** received attention for his "*good, sound judgment in the courtroom*" and for simply "*getting business done*" in a professional manner. His products liability work was strongly commended to researchers: he represents a number of Fortune 500 clients alongside his work for insurers. In addition, demonstrating his versatility, Tripp was involved in a wrongful death case for a construction manufacturer in North Dakota.
The Clients: Caterpillar; Employers Mutual Casualty; John Hancock Mutual Life Insurance; Wells Fargo Bank; Wells Fargo Home Mortgage and Auto-Owners Insurance.

Finley, Alt, Smith, Scharnberg, Craig, Hilmes & Gaffney PC
The Firm: At this 16-strong boutique specializing in litigation, all areas of dispute are covered; however, traditional areas of strength include medical malpractice, professional negligence claims and insurance-related matters. Its reputation in these areas is such that it receives a significant amount of referral work from firms in both New York and Chicago. The firm has been heavily involved in several of the landmark cases of the recent past, including the fallout from

Enron and a steady stream of tobacco and asbestos claims.

The Lawyers: **Tom Finley** registers as "*the medical malpractice czar*" for a number of his peers. His "*vintage reputation*" in the field belies a practice that is much wider, encompassing the full range of commercial litigation. Other members of the profession singled out vast experience in the courtroom as Finley's major asset. **Todd Gaffney** continues to impress other attorneys with his "*big picture understanding,*" particularly in relation to railroad and products liability litigation. His propensity to undertake the unusual was also commended. **Jack Hilmes** has a great "*presence*" and brings his "*impressive courtroom skills*" to bear on a number of malpractice cases involving medical professionals. **The Clients:** The firm defends both professional bodies and individuals in medical and legal spheres, and a wide range of clients from financial institutions to transportation companies.

Shuttleworth & Ingersoll PLC

The Firm: Harnessing the strength of the firm's business and intellectual property practice groups, the 40-strong litigation team has developed an enviable reputation in representing clients in everything from employment matters to licensing disputes. Alongside this is a growing strength in alternative dispute resolution, with a number of attorneys gaining recognition for their work in arbitration and mediation proceedings.

The Lawyers: "*Energetic*" **Bob Houghton** was praised for "*always being on top of things,*" and his experience in both the state and federal courts was highlighted to researchers. His expertise lies in both the medical malpractice and medical device litigation spheres, where he is felt to be suitably "*aggressive in defense of his client.*" **Kevin Collins**, who devotes more than a third of his practice to mediation and arbitration, was viewed as the "*standout among a pretty strong group*". Alongside a significant amount of bar association work, Collins was involved in a $20 million settlement of a claim against a manufacturer. On the personal injury front, Collins acted in a case involving the death of a young worker at a construction site, which reached a successful conclusion for his client. **John Bickel** has a broad-ranging practice, which in the past year has taken in construction litigation concerning a fire at the University of Iowa, licensing issues for a large media company, various insurance and employee disputes, and several PI cases.

The Clients: The team represents local and out-of-state businesses, including banks, insurers and companies including Gazette Communications and Oral-B Laboratories.

Whitfield & Eddy, PLC

The Firm: The 15 "*outstanding*" attorneys at this firm give such a good account of themselves in the courtroom that one competitor confessed that he feels he is "*up against a strong adversary when against them.*" Whitfield's litigation practice has broadened far beyond its traditional insurance base and is now noted for products liability, PI, IP, construction, professional malpractice and defamation among other areas.

The Lawyers: "*Top man*" **Bob Fanter**, one of only two Iowa lawyers to have been elected to the national Product Liability Advisory Council, is considered to be a leader in this arena. Fanter acts primarily for automobile and drug manufacturers; however, in the past year he has been involved in a dispute between a company in the Russian petrochemical industry and their former employees, which spanned a number of complex, interwoven disciplines including proprietary rights and IP. **David Phipps** received recommendations from clients for his "*common-sense approach,*" and from peers for his consummate professionalism, which he maintains in both state and federal courts. About half of his time is devoted to the representation of professionals, especially accountants, with the remainder including much general tort liability. In the past year, Phipps has become more involved in litigation concerning the Internet including a number of defamation and cyber-squatting issues.

The Clients: The firm represents clients from a broad array of fields including manufacturing, the professions and technology.

Band 4

Bradley & Riley, PC

The Firm: This youthful firm has a growing reputation in the litigation sector in the eastern half of Iowa. The litigation practice dovetails nicely with a strong employment practice to provide clients with a "*fair-minded, very effective*" resource for whatever contentious issue affects them.

The Lawyers: The "*creative*" and "*tenacious*" **Don Thomson** was singled out as the leading figure. His conscientious, "*thorough*" approach to general commercial and construction cases, whether at trial or appellate level, coupled with over ten years' experience as a mediator, make him a formidable force.

Brown, Winick, Graves, Gross, Baskerville and Schoenebaum PLC

See firm details p.815

The Firm: The 16 attorneys in the litigation practice of this large Des Moines firm were praised for "*knowing how to try cases to juries.*" This applies to an expansive litigation practice, which rests on both small and large disputes, with particular expertise concerning IP, employment and contractual issues.

The Lawyers: Although commentators identified no single star performer within the team, the weight of the firm's resources and the litigation team's links with the corporate arm of the firm ensure that the attorneys all "*understand business.*" They are involved both locally and nationally in arbitration and mediation as well as litigation matters. **Scott Long**, **Mike Dee** and **Rich Updegraff** were all seen to be undertaking major work.

Davis, Brown, Koehn, Shors & Roberts, PC

The Firm: Housed within one of the largest firms in Iowa, this litigation team acts both as a resource for clients attracted by the commercial prowess of the firm, and for a number of other clients attracted by a wealth of experience in several niche areas. According to peers, the 27 attorneys "*work their case effectively,*" whatever the matter at hand.

The Lawyers: "*Superb*" **David Tank** joins the tables following consistently solid client praise. About half of his time is taken up with patent litigation, for which he is known throughout the state, and as a result of which he has appeared before the Federal Court of Appeals several times. As part of his products liability practice, Tank is also Iowa counsel for American Home Products/Wyeth in defense of the diet drug Fen-Phen litigation. That representation has included the successful defense of a request for certification of a statewide class action and the disposition of over 75 individual cases. **Deborah Tharnish**, who is also recommended for employment law and is currently chair of the firm's litigation practice, has "*made her mark.*" Her work in the past year has included property tax assessment appeals, antitrust cases and coverage issues with Swiss Re.

The Clients: Clients include insurance companies, small businesses, professionals, US and foreign corporations, commercial banks, industrial companies, nonprofit organizations and educational institutions.

Dickinson, Mackaman, Tyler & Hagen, P.C.

The Firm: Active not only in Iowa but nationwide, this group of attorneys has "*the correct perspective*" and an "*awareness of the costs,*" according to satisfied clients. The team has experience in all areas from antitrust to zoning, and PI to insurance defense, and performs on all stages from appellate courts down to administrative entities. Clients noted the particularly strong link between the highly rated employment group and the litigation practice.

The Lawyers: The "*tenacious*" **Brent Appel** won the hearts of clients with his ability to correctly pick his battles and his "*understated competence,*" which ensures that he never "*overtries a case.*" His ability to relate to the Iowan juries as

All quotes in the text are from interviews with clients and competitors.

CHAMBERS USA 2005

Dutton, Braun, Staack & Hellman PLC

The Firm: At least half of the 16 attorneys in this long-established Waterloo practice are actively engaged in trial work. This consists of a mix of personal injury, medical malpractice and other professional negligence and, in the employment arena, workers' compensation issues.

The Lawyers: The acclaim reserved for "*bulldog*" **David Dutton** left researchers in no doubt as to his pedigree. He "*conveys confidence even if telling you about the weaknesses of your case*" reported clients, while his "*incredibly persistent*" and "*hard-working*" nature make him a "*more than worthy adversary*" and "*the man for tough, tough litigation.*" The breadth of his practice is staggering, encompassing (in the past twelve months alone) the representation of a municipality against a hospital corporation for their failure to keep the hospital viable, products liability issues involving motorcycle manufacturers, trade secrets litigation for the University of Iowa and PepsiCo, and a criminal case for a businessman accused of assault. If this were not enough, in the past year he has rendered expert opinions on behalf of other firms being sued on standard of care issues, and tried a PI case resulting from the collapse of an inflatable amusement.

The Clients: GE; PepsiCo; Sears Roebuck; Terex; Travelers Insurance; Kemper Insurance Companies; The Principal Financial Group and Farm Bureau Insurance.

Elderkin & Pirnie PLC

The Firm: This group of 15 lawyers is famed for its trial work across an array of commercial issues; however, peers noted a particular expertise in insurance and healthcare defense.

The Lawyers: **David Elderkin**, a "*legendary Iowa trial lawyer,*" was recommended to researchers for his role in the development of the profession throughout his long and distinguished career. He invokes a "*tremendous amount of respect*" from fellow attorneys, few of whom felt it appropriate to be described as his peer. Clearly one of a kind, **Patrick Roby** is "*totally at home in the courtroom.*" Peers speak of unforgettable performances from this "*star*" trial attorney, variously using terms such as "*physically imposing,*" "*powerful presentation*" and "*impressive and talented.*" His work in the insurance, healthcare and medical malpractice fields has established him firmly at the top of the Iowa legal scene.

The Clients: Cessna Aircraft Company, Mercy Medical Center and American Funeral Home are among the clients.

Hansen, McClintock & Riley

The Firm: The firm engages in a general trial practice, as it has done for over six decades. Seven lawyers handle all manner of disputes including professional negligence, insurance, administrative law, products liability, PI, workers' compensation, appellate practice, corporate and real estate law, probate and estates, and credit unions. The firm's practice extends to state and federal courts and administrative agencies.

The Lawyers: **John McClintock**, deemed "*a great communicator,*" was once more applauded for his involvement in the establishment of the Iowa Academy of Trial Lawyers. **David Brown** (see p.812) has earned "*about as much respect as anyone*" in the legal profession, and is renowned as the "*go-to guy for whatever is going on at Supreme Court level.*" His performance in the pressured medical malpractice sector, along with his PI practice and work for administrative bodies, resulted in plaudits from all quarters.

Simmons Perrine Albright & Ellwood P.L.C.

The Firm: Singled out by peers as having "*excellent individual trial lawyers,*" this Cedar Rapids-based firm continues to show steady growth in its litigation practice, which now boasts 20 lawyers. Primarily a defense firm, it handles almost every conceivable kind of case; however, it is frequently involved in PI, products liability and legal and medical malpractice suits.

The Lawyers: Competitors had enough faith in **Greg Lederer** to categorize him as "*the man to call when you've a problem.*" He spends more than half of his time on products liability work, including defending a brain injury case against Home Depot, where he was successful at both trial and appeal. Lederer was also recently named president elect of the International Association of Defense Counsel for 2005.

The Clients: Clients are local and national companies and include Wal-Mart.

Other Notable Practitioners

"*Class act*" **Dwight James** of The James Law Firm PC was thought to be so knowledgeable as to be named an unofficial "*dean of the trial Bar*" by peers. His commitment to the profession through work on several associations and committees and his efforts for plaintiffs in PI litigation have earned him enormous respect. **Jim Hayes** of Hayes Lorenzen Lawyers PLC was praised for his "*outstanding wins in tough cases,*" representing plaintiffs in PI litigation. "*Honorable*" and "*tenacious*" **Guy Cook** of Grefe & Sidney PLC enters the table following commendations for his commercial work at federal court level. **Nicholas Critelli** of Law Chambers Nicholas Critelli PC boasts a "*unique*" practice through his dual qualification as an English barrister and a US attorney. Critelli is "*one of the best advocates in the Midwest*" according to clients, and a "*results obtainer*" according to other attorneys. Clients recognized "*meticulous*" **Joe Gunderson** at Gunderson, Sharpe & Walke as "*a valuable resource in issues with complicated facts.*" His work for plaintiffs in all aspects of litigation was termed "*first rate.*"

REAL ESTATE

Band 1

Belin Lamson McCormick Zumbach Flynn, PC

The Firm: The market lavished praise on this six-strong team, for its "*large reach and depth of experienced real estate practitioners.*" It was especially admired for its focus on quality control and commitment to recruiting the best: "*They're very selective in who they bring in,*" said one interviewee. The group serves an impressive client base split between developers, financial institutions, contractors and individuals. It was particularly noted for its strong lender client base and is enjoying an increasing amount of retail development work. Its caseload spans the entire range of real estate work, including the acquisition of land, development, financing and maintenance of property. As local counsel for General Growth Properties, the firm oversaw the opening of Jordan Creek Town Center, and continues to be involved in zoning, land use and subdivision work for the project.

The Lawyers: Capable of guiding even the most self-reliant of clients and with a wealth of zoning experience, **Bill Bartine** won praise from developers for "*meeting everybody's needs.*" Said one, he always "*found a way on the hard issues*" and displayed an "*eagerness to get the deal done.*" "*You get no bullshit from him; you can count on

Iowa
Leading firms (Real Estate)

1 BELIN LAMSON MCCORMICK *Des Moines*
CONNOLLY, O'MALLEY, LILLIS *Des Moines*
NYEMASTER, GOODE, VOIGTS, WEST *Des Moines*

2 DAVIS, BROWN, KOEHN, SHORS *Des Moines*
LANE & WATERMAN LLP *Davenport*
SIMMONS PERRINE ALBRIGHT *Cedar Rapids*

3 BRADLEY & RILEY, PC *Cedar Rapids*
BRADSHAW, FOWLER, PROCTOR *Des Moines*
BROWN, WINICK, GRAVES, GROSS *Des Moines*
DICKINSON, MACKAMAN, TYLER *Des Moines*
MEARDON, SUEPPEL & DOWNER *Iowa City*
MOYER & BERGMAN, PLC *Cedar Rapids*
SHUTTLEWORTH & INGERSOLL PLC *Cedar Rapids*

Leading individuals (Real Estate)

1 BARTINE William *Belin Lamson, Des Moines*
DETTMANN David *Lane & Waterman, Davenport*
KUBICEK David *Simmons Perrine, Cedar Rapids*
LILLIS William *Connolly O'Malley, Des Moines*
SHARPE Jeremy *Belin Lamson, Des Moines*

2 COLACINO Antonio *Nyemaster Goode, Des Moines*
DOUGLAS Robert *Davis Brown, Des Moines*
ERICKSON David *Davis Brown, Des Moines*
HOLCOMB James *Bradshaw Fowler, Des Moines*
MOORE Dan *Berenstein Moore, Sioux City*
TYLER Paul *Dickinson Mackaman, Des Moines*

3 ANDEWEG Robert *Brown Winick, Des Moines*
LEFF Philip *Leff Haupert, Iowa City*
NELSON Stephen *Moyer & Bergman, Cedar Rapids*
POSE Christopher *Connolly O'Malley, Des Moines*
PROWELL William *Shuttleworth, Cedar Rapids*
SARCONE James *Belin Lamson, Des Moines*
SCHRAGE Russell *Nyemaster Goode, Des Moines*
SEYFER Greg *Bradley & Riley, Cedar Rapids*
SULLIVAN Jon *Dickinson Mackaman, Des Moines*

4 AUSTIN Brad *Nyemaster Goode, Des Moines*
CAMERON Streetar *Connolly O'Malley, Des Moines*
DOWNER Robert *Meardon Sueppel, Iowa City*
GREEN Mike *Brown Winick, Des Moines*
MCMENIMEN Dennis *Shuttleworth, Cedar Rapids*
MONSON Terry *Nyemaster Goode, Des Moines*
NEPPL William *Bradley & Riley, Cedar Rapids*
WINE James *Nyemaster Goode, Des Moines*

Up-and-coming individuals
HURLEY Cynthia *Bradshaw Fowler, Des Moines*

Firms and individuals are listed alphabetically in each band.

what he says," a competitor acknowledged. Bartine was responsible for the Jordan Creek project, and in the past year has been involved in a number of developments including a 75-acre shopping centre in Ames, an urbanism project in West Glen, and the relocation of the Science Center of Iowa. A typical remark on the extensive expertise and knowledge of **Jeremy Sharpe** is that "*he just knows what he is doing.*" He is well known for subdivision work for developers with large parcels of land that require mixed-use treatment. Sharpe's recent work has also includ-

ed a number of condominium developments, a golf course project and advice to both lenders and borrowers. As if this standalone work were not enough, he was heavily involved with the firm's corporate team on the sales of both Color Converting Industries and Des Moines trucking company Ruan. "*Very experienced*" **James Sarcone** has a strong presence in residential matters, where his foreclosure and relocation knowledge comes to the fore.

The Clients: Mid-America Group; Knapp Properties; GuideOne Insurance; Iowa Health System; General Growth Properties and Science Center of Iowa.

Connolly, O'Malley, Lillis, Hansen & Olson LLP

The Firm: With all eight of its attorneys practicing in this field, the market regards this "*close-knit,*" established firm as a real estate boutique. Peers speak enthusiastically of a "*detailed and extensive practice*" that is experienced in dealing with cities and governments for everything from rezoning to subdivisions. Indeed, they are seen by many as "*the go-to guys for zoning.*" The firm acts for a broad clientele including developers and retailers in an array of matters from transactions to condemnation proceedings and tax appeal work, in which they represent both landowners and assessors.

The Lawyers: **Bill Lillis** commands respect as the "*preeminent zoning attorney in the state.*" His years of experience, professional demeanor, good sense of detail and presentation style lend credence to this unofficial title, while his "*experience and reputation give his opinion weight and make bodies listen to him. He will get in front of the necessary people quickly.*" He is further admired because he is "*considerate of other counsel*" and "*keeps people in the loop.*" Known for his professional integrity, the ethical and trustworthy **Chris Pose** is gaining a reputation as the "*send man for zoning.*" Clients simply say, "*He understands what is important.*" His recent representation of statewide utility MidAmerican Energy Company involved work on the relocation of a service center, enabling a new courthouse building to be planned. Pose's involvement in environmental matters was also remarked upon. **Streetar Cameron**'s practice leans toward commercial development, mainly town houses and condominiums. Interviewees were impressed with his all-round affability, emphasis on client care, flexibility and experience in working with city councils.

The Clients: MidAmerican Energy Company; R&R Realty Group; Ronald W Cheney Revocable Trust and G&L Clothing.

Nyemaster, Goode, Voigts, West, Hansell & O'Brien, PC

The Firm: This practice, split between Des Moines and Ames, forms part of the largest law firm in Iowa. Clients regard lawyers here as reasonably priced, knowledgeable and "*very responsive.*" Their work comprises real estate exchanges, development, tax appeals, foreclosure matters, a large volume of loan financing and condominium conversions. Having "*cherry-picked*" established practitioners from elsewhere, the real estate practice is felt to be laden with good lawyers, and clients additionally noted the benefits of backup from other parts of this full-service firm.

The Lawyers: "*Easy to reach*" and with "*a good head for detail,*" **Tony Colacino** has 30 years of experience that enable him to operate at the top of the marketplace. The past twelve months have brought a significant number of acquisitions, sales and leases, as well as condemnation proceedings. In particular, he advised Wells Fargo in connection with its purchase of land from the City of West Des Moines for the development of a new corporate campus. Each year for several years, the firm has closed between 150 and 200 commercial mortgages, with a total annual loan volume in excess of £1 billion. This success is due in no small part to the following three individuals. **Russ Schrage** is "*just a top guy*" in the representation of lenders on commercial loans and mortgages, and is "*always looking to help improve things*" for clients and the profession itself. The "*influential*" **Jim Wine** won admiration for his work in the Des Moines metropolitan area, his grasp of municipal issues being viewed as his key asset. Competitors portrayed **Brad Austin** as a "*down-to-earth, thorough*" individual, crucial to the success of Nyemaster in complex commercial mortgage transactions. **Terry Monson**, meanwhile, is said to be "*a credit to the firm;*" he is involved with power and energy producers, and was especially noted for his involvement with wind farm developments.

The Clients: The firm represents independent power producers, pipeline companies, insurers, public utilities and real estate developers. Examples include EMC, City of Des Moines and GMAC Real Estate.

Band 2

Davis, Brown, Koehn, Shors & Roberts, PC

The Firm: The "*statewide exposure*" of this group of six attorneys prompted hearty recommendation from competitors, who again highlighted the firm's work in representing lenders, among them some of the largest mortgage companies in Iowa. Alongside a hefty slice of foreclosure work is a substantial body of advice to both residential and commercial developers,

810

All quotes in the text are from interviews with clients and competitors.

CHAMBERS USA 2005

and involvement in 1031 tax-deferred exchanges. The firm remains as general counsel to the Iowa Manufactured Housing Association and the Des Moines Metropolitan Planning Organization.

The Lawyers: David Erickson retains *"tireless energy"* and *"keeps his ear to the ground for changes in the law."* His visibility is enhanced through regular speaking engagements at seminars on case law updates, and peers have high regard, too, for his willingness to serve the professional community. Known mainly for his residential practice, Erickson has recently been involved for a large utility company in the acquisition of easement rights and parcels of land to facilitate the development of wind farms. He also possesses experience in dealing with nuisance claims. Being both *"hard-working"* and *"a very good technician,"* **Bob Douglas** has a number of well-satisfied clients and continues to receive admiration from peers for his *"overall knowledge and expertise."* His work for the Mercy Medical Center, his notable residential practice and his representation of a cross-section of clients in the lending and banking sector all prompted favorable comments.

The Clients: Iowa Manufactured Housing Association, Wells Fargo Mortgage and Des Moines Metropolitan Planning Organization are among the firm's clients.

Lane & Waterman LLP

The Firm: This Davenport-based group of *"excellent attorneys"* received attention for its work in both Iowa and Illinois, where the 150-year-old firm has a second office in Rock Island. The firm has been busy of late, acting for a number of well-known clients including Alcoa Employees & Community Credit Union. It has been active in the renovation and redevelopment of the old Red Stone department store, and the construction of the Mississippi Plaza, the first new office building in downtown Davenport for 20 years.

The Lawyers: The *"classy"* **David Dettman** has his *"finger on the pulse of what's going on in the state."* Equally well known for his role in the modernization of legal practices as for his client-facing activities, Dettman has been the chairman of a special committee with the remit of improving the electronic filing of real estate documents. The comments of peers point to a lawyer who is blessed with ample common sense and leadership skills. Equally impressive is *"his strong desire to achieve clients' objectives."* Dettman has acted on a number of development projects in the past year, as well as a great deal of subdivision work. He represents owners associations on matters involving their condominium blocks, seeing a project right through from acquisition of land to transfer of ownership to new tenants.

The Clients: Russell Construction; Quad City Bank & Trust; Deere & Company; Sears Manufacturing; Farm Bureau Mutual Insurance and Verizon Wireless.

Simmons Perrine Albright & Ellwood PLC

The Firm: This firm broadly divides its attorneys into business and litigation groups. A key component of the former is a burgeoning real estate practice, which operates in Iowa City and Cedar Rapids. The firm's real estate capabilities can be viewed as either stand-alone or as a part of a full-service corporate practice.

The Lawyers: David Kubicek *"would make any dream team of real estate practitioners."* His involvement in the Title Standards Committee of the Iowa Bar Association has only enhanced his reputation as an expert in title and foreclosure work. This reputation had already been built on three decades of *"meticulous and detailed"* work.

The Clients: The firm represents residential and commercial real estate developers, landlords and tenants, real estate brokers and property managers, and various mortgage lenders.

Band 3

Bradley & Riley, PC

The Firm: Operating from both Cedar Rapids, and a newly opened base in Iowa City, this expanding practice offers a full range of real estate advice from financing and development to sales and Section 1031 tax-deferred exchanges. The team received favorable comment for its reasonable approach and *"emphasis on getting deals done;"* in other words, for *"seeing the forest not the trees."*

The Lawyers: The *"experienced"* **Greg Seyfer** *"solves problems quickly and efficiently."* Residential development and subdivision projects take up the lion's share of his time, and he has been involved in almost 20 such projects in the past year. Much of the balance of his work pertains to commercial condominium development, which has included a $10 million development for a bank. Seen as both *"knowledgeable"* and *"responsive,"* **Bill Neppl** joins the tables as a result of favorable comment for his development practice.

The Clients: Clients include Guaranty Bank and Trust Company, United Fire & Casualty Company and McLeodUSA.

Bradshaw, Fowler, Proctor & Fairgrave, PC

The Firm: It may not be the largest real estate team in the state but this nine-strong group of attorneys includes, according to one commentator, *"some of my favorite lawyers."* The group represents clients on a local and national basis, and is applauded for its intelligence and adherence to principles of fairness.

The Lawyers: The group's reputation is embodied in **Jim Holcomb**, who carries 30 years of experience and knowledge with him to each transaction. His representation of the Principal Financial Group, the largest employer in Iowa, in sales and acquisitions nationally won great admiration. **Cynthia Hurley** joins the table for her work alongside Holcomb for PFG, and as a result of praise for her growing experience in the estate planning market.

The Clients: AmerUs Leasing; Earlham Savings Bank; Wells Fargo and the Principal Financial Group.

Brown, Winick, Graves, Gross, Baskerville and Schoenebaum PLC

See firm details p.815

The Firm: This team of seven broadly divides its endeavors between development work, transactions involving the acquisition or sale of property, real estate financing and real estate-related litigation. The firm also has significant experience of both tax assessment and land use issues, including environmental matters.

The Lawyers: Bob Andeweg (see p.812) rises in the tables after interviewees confirmed their respect for his development work. He acted on the purchase of an apartment complex in Des Moines for $23 million, as well as a number of redevelopment projects around the city, and a large condemnation proceeding for one of his clients. Andeweg also devotes his time to contentious matters, including contested property tax cases. *"Wonderful communicator"* **Mike Green** (see p.813), who joined the firm in the past year, secured his position in the tables following interviewees' enthusiastic endorsement of his long-established and *"rock-solid"* development practice.

Dickinson, Mackaman, Tyler & Hagen, P.C.

The Firm: This team, with *"good depth,"* has extensive experience in all aspects of real estate. Market sources noted that particular expertise is to be found in both finance and development transactions, with the representation of creditors given emphasis. Development work has involved both the public and private sectors, and attorneys at the firm appear before all relevant authorities on zoning, planning and tax assessment matters.

The Lawyers: Paul Tyler has *"seen just about everything and solves the problem".* His work for Wells Fargo and other financing work secured favourable comment from peers who noted that Tyler has *"a lot of contacts"* and *"gets things done quickly."* **Jon Sullivan**'s academic prowess underlines peers' praise for his mortgage foreclosure work. He is a regular speaker in real estate seminars, where he is *"dedicated to improving the profession."*

The Clients: US Cellular; Des Moines Area

www.ChambersandPartners.com
All quotes in the text are from interviews with clients and competitors.
811

Association of Realtors; Hills Bank & Trust Company; Waukee State Bank; Wells Fargo Home Mortgage; Iowa State Savings Bank, Knoxville; Adventure Lands of America and Wells Fargo Bank Iowa.

Meardon, Sueppel & Downer

The Firm: This team of five has a diverse practice, incorporating the representation of buyers, sellers or lenders in connection with both commercial and residential matters. It is currently involved in a number of closings, condemnation work, and the representation of property owners in highway projects around the state, and is active in redevelopment and urban renewal projects.

The Lawyers: "*Multitalented*" **Bob Downer** was singled out as the key figure at this firm. Downer, "*an excellent business generalist,*" has been involved in a number of large projects in the past year, including zoning and development work, as well as the representation of property owners before local government bodies and subdivisions of a local and industrial nature. He acted on a $25 million expansion of a retirement home in Iowa City, which necessitated the acquisition of 15 properties, the vacation of a street, rezoning and significant involvement with the local council regarding site plans. He also represents the developer behind the $180 million Iowa Environmental/Education Project to be built on a brownfield site.

Moyer & Bergman, PLC

The Firm: This two-man pairing forms part of the firm's business and tax department and concentrates on development, condemnation, estate planning and tax work. Condominium development, tax-deferred exchanges and title examination account for much of its recent work.

The Lawyers: **Stephen Nelson** has experience of everything from landlord and tenant litigation to rezoning and subdivision. His work for local developers, especially in the condominium sector, takes up the majority of his time. Peers recognized his "*long experience*" and branded him "*one of the top guys in Cedar Rapids.*"

The Clients: Bankers Trust; Fauser Oil; First Financial Center; Great America Leasing; Omega Communications and State Farm.

Shuttleworth & Ingersoll PLC

The Firm: As part of what is for some "*the best firm in Cedar Rapids,*" the team of six "*well-respected*" practitioners have capability in all aspects of real estate. The team represents residential and commercial developers, landlords and tenants, farmers, real estate brokers, property managers, and various mortgage lenders.

The Lawyers: **William Prowell** has "*extensive knowledge of both the law and the local community*" underpinning his development and leasing practice. His work for developers is on both a local and national basis, and recently involved the sale of buildings in Nevada for $20 million

while acting for a franchise restaurant business. He also acts for Ryan Companies in their construction projects and maintains a zoning practice in the local area. "*Detail-oriented*" **Dennis McMenimen** carries out large amount of development work. He acts locally for public companies, and is involved in energy assets as far afield as Wyoming and Louisiana. He also represents investors who are involved in locating and acquiring properties marketed on the Internet.

The Clients: General Growth Management; Ryan Companies; Gazette Communications; US Bank; AEGON USA; Universal Underwriters Group and local Iowa developers.

Other Notable Practitioners

Dan Moore of Berenstein, Moore, Berenstein, Heffernan & Moeller "*dominates the western part of Iowa*" from his Sioux City-based practice. His title standards work was recognized by peers, who placed him "*top of the heap*" and had a high regard for his appreciation of the other party's needs and for his ability to see beyond minor difficulties. **Phil Leff** of Leff, Haupert, Traw & Willman LLP brings a wealth of academic knowledge to his Iowa City practice. Interviewees praised his subdivision expertise and commended him for being "*a true gentleman in the profession.*"

Leaders in Iowa

ADAMS, Garth
Belin Lamson McCormick Zumbach Flynn, PC, Des Moines 515 243 7100
Recommended in Corporate/M&A

ADAMS, Helen
Dickinson, Mackaman, Tyler & Hagen, P.C., Des Moines 515 244 2600
Recommended in Employment

ANDEWEG, Robert
Brown, Winick, Graves, Gross, Baskerville and Schoenebaum PLC, Des Moines 515 242 2438
rda@ialawyers.com
Recommended in Real Estate
Practice Areas: Extensive experience in all aspects of commercial real estate law, including: development and land use; tax assessment protests and eminent domain proceedings; acquisition, sale and financing of commercial real estate; and commercial leasing.
Prof. Memberships: Polk County, Iowa State (Member, Real Estate and Title Law Section) and American Bar Associations. Iowa and National CCIM (Certified Commercial Investment Member)

Chapters. All coursework completed for CCIM designation.
Career: Joined Brown, Winick in 1987; became Partner in 1992.
Publications: Note, 35 Drake Law Review 365, 1985-86; Case Note, 35 Drake Law Review 433, 1985-86.
Personal: Past Member of the City of Urbandale Planning & Zoning Commission, and currently serves on the City of Urbandale City Council.

APPEL, Brent
Dickinson, Mackaman, Tyler & Hagen, P.C., Des Moines 515 244 2600
Recommended in Litigation

ARMENTROUT, Randall
Nyemaster, Goode, West, Hansell, and O'Brien, Des Moines 515 283 3100
Recommended in Employment

AUSTIN, Brad
Nyemaster, Goode, West, Hansell, and O'Brien, Des Moines
515 283 3100
Recommended in Real Estate

BAIER, Kelly
Bradley & Riley, PC, Cedar Rapids
319 363 0101
Recommended in Employment

BARTINE, William
Belin Lamson McCormick Zumbach Flynn, PC, Des Moines 515 243 7100
Recommended in Real Estate

BERENSTEIN, Marvin
Berenstein, Moore, Berenstein, Heffernan & Moeller, Sioux City
712 252 0020
Recommended in Corporate/M&A

BICKEL, John
Shuttleworth & Ingersoll PLC, Cedar Rapids 319 365 9461
Recommended in Litigation

BOYKEN, Quentin
Belin Lamson McCormick Zumbach Flynn, PC, Des Moines 515 243 7100
Recommended in Corporate/M&A

BROWN, David
Hansen, McClintock & Riley, Des Moines 515 244 2141
Recommended in Litigation

BROWN, Donald
Davis, Brown, Koehn, Shors & Roberts, PC, Des Moines 515 288 2500
Recommended in Corporate/M&A

BROWN, William
Brown, Winick, Graves, Gross, Baskerville and Schoenebaum PLC, Des Moines 515 242 2412
brown@ialawyers.com
Recommended in Corporate/M&A
Practice Areas: Vice Chair of Brown, Winick, Graves, Gross, Baskerville & Schoenebaum, PLC. Focuses on a corporate transactional and business planning practice, concentrating on acquisitions, divestitures, capital formation, financing and tax planning. Also has been active in legislative matters affecting small business and has successfully lobbied for several business and tax initiatives benefiting closely held business.
Prof. Memberships: American Bar Association Section on Taxation, S Corporation Committee; Iowa State Bar Association, Tax Section Council.
Career: Has been active in a wide variety of civic leadership positions with

organizations such as the Iowa Association of Business and Industry, the Iowa Taxpayers Association, the Polk-Des Moines Taxpayers Association and the United Way of Central Iowa.
Publications: 'Evaluating a Subchapter S Conversion', 37 Drake Law Review 395, 1989.
Personal: BA with honors in psychology 1974, University of Iowa; JD with high distinction 1977, University of Iowa.

CAMERON, Streetar
Connolly, O'Malley, Lillis, Hansen & Olson LLP, Des Moines 515 234 8157
Recommended in Real Estate

CARROLL, Frank
Davis, Brown, Koehn, Shors & Roberts, PC, Des Moines 515 288 2500
Recommended in Corporate/M&A

COLACINO, Antonio
Nyemaster, Goode, West, Hansell, and O'Brien, Des Moines 515 283 3100
Recommended in Real Estate

COLLINS, Kevin
Shuttleworth & Ingersoll PLC, Cedar Rapids 319 365 9461
Recommended in Litigation

COOK, Guy
Grefe & Sidney, P.L.C., Des Moines 515 245 4300
Recommended in Litigation

CORTESIO, John
Bradshaw, Fowler, Proctor & Fairgrave, PC, Des Moines 515 243 4191
Recommended in Corporate/M&A

CRITELLI, Nicholas
Law Chambers Nicholas Critelli PC, Des Moines 515 243 3122
Recommended in Litigation

CUNNINGHAM, Thomas
Nyemaster, Goode, West, Hansell, and O'Brien, Des Moines 515 283 3100
Recommended in Employment

DETTMANN, David
Lane & Waterman LLP, Davenport 563 324 3246
Recommended in Real Estate

DICKINSON, Mark
Nyemaster, Goode, West, Hansell, and O'Brien, Des Moines 515 283 3100
Recommended in Corporate/M&A

DOUGLAS, Robert
Davis, Brown, Koehn, Shors & Roberts, PC, Des Moines 515 288 2500
Recommended in Real Estate

DOWNER, Robert
Meardon, Sueppel & Downer, Iowa City 319 338 9222
Recommended in Real Estate

DRAPER, Hayward
Nyemaster, Goode, West, Hansell, and O'Brien, Des Moines 515 283 3100
Recommended in Litigation

DUTTON, David
Dutton, Braun, Staack & Hellman PLC, Waterloo 319 234 4471
Recommended in Litigation

ELDERKIN, David
Elderkin & Pirnie PLC, Cedar Rapids 319 362 2137
Recommended in Litigation

ERICKSON, David
Davis, Brown, Koehn, Shors & Roberts, PC, Des Moines 515 288 2500
Recommended in Real Estate

FANTER, Robert
Whitfield & Eddy, P.L.C, Des Moines 515 288 6041
Recommended in Litigation

FIGENSHAW, Michael
Bradshaw, Fowler, Proctor & Fairgrave, PC, Des Moines 515 243 4191
Recommended in Litigation

FINLEY, Thomas
Finley, Alt, Smith, Scharnberg, Craig, Hilmes & Gaffney PC, Des Moines 515 288 0145
Recommended in Litigation

FISCHER, Gordon
Bradshaw, Fowler, Proctor & Fairgrave, PC, Des Moines 515 243 4191
Recommended in Employment

FOLEY, Thomas
Nyemaster, Goode, West, Hansell, and O'Brien, Des Moines 515 283 3100
Recommended in Employment

GAFFNEY, Todd
Finley, Alt, Smith, Scharnberg, Craig, Hilmes & Gaffney PC, Des Moines 515 288 0145
Recommended in Litigation

GREEN, Mike
Brown, Winick, Graves, Gross, Baskerville and Schoenebaum PLC, Des Moines 515 242 2431
mgreen@ialawyers.com
Recommended in Real Estate
Practice Areas: Real estate and corporate transactional.
Prof. Memberships: American, Iowa and Polk County Iowa Bar Associations and respective sections.
Career: Concentrated practice in all aspects of the above areas from 1976 to present.

GROSS, Doug
Brown, Winick, Graves, Gross, Baskerville and Schoenebaum PLC, Des Moines 515 242 2410
gross@ialawyers.com
Recommended in Corporate/M&A
Prof. Memberships: United States District Court, Southern District of Iowa; American Bar Association; Iowa State Bar Association; Polk County Bar Association.
Career: Managing member of Brown, Winick, Graves, Gross, Baskerville & Schoenebaum, P.L.C.; Chief of Staff to Governor Terry Branstad; Director of

Business and Finance, Iowa State Board of Regents; Administrative Assistant to Governor Robert D. Ray; 2002 Republican nominee for Governor of Iowa.
Personal: BA, summa cum laude, Iowa Wesleyan College; Lydia C. Roberts fellow, Columbia University School of International Affairs; JD with honors, Drake University.

GUNDERSON, Joseph
Gunderson, Sharpe & Walke, Des Moines 515 288 0219
Recommended in Litigation

HANSELL, Edgar
Nyemaster, Goode, West, Hansell, and O'Brien, Des Moines 515 283 3100
Recommended in Corporate/M&A

HARTY, Frank
Nyemaster, Goode, West, Hansell, and O'Brien, Des Moines 515 283 3100
Recommended in Employment

HAUSER, Wade
Ahlers & Cooney PC, Des Moines 515 243 7611
Recommended in Litigation

HAYES, James
Hayes Lorenzen Lawyers PLC, Iowa City 319 887 3688
Recommended in Litigation

HILMES, Jack
Finley, Alt, Smith, Scharnberg, Craig, Hilmes & Gaffney PC, Des Moines 515 288 0145
Recommended in Litigation

HINTZE, John
Ahlers & Cooney PC, Des Moines 515 243 7611
Recommended in Corporate/M&A

HOLCOMB, James
Bradshaw, Fowler, Proctor & Fairgrave, PC, Des Moines 515 243 4191
Recommended in Real Estate

HOUGHTON, Robert
Shuttleworth & Ingersoll PLC, Cedar Rapids 319 365 9461
Recommended in Litigation

HURLEY, Cynthia
Bradshaw, Fowler, Proctor & Fairgrave, PC, Des Moines 515 243 4191
Recommended in Real Estate

JAMES, Dwight
The James Law Firm PC, Des Moines 515 246 8484
Recommended in Litigation

KENNEDY, Elizabeth
Ahlers & Cooney PC, Des Moines 515 243 7611
Recommended in Employment

KRAMBECK, James
Belin Lamson McCormick Zumbach Flynn, PC, Des Moines 515 243 7100
Recommended in Corporate/M&A

KUBICEK, David
Simmons Perrine Albright & Ellwood P.L.C., Cedar Rapids 319 366 7641
Recommended in Real Estate

LA SUER, Gene
Davis, Brown, Koehn, Shors & Roberts, PC, Des Moines 515 288 2500
Recommended in Employment

LAMSON, Jeffrey
Belin Lamson McCormick Zumbach Flynn, PC, Des Moines 515 243 7100
Recommended in Corporate/M&A

LEDERER, Gregory
Simmons Perrine Albright & Ellwood P.L.C., Cedar Rapids 319 366 7641
Recommended in Litigation

LEFF, Philip
Leff, Haupert, Traw & Willman LLP, Iowa City 319 338 7551
Recommended in Real Estate

LILLIS, William
Connolly, O'Malley, Lillis, Hansen & Olson LLP, Des Moines 515 234 8157
Recommended in Real Estate

MALHEIRO, Sharon
Davis, Brown, Koehn, Shors & Roberts, PC, Des Moines 515 288 2500
Recommended in Employment

MANSFIELD, Edward
Belin Lamson McCormick Zumbach Flynn, PC, Des Moines 515 243 7100
Recommended in Litigation

MCCLINTOCK, John
Hansen, McClintock & Riley, Des Moines 515 244 2141
Recommended in Litigation

MCCORMICK, Mark
Belin Lamson McCormick Zumbach Flynn, PC, Des Moines 515 243 7100
Recommended in Litigation

MCMENIMEN, Dennis
Shuttleworth & Ingersoll PLC, Cedar Rapids 319 365 9461
Recommended in Real Estate

MONSON, Terry
Nyemaster, Goode, West, Hansell, and O'Brien, Des Moines 515 283 3100
Recommended in Real Estate

MOORE, Dan
Berenstein, Moore, Berenstein, Heffernan & Moeller, Sioux City 712 252 0020
Recommended in Real Estate

MUCHMORE, Iris
Simmons Perrine Albright & Ellwood P.L.C., Cedar Rapids 319 366 7641
Recommended in Employment

NAYLER, Greg
Whitfield & Eddy, P.L.C, Des Moines 515 288 6041
Recommended in Employment

NELSON, Stephen
Moyer & Bergman, PLC, Cedar Rapids
319 366 7331
Recommended in Real Estate

NEPPL, William
Bradley & Riley, PC, Cedar Rapids
319 363 0101
Recommended in Real Estate

NEUMANN, Gordon
Nyemaster, Goode, West, Hansell, and
O'Brien, Des Moines
515 283 3100
Recommended in Corporate/M&A

OVERBERG, Nathan
Ahlers & Cooney PC, Des Moines
515 243 7611
Recommended in Employment

PHIPPS, David
Whitfield & Eddy, P.L.C, Des Moines
515 288 6041
Recommended in Litigation

POSE, Christopher
Connolly, O'Malley, Lillis, Hansen &
Olson LLP, Des Moines
515 234 8157
Recommended in Real Estate

PROWELL, William
Shuttleworth & Ingersoll PLC,
Cedar Rapids 319 365 9461
Recommended in Real Estate

REASONER, Carroll
Shuttleworth & Ingersoll PLC,
Cedar Rapids 319 365 9461
Recommended in Corporate/M&A

RECK, Michael
Belin Lamson McCormick Zumbach
Flynn, PC, Des Moines
515 243 7100
Recommended in Employment

REMSBURG, Edward
Ahlers & Cooney PC, Des Moines
515 243 7611
Recommended in Litigation

RILEY, Byron
Bradley & Riley, PC, Cedar Rapids
319 363 0101
Recommended in Corporate/M&A

ROBY, Patrick
Elderkin & Pirnie PLC, Cedar Rapids
319 362 2137
Recommended in Litigation

SAMSON, Russell
Dickinson, Mackaman, Tyler & Hagen,
P.C., Des Moines 515 244 2600
Recommended in Employment

SAMUELSON, Jaki
Whitfield & Eddy, P.L.C., Des Moines
515 288 6041
Recommended in Employment

SANTI, Richard
Ahlers & Cooney PC, Des Moines
515 243 7611
Recommended in Litigation

SAPP, Richard
Nyemaster, Goode, West, Hansell, and
O'Brien, Des Moines 515 283 3100
Recommended in Litigation

SARCONE, James
Belin Lamson McCormick Zumbach
Flynn, PC, Des Moines
515 243 7100
Recommended in Real Estate

SCHRAGE, Russell
Nyemaster, Goode, West, Hansell, and
O'Brien, Des Moines
515 283 3100
Recommended in Real Estate

SEYFER, Greg
Bradley & Riley, PC, Cedar Rapids
319 363 0101
Recommended in Real Estate

SHARPE, Jeremy
Belin Lamson McCormick Zumbach
Flynn, PC, Des Moines 515 243 7100
Recommended in Real Estate

SHORS, John
Davis, Brown, Koehn, Shors & Roberts,
PC, Des Moines 515 288 2500
Recommended in Corporate/M&A

STEFANI, Randall
Ahlers & Cooney PC, Des Moines
515 243 7611
Recommended in Litigation

STREIT, Gary
Shuttleworth & Ingersoll PLC, Cedar
Rapids 319 365 9461
Recommended in Corporate/M&A

SULLIVAN, Jon
Dickinson, Mackaman, Tyler & Hagen,
P.C., Des Moines 515 244 2600
Recommended in Real Estate

SWANGER, James
Belin Lamson McCormick Zumbach
Flynn, PC, Des Moines
515 243 7100
Recommended in Employment

SWINTON, David
Ahlers & Cooney PC, Des Moines
515 243 7611
Recommended in Litigation

TANK, David
Davis, Brown, Koehn, Shors & Roberts,
PC, Des Moines
515 288 2500
Recommended in Litigation

THARNISH, Deborah
Davis, Brown, Koehn, Shors & Roberts,
PC, Des Moines 515 288 2500
*Recommended in Employment,
Litigation*

THOMSON, Don
Bradley & Riley, PC, Cedar Rapids
319 363 0101
Recommended in Litigation

TRIPP, Mark
Bradshaw, Fowler, Proctor & Fairgrave,
PC, Des Moines 515 243 4191
Recommended in Litigation

TYLER, Paul
Dickinson, Mackaman, Tyler & Hagen,
P.C., Des Moines 515 244 2600
Recommended in Real Estate

WATERMAN, Thomas
Lane & Waterman LLP, Davenport
563 324 3246
Recommended in Litigation

WATERMAN, Dana
Lane & Waterman LLP, Davenport
563 324 3246
Recommended in Corporate/M&A

WATERMAN, Robert
Lane & Waterman LLP, Davenport
563 324 3246
Recommended in Litigation

WEINHARDT, Mark
Belin Lamson McCormick Zumbach
Flynn, PC, Des Moines 515 243 7100
Recommended in Litigation

WINE, James
Nyemaster, Goode, West, Hansell, and
O'Brien, Des Moines 515 283 3100
Recommended in Real Estate

ZAIGER, Mark
Shuttleworth & Ingersoll PLC,
Cedar Rapids 319 365 9461
Recommended in Employment

ZUMBACH, Steven
Belin Lamson McCormick Zumbach
Flynn, PC, Des Moines
515 243 7100
Recommended in Corporate/M&A

BROWN, WINICK, GRAVES, GROSS, BASKERVILLE & SCHOENEBAUM, P.L.C.

THE FIRM

Number of partners: 34
Number of other associates: 17

FIRM OVERVIEW: Founded in 1951, the firm offers a broad range of legal services to clients throughout Iowa, regionally and nationally. The firm's mission is to attract, retain and develop clients by providing effective and innovative solutions. The firm will provide a comprehensive range of legal services primarily to businesses, as well as to individuals in need of high quality legal services, inside and outside the state of Iowa.

MAIN AREAS OF PRACTICE:

Agribusiness: The firm serves trade associations, commodity producers, cooperatives, seed companies, genetic companies, chemical companies and biotech companies. The practice group assists clients navigating diverse federal, state and local issues such as entity organization, financing, securities laws, environmental compliance, corporate farming laws, contracts, mergers, acquisitions, joint ventures and estate and family business succession planning.

Construction Law: The firm provides legal advice and representation to everyone in the construction industry. The firm's representation includes bidding; document preparation; contract negotiation, formation and performance; warranty issues; OSHA compliance; liens; and litigation of claims and dispute resolution. The firm represents a number of construction-related trade associations in Iowa.

Corporate & Securities: The firm represents buyers, sellers and investors in mergers, acquisitions, business combinations, leverage buy-outs, ESOPs and recapitalizations. The firm advises clients regarding federal and state securities laws in connection with public offerings and private placements, annual and other periodic reports and proxy statements. The firm also advises borrowers, banks and other financial institutions on all aspects of lending transactions and various regulatory issues. The firm provides advice and consultation on choice of entity, joint venture arrangements and a wide variety of operational and strategic issues.

Employee Benefits: The firm assists clients with a wide range of benefit-related matters, including the design, establishment and maintenance of qualified retirement plans (including pension, profit sharing, ESOP and 401(k) plans).

Employment: The firm counsels both public and private employers on day-to-day employment issues such as discrimination in employment, termination and layoffs, wage and hour disputes, individual disciplinary problems, drug testing, employment and severance contracts, covenants not to compete and employee handbooks. The attorneys assist with compliance regarding a variety of state and federal laws such as workers compensation, occupational safety and health, wage and hour, and anti-discrimination statutes. The firm defends employers before a variety of local agencies, and federal and state courts, as well as representing employers in alternative dispute resolution proceedings, including mediation and arbitration.

Environmental: The firm assists clients in dealing with the wide variety of environmental challenges that face businesses and individuals. The group assists real estate developers attempting to develop industrial and commercial properties on former industrial sites and also provides advice to lenders, sellers and purchasers of industrial and commercial properties affected by potential environmental concerns. The firm provides counsel to regulated companies facing permit issues, audits, and superfund investigations and works with agricultural clients facing nuisance claims, air permitting and water permitting challenges.

Estate Planning/Retirement: The firm provides sophisticated estate and retirement planning advice, assisting clients with respect to wills; living trusts; life insurance trusts; irrevocable trusts; gifting programs; family limited partnerships; deferred compensation arrangements; gift and estate tax planning for retirement benefits; charitable planning and planning for the transition of a family or closely-held business. Members of the firm are also experienced in the administration of estates, conservatorships, and guardianships; and trust and estate litigation.

Governmental Relations: The firm represents business, agricultural and individual interests before the Iowa Legislature, the Governor's Office and numerous state, federal and local agencies and governmental subsidiaries. The firm's lobbying team of attorneys has considerable prior experience in all three branches of state government, as well as service in county and city government.

Health Law: The firm represents healthcare clients, including multi-hospital systems, community hospitals, nursing homes, physicians and physician groups. The group provides representation on a full range of health law issues, such as tax exemption, Certificate of Need, reimbursement, licensure and regulatory matters, fraud and abuse, managed care, mergers and acquisitions and physician relations.

Intellectual Property: The firm provides a range of intellectual property services and consultation pertaining to traditional copyright, trademark, patent and trade secret law. In addition, this group provides counsel on the developing e-commerce, internet and biotechnology law along with licensing and litigation expertise in all areas.

Litigation: The firm includes civil and commercial litigation in state and federal courts, appellate advocacy, arbitration/alternative dispute resolution, and administrative agency proceedings. This practice group covers a broad range of substantive areas including business torts, contracts, intellectual property, securities, employment, health care, real estate, environmental, agricultural and construction.

Real Estate: The firm provides a broad range of services to organizations and individuals who are in the business of purchasing, developing, managing, leasing and selling real estate. Clients retain the firm to guide them through the many title, environmental, land use and zoning issues involved in real estate transactions and to assist them in all legal areas relating to the utilization and management of their real property and improvements thereon, including but not limited to, taxation, tenant relations and governmental compliance.

Renewable Fuels: The firm is a leading provider of legal services to ethanol and biodiesel manufacturing companies throughout the Midwest. It develops capitalization and operating strategies for development-stage and functioning plants. The firm's reputation has resulted in assistance to dozens of ventures in nine states. It is an active member of the Renewable Fuels Association, and its lawyers are desired speakers of the industry's legal topics.

Tax: The firm provides federal, international, state and local tax consulting and routinely advises clients on tax issues related to business transactions, choice of entity, mergers, acquisitions, sales, and liquidations. The firm provides tax compliance services and represents clients before the IRS, state and local tax authorities, and in all courts.

HEAD OFFICE

IOWA
666 Grand Avenue, Suite 2000, **Des Moines**, IA 50309
Tel: 515 242 2400 **Fax:** 515 283 0231
Email: info@ialawyers.com
Website: www.ialawyers.com

BRANCH OFFICES

IOWA
616 Franklin Place, **Pella**, IA 50219
Tel: 641 628 4513 **Fax:** 641 628 8494

Regency West 5, 4500 Westown Parkway, Suite 277,
West Des Moines, IA 50266
Tel: 515 242 2400 **Fax:** 515 242 2448

CONTENTS: Corporate/M&A p.816; Employment p.817; Litigation p.819; Real Estate p.821; Individuals' Profiles p.823; Firms' Profiles p.826.

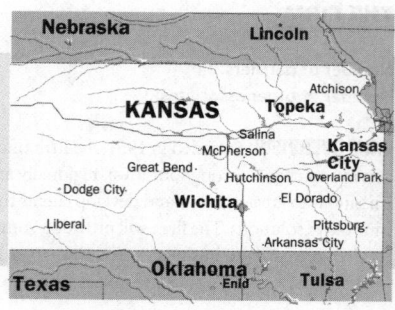

How lawyers are ranked

The opinions we gather from clients — mainly from in-house lawyers but also from other purchasers of legal services — are balanced by opinions from colleagues and competitors. Together, they provide two different perspectives — an all-round view — and biased viewpoints cancel each other out.

CORPORATE/M&A

Kansas
Leading firms (Corporate/M&A)

1 BLACKWELL SANDERS PEPER *Overland Park*
FOULSTON SIEFKIN LLP *Wichita*
STINSON MORRISON HECKER LLP *Overland Park*

2 FLEESON, GOOING, COULSON *Wichita*
LATHROP & GAGE LC *Overland Park*
POLSINELLI SHALTON WELTE *Overland Park*
SHOOK, HARDY & BACON LLP *Overland Park*
SHUGHART THOMSON *Overland Park*
TRIPLETT, WOOLF & GARRETSON LLC *Wichita*

Leading individuals (Corporate/M&A)

1 ADAMS Stephen *Blackwell Sanders*, Kansas City
ENGSTROM Eric *Fleeson Gooing*, Wichita
GARRETSON Thomas *Triplett Woolf*, Wichita
MARVIN Jack *Stinson Morrison*, Wichita
SORENSEN Harvey *Foulston Siefkin*, Wichita
SWAIN Lawrence *Shughart Thomson*, Overland Park

2 TRENKLE William *Foulston Siefkin*, Overland Park
TRIPLETT Thomas *Triplett Woolf*, Wichita
WOOD William *Foulston Siefkin*, Wichita

Firms and individuals are listed alphabetically in each band.

Band 1

Blackwell Sanders Peper Martin LLP
See firm details p.1062

The Firm: Although considered "*more of a force in Missouri,*" the corporate attorneys in Kansas have been "*particularly active over the last year.*" The corporate group at the Overland Park office in Kansas has a glittering record in the healthcare and real estate sectors and has really shown its class through involvement in some defining matters. These include the $500 million redevelopment plan for the revitalization of the downtown central headquarters of H&R Block and the $275 million IPO for Tortoise Energy Infrastructure. One of the group's greatest strengths is its ability to work cross-departmentally with other practitioners.

The Lawyers: Best known in and formally based in Kansas city, "*superb corporate attorney*"

Stephen Adams (see p.823) often divides his time between the Kansas City and Overland Park offices. Primarily representing hospitals, Adams is often seen working on healthcare joint ventures, M&A transactions and general commercial contracts. Also overlapping into real estate, Adams was recently involved in a complicated $35 million real estate financing for a public limited partnership.

The Clients: American Italian Pasta; MC Real Estate Services; Applebee's International; St. Luke's Health System; Audiovisual and Aquila.

Foulston Siefkin LLP
See firm details p.826

The Firm: This "*active business firm*" is the largest in Kansas and has more than 70 attorneys based in three offices in the state. This 23-member corporate team is "*home to some of the main players in the Kansas market*" and impressed commentators with its work for venture capitalists and family businesses. A definite leader in the field, it is "*very transactional in nature*" and has been involved in some quality work, such as private placements, securities transactions and M&A. With Kansas being the global leader in the production of general aviation aircraft, it is perhaps only natural that the firm is heavily involved in aircraft financing for some of the biggest names in the industry.

The Lawyers: "*Bright and fast transactional lawyer*" **Harvey Sorensen** (see p.824) continues to impress the market with his representation of entrepreneurs and family businesses. "*Not one to suffer fools gladly*" and "*a definite ideas guy,*" Sorensen works on taxation and M&A and gives general business advice. Last year he was appointed chair elect of World Services Group, a vast network of independent professional services firms and companies. Boasting a broad practice that encompasses real estate as well as M&A, securities, banking and franchising finance, **William Wood** (see p.825) debuts in the corporate tables this year. He acts as securities counsel to well-known public

companies and has represented three prominent franchise companies in the establishment of regional and national offerings during the year. Wood is the leader of the firm's general business group and comes highly recommended for his corporate governance advice and work for emerging businesses. "*One of the best,*" **William Trenkle** (see p.825) has also impressed onlookers. Trenkle has experience of securities, banking and business formation, although over the past few years he has been heavily involved with Nueterra Healthcare, one of the largest developers of surgical facilities in the USA. Trenkle has been doing "*a turnkey job*" on the building, licensing and operation of 50-plus new surgical facilities over the past four years.

The Clients: Nueterra Healthcare; Total Entertainment; American Restaurant Partners; LodgeWorks; Value Place; Bank of America and Boeing.

Stinson Morrison Hecker LLP
See firm details p.1069

The Firm: This firm is one of the largest, best-known corporate firms in the Midwest and is widely recommended by clients for "*the quality of its banking and corporate work*" in Kansas and Missouri. Particularly noted for its "*transactional expertise*" and "*ability to handle problem commercial loans,*" this five-member group is spread between offices in Overland Park and Wichita, from which it represents several banks and lenders. The quality of the team's real estate-related transactions was also noted. Last year the firm handled the refinancing of a gas producing company, representing the borrower in connection with the $180 million loan.

The Lawyers: Clients singled out **Jack Marvin** (see p.824) for his "*business, banking and bankruptcy knowledge, his practicality and his ability to look outside the box for alternative solutions.*" Counsel to a number of banks and financial institutions, Marvin has been heavily involved in the financing of many new hotel complexes throughout the USA.

The Clients: Commerce Bank; Central Bank and Trust; Haldex; Hillcrest Bank; Security Savings Bank and United Missouri Bank.

Band 2

Fleeson, Gooing, Coulson & Kitch, LLC

The Firm: Peers know this firm as "*one of the oldest and most prominent full-service law firms in Wichita.*" A midsized outfit, it is endorsed for its banking, bankruptcy and creditors' rights advice as well as M&A transactions. Attorneys represent some of the most familiar names in the world of banking and financial institutions. **The Lawyers:** "*Intellectual gentleman and Rhodes scholar*" **Eric Engstrom** has "*a fine reputation and a solid background.*" He was singled out for "*the quality of the bankruptcy and banking law aspects of his practice.*" Engstrom also counsels nonprofit entities on corporate and tax issues.

The Clients: American Airlines; Fidelity Bank; INTRUST Bank and Grant Thornton.

Lathrop & Gage LC

See firm details p.1064

The Firm: In the first nine months of 2004, Lathrop & Gage's corporate department was involved in transactions with an aggregate value of more than $4 billion. It serves as regional counsel to Fortune 500 companies and represents some of the largest companies in the Midwest. The Kansas corporate and general business group is home to about 12 attorneys and additionally acts for banks, commercial lenders and borrowers on the finance side. The Overland Park office was particularly commended for its "*effective handling*" of a variety of business issues, including litigation. Of the significant deals undertaken during the past year, the representation of a borrower in its $100 million secured 144A note offering is a particular highlight.

The Lawyers: Harry Wigner is a key partner in the Overland Park office. Lyle Pishny was also recommended to researchers for his tax experience and effective business planning.

The Clients: AMC Entertainment; AT&T; Bank of America; First National Bank; Butler

Manufacturing; Helena Chemical; Sprint; Time Warner Cable and The Zimmer Companies.

Polsinelli Shalton Welte Suelthaus (PSWS)

The Firm: Following its recent merger, this firm has since been named the second-fastest growing US law firm of 2004. It has two offices in Kansas and is intending to expand further. The firm has separate corporate finance, general corporate and nonprofit organizations practice groups, and acts as general counsel to more than 2000 companies throughout the Midwest, from large public companies to small and midsized regional ones. Clients recommend the attorneys for mainstream transactions and several allied areas – real estate development, partnership law and franchising and capital formations, to name a few.

The Lawyers: Stanley Woodworth is a key partner in the Overland Park office and chairs the firm's corporate finance group. His practice blends corporate finance and M&A with real estate development.

The Clients: The group represents all types of companies in industries as diverse as construction, retailing and telecom.

Shook, Hardy & Bacon LLP

See firm details p.1067

The Firm: Referred to by some peers as "*the dominant large firm,*" this international, old-line law firm has affirmed its presence in the state through "*the quality work of the Overland Park office.*" This office is home to 16 attorneys and maintains its high profile in terms of M&A, tax planning, general corporate and business litigation. The group's work in healthcare transactions and securities was also singled out for praise by clients.

The Lawyers: The key corporate contact at this firm is Bob Grossman. Also coming in for praise, Alson Martin coauthored the original Kansas Limited Liability Company Act and serves as general counsel for more than 300 privately owned businesses.

Shughart Thomson & Kilroy PC

See firm details p.1068

The Firm: This general business practice advises clients on corporate and business law, taxa-

tion and IP, and is home to "*some of the best-known names in the industry.*" The Overland Park office of this six-office firm has about 13 corporate attorneys and is described by clients as being "*excellent at everything.*" They applaud the team for being "*collegial and convivial,*" further commenting that "*it is enjoyable to work with – its attorneys are professional, knowledgeable and deserving of respect.*" The group works well in the healthcare industry and represents a number of hospitals and physicians on various corporate matters. Last year, for a credit card client, it handled a $68 million sale of a business to a publicly traded company.

The Lawyers: Clients highlight **Lawrence Swain** (see p.825) for his "*hard work, professionalism and willingness to go above and beyond the call of duty to always meet our expectations.*" Swain is managing partner of the Overland Park office, chair of the firm's business department and cochair of its IP and technology practice group. "*Always going that extra mile,*" he offers a general corporate practice with an emphasis in IP; he is thus seen as a good choice for technology companies.

The Clients: Associated Wholesale Grocers; Community Foundations of America; Black & Veatch; Encore Receivable Management; GEAR for Sports and Gill Studios.

Triplett, Woolf & Garretson LLC

The Firm: New to the corporate table for Kansas, this "*steadily growing*" Wichita firm has really impressed onlookers. As well as a business and corporate law group, the firm also has separate securities regulation, financing transactions, M&A and municipal finance teams. Approximately 15 attorneys spend a good deal of their time on business issues.

The Lawyers: **Thomas Garretson** is labeled "*one of the best business lawyers around.*" He practices in the areas of municipal finance and economic development, M&A, securities regulation and general business and corporate law. Handling M&A, tax and general business law issues, **Thomas Triplett** earns the accolade of "*one of the best tax lawyers around.*"

The Clients: Clients range from small entrepreneurial ventures through to large businesses with regional and national operations.

EMPLOYMENT

MAINLY DEFENDANT

Band 1

Foulston Siefkin LLP

See firm details p.826

The Firm: Viewed by other lawyers as "*always the prime competition*" and measured by its "*great results,*" Foulston Siefkin has a "*promi-*

nence in the market that is beyond question." The firm has separate employee benefits and ERISA groups as well as employment and labor practice groups, leading clients to remark on "*the excellent credentials*" of its attorneys. Specifically pinpointed for the strength of the employment litigation group, this firm also came in for

praise for its assistance to employers on OSHA investigations and OFCCP audits. The firm is deeply entrenched in the aircraft industry and represents some of its best-known names, including Boeing, for which it is handling three pending class actions. The firm has also been involved in some major union-organizing dri-

www.ChambersandPartners.com

All quotes in the text are from interviews with clients and competitors.

817

Kansas

Leading firms
(Employment: Mainly Defendant)

[1] **FOULSTON SIEFKIN LLP** *Wichita*
    KUTAK ROCK LLP *Wichita*
    MARTIN, PRINGLE, OLIVER, WALLACE *Wichita*

[2] **MARTIN & CHURCHILL** *Wichita*
    MORRIS, LAING, EVANS, BROCK *Wichita*
    STINSON MORRISON HECKER LLP *Wichita*

Leading individuals
(Employment: Mainly Defendant)

[1] **BABCOCK Kathleen** *Foulston Siefkin*, Wichita
    MANN Terry *Martin Pringle*, Wichita
    RUPE Alan *Kutak Rock*, Wichita
    STANLEY Douglas *Foulston Siefkin*, Wichita

[2] **CHURCHILL Stanley** *Martin & Churchill*, Wichita
    OVERMAN Robert *Morris Laing*, Wichita
    PETERSON Ken *Morris Laing*, Wichita
    SCHECK Stephanie *Stinson Morrison*, Wichita
    WORTH Diane *Morris Laing*, Wichita

[3] **HILL Donald** *Martin & Churchill*, Wichita
    MACKAY Douglas *Kutak Rock*, Wichita
    MCCLELLAN Roger *Martin Pringle*, Wichita

Up-and-coming individuals
    BAILEY Deena *Martin Pringle*, Wichita

Firms and individuals are listed alphabetically in each band.

---

ves, among them a steelworkers' contract negotiation.

The Lawyers: **Doug Stanley** (see p.824), who focuses on both employment and labor issues, is *"a quality practitioner with a down-to-earth style"* and a name associated with excellence. He has active involvement in traditional labor matters and counsels widely on employment discrimination. *"Kind, caring and rightly adored by clients,"* **Kathleen Babcock** (see p.823) continues to impress the market with her representation of public and private employers on all types of employment issue. She serves as general counsel to school districts and represents both schools and parents in special education litigation. One interviewee said: *"If I needed advice, I would call her for sure."*

The Clients: AT&T; Boeing; Cessna Aircraft Company; BAE Systems; Via Christi Health System; MEC and Coleman.

Kutak Rock LLP

The Firm: Since this *"multistate firm"* opened a Wichita office *"full of talented attorneys"* in 2003, it has impressed clients and peers in equal measure. The attorneys are experienced in defending employers in all types of litigation and are specifically recommended for their quality work in arbitration and alternative dispute resolution. A major coup for the team was being brought in to litigate a school finance lawsuit regarding children who were denied equal educational opportunities because of their race, disability or economic status. The Kansas Supreme Court recently declared state school funding inadequate and asked lawmakers to come up with a plan to add new money for K-12 education. The 18-strong team also acted on the defense of a race discrimination retaliation case that involved a public policy exception under Ohio law on the amount of damages that could be recovered.

The Lawyers: The arrival of **Alan Rupe** and his team in 2003 considerably boosted the profile of the firm. As managing partner, this *"warrior"* is admired for *"his relentless approach to cases"* and excellent record of success in the courtroom. He specializes in all types of employment discrimination and wrongful discharge claim and has a subspecialty in whistle-blowing cases. Rupe was lead counsel on the above-mentioned educational opportunities case and is a respected author. Also garnering his fair share of client praise is former public defender and *"quality counselor"* **Doug Mackay**, who is heavily involved in employment litigation. Mackay has a *"glowing national practice"* and is often found defending major corporations in federal and state courts throughout the country. He is said to excel at devising the best possible game plan for a problem.

The Clients: Schwan's Food Services; Schools for Fair Funding; Fidelity Bank and Blue Cross Blue Shield of Kansas.

Martin, Pringle, Oliver, Wallace & Bauer, L.L.P.

The Firm: This *"real strong firm,"* one of the largest in Kansas, offers legal services in Wichita and Overland Park. It is noted for its *"sheer amount of well-respected, knowledgeable attorneys"* and is considered the perfect fit for small to mid-sized companies. Traditionally strong on employment discrimination, it earned positive feedback for advice on workers' compensation and labor arbitration. Wichita is widely considered the hub of the aircraft industry and the group represents some of the biggest employers in this field, among them Raytheon Aircraft. It also comes highly recommended for FMLA work.

The Lawyers: **Terry Mann** moves up the table this year having caught the attention of clients through her *"excellent rapport"* and *"expansive reputation."* Primarily an employment discrimination defense attorney, she is deeply immersed in the aircraft industry and universally *"gets top marks"* from those with knowledge of her work. **Roger McClellan** also has a *"great reputation in the field"* and focuses his practice on employment and other types of commercial litigation. McClellan has been involved in a lot of FMLA cases of late. Making her debut as an up-and-comer is **Deena Bailey**. Described as *"very knowledgeable,"* Bailey is primarily an employment litigator, though she also takes on civil litigation. She is definitely an associate to watch.

The Clients: Raytheon Aircraft; AIG; Abercrombie RTD; Aladdin Petroleum; Lloyd's; American Investment Bank; Backwoods Equipment and Wichita Iron and Metals.

Band 2

Martin & Churchill Chartered

The Firm: This *"strong traditional labor law firm"* earned market endorsement for its advice to employers on union contracts, union strike avoidance campaigns and mergers with nonunionized companies. While it mostly undertakes traditional labor law, it also handles such employment issues as workers' compensation. It has a prolific caseload in the construction, manufacturing and healthcare industries.

The Lawyers: This group is home to a couple of the real stars of the state, **Stanley Churchill** being one of them. Widely considered *"one of the best counselors in Wichita,"* he is honored by the title *"everybody's mentor."* *"Well-respected"* **Donald Hill** was widely complimented for *"never failing to do a good job."* He practices both labor and employment law.

The Clients: Presbyterian Manors of Mid-America and Bombardier Learjet are both clients of the firm.

Morris, Laing, Evans, Brock & Kennedy, Chartered

The Firm: Representing all types of businesses, this firm is historically well known for its representation of small and midsized employers. This labor and employment group contains half a dozen dedicated attorneys split between two offices in Kansas. Clients did not perceive the division as a problem, instead choosing to refer to the firm's *"cross-departmental approach"* to practice. In addition to practicing employment law, the team represents management in labor and union negotiations, often being seen before the NRLB. In terms of employment law, attorneys are held in high regard for their work on all forms of discrimination claims and in relation to the FLSA. The team works for academic institutions, representing many colleges in the state.

The Lawyers: **Ken Peterson** comes highly recommended for *"his extraordinary ability to do well in any extremely complicated case"* and for *"always finding the right solution."* This respected litigator is capable of acting for either plaintiff or defendant. *"Real good attorney"* **Robert Overman** blends employment law with traditional labor work, although he is probably best known for the latter. Overman represents management in union negotiations and serves as a consultant to corporations on all manner of employment law issues. He has been involved with several community colleges during the past year. *"Relaxed, knowledgeable and respected attorney"* **Diane Worth** has also impressed her clients. She practices employment law (dealing particularly with discrimination matters), civil litigation and appellate law and represents management. Worth is noted for being "*particularly good at presenting herself to a group.*"

The Clients: Dillon Companies; Cargill Meat Solutions; Iowa Central Community College; Hutchinson Community College; Butler Community College and Midwest Drywall.

Stinson Morrison Hecker LLP

See firm details p.1069
The Firm: This full-service firm is one of the largest in the Midwest. It defends employers in litigation, including discrimination, harassment and retaliation claims. The employment, labor and benefits division of the firm boasts "*a real strong class action defense group*" and is well known for the quality of its FMLA advice. Like a number of its rivals, the firm frequently works within the aircraft industry.

The Lawyers: "*The person to go to with an employment problem*" is **Stephanie Scheck** (see p.824). Her peers note that she has "*a healthy*

and developing practice," adding that she is "*always up to speed.*" Scheck devotes her entire practice to employment litigation and counseling and is closely involved with the aircraft industry. Discrimination, harassment and FMLA advice are her strongest suits.

The Clients: Westar Energy; HCA; Cessna Aircraft; Protection One Alarm Monitoring; Bombardier Learjet and Commerce Bank.

LITIGATION

GENERAL COMMERCIAL

Kansas
Leading firms
(Litigation: General Commercial)

1 FOULSTON SIEFKIN LLP *Wichita*
HITE, FANNING & HONEYMAN LLP *Wichita*
SHOOK, HARDY & BACON LLP *Overland Park*
STINSON MORRISON HECKER LLP *Overland Park*

2 LATHROP & GAGE LC *Overland Park*
SHUGHART THOMSON & KILROY PC *Overland Park*
SPENCER FANE BRITT & BROWNE *Overland Park*

3 REBEIN BANGERTER PA *Dodge City*
WRIGHT, HENSON, SOMERS, CLARK *Topeka*

Leading individuals
(Litigation: General Commercial)

1 HINDERKS Mark *Stinson Morrison*, Overland Park
HITE Richard *Hite Fanning*, Wichita
REBEIN David *Rebein Bangerter*, Dodge City
STOUT Mikel *Foulston Siefkin*, Wichita

2 BADGEROW J Nick *Spencer Fane*, Overland Park
BATH Thomas *Bath & Edmonds*, Overland Park
FOCHT Jack *Foulston Siefkin*, Wichita
FOWLER Jay *Foulston Siefkin*, Wichita
HATLEY Joseph *Lathrop & Gage*, Overland Park
HONEYMAN Richard *Hite Fanning*, Wichita
MUSIL Greg *Shughart Thomson*, Overland Park
STRATTON Wayne *Goodell Stratton*, Topeka
WARTA Darrell *Foulston Siefkin*, Wichita
WRIGHT Thomas *Wright Henson*, Topeka

Leading individuals
(Litigation: Environmental)

1 EFFLANDT Charles *Foulston Siefkin*, Wichita
ERICKSON David *Shook Hardy*, Kansas City
TRIPP David *Stinson Morrison*, Kansas City

Firms and individuals are listed alphabetically in each band.

Band 1

Foulston Siefkin LLP

See firm details p.826
The Firm: The reputation of this firm, the largest in Kansas, is "*based upon a bedrock of expertise and a breadth of experience.*" With three offices across the state and more than 30 attorneys offering "*a highly professional and efficient service,*" Foulston Siefkin is short of neither resources nor know-how. The commercial and complex litigation practice group handles the full range of civil and commercial litigation, including class actions, all forms of business litigation and nearly 40 separate niche areas. The group was singled out for the "*quality and experience of the attorneys*" in environmental, healthcare and IP litigation, with clients also praising its arbitration work on professional malpractice defense.

The Lawyers: **Mikel Stout**'s (see p.825) name is "*synonymous with excellence.*" "*A pleasure to work with,*" Stout handles employment, environmental and IP litigation alongside high-value complex commercial cases. He is an active mediator and a member of the Board of Regents of the American College of Trial Lawyers. "*Superb healthcare and constitutional litigator*" **Jack Focht** (see p.823) has certainly earned his place in the table, having been prolific in the handling of government investigations, white-collar crime and the representation of public officials over the past year. In one example, he represented the County Attorney in Pratt county. Focht's position is that of special counsel to the firm's healthcare and litigation practice groups. **Jay Fowler** (see p.823) is known to be a "*tremendous trial lawyer*" with a "*wide-ranging practice*" that includes professional malpractice and tort defense. He recently successfully represented two of the businesses that were destroyed in the Hutchinson gas explosion and worked on a $94 million breach of fiduciary duty/will contest case. Continuing to make a splash, **Darrell Warta** (see p.825) impresses clients with "*his ability to effectively handle the multitude of issues often involved in high-profile cases.*" Lead trial counsel at the firm, Warta specializes in defending high-exposure personal injury, products liability and professional liability jury trials. Of the many notable cases with which he has been involved lately, standouts are his successful representation of Via Christi on two substantial matters and the positive outcome achieved for nursing clients in a medical malpractice case involving a stroke victim. Another leading individual deserving of praise is the environmental and natural resources practice group leader **Charles Efflandt** (see p.823). Noted for his "*mastery on very difficult environmental regulatory and litigious issues,*" he excels when "*dealing with the regulators and various bodies to get things done in a low-key, thoroughly professional manner.*" Efflandt represented The Coleman Company on the groundwater contamination of the Gilbert and Mosley site in Wichita and has been working on the Obee Road site in Hutchinson, a matter beset by a number of environmental and bankruptcy problems. His team is also working on a significant water rights case in an appeal to the Tenth Circuit Court of Appeals.

The Clients: Via Christi Health System; Boeing; Cessna Aircraft; Atofina Chemicals; Great West Casualty; El Paso; Johnson & Johnson; The Coleman Company; Galichia Medical Group and Delta Dental Plan of Kansas.

Hite, Fanning & Honeyman LLP

The Firm: Peers see this Wichita litigation boutique as "*stiff competition*" and clients readily agree that "*all the lawyers are very well respected.*" Unanimously thought to deserve its top slot, this firm has 18 or so attorneys, including "*some of the best litigators in the state.*" They are renowned especially for insurance and workers' compensation defense, two areas which sit within a broader general business litigation, oil and gas litigation and medical malpractice caseload. Peers took the time to remark on the group's proficiency in mediation and arbitration.

The Lawyers: "*Professional, smart, organized and effective,*" **Richard Hite** knows how to impress clients and peers. He handles all forms of general business and products liability cases and is "*quite rightly rated one of the best.*" New to the table this year is the "*well-known and well-respected*" **Richard Honeyman**, who has worked to build "*an excellent reputation as a trial lawyer*" and an equally impressive client base.

The Clients: Amoco Production; Conco Construction; Vulcan Chemicals; CNA Insurance and Farm Bureau Mutual Insurance.

Shook, Hardy & Bacon LLP

See firm details p.1067

The Firm: This international law firm is *regionally one of the most well-known litigation firms* and boasts separate business, employment, ERISA, IP and products liability subgroups. Clients pinpointed the *superb resources on offer at this firm,* and with ten offices worldwide and approximately 35 members in the litigation group, this is no overstatement of its capability. All types of business litigation are undertaken, including antitrust and securities fraud, environmental matters and complex class actions.

The Lawyers: Competitors consistently spoke highly of the chair of the environmental law section, **Dave Erickson** (see p.823). Referred to as *"one of the most accomplished environmental lawyers in the state,"* he has an impressive record in defending companies in environmental hot water. Additionally Erickson provides advice on many different types of administrative and regulatory compliance and enforcement. Gene Balloun is also deserving of mention at the Overland Park office. As one peer commented: *"When I think of this firm and great litigators, I always think of him."*

The Clients: Toshiba International; Biomat; American Airlines and Torchmark.

Stinson Morrison Hecker LLP

See firm details p.1069

The Firm: This two-office firm with approximately 16 litigators is *"a real force in Kansas."* Other firms *"definitely see them as major competition in the state."* Clients consistently speak highly of the business litigation practice division, referring in particular to the litigation avoidance advice on offer and *"the quality of the construction litigation arm."* The group represents a broad range of clients – food producers, telecom and pharmaceutical companies among them – and has strong appellate, securities and white-collar defense teams. An unusual highlight for the team was the successful representation of a class of 1200 landowners in an industrial and residential area of Kansas city. The group was defending land claims by the Wyandotte Nation and the land was valued in billions of dollars. The tribe's claims were dismissed on the basis of arguments concerning 19th century treaties.

The Lawyers: Interviewees singled out **Mark Hinderks** (see p.824) for special praise, consistently referring to his reputation as *"a hardworking and tenacious gentleman lawyer."* Hinderks' *"word is golden; he really thinks things out thoroughly and gets the job done."* He mostly concentrates on business litigation for public entities, though he has a specialty in construction cases and cochairs the firm's construction litigation practice group. Hinderks continues to represent Sprint in a number of nationwide consumer and commercial class actions and is a qualified AAA arbitrator. **David Tripp** (see p.825), meanwhile, was recommended as *"a very accomplished environmental lawyer, one of the best."* He chairs the firm's environmental law division and has been involved in several Superfund and CAA cases in the past year.

The Clients: Archer Daniels Midland; American Ingredients; Bank Midwest; Bank of America; Aventis and Sprint.

Band 2

Lathrop & Gage LC

See firm details p.1064

The Firm: Of the 275 lawyers at this seven-office national firm, about 180 are litigators. Those working from the Overland Park office are deemed to comprise a strong group, which is known for its successes in arbitration, school district and employment law litigation as well as toxic tort and IP matters. In many litigation fields, this *"excellent firm"* is frequently seen on some of the larger cases in the state. One of its recent highlights in complex commercial disputes was the successful representation of a major operator of movie theaters in a multimillion-dollar suit for liquidated damages arising from construction delays. Another highlight was the defense of a number of local school districts in a suit filed by residents questioning the legality of a tax used for the benefit of the school districts. The firm's clients prevailed on appeal and set a precedent that will be particularly important to local education interests.

The Lawyers: Interviewees say **Joseph Hatley** (see p.823) is *"doing a vigorous job as a trial attorney."* He practices in the fields of commercial litigation and telecom, education and environmental law. Of the many notable cases with which Hatley has been involved, a standout matter is his success for a group of nearly 100 corporate defendants that defeated class certification in a toxic tort suit arising from an abandoned hazardous waste disposal site.

The Clients: American Multi-Cinema; Ash Grove Cement; Burlington Northern & Santa Fe Railway Company; Blue Valley School District; Deere & Company; Extended Stay of America; Fortis Benefits Insurance; GM; Lockton Companies; Payless ShoeSource; PETsMART; Ply-Gem; Shinn Fu and Southern Farm Bureau Life Insurance.

Shughart Thomson & Kilroy PC

See firm details p.1068

The Firm: Widely regarded as *"one of the top firms,"* Shughart Thomson won unanimous recommendations for the business and healthcare litigation groups of its trial department. The healthcare group alone is home to approximately 21 attorneys. Business torts, class actions, antitrust, all forms of commercial litigation and malpractice defense work are considered strengths.

The Lawyers: **Greg Musil** (see p.824) has a name as *"a very good, wide-ranging practitioner, often found representing real estate developers and in front of Kansas board of tax appeals."* He is active in commercial litigation, property taxation and land use and zoning work.

The Clients: HCA; La Petite Academy; Gill Studios and AmeriCold Logistics.

Spencer Fane Britt & Browne LLP

The Firm: This old-line firm has four offices across the country and a strong base in Overland Park. The reputation of the litigation and dispute resolution practice group rests on the many fine attorneys noted for the quality of their commercial, construction and products liability litigation. Commentators spoke, too, of the firm's capability in terms of employment defense, environmental law and alternative dispute resolution. One highlight from the past year is the firm's work on behalf of ARY in the long-running case that arose from the bankruptcy of Krigel's, a locally owned jewelry store. The most recent decision by the Supreme Court allowed ARY to use the $7.5 million tied up in the dispute and awarded ARY three years' interest on the $1.5 million which was held in escrow pending the outcome of the case.

The Lawyers: Partner-in-charge of the Kansas office and the firm's professional responsibility counsel, **Nick Badgerow** boasts an *"exceptional reputation."* His practice encompasses many business and employment matters, including construction, trade secrets, IP, professional negligence and employment discrimination. Badgerow is also an often used expert witness in attorney liability suits.

The Clients: MGP Products; Honeywell; Life Care Centres and DoingSteel.

Band 3

Rebein Bangerter PA

The Firm: Based in Dodge City, this firm is admired for the quality of its business and commercial defense work and advice in relation to commercial agreements and all types of equipment leasing transactions. Employment litigation and more general advice concerning the cattle and oil and gas industries are among the best-known aspects of the firm's work. Last year the firm represented an area bank in a security interest priority dispute over the ownership of cattle in a feed yard. The cattle had been offered as collateral to three different banks and the feed yard itself; however, the firm's client ended up recovering over three-quarters of a million dollars.

The Lawyers: *"Very, very good and very well known,"* **David Rebein** has really impressed the market and was deemed to be *"the top lawyer in western Kansas."* As well as complex commercial and employment litigation, Rebein also practices personal injury law.

820   All quotes in the text are from interviews with clients and competitors.

CHAMBERS USA 2005

The Clients: Cargill, National Beef and Excel are three representative clients of this firm.

Wright, Henson, Somers, Clark & Bake

The Firm: A "*clear leader in the Topeka market*," this 13-attorney firm stands out for its advice on banking and business litigation for a heavily bank and insurance company-oriented client base. The firm's IP litigation practice was also identified as being worthy of praise and onlookers pointed to "*the quality and local knowledge of the attorneys.*"

The Lawyers: Much of the reputation of this group stems from "*excellent lawyer*" **Thomas Wright**, who is active in professional liability litigation and has a thriving mediation practice. Wright has been on the board of governors at the Kansas Bar Association for many years

Other Notable Practitioners

Market commentators view **Tom Bath** at Bath & Edmonds PA in Overland Park as "*the man to see if you get yourself in trouble with the Feds in northeast Kansas.*" A former assistant district attorney, Bath mainly concentrates on white-

collar crime, which involves him representing individuals and corporations on matters ranging from healthcare to tax and bank fraud. Also making his debut in the table this year is "*one hell of a lawyer*" **Wayne Stratton** of Goodell, Stratton, Edmonds & Palmer, LLP. "*It is hard to leave him out when talking about premier trial lawyers in Kansas,*" said one source. Stratton concentrates on insurance, personal injury and healthcare law. He is a former board member of a life insurance company and is regarded as "*one of the primary medical malpractice defense lawyers around.*"

REAL ESTATE

Kansas
Leading firms (Real Estate)

1	**ADAMS & JONES** *Wichita*
	LATHROP & GAGE LC *Overland Park*
	POLSINELLI SHALTON WELTE *Overland Park*
	STINSON MORRISON HECKER LLP *Leawood*
2	**FLEESON, GOOING, COULSON & KITCH** *Wichita*
	FOULSTON SIEFKIN LLP *Wichita*
	HINKLE ELKOURI LAW FIRM LLC *Wichita*
	MORRIS, LAING, EVANS, BROCK *Wichita*
	TRIPLETT, WOOLF & GARRETSON LLC *Wichita*

Leading individuals (Real Estate)

	Senior Statesman
	BOWMAN Philip *Adams & Jones*, Wichita
1	**BUCKLEY** Mert *Adams & Jones*, Wichita
	HARNDEN Ronald *Triplett Woolf*, Wichita
	HEAVEN Lewis *Lathrop & Gage*, Overland Park
	PETERSEN John *Polsinelli Shalton*, Overland Park
2	**DOERR** Brian *Duggan Shadwick*, Overland Park
	MARVIN Jack *Stinson Morrison*, Wichita
	SCHRAG Donald *Morris Laing*, Wichita
	STALLINGS John *Hinkle Elkouri*, Wichita
	STARK Stephen *Fleeson Gooing*, Wichita
	WOODWORTH Stanley *Polsinelli Shalton*, Overland Park
3	**GOODELL** Gerald *Goodell Stratton*, Topeka
	HUGHEY Roger *Adams & Jones*, Wichita
	SHORTLIDGE Neil *Stinson Morrison*, Overland Park
	VINES Monte *Adams & Jones*, Wichita
	WINN Larry *Polsinelli Shalton*, Overland Park
	WOOD William *Foulston Siefkin*, Wichita

Firms and individuals are listed alphabetically in each band.

Band 1

Adams & Jones Chartered

The Firm: Clients rated this Wichita-based firm "*top-notch in every respect*" and praised its "*accessibility, reasonable prices and concentrated real estate expertise that you can really depend on.*" Nine out the firm's 11 attorneys are dedicated to real estate and all areas of real estate law are covered. The firm represents some of the

leading names in the market and is well known for its work on office, multifamily, shopping center and other retail developments. Land use, eminent domain, loan transactions and foreclosures were also identified as strengths. Lately the firm has worked on the acquisition, development, rezoning and contractual issues surrounding a $15 million theme park project called Wild West World, located on the edge of Wichita. A further highlight for the group has been its representation of a regional hotel developer and operator on the construction of nine new hotels throughout the region.

The Lawyers: **Mert Buckley** "*is number one – he leaves no stone unturned when researching what can be done for his client.*" Such was the impression left on one interviewee, who added: "*He is a man of integrity, very honest and very easy to work with.*" Buckley, who is president of the firm, concentrates on real estate, banking, business law and bankruptcy and excels in advice on mortgage finance and land use. Clients spoke well of "*experienced real estate attorney*" **Roger Hughey**, who is known for "*his common sense and his reasonable negotiating style.*" "*Cost-conscious, exceptionally prompt in getting things done and very aware of his clients sensitivities,*" Hughey focuses on lenders in loan documentation, bankruptcy and foreclosure issues. **Monte Vines** affirms his position in the tables, with clients commenting that "*he is good at coming up with strategies*" and "*if something isn't cost-efficient, Monte will not proceed.*" Vines is often to be found resolving disputes over commercial and real estate transactions. The fourth Adams & Jones lawyer to reside in the table is senior statesman **Philip Bowman**. This established figure has "*a wealth of experience and knowledge*" and benefits from "*a very good analytical mind.*" Though Bowman undertakes work in real estate, banking, insurance and commercial litigation, he is best known for his mortgage finance practice.

The Clients: INTRUST Bank; Regency Bank; First American Title Insurance; Slawson Companies; AG Holdings and Sedgwick County.

Lathrop & Gage LC

See firm details p.1064

The Firm: The real estate group at this full-service firm acts for many notable developers, lenders and construction companies on a broad spread of acquisitions, zoning, land use, financing and construction matters. Within its portfolio of work are projects relating to large-scale entertainment complexes, shopping centers, hotels and major business parks. Many of those in the group are former city attorneys, who add "*a practical element to their advice,*" according to clients. Clients also pointed to the special talents of the attorneys handling real estate transactions in the gaming industry and golf courses. In this regard, the group continues to be involved in the development of Osage National Golf Club and Cottonwood Falls, both complex projects requiring advice on restrictive covenants, home associations and very specific golf course liability issues.

The Lawyers: "*Top-drawer, well-rounded attorney*" **Pete Heaven** (see p.823) focuses on residential and commercial development work and has a number of golf course developers on his books. "*He understands both the municipality and developer side to a deal,*" researchers were told. Heaven has been busy with a lot of commercial construction of late, including a mixed-use 4000-acre development in Johnson County.

The Clients: Rodrock Development; Atchinson, Topeka and Santa Fe Railway; Butler Real Estate; Greater Kansas City Chamber of Commerce; AMC Entertainment; Bank of America; Midland Loan Services; Block & Company; Zimmer Development; Acuff & Rhodes and Hilton Hotels.

Polsinelli Shalton Welte Suelthaus (PSWS)

The Firm: Following this firm's recent merger, the real estate team in the two Kansas offices consists of approximately 11 attorneys. Land use and real estate development matters feature heavily; advice to construction companies on environmental permitting and zoning and public-private commercial development projects are particular strengths of the group. With peers "*readily referring work to them in a conflict situation*" and clients commending "*the experienced team*," it is no surprise that the group is a leader in the state.

The Lawyers: John Petersen was universally viewed as "*a good man to deal with.*" He "*always highlights the salient issues.*" Politically well connected, Petersen concentrates on administrative and regulatory law and is held in high regard for his zoning and land use advice. "*Reliable transactional real estate attorney*" **Stanley Woodworth** is chair of the firm's corporate group and is another standout at this firm. Woodworth works on closely held businesses, M&A, residential real estate development and franchising. Also well respected by the market is the "*astute developer-oriented attorney*" **Larry Winn**. As well as real estate development in Johnson County, he deals in governmental affairs and real estate taxation. Winn is an ideal choice for residential developers looking to obtain economic incentives through either local or county government bodies.

The Clients: AG Spanos; Home Depot; Sprint and NASCAR.

Stinson Morrison Hecker LLP
See firm details p.1069

The Firm: Retaining its top slot for another year, this firm is one of the largest and best-known full-service outfits in the Midwest. Peers noted "*the strength of the firm in many practice areas, with the real estate group being no exception.*" Within the division there are separate construction and real estate lending practice groups, and the two offices in Kansas are together home to some nine dedicated practitioners. Regularly drawing on the resources of the public law and public finance division, the real estate lawyers are particularly adept at handling tax increment financing and government incentives, and are often found representing municipalities and acting on public/private projects. The team has also been deeply involved in land use litigation during the past year.

The Lawyers: Neil Shortlidge (see p.824) is portrayed as "*extremely bright, thorough and careful about how he does things.*" Clients agreed: "*It is comforting that he takes so much care.*" Shortlidge is vice chair of the firm's public law/finance division and primarily represents public sector clients on local government law issues and related litigation. One of Shortlidge's recent highlights was leading in a five-day land use trial for the City of Independence in Missouri, a case involving the traditional neighborhood developments and new urbanism projects. Also winning over clients is "*results-oriented lawyer*" **Jack Marvin** (see p.824), who is quite simply "*good to work with and a real talent.*" He

counsels a number of banks and financial institutions and has been heavily involved in the financing of new hotel complexes throughout the USA. Foreclosure litigation is another area of expertise.

The Clients: US Bancorp; SSB Realty; Corporate Woods Office Park; The Unified Government of Wyandotte County; City of Olathe; City of Overland Park; City of Lansing and the City of Bonner Springs in Kansas.

Band 2

Fleeson, Gooing, Coulson & Kitch, LLC
The Firm: The market applauded this midsized, full-service Wichita firm for the strength of its real estate development and construction group. It advises on all phases of real estate and development matters, including residential, commercial and industrial properties, and is deeply entrenched in the construction industry. A focus for the group, and the type of work most recommended by interviewees, is institutional lending, notably complex commercial real estate mortgage loans. In this regard, the group acts for the largest bank in Kansas.

The Lawyers: Fellow lawyers were quick to acknowledge "*real superstar*" **Stephen Stark**, who combines real estate transactional work with environmental law. He is held in high regard for all types of real estate financing.

The Clients: Zilkha Renewable Energy; NMF America; Bank of America; City of Wichita and GMAC.

Foulston Siefkin LLP
See firm details p.826

The Firm: This firm is the largest in Kansas, where it has three offices. Development is the firm's specialty, though much of the work of the seven-strong real estate group is in real estate financing and refinancing. The group is also known for advice to clients in the restaurant, hotel and retail sectors.

The Lawyers: "*Exceptional through and through*" and leader of the general business team, **William Wood** (see p.825) has a broad practice that encompasses securities, banking, franchising and M&A as well as pure real estate. He advises some of the best-known names in the industries in which he operates.

The Clients: Total Entertainment Restaurant, Freddy's Frozen Custard & Steakburgers and BeautyFirst are key clients of this real estate group.

Hinkle Elkouri Law Firm LLC
The Firm: Peers rate this firm as "*particularly good on real estate,*" adding that it provides "*efficient and accurate*" advice on issues relating to the development of hotels, shopping centers, commercial and office buildings, and multifam-

ily properties. Sales and purchases, leasing, financing, title issues, tax and litigation are all areas of excellence.

The Lawyers: Clients certainly hold **John Stallings** "*in the highest possible regard.*" His practice spans corporate and business law as well as real estate, where he represents investors on the purchase, development, financing and eventual sale or leasing of commercial and multifamily properties.

The Clients: Farm Credit Bank of Wichita; Chisholm Trail State Bank; AG Edwards & Sons and Stifel Nicolaus.

Morris, Laing, Evans, Brock & Kennedy, Chartered
The Firm: This "*very respected and very capable firm*" has two offices in Kansas and has seven attorneys in its real estate group. Clients include entrepreneurs, developers and financial institutions; advice is provided on the full range of issues arising out of the acquisition and divestiture of property. The group is especially admired for the depth of advice provided in terms of land use, zoning and regulatory compliance.

The Lawyers: The "*very capable, active practitioner*" **Donald Schrag** impresses clients in the areas of banking, oil and gas and corporate law as well as real estate. He has a wealth of experience in the representation of financial institutions in all types of commercial lending.

The Clients: EDO; Framatome Connectors International; PB Hoidale and Sigma Tek.

Triplett, Woolf & Garretson LLC
The Firm: Significant regional clients describe this firm as "*the best there is at closing a real estate deal.*" They also describe it as "*confident and capable.*" Attorneys act for residential, warehouse and commercial developers on the purchase and sale of properties, landlords and tenants in leasing transactions, and lenders and borrowers in deal financing.

The Lawyers: Interviewees consider "*no-nonsense*" **Ron Harnden** "*fantastic at the bargaining table.*" They say consistently that "*he is always looking out for the client's best interests while still getting on with business.*" Described as "*focused, confident and fair,*" he has "*character and honesty.*" Harnden mixes corporate and M&A with real estate work and is well known for his developer/financing practice.

The Clients: Ritchie Development; Ablah Enterprises; Flint Hills Residential Development; Key Construction; BAT and Central Mechanical Wichita.

Other Notable Practitioners
Onlookers agreed that **Gerald Goodell** at Goodell, Stratton, Edmonds & Palmer LLP in Topeka "*is very well respected, and quite rightly so.*" Frequently sought out by condominium developers and experienced in real estate trans-

822   All quotes in the text are from interviews with clients and competitors.

CHAMBERS USA 2005

actions and condemnation proceedings, Goodell also works on personal injury and malpractice cases and maintains an active involvement in the healthcare industry. **Brian Doerr** of Duggan, Shadwick, Doerr & Kurlbaum PC was routinely recommended to researchers as "*a gifted real estate attorney*" with "*a great practice.*" He acts for notable commercial real estate lenders.

Leaders in Kansas

ADAMS, Stephen
Blackwell Sanders Peper Martin LLP, Kansas City 816 983 8173
sadams@blackwellsanders.com
Recommended in Corporate/M&A
Practice Areas: Commercial transactions; healthcare; mergers and acquisitions; real estate.
Prof. Memberships: Admitted to practice in Kansas (1970) and Missouri (1971). Member, American Bar Association; American Health Lawyers Association; Greater Kansas City Society of Health Care Attorneys; Johnson County Bar Association; Kansas Bar Association; Kansas Hospital Attorneys Association; Lawyers Association of Kansas City; the Missouri Bar; and Missouri Society of Hospital Attorneys.
Career: Joined firm, 1970; named Partner, 1976.
Personal: JD, University of Kansas Law School, 1970; Member, 'Kansas Law Review', 1968-70; BS, University of Kansas, 1967.

BABCOCK, Kathleen
Foulston Siefkin LLP, Wichita
316 291 9588
kbabcock@foulston.com
Recommended in Employment
Practice Areas: Employment and labor, education/public entity, and mediation/dispute resolution. Ms Babcock advises public and private employers on the entire spectrum of employment legal issues. She regularly defends federal discrimination cases and represents public employers in First Amendment, Fourteenth Amendment, and other §1983 litigation. Ms Babcock also serves as general counsel to school districts and represents both schools and parents in special education litigation. In addition, her services as a mediator frequently are sought by litigants.
Prof. Memberships: Kansas Bar Association, Board of Governors, Secretary, Board of Discipline of Attorneys, Chair; Wichita Women Attorneys Association; Kansas School Attorneys Association.

BADGEROW, Nick
Spencer Fane Britt & Browne LLP, Overland Park 913 345 8100
Recommended in Litigation

BAILEY, Deena
Martin, Pringle, Oliver, Wallace & Bauer, L.L.P., Wichita 316 265 9311
Recommended in Employment

BATH, Thomas
Bath & Edmonds, P.A., Overland Park
913 652 9800
Recommended in Litigation

BOWMAN, Philip
Adams & Jones Chartered, Wichita
316 265 8591
Recommended in Real Estate

BUCKLEY, Mert
Adams & Jones Chartered, Wichita
316 265 8591
Recommended in Real Estate

CHURCHILL, Stanley
Martin & Churchill Chartered, Wichita
316 263 3200
Recommended in Employment

DOERR, Brian
Duggan, Shadwick, Doerr & Kurlbaum, P.C., Overland Park 913 498 3536
Recommended in Real Estate

EFFLANDT, Charles
Foulston Siefkin LLP, Wichita
316 291 9551
cefflandt@foulston.com
Recommended in Litigation
Practice Areas: Environmental law. Mr Efflandt is the Practice Group Leader of the firm's Environmental and Natural Resources Team. His practice encompasses environmental and toxic tort litigation, environmental regulatory enforcement and compliance matters and environmental issues related to business acquisitions, mergers and property transactions. Mr Efflandt represents and advises a wide variety of clients including large corporations, small and medium-sized businesses, lenders and trusts, and individuals.
Prof. Memberships: American Bar Association. Member of Section of Environment, Energy and Resources; Kansas Bar Association; Wichita Bar Association, Fee Disputes Committee; Kansas Association of Defense Counsel; Defense Research Institute.

ENGSTROM, Eric
Fleeson, Gooing, Coulson & Kitch, LLC, Wichita 316 267 7361
Recommended in Corporate/M&A

ERICKSON, David
Shook, Hardy & Bacon LLP, Kansas City
816 474 6550
derickson@shb.com
Recommended in Litigation
Practice Areas: Has devoted most of the past 15 years to environmental litigation, toxic tort litigation, environmental regulatory issues and environmental transactional issues. Has filed and defended CERCLA allocation actions involving the government and private parties.
Prof. Memberships: Admitted to practice in Missouri, Kansas and Wisconsin and before the US District Court for the Western District of Missouri, the District of Kansas and the Eastern District of Wisconsin and the US Court of Appeals for the Eighth and Tenth Circuits.
Career: Joined Shook, Hardy & Bacon, 2000 (as partner). Chair, Shook, Hardy & Bacon Environmental Section.
Publications: Missouri Environmental Law, Toxic Substances Chapter 13, 2002 Supplement; (August 2002)
Personal: JD, with distinction, University of Iowa College of Law, 1981; BA, with high honors, University of Texas at Arlington, 1978.

FOCHT, Jack
Foulston Siefkin LLP, Wichita
316 291 9519
jfocht@foulston.com
Recommended in Litigation
Practice Areas: Commercial and complex litigation, health law, mediation/dispute resolution, white-collar crime/professional responsibility, and employment and labor. Mr Focht has more than 40 years of experience as an attorney, and is a Fellow of the American College of Trial Lawyers. His practice has ranged from high-profile criminal cases to complex civil litigation. Mr Focht has directed the defense of numerous individuals and companies targeted for investigation by agencies of the state and federal government.
Prof. Memberships: American Bar Foundation, Fellow; Wichita Bar Association, President; Kansas Bar Association, President 1989-90; National Association of Criminal Defense Attorneys.

FOWLER, Jay
Foulston Siefkin LLP, Wichita
316 291 9541
jfowler@foulston.com
Recommended in Litigation
Practice Areas: Commercial and complex litigation, professional malpractice, insurance defense, and product liability. Mr Fowler's trial practice emphasizes trial of lawsuits involving commercial relationships, professional malpractice and tort defense. He frequently handles complex commercial lawsuits, intellectual property and employment disputes. He has tried high-exposure professional negligence cases and has built an extensive and respected civil litigation practice in state and federal court. He has taken in excess of 175 jury cases to verdict.
Prof. Memberships: American College of Trial Lawyers, Fellow; Kansas Bar Foundation, Fellow; American, Kansas and Wichita Bar Associations; Defense Research Institute; Kansas Association of Defense Counsel.

GARRETSON, Thomas
Triplett, Woolf & Garretson LLC, Wichita
316 630 8100
Recommended in Corporate/M&A

GOODELL, Gerald
Goodell, Stratton, Edmonds & Palmer, LLP, Topeka 785 233 0593
Recommended in Real Estate

HARNDEN, Ronald
Triplett, Woolf & Garretson LLC, Wichita
316 630 8100
Recommended in Real Estate

HATLEY, Joseph
Lathrop & Gage LC, Overland Park
913 451 5134
jhatley@lathropgage.com
Recommended in Litigation
Practice Areas: Commercial litigation, telecommunications law, education law, environmental litigation.
Career: Hatley's experience spans across a range of legal disciplines. He successfully represented the following clients: a telecommunications firm in a landmark case challenging efforts by a local city to require that firm to obtain a municipal franchise; another telecommunications firm in enforcing covenant not to compete signed by its Chief Technology Officer; an operator of motion picture theatres in a multimillion-dollar suit for liquidated damages arising from construction delays; 100 corporate defendants in defeating class certification in a toxic tort suit arising from an abandoned hazardous waste site.

HEAVEN Jr, Lewis
Lathrop & Gage LC, Overland Park
913 451 5119
pheaven@lathropgage.com
Recommended in Real Estate
Practice Areas: Real estate; land use; construction law.

Career: Heaven has represented the most prominent residential and commercial real estate developers in the Midwest for over 25 years. He served as City Attorney of the City of Merriam, Kansas, for 18 years, gaining invaluable insight into the role of government in land use. Heaven is extremely effective in presenting proposals to cities and counties on behalf of clients for planning, zoning, platting, tax increment financing, tax abatement and private activity bonds. He also serves as counsel to regional contractors and represents developers of five separate golf course communities.

HILL, Donald
Martin & Churchill Chartered, Wichita
316 263 3200
Recommended in Employment

HINDERKS, Mark
Stinson Morrison Hecker LLP,
Overland Park 913 451 8600
mhinderks@stinsonmoheck.com
Recommended in Litigation
Practice Areas: Successful prosecution and defense of cases (in court proceedings and arbitrations) involving tens and hundreds of millions of dollars on behalf of business and governmental clients, including contract disputes, telecommunications, construction, license disputes, tort actions, and land claims. Defense of class actions across the United States for major client. Co-chair of firm's Construction Litigation Practice Group and Co-General Counsel for the firm. Frequent speaker and author on professional responsibility, trial practice and construction topics.
Prof. Memberships: American College of Trial Lawyers, Fellow; Kansas Bar Association.
Personal: JD, University of Kansas (1982); BA, University of Kansas (1979).

HITE, Richard
Hite, Fanning & Honeyman LLP, Wichita
316 265 7741
Recommended in Litigation

HONEYMAN, Richard
Hite, Fanning & Honeyman LLP, Wichita
316 265 7741
Recommended in Litigation

HUGHEY, Roger
Adams & Jones Chartered, Wichita
316 265 8591
Recommended in Real Estate

MACKAY, Douglas
Kutak Rock LLP, Wichita
316 609 7900
Recommended in Employment

MANN, Terry
Martin, Pringle, Oliver, Wallace &
Bauer, L.L.P., Wichita
316 265 9311
Recommended in Employment

MARVIN, Jack
Stinson Morrison Hecker LLP, Wichita
316 265 8800
jmarvin@stinsonmoheck.com
*Recommended in Corporate/M&A,
Real Estate*
Practice Areas: Jack has served as counsel for numerous financial institutions for over 24 years. His experience includes commercial financing transactions, industrial revenue bond workouts, foreclosure/receivership litigation and bankruptcy, including chapters 7, 11 and 12. He also has significant experience with real estate transactions.
Prof. Memberships: American College of Mortgage Attorneys, Wichita Bankruptcy Council, American Bar Association.
Career: Jack is a frequent speaker on commercial finance, workouts and real estate.
Personal: JD, BS, University of Kansas.

MCCLELLAN, Roger
Martin, Pringle, Oliver, Wallace &
Bauer, L.L.P., Wichita
316 265 9311
Recommended in Employment

MUSIL, Greg L
Shughart Thomson & Kilroy PC,
Overland Park 913 451 3355
gmusil@stklaw.com
Recommended in Litigation
Practice Areas: Commercial litigation (UCC, contract, and business torts); land use, zoning and real estate development; property taxation, valuation and condemnation. Focus on land use and development and commercial litigation.
Prof. Memberships: Admitted 1983, District of Columbia (Inactive); 1987, Kansas; 1989, Missouri. Order of the Coif. Member, Editorial Board, University of Virginia Law Review, 1981-82.
Career: Joined Shughart Thomson & Kilroy PC (1987); shareholder (1992); served as a lead legislative assistant to US Senator Nancy Kassebaum Baker (R-Kansas) 1983-87; appointed by Kansas Supreme Court to the Client Protection Fund Commission (1996-2002; Chair 2001-02) and to the Continuing Legal Education Commission (2003-present).
Publications: Coauthor: Kansas Property Tax, Surviving Reappraisal and Reassessment, Journal of the Kansas Bar, March, 1988. Author: Kansas Chapter, ABA Property Tax Handbook (1995-present) and the Institute of Property Taxation annual update (1995-present).
Personal: Born Marysville, Kansas, May 23, 1957. University of Virginia, JD (1983). Kansas State University, BS, cum laude (1980). Served on the staff of US Sen. Nancy Kassebaum (R-Kan.) 1983-87 and on the Overland Park, Kansas, City Council from 1993-2001. Active in government affairs, public service, civic and charitable work and political activities at local, state and federal levels.

OVERMAN, Robert
Morris, Laing, Evans, Brock & Kennedy,
Chartered, Wichita
316 262 2671
Recommended in Employment

PETERSEN, John
Polsinelli Shalton Welte Suelthaus
(PSWS), Overland Park
913 451 8788
Recommended in Real Estate

PETERSON, Ken
Morris, Laing, Evans, Brock & Kennedy,
Chartered, Wichita
316 262 2671
Recommended in Employment

REBEIN, David
Rebein Bangerter PA, Dodge City
620 227 8126
Recommended in Litigation

RUPE, Alan
Kutak Rock LLP, Wichita
316 609 7900
Recommended in Employment

SCHECK, Stephanie
Stinson Morrison Hecker LLP, Wichita
316 265 8800
sscheck@stinsonmoheck.com
Recommended in Employment
Practice Areas: Practice concentrated in the field of employment law litigation and advising. Represents employers on employment law matters in administrative proceedings and in federal and state courts. Provides consulting, training, and audits on a variety of employment law compliance issues, including consultation in the development and implementation of personnel policies and procedures.
Prof. Memberships: Admitted to practice in Kansas and the Tenth Circuit Court of Appeals.
Personal: JD, University of Kansas (1996); BS, Business Administration, Human Resources Management, Kansas State University (1993). Selected to the Wichita Business Journal's 2003 class of '40 Under 40'.

SCHRAG, Donald
Morris, Laing, Evans, Brock & Kennedy,
Chartered, Wichita 316 262 2671
Recommended in Real Estate

SHORTLIDGE, Neil
Stinson Morrison Hecker LLP,
Overland Park 913 451 8600
nshortlidge@stinsonmoheck.com
Recommended in Real Estate
Practice Areas: Vice Chair of the firm's Public Law/Finance Division. Serves as special counsel for a number of municipalities on issues relating to land use and development, development/redevelopment incentives, annexation, public infrastructure financing and eminent domain.
Prof. Memberships: International Municipal Lawyers Association; ABA; Kansas Bar Association; Earl E. O'Connor American Inn of Court; Missouri

Bar; Missouri Municipal Attorneys Association, City Attorneys Association of Kansas, (President 2000-01); KCMBA, Local Government Law Committee (Chair 2004); Johnson County Bar Association.
Publications: Frequent speaker and author on issues of interest to local governments.
Personal: JD, University of Kansas, 1976; BA, University of Kansas, 1973.

SORENSEN, Harvey
Foulston Siefkin LLP, Wichita
316 291 9774
hsorensen@foulston.com
Recommended in Corporate/M&A
Practice Areas: Taxation, estate planning and probate, mergers and acquisitions, general business, venture capital, and family business enterprise. Mr Sorensen's practice focuses on mergers and acquisitions for public and private companies, income tax planning and inter-generational tax planning. His practice includes advising family-owned businesses through the life cycle of the business, its owners and their families.
Prof. Memberships: American College of Tax Counsel, Fellow; American Bar Association, Member, Tax Section, Agriculture Committee on Business Cooperatives, Chair-Elect; Kansas Bar Association, Member, Tax Section; Wichita Bar Association; Lex Mundi, Inc., State and Local Tax Committee, Chair; World Services Group, Director and Chair-Elect.

STALLINGS, John
Hinkle Elkouri Law Firm LLC, Wichita
316 267 2000
Recommended in Real Estate

STANLEY, Douglas
Foulston Siefkin LLP, Wichita
316 291 9502
dstanley@foulston.com
Recommended in Employment
Practice Areas: Employment and labor. Mr Stanley is Team Leader for one of the firm's two Employment Litigation Teams. He has served as chief negotiator of numerous collective bargaining agreements and advised employers in union attempts to organize groups of employees. Mr Stanley also has extensive experience in responding to unfair labor practice charges, wage and hour disputes, and employment discrimination charges before state and federal administrative agencies. Mr Stanley has tried numerous employment arbitrations in both union and non-union settings.
Prof. Memberships: American, Kansas and Wichita Bar Associations; Employment Law Section of the Kansas Bar Association, past President.

STARK, Stephen
Fleeson, Gooing, Coulson & Kitch, LLC,
Wichita 316 267 7361
Recommended in Real Estate

STOUT, Mikel
Foulston Siefkin LLP, Wichita
316 291 9516
mstout@foulston.com
Recommended in Litigation
Practice Areas: Commercial and complex litigation, environmental law, employment and labor, and mediation/dispute resolution. Mr Stout handles employment and complex commercial cases. He specializes in high-exposure litigation with an emphasis on trial practice. He is one of the most well-known trial lawyers in Kansas and has tried many of the region's high-profile employment, environmental and commercial cases. His practice includes consultation on litigation problem solving and alternative dispute resolution.
Prof. Memberships: American College of Trial Lawyers, Fellow and Board of Regents; Kansas Bar Foundation; American, Kansas and Wichita Bar Associations; Kansas Association of Defense Counsel.

STRATTON, Wayne
Goodell, Stratton, Edmonds & Palmer, LLP, Topeka 785 233 0593
Recommended in Litigation

SWAIN, Lawrence A
Shughart Thomson & Kilroy PC, Overland Park 913 451 3355
lswain@stklaw.com
Recommended in Corporate/M&A
Practice Areas: Corporate law; business law; taxation; intellectual property. Focuses in the areas of corporate and business law, mergers and acquisitions, computer law, taxation and intellectual property.
Prof. Memberships: Admitted to practice in Missouri and US Tax Court (1977); Kansas (1985). Member of The Missouri Bar (Patent, Trademark and Copyright Law Committee); past Member, Software Patent Institute's Board of Trustees; Past Vice President, Licensing

Industry Merchandisers' Association.
Career: Joined Shughart Thomson & Kilroy PC (1989); shareholder (1996). Executive Committee. Partner in charge of the Overland Park office. Cochair, Intellectual Property and Technology Practice Group.
Personal: Born Brookfield, Missouri, October 7, 1952. University of Kansas, JD (1977). University of Kansas, BS, with distinction (1974). Phi Theta Kappa. Beta Gamma Sigma. Summerfield Scholar.

TRENKLE, William
Foulston Siefkin LLP, Overland Park
913 498 2100
btrenkle@foulston.com
Recommended in Corporate/M&A
Practice Areas: Corporate, general business, taxation, banking and financial services, estate planning and probate, and health law. Mr Trenkle practices as a general business lawyer with an emphasis in taxation. Businesses he represents range from large agri-business enterprises to a healthcare facility developer. This representation includes commercial transactions, entity formation, tax planning and estate planning. He is a frequent speaker on taxation, estate planning and business topics.
Prof. Memberships: American Bar Association; Southwest Kansas and Johnson County Bar Associations; Kansas Bar Association, Tax Section - Executive Committee and past President, Corporation and Banking Section - past President.

TRIPLETT, Thomas
Triplett, Woolf & Garretson LLC, Wichita
316 630 8100
Recommended in Corporate/M&A

TRIPP, David
Stinson Morrison Hecker LLP, Kansas City 816 842 8600
dtripp@stinsonmoheck.com
Recommended in Litigation
Practice Areas: Tripp is Chair of the firm's Environmental Division and has assisted clients in environmental matters including Superfund liability issues and enforcement and permit actions involving air pollution, water pollution, toxic substances, and chemical regulation under federal, state and local laws. His experience and knowledge have been applied to issues in both administrative and judicial tribunals. Prior to joining the firm, Dave was Regional Counsel, US EPA, Region VII, where he worked for 16 years in the Enforcement Division and Office of Regional Counsel.
Personal: LLM, University of Missouri-Kansas City (1974); JD and BA, Washburn University (1971) (1968).

VINES, Monte
Adams & Jones Chartered, Wichita
316 265 8591
Recommended in Real Estate

WARTA, Darrell
Foulston Siefkin LLP, Wichita
316 291 9514
dwarta@foulston.com
Recommended in Litigation
Practice Areas: Commercial and complex litigation, professional malpractice, product liability, and mediation/ dispute resolution. Mr Warta has spent 33 years successfully trying civil lawsuits in Wichita and throughout the state of Kansas. Mr Warta is lead trial counsel specializing in defending high exposure personal injury, product liability and professional liability cases. He also serves as corporate litigation counsel in business-related trials and arbitration proceedings.
Prof. Memberships: American College of Trial Lawyers, Fellow; Federation of

Defense and Corporate Counsel; Kansas Association of Defense Counsel; American, Kansas and Wichita Bar Associations.

WINN, Larry
Polsinelli Shalton Welte Suelthaus (PSWS), Overland Park 913 451 8788
Recommended in Real Estate

WOOD, William
Foulston Siefkin LLP, Wichita
316 291 0772
bwood@foulston.com
Recommended in Corporate/M&A, Real Estate
Practice Areas: Mergers and acquisitions, securities, real estate, franchise, banking and financial services, and general business. Mr Wood has a comprehensive business practice representing public and private companies in mergers and acquisitions, creation and termination of business entities, business entity ownership issues, securities transactions, real estate transactions, franchising, venture capital investments, financing, contract negotiations and preparation, and general business matters.
Prof. Memberships: American, Kansas and Wichita Bar Associations; President and Member of Executive Committee, Kansas Bar Association Corporate Banking & Business Law Section.

WOODWORTH, Stanley
Polsinelli Shalton Welte Suelthaus (PSWS), Overland Park
913 451 8788
Recommended in Real Estate

WORTH, Diane
Morris, Laing, Evans, Brock & Kennedy, Chartered, Wichita 316 262 2671
Recommended in Employment

WRIGHT, Thomas
Wright, Henson, Somers, Clark & Bake, Topeka 785 232 2200
Recommended in Litigation

FOULSTON SIEFKIN LLP

THE FIRM

Managing Partner: Richard D Ewy
Number of partners: 49
Number of other attorneys: 26

FIRM OVERVIEW: Foulston Siefkin LLP is the largest, and one of the oldest law firms in Kansas, tracing its origins to 1919. Today the firm has over 70 attorneys, and has offices in Wichita, the state's largest city, Topeka, the state's capital, and Overland Park, the heart of commerce in the Kansas City area. Foulston Siefkin is the only Kansas member of Lex Mundi, the world's most prestigious international organization of independent law firms.

MAIN AREAS OF PRACTICE:

Administrative & Regulatory: Team members represent telecommunications companies, and gas and electric utilities, with special emphasis on rate cases and other proceedings before the Kansas Corporation Commission.
Agribusiness: Foulston Siefkin attorneys have provided counsel to the agricultural industry for more than 75 years, handling the issues that clients face in all sectors of the agribusiness industry. Clients include ranchers, farmers, meat packers, coops, and ag product suppliers and lenders.
Appellate: Foulston Siefkin attorneys have an established reputation for incisive legal writing and determined advocacy. The firm's attorneys have been counsel of record in far more reported federal and state cases in Kansas than any other firm. The appellate attorney team is experienced in complex cases and knows how to work with teams of corporate counsel and co-counsel to coordinate strategy, work allocation, and quality control.
Banking, Financial Services & Bankruptcy: Foulston Siefkin has extensive experience representing lenders, financial institutions, and other creditors in lending transactions, disputes, securities issues, loan enforcement, creditors' rights litigation, bankruptcy and bankruptcy litigation. Clients range from some of the largest financial institutions and lenders in the state to smaller community banks.
Commercial & Complex Litigation: The firm handles every variety of commercial litigation from the simple contract dispute to complex litigation, including class action, qui tam and white collar criminal defense cases. The Litigation Group includes five members of the American College of Trial Lawyers.
Construction: Attorneys assist construction industry clients with a wide range of construction projects, from conception through completion and any dispute resolution. One attorney is a graduate architect and brings unique expertise and understanding to the problems facing the construction industry.
Employment, Labor & Workers Compensation: Employment and Labor Law is one of the firm's core practice areas, with 20 attorneys that advise and represent employers in the full range of issues arising from the employer/employee relationship. The team includes the President of the Kansas Bar Association Employment Law Section and the co-editors of the Kansas Employment Law Letter, the largest circulation employment law newsletter in Kansas.
Energy: Throughout its history, Foulston Siefkin has handled the full spectrum of legal matters relating to purchase and sales, exploration, production, marketing, transportation, financing and regulation of energy and natural resources. Clients range from individual land and mineral owners, to independent oil and gas operators, both large and small, to some of the world's largest major integrated oil and gas companies.
Environmental & Water Rights: Foulston Siefkin has substantial experience in all areas of environmental law, related toxic tort litigation, regulatory and transactional areas, and water rights issues in Kansas. As important as the scope of the firm's substantive expertise, is its attorneys' practical experience and the relationships they have built with regulators, environmental consultants and other counsel on local, state, regional and national levels.

US OFFICES

KANSAS

1551 N Waterfront Parkway, **Wichita**, KS 67206
Tel: 316 267 6371 **Fax:** 316 267 6345
Email: info@foulston.com
Website: www.foulston.com

40 Corporate Woods, Suite 1050, 9401 Indian Creek Parkway,
Overland Park, KS 66210
Tel: 913 498 2100 **Fax:** 913 498 2101

555 S Kansas Ave., Suite 101, **Topeka**, KS 66603
Tel: 785 233 3600 **Fax:** 785 233 1610

Franchise: The firm has represented local, regional and national franchisors, franchisees and franchise associations in the full range of franchise law issues. Clients have included some of the best known names in the franchise business.
General Business: The firm's experience in representing a diverse range of business clients, ranging from Fortune 500 companies to sole proprietors, in local, state, regional, national, and international transactions provides a wide-ranging perspective allowing the business attorneys to find creative and resourceful solutions to business issues.
Health Law: The firm's Health Law Practice Group guides healthcare providers through the increasingly complex maze of federal and state regulations, and its relationship with the other practice groups, including taxation, general business, employment, and commercial litigation, enhances the team's ability to provide a complete solution to healthcare providers' legal requirements.
Insurance Defense: Foulston Siefkin's insurance defense attorneys have decades of experience and one of the most active trial practices in the region, defending medical malpractice actions, product liability and personal injury claims.
Mergers & Acquisitions: The firm's depth and experience in the structuring, financing and successful completion of acquisitions, divestitures, joint ventures, and other business transactions rivals that of any law firm in the region.
Taxation & Employee Benefits: The team assists individuals and businesses alike by helping to interpret, apply, and utilize the complicated rules of ERISA, the Internal Revenue Code, and applicable state laws. Foulston Siefkin's taxation services include representation before the IRS, Kansas Department of Revenue and other taxing authorities and tax agencies, including all matters of tax litigation. Seven team attorneys hold an LLM in taxation.

CLIENTS: The firm represents a broad range of clients, including major financial institutions, corporations, public utilities, insurance companies, healthcare providers, manufacturers, franchisors and franchisees, agricultural and natural resource producers and processors, professional entities, construction companies and contractors, and service providers. Clients include: AmerUs Annuity Group, AT&T Communications, Bank of America, N.A, The Boeing Company, Cessna Aircraft Company, The Coleman Company, Inc., Delta Dental Plan of Kansas, Inc., Excel Corporation, Galichia Medical Group, P.A., Koch Industries, Inc., Learjet, Inc., Neuterra Healthcare, Schaefer Johnson Cox Frey Architecture, Shelter Insurance Companies, Total Entertainment Restaurant Corp., and Via Christi Health System.

CONTENTS: Corporate/M&A p.827; Employment p.829; Environment p.832; Litigation p.834; Real Estate p.837; Individuals' Profiles p.839; Firms' Profiles p.848.

How lawyers are ranked

The opinions we gather from clients — mainly from in-house lawyers but also from other purchasers of legal services — are balanced by opinions from colleagues and competitors. Together, they provide two different perspectives — an all-round view — and biased viewpoints cancel each other out.

CORPORATE/M&A

Kentucky
Leading firms (Corporate/M&A)

1 FROST BROWN TODD LLC *Louisville*
GREENEBAUM DOLL & MCDONALD *Louisville*
STITES & HARBISON PLLC *Louisville*
WYATT TARRANT & COMBS, LLP *Louisville*

2 OGDEN NEWELL & WELCH PLLC *Louisville*
REED WEITKAMP SCHELL & VICE PLLC *Louisville*
STOLL, KEENON & PARK, LLP *Lexington*

Leading individuals (Corporate/M&A)

1 CONNER Stewart *Wyatt Tarrant*, Louisville
GLASSCOCK Ed *Frost Brown*, Louisville

2 BRADLEY Craig *Stites & Harbison*, Louisville
HELM III Kennedy *Stites & Harbison*, Louisville
LESTER David *Stoll Keenon*, Lexington
LYNDRUP Peggy *Greenebaum Doll*, Louisville
MACDONALD Alan *Frost Brown*, Louisville
MATTINGLY Patrick *Wyatt Tarrant*, Louisville
NORTHAM Patrick *Greenebaum Doll*, Louisville
SEIFFERT James *Stites & Harbison*, Louisville
STRAUS R James *Frost Brown*, Louisville
WILLIAMS Ernest *Ogden Newell*, Louisville
YOUNG Cynthia *Wyatt Tarrant*, Louisville

3 BECK Robert *Stites & Harbison*, Lexington
BECKMAN David *Frost Brown*, Louisville
CROMER Brian *Stites & Harbison*, Louisville
DIAMOND Ivan *Greenebaum Doll*, Louisville
DOLSON Scott *Frost Brown*, Louisville
GIESEL James *Frost Brown*, Louisville
HABLE Kevin *Wyatt Tarrant*, Louisville
HALLOS Jeffrey *Frost Brown*, Lexington
KEETON Charles *Frost Brown*, Louisville
KING June *Greenebaum Doll*, Louisville
RUTLEDGE Thomas *Ogden Newell*, Louisville
SCHELL Ivan *Reed Weitkamp*, Louisville
STEENROD Ralston *Stites & Harbison*, Louisville
STRENCH William *Frost Brown*, Louisville
WEITKAMP Gary *Reed Weitkamp*, Louisville

Firms and individuals are listed alphabetically in each band.

Band 1

Frost Brown Todd LLC

See firm details p.849

The Firm: Clients regard this firm as top-flight in every respect. Specific comments were made as to the "*bunch of talented attorneys on hand to deal with almost any project you can throw at them*" and the "*ability of the group to handle the most complex projects imaginable.*" Boasting over 40 dedicated attorneys across its two offices in Kentucky, and involvement in some of the most notable cases around, Frost Brown Todd affirms its position in the top tier for another year. The firm was highlighted to researchers as being exceptional on private placements of securities and registration of securities for sale to the public, although this by no means detracts from the quality of the M&A and venture capital work undertaken. The firm acted as special counsel for Brown & Williamson Tobacco in its multi-billion-dollar merger, which resulted in the formation of the second largest tobacco company in the USA, RJ Reynolds Tobacco Company. It also advised on the investment of $83.4 million by four equity funds affiliated with Onex, which acquired 28% in ResCare. Further work of significance includes the handling of the $180 million IPO of Texas Roadhouse, which, as a result, is now trading on NASDAQ.

The Lawyers: Clients could barely find enough superlatives to describe "*the extraordinarily energetic, extremely thorough, highly imaginative and incredibly reliable*" **Ed Glasscock** (see p.841). His "*strategic thinking and effective marshaling of the wealth of resources at this firm*" continue to earn him the accolade of "*probably being the number one corporate attorney in the state.*" Glasscock, cochair of the M&A section, represents both public and private companies and, following the increased volume of state M&A activity in the healthcare industry, represented ResCare in the investment detailed above. "*Solid, practical and knowledgeable transactions lawyer*" **Alan MacDonald** (see p.844) continues to earn market recommendation for "*his superb securities practice, calmness under pressure and ability to always have the answer at his fingertips.*" Though heavily focused on the representation of public companies and related securities law, MacDonald is also involved in private placements and M&A. The corporate governance element of his practice (advising both nonpublic and nonprofit entities) is developing and he also speaks on securities regulation and a variety of other issues affecting corporate entities. **Jim Straus** (see p.846) is known to be a "*multitalented financial institutions man*" who continues to impress clients with his "*invaluable knowledge of securities issues and their practical implications.*" Chair of the business/corporate department and financial institutions group, Straus is consulted widely by financial institutions and private and public companies. He has notable involvement in the food and beverage industry, representing franchisees, franchisors and corporations that purchase food and packaging for different fast food chains. Clients were also quick to recommend **Scott Dolson** (see p.841) for his "*quiet efficiency*" and ability to "*compile the most efficient means to accomplish a large number of transactions.*" A recognized expert in terms of LLC and tax work, Dolson assisted in the drafting of the statutes relating to LLCs and is widely revered for both M&A deals and his technical knowledge of the issues involved in buyouts and startups. Clients were equally quick to share their enthusiasm for **Charles Keeton** (see p.843) and his "*ability not to forget the business element to a deal.*" With a practice encompassing commercial finance, financial restructuring and e-commerce, Keeton tends to work on the private side of transactions. He co-manages the firm's commercial transactions and financial restructuring practice groups. **Jeff Hallos** (see p.842) is noted for "*his wealth of experience*" in representing lenders and borrowers, both domestically and internationally. Boasting experience that extends to infrastructure projects in Asia, he is rightly considered preeminent in the Lexington market. Hallos has continued to represent Horizon Natural

Resources in its Chapter 11 bankruptcy filing and related sale at $786 million, and has been busy with M&A and financing transactions throughout the year. A new addition to the table is "*rising corporate star*" **David Beckman** (see p.839), described by clients as "*particularly impressive on acquisitions and dispensations.*" One client commented: "*If I had to purchase or sell an entire arm of a company or handle the total sale of a business, I would use him for sure.*" Beckman is familiar with community-based financial institutions, having advised them on M&A and regulatory matters. Another new entrant to the tables is venture capital specialist and "*business incubator*" **Bill Strench** (see p.846), who was lead counsel on the Texas Roadhouse IPO. Strench is chair of the Louisville office and represents public and private companies as well as venture capital funds. Due in part to his "*tremendous securities practice*" **James Giesel** (see p.841) provides the third debut in the table this year. Clients were happy to share their thoughts on "*his knowledge of securities issues and his mastery of the resulting implications for the company on a business as well as a legal level.*" Giesel, who cochairs the public companies and securities practice group and the investment management practice group, is held in high regard for his IPO and venture capital transactions.

The Clients: Bank of Louisville; ResCare; Texas Roadhouse; Tempur-Pedic International; Horizon Natural Resources; UPS; Yum! Brands and Brown & Williamson Tobacco.

Greenebaum Doll & McDonald PLLC
See firm details p.850

The Firm: This "*definite leader in the region*" is described by clients as having "*a real forte in bankruptcy and securities law*" and boasts "*a preeminent reputation in the corporate transactional field.*" With four offices in Kentucky alone and separate corporate and securities, corporate and commercial, bankruptcy, tax and finance and development practice groups, this firm has a unity of purpose and cross-departmental philosophy which has earned it a reputation as a "*surefire leader.*" Covering a range of industries from healthcare to energy, an "*extraordinarily talented bunch of attorneys*" has been involved in many notable deals in the past year. These include acting for a large manufacturer in its sale to another large manufacturer for in excess of $75 million, and acting on the purchase of coal reserves in West Virginia worth in excess of $100 million. The firm also earned favor for its growing IP practice and was routinely described as "*an exceptional firm with a thriving corporate practice*".

The Lawyers: "*One of the leaders of the corporate Bar in Kentucky*" is **Peggy Lyndrup** (see p.844), who clients say is "*doing an outstanding job on really complex cases.*" Lyndrup is chair of the corporate and commercial practice group and is heavily involved in the representation of

the sporting goods manufacturer Hillerich & Bradsby Co. The "*thorough, confident and professional*" **Pat Northam** (see p.844) continues to impress clients and peers alike. Singled out for his "*no-nonsense approach,*" Northam handles a broad range of transactional work and has "*particular strength in the energy sector.*" Formerly in-house counsel at LG&E Energy, Northam continues to represent LG&E and many local natural resources companies. With clients quick to praise her "*far-reaching abilities,*" **June King** (see p.843) stakes her claim to a position in the table for another year. She is described as "*an excellent securities lawyer,*" and represents companies on public and private offerings and Sarbanes-Oxley Act compliance. New to the table, the "*very knowledgeable and very responsive*" **Ivan Diamond** (see p.841) concentrates on corporate and securities transactions, bank acquisitions and regulatory advice. He is chair of the financial institutions practice group and a senior member of the corporate and securities practice group.

The Clients: LG&E Energy; Papa John's International; The Kroger Co; Caldwell Tanks and Hillerich & Bradsby Co.

Stites & Harbison PLLC
See firm details p.854

The Firm: With clients commenting on "*the plethora of talented attorneys on hand*" and peers commending "*the quality of representation provided,*" this firm is rightly seen as a "*leader in the field.*" Its success rests on "*a depth of resources*" and "*a wealth of experience*" provided by 40 dedicated corporate attorneys across three offices in Kentucky. Although best known for commercial litigation, the firm also commands respect for its involvement in some of the most notable transactional matters in the state, particularly public offerings. One recent public offering and securities transaction was acting as underwriters counsel for CompuDyne. Financings and corporate governance advice are also fortes, and in terms of M&A activity, the firm handles cases on a nationwide basis. It advised, for example, on the acquisition of a Chicago-based international hotel brokerage company, on the formation of an insurance holding company and the acquisition of an insurance brokerage firm and related agencies located in the Midwest.

The Lawyers: **Craig Bradley** (see p.839) is portrayed as a "*quality, deep thinker*" who blends public company counseling with involvement in weighty transactions. In the past year he acted as investor counsel on the purchase of convertible preferred stock and common stock of ResCare by Onex Partners, and was issuer counsel for the public offering of common stock by Steel Technologies. Bradley also advised various clients on Sarbanes-Oxley compliance issues. Widely admired for his "*ability to keep bringing in the business and his activity in the community,*"

chairman of the firm **Kennedy Helm** (see p.842) retains his impressive ranking. A transactional lawyer with both broad experience and specialist knowledge in relation to airports, Helm led a number of lawyers from different firms on the $780 million Louisville Airport Improvement Program. Displaying other talents, he advised the University of Louisville Foundation during a case concerning donor privacy brought by The Courier-Journal. Dealings with **Jim Seiffert** (see p.845) lead peers to remark that it is easy to work with him and clients to speak of the "*excellent results*" he produces. Tax advice and the representation of emerging growth companies are his strongest suits, though his practice encompasses partnership law, general business advice and M&A for a variety of different entities. Seiffert was cochair of the Kentucky Limited Liability Company Act Committee, which drafted and amended said legislation. "*Well liked by clients and a fine lawyer,*" **Brian Cromer** (see p.840) is perceived as being a part of the next wave of great lawyers at this firm. His practice centers on M&A and securities, but also incorporates venture capital and general corporate advice. Currently, he chairs the business law section of the Louisville Bar Association. **Bob Beck**'s (see p.839) talents run well beyond his niche equine industry practice; this "*client-focused lawyer*" has general involvement in the corporate and financial sphere and is a member of the management committee. Adding "*an impressive amount of knowledge and experience to the team,*" **Ralston Steenrod** (see p.846) pushes his way into the rankings. His practice encompasses M&A, bank holding company formations, securities registration and exemptions and general corporate counseling.

The Clients: AEGON USA Investment Mangement; Anthem Insurance Companies; Steel Technologies; Onex Partners; CompuDyne; BellSouth; Dynegy; Regional Airport Authority of Louisville and Zurich American Insurance.

Wyatt, Tarrant & Combs LLP
See firm details p.856

The Firm: This full-service firm is widely respected for its "*no-nonsense approach to a deal*" and earned credit for "*its ability to really focus on business objectives.*" Over 30 attorneys work from four offices in Kentucky and together have the resources and experience to satisfy the complex demands of a heavyweight clientele. As well as a general business practice group, the firm fields a separate financial institutions group that serves as principal counsel to numerous institutions. Although this firm operates across a wide range of industries and undertakes the full gamut of work, it has particular strengths in healthcare, financial services and energy as well as the representation of venture capitalists and private equity investors.

The Lawyers: It is said that *"everyone in the market knows* **Stewart Conner** *from somewhere."* The chair of the firm's executive committee and key member of its general business practice group is viewed as the *"patriarch"* of the firm. *"Exuding quality",* he works on corporate finance, securities, banking and the provision of general corporate advice. He is also an author and lecturer on finance and securities matters. Cochair of the financial institutions team and *"all-round quality corporate attorney"* **Cynthia Young** makes her mark through *"her gracious representation of clients"* and her *"analytical approach to cases."* Current president-elect of the Louisville Bar Association, Young was heavily involved in the revision of Kentucky corporate statutes and boasts an impressive practice encompassing general corporate, securities and finance matters. *"Good, solid corporate lawyer"* **Pat Mattingly** is known for *"impressive business incubation and venture capital work".* This *"good man and good lawyer"* represents clients in the biotechnology and energy sectors; as well as a flourishing venture capital practice he is also active in M&A and corporate governance. Managing partner **Kevin Hable**'s practice takes in corporate law and Kentucky administrative law, with peers commenting that they would not hesitate to turn to him for advice in these areas. Hable has an active healthcare sector clientele.
The Clients: Merrill Lynch; LG&E Energy; Fruit of the Loom and First Southern Bancorp.

Band 2

Ogden Newell & Welch PLLC
See firm details p.852
The Firm: Being smaller than some of the other firms listed in no way detracts from the *"wealth of quality on offer"* at this firm. It enjoys *"an excellent reputation in the field"* and is well known for its regulatory and bond work. Clients referred to *"the ability of the firm to spend to a client's budget well and not over-man a case."* Around 15 dedicated corporate lawyers represent a range of clients, among them the Ken-

tucky Public Service Commission and Brown-Forman. In the past twelve months, the team has represented the latter client in connection with its acquisition of 55% of the stock of Tuoni e Canepa (the Italian company which produces Tuaca Liqueur). The acquisition price was approximately €61 million and the deal gave Brown-Forman full ownership of the company.
The Lawyers: *"The main guy"* is **Thomas Rutledge** (see p.845). A contributing author to the Kentucky LLC statutes, Rutledge concentrates on corporate matters, securities compliance and international law, but also works on business disputes. He has a close relationship with Brown-Forman. According to clients, **Ernest Williams** (see p.846) is *"one of the best corporate lawyers in town"* and, accordingly, he debuts in the table this year. Known for being *"knowledgeable and responsive,"* Williams practices in the area of business acquisitions, representing both buyers and sellers. He was one of the attorneys involved in the representation of the Rueff Lighting Company in connection with its sale to two local investors. Joseph Oldham also came in for market recommendation for *"his consistent delivery of excellent results".*
The Clients: Brown-Forman; ISCO Industries; Newcomb Oil Co; United Medical Corporation; Bramco LLC; Sodrel Truck Lines and Jewish Hospital Health Services.

Reed Weitkamp Schell & Vice PLLC
The Firm: Reed Weitkamp is a popular addition to this year's table. Clients of the firm commented on *"the elite status it enjoys among the firms in the Louisville area,"* and were quick to highlight *"the quality of the work and the knowledge of the lawyers."* Often representing closely held businesses, the firm has particular strength in M&A and joint venture work. It represented ResCare on its $135 million credit facility restructuring and assisted a large manufacturing company structure a change in generational control.
The Lawyers: **Ivan Schell** (see p.845) is hard to pigeonhole. He comes from a background in employee benefits advice, more than holds his

own in business planning, M&A and estate planning, and represents more than 120 medical professional groups. *"He is often seen taking the lead on various corporate matters"* and was involved in the overthrow of the board of directors of a Delaware corporation with over 200 shareholders. **Gary Weitkamp** is *"an excellent tax and corporate attorney"* who, along with Schell, enters the table for the first time. To clients, Weitkamp is *"a very effective contract negotiator and draftsman,"* known for *"the impressive amount of hours he puts in to get the deal done".* He has successfully handled the growth acquisition work for ResCare.
The Clients: The group represents many closely held companies.

Stoll, Keenon & Park, LLP
The Firm: This full-service firm is a key player in the Lexington market and home to some fine corporate attorneys. It is one of the oldest law firms in Kentucky (dating back to 1897) and the largest firm in Lexington (boasting four offices across the state). Peers were quick to comment on its impressive roster of clients and its work in the equine and coal industries. As well as a general business group, the firm is also home to a bankruptcy and financial restructuring group; commentators agree that the respective groups *"really do mesh well together."* The quality of its work in relation to estate planning and tax was also noted.
The Lawyers: Chair of the firm's business, banking and corporate department and the reason for much of the success of the group is **David Lester**. Described as *"pretty easygoing,"* he also came in for praise for *"the quality of his thinking and all-round smartness."* Lester focuses on business acquisitions, secured transactions and healthcare matters and is also a member of the equine law department.
The Clients: Keeneland Association; Lexington Herald-Leader; Lexmark International; Caterpillar; Darley Stud Management; The Jockey Club and Fifth Third Bank.

EMPLOYMENT

MAINLY DEFENDANT

Band 1

Frost Brown Todd LLC
See firm details p.849
The Firm: With rivals viewing this firm as the main competition and clients commending the quality of its lawyers and sensible billing structures, Frost Brown Todd is certainly a *"true leader in the field."* An impressive 21-lawyer team is dedicated to both traditional labor and employment law, utilizing its resources and tal-

ent to deal with the full range of issues from employment litigation to collective bargaining. The group has witnessed an increasing number of class actions and union contract negotiations in the past year and is widely admired for its work in these areas. Discrimination, sexual harassment, ADA and wrongful discharge continue to be areas of excellence, and the firm has also noticed an upturn in the number of national origin discrimination cases. Clients were quick to praise the group's advice in rela-

tion to staying union-free, commenting on attorneys' in-depth knowledge on such topics as the latest union-organizing techniques.
The Lawyers: **Patton Pelfrey** (see p.844) is *"the sort of lawyer that you really take pleasure in introducing as your lawyer."* Cochair of the firm's labor and employment department, this *"outstanding"* practitioner tends to concentrate on traditional labor matters, but is also heavily involved in employment litigation and Title VII matters, often engaging in preventative

Kentucky
Leading firms
(Employment: Mainly Defendant)

1 FROST BROWN TODD LLC *Louisville*
GREENEBAUM DOLL & MCDONALD *Louisville*

2 SMITH & SMITH ATTORNEYS *Louisville*
STOLL, KEENON & PARK, LLP *Lexington*
WYATT TARRANT & COMBS, LLP *Louisville*

3 DINSMORE & SHOHL LLP *Louisville*
OGDEN NEWELL & WELCH PLLC *Louisville*
WOODWARD, HOBSON & FULTON *Louisville*

Leading individuals
(Employment: Mainly Defendant)

1 CLEARY Richard *Greenebaum Doll, Louisville*
COCKRUM James *Frost Brown, Louisville*
GRIFFITH Richard *Stoll Keenon, Lexington*
HOPSON Edwin *Wyatt Tarrant, Louisville*
PELFREY D Patton *Frost Brown, Louisville*
SMITH III James *Smith & Smith, Louisville*
WILLIAMS Thomas *Ogden Newell, Louisville*

2 BIRCHFIELD Thomas *Greenebaum Doll, Louisville*
FLEISCHAKER Jon *Dinsmore & Shohl, Louisville*
PERRY Donna *Woodward Hobson, Louisville*
SALES Walter *Ogden Newell, Louisville*
SAVARISE Jeffrey *Greenebaum Doll, Louisville*
SHELLER John *Smith & Smith, Louisville*
SMITH Kevin *Smith & Smith, Louisville*

3 BECKER Wendy *Greenebaum Doll, Lexington*
DAWAHARE Debra *Wyatt Tarrant, Lexington*
ESCHELS Philip *Greenebaum Doll, Louisville*
HALEY III Raymond *Woodward Hobson, Louisville*
KIRK Michael *Wyatt Tarrant, Lexington*
LOVETT John *Frost Brown, Louisville*
OLDHAM Joseph *Ogden Newell, Louisville*
SANDLER David *Greenebaum Doll, Louisville*

Up-and-coming individuals
QUESENBERRY Kathryn *Woodward Hobson, Louisville*

Firms and individuals are listed alphabetically in each band.

measures to avoid litigation. **James Cockrum** (see p.840) came in for specific recommendation for his "*solid performances in court,*" and was hailed as "*just a damned good lawyer, period.*" Cockrum acts for employers in manufacturing and service industries, focusing on the development of policies that prevent litigation and advice on staying union-free. A new addition to the table this year, **John Lovett** (see p.843) is Kentucky's only charter member of the American Employment Council and is well known for his union-organizing work and preventive employment counseling.

The Clients: UPS and AK Steel are just two examples from an impressive roster of clients.

Greenebaum Doll & McDonald PLLC
See firm details p.850

The Firm: Clients say this full-service firm "*offers a great service and quality advice*" and recommend "*the wealth of resources and talented attor-*neys *on offer.*" Thought to be "*the perfect fit for midsize and large companies alike,*" this labor and employment group is one of the most substantial in the south central region, with over 20 lawyers in total. Interviewees referred to the many strengths of the group, in particular recommending it for ERISA, noncompete agreements, employment litigation and labor relations. Toyota remains a key client; the firm is outside counsel to this automotive giant in several states. As well as the automotive industry it is also involved with aluminum and steel producers, often acting on collective bargaining issues or providing advice on corporate restructuring.

The Lawyers: Richard Cleary (see p.840), the chairman of the labor and employment practice group, is a "*confident, responsive and effective attorney*" who affirms his position at the top of the table for another year. He serves an "*impressive client base,*" and self-confessed difficult clients could not praise him enough for his "*effective management, client training and friendly demeanor,*" adding that he is "*effective at taking aggressive positions when he needs to.*" As well as advising on a variety of employment and discrimination matters, Cleary has carved out a niche in the representation of aluminum and steel industries on the full range of labor relations issues. Equally as revered, **Jeff Savarise** (see p.845) is "*as good a labor and employment attorney as you will find in the state.*" Said to possess "*the highest ethical standards*" and deliver "*excellent end products,*" he also came in for praise from peers for his "*photographic memory and extraordinary competence.*" Savarise is outside counsel to Toyota and boasts a practice that, although focused heavily on employment litigation, also covers traditional labor issues. "*Real professional*" **Tom Birchfield** (see p.839) is known for "*always being there with practical answers*" and "*cutting out the theoretical stuff.*" He is widely respected for his employment litigation practice and was noted for his "*confident professionalism.*" **Philip Eschels** (see p.841) also came in for praise from clients for his "*great advice*" and flourishing litigation practice. Eschels excels in the defense of discrimination claims and has developed a niche in noncompete agreements. He was involved in the successful representation of Texas Roadhouse in the past year. **Wendy Becker** (see p.839) is an "*excellent day-to-day employment counselor*" recommended for "*her conscientious, prompt advice and general accessibility.*" Based in Lexington, she practices employment law exclusively and has extensive experience in disability discrimination. She recently acted in a Kentucky Supreme Court case that clarified the burden of proof for discrimination claims filed under the Kentucky Civil Rights Act. Finally, **David Sandler** (see p.845) debuts in the table this year after a wave of positive feedback for his labor and employment law practice. He is known for his successful track record in court and his "*wealth of experience.*" Sandler has been heavily involved in the representation of the Kroger Company.

The Clients: Toyota USA; The Kroger Company; Texas Roadhouse; American Standard; Commonwealth Industries and LG&E Energy.

Band 2

Smith & Smith Attorneys
See firm details p.853

The Firm: This "*extremely strong boutique*" is home to "*deep expertise*" and "*an impressive array of excellent attorneys*" in all facets of labor and employment law save for workers' compensation. It is well known for its litigation avoidance advice and the "*personal touch*" of attorneys who have the ability to litigate aggressively when required. Considered exceptional on the representation of small and medium-sized employers, the firm also wins work from some of the largest clients in the state.

The Lawyers: "*One of the top lawyers around,*" **Jim Smith** (see p.846) has a "*dynamite reputation.*" This "*superb practitioner*" is described as "*one sharp, hard-nosed litigator*" who "*provides an extremely good service to his clients.*" Perhaps not as well known as his brother Jim, but still "*one hell of an attorney,*" **Kevin Smith** (see p.846) also practices both labor and employment law. On the employment litigation side, "*exceptionally bright*" **John Sheller** (see p.845) continues to impress. He is known for "*pushing very hard for his clients.*"

The Clients: Small to midsized companies form the bulk of the clientele. Notable larger clients include Chubb Group and Churchill Downs.

Stoll, Keenon & Park, LLP
The Firm: "*The premier Lexington firm,*" Stoll, Keenon & Park's 14-lawyer practice group is growing in stature in the Kentucky market. This "*old-line firm certainly is moving some,*" according to commentators. It handles the full range of employment law issues, including discrimination and wage and hour disputes; in the labor arena, collective bargaining and proceedings before the NLRB are considered areas of excellence. The firm is also coming into its own in the field of immigration advice, where recent lateral hires have further strengthened an already flourishing practice. Long-standing clients agree that for "*responsiveness and a common-sense approach to dealing with really complex problems, this is the firm.*"

The Lawyers: Richard Griffith offers "*practical resolutions and client sensitivity.*" His most valuable asset is said to be the "*understanding he has of the nature of organizations, which helps him craft good arguments.*" Cochair of the employment relations department, Griffith not only "manages the troops well," but is also "an excellent litigator and counselor."

The Clients: Lexington Herald-Leader; Chrysler; Caterpillar; Keeneland Association; Kentucky Medical Services Foundation; Jim Beam Brands Company and Toyota Tsusho America.

Wyatt, Tarrant & Combs LLP

See firm details p.856

The Firm: Researchers were given ample positive feedback from clients about "the deep-rooted experience" of this seven-office firm. The employment and labor relations group operates as a subgroup of the litigation department and is comprised of 24 lawyers who work across its four Kentucky offices. Of these, the Louisville office is viewed as the strongest. Discrimination and wage and hour disputes are definite areas of excellence, and although not as obviously apparent as the employment law work, the firm also represents management in its dealings with unions. Clients heartily recommend the in-house management training and seminars on offer, especially the regularly issued updates on hot topics.

The Lawyers: **Ed Hopson** was widely recommended to researchers as a "calm, collected, responsive and very knowledgeable" attorney. One client commented: "I have yet to find a subject that he does not have the answer to or is at least very knowledgeable on." Hopson boasts a practice which encompasses both labor and employment matters, and has lately been involved in the US Court of Appeals affirmation of a judgment setting aside an arbitration award in favor of a union. Also coming in for recommendation is **Debra Dawahare**. Pinpointed for her "impressive client base," Dawahare, who is based in the Lexington office, is cochair of the practice group and concentrates on both employment law and commercial litigation. **Michael Kirk** makes his debut in the table following praise for the "great job he does in trial" and "the calming influence he exudes for his clients." His practice encompasses both labor and employment matters, though he is best known for employment litigation.

The Clients: GE; Ford; American Red Cross; Brown & Williamson Tobacco; Raytheon; DuPont; United Defense; Wal-Mart; Pernod-Ricard; Norton Healthcare and General Mills.

Band 3

Dinsmore & Shohl LLP

See firm details p.1452

The Firm: This full-service law firm, headquartered in Cincinnati, continues to expand its presence in Kentucky with two offices and "a litany of experienced local attorneys." Clients like "the sound, crisp advice in relation to First Amendment law and workers' compensation issues" and noted in particular "the impressive track record the group has in the newspaper industry." On this note, the firm represents the largest newspaper in the state and the Kentucky Press Association. Beyond newspapers, it is associated more generally with the representation of the media and communications industry in employment matters, handling cases involving religious and disability discrimination as well as wage and hour claims. The group is able to draw on the knowledge and experience of attorneys in other parts of the country, something that is seen as especially advantageous when it comes to traditional labor matters.

The Lawyers: Clients consistently referred to the managing partner of the Louisville office, **Jon Fleischaker**, as "the finest First Amendment lawyer in the state and a skilled employment litigator to boot." "Extremely deliberate" and "an absolute tank full of knowledge," Fleischaker "really understands the nature of his clients' business." Among the work he has undertaken recently, a landmark decision from the Kentucky Court of Appeal on Kentucky disability law stands out. Some of the younger members of the group were also highlighted to researchers as names to watch in the future.

The Clients: Gannet (The Courier Journal); Jewish Hospital HealthCare Services; Allstate; Winn-Dixie; Papa John's International; Media General; The Kentucky Press Association and Community Newspaper Holdings.

Ogden Newell & Welch PLLC

See firm details p.852

The Firm: This old-line firm garnered praise from clients for "its highly competent service and representation" and "excellence on the whole labor and employment package." Clients also highlighted the usefulness of the educational seminars and supervisor training on offer, noting the "preventive nature" of this advice in terms of problem avoidance. The firm is home to some exceptional specialists and, as such, has been involved in many of the defining cases seen in the state in the last year. Recent work includes acting for the defendant in Renee Jackson, et al. v United Metro Media d/b/a Job News, a wage and hour collective action brought by the company's account executives.

The Lawyers: The "consistent delivery of excellent results" and "laid-back practicality" of department head **Thomas Williams** (see p.847) was drawn to the attention of researchers. This "very personable and attentive first-rate lawyer" "thoroughly considers all angles before giving his opinion." He has been involved in the defense of several discrimination claims in the past twelve months and continues to provide training and educational seminars. Described as "very good and very active," **Walter Sales** (see p.845) debuts in the table as a result of enthusiastic support for his labor law and commercial litigation practice. Sales regularly appears before the NLRB and often works on the negotiation of union contracts. On the employment side, he has been involved in some notable discrimination cases in the past year, including the reversal of a disability discrimination jury verdict worth over half-a-million dollars. Another debutant in the table is "wonderful" **Joseph Oldham** (see p.844). Although his practice heavily overlaps with corporate, tax and estate planning, clients enthusiastically recommended him for his "exemplary" work in the field of employee benefits.

The Clients: Kindred Healthcare; University of Louisville; Safetran Systems; Water Works Supplies; Doe-Anderson; Job News; Clear Channel Communications; ISCO Industries and LG&E Energy.

Woodward, Hobson & Fulton LLP

The Firm: Although not of the size of some of the others listed, this firm boasts a ten-strong labor and employment group comprised of some "seriously top-notch lawyers." Defending employers on the full range of discrimination claims, the firm also provides day-to-day employment counseling to HR departments. It regularly appears before the NLRB on cases such as unfair labor practice charges and contract negotiations, both areas of increasing significance for the group. Peers consider the firm as "serious competition" and agree that it is one to keep an eye on.

The Lawyers: The managing partner and "the name most associated with this firm" is **Donna Perry**. As well as being "one excellent litigator," Perry is noted for her exceptional employment knowledge and expertise. She is also trained in mediation and alternative dispute resolution. Usually working more on the traditional labor side, **Ray Haley** serves as counsel to an impressive array of clients. He represents management in all areas of labor and employment law and is a committed lecturer and author. Making her debut as an up-and-comer this year is the highly recommended employment and discrimination lawyer **Kathryn Quesenberry**. Described as having a practice that is "developing nicely," Quesenberry is the current chair of the Kentucky Bar Association's labor and employment section.

The Clients: Norton Healthcare; University of Louisville; American Commercial Barge Lines; Louisville Water and Wal-Mart.

ENVIRONMENT, NATURAL RESOURCES AND REGULATED INDUSTRIES

Kentucky
Leading firms
(Environment, Natural Resources and Regulated Industries)

1 **GREENEBAUM DOLL & MCDONALD** *Lexington*
OGDEN NEWELL & WELCH PLLC *Louisville*
STITES & HARBISON PLLC *Lexington*
STOLL, KEENON & PARK, LLP *Lexington*
WYATT TARRANT & COMBS, LLP *Lexington*

2 **DINSMORE & SHOHL LLP** *Lexington*
FROST BROWN TODD LLC *Lexington*
JACKSON & KELLY PLCC *Lexington*
MIDDLETON REUTLINGER PSC *Louisville*

Leading individuals
(Environment, Natural Resources and Regulated Industries)

1 **RIGGS Kendrick** *Ogden Newell, Louisville*
WATT Robert *Stoll Keenon, Lexington*

2 **BROWN David** *Stites & Harbison, Louisville*
CRYDER Bruce *Greenebaum Doll, Lexington*
DAVIS R Eberley *Stoll Keenon, Lexington*
HATFIELD C Kent *Stoll Keenon, Louisville*
NORTHAM Patrick *Greenebaum Doll, Louisville*

3 **BENDER Jack** *Greenebaum Doll, Lexington*
CURTZ Chauncey *Dinsmore & Shohl, Lexington*
GORTON William *Stites & Harbison, Lexington*
HOFFMANN Warren *Frost Brown, Lexington*
INGRAM Lindsey *Stoll Keenon, Lexington*
OVERSTREET Mark *Stites & Harbison, Frankfort*
RHORER John *Dinsmore & Shohl, Lexington*
WARD Richard *Wyatt Tarrant, Lexington*

Firms and individuals are listed alphabetically in each band.

Band 1

Greenebaum Doll & McDonald PLLC

See firm details p.850

The Firm: This firm is "*deeply entrenched in the natural resources industry and has a tremendous amount of expertise on hand.*" Its four offices in Kentucky offer 12 attorneys in the environment and natural resources group, and together they have the resources to cope with cases at the complex end of the market. Considered pre-eminent in advising businesses on how to develop responsible environmental policies, the group also regularly assists clients with requirements for the extraction and use of natural resources, especially limestone and coal. Given that Kentucky is one of the top three coal-producing states in the USA, and with coal accounting for 97% of the state's electricity generation, this is a particularly important industry sector. Environmental litigation is another recognized forte of the team. In this regard the environmental group waste no time in drawing on the vast experience of the firm's litigation department. Finally, the work of the group in the fields of air and water quality was also commended highly.

The Lawyers: Notable industry figures describe **Pat Northam** (see p.844) as "*a real strong attorney, unflappable in any situation.*" Northam has a broad practice that includes corporate and business law as well as energy matters. He is thought to excel in all aspects. Northam has represented many of the household names in the energy sector and has recently been involved in the purchase of coal reserves in West Virginia, the speculative combined transaction value of which could reach half-a-billion dollars. **Bruce Cryder** (see p.840) is a "*superb natural resources attorney and prolific generator of business.*" Concentrating on minerals and environmental law mixed with some commercial litigation, he is widely considered to be "*one very experienced coal lawyer.*" This is no surprise as he was in-house counsel for a coal company before joining Greenebaum, and he now represents some of the best-known names in the industry. Commentators identified **Jack Bender** (see p.839) as another "*particularly strong*" attorney. Concentrating more on environmental law, Bender's practice overlaps with litigation and he is well known for his speaking engagements on topical environmental law issues. He was also singled out for his advice in relation to air and water quality issues.

The Clients: This firm represents regional producers, operators and mineral owners and regional and national natural resource companies. LG&E Energy and Big Rivers Electric Corporation are two examples.

Ogden Newell & Welch PLLC

See firm details p.852

The Firm: Peers agree that this firm is "*certainly a leading player in this niche market;*" its attorneys are widely regarded to be "*true utility specialists.*" Six dedicated attorneys work in this practice area, although they draw on the assistance of others in the firm when necessary. The utility practice group is particularly renowned for its energy, natural gas and telecommunications industry work where it has been involved in some of the defining cases in recent years. A highlight from the past twelve months was acting for LG&E and Kentucky Utilities Company on a successful application to the Kentucky Public Service Commission concerning the $101.4 million aggregate increase in gas and electric rates. A further highlight was the representation of these companies on an application for a certificate for the acquisition of four combustion turbines and a site compatibility certificate for the facility. Despite objections from certain parties, the Kentucky Commission issued the certificates and approved the acquisition.

The Lawyers: The "*calm, measured and quite exceptional regulatory attorney*" **Kendrick Riggs** (see p.845) is the main point of contact at this firm. Focusing on utility, energy and telecommunications law, Riggs also gets involved in the administrative side of these areas and is widely known as "*an outstanding public service commission lawyer.*" Riggs is head of the utilities practice group, is managing partner of the firm and has a wealth of administrative trial experience.

The Clients: LG&E Energy; Kentucky Utilities; Williams Telecommunications and Duke Energy North America.

Stites & Harbison PLLC

See firm details p.854

The Firm: Peers consider this firm "*strong on environmental and natural resources,*" while clients "*have a high regard for and good working relationship with a number of the lawyers.*" Three offices in Kentucky offer distinct environmental, natural resources and energy and mineral practice groups totaling some 20 attorneys with "*a lot of practical experience.*" Among their number are former engineers, consultants and regulatory officials. As well as providing advice on regulatory compliance, the mineral law group deals with production issues and issues surrounding supply and purchase contracts. Another specialty of the group is advice on the environmental regulation of concentrated animal feeding operations. Highlights for the team include counseling Dynegy on regulatory matters pertaining to its construction of two merchant plants in Kentucky, and representing the City of Louisville in its municipalization effort regarding LG&E Energy, in the event of its sale by E.On.

The Lawyers: This firm is home to a number of "*well-regarded, careful practitioners with a wealth of practical experience,*" and **David Brown** (see p.839) is one of them. "*A significant name in the industry,*" Brown works for the protection of electricity consumers' interests, has a thriving Kentucky Public Service Commission caseload and devotes a large segment of his practice to assisting two large aluminum smelters in procuring, negotiating and contracting power on the wholesale market. **Mark Overstreet** (see p.844) comes highly recommended by clients for his "*extensive knowledge, familiarity with local procedures and specialist regulatory appeals and utility experience.*" Based in Frankfort, the public utilities-oriented business litigator represented BellSouth in a case before the Sixth Circuit Court of Appeals last year. He was also pivotal in the representation of Kentucky Power in a challenge to a Kentucky statute, which purports to regulate how it will drop load in the event of an emergency. Peers

832

All quotes in the text are from interviews with clients and competitors.

CHAMBERS USA 2005

and clients also singled out "*busy technical lawyer*" **Bill Gorton** (see p.841) whose practice includes environmental law, natural resources, energy and surety law counseling and litigation. **The Clients:** Dynegy; LG&E Energy; BellSouth; AllTel Communications; City of Louisville and AEP.

Stoll, Keenon & Park, LLP

The Firm: Peers view this firm as "*keen competition on telecommunications, water and natural resources cases;*" certainly it is home to many of the best-known attorneys in the field. The environmental law department of this, one of the oldest law firms in Kentucky, is often found working on environmental compliance and litigation matters in the areas of mineral rights and toxic torts. The group's involvement in utility regulation is also noted.

The Lawyers: Industry figures endorsed **Robert Watt** for "*his superb work on litigation and the regulatory side*" and "*the tenacity and balanced judgment he brings to every issue.*" Focusing on utilities and complex commercial litigation, Watt often appears before the Public Services Commission and is noted for "*the quality work he does for a number of gas distribution clients.*" Another attorney picking up his fair share of client recommendation is of counsel **Eberley Davis**. A former general counsel of two large energy companies, Davis is esteemed for his wealth of practical experience and his natural resources work, especially coal-related matters. David Royse, an associate at the firm, has piqued the interest of the market with "*the number of condemnation cases he undertakes for some of the largest clients around.*" Royse handles general litigation, eminent domain, zoning, planning and land use law. **Kent Hatfield** "*spans the gamut from traditional electrical utilities to telecommunications*" and is a popular choice for referrals from peers. For this "*knowledgeable and experienced*" practitioner, utilities, energy and telecom regulation is second nature and he is familiar, too, with antitrust regulation and related litigation. The fourth name to make it into the rankings is **Lindsey Ingram**, who is noted for "*the quality of the clients he represents*" and "*the high-profile work he is often involved in.*" Concentrating on litigation and public utility law, Ingram frequently represents gas, water, electric and communication companies before the Kentucky Public Commission.
The Clients: LG&E Energy and Kentucky Utilities; Delta Natural Gas and Union Light, Heat & Power.

Wyatt, Tarrant & Combs LLP
See firm details p.856

The Firm: This full-service firm has separate environmental and mineral and energy departments and is "*historically and presently one of the strongest firms in this market.*" With four offices

across Kentucky, like rivals it has the ability to draw on the resources of other practice groups as and when needed. The mineral and energy practice group represents a wide variety of clients including owners, producers and distributors. Its work spans mineral leasing, mine safety and related litigation, mining agreements and supply contracts. In a similar vein, the environmental practice group represents a swathe of clients from manufacturers and chemical producers through to government agencies.

The Lawyers: "*Vastly experienced*" **Dick Ward** is "*widely known for his flourishing natural resources practice.*" As well as being a highly proficient litigator, he assists clients on diverse commercial transactions, including supply, lease and mining agreements.

The Clients: Arch Coal; Ashland Coal; Berwind; Drummond Company; Lodestar Energy; Rockwell International; Zeigler Coal Holding Company and Ford.

Band 2

Dinsmore & Shohl LLP
See firm details p.1452

The Firm: This firm has "*an increasing presence in the state*" and fields separate environmental, natural resources and mine safety and health administration practice groups. It is deeply involved in the mining and mineral industries and has the ability and resources to handle all issues, including the contractual arrangements and questions that arise on the leasing, extraction, purchase and sale of mineral reserves. In terms of environmental law, the team is active in the defense of Superfund and toxic tort litigation and has "*practical experience of environmental counseling.*" Public utilities matters are also handled.

The Lawyers: Said one commentator: "*The person I think of immediately is* **John Rhorer**." Based in Lexington, Rhorer combines his natural resources work with real estate and corporate transactions. His work in the coal industry is well known and he often advises minerals clients on transactional matters, including the acquisition, leasing and financing of new projects. **Chauncey Curtz**, of counsel, received warm market feedback for his work in this area. Curtz combines a natural resources practice with commercial litigation and real estate work, representing clients in every area of the ownership, extraction and sale of coal and minerals. He is the president of Coal, Energy Investments & Management, LLC.

Frost Brown Todd LLC
See firm details p.849

The Firm: This Midwest powerhouse has an "*exceptionally strong environmental practice*" and impresses the market with "*the sheer amount of resources and attorneys they can throw at a case.*"

With its two large offices in Kentucky, clients appreciate that the "*cross-departmental nature of the firm*" allows the energy and natural resources group to work closely with the plethora of allied practice groups. In the past year, attorneys have been heavily involved with the coal and electricity industries, buying and selling coal companies and mineral reserves and becoming increasingly involved in regulatory proceedings. The group has represented utilities in the financing and construction of power plants across the USA, and acted as debtors' counsel in the bankruptcy of Horizon Natural Resources, the largest ever coal company Chapter 11 bankruptcy to have occurred in the Midwest.

The Lawyers: Chairman of the energy and natural resources practice group and "*a definite name in the industry*" is **Warren Hoffmann** (see p.843). Concentrating in general corporate and commercial law with an emphasis on matters relating to the coal and electric utility industries, Hoffmann represents some of the key clients in the industry and has been involved in many of the defining cases in this area in recent years.

The Clients: Appalachian Fuels, East Kentucky Power and LG&E Energy are key clients.

Jackson & Kelly PLCC
See firm details p.1815

The Firm: Jackson & Kelly has long been known as the oldest and largest law firm in West Virginia and is now increasingly "*making its presence felt in Kentucky.*" Peers are especially aware of "*the strength of the Lexington office.*" "*Historically enjoying a strong reputation in coal,*" the firm has diversified into other natural resources, including natural gas, timber and metals. Attorneys advise on the acquisition and lease of mineral properties, associated financing arrangements, environmental permits and marketing. Backing up the natural resources practice is "*a flourishing environmental arm*" with a good capability for litigation, especially toxic tort cases.

The Lawyers: While a multitude of experienced attorneys practice in this field, clients think first of Kevin McGuire in the Lexington office. His practice encompasses business litigation as well as natural resources and environmental law. He has represented clients in state and federal courts and before the administrative agencies.

Middleton Reutlinger PSC
See firm details p.851

The Firm: This full-service Louisville firm has "*an expanding presence in this area*" and is heavily involved in environmental law and safety management, representing large industrial facilities and fossil fuel electric generating stations on the issuance and compliance of permits. Hazardous and waste management programs and violations of air and water permits are considered particular areas of excellence, although the group is also involved in Superfund and toxic tort litigation.

The Lawyers: Managing director of the firm, Charles Middleton, is the main point of contact. He has experience of Superfund litigation and the presentation of cases in the administrative arena for both land use and environmental compliance. Henry Alford was also singled out by clients for his representation of telecommunications companies and electric and water utilities before the Kentucky Public Service Commission and state and federal courts.

LITIGATION

GENERAL COMMERCIAL

Kentucky
Leading firms
(Litigation: General Commercial)
1 FROST BROWN TODD LLC *Louisville*
GREENEBAUM DOLL & MCDONALD *Louisville*
STITES & HARBISON PLLC *Louisville*
WYATT TARRANT & COMBS, LLP *Louisville*
2 MIDDLETON REUTLINGER PSC *Louisville*
OGDEN NEWELL & WELCH PLLC *Louisville*
REED WEITKAMP SCHELL & VICE *Louisville*
STOLL, KEENON & PARK, LLP *Lexington*
3 BOEHL STOPHER & GRAVES, LLP *Louisville*
DINSMORE & SHOHL LLP *Louisville*
TACHAU MADDOX HOVIOUS *Louisville*
WOODWARD, HOBSON & FULTON *Louisville*
Firms are listed alphabetically in each band.

Band 1

Frost Brown Todd LLC
See firm details p.849

The Firm: For some market commentators, this behemoth of the Midwest really does "*stand apart from the rest of the pack;*" it is "*certainly home to some fine business litigators.*" Frost Brown Todd operates from seven locations across the country and boasts two large offices in Kentucky. Home to over 140 litigators and 24 different litigation practice areas nationally, it is easy to see why the firm continues to provide the advisers of choice for some of the most notable clients in the state. It serves as national counsel to a variety of clients across a range of industries and such clients consistently referred to the "*ability of the firm to handle the really big, complex actions.*" In terms of work highlights, this "*out-front kind of a firm*" has been involved in cases producing results of national significance. To give one example, it represented LG&E Energy in litigation instigated to try and set aside a $100 million adjustment in the base electric rates approved by the Public Service Commission, the result of which impacted on all the end-users of LG&E's electricity.

The Lawyers: Chairing the litigation department is the "*very talented and very sharp*" **Winston Miller** (see p.844). Miller has a diverse practice encompassing products liability, mass tort and toxic tort litigation and is widely known for his defense of multiparty cases arising out of catastrophic losses. This "*excellent business lawyer*" has represented UPS on a variety of different commercial cases, including some relating to air routes and other assets in South America. He has also represented Equitable Resources on an assortment of legal issues. **Carl Henlein** (see p.842) also raked in praise for being "*the most creative litigator around.*" Commentators admired his "*esteemed national practice*" and "*the impressive way he fashions an argument and puts across a case.*" He too is well known for his catastrophic loss and mass disaster litigation practice. Henlein has been involved in some defining cases of late including acting as national coordinating counsel in breast implant and lead paint litigations. **Sheryl Snyder** (see p.846), chair of the appellate practice group, gathered a good volume of client approval this year. Underscoring his reputation as a "*talented constitutional and high-stakes business lawyer,*" he recently represented Governor Ernie Fletcher in a significant constitutional case. In terms of his appellate practice, in a pending copyright case before the US Court of Appeal Snyder is defending Taco Bell's use of Dinky the Chihuahua in its TV commercials. Another client favorite is the "*gregarious and charming*" **Charles Cassis** (see p.840). A "*great business generator,*" Cassis is a member of the executive committee and has a long and glittering history at the firm. Known as a "*wonderful insurance litigator,*" he is skilled in fire and explosion, products liability and toxic tort litigation. Last, but by no means least, is the "*extraordinarily promising*" **David Kaplan** (see p.843), whose practice encompasses commercial and regulatory disputes, including the representation of municipal governments. Clients say they "*certainly feel comfortable dealing with him.*" Kaplan has represented four of the largest corporations in Kentucky in a constitutional challenge to a veto of $70 million worth of corporate tax relief, the result of which is now under appeal.

The Clients: Yum! Brands; LG&E Energy; Kindred Healthcare; General Electric; Equitable Resources and UPS.

Greenebaum Doll & McDonald PLLC
See firm details p.850

The Firm: This firm moves up to the first tier of leading firms this year after calls from the market. It is identified as having "*some of the top litigators in town*" and for being "*one of the clear leaders in the region.*" The firm is widely acknowledged by rivals as being "*serious competition;*" clients, meanwhile, speak of "*the quality of its business and commercial litigation arms.*" With litigators in four offices in Kentucky, the firm can handle some of the most complex cases around, be these in the areas of bankruptcy, natural resources or general commercial litigation, to name just three. Commentators also noted the litigators' willingness to work cross-departmentally, drawing on other practice groups as and when needed. The healthcare and corporate groups were specifically mentioned in this regard.

The Lawyers: Clients fell over themselves to recommend "*ethical, sharp-witted trial attorney*" **Hiram Ely** (see p.841). They like "*his logical presentation of a case;*" "*his effortless demeanour in the courtroom*" and his "*ability to keep his powder dry and let the other side ambush themselves.*" Exuding a "*Kentuckian, confident coolness,*" he is also "*not afraid to be innovative in his approach to preventing litigation.*" Ely has a diverse practice, is a certified mediator and arbitrator and has lately served as national coordinating counsel for a notable healthcare client. **Eric Ison** (see p.843) is the esteemed chair of the litigation group. Described as a "*wonderful trial attorney with a real flair in his presentation,*" he is certainly "*a real mover and shaker who brings in a lot of business.*" "*One of the excellent attorneys in the state,*" Ison has been noted for his involvement in a couple of high-profile defamation cases recently, though his practice also encompasses products liability and appellate work. "*Excellent business litigator*" **Janet Jakubowicz** (see p.843) was also roundly applauded by clients. Noted in particular for her "*tough, fiery and well-prepared approach,*" they pointed to her "*incredible intelligence and wealth of talent.*" Hers is a business and commercial litigation practice covering securities and RICO litigation. She has been heavily involved with the representation of Papa John's International recently. Treasurer-elect of the ABA, **Bill Robinson** (see p.845) has a "*flourishing*" trial and appellate practice and works, too, on governmental affairs. Debuting in the table of leading individuals this year, **John Bush** (see p.839) is admired for "*successfully attracting good complex litigation*" and appellate matters. He was specifically singled out for his defense of antitrust, securities and general insurance cases.

The Clients: HCA; Weyerhaeuser; LifePoint Hospitals; Navistar International Transportation; Lennox International; Louisville Bedding;

Kentucky
Leading individuals
(Litigation: General Commercial)

1 CRONAN IV Charles *Stites & Harbison*, Louisville
HAYNES Greg *Wyatt Tarrant*, Louisville
REED John *Reed Weitkamp*, Louisville

2 COLLIER Philip *Stites & Harbison*, Lexington
HENLEIN Carl *Frost Brown*, Louisville
HINKLE IV Samuel *Stoll Keenon*, Louisville
KING W Gregory *Ogden Newell*, Louisville
MILLER Winston *Frost Brown*, Louisville
SNYDER Sheryl *Frost Brown*, Louisville
STOPHER Edward *Boehl Stopher*, Louisville

3 CONNOLLY Robert *Stites & Harbison*, Louisville
CORYELL II Cornelius *Wyatt Tarrant*, Louisville
ELY III Hiram *Greenebaum Doll*, Louisville
HOVIOUS Gregg *Tachau Maddox*, Louisville
ISON Eric *Greenebaum Doll*, Louisville
JAKUBOWICZ Janet *Greenebaum Doll*, Louisville
MILLIMAN James *Middleton Reutlinger*, Louisville
PITT M Stephen *Wyatt Tarrant*, Louisville
SNELL Virginia *Wyatt Tarrant*, Louisville
TACHAU David *Tachau Maddox*, Louisville

4 BALLANTINE Douglas *Ogden Newell*, Louisville
BALLANTINE John *Ogden Newell*, Louisville
BUSH John *Greenebaum Doll*, Louisville
CASSIS Charles *Frost Brown*, Louisville
CLAY Richard *Woodward Hobson*, Louisville
DOHENY Frank *Dinsmore & Shohl*, Louisville
FENZEL Mark *Middleton Reutlinger*, Louisville
GREENWELL Charles *Middleton Reutlinger*, Louisville
HALE David *Reed Weitkamp*, Louisville
MONOHAN David *Woodward Hobson*, Louisville
MURPHY Marc *Stites & Harbison*, Louisville
ROBINSON III Wm *Greenebaum Doll*, Covington
ROYSE David *Stoll Keenon*, Louisville
SHIVEL Charles *Stoll Keenon*, Lexington
THOMPSON B Todd *Thompson Miller*, Louisville

Up-and-coming individuals
KAPLAN David *Frost Brown*, Louisville

Leading individuals (Litigation: IP)
1 COX Donald *Lynch Cox*, Louisville
HIGGINS James *Middleton Reutlinger*, Louisville
WHEAT Jack *Stites & Harbison*, Louisville

Individuals are listed alphabetically in each band.

PNC Financial Services Group; Hillerich & Bradsby; Rally's Hamburger and Papa John's International.

Stites & Harbison PLLC
See firm details p.854

The Firm: This firm, one of the oldest in the USA, has "*a strong litigation component and is quite rightly listed at the top of the pack for litigation.*" Three Kentucky offices and "*a broad base covering the whole state*" provide a strong reason why clients recommend the firm – plus it fields over 30 commercial litigators with extensive experience. Traditionally strong in products liability litigation, clients additionally note the strength of the team on large class actions, a variety of business litigation and complex employment and environmental matters.

The Lawyers: Mike Cronan (see p.840) strikes the market as a "*professional, well-prepared, smooth operator*" and an "*incredibly safe pair of hands.*" His "*charismatic demeanor*" and "*expertise on heavy-duty motions*" help define his approach to a commercial litigation practice that incorporates products liability and healthcare law. He has an impressive array of clients, among them Brown-Forman and KFC. **Phil Collier** (see p.840) takes a "*details-oriented approach*" to business litigation. He is representing the Goodrich Corporation in an action involving liability for groundwater remediation costs associated with a 150-acre chemical manufacturing facility, the trial for which is scheduled for later in 2005. "*Outstanding litigator*" **Bob Connolly** (see p.840) devotes much of his time to products liability and construction law and comes highly recommended by clients. He has recently acted in a case concerning a construction accident in North Carolina involving a double fatality after an unsecured crane fell on construction workers. He is also representing the injured parties in a tank farm (petroleum storage facility) explosion in Western Kentucky. Connolly is head of the litigation department and serves as regional trial counsel to Howmedica Osteonics, a manufacturer of prosthetic devices. Maintaining his position in the table for another year is the "*highly recommended and fabulous lawyer*" **Marc Murphy** (see p.844). Murphy is the chair of the firm's white-collar crime group and, among other matters, has been heavily involved with Alsthom Power during the past year. Making his debut in the table is **Jack Wheat** (see p.846), who leads the IP and technology group and is adjunct professor of IP law at the University of Louisville.

The Clients: Yum! Brands; Goodrich; Alsthom Power; Brown-Forman; Electrolux; AEP; Regional Airport Authority of Louisville and Caldwell Energy & Environmental.

Wyatt, Tarrant & Combs LLP
See firm details p.856

The Firm: Historically the firm has been well known for the quality of its corporate practice; in recent years the litigation practice has excelled to the point where it is now readily referred to as "*a quality commercial litigation group.*" It has developed an exceptionally strong presence in the Kentucky market, with four offices across the state and approximately 60 attorneys spending the majority of their time on litigation. Clients highlighted the strength of the group in terms of banking and construction litigation and also recommended its "*strong appellate arm.*" Further praise was given for the quality of the group's work in healthcare and employment litigation.

The Lawyers: "*Top of anybody's list of all-star litigators in Kentucky*" is **Greg Haynes**, a man described as "*100% quality through and through*" and "*about as good as it gets.*" He concentrates his practice on commercial litigation and successfully represented the Housing Authority of Louisville in the dismissal of claims brought on behalf of children allegedly poisoned by exposure to lead-based paint. "*Making a good team with Haynes*" is the "*personable*" **Virginia Snell**. Chair of the appellate practice group, Snell was pinpointed by peers as "*exceptionally good on heavy-duty appellate motions*" and almost exclusively practices at this level. Covering a wide range of areas, including legal malpractice and securities fraud, she has been involved in cases for some of the largest retail and insurance companies in the USA. Another "*great attorney*" attracting plaudits is **Stephen Pitt**. Displaying variety in his work, Pitt is deemed to be "*exceptional in the fields he works in*" – complex commercial litigation, environmental and coal supply contracts issues. Moving up the table the "*very, very fine commercial lawyer*" **Corky Coryell** is "*an extraordinarily bright fellow.*" He chairs the firm's commercial litigation practice group and concentrates on banking litigation, products liability and UCC and consumer protection litigation.

The Clients: Wal-Mart; Louisville Metro Housing Authority; Churchill Downs; Destec Energy; GE; PNC Bank; Zurich North America; Heaven Hill Distilleries; Southern Baptist Theological Seminary and Thorntons.

Band 2

Middleton Reutlinger PSC
See firm details p.851

The Firm: Middleton Reutlinger graduates to the second tier of leading firms this year on the back of overwhelming client feedback. The litigation department of this full-service firm has gained respect for its pattern of "*taking into account the size of a matter, not overstaffing it and spending to a client's budget.*" Based in Louisville, this long-established law firm is widely admired not only for the myriad of talented attorneys on hand to deal with most issues, but also for "*the client-oriented*" approach it adopts. The litigators at this 38-attorney firm were especially recommended for their IP and insurance cases.

The Lawyers: Jim Milliman (see p.844) garnered universal support as "*an aggressive, passionate trial lawyer.*" Often found in the spotlight, Milliman is "*a hard fighter, who certainly is a real winner of cases.*" This in turn is "*confidence-inspiring for clients.*" He has extensive experience of class actions and trade secret cases and is a well-known figure in the defense of tobacco cases. "*Frontline guy*" and "*terrific IP litigator*"

Jim Higgins (see p.842) has been influential in the development of a large IP law group and additionally undertakes business litigation. **Charles Greenwell** (see p.842), meanwhile, has turned heads with his "*fine banking litigation practice and all-round smartness.*" This "*aggressive top-drawer commercial litigator*" debuts in the table and displays a commendable degree of flexibility, also working on medical negligence and products liability cases. **Mark Fenzel** (see p.841) had peers commenting: "*This is a lawyer I would personally hire.*" He also debuts in the table and displays a style that is described as "*not aggressive in the traditional sense, but more sober and thoughtful in his aggression, yet real effective.*" Fenzel specializes in insurance defense and commercial litigation.

The Clients: Brown & Williamson Tobacco; Chevron USA; The Kroger Company and Papa John's International.

Ogden Newell & Welch PLLC

See firm details p.852

The Firm: This is another firm that moves up the table this year following client approval for "*its excellent reputation for litigation*" and "*general responsiveness to client needs.*" Impressing clients by "*really understanding the business side to the law and taking this into account,*" this litigation group was particularly noted for medical malpractice and products liability defense. Long-standing clients could not see any need for improvement, readily recommending "*their prompt investigating, top-notch litigators and understanding of their clients' best interests.*" A highlight from the past year includes a medical malpractice action stemming from alleged negligence during leg surgery, after which the patient claimed that she suffered a nerve injury in her left arm. The jury returned a unanimous verdict for the defense.

The Lawyers: This firm is home to some of the "*stars of the state,*" and **Greg King** (see p.843) is no exception. "*A perfect gentleman on all fronts,*" King heads the litigation department and concentrates his practice in medical malpractice with a touch of products liability work. He acted on the appeal of the case of dermatologist James Green, MD, concerning his alleged negligence in allowing an unlicensed physician assistant to perform various surgical procedures. The original jury verdict was upheld on appeal and is widely considered to be a test case on how juries may respond in the future. "*A respected member of the Bar,*" **Jack Ballantine** (see p.839) is becoming increasingly involved in mediations; he mediated the claims made against the Archbishop of Louisville regarding the alleged abuse of minors and adults by various priests, and a case regarding the manufacturer of a rifle that misfired. He is also acting as co-counsel on a pending appeal of a $28 million judgment. "*Following in his father's footsteps*" and making his debut in the table is **Doug Ballantine** (see p.839). Said one commentator: "*Like his father, he is a gentleman and considers cases with a degree of sensibility.*" And from another: "*I wouldn't hesitate to use him in front of a jury; in a few years time Doug will be the guy.*" Doug Ballantine's practice covers IP, professional malpractice, toxic torts and products liability. He was involved in an interpleader action in the federal court to determine the distribution of proceeds resulting from the conversion of Anthem Insurance from a mutual insurance company to a stock insurance company.

The Clients: AP Capital Insurance; Preferred Physicians Insurance; Professional Risk Management Service; ProClaim America; American Healthcare Indemnity; Chubb Group; Norton Hospitals of Louisville and Papa John's International.

Reed Weitkamp Schell & Vice PLLC

The Firm: The third firm to climb the rankings earned enthusiastic praise for "*the delivery of high-quality written materials, general responsiveness and sensitivity to the delicate balance between the legal fees and the client's objectives.*" Though far smaller than some of the others listed, this firm has six lawyers dedicated to litigation, and peers were quick to confirm how "*well prepared, skillful and aggressive they are; they really play by the rules and get the job done.*" While the group handles a mixture of work, it was noted in particular for its IP, antitrust and employment litigation.

The Lawyers: John Reed (see p.845) was widely commended to researchers for "*his legal acumen, diligence and ethical attributes.*" "*Very sharp and never missing a trick,*" he has a broad commercial litigation practice that includes antitrust, IP and insurance coverage disputes. A new addition to the table is "*the remarkably quick study, excellent writer and courteous, respectful lawyer*" **David Hale** (see p.842). "*Most impressive in handling the daily curveballs and confrontations*" of a case, Hale represents the Official Treasurer of Kentucky and focuses on business and insurance litigation and government investigations.

The Clients: UST; ResCare; Jones Plastic & Engineering; Humana; National City Bank of Kentucky; Main Street Realty; Commonwealth of Kentucky; Kindred Healthcare; First Capital Bank of Kentucky; Fifth Third Bank of Kentucky; Massie-Clark Development Company; Northwestern Mutual Insurance Company; Landtech and Citizens Union Bank.

Stoll, Keenon & Park, LLP

The Firm: Commentators described this old-line firm as "*excellent in commercial litigation*" and noted that it "*makes its presence felt in the Lexington market.*" The reputation of the litigation group is somewhat derived from the "*fine litigators,*" but it is also due to its superb client roster. Commentators agree that IP, business and insurance defense are particular areas of excellence, with clients commending the work of the group in the equine and mineral industries. Its First Amendment litigation was also applauded, and in this and other respects, the firm continues to represent the Lexington Herald-Leader.

The Lawyers: Peers consistently referred to **Sam Hinkle** as "*an excellent trial lawyer.*" The partner-in-charge of the growing Louisville office, Hinkle is also chair of the environmental law department. With his time devoted to bankruptcy and debtor/creditor relations as well as environmental issues, one thing is certain: "*Hinkle is a very tough litigator.*" The second attorney to be endorsed by the market is **Charles Shivel**, who is especially well known for his "*depth of experience in the coal industry.*" His practice extends also to IP litigation, claims arising out of commercial bank lending and in the past year he was involved in the defense of a major dairy cooperative embroiled in antitrust charges. Following the departure of Bob Houlihan, **David Royse**'s entry maintains the firm's three-attorney stake in the table of individual litigators. Said one commentator: "*Before Bob left, I think he trained this remarkably talented lawyer whom I would recommend highly.*" In addition to general litigation, Royse works on zoning, land use and eminent domain.

The Clients: Lexmark; The Lexington Herald-Leader; Bank One and State Farm.

Band 3

Boehl Stopher & Graves, LLP

See firm details p.848

The Firm: This "*excellent litigation shop*" joins the table of leading firms following unprecedented feedback for "*some very intelligent and very personable people.*" All in all it is viewed as "*a good relationship firm.*" Almost wholly devoted to the defense of civil litigation, it is heartily recommended for products liability, toxic torts, employment disputes, IP law and professional negligence. The firm boasts 12 lawyers and ten paralegals and is considered particularly strong on "*high-risk, high-profile, voluminous cases, irrespective of subject matter.*" One recent highlight has been the defense of the Archdiocese of Louisville on 243 counts of abuse by priests; the settlement was generally considered to have been modest financially and not overly adverse in its impact on the Catholic Church.

The Lawyers: Much of the reputation of this firm is due to "*intelligent, professional Southern gentleman*" **Ed Stopher** (see p.846). "*The most effective and forceful attorney in town at present,*" according to some, "*seasoned trial attorney*" Stopher is the managing partner of the firm. He represents corporate and insurance clients in various matters including the defense of pharmaceutical-related claims, products liability and legal malpractice. He was lead counsel for CSX in a case involving the brain damage of a former employee allegedly caused by chemical cleaners in the workplace. The jury verdict favored the defense.

The Clients: CSX; Eli Lilly; Fleetwood Enterprises; LG&E Energy; Michelin North America; AIG Insurance; State Farm; National Collegiate Athletic Association and Rumpke.

Dinsmore & Shohl LLP

See firm details p.1452

The Firm: This Cincinnati-headquartered firm enters the table after receiving enthusiastic praise from commentators who recognize it to be "*a growing force in Kentucky.*" Dinsmore & Shohl is a full-service firm with two offices in Kentucky and covers some 30 or so specialist areas of litigation from antitrust to workers' compensation. It is increasingly seen as able to handle some of the more complex cases on offer, due in part to the fact that it can draw on an array of different specialists and resources from across the firm.

The Lawyers: Of the many notable attorneys in the litigation department, **Frank Doheny** is a definite standout individual. Peers recommended him to researchers as "*one hell of an attorney...an absolute star.*" Doheny concentrates in large part on the healthcare and products liability fields.

Tachau Maddox Hovious & Dickens PLC

See firm details p.855

The Firm: This firm knows how to take a "*scorched-earth, hard-ball*" approach to litigation. Market sources felt compelled to remark favorably on the "*aggression of the litigators and the excellent reputation they have in the Midwest.*" They also say it is "*the exact right size for a litigation boutique.*" A dynamic, young and up-and-coming firm, it was endorsed for its expert handling of all forms of trial work, especially commercial disputes, products liability and healthcare cases.

The Lawyers: The "*studious*" **David Tachau** (see p.846) is known for "*his astuteness, his excellent legal mind and sound judgment and the tireless way he works for his clients.*" Tachau represents plaintiffs and defendants in a range of civil matters ranging from insurance, trust and estate and healthcare litigation to employment disputes. He successfully acted as litigation counsel to PNC (as the executor of a $35 million estate) and worked on a class action securities fraud case brought against Kindred Healthcare and Ventas. A new addition to this year's table is "*street fighter*" **Gregg Hovious** (see p.843). "*Energetic and zealous in the representation of his clients,*" he too represents both plaintiffs and defendants and has numerous financial institutions and healthcare providers on his client list as well as a flourishing personal injury practice. Away from practice, Hovious lectures on lender liability matters.

The Clients: National City Corporation; The PNC Financial Services Group; JPMorgan Chase; Bank One; Huntington National Bank and Stock Yards Bank; Kindred Healthcare; ResCare and Ventas; Commonwealth Industries; GE and AEGON USA.

Woodward, Hobson & Fulton LLP

The Firm: Clients and peers hold this "*strong litigation firm*" in high regard and it enters the table accordingly. Thirteen attorneys practice litigation in a broad range of areas from insurance coverage and premises liability disputes through to complex tort litigation. Clients highlight the group's strength in employment litigation and workers' compensation claims, while peers speak of "*the fine history of good litigation*" at the firm.

The Lawyers: "*First-class litigator*" **David Monohan** would "*certainly be on my list of those who I would get to represent me,*" said one respected fellow attorney. "*He is a solid trial lawyer who is able to take on unusual things.*" Monohan's practice encompasses railroad defense, products liability, hospital defense, admiralty and professional malpractice. **Dick Clay** also came in for praise as "*a good, solid trial lawyer able to take on almost anything.*" He practices complex litigation in the fields of business disputes and healthcare as well as administrative and appellate law.

Other Notable Practitioners

Don Cox of Lynch, Cox, Gilman & Mahan, P.S.C. continues to be held in extremely high regard by the market for "*his tenacious and smart approach.*" Working mostly on litigation matters, Cox's practice spills over into commercial transactions; he is best known for his "*relentless*" representation in IP and patent disputes. He is "*certainly a worthy adversary*" and benefits from "*a good reputation for results and a loyal client base.*" **Todd Thompson** of Thompson Miller & Simpson PLC was routinely described to researchers as "*careful, methodical and always well prepared.*" Thompson does "*a lot of trial work and is well respected for the results he gets*" and "*is often found defending difficult, complex cases.*"

REAL ESTATE

Kentucky
Leading firms (Real Estate)
1 FROST BROWN TODD LLC *Louisville*
STITES & HARBISON PLLC *Louisville*
WYATT TARRANT & COMBS, LLP *Louisville*
2 GREENEBAUM DOLL & MCDONALD *Louisville*
Firms are listed alphabetically in each band.

Band 1

Frost Brown Todd LLC

See firm details p.849

The Firm: A firm that continues to impress peers and clients with "*its relationship-oriented approach and general thoroughness.*" This "*well-connected*" group numbers approximately 30 attorneys, with some ten or so devoted to real estate in Louisville alone. It earns particular praise for its development work, ground leases and zoning issues, but has the resources to allow it to cover the full gamut of practice. Highlights include representing UPS on the half-million sq ft warehouse facility linked to the UPS Worldport project in Louisville, and the Rouse Company's $123 million acquisition of a regional enclosed mall and $155 million refinancing of an existing mall.

The Lawyers: One client revealed to researchers: "*It is as much the individual attorneys as opposed to the firm itself that make this real estate group great.*" First among the most talented is **Tim Martin** (see p.844), for some "*the number one real estate attorney in Kentucky.*" Martin has involvement in some of the most complex transactions on offer; "*solid, efficient, calm, assured and available,*" he can "*translate the most complex real estate transaction into easy-to-explain plain English.*" He counsels the firm's developer and banking clients on transactional issues. **Dale Ahearn** (see p.839) has a national practice in relation to shopping centers, representing both developers and lenders as well as tenants. One client commented: "*We would definitely turn to him for any high-level work that we have.*" **Jude Clark** (see p.840) is another "*excellent real estate attorney*" who impressed commentators with his representation of lenders and developers. He has "*extensive knowledge of land use and zoning issues, as well as experience in tax credits and public finance.*" A fourth leading name is that of **Marshall Eldred** (see p.841), who is known for his devotion to the cause, frequently "*doing over and above what is called of him.*" He possesses "*really specialized technical knowledge,*" which

Kentucky
Leading individuals (Real Estate)
Senior Statesman
JOSEPH III Alfred *Stites & Harbison*, Louisville
[1] AHEARN Dale *Frost Brown*, Louisville
HADEN William *Stites & Harbison*, Louisville
MARTIN Timothy *Frost Brown*, Louisville
VINCENTI Michael *Wyatt Tarrant*, Louisville
[2] BARDENWERPER William *Bardenwerper*, Louisville
BURCHETT Angela *Stites & Harbison*, Louisville
CAMP Leo *Wyatt Tarrant*, Louisville
CLARK Jude *Frost Brown*, Louisville
ELDRED Marshall *Frost Brown*, Louisville
GATHRIGHT Joseph *Weber & Rose*, Louisville
HINES Barry *Stites & Harbison*, Louisville
PRICE Glenn *Greenebaum Doll*, Louisville
SAFFER David *Stites & Harbison*, Louisville
VICE Robert *Reed Weitkamp*, Louisville
Individuals are listed alphabetically in each band.

certainly instills confidence in the developers and lenders that instruct him on all types of real estate projects. Eldred is general counsel for the Home Builders Association of Louisville.

The Clients: Morgan Stanley; GE Capital; The Rouse Company; UPS; NTS Development Company; Hogan Development and US Bank.

Stites & Harbison PLLC
See firm details p.854

The Firm: This old-line firm retains its top slot in the table following enthusiastic praise for "*the technical expertise of attorneys who really understand the business elements of a project.*" This well-established Kentucky player operates out of three offices across the state, the main one being in Louisville. It is particularly noted for its separate real estate financing practice group and its representation of many commercial lenders, local banks and life assurance companies. Clients singled out the flourishing conduit lending practice group, much of the work of which is conducted on a national level. Low-income housing and community redevelopment are also areas of excellence.

The Lawyers: Bill Haden (see p.842) comes to the attention of clients because of his "*dedicated professionalism and the way he focuses on the business element to a deal.*" Haden has a "*terrific*" practice representing banks and other lenders, life assurance companies and borrowers; in one of his biggest deals of the year he advised the largest church in Kentucky on a $55 million loan to finance a $90 million construction project. **Alfred Joseph** (see p.843) continues to be wide-

ly admired as "*the dean of Kentucky real estate.*" Although often taking more of a back seat role on day-to-day matters, Joseph has a vast amount of knowledge in public housing projects among other things. He recently advised Louisville's housing authority on the city's Park DuValle Revitalization. A new addition to the table is **David Saffer** (see p.845). Moving from Wyatt, Tarrant & Combs to join this group, Saffer has brought experience of acting for institutional lenders in all types of commercial loans and "*gives a great boost to the conduit lending arm of the real estate finance group.*" Saffer is also former senior vice president at Ohio Valley National Bank and brings with him a great deal of "*practical experience.*" According to interviewees, **Barry Hines** (see p.842) is experienced in all forms of real estate finance and is particularly noted for his flourishing national conduit lending practice. "*Young and able partner*" **Angela Stinebruner Burchett** (see p.839) consolidates her position in the table. Her practice encompasses all forms of real estate transactions, although she is best known for financing and has recently represented Artesian Mortgage Company.

The Clients: Dixie Real Properties; SY Bancorp; JPMorgan Chase Bank; Stock Yards Bank & Trust Company; Southeast Christian Church; National City (Kentucky) and the Regional Airport Authority of Louisville.

Wyatt, Tarrant & Combs LLP
See firm details p.856

The Firm: This firm earns its top-band status for "*the wealth of resources on hand*" and attorneys' service standards. It has four offices in Kentucky and over 20 experienced lawyers form the real estate and lending practice group. Traditionally best known for its lending expertise, the group excels, too, in advice to developers on all aspects of the ownership and development of all forms of real estate.

The Lawyers: Rated very highly indeed by clients and peers, "*exceptional real estate attorney*" **Michael Vincenti** surprises no one with his top-tier position. He concentrates his practice on real estate development and commercial lending. **Leo Camp** has a great name as a result of his "*superior real estate knowledge*" and effective client representation on bigger deals. He is proficient in both general real estate and commercial lending. Arthur Rouse also picked up a fair amount of client approval for his good business mind and ability to think through the ramifications of a deal.

The Clients: Union Planters; Bank One; Houchens Industries and Schatten Properties.

Band 2

Greenebaum Doll & McDonald PLLC
See firm details p.850

The Firm: Arguably best known for the strength of the corporate group, Greenebaum fields an impressive real estate finance and development group. Clients indicate "*no hesitation*" when contemplating whether to "*send them something really complex;*" the resources on hand (four offices in Kentucky alone and an array of specialist attorneys) perhaps explains their confidence. A name for superb land use and zoning advice does not detract from its reputation for handling almost any type of real estate project from the development stage through to the eventual lease or sale.

The Lawyers: According to the market, **Glenn Price** is "*one of the best land use and zoning attorneys in the state.*" "*Extremely knowledgeable on the ins and outs*" of this area of law, his is "*a name readily associated with top-flight real estate work*" and productive negotiations over land use disputes, zone changes and permits.

The Clients: Jewish Hospital HealthCare Services; Kroger Company; Bayer Properties; HCA and the University of Louisville.

Other Notable Practitioners
Moving from Ackerson & Yann to Weber & Rose, **Joe Gathright** and his "*exceptional reputation*" continue to attract market comment. Overlapping real estate law with commercial finance and some corporate law, Gathright is considered the perfect choice for midsized real estate clients. He is said to have "*a wealth of real estate experience right at his fingertips.*" **Bill Bardenwerper** of Bardenwerper & Talbott PLLC in Louisville debuts in the tables following overwhelming support for his "*specialist zoning and land use expertise.*" In addition, he is expert in condominium law and land use litigation. Another debut in the table is **Robert Vice** of Reed Weitkamp Schell & Vice PLLC, who is considered "*Kentucky's premier lawyer for low-income housing tax credit projects.*" Vice impresses clients with "*his practical and understandable approach to the financing and syndication of these projects.*" He has further substantial experience representing community development organizations and other more mainstream real estate developers.

Leaders in Kentucky

AHEARN, Dale
Frost Brown Todd LLC, Louisville
502 568 0275
dahearn@fbtlaw.com
Recommended in Real Estate
Practice Areas: Lead counsel in development of 100+ regional shopping centers and many major industrial facilities.
Prof. Memberships: Kentucky Bar Association, 1978; International Council of Shopping Centers; CoreNet Global.
Publications: University of Kentucky, 'Use Restrictions on Real Estate'; Commercial Leasing Law and Strategy, 'Require Sublease that Protects Your Interests' (2001), 'Essential and Advanced Protections for Landlords in Subleases' (2001), 'Dealing with Landlord Default: An Introduction' (1999), 'Lessors Beware: Rejection of Lease By Lessee in Bankruptcy May Not Terminate Sublessee's Interest' (1999), 'Risk Allocation for Hazardous Substances' (1998).
Personal: Michigan State University, BA, 1975, University of Michigan, JD, 1977.

BALLANTINE, Douglas C
Ogden Newell & Welch PLLC, Louisville
502 560 4247
dballantine@ogdenlaw.com
Recommended in Litigation
Practice Areas: Concentration in commercial, intellectual property, and environmental litigation, including superfund and toxic tort matters. Experience with professional negligence litigation, especially defense of medical malpractice cases, and defense of personal injury and products liability actions.
Prof. Memberships: American, Kentucky (Chair, Continuing Legal Education Commission; Ethics Committee), and Louisville Bar Associations; Advisor Committee on Local Rules of the United States Court of Appeals for the Sixth Circuit; Kentucky Supreme Court Civil Rules Committee; Defense Research Institute; Kentucky Defense Counsel, Inc.
Personal: Indiana University (Bloomington) (JD, 1988); American University (BA, 1984). Listed in 'Best Lawyers in America,' Business Litigation.

BALLANTINE, John T
Ogden Newell & Welch PLLC, Louisville
502 560 4213
jballantine@ogdenlaw.com
Recommended in Litigation
Practice Areas: Civil, personal injury, and commercial litigation with concentration on professional liability and medical malpractice defense cases; mediation and arbitration of all types of civil cases and claims (excluding domestic relations).
Prof. Memberships: American, Kentucky, and Louisville Bar Associations; Fellow, American College of Trial Lawyers; Life Member, Judicial Conference of US Court of Appeals, Sixth Circuit; Federation of Defense and Corporate Counsel; Kentucky Defense Counsel, Inc.
Personal: Harvard Law School (LLB, 1957); University of Kentucky (AB, high distinction, 1952). Listed in 'Best Lawyers in America', Personal Injury Litigation; recipient of Kentucky Bar Association Outstanding Lawyer Award (2003).

BARDENWERPER, William
Bardenwerper & Talbott PLLC, Louisville 502 426 6688
Recommended in Real Estate

BECK Jr, Robert M
Stites & Harbison PLLC, Lexington
859 226 2336
rbeck@stites.com
Recommended in Corporate/M&A
Practice Areas: Business Service Group. Member of Management Committee. Emphasis in equine, general corporate, commercial finance, mergers and acquisitions.
Prof. Memberships: Admitted to practice in Kentucky (1975) and United States Supreme Court. Member of American, Kentucky and Fayette County Bar Associations.
Career: Member of Stites & Harbison.
Publications: Coauthor, 'Developments in Equine Breeding Syndications', University of Kentucky CLE publications, 1999.
Personal: JD, Vanderbilt University, 1975; BA, Economics, Vanderbilt University, 1971.

BECKER, Wendy
Greenebaum Doll & McDonald PLLC, Lexington 859 288 4701
wlb@gdm.com
Recommended in Employment
Practice Areas: Member in the law firm Greenebaum Doll & McDonald, PLLC. Concentrates in employment law.
Prof. Memberships: Kentucky Bar Association (Labor and Employment Law Section), Fayette County Bar Association.
Publications: 'Evaluating Employee Performance', Legal Handbook for Business, 2000, 'Workplace Harassment: Sexual, Racial and Gender' (with Julie K Hackworth), UK-CLE Monograph , 2002; 1998, 'Discrimination on the Basis of Disability' (Richard G Griffith), UK-CLE 'Employment Law Handbook', 1992; Numerous presentations in field.
Personal: University of Richmond, BA; Middlebury College, MA; University of Kentucky College of Law, JD.

BECKMAN, David
Frost Brown Todd LLC, Louisville
502 568 0374
dbeckman@fbtlaw.com
Recommended in Corporate/M&A

Practice Areas: Extensive experience in mergers and acquisitions, joint ventures, franchising, financial institutions law, and general commercial and business transactions.
Prof. Memberships: Admitted Kentucky Bar 1988. Member of American Bar Association Sections on Business Banking, Tax and Forum on Franchising.
Career: Frost Brown Todd LLC; Vice-Chair Corporate/Business Department.
Personal: JD (cum laude), Northwestern University, 1988; AB (cum laude), Harvard College, 1985.

BENDER, Jack
Greenebaum Doll & McDonald PLLC, Lexington 859 288 4607
jcb@gdm.com
Recommended in Environment, Natural Resources
Practice Areas: Mr Bender's practice involves consulting and representing clients in litigation with respect to air emission, solid and hazardous waste, and wastewater compliance and permitting issues. He also focuses his practice on the defense of tort claims alleging injury due to the release of pollutants.
Prof. Memberships: Fayette County Bar Association; Kentucky Bar Association; Air & Waste Management Association; Editor, Kentucky Air Quality Letter, a quarterly newsletter published since 1998 by Greenebaum Doll & McDonald.
Personal: Pennsylvania State University, BS, Mining Engineering; University of Kentucky, College of Law, JD.

BIRCHFIELD, Thomas J
Greenebaum Doll & McDonald PLLC, Louisville 502 587 3663
tjb@gdm.com
Recommended in Employment
Practice Areas: Member of the law firm Greenebaum Doll & McDonald, PLLC. Concentrates in the areas of labor and employment law.
Prof. Memberships: Chairperson, Employment Law Steering Committee, USLAW Network, Inc. - 2002-04, Indiana Bar Association, Labor and Employment Law Section, Kentucky Bar Association, Labor and Employment Law Section, Louisville Bar Association, Society for Human Resources Management, Kentucky State Council Member, 1999 to present.
Career: Field Examiner National Labor Relations Board, Region 25 1984-85.
Publications: 'Kentucky Employment Law Letter', M Lee Smith Publishing Co., contributing editor, 1992-present.
Personal: JD, Indiana University 1998.

BRADLEY Jr, Craig C
Stites & Harbison PLLC, Louisville
502 681 0411
cbradley@stites.com
Recommended in Corporate/M&A
Practice Areas: Business Service

Group. Practice emphasis in securities and corporate finance.
Prof. Memberships: Admitted to practice in Kentucky (1980). Member of American, Kentucky and Louisville Bar Associations, Kentucky Securities Law Legislative Advisory Committee and Drafting Committee for Kentucky Business Corporation Act.
Career: Member of Stites & Harbison. With the firm since 1980.
Personal: JD, University of Kentucky, 1980; BA, University of Virginia, 1977.

BROWN, David C
Stites & Harbison PLLC, Louisville
502 681 0421
dbrown@stites.com
Recommended in Environment, Natural Resources
Practice Areas: Kentucky Public Service Commission practice, healthcare acquisitions, commercial and business transactions and energy regulatory transactions. Certified Mediator, Private Adjudication Center, Duke University School of Law, 2002.
Prof. Memberships: Admitted to practice in Kentucky. Member of American, Kentucky and Louisville Bar Associations.
Career: Member of Stites & Harbison. Former Managing Partner. With the firm since 1964.
Personal: JD, University of Virginia, 1964; BA, Kenyon College, 1961.

BURCHETT, Angela Stinebruner
Stites & Harbison PLLC, Louisville
502 681 0542
aburchett@stites.com
Recommended in Real Estate
Practice Areas: Real Estate and Finance Service Group. Practice emphasis in conduit lending and commercial leasing.
Prof. Memberships: Admitted to practice in Kentucky (1995). Member of American, Kentucky and Louisville Bar Associations and Kentucky Chapter of Commercial Real Estate Women (Founding Member).
Career: Member of Stites & Harbison. With the firm since 1995. Selected by Business First of Louisville as Forty Under Forty.
Personal: JD, University of Louisville, 1995. BS, summa cum laude, Accounting, University of Kentucky, 1992.

BUSH, John K
Greenebaum Doll & McDonald PLLC, Louisville 502 587 3669
jkb@gdm.com
Recommended in Litigation
Practice Areas: Complex and appellate litigation (including antitrust, securities, financial institutions, intellectual property and product liability disputes).
Career: Formerly of Gibson, Dunn & Crutches, Mr Bush was one of the attorneys for President Reagan during the

Iran-Contra investigation and was also one of the attorneys who represented former Los Angeles Police Sergeant Stacey Koon in his successful sentencing appeal to the US Supreme Court in the Rodney King case. At Greenebaum Mr Bush has represented companies and individuals in complex litigation and government investigations. He has practiced before numerous trial and appellate courts at the state and federal levels throughout the country.
Personal: Vanderbilt University, BA, summa cum laude; Harvard Law School, JD, cum laude.

CAMP, Leo
Wyatt, Tarrant & Combs LLP, Louisville
502 589 5235
Recommended in Real Estate

CASSIS, Charles
Frost Brown Todd LLC, Louisville
502 568 0233
ccassis@fbtlaw.com
Recommended in Litigation
Practice Areas: Mr Cassis is a member in the Litigation Department. His practice involves general trial litigation and appellate practice.
Prof. Memberships: Kentucky Bar Foundation, Founding Member; American Bar Foundation, Fellow; US Law Firm Group; appointed to special commissions by the Governor for changes in Kentucky Legislation; Jefferson County Police Merit Board, Chairman.
Career: One of the founding partners of Brown, Todd & Heyburn PLLC, one of the legacy firms to Frost Brown Todd LLC. Instrumental in forming the Litigation Department and served as its Chairman for several years.
Personal: JD, University of Kentucky, 1963; BS, University of Kentucky, 1960.

CLARK Jr, Jude
Frost Brown Todd LLC, Louisville
502 568 0260
jclark@fbtlaw.com
Recommended in Real Estate
Practice Areas: Real estate finance; commercial finance; real estate acquisitions, dispositions, leasing and development; affordable housing tax credit investments; zoning and land use.
Prof. Memberships: Fellow, American College of Mortgage Attorneys; American Bar Association, Real Property Probate and Trust Law Section; American Bar Association Forum on Affordable Housing; Kentucky and Indiana State Bar Associations.
Career: Member, Frost Brown Todd, LLC, joined 1999; Managing Attorney, AEGON USA Realty Advisors 1992-99.
Publications: 'Between a Rock and a Hard Place: Representing Owners in SNDA Negotiations', ICSC Publications.
Personal: Born 8 August 1955; JD University of Louisville, 1981; BS University of Kentucky, 1977.

CLAY, Richard
Woodward, Hobson & Fulton LLP, Louisville 502 581 8000
Recommended in Litigation

CLEARY, Richard S
Greenebaum Doll & McDonald PLLC, Louisville 502 587 3504
rsc@gdm.com
Recommended in Employment
Practice Areas: Chairman of Labor and Employment Group. Represents employers in complex labor and employment matters, with emphasis on the labor relations implications of corporate restructurings and defense of employment and wage/hour class and collective actions.
Prof. Memberships: ABA Labor and Employment Law Section; Cochair Committee on the Development of the Law Under the NLRA 1999-2002.
Publications: 'The Developing Labor Law', BNA, co-editor 2000-02 Supplements; editor, 'Kentucky Employment Law Letter', M Lee Smith Publishers, 1991-present.
Personal: JD Georgetown University 1981; Washington and Lee University 1978 (cum laude). Born in New York; married to Helen Bragg Curtin; two children.

COCKRUM, James
Frost Brown Todd LLC, Louisville
502 568 0317
jcockrum@fbtlaw.com
Recommended in Employment
Practice Areas: Mr Cockrum practices management-side labor and employment law representing employers before federal and state courts and administrative agencies.
Prof. Memberships: Kentucky Bar Association; Louisville Bar Association.
Career: Mr Cockrum has been a member of Frost Brown Todd LLC since its inception. He joined Brown, Todd & Heyburn in 1987.
Publications: Mr Cockrum has authored private seminar publications for seminars sponsored by the Kentucky Chamber of Commerce, the University of Louisville, the University of Kentucky and other organizations.
Personal: Born 16 August 1958. JD - Indiana University (Bloomington) 1987. BA - Kentucky Wesleyan College (cum laude) 1980.

COLLIER, Philip W
Stites & Harbison PLLC, Lexington
502 681 0415
pcollier@stites.com
Recommended in Litigation
Practice Areas: Business Litigation Service Group, Liability Defense Service Group, Class Action Defense Service Group. Practice emphasis in business and insurance litigation.
Prof. Memberships: Admitted to practice in Kentucky (1979) and the United States Supreme Court. Member of American, Kentucky and Louisville Bar Associations.

Career: Member of Stites & Harbison. Member of firm's Management Committee. 24 years' trial experience in Kentucky and Tennessee state courts, Kentucky and Ohio federal district courts and the federal multidistrict panel for complex litigation. Presented oral arguments before the United States Supreme Court in Itel Containers International Corp. v Huddleston, 113 S.Ct. 1095 (US 1993). Appellate argument before Kentucky Court of Appeals, Tennessee Supreme Court and United States Court of Appeals for the 6th Circuit.
Publications: Lecturer, Kentucky Bar Association Convention, 'Disputes in Closely Held Businesses', June 2003.
Personal: JD, University of Kentucky, 1979; BA, with high distinction, University of Kentucky, 1976.

CONNER, Stewart
Wyatt, Tarrant & Combs LLP, Louisville
502 589 5235
Recommended in Corporate/M&A

CONNOLLY, Robert M
Stites & Harbison PLLC, Louisville
502 681 0424
rconnolly@stites.com
Recommended in Litigation
Practice Areas: Liability Defense Service Group, Business Litigation Service Group, Construction Service Group. Practice emphasis in product liability and personal injury defense. Litigation attorney with over 20 years' experience. Has taken more than 70 cases to trial and argued many cases before Kentucky's appellate courts.
Prof. Memberships: Admitted to practice in Kentucky (1980), 6th Circuit US Court of Appeals. Member of American, Kentucky and Louisville Bar Associations, Louisville Bar Foundation, Inc., Defense Research Institute, Kentucky Defense Council and Maritime Law Association of the United States.
Career: Member of Stites & Harbison. With the firm since 1980. Currently serves as regional trial counsel to Howmedica Osteonics (a manufacturer of prosthetic devices). Has acted as lead trial attorney in product liability and personal injury litigation in federal and state courts throughout Kentucky and in Indiana, Iowa, Tennessee and Virginia.
Publications: Reported cases: Marley Cooling Tower v Caldwell Energy & Environmental, Inc., 280 F.Supp.2d 651 (W.D. Ky. 2003); Southeastern United Medigroup, Inc. v Hughes, et al., (Ky., 952 S.W.2d 195 1997); and others.
Personal: JD, Washington and Lee University, 1980. BA, Dartmouth College, Government (Honors), magna cum laude with high distinction, 1977.

CORYELL II, Cornelius
Wyatt, Tarrant & Combs LLP, Louisville
502 589 5235
Recommended in Litigation

COX, Donald
Lynch, Cox, Gilman & Mahan, P.S.C., Louisville 502 589 4215
Recommended in Litigation

CROMER, Brian A
Stites & Harbison PLLC, Louisville
502 681 0440
bcromer@stites.com
Recommended in Corporate/M&A
Practice Areas: Business and Finance Service Group. Practice emphasis in business law, international law, secured transactions, commercial law, banking, real estate law, mergers and acquisitions, securities law and general corporate matters.
Prof. Memberships: Admitted to practice in Kentucky, 1990. Member of American, Kentucky and Louisville Bar Associations.
Career: Member of Stites & Harbison. With the firm since 1990. First National Bank of Louisville, Louisville, Kentucky, Commercial Banking Officer (1985-87), Management Training Program (1983-85).
Personal: JD, with high distinction, University of Kentucky, 1990; editor in chief, Kentucky Law Journal; Order of the Coif. BA, Business Administration, Bellarmine University, 1983.

CRONAN IV, Charles J
Stites & Harbison PLLC, Louisville
501 681 0430
ccronan@stites.com
Recommended in Litigation
Practice Areas: Business Litigation Service Group. Civil litigation with emphasis on commercial litigation, products liability and hospital medical staffs.
Prof. Memberships: Admitted to practice in Kentucky (1970). Fellow of the American College of Trial Lawyers, Member of Federation of Defense and Corporate Counsel and Defense Research Institute, Member of American, Kentucky and Louisville Bar Associations, and Kentucky Bar Foundation.
Career: US Navy Judge Advocate General's Corps, 1970-74. Joined Stites & Harbison in 1974. Managing Partner, 1994-97. Listed in The Best Lawyers in America, 1989-present.
Personal: JD, cum laude, University of Louisville, 1970. BA, Government, Wesleyan University, 1967. Married, four grown children.

CRYDER, Bruce E
Greenebaum Doll & McDonald PLLC, Lexington 859 288 4623
bec@gdm.com
Recommended in Environment, Natural Resources
Practice Areas: Mineral and environmental law; commercial law; litigation.
Prof. Memberships: Fayette County Bar Association; Kentucky Bar Association; Ohio Bar Association; American Bar Association.
Personal: Ohio University, BA (cum laude); Ohio State University, JD (cum laude).

CURTZ, Chauncey
Dinsmore & Shohl LLP, Lexington
859 425 1000
Recommended in Environment, Natural Resources

DAVIS, Eberley
Stoll, Keenon & Park, LLP, Lexington
859 231 3000
Recommended in Environment, Natural Resources

DAWAHARE, Debra
Wyatt, Tarrant & Combs LLP, Lexington
859 233 2012
Recommended in Employment

DIAMOND, Ivan M
Greenebaum Doll & McDonald PLLC, Louisville 502 587 3534
imd@gdm.com
Recommended in Corporate/M&A

Practice Areas: Corporate, securities, bank acquisitions and regulatory matters.

Prof. Memberships: Louisville Bar Association; Kentucky Bar Association; Florida Bar Association; American Bar Association.

Career: Mr Diamond has counseled clients on numerous complex corporate transactions, including initial public offerings, public and private financings, and mergers and acquisitions. He regularly advises boards of directors on corporate governance issues, regulatory and securities law compliance matters. Prior to joining Greenebaum, he served as an attorney with the Securities and Exchange Commission.

Personal: University of Florida, BA (cum laude); University of Florida, JD.

DOHENY Jr, Frank
Dinsmore & Shohl LLP, Louisville
502 540 2300
Recommended in Litigation

DOLSON, Scott
Frost Brown Todd LLC, Louisville
502 568 0203
sdolson@fbtlaw.com
Recommended in Corporate/M&A

Practice Areas: Firm Practice Leader in corporate/M&A and tax. Practice emphasis includes business and tax planning for business startups and joint ventures, representing buyers or sellers in negotiated transactions, and representing shareholders and LLC members in freeze-out transactions and owner disputes. Experience handling federal and state civil tax controversies.

Prof. Memberships: Admitted to practice in Kentucky (1982). Member of the Kentucky and Louisville Bar Associations.

Career: Frost Brown Todd LLC Member.

Publications: 'Kentucky Limited Liability Companies', 'Business Succession Planning' and 'Kentucky Corporations Handbook'.

Personal: UVA Law, Harvard College.

ELDRED Jr, Marshall Polk
Frost Brown Todd LLC, Louisville
502 568 0262
meldred@fbtlaw.com
Recommended in Real Estate

Practice Areas: Member of Commercial Transaction/Real Estate Department. He concentrates in the areas of real estate acquisition, zoning, financing, development, construction, lease and sale of the finished project and certain real estate related litigation, such as condemnation, receiverships and leasehold disputes.

Prof. Memberships: Louisville, Kentucky and American Bar Associations. Past President and current Board Member of Legal Aid Society and Isaac W Bernheim Foundation; serves as General Counsel for the Home Builders Association of Louisville and for the past 23 years.

Personal: Vanderbilt University BA, 1960 and University of Kentucky JD, 1963 (Order of the Coif and Kentucky Law Journal).

ELY III, Hiram
Greenebaum Doll & McDonald PLLC, Louisville 502 587 3562
he@gdm.com
Recommended in Litigation

Practice Areas: Experienced senior trial lawyer concentrating in business litigation, alternate dispute resolution, corporate counseling and risk management, including experience in healthcare, product liability, tax court, insurance, condemnation, antitrust, and securities matters. Lead counsel in numerous bench trials and arbitrations and in more than 50 jury trials.

Prof. Memberships: Past Chairman of Litigation Section of Louisville, Kentucky Bar Association; Past President of Louisville, Kentucky Bar Foundation; Kentucky Bar Association; American Bar Association.

Career: Law Clerk, Hon James C Turk, USDC, WD Va.

Personal: Washington & Lee University (JD 1976); Centre College of Kentucky (BA 1973). Kentucky native.

ESCHELS, Philip
Greenebaum Doll & McDonald PLLC, Louisville 502 587 3665
pce@gdm.com
Recommended in Employment

Practice Areas: Member in the law firm Greenebaum Doll & McDonald, PLLC. Concentrates in the areas of labor and employment law.

Prof. Memberships: Louisville Bar Association (Section of Labor and Employment), Kentucky Bar Association (Cochair, Section of Labor and Employment, 1992), Indiana Bar Association (Section of Labor and Employment), American Bar Association (Committee on Equal Employment Opportunity, Section of Labor and Employment).

Career: Teacher, US History, 1974-81.

Publications: 'How to Avoid Legal Problems in Hiring and Firing in Kentucky', coauthor, Greenebaum Doll & McDonald, 2002.

Personal: JD Indiana University School of Law, 1983 (cum laude); BA, Concordia College, 1974.

FENZEL, Mark S
Middleton Reutlinger PSC, Louisville
502 584 1135
mfenzel@middreut.com
Recommended in Litigation

Practice Areas: Mr Fenzel specializes in insurance defense, professional errors and omissions, school law and commercial litigation. He is chair of the firm's Insurance Practice.

Prof. Memberships: Admitted to practice in United States Supreme Court and Kentucky. Member of National School Board Association, American Bar Association, Torts and Insurance Section; Louisville Bar Foundation; Citizens for Better Judges.

Career: Mr Fenzel was involved in a landmark negligence case (Kirschner v Louisville Gas & Electric Company) and McGinnis v Taitano, involving federal procedure and international jurisdictional issues. He also handled cases involving important school law and constitutional issues. (Blau v Fort Thomas Schools, Beckham v Jefferson County Schools and Cornett v Jefferson County Schools). Mr Fenzel was an attorney with the Judge Advocate General's Corps of the US Navy. For two years he was a trial attorney at Subic Bay Naval Base in the Philippines, handling complex criminal court martials and trying cases on board ships in the Indian Ocean. Mr Fenzel was the first Special Assistant to consolidate Navy prosecution of federal crimes in San Diego County. Military awards include Navy Achievement Medal, Navy Expeditionary Ribbon and Meritorious Unit Citation.

Personal: University of Louisville School of Law; University of Kentucky (BS Accounting).

FLEISCHAKER, Jon
Dinsmore & Shohl LLP, Louisville
502 540 2300
Recommended in Employment

GATHRIGHT Jr, Joseph
Weber & Rose, Louisville
502 589 2200
Recommended in Real Estate

GIESEL, James A
Frost Brown Todd LLC, Louisville
502 568 0307
jgiesel@fbtlaw.com
Recommended in Corporate/M&A

Practice Areas: Practicing in the general corporate, transactional and securities law areas, with significant experience involving corporate governance, public offerings, banking and investment management.

Prof. Memberships: Member of Kentucky and Louisville Bar Associations; Louisville Bar Foundation, Fellow and Board Member.

Personal: Mr Giesel received his JD degree (cum laude) in 1985 from Harvard Law School and his BA degree (magna cum laude) in 1982 from Yale University.

GLASSCOCK, Ed
Frost Brown Todd LLC, Louisville
502 568 0230
eglasscock@fbtlaw.com
Recommended in Corporate/M&A

Practice Areas: Cochairman of Mergers and Acquisitions Section. Has extensive experience in mergers and acquisitions, joint ventures and venture capital transactions.

Prof. Memberships: Admitted to practice in Kentucky (1969); Chambers & Partners, Chambers USA, ranked number one Corporate/M&A attorney in Kentucky; selected and listed in Naifeh and Smith, The Best Lawyers in America (1991-2005); Kentucky Bar Association, Past Chairman, Corporations, Banking and Business Law Section; American Bar Association, Member, Mergers and Acquisitions Committee; Louisville Bar Association, Past Chairman, Corporations, Banking and Business Law Section.

Career: Joined Frost Brown Todd (FBT), formerly Brown, Todd & Heyburn, 1969; Member, 1974; Managing Partner, Brown, Todd & Heyburn 1977-2001; Co-Managing Member, FBT (2001-Present); Member, Compensation Committee, FBT.

Publications: Glasscock, Lester, Lyndrup and Tannon, Buying and Selling a Business in Kentucky', §4 & 5, (1993, University of Kentucky College of Law/Office of Continuing Legal Education); Dolson, Glasscock, et al, Buying and Selling a Business in Kentucky', §2, (2002, University of Kentucky College of Law/Office of Continuing Legal Education, 2d ed); Dolson, Glasscock, et al, 'Kentucky Corporation Law', Chapter 6, (1997, University of Kentucky College of Law/Office of Continuing Legal Education).

Personal: JD with high distinction, University of Kentucky, 1969; Order of The Coif; Kentucky Law Journal, Member of Staff; Recipient, Outstanding Student Award, University of Kentucky, Phi Delta Phi, Graduate of the Year; BS Civil Engineering, 1966.

GORTON, William T
Stites & Harbison PLLC, Lexington
859 226 2241
wgorton@stites.com
Recommended in Environment, Natural Resources

Practice Areas: Environmental, natural resources, agriculture, mining, waste, energy and surety law counseling and litigation, environmental audits and due diligence related to large natural resource and environmentally sensitive commercial transactions, drafting, analyzing legislation and participating in rulemaking on behalf of clients.

Prof. Memberships: Admitted to practice in Kentucky and Pennsylvania and state and federal courts. Member of American, Kentucky and Fayette County and Pennsylvania Bar Associations.

Career: Member of Stites & Harbison. Joined the firm in 1993. University of Kentucky, Assistant Professor in Environmental Law, College of Agriculture, Natural Resources Conservation, 1998-present.

Publications: 'A Primer for Engineering and Technical Professionals regarding Reclamation and Environmental Surety Bonds', presented at the Society of Mining, Metallurgy and Exploration Annual Meeting, Cincinnati, Ohio, 2003.

Personal: JD, University of Kentucky, 1988; BS, Man-Environment Relations with Emphasis in Natural Systems, Pennsylvania State University, 1976.

GREENWELL, Charles D
Middleton Reutlinger PSC, Louisville
502 584 1135
cgreenwell@middreut.com
Recommended in Litigation

Practice Areas: Mr Greenwell concentrates in litigation arising from complex disputes involving banking, insurance, medical and railroad industries.

Prof. Memberships: Admitted to practice in US Supreme Court. Member of Kentucky and Louisville Bar Associations; Kentucky Bar Foundation; American Bar Association, Business Law and Tort Trial and Insurance Sections; National Association of Railroad Trial Counsel, former Executive Board Member; American Trial Lawyers Association; Kentucky Academy of Trial Attorneys.

Career: Mr Greenwell won multimillion dollar recoveries for wrongful deaths for mothers and babies against three pharmaceutical manufacturers. He represented patients in Sisters of Charity Health Systems, Inc. v Raikes, KY, (Kentucky Supreme Court recognized an exception to statutory peer review privilege). Mr Greenwell was lead counsel in Kentucky's landmark lender liability and punitive damages case, (Hanson v American National Bank & Trust Co.). His experience in insurer insolvencies and liquidations includes organization, representation and successful recovery for a multi-member, multi-state creditors' group of financial institutions from 13 states. Mr Greenwell represented American International Group in a multidistrict liquidation of Delta America Re Insurance Company (Stephens v American Home Assurance Company). He successfully defended banks and insurance companies against claims of bad faith (Baldwin v North American Company for Life and Health Insurance).

GRIFFITH, Richard
Stoll, Keenon & Park, LLP, Lexington
859 231 3000
Recommended in Employment

HABLE, Kevin
Wyatt, Tarrant & Combs LLP, Louisville
502 589 5235
Recommended in Corporate/M&A

HADEN Jr, William H
Stites & Harbison PLLC, Louisville
502 681 0473
bhaden@stites.com
Recommended in Real Estate

Practice Areas: Real Estate and Finance Service Group (Chair). Practice emphasis on real estate and commercial lending, commercial leasing, tax exempt financings, general banking and corporate.

Prof. Memberships: Admitted to practice in Kentucky (1972). Member of American, Kentucky and Louisville Bar Associations, National Association of Bond Lawyers, Corporate Trust Associates and International Association of Attorneys and Executives in Corporate Real Estate, and International Council of Shopping Centers.

Career: Member of Stites & Harbison. With the firm since 1972.

Publications: Author, 'Implied Covenants of Continuous Operation in Percentage Leases: Was Charles Dickens Right?', Commercial Leasing Law & Strategy, Volume 12, Number 6, November 1999.

Personal: JD, University of Kentucky, 1972. BA, History, University of Kentucky, 1969.

HALE, David J
Reed Weitkamp Schell & Vice PLLC, Louisville 502 657 1356
dhale@rwsvlaw.com
Recommended in Litigation

Practice Areas: Member in the Litigation Section of the firm. Mr Hale concentrates his practice in business, insurance and governmental litigation.

Prof. Memberships: Kentucky, Louisville, American and Federal Bar Associations.

Career: Member, Reed Weitkamp Schell & Vice PLLC. Former Assistant US Attorney for the Western District of Kentucky, 1995-99. Significant hearing and trial experience in all divisions of District.

Personal: JD, University of Kentucky (Member, National Moot Court Team); BA, Vanderbilt University; Leadership Kentucky, 2002; Vice-Chair, Board of Directors, Kentucky Educational Television.

HALEY III, Raymond
Woodward, Hobson & Fulton LLP, Louisville 502 581 8000
Recommended in Employment

HALLOS, Jeffrey L
Frost Brown Todd LLC, Lexington
859 244 3256
jhallos@fbtlaw.com
Recommended in Corporate/M&A

Practice Areas: Vice-Chair of Corporate Department and Co-Chair of Mergers and Acquisition Practice Group. Advises clients in connection with mergers and acquisitions, corporate finance transactions, domestic and international financing transactions, and private equity investments.

Prof. Memberships: Admitted to practice in California (1989) (currently inactive), District of Columbia (1991), Kentucky (1996).

Career: Joined Frost Brown Todd LLC, 1996; Member, 1998. Previously practiced in the Los Angeles, District of Columbia and Hong Kong offices of Latham & Watkins.

Personal: Born 18 July 1963; JD (cum laude) Cornell Law School, 1988; BA Bucknell University (magna cum laude, Phi Beta Kappa), 1985.

HATFIELD, C Kent
Stoll, Keenon & Park, LLP, Louisville
502 568 9100
Recommended in Environment, Natural Resources

HAYNES, Greg
Wyatt, Tarrant & Combs LLP, Louisville
502 589 5235
Recommended in Litigation

HELM III, Kennedy
Stites & Harbison PLLC, Louisville
502 681 0449
khelmiii@stites.com
Recommended in Corporate/M&A

Practice Areas: Business Service Group. Practice emphasis in airport law, project finance, commercial banking and transportation law. Lead counsel since 1988 to the $780 million Louisville Airport Improvement Program.

Prof. Memberships: Admitted to practice in Kentucky (1968) and United States Supreme Court. Member of American, Kentucky and Louisville Bar Associations. Member of Outstanding Lawyers of America. Listed in Best Lawyers in America.

Career: Member of Stites & Harbison. Chairman of Stites & Harbison since 1997. Joined the firm in 1974.

Publications: Guest Lecturer, Aviation Law, Embry-Riddle Aeronautical University, 2000-04.

Personal: JD, University of Virginia, 1974; Order of the Coif. MA, Indiana University, 1970. BA, cum laude, Yale University, 1968.

HENLEIN, Carl
Frost Brown Todd LLC, Louisville
502 568 0348
chenlein@fbtlaw.com
Recommended in Litigation

HIGGINS Jr, James R
Middleton Reutlinger PSC, Louisville
502 584 1135
jhiggins@middreut.com
Recommended in Litigation

Practice Areas: Registered Patent Attorney. Patents, trademarks, copyrights, trade secrets, IP and commercial litigation.

Prof. Memberships: United States Supreme Court; American Bar Association, IPL Section; American Intellectual Property Lawyers Association; International Trademark Association; Kentucky Bar Association.

Career: James R Higgins, Jr founded the firm's IP law section and also handles business litigation. Mr Higgins was prevailing lead counsel for 'Victor's Little Secret' before the US Supreme Court (Mosely v Victoria's Secret). On patents, see Minco v Combustion Engineering ($28 million judgment). On trademarks, see Columbia University v Columbia/HCA Healthcare Corporation. He has been an expert witness in patent and trademark cases.

Publications: 'Top Ten Lessons Learned From Arguing a Case to the United States Supreme Court' (Kentucky Legislative Research Commission 2003); 'Impact of Mosely v Victoria's Secret on FTDA Dilution Law' (AIPLA and ABA IPL Meetings 2003); 'Victor/Victoria: How a Small Retailer Took On Giant Victoria's Secret in the US Supreme Court - And Won' (Florida Bar Association and DRI 2004).

Personal: JD, University of Louisville Law School (cum laude); BS Engineering, Alfred University. Selected 'best lawyer' in leading legal US publication; Registered Professional Engineer for Fortune 250 company for 14 years before becoming an attorney.

HINES, Barry A
Stites & Harbison PLLC, Louisville
502 681 0525
bhines@stites.com
Recommended in Real Estate

Practice Areas: Real Estate and Finance Service Group. Practice emphasis on real estate financing including construction lending and conduit loans, commercial finance including agribusiness loans and equipment leasing, real estate and banking law, and tax exempt financings including letter of credit bank and trustee representation.

Prof. Memberships: Admitted to practice in Kentucky (1993). Member of American, Kentucky and Louisville Bar Associations and Mortgage Bankers Association of America.

Career: Member of Stites & Harbison. Joined the firm in 1993. Farm Credit Administration, Louisville Office, 1987-90, Bank Examiner for the Federal Regulatory Agency of the Farm Credit System.

Publications: 'Service Contracts: Protecting Real Estate Lenders', Probate & Property, March/April 1997 (coauthor).

Personal: JD, cum laude, University of Louisville, 1993. BS, University of Kentucky, 1987.

HINKLE IV, Samuel
Stoll, Keenon & Park, LLP, Louisville
502 568 9100
Recommended in Litigation

HOFFMANN, Warren
Frost Brown Todd LLC, Lexington
859 244 3220
whoffmann@fbtlaw.com
Recommended in Environment, Natural Resources

HOPSON, Edwin
Wyatt, Tarrant & Combs LLP, Louisville
502 589 5235
Recommended in Employment

HOVIOUS, R Gregg
Tachau Maddox Hovious & Dickens PLC, Louisville 502 588 2010
ghovious@tmhd.com
Recommended in Litigation
Practice Areas: General commercial and healthcare litigation.
Career: In 2004, a Kentucky municipality engaged him to investigate improprieties by previous counsel, resulting in a substantial settlement. Previously, he successfully represented banks in lender liability actions, contract disputes and corporate takeover litigation; represented 40 Kentucky hospitals in successful class action against a regional insurer; obtained a $550,000 insurance settlement for destruction of warehoused goods in Vietnam; and obtained over $1 million in a terminated employee's arbitration. He is panel counsel for two national life insurers for ERISA and contract matters.
Personal: University of Alabama (BS, 1982); University of Kentucky (JD, 1986).

INGRAM Jr, Lindsey
Stoll, Keenon & Park, LLP, Lexington
859 231 3000
Recommended in Environment, Natural Resources

ISON, Eric
Greenebaum Doll & McDonald PLLC, Louisville 502 587 3564
eli@gdm.com
Recommended in Litigation
Practice Areas: Concentrates in commercial litigation, trial and appellate practice.
Prof. Memberships: Louisville Bar Association, Kentucky Bar Association, American Bar Association.
Career: Special Justice, Kentucky Supreme Court, 1997; Kentucky Board of Bar Examiners; admitted in Kentucky and Tennessee; past Member-in-Charge, Louisville, Member of Executive Committee and Chairman of the Litigation and Dispute Resolution Practice Group.
Personal: University of the South, BA (cum laude) 1970; Vanderbilt School of Law, JD, 1974.

JAKUBOWICZ, Janet P
Greenebaum Doll & McDonald PLLC, Louisville 502 587 3664
jpj@gdm.com
Recommended in Litigation
Practice Areas: Member, Greenebaum Doll & McDonald PLLC. Concentrates in the areas of business and commercial litigation, securities and RICO litigation and arbitration, and class action litigation.
Prof. Memberships: Member, Kentucky Defense Trial Lawyers, Louisville Bar Association (Secretary, Board of Directors), Kentucky Bar Association, American Bar Association (Subcommittee on RICO; Subcommittee on Security Trials and Takeover Litigation; Section of Corporate, Banking and Business Law).
Publications: 'The Executive Branch Code of Ethics', Election Law in Kentucky (1995); 'Survey Article-Domestic Relations', Vol. 70, 'Kentucky Law Journal', 1981-82.
Personal: University of Kentucky (JD, 1982); University of Louisville (BA, 1979).

JOSEPH III, Alfred S
Stites & Harbison PLLC, Louisville
502 681 0465
fjoseph@stites.com
Recommended in Real Estate
Practice Areas: Real Estate and Finance Service Group. Practice emphasis on commercial financing, general real estate law, affordable housing, zoning and insurance.
Prof. Memberships: Admitted to practice in Kentucky (1968) and United States Supreme Court. Member of American, Kentucky and Louisville Bar Associations and American College of Real Estate Lawyers. Listed in 'The International Who's Who of Business Lawyers'.
Career: Member of Stites & Harbison. Joined the firm in 1983. Listed in the Real Estate Lawyers section of 'The Best Lawyers in America'.
Publications: Author, Kentucky Chapter, State-By-State Guide to Commercial Real Estate Leases, Aspen Publishers, Mark Senn, editor, 2004; coauthor (with Arthur E Pape), 'Certificates of Insurance: The Illusion of Protection', Probate & Property (the magazine of the Real Property, Probate and Trust Law Section of the American Bar Association), Jan/Feb 1995 [awarded the 1995 Excellence in Writing Award by Probate & Property.]
Personal: JD, University of Michigan, 1968. BA, cum laude and Honors, Wesleyan University, 1965.

KAPLAN, David
Frost Brown Todd LLC, Louisville
502 568 0356
dkaplan@fbtlaw.com
Recommended in Litigation
Practice Areas: Commercial, regulatory, and administrative agency litigation.

Prof. Memberships: Kentucky and Louisville Bar Associations.
Career: Member in the Commercial Litigation and Appellate Groups. Specializes in commercial and regulatory matters, representation before state and federal agencies, and advising clients on administrative law and constitutional questions. Former Assistant Attorney General and counsel to the Department of the Treasury. Law clerk to Judge John Heyburn II of the US District Court for the Western District of Kentucky.
Personal: MPP, Harvard University, 1997; JD, Harvard Law School, magna cum laude, 1997; BA, University of North Carolina at Chapel Hill, 1993.

KEETON, Charles R
Frost Brown Todd LLC, Louisville
502 568 0257
ckeeton@fbtlaw.com
Recommended in Corporate/M&A
Practice Areas: Cochair of Commercial Transactions, Financial Restructuring and E-Commerce Practice Groups.
Prof. Memberships: Member American Bar Association, American Bankruptcy Institute, Kentucky Bar Association (past Chair, Commercial Law Section), and Louisville Bar Association (past Chair, Business Law Section).
Career: Joined predecessor of Frost Brown Todd LLC in 1975, became Partner January 1981.
Publications: Author, articles in various publications, recently, '10 Ways Revised Article 9 Will Change Your (Lending) Life', July 2000 Kentucky Banker; frequent seminar speaker, including sponsored by Practicing Law Institute, Kentucky Bar Association, University of Kentucky College of Law, and Louisville Bar Association. Adjunct Instructor of Law, Secured Transactions, Brandeis School of Law, University of Louisville, last taught Fall 1999.
Personal: Born 8 November 1949. Order of the Coif, 1975; JD (with High Distinction), University of Kentucky, 1975; AB (summa cum laude), Marshall University, 1972.

KING, June N
Greenebaum Doll & McDonald PLLC, Louisville 502 587 3637
jnk@gdm.com
Recommended in Corporate/M&A
Practice Areas: Member of the law firm Greenebaum Doll & McDonald, PLLC. Concentrates in the areas of securities, corporate and banking.
Prof. Memberships: Kentucky Bar Association, Louisville Bar Association, National Association of Stock Plan Professionals.
Career: Greenebaum Doll & McDonald PLLC; former Assistant General Counsel at Vencor, Inc.
Publications: 'Ethical and Practical Concerns in Attempts to Impose Contractual Limits on Attorney Liability', Midwest/Midsouth Securities Law Con-

ference, 1994; 'Public Announcements and Shareholder Communications', Midwest/Midsouth Securities Law Conference, 1996; Panelist at Corporate Management Solutions User Conference, 1995.
Personal: BM Music, JD University of Kentucky: Phi Beta Kappa; Order of the Coif.

KING, W Gregory
Ogden Newell & Welch PLLC, Louisville
502 560 4284
wgking@ogdenlaw.com
Recommended in Litigation
Practice Areas: Head of Litigation Department, concentration in defense of medical malpractice, and product liability, as well as will and trust contests, and general civil litigation. Has extensive jury trial experience, including defense of professional negligence, and plaintiff's personal injury and business fraud.
Prof. Memberships: American, Kentucky, and Louisville Bar Associations (President, 2000; Distinguished Service Award, 2005); Kentucky Academy of Trial Attorneys; Association of Trial Lawyers of America; Kentucky Defense Counsel, Inc.; Defense Research Institute.
Personal: University of Kentucky (JD, 1982); Kentucky Wesleyan College (BA, 1979). 'Best Lawyers in America', Personal Injury Litigation; Board Certified, National Board of Trial Advocates.

KIRK, Michael
Wyatt, Tarrant & Combs LLP, Lexington
859 233 2012
Recommended in Employment

LESTER, David
Stoll, Keenon & Park, LLP, Lexington
859 231 3000
Recommended in Corporate/M&A

LOVETT, John T
Frost Brown Todd LLC, Louisville
502 568 0263
jlovett@fbtlaw.com
Recommended in Employment
Practice Areas: Employment litigation, unions, and union avoidance.
Prof. Memberships: Charter Member, American Employment Law Council; Chair-Elect, Labor Lawyers Advisory Committee for the Council on Union-Free Environment (CUE); Kentucky Bar Association; US District Court, Southern District of Indiana.
Career: Law Clerk, US District Court, Western District of Kentucky (1981-82); Partner, Lovett & Lamar (1982-95); Member, Frost, Brown, Todd (1995 - present).
Personal: JD with Distinction, Order of the Coif, University of Kentucky College of Law (1981); BA, Indiana University (1978); wife, Melissa, four daughters.

LYNDRUP, Peggy B

Greenebaum Doll & McDonald PLLC,
Louisville 502 587 3626
pbl@gdm.com
Recommended in Corporate/M&A

Practice Areas: Chair of the Corporate
and Commerical Practice Group. Concentrates in the areas of corporate law;
mergers and acquisitions; international;
distribution and licensing. Corporate
Counsel to Hillerich & Bradsby, KFC
National Advertising and Rudd Equip-
ment Company. Significant representa-
tion of Japanese and other international
clients.
Prof. Memberships: Past President -
Louisville Bar Association.
Career: Greenebaum Doll & McDon-
ald; Vice President and General Counsel
- Meidinger, Inc.
Publications: 'Buying and Selling a
Business in Kentucky', 'Fiduciary Duties;
Confidentiality and Non- Competition
Agreements', 'Mergers and Acquisitions';
'Use of Delaware Corporations and
Delaware Holding Companies'.
Personal: JD (summa cum laude and
valedictorian) University of Louisville
School of Law; Harvard Law School
Program of Instruction for Lawyers -
Business Planning, Taxation of Corpo-
rate Reorganizations, Corporate Law.

MACDONALD, Alan

Frost Brown Todd LLC, Louisville
502 568 0277
amacdonald@fbtlaw.com
Recommended in Corporate/M&A

Practice Areas: Co-Chair, firm's Public
Companies and Securities Practice.
Advises on securities offerings and com-
pliance, corporate governance, mergers
and aquisitions and corporate law.
Prof. Memberships: Admitted to the
Kentucky Bar (1985). Member, Ameri-
can Bar Association, Section on Corpo-
ration, Banking and Business Law; Ken-
tucky Bar Association, Business Law
Section (Chair 2000-02); Louisville Bar
Association, Business Law Section
(Chair 1997).
Career: Joined Frost Brown Todd, 1985;
became Member 1993.
Publications: Co-author: 'Kentucky
Corporate Law' (1997); 'Limited Liability Companies in Kentucky' (2nd ed.
2000); 'Business Succession Planning'
(1998).
Personal: Born 8 June 1955. JD, Vanderbilt University, 1985; AB, Dartmouth
College, 1977.

MARTIN, Timothy

Frost Brown Todd LLC, Louisville
502 568 0274
tmartin@fbtlaw.com
Recommended in Real Estate

Practice Areas: Acquisition, zoning,
land use, financing, leasing and development of commercial, retail, residential,
industrial and office properties.
Prof. Memberships: Admitted to practice in Kentucky (1972). Member, Amer-

ican College of Real Estate Lawyers;
International Council of Shopping Cen-
ters; American, Kentucky and Louisville
Bar Associations.
Career: Joined Brown, Todd & Heyburn
(now Frost Brown Todd LLC), 1972;
became Partner, 1979; Chair of Frost
Brown Todd LLC Compensation Com-
mittee.
Publications: 'Federal Regulations
Affecting Real Estate' published by Uni-
versity of Kentucky ('Kentucky Real
Estate Law and Practice Handbook').
Personal: Born April 9, 1947. JD, Uni-
versity of Kentucky, 1972; BA, University
of Kentucky, 1969.

MATTINGLY, Patrick

Wyatt, Tarrant & Combs LLP, Louisville
502 589 5235
Recommended in Corporate/M&A

MILLER, Winston

Frost Brown Todd LLC, Louisville
502 568 0296
wmiller@fbtlaw.com
Recommended in Litigation

Practice Areas: Civil litigation includ-
ing diversified experience in products
liability, mass tort, fire and explosion,
employment and business litigation.
Prof. Memberships: American, Kentucky and Louisville Bar Associations,
Defense Research Institute, and CPR.
Career: Defending complex multi-party
cases arising out of catastrophic losses
and serial litigation. Examples (San Juan
DuPont Plaza Hotel Fire, The Breast
Implant Litigation, The Station Night
Club Fire and the West Pharmaceutical
Fire, NC). Represents manufacturers of
various products, devices, drugs, appliances, and materials. Represents area's
largest employer in employment and
business litigation.
Personal: JD University of Kentucky,
1970.

MILLIMAN, James

Middleton Reutlinger PSC, Louisville
502 584 1135
jmilliman@middreut.com
Recommended in Litigation

Practice Areas: Commercial litigation.
Prof. Memberships: Admitted to prac-
tice in United States Supreme Court.
Member of Louisville Bar Association;
Kentucky Bar Association; American
Bar Association.
Career: James E Milliman engages in a
diversified litigation practice with broad
experience in commercial and intellectual property litigation. Mr Milliman
has argued before the United States
Supreme Court. He represented Brown
& Williamson Tobacco Company in a
highly publicized case, (Brown &
Williamson Tobacco Company v
Wigand) against a whistle blower in
which he upheld the right of the company to protect its confidential information. Recently, Mr Milliman has handled
extensive election litigation. He has
experience dealing with media in high

profile cases, including the Brown &
Williamson case and his successful representation of the Governor of Kentucky
in an action to disqualify him during the
primary as a candidate. Mr Milliman's
cases have been featured in 'Time',
'Newsweek', 'Forbes', 'Business Insurance', 'The Wall Street Journal', 'USA
TODAY', 'The Sporting News', and
'ESPN's Outside the Lines'. Mr Milliman
currently serves as a commentator on a
weekly political television program, 'Hot
Button' on WAVE 3, the NBC affiliate in
Louisville.

MONOHAN, David

Woodward, Hobson & Fulton LLP,
Louisville 502 581 8000
Recommended in Litigation

MURPHY, Marc S

Stites & Harbison PLLC, Louisville
502 681 0536
mmurphy@stites.com
Recommended in Litigation

Practice Areas: Jury trial and commercial litigation. Practice emphasis on
white collar criminal litigation and complex commercial and class action
defense.
Prof. Memberships: Admitted to practice in Indiana (1984) and Kentucky
(1988). Member of American, Kentucky
and Louisville Bar Associations.
Career: Member of Stites & Harbison.
Former military prosecutor, Judge
Advocate General's Corps; former Commonwealth's Attorney. Joined the firm in
1997. Seasoned trial lawyer with over 20
years of courtroom experience, including military, handling challenging, high-
profile, and complex commercial and
white collar criminal cases.
Personal: JD, University of Louisville,
1984. BA, cum laude, University of
Notre Dame, 1981.

NORTHAM, Patrick

Greenebaum Doll & McDonald PLLC,
Louisville 502 587 3774
prn@gdm.com
Recommended in Corporate/M&A,
Environment, Natural Resources

Practice Areas: Member of the firm's
Management Committee and Corporate and Commercial Practice Group,
concentrating in corporate and business
law, mergers and acquisitions, energy
law, finance and development. Represents a variety of public and private
business clients throughout the US,
including LG&E Energy Corp., Papa
John's International, Inc. and Caldwell
Tanks, Inc. Lead counsel for numerous
domestic and international mergers,
acquisitions, divestitures, financings and
strategic alliances, including an approximate $1 billion hostile takeover of a
bankrupt rural cooperative.
Personal: JD University of Louisville,
1987; Harvard Law School Program of
Instruction for Lawyers, 1991; BA Indiana University (Phi Beta Kappa) 1984.

OLDHAM, Joseph C

Ogden Newell & Welch PLLC, Louisville
502 560 4230
jcoldham@ogdenlaw.com
Recommended in Employment

Practice Areas: Practice concentration
in estate planning and administration
and employee benefits, with an emphasis on counseling family-owned business
on succession and estate planning, business valuations, and tax savings plans.
Prof. Memberships: American, Kentucky, and Louisville Bar Associations;
Life Member, Judicial Conference of
United States Court of Appeals for the
Sixth Circuit; The Law Club.
Personal: University of Louisville Brandeis School of Law (JD, 1967); University of Virginia (BA, 1964). Listed in 'Best
Lawyers in America,' Employee Benefits
Law.

OVERSTREET, Mark R

Stites & Harbison PLLC, Frankfort
502 209 1219
moverstreet@stites.com
Recommended in Environment,
Natural Resources

Practice Areas: Civil and administrative litigation with emphasis on business
litigation, representation of utilities and
other businesses before administrative
agencies.
Prof. Memberships: Admitted to practice in Kentucky. Member of American,
Kentucky and Franklin County Bar
Associations.
Career: Member of Stites & Harbison.
Executive Partner of Frankfort, Ky.,
office. Trial practice before state and federal courts in Kentucky. Appellate arguments before Supreme Court of Kentucky, Court of Appeals of Kentucky and
US Court of Appeals for the 6th Circuit.
Publications: 'Preclusive Effect of
Administrative Agency Determinations
in Subsequent Court Proceedings,' Ken-
tucky Bar Association's Bench & Bar,
March 2004.
Personal: JD, University of Kentucky,
1980; BA, University of Kentucky, 1976.

PELFREY, D Patton

Frost Brown Todd LLC, Louisville
502 568 0252
ppelfrey@fbtlaw.com
Recommended in Employment

Practice Areas: Mr Pelfrey is Co-Chair
of Frost Brown Todd's Labor and
Employment Law Department and specializes in representing management.
Career: He has vast experience negotiating collective bargaining agreements,
handling union avoidance campaigns
and litigating cases involving all types of
employee relations issues.
Publications: Mr Pelfrey recently
authored chapters in 'The Developing
Labor Law', (various editions) - considered to be the most authoritative treatise
in the field of labor relations.
Personal: He earned the distinction of
being included in all editions of Naifeh

and Smith's 'The Best Lawyers in America' and is a Fellow of the College of Labor and Employment Lawyers.

PERRY, Donna
Woodward, Hobson & Fulton LLP, Louisville 502 581 8000
Recommended in Employment

PITT, M Stephen
Wyatt, Tarrant & Combs LLP, Louisville 502 589 5235
Recommended in Litigation

PRICE, Glenn
Greenebaum Doll & McDonald PLLC, Louisville 502 589 4200
Recommended in Real Estate

QUESENBERRY, Kathryn
Woodward, Hobson & Fulton LLP, Louisville 502 581 8000
Recommended in Employment

REED, John S
Reed Weitkamp Schell & Vice PLLC, Louisville 502 657 1313
jreed@rwsvlaw.com
Recommended in Litigation
Practice Areas: Member of Litigation Section. His practice includes commercial litigation in state and federal courts, antitrust counseling and litigation, and intellectual property litigation.
Prof. Memberships: Member of American, Kentucky and Louisville (past President) Bar Associations.
Career: Admitted to practice in Kentucky, 1974. Partner in other firms, 1979-96. Founded Reed Weitkamp Schell & Vice PLLC in 1996.
Personal: JD, University of Virginia, 1974. AB, University of Kentucky, with highest distinction, Phi Beta Kappa, 1971. He has served on a number of civic and charitable boards and is a founder and Chair of Leadership USA, Inc. Married, two children.

RHORER, John
Dinsmore & Shohl LLP, Lexington 859 425 1000
Recommended in Environment, Natural Resources

RIGGS, Kendrick R
Ogden Newell & Welch PLLC, Louisville 502 560 4222
kriggs@ogdenlaw.com
Recommended in Environment, Natural Resources
Practice Areas: Chairman of Executive Committee and Head of Utility Law Department, concentrating in representing energy and telecommunications clients before Kentucky regulatory agencies and courts, and the Virginia State Corporation Commission. Has extensive trial experience and has appeared before state and federal courts representing energy and telecommunications clients in commercial and industry disputes.
Prof. Memberships: American, Kentucky, and Virginia Bar Associations; Energy Bar Association; Energy and Mineral Law Foundation.

Personal: University of Kentucky (JD, 1982); Wittenberg University (BA, cum laude, 1979). 'Best Lawyers in America,' Public Utility Law, since 1997-98; Martindale-Hubbell AV Rating since 1996.

ROBINSON III, Wm T
Greenebaum Doll & McDonald PLLC, Covington 859 727 1336
wtr@gdm.com
Recommended in Litigation
Practice Areas: Member In Charge of Greater Cincinnati/ Northern Kentucky office and Executive Committee Member of the law firm Greenebaum Doll & McDonald, PLLC. Concentrates in civil litigation, trial and appellate practice and governmental affairs.
Prof. Memberships: Treasurer-Elect, American Bar Association, Kentucky Bar Association, Northern Kentucky Bar Association, Louisville Bar Association, Ohio State Bar Association, Cincinnati Bar Association, Kentucky Defense Counsel, Inc., Federal Bar Association.

ROYSE, David
Stoll, Keenon & Park, LLP, Lexington 859 231 3681
Recommended in Natural Resources, Litigation

RUTLEDGE, Thomas E
Ogden Newell & Welch PLLC, Louisville 502 560 4258
trutledge@ogdenlaw.com
Recommended in Corporate/M&A
Practice Areas: General business law, acquisitions and federal securities laws with concentration on the law of business organizations including structure, fiduciary duties, and disputes among owners.
Prof. Memberships: ABA Committee on Partnerships and Unincorporated Business Organizations and the Ad-Hoc Committee on Entity Rationalization. Section of Business Law Advisor to NCCUSL project to update Uniform Liability Company Act as well as drafting committees for Uniform Entity Transactions Act and Uniform Trust Act.
Publications: A national authority on business entity law, he has been published in the 'Kentucky Law Journal,' 'Business Entities,' 'The Business Lawyer,' and 'Delaware Journal of Corporate Law'.

SAFFER, David
Stites & Harbison PLLC, Louisville 502 681 0547
dsaffer@stites.com
Recommended in Real Estate
Practice Areas: Concentrates practice in real estate and lending and regularly represents institutional lenders and borrowers in all types of commercial loan transactions including complex conduit-lending transactions.
Prof. Memberships: Member of the Louisville, Kentucky, and American Bar Associations. Member of the American College of Mortgage Attorneys.
Career: Counsel to Stites & Harbison. Joined the firm in 2004.

Publications: Co-author, 'Mortgages,' UK/CLE Kentucky Real Estate and Practice Handbook, 2d Ed., 1996.
Personal: JD, cum laude, University of Louisville, 1995; BLS, summa cum laude, University of Evansville, 1992.

SALES, Walter L
Ogden Newell & Welch PLLC, Louisville 502 560 4252
wsales@ogdenlaw.com
Recommended in Employment
Practice Areas: Concentration in labor and employment and commercial litigation with regular representation of both employers and employees in cases contesting the enforcement of covenants-not-to-compete, employee breach of fiduciary duty, and employee breach of confidentiality. Has tried several cases including class action employment discrimination cases against the Equal Employment Opportunity Commission ranging from age discrimination to race, sex, sexual harassment, equal pay act, and ADA cases.
Prof. Memberships: American, Kentucky, and Louisville Bar Associations.
Personal: University of Kentucky (JD, 1973); Washington & Lee University (BA, 1970). Listed in 'Best Lawyers in America,' Labor and Employment.

SANDLER, David B
Greenebaum Doll & McDonald PLLC, Louisville 502 587 3577
dbs@gdm.com
Recommended in Employment
Practice Areas: Labor and employment law.
Career: Mr Sandler has practiced extensively before the state and federal courts, the National Labor Relations Board and various state, federal and local administrative agencies. He has broad experience in civil rights litigation and trial practice, negotiating collective bargaining agreements, conducting arbitrations, and representing employers in union organizing campaigns. He has considerable experience as a lecturer on employment law.
Personal: University of Pennsylvania, Wharton School of Finance, BS; University of Louisville School of Law, JD.

SAVARISE, Jeffrey A
Greenebaum Doll & McDonald PLLC, Louisville 502 587 3505
jas@gdm.com
Recommended in Employment
Practice Areas: Member of the law firm Greenebaum Doll & McDonald, PLLC. Concentrates in the areas of labor and employment law, with particular emphasis in representing Japanese-owned manufacturers.
Prof. Memberships: Kentucky, Louisville, Ohio, Pennsylvania and American Bar Associations (Labor and Employment Sections); American Bar Association Committee on Alternative Dispute Resolution.
Career: Frequent lecturer at business and bar association seminars.

Publications: Contributing editor, 'How Arbitration Works', Fifth Edition (BNA) 1997.
Personal: BA, John Carroll University (magna cum laude), University of Akron School of Law.

SCHELL, Ivan J
Reed Weitkamp Schell & Vice PLLC, Louisville 502 657 1341
ischell@rwsvlaw.com
Recommended in Corporate/M&A
Practice Areas: Member of Health Law, Corporate and Estate Planning Sections. His practice includes management and intergenerational transition planning for closely held businesses, medical corporation contract negotiation and government compliance, and wealth transfer planning.
Prof. Memberships: Member of American, Kentucky, Illinois and Louisville Bar Associations.
Career: Admitted to practice in Illinois, 1974, Kentucky, 1976; Founding Member Reed Weitkamp Schell & Vice 1996.
Personal: JD, University of Michigan, 1974. BS, Butler University 1968. Phi Eta Sigma. Chair, Buckhorn Children's Foundation.

SEIFFERT, James C
Stites & Harbison PLLC, Louisville 502 681 0519
jseiffert@stites.com
Recommended in Corporate/M&A
Practice Areas: Business Service Group, Tax Service Group. Practice emphasis on general corporate, business, taxation, business acquisitions and mergers.
Prof. Memberships: Admitted to practice in Kentucky and Iowa. Member of American, Kentucky, Louisville and Iowa Bar Associations.
Career: Member of Stites & Harbison. Joined the firm in 1986.
Publications: 'Physicians Beware! Dealing with Tax-Exempt Healthcare Organizations Can be Hazardous to One's Financial Health,' Journal of Kentucky Medical Association, February 1998; 'Man-O-War Restaurants, Inc. v. John Martin, Jr., Ky. Supreme Court Deals a Severe Blow to Compensatory Restricted Stock Arrangement,' Louisville Bar Association Bar Briefs, May 1997.
Personal: JD, with high distinction, University of Louisville, 1980. LLM, Taxation, University of Miami, 1981. BA, American History with minor in Education, University of Iowa, 1977.

SHELLER, John
Smith & Smith Attorneys, Louisville 502 587 0761
jsheller@smithandsmithattorneys.com
Recommended in Employment
Practice Areas: Practices in management-side labor and employment law and specializes in representing clients in employment litigation. Represents clients in federal and state courts and administrative agencies, appellate advocacy, arbitration.

Prof. Memberships: Member Louisville and Kentucky Bar Associations; Indiana State Bar Association; and State Bar of Texas Association.

Career: Joined Smith & Smith Attorneys, 1993; Partner of firm since 1995. Also practiced at Barnes & Thornsburg, Fort Wayne, Indiana, and and in-house counsel at EDS, Dallas, Texas.

Personal: BA, Ball State University (summa cum laude, 1981); JD, Indiana University (cum laude, 1984).

SHIVEL Jr, Charles
Stoll, Keenon & Park, LLP, Lexington
859 231 3000
Recommended in Litigation

SMITH, Kevin
Smith & Smith Attorneys, Louisville
502 587 0761
wks@smithandsmithattorneys.com
Recommended in Employment

Practice Areas: Practices management-side labor and employment law. Significant practice before the NLRB; representing clients in traditional labor law matters.

Prof. Memberships: Member Louisville and Kentucky Bar Associations.

Career: Law Clerk to Honorable Harry Phillips, Chief Judge, US Court of Appeals, Sixth Circuit, 1978, 1979; joined Smith & Smith Attorneys, 1979; Partner of firm since 1986. Adjunct Professor, University School of Law, 1998.

Publications: Authored numerous seminar publications and frequent presenter at labor and employment law seminars sponsored by the Kentucky Bar Association and private seminars companies.

Personal: BA, Bellarmine College (1975); JD, University of Louisville (cum laude 1978).

SMITH III, James
Smith & Smith Attorneys, Louisville
502 587 0761
jus@smithandsmithattorneys.com
Recommended in Employment

Practice Areas: Represents clients in management-side labor and employment law in all phases of labor relations. Represents clients in complex labor and employment matters, employment litigation, union conract negotiations, and union avoidance.

Prof. Memberships: Member Louisville and Kentucky Bar Associations.

Career: Joined Smith & Smith Attorneys, 1973. Partner of the firm since 1977. Adjunct professor at University School of Law, 1998.

Publications: Has authored numerous private seminar publications and frequent presenter of labor and employment law seminars sponsored by various private seminar companies.

Personal: BA, Fairfield University (1969); JD, University of Louisville (1973).

SNELL, Virginia
Wyatt, Tarrant & Combs LLP, Louisville
502 589 5235
Recommended in Litigation

SNYDER, Sheryl
Frost Brown Todd LLC, Louisville
502 568 0247
ssnyder@fbtlaw.com
Recommended in Litigation

Practice Areas: Chair of Appellate Practice Group. Extensive experience in constitutional law, state and federal; antitrust, securities, trademark, copyright and other complex business litigation.

Prof. Memberships: Bars of the Supreme Courts of the United States, Kentucky, Tennessee, Texas, and Missouri; United States Courts of Appeals for the Third, Fourth, Sixth, Seventh, Eighth, Tenth and Eleventh Circuits. Past President, Kentucky and Louisville Bar Associations.

Career: Joined Frost Brown Todd (then Brown, Todd & Heyburn) 1994. Executive Vice President and General Counsel, ICH Corporation (1990-94). Wyatt Tarrant & Combs (1973-90).

Personal: Born 11 October 1946. University of Kentucky, BA 1968, JD 1971.

STEENROD, Ralston W
Stites & Harbison PLLC, Louisville
502 681 0436
rsteenrod@stites.com
Recommended in Corporate/M&A

Practice Areas: Practice includes corporate mergers, taxable acquisitions, tax-free reorganizations, contested takeovers and general corporate. Also includes bank holding company formations, rights of dissenting shareholders and securities registration and exemptions.

Prof. Memberships: Admitted to practice in Kentucky. Member of the American, Kentucky and Louisville Bar Associations.

Career: Member of Stites & Harbison. Joined the firm in 1971.

Personal: JD, University of Louisville, 1968; AB, cum laude, English, Princeton University, 1959.

STOPHER, Edward H
Boehl Stopher & Graves, LLP, Louisville
502 589 5980
estopher@bsg-law.com
Ranked in Litigation

Practice Areas: Civil litigation and trial practice with emphasis on corporate law, Insurance law, product liability, legal malpractice and negligence matters.

Prof. Memberships: Mr Stopher is a Member of the Louisville Bar Association; Kentucky Bar Association; American Bar Association; Fellow, American College of Trial Lawyers; Fellow, International Society of Barristers; Association of Defense Trial Attorneys; Fellow, American Bar Foundation; National Association of Railroad Trial Counsel; 'Of Counsel' Committee 1993 - present; Kentucky Defense Counsel; The Law Club; The Lawyers Club. He is listed in

'The Best Lawyers in America' 1989-2005.

Career: Mr Stopher was Law Clerk to Hon James F Gordon, United States Judge Western District of Kentucky, 1968-69. He joined Boehl Stopher & Graves, LLP, in 1969 and became Partner in 1970.

Personal: BA with Honors, Davidson College, 1965; JD, University of Virginia, 1968. *This is an advert.*

STRAUS, R James
Frost Brown Todd LLC, Louisville
502 568 0221
jstraus@fbtlaw.com
Recommended in Corporate/M&A

Practice Areas: Firm Practice Chair, Financial Institutions and Franchising. Has extensive experience in banking, distribution, purchasing groups and mergers and acquisitions.

Prof. Memberships: Admitted to practice in Kentucky (1974). Member of American Bar Association Sections on Business, Banking and Anti-Trust Law, and Forum on Franchising.

Career: Joined Frost Brown Todd 1974, became Partner, 1980. Corporate Department Chair.

Personal: Born 17 August 1946. JD, University of Chicago, 1974; BA, Yale University (cum laude), 1968; Captain USMC, Vietnam Veteran; Legal Aide Society Board of Directors.

STRENCH, William
Frost Brown Todd LLC, Louisville
502 568 0207
wstrench@fbtlaw.com
Recommended in Corporate/M&A

TACHAU, David Brandeis
Tachau Maddox Hovious & Dickens PLC, Louisville 502 588 2015
dtachau@tmhd.com
Recommended in Litigation

Practice Areas: General commercial, insurance, estate and employment litigation.

Career: Recent engagements include dismissal of a RICO and fraud class action, Pratt v Ventas, Inc, 365 F3d 514 (6th Cir. 2004); successful federal jury trial yielding $28 million judgment, Monumental Life Insurance v Nationwide Retirement Solutions (WDKy 2003); and serving as litigation counsel for corporate fiduciary administering a $30 million estate involving spousal renunciation, sale of closely-held business, pursuit of legal malpractice claims, and defense of action to remove the executor.

Personal: Harvard College (AB, magna cum laude, 1978); University of Michigan (JD, 1982). Kentucky Board of Education (2002-current).

THOMPSON, B Todd
Thompson Miller & Simpson PLC, Louisville 502 585 9900
Recommended in Litigation

VICE, Robert
Reed Weitkamp Schell & Vice PLLC, Louisville 502 589 1000
Recommended in Real Estate

VINCENTI, Michael
Wyatt, Tarrant & Combs LLP, Louisville
502 589 5235
Recommended in Real Estate

WARD, Richard
Wyatt, Tarrant & Combs LLP, Lexington
859 233 2012
Recommended in Environment, Natural Resources

WATT, Robert
Stoll, Keenon & Park, LLP, Lexington
859 231 3000
Recommended in Environment, Natural Resources

WEITKAMP, Gary
Reed Weitkamp Schell & Vice PLLC, Louisville 502 589 1000
Recommended in Corporate/M&A

WHEAT, Jack A
Stites & Harbison PLLC, Louisville
502 681 0323
jwheat@stites.com
Recommended in Litigation

Practice Areas: Concentration in infringement litigation and trademark portfolio registration and maintenance. Has served as Lead Counsel in intellectual property disputes in nearly 30 states. Experience includes the ultimately successful representation of the Tennessee-based manufacturer of nationally-marketed foam athletic pads in a patent case argued at the US Supreme Court. Nelson v. Adams USA, Inc., 529 US 460 (2000).

Prof. Memberships: Admitted to practice in Kentucky and state and federal courts. Member of American, Kentucky and Louisville Bar Associations.

Career: Member of Stites & Harbison. Joined the firm in 2000. Formerly with Wheat, Smith & Beres. Adjunct professor of Intellectual Property, Louis D Brandeis School of Law at the University of Louisville.

Publications: 'To franchise or not is a big question,' Business First, August 6, 2004; 'Enforcing Rights in Derivative Works,' 1985 Section Reports, A.BA Patent, Trademark & Copyright Section; 'Copyright Law, Architects and Design Competitions: Who Owns the Copyright?' Competitions Magazine, Vol. 3, Is. 4, Winter 1994.

Personal: JD, University of Louisville, 1979; BA, Economics, Hanover College, 1976.

WILLIAMS, Ernest W
Ogden Newell & Welch PLLC, Louisville
502 560 4243
ewilliams@ogdenlaw.com
Recommended in Corporate/M&A

Practice Areas: Concentration in the area of business acquisitions with regular representation of both buyers and sellers of businesses, including asset acquisitions, stock acquisitions, mergers, establishments of joint ventures, supply and distribution agreements, and employment agreements. In an international context, has represented local businesses acquiring businesses outside of the US or establishing joint venture arrangements in foreign countries, as well as representing foreign businesses seeking to acquire or establish local operations.

Prof. Memberships: Kentucky and Louisville Bar Associations.

Personal: Harvard Law School (JD, 1975); Murray State University (BA, 1975). Listed in 'Best Lawyers in America,' Corporate, M&A and Securities Law.

WILLIAMS, Thomas M
Ogden Newell & Welch PLLC, Louisville
502 560 4279
twilliams@ogdenlaw.com
Recommended in Employment

Practice Areas: All aspects of employment itigation, counseling, and supervisor training, including class action defense and ERISA litigation.

Prof. Memberships: American Bar Association (Employment Rights and Responsibilities Subcommittee since 1999); Louisville Bar Association (VP, Board of Directors, Past Chair of Labor and Employment Section); Louisville Society for Human Resources Management (Labor Relations Chair); Society for Human Resources Management (SPHR designation).

Personal: University of Cincinnati (JD, 1990); College of William & Mary (BA, 1986). Listed in 'Best Lawyers in America,' Labor and Employment; 2002 Award for Professional Excellence by the Louisville Society for Human Resources Management.

YOUNG, Cynthia
Wyatt, Tarrant & Combs LLP, Louisville
502 589 5235
Recommended in Corporate/M&A

BOEHL STOPHER & GRAVES, LLP

THE FIRM

Executive Committee: Edward H Stopher, Larry L Johnson, Jefferson K Streepey, Robert E Stopher, Raymond G Smith
Partners: 27
Lawyers: 50

FIRM OVERVIEW: Since 1895, Boehl Stopher & Graves, LLP, has represented a wide variety of businesses all across Kentucky in State and Federal Courts. The firm's philosophy is simple: Though the firm is highly effective in the courtroom, it is more concerned with bringing matters to a satisfactory conclusion, whether it be through negotiation, mediation, arbitration, or litigation. From insurance to energy, from workers' compensation to mergers and acquisitions, the diversity of the firm's experience in civil litigation has given it the depth and breadth in the areas in which it practices.

MAIN AREAS OF PRACTICE

Civil Litigation: The firm represents clients in civil matters in just about every arena. The majority of its work has focused on product liability, toxic torts, contract disputes, corporate disputes, employment disputes, professional negligence, facility negligence, intellectual property law, and personal injury.
Workers' Compensation: The firm represents clients in the defense of workers' compensation claims.
Corporate: The firm represents buyers and sellers in various transactions including mergers, buy-outs, and other business combinations.
Trust & Estates: The firm represents individuals in the area of trust and estate planning, will preparation, execution and probate.

CLIENTS: Boehl Stopher & Graves, LLP has successfully defended corporations such as Eli Lilly and Company, CSX Transportation, Bristol-Myers Squibb, Ford, Tricon, and NCAA in high-risk, high-visibility cases. The firm has successfully defended insurance companies such as AIG, Coregis, Old Republic Companies, State Farm, and Ohio Casualty. Boehl Stopher & Graves, LLP has also defended individuals and non-profit organizations.

HEAD OFFICE

KENTUCKY
2300 AEGON Center, 400 W. Market Street, **Louisville**, KY 40202
Tel: 502 589 5980   **Fax:** 502 561 9400
Email: Louisville@bsg-1aw.com
Website: www.BSG-Law.com

BRANCH OFFICES

INDIANA
Elsby East - Suite 204, 400 Pearl Street, **New Albany**, IN 47150
Tel: 812 948 5053   **Fax:** 812 948 9233
Email: Indiana@bsg-in.com

KENTUCKY
444 West Second Street, **Lexington**, KY 40507-1009
Tel: 859 252 6721   **Fax:** 589 253 1445
Email: Lexington@bsglex.com

410 Broadway, **Paducah**, KY 42001
Tel: 270 442 4369   **Fax:** 270 442 4689
Email: rwalter@bsgpad.com

137 Main Street, Suite 200, PO Box 1139, **Pikeville**, KY 41502
Tel: 606 432 9670   **Fax:** 606 432 9680
Email: bcollier@bsgeast.com

CONTACTS

Litigation	Edward H Stopher
Workers' Compensation	Larry L Johnson
Corporate/Trust & Estates	Jefferson K Streepey

US OFFICES

NEW ALBANY

Managing Partner: Jeffrey Hansford
Number of Lawyers: 6
Office Profile: The New Albany, Indiana office is an integral part of the Greater Louisville metropolitan area providing defense representation of medical malpractice, products liability, workers' compensation, personal injury, professional liability and other litigation matters.

LEXINGTON

Managing Partner: Nolan Carter, Jr.
Number of Lawyers: 9
Office Profile: The Lexington office is strategically located 20 minutes from the state capital, Frankfort, Kentucky, and approximately 75 miles from both Louisville and Cincinnati. The office has provided a broad range of trial and appellate services since 1943.

PADUCAH

Managing Partner: Richard L Walter
Number of Lawyers: 6
Office Profile: The Paducah office has an active practice in western Kentucky and southern Illinois, including all State and Federal Courts in both jurisdictions. The Paducah office handles a wide variety of litigation, including professional liability, construction, personal injury and maritime matters.

PIKEVILLE

Managing Partner: Bayard V Collier
Number of Lawyers: 3
Office Profile: The Pikeville office handles a significant amount of workers' compensation defense cases in the heart of eastern Kentucky's coal mining region. This office's practice also includes auto and coal truck defense, school board matters and professional, products and premises liability cases.

FROST BROWN TODD LLC

THE FIRM

Managing Partners: Richard J Erickson, C Edward Glasscock

Number of partners: 190
Number of lawyers: 193

FIRM OVERVIEW: Frost Brown Todd LLC, one of the largest law firms in the Central United States, offers responsive, sophisticated legal services at rates more attractive than other national law firms. Created by the merger of two premier law firms on November 1, 2000, Frost Brown Todd is backed by the service of over 800 professionals, drawing from the foundations of legacy law firms with more than a century of service to clients. The firm meets the diverse legal challenges of local, regional and international business in over 40 different practice areas.

MAIN AREAS OF PRACTICE

Business & Corporate: Over 70 attorneys provide a full range of transactional, regulatory and other advisory services to the firm's regional, national and multinational business clients. The firm handles mergers and acquisitions, public companies and securities, tax, emerging business and venture capital, international, e-Business and technology, employee benefits and executive compensation, health law, financial institutions, investment management, public finance and governmental.

Commercial Transactions/Real Estate: The firm offers significant experience in the areas of commercial finance, financial restructuring and real estate, including financial institution regulation, equipment leasing, asset securitization, land use, economic development incentives and shopping centers/retail development.

Environmental: With one of the largest and most diverse environmental practices in the region, the firm helps clients navigate through federal, state and local environmental regulations, and assists clients in creating solutions that achieve their business objectives, avoid disputes and minimize transactional costs.

Intellectual Property: From litigation to licensing, from prosecution to unfair competition, the firm is ready to serve its clients in developing, obtaining, protecting and enforcing creative assets. After handling intellectual property litigation throughout the US for a variety of Fortune 500 clients, the firm was named one of the top 10 patent litigation firms in the US by *Managing Intellectual Property Magazine.*

Labor & Employment: Over 40 attorneys handle labor and employment issues, such as collective bargaining, employment discrimination, sexual harassment, OSHA inspections, workers' compensation, arbitration, alternative dispute resolution, wage and hour, common law employment claims and immigration.

Litigation: The firm counsels and represents a variety of clients, and has extensive experience in complex litigation, multi-party cases and class actions. The firm also has experience in the following areas: antitrust, appellate practice, banking/commercial, catastrophic loss, construction, surety and real estate, drug and medical device, fire and explosion, First Amendment, franchise and distribution, government enforcement and compliance, insurance coverage, fraud and bad faith, personal injury and tort defense, product liability, securities and professional liability, toxic tort/chemical exposure, trucking and commercial transportation and unfair competition.

Personal Planning & Family Business: The firm counsels individuals in the areas of wealth preservation and wealth transfer matters involving estate, income tax, retirement, charitable and business succession planning. Closely held businesses are served in all tax matters, ranging from choice of business structure and operational issues to the transfer, sale or liquidation of the business.

HEAD OFFICES

KENTUCKY
400 West Market Street, 32nd Floor, **Louisville**, KY 40202-3363
Tel: 502 589 5400 **Fax:** 502 581 1087
Email: info@fbtlaw.com
Website: www.frostbrowntodd.com

OHIO
2200 PNC Center, 201 East Fifth Street, **Cincinnati**, OH 45202-4182
Tel: 513 651 6800 **Fax:** 513 651 6981

BRANCH OFFICES

DISTRICT OF COLUMBIA
923 Fifteenth Street NW, **Washington**, DC 20005
Tel: 202 662 9700

INDIANA
120 West Spring Street, Suite 400, **New Albany**, IN 47150-3655
Tel: 812 948 2800 **Fax:** 812 948 7994

KENTUCKY
2700 Lexington Financial Center, **Lexington**, KY 40507-1749
Tel: 859 231 0000 **Fax:** 859 231 0011

OHIO
One Columbus, Suite 1000, 10 West Broad Street,
Columbus OH 43215-3467
Tel: 614 464 1211 **Fax:** 614 464 1737

300 North Main Street, Suite 200, **Middletown**, OH 45042-1919
Tel: 513 422 2001 **Fax:** 513 422 3010

TENNESSEE
424 Church Street, Suite 1600, **Nashville**, TN 37219-2308
Tel: 615 251 5550 **Fax:** 615 251 5551

CONTACTS

Business & Corporate	R James Straus
Commercial Trans/Real Estate	E Richard Oberschmidt
Environmental	Paul W Casper Jr
Intellectual Property	Steven J Goldstein
Intellectual Property Litigation	Arthur S Beeman, David E Schmit
International	Joseph J Dehner, Jay Middleton Tannon
Labor & Employment	Robert A Dimling, D Patton Pelfrey
Litigation	Winston E Miller
Personal Planning & Family Business	Patricia D Laub

International: Frost Brown Todd provides a wide range of legal services required by international businesses as they expand into the US and by US businesses as they market and operate abroad. The firm handles various international transactions, including direct investments, mergers and acquisitions, joint ventures, licensing, trade law compliance, as well as international commercial dispute resolution. The group's international practice concentrates on corporate, commercial, tax, intellectual property, labor and immigration law, as well as litigation and arbitration services. The firm recently received an Export Achievement Award from the US Department of Commerce in recognition of its involvement with export focused organizations.

GREENEBAUM DOLL & MCDONALD PLLC

THE FIRM

Chairman: P Richard Anderson, Jr
Number of lawyers: 185

FIRM OVERVIEW: For more than 50 years, Greenebaum has distinguished itself as a progressive business law firm committed to the practice of breakthrough law. Clients rely on Greenebaum to break through stalemates and find creative solutions to complex legal and business issues. The firm is known for getting the deal done. The firm's attorneys are licensed in more than 25 states and several international jurisdictions, and it also provides unmatched international representation through its unique TerraLex® alliance, an association of independent law firms in 87 countries.

MAIN AREAS OF PRACTICE

Regulatory & Administration: Energy; environmental and natural resources; governmental affairs; intellectual property; land use.

Corporate & Commercial: Antitrust; banking and financial companies; China; economic development and incentives; immigration; international; Japan; mergers and acquisitions; product distribution and franchising; real estate development and construction; securities; telecommunications and technology.

Estate Planning, Health & Insurance: Employee benefits; family business; general and captive insurance; health, health insurance and life sciences; privacy; wealth transfer.

Labor & Employment: Automotive; collective and class action; covenant not to compete and trade secrets; employment practices liability; labor management relations; workplace safety and health.

Litigation & Dispute Resolution: Appellate practice; alternative dispute resolution; beverage alcohol; class action defense; construction litigation law; environmental and toxic tort defense; equine; products liability; white collar crime.

Tax & Finance: Bankruptcy; bond; ERISA controversy; federal tax; finance; state and local tax; tax exempt organizations.

HEAD OFFICE

KENTUCKY
3500 National City Tower, 101 South Fifth Street, **Louisville**, KY 40202-3197
Tel: 502 589 4200 **Fax:** 502 587 3695
Website: www.greenebaum.com

BRANCH OFFICES

KENTUCKY
300 West Vine Street, Suite 1100, **Lexington**, KY 40507-1665
Tel: 859 231 8500 **Fax:** 859 255 2742

50 East RiverCenter Blvd, Suite 1800, **Covington**, KY 41011-2673
Tel: 859 655 4200 **Fax:** 859 655 4239

229 West Main Street, Suite 101, **Frankfort**, KY 40601-1879
Tel: 502 875 0050 **Fax:** 502 875 0850

OHIO
2800 Chemed Center, 255 East Fifth Street, **Cincinnati**, OH 45202-4728
Tel: 513 455 7600 **Fax:** 513 455 8500

TENNESSEE
700 Two American Center, 3102 West End Avenue, **Nashville**, TN 37203-1397
Tel: 615 760 7100 **Fax:** 615 760 7300

DISTRICT OF COLUMBIA
1146 19th Street, NW, Suite 250, **Washington**, DC 20036-3726
Tel: 202 293 7000 **Fax:** 202 293 9700

GEORGIA
1175 Peachtree Street, NE, 100 Colony Square, Suite 780, **Atlanta**, GA 30361
Tel: 770 933 6270 **Fax:** 770 675 3490

CONTACTS

Regulatory & Administration ....Carolyn M Brown
Corporate & Commercial ....Peggy B Lyndrup
Estate Planning, Health & Insurance ....John R Cummins
Labor & Employment..Richard S Cleary
Litigation & Dispute Resolution ....Mark S Riddle
Tax, Benefits & Finance ....Mark F Sommer

MIDDLETON REUTLINGER

THE FIRM

Managing Partner: Charles G Middleton III
Senior Partner: Kenneth S Handmaker, James E Milliman

Number of partners: 26
Number of other attorneys: 20

AREAS OF PRACTICE:
Litigation 50%
Intellectual Property (patents, trademarks, copyrights) 30%
Business Transactions 20%

HEAD OFFICE

KENTUCKY
2500 Brown & Williamson Tower, **Louisville**, KY 40202
Tel: 502 584 1135   **Fax:** 502 561 0442
Email: kgipson@middreut.com
Website: www.middreut.com

FIRM OVERVIEW: Middleton Reutlinger attributes its continued success to a steadfast team of attorneys who provide quality service while maintaining personalized contact. The firm's attorneys are as diverse in background as the fields of law in which they practice or the clients they represent. Yet, they share the common goals and unity of purpose which turned individual lawyers into one of Kentucky's oldest law firms. Middleton Reutlinger offers a comprehensive range of services to meet the legal needs of individuals and corporations. The firm's practice groups consistently work together to provide clients quality, full service legal representation at the most efficient cost.

MAIN AREAS OF PRACTICE:
Litigation: Middleton Reutlinger has a broad litigation practice with extensive experience including complex commercial litigation, torts litigation, intellectual property, employment law, tax and class actions, foreclosure, eminent domain, construction law, lender liability, products liability, medical malpractice, and utility regulatory. Middleton Reutlinger counsels clients on litigation issues in Kentucky, across the nation and internationally. The firm's attorneys have represented clients in many cases which have resulted in reported decisions setting legal precedent or a benchmark in the law. In one notable case, Middleton Reutlinger attorneys represented Kentucky tax payers in a class action in which the Kentucky Supreme Court held the Kentucky intangible tax on stocks and deposits (a tax enacted in 1907) discriminatory and unconstitutional. Determined under the Commerce Clause of the United States Constitution, it resulted in refunds to Kentucky taxpayers of more than $180,000,000.

Intellectual Property: The firm's intellectual property practice consists of trademark, copyright, patent, trade secrets, and internet issues. Middleton Reutlinger's patent services include evaluation of inventions for patent protection and practice before the US Patent Office, from preparation of applications through post-filing prosecution and amendments, to interferences and appeals (including the Board of Patent Appeals). In one notable case, Middleton Reutlinger secured a $28 million jury verdict, sustained in appeal, in a patent infringement action. The firm's trademark attorneys counsel clients in trademark development, clearance, and registration strategies, including preparation and assessment of trademark searches. Middleton Reutlinger files and prosecutes applications in the US Trademark Offices and in various state trademark offices. One of the firm's most recent well known trademark cases was Moseley v V Secret Catalogue, Inc., 123 S. Ct. 1115 (2003), in which the firm presented a case to the United States Supreme Court on an issue of national importance on federal trademark dilution. The firm prevailed with a 9-0 decision. The firm's copyright attorneys advise clients regarding 'fair use,' 'work made for hire,' and other copyright ownership issues, including cases involving computer software infringement.

Business Transactions: Middleton Reutlinger's attorneys have significant experience in business transactional issues including real estate, zoning, construction and land use issues, contracts, succession planning, environmental law and safety management and alcohol/beverage licensing. The firm has assisted clients with various issues at state and federal levels.

CLIENTS: Middleton Reutlinger's clients include a wide array of commercial entities for which legal services are performed in the United States and abroad. Among them is Papa John's International Inc., Brown & Williamson Holdings, Inc., Hillerich & Bradsby Co. (Louisville Slugger and Powerbuilt), Genlyte Thomas Group LLC, HCA-The Healthcare Company, The Kroger Co., Norfolk Southern Corporation, Rexam Closures, and AAF-McQuay, Inc.

INTERNATIONAL WORK: Although Middleton Reutlinger provides various legal services to clients in numerous countries, the firm is most recognized for its international work in the area of intellectual property law. The firm regularly works in obtaining patent protection in such countries as Canada, Australia, the European Patent Office, the Pacific Rim countries (including Japan, Taiwan, China, Indonesia, and Korea), Russia and many others.

MIDDLETON
REUTLINGER

OGDEN NEWELL & WELCH PLLC

THE FIRM

Chairman of the Executive Committee: Kendrick R Riggs

Number of attorneys: 40

FIRM OVERVIEW: Since 1898, Ogden Newell & Welch PLLC has provided sophisticated, practical legal counsel to clients throughout the Kentucky/Indiana region. Consciously desiring to focus on Kentucky business issues, the firm represents an exciting mix of publicly held and closely held businesses, regulated and non-regulated industries, and provides the litigation support businesses require to be competitive in the marketplace. The firm's distinctive approach to providing legal services offers both the personalized service of a mid-size firm and the knowledge and resources of a large firm. Exclusively affiliated with Meritas, the world's largest network of independent law firms, the membership provides the firm with access to over 5,000 lawyers in more than 70 countries and ensures that ON&W clients have access to some of the best legal talent wherever in the world their legal needs arise.

MAIN AREAS OF PRACTICE:

Business, Corporate & Public Finance: ON&W handles all aspects of organizing and operating a business, including choice of entity, debt and equity financing, real and personal property purchases and leases, mergers, acquisitions and divestitures. The firm represents both lenders and borrowers in connection with real estate and business loans. The securities practice includes public and private offerings under federal and state securities laws, as well as compliance with ongoing disclosure obligations and represents municipal and public authorities in public financing. The firm also provides advice on trademarks, copyrights, computer software licensing agreements, supply and distribution agreements, franchise law and antitrust concerns.

Litigation & Dispute Resolution: ON&W provides litigation services for every phase of a dispute including representing clients at trial and arguing appellate issues. Specific areas of experience include business litigation, professional malpractice defense, insurance defense, and environmental law. Attorneys in this department are trained in various forms of alternative dispute resolution.

Employer/Employee Relations: ON&W advises clients in matters of labor law and employee relations, including labor contract negotiations, resisting union organizing drives, employment discrimination, non-compete and confidentiality agreements, occupational safety and health issues, personnel policies, handbooks, and employment contracts. The firm has extensive experience in designing, implementing and qualifying retirement benefit plans, non-pension employee benefit and other executive compensation plans.

Regulatory & Utility Law: ON&W counsels energy and telecommunications utilities in regulatory, corporate and general affairs. ON&W represents clients before administrative and regulatory agencies, and provides contractual services, legislative services, trial and appellate representation.

Healthcare: ON&W advises physicians, hospitals, clinics, and other healthcare providers on business and regulatory matters. Specific experience includes certificates of need, contractual matters, joint ventures, mergers and acquisitions, facility licensure, accreditation, medical staff licensure and credentialing, healthcare payment systems and contracts, Medicare/Medicaid regulations, anti-kickback, Stark, prescription drug marketing, patient dumping and HIPAA compliance issues.

HEAD OFFICE

KENTUCKY
1700 PNC Plaza, 500 West Jefferson Street, **Louisville**, KY 40202
Tel: 502 582 1601 **Fax:** 502 581 9564
Email: onw@ogdenlaw.com
Website: www.ogdenlaw.com

CONTACTS

Business, Corporate & Public Finance	John G Treitz Jr
Litigation & Dispute Resolution	W Gregory King
Employer/Employee Relations	Thomas M Williams
Regulatory & Utility Law	Kendrick R Riggs
Healthcare	Joseph A Kirwan
Federal, State & Local Tax	Timothy J Eifler

Federal, State & Local Tax: ON&W, with extensive experience in tax planning for reorganizations, partnership transactions and individuals, represents clients in both tax planning and tax controversies before the Internal Revenue Service, the United States Tax Court and the Kentucky Board of Tax Appeals. In the state and local area, the firm routinely advises clients involving Kentucky income tax, license tax, property tax, sales and use tax, and local occupational tax issues while assisting an expanding number of clients with international tax issues.

CLIENTS: LG&E Energy LLC, Brown-Forman Corporation, Cincinnati/Northern Kentucky International Airport, United Medical Corporation, Bramco LLC, Jewish Hospital HealthCare Services, Clear Channel Radio, Sodrel Truck Lines, Inc., Paradise Tomato Kitchens, Inc., Publishers Printing, Norton Healthcare, Inc., Papa John's International, Inc., Diagnostic Imaging Alliance, ISCO Industries, Inc., Water Works, Radiology Associates, Caterpillar Inc., American Healthcare Indemnity Company.

INTERNATIONAL WORK: ON&W has represented local businesses who are acquiring businesses outside of the United States or establishing distribution or joint venture arrangements in foreign countries. The firm has also represented foreign businesses seeking to acquire or establish local operations.

SINCE 1898
OGDEN NEWELL & WELCH PLLC
ATTORNEYS FOR BUSINESS

SMITH & SMITH, ATTORNEYS

THE FIRM

Managing Partner: James U Smith, III

Number of partners: 4
Number of other lawyers: 6

AREAS OF PRACTICE:
Employment Litigation 45%
Labor Law 35%
Employment Law/Preventive Counseling 20%

FIRM OVERVIEW: Smith & Smith, Attorneys was founded in 1946 and has been at the forefront in the region in counseling public and private sector employers in all facets of labor and employment law. The firm's comprehensive labor and employment law practice includes: union avoidance; employment litigation; traditional labor law; wage and hour; in-house training; employment discrimination; and employment contracts and policies. The firm couples its goal of providing the highest quality representation of its clients with a commitment to responsive and efficient service and attention to client matters that distinguish the best small firms. The firm emphasizes consulting and advising its clients on labor and employment-related matters in an effort to avoid litigation, and on vigorously defending its clients when they are embroiled in controversies or lawsuits. Smith & Smith also is a member of Worklaw Network®, a nationwide network of independent law firms practicing exclusively in the areas of labor and employment law. Worklaw Network has 26 member firms whose approximately 340 attorneys practice in 41 states, the District of Columbia and Canada.

MAIN AREAS OF PRACTICE:
Labor Law: Smith & Smith advises and represents its clients in all phases of labor relations under the NLRA and RLA. The firm's attorneys regularly guide clients through union organizing campaigns and decertification procedures, as well as adversarial proceedings before the National Labor Relations Board. The firm also handles collective bargaining negotiations, contract administration matters and arbitrations, and other issues arising out of application of state and federal labor laws.
Employment Law/Preventive Counseling: The firm advises its clients with respect to wage and hour laws, civil rights laws, discrimination issues, wrongful discharge, employment-related torts, and employment and independent contractor agreements. Clients also seek counsel from the firm's attorneys in matters of compliance with the Americans with Disabilities Act, the Occupational Safety and Health Act, the Family and Medical Leave Act, and other federal and state employment statutes and regulations. The firm assists clients in the development and implementation of employment policies and procedures, and conducts preventive training for supervisory personnel in all aspects of the employment relationship.
Employment Litigation: Smith & Smith has an extensive Civil Litigation Practice, which encompasses representation of clients in employment law matters in state and federal trial courts, before administrative agencies, appellate advocacy, arbitration and other forms of alternative dispute resolution. A principal focus of Smith & Smith is avoiding protracted litigation and its attorneys are leaders in developing innovative defense strategies to end lawsuits at their early stages, as well as implementing preventive strategies for its clients.

HEAD OFFICE

KENTUCKY
300 South, First Trust Centre, 200 South Fifth Street,
Louisville, KY 40202
Tel: 502 587 0761   **Fax:** 502 589 5345
Email: firm@smithandsmithattorneys.com
Website: www.smithandsmithattorneys.com

CONTACTS

Labor Law . . . . .James U Smith III
Employment Law/Preventive Counseling . . . . .W Kevin Smith
Employment Litigation . . . . .John O Sheller

CLIENTS: Smith & Smith represents clients in a broad range of industries, such as utility, construction, manufacturing, retail, health care, education, chemical, banking, insurance, and transportation. The firm represents clients of every size, from small, single-site employers to large national companies. Representative clients of Smith & Smith include: Arch Chemicals, Inc.; Associated Builders & Contractors, Inc.; The Chubb Group; Churchill Downs, Inc.; Papa Johns International, Inc.; James N. Gray Company; 84 Lumber Company L.P.; Disabled American Veterans; Lindsey Wilson College; R.C. Bigelow, Inc.; Wehr Constructors, Inc.; Whayne Supply Company; Louisville Water Company; Louisville Gas & Electric Co.; United Methodist Hospital of Kentucky, Inc.; ResCare, Inc.; and T & WA, Inc.

SMITH & SMITH
ATTORNEYS

STITES & HARBISON, PLLC

THE FIRM

Chairman: Kennedy Helm, III

Number of partners: 113
Number of associates: 97
Number of counsel: 31

Email: general@stites.com
Website: www.stites.com

FIRM OVERVIEW: Stites & Harbison, PLLC, strives to be a preeminent law firm based in strategic Southeastern locations and sought by business and institutional clients nationwide for sophisticated transactions, difficult litigation and complex regulatory matters. Stites & Harbison is a full service firm practicing through departmental groupings with specialty and industry teams whose seven locations function as a single law office.

MAIN AREAS OF PRACTICE: Business and finance; business litigation; construction; creditors' rights and bankruptcy; employment; environmental; intellectual property and technology; liability defense; personal services; real estate.

CLIENTS:

REPRESENTATIVE CLIENTS: Adams USA, Inc.; Aegon USA Investment Management, Inc.; A.H. Belo Corporation; Alcoa Fujikura Ltd.; Alstom Power; Ambrake Corporation; American Electric Power Service Corporation (Kentucky Power Co.); American General Corporation; American Institute of Steel Construction, Inc.; Anthem Inc.; Bank One, Kentucky, N.A.; Baptist Healthcare System; The Beck Group; BellSouth Telecommunications, Inc.; Beverly Enterprises, Inc.; Brainstorm USA LLC; Bridgestone/Firestone, Inc.; Brown-Forman Corporation; Brown & Williamson Tobacco Corporation; Caldwell Tanks, Inc.; Catskill Development, LLC; CHA HMO, Inc.; Dynergy Power Corp.; Electrolux LLC; Fidelity National Bank; Fleet Financial Corp.; Fortune Brands; Frontier Insurance Corporation; GE Capital Corporation; GlaxoSmithKline; The Goodyear Tire & Rubber Company; International Port of Kentucky; James N. Gray Company; Holder Construction Company; ITT Financial; J.P. Morgan Mortgage Capital; Kajima Construction Services, Inc.; Kentucky Economic Development Finance Authority (KEDFA); KFC Corporation; Lexington-Fayette Urban County Airport Board; Life Insurance Company of Georgia; Louisville Regional Airport Authority; Metropolitan Nashville Airport Authority; Microsoft; Modis Professional Services, Inc.; National City Bank of Kentucky; National Health Investors, Inc.; National Renal Alliance, LLC; New Life Corporation of America; New York Department of Insurance; Northern Life Insurance Company; Pizza Magia International, LLC; Presco Steel, Inc.; Purdue Pharma LP; Regions Bank; Lin R.Rogers Electrical Contractors; Russell Athletic Corporation; Southern Land Company; Steel Technologies, Inc.; Stock Yards Bank & Trust Co.; SunTrust Bank; Synaxis Group, Inc.; ThermoView Industries, Inc.; Tricon Global Restaurants; Tyson Foods, Inc.; Union Planters Bank, N.A.; University Medical Center, Inc.; University of Kentucky; University of Louisville; Vanderbilt University; Whayne Supply Company; Zurich American Insurance Companies.

OFFICES

KENTUCKY
400 W. Market St, Suite 1800, **Louisville**, KY 40202
Tel: 502 587 3400 **Fax:** 502 587 6391

250 W. Main St, Suite 2300, **Lexington**, KY 40507
Tel: 859 226 2300 **Fax:** 859 253 9144

421 W. Main St, **Frankfort**, KY 40602
Tel: 502 223 3477 **Fax:** 502 223 4124

DISTRICT OF COLUMBIA
1200 G St, NW, Suite 800, **Washington**, DC 20005
Tel: 202 434 8968 **Fax:** 202 737 5822

GEORGIA
303 Peachtree St, NE, 2800 SunTrust Plaza, **Atlanta**, GA 30308
Tel: 404 739 8800 **Fax:** 404 739 8870

INDIANA
323 E. Court Ave, **Jeffersonville**, IN 47130
Tel: 812 282 7566 **Fax:** 812 284 5519

TENNESSEE
424 Church St, Suite 1800, **Nashville**, TN 37219
Tel: 615 244 5200 **Fax:** 615 782 2371

VIRGINIA
1199 N.Fairfax St, Suite 900, **Alexandria**, VA 22314
Tel: 203 739 4900 **Fax:** 203 739 9577

CONTACTS

Business & Finance	Robert M Beck, Jr (Lexington)
	W Thomas Halbleib, Jr (Louisville)
	Kenneth R Sagan (Lexington)
	Wynne James (Nashville)
Business Litigation	Joseph L Hamilton (Louisville)
	T Morgan Ward Jr (Louisville)
	J Clarke Keller (Lexington)
	Dianna B Shew (Nashville)
Construction	Gregory P Parsons (Lexington)
Creditors' Rights & Bankruptcy	W Robinson Beard (Louisville)
Employment, Labor & Immigration	Shannon A Hamilton (Louisville)
	Stephen H Price (Nashville)
Environmental	W Patrick Stallard (Louisville)
Intellectual Property & Technology	Jack A Wheat (Louisville)
Liability Defense	Carol D Browning (Louisville)
	John M Famularo (Lexington)
Personal Services	J David Porter (Lexington)
Real Estate	Richard W Stephens (Atlanta)
	William H Haden, Jr (Louisville)
	Stephen M Ruschell (Lexington)
	Cynthia N Sellers (Nashville)

STITES & HARBISON PLLC

ATTORNEYS

TACHAU MADDOX HOVIOUS & DICKENS PLC

THE FIRM

Founding Members: David Tachau, Victor Maddox, R Gregg Hovious
Managing Member: Dustin E Meek

Number of members: 7
Number of other attorneys: 9

AREAS OF PRACTICE:

Commercial Litigation 70%
Healthcare Litigation & Advising 10%
Plaintiff's Personal Injury Litigation 10%
Personal Injury Litigation Defense 10%

HEAD OFFICE

KENTUCKY
2700 National City Tower, **Louisville**, KY 40202-3116
Tel: 502 588 2000 **Fax:** 502 588 2020
Email: dmeek@tmhd.com
Website: www.tmhd.com

FIRM OVERVIEW: Tachau Maddox Hovious & Dickens PLC was opened in 1995 by four litigation partners from a large regional law firm, and has steadily grown by focusing on commercial litigation for businesses and individuals in Kentucky and southern Indiana. The firm also handles constitutional and public interest litigation, as well as employment matters and personal injury litigation for plaintiffs and defendants, and has several substantial healthcare clients for whom it does litigation and business counseling. The firm has enjoyed remarkable success at trials and in appeals: all seven of its partners have tried or arbitrated cases to successful awards within the last two years, and six of the partners have won state or federal appeals during that period. The firm compensates its attorneys well, and has attracted exceptionally talented lateral associates from a number of large regional and national firms.

MAIN AREAS OF PRACTICE:

COMMERCIAL LITIGATION: Tachau Maddox Hovious & Dickens handles numerous kinds of business litigation for regional and national clients:
Financial Institutions: The firm has recently represented all of the leading banking firms in the Kentucky market in complex litigation matters, including JPMorgan Chase, National City Bank, PNC Bank, Huntington National Bank, BB&T and Stock Yards Bank, in disputes involving consumer regulatory, UCC, lender liability, contract formation/breach, estate and trust/breach of fiduciary duty, letter of credit and guaranty, property rights and claims, fraud, bankruptcy and general banking matters.
General Commercial Entities: The firm handles contract performance and breach litigation, bankruptcy, commercial partnership disputes, securities and other fraud litigation, class action claims, commercial tort, and zoning and property disputes, for publicly-traded companies and other businesses such as Aegon, General Electric, Papa John's Pizza, ResCare and Ventas.
Insurance Firms: The firm has served as primary litigation counsel on various commercial, administrative and employment matters in the past decade for Neace Lukens, the largest insurance agency in the Kentucky/Indiana/Ohio region. The firm has also been engaged in other contract and insurance coverage matters for other clients, including two specialty lines managing general agents who underwrite and administer

intellectual property insurance and public employee benefits, and three substantial life and health insurers (Principal Life Insurance Co., Fortis Insurance Co., and Aegon/Life Investors Insurance Co.). The firm's agency-related work has included the successful defense of multiple errors and omissions claims, the successful prosecution and defense of multiple noncompetition covenant claims, the successful representation of various contract actions, and the successful representation of administrative matters before the Kentucky Office of Insurance.
Labor & Employment Clients: The firm provides counseling and litigation services for employers and employees on matters involving ERISA and benefits, race and gender and disability discrimination, employment contracts, independent contractor issues, restrictive covenants and non-competition agreements, and employment-related torts including defamation, interference with contractual relations and breach of fiduciary duty.
Constitutional & Public Interest Litigation: The firm has represented the state House of Representatives Minority Leader in a challenge to the constitutionality of legislative redistricting under the state constitution, successfully opposed a certiorari petition to the United States Supreme Court on behalf of the Kentucky Registry of Election Finance to defend the constitutionality of public financing of gubernatorial elections, and successfully sued the Governor and General Assembly to vindicate equal protection rights of voters to legislative redistricting, among other matters.
Healthcare Firms: The firm represents various healthcare entities, including a number on a national basis. The firm's representation includes administrative issues and Certificate of Need proceedings, government investigations and qui tam matters, physician practice issues, commercial litigation and bankruptcy matters. The firm also provides business counseling on restructuring, regulatory (including Stark and anti-kickback) analysis, and reimbursement issues. The firm's clients include Kindred Healthcare (NYSE: KND), RehabCare Group (NYSE: RHB) and Jewish Hospital Healthcare Services.
Personal Injury Litigation: The firm represents injured plaintiffs as well as serving as national coordinating counsel for certain General Electric Co. product liability litigation.

WYATT, TARRANT & COMBS, LLP

THE FIRM

Managing Partner: Kevin J Hable

FIRM OVERVIEW: With over 200 attorneys in seven offices, Wyatt, Tarrant & Combs, LLP offers a full range of legal services in Kentucky, Indiana and Tennessee. By leveraging the firm's rich heritage and tradition of excellence, the Wyatt firm has been able to continually attract top legal talent and grow its business. Attorneys in the Wyatt firm adhere to their core principles of integrity, zealous representation and absolute loyalty to clients. This discipline, combined with an overriding dedication to client service, an uncompromising commitment to quality legal work and an old fashioned work ethic are the hallmarks of the firm.

MAIN AREAS OF PRACTICE:

Business Law: Wyatt has active practices in the areas of banking, tax, public finance, venture capital, environment, real estate and lending, securities compliance, executive compensation, employee benefit plans and labor law. Wyatt counsels its clients over the entire life of the business - from selecting the form of business entity, to raising capital and financing growth (both public and private offerings), to taxation issues, to acquisition and sale transactions and other exit strategies. The firm represents a wide range of established companies (both public and closely held) and start-ups. It also represents directors, officers, majority/minority owners and entrepreneurs in connection with a range of business issues.

Commercial Litigation: Wyatt handles all types of business litigation, including class actions, multi-district litigation and other complex litigation as well as more routine matters of business litigation in both jury and non-jury settings. The firm regularly represents the interests of major businesses, individuals, professional firms and governmental entities in all varieties of disputes, including those involving contracts, antitrust, fiduciary duties, toxic torts, tortious interference with contracts, franchises, unfair competition, regulatory law, bankruptcy and creditors' rights.

Healthcare: Wyatt has significant experience in all aspects of the healthcare industry including: (i) regulatory, administrative and accreditation matters such as certificates of need, licensure, HIPAA, Medicare, Medicaid and third-party reimbursement, (ii) planning and implementation regarding corporate structure, joint ventures, sales and acquisitions and tax-exempt status, and (iii) hospital/physician/patient relationships.

Mineral & Energy: Wyatt represents owners, producers and distributors of coal, oil and gas, energy facility operators and those who provide financing, technical assistance, equipment and insurance to the mineral and energy industries. The firm handles a broad range of matters such as acquisitions and divestitures; mineral leasing; supply contracts; real and personal property issues; labor and employment; taxes; mining agreements; and disaster response consultation. The firm also frequently handles litigation matters in all of these areas before state and federal courts and regulatory agencies.

International Trade: Wyatt's Immigration Practice is very active, providing assistance with immigration, naturalization and visas. The firm also has experience with international business negotiations, acquisitions, and joint ventures, as well as multi-national sales, distribution and licensing arrangements, protection of intellectual property, and tax issues related to the foregoing.

Estate Planning: Wyatt has a large estate planning practice helping clients plan for the disposition of assets during their lifetime and at death. Primary emphasis is placed on preparation of wills, revocable and irrevocable trust agreements, prenuptial agreements and other documents that are necessary for wealth preservation, the orderly transfer of assets and the mitigation of federal and state taxes.

OFFICES

KENTUCKY

PNC Plaza, 500 West Jefferson Street, Suite 2800, **Louisville**, KY 40202-2898
Tel: 502 589 5235   **Fax:** 502 589 0309

Lexington Financial Center, 250 West Main Street, Suite 1600, **Lexington**, KY 40507-1746
Tel: 859 233 2012   **Fax:** 859 259 0649

918 State Street, **Bowling Green**, KY 42102-1220
Tel: 270 842 1050   **Fax:** 270 842 4720

The Taylor-Scott Building, 311 West Main Street, **Frankfort**, KY 40601-1807
Tel: 502 223 2104   **Fax:** 502 227 7681

TENNESSEE

1715 Aaron Brenner Drive, Suite 800, **Memphis**, TN 38120-4367
Tel: 901 537 1000   **Fax:** 901 537 1010

2525 West End Avenue, Suite 1500, **Nashville**, TN 37203-1423
Tel: 615 244 0020   **Fax:** 615 256 1726

INDIANA

The Community Bank Building, 101 West Spring Street, Suite 500
New Albany, IN 47150-3610
Tel: 812 845 3561   **Fax:** 812 949 2524

Website: www.wyattfirm.com

CONTACTS

Business Law ....Robert A Heath (Louisville)
Commercial Litigation ....Cornelius E Coryell (Louisville)
Healthcare ....Carole D Christian (Louisville)
....Theodore T Myre (Louisville)
Mineral & Energy ....Marco M Rajkovich (Lexington)
International Trade.................................Jeffrey E Wallace (Louisville)
Estate Planning ....Gordon B Wright (Louisville)

CLIENTS: Bank One, Kentucky, NA; Churchill Downs Incorporated; Brown & Williamson Tobacco Corp.; E.I. duPont de Nemours; Heaven Hill Distilleries; Jefferson County Public Schools; LG&E Energy Corp.; Norton Healthcare Inc.; Thornton Oil Corporation; Union Planters Corporation; Union Underwear Company Inc.

CONTENTS: Banking & Finance p.857; Corporate/M&A p.858; Employment p.860; Energy & Natural Resources p.862; Gaming & Licensing p.864; Litigation p.864; Real Estate p.867; Individuals' Profiles p.868; Firms' Profiles p.879.

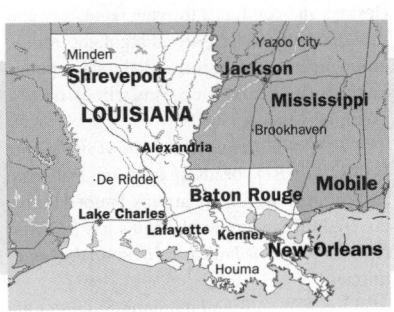

How lawyers are ranked

The opinions we gather from clients — mainly from in-house lawyers but also from other purchasers of legal services — are balanced by opinions from colleagues and competitors. Together, they provide two different perspectives — an all-round view — and biased viewpoints cancel each other out.

BANKING & FINANCE

Louisiana
Leading firms (Banking & Finance)

1
JONES WALKER WAECHTER *New Orleans*
LISKOW & LEWIS PLC *New Orleans*
PHELPS DUNBAR LLP *New Orleans*

2
CARVER DARDEN KORETZKY TESSIER *New Orleans*
CORRERO FISHMAN HAYGOOD *New Orleans*
MCGLINCHEY STAFFORD *New Orleans*

3
CHAFFE, MCCALL, PHILLIPS, TOLER *New Orleans*
PETTIETTE, ARMAND, DUNKELMAN *Shreveport*

Leading individuals (Banking & Finance)

1
CLAVERIE Philip *Phelps Dunbar, New Orleans*
STUCKEY James *Phelps Dunbar, New Orleans*
TESSIER Frank *Carver Darden, New Orleans*

2
CROMWELL David *Pettiette Armand, Shreveport*
PAGE Marshall *Jones Walker, New Orleans*
ROBERSON Tom *Jones Walker, New Orleans*
WILLENZIK David *McGlinchey Stafford, New Orleans*
WILLIS S Scott *Correro Fishman, New Orleans*
WOGAN John *Liskow & Lewis, New Orleans*

Up-and-coming individuals
LELONG Rivers *Jones Walker, New Orleans*

Firms and individuals are listed alphabetically in each band.

Band 1

Jones Walker Waechter Poitevent Carrère & Denègre, LLP

See firm details p.883

The Firm: Clients were effusive in their praise of the banking group at this large multiservice firm, painting a picture of a team that *"has a keen appreciation of what the client wants and knows how to get it."* Few sources quibbled with this *"highly impressive"* firm's top-tier ranking, one interviewee describing it as a *"powerhouse"* for structured finance. In the past year attorneys have been active on a number of fronts; they have handled public equity and debt transactions and many sophisticated bank credit facilities. The group has recently assisted Enhanced Capital with the issuing of $18 million worth of Alaba-

ma Certified Capital Companies (CAPCO) notes.

The Lawyers: A *"gifted, sought-after attorney,"* **Marshall Page** (see p.875) is renowned for his work on venture funds and bank credit facilities. Clients applauded the *"tireless enthusiasm"* of a practitioner who is *"incredibly smart and creative."* **Tom Roberson** (see p.875) is held in high esteem for his syndicated bank finance work. Interviewees remarked upon his extensive experience in the field, describing him as *"truly outstanding."* Up-and-comer **Rivers Lelong** (see p.873) makes an appearance in the tables due to market approval of his work for Hibernia National Bank.

The Clients: Bank One; Central Gulf Lines; CenturyTel; Freeport-McMoRan Copper & Gold; LCI Shipholdings; JPMorgan Chase; Superior Energy Services; Tidewater and Torch Offshore.

Liskow & Lewis PLC

The Firm: With its primary focus on banking institutions, this *"top-quality"* firm maintains its high standing in the market due to widespread approval of the banking group's *"pragmatic and committed approach."* Attorneys regularly assist in a number of diverse areas, giving regulatory compliance advice, structuring and closing secured and unsecured loans, and devising bank loan policies.

The Lawyers: Many of those interviewed highlighted **John Wogan** as the group's leading figure. *"A truly polished performer,"* Wogan has the ability to put clients at ease; *"he speaks our language,"* noted one source. Marilyn Maloney has moved to the firm's Houston office.

The Clients: CSFB, AmSouth Bank and regional banks and clients involved in the energy and minerals industries.

Phelps Dunbar LLP

See firm details p.886

The Firm: Regarded by some commentators as the *"top show in town"* on the lending side, this firm acts for most of the region's major banking institutions. Clients value the *"superior service"*

provided by attorneys, with one interviewee commenting approvingly on the *"strong sense of professionalism"* prevalent throughout the firm. In addition to work on public and private undertakings, the group is also considered highly adept at syndicated and acquisition financings.

The Lawyers: The *"practical and efficient"* **Philip Claverie** (see p.870) has an extensive practice, encompassing real estate transactions and commercial lending. He won favor with clients for his ability to explain difficult concepts clearly and concisely. **Jim Stuckey** (see p.876) is highly respected for his transactional practice. Described as a *"great technician,"* Stuckey has built up considerable expertise in UCC matters.

The Clients: The firm is predominantly known for its work with large lending institutions including: AmSouth Bank; Audubon Capital Fund; Whitney National Bank; Hibernia National Bank and IBERIABANK.

Band 2

Carver Darden Koretzky Tessier Finn Blossman & Areaux LLC

The Firm: This small New Orleans-based boutique offers particular specializations in banking and energy financing. Banks and businesses are represented in secured and unsecured lending and equipment leasing by *"a sterling group of attorneys."* Whitney National Bank is the firm's flagship client.

The Lawyers: Famed for his ability to *"get to the heart of the matter within seconds,"* **Frank Tessier** is highly respected by the market. Sources commended his credit facility work and described him as an *"exceptionally hard-working attorney."*

The Clients: Chevron Pipe Line; Deutsche Bank; Hibernia National Bank; Nexen Chemicals USA and Whitney National Bank.

Correro Fishman Haygood Phelps Walmsley & Casteix LLP

See firm details p.882

The Firm: Clients value the quality advice emanating from this commercial boutique. Its attorneys provide *"expert guidance"* on bank closings and conduct a thriving regulatory and transactional practice. Recent highlights for the group include advising on a $360 million public finance offering and counseling schools on tax-exempt financing.

The Lawyers: *"Fountain of knowledge"* **Scott Willis** (see p.877) heads up the firm's real estate and commercial finance groups. Lauded for his tax credit financing work, Willis has earned a reputation as a *"dedicated and trustworthy"* practitioner.

The Clients: ASCO; First Bank & Trust; Offshore Logistics; Robinson Lumber; S&P Cellular Holdings; US Unwired; OmniBank and Whitney National Bank.

McGlinchey Stafford

See firm details p.885

The Firm: Home to a nationally renowned consumer finance practice, this multiservice firm also hosts significant expertise in commercial lending and retail banking. The experience gained through its role as outside counsel to a number of major finance companies gives weight to one commentator's contention that the team is *"unri-*

valed in the quality and depth of its work."

The Lawyers: Although **David Willenzik**'s (see p.877) regulatory practice is highly regarded, sources also note that he has considerable experience of representing lenders. *"A master organizer,"* Willenzik operates on a truly national level and has contributed to a number of practitioner texts in the banking sphere.

The Clients: American Express; Bank of America; Bank One; Citibank; DaimlerChrysler Services; Ford Motor Credit; GE Capital; GM Finance; Toyota Motor Credit and Wells Fargo. The firm also acts for mortgage lenders and commercial finance companies.

Band 3

Chaffe, McCall, Phillips, Toler & Sarpy, LLP

See firm details p.881

The Firm: Interviewees were united in their belief that this multi service firm's finance practice merited inclusion in the rankings. The group represents borrowers and lenders in all types of commercial loan transactions. Its *"top-grade"* attorneys have impressed clients with

their *"comprehensive and authoritative"* counsel. The firm acted as the lead lender's counsel in the development of one of the largest lifestyle power centers on the Gulf Coast.

The Lawyers: Head of the firm's corporate section, Howell Crosby, is a key figure in the group's banking practice. AmSouth Bank and Hibernial National Bank are among the firm's clients.

Pettiette, Armand, Dunkelman, Woodley, Byrd & Cromwell LLP

The Firm: Based in Shreveport, this ten-attorney firm is considered the clear market leader for transactional matters in north Louisiana. With an enviable client roster that includes AmSouth and Regions Bank, this *"dynamic and resourceful"* team has expertise in commercial lending and banking-related litigation.

The Lawyers: *"Confident and assured,"* **David Cromwell** is the firm's banking specialist. With particular experience in construction financing projects, Cromwell is considered a *"strong communicator"* who demonstrates a clear understanding of the technical details.

The Clients: Clients include Regions Bank, Bank One and AmSouth Bank.

CORPORATE/M&A

Louisiana
Leading firms (Corporate/M&A)

[1]	**CORRERO FISHMAN HAYGOOD** New Orleans
	JONES WALKER WAECHTER New Orleans
[2]	**KEAN, MILLER, HAWTHORNE** Baton Rouge
	PHELPS DUNBAR LLP New Orleans
	STONE PIGMAN WALTHER New Orleans
[3]	**KANTROW SPAHT WEAVER** Baton Rouge
	MCGLINCHEY STAFFORD New Orleans
	SHER GARNER CAHILL RICHTER KLEIN New Orleans
[4]	**ADAMS AND REESE LLP** New Orleans
	LISKOW & LEWIS PLC New Orleans
	TAYLOR, PORTER, BROOKS Baton Rouge

Firms are listed alphabetically in each band.

Band 1

Correro Fishman Haygood Phelps Walmsley & Casteix LLP

See firm details p.882

The Firm: Home to the *"undisputed deans of the profession,"* this highly regarded boutique practice continues to cement its position as a major player in the Louisiana corporate market. Clients welcome the way the firm focuses on quality over quantity: *"There's no overlawyering; they pick the right people for the deal and then they just get on with it."* The firm's considerable experience in securities and M&A supports the contention of one prominent source that *"whatever the problem, there'll be an expert on hand to*

sort it out." Advice on development and growth strategies is provided to a client base that ranges from large Louisiana-based corporates to small startup entities. As well as the usual range of SEC and M&A work, recently the firm handled two interesting restructuring transactions: the first, a series of acquisitions to restructure the business and indebtedness of a foreign client's US operations; the second involved Chapter 11 proceedings for a client's wholly-owned subsidiary. The prepackaged reorganization plan for the subsidiary required the client to raise hundreds of millions of dollars.

The Lawyers: *"The three wise men of corporate Louisiana,"* **Andy Correro**, (see p.870) **Louis Fishman** (see p.871) and **Paul Haygood** (see p.872) are the firm's leading lights and have been responsible for the career development of numerous younger corporate practitioners in the state. For many interviewees, Correro *"leads the pack"* by virtue of his *"startling intelligence"* and considerable expertise in securities. In the past year he has handled a number of significant bank mergers. The *"endearing and diplomatic"* Fishman impresses both clients and peers due, in part, to his aptitude for *"articulating and framing problems in a way that makes perfect sense."* Haygood is *"excellent with the technical details"* and has recently achieved prominence in the tax-planning sphere. Blessed with *"great analytical and negotiation skills,"* Haygood *"inspires confidence"* in clients. Acknowledged to be *"an*

increasingly key figure" in the firm, **Robert Walmsley** enters this year's rankings. In the past year Walmsley has been particularly active in representing the interests of nonprofit organizations. Finally, **John Werner** (see p.877) was described as *"a breath of fresh air"* due to his ability to truly understand the client's perspective. Werner's practice focus is on energy lending.

The Clients: Amedisys; Chaffe & Associates; The Department of Treasury for the State of Louisiana; Laitram; Midsouth Bank; Offshore Logistics; Pennington Medical Foundation; Sanderson Farms; Blue Cross of Louisiana; SMG; US Unwired; Times-Picayune Publishing Corporation and Stewart Enterprises.

Jones Walker Waechter Poitevent Carrère & Denègre, LLP

See firm details p.883

The Firm: *"Head and shoulders above the rest for the big work,"* was the prevailing view of the corporate practice at this large multiservice firm. While some interviewees insisted that size is not everything, there was little disagreement that this 22-strong group *"has considerably more manpower than anyone else,"* making it *"perfectly equipped to handle any transaction, any size, at any time."* Clients commend the firm's *"unflappable and authoritative"* lawyers, reserving special praise for the group's responsiveness and efficiency. Sophisticated commercial projects are handled for an impressive client base comprised

Louisiana
Leading individuals (Corporate/M&A)

1 CORRERO Anthony *Correro Fishman*, New Orleans
FISHMAN Louis *Correro Fishman*, New Orleans
MCMILLAN II L Richards *Jones Walker*, New Orleans

2 FULLMER Mark *Phelps Dunbar*, New Orleans
HAYGOOD Paul *Correro Fishman*, New Orleans
HEARN Curtis *Jones Walker*, New Orleans
KANTROW Lee *Kantrow Spaht*, Baton Rouge
WOLFE Richard *Jones Walker*, New Orleans

3 BUTLER Patrick *Phelps Dunbar*, New Orleans
CAVERLY Joseph *Stone Pigman*, New Orleans
DILEO Anthony *Stone Pigman*, New Orleans
MILLER Ben *Kean Miller*, Baton Rouge
WHITTAKER Scott *Stone Pigman*, New Orleans

4 AGUILAR Rodolfo *McGlinchey* Baton Rouge
BOULET Virginia *Adams and Reese*, New Orleans
CAMPBELL John *Taylor Porter*, Baton Rouge
FANTACI James *McGlinchey Stafford*, New Orleans
KLEIN Steven *Sher Garner*, New Orleans
MASTERS William *Jones Walker*, New Orleans
SNYDER Charles *Milling Benson*, New Orleans
WALMSLEY Robert *Correro Fishman*, New Orleans
WERNER John *Correro Fishman*, New Orleans

Up-and-coming individuals
CURRAULT Douglas *Jones Walker*, New Orleans
ROUSSEAU Dionne *Jones Walker*, New Orleans

Leading individuals
(Corporate/M&A: Bankruptcy)

1 BARRIERE Brent *Phelps Dunbar*, New Orleans
DRAPER Douglas *Heller Draper*, New Orleans
FORSYTH David *Sessions Fishman*, New Orleans
VANCE R Patrick *Jones Walker*, New Orleans

2 CERONE Rudy *McGlinchey Stafford*, New Orleans
JONES Philip *Liskow & Lewis*, New Orleans
PATRICK III William *Heller Draper*, New Orleans

Individuals are listed alphabetically in each band.

of oil and gas, telecom, shipping and transportation companies in addition to notable financial institutions. The group also has a widely respected corporate governance practice.

The Lawyers: The "*extremely well-organized and conscientious*" **Rick McMillan** (see p.874) was the first name on most interviewees' lips when asked to list the state's outstanding corporate lawyers. McMillan "*has an incredible feel for the market*" and is said to possess "*great business acumen,*" qualities which contribute to him maintaining his top-tier ranking. His major projects in the past year have included significant securities transactions and a number of deals for stellar client McMoRan Exploration. Described as "*a hugely capable attorney*" by peers, **Dick Wolfe** (see p.878) "*continues to set the standard*" in his transactional work for public companies. Wolfe represented the controlling stockholders of Riviana Foods in the acquisition of shares by Ebro Puleva. **Curtis Hearn**'s (see p.872) increased profile in the past year has not gone unnoticed by peers who predicted an ascent "*right to the very top of the corporate pile.*" Much of Hearn's time recently has been spent on the sale to Humana of Ochsner Health Plan by Ochsner Clinic Foundation. **Bill Masters** (see p.874) enters this year's rankings following impressive market feedback. Respected for his "*refreshing common-sense approach,*" Masters undertakes a range of corporate matters for service providers, private capital portfolio companies and clients in a variety of other industries including banking. Commercial litigator **Patrick Vance** (see p.877) was singled out as a leading player in the bankruptcy arena. "*Tenacious with a capital T,*" Vance usually represents creditors. Up-and-comer **Dionne Rousseau** (see p.875) won plaudits for her expertise in public offerings; clients appreciate her "*results-focused approach.*" Last but not least, **Douglas Currault** (see p.871) also won favor with interviewees for his ability to "*talk the client's language.*" Much of Currault's business involves Freeport McMoRan.

The Clients: Freeport McMoRan; Elliott Associates; Stewart Enterprises; Enhanced Capital Partners; Horizon Offshore; SCP Pool Corporation; Superior Energy Services and CenturyTel.

Band 2

Kean, Miller, Hawthorne, D'Armond, McCowan & Jarman, LLP

The Firm: Although a significant amount of the firm's work is a result of its strong links to the chemical and refining industries, the corporate group garnered praise for its broad expertise on transactional matters across a number of fields. One prominent source insisted the firm had "*more vitality than other Baton Rouge firms;*" clients, too, were quick to comment on the "*energy and verve*" exhibited by the firm's attorneys. A significant niche has been built in the healthcare sector. Recent highlights for the group include acquisition work for The Shaw Group and Lamar Advertising.

The Lawyers: Commentators endorsed the team's head **Ben Miller** as "*a highly influential figure.*" Miller advises a range of businesses and corporate clients with regard to a variety of financing methods and the structure and formation of corporate entities.

The Clients: Lamar Advertising; Microsoft; IBM; MCI; South Baton Rouge Journal; Commercial Properties Development; Black & Decker; Sasol North America; Coca-Cola of Baton Rouge; EATEL; Albemarle Corporation; BP Amoco.

Phelps Dunbar LLP

See firm details p.886
The Firm: Benefiting from strong links with the firm's respected banking practice, the corporate group "*continues to go from strength to strength.*" Transactional work is undertaken for regional and national clients; large companies are advised on the issuance of debt and equity capital as well as M&A, and work is also carried out for private investors, underwriters and venture capital companies.

The Lawyers: The "*very reassuring*" **Mark Fullmer** (see p.872) is renowned for the quality of his securities work. "*A great guy to have in tricky situations,*" Fullmer has been representing a software solution company in a number of transactional matters over the past year. According to clients, **Patrick Butler** (see p.870) is "*always there when you need him.*" Butler has extensive experience in the purchase and sale of businesses for large public corporations as well as private firms. "*Business litigator par excellence*" **Brent Barriere** (see p.869) is ranked on the back of considerable market approval of his bankruptcy work.

The Clients: Audubon Capital Fund; Edison Chouest Offshore; Hibernia; Innovus; Isle of Capri Casinos; L&B Consulting; Waste Management and Whitney National Bank.

Stone Pigman Walther Wittmann LLC

See firm details p.887
The Firm: This commercial litigation success story has done very well to also build a fine reputation for corporate and transactional expertise. With a client roster that features many regional names, the group – now 14 strong – regularly engages in a variety of business activities for acquiring companies, venture capitalists, investment bankers and institutional private investors. Clients were quick to extol the virtues of an "*incredibly professional*" team that "*never cuts corners.*"

The Lawyers: The "*cool, calm and collected*" **Joseph Caverly** (see p.870) heads the corporate and securities practice group. Interviewees credit Caverly for much of the firm's recent success; describing him as "*the foundation figure of the firm.*" Chair of the business team **Scott Whittaker** (see p.877) is equally well respected in the market. Fêted by commentators for his "*straight-down-the-line*" pragmatism, Whittaker has recently been representing a Louisiana-based clothing manufacturer in the sale of its assets to a California-based manufacturer. Healthcare specialist **Anthony DiLeo** (see p.871) won praise from peers for his resourcefulness: "*He is able to make the best out of any bad situation,*" noted one approvingly. Much of DiLeo's work is on compliance matters for groups of physicians and hospitals, and his national arbitration practice continues to be admired.

The Clients: Avreo; Cannata's Super Markets; Capital Health Services; Lambeth House; New Orleans Coffee Works; Pelican Funding; Peter A Mayer Advertising; Selltis; Star Enterprises and Trinity Medical Management and Westway Holdings.

www.ChambersandPartners.com

All quotes in the text are from interviews with clients and competitors.

859

Band 3

Kantrow Spaht Weaver & Blitzer

The Firm: This Baton Rouge outfit conducts a mixture of litigation and transactional work. The firm's attorneys are renowned for their negotiation skills, with one source commenting on how *"they never take false positions, which makes them really easy to work with."*

The Lawyers: The leading corporate attorney is **Lee Kantrow**, whose wide-ranging practice encompasses securities law and M&As. Observers were full of praise for a *"bright and thoughtful"* practitioner who is able to *"avoid conflict by always having practical solutions at hand."*

The Clients: Air Products and Chemicals; Allied Waste Industries; American Excess Underwriters; Archer Daniels Midland; CIGNA Property and Casualty Insurance; Citizens Bank; First American Title Insurance; The Baton Rouge Clinic, AMC; The Shaw Group; United Artists Theatre Circuit and Whitney National Bank.

McGlinchey Stafford

See firm details p.885

The Firm: With three offices across the state, this firm has the resources to provide the full complement of corporate services to a healthy client base. As well as counseling on the formation and maintenance of corporations, limited liability companies, partnerships and other forms of business associations, attorneys also provide advice on M&As, divestitures of existing businesses, asset sales and purchases.

The Lawyers: **Jim Fantaci** (see p.871) is a specialist in debt restructuring and development financing. Acclaimed for his *"hugely impressive commercial knowledge,"* he has also impressed peers with his negotiation skills. *"Driving force"* **Rudy Aguilar** (see p.869) is the firm's managing partner. Much of his work in the past year has been by way of assistance to a bank holding company that was acquiring a credit facility. **Rudy Cerone**'s (see p.870) expertise lies in the business bankruptcy field. Commentators applauded his *"sound economic sense."*

Sher Garner Cahill Richter Klein McAlister & Hilbert, LLC

The Firm: Market sources were quick to report that the corporate arm of this midsized firm is *"truly making a name for itself"* due to the *"dynamic and direct"* methods employed by attorneys. Advice is given to individuals, private companies and joint ventures on a range of regional and national transactions.

The Lawyers: **Steven Klein** has *"vast knowledge"* on federal and state tax matters; much of his work involves advising on joint ventures for REITs.

The Clients: Burrus Investment Group; Darryl Berger Companies; Labyrinth HealthCare Group; Marrero Land and Improvement Association; New Orleans World Trade Center; Realm Realty; Southern Homes and Frantzen Voelker Investments.

Band 4

Adams and Reese LLP

See firm details p.879

The Firm: According to commentators, this large multiservice firm is home to a team of corporate attorneys who are *"blessed with tremendous judgment and certainty, and are never afraid to go for the jugular."* A client base that criss-crosses the country is represented on a wide range of corporate matters, such as securities regulatory work, bond financings and antitakeover protections.

The Lawyers: Peers admire the way that **Virginia Boulet** (see p.869) *"clearly knows her subject backwards,"* making her *"a great person to work with on the tricky deals."* Boulet has extensive expertise in securities and banking law.

The Clients: American Habilitation Services; Baton Rouge Neonatal; Boyd Gaming; Jeff Davis Bancshares; MJ Womack and Morgan Keegan.

Liskow & Lewis PLC

The Firm: This group splits its corporate practice between New Orleans and Lafayette. Strong links with the firm's highly respected banking and commercial groups, mean that the team of 15 *"extremely competent"* attorneys is regularly engaged on a variety of acquisition financing and related M&A matters.

The Lawyers: **Philip Jones** was singled out to researchers as *"a veritable authority on bankruptcy*

matters." Jones normally represents creditors.

The Clients: JPMorgan Chase; BP America; ChevronTexaco; Columbian Chemicals; Harrah's Casino; Hunt Oil; Shell; Whitney National Bank and Hibernia.

Taylor, Porter, Brooks & Phillips, LLP

The Firm: As an established figure in the Baton Rouge corporate sphere, this firm has been able to build up a high-profile clientele. Public projects and financings contribute to a sizable portion of the group's workload, while clients are also counseled extensively on their fiduciary obligations under state law. A recent highlight for the group was the development of a plan for the merger, with minimum tax consequences, of multiple healthcare practices into a single healthcare provider.

The Lawyers: Peers view **John Campbell** as *"a safe pair of hands"* and someone to whom they would feel extremely confident in referring work. Campbell *"effortlessly navigates his way through complex transactions"* and won plaudits for the depth of his commercial knowledge.

The Clients: Alma Plantation; AEP; Argosy Gaming; Barton Investments and Dixie Plantation; Chemical Waste Management; Chevron Products; Dow Chemical; Parish Water; Pennington Oil and Shell Pipeliney.

Other Notable Practitioners

Interviewees were unanimous in naming **Charles Snyder** (see p.876) of Milling Benson Woodward LLP as *"a true legend"* in the Louisiana corporate market. He has built up an impressively wide client base and represents healthcare providers, banks, venture capital firms and sizable corporations in large deals. **Doug Draper** and **William Patrick** of bankruptcy boutique Heller, Draper, Hayden, Patrick & Horn LLC, are seen by many peers as *"the go-to guys"* for this kind of work. Draper's *"forceful, effective style"* makes him *"the first port of call"* for matters on the debtor side, while Patrick's creditor-based practice is equally well respected. The *"incisive and insightful"* **David Forsyth** of Sessions, Fishman & Nathan LLP is another leading figure in the insolvency and bankruptcy market.

EMPLOYMENT

MAINLY DEFENDANT

Band 1

Jones Walker Waechter Poitevent Carrère & Denègre, LLP

See firm details p.883

The Firm: *"A premier firm that provides top-quality advice,"* beamed one satisfied client when questioned about their experience of the

labor and employment group at this large multiservice firm. The 20 attorneys have wide-ranging expertise in employment litigation, administrative practices, labor/management relations, employee benefits, immigration and training programs, making it hard to argue with the contention that the firm *"offers the full package and then some."* A top-tier ranking is

attained by virtue of the *"plethora of talented attorneys"* on show at the firm, many of whom have been the vanguard of the Louisiana labor and employment market for 20 years. Recent highlights include the firm's appointment as principal counsel for Sanderson Farms.

The Lawyers: **Mark Adams**' (see p.869) skill in the courtroom was noted by sources, one

Louisiana
Leading firms
(Employment: Mainly Defendant)

[1] JONES WALKER WAECHTER *New Orleans*
THE KULLMAN FIRM PLC *New Orleans*

[2] FISHER & PHILLIPS LLP *New Orleans*
PHELPS DUNBAR LLP *New Orleans*

[3] ADAMS AND REESE LLP *New Orleans*
BREAZEALE, SACHSE & WILSON *Baton Rouge*
KEAN, MILLER, HAWTHORNE *Baton Rouge*
MCGLINCHEY STAFFORD *New Orleans*
TAYLOR, PORTER, BROOKS *Baton Rouge*

Leading individuals
(Employment: Mainly Defendant)

Senior Statesman
D'ARMOND William *Kean Miller, Baton Rouge*

[1] MALONE Ernest *The Kullman Firm, New Orleans*
MCCALLA Robert *Fisher & Phillips, New Orleans*

[2] ADAMS Mark *Jones Walker, New Orleans*
ALESSANDRA Nan *Phelps Dunbar, New Orleans*
DUNCAN III Brooke *Adams and Reese, New Orleans*
JACOB Clyde *Jones Walker, New Orleans*
KIGGANS Thomas *Phelps Dunbar, Baton Rouge*
LINZY Howard *The Kullman Firm, New Orleans*
PYBURN Keith *Fisher & Phillips, New Orleans*

[3] CROCHET Vicki *Taylor Porter, Baton Rouge*
FOSTER Murphy *Breazeale Sachse, Baton Rouge*
HARTMANN Melanie *Kean Miller, Baton Rouge*
HEUSEL Cornelius *Jones Walker, New Orleans*
LEWIS Sidney *Jones Walker, New Orleans*
MALLERY Mark *McGlinchey Stafford, New Orleans*
PHARIS Michael *Taylor Porter, Baton Rouge*
PREI E Fredrick *McGlinchey Stafford, New Orleans*
SPENCER Bob *The Kullman Firm, New Orleans*

Firms and individuals are listed alphabetically in each band.

describing him as *"relentless – when he gets the bit between his teeth there's no stopping him."* Adams also counsels employers on the development of effective human resource policies, procedures and training programs. The majority of the work undertaken by the *"hugely respected"* **Sidney Lewis** (see p.873) revolves around general advice to employers on day-to-day employment situations. His client training seminars are said to be *"refreshing, innovative and very practical."* **Clyde Jacob** (see p.873) is elevated to the second tier following impressive market feedback. Seen as *"a big-time player"* by peers, Jacob was recently reappointed to the US Chamber of Commerce's Labor Relations Committee and has testified as an expert witness before Congress on a number of labor-related matters. Although principally a white-collar crime specialist, **Cornelius Heusel** (see p.872) is active in the employment sphere and has impressed competitors with his *"steely and effective litigation skills."*
The Clients: Capital City Press; Flying J; Fluor; Ochsner Clinic Foundation; Ruby Tuesday; Ruth's Chris Steak House; Turner Industries;

Ventura Foods; Wells Fargo and Freeport-McMoRan.

The Kullman Firm PLC
See firm details p.884
The Firm: Founded in 1946, this boutique firm has achieved national prominence for the quality of its labor practice. The general consensus is that the group *"still leads the way on union-related matters"* and, as such, a place in the top tier is well merited. Unionized clients are assisted with collective bargaining, grievance handling, arbitration hearings and working within the framework of a union contract. Advice is also proffered on ERISA, immigration and employee relations programs. Clients report receiving a service that was *"clear and incisive,"* and extolled the virtues of attorneys who *"get the job done to a remarkably high standard."*
The Lawyers: According to one admiring interviewee, the firm's leading light, **Ernest Malone** (see p.874), is *"so well respected that they should build a statue of him outside every Louisiana courtroom."* A *"true all-rounder,"* Malone attracted praise from every quarter, with compliments especially fulsome for his strategic planning and collective bargaining savoir faire. His litigation prowess is equally admired; in this regard he has represented employers on Title VII, age discrimination, ADA and FMLA matters plus state employment laws. The presence of two new names in the table, **Howard Linzy** and **Bob Spencer** (see p.876), reflects the firm's bench strength for union-related matters. Linzy, who won plaudits for his *"wise and considered approach,"* has been lead counsel in a large number and variety of NLRB representation and decertification elections, union-organizing drives and contract negotiations for companies. Market sources were also quick to praise the industrious nature of Spencer, describing him as *"tireless in his commitment to the cause."* He advises clients on the negotiation and administration of union contracts, the resolution of grievances, arbitrations and immigration issues.
The Clients: Clients are drawn from a range of industries – manufacturers, wholesale distributors, photo processors, oil and gas producers, banks, hospitals, construction firms and airlines.

Band 2

Fisher & Phillips LLP
See firm details p.630
The Firm: Benefiting greatly from close ties with another nine offices across the country, the New Orleans group of this national labor and employment practice is held in high esteem by the market. Litigation is an area in which it is considered to excel; one source provided impressive testimony to lawyers who *"never throw in the towel and fight hard but fair for their clients."* The group has enjoyed notable success

in matters relating to ERISA, discrimination, collective bargaining and arbitration.
The Lawyers: The market considers **Robert McCalla** (see p.874) to be *"clearly at the top of his profession"* and he accordingly retains his top-tier placing. Described by peers as *"unnervingly intelligent"* McCalla has an extensive practice in labor relations, including negotiating collective bargaining agreements in the marine and paper industries. He has also achieved prominence in defending large class actions based on race discrimination issues. **Keith Pyburn** (see p.875) is heavily involved in the collective bargaining sphere and garnered praise from clients who considered him to be *"exceptionally shrewd."*
The Clients: The client list includes Alliance, ConocoPhillips and Pan-American Life.

Phelps Dunbar LLP
See firm details p.886
The Firm: Highly respected by the market for the quality of its employment litigation practice, this firm is *"clearly on the up"* and won praise for a varied client base that includes, among others, banks, oil companies and restaurants. With offices in New Orleans and Baton Rouge the group has the resources to offer a breadth of services, such as counseling employers on disciplinary procedures and evaluations, and advising on wage and hour claims and ERISA matters.
The Lawyers: One humorous interviewee suggested that **Tom Kiggans** (see p.873) has *"such a broad range of knowledge he should go on Jeopardy."* With a practice that ranges freely across the whole labor and employment sector, there is little doubt that Kiggans is able to answer authoritatively on a host of issues. Clients painted a picture of an attorney who is both *"conscientious"* and *"able to strike up a great working relationship with everyone."* Described as an *"elegant litigator and a diligent attorney,"* **Nan Alessandra** (see p.869) climbs a tier in the rankings this year. Her employment litigation practice targets employers in the process of defending discrimination claims concerning age, sex, disability, race and religion, as well as sexual harassment cases, EEOC charges and other administrative complaints. Clients applauded the way Alessandra used strong advocacy techniques to *"dance her way through any problem that she encounters."*
The Clients: Dow Chemical; Isle of Capri Casinos; Laitram; Louisiana Lottery; Sailormen; The Shaw Group; Turner Industries; Vertex Aerospace and Domino's Pizza.

Band 3

Adams and Reese LLP
See firm details p.879
The Firm: Clients were enthusiastic about the labor and employment practice at this multidisciplinary firm, describing it as a *"breath of*

www.ChambersandPartners.com

All quotes in the text are from interviews with clients and competitors.

861

fresh air: these lawyers understand our business needs." Active in both a litigation and an advisory capacity, the team has amassed expertise on an impressive range of matters including union contract issues, unemployment compensation proceedings and discrimination claims. The group can be distinguished from others in the market by its significant niche specialization in the field of employment insurance.

The Lawyers: Brooke Duncan (see p.871) is a respected figure for union contract negotiations. Viewed by clients as a *"fantastic problem solver,"* he was recently appointed as outside general counsel for Freeman Decorating.

The Clients: The firm acts for employers in different sectors including hospitality, real estate, public education, oil and gas, maritime and software.

Breazeale, Sachse & Wilson, LLP

The Firm: Ten *"highly respected"* attorneys form the basis of this Baton Rouge practice offering services to employers of all sizes. The group won plaudits from peers for its defense of discrimination claims. One source commented that while the aggressive approach undertaken by the firm's attorneys *"might not always win friends, it sure as hell wins cases."*

The Lawyers: Murphy Foster leads the team and wins the respect of most commentators for his *"forceful"* litigation style. Foster is considered to be particularly effective in discrimination cases.

The Clients: Clients are drawn from the construction, manufacturing, transport, banking and retail sectors.

Kean, Miller, Hawthorne, D'Armond, McCowan & Jarman, LLP

The Firm: Considered by certain commentators to be the pick of the labor and employment practices in Baton Rouge, this group offers the full gamut of services to a client base featuring companies from the petrochemical and construction industries. Particularly strong in the field of union relations, the firm won market approval for its collective bargaining and grievance handling advice.

The Lawyers: Senior statesman **Bill D'Armond** has earned considerable respect; one source stated that *"he has been at the hub of labor law in Baton Rouge for the past 30 years."* D'Armond counsels clients on compliance with state and federal labor and employment laws and assists employers with the negotiation of collective bargaining agreements. **Melanie Hartmann** is active on the litigation side and has considerable experience in cases involving discrimination, sexual harassment and wrongful termination.

The Clients: American Gateway Bank; City of Baton Rouge; DSM Copolymer; ExxonMobil; Fluor; IBM; Lamar Advertising and Vulcan Materials.

McGlinchey Stafford

See firm details p.885

The Firm: This national firm with offices in Baton Rouge and New Orleans is regarded as *"a quality firm with considerable strength in depth."* Praised by clients for giving *"tremendously clear advice,"* the group works with clients on union organization avoidance, wage and hour claims, discrimination claims, employee benefits and various other labor and employment matters.

The Lawyers: Client favorite **Frederick Preis** (see p.875) is highly rated for his advisory work.

Preis is *"great at explaining tricky concepts"* and spends much of his time on supervisor training and union organizing. **Mark Mallery** (see p.874) is a new addition to the table having won significant peer approval for his work as lead counsel on a number of complex labor disputes including Sarbanes-Oxley whistle-blower complaints before the Office of Administrative Law Judges.

The Clients: ARAMARK; Interstate Warehousing; Louisiana Hotel & Lodging Association; Martin & Bayley; Namasco; OfficeMax; Target and Winn-Dixie.

Taylor, Porter, Brooks & Phillips, LLP

The Firm: Long-standing relationships with institutional and corporate clients have allowed this Baton Rouge firm to gain a significant footing in the Louisiana market. Clients are provided with a wide range of labor and employment services including the drafting and renegotiation of union contracts, the defense of disability and discrimination claims and the creation of staff handbooks.

The Lawyers: Considered *"a top man for traditional labor advice"* by commentators, **Michael Pharis** maintains his market profile and garnered praise for his *"meticulous and informed"* manner. **Vicki Crochet** was commended for her discrimination practice, one prominent source describing the quality of her advice as *"unfailingly accurate."*

The Clients: Among others the firm represents Blue Cross and Blue Shield of Louisiana, Head & Enquist Equipment and Louisiana State University.

ENERGY & NATURAL RESOURCES

Louisiana
Leading firms
(Energy & Natural Resources)
1 GORDON, ARATA, MCCOLLAM *New Orleans*
JONES WALKER WAECHTER *New Orleans*
LISKOW & LEWIS PLC *New Orleans*
2 KEAN, MILLER, HAWTHORNE *Baton Rouge*
PHELPS DUNBAR LLP *New Orleans*
SCHULLY, ROBERTS, SLATTERY *New Orleans*
STONE PIGMAN WALTHER WITTMANN *New Orleans*
Firms are listed alphabetically in each band.

Band 1

Gordon, Arata, McCollam, Duplantis & Eagan LLP

The Firm: This firm houses a highly respected energy practice group that is proficient in all forms of dispute resolution, including litigation

in state and federal courts at both trial and appellate levels, arbitration, mediation, and administrative proceedings before local, state and federal agencies such as the FERC, the US Minerals Management Service, the Louisiana State Mineral Board, the Louisiana Commissioner of Conservation and the Louisiana Public Service Commission. A considerable amount of transactional work is also undertaken.

The Lawyers: Commentators consider the *"quietly authoritative"* **John McCollam** to be a leading figure in the energy market. His practice ranges from complex energy transactions and litigation to regulatory matters. McCollam has particular expertise in litigating oil and gas disputes, including those arising from take-or-pay gas purchase and sale contracts, onshore and offshore operating agreements, mineral leases and gas balancing agreements. **Bobbi Duplantis** wins the approval of peers for his litigation

skills. *"He focuses on all the right details,"* one source emphasized. Duplantis is considered particularly adept at lease interpretation and performance issues pertaining to contract disputes affecting the oil and gas industry.

The Clients: Burlington Resources; Dominion Exploration & Production; Goodrich Petroleum and ChevronTexaco.

Jones Walker Waechter Poitevent Carrère & Denègre, LLP

See firm details p.883

The Firm: *"Clearly at the cutting edge"* was the market's verdict on this large multiservice firm. With three offices across the state, it is hard to disagree with the contention of one client that the group *"has the resources to handle anything."* Strong on both the transactional and contentious sides, a significant volume of work comes from the firm's long-standing relationship

862   All quotes in the text are from interviews with clients and competitors.

CHAMBERS USA 2005

Louisiana
Leading individuals
(Energy & Natural Resources)

1 | **ARNOLD III Edward** *Baker Donelson*, New Orleans

DUPLANTIS BJ *Gordon Arata*, New Orleans

FONTHAM Michael *Stone Pigman*, New Orleans

HUNTER Jonathon *Liskow & Lewis*, New Orleans

JAUBERT Lisa *Schully Roberts*, New Orleans

KING Katherine *Kean Miller*, Baton Rouge

MCCOLLAM John *Gordon Arata*, New Orleans

MCGUIRE Robin *Jones Walker*, Lafayette

ROSENBLUM Carl *Jones Walker*, New Orleans

WOLF Alan *Phelps Dunbar*, New Orleans

Leading individuals (Energy & Natural Resources: Marine Finance)

1 | **BENNET Blake** *Liskow & Lewis PLC*, New Orleans

BRODERS John *Jones Walker Waechter*, New Orleans

ROUSSEL James *Phelps Dunbar LLP*, New Orleans

Individuals are listed alphabetically in each band.

with the Freeport-McMoRan companies. Recent highlights include the defense of Freeport-McMoRan Energy LLC from adverse claims of ownership arising out of its construction of an offshore LNG facility.

The Lawyers: **Carl Rosenblum** (see p.875) heads up the firm's energy practice group. First and foremost a litigator, he has represented producers, pipeline and oilfield service companies and financial institutions in a variety of disputes. Clients applaud his *"keen command of the facts,"* while peers salute *"an attorney who has all the right answers."* **Robin McGuire** (see p.874) is renowned for his work on the transactional side. A former engineer, McGuire has impressed clients with his commitment and communication skills: *"He never lets you down because he's got all the angles covered."* **John Broders** (see p.870) is one of the firm's leading admiralty lawyers. His marine finance practice incorporates notable work relating to oil and gas exploration.

The Clients: McMoRan Oil & Gas; JM Huber; Massey Energy; Sundown Energy; TGS-NOPEC Geophysical; McMoRan Exploration; Global Industries; Trico Marine Assets; Tidewater and American Commercial Barge Line.

Liskow & Lewis PLC

The Firm: With its strong links to the oil and gas industry, this team of *"bright, talented lawyers"* has developed an impressive practice in the exploration and development sectors. Oil and gas producers are advised on offshore acquisitions and federal leases, and represented before the Minerals Management Service in connection with the operation of such leases. Clients were impressed with the level of professionalism evident throughout the firm and commended its *"dedicated and diligent"* attorneys.

The Lawyers: It is widely acknowledged that **Jonathon Hunter** has *"huge amounts of knowledge."* He regularly represents oil and gas producers in litigation and advises in many other contexts including the payment of royalties, lease maintenance and development, assignment of lease interests and intrastate pipeline regulatory matters. The *"economical and efficient"* **Blake Bennet** works primarily with oil and gas lenders. Clients were quick to extol the virtues of an attorney who *"truly understands our needs."*

The Clients: The firm acts for independent oil companies as well as majors including Chevron-Texaco, Shell and BP.

Band 2

Kean, Miller, Hawthorne, D'Armond, McCowan & Jarman, LLP

The Firm: Praised for *"never getting frazzled,"* this firm's regulatory practice is held in particular esteem by the market. A client base comprising large commercial and industrial users of energy, nonutility power producers and marketers, and intrastate and interstate pipelines receives advice on a variety of matters including the restructuring of the electric market, the development of electric power projects and related contractual negotiations, the negotiation of electric service agreements and state and federal regulatory compliance.

The Lawyers: The *"extremely well-connected"* **Katherine King** represents utilities and industry before the Louisiana Public Service Commission (LSPC) and the FERC. She also serves as lead counsel to the Louisiana Energy Users Group and represents electric generators and project developers in regulatory proceedings before the LPSC. Peers and clients were effusive in their praise of her style, one source describing her as *"persuasive but not pushy."*

The Clients: ExxonMobil; ChevronTexaco; ConocoPhillips; Shell; BP and CITGO Petroleum.

Phelps Dunbar LLP

See firm details p.886

The Firm: This firm has considerable expertise in electric public utility law and represents a major independent electric power producer on regulation by the Louisiana Public Service Commission, FERC and general corporate and business issues.

The Lawyers: According to peers **Alan Wolf** (see p.878) *"brings verve to everything he works on"* and has *"immense knowledge."* As director of the firm's public utilities and electric power practice, much of his work is on behalf of flagship client Cleco. **James Roussel** (see p.875) is a leading figure in the marine finance sector and has been involved in significant litigation relating to oil and gas exploration issues.

The Clients: Cleco Corporation and Cleco Power feature on the client list.

Schully, Roberts, Slattery, Jaubert & Marino

The Firm: With particular expertise in oil and gas transactions this ten-attorney practice is highly respected in the energy sector. Clients commend the team for its thorough approach, saying: *"You get the impression they have all angles covered."*

The Lawyers: Transactional lawyer **Lisa Jaubert** is *"extremely knowledgeable"* on offshore oil and gas matters.

The Clients: AROC; Amerada Hess; Apex Oil & Gas; Basin Exploration; Constellation Energy Group; Energy Partners; Energy Resource Technology; ExxonMobil; Fidelity Exploration & Production; Gryphon Exploration and Swift Energy.

Stone Pigman Walther Wittmann LLC

See firm details p.887

The Firm: This group has achieved prominence in the sector due to its impressive array of regulatory expertise. It has represented the Louisiana Public Service Commission (LPSC) as special counsel in major rate cases and in litigation involving charges paid by Louisiana customers for electric and gas services. The rate cases, and other litigation, have involved various utilities and electric and gas carriers.

The Lawyers: **Michael Fontham** (see p.872) chairs the firm's regulatory practice group; he is admired for his *"no-nonsense approach."*

The Clients: Much of the firm's work involves acting on behalf of the LPSC.

Other Notable Practitioners

Hank Arnold (see p.869) of Baker, Donelson, Bearman, Caldwell & Berkowitz PC represents landowners in connection with oil and gas leases. Arnold has impressed the market with his ability to *"get straight to the heart of the matter."*

GAMING & LICENSING

Louisiana
Leading firms (Gaming & Licensing)

[1] JONES WALKER WAECHTER *New Orleans*
MCGLINCHEY STAFFORD *New Orleans*
[2] LISKOW & LEWIS PLC *New Orleans*
PHELPS DUNBAR LLP *New Orleans*

Leading individuals
(Gaming & Licensing)

[1] DUNCAN Kelly *Jones Walker, New Orleans*
WEST Paul *McGlinchey Stafford, New Orleans*
[2] BENNET Blake *Liskow & Lewis, New Orleans*
BLACKBURN Frank *Sole Practitioner, Baton Rouge*
HARKINS Deborah *McGlinchey Stafford, New Orleans*
WALLACE Brian *Phelps Dunbar, New Orleans*

Up-and-coming individuals
BARBIN Jeff *Phelps Dunbar, Baton Rouge*

Firms and individuals are listed alphabetically in each band.

Band 1

Jones Walker Waechter Poitevent Carrère & Denègre, LLP

See firm details p.883

The Firm: Strong links with the Louisiana Gaming Control Board have enabled this firm to accumulate a wealth of regulatory knowledge. Other lawyers voiced their respect for a practice group that is *"well structured,"* while clients were more than satisfied with the firm's *"responsive, user-friendly approach."* The firm's lawyers have extensive experience advising and assisting clients on suitability applications in connection with licensing and permitting, compliance and the interpretation of the Louisiana gaming statutes and regulations.

The Lawyers: **Kelly Duncan** (see p.871) is the firm's leading light in this area of practice. He has won favor with clients for his willingness *"to go the extra mile whenever necessary."* Much of Duncan's work over the past year has related to the acquisition by Columbia Sussex of the Belle of Orleans riverboat casino from Caesars Entertainment.

The Clients: Hollywood Casino Shreveport, United States Playing Card and Maloney & Tabor.

McGlinchey Stafford

See firm details p.885

The Firm: Commentators were united in their praise for the gaming practice at this multidisciplinary firm. One source spoke glowingly of a team of attorneys who are *"intelligent and practical."* The group has extensive experience in all aspects of the industry, including riverboat gaming, land-based casinos, video poker and Native American gaming. Regularly appearing before Louisiana gaming commissions and agencies, the team has worked in connection with riverboat projects, horse racetrack projects, casino companies, casino operators, investors in gaming projects and lenders and suppliers to casino projects.

The Lawyers: **Paul West** (see p.877) is at the forefront of the firm's gaming work and represents casino owners, casino operators, financiers, gaming and nongaming suppliers and municipalities that have negotiated with gaming companies. Interviewees were impressed with his *"unique blend of dynamism and knowledge."* **Deborah Harkins** (see p.872) is held in equally high esteem by the market. She appears regularly before the Louisiana Gaming Control Board and works closely with the gaming division of the attorney general's office and Louisiana State Police, gaming division.

The Clients: Boyd Gaming and Pinnacle Entertainment feature among other big-name clients from the casino industry.

Band 2

Liskow & Lewis PLC

The Firm: This firm has achieved prominence in the market as a result of its representation of casino operators in their applications for newly issued casino licenses and their acquisitions of existing operations. Further experience in litigation resulting from gaming ventures and against gaming regulatory agencies has prompted praise from clients and peers alike. It is also worth noting that the firm's knowledge of admiralty law allows it to provide comprehensive advice regarding the maritime law implications of gaming operations conducted on water.

The Lawyers: Although **Blake Bennet** is prominent in the admiralty and energy fields, he also has an impressive gaming practice. Bennet has assisted in the financing of the construction of numerous riverboat casinos, racinos, off-track betting facilities and Native American gaming facilities.

Phelps Dunbar LLP

See firm details p.886

The Firm: Close links with the Jackson office give the firm's gaming practice group impressive reach over a number of states. Major highlights from the past year include acting as Louisiana and Mississippi regulatory counsel for Harrah's Entertainment in connection with its acquisition of Horseshoe Casino. The group also acted in a similar capacity for Penn National Gaming in its acquisition of Argosy Gaming.

The Lawyers: **Brian Wallace** (see p.877) represents an array of gaming clients on complex financial transactions, licensing and litigation. Feted for his *"tremendous work ethic,"* Wallace was recently involved in a significant refinancing in the gaming sector. Senior associate **Jeff Barbin** (see p.869), who works out of the firm's Baton Rouge office, won plaudits for his *"innovative go-getting approach."*

Other Notable Practitioners

Interviewees singled out sole practitioner **Frank Blackburn** for his work in the video poker industry. Blackburn was commended for his ability to *"remain calm and controlled even when the chips are down."*

LITIGATION

GENERAL COMMERCIAL

Band 1

Barrasso Usdin Kupperman Freeman & Sarver LLC

See firm details p.880

The Firm: Peers view this 17-attorney firm as *"top-level competition;"* clients respect the exceptional reputation the commercial litigation boutique has earned in the state. *"Full of young guns,"* this firm specializes in complex commercial cases and has particular fortes in insurance, securities and antitrust litigation. Its attorneys represent insurance companies, brokerage firms and Fortune 500 companies and are well respected for their appellate expertise and experience of defending class actions. Toxic tort litigation and securities arbitrations are also recognized areas of excellence.

The Lawyers: Clients branded this firm a *"young and fresh"* boutique, and **Judy Barrasso** (see p.869) personifies this description. *"Making waves in the profession,"* Barrasso focuses on commercial litigation, bad faith and insurance coverage disputes, but also practices in the areas of securities fraud, attorney malpractice and business torts. She was elected chair of the Louisiana Attorney Disciplinary Board during the year. The *"extremely bright, quick and attentive"* **Steven Usdin** (see p.877) was singled out for his *"wonderful instincts with the jury."* He

Louisiana
Leading firms
(Litigation: General Commercial)

1 BARRASSO USDIN KUPPERMAN *New Orleans*
JONES WALKER WAECHTER *New Orleans*
LISKOW & LEWIS PLC *New Orleans*
PHELPS DUNBAR LLP *New Orleans*
STONE PIGMAN WALTHER *New Orleans*

2 CORRERO FISHMAN HAYGOOD *New Orleans*
GAINSBURGH, BENJAMIN, DAVID *New Orleans*
GORDON, ARATA, MCCOLLAM *New Orleans*
KEAN, MILLER, HAWTHORNE *Baton Rouge*

3 BAKER, DONELSON, BEARMAN *New Orleans*
FRILOT, PARTRIDGE, KOHNKE *New Orleans*
HERMAN, HERMAN, KATZ & COTLAR *New Orleans*
MCGLINCHEY STAFFORD *New Orleans*
SHER GARNER CAHILL RICHTER *New Orleans*
TAYLOR, PORTER, BROOKS *Baton Rouge*

Leading individuals
(Litigation: General Commercial)

1 WITTMANN Phillip *Stone Pigman*, New Orleans

2 ABAUNZA Donald *Liskow & Lewis*, New Orleans
BARRASSO Judy *Barrasso Usdin*, New Orleans
BARRIERE Brent *Phelps Dunbar*, New Orleans
BROWN James *Liskow & Lewis*, New Orleans
CHEATWOOD Roy *Baker Donelson*, New Orleans
HERMAN Russ *Herman Herman*, New Orleans
LAFITTE Gene *Liskow & Lewis*, New Orleans
MCCOLLAM John *Gordon Arata*, New Orleans
MCCOWAN Charles *Kean Miller*, Baton Rouge
MEUNIER Gerald *Gainsburgh Benjamin*, New Orleans
VANCE R Patrick *Jones Walker*, New Orleans

3 EAGAN Ewell *Gordon Arata*, New Orleans
FRILOT George *Frilot Partridge*, New Orleans
GARNER James *Sher Garner*, New Orleans
HARDIN III Harry *Jones Walker*, New Orleans
JARMAN William *Kean Miller*, Baton Rouge
LUND Daniel *Montgomery Barnett*, New Orleans
MARTZELL Jack *Martzell & Bickford*, New Orleans
PHILIPS Harry *Taylor Porter*, Baton Rouge
ROSENBERG Harry *Phelps Dunbar*, New Orleans
SARVER Richard *Barrasso Usdin*, New Orleans
SWANSON James *Correro Fishman*, New Orleans
USDIN Steven *Barrasso Usdin*, New Orleans

Firms and individuals are listed alphabetically in each band.

practices commercial litigation, including insurance, securities and bank fraud. Described as an "*exceptionally knowledgeable environmental lawyer*" **Richard Sarver** (see p.876) impressed onlookers with his winning courtroom style. He specializes in complex litigation including toxic tort, environmental and products liability cases.
The Clients: 3M; Allstate; Clear Channel Communications; Gulf Insurance; Liberty Mutual; Lincoln Electric; New York Life; Occidental Chemical; Merrill Lynch; Wachovia; Viacom and Westway Holding.

Jones Walker Waechter Poitevent Carrère & Denègre, LLP
See firm details p.883

The Firm: This, the largest law firm in Louisiana, boasting three strategically located offices across the state, was routinely described as having "*a really deep and broad litigation practice.*" Home to many specialist attorneys in a variety of practice areas, the firm is deeply entrenched in securities and oil and gas litigation. It is counsel to Fortune 500 companies as well as smaller local clients and covers the full range of litigation from antitrust and securities to white-collar crime.

The Lawyers: The attorneys at this firm are viewed as "*very responsive and extremely professional,*" and the head of the litigation group **Patrick Vance** (see p.877) is no exception. A "*big-name player who routinely delivers in the courtroom,*" Vance concentrates on business litigation and creditors' rights, and is especially well respected for his "*thriving*" bankruptcy practice and his representation of Cisco Systems. **Harry Hardin** (see p.872) is the firm's senior partner and also chairs its appellate group. "*Really effective in front of a jury,*" Hardin is rated for his railroad and antitrust litigation expertise and fine reputation in general business litigation. Clients commended the breadth of his practice, noting in particular his skills at litigation avoidance.

The Clients: Aegon; Allied Waste Industries; BellSouth; El Paso Energy; ExxonMobil; Freeport McMoRan; GM; Goodyear; Marriott International; Ritz Carlton; Travelers Insurance; Wells Fargo; Westinghouse/Viacom; Universal Studios and Cisco Systems.

Liskow & Lewis PLC

The Firm: Liskow & Lewis is respected by clients for being "*strong and always knowing the right route to take with a problem.*" Its two established Louisiana offices move up into the top tier of the table, consolidating its position as a leader in the Gulf South region. Preeminent in oil and gas work, the firm is also much admired for its commercial litigation, white-collar crime defense and tax work. Class actions, environmental disputes, products liability and admiralty litigation are other recommended areas of excellence.

The Lawyers: "*Gentleman's lawyer*" and former managing partner of the firm, **Donald Abaunza** impresses clients with his "*wealth of admiralty law experience*" and ability to "*never miss a trick.*" **Gene Lafitte**, who is described simply as "*an absolute class act,*" also garnered praise for his high-level involvement in oil and gas exploration and pipeline construction issues. Lafitte is special counsel to the firm and brings with him an abundance of experience in the field. The "*smart, smooth and unruffled courtroom performer*" **James Brown** rises in this year's rank-

ings. "*On the right path to becoming one of the best,*" Brown concentrates on professional liability, especially legal malpractice, banking and contract litigation.

The Clients: Bank One; ChevronTexaco; ExxonMobil; Gaylord Chemical; Harrah's Entertainment; Hibernia National Bank; Nissan North America and Shell.

Phelps Dunbar LLP
See firm details p.886

The Firm: "*A cut above the rest,*" this firm is one of the oldest in the South and certainly has the resources to handle some of the most complex cases on offer. The firm boasts eight offices, two of them in Louisiana, and was commended by peers for "*the huge breadth of high-quality work undertaken.*" Complex commercial, torts and products liability litigation are considered particular areas of strength, although the firm offers a full range of services, including a flourishing appellate practice.

The Lawyers: "*Preeminent commercial litigator*" **Brent Barriere** (see p.869) represents clients in securities litigation, breach of contract cases, business valuation disputes and class actions. He was particularly noted for possessing "*the three 'A's every lawyer should have in his locker: attentiveness, analysis and articulacy*" and is a frequent lecturer on litigation techniques. **Harry Rosenberg** (see p.875) makes his debut in the tables for "*the truckload of litigation experience he brings to a case.*" An ex-US attorney, Rosenberg concentrates on business torts, civil rights and criminal law.

The Clients: City of Shreveport; Chubb Group; Dominion Exploration & Production; GATX; LLOG Exploration; Louisiana Sheriff's Association; Pierce Junction Petroleum; The Shaw Group and Wells Fargo.

Stone Pigman Walther Wittmann LLC
See firm details p.887

The Firm: The New Orleans firm is home to "*some of the finest advocates around*" and covers the full spectrum of litigation practice including antitrust, banking, IP, employment and securities cases. Consistently in the fray on major business cases, the firm is also considered excellent in insurance, construction and toxic tort litigation. A highlight for the team during the year was working on a case involving the release of allegedly harmful gases into the atmosphere by a refinery in Lake Charles.

The Lawyers: "*Fearless and peerless,*" **Phillip Wittmann** (see p.878) is "*a man of absolute integrity; he never quits until the job is done.*" Chair of the firm's management committee, Wittmann "*demonstrates a god-given talent in the courtroom*" and is frequently involved in the meatiest cases. He focuses on complex litigation including antitrust, products liability and toxic torts; during the past year he has been involved in tobacco cases and various other class actions as well as a number of notable disputes.

The Clients: Chevron Phillips Chemical; Endo Pharmaceuticals; International Paper; Kaiser Aluminum; Louisiana Public Service Commission; Lucent Technologies; RJ Reynolds; New York Life and New Orleans Saints.

Band 2

Correro Fishman Haygood Phelps Walmsley & Casteix LLP
See firm details p.882

The Firm: Onlookers were impressed by this firm's recent involvement in some high-profile cases. Noted in particular for securities, media and tax litigation, attorneys have also had recent success litigating products liability cases. Recent highlights for the group include representing Times-Picayune on a number of access cases, and Amedisys Securities in the defense of a class action.

The Lawyers: Head of the firm's litigation group **James Swanson** (see p.876) has cultivated a reputation as *"a smart litigator"* who can *"stand up and be counted when it's in his clients interests to do so."* Swanson has recently been acting for the Louisiana Department of Revenue.

The Clients: Amedisys; JMH Realty; The Baton Rouge Advocate; US Unwired; SMG; The Times-Picayune and Sabin, Bermant & Gould.

Gainsburgh, Benjamin, David, Meunier & Warshauer

The Firm: Displaying *"quality at every turn,"* this predominantly personal injury-oriented outfit has won plaudits for its work in the commercial litigation sphere. A stellar reputation has been cultivated in fields such as products liability, professional negligence and securities fraud. The firm is particularly active on the plaintiff side.

The Lawyers: *"Charming and charismatic"* **Gerald Meunier** was highlighted for his considerable expertise in personal injury, class actions and products liability litigation.

Gordon, Arata, McCollam, Duplantis & Eagan LLP

The Firm: Traditional strength in energy litigation has been supplemented in recent years by the growth of a well-rounded commercial practice. The firm's *"highly respected"* attorneys impressed interviewees with their *"wise and considered"* judgment on when to pursue a case and when to settle. The group often acts in utility regulation disputes and the defense of class actions.

The Lawyers: *"A legend for oil and gas matters,"* **John McCollam** also has a broad litigation practice that is the envy of many attorneys in the state. McCollam has a great ability to communi-

cate with judges and juries, one source describing his *"persuasive and personable"* style as *"a real feather in his cap."* Much of **Tim Eagan's** practice is comprised of environmental cases. He is principal litigator for Entergy and won praise from peers for his *"fantastic courtroom delivery."*

The Clients: Biloxi Marsh Land; Burlington Resources Oil; Dominion Exploration & Production; Goodrich Petroleum; Northrop Grumman; Shaw Environmental; Chevron Texaco; Swift Environmental and UHS.

Kean, Miller, Hawthorne, D'Armond, McCowan & Jarman, LLP

The Firm: Few interviewees disputed this group's position as the leading litigation firm in Baton Rouge, commending a team that is both *"resourceful and responsive."* Particular expertise in environmental litigation is to be found here, brought about through strong links with the region's oil and gas companies. The firm has been heavily involved in the recent Lake Charles litigation and won market approval for its *"steadfast commitment to getting the right result for its clients."*

The Lawyers: **Charles McCowan** is *"an expert environmental litigator"* who can be *"relentless when he gets the bit between his teeth."* McCowan has been particularly busy litigating issues pertaining to Superfund sites in the past year. One source commented that **William Jarman** *"has a mind sharper than one of James Bond's suits."* He has attained considerable market respect for his oil and gas litigation practice.

The Clients: BASF; Black & Decker; BP America; ChevronTexaco; ConocoPhillips; ExxonMobil; Formosa Plastics; IBM; IMC Global; Microsoft; The Shaw Group; CSFB; Shell and Vulcan Materials.

Band 3

Baker, Donelson, Bearman, Caldwell & Berkowitz, PC
See firm details p.1613

The Firm: A new addition to the rankings, the recently opened New Orleans office of this national firm is considered by peers to have a genuine presence in the market. Much of the group's focus is on litigation relating to the registration, issuance and underwriting of securities, corporate governance, shareholder disputes and insurance coverage.

The Lawyers: Peers applaud the fact that **Roy Cheatwood** (see p.870) is *"no shrinking violet in the courtroom,"* noting that he *"consistently gets top results for his clients."* Cheatwood recently joined the firm from Phelps Dunbar and is recognized for the quality of his appellate work.

The Clients: Entergy, Hibernia National Bank and Texas Gas Transmission all feature on the client roster.

Frilot, Partridge, Kohnke & Clements LC

The Firm: Principally renowned for the quality of its insurance work, this litigation boutique has also impressed the market with its environmental and products liability expertise. In addition, representation is provided to oil manufacturers in relation to disputes arising from naturally occurring radiation materials claims. Sources were quick to praise the *"tremendous work ethic"* exhibited by attorneys.

The Lawyers: The *"imperious"* **George Frilot** was highlighted for his advocacy skills. This *"compelling and convincing courtroom performer"* is highly regarded for his class action work.

The Clients: ChevronTexaco; ExxonMobil; GE; Medical Malpractice Insurance; Mississippi Chemical; Nintendo; Nokia and Tidewater.

Herman, Herman, Katz & Cotlar LLP

The Firm: This plaintiff firm has achieved considerable prominence in the market due to its involvement in a number of significant cases. Described as *"unnervingly good,"* attorneys have *"a reputation for excellence"* in the fields of business litigation, class actions and personal injury. Recent highlights for the group include representing Orion Refining in a $1 billion construction claim, and acting for the City of New Orleans on a claim for breach of a lease agreement.

The Lawyers: **Russ Herman** is *"tenacity personified"* in the eyes of commentators. He has been one of the main protagonists in the recent high-profile litigation against four major tobacco companies.

The Clients: The firm is well known for its work with plaintiffs in a broad range of business disputes and class actions.

McGlinchey Stafford
See firm details p.885

The Firm: Building on a national reputation for representing automobile industry clients in products liability cases, McGlinchey Stafford has a *"thriving"* litigation practice with considerable expertise in areas as diverse as pharmaceuticals and consumer finance. Three strategically located offices in the state house a group of *"streetwise and effective"* attorneys.

The Lawyers: Henri Wolbrette is a key figure in the firm's pharmaceutical litigation team.

The Clients: International clients include: International Harvester; Siemens; Suzuki; Volkswagon; Volvo and Zurich.

Sher Garner Cahill Richter Klein McAlister & Hilbert, LLC

The Firm: Formed at the end of the 1990s, this midsized firm has made *"considerable strides"* and is now regarded as *"serious competition"* by the market. Particular areas of litigation expertise include real estate, products liability and environmental matters. The group has been involved in a number of significant trials over the past year and successfully represented various nonprofit hospitals in claims against the City of New Orleans.

The Lawyers: Described as "*dynamic, diligent and dedicated,*" **James Garner** attracted praise from all quarters for the quality of his advocacy. "*Never afraid to take it to the limit,*" Garner is considered to perform especially well in insurance defense.

The Clients: AXA Corporate Solutions; Burrus Investment Group; International Rivercenter; Murphy Oil USA; Touro Infirmary; Trinity Industries and University of New Orleans Foundation.

Taylor, Porter, Brooks & Phillips, LLP

The Firm: With its long-standing reputation for "*persuasive and effective advocacy,*" this Baton Rouge firm maintains a very decent market profile for litigation practice. One of the firm's major strengths lies in the defense of class actions; its expertise has been successfully employed in defending a number of recent claims against local chemical manufacturers.

The Lawyers: **Harry Philips** is a new addition to the rankings following positive feedback for his "*ethical and professional*" style of working.

The Clients: Argosy Gaming; Baton Rouge Water Works; Bank One; BP; Entergy; Liberty Mutual; Louisiana State University; Our Lady of the Lake Hospital; Dow Chemical; Turner Industries Holdings and Yamaha Motor USA.

Other Notable Practitioners

Jack Martzell of Martzell & Bickford APC is highly respected for the breadth and depth of his litigation practice. Described by peers as "*inspirational and cerebral,*" Martzell has extensive experience in a number of areas including professional malpractice suits and ecological cases. **Daniel Lund** of Montgomery, Barnett, Brown, Read, Hammond & Mintz LLP has attained considerable acclaim for his skill in defending professional malpractice suits. An "*attorney of immense knowledge,*" Lund also has an admirable personal injury practice.

REAL ESTATE

Louisiana
Leading firms (Real Estate)

1 PHELPS DUNBAR LLP *New Orleans*
  SHER GARNER CAHILL RICHTER *New Orleans*
  STONE PIGMAN WALTHER *New Orleans*
  THE STEEG LAW FIRM LLC *New Orleans*

2 CHAFFE, MCCALL, PHILLIPS TOLER *New Orleans*
  JONES WALKER WAECHTER *Baton Rouge*
  LISKOW & LEWIS PLC *New Orleans*
  MCGLINCHEY STAFFORD *New Orleans*

Leading individuals (Real Estate)

1 BRADFORD Donald *Jones Walker, Baton Rouge*
  CLAVERIE Philip *Phelps Dunbar, New Orleans*
  SHER Leopold *Sher Garner, New Orleans*
  STEEG Robert *The Steeg Law Firm, New Orleans*
  TALLEY Susan *Stone Pigman, New Orleans*

2 CAHILL Elwood *Sher Garner, New Orleans*
  COLVIN Keith *McGlinchey Stafford, New Orleans*
  CROSBY E Howell *Chaffe McCall, New Orleans*
  KLING Neal *Sher Garner, New Orleans*
  LANDRY Charles *Jones Walker, Baton Rouge*
  REYMOND Leon *Liskow & Lewis, New Orleans*
  ROUSSEL Randy *Phelps Dunbar, Baton Rouge*
  SCHNEIDER Michael *Stone Pigman, New Orleans*

Up-and-coming individuals
  SCHMIDT Justin *Chaffe McCall, New Orleans*

Firms and individuals are listed alphabetically in each band.

Band 1

Phelps Dunbar LLP

See firm details p.886

The Firm: Phelps Dunbar retains its top-tier ranking on the back of favorable market feedback for its "*truly first-class*" team of attorneys. Commercial developments, retail-sector transactions and shopping center renovations have formed the majority of the firm's workload over the past year, with warehouse conversions becoming a significant growth area. Applauded by clients for being "*responsive and responsible,*" the group operates from Baton Rouge and New Orleans, receiving additional support from offices in Florida, Mississippi and Texas.

The Lawyers: The market noted how **Philip Claverie** (see p.870) "*always comes up with the goods for his clients.*" Principally active on the lender side, Claverie has built up expertise in the issues relating from the conversion of warehouses into condominiums. Former certified public accountant **Randy Roussel** (see p.876) enters the rankings following praise from peers. In the past year he has been heavily involved in the acquisition of sites for various restaurant chains.

The Clients: AmSouth Bank; Audubon Capital Fund; JPMorgan Chase; GHK Developments; Hibernia National Bank; IBERIABANK; Rubicon and Rutter Rex.

Sher Garner Cahill Richter Klein McAlister & Hilbert, LLC

The Firm: Although the firm is increasingly active in other sectors, it is the real estate practice that stands out for most commentators. An impressive client base of individuals, financial institutions and a range of national and international companies leaves little room for doubt that this firm merits its top-tier ranking. Those who engaged the firm applaud the "*true sense of professionalism, which runs from top to bottom.*" The firm is currently representing Gap in a nationwide lease amendment program and has also represented the New Orleans World Trade Center in the conversion of its building to a mixed-use office/hotel project through a public-private partnership.

The Lawyers: **Lee Sher** has a strong client following, a factor that interviewees put down to his "*tremendous attention to detail*" and "*clear grasp of what needs to be done and when to do it.*" Sher is involved in much of the firm's high-value transactional work and has notably been representing Academy Ltd in the acquisition and development of four new stores across the country. Entering the ranking for the first time this year is **Elwood Cahill**; interviewees admired the "*strong sense of authority*" he brings to every transaction. Commentators were also quick to compliment **Neal Kling**, describing him as a "*versatile and genuinely talented*" attorney.

The Clients: Burger King; Burrus Investment Group; Cracker Barrel Old Country Store; Greystar Development & Construction; Hertz Investment Group; Marrero Land & Improvement Association; MetLife; PMAT Real Estate Investments; Realm Realty & Management; Touro Infirmary; Southern Homes and University of New Orleans Foundation.

Stone Pigman Walther Wittmann LLC

See firm details p.887

The Firm: Although many in the market noted that the firm's main strength lies in general commercial litigation, plenty of commentators confirmed they were impressed with the expertise of the real estate group. One prominent source stated that its attorneys "*combine talent with pragmatism and are a pleasure to work with.*" Recent work has included providing counsel to lenders, developers and major tenants on a number of significant real estate transactions in Louisiana, among them hotel construction projects.

The Lawyers: **Susan Talley**'s (see p.876) practice encompasses all aspects of real estate development, including financing, leasing and purchases. Her industry and commitment were applauded by clients; she "*works like a devil*" and *"never leaves anything until the last minute."* A strong negotiator, in the past year much of Talley's time has been spent representing lenders. The *"effervescent"* **Michael Schneider** (see p.876) cochairs the firm's real estate practice. He has extensive experience in sophisticated commercial real estate transactions across the state. Clients appreciate *"that extra bit of fizz that he brings to the table."*

The Clients: The firm acts for property owners, finance companies, construction firms and developers.

The Steeg Law Firm, LLC

The Firm: This highly respected firm specializes in business and real estate matters. It won plaudits from interviewees for providing *"a personal and proactive service"* and is considered to do *"top-quality work."* Condominium developments are a specialty. The firm is also home to an in-house title insurance agency.

The Lawyers: The market views **Bob Steeg** as *"trustworthy and highly knowledgeable."* He is considered to have particular expertise in working with developers and was described by one client as *"reassuringly ahead of the game when it comes to the big transactions."*

The Clients: Bank One; Chevron USA; Entergy; First American Title Insurance; Historic Restoration; Lauricella Land; Loeb Partners Realty; The Feil Organization and Whitney National Bank; Hibernia National Bank; Magnolia Marketing; Tulane University and Corporate Realty.

Band 2

Chaffe, McCall, Phillips, Toler & Sarpy, LLP

See firm details p.881

The Firm: This *"truly innovative"* multiservice firm enter the rankings as a result of positive market feedback. The group advises on all phases of real estate transactions, including the purchase, sale, financing and leasing of commercial, industrial, retail, residential and development properties. In recent times, for example, the firm has represented a developer in a series of large mixed-use condominium projects in New Orleans.

The Lawyers: Highly regarded **Howell Crosby** (see p.871) has represented numerous lenders and developers in connection with the acquisition, divestiture, development, leasing and financing of various projects. Interviewees favored up-and-comer **Justin Schmidt**'s (see p.876) *"excellent demeanor"* and noted his strength on leasing matters.

The Clients: Home Depot; Baker Hughes; Al Copeland Enterprises; Amsdell; Kimpton Hotel and Restaurant Group and Monarch Real Estate Advisors.

Jones Walker Waechter Poitevent Carrère & Denègre, LLP

See firm details p.883

The Firm: Much of this large firm's broad real estate practice group operates from its Baton Rouge office. Work is undertaken on projects in a variety of sectors, including the residential, commercial and industrial fields. Acting on all matters from simple acquisitions to structuring large-scale developments and financings, the firm's attorneys won praise from clients for their *"keen sense of direction."*

The Lawyers: The *"extremely well-qualified"* **Donald Bradford** (see p.870) is admired for his pragmatism and has *"a tremendous working knowledge"* of the real estate sector. He practices extensively in the areas of commercial real estate lending and title law. In recent times Bradford has assisted on the development of several private golf and country clubs and industrial properties. New to this year's rankings is **Charles Landry** (see p.873), who has been instrumental in advancing many projects, including Greater Baton Rouge's hi-tech, information and entrepreneurial economic sector and the formation of the Louisiana Technology Park. Landry serves as general counsel to the Research Park Corporation.

The Clients: Columbus Properties; Department of Natural Resources; Department of Wildlife and Fisheries; Hunt Forest Products; International Paper; Jim Wilson & Associates; Piccadilly Cafeterias; Port Cargo Service; State of Louisiana; Tonti Management and Wal-Mart.

Liskow & Lewis PLC

The Firm: Principally recognized by the market for its lender representation, this *"bright and easy to work with"* group continues to benefit from its ties with the energy sector. Among the work taken on by the team recently is a hotel renovation and a project concerning the construction of large pipelines and offshore facilities.

The Lawyers: **Leon Reymond** is renowned for his work in the leasing field. Sources commended his *"exquisite judgment,"* adding that *"he knows when to stick and when to twist."* Marilyn Maloney has moved to the firm's Houston office.

The Clients: The firm acts for major financial institutions and attracts developer clients from across Louisiana and beyond.

McGlinchey Stafford

See firm details p.885

The Firm: This firm's strong regional practice is supplemented by an increasing amount of national work. Active on both the lender and developer sides, the group has earned the respect of the market for its ability to *"negotiate effectively and forcefully when the situation demands it."* Refinancing projects in the gaming sector continue to contribute heavily to the team's workload, in addition to a steady flow of low-income housing developments.

The Lawyers: Feted by peers for being *"ultra-attentive to clients,"* **Keith Colvin** is considered to be *"doing a tremendous job for the firm."* With a focus on developer-based work, Colvin has cultivated a market reputation as a strong negotiator.

The Clients: Bank One; Boyd Gaming; Cendant Timeshare Resort Group; DaimlerChrysler Services North America; Decatur Hotels; Federal National Mortgage Association; Occidental Chemical; PNC Business Credit; The Williams Companies; Toyota Motor Credit and Whitney National Bank.

868   All quotes in the text are from interviews with clients and competitors.

CHAMBERS USA 2005

Leaders in Louisiana

ABAUNZA, Donald
Liskow & Lewis PLC, New Orleans
504 581 7979
Recommended in Litigation

ADAMS, H Mark
Jones Walker Waechter Poitevent Carrère & Denègre, LLP, New Orleans
504 582 8258
madams@joneswalker.com
Recommended in Employment
Practice Areas: Partner and Chair of Jones Walker's Labor Relations and Employment Law Practice. Has successfully defended employers for 20+ years before federal and state courts, agencies, and arbitrators. Works with employers in development of creative solutions for labor and employment issues relating to mergers and acquisitions; effective HR policies, procedures and training programs; and practical and preventive strategies for dealing with HR issues from screening and hiring to discipline and termination. Frequent speaker at regional and national labor and employment law conferences and professional meetings, including American Bar Association. 'A lawyer's area of practice as stated here is one to which (s)he devotes a substantial portion of his/her professional practice and should not be considered a 'specialization' unless certified by the Louisiana Board of Legal Specialization (or similar body in any other state in which such lawyer is licensed to practice)'.
Prof. Memberships: American Bar Association, Labor and Litigation Sections; Louisiana State Bar; Mississippi State Bar. Also admitted: United States Supreme Court; United States Courts of Appeal for the Second, Fifth, Sixth, Eighth, and Eleventh Circuits; all United States District Courts in Louisiana and Mississippi. Louisiana representative to Employers Counsel Network, an association of leading labor and employment law firms in the United States and Canada.
Career: Joined Jones Walker, 1981; Partner since 1986; member of firm's Executive Committee since 2001. Mr Adams' recent accomplishments include obtaining summary judgment in favor of an international chemical manufacturing company in a 12-plaintiff employment discrimination action in federal court in Louisiana; defeating class certification and obtaining summary judgments in a 15-plaintiff employment discrimination action against a regional beverage distributor in federal court in Mississippi; and obtaining summary judgment against the Equal Employment Opportunity Commission in a representative age discrimination action on behalf of over 300 retired faculty and staff of the University of Louisiana System. In connection with the latter lawsuit, Mr Adams also successfully prosecuted a federal court action to enjoin duplicative state court litigation by two of the employees who had been represented by the EEOC.
Publications: Editor, 'Louisiana Employment Law Letter' (the leading Louisiana authority on developments and emerging trends in labor and employment law), since 1992.
Personal: Native of Mississippi; resident of New Orleans since 1981.

AGUILAR Jr, Rodolfo J
McGlinchey Stafford, Baton Rouge
225 382 3625
rudyaguilar@mcglinchey.com
Recommended in Corporate/M&A
Practice Areas: Managing Partner; maintains a corporate, business, and insurance regulatory practice; handles corporate transactions, commercial financing transactions, transactions relating to real estate development and general business matters; represents physician groups and organizations in their internal corporate structure, joint ventures and healthcare related matters; represents clients in the acquisition and formation of health, property, casualty and life insurance companies; represents the Louisiana Office of Receiverships in proceedings against insolvent insurers; represents developers and owners in the negotiation, documentation, acquisition, financing and management of various mixed use developments including hotel, retail and condominium developments.

ALESSANDRA, M Nan
Phelps Dunbar LLP, New Orleans
504 584 9297
alessann@phelps.com
Recommended in Employment
Practice Areas: Partner and Practice Coordinator of the Employment Law Group's New Orleans office. She also practices employment law out of the firm's Houston office. Her practice concentrates in labor and employment in all aspects of litigation, civil rights, constitutional law, and business litigation. She also advises clients on human resource issues and in developing employee policies and procedures. Ms Alessandra frequently provides training to clients on corporate compliance issues under federal and state law, such as workplace harassment training. Prior to joining the firm, she was Judicial Clerk to the Honorable A J McNamara and Judicial Extern to the Honorable Martin L C Feldman, both of the United States District Court for the Eastern District of Louisiana. She is a Member of the American Arbitration Association's Panel of Neutrals for employment related matters in arbitration and mediation.
Personal: Loyola University, JD, cum laude, 1985; Loyola Law Review. Hunter College in New York; University of New Orleans, BA, 1982.

ARNOLD III, Edward H.
Baker, Donelson, Bearman, Caldwell & Berkowitz, PC, New Orleans
504 566 5204
harnold@bakerdonelson.com
Recommended in Energy
Practice Areas: Extensive experience in commercial, marine and energy finance and real property acquisitions and leases. Represents owners, shipyards and lenders regarding construction, financing and operation of documented vessels. Representation of creditors, bankruptcy trustees and official committees before bankruptcy courts in Louisiana, Texas and Mississippi. Assists developers, lenders and licensed vendors regarding finance and regulatory matters in the riverboat gaming, video gaming and casino industries.
Prof. Memberships: Board Member, Turnaround Management Association Louisiana Chapter. Member, American Bankruptcy Institute. Member, Louisiana Bankers Association. Member, Maritime Law Association. Member, American, Federal and Louisiana Bar Associations.
Career: Licensed in Louisiana since 1988.

BARBIN, Jeffrey M
Phelps Dunbar LLP, Baton Rouge
225 376 0243
barbinj@phelps.com
Recommended in Gaming & Licensing
Practice Areas: Mr Barbin's practice consists of transactional and regulatory matters with emphasis on clients in the Louisiana gaming market and other substantial commercial clients. Mr Barbin handles gaming transactions requiring local gaming regulatory approvals, appearing frequently at the Louisiana Gaming Control Board. He also handles complex commercial real estate transactions including acquisitions, development, disposition, leasing, and other contracts, and often serves as local counsel in connection with large securities offerings of the firm's gaming clients. Jeff has been a guest lecturer on leases in an office practice course at the LSU Law School.
Personal: Louisiana State University, JD, 1998, BS in Finance, 1992.

BARRASSO, Judy Y
Barrasso Usdin Kupperman Freeman & Sarver LLC, New Orleans
504 589 9700
JBarrasso@barrassousdin.com
Recommended in Litigation
Practice Areas: Ms Barrasso represents clients in commercial litigation matters, including unfair trade practices, trade secret, professional liability, securities and banking, class actions, insurance coverage and insurance bad faith claims. She has been named one of the Best Lawyers in America since 2001, a Fellow of the International Society of Barristers, and to the Tulane University Law School Trial Advocacy Adjunct faculty since 1993.
Career: Ms Barrasso is a founding member of Barrasso Usdin Kupperman Freeman & Sarver, L.L.C.
Personal: JD, summa cum laude, Tulane University 1981, Order of the Coif; articles editor, Tulane Law Review.

BARRIERE, Brent B
Phelps Dunbar LLP, New Orleans
504 584 9210
barrierb@phelps.com
Recommended in Corporate/M&A, Litigation
Practice Areas: Partner in the Commercial Litigation Group, resident in the New Orleans office. He represents clients in a wide variety of commercial disputes, including securities litigation, breach of contract, business valuation disputes, and class actions. Mr Barriere has been named one of Louisiana's top 10 litigators by the National Law Journal.
Personal: Tulane University, JD, magna cum laude, 1981; Order of the Coif; Board of Editors and articles editor, Tulane Law Review. Hamilton College, BA, with honors, 1977.

BENNET, Blake
Liskow & Lewis PLC, New Orleans
504 581 7979
Recommended in Energy, Gaming & Licensing

BLACKBURN, Frank
Frank D Blackburn - Sole Practitioner, Baton Rouge 225 756 9696
Recommended in Gaming & Licensing

BOULET, Virginia
Adams and Reese LLP, New Orleans
504 585 0331
virginia.boulet@arlaw.com
Recommended in Corporate/M&A
Practice Areas: Special counsel specializing in corporate, securities and banking law. Authored numerous Louisiana banking and corporate statutes. Has represented numerous banks, securities firms and corporate firms in Louisiana and Mississippi in mergers/acquisitions, corporate restructurings, takeovers and defenses, raising capital and making investments.
Prof. Memberships: American and Louisiana Bar Associations; Association of Louisiana Bank Counsel.
Career: Admitted to Louisiana Bar in 1983. From 1983 to March 2002, served as associate, then Partner of New Orleans based firms. Director of CenturyTel, Inc, a NYSE corporation headquartered in Monroe, Louisiana.
Personal: JD (cum laude), Tulane University Law School 1983; BA Yale University 1975.

BRADFORD, Donald E
Jones Walker Waechter Poitevent Carrère & Denègre, LLP, Baton Rouge
225 248 2028
dbradford@joneswalker.com
Recommended in Real Estate

Practice Areas: All areas of commercial real estate law including acquisition and dispositions, joint ventures, secured lending, landlord and tenant relationships, architectural and construction contracts, and title insurance for office buildings, enclosed malls, lifestyle centers, planned unit developments, mixed use residential and recreational developments, and industrial developments; private and public developments. 'A lawyer's area of practice as stated here is one to which (s)he devotes a substantial portion of his/her professional practice and should not be considered a 'specialization' unless certified by the Louisiana Board of Legal Specialization (or similar body in any other state in which such lawyer is licensed to practice).'
Prof. Memberships: American Bar Association, International Council of Shopping Centers.
Career: Admitted to practice in 1966 and has continuously practiced in the area of real estate. Partner, Jones Walker. Recommended in real estate by a leading US legal publication since 1987.
Personal: Born 1941; resident of Baton Rouge, Louisiana.

BRODERS, John J
Jones Walker Waechter Poitevent Carrère & Denègre, LLP, New Orleans
504 582 8172
jbroders@joneswalker.com
Recommended in Energy

Practice Areas: Partner concentrating in all aspects of maritime and marine energy related matters with an emphasis on marine transactions, including construction of vessels, charters, services agreements, acquisitions and sales, financing and mortgages, flagging and manning, marine insurance and arbitration and related matters. 'A lawyer's area of practice as stated here is one to which (s)he devotes a substantial portion of his/her professional practice and should not be considered a 'specialization' unless certified by the Louisiana Board of Legal Specialization (or similar body in any other state in which such lawyer is licensed to practice).'
Career: Joined Jones Walker in 1971, Partner in 1976, Senior Partner in 2000.
Personal: Tulane University (BA 1971, JD 1971).

BROWN, James
Liskow & Lewis PLC, New Orleans
504 581 7979
Recommended in Litigation

BUTLER Jr, Patrick J
Phelps Dunbar LLP, New Orleans
504 584 9298
butlerr@phelps.com
Recommended in Corporate/M&A

Practice Areas: Partner in the Business Group in the New Orleans office. He practices primarily in the areas of corporate and securities law and mergers and acquisitions. Mr Butler has extensive experience in the purchase and sale of businesses (both asset and stock transactions) for large, publicly-traded corporations and for smaller, privately-held firms. He also handles federal and state securities law matters, including the registration of offerings with the Securities and Exchange Commission and state securities regulators; private placements and other transactions exempt from registration under the securities laws, disclosure requirements for companies registered under the Securities Exchange Act of 1934 and proxy contests. Mr Butler also represents issuing companies and investors in venture capital transactions, assists in the formation of joint ventures and advises clients on general corporate matters.
Personal: Duke University, JD, with honors, 1986. University of Notre Dame, BA, cum laude, 1983.

CAHILL Jr, Elwood
Sher Garner Cahill Richter Klein McAlister & Hilbert, LLC, New Orleans
504 299 2100
Recommended in Real Estate

CAMPBELL Jr, John
Taylor, Porter, Brooks & Phillips, LLP, Baton Rouge 225 387 3221
Recommended in Corporate/M&A

CAVERLY, Joseph L
Stone Pigman Walther Wittmann L.L.C., New Orleans
504 593 0845
jcaverly@stonepigman.com
Recommended in Corporate/M&A

Practice Areas: Corporate; mergers and acquisitions; securities law. Chair of the firm's Corporate and Securities Practice Group.
Prof. Memberships: Admitted to practice in Louisiana, 1985. Member of the American and Louisiana State Bar Associations and the French-American Chamber of Commerce.
Career: Joined Stone Pigman in 1985; became member in 1991.
Personal: JD (magna cum laude), Tulane University School of Law. Member of Order of the Coif and Tulane Law Review. Undergraduate and advanced degrees, the University of Notre Dame (with high honors), 1978; the London School of Economics and Political Science, 1980; the University of Oxford, 1982.

CERONE, Rudy
McGlinchey Stafford, New Orleans
504 596 2786
rcerone@mcglinchey.com
Recommended in Corporate/M&A

Practice Areas: Bankruptcy, litigation, gaming.
Prof. Memberships: American Bankruptcy Institute, American College of Bankruptcy, Bar Association of the Fifth Federal Circuit, Federal Bar, International Association of Gaming Attorneys, Louisiana Bankers Association, American Bar Association, California State Bar, Louisiana State Bar, New Orleans Bar.
Career: Bankruptcy and litigation; certified specialist in Business Bankruptcy by American Board of Certification and LA State Bar Association Board of Legal Specialization.

CHEATWOOD, Roy C
Baker, Donelson, Bearman, Caldwell & Berkowitz, PC, New Orleans
504 566 5266
rcheatwood@bakerdonelson.com
Recommended in Litigation

Practice Areas: Practice focused in commercial litigation including construction, corporate and securities, oil and gas, energy and minerals, trade secrets and legal malpractice. Representation of local, national and international concerns before trial and appellate courts as well as regulatory bodies and ADR forums.
Prof. Memberships: Member, Louisiana Board of Legal Specialization. Member, American, Federal, Louisiana State and New Orleans Bar Associations. Faculty Member, National Institute for Trial Advocacy, Trial and Deposition Programs. Master Barrister, Tulane Inn of Court. Co-author, Louisiana Courtroom Evidence.
Career: Licensed in Louisiana since 1974.
Personal: Tulane University, JD, 1974. University of South Florida, BA, 1968.

CLAVERIE Sr, Philip deV
Phelps Dunbar LLP, New Orleans
504 584 9223
claverip@phelps.com
Recommended in Banking & Finance, Real Estate

Practice Areas: Partner in the firm's Business Group in the New Orleans office. His business practice includes banking, commercial, real estate and probate. He represents various financial institutions in dozens of transactions involving financing of real estate construction, mergers and acquisitions and working capital. He also represents several real estate developers in connection with various development projects, from major office buildings to shopping centers.
Personal: Tulane University, JD, 1966; index editor, associate editor, Tulane Law Review; Order of the Coif; Phi Delta Phi; Omicron Delta Kappa. Princeton University, AB, magna cum laude, 1963.

COLVIN, R Keith
McGlinchey Stafford, New Orleans
504 586 1200
Recommended in Real Estate

CORRERO, Anthony J
Correro Fishman Haygood Phelps Walmsley & Casteix LLP, New Orleans
504 586 5253
acorrero@cfhlaw.com
Recommended in Corporate/M&A

Practice Areas: His primary practice areas include corporate and securities law, mergers and acquisitions and banking. In particular, he helps clients with SEC compliance, public and private securities offerings, the regulation of financial institutions and the buying and selling of businesses. He has advised clients in a variety of transactions, ranging in size from $3.1 billion to $100,000, including the $3.1 billion sale of First Commerce Corporation to Bank One; the purchase of Sugarland Bank by Mid-South Bancorp for $1.2 million; the $500 million purchase of Zapata Corporation by Tidewater, Inc.; the sale of VitaRx to McKesson Corporation for $62 million; the public offerings of oil and gas interests for a single client aggregating $1 billion and the private offering of oil and gas interests for a single client of $100,000; as well as initial public stock offerings for several companies.
Career: Andy has served as Chairman of the Corporate Laws Committee of the LSBA Section on Corporate and Business Law since 1998, and is a former Chairman of the Section. He has also been a Member of the Board of Directors of several private and public companies. He is a Member of the American Law Institute and Louisiana Bankers Association. He is an adjunct faculty member of both the Tulane and LSU Law Schools, where he teaches the courses in Securities Regulation and Corporation Finance. He also spent eight years as a Member of the Planning Committee of the Tulane Corporate Law Institute.
Publications: He has been the editor of the Louisiana Corporate Newsletter and co-editor of Basic Forms for Louisiana Corporations, has been listed in a leading legal publication in America, in corporate law, since that publication's inception in 1983 and has been ranked by New Orleans Magazine as one of the city's top lawyers in banking, securities and corporate law.
Personal: Andy graduated from Northeast Louisiana State College in 1962 and got his LLB degree from LSU in 1965, where he was a member of the Order of the Coif and associate editor of the 'Louisiana Law Review'.

CROCHET, Vicki
Taylor, Porter, Brooks & Phillips, LLP, Baton Rouge 225 387 3221
Recommended in Employment

CROMWELL, David
Pettiette, Armand, Dunkelman, Woodley, Byrd & Cromwell LLP, Shreveport
318 221 1800
Recommended in Banking & Finance

CROSBY, E Howell

Chaffe, McCall, Phillips, Toler & Sarpy, L.L.P., New Orleans 504 585 7212
crosby@chaffe.com

Recommended in Real Estate

Practice Areas: Partner in Real Estate Section concentrating in commercial real estate; represents developers, owners, tenants and lenders in projects including office buildings, shopping centers and malls, apartment complexes, hotels, and condominium developments.

Prof. Memberships: President - American College of Mortgage Attorneys; American College of Real Estate Lawyers; International Association of Attorneys and Executives in Corporate Real Estate; International Council of Shopping Centers; New Orleans Regional Leadership Institute.

Career: Joined Chaffe McCall in 1984 and became a Partner in 1988. Was appointed and served as an interim New Orleans City Council Member in 1999-2000.

Personal: Tulane Law School, JD 1984; Tulane Freeman School of Business, MBA 1983; admitted in Louisiana and Mississippi.

CURRAULT II, Douglas N

Jones Walker Waechter Poitevent Carrère & Denègre, LLP, New Orleans 504 582 8412
dcurrault@joneswalker.com

Recommended in Corporate/M&A

Practice Areas: Mr Currault's practice includes handling corporate and securities law matters for public and private companies. His practice focuses on SEC reporting, corporate finance, mergers and acquisitions, and corporate governance and compliance. 'A lawyer's area of practice as stated here is one to which (s)he devotes a substantial portion of his/her professional practice and should not be considered a 'specialization' unless certified by the Louisiana Board of Legal Specialization (or similar body in any other state in which such lawyer is licensed to practice)'.

Prof. Memberships: New Orleans Bar Association, Louisiana State Bar Association, Louisiana State Board of CPAs.

Career: During 2004, Mr Currault handled a variety of transactions including a $1.1 billion convertible preferred stock offering, a $140 million convertible note offering, a $350 million senior note offering, a $90 million common stock offering, and a call for redemption of $66 million of outstanding publicly traded convertible notes.

Personal: Mr Currault and his wife, Donna, have been married since 1988 and have two children, Katharine and Nicholas.

D'ARMOND, William

Kean, Miller, Hawthorne, D'Armond, McCowan & Jarman, LLP, Baton Rouge 225 387 0999

Recommended in Employment

DILEO, Anthony M

Stone Pigman Walther Wittmann L.L.C., New Orleans 504 593 0811
adileo@stonepigman.com

Recommended in Corporate/M&A

Practice Areas: Corporate and business; federal and state taxation; health and medical law.

Prof. Memberships: Admitted to practice in Louisiana, 1970 and in Washington, DC, 1972; appointed by the Louisiana Supreme Court and Member of the Committee on Admissions to Bar, as Examiner in Corporations and Securities for the Louisiana Bar Examination (1982-84); Chair of the Health Law Section, 2003-05; Chair of the Section on Corporations, Business and Securities Law, 1984; Chair of the American Bar Association, Health Law Section (Compliance, Fraud and Abuse Interest Group); New Orleans Bar Association, Executive Committee, 1986-88; Chair, Committee on Articles of Incorporation, 1991-92; American Law Institute, 1985; Louisiana Bar Association Pro Bono Publico Award, 2004.

Career: Joined Stone Pigman, 1973; became Member in 1975; Senior Law Clerk to the Honorable Alvin Rubin, US District Court, 1971-72; Law Clerk to the Honorable John Minor Wisdom, US Court of Appeals, Fifth Circuit, 1973; and adjunct professor at Tulane University School of Law.

Publications: Author of numerous articles and papers and frequent lecturer.

Personal: JD, Tulane University School of Law, 1970. Member of Order of the Coif, Tulane Law Review Board of Editors and assistant editor. LLM, Harvard Law School, 1971. BA, Tulane University, 1968.

DRAPER, Douglas

Heller, Draper, Hayden, Patrick & Horn, LLC, New Orleans 504 581 9595

Recommended in Corporate/M&A

DUNCAN, J Kelly

Jones Walker Waechter Poitevent Carrère & Denègre, LLP, New Orleans 504 582 8218
kduncan@joneswalker.com

Recommended in Gaming & Licensing

Practice Areas: Gaming law: serves as Jones Walker's Gaming Practice Chair concentrating in the representation of major casino companies, domestic and international manufacturers and suppliers, and financial institutions in connection with licensing, compliance, statutory and regulatory interpretation, administrative hearings, acquisitions, operations and financings. Admiralty, maritime and tnternational and customs law: 25 years of experience in handling marine regulatory matters, acquisitions, financings, contracts, vessel construction, lien enforcement and foreclosure, customs rulings, protests, seizures and classification disputes. 'A lawyer's area of

practice as stated here is one to which (s)he devotes a substantial portion of his/her professional practice and should not be considered a 'specialization' unless certified by the Louisiana Board of Legal Specialization (or similar body in any other state in which such lawyer is licensed to practice)'.

Prof. Memberships: Founding Member and Director of the International Masters of Gaming Law; Immediate Past Chairman of the New Orleans Bar Association Maritime and International Law Committee; Member of the following: International Association of Gaming Attorneys; American Bar Association - Sections on Admiralty and Maritime Law and Business Law - Maritime Financing and Gaming Law Committees; Maritime Law Association of the United States - Maritime Financing and Carriage of Goods Committees; New Orleans Maritime Seminar Advisory and Planning Committees; Southeastern Admiralty Law Institute; American Association of Exporters and Importers; and Association of Average Adjusters.

Career: Georgetown University (AB, cum laude, 1976); Tulane University (JD, 1979).

Publications: Member, Editorial Board, Gaming Law Review.

Personal: Born, New Orleans, Louisiana, February 22, 1954.

DUNCAN III, Brooke

Adams and Reese LLP, New Orleans 504 585 0220
brooke.duncan@arlaw.com

Recommended in Employment

Practice Areas: Partner, special business services experienced in labor and employment, management counseling, labor relations, collective bargaining, employment discrimination - agency practice, OSHA.

Prof. Memberships: Louisiana State Bar; Chairman, Louisiana State Police Commission; Louisiana Civil Service League.

Career: Proactive consulting with managers about problematic labor and employment issues to achieve positive employee relations. Counsels employers on maintaining union-free status, defending job discrimination claims, wage-hour issues, OSHA, reduction-in-force questions, compliance with workplace regulations and miscellaneous state law issues, for public and private employers.

Personal: JD, Tulane University Law School, 1986; AB, Vassar College, 1974.

DUPLANTIS, BJ

Gordon, Arata, McCollam, Duplantis & Eagan LLP, New Orleans 504 582 1111

Recommended in Energy

EAGAN, Ewell

Gordon, Arata, McCollam, Duplantis & Eagan LLP, New Orleans 504 582 1111

Recommended in Litigation

FANTACI, James

McGlinchey Stafford, New Orleans 504 596 2791
jfantaci@mcglinchey.com

Recommended in Corporate/M&A

Practice Areas: Practice includes negotiation and preparation of asset purchase, stock purchase, merger agreements for acquisition of businesses; confidential private placement memoranda; franchise agreements and disclosure documents; formation of corporations, limited liability companies and partnerships; and business restructuring. Advises on liquidations, shareholder (buy-sell) agreements, employment contracts, and other business oriented documents.

Prof. Memberships: American Bar Association, Forum on Franchising; Louisiana and Virginia Bar Associations; Jefferson Chamber of Commerce; Jefferson Parish Economic Development Commission.

Publications: Louisiana Limited Liability Company Forms and Practice Manual (1996).

Personal: Received JD from University of Virginia (1971) and BA from University of Rochester (1968).

FISHMAN, Louis Y

Correro Fishman Haygood Phelps Walmsley & Casteix LLP, New Orleans 504 586 5255
lfishman@cfhlaw.com

Recommended in Corporate/M&A

Practice Areas: Louis Fishman has since 1966 represented a variety of business clients in numerous transactions that have included mergers and acquisitions and public and private offerings of securities. He also counsels clients on business, securities and corporate law matters, including corporate governance.

Career: Louis was a founder in 1988 of Tulane's Corporate Law Institute and still serves on its Planning Committee. He has served since 1991 as a member of the Advisory Board of Editors of the 'Tulane Law Review'. He has held several key posts, including Chairman, of the Louisiana State Bar Association's Section on Corporation and Business Law and has served as a Member of that Section's Corporate Laws Committee. Louis has taught 'Corporate Governance Post Enron' at Tulane Law School, and 'Judaism and Christianity' at a Presbyterian church in New Orleans.

Publications: Louis has been listed as a top corporate lawyer in a leading legal publication in America, since that publication's first edition in 1983, and has been ranked by 'New Orleans Magazine' as one of the city's top lawyers.

Personal: Louis received his undergraduate degree in business administration from Tulane University in 1963. He received his LLB degree in 1965 from Tulane Law School, where he was a member of the Order of the Coif and editor in chief of the 'Tulane Law

Review'. He earned a Master of Laws degree in 1966 from Yale Law School, where he was a Sterling Fellow.

FONTHAM, Michael R
Stone Pigman Walther Wittmann L.L.C., New Orleans 504 593 0810
mfontham@stonepigman.com
Recommended in Energy
Practice Areas: Public utility regulation and commercial litigation.
Career: Joined Stone Pigman in 1971; became member in 1975.
Publications: Trial Technique and Evidence 2d ed (Lexis Nexis 2002); Persuasive Written and Oral Advocacy: In Trial and Appellate Courts (Aspen, 2002); and Written and Oral Advocacy (John Wiley and Sons, 1985).
Personal: JD, University of Virginia School of Law, 1971. Member of the Order of the Coif and the Virginia Law Review. Undergraduate degree from Louisiana State University.

FORSYTH, David
Sessions, Fishman & Nathan LLP, New Orleans 504 582 1500
Recommended in Corporate/M&A

FOSTER, Murphy
Breazeale, Sachse & Wilson, LLP, Baton Rouge 225 387 4000
Recommended in Employment

FRILOT, George
Frilot, Partridge, Kohnke & Clements LC, New Orleans 504 599 8000
Recommended in Litigation

FULLMER, Mark A
Phelps Dunbar LLP, New Orleans
504 584 9324
fullmerm@phelps.com
Recommended in Corporate/M&A
Practice Areas: Partner in the Business Group in the New Orleans office. He represents start-up companies as well as companies in the mature stages of their growth cycle. His practice in the area of corporate and securities includes all aspects of public and private company representation, including public offerings, private placements, and mergers and acquisitions. He has also represented both venture capital funds and investors in private equity transactions.
Personal: Louisiana State University, JD, 1976; Order of the Coif; Louisiana Law Review. University of New Orleans, BS in Accounting, 1976.

GARNER, James
Sher Garner Cahill Richter Klein McAlister & Hilbert, LLC, New Orleans
504 299 2100
Recommended in Litigation

HARDIN III, Harry S
Jones Walker Waechter Poitevent Carrère & Denègre, LLP, New Orleans
504 582 8170
hhardin@joneswalker.com
Recommended in Litigation
Practice Areas: Senior Partner concentrating in commercial business litiga-

tion, including contract, railroad, antitrust, trademark, copyright, professional responsibility and environmental law. 'A lawyer's area of practice as stated here is one to which (s)he devotes a substantial portion of his/her professional practice and should not be considered a 'specialization' unless certified by the Louisiana Board of Legal Specialization (or similar body in any other state in which such lawyer is licensed to practice)'.
Prof. Memberships: Fellow, American College of Trial Lawyers; American Judicature Society Board of Directors; American Bar Association: Board of Governors, Louisiana State Delegate (1994-2003), Fifth Circuit Representative to Standing Committee on Federal Judiciary (1998-2002), Sections of Litigation, Antitrust, Patent Trademark & Copyright, Tort & Insurance Practice; Louisiana State Bar Association past President; Louisiana Bar Foundation, past President; International Association of Defense Counsel; National Association of Railroad Trial Counsel.
Career: 1971 Jones Walker, (1973-77 1st Lt. JAG US Army), Partner in 1976; chairs Appellate Practice Group; speaks on and instructs ethics, professionalism and malpractice avoidance; Louisiana Supreme Court: Chair, Judicial Campaign Oversight Committee, Advisory Committee for Revision of Code of Judicial Conduct; listed in leading US legal publications.
Publications: Managed Care and Antitrust: The PPO Experience, ABA Press (contributing author); 'Pitfalls for In-House Counsel,' The Brief, ABA Press.
Personal: New Orleans native; BA Harvard (cum laude); JD Tulane University.

HARKINS, Deborah
McGlinchey Stafford, New Orleans
504 596 2799
dharkins@mcglinchey.com
Recommended in Gaming & Licensing
Practice Areas: Environmental, gaming, government relations, healthcare, insurance regulation and compliance.
Prof. Memberships: Louisiana Health Care Commission, Louisiana Hospital Association, Louisiana Lobbyist Association, National Health Lawyers Association, New Orleans Film and Video Corporation, Women Health Executive Network, Committee of 21, French Market Corporation Board, Vieux Carre Alliance, Lower Quarter Crime Watch.
Career: Registered lobbyist; industries represented include healthcare, insurance, environment, banking, gaming, and pharmaceutical; works with Louisiana Department of Insurance on matters including licensure, insurance regulation and compliance, managed care plans, independent review organizations and third party administrators; represents Louisiana Healthcare Commission for Commissioner of Insurance;

appears before Louisiana Gaming Control Board, works with Louisiana Attorney General Gaming Division, Louisiana State Police, Gaming Division, Public Service Commission and Louisiana Used Motor Vehicle Commission.

HARTMANN, Melanie
Kean, Miller, Hawthorne, D'Armond, McCowan & Jarman, LLP, Baton Rouge
225 387 0999
Recommended in Employment

HAYGOOD, Paul
Correro Fishman Haygood Phelps Walmsley & Casteix LLP, New Orleans
504 586 5263
phaygood@cfhlaw.com
Recommended in Corporate/M&A
Practice Areas: Mr Haygood practices in the areas of mergers and acquisitions, corporate law, securities law, probate, estate planning and trust law. He has represented clients in a variety of corporate finance and planning matters, including representing numerous financial institutions in connection with acquisition transactions involving more than $1 billion in assets; acting as lead outside counsel in connection with the corporate and securities aspects of the reorganization of a large publicly-held enterprise in what was the largest financial reorganization up to that time of a Louisiana-based company; acting as lead outside counsel in connection with the financial and corporate restructuring of a Louisiana-based, publicly-traded entity with assets in excess of $500 million; representation of an international oil and gas service company in connection with the acquisition of assets located on three different continents and totaling in excess of $40 million; and structuring estate plans for individuals having an estimated combined net worth in excess of $150 million.
Career: Like his partners, Andy Correro, Louis Fishman, and Robert Walmsley, Mr Haygood is a former Chairman of the Corporate and Business Law Section of the Louisiana State Bar Association. He also chaired for many years the Association's Bar Admission Committee that prepares the Louisiana corporation law portion of the Louisiana Bar Examination, as well as chairing for 10 years the Association's Corporate Laws Committee, which monitors the Louisiana Business Corporation Law and makes recommendations to the Louisiana Legislature with respect to changes in the Louisiana Business Corporation Law.
Publications: Mr Haygood is listed in a leading legal publication in America as one of the best lawyers in America in the area of corporate law. He has retained that listing since 1983, when that publication was first published.
Personal: Mr Haygood graduated from Louisiana State University in 1964 and received his LLB from Harvard Law

School in 1967. In addition to the practice of law, Mr Haygood also has played an active role in the civic affairs of New Orleans and Louisiana, having served as President of the Council for a Better Louisiana, as President of the New Orleans Bureau of Governmental Research, and as an active Board Member of a number of philanthropic organizations. In 1991 he chaired the New Orleans Conference on North American Free Trade. Mr Haygood also is a former Member of the Board of Supervisors of Louisiana State University and a former Member of the Board of Advisors of the National Trust for Historic Preservation.

HEARN, Curtis R
Jones Walker Waechter Poitevent Carrère & Denègre, LLP, New Orleans
504 582 8308
chearn@joneswalker.com
Recommended in Corporate/M&A
Practice Areas: Mergers and acquisitions; corporate and securities; healthcare transactions. 'A lawyer's area of practice as stated here is one to which (s)he devotes a substantial portion of his/her professional practice and should not be considered a 'specialization' unless certified by the Louisiana Board of Legal Specialization (or similar body in any other state in which such lawyer is licensed to practice)'.
Prof. Memberships: Member, American Bar Association, Negotiated Acquisitions Committee of Business Law Section.
Personal: Adjunct professor at law, mergers and acquisitions, Tulane University Law School.

HERMAN, Russ
Herman, Herman, Katz & Cotlar LLP, New Orleans 504 581 4892
Recommended in Litigation

HEUSEL, Cornelius
Jones Walker Waechter Poitevent Carrère & Denègre, LLP, New Orleans
504 582 8148
nheusel@joneswalker.com
Recommended in Employment
Practice Areas: Partner in Jones Walker's Labor Relations and Employment and White Collar Crime and Corporate Compliance Practices. 'A lawyer's area of practice as stated here is one to which (s)he devotes a substantial portion of his/her professional practice and should not be considered a 'specialization' unless certified by the Louisiana Board of Legal Specialization (or similar body in any other state in which such lawyer is licensed to practice)'.
Career: A graduate of Loyola University of New Orleans law school in 1967, Mr Heusel served for three years as a Special Agent with the Federal Bureau of Investigation. Following the FBI, he served as an Assistant District Attorney for Orleans Parish and was the Executive Assistant District Attorney in charge of capital cases. In 1972, he joined the United States Attorney's Office in New

Orleans, where he served as Chief of the Criminal Division and First Assistant US Attorney. In 1976, he received the United States Attorney General's Exceptional Service Award. Beginning in 1977, he headed the Department of Justice Organized Crime and Racketeering Strike Force with jurisdiction over the states of Texas, Louisiana, Arkansas, Mississippi, and Alabama. He also served as an Assistant Special Prosecutor appointed by the federal courts to look into allegations of corruption involving members of the White House staff. Mr Heusel has been a guest lecturer at the United States Department of Justice Trial Advocacy Institute on Trial Tactics as well as a member of the Tulane University School of Law Panel of Instructors on Trial Advocacy. Since 1979, he has primarily represented management in the field of labor relations. Joined Jones Walker in 1999.
Personal: Mr Heusel is a native of New Orleans; Loyola University (BBA, 1967); Loyola University (JD, 1967).

HUNTER, Jonathon
Liskow & Lewis PLC, New Orleans
504 581 7979
Recommended in Energy

JACOB, Clyde
Jones Walker Waechter Poitevent Carrère & Denègre, LLP, New Orleans
504 582 8230
cjacob@joneswalker.com
Recommended in Employment
Practice Areas: Clyde Jacob is a Partner in the firm's Labor Relations and Employment Law Practice. He represents employers in the field of labor relations and has assisted employers in responding to union organizing, boycotts, strikes, collective bargaining, National Labor Relations Board representation cases, and corporate campaigns throughout the United States and in Puerto Rico, Norway, and the United Kingdom. He recently helped a company prevail in the 11th largest NLRB election during 2004. He also defends employment claims. He has spoken on a national basis to employers, employer associations, and bar associations including the Inter American Bar Association and the US Chamber of Commerce. He has prepared a corporate president for testimony before the US Congress on union corporate campaigns, has twice testified as an expert before the US Congress, and has worked with and spoken before the United States Council for International Business (USCIB). 'A lawyer's area of practice as stated here is one to which (s)he devotes a substantial portion of his/her professional practice and should not be considered a 'specialization' unless certified by the Louisiana Board of Legal Specialization (or similar body in any other state in which such lawyer is licensed to practice)'.

Prof. Memberships: American Bar Association, Labor Section; Louisiana Bar Association; Virginia Bar Association; Louisiana Association of Defense Counsel (LADC); US Chamber of Commerce, Labor Relations Committee, Washington, DC; admitted to Bar, 1975, Virginia; 1976, Louisiana; also admitted: US Supreme Court; the Virginia and Louisiana Supreme Courts; and numerous Federal appellate and district courts.
Career: Law Clerk, US District Court, Eastern District of Virginia; joined Jones Walker in 1999.
Personal: Native of Norfolk, Virginia; resides in New Orleans; University of Virginia (BA, 1971; JD, 1975).

JARMAN, William
Kean, Miller, Hawthorne, D'Armond, McCowan & Jarman, LLP, Baton Rouge
225 387 0999
Recommended in Litigation

JAUBERT, Lisa
Schully, Roberts, Slattery, Jaubert & Marino, New Orleans
504 585 7800
Recommended in Energy

JONES Jr, Philip
Liskow & Lewis PLC, New Orleans
504 581 7979
Recommended in Corporate/M&A

KANTROW, Lee
Kantrow Spaht Weaver & Blitzer, Baton Rouge
225 383 4703
Recommended in Corporate/M&A

KIGGANS, Thomas H
Phelps Dunbar LLP, Baton Rouge
225 376 0247
kigganst@phelps.com
Recommended in Employment
Practice Areas: Partner and the Practice Coordinator of the Employment Law Group in the Baton Rouge office. He also practices labor and employment law out of the firm's Houston, Texas office. He has practiced labor and employment law almost exclusively since 1984. He represents primarily employers in both litigation and counseling in all areas of labor and employment, including discrimination, ERISA, sexual harassment, employee defamation, and other employment-related tort claims, employment contracts, OSHA, union matters, wage and hour, drug testing, and drafting and implementing employment policies. Mr Kiggans represents employers in a wide variety of industries, including construction, equipment rental, banks, maritime, petrochemical, oil and gas exploration and production, insurance, gaming, governmental entities, educational institutions and restaurants, and has extensive trial experience in both federal and state courts.
Personal: Louisiana State University, JD, 1984; Board of Editors, Louisiana Law

Review. Louisiana Tech University, BA, magna cum laude, 1981.

KING, Katherine
Kean, Miller, Hawthorne, D'Armond, McCowan & Jarman, LLP, Baton Rouge
225 387 0999
Recommended in Energy

KLEIN, Steven
Sher Garner Cahill Richter Klein McAlister & Hilbert, LLC, New Orleans
504 299 2100
Recommended in Corporate/M&A

KLING, Neal
Sher Garner Cahill Richter Klein McAlister & Hilbert, LLC, New Orleans
504 299 2100
Recommended in Real Estate

LAFITTE, Gene
Liskow & Lewis PLC, New Orleans
504 581 7979
Recommended in Litigation

LANDRY, Charles
Jones Walker Waechter Poitevent Carrère & Denègre, LLP, Baton Rouge
225 248 2020
clandry@joneswalker.com
Recommended in Real Estate
Practice Areas: Real estate: land use, development and finance; project development and finance. 'A lawyer's area of practice as stated here is one to which (s)he devotes a substantial portion of his/her professional practice and should not be considered a 'specialization' unless certified by the Louisiana Board of Legal Specialization (or similar body in any other state in which such lawyer is licensed to practice)'.
Prof. Memberships: Urban Land Institute; Council for a Better Louisiana; East Baton Rouge Parish Planning Commission Zoning Ordinance Task Force; LSU Foundation; Pennington Biomedical Foundation.
Career: Mr Landry is the Managing Partner of the firm's Baton Rouge offices and a member of its Executive Committee. He has represented a wide range of real estate transactions, including office buildings, shopping malls and centers, hotels, medical facilities, golf courses and golf course communities, as well as industrial and residential developments. He has also been very involved in advancing the Greater Baton Rouge's high-tech, information and entrepreneurial economic sector. He was instrumental in the formation of the Louisiana Technology Park, and serves as General Counsel to Research Park Corporation. Mr Landry has been selected annually since 1993 to be included in the publication The Best Lawyers in America as one of a few attorneys chosen in Louisiana in the area of Real Estate Law.
Publications: The Foreign Investor's Guide to the Legal Aspects of Doing Business in Louisiana, co-editor.

Personal: Louisiana State University Law School (JD, 1977); Louisiana State University (BS (Business), 1975).

LELONG, Rivers
Jones Walker Waechter Poitevent Carrère & Denègre, LLP, New Orleans
504 582 8378
rlelong@joneswalker.com
Recommended in Banking & Finance
Practice Areas: Mr Lelong's practice involves a variety of commercial transactions involving secured finance, real estate, acquisitions and divestitures of privately held companies and their assets, and the negotiation of sophisticated commercial contracts. 'A lawyer's area of practice as stated here is one to which (s)he devotes a substantial portion of his/her professional practice and should not be considered a 'specialization' unless certified by the Louisiana Board of Legal Specialization (or similar body in any other state in which such lawyer is licensed to practice)'.
Prof. Memberships: Louisiana State Bar Association.
Career: Admitted to Bar, 1990, Louisiana; Partner at Jones Walker since 1998.
Personal: Born New Orleans, Louisiana, February 14, 1965; Amherst College (BA, summa cum laude, 1987); Stanford Law School (JD 1990).

LEWIS, Sidney
Jones Walker Waechter Poitevent Carrère & Denègre, LLP, New Orleans
504 582 8352
slewis@joneswalker.com
Recommended in Employment
Practice Areas: Labor and employment law. Mr Lewis is a Partner in the firm's Labor Relations and Employment Law Practice. He is an experienced litigator in federal, state and administrative judicial forums. A large part of his practice is devoted to advising and counseling employers with respect to union organizing drives and in the development, maintenance and administration of personnel policies, procedures and employee relations to minimize exposure to litigation and union organizing. In this regard, Mr Lewis regularly conducts supervisor and management training programs. He is a frequent speaker for human resource associations, and has authored numerous articles for professional journals and other publications on a wide range of labor and employment law topics. 'A lawyer's area of practice as stated here is one to which (s)he devotes a substantial portion of his/her professional practice and should not be considered a 'specialization' unless certified by the Louisiana Board of Legal Specialization (or similar body in any other state in which such lawyer is licensed to practice)'.
Prof. Memberships: American Bar Association Labor and Employment Law Section; Louisiana State Bar Association.

Career: Admitted in Louisiana, 1985; Joined Jones Walker as Partner in 1999; Tulane School of Law, JD, 1985; University of Alabama, BA, 1982.

Publications: 'Sexual Harassment in Employment Law', BNA Books (contributing author); 'Louisiana Employment Law Letter' (associate editor); 'Jones Walker Labor and Employment Tip Sheet' (electronic newsletter) (co-editor).

Personal: Native of New Orleans, Louisiana.

LINZY, Howard

The Kullman Firm PLC, New Orleans
504 596 4105
Recommended in Employment

LUND, Daniel

Montgomery, Barnett, Brown, Read, Hammond & Mintz LLP, New Orleans
504 585 3200
Recommended in Litigation

MALLERY, Mark

McGlinchey Stafford, New Orleans
504 596 2736
mmallery@mcglinchey.com
Recommended in Employment

Practice Areas: Labor and employment.
Prof. Memberships: Program Chair, Committee on Employment Rights and Responsibilities, ABA Labor and Employment Section.
Career: Defends employers in employment litigation, including acting as lead counsel in class actions, Sarbanes-Oxley whistleblower claims, class based EEOC claims, pattern and practice cases prosecuted by the US Department of Labor's Civil Rights Center, wage and hour collective actions, hundreds of employment termination lawsuits, and prosecuting injunction proceedings against former executives and salespeople to protect trade secrets and proprietary information.
Publications: Editor in chief, Employment Termination Treatise, BNA/ABA, 2003 Supplement.
Personal: JD University of Mississippi, 1986. BBA Mississippi State University, 1983.

MALONE Jr, Ernest

The Kullman Firm PLC, New Orleans
504 596 4105
erm@kullmanlaw.com
Recommended in Employment

Prof. Memberships: ABA; LSBA; NOBA.
Career: Currently President of The Kullman Firm; shareholder since 1980.
Publications: 49 Tulane Law Review 644 (1974-75); 46 Loyola Law Review 1087 (2000).
Personal: Juris Doctorate, Tulane University School of Law; Bachelor of Science, Louisiana State University. Officer, US Army, Medical Service Corps.

MARTZELL, Jack

Martzell & Bickford, APC, New Orleans
504 581 9065
Recommended in Litigation

MASTERS, William B

Jones Walker Waechter Poitevent Carrère & Denègre, LLP, New Orleans
504 582 8278
bmasters@joneswalker.com
Recommended in Corporate/M&A

Practice Areas: Mr Masters has a broad business practice in the areas of corporate finance, mergers and acquisitions and energy. His clients include public and privately owned companies engaged in virtually all areas of the energy industry, with an emphasis on service providers, private capital portfolio companies and other businesses in a variety of industries, including banking. Mr Masters has extensive experience in public and private offerings of debt and equity securities and acts as general counsel for several public and private companies. Mr Masters also routinely structures and negotiates acquisitions and financing transactions. 'A lawyer's area of practice as stated here is one to which (s)he devotes a substantial portion of his/her professional practice and should not be considered a 'specialization' unless certified by the Louisiana Board of Legal Specialization (or similar body in any other state in which such lawyer is licensed to practice)'.
Prof. Memberships: American Bar Association, Louisiana State Bar Association and Society of Corporate Secretaries.
Career: Joined Jones Walker law firm in 1982.
Personal: London School of Economics; Tulane University, BA, 1979; George Washington University, JD, 1982.

MCCALLA, Robert

Fisher & Phillips LLP, New Orleans
504 522 3303
rmccalla@laborlawyers.com
Recommended in Employment

Practice Areas: Bob McCalla is a Senior Partner in the New Orleans office of the national law firm of Fisher & Phillips LLP, practicing exclusively in labor and employment law representing management. He has handled numerous complex individual and class action discrimination cases and Fair Labor Standards Act collective action cases and has extensive experience handling both judge trials and jury trials. Bob has negotiated many labor agreements and is experienced in advising clients in connection with strikes and corporate campaigns. He received a JD from the University of Nebraska College of Law, graduating cum laude, Order of the Coif.

MCCOLLAM, John

Gordon, Arata, McCollam, Duplantis & Eagan LLP, New Orleans
504 582 1111
Recommended in Energy, Litigation

MCCOWAN, Charles

Kean, Miller, Hawthorne, D'Armond, McCowan & Jarman, LLP, Baton Rouge
225 387 0999
Recommended in Litigation

MCGUIRE, Robin

Jones Walker Waechter Poitevent Carrère & Denègre, LLP, Lafayette
337 406 5615
rmcguire@joneswalker.com
Recommended in Energy

Practice Areas: Energy; bankruptcy, restructuring and creditors-debtors; rights; business and commercial litigations. A Partner in the firm's Energy and General Business Practice, he is an experienced transactional attorney who has also litigated various energy related matters in federal, state and bankruptcy forums. His practice focuses in the energy field representing integrated and independent oil producers, small producers, pipeline companies, end users, production purchasers and transporters, service and construction companies and large landowners. In connection with such representation, he has participated in various energy-related matters, including (1) examination of abstracts of title and preparation of title opinions for well drilling, division order and lease acquisition purposes; (2) negotiation, preparation and interpretation of various energy industry agreements and transactions, including farmout agreements, joint venture agreements, participation agreements, operating agreements, drilling contracts, contracts for the transportation, purchase and sale of production, hedging agreements, LNG related agreements, CNG related agreements, production sharing agreements, licenses, concessions, mergers and acquisitions and the provision of advices or opinions in connection with issues arising out of such activities; (3) negotiation, preparation and interpretation of agreements related to salt, coal, coal seam gas and other mining or extraction operations, including solution mining in salt domes for natural gas storage and the provision of advices or opinions in connection with issues arising out of such activities; (4) negotiation, preparation and interpretation of agreements related to electric utilities and pipelines, including acquisition of rights-of-way, purchases and leasing of facilities and the provision of advices or opinions in connection with issues arising out of such activities; (5) civil litigation related to all aspects of the oil and gas industry; and (6) bankruptcy involving energy related matters. 'A lawyer's area of practice as stated here is one to which (s)he devotes a substantial portion of his/her professional practice and should not be considered a 'specialization' unless certified by the Louisiana Board of Legal Specialization (or similar body in any other state in which such lawyer is licensed to practice)'.

Prof. Memberships: Federal Bar Association Environmental Energy Natural Resource Section; Louisiana State Bar Association, Sections of Consumer Protection and Bankruptcy Law, Environmental Law, International Law and Mineral Law; Texas Bar Association; Lafayette Parish Bar Association; Petroleum Landmen's Association of New Orleans (PLANO).
Career: Admitted in Louisiana, 1988; Admitted in Texas, 2001; Joined Jones Walker, 1988; Jones Walker Partner, 1996; Opened Jones Walker's Lafayette Office, 1991; Loyola School of Law in New Orleans, Louisiana, JD, 1988; Mississippi State University, BS in Petroleum Engineering, 1980.
Publications: A Primer on Gas Balancing, 37 Loyola Law Review 831, 1992; Penalty Issues Arising from Offshore Operations, Presented at the Rocky Mountain Mineral Law Foundation Special Institute on Oil & Gas Development on the Outer Continental Shelf; FERC Order 636 - Impacts & Implications, Presented at 2002 AAPL-OLS Committee Workshop; Oil and Gas Leasing of the Federal Outer Continental Shelf, Presented at Houston Oil & Gas Short Course; Offshore Operating Agreement - Engineering Issues, Presented at AAPL 2004 OLS Committee Workshop.

MCMILLAN II, L Richards

Jones Walker Waechter Poitevent Carrère & Denègre, LLP, New Orleans
504 582 8188
rmcmillan@joneswalker.com
Recommended in Corporate/M&A

Practice Areas: Corporate, securities, corporate finance, mergers and acquisitions, corporate governance. 'A lawyer's area of practice as stated here is one to which (s)he devotes a substantial portion of his/her professional practice and should not be considered a 'specialization' unless certified by the Louisiana Board of Legal Specialization (or similar body in any other state in which such lawyer is licensed to practice)'.
Prof. Memberships: He is past Chairman of the Corporate Law Section of the Louisiana State Bar Association and a former member of the Committee on Negotiated Acquisitions of the American Bar Association.
Career: He joined Jones Walker in 1976 after serving three years in the Navy JAG Corps and became a Partner in 1979. He served as Head of the firm's Corporate and Securities Practice from 1987-2002 and as a member and Chairman of the firm's Executive Committee from 1990 through 2002. He has broad industry experience, with significant representations of clients in banking, chemical manufacturing, computer technology, consumer services, defense contracting, manufacturing, mining, ocean shipping, offshore construction, oil and gas exploration and production, oil and gas ser-

vices, and retailing. He also has business operational experience, having served as Chairman, from 1986 through the current date and as President from 1989 through 1999, of a privately held integrated manufacturing company producing water purification equipment.
Personal: Born New Orleans, Louisiana, 1947; Washington and Lee University (BS, 1969); Tulane University School of Law (JD, 1972); Order of the Coif; US Navy Judge Advocate General's Corps (1972-75); New York University School of Law (LLM in Taxation, 1976).

MEUNIER, Gerald
Gainsburgh, Benjamin, David, Meunier & Warshauer, New Orleans
504 522 2304
Recommended in Litigation

MILLER Jr, Ben
Kean, Miller, Hawthorne, D'Armond, McCowan & Jarman, LLP, Baton Rouge
225 387 0999
Recommended in Corporate/M&A

PAGE, Marshall
Jones Walker Waechter Poitevent Carrère & Denègre, LLP, New Orleans
504 582 8248
mpage@joneswalker.com
Recommended in Banking & Finance
Practice Areas: Corporate finance; international; venture capital. 'A lawyer's area of practice as stated here is one to which (s)he devotes a substantial portion of his/her professional practice and should not be considered a 'specialization' unless certified by the Louisiana Board of Legal Specialization (or similar body in any other state in which such lawyer is licensed to practice)'.
Prof. Memberships: Louisiana State Bar Association (Chairman, International Section).
Career: Partner since 1996; University of Virginia (JD, 1988; BA, with distinction, 1985), Virginia Law Review; Jefferson Scholar; Echols Scholar; one of 50 fourth year students to live on the Lawn; Omicron Delta Kappa.

PATRICK III, William
Heller, Draper, Hayden, Patrick & Horn, LLC, New Orleans 504 581 9595
Recommended in Corporate/M&A

PHARIS, Michael
Taylor, Porter, Brooks & Phillips, LLP, Baton Rouge 225 387 3221
Recommended in Employment

PHILIPS, Harry
Taylor, Porter, Brooks & Phillips, LLP, Baton Rouge 225 387 3221
Recommended in Litigation

PREIS Jr, E Fredrick
McGlinchey Stafford, New Orleans
504 596 2716
epreis@mcglinchey.com
Recommended in Employment
Practice Areas: Heads national Labor/Employment Practice; as trial lawyer and advisor serves as lead counsel

for Fortune 500 companies, trade associations and businesses throughout the United States.
Prof. Memberships: Charter member National Academy of Hospitality Industry Attorneys; Board Member Louisiana Association of Business and Industry and Jefferson and Orleans Chambers of Commerce; Board of Editors 'The Corporate Counselor' national newsletter.
Career: Co-argued 2002 case before Louisiana Supreme Court urging New Orleans attempt to adopt minimum wage be nullified - court overwhelmingly agreed.
Personal: Prior to military service, received degrees from Louisiana State University Business Administration School and Law School.

PYBURN Jr, Keith M
Fisher & Phillips LLP, New Orleans
504 522 3303
kpyburn@laborlawyers.com
Recommended in Employment
Practice Areas: Keith Pyburn is a Partner in the New Orleans office of the national law firm of Fisher & Phillips LLP, practicing exclusively in labor and employment law representing management. He has represented management in labor relations and employment law since 1975. A former Chairman of the Labor and Employment Section of the Louisiana State Bar Association and a fellow of the College of Labor and Employment Lawyers, he is a contributing editor to Employment Discrimination Law, published by the American Bar Association's Section of Labor and Employment Law. Keith received a JD from Tulane Law School in Louisiana.

REYMOND Jr, Leon
Liskow & Lewis PLC, New Orleans
504 581 7979
Recommended in Real Estate

ROBERSON, Jr, Thomas Y
Jones Walker Waechter Poitevent Carrère & Denègre, LLP, New Orleans
504 582 8382
troberson@joneswalker.com
Recommended in Banking & Finance
Practice Areas: Mr Roberson's primary focus has been in the areas of commercial and corporate finance. He represents many of the firm's publicly-held clients in connection with structuring, negotiating and documenting syndicated credit facilities, public debt offerings and project financings. Mr Roberson has worked extensively with the treasury group of one of the firm's largest clients in connection with (among other things) a $1 billion secured working capital facility and the financing of various infrastructure projects in support of an Indonesian mining operation. He has also worked on several domestic and cross-border leveraged acquisitions. Mr Roberson also has significant experience with structured financing transactions representing various firm clients in

sale/leasebacks, inventory and accounts receivable financings/securitizations and other asset monetizations. He has also worked on, and is familiar with, standard ISDA and IFEMA agreements (and related schedules) for hedging interest rate and foreign exchange risk. 'A lawyer's area of practice as stated here is one to which (s)he devotes a substantial portion of his/her professional practice and should not be considered a 'specialization' unless certified by the Louisiana Board of Legal Specialization (or similar body in any other state in which such lawyer is licensed to practice)'.
Prof. Memberships: Louisiana State Bar Association; American Bar Association.
Career: Admitted to Bar, 1988, Louisiana; joined Jones Walker in 1988, Partner since 1996.
Personal: Born Lexington, Kentucky, January 25, 1958; University of Delaware (BS, 1980); Tulane University (JD, cum laude, 1988).

ROSENBERG, Harry
Phelps Dunbar LLP, New Orleans
504 584 9219
rosenbeh@phelps.com
Recommended in Litigation
Practice Areas: Partner in the New Orleans Commercial Litigation Practice. He concentrates his practice in the areas of business torts, trial practice, civil rights, and criminal law. Prior to joining Phelps Dunbar in 1974, Mr Rosenberg served as a judicial clerk to The Honorable Jack M Gordon, Judge, US District Court, Eastern District of Louisiana. Mr Rosenberg also served as the United States Attorney for the Eastern District of Louisiana from 1990 through 1993.
Personal: Tulane University, JD, 1972; Board of Editors and editor, Tulane Law Review. Case Western Reserve University, BA, 1969.

ROSENBLUM, Carl D
Jones Walker Waechter Poitevent Carrère & Denègre, LLP, New Orleans
504 582 8296
crosenblum@joneswalker.com
Recommended in Energy
Practice Areas: Senior litigation Partner and Chair of Jones Walker's Energy Practice Group. He devotes his time primarily to the representation of entities and individuals involved in significant oil and gas disputes. He represents independent producers, major producers, pipeline companies, oilfield service companies, seismic exploration companies, oil and gas management companies, financial institutions and significant landowners. He has addressed numerous disputes concerning the rights and obligations of parties to joint operating agreements, oil and gas leases, royalty matters, exploration agreements, gas purchase contracts, drilling contracts, pipeline right-of-way agreements, farmout agreements, gas balancing agreements, seismic permitting and

exploration agreements, and the enforcement of oil and gas liens, as well as the recognition and protection of those rights when an operator files for protection under the US Bankruptcy Code. 'A lawyer's area of practice as stated here is one to which (s)he devotes a substantial portion of his/her professional practice and should not be considered a 'specialization' unless certified by the Louisiana Board of Legal Specialization (or similar body in any other state in which such lawyer is licensed to practice)'.
Prof. Memberships: Admitted to the State Bars of Louisiana and Texas; American Bar Association; Louisiana State Bar Association; Texas State Bar Association; Federal Energy Bar Association.
Career: Joined Jones Walker, 1983; Partner since 1990.
Personal: Born 1955; married, two teenage daughters; resident of New Orleans since 1983.

ROUSSEAU, Dionne M
Jones Walker Waechter Poitevent Carrère & Denègre, LLP, New Orleans
504 582 8338
drousseau@joneswalker.com
Recommended in Corporate/M&A
Practice Areas: Corporate, securities, corporate finance, mergers and acquisitions, venture capital and corporate governance matters for public and private companies. 'A lawyer's area of practice as stated here is one to which (s)he devotes a substantial portion of his/her professional practice and should not be considered a 'specialization' unless certified by the Louisiana Board of Legal Specialization (or similar body in any other state in which such lawyer is licensed to practice)'.
Career: She joined Jones Walker in 1990 and became a Partner in 1998; Investment banker with Paine Webber Capital Markets, New York, 1985-87.
Publications: 'Overview of Recent SEC and Stock Market Rules,' 2004 Burkenroad SEC Conference; 'Corporate Governance Reform,' 2003 New Orleans Does Business Right Conference; 'Corporate Goverance in the Headlines,' 2003 UNO Energy Accounting and Technology Conference.
Personal: University of Chicago (JD 1990, Order of the Coif, Law Review); Georgetown University (BA 1985, magna cum laude, Phi Beta Kappa).

ROUSSEL, James H
Phelps Dunbar LLP, New Orleans
504 584 9260
rousselj@phelps.com
Recommended in Energy
Practice Areas: Of Counsel in the firm's New Orleans office. He practices in the areas of marine insurance coverage disputes, cargo damage claims, maritime allisions and collisions, maritime commercial transactions, ship construc-

tion, salvage drilling and sales contracts, and ocean and inland chartering agreements, and ocean and inland chartering agreements, and litigating matters arising from these transactions. He also represents general liability, marine, and P&I underwriters in regard to coverage issues involving a broad range of marine, energy, general liability, excess and umbrella forms of coverage, including representation of underwriters; interest in litigation arising out of coverage disputes.

Personal: Tulane University, JD, 1964; Phi Delta Phi; Dartmouth College, AB in History, 1961.

ROUSSEL, Randy P.
Phelps Dunbar LLP, Baton Rouge
225 376 0234
rousselr@phelps.com
Recommended in Real Estate

Practice Areas: Partner in the Business Group in the Baton Rouge office. His general business practice is concentrated in the areas of real estate, banking, and commercial transactions. Has represented Wampold Companies, Waffle House, AmSouth Bank, Whitney National Bank, Gross Builders, Inc, and a variety of multifamily and commercial developers.

Personal: Louisiana State University, JD, 1984; Louisiana Law Review; Order of Coif; Beta Alpha Psi; Louisiana Bar Association Civil Law Award for the highest grade point average in Louisiana Civil Law courses. Louisiana State University, BS, 1977. Board Member for the Louisiana Land Title Association, Baton Rouge Growth Coalition and adjunct professor at Louisiana State University Law School and Southern University Law School.

SARVER, Richard E
Barrasso Usdin Kupperman Freeman & Sarver LLC, New Orleans
504 589 9700
rsarver@barrassousdin.com
Recommended in Litigation

Practice Areas: Mr Sarver specializes in defending toxic tort, environmental and product liability cases. He has served as lead trial counsel in numerous class actions and mass joinder cases involving products liability and environmental issues. Mr Sarver also teaches trial skills and serves as an adjunct faculty member of Tulane University Law School.

Career: Mr Sarver is a founding member of Barrasso Usdin Kupperman Freeman & Sarver, L.L.C. and a former trial attorney for the US Department of Justice. He has served as lead trial counsel in jury trials in eleven different states.

Personal: JD magna cum laude, University of Michigan School of Law, 1982, Order of the Coif, Michigan Law Review.

SCHMIDT, Justin B
Chaffe, McCall, Phillips, Toler & Sarpy, L.L.P., New Orleans
504 585 7289
schmidt@chaffe.com

Recommended in Real Estate

Practice Areas: Justin B Schmidt is a Partner in the law firm of Chaffe McCall, L.L.P. in New Orleans, where he practices in the areas of commercial real estate, secured transactions and corporate and business law, with a focus on land use planning and permitting. He has represented numerous lenders and developers in connection with the acquisition, development and financing of shopping centers, office buildings, condominiums, low-income housing, restaurant and hotel developments.

Prof. Memberships: Mr Schmidt is a Member of the New Orleans, Louisiana State and American Bar Associations, where he is active in the Real Proerty and Probate Section. He is also a member of the International Council of Shopping Centers.

Career: Mr Schmidt received his BBA degree from the University of Mississippi at Oxford in 1992 and his JD degree from the Louisiana State University Paul M Hebert Law Center in 1998. Between his undergraduate work and law school, Mr Schmidt worked in the area of commercial and real estate lending at Trustmark National Bank in Jackson, Mississippi and Hibernia National Bank in New Orleans, Louisiana.

Personal: Mr Schmidt serves on the Board of Directors of the YMCA of Greater New Orleans and serves on the Building Committee of the World Trade Center in New Orleans.

SCHNEIDER, Michael R
Stone Pigman Walther Wittmann L.L.C., New Orleans
504 593 0835
mschneider@stonepigman.com
Recommended in Real Estate

Practice Areas: Real estate law; finance law; environmental law; construction law. Co-chairs the firm's Real Estate Practice and has extensive experience in the area of sophisticated commercial real estate with an emphasis on the representation of developers and owners and local counsel for national lenders.

Prof. Memberships: Admitted to practice in Louisiana, 1983. Member of the American, Louisiana, and New Orleans Bar Associations, and the International Council of Shopping Centers.

Career: Joined Stone Pigman, 1984; became member, 1990. Law clerk to Honorable Walter Marcus, Louisiana Supreme Court, 1983-84.

Personal: JD (magna cum laude), Tulane University, 1983. Member of Order of the Coif and Tulane Law Review. BA, Stanford University, 1980.

SHER, Leopold
Sher Garner Cahill Richter Klein McAlister & Hilbert, LLC, New Orleans
504 299 2100
Recommended in Real Estate

SNYDER, Charles
Milling Benson Woodward LLP, New Orleans 504 569 7000
csnyder@millinglaw.com
Recommended in Corporate/M&A

Practice Areas: Mr Snyder's practice is now primarily corporate and transactional in nature, having a more than 30 year backgound of experience in litigation, estate planning, taxes and complex financings. Mr Snyder has been listed in the Best Lawyers America since 1987 and in numerous editions of Who's Who (in the World, in America and in America Law). Milling Benson Woodward, established in 1896, is a full service civil and commercial law firm with offices in New Orleans, Lafayette and Baton Rouge, Louisiana. The firm represents business entities of all kinds, as well as individuals, foundations and other non-profit institutions. Milling Benson Woodward has been a significant part of the formation and practice of Louisiana law in such fields as tax, corporate, banking, natural resources, environmental, healthcare and estate planning. Milling is the only firm in Louisiana that is a member of TAGLaw, a network of independent law firms practicing throughout the world.

SPENCER, Bob
The Kullman Firm PLC, New Orleans
504 596 4128
rfs@kullmanlaw.com
Recommended in Employment

Practice Areas: Representing employers in a wide variety of labor and employment law matters, with special emphases on affirmative action law (including the representation of clients before the US Department of Labor, Office of Federal Contract Compliance Programs), union organizing and representation elections, Wage and Hour, ADA and FMLA compliance matters, and management training and development.

Prof. Memberships: American Bar Association, Louisiana Bar Association.

Career: Associate, The Kullman Firm: 1981-87; Shareholder, The Kullman Firm: 1987-present.

Personal: AB, Duke University, 1978; JD, University of Virginia, 1981.

STEEG, Robert
The Steeg Law Firm, LLC, New Orleans
504 582 1199
Recommended in Real Estate

STUCKEY, James A
Phelps Dunbar LLP, New Orleans
504 584 9239
stuckeyj@phelps.com
Recommended in Banking & Finance

Practice Areas: Partner in the Business Group in the New Orleans office. He practices in the areas of commercial finance, real estate, banking, and leasing. His lending practice includes representing lenders in oil and gas loans, real estate and construction financings, and secured working capital loans. He advis-

es clients in negotiations of a wide variety of contracts.

Personal: Tulane University, JD, magna cum laude, 1983; editor, Tulane Law Review; Order of the Coif. Davidson College, AB, magna cum laude, 1980; Judicial clerk to the Honorable Walter Marcus, Louisiana State Supreme Court Justice, 1983-84.

SWANSON, James R
Correro Fishman Haygood Phelps Walmsley & Casteix LLP, New Orleans
504 586 5267
jswanson@cfhlaw.com
Recommended in Litigation

Practice Areas: Mr Swanson is the Head of the firm's Litigation Section. He represents clients in a broad range of business litigation matters. He regularly represents The Times-Picayune Publishing Corporation, SMG and others. Mr Swanson has recently represented The Times-Picayune and The Associated Press in access litigation arising out of the trial of former Governor Edwin Edwards; SMG, in an arbitration brought by the New Orleans Saints alleging breaches of the Saint's lease of the Superdome; Manpower, defending hundreds of millions of dollars of claims, including class action claims, arising out of the Kaiser Plant explosion; the State of Louisiana, prosecuting corporate tax claims against Tennessee Gas, Texaco and International Paper and obtaining a $26 million jury verdict against Tennessee Gas; IBM, working with New York counsel to defend it in multidistrict patent litigation; and HPI, in the successful defense of an offshore service company in a lengthy jury trial arising out of an offshore rig explosion which caused over $20 million in property damage.

Career: Mr Swanson serves as a Director of the Louisiana Freedom of Information Coalition.

Personal: Mr Swanson received his JD, magna cum laude, from Tulane Law School, where he was a member of the Order of the Coif and an associate editor of the 'Tulane Law Review'. Mr Swanson was also winner of the Tulane Moot Court Appellate Competitions in 1986 and 1987.

TALLEY, Susan G
Stone Pigman Walther Wittmann L.L.C., New Orleans 504 593 0828
stalley@stonepigman.com
Recommended in Real Estate

Practice Areas: Real estate; finance; banking.

Prof. Memberships: Admitted to practice in Louisiana, 1981. Member of the Board of Governors of the American College of Real Estate Lawyers. Supervisory Council Member of the Real Property, Probate and Trust Law section of the American Bar Association; Vice-Chair of its Publications Committee; and a member of its Committee on

Committees, Committee on Workouts, Foreclosures and Bankruptcies and Committee on Mortgage Loan Structure and Origination. Member and US Secretary of the Anglo American Real Property Institute. Founding member of New Orleans CREW, Co-Chair of the New Orleans Bar Association Real Property Committee. Member of the American College of Mortgage Attorneys, the Council of the Louisiana State Law Institute, the Louisiana Bankers Association Bank Counsel Section and the International Council of Shopping Centers.

Career: Joined Stone Pigman, 1981; became member, 1987. Member of the firm's Management Committee.

Personal: JD (summa cum laude), Tulane University, 1981. Phi Kappa Phi, Order of the Coif, and Tulane Law Review Board of Editors, 1979-81, and Business Manager, 1980-81. BS (summa cum laude), Louisiana State University, 1978.

TESSIER, Frank
Carver Darden Koretzky Tessier Finn Blossman & Areaux LLC, New Orleans
504 585 3800
Recommended in Banking & Finance

USDIN, Steven W
Barrasso Usdin Kupperman Freeman & Sarver LLC, New Orleans
504 589 9700
susdin@barrassousdin.com
Recommended in Litigation

Practice Areas: Mr Usdin has over 20 years of experience in all types of commercial litigation matters, including intellectual property, unfair trade practices, securities, antitrust, unfair competition, insurance coverage, and oil and gas. He has extensive experience in representing clients in class actions and complex litigation and has been named one of the Best Lawyers in America since 2001.

Career: Mr Usdin is a Founding Member of Barrasso Usdin Kupperman Freeman & Sarver, L.L.C.

Personal: JD, University of Virginia School of Law, 1980; Clerk, Honorable Adrian G Duplantier, United States District Court, Eastern District of Louisiana.

VANCE, R Patrick
Jones Walker Waechter Poitevent Carrère & Denègre, LLP, New Orleans
504 582 8194
pvance@joneswalker.com
Recommended in Corporate/M&A, Litigation

Practice Areas: Business and commercial litigation, bankruptcy, restructuring and creditors-debtors rights, and appellate litigation. As a trial lawyer he has handled over three hundred plus commercial disputes in a wide variety of practice areas: antitrust, RICO, copyright infringement, Lanham Act, securities litigation, defense of class actions,

foreclosures, fraud, lender liability, banking litigation, ERISA, dealer-distributor disputes, successions, legal malpractice, expropriation, contract interpretation, partnership, utility regulation, tax, and general commercial disputes. He has over 60 reported decisions. He regularly represents secured and unsecured creditors in all types of business bankruptcy cases. He has been retained by scores of banks, telecommunication companies, international manufacturers, utilities, healthcare providers, maritime, oil and gas related industries, the music industry, casinos and insurance companies. 'A lawyer's area of practice as stated here is one to which (s)he devotes a substantial portion of his/her professional practice and should not be considered a 'specialization' unless certified by the Louisiana Board of Legal Specialization (or similar body in any other state in which such lawyer is licensed to practice)'.

Prof. Memberships: Officer and Conferee of the National Bankruptcy Conference; Fellow of the American Law Institute and American College of Bankruptcy; Past Chairman of the following: Louisiana Bankers Association, Bank Counsel Committee; Bankruptcy Litigation Subcommittee of the ABA; Louisiana State Bar Association CLE Planning Committee; Consumer Law, Bankruptcy Law and Lender Liability Law Section of the Louisiana State Bar Association.

Career: Louisiana State University (BA, with highest Honors, 1970; JD 1975); Phi Kappa Phi; Phi Beta Kappa Faculty Group Award; Member, Louisiana Law Review, 1973-75; admitted to Bar, 1975, Louisiana; Partner of firm since 1980; Section Head, Commercial Litigation (1986-91; 2003-); Chair, Executive Committee (1994-95; 1999-2000; 2004-).

Publications: Mr Vance has written 50-plus articles or seminar outlines on topics such as commercial litigation, lender liability and bankruptcy.

Personal: Born Birmingham, Alabama, February 12, 1948.

WALLACE, Brian D
Phelps Dunbar LLP, New Orleans
504 584 9204
wallaceb@phelps.com
Recommended in Gaming & Licensing

Practice Areas: Partner in the New Orleans office, concentrating on ship and gaming financing and litigation. His practice in the area of gaming law includes representing casino owners, operators, and lenders in public and private financial transactions, licensing, litigation and counseling. His practice in the area of ship financing includes, representing vessel owners, lenders, and shipyards in ship construction, sales, financing, lien enforcement, charters and related litigation.

Personal: Tulane University, New

Orleans, Louisiana, LLM in Admiralty, with distinction, 1985; Dalhousie University, Halifax, Nova Scotia, LLB, 1984; Saint Mary's University, Halifax, Nova Scotia, BS magna cum laude, 1980.

WALMSLEY, Robert
Correro Fishman Haygood Phelps Walmsley & Casteix LLP, New Orleans
504 586 5252
Recommended in Corporate/M&A

WERNER, John
Correro Fishman Haygood Phelps Walmsley & Casteix LLP, New Orleans
504 586 5252
jwerner@cfhlaw.com
Recommended in Corporate/M&A

WEST, Paul
McGlinchey Stafford, New Orleans
225 382 3636
pwest@mcglinchey.com
Recommended in Gaming & Licensing

Practice Areas: Business litigation, class action defense, corporate, gaming.

Prof. Memberships: American Bar Association, Baton Rouge Bar Association, International Association of Gaming Attorneys, Louisiana Bar Foundation, Louisiana State Bar Association.

Career: Experienced commercial litigator and one of the most recognized casino gaming attorneys in the industry; matters include riverboat and land-based casinos; racinos and video poker; represents casino owners, operators and financiers; handles negotiaions between suppliers, municipalities and gaming companies; major commercial trials (bench and bar) have involved finance companies, Fortune 500 companies, landowners, developers and growing businesses; AV rated; annually listed in 'Best Lawyers in America' by Woodward White.

WHITTAKER, Scott T
Stone Pigman Walther Wittmann L.L.C., New Orleans 504 593 0836
swhittaker@stonepigman.com
Recommended in Corporate/M&A

Practice Areas: Corporate; mergers and acquisitions; securities laws; real estate. Chair of the firm's Business Section.

Prof. Memberships: Admitted to practice in Louisiana, 1984. Member of the Louisiana State Bar Association, Section on Corporate and Business Law, and served as Chairman of the governing council of the Section in 1991-92. Chairman of the Louisiana Supreme Court Committee on Bar Admissions. From 1991 through 2004, served as Director of Testing and Examiner for the subjects of Business Entities and Negotiable Instruments on the Louisiana Supreme Court Committee on Bar Admissions. An active member of the Negotiated Acquisitions Committee of the American Bar Association. Chairman of the Subcommittee on M&A Jurisprudence, and member of the Editorial Working Group of the Task Force on the Model

Stock Purchase Agreement. Frequent lecturer and author in the area of business mergers and acquisitions.

Career: Joined Stone Pigman in 1984; became member in 1990.

Personal: JD (magna cum laude), Tulane University. Order of the Coif and Tulane Law Review Board of Editors. BA (cum laude), Tulane University, 1982.

WILLENZIK, David S
McGlinchey Stafford, New Orleans
504 596 2708
dwillenzik@mcglinchey.com
Recommended in Banking & Finance

Practice Areas: Heads Business Law Practice and focuses on banking, commercial finance, asset based lending, equipment leasing, consumer finance, and UCC litigation, defense of lender liability, consumer credit and class action claims. Clients include banks, finance companies, mortgage bankers, manufacturers, equipment lessors, insurers, venture capital companies and project finance lenders. Negotiates commercial loans, real estate, aircraft, and vessels, project finance, equipment leases, acquisition financings and letters of credit. Drafter of multistate sales, commercial and consumer finance and equipment lease documents. Initiator and primary drafter of numerous laws that apply to banking, commercial finance and consumer credit transactions. Lead effort to enact UCC Article 9 in Louisiana.

Prof. Memberships: ABA Business Law Section, Commercial Financial Services, Consumer Financial Services, Banking Law, and UCC Committees; American College of Commercial Finance Lawyers (co-founder and past President); American College of Consumer Financial Services Attorneys; American College of Mortgage Attorneys; American Law Institute; Consumer Banker's Association Lawyers Committee (past Chair); Association of Commercial Finance Attorneys (past Director); Louisiana State Law Institute UCC Committee; Louisiana Bankers Association Bank Counsel Section (past Chair); International Lawyers Network (Director).

Publications: West, 'Louisiana Secured Transactions'.

Personal: LSU Law School Board of Trustees.

WILLIS, Sterling Scott
Correro Fishman Haygood Phelps Walmsley & Casteix LLP, New Orleans
504 586 5264
swillis@cfhlaw.com
Recommended in Banking & Finance

Practice Areas: Mr Willis heads the Real Estate and Commercial Finance Groups. He practices primarily in the areas of commercial transactions, secured lending, oil and gas and commercial real estate. Mr Willis has counseled business clients in a variety of matters, including a $3 billion bank note securitization; a $150 million secured oil and gas revolving credit facility; numerous helicopter financings; the acquisition, merger and sale of numerous private and public companies; a $400 million high yield bond offering; numerous bank mergers and branch transactions; and the acquisition of the Canal Place mixed-use development in New Orleans.

Career: Mr Willis is a Member of the New Orleans, Louisiana State, and American Bar Associations. He is the Past Chairman of the ABA Real Property, Probate and Trust Law Section Committee on Legal Opinions. Mr Willis was a Member of the drafting group for the ABA/ACREL Real Estate Opinion Letter Guidelines 38 REAL. PROP. PROB. & TR. J. 241 (2003). Mr Willis is a Member of the Louisiana Bankers Association Bank Counsel Committee and a Member of the Board of Directors of the New Orleans Bureau of Governmental Research.

Publications: Mr Willis is the author of 'Article 9 Remedies' in 'West's Louisiana Statutes Annotated Code of Civil Procedure'.

Personal: Mr Willis graduated from Louisiana State University in 1980 and received his JD degree from LSU in 1983, where he was a member the Order of the Coif, and also served as an associate editor of the 'Louisiana Law Review'.

WITTMANN, Phillip A
Stone Pigman Walther Wittmann L.L.C., New Orleans 504 593 0804
pwittmann@stonepigman.com
Recommended in Litigation

Practice Areas: Commercial litigation; class actions and complex litigation; products liability; antitrust; toxic tort litigation.

Prof. Memberships: Admitted to practice in Louisiana, 1961. Immediate Past President of the New Orleans Bar Association. Served as a Member of the Civil Rules Advisory Committee of the Judicial Conference of the United States and as a Member of the House of Delegates of the American Bar Association. Chaired the Louisiana State Board of Legal Specialization and is a Member of the House of Delegates, the Continuing Legal Education Committee and the Antitrust Section of the Louisiana State Bar Association. Fellow of the American College of Trial Lawyers, the American Academy of Appellate Lawyers and the International Society of Barristers. 2000 recipient of the G Duffield Smith Outstanding Publication Award from the Defense Research Institute.

Career: Joined Stone Pigman, 1961; became member, 1963. Chair of the firm's Management Committee.

Personal: LLB, Tulane University School of Law, 1961. Phi Beta Kappa, Order of the Coif, Omicron Delta Kappa and Tulane Law Review Board of Editors. BA, Tulane University, 1956.

WOGAN, John
Liskow & Lewis PLC, New Orleans
504 581 7979
Recommended in Banking & Finance

WOLF, Alan C
Phelps Dunbar LLP, New Orleans
504 584 9316
wolfa@phelps.com
Recommended in Energy

Practice Areas: Partner in the Business Group in the New Orleans office. He practices in the areas of administrative law, electric utilities, gas utilities, and energy law, and directs the firm's public utilities and electric power practice. Prior to joining Phelps Dunbar, Mr Wolf was Senior Trial Attorney at the Office of General Counsel - Electric Rates Section, Federal Energy Regulatory Commission, and Vice-President and General Counsel, Mid Louisiana Gas Company, New Orleans, Louisiana. He has over 25 years experience in gas and electric utility matters and is a former Chair of the Electric Power Committee of the American Bar Association's Section on Natural Resources, Energy and Environmental Law and a former Chairman of the Natural Gas Rates Committee of the Federal Energy Bar Association. Mr Wolf is also a member of the Legal Committee of the Edison Electric Institute.

Personal: University of Alabama, JD, 1971; National Moot Court Team. Birmingham-Southern College, AB, 1968.

WOLFE, Richard
Jones Walker Waechter Poitevent Carrère & Denègre, LLP, New Orleans
504 582 8182
rwolfe@joneswalker.com
Recommended in Corporate/M&A

Practice Areas: Partner concentrating in corporate and securities law, particularly mergers and acquisitions, with over 35 years experience in corporate matters, including representing issuers and underwriters in initial and subsequent public equity offerings and advising public and private companies in matters involving tender offers, proxy contests, venture capital transactions, spinoffs, private offerings of securities, special litigation committees in derivative stockholder suits, foreign joint ventures, and related matters. 'A lawyer's area of practice as stated here is one to which (s)he devotes a substantial portion of his/her professional practice and should not be considered a 'specialization' unless certified by the Louisiana Board of Legal Specialization (or similar body in any other state in which such lawyer is licensed to practice)'.

Career: Joined Monroe & Lemann, New Orleans, in 1963, Partner in 1968, headed Corporate Department 1974-96; joined Jones, Walker, Waechter, Poitevent, Carrere & Denegre, LLP as Partner, 1997.

Personal: Princeton University (AB, magna cum laude, 1959); Harvard University (JD 1962); Tulane University (M Civ L 1965); Phi Beta Kappa.

ADAMS AND REESE LLP

THE FIRM

Managing Partner: Charles P Adams, Jr
Number of partners in US offices: 168
Number of other lawyers in US offices: 94

FIRM OVERVIEW: Adams and Reese is a fast-growing multi-disciplinary firm with over 260 attorneys in seven offices throughout the South Central United States and the District of Columbia. By offering legal services on a regional basis, this AMLAW 200 firm provides its clients with localized control over their legal matters, and access for clients in multiple markets where they have interests. The firm prides itself on its dedication and reputation for providing superior client service. The firm's primary commitment is to provide clients with the highest quality legal service in the most prompt, cost effective and efficient manner possible. Adams and Reese strives to foster a working environment of inclusion, understanding, respect and opportunity for all. Enriched by a diversity of backgrounds and experiences within the firm, Adams and Reese attorneys and staff are committed to helping improve the communities where they live and work. The firm dedicates time, talent and financial resources to many community outreach projects, as well as to civic and professional organizations. In recognition of these efforts, the firm was the first law firm recipient of the Excellence in Corporate Volunteerism Award presented by the Points of Light Foundation.

MAIN AREAS OF PRACTICE

Litigation: Both of the firm's founding partners were widely respected litigators involved in some of the most momentous court decisions of their time. As the firm grew, Adams and Reese earned a national reputation for outstanding trial work. Adams and Reese represents its clients before all courts, governmental regulatory bodies, tribunals, as well as alternate dispute resolution, including arbitration and mediation. The firm is experienced in an ever-increasing variety of litigation matters ranging from the simplest forms of court action, to multidistrict litigation, complex/class action claims, and mass tort litigation. Adams and Reese litigators represent clients in the following areas: commercial disputes; banking and financial matters; professional liability/D&O; antitrust and unfair competition; products liability; asbestos; pharmaceuticals; insurance; pesticides; energy and environmental; maritime; healthcare; transportation; real estate and construction; technology and telecommunications; state and local taxation; class action; appellate; arbitration and alternate dispute resolution.

Corporate/Transactions: Adams and Reese provides advice to privately and publicly held business organizations including corporations, general partnerships, limited partnerships, limited liability companies, limited liability partnerships and proprietorships. The firm counsels clients in all phases of business development and continuation, such as business organization, choice of entity, choice of jurisdiction, organizational documentation, state and federal filings, general securities, and tax issues bearing upon these types of entities. The firm also advises clients on day-to-day operations, from meetings of equity holders and management, to loans and credit facilities, to compensation and benefits. Adams and Reese clients also rely on the firm's advice on issues pertaining to directors' liability, privilege, and consulting agreements, as well as all types of commercial and financial transactions and negotiations, and the drafting and execution of all necessary documentation. The firm's corporate practice areas include: banking and finance; tax; general corporate; securities; mergers and acquisitions; bankruptcy and commercial restructuring; public finance; economic development; forestry; and real estate.

Special Business Services: Adams and Reese attorneys partner with their clients to develop and execute creative and insightful strategies which will assist in accomplishing the goals of the organization. The firm's Governmental Relations Team provides detailed representation in the public sec-

tor by integrating clients' federal, state and local business goals and participating in the legislative and executive branch processes. The team crafts and implements clear strategies and employs a broad range of public policy tools to achieve its clients objectives. On the labor and employment front, Adams and Reese clients turn to the firm to tailor policies and procedures specific to their organization. The firm represents management in all areas of employment and traditional labor law, including, employee benefits and compensation; litigation; administrative proceedings; contract compliance; and labor/management relations. Adams and Reese attorneys also represent clients in protecting their assets. The firm's Intellectual Property Team is experienced in handling all of the following: copyrights; commercial litigation; contractual negotiation, development and litigation; computer and software protection; software technology; communications law; entertainment; internet and cyberspace issues; patents; international protection; trademarks; and trade secrets.

OFFICE

LOUISIANA
One Shell Square, 701 Poydras Street, Suite 4500,
New Orleans, LA 70139
Tel: 504 581 3234   **Fax:** 504 566 0210
Website: www.adamsandreese.com
Email: info@arlaw.com

ALABAMA
Concord Center 2100 Third Avenue North, Suite 1100,
Birmingham, AL 35203
Tel: 205 250 5000   **Fax:** 205 2505034

One St. Louis Street, Suite 4500 (36602), PO Box 1348,
Mobile, AL 36633
Tel: 251 433 3234   **Fax:** 251 4387733

DISTRICT OF COLUMBIA
Market Square North, 401 9th Street, NW, Suite 610 South,
Washington, DC 20004
Tel: 202 737 3234   **Fax:** 202 737 0264

LOUISIANA
450 Laurel Street, Suite 1900, **Baton Rouge,** LA 70801
Tel: 225 336 5200   **Fax:** 225 336 5220

MISSISSIPPI
111 East Capitol Street, Suite 350 (39201), PO Box 24297,
Jackson, MS 39225
Tel: 601 353 3234   **Fax:** 601 355 9708

TEXAS
One Houston Center, 1221 McKinney, Suite 4400,
Houston, TX 77010
Tel: 713 652 5151   **Fax:** 713 652 5152

CONTACTS

Senior Partner in Charge, New Orleans ....Mark C Surprenant
Partner in Charge, New Orleans .... Edwin C Laizer
Partner in Charge, Washington, DC ....B Jeffrey Brooks
Partner in Charge, Houston ....F Lee Butler
Partner in Charge, Mobile .... W David Johnson
Partner in Charge, Birmingham .... Joe A Joseph
Partner in Charge, Jackson .... A Jerry Sheldon
Partner in Charge, Baton Rouge .... B Troy Villa

BARRASSO USDIN KUPPERMAN FREEMAN & SARVER, L.L.C.

THE FIRM

Number of members: 7
Number of other lawyers: 9

Managing Member: Steven W Usdin
Members: Judy Y Barrasso, Stephen H Kupperman, George C Freeman III, Richard E Sarver, H Minor Pipes, III, Celeste Coco-Ewing.

AREAS OF PRACTICE:
Litigation 100%

FIRM OVERVIEW: Recently founded by experienced litigators departing from an established firm, Barrasso Usdin concentrates on litigating complex civil cases throughout the Gulf South Region. The firm provides the high quality of representation expected from large firms together with responsive and efficient services provided by top tier smaller firms. The firm's lawyers are well equipped to handle complex civil cases because they always have excelled. More than 75 percent served as members of law reviews. More than half clerked for federal judges, both at the appellate and district levels.

MAIN AREAS OF PRACTICE

Class Actions/Complex Litigation: The firm regularly represents clients in a wide variety of class actions and other types of complex litigation, including mass tort cases and multidistrict litigation.
Commercial Litigation: Their attorneys have prosecuted and defended every type of commercial dispute.
Construction Litigation: Their attorneys represent general contractors, subcontractors, owners and architects in large and small disputes.
Environmental/Product Liability: The firm has successfully represented clients in environmental and product liability disputes in a myriad of forums.
Insurance Coverage & Bad Faith: Their attorneys regularly represent numerous insurers in complex declaratory judgment actions, bad faith litigation, excess judgment cases and institutional bad faith claims.
Securities Litigation & Enforcement: Their lawyers are active in every major area of securities litigation and enforcement and represent clients in federal and state courts as well as before regulatory organizations throughout the Gulf South.

CLIENTS: The firm's clients include - 3M Company, Allstate Insurance Company, Blanchard & Company, Inc., Chubb and Son, Clear Channel Broadcasting, Inc., CNA Insurance, Laitram Corporation, Liberty Mutual Insurance Corporation, Lincoln Electric Company, Morgan Keegan & Company, Inc., Smith Barney, Inc. and UBS Financial Services.

HEAD OFFICE

LOUISIANA
909 Poydras Street, Suite 1800 **New Orleans**, LA 70112
Tel: 504 589 9700   **Fax:** 504 589 9701
Website: www.barrassousdin.com

CONTACTS

Class Actions	Stephen H Kupperman
Commercial Litigation	Steven W Usdin
Construction	H Minor Pipes,III
Environmental/Product Liability	Richard E Sarver
Insurance Coverage & Bad Faith	Judy Y Barrasso
Securities Litigation/Enforcement	George C Freeman, III

BARRASSO · USDIN · KUPPERMAN
FREEMAN & SARVER, L.L.C.
- COUNSELLORS AT LAW -

CHAFFE McCALL L.L.P.

THE FIRM

Managing Partner: Corinne A Morrison

Number of members: 28
Number of other lawyers: 36

FIRM OVERVIEW: More than 64 attorneys strong, Chaffe McCall is a progressive law firm headquartered in New Orleans. Chaffe McCall has always provided high quality representation in an efficient client focused manner. Chaffe McCall's record of success in landmark litigation, as well as its political and civic endeavors, sets it apart as the exceptional New Orleans law firm a position the firm has continually earned since 1826.

MAIN AREAS OF PRACTICE

Real Estate: Chaffe McCall's Real Estate Section represents clients in a full array of real estate transactions throughout the Gulf South, including acquisitions and sales, construction and permanent financing, joint ventures and leasing transactions, as well as development, construction and real estate management, for clients such as financial institutions, investors, developers and corporations. Chaffe McCall also represents these clients in commercial real estate workouts and the enforcement of rights and remedies in foreclosure, eviction and bankruptcy and other real estate related litigation.

Business & Taxation: Chaffe McCall's Business and Taxation Section provides advice and representation in traditional areas including business formation, mergers, dispositions, stock and asset acquisitions, corporate reorganizations, dissolutions, federal and state regulations, bank governance, corporate management, franchising, entertainment law, estate planning and administration, wills, trusts, and all areas of federal, state, and local tax matters and representation in federal, state and local governmental relations, including zoning and expropriation matters and federal, state, and local constitutional and charter issues.

Labor & Employment: Chaffe McCall's Labor and Employment Law Section is a recognized leader in the field and represent clients in all aspects of employment relations law. The attorneys appear before not only state and federal courts but also before labor arbitrators and federal boards and agencies.

Commercial Litigation: Chaffe McCall's Commercial Litigation Section includes client representation in cases that arise from anti-trust, civil RICO, securities fraud, patent and trademark infringement, intellectual property disputes, unfair trade practices, dealer terminations, lender liability, professional liability, bankruptcy, mergers and acquisitions, minority shareholder rights, lease disputes, secured transactions, real-estate, fidelity and surety bonds, foreclosure and collections, tortious interference, and contract breach.

Litigation: Chaffe McCall's Litigation Section represents clients in personal injury and commercial litigation from one-plaintiff casualty cases to mass torts and class actions, representing national retailers, insurers, railroads, petrochemical companies, businesses, and individuals. A significant part of the practice is products liability litigation which includes the defense of products manufacturers.

International: Chaffe McCall's practice is international as well as national and has assisted domestic corporations in conducting business transactions abroad, and foreign corporations and law firms with business dealings in the United States.

Health Law: Chaffe McCall's Health Law Section has been involved in nearly every aspect of this technical and heavily regulated field of law.

Admiralty: Chaffe McCall's Admiralty Section has served the international and domestic shipping communities since the 1820s. Chaffe McCall attorneys represent US clients in other countries, and foreign interests in the US with a staff that is multicultural and multilingual.

Appellate: Chaffe McCall's appellate section represents clients at all levels of Louisiana and Federal appellate courts, including the United States Supreme Court. The section's attorneys work closely with fellow litigators within the firm, and co-draft appellate briefs and writ applications with other lawyers and firms who have tried cases independently.

CLIENTS: Chaffe McCall's representative client list includes major financial institutions, developers, public companies, life insurance companies, tenants, transportation and property management companies, REITS, major pharmaceutical and medical manufacturers and tobacco companies.

HEAD OFFICE

LOUISIANA
2300 Energy Centre, 1100 Poydras Street,
New Orleans, LA 70163-2300
Tel: 504 585 7000   **Fax:** 504 585 7075
Website: www.chaffe.com

BRANCH OFFICE

LOUISIANA
202 Two United Plaza, 8550 United Plaza Blvd,
Baton Rouge LA 70809
Tel: 225 922 4300   **Fax:** 225 922 4304

CORRERO FISHMAN HAYGOOD PHELPS WALMSLEY & CASTEIX, L.L.P.

THE FIRM

Number of partners: 7
Number of other lawyers: 8

FIRM OVERVIEW: Correro Fishman Haygood Phelps Walmsley & Casteix, L.L.P., was founded in the mid-1990's by the leading business and litigation lawyers from three of the largest law firms in Louisiana. Its corporate lawyers have been repeatedly recognized in national and regional publications as among the best. It regularly represents public and private companies in a variety of corporate and securities matters. It also has an extensive general business law practice that focuses on real estate, commercial transactions, commercial finance, banking, bank regulation and general contractual matters. The firm has a higher percentage of its New Orleans lawyers listed in a leading American publication of 'best lawyers' than any other firm. Four of the firm's partners are former Chairman of the Corporate and Business Law Section of the Louisiana State Bar Association. One partner was Chair of the ABA Business Law Section's Committee on Corporate Laws, and another was Chair of the ABA Real Property Section's Committee on Legal Opinions. Two partners have served, and one currently serves, on the Planning Committee of the Tulane Corporate Law Institute. One partner teaches corporate finance at Louisiana State University's Law School and securities registration at Tulane University's Law School. Another partner teaches a corporation and securities law course at Tulane University's Law School. The firm's litigators have handled some of the most challenging and interesting business litigation in their region, including representing SMG, the world's largest facilities manager, in a challenge by the New Orleans Saints of their lease of the Louisiana Superdome; IBM, in multi-district patent litigation; Manpower Inc., in the defense of class action claims arising out of the Kaiser plant explosion; *The Times-Picayune* and The Associated Press, in numerous First Amendment cases including access issues arising out of the trial of former Louisiana Governor Edwin Edwards; and the State of Louisiana, in actions to collect tens of millions of dollars of disputed taxes.

MAIN AREAS OF PRACTICE

Corporate, Securities & Corporate Finance: The firm regularly represents public and private companies in corporate and securities matters, such as public and private offerings, mergers and acquisitions, proxy contests, periodic reporting, corporate governance and general SEC compliance.

Banking: The firm is a leader among law firms representing financial institutions in Louisiana. Three partners have served on the Bank Counsel Committee of the Louisiana Bankers Association. For two years in a row the firm was ranked no. 1 in the Southwest by The Merger Strategy Report and Shushunoff Information Services in the handling of legal work associated with acquisitions of financial institutions. The firm's lawyers have been involved in at least 50 of these transactions, more by far than any other group of lawyers in the state, including the four largest bank mergers in Louisiana. The firm also routinely counsels clients regarding regulatory compliance and reorganisations, and has handled branch purchases and sales, commercial financing transactions, S-corp reorganizations, oil and gas financings, secured transactions and structured financings. Its banking clients include AmSouth Bank, Business Bank of Baton Rouge, Coastal Commerce Bank, First Bank & Trust, First Community Bank, First Guaranty Bank, Gulf Coast Bank, Liberty Bank, MidSouth Bank, Omni Bank, People's Bank of Louisiana, Resource Bank and Whitney National Bank.

Mergers & Acquisitions: The firm's corporate lawyers handle mergers and acquisitions of private as well as public companies involving both negotiated and unsolicited acquisitions, going-private transactions and acquisitions of minority interests. Lawyers in the firm have been involved in some of the largest M&A transactions in Louisiana as well as numerous others, both large and small.

Real Estate: The firm handles all aspects of commercial real estate transactions, including commercial and industrial leasing, acquisitions, financings, condominium conversions, commercial developments, oil and gas tranfers and encumbrances, timber developments and large tract opportunities. It is also experienced in transactions involving historic and low-income housing tax credits and public and private issue development bonds. Lawyers in the firm routinely advise clients on all aspects of real estate leasing, and often represent landlords and tenants in lease negotiations, including representing the landlord in major league sports leases with the NFL New Orleans Saints and the NBA New Orleans Hornets.

Litigation: The firm's litigators regularly represent The Times-Picayune Publishing Corporation in libel, defamation and invasion of privacy cases and public record and access disputes, as well as The Associated Press and Capital City Press in various access disputes. They also represent defendants in class action litigation, including mass tort and securities litigation; clients in contract disputes of various kinds, including options, purchase agreements and leases; clients in products liability and tort actions in federal and state courts throughout Louisiana and elsewhere relating to the oil industry and the various large industrial facilities located in this region; plaintiffs and defendants in securities litigation and arbitration, including broker-dealer disputes and public company disclosure; clients involved in arbitrated disputes, including proceedings administered by the American Arbitration Association, National Association of Securities Dealers and the New York Stock Exchange; and the State of Louisiana in corporate income and franchise tax matters, including obtaining a $26 million jury verdict awarding taxes, interest and penalties that is believed to be the largest jury award of its kind in Louisiana history.

Other: The firm has extensive experience in estate planning and the acquisition, sale and financing of motion picture tax credits.

CLIENTS: Some clients that have entrusted legal matters to the firm are: Amedisys, Inc., AmSouth Bank, ASCO plc, The Associated Press, Autodesk, Inc., Biloxi Marsh Lands Corporation, Blue Cross of Louisiana, Capital City Press, L.L.C., Carbo Chlorination Technologies, L.L.C., Chaffe & Associates, Inc., Enterprise Products Operating, L.P., FBT Investments, Inc., First Bank and Trust, First Guaranty Bank, Great Lakes Chemical Corporation, Gulf Coast Bank, Hibernia Southcoast Capital, Inc., High Pressure Integrity, Inc., Hirsch Investment Management, L.L.C., International Business Machines Corporation, Jefferson Capital Management, L.L.C., Kinder Morgan Energy Partners, Ltd., Laitram, L.L.C., Liberty Bank, Louisiana Companies, Mac-Re, LLC, MidSouth Bancorp. Inc., New Orleans Metropolitan Convention and Visitors Bureau, Inc., Offshore Logistics, Inc., Pennington Medical Foundation, Petrocom LLC, Resource Bankshares, Inc., Robinson Lumber Company, Inc., Sanderson Farms, Inc., SMG, Stewart Enterprises, Inc., The Times-Picayune Publishing Corporation, T.L. James & Company, Inc., Tulane University, Turbo Squid, Inc., US Unwired Inc., Waters Parkerson & Co., Inc., Whitney National Bank and Wyndham International, Inc.

HEAD OFFICE

LOUISIANA
201 St Charles Avenue, 46th Floor, **New Orleans,** LA 70170-4600
Tel: 504 586 5252   **Fax:** 504 586 5250
Website: www.cfhlaw.com

JONES WALKER WAECHTER POITEVENT CARRÈRE & DENÈGRE, LLP

THE FIRM

Management by Executive Committee
Number of partners: 109
Number of other lawyers: 105

Website: www.joneswalker.com
Email: info@joneswalker.com

FIRM OVERVIEW: Jones Walker is building partnerships and relationships. The firm is one of the most distinguished law firms in the Gulf South with nearly three dozen practice areas. Over 200 attorneys are located in Baton Rouge, Houston, Lafayette, Miami, New Orleans, and Washington, DC. Businesses routinely call on Jones Walker to handle matters of local, regional, national and international interest. The firm's continued and considered growth enables it to better serve the needs of clients, while maintaining its mission of rendering the highest standards of legal service. By understanding its clients' business and building strong, personal relationships with them, Jones Walker creates a working partnership that is concentrated on getting the best results in the most efficient manner.
Client Services: Corporate America, money center financial institutions, worldwide insurers, and small to mid-size businesses rely on the firm's creative and innovative delivery of legal services and a personalized client service approach. Jones Walker strikes a balance between the traditional one-on-one relationship of attorney and client and the demands of today's increasingly complex legal problems that often require the attention of a team of attorneys.
The Attorneys: Jones Walker attorneys are licensed to practice in 14 states, the District of Columbia, the Republic of Colombia, and the United Mexican States. The firm's attorneys are regularly published in legal, commercial, and industry journals. They are featured as speakers for professional, trade and business seminars, as well as instructing law school courses. Jones Walker attorneys are committed to improving their communities by dedicating time, talent and financial resources to many community, civic and professional organizations.

MAIN AREAS OF PRACTICE: Admiralty and maritime; antitrust and trade regulation; appellate litigation; aviation; banking; bankruptcy, restructuring and creditors-debtors rights; business and commercial litigation; class action defense; commercial lending and finance; construction; corporate and securities; emerging business; employee benefits, ERISA and executive compensation; energy; environmental and toxic torts; ERISA, life, health and disability insurance litigation; gaming; government relations; healthcare; intellectual property; international; international financial services; labor relations and employment; mergers and acquisitions; products liability; professional liability; project development and finance; public finance; real estate: land use, development and finance; tax (international, federal, state and local); telecommunications and utilities; trusts, estates and personal planning; venture capital and emerging companies; white collar crime and corporate compliance.

CLIENTS: Banking and finance; communications and technology; energy and mining; gaming; healthcare; maritime; media/advertising; manufacturing/industrial; public sector; real estate; transportation; wholesale/retail/service industries.

OFFICES

LOUISIANA
201 St Charles Avenue, **New Orleans,** LA 70170-5100
Tel: 504 582 8000   **Fax:** 504 582 8583

8555 United Plaza Boulevard, **Baton Rouge,** LA 70809-7000
Tel: 225 248 2000   **Fax:** 225 248 2010

500 Dover Boulevard, Suite 120, **Lafayette,** LA 70503-5269
Tel: 337 406 5610   **Fax:** 337 406 5620

DISTRICT OF COLUMBIA
499 South Capitol Street SW, Suite 600, **Washington,** DC 20003-4013
Tel: 202 203 1000   **Fax:** 202 203 0000

FLORIDA
601 Brickell Key Drive, Suite 500, **Miami,** FL 33131
Tel: 305 679 5700   **Fax:** 305 679 5710

TEXAS
10001 Woodloch Forest Drive, Suite 350, The Woodlands,
Houston, TX 77380
Tel: 281 296 4400   **Fax:** 281 296 4404

CONTACTS

Admiralty & Maritime	Glenn G Goodier
Corporate & Securities	Curtis R Hearn
Environmental & Toxic Tort	Michael A Chernekoff
Estates & Tax	Rudolph R Ramelli
General Business & Energy	William H Hines
Government Relations	R Christian Johnsen
Healthcare	Curtis R Hearn
	Joseph J Lowenthal Jr
Intellectual Property	Thomas K Potter III
International	Thomas F Morante
Labor Relations & Employment	H Mark Adams
Litigation	R Patrick Vance

INTERNATIONAL WORK: The firm's international attorneys have significant experience in foreign investment, corporate, commercial, financial, tax, and administrative laws and regulations relevant to global operations. Jones Walker represents clients in all forms of international transactions, including and in connection with: joint ventures; international capital markets (including issuers and underwriters on debt and equity offerings); project finance (including developers, borrowers, lenders and the World Bank); mergers and acquisitions; real estate; energy; maritime; telecommunications; international tax, tax compliance and planning; intellectual property; healthcare; antitrust and unfair trade practices; export controls; government regulation; environmental; labor and employment; and arbitration and dispute resolution. The firm has handled transactions in some 30 countries in Latin America, Europe, Asia, and Africa.

THE KULLMAN FIRM, PLC

THE FIRM

Chairman: Howard S Linzy
President: Ernest R Malone, Jr

Website: www.kullmanlaw.com

FIRM OVERVIEW: Since 1946 The Kullman Firm has represented management exclusively in the practice of labor, employment, employee benefits and related matters. From its offices in Louisiana, Alabama, and Mississippi, it counsels and represents clients throughout the US in almost every industry. The Kullman Firm attorneys practice extensively before the National Labor Relations Board (NLRB), state civil rights agencies; the Equal Employment Opportunity Commission (EEOC); OSHA; and they litigate employment related claims of all types in state and federal courts; advise clients on long- and short-term labor strategies and employment objectives; develop personnel policies and procedures; negotiate and interpret collective bargaining agreements; handle arbitration proceedings; draft affirmative action plans; and handle all forms of labor and employment litigation, including pension and benefit plan litigation. The Kullman Firm represents companies of every size ranging from large Fortune 500 to medium and small privately held companies in a wide range of industries. Its attorneys are recognized leaders in the practice of labor and employment law. The Kullman Firm prides itself on its practical approach to solving workplace problems. The firm recognizes that clients do not want to expend substantial resources to find out what they cannot do, but instead want to know how their employment objective can be lawfully achieved with minimum risk.

MAIN AREAS OF PRACTICE: The Kullman Firm strongly encourages management to reduce the risks of senseless liability and to strengthen its ability to have its decisions validated by pro-active counseling and training of all levels of management, but especially line management. The numerous federal and state labor and employment protection laws have resulted in a variety of legal actions by which employees attack management decisions. Also, union organizational drives and other labor disputes continue to attempt to disrupt or interfere with managerial initiatives and accomplishments. The Kullman Firm defends and advances management's interests in court or before agencies in a wide variety of actions, including: employment discrimination claims; retaliation and whistleblower actions; sex and other harassment cases; reasonable accommodation and other ADA matters; FMLA compliance; employment agreements; restrictive covenants; affirmative action reviews and complaints; Immigration Reform Act (IRCA) compliance; employment torts; FLSA wage and overtime actions; unfair labor practices matters before the NLRB and Section 301 actions in Court; other union contract actions; labor arbitration; and employment dispute mediations and arbitrations. Kullman Firm attorneys regularly represent management in OFCCP investigations and the drafting of affirmative action plans (AAPs) as well as advise concerning compliance issues. In today's highly competitive and electronic environment many companies find it necessary to protect their investment in human and other capital with the use of any number of tools. Kullman Firm lawyers regularly advise and draft for employers such tools as: employment agreements, handbooks and policies, and other communications about trade secrets, proprietary data, mobile equipment use, non-compete agreements, waiver of right to a jury, and any number of other critical issues. The Kullman Firm has considerable experience with the labor, employment, and benefits issues arising out of: mergers and acquisition and divestitures, relocations and shutdowns, as well other types of transactions. The Kullman Firm offers practical advice to employers in ERISA matters, including plan design, regulatory compliance, modification and implementation of benefit plans of every kind and description, in both union and non-union environments. It also defends employers and employer sponsored plans in benefits-related litigation and before government oversight agencies. The Kullman Firm lawyers regularly advise employers in wage and hour compliance, investigations, and related litigation.

CLIENTS: The Kullman Firm's clients represent a broad range of industrial, commercial and service fields including manufacturers, banks, airlines and other types of transportation, warehouses, insurance, hospitals, nursing homes, distribution, retail operations, technology, agribusiness, construction and other business interests. Specific client information is available upon request.

HEAD OFFICE

LOUISIANA
1100 Poydras Street, 1600 Energy Centre,
New Orleans, LA 70163
Tel: 504 524 4162 **Fax:** 504 596 4189
Email: erm@kullmanlaw.com

BRANCH OFFICES

ALABAMA
600 University Park Place, Suite 340, **Birmingham,** AL 35209
Tel: 205 871 5858 **Fax:** 205 871 5874
Email: eew@kullmanlaw.com

MISSISSIPPI
Court Square Towers, Suite 505, 200 6th Street North,
Columbus, MS 39701
Tel: 662 244 8824 **Fax:** 662 244-8837
Email: tbs@kullmanlaw.com

1640 Lelia Drive, Suite 120, **Jackson,** MS 39216
Tel: 601 366 2990 **Fax:** 601 366 2955
Email: rah@kullmanlaw.com

MCGLINCHEY STAFFORD

THE FIRM

Managing Partner: Rodolfo J Aguilar, Jr
Number of partners: 96
Number of other lawyers: 91

AREAS OF PRACTICE:

Commercial & Business Litigation (Defense)	22%
Financial Services	15%
Products Liability, Pharmaceutical & Medical Devices	14%
Class Action Defense & Consumer Finance Litigation	11%
Employment Law (Defense)	7%
Healthcare	5%
Public Law	5%
Real Estate (Commercial)	4%
Insurance Regulation, Compliance & Defense	3%
Admiralty	3%
Bankruptcy	3%
Environmental Law	3%
Corporate & Business Transactions	1%
Estate/Probate/Trust	1%
Government Contracts/Relations	1%
Taxation	1%
Casino Gaming	1%

MAIN AREAS OF PRACTICE

Commercial & Business Litigation: Advises clients in matters involving antitrust and trade regulation laws; pricing and product distribution; dealer terminations; unfair competition; deceptive acts and practices; advertising; patent abuse; franchising; complex multi-district and class action litigation; RICO; DOJ, and FTC investigations.

Banking & Commercial Finance: Represents financial institutions in matters involving federal and state banking laws/regulations; asset-based lending; equipment leasing; commercial loan closings; workouts; bankruptcies; loan and deposit account agreements; real estate and personal property security interests; bank holding company formations; M&A; trust powers; investment and securities activities; new product development; bank-sponsored mutual funds; insurance and annuity products.

Consumer Financial Services: Counsels the world's leading financial institutions on compliance under federal and state consumer finance laws and regulations. Services include multi-state legal surveys; design of mortgage, automobile and manufactured housing finance credit products and agreements; compliance audits and training; defense of regulatory enforcement actions and consumer credit litigation, including class actions. Affiliate MS&YB serves the residential mortgage lending industry offering outsourcing of mortgage banking functions.

Class Action Defense & Consumer Finance Litigation: Defends banks; consumer finance companies; mortgage companies; specialty and non-prime equity lenders; retailers; credit card issuers; credit insurers; property and casualty insurers; life insurers; consumer leasing companies; payday lenders; auto finance companies; insurance premium finance companies; service companies; and other consumer financial services providers in class action and multidistrict litigation involving the entire range of causes of action and emerging legal theories.

Employment Law: Representation includes affirmative action; arbitration; collective bargaining; communications and employee motivation; compensation and benefits; compliance audits; discrimination; contracts; immigration compliance; labor disputes including industry-wide, multi-state strike; management training; OSHA; personnel policies and practices; strikes and labor injunctions; unfair labor practice proceedings before the NLRB; union organizing and election proceedings; Wage and Hour investigations, and wrongful discharge.

Healthcare: Represents clients in matters involving compliance with federal and state healthcare laws and regulations, including fraud and abuse, Stark and False Claims; hospital operational and medical staff issues; licensing, including Board matters; contract matters; M&A; Medicare and other third

HEAD OFFICE

LOUISIANA
643 Magazine Street, **New Orleans**, LA 70130
Tel: 504 586 1200   **Fax:** 504 596 2800
Email: info@mcglinchey.com
Website: www.mcglinchey.com

BRANCH OFFICES

TEXAS
1001 McKinney, Suite 1500, **Houston**, TX 77002
Tel: 713 520 1900   **Fax:** 713 520 1025

2711 N. Haskell Ave, Suite 2700, LB 25, **Dallas** TX 75204
Tel : 214 257 1700   **Fax:** 214 257 1717

LOUISIANA
One American Place, 14th Floor, 301 Main Street, **Baton Rouge**, LA 70825
Tel: 225 383 9000   **Fax:** 225 343 3076

1811 Tower Drive, Suite A, **Monroe**, LA 71201
Tel: 318 651 0807   **Fax:** 318 651 0809

MISSISSIPPI
200 South Lamar Street, Suite 1100, City Centre, **Jackson**, MS 39201
Tel: 601 960 8400   **Fax:** 601 960 8406

NEW YORK
194 Washington Avenue, Suite 600, **Albany**, NY 12210 (Albany Co.)
Tel: 518 432 1200   **Fax:** 518 432 8711

OHIO
25550 Chagrin Boulevard, Suite 406, **Cleveland**, OH 44122-4640
Tel: 216 378 9905   **Fax:** 216 378 9910

CONTACTS

Banking & Commercial Finance	David S Willenzik
Commercial & Business Litigation	B Franklin Martin III
Consumer Financial Services	Bennet S Koren
Class Action & Consumer Finance Litigation	Anthony Rollo
Employment Law	E Fredrick Preis, Jr
Healthcare	Donna Guinn Klein
Real Estate	R Keith Colvin
Pharmaceutical & Medical Devices	Henri Wolbrette III
Products Liability	Michael M Noonan

party payor reimbursement issues; legislation/regulation; litigation, including professional liability; risk management and loss control, and managed care.

Real Estate: Represents developers; landlords; tenants; lenders; individual and corporate landowners; financial institutions; insurance and mortgage companies, and institutional investors. Transactions involve historical renovation and low income housing tax credits. Projects include industrial plants; merchant power and cogeneration plants; office buildings; gaming; retail and restaurant chains; wireless network sites; hotels; golf course developments; planned unit, condominium, and timeshare. Owns MACSTAM Title Company LLC, a licensed title insurance agency, and provides title abstract services through its subsidiary, Abstracts by Godail, LLC.

Products Liability: Represents foreign and domestic insurers; manufacturers and distributors in defense of manufacturer and design liability cases involving motor vehicles; electrical appliances, and chemical and industrial products. Coordinates products liability litigation for businesses regionally and nationally.

Pharmaceutical & Medical Devices: Represents major prescription pharmaceutical manufacturers and distributors in defense of claims involving prescription and over-the-counter drugs; medical and surgical devices, and implantable contraceptives. Defends clients in putative class action suits involving pharmaceutical products and in medical device litigation.

MCGLINCHEY STAFFORD PLLC

PHELPS DUNBAR

THE FIRM

Managing Partner: Richard N Dicharry
Number of partners: 98

FIRM OVERVIEW: Founded in 1853 in New Orleans, Phelps Dunbar is one of the oldest law firms in continuous practice in the South. The firm is a progressive and diverse partnership, with a practice that is international in scope. Phelps Dunbar has offices in New Orleans and Baton Rouge, Louisiana; Jackson, Tupelo, and Gulfport, Mississippi; Houston, Texas; Tampa, Florida; and London, England. Through the firm's network of regional offices, clients have access to more than 250 attorneys representing an extensive range of talent and experience. No matter how intricate a client's legal needs, the firm's professional depth and experience offer accessible, cost-effective, and reliable service. The firm continually refocuses the major practice areas to serve the changing needs of its clients community. Attorneys in all practice areas work together to provide a broad base of legal services to institutions and individuals. Phelps Dunbar handles virtually every type of civil case in federal and state courts across the region. The firm was recognized in 2002 for its efforts in diversity by receiving the Defense Research Institute (DRI) National Diversity Award. The firm was also ranked first in the nation in 2002 and 2004 and among the top three in 2003 in percentage of African-American lawyers by the *Minority Law Journal*.

CLIENTS: Clients include public and private companies, financial institutions, insurance companies, healthcare systems, educational institutions, partnerships, estates, governmental agencies and individuals.

US OFFICE CONTACTS

BATON ROUGE

City Plaza, 445 North Boulevard, Suite 701, Baton Rouge, LA 70802-5707

Office Profile: The firm's Baton Rouge office was the first regional office of Phelps Dunbar, opening in 1984. The office has experienced steady growth since its opening. With over 40 attorneys, the Baton Rouge office has become one of the largest law offices in the state capital. The firm's attorneys support clients with a full-service litigation and business practice, as well as counseling on employment, regulatory, environmental and intellectual property matters.

JACKSON

111 East Capitol Street, Suite 600, Jackson, MS 39201

Office Profile: The Jackson office opened in 1986 as a result of a merger with a firm of young attorneys who had previously been with major Jackson firms. Now, with more than 50 attorneys, the Jackson office provides full-service litigation and traditional business practice for a diverse clientele.

TUPELO

One Mississippi Plaza, 201 S. Spring Street, Seventh Floor, Tupelo, MS 38804

Office Profile: Phelps Dunbar is the only law firm with substantial offices in Tupelo, Jackson, and Gulfport Mississippi. The offices coordinate projects for many clients with legal business throughout the state. As the center of the firm's thriving healthcare practice, the Tupelo office employs attorneys well-versed in the subtleties of this constantly evolving field of law. The firm's health law attorneys represent hospitals, physicians, managed care organizations and other healthcare providers throughout the Southeast as counsel on corporate, tax and health law matters. In addition, it maintains a business and a litigation practice.

GULFPORT

NorthCourt One, 2304 1th Street, Suite 300, Gulfport, MS 39501

Office Profile: Phelps Dunbar opened its seventh office on December 1, 2000, in Gulfport, Mississippi. The Gulfport office handles business litigation, construction, real estate, financing, products liability, insurance litigation, and environmental litigation. The Gulfport office draws upon attorneys in its New Orleans and other Mississippi offices as the nature of a legal project might require.

HOUSTON

3040 Post Oak Boulevard, Suite 900, Houston, TX 77056

Office Profile: With a foundation in the strength and tradition of a law firm over a century old, the firm's Houston office is an experienced and aggressive group. Opened in 1990, the Houston office has attorneys with extensive trial, appellate and business experience supplemented by excellent academic and professional back-grounds. Consistent practice standards ensure the delivery of high quality legal services.

TAMPA

100 South Ashley Drive, Suite 1900, Tampa, FL 33602-5311

Office Profile: Phelps Dunbar extended its legal services from Texas to Florida by opening its eighth office in Tampa on April 1, 2001. The Tampa office handles admiralty and tort litigation, business, real estate, commercial litigation, insurance, and labor and employment matters, practice areas that are aligned with Florida's business community.

STONE PIGMAN WALTHER WITTMANN LLC

THE FIRM

Chair of the Management Committee: Phillip A Wittmann
Number of members: 28
Number of lawyers: 55

FIRM OVERVIEW: The New Orleans law firm of Stone Pigman Walther Wittmann LLC is an important resource for national corporations doing business in the Gulf South. 75 years of practicing law gives Stone Pigman the experience on which corporate counsel can rely. The firm possesses a deep reservoir of talent and experience in handling litigation and business matters across a wide range of industries consisting of banking and finance, construction, education, energy and natural resources, healthcare and pharmaceutical, insurance, manufacturing, media and entertainment, real estate, service, tax-exempt organizations, technology, telecommunications, transportation and utilities.

MAIN AREAS OF PRACTICE

Commercial Litigation: The firm represents defendants and plaintiffs in a variety of complex litigation matters in both state and federal courts. Firm lawyers have represented clients in cases involving class actions, multi-district litigation, professional liability, appellate procedures and other complicated cases arising from mass torts, environmental and toxic tort claims, product liability actions, consumer fraud, antitrust claims, securities claims, bankruptcy and creditors' rights, bank regulation, employment claims, healthcare regulation, utility regulation, state and federal taxation, construction, insurance regulation, gaming regulation and intellectual property disputes.

Corporate & Securities/Mergers & Acquisitions: Firm lawyers have experience in all types of corporate finance transactions, including mergers and acquisitions, reorganizations, public offerings and private placements of common and preferred stock, subordinated debentures, partnership or LLC interests, and commercial paper, medium term notes and other types of securities. The firm also has extensive experience with non-corporate entities including partnerships, limited partnerships, LLCs, registered limited liability partnerships and trusts.

Real Estate, Finance & Construction: As counsel for real estate developers, buyers, sellers, institutional lenders and major tenants, Stone Pigman lawyers have been involved in most of the commercial real estate developments that have occurred in the greater New Orleans metropolitan area over the last several decades, as well as many significant projects throughout the rest of Louisiana, the Gulf South and the United States. For owner clients, the firm offers expertise in zoning and land use, leasing, environmental matters, construction issues, acquisition techniques and cross-easements and restrictive covenants. For borrowers and lenders, Stone Pigman lawyers are proficient in current lending techniques and have an in-depth understanding of the unique issues in Louisiana lending law.

Intellectual Property & Technology: Firm lawyers advise clients in a broad range of technology-related legal services, including trademarks, copyrights, patent litigation, trade secrets and other related legal issues including unfair competition, unfair trade practices, non-competition, employee raiding, confidentiality agreements, fiduciary duties and anti-trust matters. The firm represents a diverse group of clients, from local start-ups to established international clients, in various industries.

Tax: The firm's tax practice encompasses federal, state and local taxation, and focuses on tax planning and dispute resolution. The federal Tax Practice covers corporate, partnership, limited liability company, nonprofit organization, Employee Retirement Income Security Act and executive compensation matters as well as international taxation. Stone Pigman represents taxpayers in administrative proceedings before the Internal Revenue Service and in litigation before the United States Tax Court and other

HEAD OFFICE

LOUISIANA
546 Carondelet Street, **New Orleans**, LA 70130-3588
Tel: 504 581 3200   **Fax:** 504 581 3361
Website: www.stonepigman.com

CONTACTS

Commercial Litigation	James C Gulotta Jr
Corporate & Securities/M&A	Scott T Whittaker
Real Estate, Finance & Construction	Susan G Talley
Intellectual Property & Technology	Stephen G Bullock
Tax	John W Colbert
Probate, Trusts & Estate Planning	Hirschel T Abbott
Healthcare	Anthony M DiLeo
Insurance Coverage & Regulation	Wayne J Lee
Public Utility Regulation	Michael R Fontham

federal courts. The state and local tax practice covers corporate income and franchise tax, sales and use tax, ad valorem tax and mineral severance tax. Firm lawyers represent taxpayers in administrative proceedings before the Louisiana Department of Revenue, the Louisiana Board of Tax Appeals and the Louisiana Tax Commission, and in litigation before Louisiana state courts.

Probate, Trusts & Estate Planning: Stone Pigman has an extensive probate, trust and estate practice, which involves a full range of estate planning, representation of trust beneficiaries and fiduciaries, and the establishment, qualification and representation of public and private charitable organizations.

Healthcare: Firm lawyers handle a full spectrum of litigation and business matters related to healthcare and the pharmaceutical industry for hospitals and hospital service districts; diagnostic and treatment ancillary facilities; large and small physician groups and sole practitioners; nursing homes and continuing care retirement communities; home health agencies; pharmaceutical companies; academic institutions; healthcare insurers; and medical research organizations.

Insurance Coverage & Regulation: Stone Pigman has insurance-related litigation experience with both American and London companies. Firm lawyers also have experience in insurance regulatory matters.

Public Utility Regulation: The firm's lawyers have practiced before the Louisiana Public Service Commission, United States Supreme Court, United States district and appellate courts, Federal Energy Regulatory Commission, other state public service commissions, the Securities and Exchange Commission, Federal Communications Commission and Louisiana state courts. The rate cases and other litigation have involved numerous utilities and electric, gas and telecommunications carriers.

CONTENTS: Corporate/M&A p.888; Employment p.890; Environment p.892; Litigation p.893; Real Estate p.895; Individuals' Profiles p.897; Firms' Profiles p.903.

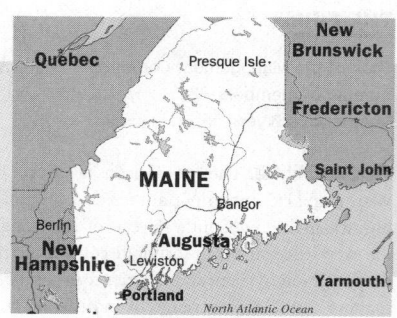

How lawyers are ranked

The opinions we gather from clients — mainly from in-house lawyers but also from other purchasers of legal services — are balanced by opinions from colleagues and competitors. Together, they provide two different perspectives — an all-round view — and biased viewpoints cancel each other out.

CORPORATE/M&A

Maine
Leading firms (Corporate/M&A)

1 PIERCE ATWOOD LLP *Portland*
　 VERRILL DANA, LLP *Portland*

2 BERNSTEIN, SHUR, SAWYER & NELSON *Portland*
　 DRUMMOND WOODSUM & MACMAHON *Portland*

3 EATON PEABODY *Bangor*
　 PRETI FLAHERTY BELIVEAU PACHIOS *Portland*
　 RUDMAN & WINCHELL LLC *Bangor*

Leading individuals (Corporate/M&A)

1 FRYER Greg *Verrill Dana*, Portland
　 HIGH Michael *Drummond Woodsum*, Portland
　 ZIMPRITCH James *Pierce Atwood*, Portland

2 CHAMPOUX David *Pierce Atwood*, Portland
　 EATON II George *Rudman & Winchell*, Bangor
　 MCKAY Daniel *Eaton Peabody*, Bangor

3 LOGIUDICE Susan *Preti Flaherty*, Portland
　 MACEWAN Alan *Verrill Dana*, Portland
　 SAUNDERS Eric *Bernstein Shur*, Portland

Leading individuals (Bankruptcy)

1 AMORY Daniel *Drummond Woodsum*, Portland
　 CLEMENT Roger *Verrill Dana*, Portland
　 KEACH Robert *Bernstein Shur*, Portland
　 MANHEIMER Jacob *Pierce Atwood*, Portland
　 MARCUS George *Marcus Clegg*, Portland

2 BOPP III Fred *Perkins Thompson*, Portland
　 MARCUS Benjamin *Drummond Woodsum*, Portland
　 MCVEIGH John *Preti Flaherty*, Portland
　 MORRELL Stephen *Eaton Peabody*, Brunswick

Firms and individuals are listed alphabetically in each band.

Band 1

Pierce Atwood LLP
See firm details p.906

The Firm: The 15-attorney corporate team at this regional giant boasts an impressive "*breadth of experience and talents*," and, according to its clients, there is "*no question they cannot address.*" This has been a busy year for the "*high-caliber*" group. It has seen a rise in minority stockholders cases, particularly following the splintering of a number of family-owned businesses. Another area of growth has been advising clients interested in purchasing family-owned businesses of various sizes. The group recently represented the three largest stockholders in a $40 million leveraged stock redemption by a privately held Maine company. Other areas of particular experience include financial services law, and the team regularly advises venture capital investors as well as the companies they are investing in. It also assists banks, insurance companies and other financial institutions, healthcare systems, investment funds and corporations of various sizes.

The Lawyers: "*Superstar*" **Jacob Manheimer** (see p.899) was applauded for his wide-ranging expertise in bankruptcy law. He advises debtors, secured and trade creditors and operating trustees on debtor-creditor relations, Chapter 11 reorganizations and commercial transactions. Dubbed the "*guru of Maine corporate law,*" **James Zimpritch** (see p.902) was described to researchers as a "*deal facilitator with sky-high credentials.*" Peers consider him a "*delight to deal with,*" while to clients he is "*focused, responsive and always congenial.*" He handles M&A, stock and asset sales, equity and debt financings and minority stockholder issues, as well as providing clients with ongoing commercial advice. Recent highlights include acting for a bank holding company in a controlled auction, which resulted in a successful merger with another publicly held bank holding company. This stock transaction was valued at $48 million, and involved negotiating agreements, executive termination provisions, option cashouts and rollovers, among other issues. Clients recommended **David Champoux** (see p.897) as "*articulate and aggressive; he knows when to get in the other side's face and when not to.*" His diverse corporate experience includes advising on acquisitions and disposals of businesses, the formation of entities and securities law.

The Clients: Maine Employers' Mutual Insurance; FNB Bankshares; Eaton Vance; Maine Mutual Group; First National Bank of Damariscotta and American Skiing.

Verrill Dana, LLP
See firm details p.908

The Firm: This corporate department of about ten attorneys was singled out for its good "*team-working approach.*" Clients particularly noted its willingness to "*employ all the resources available,*" resulting in "*the seamless handling of complex matters.*" The team's expertise spans the spectrum of corporate work, including M&A, bankruptcy and securities law. It recently advised new client First National Lincoln on the acquisition of another local bank holding company, making it the fourth largest bank in Maine. The "*excellent*" six-strong bankruptcy department, meanwhile, acts for debtors and secured creditors in Chapter 11, Chapter 7 and Chapter 13 proceedings. Recent highlights for the team include acting as lead counsel in two of the largest bankruptcies filed in Maine, namely the Bangor & Aroostook Railroad and Jackson Brook Institute. In the former, the court awarded the firm a $3 million fee enhancement, one of the largest ever awarded, for its work over five years in the Chapter 11 reorganization.

The Lawyers: "*Thorough and attentive*" **Roger Clement** (see p.897) was recommended to researchers for his "*top-drawer*" bankruptcy expertise. Clients particularly noted his high-class advocacy skills in bankruptcy-related proceedings, commenting that he is "*great on his feet.*" **Greg Fryer** (see p.898) was also enthusiastically recommended by his clients. In the words of one, "*he meets all our expectations and then some.*" Special praise was reserved for his "*creativity, tough negotiating skills and grasp of the full range of securities law matters,*" an area of particular focus for him. **Alan MacEwan**'s (see p.899) "*calmness and well-balanced judgment*" make him popular with clients. He handles a broad workload of M&A and general corporate advice.

The Clients: Over the past year the firm has attracted two new public company clients, ImmuCell and First National Lincoln. Other clients include: Chicago Title Insurance; Commonwealth Land Title Insurance; Lawyer's Title Insurance and First American Title Insurance.

Band 2

Bernstein, Shur, Sawyer & Nelson, PA

See firm details p.903

The Firm: This well-established player in the Maine corporate market was applauded for its considerable depth and resources. A sizable team handles a wide range of matters, spanning the formation of corporate entities, M&A, joint ventures, equity financing and partnership advice. Bankruptcy is a key area of focus for the firm, and it has represented clients in reorganizations, liquidations, commercial insolvencies and related litigation in the state, federal and bankruptcy courts. The corporate group serves companies from the fishing, forestry, energy and utilities, financial services and technology industries, among others, drawing its clients from both Maine and across the USA.

The Lawyers: Interviewees were full of praise for the outstanding knowledge of bankruptcy group chair **Robert Keach** (see p.898). "*He is a real student of the law,*" observed one market commentator. He has appeared before bankruptcy courts across New England, representing debtors, creditors, creditors' committees, lessors and third parties. On the corporate side, the "*outstanding*" **Eric Saunders** (see p.901) was singled out for his broad expertise.

The Clients: UnumProvident; Principal Life Insurance; Waynflete School; Georgia-Pacific; Anthem Blue Cross and Blue Shield; RJ Reynolds; Rite Aid; Northwest Airlines; McDonald's; Ford; University of Maine System; State Street Capital Markets; Citizens Financial Group and Citizens Bank New Hampshire.

Drummond Woodsum & MacMahon

See firm details p.904

The Firm: This 14-lawyer team combines considerable commercial expertise with "*excellent client care, which makes you feel so important,*" to serve clients from a broad range of industries. Typical work includes advising on corporate governance and securities issues, the formation and liquidation of companies, M&A and a variety of financings. The past year has seen it increasingly involved in out-of-state work, as the firm continues to attract a wider range of clients. For example, the team represented Vortechnics, a leading storm water technology company, in connection with a sale to CONTECH Construction Products from Cincinnati, Ohio. It also assisted the Appalachian Mountain Club with its acquisition of 37,000 acres in Maine, and the associated financing

through the use of new markets tax credits.

The Lawyers: Peers acknowledged that **Daniel Amory** (see p.897) is "*hands down the reigning Chapter 11 lawyer*" in Maine. Apart from being unusually knowledgeable in the field, he is also "*dedicated, creative and wonderful to work with.*" He operates a busy practice stretching across bankruptcy and commercial transactions. Another asset to the firm's bankruptcy group is "*practical and efficient*" **Benjamin Marcus** (see p.899). He was recommended to researchers for his "*depth of knowledge in bankruptcy matters,*" and clients appreciate the fact that "*he is always thinking of our needs.*" Clients were also full of admiration for "*conscientious and caring*" **Michael High** (see p.898). He was particularly valued for his "*tremendous legal mind – he is usually the smartest lawyer at the table.*" He devotes about three-quarters of his practice to M&A and general business law, and the rest to secured lending work.

The Clients: Banknorth; Cherryfield Foods; Citizens Bank New Hampshire; Fleet National Bank; Key Corporate Capital; Vortechnics; Workgroup Technology Partners; Oxford Networks and Stonewall Kitchen.

Band 3

Eaton Peabody

The Firm: According to clients, Bangor-based Eaton Peabody is comparable to the "*largest East Coast firms,*" in professionalism if not in size and resources. They particularly applauded the team for its "*promptness and ability to explain complex matters in layman's language.*" The seven-attorney team advises clients across Maine and beyond, providing expertise in M&A, securities issues, financing and financial services regulation. It attracts clients from a broad spectrum of industries, including manufacturing, technology, timberland, healthcare and banking. The widely admired three-attorney bankruptcy practice is well versed in the gamut of bankruptcy, insolvency and workout issues.

The Lawyers: **Daniel McKay** was rated by observers as "*highly ethical, pragmatic and good at facilitating the success of a deal.*" He typically advises smaller and midsized businesses on a wide range of commercial matters, including a range of corporate and securities transactions, as well as antitrust. The cornerstone of the firm's bankruptcy practice is **Stephen Morrell**. Clients applauded him for "*anticipating your questions and needs*" and for his creative and flexible outlook. He devotes himself to business relationship disputes and insolvency, and recently handled a Chapter 13 case involving the question of whether a creditor application by a personal injury claimant was in good faith.

The Clients: Downeast Energy & Building Supply, Downeast Toyota and Wright-Pierce feature in the client roster.

Preti Flaherty Beliveau Pachios & Haley LLP

See firm details p.907

The Firm: This "*overtly client-service oriented*" 15-lawyer corporate department handles a steady flow of corporate and commercial matters. Its clients rated it their "*first choice for their teamwork and the effort they make to understand your business.*" Typical work includes advising on business formations, securities law, venture capital matters and M&A. In addition, the firm boasts an impressive bankruptcy group, well versed in business restructuring and creditors' rights litigation. Recent highlights include acting for the management team in the MBO of Tex Tech Industries, which has a large manufacturing facility in Maine and operations in China and Taiwan. This involved obtaining and documenting debt and equity financing components, and negotiating employment and stockholder agreements.

The Lawyers: "*Client-oriented*" **Susan LoGiudice** (see p.899) was applauded by clients as a "*responsive and enthusiastic*" attorney with experience in a variety of corporate matters. **John McVeigh** (see p.899) is a highly qualified bankruptcy practitioner. He has a busy litigation practice, and handles cases concerning creditors' rights, commercial disputes and bankruptcy matters.

The Clients: The firm serves a varied client base, drawn from the healthcare, manufacturing, paper and energy industries, with a strong niche in the telecommunications sector. Examples include: Hussey Seating; Tate Access Floors; Mid-Maine Communications; Housing Initiatives of New England; Brascan; Bath Iron Works; Elmet Technologies and Unity Foundation.

Rudman & Winchell LLC

The Firm: A dedicated team of six corporate attorneys handles a busy caseload of commercial and corporate matters. Work centers on M&A and venture capital funding advice to Maine's smaller entrepreneurial private companies and midsized businesses. The firm maintains a particularly high profile in the energy, natural resources and utilities sectors, where its clients are drawn from across the USA as well as Maine.

The Lawyers: Clients praised **George Eaton** for "*adding value to business matters with his considerable knowledge and experience.*" Aside from advising on business formations, financings and M&A, he has been heavily involved this year in advising corporate clients on strategic planning.

The Clients: Fleet Bank of Maine and Merrill Merchants Bank are representative examples from a client roster that includes other names from the banking, real estate development, hospitality, manufacturing, engineering, healthcare and software industries.

Other Notable Practitioners

Many commentators consider the "*phenomenal*" **George Marcus** of Marcus, Clegg & Mistretta PA to be the "*predominant personality in Maine bankruptcy law.*" Clients specifically applauded him as "*aggressive, goal-driven, pragmatic and truly in tune to our business objectives.*" He handles a diverse commercial workload, and has particular expertise in Chapter 11 proceedings across Maine, New Hampshire, Delaware and beyond. Representative clients include UnumProvident, DIRECTV and Vision Care of Maine. Also receiving plaudits for bankruptcy expertise was **Fred Bopp** of Perkins, Thompson, Hinckley & Keddy, P.A. Interviewees rated him as "*conscientious and attentive – a real rising star.*"

EMPLOYMENT

MAINLY DEFENDANT

Maine
Leading firms
(Employment: Mainly Defendant)

[1]	**MOON, MOSS & SHAPIRO, PA** *Portland*
	PIERCE ATWOOD LLP *Portland*
[2]	**DRUMMOND WOODSUM & MACMAHON** *Portland*
	EATON PEABODY *Bangor*
[3]	**BERNSTEIN, SHUR, SAWYER** *Portland*
	PRETI FLAHERTY BELIVEAU PACHIOS *Portland*
	RUDMAN & WINCHELL LLC *Bangor*
	VERRILL DANA, LLP *Portland*

Leading individuals
(Employment: Mainly Defendant)

[1]	**MCGILL Linda** *Bernstein Shur*, Portland
	MOON Richard *Moon Moss*, Portland
[2]	**ERWIN James** *Pierce Atwood*, Portland
	JOHNSTON Thomas *Eaton Peabody*, Bangor
	MCGUIRE Frank *Rudman & Winchell*, Bangor
	MESSERSCHMIDT Michael *Preti Flaherty*, Portland
	PAYNE Clare *Eaton Peabody*, Bangor
	PRINGLE Harry *Drummond Woodsum*, Portland
	SHAPIRO Jonathan *Moon Moss*, Portland
[3]	**CURRIER Douglas** *Verrill Dana*, Portland
	DEROSBY Anthony *Pierce Atwood*, Portland
	HEWEY Melissa *Drummond Woodsum*, Portland
	JACOBS Peter *Pierce Atwood*, Portland

Up-and-coming individuals

	STOREY Anne-Marie *Rudman & Winchell*, Bangor

Firms and individuals are listed alphabetically in each band.

Band 1

Moon, Moss & Shapiro, PA
See firm details p.905

The Firm: Hailed by many commentators as Maine's leading employment boutique, the firm aims to work closely with clients to deliver a high-quality, hands-on service. The effect on it of Linda McGill's recent departure remains to be seen. However, the firm retains a wealth of talent, well versed in the gamut of employment law matters, and continues to serve a healthy stable of clients, particularly rich in municipalities. Typical work includes advising on collective bargaining agreements, wage and hour matters, OSHA, contract negotiations and the defense of discrimination and harassment claims. The provision of ongoing strategic planning and preventive training are also key features of the team's practice. Highlights include advising a large hotel on a religious accommodation matter. This concerned the beliefs of an employee, who is also a minister, colliding with a collective bargaining agreement under which he is not senior enough to take Sundays off. Recent years have also seen the group advising on employment issues arising from the stream of corporate takeovers in Maine. Clients are drawn from a spectrum of industries, both in Maine and nationally, such as healthcare systems, insurance companies, banks, nonprofits, municipalities and hospitality companies.

The Lawyers: For more than one client, **Richard Moon** (see p.900) is the "*most responsive lawyer I have worked with.*" They particularly rate his "*sound direction and intellectual advice, which he can easily translate into layman's terms and educate us in the process.*" His practice includes a mixture of consultative advice and cutting-edge employment defense. **Jonathan Shapiro** (see p.901) was applauded for his "*wealth of experience.*" He also handles a mixture of management counseling and employment defense litigation, as well as offering niche expertise advising stock analysts and portfolio managers at investment banks on employment contracts and compensation agreements.

The Clients: Chubb; Shaw's Supermarkets; Banknorth; Cumberland Farms; Starwood Hotels & Resorts Worldwide and Vital Basics.

Pierce Atwood LLP
See firm details p.906

The Firm: A team of ten labor and employment specialists here handles a remarkably wide range of matters thanks to its resources and experience. It attracts a stream of major cases, spanning discrimination and harassment litigation, FMLA, trade secrets, nonsolicitation and any other common law or statutory claims brought by employees. The firm also provides preventive training and counseling. Immigration continues to be an area of growth for the firm, and it advises US companies employing foreigners, particularly those coming from Canada. The past year has also seen the firm handling a greater number of whistle-blower cases, though better-informed management has led to a lower occurrence of sex discrimination disputes. "*I like their accuracy and efficiency,*" commented clients, who were also impressed with the team's approach to service. As one put it, "*I don't know whether we are a particularly big client for them, but they really make us feel like we are.*"

The Lawyers: According to clients, **James Erwin** (see p.898) is an "*absolute delight – he has an insightful business sense and an analytical, creative mind.*" They were particularly impressed by his "*responsiveness under immense time pressures and ability to talk a language we understand.*" He heads the firm's employment and employee benefits groups, and is widely admired for his expertise in a range of employment litigation, including harassment, age, disability, defamation and unfair discharge cases. "*Highly skilled but good fun,*" **Peter Jacobs** (see p.898) was highlighted for his "*deep understanding and ability to anticipate the opposition's moves.*" He focuses on labor law, including union negotiations, collective bargaining, organizing campaigns and NLRB proceedings. He also represents management in discrimination cases at administrative level. The majority of his client base consists of healthcare providers, based largely in Maine, but also out of state. **Anthony Derosby** (see p.897) was recommended for his expertise in OSHA and immigration matters. Clients enthusiastically praised his "*insight and experience with administrative agencies and superb delivery of the finer points to management.*"

The Clients: Maine Medical Center; Brascan; J.D. Irving, Limited; MBNA; Celerant Consulting; Bates College; IDEXX; Sappi; UnumProvident and Mercy Hospital.

Band 2

Drummond Woodsum & MacMahon
See firm details p.904

The Firm: Like the rest of the firm, Drummond Woodsum's employment department has done a "*great job of capturing the public school sector,*" observed interviewees. A loyal stable of education clients is supplemented by an impressive roster of Maine-based private employers. They are served by about 12 employment lawyers, dedicated to discrimination and harassment litigation, FMLA issues, wage and hour, and OSHA compliance. Preventive counseling is a key area of focus for the team, and clients note that it "*keeps abreast of changes and invests in our professional development to help avoid problems.*" Recent highlights include defending a client in

890

All quotes in the text are from interviews with clients and competitors.

CHAMBERS USA 2005

the US District Court in Bangor against allegations by a teacher that his First Amendment rights were violated when he was required to teach a history curriculum centered on Europe. The group also represented a school department before the Maine Human Rights Commission, in a race discrimination claim concerning bus transportation.

The Lawyers: Harry Pringle (see p.900) has impressed clients with his *"winning combination of insight, pragmatism and sympathetic listening."* He is the one they look to when *"there is a really tough employment matter to deal with; he takes the time to understand us and to find an outcome that will work."* He represents companies in employment defense matters, with a particular focus on public sector educational clients. His colleague, *"smart and tenacious"* **Melissa Hewey** (see p.898), wins the respect of the market with her mix of employment law and business litigation.

The Clients: The team acts for R. M. Davis, Fiber Materials and numerous public sector clients, particularly school districts.

Eaton Peabody

The Firm: This five-attorney labor and employment team is widely considered the best in Bangor. It is valued by clients for its *"superlative"* handling of a variety of employment law matters, thanks to its *"commitment, flexibility and depth of knowledge."* The team's workload includes advice on wage and hour matters, OSHA and discrimination claims, while a large portion of its time is devoted to preventive counseling and training on such matters as sexual harassment, discipline and terminations, all with the aim of keeping clients out of court. Aside from producing employee handbooks, advice on FMLA matters has been a key feature of the firm's work in recent months.

The Lawyers: Thomas Johnston was recommended to researchers as a *"gentlemanly but dogged litigator who is great on his feet."* According to clients, he embodies the *"perfect combination of legal knowledge and problem-solving practicality."* He represents management in discrimination cases, labor contract negotiations and union organizing campaigns, among other things. **Clare Payne** also received enthusiastic plaudits from clients. According to one, she *"has steered me and my staff through tricky currents and dangerous shoals and we have never felt that we received anything but the best advice and the most concentrated attention."* She defends management in discrimination, harassment and other claims, and provides ongoing training and advice.

The Clients: The firm represents a range of employers from across the public and private sectors.

Band 3

Bernstein, Shur, Sawyer & Nelson, PA
See firm details p.903

The Firm: The recent move of one of the sector's big names, Linda McGill, from Moon, Moss & Shapiro, caused ripples in the market and propelled her new firm into our employment rankings. This move is seen as the most obvious sign to date that the firm is dedicated to growing an important employment law department. Observers believe that the move makes sense for the firm and will be a great boost for a client base strong in both the public and private sectors. Typical work includes representing employers in the state and federal courts and before the NLRB and other bodies. It advises on, among other things, sexual harassment, recruitment, termination and severance agreements, wage and hour matters and union organization.

The Lawyers: *"Top-notch"* **Linda McGill** (see p.899) was recommended to researchers for her *"great legal skills, superb knowledge and wealth of experience"* in labor and employment law. She was particularly valued for her expertise in public sector issues, and for a consensual approach that emphasizes litigation avoidance. However, she also handles a diverse caseload of employment and labor disputes, defending discrimination and harassment claims, intellectual property and noncompete issues, and representing clients in union organizing campaigns and collective bargaining.

The Clients: Community Counseling Services; Microbac Laboratories; General Growth Properties; Homewood Benefits; Maine State Retirement System; Maine Community College System; S.R. Weiner & Associates; Town of Wiscasset; Waldo County Commissioners and York County Community Action Program.

Preti Flaherty Beliveau Pachios & Haley LLC
See firm details p.907

The Firm: Eight *"team players"* make up this *"resourceful"* employment group. The firm represents a mix of unionized and nonunionized clients in a variety of labor and employment matters, with work often cross-referred from the firm's sizable corporate and litigation departments. Following recent changes to the regulations, the team has been advising on a greater volume of wage and hour cases, as well as seeing an increase in whistle-blower matters. Recent highlights include advising a nonunionized forest products manufacturer on the effects of a significant reduction in the workforce, which involved numerous age and gender discrimination and whistle-blower claims. The client successfully defended the claims before the Maine Human Rights Commission, and there were no lawsuits filed.

The Lawyers: *"Articulate"* labor and employment expert **Michael Messerschmidt** (see p.900) was admired for his *"broad knowledge base and down-to-earth, levelheaded judgment."* The chair of the group, he devotes his time to defending employers in litigation, and counseling clients on preventive risk management, personnel policies, wage and hour issues and collective bargaining. He acts as labor counsel to the Maine Turnpike Authority, as well as serving clients from fields as diverse as manufacturing and retail, healthcare, municipal government, forestry products and communications.

The Clients: Maine Turnpike Authority; Southern Maine Medical Center; Blethen Maine Newspapers; Pride Manufacturing; Mid-Maine Communications and Bath Iron Works.

Rudman & Winchell LLC

The Firm: This team was recommended for its expertise in labor and employment law, its *"dedication to the community, and its willingness to invest in the training and education of its clients."* It acts primarily for employers in litigation and preventive training, but also represents some plaintiffs, with a particular focus on social security disability cases. The team represents clients before the state and federal courts, and other bodies, such as the Maine Human Rights Commission and the NLRB. Recent highlights include successfully obtaining a summary judgment for a university in a national origin and race discrimination claim brought by an employee.

The Lawyers: Frank McGuire (see p.899) was applauded as a *"darn good employment practitioner"* who handles a large volume of employment defense litigation and preventive counseling. Clients value his *"diligence, forthrightness and communication skills."* *"Crack-a-jack lawyer"* **Anne-Marie Storey** (see p.901) was praised for her balance of *"elegant but gutsy performances,"* and her *"professionalism and compassion."* Workers' compensation matters feature heavily in her workload, alongside advice on discrimination claims, supervisor training and employee handbooks.

The Clients: Bangor Daily News; University of Maine; St. Joseph Hospital; Sullivan & Merritt; Lafayette Hotels and Eastern Maine Healthcare Systems.

Verrill Dana, LLP
See firm details p.908

The Firm: Market sources consider this a *"well-rounded"* labor and employment practice. The ten-lawyer team handles a diverse workload, featuring OSHA compliance, harassment and discrimination claims and labor investigations and cases before the NLRB. Employment immigration is a key area of focus for the firm, and it advises employers on the yearly influxes of professional and unskilled workers into Maine. Whistle-blower discrimination has been an area of increased work over the past year, as has the provision of preventive advice on the ADA and wage disputes. The firm also boasts one of the most active employee benefits groups in New England, which has been busy of late handling cases linked to the American Jobs Creation Act 2004.

The Lawyers: Douglas Currier (see p.897) received plaudits for his expertise in labor and employment law. Clients claim that he "*always impresses with his user-friendly approach*," and "*provides balanced judgment and assertiveness without aggression.*"

The Clients: Clients are drawn from an array of industries, including healthcare, construction and education, across both Maine and the USA. Examples include: Bovis Lend Lease; Actus Lend Lease; Port of Oakland and Parsons.

ENVIRONMENT

Maine
Leading firms (Environment)

1. **PIERCE ATWOOD LLP** *Portland*
2. **BERNSTEIN, SHUR, SAWYER & NELSON** *Portland*
   EATON PEABODY *Bangor*
   PRETI FLAHERTY BELIVEAU PACHIOS *Portland*
   VERRILL DANA, LLP *Portland*

Leading individuals (Environment)

1. **AHRENS Philip** *Pierce Atwood, Portland*
   DOYLE Thomas *Pierce Atwood, Portland*
   HAMILTON P Andrew *Eaton Peabody, Bangor*
   TAYLOR William *Pierce Atwood, Portland*
2. **BROWNE Juliet** *Verrill Dana, Portland*
   KILBRETH James *Verrill Dana, Portland*
   MAHONEY Sean *Verrill Dana, Portland*
   THALER Jeffrey *Bernstein Shur, Portland*
   VAN SLYKE David *Preti Flaherty, Portland*

Firms and individuals are listed alphabetically in each band.

Band 1

Pierce Atwood LLP
See firm details p.906

The Firm: Maine's premier firm hosts its largest environmental law practice. Its 15 attorneys were hailed by clients for their "*expertise, efficiency, value for money and concise responses.*" The department is divided into areas of expertise, including air, water, wetland permitting and waste, and peers acknowledge that it is "*more specialized than we are; it has an air person, a water person and so on – just more resources.*" Recent highlights include successfully obtaining permitting for an increase of seven million cubic yards in the disposal capacity of a state-owned, privately operated landfill on behalf of Casella Waste Systems. The team also obtained the relevant permits for a new water source for Poland Spring Bottling, a complex process involving contested state administrative proceedings and a judicial appeal. The group also has a presence in New Hampshire, where its office is headed by environmental expert George Dana Bisbee.

The Lawyers: "*Aggressive but reasonable*" **Philip Ahrens** (see p.897) runs the firm's environmental department. Experienced in a broad spectrum of environmental matters, he counsels clients on regulatory and enforcement matters, particularly in the solid waste and land use spheres. Clients praised him as "*among the best; a real pleasure to work with.*" "*Technical expert*" **Thomas Doyle** (see p.898) attracted plaudits for his "*diligent*" handling of complex environmental and land use matters, while clients singled out **William Taylor** (see p.901) for his "*sterling work ethic*" and expertise in water, wetlands and natural resource matters. He was particularly commended as "*a great people person who is not afraid to argue vigorously for his clients.*"

The Clients: The team's client base includes pulp and paper companies, power producers, manufacturers, waste management companies, developers and various other corporate bodies, drawn from across New England. Examples include: Poland Spring Bottling; Casella Waste Systems; Georgia-Pacific; Gulf Island Pond Oxygenation Project Partnership; Hows Corner Superfund Site; Penobscot Bay Energy Company; GenPower; Domtar and First Hartford Realty.

Band 2

Bernstein, Shur, Sawyer & Nelson, PA
See firm details p.903

The Firm: Sources note that Bernstein Shur has been assiduously building an environmental practice in recent years, drawing upon the talents of lawyers with litigation, real estate, lobbying and regulatory expertise. The team assists individuals, businesses and municipalities with compliance or enforcement procedures relating to a wide range of environmental and land use laws and regulations. Areas of expertise include waste, water, air, toxics and wetlands.

The Lawyers: "*Perceptive and proactive*" **Jeffrey Thaler** (see p.902) has a strong litigation background, which sources say has given him "*good trial instincts.*" According to peers, he has experience of representing clients in numerous high-profile environmental proceedings. He has been particularly visible acting for groups opposing projects.

Eaton Peabody

The Firm: This four-attorney environmental practice is well known in the state for its proficiency in handling a range of natural resource and permitting matters. Much of its work concerns the operations of the Maine timberlands industry, where the firm has a long-standing history. However, it represents a broad range of commercial and industrial clients, including the developers of retail and leisure facilities, aquaculture companies and numerous municipalities across the state. The past year has seen the group advising on several redevelopment projects, such as the creation of a city park on the site of a former cardboard factory. Wetlands and water pollution permitting also feature prominently in the team's workload.

The Lawyers: Interviewees recommended **Andrew Hamilton** for his expertise in environmental and land use issues, and in particular for his profile in municipal work. Recent highlights include his involvement in the cleanup of a former battery and metals landfill, which was then developed into a softball field.

The Clients: Eastern Maine Healthcare Systems; Ocean Properties; Grant Trailer Sales; First Hartford Realty; City of Brewer and City of Bangor.

Preti Flaherty Beliveau Pachios & Haley LLC
See firm details p.907

The Firm: The compact environmental department here provides clients with advice on air, water and noise pollution, chemical regulation and land use matters. However, it is in the field of hazardous waste that the team is felt to particularly excel. It has represented clients before federal and state courts and administrative bodies, and has defended them against class actions and toxic torts litigation. It also advises on permitting, enforcement and regulatory matters.

The Lawyers: Market sources praised "*creative, informed, proactive and constructive*" **David Van Slyke** (see p.902) for his expertise in environmental matters. He has a particular name for hazardous waste issues.

Verrill Dana, LLP
See firm details p.908

The Firm: The four-attorney environment team at Verrill Dana probably provides the closest competition in the state to Pierce Atwood. It offers expertise in the full range of environmental matters and appears in much of the most interesting work. Recent examples include advising on the construction of the Maritimes & Northeast Pipeline for natural gas, spanning over 200 miles between Canada and Maine. Aside from permitting and compliance issues, environmental litigation is a key feature of the group's workload. Here it recently assisted the Maine Department of Transportation in litigation connected with a Superfund mine site in Brooksville, Maine. The team also helped to create EMSOURCE, an entity in the business of assuming environmental liabilities for compa-

nies by procuring insurance and risk transfer agreements.

The Lawyers: *"Thoughtful and effective"* **James Kilbreth** (see p.899) was enthusiastically recommended for his long-standing expertise in the field. A *"good appellate advocate,"* he is felt to be particularly strong in environmental litigation. **Juliet Browne** (see p.897) was noted for her *"track record of success"* in environmental compliance proceedings and disputes. Clients described her as *"extremely focused and articu-*

late." Interviewees also endorsed **Sean Mahoney** (see p.899) as a *"levelheaded problem solver."* His strengths lie in water pollution, hazardous waste and endangered species matters.

The Clients: Waste Management; International Paper; Bowdoin College; Maine Community College System; GAC Chemical; Great Island Development; Portland Water District and Prime Tanning.

LITIGATION

GENERAL COMMERCIAL

Maine
Leading firms
(Litigation: General Commercial)

1	PIERCE ATWOOD LLP *Portland*
2	BERNSTEIN, SHUR, SAWYER & NELSON *Portland*
	PRETI FLAHERTY BELIVEAU PACHIOS *Portland*
	VERRILL DANA, LLP *Portland*
3	BERMAN & SIMMONS *Portland*
	EATON PEABODY *Bangor*
	HARVEY & FRANK *Portland*
	NORMAN, HANSON & DETROY, LLC *Portland*
	RUDMAN & WINCHELL LLC *Bangor*

Leading individuals
(Litigation: General Commercial)

1	DETROY Peter *Norman Hanson, Portland*
	FRANK Robert *Harvey & Frank, Portland*
	HARVEY Charles *Harvey & Frank, Portland*
	KAYATTA William *Pierce Atwood, Portland*
2	CULLEY Peter *Pierce Atwood, Portland*
	PETRUCCELLI Gerald *Petruccelli Martin, Portland*
	ROBITZEK William *Berman & Simmons, Portland*
	RUBIN Peter *Bernstein Shur, Portland*
3	KILBRETH James *Verrill Dana, Portland*
	KING David *Rudman & Winchell, Bangor*
	KUBETZ Bernard *Eaton Peabody, Bangor*
	MCCARTHY John *Rudman & Winchell, Bangor*
	NEWTON Robert *Preti Flaherty, Portland*
	NYHAN Christopher *Preti Flaherty, Portland*
	PIPER Jonathan *Preti Flaherty, Portland*
	WHITE Jeffrey *Pierce Atwood, Portland*

Firms and individuals are listed alphabetically in each band.

Band 1

Pierce Atwood LLP
See firm details p.906

The Firm: Clients agree that this litigation team offers the *"best resources and depth of expertise in Maine."* The 30-strong group is experienced in the gamut of commercial disputes, including class actions and complex multistate litigation. Satisfied clients also observed that the firm is *"exceedingly good value for money,"* and has a quality equivalent to many of the country's litigation leaders. Areas

of expertise include antitrust litigation, employment, stockholder disputes and insurance defense. Intellectual property is an area of continued growth for the firm, and it advises clients in the software, life sciences and hi-tech manufacturing industries. It has been acting as lead counsel for Banknorth in a class action in the New Hampshire Superior Court. This is seeking to recover credit insurance premiums for borrowers who purchased automobiles from New Hampshire dealers and paid off the loans prior to maturity.

The Lawyers: Clients rated **William Kayatta** (see p.898) *"top of the heap"* for complex litigation, particularly major class actions. His success is based on his vast experience and skill as an *"excellent strategic thinker with a remarkable intelligence, who knows exactly when to push a point and when to compromise."* They also consider him a good person to have on your side because *"he hates to lose."* Supported by an outstanding team of lawyers, Kayatta handles an even mixture of Maine-based and out-of-state matters. *"Formidable"* **Peter Culley** (see p.897) is another *"excellent litigator."* Particular praise was reserved for his *"command of the process, insight into the way judges think, and his human touch."* His practice encompasses commercial disputes, environmental matters and personal injury litigation. **Jeffrey White** (see p.902) heads the firm's litigation department and manages an active business and antitrust caseload. According to interviewees, he possesses a *"wealth of knowledge and a truly amiable personality."*

The Clients: Anthem Insurance; CIGNA; DuPont; Enterasys Networks; Hannaford Bros.; Maine Medical Center; MBNA; Mitsubishi; UnumProvident; Verizon; Dell; Banknorth; Maine Yankee; Bushmaster Firearms; Daimler-Chrysler and the State of California.

Band 2

Bernstein, Shur, Sawyer & Nelson, PA
See firm details p.903

The Firm: About 25 quality attorneys make up this diverse litigation group. The team's work-

load encompasses all the more usual types of business and commercial dispute, as well as such niche work as antitrust, patent and trademark, ERISA and construction litigation. It is perhaps best known, however, for its impressive expertise in asbestos defense. The firm was recommended for taking an imaginative and aggressive approach to resolving complex commercial issues. Recent highlights include defending lawyers in a case brought by the participants of a health plan concerning payment to the health plan provider.

The Lawyers: **Peter Rubin** (see p.901) is renowned for his *"top-notch skills in asbestos defense work."* A *"tenacious and articulate litigator,"* his caseload includes advice on general commercial and products liability disputes.

The Clients: IDEXX Laboratories; Owens-Illinois; Travelers Insurance and UnumProvident.

Preti Flaherty Beliveau Pachios & Haley LLC
See firm details p.907

The Firm: Litigation forms a large volume of this firm's caseload, and is handled by a sizable group of 28 talented attorneys. Market sources acknowledged the team's expertise in such areas as antitrust, products liability, securities litigation and, perhaps first and foremost, healthcare and medical malpractice. The team was recently appointed by the Federal Court in Ohio as co-lead counsel to represent a class of foundry resin manufacturers against allegations of price-fixing.

The Lawyers: **Jonathan Piper** (see p.900) maintains a well-deserved reputation as a *"seasoned and aggressive"* expert in media and communications law. He has been busy recently defending six members of the media in a large libel case brought by a prominent figure against a number of government entities and media organizations. **Robert Newton** (see p.900) received glowing recommendations for his work in medical malpractice and products liability defense. Interviewees described him as *"detail-oriented and experienced at working closely with doctors."* His colleague **Christopher Nyhan** (see p.900) also garnered praise as a "*top-notch*" medical malpractice defense litigator.

The Clients: Microsoft; Visa; Nestlé Waters North America and Sherwin-Williams.

Verrill Dana, LLP
See firm details p.908

The Firm: This quality litigation department continues to climb our rankings, *en route* to a full recovery from the departures it has faced in recent times. A substantial team of 20 "*smart and classy*" attorneys was praised for taking a "*collaborative approach*" to meeting the diverse needs of local and national clients. It has long been recognized as a leader in securities litigation, and also offers expertise in antitrust, construction, bankruptcy and products liability cases. Intellectual property litigation is another important area of focus, and recent cases include a patent infringement matter concerning ski boots and apparel. The firm was lead counsel in the State of Maine's litigation against the tobacco industry, helping its client to obtain an award of approximately $1.5 billion. Other high-profile work includes successfully representing CasinosNO!, a group opposed to the building of a $600 million casino in Maine by Native American groups. Testament to the firm's continuing growth in the region is the opening of a new office in Boston, headed by senior litigation partner George Field.

The Lawyers: James Kilbreth (see p.899) enjoys a busy caseload of commercial litigation, including environmental, antitrust and securities disputes. Clients seek him out for his "*sound legal and business knowledge,*" coupled with "*common sense and great intelligence.*"

The Clients: Ford; International Paper; Waste Management; PPG Industries; Parsons; HE Sargent; Hannaford Bros.; Duke Energy; Bowdoin College; Bar Harbor Bank & Trust; Jasper Wyman & Son; Toyota; LandVest; Noranda and DeCoster Egg Farms.

Band 3

Berman & Simmons
The Firm: Market commentators praised this firm for the depth of its litigation department, which operates out of three offices across Maine, and its mixture of strategic acumen and integrity. As one source put it, the team is "*tactically strong and honorable at the same time.*" The majority of its time is devoted to representing plaintiffs in a broad spectrum of commercial litigation. This includes work in medical malpractice, personal injury and professional negligence.

The Lawyers: The "*tenacious*" William Robitzek was recommended to researchers for being "*unafraid to try a case,*" no matter how complex or important. He handles a broad range of litigation, including business torts, professional negligence and personal injury. Much of his

workload is taken on a contingency-fee basis.

The Clients: The firm represents numerous local businesses, insurance companies and individuals.

Eaton Peabody
The Firm: Ten litigation experts make up a widely admired department. They act for both defendants and plaintiffs, and have been busy over the past year handling business and real estate disputes, railroad cases and employment litigation. Other key areas of focus are products liability, First Amendment cases and personal injury work, and the team advises banks and financial institutions on a variety of matters. Recent highlights include obtaining a jury award of $640,000 for a plaintiff in a federal court personal injury case brought against a construction company.

The Lawyers: "*Commercially savvy*" **Bernard Kubetz** was recommended by market sources for his expertise in commercial litigation, including banking and personal injury cases. Clients applaud him as a "*mature and thoughtful*" attorney, who displays "*extraordinary sensitivity and judgment.*" He boasts a statewide litigation practice, as well as representing some out-of-state clients.

The Clients: GE; Fidelity Investments; New Balance Athletic Shoe and Bangor Publishing.

Harvey & Frank
The Firm: With only two lawyers, this commercial litigation boutique lacks the resources and capacity of many of its competitors. However, the quality of its "*top-notch*" attorneys earned it widespread praise. Areas of particular expertise include medical malpractice defense, personal injury, antitrust litigation and intellectual property, though it handles a broad range of general corporate and commercial disputes. The firm actively encourages the use of alternative dispute resolution, and is helping clients to resolve an increasing number of disputes through mediation. The pair advises on an even mixture of Maine-based and out-of-state litigation, and is currently representing the plaintiffs in a multi-state class action brought against a major automobile manufacturer, alleging collusive agreements preventing the importation of vehicles from Canada into the USA.

The Lawyers: **Charles Harvey** is "*extremely witty and persuasive; he has a knack of capturing a jury,*" say peers. Sources also remarked on his "*talent for getting things done in a pleasant and consensual way.*" He is particularly renowned for his expertise in medical malpractice and general commercial litigation. **Robert Frank**, meanwhile, is the quieter, more academic of the pair. He was applauded for his "*superb analysis and superior legal skills,*" and is much admired for his skill in antitrust law and trade regulation.

The Clients: Maine Community College Sys-

tem; Dead River; MaineHealth; Georgia-Pacific and Johnson Outdoors.

Norman, Hanson & DeTroy, LLC
The Firm: The bedrock of this litigation department lies in insurance defense, an area for which it received hearty praise. This is complemented by expertise in healthcare, professional liability, employment, environmental and construction litigation. The firm also enjoys a stellar reputation for its handling of complex mediation.

The Lawyers: Widely acknowledged as a "*top-grade*" litigator, **Peter DeTroy** "*possesses a broad range of litigation skills; he can handle anything in a courtroom,*" say interviewees. Clients reserved particular plaudits for his "*gift – the human touch,*" and expressed their trust in his "*excellent sense of perspective and judgment.*" He handles general business litigation, insurance, products liability and criminal defense cases.

The Clients: Acadia Insurance; AIAC; Bath Iron Works; Boise Cascade and Maine Medical Center.

Rudman & Winchell LLC
The Firm: This ten-member, Bangor-based team asserts a strong presence in the Maine litigation market. It advises on a variety of matters, including insurance defense, employment and business litigation, and often receives cross-referrals from the firm's booming transactional practice. The group increasingly employs the methods of alternative dispute resolution, especially mediation, to assist clients in complex commercial disputes. It serves a variety of companies, ranging from healthcare providers to manufacturers and a growing number of insurers.

The Lawyers: **John McCarthy**'s caseload includes employment law, insurance defense and business litigation. He is currently involved in an appeal in a complex probate dispute. Here he is defending a bank as a trustee in a case in which beneficiaries are attempting to break a trust of several million dollars. He is joined in this year's rankings by **David King**, who is an "*absolute prince*" according to peers. He advises on professional liability, personal injury, premises liability and insurance defense. Interviewees consider him an "*insightful*" advocate with a "*reliable and stable*" presence in court.

The Clients: Webber Oil; Vermont Mutual Insurance; Husson College; Bank of America; LandAmerica and a number of individuals.

Other Notable Practitioners
Gerald Petruccelli of Petruccelli Martin & Haddow LLP is an "*extraordinarily good communicator and strategist*" who has "*real presence in the courtroom.*" Clients admire his ability to be "*reasonably aggressive but conciliatory when he needs to be.*" He manages a remarkably broad caseload, employing his expertise in professional liability,

stockholder disputes, construction and insurance defense at both the first instance and appellate levels. He advises a client base of large accounting firms, contractors, liability insurers, banks, hospitals, real estate developers and pharmaceutical manufacturers.

REAL ESTATE

Maine
Leading firms (Real Estate)

[1] **BERNSTEIN, SHUR, SAWYER** *Portland*
JENSEN BAIRD GARDNER & HENRY *Portland*
PIERCE ATWOOD LLP *Portland*
VERRILL DANA, LLP *Portland*

[2] **EATON PEABODY** *Bangor*
PERKINS, THOMPSON, HINCKLEY *Portland*

[3] **DRUMMOND WOODSUM & MACMAHON** *Portland*
PRETI FLAHERTY BELIVEAU PACHIOS *Portland*
RUDMAN & WINCHELL LLC *Bangor*

Leading individuals (Real Estate)

Senior Statesman
WEBBER Walter *Jensen Baird, Portland*

[1] **KEELER Dennis** *Pierce Atwood, Portland*
MILLER Charles *Bernstein Shur, Portland*

[2] **COGGESHALL Christopher** *Verrill Dana, Portland*
COLE III Kenneth *Jensen Baird, Portland*
LEONARD III Edward *Eaton Peabody, Bangor*
OESTREICHER Charles *Verrill Dana, Portland*
SCHWARTZ Jaimie *Bernstein Shur, Portland*
SMITH Nathan *Bernstein Shur, Portland*

[3] **HUBER Karen** *Eaton Peabody, Bangor*
PIETROPAOLI Paul *Perkins Thompson, Portland*
SCANNELL Gordon *Perkins Thompson, Portland*
SHINAY Richard *Drummond Woodsum, Portland*
STEVENS Winfred *Rudman & Winchell, Bangor*
WOODBURY Judith *Pierce Atwood, Portland*

Firms and individuals are listed alphabetically in each band.

Band 1

Bernstein, Shur, Sawyer & Nelson, PA

See firm details p.903

The Firm: This multifaceted real estate practice garnered praise for its expertise in property sales and acquisitions, financing and leasing. About 15 *"attentive"* attorneys attract developers, landlords, tenants, banks and financial institutions from Maine and across the USA. Recent highlights include assisting in the acquisition and development of a 136-unit luxury apartment complex on the South Portland waterfront, involving permanent financing in excess of $15 million. This was the first residential development in Maine to benefit from tax increment financing. The team was also involved in the acquisition, financing and leasing of a former restaurant facility in Brunswick, to be developed into a food court with anchor tenants including Starbucks and Subway. Advice on low-income housing and other tax-enhanced projects features prominently in the team's workload.

The Lawyers: **Charles Miller** (see p.900) is an *"absolute pleasure to work with"* say his clients. They particularly appreciate his *"intelligence and result-oriented approach."* He represents developers, large property owners and tenants, advising on property developments, leasing and financing. **Jaimie Schwartz** (see p.901) received plaudits for his *"terrific understanding of all the legal twists and turns of the real estate profession."* His practice is focused on the acquisition, sale and development of industrial, residential and office projects. **Nathan Smith** (see p.901) completes a trio of *"high-quality"* real estate practitioners. A title expert, he is sought out by clients for his *"businesslike professionalism and grasp of the nuts and bolts of real estate transactions."* His experience spans not just the gamut of commercial real estate matters, but related environmental and conservation issues.

The Clients: Architectural Doors & Windows; ATC Realty; Bramlie; Dirigo Management; General Signal; Wal-Mart; Long Creek Properties; RiverPlace Development; Weingarten Realty Trust; CHR Realty and several Maine cities and towns.

Jensen Baird Gardner & Henry

The Firm: The firm features prominently in the Maine real estate market, and is continuing to expand, having brought on board four additional real estate attorneys over the last year. It assists clients in a range of development projects, including retail centers, offices, housing facilities and tax increment financing districts, and was also said to be *"heavily into land use and permitting."* Its client roster includes developers, local businesses, commercial lenders, landlords and tenants.

The Lawyers: *"Pragmatic and knowledgeable"* **Kenneth Cole** was recommended to researchers for his experience and skill. Peers acknowledge that he will *"work hard to structure a deal."* He was particularly recommended for his expertise in representing municipalities in real estate, land use and title matters. *"Gentlemanly"* **Walter Webber** is the *"patriarch of the practice"* who has *"seen more deals than anyone."* *"A wonderful lawyer and a very decent human being,"* he now acts as counsel to the firm, and provides expertise in a range of real estate issues, including land use and permitting.

The Clients: Stewart Title Guaranty; Banknorth; Packard Development; Commonwealth Land Title Insurance and York-Cumberland Housing Development.

Pierce Atwood LLP

See firm details p.906

The Firm: This 13-lawyer real estate team handles an assortment of transactional, title and land use matters. Clients praised the firm as *"good value for the dollar"* with a *"remarkable sense of client loyalty,"* and observed that its size and resources make it a top choice for large-scale transactions. It advises on a range of acquisitions and developments, including offices, retail centers and warehouses. For example, it recently represented major client Hannaford Bros. in its acquisition of a smaller supermarket chain with stores across Massachusetts and New Hampshire. The team also acted for Kimco Realty in connection with the financing of ten fast food stores in New York and Maine. Other recent work includes the acquisition, permitting and financing of a shopping center in Bangor.

The Lawyers: With his *"encyclopedic knowledge and creativity,"* **Dennis Keeler** (see p.898) is one of the state's *"preeminent"* real estate practitioners. He works hard for his clients to *"conclude transactions carefully, without too much hassle."* Typical work includes advice on commercial acquisitions, sales and development projects, and he has quite a focus on the retail sector. His colleague **Judith Woodbury** (see p.902) joins him in our rankings this year. Interviewees singled her out as an *"essential component"* of the team in complex real estate transactions, and she was particularly applauded by clients as a *"thorough, focused and technical"* attorney, with considerable expertise in title matters.

The Clients: The firm represents a varied client base, including supermarkets, healthcare facilities, retail centers and developers. Examples are Kimco Realty and Hannaford Bros.

Verrill Dana, LLP

See firm details p.908

The Firm: Verrill Dana enjoys a long-established profile in Maine's real estate market. A team of eight *"classy, smart and reasonable"* lawyers impresses clients with its high service standards. As one put it, *"I'm always involved, I get asked questions and can ask questions, they do what they say they will and they keep to schedule."* Areas of expertise include commercial lending, leasing and the sale and purchase of high-end residential real estate. Other typical work includes the development of manufacturing

www.ChambersandPartners.com

All quotes in the text are from interviews with clients and competitors.

895

facilities, retail centers, residential and leisure facilities and industrial parks for its client roster of landlords, tenants, lenders, developers and individuals.

The Lawyers: *"Personable and knowledgeable"* **Charles Oestreicher** (see p.900) was widely and enthusiastically recommended to researchers. *"In the mold of Walter Webber – a top notch adviser and a gentleman,"* he has a broader practice than many. This spans most aspects of real estate, such as title insurance and conservation easement work, but also stretches as far as labor negotiations. He is particularly associated with high-end residential work for wealthy clients. *"Bright and skilled"* **Chris Coggeshall** (see p.897) is *"top for leasing work – no one can touch him for that."* Peers appreciate his commitment to driving deals through: he *"focuses on re-examining issues and finding practical solutions,"* said one. Highly respected real estate practitioner Robert Patterson sadly died this year.

The Clients: GMO Renewable Resources, Portland Symphony Orchestra and LandVest feature in the firm's client base.

Band 2

Eaton Peabody

The Firm: Six attorneys devote themselves full time to real estate here. The group is widely touted as the leader in Bangor, which gives it a particularly strong foothold in timberland work. Unsurprisingly then, it handled numerous sales and acquisitions of timberland over the past year, typically ranging in value between one and 250 million dollars. However it also advises on a range of other real property matters, including development projects and commercial lending. In this latter area, the team has handled about 150 commercial loans over the past year, relating to the development of hotel complexes, condominiums and military bases, among other things.

The Lawyers: One of the *"deans of real estate"* in Maine, **Edward Leonard** won plaudits for his expertise in timberlands, natural resources and real estate lending matters. His *"prestige and general experience"* are much in demand among clients. **Karen Huber** was recommended to researchers as a *"talented lawyer with a particular specialty in timber law and a good book of business."* Her expertise and energy were admired by clients and peers alike.

The Clients: International Paper; Wagner Forest Management; Seven Islands Land; Prentiss & Carlisle; Pingree Associates; Bangor Savings Bank; Merrill Bank; Machias Savings Bank and United Kingfield Bank.

Perkins, Thompson, Hinckley & Keddy, PA

The Firm: Perkins Thompson remains a prominent player in Maine's real estate circles, and has enjoyed a busy year handling numerous property transactions. Typical matters include advice on acquiring, selling, leasing and developing various facilities. Agricultural work is considered to be a particular niche, and the group is also active in the creation of hotel and retail complexes and business campuses. As well as negotiating transaction and finance documents, the team is often also involved in environmental risk management issues and permitting.

The Lawyers: *"Bright and talented"* **Paul Pietropaoli** was applauded for his expertise in commercial real estate transactions. Market sources were particularly impressed with his *"excellent negotiating skill and ability to make things happen."* He is joined in this year's rankings by *"pragmatic transactional lawyer"* **Gordon Scannell**. He provides expertise across the spectrum of real estate matters, advising lenders, businesses and municipalities on land use, development and commercial lending issues.

The Clients: The team advises numerous businesses, developers and municipalities.

Band 3

Drummond Woodsum & MacMahon

See firm details p.904

The Firm: This compact but proactive commercial real estate team is housed within the firm's corporate department. It handles a steady stream of transactional work, including the sale, acquisition and leasing of commercial, residential and industrial real property. *"A diverse practice with strong regional clients,"* the team also offers expertise in zoning and permitting.

The Lawyers: Market commentators singled out **Richard Shinay** (see p.901) from this team, praising his talent, knowledge and hard work in the real estate arena. *"A good, pragmatic lawyer,"* he is experienced in a range of matters, including advising on mortgage foreclosures, development projects, land preservation and title

insurance matters. Sources describe him as a meticulous, *"technically oriented"* adviser with a strong background in title issues.

The Clients: The firm acts for owners, developers and lessees, and frequently assists lenders in multistate financings.

Preti Flaherty Beliveau Pachios & Haley LLC

See firm details p.907

The Firm: This four-strong team firm joins our rankings this year following widespread praise for its expertise and responsiveness. Well versed in the gamut of real estate matters, the group regularly assists clients with advice on real estate developments, leasing and financings. Recent work has included acting for a client in the refinancing and restructuring of seven low-income elderly housing projects in New Hampshire, four of which were syndicated as low-income housing tax credit properties.

The Lawyers: The real estate team includes Michael Gentile.

The Clients: Brascan Financial; Bath Iron Works; Housing Initiatives of New England and Harpers Development.

Rudman & Winchell LLC

The Firm: Market sources praised this eight-attorney real estate team as *"terrific across the board."* The firm handles a variety of real property work, including residential and commercial sales and acquisitions, leases and loan transactions, for a client base consisting of banks and lending institutions, developers, landlords, tenants and timberland managers. This last category is particularly important, as the group boasts niche expertise in assisting clients in the timberland industry, an area of high activity in Maine, which includes providing ongoing advice to a number of large pulp and paper companies.

The Lawyers: **Winfred Stevens** was warmly praised for his *"client-focused approach and excellent judgment."* Clients seek out his expertise in handling real estate transactions, financings and title insurance work.

The Clients: JD Irving; Merrill Merchants Bank; KeyBank; McPherson Timberlands; Quirk Auto Park and HO Bouchard.

Leaders in Maine

AHRENS, Philip FW
Pierce Atwood LLP, Portland
207 791 1298
pahrens@pierceatwood.com
Recommended in Environment

Practice Areas: Has concentrated on environmental matters almost exclusively since 1977. Counsels clients on complex permitting and enforcement matters before the Maine Department of Environmental Protection and Land Use Regulation Commission, and other state/federal environmental agencies. Recent successful client representation includes developers of three natural gas-fired electric generating facilities; a large-scale wind energy project; significant expansion of a major shipyard; 20-year expansion of a commercial solid waste facility; and a new major bottled water facility.
Prof. Memberships: ABA, Vice-Chair, State and Regional Environmental Cooperation Committee; Maine Bar Association.
Career: Deputy Attorney General and Chief, Natural Resources Section, Maine Attorney General's Office (1977-90).
Publications: Maine Environmental and Land Use Statutes Deskbook.
Personal: JD, University of Michigan Law School, 1975; BA, Amherst College (cum laude), 1968; US Navy, 1968-72.

AMORY, Daniel
Drummond Woodsum & MacMahon, Portland 207 772 1941
damory@dwmlaw.com
Recommended in Bankruptcy

Practice Areas: Business disputes, workouts, commercial bankruptcy proceedings and bankruptcy litigation, focusing on business reorganization, lender liability, fraudulent transfer and related issues; also has expertise in Indian law and Indian gaming.
Prof. Memberships: Fellow, American College of Bankruptcy and Member, American Bankruptcy Institute; listed in Best Lawyers in America since 1987 in the field of creditors' rights.
Career: He joined the firm in 1973; was Chair of the Bankruptcy and Reorganization Section of the Maine Bar Association 1984-85; assisted in the enactment of the Uniform Fraudulent Transfer Act and various UCC articles by the Maine legislature; and has lectured in the field of insolvency law. He served on the Committee on Local Rules, United States District Court for the District of Maine, 1985-93, and the Committee on Local Rules, United States Bankruptcy Court for the District of Maine (1995-2000).
Personal: He graduated from Yale Law School (1973) and Harvard College (1967 magna cum laude), and is active in civic affairs.

BOPP III, Fred
Perkins, Thompson, Hinckley & Keddy, P.A., Portland 207 774 2635
Recommended in Bankruptcy

BROWNE, Juliet T
Verrill Dana, LLP, Portland
207 774 4000
jbrowne@verrilldana.com
Recommended in Environment

Practice Areas: Environmental permitting, compliance and litigation. Chair, Environmental Group. Vice-Chair, Trial Department.
Prof. Memberships: Admitted to Bar: 1990, California; 1996, Maine. MSBA Natural Resources and Environmental Law Section.
Career: Skadden, Arps, Slate, Meagher & Flom (1990-93); Assistant Attorney General, Republic of Palau (1993-95); Verrill Dana (1996-present).
Publications: 'Brownfields: A Comprehensive Guide to Redeveloping Contaminated Property,' Maine Chapter, ABA Section of Natural Resources, Energy and Environmental Law (1997).
Personal: University of Michigan (BA, 1984); University of California, Boalt Hall School of Law (JD, 1990). Articles editor, California Law Review, 1989-90. Trustee, Unity College.

CHAMPOUX, David
Pierce Atwood LLP, Portland
207 791 1100
DChampoux@PierceAtwood.com
Recommended in Corporate/M&A

Practice Areas: Concentrates in corporate, finance, and general transactional representation, including all aspects of corporate, securities, and commercial law, focusing on representing corporations and individuals in a wide variety of transactional settings. Experience includes securities law, special purpose entities such as limited liability companies, M&A, venture capital financing, and SEC reporting and compliance.
Prof. Memberships: New York Bar (1985); Maine Bar (1987). Chair, Maine Bar's Business Law Section (2001).
Career: Partner, (1993-). Listed in a leading legal publication, 2003-04 edition, for corporate, M&A, and securities.
Personal: University of Virginia School of Law, JD 1984; Harvard College, AB (cum laude) 1981.

CLEMENT Jr, Roger A
Verrill Dana, LLP, Portland
207 774 4000
rclement@verrilldana.com
Recommended in Bankruptcy

Practice Areas: Chair, Bankruptcy and Commercial Law Department. Experience in representing Chapter 11 debtors-in-possession, Trustees, creditorsí committees, secured creditors, and landlords in local, regional and national Chapter 11 cases. Has represented railroads, healthcare institutions, technolo-

gy companies, manufacturers, service companies, timber companies, landlords, acquirers of assets, banks and insurance companies in bankruptcy cases, restructurings and liquidations.
Prof. Memberships: Admitted to Bar: 1991, Maine. American Bankruptcy Institute.
Career: Partner since 1997.
Publications: Going For Broke With Intellectual Property, 17 Maine Bar Journal 178 (2002).
Personal: Bowdoin College (AB, 1986); University of Maine School of Law (JD, 1991); notes editor, Maine Law Review.

COGGESHALL, Christopher J W
Verrill Dana, LLP, Portland
207 774 4000
ccoggeshall@verrilldana.com
Recommended in Real Estate

Practice Areas: Focuses on commercial real estate transactions, including negotiating, structuring and documenting commercial, retail and industrial developments, shopping centers, and office and apartment buildings. Has an extensive practice in drafting and negotiating commercial leases, acquisition documents and government-assisted housing projects.
Prof. Memberships: Admitted to Bar: 1970, Maine; 1969, New Hampshire.
Career: Partner, practicing at Verrill Dana for over 30 years.
Personal: Born: Brattleboro, Vermont, April 2, 1940. Education: Harvard Law School (LLB, 1968); Cornell University (BMetE, 1965).

COLE III, Kenneth
Jensen Baird Gardner & Henry, Portland 207 775 7271
Recommended in Real Estate

CULLEY, Peter
Pierce Atwood LLP, Portland
207 791 1288
pculley@pierceatwood.com
Recommended in Litigation

Practice Areas: Extensive experience in representing corporate interests in jury trials in all courts. Represents manufacturers, financial institutions, and professional service firms in a broad range of matters, including business litigation, professional liability and product liability actions.
Prof. Memberships: International Association of Defense Counsel; American Board of Trial Advocates; Fellow, American College of Trial Lawyers.
Career: Jacobson v Raytheon Aircraft Company: Judgment for defendant client in air-crash case; Davric v Rancourt, et al.: Successful defense of client in conspiracy and anti-trust case; Guitard v Gorham Savings Bank: Judgment for bank on all claims in a class action lawsuit; and Haines, et al. v Great Northern Paper Company: Successful defense of one of Maine's largest landowners in

breach of contract claim seeking unlimited access to 600,000 acres of Maine forest lands.
Personal: Boston University, JD 1968; University of Maine, AB 1965.

CURRIER, Douglas P
Verrill Dana, LLP, Portland
207 774 4000
dcurrier@verrilldana.com
Recommended in Employment

Practice Areas: Chair, Labor and Employment Law Department. Immigration.
Prof. Memberships: Admitted to Bar: 1985, Maine; US District Court, District of Maine. Maine State Bar Association Labor and Employment Law Section; National Association of College and University Attorneys.
Career: Having practiced law at Verrill Dana since 1985, Mr Currier has extensive experience representing employers, unionized and non-unionized, in all aspects of labor and employment law, including litigation and personnel counseling.
Personal: Born: Cleveland, Ohio, September 15, 1959. Education: Middlebury College (BA, cum laude, 1982); Ohio State University College of Law (JD, with honors, 1985).

DEROSBY, Anthony R
Pierce Atwood LLP, Portland
207 791 1343
aderosby@pierceatwood.com
Recommended in Employment

Practice Areas: Directs firm's Immigration Practice Group. Practice includes all aspects of employment and immigration law. Extensive experience in business and employment immigration as well as DOL, WHA, OSHA, and IRCA compliance, inspections and enforcement.
Prof. Memberships: Admitted in Maine (1988) and Massachusetts (1995). Member of American Bar Association, Labor and Employment Law Committee; American Immigration Lawyers Association; American Bar Association, Occupational Safety and Health Law Committee; Massachusetts State Bar Association, Employment Law Section; and Maine State Bar Association, Employment Law Committee.
Career: Joined Pierce Atwood, 1988; became Partner, 1995.
Publications: Section Editor, Wage and Hour Laws: A State-by-State Survey (ABA/BNA 2004).
Personal: JD (cum laude), University of Maine School of Law, 1988; University of North Carolina, Chapel Hill, 1980-81; BA (cum laude), Bates College, 1980.

DETROY, Peter
Norman, Hanson & DeTroy, LLC, Portland 207 774 7000
Recommended in Litigation

DOYLE, Thomas R
Pierce Atwood LLP, Portland
207 791 1214
tdoyle@pierceatwood.com
Recommended in Environment

Practice Areas: Environmental and land use law, including complex adjudicatory proceedings and corporate transactions.
Prof. Memberships: Vice-Chair, ABA's Environmental Transactions and Brownfields Committee.
Career: Successfully licensed major semiconductor fabrication facility, largest industrial investment in Maine's history; successfully licensed several high profile development projects, including energy, manufacturing, and waste facilities.
Publications: 'A Developer's Dream or Nightmare: Maine's Site Location, Storm Water, and Traffic Permitting Laws,' MSBA (2004); co-author: 'Listing Distinct Population Segments of Endangered Species: Has it Gone Too Far?', ABA's Natural Resources & Environment (2001).
Personal: Yale University, BA 1975; Suffolk University Law School, JD (cum laude)1982.

EATON II, George
Rudman & Winchell LLC, Bangor
207 947 4501
Recommended in Corporate/M&A

ERWIN, James R
Pierce Atwood LLP, Portland
207 791 1237
jerwin@pierceatwood.com
Recommended in Employment

Practice Areas: Partner and Chair, Employment Group. Representation of management in federal, state and administrative proceedings, and preventative services.
Prof. Memberships: Employment Law Alliance; ABA (Employment and Labor Relations Committee, Litigation Section); American Judicature Society (Director 2001-); American Counsel Association (Director 2002-); Maine State Bar Association; Maine Trial Lawyers Association.
Career: Assistant Attorney General, Maine (major prosecutions) (1978-83); Commissioner, Maine Human Rights Commission (1985-87).
Publications: 'Model Jury Instructions, Employment Litigation', 2d ed. (ABA 2005) (Board of Editors); 'Employment Litigation Handbook' (ABA 1998) (chapter author).
Personal: Boston University School of Law, JD 1978; Dartmouth College, AB (cum laude, High Distinction) 1975.

FRANK, Robert
Harvey & Frank, Portland
207 775 1300
Recommended in Litigation

FRYER, Gregory
Verrill Dana, LLP, Portland
207 774 4000
gfryer@verrilldana.com
Recommended in Corporate/M&A

Practice Areas: Securities, corporate, venture capital. Has represented bidder or target in every major takeover battle in Maine since 1985.
Prof. Memberships: Admitted to Bar: 1981, New York; 1983, Georgia; 1985, Maine. Maine State Bar Association: Chair, Business Law Section, (1991 and 1992); Chair, Securities Law Subcommittee (1993-); Boston Bar Association (2004-); Drafting Committee, Maine Business Corporation Act and Maine Uniform Securities Act; Board of Directors, Maine Bar Foundation (2004-).
Personal: Dartmouth College (AB, magna cum laude, 1976); Cornell University (JD, cum laude, 1979); editor, 'Cornell Law Review'.

HAMILTON, P Andrew
Eaton Peabody, Bangor
207 947 0111
Recommended in Environment

HARVEY, Charles
Harvey & Frank, Portland
207 775 1300
Recommended in Litigation

HEWEY, Melissa
Drummond Woodsum & MacMahon, Portland 207 772 1941
mhewey@dwmlaw.com
Recommended in Employment

Practice Areas: Complex civil litigation including school law and employment matters, defense against discrimination, sexual harassment and civil rights claims. Also has experience in a variety of forms of alternative dispute resolution.
Prof. Memberships: She is a Member of the Maine Trial Lawyers Association as well as the Maine State and Cumberland County Bar Associations. She serves on the Local Rules Committee of the United States District Court and is a Member of the Gignoux Inn of Court.
Career: Joined Drummond Woodsum and MacMahon in 1987 and is Chair of the Trial Services Group.
Publications: Wrote and produced training videos entitled, 'Harassment: Its about more than just sex,' 'Effective Staff evaluations: A Legal Perspective,' and 'Student Expulsions: Effective Practice and Procedures.' She is a contributing author to Maine School Law, Third Edition.
Personal: JD from University of Maine School Law (magna cum laude) 1987; BA from Wesleyan University 1980.

HIGH, Michael E
Drummond Woodsum & MacMahon, Portland 207 772 1941
mhigh@dwmlaw.com
Recommended in Corporate/M&A

Practice Areas: Represents businesses, investors, lenders and borrowers throughout New England in a wide range of corporate and commercial matters, including mergers and acquisitions, corporate finance, shareholder matters, private placements, venture capital financing, technology licensing and transfers, and intellectual property.
Prof. Memberships: Massachusetts Bar Association, 1983; Maine Bar Association, 1985; listed in a leading US legal publication and has served as Chair of the Business Law Section of the Maine State Bar Association. He was Co-Chair of a Bar Sub-committee that oversaw the adoption of Revised Article 9 in Maine, and a State Task Force Leader on the Corporate Law Revision Committee of the Business Law Section that revised and recommended the adoption of the new Maine Business Corporation Act (effective 1 July 2003).
Career: Practiced at Choate, Hall & Stewart in Boston, MA for several years before joining Drummond Woodsum and MacMahon. He is Chair of the firm's Business and Commercial Services Group.
Personal: Graduated from Cornell Law School (1983) where he was an articles editor of the 'International Law Journal'.

HUBER, Karen
Eaton Peabody, Bangor
207 947 0111
Recommended in Real Estate

JACOBS, Peter
Pierce Atwood LLP, Portland
207 791 1353
pjacobs@pierceatwood.com
Recommended in Employment

Practice Areas: Labor and employment.
Prof. Memberships: Maine Bar Association.
Career: With 30 years experience, Peter represents both unionized and non-unionized employers, including a large number of hospitals and other healthcare providers, representing employers in union organizing campaigns, union contract negotiations, unfair labor practice proceedings, grievance arbitration cases. Peter also practices in the field of discrimination law before the EEOC and state discrimination agencies.
Publications: A twice published author, Peter is the Editor of 'Maine Business and Employment Law'.
Personal: Peter attended Brown University; London School of Economics; Cambridge University; and Harvard Law School, JD 1974.

JOHNSTON, Thomas
Eaton Peabody, Bangor
207 947 0111
Recommended in Employment

KAYATTA Jr, William
Pierce Atwood LLP, Portland
207 791 1100
wkayatta@pierceatwood.com
Recommended in Litigation

Practice Areas: Complex civil litigation; class actions; life and disability.
Prof. Memberships: Fellow, American College of Trial Lawyers; Chair, Maine Professional Ethics Commission (2002); President, Maine Bar Foundation (2004).
Career: Argued UNUM v Ward to USSCT; successfully defended $846 million asset purchase deal in FPL Energy v CMP; recovered $44 million in action concerning nuclear plant decommissioning in Maine Yankee v Federal Insurance Co.; either Lead or Lead Liaison defense counsel in 3 MDL class proceedings.
Personal: Harvard Law School, 1979 (Harv L Rev 1978-79); Amherst College, 1976; Clerk, Chief Judge Frank Coffin, US 1st Circuit Court of Appeals (1980).

KEACH, Robert J
Bernstein, Shur, Sawyer & Nelson, PA, Portland 207 774 1200
rkeach@bssn.com
Recommended in Bankruptcy

Practice Areas: Chair of the Bankruptcy and Insolvency Practice Group. His practice focuses on the representation of various parties in workouts and bankruptcy cases, including debtors, creditors, creditors' committees, lessors and third parties acquiring troubled companies and/or their assets.
Prof. Memberships: Maine State Bar Association (Committee on Bankruptcy and Reorganization); American Bar Association (Section on Business, Banking and Corporations and Section on Real Estate, Probate and Trust Law); American Bankruptcy Institute (Certified Specialist, Business Bankruptcy Law, American Bankruptcy Board of Certification).
Personal: University of Maine School of Law (JD, cum laude, 1980); Univesity of Vermont (BA, magna cum laude, 1977).

KEELER, Dennis C
Pierce Atwood LLP, Portland
207 791 1331
dkeeler@pierceatwood.com
Recommended in Real Estate

Practice Areas: Chair, Real Estate Group. Practices primarily in the real estate development area, with emphasis on representing developers and owners of retail centers, office buildings, commercial projects and large residential/resort developments throughout New England and the East Coast.
Prof. Memberships: Colorado Bar (1981); Maine Bar (1984); Secretary and Member, Board of Directors of Maine Real Estate Development Association; Member, International Council of Shopping Centers.
Career: Partner (1990-). Practiced in Denver, Colorado. Selected for inclusion in a leading legal publication, 2003-04 and 2004-05 editions, for real estate law.
Personal: University of Denver, JD 1981; University of Maryland, BA 1975.

KILBRETH, James
Verrill Dana, LLP, Portland
207 774 4000
jkilbreth@verrilldana.com
Recommended in Environment, Litigation
Practice Areas: Chair, Trial Department. Complex commercial litigation, anti-trust, securities, and class actions; white collar crime; environmental.
Prof. Memberships: Admitted to Bar: 1976, District of Columbia; 1980, US Supreme Court; 1984, Maine; 1991, US District Court, District of Maine; US Court of Appeals for the DC Circuit, First, Fifth, and Eleventh Circuits. Maine State and American Bar Associations; Maine Trial Lawyers Association; Maine Equal Justice Partners Legal Panel; Gignoux Inn of Court.
Career: State of Maine, Chief Deputy Attorney General (1987-90), Deputy Attorney General (Chief, Litigation Division, 1985-86), Assistant Attorney General (Environmental Division, 1983-85), Associate, Wilmer, Cutler & Pickering, 1976-83.
Publications: 'Brownfields: A Comprehensive Guide to Redeveloping Contaminated Property,' Maine Chapter, ABA Section of Natural Resources, Energy and Environmental Law (1997); 'Minimizing Environmental Liability for Lenders and Corporate Fiduciaries in Maine,' NBI (1993).
Personal: Education: Harvard College (BA, cum laude, 1970); Northeastern University (MA, 1974); American University School of Law (JD, magna cum laude, 1976). Director and Past President, Southern Africa Legal Services and Legal Education Project.

KING, David
Rudman & Winchell LLC, Bangor
207 947 4501
Recommended in Litigation

KUBETZ, Bernard
Eaton Peabody, Bangor
207 947 0111
Recommended in Litigation

LEONARD III, Edward
Eaton Peabody, Bangor
207 947 0111
Recommended in Real Estate

LOGIUDICE, Susan E
Preti Flaherty Beliveau Pachios & Haley LLC, Portland 207 791 3000
sel@preti.com
Recommended in Corporate/M&A
Practice Areas: Chair of Preti Flaherty's Business Law Practice Group. Concentrates practice in business organizations and commercial transactions, including mergers and acquisitions, entity formation and governance, corporate finance, joint ventures, private placements and venture capital financings. She also advises family owned and closely held businesses through the life cycle of the business and on succession planning.

Prof. Memberships: Admitted to practice in Maine (1985); Maine State Bar Association, Corporate Law Section; American Bar Association, Business Law Section.
Career: Joined Preti Flaherty in 1985. Became Partner, 1992, Member, Preti Flaherty Management Committee.
Personal: Born 22 November 1957. Northeastern University JD (1985), State University of New York at Binghamton (1979).

MACEWAN, Alan D
Verrill Dana, LLP, Portland
207 774 4000
amacewan@verrilldana.com
Recommended in Corporate/M&A
Practice Areas: Business acquisitions and sales; contracts; general corporate. Has represented domestic and foreign companies, public and private, in the acquisition or divestiture of companies and divisions.
Prof. Memberships: ABA, MSBA, ABA Negotiated Acquisitions Committee. Currently serves on the Editorial Committee, ABA Model Stock Purchase Agreement Revision Task Force; served on the Committee to Revise Maine's Business Corporation Act. Admitted in New York and Maine.
Career: Partner since 1993. Chair, Business Law Department. Former Legal Counsel, Maine Governer John R McKernan, Jr (1988-91).
Publications: Has lectured and written on mergers, acquisitions and contracts. Author, Blue Sky Regulation of REG D Offerings, 'The Review of Securities & Commodities Regulation' (1985).
Personal: Syracuse University (JD, 1981); editor, 'Syracuse Law Review'; Colby College (BA, 1978).

MAHONEY, Sean
Verrill Dana, LLP, Portland
207 774 4000
smahoney@verrilldana.com
Recommended in Environment
Practice Areas: Environmental Permitting and Litigation.
Prof. Memberships: Admitted to Bar: 1992, California; 1998, Maine. Past President, MSBA Natural Resources and Environmental Law Section; Maine Trial Lawyers Association; ABA Environment, Energy, and Natural Resources Law Sections.
Career: Clerk, Judge Fred I Parker, US District Court of Vermont (1992-93); Morrison & Foerster, LLP, San Francisco, CA (1993-97); United States Peace Corps, Sri Lanka (1986-89).
Publications: Superfund Contribution Protection After The Seventh Circuits, 'Akzo v. Aigner', 9 Toxics Law Reporter 17. New Hampshire Environmental Statutes Deskbook, 2000.
Personal: Bowdoin College (AB, magna cum laude, 1986); University of Virginia (JD, 1992).

MANHEIMER, Jacob A
Pierce Atwood LLP, Portland
207 791 1338
jmanheimer@pierceatwood.com
Recommended in Bankruptcy
Practice Areas: Bankruptcy and reorganization; creditors' rights; commercial finance.
Prof. Memberships: American Bankruptcy Institute; Maine State Bar Association.
Career: Associate, Fried Frank Harris Shriver & Jacobson (1983-86); Associate, Pierce Atwood (1986-90); Partner, Pierce Atwood (1991-date).
Personal: Fordham University School of Law, JD 1983; Dartmouth College, AB 1978.

MARCUS, Benjamin E
Drummond Woodsum & MacMahon, Portland 207 772 1941
bmarcus@dwmlaw.com
Recommended in Bankruptcy
Practice Areas: Represents lenders, businesses, investors and other stakeholders in connection with troubled business enterprises, including workouts, restructurings and proceedings under Chapter 11 of the US Bankruptcy Code. Serves as general outside counsel to numerous businesses in a variety of industries including oil and gas, aquaculture, light manufacturing, automotive, insurance and hospitality.
Prof. Memberships: Maine Bar Association; American Bar Association, International Law Section; Local Rules Committee, United States Bankruptcy Court, District of Maine.
Career: Clerk, Honorable Joseph L Tauro, Chief Judge, US District Court, District of Massachusetts; joined Drummond Woodsum & MacMahon in 1997; serves on the firm's Management Committee.
Personal: Graduated from Cornell Law School in 1986, magna cum laude, where he received the Order of Coif and served as editor in chief of the Cornell Law Review.

MARCUS, George
Marcus, Clegg & Mistretta PA, Portland
207 828 8000
Recommended in Bankruptcy

MCCARTHY, John
Rudman & Winchell LLC, Bangor
207 947 4501
Recommended in Litigation

MCGILL, Linda D
Bernstein, Shur, Sawyer & Nelson, PA, Portland 207 774 1200
lmcgill@bssn.com
Recommended in Employment
Practice Areas: All aspects of public and private sector employment law; labor-management negotiations; union avoidance; defense of discrimination claims; counsel on best practices and compliance; non-competition; intellectual property.
Prof. Memberships: US Supreme Court, First Circuit; Maine State and American

Bar Associations, Labor and Employment and Women's Law Section; Maine Bar Foundation Fellow; Advisor, International Senior Lawyers Program.
Career: Chief Counsel, Governor's Office of Employee Relations (1979-84); Perkins, Thompson, Hinckley, Keddy (1984-89); Founding Partner, Moon, Moss, McGill (1989); adjunct faculty, University of Maine Law School (1994-).
Personal: JD, Northeastern University, 1978; BS (magna cum laude), Randolph-Macon Woman's College, 1971.

MCGUIRE, Frank
Rudman & Winchell LLC, Bangor
207 947 4501
fmcguire@rudman-winchell.com
Recommended in Employment
Practice Areas: Chair, Employment Law Section. His practice includes a broad range of employer representation and advice in employment, labor and personnel matters; defense of discrimination claims before agencies and courts; labor relations; arbitration; and alternative dispute resolution.
Prof. Memberships: Admitted to practice in Massachusetts in 1979; Maine in 1980. Member, Maine State and American Bar Associations, Labor and Employment Sections; Penobscot County Bar Association.
Career: 1979 graduate of Northeastern University School of Law; law clerk to Justice Francis J Quirico of Massachusetts Supreme Judicial Court, 1979-80; joined Rudman & Winchell in 1980.
Personal: Northeastern University School of Law, Boston, Massachusetts, Juris Doctor 1979; Boston College, AB Magna cum laude, 1975, Political Science. Jesuit Volunteer Corps, 1975-76. Past President, Penobscot County Bar Association.

MCKAY, Daniel
Eaton Peabody, Bangor
207 947 0111
Recommended in Corporate/M&A

MCVEIGH, John P
Preti Flaherty Beliveau Pachios & Haley LLC, Portland 207 791 3000
jmcveigh@preti.com
Recommended in Bankruptcy
Practice Areas: Bankruptcy, commercial litigation, energy litigation. Representation of major secured or unsecured creditors in bankruptcy proceedings; litigation of a wide variety of commercial disputes, including all manner of contract, commercial landlord/tenant, internal governance and close corporation, and mechanic's lien issues. Significant litigation experience representing industrial energy consumers and other parties to energy contracts. A substantial element of practice is structuring transactions in advance to avoid litigation and bankruptcy pitfalls. Practice is in all state and federal courts. Admitted to the United States Supreme Court.

Prof. Memberships: American Bankruptcy Institute; Maine State Bar (1987), Cumberland County Bar.
Career: Member, Preti Flaherty, 1996.
Personal: Born 31 July 1947, BA University of Virginia, 1969, English Dept U Va, 1972-83, JD University of Virginia, 1987.

MESSERSCHMIDT, Michael
Preti Flaherty Beliveau Pachios & Haley LLC, Portland 207 791 3000
mmesserschmidt@preti.com
Recommended in Employment
Practice Areas: Chair of firm's Labor and Employment Law Practice Group. Focuses his practice on advising and defending management in employment discrimination, harassment, and civil rights claims, including federal and state court litigation. Also has extensive experience counseling employers on EEO compliance and risk management issues, and has handled numerous arbitrations under collective bargaining agreements as well as executive compensation agreements.
Prof. Memberships: Admitted to practice in Maine (1978); Maine State Bar Association, Labor and Employment Section; American Bar Association, Labor and Employment Law Section.
Career: Assistant Attorney General, State of Maine (Criminal Division) (1978-80). Joined Preti Flaherty 1980. Became Member, 1987. Managing Partner 1991-92.
Personal: Born 22 June 1953. University of Maine School of Law, JD, 1978; Harvard College, BA (Cum Laude), 1975.

MILLER, Charles E
Bernstein, Shur, Sawyer & Nelson, PA, Portland 207 774 1200
cmiller@bssn.com
Recommended in Real Estate
Practice Areas: Managing shareholder. His practice incorporates all elements of real estate law, including the acquisition, disposition, financing, leasing, management and development of real estate. He also focuses on corporate planning, including asset and stock transactions, investment banker selection, formation of business structures, entity planning and strategy.
Prof. Memberships: American Bar (Business and Real Estate Law Section; Subcommittee on Commercial Leases), Maine State Bar (Member, Real Estate Section), and Cumberland County Bar Associations.
Personal: University of Maine School of Law (JD, cum laude, 1979); managing editor, Maine Law Review (1978-79); University of Maine (MEd, 1973); Colby College (AB, 1969).

MOON, Richard G
Moon, Moss & Shapiro, P.A., Portland 207 775 6001
rmoon@moonmoss.com
Recommended in Employment
Practice Areas: Firm practice leader in private sector labor law with an emphasis on collective bargaining, arbitrations, mergers and acquisitions and matters before the National Labor Relations Board. Extensive national experience in all employment discrimination litigation and trials, including class action employee benefits and wage and hour matters. National practice in H1-B and related business immigration matters for technology and financial sectors.
Prof. Memberships: Admitted to practice in New York (1975); Maine (1978). American Bar Association, Labor and Employment Law Section; Maine State and Cumberland County Bar Associations; Fellow, American College of Labor and Employment Lawyers. Listed in several leading US legal publications for labor and employment law and litigation expertise.
Career: Joined Carter Ledyard & Milburn (New York 1975); Joined Perkins Thompson Hinckley & Keddy (Maine 1978); Founding Partner Moon Moss (1989).
Publications: 'Winning the Battle of the Expert: Strategies for Employers in the Wake of Faragher and Ellerth', Practising Law Institute, 2000; 'Sarbanes-Oxley Act: Protection From Retaliation For Whistleblowers', Georgetown University Law Center's 21st Annual Employment & Litigation Institute, 2003.
Personal: Born Detroit, Michigan, 18 January 1947. JD, University of Michigan (1974); AB, Dartmouth College (1969).

MORRELL, Stephen
Eaton Peabody, Brunswick
207 729 1144
Recommended in Bankruptcy

NEWTON, Robert O
Preti Flaherty Beliveau Pachios & Haley LLC, Portland 207 791 3000
rnewton@preti.com
Recommended in Litigation
Practice Areas: Extensive experience before State and Federal Courts and regulatory agencies in discovery and trial of complex cases involving medical, health and environmental issues. Has acted as litigation counsel for manufacturer in extensive FIFRA action by EPA (2003); plaintiff's counsel in wrongful death action by widow of environmental engineer (2003); chief trial counsel in defense of Maine's largest toxic tort case, involving 18 Plaintiffs alleging brain cancer and related diseases (2002); trial counsel in defense of product liability action by consumers alleging repetitive stress injury by use of computer and data entry keyboards (1998).
Prof. Memberships: Admitted to practice in Colorado (1971), Maine (1996) and New Hampshire (1997). Member, Maine and New Hampshire Bar Associations, Maine Trial Lawyers Association; admitted to practice before the United States District Courts for Colorado, Maine and New Hampshire, and 10th Circuit Court of Appeals.
Career: Partner of Myrick, Newton & Sullivan, Denver, CO (1973-81); professional furniture maker and cabinetmaker, Yarmouth, ME (1981-95); became Of Counsel to Preti Flaherty in 1996, became member, 1999. Member, Preti Flaherty Recruitment Committee, 2001-present.
Personal: Born 3 April 1946. JD, University of Denver College of Law, 1971, BA Duke University, 1968.

NYHAN, Christopher D
Preti Flaherty Beliveau Pachios & Haley LLC, Portland 207 791 3000
cnyhan@preti.com
Recommended in Litigation
Practice Areas: Chair of the firm's Medical Liability Group. Extensive experience in complex medical, antitrust and products liability. Tried over 100 jury trials in state and federal courts. Has argued over 20 cases to Maine Supreme Court.
Prof. Memberships: Admitted in ME (1976), Dist. of Columbia (1998) and various federal trial and appellate courts. Maine State Bar Assn. liaison to Model Professional Liability Demonstration Project of Maine State Legislature.
Career: Joined firm in 1976, became Partner in 1980. Member or Chair, Management and Hiring Committees. Frequent lecturer to medical and professional risk associations throughout New England. Listed in 'The Best Lawyers in America.'
Personal: Born 4 February 1946; JD, University of San Francisco (1976); MA, University of California, Berkeley (1973); BA, Boston College (1968).

OESTREICHER, Charles R
Verrill Dana, LLP, Portland
207 774 4000
coestreicher@verrilldana.com
Recommended in Real Estate
Practice Areas: Real estate; real estate brokerage; land use and zoning; conservation easements. Timberland acquisitions and sales.
Prof. Memberships: Admitted to Bar: 1968, Maine. Memberships: Maine State Bar Association Real Estate & Title Section; Cumberland County Bar Association (President, 1992); New England Land Title Association; ABA Real Property, Probate & Trust Section; member, American College of Real Estate Lawyers (ACREL).
Publications: Author, 'Maine Supplement to Principles of Real Estate Law', Castle Publishing, 1986, and updates.
Personal: Born: Pittsburgh, Pennsylvania, April 8, 1942. Education: Indiana University of Pennsylvania (BS, 1964); Case Western Reserve University (JD, 1968). Phi Alpha Delta.

PAYNE, Clare
Eaton Peabody, Bangor
207 947 0111
Recommended in Employment

PETRUCCELLI, Gerald
Petruccelli Martin & Haddow LLP, Portland 207 775 0200
Recommended in Litigation

PIETROPAOLI, Paul
Perkins, Thompson, Hinckley & Keddy, P.A., Portland 207 774 2635
Recommended in Real Estate

PIPER, Jonathan S
Preti Flaherty Beliveau Pachios & Haley LLC, Portland 207 791 3000
jpiper@preti.com
Recommended in Litigation
Practice Areas: Chair of the firm's Litigation Practice Group. Extensive experience in complex litigation, international and domestic arbitration, commercial litigation, securities litigation, and libel defense work for the media.
Prof. Memberships: Admitted to practice in Maine (1976); United States (1976) and Third Circuit (2004) District Court, District of Maine (1976); United States Court of Appeals, First Circuit. Fellow, Maine Bar Foundation (since 1996); counsel member of Media Law Resource Center; Maine Civil Rules Advisory Committee (1999-2000).
Career: Law Clerk, Honorable Edward S Godfrey, Maine Supreme Judicial Court, 1976-77. Joined Preti Flaherty, 1977; became Partner, 1982. Member, Preti Flaherty Management Committee; Managing Partner, 1995-99.
Publications: Comment, The Repair Rule: Maine Rule of Evidence 407(a) and the Admissibility of Subsequent Remedial Measures in Proving Negligence, 27 Maine Law Review 255 (1975); Article, Subpoenas on the Press: The Constitutional Privilege Not to Produce, Maine Bar Journal, Vol. 2, No. 2 (1987); Contributor: Annual 50-State Survey of Libel and Privacy, Media Law Resource Center (1986 through present); 'How to Avoid Covering Your Own Trial,' Maine State Bar Association Media/Law Guide (1990).
Personal: Born 7 April 1950; JD, University of Maine School of Law (Portland), 1976; BA (magna cum laude), Bowdoin College, 1972.

PRINGLE, Harry R
Drummond Woodsum & MacMahon, Portland 207 772 1941
hrpringle@dwmlaw.com
Recommended in Employment
Practice Areas: Has extensive experience in employment litigation, labor negotiations, National Labor Relations Board and Maine Labor Relations Board proceedings, Title VII litigation, and discrimination cases before the courts, the Equal Employment Opportunity Commission and the Maine Human Rights Commission.

Prof. Memberships: Has been a member of the Board of Directors of the National School Board Association Council of School Board Attorneys. He has been listed in labor and employment law by a leading US legal publication for over 10 years, and is a fellow of the College of Labor and Employment Lawyers.
Career: Past President of the Maine Council of School Board Attorneys. He joined the firm in 1973, is a member of the firm's Board of Directors and former Chair of the Public Sector Group, has served as lead instructor for school law courses at two area universities, and is a frequent lecturer on employment law issues.
Publications: Editor of 'Maine School Law, Third Edition' co-author of 'Significant Cases in Maine School Law,' and has authored numerous articles on school and employment law issues.
Personal: He graduated from Harvard Law School (1973 cum laude) and from Princeton University (1968 magna cum laude, Phi Beta Kappa).

ROBITZEK, William
Berman & Simmons, Portland
207 774 5277
Recommended in Litigation

RUBIN, Peter J
Bernstein, Shur, Sawyer & Nelson, PA, Portland 207 774 1200
prubin@bssn.com
Recommended in Litigation
Practice Areas: Rubin's practice concentrates on complex cases involving product liability, business litigation, malpractice/P.I. claims, and defense of asbestos claims at the national level.
Prof. Memberships: Fellow, American College of Trial Lawyers and American Academy of Appellate Lawyers; advocate, American Board of Trial Advocates; member of American, Maine State, and Cumberland County Bar Associations.
Publications: Harvard Law Review and Maine Law Review.
Personal: Harvard Law School (JD, magna cum laude, 1970); Member, Harvard Law Review (1969-70); Duke University (AB, 1967); Law Clerk to the Honorable Edward T Gignoux, USDC Judge for the District of Maine, September l970 - August l971.

SAUNDERS, Eric F
Bernstein, Shur, Sawyer & Nelson, PA, Portland 207 774 1200
esaunders@bssn.com
Recommended in Corporate/M&A
Practice Areas: Business law with an emphasis on shareholder and partnership disputes, housing law with an emphasis on the acquisition and refinancing of federally subsidized housing projects, and health law with an emphasis on the structuring of multi-party transactions.
Prof. Memberships: American Bar Association; Maine State Bar Association.

Personal: Boston University (JD, 1973); Member Boston University Law Review (1972-73); Harvard University (AB, 1969).

SCANNELL, Gordon
Perkins, Thompson, Hinckley & Keddy, P.A., Portland 207 774 2635
Recommended in Real Estate

SCHWARTZ, Jaimie Paul
Bernstein, Shur, Sawyer & Nelson, PA, Portland
207 774 1200
jschwartz@bssn.com
Recommended in Real Estate
Practice Areas: Chair of the Real Estate Practice Group. He practices in several areas of real estate law, including the acquisition, disposition, financing, management and development of real estate, with particular focus on representation of landlords and tenants in commercial leasing transactions.
Prof. Memberships: Maine State Bar Association; American Bar Association (Real Property, Probate and Trust Law, Natural Resources, Energy and Environmental Law Sections).
Personal: Ohio State University College of Law (JD, with Honors, 1991); Member, Order of the Coif; Ohio State University (BA, Journalism, 1984).

SHAPIRO, Jonathan
Moon, Moss & Shapiro, P.A., Portland
207 775 6001
jshapiro@moonmoss.com
Recommended in Employment
Practice Areas: Firm practice leader in private sector employment law with extensive experience in agency and court litigation matters and employment counseling (commercial and individual) matters; safeguarding and enforcing restrictions regarding corporate property and information; internal investigations; and defending DOL, INS and other government agency audits.
Prof. Memberships: Admitted to practice in Massachusetts (1987); District of Columbia (1988); Maine (1992); New York (1997). Member: New York State and American Bar Associations (Labor and Employment Law Section; Equal Employment Opportunity Committee); District of Columbia Bar.
Career: Joined Akin Gump Strauss Hauer & Feld (Washington, DC 1987); joined Moon Moss (1992); became Partner (1996) and Managing Partner (1997) Moon, Moss.
Publications: Contributing Author, 'Cathcart and Dichter 1992 Employment at Will, State by State Survey', National Employment Law Institute.
Personal: Born Montreal, Canada, 4 October 1962. JD (with honors), Duke University (1987); BA, (with distinction) McGill University (1984).

SHINAY, Richard
Drummond Woodsum & MacMahon, Portland 207 772 1941
rshinay@dwmlaw.com
Recommended in Real Estate
Practice Areas: Represents individuals, businesses, developers, lenders, municipalities and schools in the acquisition, development, financing and sale of real estate. Also represents clients in land conservation efforts. Serves as President of Classic Title Co., a subsidiary of Drummond, Woodsum & MacMahon, overseeing the issuance of title insurance.
Prof. Memberships: American Bar Association; Maine State Bar Association; Title Standards Subcommittee, MSBA; Committee on Condominiums, Cooperatives and Associations of Co-Owners, Real Property, Probate and Trust Law Section, ABA; American Land Title Association, New England Land Title Association and the Maine Land Title Association. Legislative Committee, Maine Real Estate & Development Association.
Career: Manager/Attorney, Lawyers Title Insurance Corporation, Portland, Maine (1980-85); Drummond Woodsum & MacMahon (1985-); Former Member, South Portland Planning Board (1989-93; Chair, 1991-93) and Scarborough Planning Board (1995-2003; Chair 2000-03); Past Co-Chair, Scarborough Open Space Committee and Scarborough Growth and Services Committee; Past Chair, Scarborough Intermediate School Land Search Committee; Co-Chair, Scarborough Comprehensive Plan Revision Committee; Trustee; Scarborough Land Conservation Trust and Portland Stage Company.
Personal: University of Maine School of Law, JD 1980; Boston College, AB 1977.

SMITH, Nathan H
Bernstein, Shur, Sawyer & Nelson, PA, Portland 207 774 1200
nsmith@bssn.com
Recommended in Real Estate
Practice Areas: Nathan Smith has a broad practice which includes acquisition, development, real estate leasing and financing with particular focus on larger scale transactions, including housing projects, commercial buildings, railroads, waste to energy plants, hydro electric facilities, forest land conservation and estate properties.
Prof. Memberships: American, Maine State, and Cumberland County Bar Associations.
Career: Former: Mayor and City Councilor, Portland, Maine; Commissioner Maine State Housing Authority; lecturer on real estate law at Maine Law School.
Personal: Washington & Lee University (JD, cum laude, 1982), Omicron Delta Kappa; McMaster University (MA, 1975); University of North Carolina (BA, 1971), Phi Beta Kappa.

STEVENS, Winfred
Rudman & Winchell LLC, Bangor
207 947 4501
Recommended in Real Estate

STOREY, Anne-Marie L
Rudman & Winchell LLC, Bangor
207 947 4501
astorey@rudman-winchell.com
Recommended in Employment
Practice Areas: Her practice includes advising employers and insurers on a broad range of employment related matters, conducting preventative trainings on topics including workplace harassment, and defending claims before state and federal agencies and courts.
Prof. Memberships: Admitted to practice in Maine (1995). American Bar Association; Maine State Bar Association; John Waldo Ballou American Inn of Court. Board of Governors, Maine State Bar Association. Advisory Committee on Maine Rules of Evidence.
Career: Associate, Rella, Dostie & Tucker (1995-99); Associate and Member, Rudman & Winchell (2000-).
Publications: Author of numerous articles for employment related publications, including The Employers' Quarterly and Maine Business & Employment Law.
Personal: Vermont Law School, JD, 1995, cum laude. Middlebury College, BA, 1989. Returned US Peace Corps Volunteer. Member, Board of Directors, Literacy Volunteers of Bangor. Member, Board of Directors, Bangor Region Chamber of Commerce.

TAYLOR, William E
Pierce Atwood LLP, Portland
207 791 1213
wtaylor@pierceatwood.com
Recommended in Environment
Practice Areas: Partner, Environmental Practice Group. Represents clients before local, state, and federal administrative agencies. Practice has been devoted to matters related to water law, waste discharge, wetland and natural resource licensing, compliance counseling, rulemaking, auditing, and enforcement.
Prof. Memberships: Commissioner for State of Maine, New England Interstate Water Pollution Control Commission. Member of the Maine NPDES Advisory Group, the Maine State Wetlands Task Force, and the American and Maine State Bar Associations Natural Resourses Sections.
Publications: Authored 'Major Land Use Laws Affecting Industrial, Commercial and Residential Development in Maine,' National Business Institute, 1990, and 'Wetland Permitting in Maine,' Maine Bar Journal, September 1997. Coauthored 'A Wetlands Primer,' Natural Resources & Environment, 1992, and 'The Watershed Protection Approach,' Water Resources, Natural Resources & Environment, 1996.

Personal: Vermont Law School, JD and Masters in Environmental Law 1983; University of Massachusetts, BA (cum laude) 1980.

THALER, Jeffrey A
Bernstein, Shur, Sawyer & Nelson, PA, Portland 207 774 1200
jthaler@bssn.com
Recommended in Environment
Practice Areas: His practice includes environmental permitting and litigation, as well as litigation for commercial and professionsl disputes, insurance coverage, personal injury, and toxic tort problems.
Prof. Memberships: American Bar, Maine State Bar, and Cumberland County Bar Associations; Maine Trial Lawyers Association: Board of Governors; American Trial Lawyers Association; State Land for Maine's Future Board.
Publications: He lectures frequently and has written extensively for state and national publications on such topics as toxic torts, environmental permitting, court decisions, and legal ethics.
Personal: Yale University Law School (JD, 1977); Williams College (BA, magna cum laude with Highest Honors, 1974).

VAN SLYKE, David
Preti Flaherty Beliveau Pachios & Haley LLC, Portland 207 791 3000
dvanslyke@preti.com
Recommended in Environment
Practice Areas: Chair of firm's Environmental Law Practice Group. Focuses his practice on defense of governmental enforcement actions and toxic tort suits,

due diligence in business and lending transactions, environmental risk management and compliance counseling.
Prof. Memberships: Admitted to practice in the District of Columbia (1982), Maine; (1992), US District Court (DC 1982, Maine 1992); US Court of Appeals (First Circuit 1998). Member of Maine State Bar Association (and Natural Resources Section), American Bar Association (and Section on Environment, Energy and Natural Resources). State Law Editor, BNA Environmental Due Diligence Guide.
Career: Booz-Allen & Hamilton 1982-83; US EPA: Enforcement Attorney 1983-87, Section Chief 1987-89, Deputy Director - Hazardous Waste Division 1989-90, Director - Superfund Division, 1990-92. Preti Flaherty: Of Counsel 1992-94, Partner since 1994, Environmental Practice Group Chair since 1995.
Personal: Born 21 September 1954. JD, Syracuse University Law School 1981; BS, St. Lawrence University 1976. EPA awards: Department of Justice Commendation for Outstanding Service (1991); Assistant Administrator's Enforcement Award for Excellence (1990); Special Achievement Silver Medal (1990) and two Bronze Medals (1986 and 1988); six Superior Performance and Outstanding Achievement Awards (1984-89).

WEBBER, Walter
Jensen Baird Gardner & Henry, Portland 207 775 7271
Recommended in Real Estate

WHITE, Jeffrey M
Pierce Atwood LLP, Portland
207 791 1292
jwhite@pierceatwood.com
Recommended in Litigation
Practice Areas: Pierce Atwood Litigation Group Leader; complex, commercial, antitrust, trade regulation and intellectual property litigation.
Prof. Memberships: Fellow, Maine Bar Foundation; former Chair, Maine Bar Association CLE Committee and Director, NE Bar Association.
Career: US v American Skiing Company (merger litigation); FPL Energy v CMP (defense judgment on $846 million asset purchase contract); Maine v Sears Roebuck & Co.(defense judgment defense on Unfair Trade Practice claims involving service agreements and sales practices); Net 2 Press v 58 Dix Ave. Corp. (defense judgment on business sale contract and fraud claims); Boyle v Douglas Dynamics, LLC (summary judgment on distributorship claims).

WOODBURY, Judith Fletcher
Pierce Atwood LLP, Portland
207 791 1386
jwoodbury@pierceatwood.com
Recommended in Real Estate
Practice Areas: Partner, Real Estate Group; Chair, Title Team; Manager, Bigelow Title Company. Representation for title and conveyancing in complex commercial and residential transactions.
Prof. Memberships: Leadership Gift Co-Chair, Campaign for Justice (2005); Maine State Bar (Chair, Real Estate (1999-2000); Women's Law and Environmental Law Sections) and Cumberland County Bar Associations; Maine

Land Conservation Attorney's Network; associate, Maine Society of Land Surveyors.
Career: Assistant Attorney General, Maine (1980-83); Underwriter, Lawyers Title Insurance Corporation (1983-84); President, Casco Bay Title Company (1984-86); Attorney, Atlantic Title Company (1986-91).
Personal: University of Maine Law School, JD (1980); University of Maine, BA (highest distinction) (1976).

ZIMPRITCH, James B
Pierce Atwood LLP, Portland
207 791 1270
jzimpritch@pierceatwood.com
Recommended in Corporate/M&A
Practice Areas: Broad corporate experience. Active M&A practice. Extensive experience in corporate and securities, banking, insurance, shareholder disputes, director duties, structuring investments and general commercial law. Involved in nearly every takeover fight in Maine in last 20 years. Represents emerging, middle-market, and large publicly held companies.
Prof. Memberships: American Law Institute; ABA Corporate Laws Committee; Maine: Chair, Corporate Law Revision Committee (2000-); past Chair, Business Law Section; frequent lecturer.
Career: Partner, Pierce Atwood LLP (1978-).
Publications: 'Maine Corporation Law & Practice', the definitive treatise.
Personal: Duke Law School, JD 1973; 'Duke Law Journal', 1972-73; Dartmouth College, AB 1970.

BERNSTEIN, SHUR, SAWYER & NELSON

THE FIRM

Managing Shareholder: Charles E Miller
Senior Partner: Leonard M Nelson
President: Peter J Rubin
Number of shareholders: 54
Number of lawyers: 81

FIRM OVERVIEW: Bernstein, Shur, Sawyer & Nelson is one of northern New England's largest full service law firms, with offices in Portland and Augusta, Maine and Manchester, New Hampshire. Widely regarded as one of New England's most entrepreneurial firms, BSSN provides counsel to a diverse group of regional and international clients. BSSN is Maine's Lex Mundi affiliate.

MAIN AREAS OF PRACTICE:

Bankruptcy & Insolvency: BSSN has the largest and most experienced bankruptcy and insolvency practice group in Northern New England. The group's attorneys represent clients in reorganizations and liquidations under Chapter 11 and Chapter 7, large commercial insolvencies, and related litigation. The group's experience and expertise includes litigation involving officers' and director's liability and lender liability matters.

Construction Law: BSSN's Construction Law Group provides legal services to construction contractors and subcontractors, owners and developers of construction projects, including public sector owners, suppliers, insurers, and bonding companies. The practice covers all aspects of construction law from contract drafting, negotiation and competitive bidding issues to the development and presentation of claims, mediation, arbitration and litigation, mechanics' liens, and insurance coverage issues.

Corporate, Mergers & Acquisitions: BSSN's Business Combinations and Acquisitions Group represents bidders, investors, founders of companies, financial advisers, and other parties in privately negotiated transfers of securities or assets, leveraged buyouts, joint ventures, public-company combinations, and takeovers. BSSN attorneys assist in all aspects of mergers, acquisitions, divestitures, and joint ventures.

Education: The Education Law Practice Group represents both public and private elementary, secondary, and postsecondary educational institutions on a variety of matters including student management issues, administrative issues, and labor and employment matters.

Employment: The Employment Law Practice Group represents employers of all sizes in northern New England. The group defends employer clients in the state and federal courts, the Maine Human Rights Commission, and all other state and federal agencies that oversee labor and employment laws and regulations.

Energy: The firm's Energy Practice Group represents regional and international clients on issues relating to energy generation and distribution. Its clients are independent power producers (IPPs), small power producers and co-generators that produce electricity from renewable resources, and/or natural gas and financial institutions that have provided financing to build IPP plants; large consumers of electricity such as paper companies, water districts, or manufacturing facilities; and municipalities.

Environmental & Land Conservation: BSSN's Environmental Practice Group represents individuals, businesses, municipalities and non-profit organizations that are trying to comply with or enforce local, state or federal environmental and land use laws. The group deals with issues involving wetlands, waste disposal or recycling, water and air quality, toxics, energy production, and insurance coverage.

Governmental Relations & Legislative: BSSN understands that more law is made in the legislature and through agency rulemaking than in the courthouse. Changing the law is often more cost-effective for clients than litigating current law. Headquartered in the Capitol of Augusta, the firm's Legislative & Government Affairs Group represents BSSN's clients before the Maine Legislature and before various state and federal agencies.

Immigration: BSSN represents clients from around the world in immigration issues that include business and employment, foreign investor, family, citizenship, asylum, and deportation.

Health Law: The firm's Health Law Group represents physicians and other healthcare professionals, physical group practices and associations, hospitals, nursing homes, health agencies, pharmacies, and other healthcare providers throughout the state.

Litigation: BSSN's Litigation Practice is broad-based, with representation for both plaintiffs and defendants. The firm is involved in litigation for domestic and foreign clients, including commercial disputes, securities litigation, antitrust, business torts, energy, products liability, personal injury, real estate transactions, education, intellectual property infringement, criminal cases, constitutional issues, health, insurance, and environmental matters.

Municipal: BSSN's Municipal and Governmental Services Practice Group currently serves as general counsel to more than 55 Maine municipalities. BSSN frequently serves as special counsel to governmental entities including towns, cities, counties, school districts, sanitary and sewer districts, regional planning commissions, regional waste disposal groups, and other quasi-municipal agencies.

Real Estate: Attorneys in BSSN's Real Estate Group have expertise in all aspects of commercial real estate and a record of practical solutions to complex transactional issues. BSSN has negotiated and closed development and value-added transactions for privately and publicly held businesses, individuals, trusts, and investment partnerships involving both public and private land ownership.

Tax: BSSN's Tax Services Group provides its clients with clear approaches to the most complicated tax estate planning, business planning, succession issues, and controversies with the IRS. BSSN gives its clients practical solutions to issues involving federal, state and international taxes, estate planning matters and probate.

Technology & Intellectual Property: BSSN's Technology and Intellectual Property Group provides a wide range of expertise on the evolving legal issues surrounding today's new businesses and consumer technologies. BSSN represents technology developers as well as parties using new technologies to improve their business processes.

INTERNATIONAL WORK: BSSN's attorneys counsel clients on legal and business matters throughout the United States and in many regions of the world. The professional scope of the firm's international practice is as multi-faceted as its geographic scope, with attorneys engaging in dispute resolution, commercial negotiation, and government relations throughout the industrial and developing world.

Languages: Spanish, French, German, Italian, Japanese, and Russian.

HEAD OFFICE

MAINE
100 Middle Street, P.O. Box 9729, **Portland**, ME 04104-5029
Tel: 207 774 1200 **Fax:** 207 774 1127
Email: info@bssn.com **Website:** www.bssn.com

BRANCH OFFICES

MAINE
146 Capitol Street, **Augusta**, ME 04330
Tel: 207 623 1596 **Fax:** 207 626 0200

NEW HAMPSHIRE
Jefferson Mill Building, 670 North Commercial Street, Suite 108
PO Box 1120, **Manchester**, NH 03104
Tel: 603 623 8700 **Fax:** 603 623 7775

DRUMMOND WOODSUM & MACMAHON

THE FIRM

Managing Partner: Jerrol A Crouter

Number of shareholders: 25
Number of associates and consultants: 15

FIRM OVERVIEW: Founded in 1965, Drummond Woodsum & MacMahon is one of Maine's largest and most well respected law firms. The firm's attorneys have earned a reputation for providing high quality counsel to clients across a wide spectrum of legal practice areas. Drummond Woodsum & MacMahon's philosophy of quality, responsiveness and efficiency in the delivery of legal services to firm clients has led to the development of some of the best lawyers in the United States. The reputation of the firm's attorneys was recently recognized nationally when, in 2001 and 2002, then firm member Robert E Hirshon became the first Maine lawyer in nearly 100 years to serve as President of the American Bar Association.

MAIN AREAS OF PRACTICE:

Public Sector Group: The firm offers expertise in municipal and school law in areas including labor relations, employment matters, special education, finance, construction, employee benefits and litigation, and has litigated numerous precedent-setting cases on behalf of public sector clients. The school practice is widely recognized as pre-eminent in Maine and the school law website is nationally known.

Employment Services: The Employment Group consists of attorneys and highly skilled consultants who defend both private and public sector employers' interests. The practice includes substantial litigation in federal and state courts along with an active practice before all relevant federal and state agencies including the National Labor Relations Board, the Equal Employment Opportunity Commission, the Maine Labor Relations Board, the Maine Human Rights Commission, and other administrative bodies.

Business Services: The Business Group handles a full range of corporate and securities matters, advising clients on acquisitions and mergers, corporate tax planning and financing, multi-state financings, venture capital and private placements, and international trade. Attorneys in the firm are approved 'Red Book' bond counsel and have extensive experience in public utility law, franchising, executive compensation, foreign investment regulation, bankruptcy and securities matters, and other areas of corporate and business law.

Trial Services: The firm is involved in every type of civil litigation in federal and state courts and administrative agencies, including the United States Supreme Court. Recent cases fall into a broad range of areas including business and commercial litigation, employment, securities, intellectual property, antitrust, real estate and land use, construction disputes, product liability, bankruptcy and Native American tribal rights.

Indian Law: The Indian Practice provides legal services to Native American tribes, tribal businesses, and select developers and businesses working with tribes in the United States. Legal services include litigation in tribal, federal and state courts, economic development strategies, business transactions by and with tribes or tribal entities, tribal employment law and personnel management, developing tribal laws and governmental processes, Indian housing, federal contracting, and tribal gaming.

HEAD OFFICE

MAINE
245 Commercial Street, PO Box 9781, **Portland**, ME 04104-5081
Tel: 207 772 1941
Email: info@dwmlaw.com
Websites: www.dwmlaw.com; www.SchoolLaw.com

CONTACTS

Business Services	Michael E High
Indian Services Group	Gregory Sample
Public Sector Group	Harry R Pringle
Trial Services	Melissa Hewey

CLIENTS: Clients include Fortune 500 and private corporations throughout the US and in Canada and Great Britain, US insurance companies, commercial banks and institutions, public utilities, municipalities, private and public schools, and Native American tribes.

INTERNATIONAL WORK: The firm is the only Maine firm to be a member of Meritas, a worldwide organization that offers high-quality legal services through an integrated, yet independent, group of full-service law firms which provides clients a local contact for obtaining reliable legal services throughout the country and around the world. Membership in Meritas is by invitation only and requires firms to adhere to rigorous quality standards and a stringent code of ethics.

DRUMMOND WOODSUM & MACMAHON
Attorneys at Law

MOON, MOSS & SHAPIRO, P.A.

THE FIRM

Managing Partner: Jonathan Shapiro
Senior Partner: Richard G Moon

Number of partners: 5
Number of other lawyers: 3

HEAD OFFICE

MAINE
Ten Free Street, **Portland**, ME 04101
Mailing Address: PO Box 7250, Portland, ME 04112-7250
Tel: 207 775 6001   **Fax:** 207 775 6407
Website: www.moonmoss.com

FIRM OVERVIEW: Since1989, Moon Moss has concentrated its practice in labor and employment law on behalf of management.

MAIN AREAS OF PRACTICE:

The firm's exclusive goal is to provide the best counseling and representation to its clients to help them achieve all their business goals. To achieve that purpose, the firm's practice is organized as follows: advice concerning labor and employment law matters on behalf of unionized and non-unionized private and public sector employers, including corporate planning in mergers and acquisitions; litigation of all employment and labor related matters on behalf of management; and employee benefits and executive compensation including methods of compensation, health and retirement plan design and compliance.

Labor Relations: Moon Moss is committed to the practice of preventive labor relations through issue assessment, compliance analysis, supervisory training, policy development, and positive communications. The preservation of management rights is the firm's goal, whether prior to a union offensive or during a union-organizing campaign. The firm has assisted many employers in winning NLRB elections or in avoiding union elections altogether. Moon Moss attorneys have appeared before the National Labor Relations Board, state labor boards, and state and federal courts and have preserved operational flexibility in contract negotiations, contract administration, and grievance and arbitration proceedings. The firm has also assisted corporations in improving labor and employee relations through the creation of better policies, supervision and communication systems.

Employment: The firm's Employment Practice includes training employers and their employees in the proper handling of all employment matters, designing and implementing policies and practices, providing sound, practical advice on day-to-day personnel matters, guiding businesses through governmental audits, inspections and investigations, conducting internal corporate audits and investigations, assisting companies in safeguarding corporate property and information (including enforcing non-competition and non-solicitation agreements against former employees and competitors), as well as counseling employers on immigration matters and the employment aspects of mergers, acquisitions and divestitures.

Litigation: The attorneys at Moon Moss have been particularly successful in helping their clients in the litigation process. The firm has broad-ranging civil litigation experience. This includes all employment-related civil litigation. The firm's practice also regularly encompasses claims relating to breaches of employment contracts and restrictive covenants, breaches of an employee's fiduciary duties, and theft and/or misuse of confidential information and trade secrets. A substantial portion of litigated matters involve claims of discrimination arising out of terminations or other adverse personnel decisions as well as wage and hour disputes.

Employee Benefits & Executive Compensation: Moon Moss' Employee Benefits Practice offers a full range of legal services to its clients involving plan design and administration of pension, profit sharing, and other retirement and deferred compensation plans for both public and private employers. Moon Moss attorneys assist management in hiring and maintaining the best and the brightest executives and professionals with state-of-the-art compensation packages. The firm also advises employers when severing their relationship with top-level personnel. The firm also drafts and reviews contracts for both corporate (publicly traded and private) and individual clients.

CLIENTS: The firm's clients range from sole proprietorships to multi-state publicly traded corporations with over 100,000 employees, and include virtually every sector of the economy, from banks and hospitals to corporations involved in manufacturing, transportation, public utilities and retailing, as well as high technology companies, grocery chains, insurance companies and other service industries (including law firms). Because of the firm's reputation, several national corporations use Moon Moss for their legal work throughout New England.

MOONMOSS

Workplace Guidance and Solutions

PIERCE ATWOOD LLP

THE FIRM

Managing Partner: Bruce A Coggeshall
Senior Partner: Ralph I Lancaster, Jr
Number of partners: 70
Number of other lawyers: 43

FIRM OVERVIEW: Pierce Atwood LLP is a leading New England law firm, recognized nationally and internationally for expertise in commercial law. The firm strives to deliver the highest level of service and meet the changing and increasingly complex needs of its clients, who range from entrepreneurs and individuals to members of the Fortune 500 and foreign governments, and span a variety of traditional and emerging business sectors. Clients derive superior value from the firm's location and its high level of sophistication. Pierce Atwood Consulting provides governmental relations, public relations, and economic development.

MAIN AREAS OF PRACTICE:

Commercial Finance & Bankruptcy: Known for sophistication in complex financing transactions, leadership in creative public policy solutions to business and economic problems, and expertise in restructuring financially distressed businesses, the firm has premier practices in commercial lending, public finance and bankruptcy.

Corporate & Tax: Leading practice in acquisitions and sales of businesses, venture capital, private equity and other financing transactions, entity formation, federal and state tax, and representation of owners, directors and officers.

Employment & Employee Benefits: The group seeks to build expertise in its clients through counseling and training. Representation of management in state and federal trial, appellate, administrative and ADR proceedings; in matters arising under the NLRA and RLA (bargaining, arbitrations, board proceedings, organizing and labor disputes); in specialty areas such as benefits, immigration, FLSA, OSHA, and workers compensation; and in government relations.

Energy: The firm has built a national and international reputation serving domestic utilities, deregulated enterprises such as major merchant plants, and foreign emerging economies' need for energy market expertise. Clients are regional, national (utilities, independent project developers, lenders and investors in over 20 states), and international, including foreign governments and international financial institutions.

Environmental: The regional leader with national clients in all areas of environmental law and regulation, including land use, wastewater discharge, air emissions, solid waste, hazardous waste, chemical disclosure, wetlands, endangered species, and all other natural resources law.

Governmental Relations: In conjunction with Pierce Atwood Consulting, they combine substantive legal expertise, access to governmental leadership and a comprehensive, integrated array of complementary services such as public relations, traditional lobbying, media relations, campaigns, and stakeholder education, designed to further clients' public policy initiatives.

Intellectual Property: Intellectual property, technology, e-commerce and internet-related matters for emerging and established companies with national and international business interests. The firm manages national and international patent and trademark portfolios and litigates claims of infringement and misappropriation of all types of intellectual property.

Litigation: National and regional practice in business litigation including energy, intellectual property, white collar, products liability, environmental, ERISA, insurance and many other areas. Members include the two most recent Chief Justices of the Maine Supreme Judicial Court, a former Independent Counsel, and a past President and four Fellows of the American College of Trial Lawyers.

Real Estate: Sophisticated commercial practice includes development, financing, entity creation, taxation leasing, land use permitting and conveyancing of retail, commercial, industrial, and energy facilities and timberlands.

HEAD OFFICE

MAINE
One Monument Square, **Portland**, ME 04101
Tel: 207 791 1100   **Fax:** 207 791 1350
Email: info@pierceatwood.com   **Website:** www.pierceatwood.com

BRANCH OFFICES

MAINE
77 Winthrop Street, **Augusta**, ME 04330
Tel: 207 623 6311   **Fax:** 207 623 9367

MASSACHUSETTS
Six Harris Street, **Newburyport**, MA 01950
Tel: 978 465 9599   **Fax:** 978 465 9945

NEW HAMPSHIRE
One New Hampshire Avenue, Suite 350, **Portsmouth**, NH 03801
Tel: 603 433 6300   **Fax:** 603 433 6372

CONTACTS

Commercial Finance & Bankruptcy	Jacob A Manheimer
Corporate & Tax	David J Champoux
Employment & Employee Benefits	James R Erwin,
	Charles S Einsiedler, Jr
Energy	John W Gulliver
Environmental	Philip F W Ahrens, Thomas R Doyle
Governmental Relations	Christopher E Howard
Intellectual Property	Gloria A Pinza
Litigation	Jeffrey M White
Real Estate	Dennis C Keeler
Retail Financial Services	Richard P Hackett
State Tax	James G Good, Everett P Ingalls

Retail Financial Services: Provides transactional, regulator, compliance, operations, and dispute resolution services to lenders, deposit takers, non-deposit investment providers, and insurance producer. Also serve vendors who support these types of retail financial service companies (e.g., software companies and loan servicers).

State Tax: Expertise covers corporate structuring, M&A and other transactions, business planning, succession and estate planning, and IRS controversies, as well as all forms of taxation, including personal and corporate income tax, sales and use tax, property tax, excise tax, multistate taxation and related services such as tax controversies, transactional advice, planning, ruling requests and legislative.

CLIENTS: Include American Skiing Co., Anthem Blue Cross & Blue Shield, Banknorth, Brascan, Casella, Central Maine Power Company, Charles River Laboratories, Chittenden Bank, DaimlerChrysler, DuPont, Energy East, FPLE Seabrook, Fairchild Semiconductor, General Electric, Georgia-Pacific, Hannaford Brothers, IDEXX, J.D. Irving, Ltd., KeyBank, N.A., MBNA, Maine Medical Center, McDonald's, Poland Spring, Sappi, State of California, Tom's of Maine, UNUMProvident, USAID, Verizon, World Bank, Wright Express.

INTERNATIONAL WORK: Encompasses multilateral transactions; cross-border financings; enterprise restructuring; energy and environmental law; EU compliance; regulatory reform and compliance; competition; privatization; litigation; arbitration; cross-border boundary dispute resolution; intellectual property licensing and transfer; defense and litigation. Attorneys have worked in 50 countries.

PIERCE ATWOOD
— LLP —
ATTORNEYS AT LAW

PRETI FLAHERTY BELIVEAU PACHIOS & HALEY LLP

THE FIRM

Managing Partner: Harold C Pachios
Number of partners: 46
Number of other lawyers: 28

FIRM OVERVIEW: Preti Flaherty answers the call of a diverse business community with a sophisticated practice, international reach and multi-state experience. One of Northern New England's largest law firms, it is known for high-powered legal talent, including former Senate Majority Leader George J Mitchell, and exceptional credentials working with state and local governments.

MAIN AREAS OF PRACTICE:

Business Law: Preti Flaherty advises clients in every stage of business development. For businesses that are just beginning, the firm's attorneys have broad ranging experience navigating business formation, securities offerings, technology protection and venture capital financing. The firm can also adroitly counsel clients on the added challenges that come with growth and success such as, technology licensing, executive compensation, debt financing and counseling Boards. Those businesses that find themselves poised to move onto the regional, national or global level also turn to Preti Flaherty for counsel on mergers and acquisitions, franchising, joint ventures and strategic alliances, international transactions, commercial contracts, and tax planning.

Energy: Preti Flaherty is a national leader in the rapidly evolving US – Canada energy marketplace. The firm counsels industrial consumers, energy project developers, energy cooperatives and aggregators, energy service companies and state and local governments on the reduction of risk and cost through deregulation. The firm provides counsel on rate reductions, special rate contracts, cost of service, rate structures, customer relations and competitive relationships with, from and among utilities, energy suppliers and customers. Its attorneys also assist in the structuring of entities to finance, build, license and operate renewable and natural gas powerplants and large and small transmission lines. The firm is the national leader in the development of Regional Transmission Organizations and Independent System Operators which are responsive to the needs of customers and consumer groups.

Environmental: Preti Flaherty has one of the region's largest and most diverse environmental practices. The firm's environmental litigators, transactional attorneys and regulatory specialists advise clients on legal issues related to all aspects of environmental regulation, compliance and due diligence, including air and water pollution, hazardous waste, chemical regulation and land use controls. The firm offers in-depth experience in all phases of Federal, State and local administrative and civil judicial enforcement proceedings.

Health Law: Preti Flaherty counsels hospitals, nursing homes, home health agencies, rehabilitation centers and other healthcare facilities, as well as insurers and individual practitioners. The firm has encompassing experience dealing with emerging healthcare issues and their legal ramifications and works hard to adjust regulations and advance laws and interpretations in support of its clients' interests. Preti Flaherty provides extensive services to institutions facing increasingly complex state regulatory issues. It has represented hospitals at hearings and proceedings before the Department of Human Services and the Federal Provider Reimbursement Review Board.

Intellectual Property: The firm works with clients to develop creative and cost-effective strategies for securing, maintaining, exploiting, and enforcing a company's intellectual property assets. Trademarks, copyrights, patents or licensing issues can arise in the United States, worldwide and via the internet. The firm's attorneys register companies' assets, provide regular portfolio reviews and offer experienced insight to help make sensible decisions based

HEAD OFFICE

MAINE
One City Center, PO Box 9546, **Portland**, ME 04112-9546
Tel: 207 791 3000   **Fax:** 207 791 3111
Email: info@preti.com
Website: www.preti.com

BRANCH OFFICES

MAINE
45 Memorial Circle, PO Box 1058, **Augusta**, ME 04332-1058
Tel: 207 623 5300   **Fax:** 207 623 2914

Thirty Front Street, PO Box 665, **Bath**, ME 04530-0665
Tel: 207 443 5576   **Fax:** 207 443 6665

NEW HAMPSHIRE
57 North Main Street, PO Box 1318, **Concord**, NH 03302-1318
Tel: 603 410 1500   **Fax:** 603 410 1501

CONTACTS

Business Law	Susan LoGiudice
Energy	Anthony Buxton
Environmental	David Van Slyke
Health Law	John Doyle
Intellectual Property	Alfred Frawley
Labor & Employment	Michael Messerschmidt
Legislative, Regulatory & Governmental Services	Severin Beliveau
Litigation	Jonathan Piper

on a solid understanding of the business' goals and competitive position.

Labor & Employment: Preti Flaherty helps businesses, both in non-union and unionized settings, avoid potentially damaging situations by developing, implementing and communicating sound workplace policies and strategies. In addition to the counseling and risk prevention work the group provides, it also has extensive experience litigating claims in State and Federal courts, representing management in National Labor Relations Board proceedings and arbitrations under collective bargaining agreements, and defending charges of discrimination before the Equal Opportunity Commission and the Maine Human Rights Commission.

Legislative, Regulatory & Governmental Services: Preti Flaherty has an extensive legislative/regulatory practice. The firm's inside knowledge of public policy and the legislative process, combined with legal skills both traditional and groundbreaking, combine to create a wide range of approaches to resolving issues and influencing legislation. Many of the firm's attorneys, including Senator Mitchell, who coordinates the firm's Legislative/Regulatory Practice in Washington, DC, have actively participated in the legislative process at both State and Federal levels.

Litigation: Preti Flaherty boasts one of the largest and most respected litigation groups in northern New England. Recognizing that success is often the result of pre-litigation counseling, the Litigation Group is nonetheless equipped to advocate for its clients wherever necessary, including consensual or mandatory mediation, domestic or international arbitration, and trials in State or Federal court. The group's experience is varied and extensive, including noteworthy successes in such matters as toxic tort litigation, securities claims, professional liability litigation, construction claims, lender liability claims, injunction of governmental agencies on constitutional grounds, and libel defense of national publications. Members of the litigation group are licensed in over a dozen states and numerous Federal courts.

INTERNATIONAL WORK: Preti Flaherty works with foreign-based companies seeking to do business in the United States whether it is a straightforward joint venture or a more complex acquisition. The firm helps companies navigate the local, state and Federal legal and regulatory landscape.

VERRILL DANA, LLP

THE FIRM

Managing Partner: David E Warren
Senior Partner: Peter B Webster

Number of partners: 44
Number of other lawyers: 44

FIRM OVERVIEW: Verrill Dana, LLP is one of the leading law firms in Northern New England and the only major Maine firm with an office in Boston, Massachusetts, and Washington, DC. The firm provides sophisticated representation in a wide variety of areas, including general litigation, real estate, business law, labor and employment law, employee benefits and executive compensation, estate planning and estate administration, environmental law, land use, legislative advocacy, regulatory matters, health law, bankruptcy and commercial law, construction law, intellectual property and patents, commercial lending, financial services regulation, utilities and energy, insurance, sports law, international law, immigration, tax-exempt organizations, and charitable giving. Verrill Dana's high degree of specialization enables it to handle the most complex legal issues in an efficient and cost-effective manner.

Verrill Dana emphasizes ready access to senior attorneys in fulfilling its client service mission and employs leading edge technology to meet the needs of its attorneys and the demands of its clients. The firm's total quality management program distinguishes it from its competitors and has made a positive impact on many aspects of firm operations from client service to the mentoring of junior attorneys.

MAIN AREAS OF PRACTICE:

Business: The Business Law Group provides a wide range of corporate and transactional advice to both privately held and public companies. The group's areas of expertise include securities, tax, intellectual property and banking. Representative matters include the planning and formation of corporations, limited liability companies, professional associations, partnerships and other business entities; venture capital, commercial loans, equity offerings, bond offerings and other financing transactions; SEC compliance work; mergers, acquisitions, reorganizations and other complex corporate transactions; advice on proxy solicitations and takeover defenses; registration and licensing of trademarks, copyrights and trade secrets; business planning; and contract review.

Litigation: The firm has a sophisticated Litigation Practice in the areas of antitrust, banking, civil rights, commercial construction, complex commercial litigation, contracts, copyright, corporate and shareholder derivative actions, domestic relations, employee benefit matters, employment discrimination, environmental, health care, insurance, commercial and residential foreclosures, labor (including NLRB), land use, personal injury, products liability, RICO, securities, corporate takeover (for plaintiffs and defendants), tax and utilities. The Litigation Group has represented clients before state and federal courts at all trial and appellate levels, as well as in arbitrations and mediations.

Real Estate: The firm's Real Estate Group counsels individuals, businesses, and professional groups with respect to the ownership, purchase and sale of real estate, boundary disputes, easements, real estate trusts and a wide range of zoning matters. The group also represents lenders and developers in negotiating, structuring, and documenting commercial, retail, residential, and industrial transactions and developments, including manufacturing facilities, shopping centers, office and apartment buildings, hotels, and business and industrial parks. As an outgrowth of their financing work, the group has developed special expertise in governmental and qualified private activity bonds.

HEAD OFFICE

MAINE
One Portland Square, **Portland**, ME 04112-0586
Tel: 207 774 4000 **Fax:** 207 774 7499
Email: info@verrilldana.com
Website: www.verrilldana.com

BRANCH OFFICES

DISTRICT OF COLUMBIA
400 North Capitol Street, Suite 585, **Washington**, DC 20001-1511
Tel: 202 624 9733 **Fax:** 202 393 5218

KANSAS CITY AREA
1900 W. 47th Place, Suite 130, **Westwood**, KS 66205-1801
Tel: 913 722 9555 **Fax:** 913 722 9559

MAINE
45 Memorial Circle, **Augusta**, ME 04332-5307
Tel: 207 623 3889 **Fax:** 207 622 3117

403 Lafayette Center, **Kennebunk**, ME 04043-0147
Tel: 207 985 7193 **Fax:** 207 985 3957

MASSACHUSETTS
One Boston Place, Suite 2330, **Boston**, MA 02108
Tel: 617 367 0929 **Fax:** 617 367 0976

Employee Benefits & Executive Compensation: The firm has the preeminent Employee Benefits & Executive Compensation Department in Northern New England. The group counsels many of Maine's largest employers regarding compliance with ERISA, the Internal Revenue Code and other laws that govern the form and administration of all types of retirement plans, health plans, and fringe benefit plans. The group has represented clients in audits, investigations, and proceedings conducted by the Department of Labor, Internal Revenue Service, and Pension Benefit Guaranty Corporation. The group also prepares plan documents and advises clients regarding the design and structure of employee benefit and executive compensation plans and has special expertise regarding fiduciary oversight issues.

Estate Planning & Estate Administration: The firm's Estate Planning & Estate Administration Group is the largest in Maine, and has extensive experience in handling complex transactions which successfully combine achieving family objectives while reducing the tax impacts of family wealth transfers. The group advises individuals in formulating and implementing their financial and estate plans, including lifetime transfers to beneficiaries and charitable organizations, and planning for testamentary transfers. The group also represents individuals and professional corporate trustees in their fiduciary roles as personal representatives and trustees.

Labor & Employment: The Labor & Employment Group advises clients on all aspects of employment law, including matters involving wrongful discharge, employment discrimination, workers' compensation, wage and hour laws, employee privacy considerations, and the Occupational Safety and Health Act. The group is active in labor management relations, union negotiations, representation elections and arbitrations. The Group is also regularly involved in drafting and reviewing personnel policies, and the drafting, negotiation, and enforcement of employment contracts and non-competition agreements.

Verrill Dana LLP
Attorneys at Law

CONTENTS: Corporate/M&A p.909; Employment p.911; Litigation p.914; Real Estate p.916; Individuals' Profiles p.919; Firms' Profiles p.926.

How lawyers are ranked

The opinions we gather from clients — mainly from in-house lawyers but also from other purchasers of legal services — are balanced by opinions from colleagues and competitors. Together, they provide two different perspectives — an all-round view — and biased viewpoints cancel each other out.

CORPORATE/M&A

Maryland
Leading firms (Corporate/M&A)

1
DLA PIPER RUDNICK GRAY CARY *Baltimore*
HOGAN & HARTSON LLP *Baltimore*
VENABLE LLP *Baltimore*

2
MILES & STOCKBRIDGE PC *Baltimore*
WILMER CUTLER PICKERING HALE *Baltimore*

3
GORDON, FEINBLATT, ROTHMAN *Baltimore*
OBER KALER GRIMES & SHRIVER *Baltimore*
SAUL EWING LLP *Baltimore*
WHITEFORD, TAYLOR & PRESTON LLP *Baltimore*

Leading individuals (Corporate/M&A)

★ SMITH Robert *DLA Piper, Baltimore*

1
COOK Bryson *Venable, Baltimore*
HANKS James *Venable, Baltimore*
LOHR Walter *Hogan & Hartson, Baltimore*
SILVER Michael *Hogan & Hartson, Baltimore*
TILGHMAN Richard *DLA Piper, Baltimore*

2
FRISCH John *Miles & Stockbridge, Baltimore*
KAHN Henry *Hogan & Hartson, Baltimore*
WASHBURNE Thomas *Venable, Baltimore*
WATKINS John *Wilmer Cutler, Baltimore*
WEBB Thompson *Miles & Stockbridge, Baltimore*

3
BAADER Michael *Venable, Baltimore*
CURRAN Bob *Whiteford Taylor, Baltimore*
POLIAKOFF Abba *Gordon Feinblatt, Baltimore*

Up-and-coming individuals
ABEL Kenneth *Ober Kaler, Baltimore*
FREED Amy *Hogan & Hartson, Baltimore*

RAMIREZ John *Venable, Baltimore*

Firms and individuals are listed alphabetically in each band.

Band 1

DLA Piper Rudnick Gray Cary US LLP
See firm details p.765

The Firm: Clients described this "*deep*" practice's attorneys as being "*bright, flexible and well-rounded,*" in addition to being "*great negotiators: they know when you should hold firm or cut and run.*" Competitors called it "*a dynamic practice*

with top clients and fabulous lawyers,*" and noted that the firm's recent alliance with UK firm DLA brought an extra dimension to its "*fabulous*" corporate group. One commentator opined that the firm has "*been going increasingly upmarket, and now it's not only a national but an international player.*"

The Lawyers: "*Still a terrific lawyer*" and a "*major player in the market*" in the view of our interviewees, "*superstar*" **Jay Smith** (see p.924) is cochair of the firm's corporate and securities practice group. He advised the Rouse Company in its acquisition by General Growth Properties, and also advised Aggregate Industries and Vertis in relation to separate acquisitions. In addition to taking on more corporate governance cases of late, he also advised Human Genome Sciences and Ryland Group on separate note offerings in deals that were both worth in excess of $100 million. Competitors expressed respect for **Rich Tilghman** (see p.924) as "*a very fine securities lawyer.*" His clients include fast-expanding public and private companies. Jim Winn has recently retired from private practice.

The Clients: Recent significant work for the practice includes advising Grotech on various investments, RBC Dain Rauscher on various underwritings, and Purdue Farms on a number of acquisitions. Other clients include: Marriott International; T. Rowe Price Group; Human Genome Sciences; CSFB; Legg Mason Wood Walker; Ryland Group; Aggregate Industries and Vertis.

Hogan & Hartson LLP
See firm details p.484

The Firm: "*One of the most prominent out-of-town firms,*" according to our interviewees, the Baltimore office of this DC-based firm has been especially active in relation to M&A work and securities offerings in recent times. Peers particularly rate the practice for its presence in the public company arena, "*not only in Baltimore and DC, but nationally,*" while clients praise its "*professional*" lawyers for their "*good turnaround and creativity in the work they do.*"

The Lawyers: Described by one admiring client as "*the quarterback of our relationship with the firm,*" the "*seasoned*" **Duke Lohr** (see p.922) has "*a broad knowledge and expertise*" and is "*good as a sounding board to bounce ideas off.*" **Mike Silver** (see p.924) attracted praise from clients as one who "*really brings the full scope of his M&A and corporate securities practice to bear.*" Interviewees further noted that, despite his senior position within the team, "*he still does a lot of the work himself.*" His recent work has included advising Sienna Corporation on two large acquisitions, and advising Guilford Pharmaceuticals and Wabash National on public offerings. In addition, he represented ACA Holdings in relation to the $120 million equity capital investment in it made by Bear Stearns. Clients believe that the "*intelligent*" **Henry Kahn** (see p.922) "*has good judgment,*" "*gets the deals done*" and "*understands the business needs as well as the legal needs.*" His practice encompasses investment management, securities, M&A and corporate law. In recent times his work has included advising Mercantile Bank in relation to investment management and transactional work. He also represented SevenSpace in its acquisition by Sun Microsystems. Interviewees agreed that former SEC officer **Amy Freed** (see p.920) has "*a comprehensive knowledge of securities law nationally from both a technical and a practical standpoint.*"

The Clients: Mercantile Bank; CIENA; Guilford Pharmaceuticals; Wabash National; Baltimore Ravens; FPL Energy and Laboratory Corporation of America.

Venable LLP

The Firm: "*As conscientious and efficient as you can get*" was one appreciative client's assessment of this "*customer-centric*" practice. Another source praised its "*responsiveness and ability to understand client needs in a business setting.*" Further comment was that the practice has "*bench strength from top to bottom.*" Its expertise includes M&A, joint ventures, divestitures, reorganizations, liquidations and changes of control. The team represents public and private entities in the industrial, service and financial sectors, in addition to growth industries such as IT, Internet services, and biotech.

The Lawyers: Clients opined that practice cochair **Tuck Washburne** is *"very strong in securities, corporate governance and M&A matters,"* further noting his levels of client attentiveness. He advised Marriott in connection with its $30 million investment in Diamond Rock Hospitality. He also represented CRIIMI MAE in relation to a repayment of debt including the negotiation of a new repurchase facility and a $42 million draw under the new facility. Universally acknowledged for his expertise in Maryland corporate law, peers described **Jim Hanks** as *"the father of local counsel work"* in the state, with *"the largest practice in the cottage industry of representing mutual funds incorporated in Maryland."* Observers reported that **Bryson Cook** is *"extraordinarily smart, creative and pleasant to work with."* Clients praised the chair of the firm's corporate finance and M&A group **Michael Baader** for being *"a great relationships manager,"* who furthermore *"makes himself available and understands the client's needs in a business setting."* He represented Trios in its $60 million acquisition by SAIC. Clients believe **John Ramirez** is *"extremely diligent and fast – a terrific legal technician,"* and especially rate him for his private equity and asset-based lending expertise.

The Clients: Mercantile Bankshares; York International; Marriott International; CRIIMI MAE; Graham Packaging and 180's.

Band 2

Miles & Stockbridge PC
See firm details p.928

The Firm: In recent times this practice has seen an increasing amount of inbound investment and US M&A work for foreign corporates, in addition to continued M&A work for signature clients such as Black & Decker and US Foodservice. Clients praised it for being *"price-competitive and efficient,"* with one noting its *"refreshing sense of energy, purpose and renewal: they've had a great new leadership over the last few years."*

The Lawyers: Clients reported that firm chair **John Frisch** (see p.920) *"lives every negotiation with his clients: he cares desperately about the quality of his work and really feels his clients' pain."* One source added: *"He's a quick study and he's got good judgment and communication skills."* **Topper Webb**'s recent work has included midmarket M&A deals and acquisition financings in industries including senior living and related healthcare facilities. He has also advised in relation to a joint venture in the telecom industry, and angel investments in businesses such as technology equipment, services and distribution. In addition, he has been acting on syndi-

cated credit facilities on the borrower side for several multinational manufacturers, and acting as Maryland counsel to corporates and REITs on various transactions.

The Clients: Clients include Black & Decker, and other privately held and publicly owned enterprises engaged in a range of manufacturing, distribution, real estate development and service businesses.

Wilmer Cutler Pickering Hale and Dorr LLP
See firm details p.497

The Firm: Peers believe that this practice benefits from strong links with its *"prestigious and powerful DC office,"* and that its recent merger with Boston-based Hale and Dorr has given it a *"deeper corporate capability."* Clients praise its *"thorough and responsive"* lawyers for being *"good at taking in all the information, asking the right questions and taking a firm stance."* The Baltimore office has continued to handle M&A deals, securities offerings and compliance work for long-term public and private company clients, with increasing activity in the startup area.

The Lawyers: *"Quiet but determined"* practice head **Jay Watkins** (see p.925) *"builds up strong relationships with clients over time,"* according to peers, while clients believe he has a *"good business sense"* and *"good legal and institutional knowledge"* on the securities side in particular, in addition to being *"good at cutting through the issues and getting the answers."*

The Clients: Recent work for the practice has included representing Legg Mason in relation to its acquisition of the assets of the New York City, Philadelphia, Cincinnati and Chicago offices of Scudder Private Investment Counsel from Deutsche Bank. Other clients include: Danaher; Sinclair Broadcast Group; Calbert State Capital Partners; Camden Partners and Manugistics.

Band 3

Gordon, Feinblatt, Rothman, Hoffberger & Hollander, LLC

The Firm: Seen by competitors as being active in *"small-to-midsized matters,"* the firm's business law practice group is also noted for its securities work in particular, especially in the private company arena.

The Lawyers: Interviewees commended the practice of the chairman of the firm's business department, **Abba Poliakoff**, which focuses on technology and biotech-related corporate work. His recent work has included obtaining latter-stage private financings from venture capital groups for various companies in the biotech field. In addition, he has advised in relation to the establishment of several new technology companies, and has assisted the state department of business and economic development in

connection with the relocation of various companies to Maryland, including two medical companies, a consumer products company and a technology company.

The Clients: Advanced BioNutrition; CT Ventures; Care Advantage; World Total Return Fund; HealthSource Distributors; 1st Mariner Bank; Cambridge International and BioQuantetics.

Ober Kaler Grimes & Shriver

The Firm: Interviewees lauded this practice for its work in the financial services sector. In recent times, it has been particularly active in representing new and existing community banks, both private and publicly traded, in various capital raisings, SEC filings and public offerings, in addition to M&A work. It has also been handling private placement memoranda for various startups and growth companies, and representing private equity funds in various investments.

The Lawyers: **Ken Abel**'s practice encompasses corporate/M&A and securities. He is especially noted by peers for his work acting as local counsel for various mutual funds incorporated in the state of Maryland. His recent work includes advising the startup Loanpage.com in relation to its acquisition by a Californian venture capitalist.

The Clients: Clients include institutional and entrepreneurial clients in many industries including banking, healthcare, financial services, communications, media and entertainment, technology, advertising, wholesale/distribution, construction, and retail.

Saul Ewing LLP
See firm details p.1561

The Firm: The Baltimore office of this Philadelphia-based firm is especially rated by clients for being *"cost-effective and focused on client needs: the attorneys listen well and make sure they understand what our objective is."* Peers note the practice's transactional presence at the small-to-medium end of the market. Its work over the past year has included various M&A, joint ventures and strategic alliances, and financings.

The Lawyers: Barry Levin in the firm's Baltimore office is vice chair of its business department.

The Clients: Clients include The Baltimore Sun and various owner-managed businesses.

Whiteford, Taylor & Preston LLP

The Firm: Clients praised the lawyers of this firm's business and corporate practice for being *"diplomatic, versatile and savvy,"* adding that they *"home in on resolution issues very quickly."* Its expertise includes starting and selling businesses, succession planning, liquidation, financing, securities offerings, stockholder and employment agreements, stock incentive programs and tax planning.

910   All quotes in the text are from interviews with clients and competitors.

CHAMBERS USA 2005

The Lawyers: **Bob Curran**'s (see p.920) practice addresses M&A, strategic planning and ESOP transactions, with a focus on closely held businesses in the middle market. His recent work includes acting for a company in the document-imaging business in its estimated $70 million acquisition by a public company. He has also been representing a company in the heavy equipment distribution business in the acquisition of a company owned by another manufacturer.

The Clients: Clients include chemical manufacturers, auto parts, heavy equipment, construction, real estate companies, telecom, computer, pharmaceuticals and engineering companies, business consultants and hospitals.

EMPLOYMENT

MAINLY DEFENDANT

Maryland
Leading firms
(Employment: Mainly Defendant)

1	**DLA PIPER RUDNICK GRAY CARY** Baltimore
	MILES & STOCKBRIDGE PC Baltimore
	SHAWE & ROSENTHAL LLP Baltimore
	VENABLE LLP Baltimore
2	**MCGUIREWOODS LLP** Baltimore
	WHITEFORD, TAYLOR & PRESTON LLP Baltimore
3	**GORDON, FEINBLATT, ROTHMAN** Baltimore
	HOGAN & HARTSON LLP Baltimore
	KOLLMAN & SAUCIER PA Baltimore
	OBER KALER GRIMES & SHRIVER Baltimore
	SAUL EWING LLP Baltimore
	SEROTTE, ROCKMAN & WESTCOTT Baltimore
	TYDINGS & ROSENBERG LLP Baltimore

Firms are listed alphabetically in each band.

Band 1

DLA Piper Rudnick Gray Cary US LLP
See firm details p.765

The Firm: Heavily endorsed by our interviewees as a practice packed with "*top-notch advisers,*" it has expanded beyond its Baltimore/Maryland origins and now represents many companies on a regional and national basis. Clients commented that the practice's lawyers are "*responsive and efficient, so fees are always reasonable.*" The strategy of this practice is to build expertise across a broad range of areas, including both employment discrimination litigation and traditional labor law. The group is also well equipped to advise on OSHA claims, employee benefits issues and immigration.

The Lawyers: The "*proactive*" **Rich Hafets** (see p.921) was praised by peers for his "*experience and intelligence,*" which ensures the smooth running of complex matters, while clients noted his "*knowledge of the applicable law – you can call him with a question and get an answer on the phone.*" He has been especially active in traditional labor law in recent times, including labor arbitration and wrongful discharge matters. His litigation caseload also encompasses a variety of employment discrimination matters. **Russ Gardner**'s (see p.921) practice takes him across the USA, where he can be relied on to offer pragmatic advice on the most important of cases, particularly in the employment discrimination arena. **Emmett McGee** (see p.922) is seen to be a "*tough and real determined guy,*" with a practice encompassing employment discrimination, wage and hour issues, and affirmative action planning. **Larry Seegull** (see p.924) is carving out a reputation as "*an incredibly smart, tenacious and thorough lawyer.*" He is especially rated for his trial expertise.

The Clients: McCormick & Co; UPS; Ryland Homes; New World Pasta; Toyota; Constellation Energy; Blue Cross Blue Shield; Redland Brick; Sacks Fifth Avenue; Allied Irish Bank; Harsco; Maryland Institute College of Art; MCI; The Daily Record; Duratek and United Retail.

Miles & Stockbridge PC
See firm details p.928

The Firm: The "*thorough and practical*" attorneys based in this dedicated labor and employment group have impressed market commentators with their superb trial skills and sensitive counseling. Clients appreciate the broad experience fielded by the group. While offering expertise in discrimination litigation, the team has also advised on wage and hour issues, OSHA cases and claims brought under the ADA.

The Lawyers: Clients believe practice group leader **Kathy Pontone** (see p.923) is "*not shy about telling the client they're wrong, and what the best approach is.*" According to peers, "*her litigation skills and strategy are absolutely terrific – she prepares cases as well as anyone.*" Pontone has recently advised various securities brokerage clients and financial institutions as well as food manufacturers and other consumer products companies. **Steve Silvestri** (see p.924) has "*a strong track record of success,*" especially in the area of labor negotiations. He is also respected for his sound judgment on ERISA and employee benefits counseling. Clients believe **Steve Frenkil**'s (see p.920) "*practical judgment is exceptional, as is his sheer dedication to his clients. He will do whatever it takes using all hours of the day.*" Over the past year, he has been involved in a number of noncompete matters and wage and hour issues, as well as negotiating departure arrangements and service agreements in relation to senior executives.

The Clients: Clients include financial services companies, manufacturers, hospitality and food service providers, governments and several major educational institutions and nonprofit organizations.

Shawe & Rosenthal LLP
See firm details p.929

The Firm: Peers described this practice as "*a highly sophisticated labor and employment boutique that has been around since before the large firms began hiring labor lawyers.*" Clients appreciated that its user-friendly lawyers have "*a very inclusive and informative approach to litigation and its merits and strategies. They are very helpful: I can call them up with a quick question and they tend to answer without trying to bill me for it.*" The group shines brightest in the field of traditional labor law, collective bargaining and unfair treatment issues. It also advises on wage and hour claims and EEOC proceedings.

The Lawyers: According to sources, **Mike McGuire** (see p.922) is "*bright and analytic and can see the big picture.*" He will "*fight to the death if need be, but can also reach a pragmatic business solution too.*" His practice features a healthy mix of labor law and employment discrimination litigation. The "*highly experienced*" **Steve Shawe** (see p.924) has attracted a number of major clients, for which he undertakes cases across the USA. His recent workload has included advising healthcare organizations in relation to collective bargaining and union drives. Employment litigation specialist **Bruce Harrison** (see p.921) was described by one client as "*our first port of call*" for complex claims, while other clients valued that "*many judges think highly of him. We rely on him to take a pragmatic approach to the settlement of tricky employment issues.*" He has been representing GEICO Insurance across the country in a class action involving wage and hour claims, and also in litigation concerning whether insurance adjusters are exempt from overtime status. **Gary Simpler**'s (see p.924) expertise includes labor relations, employment discrimination, human resources advice and disputes relating to the wage and hour laws.

The Clients: The group has advised various fast-food and restaurant clients in relation to wage and hour claims, and represented a national employer in a sexual harassment litiga-

Maryland

Leading individuals

(Employment: Mainly Defendant)

1. AYRES Jeffrey *Venable*, Towson
   HAFETS Richard *DLA Piper*, Baltimore
   PONTONE Kathleen *Miles & Stockbridge*, Baltimore
   SILVESTRI Stephen *Miles & Stockbridge*, Baltimore
   TAYLOR Ronald *Venable*, Baltimore

2. AMES Robert *Venable*, Baltimore
   GARDNER Russell *DLA Piper*, Baltimore
   KELLNER Robert *Gordon Feinblatt*, Baltimore
   MCGUIRE J Michael *Shawe & Rosenthal*, Baltimore
   PALTELL Eric *Kollman & Saucier*, Baltimore
   PHELAN Jeanne *Whiteford Taylor*, Baltimore
   SEROTTE Neal *Serotte Rockman*, Baltimore
   SHAWE Stephen *Shawe & Rosenthal*, Baltimore
   TOPOLSKI Douglas *McGuireWoods*, Baltimore
   WHITE Pamela *Ober Kaler*, Baltimore
   WOLF Larry *Whiteford Taylor*, Baltimore

3. ABRAMSON Gil *Hogan & Hartson*, Baltimore
   CARRIER William *Tydings & Rosenberg*, Baltimore
   CLANCY Patrick *Venable*, Rockville
   COOPERMAN Harriet *Saul Ewing*, Baltimore
   EIDELMAN Gary *Saul Ewing*, Baltimore
   FRENKIL Steven *Miles & Stockbridge*, Baltimore
   GILLECE James *McGuireWoods*, Baltimore
   GUATTERY Peter *Whiteford Taylor*, Baltimore
   HARRISON Bruce *Shawe & Rosenthal*, Baltimore
   JOHNSTON George *Venable*, Baltimore
   MCGEE Emmett *DLA Piper*, Baltimore
   POKEMPNER Joseph *Whiteford Taylor*, Baltimore
   ROCKMAN Jeffrey *Serotte Rockman*, Baltimore
   SIMPLER Gary *Shawe & Rosenthal*, Baltimore
   VANDEUSEN Darrell *Kollman & Saucier*, Baltimore

Up-and-coming individuals

SEEGULL Larry *DLA Piper*, Baltimore

Individuals are listed alphabetically in each band.

tion. Other clients include: GEICO Insurance; May Department Stores; FedEx; Lafarge; Amtrak; MedStar Health and Chubb Insurance.

Venable LLP

The Firm: The lawyers of this large and well-established practice were described as "*responsive, knowledgeable, client-focused and easy to work with,*" while one client spoke of their efforts in "*constantly striving to give me the value for the dollar.*" The group fields specialist attorneys from its offices around the state, ensuring a breadth of coverage and access to deep resources. Employment litigation is a core area of the practice, including claims of discrimination, sexual harassment and wrongful discharge. Attorneys are also well versed in labor law issues such as collective bargaining and labor arbitrations.

The Lawyers: Based in the Towson office, **Jeff Ayres** inspires "*the utmost trust and confidence*" with his technical skill and ability to communicate complex issues effectively. He has recently been active advising in sexual harassment, age discrimination and wage and hour claims. He advised Raytheon in obtaining summary judgment in a race discrimination case where the plaintiff claimed unlawful denial of promotion. **Ron Taylor** is especially rated for his OSHA expertise, which has resulted in cases litigated on a national basis. The "*time-efficient and highly personable*" attorney impressed clients as one who "*doesn't have to spend time getting up to speed on the basics – because he's such an expert, he can get to the heart of the matter very quickly.*" He is also "*extremely responsive – you can get hold of him any time of the day or night.*" He advised PEMCO in obtaining summary judgment in a case involving claims of gender-based discrimination and harassment, and retaliatory and discriminatory discharge. **Bob Ames** has "*encountered just about everything under the sun – he's got a huge breadth of experience and combines pragmatism with aggressive presentation in litigation.*" He advised Giant Food in a race discrimination lawsuit brought by a number of current and former members of Plumbers Local Union No. 5. The "*sharp and accomplished litigator*" **George Johnston** is especially rated by clients for his discrimination claims defense. They also appreciate that he has "*developed a breadth of knowledge and provides great judgment in his advice.*" He handled the successful defense of an OFCCP enforcement action seeking substantial class damages for alleged racial discrimination in hiring of telemarketers. Clients identified **Pat Clancy** as an expert in the defense of disability discrimination claims. According to one client, he is "*an essential, invaluable resource – we've learned a lot from him over the years.*" He also "*puts in the time to learn about our organization, has a wonderful manner – he calibrates his responses to the people he's dealing with.*" His recent work includes successfully representing a software company in the defense of a wrongful termination claim brought by a former employee.

The Clients: Marriott International; Sodexho; Whiting-Turner Contracting; Mercantile Bank & Trust; MBNA; Pizzagali Construction; PEMCO and National Aquarium in Baltimore.

Band 2

McGuireWoods LLP

The Firm: Much of the firm's prominence in this market is based on its heavy diet of employment and labor litigation. Recent highlights have included employment discrimination, wrongful discharge and covenants not to compete. Clients appreciated the range of experience provided by this group and its thorough approach to cases. One client reported: "*We're highly satisfied with their work, and we're fussy!*"

The Lawyers: The "*no-nonsense*" **Jim Gillece** was described by one appreciative client as "*the best damned attorney for taking on the most diffi-*

cult issues I've ever had; there's nobody else I use for labor law.*" His recent work has included disputes faced by various hospitals, with one case involving advising a local hospital on union negotiations and a new contract for Johns Hopkins Bayview Medical Center. **Doug Topolski** is "*very in tune with the needs of sophisticated clients*" and has a focus on traditional labor law. His recent caseload has featured advice to various clients across the USA on issues of contract negotiation, union avoidance and the defense of unfair labor practice cases.

The Clients: Advertising.com; Unilever; Johns Hopkins Bayview Medical Center and DAP.

Whiteford, Taylor & Preston LLP

The Firm: Clients praised the group's attorneys for their success in "*understanding our business and culture. They give you clear directions and provide quick responses that are well researched.*" The team's recent caseload has included traditional labor relations and associated litigation, as well as negotiations with unions. Its employment litigation has featured the defense of discrimination claims, sexual harassment issues, wage and hour work and noncompete claims.

The Lawyers: Interviewees highlighted the traditional labor expertise of **Larry Wolf** (see p.925). They described him as "*really smart and strategic in his litigation efforts.*" **Joe Pokempner** (see p.923) is also a long-standing figure in the market, whose depth of experience in traditional labor law is widely respected. The "*pragmatic*" **Jeanne Phelan** (see p.923) is especially rated for her employment litigation skills. According to clients: "*You feel on a steady course with her – she gives excellent advice and ensures you stay in calm waters.*" Clients also endorsed **Peter Guattery** (see p.921) as an "*intelligent and professional*" attorney and an expert in advising employers on the hiring of foreign nationals to positions in the USA.

The Clients: Recent highlights for the practice include representing a client in the settlement of a long-running race discrimination class action lawsuit. The firm also represented an equipment manufacturer in an unfair labor practices case. Clients range from Fortune 500 companies to small, closely held businesses.

Band 3

Gordon, Feinblatt, Rothman, Hoffberger & Hollander, LLC

The Firm: This practice is noted by peers for its representation of locally focused clients and larger companies with business in the region. According to one source: "*If you have a matter in Baltimore, then this is the go-to firm.*" Attorneys advise on a balance of labor relations and employment litigation including reduction of workforce issues and discrimination claims.

The Lawyers: Our interviewees agree that

"*personable*" employment law group chair **Bob Kellner** "*really knows his stuff.*" His broad employment practice includes additional expertise in ERISA issues. His recent workload has included employment discrimination, collective bargaining and wage and hour issues.

The Clients: Mid-Atlantic Permanente Medical Group; Kennedy Krieger Institute; Henderson Webb and the Merchants Terminal.

Hogan & Hartson LLP

See firm details p.484

The Firm: Market commentators endorsed this employment group, believing that its attorneys "*bring the best business result to the problem.*" Its expertise encompasses employment discrimination, traditional labor law and general counseling. While the team in Maryland is smaller than some of its rivals, it can draw on the resources offered by this major international law firm, particularly out of the DC office.

The Lawyers: Clients appreciate that practice head **Gil Abramson** (see p.919) "*brings a good, common-sense approach to labor issues.*" They also note his success in developing a respected OSHA practice at the firm. He has been especially active for clients in the broadcasting, pharmaceutical and shipping industries, and his recent work includes advising Radio Free Europe on various discrimination, harassment and termination issues.

The Clients: Radio Free Europe; Radio Free Asia; Comcast Cable; Guilford Pharmaceuticals; Martec and Enzo Biochemicals.

Kollman & Saucier PA

The Firm: The market perception of this practice was summed up by one competitor's comment: "*We like their pedigree and their personnel – they're straight shooters.*" The group's recent work has included representing both public and private sector employers in various collective bargaining negotiations, including a major Maryland healthcare system. It also negotiated three new labor agreements for one of the largest municipalities in the state, and has been increasingly active representing employers in union-organizing activity. In addition, the attorneys are well versed in the defense of employment discrimination work, and have been particularly involved in disputes arising out of the nursing and healthcare sectors.

The Lawyers: The "*knowledgeable and pragmatic*" **Eric Paltell** was endorsed by peers as a lawyer, who is "*always up-to-date, on top of things and easy to work with.*" Clients noted that "*the great thing about Eric is that he leaves the choice to you but he helps you choose the best solu-*

tion. He never forgets who the client is and he protects our interests." **Darrell VanDeusen** has cultivated a broad employment practice, and is respected for his litigation and counseling skills on issues such as OSHA, EEOC and labor relations. "*You can trust him implicitly.*"

The Clients: Clients include businesses, associations, governmental entities and educational institutions.

Ober Kaler Grimes & Shriver

The Firm: Clients praised the lawyers of this practice for "*keeping us well informed and staying involved – it's a really transparent process.*" They also rated the detailed understanding of the law possessed by these attorneys and their thorough approach to litigation. The group is well-equipped to advise on all forms of employment discrimination litigation as well as wage and hour and wrongful dismissal claims.

The Lawyers: Chair of the firm's employment and labor group **Pam White** represents both employers and executives across a range of employment issues. Clients described her as "*brilliant at thinking through the puzzle of the case,*" and confirm that she takes an aggressive approach to litigation. Her expertise includes negotiating the resolution of disputes relating to discrimination, harassment and employment contracts.

The Clients: Clients include financial, healthcare, and construction companies and other businesses drawn from across the region.

Saul Ewing LLP

See firm details p.1561

The Firm: Clients praise this practice for giving "*value for money advice*" and a timely, responsive service. Its attorneys are highly knowledgeable and able to mediate and litigate cases at all levels. Its recent work has included noncompete work, discrimination matters, OSHA advice, wage and hour claims and affirmative action counseling.

The Lawyers: Cochair of the firm's labor, employment and employee benefits practice group **Harriet Cooperman** (see p.920) is considered a real asset to the firm and "*a good promoter for this practice.*" Her experience includes representing domestic and international corporations in labor and employment cases in both federal and state trial and appellate courts around the country. Vice office managing partner in Baltimore **Gary Eidelman** (see p.920) was praised by clients: "*He makes you feel very comfortable and at ease with the discussions*" and is "*able to answer most questions on the spot.*" He has been especially active in noncompete work

in recent times, and also successfully represented Deutsche Post Global Mail in a restrictive covenant case.

The Clients: Clients come from industries such as manufacturing, service, wholesale, automobile, technology, financial services, entertainment, and retailing, in addition to public entities and nonprofit organizations.

Serotte, Rockman & Westcott

The Firm: This specialist management boutique is rated by our interviewees as home to some of the market's real specialists: "*They are small but effective across everything they do.*" The group advises on both traditional labor law and employment discrimination, wage and hour disputes and OSHA.

The Lawyers: **Neal Serotte** is "*a decent, practical attorney and an excellent advocate for his clients.*" His practice encompasses discrimination claims, wage and hour issues and restrictive covenant litigation. Respected **Jeff Rockman** provides sound and practical advice across a range of labor and employment law issues.

The Clients: 1st Mariner Bank; AMF Bowling Centers; Anchor Motor Freight; Baltimore Aircoil; Baltimore Blast; Baltimore Spice; Benfield Electric; Cecil Community College; Cingular Wireless; Continental Realty; Fila USA; Goucher College; Griffith Energy Services; Harford Community College; Health Facilities Association of Maryland; Klein's Super Markets; Kinko's; Koons Automotive Group; Leaseway Transportation; Locke Insulators; Merrill Lynch; Pierce, Fenner & Smith; Monro Muffler Brake; NGK-Locke; Northrop Grumman; Ollie's Bargain Outlet; Polk Audio; S3 Technologies and Shopco Management.

Tydings & Rosenberg LLP

The Firm: This "*efficient*" practice was endorsed by clients as one that provides "*well-priced advice, particularly when compared with some of the larger firms in town.*" Its workload includes representing clients in covenants not to compete, wrongful discharge, and employment discrimination claims. It has also counseled clients on drug testing programs and the drafting of employee handbooks.

The Lawyers: Clients described managing partner **Bill Carrier** as a "*skilled litigator, very bright, well prepared and deliberate in approach.*"

The Clients: Adams Express; Bob Davidson Ford; Cloverland/Greenspring Farms Dairy; Hearn Kirkwood; Holly Hill Manor; IBM; MM&P MATES Program; Penn Pontiac-GMC; Sheet Metal Workers' National Pension Fund and the Classic Catering People.

LITIGATION

GENERAL COMMERCIAL

Maryland
Leading firms
(Litigation: General Commercial)

[1] **DLA PIPER RUDNICK GRAY CARY** *Baltimore*
   HOGAN & HARTSON LLP *Baltimore*
   KRAMON & GRAHAM, PA *Baltimore*
   VENABLE LLP *Baltimore*
[2] **MILES & STOCKBRIDGE PC** *Baltimore*
   ROSENBERG, MARTIN, FUNK *Baltimore*
   SAUL EWING LLP *Baltimore*
   ZUCKERMAN SPAEDER LLP *Baltimore*
[3] **BRAULT GRAHAM SCOTT & BRAULT LLC** *Rockville*
   GOODELL, DEVRIES, LEECH & DANN *Baltimore*
   GORDON, FEINBLATT, ROTHMAN *Baltimore*
   MURPHY & SHAFFER *Baltimore*
   WHITEFORD, TAYLOR & PRESTON LLP *Baltimore*

Leading individuals
(Litigation: General Commercial)

★ **GRAHAM Andrew** *Kramon & Graham, Baltimore*
[1] **BEALL George** *Hogan & Hartson, Baltimore*
   MATHIAS Robert *DLA Piper, Baltimore*
   ULWICK James *Kramon & Graham, Baltimore*
[2] **BERNSTEIN Gregg** *Zuckerman Spaeder, Baltimore*
   BETTER Herbert *Zuckerman Spaeder, Baltimore*
   BRAULT Albert *Brault Graham, Rockville*
   BURCH Francis *DLA Piper, Baltimore*
   DILLOFF Neil *DLA Piper, Baltimore*
   GATELY Mark *Hogan & Hartson, Baltimore*
   HIMELES Martin *Zuckerman Spaeder, Baltimore*
   IMMELT Stephen *Hogan & Hartson, Baltimore*
   MONK II Charles *Saul Ewing, Baltimore*
   MURPHY William *Murphy & Shaffer, Baltimore*
   ROSENBERG Ben *Rosenberg Martin, Baltimore*
   SHEA James *Venable, Baltimore*
   WRIGHT Jefferson *Miles & Stockbridge, Baltimore*
[3] **ARCHIBALD James** *Venable, Baltimore*
   CHASON James *Whiteford Taylor, Towson*
   GRAY James *Venable, Baltimore*
   LEECH Sidney *Goodell DeVries, Baltimore*
   MARTIN Gerard *Rosenberg Martin, Baltimore*
   MERKLE Craig *Goodell DeVries, Baltimore*
   NILSON George *DLA Piper, Baltimore*
   RYAN William *Whiteford Taylor, Baltimore*
   SCHATZOW Michael *Venable, Baltimore*
   SCHEELER Charles *DLA Piper, Baltimore*
   STRAIN Paul *Venable, Baltimore*
   WEINER Arnold *Weiner & Weltchek, Lutherville*

Firms and individuals are listed alphabetically in each band.

Band 1

DLA Piper Rudnick Gray Cary US LLP

See firm details p.765

The Firm: This "*top-notch*" practice possesses the depth of resources, both locally and nationally, to ensure its position as a prime choice for multistate disputes. "*It is consistently strong and has become such a national practice that its attorneys are trying a higher percentage of their cases nationally than most Maryland firms,*" acknowledged sources. And with the recent alliance with the West Coast firm, Gray, Cary, Ware & Freidenrich and the UK's DLA, its geographic reach and resources are further extended. The group's recent workload has included IP and technology litigation and disputes related to insurance and financial services.

The Lawyers: US chair of the firm's litigation practice, **Bob Mathias** (see p.922) is a "*smart, down-to-earth attorney who's not afraid to try a case.*" He also displays great trial skills as he is "*able to connect with the common juror on a very personal level.*" Interviewees described **Neil Dilloff** (see p.920) as a "*tenacious litigator,*" and particularly highlighted his understanding of complex insurance disputes. **George Nilson** (see p.923) is "*a very balanced, careful, intelligent and upright member of the Bar.*" His broad practice includes products liability claims, real estate litigation and environmental disputes. Despite his duties as the firm's managing partner, **Frank Burch** (see p.919) remains a popular choice among clients for his courtroom skills and strategic planning. He is "*a natural-born leader – a strong and trusted man who lines up everyone behind him and doesn't look back, just gets on and does it.*" **Charles Scheeler** (see p.923) can bring his superb intelligence to his cases, and according to one peer, "*many bright guys act like they're above speaking to normal human beings. Not him, though – he establishes a real rapport with juries.*" In recent times he has been representing key client MCI in various matters around the country, including criminal securities law charges filed by the Oklahoma attorney general. The case was resolved with a dismissal of all charges against the company.

The Clients: GE; MCI; Lockheed Martin; General Motors, Toyota; Deutsche Bank and Lincoln Financial.

Hogan & Hartson LLP

See firm details p.484

The Firm: Clients appreciated this firm's "*bright, hard-working and professional attorneys*" and valued the level of commitment and depth of resources that the group brings to complex commercial litigation. Competitors especially noted the practice's expertise in relation to healthcare investigations, both civil and criminal. It has also secured prominence in the representation of pharmaceuticals and biotech companies, most notably Amgen.

The Lawyers: "*A real dean of the Bar*" and a former US Attorney, **George Beall** (see p.919) is also "*a great name and a highly respected guy.*" The corporate litigation expertise of **Mark Gately** (see p.921) is widely recognized. A "*straight-talking lawyer,*" he recently advised Harmony Gold Mining in the successful defense of a challenge initiated by Gold Fields concerning a two-phase tender offer made to Gold Fields shareholders in the USA, South Africa, and other countries. The "*very cerebral*" **Steve Immelt** (see p.921) was particularly rated by our interviewees for his skillful handling of white-collar criminal investigations. "*He has the ability to work through big problems and come up with well thought-out solutions. He's smart, thorough, careful and just doesn't make mistakes.*"

The Clients: Baltimore Ravens; Amgen; Colfax; Imo Industries and Bristol-Myers Squibb.

Kramon & Graham, PA

See firm details p.927

The Firm: Clients spoke of the "*good business and courtroom sense,*" that this firm brings to its litigation. The group fields "*intelligent and thoughtful attorneys, who have the capacity to turn into very tough, hard-nosed litigators when necessary.*" The group has a wealth of experience including disputes relating to banking and securities law, construction, employment and environmental matters. Insurance coverage, products liability and professional malpractice also feature in the caseload.

The Lawyers: Interviewees endorsed the trial skills displayed by **Andy Graham** (see p.921). "*He puts the fires out.*" Graham is also "*the true lawyers' lawyer – he's the one to whom lawyers turn when they have an issue*" and a popular choice for strategic counseling on complex disputes. He has recently represented a major real estate company and a major investment house in their separate pieces of securities litigation. He has also been involved in a number of large white-collar criminal investigations, in addition to representing lawyers in malpractice cases and company executives in employment disputes. One admiring client described **Jim Ulwick** (see p.925) as "*scarily smart,*" while competitors rated him for being "*a tenacious courtroom advocate and very strategic thinker.*" His experience includes litigation relating to legal and medical malpractice, real estate and toxic tort as well as complex business litigation.

The Clients: Clients include local, national and international corporations.

Venable LLP

The Firm: This "*preeminent*" practice's expertise includes securities and antitrust matters, construction disputes, IP litigation, and bankruptcy and franchise-related cases. Clients praised its lawyers for their accessibility, while one noted, "*I give Venable very complex matters that require specialist assistance, technical matters that I want prepared well.*" The group can draw on the resources provided by the firm's network

914   All quotes in the text are from interviews with clients and competitors.

CHAMBERS USA 2005

of offices, and is well versed in state and federal trial work, as well as arbitration and mediation. **The Lawyers:** Clients spoke of the business and civil litigation expertise possessed by managing partner **Jim Shea**. "*He is smart, responsive, pleasant and not confrontational – he tries to make things work as opposed to being bombastic.*" He recently obtained judgment for a software license holder in an action by a distributor seeking to prevent the termination of its distribution rights. Clients also believe that the "*energetic and thoroughly organized*" **Jim Archibald** "*focuses on understanding as much of the factual background and pattern to the case as he can.*" He is "*an exceptional communicator and puts together a good team of lawyers, who all pull in the same direction.*" Archibald has advised a large issuer of credit cards in complex commercial litigation in the Federal Bankruptcy Court in Delaware, which arose from the bankruptcy of an airline company and involves the solicitation and transfer of 'frequent flyer' credit card account holders to a competitor. A "*real heavy hitter,*" **Jim Gray** attracted plaudits for his aggressive courtroom manner; "*he's a great trial lawyer; if you have a case where you need a bulldog, he's your guy.*" The "*versatile*" **Michael Schatzow** impresses clients with his "*command of the material*" and his "*ability to focus on what's important and develop the appropriate strategies.*" According to one client: "*He has a low-key delivery but an aura of credibility, and is a strong negotiator.*" He has recently been representing a top US corporation in high-profile bankruptcy proceedings in New York, which has involved actions against creditors to recover approximately $1.7 billion in funds transferred by the debtor prior to its bankruptcy petition. **Paul Strain** is especially rated for his expertise in products liability. John Lewin has recently retired from private practice. **The Clients:** American Standard; Cardinal Health; Ford; GM; Goodyear; Marriott International; Massachusetts Mutual Life Insurance; MBNA; Navistar International; PQ; Royal Ahold; SafeNet; US Foodservice; Wachovia and Wells Fargo.

Band 2

Miles & Stockbridge PC
See firm details p.928
The Firm: This accommodating and responsive practice has impressed clients as "*extremely client-centered; not only solving problems but also preventing them going to trial.*" Its attorneys are also technically skilled and on top of developments in the law; "*they help us define our day-to-day policies and alert us to key issues.*" The group's recent litigation workload has ranged from IP disputes to trade disputes under the UCC, antitrust matters, fraud litigation and internal corporate investigations.

The Lawyers: Head of the firm's commercial and business litigation group, **Jeff Wright** (see p.925) is "*a real professional and a very confident lawyer.*" His recent highlights include representing Calberg County in obtaining summary judgment in a dispute with a large private water utility. The matter related to the right to supply water to citizens in various areas within the county that have been the subject of new development. He also represented two individuals in a dispute relating to their sale of a printing business to a large local envelope and paper company.
The Clients: Bank of America; CitiFinancial; Black & Decker; Provident Bank of Maryland; Niro; Mercy Medical Center; M&T; Citrix Systems; Verizon; US Food Service; Lowe's and QuadraMed.

Rosenberg, Martin, Funk, Greenberg, LLP
The Firm: This respected litigation team straddles both business disputes and issues of white-collar crime and corporate investigations. Its attorneys are "*aggressive when they need to be*" and have built up a strong profile in the Maryland market. The breadth of experience available here includes contract disputes, insurance claims, professional liability and personal injury matters.
The Lawyers: **Ben Rosenberg**'s practice encompasses trial and appellate litigation, and disputes relating to antitrust, contracts, insurance and products liability. He is a "*highly respected and professional attorney,*" and a favorite among clients and peers. **Gerry Martin**'s practice encompasses both business litigation and white-collar criminal defense. "*He is a very down-to-earth guy – if you have a client who appreciates plain speaking in his lawyer, then he's your man.*"
The Clients: Clients include partnerships, corporates and individuals.

Saul Ewing LLP
See firm details p.1561
The Firm: This national firm fields a team in Baltimore that has impressed clients with its "*thorough and sophisticated advice.*" The practice has a broad geographic reach and is noted for its success in "*handling large bankruptcy cases all over the country.*" The practice also houses expertise in a range of disputes such as partnership issues, real estate issues and commercial contracts. In addition, it is also well known for its First Amendment work for various newspapers and magazines.
The Lawyers: Managing partner of the firm's Baltimore office, **Charlie Monk** (see p.922) was described by peers as "*a litigation guru,*" who manages huge cases. He is "*fabulous in the courtroom and has a tremendous work ethic.*"
The Clients: In recent times the practice has represented Owens Corning as national debtor's

counsel in its asbestos-related bankruptcy. Other clients include: The Daily Record; the Frederick News-Post; Avir Corporation and Newsweek magazine.

Zuckerman Spaeder LLP
The Firm: This practice won plaudits from clients for its "*effective, results-oriented litigators*" who "*can try cases but also get results by avoiding trials.*" In addition to trial work, the practice counsels clients involved in governmental investigations and enforcement actions.
The Lawyers: **Martin Himeles** is a "*smart and tenacious advocate.*" According to one client: "*He is able to take an esoteric and unusual point, make the judge understand it, and refute the other side's arguments, so that we ultimately prevail.*" He has handled a number of fraud and securities cases in recent times, and represented a major hospital in a commercial dispute concerning termination of a longterm contract. Market sources also highlighted **Gregg Bernstein** as "*one of the top guys in the state for white-collar criminal work,*" while **Herb Better** has "*a lot of common sense and likability – he's just the kind of person that juries warm to.*"
The Clients: Clients include Fortune 500 corporations, small and midsized public and privately held businesses, and individuals.

Band 3

Brault Graham Scott & Brault LLC
The Firm: This Rockville-based practice is especially noted for its insurance litigation work, with a particular focus on medical and professional malpractice. The attorneys here can also draw on the support of resources from the firm's offices in Washington, DC and Virginia. Its caseload includes products liability claims, general commercial and corporate disputes and real estate litigation.
The Lawyers: Market sources endorsed the deep experience possessed by the "*fantastic*" **Al Brault**. A hard-working attorney, he is "*a damned good courtroom lawyer,*" whose ability to communicate with judge and jury is widely commended.
The Clients: American Express Property and Casualty Companies; Coakley & Williams Construction; Gateway Insurance; Sterling Jewelers; GAB; Robins National America; Government Employees Insurance; Universal Underwriters Group; Colonial Penn; Integral Insurance; Medstar Health; Farm Bureau Insurance Companies; Donegal Insurance; United Services Automobile Associates (USAA); Sentry; Westchester Fire Insurance; Nations Bank; Sherwood Brands; Pohanka Auto Group; OMS National Insurance (OMSNIC).

Goodell, DeVries, Leech & Dann, LLP

See firm details p.926

The Firm: This firm is particularly rated by market observers for its professional and products liability work. Its knowledgeable attorneys can handle a range of disputes, including toxic tort and environmental matters and class action litigation.

The Lawyers: **Craig Merkle** is seen by peers to have "*terrific skills*" in relation to professional liability and medical malpractice work in particular. **Sid Leech**'s expertise encompasses advice to major corporations and insurers in products liability matters. These cases often involve the chemical, pharmaceutical, manufacturing and consumer product industries.

The Clients: Clients include businesses, banks and financial institutions, medical institutions and their directors and officers.

Gordon, Feinblatt, Rothman, Hoffberger & Hollander, LLC

The Firm: Clients endorsed the group's attorneys for their "*sharp, quick minds*" and their skillful ability to "*see all the different aspects of the problems we face.*" The team's expertise includes general commercial and construction disputes, IP, antitrust claims, environmental law and real estate disputes. Civil RICO and criminal and civil tax issues all appear on the agenda here.

The Lawyers: Lawrence Fletcher-Hill is the chair of the firm's litigation group.

The Clients: Clients include public and private entities.

Murphy & Shaffer

The Firm: This firm is a force in the region with its broad dispute resolution skills. Attorneys here attract a range of mandates from national and local companies as well as referrals from law firms outside of Maryland. The group's experience ranges from products liability defense work for some major companies, professional malpractice work, principally for lawyers, various commercial disputes, and construction and real estate matters.

The Lawyers: "*On everyone's list as a really smart guy,*" **Bill Murphy** is "*a gifted practitioner,*" reported market commentators. He is particularly rated in the area of white-collar criminal defense. A former judge, he has "*a remarkable empathy with jurors – he's not part of the normal corporate mold, but a great jury trial lawyer.*" He recently successfully tried a case for a real estate developer.

The Clients: Clients include small and mid-sized local and regional businesses, as well as Fortune 500 companies with activities in the region.

Whiteford, Taylor & Preston LLP

The Firm: Market commentators commended this litigation practice for its representation of local healthcare providers in medical malpractice work. Its broad commercial practice also encompasses disputes arising out of the finance, insurance, real estate and technology sectors. Clients reported that its "*smart and articulate*" lawyers "*always give a response that we can understand and get high marks for attention to detail.*" Peers also acknowledge: "*They know how to get through the court system efficiently and effectively.*"

The Lawyers: Clients believe that **Bill Ryan** (see p.923) is a "*clever litigator and top-notch trial lawyer. He is very poised, polished and classy with a commanding presence.*" He successfully defended a client against class action claims brought by the American Civil Liberties Union alleging that it intentionally discriminated in its public housing. He also recently won a copyright infringement case for a software developer. **Jim Chason** (see p.919) is especially respected for his medical malpractice work. According to clients, he "*takes a very keen interest in our company and our people and is very professional.*" Chason is a skilled trial lawyer, and peers rate him "*effective in front of juries – they find him appealing and believable.*"

The Clients: Clients are drawn from the technology, telecom, manufacturing, distribution, retail, municipalities, financial services and healthcare sectors.

Other Notable Practitioner

"*Superstar*" **Arnold Weiner** of Weiner & Weltcheck combines his civil litigation practice with a specialty in white-collar crime, and in both areas "*works at a very high level.*"

REAL ESTATE

Maryland
Leading firms (Real Estate)

1	**BALLARD SPAHR ANDREWS** *Baltimore*
	DLA PIPER RUDNICK GRAY CARY *Baltimore*
	VENABLE LLP *Baltimore*
2	**GORDON, FEINBLATT, ROTHMAN** *Baltimore*
	LINOWES AND BLOCHER LLP *Bethesda*
	SHULMAN, ROGERS, GANDAL, PORDY *Rockville*
3	**GALLAGHER, EVELIUS & JONES, LLP** *Baltimore*
	LENROW, KOHN & OLIVER *Baltimore*
	MCGUIREWOODS LLP *Baltimore*
	MILES & STOCKBRIDGE PC *Baltimore*
	ROSENBERG, MARTIN, FUNK *Baltimore*
	SAUL EWING LLP *Baltimore*
	WHITEFORD, TAYLOR & PRESTON LLP *Baltimore*
	WILMER CUTLER PICKERING HALE *Baltimore*

Firms are listed alphabetically in each band.

Band 1

Ballard Spahr Andrews & Ingersoll LLP

See firm details p.1541

The Firm: The real estate practice is a "*raison d'être*" for the firm, observers said, and noted that it has "*tremendous depth*" with a "*broad-based*" portfolio. It represents "*a lot of owners, developers and insurance companies*" in a range of transactions, including acquisitions, dispositions, financing and leasing. Wielding national influence in this field, it is brimming with "*top practitioners*" who participate in some of the area's most prominent projects. A significant highlight involves the Lockwood Place project, which is a mixed-use retail and office harborfront development. The team has also advised on the Silo Point project, which will involve a garage and offices on the site of several old grain silos. In addition, it has handled the Arundel Reserve project, a new development with residential, office and retail elements.

The Lawyers: "*An incredible resource,*" former Baltimore managing partner **Morty Fisher** (see p.920) was praised for his "*bird's eye view*" and his "*absolute depth of knowledge,*" interviewees said. "*He knows a number of people in the real estate community and he comes up with fast and practical solutions.*" He has represented developers, lending institutions and department stores among others. Managing partner of the firm's Baltimore office, **Ray Truitt** (see p.924) won commendation as "*a skillful lawyer*" who "*brings a positive attitude to negotiations.*" Peers believe the "*highly professional*" senior counsel **Ron Fish** (see p.920) "*knows his stuff*" and is "*always a pleasure to work with.*" His practice encompasses commercial real estate acquisitions, developments, financing, leasing and restructuring.

The Clients: Clients include developers, entrepreneurs, banks, pension funds, life insurance companies, and landlords and tenants.

DLA Piper Rudnick Gray Cary US LLP

See firm details p.765

The Firm: This real estate department proved to be a top choice due to its "*strong national practice with skilled attorneys,*" sources said. It is

916   All quotes in the text are from interviews with clients and competitors.

CHAMBERS USA 2005

Maryland
Leading individuals (Real Estate)

1 FISHER Morton *Ballard Spahr*, Baltimore
FISHMAN David *Gordon Feinblatt*, Baltimore
LEVIN Edward *DLA Piper*, Baltimore
POLLAK Mark *Wilmer Cutler*, Baltimore
SHEPHERD Kevin *Venable*, Baltimore
SHULMAN Lawrence *Shulman Rogers*, Rockville

2 CHRISS Timothy *Gordon Feinblatt*, Baltimore
FISH Ronald *Ballard Spahr*, Baltimore
OLIVER James *Lenrow Kohn*, Baltimore
RENO Russell *Venable*, Baltimore
TRUITT Raymond *Ballard Spahr*, Baltimore
WINSTON Roger *Linowes and Blocher*, Bethesda

3 KOCHANSKI David *Shulman Rogers*, Rockville
LEVINE Richard *DLA Piper*, Baltimore
MACHEN John *DLA Piper*, Baltimore
MILLSPAUGH Thomas *Wilmer Cutler*, Baltimore
WRIGHT James *Venable*, Baltimore

4 BARBUTI Thomas *Whiteford Taylor*, Baltimore
CARROLL Priscilla *Whiteford Taylor*, Baltimore
COHEN David *Linowes and Blocher*, Bethesda
GREENBERG Barry *Rosenberg Martin*, Baltimore
ISAACSON Andrew *Linowes and Blocher*, Bethesda
LEWIS Thomas *Gallagher Evelius*, Baltimore
REED Matthew *Wilmer Cutler*, Baltimore
SEARS Barbara *Linowes and Blocher*, Bethesda
SHELLEY Patrick *McGuireWoods*, Baltimore

Individuals are listed alphabetically in each band.

"*large enough that it has the capability to do all types of transactions.*" Clients praised its "*high-caliber*" cadre of "*conscientious*" operators who are of "*the highest integrity – you don't get to their position without a huge amount of talent.*" The firm's tentacles stretch nationwide through a variety of important transactions such as joint ventures, acquisitions and developments. Leasing, commercial finance and workouts also proved significant in its portfolio, while niche specialties include the taxation, environmental and regulatory aspects of real estate.

The Lawyers: **Ed Levin** (see p.922) is described by peers as "*one of the preeminent real estate lawyers in the state, without question.*" His recent work has included financing, leasing, purchase and sale transactions on behalf of clients including insurance companies, banks and individual entrepreneurs. One of his projects involved working on multistate financings for a client with a portfolio in excess of $100 million and involves a couple of dozen properties located in eight states. He also advised in relation to the sale of 80 cellular tower sites nationwide. **Jack Machen** (see p.922) "*understands client needs and how to reach a practical solution,*" according to our interviewees. "*He's a straight-up guy, very focused on client objectives, absolutely lets none of his ego get in the way.*" His recent work has included land acquisition and commercial leasing transactions. He has been advising AEGONUSA Realty Advisers in rela-

tion to commercial mortgage loans and separately advising Ryland Group on its property acquisitions. He has also been advising Struever Bros. Eccles & Rouse in relation to development work, including a sizable project in Durham, North Carolina. Especially noted for his "*sophisticated*" real estate finance practice, **Rich Levine** (see p.922) "*works with so many top developers and understands the business so well that he can break it down and make it simple for the client to understand.*"

The Clients: AEGONUSA Realty Advisers; Ryland Homes; Struever Bros. Eccles & Rouse; Constellation Real Estate and LaSalle Investment Management.

Venable LLP

The Firm: Clients praise this "*well-staffed*" practice as a top choice for "*difficult transactions,*" while competitors rate its "*knowledgeable and trustworthy senior real estate lawyers.*" Its recent work has included representing large national and multinational clients and various REITs and pension funds on real estate acquisitions and dispositions nationwide. Representing Boston Properties, the firm is handling a major lease transaction involving T. Rowe Price, the lead tenant in the premier office tower in Baltimore's Inner Harbor. In addition, it has been representing Mercantile-Safe Deposit and Trust Company in its capacity as trustee of the AFL-CIO Building Investment Trust with ongoing multimillion-dollar acquisitions and dispositions throughout the USA.

The Lawyers: Peers believe that practice cochair **Kevin Shepherd** "*gets right to the point,*" further adding that "*he writes and analyzes a lot of legislation affecting real estate. He's thoughtful, careful and diligent, and he uses these qualities in a pragmatic manner.*" He has represented the City of Rockville in a complex $350 million downtown redevelopment project involving developers Federal Realty Investment Trust (FRIT) and RD Rockville; the city is the county seat for Montgomery County, Maryland. **Ronny Reno** was described by peers as being "*one of the deans of real estate in the state,*" and represents a range of real estate developers, home builders, and lenders in the metropolitan Baltimore area. Clients described **Jim Wright** as "*pleasant, responsive and smart – a senior guy who's able to put extremely complex matters together.*" His work includes representing Marriott in its nationwide acquisition of hotels.

The Clients: City of Rockville; Mercantile-Safe Deposit and Trust Company; California State Teachers' Retirement System and Boston Properties.

Band 2

Gordon, Feinblatt, Rothman, Hoffberger & Hollander, LLC

The Firm: Clients praised this practice for its "*prompt and professional service, competitive rates and knowledge of the industry.*" Its work has included the purchase, sale and development of investment grade properties, in addition to the financing and refinancing of both new and existing projects. Representing Kimco/Mid-Atlantic Realty Trust, it orchestrated anchor leases and shopping center development work. The team has also been advising David S. Brown Enterprises in relation to both retail and office development work, and separately acted for TIA-CREF in financing and development proceedings.

The Lawyers: Real estate group chair **David Fishman** benefits from an established profile in development work as related to shopping centers, residential projects and others. **Tim Chriss** gained client confidence as "*our point person – if he left, I'd go too.*" His practice includes representing developers, lenders and governmental entities in relation to a variety of commercial real estate projects.

The Clients: The team has been representing American Port Services in land acquisition work and Bankers Association in various financings and refinancings. Other clients include Kimco/Mid-Atlantic Realty Trust; FRP; Medstar Health; Bank One; Bankers Association; David S. Brown Enterprises; Home Properties and TIAA-CREF.

Linowes and Blocher LLP

The Firm: This real estate specialist in Montgomery County has "*armies of good people*" in the field, according to our interviewees, who particularly rate its land use expertise. In this area, it is considered a powerhouse, exerting lasting influence through litigation as well as handling thorny land use and zoning problems. It is also a pioneering authority on public-private partnerships, and garnered respect in the transactional sphere through its work on projects such as shopping malls, residential developments, office parks and public buildings. Recent significant work includes advising on a $100 million tax-structured real estate sale.

The Lawyers: The "*top-flight*" **Roger Winston** is "*recognized as one of the experts in the narrow but important field of condominium law,*" according to our interviewees. **Barbara Sears** is pitched as a contending force in land use, while chair of the firm's business practice group **David Cohen** demonstrates mastery in the areas of business and tax planning for real estate developers, investors and entrepreneurs, including advice that relates to real estate acquisitions and dispositions. Rated by peers for his development work, **Andrew Isaacson** is viewed as "*a constructive problem solver.*"

The Clients: Clients include developers, builders, public or quasi-governmental entities, utility companies and local, national or international corporations and organizations.

Shulman, Rogers, Gandal, Pordy & Ecker, PA

The Firm: The practice's expertise includes acquisition, disposition and financing of real estate, predominantly for purchasers and sellers. However, the team has occasionally represented lenders, in addition to handling title insurance work. In the area of leasing, it has participated in office and retail leases, ground leases and build-to-suit leases among others. Its work often spans several states, and is blended with litigation knowledge to offer a well-rounded repertoire.

The Lawyers: Founding partner of the firm, **Larry Shulman** has been especially active in commercial leasing work. He recently negotiated a lease on behalf of Strathmore Hall Foundation, the nonprofit arts organization in charge of a major concert hall in Montgomery County. **David Kochanski** has represented home builders on both acquisitions and dispositions of real estate.

The Clients: Land America; Lawyers Title Insurance Corporation; Chicago Title Insurance; Fidelity National Title Insurance Company of New York; Conestoga Title Insurance and Republic National Title Insurance.

Band 3

Gallagher, Evelius & Jones, LLP

The Firm: Especially noted by peers for its real estate finance expertise, this firm's business and real estate transactions group has participated in residential, commercial, industrial and mixed-use real estate development projects. It often represents landlords and tenants in commercial leasing transactions. The team advised in relation to the Lexington Terrace development in Baltimore, making sure the project complied with all federal mandates and would be eligible for the maximum allowable tax credits in its financing.

The Lawyers: Described by peers as "*a major player*" in the field, **Tom Lewis** has participated in various multifamily housing and innovative mixed-use redevelopment projects in urban areas.

The Clients: The firm represented the owner of a waterfront property in the southern portion of the Inner Harbor area of Baltimore City in settling a dispute; it also handled the subsequent sale of the property. Other clients include lenders, real estate developers, equity investors, health systems, colleges and universities.

Lenrow, Kohn & Oliver

The Firm: Although smaller compared to some of its competitors, this firm nevertheless commands authority in the field. It focuses on commercial real estate, construction law, corporate and bankruptcy litigation and commercial collections. Its real estate expertise includes real estate finance, condominium law and leases and leasing.

The Lawyers: "*A practical and skilled attorney,*" **Jim Oliver** is especially noted by peers for his expertise in condominium developments.

The Clients: Chelsea Property Group; Prime Retail; Allied Domecq Retailing, USA; Baskin-Robbins; Dunkin' Donuts; Giant Food; Brookstone; Brick Bodies Health & Fitness Group; The Johns Hopkins University; Boggs & Partners Architects; Maryland Economic Development and International Design and Construction Online.

McGuireWoods LLP

The Firm: This practice encompasses real estate finance work for institutional lenders and corporate real estate work for various corporate clients. It also has expertise in office leasing and land use. Clients praised its lawyers for their "*excellence in drafting and processing,*" with one adding: "*They're good at listening to our requests and consistently keeping the deal moving forward.*"

The Lawyers: "*Able to take a complicated issue and reduce it to the core problem,*" **Pat Shelley** also attracted client commendations for "*his responsiveness – that is one of his strengths.*" With a particular niche in representing national and regional retailers, his recent work includes advising Joseph A Bank on financing and general real estate issues. Another highlight involved the Lowe's Companies on acquisition, leasing and development work.

The Clients: Clients include Lowe's Companies and Joseph A Bank.

Miles & Stockbridge PC

See firm details p.928

The Firm: Peers note that the "*driver*" of this practice is its traditional representation of a number of local banks. Clients believe its "*efficient*" lawyers "*listen well*" and "*understand client objectives.*" The firm's real estate practice comprises transactional, dispute resolution, land use and development expertise and extends to other areas. It encompasses land acquisition, contracting, construction, financing, leasing, purchase and sale advice. Other interests involve local regulatory work.

The Lawyers: Ronald Schimel in the Columbia office chairs the firm's real estate practice group.

The Clients: Clients include developers, lenders, lessors, operators and contractors.

Rosenberg, Martin, Funk, Greenberg, LLP

The Firm: This practice's expertise includes the acquisition, management, leasing and disposition of residential, commercial and investment properties. Land use and planning are also on offer at this firm. One of its drawing cards is finance, in which it represents banks and others in construction, real estate, and commercial lending.

The Lawyers: "*A high-powered local player,*" **Barry Greenberg** benefits from a practice that includes advising commercial and residential developers, investors and builders in relation to land use, financing, construction, and leasing issues.

The Clients: Clients include developers, builders, ownership entities, and individual and institutional investors, including pension advisers.

Saul Ewing LLP

See firm details p.1561

The Firm: The practice continues to represent clients, including owner-managed businesses in various zoning, development, financing, selling and leasing matters. Although its marquee name in this area – Roger Garfink – has retired from the practice, its full-service capability means that the group is able to draw from a variety of resources to maintain the level of quality that still attracts prominent clients.

The Lawyers: Barry Levin is a key member of the firm's real estate team.

The Clients: Clients include property owners and developers, institutional lenders, and other investors.

Whiteford, Taylor & Preston LLP

The Firm: This practice's recent work has included condominium development work and public-private projects in Baltimore City, including both residential and mixed-use developments. Clients rate the practice for its leasing and land use expertise in particular, and believe that its "*professional*" and "*hard-working*" lawyers "*know their subject very well*" and are "*always willing to go out there and fight for what we need.*"

The Lawyers: The firm's real estate chair **Priscilla Carroll** (see p.919) won plaudits from clients for being an excellent case manager, while **Tom Barbuti**'s (see p.919) expertise includes advising in relation to acquisitions, sales, developments, financing and leasing. He has experience in residential subdivisions, multifamily shopping centers, industrial parks and office buildings.

The Clients: The group's varied client base includes: property developers; educational establishments; retailers; financial institutions and utility companies.

Wilmer Cutler Pickering Hale and Dorr LLP

See firm details p.497

The Firm: The 2004 merger between Wilmer Cutler Pickering and Boston-based Hale and Dorr is perceived to have cemented the team's status as a substantial player in real estate law. Clients pitched the team as *"pragmatic and focused on getting results without having a national debate about it."* The practice's expertise includes advising a range of developers, major corporations, pension funds, insurance companies and investment banks in relation to real estate acquisitions and dispositions. It proved conversant in projects involving industrial, office, retail or multifamily residential developments among others. On behalf of the National Aquarium, for example, the group advised in relation to the acquisition and development of a major waterfront site for a second campus.

The Lawyers: **Mark Pollak** (see p.923) is particularly noted by competitors for his work involving *"city-related entities and bond financings"* in the real estate field. His recent work includes representing the new owner of a National Football League franchise in the financing of a new training facility. He also advised a major New York investment bank in relation to the acquisition of interests in a number of continuing care retirement communities around the country. **Ted Millspaugh** (see p.922) gained respect for his expertise concerning pension funds investing in the real estate industry, and was praised by clients for being *"excellent at getting to the heart of the matter."* He recently represented a large state pension fund and its advisers in a joint venture with one of the nation's largest retail REITs, which was created to acquire, finance and operate shopping centers throughout the USA. He also represented American Red Cross in investments by its endowment fund and retirement plan in a Harvard-sponsored opportunistic real estate fund investing in turnaround projects. **Matt Reed** (see p.923) is recommended for his *"high-level"* expertise in such areas as acquisitions, dispositions, financing, development and operation, and management. He also has interests in workouts and leasing transactions.

The Clients: Bank of America; National Aquarium in Baltimore; Morgan Stanley; American Red Cross and LaSalle Investment Management.

Leaders in Maryland

ABEL, Kenneth
Ober Kaler Grimes & Shriver, Baltimore
410 685 1120
Recommended in Corporate/M&A

ABRAMSON, Gil
Hogan & Hartson LLP, Baltimore
410 659 2723
gaabramson@hhlaw.com
Recommended in Employment
Practice Areas: EEOC, NLRB, ADEA, ADA, FLSA, OSHA, and ERISA matters. Litigates labor and employment law issues before courts and administrative agencies, including equal employment litigation, protection of intellectual property and trade secrets, restrictive covenants enforcement, wrongful discharge, wage and hour, injunctions against strikes and picketing, and enforcement of restrictive covenants. Counsels on employment practices and policies; conducts employee and management training. Handles labor arbitrations, collective bargaining, and union-organizing campaigns and unfair labor practices before the NLRB. International practice includes counseling on employment policies and operation of multijurisdictional employment laws.
Prof. Memberships: ABA; MDBA; FBA (former Chairman, Labor and Employment Law Section).
Career: Partner since 1993.
Publications: 'Protecting Your Trade Secrets Without the Inevitable Disclosure Safety Net', Labor & Employment Update, Hogan & Hartson L.L.P. (6/30/2004); 'Don't Like Court? How Mediation and Arbitration May Work for You', Hogan & Hartson L.L.P. (5/6/2004); 'Managing Your People: From Hiring to Firing and Everything In Between', Hogan & Hartson L.L.P. (5/6/2004); 'The Uncertain Fate of Gissel Bargaining Orders in the Circuit Courts of Appeal', The Labor Lawyer, Vol. 18, No. 1, Summer 2002.

Personal: Boston University School of Law (JD, 1969); State University of New York, University at Buffalo (BA, 1966).

AMES, Robert
Venable LLP, Baltimore 410 244 7400
Recommended in Employment

ARCHIBALD, James
Venable LLP, Baltimore 410 244 7400
Recommended in Litigation

AYRES, Jeffrey
Venable LLP, Towson 410 494 6200
Recommended in Employment

BAADER, Michael
Venable LLP, Baltimore 410 244 7400
Recommended in Corporate/M&A

BARBUTI, Thomas
Whiteford, Taylor & Preston LLP, Baltimore 410 347 8719
tbarbuti@wtplaw.com
Recommended in Real Estate
Practice Areas: Sophisticated, transactional commercial real estate, including purchase and sale agreements, leases, subleases, covenants, conditions and restrictions, easements, reciprocal easements, development agreements, construction contracts and financing with a concentration in development, construction and leasing of residential, commercial, retail and mixed-use projects.
Prof. Memberships: American College of Real Estate Lawyers; International Council of Shopping Centers; Urban Land Institute; National Association of Industrial and Office Properties; Maryland State Bar Association (Chair, 2005-2006, Section of Real Property, Planning and Zoning). Admitted in Maryland and Washington, DC.
Personal: JD, Rutgers University, 1974; BA, University of Maryland, 1970.

BEALL, George
Hogan & Hartson LLP, Baltimore
410 659 2715
gbeall@hhlaw.com
Recommended in Litigation
Practice Areas: Focuses on civil and criminal litigation in state and federal courts. Involved in every major contested takeover of a Maryland corporation between 1975 and 1990. Handles regulatory, compliance and criminal matters involving 'white-collar' offenses.
Prof. Memberships: Fellow, American College of Trial Lawyers; Chairman, US District Court for Maryland Magistrate Selection Panel; Co-Chairman Maryland Judicial Election Conduct Commission; permanent member of the Judicial Conference for the Fourth US Circuit Court of Appeals and of the American Law Institute.
Career: Presidential appointment as US Attorney for the District of Maryland (1970-75).
Personal: University of Virginia School of Law (JD).

BERNSTEIN, Greg
Zuckerman Spaeder LLP, Baltimore
410 332 0444
Recommended in Litigation

BETTER, Herbert
Zuckerman Spaeder LLP, Baltimore
410 332 0444
Recommended in Litigation

BRAULT, Albert
Brault Graham Scott & Brault LLC, Rockville 301 424 1060
Recommended in Litigation

BURCH Jr, Francis B
DLA Piper Rudnick Gray Cary US LLP, Baltimore 410 580 4040
frank.burch@dlapiper.com
Recommended in Litigation
Practice Areas: Litigation; class action; patent litigation; securities litigation.

Prof. Memberships: Fellow of the American College of Trial Lawyers; Member of The American Law Institute.
Career: He is joint CEO of the firm and has been listed in a leading legal publication for over ten years. He focuses on the defense and prosecution of claims under the federal securities laws, in corporate control related litigation and in a broad spectrum of business litigation, including intellectual property matters.
Personal: JD, University of Maryland; AB, Georgetown University; serves on the Boards of Johns Hopkins Medicine, and The University of Maryland Baltimore Foundation.

CARRIER, William
Tydings & Rosenberg LLP, Baltimore
410 752 9700
Recommended in Employment

CARROLL, Priscilla
Whiteford, Taylor & Preston LLP, Baltimore 410 347 8797
pcarroll@wtplaw.com
Recommended in Real Estate
Practice Areas: Complex commercial real estate transactions; public-private partnerships; developing, leasing and creatively financing commercial real estate projects.
Prof. Memberships: Urban Land Institute; International Council of Shopping Centers; Johns Hopkins University Real Estate Institute. Admitted in Maryland.
Personal: JD, University of Maryland, with honors, 1977; Johns Hopkins University; Foreign Service, US Department of State, 1996-1999.

CHASON, James R.
Whiteford, Taylor & Preston LLP, Towson 410 832 2020
jchason@wtplaw.com
Recommended in Litigation
Practice Areas: Complex litigation involving professional liability in healthcare, accounting and insurance. He has served as national counsel for

www.ChambersandPartners.com
All quotes in the text are from interviews with clients and competitors.
919

products liability cases. He has represented one of the country's leading medical institutions. He has handled over 100 jury trials during his over 25 year careeer.

Prof. Memberships: Fellow, American College of Trial Lawyers; Maryland Defense Council; Board Member, Carson Scholarship Fund. Admitted in Maryland, United States District Court for the District of Maryland, US Court of Appeals for the Fourth Circuit.

Personal: JD, with honors, University of Baltimore, 1976; BA, University of Maryland, 1973.

CHRISS, Timothy
Gordon, Feinblatt, Rothman, Hoffberger & Hollander, LLC, Baltimore
410 576 4000
Recommended in Real Estate

CLANCY, Patrick
Venable LLP, Rockville 301 217 5600
Recommended in Employment

COHEN, David
Linowes and Blocher LLP, Bethesda
301 654 0504
Recommended in Real Estate

COOK, Bryson
Venable LLP, Baltimore 410 244 7400
Recommended in Corporate/M&A

COOPERMAN, Harriet E
Saul Ewing LLP, Baltimore
410 332 8974
hcooperman@saul.com
Recommended in Employment

Practice Areas: Partner/Co-Chair of Saul Ewing's Labor and Employment Practice. Extensive experience in collective bargaining/NLRA, discrimination, harassment, tort, non-compete, and litigation. Represents private, public and nonprofit employers.

Prof. Memberships: Admitted to practice in Maryland, US Supreme Court, Fourth Circuit, US District Courts - Maryland and DC; Former Chair, Labor Section, Maryland Bar, Employer-Employee Relations Committee, ABA-TIPS.

Career: Former Vice Chair, State Higher Education Labor Relations Board; Adjunct Professor, Labor and Employment Discrimination, University of Baltimore Law School.

Publications: 'Discovery in Employment Cases', 'Unresolved Arbitration Issues,' 'Evidentiary Issues in Sexual Harassment Litigation,'

Personal: JD, University of Maryland, BS, Cornell University.

CURRAN, Bob
Whiteford, Taylor & Preston LLP, Baltimore 410 347 9472
rcurran@wtplaw.com
Recommended in Corporate/M&A

Practice Areas: Business and corporate law; mergers and acquisitions; leveraged buyouts; formation and structuring of business entities including corporations, partnerships, joint ventures, and limited

liability companies; corporate succession planning; ESOP transactions; employee benefits and executive compensation.

Prof. Memberships: American Bar Association, Maryland State Bar Association (Chair, Section of Taxation 1987-88). Admitted in Maryland.

Personal: JD, with Honors (Order of the Coif), University of Maryland School of Law, 1974; BA, University of Delaware, 1971.

DILLOFF, Neil
DLA Piper Rudnick Gray Cary US LLP, Baltimore 410 580 4138
neil.dilloff@dlapiper.com
Recommended in Litigation

Practice Areas: Insurance litigation and coverage, litigation, professional liability, construction.

Career: Experience includes significant professional malpractice liabiity litigation, particularly on behalf of lawyers, extensive construction litigation experience, and roles as lead counsel in many large, complex commercial litigation matters. He has tried more than 100 cases in state and federal courts and has won two of the largest plaintiffs' verdicts in Maryland history. He also has achieved over a dozen recoveries in excess of $1 million. He has also successfully defended law firms, insurance companies and other organizations.

Personal: JD Georgetown University; BA University of North Carolina.

EIDELMAN, Gary B
Saul Ewing LLP, Baltimore
410 332 8975
geidelman@saul.com
Recommended in Employment

Practice Areas: Partner in Saul Ewing's Labor and Employment Practice. Represents management in labor and employment law and litigation matters, including employment discrimination, sexual harassment, disability and leave, wrongful discharge, breach of contract, non-competition agreements, wage and hour, occupational safety and health, affirmative action compliance and audits, and fair housing.

Prof. Memberships: Admitted to practice in DC and Maryland; Management Co-Chair, Employment At-Will Subcommittee, American Bar Association, Labor and Employment Law Section, Employment Rights and Responsibilities Committee.

Career: Vice Office Managing Partner of Baltimore Office. Lecturer on employment law.

Personal: JD, Widener University (magna cum laude), BA, University of Maryland.

FISH, Ronald
Ballard Spahr Andrews & Ingersoll LLP, Baltimore 410 528 5617
fish@ballardspahr.com
Recommended in Real Estate

Practice Areas: He concentrates his

practice in commercial real estate acquisition, development, financing, leasing and restructuring, and represents developers, lenders, investors, landlords, tenants, and users in all areas of the real estate market.

Prof. Memberships: Member of the American College of Real Estate Lawyers since 1984 and is a member of the American Bar Association and Maryland Bar Association. He has been a lecturer on real estate law for the Maryland Institute for Continuing Professional Education of Lawyers and, for more than 10 years, he has served as an adjunct professor at the Allen Berman Real Estate Institute of Johns Hopkins University.

Career: Admitted to the Maryland Bar (1964); joined firm as Partner (1992).

Personal: LLB, cum laude, University of Maryland (1964); AB, Williams College (1961).

FISHER, Morton
Ballard Spahr Andrews & Ingersoll LLP, Baltimore 410 528 5615
fisher@ballardspahr.com
Recommended in Real Estate

Practice Areas: In his over 35 years of practice, he has been involved in every type of real estate transaction, representing developers, lending institutions, department stores, and other big box users and tenants.

Prof. Memberships: Former President of the American College of Real Estate Lawyers, former Chair of the ABA Section of Real Property Probate and Trust Law, and part-time teacher at University of Maryland School of Law. He is also a Charter Member of the American College of Construction Lawyers, a member of The American Law Institute, The Counselors of Real Estate, and the Anglo-American Real Property Institute. Mr Fisher has served in a number of leadership positions in his community including the Mayor's Advisory Council for the Downtown, the Baltimore County Economic Development Commission, and the Greater Baltimore Committee Economic Development Committee. He is currently a member of the Board of the Baltimore Downtown Partnership, a member of the Board of Trustees of the University of Maryland (Baltimore) Foundation where he is Chair of the Campus and Community Enterprise Committee and a member of the Board of the Johns Hopkins University Real Estate Institute.

Career: Admitted to the Maryland Bar (1961); admitted to the District of Columbia Bar (1978); joined as Partner (1992).

Publications: Written numerous articles appearing in various real estate publications including 'The Journal of the Section of Real Property', 'Probate and Trust Law', 'Probate & Property', 'The Practical Real Estate Lawyer', and is a contributing author to 'A Practical

Guide to Commercial Real Estate Transactions' published by ABA Publishing.

Personal: LLB, Yale Law School (1961); AB, Dartmouth College (1958).

FISHMAN, David
Gordon, Feinblatt, Rothman, Hoffberger & Hollander, LLC, Baltimore
410 576 4000
Recommended in Real Estate

FREED, Amy Bowerman
Hogan & Hartson LLP, Baltimore
410 659 2774
abfreed@hhlaw.com
Recommended in Corporate/M&A

Practice Areas: Amy Bowerman Freed's practice focuses on a wide variety of securities regulatory matters.

Prof. Memberships: National Association of Securities Dealers, National Adjudicatory Council.

Career: Amy represents issuers and investment banks in private and public offerings. She counsels boards of directors of public and private companies on corporate governance issues and provides advice on disclosure and other requirements of the securities laws. Prior to joining Hogan & Hartson, Amy was the deputy chief counsel of the Securities and Exchange Commission's Division of Corporation Finance.

Personal: University of Baltimore School of Law (JD, 1988); Tulane University (BA, 1985).

FRENKIL, Steven
Miles & Stockbridge PC, Baltimore
410 385 3758
sfrenkil@milesstockbridge.com
Recommended in Employment

Practice Areas: Advises and defends management in all areas of Labor, Employment and Human Resources Management Law.

Prof. Memberships: American Bar Association (EEO Committee); National Association of College and University Attorneys; Society for Human Resource Management; Maryland State Bar Association, Section of Labor and Employment Law (Member, Section Council); Howard County Human Resources Society (Board of Directors, Legislative Chair).

Publications: Published numerous articles. Frequently presents seminars for clients and industry groups.

Personal: George Washington University (BA, 1974 with Distinction; Phi Beta Kappa). University of Maryland School of Law (JD, 1977 with Honors).

FRISCH, John B
Miles & Stockbridge PC, Baltimore
410 385 3507
jfrisch@milesstockbridge.com
Recommended in Corporate/M&A

Practice Areas: In addition to serving as the Chairman and Chief Executive Officer of the firm, he specializes in mergers and acquisitions, securities and other business transactions. He has been responsible for acquisitions and dispositions of businesses by public and private enterprises, including the disposition of substantial international businesses. He provides general business counseling to businesses and their officers and directors, including counseling concerning fiduciary duty, corporate governance and related matters.

Career: Principal since 1990.

Personal: University of Maryland (JD, 1983); Dickinson College (BA, 1980).

GARDNER, Russell H
DLA Piper Rudnick Gray Cary US LLP, Baltimore 410 580 4154
russell.gardner@dlapiper.com
Recommended in Employment

Practice Areas: Labor and employment law; class action litigation.

Career: His practice encompasses all areas of management-side labor and employment discrimination. He regularly advises on union-avoidance matters, including representation before the National Labor Relations Board, employment discrimination and OSHA matters, and defense of employment claims, including ERISA claims, in state and federal courts across the nation. He has experience in drafting and enforcing employment agreements and non-competition agreements. He has written and lectured extensively on a variety of employment topics, particularly for the Americans with Disabilities Act.

Personal: JD, Syracuse University; BA, Alfred University.

GATELY, Mark
Hogan & Hartson LLP, Baltimore
410 659 2742
mdgately@hhlaw.com
Recommended in Litigation

Practice Areas: Focuses on complex commercial and corporate litigation, particularly in the antitrust and securities law area, and products liability. Handles significant post-closing disputes involving claims arising from large corporate transactions and hostile takeover and proxy related litigation. National products liability counsel for a major pharmaceutical company.

Prof. Memberships: Fellow, American College of Trial Lawyers; Fellow, International Academy of Trial Lawyers (Maryland State Chair); Member, Product Liability Advisory Counsel; Member, The American Board of Trial Advocates.

Career: Former Chair of the Litigation Department of a large Baltimore firm.

Publications: 'Direct and Derivative Actions of Maryland Corporation Stockholders', The Maryland Bar Journal (2/18/2004).

Personal: University of Maryland School of Law (JD, with honors, Order of the Coif).

GILLECE Jr, James
McGuireWoods LLP, Baltimore
410 659 4000
Recommended in Employment

GRAHAM, Andrew Jay
Kramon & Graham, PA, Baltimore
410 752 6030
agraham@kg-law.com
Recommended in Litigation

Practice Areas: Civil Business Litigation. Mr Graham also practices in the areas of professional liability matters, white-collar criminal litigation, trade secrets litigation, antitrust litigation, securities litigation, general civil litigation, and mediation. A lawyer's area of practice as stated here is one to which he devotes a substantial proportion of his professional practice and should not be considered a 'specialization'.

Prof. Memberships: Mr Graham is a Fellow of the American College of Trial Lawyers, and was its Maryland State Chairman from 1996-98. He is a Member of the Association of Professional Responsibility Lawyers. He is a Fellow of the American Bar Foundation. Mr Graham is a Member of, and has held various offices and board and committee positions with, the American Bar Association, the Federal Bar Association, and the Maryland and Baltimore City Bar Associations. He is the Chairman of the Maryland Bar, Ethics 2000 Committee. He is a permanent Member of the Fourth Circuit Judicial Conference. He is a founding Member of Maryland ADR Services, Inc., a nonprofit forum for alternative dispute resolution. He is a Member of Bars of Maryland, New York and the District of Columbia.

Career: Mr Graham served as a law clerk to the Honorable Alexander Harvey, II on the United States District Court for the District of Maryland. He was an Assistant United States Attorney for the District of Maryland from 1971 through 1974. Mr Graham is an active member of the Bars of Maryland, New York and the District of Columbia. He is admitted to practice before the United States Supreme Court, the United States Court of Appeals for the Fourth Circuit, and the United States District Courts for the District of Columbia, the District of Maryland, the Eastern District of New York, and the Southern District of New York.

Publications: 'The Significance of Civility', published in The Maryland Bar Journal, Volume XXXVI, Number 5, September/October 2003; 'Changes in Maryland's Rules of Professional Conduct on Horizon', published in the Bar Bulletin, December 15, 2004.

Personal: Mr Graham was born February 21, 1943. He graduated from Yale University (BA 1965) and received his law degree from the New York University School of Law (JD 1968).

GRAY, James
Venable LLP, Baltimore 410 244 7400
Recommended in Litigation

GREENBERG, Barry C.
Rosenberg, Martin, Funk, Greenberg, LLP, Baltimore 410 727 6600
Recommended in Real Estate

GUATTERY, Peter
Whiteford, Taylor & Preston LLP, Baltimore 410 347 9431
pguattery@wtplaw.com
Recommended in Employment

Practice Areas: Advice and counsel to public and private employers in employment related matters, including defense of discrimination, harassment and other employment claims; employment documentation and drafting of contracts; wage and hour; immigration and nationality law, including employer compliance, DOL investigations, and employment of foreign nationals.

Prof. Memberships: Maryland State Bar Association; American Bar Association; American Immigration Lawyers Association. Admitted in Maryland.

Personal: JD, University of Pennsylvania, 1987; BA, Johns Hopkins University, 1984.

HAFETS, Richard J
DLA Piper Rudnick Gray Cary US LLP, Baltimore 410 580 4168
richard.hafets@dlapiper.com
Recommended in Employment

Practice Areas: Labor and employment law; class action litigation.

Career: He practices in all areas of labor and employment law, including union avoidance, traditional labor-management relations, employment litigation, EEO and affirmative action, OSHA, and general personnel. He is primary labor counsel to many Fortune 500 companies, healthcare institutions, charities, and civic organizations, and represents many of the firm's significant clients. Prior to joining Piper Rudnick, he worked with the National Labor Relations Board.

Personal: JD, American University; BS, American University.

HANKS, James
Venable LLP, Baltimore 410 244 7400
Recommended in Corporate/M&A

HARRISON, Bruce S
Shawe & Rosenthal LLP, Baltimore
410 752 1040
harrison@shawe.com
Recommended in Employment

Practice Areas: Employment discrimination litigation; employment tort and contract litigation; wage and hour laws; class action litigation; family and medical leave act (FMLA); employment agreements, policies, and procedures.

Prof. Memberships: Bar Admissions: Maryland; District of Columbia; Pennsylvania; US Courts of Appeals for the 1st, 2nd, 3rd, 4th, 5th, 9th, 11th, and DC Circuits. Professional Associations: Fellow, College of Labor and Employment Lawyers, 1999-present; American Bar Association; Maryland State Bar Association

Career: Before joining the Firm in 1971, Bruce served as a senior attorney at the Equal Employment Opportunity Commission's Headquarter offices.

Publications: Bruce is editor of the 'Employment Law Deskbook' (Lexis/Matthew Bender) and has also co-authored three monographs published by Matthew Bender: 'Avoiding Employment Discrimination Charges', 'Employer Discipline and Discharge', and 'Responding to Employment Discrimination Charges'. Other publications include: 'Sexual Harassment and Related Torts - The Employer's Perspective', American Bar Association. Contributing author: 'Age Discrimination: A Legal and Practical Guide for Employers', BNA Special Report. Contributor: 'Workplace Privacy', Thompson Publishing Group. Case note editor and contributing author: 'Sexual Harassment & Discrimination Reporter', James Publishing, Inc. Board of Editors: 'Model Jury Instructions - Employment Litigation', Section of Litigation, American Bar Association. Contributor: 'Employment Litigation Handbook', Section of Litigation, American Bar Association. Member of Editorial Board and contributor: Bender's Labor & Employment Bulletin, Matthew Bender, Publishers; contributing editor: Maryland and Federal Employment Law Manual, American Chamber of Commerce Publishers. Contributor: 'Workplace Privacy', Thompson Publishing.

Personal: George Washington University School of Law, JD, cum laude, 1971; LLM Labor Law, 1975; Case Western Reserve University, BA, 1967.

HIMELES, Martin
Zuckerman Spaeder LLP, Baltimore
410 332 0444
Recommended in Litigation

IMMELT, Stephen
Hogan & Hartson LLP, Baltimore
410 659 2757
sjimmelt@hhlaw.com
Recommended in Litigation

Practice Areas: Focuses primarily on white-collar criminal litigation and complex litigation in the health and general commercial fields. His experience encompasses the conduct of internal investigations, congressional investigations, grand jury practice, defense of qui tam cases, and the development of compliance plans. Speaks and writes frequently on healthcare fraud and compliance issues.

Prof. Memberships: Member, Fourth Circuit Judicial Conference. Association memberships include: ABA Health Law Section and the National Association of College and University Attorneys.

Career: Assistant US Attorney for the District of Maryland 1979-83.

Personal: University of Maryland (JD, cum laude).

ISAACSON, Andrew
Linowes and Blocher LLP, Bethesda
301 654 0504
Recommended in Real Estate

JOHNSTON, George
Venable LLP, Baltimore 410 244 7400
Recommended in Employment

KAHN, Henry
Hogan & Hartson LLP, Baltimore
410 659 2780
hdkahn@hhlaw.com
Recommended in Corporate/M&A
Practice Areas: Henry Kahn practices in the areas of securities law and regulation (including investment management law), merger and acquisition law, and Maryland corporate law.
Career: Henry advises clients on merger and acquisition transactions, securities offerings, securities regulation matters, including Sarbanes-Oxley, and corporate governance matters. Henry also represents investment management organizations in the development of new investment products and services, as well as on governance matters and issues affecting their strategic development.
Personal: George Washington University Law School (JD, 1980); Yale University (BA, 1977).

KELLNER, Robert
Gordon, Feinblatt, Rothman, Hoffberger & Hollander, LLC, Baltimore
410 576 4000
Recommended in Employment

KOCHANSKI, David
Shulman, Rogers, Gandal, Pordy & Ecker, PA, Rockville 301 230 5200
Recommended in Real Estate

LEECH, Sidney
Goodell, DeVries, Leech & Dann, LLP, Baltimore 410 783 4000
Recommended in Litigation

LEVIN, Edward J
DLA Piper Rudnick Gray Cary US LLP, Baltimore 410 580 4700
edward.levin@dlapiper.com
Recommended in Real Estate
Practice Areas: Real estate; real estate finance.
Prof. Memberships: Member, American College of Real Estate Lawyers (ACREL).
Career: Chair, Section of Real Property, Probate and Zoning, Maryland State Bar Association (MSBA); Chair, ACREL Attorneys' Opinions Committee; Chair, Co-Chair and Steering Committee Member, projects on attorneys' opinions of MSBA, ACREL and American Bar Association (ABA); Chair and lecturer at seminars of ACREL, ABA and MSBA.
Publications: Co-author, 'Maryland Real Estate Leasing Forms - Practice'; author of articles on attorneys' opinions and other real property-related matters.

Personal: JD, University of Virginia; BA, Johns Hopkins University, with honors.

LEVINE, Richard E
DLA Piper Rudnick Gray Cary US LLP, Baltimore 410 580 4400
rich.levine@dlapiper.com
Recommended in Real Estate
Practice Areas: Business tax; real estate; corporate and securities.
Prof. Memberships: Fellow of American College of Tax Counsel.
Career: He is nationally recognized in the area of partnership and real estate taxation and represents many of the leading real estate entrepreneurs in the Maryland area. He focuses his practice on sophisticated real estate transactions which frequently involve complex tax issues. He is also listed in alternative legal publications.
Personal: JD, University of Maryland 1975; LLM, Georgetown University Law Center; BS, Mechanical Engineering, Bucknell University.

LEWIS, Thomas
Gallagher, Evelius & Jones, LLP, Baltimore 410 727 7702
Recommended in Real Estate

LOHR Jr, Walter
Hogan & Hartson LLP, Baltimore
410 659 2764
wglohr@hhlaw.com
Recommended in Corporate/M&A
Practice Areas: Represents clients in a broad range of transactions, including public and private offerings, mergers and acquisitions, and organization of partnerships and joint ventures. Also provides ongoing representation to corporations, other business enterprises, business owners and executives.
Career: Director of a Fortune 500 corporation, where he chaired the Audit Committee and currently chairs the Nominating and Governance Committee. Director of several privately-held corporations and has been a member of the advisory board of a venture capital firm sponsored by a major US life insurance company.
Personal: Princeton University (AB, 1966); Yale University (LLB, 1969).

MACHEN, John
DLA Piper Rudnick Gray Cary US LLP, Baltimore 410 580 4444
jack.machen@dlapiper.com
Recommended in Real Estate
Practice Areas: Real estate.
Career: He practices in the areas of commercial real estate financing and real estate development, including property acquisition, disposition, and leasing. He has represented lenders and developers in a variety of commercial enterprises, including shopping centers, office buildings, condominiums, townhouses, and apartments, with respect to acquisition, construction and permanent financing, syndication, leasing, sale, foreclosures, and negotiated workouts.

Personal: JD, University of Maryland; BA, Princeton University.

MARTIN, Gerard
Rosenberg, Martin, Funk, Greenberg, LLP, Baltimore 410 727 6600
Recommended in Litigation

MATHIAS, Robert
DLA Piper Rudnick Gray Cary US LLP, Baltimore 410 580 4209
robert.mathias@dlapiper.com
Recommended in Litigation
Practice Areas: Litigation; class action litigation; patent litigation; securities litigation; white –collar.
Prof. Memberships: American College of Trial Lawyers, Fellow, Complex Litigation Committee.
Career: Co-Chair of the Global Litigation Group, Chair of the US Litigation Group. His primary areas of practice are business litigation, intellectual property litigation and white-collar criminal advice to corporate clients. He has tried cases and argued appeals in the federal and state courts in a number of jurisdictions and has extensive experience with many types of alternative dispute resolution. He is listed in several leading legal publications.
Personal: JD, Harvard Law School, BA, Yale University.

MCGEE Jr, Emmett F
DLA Piper Rudnick Gray Cary US LLP, Baltimore 410 580 4211
emmett.mcgee@dlapiper.com
Recommended in Employment
Practice Areas: Labor and employment law.
Career: He represents employers in all aspects of employment law and human resource management, including employment discrimination, wage and hour issues and affirmative action planning. His practice includes litigation in state and federal courts throughout the US, as well as before administrative agencies and arbitration panels. He also has extensive experience in areas of employment contracts, trade secrets and restrictive covenants, and related litigation, as well as the litigation of ERISA claims and stock option claims.
Personal: JD, University of Virginia; BA, Johns Hopkins University.

MCGUIRE, J Michael
Shawe & Rosenthal LLP, Baltimore
410 752 1040
mcguire@shawe.com
Recommended in Employment
Practice Areas: Labor-management relations; practice before the National Labor Relations Board; collective bargaining and labor arbitration representing management; employment discrimination litigation; human resources advice and counsel; employment agreements; employment tort and contract litigation; employment handbooks, policies, and procedures; wage and hour laws; occupational safety and health

acts.
Prof. Memberships: Bar Admissions: Maryland (State and Federal); US Court of Appeals for the 4th, 9th and 11th Circuits. Professional Associations: American Bar Association; Maryland State Bar Association; Chair, Labor & Employment Law Section of Maryland State Bar Association (2004-06 Term); Maryland Association of Defense Trial Counsel.
Publications: Michael has co-authored two books, 'Employee Discipline and Discharge', and 'An Employer's Guide to the Occupational Safety and Health Act', both published by Lexis/Matthew Bender.
Personal: University of Maryland School of Law, JD, cum laude, 1978 Recipient, Joseph Bernstein Prize; University of Maryland, BA 1975.

MERKLE, Craig
Goodell, DeVries, Leech & Dann, LLP, Baltimore 410 783 4000
Recommended in Litigation

MILLSPAUGH, Thomas E D
Wilmer Cutler Pickering Hale and Dorr LLP, Baltimore
410 986 2870
thomas.millspaugh@wilmerhale.com
Recommended in Real Estate
Practice Areas: Partner in the firm's Real Estate Department and Corporate Department. Has handled real estate projects throughout the United States for pension funds, developers, lenders and other real estate investors and operators. Involved in a broad array of transactions, such as acquisitions, developments, financings, leasing transactions and dispositions. One of the team leaders managing real estate, finance and other business aspects of the startup of a $1.8 billion telecommunications company. Advised a technology corporation in the restructuring and workout of real estate obligations totaling $120 million and associated with 15 facilities throughout the United States.
Prof. Memberships: Urban Land Institute; Pension Real Estate Association; Real Property Section, Maryland State Bar Association; Advisory Board, Chicago Title Insurance Company.
Career: Has practiced real estate law for over 17 years and has experience in a wide variety of matters involving real estate investment, development, finance and operations.
Personal: University of Virginia School of Law (JD 1987); University of North Carolina at Chapel Hill (BA, with Highest Honors, 1983).

MONK II, Charles O
Saul Ewing LLP, Baltimore
410 332 8668
cmonk@saul.com
Recommended in Litigation
Practice Areas: Managing Partner of Saul Ewing's Baltimore office. Focuses on antitrust, business disputes, insolvency litigation, class actions, and regulatory.
Prof. Memberships: Admitted to prac-

tice in Maryland and before US Supreme Court; US Courts of Appeals for the Second, Third, Fourth, Fifth, Ninth, and Eleventh Circuits; US Court of Appeals for the District of Columbia; US District Courts for Districts of Columbia and Maryland. Member, American and Maryland State Bar Associations.
Career: Served as Assistant Attorney General of Maryland; Chief of the Antitrust Division, Attorney General's Office; Deputy Attorney General of Maryland.
Personal: JD, University of Maryland, AB, Brown University.

MURPHY, William
Murphy & Shaffer, Baltimore
410 783 7000
Recommended in Litigation

NILSON, George
DLA Piper Rudnick Gray Cary US LLP, Baltimore 410 580 4227
george.nilson@piperrudnick.com
Recommended in Litigation
Practice Areas: Environmental; litigation; class action litigation; state legislation and public policy; white-collar.
Career: He has had significant involvement in environmental controversies (hazardous waste, toxic torts, gasoline contamination, landfill litigation, removal of asbestos products from buildings), public and administrative law, election law controversies, tobacco litigation, cable television controversies, consumer controversies (range of regulatory and litigation issues presented by automobile dealers, condominium developers/sellers, time-share ventures and commercial lenders), zoning and litigation relating to real estate development, and complex civil litigation generally.
Personal: LLB, Yale University; BA, Master of Urban Studies, Yale School of Art and Architecture; BA, Yale College.

OLIVER, James
Lenrow, Kohn & Oliver, Baltimore
410 962 0550
Recommended in Real Estate

PALTELL, Eric
Kollman & Saucier PA, Baltimore
410 727 4300
Recommended in Employment

PHELAN, Jeanne
Whiteford, Taylor & Preston LLP, Baltimore 410 347 8738
jphelan@wtplaw.com
Recommended in Employment
Practice Areas: Management-side advice and counsel and litigation in employment-related areas, including defense of discrimination, harassment and tort claims; preparation and litigation of employment contracts, non-competition agreements, employment documents, and affirmative action plans; federal, state and local statutory compliance and litigation.
Prof. Memberships: Maryland State Bar

Association Section of Labor and Employment Law (Chair 1992-94). American Bar Association Labor and Employment Law Section. Admitted in Maryland.
Personal: JD, with Honors, University of Maryland School of Law, 1980; BS, University of Maryland, 1977.

POKEMPNER, Joseph
Whiteford, Taylor & Preston LLP, Baltimore 410 347 8739
jpokempner@wtplaw.com
Recommended in Employment
Practice Areas: Representation of employers in union-organizing campaigns and collective bargaining. representation of employers in cases before the NLRB, EEOC and other related administrative agencies.
Prof. Memberships: Maryland State Bar Association, Section of Labor & Employment (Chair 1982-84), Bar Association of Baltimore City (President 1984-85), Federal Bar Association (MD Chapter President 1979-80).
Personal: LLB, University of Maryland School of Law, 1962; BA, Johns Hopkins University, 1957.

POLIAKOFF, Abba
Gordon, Feinblatt, Rothman, Hoffberger & Hollander, LLC, Baltimore
410 576 4000
Recommended in Corporate/M&A

POLLAK, Mark
Wilmer Cutler Pickering Hale and Dorr LLP, Baltimore 410 986 2860
Mark.Pollak@wilmerhale.com
Recommended in Real Estate
Practice Areas: Partner in the firm's Real Estate Department, with more than 30 years of experience in real estate development and finance and municipal finance matters. Involved in the public financing of complex real estate projects, major sports stadiums, and the creation of public-private partnerships for development of central business districts.
Prof. Memberships: American College of Real Estate Lawyers; National Association of Bond Lawyers; American Planning Association; Board of Directors and Executive Committee for the Baltimore Children's Museum Downtown Partnership of Baltimore, Inc.
Personal: Brooklyn College (BA, cum laude, 1968); University of Pennsylvania (JD 1972; Masters in City Planning 1972).

PONTONE, Kathleen
Miles & Stockbridge PC, Baltimore
410 385 3757
kpontone@milesstockbridge.com
Recommended in Employment
Practice Areas: Labor and employment law, practice group leader; occupational safety and health, whistleblower, harassment defense and prevention; compensation litigation.
Prof. Memberships: American Bar Association; Women's Bar Association;

California Bar Association - Labor & Employment Section; US Chamber of Commerce - Labor Relations Committee and its OSHA and Wage & Hour Subcommittees; Securities Industries Association.
Career: 1978-80 Labor Counsel for Kaiser Aluminum & Chemical Corporation (Oakland, CA); 1981-92 Partner at Semmes, Bowen & Semmes (Baltimore, MD); 1992 to present, Principal at Miles & Stockbridge P.C. (Baltimore, MD). In 2004, Kathleen received the Maryland Leadership in Law Award; she was recognized by Chambers USA as a leading management-side employment lawyer in 2003; in June of 2003, she was recognized by the Baltimore Business Journal in their Who's Who in Law.
Personal: Graduated from Vassar College with AB in 1972 and Duke University School of Law with JD in 1977; Kathleen was appointed by Governor Robert Ehrlich to the Board of Directors for the Reginald F Lewis Museum of Maryland African American History & Culture; she is the Secretary, Executive Committee Member and Chair of the Roads Committee of the Valleys Planning Council.

RAMIREZ, John
Venable LLP, Baltimore 410 244 7400
Recommended in Corporate/M&A

REED, Matthew
Wilmer Cutler Pickering Hale and Dorr LLP, Baltimore 410 986 2864
Matthew.Reed@wilmerhale.com
Recommended in Real Estate
Practice Areas: Represents developers, lenders, major corporations, pension funds and other institutional investors, together with their consultants and advisors, in all areas of commercial real estate. Transactional experience is national in scope and includes acquisition, disposition, financing, development, operation, management, workout and leasing transactions involving office, industrial, mall, hotel, mixed-use, town center, transit-oriented, public-private, military redevelopment, correctional facility, golf course community, multifamily residential and diverse retail projects.
Personal: George Washington University Law School (JD 1996); Princeton University (AB 1992).

RENO, Russell
Venable LLP, Baltimore 410 244 7400
Recommended in Real Estate

ROCKMAN, Jeffrey
Serotte, Rockman & Westcott, Baltimore 410 825 7900
Recommended in Employment

ROSENBERG, Ben
Rosenberg, Martin, Funk, Greenberg, LLP, Baltimore 410 727 6600
Recommended in Litigation

RYAN Jr, William F.
Whiteford, Taylor & Preston LLP, Baltimore 410 347 8741
wryan@wtplaw.com
Recommended in Litigation
Practice Areas: Having represented domestic and international clients in various federal and many state courts, Mr Ryan concentrates on resolving complex commercial issues including corporate and contract disputes, securities and intellectual property matters. He recently won a nationally-watched landmark class action housing discrimination case for the City of Baltimore following a month-long trial, demonstrating his versatility in the courtroom. In 1999, Mr Ryan was invited to become a Fellow of the American College of Trial Lawyers, a society comprised of the top 1% of trial lawyers in the US and Canada.
Prof. Memberships: Fellow, American College of Trial Lawyers. Admitted in Maryland, Eastern District of Michigan, US Supreme Court and Circuit Courts of Appeals (2nd and 4th), as well as many state courts pro hac vice.
Personal: JD, University of Baltimore, 1979; editor in chief, Law Review; AB, with Honors, Princeton University, 1976.

SCHATZOW, Michael
Venable LLP, Baltimore 410 244 7400
Recommended in Litigation

SCHEELER, Charles P
DLA Piper Rudnick Gray Cary US LLP, Baltimore 410 580 4250
charles.scheeler@dlapiper.com
Recommended in Litigation
Practice Areas: Litigation; class action; securities litigation; white-collar.
Career: He principally engages in a commercial litigation and white-collar criminal defense practice. He has successfully litigated numerous sophisticated commercial and criminal disputes in federal and state courts, as well as in arbitration and mediation. He has represented companies and individuals in white-collar criminal investigations and prosecutions and has provided advice on a variety of substantial corporate transactions. His trial experience includes over 25 jury trials and dozens of bench trials and arbitrations.
Personal: JD, Harvard Law School; BS, University of North Carolina at Chapel Hill.

SEARS, Barbara
Linowes and Blocher LLP, Bethesda
301 654 0504
Recommended in Real Estate

SEEGULL, Larry
DLA Piper Rudnick Gray Cary US LLP, Baltimore 410 480 4253
larry.seegull@dlapiper.com
Recommended in Employment
Practice Areas: Labor and employment.
Career: He represents employers in all areas of labor and employment law. He advises clients on compliance, litigation avoidance, and limiting liability with respect to the full complement of employment decisions, ranging from hiring, leave issues, discipline and termination. He also defends clients in all types of employment-related litigation, arbitration and agency investigations, including claims of discrimination, violations of the ADA/FMLA, claims for wages, claims for breach of contract and employment-related torts.
Personal: JD, University of Michigan, BA, Michigan State University.

SEROTTE, Neal
Serotte, Rockman & Westcott, Baltimore 410 825 7900
Recommended in Employment

SHAWE, Stephen D
Shawe & Rosenthal LLP, Baltimore 410 752 1040
sshawe@shawe.com
Recommended in Employment
Practice Areas: Labor-management relations and NLRB proceedings; collective bargaining; employment discrimination; human resources advice and counsel; employment tort and contract litigation; employment handbooks, policies, and procedures; wage and hour laws; affirmative action programs; Family and Medical Leave Act; Worker Adjustment and Retraining Notification Act; appellate litigation; class actions; alternative dispute resolution.
Prof. Memberships: Bar Admissions: Maryland; US Court of Appeals for the 4th Circuit; Supreme Court of the United States. Professional Associations: American Bar Association; Maryland State Bar Association; Fellow, College of Labor and Employment Lawyers.
Career: Before joining the Firm in 1966, Stephen served as law clerk to Chief Judge Simon Sobeloff of the United States Court of Appeals for the Fourth Circuit. In 1967, he briefly left the Firm when he was appointed an Assistant United States Attorney for the District of Maryland. He held that position until 1970 when he was selected to be the first General Counsel of the Maryland Commission on Human Relations.
Publications: Stephen has authored numerous articles on labor and employment matters, including 'An Employer's Duty to Bargain Over a Decision to Subcontract' for the Harvard Legal Commentary. He was co-author of 'Avoiding Employment Discrimination Charges. for Matthew Bender & Co., Inc., and he has also written articles for the University of Baltimore Law Review on subjects ranging from concession bargaining to employment discrimination.
Personal: Education: Harvard Law School, LLB, 1965; Williams College, BA, cum laude, 1962.

SHEA, James
Venable LLP, Baltimore 410 244 7400
Recommended in Litigation

SHELLEY, Patrick
McGuireWoods LLP, Baltimore 410 659 4000
Recommended in Real Estate

SHEPHERD, Kevin
Venable LLP, Baltimore 410 244 7400
Recommended in Real Estate

SHULMAN, Lawrence
Shulman, Rogers, Gandal, Pordy & Ecker, PA, Rockville 301 230 5200
Recommended in Real Estate

SILVER, Michael J
Hogan & Hartson LLP, Baltimore 410 659 2741
mjsilver@hhlaw.com
Recommended in Corporate/M&A
Practice Areas: Michael Silver practices in the areas of corporate, securities, mergers and acquisitions, private equity and general business law. He has acted as outside counsel in a wide variety of transactions and in providing ongoing general advice to clients including CIENA Corporation, Laboratory Corporation of America Holdings, Wabash National Corporation, Guilford Pharmaceuticals Inc., ABS Capital Partners and Martek Biosciences Corporation.
Personal: Harvard University (AB, magna cum laude, 1977); University of Chicago Law School (JD, 1980).

SILVESTRI, Stephen
Miles & Stockbridge PC, Baltimore
Recommended in Employment
Practice Areas: Labor negotiations representing private and public sector employers, litigation and trials employment discrimination, WARN and ERISA benefits matters in federal courts. He is chief labor and employment counsel in the US for domestic and foreign corporations.
Prof. Memberships: American Bar Association, Maryland State Bar Association, Former Chair, Section of Labor Law, MSBA.
Career: Principal since joining Miles & Stockbridge in 1992, formerly Partner in Semmes, Bowen and Semmes.
Publications: Lectures and publishes extensively.
Personal: Former law clerk, John H Fanning, Chairman NLRB. Board of Visitors for the Columbus School of Law, The Catholic University of America.

SIMPLER, Gary
Shawe & Rosenthal LLP, Baltimore 410 752 1040
simpler@shawe.com
Recommended in Employment
Practice Areas: Labor-management relations; union avoidance, collective bargaining; employment discrimination; human resources advice and counsel; employment tort and contract litigation; covenants not-to-compete litigation; intellectual property and trade secret litigation; wage and hour laws; Family and Medical Leave Act (FMLA); Worker Adjustment and Retraining Notification Act (WARN); employment agreements, employment handbooks, policies, and procedures; appellate litigation.
Prof. Memberships: Bar Admissions: Maryland; US Courts of Appeals for the 3rd and 4th Circuits. Professional Associations: American Bar Association; Maryland State Bar Association, Member, Labor Law Section.
Publications: Gary is a contributing author to the 'Employment Law Deskbook' and 'NLRA Law & Practice', both published by Lexis/Matthew Bender.
Personal: University of Maryland School of Law, JD, cum laude, 1985; University of Maryland, BA, cum laude, 1979, Omicron Delta Epsilon, Phi Kappa Phi.

SMITH Jr, Robert (Jay) W
DLA Piper Rudnick Gray Cary US LLP, Baltimore 410 580 4266
jay.smith@dlapiper.com
Recommended in Corporate/M&A
Practice Areas: Corporate and securities; mergers and acquisitions; life sciences; corporate governance; venture capital and emerging companies.
Career: His practice focuses on public and private offerings of debt and equity securities, mergers and acquisitions, and general representation of public and private companies. A significant portion of his practice involves representation of issuers and underwriters in connection with the sale of securities by existing public companies, as well as the initial public offering of securities by emerging companies in the technology, biotechnology and real estate industries.
Personal: JD, University of Maryland; BS, The Wharton School of Finance, University of Pennsylvania.

STRAIN, Paul
Venable LLP, Baltimore 410 244 7400
Recommended in Litigation

TAYLOR, Ronald
Venable LLP, Baltimore 410 244 7400
Recommended in Employment

TILGHMAN Jr, Richard
DLA Piper Rudnick Gray Cary US LLP, Baltimore 410 580 4274
richard.tilghman@dlapiper.com
Recommended in Corporate/M&A
Practice Areas: Business and technology; biosciences; corporate and securities; mergers and acquisitions; homeland security.
Career: He practices in the area of corporate and securities law, primarily representing growth-oriented companies and underwriters in the public or private offering of equity securities. He also has substantial experience in a wide range of private and public offerings of debt and asset-backed securities, including various transactions under Rule 144A and various structured finance transactions. He currently represents a number of growth-oriented public and private companies, providing securities, corporate and general business advice.
Personal: JD, University of Maryland; BA, Union University.

TOPOLSKI, Douglas
McGuireWoods LLP, Baltimore 410 659 4000
Recommended in Employment

TRUITT, Raymond
Ballard Spahr Andrews & Ingersoll LLP, Baltimore 410 528 5629
truitt@ballardspahr.com
Recommended in Real Estate
Practice Areas: Concentrates his practice in all phases of commercial real estate including acquisition/disposition, development, structuring ownership vehicles, financing, leasing, and restructuring.
Prof. Memberships: Member of the American College of Real Estate Lawyers (ACREL), the American Bar Association and Maryland State Bar Association, and the International Council of Shopping Centers. He is the immediate past Chair of the Section Council of the Section of Real Property, Planning, and Zoning of the MSBA, and former Chair of the Code Revision Committee of the Section.
Career: Admitted to the Maryland Bar (1982); joined Ballard Spahr as Partner (1992); currently Managing Partner of the Baltimore office; previously associate (1982-89) and Partner (1990-92) at Frank, Bernstein, Conaway & Goldman. Frequent speaker for ICSC, MSBA and other professional organizations; former adjunct faculty member for the University of Baltimore School of Law and The Allen Berman Institute of Johns Hopkins University; faculty member and advisory board member for the Georgetown University Law School's Advanced Commercial Leasing Institute.
Publications: Author and contributing author to various ABA, MSBA, and ICSC periodicals.
Personal: JD, University of Virginia School of Law (1982); BA, magna cum laude, Loyola College (1979).

ULWICK, James P
Kramon & Graham, PA, Baltimore
410 752 6030
julwick@kg-law.com
Recommended in Litigation

Practice Areas: Litigation. Mr Ulwick's litigation practice is wide-ranging, including criminal and civil litigation of all kinds. Mr Ulwick has tried many cases in state and federal courts, including: banking, criminal defense, class actions, contracts, personal injury, legal and medical malpractice, RICO, construction, equal employment, real estate, securities, toxic tort, and other cases. He has extensive experience in complex cases, and he frequently appears in multidistrict litigations. A lawyer's area of practice as stated here is one to which he devotes a substantial proportion of his professional practice and should not be considered a 'specialization'.

Prof. Memberships: Mr Ulwick is a fellow in the American College of Trial Lawyers and a permanent member of the Judicial Conference for the United States Court of Appeals for the Fourth Circuit. He is a member of the Bars of Maryland, New Jersey and the District of Columbia.

Career: Upon graduation from law school, Mr Ulwick served as a judicial clerk for The Honorable Edward S Northrop, Chief Judge, United States District Court for the District of Maryland. Mr Ulwick then spent six years as a federal prosecutor; three years as an Assistant United States Attorney for the District of New Jersey (1978-81) and three years as an Assistant United States Attorney for the District of Maryland (1981-84). He joined Kramon & Graham in 1984, and became a member of the firm in 1986.

Publications: 'Producing by Mistake', Vol. 18, No. 3, Litigation, Spring 1992; 'Bank Fraud, Chapter 88, Criminal Defense Techniques', Vol. IV, Matthew Bender & Co., New York, 1991; 'The Bail Reform Act of 1984: Fundamental Changes in the Conditions and Availability of Release', 3 Barrister 16, 1985.

Personal: Mr Ulwick was born July 20, 1952. He is a 1974 graduate of the University of Massachusetts, and a 1977 graduate of the Columbus School of Law, Catholic University of America.

VANDEUSEN, Darrell
Kollman & Saucier PA, Baltimore
410 727 4300
Recommended in Employment

WASHBURNE, Thomas
Venable LLP, Baltimore 410 244 7400
Recommended in Corporate/M&A

WATKINS, John
Wilmer Cutler Pickering Hale and Dorr LLP, Baltimore 410 986 2820
John.Watkins@wilmerhale.com
Recommended in Corporate/M&A

Practice Areas: Practice focuses on securities offerings transactions, equity and debt investments, mergers and acquisitions, and real estate investment trusts (REITs). Has advised a wide range of clients on complex corporate and securities matters, and handled acquisitions and securities offerings transactions for many public and private companies. Has represented numerous investment banking firms, as well as merchant banking, private equity, and venture capital funds in connection with securities offering matters, acquisitions of controlling interests, and debt and equity investments.

Prof. Memberships: ABA Business Law Section (Venture Capital and Private Equity, Federal Regulation of Securities and Partnerships and Unincorporated Business Organizations Committees).

Career: Instructor in numerous continuing education courses in the area of corporate and securities laws.

Personal: Johns Hopkins University (BA, with honors, 1977); University of Michigan Law School (JD 1981).

WEBB, Thompson
Miles & Stockbridge PC, Baltimore
410 727 6464
Recommended in Corporate/M&A

WEINER, Arnold
Weiner & Weltchek, Lutherville
410 769 8080
Recommended in Litigation

WHITE, Pamela
Ober Kaler Grimes & Shriver, Baltimore
410 685 1120
Recommended in Employment

WINSTON, Roger
Linowes and Blocher LLP, Bethesda
301 654 0504
Recommended in Real Estate

WOLF, Larry
Whiteford, Taylor & Preston LLP, Baltimore 410 347 8747
lwolf@wtplaw.com
Recommended in Employment

Practice Areas: Labor-management relations; EEO/Discrimination claim representation; union avoidance strategies; employment claim prevention strategies.

Prof. Memberships: Maryland State Bar Association, American Bar Association. Admitted in Maryland, US Circuit Court of Appeals (DC, 3rd and 4th) and US Supreme Court.

Personal: LLB, Yale University, 1961; AB, Johns Hopkins University, 1958.

WRIGHT, James
Venable LLP, Baltimore 410 244 7400
Recommended in Real Estate

WRIGHT, Jefferson V
Miles & Stockbridge PC, Baltimore
410 385 3600
jwright@milesstockbridge.com
Recommended in Litigation

Practice Areas: Commercial and business litigation, involving the litigation and arbitration of disputes concerning business contracts and torts, class actions, securities, RICO and other fraud claims, intra-corporate and partnership disputes, internal corporate investigations, claims against or among financial institutions (lender liability, enforcement actions, inter-creditor disputes, and claims under FCRA, FDCPA, ECOA, HOEPA, TILA, UDAP and other consumer protection statutes), privacy claims, constitutional challenges, IP disputes and claims seeking injunctions or other emergency relief. He also furnishes advice to lawyers both inside and outside of his firm on matters relating to professional ethics, professional liability and corporate responsibility and liability, and occasionally serves as an expert on matters relating to business litigation and professional ethics or responsibility.

Prof. Memberships: Admitted to practice in the state and federal courts of Maryland (1981), the United States Court of Appeals for the 4th Circuit (1981) and the US Supreme Court (1995). Mr Wright is a member of the American Bar Association, Maryland State Bar Association (chair, Committee on Ethics, 1985), Bar Associations of Baltimore City and Baltimore County. Member, Judicial Nominating Commission of Maryland, as well as various professional organizations and societies.

Career: Law Clerk to J Dudley Digges of the Court of Appeals of Maryland (1979-81).

Personal: Georgetown University Law Center (JD, 1980, with honors); Tufts University (BA, 1977, with honors). Mr Wright has served as a member of his firm's Board of Directors, and as General Counsel and as chair of his firm's Ethics Committee for many years.

GOODELL, DEVRIES, LEECH & DANN LLP

THE FIRM

Managing Partner: Linda S Woolf
Senior Partner: Charles P Goodell Jr
Number of partners: 21
Number of other lawyers: 31

AREAS OF PRACTICE:

Pharmaceutical & Medical Device Litigation 35%
Medical Institutions 25%
Corporate/Commercial/Insurance 20%

FIRM OVERVIEW: Goodell, DeVries, Leech & Dann, LLP ('GDLD') was founded in 1988 by 16 lawyers who left one of Baltimore's largest firms to practice in an environment that fostered the highest quality legal representation, client service, collegiality and professionalism. The firm has expanded to over 50 lawyers without sacrificing these values. GDLD has a depth of real experience in the trial and management of complex litigation that is found in few other firms. Since the firm's inception, its attorneys have been involved in the defense and trial of pharmaceutical and medical device, healthcare, and commercial actions (including class actions and mass tort litigation) on behalf of national, regional and local clients. The firm's 'litigation-only' practice allows it to avoid many of the conflicts of interest that arise in firms with extensive corporate and transactional practices. GDLD has trial lawyers admitted to practice in Maryland, Virginia, the District of Columbia, Pennsylvania and Tennessee.

The firm's lawyers appear in court in numerous jurisdictions, from the northeast to the mid-west and throughout the south. Corporate clients frequently request that the firm staff trial teams in complex national litigation. GDLD counsels clients when sensitive business issues intersect with the company's interest in defending itself in court. The firm has been instrumental in helping its clients protect and achieve their business objectives in the course of litigation related to the acquisition or divestiture of businesses, disputes involving directors and officers, shareholders, contracts, insurance and similar matters. From its earliest days, GDLD invested significant resources and technology in order to streamline the practice of law and enhance the communications between client and counsel. GDLD's Information Service Department supports the firm's attorneys with advances in technology that extend the 'office' to wherever its lawyers need to manage large volumes of information and documents. In sum, GDLD's wealth of trial experience, central East Coast location and utilization of technology enable it to field a team of lawyers uniquely suited to achieving excellent results for its corporate clients in a cost-effective manner.

MAIN AREAS OF PRACTICE:

Pharmaceutical & Medical Device Litigation: The firm's lawyers have represented major pharmaceutical and medical device companies in product liability, class action and mass tort litigation since the 1970s. The firm has been responsible for developing successful defense strategies and nationally recognized experts in the fields of drug safety, biostatistics, health economics, epidemiology, engineering and metallurgy, protein biochemistry, hematology, toxicology, regulatory affairs and labelling. Members of the firm have served as national counsel in litigation involving pacemakers, pacemaker leads, defibrillators, HIV tainted blood products, Hepatitis C, Cipro/Avelox and other mass tort claims. They have served as regional counsel in litigation involving the Dalkon Shield, Rezulin, hormone replacement therapy medications, artificial knees, hips, and spinal devices and HIV tainted blood products. The firm's lawyers have served on national trial teams in litigation involving breast implants, the Dalkon Shield, heart valves, Rezulin, hormone replacement therapy, PPA, Baycol and diet drugs.

HEAD OFFICE

MARYLAND
One South Street 20th Floor, **Baltimore**, MD 21202
Tel: 410 783 4000   **Fax:** 410 783 4040
Email: info@gdldlaw.com.com
Website: www.gdldlaw.com

CONTACTS

Pharmaceutical & Medical Device Litigation ......Charles P Goodell Jr
Medical Institutions...Donald L DeVries Jr
Corporate/Commercial/ Insurance ....Linda S Woolf

Medical Institutions: GDLD represents health systems, medical institutions and individual hospitals on a regional and local basis. Its work for these institutions includes defending claims of professional negligence, credentialing disputes and commercial matters.

Corporate/Commercial/Insurance: The firm's attorneys have represented local, national and international clients in litigation arising from the sale of subsidiaries and business units, antitrust, theft of technology, shareholder derivative suits, claims against corporate directors and officers, trustees, security brokers, and other fiduciaries, ERISA class actions, defamation, tortious interference with contract and other business torts.

CLIENTS: The firm represents the largest pharmaceutical companies in the United States on a national and regional basis. It also represents medical systems and individual medical institutions in a variety of litigation contexts. The firm represents international, national and local corporations in corporate and commercial litigation. Finally, it represents numerous national and local companies in toxic tort litigation.

INTERNATIONAL WORK: The firm serves as international counsel for a medical device manufacturer, Accufix Research Institute, Inc. ('ARI'). The international defense of ARI by the firm has included a class action and other isolated cases pending in Canada (working with Fraser Milner Casgrain LLP), a defibrillator case in the United Kingdom (working with Taylor Wessing) and many product liability matters in France (working with Bouckaert Ormen Passemard Sportes and Proskauer Rose LLP). The firm has also assisted ARI in matters pending in Hong Kong, Israel, Japan and Australia (working with Phillips Fox and Freehills). Finally, the firm advised the officers of ARI in connection with negotiations involving agreements entered into by ARI with related corporations. The firm has represented Pacific Dunlop Limited (n/k/a Ansell Limited), an Australian corporation, in litigation arising from the sale of certain worldwide subsidiaries, including litigation in Illinois state court, federal court and bankruptcy court. The firm represents both an international mining company and one of the world's largest producers of cement and ready mix products in connection with asbestos liabilities throughout the United States. The firm represented Fireman's Fund Insurance Company in a multi-million dollar fidelity bond claim brought in Greece by a Greek subsidiary of Marriott Corporation.

KRAMON & GRAHAM P.A.

THE FIRM

Managing Principal: Philip M Andrews

Number of Members: 15
Number of other lawyers: 12

FIRM OVERVIEW: Kramon & Graham, P.A., was founded in 1975 by two former Assistant United States Attorneys to handle complex commercial litigation and significant white collar criminal matters. The firm, which has enjoyed continual growth and success since then, currently has 27 lawyers. As the firm has grown, its practice areas have expanded as well, and now include commercial real estate, corporate, insurance coverage, executive employment, and administrative law matters. In addition to their professional commitments, Kramon & Graham lawyers are actively involved in state and local civic, cultural, charitable, and political activities, and serve in leadership roles on a wide range of outside boards and committees.

MAIN AREAS OF PRACTICE:

Civil Litigation: A major portion of Kramon & Graham's practice is concentrated in business litigation, a field in which the firm is preeminent. The firm's lawyers have extensive trial and appellate experience at all levels of the federal and state court systems, as well as before administrative agencies. They have tried innumerable significant matters, involving virtually every kind of business and commercial issue. Three of the firm's members are Fellows in the American College of Trial Lawyers; four are former Assistant United States Attorneys; and three other members are former Assistant Attorneys General for the State of Maryland. Among the myriad business cases handled by Kramon & Graham lawyers are commercial disputes concerning contract, securities, fiduciary duty, unfair competition, commercial construction and residential development, trademark and copyright, trade secret, professional malpractice, technology, and attendant matters. In addition, the firm is retained to represent many lawyers and law firms on a regular basis.

Real Estate: The firm represents developers and entrepreneurs in connection with complex real estate transactions, large scale development projects, zoning and land use issues, financings, environmental issues, lending matters, and litigation involving real estate, zoning, land use, condemnation and construction matters.

Insurance Coverage & Advice: The firm maintains a sophisticated insurance practice that includes insurance coverage disputes and advice concerning general liability, excess, and umbrella policies. Kramon & Graham represents insurers in matters arising out of construction, environmental, products liability, professional liability, and other commercial disputes. The firm's practice in this area is national. It has acted as insurance liaison counsel in coverage disputes involving more than $100,000,000.00. The firm also represents insurance carriers, agents and brokers in regulatory matters before state insurance departments.

HEAD OFFICE

MARYLAND
One South Street, Suite 2600, **Baltimore**, MD 21202-3201
Tel: 410 752 6030   **Fax:** 410 539 1269
Website: www.kramonandgraham.com

CONTACTS

Administrative Law ....Philip M Andrews
Civil Litigation................................Andrew Jay Graham, James P Ulwick
Criminal Litigation ....Andrew Jay Graham, James P Ulwick
Insurance Coverage & Advice...Lee H Ogburn
Real Estate & Corporate ....Jeffrey H Scherr

Administrative Law: Among the firm's long-standing clients are entities that do business with state and local governments. Several of the firm's principals are former Assistant Attorneys General with extensive knowledge of, and familiarity with, state agencies that award contracts for privatized services, construction work, and the supply of goods and materials. The firm routinely represents clients before various state agencies in licensing and regulation matters, as well as before the Maryland State Board of Contract Appeals, which has exclusive jurisdiction of procurement disputes and state contract claims.

Corporate/Commercial: The firm represents many national and international entities, as well as regional and local businesses and entrepreneurs, in all matters relating to every kind of corporate law and business transaction. The firm's clients include professional practices such as architectural firms, law firms, medical practices, real estate services, internet services firms, wholesale distributors, manufacturers, and retail companies. The firm handles transactions that concern equity investments in businesses and real estate ventures. Kramon & Graham lawyers also do a significant amount of corporate legal planning, particularly with respect to family and closely-held businesses.

Criminal Litigation: The firm frequently represents companies, or their officers and directors, involved in federal and state criminal investigations in Maryland and other jurisdictions. Since the firm's founding, Kramon & Graham lawyers have served as lead defense counsel in many of the largest white collar criminal investigations and trials conducted in federal and Maryland courts.

MILES & STOCKBRIDGE

THE FIRM

Chairman: John B Frisch

Number of partners: 103
Number of other lawyers: 90

FIRM OVERVIEW: For more than 70 years Miles & Stockbridge attorneys have brought a deep personal commitment to serving business, corporate, non-profit and individual clients. Today their nearly 200 attorneys are both generalists – with the capacity to meet nearly every legal need – and specialists who understand the technical aspects of demanding and complex practice areas. Their eight mid-Atlantic offices have comprehensive capabilities to deliver quality work and quality service, yet they remain a humanly scaled, accessible organization with many long-term client relationships that demonstrate the firm's ability to walk in its clients' shoes.

MAIN AREAS OF PRACTICE: The firm's comprehensive business and commercial practice encompasses 15 practice groups that among them have well over 120 practice subspecialties. The broadest description of its legal services includes five wide-ranging areas of focus:

Finance: From general corporate, securities and mergers and acquisitions counsel to complex services for banks and financial institutions, the firm handles a full spectrum of transactional and capital markets needs for its clients. Its experience includes assistance with tax and creditors' rights concerns, and it also advises individuals and family-owned businesses on wealth and estate management.

Human Resources: The firm assists employers of all sizes and in all industries with the legal dimensions of human resources management in the areas of employment and labor, employee benefits and executive compensation. Although they emphasize proactive problem avoidance, they vigorously defend their clients in court and before regulatory agencies.

Litigation: The firm's comprehensive services, offered by more than 50 lawyers throughout all of the firm's offices, address general business torts and trade regulation disputes, as well as areas of emphasis like products liability, mass torts and insurance controversies. They are also skilled at domestic and international alternative dispute resolution.

Real Estate: Miles & Stockbridge assists developers, lenders, lessors, contractors and other real estate clients throughout the greater Baltimore/Washington region, from Northern Virginia to Pennsylvania. They get deals done using unsurpassed market knowledge and close working relationships with governmental entities and commercial finance institutions.

Technology: From locations in the heart of dynamic biotechnology and telecommunications centers, the firm offers intellectual property, business law and dispute resolution counsel to emerging companies and established multinational giants alike.

CLIENTS: Miles & Stockbridge is widely regarded as a leading law firm in the mid-Atlantic region that encompasses Maryland, Northern Virginia and Washington, DC. They are the choice of *Fortune* 500 industrial giants, major financial institutions, privately owned businesses as well as national and local not-for-profit organizations, and the firm's services to them in key litigation and transactional areas extend well beyond their immediate geographic base.

HEAD OFFICE

MARYLAND
10 Light Street, **Baltimore,** MD 21202-1487
Tel: 410 727 6464   **Fax:** 410 385 3700
Website: www.milesstockbridge.com

BRANCH OFFICES

MARYLAND
300 Academy Street, **Cambridge**, MD 21613-1865
Tel: 410 228 4545   **Fax:** 410 228 5652

10490 Little Patuxent Parkway, **Columbia**, MD 21044
Tel: 410 381 6000   **Fax:** 410 381 6430

101 Bay Street, **Easton**, MD 21601
Tel: 410 822 5280   **Fax:** 410 822 5450

30 West Patrick Street, **Frederick**, MD 21701
Tel: 301 662 5155   **Fax:** 301 662 3647

11 North Washington Street, **Rockville**, MD 20850
Tel: 301 762 1600   **Fax:** 301 762 0363

One West Pennsylvania Ave, **Towson**, MD 21204
Tel: 410 821 6565   **Fax:** 410 823 8123

VIRGINIA
1751 Pinnacle Drive, **McLean**, VA 22102
Tel: 703 903 9000   **Fax:** 703 610 8686

Their clients encompass 14 different industry groups, including the services sector (construction, consulting, distribution, hospitality), finance and investment, manufacturing (from consumer and industrial goods to biotechnology) and nonprofit providers of health, charitable and governmental services. Among the firm's clients are such household names as: The Black & Decker Corporation, a global consumer products manufacturer; major financial firms like Bank of America and SunTrust Bank; retailing giant Lowe's Companies, Inc.; high-profile technology leaders, including Verizon Communications and Hitachi, Ltd.

INTERNATIONAL WORK: Miles & Stockbridge advises US and multinational corporations on their transactional, investment and trade concerns worldwide, and has longstanding relationships representing non-US companies in direct investment and general business activities within the United States and North America. As members of TerraLex®, a worldwide network of independent law firms comprising 10,000 lawyers in nearly 100 countries, there are few global jurisdictions where the firm cannot provide the assistance that their clients need.

$$M \, I \, L \, E \, S \, \& \, S \, T \, O \, C \, K \, B \, R \, I \, D \, G \, E \quad \text{P.C.}$$

SHAWE & ROSENTHAL, LLP

THE FIRM

Managing Partners: Stephen D Shawe/Bruce S Harrison
Partner: J Michael McGuire

Number of partners: 10
Number of other lawyers: 5

HEAD OFFICE

MARYLAND
20 S. Charles Street, 11th Floor, **Baltimore**, MD 21201
Tel: 410 752 1040   **Fax:** 410 752 8861
Website: www.shawe.com

FIRM OVERVIEW: One of the first law firms in the country devoted exclusively to the representation of management in labor and employment matters, Shawe & Rosenthal was founded in 1947 by Earle K Shawe. Shawe & Rosenthal's practice involves both traditional labor and employment law matters, including claims brought under the Civil Rights Act, Age Discrimination in Employment Act, and the Americans with Disabilities Act. The firm defends claims involving employment discrimination, wrongful termination, defamation, ERISA, wage and hour, and occupational safety and health matters. It represents management in NLRB hearings, representation campaigns and collective bargaining negotiations. The firm provides advice and assistance in the formulation of covenants not to compete and trade secret protection commitments, and is active in litigation associated with disputes over restrictive covenants and trade secrets. The firm also provides advice and counsel in the creation of affirmation action plans and compliance with OFCCP regulations. From its inception in 1947, Shawe & Rosenthal decided to remain small (15 labor attorneys), select and centralized rather than expand into regional offices. This philosophy has contributed to a professional excellence that has attracted clients from across the nation. The firm has for decades represented many Fortune 500 companies, including some of the country's largest manufacturing, public utility, retail, healthcare and insurance concerns. Over the past three years the firm has handled two labor cases in the United States Supreme Court (Allentown Mack v NLRB, 118 S.Ct. 818 (1998) and Kolstad v American Dental Association, 527 U.S. 526 (1999)). Shawe & Rosenthal is a compact well managed organization, and is therefore able to provide clients with uniform and consistent advice, greater efficiencies in rendering services, and greater capabilities in providing short and long-term strategic planning. All of the firm's clients are represented in their general business affairs by other law firms, indeed some of the largest law firms in the country. Many of these other law firms have their own labor law sections. The firm's clients have, nonetheless, continued to turn to Shawe & Rosenthal for advice and counsel in the labor and employment field because of the firm's specialized knowledge and experience, and capability to provide advice quickly and efficiently. Members of the firm have written many publications in the employment field, including the 'Employment Law Deskbook' (1989) and two chapters in 'NLRA Law & Practice' (1991), both published by Mathew Bender. The firm also wrote the 'Maryland and Federal Employment Law Manual' (2001), published by the American Chamber of Commerce Publishers.

MAIN AREAS OF PRACTICE: Labor management relations, collective bargaining, and proceedings before the NLRB; employment discrimination; human resources advice and counsel; employment tort and contract litigation; covenants not-to-compete litigation; intellectual property and trade secret litigation; wage and hour laws (FLSA, Portal to Portal Act); Occupational Safety and Health Acts (OSHA); Affirmative Action Programs (AAPs); Family and Medical Leave Act (FMLA); Workers' Adjustment and Retraining Act (WARN); Employee Benefits/ERISA; employment agreements; employment handbooks, policies, and procedures; appellate litigation; class actions.

CLIENTS: The firm has been for many years labor and employment counsel to such large companies as Black & Decker Corp., Danaher Corp., Genesis HealthCare Corporation, GEICO, Huffy Corporation, McDonald's Corporation, The May Department Stores Co., The Federal Reserve Bank of Richmond, National Railroad Passenger Corporation (AMTRAK) and Rite Aid Corporation.

International Clients: Bermuda Hotel Association. For more than 20 years, Stephen Shawe served as chief spokesman for the Association in its collective bargaining negotiations with the union representing the Island's 3000 hotel employees. When Bermuda passed legislation requiring interest arbitration to resolve unresolved collective bargaining negotiations, Stephen presented the hotel employers' position at interest arbitration hearings in Hamilton, Bermuda.

SHAWE
ROSENTHAL LLP

CONTENTS: Antitrust p.930; Banking & Finance p.931; Bankruptcy p.934; Corporate/M&A p.937; Employment p.939; Environment p.942; Healthcare p.946; Intellectual Property p.947; Litigation p.949; Private Equity p.952; Real Estate p.956; Tax p.959; Individuals' Profiles p.961; Firms' Profiles p.980.

How lawyers are ranked

The opinions we gather from clients — mainly from in-house lawyers but also from other purchasers of legal services — are balanced by opinions from colleagues and competitors. Together, they provide two different perspectives — an all-round view — and biased viewpoints cancel each other out.

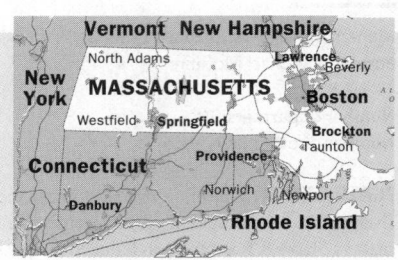

ANTITRUST

Massachusetts
Leading firms (Antitrust)
1 BINGHAM MCCUTCHEN LLP *Boston*
NUTTER, MCCLENNEN & FISH, LLP *Boston*
WILMER CUTLER PICKERING HALE *Boston*
2 CHOATE HALL & STEWART *Boston*
FOLEY HOAG LLP *Boston*
PALMER & DODGE LLP *Boston*
ROPES & GRAY LLP *Boston*

Leading individuals (Antitrust)
Senior Statesman
CURTIN John *Bingham McCutchen, Boston*
1 BURLING James *Wilmer Cutler, Boston*
GOLDBERG Daniel *Bingham McCutchen, Boston*
MILLER Michelle *Wilmer Cutler, Boston*
MOTENKO Neil *Nutter McClennen, Boston*
SCOTT Thane *Palmer & Dodge, Boston*
2 ARMISTEAD III I Cary *Ropes & Gray, Boston*
BUCHANAN Robert *Choate Hall, Boston*
PATTON William *Ropes & Gray, Boston*
SAVRIN Daniel *Bingham McCutchen, Boston*
WOOD Lisa *Foley Hoag, Boston*
Up-and-coming individuals
CONDE Kathryn *Nutter McClennen, Boston*
DOWNEY Alicia *Bingham McCutchen, Boston*
WILLIS Jane *Ropes & Gray, Boston*
Firms and individuals are listed alphabetically in each band.

Band 1

Bingham McCutchen LLP

The Firm: The depth, breadth and high quality of its antitrust and trade regulation practice make this firm a clear market leader. A substantial team of eight partners focuses on this area, covering anything from distribution counsel and M&A advice to criminal and hard-core cartel defense work. There is a considerable crossover with related areas such as franchise matters and IP. The Boston team can call on the firm's resources available nationally and internationally, and benefits from strategic affiliates

such as the Bingham Consulting Group. The practice is especially well known for representing major clients in the automotive industry. A recent highlight was representing BMW in a multidistrict class action and related actions at state level. The case concerned an alleged conspiracy and group boycott to inhibit exports from Canada to the USA. Clients recommend the group for a flexible approach and ability to "*think outside the box.*"

The Lawyers: An "*excellent*" team is spearheaded by dean of the bar **Jack Curtin**. When it comes to court representation clients seek him out for the kudos attached to the mere mention of his name. Curtin's grasp of the issues and communication skills are "*exceptional,*" they say. He was one of the attorneys who recently acted for Stop & Shop in a First Circuit appeal. "*Superb*" trial lawyer **Daniel Goldberg** "*will work on a brief until it's really excellent.*" His depth of experience across a range of industries, including as lead litigation counsel to several professional sports teams, is a major plus point for clients. He is respected for his efficient courtroom style and faultless preparation. **Daniel Savrin** also maintains a broad practice at the intersection of antitrust, white-collar crime and regulatory compliance matters. He impresses clients with his organizational skills, responsiveness and "*remarkable*" eye for detail – "*I know that nothing will fall through the cracks with him,*" said one. Savrin recently successfully resolved criminal proceedings and a related multidistrict class action for the Eastern District of Pennsylvania. Skilled litigator and new entrant **Alicia Downey** is "*absolutely the right choice for an up-and-comer,*" say clients. She is particularly noted for her distribution counseling practice.

The Clients: BMW of North America; GM; eBay; Stop & Shop; Toyota; Mitsui; Nissan North America; Freightliner; FLEXcon and Toyo Tanso.

Nutter, McClennen & Fish, LLP

The Firm: This two-partner team handles a mix of counseling and litigation work, with a special

emphasis on clients in the healthcare industry. Its expertise in these areas places it squarely on the national map. The practice is also distinguishing itself through involvement in a series of indirect purchaser class actions relating to price-fixing charges, across a range of industries (including vitamins, polyester staple, nucleotides and compact discs). Clients value the thoughtful approach and analysis of these lawyers, particularly in negotiations: "*They will not jump to conclusions but will methodically weigh up all the options for the client.*"

The Lawyers: "*Wonderful counselor*" **Neil Motenko** leads the practice and is best known for his work with healthcare providers, such as Tufts Health Plan. Clients hunt him out nationally for his "*incredible knowledge*" of the field. On the litigation side, observers agree that Motenko's understated approach belies a particularly effective courtroom presence. Recently made partner, **Kathryn Conde** is "*making her mark*" according to interviewees. Regarded as one of the bar's up-and-coming litigators, she works closely with Motenko. Recent experience has centered on price discrimination matters and a case concerning exclusionary conduct in the field of radiation oncology. She is also actively involved on the counseling side of the practice.

The Clients: Clients include ambulance companies, physicians, various healthcare organizations, hospitals, Fortune 500 companies, and a range of manufacturers, retailers and distributors.

Wilmer Cutler Pickering Hale and Dorr LLP

See firm details p.986

The Firm: Hale and Dorr's established hi-tech and IP focus combined with Wilmer Cutler Pickering's renowned regulatory expertise means the antitrust practice at the newly merged firm now has an even broader remit. On the counseling front, clients can draw on the advice of attorneys with EU expertise, not to mention benefit from cross-staffing between 20 dedicated partners. Clients point to the firm's "*highly organized*" work ethic and depth of experience. Work ranges from private litigation and government investigations to compliance issues and representing clients before the FTC and DOJ.

The Lawyers: James Burling (see p.964) and **Michelle Miller** (see p.972) are the firm's foremost practitioners in the field. Burling has recently seen an increase in private litigation work and is considered "*very insightful on FTC matters.*" He is renowned for representing hi-tech clients and "*has considerable ability when it comes to understanding business imperatives and giving practical advice.*" Miller has a foot planted firmly in both antitrust and litigation camps. She is also noted for her work in securities class actions. Described as "*an engaging communicator,*" she is valued for her "*great pragmatic advice.*" The team recently settled a significant matter for Ocean Spray Cranberries, involving claims of conspiracy and monopolization. Further highlights include acting for a technology client in an antitrust counterclaim following a patent enforcement.

The Clients: These include Penwest Pharmaceuticals; Sepracor; Avid Technology; Ocean Spray Cranberries; Wyeth; Analog Devices; Biogen IDEC; CollaGenex Pharmaceuticals and Cephalon.

Band 2

Choate Hall & Stewart

The Firm: Antitrust activity at this well-established Boston firm centers largely on the work of litigator Robert Buchanan, drawing on the strengths of the broader corporate and litigation teams where necessary. The practice spans the gamut of counseling and litigation matters with a special emphasis on the healthcare industry. The firm settled a case for a major healthcare client in an antitrust suit brought by an ambulance company, with several million dollars at stake.

The Lawyers: "*In terms of raw intellect alone he is worth his weight in gold,*" enthuse clients over **Robert Buchanan.** His practice is divided equally between antitrust litigation and counseling on the one hand and complex business litigation on the other. Consumer class actions further define Buchanan's workload. Recent highlights include acting for a hi-tech client in a

DOJ pre-merger second request, enabling the swift completion of a key transaction.

The Clients: Cape Cod Healthcare; Manulife Financial; Massachusetts Medical Society and ITA Software.

Foley Hoag LLP

The Firm: Lisa Wood's arrival from Nutter McClennen & Fish was perceived to bolster the firm's profile and it wins entry to the table accordingly. The Boston and DC offices now have three partners between them. They draw on the firm's considerable litigation resources as required, often working with its government crimes group and patent licensing attorneys. The team handles counseling and litigation surrounding antitrust, trade and broader consumer protection matters. It represents clients before judicial and administrative tribunals at all levels, and in merger and other investigations. Advice on antitrust compliance issues is also offered. Attorneys recently resolved litigation brought by a distributor against a national equipment manufacturer relating to restrictions on Internet sales. The firm also acted for a mutual fund client in a class action alleging commodities and antitrust violations.

The Lawyers: **Lisa Wood** is "*very good at taking a complex antitrust concept and translating it into business terms.*" Principally a litigator, her practice also overlaps with securities fraud issues and accountant malpractice. She has a particular interest in the workings of the Noerr-Pennington doctrine. The firm successfully obtained a motion to dismiss the majority of claims against a shopping mall developer in a recent antitrust case, involving the first application of the doctrine in New Hampshire state court.

The Clients: A diverse client base includes financial institutions, specialist producers in the high-tech, chemical and manufacturing industries, health plans, hospitals and physician groups, insurance companies, distributors and retailers, telecom clients and trade associations.

Palmer & Dodge LLP

See firm details p.984

The Firm: Three partners devote a substantial amount of time to antitrust, whether business counseling or multiparty private litigation.

Experience of government enforcement issues and investigations is also in evidence. As with the firm, the team is distinguished by its work on behalf of higher education institutions.

The Lawyers: Group chair **Thane Scott** (see p.977) impresses with his "*witty and clever*" style and "*wonderful manner with clients.*" Historically he focused on government investigations with a particular emphasis on distribution and software-related matters. Recently he represented Fidelity in the litigated Oracle/People Soft merger. Scott also provided ongoing advice to a sophisticated software manufacturer in dispute with a distributor over price competition issues.

The Clients: Fidelity; Genzyme; Risk Management Foundation; Parametric Technology and the Consortium on Financing Higher Education.

Ropes & Gray LLP

See firm details p.985

The Firm: This is another practice that has prospered on the interface between antitrust and IP law, not least since the firm recently merged with New York IP boutique Fish & Neave. The team comprises general trial lawyers focusing on antitrust work, offering an array of services across the spectrum of traditional competition law. This includes acting for clients in private disputes, FTC, DOJ and other enforcement investigations. While the team is located in Boston and the District of Columbia, the practice is increasingly global in scope.

The Lawyers: Senior figure **William Patton** (see p.974) has recently spent a lot of time on IP matters such as patent infringement litigation and associated antitrust counterclaims. "*Truly seasoned professional*" **Cary Armistead** (see p.961) chairs the firm's international practice group, counseling major corporations on a range of antitrust issues in the context of US and EU law. He is especially well regarded for the advice he provides on distribution matters. **Jane Willis** (see p.979) continues to increase her profile in the market. She is a general business litigator active on both antitrust litigation and compliance issues.

The Clients: The firm acts for a diverse range of clients, across industries such as pharmaceuticals, private equity, consumer products, healthcare and sports.

BANKING & FINANCE

Band 1

Bingham McCutchen LLP

The Firm: "*The firm to go to for complex transactions,*" this huge team "*can handle pretty much anything*" in the financial services industry. The firm is keen to emphasize its national presence and the varied deal flow that continuously filters through its extensive network of offices.

Enhanced West Coast capabilities and a growing London practice are emblematic of its far-reaching success, a background against which the Boston operation stands out in its own right. Clients speak of "*excellent quality*" and appreciate the timely delivery of documents and responsiveness of this team. Its lending and leasing prowess is well attested to. The workload also incorporates matters ranging from sophis-

ticated international financings to midmarket and smaller deals, all of which take place in a diverse range of industry settings. Considerable workout and restructuring capabilities are a further feature of the practice.

The Lawyers: "*Tough negotiator and worthy adversary*" **Neal Curtin** is "*always a favorite*" and renowned as a dean of the Bar. He is "*terrific for cross-border work*" according to interviewees.

[1]	**BINGHAM MCCUTCHEN LLP** *Boston*
	GOODWIN PROCTER LLP *Boston*
[2]	**EDWARDS & ANGELL, LLP** *Boston*
	FOLEY HOAG LLP *Boston*
	GOULSTON & STORRS *Boston*
	NUTTER, MCCLENNEN & FISH, LLP *Boston*
	PALMER & DODGE LLP *Boston*
	ROPES & GRAY LLP *Boston*
[3]	**CHOATE HALL & STEWART** *Boston*
	GALLAGHER, CALLAHAN *Boston*
[4]	**RIEMER & BRAUNSTEIN LLP** *Boston*

Leading individuals (Banking & Finance)

[1]	**SMITH Edwin** *Bingham McCutchen, Boston*
[2]	**DRAPER Thomas** *Ropes & Gray, Boston*
	KYLE Amy *Bingham McCutchen, Boston*
	SMITH Philip *Ropes & Gray, Boston*
	TICKNOR George *Palmer & Dodge, Boston*
[3]	**BERMAN David** *Riemer & Braunstein, Boston*
	HERMAN Philip *Goulston & Storrs, Boston*

Leading individuals (Banking & Finance: Corporate & Regulatory)

[1]	**BARR Lynne** *Goodwin Procter, Boston*
	COOGAN Peter *Foley Hoag, Boston*
	CURTIN Neal *Bingham McCutchen, Boston*
	MAYER William *Goodwin Procter, Boston*
[2]	**COUKOS Stephen** *Gallagher Callahan, Boston*
	EHRLICH Kenneth *Nutter McClennen, Boston*
	HANDLY Kevin *Gallagher Callahan, Boston*
	LYONS Gregory *Goodwin Procter, Boston*
	PISA Regina *Goodwin Procter, Boston*
	PRATT Carol *Foley Hoag, Boston*
[3]	**KREBS Michael** *Nutter McClennen, Boston*
	RAGALEVSKY Stanley *Kirkpatrick, Boston*
	RAPHAEL Bruce *Edwards & Angell, Boston*

Up-and-coming individuals

	STERN William *Goodwin Procter, Boston*

Firms and individuals are listed alphabetically in each band.

Indeed, Curtin has increasingly focused on international transactions, acting for Bank of America on Latin America-related matters. In Africa, he assisted Africa International Financial Holdings with Zambia National Commercial Bank and Afribank (Nigeria) privatizations. He also acted for the government and National Bank of Rwanda on the privatization of Rwanda Commercial Bank and Continental Bank of Africa. Financial services volunteer work further defines Curtin's practice. This involves providing assistance to emerging economies including Russia, Bosnia and Yemen. The *"outstanding"* **Edwin Smith** cochairs the finance group and has a hand in both front-end finance and bankruptcy matters. He *"probably knows as much about UCC as anybody in the country,"* agree sources, and is *"the person in the firm that you look to for answers to difficult questions."* Recent

work includes acting for buyers of assets out of bankruptcy and advising the agent for a syndicate of lenders on loan workouts in the Omni bankruptcy in New York. Smith *"reads judges well"* and is *"pleasant to work with,"* confirm peers. **Amy Kyle** also divides her time between straight finance and workout support. Clients like the fact she *"is able to focus on what really matters without getting caught up in the minutiae"* and has the capacity *"to think through complex issues and come up with a practical response."* She offers niche expertise when it comes to advising lead agents in transportation sector financings. A recent example involved her acting in an $850 million multicurrency international financing for Ryder System.

The Clients: Sources of instructions include banks as well as other credit providers and financial institutions, funds and private equity clients. They include: Bank of America; GE Capital; FleetBoston Financial and First & Ocean Bancorp.

Goodwin Procter LLP

See firm details p.980

The Firm: This well-respected full-service firm continues to dominate the market in corporate and regulatory arenas, making it *"one of the major practices in New England."* Banking comes under the aegis of an integrated firm-wide financial services group, serving the needs of a diverse client base that includes dealers and mutuals alongside traditional bank clients such as Citizens and State Street. As one interviewee commented: *"Goodwin deserves to be top tier thanks to its considerable portfolio and sheer number of clients."* The firm is deemed to have enhanced its national, not to mention international presence following hires in New York and DC.

The Lawyers: One interviewee described **William Mayer** (see p.972) as *"among the premier banking attorneys in the country,"* a comment typical of wide-ranging praise from peers and clients alike. Clients especially value his direct approach and *"tremendous judgment"* in the early stages of structuring a transaction: *"He doesn't waffle in terms of what's required – he knows the regulatory scheme so well that he can anticipate what's possible in negotiations."* Mayer spends a substantial portion of his time advising clients in the community bank and specialty bank sectors, whereby he boasts *"a great mixture of corporate and regulatory work."* Recent highlights include advising John Hancock Financial Services on a nationwide broker deposit program. Chair of consumer financial services **Lynne Barr** (see p.962) is nationally recognized as an expert in her field. Barr's clients include large financial institutions, financial services trade associations, mortgage companies and community institutions. She is particularly well known for her specialist regu-

latory expertise. Her practice has recently seen an increase in matters relating to electronic banking. Managing partner **Regina Pisa** (see p.974) *"inspires clients with confidence in what she's saying by the way she says it,"* say market observers. An M&A specialist, she spends the majority of her time representing financial services clients but also advises on matters such as public offerings. She is renowned for her relationship with key client Citizens and acted on its $11 billion cash acquisition of Charter One. Further recent highlights include working with Goldman Sachs on a deal involving student loan company First Marblehead. **Greg Lyons** (see p.971) chairs the group, a role in which he has *"exhibited a lot of ability and energy."* He tends to focus on sophisticated regulatory matters for the firm's larger, sophisticated clients. Rising star and *"worker bee"* **William Stern** (see p.978) is *"a major asset,"* sources report. He enters the tables for the first time following strong recommendations from clients.

The Clients: State Street Bank & Trust; Citizens Financial Group; Capital Crossing; Boston Private Financial Holdings; Mass Bankers Association and American Express.

Band 2

Edwards & Angell, LLP

The Firm: This *"decent-sized team"* continues to diversify its client base and handles *"soup-to-nuts"* work for bank and nonbank clients. The firm also boasts a substantial finance and capital markets group, spread across offices in New England, New York and Florida. A broad range of work is undertaken, with an emphasis on representing the agents and arrangers in syndicated lending transactions and real estate lending. Clients describe its lawyers as *"effective and diligent,"* finding them to *"help the client to make real practical business decisions."*

The Lawyers: **Bruce Raphael** has *"a strong M&A skill-set,"* report interviewees. Recent work includes acting for FleetBoston Financial (since acquired by Bank of America) in the acquisition of Progress Financial. He often works closely with attorneys in the firm's Rhode Island office.

The Clients: Providian Financial; AIG; Bank of America; John Hancock Life Insurance; Key-Bank; Citizens Bank; MassMutual; JPMorgan Partners; Wells Fargo; QB Insurance Group; Bear Stearns; UBS Financial Services; Brown Brothers Harriman and Textron Financial.

Foley Hoag LLP

The Firm: This corporate-oriented banking practice has achieved excellence representing the New England-based community banking industry. Recent highlights include advising Benjamin Franklin Savings Bank on its conversion from mutual to stock form prior to the acquisition of Chart Bank.

The Lawyers: Senior figure and *"outstandingly bright guy"* **Peter Coogan** *"has always had a strong presence in the banking sector."* He recently acted for Eastern Bank in its acquisition of Plymouth Savings Bank. Coogan is also renowned for his technology and startup non-bank work. **Carol Hempfling Pratt** has a similar focus to Coogan. She handles most of the regulatory compliance work, advising clients on issues such as truth-in-lending.

The Clients: Key clients include Eastern Bank, Salem Five Cents Savings Bank and Depositors Insurance Fund.

Goulston & Storrs

The Firm: This practice largely focuses on mid-market transactions across a range of industries. In line with the firm's market-leading real estate capabilities, a large part of its asset-based lending work relates to the retail and hospitality sectors. Recent highlights include working with Bank of America on financing a private equity firm's acquisition of a restaurant chain in Western USA involving multiple layers of debt and equity. The team also handles the range of corporate and regulatory work and can utilize the expertise of prominent workouts attorneys as required.

The Lawyers: **Philip Herman** wins plaudits for his responsiveness, client-oriented approach and good business judgment. One interviewee explained: *"He is very proactive at reaching out to us not to mention very intelligent and thoughtful."*

The Clients: These include commercial banks, thrifts, credit unions, investment funds and trust companies as well as officers and directors. Examples are: Citizens; Bank of America; GMAC and KeyBank.

Nutter, McClennen & Fish, LLP

The Firm: It is best known for corporate and regulatory work, while a separate group focuses on finance and bank lending. Acting as regulatory counsel to larger banks complements general corporate counsel roles with more than 30 community banks. The team has seen an increase in instructions from publicly held banks, whereby attorneys were recently involved in the recapitalization of an institution in Florida. It also continues to build its mutual bank client base.

The Lawyers: **Kenneth Ehrlich** further enhanced his presence in the community banking industry, in which he has proved *"very successful"* and *"developed a true ability to serve his clients well."* Clients emphasized his broad understanding of Massachusetts regulatory law as well as federal banking regulations, which enables him to provide clear explanations and simplify complex matters. He recently defended Commerce Bank & Trust in a significant regulatory enforcement action. Other work includes advising on the refinancing of a publicly held

bank. Described as *"a crackerjack securities and transactional lawyer,"* **Michael Krebs** enters the tables for the first time. He works almost exclusively with mutual banks, complementing Ehrlich's practice well.

The Clients: Key clients include Mellon Financial, Citizens and Banknorth.

Palmer & Dodge LLP
See firm details p.984

The Firm: Around 30 attorneys make up the finance practice, complemented by a further five workout and creditor's rights practitioners. The team also works closely with the firm's real estate department. It represents both bank and non-bank entities, with niche areas including communications sector financings. The outfit is also involved in reorganizations and leveraged buyouts. Commentators appreciate the accessibility of its partners and the ability of the group to *"provide the client with a comprehensive analysis of their position that leaves nothing to chance."* Highlights include a major financing for GE Capital, an energy company financing for Bank of America, and acting for Sheffield Steel in a substantial debt restructuring and high-yield debt issuance.

The Lawyers: *"Top-notch"* **George Ticknor** (see p.978) chairs the finance group. He focuses on syndicated acquisition financings, and has developed specialist expertise in matters involving media, communications and telecom industries. Ticknor's practice has become national in scope and he often represents companies in global debt relations. He also represents buyers of debt including major mutual funds. Clients clearly value his proactive approach and good business sense while finding him to be *"patient and effective"* in negotiations.

The Clients: Bank of America; Citizens Bank; Sheffield Steel; GE Capital; Lamar Advertising and Alta.

Ropes & Gray LLP
See firm details p.985

The Firm: Both peers and clients credit this *"profoundly talented operation"* with fielding a team of skillful financing lawyers offering *"quality from top to bottom."* As a result it *"clearly rivals the top players."* Corporate clients involved in high-yield and senior lending transactions are a key source of instructions for a practice distinguished from others by its dominant borrower focus. A top-tier funds practice means the firm's finance lawyers are also highly visible in private equity transactions nationwide.

The Lawyers: **Philip Smith** (see p.977) wins high praise from clients for his *"slick, service-oriented approach"* and *"great judgment."* Sources point to his expertise in mezzanine finance and favorable relationships with several large fund clients. Onlookers describe him as *"a deal-maker with an enormous amount of intellectual*

integrity."* Chair of debt financing **Tom Draper** (see p.966) was described as *"solid and dependable."* He was said to *"benefit from a finance practice as old as the hills."*

The Clients: Berkshire Partners; Boston Ventures; Bain Capital; Nortek; Loews; Riddell Bell and Fenway Partners are among the firm's clients.

Band 3

Choate Hall & Stewart

The Firm: This well-established full-service firm wins entry to the tables in recognition of its specialty finance group, part of a broader corporate department. A team of 16 attorneys advises banks, private equity funds and institutional investors on structuring investments and a range of finance transactions. The firm is particularly noted for niche expertise in sports sector lending. Clients highlighted the team's ability to *"diffuse tensions in complex situations."*

The Lawyers: Clients recommended the team as a whole for a *"consistently excellent"* negotiating style and an *"ability to understand the needs of the banking community."* Lyman Bullard chairs the group.

The Clients: The firm has acted for Citizens Bank; Wells Fargo; MassMutual; State Street Bank & Trust and Foothill Capital.

Gallagher, Callahan and Gartrell, PA
See firm details p.1120

The Firm: Steve Coukos, ex-Edwards & Angell partner and Kevin Handly, formerly of Goulston & Storrs, have joined forces to open the Boston office for this established New Hampshire player. This complements existing practices in Concord and Augusta. The move is designed to fill a perceived gap in serving the needs of the regional community banking market, which the firm hopes to fill by acting as *"gatekeeper"* to financial institutions. This involves handling all aspects of corporate and regulatory compliance issues as well as broader trademark, real estate and tax matters.

The Lawyers: **Steve Coukos** (see p.965) wins plaudits for his *"outstanding attention to detail and client service."* Best known historically for his work with Fleet, Coukos is focusing on developing relationships with the community banks and midmarket institutions. His experience extends to advising foreign banks on their business activities in the USA. He *"speaks our language,"* say clients, impressed by his *"great understanding of both legal and business sides."* *"Very smart"* **Kevin Handly** (see p.968) is noted for his regulatory knowledge. He has previously acted for the Federal Reserve Board in enforcement proceedings in several states. His practice encompasses advice to financial institutions on all types of M&A transaction, corporate governance and regulatory compliance issues.

Band 4

Riemer & Braunstein LLP

The Firm: A smaller shop with *"a skilled set of specialists,"* it appears in the tables for the first time following a number of strong recommendations. Commentators consider the firm a high-quality, price-sensitive alternative to some of the larger market players. Banking and finance is a core practice area. Real estate and corporate lending on the one hand and workouts on the other account form the majority of the workload. Interviewees are especially impressed with its niche expertise in retail lending on a national scale.

The Lawyers: Observers praise **David Berman** for his effective negotiating skills and strong business sense: *"He knows exactly where to press in order to guarantee deal completion."*

The Clients: Commercial banks, financial institutions and other major lenders feature on the client list.

Other Notable Practitioners

Stanley Ragalevsky (see p.974) of Kirkpatrick & Lockhart Nicholson Graham LLP enters the tables having proven himself an accomplished adviser of mutual institutions.

BANKRUPTCY

Massachusetts
Leading firms (Bankruptcy)

[1]	**GOODWIN PROCTER LLP** *Boston*
	MINTZ LEVIN COHN FERRIS GLOVSKY *Boston*
	WILMER CUTLER PICKERING HALE *Boston*
[2]	**CHOATE HALL & STEWART** *Boston*
	FOLEY HOAG LLP *Boston*
	GOULSTON & STORRS *Boston*
	HANIFY & KING *Boston*
	ROPES & GRAY LLP *Boston*
[3]	**BROWN RUDNICK BERLACK ISRAELS LLP** *Boston*
	COHN & WHITESELL LLP *Boston*
	DUANE MORRIS LLP *Boston*
	NIXON PEABODY LLP *Boston*

Firms are listed alphabetically in each band.

Band 1

Goodwin Procter LLP

See firm details p.980

The Firm: Sources are quick to highlight the breadth of experience available at the senior level in this practice, with *"true experts who can handle anything."* The practice was boosted by a new partner hire to the firm's New York operation, and is often seen on matters out of state. Clients point to the team's knowledge of international law as advantageous. A perceived reduction in visibility in the local market of late is by no means a reflection on its high-caliber individuals. Traditionally recommended for a strong debtor practice, the group also wins plaudits for its secured creditor work. Distressed M&A investing is another growing area of focus. Attorneys can draw on a wide range of resources available throughout the firm, in areas like corporate, private equity, ERISA and real estate securities. Clients are impressed by the uniformly practical approach and responsiveness of these attorneys: *"You don't feel like you're talking to a lawyer – they really understand the business we are in and how to advise us in context, which pays great dividends."*

The Lawyers: **Daniel Glosband** (see p.967) chairs a team that *"commands serious respect,"* report interviewees. He tends to act on the debtor side and is best known for his role as lead counsel in the Arthur D Little Chapter 11. He also recently acted in the successful reorganization of a major movie theater chain in the District of Delaware. Clients point to his *"cerebral approach"* and deep experience in the field: *"He has seen it all,"* they say. **Michael Pappone** (see p.973) maintains a broad practice, but has also recently been seen in debtor activity, most notably in the Bob's Stores Chapter 11. He is especially recommended for his thoughtful analysis and strategizing role: *"He will get a deep understanding of all the angles while not losing sight of a practical solution."* **Jon Schneider** (see p.976) focuses more on the money side of bankruptcy. He is typically involved in restructuring on the opposite side to the debtor, or in bringing money into troubled situations. This past year he spent a large portion of time representing a lender in a troubled condominium project. Clients find him to be *"an extremely good advocate in the courtroom."* He is also a member of the firm's leveraged finance group.

The Clients: Charlesbank Capital Partners; Bob's Stores; Arthur D Little and MHI Shipbuilding.

Mintz Levin Cohn Ferris Glovsky and Popeo PC

The Firm: There is little doubt that this firm has maintained the highest profile in the local market over the past year. It landed a number of major cases, most notably acting for the secured creditor in the International Place Chapter 11 proceeding. The practice is especially noted for its debtor work, acting for ACT, Malden Mills and Enivid (formerly Divine). It also has a national reputation in tax-exempt bonds, representing bondholders in major matters such as the United Airlines Chapter 11, and across the healthcare industry. Another focus is the growing area of insurance asbestos bankruptcies. A team of around 20 lawyers, including two in New York, can also draw on the firm's considerable litigation capacity. Clients emphasize the business sense of this *"client-savvy"* group: *"They are not so caught up in the minutiae as to lose sight of the commercial reality underpinning our needs."*

The Lawyers: Interviewees consistently recommended this superbly managed, deep team, which fields some very talented associates and has *"produced several superstars."* Clients value its responsiveness and the *"great organization"* that is in place there. *"Powerhouse"* **Rick Mikels** has built up the practice and is consistently commended for his negotiating skills. One source summed up his strengths: *"He has a winning personality that rises above the acrimony of the moment, the ability to stay focused on the deal and not get distracted by short-term thinking or petty disputes; a terrific deal-maker and strategist."* **Daniel Bleck** also has *"a real sense of the business dynamics that drive a deal,"* enthuse clients. He is actively involved in asbestos-related bankruptcy matters, acting for Liberty Mutual in a number of asbestos and mass tort Chapter 11 proceedings. His broad practice also increasingly encompasses the bond side. **William Kannel** is a new addition, following recommendations often for his work outside the state. His greatest asset is his perseverance say interviewees: *"He never gives up but will keep on plugging."* He handles almost exclusively bond work, and is best known for representing the bondholder in the United Airlines case.

The Clients: Other examples of recent work include acting for the bondholders in the following Chapter 11 proceedings: US Airways, National Benevolent Association of the Christian Church, and Alpha Housing and Health Care; as well as representing a major video game software developer in the Acclaim case; and acting for the officers in the Polaroid Chapter 11.

Wilmer Cutler Pickering Hale and Dorr LLP

See firm details p.986

The Firm: According to clients, the distinguishing feature of this *"top-notch"* practice is its consistent quality across the board, from the most senior figures down to the firm's younger players. One commentator remarked: *"No matter who you get, there is a uniform culture throughout the firm – calm, thoughtful and professional."* The recent merger widened the team's mandate,

Massachusetts
Leading individuals (Bankruptcy)

[1] COHN Daniel *Cohn & Whitesell*, Boston
GLOSBAND Daniel *Goodwin Procter*, Boston
MCCARTHY William *Ropes & Gray*, Boston
MIKELS Richard *Mintz Levin*, Boston
MURPHY Harold *Hanify & King*, Boston
POLEBAUM Mark *Wilmer Cutler*, Boston

[2] BENNETT Charles *Hanify & King*, Boston
DALEY Paul *Wilmer Cutler*, Boston
GLERUM Charles *Choate Hall*, Boston
MOORE Paul *Duane Morris*, Boston
SCHWARTZ Andrew *Foley Hoag*, Boston
SIGEL John *Wilmer Cutler*, Boston
SWAIM Hall *Wilmer Cutler*, Boston
WALLACK James *Goulston & Storrs*, Boston

[3] APPELBAUM Mitchel *Wilmer Cutler*, Boston
BALDIGA William *Brown Rudnick*, Boston
BERMAN Mark *Nixon Peabody*, Boston
BLECK Daniel *Mintz Levin*, Boston
DALE III Charles *Gadsby Hannah*, Boston
DOUGHERTY Charles *Foley & Lardner*, Boston
GOODING Douglas *Choate Hall*, Boston
KANNEL William *Mintz Levin*, Boston
LEONETTI Kenneth *Foley Hoag*, Boston
LEVINE Richard *Adler Pollock*, Boston
MONAGHAN John *Holland & Knight*, Boston
ROSNER Douglas *Goulston & Storrs*, Boston
SCHNEIDER Jon *Goodwin Procter*, Boston

Up-and-coming individuals
LYNCH Christine *Goulston & Storrs*, Boston
VENTOLA John *Choate Hall*, Boston

Individuals are listed alphabetically in each band.

further enhancing its cross-border insolvency capability and adding a New York base. While the firm itself is *"blessed with a wonderful corporate base,"* the bankruptcy and commercial group also attracts clients independently. It is particularly noted for debtor work and bondholder representation, which includes advising Boston-based mutual fund companies and New York hedge funds.

The Lawyers: Mark Polebaum (see p.974) is *"in his prime,"* agree interviewees. He stands out above all for his shrewd negotiating skills. *"Polebaum is great at achieving an outcome acceptable to all – he is the calm in the eye of the storm,"* say clients; although *"he is no shrinking violet either,"* confide peers. He acted as post-confirmation counsel to KB Toys in its Chapter 11 case, and continues to represent the bondholder committee of a Mexican satellite company. **Paul Daley** (see p.965) has a *"wealth of experience"* and *"brings good judgment and vision to a case."* Recent work includes acting on the winding down of Muro Pharmaceutical and representing the outside directors of the former Polaroid Corporation. *"Outstanding"* **John Sigel** (see p.977) is another attorney recommended for his ability to *"control diverse interests in a group set-*

ting." Clients also appreciate that he *"won't sugar-coat his advice."* Sigel works at the intersection of insolvency and commercial law, for example in the acquisition and sale of distressed companies. He recently completed a successful out-of-court restructuring. Respected senior figure **Hall Swaim** (see p.978) also maintains a broad practice and is especially noted for his representation of technology-based companies. *"Terrific"* **Mitch Applebaum** enters the tables in recognition of his *"increasingly important role"* within the team. He worked with Polebaum in the KB Toys matter and is gaining a reputation in significant bankruptcy cases.

The Clients: A broad range includes: Arch Wireless; KB Toys; PSINet; Kmart and Verizon.

Band 2

Choate Hall & Stewart

The Firm: Around 15 lawyers in the insolvency, creditors' rights and bankruptcy group handle a diverse range of work, and are said to offer *"outstanding client service."* The firm is renowned for representing secured creditors such as Citizens Bank and Bank of America as well as creditors' committees. Nationwide insurance-related work accounts for another significant portion of the workload. Peers and clients agree that the lawyers here are equally adept in negotiations (*"they bring a nice calming influence to what can be a fraught area of law"*); and in litigation (*"they are no-nonsense straight shooters when they have to be"*).

The Lawyers: Group chair **Charles Glerum** is widely respected for his deal-making ability and mediator role – *"he finds the middle ground between contentious parties and can drive through a deal that will satisfy all sides."* The team has a broad practice that tends to slant toward the fiduciary side. Glerum is increasingly called upon by the courts to act as examiner-trustee under the bankruptcy code, as in the Gitto/Global case. **Doug Gooding** led the creditor committee representation in the ACT Chapter 11, and is also heavily involved in the group's insurance-related work. Up-and-comer **John Ventola** enters the tables, recommended for his excellent writing skill and calm demeanor.

The Clients: Liberty Mutual Insurance; Citizens Bank; Computer Associates; Bank of America Business Capital; St Paul Travelers and State Street Bank.

Foley Hoag LLP

The Firm: It is deemed to have had its fair share of the market recently and is *"definitely in the mix."* Acting for the equity holders in the International Place bankruptcy was its highest profile engagement. *"Born and raised as litigators,"* the team of around ten attorneys prides itself on vigorous client representation. It handles a significant amount of creditor committee work, building on a fine reputation in the Organogen-

esis and Malden Mills cases, and currently represents creditors' committees in the RJ Development and Engage cases.

The Lawyers: Practice leader **Andrew Schwartz** is *"just a great lawyer in court,"* report interviewees. He is commended for his tenacious style and persuasiveness – *"you can tell the judges listen to him."* Meanwhile **Ken Leonetti** impresses in negotiations and *"has the ability to keep a client focused in the manner of a coach behind the scenes,"* say clients.

The Clients: The firm has also recently represented Benchmark Electronics on its purchase of the lion's share of ACT Manufacturing's assets, following Chapter 11.

Goulston & Storrs

The Firm: The team's renown extends beyond its traditional expertise in real estate-related bankruptcy matters. It has consolidated its position in the market through significant accomplishments on the debtor front, and in representing creditors' committees. A full-service firm, it acted as debtor's counsel in the High Voltage case, and advised the creditor committee in the Arthur D Little Chapter 11. Niche expertise in advising clients such as developers and investors looking to buy assets out of bankruptcy further defines the practice. The team is also recognized nationally for its work in major retail bankruptcy cases (representing landlords as well as liquidators) and works closely with the firm's commercial lawyers on lending and workout issues.

The Lawyers: Clients welcome the fact that these lawyers *"bring judgment and not just legal technical analysis to the deal table."* Department chair and *"dogged attorney"* **Jim Wallack** epitomizes this quality. He has an ability *"to digest and articulate clearly what people want, to understand the shades of gray and paint the subtleties so the client can make better decisions."* He is especially noted for his retail sector expertise. Wallack and **Doug Rosner** make a great combination according to interviewees. Rosner led on the Dehon matter. He fields experience in a myriad of bankruptcy and insolvency issues, for a range of clients. *"Smart and aggressive"* **Christine Lynch** is *"on the scene,"* agree sources. She recently made partner.

The Clients: Other significant matters include acting as debtor's counsel to Omni Facilities Services, pending in the Southern District of New York.

Hanify & King
See firm details p.981

The Firm: A specialist bankruptcy group within a compact firm, its promotion in the table reflects a robust market profile. The team of eight is *"getting a good deal of the work at the moment,"* concede peers, including representing the building owner in the International Place

www.ChambersandPartners.com

All quotes in the text are from interviews with clients and competitors.

935

bankruptcy. Acting as debtor's counsel in the Ground Round case is another highlight. Debtor representation forms a significant proportion of the workload, from Delaware to Massachusetts, from midmarket to the very large cases. Creditor committee representation is also a notable feature of the practice. These lawyers are widely respected in the community for their integrity, not to mention their ability *"to get even the messiest job done."*

The Lawyers: Firm head **Harold Murphy** (see p.973) is *"probably the best debtor's lawyer in the jurisdiction,"* agree sources. Known for being *"extremely resourceful and creative,"* he is an attorney who is *"not afraid to wade into the battle."* Interviewees were keen to ensure that the *"truly excellent"* **Charles Bennett** (see p.962) was not underrated or overshadowed by Murphy. He is distinguished from others through a unique combination of *"tough-as-nails"* litigation skill and knowledge of the bankruptcy field.

The Clients: Fort Hill Square Associates; Ground Round; Gitto/Global and Plassein International.

Ropes & Gray LLP
See firm details p.985

The Firm: This *"sophisticated, high-quality"* practice is Boston and New York based. It is often associated with work outside the state. A significant component involves servicing the firm's considerable private equity clientele, for example Bain Capital. The practice traditionally boasts a strong relationship with bondholder groups, acting for formal or informal committees in matters including Archibald Candy, Trump's Castle and York Funding. Representing the acquirers of assets out of bankruptcy proceedings is another focus area. Highlights include acting for a TJX affiliate in its acquisition of Bob's Stores in Delaware, and Genzyme in its acquisition of IMPATH in New York.

The Lawyers: *"Awesome advocate"* **William McCarthy** (see p.972) is arguably the dean of the bankruptcy Bar. Despite recently stepping down as chair, he is still the senior figure most associated with the practice and has recently represented the major investors in KB Toys and Ground Round.

The Clients: The firm also represents debtors, major institutional and trade creditors, and boards of directors.

Band 3

Brown Rudnick Berlack Israels LLP

The Firm: Its substantial team has the capacity to handle sizable cases. Around 30 lawyers operate from the firm's Boston, New York and Hartford bases, servicing a nationwide clientele. The

practice is largely focused on representing funds and other institutional and noninstitutional investors acquiring distressed companies. Recent work includes acting for the official equity committee in the Mirant case and the official creditor committee in the ATX case.

The Lawyers: **William Baldiga** is managing director of the firm's bankruptcy and finance group and is particularly noted for his creditors' rights work. He is leading the representation of the official creditor committee in the International Place proceeding. The lawyers here are especially recommended for an ability to think outside the box. *"They really do grasp the business side a bit better than others,"* remark clients.

The Clients: Areas of industry expertise include aviation, retail and gaming, as well as telecom, where attorneys acted for the buyer of Allegiance Telecom assets along the East Coast.

Cohn & Whitesell LLP

The Firm: Five attorneys at this specialist bankruptcy shop provide advice to troubled companies on the options available to them, including in Chapter 11 reorganization and out-of-court restructuring contexts. Observers pondered the effect of recent departures, but it was generally perceived the firm remains a player in the local market. Traditionally strong in debtor work, the group represents a broad range of clients involved with financially distressed companies including acquirers.

The Lawyers: *"Precocious talent"* **Daniel Cohn** is widely respected in the market. He continues to be viewed as a popular choice for debtors and a favorite referral point for larger firms in conflict situations.

The Clients: Recent work includes acting for the gas station and convenience store chain DB Companies in the sale of assets via Chapter 11.

Duane Morris LLP
See firm details p.1550

The Firm: A small team of three can call on considerable firm-wide resources at will. Around 50 attorneys in total advise on business reorganization and financial restructuring, divided between offices across the country from Delaware to San Diego. In Boston the focus slants toward the debtor side, in addition to work for secured lenders, creditors' committees and clients acquiring assets out of bankruptcy.

The Lawyers: **Paul Moore** (see p.973) is primarily a debtor's attorney, who *"combines encyclopedic knowledge of the law with a great deal of fortitude."* His litigation background also makes him *"difficult to tangle with,"* agree sources. The Med Diversified matter has continued to take up a considerable amount of his time recently.

The Clients: The firm acts for debtors, all types of interest holder, plan funders and trustees, across a broad range of industries.

Nixon Peabody LLP
See firm details p.1361

The Firm: The Boston office forms part of a national operation that *"provides clients with excellent resources throughout New England and beyond."* A seven-strong team often works together with attorneys across the firm's network of offices. Recent local-level highlights include representing franchisees in the Ground Round Chapter 11, including managing the acquisition of the franchiser's assets. Areas of emphasis include representing indenture trustees and creditors' committees.

The Lawyers: **Mark Berman** (see p.962) is *"particularly good at making sure the client understands what can be achieved."* He tends to focus on representing individual creditors in bankruptcy proceedings and recently achieved success acting for a large creditor and stockholder in the Divine Chapter 11. His practice also involves counseling parties in syndicated transactions including major hotel restructurings and financings.

The Clients: The firm acts for secured and private lenders, debtors, officers and directors, equity holders, landlords and purchasers, in workouts and bankruptcies. It has experience in industries such as manufacturing, real estate, retail and finance.

Other Notable Practitioners

Charles Dale, of Gadsby Hannah LLP, enters the tables in recognition of his increasing profile and of a practice said to be *"growing at a terrific rate."* At Foley & Lardner LLP (formerly Epstein Becker & Green) accomplished trial lawyer **Charles Dougherty** (see p.965) is described as *"an excellent strategist and imaginative thinker."* Interviewees believe his strong litigation background stands him in particularly good stead. Recent highlights include the representation of Tishman Speyer Properties in the International Place Chapter 11. **John Monaghan** (see p.972), of Holland & Knight LLP, also impresses with his *"imaginative counsel."* At Adler Pollock & Sheehan PC **Richard Levine** (see p.971) is another newcomer to the tables. A *"jack of all trades,"* he is rated for the combination of negotiating skill and ability in the courtroom – *"he can litigate better than many."*

CORPORATE/M&A

Massachusetts
Leading firms (Corporate/M&A)

1 GOODWIN PROCTER LLP *Boston*
   ROPES & GRAY LLP *Boston*
   WILMER CUTLER PICKERING HALE *Boston*

2 BINGHAM MCCUTCHEN LLP *Boston*
   FOLEY HOAG LLP *Boston*
   MCDERMOTT WILL & EMERY *Boston*
   MINTZ LEVIN COHN FERRIS GLOVSKY *Boston*
   SKADDEN, ARPS, SLATE, MEAGHER *Boston*
   WEIL, GOTSHAL & MANGES LLP *Boston*

3 CHOATE HALL & STEWART *Boston*
   PALMER & DODGE LLP *Boston*

Leading individuals (Corporate/M&A)

1 ASHER William *Choate Hall, Boston*
   BORDEN Mark *Wilmer Cutler, Boston*
   HIGGINS Keith *Ropes & Gray, Boston*
   SINGER Steven *Wilmer Cutler, Boston*

2 CABLE Stuart *Goodwin Procter, Boston*
   CHAPIN David *Ropes & Gray, Boston*
   ENGEL David *Bingham McCutchen, Boston*
   GOODMAN Louis *Skadden Arps, Boston*
   KELLER Stanley *Palmer & Dodge, Boston*
   MALT R Bradford *Ropes & Gray, Boston*
   MENNA Gilbert *Goodwin Procter, Boston*
   NUTT Robert *Ropes & Gray, Boston*
   PISA Regina *Goodwin Procter, Boston*
   REDLICK David *Wilmer Cutler, Boston*
   ROSENBLUM Peter *Foley Hoag, Boston*
   WESTRA James *Weil Gotshal, Boston*
   WIESEN Jeffrey *Mintz Levin, Boston*

3 BOTHWICK Jay *Wilmer Cutler, Boston*
   BRIGHAM Johan *Bingham McCutchen, Boston*
   BROWN Margaret *Skadden Arps, Boston*
   BROWNE Steven *Bingham McCutchen, Boston*
   COOGAN Peter *Foley Hoag, Boston*
   FELDMAN Roger *Fish & Richardson, Boston*
   JONES Barbara *Wilmer Cutler, Boston*
   KOLB William *Foley Hoag, Boston*
   RONDEAU Patrick *Wilmer Cutler, Boston*
   UTZSCHNEIDER John *Bingham McCutchen, Boston*
   WILLIAMS Samuel *Brown Rudnick, Boston*

Up-and-coming individuals
   BETTENCOURT Mark *Goodwin Procter, Boston*

Firms and individuals are listed alphabetically in each band.

Band 1

Goodwin Procter LLP
See firm details p.980

The Firm: This *"excellent, top-flight"* firm continues to be admired by competitors for its highly respected work in the corporate and M&A arena. The recent merger with New York IP boutique Fish & Neave has further raised the firm's reputation and provides the Boston-based attorneys with access to an even wider client base. *"Outstanding"* expertise in the financial services market is one of the defining strengths of this firm, and its attorneys are recognized for their success in developing a broad-based investment management practice. A national decline in the risk of leveraging real estate has resulted in prominent work for the firm's highly regarded REIT practice. For example, the team recently represented Beacon Properties in its $3.8 billion merger with Equity Office Properties and acted for Bay Apartment Communities in its $1.2 billion merger with Avalon Properties. The firm is also recommended for its work in the technology and life sciences sectors. Clients highlighted its *"collaborative nature"* and its *"creative"* use of multidisciplinary teams.

The Lawyers: *"Terrific M&A lawyer"* **Regina Pisa** (see p.974) is renowned for her work in the financial services industry where her regulatory knowledge, coupled with corporate and securities experience, is highly regarded. She is praised for balancing her management responsibilities with active work for clients, and impresses as a *"tough, sharp and entirely focused attorney."* *"Deal-doer"* **Gilbert Menna** (see p.972) has impressed clients on both sides of the negotiating table and is *"an extremely prominent player"* within the sphere of real estate capital markets. His national representation of REIT and REOC clients is widely admired. Securities and M&A specialist **Stuart Cable** (see p.964) is a *"talented attorney,"* whose recent work has included representing John Hancock and the management team in the acquisition of John Hancock Financial Services by Manulife Financial. Joining the team from the now disbanded Testa, Hurwitz & Thibeault, **Mark Bettencourt** (see p.963) is admired for *"keeping abreast of all the relevant issues."* Peers tipped him for future prominence within the corporate field, while clients appreciated his *"responsive yet non-alarmist personality"* and his ability to smoothly complete a deal.

The Clients: AvalonBay Communities; Beacon Capital Partners; Boston Properties; Citizens Bank; John Hancock Financial Services; AEW Capital Management and Inverness Medical Innovations.

Ropes & Gray LLP
See firm details p.985

The Firm: This *"preeminent"* firm is admired for its strength and depth in the M&A arena, particularly for its corporate finance expertise. The team fields *"premier practitioners"* in capital markets, mutual funds and financial services. It advises a range of clients including those listed in the Fortune 500 on securities compliance and corporate governance, including NASDAQ and Sarbanes-Oxley counseling work. The firm also boasts a developing investment management practice.

The Lawyers: *"Extremely professional and outstanding in all respects,"* **Keith Higgins** (see p.968) is a popular figure in the Massachusetts corporate market. Clients described his approach to the deal table as *"collegiate: he's a pleasure to work opposite and alongside."* **Bradford Malt** (see p.972) is renowned for his transactional expertise, which includes a preeminent reputation for private equity work. Sources credited him as central to the firm's growth in the corporate market, and he boasts an enviable client list, particularly work with major LBO funds. Senior corporate partner **Robert Nutt** (see p.973) is respected for his academic knowledge and technical understanding of the law. In addition to his expertise in corporate finance and debt restructuring, he frequently represents directors on corporate governance matters. According to clients, **David Chapin** (see p.964) is *"a very effective business counselor,"* alongside his work as a transactional lawyer. They admire his broad base of experience and appreciate his *"high-quality advice and effective judgment."*

The Clients: Bain Capital; Berkshire Partners; EMC; Merrill Lynch Private Equity Partners and Fenway Partners.

Wilmer Cutler Pickering Hale and Dorr LLP
See firm details p.986

The Firm: This recently merged firm excels in the corporate sphere where it is recommended as an *"exceptional, primary player"* that possesses a wealth of talented attorneys. According to clients, joining forces with Wilmer Cutler Pickering *"has only made Hale and Dorr stronger,"* enhancing their access to resources and skill sets. Peers also noted it as the *"firm of choice"* for corporate referrals, agreeing that its success is *"driven by the sheer quality of its lawyers."* The corporate team has a *"sophisticated ability"* to structure cross-border transactions and is commended as a significant player in the hi-tech and life sciences sectors. For example, during the past year it advised Norwood Abbey in connection with the complex cash acquisition from a subsidiary of Novartis of medical devices used for Epi-LASIK eye surgery.

The Lawyers: *"Superb"* **Mark Borden** (see p.963) possesses a *"commanding presence"* in the local market and is widely acclaimed for repeatedly *"getting a professional job done without any histrionics."* He is best known for his work in the technology sector. *"Exceptionally talented"* **Steven Singer** (see p.977) is *"one of the best biotech attorneys in the country,"* with strong business acumen and outstanding technical judgment. He has recently worked on a clutch of IPOs for pharmaceutical companies and has acted for high-profile biotech clients in two recent collaborations. Life sciences expert **David Redlick** (see p.975) *"provides practical business advice"* and is praised for his broad experience.

Clients appreciate that he is a senior attorney *"who gives his full attention to the level of detail."* With a primary focus upon M&A work in the technology sector, **Jay Bothwick** (see p.963) is a popular choice for referrals as he is *"sensible in his approach."* Clients referred to his excellent judgment and breadth of knowledge, appreciating his ability to understand the philosophy of their businesses. *"Tremendously talented and bright"* **Patrick Rondeau** (see p.975) *"knows how to get a good deal done."* He has recently represented Acopia Networks in a $25 million Series C preferred stock financing. *"Highly intelligent and accomplished in her field,"* **Barbara Jones** (see p.969) is the leader of the firm's PIPEs group, and is well versed in international M&A, securities and private equity transactions. She wins plaudits for being *"creative and thoughtful"* in her approach, and clients credit her with so much experience that *"she just seems to know what we are thinking!"*

The Clients: Adams, Harkness & Hill; America's Growth Capital; Legacy Partners Group; Needham & Co; BioSphere Medical; Transkaryotic Therapies; Millennium Pharmaceuticals; Sepracor and SkillSoft.

Band 2

Bingham McCutchen LLP

The Firm: Sources contend that this firm is *"a rising star in the market."* The 2002 merger that created Bingham McCutchen and its subsequent merger with boutique Riordan & McKenzie has *"catapulted"* the traditionally banking-focused firm onto the corporate scene and significantly expanded its national scope. The corporate group continues to develop its profile for working with entrepreneurial hi-tech and biotech clients, alongside work for high-profile private companies. It recently acted for Weston Presidio on its $550 million acquisition of Nebraska Book and advised Boston Scientific on its acquisition of Precision Vascular Systems. Clients praised the firm for its *"client-centered approach"* and sensible use of cross-departmental teams.

The Lawyers: *"Smart and fierce"* **David Engel** is respected for his energetic, hard-working style and his ability to employ an effectively *"aggressive"* stance when necessary in order to protect his client's interests. Clients find **Johan Brigham** to be *"incredibly practical and exceptionally responsive"* and commend him for *"genuinely understanding"* their businesses. He has recently advised Cytyc on its $320 million acquisition of private medical device manufacturer Novacept. *"Terrific M&A lawyer"* **John Utzschneider** is a leading figure in the corporate and securities markets. *"Thoughtful and practical"* in his work, he advised Tempur-Pedic International on its $330 million IPO. The firm's corporate team is expected to greatly benefit from the arrival of

Steven Browne, former head of the business practice group at Testa, Hurwitz & Thibeault. He is awarded *"high marks"* by clients for his ability to *"focus on the issue in hand,"* and for his communication skills and sense of humor.

The Clients: Boston Scientific; Heritage Partners; Cytyc and Raytheon.

Foley Hoag LLP

The Firm: Over three decades, this firm has developed a respected reputation among businesses in the technology sector. However, this corporate practice has proved itself to be attractive to a much broader client base; for example, it recently acted for CACI International in its $415 million acquisition of the Defense and Intelligence Group of American Management Systems. The corporate group has cultivated a cohesive team structure that can cater for a range of client needs, including business advice and counseling. Recent highlights have included advising First Essex Bancorp in its $400 million acquisition by Sovereign Bancorp and assisting Numeric Investors on its $240 million leveraged recapitalization.

The Lawyers: **Peter Rosenblum** possesses a *"low-key demeanor"* which acts as *"a secret weapon – it belies a sharp, thoughtful M&A lawyer,"* say sources. Clients appreciate his business counseling skills and his technical expertise, particularly on equity transactions. **Peter Coogan** acts on regular M&A counsel work for the firm's medical devices clients. He is also well known for his banking and corporate finance expertise. **William Kolb** is head of the M&A practice and specializes in the technology sector. He has recently represented hi-tech client CommercialWare on its transactional work.

The Clients: Numeric Investors; Charles River Associates; CACI; American Investors; Art Technology Group; First Essex Bank; CR Bard; YDI Wireless and Ascential Software.

McDermott Will & Emery
See firm details p.773

The Firm: This well-established firm is recommended by clients for its M&A expertise and, in particular, for its work on complex, national and cross-border acquisitions. The Boston office is praised for the *"high quality"* of its work and for its ability to draw on wider resources, particularly offices in Chicago and on the West Coast, when required. The corporate team has recently represented JCG in its $2.35 billion acquisition of the Eckerd drugstore operating companies from JC Penney Company. The team offers expertise in securities, private equity and corporate governance matters. These well-rounded attorneys are also able to offer strategic advice regarding the execution of clients' capital raising and corporate development plans.

The Lawyers: Dennis White heads the corporate department in the firm's Boston office. He

and the team are experienced in M&A, private placements, public offerings of equity and senior debt financings.

The Clients: A broad range of regional, US and international businesses, privately held and publicly traded corporations, venture capital-backed startups, emerging companies, financial institutions and investment banking firms make up the firm's client list.

Mintz Levin Cohn Ferris Glovsky and Popeo PC

The Firm: This firm offers a specialist focus that covers work for clients in the life sciences, biotech, information technology and hi-tech industries across the state. Clients within these sectors particularly value the collaboration between the firm's corporate and intellectual property lawyers. Recent work has included a range of activities in public and venture capital finance, including the strategic alliance between Alnylam Pharmaceuticals and Merck to develop RNA interference technology and products based on such technology. Attorneys have also advised on strategic alliances between Paratek Pharmaceuticals and Bayer to develop novel antibiotic tetracyclines. They also assisted Serono in the development of novel non-antibiotic tetracyclines.

The Lawyers: *"The real deal in the biotech field"* **Jeffrey Wiesen** has recently advised Archemix on its strategic alliance with Eyetech in order to develop novel aptamers for ophthalmic diseases. According to sources, he is a powerful practitioner who achieves *"the highest quality of work"* and inherently *"looks for real solutions to problems rather than more problems."*

The Clients: Biogen Idec; CuraGen; Archemix; Dynogen Pharmaceuticals; Hypnion; ARIAD Pharmaceuticals; Paratek Pharmaceuticals; Alnylam Pharmaceuticals and OXiGENE.

Skadden, Arps, Slate, Meagher & Flom LLP & Affiliates
See firm details p.1372

The Firm: This global heavyweight remains well respected by local clients for the work it undertakes within the region. In particular, clients described the Boston office as a credible alternative to using high-end New York lawyers and acclaimed the *"fantastic"* M&A expertise of these attorneys. Clients valued the firm's international network of offices whose resources are drawn upon as required, yet the firm maintains a cohesive, *"personal"* service. While the team's client base covers a range of industry sectors, it is particularly noted for its work in telecom and bioscience. Recent work has included regulatory compliance investigation, including matters relating to capital raising and Sarbanes-Oxley advice.

The Lawyers: Talented problem solver **Louis Goodman** (see p.967) was a popular choice for referrals who commended his deep levels of experience, especially for issues affecting public companies. Clients described **Margaret Brown** (see p.963) as a *"trusted adviser"* on general M&A and corporate finance matters. In recent years, she has developed expertise in the telecom and technology industry.

The Clients: Biogen Idec; SG Cowen Securities; EMC and Ascential Software.

Weil, Gotshal & Manges LLP
See firm details p.1378

The Firm: According to onlookers, this firm has made significant progress in the Massachusetts marketplace since its opening three years ago. This is primarily due to the fact that its practice has built up around the abilities of its individual attorneys, many of whom came from local firm Hutchins Wheeler & Dittmar in the initial merger back in 2002. As a result, clients speak highly of a local *"tailor-made"* service that operates with a national footprint and can draw upon its wider resources as required. The Boston office recently represented United Industries in its $70 million acquisition by global consumer products public company Rayovac. It also advised Thomas H Lee Partners in its $1.1 billion acquisition of Simmons Mattress.

The Lawyers: Whilst primarily renowned for his work in the private equity sphere, *"national practitioner"* **James Westra** (see p.979) is also praised for providing *"the highest quality of work across a corporate spectrum."*

The Clients: Thomas H Lee Partners; Vivendi Universal; Koch Industries; Pfizer; Highland Capital; MCI; Millennium Chemicals; Estée Lauder; Global Crossing and Reuters.

Band 3
Choate Hall & Stewart
The Firm: Observers agreed that this well-established firm *"has always been a strong proposition"* and continues to uphold its reputation for work on healthcare and pharmaceutical-related transactions. The 40-strong corporate team offers a comprehensive range of general legal services to clients across the state and beyond. Although sources claim that its *"strongest focus"* is upon the firm's private equity practice, the group also offers advice in the areas of M&A, securities, specialty finance, and business and technology.

The Lawyers: *"Dependable and technically excellent,"* **William Asher** is highly regarded for his *"pragmatic"* judgment and negotiation style. He has joined the team from the now dissolved Testa, Hurwitz & Thibeault. Sources described him as *"the most sensible lawyer I have ever dealt with."* Robert Jahrling chairs the M&A practice group. He maintains a technology-based client list of businesses in telecom, Internet infrastructure, e-health and software.

The Clients: Blue Dolphin Group; Conjoin; E5 Systems; Hammerhead Networks; Linden Technologies; Pegasystems; Platypus Technology; VenturCom and VistaCare.

Palmer & Dodge LLP
See firm details p.984

The Firm: This firm maintains its historical association with technology clients to whom it offers a range of advice including the development of founder arrangements, technology licensing, venture capital financings and IPOs. It serves a range of additional businesses on general counsel and transactional matters including publicly held and privately owned companies and nonprofit institutions.

The Lawyers: Stanley Keller (see p.969) continues to shine as the firm's leading light. Described by sources as *"intellectually skilled and exceptionally knowledgeable,"* he is highly acclaimed for his national work on corporate governance and securities issues. In particular, his position as chair of the ABA Securities Committee, which produced the ABA response to Sarbanes-Oxley, stands as testimony to his experience in this field.

The Clients: New York Stock Exchange and NASDAQ companies, growing hi-tech companies, public utilities, banks and other regulated organizations, leading educational institutions, and closely held businesses make up the firm's client base.

Other Notable Practitioners
Roger Feldman continues to develop the corporate arm of IP boutique Fish & Richardson, which was set up in 2002. He has maintained a loyal client base since his time at Bingham McCutchen and continues to focus upon M&A and securities law transactions, where he is admired for his practical approach. He has recently represented LeCroy on a follow-on public offering of common stock and in its subsequent cash acquisition of Computer Access Technology. *"Smart, practical and results-oriented,"* **Sam Williams** is managing director of the corporate department at Brown Rudnick Berlack Israels LLP and is recommended for his broad corporate experience. Alongside M&A transactions, his regular work includes the representation of issuers and underwriters in IPOs. He offers extensive experience in private placement transactions and a national practice, which provides a variety of work covering equity and securities. Sources describe him as *"always a pleasure to deal with."*

EMPLOYMENT

MAINLY DEFENDANT

Massachusetts
Leading firms
(Employment: Mainly Defendant)

1	**FOLEY HOAG LLP** *Boston*
	ROPES & GRAY LLP *Boston*
	SEYFARTH SHAW LLP *Boston*
2	**GOODWIN PROCTER LLP** *Boston*
	LITTLER MENDELSON PC *Boston*
	WILMER CUTLER PICKERING HALE *Boston*
3	**JACKSON LEWIS** *Boston*
	MINTZ LEVIN COHN FERRIS GLOVSKY *Boston*
	MORGAN, BROWN AND JOY LLP *Boston*

Firms are listed alphabetically in each band.

Band 1
Foley Hoag LLP
The Firm: This *"first-rate"* firm offers *"the corporate client's dream service,"* with its winning combination of breadth of expertise and partner accessibility. Features of the 20-strong labor and employment practice that win it praise include that it *"never overstaffs matters"* and that it produces a *"quality work product at a reasonable cost."* Clients were especially impressed by the pragmatism of team members and their responsiveness and client-oriented approach. The classic range of work is undertaken, with a particular emphasis on traditional labor law, and the team represents clients in bargaining negotiations and NLRB proceedings. Recent

litigation included a major wage and hour dispute and high-profile appellate court cases. Attorneys have also been actively involved in various ERISA litigations. The unit acts for clients across New England and nationally.

The Lawyers: *"Ethical and talented"* **Arthur Telegen** continues to be seen as the dominant force in this practice. Known for *"the oftentimes ferocious defense"* of his clients, he is also a lawyer who *"has the business sense to resolve issues rationally and efficiently, in a way that is most beneficial to the client."* He tends to handle more traditional labor work and counts large corporates such as Verizon and Anheuser-Busch among his clients. Recent work includes advising a multinational client on the labor law issues surrounding a subcontract between a company

Massachusetts

Leading individuals

(Employment: Mainly Defendant)

[1] ALFRED Richard *Seyfarth Shaw*, Boston
CASEY David *Littler Mendelson*, Boston
GORDON Robert *Ropes & Gray*, Boston
LUKEY Joan *Wilmer Cutler*, Boston
ROSS Nelson *Ropes & Gray*, Boston
TELEGEN Arthur *Foley Hoag*, Boston
WARD Richard *Ropes & Gray*, Boston

[2] AMBASH Joseph *Seyfarth Shaw*, Boston
BENOIT Wilfred *Goodwin Procter*, Boston
BURGER Sharon *Nutter McClennen*, Boston
DAMON Lisa *Seyfarth Shaw*, Boston
FORMAN Adam *Littler Mendelson*, Boston
JOY Robert *Morgan Brown*, Boston
KOFFEL William *Foley Hoag*, Boston
MALONE Judith *Palmer & Dodge*, Boston
NAGLE James *Goodwin Procter*, Boston
RIZZOTTI Anthony *Ropes & Gray*, Boston
WELSH John *Bello Black*, Boston

[3] BUCKING James *Foley Hoag*, Boston
COHEN Bret *Mintz Levin*, Boston
GAULT Robert *Mintz Levin*, Boston
HIRSCH Jeffrey *Robinson & Cole*, Boston
JACOBS Neil *Wilmer Cutler*, Boston
JOY William *Morgan Brown*, Boston
PERRY Christopher *Littler Mendelson*, Boston
PICKETT Andrew *Jackson Lewis*, Boston
SHEPHERD Jay *Shepherd Law Group*, Boston
SUNSHINE Ilene *Sullivan & Worcester*, Boston
WEINSTEIN Jerome *Sullivan Weinstein*, Boston

Up-and-coming individuals

GODDARD Jennifer *Goddard Law Office*, Needham

Individuals are listed alphabetically in each band.

regulated by the NLRA and a company regulated by the Railway Labor Act. A former trial attorney with the US Department of Labor, **William Koffel** also wins plaudits for his sound judgment and thoughtful approach. A notable area of his practice involves representing clients before the various state and federal agencies and courts in significant discrimination cases. **James Bucking** focuses on the traditional labor side, where his "*aggressive, yet practical manner*" serves clients particularly well.

The Clients: Clients span a range of industries and include: Verizon; General Dynamics; Anheuser-Busch; Polaroid; Genzyme; Intel; Bath Iron Works and National Energy. Healthcare, financial services, hospitality, transportation, education, manufacturing and the public sector are all fields in which attorneys are actively involved.

Ropes & Gray LLP

See firm details p.985

The Firm: Sources agree this "*fantastically polished group*" offers a breadth of expertise that is difficult to beat. Clients greatly appreciate its strength in ancillary areas such as pension plans and tax. The practice divides fairly evenly between general client counseling, conventional old-style labor work, and the range of employment-related litigation. An uptake in ERISA-related litigation and wage and hour class actions has further defined the workload of late. Representing clients in collective bargaining, particularly in the healthcare industry, is a key specialty of this group. One of the group's 15 lawyers is "*always available,*" say clients. As one interviewee explained: "*They manage to make us feel as though we are their only client – as big as the firm is, the level of service is superb.*"

The Lawyers: Hugely respected **Robert Gordon** (see p.967) is clearly a standout figure, first and foremost for his "*superb intellect.*" Clients also refer to his excellent knowledge, preparation and savvy approach to problem solving: "*He always keeps the client's goals in mind.*" Gordon is also "*not afraid to try a case,*" say peers. His practice comprises both counseling and litigation, usually on the nonunionized side. He recently defended a major client in an ERISA class action, potentially with billions of dollars at stake, concerning a cash-balance pension plan. Senior figure **Richard Ward** (see p.979) wins plaudits for his "*doggedness and really sound judgment.*" His practice focuses on employment litigation and labor arbitration. "*Tremendous negotiator*" and department chair **Nelson Ross** (see p.975) mostly concentrates on representing clients in collective bargaining. Recent highlights include successfully defending Reebok before the NLRB against an effort by the Teamsters Union to unionize employees at one of Reebok's distribution centers. Acting for clients in the healthcare industry is an area of emphasis for Ross, in accordance with a firm-wide focus on the sector. This is an area where he has recently been appointed special counsel on strategic labor relations on several occasions. Clients value the fact that he "*respects, and has an incredible understanding of, the other side.*" His "*real-world orientation of how to apply the law to a business problem*" came in for further praise. "*Superb*" **Tony Rizzotti** (see p.975) is "*the real deal.*" While benefiting from the influence of Ross, he is "*very strong and senior in his own right,*" say clients. His "*ability to convey the most complex information in a crisp way that clients will understand,*" attracted further plaudits. Rizzotti is also considered an attractive advocate in the most sensitive matters.

The Clients: Caritas Christi Health Care, Reebok and Partners HealthCare feature in a diverse client list that includes Fortune 500 companies across a range of industries. Educational and nonprofit entities are further sources of instructions.

Seyfarth Shaw LLP

See firm details p.777

The Firm: Clients expressed their satisfaction at working with lawyers who are easy to talk to and "*won't let raging egos get in the way.*" The combination of a national presence and expertise at the local level is considered a major boon for larger clients requiring a seamless service nationwide. Boston, one of the firm's ten office locations throughout America, fields about 20 attorneys, who were praised for "*terrific customer service.*" With labor and employment law among the firm's core practice areas, the workload comprises counseling and labor relations issues as well as a burgeoning employment litigation caseload. Recent successes include defending a major retailer in a first impression religious discrimination case. Attorneys have also achieved notable victories in wage and hour class actions relating to tipping in the hospitality industry. The firm's separate immigration group also came in for praise.

The Lawyers: "*Extremely high-quality*" **Richard Alfred** maintains a high profile in the market. Although primarily a litigator, he counsels clients on the range of employment law issues and has "*real breadth to his practice.*" Clients particularly value his responsiveness and consider him "*at the top when it comes to devotion.*" They also point to his "*wonderful mix of technical mastery and practical business sense.*" Recent work ranges from major noncompete cases to age discrimination lawsuits, with class actions involving wage and hour issues also featuring. **Lisa Damon**'s key strength is her practicality, say clients: "*She has a keen understanding of the importance of viewing matters from a business perspective and always provides a balanced judgment.*" Discrimination litigation and counseling are her main areas of focus, with an emphasis on retail and supermarket clients. "*Terrific*" **Joseph Ambash** concentrates on traditional labor work and the defense of discrimination and wrongful discharge claims. He is noted for a creative approach to problem solving, which makes him particularly suited to acting as a negotiator in collective bargaining agreements.

The Clients: Gillette; Motorola; Abbott Laboratories; Brown University; Accenture; Bain & Company; MKS Instruments; Boston Harbor Hotel; Lehman Brothers; Liberty Mutual; Staples; Stop & Shop; Cognex; Costco; Delta Air Lines; United Air Lines; UnitedHealth Group; University of Massachusetts; Whole Foods Market; Yale University; Deluxe Corporation; Greyhound Lines; Hilton Hotels; Legal Sea Foods; Marriott International; The Palm Restaurant; Robert Half International and The Wang Center for the Performing Arts.

Band 2

Goodwin Procter LLP

See firm details p.980

The Firm: As a leader in corporate and litigation arenas, the firm often acts for larger corporate clients when it comes to labor and employment law issues. Clients benefit from the spread of expertise available firm wide, with

ERISA and employee benefits attorneys receiving special mention. (Readers should refer to the separate Tax: Employee Benefits section for specific individuals.) Clients value the careful, thoughtful style of its lawyers. One commented: "*You don't feel as though you are reinventing the wheel with them.*" Areas of strength include whistle-blower litigation, affirmative action and OSHA issues, as well as matters involving the FMLA and FLSA. Recent successes include resolving several challenging discrimination and harassment suits. Attorneys have also seen an increase in noncompete litigation.

The Lawyers: Practice chair **James Nagle** (see p.973) "*understands all the nuances of what has become a highly technical field.*" Clients also refer to his "*confident air, which provides instant comfort.*" His broad practice encompasses traditional labor law, the range of employment litigation and a focus on issues arising from the dismissal of highly compensated executives. Nagle was recently involved in a breach of fiduciary duty case, and prevailed in a motion to dismiss a case under Sarbanes-Oxley. This last year his practice has seen an increase in whistle-blower claims. Clients praised **Bill Benoit** (see p.962) for his "*flexible approach and limitless capacity for adapting to rapidly changing situations.*" He was also credited with a sense of humor. Counseling clients on issues such as workforce restructuring and severance accounts for a large portion of Benoit's practice. Like his colleagues, he also handles employment disputes of all kinds, including recent noncompete disputes and a sexual orientation discrimination matter. He also tends to get involved on the traditional labor law side of the practice, and recently negotiated some collective bargaining agreements.

The Clients: Boston Scientific; Beacon Capital Partners; Hewlett-Packard; Fidelity Investments and Invensys.

Littler Mendelson PC

The Firm: This national labor and employment boutique is considered to have consolidated its position in the market, having "*put together a team of lawyers with impressive track records*" since the Boston office was formed just over a year ago. Now with about ten attorneys and growing, it is able to draw on the resources and specialist expertise of the firm's 400-lawyer national network. Examples of recent work include involvement in a nationwide wage and hour class action filed in California. The practice divides between employment litigation, discrimination, wrongful termination, noncompete and ERISA matters, counseling and all aspects of traditional labor law.

The Lawyers: David Casey is "*a shining star,*" agree sources. A respected trial lawyer, he impresses with "*a combination of intellect, wit and charm.*" One major client hinted at the breadth of Casey's practice, praising his flare for

presenting points of complex international law to the jury. Recent work includes a major reduction in force case and the successful defense of a client in a high-stakes contractual competition dispute involving a former in-house lawyer. The team has been boosted by the arrival of "*phenomenal resource*" **Adam Forman** from the now defunct Testa Hurwitz & Thibeault. He "*won't try and fit a square peg in a round hole,*" say clients, who clearly value his flexible thinking and business-minded advice. He recently defended a public company in noncompete litigation before a federal court in Manhattan, achieving a consent decree after a hearing of just one day. **Christopher Perry** provides counsel and litigates on a wide range of issues. He has recently been involved in some significant trade secret and noncompete litigation.

The Clients: Partners HealthCare; Aspen Technology; Casual Male; Cookson America; Family Dollar; Hewlett-Packard; Lowes; State Street Bank; Taco Bell; Viacom; Zurich North America; Abbott Laboratories; Allmerica Financial; WellCare; Bose Corporation; Buckingham Browne & Nichols School; Cisco; Compass Group; Cytyc Corporation; El Paso Energy; EMC; Emerson Hospital; Cybermark; Friendly's Ice Cream; General Mills; Hudson Highland Group; Infinity Pharmaceuticals and US Airways.

Wilmer Cutler Pickering Hale and Dorr LLP

See firm details p.497

The Firm: A Boston team of about ten attorneys works closely with lawyers in the firm's other US offices. With the international labor and employment group based in London, the firm has considerable capacity for serving clients globally. Its strength in areas such as corporate law, IP and litigation means it can provide a seamless overall service to a large clientele, using a wealth of experience across the board. Clients appreciate that its lawyers "*will not push you into litigation,*" but rather take a thoughtful, analytical approach to problem solving. The practice breaks down into training and counseling, litigation and, though not a major area of focus, some traditional labor law. It has seen an increase in whistle-blower claims since the Sarbanes-Oxley Act. It also offers cutting-edge performance management training. Recent work included a number of wage and hour class actions and numerous discrimination cases. The merger of Hale and Dorr with Wilmer Cutler Pickering added some executive compensation specialists from the Wilmer side. The Boston team also boasts immigration expertise.

The Lawyers: As an "*extremely experienced*" litigator who does not focus exclusively on employment, **Joan Lukey** (see p.971) is unique to the table. Many aspects of her general commercial litigation practice have an employment angle and she is one of the few lawyers who will

act for both sides in employment matters. High-stakes litigation, including the representation of senior management, accounts for most of Lukey's practice. A prominent face on the Boston legal scene, she is described as "*a confident, inspiring figure with a total command of the situation.*" Clients praised **Neil Jacobs** (see p.969) for his technical ability and "*superb judgment.*" They were impressed by his tendency "*not to run up the clock but instead focus on getting the outcome you want.*" He recently favorably resolved various wage and hour class actions and is noted for his work with the Boston Celtics.

The Clients: Clients include AstraZeneca, Red Hat and Thermo Electron.

Band 3

Jackson Lewis

The Firm: The "*terrific*" Boston branch of this national labor and employment boutique fields 18 lawyers. It is perceived to provide a value-for-money product to clients. There are 20 offices coast to coast offering the broadest range of services across the spectrum of labor and employment law. These include services in the specialty areas expected of a boutique practice and niche expertise in drug testing and substance abuse management. Interviewees point to a seasoned group of practitioners with the experience and good judgment to provide clients with practical solutions.

The Lawyers: A "*talented*" team includes Boston office managing partner and "*top-quality*" litigator **Andrew Pickett**. His practice encompasses areas such as reductions in force and trade secret disputes. He is also actively involved in alternative dispute resolution.

The Clients: Clients include a mix of public and private companies and nonprofit entities.

Mintz Levin Cohn Ferris Glovsky and Popeo PC

The Firm: This employment, labor and benefits group has been enhanced over the past year following a number of hires, not to mention increased capability in New York and Reston, Virginia. The workload runs the gamut of classic labor and employment law, with a litigation bent. The representation of clients setting up businesses in the USA from the UK and Europe, Israel and Canada is a distinctive feature of the practice. A team of 12 in Boston incorporates an integrated benefits group, and can draw on the expertise of the firm's immigration law department. Attorneys have continued to see a large number of noncompete and trade secrets cases and have succeeded in dismissing numerous matters before the Massachusetts Commission Against Discrimination.

The Lawyers: Clients value group chair **Robert Gault** for his "*exceedingly rigorous*" approach and ability to "*cut to the bottom line while ensuring that* the client understands the nuances of a situation and how it will affect their business." Coming from a litigation background, Gault maintains a broad practice spanning the range of classic labor and employment law. The practice of recent Pepe & Hazard recruit **Bret Cohen** comprises a mix of counseling and litigation. Recent successes include victory for a client at jury trial where the plaintiff demanded millions of dollars in unpaid commission. Cohen is a particular favorite with smaller clients, who value highly his empathy and ability to navigate them through unfamiliar territory "*without bulldozing the client into a decision they do not want to make.*"

The Clients: It is not unusual for the team to be advising the firm's corporate clients on the employment law implications of an M&A deal. Clients come from sectors such as hi-tech and biotech, financial and professional services, hospitality, manufacturing and education.

Morgan, Brown and Joy LLP

See firm details p.983

The Firm: This "*impressive*" 25-member boutique is well established in the Boston market, acting for a range of clients across New England and beyond. The operation offers a wide array of services that span the spectrum of labor and employment law. Clients rate these lawyers for their oral advocacy skill and "*extremely thorough*" preparation before the various courts and agencies. They also point to the quality of written work it produces. The group is particularly strong on issues of pure labor law.

The Lawyers: Although the departure of Jim Paulson was considered a blow to the firm, litigator **Robert Joy** remains a key figure who impresses whether counseling or litigating. **William Joy** is "*a real craftsman*" and is noted for his experience in labor management relations.

The Clients: GE; Harvard University; AT&T; AMICA Mutual Insurance; Bloomingdale's; Boston Scientific; Lucent Technologies; Oracle; Progress Software; Brandeis University; Duke Energy; Electronic Data Systems; Martha's Vineyard and Nantucket Steamship Authority; Enter-

gy; Federal Express; The Home Depot; Kraft Foods; Macy's; Delta Air Lines; New England Cable News; Sepracor; South Shore Hospital; Town of Wellesley and University of Vermont.

Other Notable Practitioners

At Nutter McClennen & Fish LLP, **Sharon Burger** is praised for her personable style and excellent work ethic. A partner in the firm's litigation department, she handles a mix of employment, general commercial and product liability litigation. Her broad experience includes defending management against discrimination claims, wrongful discharge, sexual harassment and retaliation allegations. **Judith Malone** (see p.971) is one of five labor and employment lawyers within the litigation group at Palmer & Dodge LLP and maintains a broad practice. She is "*extremely insightful,*" say clients, referring to her ability to "*defuse legal situations and come to a beneficial result for the client.*" Recent highlights include favorably settling a piece of noncompete litigation and defending the client in a wage and hour case of first impression argued in front of the US Supreme Court. Malone is also known for her schools and colleges practice and represents clients such as Boston College, Northeastern University and Williams College. **John Welsh** is now at boutique shop Bello, Black & Welsh LLP following the dissolution of Testa Hurwitz & Thibeault. He wins plaudits for his ability "*to provide answers straight away from the top of his head*" and to produce balanced assessments based on his knowledge and experience. His practice has traditionally covered a fair amount of counseling, litigation and labor law, often representing clients out of state. He has recently been involved in a number of successful labor contract negotiations, and acted for a telecom client in a mass layoff case before the NLRB. **Jay Shepherd** (see p.977) of the Shepherd Law Group, P.C. enters the table for the first time following strong recommendations for his expertise in the area of noncompete litigation. Described by one client as "*an absolute rock star,*" he is rated for a creative approach and excellent negotiating skills. At

Sullivan Weinstein & McQuay, **Jerome Weinstein** "*is just one of those guys you can't help respecting.*" He boasts expertise across the spectrum, having acted for a wide range of clients, whether unionized or nonunionized. Representative matters include collective bargaining, unfair labor practice cases, defense against discrimination and wrongful discharge, and involvement in labor arbitrations. At Sullivan & Worcester **Ilene Robinson Sunshine** "*just gives such wonderful, practical advice to her clients,*" a quality noted by peers and clients alike. As one client commented: "*She is able to step outside her ivory tower and put herself in her client's situation.*" Her practice includes significant discrimination litigation. Recent work has included a large disabilities discrimination case and litigation involving contract and tort claims. Clients emphasized that her strong litigation background provides a basis for solid and rapid guidance when it comes to counseling. "*Creative problem solver*" **Jeff Hirsch** (see p.968) cochairs the firm-wide labor, employment and benefits group at Robinson & Cole LLP. Clients find him "*incredibly responsive*" and particularly adept at handling what can often be sensitive issues. His practice has seen an increase in collective bargaining work. Hirsch recently served as chief union negotiator for a manufacturing company in Connecticut. **Jennifer Goddard**, formerly of Testa, Hurwitz & Thibeault, is rated for her business-minded approach and "*ability to talk the client through the various options in a refreshingly 'unlegal' way.*" She is currently solo practitioner at her newly established Goddard Law office in Needham, Massachusetts. Her broad practice encompasses counseling and litigation, acting for senior executives in employment negotiations and advising clients on affirmative action issues and government audits. Recent work has included defending a public company in a sexual harassment suit where the plaintiff is still employed by the company, and representing a company in two lawsuits, one in Pennsylvania, brought by a salesperson alleging unpaid commissions.

ENVIRONMENT

Band 1

Foley Hoag LLP

The Firm: "*For depth and caliber they are in a class of their own.*" There is no doubt among commentators that this substantial practice is one of the premier outfits in town. Sources talk of a cohesive team structure that ensures uniformly excellent quality from top to bottom (the associates here picked up high praise from clients). This "*formidable*" group undertakes the full range of matters, including brownfield redevelopment, contamination cleanup, Superfund

and environmental insurance coverage litigation. Distinguishing features are its work for public and redevelopment authorities and power plants. The team has experienced an increased caseload derived from the renewable energy sector, in addition to its waste-to-energy and conventional energy client base. Clients value the practicality and attention to detail delivered by attorneys, who "*never miss a trick,*" and have "*an unbelievable grasp of the facts of each case.*"

The Lawyers: "*Extremely experienced*" practitioner **Laurie Burt** is a widely respected figure in the industry. Credited with "*building up the prac-*

tice and allowing others to develop beneath her,*" she focuses on the cleanup of contaminated property, hazardous waste, Superfund law and matters involving the raft of environmental rules and regulations. Peers and clients describe her as "*a shrewd and tough negotiator, who simply knows the law and knows the people.*" Recent work has included use of innovative cleanups and public-private partnerships for highly contaminated sites. **Seth Jaffe** is "*effective on a variety of fronts.*" Considered by many to be a first-rate environmental litigator, he has also advised on auditing and compliance-related

connection with permitting approvals for expansion into the waterfront. A broad range of clients includes Verizon; National Energy & Gas Transmission; Newark Group; Allied Waste Industries; American Ref-Fuel; Cornell Dubilier Electronics; NiSource Corporate Services and the Institute of Contemporary Art.

Goodwin Procter LLP
See firm details p.980

The Firm: Sources identified this firm as a major force that "*has put energy and resources*" into its environmental practice and fields "*a group of excellent individuals.*" The group has a special focus on energy and power generation-related work, most notably in the nuclear power area. A large team works for major client Entergy Nuclear on the range of acquisitions, operational and litigation matters. Traditionally strong in the real estate arena, the firm is also home to a separate permitting and development group that works at the intersection of real estate and environment. Linked to this, an increasingly active part of the practice revolves around the environmental aspects of transactions, for example due diligence, compliance and insurance-related matters. Superfund, Chapter 21E and brownfield work are also found on the agenda. Market observers await the effect of the firm's recent merger with DC litigation boutique Shea & Gardner.

The Lawyers: "*Terrific*" **Christopher Davis** (see p.965) is the real star of the team. "*He has so much experience to draw on and operates at such a high level that he can answer any number of different questions,*" reported interviewees. A thoughtful lawyer, he is "*constructive and creative*" when pursuing his clients' interests. On the transactional side, Davis recently led the environmental due diligence for a large REIT that had purchased about 100 hotel sites across 20 states in a very short space of time. He is also advising Kerr-McGee Chemical on the investigation and cleanup of a former munitions manufacturing facility. "*Absolutely fantastic*" **Elise Zoli** (see p.979) is recognized for the efforts she has made in building up the firm's nuclear power practice and relations with Entergy Nuclear. At the crossover of environmental and energy law, her work ranges from acquisition and due diligence to environmental insurance coverage.

The Clients: Cabot; GE; Hewlett-Packard; Honeywell; Kraft; Mitsubishi; Newmont Mining; Prudential; UniFirst; Unisys and Watts Water Technologies.

Band 2

McDermott Will & Emery
See firm details p.773

The Firm: This firm occupies a unique position in the Boston market: although it does act for clients throughout the New England region, the team is most closely associated with the work it handles on a national, and international, scale. The integrated environmental practice group spans offices in Boston, New York, Washington DC, Los Angeles and Chicago. A broad practice includes environmental litigation, much of which is toxic tort, regulatory compliance, and due diligence-related activity. The "*smart, knowledgeable and practical*" team can also draw on the strength of a separate OSHA practice. In Boston, the focus is more on regulatory matters, where "*for the level of regulatory work they get, you would think they were in DC.*" This is a team that "*knows how to get you from A to B*" and "*will not leave you with a bad taste in your mouth on the other side,*" say observers.

The Lawyers: Susan Cooke (see p.964) heads the firm's national environmental practice group. She is considered one of the deans of the Boston environmental bar and "*a real generalist with an impressive resume for dealing with every kind of environmental problem.*" Well versed in regulatory issues, Cooke recently advised on due diligence matters for a Canadian client in the acquisition of a large drug store chain. "*Brilliant*" **Jeffrey Bates** (see p.962) has "*a wealth of experience*" and is the key figure associated with the firm's international environmental expertise. He maintains a broad practice, and is noted in particular for his insurance-related work. He has been actively involved in matters relating to the polychlorinated biphenyl contamination of the Fox River in Wisconsin. Sources rate his "*great judgment*" and "*practical way of thinking things through.*"

The Clients: The team represents a truly diverse set of clients, from individuals and small businesses, to US and foreign multinationals, governments and nongovernmental organizations.

Mintz Levin Cohn Ferris Glovsky and Popeo PC

The Firm: This "*superb*" firm fields an impressive stand-alone environmental practice. Clients endorsed its combination of specialist expertise and excellent connections with the state and federal decision makers. The team advises on regulatory and permitting issues and brownfield redevelopment. It also represents national chains in identifying sites for development and sale. Clients value the detail-oriented approach of these lawyers, who "*will analyze every nuance*" and "*convert their legal knowledge to provide real results for a real world.*" In litigation, they are considered tough operators who are "*always five steps ahead of the opponent.*"

The Lawyers: Ralph Child is widely respected for his regulatory expertise. As former general counsel to the Massachusetts Department of Environmental Protection, he is "*great at getting through to the right people.*" He represents international power generation company Mirant on the renewal of complex federal permits for cooling water discharges at its various plants. Clients value his responsiveness and "*ability to*

Massachusetts
Leading firms (Environment)

1 FOLEY HOAG LLP *Boston*
　GOODWIN PROCTER LLP *Boston*

2 MCDERMOTT WILL & EMERY *Boston*
　MINTZ LEVIN COHN FERRIS GLOVSKY *Boston*
　MOEHRKE, MACKIE & SHEA PC *Boston*
　WILMER CUTLER PICKERING HALE *Boston*

3 GOULSTON & STORRS *Boston*
　NUTTER, MCCLENNEN & FISH, LLP *Boston*

4 ANDERSON & KREIGER LLP *Cambridge*
　BERNSTEIN, CUSHNER & KIMMELL PC *Boston*
　BOWDITCH & DEWEY LLP *Worcester*
　BROWN RUDNICK BERLACK ISRAELS LLP *Boston*
　CHOATE HALL & STEWART *Boston*
　DLA PIPER RUDNICK GRAY CARY *Boston*

Leading individuals (Environment)

1 BATES Jeffrey *McDermott Will, Boston*
　BURT Laurie *Foley Hoag, Boston*
　CHILD Ralph *Mintz Levin, Boston*
　COOKE Susan *McDermott Will, Boston*
　DAVIS Christopher *Goodwin Procter, Boston*
　JAFFE Seth *Foley Hoag, Boston*

2 ABELSON Ned *Goulston & Storrs, Boston*
　GOODHEART Lisa *DLA Piper, Boston*
　KAHN Adam *Foley Hoag, Boston*
　KIRSCH Robert *Wilmer Cutler, Boston*
　LEON Michael *Nutter McClennen, Boston*
　LEONARD Stephen *Brown Rudnick, Boston*
　MACKIE Thomas *Moehrke Mackie, Boston*
　PORTER Jeffrey *Mintz Levin, Boston*
　RYAN Mary *Nutter McClennen, Boston*

3 ANGLEHART Donald *Gadsby Hannah, Boston*
　COX Robert *Bowditch & Dewey, Worcester*
　HACKNEY Hamilton *Choate Hall, Boston*
　KIMMELL Kenneth *Bernstein Cushner, Boston*
　KREIGER Arthur *Anderson & Kreiger, Cambridge*
　PENTZ Martin *Nutter McClennen, Boston*
　RIKLEEN Lauren *Bowditch & Dewey, Framingham*
　SANOFF Robert *Foley Hoag, Boston*
　SHEA John *Moehrke Mackie, Boston*
　ZOLI Elise *Goodwin Procter, Boston*

Firms and individuals are listed alphabetically in each band.

---

work. He is "*an aggressive but reasonable advocate, who knows how to step back and be objective.*" "*Worker bee*" **Adam Kahn** chairs the environmental group and maintains a diverse practice with a special emphasis on the siting, permitting and operation of energy facilities. Recent matters include handling the environmental aspects of the $1 billion plus sale of energy facilities for power generator client USGen New England. He is also involved in land use and development-related work. "*Thoughtful and sophisticated*" advocate **Robert Sanoff** enters the tables this year following strong recommendations in the area of defense litigation, in particular cases relating to insurance coverage and hazardous waste.

The Clients: On the development side, the group has recently represented two museums in

find win-win solutions." They also find that he works well as part of a broader team. Child was lead permitting counsel to the Maritimes and Northeast Pipeline Project, which crosses 19 towns and cities across the state. "*Practical and service-oriented*" **Jeffrey Porter** "*holds his own with the best of them*," according to clients. His practice encompasses brownfield sites and hazardous waste work, and the defense of contamination claims. Best known for his relationship with GE, Porter regularly advises this client on its aircraft engines and energy businesses. Clients find that "*he is very plugged in to what the regulators are up to*" and "*he knows when to push an issue and when not to.*"

The Clients: GE; CVS; Mirant; Cargill; Nestlé Waters North America; Maritimes and Northeast Pipeline Project and Allied Domecq.

Moehrke, Mackie & Shea, PC

The Firm: This respected boutique is best known for its niche in representing major players in the solid and hazardous waste manufacturing industries. The practice breaks down into the three main areas: litigation, transactional matters and issues of compliance. Attorneys are well equipped to advise on permitting and licensing at all regulatory levels, and the team fields special expertise in wetlands and waterways. Interviewees agree that this is the firm of choice "*if you need to get something done at the local level.*"

The Lawyers: **Thomas Mackie** stands out for his experience in permitting and facility acquisition for waste management clients. "*His strong knowledge of the law and local processes makes him a vital partner when seeking local approvals,*" sources say. Peers find him a tough adversary ("*he can withstand the knocks in litigation*") but also a balanced and versatile lawyer who will "*work things out creatively.*" He has recently conducted negotiations for a waste management client in matters relating to its expansion program, including liaising with a number of town boards. **John Shea** enters the tables following recommendations for his land use development and permitting practice. The highlight of his year has been successfully representing a major national real estate developer in the building of 200 luxury homes in Walpole. The project has involved complex permitting and litigation before multiple forums over a number of years. That Shea is "*an excellent attorney, well respected by the regulators*" is a major plus point for clients.

The Clients: The firm represents businesses and industries across Massachusetts, and occasionally on a regional basis. Solid, hazardous and other waste facility operators, manufacturers, property owners and developers are among the client base.

Wilmer Cutler Pickering Hale and Dorr LLP

See firm details p.497

The Firm: The stand-alone environmental practice belonging to this newly merged national firm is spread between the Boston and DC offices, with about six attorneys working out of Boston. Defending clients against government enforcement actions forms the bulk of the workload, making the team an obvious choice for substantial claims at state or federal level. The caseload includes assisting clients in high-stakes criminal litigation, where the environmental lawyers will typically work together with the firm's white-collar specialists. Attorneys recently settled one of the most significant environmental prosecutions in New England, following a three-year civil and criminal investigation concerning a multinational electronics manufacturer. On the transactional side, the team is busy obtaining permits for the development of facilities, ranging from an offshore wind power plant to work for a large solid waste company.

The Lawyers: "*Politically savvy*" department chair **Robert Kirsch** (see p.970) stands out as the key figure in the market. Recognized most for his work on the litigation and enforcement side, he typically defends clients against violation charges brought by the government and private parties. He also advises companies, in particular utilities, with issues relating to the permitting of new projects. Another facet to Kirsch's practice involves acting as common counsel in significant Superfund proceedings. He recently negotiated for a group of 28 companies on various issues arising at the Sutton Brook Superfund site. Clients value his "*level-headed, calm approach in negotiations*" and "*ability to come to a solution that is beneficial to both sides.*"

The Clients: National Grid; Lowe's Companies; BBA US Holdings; Casella Waste Systems and Textron Systems.

Band 3

Goulston & Storrs

The Firm: By virtue of its excellent reputation in the real estate arena, this firm naturally offers an attractive overall package to clients on a broad range of environmental issues. A substantial proportion of the mainly transactional workload involves contaminated property development, and the team is especially highly regarded for its brownfield practice, both locally and nationally. The environmental team does take on work that is stand-alone in nature, and has seen an increase in its insurance coverage work of late. Recent highlights include representing Boston Redevelopment Authority in the due diligence, cost recovery and litigation related to the Boston Convention and Exhibition Center project, and advising National Development Associates in ongoing environmental issues surrounding the former Industri-Plex federal Superfund site at Woburn, MA. Clients in particular point to an attentive and responsive team of lawyers.

The Lawyers: **Ned Abelson** won strong recommendations for his "*sophisticated*" practice. He is one of three partners in the firm's environmental group and is particularly well respected in the community for his brownfield redevelopment expertise. Clients clearly value his "*extensive level of knowledge and experience,*" while peers find that he "*keeps you on your toes on the other side.*"

The Clients: Nordblom Company; Brownfields Recovery; BJ's Wholesale Club; New England Patriots; SR Weiner & Associates; Avalon Bay Communities; Citizens Bank and Beacon Capital.

Nutter, McClennen & Fish, LLP

The Firm: An "*excellent*" practice group of about 12 attorneys handles the full range of environmental matters, with an emphasis on solid waste regulation, water and air pollution control, and land use matters. The land use practice benefits from the support of the firm's respected real estate group. The team also represents a number of oil companies in petroleum facility remediation work and acts for redevelopment authorities on brownfield projects. The environment attorneys are able to draw on the interdisciplinary strength available across the firm when advising clients.

The Lawyers: **Michael Leon** chairs the environmental practice group and is commended for a practical and business-oriented approach. According to interviewees, "*He doesn't get bogged down with the technical details.*" His practice is at the intersection of environmental and land use management, where he is regularly involved on the environmental permitting side of urban development projects. Superfund and solid and hazardous waste regulation are also active areas of focus. Leon recently negotiated a settlement with the EPA for a large company that had allegedly violated the Toxic Substances Control Act. "*Zealous advocate*" **Mary Ryan** has "*seen it all and done it all,*" say peers. She has recently been acting for Tritown Development in efforts to obtain transfers of property from the US Navy. Litigator **Martin Pentz** enters the tables following numerous recommendations for his environmental insurance coverage practice. He is described as "*very precise and focused on the details*" and has also been involved in hazardous waste cleanup matters.

The Clients: The team continues to represent a real mix of public and private clients, predominantly based in the New England region. They range from municipalities and nonprofit institutions to manufacturers and national and international conglomerates.

Band 4

Anderson & Kreiger LLP

The Firm: This well-respected Cambridge-based boutique specializes in environmental, land use and municipal law. A team of four partners has

944

All quotes in the text are from interviews with clients and competitors.

CHAMBERS USA 2005

secured a reputation for its litigation skills and is described as "*a preeminent force*" on the plaintiff side. It represents citizen groups, conservation commissions and municipalities, in addition to landowner and developer clients. Recent matters include hazardous waste and oil contamination, insurance review and cases relating to clean water and wetlands. The team has developed specialist expertise in the contamination issues surrounding manufactured gas plants.

The Lawyers: "*Knowledgeable and experienced*" **Arthur Kreiger** is particularly endorsed for his work representing citizen groups on zoning issues, although he maintains a broad environmental and land use practice.

The Clients: The City of Cambridge and the towns of Acton, Wrentham, Norfolk, Belmont and Wakefield feature on the client list. The firm also acts for a number of oil companies.

Bernstein, Cushner & Kimmell PC

The Firm: This growing practice enters the tables for the first time following a number of strong recommendations, in particular for its work with citizen groups. This compact team handles a mix of corporate, regulatory and litigation matters. Work ranges from permitting, regulatory compliance and risk counseling to representation in judicial and administrative proceedings such as wetlands appeals. Brownfield development is a particular area of focus, and clients especially benefit from the deep public sector experience of a number of the attorneys in this team. Examples of recent cases include advising the Pittsfield Economic Development Authority in a brownfield redevelopment plan, following polychlorinated biphenyl contamination of industrial property in the City of Pittsfield.

The Lawyers: Interviewees picked highlighted senior lawyer **Kenneth Kimmell** for his effectiveness at representing citizens. His practice also extends to real estate and commercial litigation. He is commended for his "*excellent preparation*" and his ability to perform well in a courtroom.

The Clients: The firm acts for businesses, landowner/developers, towns and cities, state governments, environmental groups and other nonprofit organizations.

Bowditch & Dewey LLP

The Firm: Sources agree that clients looking for representation in the center of the state should consider this respected firm. A new Boston base complements the firm's existing offices in Framingham and Worcester, with five partners concentrating exclusively on environmental matters. One of the strengths of the practice is the representation of nonprofit clients such as educational establishments and hospitals, in addition to its ability to serve a corporate client base. The group is well versed in environmental litigation, permitting, compliance and government enforcement. Attorneys are currently

working with several Massachusetts hospitals in relation to internal compliance development and assisting a number of municipalities on environmental enforcement issues. The team offers additional strength in brownfield matters and in mediation.

The Lawyers: **Robert Cox** is "*a class act*," enthused clients, impressed with his knowledge base, communication skills and "*ability to cut right to the heart of the matter*." He maintains a broad-based practice and is especially noted for representing clients in Chapter 21E private party litigation. **Lauren Stiller Rikleen** "*has worked in pretty much every context*," say peers. She focuses on negotiation, compliance and enforcement issues, and currently serves as mediator in environmental and land use issues.

The Clients: Harvard University; Boston College; Boston University and Children's Hospital and Wyman-Gordon.

Brown Rudnick Berlack Israels LLP

The Firm: The environmental practice is closely associated with the firm's corporate and real estate departments, providing advice to clients on the environmental aspects of acquisitions and development projects. These typically involve due diligence, liability issues and land use permitting. However, the small team does take on work on a stand-alone basis, and has particular expertise in representing energy companies. Attorneys successfully negotiated on behalf of client Millennium Power Partners to secure additional emissions credits worth up to $1 million, allocated by the Massachusetts DEP. The team is also experienced in representing clients before the regulatory agencies on enforcement matters and in environmental litigation.

The Lawyers: **Stephen Leonard** is the team's standout figure. His previous government experience adds an extra dimension to his practice: "*He is in touch with what's going on politically, as well as legally*," remarked clients. He continues to act for LNR in the acquisition of the South Weymouth Naval Air Station from the US government, and is also defending Massachusetts Bay Transportation Authority against allegations that the construction of a subway station entrance with disabled access is obscuring the view of a historic church.

The Clients: The firm represents a mix of clients, including developers, state agencies, manufacturers, municipalities and individuals.

Choate Hall & Stewart

The Firm: The environmental practice at this traditional Massachusetts firm is recognized for its increasing visibility in the market. A team of eight attorneys handles a wide range of matters at the intersection of land use and environmental law at state and federal levels. These include hazardous and solid waste, asbestos abatement, air and waste water emissions, and toxic chemicals.

The Lawyers: Sources endorsed **Hamilton Hackney** for his "*ability to get to the substance of the matter and offer practical solutions*." He cochairs the firm's environmental and land use group and handles a mix of administrative, transactional and litigation matters. He is especially noted for his work in the toxic tort and hazardous waste areas, and regularly acts for clients acquiring and selling brownfield designated sites.

The Clients: Massachusetts Turnpike Authority; Harvard University; Cape Cod Commission; Museum of Fine Arts; Amtrak; Bayer; Martha's Vineyard Commission and Agfa.

DLA Piper Rudnick Gray Cary

See firm details p.765

The Firm: While the Washington DC office forms the hub of the firm's environmental operation, the small team in Boston wins acclaim from clients for its ability to work seamlessly with lawyers in the firm's real estate, energy and litigation departments. Attorneys represent real estate and energy clients in mediation and in the full range of environmental disputes before the courts and administrative agencies. Particular areas of specialty are private cost recovery litigation and permit appeals, an area closely linked to the firm's notable strength in the land use area. For example, attorneys are currently handling the waterways permit appeal for the North Point project. The firm acts for commercial real estate developers, municipal facility operators and major utilities clients in Boston and across New England. Environmental insurance work forms the backbone of the practice, and the team also advises clients in connection with ongoing contamination cleanup matters.

The Lawyers: **Lisa Goodheart** (see p.967) is considered a "*star*" in the area of environmental and land use litigation. Peers describe her as "*tough as nails, but extremely fair*," while clients find her to be "*the antithesis of the arrogant litigator*." She is currently defending a number of clients in Chapter 21E response cost recovery claims, and continues to act for a municipal waste water commission concerning challenges to operating permits. Gregory Bialecki is another key member of the team, and is recommended in the separate land use section in the real estate chapter.

The Clients: Channel Fish; Congress Group; Edgartown Wastewater Commission; Hobbs Brook Management; Lyme Properties and New England Fertilizer Company.

Other Notable Practitioners

At Gadsby Hannah LLP, **Donald Anglehart** is considered "*a real force*." He is particularly experienced at defending clients in enforcement and permitting actions involving the EPA and Massachusetts DEP, in addition to private party litigation.

HEALTHCARE

Massachusetts
Leading firms (Healthcare)

[1] MCDERMOTT WILL & EMERY *Boston*
ROPES & GRAY LLP *Boston*

[2] BROWN RUDNICK BERLACK ISRAELS LLP *Boston*
CHOATE HALL & STEWART *Boston*
MINTZ LEVIN COHN FERRIS GLOVSKY *Boston*

Leading individuals (Healthcare)

[1] GARVIN Michele *Ropes & Gray, Boston*
HEIDT Jeffrey *Ropes & Gray, Boston*
JEDREY Christopher *McDermott Will, Boston*
ROBLE Daniel *Ropes & Gray, Boston*
WEINER Stephen *Mintz Levin, Boston*

[2] BERNSTEIN Stephen *McDermott Will, Boston*
BLAU Michael *McDermott Will, Boston*
BRAUN Peter *McDermott Will, Boston*
KNOWLTON William *Ropes & Gray, Boston*
LITWAK Lawrence *Brown Rudnick, Boston*
OGILBY Anne *Ropes & Gray, Boston*
SOLT Christine *Choate Hall, Boston*

Firms and individuals are listed alphabetically in each band.

Band 1

McDermott Will & Emery

See firm details p.773

The Firm: As one of America's best-established industry advisers, the firm offers clients over 50 years of experience in healthcare policy and legislation. The Boston team provides regulatory and transactional advice to leading healthcare organizations. Its attorneys are also skilled in providing cutting-edge advice in areas such as image technology and the use of health information for research processes. With additional offices in Chicago, Los Angeles, Miami, New York City, and Washington DC, clients appreciate the team's *"local knowledge,"* coupled with its judicious use of national and international resources. Its work on the interface between academia and industry is considered unique. The team actively advises clients in research contexts, including those engaged in European drug development and related clinical trials. The group is further lauded for its broad client base. Niche areas include assisting with the amalgamation of teaching hospitals and medical schools as well as advising physician groups.
The Lawyers: *"Cream of the crop,"* **Chris Jedrey** (see p.969) is highly regarded for his traditional healthcare practice in the nonprofit sector. Rated for his versatility, *"breadth of knowledge"* and listening skills, market sources have *"tremendous respect"* for Jedrey's *"incredible integrity."* Dubbed a *"godsend"* by clients who appreciate his down-to-earth nature, he is further recommended for his outstanding tax expertise. Recent work has included a tax reorganization plan for Blue Cross and Blue Shield. Jedrey also

advised St Peters Hospital on the termination of its relationship with Robert Wood Johnson medical school. According to onlookers, the *"piercingly sharp"* **Stephen Bernstein** (see p.963) is *"superb to work with"* on both local and national matters. According to sources, his application of healthcare law is informed by a *"deep understanding"* of the industry. He is praised for his adaptable advisory style, deemed to make Bernstein equally at home whether dealing with government regulators, insurers or clients. Recommended for his work with physician groups, **Michael Blau** (see p.963) enjoys a strong reputation in the Massachusetts healthcare market. Onlookers rated his willingness to *"roll his sleeves up and fight in the dirt"* for the benefit of his clients' interests. *"Excellent"* practitioner **Peter Braun** (see p.963) is renowned for his experience with insurers and managed care organizations. He is also rated for his work with community hospitals.
The Clients: Genentech; IMS Health; Harvard University; Physician's Organization at Children's Hospital of Boston; Massachusetts Eye & Ear Infirmary; Caritas Medical Group; Dana-Farber/Partners Cancer Care; HealthOne Care System; St Peter's University Hospital and ChartOne.

Ropes & Gray LLP

See firm details p.985

The Firm: This *"outstanding"* Massachusetts firm is one of the state's original healthcare players and has served regional clients for over twenty years. A popular choice in Boston, long-term relationships with Children's Hospital and NYU Hospitals Center have placed them on the national map. Since working on the formation of the first HMO in New England, the firm has built up a formidable reputation for advising on managed care plans and provider networks. It offers acquisition and regulatory advice to hospitals and physician practices, alongside expertise in bond financing, disaffiliations and joint ventures. The *"terrific"* healthcare team also advises on a range of non-profit entities. Its workload in this field amounts to one of the largest exempt organization tax practices in the USA. Clients include academic medical centers and troubled institutions. The firm also offers a well-regarded Health Insurance Portability and Accountability Act (HIPAA) compliance service. Sources praise its diverse range of expertise, describing its attorneys as *"exceptionally well seasoned."* The department's experience of representing institutions on a national scale is perceived as *"a huge advantage."*
The Lawyers: *"Smart and pragmatic,"* chair of the healthcare group **Michele Garvin** (see p.967) excels in healthcare sector governance and compliance issues. Having *"grown up"* in the managed care sector, she is highly recom-

mended for advising physician groups and for her healthcare regulation expertise at both state and federal level. Clients praise Garvin's *"fabulous business sense, remarkable negotiation style and tremendous ability to distill a lot of rhetoric"* in order to get to the legal issues at the heart of a matter quickly. *"Extraordinarily smart"* **Jeffrey Heidt** (see p.968) is counted as *"one of the original members of the Massachusetts healthcare Bar"* and his recent arrival from Choate Hall & Stewart is expected to bolster this team further. Recommended primarily as a reimbursement specialist, he is also admired for his wealth of experience and as an indispensable resource. Clients value his *"creative"* advice and *"impeccable reputation for integrity."* *"Healthcare giant"* **Daniel Roble** (see p.975) is lauded by sources as *"one of America's most prominent attorneys in the field."* His *"first-class"* practice specializes on the nonprofit sector, where he *"combines cutting-edge experience of policy issues with an awareness of the bigger picture."* *"Bright, thoughtful"* attorney **William Knowlton** (see p.970) is admired for his work with state medical centers and physician groups. With a regulatory focus, clients value his experience as a corporate lawyer well attuned to healthcare. Sources deemed his *"strong background"* in nonprofit tax law particularly beneficial. *"Terrific"* **Anne Ogilby** (see p.973) is highly recommended for her public financing expertise, particularly hospital bond work. Rated by one client as *"the brightest attorney I've ever come across,"* sources also have *"huge respect"* for her advocacy skills – *"she knows which points are worth fighting over."*
The Clients: Academic medical centers; community hospitals; pharmaceutical companies and pharmacy benefit managers; managed care organizations; insurance companies; healthcare provider organizations; physician practice groups; healthcare technology and biomedical companies and long-term care and skilled nursing home providers.

Band 2

Brown Rudnick Berlack Israels LLP

The Firm: This healthcare team was billed as a *"well-rounded"* practice that offers a range of expertise and a multidisciplined approach to clients' needs. With offices in Boston, Providence and Hartford, the team has a strong regional presence and is credited with the formation of some of New England's largest physician practices and networks. Specialties include M&A, affiliations and joint ventures for private medical institutions, public healthcare entities and tax-exempt organizations. The team also advises on compliance, particularly in relation to HIPAA privacy and medical records requirements. Praised for its client focus, sources particularly value the group's *"refreshingly prompt response times."*

The Lawyers: *"Steady and tenacious,"* **Lawrence Litwak** was credited with *"a wealth of valuable experience"* in the healthcare arena, reported sources. With extensive industry experience, he is noted for completing a *"ton of deals"* on behalf of clients including medical centers, hospitals and physician groups.

The Clients: Community and academic hospitals; clinics and community health centers; home health providers; physician group practices; long-term care and assisted living facilities; medical billing companies; ambulance companies and integrated healthcare networks and systems.

Choate Hall & Stewart

The Firm: This *"terrific firm"* is a long-term player in the local market that boasts *"exceptional alumni"* in the healthcare arena. The core healthcare team can draw on flexible, cross-departmental resources as required. It is known for its long history of working with community hospitals across Massachusetts. It also advises provider hospitals outside the state and is recommended for its advice on tax matters, alongside medicare and payment issues. The *"committed"* team also offers a range of corporate and general governance advice to institutional clients. Sources recommended the firm's *"unique"* ability to handle novel patient situations, providing *"rapid advice on request at any time of day."*

The Lawyers: *"Smart and focused,"* **Christine Solt** balances a healthcare practice with white-collar crime advice. Noted for her ability with mental health privacy information, she focuses upon government enforcement matters and has recently advised on human research issues, including clinical trials. Clients appreciate her *"reliability and responsiveness,"* not to mention *"raw intelligence"* and technical ability.

The Clients: Saints Memorial Medical Center; Martha's Vineyard Hospital; Tufts Associated Health Plans; Cambridge Health Alliance; Holy Family Hospital and Medical Center; Baystate Health Systems; Cape Cod Healthcare; Health Dialog; Harvard University and Massachusetts General Hospital.

Mintz Levin Cohn Ferris Glovsky and Popeo PC

The Firm: *"One of the authentic healthcare powerhouses"* in Massachusetts was the verdict returned by interviews. The firm was among the first in the region to *"embrace healthcare"* as a dedicated practice area. As a result of its *"many long-term relationships"* with hospital systems, managed care organizations and long-term care providers, the firm has developed a national presence. Additional clients include physician groups and military hospitals. Involvement in M&A, strategic partnerships, joint ventures and affiliation arrangements also contributes to the workload. Expertise in statutory advice, with several healthcare attorneys who have previously served state and federal regulatory bodies, is another draw for clients.

The Lawyers: *"Capable and well-connected,"* **Stephen Weiner** is admired for the diversity of clients he represents. Recommended as a *"highly effective"* attorney in the representation of large healthcare organizations, he frequently advises on hospital structuring and restructuring work.

The Clients: Brigham and Women's/Faulkner Hospitals; Massachusetts General Hospital; North Shore Medical Center; Newton Wellesley Hospital; McLean Hospital; Spaulding Rehabilitation Hospital; Dana-Farber/Partners CancerCare and Partners Community HealthCare.

INTELLECTUAL PROPERTY

Massachusetts
Leading firms (Intellectual Property)

1	WILMER CUTLER PICKERING HALE *Boston*
2	FISH & RICHARDSON *Boston*
	FOLEY HOAG LLP *Boston*
	GOODWIN PROCTER LLP *Boston*
3	CHOATE HALL & STEWART *Boston*
	PROSKAUER ROSE LLP *Boston*

Firms are listed alphabetically in each band.

Band 1

Wilmer Cutler Pickering Hale and Dorr LLP

See firm details p.497

The Firm: This *"top-notch"* general practice firm wins plaudits for having grown *"head and shoulders"* above IP boutiques in the region. Praised for its *"high-caliber"* work, Hale and Dorr has, through its merger with Wilmer Cutler Pickering, succeeded in *"enhancing its client base"* and dispelling any doubt that it is *"a truly national firm."* Indeed, a significant portion of its work now takes place outside New England as the IP team advises a number of Fortune 500 companies and European clients. With *"a solid cast of attorneys at all levels,"* the group is commended for its *"extraordinary bench strength,"* not to mention knowledge and experience. It remains *"eagerly sought after"* in the pharmaceutical sector, where it assists a significant number of start-up companies alongside established public companies. *"Thoughtful"* attorneys are praised for their detail orientation, *"leaving no stone unturned"* on a range of work including patent prosecution, litigation and licensing, trademarks and client counseling. In particular, the department's litigation specialists stand out, not least *"because they win"* say clients. The team has recently represented EMC in a two-week jury trial against Hewlett-Packard where all three asserted patents were found infringed and valid. Clients refer to a significant degree of *"added value simply by mentioning the firm's name"* in a patent licensing context. Market onlookers claimed the group's levels of client support to be *"just unparalleled"* both within the state and beyond.

The Lawyers: *"Unflappable superstar"* **William Lee** (see p.962) is hailed by clients as *"the best IP trial lawyer in the business"* with an *"outstanding track record"* in district court litigation. *"Incredibly bright and perceptive,"* he is praised by sources for his strategic use of *"winning arguments"* and his *"wonderful manner."* Lee is credited with taking his firm *"to new heights"* and is particularly admired by pharmaceutical clients for his successful *"integration of science and law."* According to market sources, his *"unequalled"* ability to understand technology at *"a very, very high level"* marries well with his efficiency at explaining it *"in crystal-clear terms"* to an audience. *"Articulate and proactive,"* not to mention boasting international IP experience, **Peter Dichiara** (see p.965) focuses on electrical engineering technologies, computer technologies and nanotechnology. Viewed by clients as *"a natural extension to our team,"* he is adept at *"seeing both the big picture and the small details."* Clients particularly value his background in engineering. He was described by one source as *"the smartest technology lawyer I have ever seen."* *"Remarkably efficient,"* **David Bassett** (see p.962) is commended for his *"excellent attention to detail."* Clients admired his poise in the courtroom, where he demonstrates a style that is *"firm but not combative."* He is especially admired for his *"thorough"* and *"insightful"* patent infringement work for the biotech industry. *"Big-picture thinker"* **Wayne Kennard** (see p.970) is recommended for his *"brilliant, creative mind"* and *"ton of experience."* Though he is renowned for a *"strategic"* focus on patent prosecution, clients also appreciate his ability to *"understand our litigation needs"* and note the *"breadth, depth and speed"* of his work. *"Excellent"* attorney **James Lampert** (see p.962) is praised for his *"unparalleled depth"* of knowledge and experience within the licensing field.

Massachusetts
Leading individuals
(Intellectual Property)

★ LEE William *Wilmer Cutler*, Boston

1 BAUER Steven *Proskauer Rose*, Boston
FRANK Robert *Choate Hall*, Boston
HILLMAN Robert *Fish & Richardson*, Boston
PORCELLI Frank *Fish & Richardson*, Boston
WARE Donald *Foley Hoag*, Boston

2 ARNOLD Beth *Foley Hoag*, Boston
BASSETT David *Wilmer Cutler*, Boston
DICHIARA Peter *Wilmer Cutler*, Boston
DOWNS J Anthony *Goodwin Procter*, Boston
HENNESSEY Gilbert *Fish & Richardson*, Boston
KLINE Douglas *Goodwin Procter*, Boston
PASTERNACK Sam *Choate Hall*, Boston
WARE Paul *Goodwin Procter*, Boston

3 CAPRARO Joseph *Proskauer Rose*, Boston
CHARKOUDIAN Stephen *Goodwin Procter*, Boston
ENGLANDER John *Goodwin Procter*, Boston
FRANK Steven *Goodwin Procter*, Boston
JARRELL Brenda *Choate Hall*, Boston
KENNARD Wayne *Wilmer Cutler*, Boston
LAMPERT James *Wilmer Cutler*, Boston
LAPORTE Claire *Foley Hoag*, Boston
REMIS Shepard *Goodwin Procter*, Boston
SCHERKENBACH Frank *Fish & Richardson*, Boston
SELWYN Mark *Wilmer Cutler*, Boston
STEINBERG Donald *Wilmer Cutler*, Boston
STONER Wayne *Wilmer Cutler*, Boston
TURANO Thomas *Kirkpatrick & Lockhart*, Boston

Individuals are listed alphabetically in each band.

"Practical, pragmatic and business-oriented," he is respected for his *"timeliness and communication skills."* According to commentators, **Mark Selwyn** (see p.977) is *"advancing well in an understudy role"* to Bill Lee. Noted for his *"impressive"* teamwork skills and *"excellent"* communication with clients, he is recommended for being *"incredibly diligent"* in his work with patents. *"Outstanding"* **Wayne Stoner** (see p.978) has impressed market sources for *"knowing his cases backwards,"* particularly during complex litigation. Clients profess *"complete confidence"* in his patent advice and advocacy, which is *"always competent and clear."* *"Terrific adviser"* **Donald Steinberg** (see p.977) wins plaudits from clients for *"going the extra mile to understand our technical issues."* He specializes in patent work relating to computer networks and systems, including cell phone technology and digital cameras. In the courtroom he is admired for *"distilling the facts efficiently,"* making them easily understandable for the jury.

The Clients: Wyeth; Intel; Procter & Gamble; GM; EMC; Boston Scientific; GE; Disney; GlaxoSmithKline; Biogen; Nantero and Analog Devices.

Band 2

Fish & Richardson

The Firm: This specialist firm boasts a *"big biotech presence"* and *"hits the ground running"* with its technology know-how. It is highly recommended within Massachusetts for its expertise in patent applications and prosecutions. The team also boasts significant experience in patent infringement litigation. According to onlookers, the strategic development of corporate and commercial litigation services within this IP boutique has broadened its client base. The team recently defended Microsoft in a federal jury trial concerning a patent infringement claim against Arendi Holdings and Arendi USA. Part of a network of eight offices across the USA, the Boston team is valued by clients for its ability to draw on national resources as required.

The Lawyers: *"Excellent"* patent litigator **Robert Hillman** maintains a strong national reputation as the firm's primary *"go-to guy"* for complex cases. With significant experience in representing plaintiffs and defendants in jury trials, he regularly appears in the courts of Delaware and Texas. *"Skillful and accomplished,"* **Frank Porcelli** impressed interviews with his appellate practice, which focuses on patent infringement litigation. Clients value his technical expertise and *"tremendous"* advocacy skills. His *"understanding of the personal dynamics"* in a courtroom situation came in for special praise. The *"highly recommended"* **Gilbert Hennessey** continues to win plaudits for maintaining an international practice that balances IP prosecution and litigation work. He is also admired for his expertise as a registered patent attorney. *"Bright and well organized,"* **Frank Scherkenbach** is a well-respected patent litigator who recently relocated from the firm's California office. His previous Silicone Valley experience has contributed to an *"unparalleled"* understanding of the chemical and pharmaceutical industries.

The Clients: Mayo Foundation for Medical Education and Research; Intel; SeaChange International; Rollerblade and Massachusetts General Hospital.

Foley Hoag LLP

The Firm: This *"terrific"* team is commended for its broad expertise across patent prosecution, application and opinion work, particularly within the biotech field. It prides itself on *"seamlessly combining the advice of both top-notch attorneys and in-house scientists,"* enhancing the pharmaceutical development expertise on which much recent activity has centered. The firm has continued to advise a parade of biotech heavyweights including Amgen, Biogen, Genzyme and Genentech in a high-profile biotech patent case against Columbia University. Clients reported a *"huge degree of confidence"* in a team that offers *"a deep bench"* of attorneys with *"highly relevant technical knowledge"* in the life sciences field. It is valued for offering a *"competent, thorough and cost-effective"* service, coupled with *"a judicious use of resources."* According to one client, its attorneys do not *"over-lawyer – they do a great job without turning over every stone unnecessarily."*

The Lawyers: *"Powerful courtroom persona"* **Donald Ware** is *"an excellent strategist"* who maintains an *"outstanding"* reputation for his work in patent litigation. Head of the firm's IP practice, he is described by one peer as *"the most analytical litigator I've come across."* Ware has *"a total command of all the aspects of the case"* and *"the capacity to figure out its breakpoints."* *"Bright, knowledgeable"* patent prosecution team leader **Beth Arnold** is recommended for her corporate awareness and *"strategic development"* advice. Alongside her *"scientific prowess"* in life sciences, particularly within the drug development arena, clients praise her communication skills. *"Incredibly intellectual, competent and thorough,"* **Claire Laporte** is praised for her work in the medical devices sphere. Her *"analytical mind"* is coupled with a *"terrific demeanor in front of a jury."* In particular, clients value her *"unique"* ability to *"slice through adversarial matters"* to aid efficiency in the courtroom.

The Clients: Baxter; Becton, Dickinson and Company; Genzyme; Pfizer; Bristol-Myers Squibb; CR Bard; Harvard University and Massachusetts Institute of Technology.

Goodwin Procter LLP
See firm details p.980

The Firm: Whilst this firm is not perceived as one of the state's traditional patent outfits, it wins plaudits for its *"great combination"* of general trial skills and life sciences technical know-how. According to market onlookers, the recent arrival of attorneys from the now defunct firm Testa Hurwitz & Thibeault has bolstered the team. The IP practice is supported by the firm's *"outstanding"* litigation department, providing it with a *"terrific"* patent litigation capability. Clients also rate the department's trademark and copyright services. The Boston office's close links with counterparts in New York and Washington, DC, are perceived as an asset by the firm's national clients. Admired for its teamwork, the *"high-energy, diverse and extremely capable"* group is credited with repeatedly producing *"strong results."* Recent work included enforcing 14 different patents for Medical Innovations and advising Applied Materials in California with regard to ongoing patent litigation in Korea and Taiwan.

The Lawyers: *"Exemplary trial lawyer"* **Paul Ware** (see p.979) is *"one of best cross-examiners in business."* In balancing his IP work with a general commercial litigation practice, he brings *"impressive intellect"* and *"exceptional"*

948   All quotes in the text are from interviews with clients and competitors.

CHAMBERS USA 2005

advocacy skills to complex scientific issues. "*Absolutely superb*" litigator **Anthony Downs** (see p.966) is recommended as a "*bright, seasoned*" attorney who is "*always fair.*" "*Exceptionally good on his feet*" in the courtroom, he is appreciated by clients for his willingness to "*get down in the dirt*" in order to fight their corner in patent infringement cases. "*Aggressive*" former Testa Hurwitz & Thibeault lawyer **Douglas Kline** (see p.970) is a respected patent litigator who possesses "*a good skills set, a strong demeanor and presence in the courtroom.*" "*He goes for the jugular*" and often "*leaves the other party no escape route.*" Clients appreciate his engineering background, along with his "*deep knowledge*" of their IP portfolios. Patent litigation manager **John Englander** (see p.966) is said to "*dig deep into the trenches*" of IP administration. His efficient teamwork skills are noted by sources who credit him with "*the groundwork behind the court mouthpiece.*" "*Diligent and client-oriented*" **Shepard Remis** (see p.975) brings his experience in products liability to the IP arena. According to sources, he is a "*hands-on*" patent litigator with the ability to "*anticipate client concerns*" effectively. **Stephen Charkoudian** (see p.964) won plaudits for his negotiation skills and levels of commitment and responsiveness. He has a knack for "*grasping complex terms and conveying them back to the layman.*" Former Testa Hurwitz & Thibeault attorney **Steven Frank** (see p.966) is commended for his communication skills and "*depth of understanding.*" With a "*strategic*" approach to patent prosecution, he is admired by sources for his appreciation of the business implications facing IP clients.

The Clients: GE; Teva Pharmaceuticals; Applied Materials; Boston Scientific; VICOR; Medical Innovations and Hewlett-Packard.

Band 3

Choate Hall & Stewart

The Firm: This "*technically astute*" firm remains a "*major player*" in the Massachusetts IP market. A popular choice for peer referrals, it is admired for its "*talented*" attorneys, specialized patent agents and staff scientists. With highly qualified personnel in the fields of biotechnology, chemistry, engineering and material science, it is especially popular with regional clients in the healthcare and life sciences industries. As a "*well-established*" practice it offers advice in both patent prosecution and litigation, alongside strategic IP counseling to established companies, universities and start-ups. Working closely with the corporate department, the team also offers varied expertise in the trademark sphere.

The Lawyers: "*Top-tier*" IP specialist **Robert Frank** is an "*impressive*" practitioner who is acclaimed for his litigation skill. A popular attorney for referrals, sources note his "*outstanding court demeanor*" and "*excellent judgment.*" "*Experienced and knowledgeable*" senior attorney **Sam Pasternack** is rated for his "*depth of understanding,*" which is largely attributed to his engineering background. With "*great opinion work under his belt,*" he is highly recommended for his "*practical*" advisory skills. "*Brilliant*" **Brenda Jarrell** is "*one of the top life sciences patent prosecutors in the city.*" "*Diligent, smart and technically strong,*" she is a scientist tipped to be a future leader in the field.

The Clients: Massachusetts Institute of Technology; Microsoft; Hewlett-Packard; EMC; Harvard University and Massachusetts General Hospital.

Proskauer Rose LLP

See firm details p.1365

The Firm: This "*developing*" Massachusetts IP practice has been shaped by last year's arrivals from the now defunct legal outfit Testa Hurwitz & Thibeault. Although the national firm is new to Boston, onlookers agree it is a prominent player in the market that is tipped to grow. The firm's established experience in entertainment, sport and music is now combined with "*some of the best and brightest*" local lawyers on the biotech and software side. Alongside New England-based technology companies, the firm advises clients across the USA on patent litigation and prosecution, copyright and trademark issues. Clients praise the strength of "*creative*" senior and mid-level attorneys who don't "*over-lawyer*" while remaining "*business-focused.*" They "*won't force the law down our throats,*" said one source.

The Lawyers: "*Tenacious, energetic*" and popular with clients, patent litigation head **Steven Bauer** (see p.962) is "*up there with the luminaries in the field.*" Sources appreciate his level of commitment to their cause and "*aggressive*" defense of their interests – "*he will push his head through a brick wall for you.*" While winning plaudits for his ability to "*resolve a dispute before it turns into a multi-million-dollar case,*" he was also commended in the courtroom for "*getting to the core weakness of the opposition's case and drilling in on it.*" "*Competent and bright,*" **Joseph Capraro** (see p.964) leads the firm's portfolio development and patent prosecution specialties. He is particularly recommended for his work on patent disclosure and trademarks. Praised for the depth of his technical expertise, he is credited with bringing "*significant value*" to clients' IP portfolios.

The Clients: RSA Security; Descartes Systems Group; Bessemer Ventures Partners; Helicos Biosciences; MKS Instruments; Hypertherm and Candela.

Other Notable Practitioners

"*Excellent*" former Testa Hurwitz & Thibeault patent prosecutor **Tom Turano** (see p.978) was described as "*well versed on technical issues.*" Clients praised him further for being "*very quick on his feet*" and for "*thinking outside the box.*" Turano now practices with Kirkpatrick & Lockhart, Nicholson Graham LLP.

LITIGATION

Band 1

Goodwin Procter LLP

See firm details p.980

The Firm: Litigation is a key focus of this full-service firm, which has been boosted by its recent merger with DC litigation boutique Shea & Gardner, and the arrival of a number of respected litigators from dissolved firm Testa Hurwitz & Thibeault. An "*absolutely top-notch*" team covers anything from general commercial and IP to products liability, white-collar crime and securities litigation. Clients benefit from the big-firm resources available, emphasizing the operation's national and even international capabilities. They are also quick to stress the firm's top-to-bottom quality and praise its "*impressive body of skilled associates.*" The efficient management structure came in for further commendation, as did the team's excellent preparation which enables it "*always to be seven steps ahead of the other side.*"

The Lawyers: Leading the charge is "*stellar trial attorney*" and department chair **Paul Ware** (see p.979). A seasoned litigator with a considerable breadth of experience, he is especially recommended for his practical approach and "*excel-*

GENERAL COMMERCIAL

lent strategic vision." Ware led advice to Harvard University on a federal government procedure under the False Claims Act relating to a contract with USAID concerning Russian market reform programs. "*Great crisis manager*" **Ken Felter** (see p.966) sustains a broad commercial practice, incorporating disciplines ranging from complex financial litigation to disputes over trade secrets. One client likened his courtroom style to a panther: "*He doesn't throw his arms in the air – he is just very subtle, then pounces and goes in for the kill.*" Felter also impresses with thorough preparation and thorough attention to detail.

Massachusetts

Leading firms

(Litigation: General Commercial)

1 GOODWIN PROCTER LLP *Boston*
  ROPES & GRAY LLP *Boston*
  WILMER CUTLER PICKERING HALE *Boston*

2 BINGHAM MCCUTCHEN LLP *Boston*
  FOLEY HOAG LLP *Boston*
  GOULSTON & STORRS *Boston*
  MINTZ LEVIN COHN FERRIS GLOVSKY *Boston*

3 FOLEY & LARDNER *Boston*
  HOLLAND & KNIGHT LLP *Boston*
  MCDERMOTT WILL & EMERY *Boston*
  SHERIN AND LODGEN LLP *Boston*
  TODD & WELD LLP *Boston*

Firms are listed alphabetically in each band.

Ken Parsigian (see p.974) stands out in products liability terms for his creative, out-of-the-box approach: "*If there's a defense out there, he'll find it!*" He continues to act for Philip Morris in international contraband scenarios, and has been involved in a series of manganese welding fume cases. Parsigian also won accolades for consistently "*striking a good rapport with the judge.*" "*Great thinker*" **Tony Downs** (see p.966) is credited with "*acquiring a strong skill in complex litigation,*" and also recommended for his IP expertise. **Stephen Poss** (see p.974) was identified as something of a national Sarbanes-Oxley expert. He has defended companies in securities class actions, recently achieving a major victory for General Cinema in a securities fraud case. Poss also helps clients with SEC and other investigations. "*Extremely hard-working*" **James Dittmar** (see p.965) is the "*go-to-guy*" for securities mutual fund work. He is someone who is "*able to immediately delve into a complex issue without preparation*" and who has "*a very commanding courtroom presence.*" The securities group has been further strengthened by the arrival of former Testa Hurwitz & Thibeault attorney **Brian Pastuszenski** (see p.974). He wins acclaim for developing a securities litigation practice that incorporates significant national cases. He also defends shareholders and advises businesses on corporate governance and risk mitigation issues. He is especially well suited to dealing with board and committee members, because "*he has a way of asking questions without causing friction.*" **David Apfel** (see p.961) is in the firm's white-collar crime and government investigations group. He is "*particularly effective in organizing a large litigation team*" and achieved high visibility upon defending Martha Stewart's accountant at trial. The white-collar team has also been boosted by Testa arrival **Joseph Savage** (see p.976), who "*consistently displays excellent judgment when dealing with the government agencies.*"

The Clients: A client list with many Fortune 100 and 500 companies includes: GE; Philip Morris; Citizens Financial Group; Fidelity Investments; Harvard University and Boston College.

Ropes & Gray LLP
See firm details p.985

The Firm: An already talented and widely respected team of litigators is perceived as having gone from strength to strength following the firm's merger with New York IP boutique Fish & Neave. This bolstered its capabilities in areas such as hi-tech and biotech. Recent involvement in countless investigations and litigations on behalf of mutual fund and investment management clients reflects the firm's substantial corporate and securities leverage. Around eight partners spend most of their time on such matters. In addition to expertise in the gamut of general commercial litigation, including labor and employment issues, niche white-collar crime and insurance coverage expertise is on offer.

The Lawyers: "*Exceptional*" **John Donovan** (see p.965) instills instant confidence in clients, due not least to his experience base and sound judgment. His practice comprises mainly securities, stockholder and corporate work. Donovan has advised on a case involving the reorganization of Genzyme and is recognized for a tough, no-nonsense approach that "*cuts to the heart of the matter.*" **John Montgomery** (see p.973) is a new entry to this year's table following numerous recommendations. He has "*enormous integrity,*" say peers, and is especially noted for his leadership qualities. Interviewees tend to mention **Michael Fee** (see p.966) and **Joan McPhee** (see p.972) in the same breath when referring to the firm's strength in white-collar crime. The "*tenacious*" Fee is described as "*a relentless advocate for his clients,*" while McPhee is noted for her practical and thoughtful approach. Senior figure and general commercial litigator **Paul Galvani** (see p.967) is perceived as having made his name in major environmental cases. He stands out as "*a great strategist,*" say peers, who wouldn't hesitate to refer work to him.

The Clients: In accordance with the firm's widely respected healthcare sector prowess, the team acts for numerous hospitals and other healthcare providers. Public companies, mutual funds, government agencies, universities and colleges, insurers and reinsurers, financial institutions and manufacturers are also clients.

Wilmer Cutler Pickering Hale and Dorr LLP
See firm details p.497

The Firm: "*I haven't dealt with anyone in that Boston office who isn't terrific!*" enthused one client, expressing a sentiment shared by peers and clients alike. The merger of Hale and Dorr with DC-based Wilmer Cutler Pickering provided a team already "*able to tackle extremely large litigation*" with additional horsepower. Interviewees highly valued the strategic thinking invested in structuring teams of technically accomplished lawyers, branding the department a "*wonderful organization.*" IP, securities and white-collar crime were all areas in which it won special praise.

The Lawyers: **Joan Lukey** (see p.971) is clearly a gifted trial lawyer who carries great credibility among the profession. She has increasingly focused on products liability work while continuing to be involved in major employment cases representing both defendants and plaintiffs. General commercial litigation often involving a pronounced employment aspect also features in Lukey's practice. Interviewees described her as "*a stylish performer with an impeccable reputation for quality,*" pointing to excellent cross-examination skills and an ability to form winning rapports with judge and jury. Securities guru **Jeff Rudman** (see p.976) "*knows how to get results with the SEC.*" Clients value the fact that he "*won't play politics but will tell it how it is.*" Rudman can call on the resources of a large and successful team, securities litigation being a major feature of the Boston practice. **Jack Fabiano** (see p.966) is an all-round lawyer who "*tries a great case.*" He handles a diverse range of work, with a recent focus on telecom sector litigation. White-collar crime expert **Robert Keefe** (see p.969) "*has a very practical approach in an area of law that terrifies people.*" He "*has an ability to fight the government in an amiable and disarming manner,*" say peers. "*Extremely diligent*" **Karen Green** (see p.967) largely represents corporations in federal criminal investigations, particularly involving alleged healthcare and securities fraud, political corruption and espionage. She is "*a quick study on the facts,*" say clients. **Daniel Halston** (see p.968) also enters the tables for the first time following a number of strong recommendations. He is especially noted for a methodical approach that "*neglects not a single detail*" while "*always managing to avoid getting lost among the trees.*" He has worked extensively on securities class action cases, in addition to broader commercial litigation.

The Clients: John Hancock; Sonus Networks; Red Hat and Fidelity Investments.

Band 2

Bingham McCutchen LLP
The Firm: This firm of "*extremely smart*" lawyers has tended to resist the trend of specialization, maintaining a truly mixed litigation practice. The team recently saw an increase in securities, broker-dealer and mutual fund work. It continues to handle significant energy and construction-related disputes, including the litigation surrounding Boston's Big Dig. Other

950

All quotes in the text are from interviews with clients and competitors.

CHAMBERS USA 2005

Massachusetts
Leading individuals
(Litigation: General Commercial)

Senior Statesman
POPEO R Robert *Mintz Levin*, Boston

[1] DONOVAN John *Ropes & Gray*, Boston
KEATING Michael *Foley Hoag*, Boston
LUKEY Joan *Wilmer Cutler*, Boston
RENEHAN Richard *Goulston & Storrs*, Boston
TODD Owen *Todd & Weld*, Boston
WARE Paul *Goodwin Procter*, Boston

[2] FELTER J Kenneth *Goodwin Procter*, Boston
GALVANI Paul *Ropes & Gray*, Boston
KOCIUBES Joseph *Bingham McCutchen*, Boston
MULDOON Robert *Sherin and Lodgen*, Boston
PEARLSTEIN Mark *McDermott Will*, Boston
PIERCE Rudolph *Goulston & Storrs*, Boston

[3] BARSHAK Edward *Sugarman Rogers*, Boston
DOWNS J Anthony *Goodwin Procter*, Boston
FABIANO John *Wilmer Cutler*, Boston
HALSTON Daniel *Wilmer Cutler*, Boston
LANE Roger *Greenberg Traurig*, Boston
LEIBENSPERGER Edward *McDermott Will*, Boston
MAHONY Gael *Holland & Knight*, Boston
MONTGOMERY John *Ropes & Gray*, Boston
PARSIGIAN Kenneth *Goodwin Procter*, Boston
POSS Stephen *Goodwin Procter*, Boston
TUTEUR Michael *Foley & Lardner*, Boston

Leading individuals
(Litigation: White-Collar Crime
& Government Investigations)

[1] APFEL David *Goodwin Procter*, Boston
FEE Michael *Ropes & Gray*, Boston
GREEN Karen *Wilmer Cutler*, Boston
KEEFE Robert *Wilmer Cutler*, Boston
MCPHEE Joan *Ropes & Gray*, Boston
PEARLSTEIN Mark *McDermott Will*, Boston
SAVAGE Joseph *Goodwin Procter*, Boston

Leading individuals
(Litigation: Securities)

[1] DITTMAR James *Goodwin Procter*, Boston
DONOVAN John *Ropes & Gray*, Boston
PASTUSZENSKI Brian *Goodwin Procter*, Boston
POSS Stephen *Goodwin Procter*, Boston
RUDMAN Jeffrey *Wilmer Cutler*, Boston
Individuals are listed alphabetically in each band.

thriving areas of practice include antitrust litigation. Clients appreciate the accessibility of the service provided and the fact that "*You don't feel like you are being double-billed.*"
The Lawyers: **Joe Kociubes** is recommended for his excellent judgment and courtroom demeanor: "*He is not arrogant, but very professional and civil, and always thoroughly prepared.*" His varied practice encompasses a range of matters, from consumer class actions to large tax cases to disputes over employee bonuses. He also acts as a mediator and arbitrator. Clients would

"*refer to him in a heartbeat*" thanks to his excellent trial skills, good business sense and ability to communicate.
The Clients: Bain & Company and Boston Scientific feature in a diverse client list that includes a large number of Fortune 500 companies. National and international businesses in service and manufacturing industries as well as government and nonprofit entities are also a source of instructions.

Foley Hoag LLP
The Firm: About 80 attorneys focus on general business litigation with an emphasis on patent defense and prosecution, securities (particularly on behalf of accountant clients) and white-collar investigations. The firm is noted for its appellate work and also heavily involved in employment disputes. Clients consider its litigators "*aggressive without being overbearing*" and also appreciate their accessibility and pragmatic approach.
The Lawyers: **Michael Keating** is "*one of the very best,*" according to sources. Well liked by judges, he tends to be brought in on sensitive issues for his judgment, integrity and reputation.
The Clients: The firm acts for national and international businesses, largely based in the New England region, as well as individuals. Clients include: Baxter Healthcare; Varian Semiconductor; Boston Communications Group and Electro Scientific Industries.

Goulston & Storrs
The Firm: A sizeable team handles general business litigation and is renowned for its involvement in real estate sector disputes such as land damage cases. Professional malpractice defense is another major area of focus.
The Lawyers: "*Consummate trial practitioner*" **Richard Renehan** is the standout name at this practice. "*Probably one of the most respected lawyers in town,*" he is said to have "*a lot of jury appeal.*" Noted for his experience across the board, Renehan is best known for professional malpractice defense work. As one client commented: "*He really is very gifted in understanding the strengths and weaknesses of a case and how matters will unfold in the court setting.*" Splitting his time between Boston and DC, former Superior Court judge **Rudi Pierce** is also well respected. He handles a range of litigation, often with a slant toward the firmwide real estate focus. Recent work has included acting for Massachusetts Bay Transportation in two First Amendment cases in the First Circuit Court of Appeals.
The Clients: Further clients include Boston Redevelopment Authority and numerous leading law firms.

Mintz Levin Cohn Ferris Glovsky and Popeo PC
The Firm: Its department sustains a prestigious position in the litigation arena. Praise for the operation focuses on its breadth of practice and depth of experience, especially when it comes to handling complex business disputes. The team is also particularly adept when it comes to political sensitivities, and can use the press and government relations expertise of its affiliate group ML Strategies. The practice runs the gamut, from class actions and environmental litigation to breaches of fiduciary duty and white-collar criminal defense.
The Lawyers: "*Fantastic negotiator*" and firm chairman **Bob Popeo** enters the senior statesman category in recognition of his role as rainmaker and distinguished trial lawyer. "*There is no one who better knows their way around a courtroom or is better prepared,*" sources report.
The Clients: Members of the firm represent clients across a range of industries, from individuals to multinationals. Massachusetts General Hospital and AOL (now Time Warner) are examples.

Band 3

Foley & Lardner
See firm details p.1828
The Firm: Foley & Lardner recently acquired Epstein Becker & Green's Boston office in its entirety, in a move designed to consolidate its presence in the commercial litigation, private equity and life sciences fields. This "*excellent team with a fine reputation*" prides itself on being able to offer clients a hands-on approach. Healthcare litigation is an area of special emphasis – attorneys are currently representing six major health insurers in a multibillion national class action in Florida. White-collar criminal defense is a small yet significant part of the practice, focusing on investigations in the securities and financial markets.
The Lawyers: Former Assistant US Attorney **Michael Tuteur** (see p.978) is praised for his "*business head*" and creative problem-solving ability. He practices a mix of general commercial and white-collar litigation and is especially valued for a practical and client-oriented approach.
The Clients: Harvard University; Blue Cross Blue Shield of Massachusetts; Boston Consulting Group; Mutual of America; Sandler Systems; Massachusetts Housing Finance Agency; Harvard Vanguard Medical Associates; National Lumber; CIGNA and Coldwell Banker.

Holland & Knight LLP
See firm details p.1352
The Firm: With litigation a key focus for this international player, the 45 attorneys in the firm's Boston office handle a predictably broad

spread of work. According to clients, the main strength is that *"they have enough staff to jump into any situation that arises."* The practice covers, inter alia, white-collar crime and government investigations, appellate work, consumer and securities class actions, insurance coverage and real estate litigation.

The Lawyers: Senior figure **Gael Mahony** (see p.971) *"still likes to get in there and try cases."* Appellate work accounts for a large proportion of his workload, and he has a particularly impressive track record within the Puerto Rican court system.

The Clients: These include Fortune 500 companies, government bodies and nonprofit organizations.

McDermott Will & Emery

See firm details p.773

The Firm: There are about 40 attorneys in the firm's trial department in Boston, a practice notable for strength in the white-collar criminal defense area. In addition to general business litigation, areas of emphasis include professional malpractice defense and, on a nationwide level, pharmaceutical and biotech litigation. That the firm's Boston attorneys are able to draw on resources available across its substantial network is considered an advantage.

The Lawyers: Consistently displaying *"excellent judgment,"* **Edward Leibensperger** (see p.971) is first and foremost respected as a highly talented trial lawyer. He recently moved from Nutter McLennan & Fish to become national cochair of McDermott's professional liability practice. Leibensperger won special praise for his defense of accountants and large accountancy firms. The *"incredibly hard-working"* former First Assistant US Attorney **Mark Pearlstein** (see p.974) is most often associated with white-collar criminal defense. In court he *"keeps his ego under control"* and has an ability *"to go for the jugular in a civil and practical way."* A large part of his practice

involves government enforcement procedures, ranging from criminal investigations to purely civil matters. He also handles various general commercial litigation matters. Recent work includes representing GE in a case arising out of a fatal airplane crash.

The Clients: GE, Dynamics Research and Massachusetts Port Authority feature on the client list.

Sherin and Lodgen LLP

The Firm: Litigation is a core practice area for this compact outfit. Most of its workload comprises complex business disputes, with special emphasis on real estate as well as advising Massachusetts agencies, towns and cities involved in major construction projects. Legal malpractice defense is also a major feature of the practice. Attorneys recently saw an increase in corporate litigation involving the control of companies and rights of shareholders, securing victory for a client in Connecticut concerning the ownership of a hi-tech company. Other recent successes include a major victory for Volvo in the Massachusetts Supreme Judicial Court.

The Lawyers: **Robert Muldoon** is quite simply recommended for the quality of his lawyering and of his trial and personal skills. He is particularly noted in the area of legal malpractice defense. The firm has acted for some of the major law firms in the region in this regard.

The Clients: Teva Pharmaceuticals; Haemonetics; The Beal Companies; Stop & Shop; Volvo North America; Royal Ahold and Wachovia.

Todd & Weld LLP

The Firm: This *"excellent"* trial boutique houses about 30 *"tremendous advocates"* who handle every type of litigation, not to mention settlement negotiations, mediation and arbitration. It acts for both plaintiffs and defendants. Heavy involvement in complex commercial litigation is punctuated by appearances in construction

cases including on behalf of the principal contractors in Boston's Big Dig. Professional and legal malpractice also contributes to the workload. Notable highlights include successfully defending Subaru of New England in a class action brought by its dealers. The firm also achieved several significant results for plaintiffs in products liability and medical malpractice suits. Peers are full of praise for the firm's presentation of cases, declaring it *"very well plugged in politically – if you have a PR or government regulation issue, they are the ones to go to."*

The Lawyers: **Owen Todd** is *"a litigator par excellence."* A former Superior Court judge, he is widely respected for his strategic vision and no-nonsense approach. In addition to conducting complex business litigation, Todd represents legal professionals before disciplinary boards.

The Clients: The team is brought in at the litigation stage and therefore acts for all types of clients, frequently taking on referrals from the larger firms and coming up against national players on the opposing side.

Other Notable Practitioners

Previously the litigation chair at the now defunct Testa firm, **Roger Lane** (see p.970) at Greenberg Traurig LLP *"knows when to hold them down and when to fold them,"* say clients. His practice encompasses general business litigation, corporate governance and acting for boards of directors on fiduciary duty issues. In risk management contexts, clients specifically referred to his ability to keep them out of court. Lane's insight into the thinking of the other parties is such that *"he can bring creative and thoughtful win-win solutions to the table."* Senior figure **Edward Barshak** at trial firm Sugarman, Rogers, Barshak & Cohen, PC *"has a wonderful touch, especially with regard to charming the jury."* He defends lawyers and physicians before their respective disciplinary authorities, as well as being involved in significant commercial litigation.

PRIVATE EQUITY

BUYOUTS & VENTURE CAPITAL INVESTMENT

Massachusetts

Leading firms (Private Equity: Buyouts & Venture Capital Investment)

1	**GOODWIN PROCTER LLP** *Boston*
	ROPES & GRAY LLP *Boston*
	WEIL, GOTSHAL & MANGES LLP *Boston*
2	**BINGHAM MCCUTCHEN LLP** *Boston*
	MCDERMOTT WILL & EMERY *Boston*
	WILMER CUTLER PICKERING HALE *Boston*
3	**CHOATE HALL & STEWART** *Boston*
	EDWARDS & ANGELL LLP *Boston*
	FOLEY HOAG LLP *Boston*
	MORSE, BARNES-BROWN *Waltham*

Firms are listed alphabetically in each band.

Band 1

Goodwin Procter LLP

See firm details p.980

The Firm: In the final stages of this year's research, significant changes to the Massachusetts private equity market occurred in the wake of Testa Hurwitz & Thibeault's dissolution. Goodwin Procter is one of a number of firms to benefit from the distribution of its attorneys, notably specialists in the venture capital and buyouts arena. Furthermore, the lateral hire of several attorneys from McDermott Will & Emery has compounded the firm's increased

private equity potential. According to clients, one distinguishing feature of the group's previous success has been to offer a *"comprehensive service to all business models"* such as those requiring venture capital work or advice on buyouts. It combines work with investors with a highly regarded practice in the emerging growth market, particularly with businesses in the life sciences sector. Attorneys are also well equipped to handle mature stage private equity work for traditional healthcare clients such as dental practices, surgeries and nursing homes. Although changes to this department are relatively new, onlookers predict that the quality and

Massachusetts

Leading individuals (Private Equity: Buyouts & Venture Capital Investment)

1
BORDEN Mark *Wilmer Cutler*, Boston
CHAPIN David *Ropes & Gray*, Boston
ROSENBLUM Peter *Foley Hoag*, Boston
WESTRA James *Weil Gotshal*, Boston

2
EGAN III John *Goodwin Procter*, Boston
HESSION John *McDermott Will*, Boston
HODGES TAYLOR Laura *Goodwin Procter*, Boston
LECLAIRE John *Goodwin Procter*, Boston
MALT R Bradford *Ropes & Gray*, Boston
SCHNOOR William *Goodwin Procter*, Boston
WOLF Robert *Bingham McCutchen*, Boston

3
CHORY John *Wilmer Cutler*, Waltham
MEDAGLIA Anthony *Goodwin Procter*, Boston
MEREDITH Steven *Edwards & Angell*, Boston
MORREALE Justin *Bingham McCutchen*, Boston
PACI Victor *Bingham McCutchen*, Boston
PENDLETON Lea *Morse, Barnes-Brown*, Waltham
RONDEAU Patrick *Wilmer Cutler*, Boston
STILLWELL R Newcomb *Ropes & Gray*, Boston

Up-and-coming individuals

FRENCH Marilyn *Weil Gotshal*, Boston
KENDALL Michael *Goodwin Procter*, Boston

Individuals are listed alphabetically in each band.

breadth of its new arrivals will catapult the firm into a premiere league of its own.

The Lawyers: From Testa Hurwitz, the group this year welcomed **William Schnoor** (see p.976) to its ranks. He enjoys a well-established reputation in the market and is a popular point of referral among peers. "*He really has what it takes and produces work of a great quality,*" reported one observer, while clients praised his "*ability to put his arms around a project and deliver a solution.*" The arrival of former McDermott Will & Emery lawyer **John Egan** (see p.966) is reported as a triumph for the team. A popular port of call for referrals with a specialty in late stage private equity for startup IT companies, he is experienced in software and network securities. Viewed as "*exceptionally knowledgeable*" about the technology and venture capital markets, he is also admired for his presentation skills. With a reputation for "*handling unruly situations,*" **Laura Hodges Taylor** (see p.968) has cultivated a loyal following. A good listener, she is "*articulate, knowledgeable and thorough,*" and is acclaimed for her work in hedge funds and real estate investments. **John LeClaire** (see p.970) wins plaudits for his experience of later stage buyouts and for his outstanding negotiation skills. Clients described him as "*a real people person*" who is "*a pleasure to work with.*" Clients single out **Anthony Medaglia** (see p.972) as the "*go-to guy in Boston*" for his "*wonderful mix of legal acumen and practical business sense.*" He combines his work on venture capital transactions with expertise in

general corporate work. **Michael Kendall** (see p.970) mixes experience in later stage investment and buyouts with venture capital work, where he has recently represented emerging companies.

The Clients: TA Associates; AIG; Alta Communications; Matrix Partners; Charlesbank Capital Partners; Behrman Capital and Fidelity Investments.

Ropes & Gray LLP
See firm details p.985

The Firm: There is "*absolutely no question*" that this firm is "*top of the class*" for private equity transactions, say peers. Clients endorsed the LBO know-how displayed by these attorneys and particularly their experience with later-stage companies. A joining of forces with IP boutique Fish & Neave has followed this firm's merger with private equity specialists Reboul, MacMurray, Hewitt & Maynard, thus enhancing the firm's New York profile. Its impressive client base stretches across the USA and overseas. The firm has recently acted for BainCapital on the $2.15 billion buyout of UGS PLM Solutions from public company EDS – one of the largest technology buyouts in history.

The Lawyers: "*Brilliant*" **David Chapin** (see p.964) comes highly recommended by clients for his expertise on private equity buyouts. They appreciate that his experience in this market enables him to see all sides to a transaction. Among his clients are funds such as Berkshire Partners and financial investors and underwriters such as Goldman Sachs. While **Brad Malt** (see p.972) now provides a greater degree of strategic advice to clients in line with his management role at the firm, he continues to be a formidable player in the private equity market. His prominence is assured as a result of his long-standing client relations with BainCapital. Peers credit him with outstanding buyout expertise, claiming that he was undertaking complex LBO work "*before we had even defined leveraged buyouts.*" **Newcomb Stillwell** (see p.978) impresses with his negotiation skills and is said to possess "*the ability to organize and run major deals smoothly.*" Clients value his conscientiousness in "*covering all of the details*" and appreciate his perseverance at "*sticking with a deal in order to get it closed as quickly as possible.*"

The Clients: Fenway Partners is key a client of this practice.

Weil, Gotshal & Manges LLP
See firm details p.1378

The Firm: In Boston, the firm fields "*impressive*" teams dedicated to buyouts and venture capital investment respectively. Clients appreciate that, while the practice group is truly international in resources, it has not forgotten the Massachusetts marketplace. In the USA alone, this firm is "*a formidable power*" when linked

with attorneys in New York and Texas. For example, the Boston team recently joined forces with the Dallas branch to represent Thomas H Lee Partners in its acquisition of REFCO, valued at $2.25 billion. Its strong international footprint and "*one-firm approach*" enable the team to work with US investors on overseas investments. Clients continue to praise the "*local understanding*" of the firm's attorneys and allied departments. The tax team especially has been recognized for its success in working cohesively with the private equity transactional attorneys.

The Lawyers: Described by one client as "*the best attorney I have ever worked with,*" **James Westra** (see p.979) is credited with the development of his respected private equity practice. According to clients, he is a "*thoughtful and detail-oriented attorney,*" who "*inspires great confidence*" particularly for company and early-stage capital work. He combines the respect of peers for his professionalism with the loyalty of a client base that values his success in "*just getting the deal done!*" **Marilyn French** (see p.967) is showing great promise for the volume of transactions that she has already undertaken in the private equity arena, particularly work with major client Thomas H Lee Partners. Clients describe her as "*extremely versatile,*" working easily with equity sponsors and management teams alike.

The Clients: Summit Partners; Highland Capital; United Industries and Berkshire Partners.

Band 2

Bingham McCutchen LLP

The Firm: According to onlookers, this firm has becoming increasingly visible in the Massachusetts market since Bingham Dana's 2002 merger with McCutchen, Doyle, Brown & Enersen. Its subsequent acquisition of Los Angeles venture capital boutique Riordan & McKinzie has been viewed as a striking strategic move, which is already starting to pay dividends. Investors speak highly of the national reach achieved by this group, and endorse its technical understanding of private equity transactions, in particular early-stage and registration work.

The Lawyers: Market sources described **Rob Wolf** as the firm's "*go-to guy for buyouts – very bright and technically sound.*" He is a fine deal-doer, who is equally well known for his public company advice. Senior figure in the market **Justin Morreale** is credited with "*building up the practice*" to date and is praised for his business acumen. **Victor Paci** is well respected in the investment community for "*understanding real business issues whilst ensuring that everything is buttoned down from a legal perspective.*" Recent work has included advising private equity groups and real estate investment trusts on their investments.

The Clients: Clients include BancBoston Capital, Heritage Partners and Weston Presidio.

McDermott Will & Emery

See firm details p.773

The Firm: Clients working with software, IT services and wireless technology expressed their admiration for this group's "*superb understanding*" of technology issues. The team advises on a broad range of transactions such as those in the venture capital sphere, buyouts and late-stage private equity deals. Clients appreciate the firm's international footprint, which provides a "*seamless*" service for clients requiring work beyond the state. Locally, clients feel that the private equity group offers "*added value*" through its interfacing with colleagues in the corporate and IP departments to provide a cohesive package. The team has recently advised Boston-based venture capital fund Oxford Bioscience Partners in the disposition of some of its portfolio companies, including the $140 million sale of Percutaneous Valve Technologies to Edwards Lifesciences.

The Lawyers: While sources lament the departure of John Egan to rival firm Goodwin Procter, the department's new key contact, "*smart, practical lawyer*" **John Hession** (see p.968), is also highly recommended. Renowned for his early-stage venture capital work, he is particularly active within the hi-tech industry, say onlookers. Clients "*couldn't ask for a better business attorney*" and value him for "*understanding the deeper aspects of an organization,*" as well as being able to prevent "*legal pitfalls.*"

The Clients: Clients include Authentica, Q1 Labs and Raptor Systems.

Wilmer Cutler Pickering Hale and Dorr LLP

See firm details p.497

The Firm: This firm is highly regarded for its ability to provide strategic advice to companies that require private equity financing and is noted by clients as "*by far the state's most prevalent firm in the venture capital market.*" The firm maintains its "*formidable*" reputation for serving clients in the technology sector. It is particularly admired for its ability to work on early-stage and startup companies, which are spin-offs from universities in the region, such as Massachusetts Institute of Technology and Harvard University.

The Lawyers: Alongside a reputation among clients as "*Boston's number-one corporate lawyer,*" **Mark Borden** (see p.963) has experience in a range of private equity transactions. He is particularly admired for his expertise on venture capital investments. **John Chory** (see p.964) has developed a practice that focuses on the ven-

ture-backed financing of early-stage companies. He is also regarded as "*the firm's public face*" for private equity deals. **Patrick Rondeau** (see p.975) has marked out a strong presence in the Massachusetts venture capital market. Peers find him "*easy to work with*" and are impressed by his ability "*to avoid making a big fuss – he gets the job done.*"

The Clients: Venture-backed companies and venture capital firms in industries such as software, semiconductors and electronics, telecom and networking, life sciences and medical devices.

Band 3

Choate Hall & Stewart

The Firm: Onlookers identified the firm's success in developing some key clients and acknowledged that it has fast become a "*very real contender*" in the Massachusetts private equity market. Alongside the acquisition and investment of target businesses, the team advises clients on exit strategies. The team is also able to provide assistance with related areas of law such as equity and compensation arrangements for management teams. Recent highlights have included the representation of Boston Ventures in the sale of its portfolio company Marshall & Swift to MacDonald Dettwiler for $250 million in cash and an additional contingent payment of up to $90 million. It also advised Riverside Partners in the merger of its portfolio company Microflex with FoodHandler. The firm also offers advice on the structuring of investment funds.

The Lawyers: Stephen Cohen chairs the private equity group and is experienced on mid-market to large funds.

The Clients: Advent International; Boston Ventures; Greylock Management; Heritage Partners; Highland Capital Partners and Summit Partners.

Edwards & Angell, LLP

The Firm: This full-service firm has secured a fine reputation in the state with its private equity work for telecom and broadcasting clients. According to sources, the team is best known for its expertise in venture capital financing, particularly for startups and emerging companies. Its client-focused lawyers are praised for their technical ability and communication skills.

The Lawyers: Observers described **Steven Meredith** as "*the real strength of Edwards & Angell – without question.*" He is highly respected for his

experience with media clients. Both clients and peers appreciate the sense of humor and reasonable attitude that he brings to the deal table.

The Clients: Columbia Capital, Spectrum Equity Investors and MC Venture Partners are key clients at this firm.

Foley Hoag LLP

The Firm: One distinguishing feature of this firm's private equity practice is its high-quality work with clients in the biotech and life sciences sectors. Clients are well served by the firm's Route 128 office location. They also appreciate its significant number of non-lawyers who are on hand to assist with detailed transactions. The collaborative private equity team is admired for its "*practical understanding of client needs*" and is described as being among the state's original founders of "*serious*" venture capital work. The team comes highly recommended for its late-stage venture capital work.

The Lawyers: Sources identified talented **Peter Rosenblum** as the firm's leading name for venture capital and private equity work.

The Clients: Polaris Venture Partners; TechnoVentures; Argo GSM; CommonAngels and Skyline Ventures.

Morse, Barnes-Brown & Pendleton PC

The Firm: This "*organically growing*" firm punches above its weight as one of the top firms in the eastern region, and yet manages this feat with a team size smaller than its direct competitors. Popular among venture-backed companies, the firm has over the past decade developed a practice that blends private equity and venture capital advice. The team is renowned for its work with early-stage companies and angel investors. Recent work has included a high number of convertible preferred stock transactions and several convertible debt transactions. The team continues to impress technology clients – many of whom are well served by its convenient Route 128 location – with its alternative approach and "*reasonable*" billing structure.

The Lawyers: "*Smart and practical*" **Lea Pendleton** (see p.974) offers expertise in venture capital financings and has undertaken recent work for clients in the medical devices sphere. He is experienced at working with both companies and investors.

The Clients: Egan-Managed Capital; Konarka Technologies; OATSystems; Axia Partners; Windspeed and Julius Koch USA.

PRIVATE EQUITY

FUND FORMATION

Band 1

Proskauer Rose LLP

See firm details p.1365

The Firm: Following the vote to disband Testa, Hurwitz & Thibeault, the core of its fund formation team joined this firm, catapulting it into the heart of the Boston private equity market. Sources across the USA agree that this group combines some of the *"deepest and most experienced in the country."* While winning national plaudits for its expertise, particularly along the West Coast, the team also attracts global recognition for its fund work in Germany, Israel and the UK. A major player in the state's private equity market, the group has attracted a loyal following of venture funds, institutional investors, and limited partnerships based within Massachusetts. According to sources, *"knowledgeable and technically experienced"* attorneys at the firm remain *"head and shoulders above the rest."*

The Lawyers: **Robin Painter** (see p.973) is widely recognized for her expertise in international venture capital fund formation. She recently assisted Charles River Ventures in forming their twelfth fund and represented a syndicate of blue-chip foundations and university endowments. *"Exceptionally bright"* **David Tegeler** has impressed market commentators with detailed knowledge of venture capital fund formation work. He is experienced in representing both general and limited partners. *"Absolutely outstanding"* **Daniel Finkelman** (see p.966) is an established figure in the private equity market. Clients appreciate that he has an

"understanding of the science of fund formation" that is so deep that he *"knows what everyone else is doing as well."* *"Excellent and trusted counselor"* **Malcolm Nicholls** (see p.973) is tipped to be a prominent player as he continues to gain experience across the breadth of private equity fund formation advice. He has represented private equity fund managers in both domestic and foreign fund formation projects, alongside his work with institutional investors and investment advisers. Among peers, he wins plaudits for being *"reasonable and easy to deal with."*

The Clients: A range of international general and limited partners are represented by the team, alongside institutional investors.

Ropes & Gray LLP

See firm details p.985

The Firm: The recent merger with New York IP boutique Fish & Neave has further raised this firm's national reputation. Home to *"just outstanding"* practitioners, who regularly work for clients in New York, the firm is rated among the most active private equity fund formation players in the USA. The sheer volume of its fund organization work, coupled with its representation of *"a dominant share"* of institutional investors in transactions, sets the team apart from its competitors. The group is highly rated for advice on the formation of venture capital and LBO funds. It is also recognized for its representation of limited partners and mutual funds.

The Lawyers: *"Excellent, excellent private equity attorney"* **Larry Jordan Rowe** (see p.976) is praised for his fund work with investors and high-profile limited partners. He commands respect for being *"a tough but level headed negotiator"* in meeting the needs of his clients. According to sources, **Bradford Malt** (see p.972) is *"father of the firm's private equity practice"* and has *"grown up in this industry."* A senior counselor at the firm, he brings his astute judgment and strategic advice to issues relating to the structuring of funds.

The Clients: BainCapital; Fenway Partners; Thomas H Lee Partners; Welsh, Carson, Anderson & Stowe; Saunders Karp & Megrue; Goldman Sachs and Merrill Lynch.

Band 2

Goodwin Procter LLP

See firm details p.980

The Firm: This firm offers unique expertise in real estate investment for private equity funds. For example, it advised Kimco Realty on its $100 million dedicated real estate fund. In particular, its focused fund formation team has a highly regarded national reputation for its work in REITs and REOCs. Further recent highlights have included advice to HEI Hospitality Fund

on a $250 million hotel investment fund and acting for Friend Skoler Equity Investors on its $250 million midmarket LBO fund. The firm also offers expertise in investment management.

The Lawyers: Clients respect **David Watson** (see p.979) as an *"extremely knowledgeable"* practitioner renowned for his work on real estate funds. Peers rate the quality of his work within this specialist arena. He has recently assisted Beacon Capital Strategic Partners III in raising its $1 billion real estate opportunity fund.

The Clients: Advent International; Beacon Capital Partners; Friend Skoler & Co; GMO Renewable Resources; Great Hill Partners; Kimco Realty and RREEF America.

Weil, Gotshal & Manges LLP

See firm details p.1378

The Firm: Since its arrival in Massachusetts through merger less than three years ago, this firm has built on the existing resources and forged strong links with the teams in Texas and New York and attorneys across Europe, particularly London. The team is particularly renowned for its buyout fund representation. Clients appreciate the firm's *"international depth,"* although the Boston office continues to successfully foster a *"regional identity"* that has ensured the loyalty of its existing client base.

The Lawyers: Senior practitioner **Charles Robins** (see p.975) continues to be involved in the counseling and representation of private equity firms, especially with regard to strategic issues.

The Clients: Berkshire Partners, TH Lee Putnam Ventures and Thomas H Lee Partners are key clients of this firm.

Wilmer Cutler Pickering Hale and Dorr LLP

See firm details p.497

The Firm: According to sources, Hale & Dorr's merger with Wilmer Cutler has added *"an extra layer of quality and volume"* to a fund formation practice that *"wasn't huge but was great quality."* With a diverse geographical client base, the firm often undertakes work on funds run out of eastern and central Europe, in addition to those in New England and across the USA. The attorneys here are admired for their *"deep market knowledge,"* tax expertise and, most particularly, their client-oriented approach. The lawyers are respected by the venture capital and investor communities alike, and possess an excellent understanding of the hi-tech and biotech industries.

The Lawyers: This team has been bolstered by the recent arrival of its new head of private equity, *"top-class"* **Tom Beaudoin** (see p.962) from Testa, Hurwitz & Thibeault. Sources valued him for his experience with venture capital funds and pointed to his impressive client rostra and his *"endless amounts of energy."* **Sarah Rothermel**

www.ChambersandPartners.com
All quotes in the text are from interviews with clients and competitors.
955

(see p.976) is *"a zealous advocate for her clients,"* who stands out as *"someone who really knows how to handle private equity deals."* She adopts an *"extremely reasonable"* position in deal negotiations and maintains excellent judgment, particularly in her work with investment banks.

The Clients: Alpha Associates; John Hancock; Greylock Partners; Matrix Partners and Valhalla Partners.

REAL ESTATE

Massachusetts
Leading firms (Real Estate)

[1]	**DLA PIPER RUDNICK GRAY CARY** *Boston*
	GOODWIN PROCTER LLP *Boston*
	GOULSTON & STORRS *Boston*
[2]	**WILMER CUTLER PICKERING HALE** *Boston*
[3]	**NUTTER, MCCLENNEN & FISH, LLP** *Boston*
	PALMER & DODGE LLP *Boston*
[4]	**BINGHAM MCCUTCHEN LLP** *Boston*
	BROWN RUDNICK BERLACK ISRAELS *Boston*

Leading individuals (Real Estate)

[1]	**FISHMAN Robert** *Nutter McClennen, Boston*
	GLAZER Michael *Goodwin Procter, Boston*
	KRASNOW Jordan *Goulston & Storrs, Boston*
	ROTTENBERG Alan *Goulston & Storrs, Boston*
	SURKIN Elliot *DLA Piper, Boston*
[2]	**BARKER Christopher** *Goodwin Procter, Boston*
	BLOCH Thomas *Goulston & Storrs, Boston*
	HAROZ Michael *Goulston & Storrs, Boston*
	MITCHELL Beth *Nutter McClennen, Boston*
	RATTIGAN John *Palmer & Dodge, Boston*
	RUDMAN Richard *DLA Piper, Boston*
	SIRKIN Joel *Wilmer Cutler, Boston*
	SULLIVAN John *DLA Piper, Boston*
[3]	**BACHMAN Katharine** *Wilmer Cutler, Boston*
	CHRISTIAN Joseph *Wilmer Cutler, Boston*
	FORBUSH III William *DLA Piper, Boston*
	GREEN Barry *Goulston & Storrs, Boston*
	JAKUBOWSKI Paul *Wilmer Cutler, Boston*
	KAY Minta *Goodwin Procter, Boston*
	KWASNICK Raymond *Goulston & Storrs, Boston*
	MOFFATT Maura *Goodwin Procter, Boston*
	O'REILLY William *Wilmer Cutler, Boston*
	RECK Joel *Brown Rudnick, Boston*
	ROBINSON Marcia *Bingham McCutchen, Boston*
	SCHWARTZ Paul *Goodwin Procter, Boston*
	TOELKE Richard *Bingham McCutchen, Boston*

Up-and-coming individuals

	HOWELL Geoffrey *DLA Piper, Boston*
	TRIBUSH Bruce *Goodwin Procter, Boston*

Firms and individuals are listed alphabetically in each band.

Band 1

DLA Piper Rudnick Gray Cary
See firm details p.765

The Firm: Competitors concede that this national player is *"a real force"* in the local market, typically acting for owner/developers on complex urban projects. Real estate is a core practice area for the firm. Its 20-strong team in Boston can draw on coast-to-coast resources, giving it substantial domestic and international capability. Clients talk of lawyers *"who want to do deals, not prove how smart they are."* That the entire operation is geared toward quality representation was also stressed. In addition to serving a strong developer client base the firm acts for institutional investors, including pension funds and publicly traded real estate companies.

The Lawyers: *"Formidable thinker and manager"* **Elliot Surkin** (see p.978) heads the Boston office and personifies the deal-making ability of this team. He has acted as general real estate counsel for many of the major development projects in the Boston area including North Point and Fan Pier. He was also involved in the sale of the Providence Place Mall, one of the largest retail shopping centers in New England, for over $500 million. *"Sharp and practical"* **Richard Rudman** (see p.976) was deemed to *"represent clients vigorously to great effect."* He usually acts for developers. Highlights of this work have included the redevelopment of Lovejoy Wharf. Rudman also keeps a hand in on the institutional investor front, recently representing Washington DC client ASB Capital Management in several joint venture investments. Clients welcome his business approach and find his local authority contacts *"add value"* when it comes to the approval process. **John Sullivan** (see p.963) is known for the commercial real estate aspects of his capital markets practice. He acts for a number of sophisticated investors on deals that often take him out of state. Clients said *"he is not easily flustered"* in negotiations and brings *"good business sense"* to the table. Sullivan recently closed a large transaction involving over 30 industrial properties in multiple states and acted for the equity capital provider in a New Jersey joint venture apartment/condominium project. Representing pension fund advisers is another forte of his. **William Forbush** (see p.966) divides his practice between financing and commercial leasing. He handles all kinds of finance projects for major institutional clients, such as AEW Capital Management, and also boasts long-established client relations with several downtown office tower owners. He handled the leasing and structuring for the development of an office building at 100 Cambridge Street. Sources singled out **Geoffrey Howell** (see p.968) as an up-and-coming talent. His practice focuses on development and leasing work for regional and national developers operating in Boston and New England. On the leasing side he has a niche biotech laboratory practice: as primary leasing counsel for Lyme Properties he helped negotiate a major anchor lease for a medical and laboratory building at the Blackfan Research Center. He is also leasing counsel to Science Park and handled a substantial amount of work for several real estate fund management clients. **Gregory Bialecki** (see p.963) is recommended in the land use area in recognition of his *"enormous experience in waterfront work."* His practice spans the permitting, construction and development of major projects, for example Fan Pier and North Point.

The Clients: The Congress Group; The Davis Companies; Tishman Speyer Properties; Lyme Properties; AEW Capital Management; Fidelity Investments and Charlesbank Capital Partners.

Goodwin Procter LLP
See firm details p.980

The Firm: This full-service operation retains its top spot, not least on the basis of consistent commendation of its flair for handling capital-raising matters and REITs. This dovetails nicely with the firm's corporate standing and with recommended corporate lawyer Gil Menna being described as *"the god of REITs on a national basis."* Clients acknowledged numerous other strengths, including in pure real estate matters. Its broad client base and *"tremendous amount of expertise"* mean this substantial team can assist on *"every type of deal you can imagine,"* enthuse clients. The real estate lawyers draw on considerable expertise available elsewhere in the firm, including in ancillary areas such as tax.

The Lawyers: Clients applaud a team described as *"talented at every level"* that will *"work unbelievably hard to gets things done."* Highly respected **Michael Glazer** (see p.967) chairs the real estate investment management practice. He acts for a number of real estate investors, funds and advisers in complex transactions on a national basis. Recent matters include representing SSR Realty Advisors in numerous joint ventures nationwide. Peers consider Glazer *"a pleasure to have on the other side; a smart and practical attorney who is focused on the client's needs and closing the transaction."* **Christopher Barker** (see p.961) is overall head of the firm's real estate group. He has primarily concentrated on transactions in the investment management and public REIT arena. He also fields niche expertise in the hospitality industry, closing over $1 billion in hotel

Massachusetts
Leading individuals
(Real Estate: Zoning/Land Use)

1 **BIALECKI** Gregory *DLA Piper*, Boston
FISHMAN Robert *Nutter McClennen*, Boston
HALEY Joseph *Goodwin Procter*, Boston
HEALY Martin *Goodwin Procter*, Boston
HUSID Douglas *Goulston & Storrs*, Boston
KIEFER Matthew *Goulston & Storrs*, Boston
LYMAN R Jeffrey *Goodwin Procter*, Boston
NYLEN Richard *Lynch DeSimone*, Boston
PUTZIGER Myrna *Rubin and Rudman*, Boston
TWOHIG John *Goulston & Storrs*, Boston

Individuals are listed alphabetically in each band.

transactions in the past year alone. **Paul Schwartz** (see p.976) focuses on the range of issues affecting clients in the real estate investment management business, including capital raising and investing, and the compensation of senior personnel. Clients consider him "*a natural*" when it comes to fund formation: "*When he talks you know that he has understood the ramifications instantly.*" **Minta Kay** (see p.969) is recognized as a "*tough negotiator.*" She is especially known for representing investors and finance clients in complex transactions across a range of property types. **Maura Griffith Moffatt** (see p.972) "*has the biggest rising star next to her name,*" according to peers, whom she impressed with a combination of common sense, intuitiveness and great sense of humor. She is said to be particularly well connected in the market and "*clearly relied on heavily.*" Up-and-comer **Bruce Tribush** (see p.978) enters the tables for the first time following strong recommendations. He "*understands the issues facing developers*" and is considered "*a facilitator in terms of seeing a complicated transaction through to the end.*" Senior figure **Joseph Haley** (see p.968) acts mostly on the developer side, increasingly on permitting and land use issues, overseeing projects from the planning to construction stage. One client commented: "*What makes him a unique lawyer is that he understands the business side – he doesn't go in with blinders on but knows how to strategize.*" **Martin Healy** (see p.968) is a land use attorney specializing in environmental law. He heads the firm's real estate development and permitting practice group. Healy's recent focus has been on the land use/zoning aspects of complex development projects. He also acts for a major waste management client in connection with the permitting of new landfill areas. Clients value his creative approach and find that "*he just knows the whole process extremely well.*" Permitting lawyer **Jeffrey Lyman** (see p.971) is "*a rising star on the scene,*" say peers. Considered an expert when it comes to complex ocean front regulations, he formerly worked at the Massachusetts EPA and is "*well tuned to political sensitivities.*" He has recently been working on all kinds of permitting

issues for a golf course, luxury home and conference center development on the North Shore.
The Clients: AEW Capital Management; SSR Realty Advisors; Fidelity Investments; The Wilder Companies; Four Seasons; Prudential Real Estate Investors; La Quinta; Millennium Partners; Beacon Capital Partners; Equity Office Properties; HEI Hospitality; Wyndham Hotels & Resorts; Leggat McCall Properties and Cabot Properties.

Goulston & Storrs

The Firm: The sheer size of its real estate group is enough to separate it from competitors. As a result "*in terms of the raw number of deals, it would be hard to beat.*" The team handles a diverse range of work, but is probably best known for its "*hands-on*" development expertise, acting for most of the major developers in the region. Clients talk of a "*prompt and professional*" service, while peers repeatedly emphasize: "*These are serious lawyers doing the high-profile deals.*" On the financing front the firm acts for lenders and borrowers, providing an extra perspective that clients find particularly useful.
The Lawyers: A deep bench begins with **Jordan Krasnow** and **Alan Rottenberg**, "*two of the great real estate lawyers in town.*" Krasnow spends a substantial amount of time representing Beacon Capital Partners and AvalonBay in significant transactions on local and national levels, recently handling the disposition of multiple assets in Washington DC involving complex tax issues. He stands out for his deal-making ability and "*is always at the top of a conflict list.*" Clients appreciate the fact that he will "*roll up his sleeves and actually do the work himself.*" Rottenberg focuses on the owner side, working on a mix of large projects that often involve complex public/private financing. He recently spent a considerable amount of time representing New England Development on the Pier 4 mixed-use project. He is an attorney who "*really understands the overall goal and needs of the client.*" **Michael Haroz** "*is just so damn smart,*" say peers. His practice is split between lender and developer matters, with a recent emphasis on the latter. Major projects where Haroz was involved include Boston's Convention Center Hotel and a mixed-use commercial development outside the District of Columbia. He has also assisted with various construction loans in the Boston area and represented the lead lender in a mixed-use condominium project in Florida. Clients particularly value his thoroughness: "*When you get something from him, you just know it is done right.*" **Thomas Bloch** is "*very much a deal-maker,*" agree interviewees. He advises developers and entrepreneurs on the structuring and financing of real estate transactions, and recently represented foreign inbound investors in US real estate, for example German funds. "*Bright*" **Raymond Kwasnick** specializes in leasing and construc-

tion but has seen his practice broaden over the past year to include more general real estate transactions such as representing State Street Bank in the sale of two of its buildings. Other work includes representing Partners HealthCare on leasing and construction issues relating to a research and lab facility in Charles River Plaza. "*Incredibly smart*" **Barry Green** is a newcomer to the table following a number of compelling recommendations. He is credited with attracting overseas investor clients and increasingly "*getting involved in sophisticated transactions.*" Interviewees described him as "*full of energy; he gets thousands of things done and does them all very well.*" The firm's expertise across the spectrum of real estate law makes it a natural choice for land use matters. **Douglas Husid** advises clients on the development and permitting of major projects, including the Boston Convention Center. His previous experience at the Executive Office of Transportation and Construction and involvement in the Central Artery project make him an excellent negotiator. **Matthew Kiefer** is "*a big-picture lawyer*" typically advising on planning issues surrounding complex urban projects. Recent work includes the proposed master plan redevelopment of the Boston Museum of Fine Arts. "*Terrific*" **John Twohig** leads on permitting in the Pier 4 development project and is known for taking the New England Patriots through the approval process for building the Gillette Stadium.
The Clients: New England Development; Boston Properties; SR Weiner; The Green Company; Beacon Capital Partners; John Hancock; Samuels & Associates; Boston Redevelopment Authority; Winn Development Company and Northland Investment Corporation.

Band 2

Wilmer Cutler Pickering Hale and Dorr LLP
See firm details p.497
The Firm: Real estate may not be the focal point for this recently merged giant, but a sizeable team nevertheless retains a prominent position in the market and a diverse client following. Eleven partners in Boston have been bolstered by the addition of a group from the former Wilmer Cutler's Baltimore base, a move expected to enhance the outfit's national and international footprints. Institutional debt and equity, development and capital management are the core areas besides corporate support and an increasing amount of international work. The firm's full-service capability is a major advantage for clients, who appreciate the responsiveness and creative approach of these lawyers. As one interviewee explained: "*I don't have to chase them for esoteric tax or environmental advice, because they always have a specialist on hand.*" Another remarked on "*the refreshing willingness*

of lawyers firm-wide to foster a cross-disciplinary approach that best serves the interests of clients."

The Lawyers: Department chair **Joel Sirkin** (see p.977) is a respected senior member of the team. He focused recently on institutional investment matters while continuing to act as general real estate counsel to Berkshire Income Realty. Sirkin also represented numerous banks and financial institutions in statewide and nationwide projects including Fidelity Investments and AEW Capital Management. In line with the firm's reputation in the biotech field, he served as lead counsel for Novartis in the development of its biomedical research headquarters in Cambridge (Massachusetts). *"Technically excellent"* **Katharine Bachman** (see p.961) maintains a broad practice spanning development and permitting, financing, acquisition and sales, and leasing. She was recently involved in several affordable housing projects under the federal low income tax credit program, and handled a number of acquisitions for a REIT investing in life science facilities across New England. Clients describe her as *"a deal-doer – not one for picking non-essential fights with opposing counsel."* **Joseph Christian** (see p.964) is most associated with the team's international exposure. He recently closed the initial phase of financing for the development over a ten-year period of a new city in Korea on behalf of the first ever US/South Korean real estate venture. He is especially recommended for his *"ability to capture the practical business aspects of a transaction."* Generalist **William O'Reilly** (see p.973) is *"exceptional – a true businessman's lawyer,"* according to clients, who welcome his *"ability to couch issues in the broader context for the client."* New entrant **Paul Jakubowski** (see p.969) has impressed peers across the table. He enjoys a rising profile in the market and recently acted for a national retailer in a series of site acquisitions and associated development issues.

The Clients: New institutional clients include LaSalle Investment Management. Firm members represented LaSalle Investment Management and its pension fund clients in billions of dollars' worth of property transactions across the USA. Recent development highlights include representing Equity Office Properties in the redevelopment of Russia Wharf, a mixed-use waterfront complex in Boston. Other clients include Campanelli Companies, Alexander Real Estate Equities and Trinity Financial.

Band 3

Nutter, McClennen & Fish, LLP

The Firm: There are about 25 attorneys in this well-respected practice, dividing their time fairly evenly between landowner/developer and lender work. On the development front the team advises private developers and nonprofit organizations on major projects, most notably in the healthcare and education sectors. The firm is particularly well known for the expertise of its separate land use group, which is considered to add value to a transaction. On the lender side it has seen an increase in the representation of banks in the Boston area, including KeyBank, Eastern Bank and Anglo Irish Bank. Significant work for several major life assurance companies also contributed to recent activity. Clients particularly recommended these attorneys for their low-key, efficient approach to handling potentially tricky situations.

The Lawyers: **Robert Fishman** is *"one of those competent professionals who you know with confidence will analyze intelligently and get the job done,"* say peers. As chair of the land use group, his practice focuses primarily on owner/developer advice and recently featured substantial permitting work. The past year also saw Fishman handle several large financings for institutional clients. Significant matters include negotiating with the City of Boston regarding zoning approvals for the mall redevelopment at Boston's Assembly Square, and handling zoning and permitting for the Station Landing project, an example of *"smart growth"* development. Acting for nonprofit clients is another growing source of instructions for Fishman and recently included assisting a nursing home organization with developing a major assisted living facility in a Boston suburb. The *"terrific"* **Beth Mitchell** advises on large acquisitions and financings, particularly construction and permanent financings for new apartment and retail projects. She usually acts for the lender and is especially valued in complex, multiparty transactions, where she *"does an excellent job of herding a group of cats through the same door."* Mitchell recently represented a consortium of lenders in the construction/permanent mortgage financing of the Trilogy project in Boston's Fenway district. She also continues to represent South Shore Tri-Town Development Corporation in the redevelopment of the former South Weymouth Naval Air Station.

The Clients: Anglo Irish Bank; Connecticut General Life Insurance; GMAC Commercial Mortgage and New York State Teachers' Retirement System.

Palmer & Dodge LLP

See firm details p.984

The Firm: This team of 21 continues to stand out against the Boston legal scene for its involvement in public-private enterprises. Private developer clients found a wealth of experience of dealing with public agencies and redevelopment authorities especially useful, particularly during the initial permitting and approval stages of a project. Three core areas are real estate development and finance, construction and public projects, and the representation of colleges and universities (Tufts University is a recent addition to the client base). The firm has also expanded its related airport practice by creating outposts in Washington and New York. While the majority of work is undertaken for clients in the New England region, niche expertise in major infrastructure projects often takes the team further afield. This has recently included instructions on a multibillion-dollar subway tunnel project in New York.

The Lawyers: Standout figure **John Rattigan** (see p.975) is *"just an excellent, practical real estate attorney."* Concentrating on private developer advice, he continues to assist Millennium Partners-Boston on several major projects, and has been working with national retail real estate company Edens & Avant on developing two strip shopping centers. Peers consider him *"a pleasure to work with – someone who will strive to make the deal happen."* A new strand to his practice involved acting for a German investment fund in its acquisition of a mall in Rhode Island.

The Clients: The firm advises public authorities, businesses, institutional landowners and private developers. These include: Port Authority of Oakland; Millennium Partners-Boston; Hines; Massachusetts Port Authority; Edens & Avant and Massachusetts Convention Center Authority.

Band 4

Bingham McCutchen LLP

The Firm: Its corporate prowess makes the firm well positioned to advise on the full range of complex real estate financing matters, the area in which it is best known. It acts for a wide variety of clients and has seen an increase in owner/developer activity spanning the *"soup to nuts"* issues for both large institutional clients and small real estate developers. Though the bread-and-butter work tends to be local, lawyers act for a couple of REITs buying on a national basis.

The Lawyers: **Rich Toelke** is particularly admired for his deal-making abilities. He has been heavily involved in representing joint ventures. He acted for Berkeley Investments and Starwood Capital Group in the redevelopment of Worcester Mall. Toelke also assisted Essex River Ventures and equity partner The Praedium Group in the acquisition and financing of Lexington Corporate Center. *"Excellent"* **Marcia Robinson** is key player in the Boston office. She enters the tables this year having acted for the likes of Harvard University and Boston Scientific.

The Clients: The firm advises lenders, developers, pension fund advisers, REITs, banks and corporations on a range of transactions and property types.

Brown Rudnick Berlack Israels LLP

The Firm: Although some market observers feel the firm's profile in real estate is losing out to its bankruptcy profile, this multidisciplinary team continues to handle a wide variety of work for a diverse client base, across New England and increasingly nationwide. Clients acknowledge having access to lawyers in the firm's Hartford and Providence bases as a benefit. Attorneys are also available in offices in New York, Washington and London. The firm continues to act for LNR Properties on the mixed-use redevelopment of South Weymouth Naval Air Station. This experience has led to similar work, advising Carabetta Enterprises and The Shaw Group on the privatization of over 10,000 housing units on a number of military bases nationwide. Niche areas include affordable housing and retail development, for the likes of national retailers

Target Stores, Staples, and Bed Bath & Beyond. Its expertise in structured 1031 tax-free exchange transactions has also been in demand recently. **The Lawyers:** Clients refer to *"a nicely assembled team,"* with immediate partner accessibility and high-quality associates. They are especially impressed by the personal service they receive and the fact that these attorneys *"are very well connected in the market."* **Joel Reck** is real estate department chair and considered the go-to figure for strategic advice on large projects. He maintains a generalist practice, with a recent focus on development, acquisitions and sales. **The Clients:** Spaulding & Slye Colliers; KBS Realty Advisors; Teradyne; Brooks Automation; Kendall Companies; Tyco; Sun Microsystems; Boston, Cambridge and Somerville housing authorities; East Boston Community Development Corporation and Rogerson Communities.

Other Notable Practitioners

"Terrific" **Myrna Putziger** at Rubin & Rudman LLP is clearly a name in land use and one of the stronger practitioners for permitting at the local level. Her practice includes zoning, subdivision, environmental and title review and permitting. **Chip Nylen** (see p.963), of smaller shop Lynch DeSimone & Nylen LLP, enters the table in recognition of his deep experience and knowledge in the often complex area of wetlands and Chapter 91 permitting, in particular relating to development on the oceanfront. Interviewees describe him as *"a great practitioner with a practical approach to regulatory issues – he doesn't throw the kitchen sink at a case but uses smarter resources to get to the heart of the matter."*

TAX

Massachusetts
Leading firms (Tax)

1	**GOODWIN PROCTER LLP** *Boston*
	ROPES & GRAY LLP *Boston*
	WILMER CUTLER PICKERING HALE *Boston*
2	**BINGHAM MCCUTCHEN LLP** *Boston*
3	**FOLEY HOAG LLP** *Boston*
	SULLIVAN & WORCESTER LLP *Boston*

Leading individuals (Tax)

1	**BROWN John** *Bingham McCutchen*, Boston
	CUBELL Howard *Goodwin Procter*, Boston
	SHAY Stephen *Ropes & Gray*, Boston
2	**ELFMAN Eric** *Ropes & Gray*, Boston
	RITT Roger *Wilmer Cutler*, Boston
	WATSON Rom *Ropes & Gray*, Boston
3	**ABRAMS Donald-Bruce** *Bingham* Boston
	BENJAMIN William *Wilmer Cutler*, Boston
	BURKE Robert *Wilmer Cutler*, Boston
	CORCORAN William *Osler Hoskin & Harcourt*, New York
	DAVIS Michael *Sullivan & Worcester*, Boston
	GIULIANI Richard *Wilmer Cutler*, Boston
	JOHNSTON Susan *Ropes & Gray*, Boston
	LEICH Christopher *Ropes & Gray*, Boston
	MARETT Louis *Choate Hall*, Boston
	MAY Arnold *Proskauer Rose*, Boston
	SCHNALL Matthew *Bingham McCutchen*, Boston
	SCHNEIDMAN Leonard *Foley Hoag*, Boston
	WHITLEDGE William *Goodwin Procter*, Boston

Leading individuals
(Tax: Employee Benefits)

1	**CLEARY John** *Goodwin Procter*, Boston
	HUGG Joseph *DLA Piper*, Boston
	ISAIA Russell *Bingham McCutchen*, Boston
	SCHMIDT William *Wilmer Cutler*, Boston
	ZORN Jonathan *Ropes & Gray*, Boston

Firms and individuals are listed alphabetically in each band.

Band 1

Goodwin Procter LLP
See firm details p.980

The Firm: The firm's *"very significant"* tax group, comprising around 15 lawyers, continues to win praise from all quarters. A transactions-oriented practice reflects the firm's undisputed strength in corporate and real estate arenas. Its celebrated specialist REIT expertise gives the operation an added edge. Private equity-related tax work, both fund formation and transactional, is a major focus for the group. Providing general *"catch-all"* corporate tax advice to US and foreign businesses on a state, federal and international level also accounts for a considerable portion of the workload. Clients highlighted the responsiveness of its lawyers – *"they do what they say they're going to do, when they say they will"* – and find that the team is *"very quick at sizing up a situation and instantly identifying any problems that might exist."* That the expertise of an integrated ERISA and employee benefits group is on hand as required was also considered an advantage.

The Lawyers: *"Can-do"* group chair **Howard Cubell** (see p.965) personifies the creative quality of this *"deep"* team. Describing him as *"a very bright and pleasant individual,"* clients like the fact that Cubell's style borders on the aggressive – *"he is not overly cautious and will push things close to the line, but he has a lot of integrity and will always back his judgments with opinions."* His practice focuses largely on the structuring and sale of private equity investments, in addition to the general mix of M&A tax-related advice. Recent highlights including representing TA Associates in the $240 million recapitalization of Numeric Investors. An increase in private

equity transactions overseas has been a recent feature of Cubell's practice. **William Whitledge** (see p.979) boasts *"an exceptional combination of technical skill and practical business judgment,"* sources report. His practice reflects that of the team as a whole, encompassing private equity, real estate finance and M&A work. He recently acted for Arclight Capital Partners and Medical Facilities Corp. in the first two public offerings of income preferred securities in Canada by US businesses. Marian Tse and **John Cleary** (see p.964) are key figures on the ERISA/employee benefits side. Tse chairs the group and focuses primarily on executive compensation issues, while Cleary *"combines the technical mind of an MIT grad with that of a Yale Law School grad:"* skills that make him the go-to guy for advice on sophisticated, complex structures.

The Clients: Many clients are based around Boston's financial money management center. Examples are Beacon Capital Strategic Partners; Morgan Stanley; Citizens Financial Group; Kimco Realty and Boston Properties.

Ropes & Gray LLP
See firm details p.985

The Firm: Researchers were left in no doubt as to the firm's strength in the field. Boasting over 50 lawyers, this tax and benefits practice offers *"such depth right across the tax spectrum – they simply have it all covered."* Clients hold its deeply experienced lawyers in high regard. Many team members have previously held positions in government. That the firm offers a local service described as *"comparable to the largest firms, but without the hierarchy,"* was also considered an attractive attribute. Its prowess in domestic tax issues is complemented by an accomplished international tax practice. Traditionally thought to derive considerable leverage from its impressive stable of private equity clients, the firm recently boosted its life sciences profile upon merging with New York IP boutique Fish & Neave. Clients especially value the ability of this team to *"think outside the box"* on complex issues. Recent highlights include advising Bain Capital in the acquisition of Loews Cineplex Entertainment.

The Lawyers: *"All-round excellent lawyer"* **Stephen Shay** (see p.977) is extremely well regarded for his substantial international tax expertise. He *"brings a lot to the table based on his IRS background,"* say clients, and frequently advises on matters such as transfer pricing, foreign tax credits and withholding taxes. Clients clearly value his thorough and strategic approach. **Rom Watson** (see p.979) also wins plaudits for his international practice. His previous experience as associate international tax counsel at the US Department of the Treasury means that he *"is especially astute at identifying the relevant issues."* His key strength is his practicality, agree clients. Watson has particular expertise relating to the tax aspects of securities lending and financial products. **Eric Elfman** (see p.966) *"is one of the foremost authorities on US corporate taxation,"* according to sources. He continues to advise a large number of clients in the life science and private equity sectors. Recent work included the Loews acquisition, the recapitalization and IPO of Domino's Pizzas and working as special tax counsel with a New York firm on one of the growing number of so-called 'club deals' to have taken place recently. He has also been busy advising Genzyme on the tax aspects of its acquisition of ILEX. Clients found that Elfman's previous government experience helps considerably in practical dealings with the government. *"Savvy"* **Susan Johnston** (see p.969) heads the department and *"has a unique ability to take very complex concepts and communicate them in such a way that a lay person can understand them."* She concentrates her practice on the regulated investment and mutual fund area, frequently advising on the tax implications in complex fund structures and reorganizations. She is *"incredibly knowledgeable,"* report clients, especially in the arena of financial services and complex derivative instruments. **Christopher Leich** (see p.971) is respected for his transactional tax practice, and also highly valued for his *"ability to explain complex matters to someone who isn't a tax specialist."* Recent work highlights include acting for Bain in the acquisition of Dollarama's business operations, including liaising with Luxembourg and Canadian counsel. **Jonathan Zorn** (see p.979) is a *"smart guy"* when it comes to employee benefits and compensation issues.

The Clients: BainCapital; Millipore; Genzyme; Gillette; Timberland; Silver Lake Partners; Fenway Partners; Softbank Capital Partners; Brooks Automation; EMC; Barclays Global Investors; Columbia Management Group; State Street Bank & Trust Company and Harvard Management.

Wilmer Cutler Pickering Hale and Dorr LLP

See firm details p.936759

The Firm: This newly merged firm moves up the table in recognition of its increased visibility in the market and on account of the large proportion of its tax specialists attracting recommendations. Special mention must be made of the strong bench of junior partners and associates here, who picked up high praise from clients for their *"ability to distill complex facts and communicate technical regulations in a way that all parties can really understand."* The merger added critical mass and created the potential to service a new high-end client base, thanks to Wilmer Cutler's connections in DC. A primarily transaction-driven practice supports the firm's renowned corporate department in M&A deals. Fund formation, partnership tax and other specialty areas such as ERISA, employee benefits and executive compensation are also integral to the operation.

The Lawyers: There was strong consensus that **Roger Ritt** (see p.975) is the most well-known M&A tax expert in the Boston office. Clients value his creative approach and the fact that he *"refuses to give up in a situation."* He also advises mutual fund complexes on taxation issues. Recent work includes advising Modus Media on the tax aspects of its acquisition by CMGI. **William Benjamin** (see p.962) wins plaudits for his distinctly international tax practice. He acts for both US businesses abroad and foreign clients doing business in the USA. Recent work included advising an Australian client on the acquisition of assets in Switzerland, and a US company doing business in China. **Robert Burke** (see p.964) is a *"guru"* when it comes to the taxation of partnerships and limited liability companies, especially in relation to complex real estate and hedge fund investment activity. **Richard Giuliani** (see p.967) impresses with his detail-oriented approach and knowledge base, particularly at the state and local level. His broad practice encompasses transactional work, significant controversy matters and advising mutual funds on tax planning. **William Schmidt** (see p.976) enters the table following recommendations for his compensation law expertise. This includes advising investment management clients of their responsibilities under ERISA. He has advised pension plan providers and acted for clients in relation to ESOPs.

The Clients: The firm's client base revolves around technology and life science entities operating on a national and global scale. These clients tend to be based around Boston and DC. Examples include: DoubleClick; Bookham Technology; Netegrity and M-Audio.

Band 2

Bingham McCutchen LLP

The Firm: Sources agree that this is the firm you would seek out in New England for its experience base in federal and state tax controversy work. The team represents clients in courts and administrative proceedings, as well as in dealings with the Internal Revenue Service and Massachusetts Department of Revenue. Recent work included a number of major representations at the Massachusetts Appellate Tax Board. Clients talk of *"user-friendly"* lawyers, who are *"extremely dependable."* The practice also extends to the range of transaction-related tax advice that, given the firm's *"wonderful"* corporate client base, is an area of expertise in constant demand.

The Lawyers: *"Superb"* **John Brown** leads the practice and *"does an outstanding job at securing positive outcomes in situations of controversy."* He has an excellent reputation in this area of law and is considered *"a key component of the brain trust"* at the firm. Clients agree that **Donald-Bruce Abrams'** engineering background enables him to *"combine sophisticated technical skills with a pragmatic commercial outlook."* The two often cooperate on controversy matters, whereby their appellate experience is *"unsurpassed."* Abrams also maintains a broad transactions-based practice. **Matthew Schnall** is another integral member of the team. He was deemed to be *"building his practice nicely,"* handling a diverse mix of work, from controversies to transactional tax planning and advising on tax-exempt bond financing. **Russell Isaia** is recognized for his strength in employee benefits and executive compensation.

The Clients: Boston Scientific; PerkinElmer; Harvard University; Raytheon Company; National Grid USA; Bank of America; Invensys and AT&T.

Band 3

Foley Hoag LLP

The Firm: Clients perceive the relatively compact nature of this transactions-oriented group to be capable of casting a fresh eye on matters and offer an innovative approach. Key areas of expertise include international tax planning, not to mention advising hedge and other investment funds. A distinctive niche in representing US entities investing in forestry plantations and other natural resources in the Southern Hemisphere further defines the practice. It also advises high net-worth individuals.

The Lawyers: *"Creative"* **Leonard Schneidman** is noted for his international tax-planning expertise and is a former chair of the firm's tax department. The main thrust of his practice involves assisting US clients doing business abroad, particularly in Europe, and counseling foreign clients coming into the US.

The Clients: Other clients include Millicom International Cellular and Global Forest Partners.

Sullivan & Worcester

The Firm: Tax is one of the key focus areas for the firm, which fields offices in Boston, New York and Washington DC. A versatile team of more than 20 lawyers handles a variety of matters, from corporate taxation and cross-border planning to federal and state controversy work, as well as planning for charitable trusts. The firm also boasts a separate trusts and estates practice.

The Lawyers: Senior figure **Michael Davis** heads up the group and has a wealth of experience, particularly when it comes to income tax and estate planning. His clients tend to be owners of closely held businesses, and those with large holdings of real estate and S corporation stock.

The Clients: Fortune 500 companies; entrepreneurs; financial institutions; closely held businesses; hedge funds; LBO and venture capital funds, and REITs.

Other Notable Practitioners

The following recommended attorneys have joined new firms following the dissolution of Testa, Hurwitz & Thibeault LLP. *"Exceptionally bright and practical"* **Louis Marett**, former chair of Testa's tax department, is now a partner in Choate Hall & Stewart's private equity practice group. Clients like the fact that he *"won't come into a transaction with specialist blinders on, but will look at the whole picture, not just the tax aspects."* He acts primarily for technology companies and associated investors, providing domestic and cross-border transactional support. He also advises on executive compensation issues. Recent work includes acting for Sand Video during its acquisition by Broadcom Corporation and advising Bessemer Venture Partners on the formation of Bessemer Venture Partners VI. *"Incredibly practical"* **Arnold May** (see p.972) is *"the first person I would turn to if the IRS came knocking,"* enthused one satisfied interviewee. This comment articulated the instant trust that May typically instills in his clients. He is one of a group of

Testa lawyers who moved over to bolster the new Boston office of Proskauer Rose LLP. May works at the interface of taxation and private equity, acting for institutional investor and fund clients on a national scale. Clients noted that he is *"not abrasive"* when dealing with other attorneys, and will *"look at a problem from all sides, then come up with creative ways of avoiding trouble."* Prior to going to press, **William Corcoran** relocated to Osler, Hoskin & Harcourt LLP in New York. He enters the table for the first time following recommendations for his cross-border tax planning expertise, in particular relating to transactions in Canada and Ireland. *"Bright and creative,"* he acts for private equity funds and investors and is also noted for his advice on the tax aspects of compensation strategies. **Tony Hugg** (see p.968) , now at DLA Piper Rudnick Gray Cary US LLP, is *"a superb attorney; smart, cost-conscious and thorough."* He is especially noted for his ERISA/employee benefits expertise. Clients like the fact that he is *"willing to engage in a back-and-forth discussion with the client."*

Leaders in Massachusetts

ABELSON, Ned
Goulston & Storrs, Boston
617 482 1776
Recommended in Environment

ABRAMS, Donald-Bruce
Bingham McCutchen LLP, Boston
617 951 8000
Recommended in Tax

ALFRED, Richard
Seyfarth Shaw LLP, Boston
617 946 4800
Recommended in Employment

AMBASH, Joseph
Seyfarth Shaw LLP, Boston
617 946 4800
Recommended in Employment

ANGLEHART, Donald
Gadsby Hannah LLP, Boston
617 345 7000
Recommended in Environment

APFEL, David J
Goodwin Procter LLP, Boston
617 570 1000
dapfel@goodwinprocter.com
Recommended in Litigation
Practice Areas: Mr Apfel is an experienced trial lawyer who defends individuals and entities in criminal and complex civil litigation. His areas of expertise are white collar crime, including insider trading and money laundering; government investigations, especially Department of Justice, US Attorneys Offices, SEC and NASD investigations; the federal False Claims Act; the federal Racke-

teer Influenced and Corrupt Organizations Act (RICO); and multi-dimensional business litigation. He also specializes in land use litigation.
Prof. Memberships: Massachusetts State 'Murder List': Member Attorney; US District Court's 'CJA Panel': Member Attorney.
Personal: JD, Northeastern University School of Law, 1987; BA, Swarthmore College, 1974.

APPELBAUM, Mitchel
Wilmer Cutler Pickering Hale and Dorr LLP, Boston 617 526 6713
mitchel.appelbaum@wilmerhale.com
Recommended in Bankruptcy
Practice Areas: Practice focuses on matters involving the financial restructuring of corporate clients, including the use of Chapter 11, secured lending, lease arrangements and other commercial transactions for clients. Advises variety of clients on acquisition of troubled companies through section 363 sales, and has counseled various secured and unsecured creditors with respect to bankruptcy, workout and restructuring matters.
Prof. Memberships: Turnaround Management Association; American, Massachusetts and Boston Bar Associations; Board of Directors, The Lawyers Clearinghouse for Homelessness and Affordable Housing, Inc.
Career: Admitted to Massachusetts Bar. Joined firm in 1991.
Personal: Boston University School of Law (JD); Brandeis University (BA).

ARMISTEAD III, I Cary
Ropes & Gray LLP, Boston
671 951 7832
cary.armistead@ropesgray.com
Recommended in Antitrust
Practice Areas: Counsels domestic and multinational corporations regarding corporate legal matters, the antitrust laws of the US, and the competition laws of European Union and other nations in: joint ventures, mergers, acquisitions, and divestitures; acquisition and licensing of intellectual property rights; distribution of products and services. Assists high-technology and other clients with domestic and international commercial matters including technology transfers, distribution and licensing agreements, and other complex business arrangements.
Career: District of Columbia Bar (1970). Massachusetts Bar (1979). Partner, Ropes & Gray (1996).
Personal: JD, cum laude, Columbia Law School (1970). BA, Economics, Michigan State University (1967).

ARNOLD, Beth
Foley Hoag LLP, Boston
617 832 1000
Recommended in Intellectual Property

ASHER Jr, William
Choate Hall & Stewart, Boston
617 248 5000
Recommended in Corporate/M&A

BACHMAN, Katharine E
Wilmer Cutler Pickering Hale and Dorr LLP, Boston 617 526 6216
katharine.bachman@wilmerhale.com
Recommended in Real Estate
Practice Areas: Vice-Chair of firm's Real Estate Department. Practice covers broad spectrum of real estate development and financial transactions, including representation of investors and developers in office, industrial, R&D facilities and residential developments. Represents institutional lenders in loan collection matters and landlords and tenants in commercial leasing matters (including high technology and biotechnology facilities). Special interest in projects involving public/private partnerships and affordable housing.
Prof. Memberships: New England Regional Advisory Committee of The Trust for Public Land; Trustee, Dickinson College.
Career: Admitted to Massachusetts Bar.
Personal: New York University School of Law (JD); Dickinson College, (BA, summa cum laude).

BALDIGA, William
Brown Rudnick Berlack Israels LLP, Boston 617 856 8200
Recommended in Bankruptcy

BARKER, Christopher
Goodwin Procter LLP, Boston
617 570 1000
cbarker@goodwinprocter.com
Recommended in Real Estate

Practice Areas: Mr Barker has particular expertise in representing tax-exempt entities in structuring and implementing debt and equity investments in real estate and in real estate operating companies. His practice, national in scope, involves representing institutional investors, public and private real estate operating companies and lenders in a wide range of real estate activities. Clients include: Charlesbank Capital Partners, AEW Capital Management, Fidelity Investments Real Estate Group, Westcor Partners, Beacon Capital Partners, AMB Properties, La Quinta Hotels, Wyndham Hotels, Leggat McCall Properties and Liberty Properties.
Personal: JD, Harvard Law School, 1985; BA, Brown University, 1982 (magna cum laude).

BARR, Lynne
Goodwin Procter LLP, Boston
617 570 1000
lbarr@goodwinprocter.com
Recommended in Banking & Finance
Practice Areas: Ms Barr advises banks, bank holding companies, brokerage concerns, mortgage companies, trade associations and other entities on general corporate matters, including the operation and offering of their products and services, particularly in the context of federal and state regulation of financial institutions and their activities. She has extensive experience in credit and mortgage lending matters, fair lending and equal credit opportunity issues, credit and deposit services, electronic banking and Internet services, and insurance products.
Personal: JD, George Washington University, 1975 (with honors); BA, George Washington University, 1972.

BARSHAK, Edward
Sugarman, Rogers, Barshak & Cohen, PC, Boston 617 227 3030
Recommended in Litigation

BASSETT, David
Wilmer Cutler Pickering Hale and Dorr LLP, Boston 617 526 6259
david.bassett@wilmerhale.com
Recommended in Intellectual Property
Practice Areas: Practice concentrates on intellectual property litigation, particularly on biotechnology patent disputes. Represents clients in wide variety of other business disputes, including breach of contract, Lanham Act and Internet-related claims. Covers all facets of litigation, including discovery, settlement, alternative dispute resolution, trials and appeals.
Prof. Memberships: American and Massachusetts Bar Associations; Co-Chair, Intellectual Property Litigation Committee of the Boston Bar Association.
Career: Admitted to Massachusetts Bar and Indiana Bar. Joined firm in 1989.
Personal: Harvard Law School (JD, cum laude); Editor, 'Harvard Law

Review'; Finalist, Ames Moot Court Competition; Indiana University (BA, with Honors and Distinction National Merit Scholarship).

BATES, Jeffrey
McDermott Will & Emery, Boston
617 535 4068
jbates@mwe.com
Recommended in Environment
Practice Areas: Practices international and environmental law. Has provided counsel to corporations, environmental organizations and governments in connection with international law, environmental litigation, due diligence, product roll-outs, compliance, cleanups, Brownfields development, insurance coverage and products, corporate and governmental policy, and legislation and rule-making worldwide. Has considerable experience with high profile, complex litigation and controversies. Currently acting for Italian and Swiss bondholders in Argentina Sovereign Debt Default litigation and providing insurance structuring advice on redevelopment of 270 railyard in Sacramento, California. Served as counsel on Doe v Milošević (human rights and war crimes violations in Kosovo); New Bedford Harbor, Boston Harbor and Lower Fox River (Wisconsin) litigation and cleanup; Woburn, Massachusetts litigation and cleanup featured in book and film, 'A Civil Action'; appeal of EPA rule implementing WTO Gasoline Standards decision; Caspian Sea delimitation; and anti-corruption matters for Bosnian President, Prime Minister and UN Ambassador.
Prof. Memberships: Admitted to practice before US Supreme Court, US District Court for the District of Massachusetts, US Court of Appeals for the First Circuit, US Court of Appeals for the District of Columbia and Supreme Judicial Court of Massachusetts.
Personal: Earned BA from Colgate University and JD from University of Virginia Law School.

BAUER, Steven M
Proskauer Rose LLP, Boston
617 526 9700
sbauer@proskauer.com
Recommended in Intellectual Property
Practice Areas: A Partner in Proskauer Rose's Patent Litigation Dispute Resolution Group and Head of the firm's Boston office. He has over 20 years of experience concentrating exclusively in complex patent and other intellectual property enforcement, litigation and dispute resolution. He has been lead trial counsel in litigations involving medical devices; software, encryption and business method processes; high-energy plasma systems; telecommunications and cable industry technology; nanotechnology; polymer chemistry; blood gas and genetic testing kits; high temperature superconductors; and digital compression techniques.

Prof. Memberships: An active member of the Roster of Neutrals of the American Arbitration Association; is vice-chair of the Litigation Committee of the Intellectual Property Owners' Association; was an Editor of the AIPLA Quarterly Journal.
Publications: He has published a number of papers, speaks regularly to leading patent law and industry groups (e.g., The Sedona Conference, MIT Sloan School, National Bureau of Economic Research, MCLE, BU Law School, BC Law School), and has been quoted often in the national press on intellectual property issues (e.g., 'The Economist', Associated Press, 'InfoWorld', 'Boston Business Journal' and Reuters.)
Personal: Boston University Sschool of Law, JD, 1983. Massachusetts Institute of Technology, MS, 1980. Massachusetts Institute of Technology, BS, 1979.

BEAUDOIN, Thomas A
Wilmer Cutler Pickering Hale and Dorr LLP, Boston 617 526 6661
thomas.beaudoin@wilmerhale.com
Recommended in Private Equity
Practice Areas: Firm's Fund Formation Group Chair. Advises US and non-US fund managers, institutional investors and investment advisers on broad range of issues, including capital formations, secondary transactions, portfolio investments, internal governance and administration, and divestments and distributions.
Prof. Memberships: American Bar Association; Massachusetts Bar Association; Boston Bar Association.
Career: Admitted to Massachusetts Bar. Partner at Testa, Hurwitz & Thibeault, LLP before joining firm in 2004.
Publications: Frequent lecturer and panelist at private equity industry-sponsored events (US and abroad); writes for several prominent private equity publications.
Personal: George Washington University Law School (JD, with Honors); Boston University (BA, cum laude).

BENJAMIN, William
Wilmer Cutler Pickering Hale and Dorr LLP, Boston 617 526 6318
william.benjamin@wilmerhale.com
Recommended in Tax
Practice Areas: Advises on legal and tax aspects of international business transactions. Represents US companies in connection with their activities outside the US, and foreign businesses and individuals with respect to their activities in the US.
Prof. Memberships: New England Regional Council of the International Fiscal Association; Editorial Advisory Board of Practical U.S./International Tax Strategies; International Bar Association; American Bar Association; Massachusetts Bar Association.
Career: Admitted to Massachusetts Bar, New York Bar, United States Tax Court. Joined firm in 1982.

Personal: Harvard Law School (JD, cum laude); Graduate Institute of International Studies, Fulbright Scholar; Princeton University (BA, summa cum laude).

BENNETT Jr, Charles R
Hanify & King, Boston 617 423 0400
crb@hanify.com
Recommended in Bankruptcy
Practice Areas: Complex commercial litigation involving financial institutions, contracts and corporate issues, including directors' and officers' claims and insolvency. The current focus of his practice is on rights and remedies for debtors and creditors in corporate Chapter 11 cases. Mr Bennett has substantial experience in banking and lending litigation representing both borrowers and banking institutions in commercial disputes, and has tried numerous jury and jury-waived cases concerning business torts, unfair trade practices, and insolvency issues.
Prof. Memberships: American Bankruptcy Institute, Massachusetts and Boston Bar Associations.
Career: Massachusetts Bar, New Hampshire Bar, Rhode Island Bar.
Personal: JD, Boston College Law School (1974); BA, cum laude, Boston College (1970).

BENOIT, Wilfred
Goodwin Procter LLP, Boston
617 570 1000
wbenoit@goodwinprocter.com
Recommended in Employment
Practice Areas: Mr Benoit has represented management in all types of labor and employee relations disputes since 1975. He also has extensive employment litigation and alternative dispute resolution experience. He has successfully defended companies across a broad spectrum of industries in suits involving a wide variety of wrongful discharge and employment discrimination issues, including disparate treatment, sexual and racial harassment, equal pay, reasonable accommodation of disabilities and age discrimination claims arising out of reductions in force.
Personal: JD, University of Michigan Law School, 1973 (cum laude); BA, University of Notre Dame, 1970 (cum laude).

BERMAN, David
Riemer & Braunstein LLP, Boston
617 523 9000
Recommended in Banking & Finance

BERMAN, Mark N
Nixon Peabody LLP, Boston
617 345 6037
mberman@nixonpeabody.com
Recommended in Bankruptcy
Practice Areas: Chapter 11 reorganizations, Chapter 7 liquidations, out-of-court workouts. Represents public/private companies, debtors, trustees, committees, secured and unsecured credi-

tors, equity, directors, consultants, liquidators, purchasers of assets/businesses.
Prof. Memberships: Admitted to practice in MA, US District Court (MA), US Court of Appeals (First Circuit), US Supreme Court. Boston Bar Association (former Chair Business Law Section and Bankruptcy Committee). American Bar Association, American Bankruptcy Institute (Ed. ABI World). Client Security Board (former vice chairman, secretary, and treasurer). Instructor in Business and Credit Law for National Association of Credit Management. Fellow, American College of Bankruptcy.
Personal: Boston College, JD; Northwestern University, BA.

BERNSTEIN, Stephen W
McDermott Will & Emery, Boston
617 535 4062
sbernstein@mwe.com
Recommended in Healthcare
Practice Areas: Co-Chair of HIPAA Practice and Health Transactions Practice. Specializes in e-health, health related matters impacted by the internet, and HIPAA, and M&As, affiliations and joint ventures in hospital and physician areas; fraud, abuse and Stark issues; and related licensing and regulatory matters. Has experience working with pharmaceutical, biotech, device companies, health care providers and insurers concerning uses of health information and tissue samples for clinical and database research, patient registries and marketing matters. Representative clients include: Genentech, Inc., Cardinal Health, Inc., Harvard University, IMS Health, Inc., Physicians' Organization at Children's Hospital, ChartOne, Inc., Massachusetts Eye & Ear Infirmary, Caritas Christi Health System and its affiliates, and The Massachusetts eHealth Collaborative.
Prof. Memberships: Member of Massachusetts, District of Columbia and California bars. Chaired Boston Bar Association's HIPAA/State Law Task Force's subcommittee on preemption, previously member of Massachusetts Medical Society's HIPAA speakers bureau. Member of the American Health Lawyers Association and its Health Information Technology Practice Group.
Career: Completed internships with British National Health Service and US House of Representatives Subcommittee on Health and Long-Term Care.
Personal: Earned JD (cum laude) in 1988 from Boston College Law School, and AB (magna cum laude) in 1985 from Duke University.

BETTENCOURT, Mark
Goodwin Procter LLP, Boston
617 570 1000
mbettencourt@goodwinprocter.com
Recommended in Corporate/M&A
Practice Areas: Mr Bettencourt concentrates his practice on general corporate and securities law and has extensive

experience in mergers and acquisitions, public offerings, private placements of debt and equity securities, securities law compliance, and technology transfer and licensing. He represents start-up, private and public companies in a wide range of industries, including software, hardware, networking equipment, information services and healthcare. He has worked with numerous companies from their initial financing through successful initial public offerings or acquisitions.
Personal: JD, New York University School of Law, 1994 (cum laude); BA, University of Notre Dame, 1991 (with high honors).

BIALECKI, Gregory
DLA Piper Rudnick Gray Cary, Boston
617 406 6019
gregory.bialecki@dlapiper.com
Recommended in Real Estate
Practice Areas: Real estate; state legislation and public policy.
Career: His practice is focused on permitting, construction, and development of large mixed-use urban redevelopment projects. His work frequently involved technical and strategic advice on sophisticated land use and environmental regulation matters. His clients include nonprofit organizations and governmental agencies engaged in land conservation and open space protection.
Personal: JD, Harvard Law School; BA, Harvard University.

BLAU, Michael L
McDermott Will & Emery, Boston
617 535 4010
mblau@mwe.com
Recommended in Healthcare
Practice Areas: Chairs health department's planning committee. Represents a variety of for-profit and non-profit health care organizations. Advises on corporate and regulatory matters, including mergers, acquisitions and affiliations, managed care contracting, and forming provider groups, networks, alliances, health plans and joint ventures. Has experience in advising and financing health related companies. Represents clients in health care-related investigations, and administrative and judicial proceedings.
Prof. Memberships: Past Chair of Health Law Section of Boston Bar Association (BBA) and serves on its Steering Committee and co-chairs BBA's Child Mental Health Task Force. Member of Curriculum Advisory Committee of Massachusetts Continuing Legal Education, Inc. and annually chairs health law programs for MCLE and BBA. Serves as Chairman of the board of Project HEALTH, a national charity that develops and operates volunteer programs in conjunction with academic institutions to improve the health status of impoverished children with chronic medical conditions. Member of Health Lawyer's Association, and health law committees

of American Bar Association, Massachusetts Bar Association and Boston Bar Association.
Publications: Recently co-authored a book entitled 'Developing and Managing Physician Networks' (Thompson Publishing).
Personal: Earned JD (cum laude) in 1979 from Georgetown University Law Center, and AB (magna cum laude) in 1976 from Harvard College.

BLECK, Daniel
Mintz Levin Cohn Ferris Glovsky and Popeo PC, Boston 617 542 6000
Recommended in Bankruptcy

BLOCH, Thomas
Goulston & Storrs, Boston
617 482 1776
Recommended in Real Estate

BORDEN, Mark
Wilmer Cutler Pickering Hale and Dorr LLP, Boston 617 526 6675
mark.borden@wilmerhale.com
Recommended in Corporate/M&A, Private Equity
Practice Areas: Member of the firm's Management Committee and Co-Chair of the Corporate Department. Practice concentrates primarily in the areas of securities law, corporate finance and acquisitions; has over 25 years experience in representing public companies; represented companies and underwriters in over 100 public offerings; has extensive experience both in structuring acquisitions and in designing defenses against unsolicited takeovers.
Career: Admitted to Massachusetts Bar. Joined firm in 1976.
Publications: Co-author of 'Start-up Companies - Planning, Financing and Operating the Successful Business', published by Law Journal Seminars Press.
Personal: Harvard Law School (JD); Yale University (BA, summa cum laude).

BOTHWICK, Jay
Wilmer Cutler Pickering Hale and Dorr LLP, Boston 617 526 6526
jay.bothwick@wilmerhale.com
Recommended in Corporate/M&A
Practice Areas: Member of the firm's Executive Committee and Chair of the firm's Mergers and Acquisitions Group. Practice focuses on mergers and acquisitions; significant experience in venture capital and corporate finance transactions. Advised public and private companies, both domestically and overseas, in mergers and acquisitions, tender and exchange offers, proxy contests and public and private offerings.
Prof. Memberships: American, Massachusetts and Boston Bar Associations; Negotiated Acquisitions Committee of the Business Law Section of the American Bar Association.
Career: Admitted to Massachusetts Bar. Joined firm in 1981.
Personal: Columbia Law School (JD);

Bowdoin College (AB, summa cum laude, Phi Beta Kappa).

BRAUN, Peter
McDermott Will & Emery, Boston
617 535 4032
pbraun@mwe.com
Recommended in Healthcare
Practice Areas: Member of the Health Department. Has significant experience in general counsel, corporate and regulatory matters affecting hospitals and other aspects of the health care industry. Has assisted in a substantial number of corporate restructurings, joint ventures and tax-exempt bond financings involving health care industry clients.
Personal: Earned JD from Franklin Pierce Law Center in 1979, and earned BA in 1971 from Oberlin College.

BRIGHAM, Johan
Bingham McCutchen LLP, Boston
617 951 8000
Recommended in Corporate/M&A

BROWN, John
Bingham McCutchen LLP, Boston
617 951 8000
Recommended in Tax

BROWN, Margaret A
Skadden, Arps, Slate, Meagher & Flom LLP & Affiliates, Boston
617 573 4815
mabrown@skadden.com
Recommended in Corporate/M&A
Practice Areas: Counsels on a wide variety of corporate matters, concentrating on merger and acquisition transactions, corporate financings and corporate governance matters. Represents various venture capital investors and start-up companies and has been underwriter's and issuer's counsel in a number of public offerings of debt and equity securities. Has also worked on a number of proxy contests and consent solicitations, as well as restructurings of publicly held debt securities.
Career: JD, Boston College Law School, 1979 (cum laude; Articles Editor, 'Boston College Law Review'); BA, Holy Cross College, 1976.

BROWNE, Steven
Bingham McCutchen LLP, Boston
617 951 8000
Recommended in Corporate/M&A

BUCHANAN Jr, Robert
Choate Hall & Stewart, Boston
617 248 5000
Recommended in Antitrust

BUCKING, James
Foley Hoag LLP, Boston
617 832 1000
Recommended in Employment

BURGER, Sharon
Nutter, McClennen & Fish, LLP, Boston
617 439 2000
Recommended in Employment

BURKE, Robert
Wilmer Cutler Pickering Hale and Dorr LLP, Boston 617 526 6470
robert.burke@wilmerhale.com
Recommended in Tax

Practice Areas: Practice concentrates on the taxation of partnerships and limited liability companies engaged in investment activities (including real estate, venture capital and "hedge fund" activities) and business operations as well as on corporate restructurings, acquisitions, and dispositions and the taxation of financial instruments.
Prof. Memberships: Member of the American Bar Association's Section on Taxation; serves on its Committee on Partnerships and Subcommittee on Partnership Allocations.
Career: Admitted to Massachusetts Bar.
Personal: Williams College (BA, magna cum laude, Phi Beta Kappa); Cornell University Law School (JD, magna cum laude); Boston University School of Law (LLM in taxation).

BURLING, James
Wilmer Cutler Pickering Hale and Dorr LLP, Boston 617 526 6416
james.burling@wilmerhale.com
Recommended in Antitrust

Practice Areas: Co-Chair of firm's Antitrust and Competition Department. Concentrates in antitrust litigation and merger clearance for high technology clients, particularly in computer, Internet, biotech and pharmaceutical industries. Represents clients in private litigation, in responding to government antitrust investigations, and before the Department of Justice and Federal Trade Commission in Hart-Scott-Rodino review of mergers and acquisitions.
Prof. Memberships: American Bar Association Antitrust Section; Boston Bar Association Antitrust Committee; Massachusetts Bar Association.
Career: Admitted to Massachusetts Bar, United States Supreme Court. Joined firm in 1978 after two years with the Federal Trade Commission.
Personal: Harvard Law School (JD); Grinnell College (AB).

BURT, Laurie
Foley Hoag LLP, Boston 617 832 1000
Recommended in Environment

CABLE, Stuart M
Goodwin Procter LLP, Boston
617 570 1000
scable@goodwinprocter.com
Recommended in Corporate/M&A

Practice Areas: Mr Cable represents as outside general counsel a wide array of public and private companies involved in diverse businesses, including those involving life sciences, optical components, semiconductors, professional services, alternative energy and software. His transactional practice is focused on public offering transactions, negotiating, structuring and implementing strategic acquisitions and private place-ments of equity and debt.
Prof. Memberships: The Buckingham, Browne and Nichols School: Chairman of the Board of Trustees; Beth Israel Hospital: Trustee.
Personal: JD, Columbia Law School, 1979; MBA, Amos Tuck School of Business Administration at Dartmouth College, 1976; AB, Dartmouth College, 1975 (magna cum laude).

CAPRARO Jr, Joseph A
Proskauer Rose LLP, Boston
617 526 9800
jcapraro@proskauer.com
Recommended in Intellectual Property

Practice Areas: A Partner in the Patent Law and Intellectual Property Practice Groups at Proskauer Rose LLP. He provides clients with practical legal advice across the entire spectrum of intellectual property areas. He represents technology start-ups as well as private and public emerging technology companies, and spends much of his time working with companies having products in the engineering arts, with particular emphasis on plasma devices, semiconductor equipment, power supplies, medical lasers, image processing devices, optical components, medical devices, alternative energy technologies, financial services software, and telecommunications devices and software. He works closely with clients in developing national and international patent and trademark portfolios. His experience in the area of patent prosecution includes basic prosecution issues as well as patent reissue and re-examination proceedings in the United States and in patent opposition proceedings throughout the world. He has extensive experience in the area of technology and intellectual property licensing, and has also participated in numerous intellectual property litigations and in alternative dispute resolution of intellectual property matters, involving patents, trademarks, copyrights and trade secrets.
Personal: Suffolk University Law School, JD, cum laude, 1993. Tufts University, BS, magna cum laude, 1985.

CASEY, David
Littler Mendelson PC, Boston
617 217 2831
Recommended in Employment

CHAPIN, David C
Ropes & Gray LLP, Boston
617 951 7371
david.chapin@ropesgray.com
Recommended in Corporate/M&A, Private Equity

Practice Areas: Member of the firm's Policy Committee and the Strategic Development Partner at Ropes & Gray. Specializes in private equity transactions, securities law and mergers and acquisitions involving public companies. Practice includes representing private equity sponsors, issuers of high-yield debt, underwriters of debt and equity securities, and purchasers of high-yield "144A" debt offerings. Broad experience representing clients in financial and strategic transactions.
Career: Massachusetts Bar (1980). Partner, Ropes & Gray (1989).
Personal: JD, cum laude, Harvard Law School (1980). BA, summa cum laude, Lafayette College (1976).

CHARKOUDIAN, Stephen G
Goodwin Procter LLP, Boston
617 570 1000
scharkoudian@goodwinprocter.com
Recommended in Intellectual Property

Practice Areas: Mr Charkoudian's practice encompasses a broad range of intellectual property and technology matters, including advising clients on intellectual property protection, technology licensing and transfers, product development and distribution, mergers and acquisitions of technology companies, technology joint ventures, and venture capital transactions. He has represented high-tech, life sciences, private equity and venture capital firms, emerging growth companies and other clients in intellectual property matters, including issues relating to patents, trademarks, copyrights and trade secrets.
Personal: JD, American University, Washington College of Law, 1992 (cum laude); BA, Boston College, 1987 (cum laude).

CHILD, Ralph
Mintz Levin Cohn Ferris Glovsky and Popeo PC, Boston 617 542 6000
Recommended in Environment

CHORY, John
Wilmer Cutler Pickering Hale and Dorr LLP, Waltham
718 966 2001
john.chory@wilmerhale.com
Recommended in Private Equity

Practice Areas: Partner in charge of the firm's Waltham office. Advises both private and public companies in the areas of initial- through late-stage venture capital financings, public offerings of securities, mergers and acquisitions, technology licensing and securities law. Also advises many entrepreneurs in early-stage company formation and strategy.
Prof. Memberships: Advisory Board of MIT Enterprise Forum.
Publications: Lectures frequently and has had several articles published on legal issues facing emerging companies.
Personal: Harvard Law School (JD 1988); Golden Gate University (MBA 1984); US Military Academy, West Point (BS 1980).

CHRISTIAN, Joseph J
Wilmer Cutler Pickering Hale and Dorr LLP, Boston 617 526 6947
joseph.christian@wilmerhale.com
Recommended in Real Estate

Practice Areas: Chair of firm's Real Estate Capital Management Group and Institutional Investment Group. Has handled acquisition, management and disposition of real estate assets in all major US markets, representing investment advisory firms, operating companies, tax-qualified and public pension and profit-sharing plans, financial institutions, real estate investment trusts and individuals. Areas of legal expertise include equity and debt financings, real estate and land-use law, environmental law, insurance company separate accounts, taxation of tax-exempt entities, and rules governing real estate investment trusts.
Career: Admitted to Massachusetts Bar. Joined firm in 1994.
Personal: Northeastern University School of Law (JD); Catholic University (BA).

CLEARY, John
Goodwin Procter LLP, Boston
617 570 1000
jcleary@goodwinprocter.com
Recommended in Tax

Practice Areas: Mr Cleary specializes in all aspects of ERISA and employee benefits. He represents numerous employers in connection with their employee benefit requirements, including qualified and nonqualified retirement plans, welfare plans and executive compensation. Mr Cleary has particular experience with respect to issues arising in connection with corporate and real estate transactions and under Title I of ERISA.
Prof. Memberships: Government Affairs Committee of the Pension Real Estate Association: Member; New England Employee Benefits Council: Former Director.
Personal: JD, Harvard Law School, 1974 (magna cum laude); MA, Yale University, 1970; BS, Massachusetts Institute of Technology, 1968.

COHEN, Bret
Mintz Levin Cohn Ferris Glovsky and Popeo PC, Boston 617 542 6000
Recommended in Employment

COHN, Daniel
Cohn & Whitesell LLP, Boston
617 951 2505
Recommended in Bankruptcy

CONDE, Kathryn
Nutter, McClennen & Fish, LLP, Boston
617 439 2000
Recommended in Antitrust

COOGAN, Peter
Foley Hoag LLP, Boston 617 832 1000
Recommended in Banking & Finance, Corporate/M&A

COOKE, Susan
McDermott Will & Emery, Boston
617 535 4012
scooke@mwe.com
Recommended in Environment

Practice Areas: Has worked on environmental and health and safety matters worldwide. Practice includes regulatory analyses and counseling, enforcement actions, permitting activities, Brownfields redevelopment, land use and environmental issues in transactions, and legislative and regulatory proposals. Work has covered site cleanups and liability actions at contaminated sites including service as coordinating counsel in Superfund negotiations; Brownfields redevelopment projects; EHS audits; due diligence reviews and permitting of industrial, commercial, and large residential properties, including development of environmental opinion format for transactions; chemical regulation and use, including procurement of first waiver under state chemical regulation law to expedite construction of industrial facility and first US exemption from premanufacture notification requirements under federal Toxic Substances Control Act. Clients include major manufacturers and energy, technology, and health sector companies.

Prof. Memberships: Admitted to practice in Massachusetts and before US Patent and Trademark Office. Chaired Hazardous Waste Subcommittee of American Bar Association Business Law Section's Environmental, Energy, and Natural Resources Law Committee.

Publications: General editor and principal author of five volume treatise on hazardous waste and Superfund law; co-editor of two editions of 'Massachusetts Environmental Law Handbook'.

Personal: BA, Chemistry, Emmanuel College; JD, Boston University; special student, Electrical Engineeering, MIT.

CORCORAN, William
Osler, Hoskin & Harcourt LLP, New York
212 867 5800
Recommended in Tax

COUKOS, Stephen J
Gallagher, Callahan and Gartrell, PA,
Boston 877 426 5347
coukos@gcglaw.com
Recommended in Banking & Finance

Practice Areas: Advises public and private companies on strategic transactions, corporate and regulatory matters, securities law compliance and corporate governance issues.

Prof. Memberships: American and Boston Bar Associations; co-chair of Banking and Financial Services Committee of Business Law Section of Boston Bar Association.

Publications: Frequent author and speaker on corporate and banking topics; recent articles and presentations have addressed mergers and acquisitions, strategic thinking for mutual institutions, recent developments in banking regulation and credit union conversions.

Personal: Stanford Law School, JD, 1986; Trinity College (CT), BA, 1981 (Phi Beta Kappa)

COX Jr, Robert
Bowditch & Dewey LLP, Worcester
508 791 3511
Recommended in Environment

CUBELL, Howard
Goodwin Procter LLP, Boston
617 570 1000
hcubell@goodwinprocter.com
Recommended in Tax

Practice Areas: Mr Cubell's practice focuses on the development of innovative tax strategies for various domestic and international business transactions and collective investment vehicles. He has been at the forefront in developing creative structures for private equity funds to use in doing leveraged buyouts overseas and for making investments in domestic pass-through entities such as Subchapter S corporations, partnerships and LLCs.

Personal: JD, Boston University School of Law, 1973; BA, University of Michigan, 1970; New York University Graduate Tax Program.

CURTIN, John
Bingham McCutchen LLP, Boston
617 951 8000
Recommended in Antitrust

CURTIN, Neal
Bingham McCutchen LLP, Boston
617 951 8000
Recommended in Banking & Finance

DALE III, Charles
Gadsby Hannah LLP, Boston
617 345 7000
Recommended in Bankruptcy

DALEY, Paul
Wilmer Cutler Pickering Hale and Dorr
LLP, Boston 617 526 6720
paul.daley@wilmerhale.com
Recommended in Bankruptcy

Practice Areas: Focuses practice in bankruptcy and commercial law, including representation of boards of directors, debtors, creditors' committees, trustees, secured and unsecured creditors in Chapter 11 reorganizations and Chapter 7 liquidations. Represents third parties acquiring debtors or assets in Chapter 11 reorganizations under Section 363 sales, and both debtors and creditors in common law practices including commercial litigation. Considerable experience in the areas of commercial finance, secured lending, venture capital, mergers and acquisitions, trade secret protection, licensing, franchising, and the Uniform Commercial Code matters often involved in commercial transactions and reorganizations.

Prof. Memberships: American Bar Association; Boston Bar Association; International Bar Associations; American Bankruptcy Institute; Commercial Law League; Legal Fee Arbitration Board of the Massachusetts Bar Association (MBA).

Career: Admitted to Massachusetts Bar,

New York Bar and United States Supreme Court. Joined firm in 1973.
Personal: Harvard Law School (JD); Harvard Business School (MBA); Boston College (AB).

DAMON, Lisa
Seyfarth Shaw LLP, Boston
617 946 4800
Recommended in Employment

DAVIS, Christopher P
Goodwin Procter LLP, Boston
617 570 1000
cdavis@goodwinprocter.com
Recommended in Environment

Practice Areas: Mr Davis is a nationally recognized Superfund practitioner and environmental litigator, who has represented potentially responsible parties at more than 50 federal and state Superfund sites throughout the northeastern United States. He served as trial counsel in the first governmental and private Superfund trials and has litigated a number of prominent CERCLA cases and had mediated complex, multiparty environmental disputes.

Prof. Memberships: Keystone Conference on Environmental Law: Chair; Massachusetts Waste Cleanup Advisory Committee: Member; Toxics Law Reporter: Advisory Board Member.

Personal: JD, Harvard Law School, 1980; AB Dartmouth College, 1976.

DAVIS, Michael
Sullivan & Worcester, Boston
617 338 2800
Recommended in Tax

DICHIARA, Peter M
Wilmer Cutler Pickering Hale and Dorr
LLP, Boston 617 526 6466
peter.dichiara@wilmerhale.com
Recommended in Intellectual Property

Practice Areas: Chair of firm's Nanotechnology Practice Group. Practice focuses on obtaining and enforcing intellectual property rights, with an emphasis on the electronics, communications and computer industries. Has litigated patents and trade secrets relating to communication systems, computer software, storage systems, electronic circuits and semiconductor manufacturing equipment. Has prepared infringement and validity opinions and has advised clients on portfolio strategy, risk assessment and design-around strategies.

Prof. Memberships: Mass Nanotech Exchange, board member.

Career: Admitted to Massachusetts Bar, United States Patent and Trademark Office. Joined firm in 1997.

Personal: Boston University School of Law (JD); Boston University (BS, Computer Engineering).

DITTMAR, James S
Goodwin Procter LLP, Boston
617 570 1000
jdittmar@goodwinprocter.com
Recommended in Litigation

Practice Areas: Mr Dittmar focuses his practice on complex business litigation with particular emphasis on securities litigation; civil litigation and regulatory investigations and enforcement proceedings involving asset management and other capital markets financial services; civil litigation and regulatory investigations and enforcement proceedings under ERISA; and corporate transaction, control and governance disputes. His practice concentrates on class actions, derivative actions, and multiproceeding litigations including federal multi-district litigation and simultaneous federal and state court actions.

Personal: JD, Harvard Law School, 1972 (cum laude); MSc, London School of Economics, 1967; BA, Amherst College, 1966 (magna cum laude).

DONOVAN, John
Ropes & Gray LLP, Boston
617 951 7566
john.donovan@ropesgray.com
Recommended in Litigation

Practice Areas: Business litigation, including corporate and securities matters, class actions, disputes in connection with mergers and acquisitions, other complex business transactions. Expertise in corporate and securities litigation as a result of successfully defending high tech corporations, 'old economy' issuers, underwriters and financial services companies in litigation. Appeared and argued such cases in dozens of state and federal jurisdictions, producing successful results at both trial and appellate court levels.

Career: Massachusetts Bar (1981). New York Bar (2003). Partner, Ropes & Gray (1990).

Personal: JD, summa cum laude, Boston College Law School (1981). Undergraduate degree, cum laude, Harvard College (1975).

DOUGHERTY, Charles R
Foley & Lardner, Boston 617 342 4053
cdougherty@foley.com
Recommended in Bankruptcy

Career: Charles R. Dougherty, a partner in the Boston office of Foley & Lardner LLP, is a member of the Business Reorganizations Practice Group. Mr Dougherty is a business lawyer whose practice focuses on troubled companies. In addition to working with companies facing serious financial challenges, he advises creditors holding the debt of troubled companies and equity holders of companies in financial difficulty. Mr Dougherty received his JD from Boston University School of Law in 1980, magna cum laude. His BA degree is from Hampshire College in 1975.

DOWNEY, Alicia
Bingham McCutchen LLP, Boston
617 951 8000
Recommended in Antitrust

DOWNS, J Anthony
Goodwin Procter LLP, Boston
617 570 1000
jdowns@goodwinprocter.com
Recommended in Intellectual Property, Litigation

Practice Areas: Mr Downs practices general civil litigation, with specialization in patent, copyright, antitrust/competition law, securities and other complex commercial litigation. He has represented individuals and entities in a wide variety of commercial disputes and business litigation. He also has extensive experience in arbitration and other alternative dispute resolution procedures. Clients include General Electric, Applied Materials, Inverness Medical Innovations and Boston Scientific.
Personal: JD, University of Chicago Law School, 1986 (cum laude); AB, Princeton University, 1982 (magna cum laude).

DRAPER, Thomas B
Ropes & Gray LLP, Boston
617 951 7430
thomas.draper@ropesgray.com
Recommended in Banking & Finance
Practice Areas: Broad range of experience in financing transactions. Coordinator for firm debt financing practice group. Represents lenders and borrowers in many large financings, with emphasis on leveraged acquisitions and financial sponsor transactions. Also represents collateralized loan obligation funds and venture capitalists in investments in startup and middle-market companies. Has taught commercial lending at Boston University School of Law and has chaired panels for numerous continuing legal education programs about financing transactions.
Career: Texas Bar (1979). Massachusetts Bar (1980). Partner, Ropes & Gray (1989).
Personal: JD, University of Texas School of Law (1979). Undergraduate degree, cum laude, Yale University (1975).

EGAN III, John J
Goodwin Procter LLP, Boston
617 570 1000
jegan@goodwinprocter.com
Recommended in Private Equity
Practice Areas: Mr Egan's practice involves early and late-stage venture financings, leveraged recapitalizations and buyouts, IPOs, mergers and acquisitions, joint ventures, strategic licensing and the general representation of public and private emerging growth companies in industries ranging from enterprise software, networking, security and business services to communications, media and life sciences. He also represents numerous venture capitalists, private equity investors and investment banks and has extensive experience in intellectual property and licensing issues.
Personal: JD, Boston University School of Law, 1984; AB, Brown University, 1981.

EHRLICH, Kenneth
Nutter, McClennen & Fish, LLP, Boston
617 439 2000
Recommended in Banking & Finance

ELFMAN, Eric M
Ropes & Gray LLP, Boston
617 951 7298
eric.elfman@ropesgray.com
Recommended in Tax
Practice Areas: Federal and corporate tax practice focusing on transactions, planning, tax audit and controversy matters; extensive experience in structuring acquisitions, mergers, leveraged buyouts, recapitalizations, preferred stock financings and spin-off transactions, venture capital and private equity deals, technology licensing transactions for biotechnology and life science companies.
Career: California Bar (1980). Massachusetts Bar (1986). Certified Public Accountant (Pennsylvania, 1977). Partner, Ropes & Gray (1999). Previously Attorney-Advisor in the US Treasury's Office of Tax Policy.
Personal: JD, George Washington University Law School (1980). MS, Accounting, University of Pennsylvania Wharton Graduate School (1976). BS, Economics, University of Pennsylvania Wharton Graduate School (1975).

ENGEL, David
Bingham McCutchen LLP, Boston
617 951 8000
Recommended in Corporate/M&A

ENGLANDER, John
Goodwin Procter LLP, Boston
617 570 1000
jenglander@goodwinprocter.com
Recommended in Intellectual Property
Practice Areas: Mr Englander's practice focuses on complex commercial litigation, with an emphasis on patent litigation. He also has extensive experience in banking and financial services litigation, including in particular class action defense. He has litigated cases involving all manner of commercial disputes, business torts, and unfair trade practices claims. In addition, Mr Englander has been counsel in patent infringement cases involving clients including Applied Materials, Inc., Brooktrout Technology, Inc. and GE-Interlogix and has represented various medical/pharmaceutical companies including ViaCell and TEVA Pharmaceuticals, USA Inc.
Personal: JD, Boston University Law School, 1983; BS, Cornell University, 1980.

FABIANO, John G
Wilmer Cutler Pickering Hale and Dorr LLP, Boston 617 526 6612
jack.fabiano@wilmerhale.com
Recommended in Litigation
Practice Areas: Has tried more than 100 jury and non-jury cases before state and federal courts; and administrative hearings and arbitrations in both the US and the UK. Specializes in complex commercial litigation and has trial experience in a variety of areas including wrongful death and personal injury, medical malpractice, legal malpractice, insurance, strategic consulting, securities, fraudulent conveyance, ERISA, oil and gas, partnership disputes, employment disputes, banking, real estate, insurance, professional baseball, professional hockey and academic tenure.
Prof. Memberships: Fellow of the American College of Trial Lawyers.
Career: Admitted to Massachusetts Bar.
Personal: Harvard Law School (JD); Harvard College (AB).

FEE, Michael K
Ropes & Gray LLP, Boston
617 951 7607
michael.fee@ropesgray.com
Recommended in Litigation
Practice Areas: Represents clients in criminal litigation and counsels clients in federal and state investigations. Handles civil litigation matters, many of which are related to government enforcement. Defended numerous clients in matters involving health care, securities, investment adviser regulation, export law, public corruption and campaign finance law.
Career: Massachusetts Bar (1985). Prosecutor, Public Integrity Section, Criminal Division, US Department of Justice (1985-1989). Partner, Ropes & Gray (1993).
Personal: JD, magna cum laude, Boston College Law School (1984). AB, magna cum laude, Boston College (1981).

FELDMAN, Roger
Fish & Richardson, Boston
617 542 5070
Recommended in Corporate/M&A

FELTER, John Kenneth
Goodwin Procter LLP, Boston
617 570 1000
kahuna@goodwinprocter.com
Recommended in Litigation
Practice Areas: Mr Felter is an experienced trial attorney who has tried numerous cases in federal and state trial courts. He has also frequently presented oral arguments before federal and state appellate courts. Mr Felter's practice is concentrated in the areas of complex commercial, land use, products liability, sports and entertainment, and college and university litigation.
Prof. Memberships: American College of Trial Lawyers: Fellow; National Association of College and University Attorneys: Member; Greater Boston Legal Services: Board of Directors.
Personal: JD, Harvard Law School, 1975 (cum laude); MA in Economics, Boston College, 1972; BA, Boston College, 1972 (magna cum laude).

FINKELMAN, Daniel P
Proskauer Rose LLP, Boston
617 526 9755
dfinkelman@proskauer.com
Recommended in Private Equity
Practice Areas: A Partner at Proskauer Rose, he has over 25 years of experience in the private equity field. He concentrates in the representation of private equity funds, including independent venture capital funds, corporate-sponsored venture capital funds, offshore and multi-national venture capital funds, and fund-of-funds. He also represents institutional fund investors. His principal activities on behalf of funds have included capital formations, portfolio investments, sales and distributions, internal governance, secondary transactions, and administration. He has represented funds in raising over $15 billion of committed capital.
Personal: Columbia University School of Law, JD, 1972; Harlan Fiske Stone Scholar. Columbia University, MBA, 1972. Clark University, AB, cum laude, 1968; Phi Beta Kappa.

FISHMAN, Robert
Nutter, McClennen & Fish, LLP, Boston
617 439 2000
Recommended in Real Estate

FORBUSH III, William B
DLA Piper Rudnick Gray Cary, Boston
617 406 6021
william.forbush@dlapiper.com
Recommended in Real Estate
Practice Areas: Real estate.
Career: Concentrates on commercial real estate work representing institutional investors acquiring, financing, restructuring, and selling commercial properties; owners and developers of downtown high-rise office towers and mixed-use projects; and landlords and tenants in major leases of office, retail and industrial properties. He has represented opportunity funds, private investors, and public REITs investing in, selling, and financing national real estate portfolios. He has been a guest lecturer at the Massachusetts Institute of Technology's Center for Real Estate.
Personal: JD, Harvard Law School (cum laude); BA, Harvard College (magna cum laude).

FORMAN, Adam
Littler Mendelson PC, Boston
617 217 2831
Recommended in Employment

FRANK, Robert
Choate Hall & Stewart, Boston
617 248 5000
Recommended in Intellectual Property

FRANK, Steven J
Goodwin Procter LLP, Boston
617 570 1000
sfrank@goodwinprocter.com
Recommended in Intellectual Property
Practice Areas: Mr Frank focuses on advising clients in all areas of intellectual

property law, with emphasis on patent prosecution, analysis of infringement and related issues, copyright questions, and the drafting and negotiation of agreements relating to the transfer or license of intellectual property. He has significant experience with general IP diligence, both in investment and M&A contexts. Mr Frank has negotiated multimillion-dollar domestic and cross-border licenses, as well as technology-transfer agreements involving leading universities and research institutions.

Personal: JD, Harvard Law School (cum laude), 1986; ScB in Chemistry, Brown University (magna cum laude), 1983.

FRENCH, Marilyn
Weil, Gotshal & Manges LLP, Boston
617 772 8319
marilyn.french@weil.com
Recommended in Private Equity
Practice Areas: Private equity, fund formation and mergers and acquisitions.
Career: Ms French's practice focuses on private equity, fund formation, mergers and acquisitions. She represents some of the country's leading private equity firms. Recent transactions include representing Thomas H Lee Partners in its buyouts of Michael Foods, Simmons and Progressive Mouldings; Berkshire Partners in its investment in Acosta; and Summit Partners in the acquisition of Tippmann Sports. She also represents portfolio companies in connection with corporate counseling, acquisitions and liquidity events.
Personal: Boston College Law School (JD, cum laude, Order of the Coif, 1990); Hofstra University (BA, cum laude, 1987).

GALVANI, Paul
Ropes & Gray LLP, Boston
617 951 7543
paul.galvani@ropesgray.com
Recommended in Litigation
Practice Areas: Extensive practice in environmental law, commercial litigation, and intellectual property matters. Experienced trial lawyer who has served as defense counsel in complex commercial and white collar litigation, including in securities, patent, and natural resource damage cases. Represented potentially responsible parties in numerous CERCLA matters. Written and lectured extensively on litigation.
Career: Former law clerk and assistant United States Attorney in the Southern District of New York. Massachusetts Bar (1964). New York Bar (1965). Partner, Ropes & Gray (1975).
Personal: JD, cum laude, Harvard Law School (1964). Undergraduate degree, magna cum laude, Phi Beta Kappa, Williams College (1960).

GARVIN, Michele M
Ropes & Gray LLP, Boston
617 951 7495
michele.garvin@ropesgray.com
Recommended in Healthcare

Practice Areas: Focused on general federal and state regulatory compliance and transactional matters including clinical joint ventures, governance, physician integration and managed care issues. Practiced in the health law field since 1987 and has represented a wide range of health care industry representatives including health plans, academic medical centers, community hospitals, faculty practice plans, physician group practices, and pharmaceutical manufacturers.
Career: Massachusetts Bar (1988). Partner, Ropes & Gray (1996).
Personal: JD, Suffolk University Law School (1987). PhD, Boston College (1981). BA, College of William and Mary (1974).

GAULT, Robert
Mintz Levin Cohn Ferris Glovsky and Popeo PC, Boston 617 542 6000
Recommended in Employment

GIULIANI, Richard
Wilmer Cutler Pickering Hale and Dorr LLP, Boston 617 526 6435
richard.giuliani@wilmerhale.com
Recommended in Tax
Practice Areas: Firm's State and Local Tax Group Chair. Experienced in all areas of tax law including federal and state income taxation and state sales and use taxes. Handles corporate, partnership and individual federal and state tax matters; tax dispute advocacy in administrative and judicial forums; tax planning. Represented clients before the Internal Revenue Service Appeals Office; US Tax Court; Massachusetts Appellate Tax Board; Massachusetts courts.
Prof. Memberships: Extensive work with Boston Bar Association, Massachusetts Taxpayers Foundation, Massachusetts Department of Revenue.
Career: Admitted to Massachusetts Bar. Joined firm in 1970.
Personal: Harvard Law School (JD); Harvard College (BA, cum laude).

GLAZER, Michael
Goodwin Procter LLP, Boston
617 570 1000
mglazer@goodwinprocter.com
Recommended in Real Estate
Practice Areas: Mr Glazer specializes in real estate, commercial finance, joint ventures and leasing. He has developed special expertise in the areas of joint ventures, creative debt structuring and investments by tax-exempt investors, such as pension funds and endowments. In addition, he helps clients structure complex debt and equity transactions specifically targeted to the needs of these institutional investors and has extensive leasing experience representing both landlords and tenants of office, flex, industrial and retail space.
Personal: JD, Boston University Law School, 1973; BS, in Economics, Wharton School, University of Pennsylvania, 1970.

GLERUM, Charles
Choate Hall & Stewart, Boston
617 248 5000
Recommended in Bankruptcy

GLOSBAND, Daniel
Goodwin Procter LLP, Boston
617 570 1000
dglosband@goodwinprocter.com
Recommended in Bankruptcy
Practice Areas: Mr Glosband's primary areas of practice are insolvency and reorganization. He represents secured and unsecured creditors, committees and debtors in workouts and proceedings under the Bankruptcy Code. Mr Glosband also acts as an adviser to the US State Department and the American Law Institute on international insolvency projects. He has worked with lenders and debtors in major real estate, retail and technology oriented reorganizations; parties to significant contracts with debtors in reorganization; and defendants in complex Bankruptcy Court litigation.
Personal: JD, Cornell University, 1969; BA, University of Massachusetts, 1966.

GOLDBERG, Daniel
Bingham McCutchen LLP, Boston
617 951 8000
Recommended in Antitrust, Sport

GOODHEART, Lisa
DLA Piper Rudnick Gray Cary, Boston
617 406 6023
lisa.goodheart@dlapiper.com
Recommended in Environment
Practice Areas: Environmental, litigation and real estate.
Prof. Memberships: Co-Chair of the Boston Bar Association's Environmental Law Section; New England Women in Real Estate.
Career: Trial lawyer concentrating in environmental, real estate and business disputes. She has been named as one of 10 'Lawyers of the Year' in a leading American legal publication, and as one of the top 50 women in 'Super Lawyers' in Massachusetts.
Personal: JD, University of Pennsylvania Law School, cum laude; BA, Williams College, cum laude, Phi Beta Kappa.

GOODING, Douglas
Choate Hall & Stewart, Boston
617 248 5000
Recommended in Bankruptcy

GOODMAN, Louis A
Skadden, Arps, Slate, Meagher & Flom LLP & Affiliates, Boston
617 573 4830
lgoodman@skadden.com
Recommended in Corporate/M&A
Practice Areas: Head of Skadden's Boston office. Advises on a wide range of corporate matters, from financings, acquisitions and restructurings to white collar criminal defense. For many years, has represented clients in some of their most significant transactions – many

that have industry-wide and sometimes worldwide significance.
Career: JD, Harvard Law School, 1969; MA, Harvard University, 1966; AB, Columbia College, 1965.
Publications: Author, 'Takeover Strategies & Responses: The Battle for Corporate Control'.

GORDON, Robert B
Ropes & Gray LLP, Boston
617 951 7442
robert.gordon@ropesgray.com
Recommended in Employment
Practice Areas: Advising, defending management in employment discrimination, wrongful discharge, employee privacy, defamation, employee benefits, wage and hour, non-competition, trade secret litigation. Counsels on employee discipline and discharge, reductions in force, executive employment and separation agreements, sexual harassment and other internal investigations, and compliance issues under Americans with Disabilities Act, Family and Medical Leave Act, Worker Adjustment Retraining and Notification Act, and Fair Labor Standards Act.
Career: Massachusetts Bar (1986). Rhode Island Bar (1991). Connecticut Bar (1995). Partner, Ropes & Gray (1995).
Personal: JD, cum laude, University of Michigan Law School (1986). BA, Phi Beta Kappa, Wesleyan University (1983).

GREEN, Barry
Goulston & Storrs, Boston
617 482 1776
Recommended in Real Estate

GREEN, Karen F
Wilmer Cutler Pickering Hale and Dorr LLP, Boston
617 526 6207
karen.green@wilmerhale.com
Recommended in Litigation
Practice Areas: Co-chair of firm's Litigation Department; member of firm's Executive Committee. Practice concentrates on complex business litigation, including the defense of white-collar criminal investigations and litigation. Extensive experience representing companies and corporate officers and directors in parallel civil and criminal proceedings alleging health care fraud, securities fraud, government contracting fraud, consumer fraud and mail and wire fraud. Has conducted corporate internal investigations, and provided advice on establishment of corporate compliance programs.
Prof. Memberships: Fiduciary Trust Company, Director.
Career: Admitted to Massachusetts Bar. Joined firm in 1982.
Personal: Harvard Law School (JD, cum laude); Radcliffe College (AB, magna cum laude).

HACKNEY, Hamilton
Choate Hall & Stewart, Boston
617 248 5000
Recommended in Environment

HALEY, Joseph
Goodwin Procter LLP, Boston
617 570 1000
jhaley@goodwinprocter.com
Recommended in Real Estate
Practice Areas: Mr Haley's practice focuses on real estate development, as well as on acquisitions, dispositions, equity and mortgage financing, master planning, permitting, environmental law and leasing. He has extensive experience in urban and suburban office, retail, industrial, residential, mixed-use and specialty real estate product types. He represents many of the large development firms (both private and public), lenders and institutional owners in Boston, New England and the United States.
Prof. Memberships: American College of Real Estate Lawyers: Member; Abstract Club of Boston: Member.
Personal: JD, Cornell Law School, 1963; BA, University of Maine, 1960.

HALSTON, Daniel W
Wilmer Cutler Pickering Hale and Dorr LLP, Boston 617 526 6654
daniel.halston@wilmerhale.com
Recommended in Litigation
Practice Areas: Focuses practice on securities litigation, general commercial litigation and administrative law disputes. Handles wide range of complex litigation matters, including securities fraud class actions, derivative litigation, M&A disputes, investment advisor claims, closely-held corporation disputes, proxy contests, non-competition claims, trade secret claims, software license and development disputes, and wide variety of public law matters. Represents clients in internal investigations and before the SEC, NASD and state regulatory agencies.
Prof. Memberships: American, Massachusetts and Boston Bar Associations; Director, Massachusetts Appleseed Center for Law and Justice.
Career: Admitted to Massachusetts Bar.
Personal: Boston University School of Law (JD); Vassar College (AB).

HANDLY, Kevin
Gallagher, Callahan and Gartrell, PA, Boston 877 426 5347
handly@gcglaw.com
Recommended in Banking & Finance
Practice Areas: Bank regulatory, mergers and acquisitions, corporate, securities, litigation, administrative law.
Career: Assistant District Attorney, Brooklyn, New York, 1979-82; Senior Attorney, Federal Reserve Board, Legal Division, Washington, D.C., 1982-87; Partner, Goodwin Procter & Hoar, Boston, MA, 1987-95; Partner, Peabody & Brown, Boston, MA, 1995-2000; Director, Goulston & Storrs, P.C., Boston, MA, 2001-04; Shareholder-

Director, Gallagher Callahan & Gartrell, P.A., 2005-present; Lecturer on Financial Institutions Mergers & Acquisitions Law, Morin School of Banking and Financial Law, Boston University Law School, 2002-present.

HAROZ, Michael
Goulston & Storrs, Boston
617 482 1776
Recommended in Real Estate

HEALY, Martin
Goodwin Procter LLP, Boston
617 570 1000
mhealy@goodwinprocter.com
Recommended in Real Estate
Practice Areas: Mr Healy's practice concentrates on providing acquisition, due diligence and permitting advice for complex development projects. His current/past projects include the Boston Logan Airport modernization which has been challenged continuously throughout its lifetime, the permitting of the Central Artery/Tunnel Project, the renovation of Millennium Place, including the overhaul of the Boston Ritz Carlton and involvement with commercial property projects in and around the Boston area. He is the editor of and a contributing author for the Massachusetts Zoning Manual.
Personal: JD, Boston College Law School, 1975 (cum laude); BA, Boston College, 1972 (summa cum laude).

HEIDT, Jeffrey L
Ropes & Gray LLP, Boston
617 248 5108
jeffrey.heidt@ropesgray.com
Recommended in Healthcare
Practice Areas: Mixture of corporate, regulatory and financial matters. Majority of clients are hospitals, health systems and their affiliated education and business institutions, some of which he has worked with for over three decades.
Career: Massachusetts Bar (1970). Partner, Ropes & Gray (2005).
Personal: JD, Harvard Law School (1970). AB, high honors in Philosophy, Brown University (1967).

HENNESSEY, Gilbert
Fish & Richardson, Boston
617 542 5070
Recommended in Intellectual Property

HERMAN, Philip
Goulston & Storrs, Boston
617 482 1776
Recommended in Banking & Finance

HESSION, John
McDermott Will & Emery, Boston
617 535 4460
jhession@mwe.com
Recommended in Private Equity
Practice Areas: Represents emerging-growth companies, principally in software, medical devices, life sciences, telecommunications and electronic commerce fields, as well as venture capital funds in the investment process in

these sectors. Practice includes both start-up and public company work; equity-based compensation strategies; public offerings, representing either underwriters or companies; acquisitions and divestitures, representing either buyers or sellers; corporate partnering, joint ventures and other strategic alliances involving technology transfers; hardware and software license and distribution arrangements; and venture capital financings of technology companies, representing either funds or companies.
Prof. Memberships: Member of the National Venture Capital Association (NVCA) Drafting Committee creating a set of standard transaction documents for venture capital investments.
Personal: Earned JD (cum laude) from Boston College Law School, and BA (summa cum laude and Phi Beta Kappa) from University of Notre Dame. Prior to joining legal field, was a sales representative with Burroughs Corporation, a Fortune 500 manufacturer of computer hardware, where he achieved Burroughs' Legion of Honor award for one of the top-performing sales representatives in the company; a high school English teacher; and a carpenter in Ireland.

HIGGINS, Keith
Ropes & Gray LLP, Boston
617 951 7386
keith.higgins@ropesgray.com
Recommended in Corporate/M&A
Practice Areas: Over 20 years experience counseling public companies in securities offerings, mergers and acquisitions and corporate governance. Represents underwriters in public and private securities offerings. Recognized as a top IPO lawyer in the country.
Career: Massachusetts Bar (1982). Partner, Ropes & Gray (1991).
Personal: JD, summa cum laude, Boston University School of Law (1982). MA, University of Virginia (1975). BA, Phi Beta Kappa, Florida State University (1973).

HILLMAN, Robert
Fish & Richardson, Boston
617 542 5070
Recommended in Intellectual Property

HIRSCH, Jeffrey L
Robinson & Cole LLP, Boston
617 557 5915
jhirsch@rc.com
Recommended in Employment
Career: Jeffrey Hirsch deals extensively in labor and employment law, representing and advising union and non-union employers in organizing campaigns, labor negotiations and arbitration, OSHA, wage and hour, wrongful discharge and sexual harassment cases. He has appeared before the National Labor Relations Board, OSHA, the US Department of Labor, and state and federal courts. He has written five books including the 'Occupational Safety and Health

Handbook' and the 'Labor and Employment Handbook' for Massachusetts, Connecticut, New Hampshire and Rhode Island. Mr Hirsch received his BS from Cornell University School of Industrial and Labor Relations and his JD from Boston University.

HODGES TAYLOR, Laura
Goodwin Procter LLP, Boston
617 570 1000
lht@goodwinprocter.com
Recommended in Private Equity
Practice Areas: Ms Hodges Taylor focuses on corporate finance and securities law, as well as on limited partnerships, REITs and business trusts in a variety of industries. She has extensive experience in representing institutional investors in structuring and effecting investments. She also represented issuers, financial advisors and investors in restructurings such as exchange offers, tender and self-tender offers, going private transactions, rights offerings and leveraged buyouts. Ms Hodges Taylor is the co-author of 'Massachusetts Business Lawyering'.
Personal: JD, Harvard Law School, 1982; BA, Wellesley College, 1977.

HOWELL, Geoffrey A
DLA Piper Rudnick Gray Cary, Boston
617 406 6108
geoff.howell@piperrudnick.com
Recommended in Real Estate
Practice Areas: Real estate.
Career: Concentrates on real estate development, finance and leasing and has represented regional and national owners and developers in a broad variety of real estate transactions, including the development and operation of hotels, multi-tenant and build-to-suit office buildings, large mixed use projects, and laboratory/research facilities; the development of a national rooftop leasing program; the permitting of one of the largest residential developments in the Commonwealth of Massachusetts; the expansion of an urban renewal project; and the acquisition of a horse racing track.
Personal: JD, Boston College Law School (magna cum laude); BA, Wesleyan University.

HUGG, Joseph A
DLA Piper Rudnick Gray Cary, Boston
617 406 6052
joseph.hugg@dlapiper.com
Recommended in Tax
Practice Areas: Tax, employee benefits and ERISA.
Prof. Memberships: American Bar Association (Tax Section); Massachusetts and Boston Bar Associations.
Career: He assists US and international clients in structuring venture capital and other private equity funds to comply with tax and pension regulations, including ERISA. He also advises fund clients on the tax and ERISA aspects of portfolio investments. In addition, he

provides advice on executive compensation and employee benefits.
Personal: LLM (Taxation), New York University School of Law; JD, Harvard Law School; BA, Georgetown University.

HUSID, Douglas
Goulston & Storrs, Boston
617 482 1776
Recommended in Real Estate

ISAIA, Russell
Bingham McCutchen LLP, Boston
617 951 8000
Recommended in Tax

JACOBS, Neil
Wilmer Cutler Pickering Hale and Dorr LLP, Boston 617 526 6970
neil.jacobs@wilmerhale.com
Recommended in Employment
Practice Areas: Extensive experience in negotiation and administration of collective bargaining agreements; employment and labor law litigation in state and federal courts; and administrative proceedings before state and federal fair employment agencies. Lead trial or appellate counsel in major employment litigation involving ERISA litigation; unfair labor practice proceedings before the National Labor Relations Board and in US Courts of Appeals; predatory hiring cases; employee theft of trade secrets; wrongful discharge litigation; and discrimination litigation.
Prof. Memberships: American Bar Association's Developing Labor Law Committee.
Career: Admitted to Massachusetts Bar. Joined firm in 1977.
Personal: Harvard Law School (JD); Harvard College (AB).

JAFFE, Seth
Foley Hoag LLP, Boston
617 832 1000
Recommended in Environment

JAKUBOWSKI, Paul
Wilmer Cutler Pickering Hale and Dorr LLP, Boston 617 526 6948
paul.jakubowski@wilmerhale.com
Recommended in Real Estate
Practice Areas: Practice focuses on all aspects of real estate law, including sales and acquisitions, joint ventures, financing, development and leasing. Has numerous real estate groups as clients, including national retailers, pension fund advisors, an industrial real estate investment trust (REIT), foreign investors in US real estate, and value-added funds. Counsels many of firm's corporate clients on real estate and leasing matters, including credit tenant leases.
Prof. Memberships: Boston, Massachusetts and American Bar Associations; Real Estate Finance Association; National Association of Industrial and Office Properties.
Career: Admitted to Massachusetts Bar.
Personal: Harvard Law School (JD); University of Pennsylvania (BA).

JARRELL, Brenda
Choate Hall & Stewart, Boston
617 248 5000
Recommended in Intellectual Property

JEDREY, Christopher M
McDermott Will & Emery, Boston
617 535 4405
cjedrey@mwe.com
Recommended in Healthcare
Practice Areas: Co-Chair of Boston Health Law Practice, and Co-Chair of Academic Medical Center Practice. Concentrates on federal and state health care regulatory matters, including anti-kickback and Stark law requirements. Focuses on federal, state and local tax exemption requirements, and charitable trust and corporation law. Represents clients in hospital and physician practice mergers, joint ventures among health care providers, purchases and sales of physician practices, and sales of non-profit assets and operations to for-profit companies. Has assisted hospitals and health maintenance organizations with organization, restructuring and "spin off" of affiliated practices. Represents academic medical centers on compliance with HHS requirements for human subjects research and IRS requirements for tax-exempt organizations, including incentive compensation plans for physicians. Advises tax-exempt organizations with respect to requirements for tax-exempt status.
Prof. Memberships: Co-Chairman of Health Care Law Subcommittee of American Bar Association Exempt Organizations Committee, Fellow of American Bar Foundation, member of Massachusetts Attorney General's Advisory Committee on Public Charities and lecturer on Law, Boston University.
Personal: Earned JD in 1984 from Boston College Law School; earned PhD in 1977 and MA in 1972 from Harvard University; and BA in 1971 from University of Massachusetts. Liberal Arts Fellow, Harvard Law School (1980-81).

JOHNSTON, Susan A
Ropes & Gray LLP, Boston
617 951 7301
susan.johnston@ropesgray.com
Recommended in Tax
Practice Areas: Specializes in the taxation of regulated investment companies (including mutual funds), other pooled investment vehicles and financial products. Speaks and writes extensively on the taxation of regulated investment companies (mutual funds), international tax law, and state tax matters.
Career: Massachusetts Bar (1978). Partner, Ropes & Gray (1987). Head of Ropes & Gray's Tax & Benefits Department. Member, Investment Company Institute Tax Advisory Board (1988-present).
Personal: JD, Harvard Law School (1978). BA, Wellesley College (1975).

JONES, Barbara
Wilmer Cutler Pickering Hale and Dorr LLP, Boston 617 526 6490
barbara.jones@wilmerhale.com
Recommended in Corporate/M&A
Practice Areas: Extensive experience in international corporate finance, including private equity, initial public offerings, mergers and acquisitions and government privatizations. Maintains a diverse corporate and securities law practice across industry groups, emphasizing complex international and domestic transactions, including private and public financings, dual listings, and mergers and acquisitions. Regularly serves as counsel to leading investment banks and financial institutions, as well as public and private companies in life sciences and biotechnology, information technology, energy, telecommunications, media, entertainment and sports.
Prof. Memberships: American Bar Association, Co-Chair of the ABA Subcommittee on International Securities Matters; Board of Visitors of Pepperdine University School of Law; Board of Directors of Teams of Angels, Inc.; Congress of Fellows of the Center for International Legal Studies; Sports Lawyers Association; National Sports Marketing Network; International Bar Association; California Bar Association; Massachusetts Bar Association; Boston Bar Association; Society for English and American Lawyers.
Career: Admitted to Massachusetts Bar and California Bar. Joined firm in 2003, after heading Kirkland & Ellis's capital markets practice in Europe.
Personal: Pepperdine University School of Law (JD, magna cum laude); Michigan State University (BA, Honors).

JOY, Robert
Morgan, Brown and Joy LLP, Boston
617 523 6666
Recommended in Employment

JOY, William
Morgan, Brown and Joy LLP, Boston
617 523 6666
Recommended in Employment

KAHN, Adam
Foley Hoag LLP, Boston 617 832 1000
Recommended in Environment

KANNEL, William
Mintz Levin Cohn Ferris Glovsky and Popeo PC, Boston 617 542 6000
Recommended in Bankruptcy

KAY, Minta E
Goodwin Procter LLP, Boston
617 570 1000
mkay@goodwinprocter.com
Recommended in Real Estate
Practice Areas: Ms Kay's practice focuses on a variety of commercial real estate transactions, concentrating on real estate securities and capital markets, real estate finance and investment, property acquisitions, leasing and sales, and debt and equity restructuring. She has extensive experience in representing investors in complex joint venture and limited partnership transactions to acquire or develop properties as well as with commercial real estate loan and equity investment restructuring.
Personal: JD, Columbia University School of Law, 1986; BA, Barnard College, 1983 (magna cum laude).

KEATING, Michael
Foley Hoag LLP, Boston 617 832 1000
Recommended in Litigation

KEEFE, Robert D
Wilmer Cutler Pickering Hale and Dorr LLP, Boston 617 526 6334
robert.keefe@wilmerhale.com
Recommended in Litigation
Practice Areas: Co-Chairman of the firm's Government Investigations and Litigation Group. Has a complex general litigation practice which includes extensive white collar criminal defense work, general commercial litigation, civil rights and environmental cases. Has worked on large commercial disputes and antitrust lawsuits; advised companies in connection with internal investigations on topics ranging from environmental, bankruptcy and fraud issues; represented number of individuals before state and federal grand juries and represented companies and individuals charged with state and federal crimes involving violations of the federal health laws, FDA laws, federal and state banking laws, federal and state housing laws, customs law, and federal and state laws protecting intellectual property rights.
Prof. Memberships: American, Massachusetts and Boston Bar Associations.
Career: Admitted to Massachusetts Bar. Was an attorney in the Criminal Division of the Department of Justice, prior to joining the firm in 1974.
Personal: Boston College Law School (JD, summa cum laude, Order of the Coif); Harvard College (BA, cum laude).

KELLER, Stanley
Palmer & Dodge LLP, Boston
617 239 0217
skeller@palmerdodge.com
Recommended in Corporate/M&A
Practice Areas: Has extensive, high-level experience in business and securities law matters involving emerging and public companies; financial transactional work involving public and private entities, banks, energy and utility companies, developers and governmental agencies, including representing issuers, underwriters, financial institutions and investors; and mergers and acquisition transactions. Advises companies, boards, board committees and special committees on corporate governance issues, transactional matters and special investigations. Has been Chair of the American Bar Association's Business Law Section Committee on Federal Regulation of Securities, a special adviser to

the ABA Task Force on Corporate Responsibility and reporter for the ABA Task Force on Implementation of the Section 307 Attorney Professional Conduct Rules. Co-Chair of the Boston Bar Association's Task Force on Revision of the Massachusetts Business Corporation Law, former Chair of the BBA's Business Law Section, Corporation Law Committee, and Legal Opinions Committee, and a member of the TriBar Opinion Committee.

Prof. Memberships: American Bar Association, Boston Bar Association.
Career: Joined Palmer & Dodge in 1962; Partner since 1969.
Publications: Has written and edited many articles and treatises on corporate and securities law matters. They include 'Massachusetts Business Lawyering', a three-volume treatise published by MCLE (editor); 'International Securities Law Handbook', published by Graham & Trotman, Ltd. (co-editor); and 'Massachusetts Limited Liability Company Forms and Practice Manual', published by Data Trace Publishing Co. (co-author). Most recently, has written a number of articles and chaired several programs on the impact of the Sarbanes-Oxley Act of 2002 and related SEC and stock exchange initiatives and how they have dramatically changed the landscape for corporate governance and disclosure requirements. He is co-editor of 'The Practitioner's Guide to the Sarbanes-Oxley Act' published by ABA-CLE. Sought out as an expert on securities issues by local and national media.
Personal: Columbia University, AB, 1959; Harvard Law School, LLB, magna cum laude, 1962.

KENDALL, Michael J
Goodwin Procter LLP, Boston
617 570 1000
mkendall@goodwinprocter.com
Recommended in Private Equity
Practice Areas: Mr Kendall focuses his corporate finance and securities practice on representing private equity and venture capital firms in connection with early and later stage investments, leveraged recapitalizations and buyouts, as well as counseling a variety of emerging companies. He has substantial experience representing issuers and underwriters in initial and follow-on public offerings, public and private mergers and acquisitions, and advising public companies on SEC reporting and other general corporate matters.
Personal: JD, Boston University School of Law, 1993 (magna cum laude); MBA, Boston University Graduate School of Management, 1994; BA, Tufts University, 1990.

KENNARD, Wayne M
Wilmer Cutler Pickering Hale and Dorr LLP, Boston 617 526 6183
wayne.kennard@wilmerhale.com
Recommended in Intellectual Property

Practice Areas: Practice focuses on representing high-tech start-up and established companies in full range of intellectual property (IP) matters, including obtaining patent, trademark, and copyright protection, licensing IP, trade secret protection and protection of plaintiffs' and defendants' rights in IP through litigation. Experienced in obtaining IP protection, licensing, and litigation in computer hardware, software, electrical, electronics technology, and the mechanical and electromechanical technology areas. Extensive experience advising US and international companies on US and international IP issues.
Career: Admitted to Massachusetts, District of Columbia, New York and Pennsylvania Bars.
Personal: George Washington University Law School (JD); US Naval Academy (BS).

KIEFER, Matthew
Goulston & Storrs, Boston
617 482 1776
Recommended in Real Estate

KIMMELL, Kenneth
Bernstein, Cushner & Kimmell PC, Boston 617 236 4090
Recommended in Environment

KIRSCH, Robert
Wilmer Cutler Pickering Hale and Dorr LLP, Boston 617 526 6779
rob.kirsch@wilmerhale.com
Recommended in Environment
Practice Areas: Chair of firm's Environmental Department and member of Litigation Department. Represents clients in wide range of environmental defense, counseling and permitting contexts. Helps industry clients in high tech, energy, life science, property management, waste management and manufacturing sectors to manage their environmental risks and liabilities quickly and cost effectively. Has defended clients involved in criminal, civil and administrative investigations and enforcement proceedings.
Prof. Memberships: American, Boston and New Hampshire Bar Associations.
Career: Admitted to Massachusetts and New Hampshire Bars. Joined firm in 1983.
Personal: Cornell Law School (JD, cum laude); Middlebury College (BS, cum laude, Phi Beta Kappa).

KLINE, Douglas J
Goodwin Procter LLP, Boston
617 570 1000
dkline@goodwinprocter.com
Recommended in Intellectual Property
Practice Areas: Mr Kline practices within all aspects of intellectual property litigation, particularly patent infringement matters and disputes related to the enforcement of intellectual property rights. He advises inventors, companies, investors and underwriters concerning

patent enforcement and infringement risks. He advises clients regarding technology transfer, including the negotiation and drafting of all forms of related agreements such as patent licenses and technology development and license agreements. He also works with clients to develop patent portfolio development strategies, and oversees the preparation and prosecution of patent applications.
Personal: JD, Suffolk University Law School, 1990 (magna cum laude); BS, Tufts University, 1984.

KNOWLTON, William A
Ropes & Gray LLP, Boston
617 951 7496
william.knowlton@ropesgray.com
Recommended in Healthcare
Practice Areas: Counsels academic medical centers, community hospitals, faculty practice plans, physician groups, managed care organizations, healthcare investment firms, pharmaceutical companies, biotechnology companies, and healthcare information technology companies on business and regulatory matters, helping them find practical solutions to difficult issues in a complex healthcare industry environment.
Career: Massachusetts Bar (1982). District of Columbia Bar (1998). Partner, Ropes & Gray (1991).
Personal: JD, University of Virginia School of Law (1982). BA, Yale University (1977).

KOCIUBES, Joseph
Bingham McCutchen LLP, Boston
617 951 8000
Recommended in Litigation

KOFFEL, William
Foley Hoag LLP, Boston 617 832 1000
Recommended in Employment

KOLB, William R
Foley Hoag LLP, Boston 617 832 1000
Recommended in Corporate/M&A

KRASNOW, Jordan
Goulston & Storrs, Boston
617 482 1776
Recommended in Real Estate

KREBS, Michael
Nutter, McClennen & Fish, LLP, Boston
617 439 2000
Recommended in Banking & Finance

KREIGER, Arthur
Anderson & Kreiger LLP, Cambridge
617 252 6575
Recommended in Environment

KWASNICK, Raymond
Goulston & Storrs, Boston
617 482 1776
Recommended in Real Estate

KYLE, Amy
Bingham McCutchen LLP, Boston
617 951 8000
Recommended in Banking & Finance

LAMPERT, James
Wilmer Cutler Pickering Hale and Dorr LLP, Boston 617 526 6456
james.lampert@wilmerhale.com
Recommended in Intellectual Property
Practice Areas: Chair of firm's Intellectual Property Department; member of Litigation and Corporate Departments and member of the Technology Transfer Section within the International Group. Has extensive experience in areas of patent, trademark, copyright, trade secret and unfair competition matters.
Career: Admitted to Massachusetts Bar, United States Supreme Court, and United States Patent and Trademark Office. Joined firm in 1985; was an adjunct professor of law at Boston University School of Law and, for 15 years, taught courses on patent law and trademarks and copyrights.
Personal: Harvard Law School (JD, magna cum laude); Massachusetts Institute of Technology (BS, Mechanical Engineering).

LANE, Roger
Greenberg Traurig LLP, Boston
617 310 6006
laner@gtlaw.com
Recommended in Litigation
Practice Areas: Litigation.
Publications: Author, 'Managing Risks in Distressed Companies – Director Duties to Shareholders, Creditors and Employees,' The Venture Capital Review, Fall 2001.
Personal: JD, cum laude, Harvard University Law School. BA, with high honors, with highest distinction, University of Michigan. Phi Beta Kappa.

LAPORTE, Claire
Foley Hoag LLP, Boston 617 832 1000
Recommended in Intellectual Property

LECLAIRE, John R
Goodwin Procter LLP, Boston
617 570 1000
jleclaire@goodwinprocter.com
Recommended in Private Equity
Practice Areas: Mr LeClaire's private equity work includes leveraged recapitalizations, buyouts and minority investments, both in later stage situations and earlier stage ventures, for leading private equity firms throughout the country. He also specializes in the representation of emerging growth companies in sectors such as technology and information services, health care, financial services and consumer products. Involvement with above-mentioned clients focuses on strategic counsel, mergers and acquisitions, equity and executive compensation programs, and going-private transactions.
Personal: JD, Boston University School of Law, 1982 (magna cum laude); AB, Brown University, 1979 (magna cum laude).

LEE, William F
Wilmer Cutler Pickering Hale and Dorr LLP, Boston 617 526 6556
william.lee@wilmerhale.com
Recommended in Intellectual Property
Practice Areas: Firm's Co-Managing Partner. Concentrates practice on intellectual property and commercial litigation. Has extensive trial experience. Has acted as lead trial counsel in patent litigation concerning genetically engineered tomato product; a trial involving the right to manufacture and sell recombinant erythropoietin; a trial before the International Trade Commission involving $3 billion of commerce; and trials in federal court involving laser optics, video conferencing, remote data storage, secure Internet communicator, dye chemistry, high-speed chromatography and medical devices.
Prof. Memberships: Fellow of American College of Trial Lawyers; served as visiting professor at Harvard Law School; Advisory Committee of the Court of Appeals for the Federal Circuit; US District Court of Massachusetts' Advisory Committee; serves on the US District Court for the District of Delaware's Intellectual Property Advisory Committee; appointed by governor of Massachusetts to serve on a special Judicial Nominating Committee for selection of judges for the Massachusetts Supreme Judicial Court; elected to Board of Overseers, Harvard University; Visiting Committee, Cornell Law School.
Career: Admitted to Massachusetts Bar and United States Supreme Court. Joined firm in 1976.
Personal: Cornell Law School (JD, magna cum laude, Order of the Coif); Cornell Business School (MBA, with Distinction); Harvard College (AB, magna cum laude).

LEIBENSPERGER, Edward P
McDermott Will & Emery, Boston
617 535 4046
eleibensperger@mwe.com
Recommended in Litigation
Practice Areas: Focuses on litigation and trial of general business, securities, corporate governance, and professional liability cases. Experience includes trials of numerous jury cases in both state and federal courts. Appears regularly in courts on preliminary injunctions, motions and jury-waived hearings. Has handled appeals in US Court of Appeals for the First and Second Circuits and Massachusetts Supreme Judicial Court and Appeals Court. Has tried to a successful jury verdict several accounting malpractice cases, and corporate and commercial cases. Has represented defendants in private securities litigation and before Securities and Exchange Commission. Has represented plaintiffs in business cases, obtaining settlements and verdicts in multi-million dollar range.
Prof. Memberships: Fellow of American College of Trial Lawyers since 1995. Served as Member of Governing Council of American Bar Association's Section of Litigation and co-chair of Committee on Corporate Counsel. Currently President-elect of Boston Bar Association, and previously served as chair of BBA's Litigation Section and Professional Liability Committee.
Personal: Earned JD (summa cum laude) in 1974 from Ohio State University College of Law, and BA (magna cum laude) in 1970 from Muskingum College. Admitted to practice before the US Supreme Court.

LEICH, Christopher M
Ropes & Gray LLP, Boston
617 951 7279
christopher.leich@ropesgray.com
Recommended in Tax
Practice Areas: Corporate and partnership federal income taxation. Practice substantially devoted to private equity sponsors and investors, including Bain Capital, Silver Lake Partners, Berkshire Partners, Weston Presidio Capital, and Merrill Lynch Investment Managers. Extensive experience structuring private equity funds, hedge funds, CBO funds, and funds of funds. Regularly advises domestic and cross-border M&A transactions, joint ventures, and spin-offs, as well as public offerings of equity and debt securities.
Career: Massachusetts Bar (1987). District of Columbia Bar (1987). Partner, Ropes & Gray (1996).
Personal: JD, cum laude, Harvard Law School (1987). BPhil, Oxford University (1987). BA, high honors, Swarthmore College (1975).

LEON, Michael
Nutter, McClennen & Fish, LLP, Boston
617 439 2000
Recommended in Environment

LEONARD, Stephen
Brown Rudnick Berlack Israels LLP, Boston 617 856 8200
Recommended in Environment

LEONETTI, Kenneth
Foley Hoag LLP, Boston 617 832 1000
Recommended in Bankruptcy

LEVINE, Richard
Adler Pollock & Sheehan PC, Boston
617 603 0556
rlevine@apslaw.com
Recommended in Bankruptcy
Practice Areas: Bankruptcy, business and corporate, litigation, creditors' rights.
Prof. Memberships: American College of Bankruptcy, Future of the College Committee.
Career: A Partner in the Corporate Group, he represents a variety of parties, including lenders, debtors-in-possession, trustees, creditors' committees, and principals in connection with bankruptcy proceedings (especially Chapter 11) and out-of-court work-outs. He also represents prospective acquirers of assets from insolvent companies or companies in bankruptcy proceedings. He is an expert witness on bankruptcy and ethical matters and frequently lectures on commercial matters, including the liability of officers and directors of companies in precarious financial conditions.

LITWAK, Lawrence
Brown Rudnick Berlack Israels LLP, Boston 617 856 8200
Recommended in Healthcare

LUKEY, Joan
Wilmer Cutler Pickering Hale and Dorr LLP, Boston 617 526 6798
joan.lukey@wilmerhale.com
Recommended in Employment, Litigation
Practice Areas: Concentrates practice in commercial and employment litigation. Highly regarded trial attorney; tried more than 50 federal and state cases, predominantly to juries. Experienced appellate advocate; argued approximately 15 cases before US Court of Appeals for the First Circuit, and approximately 35 cases before state appellate courts in Massachusetts and New Hampshire.
Prof. Memberships: Boston Bar Association (President, 2000-01); American College of Trial Lawyers (elected, 1991); International Academy of Trial Lawyers (elected to Fellowship).
Career: Admitted to Massachusetts Bar, New Hampshire Bar and US Supreme Court. Joined firm in 1974.
Personal: Boston College Law School (JD); Smith College (BA).

LYMAN, R Jeffrey
Goodwin Procter LLP, Boston
617 570 1000
rlyman@goodwinprocter.com
Recommended in Real Estate
Practice Areas: Mr Lyman represents clients in all aspects of commercial real estate development and permitting. His practice often involves cutting-edge permitting and environmental issues and he is widely sought after on complex matters relating to environmental impact assessment, wetlands and waterways work, brownfields redevelopment, regulatory takings litigation, and master plan implementation. He has successfully permitted projects under innovative zoning regulations. Mr Lyman has worked with clients building office, multi-family residential, industrial and recreational facilities in urban, suburban and rural locations.
Personal: JD, Vermont Law School, 1993 (magna cum laude); BA, Harvard College, 1986 (cum laude).

LYNCH, Christine
Goulston & Storrs, Boston
617 482 1776
Recommended in Bankruptcy

LYONS, Gregory
Goodwin Procter LLP, Boston
617 570 1000
glyons@goodwinprocter.com
Recommended in Banking & Finance
Practice Areas: Mr Lyons' practice concentrates principally in the banking area, engaging in US and foreign bank regulatory, formation, merger, conversion, structuring and securities work, risk capital and trust matters, as well as general corporate and securities law matters. He has represented financial institutions before the Federal Deposit Insurance Corporation, the Federal Reserve Board, the Office of Comptroller of the Currency, the Office of Thrift Supervision, the Securities and Exchange Commission, and state banking and securities regulatory agencies.
Personal: JD, Boston University School of Law, 1990 (magna cum laude); BA, Wesleyan University, 1987.

MACKIE, Thomas
Moehrke, Mackie & Shea, P.C., Boston
617 266 5700
Recommended in Environment

MAHONY, Gael
Holland & Knight LLP, Boston
617 523 2700
gael.mahony@hklaw.com
Recommended in Litigation
Practice Areas: Partner in the Litigation Section, specializing in complex business and appellate cases. His high-profile clients include such companies as Volvo and the Hyatt Hotel chain. In a 'Boston Magazine' survey of Boston lawyers he was named the lawyer of choice for "betting the company" cases. Mahony is a Member and former President of the American College of Trial Lawyers, an invitation-only organization of top litigators across the country. He is a graduate of Yale University and Harvard Law School.

MALONE, Judith
Palmer & Dodge LLP, Boston
617 239 0321
jmalone@palmerdodge.com
Recommended in Employment
Practice Areas: Counsels employers on issues ranging from organizational restructuring to individual termination cases, and on policies and practices to deal with current employment issues. Litigates employment-related claims in both state and federal court, and has represented clients in a variety of discrimination actions, including claims involving race, sex, national origin, disability, sexual harassment, and age discrimination. Represents employers before administrative agencies and conducts employment-law seminars for employers. Has also conducted a number of investigations for employers in the areas of sexual harassment and discrimination.
Prof. Memberships: American Bar Association, Massachusetts Bar Association.

Career: Joined Palmer & Dodge in 1985; Partner since 1990.
Personal: University of Massachusetts, BA, magna cum laude, 1973; Boston College Law School, JD, magna cum laude, 1978.

MALT, R Bradford
Ropes & Gray LLP, Boston
617 951 7318
bradford.malt@ropesgray.com
Recommended in Corporate/M&A, Private Equity
Practice Areas: Concentrates in corporate finance and mergers and acquisitions. Represents a variety of private and public equity clients in fundraising and investment activities. Clients include leveraged buyout funds, hedge funds, CBO funds, fund-of-funds, mezzanine funds, pension funds, alternative investment funds and investors. Expertise advising fund sponsors in connection with fundraising, strategic initiatives, relationships among partners, organizational structure, effective policies and procedures, and operational matters. A founder of the Private Equity Practice at Ropes & Gray.
Career: Massachusetts Bar (1979). Partner, Ropes & Gray (1987).
Personal: JD, cum laude, Harvard Law School (1979). AB, magna cum laude, Harvard College (1976).

MARETT, Louis
Choate Hall & Stewart, Boston
617 248 5000
Recommended in Tax

MAY, Arnold P
Proskauer Rose LLP, Boston
617 526 9757
amay@proskauer.com
Recommended in Tax
Practice Areas: A Partner in the firm's Tax Department and a member of the Private Investment Funds Group. His practice focuses on tax planning for private equity fund managers in connection with their fund-raising and internal organizational matters, as well as investment activities. In addition, he represents US and non-US investors in connection with their investments in venture capital funds, buyout funds, hedge funds and other investment partnerships. In this capacity, as well as in connection with advising private equity funds with respect to their investment activities, he regularly advises on international tax issues that arise in connection with investments in the US by non-US investors (including non-US investors subject to special US tax treatment, such as governmental pension plans and tax-exempt organizations), as well as investments outside of the US by US persons. He also has significant experience structuring tax-free and taxable mergers and acquisitions (including cross-border transactions), equity compensation arrangements and innovative financing techniques for investments in

tax transparent entities such as partnerships, limited liability companies and Subchapter S corporations.
Personal: University of Florida College of Law, LLM, 1994. University of San Diego School of Law, JD, 1993. Rutgers College, BA, 1990.

MAYER, William
Goodwin Procter LLP, Boston
617 570 1000
wmayer@goodwinprocter.com
Recommended in Banking & Finance
Practice Areas: Mr Mayer has handled a wide variety of transactions including mergers, acquisitions, public and private offerings of debt and equity securities, stock conversions, bank and holding company formations and reorganizations of financial institutions and holding companies. He regularly advises clients on bank regulatory matters involving state and federal law.
Prof. Memberships: Center for Banking & Financial Law Studies (Boston University): Board of Advisors.
Personal: JD, Virginia Law School, 1977; MS, University of Dar es Salaam, Tanzania, 1974; AB, Dartmouth College, 1973 (summa cum laude).

MCCARTHY, William
Ropes & Gray LLP, Boston
617 951 7466
william.mccarthy@ropesgray.com
Recommended in Bankruptcy
Practice Areas: Represents debtors and creditors in reorganization cases throughout the United States and has lectured extensively on debtor/creditor relationships to business and professional groups. Represented debtors in cases in Massachusetts, Delaware and New York; boards of directors; major creditors in Chapter 11 cases; and bidders for assets of Chapter 11 debtors.
Career: Massachusetts bar (1970). Partner, Ropes & Gray (1979).
Personal: JD, cum laude, Harvard Law School (1970). BA, College of the Holy Cross (1967).

MCPHEE, Joan
Ropes & Gray LLP, Boston
617 951 7535
joan.mcphee@ropesgray.com
Recommended in Litigation
Practice Areas: Specializes in white collar criminal matters and complex civil litigation. Represents clients in criminal litigation, enforcement actions, and federal and state grand jury investigations involving health care fraud, securities fraud, bank fraud, contract fraud, RICO violations, mail and wire fraud, and export control violations.
Career: Massachusetts Bar (1986). New York Bar (1986). Rhode Island Bar (1991). Partner, Ropes & Gray (1993).
Personal: JD, magna cum laude, Harvard Law School (1984). BA, Phi Beta Kappa, Princeton University (1980).

MEDAGLIA, Anthony
Goodwin Procter LLP, Boston
617 570 1000
amedaglia@goodwinprocter.com
Recommended in Private Equity
Practice Areas: Mr Medaglia focuses his practice on the representation of technology companies – both public and private; private equity; mergers and acquisitions; public and private sales of securities; corporate buyouts and reorganizations; and transactions involving intellectual property. He has extensive experience representing hedge funds, investment advisors and venture capitalists. He has structured, negotiated and closed numerous strategic transactions for a diverse group of clients.
Personal: LLB, Harvard Law School, 1965; AB, Harvard College, 1959.

MENNA, Gilbert
Goodwin Procter LLP, Boston
617 570 1000
gmenna@goodwinprocter.com
Recommended in Corporate/M&A
Practice Areas: Mr Menna has extensive experience representing public and private issuers (ranging from emerging to NYSE-listed public companies), investors (private and institutional), underwriters and placement agents in all types of equity and debt securities, including sophisticated convertible and exchangeable securities with a broad range of economic, substantive and tax-sensitive terms. He's nationally recognized for his representation of publicly traded real estate operating companies.
Prof. Memberships: NYU Real Estate Institute REIT's Center: Board of Directors; NAREIT: Board Member; ULI: Member.
Personal: JD, Georgetown University Law Center, 1982; MLT, Georgetown University Law Center, 1983; BA, Syracuse University, 1978 (magna cum laude).

MEREDITH, Steven
Edwards & Angell, LLP, Boston
617 439 4444
Recommended in Private Equity

MIKELS, Richard
Mintz Levin Cohn Ferris Glovsky and Popeo PC, Boston 617 542 6000
Recommended in Bankruptcy

MILLER, Michelle
Wilmer Cutler Pickering Hale and Dorr LLP, Boston
617 526 6116
michelle.miller@wilmerhale.com
Recommended in Antitrust
Practice Areas: Vice-Chair of firm's Litigation Department and Antitrust and Competition Department; member of firm's Executive Committee. Concentrates practice on complex commercial litigation and on providing advice to clients on antitrust compliance issues and strategies for avoiding litigation. Litigates in federal and state courts. Repre-

sents clients before the Federal Trade Commission and the Antitrust Division of the Department of Justice in connection with mergers and other government investigations.
Prof. Memberships: American Bar Association; former Co-Chair of Boston Bar Association's Antitrust Committee.
Career: Admitted to Massachusetts Bar. Joined firm in 1980.
Personal: Boston College Law School (JD); Boston University (BA).

MITCHELL, Beth
Nutter, McClennen & Fish, LLP, Boston
617 439 2000
Recommended in Real Estate

MOFFATT, Maura Griffith
Goodwin Procter LLP, Boston
617 570 1000
mmoffatt@goodwinprocter.com
Recommended in Real Estate
Practice Areas: Ms Moffat focuses on commercial real estate transactions, with an emphasis on real estate investment management and finance, capital markets and real estate securities. Her national real estate practice includes property acquisitions, leasing and sales, and debt and equity investments and restructurings. She represents investors, including pension fund advisors and their institutional investors, banking institutions, insurance companies, public and private operating companies and private real estate investors and real estate investment fund sponsors.
Prof. Memberships: ULI: Member; Real Estate Finance Association of the Greater Boston Real Estate Board: Member; NAIOP: Member.
Personal: JD, Georgetown University Law Center, 1991 (cum laude); BS, Georgetown University's College of Arts and Sciences, 1988.

MONAGHAN, John J
Holland & Knight LLP, Boston
617 523 2700
john.monaghan@hklaw.com
Recommended in Bankruptcy
Practice Areas: Practice Group Leader of the firm's National Corporate Restructuring, Bankruptcy and Creditor' Rights Group. His extensive bankruptcy practice has involved representation of a wide range of clients, including Chapter 11 debtors, creditors' committees, equity committees, lenders, landlords, licensors, trustees, parties to prepetition contracts and leases, defendants in adversary proceedings and unsecured creditors. He is particularly focused on representing major case participants in complex commercial Chapter 11 cases. He advises clients on the business aspects of bankruptcy and workouts, and represents clients in matters in the Bankruptcy Court as well as in other state and federal courts.

MONTGOMERY, John T
Ropes & Gray LLP, Boston
617 951 7565
john.montgomery@ropesgray.com
Recommended in Litigation
Practice Areas: Complex civil litigation with emphasis on trials and appeals in high profile cases involving novel or publicly sensitive issues. Practice includes a variety of complex matters involving securities, pharmaceutical pricing, intellectual property, insurance coverage, commercial tort, product liability, ERISA, and regulatory matters. Tried cases and argued appeals in state and federal courts in Maine, Massachusetts, Illinois, New York, New Jersey, and Washington, DC. Argued two successful appeals in the United States Supreme Court.
Career: Massachusetts Bar (1975). Partner (1985) and Managing Partner (2004), Ropes & Gray.
Personal: JD, Boston College Law School (1975). BA, University of Michigan (1969).

MOORE, Paul D
Duane Morris LLP, Boston
617 289 9230
pdmoore@duanemorris.com
Recommended in Bankruptcy
Practice Areas: Paul D Moore focuses his practice on business reorganization, bankruptcy law and litigation and loan workouts. He represents debtors in possession and Chapter 11 trustees in a wide range of reorganization cases under Chapter 11 of the Bankruptcy Code pending in various jurisdictions, including Delaware, as well as Massachusetts. He also represents creditors in bankruptcy and loan workout matters.
Prof. Memberships: American Bar Association; Massachusetts Bar Association; Boston Bar Association; American Bankruptcy Institute.
Career: Admitted to practice in the Commonwealth of Massachusetts; the Supreme Court of the United States; the United States Court of Appeals for the First Circuit; and the United States District Court for the District of Massachusetts. Duane Morris LLP, Partner, 1999-present; Choate, Hall & Stewart, Boston, Massachusetts, Partner, 1990-99; Foley, Hoag & Eliot, Boston, Massachusetts, Partner, 1982-90, Associate, 1979-82; Testa, Hurwitz & Thibeault, Boston, Massachusetts, Associate, 1976-79.
Personal: Boston College Law School, JD, 1976; Boston College, BS, 1973.

MORREALE, Justin
Bingham McCutchen LLP, Boston
617 951 8000
Recommended in Private Equity

MOTENKO, Neil
Nutter, McClennen & Fish, LLP, Boston
617 439 2000
Recommended in Antitrust

MULDOON Jr, Robert
Sherin and Lodgen LLP, Boston
617 646 2225
Recommended in Litigation

MURPHY, Harold B
Hanify & King, Boston
617 423 0400
hbm@hanify.com
Recommended in Bankruptcy
Practice Areas: Leads Hanify & King's Bankruptcy and Financial Restructuring Group. Specializes in bankruptcy and commercial law including the representation of debtors, creditors' committees, trustees and creditors in Chapter 11 reorganizations and Chapter 7 liquidations. Mr Murphy has been appointed as trustee, examiner and receiver in various bankruptcy and non-bankruptcy corporate restructurings and liquidations. He has had considerable experience in the areas of commercial finance and litigation as well as matters involving secured lending, mergers and acquisitions, and the Uniform Commercial Code.
Prof. Memberships: American, Boston and Massachusetts Bar Associations; Turnaround Management Association; American Bankruptcy Institute.
Career: Founder and Director of Hanify & King's Bankruptcy and Financial Restructuring Group.
Personal: JD, Suffolk University Law School (1981); AB, cum laude, Harvard College (1977).

NAGLE, James
Goodwin Procter LLP, Boston
617 570 1000
jnagle@goodwinprocter.com
Recommended in Employment
Practice Areas: Mr Nagle focuses on defending corporations against claims made by employees. He practices in state and federal courts, as well as before a variety of administrative agencies. He is experienced in litigating complex age, sex, race and disability discrimination claims, as well as in defending wrongful discharge, civil rights, employee privacy and drug-testing cases. He also has experience negotiating and litigating issues related to the termination of highly compensated executives.
Personal: JD, Georgetown University Law Center, 1980 (magna cum laude); MPA, American University, 1976; BA, Georgetown University, 1974 (magna cum laude).

NICHOLLS III, Malcolm B
Proskauer Rose LLP, Boston
617 526 9787
mnicholls@proskauer.com
Recommended in Private Equity
Practice Areas: A Partner in the firm's Corporate Department and a member of the Private Investment Funds Group. He concentrates in the areas of corporate and securities law, with a particular emphasis on private equity transactions. His experience includes representation of private equity fund managers and

investors in both US and non-US fund formation projects, portfolio company investments, and management and governance issues.
Prof. Memberships: A member of the American Bar Association and Boston Bar Association. He was admitted to the New York Bar in 1995, the US District Court, Southern District of New York, in 1995 and the Massachusetts Bar in 1996.
Personal: Boston University School of Law, JD, 1994. University of New Hampshire, BA, magna cum laude, 1991.

NUTT, Robert L
Ropes & Gray LLP, Boston
617 951 7384
robert.nutt@ropesgray.com
Recommended in Corporate/M&A
Practice Areas: Transactions lawyer, experienced at marshalling resources of Ropes & Gray in complex capital markets transactions. Represents primarily investment advisors, investment banking firms and private equity clients. Represents committees of public bondholders in large case debt restructurings and directors of publicly traded companies. Specialist in corporate, commercial, and insolvency law.
Career: Massachusetts Bar (1971). New York Bar (1971). Partner, Ropes & Gray (1979).
Personal: JD, cum laude, University of Pennsylvania Law School (1970). BA, summa cum laude, Grove City College (1967).

NYLEN Jr, Richard
Lynch DeSimone & Nylen LLP, Boston
617 348 4500
Recommended in Real Estate

OGILBY, Anne Phillips
Ropes & Gray LLP, Boston
617 951 7472
anne.ogilby@ropesgray.com
Recommended in Healthcare
Practice Areas: Principally responsible for capital financings undertaken on behalf of the firm's healthcare and higher education clients, including over a hundred tax-exempt and taxable borrowings. Serves routinely as underwriter's counsel and counsel to financially distressed non-profit corporations. Broadly involved in corporate transactions, including acquisitions and divestitures of healthcare and other non-profit corporations and the development and break-up of multi-provider delivery systems. General corporate counseling for non-profit corporations, including endowment issues.
Career: Massachusetts Bar (1985). New York Bar (2004). Partner, Ropes & Gray (1993).
Personal: JD, University of Virginia School of Law (1984). BA, Harvard College (1980).

O'REILLY Jr, William R
Wilmer Cutler Pickering Hale and Dorr LLP, Boston 617 526 6210
william.o'reilly@wilmerhale.com
Recommended in Real Estate
Practice Areas: Vice-chair of the firm's Real Estate Department. Practice focuses on all aspects of real estate law, including permitting, development, construction, financing, purchase and sales and leasing. Has served as counsel for a broad range of clients, including numerous office, R&D and multi-family developers, retailers, corporations and non-profit institutions for nearly 25 years.
Prof. Memberships: Tufts University (Trustee); The American College of Real Estate Lawyers (Member).
Career: Admitted to Massachusetts Bar. Joined the firm in 1980.
Personal: Georgetown University Law Center (JD, magna cum laude); Tufts University (BA, summa cum laude with Special Honors).

PACI, Victor
Bingham McCutchen LLP, Boston
617 951 8000
Recommended in Private Equity

PAINTER, Robin A
Proskauer Rose LLP, Boston
617 526 9790
rpainter@proskauer.com
Recommended in Private Equity
Practice Areas: Partner at Proskauer Rose, LLP. Concentrates in the areas of corporate and securities law with a particular emphasis on private equity. Her experience includes representation of private equity fund managers in capital formations, portfolio investments and governance issues, and institutional investors and investment advisers in the private equity field.
Prof. Memberships: Member of the American Bar Association, the Boston Bar Association and the Massachusetts Bar Association. Admitted to the Massachusetts Bar in 1985 and the US District Court, District of Massachusetts in 1986.
Career: Frequently speaks nationally and internationally on private equity related issues and is also a frequent contributor to publications in the venture capital field.
Personal: Received her BA, cum laude, from Northwestern University in 1982. In 1985, received her JD, cum laude, from Boston College School of Law where she also served as editor for the 'Boston College International' and 'Comparative Law Review'.

PAPPONE, Michael
Goodwin Procter LLP, Boston
617 570 1000
mpappone@goodwinprocter.com
Recommended in Bankruptcy
Practice Areas: Mr Pappone concentrates in commercial insolvency and reorganization law. His practice spans the spectrum of representing principal

parties in large corporate reorganizations to out-of-court workouts for smaller entrepreneurial companies, including representation of equipment lessors, landlords, asset acquirers, creditors' committees or committee members, court-appointed trustees and entities involved in leveraged buyouts. Also advises clients on commercial and insolvency issues arising in corporate restructurings, financings and securitization transactions.

Prof. Memberships: American College of Commercial Finance Lawyers: Member; American Bar Foundation: Fellow; American College of Bankruptcy: Fellow.

Personal: JD, Harvard Law School, 1973; AB, University of California, Berkeley, 1970.

PARSIGIAN, Kenneth
Goodwin Procter LLP, Boston
617 570 1000
kparsigian@goodwinprocter.com
Recommended in Litigation

Practice Areas: Mr Parsigian represents clients in both civil and criminal matters, with a primary focus on complex products liability, mass tort and RICO litigation. He also advises clients on product warnings and compliance with laws and regulations concerning product safety, import-export procedures and anti-money laundering programs. He has served as Lead Counsel for Philip Morris USA, and National Coordinating Counsel for the tobacco industry in more than 60 suits across the country involving claims for more than $100 billion in damages.

Personal: JD, Boston University School of Law, 1987 (magna cum laude); BA, University of Michigan, 1983.

PASTERNACK, Sam
Choate Hall & Stewart, Boston
617 248 5000
Recommended in Intellectual Property

PASTUSZENSKI, Brian
Goodwin Procter LLP, Boston
617 570 1000
bpastuszenski@goodwinprocter.com
Recommended in Litigation

Practice Areas: Mr Pastuszenski has achieved national prominence in the defense of securities class action and shareholder litigation matters and proceedings brought by the SEC and other regulatory organizations, and the related insurance and indemnification issues that such matters involve. His practice is concentrated in the areas of securities class action and shareholder litigation defense, defense of SEC proceedings, internal corporate investigations, corporate governance and compliance matters, merger and acquisition-related litigation, and other high-stakes business litigation.

Personal: JD, Cornell Law School, 1981 (magna cum laude, Order of the Coif); BA, Dartmouth College, 1978 (summa cum laude).

PATTON, William
Ropes & Gray LLP, Boston
617 951 7572
william.patton@ropesgray.com
Recommended in Antitrust

Practice Areas: Many years of experience in general litigation, including antitrust litigation. Advises and represents clients in a wide range of antitrust matters including private disputes and Department of Justice, FTC, and state law enforcement investigations. Significant trial and appellate experience before the Supreme Judicial Court, the Federal Courts of Appeals, and the United States Supreme Court.

Career: Massachusetts Bar (1969). Maine Bar (1969). Assistant to the Solicitor General of the US (1973-75). Partner, Ropes & Gray (1977).

Personal: JD, Duke University School of Law (1968). BA, Yale University (1965).

PEARLSTEIN, Mark W
McDermott Will & Emery, Boston
617 535 4425
mpearlstein@mwe.com
Recommended in Litigation

Practice Areas: Concentrates practice on white-collar criminal defense, the defense of actions brought by the SEC, complex commercial litigation, arbitration and internal investigations. Has significant experience in corporate criminal investigations, and served as Acting US Attorney responsible for negotiating what was then the largest resolution of a health care fraud case.

Prof. Memberships: Served on the Massachusetts Supreme Judicial Court's Web Advisory Board and on the Committee to Revise the Local Rules of the US District Court for the District of Massachusetts. Appointed by the US District Court for the District of Massachusetts to serve on its Criminal Justice Act panel of defense attorneys.

Career: Served as federal prosecutor in Boston's US Attorney's Office (1989-2000). Litigated a range of civil and criminal matters and tried a number of complex white-collar crime cases. Served as Chief of the Office's Economic Crimes Unit (1994-96), and was the First Assistant US Attorney (1996-2000) supervising the Civil and Criminal Divisions of the US Attorney's Office. Received the Attorney General's Award for Exceptional Service, the highest award presented by the Department of Justice.

Personal: Earned AB, Phi Beta Kappa in political science, from the University of Michigan, and JD, cum laude, from Harvard Law School.

PENDLETON, Lea B
Morse, Barnes-Brown & Pendleton PC, Waltham 781 622 5930
lbp@mbbp.com
Recommended in Private Equity

Practice Areas: For over 20 years, Lea has represented venture capital firms in

their investments in their portfolio companies, and venture capital backed companies. In addition to his investment work, his experience includes business structuring, corporate finance, buyouts, mergers and acquisitions, and project finance. He is a frequent speaker and writer on issues relating to venture capital finance and the organization of new businesses. He is a member of the Corporate Law Committee of the Boston Bar Association and of the Business Section of the American Bar Association. Lea is a graduate of Yale College and Yale Law School.

PENTZ, Martin
Nutter, McClennen & Fish, LLP, Boston
617 439 2000
Recommended in Environment

PERRY, Christopher
Littler Mendelson PC, Boston
617 217 2831
Recommended in Employment

PICKETT, Andrew
Jackson Lewis, Boston 617 367 0025
Recommended in Employment

PIERCE, Rudolph
Goulston & Storrs, Boston
617 482 1776
Recommended in Litigation

PISA, Regina M
Goodwin Procter LLP, Boston
617 570 1000
rpisa@goodwinprocter.com
*Recommended in Banking & Finance,
Corporate/M&A*

Practice Areas: Ms Pisa serves as Chairman and Managing Partner of Goodwin Procter LLP. Her practice focuses on the financial services area, representing banks and investment companies. She has recently concentrated on mergers and acquisitions of banks and financial institutions. She also represents banks and financial institutions on a wide variety of other matters, including corporate and board governance issues, capital raising, and general corporate and securities law issues.

Prof. Memberships: Citizens Financial Group, Inc.: Board of Directors; Boys and Girls Club of America: Board of Trustees; Easter Seals Society of Massachusetts: Board of Directors; Simmons College: Board of Trustees.

Personal: JD, Georgetown University Law Center; BA, MA, Oxford University, St Hilda's College; AB, Harvard University.

POLEBAUM, Mark
Wilmer Cutler Pickering Hale and Dorr LLP, Boston 617 526 6792
mark.polebaum@wilmerhale.com
Recommended in Bankruptcy

Practice Areas: Partner and Co-Chair of the firm's Bankruptcy and Commercial Department. Practice focuses on out-of-court restructurings and Chapter 11 reorganizations, with an emphasis on representation of debtors and bond-

holders. Has represented private and public companies in the technology, retail, telecommunication and manufacturing sectors and bondholder committees for companies in the aviation, satellite, technology, energy and manufacturing sectors.

Prof. Memberships: American College of Bankruptcy; American Bankruptcy Institute.

Career: Admitted to Massachusetts Bar. Joined the firm in 1979.

Personal: New York University School of Law (JD, Order of the Coif); Middlebury College (BA, summa cum laude, Phi Beta Kappa).

POPEO, R Robert
Mintz Levin Cohn Ferris Glovsky and Popeo PC, Boston 617 542 6000
Recommended in Litigation

PORCELLI, Frank
Fish & Richardson, Boston
617 542 5070
Recommended in Intellectual Property

PORTER, Jeffrey
Mintz Levin Cohn Ferris Glovsky and Popeo PC, Boston 617 542 6000
Recommended in Environment

POSS, Stephen D
Goodwin Procter LLP, Boston
617 570 1000
sposs@goodwinprocter.com
Recommended in Litigation

Practice Areas: Mr Poss has a national business litigation and counseling practice, particularly in the areas of securities class action defense, SEC disclosure and corporate governance issues, complex business litigation, mergers and acquisitions, contests for corporate control and intellectual property disputes. He represents venture capital and private equity firms in connection with deal protection, IPO issues, shareholder disputes and transactional litigation and also handles complex business litigation and arbitrations.

Prof. Memberships: The SEC Institute: Advisory Board Member.

Personal: JD, University of Chicago Law School, 1981; BA, Amherst College, 1978 (magna cum laude).

PRATT, Carol
Foley Hoag LLP, Boston
617 832 1000
Recommended in Banking & Finance

PUTZIGER, Myrna
Rubin and Rudman LLP, Boston
617 330 7000
Recommended in Real Estate

RAGALEVSKY, Stanley V
Kirkpatrick & Lockhart Nicholson Graham LLP, Boston 617 951 9203
sragalevsky@klng.com
Recommended in Banking & Finance

Practice Areas: Legal problems of financial institutions – capital adequacy, regulatory compliance, safety and soundness, governance, anti-money laundering,

charterings, holding companies, third party outsourcing, mergers and restructurings, asset securitization, loan and investment issues, examination problems, bank policies, risk management issues, lending process issues like loan participations, problem loans and loan workouts, financial institution insolvencies and regulatory enforcement orders.
Prof. Memberships: ABA, Boston Bar Association, Massachusetts Bankers Association.
Career: Partner since 1981.
Publications: Has lectured and written extensively on US financial institution matters for numerous financial services organizations and publications.
Personal: Harvard Law School (1973); Boston College (1970) (magna cum laude)

RAPHAEL, Bruce
Edwards & Angell, LLP, Boston
617 439 4444
Recommended in Banking & Finance

RATTIGAN, John
Palmer & Dodge LLP, Boston
617 239 0368
jrattigan@palmerdodge.com
Recommended in Real Estate
Practice Areas: Has over 20 years of experience representing developers and other property owners in the acquisition, financing and development of major real estate projects. Acts as counsel to national and regional lenders in connection with construction, permanent and revolving credit loans, having principal amounts ranging from $4 million - $300 million and in connection with loan workouts and enforcement of remedies. Represents landowners in the sale of development parcels to developers, institutions in connection with land acquisition and construction, and public authorities in connection with the development of their properties.
Prof. Memberships: Boston Bar Association, Massachusetts Bar Association.
Personal: Merrimack College, AB, summa cum laude, 1979; University of Virginia School of Law, JD, 1982.

RECK, Joel
Brown Rudnick Berlack Israels LLP, Boston 617 856 8200
Recommended in Real Estate

REDLICK, David
Wilmer Cutler Pickering Hale and Dorr LLP, Boston 617 526 6434
david.redlick@wilmerhale.com
Recommended in Corporate/M&A
Practice Areas: Partner in the firm's Corporate Department; Co-Chair of the Life Sciences Group; former Co-Chair of Hale and Dorr's Corporate Department. Practice focuses on corporate and securities law, with an emphasis on public offerings, corporate collaborations, mergers and acquisitions and venture capital transactions. Has served as counsel for broad range of clients, including

public companies, private high technology and medical technology companies, investment banks, venture capital funds, and real estate development and finance companies for almost 30 years.
Prof. Memberships: Board of Associates of the Whitehead Institute for Biomedical Research (affiliated with The Massachusetts Institute of Technology); Executive Committee of the Board of Directors of the Greater Boston Chamber of Commerce; guest lecturer at Kellogg School of Management at Northwestern University on subject of biotechnology initial public offerings; former trustee of the Massachusetts College of Art.
Career: Admitted to Massachusetts Bar. Joined the firm in 1975.
Personal: Harvard Law School (JD, cum laude); University of Wisconsin (BA, Class Valedictorian, Phi Beta Kappa).

REMIS, Shepard M
Goodwin Procter LLP, Boston
617 570 1000
sremis@goodwinprocter.com
Recommended in Intellectual Property
Practice Areas: Mr Remis has practiced extensively in the areas of intellectual property litigation and Internet and e-commerce litigation, products liability and mass torts litigation and complex commercial litigation. He has extensive experience in trying cases, both to courts and juries, as well as in the full range of ADR procedures, including mediations and arbitrations. His practice includes counseling clients on ways to prevent or limit exposure to litigation or claims.
Prof. Memberships: American Intellectual Property Law Association: Member; Defense Research Institute: Member; CPR Institute for Dispute Resolution: Member.
Personal: LLB, Columbia Law School, 1967; AB, Bowdoin College, 1964.

RENEHAN, Richard
Goulston & Storrs, Boston
617 482 1776
Recommended in Litigation

RIKLEEN, Lauren
Bowditch & Dewey LLP, Framingham
508 879 5700
Recommended in Environment

RITT, Roger M
Wilmer Cutler Pickering Hale and Dorr LLP, Boston 617 526 6475
roger.ritt@wilmerhale.com
Recommended in Tax
Practice Areas: Practice focuses on taxable and tax-free mergers and acquisitions, spin-offs, compensation planning, federal and state tax controversies, and bankruptcies and workouts. Successfully represented many of firm's clients at US Tax Court, IRS appeals, Supreme Judicial Court of Massachusetts, Massachusetts Appellate Tax Board and Massachusetts Department of Revenue.
Prof. Memberships: American Bar

Association's Section on Taxation (Chairman, Committee on Corporate Tax's Carryovers Subcommittee); Executive Committee of the Federal Tax Institute of New England; The Foundation for Tax Education (Co-Founder, Treasurer).
Career: Admitted to Massachusetts Bar.
Personal: Boston University School of Law (JD, LLM); University of Pennsylvania (BA, with Honors).

RIZZOTTI, Anthony
Ropes & Gray LLP, Boston
617 951 7954
anthony.rizzotti@ropesgray.com
Recommended in Employment
Practice Areas: Maintains broad labor and employment practice including government and administrative litigation (class actions, discrimination, non-compete, trade secret and Sarbanes-Oxley), labor arbitration, and collective bargaining. Conducts internal investigations on issues such as sexual harassment and misappropriation of confidential information. Provides day-to-day advice on broad ranges of labor and employment issues, trains clients on issues such as sexual harassment prevention, and assists clients in drafting agreements, handbooks, plans and policies.
Career: Massachusetts Bar (1992). New York Bar (2002). Rhode Island Bar (2004). Partner, Ropes & Gray (2003).
Personal: JD, cum laude, Boston College Law School (1992). Undergraduate, Boston College (1989).

ROBINS, Charles W
Weil, Gotshal & Manges LLP, Boston
617 772 8302
charles.robins@weil.com
Recommended in Private Equity
Practice Areas: Private equity and corporate.
Career: Mr Robins focuses on private equity and corporate. He was an early participant in private equity, representing clients in the late 1960's and early 1970's in structuring leveraged buyouts. He established a practice involving fund formation and administration, as well as portfolio company engagements and dispositions. He represented Tom Lee in forming Thomas H Lee Partners and advised Berkshire Partners in its formation. A recent fund formation was Thomas H Lee Equity Partners V L.P., a $6.3 billion buyout fund.
Personal: Columbia University School of Law (JD, 1964); Bates College (BA, 1961).

ROBINSON, Marcia
Bingham McCutchen LLP, Boston
617 951 8000
Recommended in Real Estate

ROBLE, Daniel T
Ropes & Gray LLP, Boston
617 951 7476
daniel.roble@ropesgray.com
Recommended in Healthcare

Practice Areas: Structuring pay-for-performance and gainsharing initiatives involving hospitals and physicians. Redefines relationships between academic medical centers and faculty practice plans, creating innovative relationships based on quality initiatives among hospitals, physician groups and managed care organizations, assisting hospitals with governance reconfiguration following Sarbanes-Oxley, helping home healthcare organizations with acquisitions and divestitures, dealing with healthcare organizationsí fiscal distress, creating joint ventures among media organizations, healthcare consumer organizations and data collection entities. Serves as trustee and counsel to: The Leapfrog Group; Jackson Hole Group.
Career: Massachusetts Bar (1975). Partner, Ropes & Gray (1984).
Personal: JD, University of Virginia School of Law (1975).

RONDEAU, Patrick J
Wilmer Cutler Pickering Hale and Dorr LLP, Boston 617 526 6670
patrick.rondeau@wilmerhale.com
Recommended in Corporate/M&A, Private Equity
Practice Areas: Vice-Chair of firm's Corporate Department; Co-Chair, Venture Capital Group. Practice focuses on venture capital and start-up company work, public offerings, mergers and acquisitions, and general corporate and securities work. Advises significant number of venture-backed companies and represents variety of venture capitalists in their investments in portfolio companies. Public offering experience includes variety of types of public offerings, and representation of both issuers and underwriters.
Prof. Memberships: National Venture Capital Association task force on Model Financing Documents.
Career: Admitted to Massachusetts Bar. Joined firm in 1984 and Partner since 1992.
Personal: Harvard Law School (JD); Williams College (BA).

ROSENBLUM, Peter
Foley Hoag LLP, Boston
617 832 1000
Recommended in Corporate/M&A, Private Equity

ROSNER, Douglas
Goulston & Storrs, Boston
617 482 1776
Recommended in Bankruptcy

ROSS, Nelson G
Ropes & Gray LLP, Boston
617 951 7450
nelson.ross@ropesgray.com
Recommended in Employment
Practice Areas: Advises employers, particularly in the health care industry and higher education. Extensive experience advising employers on a wide spectrum of todayís labor and employment

issues. Regularly represents clients before the National Labor Relations Board. Special expertise in collective bargaining negotiations, both traditional and interest-based and developing labor relations strategies for organizations. Chief negotiator in many complex, high stakes negotiations. Represented several health care employers who were parties to the precedent-setting nine-year master agreement dealing with system-wide labor issues.
Career: Massachusetts Bar (1964). Partner, Ropes & Gray (1976).
Personal: JD, Boston College Law School (1964). Undergraduate, Boston University (1960).

ROTHERMEL, Sarah
Wilmer Cutler Pickering Hale and Dorr LLP, Boston 617 526 6512
sarah.rothermel@wilmerhale.com
Recommended in Private Equity
Practice Areas: Vice-Chair of the firm's Fund Formation Group; member of the Venture Capital Financing Group and Executive Committee. Represents principally private investment entitles, including venture capital funds. Also represents LLCs, partnerships, joint ventures and closely-held non-corporate businesses engaged in all types of business activities. Advises clients on all aspects of organization, management, operation and regulatory compliance.
Prof. Memberships: American Bar Association; Massachusetts Bar Association; Boston Bar Association; Private Equity CFO Organization (advisory board member).
Career: Admitted to Massachusetts Bar. Joined the firm in 1981.
Personal: Boston University School of Law (JD, magna cum laude); Wellesley College (BA).

ROTTENBERG, Alan
Goulston & Storrs, Boston
617 482 1776
Recommended in Real Estate

ROWE, Larry Jordan
Ropes & Gray LLP, Boston
617 951 7407
larry.rowe@ropesgray.com
Recommended in Private Equity
Practice Areas: Specializes in structuring and analyzing private debt and equity investments, investment fund formation and investments, leveraged buyouts, venture capital investments, and international transactions. Extensive experience in organizing funds of funds. Clients include some of the largest endowment funds in the country, funds of funds, investment funds and other institutional investors and advisers.
Career: Massachusetts Bar (1985). Partner, Ropes & Gray (1993).
Personal: JD, Harvard Law School (1984). MPP, Harvard University (1984). Undergraduate degree, summa cum laude, Phi Beta Kappa, Dartmouth College (1980).

RUDMAN, Jeffrey
Wilmer Cutler Pickering Hale and Dorr LLP, Boston 617 526 6912
jeffrey.rudman@wilmerhale.com
Recommended in Litigation
Practice Areas: Partner in the firm's Litigation Department and a Co-Chair of the Securities Department. Nationally recognized authority on defending shareholder class and derivative actions and the related tasks of defending Securities and Exchange Commission investigations and pursuing directors' and officers' insurance coverage. Has represented numerous public or mutual companies and/or their officers and directors charged with various alleged misrepresentations or breaches of duty.
Prof. Memberships: Boston Public Library, Boston Museum Project (Trustee); served on many charitable boards, including the Board of Directors of the Association of American Rhodes Scholars; the Boston Public Library Foundation; Buckingham, Browne & Nichols School and the WGBH Advisory Board. For the past quarter century, has administered the Rhodes Scholarship selection process for Maine, New Hampshire, Massachusetts, Rhode Island, Connecticut and, more recently, New Jersey. Also lectures on securities litigation, insurance coverage, duties of disclosure and corporate governance for several organizations throughout the country.
Career: Admitted to Massachusetts Bar. Joined firm in 1975.
Personal: Harvard Law School (JD); First in Honours School of Modern History (BA); Oxford University Rhodes Scholar; Columbia College (AB, Phi Beta Kappa).

RUDMAN, Richard
DLA Piper Rudnick Gray Cary, Boston
617 406 6027
richard.rudman@dlapiper.com
Recommended in Real Estate
Practice Areas: Real estate.
Prof. Memberships: American College of Real Estate Lawyers.
Career: Focuses his practice on real estate development and finance, property acquisition, leasing, land use and environmental regulation, joint venture arrangements, and construction and design agreements. He has represented the developers of several downtown office towers, and has extensive experience in build to suit developments, hotels, and multi-family apartment projects, including projects with complicated phasing arrangements, environmentally contaminated sites and public/private development agreements. He is listed in a leading American legal directory.
Personal: JD, Harvard University (1982), cum laude; BA, Yale College (1979), summa cum laude.

RYAN, Mary
Nutter, McClennen & Fish, LLP, Boston
617 439 2000
Recommended in Environment

SANOFF, Robert
Foley Hoag LLP, Boston 617 832 1000
Recommended in Environment

SAVAGE, Joseph
Goodwin Procter LLP, Boston
617 570 1000
jsavage@goodwinprocter.com
Recommended in Litigation
Practice Areas: Mr Savage concentrates his practice on complex civil litigation, white collar criminal defense and governmental investigations work. His practice involves representing individuals and companies in a wide variety of fraud, tax, public corruption, health care, securities, environmental and other investigations by federal, state and local law enforcement and government regulators. He has also handled sophisticated trade secret, Lanham Act, RICO, consumer fraud and other civil litigation, including multi-district class action litigation and has experience in litigating complex white collar criminal matters including fraud, tax, securities, healthcare, RICO, health and safety act, money laundering and public corruption matters.
Personal: JD, University of Virginia School of Law, 1981 (Order of the Coif); BA, Harvard College, 1978 (magna cum laude).

SAVRIN, Daniel
Bingham McCutchen LLP, Boston
617 951 8000
Recommended in Antitrust

SCHERKENBACH, Frank
Fish & Richardson, Boston
617 542 5070
Recommended in Intellectual Property

SCHMIDT, William
Wilmer Cutler Pickering Hale and Dorr LLP, Boston 617 526 6946
william.schmidt@wilmerhale.com
Recommended in Tax
Practice Areas: Compensation law, including employee-benefits plans and executive compensation. Has assisted pension plan providers in structuring investment vehicles; represented many such providers in connection with pension plan investments. Represents clients in financings in which a pension plan provider is party. Expert in matters of professional corporations, personal domestic tax planning and estate planning. Has represented many clients in establishment of employee stock ownership plans (ESOPs).
Prof. Memberships: American, Massachusetts, and Boston Bar Associations.
Career: Admitted to Massachusetts Bar; United States Tax Court. Joined firm in 1976.
Personal: Georgetown University Law Center (JD); University of Chicago (MS); Yale University (BS).

SCHNALL, Matthew
Bingham McCutchen LLP, Boston
617 951 8000
Recommended in Tax

SCHNEIDER, Jon
Goodwin Procter LLP, Boston
617 570 1000
jschneider@goodwinprocter.com
Recommended in Bankruptcy
Practice Areas: Mr Schneider's practice focuses on creditors' rights, secured transactions, acquisitions and insolvency matters, including representation of lenders in loan transactions, workouts and bankruptcy; bondholders in restructurings; businesses in connection with financial restructurings and acquisitions; investors in connection with buyouts and turn-arounds; and unsecured creditors in connection with bankruptcy proceedings. Practice also involves leveraged buyouts and financially troubled situations.
Prof. Memberships: American College of Bankruptcy: Fellow; Massachusetts Certified Development Corporation: Director; American Bankruptcy Institute: Member.
Personal: JD, Boston College, 1968; BS, Boston College, 1965.

SCHNEIDMAN, Leonard
Foley Hoag LLP, Boston
617 832 1000
Recommended in Tax

SCHNOOR, William
Goodwin Procter LLP, Boston
617 570 1000
wschnoor@goodwinprocter.com
Recommended in Private Equity
Practice Areas: Mr Schnoor concentrates his practice in the areas of business and securities law, private equity and acquisitions. He has 21 years of experience in representing start-up, private and public companies in a wide range of industries. He has worked with numerous companies from their initial financing through successful initial public offerings or acquisitions. His practice also includes: assisting with cross-border financings and acquisitions; representing investment banks in connection with underwritten offerings and their activities as financial advisors to companies engaged in mergers and acquisitions; and representing numerous private equity clients in connection with their own fund-raising and organizational issues.
Personal: JD, Yale University, 1983; BA, Yale College, 1980 (summa cum laude).

SCHWARTZ, Andrew
Foley Hoag LLP, Boston
617 832 1000
Recommended in Bankruptcy

SCHWARTZ, Paul D
Goodwin Procter LLP, Boston
617 570 1422
pschwartz@goodwinprocter.com
Recommended in Real Estate

Practice Areas: Mr Schwartz concentrates on private market finance with emphasis on the real estate industry, including collective investment vehicles for institutional investors, joint ventures, participating and mezzanine debt, and REIT investments. He is familiar with integrating the UBTI, REIT and other tax, ERISA, Investment Company Act, and other securities law aspects of investments by ERISA plans and registered investment companies.

Prof. Memberships: Pension Real Estate Association; MIT Center for Real Estate; Real Estate Finance Association.

Personal: JD, Harvard Law School, 1978 (magna cum laude); Masters in Architecture, MIT, 1976; BA, Connecticut College, 1973 (magna cum laude).

SCOTT, Thane
Palmer & Dodge LLP, Boston
617 239 0154
tscott@palmerdodge.com
Recommended in Antitrust

Practice Areas: Concentrates practice in antitrust and trade regulation. Has counseled industry leaders and litigated prominent cases that define modern antitrust law. Has served as lead or liaison counsel in numerous multi-district, complex, or class action cases, as well as representing clients during the course of government investigations. Frequently litigates complex cases among business rivals as well as defending class actions involving antitrust and business tort claims, and he has served as an expert witness in federal litigation involving distribution. Actively litigates cases in both state and federal courts. Admitted to practice before a wide variety of federal courts including the United States Supreme Court.

Prof. Memberships: American Bar Association, Boston Bar Association, Massachusetts Bar Association.

Career: Joined Palmer & Dodge in 1986; Partner since 1989.

Personal: State University of New York at Albany, BA, cum laude, 1974; Boston College Law School, JD, cum laude, 1980.

SELWYN, Mark D
Wilmer Cutler Pickering Hale and Dorr LLP, Boston 617 526 6923
mark.selwyn@wilmerhale.com
Recommended in Intellectual Property

Practice Areas: Has represented wide range of commercial interests, concentrating in patent litigation, government investigations, securities and consumer class actions. Also represented clients before the SEC, NASD and state regulatory agencies.

Career: Admitted to Massachusetts Bar and New York Bar. Served as a law clerk to Hon. Naomi Reice Buchwald on the US District Court for the Southern District of New York prior to joining the firm in 1994.

Publications: 'Higher Education Under

Fire: The New Target of Antitrust,' 26 Colum. J. L. & Soc. Probs. 117 (1992).

Personal: Columbia Law School (JD); Harvard College (AB, magna cum laude).

SHAY, Stephen
Ropes & Gray LLP, Boston
617 951 7302
stephen.shay@ropesgray.com
Recommended in Tax

Practice Areas: Extensive international tax experience advising clients including large and medium-sized multinational companies, financial institutions, and global investors on issues such as foreign tax credits, deferral of US taxation, foreign currency gains and losses, withholding taxes and financial product issues. Regularly advises clients on transfer pricing issues. Has successfully resolved numerous transfer pricing controversies with the IRS. Advises high net worth clients on cross-border income tax planning.

Career: New York Bar (1977). Massachusetts Bar (1991). International Tax Counsel, US Department of the Treasury. Partner, Ropes & Gray (1987).

Personal: JD, Columbia Law School (1976). MBA, Columbia Business School (1976).

SHEA, John
Moehrke, Mackie & Shea, P.C., Boston
617 266 5700
Recommended in Environment

SHEPHERD, Jay
Shepherd Law Group, P.C., Boston
617 439 4200
js@sheplawgroup.com
Recommended in Employment

Practice Areas: Specializes in noncompete and trade secret litigation. Protects employers from employee lawsuits and commercial espionage. Advocates for employers before state and federal courts and administrative agencies.

Prof. Memberships: Massachusetts (Chair, Employment Law Practice Group, 2003-04) and Boston (Member, Labor & Employment Law Steering Committee, 2003-05) Bar Associations; ABA.

Career: Principal since 1998. Bar admissions: Massachusetts (1994), US District Court (Mass. 1995), First Circuit Court of Appeals (1996), US Supreme Court (2000). Named one of five 'Up and Coming Lawyers' by Massachusetts Lawyers Weekly (2004) and a 'Rising Star' by Law & Politics Magazine (2005).

Publications: Author: Noncompete Nonstarters: Avoiding the Seven Biggest Drafting Mistakes, 'New England In House,' October 2004; The Role of Managers in U.S. Employment Law, in 'Business Guide USA' (Frankfurt, 2000); An Employment Lawyer's Guide to ERISA Preemption, in 'Wrongful Termination Update,' MCLE 1998 & 1999. Contributing Author: 'Employee Benefits Law,' 2d Ed., 2000 Supp. (ABA, 2000). Co-

Author: Keeping Your Clients Competitive: Practice Points for Breaking Non-competes, 'Massachusetts Bar Association Section Review,' 2003; Navigating Noncompetes: Ten Tips for In-House Counsel, 'Massachusetts Bar Association Section Review,' 2002.

Personal: Boston College Law School (JD, cum laude, 1994); Johns Hopkins University (BA, 1988). Married, two daughters.

SIGEL, John
Wilmer Cutler Pickering Hale and Dorr LLP, Boston 617 526 6728
john.sigel@wilmerhale.com
Recommended in Bankruptcy

Practice Areas: Co-Vice-Chair of firm's Bankruptcy and Commercial Department. Commercial law focus, advising clients on secured and unsecured lending and debt issuance, Chapter 11 reorganizations and Uniform Commercial Code. Expert in matters relating to debt financings of public and private companies and acquisitions and sales of distressed companies. Represented many clients in negotiating credit facilities with institutional lenders, including private placement of debt securities; advised corporate clients in connection with public offering of debt securities.

Prof. Memberships: Massachusetts and Boston Bar Associations.

Career: Admitted to Massachusetts Bar. Joined firm in 1980.

Personal: Cornell Law School (JD); Middlebury College (BA).

SINGER, Steven
Wilmer Cutler Pickering Hale and Dorr LLP, Boston 617 526 6410
steven.singer@wilmerhale.com
Recommended in Corporate/M&A

Practice Areas: Vice chair of the firm's Corporate Department; co-chair of the firm's Life Sciences Group. Has served as counsel for public and private companies in the life sciences sector, including biotechnology, medical device and pharmaceutical companies. Practice focuses on joint ventures and strategic alliances, corporate and securities laws, public offerings and venture capital transactions.

Prof. Memberships: American Bar Association; Massachusetts Biotechnology Council; Biotechnology Industry Organization; Board of Overseers of Beth Israel Deaconess Medical Center.

Career: Admitted to Massachusetts Bar. Joined the firm in 1979.

Personal: Harvard Law School (JD, magna cum laude); Tufts University (BA, summa cum laude).

SIRKIN, Joel
Wilmer Cutler Pickering Hale and Dorr LLP, Boston 617 526 6279
joel.sirkin@wilmerhale.com
Recommended in Real Estate

Practice Areas: Chair of firm's Real Estate Department; member of firm's Executive Committee and Real Estate

Capital Markets Committee. Has represented clients in acquisition, development, and financing of apartment projects, hotels, office buildings, and shopping centers in over 25 states. Major projects include: acquisition, repositioning, and sale of portfolio of 14 Boston office properties for overseas investor group; and the implementation of regional partner UPREIT strategy for major multifamily REIT client. Has been involved in development of Boston office towers and several major suburban office parks.

Career: Admitted to Massachusetts Bar.

Personal: Harvard Law School (JD); Johns Hopkins University (BA).

SMITH, Edwin
Bingham McCutchen LLP, Boston
617 951 8000
Recommended in Banking & Finance

SMITH, Philip
Ropes & Gray LLP, Boston
617 951 7744
philip.smith@ropesgray.com
Recommended in Banking & Finance

Practice Areas: Leveraged buyout and private equity transactions including debt and equity components of these matters. Extensive experience in structuring syndicated bank credits, leveraged leases, mezzanine capital transactions, and high-yield debt plus experience with acquisitions and public and private preferred stock financings. Experience includes acquisitions and financings on national and international levels in manufacturing, distribution, leasing, motion picture and entertainment industries. Has developed educational seminars and lectured extensively on financing and leverage buy out transactions.

Personal: JD, Order of the Coif, University of Virginia School of Law (1966). Undergraduate degree, cum laude, Williams College (1963).

SOLT, Christine
Choate Hall & Stewart, Boston
617 248 5000
Recommended in Healthcare

STEINBERG, Donald R
Wilmer Cutler Pickering Hale and Dorr LLP, Boston 617 526 6453
donald.steinberg@wilmerhale.com
Recommended in Intellectual Property

Practice Areas: Vice-Chair of firm's Intellectual Property Department. Practice focuses on advising clients on intellectual property matters, obtaining patent and trademark protection, and intellectual property litigation. Has extensive experience before the Trademark Trial and Appeal Board, including successful trials of opposition and cancellation proceedings involving medical devices and games.

Prof. Memberships: Intellectual Property Owners Association's Trademark Law Committee; New England School

of Law (adjunct faculty member).
Career: Admitted to Massachusetts Bar and United States Patent and Trademark Office. Joined the firm in 1994.
Personal: Harvard Law School (JD, cum laude); Princeton University (BSE, magna cum laude, Phi Beta Kappa).

STERN, William E
Goodwin Procter LLP, Boston
617 570 1000
wstern@goodwinprocter.com
Recommended in Banking & Finance
Practice Areas: Mr Stern works on transactional and regulatory matters with particular emphasis on transactions involving the creation of new bank charters and charter conversions and assisting clients in choosing and structuring the most appropriate bank charter for their business needs. He advises clients on bank regulatory matters relating to domestic and foreign investments and activities, including merchant banking and other passive investments, personal and real property leasing, lending, captive reinsurance, trust department and other asset management operations, and other types of financial activities.
Personal: JD, George Washington University, 1996 (with high honors); BA, Hamilton College, 1993 (summa cum laude).

STILLWELL, R Newcomb
Ropes & Gray LLP, Boston
617 951 7316
newcomb.stillwell@ropesgray.com
Recommended in Private Equity
Practice Areas: Co-Head of the Ropes & Gray Private Equity Group. Deep experience in mergers and acquisitions and related financings including cross-border transactions (Canada, Mexico, Europe). Serves on the Board of Directors and is the Vice-Chairman of the Volunteers of America of Massachusetts, Incorporated.
Career: Massachusetts Bar (1984). Partner, Ropes & Gray (1993).
Personal: JD, cum laude, Harvard Law School (1984). AB, magna cum laude, Princeton University (1979).

STONER, Wayne L
Wilmer Cutler Pickering Hale and Dorr LLP, Boston 617 526 6863
wayne.stoner@wilmerhale.com
Recommended in Intellectual Property
Practice Areas: Partner in the firm's Litigation Department and Co-Chair of the firm's Intellectual Property Litigation Group. Practice focuses on patent litigation and strategy. Has represented a broad range of clients, including in jury and bench trials and appeals, in diverse technologies such as lasers, medical devices, semiconductor processing, integrated circuits and telecommunications. Practices in courts nationwide and before the US International Trade Commission.
Prof. Memberships: Faculty, Harvard Law School Trial Advocacy Program.
Career: Admitted to Massachusetts Bar.

Joined the firm in 1986.
Personal: University of Pennsylvania Law School (JD); University of Denver (BA, Phi Beta Kappa).

SULLIVAN, John L
DLA Piper Rudnick Gray Cary, Boston
617 406 6029
john.sullivan@dlapiper.com
Recommended in Real Estate
Practice Areas: Real estate.
Career: Broad-ranging practice that encompasses all aspects of commercial real estate, with a particular emphasis representing public and private pension plans, opportunity funds, investment advisors and other sophisticated investors in debt, equity, hybrid and joint venture transactions throughout North America.
Personal: JD, Cornell University, cum laude; BA, College of the Holy Cross, summa cum laude.

SUNSHINE, Ilene Robinson
Sullivan & Worcester, Boston
617 338 2800
Recommended in Employment

SURKIN, Elliot
DLA Piper Rudnick Gray Cary, Boston
617 406 6030
elliot.surkin@dlapiper.com
Recommended in Real Estate
Practice Areas: Real estate.
Prof. Memberships: American College of Real Estate Lawyers; American Law Institute.
Career: Real estate development, finance and taxation. General counsel to many of Boston's significant office, mixed-use and retail projects. He has taught full semester courses in real estate development and finance at Harvard Law School and MIT's Center for Real Estate throughout his career.
Publications: 'When Joint Venturers Can't Agree: The Buy-Sell Revisited,' and 'How Do I Get Out of Here? A discussion of Exit Strategies in Closely-Held Real Estate LLCs'.
Personal: LLB, Harvard Law School, magna cum laude; AB, Princeton University, magna cum laude.

SWAIM, Hall
Wilmer Cutler Pickering Hale and Dorr LLP, Boston 617 526 6716
hall.swaim@wilmerhale.com
Recommended in Bankruptcy
Practice Areas: Partner in firm's Bankruptcy and Commercial Department. Practice focuses on commercial law, with an emphasis on Chapter 11 reorganizations, out-of-court restructurings, loan documentation, workouts and contract negotiations, with emphasis on technology-based companies and technology transfer.
Prof. Memberships: American, Massachusetts and Boston Bar Associations; Commercial Law League; American Bankruptcy Institute; New England Chapter of Turnaround Management Association (board member, former

President).
Career: Admitted to Massachusetts, Colorado, New York and Texas Bars; United States Supreme Court; United States Patent and Trademark Office. Joined firm in 1971.
Personal: New York University School of Law (JD); Colorado School of Mines (Geophysical Engineer).

TEGELER, David W
Proskauer Rose LLP, Boston
617 526 9795
dtegeler@proskauer.com
Recommended in Private Equity
Practice Areas: Partner at Proskauer Rose LLP. Concentrates in the areas of corporate and securities law, with a particular emphasis on private equity transactions. His experience includes representation of private equity fund managers in capital formations, portfolio investments and governance issues, and institutional investors and investment advisers in the private equity field.
Prof. Memberships: Member of the American Bar Association and the Business Law Division of the Massachusetts Bar Association. Is admitted to the Massachusetts Bar (1989). Has served on numerous panels in the US and Europe discussing issues related to private equity fund formations.
Personal: Received his BA from Middlebury College in 1985 and his JD from Vanderbilt University School of Law in 1989 where he was an editor of the 'Vanderbilt Journal of Transnational Law'.

TELEGEN, Arthur
Foley Hoag LLP, Boston 617 832 1000
Recommended in Employment

TICKNOR, George
Palmer & Dodge LLP, Boston
617 239 0357
gticknor@palmerdodge.com
Recommended in Banking & Finance
Practice Areas: Represents public companies with complex debt structures in connection with high yield and convertible note issuances, private equity, sponsor, and other investor groups making investments and acquisitions. Also represents banks and financial institutions in financings with emphasis on acquisition financing. Has been involved in acquisitions and financings in a broad range of industries with special focus on the media, communications and telecommunication sectors. Experience also encompasses public debt issues and restructurings, second lien financings, securitizations, and mezzanine financings. Represents private equity portfolio companies and other operating companies in a range of industries including communications, steel, financial services, and investment management. Chair of the firm's Finance Group and the Media and Communications Group.
Prof. Memberships: American Bar Association, Boston Bar Association.

Career: Joined Palmer & Dodge in 1991; Partner since 1993.
Personal: Harvard University, BA, magna cum laude, 1977; University of Virginia School of Law, JD, 1983.

TODD, Owen
Todd & Weld LLP, Boston
617 720 2626
Recommended in Litigation

TOELKE, Richard
Bingham McCutchen LLP, Boston
617 951 8000
Recommended in Real Estate

TRIBUSH, Bruce
Goodwin Procter LLP, Boston
617 570 1000
btribush@goodwinprocter.com
Recommended in Real Estate
Practice Areas: Mr Tribush represents commercial lenders and borrowers in secured and unsecured credit facilities, construction loans, permanent loans, bridge loans, mezzanine debt transactions, loan participations and loan restructurings; owners and developers in the acquisition, financing and development of real estate; owners, developers, lenders, design professionals and construction professionals in design and construction matters; landlords and tenants in commercial leasing transactions; and institutional and private investors in debt and equity real estate investments.
Personal: JD, Fordham University, 1990; BS, Cornell University, 1987.

TURANO, Thomas A
Kirkpatrick & Lockhart Nicholson Graham LLP, Boston 617 261 3148
tturano@klng.com
Recommended in Intellectual Property
Practice Areas: Intellectual property counseling, patent and trademark prosecution, licensing, opinions, transactional due diligence and litigation; counseling both international and US clients on creating a patent portfolio that will maximize the business value of a company's intellectual property in the individual jurisdictions of interest; practice in both health science-related and high tech-related technologies.
Personal: JD, Suffolk University Law School (1988); MS, Worcester Polytechnic Institute (1984) (Electrical Engineering); MS, Brown University (1983) (Biology); MS, University of Rhode Island (1975) (Biophysics); BS, University of Rhode Island (1971) (Physics).

TUTEUR, Michael
Foley & Lardner, Boston
617 342 4016
mtuteur@foley.com
Recommended in Litigation
Career: Michael J Tuteur is Partner in the Boston office of Foley & Lardner (general commercial litigation). Mr Tuteur's practice concentrates on complex commercial litigation, internal investigations and white-collar criminal defense. Mr Tuteur has litigated a num-

ber of high-profile litigations and arbitrations, including cases featured in the 'Wall Street Journal', 'Boston Globe' and Canada's 'Globe & Mail'. He also represents organizations and corporate officers and directors in connection with criminal and civil investigations involving alleged health care fraud, securities fraud, mutual fund regulatory violations and banking infractions. Mr Tuteur's JD was conferred magna cum laude from Harvard Law School (1984).

TWOHIG, John
Goulston & Storrs, Boston
617 482 1776
Recommended in Real Estate

UTZSCHNEIDER, John
Bingham McCutchen LLP, Boston
617 951 8000
Recommended in Corporate/M&A

VENTOLA, John
Choate Hall & Stewart, Boston
617 248 5000
Recommended in Bankruptcy

WALLACK, James
Goulston & Storrs, Boston
617 482 1776
Recommended in Bankruptcy

WARD, Richard
Ropes & Gray LLP, Boston
617 951 7444
richard.ward@ropesgray.com
Recommended in Employment
Practice Areas: Provides counsel on employment issues and litigates employment disputes at the trial and appellate level. Specializes in employment litigation, including the trial of discrimination, civil rights, contract and public employment cases, and labor arbitrations. Member of the Labor and Employment Law Section and the Equal Employment Opportunity Committee of the American Bar Association. Elected as a Fellow in the prestigious College of Labor and Employment Lawyers. Writes and lectures on emerging employment law issues.
Career: Massachusetts Bar (1967). Partner, Ropes & Gray (1977).
Personal: LLB, cum laude, Harvard Law School (1967). AB, magna cum laude, Boston College (1964).

WARE, Donald
Foley Hoag LLP, Boston
617 832 1000
Recommended in Intellectual Property

WARE, Paul
Goodwin Procter LLP, Boston
617 570 1000
pware@goodwinprocter.com
Recommended in Intellectual Property, Litigation
Practice Areas: Mr Ware is an experienced trial lawyer, having tried numerous civil and criminal cases to conclusion throughout the country. His principal practice is intellectual property, including patent and other complex

technology-related litigation. Mr Ware served as lead trial counsel for the prosecution of the CIA chief of European Operations in the Iran Contra Affair and as Special Counsel to the Massachusetts Commission on Judicial Conduct.
Prof. Memberships: American College of Trial Lawyers: Fellow; Supreme Judicial Court Historical Society: Board of Overseers; Social Law Library: Trustee.
Personal: LLB, University of Pennsylvania, 1969; AB, University of Notre Dame, 1966.

WATSON, David
Goodwin Procter LLP, Boston
617 570 1000
dwatson@goodwinprocter.com
Recommended in Private Equity
Practice Areas: Mr Watson's practice focuses on public and private securities offerings, private fund formation, partnership law, public and private mergers and acquisitions, securities law compliance for public companies and general corporate matters. His experience in the fund formation area includes establishing private funds through US and international securities offerings, organizing fund manager and sponsor entities, advising fund managers and sponsors in establishing compensation structures and internal operating policies, representing funds and investors and restructuring the terms of existing investment funds.
Personal: JD, Harvard Law School, 1988 (cum laude); BA, University of Maine, 1985 (salutatorian).

WATSON, Rom P
Ropes & Gray LLP, Boston
617 951 7672
rom.watson@ropesgray.com
Recommended in Tax
Practice Areas: Extensive experience in the international tax area, advising clients including large and medium-sized multinational companies, global investors, and financial institutions. Specializes in the areas of cross-border financial products, transfer pricing, and multinational transactions. Practiced in the Office of Tax Policy at the US Department of the Treasury (1988-91), and was appointed Associate International Tax Counsel.
Career: Massachusetts Bar (1985). Partner, Ropes & Gray (1993).
Personal: JD, cum laude, Boalt Hall School of Law, University of California at Berkeley (1983). AB, Phi Beta Kappa, Stanford University (1979).

WEINER, Stephen
Mintz Levin Cohn Ferris Glovsky and Popeo PC, Boston 617 542 6000
Recommended in Healthcare

WEINSTEIN, Jerome
Sullivan Weinstein & McQuay, Boston
617 348 4300
Recommended in Employment

WELSH, John
Bello, Black & Welsh, LLP, Boston
617 247 4100
Recommended in Employment

WESTRA, James
Weil, Gotshal & Manges LLP, Boston
617 772 8377
james.westra@weil.com
Recommended in Corporate/M&A, Private Equity
Practice Areas: Mr Westra's diverse corporate practice includes private equity, mergers and acquisitions, financings, general corporate and corporate governance matters.
Career: Mr Westra regularly represents leading private equity and venture firms in acquiring and investing in public and private companies in the US and Europe. He also represents numerous public companies on general corporate matters, financings and merger & acquisition transactions. Mr Westra regularly serves as counsel to boards of directors and board committees with respect to corporate governance matters.
Personal: Boston University School of Law, JD; Harvard University, AB.

WHITLEDGE, William H
Goodwin Procter LLP, Boston
617 570 1000
wwhitledge@goodwinprocter.com
Recommended in Tax
Practice Areas: Mr Whitledge specializes in corporate, partnership, foreign and general business taxation. He spends a substantial amount of time structuring international and domestic business transactions, including mergers, acquisitions, financings, dispositions, reorganizations and other business restructurings, and venture capital investments. He also has extensive experience in structuring collective investment vehicles with tax-exempt, foreign and domestic investors, including RICs, REITs and pension investments from an unrelated business taxable income perspective.
Personal: LLM, New York University, 1985; JD, Columbia University, 1980; BA, Michigan State University, 1976.

WIESEN, Jeffrey
Mintz Levin Cohn Ferris Glovsky and Popeo PC, Boston 617 542 6000
Recommended in Corporate/M&A

WILLIAMS, Samuel
Brown Rudnick Berlack Israels LLP, Boston 617 856 8200
Recommended in Corporate/M&A

WILLIS, Jane E
Ropes & Gray LLP, Boston
617 951 7603
jane.willis@ropesgray.com
Recommended in Antitrust
Practice Areas: Specializes in complex commercial litigation. Experienced in antitrust law, intellectual property and trademark matters, and merger and acquisition-related disputes. Regularly

provides advice and counseling regarding fiduciary duty issues and competition law matters. Clients include publicly-traded corporations, privately-held businesses, and private equity funds involved in the consumer products, sports, high technology, and financial services industries.
Career: Massachusetts Bar (1994). Partner, Ropes & Gray (2003).
Personal: JD, magna cum laude, Harvard Law School (1994). Undergraduate degree, Phi Beta Kappa, Harvard University (1991).

WOLF, Robert
Bingham McCutchen LLP, Boston
617 951 8000
Recommended in Private Equity

WOOD, Lisa
Foley Hoag LLP, Boston
617 832 1000
Recommended in Antitrust

ZOLI, Elise
Goodwin Procter LLP, Boston
617 570 1000
ezoli@goodwinprocter.com
Recommended in Environment
Practice Areas: Ms Zoli specializes in the areas of energy, environmental and development law. She has extensive experience in the transfer, permitting and development of energy projects, particularly electric-generating and natural-gas-pipeline facilities. Ms Zoli's recent energy work includes development and acquisition advice, compliance counseling and litigation services on behalf of nuclear-powered, fossil-fuel and wind-turbine electric-generating stations, and strategic counseling for a leading 'Green tag' provider. She has done extensive work on the assessment and permitting of redevelopment projects involving complex sites, including former nuclear assets.
Personal: JD, University of Pennsylvania Law School, 1990; BA, Duke University, 1987 (magna cum laude).

ZORN, Jonathan
Ropes & Gray LLP, Boston
617 951 7299
jonathan.zorn@ropesgray.com
Recommended in Tax
Practice Areas: Teaches in the Boston University Graduate Tax Program on employee benefits. Has participated as a speaker in continuing legal education programs for the Boston Bar Association and the Federal Tax Institute of New England, among others.
Career: Massachusetts Bar (1982). Partner, Ropes & Gray (1991).
Personal: JD, Yale Law School (1982). BA, Indiana University (1972).

GOODWIN PROCTER LLP

THE FIRM

Chairman & Managing Partner: Regina M Pisa
Partners nationwide: 190
Total attorneys: 600

FIRM OVERVIEW: Goodwin Procter LLP is one of the nation's leading law firms, with more than 600 attorneys and offices in Boston, New York, New Jersey and Washington, DC. The firm combines in-depth legal knowledge with practical business experience to deliver innovative solutions to complex legal problems. It provides corporate, litigation and real estate services to clients ranging from emerging companies to Fortune 500 multinationals, with a focus on matters involving private equity, real estate capital markets, financial services, intellectual property and products liability. Goodwin Procter understands that people are its most important asset. Consequently, the firm devotes considerable resources to recruiting, training and retaining its lawyers and staff. The firm hires talented, motivated people committed to a culture based on teamwork. Goodwin Procter has long been committed to establishing a diverse workplace reflective of today's society. The firm is one of only a handful of comparably sized law firms in the United States to have a woman acting as chairman and managing partner. A number of the firm's partners serve or have served as leaders of minority law associations, and Goodwin Procter is a founding member of a group known nationally for helping law firms recruit and retain minority lawyers. The firm believes strongly in its obligations as a corporate citizen and is dedicated to community service. Through its longstanding and extensive pro bono program, the firm strongly encourages its legal staff to assist those unable to afford legal representation.

MAIN AREAS OF PRACTICE: Work includes corporate, litigation, real estate, financial services, intellectual property, products liability, energy, transportation, private equity, real estate capital markets, tax, ERISA and employee benefits, labor and employment, environmental, and estate planning.
Business Law: The Business Law Practice offers a multidisciplinary approach and strong industry focus, combined with a formidable tax capability. Goodwin Procter consistently ranks among the nation's leaders in financial services and REIT transactions, and its Private Equity and Intellectual Property Practices are among the firm's fastest-growing areas.
Litigation: The firm's Litigation Practice assists clients in complex, contested matters around the country. Its attorneys provide counsel on litigation avoidance and control, risk management and dispute resolution, and its work includes appearing before state and federal courts - including matters at the appellate level. A number of litigators have served as Assistant United States Attorneys, and three federal district court judges are former partners of the firm.

CLIENTS: Goodwin Procter maintains a diverse client base, with clients ranging from entrepreneurial emerging companies to established multinationals. The firm's clients present complex issues and expect cost-effective results to be delivered under tight deadlines. Client service begins with knowing the client, knowing their business and knowing their competitors. With this information, the firm's attorneys are able to leverage their specialized skills and expertise to deliver responsive, knowledgeable and practical legal advice. The firm maximizes its practice efficiency by focusing on effective use of technology and knowledge management.

HEAD OFFICE

MASSACHUSETTS
Exchange Place, **Boston**, MA 02109
Tel: 617 570 1000 **Fax:** 617 523 1231
Email: rpisa@goodwinprocter.com
Website: www.goodwinprocter.com

BRANCH OFFICES

DISTRICT OF COLUMBIA
901 New York Avenue, NW **Washington**, DC 20001
Tel: 202 346 4000 **Fax:** 202 346 4444
Email: jaldock@goodwinprocter.com

NEW JERSEY
103 Eisenhower Parkway, **Roseland**, NJ 07068
Tel: 973 992 1990 **Fax:** 973 992 4643
Email: mhildebrand@goodwinprocter.com

NEW YORK
599 Lexington Avenue, **New York**, NY 10022
Tel: 212 813 8800 **Fax:** 212 355 3333
Email: asolecki@goodwinprocter.com

CONTACTS

Boston	Regina M Pisa
Roseland	Mary Hildebrand
New York	Albert Solecki
Washington, DC	John Aldock

GOODWIN
PROCTER

HANIFY & KING

THE FIRM

Managing Partner: James Coyne King
Executive Director: Charles F McCannon, Jr

Number of partners: 14
Number of lawyers: 35

FIRM OVERVIEW: Since 1980 Hanify & King has met the legal needs of individuals, small businesses and large corporations by delivering on-target solutions in a focused and cost-effective manner. Hanify & King attorneys represent clients in areas ranging from commercial litigation and bankruptcy and financial restructuring to business formation and labor and employment. Clients include private and public corporations, investment partnerships, government agencies, Fortune 500 companies, individuals and non-profit organizations. Hanify & King's sensible approach to legal guidance is embodied in its 14 partners and 21 associates and reflected in its ongoing investment in the most current technology available to the legal profession. This commitment to technology allows Hanify & King attorneys to build evidentiary databases and offer interactive documents that allow for immediate access to critical case information, thereby truncating the time between the onset of a client's problem and its resolution. Exceptional legal talent and catered client service have earned Hanify & King a reputation as a top-notch mid-sized firm.

MAIN AREAS OF PRACTICE

Litigation: Litigation is Hanify and King's largest practice area, and its attorneys appear before state and federal courts and administrative agencies with an 'at trial' success rate of 85 percent or higher. Several cases tried by Hanify and King attorneys have set legal precedents in areas such as intellectual property, business fraud, bankruptcy, leveraged buyouts, professional malpractice and employment. The firm's litigation attorneys, led by co-founder John D Hanify, work with clients outside the courtroom as well, guiding them through critical cost/benefit decisions. The wide-ranging civil litigation practice group offers expertise in the following areas: financial representations, warranty and fraud claims, business divorce and intra-entity disputes, real estate development, ownership and construction disputes, labor and employment, intellectual property claims, insolvency, public and administrative law and fiduciary duty and professional liability claims.

Bankruptcy & Financial Restructuring: The Bankruptcy and Financial Restructuring Group represents debtors, creditors and creditors' committees, estate fiduciaries, investors in formal insolvency proceedings and out-of-court workouts throughout the United States. Led by Harold B Murphy, recognized in two leading legal publications including Chambers USA, America's Leading Business Lawyers, Hanify & King bankruptcy lawyers have been nationally recognized for delivering superior results in a timely and cost-effective manner and include former law clerks to bankruptcy judges and attorneys with the Office of the United States Trustee. Hanify and King's Bankruptcy practice is regularly called upon to serve as estate representatives and counsel in Chapter 7 and 11 cases. The group has represented clients in all types of businesses including real estate, hospitality, healthcare, technology, telecommunications, manufacturing, and retail.

Business & Real Estate: The Business and Real Estate Practice at Hanify and King represents clients in mergers and acquisitions and in the purchase and sale of business assets. Hanify and King's business and real estate attorneys provide counsel to owners and investors in the sale, acquisition, development, zoning, and leasing of commercial real estate. Robert E Richards, Jr heads this practice area and has compiled a team of professionals who are able to negotiate complex transaction documents and navigate due diligence reviews, employment issues, debt and equity structures, licensing or transfer of intellectual property, business organization and commercial loans.

HEAD OFFICE

MASSACHUSETTS
One Beacon Street, 21st Floor, **Boston**, MA 02108-3107
Tel: 617 423 0400 **Fax:** 617 423 0498

Website: www.hanify.com

CONTACTS

Litigation	John D Hanify
Bankruptcy & Financial Restructuring	Harold B Murphy
Business & Real Estate	Robert E Richards, Jr
Labor & Employment	Terence P McCourt
Alternative Dispute Resolution	David Lee Evans

Labor & Employment: In conjunction with the firm's Litigation Practice, Hanify and King's Labor and Employment Group, headed by Terence P McCourt, counsels both public and private sector employers to ensure that the myriad legal requirements concerning personnel practices do not distract them from achieving their business objectives. Hanify and King handles union petitions, unfair labor practice charges, collective bargaining negotiations and contract arbitrations. The group's in-depth knowledge of proceedings under the jurisdiction of the National Labor Relations Board is why Hanify and King is frequently called upon to advise businesses on maintaining union-free status.

Alternative Dispute Resolution: Hanify and King's Alternative Dispute Resolution Practice stems from the firm's expertise inside the courtroom. Hanify and King's attorneys are experienced trial attorneys, however, they understand that not all cases need to be settled in court. The firm encourages clients involved in cases with potential or actual litigation to explore the benefits of alternative dispute resolution. The Alternative Dispute Resolution Group, headed by David Lee Evans, has settled countless business disputes through mediation, arbitration or other informal dispute resolution proceedings, bringing conflicts to a quick and less expensive resolution. Attorneys at Hanify and King have served in approximately 100 cases for the American Arbitration Association's Commercial and Large, Complex Case Panels. The firm also co-founded the Technology Company Mediation Program for the Massachusetts Software and Internet Council. Hanify and King's Alternative Dispute Resolution Group has successfully handled the legal needs of deadlocked corporations, professional malpractice and intellectual property claims and complex business disputes.

KIRKPATRICK & LOCKHART NICHOLSON GRAHAM LLP

THE FIRM

**Chairman of the Management Committee &
Managing Partner:** Peter J Kalis
Number of partners: 323
Number of other lawyers: 627

Website: www.klng.com

FIRM OVERVIEW: Kirkpatrick & Lockhart Nicholson Graham LLP (K&LNG) – the product of one of the largest Anglo-American legal combinations in history on January 1, 2005 – comprises 950 lawyers who practice from offices throughout the US and in London, England. K&LNG represents entrepreneurs, growth and middle-market companies and leading global corporations in every major industry group. The firm practices across all legal disciplines within the corporate, litigation and regulatory fields. K&LNG's extensive knowledge about the business sectors in which our clients operate enables the practice to be at once regional, national and international in scope, cutting edge, complex, and dynamic. K&LNG was the only law firm in the world to receive the CIO Magazine CIO 100 Award for three consecutive years, while the official publication of the Minority Corporate Counsel Association selected K&LNG as one of only four American law firms to feature for their innovative diversity initiatives.

MAIN AREAS OF PRACTICE:

Corporate: K&LNG practices law on an integrated and firm-wide basis. The multi-office, international corporate and transactional practice is one of the most substantial in the profession. The firm closed over 100 M&A transactions last year, and is perennially a leader as issuer's counsel in equities issued by corporate clients, both in terms of number of transactions and proceeds. K&LNG has completed hundreds of public debt and equity offerings over the last decade.

Litigation: K&LNG's litigation engagements including, among other substantive areas, insurance coverage, intellectual property, real estate, white-collar criminal, construction, professional liability, environmental, toxic tort, products liability, franchise, tax, bankruptcy and insolvency, antitrust and competition, employment, benefits, and securities fraud are among the largest and most attractive enjoyed by any law firm. The firm has been rated a leading practice in the representation of corporate policyholders in the insurance coverage area, and as a leading litigation firm for the financial sector. It is active in jurisdictions around the US and in the UK as well as in various international arbitration forums.

Regulatory: K&LNG's Regulatory Practice cuts across the many disciplines that require highly specialized knowledge and experience to address governmental regulation of the private markets. The firm's lawyers regularly represent clients before regulatory bodies in both the US and the UK. Its premier regulatory practice is in the diversified financial services area. K&LNG represents a large majority of the major financial institutions and securities firms in a variety of disciplines, and the investment management practice is a perennial leader. Many of the firm's practice leaders as well as more junior lawyers have governmental experience that enhances their ability to serve K&LNG's clients in regulatory fields, while others have held prominent positions in regulated industries.

Emerging Practices: The firm continuously allocates resources so that its capabilities reach to the forefront of emerging disciplines. K&LNG's Intellectual Property Practice, with approximately 100 practicing lawyers, and its Technology Practice, serving growth companies in disciplines such as biotechnology, internet services, medical devices, and information systems, are examples of how this investment has borne fruit. Most frequently, the firm continues to recruit lateral partners in such disparate fields as structured finance, bankruptcy, real estate, food and drug, ERISA litigation, Small Business Administration financing, telecommunications, project finance, intellectual property, private equity, trademarks, employment and public sector technology to address the evolving needs of its

OFFICES

CALIFORNIA
10100 Santa Monica Boulevard, 7th Floor, **Los Angeles**, CA 90067
Tel: 310 552 5000 **Fax:** 310 552 5001

Four Embarcadero Center, 10th Floor, **San Francisco**, CA 94111
Tel: 415 249 1000 **Fax:** 415 249 1001

DISTRICT OF COLUMBIA
1800 Massachusetts Avenue, NW, 2nd Floor, **Washington**, DC 20036-1221
Tel: 202 778 9000 **Fax:** 202 778 9100

FLORIDA
Miami Center, 201 South Biscayne Boulevard, 20th Floor,
Miami, FL 33131-2399
Tel: 305 539 3300 **Fax:** 305 358 7095

MASSACHUSETTS
75 State Street, **Boston**, MA 02109
Tel: 617 261 3100 **Fax:** 617 261 3175

NEW JERSEY
One Newark Center, 10th Floor, **Newark**, NJ 07102-5252
Tel: 973 848 4000 **Fax:** 973 848 4001

NEW YORK
599 Lexington Avenue, **New York**, NY 10022-6030
Tel: 212 536 3900 **Fax:** 212 536 3901

PENNSYLVANIA
Payne Shoemaker Building, 240 North Third Street,
Harrisburg, PA 17101-1507
Tel: 717 231 4500 **Fax:** 717 231 4501

Henry W. Oliver Building, 535 Smithfield Street, **Pittsburgh**, PA 15222-2312
Tel: 412 355 6500 **Fax:** 412 355 6501

TEXAS
2828 North Harwood Street, Suite 1800, **Dallas**, TX 75201-6966
Tel: 214 939 4900 **Fax:** 214 939 4949

INTERNATIONAL OFFICES

The firm also has an office in London, UK

clientele. The firm strives to maintain a creative, interdisciplinary approach to the practice, as evidenced by the extraordinary convergence of disciplines that permitted its K&LNG colleague, former US Attorney General Dick Thornburgh, to act as the court appointed Examiner in the WorldCom bankruptcy proceeding – the largest bankruptcy in US history – and the firm itself to act as his counsel.

CLIENTS: K&LNG currently represents or recently has performed projects for over half of the FORTUNE 100; 21 of the 25 largest mutual fund complexes or their investment managers; and 18 of the 20 largest US bank holding companies or their affiliates. Representative clients include Alcoa, Bank of America, DuPont, Fidelity, Halliburton, Mellon, PPG, United Technologies, Wachovia, and World Wrestling Entertainment. The firm is a multiple winner of DuPont's Meeting the Challenge Award for its 'remarkable and extraordinary accomplishments' for that client, and is the only law firm on which PPG Industries has conferred its Excellent Supplier Award.

INTERNATIONAL WORK: With offices throughout the US and in London, K&LNG represents clients across North America and the United Kingdom on matters that span the globe. K&LNG's primary working language is English, but the firm has attorneys fluent in Afrikaans, Chinese (Mandarin), Farsi, French, German, Greek, Hebrew, Hindi, Italian, Japanese, Korean, Polish, Portuguese, Russian and Spanish. Various members of the firm have foreign degrees, which enable them to take into account legal and cultural differences in representing the firm's clients in international transaction and litigation matters worldwide.

MORGAN, BROWN & JOY LLP

THE FIRM

Managing Partner & Chairman of Management Committe: Robert P Joy

Number of partners: 16
Number of other lawyers: 15

FIRM OVERVIEW: Founded in 1923, Morgan, Brown & Joy is New England's oldest and largest management-side employment law firm. The firm's continued success can be credited to its ability to respond rapidly to changes in the law and the workplace. Morgan, Brown & Joy credits its distinguished history and longevity to the value and return on investment that it provides employers. The firm represents clients before courts at all levels, including the United States Supreme Court as well as state and federal agencies. Clients range from Fortune 100 corporations to small businesses and across all sectors of the economy including retailing, technology, biotechnology, healthcare, colleges and universities, utilities, insurance, banking, government and manufacturing. Morgan, Brown & Joy's focus is on anticipating and finding solutions to the ever-expanding range of employment-related legal issues in order to avoid the time and cost of litigation. When litigation becomes necessary, the firm aggressively defends its clients and has a proven record of litigation success.

MAIN AREAS OF PRACTICE:

Labor & Employment: Morgan, Brown & Joy's services include advice on all aspects of workplace discrimination, harassment or retaliation issues; collective bargaining and labor-management relations; reductions in force and terminations; FLSA; NLRA; FMLA; ERISA; OFCCP; worker's compensation; business tort and contract litigation including trade secrets, non-competition agreements and individual employment contracts.

Employment Counsel & Legal Advice: Morgan, Brown & Joy focuses on anticipating and finding solutions to the ever-expanding range of employment-related legal issues in an effort to avoid the time and cost of litigation. Its services include: advice on all aspects of workplace discrimination, harassment or retaliation issues; comprehensive counsel on labor-management relationships; advice on reductions in force, terminations and handling employee complaints; expertise on changes in business operations and labor contracts due to mergers and acquisition; counsel on FMLA, wage and hour issues, workers' compensation claims and ERISA, and the ever-increasing list of employment-related laws; guidance on the complex set of laws and regulations governing employee illness, injury, disability and medical leaves; business tort and contract litigation including trade secrets, non-competition agreements and individual employment contracts.

HEAD OFFICE

MASSACHUSETTS
200 State Street, **Boston**, MA 02109-2605
Tel: 617 523 6666   **Fax:** 617 367 3125

Website: www.morganbrown.com

CONTACTS

Head Office ....Robert P Joy

Litigation: Morgan, Brown & Joy attorneys are not only expert advisors in employment law, but also experienced litigators. When the same team of attorneys handles the case from inception to the courtroom, they bring complete knowledge of the case along with skills in negotiation, mediation and alternative dispute resolution that can help minimize the most abrasive and expensive litigation. When litigation becomes necessary, the firm aggressively defends its clients in all of the employment areas about which they provide advice and counsel.

Prevention & Training: Morgan, Brown & Joy emphasizes the importance of seeking legal advice at the earliest possible time. Because the prevention of claims is preferable to the defense of claims, they offer the following services: its audit and training team reviews clients' policies and practices and provides training to the workforce on how to avoid litigation or other adverse legal consequences; human resource support includes employee handbooks and counsel on a range of personnel policies.

Labor Law: Resolution of labor disputes is its primary objective, and they support employers with counsel and litigation related to: unfair labor practice charges; negotiations of collective bargaining agreements; grievance and arbitration; National Labor Relations Act (NLRA) and state labor law matters, including union organizing issues and union avoidance strategy.

Employment Law Leadership: Morgan, Brown & Joy holds the distinction of having two partners who have served as Chairman of the Labor and Employment Law Section of the American Bar Association. Its attorneys are active in the American Bar Association and the Massachusetts Bar Association, as well as national organizations in specific industries such as the National Association of College and University Attorneys and the National Retail Federation. Its attorneys frequently serve as faculty members of educational programs sponsored by these and other organizations. Morgan, Brown & Joy attorneys are members of multiple state bars including California, Connecticut, Georgia, Massachusetts, New Hampshire, New York, Ohio, Pennsylvania, Rhode Island and Vermont.

PALMER & DODGE LLP

THE FIRM

Managing Partner: Jeffrey F Jones
Executive Director: Ross W Farrer
Number of partners: 68
Number of other lawyers: 112

FIRM OVERVIEW: Palmer & Dodge provides a broad spectrum of legal services to its diversified client base. The firm's practice ranges from sophisticated corporate transactions and complex civil litigation to private trust matters, with a number of focused specialties, including technology-based companies, bank and institutional finance, general and transactional representation of closely held businesses, real estate development, antitrust, public finance, schools and colleges, insurance coverage and defense, and airport law and international representation.

MAIN AREAS OF PRACTICE:

Corporate & Securities: Counsels corporations, officers and directors, and major shareholders on securities transactions and compliance with disclosure requirements and insider trading issues. Extensive experience in a broad number of areas, including: public offerings of securities, private placements, 1934 Act compliance, underwriter representation, mergers and acquisitions, joint ventures and strategic alliances, corporate governance, international transactions, and commercial transactions.

Finance & Creditors' Rights: Represents banks, insurance companies, finance companies, and other institutional sources of financing, individually and as agents or participants in lending groups, in connection with various secured (including asset based) and unsecured financings. Represent lenders at all tiers of the capital spectrum: senior, mezzanine, subordinated, and equity levels.

Life Science: Advises life science companies on all legal issues, including corporate formation and governance, intellectual property strategy and positioning, institutional and corporate licensing, patent prosecution, patent due diligence, patent opinions and patent enforcement, strategic alliances and other partnering arrangements, venture capital financings, public offerings, and mergers and acquisitions.

Private Equity & Venture Capital: Represents private equity investor groups and venture capital firms in their portfolio investment, fund raising, and management activities. Significant experience representing public and private emerging growth and established companies in the life sciences, internet, telecommunications, media, communications, and information technology industries.

Tax & Benefits: Assists clients in structuring a wide variety of transactions, including mergers and acquisitions, corporate finance, formation of, or investment in, pass-through entities, including joint ventures, private equity funds, and real estate syndications. The practice also includes employee benefits and executive compensation.

Public Finance: Represents issuers, underwriters, borrowers, and purchasers in public finance transactions. The practice encompasses a full range of governmental financings and tax-exempt borrowings for qualifying businesses, including healthcare, educational, cultural, and other charitable institutions. Represent states, cities and towns, public authorities, commissions, and other public bodies in legislative and regulatory matters.

Public Projects: Provides legal services to state agencies, municipalities and public authorities. Advise clients on the planning, financing, design, procurement, construction and operation of publicly owned facilities, including transportation facilities, schools, sports and convention facilities, water and wastewater infrastructure, solid waste facilities and other public sector projects.

Real Estate Development & Finance: Advises clients through all aspects of land use and development. Development experience includes waterfront projects, mixed-use downtown hotels, residential and commercial condo-

miniums, air-rights projects, redevelopment of existing buildings, subsidized rental housing, university buildings, and state-of-the-art biotechnology facilities, shopping centers, multi-family housing, office park developments, and the siting of wireless telecommunications towers.

Commercial Litigation: Provides expertise in litigation, alternative dispute resolution, and related counseling and advice involving a broad spectrum of substantive areas including: antitrust and unfair competition, bankruptcy and creditors' rights, breach of contract, commercial fraud and misrepresentation, construction, defamation and media law, employment, product liability, premises liability, professional negligence, and securities.

Insurance Coverage: Represents and counsels members of the insurance industry on the state, regional, and national levels on a wide variety of matters including litigation, litigation avoidance, regulatory proceedings, and business issues of all kinds.

Patent Litigation: The Intellectual Property Litigation Group litigates patent cases ranging from a straight-forward simple case to the most complex. The practice spans a vast range of industries and technologies, including biotechnology, chemistry, pharmaceuticals, medical and mechanical devices, electronics, and computer technology.

Private Client: The firm's attorneys and other professionals are available to assist clients with their personal financial, tax, and estate planning decisions. The group offers extensive experience in dealing with the personal financial affairs of individual clients, including preparation of comprehensive estate plans for clients.

Schools & Colleges: Palmer & Dodge LLP has a long tradition of representing educational institutions of all sizes, from small independent schools and private colleges to large universities. In a number of situations the firm serves as general counsel to the institution, and works directly with the operating administrative officers.

Airport Group: Palmer & Dodge has one of the largest and fastest growing airport practices in the country, representing owners and operators of airports of all sizes across the country. The firm's Airport Group has experience with a full array of regulatory, financial, and operational matters, including rates and charges, regulatory compliance, airport-airline agreements, fueling issues, airport development, environmental compliance and remediation, public finance, litigation and appeals, and leasing and concessions.

International: Provides legal services for domestic clients transacting business overseas, and for foreign companies entering and establishing business in the United States. The firm is an active member of The World Law Group, a network of law firms with attorneys in commercial centers throughout the world.

HEAD OFFICE

MASSACHUSETTS
111 Huntington Avenue at Prudential Center, **Boston**, MA 02199
Tel: 617 239 0100   **Fax:** 617 227 4420
Email: webmaster@palmerdodge.com
Website: www.palmerdodge.com

BRANCH OFFICES

NEW YORK
730 5th Avenue, 9th Floor, **New York**, NY 10019
Tel: 212 659 7722   **Fax:** 212 659 7805

DISTRICT OF COLUMBIA
1776 I Street NW, **Washington**, DC 20006
Tel: 202 756 1486   **Fax:** 202 756 1301

PALMER & DODGE LLP

ROPES & GRAY LLP

THE FIRM

Chairman: R Bradford Malt
Managing Partner: John T Montgomery

Number of partners: 243
Number of lawyers: 473

AREAS OF PRACTICE:

Corporate	39%
Fish & Neave IP Group of Ropes & Gray	33%
Litigation	11%
Tax & Benefits	6%
International	5%
Private Client Group	3%
Bankruptcy & Business Restructuring	2%
Labor & Employment	2%

FIRM OVERVIEW: Ropes & Gray LLP provides comprehensive legal services to leading businesses around the world. Clients benefit from the firm's expertise combined with unwavering standards for integrity, service, and responsiveness. With offices in preeminent centers of finance, technology and government, Ropes & Gray is ideally positioned to address today's most pressing legal and business issues. More than 750 lawyers and professionals provide comprehensive legal services from its facilities in Boston, New York, Palo Alto, San Francisco, Providence, Washington, DC and London.

MAIN AREAS OF PRACTICE

Corporate: The Corporate Practice is Ropes & Gray's largest practice area and includes practices in debt financing, government relations and regulatory, healthcare, intellectual property and rights management, investment management, life sciences, private equity, public finance, real estate, securities and public companies, sports law, technology company, and venture capital.

Intellectual Property: The Fish & Neave IP Group of Ropes & Gray has earned national prominence in every area of intellectual property law. Its expertise includes patent prosecution, copyrights and trademarks, protection of trade secrets, and licensing, litigation and financial transactions involving intellectual property assets.

Litigation: The Ropes & Gray Litigation Practice is one of the largest in New England. The firm's litigators practice in the following areas: alternative dispute resolution, antitrust, bankruptcy, commercial and business, environmental, government contracts, government enforcement, healthcare, insurance, intellectual property and technology litigation, investigative services, labor and employment, and securities and corporate.

Tax & Benefits: The Ropes & Gray Tax Practice has experience in virtually every area of state and federal taxation, including corporate acquisitions, mergers and reorganizations, domestic and international joint ventures, registered and unregistered investment funds, executive compensation and benefits, tax-exempt municipal bonds, utilization of investment and research credits and tax-exempt organizations. The firm's Employee Benefits Practice offers guidance across the entire range of benefits planning, implementation, administration, compliance and tax matters.

International: The Ropes & Gray International Practice meets the diverse needs of global clients. Its international work spans all areas of the firm's practice – from corporate transactions, finance and tax planning, to international litigation and commercial arbitration. The firm has deep experience in international investments, mergers, acquisitions, alliances, intellectual property and investment management.

Private Client Group: The Ropes & Gray Private Client Group has represented individuals and families for more than a century and today has one of the largest practices of its kind in the United States. The firm's practice is primarily focused on four areas: estate planning, estate settlement, trust administration, and general matters involving the appointment of fiduciaries and resolution of disputes over wills and trusts.

Bankruptcy & Business Restructuring: Ropes & Gray lawyers have extensive experience in the areas of insolvency and bankruptcy law. They have represented debtors, creditors' committees, secured lenders and other major players, including sources of new capital, in major reorganization cases throughout the US. The firm's attorneys help clients in formulating, negotiating, and documenting complex economic and legal solutions to business and personal insolvency problems.

Labor & Employment: The Labor and Employment Practice handles all types of issues arising under federal and state labor and employment laws, including labor relations, fair labor standards, civil rights, equal employment and OSHA. Work also covers the individual employment relationship from compensation to non-competition and protection of trade secrets. Ropes & Gray also advises on employee relations matters.

HEAD OFFICE

MASSACHUSETTS
One International Place, **Boston**, MA 02110-2624
Tel: 617 951 7000 **Fax:** 617 951 7050
Website: www.ropesgray.com

BRANCH OFFICES

NEW YORK
45 Rockefeller Plaza, **New York**, NY 10111-0087
Tel: 212 841 5700 **Fax:** 212 841 5725

Avenue of the Americas, **New York**, NY 10020-1105
Tel: 212 596 9000 **Fax:** 212 596 9090

CALIFORNIA
525 University Avenue, Suite 3000, **Palo Alto**, CA 94301-1917
Tel: 650 617 4000 **Fax:** 650 617 4090

One Embarcadero Center, Suite 2200, **San Francisco**, CA 94111-3627
Tel: 415 315 6300 **Fax:** 415 315 6350

WASHINGTON
One Metro Center, 700 12th Street, NW, Suite 900,
Washington, DC 20005-3948
Tel: 202 508 4600 **Fax:** 202 508 4650

CONTACTS

Corporate	Ivor Cary Armistead, III, Dwight W Quayle
Intellectual Property	Edward G Black, Peter M Brody, James F Haley, Jr, Robert C Morgan
Litigation	Denise Loring, Lisa Ropple, Roscoe Trimmier, Jr
Tax & Benefits	Susan A Johnston
International Group	Ivor Cary Armistead, III, Adolfo R Garcia; John Reboul
Private Client Group	Robert N Shapiro
Labor & Employment	Peter L Ebb; Nelson G Ross
Bankruptcy & Business Restructuring	Stuart Hirshfield, Steven T Hoort

ROPES & GRAY

WILMER CUTLER PICKERING HALE AND DORR LLP

THE FIRM

Co-managing Partners: William F Lee, William J Perlstein
Email: law@wilmerhale.com
Website: www.wilmerhale.com

FIRM OVERVIEW: Wilmer Cutler Pickering Hale and Dorr LLP offers unparalleled legal representation across a comprehensive range of practice areas that are critical to the success of its clients. The firm has over a thousand lawyers operating in five countries and practices at the very top of the legal profession. With a practice unsurpassed in depth and scope by any other major firm, it has the ability to anticipate obstacles, seize opportunities and get the case resolved or the deal done – and the experience and know-how to prevent it from being undone. Wilmer Cutler Pickering Hale and Dorr was formed in May 2004 through the merger of two of the nation's leading law firms, Hale and Dorr LLP and Wilmer Cutler Pickering LLP. The formation of the new firm fused two storied pro bono and public service traditions. This commitment continues to be an integral part of the cultural fabric of the firm.

MAIN AREAS OF PRACTICE:

Antitrust & Competition: With more than 50 years' experience and over 75 competition lawyers in the US and Europe, the firm has secured antitrust clearance for hundreds of complex mergers and joint ventures, helped clients avoid fines and prison terms in many cartel investigations, and won numerous victories for clients in private and government litigation.

Aviation: Regarded as having one of the world's premier commercial aviation practices, the firm advises airlines, airports, associations and governments on aviation-specific legal and policy issues, from certification to licensing to enforcement. It provides strategic counseling on litigation and dispute resolution, aircraft acquisition and finance transactions, joint ventures, and bankruptcy, tax and distribution issues.

Bankruptcy & Commercial: Named by *Business Week* as one of the 'top bankruptcy shops' in the United States, the firm has broad experience representing debtors, creditors and creditors' committees in bankruptcy, insolvency and debt restructuring matters, and in related litigation and commercial transactions.

Communications: Wilmer Hale has played a major role in shaping the rules governing the wireline and wireless telecommunications, e-commerce and mass media industries. When important issues and transactions arise in these fiercely competitive industries, companies turn to them for the highest quality representation and effective problem solving.

Corporate: The firm is widely recognized for its preeminence in the representation of technology and life sciences companies in the US and Europe. Its corporate lawyers are renowned for their work in initial public offerings, venture capital and private equity, mergers and acquisitions, strategic alliances, corporate governance matters and the representation of start-up companies.

Defense, National Security & Government Contracts: With extensive experience serving in senior national security posts in the US government, their lawyers provide regulatory, legislative, transactional and enforcement advice to clients supplying products and services to military, governmental and commercial customers worldwide.

Environmental: Clients rely on the firm to address complex environmental liabilities, permit key operations and understand evolving environmental laws.

FDA: The firm's FDA Practice includes considerable experience before the FDA and other administrative agencies, Congress and the federal courts.

Financial Institutions: Over the past 30 years, the firm has built a practice of extensive breadth and depth in regulatory, transactional and litigation matters for banks and other financial institutions.

Intellectual Property: The Intellectual Property Practice serves as a one-stop solution for clients' intellectual property prosecution, litigation and licensing needs in the US and Europe. In 2004, *The American Lawyer* recognized Wilmer Hale for having one of the top IP litigation departments in the US, and *IP Law and Business* named it one of the top ten US law firms for biotech patent prosecution.

International Trade & Market Access: Recognized as one of the world's leading trade law firms, Wilmer Hale represents clients from the US, EU and more than 30 other countries before administrative, judicial and legislative bodies across the globe, as well as in proceedings under the WTO, NAFTA and the World Customs Organization.

Labor & Employment: With capabilities including comprehensive labor and employment law counseling, employment litigation and custom-designed training programs, the firm offers clients in the US and Europe practical solutions for effectively dealing with employment issues and achieving their business objectives.

Litigation & Arbitration: The firm's preeminent Litigation Practice is widely recognized for its excellence in civil and criminal trial and appellate litigation, as well as in intellectual property and securities litigation. In addition, it has one of the world's leading international arbitration practices. Many of its litigators formerly held senior government positions and have particular expertise in litigation strategies designed to advance clients' objectives in regulatory and political arenas.

Private Client: Attorneys in the Private Client Group advise clients on gift, estate and income taxation, sophisticated gifting and diversification strategies, private philanthropy, trusts and fiduciary investments, and the administration of estates.

Real Estate: The firm has extensive expertise in real estate capital management, institutional and pension fund equity and debt investment, development and permitting, leasing and foreign investment.

Tax: The firm's top-ranked Tax Practice includes lawyers recognized by *Who's Who Legal* as among 'the world's leading tax practitioners.' It handles all aspects of domestic and international tax advice for public and private companies, non-profit organizations and individuals.

OFFICES

DISTRICT OF COLUMBIA
2445 M Street, NW **Washington**, DC 20037-1420
Tel: 202 663 6000 **Fax:** 202 663 6363

The Willard Office Building, 1455 Pennsylvania Avenue, NW, **Washington**, DC 20004
Tel: 202 942 8400 **Fax:** 202 942 8484

MARYLAND
100 Light Street, **Baltimore**, MD 21202
Tel: 410 986 2800 **Fax:** 410 986 2828

MASSACHUSETTS
60 State Street, **Boston**, MA 02109
Tel: 617 526 6000 **Fax:** 617 526 5000

Hale and Dorr Venture Group, Bay Colony Corporate Center, 1100 Winter Street, **Waltham**, MA 02451
Tel: 781 966 2000 **Fax:** 781 966 2100

NEW YORK
399 Park Avenue, **New York**, NY 10022
Tel: 212 230 8800 **Fax:** 212 230 8888

VIRGINIA
1600 Tysons Boulevard, Suite 1000, **McLean**, VA 22102
Tel: 703 251 9700 **Fax:** 703 251 9797

Reston Town Center, 11951 Freedom Drive, **Reston**, VA 20190
Tel: 703 654 7000 **Fax:** 703 654 7100

INTERNATIONAL OFFICES

The firm has offices in Beijing, Berlin, Brussels, London, Munich and Oxford.

CONTENTS: Banking & Finance p.987; Corporate/M&A p.988; Employment p.991; Litigation p.993; Real Estate p.995; Individuals' Profiles p.998; Firms' Profiles p.1001.

How lawyers are ranked

The opinions we gather from clients — mainly from in-house lawyers but also from other purchasers of legal services — are balanced by opinions from colleagues and competitors. Together, they provide two different perspectives — an all-round view — and biased viewpoints cancel each other out.

BANKING & FINANCE

Michigan
Leading firms (Banking & Finance)

1. **BODMAN LLP** *Detroit*
   DICKINSON WRIGHT PLLC *Detroit*
2. **MILLER, CANFIELD, PADDOCK** *Detroit*
   VARNUM, RIDDERING, SCHMIDT *Grand Rapids*
   WARNER NORCROSS & JUDD LLP *Grand Rapids*

Leading individuals (Banking & Finance)

1. **SHIELD William** *Dickinson Wright, Detroit*
   SHULMAN Larry *Bodman LLP, Detroit*
2. **BREAY James** *Warner Norcross, Grand Rapids*
   DIEHL Robert *Bodman LLP, Detroit*
   JOHNSON Donald *Varnum Riddering, Grand Rapids*
   MCLEOD David *Miller Canfield, Detroit*
   RIBACK Ronald *Miller Canfield, Troy*
   SHEVNOCK Colleen *Dickinson Wright, Detroit*

Firms and individuals are listed alphabetically in each band.

Band 1

Bodman LLP

The Firm: This *"historically strong"* firm draws clients by deftly catering to a *"cradle-to-grave"* range of transactions. It offers unparalleled depth in the loan origination and regulatory areas, particularly on behalf of financial institutions. Clients appreciate its ability to get to the crux of the issue and *"prevent valuable time loss."* Another client added: *"The bench is one that is full of rising stars."* In 2004, the group structured, documented and negotiated more than 500 commercial and real estate credit facilities. It represented a Michigan de novo bank and its parent company in all aspects of its new entity formation and the sale of $10 million in equity securities. Acting for Comerica, the team assisted on a $15 million debtor-in-possession loan to the Ohio-based Buffalo Molded Plastics.
The Lawyers: **Larry Shulman** was highlighted for his ability to *"get the deals done well, effectively and efficiently."* Representing lenders in the loan origination area, he focuses on midmarket transactions. He also benefits from *"legal and technical knowledge that really stands out,"* sources said. Loan workouts, contracts and lender liability issues are some facets of his practice. **Robert Diehl** won praise for his *"high standard of work"* – commentators said. *"He's as good as they get."* Diehl boasts extensive experience in the loans arena, and his practice also involves representing financial institutions in bankruptcy proceedings. In 2004 he represented JPMorgan Chase as agent for a group of lenders with respect to a $25 million syndicated loan to a fast-food chain.
The Clients: Comerica; Standard Federal Bank; Fifth Third Bank; National City Bank; TCF National Bank; Huntington National Bank and Bancorp.

Dickinson Wright PLLC

The Firm: This firm was endorsed for its *"strong business-oriented approach to practicing law, leading to an impressive understanding of financial institutions."* Noted by clients as having *"one of the best"* teams, it received impressive commendation for its work on behalf of JPMorgan Chase. With 35 attorneys, the firm commands respect on a variety of work in the commercial finance area, including credit agreements, subordinate debt agreements, preferred stock-related structures and other loan-related proceedings.
The Lawyers: *"Head and shoulders above the rest,"* **William Shield** was pitched as a *"great technician"* who is especially distinguished for his *"really phenomenal ability to break through the logjams."* Handling a wide-ranging workload, his work centers on various complex lending structures, including syndicated and leveraged financing. Clients appreciate his *"real involvement in the business issues"* of a deal, adding that it was *"almost as if he worked for us."* **Colleen Shevnock's** *"excellent knowledge and experience"* in the banking sector ensures her prominence. She delivers *"practical solutions,"* particularly as related to commercial lending, securitization and syndicated financing. She also has experience with foreign currency facilities, working capital financing and letters of credit.
The Clients: JPMorgan Chase; Standard Federal Bank; National City Bank; Fifth Third Bank; Citizens Bank; Borders Group and Visteon.

Band 2

Miller, Canfield, Paddock and Stone, PLC
See firm details p.1004

The Firm: This *"well-established and traditionally strong"* firm has more than 30 lawyers carrying out transactions on a domestic, national and international level. Commentators praised its proficiency on a range of transactions, including acting for a bank group in a $45 million export financing facility involving a Mexican manufacturing company. It also counseled a lead bank as part of a group that provided $55 million in coordinated bilateral facilities to an automotive supplier.

The Lawyers: Department leader **Dave McLeod** carries out a variety of work in the financial institutions, commercial, real estate and banking transactional area. Deemed an *"excellent lawyer,"* one of his strongest attributes is his *"personable, professional and timely"* delivery of legal advice. Known as *"the attorney around town to do a lot of loan origination work,"* he acted as counsel for a bank group providing a $125 million mortgage warehouse facility for a mortgage lender. He also counseled a bank group providing $50 million revolving credit and letter of credit facilities to an automotive supplier. *"One that knows the ins and outs of the banking practice,"* **Ronald Riback** is respected as a *"well-seasoned, experienced lawyer."* His *"consistent and nonconfrontational style"* draws loyalty from clients and ensures his prominence in the practice group. Recent transactions include counseling lenders in a syndicated term loan facility agreement. In addition, he advised the lender in a construction and end-mortgage financing of a regional exposition center.

The Clients: Comerica; TCF National Bank; Standard Federal Bank; Fifth Third Bank; National City Bank and National City Bank of the Midwest.

Varnum, Riddering, Schmidt & Howlett LLP

The Firm: *"One of the chief players"* in western Michigan, the firm offers *"prompt service"* and *"provision of sound legal and business advice,"* particularly as related to the banking aspects associated with real estate law. The firm has also continued to act for municipal clients in the bond financing area. On behalf of Independent Bank Corporation, it orchestrated two separate institution acquisitions located in the northern Michigan and Detroit areas. In 2004, the group also participated in two separate State of Michigan bond issues aggregating more than $230 million. In another highlight, it represented three financial institutions in separate issues of privately placed trust-preferred securities.

The Lawyers: With *"thorough knowledge of banking-related issues and regulations,"* **Donald Johnson** is highly regarded for his *"excellence, honesty and good business judgment."* His extensive workload includes bank regulatory and structuring matters. For example, he assisted Firstbank on a buy-back concerning a public tender offer.

The Clients: Huntington Bank; Pavilion Bancorp; Standard Federal Bank; Independent Bank; Macatawa Bank and Firstbank.

Warner Norcross & Judd LLP

The Firm: This group's continued representation of the Michigan Bankers Association kept them *"in the front line of industry development,"* analysts said. It plays a significant role in banking-related regulations, for example, testifying before legislative committees on behalf of the banking industry. Noted by researchers as a leader in western Michigan, the firm has recently acted in five trust-preferred offerings and separately advised on substituting long-term debts as equity. It has also handled substantial commercial lending transactions and tax-exempt financing transactions.

The Lawyers: The chair of the firm's commercial finance and commercial transactions practice, **James Breay** is also general counsel to the Michigan Bankers Association. Described as being *"remarkably clued up in his field of practice,"* he attracts client devotion by *"knowing how to deal with complicated issues – and complicated people."* He regularly advises on a number of regulatory issues, in addition to his involvement in drafting revisions to the state's banking law.

The Clients: Clients include Fifth Third Bank and Chemical Financial.

CORPORATE/M&A

Michigan
Leading firms (Corporate/M&A)
1   HONIGMAN MILLER SCHWARTZ *Detroit*
2   BUTZEL LONG *Detroit*
DICKINSON WRIGHT PLLC *Detroit*
DYKEMA GOSSETT PLLC *Detroit*
MILLER, CANFIELD, PADDOCK *Detroit*
3   BODMAN LONGLEY & DAHLING LLP *Ann Arbor*
CLARK HILL PLC *Detroit*
VARNUM, RIDDERING, SCHMIDT *Grand Rapids*
WARNER NORCROSS & JUDD LLP *Grand Rapids*
4   BARNES & THORNBURG *Grand Rapids*
FOLEY & LARDNER *Detroit*
JAFFE, RAITT, HEUER & WEISS, PC *Detroit*
MILLER, JOHNSON, SNELL *Grand Rapids*
Firms are listed alphabetically in each band.

Band 1

Honigman Miller Schwartz and Cohn

The Firm: With one of the strongest indigenous practices, this *"firm of choice"* remains the *"one to beat"* in the corporate/M&A sector. The quality of the overall team often stands out as its distinguishing feature, while an *"extensive stable of clients"* means that it inevitably gets involved in some of the region's most notable transactions. The *"exceptional"* team is further enhanced by the arrival of eight members to the new intellectual property group. It also continues to be a contender in the securities and finance arena, carrying out multiple public debt offerings in excess of $2 billion. Restructurings and recapitalizations also feature in its smorgasbord, along with other structures such as joint venture formations. Its extensive experience includes work in India and China.

The Lawyers: Legendary **Cyril Moscow** continues to represent clients on a consultation basis, while **Alan Schwartz** garnered respect for his agile handling of corporate and securities matters. The firm's chairman and CEO participated in the acquisition of the Cleveland Cavaliers basketball team. *"Besides being an excellent lawyer,"* commentators said, *"he's also a very savvy businessman."* **David Foltyn** has become increasingly prominent in the practice as another *"key"* member of the firm. His skills as an *"impressive deal-maker and organizer"* were particularly noted, as was his *"brilliance, pure ability and sharp"* character. His practice illustrates a *"level of sophistication"* that ensures his distinction in a firm with a strong pool of talent. Continuing to represent the corporate matters of Pulte Homes, he was involved in their acquisition of the largest home builder in New Mexico. **Donald Kunz**'s *"common-sense"* approach was distinguished, analysts said. He exhibits a *"respectful balance of costs against levels of effort and the nature of transactions."* He was involved in a series of public offerings – including a public offering of $100 million of preferred shares, a $75 million acquisition involving companies that manufacture building components, and a $50 million sale of an Internet automotive-related business.

The Clients: Pulte Homes; Taubman Centers; Ramco-Gershenson Properties Trust; Sorenson Capital Partners and Huron Capital Partners.

Band 2

Butzel Long
See firm details p.1002

The Firm: The firm is recognized as having expertise in acting for midmarket companies and the manufacturing sector, with additional expertise in technology. Clients remarked the practice was *"solid for day-to-day needs"* and possessed a depth of experience in M&A, finance, corporate governance and securities. Clients appreciate the team's *"measured and timely responses."* Some noteworthy transactions include a $200 million recapitalization for an information technology service provider and a separate $52 million ESOP acquisition and debt refinancing for a maker of industrial manufacturing machinery. The team also participated in some significant bankruptcy-related purchases for a pharmaceutical company.

The Lawyers: **Justin Klimko** (see p.999) is especially noted for his *"encyclopedic legal knowledge"* and experience in securities regulation. Clients said he can tackle *"any project thrown at him,"* parlaying a *"low-key, yet very effective"* style into legal advantages. Others praised his *"meticulous and thorough understanding of their business needs."*

The Clients: Covansys; Besser; Dunham's Athleisure and Michigan Rivet.

Dickinson Wright PLLC

The Firm: In addition to private equity companies, this firm's clientele covers a variety of business sectors, with deals transpiring on domestic and national levels. *"Definitely leading competitors within the market,"* the *"sophisticated"* group

Michigan
Leading firms (Corporate/M&A)

Senior Statesmen
MOSCOW Cyril *Honigman Miller*, Detroit
SEMPLE Lloyd *Dykema Gossett*, Detroit

[1] **FOLTYN David** *Honigman Miller*, Detroit
JOSWICK David *Miller Canfield*, Troy
KUNZ Donald *Honigman Miller*, Detroit
LARSEN Tracy *Barnes & Thornburg*, Grand Rapids

[2] **AMMON Jeffrey** *Miller Johnson*, Grand Rapids
DAMSCHRODER Timothy *Bodman Longley*, Ann Arbor
DAUGHERTY Patrick *Foley & Lardner*, Detroit
KLIMKO Justin *Butzel Long*, Detroit

[3] **BERNARD J Michael** *Dykema Gossett*, Detroit
BOLTON Richard *Dickinson Wright*, Detroit
DEITCH Laurence *Bodman LLP*, Detroit
JAFFE Ira *Jaffe Raitt*, Detroit
JOHNSON Donald *Varnum Riddering*, Grand Rapids
MAKENS Hugh *Warner Norcross*, Grand Rapids
MCCALLUM Charles *Warner Norcross*, Grand Rapids
MINKUS Daniel *Clark Hill*, Detroit
OOSTERHOUSE Carl *Varnum Riddering*, Grand Rapids
RENTENBACH Paul *Dykema Gossett*, Detroit
SCHWARTZ Alan *Honigman Miller*, Detroit

Individuals are listed alphabetically in each band.

comprises a *"strong set of individuals."* Its combination of *"accuracy"* and *"timely delivery"* impresses clients, who have retained the team on such prominent transactions as the Huron Fund's $150 million private equity transaction. In addition it represented Plastech Engineered Products in its acquisition of LDM Technologies valued at more than $200 million.

The Lawyers: Director of the firm's corporate, corporate finance and securities group, **Richard Bolton** is highly regarded for his wealth of knowledge. Described as a *"good business-getter,"* he is particularly skilled in the private equity and venture capital arenas. In addition to the Plastech Engineered Products' takeover of LDM Technologies, he has also completed multiple mezzanine finance transactions and continued to structure substantial private equity transactions.

The Clients: Qualitor; The Peninsula Fund; Huron Capital Partners and Wind Point Partners.

Dykema Gossett PLLC
The Firm: Clients were particularly impressed by the *"level of expertise and innovative ideas brought to the table."* The group remains a principal player in the market for its adroit handling of a range of corporate issues. Offering corporate legal services to both domestic and foreign entities, it has broad experience that includes M&A, securitization and corporate governance. Some of the firm's recent work includes certain acquisitions involving Marine Innovations Warranty. In addition, it has also helped orchestrate a number of IPOs.

The Lawyers: Lloyd Semple, the firm's chairman emeritus, brings to bear more than 40 years of experience. Though not involved in the firm's day-to-day activities, Semple continues to offer selective clients advice on a consultation basis in addition to serving as a law professor at the University of Detroit. **Paul Rentenbach** also won respect with his *"understated"* yet *"more than capable style."* He is commended for his extensive knowledge of publicly traded companies in a variety of industries – including automotive, retail and technology. He's *"not one to pound the table,"* commentators said: *"But rather, he uses the force of logic to be persuasive."* He continues to advise prominent clients such as Kaydon and Saga Communications. **Michael Bernard**, leader of the corporate finance practice group, is described as *"a good egg"* whose practice involves business planning, general corporate and securities.

The Clients: Bank One; UPS; Kaydon; Saga Communications; Franklin Enterprises and Sears.

Miller, Canfield, Paddock and Stone, P.L.C.
See firm details p.1004

The Firm: The largest law firm in Michigan, this *"selection of first-rate lawyers"* is chosen for its practical solutions to complex business problems, commentators said. The practice also won praise for having the *"wide and diverse skills to deal with the big utility companies,"* and for an equally impressive *"timeliness."* Covering a full range of corporate services, it has handled M&A, joint ventures, securities regulatory proceedings and corporate compliance issues. Corporate governance is also a strong suit, as are other specialties in such areas as franchising, antitrust and government contracts.

The Lawyers: David Joswick is regarded as a leader in the corporate field due to attributes including *"great style and great expertise,"* peers said. Recognized as being *"extremely innovative,"* he delivers *"great strategic vision."* In 2004, Joswick closed a $30 million deal involving the rehabilitation of a bank holding company by raising equity and changing its management. He additionally implemented a new business plan for Mackinac Financial.

The Clients: Tecumseh Products, Mackinac Financial and DaimlerChrysler are among the firm's highly regarded clientele.

Band 3

Bodman Longley & Dahling LLP
The Firm: This firm's long-standing relationship with the automotive industry still thrives, yet it has expanded its legal influence to include work on behalf of clients in communications and media, computer software, biotech and banking. Other interests involve the insurance,

securities and manufacturing sectors. Although the firm's corporate practice is smaller than some of its competitors, it often wins praise as the *"preferred choice in the tenor of the deal."* It continues to represent major automotive suppliers in M&A and divestitures. Representing the holding company for a southeast Michigan national bank, it participated in the $82.2 million acquisition by an out-of-state purchaser in a cash and stock transaction. Other features include debt and equity investments, representing either investors or issuers.

The Lawyers: Timothy Damschroder garnered respect as an *"exceptional lawyer"* with a *"vibrant M&A practice."* With *"special expertise in the technology sector that is unparalleled,"* this practical lawyer demonstrates *"an enormous capacity for work done well and promptly."* He successfully closed several M&A transactions including the purchase of a minority equity investment in a Chinese manufacturing business. Another highlight involved the sale of a Dominican Republic cigar manufacturer. *"Collaborative rather than confrontational,"* **Laurence Deitch** is praised for being *"quietly effective for clients,"* a quality that is particularly suited to Michigan's more relaxed style. Political connections further bolstered his status, along with his participation in such prominent work as Larson's sale of its statewide and overseas outsourcing operations to a New York-based private entity.

The Clients: Lear; Freudenburg-NOK General Partnership; Larson; Detroit Diesel; RW Automotive; Pulte Homes; St Marys Cement and Caraco Pharmaceutical Laboratories.

Clark Hill PLC
The Firm: The firm's ability to *"respond quickly, methodically and thoroughly to client needs"* attracts a loyal following. In addition, its range of legal proficiency spans many different facets of corporate law. It has represented Severstal North America in a joint venture with US Coking Group; the transaction was estimated to exceed $200 million. The group also represented Universal Truckload Services in a $115 million offering of common stock. In another highlight, it advised Metropolitan Life Insurance and Massachusetts Mutual Life Insurance as co-lenders in a $92 million refinancing of a four-building complex.

The Lawyers: Daniel Minkus is experienced in representing minority business enterprises (MBEs) as part of a broader remit. His *"business-oriented"* style is suited to a variety of clients, who often approach him as a *"sounding board"* on complex problems.

The Clients: Severstal North America; Elopak; Johnston Lewis Associates; Trettco; Universal Truckload Services; Metropolitan Life Insurance and Dale Industries.

Varnum, Riddering, Schmidt & Howlett LLP

The Firm: *"A leading firm"* in western Michigan, the team of *"intelligent"* and *"knowledgeable"* lawyers *"always meets expectations,"* commentators said. The day-to-day focus is on M&A and equity offerings among other corporate services. The group represented Metropolitan Title in its sale to First American. In another highlighted transaction, the team represented Applied Films in its acquisition of the In-Line Systems division of Helix Technology in Taiwan.

The Lawyers: Newly appointed chair of the corporate practice group, **Carl Oosterhouse**'s practice includes M&A, business planning and tax as well as other expertise. Described as *"on the ball"* when dealing with business transactions, he was retained to represent Healthcare Solutions in a considerable $120 million sale. **Donald Johnson** is a *"much-respected lawyer in the west of the state"* whose practice centers on financial institutions, including transactions involving the formation of French banks within Europe.

The Clients: Donnelly, Healthcare Solutions, and other publicly traded and privately held companies form the backbone of the firm's client list.

Warner Norcross & Judd LLP

The Firm: With four Michigan offices – including Grand Rapids, Metro Detroit, Muskegon and Holland – this firm continues to *"stand out"* as holding a *"lock on the west side of the state."* It was noted as having *"top practitioners"* and offering an *"experienced and professional"* service. A broad spectrum of businesses depends on its legal proficiency in a wide variety of corporate matters, M&A and reorganizations.

The Lawyers: Considered the *"dean on the west side of the state,"* **Hugh Makens** has *"real expertise when it comes to securities law,"* industry analysts said. *"Hard-working, dedicated and well-respected,"* he also chairs the firm's broker-dealer/investment advisers practice group. Regarded as a *"strong and experienced lawyer,"* **Charles McCallum** continues to counsel corporate management in M&A, corporate finance and various other general commercial transactions. The chair of the firm's international business group, he often assists US companies overseas and advises non-US firms regarding their US operations.

The Clients: Clients include multinational corporations and emerging growth companies.

Band 4

Barnes & Thornburg

The Firm: This firm's corporate/M&A practice has acquired increased depth with the addition of Tracy Larson, and leading industry analysts praise its *"high-quality"* team. *"It has been great for them and is helping to make them a significant firm."* Although smaller than other heavyweights, the firm impresses with quality and quantity on a domestic, national and international level. In 2004, it handled more than 50 M&A transactions outside the country. In addition, the group acted for Wolverine World Wide in its acquisition of the Sebago shoe company. The firm also enjoys a strong relationship with several Berkshire Hathaway companies, and separately handled several significant transactions for the UK-based Novar.

The Lawyers: Regarded as *"one of the shining stars,"* **Tracy Larsen** is praised as one of the *"most dynamic M&A lawyers in Michigan."* Larsen exhibits an enormous clientele, particularly in the banking community. His *"intense, tenacious and aggressive"* capacity as a lawyer is illustrated by such transactions as BISSELL Homecare's $62 million acquisition of the Woolite rug and upholstery business from Playtex Products. In 2004, he advised on more than 25 M&A and equity/mezzanine financing transactions involving a total consideration of more than $3 billion.

The Clients: The firm has represented BISSELL Homecare, Wolverine World Wide and Novar. Others range from startups to large corporations involved in domestic, national and international matters.

Foley & Lardner

See firm details p.1828

The Firm: One of the nation's most established law firms, its Michigan branch is a relative newcomer but one that is making a splash in the market; so much so that it is now *"exporting"* work to other branches. With a practice that includes corporate governance matters and asset security, this team is able to draw on the strength of an extensive international network. Its team of attorneys delivers *"great technical knowledge and expertise,"* commentators said.

The Lawyers: The premier corporate/M&A lawyer in the firm's Michigan office, **Patrick Daugherty** (see p.998) is *"definitely building his reputation"* statewide, focusing on IPOs, private equity fund formations and client relationship management. He was deemed *"very practical and business-oriented,"* providing clients with a *"good understanding of issues that should be taken into account."*

The Clients: Tyco, Veri-Tech (a subsidiary of Noble International) and Builders Insurance Group are examples of the firm's notable clientele.

Jaffe, Raitt, Heuer & Weiss, PC

The Firm: A firm respected for its midmarket strength, it caters to the diverse legal and business requirements of enterprises engaged in a variety of industries. The group provides expertise in matters including M&A, securities, corporate governance and joint ventures. It is also supported by experience in related areas such as antitrust and partnership issues.

The Lawyers: *"Household-name"* **Ira Jaffe** was accredited as *"a superb businessman and lawyer."* He is *"loved by clients"* for his practical approach to corporate law, often undertaking transactions related to finance, securities or restructuring.

The Clients: The firm has represented Crawford Realty Group and Northern Equities Group among other companies.

Miller, Johnson, Snell & Cummiskey, PLC

The Firm: Although smaller in comparison to the other leading Grand Rapids firms, it won client loyalty with its *"entrepreneurial"* spirit that often results in *"good ideas brought to the table."* In addition, clients appreciate the *"great rate."* This practice continues to encompass a wide variety of matters including commercial agreements and entity formations as related to corporations, limited liability companies, general and limited partnerships, and joint ventures. Representing Siemens, the team helped negotiate a development agreement with the City of Grand Rapids; the deal involved an acquisition of land as well as a negotiation of various tax incentives and tax increment financing.

The Lawyers: With a practice that centers on significant economic development projects, **Jeffrey Ammon** is accredited as a *"terrific"* and *"sophisticated"* operator who provides *"the best methods"* to deal with complex problems. He has assisted Kellogg in its negotiation of local and state economic development incentives in connection with its relocation of a division from Illinois to Michigan. In addition, he assisted Stryker in negotiating a package of incentives in connection with the acquisition of land for a major development project.

The Clients: The team has advised Kellogg, Siemens and Stryker as well as other corporations, partnerships and family-owned businesses.

990   All quotes in the text are from interviews with clients and competitors.

CHAMBERS USA 2005

EMPLOYMENT

MAINLY DEFENDANT

Michigan
Leading firms
(Employment: Mainly Defendant)

[1] **KIENBAUM OPPERWALL HARDY** Birmingham
MILLER, CANFIELD, PADDOCK Detroit
VERCRUYSSE MURRAY & CALZONE Bingham Farms

[2] **BRADY HATHAWAY BRADY & BRETZ** Detroit
BUTZEL LONG Detroit
DICKINSON WRIGHT PLLC Detroit
DYKEMA GOSSETT PLLC Detroit
VARNUM, RIDDERING, SCHMIDT Grand Rapids

[3] **CLARK HILL PLC** Detroit
MILLER, JOHNSON, SNELL Grand Rapids
WARNER NORCROSS & JUDD LLP Grand Rapids

Leading individuals
(Employment: Mainly Defendant)

[1] **KIENBAUM** Thomas Kienbaum Opperwall, Birmingham
RITOK Joseph Dykema Gossett, Detroit
VERCRUYSSE Robert Vercruysse, Bingham Farms

[2] **BARNES** Thomas Varnum Riddering, Grand Rapids
BRETZ Daniel Brady Hathaway, Detroit
CALZONE David Vercruysse Murray, Bingham Farms
DICKSON Andrea Roumell Butzel Long, Detroit
GIVENS Leonard Miller Canfield, Detroit
HANCOCK John Butzel Long, Detroit
HARDY Elizabeth Kienbaum Opperwall, Birmingham
HOWLETT Timothy Dickinson Wright, Detroit
MARCH Jon Miller Johnson, Grand Rapids
MURRAY Gregory Vercruysse, Bingham Farms
NORRIS Megan Miller Canfield, Detroit

[3] **BATTEN** Fred Clark Hill, Detroit
DONATI Donna Miller Canfield, Detroit
HATHAWAY Thomas Brady Hathaway, Detroit
KHOREY David Varnum Riddering, Grand Rapids
MURPHY Lawrence Varnum Riddering, Grand Rapids
NIEHOFF Leonard Butzel Long, Detroit
SERYAK Richard Miller Canfield, Detroit
SOUBLY Diane Vercruysse Murray, Bingham Farms
WATSON Jerome Miller Canfield, Detroit

Firms and individuals are listed alphabetically in each band.

Band 1

Kienbaum Opperwall Hardy & Pelton P.L.C.
See firm details p.1003
The Firm: "Responsive and efficient," the team impresses market commentators with its "premier-quality advice, good judgment and hardworking philosophy." Although best known for its distinguished employment litigation practice, the firm also advises employers on traditional labor relations. Its client base extends from independently owned businesses and educational institutions to large regional businesses. Attorneys also represent corporate institutions of the caliber of Ford and Wal-Mart.

The Lawyers: "Brilliant and tenacious" **Thomas Kienbaum** (see p.999) possesses years of experience and an "extensive knowledge and comprehensive understanding of all issues," interviewees said. Good political connections bolster his reputation within the state and beyond. In 2004, he advised on a significant number of retirement health claims for El Paso and was involved in decertifying a class action brought against Ford and Wal-Mart. Peers endorsed "top lawyer" **Elizabeth Hardy** (see p.999) for her "great attention to detail and passion for her work. She is always looking for a strategy and this keeps her winning," clients said. Experienced at both trial and appellate level, she additionally counsels clients on preventive measures. She was recently involved in the reversal by the Michigan Supreme Court of a $21 million award for sexual harassment against DaimlerChrysler.

The Clients: DaimlerChrysler; Starwood Hotels & Resorts; Detroit Edison; PepsiCo and Detroit Diesel.

Miller, Canfield, Paddock and Stone, P.L.C.
See firm details p.1004
The Firm: This "top-of-the-league" full-service firm wins market plaudits for "its assembly of impressive lawyers and encompassing field expertise." The group handles a wide variety of "very satisfied" public sector and private sector clients ranging from corporations to municipalities and public bodies. Among its recent highlights, the firm settled a significant multiplaintiff racial harassment case on behalf of a contractor company. Attorneys also represented the same client in a high-profile employee fatality case during the construction of a public sports facility. They have continued to guide a large school district through a termination and criminal investigation related to an alleged embezzlement by a high-level administrator, and remain as outside general counsel to Northern Michigan University.

The Lawyers: Group leader **Leonard Givens** is widely respected as "one of the experts in traditional labor law." His years of experience combine with an "innate ability," report clients. In 2004, he was involved in an SEC glass-ceiling audit for Comerica, and advised the City of Detroit on labor issues. Givens also represented clients in a number of lawsuits claiming wrongful termination and harassment. As "one of the most capable litigators around," co-group leader **Megan Norris**'s focus includes issues involving the ADA, wrongful discharge, sexual harassment and workers' compensation. "Skilled litigator and proficient counsel" **Jerome Watson** is experienced in discrimination, breach of contract and wrongful dismissal. He has recently acted on a major case involving racial harassment claims

for Hunt Construction Group. A further highlight is his defense of a highly publicized lawsuit challenging the governance structure of Southeast Michigan Council of Governments (SEMCOG). Watson's major client continues to be Detroit Public Schools. **Donna Donati** is "a very tough and smart lawyer," who impressed employers in both the public and private arenas. Over the past year, she has acted in litigation involving SEMCOG. Respected **Richard Seryak** has a depth of experience in wrongful discharge and employment discrimination cases.

The Clients: Comerica; Detroit Edison; Detroit Public Schools; SEMCOG; Hunt Construction Group and Northern Michigan University.

Vercruysse Murray & Calzone, PC
The Firm: "Cream of the crop," this boutique was highly endorsed by market observers for its "depth, breadth and consistency of high-quality advice resulting from longtime expertise." Its 16 lawyers represent management in the traditional labor field and undertake substantial litigation of discrimination and sexual harassment claims and ERISA matters. It is described by peers as having the "top defense lawyers in the state." One interviewee remarked: "They definitely have some great lawyers, any number of which I would be glad to have represent me." Moreover, these attorneys are noted for the "freshness, energy and great problem-solving skills" they bring to the negotiating table.

The Lawyers: Highly respected firm president **Robert Vercruysse** stands out as a leading labor and employment lawyer. In addition to his "great advocacy skills," he was marked out as a great problem solver. His loyal client following includes manufacturers, educational institutions, television stations, financial institutions and hospitals. Clients remarked that they "would not hesitate to call him" for advice on the most complex of issues. "Incredibly talented" **David Calzone** was highlighted for his impressive trial skills. His practice involves discrimination litigation, appellate matters and complex class actions. "One of the strongest in the firm," **Gregory Murray** acts on behalf of employers in a variety of employment matters. Leading analysts noted his particular expertise in healthcare and hospital issues. Litigator **Diane Soubly** is an erudite adviser, who represents clients in wrongful discharge, employment discrimination claims, ERISA litigation and sexual harassment investigations.

The Clients: Comerica; Detroit Diesel; CDI Professional Services; Chubb Group; Central Michigan University; Detroit Newspapers; Penske; Home Depot and Northwest Airlines

Band 2

Brady Hathaway Brady & Bretz

See firm details p.1001

The Firm: Market sources agreed this boutique firm was "*highly accomplished and very much a player within the state.*" Clients rated its nine-member team as "*specialized folks not spreading themselves too thin,*" and felt they benefited from a "*more nimble and responsive*" approach to case management. Attorneys here possess "*impressive technical knowledge*" and an ability to maintain the confidence of large-scale clients. The team concentrates on discrimination litigation and wrongful termination, while remaining prominent for its advice on union relations and traditional labor law matters.

The Lawyers: "*Top-flight*" lawyer **Daniel Bretz** (see p.998) is regarded as a key member of the firm. He divides his practice between employment litigation, civil rights issues and traditional labor work. "*Obviously knowledgeable, he's a good guy to have in your corner,*" reported clients. He recently successfully acted in a case in which the Michigan Supreme Court granted a decision in favor of his construction company client following a defamation and tortious interference claim against a union. **Thomas Hathaway** displays "*superb skills and an excellent trial demeanor.*" He provides litigation counsel to national companies and local businesses, advising on constitutional law, labor and employment matters. He has tried cases in federal and state courts around the USA including Florida, New Mexico and the US Supreme Court.

The Clients: J&J Construction; Kinsman Lines; Michigan State University Foundation; Schering-Plough; Wolverine Technologies; Shaw Industries; Wayne State University; Compuware; Botsford General Hospital; Detroit Metropolitan Bar Association and Trinity Health.

Butzel Long

See firm details p.1002

The Firm: This employment and labor law practice comprises 45 attorneys, who are committed to the provision of a full service to clients. Such resources and breadth of expertise makes this firm "*a noteworthy contender*" within the state. Its attorneys emit "*a real feel that they enjoy practicing law together*" and impress through their "*real passion for high-quality client service.*" The group serves a broad base of clients in the public and private sectors.

The Lawyers: "*Highly capable*" **Andrea Dickson** (see p.998) won plaudits for her work in sex, race, and disability discrimination and her expertise in medical leave disputes. Over the past year she has carried out substantial work for MGM Mirage and Marriott Hotels, and she continues to act for the University of Michigan. **John Hancock**'s (see p.999) broad experience encompasses collective bargaining negotiations,

employment litigation and OSHA claims. He has recently advised a number of hospitals and manufacturers in the automotive industry on employment issues. **Leonard Niehoff** (see p.1000) is best known for his work with public schools, municipal bodies and public utilities. But his clientele is far broader and spans a variety of industries from casinos to steel plants.

The Clients: UPS; Standard Federal Bank; MGM Mirage; Marriott Hotels; Marshall Field's and Citigroup.

Dickinson Wright PLLC

The Firm: This full-service firm houses a substantial employment litigation practice that has attracted "*an impressive stable of clients.*" Its caseload covers all employment law matters, with emphasis on discrimination litigation before the state and federal courts. The group also provides preventive counseling, and is well equipped to advise on immigration, employee benefits and labor relations.

The Lawyers: **Timothy Howlett** gathered admiration as a well-rounded lawyer, who is "*skilled in every respect.*" Peers also described him as "*professional, trustworthy and knowledgeable,*" while clients said they could "*always count on him.*" Best known for his expert counseling and skill in handling appellate matters, he has worked with clients such as the University of Michigan and Borders Group. Over the past year, Howlett has also advised new client Kmart.

The Clients: Borders Group; Carhartt; Central Transport; Dow Chemical; Lawrence Technological University; Magna International; University of Michigan; AG Simpson Automotive; CenturyTel; DuPont; Ford; Michigan Road Builders Association; SBC Michigan and MGM Grand Detroit Casino.

Dykema Gossett PLLC

The Firm: The remit of this full-service firm extends to all facets of labor and employment law. The group is distinguished by its litigation prowess, and over the past twelve months has assisted clients in the retail, manufacturer, construction and healthcare industries within Michigan. Attorneys have additionally advised on traditional labor matters during union labor negotiations and continued to advise on non-compete issues and wrongful termination.

The Lawyers: "*Class act and a well-seasoned attorney*" **Joseph Ritok** was highly acclaimed. He is very professional and possesses a wealth of experience in the sector. He has represented clients in the Michigan retail industry.

The Clients: University of Michigan; UPS; Standard Federal Bank; Citigroup; Marshall Field's; Bank One and Ann Arbor Public Schools.

Varnum, Riddering, Schmidt & Howlett LLP

The Firm: This Grand Rapids heavyweight stood out as a principal player in the west of the state. It fields more than 30 "*highly skilled and hard-working*" attorneys in the labor and employment practice team. Expertise ranges from employee benefits issues to workers' compensation and immigration. The group also provides litigation and labor law advice to the needs of Fortune 500 companies and smaller retail establishments in the region and beyond. Of late, it has advised on a number of health benefit cases for large manufacturing companies in the Midwest involving class actions in the federal courts. Attorneys have also advised clients in the food service and transportation sectors.

The Lawyers: **Thomas Barnes** garners respect as an "*experienced, clued-up and constructive*" lawyer. His practice encompasses employee benefits, the defense of discrimination claims and union negotiations. He regularly works with federally recognized tribes and is familiar with the specialist labor issues confronting American Indians. Chair of the practice, **David Khorey**'s expertise spans the areas of labor law and employer/employee relations. In the past year he has concentrated his practice on labor law issues, including proceedings before the NLRB. **Lawrence Murphy** is a "*dynamite lawyer.*" His broad practice covers both employment litigation and labor law issues for management clients.

The Clients: Clients range from large corporations and universities to small retailers and service firms; and public, private, union and nonunion employers throughout the Midwest and across the country.

Band 3

Clark Hill PLC

The Firm: With 25 lawyers acting in the practice area, its broad remit includes expertise in the areas of employee benefits, employment litigation, collective bargaining, workers' compensation and OSHA matters. Skilled in the defense of management, the firm has also provided employment counsel to the Michigan Manufacturers Association and the American Society of Employers. It frequently appears as *amicus curiae* before the Michigan state and federal courts.

The Lawyers: Sources recommended **Fred Batten** as an "*incredibly committed lawyer – he pretty much knows everything about labor law matters.*" An experienced advocate, he has represented management, including Fortune 500 entities and nonprofit organizations in collective bargaining and other union relations issues. He has successfully represented employers in variance and contested citation proceedings before the Board of Health and Safety Compliance and Appeals.

Miller, Johnson, Snell & Cummiskey, PLC

The Firm: The employment practice group at this firm was commended for its success in producing a *"number of fabulous lawyers."* With 35 lawyers working in the employment practice, it has the resources to handle most issues from advising on employment litigation to negotiating union workouts. Market sources commented that a track record of complex cases has *"given them expertise in discrimination cases."* Client representation spans a diverse set of sectors. The team has advised a number of office furniture manufacturers in employment matters and recently assisted model appliance manufacturer Stryker. It also continues to advise Gordon Food Service, one of the firm's largest clients, on employment law matters.

The Lawyers: **Jon March** is a *"very, very fine attorney and litigator."* Although his is a broad-based trial practice, the past year has seen him concentrating on facilitations and alternative dispute resolution. Clients spoke of his excellent legal skills and were *"impressed with his conduct toward the other parties"* in disputes. He combines his defense of sexual harassment claims, covenants not-to-compete, and race discrimination claims with a general litigation practice.

The Clients: The firm represents manufacturers, financial institutions, retailers and wholesalers, hospitals, professional corporations, nonprofit agencies, school districts, and other governmental entities.

Warner Norcross & Judd LLP

The Firm: Sources recognized that this firm has established a strong employment law practice in the west of the state. Although they represent more employers in the private sector, they are nonetheless respected by their corporate clients in the public sector as well. Attorneys here are well versed in a range of employment relations issues, advising on union-organizational efforts, collective bargaining and other labor law-related issues. They also advise management on occupational health and safety laws.

LITIGATION

Michigan
Leading firms
(Litigation: General Commercial)

1	BUTZEL LONG *Detroit*	
	DICKINSON WRIGHT PLLC *Detroit*	
	HONIGMAN MILLER SCHWARTZ *Detroit*	
	MILLER, CANFIELD, PADDOCK *Detroit*	
2	BARRIS, SOTT, DENN & DRIKER, PLLC *Detroit*	
	DYKEMA GOSSETT PLLC *Detroit*	
3	BODMAN LLP *Detroit*	
	MILLER, JOHNSON, SNELL *Grand Rapids*	
	VARNUM, RIDDERING, SCHMIDT *Grand Rapids*	
	WARNER NORCROSS & JUDD LLP *Grand Rapids*	
4	CLARK HILL PLC *Detroit*	
	KERR RUSSELL & WEBER *Detroit*	
	YOUNG & SUSSER PC *Southfield*	

Firms are listed alphabetically in each band.

Band 1

Butzel Long
See firm details p.1002

The Firm: A *"principal competitor in the high-end market,"* agreed peers; this litigation department is home to an array of *"first-class, skillful lawyers."* Its breadth of resources provides *"a comprehensive service to clients"* across the range of commercial and white-collar criminal disputes. Its recent caseload has included antitrust, IP litigation, insurance coverage, and products and professional liability claims. Its media practice also attracted plaudits and clients endorsed the firm as *"the first choice for local counsel in media matters."*

The Lawyers: An excellent litigator, **David DuMouchel** (see p.999) is highly respected by judges, peers and clients for his *"amazing ability to make sense of the federal and state criminal processes."* He has the ability to communicate complex issues to the jury and this ensures the smooth running of a case. He has recently acted in one of the largest federal healthcare trials in the USA. *"At the very top of his field,"* **Philip Kessler** (see p.999) combines an impressive caseload with his duties as president of the firm. He possesses extensive experience before state and federal courts covering the many areas of business litigation. Chair of the firm, **Richard Rassel** (see p.1000) also undertakes managerial duties alongside his active litigation and mediation practice. A *"top-class litigator and strategic adviser,"* he principally represents suppliers of the automotive community. **Edward Kronk** (see p.1000) is *"someone who can simplify things and capture an audience."* His practice focuses on products liability defense, commercial litigation and securities dealer litigation.

The Clients: University of Michigan; the Sunflower Group; Ferndale Laboratories and Michigan Press Association.

Dickinson Wright PLLC

The Firm: The *"impressive volume and depth"* of this firm's litigation practice ensures its prominence within the Detroit market. The group has remained *"on top of its game"* by producing attorneys that are *"high quality, both intellectually and ethically,"* say clients. Its expertise across the board was also heavily endorsed. The practice encompasses a variety of commercial disputes including nationwide class actions and multidistrict litigation. The firm has also witnessed an increase in its white-collar crime caseload.

The Lawyers: Prominent in the civil litigation arena, **Lawrence Campbell** was commended for his *"effective courtroom presence."* His organizational skills and thorough preparation have impressed many. A *"bright and tenacious"* attorney, his wealth of knowledge is *"well respected by judges and opposing counsel."* Described as *"highly knowledgeable,"* **John Scott** handles a variety of disputes, including civil and appellate litigation. Business litigator **Ed Pappas** has joined this group from Miro Weiner & Kramer. An *"exceptionally talented attorney,"* his practice

GENERAL COMMERCIAL

encompasses corporate partnership and shareholder dispute litigation with an additional interest in products liability claims.

The Clients: William Beaumont Hospital; Ford; Kmart; Mellon Mortgage; Northwest Airlines; Automobile Club of Michigan; Blue Cross Blue Shield of Michigan; Florists' Transworld Delivery; Michigan Funeral Directors Association; ROSS Controls; SY Systems Technologies and Toyoda Gosei North America.

Honigman Miller Schwartz and Cohn

The Firm: The recruitment of attorneys from Miro Weiner & Kramer has increased the firm's litigation capacity. Such depth of resources ensures that this leading firm remains *"one of the principal players in the state."* It handles various types of high-end business and contractual disputes for a healthy number of Fortune 500 clients. Its *"accomplished lawyers"* have developed niche expertise in disputes arising out of such sectors as pharmaceuticals and the media. The group is also one of the few in Michigan that has the expertise to deal with election litigation. Recent highlights include the representation of Kmart in a series of complex cases against Capital One.

The Lawyers: *"Top-flight litigator"* **Joseph Aviv** joined the firm in December 2004, adding *"increased depth and greater capabilities to the group."* Clients described him as simply *"one of the smartest people I have ever met."* His practice includes shareholder class actions, and complex commercial disputes as well as a domestic relations practice. He is well known for his representation of the Taubman Centers. Chair of the firm's litigation department, **Norman Ankers** is an effective litigator, whose good staffing of cases and broad experience are widely recognized. He acts in shareholder and partnership disputes, trade secrets and complex contractual disputes. According to clients, turning to **Raymond Henney**

Michigan
Leading individuals
(Litigation: General Commercial)

★ **DRIKER Eugene** *Barris Sott*, Detroit

[1] **CAMPBELL Lawrence** *Dickinson Wright*, Detroit
  KESSLER Philip *Butzel Long*, Detroit
  VON ENDE Carl *Miller Canfield*, Detroit

[2] **AVIV Joseph** *Honigman Miller*, Detroit
  HAFFEY Dennis *Dykema Gossett*, Detroit
  POZZA Jr Clarence *Miller Canfield*, Detroit
  RASSEL Richard *Butzel Long*, Detroit
  SCOTT John *Dickinson Wright*, Detroit
  WOODS Sharon *Barris Sott*, Detroit
  YOUNG Rodger *Young & Susser*, Southfield

[3] **ANKERS Norman** *Honigman Miller*, Detroit
  DOZEMAN Douglas *Warner Norcross*, Grand Rapids
  FEENEY James *Dykema Gossett*, Bloomfield Hills
  HENNEY Raymond *Honigman Miller*, Detroit
  KAY Richard *Varnum Riddering*, Grand Rapids
  KRONK Edward *Butzel Long*, Detroit
  MUTH Jon *Miller Johnson*, Grand Rapids
  PAPPAS Edward *Dickinson Wright*, Detroit
  SANKBEIL William *Kerr Russell*, Detroit
  ZUCKERMAN Richard *Honigman Miller*, Detroit

Leading individuals
(Litigation: White-Collar Crime & Government Investigations)

[1] **CRANMER Thomas** *Miller Canfield*, Detroit
  DUMOUCHEL David *Butzel Long*, Detroit
  ZUCKERMAN Richard *Honigman Miller*, Detroit

Individuals are listed alphabetically in each band.

for advice is "*great for the company's reputation, due to his superb understanding of business practices.*" His broad commercial practice includes significant experience in the securities field, including enforcement actions by the SEC. **Richard Zuckerman** has won fans with his "*outstanding trial capabilities.*" Over the past year, he provided independent counsel to a number of public companies within Detroit during their investigations. He additionally acted in computer litigation for a public computer company and continued with more traditional work in the antitrust area.

The Clients: The firm retains its strong relationships with Detroit's leading companies and international players such as Philip Morris and Hewlett-Packard. Clients include individuals and small to midsized entities through to national and multinational companies.

Miller, Canfield, Paddock and Stone, PLC
See firm details p.1004

The Firm: "*Great strength and presence in the high end of the market,*" underscores this litigation practice. Clients spoke of its provision of "*first-rate services and a deep understanding of litigation matters.*" The group has expertise in all aspects of litigation before both state and federal courts. Over the year, the team has defended consumer financial class actions in Maryland and DC for Ford Motor Credit. Attorneys additionally represented the City of Midland, Michigan in connection with matters concerning a property valuation. Other highlights from 2004 include a role as co-counsel in Compuware v IBM and the defense of a major utility in a case against 400 employees seeking $100 million of overtime pay under the Fair Labor Standards Act. The firm was also noted for its strong white-collar crime practice.

The Lawyers: **Carl von Ende** "*commands great admiration as a trial lawyer.*" His effective strategies in court win him respect from judges and acclaim from market commentators. His broad practice encompasses IP, banking and securities disputes, tax and construction matters. He defeated a motion for a preliminary injunction in a $4 billion hostile takeover bid for the Taubman Centers, and was also successful in a significant case on behalf of Michigan State Housing Development Authority. **Clarence Pozza**'s practice encompasses commercial, securities (he has carried out an arbitration before the NYSE) and insurance litigation. In 2004, he advised Equitable in its defeat of a $45 million claim by a former shopping mall tenant. **Thomas Cranmer** combines his work in the commercial litigation field with white-collar crime defense. He joined the practice group in November 2004 from Miro Weiner & Kramer and brings to the firm his "*excellent manner with clients and expertise in the courtroom.*" He has successfully handled healthcare and securities fraud matters in addition to environmental and antitrust violations.

Band 2

Barris, Sott, Denn & Driker, PLLC

The Firm: A widely respected litigation practice provides the foundation for this midsized firm. A "*major player,*" clients identified its ability to field talented litigators with strong advocacy skills. Attorneys here are also experienced in arbitration and mediation. The group secured a federal court decision in Detroit, upholding a $12.5 million arbitration award against a brokerage house. It also carries out significant disputes on behalf of 3M.

The Lawyers: Michigan's "*premier litigator*" **Eugene Driker** received the highest accolades from experts within the field, being well versed in commercial disputes and appellate matters. Peers "*would refer to him in a heartbeat*" and praised his "*sophisticated practice – he's a great person to have on the other side of the table.*" His trial skills are commended for attaining the respect of judges. Driker recently acted for the State of Michigan in a constitutional challenge to agreements between the state and four Indian tribes that provide for casino gaming on tribal land. "*Exceptional trial lawyer*" **Sharon Woods** chairs the firm's litigation department. Her practice encompasses complex commercial disputes, construction, securities and IP litigation as well as employment matters. She is also experienced in class actions and professional malpractice defense.

The Clients: GM; DTE Energy; Dow Chemical; State of Michigan; Wayne State University; Ford and City of Detroit.

Dykema Gossett PLLC

The Firm: This full-service firm's litigation practice comprises 160 lawyers. Market commentators highlighted the firm's expertise in business litigation and noted a growing national products liability practice that handles actions arising from the automotive industry and pharmaceutical products. "*A top-level competitor,*" this group advises national Fortune 500 clients, such as Ford. Its attorneys are described as "*high-quality litigators with intellectual and ethical strengths.*"

The Lawyers: **Dennis Haffey** "*impresses with his courtroom bearing and his robust advocacy,*" reported sources. Head of the department, he acts on high-end commercial litigation in both state and federal courts. He shares with **Jim Feeney** a "*thoroughness in his case preparation and a deep understanding of the law.*" Feeney's representative clients include automobile manufacturers, media companies and pharmaceutical companies.

The Clients: The firm caters to the needs of clients in a variety of sectors including retail, banks, insurance, manufacturing, utilities, and contractors, in addition to representing small businesses, partnerships and individuals.

Band 3

Bodman LLP

The Firm: Although it is not as large as other Detroit heavyweights, clients praised the "*rich pedigree*" of the litigators based in this department. "*They have a tremendous set of skills.*" The clientele here spans from local entrepreneurs to Fortune 500 companies, which ensures the group experiences a variety of cases. Highlights from the past twelve months include successfully defending one of the nation's largest financial advisers to state and local governments in a trade secrets case. The group has also defended the financial arm of a major auto manufacturer in US district court proceedings in Detroit against claims made by a software supplier seeking up to $800 million in damages.

The Clients: Comerica; Lear; DaimlerChrysler; Henry Ford Health System; Burger King; Cendant Car Rental Group; Comcast; Roman Catholic Archdiocese of Detroit; Detroit Lions; Blue Cross Blue Shield of Michigan; Outdoor Advertising Association of Michigan; Freudenberg-NOK General Partnership; Citicorp and Symantec.

Miller, Johnson, Snell & Cummiskey, PLC

The Firm: This Grand Rapids practice group *"has made its presence felt"* with an increasing role in high-profile and complex disputes. The group's antitrust and criminal litigation expertise was especially noted, as was its ability to staff cases efficiently. The lawyers are also endorsed for their *"broad abilities, courtroom skills and professionalism."* The group's caseload features antitrust, banking and securities disputes and claims arising from the insurance sector.

The Lawyers: Skilled trial lawyer **Jon Muth** *"instantly comes to mind as a fine litigator,"* sources said. He is also respected for his mediation experience and work on employment-related disputes.

The Clients: Major national and international corporations, local and regional businesses, and individuals.

Varnum, Riddering, Schmidt & Howlett LLP

The Firm: A *"major player"* in both criminal and civil litigation, the firm fields more than 30 lawyers handling all aspects of litigation for corporations from across the region. In the past year, the firm represented Ford in a $50 million dispute regarding its provision of frames to DaimlerChrysler. The firm also handled three large employee benefits disputes for North Carolina company Mark 4 and continues to represent a large trucking company in all its litigation nationally.

The Lawyers: Head of the litigation group, **Dick Kay** has an excellent reputation for his work in commercial disputes, construction litigation, employment matters and products liability. A registered patent attorney, he is also well equipped to advise on IP matters.

The Clients: Herman Miller; Ford; Gentex and Tower Automotive.

Warner Norcross & Judd LLP

The Firm: The firm devotes approximately one-third of all its lawyers to dispute resolution. Its caseload covers general commercial litigation as well as more specialist issues such as IP, securities and, particularly over the past year, construction litigation. In a recent highlight, the group has acted as lead counsel for Wrench LLC against Taco Bell in a breach of implied contract case involving the Taco Bell Chihuahua advertising campaign. It obtained a jury verdict for Wrench of more than $30 million. Clients commended the *"exceptional trial skills"* of these attorneys, and the depth of the whole team.

The Lawyers: *"Highly respected"* **Douglas Dozeman** chairs the firm's practice group. He is well versed in state and federal litigation, handling disputes arising out of the technology, construction and IP arenas.

The Clients: The firm's clientele ranges from large national corporations to smaller partnerships and individuals.

Band 4

Clark Hill PLC

The Firm: Sources credited this firm with *"truly building up and making its presence felt"* within Michigan. A sizable department, it serves clients in the full range of trial, litigation and alternative dispute resolution. Attorneys here have experience in construction disputes arising out of the power sector, and claims relating to manufacturing plants, commercial buildings, hospitals and airports. An additional aspect to this practice is its substantial volume in the defense of insurance-related disputes.

The Clients: The firm represents national and local businesses, individuals, and governmental agencies, in federal, state and local courts.

Kerr Russell & Weber

The Firm: This smaller firm is home to a litigation department that has the experience to advise on a range of commercial disputes, such as antitrust and IP cases, insurance coverage claims and shareholder disputes. Its attorneys are also well equipped to advise on mediations and other forms of dispute resolution.

The Lawyers: *"Gentleman and scholar"* **William Sankbeil** is respected as an excellent commercial litigator. He is especially commended for his deep knowledge of antitrust matters.

The Clients: The firm advises corporations of all sizes, partnerships and individuals.

Young & Susser PC Attorneys and Counselors

The Firm: This complex litigation boutique has secured a name for itself in Michigan and beyond. Its *"practical approach"* to dispute resolution is widely admired, as are the extensive trial skills displayed by its attorneys. The group has a breadth of experience and can advise on a range of disputes, such as antitrust, IP and malpractice issues or litigation arising out of the real estate and hi-tech sectors. In a recent highlight, the group successfully represented Ferris in a dispute with a Japanese trading company, Nissho Iwai American, concerning monies owed following the purchase of a leasing company.

The Lawyers: Market sources described *"terrific lawyer"* **Rodger Young** as a trusted and highly skilled litigator. He has a command of the courtroom and a broad practice that ensures he can handle disputes from all manner of industries.

The Clients: The firm's clients include Algonquin Automotive; Aon Consulting; Kojaian Companies; Pullman Industries and Teleflex.

REAL ESTATE

Band 1

Honigman Miller Schwartz and Cohn

The Firm: This broad-based real estate department *"brings to the table everything a real estate client could wish for."* With a group of 41 *"top-quality"* attorneys, the firm houses the largest real estate transactional department in Michigan. The attorneys here are distinguished for their *"strong levels of commitment to clientele,"* and, according to clients, have *"cultivated a culture where they have strength at all positions."* Responsiveness and the ability to complete deals quickly are also appreciated. The bulk of the

practice rests predominantly on the developer side and its caseload stretches beyond the state boundaries with numerous land sales, financings and acquisitions occurring on a national level. Recent examples include an $850 million financing for a multiphase condominium project in Nevada, and advice on a $240 million secured and unsecured financing for a shopping center REIT. The group has also advised on an $80 million land sale in California, and continues to carry out high-end work for GM.

The Lawyers: Peers and clients alike singled out star practitioner **Lawrence McLaughlin** for his *"intelligence, experience and unmatchable expertise"* in the playing field. Clients described him

as *"loyal, sincere and extremely hard working."* His practice encompasses the full range of real estate matters, and includes a specialty in construction litigation. Over the past year, he has advised on the East Riverfront redevelopment project and represented developer The Mills Corporation on a number of its significant redevelopment projects. He has additionally continued to represent key client Taubman in various transactions. **Richard Burnstein** is a renowned practitioner who *"adds a ton of class to the firm."* Clients appreciate his ability to *"use the law's instruction and make exceptional deals out of it."* He adopts a common-sense approach to deals and has been heavily involved in the developer

Michigan
Leading firms (Real Estate)

1 **HONIGMAN MILLER SCHWARTZ** *Detroit*

2 **DAWDA, MANN, MULCAHY** *Bloomfield Hills*
   DICKINSON WRIGHT PLLC *Detroit*
   MILLER, CANFIELD, PADDOCK *Detroit*

3 **BARRIS, SOTT, DENN & DRIKER, PLLC** *Detroit*
   BUTZEL LONG *Detroit*
   CLARK HILL PLC *Detroit*
   DYKEMA GOSSETT PLLC *Detroit*
   JAFFE, RAITT, HEUER & WEISS, PC *Detroit*
   KERR RUSSELL & WEBER *Detroit*
   MADDIN, HAUSER, WARTELL, ROTH *Southfield*

Leading individuals (Real Estate)

★ **MCLAUGHLIN Lawrence** *Honigman Miller, Detroit*

1 **BROMBERG Stephen** *Butzel Long, Bloomfield Hills*
   DAWDA Edward *Dawda Mann, Bloomfield Hills*
   DUNN William *Clark Hill, Detroit*

2 **BARRIS William** *Barris Sott, Detroit*
   CANDLER James *Dickinson Wright, Detroit*
   DAWSON Stephen *Dickinson Wright, Bloomfield Hills*
   MADDIN Michael *Maddin Hauser, Southfield*
   SALESIN Lowell *Maddin Hauser, Southfield*
   ZUSSMAN Richard *Jaffe Raitt, Detroit*

3 **ADAMS James** *Dykema Gossett, Detroit*
   BURNSTEIN Richard *Honigman Miller, Detroit*
   HODESS Ronald *Miller Canfield, Troy*
   KOLTUN Timothy *Clark Hill, Detroit*
   LEWIS Denise *Honigman Miller, Detroit*
   MULCAHY Michael *Dawda Mann, Bloomfield Hills*
   NIX II Robert *Kerr Russell, Detroit*
   PIGGOTT Cameron *Dykema Gossett, Bloomfield Hills*
   SIMPSON James *Miller Canfield, Troy*
   WINOKUR Laurence *Dickinson Wright, Detroit*

Up-and-coming individuals
   ZELENOCK Katheryne *Miller Canfield, Troy*

Firms and individuals are listed alphabetically in each band.

has impressed many commentators, and with over half the lawyers focused on real estate: "*It's nice to see a firm specializing rather than trying to spread itself too thin,*" was a common reaction among clients. It has the capacity to attract major developers and users of real estate, including such names as Wal-Mart. For example attorneys completed numerous purchase/ground lease transactions for Wal-Mart and for Home Depot. Further recent highlights include the sale and leaseback of several Ford parts and distribution centers across the USA. The group also advised on the restructuring of a loan for a major office building in Detroit, and carried out 40 lease transactions for AMB Property's industrial portfolio across Chicago, Columbus and Cincinnati.

The Lawyers: Sources agreed that **Edward Dawda** has ensured this firm develops "*in leaps and bounds.*" One of the market's hardest working lawyers, clients preferred him "*in high-level and complicated transactions, due to his extremely strong management abilities, resourcefulness and flexibility with changeable requirements.*" He brings a win-win attitude to business negotiations and is respected for his representation of Wal-Mart. Of late, he has represented retailers and automobile manufacturers in their acquisitions and advised on construction and finance issues arising out of the sector. **Michael Mulcahy**'s strengths include the structuring of real estate transactions, including expertise in leveraged finance. He has acted in the land acquisition, development, construction and financing associated with the Royal Park Hotel, in the suburbs of Detroit. He has also been involved in the refinancing of a large office building in downtown Detroit.

The Clients: Wal-Mart; Comerica; Charter One; Fifth Third Bank; Republic Bank and The BOSC Group.

Dickinson Wright PLLC

The Firm: New depth has been added to this firm's real estate department with the addition of four members to the team. Experienced across a wide range of disciplines, these attorneys are "*high-quality technicians and pleasurable to deal with,*" reported clients. Their "*integrity and ethical stances*" on issues are also appreciated. Historically strong in lender representation, the group has struck a balance with its representation of corporate clients in real estate transactions and developers.

The Lawyers: **Steve Dawson** was distinguished as "*an expert with widespread knowledge of real estate matters.*" Clients considered his advice to be "*highly ethical and honest and always accurate.*" He represented AISIN Holdings of America in an 800-acre acquisition in Livingston County. He orchestrated the rezoning of this land for use in test track research. He also established an industrial development district gaining incentives from local government. **James Candler** combines an "*appealing, proactive style and excellent technical skills.*" He is "*not afraid of getting into the trenches and doing the groundwork*" and impresses with the thoroughness of his advice. He was recently involved in the planning of a proposed renovation of the Michigan Central Depot into new headquarters for the Detroit Police Department. He additionally carried out extensive acquisition and construction work on behalf of MGM Mirage related to its casino in Detroit. The recruitment of **Laurence Winokur** extends the remit of the practice to include increased developer representation. A deal-savvy lawyer, he "*knows his way around issues,*" and is particularly commended for his work in the retail and shopping center sector.

The Clients: Borders Group; Pacific Life Insurance; DaimlerChrysler Services North America; JPMorgan Chase; Liberty Property Trust; Connecticut General Life Insurance; MGM Mirage; Turner Construction; Finsilver/Friedman Management and Falcon Center Properties.

Miller, Canfield, Paddock and Stone, PLC

See firm details p.1004

The Firm: One of the leading firms in Michigan, this highly respected real estate department has weathered the departure of top practitioner Stephen Palms to McKinley Associates. The group impresses clients with its "*consistently high-quality advice*" and thorough drafting skills. The group has attracted a loyal following among leading banks and has represented a large stable of municipal clients – including all Michigan universities – on public-private partnership issues. The group also advised on a proposed $140 million mixed-use retail development in Ann Arbor in which the Michigan Economic Growth Authority approved $60 million of brownfield redevelopment subsidies. Attorneys further advised an international management firm on Ford Field football stadium and the Northwest Airlines Midfield Terminal project.

The Lawyers: Clients appreciate that group leader **Ronald Hodess** takes the time to "*learn the idiosyncrasies of our business – it makes him a better adviser.*" He received accolades for his "*innovative thought process*" and extensive experience. Hodess has acted on a substantial number of real estate and construction projects including the Hilton Garden project for Bank of America, and assisted Champion Enterprises in their national housing projects. He also represented the developers in issues relating to the Ford Field stadium, a $350 million project. **Jim Simpson** was described to researchers as a "*flexible adviser – able to project an aura of calm through tough and complex negotiations.*" Skilled in finance matters, he has advised Wells Fargo and LaSalle Bank on the structuring of

arena, including advice to Taubman. Commentators recognized **Denise Lewis**'s success in building a sizable practice both in the state and beyond. She is "*intelligent and highly proficient,*" and recently counseled in the development and construction of the $350 million new headquarters building for Compuware. Lewis also advised on the Book-Cadillac project, the restructuring of a landmark hotel in Detroit.

The Clients: Ramco-Gershenson Properties Trust; Larson Realty Group; Kmart; Federal Reserve Bank of Chicago; Detroit Economic Growth; The Sterling Group; Biltmore Properties; GM and Compuware.

Band 2

Dawda, Mann, Mulcahy & Sadler PLC

The Firm: An "*excellent midsized boutique,*" DMMS was rated for its high degree of transactional experience. Its commitment to the sector

international finance programs. According to clients, **Kathy Zelenock** "*always covers the bases – nothing falls through cracks.*" Extremely well prepared and "*tough when she needs to be,*" Zelenock has impressed with her work on sizable commercial real estate financings.

The Clients: The group has advised on commercial mortgage loans of various property types across the country for national, regional and local lenders. Example of its clients include: Wells Fargo; LaSalle Bank; Champion Enterprises; Burton-Katzman Development; Siemens; Goldfarb Bonding Agency; Hunt Corporation; Turner Construction; Bank of America and Kmart.

Band 3

Barris, Sott, Denn & Driker, PLLC

The Firm: Although smaller in size than some of its direct rivals, this firm is credited with having made a "*real impact,*" especially within the local real estate community. The team possesses a "*thorough understanding of the issues*" and is experienced in both real estate development and financing issues. Its "*low-key but high-caliber*" advice has attracted a healthy client list comprising banks and other financial institutions, developers and contractors.

The Lawyers: "*Top-notch lawyer*" **William Barris** is endorsed for "*bringing not only legal skills, but great business acumen to the deal table.*" Sources also commended his involvement in local issues and described him as "*a dean of the community.*" Much of his workload over the past year has involved the representation of key developer client Kojaian Companies.

The Clients: The firm's client roster features banks and developers.

Butzel Long

See firm details p.1002

The Firm: The real estate practice of this respected Detroit firm is able to call upon "*strong capabilities across the board.*" Its wide experience has elicited "*allegiance from its devoted developer clients,*" agreed sources. The team is widely regarded for its adeptness in all aspects of loan enforcement and land use issues for a clientele that spans major urban redevelopers to residential developers. Recently, the firm has been active in redevelopment issues, advising on the conversion of some Detroit public housing into a mixed income development project.

The Lawyers: The "*model of a practitioner,*" **Steve Bromberg** (see p.998) commands the highest respect and "*top accolades*" within the local real estate community for his experience and effective handling of complex cases. In 2004, he advised on the refinancing of leading hotels, alongside his work for various banks, shopping centers and mobile home parks. Rehabilitation projects for Detroit Housing Commission have

also benefited from his years of development experience.

The Clients: The firm represents an assortment of developers, contractors, lenders and investors.

Clark Hill PLC

The Firm: This group's practice encompasses "*all forms and facets*" of real estate law and provides "*honest, straightforward, customer service-oriented advice.*" It participates in multistate transactions as counsel to both borrowers and lenders and also represents developers in structuring, financing and leasing issues. In a recent highlight, the group represented a national quasi-governmental entity in a $50 million sale of a 1000-unit multifamily development. Attorneys also advised on the development and opening of Campus Martius Park in downtown Detroit for a public nonprofit foundation. Corporate real estate issues can also be found in the group's workload. For example, the team has advised in a number of investor acquisitions in New York and Chicago, and represented the YMCA of Metropolitan Detroit in site acquisition, public development agreements, and the construction of its new Detroit downtown facility. The project is valued at $30 million.

The Lawyers: "*Nationally renowned,*" **William Dunn** has played a part in pioneering Michigan real estate law. He "*knows everything about everything,*" said sources, and he advises on workouts, leasing and acquisitions. Dunn recently acted in the acquisition of a 560-acre site in Wayne County, and he continues to represent the City of Detroit as special real estate counsel. The "*first-rate*" transactional experience of **Timothy Koltun** has won him a following among peers and clients. He has advised Becker Ventures and can count major developer Centex Homes as an active client.

The Clients: Retirement System of the City of Detroit; Metropolitan Life Insurance; General Growth Properties; Disney; AIMCO; Freddie Mac; Crown Enterprises; SPX and Lincoln National Life Insurance.

Dykema Gossett PLLC

The Firm: This Detroit firm retains its powerful presence in the local market, advising clients on an extensive range of real estate matters. "*The team combines technical knowledge with an understanding of how we run our business,*" clients said. Among the group's recent highlights is its work on the sale of Marshall Field's department store. Attorneys here also acted for long-standing client Turner Construction in an arbitration in Bay City, and recently closed the acquisition of a dozen airport parking lots around the USA for its client. In the land use sphere, the group is advising on a conservation easement for more than 250,000 acres of land in Michigan.

The Lawyers: **James Adams** is leader of the real estate practice group. An "*accomplished and*

highly intelligent lawyer," clients additionally praised "*his concern for their business as well as the legal issues.*" He is real estate counsel for Pfizer and has advised in lease negotiations and tenant disputes for a Miami client. **Cameron Piggott** garnered respect for his "*creative thinking*" and ability to bring a deal to its conclusion through his "*excellent long-term perspective.*" He recently assisted a school district in conducting a $200 million program to renovate existing buildings and construct a new high school. He additionally negotiated a development agreement with a municipality involving a $60 million mixed-use project in North Michigan.

The Clients: The group has advised Kmart on its leasehold dispositions. Other clients include: Turner Construction; Finsilver/Friedman Management; Victor International; Eaton; Metro Cars and Silverman Development.

Jaffe, Raitt, Heuer & Weiss, PC

The Firm: This "*entrepreneurial, midsized firm*" benefits from a bounty of loyal customers. It undertakes real estate transactions and developments on a national level. For example, the team advised on the financing for 53 manufactured home communities spread throughout the USA, in a deal valued at $490 million. A further highlight was its advice on the conversion of a commercial purpose building into a condominium in a multifaceted transaction.

The Lawyers: **Richard Zussman** possesses "*sharp negotiation skills,*" and wins fans with his high degree of professionalism and efficient handling of deals. His practice focuses on commercial real estate development and related transactional matters. He recently completed a $390 million financing for 34 home communities spread throughout the USA.

The Clients: Sun Communities; The Farbman Group; Ram Real Estate; The Fisher Group; Sillman Enterprises; Uniprop; Crawford Realty Group; The Somerset Collection; Frankel & Associates; Northern Equities Group; Princeton Enterprises; Edgemere Enterprises and Amson Dembs.

Kerr Russell & Weber

The Firm: Smaller than some of its rivals in the market, this firm's real estate practice is endorsed as a highly commercial operation that is a popular choice for private developers and contractors. The bulk of the practice revolves around business and commercial property work. Its attorneys are well equipped to advise on leasing and financing issues, real estate development and construction matters.

The Lawyers: **Robert Nix** was described to researchers as "*a wonderful transactional lawyer.*" Proficient in negotiations, this "*dedicated lawyer*" was commended for his thoroughness and commitment to deals.

The Clients: On the client roster are private

developers, municipalities with public-private mixed-use development projects in addition to construction contractors, subcontractors and developers.

Maddin, Hauser, Wartell, Roth & Heller PC

The Firm: Representing both banks and developers, this firm secures preference among clients for its "*responsiveness, trustworthiness and efficiency in matters.*" It impresses with its practical

approach to negotiations; it is "*fair to both sides, starting in the middle rather than at opposite ends of the spectrum,*" clients said. The team also displays "*a high-quality standard of work.*" Over the past year, the group advised on the acquisition of 23 multifamily block properties in a $110 million transaction.

The Lawyers: A "*prominent figure*" in the field, **Michael Maddin** is an "*attentive and astute adviser.*" He was particularly noted for his work in commercial leasing and matters related to

mobile home parks. The "*extremely smart*" **Lowell Salesin** is "*an exceptional deal-maker.*" Clients appreciate his ability "*to provide options and find resolutions to any problem.*" He has acted for Fifth Third Bank in a number of property financings.

The Clients: The Kroger Company; Fifth Third Bank; RHP Properties and Huntington National Bank.

Leaders in Michigan

ADAMS, James
Dykema Gossett PLLC, Detroit
313 568 6800
Recommended in Real Estate

AMMON, Jeffrey
Miller, Johnson, Snell & Cummiskey, P.L.C., Grand Rapids 616 831 1700
Recommended in Corporate/M&A

ANKERS, Norman
Honigman Miller Schwartz and Cohn, Detroit 313 465 7000
Recommended in Litigation

AVIV, Joseph
Honigman Miller Schwartz and Cohn, Detroit 248 646 2400
Recommended in Litigation

BARNES, Thomas
Varnum, Riddering, Schmidt & Howlett LLP, Grand Rapids 616 336 6000
Recommended in Employment

BARRIS, William
Barris, Sott, Denn & Driker, PLLC, Detroit 313 965 9725
Recommended in Real Estate

BATTEN, Fred
Clark Hill PLC, Detroit 313 965 8300
Recommended in Employment

BERNARD, J Michael
Dykema Gossett PLLC, Detroit
313 568 6800
Recommended in Corporate/M&A

BOLTON, Richard
Dickinson Wright PLLC, Detroit
313 223 3500
Recommended in Corporate/M&A

BREAY, James
Warner Norcross & Judd LLP, Grand Rapids 616 752 2000
Recommended in Banking & Finance

BRETZ, Daniel J
Brady Hathaway Brady & Bretz, Detroit
313 965 3700
dbretz@bradyhathaway.com
Recommended in Employment
Practice Areas: Employment law consultation and litigation, including dis-

crimination, harassment, retaliation, whistleblower, breach of contract and trade secret claims. Labor law consultation and litigation, including NLRB investigations and trials, union election campaigns, collective bargaining negotiations, grievance arbitrations and contract administration. Extensive defamation and First Amendment trial and appellate experience.
Prof. Memberships: ABA (Member EEO SubCommittee, 1990-present); State Bar of Michigan (Member Labor and Employment Law Section Committee, 2001-present); American Employment Lawyers Council, (Member 1997-present).
Career: Founding Partner (1989).
Publications: Has lectured extensively before the ABA, State Bar of Michigan and Michigan ICLE groups. Author: 'FMLA Litigation, Employment Law in Michigan, An Employer's Guide, ICLE' (2d ED. in publication).
Personal: University of Michigan, AB; Wayne State University Law School, JD.

BROMBERG, Stephen A
Butzel Long, Bloomfield Hills
248 258 1616
bromberg@butzel.com
Recommended in Real Estate
Practice Areas: Represents borrowers and institutional lenders, purchasers and sellers, non profit entities and contractors and owners in all types of office, commercial, shopping center, apartment and subdivision matters, and major construction and zoning matters and workouts, reorganizations and foreclosures.
Prof. Memberships: President, American College of Mortgage Attorneys (ACMA). Member: American Judicature Society, American College of Real Estate Lawyers. Past Chair, Real Property Law Section of the State Bar of Michigan.
Career: Senior Attorney, Butzel Long. Past Director and past President, Butzel Long.
Personal: University of Michigan, 1952, with distinction, (Phi Beta Kappa). The University of Michigan Law School (JD, 1954).

BURNSTEIN, Richard
Honigman Miller Schwartz and Cohn, Detroit 313 465 7000
Recommended in Real Estate

CALZONE, David B
Vercruysse Murray & Calzone, PC, Bingham Farms 248 540 8019
Recommended in Employment

CAMPBELL, Lawrence
Dickinson Wright PLLC, Detroit
313 223 3500
Recommended in Litigation

CANDLER, James
Dickinson Wright PLLC, Detroit
313 223 3500
Recommended in Real Estate

CRANMER, Thomas
Miller, Canfield, Paddock and Stone, P.L.C., Detroit 313 963 6420
Recommended in Litigation

DAMSCHRODER, Timothy
Bodman Longley & Dahling LLP, Ann Arbor 734 761 3780
Recommended in Corporate/M&A

DAUGHERTY, Patrick D
Foley & Lardner, Detroit 313 442 6495
pdaugherty@foley.com
Recommended in Corporate/M&A
Career: Patrick Daugherty is a Partner in Foley & Lardner's Business Law Department. Mr Daugherty directs multi-office, multi-disciplinary teams of lawyers in the planning and execution of public and private offerings of equity and debt securities, structured financings, tender offers, exchange offers, restructurings, recapitalizations, mergers, acquisitions, divestitures, management buyouts, 'going private' transactions and corporate governance assignments. He regularly coaches corporate boards and committees to make business decisions that comply with the Sarbanes-Oxley Act, securities laws, stock exchange rules, corporate codes and best practices. He received his law degree, cum laude, from Cornell in 1981.

DAWDA, Edward
Dawda, Mann, Mulcahy & Sadler PLC, Bloomfield Hills 248 642 3700
Recommended in Real Estate

DAWSON, Stephen
Dickinson Wright PLLC, Bloomfield Hills
248 433 7200
Recommended in Real Estate

DEITCH, Laurence
Bodman LLP, Detroit 313 259 7777
Recommended in Corporate/M&A

DICKSON, Andrea Roumell
Butzel Long, Detroit 313 983 7440
dickson@butzel.com
Recommended in Employment
Practice Areas: Labor and employment litigation matters, representing both public and private sector organizations. Representation includes employment discrimination litigation, labor-related administrative agency proceedings, sexual harassment and wrongful discharge. Preventative counseling and training in employment and personnel-related issues.
Prof. Memberships: Past Chair, State Bar of Michigan Labor and Employment Law Council.
Career: Shareholder, Butzel Long.
Publications: Chapter author, ICLE Employment Law in 'Michigan Labor Law Handbook'.
Personal: Smith College (BA, 1978). Wayne State University Law School (JD, 1981). Judicial Clerk to Honorable Robert B Burns of the Michigan Court of Appeals.

DIEHL Jr, Robert
Bodman LLP, Detroit 313 259 7777
Recommended in Banking & Finance

DONATI, Donna
Miller, Canfield, Paddock and Stone, P.L.C., Detroit 313 963 6420
Recommended in Employment

DOZEMAN, Douglas.
Warner Norcross & Judd LLP, Grand Rapids 616 752 2000
Recommended in Litigation

DRIKER, Eugene
Barris, Sott, Denn & Driker, PLLC,
Detroit 313 965 9725
Recommended in Litigation

DUMOUCHEL, David F
Butzel Long, Detroit 313 225 7004
dumouchd@butzel.com
Recommended in Litigation
Practice Areas: Criminal defense, pro-
fessional licensure, criminal healthcare
matters, internal corporate investiga-
tions and compliance. Federal Bar Asso-
ciation Leonard Gilman Award, out-
standing criminal law practitioner, East-
ern District of Michigan (1986).
Prof. Memberships: Member: Rules
Advisory Committee, US District Court,
Eastern District of Michigan; US District
Court Committee, Magistrate Program
Evaluation; American Law Institute
Advisory Committee, Restatement of the
Law Governing Lawyers; American Col-
lege of Trial Lawyers; State Bar of Michi-
gan Criminal Code Revision Committee,
US Courts Committee, Grievance Com-
mittee; National Association of Criminal
Defense Lawyers, Director (1981). Chair:
Federal Bar Association Crime Defense
Committee; Michigan Attorney Griev-
ance Commission, 1978-85. Master of
Bench Emeritus, American Inn of Court
Ch. XI. Fellow, American Bar Founda-
tion, Michigan State Bar Foundation.
Career: Shareholder, Butzel Long.
Chair, corporate compliance and crimi-
nal defense.
Publications: 'Victim Witness Protec-
tion Act', Federal Bar Association
National Commission, 1985; 'Subpoe-
naing Lawyers', Criminal Justice Section,
Federal Bar Association, 1986; 'Plea
Negotiation', White-Collar Crime Semi-
nar, Federal Bar Association, 1986;
'Grand Jury Practice', Federal Bar Asso-
ciation, 1986-present; 'Grand Jury Prac-
tice', US District Court, New Lawyer
Seminar, 1986-present.
Personal: University of Detroit (MA,
1972). Wayne State University Law
School (JD, cum laude, 1975).

DUNN, William
Clark Hill PLC, Detroit 313 965 8300
Recommended in Real Estate

FEENEY, James
Dykema Gossett PLLC, Bloomfield Hills
248 203 0700
Recommended in Litigation

FOLTYN, David
Honigman Miller Schwartz and Cohn,
Detroit 313 465 7000
Recommended in Corporate/M&A

GIVENS, Leonard
Miller, Canfield, Paddock and Stone,
P.L.C., Detroit 313 963 6420
Recommended in Employment

HAFFEY, Dennis
Dykema Gossett PLLC, Detroit
313 568 6800
Recommended in Litigation

HANCOCK Jr, John P
Butzel Long, Detroit 313 225 7021
hancock@butzel.com
Recommended in Employment
Practice Areas: Employment litigation,
OSHA litigation, arbitrations, collective
bargaining negotiations and counseling
for various industries, public schools,
municipalities and public utilities. Trials
and hearings before the NLRB, multiple
state agencies and over 400 arbitrations
for clients.
Prof. Memberships: Past Chair, State
Bar of Michigan Labor and Employ-
ment Section. Member, American Bar
Association, Detroit Bar Association,
and Michigan Council of School Attor-
neys. Fellow, College of Labor and
Employment Attorneys. Board Member,
National Safety Council of Southeastern
Michigan.
Career: Shareholder, Butzel Long.
Publications: Articles/presentations on
numerous workplace issues.
Personal: University of Notre Dame
(BA, 1970). Duke University Law School
(JD, 1973).

HARDY, Elizabeth P
Kienbaum Opperwall Hardy & Pelton
P.L.C., Birmingham 248 645 0000
ehardy@kohp.com
Recommended in Employment
Practice Areas: Employment litigation,
preventative counseling and appellate work.
Prof. Memberships: Member, Model
Civil Jury Instruction Committee
(Michigan Supreme Court appointee)
(2005-); Co-Chair, Judicial Qualifica-
tions Committee, State Bar of Michigan
(1998-September, 2004); Member, Judicial Selection Committee, State Bar of
Michigan (1991-1994; 1996-2004);
Member, LAWPAC Board of Directors
(1996-2002); Co-Chair, Professionalism
Committee, Oakland County Bar Asso-
ciation (1995-1996).
Career: George Washington University
(BA, with high honors, 1978); Wayne
State University (JD, 1984); editor in
chief, 'Wayne Law Review' (1983-84);
named 'One of Detroit's Most Influen-
tial Women,' Crain's Detroit Business,
1997; named 'Lawyer of the Year,' Michi-
gan Lawyers Weekly, 2004. Public Office:
Member 1991-, Chair 1995-97, Wayne
State University Board of Governors;
Chair 1996-97, Presidential Selection
Advisory Committee, Wayne State Uni-
versity. Member 2001-03, State Board of
Canvassers; Member 1996-98, Detroit
Medical Center Board of Trustees;
Member 1998-2001, Karmanos Cancer
Institute Board of Trustees and Execu-
tive Committee; Member 1995, Gover-
nor Engler's Task Force on Election Law
Reform. Partner, Dickinson Wright
Moon VanDusen & Freeman, 1990-97;
founding partner, Kienbaum Opperwall
Hardy & Pelton, PLC, 1997-.
Publications: Numerous papers pre-
sented on behalf of the State Bar Labor
& Employment Law Section and the

National Employment Law Institute,
Denver, CO.
Personal: Born in Traverse City, Michigan,
1955; married to Thomas G Kienbaum.

HATHAWAY, Thomas
Brady Hathaway Brady & Bretz, Detroit
313 965 3700
Recommended in Employment

HENNEY, Raymond
Honigman Miller Schwartz and Cohn,
Detroit 313 465 7000
Recommended in Litigation

HODESS, Ronald E
Miller, Canfield, Paddock and Stone,
P.L.C., Troy 248 879 2000
Recommended in Real Estate

HOWLETT, Timothy
Dickinson Wright PLLC, Detroit
313 223 3500
Recommended in Employment

JAFFE, Ira
Jaffe, Raitt, Heuer & Weiss, PC, Detroit
313 961 8380
Recommended in Corporate/M&A

JOHNSON, Donald
Varnum, Riddering, Schmidt & Howlett
LLP, Grand Rapids 616 336 6000
*Recommended in Banking & Finance,
Corporate/M&A*

JOSWICK, David
Miller, Canfield, Paddock and Stone,
P.L.C., Troy 248 879 2000
Recommended in Corporate/M&A

KAY, Richard
Varnum, Riddering, Schmidt & Howlett
LLP, Grand Rapids 616 336 6000
Recommended in Litigation

KESSLER, Philip J
Butzel Long, Detroit 313 225 7018
kessler@butzel.com
Recommended in Litigation
Practice Areas: Prosecution and
defense of a wide variety of business disputes on behalf of individuals, partnerships, and private and public corporations. Antitrust litigation, audit malpractice, bankruptcy litigation, contract
litigation, corporate control contests,
distributorship litigation, false advertising claims, health care and pharmaceutical counseling and litigation; intellectual
property litigation (including copyright,
trademark, trade secrets and unfair
competition and patent infringement
claims), intra-corporate and partnership
disputes, merger and acquisition-related
litigation, probate and trust litigation
and securities fraud claims. United
States Court of Appeals for the Sixth
Circuit, the Michigan Court of Appeals,
the United States District Court for the
Eastern and Western Districts of Michigan and multiple county Circuit Courts.
Prof. Memberships: Life Member, United States Court of Appeals, Sixth Circuit
Judicial Conference. Fellow, American
College of Trial Lawyers. Fellow, Inter-

national Society of Barristers. Fellow,
American Bar Foundation. Fellow,
Michigan State Bar Foundation. Mem-
ber and Chair, Local Rules Advisory
Committee, United States District Court
for the Eastern District of Michigan.
Career: President, Butzel Long. Mem-
ber, Board of Directors.
Personal: The University of Michigan
(1969, AB, with distinction). School of
Law of the University of California at
Berkeley (1972).

KHOREY, David
Varnum, Riddering, Schmidt & Howlett
LLP, Grand Rapids 616 336 6000
Recommended in Employment

KIENBAUM, Thomas
Kienbaum Opperwall Hardy & Pelton
P.L.C., Birmingham 248 645 0000
tkienbaum@kohp.com
Recommended in Employment
Practice Areas: Employment litigation
with emphasis on complex or class
actions; traditional labor relations.
Prof. Memberships: State Bars of
Michigan and Illinois; Fellow, American
and State Bar of Michigan Foundations;
College of Labor and Employment
Lawyers; Advisory Board, National
Employment Law Institute; Former
President of the State Bar of Michigan.
Career: BA, University of Michigan,
1965; JD, Magna Cum Laude (Order of
the Coif) Wayne State University, 1968;
associate, partner and Chair of Employment Practices Group, Dickinson
Wright Moon Van Dusen & Freeman,
1968-97; founding partner, Kienbaum
Opperwall Hardy & Pelton, PLC, 1997-
present.
Publications: Various, including papers
presented on behalf of the National
Employment Law Institute, and Institute of Continuing Legal Education.
Personal: Born in Berlin, Germany,
1942; married to Elizabeth Hardy,
founding partner, Kienbaum Opperwall
Hardy & Pelton, PLC .

KLIMKO, Justin
Butzel Long, Detroit 313 225 7037
klimkojg@butzel.com
Recommended in Corporate/M&A
Practice Areas: Extensive experience in
securities regulation, corporate financing, mergers and acquisitions and general corporate matters. Specific experience
with biotechnology and life sciences
companies. Focuses on securities regulation matters for publicly and privately
held companies. Planning, negotiating
and implementing various types of
merger and acquisition transactions,
representing both acquiring and
acquired companies. Significant experience advising and representing special
committees of boards of directors.
Prof. Memberships: Past Chair, State
Bar of Michigan Business Law Section.
Co-Chair, Business Law Section, Corporate Laws Committee. Past Chair, Busi-

ness Law Section, Ad Hoc Committee on Legal Opinions in Business Transactions. Member, American Bar Association, Legal Opinions Committee, Negotiated Acquisitions Committee, and Federal Regulation of Securities Committee.
Career: Shareholder, Butzel Long. Practice Group Manager - transaction and finance.
Publications: Frequent lectures and articles on business law subjects and has served as general editor of a treatise on Michigan Business Forms and a contributing author for a treatise on Michigan contract law.
Personal: Ohio University (BA, summa cum laude, 1977). Duke University (JD, with distinction, 1980).

KOLTUN, Timothy
Clark Hill PLC, Detroit 313 965 8300
Recommended in Real Estate

KRONK, Edward M
Butzel Long, Detroit 313 225 7017
kronk@butzel.com
Recommended in Litigation
Practice Areas: Litigation involving products liability defense, commercial litigation and securities dealer litigation.
Prof. Memberships: State Bar of Michigan; teaching with the Michigan Institute for Continuing Legal Education; faculty of the National Institute of Trial Advocacy; member and past presdident of the Eastern District of Michigan Chapter of the Federal Bar Association; past president of the Michigan Defense Trial Counsel; fellow of the American College of Trial Lawyers; and listed in 'Best Lawyers in America.'
Career: Shareholder, Butzel Long.
Personal: University of Michigan (JD 1971); College of the Holy Cross (AB 1968).

KUNZ, Donald
Honigman Miller Schwartz and Cohn, Detroit 313 465 7000
Recommended in Corporate/M&A

LARSEN, Tracy
Barnes & Thornburg, Grand Rapids 616 742 3930
Recommended in Corporate/M&A

LEWIS, Denise
Honigman Miller Schwartz and Cohn, Detroit 313 465 7000
Recommended in Real Estate

MADDIN, Michael
Maddin, Hauser, Wartell, Roth & Heller PC, Southfield 248 354 4030
Recommended in Real Estate

MAKENS, Hugh
Warner Norcross & Judd LLP, Grand Rapids 616 752 2000
Recommended in Corporate/M&A

MARCH, Jon
Miller, Johnson, Snell & Cummiskey, P.L.C., Grand Rapids 616 831 1700
Recommended in Employment

MCCALLUM, Charles
Warner Norcross & Judd LLP, Grand Rapids 616 752 2000
Recommended in Corporate/M&A

MCLAUGHLIN, Lawrence
Honigman Miller Schwartz and Cohn, Detroit 313 465 7000
Recommended in Real Estate

MCLEOD, David
Miller, Canfield, Paddock and Stone, P.L.C., Detroit 313 963 6420
Recommended in Banking & Finance

MINKUS, Daniel
Clark Hill PLC, Detroit 313 965 8300
Recommended in Corporate/M&A

MOSCOW, Cyril
Honigman Miller Schwartz and Cohn, Detroit 313 465 7000
Recommended in Corporate/M&A

MULCAHY, Michael
Dawda, Mann, Mulcahy & Sadler PLC, Bloomfield Hills 248 642 3700
Recommended in Real Estate

MURPHY, Lawrence
Varnum, Riddering, Schmidt & Howlett LLP, Grand Rapids 616 336 6000
Recommended in Employment

MURRAY, Gregory
Vercruysse Murray & Calzone, PC, Bingham Farms 248 540 8019
Recommended in Employment

MUTH, Jon
Miller, Johnson, Snell & Cummiskey, P.L.C., Grand Rapids 616 831 1700
Recommended in Litigation

NIEHOFF, Leonard M
Butzel Long, Detroit 734 213 3625
niehoff@butzel.com
Recommended in Employment
Practice Areas: Litigation, involving media law, higher education law, civil rights, constitutional law, First Amendment and employment issues.
Prof. Memberships: Member of the First Amendment and Media Litigation Section of the American Bar Association and National Association of College and Unviersity Attorneys. Board Member C.S. Mott Children's Hospital, the Michigan Theater Foundation and the University Musical Society.
Career: Shareholder, Butzel Long.
Personal: University of Michigan (JD 1984); University of Michigan (BA 1981).

NIX II, Robert
Kerr Russell & Weber, Detroit 313 961 0200
Recommended in Real Estate

NORRIS, Megan
Miller, Canfield, Paddock and Stone, P.L.C., Detroit 313 963 6420
Recommended in Employment

OOSTERHOUSE, Carl
Varnum, Riddering, Schmidt & Howlett LLP, Grand Rapids 616 336 6000
Recommended in Corporate/M&A

PAPPAS, Edward H
Dickinson Wright PLLC, Detroit 313 223 3500
Recommended in Litigation

PIGGOTT, Cameron
Dykema Gossett PLLC, Bloomfield Hills 248 203 0700
Recommended in Real Estate

POZZA Jr, Clarence
Miller, Canfield, Paddock and Stone, P.L.C., Detroit 313 963 6420
Recommended in Litigation

RASSEL, Richard E
Butzel Long, Detroit 313 225 7014
rassel@butzel.com
Recommended in Litigation
Practice Areas: Business litigation, concentration in media law, libel and slander law, and complex business disputes. Certified Judge Advocate for the US Navy Judge Advocate School.
Prof. Memberships: Chair, Multi-Disciplinary Practice Committee, State Bar of Michigan. Past Chair, Media and Law Committee, State Bar of Michigan. Vice-Chair, Media and Law Committee, ABA; Chair, Tort Reform Committee, Media Law Resource Center; Chair, Administrative Committee of Lex Mundi. Fellow, American College of Trial Lawyers.
Career: Chairman and CEO, Butzel Long.
Publications: Numerous professional publications and presentations
Personal: University of Notre Dame (BA, 1964). University of Michigan Law School (JD, 1966).

RENTENBACH, Paul
Dykema Gossett PLLC, Detroit 313 568 6800
Recommended in Corporate/M&A

RIBACK, Ronald
Miller, Canfield, Paddock and Stone, P.L.C., Troy 248 879 2000
Recommended in Banking & Finance

RITOK, Joseph
Dykema Gossett PLLC, Detroit 313 568 6800
Recommended in Employment

SALESIN, Lowell
Maddin, Hauser, Wartell, Roth & Heller PC, Southfield 248 354 4030
Recommended in Real Estate

SANKBEIL, William
Kerr Russell & Weber, Detroit 313 961 0200
Recommended in Litigation

SCHWARTZ, Alan
Honigman Miller Schwartz and Cohn, Detroit 313 465 7000
Recommended in Corporate/M&A

SCOTT, John
Dickinson Wright PLLC, Detroit 313 223 3500
Recommended in Litigation

SEMPLE, Lloyd
Dykema Gossett PLLC, Detroit 313 568 6800
Recommended in Corporate/M&A

SERYAK, Richard
Miller, Canfield, Paddock and Stone, P.L.C., Detroit 313 963 6420
Recommended in Employment

SHEVNOCK, Colleen
Dickinson Wright PLLC, Detroit 313 223 3500
Recommended in Banking & Finance

SHIELD, William
Dickinson Wright PLLC, Detroit 313 223 3500
Recommended in Banking & Finance

SHULMAN, Larry
Bodman LLP, Detroit 313 259 7777
Recommended in Banking & Finance

SIMPSON, James
Miller, Canfield, Paddock and Stone, P.L.C., Troy 248 879 2000
Recommended in Real Estate

SOUBLY, Diane
Vercruysse Murray & Calzone, PC, Bingham Farms 248 540 8019
Recommended in Employment

VERCRUYSSE, Robert
Vercruysse Murray & Calzone, PC, Bingham Farms 248 540 8019
Recommended in Employment

VON ENDE, Carl
Miller, Canfield, Paddock and Stone, P.L.C., Detroit 313 963 6420
Recommended in Litigation

WATSON, Jerome
Miller, Canfield, Paddock and Stone, P.L.C., Detroit 313 963 6420
Recommended in Employment

WINOKUR, Laurence
Dickinson Wright PLLC, Detroit 313 223 3500
Recommended in Real Estate

WOODS, Sharon
Barris, Sott, Denn & Driker, PLLC, Detroit 313 965 9725
Recommended in Litigation

YOUNG, Rodger
Young & Susser PC Attorneys and Counselors, Southfield 248 353 8620
Recommended in Litigation

ZELENOCK, Katheryne L
Miller, Canfield, Paddock and Stone, P.L.C., Troy 248 879 2000
Recommended in Real Estate

ZUCKERMAN, Richard
Honigman Miller Schwartz and Cohn, Detroit 313 465 7000
Recommended in Litigation

ZUSSMAN, Richard
Jaffe, Raitt, Heuer & Weiss, PC, Detroit 313 961 8380
Recommended in Real Estate

BRADY HATHAWAY BRADY & BRETZ, P.C.

THE FIRM

Founding Partners: John F Brady, Thomas M J Hathaway,
Thomas P Brady, Daniel J Bretz

Number of partners: 6

Number of associates: 3

HEAD OFFICE

MICHIGAN
535 Griswold Street, 1330 Buhl Building, **Detroit**, MI 48226
Tel: 313 965 3700   **Fax:** 313 965 2830
Email: brady@bradyhathaway.com
Website: www.bradyhathaway.com

FIRM OVERVIEW: Founded in 1989, Brady Hathaway Brady & Bretz, P.C. ('Brady Hathaway') specializes in counseling and representing management in all aspects of labor and employment law. Brady Hathaway has proven expertise in the areas of employment counseling and litigation, labor law, general litigation and appellate law. The firm has a national reputation as 'The Employer's Lawyer.' In terms of size, the firm is comparable to a labor and employment department found in large 'general practice' law firms. Yet, unlike many big firms, all of the attorneys at Brady Hathaway are specialized litigators with 'first chair' experience in some of the regions most complex and high profile cases. Collectively, the members of Brady Hathaway possess over 135 years of concentrated experience. Clients of all sizes appreciate the value added by having nimble and responsive attorneys who have a proven track record in handling their particular employment matter. The attorneys at Brady Hathaway place a strong emphasis on prompt and open communication at all levels with clients. The firm is committed to premier investigation, reporting and handling of sensitive legal matters. The goal is a cost-effective deployment of veteran legal talent specializing in a complex and fluid area of the law.

MAIN AREAS OF PRACTICE:

Employment Law Experience: In the area of civil rights and employment litigation, the attorneys at Brady Hathaway have successfully defended clients against lawsuits alleging discrimination, harassment, breach of express or implied contract, public policy discharge, promissory estoppel, whistleblower, retaliation, defamation, interference with a contract, misrepresentation, fraud, and invasion of privacy. Brady Hathaway has represented employers faced with single-plaintiff suits as well as complex multi-plaintiff and class action proceedings. Brady Hathaway has strong credentials at all levels of federal and state trial and appellate courts. The firm has also appeared in other forums including employment discrimination administrative tribunals such as the EEOC, the Michigan Department of Civil Rights, and various other states' Civil Rights agencies. The firm counsels clients on a daily basis and has conducted investigations into sexual and racial harassment complaints. The firm has extensive experience with affirmative action plans and was the first law firm to successfully certify a client's affirmative action plan with the Michigan Department of Civil Rights. While most of the firm's practice is centered in Michigan, it has represented clients nationwide and has rendered employment advice based on the law of other states including Alabama, Arizona, California, Colorado, Florida, Georgia, Illinois, Indiana, Iowa, Kansas, Massachusetts, Michigan, Minnesota, Missouri, New York, North Carolina, Ohio, Pennsylvania, Texas and Utah.

Brady Hathaway develops, drafts, and reviews employment manuals and policies regarding all facets of employment law, including harassment, equal employment opportunity, at-will employment, employee evaluations, fringe benefits, drug testing, sick leave, rules of conduct, attendance control, and the Family and Medical Leave Act. The firm has also worked with management to develop and defend high-level employment contracts, such as stock option agreements, change of control contracts, and covenants regarding confidentiality, trade secrets and competition.

Labor Law Experience: Brady Hathaway possesses some of the leading traditional labor lawyers in the region. The firm has extensive trial and investigatory experience before the National Labor Relations Board (NLRB) and the Michigan Employment Relations Commission (MERC).

The firm has also handled numerous union organizational campaigns, and provides key supervisor training, development of policies, and advice on sound, practical employment relations. Brady Hathaway represents numerous private and public employers in collective bargaining negotiations. In the role of chief negotiator, the firm has negotiated labor contracts that meet the client's economic and efficiency objectives while maintaining labor peace. The firm's attorneys have also handled a broad range of traditional labor matters for governmental and nonprofit entities, including interest-based bargaining, 'Act 312 arbitrations,' mediation-based bargaining, and fact-finding proceedings. The firm also advises clients on the administration of collective bargaining agreements and the drafting of contract language to avoid unnecessary grievances. The firm has tried hundreds of contract interpretation and discipline arbitrations.

General Legal Experience: Brady Hathaway is 'AV' rated (the highest rating available) in the Martindale-Hubbell Law Firm Directory. Each of the five shareholders is also 'AV' rated, as are two of the firm's associates. Martindale-Hubbell is the facilitator of a peer review process that rates lawyers in two categories - legal ability and general ethical standards.

In a recent edition of The Best Lawyers of America, 14 attorneys were listed as 'the best' management and labor employment lawyers in the Metropolitan Detroit area. Two of those 14 are members of Brady Hathaway.

CLIENTS: Brady Hathaway has represented a broad range of clients from small local firms to large national and international businesses. The firm has been selected as panel counsel by several insurance firms to defend profit and nonprofit entities under employment practices liability insurance policies. The firm is frequently selected by other attorneys and judges to represent and counsel their law firms and legal entities in labor and employment matters, from representing more than 30 law firms, as well as the Michigan State Court Administrative Office, the 24th, 34th and 36th District Courts, the Detroit Metropolitan Bar Association and the Michigan Attorney Grievance Commission. Included in the firm's national clients are ACE USA, Atlantic Coast Airlines, The Bartech Group, CertainTeed Corporation, Compuware Corporation, Cooper Standard Automotive, Inc., Florists TransWorld Delivery, Inc., Honeybaked Ham Company, K-Mart Corporation, Modis Professional Services, Inc., Pall Corporation, Paul Arpin Van Lines, Inc., R.L. Polk and Company, Schering-Plough Corporation, Shaw Industries, Inc., Spirit Airlines, Inc., Sprint, TI Group Automotive Systems, Tiffany & Company, U-Haul International, USF Holland, Inc., Walbridge Aldinger, and Wallside Windows.

Brady Hathaway has a particular expertise in representing health care providers. The firm represents Trinity Health Systems, St. Joseph Mercy Oakland Hospital, St. Mary's of Livonia Hospital, St. Joseph Mercy Ann Arbor Hospital, Battle Creek Health Systems, Ascension Health, Botsford General Hospital, Mercy Memorial Hospital, Community Emergency Medical Services, and a number of nursing homes. Among the governmental and nonprofit clients of the firm are Macomb Community College, Oakland Community College, Wayne County Community College, Wayne State University, Eastern Michigan University Foundation, Michigan State University Foundation, the School Districts of Detroit, Bloomfield Hills, Highland Park and Riverview, Genesee County, the Cities of Hazel Park, Highland Park, Novi, Royal Oak, Troy, Oklahoma City, Oklahoma and Colorado Springs, Colorado and, the Townships of Northville, Plymouth and Shelby.

BUTZEL LONG

THE FIRM

Chairman & CEO: Richard E Rassel
President: Philip J Kessler
Chief Marketing Officer: Joseph J Melnick

Number of partners: 109
Number of other lawyers: 100

AREAS OF PRACTICE:

Litigation 35%
Corporate/Tax/Real Estate/Wealth Planning 35%
Labor/Employment/Benefits/Immigration 30%

FIRM OVERVIEW: The firm is one of Michigan's leading law firms, with over 200 lawyers and seven offices in Michigan and Florida and two alliance offices in Beijing and Shanghai. Since its founding in 1854, the firm has played a prominent role in the development of Michigan as a research, industrial and manufacturing center. The firm strives to be on the cutting edge of significant trends and developments in the business world including advanced technology and manufacturing, e-commerce, internet law, and global operations and transactions. The firm's approach is to provide a personalized attorney-client relationship based on a recognition of, and responsiveness to, each client's unique concerns and requirements. It seeks a clear understanding of the business needs of each client through industry-focused research, knowledge management and partnering relationships. A distinguishing advantage of the firm is a commitment to providing 'value added' counseling and advice to its clients. It is dedicated to providing full value for every dollar invested in legal services. Fees and billing mechanisms are structured to fit each client's situation. The firm's clients can expect superlative service and uncompromising work quality delivered in a cost-effective manner.

MAIN AREAS OF PRACTICE:

Litigation: Litigation remains one of the firm's core practice strengths throughout its 150 year history. Several areas of concentration provide representation throughout the United States. The firm continues its tradition of landmark, precedent setting matters in litigation. The practice consists of skilled attorneys who by expertise and experience specialize in finding solutions for disputes arising out of business transactions and operations. The range of business matters include complex business disputes, IP litigation, product liability, class actions, antitrust and constitutional law.
Corporate/Tax/Real Estate/Wealth Planning: The firm has a reputation as leader on all types of transaction and compliance issues. Representative clients include Fortune 500 companies; non-US global concerns; private companies; technology and service companies; business start-ups. The firm maintains a depth of experience in all areas of corporate advice and counsel.
Labor/Employment/Benefits/Immigration: The firm is the established leader in all areas of workforce issues. Clients from around the globe are advised on all aspects of employment concerns. Former partner is Chair of the US National Labor Relations Board. The firm maintains the largest immigration and employee benefits practices in Michigan.

HEAD OFFICE

MICHIGAN
150 West Jefferson, Suite 100, **Detroit**, MI 48226
Tel: 313 225 7000   **Fax:** 313 225 7080
E-mail: info@butzel.com
Website: www.butzel.com

BRANCH OFFICES

FLORIDA
1200 North Federal Highway, Suite 420, **Boca Raton**, FL 33432
Tel: 561 368 2151   **Fax:** 561 368 4668

801 Laurel Oak Drive, Suite 705, **Naples**, FL 34108
Tel: 239 597 4500   **Fax:** 239 597 5623

MICHIGAN
350 S. Main Street, Suite 300, **Ann Arbor**, MI 48104
Tel: 734 995 3110   **Fax:** 734 995 1777

100 Bloomfield Hills Parkway, Suite 200, **Bloomfield Hills**, MI 48304
Tel: 248 258 1616   **Fax:** 248 258 1439

25 West 8th Street, Suite 200, **Holland**, MI 49423
Tel: 616 396 8860   **Fax:** 616 396 1771

110 West Michigan Avenue, Suite 1100, **Lansing**, MI 48933
Tel: 517 372 6622   **Fax:** 517 372 6672

INTERNATIONAL OFFICES

The firm also has alliance offices in Beijing and Shanghai.

INTERNATIONAL WORK: The firm has broad experience in all manner of international issues. A cross-disciplinary Global Trade and Transactions Group represents client interests throughout the world. The firm has developed a thriving Global Automotive Practice. The firm's lawyers serve as key advisors to automotive companies from Canada, the UK, France, Germany, other European suppliers, Japan, Korea and China. Special focus on developing economies of China and Mexico. Recently formed China Alliance to provide on-the-ground capabilities in Shanghai and Beijing. A founding member of Lex Mundi, a firm shareholder is the past Chair of the organization. Firm shareholder named by British Consulate as Honorary Consul of the United Kingdom for Michigan and is President of the Michigan Chapter of the British American Business Council. The firm has the largest immigration practice in Michigan serving in-bound and outbound business executives and engineers and their families. They serve as North American counsel to several non-US based multinationals.

BUTZEL LONG
ATTORNEYS AND COUNSELORS

KIENBAUM OPPERWALL HARDY & PELTON, P.L.C.

THE FIRM

Managing Partner: Thomas G Kienbaun
Administrative Partner: Eric J Pelton

Number of partners: 4
Number of other lawyers: 10

FIRM OVERVIEW: With offices in Oakland County and Detroit, Michigan, Kienbaum Opperwall Hardy & Pelton, P.L.C. specializes in counseling and representing management clients in all facets of employment and labor law, including discrimination and wrongful discharge litigation, traditional labor relations, employment contracts and policies, trade secret and covenant not to compete issues, alternative dispute resolution, ERISA litigation, appellate practice, and preventive counseling. Working in partnership with its clients, the firm assists employers in meeting the challenges of the contemporary workplace, which involves a myriad of federal and state statutes, as well as countless other legal, practical, and business issues.

The firm's distinctive 'boutique' practice style and philosophy offer its clients a highly focused, proactive, strategic, and resource-conscious approach to avoiding if possible, confronting when necessary, and efficiently resolving the many workplace issues and claims that face American employers today. A sizable segment of the practice consists of complex multi-state litigation including class action lawsuits brought under various labor and employment statutes or theories. The firm represents many clients on a regional or national basis.

The firm was founded in May 1997 by four partners from a major Detroit law firm, and all of its attorneys have substantial large-firm, large-corporation, or equivalent experience. All the firm's attorneys have devoted their careers to this specialized field and do not have to 'reinvent the wheel' with each new representation. In addressing the needs for each client and each representation, the firm draws on its attorneys' individual talents and wide-ranging experiences in the field to deliver large-firm effectiveness at small-firm cost-efficiencies that it passes on to its clients.

Among the firm's members are several of the region's most recognized and successful employment and labor attorneys, who are frequent lecturers for the prestigious National Employment Law Institute and other business education programs. The firm also publishes a periodic newsletter, *Employment and Labor Law Insight*, to keep its clients informed of developments in this fast-moving field.

MAIN AREAS OF PRACTICE: Kienbaum Opperwall Hardy & Pelton, P.L.C. provides employment and labor law services in the following areas:
Preventive Counseling: Personnel policies and handbooks; workforce reductions; sexual harassment; employee discipline and terminations; workplace investigations; affirmative action; supervisory training; employment contracts; covenants not to compete; arbitration procedures; wage and hour compliance; disability and family leave issues; drug and alcohol issues.

HEAD OFFICE

MICHIGAN
325 South Old Woodward Avenue, **Birmingham**, MI 48009
Tel: 248 645 0000   **Fax:** 248 645 1385

Website: www.kohp.com
Email: kohpinfo@kohp.com

BRANCH OFFICE

MICHIGAN
660 Woodward Avenue, Suite 1037, **Detroit**, MI 48226
Tel: 313 961 3926   **Fax:** 313 961 3945

Employment Litigation: Wrongful discharge and discrimination suits; defamation and other workplace torts; injunction suits; administrative claims; appeals; alternative dispute resolution.
Traditional Labor Relations: Union organizing; collective bargaining; contract administration and arbitration; NLRB matters; specialized labor injunctions; interest arbitrations.

CLIENTS: American General Corporation; Avis Rent A Car System, Inc.; Blue Cross Blue Shield of Michigan; College for Creative Studies; Comcast Cable Communications, Inc.; Crain Communications, Inc.; DaimlerChrysler Corporation; DaimlerChrysler Services; Deloitte & Touche; DTE Energy Company, Inc.; Eaton Corporation; Federal-Mogul Corporation; Ford Motor Company; The Hertz Corporation; Pepsi Bottling Group, Inc.; Rent-A-Center, Inc.; U-Haul International; Vance International; Wal-Mart Stores, Inc.; YUM Brands, Inc.

KIENBAUM OPPERWALL
HARDY & PELTON, P.L.C.
ATTORNEYS AND COUNSELORS

MILLER, CANFIELD, PADDOCK AND STONE, P.L.C.

THE FIRM

Chief Executive Officer: Thomas W Linn
Deputy CEO: Beverly Hall Burns
Attorneys: 330
Legal assistants: 50+
Support staff: 300+

FIRM OVERVIEW: Founded in 1852, Miller, Canfield, Paddock and Stone, P.L.C., is one of the largest and longest established law firms in Michigan. With eight offices in Michigan, and other offices in New York City, Washington, DC, Pensacola, Florida, Windsor, Ontario, Canada, and in Gdynia, Katowice, and Warsaw, Poland, Miller Canfield provides a broad range of integrated services to meet the needs of clients. Working together with the US offices, the offices in Poland expand the firm's reach to clients throughout Eastern Europe, and the Windsor, Ontario office broadens the firm's ability to offer clients seamless cross-border representation to organizations interested in doing business in North America. Miller Canfield's leadership position is an advantage it shares with each of its clients. Currently, Miller Canfield represents seven of the top 10 Fortune 500 companies and over 20% of the overall list. For nearly 75 years, the firm has served as Martindale-Hubbell's reviser law firm for the state of Michigan's law section. Several of the firm's attorneys belong to prestigious American Colleges, including the College of Labor and Employment Lawyers, and the American Colleges of Bond Counsel, Employee Benefits, Tax Counsel, Trial Lawyers, and Trust and Estate Counsel.

MAIN AREAS OF PRACTICE: The practice groups of the firm are: bankruptcy; business and finance; environmental and regulatory; federal tax and employee benefits; financial institutions/transactions; healthcare; intellectual property and information technology; international business; labor and employment; litigation, including dispute resolution, product litigation and torts, product safety, and state and local tax; personal services; public law; and real estate. Other specialty areas include assisted living facilities; automotive; aviation and transportation; Canadian law; capital markets lending; construction; corporate discovery management; criminal defense; export control; governmental entities; high-technology ventures; housing; immigration; insurance; international trade and customs and tax and transfer pricing; minority business; nonprofit and charitable organizations; professional firms; schools; and telecommunications. For contact information, visit www.millercanfield.com.

CLIENTS: The firm represents clients diverse in size and character. Attorneys represent individuals in their personal and business concerns, trusts and estates, publicly traded and multinational companies, and many startup, small- and medium-sized businesses. Clients also include public bodies such as the state of Michigan and many of its agencies, authorities and universities, cities, counties, townships, school and community college districts, and special authorities throughout the state. The firm represents many nonprofit, tax-exempt institutions, such as hospitals, charitable corporations and professional associations.

INTERNATIONAL WORK: The firm has dedicated an entire practice group, the International Business Group, to provide legal services to US and foreign multinational companies, banks, and other clients whose business affairs are tied to the increasingly interdependent world economy. The firm handles work in Arabic, Danish, Dutch, French, German, Greek, Haitian Creole, Hebrew, Hindi, Italian, Japanese, Macedonian, Norwegian, Polish, Portuguese, Punjabi, Russian, Spanish, Swedish, Ukrainian and Yiddish.

HEAD OFFICE

MICHIGAN
150 W. Jefferson, Suite 2500, **Detroit,** MI 48226
Tel: 313 963 6420
Email: linn@millercanfield.com
Website: www.millercanfield.com

OTHER US OFFICES

MICHIGAN
101 North Main Street, 7th Floor, **Ann Arbor,** MI 48104
Tel: 734 663 2445

99 Monroe Avenue, NW, Suite 1200, **Grand Rapids,** MI 49503
Tel: 616 454 8656

444 West Michigan Avenue, **Kalamazoo,** MI 49007
Tel: 269 381 7030

One Michigan Avenue, Suite 900, **Lansing,** MI 48933
Tel: 517 487 2070

840 West Long Lake Road, Suite 200, **Troy,** MI 48098
Tel: 248 879 2000

FLORIDA
25 West Cedar Street, Suite 500, **Pensacola,** FL 32501
Tel: 850 469 1088

NEW YORK
1450 Broadway, 41st Floor, **New York,** NY 10018
Tel: 212 704 4400

DISTRICT OF COLUMBIA
1900 K Street, NW, Suite 880, **Washington,** DC 20006
Tel: 202 429 5575

INTERNATIONAL OFFICES

The firm also has offices in Windsor, Ontario, Canada and in Gdynia, Katowice, and Warsaw, Poland.

CONTACTS

Detroit	Thomas Parachini
Ann Arbor	Timothy Sochocki
Grand Rapids	Mark Putney
Kalamazoo	John Campbell
Lansing	Michael Atkins
Troy	Kenneth Konop
Pensacola	Richard Lott
New York	Gregory Curtner
Washington, DC	John Renken

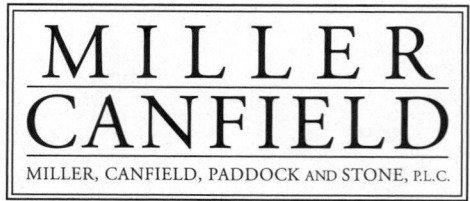

MILLER CANFIELD
MILLER, CANFIELD, PADDOCK AND STONE, P.L.C.

MINNESOTA

CONTENTS: Corporate/M&A p.1005; Employment p.1007; Litigation p.1010; Real Estate p.1014; Individuals' Profiles p.1017; Firms' Profiles p.1022.

How lawyers are ranked

The opinions we gather from clients — mainly from in-house lawyers but also from other purchasers of legal services — are balanced by opinions from colleagues and competitors. Together, they provide two different perspectives — an all-round view — and biased viewpoints cancel each other out.

CORPORATE/M&A

Minnesota
Leading firms (Corporate/M&A)

1 DORSEY & WHITNEY LLP *Minneapolis*
FAEGRE & BENSON LLP *Minneapolis*

2 KAPLAN, STRANGIS & KAPLAN *Minneapolis*
OPPENHEIMER WOLFF & DONNELLY *Minneapolis*

3 BRIGGS AND MORGAN *Minneapolis*
FREDRIKSON & BYRON PA *Minneapolis*
GRAY, PLANT, MOOTY, MOOTY *Minneapolis*
LEONARD, STREET AND DEINARD *Minneapolis*
LINDQUIST & VENNUM PLLP *Minneapolis*

4 HENSON & EFRON *Minneapolis*
LOMMEN, NELSON, COLE *Minneapolis*

Leading individuals (Corporate/M&A)

1 GARON Philip *Faegre & Benson, Minneapolis*
ROSENBAUM Robert *Dorsey & Whitney, Minneapolis*
SCALLEN Timothy *Oppenheimer Wolff, Minneapolis*
SHARPE W Smith *Faegre & Benson, Minneapolis*
STRANGIS Ralph *Kaplan Strangis, Minneapolis*

2 CUTLER Kenneth *Dorsey & Whitney, Minneapolis*
ENGLER Bruce *Faegre & Benson, Minneapolis*
HUMPHREY Andrew *Faegre & Benson, Minneapolis*
KAPLAN Samuel *Kaplan Strangis, Minneapolis*
LIBBEY Keith *Fredrikson & Byron, Minneapolis*
MACHMEIER Bruce *Oppenheimer Wolff, Minneapolis*
SHERMAN Morris *Leonard Street, Minneapolis*

3 BUSCH William *Faegre & Benson, Minneapolis*
CLEVELAND Christopher *Briggs, Minneapolis*
COSTLEY Kevin *Lindquist & Vennum, Minneapolis*
EFRON Stanley *Henson & Efron, Minneapolis*
GORDON Avron *Briggs and Morgan, Minneapolis*
KAUFMAN D William *Oppenheimer Wolff, Minneapolis*
LETSCHER Tom *Oppenheimer Wolff, Minneapolis*
MOORSE Charles *Lindquist & Vennum, Minneapolis*
PAYNE William *Dorsey & Whitney, Minneapolis*
STAGEBERG Roger *Lommen Nelson, Minneapolis*
VANDER HAAR David *Faegre & Benson, Minneapolis*
WEITZ Mark *Leonard Street, Minneapolis*

Up-and-coming individuals

KOZACHOK Steve *Dorsey & Whitney, Minneapolis*
STANCHFIELD Mike *Faegre & Benson, Minneapolis*

Firms and Individuals are listed alphabetically in each band.

Band 1

Dorsey & Whitney LLP

The Firm: This truly international practice continues to have *"a presence that is hard to ignore."* Interviewees spoke of its twin-pronged approach: geographical spread and diversity of practice – *"virtually any specialty area is covered."* In particular, the team excels in the capital markets arena, where, as a result of recent recruitment, strong links are maintained with the firm's London office. The firm represented UnitedHealth Group in the permanent financing for its acquisition of Oxford Health Plans, advising in connection with an SEC-registered debt offering of $1.5 billion senior notes. A recovering M&A market has involved the firm in a number of notable transactions.

The Lawyers: *"Standout"* **Robert Rosenbaum**'s *"great knowledge of the law and facts"* and *"good interpersonal skills"* allow him to *"see where he can push"* when negotiating a deal. Clients acknowledge his ability to *"seize an opportunity"* and have instructed him on both acquisitions and public company compliance, and advisory matters. He advised Deluxe Corp in its acquisition of a public company for $600 million through a negotiated tender offer, and acted in the formation of The Mosaic Company, which involved the combination of other business entities. **Ken Cutler**, whose forte is the representation of emerging companies, *"has all the necessary attributes,"* including *"effective negotiating skills and a great personality."* His work, predominantly for companies in the technology sector, recently included advising Endocardial Solutions in its $273 million acquisition by St. Jude Medical, and High Jump Software in its acquisition by 3M, alongside a number of venture financing projects. **Bill Payne**, chair of the M&A practice, *"has seen every type of deal going"* and his direct approach *"cuts through the crap."* His work for Schwan Food attracted substantial praise. **Steve Kozachok**'s practice is quickly gaining the attention of an appreciative market.

He joins the table for his work on high-profile acquisitions, emerging companies and venture capital financing.
The Clients: US Bancorp; UnitedHealth Group; ADC Telecommunications; Southern MN Beet Sugar Coop; Hormel Foods and SuperValu.

Faegre & Benson LLP
See firm details p.1022
The Firm: An *"outstanding"* 60-strong group that is *"excellent on all aspects of corporate law,"* according to clients. The firm's place at the head of the market has been cemented by *"a strong core group of practitioners"* working for *"a blue-chip list of clients."* Dominance in the M&A field was underlined by the firm's representation of Target in its sale of the Marshall Field's department store chain to May Department Stores for $3.2 billion. The team has vast experience in general corporate counseling, acting as general counsel for a number of public companies such as Wilsons Leather and Hutchinson Technology; and advises on regulatory compliance for clients ranging from emerging companies to staples of the Fortune 100.

The Lawyers: **Phil Garon** (see p.1018) *"never loses track of a single detail"* even on the largest deals, say clients. *"His work product and practical analysis stands up to anyone in the world"* as he *"leaves no stone unturned."* Even peers branded him *"the top corporate lawyer in Minnesota"* and a guy who has *"both literally and metaphorically written the book on corporate law."* Garon's work serves only to reinforce these remarks. In the past year he has acted on the sale of the Mervyn's department store chain by Target to Sun Capital Partners and other financial investors for more than $1.6 billion; the acquisition of High Jump Software for 3M; and the completion of The St. Paul Companies/Travelers Property Casualty merger, valued at nearly $18 billion. **Kris Sharpe** (see p.1020), who heads the corporate department, is acknowledged by clients as *"a very talented guy for esoteric questions"* and

applauded by competitors for his ability to "*see his way to solutions.*" Sharpe handles both securities work, where he was involved in a $210 million IPO for Life Time Fitness; and M&A, where his work included the purchase of Optika by his client Stellent for $60 million. **Andrew Humphrey** (see p.1018), the man responsible for the firm's emerging company work, has used the upturn in the economy to carry out financing transactions and venture financing rounds for clients including Better Life Media. He also handles a range of corporate work for clients such as General Mill and ShopNBC. **Bruce Engler** (see p.1017) debuts in the tables following a hugely successful year for his private equity LBO practice. He was responsible for the $105 million IPO of long-term client Gander Mountain and handled four private equity LBO deals during 2004 with a total transaction value exceeding $500 million. **Bill Busch** (see p.1017) has "*a practical approach to business issues,*" which he employs in his M&A practice and his representation of the Minnesota Twins and Minnesota Vikings. The profession recommended him for his expertise in both the media and professional sports contexts. **David Vander Haar** (see p.1020) is active in the legislative arena but maintains a strong M&A practice, which has included work with Garon on the sale of publicly held International Multifoods to publicly held JM Smucker for stock and cash totaling $840 million. His drafting skills and securities work were also praised. Another newcomer to the tables, **Mike Stanchfield** (see p.1020) won clients' admiration for being "*practical and not over-lawyering.*" He possesses "*all the earmarks of a guy that will be very successful.*"
The Clients: American Express; Bemis; Guidant; Hutchinson Technology; Land O' Lakes; 3M; Norwest Equity Partners; Piper Jaffray; The St. Paul Travelers Companies; Target; Tennant and Wells Fargo.

Band 2

Kaplan, Strangis & Kaplan
The Firm: This corporate boutique "*punches well above its weight.*" Despite fielding a team of only 14 attorneys, the firm is consistently employed in high-profile transactions and sophisticated deals, tackling M&A, securities, tax, business planning and corporate governance as part of an "*outstanding practice.*"
The Lawyers: **Ralph Strangis** and **Samuel Kaplan** provide "*great strength at the top.*" The "*stellar*" Strangis is viewed as "*the deal-maker*" in the state, and, more broadly, "*a leading light in the community.*" His "*sage business advice*" is based on his experience as both a lawyer and a seasoned board member, which enables him "*to relate to clients' needs and translate them into actions.*" Kaplan, too, maintains a presence on the board of a public company. This involve-

ment underscores his "*client-oriented*" approach to a legal practice that encompasses M&A, securities and joint venture enterprises.
The Clients: The firm addresses the needs of a broad range of industries on a local, regional and national basis.

Oppenheimer Wolff & Donnelly LLP
The Firm: Drawing on a 40-strong team, the corporate finance and transactions practice continues to perform well and boasts an enviable reputation across the board in corporate matters, most notably joint venture agreements and securities work, with the medical technology sector benefiting in particular. Clients made plain their appreciation for the "*good group of core corporate lawyers*" with whom they have "*strong relationships.*" The team flexed its M&A muscle while representing Honeywell in the sale of its security monitoring business to GTCR for $315 million.
The Lawyers: **Tim Scallen**'s major focus is M&A. Alongside work on the Honeywell transaction, he advised Ecolab during its acquisition of Alcide for $60 million and led the representation of ADC Telecommunications in its sale of Broadband Access Systems to BigBand Networks. "*Well known for client loyalty,*" Scallen is appreciated by clients for his "*practical business sense and focus.*" "*Levelheaded*" **Bruce Machmeier** "*knows his way around the corporate legislation*" and, according to one satisfied client, compounds this academic footing with "*an understanding of business generally and our business specifically.*" Machmeier is an experienced operator on both M&A and securities work, especially that involving private equity funds. A highlight from the past year was Arizant's $225 million sale to an entity controlled by Citigroup Venture Capital Equity Partners. **Tom Letscher**, cochair of the firm's medical technology industry group, concentrates on the representation of emerging companies. This involves assistance with financing, acquisitions, licensing and day-to-day counseling. A $17.5 million venture capital round was recently completed on behalf of CoAxia. **Bill Kaufman** is newly ranked in the tables. He is very much involved in private investment and emerging company work, representing venture capital, midmarket and early-stage companies.
The Clients: ADC Telecommunications; Arizant; American Medical Systems; Ceridian; Ecolab; ev3; Honeywell; Toro; Nash Finch and Split Rock Partners.

Band 3

Briggs and Morgan, Professional Association
The Firm: Within this "*old-line St. Paul firm,*" a 25-strong business law section, now based in Minneapolis, is supplemented by a reputable

banking practice and a public finance sector team. Further assistance is granted from the business litigation and trade regulation departments of the firm. Ensuring clients' compliance with the stipulations of the Sarbanes-Oxley Act has become a particular focus of late.
The Lawyers: **Chris Cleveland** divides his time between advising public companies of their reporting obligations and assisting them with projects ranging from private placements of debt and equity to M&A. He has gained peers' attention for his knowledge of securities and regulatory matters, and for executing a substantial amount of work for operators of mutual funds. Clients turn to **Av Gordon**, who debuts in the tables, when in need of someone "*very knowledgeable about the Minnesota Business Corporation Act.*" His extensive practice takes in the full spectrum of business-related advice, though he does have a niche in the counseling of issuers and underwriters in public offerings, private placement and venture capital financing. His deal-making activity has brought him into contact with clients from sectors including medical device, medical products distribution, food service and manufacturing.

Fredrikson & Byron PA
The Firm: With more than 40 attorneys active in the three key areas of M&A, private financing and corporate governance, business continues to flow from all manner of enterprises, from startups to established Fortune 500 companies. In particular, the firm has clout in the medical products sphere and enjoys a strong reputation for its work in educating board members on corporate governance issues. A strong banking practice is also considered a hallmark.
The Lawyers: **Keith Libbey** "*has been a leader for a long time*" especially in M&A, where his expertise in the medical technology field is put to use by clients such as Medtronic. Interviewees remarked how he makes good use of his knowledge of the international business community.
The Clients: The client base includes manufacturers and marketers of a variety of industrial, commercial, medical and consumer products; insurance agencies; engineering and consulting firms; venture capital investors; computer software companies and biotech companies.

Gray, Plant, Mooty, Mooty & Bennett, PA
The Firm: Active across the Midwest, the 25 attorneys of the business law transactions group have forged links with firms beyond the region to ensure that clients receive local knowledge, whatever the size of a deal. Although unwilling to single out a star, commentators found the distinguishing feature of the practice as a whole to be a "*not flashy but effective and intelligent*" approach. The firm has a number of impressive clients, including Dairy Queen, and its work for

franchisers and emerging businesses has not gone unnoticed.

The Clients: NRG Energy and Dairy Queen are among the household names represented by the firm.

Leonard, Street and Deinard Professional Association

The Firm: Usually described as a midmarket operator, the corporate half of this long-established firm is nevertheless involved in some major transactions. "*Visible throughout Minnesota,*" the corporate team undertakes work for Taylor Corp and a number of other large corporations situated outside Minneapolis. The Washington-based office handles a large volume of work for regulated public utility and energy generators. Competitors acknowledge that they "*always feel they are dealing with strong attorneys,*" a view that is reinforced by the team's participation in the closing of a $250 million credit agreement refinancing for Hubbard Broadcasting, and the representation of Allianz Life in the sale of its US life reinsurance business for $310 million.

The Lawyers: Labeled "*the tiger,*" **Moe Sherman** is equally at home in the cut and thrust of acquisition work, including a $200 million acquisition on behalf of Computer Network Technology, and corporate counseling, where his years of experience have gained him a loyal client following. A constant stream of shareholder disputes, and a trust dispute involving more than $1 billion, has occupied Sherman in the past year. "*Headliner*" **Mark Weitz** has a long-standing reputation for securities work (he was responsible for the second largest IPO in Minnesota history), though interviewees also commented on his skills in transactional work generally and his involvement with regional brokers specifically. His "*excellent legal skills*" are matched by "*an equally strong ability with clients.*"

The Clients: Allianz Life; American Express Tax and Business Services; Buffets; LodgeNet

Entertainment; Marvin Windows; Michael Foods and CNT.

Lindquist & Vennum PLLP
See firm details p.1023

The Firm: Peers noted the "*good local and regional reputation*" of this firm. Acting for both public and private companies, it dispenses advice on securities, acquisitions, corporate governance and finance difficulties. In addition, the team acts as outside counsel for a number of public companies. The development of industry-specific practice groups (especially those of life sciences, banking and agriculture) has facilitated the team's instruction in matters as diverse as ethanol plants and midmarket banking deals. The breadth of its expertise was demonstrated by the sale of Community First Bank for $1.2 billion, some 17 years after the firm had been involved in setting up the company.

The Lawyers: **Kevin Costley** (see p.1017) is heavily involved in the banking sector of the team. His representation of financial institutions extends to financing, acquisition, taxation and expansion strategies, and is illustrated by his work with Community First Bank. **Chuck Moorse** (see p.1019) is "*a straightforward, good, practical business lawyer,*" primarily employed by public companies (keen to tap into his corporate governance expertise) to serve as outside counsel. During his relationship with a major sports retailer, its business has grown from one store to more than 30 in just seven years, resulting in Moorse's involvement in financings to support the expansion.

Band 4

Henson & Efron
The Firm: With a background in both deal-making and the financing of transactions, this team of 15 is routinely hired to smooth working capital credit facilities, acquisition financing, project financing, letters of credit and capital equipment leasing. A boon in M&A encouraged

a busy year for a group that was favorably compared with firms with much greater manpower. Business entity formation and tax structures were pitched as strengths of the practice.

The Lawyers: Also experienced in employment law, **Stanley Efron** is a "*tough negotiator.*" Efron can cite public offerings, tax and estate planning for high-profile individuals, and the status of general counsel to organizations up to a value of $3 billion as standout features of his recent resume.

The Clients: Charitable organizations join companies of all types on the client roster.

Lommen, Nelson, Cole & Stageberg, PA

The Firm: Frequently drafted in as "*special M&A counsel*" by companies on the verge of sale, this group of eight attorneys plans each stage of the transaction from due diligence through to the execution of acquisition documents, paying particular attention to the tax aspects of the deal. Midmarket, privately held companies compose the bulk of the team's work that recently saw several acquisitions, notably the sale of a medical company to a Toronto-based buyer.

The Lawyers: **Roger Stageberg** "*has a great reputation for smaller clients.*" His largest current client is Kulkoni, based in Frankfurt, which he assisted in closing a $16 million refinancing in Houston with lending institutions from Chicago and Germany. Other clients are drawn from the computer, electronics and medical products industries, with an emphasis on start-up or closely held enterprises.

The Clients: Although the focus of the firm is very much on small, Minnesota companies, international conglomerates and national financial institutions have also sought advice from the team.

EMPLOYMENT

MAINLY DEFENDANT

Band 1

Dorsey & Whitney LLP
The Firm: Some 25 attorneys at this Minneapolis Goliath band together to form an "*analytical and thoughtful team*" that is unafraid to "*dig in and get involved in order to deliver the goods.*" Regarded by peers as a formidable opponent, the full-service employment practice is complemented by a seven-strong group focusing on labor relations, to which clients turn on the "*specialized, prickly issues.*" An interdisciplinary approach and "*good bench strength*" ensure

that clients are also advised on all relevant tax and benefits issues. Alongside attorneys' legal capabilities, clients were keen to emphasize the "*responsive, friendly persona*" of the practice.

The Lawyers: "*Rock solid*" **Robert Reinhart** "*does not let his ego get in the way of doing a great job for clients.*" More than 30 years of experience have forged a "*powerful combination*" of legal knowledge and trial ability, which Reinhart applies to his employment litigation practice. Recently, he defended Wal-Mart in a class action concerning paid work-breaks, and he has handled an increasing volume of matters focused on

overtime pay. "*Principled*" **Bob Hobbins** "*always has the definitive answer*" for his clients. Interviewees noted "*a lot of Midwestern common sense*" in Hobbins' approach, and some place "*more confidence in him than in anyone else in the country.*" His practice encapsulates both employment issues, which saw him travel coast to coast in the defense of class actions and arbitrations, and labor issues including executive employment matters and separations. Hobbins is commonly drafted in to assist in the due diligence on M&A transactions. **Doug Christensen** is "*great for getting things going,*" thanks to his

Minnesota
Leading firms
(Employment: Mainly Defendant)

[1] DORSEY & WHITNEY LLP Minneapolis

[2] BRIGGS AND MORGAN Minneapolis
FAEGRE & BENSON LLP Minneapolis
FELHABER, LARSON, FENLON Minneapolis

[3] FREDRIKSON & BYRON PA Minneapolis
GRAY, PLANT, MOOTY, MOOTY Minneapolis
LEONARD, STREET AND DEINARD Minneapolis
RIDER, BENNETT, EGAN & ARUNDEL Minneapolis
SEATON, BECK, PETERS, BOWEN Minneapolis

Leading individuals
(Employment: Mainly Defendant)

[1] DAVIES Scott *Briggs and Morgan*, Minneapolis
HOBBINS Robert *Dorsey & Whitney* Minneapolis
HUNTRODS Ann *Briggs and Morgan* St Paul
REINHART Robert *Dorsey & Whitney* Minneapolis
ROSS Richard *Fredrikson & Byron* Minneapolis

[2] CARRON Reid *Faegre & Benson*, Minneapolis
CHRISTENSEN Douglas *Dorsey*, Minneapolis
D'AQUILA Barbara *Flynn Gaskins*, Minneapolis
DAWSON James *Felhaber Larson*, Minneapolis
HALVERSON Jan *Felhaber Larson*, Minneapolis
LANGEVIN Judith *Gray Plant*, Minneapolis
STUMO Mary *Faegre & Benson*, Minneapolis
ZECH Paul *Felhaber Larson*, Minneapolis

[3] GINSBURG Roy *Dorsey & Whitney*, Minneapolis
GOTTSCHALK Steve *Dorsey & Whitney*, Minneapolis
MERLEY Dennis *Felhaber Larson*, Minneapolis
MRKONICH Marko *Littler Mendelson*, Minneapolis
NOECKER Kathlyn *Faegre & Benson*, Minneapolis
PHILLIPS Penny *Felhaber Larson*, Minneapolis
RADOLINSKI Anne *Fredrikson & Byron*, Minneapolis
RAPHAN Melissa *Dorsey & Whitney*, Minneapolis
ROBINER Susan *Leonard Street*, Minneapolis
ROBY, Joseph *Johnson Killen*, Duluth
SEATON Doug *Seaton Beck*, Minneapolis
SNYDER Stephen *Gray Plant*, Minneapolis
STENMOE Gregory *Briggs and Morgan*, Minneapolis
THOMPSON John *Rider Bennett*, Minneapolis
WILLE Karin *Briggs and Morgan*, Minneapolis
ZEGLOVITCH Robert *Leonard Street*, Minneapolis

Up-and-coming individuals
ENG Holly *Dorsey & Whitney*, Minneapolis

Firms and Individuals are listed alphabetically in each band.

determination "*not to fight just for the sake of it.*" He practices in all areas of labor and employment law for management, including union-organizing attempts and collective bargaining, but won special acclaim for his litigation prowess. **Roy Ginsburg** is "*a pillar in the employment community.*" A past chair of the firm's employment law practice group, he undertakes litigation defense in individual, multiparty and class-wide claims of a discriminatory, harassment or common law nature. His knowledge of noncompetition and fiduciary duties drew special praise. **Melissa Raphan** is

"*relentless*" in the defense of her clients, and "*impresses in difficult situations.*" Handling all types of employment dispute, she has gained a significant amount of experience in the financial services industry. Clients recognize **Steve Gottschalk**, chair of the employee benefits group, as "*one of the few attorneys who can take pension law and turn it into everyday English.*" His "*logical approach*" to employee retirement, welfare plans and executive compensation plans ensures that "*what you want to accomplish is achieved in a plan document.*" **Holly Eng** joins the tables as someone who is "*going to play a big part in the firm.*" Primarily a litigator, her recent workload has covered discrimination and matters generated by Sarbanes-Oxley legislation.

The Clients: Mayo Clinic and Mayo Foundation; NRG Energy; Cargill; Wal-Mart and Cisco Systems.

Band 2

Briggs and Morgan, Professional Association

The Firm: In offices in both St. Paul and Minneapolis, this group of more than 20 attorneys has "*a really strong and long-lasting presence in labor and employment.*" Several interviewees commented on the "*seasoned*" and "*experienced*" nature of the practice, which embraces both labor relations and employment litigation in such a way as to "*consider the overall needs of clients.*" The depth of the team's resources is well demonstrated by its labor practice, where specialist knowledge of the Railway Labor Act is to be found. On employment matters, attorneys handle litigation in state and federal courts as well as before local, state, and federal agencies, with the team enjoying a successful run in the defense of discrimination claims in the past year.

The Lawyers: Known to be a "*superb trial lawyer,*" **Scott Davies** "*does not try cases merely to show off, and always acts in the best interests of his clients.*" Trial skills have also generated a flow of mediation work for Davies, who, as a board member, has a first-hand understanding of the challenges facing businesses. The past year has seen Davies involved in Title VII race and sex discrimination matters, defending claims brought by dismissed executives, representing sections of the poultry industry against class actions, and the successful maintenance of a challenged ERISA preemption for AT&T. St. Paul-based **Ann Huntrods** has developed "*a sense of what is typical and what is important*" and is "*devoted to her clients.*" Chair of the employment practice, she is an "*astute giver of advice on regulatory issues*" and has kept pace with the increasing tendency for plaintiffs to rely on expert evidence. A regular speaker on ADA and FMLA issues, she concentrates on discrimination and harassment. "*Thoughtful*" **Gregory Stenmoe** continues to impress observers with

his sexual harassment litigation and training. He is recognized for his work on both discrimination and covenant noncompete cases and "*presents well in court.*" **Karin Wille** "*makes great calls*" for her clients. With prior experience as in-house counsel at Target, she has ample expertise in training and counseling, which goes some way to explaining why she has gained the trust of employers in several fields, notably higher education.

The Clients: Carlson; Northwest Airlines; Ceridian; AT&T; Federated Insurance; PepsiCo and Conseco.

Faegre & Benson LLP
See firm details p.1022

The Firm: Offering 23 "*flexible, nimble and responsive*" attorneys, the labor and employment group at this firm advises management on all aspects of business, and places specific emphasis on preventive advice and the review of company employee procedures. A "*major player*" in both traditional labor issues, such as collective bargaining, and the growing raft of employment matters, such as wage and hour concerns, the group is supplemented by dedicated teams in both employee benefits and immigration law. Also actively involved in assisting the firm's corporate department on transactional matters, it has become adept at dealing with service contracts for executives. Among the firm's core clients is an international delivery service for which it is the main regional counsel on labor and employment matters in six Midwestern states.

The Lawyers: Among those highlighted for their "*commitment to excellent service,*" **Mary Stumo** (see p.1020) adopts a "*take-no-prisoners approach to litigation.*" Her depth of experience and command of the practice area were identified as key assets, and were tested recently in the successful defense of a whistle-blowing and assault and battery claim. As "*one of the top guys in town,*" **Reid Carron** (see p.1017) always shows "*common sense*" in his labor-centered practice. He is a veteran of organizing defenses and countless unfair labor practice disputes, collective bargainings and decertification elections. **Kathy Noecker** (see p.1019) heads the department and is called upon by clients in the retail, media and technology sectors. She has been instrumental in smoothing through executive transitions for public companies, including the drafting of separation agreements and contracts for incoming executives.

Felhaber, Larson, Fenlon & Vogt, PC

The Firm: Labor and employment have been "*the substantial specialization of the firm for a long, long time,*" claimed interviewees. It is therefore no surprise that clients found a "*well-connected*" practice, which "*understands business and its environment.*" Dividing time roughly

1008   All quotes in the text are from interviews with clients and competitors.

CHAMBERS USA 2005

equally between traditional labor law and employment matters, the 22-strong team recently advised the six major hospital systems in the Twin Cities in negotiations with unions representing nurses, service workers and pharmacists. Indeed healthcare entities have come to regard Felhaber as the "*go-to firm.*"

The Lawyers: **Paul Zech**, chair of the firm's labor and employment section, is a "*high-energy guy.*" Attracting favorable comment for his "*broad exposure to industrial issues,*" Zech is well equipped for employment litigation. He successfully defended Supervalu in the Eighth Circuit Court of Appeals in a disability discrimination case concerning an epilepsy sufferer. **Jan Halverson** continues with an increasingly rare practice, which combines both labor and employment matters. A substantial portion of his time is spent addressing employment issues, including unfair labor practices, for a number of healthcare entities. Halverson "*adapts to what his client wants to achieve*" and "*understands the basic needs of parties.*" Further, "*his gentle style allows him to deliver difficult messages in a reasonable way.*" Clients regret that **Jim Dawson** is also "*something of a dying breed*" given his equal familiarity with labor and employment concerns. "*Not afraid to play hardball,*" the "*aggressive*" Dawson "*appreciates the diversity of our business,*" reported one client. Primarily a counselor with an eye on risk prevention, **Dennis Merley** is regarded by clients as "*an expert on EEOC affirmative action issues.*" He advises management on a broad range of workplace issues, including discrimination, minimum wage and overtime, downsizing and severance agreements. **Penny Phillips** is "*emerging as a great lawyer,*" particularly with respect to the FLSA, an area in which she is "*very well versed.*"

The Clients: Among those who commonly turn to the firm for advice are the management of retailers, healthcare entities and public sector operators.

Band 3

Fredrikson & Byron PA

The Firm: This nine-attorney team was singled out for its responsiveness to client needs: "*They don't rely on doing everything the same way as last time.*" An emphasis is placed on offering clients advice by way of the creation and application of policies, apprising them of changing law and assisting with issues such as discipline. Recent instructions concern the FMLA, where attorneys are said to be adept at discerning employers' day-to-day obligations.

The Lawyers: **Richard Ross** "*works his butt off.*" A "*gifted trial attorney,*" according to clients, he is described by peers as "*one of the most tenacious human beings in the world.*" Ross additionally provides "*solid leadership*" of the

department, and recently saw an upturn in union activity among his widely drawn clientele. His failure to appear at trial in the past year is due to his having prevailed on motions for summary judgment, including a number of sexual harassment and age discrimination claims. Although experienced in litigation, it is counseling that has occupied much of **Anne Radolinski**'s time and turned heads in the market recently. Her 20 years of experience and "*sophisticated understanding of client issues*" aid those she represents, among them employers, individuals, company officers and directors.

The Clients: Healthcare institutions, manufacturers and educational institutions are among the broad range of individuals, companies and governmental bodies to benefit from the team's advice.

Gray, Plant, Mooty, Mooty & Bennett, PA

The Firm: Insistent that its 13 attorneys should operate on both sides of the counseling/litigation coin, the firm adopts a holistic approach to employment practice. Acting for all manner of employers, but with particular knowledge of the franchiser, higher education and healthcare sectors, the team has been heavily involved in noncompete claims in the past twelve months. The same period has also brought victories in a race discrimination trial in Ohio and a workers' compensation trial in Texas. The group is also a member of the International Employment Law Alliance, which has recently developed theater-based training for clients.

The Lawyers: **Judith Langevin** remains chair of the practice group and reinforces "*substantive expertise*" with "*creative, groundbreaking work in the nonlitigation strand of employment law.*" Her litigation and counseling work each have an emphasis on discrimination and sexual harassment. **Stephen Snyder** concentrates on complex litigation and maximizes his 32 years of experience in his class actions. Snyder was involved in a dispute between 2000 employees and Northwest Airlines over $75 million worth of shares issued following the demutualization of Prudential.

The Clients: St. Olaf College; University of Minnesota Physicians; National American University; Cargill; Taylor Corporation; US Trust; Tastefully Simple; International Dairy Queen and Owens Companies.

Leonard, Street and Deinard Professional Association

The Firm: This full-service employment law department comprises 16 individuals, not including a further specialized group of three attorneys dealing exclusively with immigration law. Regular representations cover discrimination, harassment, contractual disagreements, employment-related torts and noncompete

defense. New overtime regulations and an increase in class action litigation have ensured a busy year for the department.

The Lawyers: "*Creative thinker*" **Susan Robiner** has "*an effective, persuasive style.*" Her work straddles employment litigation and intellectual property, such that she is now renowned for her expertise on trade secrets and noncompete matters. Her clients include businesses involved in heavy manufacturing, sales and higher education, a number of which have engaged her in a variety of recategorization exercises to ensure compliance with overtime regulations. **Robert Zeglovitch** wins applause for a discrimination practice that involves him in day-to-day counseling and has taken him to court in precedent-setting scenarios.

The Clients: Land O'Lakes; St. Jude Medical; Canadian Pacific Railway; Honeywell; General Mills; LexisNexis; JC Penney Company; Taylor Corporation; Pentair; HB Fuller; Gustavus Adolphus College; Cargill and Prudential.

Rider, Bennett, Egan & Arundel, LLP

The Firm: Active in both traditional labor and employment markets, this firm represents executive management, supervisory personnel and human resources professionals in the public and private sectors. It hosts seminars and in-house training sessions on a variety of topics and also publishes newsletters for clients. The firm's wholly owned subsidiary, Critical Measures, offers both training and consulting.

The Lawyers: **John Thompson**, as might be expected from the author of a textbook on employment law, is an "*expert advice-giver.*" His experience as in-house counsel with 3M has spawned "*a good sense of what clients want.*" Thompson is considered an expert on workplace violence, an area in which he enjoys a national reputation.

The Clients: The firm counsels businesses in both the public and private sectors.

Seaton, Beck, Peters, Bowen & Feuss

The Firm: "*One of the best boutiques,*" with all 11 "*excellent*" attorneys dedicated to representing employers. Lately work has included acquisition and reduction in force planning, the drafting and enforcement of noncompete agreements, major union campaigns, and the defense of discrimination and ERISA claims. One client claimed that he turned to the firm when in need of someone "*to play hardball with the unions.*" Clients come from all commercial sectors, though notably from manufacturing, transportation and distribution, mining, construction, food processing, education and retailing.

The Lawyers: Founding shareholder **Doug Seaton** fuses the "*highly intellectual*" approach one would expect from the holder of a PhD in

labor relations with an *"effective, persuasive style"* in the courtroom and in negotiations, thus making him *"one of the premier guys in town."*
The Clients: Alliant Techsystems; United Hardware; Corporate Express Office Products; American Appraisal Associates; General Nutrition; Holiday Inn; Barton Sand & Gravel; Bauerly; Weis Builders; M&I Bank and INVESCO.

Other Notable Practitioners

"Tigerish" **Barbara D'Aquila** of Flynn, Gaskins & Bennett is proclaimed as *"the preeminent management attorney in town."* She handles *"sophisticated"* cases and is equally well thought of in litigation, counseling and mediation. **Marko Mrkonich** heads up national player Littler Mendelson PC's *"successful"* Minneapolis office. His employment work, both in litigation and advisory is *"achieving prominence."*

Mrkonich regularly speaks on a wide variety of employment topics to legal, human resource and other business audiences. **Joseph Roby** of Johnson Killen & Seiler, the oldest law firm in Duluth *"would be a top guy anywhere."* Commentators pointed to his *"exceptional knowledge"* and ability to be *"an effective advocate while maintaining a professional demeanor towards opposing counsel and parties."*

LITIGATION

GENERAL COMMERCIAL

Minnesota
Leading firms
(Litigation: General Commercial)

[1]	**DORSEY & WHITNEY LLP** *Minneapolis*
	FAEGRE & BENSON LLP *Minneapolis*
	ROBINS KAPLAN MILLER & CIRESI *Minneapolis*
[2]	**ANTHONY OSTLUND & BAER** *Minneapolis*
	GREENE ESPEL PLLP *Minneapolis*
[3]	**BRIGGS AND MORGAN** *Minneapolis*
	FREDRIKSON & BYRON PA *Minneapolis*
	KELLY & BERENS PA *Minneapolis*
	LEONARD, STREET AND DEINARD *Minneapolis*
	LINDQUIST & VENNUM PLLP *Minneapolis*
	MASLON EDELMAN BORMAN *Minneapolis*
[4]	**BASSFORD REMELE** *Minneapolis*
	GRAY, PLANT, MOOTY, MOOTY *Minneapolis*
	OPPENHEIMER WOLFF & DONNELLY *Minneapolis*
	WINTHROP & WEINSTINE *Minneapolis*

Firms are listed alphabetically in each band.

Band 1

Dorsey & Whitney LLP

The Firm: *"Its size matters,"* claimed one commentator regarding the litigation group within the largest firm in Minnesota. Indeed, Dorsey *"can bring resources to any task or matter that no one else can match."* Showing that quality is equally as important as quantity, the group comprises *"a hard-to-replicate collection"* of *"well-trained litigators covering all specialties."* Talent across the board was confirmed by interviewee praise for everything from healthcare and medical malpractice suits to insurance and securities cases. Standout work in the past year included the representation of 382 sugar beet farmers against their insurance companies in a two-tiered litigation/arbitration proceeding in which the firm's clients won almost $40 million.
The Lawyers: Benefiting from *"a tremendous memory,"* **Roger Magnuson** is regarded as being simultaneously both *"polished"* and *"ferocious."* He is clearly a man able to adapt his talents to the needs of a case, and as head of the firm's strategic litigation group, Magnuson often undertakes high-profile work nationally and

even internationally. Peers couldn't fail to notice his recent success in the Mall of America litigation, where he won a complete victory for his clients. He represented the Minnesota Twins in litigation concerning broadcasting rights with Fox Sportsnet, and has considerable experience of white-collar crime. **Thomas Tinkham**, chair of the commercial litigation group, has such depth of knowledge that clients feel he will *"do a good job whatever legal issues surface in the case."* His familiarity with the Minnesota legal scene allows him to *"pull things together brilliantly,"* and, despite his seniority, he is still *"very hands-on. Tom doesn't sit back and let the juniors get on with it,"* which clients say provides *"a certainty that you will get high-level attention to your case."* Tinkham acted in a tax refund claim for Mayo Clinic, securing an exception worth more than $50 million, and is currently involved in an arbitration on behalf of the Airline Pilots Association concerning the ownership of $70 million of Prudential stock acquired by Northwest Airlines. **Richard Solum**'s star is *"rising in the community as a mediator."* A former district judge, with 32 years' experience under his belt, he advises US Bank on diverse issues and earned plaudits for his enthusiasm to always *"get on with the next challenge."* Pitched by clients as *"one of the best commercial litigators in the state"* **Paul Klaas** *"lives up to his name."* He serves as lead counsel in a cross-section of matters, among them IP, commercial, technology and medical malpractice. A leader in healthcare work, Klaas also finds time to counsel Disney and ABC. **Craig Diviney** heads the Minneapolis IP practice. A *"skillful, honest and successful litigator,"* Diviney also counsels on litigation avoidance. In the past year, most of his time was devoted to a series of cases for Syngenta, involving licensing arrangements and disputes with Monsanto; and more generally, his life sciences knowledge is appreciated by clients who produce medical devices and agricultural products. Diviney recently had a $35 million verdict for Cargill concerning a purchase agreement affirmed on appeal.
The Clients: US Bank; Cargill; UnitedHealth Group; Qwest; Northwest Airlines and SuperValu.

Faegre & Benson LLP

See firm details p.1022
The Firm: The *"silk-stocking"* firm in the state fields 75 litigators. One commentator enthused that *"everybody I know or have worked with is absolutely first rate,"* including *"a great stable of young associates."* Attracted to a practice where people *"don't play games,"* and instead offer *"the highest standards technically and ethically,"* clients bring a full complement of matters to the firm. Securities, trade secrets and insurance coverage have occupied the team heavily in the recent past, helping it to reach its place at the head of the market.
The Lawyers: *"Top dog"* **Jerry Snider** (see p.1020) is recognized as *"a great jury trial lawyer."* Combining *"tremendous intelligence and a great deal of experience,"* Snider mainly handles complex civil litigation and appellate work. He recently acted in a large shareholder-rights matter concerning a dispute over the value of a business, and has a who's who list of clients, including Abbott Laboratories, American Express, IBM, Target and Koch Industries. Snider also has experience in the employment arena and an in-depth knowledge of Indian and Tribal Law. **Brian O'Neill** (see p.1019) *"gets to the heart of matters quickly in order to represent clients vigorously."* With trial experience across the country, O'Neill made *"a tremendous splash"* in the litigation arising from the Exxon Valdez oil spill in Alaska. His knowledge of complex commercial disputes, intellectual property and environmental law continues to win the hearts of clients. **Jim Volling** (see p.1020), head of the firm's business litigation group, debuts in the tables. His broad-based litigation practice comprises several key elements: securities and shareholder litigation, antitrust and white-collar criminal defense. The past year saw Volling act for Wells Fargo in consumer class actions and represent Ashland in a criminal environmental matter, and also brought involvement in the litigation resulting from the failure of MJK Clearing. **Charles Webber** (see p.1020) is *"going to be a big, big star."* Though he appears on the full gamut of general commercial work, his practice centers on the representation of financial insti-

Minnesota
Leading individuals
(Litigation: General Commercial)

1 ANTHONY Joseph *Anthony Ostlund*, Minneapolis
CIRESI Michael *Robins Kaplan*, Minneapolis
FRASER Thomas *Fredrikson & Byron*, Minneapolis
KELLY Timothy *Kelly & Berens*, Minneapolis
LUGER Andrew *Greene Espel*, Minneapolis
MAGNUSON Roger *Dorsey & Whitney*, Minneapolis
PENTELOVITCH William *Maslon*, Minneapolis
REMELE Lewis *Bassford Remele*, Minneapolis
SNIDER Jerry *Faegre & Benson*, Minneapolis

2 FLEMING Terrence *Lindquist & Vennum*, Minneapolis
KEYES Jeffrey *Briggs and Morgan*, Minneapolis
SIMONSON James *Gray Plant*, Minneapolis
SOLUM Richard *Dorsey & Whitney*, Minneapolis
TINKHAM Thomas *Dorsey & Whitney*, Minneapolis

3 FIELD Lawrence *Leonard Street*, Minneapolis
FRUTH Terence *Fruth Jamison*, Minneapolis
IHRIG Richard *Lindquist & Vennum*, Minneapolis
KLAAS Paul *Dorsey & Whitney*, Minneapolis
MARK Richard *Briggs and Morgan*, Minneapolis
NOTEBOOM Todd *Leonard Street*, Minneapolis
O'NEILL Brian *Faegre & Benson*, Minneapolis
OSTLUND Richard *Anthony Ostlund*, Minneapolis
VOLLING James *Faegre & Benson*, Minneapolis
WEBBER Charles *Faegre & Benson*, Minneapolis
WEINSTINE Robert *Winthrop & Weinstine*, Minneapolis
WILDUNG Wendy *Faegre & Benson*, Minneapolis

Up-and-coming individuals
BRENNA Nathan *Anthony Ostlund*, Minneapolis

Individuals are listed alphabetically in each band.

tutions and banking entities, including Wells Fargo, Koch Industries and US Bank. He assisted the latter in connection with a large arbitration in the past year. **Wendy Wildung** (see p.1021) has "*a great success rate*," according to her clients. Again, despite being able to undertake almost any litigious matter, including real estate litigation and intellectual property, Wildung's emphasis is on securities-related litigation. She handles the defense of consumer fraud and financial irregularity allegations for boards of directors, which commonly involves extensive interaction with investigative and regulatory authorities. **Ken Liebman** (see p.1018) heads the firm's international IP practice group. His own practice focuses on patent litigation, where he represents two medical device colossi, Guidant and Zimmer Spine. He also acts for Hutchinson Technology, the world's leading supplier of suspensions for disk drives, and the University of Minnesota, for which he secured a $300 million settlement from Glaxo Wellcome recently. A "*commanding presence*," **David Gross** (see p.1018) has "*an instinct for the battle of IP litigation*." 3M, Guidant, Hutchinson Technology and the Mayo Foundation have all been lured by the skills of this lecturer in the art of trial practice. Gross was lead trial counsel for Wyeth in the billion-dollar trade secrets case Wyeth v

Natural Biologics and argued the appeal in early 2005. **Randall Kahnke** (see p.1018) joins the tables on the back of praise for his "*impressive, polite persistence*" which has secured favorable verdicts at trial and arbitration for his medical and technological clients.

The Clients: IBM; General Mills; US Bank; Wells Fargo; Koch Industries; Cargill; University of Minnesota; CSC Credit Services; DuPont; Mathy Construction; Cardiac Rhythm Management; Acorn Cardiovascular; Centerpulse USA and Hutchinson Technology.

Robins Kaplan Miller & Ciresi

The Firm: This firm received numerous client acknowledgements for the quality of its trial work: "*They are great at presenting a case and focusing on important issues.*" Clients additionally took time to praise the quality of the firm's support staff, who include relevantly qualified science advisers. The firm acts for both plaintiffs and defendants, its largest cases most commonly being in the fields of IP and products liability.

The Lawyers: "*Major gunslinger*" **Michael Ciresi** is "*top of the form.*" His approach to litigation has engineered results that "*stand up against anyone in the country.*" Ciresi's trial practice focuses on products liability, intellectual property and complex strategic litigation; in each area his experience in representing plaintiffs is held in the same high regard as his counseling of defendants. A formidable opponent, Ciresi always "*gets the most out of a case.*" **Martin Lueck** is an IP litigator known to be "*very good at boiling things down for juries.*" This has led to some "*spectacular results for clients,*" including Honeywell, and a jury verdict in favor of Eolas Technologies and the University of California on issues of infringement, validity, and damages in the region of $520 million. Keen to stress that these are not freak results, peers enviously noted that "*he wins a lot.*" **Ron Schutz**'s trial experience has earned him a reputation as "*one of the most successful IP lawyers in the country.*" Schutz, chair of the firm's IP litigation department, has won a series of huge victories running to hundreds of millions of dollars.

The Clients: The firm's clients include a number of well-known technology-led companies, manufacturers and insurers.

Band 2

Anthony Ostlund & Baer

The Firm: A team of 22 attorneys form this "*litigation powerhouse.*" Concentrating solely on litigation, the firm offers advice across a wide variety of matters including securities, shareholder, employment, professional negligence and unfair competition. Recent actions include the representation of AIG, Northwestern Mutual Life and several hedge funds in connection with the collapse of Adelphia and HealthSouth,

where hundreds of millions of dollars are at stake. With a style that is "*aggressive without crossing the line,*" the firm gets the results necessary to carry off what some commentators observe to be a confident "*strut.*" The past year saw a $10 million judgment for a client in an arbitration before a panel of the National Association of Securities Dealers, the third largest of its kind in the USA.

The Lawyers: **Joe Anthony** is "*just so damn good.*" A "*street-smart*" operator who "*has all the tools,*" Anthony draws clients from across the country who are "*eager to tap into expertise that doesn't exist locally.*" Embroiling himself in complex securities and IP disputes, he was successful in two Minnesota Supreme Court cases in 2004, one concerning the rights of corporations and their directors and the other the rights of parties in real estate disputes. "*Technically superior*" **Richard Ostlund** is recommended by clients for complex commercial litigation. He is currently handling three major matters with claims in excess of $30 million for clients including Cardiovention/Medtronic and AXA, as well as one in excess of $300 million for NeoNetworks. **Nathan Brenna**, who debuts in the tables, represents companies and individuals in all aspects of business litigation. Brenna's hardworking style has caught the attention of peers, who conclude, "*He's going to go far.*"

The Clients: The firm's client roster includes Miller Meester Advertising, Minnesota Twins Partnership and Onvoy.

Greene Espel PLLP

The Firm: A "*clear cut above,*" this litigation boutique "*only recruits the absolute top talent*" to maintain its reputation as "*a highly selective and gifted group of lawyers.*" Harnessing the talents of 19 "*top-to-bottom better*" attorneys, the firm exercises its muscle in all major areas of work including commercial and contractual disputes, employment, environmental and product liability. Commentators further remarked on a particular niche in public sector litigation. Recent action has included representing universities in construction disputes, defending a healthcare executive in a white-collar criminal case, and a continual flow of professional negligence work for accountancy professionals.

The Lawyers: The claim that **Andrew Luger** is "*more comfortable in a courtroom than he is relaxing at home in his living room*" is indicative of the admiration of commentators for this "*quintessential, successful litigator.*" Luger brings a "*dynamic, bubbly, East Coast brash*" to proceedings and divides his time equally between complex business litigation and white-collar crime investigations, where his background as a US attorney stands him in good stead. In the past year he has represented several large corporations that were investigating allegations of wrongdoing by their own employees, and

Minnesota
Leading individuals (Litigation: IP)

[1] ALLGEYER David *Lindquist & Vennum*, Minneapolis
CARLSON Alan *Carlson Caspers*, Minneapolis
CIRESI Michael *Robins Kaplan*, Minneapolis
DIVINEY Craig *Dorsey & Whitney*, Minneapolis
GROSS David *Faegre & Benson*, Minneapolis
HEIN Laura *Gray Plant*, Minneapolis
LIEBMAN Kenneth *Faegre & Benson*, Minneapolis
LUECK Martin *Robins Kaplan*, Minneapolis
MCDONALD Daniel *Merchant & Gould*, Minneapolis
SCHUTZ Ron *Robins Kaplan*, Minneapolis

Up-and-coming individuals
KAHNKE Randall *Faegre & Benson*, Minneapolis

Leading individuals
(Litigation: Appellate)

[1] HERR David *Maslon Edelman*, Minneapolis
Individuals are listed alphabetically in each band.

defended a large financial client in a securities fraud case.

The Clients: The firm acts for some of the nation's largest retail, medical device, insurance and banking entities, as well as counseling local and start-up enterprises.

Band 3

Briggs and Morgan, Professional Association

The Firm: Lauded by Fortune 500 clients for its ability to maneuver clients out of tight situations with "*good, sound legal theories,*" the litigation department at this firm is permeated by "*a great sense of integrity.*" Employing around 50 litigators, the firm has a background in class action work brought under federal and state securities, and consumer and banking statutes as well as common law. It recently advised dozens of mortgage bankers in connection with the defense of class actions in 14 states, including cases that raised challenges to escrow practices. The firm's appellate strength was demonstrated in a major coverage dispute following a $29 million jury verdict in favor of its client.

The Lawyers: The "*unflappable*" **Jeffrey Keyes** is "*one cool customer.*" Peers recognized his academic and practical expertise in trial situations and on franchising and antitrust issues. Commentators viewed his argument in the Supreme Court concerning an asylum seeker from Somalia as "*a credit to the profession.*" **Richard Mark**, the president of the firm, "*can try anything.*" His broad-based litigation practice has taken him into almost every conceivable business litigation area, including securities fraud, minority shareholder disputes, insurance coverage, white-collar crime, lender liability and general bank litigation. Regardless of the matter at hand, Mark "*spends a lot of time researching the area thus ensuring that he only speaks in a knowledgeable way.*"

The Clients: The firm is retained by clients of all shapes and sizes, and from a range of industries including medical devices, manufacturing and financial services.

Fredrikson & Byron PA

The Firm: Now with around 60 attorneys involved to a greater or lesser extent, the litigation practice continues to expand to handle an increased workload, particularly in IP matters. Enlisted in all types of commercial disputes, the firm spends a great deal of time advising on securities, shareholder and partnership issues, real estate litigation, noncompete and trade secrets, and professional liability work. It also taps into an extensive knowledge of alternative dispute resolution, and was recently engaged in a multimillion-dollar breach of contract arbitration. Crucially, clients say the firm's consideration of their interests extends to the bottom line: "*They are great at understanding the business and asking questions about the scope of the project so that they can keep the bill down.*"

The Lawyers: **Tom Fraser** was "*born to be a trial lawyer. He says what he has to say in an organized manner, and people listen.*" Fraser concentrates on shareholder and partnership disputes, the representation of Mayo Clinic in medical malpractice work, and also serves as a neutral arbitrator in internal investigations, where he is gaining a reputation as a man who is "*effective in bringing people together.*"

The Clients: The firm represents major companies from a variety of spheres, including banking and financial services, chemicals, energy, biotech, media and healthcare.

Kelly & Berens PA

The Firm: The 12 lawyers in this team continue to win praise for their work on complex commercial litigation.

The Lawyers: **Tim Kelly** is "*on everyone's shortlist of who to go to.*" His "*straight-shooting*" approach allows him to "*get to the heart of the issue.*" Commentators perceive that he is still "*doing most of the heavy lifting*" at the firm, and note that "*he can try any kind of case.*" Clients highlighted Kelly's skill in both trial and arbitration situations.

The Clients: TCF Financial; Regis; Allianz Life Insurance; Inter-Regional Financial Group; Guidant; Ceridian and BankFIRST.

Leonard, Street and Deinard Professional Association

The Firm: Around half of the firm's 190 employees are engaged in litigation, and the firm has a wealth of knowledge in class action, environmental and construction cases. Attorneys have been involved in several significant actions of late: the representation of Honeywell International in a variety of matters throughout the USA involving construction law claims; success-

fully advising three trust beneficiaries in a dispute with six other beneficiaries involving a family trust valued at more than $900 million; and the defense of Microsoft in a class action in state court involving alleged violations of Minnesota antitrust laws.

The Lawyers: **Lawrence Field** maintains a reputation as an "*extremely knowledgeable*" attorney who is "*efficient in getting cases against his clients dismissed in the early stages.*" His forte is in shareholder and class action litigation, where he led the defense of Allianz Life Insurance in class actions in state courts in Minnesota, California and Louisiana. Alongside his continuing representation of Simon Property Group, North America's largest publicly traded retail REIT, in an ownership dispute involving the Mall of America, Field acted for Heartland Advisors in a securities fraud case brought by the SEC in federal district court in Wisconsin. Opponents underestimate the "*phenomenal*" **Todd Noteboom** at their peril. On the surface "*unassuming and nonthreatening,*" he can "*dismantle*" arguments, clients say, and is "*as good as anyone in the country*" on his feet. Noteboom was lead counsel in the defense of State Farm Insurance in a class action in state court in Minnesota involving rates charged for homeowners' insurance and damage claims in the tens of millions of dollars. The trial court granted a motion for summary judgment and dismissed the plaintiffs' claims.

The Clients: Allianz Life Insurance; Simon Property Group; Kodak; Texas Instruments; Microsoft; State Farm Insurance; Honeywell International and Soo Line Railroad.

Lindquist & Vennum PLLP

See firm details p.1023

The Firm: At this strong operator in the mid-market sector, around 60 attorneys act across the board in commercial litigation to advise clients on everything from securities litigation to white-collar crime. Peers commented on a growing presence in the antitrust area and an established securities practice. Further work derives from the firm's corporate reputation and a well-developed IP practice group. The latter predominantly handles matters for the medical device, computer, software and agricultural device industries.

The Lawyers: **Terrence Fleming** (see p.1017) is the present "*star*" of the team, according to interviewees. Active nationally, Fleming boasts expertise in shareholder litigation, M&A litigation and regulatory proceedings. His success in these areas is due in no small part to his uncanny ability "*to get judges going his way.*" **Richard Ihrig**'s (see p.1018) practice revolves around the counseling of clients on large-scale class actions. His knowledge of the intricacies involved in the reorganization of staff and assets makes him a valuable ally in times of change for businesses, while his work in the antitrust field has gained the respect of significant customers of the chemical products, vitamins, rubber and cardboard industries. "*Well-spoken*" **David Allgeyer** (see p.1017) was identified as the outstanding member of the firm's seven-person IP litigation department. His practice revolves around IP litigation, predominantly for the medical technology industry, but he has found himself embroiled in disputes concerning agricultural devices. Commentators confirm that, with "*a ton of experience*" and "*an effective communication style,*" he is "*fun to be involved with.*"

The Clients: AG Edwards & Sons; Dain Rauscher; Piper Jaffray and UBS PaineWebber.

Maslon Edelman Borman & Brand, LLP

The Firm: Now expanded to more than 40 attorneys, the firm's litigation group, which is "*dominated by some of the best trial lawyers in town,*" continues to place emphasis on the representation of business entities in complex litigation. Recent work includes ownership, construction, insurance coverage and product liability disputes, particularly for the medical device industry. An increasingly large slice of the group's time is awarded to the defense of class actions, while the trial practice is further supported by a renowned appellate ability.

The Lawyers: **Bill Pentelovitch** is a "*powerful*" presence on the Minnesota trial scene where his "*focused, super-aggressive*" style is the key to unlocking difficult matters. Pentelovitch handles the entire scope of commercial litigation, but undertakes a growing volume of IP work. His recent involvement in Afremov v Amplatz, a dispute between owners of a medical device company, generated a groundbreaking precedent, and he remains national counsel for Medtronic on noncompete cases. Clients attribute his success to "*a unique combination possessed by a very small group of people across the country: he is an exceptional strategist, a superb legal analyst, and a formidable trial lawyer.*" **David Herr** leads the appellate practice and is chairman of the American Academy of Appellate Lawyers. Peers remarked that it was "*typical to call Herr in*" when "*looking for someone to appeal a case that's in trouble.*"

The Clients: Attracting business from all corners of industry, among others the firm acts for medical device manufacturers, construction companies and banking and insurance entities.

Band 4

Bassford Remele, A Professional Association

The Firm: Established in 1882, this "*highly professional and very skillful*" firm features nationally recognized manufacturing corporations, insurance companies, healthcare providers and

one of the largest agricultural and food product companies in the world among its clients. Though all areas of business litigation are handled, the team's IP and securities expertise attracted especially favorable comment.

The Lawyers: **Lewis Remele** (see p.1019) is "*in a league of his own.*" Bringing wisdom and practical experience to his trial practice, he is "*extremely comfortable on his feet and has a charming way of cross-examining.*" If this were not enough, he enjoys a reputation as "*the world's nicest guy;*" "*he has enormous skill in the communication of complicated ideas and can bring people together.*" These talents have allowed Remele to establish a highly successful line in alternative dispute resolution.

The Clients: Metropolitan Council; Minnesota Lawyers Mutual; New Access Communications; ConAgra Foods; Murphy Oil; Kone; Cummins Engine; Bor-Son Construction and Upsher-Smith Laboratories.

Gray, Plant, Mooty, Mooty & Bennett, PA

The Firm: Founded in 1866, the firm has the longest continuing existence of any law firm in Minnesota. With "*quality running through the firm,*" the trial and litigation department engages over 60 individuals, subdivided into 12 practice groups. It has a national presence in franchise work, a burgeoning securities group, a dedicated IP group and an antitrust and products liability defense team that is highly regarded by the market. The firm represented Teachers Insurance & Annuity Association, one of the largest pension funds in the country, in a major foreclosure action in Minnesota. The franchise team won a major case in Ohio for Country Kitchen International, both defeating a claim against the client by a franchisee and obtaining a $500,000 award against the franchisee.

The Lawyers: "*Real thinker*" **Jim Simonson** is "*the master*" to his clients. Clients say he puts effort into "*understanding the culture and business climate of the company;*" peers claim he possesses "*great judgment about what appeals to a jury and how to present a case.*" Simonson is counseling General Motors in class action litigation that challenges GM's pricing and distribution practices, and has represented Bridgestone/Firestone on claims concerning tire safety. He continues to defend clients in residual tobacco litigation, including both personal injury and price-fixing aspects. **Laura Hein** acts for franchisers, printers and publishers, manufacturers and the hospitality industry in her counseling and IP infringement work. A recent highlight was Mid-List Press v Nora, which affirmed a grant of summary judgment in favor of a literary publisher against its former director and officer on claims for trademark infringement and breach of fiduciary duty.

The Clients: Teachers Insurance & Annuity Association; GM; RJ Reynolds; HEI; Bridge-

stone/Firestone; Experian; Bayer; Laidlaw Transit Services; Ford; Carlson; Cargill; UniCare and the City of Bloomington.

Oppenheimer Wolff & Donnelly LLP

The Firm: More than 40 lawyers constitute the business litigation department, which has survived the firm's recent size reduction and continues to provide top-level advice to clients on the full range of corporate disputes. Significant experience is to be found in securities and D&O cases, claims centering on fiduciary duties, government investigations, insurance litigation and class actions. Mass tort and mass disaster trials are a specialty for which the firm has gained national prominence.

The Clients: The firm advises clients from the manufacturing, financial services, technology and healthcare industries.

Winthrop & Weinstine, A Professional Association

The Firm: Armed with the expertise of 28 "*excellent, aggressive*" attorneys, the litigation department of this Minneapolis-based firm is well placed to deal with all manner of issues ranging from contractual disputes to fiduciary duties, and boasts experience in franchise, insurance and construction litigation.

The Lawyers: Commentators were keen to identify **Robert Weinstine** as "*a very dogged litigator who gives it all he's got.*" They confirm that Weinstine's tough approach serves his clients well. He has a wide-ranging commercial litigation practice and is applauded especially for antitrust, securities and construction disputes.

The Clients: Among clients of the firm are Alliant Techsystems; Merrill Lynch; Wells Fargo; GMAC; Medtronic; US Bank and Saab Aircraft.

Other Notable Practitioners

Terence Fruth of Fruth, Jamison and Elsass is "*the voice of experience*" in Minnesota. Typically embroiled in litigation with a shareholder or healthcare element, Fruth prevailed against the SEC in an enforcement proceeding tried before a jury in federal court. **Alan Carlson**, of IP litigation boutique Carlson, Caspers, Vandenburgh & Lindquist, is "*probably the most experienced IP guy in town*" and has seen every type of case. His clients have "*well-placed trust in him,*" while peers underlined his jury trial ability, noting how his knowledge of the law allows him to "*pitch his tone to the needs of the case.*" "*Tough but fair*" **Dan McDonald** of Merchant & Gould is "*an all-around great lawyer.*" His IP litigation practice focuses on electronics, computer, and Internet issues and has resulted in some "*significant verdicts*" in the past year.

All quotes in the text are from interviews with clients and competitors.

REAL ESTATE

Minnesota
Leading firms (Real Estate)

1 DORSEY & WHITNEY LLP *Minneapolis*
FAEGRE & BENSON LLP *Minneapolis*
LEONARD, STREET AND DEINARD *Minneapolis*

2 BRIGGS AND MORGAN *Minneapolis*
FREDRIKSON & BYRON PA *Minneapolis*
GRAY, PLANT, MOOTY, MOOTY *Minneapolis*
OPPENHEIMER WOLFF *Minneapolis*

3 FABYANSKE, WESTRA & HART PA *Minneapolis*
FELHABER, LARSON, FENLON *Minneapolis*
LINDQUIST & VENNUM PLLP *Minneapolis*
RAVICH MEYER KIRKMAN MCGRATH *Minneapolis*
WINTHROP & WEINSTINE *St Paul*

Leading individuals (Real Estate)

1 COOK Jay *Dorsey & Whitney, Minneapolis*
EIDE David *Felhaber Larson, Minneapolis*
FERRELL Charles *Faegre & Benson, Minneapolis*
HAMEL Mark *Dorsey & Whitney, Minneapolis*
KONECK John *Fredrikson & Byron, Minneapolis*
WHEATON John *Faegre & Benson, Minneapolis*

2 CHRISTY Angela *Faegre & Benson, Minneapolis*
FINLEY Joseph *Leonard Street, Mankato*
HAYNOR Charles *Briggs and Morgan, Minneapolis*
KELLEY David *Leonard Street, Minneapolis*
KEPPLE Lloyd *Oppenheimer Wolff, Minneapolis*
MASSOPUST Richard *Oppenheimer, Minneapolis*
MAYERLE Thomas *Faegre & Benson, Minneapolis*
NORWICH Donald *Oppenheimer Wolff, Minneapolis*
ODLAUG Bruce *Lindquist & Vennum, Minneapolis*
THIEL John *Gray Plant, Minneapolis*
WESTRA Mark *Fabyanske Westra, Minneapolis*

3 COLE Dan *Briggs and Morgan, Minneapolis*
PARSONS Chuck *Moss & Barnett, Minneapolis*
RAVICH Paul *Ravich Meyer, Minneapolis*
WILHELMY Thomas *Fredrikson & Byron, Minneapolis*

Firms and Individuals are listed alphabetically in each band.

Band 1

Dorsey & Whitney LLP

The Firm: Meeting the growing real estate sector in Minnesota head on, this 30-strong group has developed several specialist teams, each with a particular market focus and "*brimming with talent.*" In the areas of development, real estate finance, corporate real estate management and investment real estate, "*they know the terrain involved in larger deals.*" A growing area of expertise is that of mixed-use development, including the Saint Anthony's Silver Lake Village project, which has new retail and office space, 261 rental units and approximately 350 flats and townhouses. The project combined real estate, land use, environmental, public finance and municipal law expertise. Competitors cite the firm's "*huge resources*" as an obvious strength and client confidence is such that "*you could take*

anything to them and know they would deal with it properly."
The Lawyers: **Jay Cook** "*has the experience and patience to get over bumps in the road.*" As a "*problem solver*" with "*a strong desire to get the deal done,*" he is always "*totally in control.*" Cook's practice has a strong transactional core, and he has recently been involved in the $600 million development project to be built along the Hiawatha Light Rail line in Bloomington, which will include office space, residential housing and a 700-room hotel and resort. His work on the Lewis and Clark Rural Water System has also attracted attention: the system will provide safe, reliable drinking water to approximately 200,000 people in South Dakota, Iowa and Minnesota. Chair of the practice group, the "*unflappable*" **Mark Hamel** is "*a businessman's lawyer*" who "*sees the big picture and gets to the heart of the matter.*" He devoted himself to the 322-acre Ramsay Town Center project, which has approximately 2000 housing units, and is in charge of Presbyterian Homes & Services' $50 million senior community development in North Oaks. Ranked for his land use work, **Jay Lindgren** has an impeccable pedigree. As a former CEO of the Metropolitan Council, his experience of land use, planning and other public and development issues is vast.
The Clients: The team attracts clients from both developing and lending backgrounds, including several national financial institutions, and manages the real estate assets of companies in a diverse range of industries.

Faegre & Benson LLP
See firm details p.1022

The Firm: This 25-attorney unit "*should be the first port of call for all real estate work,*" according to satisfied clients, who attest that "*the attorneys have all the legal knowledge you would need.*" Among their top qualities is an ability to "*cut through the layers of minutiae,*" to "*be proactive in letting clients know what is happening on a transaction*" and to "*never sacrifice excellence, whatever the time frame.*" A growing emphasis on areas such as affordable housing, land use and equity investments has not come at the expense of the fundamentals: the firm acted for General Mills in structuring and documenting the sublease of Pillsbury's headquarters in downtown Minneapolis, receiving an award from the National Association of Industrial and Office Properties for its efforts.
The Lawyers: "*Objective-oriented*" **Charles Ferrell** (see p.1017) "*gets the difficult deals done – nothing is too complicated for him*" and he just "*zeros in on the important issues.*" His practice is very broad in nature, though a number of commentators noted particular excellence in development and leasing matters. Ferrell teamed up

with **John Wheaton** (see p.1021) to advise Allina Health Systems as anchor tenants of Midtown Exchange, a 500,000-sq-ft redevelopment. Together the pair are "*a practical and technical powerhouse that can see all aspects of the deal,*" and each garnered praise for maintaining a sense of humor and perspective in the heat of a deal. "*Creative problem solver*" Wheaton "*never disappoints you,*" according to clients, who cited his ability to meet deadlines, mitigate risks and "*run the show*" as his key strengths. His is a development, leasing and financing practice, and recently he took the lead role representing Capella Education in its headquarter lease of over 200,000 sq ft. Wheaton and **Tom Mayerle** (see p.1019), head of the real estate practice group, led the teams involved in Target's sale of Marshall Field's and Mervyn's for a combined total of $5 billion. Mayerle, whose expertise in the development and leasing of retail and shopping centers was firmly endorsed by peers, retains an enviable clientele because he "*understands all the twists and turns*" and "*brings the breadth of issues to you.*" **Angela Christy** (see p.1017), who recently acted on the $7.5 million renovation of the vacant St Barnabas hospital building in downtown Minneapolis, is regarded as "*the premier attorney in the state for affordable housing.*" Christy is a former chair of the ABA forum on affordable housing and community development law. "*The brownfields guy,*" **John Herman** (see p.1018) has long been involved in regeneration and redevelopment and has scores of projects to his name: housing, commercial, public and historical buildings among them. **Becky Rom** (see p.1020) has been working with the firm on development, land use, administrative and environmental matters for more than 25 years. Peers say she "*always finds a way to get a deal done;*" clients value her "*wealth of knowledge in municipal land use and environmental matters. She led us through the zoning process and was key to getting things done.*"
The Clients: Cargill; 3M; Target; General Mills; Park Nicollet; Hines; Brookfield Development; Gander Mountain and Metropolitan Airports Commission.

Leonard, Street and Deinard Professional Association
The Firm: A firm recognized to possess a true concentration of knowledge in real estate matters; Leonard Street has 30 attorneys who are "*excellent top to bottom.*" Covering all bases, the group grabs a large slice of the development work in the Twin Cities and beyond, and adds depth to its services through the involvement of environmental and tax groups. This interdisciplinary approach results in an ability to act in a variety of specialist areas, such as planned residential communities, real estate partnerships

and joint ventures, secondary mortgage market transactions, brownfield redevelopments and REITs. An identifiable niche lies in the representation of financial institutions, including Marshall & Ilsley in its lending transactions to buyers, owners and developers of commercial real estate.

The Lawyers: *"Straight shooter"* **David Kelley** adds a *"magic touch"* to his work for lenders. As *"one of the most technically precise lawyers,"* his knowledge of lending attracts national and state banks, investment banks, insurance companies and municipal agencies to the firm. His work in the past year included representing the Minneapolis Department of Community Planning and Economic Development in the workout of a defaulted loan on a high-profile downtown retail property. *"Crackerjack"* **Joseph Finley** found favor among peers for his *"high-energy,"* broad-based practice. His ability to *"sell his client's point of view"* was tested recently in the sale of Quadion's corporate headquarters building and manufacturing facility in St. Louis Park, and the purchase of its new office building and laboratory space in Plymouth. Alongside leasing and financing work, Finley represents owners of undeveloped land and gets involved in zoning, brownfield and land use issues.

The Clients: Marshall & Ilsley, Minneapolis Department of Community Planning and Economic Development, and Quadion feature on the client list.

Band 2

Briggs and Morgan, A Professional Association

The Firm: The 22 attorneys in this established real estate group concentrate on two major areas: the representation of developers in acquisitions, dispositions and financing; and the representation of banks and lending institutions in an array of concerns including the securitization of mortgage-backed loans, secondary market programs and tax increment financing. There is department-wide breadth of knowledge in everything from environmental law to partnerships and joint venture agreements, all of which enables the firm to be a key performer both inside and beyond the state borders.

The Lawyers: *"Main player"* **Chuck Haynor** is involved on both the development and finance

sides of the practice. He advised a national developer on a 290-unit condominium project and a borrower in connection with the $100 million financing of a shopping center in Portland, Oregon. However, it is lending work that interviewees identified as his greatest strength. In this he is *"a firm but fair, honest negotiator."* **Dan Cole** who combines an extensive knowledge of environmental law with his real estate practice, joins him in the tables. Cole, based in the St. Paul office, won praise for his financing advice, where he is *"right at the top creatively in terms of getting the job done."*

The Clients: The firm acts for all major players in the real estate industry, including large and small corporate developers, lenders, city governments, school districts, retail and entertainment companies, and developers of multiple-unit projects.

Fredrikson & Byron PA

The Firm: Expanding rapidly in the past two years and viewed as an *"up-and-comer"* in the market, the team has a growing reputation in all aspects of real estate advice. Its numerical strength is reflected by its involvement in significant development projects; for example, the firm made a decisive contribution towards the downtown Minneapolis Target store and office complex and the Alliance Pipeline. As well as widespread recognition for the breadth of experience within the group, special plaudits were reserved for attorneys' activities in land use and real estate dispute resolution.

The Lawyers: **John Koneck** inspires such confidence that commentators *"would put their life in his hands."* In a rare practice, he splits his time between transactional matters and real estate disputes. The latter has provided Koneck with substantial exposure to bankruptcy and debtor/creditor law, where his *"calming effect"* and understanding of *"the interplay between a client's business and a client's legal quest"* are showcased. *"Top-notch"* **David Sellergren** is *"the go-to guy for land use work."* He has spearheaded an upturn in this area at the firm, capitalizing on the booming market. Sellergren focuses on development and redevelopment approvals for all commercial land use types, environmental reviews and permits, and residential/mixed-use development. **Tom Wilhelmy** is viewed by commentators as *"one of the smartest guys in the Twin Cities;"* they recognize the strength of his analytical skills and the national scope of his property valuation and commercial property tax appeals practice. He can be aggressive when necessary in negotiated and litigated proceedings.

The Clients: Town and Country Homes; DR Horton; Newland Communities; Chesapeake Companies; Buffalo Wild Wings and Ryan Companies US.

Gray, Plant, Mooty, Mooty & Bennett, PA

The Firm: Employing around 20 lawyers, this full-service operation draws clients from developers to governmental agencies, and from builders to investors. Boasting expertise in both commercial and residential real estate, recent experience has included obtaining financing, the remediation of environmentally contaminated property, and real estate tax protests on behalf of the owners of numerous hotels, shopping centers, offices, warehouses and multiple residential buildings.

The Lawyers: *"Gentleman"* **John Thiel** *"doesn't miss anything and just doesn't make mistakes."* Bringing 30 years of experience to the table, he devotes a large part of his time seeking a reduction in real estate taxes for his broad raft of clients. Large loan transactions for institutional lenders and complex debt restructuring have made up the balance of his work in the recent past.

The Clients: The firm acts for developers of significant suburban retail, office, industrial and residential developments, as well as the lenders, builders and contractors involved in such projects.

Oppenheimer Wolff & Donnelly LLP

The Firm: Though capable of offering a full-service real estate practice, the 30 real estate practitioners at this firm are heavily oriented towards the representation of financial institutions. Recognized by commentators to be *"the dominant player in the financial arena,"* the firm engages in all significant aspects of work for life insurance vehicles, and investment banking and mortgage banking houses. Mortgage lending, conduit financing, loan participation and syndication, and joint venture work have become second nature to the group.

The Lawyers: *"Ace in the pack"* **Lloyd Kepple** *"always has clients' concerns in mind."* Kepple acts for a number of major national equity investors, lenders and institutional investors, who have propelled him into *"big-ticket"* mortgage work and substantial acquisitions and sales, notably a multilevel parking facility and large office blocks. It was, however, his keen knowledge of the tax minefield that most commended him to peers and clients. **Richard Massopust** is the *"prototype lender's counsel."* His work, particularly in large-scale conduit financing, has been the driving force behind the firm's reputation in the area. Crucially he *"knows how and when to say no."* **Donald Norwich** impresses by being *"smart, fast and decisive,"* and is known for his determined support of his client's position. His work on syndicated loans has a national flavor; Norwich acted on hotel projects in California, ethanol plants in Kansas, Iowa and South Dakota and a marina in Florida.

The Clients: Accenture; ADC; American Express; United Airlines and GE Transportation.

Band 3

Fabyanske, Westra & Hart PA

The Firm: Despite fielding a smaller team than many of its competitors, this firm continues to attract clients based on its excellent reputation for all aspects of real estate work. Representing commercial developers, lenders and entrepreneurs, the firm dispenses advice on properties varying from basic land developments to industrial, office and retail facilities. The firm was also singled out for its knowledge of construction law.

The Lawyers: **Mark Westra** is *"the consummate businessman's lawyer"* as his years of experience have given him *"a very good head for business points."* Westra advises lenders and developers on finance issues, including revolving credit, acquisition finance, and term and asset-based loans, assisting them in the development of shopping centers, retail projects and condominiums.

The Clients: Cargill Financial Services; Integroup Realty Trust; APEX Asset Management; Tanurb Developments; Eagle Ridge Partners and Trammell Crow.

Felhaber, Larson, Fenlon & Vogt, PC

The Firm: With around 15 lawyers involved to some extent in the practice, this midmarket enterprise devotes much of its efforts to development. Recent projects include detached homes, townhouse flats, and mixed-use retail and residential developments. The firm also acts for both lenders and borrowers in real estate-related finance, and defends developers against claims of construction defects by homeowners. Major work in the past year included a $200 million refinancing for a client with manufacturing and distribution plants in 13 states, and redevelopment projects as far afield as Missouri.

The Lawyers: **David Eide** is *"Mr. Condominium."* His work in structuring and financing multifamily housing and commercial developments has accorded him *"the premier position in*

his niche" in the state. Clients and others in the profession view him, in equal measure, as a resource for complex questions relating to common interest communities and condominium work. Clients claim: *"He gets his thinking cap on"* to produce *"creative drafting that ties up the loose ends."* The past year has seen Eide consolidate his reputation with a ten-block residential tower project in the Twin Cities area and several master-planned communities.

The Clients: American Building Contractors; Builders Association of the Twin Cities; Derrick Construction; GRECO Group; Opus Northwest; Pratt Homes and Shamrock Development.

Lindquist & Vennum PLLP
See firm details p.1023

The Firm: The market viewed this team of 13 as having benefited hugely from the firm's increased focus on real estate in the recent past. The firm is now more than capable of addressing common real estate difficulties and transfers; further its blossoming experience in more nuanced areas, such as planning, zoning and environmental impact law, guarantees the breadth of expertise required to resolve the most complex of transactions.

The Lawyers: **Bruce Odlaug** (see p.1019) is credited by many as the man who *"put the firm on the map in real estate."* He handles all commercial real estate issues, representing both financial lending institutions and developers; however, peers hold his tax dispute work in particularly high esteem – crucially, *"he helps people pay less."*

The Clients: The firm serves a mix of lenders, investors, owners and managers of property, and developers of a range of different property types.

Ravich Meyer Kirkman McGrath & Nauman, PA

The Firm: This boutique of seven attorneys has developed a niche in bankruptcy and corporate transactions, and handles pure real estate matters with aplomb. Relied upon by users, developers, investors, managers and syndicates, the team handle purchase and sale transactions (including Section 1031 exchange transactions),

leases and development activities. Should a matter require it, advice is also available on planning and negotiation with cities and other local government entities.

The Lawyers: **Paul Ravich** practices in the areas of real estate, business and finance law, representing small to midsized businesses and their owners, as well as real estate users, developers, investors, managers and syndicators. In recent years, he has utilized his financial background to represent distressed corporations and real estate owners as well as companies attempting to benefit from such distress.

The Clients: The firm acts for local and national companies with real estate interests, and is well known for its work on sales out of bankruptcy to maximize the value of estates.

Winthrop & Weinstine, A Professional Association

The Firm: This small firm, highly regarded for its work on behalf of lending institutions, *"doesn't create road-blocks."* Maintaining links with all sectors of the real estate industry, the group is retained on the full range of transactions from dispositions for local real estate entrepreneurs to complex zoning and low-income housing matters requiring extensive cooperation with governmental authorities.

The Clients: The firm's client base includes individual real estate developers, equity investors, homeowners' associations, nonprofit entities and other institutions.

Other Notable Practitioners
Market observers singled out **Chuck Parsons** of Moss & Barnett as *"a super-nice guy"* who *"always sheds light on a situation."* A real estate generalist, his broad knowledge is also put to use in the legislative context. **Bruce Malkerson** of Malkerson, Gilliland, Martin in Minneapolis is a top choice for land use issues. According to peers: *"People pick Bruce if they think there might be a dispute."* His attributes are obvious: *"He has great attention to detail – he's a lawyer's lawyer in his area; his expertise is incredible; and he has a very strong reputation on the government side. He's almost feared he's respected that much."*

Leaders in Minnesota

ALLGEYER, David
Lindquist & Vennum PLLP, Minneapolis
612 371 3216
dallgeyer@lindquist.com
Recommended in Litigation
Practice Areas: David practices in the areas of intellectual property litigation, arbitration and commercial litigation. He has successfully litigated cases in the state and federal courts involving patents, trademarks, trade secrets and copyright issues as well as matters regarding contractual obligations and the Uniform Commercial Code relating to software and manufacturing devices. He also helps clients identify and deal with licensing and other intellectual property law matters as well as contractual issues and business disputes.
Personal: University of Minnesota Law School (JD, magna cum laude, 1980). University of Minnesota (BA, 1975).

ANTHONY, Joseph
Anthony Ostlund & Baer, Minneapolis
612 349 6969
Recommended in Litigation

BRENNA, Nathan
Anthony Ostlund & Baer, Minneapolis
612 349 6969
Recommended in Litigation

BUSCH, William
Faegre & Benson LLP, Minneapolis
612 766 8809
WBusch@faegre.com
Recommended in Corporate/M&A
Practice Areas: Advertising; corporate and business enterprises; corporate finance and securities; executive compensation; joint ventures; leveraged acquisitions; M&A; private debt and equity financings; shareholder agreements; media and professional sports.
Prof. Memberships: American Society of Corporate Secretaries.
Career: Current member of firm's Management Committee; acquisition of Minnesota Timberwolves professional basketball franchise from the National Basketball Association; sale of Forward Communications Corporation (including six television stations, eight radio stations and a newspaper) to Wesray Communications, Inc.
Personal: BA, University of St Thomas; JD, University of Minnesota, magna cum laude; MBA, University of Minnesota.

CARLSON, Alan
Carlson, Caspers, Vandenburgh & Lindquist, Minneapolis 612 436 9600
Recommended in Litigation

CARRON, Reid
Faegre & Benson LLP, Minneapolis
612 766 7428
RCarron@faegre.com
Recommended in Employment

Practice Areas: Collective bargaining; opposing union organizing campaigns; unfair labor practice charges; decertification elections; strike planning and operations; labor issues associated with M&A; arbitrations; employment agreements.
Prof. Memberships: American Bar Association; Minnesota State Bar Association.
Career: Former Head of the Faegre & Benson Labor and Employment Law Group, which offers among the largest teams of full-time labor and employment lawyers and litigators in the Midwest and Rocky Mountain regions.
Publications: The Employer's Duty to Supply Financial Information to the Union, The Labor Lawyer.
Personal: BA, Southeast Missouri State University, magna cum laude; JD, University of Missouri-Columbia, cum laude.

CHRISTENSEN, Douglas
Dorsey & Whitney LLP, Minneapolis
612 340 2600
Recommended in Employment

CHRISTY, Angela
Faegre & Benson LLP, Minneapolis
612 766 6833
achristy@faegre.com
Recommended in Real Estate
Practice Areas: Affordable housing; low-income housing tax credit; Indian/tribal law.
Prof. Memberships: ABA Forum on Affordable Housing and Community Development Law (Past Chair); Minnesota Certified Real Property Specialist.
Career: Angela's practice focuses on affordable housing, particularly tax credit transactions. She has represented non-profit and for-profit developers, investors and governmental entities in more than 150 tax credit transactions throughout the United States. She also has represented numerous contractors and developers regarding construction documents for housing, office buildings and other developments.
Personal: BA, North Dakota State University; JD, University of Minnesota, cum laude.

CIRESI, Michael
Robins Kaplan Miller & Ciresi,
Minneapolis 612 349 8500
Recommended in Litigation

CLEVELAND, Christopher
Briggs and Morgan, Professional Association, Minneapolis
612 977 8400
Recommended in Corporate/M&A

COLE, Dan
Briggs and Morgan, Professional Association, Minneapolis 612 977 8400
Recommended in Real Estate

COOK, Jay
Dorsey & Whitney LLP, Minneapolis
612 340 2600
Recommended in Real Estate

COSTLEY, Kevin
Lindquist & Vennum PLLP, Minneapolis
612 371 3547
kcostley@lindquist.com
Recommended in Corporate/M&A
Practice Areas: Kevin specializes in representing financial institutions in mergers and acquisitions, capital financing plans, and business expansion strategies. Most of his clients are independent community banks located in the Upper Midwest.
Personal: University of Minnesota School of Law (JD, 1975; editor, Minnesota Law Review; Order of the Coif). University of California at Los Angeles (BA, summa cum laude, 1971). Before joining Lindquist & Vennum, he clerked for Justice Harry MacLaughlin of the Minnesota Supreme Court.

CUTLER, Kenneth
Dorsey & Whitney LLP, Minneapolis
612 340 2600
Recommended in Corporate/M&A

D'AQUILA, Barbara
Flynn, Gaskins & Bennett, Minneapolis
612 333 9500
Recommended in Employment

DAVIES, Scott
Briggs and Morgan, Professional Association, Minneapolis 612 977 8400
Recommended in Employment

DAWSON, James
Felhaber, Larson, Fenlon & Vogt, PC, Minneapolis 612 339 6321
Recommended in Employment

DIVINEY, Craig
Dorsey & Whitney LLP, Minneapolis
612 340 2600
Recommended in Litigation

EFRON, Stanley
Henson & Efron, Minneapolis
612 339 2500
Recommended in Corporate/M&A

EIDE, David
Felhaber, Larson, Fenlon & Vogt, PC, Minneapolis 612 339 6321
Recommended in Real Estate

ENG, Holly
Dorsey & Whitney LLP, Minneapolis
612 340 2600
Recommended in Employment

ENGLER, Bruce
Faegre & Benson LLP, Minneapolis
612 766 8811
bengler@faegre.com
Recommended in Corporate/M&A
Practice Areas: Corporate counseling, finance and securities, debt and equity financing, institutional private placement financing, issuance of securities,

leveraged acquisitions, mergers and acquisitions, public and private securities offerings
Career: He focuses on mergers and acquisitions, public and private securities offerings, institutional private placement financing, and general corporate counseling. Regarding M&A, Bruce has represented buyers, sellers and institutional investors in various public and private transactions. He's had primary or significant responsibility for more than 45 acquisition transactions with an aggregate transaction value exceeding 3.5 billion dollars.
Personal: BA, Creighton University, summa cum laude; JD, University of Michigan, magna cum laude.

FERRELL, Charles
Faegre & Benson LLP, Minneapolis
612 766 7531
cferrell@fagre.com
Recommended in Real Estate
Practice Areas: Commercial real estate; sports law; real estate development; debt and equity financing.
Prof. Memberships: American College of Real Estate Lawyers; Building Owners and Managers Association.
Career: Has represented: US Bank (Minneapolis); Norwest Center (Minneapolis); University of Arizona Science and Technology Park (Tucson); Niketown (Seattle); Rich Stadium (Buffalo); Target Center (Minneapolis); Major Workout (California, Texas and Pennsylvania). Pro bono areas include environmental law and lease representation for civic groups.
Publications: 'Form of Commercial Lease', Minnesota Continuing Legal Education.
Personal: BS, Cornell University, with distinction; JD, University of Michigan, Law Review, magna cum laude, Order of the Coif.

FIELD, Lawrence
Leonard, Street and Deinard Professional Association, Minneapolis
612 335 1500
Recommended in Litigation

FINLEY, Joseph
Leonard, Street and Deinard, Professional Association, Mankato
507 345 1179
Recommended in Real Estate

FLEMING, Terrence
Lindquist & Vennum PLLP, Minneapolis
612 371 3248
tfleming@lindquist.com
Recommended in Litigation
Practice Areas: Terry represents parties in cases involving commercial fraud including, shareholder derivative and shareholder class actions, merger and acquisition litigation, regulatory proceedings, investor-broker and law firm disputes, and minority shareholder dis-

putes. He also works as an arbitrator, mediator and expert witness in these areas. He represents parties in regulatory proceedings involving insider trading, securities fraud, accounting issues, and investor complaints before the SEC, NASD and state regulatory entities. Terry has represented parties in more than 100 completed jury and court trials, arbitrations, mediations and regulatory proceedings.
Personal: Harvard Law School (JD, 1981). College of St. Thomas (BA, 1978).

FRASER, Thomas
Fredrikson & Byron PA, Minneapolis
612 492 7000
Recommended in Litigation

FRUTH, Terence
Fruth, Jamison & Elsass, Minneapolis
612 344 9700
Recommended in Litigation

GARON, Philip S
Faegre & Benson LLP, Minneapolis
612 766 8101
PGaron@faegre.com
Recommended in Corporate/M&A
Practice Areas: Corporate finance and securities; corporate governance; hostile takeover defense; M&A.
Prof. Memberships: Minnesota State Bar Association, Business Law Section - Former Chair.
Career: Phil is a Partner in Corporate Group and is former Chair of the firm's Management Committee. He focuses upon corporate matters, public and private mergers and acquisitions, private financings and hostile takeover defense.
Publications: 'Minnesota Corporation Law and Practice', West Publishing Company.
Personal: BA, University of Minnesota, Phi Beta Kappa, summa cum laude; JD, University of Minnesota, Law Review (Associate Editor), Order of the Coif, summa cum laude.

GINSBURG, Roy
Dorsey & Whitney LLP, Minneapolis
612 340 2600
Recommended in Employment

GORDON, Avron
Briggs and Morgan, Professional Association, Minneapolis 612 977 8400
Recommended in Corporate/M&A

GOTTSCHALK, Steve
Dorsey & Whitney LLP, Minneapolis
612 340 2600
Recommended in Employment

GROSS, David
Faegre & Benson LLP, Minneapolis
612 766 7804
dgross@faegre.com
Recommended in Litigation
Practice Areas: Intellectual property litigation, civil trial practice.
Career: David was lead trial counsel for Wyeth in the billion-dollar trade secret case, Wyeth v Natural Biologics, Inc.

Court granted a permanent injunction prohibiting the defendant from developing a generic version of Wyeth's product Premarin. As a result, David was named one of 15 'Attorneys of the Year' by Minnesota Lawyer, and the case was profiled in a page one story in the National Law Journal.
Publications: 'The Power Trial Method'.
Personal: BA, University of Minnesota, Phi Beta Kappa, summa cum laude; JD, Harvard University, magna cum laude.

HALVERSON, Jan
Felhaber, Larson, Fenlon & Vogt, PC, Minneapolis 612 339 6321
Recommended in Employment

HAMEL, Mark
Dorsey & Whitney LLP, Minneapolis
612 340 2600
Recommended in Real Estate

HAYNOR, Charles
Briggs and Morgan, Professional Association, Minneapolis 612 977 8400
Recommended in Real Estate

HEIN, Laura
Gray, Plant, Mooty, Mooty & Bennett, PA, Minneapolis 612 632 3000
Recommended in Litigation

HERMAN, John
Faegre & Benson LLP, Minneapolis
612 766 8908
jherman@faegre.com
Recommended in Real Estate
Practice Areas: Real estate, development and finance, government relations, environmental law, land use/zoning/ environmental review, government regulation of business and commerce.
Career: He focuses on real estate development and finance, legislative and government relations and environmental/ land use law. He's been a central figure in Minnesota real estate development and environmental policy for more than 25 years. Represents developers of numerous large commercial projects including retail, restaurant, entertainment and office including Block E, City Center, General Mills Headquarters, Walker Art Center Complex, Graco Corporate Headquarters, Stinson Technology Corridor, and Riverplace.
Personal: BA, Yale University, cum laud; JD, Harvard University.

HERR, David
Maslon Edelman Borman & Brand, LLP, Minneapolis
612 672 8200
Recommended in Litigation

HOBBINS, Robert
Dorsey & Whitney LLP, Minneapolis
612 340 2600
Recommended in Employment

HUMPHREY, Andrew
Faegre & Benson LLP, Minneapolis
612 766 8816
AHumphrey@faegre.com
Recommended in Corporate/M&A

Practice Areas: Frequently advises public and private companies in their organization and corporate governance, ongoing business review and documentation, contractual negotiations, obligations of directors and officers, relations with shareholders, capitalization and securities issuances. Lead counsel in multiple venture capital transactions.
Publications: 'Strategies' business column, The Business Journal; contributing editor, Encyclopedia of Venture Capital; 'When the Going Gets Tough', Trends; 'Venture Finance in the 'New' New Economy', Minnesota Technology; 'Antitrust Jurisdiction and Remedies in an Electric Utility Price Squeeze', University of Chicago Law Review.
Personal: BA, Amherst College, cum laude; JD, University of Chicago, Law Review (comment editor).

HUNTRODS, Ann
Briggs and Morgan, Professional Association, St Paul 651 808 6600
Recommended in Employment

IHRIG, Richard
Lindquist & Vennum PLLP, Minneapolis
612 371 3257
rihrig@lindquist.com
Recommended in Litigation
Practice Areas: Rich resolves commercial disputes, particularly large scale class actions and multi-party disputes that present difficult jurisdiction, liability and damage issues. He has extensive experience in the electric utility, consumer, finance, airline and health care industries. He also handles major antitrust cases. Rich is currently representing major drug store chains and more than 150 animal feed manufacturers on price fixing and market allocation claims against several vitamin manufacturers.
Personal: University of Minnesota Law School (JD, magna cum laude, 1973). Gustavus Adolphus College (BA, cum laude, 1970).

KAHNKE, Randall
Faegre & Benson LLP, Minneapolis
612 766 7658
RKahnke@faegre.com
Recommended in Litigation
Practice Areas: Complex business litigation, intellectual property litigation.
Prof. Memberships: Past President and a Member of the Board of Directors of the Minnesota Chapter of the Federal Bar Association.
Career: Randy has extensive consulting, pretrial, and trial experience with complex commercial and intellectual property disputes. Randy has been the lead attorney at numerous trials and arbitrations, and is a frequent lecturer on issues related to complex business disputes and intellectual property litigation.
Personal: BA, University of St. Thomas, summa cum laude; JD, University of Minnesota, cum laude, Law Review.

KAPLAN, Samuel
Kaplan, Strangis & Kaplan, Minneapolis 612 375 1138
Recommended in Corporate/M&A

KAUFMAN, D William
Oppenheimer Wolff & Donnelly LLP, Minneapolis 612 607 7000
Recommended in Corporate/M&A

KELLEY, David
Leonard, Street and Deinard Professional Association, Minneapolis
612 335 1500
Recommended in Real Estate

KELLY, Timothy
Kelly & Berens P.A., Minneapolis
612 349 6171
Recommended in Litigation

KEPPLE, Lloyd
Oppenheimer Wolff & Donnelly LLP, Minneapolis 612 607 7000
Recommended in Real Estate

KEYES, Jeffrey
Briggs and Morgan, Professional Association, Minneapolis 612 977 8400
Recommended in Litigation

KLASS, Paul
Dorsey & Whitney LLP, Minneapolis
612 340 2600
Recommended in Litigation

KONECK, John
Fredrikson & Byron PA, Minneapolis
612 492 7000
Recommended in Real Estate

KOZACHOK, Steve
Dorsey & Whitney LLP, Minneapolis
612 340 2600
Recommended in Corporate/M&A

LANGEVIN, Judith
Gray, Plant, Mooty, Mooty & Bennett, PA, Minneapolis 612 632 3000
Recommended in Employment

LETSCHER, Tom
Oppenheimer Wolff & Donnelly LLP, Minneapolis 612 607 7000
Recommended in Corporate/M&A

LIBBEY, Keith
Fredrikson & Byron PA, Minneapolis
612 492 7000
Recommended in Corporate/M&A

LIEBMAN, Kenneth A
Faegre & Benson LLP, Minneapolis
612 766 8800
KLiebman@faegre.com
Recommended in Litigation
Practice Areas: Intellectual property; patent litigation; trade secret litigation; copyright litigation; trademark litigation; medical technology; information technology.
Career: Chair of the firm's Intellectual Property Group. His focus is on the representation of companies in the medical technology and information technology fields. Was lead counsel for the University of Minnesota in its patent licensing litigation against Glaxo Wellcome over

the AIDS drug ZiagenTM. Case settled with the defendant recognizing the validity of the University's patents and agreeing to pay royalties estimated to total $300 million.

Personal: BA, Columbia University, Phi Beta Kappa, summa cum laude; JD, Yale University.

LINDGREN, Jay
Dorsey & Whitney LLP, Minneapolis
612 340 2600
Recommended in Real Estate

LUECK, Martin
Robins Kaplan Miller & Ciresi, Minneapolis 612 349 8500
Recommended in Litigation

LUGER, Andrew
Greene Espel PLLP, Minneapolis
612 373 0830
Recommended in Litigation

MACHMEIER, Bruce
Oppenheimer Wolff & Donnelly LLP, Minneapolis 612 607 7000
Recommended in Corporate/M&A

MAGNUSON, Roger
Dorsey & Whitney LLP, Minneapolis
612 340 2600
Recommended in Litigation

MALKERSON, Bruce
Malkerson, Gilliland, Martin, Minneapolis 612 344 1111
Recommended in Real Estate

MARK, Richard
Briggs and Morgan, Professional Association, Minneapolis 612 977 8400
Recommended in Litigation

MASSOPUST, Richard
Oppenheimer Wolff & Donnelly LLP, Minneapolis 612 607 7000
Recommended in Real Estate

MAYERLE, Thomas M
Faegre & Benson LLP, Minneapolis
612 766 7228
TMayerle@faegre.com
Recommended in Real Estate

Practice Areas: General commercial real estate and corporate real estate.
Career: Tom is the Head of Faegre's Real Estate Group. He has developed expertise across the broad spectrum of commercial real estate, with particular emphasis on the development, purchase, sale, leasing and financing of office building and shopping center projects. Tom is a member of the American College of Real Estate Lawyers and has been included since 1983 in the listing of Minnesota real estate lawyers in 'The Best Lawyers in America.'
Personal: AB, Dartmouth College; JD, University of Minnesota, Law Review, magna cum laude, Order of the Coif.

MCDONALD, Daniel
Merchant & Gould PC, Minneapolis
612 332 5300
Recommended in Litigation

MERLEY, Dennis
Felhaber, Larson, Fenlon & Vogt, PC, Minneapolis 612 339 6321
Recommended in Employment

MOORSE, Charles
Lindquist & Vennum PLLP, Minneapolis
612 371 5771
cmoorse@lindquist.com
Recommended in Corporate/M&A

Practice Areas: Chuck advises public and private companies across various industry groups on matters including mergers and acquisitions, venture financing, public offerings, corporate governance and securities regulation. On the M&A side, Chuck represents both buyers and sellers of privately and publicly held companies across a range of industry groups, including high technology, manufacturing, retailing, financial services, medical devices, OTC products, consulting and contract services. In his general corporate practice, Chuck serves as outside general counsel to mid-cap publicly and privately held companies.
Personal: William Mitchell College of Law (JD, magna cum laude, 1986). Saint John's University (BS, cum laude, 1981).

MRKONICH, Marko
Littler Mendelson, A Professional Corporation, Minneapolis 612 630 1000
Recommended in Employment

NOECKER, Kathlyn E
Faegre & Benson LLP, Minneapolis
612 766 8604
KNoecker@faegre.com
Recommended in Employment

Practice Areas: International and domestic labor and employment law and executive compensation.
Prof. Memberships: Kathy leads Faegre's Labor and Employment Group and practices in Executive Compensation and Emerging Business Groups. Kathy works extensively with employers of all sizes to advise them regarding complex workplace laws. A significant portion of Kathy's practice involves the negotiation and preparation of employment, compensation and separation arrangements for executives. She also counsels clients on employee discipline and discharge decisions, personnel policies, disability accommodation, sexual harassment investigations, reductions-in-force, and on employment issues arising out of corporate transactions.
Personal: BA, College of St. Catherine; JD, Georgetown University.

NORWICH, Donald
Oppenheimer Wolff & Donnelly LLP, Minneapolis 612 607 7000
Recommended in Real Estate

NOTEBOOM, Todd
Leonard, Street and Deinard Professional Association, Minneapolis
612 335 1500
Recommended in Litigation

ODLAUG, Bruce
Lindquist & Vennum PLLP, Minneapolis
612 371 5792
bodlaug@lindquist.com
Recommended in Real Estate

Practice Areas: Bruce's practice involves all aspects of commercial real estate representing both financial lending institutions and developers. He has counseled property owners regarding zoning and land use matters as well as landlord and tenant representation and eminent domain proceedings. He is a certified real estate specialist.
Prof. Memberships: Hennepin County Bar Association. Minnesota State Bar Association. American Bar Association.
Personal: University of Minnesota Law School (LLB, 1965). University of Notre Dame (BBA, 1962).

O'NEILL, Brian B
Faegre & Benson LLP, Minneapolis
612 766 8318
BONeill@faegre.com
Recommended in Litigation

Practice Areas: Trial practice and appellate practice.
Prof. Memberships: American College of Trial Lawyers (State Chair). Board of Visitors, University of Michigan Law School, 1994-present. Board of Directors, Defenders of Wildlife, 1984-present.
Career: Significant trials and appeals include: Peterson v BASF; Pioneer Hi-Bred International Inc. v Monsanto Company; Lujan v Defenders of Wildlife, 504 US 555 (1992) (application of Endangered Species Act to US projects overseas; standing).
Personal: BS, United States Military Academy, served to Captain, US Army; JD, University of Michigan, Law Review, magna cum laude, Order of the Coif.

OSTLUND, Richard
Anthony Ostlund & Baer, Minneapolis
612 349 6969
Recommended in Litigation

PARSONS, Chuck
Moss & Barnett, A Professional Association, Minneapolis 612 347 0300
Recommended in Real Estate

PAYNE, William
Dorsey & Whitney LLP, Minneapolis
612 340 2600
Recommended in Corporate/M&A

PENTELOVITCH, William
Maslon Edelman Borman & Brand, LLP, Minneapolis 612 672 8200
Recommended in Litigation

PHILLIPS, Penny
Felhaber, Larson, Fenlon & Vogt, PC, Minneapolis 612 339 6321
Recommended in Employment

RADOLINSKI, Anne
Fredrikson & Byron PA, Minneapolis
612 492 7000
Recommended in Employment

RAPHAN, Melissa
Dorsey & Whitney LLP, Minneapolis
612 340 2600
Recommended in Employment

RAVICH, Paul
Ravich Meyer Kirkman McGrath & Nauman, PA, Minneapolis
612 332 8511
Recommended in Real Estate

REINHART, Robert
Dorsey & Whitney LLP, Minneapolis
612 340 2600
Recommended in Employment

REMELE Jr, Lewis A
Bassford Remele, A Professional Association, Minneapolis
612 333 3000
lewr@bassford.com
Recommended in Litigation

Practice Areas: Civil trial practice involving commercial litigation including contract disputes, securities, fiduciary and shareholder disputes, class actions, trust and estates litigation, professional liability, employment, personal injury and insurance coverage. Clients include Minnesota Lawyers Mutual Insurance Company; Illinois Tool Corporation; Medica Health Plan; URS; American National Can; Con Agra; Metropolitan Council; St. Paul Travelers Companies; and Advance PCS. Appointed Special Master, United States District Court, District of Minnesota, for In Re Baycol Litigation. Appointed Special Master, Hennepin County District Court, for In Re Soo Line Derailment Litigation.
Prof. Memberships: Minnesota State Bar Association (past President); Fellow of the American College of Trial Lawyers, American Board of Trial Advocates and American Bar Foundation; Hennepin County Bar Association (past President).
Career: Admitted to Minnesota state and federal courts, Eighth Circuit Court of Appeals and United States Supreme Court. Shareholder with BASSFORD REMELE since 1989; chief executive officer, 2001-04. Listed in leading American publications. Best lawyer in Minnesota by 'Minnesota Law & Politics', 2001-04.
Personal: JD, Creighton University (cum laude); BA, Harvard University (magna cum laude).

ROBINER, Susan
Leonard, Street and Deinard Professional Association, Minneapolis
612 335 1500
Recommended in Employment

ROBY, Jr, Joseph
Johnson Killen & Seiler, Duluth
218 722 6331
Recommended in Employment

ROM, Rebecca L
Faegre & Benson LLP, Minneapolis
612 766 7231
rrom@faegre.com
Recommended in Real Estate

Practice Areas: Becky has practiced with the Real Estate, Environmental, Administrative Law and Litigation Groups at Faegre & Benson's Minneapolis office since 1979. Her practice is focused primarily on commercial real estate.
Prof. Memberships: Alaska Coalition of Minnesota, Founder and Chair 1995-present. The Wilderness Society, member, Governing Council 1996-present, Chair 2002-present.
Career: In 1999, Becky was named by Citybusiness as one of the 25 Most Influential Women in Business in the Twin Cities. She also received the John C Benson Pro Bono Award.
Personal: BA, Mount Holyoke College; JD, William Mitchell College of Law, cum laude.

ROSENBAUM, Robert
Dorsey & Whitney LLP, Minneapolis
612 340 2600
Recommended in Corporate/M&A

ROSS, Richard
Fredrikson & Byron PA, Minneapolis
612 492 7000
Recommended in Employment

SCALLEN, Timothy
Oppenheimer Wolff & Donnelly LLP, Minneapolis 612 607 7000
Recommended in Corporate/M&A

SCHUTZ, Ron
Robins Kaplan Miller & Ciresi, Minneapolis 612 349 8500
Recommended in Litigation

SEATON, Doug
Seaton, Beck, Peters, Bowen & Feuss, Minneapolis 952 896 1700
Recommended in Employment

SELLERGREN, David
Fredrikson & Byron PA, Minneapolis
612 492 7000
Recommended in Real Estate

SHARPE, W Smith 'Kris'
Faegre & Benson LLP, Minneapolis
612 766 6828
KSharpe@faegre.com
Recommended in Corporate/M&A

Practice Areas: Corporate finance and securities; mergers and acquisitions; private debt and equity financings; venture capital financing; entrepreneurial and emerging companies.
Career: Kris represents a number of companies in their development stage prior to going public. Representation of such companies involves their formation, private placement financings, creation of employee benefit plans, coordination of other legal service specialties (e.g., intellectual property), and general corporate counseling, including attendance at board meetings.

Personal: BA, Columbia University, Phi Beta Kappa, summa cum laude; JD, Yale University.

SHERMAN, Morris
Leonard, Street and Deinard Professional Association, Minneapolis
612 335 1500
Recommended in Corporate/M&A

SIMONSON, James
Gray, Plant, Mooty, Mooty & Bennett, PA, Minneapolis 612 632 3000
Recommended in Litigation

SNIDER, Jerry W
Faegre & Benson LLP, Minneapolis
612 766 7816
jsnider@faegre.com
Recommended in Litigation

Practice Areas: Antitrust and trade regulation. Civil, commercial and complex employment, Indian/tribal law and intellectual property. Trial and appeals of complex civil cases.
Career: Member of firm's Management Committee. Representative clients include Abbott Laboratories, Inc., American Express Financial Corporation, Archer Daniels Midland ('ADM'), Battenfeld of America, Inc., International Business Machines Corp. ('IBM'), Old Republic Title Insurance Company, Parke, Davis & Co., The Pillsbury Company, Target Corporation.
Personal: BS, Wake Forest University; JD, University of Houston, Law Review (articles editor).

SNYDER, Stephen
Gray, Plant, Mooty, Mooty & Bennett, PA, Minneapolis 612 632 3000
Recommended in Employment

SOLUM, Richard
Dorsey & Whitney LLP, Minneapolis
612 340 2600
Recommended in Litigation

STAGEBERG, Roger
Lommen, Nelson, Cole & Stageberg, P.A., Minneapolis 612 339 8131
Recommended in Corporate/M&A

STANCHFIELD, Mike
Faegre & Benson LLP, Minneapolis
612 766 7764
MStanchfield@faegre.com
Recommended in Corporate/M&A

Practice Areas: Corporate, mergers and acquisitions.
Career: Mike is a Partner in Faegre's Corporate Group. His practice is focused on the areas of mergers and acquisitions, corporate governance, takeover preparedness, public securities offerings, private financings, and general corporate counseling. Mike has handled major M&A transactions in recent years for companies like Marshall Fields, St. Paul Companies, Guidant, Archer-Daniels-Midland, Graco, ReliaStar, Lutheran Brotherhood, and many others.
Publications: 'Voting Lock-Ups and Sales of Partially Owned Subsidiaries:

Can Stockholders Love a Deal Too Early and Too Much?' - Winner, 2003 Burton Award for Legal Writing.
Personal: BA, University of Minnesota; JD, Harvard University.

STENMOE, Gregory
Briggs and Morgan, Professional Association, Minneapolis 612 977 8400
Recommended in Employment

STRANGIS, Ralph
Kaplan, Strangis & Kaplan, Minneapolis 612 375 1138
Recommended in Corporate/M&A

STUMO, Mary
Faegre & Benson LLP, Minneapolis
612 766 8115
mstumo@faegre.com
Recommended in Employment

Practice Areas: Employment and employment litigation.
Prof. Memberships: Minnesota Women Lawyers.
Career: Mary's practice focuses on employment-related litigation including claims related to all types of discrimination (sexual harassment, age, race, sex and disability), breach of contract, defamation, whistleblowing, and non-compete agreements, up to and including multiple jury trials. Member of firm's Management Committee.
Publications: Chapter 21, Using Psychiatric and Psychology Experts at Trial: 'Defense Perspective, Litigating the Sexual Harassment Case' (ABA Book) (1999); 'Forum: Sexual Harassment News for Employers', CityBusiness (1998).
Personal: BS, University of Wisconsin, with honors; JD, University of Minnesota, cum laude.

THIEL, John
Gray, Plant, Mooty, Mooty & Bennett, PA, Minneapolis 612 632 3000
Recommended in Real Estate

THOMPSON, John
Rider, Bennett, Egan & Arundel, LLP, Minneapolis 612 340 7951
Recommended in Employment

TINKHAM, Thomas
Dorsey & Whitney LLP, Minneapolis
612 340 2600
Recommended in Litigation

VANDER HAAR, David
Faegre & Benson LLP, Minneapolis
612 766 8705
DVanderHaar@faegre.com
Recommended in Corporate/M&A

Practice Areas: Public and private mergers and acquisitions, joint ventures, strategic alliances and other collaborations, general corporate counseling, antitrust counseling in connection with mergers and acquisitions, and hostile takeover defense.
Prof. Memberships: He is currently Chair of the Minnesota Bar Association's Standing Committee on the Minnesota Business Corporation Act, Chair

of the Corporate Law Section of the Minnesota Bar Association's Business Law Section and a Member of the Section's Executive Committee.
Publications: Drafted changes to substantial portions of the 'Minnesota Business Corporation Act'.
Personal: BA, Hope College; JD, University of California, Berkeley.

VOLLING, James
Faegre & Benson LLP, Minneapolis
612 766 7758
JVolling@faegre.com
Recommended in Litigation

Career: Jim is the Head of the firm's Business Litigation Group. For more than two decades, he has represented clients in a wide variety of complex commercial disputes valued up to several hundred million dollars. Jim has appeared in state and federal trial courts in every region of the country and has argued appeals in several federal and state appellate courts. His broad-based experience includes extensive work in antitrust, securities and shareholder litigation, consumer class actions, False Claims Act, RICO, lender liability, breach of contract, breach of warranty, and lender liability.
Personal: AB, Harvard University; JD, The George Washington University.

WEBBER, Charles F
Faegre & Benson LLP, Minneapolis
612 766 8719
Cwebber@faegre.com
Recommended in Litigation

Practice Areas: Bankruptcy litigation; foreclosures and workouts; and receiverships.
Career: Chuck Webber is a commercial litigator. He has litigated in a wide variety of commercial contexts, especially the areas of financial services, consumer protection laws, and commercial contracts. Chuck recently successful defended one of the nation's largest refining companies in a whistleblower trial that was named one of the top defense verdicts of the year by The National Law Journal.
Personal: BA, University of Minnesota, Phi Beta Kappa, summa cum laude; JD, University of Chicago, Law Review (associate managing editor), Order of the Coif, with honors.

WEINSTINE, Robert
Winthrop & Weinstine, A Professional Association, Minneapolis
612 347 0700
Recommended in Litigation

WEITZ, Mark
Leonard, Street and Deinard Professional Association, Minneapolis
612 335 1500
Recommended in Corporate/M&A

WESTRA, Mark
Fabyanske, Westra & Hart PA, Minneapolis 612 359 7600
Recommended in Real Estate

WHEATON, John
Faegre & Benson LLP, Minneapolis
612 766 7761
JWheaton@faegre.com
Recommended in Real Estate
Practice Areas: Banking; real estate litigation; construction law.
Prof. Memberships: Admitted to Practice in Minnesota.
Career: Represented a national bank in the sale of its downtown headquarters building in the midst of pending condemnation proceedings. Placement of development and construction loans, and the later closing of securitized, permanent financing, for Dain Bosworth Plaza, a vertical retail and high-rise office project in Minneapolis.

Publications: Speeches on various topics at Advanced Legal Education Seminars and Bar Association Groups.
Personal: BA, Northwestern University, with honors; JD, University of Minnesota, magna cum laude.

WILDUNG, Wendy J
Faegre & Benson LLP, Minneapolis
612 766 7759
WWildung@faegre.com
Recommended in Litigation
Practice Areas: Business torts; litigation; securities law.
Prof. Memberships: American Bar Association; Federal Bar Association; Hennepin County Bar Association; Minnesota State Bar Association; Securities Industry Association Division of Legal and Compliance.

Career: Defending securities broker-dealers and financial advisors against claims brought by customers involving purchases and sales of stocks, bonds, mutual funds, option contracts, and commodities futures contracts. Defending corporations against shareholder suits arising out of leveraged buy-outs and going-private transactions. Defending publicly-held corporations, and their officers and directors, in hostile takeover litigation.
Personal: BA, University of Minnesota, magna cum laude, Phi Beta Kappa, JD, Harvard University.

WILHELMY, Thomas
Fredrikson & Byron PA, Minneapolis
612 492 7000
Recommended in Real Estate

WILLE, Karin
Briggs and Morgan, Professional Association, Minneapolis 612 977 8400
Recommended in Employment

ZECH, Paul
Felhaber, Larson, Fenlon & Vogt, PC, Minneapolis 612 339 6321
Recommended in Employment

ZEGLOVITCH, Robert
Leonard, Street and Deinard Professional Association, Minneapolis
612 335 1500
Recommended in Employment

FAEGRE & BENSON LLP

THE FIRM

Managing Partners: Thomas G Morgan (Chair), John D Shively, Jerry W Snider, Charles S Ferrell, Jack M Fribley, Mary E Stumo, William R Busch, Michael S McCarthy, Winthrop A Rockwell

Number of partners in the US: 228
Number of other lawyers in US Offices: 168

FIRM OVERVIEW: The firm offers clients more than 460 lawyers in a full range of practice groups, with experience handling legal matters throughout the United States, as well as Europe and Asia. The firm is one of the 100 largest law firms in the US. In 2002-04, an independent survey of corporate counsel in Fortune 1000 companies throughout the US ranked Faegre & Benson among the top 20 law firms in the country for client service. Faegre & Benson is also a member of two consortiums that provide access to a national and worldwide network of experienced commercial lawyers, the United States Law Firm Group and The World Law Group. Faegre & Benson received several prestigious honors in 2004. The firm scored 100% on the HRC (Human Rights Campaign) Corporate Equality Index; and was recognized by the Minority Corporate Counsel Association's Sager Award for efforts to recruit and retain minorities and women.

MAIN AREAS OF PRACTICE:

Corporate: Offering one of the most sophisticated corporate legal teams in the nation, Faegre & Benson regularly handles complex finance and securities transactions for leading regional and national companies. The firm handled mergers and acquisitions for companies such as Target Corporation, International Multifoods, St. Paul Companies, Inc., Fair Isaac Corporation, Norwest Equity Partners, Guidant, American Express, Piper Jaffray, Cowles Media Company, ReliaStar, Archer-Daniels-Midland, Bemis, and Land O'Lakes, in transactions totaling more than $30 billion. The firm offers among the largest and most experienced corporate finance teams in both the Minnesota and Colorado regions and highly regarded corporate experience in London, Frankfurt, Shanghai, and Des Moines. Highlights for the firm in 2004 include representing Target Corporation and International Multifoods in M&A deals totaling almost $6 billion. Faegre & Benson also represented clients in a string of IPOs worth over $1 billion.

Intellectual Property: Faegre & Benson offers one of the largest teams of intellectual property lawyers in the central US, with experience handling complex litigation and transactions for clients ranging from multinationalcorporations to high-technology entrepreneurs. The IP team includes 70 lawyers in the US, Europe, and Asia, including 20 registered patent attorneys. Many of its lawyers offer educational and professional experience unique to the intellectual property needs of specific industries, including backgrounds in chemical and electrical engineering, biotechnology, microbiology, physics, and computer science. Its size and depth gives a level of IP expertise that is comparable to leading 'boutique' IP firms, while offering clients the resources of one of the most respected corporate and litigation firms in the US.

Litigation: Faegre & Benson offers a large litigation team, with experience litigating at every level of the state and federal court systems, including the US Supreme Court. The firm regularly litigates in product liability, intellectual property, toxic torts, securities, employment law, class actions, multidistrict litigation, insurance, antitrust, bankruptcy, franchise and dealer disputes, construction, contract and other commercial litigation. The firm's lawyers have litigated matters in nearly every US state, plus the UK, Europe and Asia. Its team includes highly experienced trial lawyers; litigation managers; lawyers with special expertise with expert witnesses and Daubert challenges; lawyers with extensive experience handling mediations and arbitrations; as well as one of the nation's most advanced in-house technology departments for managing litigation. The firm achieved significant successes for clients Novartis and BASF. The firm was engaged as national

HEAD OFFICE

MINNESOTA
2200 Wells Fargo Center, 90 South Seventh Street,
Minneapolis, MN 55402
Tel: 612 766 7000   **Fax:** 612 766 1600
Website: www.faegre.com

BRANCH OFFICES

COLORADO
1900 Fifteenth Street, **Boulder,** CO 80302
Tel: 303 447 7700   **Fax:** 303 447 7800

3200 Wells Fargo Center, 1700 Lincoln Street, **Denver,** CO 80203
Tel: 303 607 3500   **Fax:** 303 607 3600

IOWA
Suite 3100, 801 Grand Avenue, **Des Moines,** IA 50309
Tel: 515 248 9000   **Fax:** 515 248 9010

INTERNATIONAL OFFICES

The firm also has offices in London, Frankfurt and Shanghai.

CONTACTS

Banking-Commercial	Michael R Stewart
Construction Law	William R Joyce
Corporate-Finance	W Smith 'Kris' Sharpe
Employee Benefits	Richard A Nelson
Health Care/Nonprofit Organizations	Jay D Christiansen
Intellectual Property	Kenneth A Liebman
Labor & Employment Law	Kathlyn E Noecker
Litigation	James A O'Neal
Real Estate	Thomas M Mayerle
Tax	John K Steffen
Trusts & Estates	David J Shannon

counsel to defend multiple class actions involving the well known A.D.D. medication Ritalin®, and succeeded in achieving the dismissal of all five actions. Additionally the firm defeated certification of a class and achieved summary dismissal of all claims against BASF in federal court in Arkansas.

CLIENTS: Faegre & Benson has been a leader in developing the concept of law firm partnering. The firm has for several years been one of a small number of firms selected by DuPont to serve as a preferred legal provider in its innovative 'DuPont Legal Model'. The firm has developed similar relationships on a national and multi-state basis with companies such as Guidant (primary outside counsel), Target (primary outside counsel), American Express (preferred litigation and M&A provider), UPS (principal outside counsel for many practice areas in a multi-state region) and Cargill, as one of two national preferred legal providers.

INTERNATIONAL WORK: Faegre & Benson offers sophisticated legal counsel for companies doing business around the world and has handled legal matters in more than 60 countries. The firm's clients range in size from multinational corporations to small and mid-sized companies establishing or expanding their operations overseas. In London, the firm offers the services of 35 English solicitors with extensive experience representing US businesses in England and Europe. Faegre & Benson offers a substantial German law capability through its merger in 2001 with a respected Frankfurt firm. Faegre & Benson opened its Shanghai office in 2001. The firm offers legal professionals based in both the US and China who have extensive experience dealing with the Chinese legal, business, and political systems.

LINDQUIST & VENNUM PLLP

THE FIRM

Managing Partner: Daryle L Uphoff
Number of partners in US office: 116
Number of other attorneys in US office: 64

FIRM OVERVIEW: Lindquist & Vennum is a business-oriented, general practice law firm with approximately 180 attorneys in Minnesota and Colorado. The firm is known for its extensive corporate finance, banking and complex commercial litigation practices as well as its agribusiness and life sciences industry-focused groups. Of note are its practices in white collar and regulatory defense, securities litigation and bankruptcy.

MAIN AREAS OF PRACTICE:

Corporate & Business: The firm's corporate business attorneys serve as outside counsel to over 30 public companies in the middle market. In the past 12 months, the group has been involved in a number of IPOs representing both issuers and underwriters. The firm has been very active with its private equity clients and has completed a number of significant M&A transactions.

Agribusiness & Cooperatives: The firm has a national practice representing the interests of agribusinesses and cooperatives. Lindquist & Vennum assists traditional agribusiness clients and has helped shape the 'value-added' movement in agriculture, created by agricultural producers seeking new markets for their commodities through ownership of processing and distribution facilities.

Life Sciences: The firm's Life Sciences Group provides experienced legal services to clients in the healthcare, pharmaceutical, biotech and device industries. Clients range in size from start-up ventures to mature, publicly traded companies. They work with clients in the areas of private capital, venture finance and public offerings, distribution and licensing, intellectual property protection, non-competition, confidentiality and employment matters, health plans and benefits, regulatory matters and litigation.

Financial Institutions: National in scope and serving clients representative of the largest and smallest members of the industry, the firm's Financial Institutions Practice Group has remained on the forefront of issues affecting commercial banks and savings associations in a time of change and challenge. In the last five years, the firm has represented more institutions in mergers and acquisitions than any other law firm in its Federal Reserve District and is among the leading national firms in this practice.

Complex Commercial Litigation: The firm's Commercial Litigation Group has extensive experience in the litigation, resolution and prevention of business-related disputes. The firm is particularly well-known for its work in antitrust, insurance coverage, securities fraud and shareholder disputes.

Securities Litigation: The relationship between investors and their brokerages has always been fragile, but the current state of the stock market has created an unprecedented rash of complaints and filings. The firm represents brokerage firms, brokers and customers in a wide variety of investment and securities-related issues. In addition to arbitration and litigation matters, they counsel clients in regulatory compliance and represent clients in administrative and regulatory matters, including investigations conducted by governmental and self-regulatory organizations.

Bankruptcy: The firm is recognized as having one of the premier bankruptcy practices in the Upper Midwest and the Rocky Mountain regions. The group has a wide range of experience including the landmark Marathon Oil and Kaiser Steel/Kaiser Coal cases.

White Collar & Regulatory Defense: The White Collar and Regulatory Defense Practice Group is a nationally recognized team of experienced trial lawyers who represent both corporations and individuals involved with increasingly complex criminal, regulatory and civil fraud investigations and lawsuits. Its attorneys include a number of formal federal prosecutors.

HEAD OFFICE

MINNESOTA
4200 IDS Center, 80 South Eighth Street, **Minneapolis,** MN 55402
Tel: 612 371 3211   **Fax:** 612 371 3207
Website: www.lindquist.com

BRANCH OFFICES

COLORADO
600 17th Street, Suite 1800 South, **Denver**, CO 80202
Tel: 303 573 5900   **Fax:** 303 573 1956

CONTACTS

Agribusiness & Cooperatives	Mark Hanson
Antitrust	Mark Jacobson
Bankruptcy	James Lodoen
Complex Commercial Litigation	Wallace Hilke
Corporate & Business	Dennis O'Malley
Emerging Companies	Jeffrey Saunders
Employee Benefits	Robert Hartman
Life Sciences	Barbara Lano Rummel
Financial Institutions	Kevin Costley
Insurance Coverage	James Reuter
Intellectual Property	Bruce Little
Labor & Employment	Nancy Vollertsen
Litigation	James McCarthy
Mergers & Acquisitions	Richard McNeil
Real Estate	Michael Margulies
Securities Litigation	William Stute
Trusts & Estates	Mavis Van Sambeek
White Collar & Regulatory Defense	William Michael

Real Estate: The firm represents owners, managers, investors and developers of commercial, industrial and mixed-use properties. Projects range from raw land to shopping centers to downtown office complexes. Its practice includes extensive experience in real estate transfers, leasing, financing, land development, construction and environmental compliance.

Labor & Employment: The firm provides a wide range of services to businesses concerning employment issues. For several years, they have collaborated with the state of Minnesota to create the publication, 'An Employer's Guide to Employment Law Issues in Minnesota.' This is one of the premier employment law resources used by Minnesota businesses and state agencies.

Intellectual Property: The firm's intellectual property attorneys counsel clients to protect, develop and exploit their intellectual property assets to the fullest. Its practice areas include a full range of protection of rights in copyrights, trademarks, trade names, domain names, advertising compliance, trade secret protection and patent, trademark, copyright, trade secret and related litigation.

INTERNATIONAL WORK: The firm is regularly involved in assisting clients in the expansion of their international activities. These efforts include: strategic alliances, including joint ventures for product development and distribution; foreign distributors; foreign manufacturing operations; OEM manufacturing; private label manufacturing; raw materials supply; dispute resolution and acquisition of foreign companies and product lines. The firm's reach is extended globally through our membership in The Appleton Group Legal Network (TAGLaw). Founded in 1998, TAGLaw is a worldwide network of 125 prominent, high-quality law firms. Lindquist & Vennum has been a member since TAGLaw's initial year.

CONTENTS: Corporate/M&A p.1024; Employment p.1026; Litigation p.1028; Real Estate p.1031; Individuals' Profiles p.1032; Firms' Profiles p.1037.

How lawyers are ranked

The opinions we gather from clients — mainly from in-house lawyers but also from other purchasers of legal services — are balanced by opinions from colleagues and competitors. Together, they provide two different perspectives — an all-round view — and biased viewpoints cancel each other out.

CORPORATE/M&A

Mississippi
Leading firms (Corporate/M&A)

1 BRUNINI, GRANTHAM, GROWER *Jackson*
BUTLER, SNOW, O'MARA, STEVENS *Jackson*

2 BAKER, DONELSON, BEARMAN *Jackson*
MCGLINCHEY STAFFORD PLLC *Jackson*
PHELPS DUNBAR LLP *Jackson*
WATKINS & EAGER PLLC *Jackson*
WATKINS LUDLAM WINTER & STENNIS *Jackson*
WISE CARTER CHILD & CARAWAY *Jackson*

Leading individuals (Corporate/M&A)

1 CANNADA Barry *Butler Snow, Jackson*
CHATHAM Henry *Wise Carter, Jackson*
DRINKWATER Robert *Brunini Grantham, Jackson*
HISE Daniel *Butler Snow, Jackson*

2 BUSH III F M *Phelps Dunbar, Tupelo*
FAIR George *Watkins & Eager, Jackson*
GRISHMAN David *Watkins Ludlam, Jackson*
HAFTER Jerome *Phelps Dunbar, Jackson*
HODGE Clifton *Phelps Dunbar, Jackson*
LAZARUS Robert *Watkins Ludlam, Jackson*
PAINTER William *Baker Donelson, Jackson*
WEEMS Walter *Brunini Grantham, Jackson*

3 CLARK Donald *Butler Snow, Jackson*
JACOBS Gina *Watkins Ludlam, Jackson*
MARTIN David *Watkins Ludlam, Jackson*
MENDENHALL William *McGlinchey Stafford, Jackson*
TAYLOR Zachary *Watkins Ludlam, Jackson*

Leading individuals
(Gaming & Licensing)

1 ANDRESS Scott *Balch & Bingham, Jackson*
HISE Daniel *Butler Snow, Jackson*
MCDANIEL Dan *Phelps Dunbar, Jackson*
SHEPHERD III Thomas *Watkins Ludlam, Jackson*

Leading individuals (Bankruptcy)

1 BYRD Robert *Byrd & Wiser, Biloxi*
GENO Craig *Harris & Geno, Jackson*
O'MARA James *Phelps Dunbar, Jackson*
ROSENBLATT Stephen *Butler Snow, Jackson*

Firms and individuals are listed alphabetically in each band.

Band 1

Brunini, Grantham, Grower & Hewes PLLC
See firm details p.1037

The Firm: This outfit comprises 15 corporate and commercial attorneys who advise a "*wonderful stable of clients*" from small businesses and entrepreneurs to traditional institutional clients, statewide, nationally and internationally. Peers admire their "*ability to stay on top in terms of clients and quality,*" while clients confirm they turn to Brunini for its "*overall strength*" and with utmost "*confidence that it will handle a commercial project well.*"

The Lawyers: Bob Drinkwater (see p.1033) is a man who "*doesn't chase rabbits, stays focused on the important issues and provides solutions that work.*" With his two decades of experience, interviewees insist that he is "*one of the most respected corporate lawyers in the state.*" To support this, they cite his knowledge of both the law and his clients, and draw further attention to his "*impeccable integrity,*" "*attention to detail*" and "*prompt turnaround.*" Interviewees additionally note that he is very compatible with **Walter Weems** (see p.1036), who has a "*wealth of experience*" in the timber and poultry industries. Within the latter, he represents Tyson Foods and Peco Foods among others, yet he also finds the time to "*show up in a lot of different types of transactions.*" Weems is described as "*a smart and conscientious lawyer*" with an affable personality and admirable work ethic.

The Clients: Trustmark National Bank; St Dominics Hospital; Cellular South; John Hancock Life Insurance; Pipeline Companies; BFI Waste Management; Tyson Foods; Chevron USA; Reliant Energy; Peco Foods and Kalmine.

Butler, Snow, O'Mara, Stevens & Cannada PLLC
See firm details p.1038

The Firm: As a result of the size and consequent resources of this large local firm, Butler Snow is said to be able "*to pull in all the experts that are needed*" in connection with its varied transactional practice. Clients view this unity as "*cost effective,*" adding that they find the attorneys' creative and pragmatic approach "*refreshing.*" A team of "*younger, aggressive attorneys*" reportedly has "*excellent credentials in anything from oil and gas to healthcare.*" Recently it has represented a top-50 firm of CPAs in its corporate restructuring and acquisition interests.

The Lawyers: Barry Cannada (see p.1032) is a former investment banker and accountant who combines this experience with his legal practice to handle many of the largest acquisitions in the South. He still maintains a foothold in the business world generally, yet he can more commonly be found using his "*enormous energy*" to advise accounting firms on anything from acquisitions to financing. Beyond this, Cannada is noted for a personality that is "*comfortable for people to work with*" and for his "*ability to apply his expertise in a practical manner.*" **Dan Hise** (see p.1034) has a strong gaming practice, which boasts big-name clients such as Harrah's and MGM, testifying to the high esteem in which he is held. Various adjectives are used to describe this lawyer who "*has been on all the corporate law committees;*" all are decidedly positive. Clients report they are completely satisfied with the services of this "*congenial*" and "*extremely knowledgeable*" lawyer, whose strengths also include a "*deliberative, detail-oriented approach*" and professional demeanor. **Don Clark** (see p.1032) is a prominent municipal bond lawyer described as "*truly excellent in this business.*" He has a vibrant practice serving as bond, underwriter and trustee's counsel and, over the course of his career, has gained a great deal of expertise in advice to governmental and healthcare entities. Chair of the firm **Stephen Rosenblatt** (see p.1035) boasts a successful bankruptcy practice focused on secured and unsecured creditors. Over the past year this "*extremely experienced and knowledgeable gentleman*" has acted as creditors' counsel for the lead bank in the Mississippi

Chemical Corporation case and dealt with bankruptcy matters in Memphis and New Orleans.

The Clients: Amsouth Bank; Beau Rivage Resorts; Cooperative Association of Tractor Dealers; FNC; U-Save Auto Rental of America; Oxford Publications; Horne CPA Group; Harrah's and MGM.

Band 2

Baker, Donelson, Bearman, Caldwell & Berkowitz, PC
See firm details p.1613

The Firm: This regionally focused law firm is billed as the largest between Atlanta and Dallas. The office setup allows seamless communication and integration with other branches spread across the Southeast, including the latest location, recently opened in New Orleans. The Jackson team is noted specifically for its tax and healthcare capabilities, and generally for its joint venture, acquisition, disposal and private equity investment work. Clients report that they *"respect and have confidence"* in the abilities and *"great integrity"* of this *"excellent firm."*

The Lawyers: William Painter (see p.1035) was singled out as an *"analytical, creative lawyer with a broad base of experience."* Known best for his tax practice, Painter is also well thought of as a transactional lawyer with strong leanings toward strategic initiatives and healthcare. In the healthcare arena, clients report that he maintains and advises *"first-rate clients,"* and has recently been involved in a number of physician/hospital joint venture deals. Beyond healthcare, over the last two years he has represented a wireless company in negotiating a settlement of complex litigation in excess of $100 million.

The Clients: Clients come from diverse fields and include physicians, public and private healthcare companies, business interests and high net-worth individuals.

McGlinchey Stafford, PLLC
See firm details p.885

The Firm: The five partners in this firm's business group concentrate on representing local businesses and act as local counsel for national entities. Their practice includes commercial financing and development, corporate formations and insurance regulatory work. Unusually for a small office such as this – it is an outpost of the firm's New Orleans headquarters – its practice includes some bond work.

The Lawyers: William Mendenhall's (see p.1035) practice spans general corporate transactions and commercial real estate work. Interviewees identify him as *"very easy to get along with"* and a *"first-rate thinker."* He is a member of the Secretary of State's Business Law Advisory Group and is further praised by interviewees as *"diligent and responsible."*

The Clients: Raising Canes Restaurants; The Gulf Group: RPM Pizza; O'Keefe Foundation.

Phelps Dunbar LLP
See firm details p.886

The Firm: This large firm is headquartered in Louisiana and has a strong presence across the Southeast, with offices in Gulfport, Tupelo and Jackson. Its reach extends across the Atlantic, where it has established an office in London, England. Clients confirm that it has *"a large resource pool to draw on"* and a *"broad array of experts,"* enabling it to provide a high-quality, comprehensive corporate service. The Jackson practice covers commercial contracts, M&A, corporate finance, bankruptcy, tax, securities, IP, gaming and regulatory work. With Mike Bush at the helm, the Tupelo office has a notable leaning towards healthcare.

The Lawyers: Clifton Hodge's (see p.1034) extensive knowledge of Mississippi's corporate scene has been strengthened and refined over three decades of practice. Having taught in the field, he is recognized as *"the best for securities,"* and has recently been advising directors on their fiduciary duties. Hodge is commended for his *"experience and background, demeanor and knowledge,"* which remain current in the transactional sphere despite a move on his part to focus more on litigation. Interviewees report that **James O'Mara** (see p.1035) excels at complicated bankruptcy deals and creditors' rights. As such, he is primarily seen as *"an insolvency guy"* with much expertise and experience in this field; however, he also handles loan workouts, secured lending and commercial litigation with authority. He is valued by his clients for *"expressing himself well and going to the heart of the issue."* They say *"if you give him a problem, he has the experience and knowledge to solve it."* **Jerry Hafter**'s (see p.1034) practice operates on a national and international level, focusing on contract work, business organization, technology and IP licensing. An expert on Article 9 of the UCC, one of his roles is as general outside counsel for Delta and Pine Land Company, the world's largest cottonseed business, which recently made a $46.8 million acquisition of biotech licenses from Syngenta. Sources report that he possesses *"an excellent legal mind"* and *"will round up the resources necessary to get the job done."* Furthermore, clients find his *"passionate commitment to getting the job done right"* wholly refreshing. The *"extremely bright"* **Frederick Bush** (see p.1032) is the managing partner of the Tupelo office and has carved out a reputation as *"an excellent counselor"* with *"good judgment."* He concentrates on providing corporate advice to the manufacturing, healthcare and banking industries and the market also recognizes him as an authority on municipal finance-related issues. **Dan McDaniel** (see p.1035) has been working in the gaming arena

since the industry began in Mississippi; he has since developed a comprehensive practice both in Louisiana and Mississippi acting for manufacturers, distributors and individuals. This *"diligent regulatory lawyer"* is applauded for his *"strong character,"* knowledge and *"integrity."* He will take over as president of the International Association of Gaming Attorneys in October 2005 and is currently advising Penn National Gaming on its acquisition of Argosy.

The Clients: Delta and Pine Land; Southern Farm Bureau Insurance Companies; Mississippi Chemical; Viking Range; Isle of Capri Casino; Wal-Mart; BancorpSouth.

Watkins & Eager PLLC
See firm details p.1040

The Firm: This firm's practice is traditionally oriented towards litigation yet has a successful and growing business practice. The February 2004 acquisition of a five-attorney real estate firm has served to further strengthen their breadth and transactional capabilities. The market acknowledges the team's *"good judgment and good sense"* and for consequently *"knowing when to push."* Furthermore, clients are *"impressed by the attorneys' willingness and effort."*

The Lawyers: Watkins & Eager's main business lawyer, **George Fair**, has a general business and commercial practice, with a particular emphasis on transactional, public utility and finance matters. Clients like his adroitness at protecting their interests and his *"sensitivity to the prevailing needs"* in corporate transactions.

The Clients: Pruitt Companies; Willmut Gas; Knobias Holdings; Blossman Gas and La-Z-Boy.

Watkins Ludlam Winter & Stennis, P.A
See firm details p.1041

The Firm: The firm is described as *"a general hospital to the corporate world"* as, alongside traditional M&A, it has strong public finance, gaming, and private sector banking and finance practices. Furthermore, clients consider it the *"top insurance regulatory firm around,"* and its long history of public service-based activities confers it with a niche in this market. The crown jewel on the client book is Nissan, which chose the firm when it opened a plant in Mississippi a few years ago. A number of attorneys on this 34-strong corporate team have tax qualifications, and clients praise the team as a whole for being *"extremely professional and highly responsive."*

The Lawyers: David Grishman (see p.1033) has *"good tax expertise"* and a reputation as a very good business lawyer with a great deal of experience in representing entrepreneurs in particular. His clients say *"he cares about your situation,"* is *"readily available"* as well as *"very knowledgeable and practical."* Currently he is undertaking general syndication and franchise work in the development of a food franchise for

Catfish One. Known for his "*great knowledge and people skills,*" **David Martin**'s (see p.1034) focus is on insurance regulatory law as well as corporate and finance transactions. Recently he advised on over $1 billion of student loan-related securitized financing. Clients report that he displays "*excellent attention to detail*" and is "*really involved in the community.*" **Zachary Taylor** (see p.1036) excels at sophisticated finance transactions, several interviewees noting his particular experience in public sector financing. In 2004 he advised Madison Square Redevelopment Authority and assisted Mississippi Higher Education Authority with $100 million worth of student loan bond issues. **Gina Jacob** (see p.1034) is described as "*an extremely top-notch M&A lawyer.*" Her clients include American Manufacturing and Colony Resorts, and she recently represented a venture capital firm in its acquisition of a furniture enterprise. Interviewees report that she is "*very bright, very thorough*" and that her work is "*of an extremely high standard.*" The market places **Robert Lazarus** (see p.1034) "*head and shoulders above the rest*" in the field of municipal and corporate finance. Able to handle large and complex matters, he was selected by Nissan as its Mississippi counsel

after its substantial investment in the state. **Thomas Shepherd** (see p.1036) has a broad gaming industry practice. He is able to "*blend his technical knowledge with ability,*" and has been representing Caesars Entertainment in its sale of the company to Harrah's Entertainment, a transaction valued at $10 million. He was also Mississippi counsel for Pinnacle Entertainment throughout its $400 million refinancing and is representing Mikohn Gaming's corporate and antitrust-related legal interests. Clients commended him for being "*sensitive to ethical issues and involved in the community.*"

The Clients: Nissan; Caesars Entertainment; Pinnacle Entertainment; Colony Capital and Resorts International Hotel; Mikhon Gaming; Catfish One; Mississippi Life & Health Insurance Guaranty Association; Comprehensive Health Insurance Risk Pool Association; GE Medical Protective Company; American Fidelity Insurance and Education Services Foundation.

Wise Carter Child & Caraway, Professional Association

The Firm: **Henry Chatham**'s practice runs the gamut from business transactions to corporate litigation. He is recognized as exceedingly bright,

"*very well informed*" and "*meticulous.*" He "*puts a lot of research and forethought*" into what he does and is especially knowledgeable on business organization and securities law matters.

Other Notable Practitioners

Scott Andress (see p.1032) of Balch & Bingham has built "*effective relationships with the commissioners and key staff members*" as well as acquiring a "*thorough knowledge of the code in this area.*" He has been working on the regulatory approvals associated with development of both the Hard Rock Casino in Biloxi and the Silver Slipper Gambling Hall and Saloon in Hancock County. "*Versatile*" **Bob Byrd** of Byrd & Wiser is considered the most respected bankruptcy lawyer in the southern part of the state" and has "*good relationships with the judges.*" His practice caters to both consumers and businesses; over the past year he acted on multiple equitable estoppel cases and represented Friede Goldman in a Chapter 11 reorganization. **Craig Geno** of Harris & Geno PLLC is admired for the sheer volume and high quality of his work in Chapter 11 debtor cases. "*Very well respected by both lawyers and judges*" his work also encompasses creditor, trustee and committee work.

EMPLOYMENT

MAINLY DEFENDANT

Mississippi
Leading firms
(Employment: Mainly Defendant)

1	PHELPS DUNBAR LLP *Jackson*
2	BALCH & BINGHAM *Jackson*
	THE KULLMAN FIRM *Jackson*
	WATKINS & EAGER PLLC *Jackson*
3	BUTLER, SNOW, O'MARA, STEVENS *Jackson*
	WATKINS LUDLAM WINTER, PA *Jackson*
	WISE CARTER CHILD & CARAWAY *Jackson*

Leading individuals
(Employment: Mainly Defendant)

1	MILAM Kenneth *Watkins & Eager, Jackson*
	SILER Thomas *Phelps Dunbar, Jackson*
	SMITH Taylor *The Kullman Firm, Columbus*
2	ADAMS Joseph *Phelps Dunbar, Jackson*
	CRUTCHER Pepper *Balch & Bingham, Jackson*
	FRIEDMAN Gary *Phelps Dunbar, Jackson*
	MOELLER Armin *Balch & Bingham, Jackson*
3	IRBY Peyton *Watkins Ludlam, Jackson*
	WALKER Jeffrey *Butler Snow, Jackson*
	WALLACE Barbara *Wise Carter, Jackson*

Firms and individuals are listed alphabetically in each band.

Band 1

Phelps Dunbar LLP
See firm details p.886

The Firm: The large labor and employment group at this firm comprises 14 "*superior and attentive*" lawyers working from Jackson with others in offices across the Deep South. Their expertise covers every aspect of constitutional defense, labor and employment law, and this "*accomplished*" team boasts a healthy client roster, including Fortune 500 companies based in the region and a substantial number of local employers. A large proportion of these clients are involved in the healthcare, automobile, manufacturing, gaming and hospitality industries.

The Lawyers: **Gary Friedman** (see p.1033) benefits from a "*world of experience*" and handles employment law matters up to and including appellate level. His practice is also focused on the resolution of civil rights disputes on behalf of cities and counties, and he serves as general counsel to the Mississippi Municipal Liability Plan, the Mississippi Municipal Workers' Compensation Group and the Mississippi Drug Testing Consortium. This lawyer's "*great judgment*" has most recently been exercised in

fiduciary duty cases, ensuring enforcement of non compete agreements and wrongful termination cases. Interviewees praise him for being "*efficient at getting to a final resolution.*" **Tommy Siler**'s (see p.1036) forte is the defense of wrongful dismissal cases, though his practice extends to collective bargaining, arbitration and counseling employers on policy and day-to-day decisions. Interviewees admire his "*ability, ethics and integrity*" as well as his "*methodical and thorough*" approach. These attributes may have inspired Frito-Lay and Georgia-Pacific to solicit his assistance in their recent defense of employment discrimination claims. **Joseph Adams** (see p.1032) is a "*shining star on his way up,*" well known for his representation of school districts, such as Rankin County. He is much liked by clients for being "*conscientious,*" "*excellent in his field*" and "*honest.*" Adams' specialties include standard Title VII discrimination cases, sexual harassment claims, wage and hour disputes and the representation of hospitals in employment matters.

The Clients: Mississippi Municipal Workers' Compensation Group; Frito-Lay; Georgia-Pacific; Philip Morris and True Temper Sports.

Band 2

Balch & Bingham
See firm details p.127
The Firm: This group of "*highly qualified attorneys*" is currently focusing its energy on the litigation of employment discharge disputes in state and federal courts, collective bargaining negotiations and the defense of discrimination charges before the EEOC. A large part of its daily practice is also devoted to warding off future problems through training and counseling employers, and it boasts a strong labor practice, despite the decline in demand for such services. Clients say the experienced lawyers here give "*a personal touch to cases*" and "*lots of feedback.*"
The Lawyers: Clients describe **Pepper Crutcher** (see p.1033) as a "*charismatic, responsive and smart*" attorney. Praise is leveled at both his knowledge base and his "*experience and demeanor with clients and adversaries.*" Clients turn to him for assistance with union contract negotiations and grievance arbitrations, drug testing disputes, discrimination and wrongful discharge claims, and state whistleblower cases. Meanwhile, **Armin Moeller** (see p.1035) is a bright guy who certainly "*knows the intricacies of the law*" and "*keeps himself well informed on the trends and developments*" in this area. "*An experienced lawyer,*" his practice centers on labor issues, arbitrations, collective bargaining and litigation. Clients say, "*It is so refreshing that he looks at things from a company's standpoint.*"
The Clients: Horseshoe Gaming; L-3 Communications; Hattiesburg Clinic; Delta Air Lines; Telapex; Minact; Jackson State University; La-Z-Boy; Delta Oil Mill; Mississippi Power; Cingular Wireless; Clorox Products Manufacturing and Merit Electrical.

The Kullman Firm A Professional Law Corporation
See firm details p.884
The Firm: One of the country's original labor law firms, this boutique practice handles the full range of labor and employment-related issues, including representation before the NLRB, contract negotiations, grievance procedures, arbitration, management advice and defense under the various anti-discrimination laws. It further advises on ERISA and civil rights issues. This complete practice is chosen by clients, among other reasons, for its "*national reputation of excellence in union avoidance,*" and praise is also leveled at its geographical scope, professionalism and "*excellence of advice and counsel.*" Kullman's history and fine reputation ensure that it boasts many old-line Mississippi clients.
The Lawyers: With his US Supreme Court track record, **Taylor Smith** (see p.1036) is "*a veteran lawyer who has seen it all.*" His focus is mainly

labor arbitration hearings, union election campaigns, training and decertification; yet he is also involved in mainstream employment discrimination cases. Clients appreciate that, as lead attorney, he can draw on all the resources and the high market respect afforded to the firm.
The Clients: AmeriCold Logistics; Weyerhaeuser; Sanderson Plumbing Products; WG Yates & Sons Construction; Babcock & Wilcox; Artex International; Columbus and Greenville Railway; Cooper Tire & Rubber; The City of West Point and Flexible Flyer.

Watkins & Eager PLLC
See firm details p.1040
The Firm: As the oldest law firm in Jackson, Watkins & Eager's labor and employment group benefits from an enviable client base and an established local reputation, especially in the insurance defense and corporate/commercial fields. Sources report that its labor and employment law team is equipped with "*vast experience and great judgment.*"
The Lawyers: With his "*great personality and good business sense,*" **Kenny Milam** has built himself a strong reputation, notably for his handling of union election campaigns. He has an excellent rapport with his clients, who describe him as a good communicator and "*excellent at handling conflict situations.*" These days he is more involved in mediation and is applauded for his deftness and ability in this regard.
The Clients: Fleetwood Homes; Hunter Engineering; Kuhlman; La-Z-Boy; Mississippi Baptist Health Systems and Sherwin-Williams.

Band 3

Butler, Snow, O'Mara, Stevens & Cannada, PLLC
See firm details p.1038
The Firm: This large and "*rapidly expanding*" labor and employment group has a broad practice. It recently represented Kroger and Dillard's against wrongful discharge claims, defended clients against union organizing campaigns and fought off unfair labor practice charges. The group benefits from the firm's status as a full-service outfit and its strong Memphis office.
The Lawyers: The market identifies **Jeff Walker** (see p.1036) as "*very knowledgeable on this area of the law.*" His practice spans both labor and employment law and boasts "*supportive backup*" alongside "*a good stable of clients.*" He is involved in matters related to the NLRA, claims of wrongful discharge and discrimination, as well as ERISA, OSHA and wage and hour matters.
The Clients: All American Moving; Alliant Aerospace Company; Baxter Healthcare; Ergon; MMC Materials and Tenet Healthcare.

Watkins Ludlam Winter & Stennis, PA
See firm details p.1041
The Firm: The team of eight lawyers do the "*full panoply*" of labor and employment matters. Their focus is traditional labor law, employment litigation, OSHA, wage and hour disputes and affirmative action plans. A substantial part of the practice of these "*prominent and accomplished attorneys*" is also geared toward drafting employer handbooks and advising clients regarding ERISA and executive employment matters. There is no single typical industry from which clients are derived, as they run the gamut from shippers to manufacturers to healthcare companies and resorts.
The Lawyers: One quarter of **Peyton Irby**'s (see p.1034) practice is devoted to traditional labor law and union issues; the rest comprises general employment matters, such as advising on employer handbooks and contracts, wage and hour-related matters, affirmative action plans and equal opportunities litigation. Clients speak of his "*priceless experience*" on the NLRB, confirming that he is an all-around "*highly valuable resource.*"
The Clients: Bankers Compliance Task Force; Dynasteel; Caesar's Entertainment; City of Olive Branch, Mississippi; Nissan North America; Sunbeam Products; Brown Bottling Group; Turan-Foley Chevrolet Buick and Mtek.

Wise Carter Child & Caraway, Professional Association
The Firm: The three partners at this firm have a "*comprehensive knowledge*" of all areas of employment law. Their practice includes counseling, administrative proceedings, mediation, arbitration and litigation. It is purely a reflection of the current market that relatively little labor work is undertaken; however, the attorneys do have ample experience and capabilities in this field. They are currently heavily involved in discrimination law, in particular with regard to race discrimination and sexual harassment cases.
The Lawyers: A member of the US Congress' Office of Compliance, the "*extremely intelligent*" **Barbara Wallace** expresses evident enthusiasm for her work, which includes counseling, mediation, arbitration and litigation. Defending a client in a race discrimination case filed by 84 employees constitutes the core of her current practice, though she is also seeing more litigation under the ADA. Clients describe her as "*a tremendous lawyer at the top of her field,*" and appreciate her unfaltering knowledge of the law's perpetual evolution.
The Clients: Clients include Gold Strike Casino and Resort, Sanderson Farms and Entergy Operations.

LITIGATION

GENERAL COMMERCIAL

Mississippi
Leading firms
(Litigation: General Commercial)

1 PHELPS DUNBAR LLP *Jackson*
  WATKINS & EAGER PLLC *Jackson*

2 BAKER, DONELSON, BEARMAN *Jackson*
  BRADLEY ARANT ROSE & WHITE LLP *Jackson*
  BRUNINI, GRANTHAM, GROWER *Jackson*
  BUTLER, SNOW, O'MARA, STEVENS *Jackson*

3 FORMAN PERRY WATKINS KRUTZ *Jackson*
  MITCHELL, MCNUTT & SAMS PA *Tupelo*

4 LATHAM & BURWELL PLLC *Ridgeland*
  WATKINS LUDLAM WINTER & STENNIS *Jackson*
  WISE CARTER CHILD & CARAWAY *Jackson*

Leading individuals
(Litigation: General Commercial)

★ DRINKWATER Wayne *Bradley Arant, Jackson*

1 CORLEW John *Watkins & Eager, Jackson*
  PERRY Alan *Forman Perry, Jackson*
  SHAPLEY Christopher *Brunini Grantham, Jackson*
  ULMER Michael *Watkins & Eager, Jackson*

2 ANDERSON Reuben *Phelps Dunbar, Jackson*
  BASS Ross *Phelps Dunbar, Jackson*
  FORD Barry *Baker Donelson, Jackson*
  GALLOWAY Robert *Butler Snow, Gulfport*
  GOODMAN William *Watkins & Eager, Jackson*
  HENEGAN John *Butler Snow, Jackson*
  HODGE Clifton *Phelps Dunbar, Jackson*
  JONES Walker *Baker Donelson, Jackson*
  KAUFMAN David *Brunini Grantham, Jackson*
  REED William *Baker Donelson, Jackson*
  SAMS L F *Mitchell McNutt, Tupelo*
  WALLACE Michael *Phelps Dunbar, Jackson*
  WELCH W Scott *Butler Snow, Jackson*

3 AYERS David *Watkins & Eager, Jackson*
  CAMPBELL Roy *Bradley Arant, Jackson*
  DOVE Luke *Dove and Chill, Jackson*
  GIBBS Robert *Brunini Grantham, Jackson*
  GRAHAM Collier *Wise Carter, Jackson*
  JONES Christy *Butler Snow, Jackson*
  LATHAM William *Latham & Burwell, Ridgeland*
  STEPHENSON III Paul *Watkins & Eager, Jackson*

Leading individuals
(Litigation: Appellate)

1 DRINKWATER Wayne *Bradley Arant, Jackson*
  MUNFORD Luther *Phelps Dunbar, Jackson*

2 BANKS Fred *Phelps Dunbar, Jackson*
  HENEGAN John *Butler Snow, Jackson*
  PERRY Alan *Forman Perry, Jackson*
  WALLACE Michael *Phelps Dunbar, Jackson*

Leading individuals
(Litigation: Construction)

1 MOCKBEE David *Mockbee Hall, Jackson*

Firms and individuals are listed alphabetically in each band.

Band 1

Phelps Dunbar LLP
See firm details p.886
The Firm: This top-tier firm covers everything from environmental and commercial litigation to employment disputes. Despite wider professional and political efforts to minimize the state's reputation as a *"torts magnet,"* Phelps Dunbar still reports a strong market for mass tort actions, and their defense. Reflecting this situation, it has recently been involved in asbestos and pharmaceutical litigation, including defending the well-publicized diet drug Fen-Phen. Clients reported that they chose the firm for its *"reasonably aggressive approach for a conservative town"* and its *"creative, professional"* working style.
The Lawyers: **Reuben Anderson**'s (see p.1032) three decades in the legal community have produced *"a major talent in the courtroom."* A former US Supreme Court judge, he is blessed with both cool judgment and quick thinking. With a distinguished career behind him, he is greatly valued by clients for his experience and ability to capture the court's attention. Managing partner **Rick Bass**'s (see p.1032) forte is products liability litigation and his specialty is settling mass tort litigation through class settlement actions. Clients like the fact that he *"knows the playing field in Mississippi."* The market expects to see a lot more of **Cliff Hodge** (see p.1034) on the litigation circuit, after a concerted decision on his part to move away from his corporate law practice. Over the past year, this has meant involvement in a dealer/franchise dispute representing West Implement. A former business law lecturer, he has *"thorough knowledge and understanding"* of the corporate world, making him an excellent choice for commercial disputes. Clients note that Hodge *"does his homework"* and *"communicates well."* **Luther Munford**'s (see p.1035) practice orbits almost exclusively around appellate and First Amendment work. He has taken his extensive knowledge to print and written books on Mississippi's appellate law. His *"ability to see the big picture,"* the respect he commands throughout the 5th Circuit and his excellent brief-writing skills combine to convince clients he is *"the best appellate man in the state."* *"Good at outwitting his opponent,"* **Mike Wallace** (see p.1036) is also best known for his appellate work and represents clients such as Philip Morris, Ford and Chevron USA. He has recently defended lawsuits filed by landowners objecting to the use of land for telecom purposes, and is also handling an arbitration for BellSouth. Furthermore, he lends his considerable talents to working with other sectors, for example healthcare, where he represents Mississippi Baptist Hospital. Former Supreme Court judge **Fred Banks** (see p.1032) is lauded for his *"good judgment"* and *"excellent understanding of the law."* Widely recognized as extraordinarily smart, the core of his practice centers on commercial litigation. However, he is also noted for his strong appellate and alternative dispute resolution work.
The Clients: BancorpSouth; Philip Morris; GE; BellSouth; Wells Fargo; St. Paul Insurance; Interstate Fibernet; Wachovia and North Mississippi Medical Center.

Watkins & Eager PLLC
See firm details p.1040
The Firm: Historically one of the state's leading litigation firms, this group of 60 litigators handles any and all civil litigation, yet is best known for products liability, toxic torts, pharmaceutical and finance-related cases. Clients are drawn to its twin talents: *"subject matter expertise"* and *"depth of knowledge on Mississippi laws and local courts."*
The Lawyers: Like many in this group, **John Corlew** is riding the residual wave of mass tort litigation, notably in defense of claims involving silica and lead paint contamination. He also defends individual commercial claims and is doing all of the above very well in the eyes of clients, who believe *"his practicality really sets him apart."* Such client loyalty can be, in part, attributed to his ability to *"communicate with all personalities"* and try cases all over the state. **Mike Ulmer**'s practice has evolved from insurance defense and automotive industry representation to his current focus on the tobacco industry and involvement in mass tort litigation. In defending claims against 6000 plaintiffs on behalf of welding clients, he has been involved in more than 80 related cases. The Ford Motor Company also ranks among Ulmer's clients. *"Tenacity and experience"* combined with the fact that *"juries just love this guy"* help to explain his success. *"The dean of all practicing lawyers in Mississippi,"* **Bill Goodman** has established an outstanding reputation for himself over his 50 years of general civil defense work. Now an effective rainmaker, he still advises on business, commercial and banking litigation. Many comment on the *"steam and energy"* that keeps him active as one of the *"smartest, most accomplished"* lawyers in Mississippi. **David Ayers** is a *"well-prepared"* products defense lawyer. Described as *"a light"* that *"navigates [clients] through tough lawsuits,"* he displays *"outstanding"* ability and knowledge of products liability law and the Mississippi courts. *"Fine lawyer and great technician"* **Paul Stephenson** is identified as the firm's standout business and commercial litigator. He is known for his work representing financial institutions and has most recently been working on class action and fraud cases in this industry.
The Clients: Trustmark National Bank; Bridgestone Tires; Toyota; Tyson Foods; RJ Reynolds; Chevron USA; Lincoln Electric and BOC.

Band 2

Baker, Donelson, Bearman, Caldwell & Berkowitz PC
See firm details p.1613

The Firm: A part of one of the fastest growing firms in the USA, this litigation group boasts a great regional and local practice in addition to an impressive client roster. Its primary focus is products liability, most notably within the automotive and pharmaceutical spheres. It is in this capacity that the firm is general counsel for Ford, Abbott Laboratories and Bristol-Myers Squibb to name but three of its most recognizable clients. The firm also boasts a white-collar crime section and is heavily involved in toxic torts, mass torts, insurance defense, employment, healthcare, antitrust, commercial and franchise litigation. Contented clients applaud the high quality of work that this *"efficient"* firm turns out and recommend its *"broad base of capable, aggressive litigators."*

The Lawyers: **Walker Jones**' (see p.1034) practice centers on products liability and environmental contamination litigation. Over the past year, this *"likable, big-picture guy"* has been busy with pharmaceutical products liability litigation, automotive trial work for Ford and insurance underwriter work for Lloyd's. His *"excellent persuasive abilities"* and aptitude for organizing and strategizing render him an outstanding litigator; clients view his knowledge of Mississippi courts as *"a wonderful resource."* **Barry Ford** (see p.1033) works closely with Jones, and together they make *"a dynamite team."* A former circuit court judge, Ford uses his *"superb trial skills"* to represent such household names as Ford, Chrysler and 3M. His practice focuses on products liability, general torts, mass torts, insurance defense and commercial litigation. Clients say he possesses *"the highest ethical standards and sterling character."* The firm's president, **William Reed** (see p.1035) is recognized for his political connections and for being *"an extremely competent litigator."* Although somewhat constrained by the commitments of management, his work lies in the areas of commercial litigation and products liability. Recently this *"bright and well-rounded"* attorney has been working on a franchise agreement for Cendant and a large insurance dispute for Linux International.

The Clients: Ford; Philip Morris; 3M; Monsanto; AmSouth Bank; First Tennessee Bank; Lloyd's; Abbott Laboratories and Bristol-Myers Squibb.

Bradley Arant Rose & White LLP
See firm details p.128

The Firm: Clients say the 16 lawyers at this specialist litigation firm have a winning formula – *"thinking strategically about legal issues while keeping an eye on cost."* The *"first-rate team"* typically concentrates on commercial and environmental litigation, appellate matters, products liability and antitrust cases. The firm is also known for its involvement in asbestos and silica claims. Admired for its *"extensive national capabilities,"* it represents expansive companies such as Equitable, New England Mutual, Caterpillar and 3M.

The Lawyers: According to sources, **Wayne Drinkwater** (see p.1033) *"is the tops. Period."* A former clerk for the US Supreme Court, he is an all-rounder who has the ability to communicate with judge, jury and appellate court with equal ease. Indeed, interviewees universally agreed that he is one of the top appellate lawyers in Mississippi: *"He really knows how to protect his clients on appeal."* *"Tremendous intellect, a fantastic resume and good judgment"* further strengthen his capabilities and furnish his reputation. Clients shower him with compliments concerning his oral advocacy skills and ability to effectively plan for both short and long-term eventualities. **Roy Campbell** (see p.1032) is best known for insurance defense, products liability and commercial litigation. This *"highly experienced attorney"* has recently been involved in defending insurance companies against claims of bad faith. He is also licensed to practice in Tennessee.

The Clients: Caterpillar; MONY; New England Mutual; AXA; 3M; Progressive Casualty Insurance; Chicago Bridge & Iron; Vulcan Materials; Dryvit Systems; Delta & Pine Land; Honda and ConAgra Foods.

Brunini, Grantham, Grower & Hewes PLLC
See firm details p.1037

The Firm: This old-line firm boasts *"a great core group of hard-working litigators"* and a healthy local client roster. Its diverse practice takes in mass torts, products liability and chemical and toxic torts alongside a substantial share of business and consumer fraud litigation. As an *"excellent one-stop shop,"* it is also active in environmental cases and an increasing amount of healthcare and nursing home litigation. Attorneys have the *"requisite connections and ability"* to represent the interests of noteworthy clients, including the state's largest employer, bank and health insurer.

The Lawyers: The practice of *"likable, affable and talented"* **Chris Shapley** (see p.1035) is concentrated on pharmaceutical, consumer fraud and environmental litigation. Working on cases for Purdue Pharma, Trustmark National bank and Blue Cross has kept this *"bright, competent, good guy"* occupied over the past year. Shapley is cited as one of the main reasons behind the firm's growing reputation; he is admired for being *"able to go at all levels,"* for knowing the judges and, quite simply, for being *"excellent in the courtroom."* When the former CEO of WorldCom was looking for legal representation, he chose *"spectacular"* **David Kaufman** (see

p.1034). Although still involved in the litigation resulting from the WorldCom collapse, Kaufman has recently taken on welding fume mass tort litigation for BOC and a poultry-related litigation for Choctaw Maid Farms. He is also Mississippi trial counsel for CenterPoint Energy and Harrah's Entertainment. Kaufman displays *"great demeanor and ability"* in the courtroom, more specifically *"charisma that exudes confidence."* Clients choose **Robert Gibbs** (see p.1033) for the *"solid head on his shoulders"* and the respect he commands from both judges and juries alike. A former Hinds County circuit court judge, he has extensive trial experience and proves *"a mighty advocate for his clients."*

The Clients: Purdue Pharma; GlaxoSmithKline; CenterPoint Energy; Aventis; Northrop Grumman; Choctow Maid Farms; Harrah's Entertainment; Kerr McGee; Textron; North Safety; Koppers; Trustmark National Bank; Beverly Enterprises and Marina.

Butler, Snow, O'Mara, Stevens & Cannada, PLLC
See firm details p.1038

The Firm: Sources describe this large Mississippi outfit as an *"outstanding institutional firm."* It makes regular appearances on the shortlist for major pieces of litigation and is involved in a broad array of mass tort actions, including asbestos, silica and pharmaceutical matters. With respect to mass torts, the *"creative and industrious"* team has handled a number of appeals to the US Supreme Court on issues of joinder and venue. These efforts culminated in a significant change in the law in this area. Aside from mass torts, the firm undertakes a significant amount of commercial, maritime and employment litigation, and still finds time to provide governmental defense to more than half the counties in the state.

The Lawyers: **Bob Galloway** (see p.1033) in the Gulf Coast office is smart, experienced and *"always exceptionally well prepared."* One interviewee explained: *"Smart folks have IQ, but he has both IQ and EQ"* alongside *"impeccable judgment."* The main components of his broad practice are products liability, mass torts and employment litigation. To all of these areas, clients report he brings *"maturity and an understanding of the business world."* The *"incredibly bright"* **John Henegan** (see p.1034) works on complex commercial cases, defamation and antitrust litigation, together with telecom matters for clients such as BellSouth. However, it is his First Amendment and appellate work that compels the market to offer the most prolific praise. In sum, clients are bowled over by the intelligence and ability of this *"fine attorney."* The chair of the litigation department and a former president of the State Bar Association, **Scott Welch** (see p.1036), concentrates on commercial transportation, products liability and environmental cases. Sources consider him a *"tremendous lawyer,"* saying: *"He knows the law and is up on the issues."* As if this were not enough, he is also known for *"excellent presentation in front of the jury."* **Christy Jones** (see p.1034) represents pharmaceutical and medical device companies in products liability matters. She has recently been working on the case of Janssen Pharmaceutical v Robert Bailey, in which the court reversed a $100 million verdict against Johnson & Johnson. The six other decisions related to this case resulted in a significant change in the law regarding venue provisions and Rule 20. Clients are profuse in their flattery, and recommend Jones' *"excellent work ethic."*

The Clients: American General Finance; AmSouth Bank; Baxter Healthcare; Johnson & Johnson; Milacron; Merck; Wyatt Ayerst Pharmaceuticals; FMC and MGM Mirage.

Band 3

Forman Perry Watkins Krutz & Tardy LLP
See firm details p.1039

The Firm: Litigating throughout the state on behalf of both local and national clients, this *"experienced, premier defense firm"* has a general civil practice that leans toward mass torts, environmental and commercial litigation. Acclaimed as *"the leading light in asbestos and silica cases,"* the team recently obtained the keynote Mangialardi decision, thereby enabling its client to benefit from thousands of dismissals from asbestos cases filed against it.

The Lawyers: Equipped with an accounting background, **Alan Perry** (see p.1035) *"gets straight to the root of the problem"* and then offers practical, as opposed to theoretical, solutions. He focuses on commercial litigation and has recently represented an accounting firm on issues related to its dissolution in Chancery Court. Wielding a *"piercing intellect,"* he represents clients such as Community Bank, Central Industries and AT&T Wireless in commercial litigation.

The Clients: Georgia-Pacific; Jacuzzi; BP America; Liberty Mutual and Owens-Illinois.

Mitchell, McNutt & Sams PA

The Firm: The firm maintains a strong regional presence through offices in Tupelo, Columbus, Corinth, Oxford, Memphis and Jackson. The varied practice of this *"fine group of knowl-*edgeable and experienced lawyers"* is centered on civil litigation, including business, professional liability, railroad defense, toxic torts and pharmaceutical litigation.

The Lawyers: Based in Tupelo, the *"simply fabulous"* **Sandy Sams** is admired by peers for his *"thoughtful and thorough"* work. His practice encompasses complex commercial litigation, products liability, construction, and professional liability litigation. Clients say they are fully aware that this man of *"integrity"* possesses *"the highest standard of ethics."*

The Clients: BDO Siedman; Harrah's Entertainment; Merchants & Farmers Bank; FL Crane & Sons; Franklin Corporation and North Mississippi Medical Center.

Band 4

Latham & Burwell PLLC

The Firm: This five-partner outfit commands respect from peers for its business and commercial, contractual dispute, employment and PI litigation successes. Its wide-ranging capabilities are reflected in its client roster, which includes individuals, large national corporations and all manner of organizations in between. Sources report that this *"extremely competent and resolutely ethical"* group excels at both the trial and appellate level.

The Lawyers: *"Tough as nails"* **Larry Latham** is recognized as a worthy opponent in the courtroom. His practice, currently more focused on mediations and arbitrations, greatly benefits from his *"warrior smarts"* and *"sound judgment."*

The Clients: The firm acts for individuals, financial institutions and corporations, including: Mississippi Valley Title Insurance; Scott Regional Hospital; Shell; Northern Trust Bank; State Bank & Trust and Western Atlas.

Watkins Ludlam Winter & Stennis PA
See firm details p.1041

The Firm: A firm that is perhaps more established in transactional and real estate work, their litigation practice has, nonetheless, stood the test of time. As one of Mississippi's old-line firms, it boasts a great deal of experience with public bodies. Owing to its full-service nature and network of offices across Mississippi and Louisiana, it has a substantial breadth of resources at its disposal. Its practice encompasses everything from general commercial cases to business torts,

insurance, products liability, antitrust and workers' compensation.

The Lawyers: Neville Boschert is the chair of the litigation practice group. He practices in the areas of antitrust, business torts, insurance, general commercial and products liability litigation.

The Clients: American National Insurance; Hartford Mutual; City of Olive Branch and Mississippi Baptist Health Systems.

Wise Carter Child & Caraway, Professional Association

The Firm: This old-line firm commands respect from the market for its *"large base of good litigators."* Areas of focus include maritime, insurance coverage, professional liability, general commercial and products liability; however, the group is particularly strong in the defense of public utilities and railroads. It is also noted for the strong reputation it has developed in the medical malpractice area.

The Lawyers: **Collier Graham** defends products and professional liability claims, in addition to litigating toxic, healthcare and environment-related matters. Sources admire the fact that *"he can go into very difficult courthouses and come out a winner."*

The Clients: Rankin Medical Center; Jackson National Life Insurance; Sprint Communications and Johnson & Johnson.

Other Notable Practitioners

David Mockbee of Mockbee Hall & Drake PA is *"at the top of the heap on construction litigation and arbitration."* Identified as *"a superb lawyer"* who specializes in representing architects, engineers, subcontractors and general contractors, he has recently been involved in litigation over a major league baseball park concerning steel fabrication issues. Clients described him as *"a most tenacious guy,"* who *"doesn't leave a stone unturned."* Mockbee represents Johnson Bailey Henderson McNeel Architects, Steel Service, Mountain Construction and Aceros Prefabricados among others. The market also singles out **Luke Dove** of Dove & Chill as a bright, effective litigator with *"excellent legal strategy."* His practice focuses on complex commercial litigation and products liability in both state and federal courts.

REAL ESTATE

Mississippi
Leading firms (Real Estate)

[1] BUTLER, SNOW, O'MARA, STEVENS *Jackson*

WATKINS LUDLAM WINTER & STENNIS *Jackson*

[2] BRUNINI, GRANTHAM, GROWER *Jackson*

WATKINS & EAGER PLLC *Jackson*

Leading individuals (Real Estate)

[1] CANNADA Don *Butler Snow*, Jackson

[2] CLEMENT Rodney *Brunini Grantham*, Jackson

DAVIS Mark *Watkins Ludlam*, Jackson

GUNN Paul *Watkins & Eager*, Jackson

SMITH III William *Watkins & Eager*, Jackson

TOHILL Jim *Watkins Ludlam*, Jackson

Firms and individuals are listed alphabetically in each band.

Band 1

Butler, Snow, O'Mara, Stevens & Cannada PLLC

See firm details p.1038

The Firm: This large, full-service firm offers its real estate practice a great deal of support both from other departments and its regional network of offices. As many as ten attorneys work in the practice group, their work ranging from purchasing through to financing, leasing and sales. The group is bursting with expertise on retail, residential, casino and office developments, and recently facilitated one of the largest property assemblages in the Southeast for Wal-Mart. Clients confirm the group "*is not out to score points, but looks for a solution*," and consequently focuses on "*getting the deal done.*"

The Lawyers: Don Cannada (see p.1032) is viewed as "*the top gun in the biggest firm in the state.*" Applauded by clients for his "*expertise, thoroughness and pragmatism*," he is regarded by his peers as "*an experienced lawyer, able to handle many complex issues,*" including tax and public finance. He has recently been advising on the sale and development of various shopping centers, facilitating construction loans and working on the first ever receipt of $6 million of bonds under Mississippi's public improvement district statutes.

The Clients: Canebrake Development Company; Wal-Mart; Luckney LLC; Magazine Street Interests and Reunion.

Watkins Ludlam Winter & Stennis PA

See firm details p.1041

The Firm: Watkins Ludlam's practice is statewide, from the Memphis suburban area to Jackson and the Gulf Coast. It leans toward the representation of commercial developers and lenders in negotiating purchase and sale contracts, leases and loan documentation. The firm additionally handles its fair share of public work, which sees it structuring public and private financing and development ventures in state. Clients appreciate attorneys' "*attention to detail, high-quality, customer-oriented service*" and commitment to keeping up-to-date with all the latest developments.

The Lawyers: Mark Davis (see p.1033), an all-around "*great lawyer and good guy,*" practices commercial real estate and is especially known for his construction and development work. Clients regard him as a "*sophisticated,*" and "*dependable*" attorney, whom they would be lost without. "*Student of the law*" **Jim Tohill** (see p.1036) is "*extremely knowledgeable.*" Over the past year he has been representing Pearl Valley Water, restructuring loan documentation as well as leasing and developing both a neighborhood commercial development and a major mariner complex.

The Clients: State Street; Mattiace Properties; Homewood Company; Mississippi Baptist Health Systems; Reunion; Magazine Street Interests; Pearl River Valley Water Supply District and Wal-Mart.

Band 2

Brunini, Grantham, Grower & Hewes PLLC

See firm details p.1037

The Firm: This older, established firm boasts a good base of local clients and a team of "*courteous and professional real estate lawyers.*" It has a historic connection to the energy industry in Mississippi, yet its practice has broadened to cater for various industry sectors. To demonstrate, a handsome client roster currently includes the largest bank, private hospital and land developer in the state. Its real estate capabilities are wide ranging, encompassing acquisitions and sales, financing, development, leasing, foreclosures and bankruptcies.

The Lawyers: Rodney Clement (see p.1032) is well known in the land use and planning arena as "*a trustworthy lawyer*" who is "*easy to get along with.*" Fully au fait with real estate trends and admired as "*a good detail person and an excellent negotiator,*" he has recently represented Lowe's in their development of a new store, and General Electric Capital Corporation in its guise as lender. The past year has also seen him working on a string of financings, as well as assisting with the acquisition of multiple retail franchises.

The Clients: Cellular South; Mattiace Properties; St. Dominic's Health Services; Trustmark National Bank and Ingalls Shipbuilding.

Watkins & Eager PLLC

See firm details p.1040

The Firm: Having been joined by attorneys from Taylor Covington in February 2004, Watkins & Eager continues its evolution from a corporate boutique into a broader-based firm. Its roster of clients turn to it for "*quality, professional legal representation and excellent customer service,*" finding an outfit that is capable of handling all aspects of real estate. It is particularly well regarded for its work with local developers.

The Lawyers: Paul Gunn is "*one of the smartest*" real estate lawyers in Mississippi. He "*speaks with authority about the law*" and is especially strong on construction matters and affordable housing tax credits. His "*intricate knowledge,*" "*excellent advice*" and ability to "*get through difficult situations*" make him a go-to real estate man. Clients also feel very comfortable with the "*extremely dependable,*" "*hard-working and responsive*" **William Smith**. Interviewees report that the development aspect of his practice is greatly assisted by his ability to "*identify easily with local developers.*" He is further identified as a lawyer with "*first-class negotiating and drafting skills.*"

The Clients: The Park Companies; BankPlus; One Capital Advisors; SouthTrust Bank and Evans Brothers Investments.

Leaders in Mississippi

ADAMS, Joseph Lee
Phelps Dunbar LLP, Jackson
601 360 9708
adamsjo@phelps.com
Recommended in Employment

Practice Areas: Partner in the Labor and Employment Group in the Jackson office. He has extensive experience in litigating Wage and Hour Collective Actions. He practices in the areas of Civil Rights and Title VII, as well as the Age Discrimination in Employment Act and the Americans with Disabilities Act.
Personal: University of Mississippi, JD, cum laude, 1997; associate editor, Mississippi Law Journal. Mississippi State University, BBA, magna cum laude, 1994.

ANDERSON, Reuben V
Phelps Dunbar LLP, Jackson
601 360 9339
andersor@phelps.com
Recommended in Litigation

Practice Areas: The first African-American Supreme Court Justice in Mississippi, and a Partner in the General Litigation Group in the Jackson office. He practices in the areas of commercial litigation, regulatory and governmental matters and gaming. In addition to his work at the firm, he has cultivated a professional resume spanning three decades of legal service. Key positions have included the Jamie L Whitten Chair of Law and Government at the University of Mississippi, Fall of 1995 and Mississippi Supreme Court Justice, 1985-90.
Personal: University of Mississippi, JD, 1967. Tougaloo College, BA, 1964.

ANDRESS, Scott
Balch & Bingham, Jackson
601 965 8160
sandress@balch.com
Recommended in Gaming & Licensing
Practice Areas: Gaming; litigation.
Prof. Memberships: American Bar Association; Mississippi Bar Association; Hinds County Bar Association; International Association of Gaming Attorneys.
Career: Scott Andress' practice focuses primarily on gaming law, corporate law, commercial transactions, commercial litigation, intellectual property and environmental law. Mr Andress began his career as a management information consultant in New Orleans, Louisiana, and Washington, DC. Along with the handling of general corporate, transactional, environmental, intellectual property and commercial litigation matters, Mr Andress' practice includes the regular representation of privately owned and publicly traded casino operators, gaming equipment manufacturers and distributors, and landowners in the following areas: gaming compliance, gaming permitting and approvals, gaming litigation.

Personal: Born: April 21, 1964; education: Tulane University (JD, cum laude, 1992); Louisiana State University (BS, 1986).

AYERS, David
Watkins & Eager PLLC, Jackson
601 948 6470
Recommended in Litigation

BANKS Jr, Fred L
Phelps Dunbar LLP, Jackson
601 360 9356
banksf@phelps.com
Recommended in Litigation

Practice Areas: Partner in the General Litigation Group in the Jackson office. He is a former Presiding Justice of the Mississippi Supreme Court and retired from that position in October 2001. He was appointed to the Mississippi Supreme Court in 1991 and served on that court for 11 years. He served as a circuit judge in Hinds and Yazoo counties for six years before that. From 1976 until 1985, Mr Banks served in the Mississippi House of Representatives where he served as Chair of the Ethics Committee, a Judiciary Committee and the Legislative Black Caucus. Mr Banks also served as a Member of the Mississippi Board of Bar Admissions from 1978-80, and as a member of a number of advisory commissions at the state and federal level. He practices in the areas of commercial litigation, alternative dispute resolution, legislative and governmental relations and appellate law.
Personal: Howard University, JD, cum laude, 1968; Civil Rights and Book Reviews Editor, Howard Law Journal; Howard University, BA in Administration (Accounting), 1965.

BASS Jr, Ross F
Phelps Dunbar LLP, Jackson
601 360 9332
bassr@phelps.com
Recommended in Litigation
Practice Areas: Managing Partner of the firm's Jackson office and regional Practice Coordinator of the firm's Commercial Litigation Practice Group. He practices in the area of complex business and product liability litigation and has substantial experience in the defense of financial institutions and the litigation and settlement of class actions. Admitted in Mississippi and Georgia in 1973 and the US Supreme Court in 1977.
Personal: University of Mississippi, JD, with honors, 1973; editor in chief, Mississippi Law Journal. Vanderbilt University; Belhaven College, BA, 1970.

BUSH III, F M
Phelps Dunbar LLP, Tupelo
662 690 8136
bushm@phelps.com
Recommended in Corporate/M&A
Practice Areas: Managing Partner of the Tupelo office. He concentrates in the

areas of corporate and business law. He has provided corporate and business representation for many corporations, concentrating primarily in the industries of manufacturing, healthcare, and banking. Mr Bush has served as outside counsel to the largest hospital system in Mississippi for over 20 years. In addition, he provides ongoing corporate counsel to approximately 20 business corporations in Mississippi and is local counsel to several large out-of-state public companies. He has represented out-of-state companies in locating or expanding facilities in Mississippi, particularly with a view toward maximizing tax and other incentives offered by the State of Mississippi. Mr Bush has also worked in the area of municipal finance, having served as underwriters' counsel, bond counsel, and trustees' counsel. He has represented both buyers and sellers in a variety of acquisition transactions involving public and private companies in taxable and tax-free transactions.
Personal: Harvard University, LLM, 1972; University of Mississippi, JD, 1969; editor in Chief, Mississippi Law Journal. Brown University, BA, 1967.

BYRD, Robert
Byrd & Wiser, Biloxi
228 432 8123
Recommended in Bankruptcy

CAMPBELL, Roy
Bradley Arant Rose & White LLP, Jackson 601 592 9934
rcampbell@bradleyarant.com
Recommended in Litigation
Practice Areas: Partner in general civil litigation, with emphasis in product liability and personal injury.
Prof. Memberships: Admitted, Mississippi (1975) and Tennessee (1999). Member, American Board of Trial Advocates, Mississippi Bar Foundation, International Association of Defense Counsel, Board of Governors of Fifth Circuit Bar Association.
Personal: University of Mississippi, JD, 1975; Vice-Chairman, Moot Court Board; Davidson College, BA, 1972.

CANNADA, Barry
Butler, Snow, O'Mara, Stevens & Cannada, PLLC, Jackson 601 985 4535
barry.cannada@butlersnow.com
Recommended in Corporate/M&A
Practice Areas: Business planning and operations, business structure and capitalization and mergers and acquisitions.
Prof. Memberships: The Mississippi Bar, National Lawyers Association, American Bar Association.
Career: Listed in The Best Lawyers in America; former consultant to a national investment banking firm; negotiated substantial specialized financing transactions for transportation related entities; President and General Counsel of local, privately-held holding company;

assisted in the preparation of public issuances of high yield debt and preparation for a public offering of equities.
Personal: The University of Mississippi, JD, cum laude, 1980; BBA, magna cum laude, 1977.

CANNADA, Don
Butler, Snow, O'Mara, Stevens & Cannada, PLLC, Jackson 601 985 4510
don.cannada@butlersnow.com
Recommended in Real Estate
Practice Areas: Commercial law and lending, real estate transactions and financing, mergers and acquisitions.
Prof. Memberships: Hinds County Bar Association, The Mississippi Bar, the Business Law, Real Property and Probate and Trust sections of American Bar Association, National Association of Bond Lawyers, American Land Title Association, officer of Tri-County Real Estate Association.
Career: Practice Group Leader for Financial Services group, elected to membership in American College of Real Estate Lawyers, former Chairman of the Mississippi College School of Law Annual Real Estate Seminar, listed in 'Best Lawyers in America'.
Personal: Vanderbilt University, JD, 1978; The University of Mississippi, BBA, 1975.

CHATHAM, Henry
Wise Carter Child & Caraway, Professional Association, Jackson
601 968 5500
Recommended in Corporate/M&A

CLARK, Donald
Butler, Snow, O'Mara, Stevens & Cannada, PLLC, Jackson 601 985 4586
don.clark@butlersnow.com
Recommended in Corporate/M&A
Practice Areas: Municipal bonds, healthcare transactions, governmental affairs.
Prof. Memberships: Hinds County Bar Association, The Mississippi Bar, Mississippi Association of County Board Attorneys, American Bar Association, National Association of Bond Lawyers.
Career: Chairman of Business Department, former Practice Group Leader of Public Finance and Governmental Affairs group, former Special Assistant Attorney General for Mississippi, represented State of Mississippi and advised county and municipal governments and officials and served as bond counsel, underwriter's counsel and trustee's counsel to government entities.
Personal: The University of Mississippi, JD, 1973; the University of Southern Mississippi, BS, 1971.

CLEMENT, Rodney
Brunini, Grantham, Grower & Hewes, PLLC, Jackson 601 948 3101
rclement@brunini.com
Recommended in Real Estate
Practice Areas: Real estate, land use, secured financing.

Prof. Memberships: American College of Real Estate Lawyers, American College of Mortgage Attorneys, Best Lawyers in America (real estate).
Career: Admitted to The Mississippi Bar in 1983. Brunini, Grantham, Grower & Hewes, PLLC, 1983-present. President of Real Property Section of The Mississippi Bar, 2002-03.
Publications: Revised Article 9 and Real Property, 36 Real Property, Probate and Trust Journal 513 (Fall 2001)(co-author); Enforcing Security Interests in Personal Property in Mississippi, 67 Mississippi Law Journal 43 (Fall 1997).
Personal: BA, Millsaps College,1980; JD,Washington & Lee University, 1983.

CORLEW, John
Watkins & Eager PLLC, Jackson
601 948 6470
Recommended in Litigation

CRUTCHER Jr, Pepper
Balch & Bingham, Jackson
(601) 965-8158
pcrutcher@balch.com
Recommended in Employment
Practice Areas: Labor and employment; litigation; antitrust; intellectual property.
Prof. Memberships: Mississippi Bar; Louisiana Bar Association; Federalist Society of Mississippi; Federalist Society for Law and Public Policy Studies; Fifth Circuit Bar Association.
Career: R Pepper Crutcher, Jr for more than 20 years, has advised and represented employers in defense of their lawful discretion to hire, direct, and discharge their employees. This practice has involved him in continuing litigation in state and federal courts, predominantly in Mississippi and Louisiana, and administrative litigation and investigations conducted by the National Labor Relations Board. Pepper's regular practice includes the drafting and enforcement of confidential non-union employment dispute arbitration agreements, traditional arbitration of union contract grievances, and negotiation of traditional labor agreements. He also frequently presents continuing education programs for clients and industry groups and has testified before subcommittees of the Mississippi Legislature on related topics.
Personal: Born: October 12, 1957; education: University of Virginia (JD, 1982); University of Mississippi (BA, magna cum laude, 1979).

DAVIS, Mark
Watkins Ludlam Winter & Stennis, P.A.
Jackson 601 949 4909
mdavis@watkinsludlam.com
Recommended in Real Estate
Practice Areas: Shareholder in the Business Solutions Practice Group, focusing his practice in real estate and commercial finance transactions.
Prof. Memberships: Member: The Mississippi Bar (Past Chair of the Real Property Section), Hinds County and Ameri-

can Bar Associations, International Council of Shopping Centers.
Career: Admitted to The Mississippi Bar in 1984. Member of the Board of Directors and attorney with Watkins Ludlam Winter & Stennis, P.A.
Personal: Cumberland School of Law (JD, summa cum laude, 1984) and Samford University (BA, magna cum laude, 1981). Managing editor of the 'Cumberland Law Review'.

DOVE, Luke
Dove and Chill, Jackson
601 352 0999
Recommended in Litigation

DRINKWATER, Robert
Brunini, Grantham, Grower & Hewes, PLLC, Jackson 601 960 6852
bdrinkwa@brunini.com
Recommended in Corporate/M&A
Practice Areas: Corporations, mergers and acquistions, securities, real estate, business entities, banking, finance and commercial transactions.
Career: Mr Drinkwater has specialized in commercial law since beginning practice in 1977. In recent years his practice has focused on banking, finance and commercial real estate.

DRINKWATER, Wayne
Bradley Arant Rose & White LLP, Jackson
601 592 9911
wdrinkwater@bradleyarant.com
Recommended in Litigation
Practice Areas: Senior Partner, general civil litigation. Extensive experience in commercial litigation and appellate practice.
Prof. Memberships: Admitted, Mississippi (1974). Member, American College of Trial Lawyers; American Academy of Appellate Lawyers; American Law Institute; American Bar Association.
Career: Joined Bradley Arant, 2001; Member, Executive Committee and Litigation Practice Group. Former law clerk to Chief Justice Warren E Burger, United States Supreme Court; and Chief Judge William C Keady, United States District Court for Northern District of Mississippi.
Personal: Born 20 February 1949. JD (summa cum laude), University of Mississippi, 1974, BA (summa cum laude), University of Mississippi, 1971.

FAIR, George
Watkins & Eager PLLC, Jackson
601 948 6470
Recommended in Corporate/M&A

FORD, Barry
Baker, Donelson, Bearman , Caldwell & Berkowitz, PC, Jackson 601 351 8925
bford@bakerdonelson.com
Recommended in Litigation
Practice Areas: Practice concentrated in general civil litigation and white collar defense. Prior to joining Baker Donelson, Judge Ford served three terms as Circuit Court Judge for the First Circuit Court District, the largest Circuit Court

District in Mississippi. During this time he served for approximately five years as the Circuit Judges' representative on the Board of Governors, the governing body of all state, county and youth court judges in Mississippi.
Prof. Memberships: Member, Mississippi and Magnolia Bar Associations. Barrister, American Inns of Court. Recipient, Drum Major for Justice Award. Graduate, National Judicial Council.
Career: Licensed in Mississippi since 1979.

FRIEDMAN, Gary E
Phelps Dunbar LLP, Jackson
601 360 9355
friedmag@phelps.com
Recommended in Employment
Practice Areas: Partner and Practice Coordinator of the Labor and Employment Group in the Jackson office. He is general counsel to the Mississippi Municipal Liability Plan, the Mississippi Municipal Workers' Compensation Group, and the Mississippi Drug Testing Consortium. Has assisted public and private employers throughout the state in matters involving labor and employment problems.
Personal: University of Mississippi, JD, with distinction, 1982; articles editor, Mississippi Law Journal; Phi Delta Phi. Georgia Institute of Technology, BS in Industrial Engineering, 1971.

GALLOWAY, Robert
Butler, Snow, O'Mara, Stevens & Cannada, PLLC, Gulfport 228 575 3019
bob.galloway@butlersnow.com
Recommended in Litigation
Practice Areas: Product liability, commercial litigation, maritime litigation, professional liability defense, healthcare law.
Prof. Memberships: Harrison County Bar Association, The Mississippi Bar, Mississippi Defense Lawyers Association, American Bar Association, Defense Research Institute, Maritime Law Association of the United States, International Association of Defense Counsel, American Board of Trial Advocates.
Career: Principle Attorney for Memorial Hospital at Gulfport 20+ years, Fellow in American College of Trial Lawyers and past Chairperson of State Committee, Fellow and past President of The Mississippi Bar Foundation, frequent law school lecturer, listed in 'Best Lawyers in America'.
Personal: The University of Mississippi, JD, 1967; BA, 1964.

GENO, Craig
Harris & Geno PLLC, Jackson
601 948 0048
Recommended in Bankruptcy

GIBBS, Robert
Brunini, Grantham, Grower & Hewes, PLLC, Jackson 601 960 6861
rgibbs@brunini.com
Recommended in Litigation

Practice Areas: Personal injury, mass torts and professional product liability; commercial litigation; environmental litigation; alternative dispute resolution (ADR); white collar criminal defense.
Prof. Memberships: Mississippi Bar Association, Magnolia Bar Association; Hinds County Bar Association; National Bar Association; Bar Association of the Fifth Circuit, Past President; Charles Clark Chapter, American Inns of Court, President 1999-2001; Model Civil Jury Instruction Committee; Law Alumni Board, University of Mississippi; People's Law School, Presenter; American Bar Association, Law School Site Accreditation Team Member; Mississippi Bar Foundation, President; Mississippi Supreme Court, Task Force on Gender Fairness; Board of Governors of the Fifth Circuit Bar, President 2000-02; Court Liaison and Judicial Administration Committee of the Mississippi Bar, Chairperson, 1999-2001; Bar Commissioner, Mississippi Bar; Mississippi Supreme Court, Commission of Bar Admission Review.
Career: Robert has worked as Staff Attorney for Southeast Mississippi Legal Services, Assistant District Attorney for the Eleventh Circuit District, and Deputy Attorney General for the State of Mississippi. In 1991, Robert became Hinds County Circuit Court Judge, a position he held until 1998. In 1998 he joined the Brunini firm, practicing areas including alternative dispute resolution, criminal litigation, mass tort litigation, product liability and white collar criminal defense.
Publications: On Faculty Excellence in Judicial Education, 1996, National Council of Juvenile and Family Court Judges, Reno Nevada.
Personal: Tougaloo College (BS, Cum Laude, 1975; University of Mississippi (JD, 1979); National Judicial College, Reno, Nevada (Graduate 1991, 1993).

GOODMAN Jr, William
Watkins & Eager PLLC, Jackson
601 948 6470
Recommended in Litigation

GRAHAM, Collier
Wise Carter Child & Caraway, Professional Association, Jackson
601 968 5500
Recommended in Litigation

GRISHMAN, David
Watkins Ludlam Winter & Stennis, P.A.
Jackson 601 949 4770
dgrishman@watkinsludlam.com
Recommended in Corporate/M&A
Practice Areas: Shareholder in the Business Solutions Practice Group, focusing his practice in federal, state and local taxation; corporations; trusts and estates; real estate syndication; and franchising.
Prof. Memberships: Fellow: American College of Trust and Estate Counsel, American College of Tax Counsel, Mississippi Bar Foundation; Member: The

Mississippi Bar, State Bar of Texas, American Bar Association (Business Law; Real Property, Probate and Trust Law; Taxation; and Forum Committee on Franchising).
Career: Admitted to the Mississippi and Texas Bars in 1971.
Personal: University of Alabama (BA, 1966; JD, 1970) and New York University (LLM in Taxation, 1971).

GUNN, Paul
Watkins & Eager PLLC, Jackson
601 948 6470
Recommended in Real Estate

HAFTER, Jerome C
Phelps Dunbar LLP, Jackson
601 360 9347
hafterj@phelps.com
Recommended in Corporate/M&A
Practice Areas: Partner in the Business Group in the Jackson office. He practices in the areas of business and corporate law, agricultural law, biotechnology, acquisitions, bankruptcy, taxation, casino gaming, intellectual property licensing, international transactions and commercial litigation. Served as a law clerk to Judge Charles Clark, United States Court of Appeals, Fifth Circuit in 1972-73. Admitted to practice in Mississippi.
Personal: Yale University, JD, 1972; associate editor, Yale Law Journal. Oxford University, MA, 1974, BA, first class honours, 1969. Rice University, BA, summa cum laude, 1967. Chair, Mississippi Board of Bar Admissions (1979-2002) and National Conference of Bar Examiners (1998-99).

HENEGAN, John
Butler, Snow, O'Mara, Stevens & Cannada, PLLC, Jackson 601 985 4530
john.henegan@butlersnow.com
Recommended in Litigation
Practice Areas: Antitrust, defamation, privacy and all media-related matters, patent and intellectual property, telecommunications, constitutional law, complex commercial litigation, all aspects of federal and state appellate practice.
Prof. Memberships: Hinds County Bar Association, The Mississippi Bar, Federal Bar Association, Antitrust, Litigation and Patent and Copyright sections of American Bar Association, Media Law Resource Center.
Career: Practice Group Leader of Commercial Litigation group, served as Executive Assistant and Chief of Staff to former Mississippi Governor William Winter, co-authored several legal articles, awarded Distinguished Service Award by Hinds County Bar Association.
Personal: The University of Mississippi, JD, with honors, 1976; BA, 1972.

HISE, Daniel G
Butler, Snow, O'Mara, Stevens & Cannada, PLLC, Jackson 601 985 4509
dan.hise@butlersnow.com
Recommended in Corporate/M&A, Gaming & Licensing

Practice Areas: Securities law, gaming law, corporate transactions.
Prof. Memberships: Business Law and Gaming Law sections of The Mississippi Bar, Business Law section of American Bar Association, the International Association of Gaming Attorneys.
Career: Listed in 'The Best Lawyers in America,' founding member and past Chairman of the Secretary of State's Business Law Advisory Group, serves as Mississippi Liaison to the State Regulations of Securities Committee, represented the two largest casino operating companies, Mississippi College School of Law's 1999 Outstanding Alumnus.
Personal: Mississippi College, JD, with special distinction, 1985; Tulane University, PhD, 1973; the University of California, Berkeley, BA, 1965.

HODGE Jr, E Clifton
Phelps Dunbar LLP, Jackson
601 360 9331
hodgec@phelps.com
Recommended in Corporate/M&A, Litigation
Practice Areas: Partner in the General Litigation Group in the Jackson office. He practices in the areas of commercial litigation and business transactions. His litigation practice involves many types of business disputes and corporate and securities matters, including breach of contract claims and business torts such as breach of fiduciary duty and wrongful interference with business relations. Frequently advises corporate boards of directors concerning duties and responsibilities of board members, corporate procedure, and board decisions concerning threatened litigation.
Personal: Harvard University, LLM (concentration on corporate law), 1970. University of Mississippi, JD, 1967; assistant editor, Mississippi Law Journal. University of Mississippi, BBA in Accounting, 1964.

IRBY, Peyton
Watkins Ludlam Winter & Stennis, P.A. Jackson 601 949 4810
pirby@watkinsludlam.com
Recommended in Employment
Practice Areas: Shareholder in the Labor & Employment Practice Group, focusing his practice in labor matters, NLRB litigation, employment law and related litigation.
Prof. Memberships: Fellow: College of Labor & Employment Lawyers; Member: The Mississippi Bar (Past Chair, L&E Law Section), American & Federal Bar Associations.
Career: Admitted to The Mississippi Bar in 1970. Co-Chair of the Labor & Employment Practice Group and attorney with Watkins Ludlam Winter & Stennis, P.A.
Publications: Editor, Mississippi Employment Law Letter; 'The Americans with Disabilities Act: The Employer's Perspective,' 11 Miss.C.L.Rev.263

(1991).
Personal: University of Mississippi (JD, 1970) and Mississippi State University (BS, 1967).

JACOBS, Gina
Watkins Ludlam Winter & Stennis, P.A. Jackson 601 949 4705
gjacobs@watkinsludlam.com
Recommended in Corporate/M&A
Practice Areas: Shareholder in the Business Solutions Practice Group, focusing her practice in corporate law, commercial finance, mergers and acquisitions, and health law.
Prof. Memberships: Member: The Mississippi Bar, American Bar Association, American Health Lawyers Association, Jackson Young Lawyers Association (past member, Board of Directors, and Secretary), Mississippi Secretary of State's Business Law Advisory Group.
Career: Admitted to The Mississippi Bar in 1983. Chair of the Business Solutions Practice Group and attorney with Watkins Ludlam Winter & Stennis, P.A.
Personal: University of Mississippi (JD, magna cum laude, 1983; BBA, summa cum laude, 1980).

JONES, Christy
Butler, Snow, O'Mara, Stevens & Cannada, PLLC, Jackson 601 985 4523
christy.jones@butlersnow.com
Recommended in Litigation
Practice Areas: Drug and medical device litigation, product liability, professional liability, toxic and mass tort.
Prof. Memberships: The Mississippi Bar, American Bar Association, Defense Counsel Trial Academy, International Association of Defense Counsel, Trial Attorneys of America, Bar Association of the Fifth Federal Circuit.
Career: Chair of Litigation Department, Fellow of American College of Trial Lawyers and the American Bar Association Foundation, listed in 'The Best Lawyers in America,' listed in 'Who's Who Among International Product Liability Lawyers,' former Chair of Drug and Device Committee of the Defense Research Institute.
Personal: University of Arkansas, JD, with high honors, 1977; BA, 1974.

JONES, Walker
Baker, Donelson, Bearman, Caldwell & Berkowitz, PC, Jackson 601 351 2413
wjones@bakerdonelson.com
Recommended in Litigation
Practice Areas: Cochair of Baker Donelson's Product Liability/Tort Group. Practice concentrated in insurance, commercial and product liability litigation. Extensive experience handling mass tort defense, construction law and chemical/toxic tort litigation.
Prof. Memberships: American, Mississippi, Texas and Tennessee Bar Associations (Member, Sections on Litigation, Public Contract Law, Tort and Insurance Practice). Member, Trial Attorneys of America, The American Board of Trial

Advocates, International Association of Defense Counsel and Maritime Law Association of the United States.
Career: Licensed in Mississippi since 1973, Texas since 1996 and Tennessee since 1997.

KAUFMAN, David
Brunini, Grantham, Grower & Hewes, PLLC, Jackson 601 960 6873
dkaufman@brunini.com
Recommended in Litigation
Practice Areas: General civil litigation, including complex commercial and mass tort cases, antitrust, toxic exposure, business torts, product liability, and premises liability.
Prof. Memberships: American College of Trial Lawyers; American Board of Trial Advocates; International Association of Defense Counsel; Hinds County Bar Association (Secretary).
Career: He has been practicing litigation exclusively since joining the Brunini firm in 1978.
Publications: He has spoken at a number of trial practice and toxic exposure seminars and has been an invited lecturer at a number of trial practice classes at area law schools.
Personal: University of Mississippi (BBA, 1975); University of Mississippi (JD, 1978).

LATHAM, William
Latham & Burwell PLLC, Ridgeland
601 981 4470
Recommended in Litigation

LAZARUS, Robert
Watkins Ludlam Winter & Stennis, P.A. Jackson 601 949 4930
blazarus@watkinsludlam.com
Recommended in Corporate/M&A
Practice Areas: Shareholder in the Education, Environmental and Government Law Practice Group, focusing his practice in corporate finance and state and local government finance.
Prof. Memberships: Member: The Mississippi Bar, American Bar Association, National Association of Bond Lawyers, Ohio State Bar (inactive status).
Career: Admitted to the Ohio State Bar in 1976 and The Mississippi Bar in 1982. Attorney with Watkins Ludlam Winter & Stennis, P.A.
Personal: Boston University School of Law (JD, cum laude, 1976) and Dartmouth College (AB, magna cum laude, 1973).

MARTIN, David L
Watkins Ludlam Winter & Stennis, P.A. Jackson 601 949 4901
dmartin@watkinsludlam.com
Recommended in Corporate/M&A
Practice Areas: Shareholder in the Regulated Industries Practice Group, focusing his practice in insurance law (corporate, regulatory and insolvency).
Prof. Memberships: Member: The Mississippi Bar (Past Chair, Business Law Section), American Bar Association,

Federation of Regulatory Counsel.
Career: Admitted to The Mississippi Bar in 1976. Chair of the Regulated Industries Practice Group, former CEO and attorney with Watkins Ludlam Winter & Stennis, P.A.
Publications: 'Arbitrating Insurance Disputes in Mississippi: Insurance Commissioner's Authority,' Federation of Regulatory Counsel Quarterly Journal of Insurance Law and Regulation (Dec 2002).
Personal: University of Virginia (JD, 1976) and Millsaps College (BA, 1969).

MCDANIEL Jr, Dan M
Phelps Dunbar LLP, Jackson
601 360 9367
mcdaniel@phelps.com
Recommended in Gaming & Licensing
Practice Areas: Partner in the firm's Jackson, Mississippi, office. He manages Phelps Dunbar's Gaming Practice in all states in which the firm has offices - Mississippi, Louisiana, Texas and Florida. Mr McDaniel, currently Vice President for the International Association of Gaming Attorneys, represents both domestic and international clients (including casinos, manufacturers, distributors, lessors, shareholders, officers, directors, key employees and other persons) before gaming authorities with regard to licensing, registration, findings of suitability, transfers of ownership, work permits, patron disputes, investigations, disciplinary proceedings and other regulatory matters. He has also represented clients in several other states regarding proposed gaming legislation and has testified as an expert witness before numerous legislative committees.
Personal: University of Mississippi, JD, 1973. University of Southern Mississippi, BS, 1971.

MENDENHALL, William
McGlinchey Stafford, PLLC, Jackson
601 960 8400
bmendenhall@mcglinchey.com
Recommended in Corporate/M&A
Practice Areas: Partner in the business section concentrating in corporate practice, business transactions and commercial real estate.
Prof. Memberships: The American Bar Association, the Hinds County Bar Association, and the Mississippi Bar.
Career: Admitted to the Mississippi Bar in 1984. Former Chairman of Mississippi Law Institute. In 1993, appointed by Secretary of State Dick Molpus to the Secretary of State's Business Law Advisory Group and currently serves as Chairman of Corporate Laws Subcommittee.
Personal: Received a JD (cum laude) in 1984, and a BBA (magna cum laude) in 1980 from the University of Mississippi. Named in leading US legal publication.

MILAM, Kenneth
Watkins & Eager PLLC, Jackson
601 948 6470
Recommended in Employment

MOCKBEE, David
Mockbee Hall & Drake, Jackson
601 353 0035
Recommended in Litigation

MOELLER Jr, Armin J
Balch & Bingham, Jackson
601 965 8156
amoeller@balch.com
Recommended in Employment
Practice Areas: Labor and employment; healthcare; litigation; technology.
Prof. Memberships: Mississippi Defense Lawyers Association; Mississippi Bar; American Bar Association Developing Labor Law Committee; College of Labor and Employment Law.
Career: Armin J Moeller, Jr's practice concentrates on labor relations and the defense of adverse employment decisions; litigation; drafting and negotiating contracts, including information technology project agreements; and litigation claims against information technology companies. Mr Moeller represents employers in maintaining non-union status; collective bargaining negotiations and arbitration; race, sex, religion, age, disability, sexual/workplace harassment discrimination and retaliation claims; handling EEOC, NLRB, OSHA and other administrative claims through judicial process; drafting employment, severance, noncompetition and confidentiality contracts; and affirmative action and OFCCP compliance. Mr Moeller has been listed in The Best Lawyers in America since 1989.
Personal: Born: June 18, 1947; education: Louisiana State University (JD, Phi Alpha Delta, 1972); Tulane University (BA, 1989).

MUNFORD, Luther T
Phelps Dunbar LLP, Jackson
601 360 9364
munfordl@phelps.com
Recommended in Litigation
Practice Areas: Appellate litigation, media law, constitutional litigation. Author, Mississippi Appellate Practice (2001). Adjunct professor, Mississippi College School of Law. Formerly: President, American Academy of Appellate Lawyers; Member, Advisory Committee on Appellate Rules to Judicial Conference of the United States; Chair, Alumni Association of Princeton University; law clerk, US Supreme Court Justice Harry A Blackmun, US Fifth Circuit Judge Paul H Roney.
Personal: University of Virginia, JD, 1976; Oxford University, BA, 1973; Princeton University, AB, 1971.

O'MARA, James W
Phelps Dunbar LLP, Jackson
601 360 9720
omaraj@phelps.com
Recommended in Bankruptcy
Practice Areas: Partner in the Business Group of the Jackson office. He practices in the areas of business bankruptcy and creditors' rights, loan workouts, secured lending, commercial litigation and business transactions.
Personal: University of Mississippi, JD, with distinction, 1967; editor in chief, Mississippi Law Journal; Phi Delta Phi; Phi Kappa Phi; Omicron Delta Kappa. University of Mississippi, BA, 1962.

PAINTER, William
Baker, Donelson, Bearman, Caldwell & Berkowitz, PC, Jackson 601 351 2425
wpainter@bakerdonelson.com
Recommended in Corporate/M&A
Practice Areas: Practice concentrated in corporate transactions, tax and health care restructuring. Extensive experience in employee benefits and deferred compensation; federal, state and local taxation; securities and trusts and estates.
Prof. Memberships: Fellow, American College of Trust and Estate Counsel. Fellow, American College of Tax Counsel. Former Chair, Mississippi Secretary of State's Task Force on Business Law Reform. Former Chair, Mississippi Secretary of State's Business Law Advisory Group. Member, American, Mississippi and Hinds County Bar Associations.
Career: Licensed in Mississippi since 1974 and US Tax Court since 1975.

PERRY, Alan W
Forman Perry Watkins Krutz & Tardy LLP, Jackson 601 960 8600
aperry@fpwk.com
Recommended in Litigation
Practice Areas: Mr Perry is involved in a wide variety of complex commercial and corporate litigation, including disputes related to environmental matters, professional liability of accountants and lawyers, and the obligations of corporate directors and officers. He frequently advises corporate boards of directors on corporate governance matters and potential litigation.
Prof. Memberships: Member, Lawyers Advisory Committee, United States Court of Appeals, Fifth Circuit; former Member, Standing Committee of Rules and Procedure of the Judicial Conference of the United States.
Career: Clerked for Judge Charles Clark, United States Court of Appeals, Fifth Circuit (1972-73); founding Partner of Forman Perry Watkins Krutz & Tardy, 1986.
Personal: Awarded JD, magna cum laude, Harvard Law School, 1972, receiving the Fay Diploma as first in class. Served as editor and senior editor, Harvard Law Review. Awarded BBA (Accountancy), summa cum laude, University of Mississippi, 1969. Awarded Silver Medal for second highest grade in the United States on CPA Examination. Director of BancorpSouth, Inc.

REED, William
Baker, Donelson, Bearman, Caldwell & Berkowitz, PC, Jackson 601 351 2410
wreed@bakerdonelson.com
Recommended in Litigation
Practice Areas: Chief Operating Officer of Baker Donelson. Practice concentrated in products liability, toxic tort, insurance and franchise litigation. Mr Reed has litigated commercial and tort cases in federal and state courts in ten states and has handled appeals in Mississippi and four federal circuits.
Prof. Memberships: Fellow, Mississippi Bar Foundation. Member, American (Tort and Insurance Practice Section and Forum on Franchising), Hinds County and Mississippi (Health Law Section) Bar Associations. Member, American Health Lawyers Association, Bar Association of the Fifth Federal Circuit and International Association of Defense Counsel. United States Army (1972-74).
Career: Licensed in Mississippi since 1977.

ROSENBLATT, Stephen W
Butler, Snow, O'Mara, Stevens & Cannada, PLLC, Jackson 601 985 4504
steve.rosenblatt@butlersnow.com
Recommended in Bankruptcy
Practice Areas: Bankruptcy, creditors' rights, commercial litigation, loan workouts and restructuring, commercial transactions and contracts, corporate law.
Prof. Memberships: The Mississippi Bar, American Bankruptcy Institute, Mississippi Bar Foundation, Lex Mundi College of Mediators.
Career: Chairman of Executive Committee, listed in 'The Best Lawyers in America,' lecturer and panelist at CLE programs, founding member and past President of the Mississippi Bankruptcy Conference, Fellow in the Mississippi Bar Foundation, past President of Mississippi Young Lawyers Association and the Jackson Young Lawyers Association, experience as mediator in alternative dispute resolution.
Personal: The University of Mississippi, JD, with honors, 1975; Vanderbilt University, BA, 1970.

SAMS Jr, L F
Mitchell, McNutt & Sams PA, Tupelo
662 842 3871
Recommended in Litigation

SHAPLEY, Christopher
Brunini, Grantham, Grower & Hewes, PLLC, Jackson
(601) 960-6875
cshapley@brunini.com
Recommended in Litigation
Practice Areas: General civil litigation, including environmental, pharmaceutical, business, healthcare, mass torts and personal injury.
Prof. Memberships: American College of Trial Lawyers (1995); American Board of Trial Advocates (2000); International Association of Defense Counsel (2001).
Career: He has been practicing litigation exclusively since joining the Brunini firm in 1976.
Publications: 'ABA Antitrust Law Sections, State Antitrust Practice and Statutes (1990)', Chapter 26 - Mississippi, p. 26-1.

Personal: Mississippi State University (BS cum laude 1973); University of Mississippi (JD 1976).

SHEPHERD III, Thomas B
Watkins Ludlam Winter & Stennis, P.A, Jackson 601 949 4711
tshepherd@watkinsludlam.com
Recommended in Gaming & Licensing
Practice Areas: Shareholder in the Regulated Industries Practice Group, focusing his practice in corporate law and gaming law.
Prof. Memberships: Member: The Mississippi Bar, American Bar Association, International Association of Gaming Attorneys (Board of Trustees), Mississippi Secretary of State's Business Law Advisory Group (Chairman).
Career: Admitted to The Mississippi Bar in 1984. CEO and attorney with Watkins Ludlam Winter & Stennis, P.A.
Publications: Mississippi Corporations—Formation and Operation With Forms (The Harrison Company, 2002); Mississippi Chapter, International Casino Law (University of Nevada Reno, 1999).
Personal: Washington & Lee University (JD, cum laude, 1984) and University of Mississippi (BBA, cum laude, 1980).

SILER Jr, W Thomas
Phelps Dunbar LLP, Jackson
601 360 9357
silert@phelps.com
Recommended in Employment
Practice Areas: Partner and the Regional Practice Coordinator of the firm's Labor and Employment Practice Group. He serves as a Member of the firm's Policy and Planning Committee. Since 1983, his practice has been concentrated in the representation of management in labor and employment law matters, and in the defense of civil rights issues. Among other matters, Mr Siler has represented employers in Title VII, ADEA, ADA, FLSA, FMLA, OSHA, ERISA, as well as matters involving the NLRA and LMRA. He also has handled a variety of issues arising under the United States Constitution. In more than 20 years of practice Mr Siler has litigated numerous jury trials in the Federal Court system.
Personal: University of Mississippi, JD, with distinction, 1983; assistant editor, Mississippi Law Journal; Millsaps College, BBA, 1979; Past President of the Mississippi Defense Lawyer's Association and Vice-Chairman of the IADC's Employment Law Committee.

SMITH, Taylor
The Kullman Firm A Professional Law Corporation, Columbus
662 244 8824
tbs@kullmanlaw.com
Recommended in Employment
Practice Areas: Throughout his career, Taylor Smith has represented employers in all types and aspects of labor and employment law matters. He has exten-

sive litigation experience in both bench and jury trials involving claims of sexual harassment, wrongful discharge, and breach of employment contracts, as well as extensive experience in litigating race, sex, age, and disability discrimination lawsuits. He regularly provides training and counseling for supervisors, managers, and executives regarding various aspects of federal and state laws, as well as Human Resource policies, procedures, and practices. Additionally, Mr Smith has extensive experience in representing employers before the National Labor Relations Board, including union representation elections, litigation of unfair labor practice charges, negotiation of collective bargaining agreements, and handling of arbitration cases in this sector.
Prof. Memberships: Taylor Smith is a Member of the American Bar Association (Section: Labor and Employment Law); the Mississippi Defense Lawyers Association; the American Academy of Hospital Attorneys; and is a Fellow of the American College of Trial Lawyers. He has spoken at numerous employment seminars. He is admitted to practice before the United States Supreme Court, the Courts of Appeal for the Fifth and Eleventh Circuits, all courts in the state of Mississippi and the United States District Courts for the Northern and Southern Districts of Mississippi.
Career: Taylor Smith graduated from Mississippi State University in 1962 with honors. He received a JD degree from the University of Mississippi Law School in 1964 and was a member of the Miss. Law Journal, serving as article editor. He has been practicing law in excess of 40 years and is a shareholder in The Kullman Firm, a firm founded in 1946 and devoted exclusively to the representation of management in labor and employment matters.

SMITH III, William
Watkins & Eager PLLC, Jackson
601 948 6470
Recommended in Real Estate

STEPHENSON III, Paul
Watkins & Eager PLLC, Jackson
601 948 6470
Recommended in Litigation

TAYLOR, Zachary
Watkins Ludlam Winter & Stennis, P.A, Jackson 601 949 4860
ztaylor@watkinsludlam.com
Recommended in Corporate/M&A
Practice Areas: Shareholder in the Education, Environmental and Government Law Practice Group, focusing his practice in state and local government finance.
Prof. Memberships: Member: The Mississippi Bar, American Bar Association.
Career: Admitted to The Mississippi Bar in 1977. Attorney with Watkins Ludlam Winter & Stennis, P.A.

Personal: University of Mississippi (JD, magna cum laude, 1977) and Harvard University (BA, cum laude, 1973).

TOHILL, Jim
Watkins Ludlam Winter & Stennis, P.A, Jackson 601 949 4790
jtohill@watkinsludlam.com
Recommended in Real Estate
Practice Areas: Shareholder in the Business Solutions Practice Group, focusing his practice in real estate and commercial finance.
Prof. Memberships: Fellow: American College of Mortgage Attorneys, American College of Real Estate Lawyers; Member: The Mississippi Bar (Past Chair, Real Property Section), American Bar Association, Hinds County Bar Association.
Career: Admitted to The Mississippi Bar in 1974. Former CEO and attorney with Watkins Ludlam Winter & Stennis, P.A.
Personal: University of Mississippi (JD, cum laude, 1974) and Millsaps College (BA, 1969).

ULMER, Michael
Watkins & Eager PLLC, Jackson
601 948 6470
Recommended in Litigation

WALKER, Jeffrey A
Butler, Snow, O'Mara, Stevens & Cannada, PLLC, Jackson
601 985 4558
jeff.walker@butlersnow.com
Recommended in Employment
Practice Areas: Collective bargaining, labor arbitration, union organizing campaigns, unfair labor practice charges, preventive labor relations, other matters arising under National Labor Relations Act.
Prof. Memberships: Labor and Employment Law section of The Mississippi Bar, Mississippi Defense Lawyers Association, Labor and Employment and Litigation sections of American Bar Association, Defense Research Institute.
Career: listed in 'The Best Lawyers in America,' Fellow of the College of Labor and Employment Lawyers, frequent speaker at labor and employment seminars, made presentations at Mississippi Manufacturers Association and Mississippi Bankers Association seminars.
Personal: The University of Mississippi, JD, 1978; the University of Wisconsin-Madison, BS, 1975.

WALLACE, Barbara
Wise Carter Child & Caraway, Professional Association, Jackson
601 968 5500
Recommended in Employment

WALLACE, Michael B
Phelps Dunbar LLP, Jackson
601 352 2300
wallacem@phelps.com
Recommended in Litigation
Practice Areas: Partner in the General Litigation Group in the Jackson office. He was admitted to the Mississippi Bar

in 1976. In 1999, he served as Special Impeachment Counsel to Senate Majority Leader Trent Lott for the impeachment trial of President Clinton. His practice is concentrated in commercial litigation at the trial and appellate levels. He also has wide experience in litigating constitutional claims and election disputes. Prior to joining Phelps Dunbar, Mr Wallace served as a law clerk to Justice Harry G Walker, Supreme Court of Mississippi, from 1976-77, and to Associate Justice William H Rehnquist, Supreme Court of the United States, from 1977-78. He chairs DRI's Appellate Advocacy Committee and is a member of the American Academy of Appellate Lawyers.
Personal: University of Virginia, JD, 1976; Law Review; Order of the Coif. Harvard University, BA in Government, cum laude, 1973.

WEEMS, Walter S
Brunini, Grantham, Grower & Hewes, PLLC, Jackson 601 960 6863
wweems@brunini.com
Recommended in Corporate/M&A
Practice Areas: Corporate; mergers and acquisitions; real estate.
Prof. Memberships: American Bar Association; Mississippi Bar.
Career: With Brunini Grantham Grower & Hewes from 1978-present.
Personal: JD from Vanderbilt Law School 1977 (first honors; Order of Coif). BA from Vanderbilt University 1974 (Magna cum Laude; phi beta kappa).

WELCH, W Scott
Butler, Snow, O'Mara, Stevens & Cannada, PLLC, Jackson
601 985 4516
scotty.welch@butlersnow.com
Recommended in Litigation
Practice Areas: Commercial transportation litigation, insurance coverage matters, environmental litigation, product liability litigation.
Prof. Memberships: The Mississippi Bar, Mississippi Defense Lawyers Association, American Bar Foundation, International Association of Defense Counsel, Trucking Industry Defense Association, Defense Research Institute, Bar of United States Supreme Court.
Career: former President of American Board of Trial Advocates, Fellow of American College of Trial Lawyers, Mississippi State Delegate to American Bar Association House of Delegates, listed in 'The Best Lawyers in America,' 40+ years trial and appellate experience.
Personal: The University of Mississippi, LLB, with distinction, 1964; the University of the South, BA, cum laude, 1961.

BRUNINI, GRANTHAM, GROWER & HEWES, PLLC

THE FIRM

Managing Partner: Walter S Weems
Number of partners: 41
Number of other lawyers: 26

FIRM OVERVIEW: A singular focus on Mississippi makes the Brunini firm unique among many of the law firms with offices in Mississippi and its capital city, Jackson. The firm was founded in the 1880s, and it has long been recognized as being at the top of the legal profession in Mississippi. In addition to being a well established firm, the Brunini firm is also dynamic, having made significant strides towards achieving the diversity necessary to reflect Mississippi's populace. The firm's clientele includes numerous Fortune 500 companies, as well as many of Mississippi's largest employers, its largest bank and its largest health insurer. The Brunini firm knows and understands Mississippi's legal and business environment.

MAIN AREAS OF PRACTICE

General & Commercial Litigation: Chambers USA recognizes Brunini trial lawyers Chris Shapley, Robert Gibbs and David Kaufman as three of the best litigators in Mississippi. Brunini's trial lawyers handle a wide range of matters, including litigation involving complex commercial transactions, mass torts, environmental issues, pharmaceutical products, consumer fraud, construction disputes, employment discrimination, products liability, medical malpractice, nursing homes, breach of contract, antitrust, securities fraud, business torts, taxation, and white collar crime. The firm's trial lawyers have extensive experience in state and federal trial and appellate courts in Mississippi and have served as lead counsel in some of Mississippi's largest and most complex litigation.

Environmental Law & Litigation: The firm's Environmental Practice Group is acknowledged as a statewide leader. One of the firm's attorneys currently serves as chair of the environmental section of the Mississippi Bar. The firm's attorneys have extensive experience in both environmental litigation and regulatory proceedings and have defended numerous enforcement actions instituted by the United States Department of Justice, Region IV of the Environmental Protection Agency, and the Bureau of Pollution Control. The firm has also obtained numerous environmental permits for its clients in proceedings before the Mississippi Environmental Quality Permit Board. The firm also has extensive experience in defending multi-plaintiff and class action lawsuits alleging harm from releases of hazardous substances, hazardous waste, and petroleum products.

Healthcare Law & Litigation: The firm has a comprehensive healthcare practice, representing hospitals, physician groups, nursing homes, and other healthcare providers. The firm has broad experience in administrative proceedings and litigation concerning Certificates of Need, Medicaid fraud, nursing home care, fraud and abuse-Stark II, private inurement, and other legal issues facing the healthcare industry.

Business & Commercial: Chambers USA recognizes Robert Drinkwater, Walter Weems and Rodney Clement as leading Mississippi business lawyers. Other Brunini business lawyers are recognized among their peers as leaders in their respective areas of business expertise. The firm's expertise includes general corporate law, mergers and acquisitions, public and industrial development financing and tax incentives, securities regulation, banking, real estate transactions, insurance regulation, syndication, estate planning, and corporate and personal taxation.

Public Industrial Development & Tax Incentives: The firm's representation in tax-exempt financing has included bonds issued by the State of Mississippi and various instrumentalities of the State, municipalities, counties, junior and senior colleges, and public school districts. In addition, the firm has extensive experience in state and local industrial and economic development financing with state and federal tax incentives.

HEAD OFFICE

MISSISSIPPI
248 East Capitol Street, **Jackson**, MS 39201
Tel: 601 948 3101 **Fax:** 601 960 6902
Website: www.brunini.com

BRANCH OFFICE

MISSISSIPPI
1710 Jackson Avenue, **Pascagoula**, MS 39567
Tel: 228 696 0044 **Fax:** 228 696 0223

CONTACTS

General & Commercial Litigation ....Chris Shapley, Robert Gibbs
....David Kaufman
Business & Commercial ....Robert Drinkwater, Walter Weems
....Rodney Clement, Leigh Allen
Taxation ....Louis Fuller, Jody Varner
Labor & Employment ....Brooks Eason, Anne Sanders
....Stephen Carmody
Construction ....Ron Yarbrough, Samuel Kelly
Public Industrial Development & Tax Incentives ......Wilson Montjoy
....Louis Fuller
Environmental Law & Litigation ....John Milner, Trudy Fisher
....Chris Shapley, David Kaufman
Healthcare Law & Litigation ....Edmund L Brunini, Jr, Chris Shapley,
....John E Wade, Kathryn R Gilchrist
Public Utilities & Telecommunications ....Wilson Montjoy,
....James L Halford, Charles L McBride, Jr

Public Utilities & Telecommunications: The firm practices extensively before the Mississippi Public Service Commission, representing a number of intrastate pipeline companies and telecommunications, gas, water and sewer companies. The firm has served as counsel in administrative proceedings and litigation regarding rates and service and application for certificates of public convenience and necessity for the construction of electric generation facilities, natural gas transmission and distribution facilities, underground natural gas storage facilities and telecommunications facilities.

Labor & Employment: The firm's labor and employment attorneys represent employers' interests both in litigation and in a broad array of state and federal administrative settings. In addition, the firm's employment attorneys advise and assist employers with a variety of other employment issues.

Construction Law & Litigation: The firm's construction attorneys have a vast range of experience representing owners, contractors, subcontractors, and sureties in the construction industry. Specifically, the firm's experience includes drafting and negotiating contract agreements, preparing and presenting construction claims, bid protests, business consultation, project workouts and mediation, arbitration or litigation of claims and disputes which arise in the course of construction projects.

CLIENTS: Trustmark National Bank; Northrup Grumman (Ingalls Shipbuilding); Blue Cross Blue Shield of Mississippi; Kerr-McGee Corporation; Purdue Pharma, L.P.; Cendant Corporation; Cellular South, Inc.; AT&T; St. Dominic Health Services, Inc.; CenterPoint Energy; Choctaw Maid Farms, Inc.; Textron; Beverly Enterprises; and Mariner Healthcare.

BUTLER, SNOW, O'MARA, STEVENS & CANADA PLLC

THE FIRM

Firm Chair: Stephen W Rosenblatt

Number of partners : 70
Number of other lawyers : 86

FIRM OVERVIEW: For 50 years, Butler Snow has been a leading presence in the field of law. With offices in Jackson, Mississippi, on the Gulf Coast of Mississippi, and in Memphis, Tennessee, Butler Snow provides legal services to many of the nation's leading businesses, as well as to individuals. Butler Snow represents a variety of clients across a multitude of industry sectors in both the litigation and business practice areas.

MAIN AREAS OF PRACTICE:

Appellate & Written Advocacy: Since the firm's inception, Butler Snow has enjoyed an extensive federal and state appellate practice, often involving cases raising novel or complex legal issues, in all fields of law.

Commercial Litigation: Butler Snow's Commercial Litigation Practice is led by some of the firm's most experienced trial lawyers. Although the firm's size and formidable litigation resources attract a significant number of representations in large commercial disputes, basic contract and business dissolution matters continue to be a significant part of the commercial litigation practice.

General Litigation: Butler Snow's General Litigation Group represents a wide variety of clients in litigated matters in both state and federal court, including personal injury, insurance coverage/bad faith, trucking and motor home matters.

Healthcare Litigation: Butler Snow's Healthcare Litigation Group regularly represents a wide variety of professionals, providers and businesses in the healthcare field on a national, regional and statewide basis, including physicians and medical practices, hospitals and hospital systems, and companies providing products and services, pharmaceuticals and medical devices.

Product Liability: Butler Snow has a long history of representing both manufacturers and sellers in product liability litigation in the state and federal courts of the United States and abroad. Butler Snow attorneys have experience which permits them to work equally well with the design engineers and the operators in the field.

Toxic & Environmental Torts: From dioxin to PCBs, HCL, agricultural chemicals and other substances, Butler Snow has successfully defended toxic tort cases across the United States. The firm has tried many cases to verdict and trials range from one plaintiff to several thousands.

BUSINESS

Corporate Services: The firm's business attorneys are regularly engaged in offering counsel regarding the formation and operation of and transactions involving corporations and other business entities. Clients include entities of widely varying sizes and sophistication.

Financial Services: Butler Snow's Banking & Financial Services Group serves a large and growing number of financial services providers throughout Mississippi and the nation. Butler Snow attorneys have wide-ranging experience as in-house bank lawyers and with the Comptroller of the Currency. They serve as counsel to the Mississippi Regulatory Compliance Group (a coalition of some 40 banks).

Government & Administrative: Butler Snow has a team of lawyers with a unique combination of experience in representation of governmental entities. This includes attorneys from commercial and general litigation groups and the business department who have handled matters from the local, state, regional and national levels.

HEAD OFFICE

MISSISSIPPI
AmSouth Plaza, 17th Floor, 210 East Capitol Street,
PO Box 22567, **Jackson**, MS 39225
Tel: 601 948 5711 **Fax:** 601 985 4500
Email: info@butlersnow.com
Website: www.butlersnow.com

Health & Technology: Butler Snow's Healthcare Group regularly represents a wide variety of professionals, providers and businesses in the healthcare field on a national, regional and statewide basis. As relates to the firm's Technology Practice, Butler Snow's attorneys are experienced in computer software and technology licensing, electronic commerce, multimedia issues, and technology transfer issues.

Labor & Employment: Butler Snow represents private and public sector employers in every aspect of the employment relationship. Butler Snow represents clients in employment-related matters throughout the United States, and adheres to a philosophy that preventive advice and action are the most efficient means for resolving and preventing workplace disputes.

Public Finance: Butler Snow enjoys a comprehensive and diverse public finance practice ranging from all forms of state and municipal bonds and obligations to the full complement of techniques available to finance healthcare, industrial/economic development, exempt facilities, utilities and housing.

Real Estate: Butler Snow has maintained a substantial and diverse real estate practice since the inception of the firm. The firm provides a full range of services to clients, from the initial purchase of real property, to the development, financing and leasing stages, and through the sale or syndication of such real property.

Trust & Estate: Butler Snow advises fiduciaries involved in the administration of estates and trusts. Two of the firm's attorneys in this practice area have been honored by induction into the prestigious American College of Trust and Estate Counsel.

CLIENTS: Butler Snow represents a wide range of clients which includes pharmaceutical companies, health care providers, insurance companies, government and government related entities, transportation and financial services organizations.

INTERNATIONAL WORK: Butler Snow attorneys have represented clients in trade matters before the US International Trade Commission, the US Department of Commerce and have been involved in disputes in the World Trade Organization. The firm's network of foreign associates enables them to coordinate their clients' legal and regulatory needs. Butler Snow also serves as national counsel for some clients whose businesses are conducted internationally and has represented clients in various parts of the world.

**BUTLER, SNOW,
O'MARA, STEVENS
& CANNADA, PLLC**

ATTORNEYS AT LAW

FORMAN PERRY WATKINS KRUTZ & TARDY LLP

THE FIRM

Firm Management: Executive Committee: Richard L Forman, Walter G Watkins Jr, Fred Krutz, Steven M Hendrix

Number of partners: 24
Number of other lawyers: 93

FIRM OVERVIEW: Forman Perry Watkins Krutz & Tardy LLP is a general civil practice firm with a strong emphasis in tort, environmental and commercial litigation. Founded in Jackson, Mississippi in 1986, Forman Perry has grown to more than 100 lawyers in four cities. Forman Perry litigates throughout the United States for both local and national clients, handling virtually every type of litigation from simple negligence claims to complex commercial litigation and mass tort claims involving thousands of plaintiffs. Lawyers within the firm also provide a wide spectrum of legal services in a number of other areas, including corporate law, commercial lending, bankruptcy, securities, commercial real estate, public utilities, antitrust and administrative law. Forman Perry utilizes the latest technology to handle all aspects of litigation, from discovery through trial, and maintains an extensive medical library and expert deposition depository. The firm has a strong belief in obtaining the best possible results for its clients at the least possible cost, and all management decisions are made with that goal in mind.

MAIN AREAS OF PRACTICE

LITIGATION

Class Actions: Forman Perry's attorneys have extensive experience in class action litigation, litigating the issues of class certification, class and merits discovery, and negotiating and obtaining approval for class settlements. Forman Perry's attorneys also have extensive experience in appellate practice involving all aspects of class action litigation.

Commercial Disputes: Attorneys in the firm are experienced in handling a full range of complex commercial disputes, and understand and appreciate the factually complex business, financing and operational issues which are at the core of most commercial disputes. Forman Perry has extensive experience representing individuals, partnerships, and publicly-traded and privately-held corporations, and represents clients involved in: lending and public finance, transportation, telecommunications, real estate, public utilities, securities, technology, manufacturing and distribution, and others. Forman Perry regularly represents clients in state and federal courts and before administrative agencies in matters involving lender liability claims, contract disputes, shareholder disputes, securities fraud, trade regulation, antitrust claims, debtor-creditor disputes, and others.

Drugs & Medical Devices: Attorneys in the firm have been involved in all aspects of drug and medical device litigation, defending a broad array of pharmaceutical claims, and acting as national coordinating counsel in medical device litigation.

Environmental & Toxic Torts: Forman Perry is actively involved in defending numerous environmental and toxic torts including asbestos, silica, welding rod, lead paint, mold, PVC, PCB and wood preservation. Forman Perry's presence in asbestos litigation on the local and national fronts is unparalleled. The firm represents over 180 asbestos clients in Mississippi and is handling more than 250,000 individual claims nationwide, representing clients in 23 states, with particular emphasis in Texas and Louisiana. Forman Perry lawyers serve as national counsel and national trial counsel to a number of asbestos defendants. Forman Perry is also extensively involved in silica litigation nationally, representing numerous defendants and acting as national counsel for several silica defendants. Forman Perry's litigation experience also includes defense of claims of alleged environmental contamination from industrial and oilfield operations involving various chemicals, including PCBs, BTEX/TPH, heavy metals, saltwater and naturally-occurring radiation materials ('NORM').

Insurance: Forman Perry represents insurance companies in many different facets, including third-party and first-party claims, coverage-related issues, claims involving commercial general liability (CGL), property, casual, automobile, environmental and fleet insurance.

Products Liability: From the firm's inception, Forman Perry has enjoyed a close working relationship with manufacturers and insurers in defending products liability cases, successfully defending a full spectrum of products liability cases.

Professional Negligence: The firm handles professional negligence claims including claims alleging accounting, legal and medical malpractice. The firm's litigation attorneys who handle accounting negligence claims are certified public accountants who have practiced in major public accounting firms.

BUSINESS & CORPORATE PRACTICE

General: Forman Perry's Business and Corporate Practice includes representation of both privately-held and publicly-traded corporations in a wide variety of industries. The firm regularly provides counsel to banks and financial institutions, institutions of higher learning, REITs, manufacturers and distributors, private foundations, public utilities, telecommunications companies and other businesses, working closely with clients to understand and analyze the legal and business issues behind a deal to provide clients with creative, cost-effective strategies and solutions for complex transactions.

Lending: The firm regularly represents community, state and national banking institutions in connection with commercial lending activities, including large multi-state financings. Forman Perry also represents insurance companies and other national financing institutions as both lead and local counsel with respect to loans in Mississippi.

Real Estate: Forman Perry's commercial Real Estate Practice is national in scope, the firm regularly represents NYSE-listed REITs and other companies in connection with acquisitions, dispositions and financings. Forman Perry attorneys also have extensive leasing expertise representing publicly-traded companies on a national basis.

Transactions/Securities: Forman Perry has substantial experience representing buyers and sellers in major transactions ranging from asset and stock transactions to mergers, acquisitions and corporate reorganizations, including experience in both registered and exempt offerings.

HEAD OFFICE

MISSISSIPPI
City Centre, 200 South Lamar Street, Suite 100, **Jackson**, MS 39201
Tel: 601 960 8600   **Fax:** 601 960 8613
Website: www.fpwkt.com
Mailing Address: PO Box 22608 Jackson, MS 39225-2608

BRANCH OFFICES

LOUISIANA
1515 Poydras Street, Suite 1300, **New Orleans**, LA 70112
Tel: 504 799 4383   **Fax:** 504 799 4384

TEXAS
Bryan Tower, Suite 1300, 2001 Bryan Street, **Dallas**, TX 75201
Tel: 214 905 2924   **Fax:** 214 905 3976

1717 St. James Place, Suite 600, **Houston**, TX 77056
Tel: 713 402 1717   **Fax:** 713 621 6746.

CONTACTS

Mass Tort Litigation ....Richard L Forman, Walter G Watkins, Jr
Commercial Litigation ....Alan W Perry
General Litigation ....Fred Krutz
Toxic Tort & Environmental Litigation ....Thomas W Tardy, III
....Walter G Watkins, Jr

WATKINS & EAGER PLLC

THE FIRM

Managing Member: Paul H Stephenson III
Senior Member: William F Goodman Jr

Number of members : 45
Number of other lawyers : 34

OFFICE

MISSISSIPPI
The Emporium Building, Suite 300, 400 East Capitol Street,
Jackson, MS 39205
Tel: 601 948 6470   **Fax:** 601 354 3623
Website: www.watkinseager.com

FIRM OVERVIEW: Watkins & Eager PLLC is a full service, diversified law firm. The firm began in 1895 when William Hamilton Watkins became the twentieth lawyer at the Jackson Bar. The influential career of Will Watkins spanned 64 years during which he argued over 20 cases before the Supreme Court of the United States. Pat H Eager Jr joined Will Watkins in 1916 and practiced with the firm until his death in 1970. Pat Eager was recognized as a premier trial lawyer who served as president of the International Association of Defense Counsel (1943-44) and who was Mississippi's initial invitee into the American College of Trial Lawyers. For several decades the image of the firm was heavily influenced by two of Will Watkins' children. Elizabeth Watkins Hulen, an outstanding appellate advocate, was the first woman in Mississippi history to argue before the Supreme Court of the United States. Thomas H Watkins earned a national reputation in the representation of corporate and governmental clients. Will Watkins' grandson, William F Goodman Jr, is the firm's senior member and is one of only a few Mississippi lawyers who is a member of both the American College of Trial Lawyers and the American Academy of Appellate Lawyers. Charles Clark, another active member, is the retired Chief Judge of the United States Court of Appeals for the Fifth Circuit and is also a member of both the American College of Trial Lawyers and the American Academy of Appellate Lawyers. Four other members are also Fellows in the American College of Trial Lawyers. Others are fellows of the American College of Trust and Estate Counsel and American College of Employment Lawyers. Many others have contributed and continue to contribute to the growth and progress of the firm that now enjoys an extensive corporate and business practice in addition to its broad trial and appellate practice.

MAIN AREAS OF PRACTICE:

Commercial & Business Litigation: The firm's involvement in the rapidly expanding areas of contract and business litigation and arbitration addresses a large variety of commercial controversies and business tort disputes as well as litigation involving issues of antitrust, lender liability, consumer fraud, and securities. Several members of the firm have served as arbitrators and mediators of various business disputes.

Tort/Mass Tort Litigaton: Firm lawyers defend tort claims of all types. A substantial part of the firm's tort practice is the defense of product liability actions, representing a number of manufacturers of aircraft, automotive products, chemicals, farm implements, firearms, heavy equipment, tires, tools, medical devices, and pharmaceuticals throughout the state and beyond its borders. The firm's lawyers have also assumed key defense roles on a local, regional and national basis, in mass tort litigation of matters such as pharmaceutical products, breast implants, dioxin, asbestos, and welding. The defense of professional malpractice claims against doctors, dentists, lawyers, architects, engineers and accountants is another significant segment of the firm's tort practice.

Banking & Consumer Finance: The firm has represented various financial institutions both in and out of state, maintaining a regular clientele of the state's leading financial institutions. The firm's banking work includes litigation, transactional advice and counsel, opinions and drafting bank forms and loan workouts.

Corporate: The firm's Corporate Practice covers a wide range of areas including mergers and acquisitions, commercial finance, the formation of and counsel to business entities, and the drafting of commercial contracts.

Tax: The firm has six lawyers who are experienced tax attorneys. Three lawyers are also CPAs. In addition to providing tax counsel and advice to businesses and individuals, firm members have also represented clients in tax disputes before the IRS, the State Tax Commission and local public bodies.

Wills, Trusts & Estates: Estate planning, wills, trusts and probate are an integral part of the firm's practice.

Public Utility Law: The firm has historically represented utilities before the Public Service Commission, which regulates public utilities in Mississippi.

Construction Law: The firm has represented owners, architects and engineers, contractors and sureties in construction disputes and projects and their business activities.

Bankruptcy: The firm has represented various lenders and other creditors in workouts and in bankruptcy proceedings.

Labor & Employment: The firm possesses considerable experience in representation of management in various employer related transactions and disputes, including, day to day employment issues, litigation, collective bargaining and proceedings before the federal and state regulatory bodies.

Environmental: The firm's Environmental Practice includes representation of clients in litigation in both federal and state courts, as well as before the MS Department of Environmental Quality, the EPA and other administrative agencies. Representation includes the defense of toxic claims, environmental permitting and compliance matters, and negotiating and drafting of environmental related contract provisions.

Real Estate: The firm has a broad Real Estate Practice. In January 2004, the members of Taylor, Covington & Smith, P.A., a firm known for its real estate practice, joined the firm and added extensive expertise in real estate matters. The Real Estate Practice now includes representation of local residential and commercial developers, and involves new urbanism, multifamily and commercial developments in Mississippi and neighboring states. The firm also serves as local counsel for numerous out of state lending institutions and has experience in eminent domain proceedings.

Insurance: The firm has considerable experience in insurance matters. Firm members possess experience in handling claims involving fire, property, casualty, workers' compensation, fidelity and surety, officers and directors, errors and omissions, as well as life, health and accident matters/insurance.

Government: The firm has traditionally represented a number of governmental bodies on various matters, including annexation, public finance and housing.

CLIENTS: Watkins & Eager's client base includes major manufacturers, employers, contractors, real estate developers, public utilities, oil and gas producers and refiners, banks and financial institutions, cable television operators, telecommunication providers, insurers and government entities on the federal, state, county and municipal levels.

Free background information is available upon request from M Binford Williams at the above address.

WATKINS LUDLAM WINTER & STENNIS, P.A.

THE FIRM

Chief Executive Officer: Thomas B Shepherd III
Senior Shareholders: William F Winter, John Hampton Stennis
Number of shareholders: 54
Number of non-shareholders: 26

FIRM OVERVIEW: Founded in 1905, Watkins Ludlam Winter & Stennis, P.A. has grown into a comprehensive, business-oriented law firm. The firm is one of the largest and most established full-service law firms in the State of Mississippi, with 80 attorneys, licensed in 10 states and the District of Columbia, and graduates of 38 different law schools, colleges and universities. The firm is a member of Meritas, the world's largest affiliation of business law firms. Meritas member firms provide business clients worldwide access to sophisticated legal advice and exceptional service. The firm is also a member of the State Capital Law Firm Group, an organization comprised of leading domestic and international law firms occupying leadership positions in their respective states and countries.

MAIN AREAS OF PRACTICE:

Antitrust, Business Tort & Commercial Litigation: For many decades the firm has litigated substantial matters involving business disputes of virtually every nature, ranging from antitrust to business torts and RICO. The firm's litigation attorneys also have in-depth knowledge of industries including computers and information technology, finance, financial institutions, communications, advertising, mining, oil and gas and agricultural products.

Bankruptcy & Creditors' Rights: The general practice of the firm includes extensive representation of local, regional, national, and international companies in a full range of bankruptcy matters and creditors' rights.

Construction Law: The group's attorneys have extensive experience in drafting construction contracts in both the private and governmental arenas and in representing owners, contractors and insurers in construction contract disputes and litigation. The group's attorneys have advised clients concerning and preparing fixed, design/build, unit price, construction management and cost plus contracts.

Environmental: The firm's work includes the performance of environmental due diligence in connection with financing, mergers and acquisitions, industrial and municipal development and real property transfers.

Federal, State & Local Taxation: Members of the firm's Tax Practice Group concentrate on federal, state and local tax matters of all types, including income and estate tax planning, administrative controversies and appeals (including employment and excise tax matters), litigation of tax cases in federal and state courts, and legislative counseling and representation on industry and client-specific issues.

Financial Institutions: The firm represents numerous financial institutions (including commercial banks, savings institutions and small loan companies) throughout the Southeast. The firm also represents holding companies owning financial institutions and helped establish many of these holding companies.

Gaming & Resort: The firm represents businesses and individuals in all aspects of gaming licensing, process and related approval processes and regulatory compliance. Because of the firm's diversity of experiences and backgrounds, it is able to work with its gaming clients to address the entirety of their regulatory, corporate, finance, taxation and litigation needs.

Insurance Litigation: The firm undertakes, both statewide and regionally, insurance-based representation of manufacturers, financial institutions, retailers, public entities and officials, medical professionals, health care facilities, common carriers, utilities, and individuals, as well as various entities engaged in interstate and intrastate transportation, commerce, gaming, agribusiness, construction and specialized industries.

Labor & Employment: The attorneys in the L&E Group are among the most experienced in the nation in labor and employment law matters,

HEAD OFFICE

MISSISSIPPI
Jackson Office, 633 North State Street (39202), PO Box 427, Jackson, MS 39205-0427
Tel: 601 949 4900 **Fax:** 601 949 4804
Website: www.watkinsludlam.com

BRANCH OFFICES

MISSISSIPPI
Memphis Metropolitan Office, 6897 Crumpler Boulevard, Suite 100, PO Box 1456, **Olive Branch**, MS 38654
Tel: 901 526 1312 **Fax:** 662 895 5480

Mississippi Gulf Coast Office, One Hancock Plaza, 2510 14th Street, Suite 1010 (39501), PO Drawer 160, **Gulfport**, MS 39502
Tel: 228 864 3094 **Fax:** 228 864 0516

LOUISIANA
New Orleans Office, Poydras Center, 650 Poydras Street, Suite 1020, **New Orleans**, LA 70130
Tel: 504 522 8788 **Fax:** 504 522 8865

such as NLRB matters and litigation, OSHA investigations and litigation, complex EEO litigation, and counseling employers and litigating issues such as wage and hour, FMLA, ADA and employment contract issues. Firm attorneys regularly provide employers with training on harassment, workplace violence, and overall human resource policies.

Legislative & Governmental Relations: The firm's attorneys help clients to formulate well adapted strategies that will be clearly understood; provide monitoring, tracking and analysis of legislative and regulatory developments; help clients to develop legislative and regulatory relationships; serve as registered lobbyists when required; and generally assist clients in communicating more effectively their viewpoints with respect to issues.

Mergers & Acquisitions: The firm has extensive experience in buying, selling and combining companies across a broad spectrum of industries, including banking, insurance, gaming, telecommunications, manufacturing, retail and healthcare. It has represented both buyers and sellers of family owned businesses to publicly traded companies in all types of transactions, including stock acquisitions, asset acquisitions, mergers, going private transactions, corporate spin offs, bids, leveraged buy outs, recapitalizations and restructurings.

Public Finance: In the 1960s the firm became Mississippi's first nationally recognized bond counsel. The firm served as underwriter's counsel for the first industrial development revenue bonds issued in Mississippi in 1961, and public finance has been a central part of the firm's practice ever since. The Public Finance Practice Group is supported by the firm's Tax and Securities Practice, which is the largest in Mississippi.

Real Estate & Commercial Finance Transactions: The firm has extensive experience in real estate development and commercial finance transactions of all descriptions and has represented developers and lenders in some of the most substantial and sophisticated projects in Mississippi.

Securities: The Securities Practice has handled billions of dollars of equity and debt offerings, including initial public offerings and other SEC registered securities offerings, as well as private placements and other exempt offerings. The firm has guided public and private companies, underwriters and securities owners through securities law compliance issues.

CONTENTS: Corporate/M&A p.1042; Employment p.1045; Litigation p.1048; Real Estate p.1052; Individuals' Profiles p.1055; Firms' Profiles p.1062.

How lawyers are ranked

The opinions we gather from clients — mainly from in-house lawyers but also from other purchasers of legal services — are balanced by opinions from colleagues and competitors. Together, they provide two different perspectives — an all-round view — and biased viewpoints cancel each other out.

OVERVIEW: Geographically and legally, the markets in Kansas and Missouri are closely linked and, in certain instances, merge. For example, an attorney admitted to practice in Missouri is also registered for Kansas. And one of the main commercial centers, Kansas City, straddles the state line. For this edition of Chambers USA, we asked leading clients and attorneys across both states whether it would be appropriate to combine our coverage of these states. Our commentators felt there was sufficient distinction and state-specific expertise to warrant separate chapters. However, we encourage readers to refer to the Kansas chapter to gain the full picture of legal services across this region.

CORPORATE/M&A

Missouri
Leading firms (Corporate/M&A)

1 BLACKWELL SANDERS PEPER *Kansas City*
  BRYAN CAVE LLP *St. Louis*
  SONNENSCHEIN NATH & ROSENTHAL *Kansas City*
  STINSON MORRISON HECKER LLP *Kansas City*

2 ARMSTRONG TEASDALE LLP *St. Louis*
  LATHROP & GAGE LC *Kansas City*
  POLSINELLI SHALTON WELTE *Kansas City*
  THOMPSON COBURN LLP *St. Louis*

3 HUSCH & EPPENBERGER LLC *Kansas City*
  LEWIS, RICE & FINGERSH LC *St. Louis*
  SHOOK, HARDY & BACON LLP *Kansas City*
  SHUGHART THOMSON & KILROY PC *Kansas City*
  SPENCER FANE BRITT & BROWNE *Kansas City*

Firms are listed alphabetically in each band.

Band 1

Blackwell Sanders Peper Martin LLP

See firm details p.1062

The Firm: Clients described this corporate powerhouse as "*the clear market leaders,*" while peers acknowledged its attorneys as "*always the stiffest of competition*" in the most complex of transactions. Clients referred to "*the client-oriented philosophy and effective cost management*" produced by the group and its success in breeding a "*wealth of professional and knowledgeable attorneys.*" The firm houses over 50 attorneys dedicated to M&A, securities and tax law, as well as venture capital and private equity financing. Their expertise covers a range of industries, including energy and public utilities, telecom, and the restaurant and healthcare sectors, and they represent some of the most notable companies in each. Highlights in the past year include handling acquisition work for the world's largest casual dining restaurant, Applebee's, and advice on the $120 million acquisition of 22 golf courses in Texas. The group also advised on the creation of a novel template mutual fund in relation to the public offering of Tortoise Energy Infrastructure, which is now trading on the New York Stock Exchange.

The Lawyers: "*The real deal,*" **Ralph Wrobley** (see p.1061) is a senior corporate partner at the firm, and roundly applauded for "*his outstanding talents*" and "*ability to always remember the business side to a deal as well as the legal issues.*" Wrobley is active in M&A, especially representing midmarket entrepreneurial companies, and possesses a wealth of experience on both domestic and international issues. He recently acted on a complex $22 million M&A involving a supplier and manufacturer to the construction industry. Having moved to the Kansas City office during the year, "*excellent corporate healthcare lawyer*" **Stephen Adams** (see p.1055) is certainly a welcome addition to this group. He represents hospitals and related healthcare clients on joint ventures and M&A, combining his work is this practice with his duties as manager of the Overland Park office. Adams' practice also contains elements of real estate law and he has advised on a complex $35 million real estate financing for a public limited partnership during the past year. An "*outstanding lawyer,*" **Gary Gilson** (see p.1057) has impressed peers with "*his common sense and judgment in mixing business advice with legal advice.*" Gilson counsels corporate issuers and underwriters in public offerings, and advises on corporate governance and transactional issues all over the country. He represented the individual behind the John Q Hammonds Hotel chain during the year and worked on a large strategic project for H&R Block. The "*very knowledgeable*" **Jim Ash** (see p.1055) has won a loyal following for "*the excellent work he does – his personable, far-sighted approach and all-round understanding of the deal.*" Ash focuses on M&A and securities law, often relating to the technology and restaurant industries. He has counseled key client Applebee's International in corporate matters and advised on large transactions in the telecom industry during the year. Clients endorsed **Jason Reschly** (see p.1060) for his expert advice and "*fine reputation in the field.*" Reschly is a taxation specialist, who also advises on agribusiness and energy and public utility law. He advised on the public offering of Tortoise Energy Infrastructure. Making his debut in the tables this year is "*recognized up-and-comer with a real future ahead of him*" **Steven Carman** (see p.1055). Concentrating on M&A, technology and securities law, Carman has a firm grasp of the technical issues and is noted for his experience in the venture capital arena.

The Clients: Applebee's International; American Italian Pasta Company; Tortoise Energy Infrastructure; MC Real Estate Services; Saint Luke's Health System; Aquila; Ash Grove Cement; Associated Wholesale Grocers; Energy West; Huntco Steel; Kansas City Royals; Lady Baltimore Foods and Kansas Farm Bureau.

Bryan Cave LLP

The Firm: Clients commended this large full-service firm for "*its broad range of expertise, the tremendous amount of resources on offer and its general efficiency in getting things done.*" These blue-chip clients also noted "*the tremendous service and provision of legal solutions in a variety of arenas.*" Attorneys here represent local and

Missouri
Leading individuals (Corporate/M&A)

Senior Statesman

NIXON Richard *Stinson Morrison*, Kansas City

[1] ADAMS Stephen *Blackwell Sanders*, Kansas City
ASH James *Blackwell Sanders*, Kansas City
GILSON Gary *Blackwell Sanders*, Kansas City
GRANDA John *Stinson Morrison*, Kansas City
LENTS Donald *Bryan Cave*, St. Louis
MEDVED Joseph *Lathrop & Gage*, Kansas City
NOUSS James *Bryan Cave*, St. Louis
VAN DYKE Thomas *Bryan Cave*, Kansas City
WROBLEY Ralph *Blackwell Sanders*, Kansas City

[2] FISHER Robert *Sonnenschein Nath*, Kansas City
FITZGERALD Robert *Shughart Thomson*, Kansas City
FRETWELL Norman *Spencer Fane*, Kansas City
HEETER James *Sonnenschein Nath*, Kansas City
HUNTER Robert *Stinson Morrison*, Kansas City
LAUSE Michael *Thompson Coburn*, St. Louis
LITZ Thomas *Thompson Coburn*, St. Louis
MONROE C Robert *Stinson Morrison*, Kansas City
O'CONNELL Mary *Husch & Eppenberger*, Kansas City
POLSINELLI James *Polsinelli Shalton*, Kansas City
PRUELLAGE John *Lewis Rice*, St. Louis
STAHL Thomas *Armstrong Teasdale*, Kansas City

[3] BARTELSMEYER Fred *Bryan Cave*, St. Louis
CARMAN Steven *Blackwell Sanders*, Kansas City
ESSIG Leonard *Lewis Rice*, St. Louis
EVANS Craig *Shook Hardy*, Kansas City
FRIZELL Edward *Polsinelli Shalton*, Kansas City
JONES Steve *Armstrong Teasdale*, St. Louis
KEIM Robert *Kutak Rock*, Kansas City
MARVIN John *Sonnenschein Nath*, Kansas City
MINOGUE Thomas *Thompson Coburn*, St. Louis
RESCHLY Jason *Blackwell Sanders*, Kansas City
SEABAUGH William *Bryan Cave*, St. Louis
STEPLETON James *Husch & Eppenberger*, St. Louis
WERTS Dale *Lathrop & Gage*, Kansas City

Individuals are listed alphabetically in each band.

international clients in securities law and complex M&A, and have carved out a reputation for the firm as "*the dominant player in St. Louis.*" Their expertise in handling IPOs has made these attorneys the go-to figures for such issuance. The team also counsels public companies on regulatory matters associated with securities such as stock repurchase programs. The group has of late provided transactional advice to Monsanto and represented the now defunct Farmland Industries in its bankruptcy.

The Lawyers: Thomas Van Dyke (see p.1061) is "*the dean of this corporate practice – a highly poised and professional attorney.*" He "*certainly knows how to get the deal done*" and "*has the guts to give a strong opinion.*" A corporate attorney who is "*full of integrity,*" Van Dyke is heavily engaged in advice to corporate management on LBOs and the formation of business entities and is well versed in the portfolio management of private equity funds. Clients also roundly applauded the "*absolutely first-rate*"

James Nouss (see p.1060), who is co-leader of the corporate finance and securities group. Nouss concentrates on corporate finance and M&A, including issues ranging from venture capital through to IPOs. Deeply entrenched in the biotechnology field, this "*serious player in the market*" was involved in taking Stereotaxis public during the year by way of a $47 million share offering. Chairman of the firm **Don Lents** (see p.1058) impresses clients as "*not only the smartest lawyer around, but also one of the most reasonable and persuasive.*" He is coauthor of a leading treatise on Missouri corporate law and practice, and is often called on by committees and board members to provide corporate governance counseling. **Bill Seabaugh** (see p.1060) is "*an extremely talented and creative corporate lawyer who constantly strives to find cost-efficient solutions to complex legal issues.*" Clients describe him as "*the consummate business partner – proactive and never losing focus of our business goals.*" Seabaugh is the co-leader of the transactions group and represents, among others, Emerson Electric and Sporlan Valve. The "*very knowledgeable business lawyer*" **Fred Bartelsmeyer** (see p.1055) was also highlighted by clients for his expertise on cross-border and international M&A and technology transactions.

The Clients: Emerson Electric; Brown Shoe; Ralcorp Holdings; NS Group; Sporlan Valve; Monsanto; Sigma-Aldrich; Stereotaxis; AG Edwards; Oakwood Medical Investors and C3 Capital Partners.

Sonnenschein Nath & Rosenthal
See firm details p.779

The Firm: This firm is "*in the upper echelon of firms competing for the top work in the state.*" It is held in high regard for its "*really strong representation of large public companies in Kansas City.*" This corporate group operates from offices in St. Louis and Kansas City and fields nearly 30 specialist attorneys in Missouri alone. The corporate and securities group encompasses the range of transactional activities and has extensive experience handling M&A, debt financings and joint ventures. Commentators also praise the firm's prowess in M&A transactions arising out of the healthcare and technology sectors.

The Lawyers: Commentators roundly applauded **Bob Fisher** as a highly skilled attorney, who "*brings a lot of business to the table.*" He concentrates on complex M&A and debt financing, joint ventures and strategic alliances, representing one of the nation's most active midmarket private equity firms. **James Heeter** (see p.1057) stands out in the market with his "*effective handling of client relations and personable approach to business negotiations.*" Active in corporate and healthcare law, Heeter also advises public companies on corporate governance issues and policy strategy. **John Marvin** (see p.1058) also came highly recommended by

clients for his expertise in securities issues. He also counsels startup companies and venture capital investors in the emerging growth sectors.
The Clients: H&R Block; Monsanto; American Safety Razor; Waddell & Reed and Jordan Industries.

Stinson Morrison Hecker LLP
See firm details p.1069

The Firm: The general business division of this firm, which combines the forces of three offices in the state, fields about 34 dedicated attorneys. "*A major player, it has come through its merger well and is happily getting great work,*" market commentators said. Its depth of resources is one of the distinguishing features of this practice group, and the corporate attorneys can draw on the support of separate bankruptcy and creditors' rights, and financial services practice groups. "*They have strength and depth in all areas.*" Among the many notable cases undertaken by the group over the past year was acting for Midland Loan Services on multiple securitizations of mortgage-backed loans. The team also represented Inergy on various corporate issues, the most notable of which was the $475 million acquisition of Star Gas.

The Lawyers: John Granda (see p.1057) "*certainly does bring a lot of experience with him and enjoys a fine reputation.*" A skilled transactional attorney, he is chairman of the firm's corporate finance division and cochairman of the firm's corporate accountability division. Granda was recently involved in the $140 million offering of convertible debentures for Euronet Worldwide. **Bob Monroe** (see p.1059) is chairman of the firm's financial services division and was often mentioned "*as a definite inclusion in anybody's corporate dream team.*" He represents financial institutions and financial holding companies and possesses a wealth of experience in reviewing agreements that banks enter into, such as complex loan structures. **Robert Hunter** (see p.1058) is trusted as a "*meticulous corporate lawyer*" and chair of the firm's general business division. He serves as general counsel to several companies in Kansas City, and has advised on several private equity investments and sales and purchasers, including assets in the real estate sector. Commentators agree that "*classic M&A attorney*" **Richard Nixon** (see p.1060) is a force to be reckoned with. This senior statesman has experience in representing private and publicly held companies in acquisitions, dispositions and strategic joint ventures. His breadth of experience and highly professional reputation have made him a popular port of call for some of the market's most important clients.
The Clients: Block Financial; Bank of America; Cerner; Gold Banc; Midland Loan Services; Sprint; LabOne; Haldex; Quest Resources; Inergy; H&R Block; Euronet Worldwide; CIT Group and Archer Daniels Midland.

www.ChambersandPartners.com
All quotes in the text are from interviews with clients and competitors.
1043

Band 2

Armstrong Teasdale LLP

The Firm: This respected firm has won the loyalty of the region's leading clients with its responsive service and understanding of business issues. The firm is recommended for its presence in the St. Louis market. However, it fields three offices across the state, housing about 100 attorneys in the business services department. Such depth of resources gives the firm the firepower needed to handle a volume of deals across the state and beyond. Peers noted *"its quality representation of significant private companies"* and its work on M&A and regulatory matters for public companies. The recent caseload of the group includes the representation of clients before the Federal Reserve Board and Federal Deposit Insurance Corporation.

The Lawyers: Commentators agree that **Thomas Stahl** *"is an excellent lawyer who handles complex situations and consistently gets good results."* Stahl's practice incorporates business formation and strategic planning, M&A and shareholders issues. **Steve Jones** *"is one of the leaders in the corporate market"* and closely associated with the continued success of this group. He combines corporate and securities law with involvement in real estate transactions.

The Clients: Among others, the firm represents banks and pharmaceutical companies.

Lathrop & Gage LC

See firm details p.1064

The Firm: This busy group is housed in the third largest firm in Kansas City, and viewed by peers as *"the main competition on many deals."* From the firm's four offices across the state, a practice of about 35 lawyers covers the full range of business services for clients from the agribusiness and farming, biotechnology and entertainment and sports industries. In the first nine months of 2004, this corporate department was involved in transactions with an aggregate value of more than $4 billion. For example, it represented AMC Entertainment on a new revolving credit facility of $170 million. Well versed in media and entertainment issues, the team can also list Chingy, the performance artist, as a corporate client.

The Lawyers: Commentators agree that **Joseph Medved** (see p.1059) *"would definitely be in anyone's list of leading corporate attorneys"* in recognition of his broad skill base and ability to manage complex transactions. He is a member of the firm's executive committee and chairman of the Greater Kansas City Foreign Trade Zone. Chair of the corporate department **Dale Werts** (see p.1061) is *"a fine attorney of good stature,"* who specializes in corporate finance, M&A and corporate governance. He possesses a subspecialty in cases involving life insurance companies, and was co-lead counsel on the representation of a financial services holding company in its split-off to form an insurance premium financing company.

The Clients: AMC Entertainment; AT&T; Bank of America; Butler Manufacturing; MGP Ingredients; Sprint; Time Warner Cable and the Zimmer Companies.

Polsinelli Shalton Welte Suelthaus (PSWS)

The Firm: Market sources commended the success of this firm's recent merger and described it as one of the fastest growing firms in the region. It handles a broad spectrum of corporate matters including M&A, shareholder disputes, corporate restructurings and public offerings for a variety of Fortune 500 and mid-sized companies. Clients are *"very pleased with the cross-departmental nature of the firm"* and pinpointed healthcare, IP and banking as particular strengths. The group is also well equipped to handle tax and employee benefits and executive compensation matters.

The Lawyers: The *"extraordinarily able lawyer"* **Jim Polsinelli** advises on M&A, business succession planning and bankruptcy. He is *"ever the consummate professional and great with clients."* Clients endorsed **Tripp Frizell** for his *"all-round grasp of all the issues involved in a case."* His broad commercial practice covers corporate and real estate transactions, franchise law and acquisitions arising out of the healthcare sector.

The Clients: CommuniTech.Net; eScout; Sunflower Group; Fidelity Brokerage Services; First American Capital; Kansas Venture Capital; KeyBank; Kansas Turnpike Authority; Kessinger/Hunter & Company; Medi-Flex Hospital Products and MorAmerica Capital.

Thompson Coburn LLP

See firm details p.1071

The Firm: Other firms see this 140-member transactional practice as a key competitor with its *"excellent individual lawyers and full-service capabilities."* The firm is home to a number of M&A and securities specialists. It also fields attorneys dedicated to public finance and the representation of financial institutions. Among recent highlights, the group has advised one of the largest privately held companies in the state, Maritz, on corporate restructuring and litigation among its shareholders. The firm is also primary outside general counsel for Enterprise Rent-A-Car, and has advised this client on IP and general corporate matters during the past year.

The Lawyers: **Michael Lause** (see p.1058) is the administrative head of the corporate department of the firm and chairman of the firm's public finance and public law practice area. Highlighted as *"an excellent and knowledgeable public finance lawyer,"* he is highly respected for his expertise in tax-exempt bonds and related governmental issues. Clients were quick to recommend **Tom Litz** (see p.1058) as an *"experienced and insightful business lawyer, conversant in corporate governance matters and M&A."* Cochair of the firm's corporate finance and securities group, he advises on securities regulation and business organizations, M&A and share offerings. Respected **Tom Minogue** (see p.1059) is chairman of the firm and concentrates on general corporate law and finance.

The Clients: AG Edwards & Sons; BC Ziegler; Commerce Bank; Stern Brothers & Co.; Missouri Health & Educational Facilities Authority; Missouri Higher Education Loan Authority; Missouri State Employees' Retirement System; University of Missouri; Enterprise Rent-A-Car; Maritz; UniGroup; US Bank and Wells Fargo.

Band 3

Husch & Eppenberger, LLC

The Firm: Commentators were quick to highlight the number of *"great transactional lawyers at this full-service law firm."* The firm comprises 100 attorneys, who are respected for their sound business judgment and broad corporate advice. M&A, venture capital, and securities issuance are all to be found on the agenda here. Attorneys are also skilled in healthcare transactions and tax-exempt financing arising out of the real estate market.

The Lawyers: The *"technically proficient"* **Jim Stepleton** is respected for his wide-ranging experience in M&A and private equity transactions. Also impressing market sources is **Mary Anne O'Connell**. Peers expressed their willingness to *"sing her praises – she has a fine reputation and great range of abilities."* She works out of both the St. Louis and Kansas City offices, and advises on private equity matters, public company transactions and corporate governance.

The Clients: John Q. Hammons Hotels; Olin; Monsanto and Capital for Business.

Lewis, Rice & Fingersh LC

See firm details p.1065

The Firm: This firm has six offices strategically located across Missouri and was particularly commended for *"the strength and good reputation of the group among the local and regional banks."* These talented attorneys have attracted a wide range of clients, which they advise on bankruptcies, tax and municipal finance as well as corporate and bank lending transactions. The group is also well versed in employee benefits issues and the development of e-commerce.

The Lawyers: **John Pruellage** (see p.1060) is *"one of the leaders in the St. Louis corporate community."* He remains best known for his representation of banks and financial institutions on bank lending, and corporate M&A issues. **Leonard Essig** (see p.1056) is recognized for *"his quality M&A advice"* in the technology sector. He also provides clients with banking and general corporate advice.

The Clients: Clients include Blue Cross Blue Shield of Missouri, RightCHOICE Managed Care and St. Anthony's Medical Centre.

Shook, Hardy & Bacon LLP

See firm details p.1067

The Firm: Although this firm is best known for the prowess of its litigation practice, commentators agree that the Kansas City office is "*a definite corporate player in the state.*" A regional and national presence, this firm was noted for its M&A, joint ventures, strategic alliances and securities advice to publicly held and private entities. Loan documentation and business estate planning are also key elements of the corporate practice here.

The Lawyers: The "*excellent corporate attorney*" **Craig Evans** (see p.1056) is chair of the firm's corporate finance and banking practice group and focuses on M&A, securities, corporate governance matters and technology-driven joint ventures.

The Clients: Bank of America; Barkley Evergreen & Partners; BAT; Businessmen's Assurance Company of America and Deutsche Financial Services.

Shughart Thomson & Kilroy PC

See firm details p.1068

The Firm: Onlookers agree that this 30-strong corporate practice is "*a real force*" in public M&A, joint ventures, private equity and tax. The firm is closely associated with the construction and healthcare industries, although it advises a much broader clientele. This general business group covers the full range of issues from banking to municipal finance, representing some of the household names in the state. Among the firm's recent highlights is its advice to public libraries on structured transactions.

The Lawyers: Peers agreed that **Bob Fitzgerald** (see p.1057) is a "*superb, well-regarded lawyer*" and deserving of recognition for his broad business practice. Among his recent caseload have been issues of real estate law and taxation as well as major business acquisitions and sales on various projects.

The Clients: Carondelet Health; Chicago Title Insurance; Commerce Bank; Dickinson Financial; DST Realty; Kansas City Southern Railway; Stormont-Vail HealthCare; Mission Bank; United Missouri Bank and Walton Construction.

Spencer Fane Britt & Browne LLP

The Firm: This old-line law firm has offices in Kansas City and St. Louis and "*its independence in not following the trend to merge has ensured*

consistent quality for many years.*" Although it is perhaps best known for the strength of the labor and employment group, onlookers agreed, "*They have a series of niche corporate practices doing excellent work.*" Attorneys here are experienced in loan work for banks, and advise a client base that ranges from small startup entities to large public companies on corporate M&A and strategic growth options.

The Lawyers: Peers readily recommended **Norm Fretwell** as "*the shining star of this group.*" A member of the firm's executive committee, Fretwell is also the leader of the financial services group and impresses with "*the fine loan work he does for financial institutions.*"

The Clients: Allied Waste Industries; American Century Investments Company; Birch Telecom; Commerce Bank; Gannett Satellite Information Network; Kansas City Power & Light and Procter & Gamble.

Other Notable Practitioners

Robert Keim (see p.1055) of Kutak Rock LLP also roused interest from commentators during the research this year. Particularly impressing peers for his "*superb transactional practice,*" Keim represents businesses on acquisitions and sales, joint ventures and financing relating to ongoing and startup businesses.

EMPLOYMENT

MAINLY DEFENDANT

Missouri
Leading firms
(Employment: Mainly Defendant)

[1] **BLACKWELL SANDERS PEPER** *Kansas City*

[2] **BRYAN CAVE LLP** *St Louis*
LATHROP & GAGE LC *Kansas City*
SHOOK, HARDY & BACON LLP *Kansas City*
STINSON MORRISON HECKER LLP *St Louis*
THOMPSON COBURN LLP *St Louis*

[3] **ARMSTRONG TEASDALE LLP** *Kansas City*
CONSTANGY, BROOKS & SMITH, LLC *Kansas City*
FISHER & PHILLIPS LLP *Kansas City*
GREENSFELDER, HEMKER & GALE, PC *St Louis*
HUSCH & EPPENBERGER LLC *St Louis*
MCMAHON BERGER HANNA LINIHAN *St Louis*
SPENCER FANE BRITT & BROWNE *Kansas City*

Firms are listed alphabetically in each band.

Band 1

Blackwell Sanders Peper Martin LLP

See firm details p.1062

The Firm: This firm is "*a real force to contend with in Missouri,*" said market observers. It fields three offices in the state and retains its preemi-

nence in the field through work on the most significant cases related to the market's largest clients. Striding ahead of the pack, this 30-member labor and employment practice "*has an unparalleled depth in labor and employment law.*" Employment litigation is a key strength and attorneys are well versed in the use of dispute resolution procedures to avoid court litigation. The team has experience of class actions and multiple plaintiff cases such as sexual harassment claims. It is the main outside counsel on employment matters for Hallmark Cards and obtained a successful jury verdict for the Kansas City Star during the past year. Attorneys are also experienced in traditional labor law issues, such as collective bargaining and union relations.

The Lawyers: An "*accommodating and very professional attorney – dean of the employment Bar,*" **John Phillips** (see p.1060) was heavily endorsed for his expertise in alternative dispute resolution. Although experienced in labor law, he concentrates much of his practice on the defense of national class actions and individual discrimination claims. The "*top-notch*" **Robert Tomaso** (see p.1061) is highly regarded for his labor and employment practice for closely held businesses and is managing partner of the St. Louis office. Thoroughly experienced in

employment discrimination jury trials, Tomaso also provides clients with regulatory advice and representation before the NLRB.

The Clients: Kansas City Star; Commerce Bank; Saint Luke's Health System; Applebee's; Harcros Chemicals; Chubb Group; Jacobs Engineering Group; Hallmark Cards; CCP Industries and Maytag.

Band 2

Bryan Cave LLP

The Firm: One of the largest in the state, this firm "*provides excellent advice and counsel*" in labor and employment matters, reported clients. Deeply entrenched in the state and well respected for its traditional labor law practice, this firm was praised by clients for its "*expertise in representing major companies from minor to very complex matters.*" These attorneys "*protect our interests and forthrightly address all the issues of a case.*" Attorneys here also have the added benefit of drawing on the resources of a nationwide office network and regularly counsel and litigate across the spectrum of discrimination claims. A highlight for the team includes serving as outside legal adviser to ABB in the ongoing labor dispute with the United Auto Workers

www.ChambersandPartners.com

All quotes in the text are from interviews with clients and competitors.

1045

Missouri

Leading individuals

(Employment: Mainly Defendant)

1
MARTUCCI William *Shook Hardy*, Kansas City
PHILLIPS John *Blackwell Sanders*, Kansas City
ROWE Jack *Lathrop & Gage*, Kansas City

2
DONNELLY Paul *Stinson Morrison*, Kansas City
FINUCANE Brian *Fisher & Phillips*, Kansas City
HUNTER Jerry *Bryan Cave*, St. Louis
JANOWITZ Robert *Constangy Brooks*, Kansas City
MCCARTHY Thomas *McMahon Berger*, St Louis
TOMASO Robert *Blackwell Sanders*, St. Louis
VERING III John *Armstrong Teasdale*, Kansas City

3
COLLINS Dennis *Greensfelder Hemker*, St. Louis
DONNELLY Dennis *Bryan Cave*, St. Louis
GODINER Clifford *Thompson Coburn*, St. Louis
JAUDES Richard *Thompson Coburn*, St. Louis
MCNAMARA Rosalee *Lathrop & Gage*, Kansas City
ORTBALS Mary *Greensfelder Hemker*, St. Louis
WING David *Spencer Fane*, Kansas City
YATES Jack *Husch & Eppenberger*, Kansas City

Individuals are listed alphabetically in each band.

International union. In the employment law sphere, the team also obtained summary judgment in the representation of ABB in a disability discrimination case.

The Lawyers: Labor law specialist and "*one of the best lawyers in the state*" is **Jerry Hunter** (see p.1058). He advises on labor relations and regularly appears before the NLRB and the EEOC. Hunter has successfully represented Wells Fargo Home Mortgage in a case involving the employment status of a temporary agency worker. **Dennis Donnelly** (see p.1056) is an "*extremely smart guy who knows his onions.*" He has developed a respected trial practice defending employers in employment discrimination claims, workforce reduction, wrongful discharge and ERISA litigation.

The Clients: ABB; Waste Management; State Farm Mutual Automobile Insurance; Wells Fargo Home Mortgage and Lyondell-CITGO Refining LP.

Lathrop & Gage LC

See firm details p.1064

The Firm: This firm has devoted its resources to create one of the largest labor and employment practices in the state with over 25 dedicated attorneys. It counsels and represents employers across the country in employment discrimination claims, wrongful discharge, breach of contract and the raft of traditional labor matters. The group witnessed an upturn in wage and hour claims and OFCCP audits. Highlights for the team include obtaining a successful jury verdict for the employer in a pregnancy discrimination case and obtaining summary judgment for a food industry client in an alleged race discrimination action before the Kansas Human Rights Commission.

The Lawyers: **Jack Rowe** (see p.1060) is "*one of the best-known employment attorneys around*" and has continued to impress clients with the breadth of his expertise. He recently obtained summary judgment for a railroad client in an alleged age discrimination case in the US District Court of Kansas. Also making an impression is the "*well-rounded and likable*" **Rosalee McNamara** (see p.1059). Her practice covers all forms of employment discrimination and counseling, training and investigations. The head of the department is Robert McKinley, who specializes in labor and employment law as well as employee benefits and fiduciary litigation.

The Clients: Allied Waste Industries; AMC Entertainment; Butler Manufacturing; Colgate-Palmolive and Harley-Davidson.

Shook, Hardy & Bacon LLP

See firm details p.1067

The Firm: According to one client, "*this firm is definitely one of the leaders in the state*" for employment and labor issues. It has secured a national reputation with its advice on large, complex class actions. Its dedicated employment law specialists can also draw on the support of a separate employee benefits and ERISA litigation practice group. The combined teams consist of about 30 attorneys, and clients were quick to praise the strength in depth of the firm. Attorneys here also excel in their counseling on federal compliance issues and employee benefits programs.

The Lawyers: **Bill Martucci** (see p.1058) garnered overwhelming feedback for "*his great knowledge in the employment arena, his ability to relate well to clients and winning personality in the courtroom.*" He is "*well informed and well respected,*" and focuses on complex class actions and ERISA matters.

The Clients: Verizon; Honeywell; Centerpulse and Ferrell Gas.

Stinson Morrison Hecker LLP

See firm details p.1069

The Firm: Clients were quick to endorse this group as one of the best around, appreciating the "*high-quality services rendered, the impressive level of professional knowledge, the effective communication with the client, and conservative and efficient staffing of a case.*" This full-service operation is one of the largest in the Midwest. A "*classy outfit, integrating well,*" it houses 22 dedicated lawyers and handles ERISA and employment litigation and policy counseling. One client even went as far as to say: "*It is actually a pleasure to sign the checks and pay the bill as you know that you would have been a lot worse off had you not used them.*" Highlights in the year include continuing to defend Deluxe in a long-standing nationwide class action.

The Lawyers: **Paul Donnelly** (see p.1056) has impressed clients for "*always understanding what it is a client wants and doing his best to meet their objectives.*" According to one source: "*You would love to have him in the courtroom with you, and yet you would also love to go fishing with him.*" Donnelly is chair of the firm's employment litigation division and has been heavily involved in the putative nationwide class action brought against Deluxe. He is also recognized for his work on behalf of the purebred cattle industry and for representing international air carriers in actions brought under the Railway Labor Act.

The Clients: Hallmark Cards; Chubb Group of Insurance Companies; MCI; American Airlines; Cerner; US Bancorp and American Academy of Family Physicians.

Thompson Coburn LLP

See firm details p.1071

The Firm: Clients spoke of their loyalty to this group's lawyers because of "*the quality of their work, and the highly responsive, strategic and practical nature of the advice provided.*" The labor and employment practice group of 20 dedicated lawyers has carved a strong reputation in St. Louis. Employment litigation, and union negotiations and labor grievances are considered particular areas of strength. An emerging specialty for the group is advice on immigration law, while ERISA and employee benefits expertise adds a further string to its bow. The group has been heavily engaged in matters arising out of the railroad industry, representing employers on union relations in the transportation industry.

The Lawyers: Clients likened **Cliff Godiner** (see p.1057) to "*a good strategist with a workable plan for each case.*" He possesses a "*great analytical ability,*" and is particularly known for his expertise in issues related to the Railway Labor Act. This "*able trial attorney*" splits his practice between defense employment discrimination suits and representing railroad clients with union-related issues. **Richard Jaudes** (see p.1058) is chair of the labor and employment group. He impresses clients with his smooth handling of complex discrimination litigation and wins plaudits for the supervisor training programs he presents. Highlights during the year include representing the Saint Louis Symphony Orchestra on union organization issues and representing BUNZL Distribution on collective bargaining and union grievance arbitrations.

The Clients: Union Pacific; ACF Industries; Monsanto; BUNZL Distribution and Baldor Electric.

Band 3

Armstrong Teasdale LLP

The Firm: Competitors agree: "*This firm has a good diverse client base and a wealth of concentrated expertise.*" This employment and labor department is home to 13 specialist attorneys,

1046

All quotes in the text are from interviews with clients and competitors.

CHAMBERS USA 2005

who are skilled in litigation arising out of discrimination claims, immigration issues, and NLRB proceedings. Attorneys also provide employment-related training and counseling. A highlight for the team includes obtaining summary judgment on behalf of UPS in a nationwide class action alleging race discrimination in promotions, pay and working conditions.

The Lawyers: "*Super lawyer*" **John Vering** is vice chairman of the employment and labor law practice group in the Kansas City office. He represents employers in the defense of discrimination claims and serves as an arbitrator and mediator for the AAA.

The Clients: Clients include Columbia Public Schools, IBM and General Mills.

Constangy, Brooks & Smith, LLC
The Firm: This management-only labor and employment law firm handles a range of wage and hour claims, workers' compensation issues and employment litigation, but is best known for its "*history of excellence in traditional labor law*." This national boutique has an increasing presence in the state with an expanding office in Kansas City. Clients pointed to the "*advantage this firm has in drawing on the resources across the 14 offices in the USA.*" Class actions are another recognized strength of this 12-strong group and during the past year it has defeated class certification in a multimillion-dollar class action involving allegations of off-the-clock work and falsification of time records by management.

The Lawyers: **Robert Janowitz** is "*one of the best-known names in the state for traditional labor law*" and manages the Kansas City office. He is a senior litigator, who advises on all aspects of proceedings before the NLRB for clients in the healthcare, transportation, construction, retail and entertainment industries.

The Clients: Associated Builders & Contractors; Four Seasons; Greater Kansas City Community Foundation; McDonald's and Marriott Hotels.

Fisher & Phillips LLP
See firm details p.630

The Firm: From March 2005, Bioff Finucane Coffey Holland & Hosler LLP merged with Fisher & Phillips LLP. The firm is "*definitely one to watch for the future.*" Clients agree that it will be interesting to see how the merger affects it, but report "*it is certain to increase its presence in the state*". This Kansas City-based team can now draw on the support of a network of offices in 14 cities across the USA. It exclusively represents

management in labor and employment law, with wrongful discharge, discrimination and wage and hour litigation as its recognized areas of excellence. Commentators agreed that it is "*the impressive client base*" and employment litigation arm that really set it apart.

The Lawyers: Competitors "*would happily refer work to* **Brian Finucane** (see p.1056) *safe in the knowledge that he would take care of it.*" He is "*an incredible hard worker who really knows his stuff*" and an experienced trial attorney.

The Clients: ADT; GE Capital; Sutherland Lumber; Interstate Brands; Farmers; Neighbors Construction; TAMKO Asphalt Products; Sprint; Louis Dreyfus and Deffenbaugh Industries.

Greensfelder, Hemker & Gale, PC
The Firm: This St. Louis-based full-service law firm "*has a real presence in the state*" with its 14 highly talented labor and employment attorneys. The group is well versed in advising management in labor relations and in the defense of employment discrimination, harassment and wrongful termination claims. Noted for the "*quality of the labor relations advice*," this group also fields specialists in employee benefits litigation.

The Lawyers: According to peers, **Mary Beth Ortbals** is "*a leading choice for referrals in the state.*" She advises on labor relations and represents management in employment law litigation and in developing union avoidance strategies. **Dennis Collins** possesses the "*effective knack of keeping control of a case.*" Chairman of the labor and employment practice group, he has a broad-based litigation and advisory practice.

The Clients: The firm represents clients in the healthcare and hospital, grocery, manufacturing, technology and securities industries.

Husch & Eppenberger, LLC
The Firm: This full-service law firm operates from four offices spread across the state and fields about 30 labor and employment attorneys. National in scope, this group represents a diverse clientele ranging from small businesses to large publicly held corporations from many industries. Proficient in labor negotiations and proceedings before the NLRB, the group also excels in the defense of discrimination claims. Attorneys counsel clients on affirmative action plans and provide FMLA training. A recent litigation victory for the group was the successful defense of GlaxoSmithKline Consumer Healthcare in an employment discrimination action arising out of a termination.

The Lawyers: Chair of the labor and employment practice group **Jack Yates** impressed interviewees with his "*quality representation of significant clients.*" Yates has vast experience in class actions, discrimination claims and employment policy counseling.

The Clients: Clients include Securicor Wireless Holdings, Sprint and Tyson Foods.

McMahon Berger Hanna Linihan Cody & McCarthy, A Professional Corporation
See firm details p.1066

The Firm: Market commentators endorsed the labor law expertise displayed by this sizable boutique. A group of 26 attorneys proves "*tough competition*" for many peers with its long track record of representing companies in unfair labor practice proceedings before the NLRB. This group has carved a name for itself with high-quality litigation experience across a range of matters such as the defense of class actions and ERISA litigation.

The Lawyers: **Thomas McCarthy** is "*a talented and really experienced lawyer,*" said interviewees. He has advised sizable national and international clients on employment litigation and proceedings before the NLRB.

The Clients: AT&T; Bodine Aluminum (a subsidiary of Toyota Motor Corporate Services of North America); Brinker International; Cooper Industries; Dana; EDS and Emerson Electric.

Spencer Fane Britt & Browne LLP
The Firm: "*This firm's real claim to fame is on the labor side, where they have extremely strong skills,*" said interviewees. A dedicated group of 42 attorneys is spread across offices in Kansas City and St. Louis. The team is best known for its advice on union avoidance and unfair labor practice proceedings. However, attorneys are well equipped to handle employment litigation and regulatory compliance issues for clients across a wide array of industries. The firm has developed a niche in the healthcare and trucking industries.

The Lawyers: **Dave Wing** represents management in litigation and traditional labor law matters, providing advice on human resources policies. A portion of his workload derives from hospitals and other healthcare organizations.

The Clients: Community Health Group; Century Business Services; Hy-Vee and Lucent Technologies.

LITIGATION

GENERAL COMMERCIAL

Missouri
Leading firms
(Litigation: General Commercial)

[1] BERKOWITZ STANTON BRANDT *Kansas City*
BRYAN CAVE LLP *St. Louis*
ROUSE HENDRICKS GERMAN MAY PC *Kansas City*
SHOOK, HARDY & BACON LLP *Kansas City*
SHUGHART THOMSON & KILROY PC *Kansas City*
THOMPSON COBURN LLP *St. Louis*

[2] ARMSTRONG TEASDALE LLP *St. Louis*
BLACKWELL SANDERS PEPER *Kansas City*
HUSCH & EPPENBERGER LLC *Kansas City*
LATHROP & GAGE LC *Kansas City*
POLSINELLI SHALTON WELTE *Kansas City*
STINSON MORRISON HECKER LLP *Kansas City*

[3] DEACY & DEACY LLP *Kansas City*
GALLOP, JOHNSON & NEUMAN LC *St. Louis*
KOHN, SHANDS, ELBERT, GIANOULAKIS *St. Louis*
LEWIS, RICE & FINGERSH LC *St. Louis*
SONNENSCHEIN NATH & ROSENTHAL *Kansas City*
SPENCER FANE BRITT & BROWNE *Kansas City*
WYRSCH HOBBS & MIRAKIAN PC *Kansas City*

Firms are listed alphabetically in each band.

Band 1

Berkowitz Stanton Brandt Williams & Shaw LLP

The Firm: This Kansas City-based firm "*is one of the best commercial litigation boutiques around*" and was routinely described as the number-one player by both clients and peers. Clients spoke of the "*astounding results achieved in the courtroom*" and endorsed the wealth of talented attorneys on hand to deal with any type of case. This 30-member litigation team represents clients in state and federal trial and appellate court proceedings across the USA. Its areas of experience include antitrust and class actions, healthcare disputes, securities litigation and fraud. Attorneys are also well versed in alternative dispute resolution.

The Lawyers: Sources described **David Oliver** as "*fabulous – the personification of professional politeness all the time and a real smooth courtroom performer.*" Oliver primarily handles complex commercial disputes and has a particular forte in class action defense. A "*skilled trial lawyer,*" **Roger Stanton** has also impressed clients with his national products liability and healthcare management litigation experience. He is well equipped to advise on the defense of class actions. "*Superb white-collar practitioner*" **Jim Eisenbrandt** "*is the immediate name that springs to mind,*" reported sources. He has experience in major federal investigations and medical fraud and abuse claims. **Barney Berkowitz** is "*one of the most readily recognized names in the industry.*" His broad expertise features securities, banking, professional liability and insurance

coverage litigation. He is also a well-respected mediator and arbitrator.

The Clients: Ford; BMW North America; Morgan Stanley Dean Witter; KPMG; ONEOK; Prudential Securities; Kawasaki Motors Manufacturing USA and UBS Financial Services.

Bryan Cave LLP

The Firm: This international firm has 15 offices across the world and three offices in Missouri, which house dispute resolution resources. Clients were quick to recommend the strength of the business litigation and appellate arms of the firm and found its attorneys to be "*exceedingly proficient, professional, courteous, responsive and leaders in their respective fields.*" They agreed, "*this firm is one of the first to call for complex or governmental litigation.*" The litigation group represents clients in banking matters, creditors' rights and products liability disputes. Of the many notable cases undertaken by this firm during the year, one highlight is its successful defense of Ford in litigation surrounding the alleged fire risk of Crown Victoria police cars following high-speed rear collisions.

The Lawyers: Of the "*many remarkable attorneys*" at this firm, **Craig O'Dear** (see p.1060) stands out as the "*serious lawyer who tries cases to a jury all over the country.*" He has "*a winning manner with the jury,*" and has represented World Wrestling Entertainment in a contribution action against British manufacturer Lewmar to recover a substantial portion of an $18 million settlement WWE paid to the family of the wrestler Owen Hart, the 'Blue Blazer', who died during a performance in 1999. O'Dear's practice encompasses commercial and products liability litigation and "*you certainly can't quibble with his impressive track record.*" The "*fair-minded, personable and professional*" **Irvin Belzer** (see p.1055) has also impressed clients for "*his ability to relate to people*" and his representation of financial institutions and healthcare-related clients. Belzer is the managing partner of the Kansas City office and co-leader of the commercial litigation group. **Thomas Walsh** (see p.1061) is described as "*probably one of the leading appellate lawyers in the country.*" He is the leader of the appellate client service group, and he recently worked on upholding the $75 million verdict for breach of contract against a GE subsidiary for Biomedical Systems. The Kansas City head of the bankruptcy, restructuring and creditors' rights group, **Larry Frazen** (see p.1057), is widely respected for his dedication to clients. He represented Farmland Industries in the largest Chapter 11 proceedings ever to be filed in the Western District of Missouri, of which the assets alone were worth $2.3 billion. Sources also recognized "*one of the state's great up-and-*

coming lawyers" in **Bob Hoffman** (see p.1057). Hoffman has been involved in a complex real estate fraud case during the past year, while his broad business litigation practice often overlaps with employment law disputes. **Dan Ball** (see p.1055) is a "*fine trial lawyer*" and group leader of the products liability client service group. He specializes in class and derivative actions and commercial litigation. "*Superb white-collar crime attorney*" **Ed Dowd** (see p.1056) has impressed clients for his federal litigation practice. During the past year, Dowd has advised US congressman and presidential candidate Richard Gephardt, and also assisted the Missouri Development Finance Board in relation to a redevelopment of a downtown area.

The Clients: Sprint; H&R Block; Bank of New York; Boeing; DaimlerChrysler; Ford; Bank of America; Monsanto; Wells Fargo; Commerce Bank; Lucent Technologies; Pulitzer Publishing; Merck; Missouri Development Finance Board; HCA and GMAC.

Rouse Hendricks German May PC

The Firm: This Kansas City-based firm "*is one of the best commercial litigation boutiques around.*" The high caliber of its attorneys and their thorough approach to complex litigation has convinced many that this firm is "*at the top of the heap for sure.*" The team represents individuals and small and large business entities alike in a range of disputes including antitrust, securities disputes, products liability and white-collar crime. The 14 dedicated attorneys are also well equipped to handle class actions.

The Lawyers: Clients and peers described **Charles German** as "*the cream of the crop.*" He is "*a consummate professional, smart and always on top of the situation.*" His broad commercial caseload encompasses securities and healthcare litigation, although he is best known for "*his flourishing white-collar crime practice.*"

The Clients: Coca-Cola; Employers Reinsurance; Fru-Con Construction; Goodyear; Health Midwest; Hoechst Marion Roussel; Hutchens Industries; Kelly-Springfield Tire & Rubber; Southwestern Bell Yellow Pages; Stamina Products and Valley View State Bank.

Shook, Hardy & Bacon LLP

See firm details p.1067

The Firm: Heavily geared towards litigation, this firm is "*unparalleled in terms of skill and the ability to go to trial and get good results,*" claimed sources. Rivals describe the firm as "*tremendous competition,*" because of its ability to draw on approximately 200 litigation attorneys. The group in Missouri covers the full range of litigation from employment to IP and securities disputes. The firm is internationally respected for its "*exceptional products liability expertise,*"

Missouri
Leading individuals
(Litigation: General Commercial)

★ **WARD R Lawrence** *Shughart Thomson*, Kansas City

[1] **EVERSON David** *Stinson Morrison*, Kansas City
GERMAN Charles *Rouse Hendricks*, Kansas City
GRIFFIN James *Blackwell Sanders*, Kansas City
SAMPSON William *Shook Hardy*, Kansas City
TRIPP David *Stinson Morrison*, Kansas City
VOIGTS Gene *Shook Hardy*, Kansas City

[2] **ADAMS Robert** *Shook Hardy*, Kansas City
BELZER Irvin *Bryan Cave*, Kansas City
BERKOWITZ Lawrence *Berkowitz*, Kansas City
BROWN Spencer *Deacy & Deacy*, Kansas City
DALGLEISH Douglas *Lathrop & Gage*, Kansas City
DEAN Cathy *Polsinelli Shalton*, Kansas City
KAPLAN Harvey *Shook Hardy*, Kansas City
KOHN Alan *Kohn Shands*, St. Louis
O'DEAR Craig *Bryan Cave*, Kansas City
OLIVER David *Berkowitz Stanton*, Kansas City
PRICE James *Spencer Fane*, Kansas City
SHORT Barry *Lewis Rice*, St. Louis
STANTON Roger *Berkowitz Stanton*, Kansas City
VIRTEL James *Armstrong Teasdale*, St. Louis
WALSH Thomas *Bryan Cave*, St Louis
WOLF Jerome *Sonnenschein Nath*, Kansas City

[3] **BALL Dan** *Bryan Cave*, St. Louis
BASH Roy *Shughart Thomson*, Kansas City
BECK William *Lathrop & Gage*, Kansas City
BETHUNE Scott *Davis Bethune*, Kansas City
CARNEY Thomas *Husch & Eppenberger*, St. Louis
DAVIS Grant *Davis Bethune*, Kansas City
FRAZEN Laurence *Bryan Cave*, Kansas City
GIANOULAKIS John *Kohn Shands*, St. Louis
GOLDMAN Joel *Husch & Eppenberger*, Kansas City
HOFFMAN Robert *Bryan Cave*, Kansas City
HUNT Jeffrey *Gallop Johnson*, St. Louis
KOKORUDA Thomas *Shughart Thomson*, Kansas City
MASSEY Ray *Thompson Coburn*, St. Louis
NEWBOLD J William *Thompson Coburn*, St. Louis
REBEIN Joseph *Shook Hardy*, Kansas City
WELSH Russell *Polsinelli Shalton*, St. Louis

Leading individuals
(Litigation: White-Collar Crime &
Government Investigations)

[1] **AISENBREY John** *Stinson Morrison*, Kansas City
ANKNEY Gordon *Thompson Coburn*, St. Louis
BRADSHAW II Jean *Lathrop & Gage*, Kansas City
DEMERATH Jeffrey *Greensfelder Hemker*, St. Louis
DOWD Edward *Bryan Cave*, St. Louis
EISENBRANDT James *Berkowitz Stanton*, Kansas City
GERMAN Charles *Rouse Hendricks*, Kansas City
HOBBS James *Wyrsch Hobbs*, Kansas City
SHORT Barry *Lewis Rice*, St Louis
WYRSCH James *Wyrsch Hobbs*, Kansas City

Individuals are listed alphabetically in each band.

particularly in the fields of tobacco and pharmaceuticals. The group also stands apart from the market due to its ability to coordinate and manage complex litigation through its international network of offices.

The Lawyers: This firm is well known for producing a breed of "*high-powered trial lawyers*" and **Bill Sampson** (see p.1060) is no exception. This "*great practitioner*" impresses with his skillful handling of business, products liability and construction law disputes. A past president of the Defense Research Institute, Sampson is respected for his glittering track record. **Gene Voigts** (see p.1061) is the firm's vice chair and was routinely commended as "*a legend in the courtroom.*" Voigts has a long-standing reputation for success in products liability and white-collar crime litigation. The "*high-quality*" **Harvey Kaplan** (see p.1058) chairs the firm's pharmaceutical and medical devices litigation division. According to onlookers, he is "*outstanding at what he does and manages to run a tight ship.*" **Rob Adams** (see p.1055) focuses on IP, products liability and tort litigation, and has carved out a reputation as a go-to lawyer for patent litigation and disputes in the automotive sector. A "*fine trial lawyer,*" **Joe Rebein** (see p.1060) is chair of the firm's general litigation division. His is a diverse practice which includes antitrust and securities litigation, white-collar criminal defense and complex class actions.

The Clients: Eli Lilly; DuPont; Sanofi-Synthelabo; Aventis Pharmaceuticals; BAT and Pharmacia.

Shughart Thomson & Kilroy PC
See firm details p.1068

The Firm: This 80-strong litigation practice was commended by clients for "*the array of diverse knowledge on offer*" and, in particular, "*the efficient handling of the most complex issues.*" Although broad in its reach, the firm is especially endorsed for its expertise in construction and healthcare litigation and has developed thriving products liability, environmental and IP litigation practices. Clients were also quick to point out the wealth of trial and appellate experience these attorneys possess. A highlight for the team during the past year includes successfully acting for Kansas City Power & Light in a multimillion-dollar suit against its liability carriers for an explosion that occurred at its Hawthorne generating station.

The Lawyers: The "*dean of the Missouri litigation Bar*" and "*the star of the show,*" **Lawrence Ward** (see p.1061) has impressed all quarters of the market. According to peers, he has "*the heart of a commando and is as honest as the day is long,*" while clients described him as "*this rare individual with a great analytical ability to reduce big problems to smaller, bite-sized ones – he has a glittering track record behind him.*" Ward is chairman of the firm and the business litigation group and, inter alia, has experience in antitrust, fraud, securities and professional negligence litigation. Clients also highlighted **Thomas Kokoruda** (see p.1058) as "*a particularly effective attorney, who is very creative and aggressive.*" A talented trial lawyer, he has developed a respected niche in healthcare and hospital law litigation and also handles catastrophic disaster litigation. Highlights during the year include representing Health Midwest in a suit filed by entities relating to the propriety of sale of non-profit companies to for-profit companies. Kokoruda was also involved in contractual disputes concerning the Hospital Corporation of America, physicians and other hospitals. **Roy Bash** (see p.1055) is chair of the construction practice group and concentrates on construction and professional liability litigation. Representing some of the best-known names in the construction industry, Bash resolved by negotiation a significant mold-contaminated construction project case during the past year. He is highly respected for his sensible judgment and arbitration and mediation skills.

The Clients: HCA; H&R Block; Black & Veatch; BlueCross/BlueShield of Kansas City; JE Dunn Construction and Kansas City Power & Light.

Thompson Coburn LLP
See firm details p.1071

The Firm: This respected litigation group is certainly "*home to exceptional lawyers who know what they are doing in a courtroom.*" The firm fields dedicated appellate, business, real estate, products liability and railroad litigation practice groups. However, it is probably best known for the work of the tobacco litigation group. Market commentators believe that the group's extensive trial skills ensure that it excels in all forms of litigation matters, but the areas of antitrust, banking and insurance were particularly noted. The caseload here also features a significant proportion of admiralty law and white-collar crime disputes.

The Lawyers: **Ray Massey** (see p.1059) was universally commended by clients for "*the good job he does, his knowledgeable, down-to-earth approach and his way of explaining things in terms that clients can understand.*" Chairman of the litigation department, he has been engaged in heavy-duty business trials and environmental cases during the year and is admiralty counsel to some of the top names in the maritime world. Also impressing clients is "*the excellent and very experienced*" **Gordon Ankney** (see p.1055). "*He really knows how to try a case*" and concentrates his practice on white-collar crime, commercial and environmental tort litigation. **Bill Newbold** (see p.1059) has been heavily involved in trying large complex cases for major clients of late, such as his representation of Lorillard Tobacco in the $280 billion racketeering case against the tobacco industry. This is the largest such trial to be witnessed in the USA.

The Clients: AIG; American Commercial Barge Line; Lorillard Tobacco; Cargill and London Underwriters.

Band 2

Armstrong Teasdale LLP

The Firm: This *"substantial trial team"* is spread across three offices located in the state and comprises over 100 dedicated litigators. Market sources also identified the breadth of this litigation practice, which boasts attorneys who can take on any number of disputes. The caseload here ranges from antitrust through to construction and healthcare litigation. The team is also noted for its track record in IP, products liability and contract disputes. Alternative dispute resolution and appellate law are also areas embraced by this group.

The Lawyers: *"Top-flight business trial lawyer"* **James Virtel** garnered kudos during research this year for being *"one hell of a commercial trial lawyer."* He is cochair of the litigation department and has cultivated broad business litigation practice that covers environmental law, products liability and insurance coverage liability litigation.

The Clients: Clients are drawn from a wide range of industries such as banking and finance, manufacturing and transportation.

Blackwell Sanders Peper Martin LLP

See firm details p.1062

The Firm: This firm houses over 100 litigators and has a long-established reputation for high-profile antitrust and bankruptcy cases as well as complex class actions. Of the many areas of litigation covered by this firm, clients noted IP, securities law and complex commercial class actions as particular strengths. Highlights during the year include representing a charitable hospital in a suit alleging that it had not fulfilled the tax and other obligations required of it.

The Lawyers: *"Very bright and quick on his feet,"* **James Griffin** (see p.1057) is widely admired by clients for his detailed approach to dispute resolution, which makes him a popular choice for *"tough cases that are complex in nature."* He recently acted in a case that involved shareholders' claims that mutual fund fees were excessive.

The Clients: AG Edwards & Sons; Stifel Nicolaus & Company; The Kansas City Star and Saint Luke's-Shawnee Mission Health System.

Husch & Eppenberger, LLC

The Firm: This full-service firm has four offices strategically spread across the state with more than 150 attorneys who can provide litigation support. The general business litigation group handles a wide range of complex matters, and is held in high regard for its class action, business litigation and products liability expertise. Commentators also noted the firm's involvement in appellate matters.

The Lawyers: Peers singled out **Joel Goldman** for the *"huge volume of cases he can handle."* His wide-ranging experience encompasses asbestos-related cases, products liability and toxic torts defense. Of late, Goldman has served as national and regional products liability defense counsel in claims related to medical and consumer products. **Thomas Carney** is chair of the litigation department. He has impressed interviewees with his success in winning jury verdicts across a range of general business, products liability and toxic tort litigation.

The Clients: Monsanto, Olin Corporation and various local and national financial and healthcare institutions are clients of the group.

Lathrop & Gage LC

See firm details p.1064

The Firm: Clients praised this law firm as *"having enough variety and being big enough to effectively handle anything – they constantly come up with successful results."* With over 180 litigation attorneys, the firm has *"talent and ability in abundance."* Clients were also keen to point out its ability *"to do a good job handling the files at competitive prices."* The department is split into dedicated groups: bankruptcy and creditors' rights; business litigation; environmental law; labor and employment and torts litigation. Clients agree that *"the knowledge is high in all."* The defense of manufacturers in products liability litigation and environmental litigation are particular areas of excellence.

The Lawyers: Clients described **Douglas Dalgleish** (see p.1056) as *"a very bright and talented trial attorney who really gets the job done. He has the ability to effectively convey a message to a jury."* Dalgleish's practice focuses on business, products liability and tort litigation. He recently defended major landowners against attempts by an Indian tribe under ancient treaties to reclaim a major portion of modern-day Kansas. *"Impressive attorney"* **William Beck** (see p.1055) is typically found in environmental, natural resources and insurance-related litigation and has a particular forte in landfill and Superfund matters, especially those involving swine farms and animal waste. Highlights include working on the Yeoman Creek Superfund site in Illinois and advising on claims against an insurance company involving the settlement of a wrongful imprisonment case for a client falsely convicted of capital murder. Also garnering client approval during the year is **Jean Paul Bradshaw**. Peers commented: *"I immediately think of him when I think of good white-collar criminal defense attorneys."* He is well-known for his advice in healthcare fraud and internal corporate investigations.

The Clients: Allied Waste Industries; American Cyanamid; American Multi-Cinema; Armco; Burlington Northern and Santa Fe Railway; Fortis Benefits Insurance; Payless ShoeSource; Colgate-Palmolive and GM.

Polsinelli Shalton Welte Suelthaus (PSWS)

The Firm: A recent merger has provided extra resources for this litigation department, which is viewed as a *"major player in the state."* Attorneys here represent clients in a wide range of industries. A group of 45 specialists has won a loyal following for its work in commercial disputes, construction law, healthcare and insurance coverage. Clients also noted the group's niche in the pharmaceuticals sector.

The Lawyers: **Cathy Dean**, chair of the litigation department, stands out as an experienced trial lawyer, particularly for disputes related to the pharmaceuticals sector. Dean has experience in antitrust, products liability and taxation disputes. Making his debut in the tables this year is chairman and CEO of the firm **Russell Welsh**. Peers were quick to say: *"If I had a piece of commercial litigation I would definitely consider him"* and highly recommended his *"integrity and the tenacious yet charming approach that he adopts in court."* Welsh is well-versed in products liability, business torts, trade secrets, commercial and bankruptcy litigation.

The Clients: Bayer; Bristol-Myers Squibb; Honeywell; University of Kansas Hospital Authority and Healthcare USA.

Stinson Morrison Hecker LLP

See firm details p.1069

The Firm: Clients endorsed the litigation group's broad coverage and ability to handle the most complex of cases, while peers pointed to the professional approach displayed *"by some of the best of the Bar."* Prominent in antitrust, IP, environmental and white-collar criminal disputes, the group was also recommended for the quality of its appellate arm and securities litigation practice group. A caseload of healthcare and insurance industries-related disputes has also underlined the trial skills of these attorneys. As well as working on Superfund cases, further highlights for the group include the defense of a major pharmaceutical manufacturer in individual and class action suits over alleged antitrust violations in the settlement of patent litigation.

The Lawyers: Sources described **David Everson** (see p.1056) as *"a real bright guy with a substantial following."* He has been heavily involved in antitrust litigation during the year, alongside his steady diet of IP (often for pharmaceuticals companies), commercial and white-collar criminal litigation. *"One of the most accomplished environmental lawyers in the state,"* **David Tripp** (see p.1061) is chair of the firm's environmental law division. He advises on Superfund and CAA cases, EPA disputes and matters relating to the financing of development projects. *"The real deal,"* **John Aisenbrey** (see p.1055) is a talented white-collar criminal specialist who combines this practice with his complex commercial case-

1050   All quotes in the text are from interviews with clients and competitors.

CHAMBERS USA 2005

load. A former federal prosecutor, Aisenbrey is also well known for his products liability experience and he was recently involved in a dispute between a reinsurer and an insurance company over coverage for losses sustained in a non-standard automobile insurance program in New York.

The Clients: Aventis Pharmaceuticals; Hallmark Cards; Crown Equipment; ERC; Players Reinsurance; Gold Banc; C&H Distributors and Pepsi-Cola.

Band 3

Deacy & Deacy LLP

The Firm: This firm has lived up to its glowing reputation in defense litigation during the year and was singled out for "*its quite exceptional work in the insurance field.*" Comprising about 11 attorneys, this firm also litigates in the areas of antitrust, securities and railroad law.

The Lawyers: "*One of the best all-round trial lawyers in the city,*" **Spencer Brown** is "*tenacious and trustworthy – he has a terrific way with judge and jury and is universally well respected,*" reported sources. Business torts, securities and asbestos litigation cases are particular areas of excellence for this "*no-nonsense trial lawyer.*"

The Clients: BellSouth; Burlington Northern and Santa Fe Railway; Cessna; Continental Western Insurance; Hyatt; Illinois Central Railroad; CIGNA; Lexington Insurance; Missouri Insurance Guaranty Association; Pitney Bowes and Southwestern Bell.

Gallop, Johnson & Neuman LC

The Firm: This firm is home to 80 attorneys, 23 of which are dedicated to litigation services. A real presence in St. Louis, the team is well known for its effective handling of a variety of complex commercial disputes. Attorneys are involved in antitrust, insurance, licensing and fraud litigation. A recent highlight for the group was obtaining an $8.5 million judgment in a pension and ERISA severance benefit case.

The Lawyers: Sources were quick to highlight the "*superb technical ability*" of **Jeffrey Hunt**. He practices in environmental law, products liability, medical malpractice and complex commercial litigation. He has attracted a number of clients from the manufacturing and healthcare industries.

The Clients: Attorneys act for local and national financial services companies, manufacturers, energy corporates and food processors as well as Fortune 100 companies.

Kohn, Shands, Elbert, Gianoulakis & Giljum,LLP

The Firm: This "*very fine, well-rounded trial firm*" undertakes business and commercial litigation such as securities disputes, insurance coverage claims and employment discrimination

defense. Based in St. Louis, it comprises about 16 attorneys in a team that also excels in appellate matters and legal and accounting malpractice defense.

The Lawyers: The "*excellent*" **Alan Kohn** impresses with a practice heavily concentrated on securities litigation and legal malpractice defense. He is also well versed in the defense of class actions. The "*experienced, talented trial lawyer*" **John Gianoulakis** has developed a broad commercial practice but is perhaps best known for his "*thriving appellate and malpractice caseload.*"

Lewis, Rice & Fingersh LC
See firm details p.1065

The Firm: This old-line, full-service law firm operates from six offices positioned across the state and fields 60 dedicated litigation attorneys. "*Home to some good trial lawyers,*" this firm was particularly respected for its experience in admiralty, antitrust, environmental, IP and securities disputes. Insurance defense and complex nationwide class actions are also noted areas of excellence.

The Lawyers: A skilled trial lawyer, **Barry Short** (see p.1060) is a key figure at the Bar. He combines his commercial litigation practice in antitrust, environmental and toxic tort law with a respected white-collar crime caseload.

The Clients: Bank of America; Daimler-Chrysler; Doe Run; St. Louis Post-Dispatch; The Stanley Works; RightCHOICE Managed Care; Pioneer Hi-Bred International; True Fitness Technology and Owens Corning Fiberglass.

Sonnenschein Nath & Rosenthal
See firm details p.779

The Firm: The litigation and business regulation practice group at this firm was praised for its ability to draw on a national network of offices to work jointly on major litigation matters. With 27 dedicated litigation attorneys in Missouri alone, this firm has the resources to handle the more complex disputes. Insurance coverage and financial litigation are considered key strengths, and the firm is well equipped to advise on antitrust, real estate and construction and white-collar criminal matters. Of the many notable recent cases undertaken by the team a highlight was representing The Allstate Corporation in a federal antitrust suit against several major insurers.

The Lawyers: **Jerome Wolf** (see p.1061) has a wealth of trial experience. Head of the Kansas City litigation group, he is experienced across a range of dispute matters and can also advise on alternative dispute resolution tools.

The Clients: CNA Insurance; Sun Microsystems; Lafarge North America and Duke Energy.

Spencer Fane Britt & Browne LLP

The Firm: An old-line law firm with offices in Kansas City and St. Louis, its 50 dedicated litigators have secured a strong reputation for their trial expertise. Environmental law, insurance coverage litigation and contract disputes form the backbone of this practice. The group is also fully conversant with the effective use of arbitration and mediation to resolve complex business disputes.

The Lawyers: Chair of the firm's environmental law group, **Jim Price** was hailed by peers as "*an excellent environmental litigator, always at the centre of the action.*" He advises on compliance and regulatory issues related to air, water and waste. Superfund proceedings, RCRA corrective action and insurance coverage litigation are also key areas of his practice.

The Clients: Attorneys act for clients in the telecom, environmental, media and manufacturing sectors.

Wyrsch Hobbs & Mirakian PC

The Firm: This law firm places a great emphasis on complex civil and criminal litigation. Onlookers were quick to recommend the firm's representation of clients in business and commercial litigation, such as tax, antitrust, PI and real estate litigation. Also noteworthy, "*white-collar criminal defense is a real forte of this firm.*" Based out of Kansas City, this firm fields ten attorneys, who all have experience on high-profile litigations.

The Lawyers: **James Hobbs** is best known for his sound judgment and ability to handle complex white-collar criminal cases, as well as antitrust, professional licensing and business and commercial law. Hobbs also has experience in the areas of political corruption, the criminal enforcement of environmental laws and healthcare prosecutions. "*Dean of the Bar*" **James Wyrsch** (see p.1061) is president of the firm and comes highly recommended for "*his visibility in the legal community and his commitment to the Bar.*" Wyrsch has vast experience in complex criminal matters, defending cases in the areas of antitrust, bank and wire fraud, tax, healthcare and environmental law.

The Clients: Clients are drawn from an array of industries, including the roofing, telecommunications, real estate, marketing, insurance and securities industries.

Other Notable Practitioners

Scott Bethune of Davis Bethune & Jones, L.L.C. was often described as "*doing a good job for his clients – he's great at making presentations in court.*" His practice encompasses automotive litigation, lead paint and other products liability, medical and professional negligence. His colleague **Grant Davis** came highly recommended to researchers for "*his wonderful reputation and history of success.*" He devotes much of his prac-

www.ChambersandPartners.com
All quotes in the text are from interviews with clients and competitors.
1051

tice to professional negligence claims. **Jeffrey Demerath** of Greensfelder, Hemker & Gale, PC is a widely respected white-collar criminal attor-ney. Co-manager of the litigation practice group, Demerath is a former assistant US attor-ney for the District of Columbia and represents corporations and individuals in white-collar criminal cases.

REAL ESTATE

Missouri
Leading firms (Real Estate)

[1] **BLACKWELL SANDERS PEPER** *Kansas City*
LEWIS, RICE & FINGERSH, LC *Kansas City*
STINSON MORRISON HECKER LLP *Kansas City*

[2] **BRYAN CAVE LLP** *St. Louis*
LATHROP & GAGE LC *Kansas City*
POLSINELLI SHALTON WELTE *Kansas City*
WHITE GOSS BOWERS MARCH *Kansas City*

[3] **ARMSTRONG TEASDALE LLP** *St. Louis*
GREENSFELDER, HEMKER & GALE, PC *St. Louis*
KING HERSHEY *Kansas City*
SHUGHART THOMSON & KILROY PC *Kansas City*
THOMPSON COBURN LLP *St. Louis*

Leading individuals (Real Estate)

[1] **CARR William** *Lewis Rice, Kansas City*
DIGIOVANNI Peter *Lewis Rice, Kansas City*
FRANTZE David *Stinson Morrison, Kansas City*
KING Richard *King Hershey, Kansas City*
MILLER Charles *Lewis Rice, Kansas City*

[2] **DAGENAIS Don** *Lathrop & Gage, Kansas City*
FITZGERALD Robert *Shughart Thomson, Kansas City*
FLANIGAN Daniel *Polsinelli Shalton, Kansas City*
HAINES Lisa *Polsinelli Shalton, Kansas City*
KENNEDY Donald *Greensfelder Hemker, St. Louis*
MCNEARNEY John *Blackwell Sanders, St. Louis*
MUELLER Kathleen *Blackwell Sanders, St. Louis*
MURRAY George *Bryan Cave, Kansas City*
SHALTON Lonnie *Polsinelli Shalton, Kansas City*
SHTEAMER Michael *Shughart Thomson, Kansas City*
SPARKS Stephen *Bryan Cave, Kansas City*

Firms and individuals are listed alphabetically in each band.

Band 1

Blackwell Sanders Peper Martin LLP

See firm details p.1062

The Firm: This "*substantial real estate group*" of 34 dedicated real estate attorneys has impressed sources with "*its unparalleled reputation and experience in urban real estate redevelopment.*" Clients spoke of the quality of the group's real estate financing and its advice on the leasing of commercial and retail property, particularly the redevelopment of older buildings. Attorneys also provide regional and national clients with "*high-quality advice*" on securitizations and zoning and land use issues. The caseload during the past year has included advice on the rede-velopment of the South Loop area, the biggest redevelopment project in the history of down-town Kansas City. Further highlights include

representing Principal Life Insurance in its $200 million of securitized commercial real estate loans.

The Lawyers: **John McNearney** (see p.1059) is "*a great lawyer.*" Clients say: "*He is practical and does not get hung up on the pointless details.*" Clients feel that his background as in-house counsel is a distinct advantage. He advises on real estate finance, mostly representing financial institutions and is chair of the firm's real estate department. One recent highlight is his advice to AXA Financial in the disposition and acqui-sition related to its $500 million agricultural loan portfolio. **David Fenley** (see p.1056) is a skilled land use and zoning attorney, who advis-es on real estate development land use and tax incentive packages between developers and gov-ernment bodies. Peers described him as "*a wel-come addition to anyone's real estate dream team; he really does attract some fine clients.*" Fenley is the real estate development counsel for H&R Block, and is currently working on a $500 mil-lion multifamily and entertainment redevelop-ment project of downtown Missouri. Also making waves with clients is the "*very practical*" **Kathleen Mueller** (see p.1059). She is "*a straight-ahead lawyer who does a good job and handles herself with diplomacy*" in her practice that features real estate finance and the repre-sentation of closely held companies.

The Clients: Aquila; AG Edwards & Sons; Fed-eral Reserve Bank of St. Louis; H&R Block; Highwoods Properties; Principal Life Insurance; AXA Financial; Keystone Bank; JC Nichols and Jacobs Engineering Group.

Lewis, Rice & Fingersh, LC

See firm details p.1065

The Firm: Clients agree that this firm has devel-oped "*a good real estate presence – they are as strong as anyone in the market,*" while peers "*reg-ularly see them on the other side of the best work in the state.*" This full-service law firm can boast six strategically positioned offices across the state and has an established presence in St. Louis with some of the finest real estate attorneys in the state. The real estate is home to approximately 18 dedicated real estate lawyers. Clients were quick to highlight the cross-departmental resources and expertise provided: "*Specialists are on hand in any sort of real estate problem.*" The group acts for lenders, borrowers and commer-cial developers on leasing, zoning, acquisition finance and governmental approval work. Dur-ing the past year, the team has been heavily

involved in the redevelopment of malls and 'new urbanism' projects. An example of the latter is its advice in relation to Park Place, the mixed-use new urbanism project containing over a million square feet of buildings.

The Lawyers: Commentators agreed that **Bill Carr** (see p.1055) is "*one of the most prominent real estate attorneys in town.*" One source high-lighted that "*he really knows what is important and when you deal with him you get right to the point of the case, which is good for all parties.*" He has recently represented a company that pur-chased oil refineries and pipelines that ran through Oklahoma, in a complex $300 million project involving acquisition and finance issues. A "*wonderful commercial real estate lawyer,*" **Charles Miller** (see p.1059) garnered praise for his general real estate practice, particularly his "*quality representation of developers.*" His high-lights include representing the developer of the Antioch Center Mall, a $70 million redevelop-ment project in Kansas City. Miller also worked on the redevelopment of several blocks of the Accardo Arts & Design district in the Crossroads of Kansas City. **Peter DiGiovanni** (see p.1056) "*gets right to the point of a case and always protects his clients' interests.*" He is experienced in com-mercial and residential development projects, and is often found representing tenants and developers in large, complex cases. DiGiovanni advised on the development of a new regional mall in Pittsburgh for the Mills Corporation, a project involving over a million square feet.

The Clients: AMC Entertainment; Sprint Spectrum; US Bank; Mills; Westfield; Helzberg Diamonds; T-Mobile; Landmark Theaters; VeriSign; AMLI Residential Properties and Pulte Homes.

Stinson Morrison Hecker LLP

See firm details p.1069

The Firm: This firm has three offices in the state and was routinely described by sources as "*definitely top of the heap because of its superb, well-rounded real estate department.*" The real estate group is subdivided into construction and real estate lending practice groups and fields about 18 specialists in Missouri alone. Attorneys here act for lenders on significant conduit finance structuring, old building conversion deals and acquisition financing. A recent high-light for the team includes representing Cordish in the $330 million retail development of the seven-square block Kansas City Live! entertain-ment district. It also worked on the develop-

Missouri
Leading individuals
(Real Estate: Zoning/Land Use)

[1]	**FENLEY** David *Blackwell Sanders*, Kansas City
	KING Richard *King Hershey*, Kansas City
	WHITE Michael *White Goss*, Kansas City
[2]	**BOWERS** James *White Goss*, Kansas City
	FREILICH Robert *Freilich Leitner*, Kansas City
	MARCH Aaron *White Goss*, Kansas City
	NESTER Daniel *Bryan Cave*, St Louis
	RIFFEL Jerome *Lathrop & Gage*, Kansas City

Individuals are listed alphabetically in each band.

ment of the $250 million Sprint center arena located in downtown Kansas City. The department is also the national real estate counsel for Entertainment Properties Trust, one of the largest REITs in the country.

The Lawyers: The *"accomplished"* **David Frantze** (see p.1057) impressed clients and peers alike for his *"achievements on the biggest projects around"* and *"his exceptional economic development practice."* Frantze is chair of the real estate practice division and represents developers, property owners and tenants in development projects, particularly those that include the use of incentives. He also represents the Kansas City Royals baseball club in connection with its stadium leases and real estate activities.

The Clients: DeBruce Grain; Federal Reserve Bank of Kansas City; Cordish; Entertainment Properties Trust; Anschutz Entertainment Group; Kansas City Royals and BST Realty.

Band 2

Bryan Cave LLP

The Firm: This large, full-service firm has impressed onlookers not only for *"the amount of top-notch attorneys"* it possesses, but also for *"the sheer number of large projects it has secured."* The firm has three offices in the state, but was particularly noted for *"the strength and resources of the St. Louis office,"* which draws on its respected corporate department. Real estate litigation, zoning and land use and corporate real estate transactions were highlighted as areas of strength, while attorneys are also able to advise on construction and project finance. The group recently negotiated the contracts and design and build of a 250,000-sq-ft distribution center for Watson Pharmaceuticals. A further highlight for the firm is its representation of the developer and seller in the redevelopment and sale (for $235 million) of the Saint Louis Galleria, which covers nearly 50 acres of land and has 180 stores, 18 restaurants, a six-screen theater and structured parking.

The Lawyers: **George Murray** (see p.1059) is co-leader of the real estate development, construction and project finance group. A leading figure in the state, he concentrates on the struc-

turing and implementation of development projects. He represented Farmland Industries in the sale in excess of $450 million of real estate assets comprising more than 23 properties in eight states. Murray also worked on the leasing and disposition of the renovated old Edison Brothers office tower building in downtown St. Louis, a project involving over 400,000 sq ft of real estate. Finance specialist **Steve Sparks** (see p.1060) impresses with *"the high quality of his bond work and real estate finance."* **Dan Nester** (see p.1059) is *"one heck of a land use attorney; a real dynamo."* He obtained a conditional use permit for the construction and operation of a large mausoleum in the City of Creve Coeur, and acquired and rezoned a new branch of West Pointe Bank in Illinois.

The Clients: Sara Lee; Emerson Electric; Merrill Lynch; Lucent Technologies; Watson Pharmaceuticals; Pulte Homes; Rave Motion Picture Theaters; Sunrise Assisted Living; West Pointe Bank; Forever Enterprises and Monsanto.

Lathrop & Gage LC
See firm details p.1064

The Firm: This *"busy, well-rounded firm"* is widely respected for its wealth of experience in commercial and residential acquisitions, leasing, development and land use work. It produces *"practical, experienced attorneys,"* who have attracted national developers, lenders and construction companies on to the client roster. Thirty attorneys devote most of their time to real estate. Work involving government incentives, advice on shopping centers and lease negotiations are areas of strength. Highlights include representing Lafarge in its 1000-acre, $150 million development of a state-of-the-art cement manufacturing facility. The team also negotiated a process through which the GSA and the IRS were able to achieve congressional authorization for a long-term lease for the IRS service center, allowing the US Postal Service to find a better use for an older facility and the IRS to open a new service center.

The Lawyers: **Don Dagenais** (see p.1056) was commended to researchers as *"a cutting-edge attorney"* for his work in commercial sales and purchases, construction law and zoning. Highlights include representing developers and lenders on the conversion of old commercial buildings into condominiums and representing a large retailer in lease negotiations. **Jerome Riffel** (see p.1060) is an expert on zoning and economic development incentives. He is lead counsel for Children's Mercy Hospital in Kansas City, general real estate counsel for the Kansas City Area Transportation Authority and serves as lead counsel for a riverboat gaming facility on the Missouri River.

The Clients: Butler Real Estate; GM; AMC Entertainment; Zimmer Development; Hilton Hotels; Children's Mercy Hospital; Kansas City

Area Transportation Authority; First Bank of Missouri and JCPenney.

Polsinelli Shalton Welte Suelthaus (PSWS)

The Firm: *"Always involved in a piece of the action,"* this group is a popular choice for financial institutions and corporate entities involved in acquisitions and real estate finance. Such success is illustrated by the firm's advice on closing commercial mortgage loans worth over $400 million in the past twelve months alone. Tax increment financing, zoning and land use, and acquisitions and dispositions are all found in the workload of this 40-member group.

The Lawyers: The *"highly capable"* **Lonnie Shalton** is held in high regard for his *"negotiation skills and his broad experience."* He has assisted in the acquisition, development, government approval and financing of several key projects during the year. Clients value **Daniel Flanigan** for *"his specialist expertise in handling large real estate loans for national clients."* He is chair of the real estate and financial services department. **Lisa Haines** continues to make her mark on this sector as chair of the firm's real estate transactions and commercial lending group. Haines advises on commercial lending and creditors' rights and is well versed in the formation of homes and condominium associations.

The Clients: KeyBank; Wells Fargo; Bridger Commercial Funding; CSFB; International Speedway; Target; Costco and AG Spanos.

White Goss Bowers March Schulte & Weisenfels, A Professional Corporation

The Firm: Clients and peers singled this firm out as *"the number one firm for zoning and land use"* and recognized its skills in handling tax incentives and development approvals. Home to 15 dedicated attorneys, this firm concentrates in the areas of development, land use and tax credit financing. The firm is well known for representing developers on city approval work and public-private economic partnerships.

The Lawyers: *"One of the best in the state"* for land use and zoning issues is **Mike White**. Sources also endorsed him as *"good at getting the work completed in a timely fashion for his clients."* His caseload also includes eminent domain, public finance and government approval work. Also making waves with clients during the year is *"bulldog"* **James Bowers**. *"If you have a case involving zoning, land use or real estate litigation, you should choose him to fight your corner."* **Aaron March** was described to researchers as *"one to watch."* He is *"careful, thorough and well liked."*

The Clients: Knight Ridder, Home Depot and Target are just a few representative clients.

Band 3

Armstrong Teasdale LLP

The Firm: This firm has three offices across the state, although it was particularly pinpointed for the "*strength and depth*" of the St. Louis office. It represents national and local developers, lenders and governmental entities in all areas of real estate law. This real estate group garnered praise for its cross-departmental ethos, often drawing on the experience of the public law and finance and litigation practice groups as and when the case dictates. The real estate group has over 30 dedicated members advising on development projects and land use disputes. Recent highlights include representing Mills in the development of a 250-acre regional outlet mall and entertainment site, and working on the development of the St. Louis Cardinals' new downtown stadium.

The Lawyers: Timothy Tryniecki is the leader of the firm's real estate practice group and the main point of contact at this firm.

The Clients: Mills, Ameren and Centocor are just a few representative clients of this real estate group.

Greensfelder, Hemker & Gale, PC

The Firm: This firm has successfully secured "*an established presence*" in the St. Louis market. Clients valued the concentrated areas of expertise this firm has to offer and particularly noted the high caliber of its advice on real estate development, finance and transactional work. Zoning, land use and commercial leasing were also highlighted as strengths of this 13-strong group.

The Lawyers: Respected **Donald Kennedy** is the manager of the firm's real estate practice group and a popular port of call for referrals from peers. He practices in all aspects of real estate transactions including leasing, development, financing and zoning.

King Hershey, A Professional Corporation

See firm details p.1063

The Firm: This firm stands out with its "*good, strong team of real estate attorneys who are always good to work with.*" The group's expertise in incentives and zoning issues is a distinguishing feature. However, this Kansas City-based firm provides representation in all aspects of commercial real estate law for developers, lenders, builders and municipalities. Of late, the group has been involved in tax increment financing, redevelopment projects and work in neighborhood improvement districts. The structuring of public-private financing for real estate development projects is another recognized forte of this firm.

The Lawyers: Market sources agreed that **Richard King** (see p.1058) is a leader for zoning and land use issues in the state. Chairman and CEO of the firm, King is "*politically well connected*" and widely considered an expert on the structuring of public-private finance transactions, government finance projects and land use. King is a former mayor of the City of Independence and the current president elect of the Missouri Economic Development Financing Association.

The Clients: City of Boonville; City of Fulton; City of Kirksville; Clay County, Missouri; Economic Development Corporation of Kansas City; Land Clearance for Redevelopment Authority of Kansas City, Missouri; Prairie View Development; Quality Hill Redevelopment and Security Bank of Kansas City.

Shughart Thomson & Kilroy PC

See firm details p.1068

The Firm: Although real estate is not the mainstay of this firm, sources acknowledged its "*emerging presence in the state – they are often found competing for the major deals.*" The group serves clients in all phases of real estate transactions from acquisition and construction to operation and eventual sale. The ten dedicated attorneys also work closely with the construction group at the firm. The recent caseload has featured advice to business developers on such projects as hotels, multifamily complexes and golf courses.

The Lawyers: **Robert Fitzgerald** (see p.1057) was routinely described as a "*quality corporate lawyer with a flourishing real estate practice.*" He has secured the loyalty of a wide variety of clients who conduct real estate transactions all around the country. Fitzgerald is also well known for his work in relation to real estate venture formations. The "*talented, younger real estate attorney*" **Michael Shteamer** (see p.1060) has impressed with his work in real estate and financing issues. He can often be found representing lenders and developers in negotiating commercial real estate loans, workouts and leasing arrangements as well as resolving environmental issues that relate to real estate law.

Thompson Coburn LLP

See firm details p.1071

The Firm: This St. Louis-based firm was highly recommended by clients and peers for its "*long-established reputation*" in real estate transactional and development work. The firm benefits from its strong regional ties and is also developing a healthy national practice, representing developers across the country. About 22 real estate attorneys handle transactions for commercial, industrial and multifamily properties in 47 states. Attorneys also represent borrowers and lenders in transactions involving commercial, industrial and multifamily properties.

The Lawyers: Daniel Engle and Paul Macon jointly head up this real estate group and are believed to set the standards for this "*high-quality practice.*"

The Clients: Barry-Wehmiller; Mills; US Bancorp; Hardee's; Savvis Communications; Clayco Construction; United Industries and Sam's Club.

Other Notable Practitioners

Robert Freilich of Freilich, Leitner & Carlisle was roundly applauded as "*a national hotshot in representing cities and municipalities in zoning and planning issues.*" Renowned for his urban planning expertise, he is also skilled in city subdivisions and municipal growth management strategies. Commentators described him as "*a real smart academic*" and "*a recognized expert on encouraging the use of infrastructure to contain the urban sprawl.*"

Leaders in Missouri

ADAMS, Robert
Shook, Hardy & Bacon LLP, Kansas City
816 474 6550
rtadams@shb.com
Recommended in Litigation
Practice Areas: Practices in products liability litigation, intellectual property litigation, insurance coverage litigation and tort litigation. Has tried more than 25 jury trials in several different states, primarily in the areas of automobile litigation and patent litigation. Has made numerous appellate arguments in appellate courts throughout the country.
Prof. Memberships: Admitted to practice in Missouri and before the US Court of Appeals for the Fourth and Eighth Circuits. Member of Federation of Defense and Corporate Counsel and Board Member of Missouri Organization of Defense Lawyers.
Career: Joined Shook, Hardy & Bacon, 1987; became Partner, 1994. Chair, Shook, Hardy & Bacon Tort Section. Member, Shook, Hardy & Bacon Executive Committee.
Publications: Juror Non-Disclosure, 'MODL Journal' (April 2000); Practical Aspects of the Revisions to the Federal Rules of Civil Procedure, 'Journal of the Missouri Bar' (1994).
Personal: JD, University of Missouri-Columbia Law School, 1987; BA, University of Kansas, 1984.

ADAMS, Stephen
Blackwell Sanders Peper Martin LLP, Kansas City 816 983 8173
sadams@blackwellsanders.com
Recommended in Corporate/M&A
Practice Areas: Commercial transactions; healthcare; mergers and acquisitions; real estate.
Prof. Memberships: Admitted to practice in Kansas (1970) and Missouri (1971). Member, American Bar Association; American Health Lawyers Association; Greater Kansas City Society of Health Care Attorneys; Johnson County Bar Association; Kansas Bar Association; Kansas Hospital Attorneys Association; Lawyers Association of Kansas City; the Missouri Bar; and Missouri Society of Hospital Attorneys.
Career: Joined firm, 1970; named Partner, 1976.
Personal: JD, University of Kansas Law School, 1970; Member, 'Kansas Law Review', 1968-70; BS, University of Kansas, 1967.

AISENBREY, John C
Stinson Morrison Hecker LLP, Kansas City 816 842 8600
jaisenbrey@stinsonmoheck.com
Recommended in Litigation
Practice Areas: Focuses on commercial litigation and white collar crime. Provides representation in complex commercial, civil RICO and fraud matters, federal criminal investigations and prosecutions, and internal investigations.

Also defends manufacturers in product liability actions.
Prof. Memberships: Admitted in Missouri and Kansas. International Association of Defense Counsel, National Association of Criminal Defense Lawyers, American Bar Association.
Career: Former Assistant United States Attorney, District of Columbia. Was law clerk to Judge Roger Robb, US Court of Appeals for DC Circuit. Former adjunct law professor at University of Missouri-Kansas City School of Law.
Personal: JD, Georgetown University, 1977; AB, Cornell University, 1969.

ANKNEY, Gordon L
Thompson Coburn LLP, St Louis
314 552 6003
gankney@thompsoncoburn.com
Recommended in Litigation
Practice Areas: Co-Chairman of firm's White Collar Practice. Has extensive experience as a trial lawyer in white collar criminal cases, as well as civil commercial litigation.
Career: Spent 12 years as special prosecutor in St. Louis, Missouri. In private practice, he has tried cases to juries involving allegations of fraud, securities violations, false test reports, nuisance, anti-trust, government false claims, taxation, negligence, bid-rigging and whistle-blower claims. His trials have taken place in federal and state courts, including: Missouri, Illinois, Kansas, Alabama and Maryland. Has made extensive use of computers in trials, especially in US v Thermal Science, Inc., USDC Maryland.

ASH, James
Blackwell Sanders Peper Martin LLP, Kansas City 816 983 8137
jash@blackwellsanders.com
Recommended in Corporate/M&A
Practice Areas: Mergers and acquisitions; securities.
Prof. Memberships: Admitted to practice in Missouri (1981). Member, American Bar Association, Sections on Business Law and Intellectual Property Law, and the Missouri Bar.
Career: Joined firm as Partner, 1993. Chair, Blackwell Sanders Peper Martin Corporate Department, 2000-present.
Personal: JD, University of California at Los Angeles, 1981; Member, Order of the Coif and 'Law Review'; Editor, University of California at Los Angeles 'Alaska Law Review'; BA, University of California at Los Angeles (summa cum laude), 1978.

BALL, Dan
Bryan Cave LLP, St Louis
314 259 2000
Recommended in Litigation

BARTELSMEYER, Fred
Bryan Cave LLP, St Louis
314 259 2000
Recommended in Corporate/M&A

BASH, Roy
Shughart Thomson & Kilroy PC, Kansas City 816 395 0633
rbash@stklaw.com
Recommended in Litigation
Practice Areas: Business litigation, construction industry, construction litigation. Represents architects and engineers, public and private owners, general contractors and specialty contractors in various construction related business matters. Also handles litigation and dispute resolution issues.
Prof. Memberships: American Arbitration Assocition. Has served as arbitrator or mediator on a number of occasions, including arbitration of a commercial dispute regarding an international licensing agreement for computer software. American Bar Association Forum on the Construction Industry. The Missouri Bar.
Career: Joined Shughart Thomson & Kilroy in 1990 as Shareholder/Director. Chair, Construction Practice Group. Member, Executive Committee. 1974 court admissions in Iowa and Missouri.
Personal: Born in Oklahoma City, Oklahoma. University of Iowa, BBA with High Distinction, 1971. University of Iowa, JD 1974. Phi Delta Phi, President, 1973-74.

BECK, William G
Lathrop & Gage L.C., Kansas City
816 460 5811
bbeck@lathropgage.com
Recommended in Litigation
Practice Areas: Environmental, insurance and other complex litigation.
Career: Beck devotes his practice to resolving complex environmental liabilities and insurance claims. His environmental experience includes matters relating to the generation, transportation, treatment, storage, disposal, cleanup and taxation of hazardous and solid waste, including acquisition, permitting, operational, corrective action, closure, financial assurance and post-closure issues for both sanitary landfills and hazardous waste facilities. He successfully represents policyholders seeking to enforce coverage for environmental damages and defends toxic tort lawsuits claiming personal injury, death and property damage due to chemical exposure. He has experience in insurance archeology, claims resolution and coverage litigation.

BELZER, Irvin
Bryan Cave LLP, Kansas City
816 374 3200
Recommended in Litigation

BERKOWITZ, Lawrence
Berkowitz Stanton Brandt Williams & Shaw LLP, Kansas City 816 561 7007
Recommended in Litigation

BETHUNE, Scott
Davis Bethune & Jones, L.L.C., Kansas City 816 421 1600
Recommended in Litigation

BOWERS, James
White Goss Bowers March Schulte & Weisenfels, A Professional Corporation, Kansas City 816 753 9200
Recommended in Real Estate

BRADSHAW II, Jean Paul
Lathrop & Gage L.C., Kansas City
816 460 5507
jpbradshaw@lathropgage.com
Recommended in Litigation
Career: Bradshaw's practice includes white-collar criminal defense, healthcare fraud and abuse, internal corporate investigations, the establishment of corporate preventative law programs that comply with federal requirements and complex commercial litigation. His experience includes: United States Attorney, Western District of Missouri, 1989-93; formed first healthcare fraud task force in Missouri in 1992; Chairman-Elect and Member, United States Attorney General's Advisory Committee - Subcommittees on Sentencing Guidelines, Office Management and Budget, 1991-93; Member, Economic Crimes Council, US Department of Justice, 1989-93; Member, Governor's Commission on Crime, 1989-93; and Special Assistant Attorney General State of Missouri, 1985-89.

BROWN, Spencer
Deacy & Deacy LLP, Kansas City
816 421 4000
Recommended in Litigation

CARMAN, Steven F
Blackwell Sanders Peper Martin LLP, Kansas City 816 983 8153
scarman@blackwellsanders.com
Recommended in Corporate/M&A
Practice Areas: M&A, securities, technology, general corporate.
Prof. Memberships: The Missouri Bar.
Career: Joined firm as Partner, 1995.
Personal: JD, University of Pennsylvania, 1985; MBA, Wharton School of Business at the University of Pennsylvania, 1985; BA, Hamilton College, 1981.

CARNEY, Thomas
Husch & Eppenberger, LLC, St Louis
314 421 4800
Recommended in Litigation

CARR, William E
Lewis, Rice & Fingersh, L.C., Kansas City 816 472 2503
wecarr@lrf-kc.com
Recommended in Real Estate
Practice Areas: Recognized as a leader in the practice of commercial real estate, including finance, development, acquisitions and sales, joint ventures and leasing; worked on projects throughout the United States and in Europe and Asia.

Prof. Memberships: Admitted to practice in Missouri and Kansas (1971). Member, Kansas City Metropolitan Bar Association (Past Chairman, Real Estate Section and Managing Partners Section); Member, American College of Real Estate Lawyers (Chairman, Leasing Committee); Member of Advisory Board, Georgetown University Law School Advanced Commercial Leasing Institute.
Career: Joined Brown, Koralchik & Fingersh, predecessor to Lewis, Rice & Fingersh in 1973; former Chairman, Real Estate Department; Managing Member of Kansas City office, 1997 to present.
Publications: Co-author, 'The International Practice of Real Estate,' Probate & Property, September/October 1996, The Magazine of Real Property, Probate and Trust Law Section of the American Bar Association (Recipient of the 1996 Excellence in Writing Award). Author, 'Negotiation of Commercial Leases,' the Commercial Property Lease, 1993 American Bar Association Section of Real Property, Probate and Trust Law. Author, 'Boxed In: The Rise of the Box Store and the Downfall of the Traditional Shopping Center Lease,' American College of Real Estate Lawyers, Spring 2001, Williamsburg, VA, published as part of the ACREL Papers by ALI-ABA.
Personal: Born July 20, 1946, JD, University of Chicago Law School, 1971; AB, University of California at Berkeley, 1968.

COLLINS, Dennis
Greensfelder, Hemker & Gale, P.C.,
St Louis 314 241 9090
Recommended in Employment

DAGENAIS, Don F
Lathrop & Gage L.C., Kansas City
816 460 5715
ddagenais@lathropgage.com
Recommended in Real Estate
Practice Areas: Real estate and financial institutions.
Career: Dagenais handles real estate and other asset-based lending work for banks, savings and loan associations, savings banks and other commercial lenders. The types of projects involved in this work include apartment complexes, shopping centers, office buildings, warehouse/industrial projects, retail stores and nursing homes. He also practices construction law, zoning, foreclosures and loan workouts, ADA requirements pertaining to commercial space, and other related issues. He was selected as 'Best of the Bar', Kansas City Business Journal, 2003-04 and a 'Leading Lawyer' by Chambers USA, 2003, 2004 and 2005.

DALGLEISH, Douglas
Lathrop & Gage L.C., Kansas City
816 460 5708
ddalgleish@lathropgage.com
Recommended in Litigation
Practice Areas: Tort litigation, business litigation, personal injury/products liability.

Career: Dalgleish is an experienced trial attorney and a member of the American Board of Trial Advocates, which reflects his high personal character, honorable reputation and proficiency as a trial lawyer. He was named 'Best Lawyers in America', 2005-06; 'Best of the Bar' by the Kansas City Business Journal, 2004; and was a 'Top Lawyer Under 40' by Missouri Lawyers Weekly. He handles cases including breach of contract, personal injury, product liability, premises liability, FELA litigation, employee injuries, misappropriation of trade secrets, employee solicitation, and Trademark Trial and Appeal Board litigation.

DAVIS, Grant
Davis Bethune & Jones, L.L.C.,
Kansas City 816.421.1600
Recommended in Litigation

DEAN, Cathy
Polsinelli Shalton Welte Suelthaus
(PSWS), Kansas City 816 753 1000
Recommended in Litigation

DEMERATH, Jeffrey
Greensfelder, Hemker & Gale, P.C.,
St Louis 314 241 9090
Recommended in Litigation

DIGIOVANNI, Peter
Lewis, Rice & Fingersh, L.C.,
Kansas City 816 472 2504
pmdigiovanni@lrf-kc.com
Recommended in Real Estate
Practice Areas: Development, acquisition and disposition of commercial real estate, including regional malls, office buildings and mixed use projects. Has extensive experience in negotiation of regional mall department store REA's and substantial retail and office leases.
Prof. Memberships: Admitted to practice in Missouri (1977) and Kansas (1983). Member of the American College of Real Estate Lawyers; Member, Missouri Bar Association, Kansas Bar Association, Kansas City Metropolitan Bar Association (former Chair of the Real Estate Section).
Career: Joined Brown, Koralchik and Fingersh (predecessor to Lewis, Rice & Fingersh) in 1976, became Partner in 1980; Adjunct Professor of Law (Real Estate Development and Finance), University of Kansas School of Law, 1985-87 and 2000-02.
Publications: Alternate Methods of Financing the Sale and Purchase of Single Family Residences: Representing the Buyer and the Seller, 'Journal of the Kansas Bar Association', Fall, 1981.
Personal: Born June 5, 1948; JD University of Kansas School of Law (Order of the Coif and Law Review) 1976; BA University of Kansas 1971.

DONNELLY, Dennis
Bryan Cave LLP, St Louis
314 259 2000
Recommended in Employment

DONNELLY, Paul
Stinson Morrison Hecker LLP,
Kansas City 816 842 8600
pdonnelly@stinsonmoheck.com
Recommended in Employment
Practice Areas: Donnelly serves as lead counsel in both jury and bench trials in federal and state courts throughout the multi-state region, representing employers in federal discrimination class actions and individual and multi-plaintiff actions. He regularly counsels employers and senior management with respect to executive compensation issues as well as basic employment law issues. Donnelly is Chair of the firm's Employment Litigation Division.
Prof. Memberships: American Employment Law Council; Federal Practice Committee, Western District of Missouri; The Missouri Bar.
Personal: JD, St. Louis University (1973); BA, St. Louis University (1970).

DOWD Jr, Edward
Bryan Cave LLP, St Louis
314 259 2000
Recommended in Litigation

EISENBRANDT, James
Berkowitz Stanton Brandt Williams &
Shaw LLP, Kansas City 816 561 7007
Recommended in Litigation

ESSIG, Leonard
Lewis, Rice & Fingersh LC, St Louis
314 444 7600
Recommended in Corporate/M&A

EVANS, Craig
Shook, Hardy & Bacon LLP, Kansas City
816 474 6550
cevans@shb.com
Recommended in Corporate/M&A
Practice Areas: Practice focuses on mergers and acquisitions involving public and private companies, public and exempt offerings of securities, securities law compliance, technology driven joint ventures and strategic alliances and corporate governance matters, including takeover defense planning and implementation for public companies.
Prof. Memberships: Admitted to practice in Missouri and Texas.
Career: Joined Shook, Hardy & Bacon, 2002 (as Partner). Chair, Shook, Hardy & Bacon Business Law Division and Corporate Finance and Banking Section.
Publications: Co-author, Developing a Flexible and Reliable Crisis Management Plan, 'The Metropolitan Corporate Counsel' (October and November 2004). What You Need to Know About the Sarbanes-Oxley Act, 'The Metropolitan Corporate Counsel' (October 2002). The Uniform Commercial Code - Article 8 - Investment Securities, 'West Missouri Practice Transaction Guide' (2001).
Personal: JD, University of Kansas School of Law, 1985; BA, William Jewell College, 1982.

EVERSON, David
Stinson Morrison Hecker LLP,
Kansas City 816 842 8600
deverson@stinsonmoheck.com
Recommended in Litigation
Practice Areas: Everson handles a wide range of civil and criminal business litigation, including antitrust and intellectual property, in state and federal courts. He has lectured and appeared on panels across the country, having made presentations at the ABA Antitrust Meeting, the New England Conference on Antitrust and the Southeastern Criminal Defense Seminar.
Prof. Memberships: IOLTA, Board Member; Legal Aid of Western Missouri; The Missouri Bar; University of Michigan Board of Visitors.
Personal: JD, University of Michigan (1971); AB, University of Missouri (1966).

FENLEY, David A
Blackwell Sanders Peper Martin LLP,
Kansas City 816 983 8134
dfenley@blackwellsanders.com
Recommended in Real Estate
Practice Areas: Real estate.
Prof. Memberships: Admitted to practice in Missouri (1979), US District Court, District of Western Missouri (1979), and US Tax Court (1980). Member, American Bar Association, Sections on Real Property, Probate & Trust Law, and Taxation; American College of Real Estate Lawyers; Kansas City Metropolitan Bar Association; Lawyers Association of Kansas City; and the Missouri Bar.
Career: Joined firm, 1980; named Partner, 1985; named firm Chairman, 2000.
Personal: JD (with honors), Washburn University, 1979, assistant notes editor, 'Washburn Law Journal'; BBA (cum laude), Washburn University, 1976; Certified Public Accountant (Missouri), 1980.

FINUCANE, Brian J
Fisher & Phillips LLP, Kansas City
816 842 8770
bfinucane@laborlawyers.com
Recommended in Employment
Practice Areas: Brian Finucane is Managing Partner of the Kansas City regional office of Fisher & Phillips LLP, a national law firm practicing exclusively in labor and employment law representing management. He represents employers before state and federal courts and administrative agencies, including the Equal Employment Opportunity Commission, Department of Labor, and National Labor Relations Board. He served as Chairperson of the Missouri Bar Labor Law Committee, member of the Heartland Labor and Employment Law Institute, and contributing editor to The Developing Labor Law. Brian received BS and JD degrees from the University of Missouri-Columbia (Order of the Coif).

FISHER, Robert
Sonnenschein Nath & Rosenthal,
Kansas City 816 460 2400
Recommended in Corporate/M&A

FITZGERALD Jr, Robert E
Shughart Thomson & Kilroy PC,
Kansas City 816 421 3355
rfitzgerald@stklaw.com
*Recommended in Corporate/M&A,
Real Estate*

Practice Areas: Business law; taxation;
real estate; corporate transactions. Has
practiced law in Kansas City, Missouri,
for more than 31 years. Represents
clients in business transactions ranging
from corporate acquisitions to regulatory enforcement. Handles major business
acquisitions and sales with such divergent projects as real estate general partnerships, dealership purchases and sales,
construction business sales, statutory
reorganizations of Missouri political
subdivisions and real estate venture formations.
Prof. Memberships: The Missouri Bar
(President's Award for 'Outstanding
Contributions' to the Bar; Vice-Chair,
Corporation Committee.) American
Bar Association. Kansas City Metropoli-
tan Bar Association. Arbitrator for the
American Arbitration Association and
the National Association of Securities
Dealers. 'Chambers USA 2003-2004
America's Leading Business Lawyers.'
Has served extensively on securities and
corporate committees with the Missouri
Secretary of State's office.
Career: Joined Shughart Thomson &
Kilroy PC as a shareholder in 1995.
Member of the firm's finance commit-
tee.
Publications: 'Taxes in Your Practice' col-
umn, 'Journal of Missouri Bar', 1982-98.
Personal: Born Chicago, Illinois, Febru-
ary 22, 1949. St Louis University, JD
(1974). St Benedict's College, AB summa
cum laude (1971). Judicial Clerkship:
Honorable George G Gunn, Jr, Missouri
Court of Appeals, St Louis (1972-73).

FLANIGAN, Daniel
Polsinelli Shalton Welte Suelthaus
(PSWS), Kansas City 816 753 1000
Recommended in Real Estate

FRANTZE, David
Stinson Morrison Hecker LLP,
Kansas City 816 842 8600
dfrantze@stinsonmoheck.com
Recommended in Real Estate

Practice Areas: Land use and development, leasing, real estate lending. Chair
of the Real Estate Practice Division. Represents developers, property owners,
tenants, municipalities and non-profits.
Expertise in using development incentives such as tax increment financing
and tax abatement. Counsel to both
developers and municipalities in forming public/private partnerships.
Prof. Memberships: ABA, Real Property Section, Probate and Trust Law;
American College of Real Estate

Lawyers; The Missouri Bar, Property
Law Committee.
Personal: JD, University of Missouri-
Kansas City, with distinction, 1981; BA,
Avila University, magna cum laude,
1976. Adjunct professor at UMKC
School of Law, taught real estate finance
and development law.

FRAZEN, Laurence
Bryan Cave LLP, Kansas City
816 374 3200
Recommended in Litigation

FREILICH, Robert
Freilich, Leitner & Carlisle, Kansas City
816 561 4414
Recommended in Real Estate

FRETWELL, Norman
Spencer Fane Britt & Browne LLP,
Kansas City 816 474 8100
Recommended in Corporate/M&A

FRIZELL, Edward
Polsinelli Shalton Welte Suelthaus
(PSWS), Kansas City 816 753 1000
Recommended in Corporate/M&A

GERMAN, Charles
Rouse Hendricks German May PC,
Kansas City 816 471 7700
Recommended in Litigation

GIANOULAKIS, John
Kohn, Shands, Elbert, Gianoulakis &
Giljum,LLP, St Louis 314 241 3963
Recommended in Litigation

GILSON, Gary
Blackwell Sanders Peper Martin LLP,
Kansas City 816 983 8141
ggilson@blackwellsanders.com
Recommended in Corporate/M&A

Practice Areas: Mergers and acquisitions; securities; venture capital/private
equity financing and funds; commercial
transactions.
Prof. Memberships: Admitted to practice in Missouri (1981), Kansas (1985),
and Nebraska (1995). Member, American Bar Association; the Association for
Corporate Growth; Kansas Bar Association; the Missouri Bar; National Association of Small Business Investment
Companies; and Nebraska State Bar
Association.
Career: Joined firm as Partner, 1993;
founding and Managing Partner, Blackwell Sanders Omaha office, 1995-97.
Publications: Author, Chapter 5, General Corporate Actions and Operations,
'Missouri Bar Association Business
Organizations Deskbook' (1998).
Personal: JD, University of Nebraska at
Lincoln, 1981; BS, University of Nebras-
ka at Lincoln, 1978.

GODINER, Clifford A
Thompson Coburn LLP, St Louis
314 552 6433
cgodiner@thompsoncoburn.com
Recommended in Employment

Practice Areas: Represents employers
in all facets of labor and employment
law, including employment discrimina-

tion, wrongful discharge, and non-compete litigation. He has handled and tried
cases in federal and state courts. Experience in union-managment relations,
especially under the Railway Labor Act.
Prof. Memberships: Admitted in Missouri. Member of Bar of Seventh,
Eighth, Tenth, and DC Circuit Courts of
Appeals.
Career: Joined Thompson Coburn LLP
in 1997 (as a Partner). Adjunct professor
at Saint Louis University School of Law,
Center for Employment Law since 1992.
Personal: JD, magna cum laude, University of Michigan Law School (1986);
BA, Wesleyan University (1983).

GOLDMAN, Joel
Husch & Eppenberger, LLC,
Kansas City 816 421 4800
Recommended in Litigation

GRANDA, John A
Stinson Morrison Hecker LLP,
Kansas City 816 842 8600
jgranda@stinsonmoheck.com
Recommended in Corporate/M&A

Practice Areas: Chairman of Corporate Finance Division and Co-Chairman
of Corporate Accountability Division.
Serves as outside general counsel to a
wide range of publicly- and privately-
held businesses, including many of
Kansas City's largest companies. Extensive experience in large and complex
transactions (with size of deals in excess
of $5 billion), including public and pri-
vate offerings of debt and equity securities, mergers, acquisitions, tender offers,
proxy contests, takeover defense, spin-
offs, recapitalizations, going private,
venture capital, joint ventures, strategic
alliances, SEC reporting, compliance
programs and corporate governance.
Prof. Memberships: American Bar
Association, The Missouri Bar, Kansas
City Metropolitan Bar Association,
American Society of Corporate Secretaries, Associate for Corporate Growth,
and International Trade Club.
Career: Former Counsel to SEC Commissioner and Special Counsel in SEC's
Division of Corporation Finance over a
five-year period.
Publications: Contributing author,
'Missouri Methods of Practice: Transaction Guide.' Numerous papers for pro-
grams on securities, mergers and acquisitions and governance sponsored by:
Practicing Law Institute; Iowa, Kansas
and Missouri Bar Associations; KPMG
Audit Committee Roundtable; and several law schools, including Universities
of Iowa, Kansas and Missouri.
Personal: LLM, Taxation, Georgetown
University (1979); JD, University of
Iowa, with distinction (1975); Master's
(1972) and Bachelor's (1971) in Business Administration, University of Iowa.

GRIFFIN, James
Blackwell Sanders Peper Martin LLP,
Kansas City 816 983 8199
jgriffin@blackwellsanders.com
Recommended in Litigation

Practice Areas: Business and commercial litigation; products liability.
Prof. Memberships: Admitted to practice in Kansas (1985) and Missouri
(1983). Fellow, American College of Trial
Lawyers. Member, Defense Research
Institute and Kansas Bar Association.
Career: Joined firm, 1983; named Partner, 1990; Chair, Litigation Department,
2003.
Publications: Author, An Analysis of the
Admissibility of Expert Opinion Testimony in Kansas State Courts After Kuhn
v Sandoz Pharmaceuticals, 'Journal of
the Kansas Bar Association' (February
2002); and Class Action Trials Commonly Deprive Defendants of Due
Process, 'Washington Legal Foundation'
(November 2001).
Personal: JD, University of Virginia,
1983; BS (cum laude), Kansas State University, 1980.

HAINES, Lisa
Polsinelli Shalton Welte Suelthaus
(PSWS), Kansas City 816 753 1000
Recommended in Real Estate

HEETER, James
Sonnenschein Nath & Rosenthal,
Kansas City 816 460 2452
jheeter@sonnenschein.com
Recommended in Corporate/M&A

Practice Areas: 30 years of corporate
and healthcare experience. Experience
in M&A, debt financings and start-ups.
Works with executives, directors and
shareholders as general counsel to
diverse businesses, including a major
local hospital, and special counsel to
other Midwest hospitals. Represents
some of the area's fastest-growing businesses; physician groups; state and local
governments in 'privatizing' healthcare
facilities and services.
Prof. Memberships: Member, ABA,
Missouri Bar, Kansas City Metropolitan
Bar Association, American Academy of
Healthcare Attorneys, National Health
Lawyers Association, Missouri and
Kansas City societies of hospital attorneys.
Personal: Harvard Law School, JD cum
laude. University of Missouri-Columbia,
AB with honors.

HOBBS, James
Wyrsch Hobbs & Mirakian PC,
Kansas City 816 221 0080
Recommended in Litigation

HOFFMAN, Robert
Bryan Cave LLP, Kansas City
816 374 3200
Recommended in Litigation

HUNT, Jeffrey
Gallop, Johnson & Neuman LC,
St Louis 314 615 6000
Recommended in Litigation

HUNTER, Jerry
Bryan Cave LLP, St Louis
314 259 2000
Recommended in Employment

HUNTER, Robert
Stinson Morrison Hecker LLP,
Kansas City 816 842 8600
rhunter@stinsonmoheck.com
Recommended in Corporate/M&A
Practice Areas: Chairman of the firm's
General Business Division. Serves as
outside general counsel for several
Kansas City-based companies and provides assistance on real estate transactions and commercial leasing, commercial finance, acquisitions and sales, and
general corporate matters. Regularly represents entrepreneurs and venture capital
investors in structuring venture capital
investments. Counsels closely-held businesses on business and transaction matters, including contracts, real estate leasing, acquisitions and divestitures.
Prof. Memberships: ABA, Corporate
Law Committee; Kansas Bar Association, Corporate Law Committee; Missouri Bar.
Career: Centurions Leadership Training
Program (2000); Up and Comers Award
(2000).
Personal: JD, Kansas University, 1989;
BS, Kansas University, 1986.

JANOWITZ, Robert
Constangy, Brooks & Smith, LLC,
Kansas City 816 472 6400
Recommended in Employment

JAUDES, Richard E
Thompson Coburn LLP, St Louis
314 552 6431
rjaudes@thompsoncoburn.com
Recommended in Employment
Practice Areas: Chairman of firm's
Labor and Employment Group. Practice
focuses on employment litigation and
traditional labor relations. National
experience in federal employment litiga-
tion, negotiating collective bargaining
agreements and union avoidance.
Prof. Memberships: Admitted to prac-
tice in Missouri.
Career: Joined and formed Labor and
Employment Department at Peper,
Martin, Jensen, Maichel and Hetlage.
Joined Thompson Coburn LLP in 1997
as Partner.
Personal: JD (with honors) Saint Louis
University Law School, 1968; BS (with
honors) Saint Louis University, 1965.

JONES, Steve
Armstrong Teasdale LLP, St Louis
314 621 5070
Recommended in Corporate/M&A

KAPLAN, Harvey
Shook, Hardy & Bacon LLP, Kansas City
816 474 6550
hkaplan@shb.com
Recommended in Litigation
Practice Areas: Is well known for
defending pharmaceutical and medical
device companies in products liability

litigation and has played a prominent
role in national litigation involving oral
contraceptives; hip and knee implants;
diethylstilbestrol (DES); DTP, hepatitis,
polio and flu vaccines; IUDs; ophthalmic products; migraine drugs; diet
drugs; analgesics and anti-rheumatic;
diabetic drugs; diet drugs; anti-rejection
drugs; and antihistamines.
Prof. Memberships: Admitted to prac-
tice before the Supreme Court of the
United States; the United States Court of
Appeals for the Fifth, Sixth, Eighth,
Ninth and Tenth Circuits; the United
States Tax Court; the Missouri Supreme
Court; and the federal courts of Mis-
souri, Kansas, Arizona and Nebraska.
Fellow of International Academy of Trial
Lawyers (board member), International
Society of Barristers and American Bar
Foundation. Member of International
Association of Defense Counsel
(IADC).
Career: Joined Shook, Hardy & Bacon,
1970; became Partner, 1974. Chair,
Shook, Hardy & Bacon Pharmaceutical
and Medical Device Litigation Division.
Member, Shook, Hardy & Bacon Execu-
tive Committee.
Publications: United States Q&A Chap-
ter, Global Counsel: 'Life Sciences Indus-
try Report 2004/05'; Avoiding/Minimiz-
ing the Risk of Punitive Damages, 'Glob-
al Legal Group: The International Comparative Legal Guide to: Product Liability 2004'; USA Chapter 30 in 'Global
Legal Group: The International Comparative Legal Guide to: Product Liability 2004'.
Personal: JD, University of Missouri-
Columbia School of Law, 1968; BS,
(Pharm.) University of Michigan, 1965.

KEIM, Robert
Kutak Rock LLP, Kansas City
816 960 0090
Recommended in Corporate/M&A

KENNEDY, Donald
Greensfelder, Hemker & Gale, P.C.,
St Louis 314 241 9090
Recommended in Real Estate

KING, Richard A
King Hershey, A Professional Corpora-
tion, Kansas City 816 842 3636
rking@kinghershey.com
Recommended in Real Estate
Practice Areas: Real estate develop-
ment, public/private finance, state and
local taxation.
Prof. Memberships: American Bar
Association, National Association of
Bond Lawyers, International Association
of Gaming Attorneys, Missouri Bar
Assocation, Kansas City Bar Association,
Eastern Jackson County Bar Associatin.
Career: Chairman and CEO, King Her-
shey, Kansas City, Missouri, 1988-date;
Partner, Smith Gill Fisher and Butts,
Kansas City, Missouri 1985-87; Director
of Revenue, State of Missouri 1982-85;
Executive Assistant to the Governor of

Missouri 1981-82; Partner, Cochran,
Kramer, Kapke, Willerth and King, Independence, Missouri, 1979-80; Partner,
Constance Slayton Stewart & King,
Independence, Missouri 1973-79.
Personal: Mayor, Independence, Missouri, 1974-78; President, Missouri Economic Development Financing Association, 1999-2001.

KOHN, Alan
Kohn, Shands, Elbert, Gianoulakis &
Giljum,LLP, St Louis 314 241 3963
Recommended in Litigation

KOKORUDA, Thomas G
Shughart Thomson & Kilroy PC,
Kansas City 816 374 0513
tkokoruda@stklaw.com
Recommended in Litigation
Practice Areas: Healthcare; hospital
law; litigation. Focuses his trial practice
primarily on commercial healthcare liti-
gation, physician malpractice and med-
ical staff privilege litigation.
Prof. Memberships: Admitted to Mis-
souri Bar (1972). Member Kansas City
Metropolitan Bar Association (Executive
Committee, 1986-94; President, 1993);
National Health Lawyer Association;
Missouri Society of Hospital Attorneys;
American College of Legal Medicine.
Fellow, American College of Trial
Lawyers. Phi Delta Phi. Member, Board
of Governors, University of Kansas
School of Law (1991-93); Missouri
Supreme Court Civil Jury Study Com-
mittee (2000-01). Listed in healthcare
section of leading legal publication.
Career: Joined Shughart Thomson &
Kilroy, 1972; shareholder, 1976. Execu-
tive Committee (Executive Vice Presi-
dent.) Chair, Litigation Department and
Healthcare Litigation Group; Vice-
Chair, Hospital Law Group.
Publications: Author: 'Pleadings' in
Missouri Trial Practice Essays, 57
UMKC Law Review 736, Summer, 1989.
Personal: Born Kansas City, Kansas,
January 14, 1947. University of Kansas,
JD (1972). University of Kansas, BS
(1968).

LAUSE, Michael F
Thompson Coburn LLP, St Louis
314 552 6069
mlause@thompsoncoburn.com
Recommended in Corporate/M&A
Practice Areas: Chairman of firm's
Corporate Department. Legal practice is
focused in areas of finance and corporate law. He has special concentrations
in areas of public finance and in the representation of governmental and nonprofit entities and of financial institutions interacting with such entities.
Career: Thompson Coburn LLP (1973-
present). He serves as outside general
counsel to various entities.

LENTS, Donald
Bryan Cave LLP, St Louis
314 259 2000
Recommended in Corporate/M&A

LITZ, Thomas A
Thompson Coburn LLP, St Louis
314 552 6072
tlitz@thompsoncoburn.com
Recommended in Corporate/M&A
Practice Areas: Co-Chairman of firm's
Corporate and Securities Group; member of firm's Management and Executive
Committees. Concentrates practice in
corporate and securities law, and mergers and acquisitions. Over 20 years of
experience representing issuers and
underwriters in public and private offerings of securities, and public and privately held companies in mergers, acquisitions and securities law compliance.
Experience representing private equity
funds in syndication and portfolio
investments and dispositions.
Prof. Memberships: Admitted to practice in Missouri and Illinois.
Career: Thompson Coburn LLP (1982-
present).
Personal: JD, cum laude, Georgetown
University Law Center (1982); BSBA
Finance, magna cum laude, Georgetown
Univeristy (1979).

MARCH, Aaron
White Goss Bowers March Schulte &
Weisenfels, A Professional Corporation,
Kansas City 816 753 9200
Recommended in Real Estate

MARTUCCI, William
Shook, Hardy & Bacon LLP, Kansas City
816 474 6550
wmartucci@shb.com
Recommended in Employment
Practice Areas: Practice focuses on
complex class action litigation, employment discrimination, wage and hour litigation, ERISA litigation and covenants
not to compete. Has successfully defended various employment lawsuits and
written and lectured extensively on
employment law issues throughout the
country. Practices exclusively on behalf
of management in connection with
national employment litigation and policy matters.
Prof. Memberships: Member of Eighth
Circuit Model Federal Civil Jury
Instructions Subcommittee and National Human Resources Policy Board of
Commerce Clearing House (CCH).
Listed in 'The Best Lawyers in America.'
Career: Joined Shook, Hardy & Bacon,
2000 (as partner). Practice Leader,
Shook, Hardy & Bacon National
Employment Litigation and Policy
Group.
Personal: Executive Education, Harvard
Business School, 1997; LLM, George-
town University Law Center, 1981; JD,
with honors, Leflar Law Center, Univer-
sity of Arkansas, 1977; AB, magna cum
laude, Rutgers College, 1974.

MARVIN, John
Sonnenschein Nath & Rosenthal,
Kansas City 816 460 2513
jmarvin@sonnenschein.com
Recommended in Corporate/M&A

Practice Areas: Has 40+ years of experience, primarily in securities and general corporate law, encompassing IPOs, after-market trading and control compliance, proxy solicitation, takeover defense and corporate transactions. Counsels public company boards and management governance.

Prof. Memberships: Law professor at two law schools; State Board of Law Examiners; Director, Chamber of Commerce of Greater Kansas City; Member, several bar associations.

Personal: University of Missouri at Kansas City, BBA, JD, with distinction, Omicron Delta Kappa, Law Review Editor, National Moot Court Team; New York University, LLM, honors.

MASSEY, Raymond L
Thompson Coburn LLP, St Louis
314 552 6075
rmassey@thompsoncoburn.com
Recommended in Litigation
Practice Areas: Chairman of firm's Litigation Department and Admiralty Group. Concentrates practice in litigation affecting heavy industry, including vessels, marine contracts and serious personal injury as well as litigation involving complex tort, environmental and contract issues. Taken significant jury and non-jury trials to verdict in state and federal courts and is often selected by the assured as counsel where a loss is subject to insurance in complex litigation.

Prof. Memberships: Admitted to practice in Missouri, Illinois and Texas. Proctor Member and past Director of Maritime Law Association of the United States.

MCCARTHY, Thomas
McMahon Berger Hanna Linihan Cody & McCarthy, A Professional Corporation, St Louis 314 567 7350
Recommended in Employment

MCNAMARA, Rosalee M
Lathrop & Gage L.C., Kansas City
816 460 5604
rmcnamara@lathropgage.com
Recommended in Employment
Practice Areas: Employment litigation, labor law, general employment counseling.
Career: McNamara represents clients in employment matters throughout the US. She was selected as 'Leading Lawyer' by Chambers USA, 2004-05 and has received Martindale Hubbell's highest rating, the 'AV Rating'. She has defended complaints of alleged employment discrimination and has handled court and jury trials in federal and state court. Her litigation and counseling experience includes sexual harassment, ADA, race, age, sex, national origin, and religious discrimination, FMLA and related issues, wage and hour laws, hiring and reference procedures, employee discipline and termination, and employee drug/alcohol testing policies and procedures.

MCNEARNEY, John
Blackwell Sanders Peper Martin LLP,
St Louis 314 345 6415
jmcnearney@blackwellsanders.com
Recommended in Real Estate
Practice Areas: Real estate; creditors' rights and bankruptcy; financial institutions.
Prof. Memberships: Admitted to practice in Illinois (1984) and Missouri (1983). Member, American Agricultural Law Association; American Bankruptcy Institute; American Bar Association; Bar Association of Metropolitan St. Louis; CORENET Global; Illinois State Bar Association; Life Skills Foundation; and the Missouri Bar.
Career: Named Partner, 1993; Chair, Real Estate Department.
Publications: Author, 'Anatomy of a Mortgage: A Primer on Real Estate Finance', 'American Bar Association' (2000); and Real Estate Financing, Chapter 9 of 'Missouri Real Estate Practice', Fourth Edition (2000).
Personal: JD, Northwestern University, 1983; BA, University of Virginia, 1979.

MEDVED, Joseph W
Lathrop & Gage L.C., Kansas City
816 460 5824
jmedved@lathropgage.com
Recommended in Corporate/M&A
Practice Areas: Corporate and general business; corporate finance; mergers and acquisitions; securities.
Career: Medved represents clients in transactions in mergers and acquisitions and corporate finance, including asset purchases and sales, stock purchases and sales, mergers, joint ventures, tender offers, bank financings, public and private stock offerings, and public and private debt offerings. His transactions range from the $200 million range to the billion dollar range. He is engaged in a broad corporate and business practice, representing public and private companies. Medved is a member of the firm's Executive Committee and Chairman of the Greater Kansas City Foreign Trade Zone.

MILLER, Charles F
Lewis, Rice & Fingersh, L.C.,
Kansas City 816 472 2512
cfmiller@lrf-kc.com
Recommended in Real Estate
Practice Areas: Real estate law, including acquisition, sales, financing, leasing, construction, development, redevelopment, incentives, zoning, other governmental approvals and joint ventures.
Prof. Memberships: American College of Real Estate Lawyers; Missouri Economic Development Finance Association; NAIOP Association of Commercial Real Estate, local Board of Directors; Missouri Bar Association, Property Law Committee; Kansas City Metropolitan Bar Association, Real Estate Law Committee (Past Chairman); Board of Editors (past), Shopping Center Legal

Update; International Council of Shopping Centers; Greater Kansas City Chamber of Commerce, Kansas City, Missouri Committee; Downtown Council of Kansas City (Executive Committee Member) and other civic and professional organizations.
Career: Joined Brown, Koralchik & Fingersh 1979 (predecessor to Lewis, Rice & Fingersh, L.C.); Chairman of Real Estate Department; Member of Executive Committee; past Adjunct Professor of law, UMKC Law School; regular speaker at legal and real estate industry events and seminars, including Using Development Incentives (2003), Are Easements Easy (2003), Overview of Economic Development Financing Tools in Missouri (Missouri Economic Development Finance Association 2003), and Case Study of Missouri and Kansas Development Incentives (Missouri Economic Development Finance Association 2003).
Publications: Missouri Provides Condemnation Powers and Real Estate Tax Abatement for Developers, 'Shopping Center Legal Update', Summer, 1986. Landlord's Duty to Relet When a Tenant Abandons Leased Property, 43 'Missouri Law Review' 359. Information for the Attorney Representing a Landowner in an Oil and Gas Lease Transaction, 'Journal of The Missouri Bar', Vol. 38, No. 5.
Personal: Born September 25, 1953. JD University of Missouri Law School, 1979, Law Review Board of Editors; AB Political Science, University of Missouri, 1976 (summa cum laude), Phi Beta Kappa.

MINOGUE, Thomas J
Thompson Coburn LLP, St Louis
314 552 6080
tminogue@thompsoncoburn.com
Recommended in Corporate/M&A
Practice Areas: Chairman of Thompson Coburn LLP. Legal practice is principally concentrated in the areas of corporate law and finance. Over 25 years of experience in mergers and acquisitions, leveraged buyouts, joint ventures, shareholder relations and redemptions, commercial finance (representing borrowers and lenders), private placements, secured and unsecured lending and lease financing. Successfully concluded multiple transactions involving dollar amounts in excess of $1 billion.
Prof. Memberships: Admitted to practice in Missouri and Illinois.
Career: Thompson Coburn LLP (1979-present); Acting General Counsel, Mercantile Bancorporation (1990).
Personal: JD, cum laude, Harvard Law School (1979); BA Economics, summa cum laude, UM-St. Louis (1976).

MONROE, C Robert
Stinson Morrison Hecker LLP,
Kansas City 816 842 8600
bmonroe@stinsonmoheck.com
Recommended in Corporate/M&A

Practice Areas: Chairman of the firm's Financial Services Division. Counsel to over 100 financial institutions and financial holding companies. Has significant experience in company mergers, bank and bank holding company formations, branch acquisitions, converting to S-Corporations, regulatory orders and bank examination issues.
Prof. Memberships: ABA, Banking Law Committee; Kansas Bar Association; Missouri Bar; Missouri Bankers Association; Kansas Bankers Association; Illinois Bankers Association; New York Bankers Association.
Career: Listed in 'Best Lawyers in America.'
Publications: Frequent lecturer and author on banking issues.
Personal: JD, St. Louis University School of Law, cum laude, 1975; BA, Westminster College, 1968.

MUELLER, Kathleen T
Blackwell Sanders Peper Martin LLP,
St Louis 314 345 6491
kmueller@blackwellsanders.com
Recommended in Real Estate
Practice Areas: Real estate, finance and lending, closely held businesses.
Prof. Memberships: American Bar Association, Bar Association of Metropolitan St. Louis, International Association of Attorneys and Executives in Corporate Real Estate (AECRE), The Missouri Bar, St. Louis Leadership Program.
Career: Joined firm as associate, 1980; named Partner, 1987.
Personal: JD, Washington University 1980, Order of the Coif. Washington University Law Quarterly; BA, Maryville University, summa cum laude, 1976.

MURRAY, George
Bryan Cave LLP, Kansas City
816 374 3200
Recommended in Real Estate

NESTER, Daniel
Bryan Cave LLP, St Louis
314 259 2000
Recommended in Real Estate

NEWBOLD, J William
Thompson Coburn LLP, St Louis
314 552 6088
wnewbold@thompsoncoburn.com
Recommended in Litigation
Practice Areas: For over 37 years, he has tried complex cases for major companies before state and federal courts in the US. He is one of the lead counsel in United States of America v. Philip Morris USA Inc., f/k/a Philip Morris Inc., et al., that began on September 21, 2004.
Prof. Memberships: Admitted to practice in Missouri, Illinois and various federal and appellate courts. Member, American College of Trial Lawyers and International Society of Barristers.
Career: Thompson Coburn LLP (1979-present).
Personal: JD, University of Missouri-Columbia School of Law, 1967.

NIXON, Richard
Stinson Morrison Hecker LLP,
Kansas City 816 842 8600
dnixon@stinsonmoheck.com
Recommended in Corporate/M&A
Practice Areas: Serves clients in general
business matters, including organizational and financing matters, day-to-day
operational/legal issues, acquisitions and
selling the business. Represents private
and publicly held companies in acquisitions, dispositions, debt and equity
financing, and joint ventures. Has
worked extensively with not-for-profit
and cooperative organizations.
Prof. Memberships: ABA, Business Law
Committee; Missouri Bar, Business Law
Committee.
Career: Has served as general counsel to
several of the firm's mid-sized clients.
Listed in 'Best Lawyers in America' since
1987; held several leadership roles with
the firm.
Personal: JD, University of Missouri,
1969; MA, Florida State University,
1966; AB, William Jewell College, 1964.

NOUSS, James
Bryan Cave LLP, St Louis
314 259 2000
Recommended in Corporate/M&A

O'CONNELL, Mary
Husch & Eppenberger, LLC,
Kansas City 816 421 4800
Recommended in Corporate/M&A

O'DEAR, Craig
Bryan Cave LLP, Kansas City
816 374 3200
Recommended in Litigation

OLIVER, David
Berkowitz Stanton Brandt Williams &
Shaw LLP, Kansas City 816 561 7007
Recommended in Litigation

ORTBALS, Mary
Greensfelder, Hemker & Gale, P.C.,
St Louis 314 241 9090
Recommended in Employment

PHILLIPS, John R
Blackwell Sanders Peper Martin LLP,
Kansas City 816 983 8119
jphillips@blackwellsanders.com
Recommended in Employment
Practice Areas: Labor and employ-
ment; alternative dispute resolution.
Prof. Memberships: Admitted to prac-
tice in Missouri (1971) and US Supreme
Court (1976). Fellow, American College
of Trial Lawyers. Member, American Bar
Association; Kansas City Metropolitan
Bar Association; Lawyers Association of
Kansas City; the Missouri Bar.
Career: Joined firm, 1971; named Part-
ner, 1976.
Publications: Author, Mediation from
the Perspective of Defense Counsel,
'Journal of the Kansas Trial Lawyers
Association' (2003); and Mediation as
One Step in Adversarial Litigation, 'Jour-
nal of Dispute Resolution' (2002).
Personal: JD (cum laude), University of

Missouri at Columbia, 1971; BS (cum
laude), University of Missouri at
Columbia, 1968.

POLSINELLI, James
Polsinelli Shalton Welte Suelthaus
(PSWS), Kansas City 816 753 1000
Recommended in Corporate/M&A

PRICE, James
Spencer Fane Britt & Browne LLP,
Kansas City 816 474 8100
Recommended in Litigation

PRUELLAGE, John
Lewis, Rice & Fingersh LC, St Louis
314 444 7600
Recommended in Corporate/M&A

REBEIN, Joseph
Shook, Hardy & Bacon LLP, Kansas City
816 474 6550
jrebein@shb.com
Recommended in Litigation
Practice Areas: Specializes in complex
litigation. Serves as lead trial counsel in
complex cases, including antitrust and
securities class actions. Has tried both
federal and state trials, NASD arbitrations, general civil arbitrations, administrative proceedings before state and federal regulatory bodies and CFTC
enforcement actions.
Prof. Memberships: Admitted to practice in Missouri and before the US
Court of Appeals for the Sixth, Eighth
and Tenth Circuits; and the US District
Court for the Western District of Missouri, the District of Kansas, the Eastern
and Western Districts of Wisconsin, the
Southern and Northern Districts of Mississippi, the Northern District of Illinois,
the District of Nebraska and the District
of Connecticut. Member of the Defense
Research Institute and the American Bar
Associations's Antitrust Section and
Securities Litigation Section.
Career: Joined Shook, Hardy & Bacon,
1985; became Partner, 1992. Chairman,
Shook, Hardy & Bacon General Litiga-
tion Division. Firm's member of the
CPR Institute for Dispute Resolution.
Publications: Co-author, Derail the
Runaway Jury by Promoting Jury Ser-
vice within Corporate America:
Employers Should Support Jury Service
- Here Is How, 'The Metropolitan Cor-
porate Counsel' (November 2003).
Personal: JD, University of Kansas
School of Law, 1985; BS, University of
Kansas, 1982.

RESCHLY, Jason
Blackwell Sanders Peper Martin LLP,
Kansas City 816 983 8170
jreschly@blackwellsanders.com
Recommended in Corporate/M&A
Practice Areas: Taxation; agribusiness;
energy and public utility.
Prof. Memberships: Admitted to prac-
tice in Missouri (1981). Member of
American Bar Association and the Mis-
souri Bar.
Career: Joined firm as Partner, 2002.
Certified Public Accountant (Missouri).

Personal: JD (cum laude), University of
Missouri at Columbia, 1981, Order of
the Coif; BS (magna cum laude), University of Colorado, 1977.

RIFFEL, Jerome
Lathrop & Gage L.C., Kansas City
816 460 5712
jriffel@lathropgage.com
Recommended in Real Estate
Practice Areas: Real estate, public law,
business litigation, government relations.
Career: Riffel is one of the most experienced real estate attorneys in the region.
He serves on organizations such as the
Executive Committee of the Downtown
Council and is former City Councilman
for Kansas City, Mo. Riffel handles Tax
Increment Financing Development,
urban redevelopment, land clearance,
condemnation, special business districts,
economic development incentives, and
all aspects of land use planning and
development. He was honored as 'Best
of the Bar', Kansas City Business Journal,
2003-04; 'Leading Lawyer' by Chambers
USA 2004 and 2005; and has a Martindale Hubbell AV Rating.

ROWE, Jack D
Lathrop & Gage L.C., Kansas City
816 460 5607
jrowe@lathropgage.com
Recommended in Employment
Practice Areas: Employment and labor
relations.
Career: Rowe represents management
and the business sector in equal employment opportunity, personnel relations
and traditional labor matters, including
federal, state and local agency investigations and hearings, court actions and
day-to-day counseling. His practice
involves consultation concerning and
litigation defense of complex employment, personnel and labor relations
issues, including union elections, negotiations and arbitrations, reductions in
force, discipline and discharge, pay practices, affirmative action, ERISA, OSHA,
government complaints, compliance
reviews. Honors include 'Leading
Lawyer' by Chambers USA, 2004-05;
Best Lawyers in America, 2005-06, 2003-
04; 'Best of the Bar', The Kansas City
Business Journal, 2003-04.

SAMPSON, William
Shook, Hardy & Bacon LLP, Kansas City
816 559 2482
wsampson@shb.com
Recommended in Litigation
Practice Areas: Complex litigation,
antitrust and business torts. Has tried
more than 80 jury cases in federal, state
and military courts and tribunals and
has been active nationally and internationally in the defense of civil litigation.
Listed in 'The Best Lawyers in America.'
Prof. Memberships: Admitted to practice in Kansas and before the US Court
of Appeals for the Eighth and Tenth Circuits. Member Association of Defense

Trial Attorneys and Fellow of American
Bar Foundation. Appointments: Presi-
dent, Defense Research Institute.
Career: Joined Shook, Hardy & Bacon,
1987; became Partner, 1989. Has an
extensive teaching background.
Publications: Principal Author, 'Kansas
Trial Handbook' (1997); Excellence at
DRI, 'For The Defense' (November
2003); Shively's Got a Brand New Firm,
'For The Defense' (March 2003).
Personal: JD, University of Kansas
School of Law, 1971; BA (with honors in
history), University of Kansas, 1968.

SEABAUGH, William
Bryan Cave LLP, St Louis
314 259 2000
Recommended in Corporate/M&A

SHALTON, Lonnie
Polsinelli Shalton Welte Suelthaus
(PSWS), Kansas City 816 753 1000
Recommended in Real Estate

SHORT, Barry
Lewis, Rice & Fingersh LC, St Louis
314 444 7600
Recommended in Litigation

SHTEAMER, Michael B
Shughart Thomson & Kilroy PC, Kansas
City 816 374 0586
mshteamer@stklaw.com
Recommended in Real Estate
Practice Areas: Real estate; banking;
corporate law; business law. Has practiced law in Kansas City, Missouri for
more than 28 years. Represents a diverse
clientele ranging from entrepreneurs,
developers, syndicators, financial institutions, and insurance companies. Expertise encompasses negotiating, documenting, and closing commercial real
estate acquisitions, dispositions, workouts, foreclosure, leases, secured private
and public financing, credit facilities,
environmental, zoning and construction.
Prof. Memberships: The Missouri Bar;
Kansas City Metropolitan Bar Association.
Career: Joined Shughart Thomson &
Kilroy PC as a shareholder in 1995.
Personal: Born Kansas City, Missouri
July 7, 1951. Tulane University, JD, 1973;
BA, 1976.

SPARKS, Stephen
Bryan Cave LLP, Kansas City
816 374 3200
Recommended in Real Estate

STAHL, Thomas
Armstrong Teasdale LLP, Kansas City
816 221 3420
Recommended in Corporate/M&A

STANTON, Roger
Berkowitz Stanton Brandt Williams &
Shaw LLP, Kansas City
816 561 7007
Recommended in Litigation

STEPLETON, James
Husch & Eppenberger, LLC, St Louis
314 421 4800
Recommended in Corporate/M&A

TOMASO, Robert
Blackwell Sanders Peper Martin LLP,
St Louis 314 345 6433
rtomaso@blackwellsanders.com
Recommended in Employment
Practice Areas: Labor and employment; closely held businesses; education.
Prof. Memberships: Admitted to practice in Missouri (1989) and US Supreme Court. Member of American Bar Association and Bar Association of Metropolitan St Louis.
Career: Named as Partner, 1997; Member, Advisory Board Committee, 2000-03; Managing Partner of St Louis office, 2003-present.
Personal: JD, University of Virginia, 1989; BA (summa cum laude), Washington & Lee University, 1985.

TRIPP, David
Stinson Morrison Hecker LLP,
Kansas City 816 842 8600
dtripp@stinsonmoheck.com
Recommended in Litigation
Practice Areas: Tripp is Chair of the firm's Environmental Division and has assisted clients in environmental matters including Superfund liability issues and enforcement and permit actions involving air pollution, water pollution, toxic substances, and chemical regulation under federal, state and local laws. His experience and knowledge have been applied to issues in both administrative and judicial tribunals. Prior to joining the firm, Dave was Regional Counsel, US EPA, Region VII, where he worked for 16 years in the Enforcement Division and Office of Regional Counsel.
Personal: LLM, University of Missouri-Kansas City (1974); JD and BA, Washburn University (1971)(1968).

VAN DYKE, Thomas
Bryan Cave LLP, Kansas City
816 374 3200
Recommended in Corporate/M&A

VERING III, John
Armstrong Teasdale LLP, Kansas City
816 221 3420
Recommended in Employment

VIRTEL, James
Armstrong Teasdale LLP, St Louis
314 621 5070
Recommended in Litigation

VOIGTS, Gene
Shook, Hardy & Bacon LLP, Kansas City
816 474 6550
gvoigts@shb.com
Recommended in Litigation
Practice Areas: Products liability litigation and business litigation. Has appeared in various civil (products liability, professional liability and commercial litigation) and criminal cases in state and federal courts. Has also argued cases at all levels of the state and federal appellate systems, including the US Supreme Court.
Prof. Memberships: Admitted to practice in Missouri and before the US

Court of Appeals for the Fifth and Eighth Circuits and the US Supreme Court. Member of American Bar Association, The Missouri Bar, Kansas City Metropolitan Bar Association, The Lawyers Association of Kansas City and Missouri Organization of Defense Lawyers. Appointment: Member, Advisory Group appointed by the US District Court for the Western District of Missouri under the Civil Justice Reform Act of 1990.
Career: Joined Shook, Hardy & Bacon, 1973; became Partner, 1975. Firm's General Counsel and member of Executive Committee.
Personal: LLB, University of Missouri-Kansas City School of Law, 1964; BA, William Jewell College, 1961.

WALSH, Thomas
Bryan Cave LLP, St Louis
314 259 2000
Recommended in Litigation

WARD, R Lawrence
Shughart Thomson & Kilroy PC,
Kansas City 816 421 3355
lward@stklaw.com
Recommended in Litigation
Practice Areas: Trial practice; commercial litigation; securities; class actions; antitrust. Has spent over 35 years trying cases and arguing appeals in both state and federal courts around the country. Substantive areas of trial and appellate experience include antitrust, business tort and commercial claims, fraud, securities, franchise litigation, fiduciary duty claims, lender liability, shareholder derivative cases, class actions, professional negligence, intellectual property, environmental law, employment law, product liability and personal injury. Client representation includes accounting and law firms, the trucking industry, cable television, the banking industry, national computer companies, pharmaceutical drug manufacturers, utilities and various other manufacturers.
Prof. Memberships: Admitted to Missouri Bar (1961); US Supreme Court. Fellow: American College of Trial Lawyers; Kansas City Metropolitan Bar Association (President, 1983) and American Bar Association (State Delegate, 1993-98; American Bar Foundation); The Missouri Bar (Lon O. Hocker Memorial Trial Lawyer Award); Trustee, Missouri Bar Foundation (Missouri Bar Foundation Purcell Professionalism Award, 1997). Phi Alpha Delta. Listed in business litigation, personal injury litigation, and antitrust law sections of leading legal publication. 'Chambers USA 2003-2004 America's Leading Business Lawyers.'
Career: Joined Shughart Thomson & Kilroy PC (1961); shareholder (1963). Executive Committee (Firm Chairman); Chair Business Litigation Group.
Personal: Born Kansas City, Kansas, May 19, 1936. University of Missouri at

Kansas City, JD (1961). University of Missouri at Kansas City, BBA (1959). Named Practitioner of the Year (1996) Law Alumni, University of Missouri at Kansas City. President, Law Foundation of the University of Missouri at Kansas City (1984-86).

WELSH, Russell
Polsinelli Shalton Welte Suelthaus
(PSWS), St Louis 314 231 1950
Recommended in Litigation

WERTS, Dale A
Lathrop & Gage L.C., Kansas City
816 460 5828
dwerts@lathropgage.com
Recommended in Corporate/M&A
Practice Areas: Corporate and general business.
Career: Werts specializes in corporate and general business, corporate finance, mergers and acquisitions and corporate governance. He represents public and private clients in connection with finance, operational and transactional needs. Werts represents buyers and sellers in connection with their purchases and sales of stock and assets in regulated and unregulated businesses. He handles financing transactions for lenders and investors and for borrowers and targets. His corporate finance expertise includes advising clients concerning venture capital and angel investments, PIPEs, private placements of debt and equity, bank financings and asset based lending.

WHITE, Michael
White Goss Bowers March Schulte & Weisenfels, A Professional Corporation, Kansas City 816 753 9200
Recommended in Real Estate

WING, David
Spencer Fane Britt & Browne LLP,
Kansas City 816 474 8100
Recommended in Employment

WOLF, Jerome
Sonnenschein Nath & Rosenthal,
Kansas City 816 460 2420
jwolf@sonnenschein.com
Recommended in Litigation
Practice Areas: Firm marketing committee chair and Kansas City litigation group head. Concentrates in civil and commercial litigation. Experience in environmental, antitrust, intellectual property, franchise litigation, construction litigation and alternative dispute resolution. Founding Managing Partner of Kansas City office and member of firm's Management Committee.
Prof. Memberships: Past President, Kansas City Bar Association; Founding President, Kansas City Bar Foundation; Member, Center for Public Resources National Commission to Study Arbitration; Chairman, Civil Justice Reform Act of 1990 Advisory Group, US District Court, Western District of Missouri.
Personal: Harvard Law School, JD. Yale University, BA magna cum laude, Phi Beta Kappa.

WROBLEY, Ralph
Blackwell Sanders Peper Martin LLP,
Kansas City 816 983 8111
rwrobley@blackwellsanders.com
Recommended in Corporate/M&A
Practice Areas: Commercial transactions; energy and public utility; international; mergers and acquisitions.
Prof. Memberships: Admitted to practice in Missouri (1962). Vice-President, Council on Education. Chair, Mid-America Coalition on Healthcare; Citizens Association of Kansas City; and Public Housing Authority of Kansas City. Trustee and Chair, Clearinghouse of Mid-Continent Foundations. Vice-Chair, Center for Business Innovation. Legal Committee Member, National Automated Clearinghouse. Member, Civic Council of Kansas City.
Career: Joined firm as Partner, 1992; Member, Blackwell Sanders Peper Martin Executive Committee, 1992-2000; Chair, Blackwell Sanders Peper Martin Corporate Department, 1992-2000.
Personal: JD, University of Chicago, 1962; BA, Yale University, 1957.

WYRSCH, James R
Wyrsch Hobbs & Mirakian PC,
Kansas City 816 221 0080
jimwyrsch@whmlaw.net
Recommended in Litigation
Practice Areas: White-collar criminal defense; complex litigation.
Prof. Memberships: Admitted to practice in Missouri, 1966, and numerous federal courts; member, MO Supreme Court Procedures Committee, and Subcommittee to Draft Model Criminal Instructions for 8th Circuit Federal District Courts; Advocate, American Board of Trial Advocates; Fellow, American College of Trial Lawyers; Life Fellow, American Bar Foundation; Senior Counsel, College of Master Advocates and Barristers; adjunct professor, University of Missouir-Kansas City Law School.
Career: President, Wyrsch Hobbs & Mirakian, P.C. (and predecessors), 1970 to present.
Publications: Co-author 'Missouri Criminal Trial Practice', 1994, and numerous articles in professional journals.
Personal: Born 23 February 1942; BA, Notre Dame University, 1963; JD, Georgetown University, 1966; LLM in Trial Practice, University of Missouri-Kansas City, 1972.

YATES, Jack
Husch & Eppenberger, LLC,
Kansas City 816 421 4800
Recommended in Employment

BLACKWELL SANDERS PEPER MARTIN LLP

THE FIRM

Chairman: David A Fenley

Number of partners: 137
Number of other lawyers: 151

FIRM OVERVIEW: With 288 attorneys and over 40 practice concentrations, the firm is one of the leading commercial law firms in the central Midwest and is recognized for its transactional and litigation practices. *Corporate Board Member* magazine has consistently ranked Blackwell Sanders as one of the 'Best Corporate Law Firms in America'.

MAIN AREAS OF PRACTICE: Mergers and acquisitions, corporate finance, business and commercial litigation, labor and employment, intellectual property and intellectual property infringement litigation, real estate, international and governmental affairs.

Corporate: Corporate attorneys represent globally known companies, including New York Stock Exchange and NASDAQ listed companies. Because of the diversity of clients and the complexity of their transactions, the firm has nurtured unique legal experiences and earned a national reputation in securities, mergers and acquisitions, and secured and unsecured financing transactions. The sophistication of the firm's transactional work has enabled it to gain distinction in industries such as energy and public utility, agribusiness, healthcare, specialty retailing, manufacturing, financial institutions, telecommunications, franchising and distribution, and transportation.

Litigation: The firm's litigation attorneys have attained hard-earned reputations for winning crucial, complex business verdicts. Litigators focus on complex areas of the law, including antitrust, bankruptcy, class actions, corporate governance, securities, intellectual property and white collar crime. Experiences in industry sectors such as energy and public utility, agribusiness, healthcare, construction, transportation, securities and insurance enable the firm's trial attorneys to quickly assess regulatory and operating litigation exposure.

Labor & Employment: The firm's Labor and Employment Department is anchored by experienced attorneys. They have guided leading employers, including *Fortune* 500 companies, both regionally and nationally, in labor and employment matters. Labor and employment representations include traditional labor involving labor negotiations, defense of NLRB allegations, strikes and strike preparation, arbitrations and union prevention, as well as defense of employment discrimination litigation, Wage and Hour audits, OSHA/MSHA safety and OFCCP Affirmative Action program audits.

Real Estate: The firm's Real Estate Practice is one of the most diverse in the Midwest. Attorneys represent regional and national clients active in real estate investment, development, financing and leasing. Real estate services range from traditional purchases and sales, leases and financings to complex national mortgage loan and mortgage securitization programs. Real estate attorneys have structured and negotiated developments in the urban core districts of Kansas City, Omaha and St. Louis and secured crucial economic development incentives that serve as the cornerstone for competitive project development.

CLIENTS: The firm represents *Fortune* 500, multi-national and some of the largest privately held companies in the United States. Many of these clients are global leaders in their industries, including agribusiness, energy, finance, manufacturing, specialty retailing, consulting, design and engineering, and real estate lending.

HEAD OFFICE

MISSOURI
4801 Main Street, Suite 1000, **Kansas City**, MO 64112
Tel: 816 983 8000   **Fax:** 816 983 8080
Email: info@blackwellsanders.com
Website: www.blackwellsanders.com

BRANCH OFFICES

DISTRICT OF COLUMBIA
1737 H Street, NW, Suite 300, **Washington**, DC 20006
Tel: 202 378 2300   **Fax:** 202 378 2319

MISSOURI
720 Olive Street, Suite 2400, **St Louis**, MO 63101
Tel: 314 345 6000   **Fax:** 314 345 6060

901 St. Louis Street, Suite 1900, **Springfield**, MO 65806
Tel: 417 268 4000   **Fax:** 417 268 4040

NEBRASKA
1620 Dodge Street, Suite 2100, **Omaha**, NE 68102
Tel: 402 964 5000   **Fax:** 402 964 5050

INTERNATIONAL OFFICES

The firm also has an office in London.

CONTACTS

Corporate Finance & M&A	Jim Ash
Litigation	Jim Griffin
	Jeff Kalinowski (St Louis)
Intellectual Property	Sam Digirolamo (St Louis)
	Michael Kahn (St Louis)
Energy	William Demarest (DC)
Real Estate	Dave Fenley
	John McNearney (St Louis)
Labor & Employment	Paul Pautler
	John Phillips
	Terry Potter (St Louis)
Governmental Affairs	Steve Kupka (DC)
International	John Mandelbaum (London)

INTERNATIONAL WORK: The firm's international practice involves representing United States-based clients with the conduct of their businesses in other countries, including: acquisitions and joint ventures; establishing US subsidiaries in foreign countries; establishing overseas dealerships; and arbitrating international disputes under all major dispute systems (including the rules of the International Chamber of Commerce).

BLACKWELL SANDERS PEPER MARTIN
LLP

KING HERSHEY, PC

THE FIRM

Managing Partner: Richard A King, Chairman & CEO

Number of partners: 9
Number of other lawyers: 10

FIRM OVERVIEW: Founded in 1988, King Hershey has developed a reputation as a law firm that finds innovative solutions to complex legal issues facing their clients. Local governments, developers, financial institutions and other businesses bring real estate development, public/private finance, litigation and business challenges to King Hershey. The firm has a diverse practice emphasizing real estate development, public finance and general commercial real estate law.

MAIN AREAS OF PRACTICE:

Economic Development Practice: The firm's Development Practice emphasizes public finance and real estate development. The firm has extensive experience in municipal law, including tax increment financing (TIF) and other forms of municipal finance. King Hershey is known for its ability to assist in the structuring of complex public/private financing partnerships for development projects. The firm has been responsible for several major legislative initiatives in Missouri during the past decade, including an extensive amendment of the Missouri Transportation Development District Act, enactment of the Community Improvement District Act, and modification of the Missouri Tax Increment Financing Act. These tools are key to the firm's ability to craft innovative public/private financing partnerships for development projects. King Hershey has a unique 'vertical integration' of its practice, allowing the same attorneys to handle planning, structuring and financing complex public/private financed transactions. While most law firms have different attorneys handle zoning and plan approvals, tax increment financing or other public assistance tools and the issuance of municipal bonds related to a project, attorneys in King Hershey's economic development practice handle all aspects of these complex matters, creating efficiency and saving duplication of effort.

Commercial Real Estate: The firm maintains one of the Midwest region's most active commercial real estate practices, providing representation in all aspects of real estate law to developers, non-profit organizations, syndication groups, lenders, landlords, builders, title insurance companies and municipalities. King Hershey is recognized for its expertise in innovative real estate financing techniques and has been instrumental in some of the region's most notable development projects, including Quality Hill, the Jazz District, Park Central Plaza and Ameristar Casino in Kansas City, the Mall at Fall Creek in Blue Springs, Missouri, and Bolger Square, the Independence Regional Medical Center and Hartman Heritage Park in Independence, Missouri. The firm is general counsel to the Land Clearance for Redevelopment Authority of Kansas City, for which it performs urban redevelopment and municipal finance services. King Hershey also represents a number of real estate lending institutions. The firm is experienced in the representation of public agencies and developers in regard to tax increment financing, transportation development districts, neighborhood improvement districts, community improvement districts, Missouri '353' urban development projects and taxable bonds to fund development. King Hershey also represents organizations that own real property, including organizations that operate a variety of multi-family complexes, golf courses and historic structures.

HEAD OFFICE

MISSOURI
2345 Grand Boulevard, Suite 2100, **Kansas City**, MO 64108
Tel: 816 842 3636   **Fax:** 816 842 2414
Website: www.kinghershey.com

Bond Practice: King Hershey has an active bond practice, providing representation in all aspects of municipal bond transactions and other public/private financing transactions. The firm has served as underwriter's counsel and bond counsel on municipal bond offerings as well as acting as issuer's counsel to both public and not-for-profit agencies. King Hershey is listed as nationally recognized bond counsel in the Bond Buyer's Municipal Market Place, commonly known as the 'Red Book'.

Litigation: King Hershey provides complete civil and criminal federal and state court litigation services in Kansas and Missouri including mediation and appellate practice. The firm provides litigation expertise and representation in administrative hearings in a variety of areas including: banking, bankruptcy, business, commercial, construction law, real estate and taxation.

Alternative Dispute Resolution: The firm provides services for any type of alternative dispute resolution and acts as a neutral, including areas of mediation and arbitration.

CLIENTS: King Hershey represents a wide variety of both public and private clients including the Economic Development Corporation of Kansas City, Missouri; HCA, Inc; the Jazz District Redevelopment Corporation; Nextel Communications; the Port Authority of Kansas City, Missouri and Wolfe Automotive Group.

King Hershey
ATTORNEYS AT LAW

LATHROP & GAGE L.C.

THE FIRM

Managing Partner: Thomas S Stewart
Number of partners worldwide: 147
Number of other lawyers worldwide: 133

FIRM OVERVIEW: With 280 attorneys, Lathrop & Gage is now the third largest firm in Kansas City, making it one of the largest in the state. In the past year, the firm has grown 20% in part due to an increase in business and tort litigation and intellectual property practice areas. More than 150 of the firm's attorneys have received Martindale-Hubbell's highest rating, dozens are listed in *"Best Lawyers in America"*, two of the firm's litigators have been inducted into the American College of Trial Lawyers, and Lathrop consistently ranks as one of the best litigation and corporate firms in the Midwest. From January 2004 – October 2004, the firm's Corporate Practice was involved in transactions with an aggregate value of more than $4 billion dollars. Lathrop ranked 170 in the *National Law Journal*'s 2003 survey of the nation's largest firms. Founded in 1873, the firm is considered the oldest firm west of the Mississippi River and still represents its first-ever client, Burlington Northern & Santa Fe Railway. The firm's core practice areas are business and tort litigation, intellectual property, corporate, environmental, labor and employment, healthcare, real estate, financial institutions, tax, bankruptcy/creditors' rights, and wealth strategies.

MAIN AREAS OF PRACTICE:

Litigation: Lathrop & Gage has one of the largest and most experienced litigation departments in the region with over 170 litigators specializing in business litigation, class actions and multiparty litigation, intellectual property, employment law, tort, trade secrets and covenants not to compete, and bankruptcy. In August 2004, the firm successfully represented victims of the largest cattle fraud case in history, which resulted in a $4.2 million settlement. The firm also successfully represented Payless Shoe-Source in a proxy fight with a group of dissident shareholders who solicited proxies from shareholders in an attempt to elect members to Payless's nine-member board of directors. The firm's tort litigation attorneys have handled cases resulting in significant changes in tort law, including the adoption of the concept of comparative negligence in Missouri and significant changes in the Kansas comparative negligence law. The attorneys have defended numerous high-profile medical malpractice cases as well as cases of first impression. In 2004, attorneys in this group won a class action suit against 300 property owners brought by the Wyandotte Nation Indian Tribe claiming original title to 1920 acres in Kansas City, Kansas, including General Motor Corporation's automotive production facility.

Intellectual Property: Lathrop & Gage has the largest intellectual property (IP) practice of any Kansas City-based law firm with 40 attorneys devoted to this practice who are backed by a general litigation practice with over 170 attorneys. Attorneys practice in every area of IP including litigation, patent, trademark, copyright, trade secret, and licensing law and have helped to shape IP law through their involvement in landmark trademark and false advertising cases involving Thermos®, Monopoly, Eveready Battery and Weight Watchers®. The firm has represented many well-known clients with complex IP issues including Payless ShoeSource, Dear Abby, AMC Entertainment Inc. and Yahoo! Inc.

Corporate: From January 2004 – October 2004, the firm was involved in transactions with an aggregate value of more than $4 billion dollars. *Corporate Board Member* magazine recently featured Lathrop & Gage among the top corporate practices in the country. The firm represents many of the largest companies headquartered in the region and serve as regional counsel to *Fortune 500* companies with a Midwest presence.

Environmental: Recently the firm has collected more than $100 million for clients from insurance carriers for historic contamination. Addition-

ally, the firm has successfully defended clients in more than 60 Superfund matters, closing landfill sites in 18 states. The firm boasts one of the nation's strongest environmental law practices, providing counsel to businesses on federal and state environmental laws and regulations.

Labor & Employment: Lathrop & Gage counsels and represents *Fortune 500* employers across the country in complex matters. During 2004, the department obtained several summary judgment and trial successes, most recently a jury verdict for the employer in a case claiming pregnancy discrimination.

Real Estate: The firm's attorneys have been instrumental in developing and financing numerous local and national commercial real estate projects, including large-scale entertainment complexes, shopping centers, hotels and major business parks. Recently the firm negotiated a process through which the GSA and the IRS were able to achieve congressional authorization and approval for a long-term lease for the IRS Service Center, allowing the Postal Service to find better use for an older facility and the IRS to open a new service center. Additionally, the firm represented the Kansas and Missouri Union Station Bistate Commission to fund $118 million of a $256 million project to renovate Kansas City's historic Union Station and create a world-class science museum. The intermodal portion of the project was funded significantly by federal DOT grants totaling $29 million, together with an additional $10 million from four other federal agencies. The firm participated in all aspects of the project.

HEAD OFFICE

MISSOURI
2345 Grand Boulevard, **Kansas City**, MO 64108

OTHER OFFICES

COLORADO
4845 Pearl East Circle, **Boulder**, CO 80301

KANSAS
10851 Mastin Boulevard, **Overland Park**, KS 66210

MISSOURI
314 East High Street, **Jefferson City**, MO 65101

1845 South National, **Springfield**, MO 65808

10 South Broadway, **St Louis**, MO 63102

NEW YORK
230 Park Avenue, **New York**, NY 10169

AFFILIATE OFFICE

DISTRICT OF COLUMBIA
Lathrop & Gage DC, PLLC 1300 Eye Street, NW, **Washington, DC** 20005

FIRM CONTACTS

Thomas S Stewart
Tel: 800 476 4224   **Website:** www.lathropgage.com

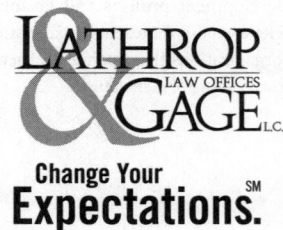

LEWIS, RICE & FINGERSH, LC

THE FIRM

Managing Partner, St Louis: John K Pruellage
Managing Partner, Kansas City: William E Carr

FIRM OVERVIEW: The law firm of Lewis, Rice & Fingersh, LC traces its history to the founding of Lewis & Rice in St Louis during 1909 and of Brown, Koralchik & Fingersh in Kansas City during 1948. In August 1989, the two firms merged to form the present organization, having offices in Creve Coeur, Jefferson City, Kansas City, St Louis and Washington, Missouri; Leawood, Kansas and Belleville, Illinois. With more than 170 lawyers practicing in all of the major legal specialty areas, Lewis, Rice & Fingersh is not only a leading regional firm but has a broad base of national clients as well, who draw upon its talents in such diverse areas as admiralty, antitrust, corporate, heathcare, intellectual property, labor and employment, litigation, estate planning, tax and real estate.

MAIN AREAS OF PRACTICE:

Corporate/Business, Tax & Estate Planning: The firm's Corporate Practice encompasses many disciplines, including banking, securities, corporate finance, mergers and acquisitions, healthcare, bankruptcy, closely-held businesses, employee benefits and e-commerce. The firm serves the diverse needs of public and private businesses of all sizes and in all industries. The attorneys in the firm's Tax Department handle a variety of federal, state and local matters involving tax planning and tax disputes. The firm's estate planning attorneys advise clients regarding individual tax and estate planning, prenuptial agreements, charitable giving and intrafamily wealth transfers.

Litigation & Labor: The firm's Litigation Department represents clients in all types of commercial disputes, including claims brought under general contract law, business tort law, insurance policies, the Uniform Commercial Code, federal and state securities laws, lender liability and class action representations. The department has extensive experience in complex litigation, which often requires in-depth review and analysis of thousands of documents, and in alternative dispute resolution techniques. The Labor and Employment Group represents management in employment-related litigation in federal and state courts in actions involving Title VII, the ADA, the ADEA, ERISA, the FMLA, the PDA, state anti-discrimination statutes, and various state law theories, such as wrongful discharge claims and non-competition disputes.

Real Estate: The firm's Real Estate Practice includes representation of lenders, developers, institutional investors, contractors, architects, investment advisors, mortgage bankers, brokers and tenants. The department has extensive experience in financing, development, acquisition, joint ventures, taxation, leasing, environmental law, zoning, and work-outs, involving complex, large-scale transactions of all kinds and in nearly every state, as well as several foreign countries. A significant number of attorneys within the department have been recognized by inclusion in, for example, the American College of Real Estate Lawyers, and several leading legal publications, as well as being called upon to teach their specialty at area law schools.

MAIN OFFICES

MISSOURI
500 N Broadway, Suite 2000, **St Louis**, MO 63102
Tel: 314 444 7600 **Fax:** 314 241 6056
Website: www.lrf.com

1010 Walnut, Suite 500, **Kansas City**, MO 64106
Tel: 816 421 2500 **Fax:** 816 472 2500
Email: firm@lrf-kc.com

OTHER OFFICES

ILLINOIS
325 S. High Street, **Belleville**, IL 62220
Tel: 618 234 8636

KANSAS
7015 College Boulevard, Suite 135, **Overland Park**, KS 66211
Tel: 913 381 8898

MISSOURI
555 N New Ballas Road, Suite 260, **Creve Coeur**, MO 63141
Tel: 314 569 2262

221 E Capitol Avenue, **Jefferson City**, MO 65101
Tel: 573 893 7724

1200 Jefferson; PO Box 1040, **Washington**, MO 63090
Tel: 636 239 7747

10034 N. Ambassador Drive, **Kansas City**, MO 64153
Tel: 816 891 9390

CONTACTS

Chairman Business, Tax & Estate Planning ....Stanley C Johnston, Kansas City
Chairman Corporate Department ....Joseph H Weyhrich, St Louis
Chairman Estate Planning Department ....Michael D Mulligan, St Louis
Chairman Litigation & Labor Department ....Andrew Rothschild, Kansas City
Chairman Real Estate Department ....Charles F Miller, Kansas City
Chairman Tax Department ....Lawrence H Weltman, St Louis

MCMAHON, BERGER, HANNA, LINIHAN, CODY & MCCARTHY

THE FIRM

Managing Partner: Thomas O McCarthy

Number of partners: 17
Number of other lawyers: 11

FIRM OVERVIEW: Established in 1955, McMahon, Berger, Hanna, Linihan, Cody & McCarthy is a nationally recognized labor and employment law firm whose practice is devoted to representing management in labor and employment law matters throughout the United States. The firm's philosophy is one of commitment to the highest standards of integrity, quality and service with the achievement of practical, business-oriented results in a cost efficient manner. The firm provides comprehensive labor and employment advice and services to both public and private employers in virtually all areas, including employment litigation, traditional labor matters, employee benefits and health and safety matters.

MAIN AREAS OF PRACTICE:

Employment: McMahon Berger advises clients in establishing policies and procedures to ensure compliance with various federal, state and local non-discrimination laws, as well as assisting them in formulating strategies to maintain a productive workplace environment and minimize the risk of employment litigation. The firm's attorneys regularly teach labor and employment law courses and chair and speak at seminars and workshops on labor, employment and employee benefits topics. McMahon Berger regularly represents clients before federal administrative agencies including EEOC, OFCCP, OSHA and Department of Labor, as well as state and local agencies dealing with the same type issues.

Traditional Labor: In court, in negotiations, in arbitration and before government agencies such as the NLRB and NMB, McMahon Berger advises and represents clients in all phases of traditional labor law. Collectively the firm's partners have many years of experience handling and solving the most difficult labor problems faced by employers under the NLRA and RLA. The firm also provides advice on a wide variety of business related labor issues including mergers and acquisitions, relocation and closures.

Litigation: McMahon Berger represents clients before state and federal trail and appellate courts throughout the nation, up to and including the United States Supreme Court. The firm's seasoned litigators routinely try to verdict all types of employment cases, including discrimination, harassment, retaliation, wrongful discharge, breach of contract, breach of non-complete agreements, and employee benefit claims. McMahon Berger also has extensive experience representing and defending clients in class actions involving claims of employment discrimination as well as breach of the FLSA, WARN and ERISA.

Employee Benefits: McMahon Berger's employee benefits attorneys advise clients on design and implementation of employee benefit plans and compliance with IRS, DOL and PBGC requirements.

CLIENTS: Ameren UE; Bodine Aluminum, Inc. (A Subsidiary of Toyota Motor Corporate Services of North America, Inc.) Brinker International; Crane Co.; Emerson Electric Co.; Enterprise Rent-A-Car; Federal Mogul; Harbour Group Companies; Integram St. Louis Seating, a division of Intier Automotive; Kellwood Co.; Tyco Heathcare/ Mallinckrodt, Inc.; Prairie Farms Dairy, Inc.; Ralston Purina; Sara Lee Bakery Group; Sigma-Aldrich Corp; Smurfit Stone Container Corp.; SuperValu, Inc. and its subsidiary Shop 'n Save Warehouse Foods, Inc.

HEAD OFFICE

MISSOURI
2730 North Ballas Road, **St. Louis**, MO 63131
Tel: 314 567 7350   **Fax:** 314 567 5968
Website: www.mcmahonberger.com

BRANCH OFFICES

ILLINOIS
400 North Bluff Road, **Collinsville**, IL 62234
Tel: 618 345 5822   **Fax:** 618 345 6483

SHOOK, HARDY & BACON LLP

THE FIRM

Chairman: John F Murphy

Number of partners & counsel: 240
Number of attorneys: 502

FIRM OVERVIEW: International law firm Shook, Hardy & Bacon LLP (SHB) possesses a legacy spanning more than a century. Established in Kansas City in 1889, the firm today has more than 500 attorneys and more than 1,200 employees worldwide. SHB's efficiencies and innovations have evolved over time, yet the foundational beliefs in working for the client's best interest have remained, and are reflective by the firm's representation of many of the nation's major corporations included in *Fortune's* elite top 100. SHB's culture and values focus on the firm's collective and collaborative strengths within the firm's practice areas. This strength creates a strong global stance, which serves clients around the world.

MAIN AREAS OF PRACTICE:

Litigation: The legacy of Shook, Hardy & Bacon (SHB) spans more than a century, being the firm of choice for corporations facing high-stakes litigation. SHB attorneys are nationally noted and have tried cases to verdict or to judgment in virtually every substantive area of law and business segment including the following: antitrust, corporate finance, employee benefits, employment litigation and policy, environmental, ERISA, healthcare, intellectual property, pharmaceutical and medical device, products liability, public policy, securities, tax and tort litigation. Many litigation cases also involve class actions, where SHB attorneys are at the forefront in efforts to reform the class action device and its application. SHB has played a key role in developing potential revisions to federal and state court class action rules, including developing legislation to curtail the increasingly common abuses of class action. In recent years, SHB attorneys have also filed *amicus* briefs on behalf of organizations involved in high-profile appeals that raise significant class action-related policy questions.

Corporate Finance & Banking: Attorneys in SHB's Corporate Finance and Banking Section concentrate their practices in mergers and acquisitions, joint ventures, strategic alliances, securities matters, private equity and financing transactions, commercial finance and banking and the general representation of publicly-held and private entities. The firm's corporate finance attorneys are experienced in all aspects of corporate transactions, including private placements; mergers, acquisitions and divestitures; joint ventures; distributorships; public offerings; tender offers; venture capital financing; equity and debt restructuring; project finance; workouts; corporate governance; and general corporate law. SHB's banking and commercial law attorneys counsel local, national and international financial institutions and corporate borrowers on loan transactions and regulatory issues and are nationally recognized experts in various areas of commercial law.

HEAD OFFICE

MISSOURI
2555 Grand Boulevard, **Kansas City**, MO 64108-2613
Tel: 816 474 6550   **Fax:** 816 421 5547

BRANCH OFFICES

CALIFORNIA
Jamboree Center, 5 Park Plaza, Suite 1600, **Irvine**, CA 92614-2546
Tel: 949 475 1500   **Fax:** 949 475 0016

333 Bush Street, Suite 600, **San Francisco**, CA 94104-2828
Tel: 415 544 1900   **Fax:** 415 391 0281

DISTRICT OF COLUMBIA
Hamilton Square, 600 14th Street, NW, Suite 800,
Washington, DC 20005-2004
Tel: 202 783 8400 **Fax:** 202 783 4211

FLORIDA
Miami Center, Suite 2400, 201 South Biscayne Boulevard,
Miami, FL 33131-4332
Tel: 305 358 5171   **Fax:** 305 358 7470

100 North Tampa Street, Suite 2900, **Tampa**, FL 33602-5810
Tel: 813 202 7100   **Fax:** 813 221 8837

KANSAS
84 Corporate Woods, 10801 Mastin, Suite 1000,
Overland Park, KS 66210-1697
Tel: 913 451 6060   **Fax:** 913 451 8879

TEXAS
JP Morgan/Chase Tower, 600 Travis Street, Suite 1600,
Houston, TX 77002-2911
Tel: 713 227 8008   **Fax:** 713 227 9508

INTERNATIONAL OFFICES

The firm also has offices in Switzerland and the United Kingdom.

CONTACTS

Missouri	John F Murphy
District of Columbia	Michelle R Mangrum
Kansas	Ron Bodinson
Miami	Kenneth J Reilly
Orange County	Michelle M Fujimoto
San Francisco	Shannon L Spangler
Tampa	Daniel F Molony
Texas	Gene M Williams

SHUGHART THOMSON & KILROY

THE FIRM

Chairman: R Lawrence Ward
Managing Partner: John M Kilroy, Jr
Denver Managing Partner: G Stephen Long
Overland Park Managing Partner: Lawrence A Swain
Phoenix/Tucson Managing Partner: Brian Michael Goodwin
Springfield Managing Partner: Thomas J O'Neal
St. Joseph Managing Partner: Thomas D Watkins

Shareholders: 96
Of Counsel: 26
Associates: 52

FIRM OVERVIEW: Shughart Thomson & Kilroy is a full service law firm, with more than 170 attorneys in six offices in the US. Attorneys and staff members from multiple offices work together to serve a broad range of corporate, institutional and individual clients across the United States and throughout the world. The firm's affiliation with Mackrell International, a worldwide association of independent law firms, enhances its global reach.

MAIN AREAS OF PRACTICE:

Commercial Litigation: Shughart Thomson & Kilroy is one of the region's best known trial law firms and includes five members of the American College of Trial Lawyers. More than a fourth of the firm's attorneys are involved in business litigation in federal and state courts. The firm is known for its outstanding trial results in all types of commercial disputes, including contract cases, fraud, business torts of many kinds and high profile contingent fee cases. The firm also has strong appellate and alternative dispute resolution practices.

Healthcare Business & Litigation: The firm's trial attorneys include members of the American College of Legal Medicine and healthcare professionals who entered the practice of law after they had established medical careers. The firm's services include: direct representation of healthcare institutions, healthcare labor law, and healthcare antitrust. The firm has over 60 years experience developing healthcare organizations and addressing the business challenges in the highly regulated healthcare industry.

Construction & Real Estate: Shughart Thomson & Kilroy's Construction attorneys represent five of ENR's Top 225 Global Contractors and two of the largest transit projects in the nation. The group handles construction business matters as well as multimillion-dollar lawsuits, appeals and arbitration, in state and federal courts, and before government administrative appeals boards. Shughart's real estate attorneys serve major developers and lenders nationwide in all phases of real property acquisition, entitlement, construction, operation and sale, and all the interrelated financing that occurs in these transactions.

General Business: The firm is highly regarded in general business law, and assists clients with: forming business enterprises, employee benefits planning, labor law, commodities and securities, government lobbying, tax, real estate, franchising, insurance, estate and succession planning, public finance and municipal bonds, bankruptcy and reorganization, and mergers and acquisitions.

Labor & Employment: Shughart Thomson & Kilroy's Labor and Employment Law Team is experienced in representing management in all employment issues including union elections, collective bargaining and arbitration, equal employment opportunity litigation (age, sex, race, disability etc.), affirmative action, wage and hour, occupational safety and Health (OSHA), drug testing, employment contracts, and noncompete agreements. The firm advises clients on claim prevention and are experienced litigators when the need arises.

HEAD OFFICE

MISSOURI
Twelve Wyandotte Plaza, 120 West 12th Street, **Kansas City**, MO 64105
Tel: 816 421 3355 **Fax:** 816 374 0509
Email: solutions@stklaw.com **Website:** www.stklaw.com

BRANCH OFFICES

ARIZONA
3636 North Central Avenue, Suite 1200, **Phoenix**, AZ 85012
Tel: 602 650 2000 **Fax:** 602 264 7033

COLORADO
1050 17th Street, Suite 2300, **Denver**, CO 80265
Tel: 303 572 9300 **Fax:** 303 572 7883

KANSAS
9225 Indian Creek Parkway, **Overland Park**, KS 66210
Tel: 913 451 3355 **Fax:** 913 451 3361

MISSOURI
Hammons Tower, 901 St. Louis Avenue, Suite 1200, **Springfield**, MO 65806
Tel: 417 869 3353 **Fax:** 417 869 9943

3101 Frederick Avenue, **St Joseph**, MO 64506
Tel: 816 364 2117 **Fax:** 816 279 3977

CONTACTS

Commercial Litigation	R Lawrence Ward
Construction	Roy Bash
General Business	Jacob W (Jeb) Bayer Jr
Healthcare	Randal L Schultz/Thomas G Kokoruda
Intellectual Property	Lawrence A Swain/Russell S Jones Jr
Labor & Employment Law	W Terrence Kilroy
Real Estate	Daniel T Murphy
Tort	Robert A Henderson

CLIENTS: Alstom Power, Inc.; Associated Wholesale Grocers, Inc.; Black & Veatch; Blue Cross and Blue Shield of K.C.; Burns & McDonnell Engineering Co.; Commerce Bank; Crane Plumbing; Dickinson Financial Corporation; DST Realty, Inc.; Heartland Regional Medical Center; HCA, Inc.; H&R Block; J.E. Dunn Construction; Jack Henry & Associates, Inc.; Kansas City Power & Light; Kansas City Public Library; Kansas City Southern Railway; Major League Baseball Players Association; New Directions Behavioral Health, L.L.C.; New Prime, Inc.; Northwest Missouri State University; Olathe Medical Center; Sprint Corp.; St. Joseph Health Center; Stormont Vail Regional Healthcare; United Missouri Bank; U.S. Bank; Banner Health System; City of Phoenix; Swift Transportation; Valley Metro Rail, Inc.; Colorado Surgical Services; Horizon Organic Holding Corporation.

Law Offices

SHUGHART THOMSON & KILROY P.C.

Consider it done.

STINSON MORRISON HECKER LLP

THE FIRM

Managing Partner: Mark S Foster

Total number of US partners: 211
Number of other lawyers in US offices: 112

Website: www.stinsonmoheck.com

FIRM OVERVIEW: Stinson Morrison Hecker LLP has corporate and litigation experience in every aspect of business and commercial enterprise including agriculture, aviation, construction, corporate finance, e-commerce, financial institutions, healthcare, real estate, intellectual property, environmental, manufacturing, municipalities, pharmaceuticals, sports, telecommunications and utilities, among others. The firm has offices throughout the Midwest as well as Phoenix and Washington, DC. It represents local, national, and international clients including Fortune 50 corporations, small businesses and individuals, publicly and privately-held companies, municipalities and not-for-profits.

MAIN AREAS OF PRACTICE:

Bankruptcy & Creditors' Rights: The firm's expertise includes business litigation, reorganizations, liquidations and foreclosures for secured and unsecured creditors, debtors, trade creditors, unsecured creditor and equity committees, trustees, buyers, and landlords.

Business Litigation: The firm litigates in all aspects of business litigation including antitrust, banking, securities, construction, corporate governance, trade secrets and non-compete agreements, as well as white collar criminal defense in state and federal courts throughout the nation.

Corporate Finance: The scope of this practice includes financing and securities law compliance, M&A, asset securitizations and structured finance, corporate governance, investment management, and venture and private equity capital. The practice includes representation of more than 20 publicly-held companies which run the gamut in size and industry as well as broker dealer, investment companies, investment advisors, merchant bankers, venture capital and private equity funds, and other participants in the capital market.

Employee Benefits Planning & Litigation: The firm has extensive experience in handling benefits issues in mergers, acquisitions and corporate transactions as well as securities issues which can impact employee benefits. The firm is well-versed in all types of employee benefits matters ranging from the drafting of simple benefit documents to assisting in the administration of ongoing benefit plans. Additionally, the firm has attorneys experienced in employee benefits litigation, defending employee benefit plans, their sponsors, administrators and fiduciaries from alleged violations of ERISA.

Employment Law: The firm assists clients with employment handbooks, policies and practices, EEOC charges of discrimination and retaliation, conducting investigations, wage and hour, discipline and termination, OSHA and government and administrative proceedings, human resource audits, consulting and training, workplace violence and embezzlement matters.

Employment Litigation: The firm represents management clients on the full scope of employment litigation and claims, including discrimination claims under federal, state and local discrimination laws, eg, Title VII, ADA, ADEA; wrongful termination; whistleblowing; and compliance issues and claims under Federal employment statutes, such as FLSA, FMLA, NLRA, OSHA, ERISA, OWBPA, COBRA, HIPAA, IRCA, OFCCP, WARN, and claims under equivalent state statutes.

Energy & Telecommunications: The firm has extensive experience representing clients before federal and state regulatory agencies, including FERC, involving the electric, hydroelectric and natural gas industries. It

HEAD OFFICE

MISSOURI
1201 Walnut, Suite 2900, **Kansas City**, MO 64106-2150
Tel: 816 842 8600   **Fax:** 816 691 3495
Email: info@stinsonmoheck.com

BRANCH OFFICES

ARIZONA
1850 North Central Avenue, Suite 2100, **Phoenix**, AZ 85004-4584
Tel: 602 279 1600   **Fax:** 602 240 6925

KANSAS
9 Corporate Woods, Suite 450, 9200 Indian Creek Parkway,
Overland Park, KS 66210-2008
Tel: 913 451 8600   **Fax:** 913 451 6352

600 Commerce Bank Center, 150 North Main, **Wichita**, KS 67202-1320
Tel: 316 265 8800   **Fax:** 316 265 1349

MISSOURI
230 West McCarty Street, **Jefferson City**, MO 65101
Tel: 573 636 6263   **Fax:** 573 636 6231

100 South 4th Street, Suite 700, **St Louis**, MO 63102
Tel: 314 259 4500   **Fax:** 314 259 4599

NEBRASKA
1299 Farnam Sreet, Suite 1501, **Omaha**, NE 68102
Tel: 402 342 1700   **Fax:** 402 930 1701

DISTRICT OF COLUMBIA
1150 18th Street, NW, Suite 800, **Washington**, DC 20036-3816
Tel: 202 785 9100   **Fax:** 202 785 9163

CONTACTS

Business Litigation	Robert L Driscoll
Corporate Finance	John A Granda
Bankruptcy & Creditors' Rights	Mark Shaiken
Employee Benefits	Thomas R Brous
Employment & Labor	David A Selden
Employment & Litigation	Paul E Donnelly
Energy & Telecommunications	Kelly A Daly
Environment & Natural Resources	David R Tripp
Financial Services	C Robert Monroe
General Business	Robert C Hunter
IP&T	J David Wharton
Public Law & Finance	Stephen P Chinn
Real Estate	David W Frantze
Tax, Trusts & Estates	Paul E McLaughlin

also represents clients on regulatory and transactional matters relating to the transportation of crude oil and petroleum products. The firm advises on state and federal telecom regulatory law, as well as matters involving the negotiation and documentation of interconnection agreements, regulatory compliance and authorization, right of way litigation, and bankruptcy of telecom service providers.

Environment & Natural Resources: The firm provides local, regional, and national environmental representation to businesses at all levels including the energy sector, public utilities, agricultural enterprises, industrial and manufacturing concerns, lending institutions and governmental agencies. The firm also represents clients in regulatory compliance and rulemaking, administrative hearings, Superfund and toxic tort litigation and insurance coverage.

STINSON MORRISON HECKER LLP cont'd

Financial Services: The firm helps all types of financial companies to ensure compliance with federal and state regulations and to achieve their business objectives. This help includes, without limitation, commercial lending matters such as loan syndications and Article 9 of the UCC; M&A transactions; reverse stock splits; bank and holding company formations; succession planning; S-Corp conversions; regulatory issues involving the issuance of trust preferred securities; broker/dealer and insurance networking arrangements; assistance in the negotiation of bank regulatory orders; officer and director training; dealing with corporate governance issues involving financial companies (public and non-public); and federal and state regulatory compliance.

General Business: The firm is recognized as one of the most experienced and respected business law firms in the United States and focuses on all areas relevant to modern business. These include agribusiness, healthcare, international law, mergers and acquisitions, closely-held businesses, Indian law and sports law.

Intellectual Property: The firm has broad experience in patents, trademarks, copyrights and trade secrets; media and advertising; e-commerce, technology and outsourcing; and intellectual property and technology litigation in courts throughout the United States.

Product Liability: The firm defends manufacturers, designers, and distributors in product liability litigation at the state and federal level throughout the United States. The practice involves a wide variety of products, including industrial trucks, over-the-road trucks, cranes, natural gas and liquified petroleum gas, aircraft, motorcycles, radiant heaters, forklifts, medical devices, seat belts, agricultural products, asbestosis, silicosis, and more. In addition to product liability defense, the firm counsels clients on the product liability safety and prevention, warnings and instructions for the proper and safe use of products, and adjustment and management of claims.

Public Law & Finance: The division is composed of 12 attorneys who have extensive experience in the full range of public law issues: including land use; economic development incentives; public facility financing; environmental and storm water management; home rule and general governmental powers; annexation and boundary adjustments; eminent domain; and open records and public meetings. Members of the division also have impressive code drafting and public law litigation experience. The division members expertise also encompasses all of the various types of municipal finance, including general and special obligation bonds, utility revenue bonds, single and multi-family housing bonds, municipal lease financings, economic development bonds, industrial development bonds and tax increment financings.

Real Estate: The firm's Real Estate Practice focuses on real estate development (office buildings, shopping centers, industrial and multi-family and single family residential projects), including the use of economic development incentives; acquisitions and sales; mortgage lending; conduit lending and securitization; historic preservation; tax credits; public/private partnerships; leasing (retail/commercial); gaming and liquor licensing issues; real estate litigation and condemnation.

Tax, Trusts & Estates: The firm's Tax Practice focuses on planning and implementing strategies to reduce the tax burden borne by businesses, individuals and their estates and also includes representation of taxpayers in litigation and administrative appeals. The Tax Practice encompasses: transactional work such as business acquisitions and sales of businesses; pass-through entity planning, formation and preparation of related documentation for limited liability companies, limited liability partnerships, limited and general partnerships, joint ventures and S-corporations; and the use of family-limited partnerships and other entities to enhance the growth of family assets and reduce the tax burden of business interests on the estates of the senior generation.

CLIENTS: Aventis Pharmaceuticals, Inc.; Rawlings Sporting Goods, Inc.; BHA Group, Inc.; Cerner Corporation; Cessna Aircraft Company; H&R Block; Inergy Partners, LLC; Midland Loan Services, Inc.; Sprint Corporation; LabOne, Inc.

INTERNATIONAL WORK: The firm provides representation to many of its clients in international areas including contracts and related transactional issues, trade issues, banking and taxation, litigation and business-related immigration. Several attorneys in the firm offer non-English language expertise in a variety of major languages including French, Spanish, Russian, Portuguese, Japanese and Korean.

STINSON
MORRISON
HECKER LLP

THOMPSON COBURN LLP

THE FIRM

Chairman: Thomas J Minogue

Number of partners: 169
Number of other attorneys: 121

FIRM OVERVIEW: Thompson Coburn LLP is a full-service law firm that was established in 1996 with the merger of two of St. Louis' most respected law firms –Thompson & Mitchell and Coburn & Croft. According to the *St. Louis Business Journal*, Thompson Coburn is the largest law firm in the St. Louis metropolitan area. The firm is regularly ranked among top law firms nationwide in the application of client-focused technology and is constantly pursuing initiatives designed to enhance its client service capabilities.

MAIN AREAS OF PRACTICE: Through its St. Louis headquarters, Thompson Coburn provides services across a full range of legal specialties and industry sectors, including:

Corporate & Securities: For businesses of all sizes, from large publicly owned corporations listed on the New York Stock Exchange to mid- and small-cap companies, the firm provides creative solutions in areas of corporate and securities counseling, public and private offerings of debt and equity securities, and mergers and acquisitions.

Financial Services: The firm serves a full spectrum of financial institutions, including commercial banks, investment banks, governmental financial institutions, venture capitalists, pension funds, investment advisors and fund managers. Services cover a complete range of transactional, regulatory and advisory legal matters.

Healthcare: The firm provides a full range of legal services to meet the needs of healthcare industry clients, including ambulatory surgery centers, durable medical equipment suppliers, health insurers, hospitals and their medical staffs, managed care organizations, nursing homes, professional associations, staffing agencies and third-party administrators.

Intellectual Property: With one of the region's largest IP practices, the firm serves clients in the areas of patent, trademark, copyright, trade secret protection, Internet and new media, electronic commerce, software licensing and false advertising.

Labor & Employment: Thompson Coburn has a team of more than 20 attorneys who practice labor and employment law exclusively. They handle traditional contract negotiations and union organizing matters, as well as provide advice and counsel on issues such as terminations and lay-offs, and protection of intellectual property rights through post-employment restrictions.

Litigation: The firm handles a broad range of business, product and mass litigation matters. This group includes a wealth of accomplished trial lawyers who are skilled in the intricacies of class action and other complex litigation of all types.

Real Estate: The firm has a strong regional and national real estate practice. Since 2000, the firm has handled transactions for commercial, industrial and multi-family properties in 47 states valued at more than $1 billion.

Other Practice Areas: Admiralty; bankruptcy; corporate compliance; construction; employee benefits; environmental; government contracts; private client services; product liability; public finance/law; railroad; tax; tobacco and toxic tort.

Washington, DC Office: With a strong focus on transportation, the firm's Washington, DC office serves clients throughout the country on matters that involve direct dealings with Federal agencies and the US Congress. Areas of special concentration in the transportation field include marine, aviation, surface, public transit and infrastructure. The firm's Washington, DC office also includes attorneys with experience in litigation, government contracts, international commerce, and postal and utilities regulations.

Southern Illinois Office: With only a small faction the nation's population, this portion of the country attracts more class actions each year than many of the nation's most populous communities. Attorneys in the firm's Illinois office have experience handling a wide range of class action matters, including product liability, FELA, labor and retaliatory discharge, Railway Labor Act, and matters for insurance companies and financial institutions.

CLIENTS: The firm serves a broad spectrum of regional and national clients, including A.G. Edwards & Sons, Inc., Bunzl USA, Inc., Charter Communications, Inc., DaimlerChrysler Corp., Enterprise Rent-A-Car Co., ExxonMobil Corp., KV Pharmaceutical Co., Lorillard Tobacco Co., Maritz Inc., Peabody Holding Co., Inc., SBC Communications, Inc., Stifel Nicolaus & Company, Union Pacific Railroad Co., UniGroup, Inc., and U.S. Bank, N.A.

INTERNATIONAL WORK: Increasingly, Thompson Coburn handles matters for US-based clients that are international in scope. In addition, it is the only firm in the Midwest to be a member of Globalaw Limited, an international network of attorneys and law firms. Through Globalaw, the firm can connect clients with more than 2,600 attorneys in 75 jurisdictions around the world.

HEAD OFFICE

MISSOURI
One US Bank Plaza, **St. Louis**, MO 63101-1611
Tel: 314 552 6000 **Fax:** 314 552 7000
Website: www.thompsoncoburn.com

BRANCH OFFICES

DISTRICT OF COLUMBIA
1909 K Street, N.W., Suite 600, **Washington**, DC 20006-1167
Tel: 202 585 6900 **Fax:** 202 585 6969

ILLINOIS
525 West Main Street, **Belleville**, IL 62220-1547
Tel: 618 277 4700 **Fax:** 618 236 3434

CONTACTS

St. Louis – Corporate	Michael F Lause
St. Louis – Litigation	Raymond L Massey
Washington, DC	Warren L Dean, Jr
Southern Illinois	Thomas W Alvey, Jr

THOMPSON COBURN LLP

CONTENTS: Corporate/M&A p.1072; Employment p.1073; Litigation p.1074; Natural Resources & Environment p.1077; Real Estate p.1078; Individuals' Profiles p.1079.

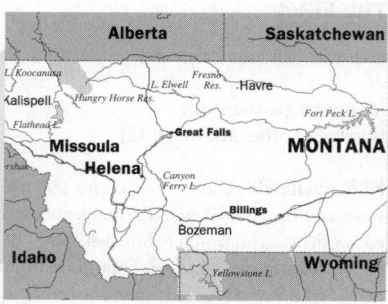

How lawyers are ranked

The opinions we gather from clients — mainly from in-house lawyers but also from other purchasers of legal services — are balanced by opinions from colleagues and competitors. Together, they provide two different perspectives — an all-round view — and biased viewpoints cancel each other out.

CORPORATE/M&A

Montana
Leading firms (Corporate/M&A)

1. **CROWLEY, HAUGHEY, HANSON, TOOLE** Billings
   DORSEY & WHITNEY LLP Great Falls
   GARLINGTON, LOHN & ROBINSON Missoula
2. **BOONE, KARLBERG PC** Missoula
   CHRISTIAN, SAMSON, JONES Missoula
   HOLLAND & HART LLP Billings

Leading individuals (Corporate/M&A)

1. **CHISHOLM David** Christian Samson, Missoula
   ELLINGSON Mae Nan Dorsey & Whitney, Missoula
   LAMDIN III William Crowley Haughey, Billings
   MANNING John Dorsey & Whitney, Great Falls
2. **BOONE Thomas** Boone Karlberg, Missoula
   BROWN Stephen Garlington Lohn, Missoula
   CHUMRAU Gary Garlington Lohn, Missoula
   HINGLE Charles Holland & Hart, Billings
   PETERSEN Larry Holland & Hart, Billings

Firms and individuals are listed alphabetically in each band.

Band 1

Crowley, Haughey, Hanson, Toole & Dietrich, PLLP

The Firm: This Billings-headquartered firm is acknowledged to be among the very best in the State of Montana for corporate transactions and general commercial advice. An old firm with five offices throughout the state and another in North Dakota, it is one of the largest in the northern Rocky Mountains region. The "*smart and business-minded*" attorneys in the corporate and commercial group additionally offer expertise in banking and finance, commercial real estate transactions, tribal business and bankruptcy matters. The team is presently representing a Montana bank in the finalization of a $10 million term-loan facility to a Montana Indian tribe.

The Lawyers: According to clients, **Bill Lamdin** is one of the most knowledgeable and experienced lawyers around. Clients say he is articulate and straight to the point, confirming his "*great practical knowledge of banking and the purpose behind any deal.*" He is famous for his extensive knowledge of the business of each and every client he works for, and recently closed a $14 million revolving line of credit facility to a publicly traded coal company on behalf of a Montana bank.

The Clients: First Interstate Bank; Stockman Bank; The Bank of Baker and Blue Cross and Blue Shield of Montana.

Dorsey & Whitney LLP

The Firm: Dorsey & Whitney attorneys handle a range of corporate work from startups and venture capital to M&A. The firm is known for its emphasis on technology clients and advised on the recent IPO of RightNow Technologies. Even though the firm has closed its Billings office, it is nevertheless active in the Montana marketplace through its two offices in Great Falls and Missoula.

The Lawyers: "*A superb communicator*" and the partner in charge of the Montana offices, **John Manning** "*takes the time to look into the business he is dealing with to enable him to give very specific advice.*" He works with a talented pool of attorneys, from which interviewees say he can always find the right person for the right problem. In terms of securities work, he is described as simply "*brilliant.*" Manning is perhaps best known for his work with emerging companies, though he also represents public companies, investors, banks and underwriters. Fellow partner **Mae Ellingson**, who operates out of the Missoula office, is considered by peers to be "*probably the best bond attorney in the state.*" Her practice encompasses legislative as well as transactional advice, and she has represented many governmental bodies.

The Clients: Among the numerous private and public companies the firm represents are Right-Now Technologies, DA Davidson & Co and United Financial Corp.

Garlington, Lohn & Robinson, PLLP

The Firm: "*Probably the best firm in Missoula,*" said one client of this well-established western Montana outfit. It provides a comprehensive service in the corporate and commercial sphere and offers a number of specialist lawyers. Acting for clients across the state, the firm recently represented the Yellowstone Mountain Club on one of its biggest deals yet.

The Lawyers: **Steve Brown** is a dynamic lawyer with a specific interest in environmental law, natural resources and land use. Even those who have not worked with him admit that his reputation alone "*sends positive vibes.*" His regulatory and transactional advice covers permitting, enforcement actions and Superfund matters, and is directed at both public and private concerns. **Gary Chumrau** has made a name for himself though his work with clients in the healthcare sector and counts many medical practices, hospitals and similar organizations among his clients.

The Clients: Milwaukee Railroad; Mountain Water Company; Yellowstone Mountain Club and The Sterling Group.

Band 2

Boone, Karlberg PC

The Firm: This Missoula firm acts for a broad client base ranging from small entities to large corporates and banks. Attorneys here are said by peers to be prompt and accurate with an unpretentious and yet creative approach to business transactions.

The Lawyers: President of the firm **Tom Boone** "*would be at the top of my list,*" said one commentator. This "*ethical*" lawyer has many years of experience and is involved with several regional corporations on a fairly regular basis, advising on general corporate, real estate and planning matters. He recently advised on the disposal of a successful dental practice by way of the sale of corporate assets with an employment agreement and a covenant not to compete.

The Clients: Ronan State Bank; Jore Corporation; First Security Bank; BJ's Metalworks; Ingersoll-Rand and Sun Mountain Sports.

Christian, Samson, Jones & Chisholm, PLLC

The Firm: This smaller Missoula firm blends younger business attorneys with established practitioners to create a recognized name for dynamism and wisdom. It does an "excellent job" in banking and bankruptcy matters.

The Lawyers: Of "courteous and professional" David Chisholm, commentators say that he is "a quality guy with a heavy dose of pragmatism." At his best on banking matters, "his goal is always to get the transaction completed."

The Clients: First Interstate Bank; American Bank of Montana; Stockman Bank of Montana; Rocky Mountain Bancorporation; Rocky Mountain Bank and The Bridger Company.

Holland & Hart LLP

See firm details p.325

The Firm: A range of experience, extending from operating agreements to M&A, bankruptcy and IP, together with specialized industry knowledge, makes this small Billings firm "one of the toughest in town." Tax planning and natural resources are key focus areas.

The Lawyers: Charles Hingle (see p.1080) is regarded as "a very smart and solid lawyer with good technical skills." Best known for his bankruptcy practice, he is effective in banking, real estate and commercial litigation too. Larry Petersen (see p.1080) drew high praise from clients and other lawyers; he is a powerful negotiator, "very influential" and has "great business acumen."

The Clients: Clients include Ballard Petroleum, Wesco Resources and Double D Energy.

EMPLOYMENT

MAINLY DEFENDANT

Montana
Leading firms
(Employment: Mainly Defendant)

1. CROWLEY, HAUGHEY, HANSON, TOOLE *Billings*
   GARLINGTON, LOHN & ROBINSON *Missoula*
   HOLLAND & HART LLP *Billings*
2. BROWN LAW FIRM PC *Billings*
   DORSEY & WHITNEY LLP *Great Falls*
   GOUGH, SHANAHAN, JOHNSON *Helena*
   HUGHES, KELLNER, SULLIVAN & ALKE *Helena*
   UGRIN, ALEXANDER, ZADICK *Great Falls*
   WORDEN THANE PC *Missoula*

Leading individuals
(Employment: Mainly Defendant)

1. BENDER Jeanne *Holland & Hart, Billings*
   FETSCHER Candace *Garlington Lohn, Missoula*
   LEHMAN Steven *Crowley Haughey, Billings*
   SULLIVAN John *Hughes Kellner, Helena*
   ZADICK Gary *Ugrin Alexander, Great Falls*
2. HATTERSLEY III Thomas *Gough Shanahan, Helena*
   HERINGER Michael *Brown Law Firm, Billings*
   KUTZMAN John *Dorsey & Whitney, Great Falls*
   LENNON Maureen *Garlington Lohn, Missoula*
   THANE Jeremy *Worden Thane, Missoula*

Up-and-coming individuals
CHRISTENSEN Amy *Hughes Kellner, Helena*
FRANCE Lucy *Garlington Lohn, Missoula*

Firms and individuals are listed alphabetically in each band.

Band 1

Crowley, Haughey, Hanson, Toole & Dietrich, PLLP

The Firm: The firm's labor and employment law practice is among the largest and most established in the state. The team has experienced a substantial increase in the number of wrongful discharge and discrimination cases, recently defending a banking client in one such matter. In another case it defended the Great Falls Pre-Release Center from a claim alleging sex discrimination.

The Lawyers: Steve Lehman is admired by clients for his intellect and knowledge, and by his peers for his good judgment and candidness. These traits combine to make Lehman "a very effective litigator." He is especially adept at advising on employee relations and how to avoid wrongful discharge and discrimination claims.

The Clients: The Bank of Baker; First Interstate Bank; City of Billings; CTA and MDU Resources Group and Stockman Bank.

Garlington, Lohn & Robinson, PLLP

The Firm: Besides litigating discrimination and wrongful discharge matters, the firm's seven-partner employment law team spends time counseling clients on employment policies and contracts, including noncompete clauses. In turn, clients consider the team to be "organized and efficient" and extremely "service-oriented." One commentator revealed how "the firm appears to have a well-rounded staff with a good knowledge of industry specifics."

The Lawyers: Candace Fetscher is known for her meticulous approach and "amazing grasp of the area;" according to one source, "she does an excellent job of educating clients." Some attorneys label her as "the top person" in Missoula, not only for labor and employment law but also for medical malpractice and healthcare matters. Acclaimed for her "remarkable work," Maureen Lennon is a "great problem solver." She is first and foremost a litigator, whose practice has a heavy emphasis on employment law. Finally, younger attorney Lucy France is applauded for being "extremely competent and efficient." Her practice encompasses all aspects of employment law, both counseling and litigation.

The Clients: Tamarack Management; Community Medical Centre; Marcus Daly Hospital; Clark Fork Valley Hospital; Beach Transportation; Southgate Mall and the Yellowstone Club.

Holland & Hart LLP

See firm details p.325

The Firm: There are two partners and two associates working on employment matters at the Holland & Hart's Billings office. The past year has brought a number of disability discrimination cases, on which the firm has a good record of settlement. The team was successful in obtaining summary judgment in two separate employment-related tort cases brought against two of its clients, a utility and a mining company.

The Lawyers: According to clients, one-of-a-kind Jeanne Bender (see p.1079) has "great practical knowledge and is realistic when advising on a situation." Peers, too, admit that "not many people have as much knowledge as she has." She recently obtained favorable results in four disability and sex discrimination cases before the Montana Human Rights Commission. Her practice encompasses not only employment law, both litigation and counseling, but also natural resources and general commercial matters.

The Clients: Ballard Petroleum; Wesco Resources; Stockman Bank; Security Armored Express; Northern Directory Publishing and 3 Rivers Communications.

Band 2

Brown Law Firm PC

The Firm: A highly qualified and competent Billings firm, Brown has caught the attention of the market for its broad-ranging litigation prowess. It is also highly regarded in the labor and employment law field.

The Lawyers: Michael Heringer is an excellent all-round litigator, who handles his clients with great care and shows charisma in front of a jury. His charm works on peers too; they describe him as "a very likable guy" and "a gentleman" who "thinks on his feet." Heringer was praised especially for his experience on workers' compensation.

www.ChambersandPartners.com
All quotes in the text are from interviews with clients and competitors.
1073

Dorsey & Whitney LLP

The Firm: The Great Falls office of this international firm benefits from the technical and staff support of their many offices spread across the USA. The labor and employment team represents a variety of clients, including regional and national employers as well as individuals.

The Lawyers: **John Kutzman** is a *"very bright attorney,"* who deals with a considerable number of wage and hour issues and wrongful discharge cases both at trial and on appeal. He recently worked on a brief of appeal for a summary judgment for Bombardier Motor.

The Clients: The team represents various regional and national businesses.

Gough, Shanahan, Johnson & Waterman

The Firm: The firm represents market leaders in a variety of industries, though its market position is more usually attributed to its relationships with natural resources and technology industry clients. Six attorneys are active in the employment and labor law field, particularly so on collective bargaining and cases of wrongful discharge and discrimination.

The Lawyers: **Tom Hattersley** has a fine reputation for representing major mining companies. He has been practicing in this area for almost 20 years and is additionally known for his work on issues such as civil rights and safety compliance. Depth of knowledge together with the breadth of experience make him *"a top-notch lawyer,"* and commentators appreciate his *"straightforward"* manner.

The Clients: The firm represents a range of industrial and commercial employers.

Hughes, Kellner, Sullivan & Alke

The Firm: The firm's employment lawyers deal with large local and statewide clients, who confirm there are two key things they admire most about their advisers: the quality of legal analysis and the team's dexterity in handling matters like discrimination or wrongful discharge.

The Lawyers: **John Sullivan** has *"a great legal mind"* and long experience counseling employers. Sources describe him as being *"tremendously knowledgeable and thoughtful"* with *"good judgment."* Besides litigating, he is also involved in a good deal of mediation and arbitration. **Amy Christensen** is an *"amazingly bright"* up-and-comer. She handles cases with great accuracy and confidence: *"She knows what she's doing."*

The Clients: Shodair Children's Hospital; Carroll College; Morrison-Maierle Engineering; Mergenthaler Transfer & Storage; Montana School Services Foundation; Montana Education Association and Montana State University.

Ugrin, Alexander, Zadick & Higgins, PC

The Firm: This Great Falls outfit has a notable profile in labor and employment law. It has been busy representing Liberty County in litigation with the Teamsters Union over benefits, and Northern Rockies Medical Center in labor negotiations and an arbitration concerning a discharged employee.

The Lawyers: Though he does not work exclusively in this field, **Gary Zadick** has the perfect combination of employment knowledge and trial capability. *"Very professional, extremely bright and detail conscious"* is how the market describes him, while taking the time to also acknowledge his status as a *"tremendously skilled mediator."*

The Clients: Chotaeu; BMC West/Poulsens; Herberger Department Store; Smith's Food & Drug Stores and Albertson's.

Worden Thane PC

The Firm: Missoula-based Worden Thane's employment practice focuses on matters such as discrimination and wrongful discharge cases, wage and hour disputes, labor negotiations and contract negotiations on behalf of employers. The team has been described as being very thorough, sharp and efficient and has had a busy past twelve months. The team recently represented the St Patrick Hospital and Health Sciences Center in the negotiation of a collective bargaining agreement with registered nurses.

The Lawyers: A long-established, traditional labor lawyer, **Jeremy Thane** is considered to be *"the go-see man for union matters."* He has recently been providing advice regarding collective bargaining agreements for various members of the Employers Association of Western Montana, and represented Missoula Cartage Company on collective bargaining over a contract renewal. During the period of the negotiations, several unfair labor practice charges had to be defended and the employees filed a petition with the NLRB seeking an election to decertify the union.

The Clients: The firm represents St Patrick Hospital, Glendive Medical Center and Montana Nurses' Association, among others.

LITIGATION

GENERAL COMMERCIAL

Montana
Leading firms
(Litigation: General Commercial)

1
CHRISTENSEN, MOORE, COCKRELL *Kalispell*
CROWLEY, HAUGHEY, HANSON, TOOLE *Billings*
GARLINGTON, LOHN & ROBINSON *Missoula*

2
BOONE, KARLBERG PC *Missoula*
DORSEY & WHITNEY LLP *Great Falls*
EDWARDS FRICKLE ANNER-HUGHES *Billings*
POORE, ROTH & ROBINSON, PC *Butte*

3
BROWN LAW FIRM PC *Billings*
GOETZ, GALLIK & BALDWIN, PC *Bozeman*
GOUGH, SHANAHAN, JOHNSON *Helena*
LEWIS & SLOVAK PC *Great Falls*

4
BROWNING, KALECZYC, BERRY & HOVEN *Helena*
HOLLAND & HART LLP *Billings*
HUGHES, KELLNER, SULLIVAN & ALKE *Helena*
UGRIN, ALEXANDER, ZADICK *Great Falls*

Firms are listed alphabetically in each band.

Band 1

Christensen, Moore, Cockrell, Cummings & Axelberg PC

The Firm: Charging into the top band of the table is a team of six attorneys who defend clients in all types of civil trial and appellate litigation. Christensen Moore is recognized as the firm to go to for medical malpractice defense. In 2004, its attorneys successfully defended an orthopedic surgeon in a Missoula federal court case. The allegation of negligent treatment and care made by a 62-year-old skier was rejected by the jury.

The Lawyers: **Dana Christensen** is a thorough, well-organized lawyer with a *"terrific presence in court."* As one commentator put it. *"He is smooth, earnest and extremely smart: he has a lethal combination of qualities!"* Christensen has seen an increase in the volume of medical malpractice claims on his desk, but continues to work on diverse commercial disputes for corporate clients. **Mikel Moore** can commonly be found defending resorts in ski area liability cases, though he also deals with governmental tort claims, insurance bad faith and employment litigation. He is said to be extremely focused and a man who *"gets things done."* **Tracy Axelberg** is known for his mediation work, with many regarding him as *"the best mediator in the state."* Beyond this, he has been dealing with litigation concerning professional negligence, construction defects and insurance defense.

The Clients: St. Paul; The Doctors Company; Ophthalmic Mutual Insurance Company; Allstate; State Farm; AIG; USAA; Unum Life Insurance Company and CNA Insurance Companies.

Crowley, Haughey, Hanson, Toole & Dietrich, PLLP

The Firm: Crowley's 50-attorney department is the biggest in the state and covers all aspects of litigation from its five offices. In the past year

1074   All quotes in the text are from interviews with clients and competitors.

CHAMBERS USA 2005

Montana
Leading individuals
(Litigation: General Commercial)

Senior Statesman
JONES William *Garlington Lohn*, Missoula

[1] CHRISTENSEN Dana *Christensen Moore*, Kalispell
COX Randy *Boone Karlberg*, Missoula
GOETZ James *Goetz Gallik*, Bozeman
GRAHAM Gary *Garlington Lohn*, Missoula
LEWIS Tom *Lewis & Slovak*, Great Falls
ROBINSON Donald *Poore Roth*, Butte
STRONG Keith *Dorsey & Whitney*, Great Falls

[2] EDWARDS A Clifford *Edwards Frickle*, Billings
KELLNER Stuart *Hughes Kellner*, Helena
MAYNARD Joe *Crowley Haughey*, Billings
MOORE Mikel *Christensen Moore*, Kalispell
SHERIDAN Robert *Garlington Lohn*, Missoula
TALEFF Ward *Alexander Baucus*, Great Falls
WATERMAN Ronald *Gough Shanahan*, Helena
WELSCH Thomas *Poore Roth*, Butte

[3] ANNER-HUGHES Roberta *Edwards Frickle*, Billings
AXELBERG Tracy *Christensen Moore*, Kalispell
DALY Lawrence *Garlington Lohn*, Missoula
HINGLE Charles *Holland & Hart*, Billings
KALECZYC Stanley *Browning Kaleczyc*, Helena
MACDONALD Terry *Garlington Lohn*, Missoula
O'CONNELL Barry *Moore O'Connell*, Bozeman
PFENNIGS Robert *Jardine Stephenson*, Great Falls
SULLIVAN Robert *Boone Karlberg*, Missoula
UGRIN Neil *Ugrin Alexander*, Great Falls

Up-and-coming individuals
MCINTOSH Ian *Crowley Haughey*, Bozeman
WESTESEN Neil *Crowley Haughey*, Bozeman

Individuals are listed alphabetically in each band.

attorneys have tackled many workers' compensation, medical malpractice and contract disputes. The law firm is representing the officers of Touch America Holdings who attempted a transition from a utility to a dotcom and went into bankruptcy. The case seeks return of several million dollars paid in 'golden parachutes'.
The Lawyers: Clients say **Joe Maynard** "*supersedes all other lawyers*," while peers note how hard he works to settle a case. Maynard excels in personal injury, contractual disputes and medical malpractice. "*In a few years we will be talking about* **Ian McIntosh**," one attorney predicted of the lawyer who enters the tables this year. His practice incorporates general civil litigation and more specialist areas such as products liability or casualty insurance defense. Another up-and-comer is **Neil Westesen**, whom a client described as "*one of the best lawyers at Crowley*." This smart trial attorney practices in construction law, Indian law and commercial litigation.
The Clients: Clients include local, national and international businesses and corporations.

Garlington, Lohn & Robinson, PLLP
The Firm: Dubbed "*the best of the west*" by a Montana competitor, this firm's litigation team has represented many of the state's leading companies in complex disputes. As is to be expected of the second-largest firm in Montana, Garlington has a large and prestigious client base that includes insurance companies and banks, many of them nationwide organizations. Its attorneys are said to be bright, extremely hard working and client-focused.
The Lawyers: **William Jones** is a "*highly skilled*" civil litigation lawyer, who focuses primarily on products liability, major negligence and insurance bad-faith cases. This "*unparalleled*" litigator has "*tried more cases than anyone else in the state*" and does a "*tremendous job*." **Gary Graham** is a man with "*judgment and common sense*." He has a well-seasoned reputation for combining trial skills and legal knowledge to great effect, and in court he is "*smooth and extremely well spoken*." Clients like the fact that he "*doesn't get lost in details*." Graham handles everything from general negligence claims, products liability and toxic torts through to ERISA. "*Brilliant*" **Robert Sheridan** is a "*solid guy*" whose top priority is always "*to get the case resolved*." He has taken on the role of mediator in the latter part of a 30-year career in which he has handed civil trial litigation and appellate matters at both state and federal level. The firm's managing partner, **Lawrence Daly**, is a hard-working, thorough attorney who is "*very good at developing a case*." His practice is broad ranging, and he has worked on some high-profile, complex cases lately. **Terry MacDonald** "*will be the leader of the next generation*," said a lawyer from a rival firm. His practice is also wide in scope, incorporating commercial litigation, toxic torts, personal injury and employment law.
The Clients: The firm advises regional and national clients from a variety of industry sectors.

Band 2

Boone, Karlberg PC
The Firm: Boone, Karlberg is depicted as "*a very clever firm in the west of Montana*." The litigation team is comprised of eight attorneys and is closely associated with railroad cases. It recently completed work on a lengthy bad-faith contract termination claim against the State of Montana, in which it represented the state.
The Lawyers: Fearless and successful, **Randy Cox** is considered by other members of the bar to be a "*worthy adversary*" and "*the full package*." This great legal scholar is especially thorough when it comes to preparing cases: "*If there is a way to win the case, Randy will find it*." He is at his best on toxic torts, products liability, professional negligence and, perhaps his strongest suit, railroad litigation. **Robert Sullivan** is a "*seasoned, bright and hard-working attorney*," who is at his finest in the courtroom. His trial experience is practically boundless, and he is familiar with all forums up to and including the US Court of Appeal.
The Clients: Montana Rail Link; Farmers Alliance Mutual Insurance; State of Montana; Burlington Northern Santa Fe Railway; Sterling Savings Bank and First Interstate Bank.

Dorsey & Whitney LLP
The Firm: The firm deals with general commercial, securities and derivatives lawsuits as well as some white-collar crime. In the area of professional negligence, it recently met with success when defending another law firm in a malpractice case. Although the firm's main activity takes place in Great Falls, its one-man Missoula practice is also busy and widely respected.
The Lawyers: Dorsey's man in Missoula is the "*intuitive*" **Keith Strong**, a bright and industrious attorney, sometimes referred to as "*the lawyers' lawyer*." He is famous for his soft manner with juries, but can be suitably aggressive in negotiations. Strong's practice encompasses commercial and securities litigation and white-collar criminal defense. Those who work with or against him agree with his reputation for high standards and describe him as a "*tremendous lawyer*."
The Clients: The firm's base of financial and investment, technology, energy, life sciences and emerging company clients is reflected in its litigation clientele.

Edwards Frickle Anner-Hughes & Cook
The Firm: This Billings plaintiff firm is small but packed with "*energetic people*" who are regularly engaged in litigation with major insurance companies and corporates. Serious personal injury and wrongful death as a result of product defects, toxic torts and transportation disasters are specialities.
The Lawyers: **Clifford Edwards** is one of the most successful plaintiff lawyers in Montana, perhaps because "*he is very technical, very good at preparing cases – lining up the facts, etc*," and is then "*extremely smooth in court*," doubtless due to his "*incredible jury appeal and great gut instincts*." While excelling in personal injury, specifically brain and spinal cord injuries, he is also a respected general civil litigator, and, not content with life as an attorney, Edwards runs a renowned Angus ranch and an air charter business. His right-hand woman is name partner **Bobby Anner-Hughes**. She is "*strong on the law*," has good judgment and is an "*excellent writer*."

Poore, Roth & Robinson, PC
The Firm: The ten-partner litigation team accounts for the majority of the firm, a fact that reflects its long-established litigation bent. Defending insurance companies against all types of claim, not least personal injury and medical malpractice suits, and entering the fray

in sex discrimination cases for employer clients, attorneys are not afraid of a set-to in court.

The Lawyers: *"Tenacious"* **Donald Robinson** is considered *"a real bulldog."* He tries case after case, yet does not tire of immersing himself deeply in the law and expertly juggling with the facts. *"He's my favorite,"* said one top-level rival; and from another, *"I can't say enough good things about him."* Robinson has what can only be described as an extremely broad litigation practice. For a complicated case, **Thomas Welsch** *"is your man"*, according to a number of commentators. Clients use him again and again because *"he is quick and accessible,"* provides a thorough analysis of a case and *"knows what he is doing."*

The Clients: Clients include Continental Western Insurance, Safeco Life and The Doctors' Company.

Band 3

Brown Law Firm PC

The Firm: This Billings firm is an established part of the Montana litigation scene. Its work is wide ranging, with attorneys handling cases in the fields of general civil litigation, medical malpractice, professional negligence, insurance coverage and employment law.

The Lawyers: Michael Heringer, who is ranked in the employment law section, is the lead name in the litigation practice.

The Clients: The firm acts for a number of insurance companies and well-known corporates.

Goetz, Gallik & Baldwin, PC

The Firm: First and foremost a litigation firm, this Bozeman outfit boasts a small but dedicated team. It recently worked on a case for an aircraft charter company that rejected two defective aeroplanes, and completed a jury trial on a construction case concerning defective custom-fabricated windows. Attorneys additionally settled a complicated malpractice case.

The Lawyers: **James Goetz** is in his element handling complex commercial cases. While he can be *"extremely technical"* and, when necessary, *"very aggressive,"* he is *"always polished."* Experienced in the lower courts and *"a terrific appellate lawyer,"* Goetz's practice encompasses constitutional, criminal, environmental and plaintiff personal-injury work in addition to general commercial and business litigation.

The Clients: Edwards Jet Center; Confederated Salish and Kootenai Tribes; Flathead Reservation and Blue Cross and Blue Shield of Montana.

Gough, Shanahan, Johnson & Waterman

The Firm: The firm's pedigree is an illustrious one and is closely tied to the state's natural resources. Despite a slowdown in the mining sector, there remains a substantial amount of work for Gough Shanahan, which has a major interest in mining and all related legal disciplines, including environmental law. Insurance defense, health and safety litigation, employment cases and general commercial disputes all keep a substantial litigation bench active in the Montana courts, at both state and federal levels.

The Lawyers: Senior figure **Ronald Waterman** is applauded by peers for his ability to resolve complex cases and his equal adeptness in acting for both plaintiffs and defendants. His trial experience is particularly wide in scope.

Lewis & Slovak PC

The Firm: The Great Falls plaintiff firm of Lewis & Slovak has gained a reputation for its statewide civil litigation practice, covering among other things insurance law, personal injury, toxic tort, products liability and workers' compensation. It recently convinced a jury to return a verdict ordering Texaco to pay over $40 million in cleanup costs and damages following a pipeline leak in 1955.

The Lawyers: Managing partner **Tom Lewis** has impressed the market with his tenacity and *"outstanding trial skills."* Peer recommendations see this *"very creative lawyer"* rising to the top band of the table.

The Clients: The firm represents plaintiffs, including corporate clients.

Band 4

Browning, Kaleczyc, Berry & Hoven PC

The Firm: Attorneys at the Helena firm handle almost all types of litigation and appellate work, including general commercial cases, medical malpractice, municipal liability, products liability and workers' compensation. Of late they have represented clients on complex commercial cases involving bankruptcy and securities matters.

The Lawyers: *"Highly competent"* founding member **Stanley Kaleczyc** is the chair of the firm's busy commercial group and has represented leading businesses in the telecommunication and transportation industries.

The Clients: Northwestern Corp and Montana Municipal Insurance Authority are among the firm's clientele.

Holland & Hart LLP

See firm details p.325

The Firm: As the largest firm in the Rocky Mountain Region, Holland & Hart fields many experienced litigators across its seven offices. Undoubtedly benefiting from the back up of colleagues out of state, the Billings' office provides quality, full-service representation to a whole range of businesses.

The Lawyers: **Charles Hingle** (see p.1080) primarily handles bankruptcy matters and is as admired for his transactional and advisory practice as he is for his litigation practice.

The Clients: The firm represents local, national and international companies.

Hughes, Kellner, Sullivan & Alke

The Firm: A smaller Helena-based firm specializing in personal injury and insurance defense, employment law and business law.

The Lawyers: **Stuart Kellner**'s name is known around the state, and for all the right reasons. While perceived to be *"very thorough and capable in court,"* he is more usually mentioned in relation to his mediation practice: he is *"always on the shortlist for mediation cases."*

The Clients: Chubb Group; Montana Children's Home & Hospital; Montana Department of Commerce; Qwest Corporation and Dick Anderson Construction.

Ugrin, Alexander, Zadick & Higgins, PC

The Firm: This Great Falls firm tries civil cases in both state and federal courts. Its work includes insurance, products liability, medical malpractice and healthcare law, personal injury and employment law.

The Lawyers: **Neil Ugrin** is considered an *"outstanding lawyer."* He is famous for his healthcare litigation and medical malpractice defense, representing a great number of doctors and hospitals across the state.

The Clients: Capitol Indemnity Group; Chrysler; City of Great Falls; Brunswick Corp and Mountainview Medical Center.

Other Notable Practitioners

Ward Taleff of Alexander, Baucus, Taleff & Paul PC is considered one of the best litigators in Great Falls. His peers portray him as *"a very thorough attorney"* with broad experience: *"He is a genius!"* insisted one client. **Barry O'Connell** of Moore, O'Connell & Refling PC is a client-focused, cost-effective and a smart general civil litigator according to interviewees. **Robert Pfennigs** of Jardine, Stephenson, Blewett and Weaver PC specializes in product liability and general negligence. He recently represented a client in a successful action against the Montana Power Company.

1076   All quotes in the text are from interviews with clients and competitors.

CHAMBERS USA 2005

NATURAL RESOURCES & ENVIRONMENT

Montana
Leading firms
(Natural Resources & Environment)

[1] BROWNING, KALECZYC, BERRY & HOVEN *Helena*
CHRISTENSEN, MOORE, COCKRELL *Kalispell*
CROWLEY, HAUGHEY, HANSON, TOOLE *Billings*
DONEY, CROWLEY, BLOOMQUIST, PAYNE *Helena*
GARLINGTON, LOHN & ROBINSON *Missoula*
GOUGH, SHANAHAN, JOHNSON *Helena*
HOLLAND & HART LLP *Billings*

Leading individuals
(Natural Resources & Environment)

[1] BROWN Stephen *Garlington Lohn, Missoula*
COCKRELL Dale *Christensen Moore, Kalispell*
CROWLEY Frank *Doney Crowley, Helena*
FOSTER Stephen *Holland & Hart, Billings*
JOSCELYN Alan *Gough Shanahan, Helena*
QUANDER Don *Holland & Hart, Billings*
RUFFATTO Steven *Crowley Haughey, Billings*

[2] BERRY Leo *Browning Kaleczyc, Helena*
LEE John *Crowley Haughey, Billings*
METROPOULOS Jon *Gough Shanahan, Helena*
ROSS John *Brown Law Firm, Billings*

Up-and-coming individuals
WADE Steven *Browning Kaleczyc, Helena*

Firms and individuals are listed alphabetically in each band.

Band 1

Browning, Kaleczyc, Berry & Hoven PC

The Firm: Situated in Helena, this 22-attorney firm has one of the largest practice groups in Montana. The team's principal areas of expertise include Superfund, water law, environmental and natural resources litigation and environmental permitting and compliance. Its six lawyers represent federal and state agencies as well as public interest groups across the state and beyond.
The Lawyers: At the head of the environment practice group, **Leo Berry** is one of the most knowledgeable lawyers in Helena. His experience serving as the Montana Commissioner of State Lands and the Director of the Department of Natural Resources and Conservation make him an ideal lobbyist. His practice areas include Superfund, environmental and natural resources litigation, government relations and administrative proceedings. **Steven Wade** is a *"young, thorough, sharp and focused"* environmental litigator who deals with a variety of commercial clients. He additionally counsels on regulatory issues, hazardous waste and air quality.
The Clients: The Burlington Northern and Santa Fe Railway; ConocoPhillips; Bull Mountain Development; NorthWestern Energy; Columbia Falls Aluminum and Great Northern Power.

Christensen, Moore, Cockrell, Cummings & Axelberg PC

The Firm: Kalispell-based Christensen Moore offers a well-honed, one-man practice providing in-depth advice on natural resources and environment law, including cleanup, toxic tort and clean air and water issues. Timber and mining concerns have beaten a path to the firm's door.
The Lawyers: Popular **Dale Cockrell** calls the shots in this field of work. A vast amount of experience working for natural resources clients, clear dedication and sheer hard work make him one of the best in the state, a fact that has not escaped the notice of rivals. Cockrell is devoting an increasing amount of time to defending clients from claims relating to toxic tort or clean air and water issues.
The Clients: Homestake Mining Company and Noranda Minerals are among the firm's clients.

Crowley, Haughey, Hanson, Toole & Dietrich, PLLP

The Firm: Billings-based and with nine attorneys working on environment and natural resources matters, this practice group is one of the largest in Montana. Between them, its lawyers have admirable breadth of experience and are regarded as efficient in their way of working. Mining law, Superfund, oil and gas and natural resources litigation all feature on the menu.
The Lawyers: *"Highly respected in the mining business,"* **Steve Ruffatto** is possibly the best-known oil, gas and mining attorney in the state. He has substantial experience in Superfund (CERCLA and CECRA) and clients portray him as a pragmatic, responsive character who never forgets to *"take into account the commercial realities of any deal."* Though younger, **John Lee** also has a wealth of experience and is known for his practical, as opposed to purely legal, advice. Working primarily on oil and gas matters, he has recently been representing Headington Oil.
The Clients: Nexen Oil & Gas USA; Noranda; Consol Energy; Merchant Banking; Headington Oil; Lyco Energy; Newmont Mining Company.

Doney, Crowley, Bloomquist, Payne & Uda, PC

The Firm: This firm's Helena base has boosted its lobbying capability, an aspect of practice that one client felt it managed *"superbly."* Besides regulatory work, the team covers all facets of environment and natural resources law, and represents many corporations on matters relating to water quality, contamination, solid waste and resource development.
The Lawyers: **Frank Crowley** is *"a very ethical attorney"* who shows *"great respect for his clients."* Proficient in both environment and natural resources matters, his time is spent on everything

from hazardous waste and air quality issues to environmental auditing. His water rights practice is arguably the strongest in Montana.
The Clients: The firm represents both private and public sector clients, including the Montana Department of Environmental Quality.

Garlington, Lohn & Robinson, PLLP

The Firm: Representing large corporations on environment and natural resources issues, the two-partners-and-one-associate team have recently worked on one of the largest settlements with the EPA. It has also represented the State of Montana on some of its cleanup cases and secured permits for large resorts.
The Lawyers: After nearly 15 years in the business, environmental specialist **Stephen Brown** does *"an excellent job."* Advising on everything from water rights to Superfund, and boasting excellent lobbying skills, Brown is felt by some to have an academic approach, though they stress that this only serves to enhance his appeal.
The Clients: Mountain Water Company; Louisiana-Pacific Corporation; Roseburg Forest Products; Yellowstone Mountain Club; Spanish Peaks Resort; Bitterroot Resort; The Sterling Group; Avista and the State of Montana.

Gough, Shanahan, Johnson & Waterman

The Firm: Lawyers at this Western Montana firm are said to be excellent at handling water rights and water quality issues. Based in Helena, the team incorporates regulatory advice and lobbying into its practice.
The Lawyers: Market sources lined up to praise the considerable knowledge and experience of **Alan Joscelyn**. He was described by one as *"a brilliant lawyer with a lot of experience in the mining business,"* and by another as *"the best in coal-bed methane cases,"* which have become a major issue lately. The strength of these plaudits aside, mining is just one aspect of his broad environment and natural resources practice. Involved in regulatory matters on a regular basis, **Jon Metropoulos** is an *"excellent,"* young and dynamic attorney, who is known for his work on water matters and the concerns of Indian tribes. Metropoulos has also involved himself in coal-bed methane litigation.
The Clients: The firm represents Magellan Resources, Montana Mining Association and Rocky Mountain Power.

Holland & Hart LLP
See firm details p.325
The Firm: Regional giant Holland & Hart's Montana practice provides a specific service to high-end clients in areas such as title research and land ownership, energy management and energy contracts. The firm has recently repre-

sented ARCO on a case involving the recovery of cleanup costs worth $700 million.

The Lawyers: **Don Quander**'s (see p.1080) *"extraordinary industrial intelligence"* enables him to have *"a firm grasp of the end-use requirements of a company;" "he understands the process, not just the contract,"* revealed one satisfied client. This extremely thorough attorney centers his practice on energy-related issues (contract nego-

tiations and regulatory matters) plus air quality work. Representing a substantial number of large mining companies, **Steve Foster** (see p.1080) has participated in environmental litigation, coal-bed methane and Superfund cases for more than 30 years.

The Clients: ARCO; ExxonMobil; Smurfit-Stone Container and Stillwater Mining.

Other Notable Practitioners

John Ross of the Brown Law Firm PC in Billings has been involved in environment and natural resources law since the 1970's. Combining experience with intelligence, he deals with a substantial number of NEPA cases. Clients include Brenntag in New York and Pioneer Natural Resources in Texas.

REAL ESTATE

Montana
Leading firms (Real Estate)

1. **BOONE, KARLBERG PC** *Missoula*
   CROWLEY, HAUGHEY, HANSON, TOOLE *Billings*
   GARLINGTON, LOHN & ROBINSON *Missoula*
2. **CHRISTENSEN, MOORE, COCKRELL** *Kalispell*
   HEARD & HOWARD *Columbus*
   MOULTON, BELLINGHAM, LONGO *Billings*
3. **MOORE, O'CONNELL & REFLING PC** *Bozeman*
   SULLIVAN, TABARACCI AND RHOADES *Missoula*
   WORDEN THANE PC *Missoula*

Leading individuals (Real Estate)

1. **CUMMINGS Stephen** *Christensen Moore, Kalispell*
   DOCKERY Michael *Crowley Haughey, Billings*
   KNIGHT Robert *Sole Practitioner, Missoula*
   SULLIVAN Zane *Sullivan Tabaracci, Missoula*
   WAGNER William *Garlington Lohn, Missoula*
2. **BOONE Thomas** *Boone Karlberg, Missoula*
   HEARD Richard *Heard & Howard, Columbus*
   HOWARD Douglas *Heard & Howard, Columbus*
   JONES John *Moulton Bellingham, Billings*
   KARELL Allan *Crowley Haughey, Billings*
   MCELYEA Russell *Moore O'Connell, Bozeman*
   STENSLAND Dean *Boone Karlberg, Missoula*

Firms and individuals are listed alphabetically in each band.

Band 1

Boone, Karlberg PC

The Firm: The five-attorney real estate team within this full-service firm has developed a niche in ranch transactions. The team acted for the seller of a 600-plus-acre recreational and operating ranch, and is in the process of handling ranch sales with tax-free exchanges. Clients trust the team and other attorneys feel more than comfortable referring work to it.

The Lawyers: Also ranked in the corporate table, experienced all-rounder **Thomas Boone** has proved himself *"a first-rate real estate lawyer."* He is known for his tenacity and determination to see a deal through to completion, and has engendered great loyalty from clients. He was recently involved as the attorney for the seller of a 3300-acre ranch. Skilled in both litigation and transactional matters, **Dean**

Stensland does some *"brilliant work"* in real estate. His peers are convinced that, given a little more time, he is destined for the first tier of the table.

The Clients: Hi-Noon Petroleum; Farmers Alliance Mutual Insurance Company; Montana Rail Link; Sterling Savings Bank and First Interstate Bank.

Crowley, Haughey, Hanson, Toole & Dietrich, PLLP

The Firm: This firm's real estate practice focuses mainly on commercial and agricultural transactions, including subdivision, development, finance and bankruptcy proceedings, commonly representing creditors. Clients regard its work as being outstanding, saying of attorneys, *"they are good at keeping things simple."* Other lawyers would not hesitate to outsource work to the firm.

The Lawyers: **Michael Dockery**, *"one of the best real estate lawyers on the market,"* is at home on both transactional and litigation matters. He is very bright, *"smooth and attentive"* and *"a few dollars go a long way with him."* **Allan Karell**, too, has a strong reputation. Depicted as a *"solution-oriented attorney,"* his practice encompasses agricultural loans and farm, ranch and business sales.

The Clients: Streeter Brothers Mortgage Corp; Big Sky Economic Development Authority; First Interstate Bank of Commerce; First American Title Insurance Company; Fidelity National Title Insurance Company and Chicago Title Insurance Company.

Garlington, Lohn & Robinson, PLLP

The Firm: An increasing amount of real estate-related litigation has not diminished the transactional, land use and permitting capabilities of this Missoula firm. Research threw up a large volume of favorable client comment for a practice group that is regarded as having some of the most *"amazing people in Missoula"* and a very strong support team.

The Lawyers: **William Wagner** is a *"solid lawyer who really understands the law and how to implement it."* Clients trust his 30-odd years of experience and peers confirm that *"he works really hard for his people."* He is *"professional,*

thorough and always available when you need him," furthermore, *"he will get you the result you want!"*

The Clients: Maloney Properties; Canyon Resources; Alternative Service Concepts and Mountain Water Company.

Band 2

Christensen, Moore, Cockrell, Cummings & Axelberg PC

The Firm: This Kalispell firm is considered to be very professional; quite simply, its lawyers *"know what they're doing."* Besides general real estate matters, its team also deals with estate planning, environmental and natural resources. It is said of the firm that it has involvement in almost every resort development in the state.

The Lawyers: **Stephen Cummings** is a *"convincing and effective"* attorney who *"never leaves a problem unsolved."* Garnering a considerable amount of deep-felt praise from peers and clients, this is a lawyer who is *"always calm under pressure"* and *"a man of his word."* Cummings handles all aspects of real estate for his clients, who include the developers of recreational and luxury properties and homeowners' associations.

The Clients: Winter Sports Inc; USAA Insurance; The Doctors Company; American International Group and ITT Hartford.

Heard & Howard

The Firm: The practice of this smaller Columbus law firm incorporates a broad spectrum of areas including banking and finance, litigation and bankruptcy, as well as transactional real estate. It is the combination of breadth of knowledge and litigation skills that draws plaudits.

The Lawyers: Praise for the eponymous **Richard Heard** came in many forms, from the no-nonsense *"he gets to the point, he solves problems and does deals"* to the more sophisticated description of his style as *"refined."* His peers admire his practical and pragmatic approach to deals and know him best for agricultural matters. The second name partner, **Douglas Howard**, is a very solid practitioner with *"real depth of knowledge."* He spends more time on lit-

1078   All quotes in the text are from interviews with clients and competitors.

CHAMBERS USA 2005

igation than on the transactional side of real estate business.

The Clients: The firm advises local, regional and national clients.

Moulton, Bellingham, Longo & Mather, PC

The Firm: From residential services to individuals right through to large ranch and commercial acquisitions and developments, attorneys at the Moulton firm have made their mark. They are known to offer effective tax advice in conjunction with real estate transaction support and have an established niche in the healthcare sector. The firm was recently involved in four separate joint ventures between hospitals in Billings, Bozeman and Helena.

The Lawyers: **John Jones**' practice encompasses health sector-related work, probate and estate planning, business sales and acquisitions, and tax issues. Of Jones, who is popular among his peers because he is always pleasant to deal with, one source confirmed, *"the client's interests are always best served with him."*

The Clients: Video Library, St Vincent Healthcare and West Park Hospital all feature on the client roster.

Band 3

Moore, O'Connell & Refling PC

The Firm: In the words of one commentator, the firm is *"very good at keeping its clients out of the soup."* This Bozeman firm's real estate practice focuses on commercial developments, large ranches and ski resorts. The team of seven attorneys also deal with environmental law, water rights and banking, personal injury and products liability.

The Lawyers: **Russ McElyea** is a *"very bright and knowledgeable lawyer,"* whose real estate practice additionally encompasses water and land use issues plus real estate finance. His client base ranges from ski resorts to ranch owners and all agree that he is one of the best attorneys in Bozeman. Other lawyers happily refer work to him.

The Clients: Other clients include Moonlight Basin Ranch, Scottsdale Insurance and National Casualty Insurance.

Sullivan, Tabaracci and Rhoades PC

The Firm: This full-service firm is especially known for its strength in litigation, though a number of its *"very bright attorneys"* represent clients across the state on real estate matters including acquisitions, developments and financings.

The Lawyers: **Zane Sullivan**'s three decades of experience, including time spent working in the title insurance industry, have rendered him a *"tough, knowledgeable and widely respected attorney."* His practice has a strong slant towards residential matters, though he also has the loyalty of many commercial developers and owners. When not driving transactions or litigating, Sullivan runs seminars for realtors across the state.

The Clients: Circle H Ranch; Sage Development; Keystone Homes; Chevy Chase Bank and Missoula Airport Authority.

Worden Thane PC

The Firm: Though dealing mainly with commercial real estate transactions, the volume of related litigation handled by attorneys has increased recently. The team recently represented the owner of a large parcel of land on the west side of Swan Lake in litigation concerning access along the United States Forest Service's Bug Creek Road, about 1.5 miles of which runs through its client's property and is used to gain access to about 100 parcels of land.

The Lawyers: Peter Dayton and Ronald Bender are known for their work in real estate, corporate and business transactions. They specialize in conservation easements and road law. Litigation also features in the workload of these two attorneys: Bender has been representing the American West Bank in foreclosure of a $6.2 million loan on a large ranch adjacent to Missoula.

The Clients: First American Title Insurance Company; Missoula County Public Schools; First National Bank of Montana and WGM Group.

Other Notable Practitioners

Robert Knight is a sole practitioner *"who leaves nothing to chance"* and focuses on large ranch, commercial and recreational property transactions. The Hilton Garden Inn project is just one of the many complex transactions he has worked on. This outstanding lawyer is very detail conscious and inspires great confidence: *"He is an institution in the real estate business in Montana."*

Leaders in Montana

ANNER-HUGHES, Roberta
Edwards Frickle Anner-Hughes & Cook, Billings 406 256 8155
Recommended in Litigation

AXELBERG, Tracy
Christensen, Moore, Cockrell, Cummings & Axelberg PC, Kalispell
406 751 6000
Recommended in Litigation

BENDER, Jeanne Matthews
Holland & Hart LLP, Billings
406 252 2166
jbender@hollandhart.com
Recommended in Employment
Practice Areas: Partner practicing in commercial and natural resources litigation, and employment counseling and litigation. Has represented commercial and nonprofit entities in a variety of claims including breach of contract,

wrongful discharge, discrimination, wage and hour claims and labor issues. Regularly makes presentations on sexual harassment, wrongful discharge, discrimination, fair labor standards and related topics.
Prof. Memberships: Member of the American Bar Association Foundation; Montana Bar Association; American Bar Association; ABA sections on Litigation and Labor and Employment Law and Torts and Insurance Law; and the Montana Defense Trial Lawyers Association. Appointments: Past President, Montana Association of Female Executives.
Career: Admitted to the Montana (1985) and Colorado (1988) Bars, the United States District Court and the Ninth Circuit Court of Appeals.
Publications: Editor, Montana Employment Law Letter, published monthly by

M Lee Smith Publishers and Printers (Nashville). 50-State Survey: Employment Libel and Privacy Law, Montana chapter, Libel Defense Resource Center, 2004.
Personal: Received a JD (1985) and a BA (1965) from the University of Montana.

BERRY, Leo
Browning, Kaleczyc, Berry & Hoven PC, Helena 406 443 6820
Recommended in Natural Resources

BOONE, Thomas
Boone, Karlberg PC, Missoula
406 543 6646
Recommended in Corporate/M&A, Real Estate

BROWN, Stephen
Garlington, Lohn & Robinson, PLLP, Missoula 406 523 2500
Recommended in Corporate/M&A, Natural Resources

CHISHOLM, David
Christian, Samson, Jones & Chisholm, PLLC, Missoula 406 721 7772
Recommended in Corporate/M&A

CHRISTENSEN, Amy
Hughes, Kellner, Sullivan & Alke, Helena 406 442 3690
Recommended in Employment

CHRISTENSEN, Dana
Christensen, Moore, Cockrell, Cummings & Axelberg PC, Kalispell
406 751 6000
Recommended in Litigation

CHUMRAU, Gary
Garlington, Lohn & Robinson, PLLP,
Missoula 406 523 2500
Recommended in Corporate/M&A

COCKRELL, Dale
Christensen, Moore, Cockrell, Cummings & Axelberg PC, Kalispell
406 751 6000
Recommended in Natural Resources

COX, Randy
Boone, Karlberg PC, Missoula
406 543 6646
Recommended in Litigation

CROWLEY, Frank
Doney, Crowley, Bloomquist, Payne &
Uda, P.C., Helena 406 443 2211
Recommended in Natural Resources

CUMMINGS, Stephen
Christensen, Moore, Cockrell, Cummings & Axelberg PC, Kalispell
406 751 6000
Recommended in Real Estate

DALY, Lawrence
Garlington, Lohn & Robinson, PLLP,
Missoula 406 523 2500
Recommended in Litigation

DOCKERY, Michael
Crowley, Haughey, Hanson, Toole &
Dietrich, PLLP, Billings
406 252 3441
Recommended in Real Estate

EDWARDS, A Clifford
Edwards Frickle Anner-Hughes & Cook,
Billings 406 256 8155
Recommended in Litigation

ELLINGSON, Mae
Dorsey & Whitney LLP, Missoula
406 721 6025
Recommended in Corporate/M&A

FETSCHER, Candace
Garlington, Lohn & Robinson, PLLP,
Missoula 406 523 2500
Recommended in Employment

FOSTER, Stephen H
Holland & Hart LLP, Billings
406 252 2166
sfoster@hollandhart.com
Recommended in Natural Resources
Practice Areas: Mr Foster has experience in environmental and commercial litigation in state and federal courts (jury and non-jury), and has contested matters before administrative agencies. His current practice is heavily focused on CERCLA natural resource damage and cost-recovery cases. His recent practice has also included toxic tort, products liability, and legal malpractice defense. He was lead defense counsel in U.S. v ARCO and State of Montana v ARCO, two major federal court cases involving the largest superfund sites in the United States.
Prof. Memberships: Member of the American Bar Association, Sections on Litigation and Natural Resources; State Bar of Montana; Yellowstone County

Bar Association; American College of Trial Lawyers; Montana Supreme Court Commission on Rules of Evidence; and the American Board of Trial Advocates.
Career: Prior to joining Holland & Hart, Mr Foster served as senior counsel for Atlantic Richfield Company, and as a law clerk to the Honorable James R Browning, US Court of Appeals for the Ninth Circuit.
Personal: Received a JD with honors from the University of Montana (1963), and a BS from Montana State University (1960).

FRANCE, Lucy
Garlington, Lohn & Robinson, PLLP,
Missoula 406 523 2500
Recommended in Employment

GOETZ, James
Goetz, Gallik & Baldwin, PC, Bozeman
406 587 0618
Recommended in Litigation

GRAHAM, Gary
Garlington, Lohn & Robinson, PLLP,
Missoula 406 523 2500
Recommended in Litigation

HATTERSLEY III, Thomas
Gough, Shanahan, Johnson & Waterman, Helena 406 442 8560
Recommended in Employment

HEARD, Richard
Heard & Howard, Columbus
406 322 4429
Recommended in Real Estate

HERINGER, Michael
Brown Law Firm PC, Billings
406 248 2611
Recommended in Employment

HINGLE, Charles
Holland & Hart LLP, Billings
406 252 2166
chingle@hollandhart.com
*Recommended in Corporate/M&A,
Litigation*
Practice Areas: A Partner whose practice focuses on business bankruptcy and creditors' rights, but with extensive experience in banking, real estate and commercial litigation. He has been certified as a business bankruptcy specialist by the American Board of Certification since 1993.
Prof. Memberships: Member of the Louisiana State Bar Association; Montana State Bar Association; Wyoming State Bar Association; American Bankruptcy Institute; and the Roster of Neutrals, American Arbitration Association.
Career: Admitted to the Louisiana (1976), Montana (1980), and Wyoming (1996) State Bars.
Personal: Received a JD from Louisiana State University (1976) and a BA from Tulane University (1972).

HOWARD, Douglas
Heard & Howard, Columbus
406 322 4429
Recommended in Real Estate

JONES, John
Moulton, Bellingham, Longo & Mather,
PC, Billings 406 248 7731
Recommended in Real Estate

JONES, William
Garlington, Lohn & Robinson, PLLP,
Missoula 406 523 2500
Recommended in Litigation

JOSCELYN, Alan
Gough, Shanahan, Johnson & Waterman, Helena 406 442 8560
Recommended in Natural Resources

KALECZYC, Stanley
Browning, Kaleczyc, Berry & Hoven PC,
Helena 406 443 6820
Recommended in Litigation

KARELL, Allan
Crowley, Haughey, Hanson, Toole &
Dietrich, PLLP, Billings
406 252 3441
Recommended in Real Estate

KELLNER, Stuart
Hughes, Kellner, Sullivan & Alke,
Helena 406 442 3690
Recommended in Litigation

KNIGHT, Robert
Robert M. Knight, Missoula
406 721 5440
Recommended in Real Estate

KUTZMAN, John
Dorsey & Whitney LLP, Great Falls
406 727 3632
Recommended in Employment

LAMDIN III, William
Crowley, Haughey, Hanson, Toole &
Dietrich, PLLP, Billings
406 252 3441
Recommended in Corporate/M&A

LEE, John
Crowley, Haughey, Hanson, Toole &
Dietrich, PLLP, Billings
406 252 3441
Recommended in Natural Resources

LEHMAN, Steven
Crowley, Haughey, Hanson, Toole &
Dietrich, PLLP, Billings
406 252 3441
Recommended in Employment

LENNON, Maureen
Garlington, Lohn & Robinson, PLLP,
Missoula 406 523 2500
Recommended in Employment

LEWIS, Tom
Lewis & Slovak PC, Great Falls
406 761 5595
Recommended in Litigation

MACDONALD, Terry
Garlington, Lohn & Robinson, PLLP,
Missoula 406 523 2500
Recommended in Litigation

MANNING, John
Dorsey & Whitney LLP, Great Falls
406 727 3632
Recommended in Corporate/M&A

MAYNARD Jr, Joe
Crowley, Haughey, Hanson, Toole &
Dietrich, PLLP, Billings
406 252 3441
Recommended in Litigation

MCELYEA, Russell
Moore, O'Connell & Refling PC,
Bozeman 406 587 5511
Recommended in Real Estate

MCINTOSH, Ian
Crowley, Haughey, Hanson, Toole &
Dietrich, PLLP, Bozeman
406 556 1430
Recommended in Litigation

METROPOULOS, Jon
Gough, Shanahan, Johnson & Waterman, Helena 406 442 8560
Recommended in Natural Resources

MOORE, Mikel
Christensen, Moore, Cockrell, Cummings & Axelberg PC, Kalispell
406 751 6000
Recommended in Litigation

O'CONNELL, Barry
Moore, O'Connell & Refling PC,
Bozeman 406 587 5511
Recommended in Litigation

PETERSEN, Larry
Holland & Hart LLP, Billings
406 252 2166
lpetersen@hollandhart.com
Recommended in Corporate/M&A
Practice Areas: Mr Petersen's practice focuses on tax, estate planning, real estate, natural resources, mergers, and acquisitions. He has extensive experience with probates; formation of LLC's, partnerships and corporations; coal leasing, acquisitions, and entity formations; purchase and sale of oil and gas and entity formation; and healthcare.
Prof. Memberships: American Bar Association, Montana Bar Association, Yellowstone County Bar Association, ACTEC.
Career: Admitted to Montana Bar (1967).
Personal: Received a JD from University of Montana (1967), a BS in Economics from the Wharton School at the University of Pennsylvania (1964), and an LLM from New York University (Taxation, 1970).

PFENNIGS, Robert
Jardine, Stephenson, Blewett and
Weaver, P.C., Great Falls
406 727 5000
Recommended in Litigation

QUANDER, Don
Holland & Hart LLP, Billings
406 252 2166
DQuander@hollandhart.com
Recommended in Natural Resources
Practice Areas: Partner addressing the full range of regulatory issues resulting from natural gas and electric power industry restructuring, including transmission, wholesale, and retail contract-

ing and determination of transition costs. Experience in environmental permitting and compliance for power projects, mining, wood projects, refining and other and other industrial facilities. Has been instrumental in the drafting of facility siting and environmental laws in several western states.

Prof. Memberships: Member of the American Bar Association; Montana Bar Association; Colorado Bar Association; Montana, Colorado, and ABA sections on Administrative Law and on Natural Resources, Energy, and Environmental Law; State Industrial Utility Group Lawyers; Director of the Western Environmental Trade Association; Director of Energy Share Montana.

Career: Admitted to the Colorado (1978) and Montana (1985) Bar Associations.

Personal: Received a JD (1978) from Harvard and the University of Chicago Law Schools and a BA (1974) from the University of Chicago.

ROBINSON, Donald
Poore, Roth & Robinson, P.C., Butte
406 497 1200
Recommended in Litigation

ROSS, John
Brown Law Firm PC, Billings
406 248 2611
Recommended in Natural Resources

RUFFATTO, Steven
Crowley, Haughey, Hanson, Toole & Dietrich, PLLP, Billings
406 252 3441
Recommended in Natural Resources

SHERIDAN, Robert
Garlington, Lohn & Robinson, PLLP, Missoula 406 523 2500
Recommended in Litigation

STENSLAND, Dean
Boone, Karlberg PC, Missoula
406 543 6646
Recommended in Real Estate

STRONG, Keith
Dorsey & Whitney LLP, Great Falls
406 727 3632
Recommended in Litigation

SULLIVAN, John
Hughes, Kellner, Sullivan & Alke, Helena 406 442 3690
Recommended in Employment

SULLIVAN, Robert
Boone, Karlberg PC, Missoula
406 543 6646
Recommended in Litigation

SULLIVAN, Zane
Sullivan, Tabaracci and Rhoades PC, Missoula 406 721 9700
Recommended in Real Estate

TALEFF, Ward
Alexander, Baucus, Taleff & Paul PC, Great Falls 406 761 4800
Recommended in Litigation

THANE, Jeremy
Worden Thane PC, Missoula
406 721 3400
Recommended in Employment

UGRIN, Neil
Ugrin, Alexander, Zadick & Higgins, PC, Great Falls 406 771 0007
Recommended in Litigation

WADE, Steven
Browning, Kaleczyc, Berry & Hoven PC, Helena 406 443 6820
Recommended in Natural Resources

WAGNER, William
Garlington, Lohn & Robinson, PLLP, Missoula 406 523 2500
Recommended in Real Estate

WATERMAN, Ronald
Gough, Shanahan, Johnson & Waterman, Helena 406 442 8560
Recommended in Litigation

WELSCH, Thomas
Poore, Roth & Robinson, P.C., Butte
406 497 1200
Recommended in Litigation

WESTESEN, Neil
Crowley, Haughey, Hanson, Toole & Dietrich, PLLP, Bozeman
406 556 1430
Recommended in Litigation

ZADICK, Gary
Ugrin, Alexander, Zadick & Higgins, PC, Great Falls 406 771 0007
Recommended in Employment

CONTENTS: Corporate/M&A p.1082; Employment p.1083; Litigation p.1084; Real Estate p.1086; Individuals' Profiles p.1087.

How lawyers are ranked

The opinions we gather from clients — mainly from in-house lawyers but also from other purchasers of legal services — are balanced by opinions from colleagues and competitors. Together, they provide two different perspectives — an all-round view — and biased viewpoints cancel each other out.

CORPORATE/M&A

Nebraska
Leading firms (Corporate/M&A)

1 BAIRD, HOLM, MCEACHEN, PEDERSEN *Omaha*
BLACKWELL SANDERS PEPER MARTIN *Omaha*
FRASER STRYKER LAW FIRM *Omaha*
MCGRATH NORTH MULLIN & KRATZ PC *Omaha*

2 ABRAHAMS KASLOW & CASSMAN LLP *Omaha*
CLINE, WILLIAMS, WRIGHT, JOHNSON *Lincoln*
KOLEY JESSEN PC *Omaha*
KUTAK ROCK LLP *Omaha*

3 ERICKSON & SEDERSTROM, PC *Omaha*
WOODS & AITKEN LLP *Lincoln*

Leading individuals (Corporate/M&A)

1 DIXON Joyce *Blackwell Sanders, Omaha*
FREEMAN Robert *Fraser Stryker, Omaha*
HEFFLINGER David *McGrath North, Omaha*
KASLOW Howard *Abrahams Kaslow, Omaha*

2 BURT Donald *Cline Williams, Lincoln*
GEHRING Stephen *Cline Williams, Omaha*
JESSEN Paul *Koley Jessen, Omaha*
RICHARDSON Todd *Blackwell Sanders, Omaha*
ZEILINGER John *Baird Holm, Omaha*

3 BASS Jo *Kutak Rock, Omaha*
HANDLOS Bryan *Kutak Rock, Omaha*
HERDZINA John *Abrahams Kaslow, Omaha*
SEDERSTROM Charles *Erickson & Sederstrom, Omaha*
STRASHEIM Jerrold *Baird Holm, Omaha*
TURNER Steven *Baird Holm, Omaha*

Firms and individuals are listed alphabetically in each band.

Band 1

Baird, Holm, McEachen, Pedersen, Hamann & Strasheim LLP

The Firm: This full-service firm has a "*superb*" corporate team, which handles a range of business matters from internal restructuring to M&A. However, it is in all things related to banking and finance that the firm particularly shines, winning acclaim from clients, who often retain its cadre of "*young and effective*" lawyers on a variety of complex proceedings. It enjoys an established reputation in corporate securities in addition to delivering expertise in areas such as banking regulatory law, loan issues and foreclosures.

The Lawyers: "*Outstanding*" **John Zeilinger** handles M&A, banking and corporate securities among other issues. He attracts clients partly through his deep knowledge of banking law, which melds with an ability to pick out the "*business issues.*" With a background in bankruptcy law, **Jerrold Strasheim** focuses on commercial litigation in federal and state courts involving such disputes as breach of contract, business torts and accounting malpractice. Meanwhile, "*top*" bankruptcy and corporate finance attorney **Steve Turner** has been attracting national clients with his handling of sophisticated financial methods.

The Clients: The firm has represented many financial institutions in the Midwest, including Great Western Bancorporation and River Valley Bancorp.

Blackwell Sanders Peper Martin LLP

See firm details p.1062

The Firm: This "*top of the line*" corporate firm has both a local and a national presence in the field, working with public and private companies on high-profile acquisitions, IPOs, loan transactions and securitizations. Clients appreciate the firm's ability to combine "*great depth and sophistication*" with good local knowledge. It also appears to have "*experts in every area,*" so it doesn't have to search far to find solutions to complex problems.

The Lawyers: Joyce **Dixon**'s (see p.1088) excellent reputation is forged from a legal smorgasbord of work in such areas as M&A, public offerings, commercial lending and large-scale asset securitization. "*Bright, practical and very capable,*" she is a key player in the firm's relationships with significant clients such as Commercial Federal Bank and World's Foremost Bank. Meanwhile, the reputation of younger partner **Todd Richardson** (see p.1088) in M&A continues to thrive with excellent recommendations from corporate clients in the areas of M&A, company formations and various financing transactions. He also boasts a specialty in IP-related proceedings, including software development agreements.

The Clients: Government Properties Trust; Commercial Federal Bank; World's Foremost Bank; Empire Fire & Marine Insurance; First National Bank of Omaha; InfiBank; Gordmans; Diversified Financial Services and Commercial Federal Bank.

Fraser Stryker Law Firm

The Firm: This "*client-centered*" group continues to build on its regional reputation as an "*efficient and perceptive*" service centered on issues including the negotiation of M&A and financing agreements. Pitched as a "*top-notch*" operation, the team also offers expertise on compliance and other regulatory matters. The firm's reputation is established from a broad array of experience, including corporate formations, in addition to an established profile in banking-related proceedings.

The Lawyers: **Bob Freeman** earned praise as a "*brilliant*" general corporate lawyer who attracts clients with his practical negotiating and planning skills. One signature project was the $220 million convention center called Qwest Center Omaha, which opened in September 2004. He is also active in a broad range of counseling and strategic work.

The Clients: Omaha's Children's Hospital; Oakview Construction; Level 3 Communications; WorldCom and Goodyear.

McGrath North Mullin & Kratz PC

The Firm: Another major corporate player in Oklahoma, the group continues to enjoy a fine reputation in its market, particularly for its work with top US food producer ConAgra Foods. Its M&A team advises public and private companies on business purchases and sales, reorganizations and redemptions. The firm's corporate experience also includes entity formations, corporate governance and various issues affecting private businesses. Further enhancing its strength is proficient expertise in related areas such as tax and litigation.

The Lawyers: **David Hefflinger** continues to garner praise as an "*exceptionally bright, sound business lawyer*" with expertise in business planning and high-level corporate work.

The Clients: In addition to anchor client ConAgra Foods, the team has represented companies in the manufacturing, finance, retail, insurance, real estate and technology sectors.

Band 2

Abrahams Kaslow & Cassman LLP

The Firm: This "*compact*" firm often delivers legal potency that far outstrips its size. Catering to a full range of clients' corporate needs, it provides a service that was described as "*responsive, practical and personal.*" The focus is on business transactions such as M&A and company formations. The firm also acts as local counsel for lenders based outside Nebraska.

The Lawyers: **Howard Kaslow** is revered as an "*exceptionally bright*" practitioner whose experience equips him to give "*practical, usable advice*" on SEC and corporate matters. "*An exceptionally good, practical lawyer,*" **John Herdzina** won praise from clients for "*getting to the issues quickly.*" One commented: "*He's a deal-maker, not a deal-breaker.*"

The Clients: The firm has advised financial institutions among other clients across the Midwest, including SITEL, Tenaska and American National Bank.

Cline, Williams, Wright, Johnson & Oldfather LLP

The Firm: A well-established firm in Lincoln for more than a century, Cline Williams brings to the negotiation table a reputation for "*high-quality*" business and commercial practice. Its lawyers offer "*solid judgment and good technical knowledge*" on a broad range of corporate law, including M&A.

The Lawyers: **Donald Burt** maintains an established reputation in general corporate law, with particular strengths in securities. He and **Stephen Gehring** offer more than 60 years of experience in the field between them.

The Clients: GM; Cargill; ConocoPhillips and Wells Fargo Bank Nebraska.

Koley Jessen PC

The Firm: This growing Omaha-based firm continues to forge a fine reputation in the market, with a team of more than 20 attorneys handling business finance and federal and state regulatory compliance proceedings. Its impressive portfolio also includes a broad range of tax, general corporate and M&A transactions. The firm's clientele tends to be weighted toward the more regional financial institutions and related businesses. Considered effective strategists by market analysts, the group's lawyers do a "*capable, effective job of representing clients.*"

The Lawyers: **Paul Jessen** is recognized as by far the firm's "*top corporate strategic lawyer.*" Clients appreciate his commitment to stay "*on top of the developments in corporate matters,*" including securities law.

The Clients: CitiCapital; First Nebraska Trust; Five Points Bank; Carlson Systems; Security National Bank of Omaha and World Investments.

Kutak Rock LLP

The Firm: The Omaha office of this national player has successfully established a corporate finance practice, handling a large volume of SEC compliance work. Though its drawing card is securities expertise, the group also carries out other business transactions such as M&A for major public and private companies across the region.

The Lawyers: Commentators recognized the "*understated, very professional*" **Bryan Handlos** as a "*wonderful*" candidate for regulatory and technology proceedings. He also won respect for bringing "*tons of experience*" particularly to banking M&A. **Jo Bass** garnered equally positive comment for her asset securitization work, often producing "*knowledgeable*" advice on the issuer and credit enhancement side.

The Clients: The firm has counseled bank holding companies, major credit card issuers and a Fortune 500 data processing and financial services organization among others.

Band 3

Erickson & Sederstrom, PC

The Firm: A full-service firm with offices in Lincoln and Omaha, this corporate team has a long-standing reputation in M&A and associated transactions such as reorganizations. Other interests involve franchise arrangements, tax-exempt organizations and securities law. In a more recent development, the firm has won commendation for its work on behalf of the healthcare sector.

The Lawyers: "*Rainmaker*" **Charles Sederstrom**, who heads the firm, has maintained his position "*at the forefront of legal developments*" by successfully representing clients such as bankers, lenders and healthcare organizations.

The Clients: These comprise healthcare conglomerates, regional manufacturers, retailers and other companies.

Woods & Aitken LLP

The Firm: This "*high-class, old-line*" law firm is highly regarded "*on any level,*" although its corporate section particularly stands out for its specialist knowledge in such areas as government contracts, construction law, telecom, banking and tax. Another feature is its experience in company formations and bankruptcy law. Further bolstering its strength is a new office in Omaha, which has allowed the team to extend its "*excellent all-round*" practice.

The Lawyers: Lee Merritt leads a team of about ten attorneys providing advice regarding banking, tax and international planning among other corporate issues.

The Clients: HyGain Electronics; Sanitary and Improvement District No. 7; Gateway Realty; J & E Cattle; Rose Equipment; Wanek Furniture and Appliances; ALLTEL and Citizens Communications.

EMPLOYMENT

MAINLY DEFENDANT

Band 1

Baird, Holm, McEachen, Pedersen, Hamann & Strasheim LLP

The Firm: One of Nebraska's largest dedicated employment practices; the Omaha-based firm manages to combine "*wealth of experience*" with focused pragmatism. Working in both the private and public sectors, the team offers a "*whole gamut*" of labor and employment expertise. Employee benefits is another feature of its repertoire, including ERISA lawsuits that have become more prevalent nationwide.

The Lawyers: **Chris Hedican** won plaudits as a "*bright and talented attorney*" as well as a "*strong advocate*" who "*gets good results.*" The backbone of his practice is employment-related litigation such as disputes involving employee benefits issues. With 18 years of experience in the field, **Randy Stevenson** has been called "*the man to send labor matters to,*" while **Jonathan Breuning** benefits from a focus on the healthcare sector. Traditional labor specialist **Scott Moore** also continues to enjoy an established reputation in the field.

The Clients: Wal-Mart; MSI Systems Integrators; FBG Services and Gordmans.

Nebraska
Leading firms
(Employment: Mainly Defendant)

1 BAIRD, HOLM, MCEACHEN, PEDERSEN *Omaha*
FRASER STRYKER LAW FIRM *Omaha*
MCGRATH NORTH MULLIN & KRATZ PC *Omaha*

2 BERENS & TATE PC *Omaha*
HARDING SHULTZ & DOWNS *Lincoln*
LAMSON, DUGAN & MURRAY, LLP *Omaha*

Leading individuals
(Employment: Mainly Defendant)

1 BARRETT Patrick *McGrath North, Omaha*
HEDICAN Chris *Baird Holm, Omaha*
ROSSITER Robert *Fraser Stryker, Omaha*
ROZMARIN George *Fraser Stryker, Omaha*

2 BOGUE Stevenson *McGrath North, Omaha*
HARDING William *Harding Shultz, Lincoln*
LOUDON Timothy *Berens & Tate, Omaha*
MILLER Roger *McGrath North, Omaha*

3 BREUNING Jonathan *Baird Holm, Omaha*
MCGRATH Brian *Lamson Dugan, Omaha*
MOORE Scott *Baird Holm, Omaha*
SHULTZ Jack *Harding Shultz, Lincoln*
STEVENSON Randy *Baird Holm, Omaha*

Firms and individuals are listed alphabetically in each band.

Fraser Stryker Law Firm

The Firm: Also *"leading the line"* in employment law in Omaha is Fraser Stryker, which often represents employers on a range of issues such as work-related policies and other preventative measures. The team is a first stop for *"high-profile employment litigation,"* NLRB proceedings, OSHA regulations, and wage-and-hour issues. Union organization and other labor-related matters also feature. The team is viewed as a *"top-drawer group at the cutting edge of employment law."*

The Lawyers: **Robert Rossiter** was recognized as *"one of the best, if not the best around"* for employment law. He expertly melds *"a strong knowledge of the law"* with litigation agility, *"translating academic prowess into successful results."* With *"flawless"* knowledge of employment law, **George Rozmarin** *"stands right at the top"* for his labor-related work.

The Clients: Avaya, Level 3 Communications

and Omaha Public Power District are among the firm's distinguished clientele.

McGrath North Mullin & Kratz PC

The Firm: With seven attorneys in its labor and employment section, this firm is noted particularly for its excellence in the traditional labor area. Though the practice offers a broad array of services, it remains most noted for its dispute resolution expertise on behalf of an enviable clientele. A jewel in its crown involves an eighth Circuit Court of Appeals victory pertaining to a punitive damages case.

The Lawyers: Renowned as an *"extremely intelligent, practical attorney,"* **Patrick Barrett** earned respect as a *"strong advocate"* who often wins cases for his clients. In addition, he also advises on collective bargaining and OSHA proceedings. **Stevenson Bogue** reaped plaudits for his employment discrimination expertise, while the *"gregarious and well-resourced"* **Roger Miller** spends most of his time on NLRA matters in addition to various arbitration proceedings arising from collective bargaining issues.

The Clients: The team's client base includes ConAgra Foods, Physicians Mutual Insurance and Mutual of Omaha Insurance.

Band 2

Berens & Tate PC

The Firm: Boasting an exceptional 14 dedicated labor and employment attorneys, this firm is pitched as one of the region's best-known employment specialists. Its *"strong team"* deals exclusively with labor and employment matters from a private company management perspective, covering a broad spectrum of issues including NRLA, employment practices liability insurance (EPLI), union elections and alternative dispute resolution.

The Lawyers: In addition to being *"one of the best discrimination lawyers in town"*, **Timothy Loudon** also benefits from his *"bright, congenial, straight-shooting"* style. His expertise includes contract negotiations, labor agreements, EPLI defense work and arbitration. He also has knowledge of federal white-collar exemptions. Chris Hoyme has a successful practice that stretches into the outlying states, often advising

on the establishment of human resources systems. Jo Dreesen is one of the premier lawyers to represent unionized employers in addition to other labor-related issues such as OSHA.

The Clients: DRM; American National Bank; Wal-Mart; SITEL; Travelers Insurance and Nucor.

Harding Shultz & Downs

The Firm: Based in Lincoln, the firm's mixture of public and private sector clients earned them a *"hard-to-beat"* reputation regarding preventative maintenance and unfair labor practice defense work. Its success also stems from its cultivated force in dispute resolution, handling a variety of matters including employment-related discrimination and wrongful discharge.

The Lawyers: **William Harding**'s reputation is partly based on his *"cutting-edge"* union work, both in the public and private sectors. Harding has defended clients against unfair labor practice charges among other crucial matters. *"Dedicated and thorough"* **Jack Shultz** focuses on the telecom area, and his expertise includes regulatory proceedings.

The Clients: The firm frequently represents school districts, as well as other public and private entities in such sectors as distribution, retail, manufacturing, hi-tech, healthcare and energy.

Lamson, Dugan & Murray, LLP

The Firm: This flourishing team exhibits good all-around experience, offering employers a full service that includes litigation, training, policy review and human resource counseling. It also handles assignments relating to traditional union representation. Clients appreciate its commitment to provide partner-level involvement, ensuring that they *"won't be passed down to a junior associate on day two."*

The Lawyers: A *"tenacious"* attorney, **Brian McGrath** frequently advises and represents major corporations such as McDonald's on litigation among other issues. He has appeared before federal and state courts, defending clients against discrimination suits and others. Another feature of his practice is alternative dispute resolution.

The Clients: McDonald's; Shopko Stores; Eaton and The Gallup Organization.

LITIGATION

GENERAL COMMERCIAL

Band 1

Baird, Holm, McEachen, Pedersen, Hamann & Strasheim LLP

The Firm: The team of 14 advocates cements its position as one of Nebraska's leading litigation groups, *"excelling over a broad range of commer-*

cial issues." The firm caters to a wide corporate and general commercial client base, and is able to take on work in such diverse spheres as IP disputes, bankruptcy, and employment. Other interests include tax, antitrust and securities litigation.

The Lawyers: **Thomas Johnson** is considered to be a *"top-notch"* lawyer by his peers and has a

practice that takes into consideration insurance defense and commercial contracts. He has experience in medical technology issues and has also litigated in the energy sector. **Bill Dittrick** has a reputation as a *"smart"* advocate with *"a ton of experience"* in court, while **Kirk Blecha** won a celebrated eighth Circuit Court of Appeals vic-

Nebraska
Leading firms
(Litigation: General Commercial)

1 BAIRD, HOLM, MCEACHEN, PEDERSEN *Omaha*
CLINE, WILLIAMS, WRIGHT, JOHNSON *Lincoln*
FRASER STRYKER LAW FIRM *Omaha*
MCGRATH NORTH MULLIN & KRATZ PC *Omaha*

2 BLACKWELL SANDERS PEPER MARTIN *Omaha*
ERICKSON & SEDERSTROM, PC *Omaha*
KUTAK ROCK LLP *Omaha*
LAMSON, DUGAN & MURRAY, LLP *Omaha*

Leading individuals
(Litigation: General Commercial)

1 MEUSEY Joseph *Fraser Stryker, Omaha*
PETERSON Alan *Cline Williams, Lincoln*

2 BAUSCH James *Cline Williams, Omaha*
CULHANE Thomas *Erickson & Sederstrom, Omaha*
DAHLK Thomas *Blackwell Sanders, Omaha*
DITTRICK William *Baird Holm, Omaha*
FITZGERALD James *McGrath North, Omaha*

3 BROWNRIGG John *Erickson & Sederstrom, Omaha*
KAUFFMAN Fred *Cline Williams, Omaha*
KNOWLES Leo *McGrath North, Omaha*
MARK Wayne *Fraser Stryker, Omaha*
MCLEAY Bart *Kutak Rock, Omaha*

Leading individuals (Litigation: IP)

1 ACKERMAN Jill *Baird Holm, Omaha*
DOMINA David *Domina Law, Omaha*
PASSARELLI John *McGrath North, Omaha*
THOMTE Dennis *Thomte Mazour, Omaha*

Leading individuals
(Insurance: Dispute Resolution)

1 LAMSON William *Lamson Dugan, Omaha*

2 BLECHA Kirk *Baird Holm, Omaha*
JOHNSON Thomas *Baird Holm, Omaha*
KINNEY Michael *Cassem Tierney, Omaha*

Firms and individuals are listed alphabetically in each band.

tory and a substantial award for his client in the case of Schoch v InfoUSA. In the field of IP, the firm boasts **Jill Robb Ackerman**, a *"tenacious, yet methodical"* litigator who has expanded her practice into trademarks, copyright and patents both locally and regionally.

The Clients: The firm's litigation clients include: Tenaska; Woodmen of the World Life Insurance; Nebraska Methodist Health System and IBP.

Cline, Williams, Wright, Johnson & Oldfather LLP

The Firm: This well-established firm has a set of *"very fine trial lawyers"* working out of its Lincoln and Omaha offices. Commentators confirmed that the team, which includes about 20 litigators, has *"outstanding experience"* in a wide range of contentious issues, including First

Amendment, securities, TMT representation and complex commercial disputes. Environmental law, antitrust and medical malpractice work also feature among other expertise.

The Lawyers: Market sources agree that **Alan Peterson**, one of the state's most accomplished litigators, has handled some of Nebraska's most important trials. Peterson has *"the experience to take on constitutional-type cases and appellate work,"* as well as having a well-rounded media practice that involves newspapers and television stations. **Jim Bausch** also continues to impress as an *"experienced, excellent lawyer"* handling securities and commercial contract cases. *"Well-regarded"* **Fred Kauffman** maintains a notable presence in medical and legal malpractice defense work, in addition to his niche specialty in antitrust.

The Clients: Lincoln Journal Star; University of Nebraska; Central Interstate Low-Level Radioactive Waste Commission (CIC); Nebraska Press Association; Nebraska Medical Association; Viacom and GM.

Fraser Stryker Law Firm

The Firm: Omaha stalwart Fraser Stryker is able to boast more than 20 trial lawyers and a solid stable of clients to affirm its status as one of Nebraska's top choices for dispute resolution. Market observers endorsed the indisputable *"high quality"* of its top litigators, bolstered by the high ratio of courtroom experience linked to insurance defense. Its excellent profile in the Omaha market also depends on other types of litigation, including complex commercial cases.

The Lawyers: **Joe Meusey** garnered respect as a *"seasoned trial lawyer with very good judgment"* and *"a way with a jury,"* consistently impressing peers and clients in equal measure. His practice takes into account major constitutional and commercial cases as well as class action litigation and some personal injury lawsuits. **Wayne Mark** earned confidence with a combination of *"excellent people skills and organizational aptitude."* He is regularly involved in the negotiation of construction and design agreements.

The Clients: The State of Nebraska; Minnesota Lawyers Mutual; Omaha Public Power District; Level 3 Communications and State Farm.

McGrath North Mullin & Kratz PC

The Firm: Based in Omaha with a team of more than 30 litigators, this firm maintains a strong client base that includes multinational corporations with ties to Nebraska. Indeed, as the state's second largest law firm, it is able to take on cases of almost any size and naturally gravitates toward the more complex measures. Its *"seasoned trial lawyers"* command respect in such areas as employment, product liability and white-collar crime.

The Lawyers: **James Fitzgerald** won plaudits as *"one of the smartest lawyers out there,"* regu-

larly handling complex litigation for major corporate clients such as ConAgra Foods. Peers were in awe of his intellectual fortitude, adding that he *"gets it, and gets it quick."* His practice also includes fraud and some toxic tort work. With more than 30 years of experience in commercial disputes, **Leo Knowles** is another market favorite. His caseload involves fraud, contract and shareholder disputes. He also has a strong reputation in mediation. In IP, **John Passarelli** stands out as *"one of the top IP people"* in the state, taking on cases throughout the region and beyond.

The Clients: ConAgra Foods; Rolex; Automobile Association of America; First National Bank of Omaha; Farm Credits Services of America and Valmont Industries.

Band 2

Blackwell Sanders Peper Martin LLP

See firm details p.1062

The Firm: One of the strengths of this corporate firm is its ability to augment an 11-strong Omaha litigation team with personnel drawn from more than 100 litigation experts across the Midwest and additional bases in DC and London. This gives it the flexibility to provide active litigating capacity to its sophisticated corporate practice. Work undertaken by the group has included a large volume of securities and shareholder litigation as well as complex antitrust, real estate, lender liability and contract disputes.

The Lawyers: **Thomas Dahlk** (see p.1087) has the respect of the market for his *"excellent judgment"* in business litigation, having achieved successful results in substantial securities, civil RICO and business tort cases. Other features of his practice involve defamation, professional malpractice, appellate and white-collar crime.

The Clients: Roberts Dairy; Waddell & Reed Financial Services; The Gallup Organization; QA3 Financial; AGP and Gordmans.

Erickson & Sederstrom, PC

The Firm: With offices in Omaha and Lincoln and a team of 11 trial lawyers, this firm has a strong reputation in insurance defense, representing plaintiffs and defendants. It has also begun to make inroads into a wider range of commercial disputes such as workers compensation and other complex litigation.

The Lawyers: *"Bright and well-prepared"* **Thomas Culhane** has the backing of the market for his *"good judgment."* He regularly appears in commercial trials, and specializes in contractor representation in construction litigation. **John Brownrigg** is considered a strong contender in complex mediation and arbitration matters.

The Clients: The firm acts for healthcare, construction and insurance companies among others.

Kutak Rock LLP

The Firm: Founded in Omaha, the team here has grown over the years to become a national firm with a broad client base that involves companies of all sizes, including some of the world's largest corporations. Unsurprisingly then, it can handle litigation ranging from antitrust to white-collar crime. IP disputes, reinsurance, construction and business torts have also featured.

The Lawyers: The firm's national reach means that exposure to the local market is somewhat limited, commentators said. But among its cadre of litigators, **Bart McLeay** dazzles as a *"well-prepared"* trial lawyer with *"lots of experience and good judgment."*

The Clients: These include multinational giant Wal-Mart and First National Bank of Omaha.

Lamson, Dugan & Murray, LLP

The Firm: Despite its smaller size, this 28-lawyer firm packs a punch with its litigation prowess with more than 12 dedicated trial lawyers catering to a broad array of industrial and commercial clients. Its smorgasbord has included legal battles involving professional liability, product liability and various other commercial disputes. The litigation team is further supported by corporate specialists in areas such as M&A, tax and employment.

The Lawyers: **William Lamson** was reckoned to be *"one of the best litigation lawyers around,"* observers said. He *"tries more cases than most others,"* often veering towards insurance, including medical malpractice defense.

The Clients: The team has counseled Dow Chemical; GM; Nebraska Public Power District and Union Pacific Railroad.

Other Notable Practitioners

David Domina of Domina Law pc LLO is a *"well-regarded"* trial lawyer whose broad litigation practice often relates to complex civil and criminal cases across the nation. **Michael Kinney** of Cassem Tierney Adams Gotch & Douglas is known for his successful business and insurance litigation practice. He was described as a *"tenacious trial lawyer"* with a *"gentlemanly demeanor."* Working out of Omaha, leading IP specialist **Dennis Thomte** of Thomte, Mazour & Niebergall LLC won commendation for his expertise in patent law.

REAL ESTATE

Nebraska
Leading firms (Real Estate)

1 FULLENKAMP, DOYLE & JOBEUN *Omaha*
PANSING HOGAN ERNST & BACHMAN *Omaha*

2 BAIRD, HOLM, MCEACHEN, PEDERSEN *Omaha*
FRASER STRYKER LAW FIRM *Omaha*
KUTAK ROCK LLP *Omaha*
MCGRATH NORTH MULLIN & KRATZ PC *Omaha*

3 BLACKWELL SANDERS PEPER MARTIN *Omaha*
CROKER, HUCK, KASHER, DEWITT *Omaha*
GROSS & WELCH, PC *Omaha*

Leading individuals (Real Estate)

1 BACHMAN John *Pansing Hogan, Omaha*
DYE Scott *Baird Holm, Omaha*
FULLENKAMP John *Fullenkamp Doyle, Omaha*
HAMANN Lee *McGrath North, Omaha*
RIEKE Robert *Fraser Stryker, Omaha*

2 ANDERSON Richard *Croker Huck, Omaha*
BUSER James *Pansing Hogan, Omaha*
CURRY Michael *Kutak Rock, Omaha*
HUCK Robert *Croker Huck, Omaha*
JOBEUN Larry *Fullenkamp Doyle, Omaha*
KATELMAN John *Blackwell Sanders, Omaha*
KRITENBRINK Lawrence *Baird Holm, Omaha*

Leading individuals
(Real Estate: Zoning/Land Use)

1 FULLENKAMP John *Fullenkamp Doyle, Omaha*
HOGAN III Dennis *Pansing Hogan, Omaha*

2 DYE Scott *Baird Holm, Omaha*
HUCK Robert *Croker Huck, Omaha*
SLUSKY Jerry *Gross & Welch, Omaha*

Firms and individuals are listed alphabetically in each band.

Band 1

Fullenkamp, Doyle & Jobeun

The Firm: This team of dedicated real-estate lawyers continues to excel in its chosen field of development work. It is regularly immersed in high-profile development projects, including brownfield sites. In addition, the team's established profile means that it is often retained on regional residential projects. The practice also incorporates zoning, planning and lobbying as part of a broader remit that includes setting up concomitant administrative entities.

The Lawyers: **John Fullenkamp** has long been a *"leading light"* in this field, doing *"more zoning and planning work than anyone in the city."* He also benefits from enduring relationships with the area's planning board and *"knows who to work with"* within government agencies on the various zoning issues. **Larry Jobeun** is said to be *"following Fullenkamp's footsteps"* in delivering quality advice.

The Clients: The firm's client base includes regional developers, telecom companies and local utility companies.

Pansing Hogan Ernst & Bachman LLP

The Firm: This firm also handles a large volume of development work and related matters, including some high-end commercial real estate projects. The firm has assisted on residential subdivisions, retail centers and office buildings. Highlights include the Village Point among other developments, and the firm has also seen an uptake in private placements and syndication work.

The Lawyers: **John Bachman** earned accolades in the area of structured acquisitions in addition to his development work, while **Dennis Hogan** concentrates almost entirely on representing developers. He has a *"loyal following"* and is reckoned to be a key player in the firm's overall success in this field. **Jim Buser**, recognized by some as *"heir apparent"* to his more senior colleague Denny Hogan, has a broad-based practice that also includes representing some of the larger banks.

The Clients: Lanoha; Horgan Development; Lerner; Rogers and Papillion.

Band 2

Baird, Holm, McEachen, Pedersen, Hamann & Strasheim LLP

The Firm: This firm's real estate team caters to institutional clients across the country, handling large and complex acquisitions, and planning and development projects. In one prominent transaction, it advised Omaha Public Schools on the acquisition of a private high school in a $250 million project. The firm's breadth and experience attracts a variety of clients who depend on its resources to tackle the more complicated cases.

The Lawyers: **Scott Dye** counts among his institutional clients some of Nebraska's largest hospitals and public school districts. The *"reliable deal-maker"* undertakes leasing, sales and acquisitions in addition to various construction and tax-related advice. Commanding a more statewide reputation is **Lawrence Kritenbrink**, who handles all aspects of real estate work, including mortgage financing.

The Clients: Omaha Public Schools; Airlite Plastics; First Data Resources; Nebraska Methodist Health System and Great Western Bank.

Fraser Stryker Law Firm

The Firm: This firm's dedicated real estate team of four attorneys continues to impress the market with its capacity to handle potentially complicated transactions, including subdivisions. Its experience also involves lenders and financial institutions in an array of real estate transactions. One of its principal clients is Noddle Development, which focuses on shopping centers and office buildings.

The Lawyers: **Robert Rieke** earned plaudits as *"the go-to guy for real estate transactions."* Clients including lenders and developers appreciate his *"good, prompt and aggressive"* approach.

The Clients: These include savings and loan associations, financial institutions, national mortgage bankers and insurance companies.

Kutak Rock LLP

The Firm: This national firm's real estate team of about 25 lawyers serves a stable of multinational corporations, counseling on acquisitions, developments, and related financial advice. Another drawing card is its established command of the structured finance market as related to real estate. In this area, it is able to call on a host of specialist experience including tax, banking and bankruptcy.

The Lawyers: **Mike Curry** is one of Kutak's leading real estate practitioners, representing financial institutions around the country. *"At the top of the Nebraska list,"* his expertise is often rendered on complex structure finance transactions and workouts as related to real estate.

The Clients: Clients include prominent developers, retailers, investment funds, financial institutions and others.

McGrath North Mullin & Kratz PC

The Firm: The firm's seven real estate practitioners carry out a full gamut of real estate transactions for its national client base, offering practical experience in such areas as the acquisition and disposition of properties. The team offers financing expertise to borrowers, lenders and other participants. In addition, it advises on property developments including planning and zoning proceedings, whether for industrial, commercial or residential use.

The Lawyers: *"Practical and well versed,"* Lee Hamann *"knows how to make a deal"* and brings a *"high degree of credibility"* to institutional real estate work. Among others, he advises corporate giants such as ConAgra Foods.

The Clients: ConAgra Foods; PJ Morgan Real Estate; McCarthy & Co and Valmont Industries.

Band 3

Blackwell Sanders Peper Martin LLP

See firm details p.1062

The Firm: This firm's major corporate real estate clients hailed the team's performance on commercial acquisitions, sales and leasing transactions. Its role in several prominent downtown development projects also won recognition, as did its expert knowledge on the finance aspects of the deal, including complex mortgage securitization.

The Lawyers: **John Katelman** (see p.1088) represents lenders and other commercial entities in various leases, development projects and other proceedings. A feather in his cap involves an acquisition for No Frills Supermarkets. A *"solid real estate lawyer"* who is *"good on documentation"* and *"big projects,"* he has also represented Pacific Life Insurance.

The Clients: Wells Fargo; First National Bank of Omaha; Centris Federal Union; Grubb & Ellis/Pacific Realty; The Gallup Organization; First Data Resources; No Frills Supermarkets and Pacific Life Insurance.

Croker, Huck, Kasher, DeWitt, Anderson & Gonderinger, PC

The Firm: This firm carries out transactional work for lenders, title companies, builders, real estate brokers, and private individuals in a bevy of real estate matters including sales, purchases and foreclosures. It is also commended for its financing expertise, and regularly assists on municipal zoning proceedings.

The Lawyers: **Robert Huck** has a development practice that originated in residential work, but has successfully diversified into the commercial arena, while **Richard Anderson** is a *"personable"* and *"very diligent"* real estate lawyer who delivers quality transactional and financing advice.

The Clients: Bancroft Property & Casualty; Marathon Realty; Noddle Development and NP Dodge.

Gross & Welch, P.C.

The Firm: This firm's success is illustrated through its participation in some of Nebraska's largest construction projects in addition to a typical mixture of zoning and land-use proceedings, purchase agreements and financing transactions. It recently represented Oriental Trading in the development of its 1.2 million sq ft warehouse and distribution center. Commentators particularly value the team's *"close cooperation"* with all the concerned parties in a large development.

The Lawyers: With 25 years of expertise in zoning and municipal law, **Jerry Slusky** garnered acclaim as an attorney who not only brings a *"developer's knowledge"* to a real estate deal, but also provides *"practical answers"* to thorny problems.

The Clients: The firm has represented Oriental Trading, Boys & Girls Club of Omaha and Omaha Housing Authority.

Leaders in Nebraska

ACKERMAN, Jill
Baird, Holm, McEachen, Pedersen, Hamann & Strasheim LLP, Omaha
402 344 0500
Recommended in Litigation

ANDERSON, Richard
Croker, Huck, Kasher, DeWitt, Anderson & Gonderinger, P.C., Omaha
402 391 6777
Recommended in Real Estate

BACHMAN, John
Pansing Hogan Ernst & Bachman LLP, Omaha 402 397 5500
Recommended in Real Estate

BARRETT, Patrick
McGrath North Mullin & Kratz PC, Omaha 402 341 3070
Recommended in Employment

BASS, Jo
Kutak Rock LLP, Omaha
402 346 6000
Recommended in Corporate/M&A

BAUSCH, James
Cline, Williams, Wright, Johnson & Oldfather LLP, Omaha 402 397 1700
Recommended in Litigation

BLECHA, Kirk
Baird, Holm, McEachen, Pedersen, Hamann & Strasheim LLP, Omaha
402 344 0500
Recommended in Insurance

BOGUE, Stevenson
McGrath North Mullin & Kratz PC, Omaha 402 341 3070
Recommended in Employment

BREUNING, Jonathan
Baird, Holm, McEachen, Pedersen, Hamann & Strasheim LLP, Omaha
402 344 0500
Recommended in Employment

BROWNRIGG, John
Erickson & Sederstrom, PC, Omaha
402 397 2200
Recommended in Litigation

BURT, Donald
Cline, Williams, Wright, Johnson & Oldfather LLP, Lincoln
402 474 6900
Recommended in Corporate/M&A

BUSER, James
Pansing Hogan Ernst & Bachman LLP, Omaha 402 397 5500
Recommended in Real Estate

CULHANE, Thomas
Erickson & Sederstrom, PC, Omaha
402 397 2200
Recommended in Litigation

CURRY, Michael
Kutak Rock LLP, Omaha
402 346 6000
Recommended in Real Estate

DAHLK, Thomas
Blackwell Sanders Peper Martin LLP, Omaha 402 964 5031
tdahlk@blackwellsanders.com
Recommended in Litigation
Practice Areas: Business and commercial litigation; securities industry regulation and litigation.
Prof. Memberships: Admitted to practice in Nebraska Supreme Court (1977)

and US Supreme Court (1992). Member, American Bar Association, Section on Litigation; Nebraska Association of Trial Attorneys; and Omaha Bar Association. Fellow, Nebraska State Bar Foundation, 1999.
Career: Joined firm as Partner, 1998; Office Managing Partner, Omaha, 2003-present.
Publications: Author, 'Class Actions - The Nebraska Procedure', 'Nebraska Law Review' (1982); and 'Real Estate Partnerships and the Securities Laws: A Primer', 'Creighton Law Review' (1982).
Personal: JD (magna cum laude), Creighton University, 1977; BA (with distinction), University of Wisconsin, 1974.

DITTRICK, William
Baird, Holm, McEachen, Pedersen, Hamann & Strasheim LLP, Omaha 402 344 0500
Recommended in Litigation

DIXON, Joyce A
Blackwell Sanders Peper Martin LLP, Omaha 402 964 5020
jdixon@blackwellsanders.com
Recommended in Corporate/M&A
Practice Areas: Finance and lending; mergers and acquisitions; real estate.
Prof. Memberships: Admitted to practice in Nebraska (1975), US District Court of Appeals, Eighth Circuit; and US District Court, District of Nebraska. Member, American Bar Association, Sections on Local Government and Banking, Business and Bankruptcy, and Law Practice Management; Nebraska State Bar Association, Committees on Budget and Inquiry for Second Judicial District; and Omaha Bar Association.
Career: Joined firm as Partner, 2000; Member, Advisory Board Committee, 2003-present.
Personal: JD (summa cum laude), Creighton University, 1975; editor in chief, 'Creighton Law Review;' BA (with high honors), University of Illinois.

DOMINA, David
Domina Law pc LLO, Omaha 402 493 4100
Recommended in Litigation

DYE, Scott
Baird, Holm, McEachen, Pedersen, Hamann & Strasheim LLP, Omaha 402 344 0500
Recommended in Real Estate

FITZGERALD, James
McGrath North Mullin & Kratz PC, Omaha 402 341 3070
Recommended in Litigation

FREEMAN, Robert
Fraser Stryker Law Firm, Omaha 402 341 6000
Recommended in Corporate/M&A

FULLENKAMP, John
Fullenkamp, Doyle & Jobeun, Omaha 402 334 0700
Recommended in Real Estate

GEHRING, Stephen
Cline, Williams, Wright, Johnson & Oldfather LLP, Omaha 402 397 1700
Recommended in Corporate/M&A

HAMANN, Lee
McGrath North Mullin & Kratz PC, Omaha 402 341 3070
Recommended in Real Estate

HANDLOS, Bryan
Kutak Rock LLP, Omaha 402 346 6000
Recommended in Corporate/M&A

HARDING, William
Harding Shultz & Downs, Lincoln 402 434 3000
Recommended in Employment

HEDICAN, Chris
Baird, Holm, McEachen, Pedersen, Hamann & Strasheim LLP, Omaha 402 344 0500
Recommended in Employment

HEFFLINGER, David
McGrath North Mullin & Kratz PC, Omaha 402 341 3070
Recommended in Corporate/M&A

HERDZINA, John
Abrahams Kaslow & Cassman LLP, Omaha 402 392 1250
Recommended in Corporate/M&A

HOGAN III, Dennis
Pansing Hogan Ernst & Bachman LLP, Omaha 402 397 5500
Recommended in Real Estate

HUCK, Robert
Croker, Huck, Kasher, DeWitt, Anderson & Gonderinger, P.C., Omaha 402 391 6777
Recommended in Real Estate

JESSEN, Paul
Koley Jessen P.C., Omaha 402 390 9500
Recommended in Corporate/M&A

JOBEUN, Larry
Fullenkamp, Doyle & Jobeun, Omaha 402 334 0700
Recommended in Real Estate

JOHNSON, Thomas
Baird, Holm, McEachen, Pedersen, Hamann & Strasheim LLP, Omaha 402 344 0500
Recommended in Insurance

KASLOW, Howard
Abrahams Kaslow & Cassman LLP, Omaha 402 392 1250
Recommended in Corporate/M&A

KATELMAN, John
Blackwell Sanders Peper Martin LLP, Omaha 402 964 5010
jkatelman@blackwellsanders.com
Recommended in Real Estate
Practice Areas: Real estate; commercial transactions; financial institutions; mergers and acquisitions.
Prof. Memberships: Admitted to practice in Nebraska (1973) and US District Court, District of Nebraska (1973). Member, American Bar Association,

Sections on Real Property and Probate and Trust Law; Nebraska State Bar Association; and Omaha Bar Association.
Career: Joined firm as Partner, 1996.
Personal: JD, Creighton University, 1972; BS, University of Nebraska, 1970.

KAUFFMAN, Fred
Cline, Williams, Wright, Johnson & Oldfather LLP, Omaha 402 397 1700
Recommended in Litigation

KINNEY, Michael
Cassem Tierney Adams Gotch & Douglas, Omaha 402 390 0300
Recommended in Insurance

KNOWLES, Leo
McGrath North Mullin & Kratz PC, Omaha 402 341 3070
Recommended in Litigation

KRITENBRINK, Lawrence
Baird, Holm, McEachen, Pedersen, Hamann & Strasheim LLP, Omaha 402 344 0500
Recommended in Real Estate

LAMSON, William
Lamson, Dugan & Murray, LLP, Omaha 402 397 7300
Recommended in Insurance

LOUDON, Timothy
Berens & Tate PC, Omaha 402 391 1991
Recommended in Employment

MARK, Wayne
Fraser Stryker Law Firm, Omaha 402 341 6000
Recommended in Litigation

MCGRATH, Brian
Lamson, Dugan & Murray, LLP, Omaha 402 397 7300
Recommended in Employment

MCLEAY, Bart
Kutak Rock LLP, Omaha 402 346 6000
Recommended in Litigation

MEUSEY, Joseph
Fraser Stryker Law Firm, Omaha 402 341 6000
Recommended in Litigation

MILLER, Roger
McGrath North Mullin & Kratz PC, Omaha 402 341 3070
Recommended in Employment

MOORE, Scott
Baird, Holm, McEachen, Pedersen, Hamann & Strasheim LLP, Omaha 402 344 0500
Recommended in Employment

PASSARELLI, John
McGrath North Mullin & Kratz PC, Omaha 402 341 3070
Recommended in Litigation

PETERSON, Alan
Cline, Williams, Wright, Johnson & Oldfather LLP, Lincoln 402 474 6900
Recommended in Litigation

RICHARDSON, Todd
Blackwell Sanders Peper Martin LLP, Omaha 402 964 5032
trichardson@blackwellsanders.com
Recommended in Corporate/M&A
Practice Areas: Commercial transactions; closely held businesses; mergers and acquisitions; securities; venture capital/private equity financing and funds.
Prof. Memberships: Admitted to practice in Nebraska (1991). Board of Directors, American Society of Corporate Secretaries, Rocky Mountain Chapter; and Midlands Venture Forum, Chair of Presentations Committee.
Career: Joined firm as Partner, 1998.
Personal: JD (with highest distinction), University of Nebraska at Omaha, 1991; Editor in chief, 'Nebraska Law Review'; BS and BA (magna cum laude), University of Nebraska at Omaha, 1988.

RIEKE, Robert
Fraser Stryker Law Firm, Omaha 402 341 6000
Recommended in Real Estate

ROSSITER, Robert
Fraser Stryker Law Firm, Omaha 402 341 6000
Recommended in Employment

ROZMARIN, George
Fraser Stryker Law Firm, Omaha 402 341 6000
Recommended in Employment

SEDERSTROM, Charles
Erickson & Sederstrom, PC, Omaha 402 397 2200
Recommended in Corporate/M&A

SHULTZ, Jack
Harding Shultz & Downs, Lincoln 402 434 3000
Recommended in Employment

SLUSKY, Jerry
Gross & Welch, P.C., Omaha 402 392 1500
Recommended in Real Estate

STEVENSON, Randy
Baird, Holm, McEachen, Pedersen, Hamann & Strasheim LLP, Omaha 402 344 0500
Recommended in Employment

STRASHEIM, Jerrold
Baird, Holm, McEachen, Pedersen, Hamann & Strasheim LLP, Omaha 402 344 0500
Recommended in Corporate/M&A

THOMTE, Dennis
Thomte, Mazour & Niebergall, L.L.C., Omaha 402 392 2280
Recommended in Litigation

TURNER, Steven
Baird, Holm, McEachen, Pedersen, Hamann & Strasheim LLP, Omaha 402 344 0500
Recommended in Corporate/M&A

ZEILINGER, John
Baird, Holm, McEachen, Pedersen, Hamann & Strasheim LLP, Omaha 402 344 0500
Recommended in Corporate/M&A

CONTENTS: Corporate/M&A p.1089; Employment p.1091; Environment p.1093; Gaming & Licensing p.1094; Litigation p.1095; Real Estate p.1098; Individuals' Profiles p.1101; Firms' Profiles p.1104.

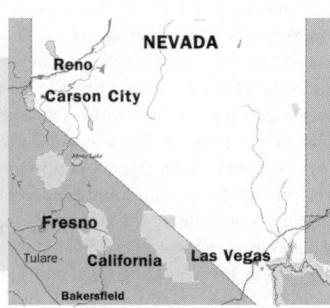

How lawyers are ranked

The opinions we gather from clients — mainly from in-house lawyers but also from other purchasers of legal services — are balanced by opinions from colleagues and competitors. Together, they provide two different perspectives — an all-round view — and biased viewpoints cancel each other out.

CORPORATE/M&A

Nevada
Leading firms (Corporate/M&A)

1   LIONEL SAWYER & COLLINS *Las Vegas*
    SCHRECK BRIGNONE *Las Vegas*

2   HALE LANE PEEK DENNISON AND HOWARD *Reno*
    JONES VARGAS *Las Vegas*
    KUMMER KAEMPFER BONNER *Las Vegas*
    WOODBURN AND WEDGE *Reno*

Leading individuals (Corporate/M&A)

1   FOWLER John *Woodburn and Wedge*, Reno
    GARCIA David *Hale Lane*, Reno
    SCHULHOFER Ellen *Schreck Brignone*, Las Vegas
    ZUCKER Jeffrey *Lionel Sawyer*, Las Vegas

2   BONNER Michael *Kummer Kaempfer*, Las Vegas
    JONES Leslie *Schreck Brignone*, Las Vegas
    WOLOSON Kenneth *Haney Woloson*, Las Vegas

3   BARNARD Gregg *Woodburn and Wedge*, Reno
    GOLDSTEIN Mark *Lionel Sawyer*, Las Vegas
    KIM Robert *Kummer Kaempfer*, Las Vegas
    VERMEYS Sonia *Schreck Brignone*, Las Vegas

Up-and-coming individuals
    BATTCHER Frederick *Hale Lane*, Reno
    NEWMAN James *Hale Lane*, Reno
    SAVAGE NELSON Elizabeth *Schreck*, Las Vegas

Firms and individuals are listed alphabetically in each band.

Band 1

Lionel Sawyer & Collins

The Firm: Interviewees confirmed this firm's position as one of the "*preeminent*" firms in Nevada of the past 25 years, commending its "*highly professional*" attorneys and broad range of corporate skills. More than 85 attorneys are housed in the firm's three Nevada offices and its Washington DC base. With such a wealth of resources, the firm is retained by some of the state's highest profile real estate developers, corporations and gaming/hotel resorts, and those investors focused on the gaming industry. Moreover, the team continues to be at the forefront of the consolidation in the hotels sector, assisting clients of the caliber of MGM Mirage and Mandalay Resort Group in their merger efforts. The firm has also picked up on the rapid increase in condominium developments and financing, another major trend affecting both the corporate and real estate fields. Attorneys are often called upon to provide opinions on Nevada law for those large transactions involving major and national banks.

The Lawyers: Sources commend **Jeff Zucker** as a "*perfectionist for detail*," who has always been in the "*top league of attorneys*" in the field. Chair of the business law department, he has been largely responsible for the firm's involvement in a host of significant residential housing development deals, joint ventures and project financings. He also advised on the Marriott Hotel and the Diamond/Nevada Resort Properties Polo Towers Limited Partnership for the construction of a timeshare project. The "*highly capable and talented*" **Mark Goldstein** draws his clientele primarily from the gaming industry but represents a host of clients from other sectors. For example, he advised a nonprofit Catholic health system on the development of its latest health facility in Nevada. His caseload has also included the revision of agreements between MGM and Mandalay Resort Group to ensure that they conformed to Nevada law and to win approvals from shareholders and Nevada regulatory bodies. Most recently, he negotiated a licensing agreement with Playboy Enterprises for the opening of a Playboy-branded club, casino and store at the Palms Casino Resort.

The Clients: Over the past year, Jeff Zucker and his team have acted as Nevada counsel in the $1.3 billion merger between a major, diversified gaming casino operator, Boyd Gaming, and Coast Casinos, a leader in the Las Vegas locals sector. This merger will create one of the most diversified casino companies in the USA with 17 casino entertainment facilities. Other clients of the firm include: Caesars Entertainment; Bank of America; Hilton Grand Vacations and Aztar (Tropicana Hotel).

Schreck Brignone

The Firm: Clients "*think the world*" of this firm's corporate practice highlighting its strength in corporate transactions, such as refinancing projects and M&A. The Las Vegas-based team recently acted as Nevada counsel in the acquisition of the Desert Inn hotel property by Steve Wynn and the subsequent financings by Wynn Resorts of the Le Reve resort/casino project. The firm was also instrumental in the acquisition of Mirage Resorts, incorporated by MGM to form MGM Mirage. Sources identified the firm's "*outstanding*" connections in the hotel industry as a distinguishing feature that has ensured it a steady flow of work in that sector. At the start of 2004, the firm represented Harrah's Entertainment in the acquisition of assets (including IP rights) belonging to the Horseshoe Club. The transaction was consummated on a fast-track basis, ensuring that issues relating to creditors and the hiring of employees were quickly addressed. Additional transactions on behalf of Harrah's Entertainment include representation in its acquisition of the Showboat and Rio hotels.

The Lawyers: Sources commended **Ellen Schulhofer** as a lawyer of substance, who "*understands details, gets projects done quickly and is also a brilliant strategist.*" Some dubbed her "*the best transactional attorney in Las Vegas*," and she has been able to cement the firm's reputation as a major political player in the field. She regularly contributes to the drafting of legislation relating to fiduciary duties indemnification and stockholder rights plans. Clients also pointed to her expertise in county zoning ordinances and regulatory matters. Additionally, she advises on SEC and financing issues for Wynn Las Vegas. **Leslie Terry Jones** has a talent for "*catching things that nobody else catches.*" Among his most notable engagements has been his representation of Steve Wynn in the purchase of the Desert Inn hotel and golf course. Jones also served as local real estate counsel in the financing for the Le Reve project by Wynn Resorts, and advised Phillip Ruffin in his joint venture with the Trump Organization. The "*highly organized*" **Sonia Vermeys** provides her clients with "*timely, direct and cost-efficient advice.*" Licensing issues lie at the heart of her practice, and she recently represented Phillip Ruffin and his subsidiary entities in two significant financings and advised on his partnership with Donald Trump for the development of a condominium project adjacent to the New Frontier. She is currently representing Wynn Las Vegas in connection with its Clark County privileged, regulated and general business licenses. Sources picked out the "*impressive*" **Elizabeth Savage Nelson** as one of the rising stars at the firm. She was involved in the reorganization of American Nevada and certain of its affiliates and subsidiaries. Her practice also focuses on administrative law and she has represented clients before the Nevada State Gaming Control Board.

The Clients: Harrah's Entertainment; Caesars Entertainment; The Greenspun Companies/ American Nevada and Pinnacle Entertainment.

Band 2

Hale Lane Peek Dennison and Howard

The Firm: The 12-strong corporate team is known for providing "*top representation in the state for its high degree of focus and experience*" in transactional law including the structuring of complex M&A. The firm has its roots in the real estate market and has expanded significantly to house attorneys well versed in all types of business and commercial transactions and commercial litigation. A diverse practice incorporates areas ranging from general corporate law to tax planning, securities and healthcare. The ability to combine such skills enables these lawyers to deal regularly with all aspects of stock purchases, M&A, buyouts and recapitalizations. On the securities side, the attorneys are frequently called to assist in venture capital financing, either as counsel to the company receiving the funds or as counsel to the investors.

The Lawyers: The "*exceptional*" **David Garcia** has the ability "*to bring people together.*" Clients also describe him as "*perceptive – he gets to the essence of the issues.*" Venture capital financing, M&A and public and private security offerings are key features of his practice. He is particularly versed in the structuring of corporate partnering transactions and licensing agreements. According to sources he is "*one of the best in the state for SEC issues.*" The "*extremely responsive, thorough and detailed*" **James Newman** was also praised for being "*in tune with the latest developments.*" He has particular expertise in representing technology and manufacturing clients owing in part to his background as a sales and marketing manager at a large Fortune 500 company. Clients endorsed **Fritz Battcher**'s knowl-

edge of M&A and securities law, describing him as "*a go-getting type: open minded and very involved with his clients' business.*"

The Clients: Bank of America, the Venetian Hotel and the Southern Nevada Water Authority are key clients of the firm.

Jones Vargas

The Firm: One of the oldest in Nevada, the firm is also well known for its long-standing client relationships. The corporate practice is staffed with 11 attorneys, who are fully equipped to handle a range of corporate issues, such as limited liability company and real estate transactions. The firm's size enables it to specialize in certain areas of practice, such as complex financing transactions and municipal finance. Operating out of its Las Vegas and Reno offices, the firm serves clients, which range from small businesses to large corporations and institutions. It also has a niche clientele in state and local bond issuers as well as underwriters.

The Lawyers: A number of the team's attorneys have more than 30 years of experience in the field and a distinct expertise in transactional law including securities and corporate finance and M&A. Partner Craig Norville is particularly active in these areas of the law and he also frequently advises on developments such as the enactment and effects of the Sarbanes-Oxley Act.

The Clients: Business Bank of Nevada; Las Vegas Chamber of Commerce; Lehman Brothers and Wells Fargo.

Kummer Kaempfer Bonner & Renshaw

See firm details p.1105

The Firm: One of Nevada's largest firms, it is home to "*high-quality*" attorneys, who are respected for their expertise in securities transactions, the structuring of IPOs and all aspects of compliance with SEC requirements. The team has attracted a diverse range of public and private companies in transactions ranging from M&A to divestures. Recent highlights for the group have included the representation of Rio Hotel & Casino in its acquisition by Harrah's Entertainment. Additionally, the firm has been involved in the transportation sector, as shown by the team's advice on the acquisition of the monorail system from MGM Grand and Park Place Entertainment by Las Vegas Monorail.

The Lawyers: Clients and peers alike view managing partner **Michael Bonner** (see p.1101) as an "*absolute fixture in the Las Vegas corporate market.*" Known for his "*cool manner no matter what the disaster,*" Bonner is well versed in IPO and securities transactions, as well as in the counseling of publicly held companies on disclosure. He advises high-profile clients such as Monarch Casino & Resort and Gaming Partners International on the prepara-

tion of reports to the SEC. **Robert Kim** (see p.1102) has "*firmly established*" his reputation in the market through his strong track record on the structuring of IPOs, private placements and corporate governance issues. He also assists emerging growth companies in various financing projects.

The Clients: The firm's client base includes businesses in the hotel and gaming sector including Monarch Casino & Resort and Rio Hotel & Casino. Additionally, it has a solid client base in the gaming-manufacturing sector where it represents Paul-Son Gaming and ITT. Other clients include Atlantis Casino Resort, which the firm has advised on various licensing matters.

Woodburn and Wedge

See firm details p.1106

The Firm: Interviewees highlighted the corporate team, housed in Nevada's oldest firm, for its skilled attorneys, who possess a "*wealth of knowledge and deep experience.*" From its two offices in Reno, the firm concentrates on corporate finance, such as the representation of a large southeastern Nevada utility company on the issuance of equity and debt. Attorneys also spend a substantial portion of their time advising a licensing company that has opened medical facilities for the elderly on properties across the USA. The firm also serves as counsel for many publicly traded corporations including Sierra Pacific Resources and Tenet Healthcare.

The Lawyers: Sources praised **John Fowler** (see p.1102) for his "*incredible attention to detail*" and for "*asking all the tough questions that need to be asked.*" He is experienced in federal laws and requirements, and won great acclaim for his revision of Nevada corporate legislation. The bulk of his practice consists of advising lenders on Nevada corporate matters, which include mostly public and private equity issues. He also represents local public agencies including the Regional Transportation Commission of County Washoe and the local bus system, as well as large utility companies. The "*very sharp*" **Gregg Barnard** (see p.1101) is best known for his representation of Sierra Pacific Resources and its subsidiary, the Sierra Pacific Power Company, providing advice on various long-term financing activities. His practice is nationwide in scale, and he advises several nationwide commercial lenders.

The Clients: The Regional Transportation Commission of Washoe County; Sierra Pacific Resources; Belco Oil&Gas; and various banks and consortiums.

Other Notable Practitioners

Ken Woloson of Haney, Woloson & Mullins has impressed many as a "*very knowledgeable and creative*" lawyer who "*really knows his stuff.*" He serves as local and general counsel in M&A and leasing issues, often derived from the real estate sector. He is also extensively involved in the gaming industry having represented clients such as the Gold Rush and Magic Star Casinos. Recently, he represented a publicly traded company in its acquisition of a formerly distressed gaming property.

EMPLOYMENT

MAINLY DEFENDANT

Nevada
Leading firms
(Employment: Mainly Defendant)

1	**KAMER ZUCKER & ABBOTT** Las Vegas
2	**DLA PIPER RUDNICK GRAY CARY** Las Vegas
	FISHER & PHILLIPS LLP Las Vegas
	LIONEL SAWYER & COLLINS Las Vegas
	SCHRECK BRIGNONE Las Vegas
	SMITH & KOTCHKA LTD Las Vegas
3	**KIRSHMAN HARRIS & ROSENTHAL** Las Vegas
	LITTLER MENDELSON PC Las Vegas

Leading individuals
(Employment: Mainly Defendant)

Senior Statesman
EFROYMSON Kevin Sole Practitioner, Las Vegas

1	**COLE Howard** Lionel Sawyer, Las Vegas
	KAMER Gregory Kamer Zucker, Las Vegas
	MOSS Gary DLA Piper, Las Vegas
	ZUCKER Carol Kamer Zucker, Las Vegas
2	**KIRSHMAN Norman** Kirshman Harris, Las Vegas
	RICCIARDI Mark Fisher & Phillips, Las Vegas
	SMITH Gregory Smith & Kotchka, Las Vegas
	YOUCHAH Elayna Schreck Brignone, Las Vegas
3	**ABBOTT Scott** Kamer Zucker, Las Vegas
	HICKS Patrick Littler Mendelson, Reno
	KOTCHKA Malani Smith & Kotchka, Las Vegas
	MORGAN Ann Jones Vargas, Reno
	PAUSTIAN Kathleen Allf Paustian, Las Vegas

Up-and-coming individuals
KELLER Edwin Kamer Zucker, Las Vegas

Leading individuals
(Employment: Mainly Defendant ERISA)

1	**BRIGNONE Andrew** Schreck Brignone, Las Vegas

Firms and individuals are listed alphabetically in each band.

Band 1

Kamer Zucker & Abbott

The Firm: A "*definite leader*" in employment and labor law, the firm is widely recognized for its "*consistently excellent services*" and the "*loyal support*" it shows to its clients. Clients also commented that they trusted the dedication and broad knowledge shown by these attorneys with some pitching this as their "*first-choice firm.*" The firm has maintained an extensive practice in all areas of traditional labor law, such as in the representation of employers before the NLRB. One recent highlight was the group's successful resolution of a 63-day hearing before the NLRB involving the closure of a

facility on the West Coast. The firm also boasts a vibrant employment litigation practice, representing both public and private employers before bodies such as the US Supreme Court and the Ninth Circuit Court of Appeals. Recently, the firm has been heavily involved in representing employers in discrimination, sexual harassment and retaliation charges, and has undertaken First Amendment and civil rights law issues.

The Lawyers: Clients and peers alike singled out **Greg Kamer** as "*a tough advocate, passionate about representing his clients' best interests.*" Kamer's in-depth knowledge of labor law has also helped him cement the group's understanding of NLRB proceedings. He also handles all aspects of employment litigation for a client list that includes hotel and casino giants such as MGM Mirage, as well as healthcare facilities, financial institutions and government entities. Additionally, he serves as mediator and arbitrator for the Mountain States Employment Panel of the AAA. **Carol Zucker** is "*always well prepared and thoughtful and therefore a complete attorney.*" She spends most of her time handling employment discrimination suits involving sexual harassment, race or age discrimination. Her 20-year career includes a number of high-profile successes such as the 2001 Clark County School District v Breeden sexual harassment case before the US Supreme Court. Her work on the development of in-house training programs is also appreciated by clients. **Ed Keller** is a "*star of the future,*" agree sources. He is particularly active on the labor law side of the practice representing clients on issues such as union organizing, labor relations and arbitration proceedings. **Scott Abbott** has made an impact on the labor law market with sources commending his ability to be "*smart and aggressive, while remaining soft-spoken and levelheaded.*" Clients also appreciate that he can "*zero in on central issues and convey them in a terminology that everybody can understand.*"

The Clients: Alliance Gaming; Ameristar Casinos; Bellagio; Golden Nugget Hotel & Casino and Clark County School District.

Band 2

DLA Piper Rudnick Gray Cary
See firm details p.765

The Firm: The firm houses a "*deep bench of extremely professional attorneys*" in its Las Vegas office and has the ability to call upon increased national and international resources following

its recent mergers. National clients report that they "*wouldn't go anywhere else*" and endorse the client-focused service provided by the group. The four-attorney team (which includes an associate in the bankruptcy law practice) exclusively specializes in labor and employment law. Traditional labor law is a key area of strength, and one marked by significant successes this year. The firm prevailed in a complex jurisdictional dispute between two unions and its client relating to the construction of the Mandalay Bay Convention Center. The case was taken before the NLRB and decided under an infrequently used federal law provision. In another matter, the team successfully represented a Washington state-based timber company in an arbitration under a collective bargaining agreement, which arose out of the sale of the company.

The Lawyers: Both peers and clients were full of praise for **Gary Moss** (see p.1103), who has an "*ability to persuade people like nobody else in Las Vegas.*" Interviewees also remarked that he attracts a great level of respect from unions for his "*political astuteness*" and the "*tremendous experience and knowledge*" he brings to the negotiating table. Moss spends most of his time in traditional labor law matters. In addition to having successfully concluded the NLRB hearing related to the Mandalay Bay Center, he has successfully negotiated various collective bargaining agreements. Three of these negotiations, which were all contentious and high profile in nature, were on behalf of clients from Southern California.

The Clients: Aircraft Services International; Cintas; Gucci America; MGM Mirage and the Sahara Hotel & Casino.

Fisher & Phillips LLP
See firm details p.630

The Firm: The national resources available to this respected team distinguishes it in the Nevada market. Interviewees also highlighted its "*well-qualified*" attorneys and dedicated client service. With offices across the USA reaching from Chicago and Atlanta to San Diego, the firm has established roots in Las Vegas with its representation of employers in complex labor and employment matters. The team has experienced an upturn in union-organizing cases; for example, it handled several legal actions involving the obtaining of injunctions before expected strikes. More than half the firm's practice also focuses on employment litigation in areas such as wrongful termination, retaliation, sexual harassment and age discrimination.

The Lawyers: Interviewees most frequently commented on **Mark Ricciardi**'s (see p.1103) advocacy strengths, describing him as *"always aggressively defending his clients."* He has had great successes in protecting clients during strike actions and has litigated unfair labor practice charges and union election objections before the NLRB. A portion of his practice is dedicated to supervisory training in the areas of discrimination and harassment awareness, as well as union avoidance and employment law compliance.

The Clients: The firm's clients include hospitals, casinos, restaurants and government contractors for the Department of Energy.

Lionel Sawyer & Collins

The Firm: Market observers characterized this team as *"excellent at everything."* The practice has witnessed marked increases in employment discrimination suits, particularly in the areas of sexual harassment and wrongful termination. The firm achieved a significant victory in one such claim on behalf of the telecom giant AT&T, following a class action filed in New Jersey. Within the realm of traditional labor law, the team assisted in decertifying a large gaming and manufacturing union, and has also negotiated a number of collective bargaining agreements for its clients.

The Lawyers: The *"studious, diligent and extremely knowledgeable"* **Howard Cole** drew praise from interviewees for his extensive trial experience and his skill in handling arbitration proceedings. He has been particularly busy in the area of wage and hour laws, alongside his work on employee benefit matters, contract administration, and discipline and discharge issues. Among his most significant clients is the state's biggest laundry operator, for which he handles most of its employment law work.

The Clients: The firm's clients are diverse, running the gamut from the airline industry to restaurants, golf courses and major developers. Examples include: AT&T; MGM Mirage; Venetian Casino Resort and Southern Union.

Schreck Brignone

The Firm: The five-attorney strong group has impressed market sources with its strong niche in employee benefits matters, alongside its broader employment litigation practice. The healthcare sector is a particular area of focus for the practice following a significant increase in the number of lawsuits filed. For instance, the firm has recently been successful in the Ninth Circuit in the area of delinquent employee contributions. Additionally, its attorneys have extensive experience representing employers against claims such as breach of contract, civil conspiracy and intentional infliction. The group's regular workload also includes the provision of advice to clients on the structuring of downsizing agreements designed to avoid discrimination litigation.

The Lawyers: Interviewees endorsed **Andrew Brignone** as a leading light in the employee benefits field and related ERISA litigation. His powerful trial skills and his *"outstanding grasp of the law"* have also secured him a following. Brignone has advised employers on contributions to retirement savings funds, and more recently, been retained by clients in the healthcare industry on various litigation matters. He also regularly conducts employment seminars and workshops on topics ranging from sexual harassment to progressive discipline. The *"finely skilled"* **Elayna Youchah** is an *"ethical attorney and entirely dedicated"* to her work. Interviewees also stressed the excellence of her research and written work. She focuses on employment litigation such as disability discrimination.

The Clients: Clients include multinational defense contractors, hotel/casinos, healthcare providers and the construction industry.

Smith & Kotchka Ltd

The Firm: The *"well-respected"* firm has caught the attention of the market with its success in attracting an enviable client base, which in the eyes of some commentators belies its relatively small team size. The team of two partners and one associate specializes in employment litigation as well as labor law, especially union contract negotiations and bargaining laws. A good portion of the firm's client base is drawn from the convention industry, and has provided the team with a steady flow of matters related to contract negotiations. Additional areas of expertise include industrial insurance compensation, employee benefits and labor-management relations. The firm also regularly represents public agencies on such matters.

The Lawyers: Sources were quick to identify this firm's *"high-quality duo."* **Gregory Smith** stands out for his labor law expertise and interviewees were particularly impressed with his writing skills and his presentation of cases. He is heavily involved in contract negotiations and bargaining laws, often for convention industry clients. The *"outstanding"* **Malani Kotchka** is renowned for her workers' compensation track record as well as her experience in employment litigation, particularly as relates to sexual harassment matters.

The Clients: The firm's client base is derived from, among others, the convention and construction industries, hotels and casinos, and public agencies.

Band 3

Kirshman Harris & Rosenthal

The Firm: The five-attorney team is particularly known for its excellent labor law practice, where it has been able to establish a good rapport with trade unions. The firm has extensive experience practicing before state and federal courts, the NLRB, the Nevada Equal Rights Commission, as well as various other federal and state agencies. Additionally, the attorneys regularly argue cases involving sexual harassment, all forms of discrimination and hiring and termination issues on behalf of their clients.

The Lawyers: A *"classic labor lawyer and extremely knowledgeable"* **Norman Kirshman** has more than 20 years of experience, primarily representing clients from the public as well as the private sectors in collective bargaining, arbitration and NLRB proceedings. Additionally, he is highly experienced in civil litigation and has represented clients before the Nevada Equal Rights Commission.

The Clients: The firm's clients are drawn primarily from the residential, commercial and industrial construction sectors as well as the hotel, casino and gaming sectors. The group is also strong in the public sector representing municipalities and trade associations.

Littler Mendelson PC

The Firm: A national employment and labor law powerhouse, this firm is recognized for its *"depth of talent and very knowledgeable attorneys."* The group of 14 lawyers in the Las Vegas office is heavily involved in Title VII employment law work, and has developed an active litigation practice dealing with harassment and discrimination claims. Attorneys are also well versed in wage and hour laws and other issues relating to traditional labor law. The team has represented its clients before local state tribunals such as the Nevada Equal Rights Commission, as well as out-of-state courts such as in California.

The Lawyers: The *"highly talented, thorough and responsive"* **Patrick Hicks** is widely respected for his trial expertise. He focuses his practice on employment litigation, counseling clients on wrongful dismissal claims, discrimination litigation and matters relating to the ADA and the FMLA.

The Clients: The firm's employer clients are drawn from a wide variety of industries ranging from the advertising to the hospitality sector and including hotels, restaurants and wineries. Additionally, the group represents numerous financial institutions as well as nonprofit organizations.

Other Notable Practitioners

The *"experienced and dynamic"* **Kathleen Paustian** of Allf, Paustian & Szostek is renowned for her work on employment discrimination lawsuits and for her eight-year defense of the Metropolitan Police Department in a case involving the demotion of a police officer. Additionally, she has dealt with civil court cases revolving around family law. The bulk of her clients are midsized companies as well as employees and government agencies. The *"dean of Nevada labor law,"* sole practitioner **Kevin Efroymson** continues to impress sources with his "*amazing memory, great recollection of details*" and "*superb approach to the courtroom.*" He "*knows everybody in town,*" and acts as chief negotiator for all Las Vegas strip casinos and hotels. Interviewees commended

Ann Morgan of Jones Vargas for her expertise in employment litigation. Presently, she is handling two cases of wrongful termination involving issues of workplace violence. Additionally, she successfully represented a number of public

institutions in relation to employee contracts and regularly provides advice to both private and public sector companies on disciplinary actions.

ENVIRONMENT

Nevada
Leading firms (Environment)

[1]	LIONEL SAWYER & COLLINS *Reno*
	MARSHALL HILL CASSAS & DE LIPKAU *Reno*
	WOODBURN AND WEDGE *Reno*
[2]	ALLISON, MACKENZIE, RUSSELL *Carson City*
	MCDONALD CARANO WILSON MCCUNE *Reno*
	SANTORO, DRIGGS, WALCH *Las Vegas*

Leading individuals (Environment)

[1]	DE LIPKAU Ross *Marshall Hill, Reno*
	DEPAOLI Gordon *Woodburn and Wedge, Reno*
[2]	HILL Earl *Marshall Hill, Reno*
	SAVELY Carl *Lionel Sawyer, Reno*
	WALCH Greg *Santoro Driggs, Las Vegas*
[3]	BULLEN Linda *Lionel Sawyer, Las Vegas*
	HARRISON Sylvia *McDonald Carano, Reno*
	PETERSON Karen *Allison MacKenzie, Carson City*

Firms and individuals are listed alphabetically in each band.

Band 1

Lionel Sawyer & Collins

The Firm: This "*prestigious*" firm fields a team of "*highly accomplished lawyers*" dedicated to environmental law. The vast majority of the group's workload is formed by air permission and air violations-related issues. Water-related work and public land use matters are also high on the agenda. Over the past year, the firm has been involved in negotiating a number of groundwater registration permits on behalf of Clark County. The team also represents commercial mobile radio and telephone service providers in rate hearings and the establishment of tariff schedules.

The Lawyers: The "*highly respected expert*" **Carl Savely** has developed a broad ranging practice that sees work on commercial transactions and permitting matters. He has a wealth of experience in dealing with the State Engineer's office, and he advises clients from the mining, chemical manufacturing, industrial and land development industries. Additionally, Savely represents a significant number of the co generation, geothermal and independent power producers operating within Nevada. The "*engaging and highly competent*" **Linda Bullen** advises extensively on complex and state and federal environmental matters. She has a niche practice in hazardous waste, water and air issues and is fully equipped to handle jury trials.

The Clients: Among the firm's top clients are public authorities such as Clark County and various companies in the construction industry.

Marshall Hill Cassas & De Lipkau

The Firm: This firm leads the way in water rights law, acknowledged sources. Its respected natural resources practice incorporates water rights, mining and public lands as well as other aspects of environmental disputes and counselling. Attorneys here have also cultivated a substantial political and legislative experience, having been responsible for the drafting of some of the state's most significant documents, while others have served on various water rights subcommittees. A strong public utilities practice, which incorporates gas, water, electric and cooperatives rights, ensures that this firm can provide the broadest range of services and expertise.

The Lawyers: According to interviewees **Ross de Lipkau** is "*forceful in defense of his clients;*" a stance that has ensured him the deference of both peers and governmental bodies in the field of water rights. His work also includes environmental permitting and litigation and he has taken his experience acquired in practice to public life having served as a member of the Water Rights subcommittee of the American Mining Congress. **Earl Hill** is "*always outstanding person to work with*" and has represented clients in the mining industry for over 20 years. He has also served as special counsel to the Nevada State Engineer.

The Clients: City of Las Vegas, Las Vegas Water Valley District and Muddy Valley Irrigation are key clients of the firm.

Woodburn and Wedge

See firm details p.1106

The Firm: This "*top-notch*" firm "*has a historic reputation*" within the mining industry, having represented such clients since 1917. These "*well-qualified*" attorneys have been extensively working on the Walker River Basin project as part of a group that advocated on behalf of several counties claiming rights to the water use of Walker Lake. This matter is currently at the negotiation stage and could potentially go to litigation. Attorneys are also involved in issues relating to surface water, another crucial matter with far-reaching environmental implications for the state. The group also represents clients in disputes with the Bureau of Land Management

and in private mining claims disputes before the state and federal courts.

The Lawyers: Gordon De Paoli (see p.1101) impresses many as one of the premier water rights lawyers in the state. Clients described him as "*incredibly energetic, intellectually precise*" and pointed to his skills as a "*very talented author of written documents.*" He was instrumental in the recently passed Truckee River Operating Agreement, which provides that a permanent allocation of water in the Lake Tahoe, Truckee River and Carson River basins between California and Nevada will take effect. De Paoli has extensively advised on the Walker River Basin especially advocating additional water rights for an Indian reservation.

The Clients: The firm's client base includes a significant number of public authorities such as the City of Reno; Washoe County; Truckee Meadows Water Authority, and Walker River Irrigation District. Additionally, the firm's long-standing ties to the mining industry include clients such as Placer Dome US, Amax Gold and Glamis Gold. The firm also has extensive experience representing both borrowers and lenders in gold loan financings.

Band 2

Allison, MacKenzie, Russell, Pavlakis, Wright & Fagan, Ltd

The Firm: The Carson City-based firm houses a 14-strong team that specializes in administrative law and public utility law, and has a special expertise in water rights. Additionally, the attorneys are well equipped to handle both state and federal courts trials and are involved in a range of compliance, permitting and regulatory issues surrounding environmental law and land use.

The Lawyers: The "*talented*" **Karen Peterson** predominantly represents the firm's public entities in the state such as the State of Nevada Environmental Protection Division and the Public Service Commission of Nevada, which she has represented in court on several occasions. Peterson also has a specialty in telecom law and water rights, one of her marquee clients being the Department of Water Resources.

The Clients: Nevada Land & Resource; Northern Nevada Industrial & Electric Users; Anderson Engineering and Washoe County Utility Division.

McDonald Carano Wilson McCune Bergin Frankovich & Hicks LLP

The Firm: This Reno powerhouse fields one of the leading natural resources practices in Southern Nevada. The firm handles environmental issues relating to all types of commercial transactions including the management of environmental due diligence. Other areas of expertise include compliance and permitting, environmental torts, water rights as well as mining and energy law. The attorneys are also regularly involved in appeals proceedings before the Interior Board of Land Appeals.

The Lawyers: Experienced **Sylvia Harrison** has been a partner in the firm since 1994 and came to the law from a background in geology. She principally handles environmental aspects of complex commercial transactions and bankruptcies, and is experienced in complex, high exposure environmental cases including the

defense of the Resource Conservation and Recovery Act citizen suits, EPA matters and state enforcement actions.

The Clients: CH2M Hill Engineers, Time Oil, and State Industries are key clients of this firm.

Santoro, Driggs, Walch, Kearney, Johnson & Thompson

The Firm: The 1996-launched firm places high importance on its natural resources practice, which is equipped with a team that comes from a strong science background. The team has significant experience in the purchase and sale of Nevada groundwater rights, in the analysis and perfection to title to water rights as well as in the negotiation of complex arrangements for the purchase of delivery of fresh or reclaimed water. Additionally, the team deals on an everyday basis with the Nevada State Engineer and has developed and maintained important relationships

with each of the Southern Nevada local governments and the Southern Nevada Water Authority.

The Lawyers: Greg Walch heads the natural resources practice. Having started his career as an engineer, he moved to Las Vegas in the early 1990s and started his water law practice that advises clients from the agriculture and mining sectors to regulated water suppliers. Over the years, he has expanded his practice to include power, chemical manufacturing and municipal clients. Recently, he has been involved in a 61-acre regeneration project with a group of developers based in New York.

The Clients: Real estate developers such as Sands Gravel, chemical manufacturers like America Pacific, the Nevada Department of Transportation and Las Vegas home builders feature on the client list.

GAMING & LICENSING

Nevada
Leading firms (Gaming & Licensing)

1. **LIONEL SAWYER & COLLINS** *Las Vegas*
   SCHRECK BRIGNONE *Las Vegas*
2. **GORDON & SILVER LTD** *Las Vegas*
   MCDONALD CARANO WILSON *Las Vegas*
3. **CURRAN & PARRY** *Las Vegas*
   JONES VARGAS *Las Vegas*

Leading individuals
(Gaming & Licensing)

1. **ARRAJJ David** *Schreck Brignone*, Las Vegas
   FAISS Robert *Lionel Sawyer*, Las Vegas
   SCHRECK Frank *Schreck Brignone*, Las Vegas
2. **ALONSO Michael** *Jones Vargas*, Reno
   CABOT Anthony *Lionel Sawyer*, Las Vegas
   HICKS Alvin *McDonald Carano*, Reno
   SILVER Jeffrey *Gordon & Silver*, Las Vegas
3. **CURRAN William** *Curran & Parry*, Las Vegas
   GIORDANO P Gregory *Lionel Sawyer*, Las Vegas

Firms and individuals are listed alphabetically in each band.

Band 1

Lionel Sawyer & Collins

The Firm: A *"great history"* in gaming law marks this firm out as one of the leaders in the state. It has cultivated a loyal clientele that ensures attorneys here are some of the *"busiest around; this makes them the most comprehensively knowledgeable."* The firm has greatly benefited from the upsurge in consolidations in the gaming industry, for example representing MGM in its acquisition of Mirage. Another significant client for the firm has proved to be Barrack Gaming on whose behalf the attorneys

obtained licenses to acquire seven casinos in Las Vegas. Additionally, the firm handles all gaming matters for the large restaurant chain Hooters, representing it in all commercial dealings in anticipation of the opening of its first casino. The team also takes a great interest in technological innovations in gaming law, and has developed a niche in Internet gaming.

The Lawyers: Market commentators described **Bob Faiss** as the *"patriarch"* of gaming law in the state and beyond: *"Highly skilled, confident, and as good as they come."* An expert on the Nevada Gaming Control Act, Faiss has represented the gaming industry in the Nevada State Legislature for the past 26 years. He represents the most prominent names among the large casino operators, slot machine manufacturers, casino suppliers and the hotel industry. Also on his resume is his advisory role to the US Treasury as the representative of the US casino industry and his position as an adjunct professor at the University of Nevada. **Anthony Cabot** brings a *"tremendous experience and professional approach"* to his gaming law practice. He is widely recognized as the leading light on Internet gaming, sweepstakes and contests. He has extensively represented Hooters in relation to the opening of its first casino nationwide and has recently been retained by the attorney general's office in Texas to authorize gaming in the state for the first time in its history. **Greg Giordano** *"understands the law and how to negotiate in the gaming world,"* agreed sources. His practice concentrates on publicly traded corporations and regulatory compliance. Giordano also has extensive experience in public office and is regularly asked to lecture on various aspects of gaming law.

The Clients: Playboy Enterprises; Mandalay Resort Group; MGM Mirage; Caesars Entertainment; Anchor Gaming and Venetian Resort Casino.

Schreck Brignone

The Firm: Clients were quick to commend this firm as *"the place to go for high-quality gaming law advice,"* and for some, *"no one will do a better job."* The firm has great expertise in Nevada gaming laws, compliance issues and corporate licensing matters. Among the team's highlights is its recent representation of the purchaser of the Aladdin Hotel, taking this major player out of the bankruptcy proceedings that has dogged it since 2001 and providing a significant boost to the Las Vegas strip. Wynn Resorts is the firm's marquee client, and attorneys here represent this group on its refinancing and development issues. The attorneys also have extensive experience in the field of gaming regulation and legislation drafting and regularly provide advice to large clients in relation to legislative activity in several domestic and foreign jurisdictions.

The Lawyers: Clients and peers were full of praise for the *"dean of gaming law"* **Frank Schreck** who *"understands the gaming environment like nobody else."* They find him experienced and pragmatic as well as *"solutions-oriented and accessible."* His former role at the Nevada Gaming Commission has provided him with an enviable understanding of such bodies and this knowledge has proved attractive to many of the premier public and private gaming companies involved in licensing matters and regulatory compliance. Most recently, he acted as a legal adviser to Macao government officials in their efforts to assess new regulations for the licensing of gaming establishments in Macao. He counsels Wynn Resorts on all aspects of its gaming transactions. **David Arrajj** forms *"a formidable duo"* with Frank Schreck. Interviewees endorsed him as a *"phenomenal attorney, technically superb"* in personal licensing applications. A former in-house counsel for Hilton Gaming and Park Place, he represents gaming clients on licensing, regulatory investigation and compliance matters, as well as their corporate transactions. His clients include Caesars and Harrah's Entertainment, and he was among the principal drafters of new institutional investment regulations in nonpublic companies that became effective in July 2000.

The Clients: Harrah's Entertainment; Caesars Entertainment; MGM Mirage; Circus Circus; Aristocrat Technologies; Mandalay Resort Group and Wynn Resorts.

Band 2

Gordon & Silver Ltd

The Firm: The respected Las Vegas-based firm is well known for its high-profile clientele, secured by attorneys who are well versed in gaming, liquor and professional license applications. The team regularly represents clients before various public agencies, public boards and commissions. The firm is also distinguished by its foray into areas such as Native American law and Internet gaming. As part of such expansion, the team is advising several Class III gaming operators, who are seeking business opportunities in other states. Further areas of activity include Internet gaming and gaming technology companies who are looking into business opportunities in the State of Nevada.

The Lawyers: Sources pointed to **Jeffrey Silver**'s *"excellent work and thorough knowledge"* in representing clients in the hotel industry. For example, he advises Hard Rock Hotel on its day-to-day issues as well as complex matters. He frequently appears before state, county and municipal authorities involved in the licensing process. Increasingly, Silver has been advising on issues relating to Internet gaming and is well versed in related taxation issues.

The Clients: Hard Rock Hotel; Riviera Hotel; Gaming Laboratories International; Applebee's International and California Pizza Kitchen.

McDonald Carano Wilson McCune Bergin Frankovich & Hicks LLP

The Firm: The market leader in Reno, attorneys here work together with the Las Vegas office to form one of the largest departments in the state. A group of five dedicated attorneys practice gaming law on a full-time basis. In line with the general trend toward major consolidations in the hotel and entertainment sector, attorneys have continued to secure the loyalty of the major gaming conglomerates. Additionally, the firm has a large client base among the game machine manufacturing industry, representing some of the best-known operators, including the state's largest Native American gaming operation. In a recent highlight, the team advised Goldman Sachs on the refinancing of the Venetian Hotel, a project of significant implication for the Las Vegas strip.

The Lawyers: The *"highly competent and very experienced"* **AJ (Bud) Hicks** practices in all areas of gaming law, taking a specific interest in the gaming manufacturing sector where he represents industry giants such as Universal Distributing of Nevada. Over the course of his career, he has represented both publicly traded companies and privately owned gaming establishments. Hicks is also a consultant to the investment banking and lending industry, regularly serving as Nevada counsel on large transactional matters and related financings.

The Clients: Universal Distributing of Nevada; Bank One; Eldorado Hotel & Casino; Fort Mohave Indian Tribe and Valley National Financial Services.

Band 3

Curran & Parry

See firm details p.1104

The Firm: Perhaps best known for its administrative department, this Las Vegas firm, founded in 1994, has extensive experience in all areas of business litigation. It serves various clients in

the development industry, who are involved in casino-related projects, providing advice on a full range of gaming law issues. The five-attorney team is also respected for its role in the Las Vegas public community with several of its members sitting on compliance committees.

The Lawyers: According to sources, founder of the firm **Bill Curran** is a *"great guy to work with"* and a long-standing member of the Las Vegas legal community. Alongside his extensive experience in zoning and administrative matters, Curran has cultivated a broad base of experience through his roles as chair of various gaming regulatory committees.

The Clients: Alamo Rent A Car, International Construction and Sprint PCS are examples of this firm's client base.

Jones Vargas

The Firm: According to peers: *"Clients gravitate toward the firm because of its established reputation."* The firm is widely recognized for its expertise in general administrative law, land use matters, lobbying and government affairs. Recently, its attorneys have been instrumental in the securing of local ordinances to allow the licensing of the Downtown Executive Center, the Mandalay Resort and Harrah's Entertainment. Attorneys are particularly versed in government affairs, many of them having served previously in government positions before joining the firm.

The Lawyers: Labeled *"the future star"* of gaming law, **Michael Alonso** heads up the practice at the firm. He is respected for his political lobbying work, an activity that sees him appear before the Nevada Legislature and local governing bodies on a regular basis. Alonso's advice has also been instrumental in the approval of certain tax rates by the City of Reno for several casino projects. Additionally, he has been responsible for the licensing of a substantial number of individual public gaming companies.

The Clients: Harrah's Entertainment; International Game Technology; MTR Gaming Group; Pioneer Gambling Hall and Station Casinos.

LITIGATION

Band 1

Campbell & Williams

The Firm: Although smaller in size than some of its direct competitors, this firm's focus on its high-quality reputation and visibility in a *"handful of top-notch"* cases stands it in good stead. Sources endorse the *"highly professional and ethical"* lawyers in this four-attorney team. Catastrophic personal injury and wrongful

death cases are handled alongside a broad commercial litigation, white-collar crime defense and First Amendment law practice. The firm has also cultivated a renowned appellate practice.

The Lawyers: **Donald Campbell** has a *"wonderful reputation with the courts,"* not least as a result of his many successes over the years in representing both plaintiffs and defendants. Interviewees report that he handles complex jury trials in a *"fearless and highly professional*

GENERAL COMMERCIAL

manner," while his aggressive defense of his clients is widely recognized. Campbell continues to lead this *"formidable"* team in all litigation matters. His partner, **Colby Williams** is especially regarded as an astute attorney, whose *"thorough approach"* and understanding of the details to a case make him a popular choice.

The Clients: Medical facilities and healthcare providers, car manufacturers and high-end retailers feature on the client list.

Nevada
Leading firms
(Litigation: General Commercial)

1 **CAMPBELL & WILLIAMS** Las Vegas
   HARRISON, KEMP & JONES LLP Las Vegas
   JONES VARGAS Las Vegas
   LIONEL SAWYER & COLLINS Las Vegas

2 **HALE LANE PEEK DENNISON AND HOWARD** Reno
   MORRIS PICKERING & SANNER Las Vegas
   SCHRECK BRIGNONE Las Vegas

3 **JOLLEY, URGA, WIRTH & WOODBURY** Las Vegas
   KUMMER KAEMPFER BONNER Las Vegas
   LAXALT & NOMURA Reno
   LEWIS AND ROCA Las Vegas
   MCDONALD CARANO WILSON MCCUNE Reno
   ROBISON, BELAUSTEGUI, SHARP & LOW Reno
   SANTORO, DRIGGS, WALCH, KEARNEY Las Vegas

Leading individuals
(Litigation: General Commercial)

1 **CAMPBELL Donald** Campbell & Williams, Las Vegas
   JONES J Randall Harrison Kemp, Las Vegas
   KENNEDY Dennis Lionel Sawyer, Las Vegas

2 **FERENBACH Cam** Lionel Sawyer, Las Vegas
   HARRISON Kirk Harrison Kemp, Las Vegas
   HEINZ Von Lewis and Roca, Las Vegas
   HEJMANOWSKI Paul Lionel Sawyer, Las Vegas
   LAXALT Bruce Laxalt & Nomura, Reno
   LENHARD Kirk Jones Vargas, Las Vegas
   MORRIS Steve Morris Pickering, Las Vegas
   PEEK J Stephen Hale Lane, Las Vegas
   PISANELLI James Schreck Brignone, Las Vegas
   SANTORO Nicholas Santoro Driggs, Las Vegas
   WILLIAMS J Colby Campbell & Williams, Las Vegas

3 **GORDON Andrew** McDonald Carano, Las Vegas
   JOLLEY R Gardner Jolley Urga, Las Vegas
   KUMMER Thomas Kummer Kaempfer, Las Vegas
   ROBISON Kent Robison Belaustegui, Reno
   URGA William Jolley Urga, Las Vegas

Up-and-coming individuals
   BICE Todd Schreck Brignone, Las Vegas

Firms and individuals are listed alphabetically in each band.

Harrison, Kemp & Jones, LLP

The Firm: The five-attorney team is staffed with *"highly professional"* lawyers who are *"a real pleasure to deal with,"* and are well equipped to handle a wide range of disputes. The team is particularly known for its representation of large hotels, such as Caesars, and as such are a presence in the real estate market. Other clients include developers involved in large contract disputes, and local municipalities engaged in land disputes. Frequently, the attorneys also get involved in complex class actions where they have experience on both the plaintiff and defense side. Additionally, the firm serves clients outside of the state; for example attorneys are heavily involved in the defense of an energy company based in California. In somewhat of a niche area, the team represents physicians with large practices in negligence cases against former patients.

The Lawyers: A *"brilliant trial lawyer"* **Randall Jones** has impressed sources with his courtroom presence; he *"speaks with authority, develops strategies very effectively and is always conscientious in his decision-making."* Jones is well versed in real estate litigation, in which he represents some of the largest landowners in Las Vegas. Another important area of his practice is the energy sector. The *"highly effective"* **Kirk Harrison** is heavily involved in litigation arising out of large commercial developments such as the Venetian Hotel project, which consumes the majority of his time. His remaining focus is spent on the construction industry, where he defends various trade and general contractors, for example the City of Las Vegas. In addition, he is increasingly active in mediation and arbitration proceedings and mediates one or two cases each month.

The Clients: City of Las Vegas; Caesars; Las Vegas Hilton; MacDonald Properties and Pacific Properties & Development.

Jones Vargas

The Firm: This is the second largest firm in the state, with dedicated litigators based in both Las Vegas and Reno. It concentrates its disputes practice on trial work in all state and federal courts in Nevada, as well as appellate work before the Supreme Court of Nevada and the Ninth Circuit Court of Appeals. The firm has also made itself a name in representing the entire gamut of clients ranging from individuals and small businesses to large corporations and institutions. Marquee clients include Airport Authority of Washoe County, Lehman Brothers and Station Casinos.

The Lawyers: Portrayed as a *"standout trial lawyer"* **Kirk Lenhard** has won much acclaim for his track record before a jury. He combines an *"easy and relaxed"* persona with a *"cutthroat attitude,"* in the defense of his clients. Peers also recognize that he is backed by a strong supporting team of attorneys. At present, Lenhard is heavily involved with the representation of the McCarran airport in Las Vegas, while his experience also includes the representation of casinos, large commercial entities, other lawyers and premier client, Bank of America.

The Clients: Further names found on the client roster include Mandalay Bay Resorts and JPMorgan Securities.

Lionel Sawyer & Collins

The Firm: A *"powerful name in Nevada,"* the firm has impressed our sources with the strength and depth of its litigation practice. Indicative of the overall trend toward increased complex litigation, the firm has represented major real estate developers in disputes arising out of office projects as well as companies involved in equipment manufacturing. A further area of increased focus has been mass tort actions, for example, the firm has recently been engaged in class actions involving faulty electronic gaming devices, scoring an important victory for the gaming industry in the Ninth Circuit Court of Appeals. Medical malpractice-related insurance disputes within the State of Nevada are also high on the agenda here.

The Lawyers: Market commentators were quick to point to the *"brilliant"* **Dennis Kennedy** for his *"great courtroom aplomb."* A good portion of his practice is devoted to large class action suits and complex multiparty litigation with a special emphasis on the tobacco and pharmaceutical industries. He secured an important victory for manufacturers of gaming devices in the Ninth Circuit Court of Appeals against a class of plaintiffs claiming alleged fraud as a result of faulty machines. He also has a specialty in medical malpractice insurance and is heavily involved in a number of challenging cases related to the herbal drug ephedra. Interviewees singled out *"academic"* **Cam Ferenbach** for his *"great intellectual ability and effectiveness at the appellate stage."* Most recently, he has been involved in a high-profile medical malpractice case involving the diabetes drug Rezulin, which has resulted in FDA investigations and its ultimate withdrawal. Additionally, he successfully handled an employment litigation suit on behalf of the Culinary Workers Union, the country's largest hotel and restaurant employees union. Clients praised **Paul Hejmanowski** as *"the best attorney"* they'd *"ever seen; he communicates clearly without getting into technical jargon."* He represents companies that are heavily involved in the real estate developments, often office projects, as well as companies involved in equipment manufacturing. One of his most high-profile clients is the boxing promoter Don King.

The Clients: St. Paul Insurance; International Game Technology; Sunrise Hospital & Medical Center and Hanson Properties.

Band 2

Hale Lane Peek Dennison and Howard

The Firm: While many sources pointed to this firm as one of the main competitors in the market, much of its profile rests with the reputation of lead litigation partner, Stephen Peek. The litigation practice consists of 27 full-time attorneys across three offices in the state, and is well equipped to handle a broad range of disputes. The firm's representation of e-commerce companies, hotels, casinos and major developers is widely recognized. In the largest jury trial in Nevada State Court, the group won a significant jury verdict on behalf of its developer client against subcontractors. The attorneys are heavily involved in litigation emanating from the 2002 energy crisis, focusing on issues such as the regulation of electric utilities for the state.

The Lawyers: The *"fierce and tenacious"* **Stephen Peek** is based in the firm's Reno office, from which he continues to handle the firm's most significant cases and trials. In addition to his real estate and energy sector expertise, he is increasingly engaged in discovery issues, especially electronic data.

The Clients: Southern Nevada Water Authority; Bank of America; Venetian Resort Hotel & Casino and Golden Nugget.

Morris Pickering & Sanner

The Firm: Described as a firm *"packed with brilliant lawyers,"* this four-partner litigation team handles complex litigation for private and public entities, and represents regional as well as national clients. It specializes in areas of civil litigation ranging from products liability, antitrust and securities fraud to First Amendment and employment matters. The firm has also represented a number of high-profile clients in cases that were of statewide importance, such as the Hilton takeover litigation, during which the firm represented the hotel chain.

The Lawyers: Sources described **Steve Morris** as *"a brilliant trial lawyer and a tough negotiator,"* who is best known for his track record in handling highly complex lawsuits. He has defended claims against pharmaceutical companies, medical devices and automobile manufacturers, as well as hospitals and insurers in coverage disputes. Additionally, he has a niche practice in natural resources litigation having represented landowners in disputes arising out of the mining sector.

The Clients: Hard Rock Cafe Hotel and Casino; Harrah's Entertainment; Honeywell International and Prudential.

Schreck Brignone

The Firm: Attorneys at this firm are well versed in proceedings before state and federal courts, including appellate matters. The team is particularly commended for its substantial experience in the areas of complex litigation and class actions. Its caseload is wide-ranging in nature, and often involves bankruptcy and securities law, First Amendment issues and tort litigation. Some of the group's most notable engagements include the representation of major hotel properties in disputes arising out of the development of new hotels and resort projects.

The Lawyers: **James Pisanelli** has won a loyal client following thanks to his *"intelligent and pragmatic approach – he does a good job in difficult circumstances."* His practice encompasses commercial litigation, construction and healthcare law. Pisanelli has also made a name for himself in the alternative dispute resolution field

by handling a creditor's rights-related action for Interstate Bank of Arizona, which saw him obtain a judgment in the upper region of $18 million. Interviewees endorsed **Todd Bice**'s *"strong client relations,"* while clients reported that they *"heavily rely upon him"* for his sound judgment. He recently obtained preliminary injunctions on behalf of hotel casinos such as Harrah's, Circus Circus and Treasure Island in disputes with advertisers and street vendors who attempted to distribute commercial handbills and merchandise on the sidewalks surrounding these resorts.

The Clients: One of the firm's marquee clients is Nevada's largest HMO, which the firm has represented in many of its commercial disputes. Other clients include: MGM Mirage; Station Casinos; Titanium Metals and Wynn Resorts.

Band 3

Jolley, Urga, Wirth & Woodbury

The Firm: This firm has a broad geographic reach with offices in Boulder, CO, and Las Vegas. Attorneys specialize in a multitude of civil law areas including business and commercial litigation, administrative law, IP and domestic relations. The recent caseload here has included environmental law disputes, real estate and personal injury litigation. The firm's attorneys are also active in public office: one member has recently been re-elected to his 16th year as Clark County Commissioner, while a partner has completed service as a six-year member of the Nevada Gaming Commission.

The Lawyers: *Founding member* **Gardner Jolley**'s extensive experience encompasses banking and commercial litigation, as well as environmental and real estate disputes. Probate law is a further specialty; and Jolley has advised on the estates of key players in the Las Vegas hotel scene. Interviewees also commended **William Urga** as *"an articulate, reasonable, civil and undeniably effective attorney."* After six years on the Nevada Gaming Commission, he returned to full-time practice in 1997. He is particularly well versed in business litigation and gaming law and occasionally also handles employment litigation trials. Urga's handling of the Pyramid Scheme investigation, which saw the investors recovering $18 million in reimbursement checks, won him high acclaim in recent times.

The Clients: Clients include Fortune 500 companies, large financial institutions and local contractors and business developers.

Kummer Kaempfer Bonner & Renshaw

See firm details p.1105

The Firm: Market commentators acknowledged that this firm *"truly excels"* at government affairs and land use and, despite some losses to its litigation department in recent times, remains a

real force. A team of 17 attorneys specializes in professional responsibility litigation, especially in attorney and accountant liability. The firm is also widely recognized for its niche practice in aviation litigation. With the recent opening of the Reno office, the firm is expanding the reach of its practice into Northern Nevada. The firm is also a market leader in the state for e-commerce and technology startups.

The Lawyers: Head of the litigation practice, **Thomas Kummer** (see p.1102) has represented some of the largest insurance companies nationwide in lawsuits involving coverage issues, errors and omissions, and bad faith claims. He is also experienced in aviation law and regularly advises clients on matters relating to this specialized area.

The Clients: ITT Corporation; Wal-Mart; Rio Hotel & Casino and USA Capital First Trust Deed Fund.

Laxalt & Nomura

The Firm: Although smaller in size, this firm provides expertise in all areas of civil law such as construction, legal malpractice defense and civil rights law. The firm has a total of 18 lawyers and six insurance industry paralegals, who continue to be known for their aggressive trial approach and for the diverse clientele they represent. Clients range from insurance industry giants to large manufacturers and banks, and include a number of national businesses.

The Lawyers: The *"highly effective"* **Bruce Laxalt** brings to the practice significant experience in public life having previously practiced as chief deputy district attorney in Reno. Laxalt divides his time between the firm's Las Vegas and Reno offices, and is praised for the aggressive and proactive approach to litigation.

The Clients: In the insurance industry, the firm actively represents giants such as Allianz Life Insurance, Allstate and Pioneer Life Insurance. Additionally, the firm's heavyweight clients in the manufacturing and banking industries include ARAMARK, Washington Mutual Bank and Wells Fargo.

Lewis and Roca

The Firm: Sources endorsed this *"well-rounded, well-connected"* firm, agreeing that its top-notch litigation practice has made an impact on the market since the opening of the Las Vegas office in 1996. With headquarters in Arizona, the firm has expanded its operations into Nevada, where it now houses four attorneys, who advise on IP litigation and business transactions. Recent highlights for the group have included the representation of a New York law firm in relation to the firm's alleged improper accounting advice practices. The team has also handled shareholder disputes between two large financial institutions.

The Lawyers: Clients had much enthusiasm for **Von Heinz**, who they described as having "*technical proficiency in all areas of the law – he can take a case from top to bottom.*" He combines "*excellent people skills mixed in with street smarts.*" Heinz spends a large portion of his time representing law firms across the USA on issues ranging from erroneous tax practices to illegal accounting methods. Additionally, he has handled white-collar crime matters for the financial services industry and frequently gets involved in the representation of Fortune 500 shareholder disputes. Heinz has also made inroads in the hospitality industry where he recently started representing a high-profile California-based restaurant group.

The Clients: Unum Life Insurance, Aetna and Wolfgang Puck Group are key clients of this firm alongside large retailers.

McDonald Carano Wilson McCune Bergin Frankovich & Hicks LLP

The Firm: This Reno "*heavyweight*" continues to house a busy commercial litigation department that has been engaged in a large number of real estate disputes over recent months. Totaling 22 attorneys, the team also places great emphasis on landlord and tenant work representing primarily the landlord side in commercial retail disputes. Other areas of experience include insurance and construction law where the firm currently represents a large insurance company and a hotel/casino. Increasingly, in line with current trends in the state, the attorneys are engaged in alternative dispute resolution such as mediation.

The Lawyers: The "*top-flight*" **Andrew Gordon** is known among his peers for making "*well-crafted, conscientious*" arguments. Aside from handling a substantial number of real estate disputes, he also increasingly serves as arbitrator in private arbitrations. Recently, he has acted for clients in the public sector, such as the Department of State, on premise liability and compliance with health and safety regulations. His other clients include medical manufacturers, who he represents in products liability disputes, hotels and casinos in construction litigation, and landlords in commercial disputes.

The Clients: The client list features Reno/Sparks Association of Realtors, Eldorado Hotel & Casino and Haydon Building.

Robison, Belaustegui, Sharp & Low

The Firm: This midsized firm fields a team of seven that focuses its practice on commercial litigation, representing both plaintiffs and defendants. The firm is representing Sierra Gateway in the Gateway v Landmark Homes case. The client is seeking total damages worth $135 million against the defendant company, which stands accused of having deprived the client of the opportunity of forming a joint venture to develop a prime real estate project in the Reno area. The firm has also represented Edgewood Properties against AG Spanos in a matter involving $5 million in damages caused by subsidence of inadequate soils at a 240-apartment complex.

The Lawyers: Clients valued **Kent Robison** for his "*never condescending attitude*" and his ability to make "*complex legal jargon look simple.*" A respected trial lawyer, Robison has been engaged in a lengthy defamation suit involving the medical profession, in which he won $18 million on behalf of his physician client who had fallen victim to a malicious peer review process. He has also been involved in complex arbitration proceedings for $4.5 million on behalf of a large medical provider before the AAA.

The Clients: The group's clients include: Mandalay Resort Group; Edgewood Properties; Reno Development and Specialty Mortgage Trust.

Santoro, Driggs, Walch, Kearney, Johnson & Thompson

The Firm: Interviewees agreed that this firm is "*on the ascendancy,*" not least on account of its "*accomplished litigators.*" Real property disputes and commercial torts are two key areas of practice, although the group's caseload is far broader and encompasses tax-related disputes, natural resources issues and workers compensation. Formed in 1996, the firm houses 34 attorneys, who are respected for their involvement with the local community and businesses active in Nevada.

The Lawyers: **Nick Santoro** is credited as the driving force behind this practice. Clients appreciated his efforts to "*consistently maintain the quality of the firm,*" and endorsed his litigation skills; he is "*highly convincing at closing argument.*" Santoro represents numerous national and local clients on matters running the gamut from commercial law to personal injury cases.

The Clients: Alexis Park Resort Hotel; Auto Nation Financial Services; American West Homes and the City of North Las Vegas.

REAL ESTATE

Nevada **Leading firms** (Real Estate)

1   **GOOLD PATTERSON ALES ROADHOUSE** *Las Vegas*
     JONES VARGAS *Las Vegas*
     KUMMER KAEMPFER BONNER *Las Vegas*
     LIONEL SAWYER & COLLINS *Las Vegas*

2   **ALLISON, MACKENZIE, RUSSELL** *Carson City*
     HALE LANE PEEK DENNISON AND HOWARD *Reno*
     MCDONALD CARANO WILSON MCCUNE *Reno*
     RICE SILBEY REUTHER & SULLIVAN *Las Vegas*
     SANTORO, DRIGGS, WALCH, KEARNEY *Las Vegas*
     SCHRECK BRIGNONE *Las Vegas*
     SNELL & WILMER LLP *Las Vegas*

3   **DEANER, DEANER, SCANN, MALAN** *Las Vegas*   **GORDON & SILVER LTD** *Las Vegas*
Firms are listed alphabetically in each band.

Band 1

Goold Patterson Ales Roadhouse & Day

The Firm: Sources identified this "*first-class*" real estate practice for its breadth of coverage, which includes sales, financings and leasing. Formed in 1988, the firm houses 11 attorneys who dedicate their time to real estate transactions and related civil litigation. Additionally, the attorneys frequently advise on the negotiation and performance of construction contracts and other real and personal property matters.

The Lawyers: At the "*top of the heap*" is **Barry Goold** (see p.1102). As one of two cofounders of the practice, he has built up a sizable Reno real estate practice. He devotes most of his practice to sales and financial real estate transactions, while the remaining portion is made up of landlord and tenant matters and leasing issues. Clients commended him for his "*excellent knowledge of the law, great understanding of business and incredible experience in the field.*"

Serving as director of the practice, **Jeffrey Patterson** (see p.1103) focuses on all aspects of commercial real estate law. Much of his workload involves representing landlords and creditors in bankruptcy proceedings.

The Clients: Desert Oak Development; Southwest Homes; USA Capital and WestMark Homes.

Jones Vargas

The Firm: The respected firm has maintained its enviable client base, drawn from the gaming and real estate sector, despite the departure of several of its partners. The firm's diverse clientele includes master-planned community developers, home builders and commercial developers, as well as resort hotels, casinos and banks. The attorneys have frequently participated in loan workouts and have worked with builders to create and finance new communities throughout the valley.

The Lawyers: **Michael Buckley** impresses with his "*encyclopedic knowledge on condominiums*

Nevada
Leading individuals (Real Estate)

1 BUCKLEY Michael *Jones Vargas*, Las Vegas	
DENNISON Karen *Hale Lane*, Reno	
GOOLD Barry *Goold Patterson*, Las Vegas	
ZUCKER Jeffrey *Lionel Sawyer*, Las Vegas	
2 CURTIS Patricia *Snell & Wilmer*, Las Vegas	
MACE James *Snell & Wilmer*, Las Vegas	
RICE Stephen *Rice Silbey*, Las Vegas	
WHITTEMORE David *Lionel Sawyer*, Las Vegas	
3 BERGIN Leo *McDonald Carano*, Reno	
DRIGGS J Douglas *Santoro Driggs*, Las Vegas	
FRANKOVICH John *McDonald Carano*, Reno	
JONES Leslie *Schreck Brignone*, Las Vegas	
NOVACEK Stephen *Hale Lane*, Reno	
PATTERSON Jeffrey *Goold Patterson*, Las Vegas	
SHARP F DeArmond *Robison Belaustegui*, Reno	
YOKEN Stephen *Snell & Wilmer*, Las Vegas	

Leading individuals
(Real Estate: Zoning/Land Use)

1 FIORENTINO Mark *Kummer Kaempfer*, Las Vegas	
KAEMPFER Christopher *Kummer Kaempfer*, Las Vegas	

Individuals are listed alphabetically in each band.

and homeowners' associations." He is the most visible face at the practice, and continues to represent the firm's high-profile clientele in all its key projects. Most prominently, he was a major force in the creation of the franchise and real estate rights that led to the construction and completion of the Las Vegas Monorail. In 2003, Buckley was appointed chair of the Nevada Commission for Common Interest Communities by the governor of the state.
The Clients: Clients include major real estate developers such as Gypsum Construction and Reynolds Construction, as well as large title companies and lenders such as Chicago Title Insurance and National Title.

Kummer Kaempfer Bonner & Renshaw

See firm details p.1105
The Firm: While the firm continues to be best known for its "*extremely influential*" zoning and land use practice, it maintains a far broader transactional and development practice. Attorneys have represented owners, developers, tenants and financiers in a variety of real estate transactions and financings. The team also has significant experience counseling clients on personal and entity tax. As part of its famed land use and zoning departments, the attorneys have in-depth experience drafting ordinances, legislation and regulations on a host of zoning, gaming and general business issues.
The Lawyers: The "*superb*" **Mark Fiorentino** (see p.1101) is one of the highest profile attorneys in the state on zoning and land use issues. His extensive experience includes the handling

of state and local gaming licenses as well as tax matters. Fiorentino regularly represents clients on projects involving construction defects, water rights and land development. Fiorentino led the firm's legislative lobbying team at the Nevada legislature in Carson City in 2001 and 2003. **Christopher Kaempfer** (see p.1102) is "*the go-to attorney if you want a development in Clark County.*" He has a wealth of experience in land use law that spans more than 20 years and has argued cases of far-reaching implications on land use law in both state and federal court.
The Clients: DP Partners; Las Vegas Monorail; Mandalay Resort Group; TNT North American Group and USA Commercial Mortgage.

Lionel Sawyer & Collins

The Firm: For many commentators, this firm remains the "*first choice*" for real estate matters because of its "*preeminence and high-quality attorneys.*" The firm has been busy of late in several financings involving the hotel and gaming industry. For example, it was a key player in the refinancing of the Venetian convention center. Attorneys are involved in the refinancing of the Grand Canal shopping center, which has a total worth of $66 million. The condominium-building boom in the state has also benefited the team's workflow, as it is advising a number of developers on projects of this kind. A further highlight has been advice on the joint venture between the Marriott Hotel and a local developer for the construction of a local timeshare project.
The Lawyers: According to market sources, **Jeffrey Zucker** has "*always been one of the top attorneys in the field.*" Known for his "*deep intelligence and perfectionism*" as a lawyer, he has lately advised on the boom in the condominium market, representing more condominium developers than ever before. He acted as Nevada counsel for Boyd Gaming in its merger with Coast Casinos and was also a key player in the joint venture agreement for the construction of a timeshare project. His extensive clientele includes many hotels, real estate developers, financial institutions and healthcare providers. The "*tremendously experienced and highly professional*" **David Whittemore** advised on the refinancing of the Venetian Resort Hotel & Casino convention center. More recently, he closed the deal on the sale of the Grand Canal shopping center. Additionally, he has closed a number of apartment projects for another major developer and is working on a housing deal for the Department of Prisons.
The Clients: MGM Grand Hotel/Casino; Mandalay Resort Group; Caesars Entertainment; First Republic Bank; Baxter Healthcare and Hanson Properties North America.

Band 2

Allison, MacKenzie, Russell, Pavlakis, Wright & Fagan, Ltd

The Firm: The firm is considered a "*prime real estate practice in Northern Nevada*" by market observers. Its high-profile real estate work on behalf of both state and national clients is run alongside a respected business litigation and administrative law practice. The team also acts as general counsel for public authorities such as the Carson City School District and the Nevada State Board of Accountancy, and health providers such as the Carson-Tahoe Hospital. The firm also has a niche practice within natural resources and environmental law, handling water law matters.
The Lawyers: The real estate practice is led by James Cavilia, who handles all aspects of real estate development and land use as well as bankruptcy and business law.
The Clients: David Walley's Resort; Las Vegas Paving; Oxbow Power Services; Carriage House Timeshare Association and Quintus Resorts.

Hale Lane Peek Dennison and Howard

The Firm: This "*absolutely superb*" firm has always placed real estate law at the core of its practice. The attorneys regularly advise real estate developers, purchasers, sellers and title companies. As a result of the influx of real estate developers into the state, the firm captured many new and expanding businesses as clients. The firm is also respected for its experienced finance department representing many local, national and international financial institutions.
The Lawyers: Clients especially praised the "*creative, ethical and knowledgeable*" **Karen Dennison** for her "*strong orientation toward getting the deal done.*" Her 30 years' experience encompasses real property development, leasings and financings. She has advised on developments in the leisure sector, such as timeshare properties, golf courses, industrial parks and shopping centers. **Stephen Novacek** has an expertise in real estate financings, planned residential and mixed-use communities and office project acquisitions.
The Clients: Office, retail and timeshare developers, large financial institutions and banks, and major lending and borrowing institutions are all found among the firm's clients.

McDonald Carano Wilson McCune Bergin Frankovich & Hicks LLP

The Firm: The past year has seen Reno turn into a hot residential market with estimates of housing development projects having risen by 30-35%. This firm has capitalized on the increased activity, advising both buyers and sellers in the purchase and sale of developed and undeveloped commercial and residential real property. Two highlights for the team have been its handling of a sale of a casino and the sale of a $35 million hospital and adjoining office space. Furthermore, the firm fields a respected land use department that advises on zoning, entitlements and use permits.

The Lawyers: Former managing partner **Leo Bergin** primarily focuses his work on real estate, securitization issues and agricultural law. Of late, he has handled the sale of a major local casino and a $35 million hospital and its adjoining office space. Bergin represents title companies in land disputes as well as title insurers and banks. Sources believe that **John Frankovich** "*dominates the real estate and land planning scene in Northern Nevada.*" He combines his work on real estate development and financing with litigation and public utilities law.

The Clients: Associated General Contractors of America; Clark & Sullivan; First Security Bank and Sun State Bank.

Rice Silbey Reuther & Sullivan LLP

The Firm: Formed in April 2004, this is a group of four partners, all of whom are former members of prominent Las Vegas law firms. An "*impressive offering,*" it is fast becoming a "*definite player*" in the Las Vegas real estate market. Among the firm's most prominent transactions has been a purchase agreement for a company that acquired a 2000-hectare plot of land in one of the largest brownfield redevelopment schemes in the USA.

The Lawyers: **Stephen Rice**, one of the founding partners, is a prominent figure in the market following his top-flight practice at Jones Vargas. Clients point to his "*outstanding deal-making qualities*" and his "*excellent business sense*" as major drawing cards. Since the launch of his firm, Rice has continued his involvement in market-leading transactions and recently closed a property transaction for an urban village project, which will incorporate a mixture of retail, gaming and residential uses.

The Clients: Clients include large furniture retailers and marts such as the World Market Center, which is attracting considerable business to the Las Vegas Valley. The firm also works with real estate developers such as Crescent Real Estate Equities, technology consulting firms and providers such as Cintra, and local leaders in residential development such as the American Nevada Corporation.

Santoro, Driggs, Walch, Kearney, Johnson & Thompson

The Firm: Market sources were quick to point to the firm's experienced real estate department, which continues to play an important role in developments across Nevada. Attorneys concentrate on real property acquisition and associated environmental, water and land use matters, as well as business organization and

operational issues. The firm's clients include national lenders, and prominent Las Vegas construction and home-building companies. The team of two full-time real estate partners and three associates can draw upon construction, finance and M&A specialists.

The Lawyers: Interviewees asserted their favorable impression of **Douglas Driggs** praising his "*real know-how of the field.*" Driggs represents several of Nevada's largest commercial and residential developers and advised on the development of the state's major shopping centers, hotels, office buildings and apartment complexes.

The Clients: American West Homes; Greystone Homes; Republic Mortgage and Pinnacle Entertainment.

Schreck Brignone

The Firm: Market sources endorsed the extensive experience possessed by these attorneys, and the firm's ability to effectively staff large real estate transactions. The attorneys are particularly active in the gaming sector where they have been involved in the acquisition and financing of resort hotel casino properties. Among its most prominent transactions has been its representation of Mirage Resorts in the acquisition of various properties, including the Golden Nugget and the Bellagio site. The team has also been active in the healthcare sector, having represented Sierra Health Services for a number of years in all its real estate transactions.

The Lawyers: Equipped with long-standing experience in the field, **Leslie Terry Jones** continues to enjoy a "*formidable*" reputation in the marketplace. Jones has represented the firm's major clients, such as Mirage Resorts and Caesars Entertainment in real property transactions. He recently acted as local real estate counsel in financing transactions for the Le Reve project by Wynn Resorts. He was also counsel to Phillip Ruffin in his joint venture project with the Trump Organization.

The Clients: Sierra Health Services; Goldman Sachs; MGM/Mirage; Wynn Resorts and Hard Rock Cafe.

Snell & Wilmer LLP
See firm details p.167

The Firm: According to market sources, the firm has "*significantly gained in strength*" since the opening of its newest office in Las Vegas. The attorneys' experience ranges from transactions involving educational facilities and industrial parks to resorts and hotels. Most recently, the firm closed a $46 million construction loan to a Nevada-based developer. Currently, the team's 12 attorneys are engaged in the acquisition of the lease for a major shopping center in Las Vegas, which is due to be opened in April 2005.

The Lawyers: The firm has greatly benefited from the arrival of **James Mace** (see p.1103)

from Gordon & Silver, who has brought to the practice "*a unique perspective and expertise*" on condominium development. He is presently involved in the acquisition of the lease of a shopping center due to be opened in the near future. The "*wonderful*" **Patricia Curtis** (see p.1101) is widely recognized for her detailed understanding of the market, having worked as in-house counsel at Caesars Entertainment. Her practice focuses on real estate financing with an emphasis on asset secured and unsecured loans and lines of credit. Interviewees commented on **Stephen Yoken**'s (see p.1103) strength on the transactional side of the market, especially lending issues. Since 2004, when he joined the firm alongside James Mace, his arrival has contributed to the increase in the firm's profile, market sources agree.

The Clients: Clients include real estate developers such as Centex Destination Properties, construction management companies such as Kitchell Contractors, and title insurance companies such as Land America Lawyers.

Deaner, Deaner, Scann, Malan & Larsen

The Firm: This 1971-founded entity has cultivated a reputation in the market, housing a sensible and practical real estate team that can support clients on all aspects of real estate law, including zoning law and finance issues. Over the years the firm has grown to incorporate six full-time attorneys, who advise clients from the construction, banking and real estate development industries.

The Lawyers: Founder Charles Deaner is the key contact for advice on all aspects of real estate law.

The Clients: Clients include important financial institutions such as the Clark County Credit Union, title companies such as Land Title of Nevada, and real estate developers such as John Laing Homes, as well as public regeneration authorities such as the North Las Vegas Redevelopment Agency.

Gordon & Silver Ltd

The Firm: Despite the recent departures of two of its partners, the firm remains active in the market, particularly representing condominium developers in their latest Las Vegas projects. Of late, the seven-member team has been extensively involved in negotiations for the acquisition of a major slot machine operator, which was recently sold to another client of the firm, Alliance Gaming. The attorneys also regularly represent hotel casinos and assist companies in Chapter 11 bankruptcy proceedings.

The Lawyers: The team is headed by Richard Galin, who advises on the negotiating and drafting of agreements for purchases and sales of businesses as well as M&A.

The Clients: Clients include Hard Rock Cafe, Riviera Hotel & Casino and the Nevada Title Company.

Other Notable Practitioners

Interviewees highlighted the "*great deal-making skills*" of **F DeArmond Sharp** (see p.1103) at

Robison, Belaustegui, Sharp & Low. He combines his transactional real estate workload with a general commercial litigation practice.

Leaders in Nevada

ABBOTT, Scott
Kamer Zucker & Abbott, Las Vegas
702 259 8640
Recommended in Employment

ALONSO, Michael
Jones Vargas, Reno 775 786 5000
Recommended in Gaming & Licensing

ARRAJJ, David
Schreck Brignone, Las Vegas
702 382 2101
Recommended in Gaming & Licensing

BARNARD, Gregg
Woodburn and Wedge, Reno
775 688 3025
gbarnard@woodburnandwedge.com
Recommended in Corporate/M&A
Practice Areas: Practicing primarily in corporate law, with extensive experience in corporate mergers and acquisitions and financing transactions, and real estate acquisition, development, sale and finance. Representative clients include Advanta Corp., AIG, Barker-Coleman Communities, Bombardier Transportation Inc., General Growth Properties, Glamis Gold, Inc., Household Finance Corporation, JPMorgan, Macquarie Capital, Magnum Hunter Resources, Marlin Leasing Inc., Nevada Power Company, Placer Dome US Inc., Sierra Pacific Resources, Sierra Pacific Power Company, Tanamara Development, Tenet Healthcare Corporation, The Outdoor Channel, The Trust Company of the West.
Prof. Memberships: Member of the Executive Committee for the Business Law Section of the State Bar of Nevada and the American Bar Association.
Career: Shareholder and member of the Board of Directors of the law firm of Woodburn and Wedge, Nevada's oldest law firm.
Personal: JD, Willamette University (1991), BA University of Nevada-Reno.

BATTCHER, Frederick
Hale Lane Peek Dennison and Howard, Reno 775 327 3000
Recommended in Corporate/M&A

BERGIN, Leo
McDonald Carano Wilson McCune Bergin Frankovich & Hicks LLP, Reno
775 788 2000
Recommended in Real Estate

BICE, Todd
Schreck Brignone, Las Vegas
702 382 2101
Recommended in Litigation

BONNER, Michael J
Kummer Kaempfer Bonner & Renshaw, Las Vegas 702 792 7000
mbonner@kkbr.com
Recommended in Corporate/M&A
Practice Areas: Managing Partner. Practice concentration in business transactions, securities and gaming law. Has acted as counsel on IPOs, follow on offerings, private placements, M&A and restructuring transactions. Has counseled publicly held companies on federal securities law disclosure and corporate governance matters, including Rio Hotel & Casino, Inc., Paul-Son Gaming Corporation (now Gaming Partners International Corp.) and Monarch Casino & Resort, Inc. Has counseled acquirors and acquirees in M&A, roll-ups and other acquisition-related transactions. Has represented hotel-casino resort operators, including ITT Corporation, Atlantis Casino Resort (Reno), Rio Suite Hotel Casino, Casablanca Resorts, Aladdin Hotel & Casino, as well as manufacturers, suppliers, lenders and officers and directors in transactional and licensing approvals before the Nevada Gaming regulatory agencies.
Prof. Memberships: Former Chairman, Corporations Sub-Committee, Business Law Committee, State Bar of Nevada; former Vice-Chairman, Southern Nevada Disciplinary Board, State Bar of Nevada; Executive Committee, Nevada Development Authority; Member, International Association of Gaming Attorneys and Young President's Organization.
Career: Admitted to Nevada Bar (1981). Founding stockholder of Kummer Kaempfer Bonner & Renshaw (1994) and stockholder of predecessor firm.
Personal: Las Vegas native; JD, University of California, Los Angeles (1981); BS (High Distinction), University of Nevada, Las Vegas (1978).

BRIGNONE, Andrew
Schreck Brignone, Las Vegas
702 382 2101
Recommended in Employment

BUCKLEY, Michael
Jones Vargas, Las Vegas
702 734 2220
Recommended in Real Estate

BULLEN, Linda
Lionel Sawyer & Collins, Las Vegas
702 383 8888
Recommended in Environment

CABOT, Anthony
Lionel Sawyer & Collins, Las Vegas
702 383 8888
Recommended in Gaming & Licensing

CAMPBELL, Donald
Campbell & Williams, Las Vegas
702 382 5222
Recommended in Litigation

COLE, Howard
Lionel Sawyer & Collins, Las Vegas
702 383 8888
Recommended in Employment

CURRAN, William
Curran & Parry, Las Vegas
702 471 7000
Recommended in Gaming & Licensing

CURTIS, Patricia
Snell & Wilmer LLP, Las Vegas
702 784 5226
pcurtis@swlaw.com
Recommended in Real Estate
Practice Areas: Practice concentrated in real estate financing and development. Represents developers of commercial, residential, condominium and mixed-use projects and assisted living communities, as well as a variety of local, regional and national lenders and borrowers in financing transactions.
Prof. Memberships: State Bar of Nevada; Clark County Bar Association; American Bar Association (Business Law and Real Estate Sections); Urban Land Institute, Las Vegas Chapter; National Association of Industrial and Office Parks, Las Vegas Chapter; Commercial Real Estate Women of Southern Nevada.
Personal: Member of Executive Board, Communities in Schools of Southern Nevada.

DE LIPKAU, Ross
Marshall Hill Cassas & De Lipkau, Reno 775 323 1601
Recommended in Environment

DENNISON, Karen
Hale Lane Peek Dennison and Howard, Reno 775 327 3000
Recommended in Real Estate

DEPAOLI, Gordon
Woodburn and Wedge, Reno
775 688 3000
gdepaoli@woodburnandwedge.com
Recommended in Environment
Practice Areas: Water law, real estate law and civil litigation.
Prof. Memberships: American Bar Association; State Bar of Nevada; Washoe County Bar Association.
Career: Shareholder for 28 years in the law firm of Woodburn and Wedge; Chairman, Nevada Standing Committee on Judicial Ethics and Election Practices.

Publications: 'Federal and Indian Reserved Water Rights - The Nevada Experience,' presented at 1998 Nevada Water Law Conference.
Personal: JD, University of Colorado (1972) (Order of the Coif); BA, University of Nevada (1969) (High Distinction).

DRIGGS, Douglas
Santoro, Driggs, Walch, Kearney, Johnson & Thompson, Las Vegas
702 791 0308
Recommended in Real Estate

EFROYMSON, Kevin
Kevin C Efroymson, Las Vegas Null
Recommended in Employment

FAISS, Robert
Lionel Sawyer & Collins, Las Vegas
702 383 8888
Recommended in Gaming & Licensing

FERENBACH, Cam
Lionel Sawyer & Collins, Las Vegas
702 383 8888
Recommended in Litigation

FIORENTINO, Mark H
Kummer Kaempfer Bonner & Renshaw, Las Vegas 702 792 7000
mfiorentino@kkbr.com
Recommended in Real Estate
Practice Areas: Partner/Head of Land Use and Government Affairs Practice. Practices extensively before the Nevada State Legislature and local government authorities on land use, zoning, licensing and general business matters. Substantial experience with zoning matters, state and local gaming license and tax matters. Drafts ordinances, legislation, and regulations on a variety of zoning, gaming and general business issues. Represents Focus Property Group, Howard Hughes Corporation, Boyd Gaming Corporation, The Related Companies, Republic Services, Sierra Health Services, Chelsea Property Group, Pulte Homes, Astoria Homes, and Lamar Advertising. Registered lobbyist with the Nevada State Legislature, Clark County and Cities of Las Vegas and Henderson.
Prof. Memberships: Member, American Bar Association, Clark County Bar Association, International Association of Gaming Attorneys. Served as Circuit Governor, Law Student Division, American Bar Association, Former Member, Clark County Comprehensive Planning Steering Committee. Served on Clark County Committee rewriting the County's Zoning Code and City of Las Vegas Master Plan Committee.

Career: Admitted to Nevada Bar (1992); Partner, Kummer Kaempfer Bonner & Renshaw 1999); former associate, Lionel, Sawyer & Collins (1992-95).

Publications: Member, Drake University Law Review. Published article on federal preemption of tobacco litigation. Contributing author to International Casino Law (1993) and Nevada Gaming Law (1995).

Personal: JS-Drake University (1992); BS-Arizona State University (1986).

FOWLER, John

Woodburn and Wedge, Reno
775 688 3000
jfowler@woodburnandwedge.com
Recommended in Corporate/M&A

Practice Areas: Business organizations, corporate governance, mergers and acquisitions, real estate and other business transactions, government procurement.

Prof. Memberships: State Bar of Nevada; Member, Executive Committee, Business Law Section, State Bar of Nevada 1992-; Chair 1992-2004; American Bar Association, Section on Business Law, Section on Real Property, Probate and Trusts.

Career: Associate, Vargas & Bartlett (1977-81); Partner, Vargas & Bartlett (1981-94); Partner, Marshall, Hill, Cassas & deLipkau (1994-2003); Partner, Woodburn and Wedge (2003-present).

Publications: Study of Nevada Corporate Law, Vargas & Bartlett, 1990. Managing editor and co-author; prepared under contract for the Nevada Secretary of State. Two articles on Nevada Corporate Law: Vargas & Bartlett, 1991 (co-author) 'Business Law in the Legislature', 'Nevada Lawyer', July, 2003, p13.

FRANKOVICH, John

McDonald Carano Wilson McCune Bergin Frankovich & Hicks LLP, Reno
775 788 2000
Recommended in Real Estate

GARCIA, David

Hale Lane Peek Dennison and Howard, Reno 775 327 3000
Recommended in Corporate/M&A

GIORDANO, Gregory

Lionel Sawyer & Collins, Las Vegas
702 383 8888
Recommended in Gaming & Licensing

GOLDSTEIN, Mark

Lionel Sawyer & Collins, Las Vegas
702 383 8888
Recommended in Corporate/M&A

GOOLD, Barry

Goold Patterson Ales Roadhouse & Day, Las Vegas 702 436 2600
bgoold@goldpatterson.com
Recommended in Real Estate

Practice Areas: Barry Goold's practice is focused on commercial real estate. He handles a variety of transactions, including purchases and sales of unimproved real property, shopping centers, apartment complexes and hotels. He also handles landlord/tenant disputes, negotiation of leases (especially 'Big Box' leas-

es), and preparation of commercial covenants, conditions and restrictions. He represents owners of master-planned communities and developers of all kinds. (For example, the firm represents more than a dozen homebuilders). Mr Goold has an extensive practice representing lenders and commercial borrowers in loans secured by real property. Mr Goold also has a considerable practice in construction law, negotiating agreements with architects and contractors for his developer clients.

Prof. Memberships: American Bar Association, State Bar of Nevada, Clark County Bar Association, State Bar of California (inactive).

Career: Barry Goold is the chief executive officer of Goold Patterson Ales Roadhouse & Day, which he co-founded with Jeffrey D Patterson in 1988. He has practiced in Las Vegas, Nevada for over 25 years. Mr Goold has been named in every consecutive edition of a leading US legal publication. He has given many seminars, and serves as an expert witness in complex real estate litigation.

Personal: Barry Goold received his undergraduate degree (with distinction) from UC Berkeley in 1974 (Phi Beta Kappa), and his JD degree from UC Berkeley (Boalt Hall) in 1977. While attending Boalt Hall, he clerked for Melvin Belli, and also clerked for consumer-law specialist Robert A Goldstein. He is admitted to practice in California (1977) and Nevada (1978). From February 1978 through July 1982, he was an associate commercial attorney with Lionel Sawyer & Collins. He broadened his commercial practice as a director in the firm of Smith, Goold & Kotchka prior to founding Goold Patterson Ales Roadhouse & Day.

GORDON, Andrew

McDonald Carano Wilson McCune Bergin Frankovich & Hicks LLP, Las Vegas 702 873 4100
Recommended in Litigation

HARRISON, Kirk

Harrison, Kemp & Jones, LLP, Las Vegas 702 385 6000
Recommended in Litigation

HARRISON, Sylvia

McDonald Carano Wilson McCune Bergin Frankovich & Hicks LLP, Reno
775 788 2000
Recommended in Environment

HEINZ, Von

Lewis and Roca, Las Vegas
702 949 8200
Recommended in Litigation

HEJMANOWSKI, Paul

Lionel Sawyer & Collins, Las Vegas
702 383 8888
Recommended in Litigation

HICKS, Alvin

McDonald Carano Wilson McCune Bergin Frankovich & Hicks LLP, Reno
775 788 2000
Recommended in Gaming & Licensing

HICKS, Patrick

Littler Mendelson PC, Reno
775 348 4888
Recommended in Employment

HILL, Earl

Marshall Hill Cassas & De Lipkau, Reno 775 323 1601
Recommended in Environment

JOLLEY, Gardner

Jolley, Urga, Wirth & Woodbury, Las Vegas 702 699 7500
Recommended in Litigation

JONES, Randall

Harrison, Kemp & Jones, LLP, Las Vegas 702 385 6000
Recommended in Litigation

JONES, Leslie

Schreck Brignone, Las Vegas
702 382 2101
Recommended in Corporate/M&A, Real Estate

KAEMPFER, Christopher

Kummer Kaempfer Bonner & Renshaw, Las Vegas 702 792 7000
ckaempfer@kkbr.com
Recommended in Real Estate

Practice Areas: Senior Partner/Founder of the Land Use and Governmental Relations Department. Nearly 25 years representing development clients in Nevada. Personally argued precedent setting land use cases in both state and federal court. Registered lobbyist with the City of Las Vegas and Clark County, Nevada. Representative clients include Wal-Mart, Home Depot, Marnell Corrao, Pulte Homes, Las Vegas 51s Baseball Club, Olympia Group, CamCo, Inc. (SuperPawn) and Atlantic Richfield. Since 1977, represented numerous general contractors and subcontractors in Nevada, including Marnell Corrao (and its predecessor, Corrao Construction Company). As legal counsel for Marnell Corrao, negotiated construction contracts totaling nearly two billion dollars.

Prof. Memberships: Member, American Bar, Clark County Bar, Nevada and California State Bar Associations; admitted to practice in United States District Courts for State of Nevada.

Career: Admitted to Nevada Bar (1976); California Bar (1975); Clerked in United States District Court for the Honorable Judge Roger D Foley (1975-76); District Counsel for the State of Nevada for the United States Small Business Administration (1976-77); founding Partner, Kummer Kaempfer Bonner & Renshaw (1993); former Partner, predecessor firm Vargas & Bartlett (1982-93).

Personal: JD, University of the Pacific, McGeorge School of Law (1975); BA, University of Nevada, Las Vegas (1971).

KAMER, Gregory

Kamer Zucker & Abbott, Las Vegas
702 259 8640
Recommended in Employment

KELLER, Edwin

Kamer Zucker & Abbott, Las Vegas
702 259 8640
Recommended in Employment

KENNEDY, Dennis

Lionel Sawyer & Collins, Las Vegas
702 383 8888
Recommended in Litigation

KIM, Robert C

Kummer Kaempfer Bonner & Renshaw, Las Vegas 702 792 7000
rkim@kkbr.com
Recommended in Corporate/M&A

Practice Areas: Partner. Practice includes general corporate, transactional, securities and gaming law, with focus on corporate governance, entity formation, public company compliance, private placements and contracts. Prior transactions include: VendingData Corporation (2003 $27.5 million equity offering); USA Capital First Trust Deed Fund, LLC (2002 $120 million equity offering); eRoomSystem Technologies, Inc. (2000 IPO); Carefree Holdings Limited Partnership (1999 $60 million roll-up transaction); Rio Hotel & Casino, Inc. (1998 $1.0 billion acquisition by Harrah's Entertainment, Inc.); and ITT Corporation (1997 takeover defense).

Prof. Memberships: Member, State Bar of Nevada, State Bar of California and American Bar Association; Chairman, Executive Committee, Business Law Section, State Bar of Nevada (committee responsible for proposing and preparing amendments to Nevada's business entity statutes). President and Co-Founder, Asian Bar Association of Las Vegas.

Career: Admitted to Nevada Bar (1996) and California Bar (1998).

Publications: Authored articles for Nevada Business Journal and American Bankruptcy Institute Journal. Speaker at seminars on business entity selection, limited-liability companies and venture capital.

Personal: JD and MBA, University of Southern California (1996); BA, Government, Cornell University (1992). Born in New York, New York.

KIRSHMAN, Norman

Kirshman Harris & Rosenthal, Las Vegas 702 384 3877
Recommended in Employment

KOTCHKA, Malani

Smith & Kotchka Ltd, Las Vegas
702 382 1707
Recommended in Employment

KUMMER, Thomas F

Kummer Kaempfer Bonner & Renshaw, Las Vegas 702 792 7000
tkummer@kkbr.com
Recommended in Litigation

Practice Areas: Senior litigation Partner and Chair of Litigation Department. Practice concentration encompasses business/commercial, professional malpractice, solid waste/resource recovery and aviation litigation. Has represented

ITT Corporation (1997 hostile takeover), Exxon Mobil, Republic Services, Aerospatiale, US Aviation Underwriters, General Growth Properties, Inamed Corporation and Las Vegas Metropolitan Police Department. Has appeared in US and Nevada District Court, the 9th Circuit Court of Appeals, and the Nevada Supreme Court. **Prof. Memberships:** State Bar of Nevada; American Bar, Clark County Bar and American Trial Lawyers Associations; Defense Research Institute; served for eight years on the Ethics and Professional Responsibility Committee of the State Bar of Nevada, three years as Committee Chair; appointed by the Nevada Supreme Court to act as a Supreme Court Settlement Conference Judge. **Career:** St Louis University, BSC (1965) and JD (1968). Admitted to Missouri Bar (1968-inactive) and Nevada Bar (1971). Founding Partner, Kummer Kaempfer Bonner & Renshaw (1994); former Partner, predecessor firm (1982-94, Vargas & Bartlett). **Personal:** Active member of Las Vegas community, participates in various community and church organizations. Currently serves as Board Member and legal counsel to HELP of Southern Nevada.

LAXALT, Bruce
Laxalt & Nomura, Reno
775 322 1170
Recommended in Litigation

LENHARD, Kirk
Jones Vargas, Las Vegas
702 734 2220
Recommended in Litigation

MACE, James
Snell & Wilmer LLP, Las Vegas
702 784 5227
jmace@swlaw.com
Recommended in Real Estate
Practice Areas: Practice concentrated in complex real estate development, including mixed use, high rise condominium and condominium hotel projects. **Prof. Memberships:** American Bar Association (Business Law Section, Real Property Section, and Probate and Trust Section); New York Bar Association; Florida Bar Association; Nevada Bar Association; Clark County Bar Association.

MORGAN, Ann
Jones Vargas, Reno
775 786 5000
Recommended in Employment

MORRIS, Steve
Morris Pickering & Sanner, Las Vegas
702 474 9400
Recommended in Litigation

MOSS, Gary
DLA Piper Rudnick Gray Cary US LLP, Las Vegas 702 737 3433
gary.moss@dlapiper.com
Recommended in Employment
Practice Areas: Labor and employment. **Career:** His labor and employment law practice includes federal and state court

employment discrimination and wrongful discharge litigation, collective bargaining negotiations, arbitrations, union organizing campaigns, cases before federal and state administrative agencies, wage and hour matters, and labor and employment law issues relating to sales, mergers, acquisitions, shutdown and bankruptcies. He has extensive experience in advising clients regarding strikes and other forms of labor disputes, union organizing attempts, corporate campaigns, and arbitration of disputes arising under collective bargaining agreements. **Personal:** JD, University of Iowa; BA, University of Illinois.

NEWMAN, James
Hale Lane Peek Dennison and Howard, Reno 775 327 3000
Recommended in Corporate/M&A

NOVACEK, Stephen
Hale Lane Peek Dennison and Howard, Reno 775 327 3000
Recommended in Real Estate

PATTERSON, Jeffrey
Goold Patterson Ales Roadhouse & Day, Las Vegas 702 436 2600
jpatterson@gooldpatterson.com
Recommended in Real Estate
Practice Areas: Jeffrey Patterson has practiced in Las Vegas, Nevada for over 23 years, focusing primarily on commercial real estate. He handles a variety of transactions, including the purchase, sale and financing of unimproved real property, shopping centers, apartment complexes and hotels. He also handles lease negotiations and drafting, and landlord and tenant disputes. Mr Patterson also devotes a portion of his practice to representing landlords and lenders in bankruptcy proceedings. **Prof. Memberships:** American Bar Association, State Bar of Nevada, Clark County Bar Association. **Career:** Jeffrey Patterson co-founded Goold Patterson Ales Roadhouse & Day with Barry Goold in 1988. Mr Patterson has spoken at a number of seminars on commercial leasing and evictions. Recently, Mr Patterson handled two separate hotel transactions. **Personal:** Jeffrey Patterson received his undergraduate degree (with honors) from the University of Michigan in 1978, and his Juris Doctor degree from the University of San Diego School of Law in 1981. He was admitted to practice in the State of Nevada in 1981. From September 1981 to December 1982, he was a Nevada Deputy Attorney General. Mr Patterson was the senior commercial associate at Smith Goold & Kotchka from 1983-88, prior to founding Goold Patterson Ales Roadhouse & Day.

PAUSTIAN, Kathleen
Allf Paustian & Szostek, Las Vegas
702 307 5001
Recommended in Employment

PEEK, Stephen
Hale Lane Peek Dennison and Howard, Las Vegas 702 222 2500
Recommended in Litigation

PETERSON, Karen
Allison, MacKenzie, Russell, Pavlakis, Wright & Fagan, Ltd, Carson City
775 687 0202
Recommended in Environment

PISANELLI, James
Schreck Brignone, Las Vegas
702 382 2101
Recommended in Litigation

RICCIARDI, Mark J
Fisher & Phillips LLP, Las Vegas
702 252 3131
mricciardi@laborlawyers.com
Recommended in Employment
Practice Areas: Mark Ricciardi is a Partner in the Las Vegas office of the national law firm of Fisher & Phillips LLP, practicing exclusively in labor and employment law representing management. He represents hotels, casinos and other businesses in labor and employment matters and is one of the leading authorities in Nevada on wage-hour law. Mark has successfully tried jury and bench trials in wrongful termination, retaliation, sexual harassment, discrimination, and wage-hour claims. He has also litigated unfair labor practice charges and union election objections before the NLRB. He received an MBA and a JD from Washington University-Missouri.

RICE, Stephen
Rice Silbey Reuther & Sullivan LLP, Las Vegas 702 732 9099
Recommended in Real Estate

ROBISON, Kent
Robison, Belaustegui, Sharp & Low, Reno 775 329 3151
Recommended in Litigation

SANTORO, Nicholas
Santoro, Driggs, Walch, Kearney, Johnson & Thompson, Las Vegas
702 791 0308
Recommended in Litigation

SAVAGE NELSON, Elizabeth
Schreck Brignone, Las Vegas
702 382 2101
Recommended in Corporate/M&A

SAVELY, Carl
Lionel Sawyer & Collins, Reno
775 788 8666
Recommended in Environment

SCHRECK, Frank
Schreck Brignone, Las Vegas
702 382 2101
Recommended in Gaming & Licensing

SCHULHOFER, Ellen
Schreck Brignone, Las Vegas
702 382 2101
Recommended in Corporate/M&A

SHARP, DeArmond
Robison, Belaustegui, Sharp & Low, Reno 775 329 3151
Recommended in Real Estate

SILVER, Jeffrey
Gordon & Silver Ltd, Las Vegas
702 796 5555
Recommended in Gaming & Licensing

SMITH, Gregory
Smith & Kotchka Ltd, Las Vegas
702 382 1707
Recommended in Employment

URGA, William
Jolley, Urga, Wirth & Woodbury, Las Vegas 702 699 7500
Recommended in Litigation

VERMEYS, Sonia
Schreck Brignone, Las Vegas
702 382 2101
Recommended in Corporate/M&A

WALCH, Greg
Santoro, Driggs, Walch, Kearney, Johnson & Thompson, Las Vegas
702 791 0308
Recommended in Environment

WHITTEMORE, David
Lionel Sawyer & Collins, Las Vegas
702 383 8888
Recommended in Real Estate

WILLIAMS, Colby
Campbell & Williams, Las Vegas
702 382 5222
Recommended in Litigation

WOLOSON, Kenneth
Haney, Woloson & Mullins, Las Vegas
(702) 474-7557
Recommended in Corporate/M&A

YOKEN, Stephen
Snell & Wilmer LLP, Las Vegas
702 784 5235
syoken@swlaw.com
Recommended in Real Estate
Practice Areas: Practice concentrated in real estate, including purchases, sales, leasing, and development issues; real estate finance, including construction loans, acquisition and development loans, permanent loans, problem loan restructuring, creditors rights issues, and foreclosures; affordable housing and redevelopment projects; and other business and contract law matters. **Prof. Memberships:** State Bar of Nevada; State Bar of California; American Bar Association; Clark County Bar Association.

YOUCHAH, Elayna
Schreck Brignone, Las Vegas
702 382 2101
Recommended in Employment

ZUCKER, Carol
Kamer Zucker & Abbott, Las Vegas
702 259 8640
Recommended in Employment

ZUCKER, Jeffrey
Lionel Sawyer & Collins, Las Vegas
702 383 8888
Recommended in Corporate/M&A, Real Estate

CURRAN & PARRY

THE FIRM

Managing Partners: William P Curran
Stanley W Parry

Number of partners: 2
Number of other lawyers: 3

HEAD OFFICE

NEVADA
Bank of America Plaza, 300 South 4th St, Suite 1201,
Las Vegas, NV 89101
Tel: 702 471 7000 **Fax:** 702 471 7070
Website: www.curranparry.com
Email: curranparry@curranparry.com

FIRM OVERVIEW: Curran & Parry serves the business, financial, gaming, entertainment, real estate development and construction industries in the areas of litigation, business transactions, and on issues involving government and administrative law such as zoning, land use development, privileged licensing and regulatory compliance. As a small firm, Curran & Parry provides high quality and selective legal representation backed by many years of professional expertise in both the legal and the political environments of the State of Nevada. The foundational culture of the firm is its unwavering commitment to the highest standards of service, integrity and professionalism.

Bill Curran's 10 years as County Counsel to the Clark County Commission and numerous other local government entities, and subsequent 10-year membership on the Nevada Gaming Commission, including eight years as Chairman, give him inside knowledge of the government process in Nevada. This, coupled with his reputation for diligence and an extensive network of key contacts, enables him to provide uniquely effective representation on matters involving state and local government affairs. His service as President of the State Bar of Nevada and membership on the boards of directors of several corporate and non-profit organizations reflect his active involvement in the Las Vegas community.

Stan Parry's service as a trial attorney in the Civil Division of the District Attorney's office and on the US Department of Justice Organized Crime Strike Force has earned him countless honors as a tireless, aggressive and highly successful litigator. He is also active in a number of community organizations.

Other firm attorneys have served as law clerks to federal trial and appellate courts, as Supervising Chief Deputy Attorney General for the State of Nevada, as General Counsel and Corporate Counsel of several major publicly traded hotel-gaming companies, and as a professor at the University of Nevada, Las Vegas. This wealth of government, corporate and litigation experience, coupled with a Martindale Hubble A-V rating, assures clients unparalleled legal advocacy with the personal attention unique to a small firm.

MAIN AREAS OF PRACTICE:

Business: Curran & Parry represents clients on a wide variety of operational and strategic business issues, including the structuring and formation of business entities, commercial transactions and contracts, real estate transactions, commercial leases, regulatory requirements, and contractual employment matters such as executive employment and severance agreements. Due to the firm's extensive number of gaming clients, it provides expert operational advice for the complicated regulatory requirements of a gaming-related business.

Litigation: The firm practices predominantly civil business litigation in state, federal and appellate courts. Litigation areas include real estate litigation, administrative and regulatory matters, business entity member disputes, shareholder derivative lawsuits, business contracts and torts, eminent domain, complex personal injury matters, construction litigation, and title insurance defense.

Gaming Licensing: The State of Nevada and each local government in Nevada have adopted complex regulatory schemes and procedures for obtaining gaming licenses and for regulatory compliance. Curran & Parry specializes in assisting its clients navigate this multi-jurisdictional regulatory process, both pre-licensing and post-licensing. Bill Curran has been recognized as one of Nevada's foremost gaming attorneys. In an industry where the value of experience and knowledge of institutional history is critical, his background as a regulator and as private counsel to gaming licensees makes him one of the most sought after representatives for applicants to the gaming industry. He serves as a member of several casinos' regulatory compliance committees and is frequently called upon to assist as an advisor to Wall Street investment firms as an expert witness in gaming litigation, and as a consultant for emerging gaming jurisdictions.

Land Use/Zoning: With thousands of people moving into Southern Nevada monthly for residential and new commercial opportunities, local municipalities struggle to address growth issues. Curran & Parry's breadth of experience on the inside makes it a prudent choice for clients seeking to obtain approvals for land development and related entitlements. Curran & Parry is recognized as one of the few local firms specializing in land use matters and represents numerous land owners, investors and developers on such matters.

Administrative & Government Relations: A significant number of Curran & Parry's clients have matters requiring favorable City Council, County Commission, or State agency action. In addition to privileged licenses such as liquor and gaming, Curran & Parry represents corporations and individuals in matters relating to public policy advocacy and legislative relations. Work with other professionals such as corporate counsel, out of state counsel, CPA's, engineers, public relations firms and the media are routine.

Construction & Development: The firm's clients include real estate developers, general contractors and sub-contractors for whom it provides a wide array of legal advice and services, including zoning applications, contract drafting and review, insurance review and advice, public works bid disputes, construction defect representation, litigation, and alternative dispute resolution.

CLIENTS: CH2M Hill, Dupont Flooring, Enoitalia S.P.A., an Italian Corporation, Henry Brent Company/Lady Luck Casino, Hotspur/JW Marriott, Interstate Brands Corporation, Lawyers Title Company, Majestic Las Vegas/Conrad Hilton Hotel, Meadow Gold Dairy, Nevada Power Company, Sletten Construction Company, Southern California Edison.

KUMMER KAEMPFER BONNER & RENSHAW

THE FIRM

Managing Partner: Michael J Bonner

Number of partners: 15
Number of other lawyers: 30

AREAS OF PRACTICE:
Corporate/Real Estate/Transactional/SEC & Gaming 44%
Governmental Affairs/Zoning/Land Use/Licensing 29%
Commercial/Complex Litigation 27%

HEAD OFFICE

NEVADA
3800 Howard Hughes Parkway, Seventh Floor, **Las Vegas**, NV 89109-0907
Tel: 702 792 7000 **Fax:** 702 796 7181
Email: info@kkbr.com
Website: www.kkbr.com

BRANCH OFFICE

NEVADA
5250 S. Virginia Street, Suite 220, **Reno**, NV 89502
Tel: 775 852 3900 **Fax:** 775 852 3982

FIRM OVERVIEW: Kummer Kaempfer Bonner & Renshaw (KKB&R) is one of Nevada's largest law firms and a prominent force in the fastest growing state in the US, with offices in Las Vegas as well as Reno/Carson City. The firm's lawyers have had the honor and privilege to counsel many corporations, successful business owners, corporate executives and high-net worth individuals on their legal needs in Nevada. Founded in 1994, the firm's attorneys include a former United States Congressman, a Nevada State Senator, and a former Deputy Secretary of State. Firm attorneys are active members of committees of the State Bar of Nevada, participate in the drafting of new business legislation, and are sought after as lecturers on local, regional and national legal topics. The firm believes that the basic elements of its success - a focus on the client, instead of the lawyer, and a commitment to results - are values that businesses identify with and share. The firm serves a diverse group of local, regional, national and international clients, including publicly- and privately-held business organizations, institutions, private individuals and non-profit organizations. The industries that the firm serves, among others, include: real estate development; hospitality; gaming; manufacturing; service; high technology.

MAIN AREAS OF PRACTICE

Corporate/Real Estate/Transactional/Securities & Gaming: KKB&R's attorneys are recognized to be among the best corporate and transactional lawyers in Nevada and have participated in a broad range of business transactions including complex merger and acquisition matters. The firm has the premier Nevada-based practice in federal and state securities law representation, having handled initial public offerings, private and public debt and equity securities offerings, development stage and venture capital financings and comprehensive corporate and business entity counseling and representation for issuers, underwriters, investors and lenders. KKB&R has represented owners, developers, tenants and financiers in a multitude of real estate transactional and financing matters with significant experience in drafting and negotiating agreements for a variety of clients, projects and industries. KKB&R represents clients in all aspects of Nevada's gaming regulatory matters including license and disciplinary proceedings.

Commercial/Complex Litigation: KKB&R's trial and appellate attorneys have reputations for litigation excellence. Litigation areas include business disputes, professional responsibility litigation (including attorney and accountant liability), alternative dispute resolution, employment litigation, administrative and regulatory matters, construction litigation, general insurance litigation (including coverage issues), securities litigation, real estate litigation, receiverships and aviation litigation.

Governmental Relations, Land Use, Zoning & Licensing, & Public Utilities: KKB&R is the unquestioned leader representing developers and other businesses in the Las Vegas Metropolitan area before governmental bodies on licensing, planning, zoning, and building matters. The firm's Legislative Affairs Team provides select clients with legislative representation before the Nevada State Legislature. The firm also has affiliate relationships in Washington, DC for federal legislative and administrative representation. KKB&R's Public Utility practice includes representation of clients before the Public Utilities Commission of Nevada on matters that address the purchase, sale and distribution of gas, water and electricity, including all forms of renewable energy such as solar, wind, geo-thermal and biomass. The firm represents land developers, private individuals and large users and purchasers of water and electricity throughout the state. In addition, the firm represents clients before the State Water Engineer on matters that are exclusively related to the procurement of water.

Meritas: KKB&R is the Las Vegas, Nevada member firm of Meritas, an international affiliation of business law firms. Meritas is a worldwide alliance consisting of 5,140 lawyers in 175 business law firms located in 55 countries around the world, each working together to provide clients the best of both worlds: a local legal partner with deep international resources. The alliance has a 12 year record of successful co-operation, offering clients the ability to access high quality legal service worldwide supported by a common technology platform. Membership is by invitation only and firms are subject to a rigorous selection and ongoing monitoring process. (www.meritas.org)

CLIENTS: Clients include Aerospatiale; Archon Corporation; Astoria Homes; BHRE, LLC; Boyd Gaming Corporation; Camco, Inc; Casablanca Resorts; Chelsea Property Group; Cole Industries; Exxon-Mobil Corporation; Focus Property Group; Gaming Partners International Corp.; Herbst Gaming, Inc; Kinder Morgan Energy Partners, LP; Lamar Advertising; Marnell Corrao Associates, Inc; Marshall Management Company; Molasky Companies; Monarch Casino & Resort, Inc; Nevada Contractors Insurance Co.; Nevada Development Authority; Nevada Power; Newmont Mining Corp.; Pulte Homes; Reading International, Inc; Republic Services of Southern Nevada; Olympia Land Corporation (Southern Highlands); US Aviation Underwriters; USA Capital, Inc; VendingData Corporation; Zurich-American Insurance Co.

The Law Firm of
Kummer Kaempfer Bonner & Renshaw

WOODBURN AND WEDGE

THE FIRM

Managing Shareholder: John F Murtha
Number of shareholders: 13
Number of other lawyers: 6

AREAS OF PRACTICE:

Corporate, General Business, Partnerships 35%
Litigation 25%
Family Law 13%
Wills, Estate Planning, Estates, Trust Admin. 10%
Bankruptcy 4%
Mining, Natural Resources & Utilities 4%
Real Estate. 3%
Misc., including Taxation, Labor & Criminal 6%

HEAD OFFICE

NEVADA
6100 Neil Road, Suite 500, **Reno**, Nevada 89511-1149
Tel: 775 688 3000 **Fax:** 775 688 3088
Email: www.jfowler@woodburnandwedge.com
Website: www.woodburnandwedge.com

FIRM OVERVIEW: Woodburn and Wedge is one of Reno's largest law firms with its office located in the Sierra Plaza in Southeast Reno. Woodburn and Wedge is a general practice law firm which has developed a strong corporate and business clientele, especially among mining, utility and real estate companies. Although Woodburn and Wedge maintains a general law practice, its attorneys concentrate on litigation, corporate law, commercial law, real estate law, mining law, water law, environmental law, bankruptcy, utility law, and public and private land use law. The firm also has broad experience in estate planning, family law, probate and tax law.

MAIN AREAS OF PRACTICE:

Litigation: Woodburn and Wedge handles a broad range of matters, from the largest and most complex commercial disputes to smaller, more specialized matters. The firm serves clients in all facets of litigation including, contracts, real property, construction, insurance coverage, securities, and franchises.

Business & Commercial: Woodburn and Wedge is counsel to a variety of corporations and other entities conducting business in Nevada or requiring guidance on tax and legal concerns regarding their contemplated commercial activities. The firm counsels on business organization, mergers, acquisitions and licensing. Woodburn and Wedge is frequently called upon to render advice and give opinions on multi-million dollar corporate finance and securitization issues and is recognized as one of the principal Nevada law firms in the mergers and acquisitions arena. Shareholders of the firm are members of the Executive Committee of the Nevada Bar Association's Business Law Section and of the Business Entities Subcommittee, and the firm is active in drafting and seeking changes to the Nevada law governing business organizations.

Real Estate: Woodburn and Wedge represents individual and institutional investors, asset managers, developers, lenders, and homeowners and condominium associations. The firm's real estate attorneys advise clients with respect to acquisitions and complex financing transactions, landlord-tenant disputes, complex commercial leasing, and contract negotiations. Attorneys are intimately involved in assisting and advising residential and commercial developers on state and local requirements, in preparing master plans for planned unit developments, in drafting and negotiating development agreements, implementing residential and commercial CC&Rs, and in representing clients before planning commissions, city councils, and county commissions.

Tax Law & Litigation: Woodburn and Wedge's Tax Practice Group provides tax services to individuals, partnerships, limited liability companies, corporations, trusts and tax-exempt organizations with respect to federal income, gift, and estate tax. Services provided by Woodburn and Wedge include: state and federal tax litigation, partnership, LLC and corporate tax planning, Subchapter S tax planning, estate and gift tax planning, Cal-

ifornia and Nevada state tax matters, keeping clients abreast of new tax laws and regulations, structuring complex transactions, creation and implementation of trusts and wills, and representation of clients before the Internal Revenue Service. One member of the firm has received an LLM degree in tax law, one is a CPA and those two lawyers are admitted to the Bar of the United States Tax Court.

Natural Resources & Environmental: Woodburn and Wedge represents clients in virtually all areas of natural resources or environmental concerns, including water law, geothermal law and mining law. Woodburn and Wedge is nationally recognized as one of the West's pre-eminent natural resources law firms. The firm helps its clients obtain necessary permits, and develop and implement strategies for compliance. Woodburn and Wedge has extensive experience in hard rock minerals transactions, including the preparation of mineral leases, joint venture agreements, exploration agreements, and development agreements. The firm has extensive experience representing both lenders and borrowers in gold loan financings. The firm represents its natural resources clients in disputes with the Bureau of Land Management and in private mining claims disputes before the state and Federal courts. The firm has extensive knowledge of Nevada water rights law and is intimately familiar with the regulations and procedures adopted by the Nevada State Water Engineer in issuing water permits and in transferring water rights. The firm has extensive hands-on experience in the application of Federal Court decrees adjudicating water right entitlements to Nevada's major rivers.

Construction: Woodburn and Wedge represents numerous general contracting and subcontracting firms in the State of Nevada. Woodburn and Wedge attorneys have experience in all facets of construction law, including contract negotiation, performance, enforcement of lien rights and payment or settlement of disputed claims. The firm has served as both defense counsel and as plaintiff's counsel in numerous construction defect litigation matters. The firm has extensive experience in the licensing of contractors and in representation of contractors before the Nevada State Contractors' Board.

Public & Private Land Use: Woodburn and Wedge is widely recognized for its unique and sophisticated perspective in assisting and advising property owners on sensitive zoning, permitting, and public trust issues. The firm is involved in all stages of the land development process, including drafting and seeking changes in federal, state or local law and counseling and representation before administrative agencies.

Banking & Finance: Woodburn and Wedge assists banking and finance clients in all aspects of their business operations including negotiation and documentation of loans, financial institution formation and regulations, consumer credit regulation, Uniform Commercial Code compliance, and workouts and foreclosures. The firm has extensive experience in the creditor representation of financial institutions and other lenders in bankruptcy matters and in commercial litigation.

CONTENTS: Corporate/M&A p.1107; Employment: p.1109; Litigation: p.1111; Real Estate p.1114; Individuals' Profiles p.1116; Firms' Profiles p.1120.

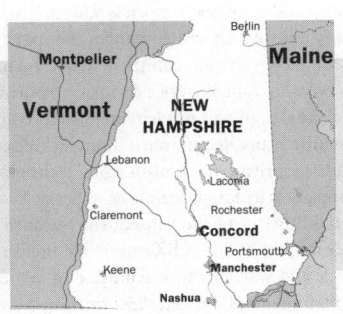

How lawyers are ranked

The opinions we gather from clients — mainly from in-house lawyers but also from other purchasers of legal services — are balanced by opinions from colleagues and competitors. Together, they provide two different perspectives — an all-round view — and biased viewpoints cancel each other out.

CORPORATE/M&A

New Hampshire
Leading firms (Corporate/M&A)

1. **MCLANE, GRAF, RAULERSON** *Manchester*
   SHEEHAN PHINNEY BASS + GREEN PA *Manchester*
2. **COOK, LITTLE, ROSENBLATT** *Manchester*
   DEVINE MILLIMET & BRANCH PA *Manchester*
   NIXON PEABODY LLP *Manchester*
3. **HINCKLEY, ALLEN & SNYDER LLP** *Concord*
   ORR & RENO PA *Concord*

Leading individuals (Corporate/M&A)

1. **REISCHE Alan** *Sheehan Phinney, Manchester*
   SAMUELS Richard *McLane Graf, Manchester*
2. **CASTALDO Neil** *Hinckley Allen, Concord*
   COHEN Steven *Devine Millimet, Manchester*
   COOK James *Cook Little, Manchester*
   HOOD James *Nixon Peabody, Manchester*
   LITTLE Curtis *Cook Little, Manchester*
3. **BURGER Peter** *Orr & Reno, Concord*
   BURKE Steven *McLane Graf, Manchester*
   DI CROCE Camille *Devine Millimet, North Hampton*
   DROOFF Michael *Sheehan Phinney, Manchester*
   ELLISON Scott *Devine Millimet, North Hampton*
   MANSON Tom *Cook Little, Manchester*
   MCCUE Mark *Sheehan Phinney, Manchester*
   SKLAR Daniel *Nixon Peabody, Manchester*

Up-and-coming individuals

   TAUB Philip *Nixon Peabody, Manchester*

Leading individuals (Tax)

1. **ARDINGER William** *Rath Young, Concord*
   COHEN Steven *Devine Millimet, Manchester*
2. **BURKE Steven** *McLane Graf, Manchester*
   LAW David *Cleveland Waters, Concord*
   SPARKMAN Jon *Devine Millimet, North Hampton*

Leading individuals (Government Relations)

1. **RATH Thomas** *Rath Young, Concord*

Leading individuals (Bankruptcy)

1. **SKLAR Daniel** *Nixon Peabody, Manchester*

Firms and individuals are listed alphabetically in each band.

Band 1

McLane, Graf, Raulerson & Middleton Professional Association
See firm details p.1121

The Firm: Well established and respected in the business community, the firm's corporate practice retains its place at the forefront of the New Hampshire market through a combination of strong leadership, bench depth and the availability of ancillary support throughout the firm. A substantial team services the full range of general business needs, including formation and contracts, corporate governance, purchase and sale, debt and equity finance, and public and private stock and equity offerings. Specialist expertise in securities law and a separate state and federal tax practice are notable drawing cards for clients, who appreciate the big-picture thinking of these lawyers. "*I like the fact that they look at a transaction from a business perspective, instead of dealing with the minutiae. It makes such a big difference,*" said one.

The Lawyers: "*Excellent business lawyer*" **Richard Samuels** (see p.1118) chairs the corporate department and is especially recommended for his expertise in the securities area. Clients find that he "*knows how to balance risk and reward to get the deal done.*" Samuels has been involved in a number of public offerings in the past year, including representing a municipal water department in a $38 million municipal revenue bond offering, the proceeds of which are being used to finance improvements to water treatment facilities. He also recently acted for Great Bay Hydro, a subsidiary of BayCorp Holdings, in its acquisition of multiple hydro-electric generating facilities in Vermont from Citizens Communications. **Steven Burke** (see p.1116) combines a "*great tax background*" with a "*real ability for corporate work.*" He chairs the firm's tax group and concentrates his practice on the financial and tax-driven elements of business transactions. Areas of focus include corporate governance, ESOPs, employee benefits, and state and federal tax planning. Burke recently represented a major seafood harvester and distributor in a $20 million private placement securities transaction, and advised on a number of management buyouts using leveraged ESOPs.

The Clients: Although traditionally associated with the state's larger, old-line client base of manufacturing and utilities industries, the firm also represents emerging businesses and fields a separate small-business law group. Clients range from closely held entities to regional, national and multinational corporations. They include: BayCorp Holdings; KeyBank; International Paper; Hitchiner Manufacturing; Hanover Water Works; Manchester Water Works; KeySpan Energy Delivery New England; Constellation Energy Group; Algonquin Power Income Fund; Concord Steam; Verizon Communications and Pennichuck.

Sheehan Phinney Bass + Green PA
See firm details p.1122

The Firm: A dominating presence at the New Hampshire corporate Bar, this deep team "*operates in a different league.*" Work ranges from handling clients' most fundamental business needs to complex financings and M&A. The practice distinguishes itself from most through its strength in securities-related transactions and an international business capability. Clients appreciate the professionalism and responsiveness of the lawyers here, with their conservative, yet proactive approach to deal-making.

The Lawyers: "*Polymath*" **Alan Reische** (see p.1118) is the firm's standout individual in the corporate arena and is generally considered one of the leading and most senior business lawyers in the state. Generally acknowledged as a top name in the state, Reische is "*an effective negotiator, a skillful problem solver, and great for bouncing ideas off.*" His practice has become increasingly focused on strategic planning and corporate governance issues for privately owned companies, for example relating to the impact of Sarbanes-Oxley. A newcomer to the tables, young partner **Michael Drooff** (see p.1116) wins plaudits for his *"incredible skill set,"* particularly in securities-related matters. His practice encompasses private company M&A, finance and venture capital, public company reporting, and the design and implementation of equity incentive plans. Recent transactions include acting for a private medical-imaging technology company in a recapitalization of its Series A Preferred Stock, and the subsequent issuance of $3.5 million of Series B Convertible Preferred Stock and warrants to a syndicate of venture capital investors. An *"excellent problem solver"* **Mark McCue** (see p.1118) is another new entry this year. His practice focuses on providing organizational and transactional planning advice to privately held businesses, professionals and healthcare institutions, including a specialty in tax-exempt bond financing. He recently acted for an airway corporation in a multiparty merger and reorganization in the private aircraft industry.

The Clients: This full-service firm boasts a truly diverse client base, from small businesses to international concerns, municipalities, and religious and nonprofit organizations.

Band 2

Cook, Little, Rosenblatt & Manson PLLC

The Firm: This practice might be smaller than others, but a roster of talented individuals ensures it continues to punch above its weight, and peers acknowledge the firm has *"carved out an effective niche in the market."* The corporate group caters to the full range of general business needs, with a unique emphasis on entrepreneurs and technology-based clients. It follows that IP protection and software and technology licensing are notable areas of strength, as are other discrete areas such as ESOPs. Commercial lending is another major feature of the practice and attorneys recently represented the lead bank in a $115 million syndicated loan. Clients identified the team's practical approach as a major plus point for the practice: *"They don't overanalyze to generate fees – they have a much better understanding of the business climate."*

The Lawyers: Key individual **James Cook** was identified as *"the go-to person in the community for hi-tech clients."* He is highly valued for his depth of experience and his ability to *"relate instantly to the situation at hand."* **Curtis Little** is best known for representing banks and financial institutions in corporate and transactional matters. He is described as *"one of the best"* for high-end, commercial loan work, where he *"cuts to the chase without getting bogged down with immaterial issues."* *"Top-notch"* **Tom Manson** is a new addition to this year's tables. His practice comprises a mix of banking and standard corporate work and he counts major natural gas

supplier Eastern Propane among his clients. Examples of recent work for the team include representing an early stage company in an angel investment-financing round, and acting for a client in the acquisition of a manufacturing product line.

The Clients: Bank of America (formerly Fleet Bank); Citizens Bank; Banknorth; Chittenden Bank; Sovereign Bank; Eastern Propane; Providus Software Solutions; Pragmatech Software; Geophysical Survey Systems; Powerspan and Peterboro Basket.

Devine Millimet & Branch PA

The Firm: A premier New Hampshire firm with an ever-increasing profile in the corporate arena. There are nine partners heading up the M&A and corporate finance work in the firm's Manchester office, assisted by a regional spread of expertise across Massachusetts, Maine and Rhode Island. A *"great pool of young talent"* bolsters the team's strength in the field. As one interviewee explained: *"They have resources beyond the individual leaders, which let them handle sophisticated work."* The team acts for clients across sectors such as utilities, hi-tech, radio and telecom, distribution and retail. Banking work forms a significant part of the corporate practice and the firm is one of only a few in the state authorized to act as bond counsel. Attorneys recently represented the buyer of the largest paper mill and employer in the state, which was purchased out of bankruptcy.

The Lawyers: *"Excellent"* **Steven Cohen** continues to be recognized as the standout performer in this team. A CPA with a strong tax background, his broad-based practice spans general corporate representation, M&A, and business and estate planning for closely held businesses. He recently represented a large regional software company in its sale to Oracle for $10 million and represented the purchaser of a retail distribution company for $11 million. Peers and clients describe him as *"a very hands-on attorney, who always has his clients' interests at heart."* Cohen works closely with fellow tax specialists and *"heavy hitters"* **Scott Ellison** and **Jon Sparkman**, whose practices comprise a mix of general corporate and M&A work. Both are recommended as lawyers who *"balance well the need of the client with the need to get the deal done."* *"Extremely thorough"* **Camille Di Croce** also enters the tables this year following strong recommendation from clients. She chairs the firm's finance practice group and handles a broad spectrum of bank and borrower work, including a niche in real estate finance. Clients welcome her *"ability to get things done, and get them done fast."*

The Clients: Insight Technology; Rockingham Ventures; Robbins Auto Parts; CB Sullivan; US Trust and Bank of America.

Nixon Peabody LLP

See firm details p.1361

The Firm: Although viewed by some observers as an interloper in the New Hampshire market, it is clear that clients value the combination of national strength and local access available at this practice. As one interviewee commented: *"I find it comforting that they have lawyers available if I have a problem in New York."* On the other hand, smaller clients are not put off by the firm's wider aspirations, with one stating: *"I know I am probably small fry to them, but they are always there when I need them."* Half of the 20 lawyers based in the Manchester office focus on corporate work, with practice groups run on a firm-wide basis. The group handles a mix of midmarket M&A and corporate finance, representing a range of local regional clients as well as larger Boston and New York-based corporations. In addition to its national network of 14 offices, the firm is distinguished by a dominant presence in the bankruptcy field.

The Lawyers: **James Hood** (see p.1117) chairs the firm's national financial services practice group. He primarily acts for medium to large, privately owned corporations on issues ranging from equity finance to corporate governance and M&A. Peers and clients alike point to his no-nonsense approach to deal-making: *"He will give it to you straight and cut to the deal."* Hood recently represented a nationally known, hi-tech client in negotiating and closing a large cash-out merger involving a national competitor. There is little doubt that **Daniel Sklar** (see p.1118) is the premier individual in the state for bankruptcy work. Extolled by clients as *"extremely practical with a real sense for business and logic,"* Sklar is *"the one you want in complex and troubling situations."* Sklar heads up the bankruptcy group and divides his time between Chapter 11 matters and general corporate representation. He recently acted for two major creditors in the Kmart bankruptcy and represented the developer of a major golf course and housing development in a successful reorganization and sale. Up-and-coming player **Philip Taub** (see p.1119) enters the tables following general acclaim for his *"innate ability to put potential risks into perspective for the client."* He has developed a significant corporate and business practice and recently picked up work for specialty retailer Brookstone.

The Clients: The team represents varying clients throughout the state and Northern New England, across a range of industry sectors.

Band 3

Hinckley, Allen & Snyder LLP

The Firm: A niche player in the New Hampshire market, the small corporate team can draw on resources available in the larger Boston and Rhode Island bases. Although perhaps lacking the depth of some of its rivals, the firm earns praise from clients for the wealth of specialist knowledge available on a regional basis. The focus is on midmarket M&A, benefits and tax planning, antitrust and general corporate matters, with a well-recognized subspecialty in the healthcare arena.

The Lawyers: "*Top-drawer lawyer*" **Neil Castaldo** is one of two partners in the Concord office. Interviewees feel he stands out from the crowd for his practical approach and ability to explain the law to lay people. "*He's probably the best business attorney in the USA!*" enthused one client. "*Some lawyers have a tendency to kill the deal, but with Neil I can go to him and say 'make it work,' and he does.*" Recent matters include representing a number of hospitals in purchasing the assets or leasing the services of more than ten physician group practices throughout New Hampshire. Castaldo also acted for a major client in the preparation and submission of an advisory opinion to the US Federal Trade Commission, seeking approval of certain business practices. The process resulted in a no action decision by the FTC.

The Clients: Dartmouth-Hitchcock Medical Center; Bank of America; Hasbro; Citizens Bank; New Hampshire Higher Education Loan;

CVS/pharmacy; Modern Continental Construction; Textron and Eagle Publications.

Orr & Reno PA

The Firm: This highly respected Concord firm is less visible perhaps in the corporate arena than in its traditionally strong suit of litigation. However, the team has seen an upswing in M&A activity this year and distinguishes itself from others for its strength in representing foreign-owned subsidiaries (Lindt features on the client list) and foreign entities setting up business in the USA. Specialist expertise ranges from commercial real estate and bankruptcy through to the hospitality and healthcare industries. Recent transactions include the sale of a recreational gun manufacturing company for $38 million and a $9 million bond financing for a hospital.

The Lawyers: "*Top-notch*" **Peter Burger** is the figure most associated with the firm's corporate profile. Interviewees describe him as "*a deal-doer who won't insert his ego into a transaction*" and "*someone who grasps the broader international context of a deal.*" Clients value his responsiveness and no-nonsense approach. Burger continues to see a steady flow of German work in his practice.

The Clients: Leading names include Lindt & Sprüngli, Audley Construction and Steenbeck & Sons.

Other Notable Practitioners

In dealings with the state government, **Thomas Rath**, of Concord firm Rath, Young & Pignatelli PA, is the one to turn to, say interviewees. Founder of "*the most effective lobbying firm in the state,*" Rath is "*Mr Politician – extremely well connected and a very fine lawyer besides.*" At the intersection of business, law and public policy, the firm's government relations group represents a broad range of clients appearing before the New Hampshire government. "*Grade A, quality player*" **William Ardinger**, of the same firm, wins plaudits for his expertise in state and federal tax matters, including multijurisdictional transaction planning and federal and state tax controversies. In the same vein as Rath: "*If you want to get the law changed, he's the one to go to.*" At Cleveland, Waters & Bass PA, low-key operator and "*superb*" tax lawyer **David Law** is recommended for his employee benefits and ERISA expertise. One peer remarked: "*This is a complex area that so many lawyers can get wrong – David simply gets it right.*"

EMPLOYMENT

MAINLY DEFENDANT

New Hampshire
Leading firms
(Employment: Mainly Defendant)

1	DEVINE MILLIMET & BRANCH PA *Manchester*	
	FLYGARE SCHWARZ & CLOSSON PLLC *Exeter*	
	GALLAGHER, CALLAHAN *Concord*	
2	MCLANE, GRAF, RAULERSON *Manchester*	
	ORR & RENO PA *Concord*	
	SHEEHAN PHINNEY BASS + GREEN PA *Manchester*	
3	SULLOWAY & HOLLIS PLLC *Concord*	

Leading individuals
(Employment: Mainly Defendant)

1	BROTH Mark *Devine Millimet, North Hampton*	
	FLYGARE Thomas *Flygare Schwarz, Exeter*	
	JOHNSTONE Andrea *Gallagher Callahan, Concord*	
2	FORD Debra *Devine Millimet, Manchester*	
	JOHNSON Linda *McLane Graf, Manchester*	
	KAPLAN Edward *Sulloway & Hollis, Concord*	
	REIDY James *Sheehan Phinney, Manchester*	
	RICE Emily *Orr & Reno, Concord*	
3	BLACKMER Jill *Orr & Reno, Concord*	
	CLOSSON Tom *Flygare Schwarz, Exeter*	
	DYLESKI-NAJJAR Debra *Hinckley Allen, Concord*	
	MOECKEL Jennifer *Devine Millimet, North Hampton*	

Firms and individuals are listed alphabetically in each band.

Band 1

Devine Millimet & Branch PA

The Firm: Consistently recommended for the depth and diversity of its labor, employment and employee benefits group, this firm offers clients a regional presence with three offices across New Hampshire and an additional base in northern Massachusetts. Work is divided equally between counseling and litigation, and, more unusually for this market, almost one-third of the practice comprises traditional labor law. The team of ten has seen a busy year, successfully defending clients in numerous wage and hour, whistle-blower, and discrimination cases.

The Lawyers: "*Extremely knowledgeable*" **Mark Broth** continues to be cited a standout industry figure and is credited with building up the practice. He is especially noted for his labor relations expertise, and boasts a "*wonderful ability to interpret the law to lay clients.*" Group chair **Debra Weiss Ford** is an experienced trial lawyer who runs the gamut of employment litigation. In mediation, she is "*willing to take a tough stand when needed, but is well reasoned in her judgment.*" She also takes on some counseling and union work. Clients point to her down-to-earth approach and the instant trust she instills: "*She's the most compassionate lawyer I have ever met. I*

feel as if I am her only client and I know I will have her undivided attention.*" A new addition to the tables, **Jennifer Shea Moeckel** was recommended for her counseling practice, which touches on all aspects of the employment relationship. Clients depend on her calming influence in potentially stressful situations and her "*ability to play devil's advocate by looking at both sides of the story.*" She also represents clients in litigation at administrative agency level, for example before the EEOC.

The Clients: Clients range from small family businesses to Fortune 500 companies, including auto dealerships (almost a niche focus for this firm), healthcare institutions, manufacturers and municipal bodies.

Flygare Schwarz & Closson PLLC

The Firm: The only true employment law boutique in the tables, this three-partner firm is highly recommended for its quality of representation and an excellent client base. The full range of work is undertaken, from counseling to litigation and arbitration. Noncompete covenants and executive employment agreements are particular areas of focus.

The Lawyers: Frequently seen acting on behalf of educational institutions, **Thomas Flygare** spends a significant proportion of his practice handling collective bargaining agreements.

Clients value the fact that he "*provides clear explanations as to the business alternatives*" and "*gets the job done with no publicity.*" Peers respect his considerable knowledge base and "*ability to navigate through a problem to find a helpful solution for both sides.*" "*Terrific*" trial attorney **Tom Closson** enters the tables this year following numerous recommendations. Both he and fellow attorney, Dan Schwarz, play an active role in representing clients in arbitration proceedings.
The Clients: A large proportion of the practice involves representing public sector, nonprofit clients, including schools, colleges and universities, cities, healthcare institutions and charitable agencies.

Gallagher, Callahan and Gartrell, PA
See firm details p.1120
The Firm: This strong seven-attorney team services clients across New England from offices in Concord and Augusta, Maine. The focus is on providing support to businesses from a compliance and risk management perspective, including training and assistance with labor relations issues. The team also represents management in court and at state and federal agency level. Attorneys work together with the firm's taxation experts to provide advice on a wide range of employee benefits and ERISA matters. Peers speak of a group with "*great leadership and great backup.*"
The Lawyers: The firm's premier position in this field is linked largely to the reputation of "*all-around terrific*" lead employment lawyer **Andrea Johnstone**, whom many consider to be "*at the very top of her game.*" Best known for her risk management role, Johnstone also handles a fair amount of litigation and labor relations work. She recently successfully represented FedEx in the US District Court in a disabilities discrimination case involving one of its drivers. Peers acknowledge her huge breadth of experience and "*ability to assess objectively the strengths and weaknesses of each case.*"
The Clients: The team's client base cuts across the full range of industry sectors, from banking and hi-tech to educational institutions and nonprofit entities.

Band 2

McLane, Graf, Raulerson & Middleton Professional Association
See firm details p.1121
The Firm: This heavyweight New Hampshire firm draws on core interdisciplinary strengths to provide a comprehensive service to a broad range of clients. With an emphasis on straight employment law, as opposed to the traditional labor side, the team offers advice on everything from policy drafting, training and day-to-day consultation to litigation at every level. The firm distinguishes itself from others in the market

through its independent-school law practice, where attorneys are able to provide specialist advice to educational clients on the unique issues that arise in the employment law context.
The Lawyers: "*Talented*" **Linda Johnson** (see p.1117) cochairs the employment law practice. She is especially noted for her strong cadre of private-school clients and is chair of the firm's independent-school law practice. Although primarily a civil litigator, she also assists clients with in-house training and policy formulation. Clients appreciate her responsiveness and "*ability to blend the legal and practical perspectives.*" The firm's attorneys have recently acted for clients in a range of harassment and discrimination claims, wage and hour audits, and complaints over employee retirement plans.
The Clients: Bauer NIKE Hockey; Citronics; Kluber Lubrications; Polyonics; Poultry Products and St. Paul's School.

Orr & Reno PA
The Firm: The employment law group at this "*top-notch*" firm comprises six attorneys handling an even mix of counseling and litigation. The practice is distinguished by its immigration law expertise and increasing focus on alternative dispute resolution and mediation. Attorneys have also been particularly active recently in front of New Hampshire's Human Rights Commission.
The Lawyers: "*First-rate*" trial attorney **Emily Rice** epitomizes the firm's traditional strength in the litigation arena. "*She could be a judge,*" enthused one peer. Employment law is only one focus of her eclectic practice, which also includes commercial litigation and medical malpractice defense. Known among clients as a "*quick study,*" Rice "*sees instantly how a particular issue fits into the larger picture.*" A solid practitioner with an excellent reputation, **Jill Blackmer** concentrates on the counseling side where she "*definitely knows her stuff.*" Highly respected commercial litigator Martha Van Oot is an additional valuable resource for clients. Both attorneys recently defended a manufacturing company in claims arising out of a noncompetition agreement.
The Clients: Rite Aid; Shaw's Supermarkets; Lindt & Sprüngli (USA); Rent-A-Center; Clear Channel; Precitech; National Grange Mutual Insurance; Laidlaw Transit and Blockbuster.

Sheehan Phinney Bass + Green PA
See firm details p.1122
The Firm: Another New Hampshire mainstay, this well-respected firm maintains an additional base in Boston. The focus here is on the counseling and risk management side, although the team also provides the full range of litigation services where necessary. Clients prize the group's ability to draw on specialist resources available within the rest of the firm, for example where there is an overlap with tax matters.

The Lawyers: Clients consistently singled out group chair and "*excellent trainer*" **Jim Reidy** (see p.1118) for his wealth of experience and responsiveness to their needs: "*I know that his response will always be over and above – he will follow up on a point and tell me exactly what I need to know and how it is relevant to our business.*" He recently assisted an out-of-state employer in successfully resolving a matter with the New Hampshire Department of Labor involving alleged violations of state wage and hour laws.
The Clients: As well as acting for an emerging client base, the firm represents some of the major businesses in the state. Representative clients include: Avis; BioSan Laboratories; Bottomline Technologies; Colby-Sawyer College; Easter Seals New Hampshire; Elliot Hospital; Felton Brush; Macmillan Construction; Town of Milford; New London Hospital; New Hampshire Retirement System; Nobis Engineering; PC Connections; Rockingham County; Southern New Hampshire University; Stonyfield Farm; Wal-Mart and Yankee Publishing.

Band 3

Sulloway & Hollis PLLC
The Firm: A team of seven attorneys at this Concord practice acts for unionized and nonunionized clients across a range of employment issues, from policy formation and handbook interpretation to the investigation and defense of harassment and discrimination claims. Practitioners regularly appear before both state and federal courts and administrative agencies.
The Lawyers: Litigator **Edward Kaplan** stands out for his work with school districts and public authorities. One client summed up his strengths: "*A skilled negotiator and effective fact finder, who keeps us informed all the way. He's great at representing the client's interests in this delicate area of the law.*"
The Clients: In addition to school districts, the team also acts for municipalities, hospitals and other medical institutions, as well as corporate entities.

Other Notable Practitioners
Debra Dyleski-Najjar, of regional firm Hinckley, Allen & Snyder LLP, enters the tables this year following strong commendation of her work in this area. Her generalist practice covers all aspects of employment law, with a recent emphasis on the litigation side. She earned two victories in ERISA litigation in the Federal District Court concerning the termination of retiree health benefits, and has also been involved in defending a number of discrimination claims.

LITIGATION

GENERAL COMMERCIAL

New Hampshire
Leading firms
(Litigation: General Commercial)

1. MCLANE, GRAF, RAULERSON *Manchester*
   ORR & RENO PA *Concord*
2. DEVINE MILLIMET & BRANCH PA *Manchester*
   NIXON PEABODY LLP *Manchester*
   SHEEHAN PHINNEY BASS + GREEN PA *Manchester*
3. COOK, LITTLE, ROSENBLATT *Manchester*
   D'AMANTE COUSER STEINER *Concord*
   GALLAGHER, CALLAHAN *Concord*
   HINCKLEY, ALLEN & SNYDER LLP *Concord*
   NELSON KINDER MOSSEAU *Manchester*
   SULLOWAY & HOLLIS PLLC *Concord*
   UPTON AND HATFIELD LLP *Concord*
   WADLEIGH, STARR & PETERS PLLC *Manchester*
   WIGGIN & NOURIE *Manchester*

Leading individuals
(Litigation: General Commercial)

Senior Statesman
MIDDLETON Jack *McLane Graf*, Manchester

1. FELMLY Bruce *McLane Graf*, Manchester
   GLAHN III Wilbur *McLane Graf*, Manchester
   HARVELL Michael *Sheehan Phinney*, Manchester
   HILLIARD Russell *Upton and Hatfield*, Concord
   SNOW Ronald *Orr & Reno*, Concord
   VAN OOT Martha *Orr & Reno*, Concord
2. CALLAHAN Michael *Gallagher Callahan*, Concord
   CHAPMAN William *Orr & Reno*, Concord
   HIGGINS James *Sheehan Phinney*, Manchester
   RICE Emily *Orr & Reno*, Concord
   VICINANZO David *Nixon Peabody*, Boston
   WHEAT James *Wadleigh Starr*, Manchester
   WOLOWITZ David *McLane Graf*, Portsmouth
3. CONNOLLY Michael *Hinckley Allen*, Concord
   COUSER Richard *D'Amante Couser*, Concord
   DANENBARGER Wright *Wiggin & Nourie*, Manchester
   DONOVAN Thomas *McLane Graf*, Manchester
   FITZGERALD Kevin *Nixon Peabody*, Manchester
   MOORE George *Devine Millimet*, Manchester
   MOSSEAU Peter *Nelson Kinder*, Manchester
   ROSENBLATT Arnold *Cook Little*, Manchester

Leading individuals (Litigation: Medical Malpractice Defense)

★ SNOW Ronald *Orr & Reno*, Concord
1. FRIBERG Sr John *Wadleigh Starr*, Manchester
   LEHMAN Michael *Sulloway & Hollis*, Concord
   MOSSEAU Peter *Nelson Kinder*, Manchester
   PIGNATELLI Michael *Rath Young*, Concord

Firms and individuals are listed alphabetically in each band.

Band 1

McLane, Graf, Raulerson & Middleton Professional Association
See firm details p.1121

The Firm: Clients applaud this premier litigation practice for excellent service and a real *"team approach."* Said one: *"I like the way they partner on litigation matters. I feel like we are working together and they deal with me as a colleague."* Sources also point to the depth and variety of expertise available within this sizable team, and the additional advantage of a strong core group of corporate attorneys. The quality of representation goes right the way through the firm, from top to bottom. Clients also offered praise for the practice's support staff, who are *"sharp, attentive, and always on hand to help."* The group undertakes all manner of litigation, acting increasingly on a multijurisdictional basis. Arbitration and mediation are important features of the practice.

The Lawyers: There is certainly no shortage of talent in this team. At the helm is *"premier litigator"* **Bruce Felmly** (see p.1117), *"the biggest of the big guns with a personality to match."* His commercial practice has witnessed an increase in environmental claims. He continues to represent EnergyNorth (KeySpan Energy Delivery) in multiple cases involving industrial contamination and insurance coverage issues. Felmly recently won a landmark decision in the New Hampshire Supreme Court. Clients find him *"very tuned into our business,"* while peers note that *"he is not a lone ranger, but works very well with co-counsel."* Senior department member and *"dean of trial lawyers"* **Jack Middleton** (see p.1118) maintains a broad practice, which ranges from tax abatement and land use litigation to legal malpractice defense, appellate and alternative dispute resolution work. He is currently representing key client Verizon New England in an ongoing tax abatement case. Clients and peers are *"thrilled to have him on the case."* **Wilbur Glahn** (see p.1117) has a *"crispness and style about him that elevates him to the next level when dealing with judges,"* clients say. He recently represented broadcaster CBS in a trademark and copyright infringement action. **David Wolowitz** (see p.1119) maintains an eclectic practice comprising church and school law, commercial, employment and probate litigation. This mix is particularly valuable to clients: *"The fact that he has that broad range means he is able to offer a holistic approach."* Wolowitz continues to act for Bauer NIKE and recently secured the dismissal of an action against an auction house to prevent the auction of valuable heirlooms. Sources agree that the defining quality of Wolowitz is his *"firm yet noncombative approach that walks a good balance between being*

a wonderful advocate for the client, while respecting opposite counsel." **Thomas Donovan** (see p.1116) wins plaudits for his *"creative approach to client relations"* and his thorough preparation and analysis. He is especially recognized for a strong IP litigation practice.

The Clients: Abbott Laboratories; BAE SYSTEMS; Bauer NIKE Hockey USA; Bayer; Chicago Title Insurance; Dartmouth College; Irving Oil; KeyBank; KeySpan Energy Delivery and Verizon.

Orr & Reno PA

The Firm: This traditional Concord firm has always been synonymous with its preeminent litigation practice. Sources point to a *"deep senior bench of true trial lawyers, with no drop-off in quality."* The team typically handles a wide range of litigation, with a particularly strong reputation in medical malpractice defense, a niche specialty in First Amendment cases, and an increasing focus on alternative dispute resolution. Peers praise a group of attorneys who *"don't just understand the law in their own jurisdiction, but also the wider implications."*

The Lawyers: **Ronald Snow** is *"the real deal,"* according to interviewees: *"He is one of those rare lawyers who actually knows how to try cases and has a really serious trial record under his belt."* His practice divides evenly between medical malpractice defense (where he is considered *"the dean"* in the state) and general commercial litigation. In addition to trying four significant medical malpractice cases, he recently acted for several reinsurance companies in the liquidation of Home Insurance, represented a national car manufacturer in a RICO case and successfully codefended an airplane owner in a wrongful death action. *"Outstanding"* **Martha Van Oot** maintains a broad business litigation practice, with an additional emphasis on employment-based litigation. She was one of the attorneys defending a manufacturing company in claims arising out of a noncompetition agreement. Van Oot has also been representing a foreign bank in civil forfeiture proceedings brought by the federal government. She is a great person to consult, say peers, because *"she always has that extra thought that nobody else has."* **Emily Rice**'s eclectic practice encompasses employment, medical and professional malpractice defense, and other general commercial litigation. Peers and clients alike are full of praise for her trial skills: *"She thrives in stressful situations and will always face a courtroom without trepidation."* Rice recently defended a manufacturing company in a products liability and breach of warranty case. New entrant **William Chapman** is *"probably the best person in the state for First Amendment work,"* according to clients. He is credited with building an excellent practice and has counseled a large

www.ChambersandPartners.com
All quotes in the text are from interviews with clients and competitors.
1111

number of local and national media publications.

The Clients: Dartmouth-Hitchcock Clinic; Oracle; Sears Roebuck; Raytheon Aircraft; Liberty Mutual Insurance; Presstek; Subaru of New England; University System of New Hampshire; Chittenden Bank and PaxWorld Balanced Fund.

Band 2

Devine Millimet & Branch PA

The Firm: A well-respected team of around 15 core litigators runs the gamut, representing a broad range of businesses and professionals at all levels, including in the United States Supreme Court. The firm is particularly recommended in the field of insurance defense and its reach extends beyond New England. Observers agree that a strong showing in the corporate arena adds to the effectiveness of the firm's litigation profile. Recently attorneys successfully quashed a stockholder lawsuit in a piece of merger litigation.

The Lawyers: George Moore is the name most associated with the firm's work in this area. Interviewees describe him as *"adept at complex litigation."* Having taken on the task of developing the firm's Massachusetts litigation practice (a team of four currently handles this work in the Andover office), Moore's time is divided between representing clients in both states. IP, securities and hi-tech matters have recently featured on his agenda. Ovide Lamontagne chairs the litigation practice group from the firm's Manchester headquarters.

The Clients: A broad client base ranges from individuals to large commercial concerns as well as educational, charitable and financial institutions.

Nixon Peabody LLP

See firm details p.1361

The Firm: Ten litigators in the Manchester office benefit from the wider resources available across the firm's national network. Clients deem the practice a *"one-stop shop,"* where *"everyone is a specialist."* The mix of local and national seems to work well – while smaller clients *"feel as though we are their biggest client in the world,"* larger businesses welcome the fact that these lawyers *"actually talk to each other and make the effort to function like a business unit."* Areas of focus include financial services and securities, antitrust, government investigations and white-collar, IP, professional liability and international arbitration.

The Lawyers: *"Effective negotiator"* Kevin Fitzgerald (see p.1117) heads the litigation department and is managing partner of the firm's Manchester office. He is *"as good as any"* in a courtroom, say clients, who are impressed with his ability to *"grasp whole concepts in very short spaces of time."* A broad practice encompasses financial services and insurance coverage

issues, employment defense and a subspecialty in directors' and officers' litigation (he is *"the ideal CEO/CFO sounding board,"* report clients). Fitzgerald worked as litigation counsel to Kodak in a matter arising out of the Kmart bankruptcy in Chicago. *"Outstanding"* David Vicinanzo (see p.1119) enters the tables this year based on particularly strong recommendations for his business crime practice. Noted for his career in the US Attorney's Office, he is known as a lawyer who *"has taken many cases all the way through the process and can keep an eye on the endgame."*

The Clients: Kodak; Starwood Hotels; Riverstone Resources; Bausch & Lomb; Corning; Putnam Investments; KeyBank; St Mary's Bank; Sovereign Bank; Catholic Diocese; Nordica; Annalee Dolls; Coca-Cola; SIGARMS; Booth Creek Ski Holdings; Jet Blue; John Hancock and Brand Partners.

Sheehan Phinney Bass + Green PC

See firm details p.1122

The Firm: This is a firm well known for its prowess in the corporate field, a strength that is reflected when it comes to business litigation. There are 15 lawyers in the group, based in offices in Manchester, Concord and Boston. Work cuts across the various practice areas, including employment, tax, mergers, securities and environmental; while practitioners are visible acting both locally and on an international, cross-jurisdictional basis. The methodical approach of these attorneys is highly valued by clients.

The Lawyers: *"Impressive"* Michael Harvell (see p.1117) is *"quick to identify the key issues in a case,"* report interviewees. His practice has an emphasis on partnership and stockholder disputes, and he has recently undertaken a fair amount of litigation in the tax and environmental areas. Another leading figure in the team, James Higgins (see p.1117) earns acclaim as a *"dogged tactician."* Peers call him their referral of choice for a tricky corporate governance dispute, although this is just one element of a much broader practice. One interviewee summed up his strengths: *"He has a good sense of the value of a case and when it's appropriate to do a deal – a worthy opponent and codefendant."*

The Clients: In keeping with its New Hampshire base, the practice represents a diverse mix of clients, from small, closely held businesses to large institutions. These include banks and other commercial lenders, hospitals and other healthcare providers, manufacturers, insurers, colleges and other nonprofit organizations.

Band 3

Cook, Little, Rosenblatt & Manson PLLC

The Firm: This small, yet highly respected player fields two full-time business litigators. The

practice has established a reputation for its representation of entrepreneurial and technology-based companies, both in and around New Hampshire. Areas of expertise include IP, software and technology disputes, breach of fiduciary duty, securities arbitration, noncompetition and other contractual issues.

The Lawyers: Experienced attorney Arnold Rosenblatt is the main name associated with the litigation side of the practice. Peers describe him as a *"thorough, quality lawyer, who serves his clients well,"* while clients find his practical, non-adversarial approach particularly effective. He recently defended a client in a trade dress and copyright claim in the federal court, and settled a long-standing matter involving claims of breach of fiduciary duty.

The Clients: The client base ranges from startups to larger, established concerns, including hi-tech and low-tech industries.

D'Amante Couser Steiner Pellerin, PA

The Firm: *"A small but exceedingly successful practice,"* according to sources, with civil litigation comprising one of its core practice areas. The firm is undergoing growth, and currently maintains two full-time litigators. Plaintiff commercial representation is a key area of strength. Practice areas covered include real estate, employment, probate, and environmental and personal injury.

The Lawyers: *"A venerable presence at the trial Bar,"* Richard Couser recently joined the firm from New Hampshire giant Orr & Reno. Interviewees attribute his effectiveness in the courtroom to a *"low-key, methodical approach"* and an *"unflappable"* character. He recently acted in a major seven-figure commercial case, representing a medical group in connection with a failed hospital merger. In addition to his trial practice, Couser also counsels churches and other religious and nonprofit organizations.

The Clients: Target; Lowes; Rite Aid; Toys 'R' Us; BJ's Wholesale Club; Shaw's Supermarkets; Chicago Title; Brooks Pharmacy; Burger King; Laconia Savings Bank; Concord Hospital and Pizza Hut.

Gallagher, Callahan and Gartrell, PA

See firm details p.1120

The Firm: The trial and appellate practice at this highly regarded Concord firm comprises four primary litigators, who are additionally supported by a strong labor and employment law team. A range of general commercial litigation is undertaken, for example in the areas of environmental law, financial services and professional misconduct. Representation of clients in insurance coverage disputes is a particular strength of the team. The firm also operates from an office in Augusta, Maine.

The Lawyers: Founding partner and senior

1112   All quotes in the text are from interviews with clients and competitors.

CHAMBERS USA 2005

litigator **Michael Callahan** (see p.1116) is described as "*an extremely accomplished trial lawyer, who has handled every kind of case you can imagine.*" Recently he successfully resolved a significant class action lawsuit for a large commercial client.

The Clients: The firm acts for clients on both a regional and national basis, across a range of industry sectors.

Hinckley, Allen & Snyder LLP

The Firm: The Concord operation of this regional player is a small one, with two former prosecutors handling the litigation side of the practice. However, the depth of resources and wider profile of the firm means it "*attracts a more sophisticated client base,*" say observers, and the team is able to draw on the considerable support available in the Boston office. Practitioners undertake a broad variety of civil and commercial litigation and boast particular strength in white-collar defense.

The Lawyers: Michael Connolly's practice spans both New Hampshire and Massachusetts, where he handles an even mix of commercial disputes and the defense of companies and individuals in white-collar crime matters. He is highly rated for "*superb client skills*" and the ability to work "*wonderfully and collaboratively with co-counsel.*" A substantial portion of his time has been spent representing a large pharmaceutical company in an ongoing products liability matter. He also acts for many companies in breach of contract disputes, and has an active construction litigation practice, representing public contractors and private parties. Recent highlights include representing a London-based auto distributor in an action against Chrysler, based on promissory estoppel.

The Clients: Bread-and-butter work tends to be for smaller New England companies, although the firm has also represented global corporations in litigation potentially worth around half a billion dollars.

Nelson Kinder Mosseau & Saturley PC

The Firm: This is a "*progressive*" boutique of 28 trial lawyers, with offices in Manchester and Boston. Particular areas of strength include medical malpractice defense, construction (the firm has recently handled two major cases in this area, one of which was resolved through mediation), environmental and employment matters. The firm acted as local counsel for a major gasoline manufacturer and distributor in successfully removing a series of cases to be consolidated and litigated in New York.

The Lawyers: Peter Mosseau maintains an eclectic practice, which encompasses medical malpractice defense, general commercial disputes, defamation, and acting as local counsel on class actions. He wins particular acclaim for

his medical malpractice and professional misconduct expertise. Peers describe him as "*an extremely bright, common-sense attorney, with considerable trial experience.*"

The Clients: The firm acts for businesses and individual clients on a state, regional and national basis.

Sulloway & Hollis PLLC

The Firm: A "*top-quality*" firm handling a wide range of business litigation, spanning products and professional liability, insurance coverage and environmental, workers' compensation and defamation. Class actions are a substantial feature of the practice, which distinguishes itself through a first-class medical and healthcare malpractice defense capability. The firm also boasts an active appellate practice. Recent highlights for this sizable team include representing clients in several substantial insurance class actions, and handling a significant piece of commercial litigation for a large healthcare manufacturer.

The Lawyers: "*Outstanding*" **Michael Lehman** heads up the firm's medical malpractice and physician advocacy group. He is a widely respected figure in the field of medical malpractice litigation and represents a range of healthcare institutions and professionals, for whom he also takes on a risk management role. The remainder of his litigation practice comprises products liability defense, including drug and medical device cases, and the defense of clients in aircraft accident litigation. Peers describe the team as "*excellent trial lawyers with very good pretrial strategy, who will exercise good judgment quickly in a trial.*" Highly regarded practitioner Robert Larsen recently took an of counsel role within the firm and remains a valuable resource to the team.

The Clients: Public Service Company of New Hampshire; Amica Mutual Insurance; Medical Malpractice Joint Underwriting Association; New Hampshire Medical Society; Chicago Title Insurance; Merrill Lynch; Citizens Bank New Hampshire; Liberty Mutual Insurance; CNA Insurance; Concord School District; AIG; Dartmouth-Hitchcock Medical Center; Keane; Swenson Granite and Southworth-Milton.

Upton and Hatfield LLP

The Firm: This well-respected Concord practice offers a range of expertise across the spectrum of business litigation. Areas of focus include antitrust, partnership and insurance coverage, employment, medical and professional malpractice, class actions and breaches of fiduciary duty.

The Lawyers: The firm's reputation in the litigation arena is largely linked to the profile of "*consummate professional and outstanding trial lawyer*" **Russell Hilliard**. He wins plaudits for his professional conduct practice and expertise

in alternative dispute resolution. Peers highlight his considerable trial experience and reputation for quality preparation. He is also "*a pleasure to try a case with,*" they say.

The Clients: The firm represents a mix of businesses and individuals across the state.

Wadleigh, Starr & Peters PLLC

The Firm: A sizable civil litigation team handles a wide range of matters before the state and federal courts, from smaller cases for individual clients through to complex business disputes. The practice is especially noted in the areas of insurance and medical malpractice defense, reflecting the firm's established relationship with several of the state's major healthcare providers and professionals. Other areas of expertise include construction and land-use planning litigation.

The Lawyers: "*Top-notch*" **James Wheat** is recommended for his trial experience in both the broader commercial litigation and insurance defense fields. He wins plaudits for his "*excellent people skills*" and analytical approach, and is considered to be a tough opponent. **John Friberg**'s experience is such that "*you know you're going to have a battle with him.*" He is one of the senior members of the team and is considered to be "*one of the outstanding medical malpractice practitioners in the state,*" according to interviewees.

The Clients: Manufacturers, insurers, hospitals, school districts, physicians and other professionals feature on the client list.

Wiggin & Nourie

The Firm: Insurance defense work is a mainstay of this firm, which boasts a separate insurance services group. On the general commercial side, the practice covers construction litigation, stockholder and contract disputes, IP litigation, and trusts, estates and valuation issues. Recently attorneys successfully completed the first stage of litigation for Sprague Energy against the Boston & Maine Railroad, involving right-of-way access to Sprague's facilities. A distinguishing feature of the practice is its representation of automobile dealers – a team from the firm is currently litigating a multimillion-dollar class action on behalf of New England Subaru dealers against the New England Subaru distributor. Clients are especially impressed with the excellent service and responsiveness of these lawyers, and feel that they are receiving a top-quality, value-for-money product.

The Lawyers: Wright Danenbarger is considered to be one of the more experienced litigators in the state. The majority of his practice is business litigation, although he also has a focus on personal injury plaintiff matters. His broad commercial practice includes representing developers in construction, planning and zoning litigation (an engineering degree is said to have given him an "*excellent technical grasp*" of the issues), as well as acting for stockholders in corporate disputes, and IP litigation. He also represents doctors in front of licensing boards. **The Clients:** Associated Grocers of New England; Conproco; Crotched Mountain Foundation; Eckman Construction; New Hampshire Automobile Dealers Association; Sprague Energy and FleetBoston Financial. Among the firm's insurer clients are: Allstate; Concord Group; Merchants; Progressive; State Farm and Vermont Mutual.

Other Notable Practitioners

At Rath, Young & Pignatelli PA, founding partner and litigation head **Michael Pignatelli** was singled out as "*a first-rate litigator for medical malpractice defense.*" He also maintains a broader commercial litigation practice and has been involved in a number of complex multiparty actions, both in New Hampshire and further afield.

REAL ESTATE

New Hampshire
Leading firms (Real Estate)

1 MCLANE, GRAF, RAULERSON *Manchester*
  SHEEHAN PHINNEY BASS + GREEN *Manchester*

2 DEVINE MILLIMET & BRANCH PA *Manchester*
  GALLAGHER, CALLAHAN AND GARTRELL *Concord*
  SULLOWAY & HOLLIS PLLC *Concord*
  UPTON AND HATFIELD LLP *Concord*
  WADLEIGH, STARR & PETERS PLLC *Manchester*

3 D'AMANTE COUSER STEINER PELLERIN *Concord*
  DAVIS & BOGHIGIAN, PC *Nashua*
  DONAHUE, TUCKER & CIANDELLA *Exeter*
  NUNGESSER & HILL *Meredith*
  WINER & BENNETT LLP *Nashua*

Leading individuals (Real Estate)

1 DAVIS Jefferson *Davis & Boghigian, Nashua*
  IMSE Peter *Sulloway & Hollis Concord*
  MANCHESTER Susan *Sheehan, Manchester*
  ROTCH Peter *McLane, Graf, Raulerson, Manchester*
  TUCKER William *Wadleigh, Starr & Peters, Manchester*

2 D'AMANTE Raymond *D'Amante Couser, Concord*
  GARTRELL Donald *Gallagher, Callahan, PA, Concord*
  HILL Douglas *Nungesser & Hill, Meredith*
  POULOS Denise *Donahue, Tucker, Exeter*
  RAYMOND James *Upton and Hatfield, Concord*
  UPTON II Robert *Upton and Hatfield, Concord*
  WESTGATE J Bradford *Winer & Bennett, Nashua*

Firms and individuals are listed alphabetically in each band.

Band 1

McLane, Graf, Raulerson & Middleton Professional Association
See firm details p.1121
The Firm: Retaining its well-deserved place at the top of the table, this team of four continues to stand out for its excellent deal-making ability. Clients rave: "*They're well prepared and focused on the important issues, so you won't end up spinning your wheels. They simply get the deal done.*" The group handles a wide range of matters, from all aspects of the development process through to sophisticated real estate financings. The availability of ancillary support across the firm adds depth to the practice. The real estate team draws on the strength of the tax depart-

ment when handling Section 1031 exchanges, and has access to a highly regarded environmental group. Clients include landowners and developers, lenders and borrowers.
The Lawyers: Peter Rotch (see p.1118) heads up the real estate and commercial lending department and is widely respected in the industry as "*a terrific deal-maker.*" He maintains a broad practice, with a recent focus on commercial industrial development, land use and planning issues, as well as straight acquisition work. Recent matters include representing the purchaser of land for a mini-mall development using a Section 1031 exchange.
The Clients: BayCorp Holdings; Chicago Title Insurance; Community Bank & Trust; Citizens Bank; City of Portsmouth; GE Capital; Heidelberg Web Systems; Hyundai; Manchester Water Works; Microsoft; Monadnock Paper Mills; Nashua Motor Express; Pfeiffer Vacuum Technology; Summit Packaging Systems and Synagro Technologies.

Sheehan Phinney Bass + Green PA
See firm details p.1122
The Firm: Another visible presence in the market, this strong team handles the "*soup to nuts*" of commercial development matters, offering a niche practice in condominium law and specialist expertise in affordable housing. Clients value the responsiveness of the lawyers here, and the fact that the real estate team can draw on the strength of resources available across the firm, in particular the environmental and litigation departments. Attorneys have recently seen an increase in zoning work and appeals, and represented the Fisher Cats baseball team in a complex land redevelopment. Peers find it a pleasure to work with a team of professionals of such "*uniformly high level of expertise.*"
The Lawyers: Group chair **Susan Manchester**'s (see p.1118) real estate and lending practice encompasses land use and title issues, and a focus on condominium development. "*A strong negotiator who won't get pushed around,*" Manchester is in demand as "*the one to bring to the table in contentious situations.*" She continues to represent Pease Development Authority in ongoing matters concerning the redevelopment

of a former air force base, including complex title issues.
The Clients: Manchester Neighborhood Housing Services; Citizens Bank; City of Keene; Summit Packaging Systems; ABN AMRO; Families in Transition; Tyco International; The Nature Conservancy; Trust for Public Lands; Bio Energy; Maritimes and Northeast Pipelines; Rymes Heating Oil; Ocean National and Macmillan Construction.

Band 2

Devine Millimet & Branch PA
The Firm: This well-respected practice maintains seven attorneys in the New Hampshire office and provides additional coverage from the firm's Massachusetts base. The team runs the gamut of real estate development, from shopping center projects to nonprofit hospital work and affordable housing. Attorneys also act for lenders and borrowers on the complex financial aspects of real estate transactions. Clients benefit from the firm's interdisciplinary approach, with discrete specialties available in areas such as municipal bonds, tax credits, smart growth and telecom (the firm continues to take on a lot of cell tower work). A lobbying office in Concord also means that the firm is uniquely positioned to advise on local regulatory land use matters. The lawyers here are praised for being thorough, yet speedy. "*You get what you need, and you get it quickly,*" report clients. Recent work includes representing the buyer in the acquisition of a paper mill, involving issues of potential environmental contamination.
The Lawyers: Highly rated finance attorney Camille Di Croce (recommended in corporate/M&A) is considered a real force in the field of real estate lending. Robert Lavoie chairs the group from the firm's Andover office.
The Clients: Classic real estate developers, borrowers and lenders across New England feature on the client list.

Gallagher, Callahan and Gartrell, PA
See firm details p.1120
The Firm: The firm's land use practice spans the areas of real estate development and financing,

environmental law, municipal, and condominium and resort law. Five attorneys work exclusively in this group, typically representing major commercial lenders and developers, most notably in the retail, utility and timeshare industries across New England. The team has seen increased activity representing property owners in tax abatement litigation, in some cases directly resulting in the redefinition of land use standards.

The Lawyers: "*Top-notch*" founding partner **Donald Gartrell** (see p.1117) is especially noted for his municipalities practice and advises boards in a number of towns. According to observers, this experienced practitioner is "*constantly looking at the bottom line, but in a fair and environmentally sensitive way.*" He is one of the attorneys involved in extensive site development permitting with municipalities and state agencies for the construction and redevelopment of major commercial retail centers and industrial sites.

The Clients: The firm has represented Citizens Bank; Nike; Manchester Sand & Gravel; BAE SYSTEMS; PIKE Industries; Bank of New Hampshire; Demoulas Super Markets; Granite State Concrete; Providian National Bank; Dartmouth College; PNGTS; Southern New Hampshire Bank & Trust; Concord Monitor and Thermal Technology.

Sulloway & Hollis PLLC

The Firm: A core group of three attorneys covers the spectrum of real estate issues associated with commercial and large-scale residential development, with particular expertise in site acquisition and the permit approval process. The firm has an established relationship with a number of title insurance companies, and recently provided local representation to Chicago Title Insurance in connection with a major claim after mechanics' liens were filed against a property insured under one of the company's policies. The core team draws on the firm-wide expertise in the areas of utilities and tax abatement. Other recent matters include representing an out-of-state lender in connection with the sale/leaseback financing of a $10 million industrial facility, and acting for John Hancock Life Insurance on the sale of tracts of timber land in northern New Hampshire.

The Lawyers: Team leader **Peter Imse** continues to be viewed as a major player. He typically handles land use and permitting matters, and has seen an increasing amount of work in the nonprofit sector of late. The firm is representing a nonprofit corporation in connection with site acquisition and permit approvals for a new community center facility. Imse is also a "*condo guru,*" according to peers, who find him to be a worthy opponent. Said one: "*If you're opposite him you know you'll get a reasonable outcome without reinventing the wheel.*"

The Clients: John Hancock Life Insurance; Konover & Associates; City of Concord; Kearsarge/Lake Sunapee Community Center and Chicago Title Insurance.

Upton and Hatfield LLP

The Firm: While the firm has the ability to handle a wide array of pure real estate transactional work, its "*top-notch knowledge and experience base*" in municipal law is the feature that really marks this practice out from its competitors. Attorneys act for towns and cities on land use, development and property taxation issues before the various administrative and judicial bodies. Clients especially rate the forthright, common-sense approach of these lawyers: "*They tell us when we have a case and when we have a dog, and will cut to the meat of the issue very quickly.*"

The Lawyers: "*Highly skilled*" **Robert Upton** occupies a unique spot in the tables. He has a substantial practice representing municipalities in tax abatement proceedings in addition to matters concerning large utilities and special purpose properties across New England. Recent significant highlights include representing the City of Nashua in an eminent domain proceeding against Pennychuck, and defending the owner in a tax abatement appeal involving a combined cycle gas power plant in the Town of Londonderry. **James Raymond** is a key figure on the transactional side of the practice, which encompasses the full range of traditional real estate advice for a diverse cross section of clients.

The Clients: City of Nashua, Town of Londonderry and Town of Newington feature on the client list.

Wadleigh, Starr & Peters PLLC

The Firm: This highly regarded firm comprises a team of four "*extremely competent*" attorneys with a broad range of experience across the real estate, corporate, commercial and banking fields. The work ranges from small-scale residential property transactions to sophisticated corporate representation. Clients are full of praise for a team that "*takes time to understand our business and really listens to what we're trying to achieve.*"

The Lawyers: "*Probably one of the best dealmakers in the state,*" **William Tucker** stands out as the premier figure in the group. Noted for his work in development and lending transactions Tucker has the "*ability to cut through the legal mumbo-jumbo and get people to be practical – if the two sides are knocking heads, he can get everybody calmed down and make the deal happen.*"

The Clients: The client base ranges from individuals to corporate developers, and private and institutional lenders. A broad spectrum of sector representation includes finance, healthcare, retail, manufacturing, local government and education.

Band 3

D'Amante Couser Steiner Pellerin, PA

The Firm: A team of two at this small Concord-based practice handles all aspects of the real estate development process, including construction financing. The practice covers every type of development, from retail centers, restaurants and affordable housing to luxury apartments, golf courses, ski areas, hospital complexes, mobile home parks and office buildings. The team typically acts for the developer or end user, but also represents the contractor, seller or lender in transactions. Extensive knowledge and experience of local land use issues is a major drawing card for clients.

The Lawyers: **Raymond D'Amante** wins high praise from clients for his "*extraordinary*" knowledge of the local regulatory environment. He frequently appears before zoning and planning boards and other governmental bodies, where his preparation and presentation is described as "*flawless.*" D'Amante's engineering background earns points with developer clients who appreciate his grasp of technical issues. Recent matters include obtaining various approvals and negotiating the project financing documentation for a retail complex that includes a Target, Staples, McDonald's, Bed Bath & Beyond and Home Depot. The team also recently obtained approvals for the 70,000-sq-ft Payson Center for Cancer Care at Concord Hospital.

The Clients: Capital Region Health Care; The Grappone Companies; Lowe's Home Improvement Centers and BJ's Wholesale Clubs.

Davis & Boghigian, PC

The Firm: This "*small, yet highly skilled*" Nashua-based boutique retains a visible profile in the niche area of real estate lending. Despite its size, this two-partner practice continues to be the firm of choice for a large number of well-known local financial institutions, and also handles the general acquisition and sale of commercial property.

The Lawyers: "*Lending guru*" **Jefferson Davis** wins the respect of peers, who "*wouldn't hesitate to pick up the phone and bounce ideas off him,*" while clients appreciate his detail-oriented approach and willingness to roll up his sleeves on a transaction.

The Clients: An impressive roster includes: Banknorth; Sovereign Bank; Centrix Bank & Trust; New Hampshire Bank & Trust; First National Bank of Ipswich; Lawyers Title Insurance; Community Bank & Trust and Fleet Bank.

Donahue, Tucker & Ciandella

The Firm: This small shoreline firm enters the tables following particularly strong recommendations for its "*excellent*" municipal law practice and related real estate expertise. A team of approximately eight attorneys handles transactional, development and financing work for a mix of clients throughout New England. The team's expertise in municipal law makes it especially well suited to representing clients in front of local land use boards.

The Lawyers: *"Fantastic"* **Denise Poulos** wins plaudits from clients for her practical approach: *"She doesn't waste time talking semantics."* Based in the firm's Portsmouth office, she represents developers, lenders and borrowers in complex real estate and secured lending transactions.

The Clients: Clients range from individuals and small businesses to municipalities and large institutions based in New Hampshire and regionally.

Nungesser & Hill

The Firm: This established Meredith-based boutique is best known for its development work in New Hampshire's Northern Lakes region. A small team provides a range of real estate-related advice, including land planning, zoning and environmental regulation, and also handles related issues of trusts and estate planning.

The Lawyers: Group head **Douglas Hill** is the firm's most prominent personality. He is highly respected for his specialist knowledge and profile in the field of lakeside community and vacation property development. One interviewee explained: *"This is an area of real estate with its own subculture and problems, and Doug simply knows his way around the law."*

The Clients: The firm represents a cross section of New Hampshire landowners, municipalities and businesses.

Winer & Bennett LLP

The Firm: There are six attorneys in this Nashua-based practice handling the range of real estate-related matters. These include commercial and residential development, condominium law, leasing, loan workouts, acquisition and sale, zoning and planning issues, and litigation.

The Lawyers: **Bradford Westgate** is the standout figure in the team and is especially noted for his zoning and land use expertise. Typically acting for the developer, *"he will get totally consumed in a transaction."* Peers note: *"He is so thorough and knowledgeable that you can call him up and he will know the thing inside out."*

The Clients: The firm has acted for a mix of local, national and multinational concerns.

Leaders in New Hampshire

ARDINGER, William
Rath, Young and Pignatelli, Professional Association, Concord
603 226 2600
Recommended in Tax

BLACKMER, Jill
Orr & Reno PA, Concord
603 224 2381
Recommended in Employment

BROTH, Mark
Devine Millimet & Branch PA, North Hampton 603 964 4990
Recommended in Employment

BURGER, Peter
Orr & Reno PA, Concord
603 224 2381
Recommended in Corporate/M&A

BURKE, Steven M
McLane, Graf, Raulerson & Middleton Professional Association, Manchester
603 628 1454
steve.burke@mclane.com
Recommended in Corporate/M&A, Tax
Practice Areas: Concentrates on M&As and business ventures, including tax implications of transactions, ESOPs, pension plans, ERISA, executive compensation and corporate governance arrangements. Advises on tax and estate planning for business owners, IRS and state tax matters. Steve is a CPA.
Prof. Memberships: New Hampshire and Massachusetts Bars, New Hampshire Society of CPAs, AICPA, American College of Tax Counsel.
Career: Shareholder, Director, Tax Department Chair; Past President and Board of Directors-NHSCPA; Past President-Tax Section NH Bar; Past President and Treasurer-NH Employee Benefits Council; Adjunct Professor-Franklin Pierce Law School. Listed in a leading US legal publication.

Personal: BA, Bates College, 1981; MBA, University of Lowell, 1984; JD Franklin Pierce Law School, 1987; LLM in Taxation, Boston University School of Law, 1990.

CALLAHAN, Michael
Gallagher, Callahan and Gartrell, PA, Concord 800 528 1181
callahan@gcglaw.com
Recommended in Litigation

CASTALDO, Neil
Hinckley, Allen & Snyder LLP, Concord
603 225 4334
Recommended in Corporate/M&A

CHAPMAN, William
Orr & Reno PA, Concord
603 224 2381
Recommended in Litigation

CLOSSON, Tom
Flygare Schwarz & Closson PLLC, Exeter 603 778 7300
Recommended in Employment

COHEN, Steven
Devine Millimet & Branch PA, Manchester 603 669 1000
Recommended in Corporate/M&A, Tax

CONNOLLY, Michael
Hinckley, Allen & Snyder LLP, Concord
603 225 4334
Recommended in Litigation

COOK, James
Cook, Little, Rosenblatt & Manson PLLC, Manchester 603 621 7100
Recommended in Corporate/M&A

COUSER, Richard
D'Amante Couser Steiner Pellerin, P.A., Concord 603 224 6777
Recommended in Litigation

D'AMANTE, Raymond
D'Amante Couser Steiner Pellerin, P.A., Concord 603 224 6777
Recommended in Real Estate

DANENBARGER, Wright
Wiggin & Nourie, Manchester
603 669 2211
Recommended in Litigation

DAVIS, Jefferson
Davis & Boghigian, PC, Nashua
603 595 0210
Recommended in Real Estate

DI CROCE, Camille
Devine Millimet & Branch PA, North Hampton 603 964 4990
Recommended in Corporate/M&A

DONOVAN, Thomas J
McLane, Graf, Raulerson & Middleton Professional Association, Manchester
603 628 1337
tom.donovan@mclane.com
Recommended in Litigation
Practice Areas: Handles intellectual property litigation and complex commercial disputes, with a focus on patent, trademark and trade secret litigation involving computer software and related businesses. Recent matters have involved Microsoft, Sandia Laboratories and Micromuse.
Prof. Memberships: Admitted to practice before New Hampshire state and federal courts, as well as federal courts in Massachusetts, Indiana and Colorado, as well as the First and Federal Circuits. Former Chair of New Hampshire Bar Association Business Litigation Section. Commercial arbitrator, American Arbitration Association.
Career: Shareholder and Director since 1985; current Chair of management committee.

Publications: 'Cybersmears and Cyber-Attacks: Protecting Your Company', Association of Corporate Counsel (2003).
Personal: Harvard College, BA magna cum laude 1975; University of Pennsylvania Law School, JD 1978.

DROOFF, Michael J
Sheehan Phinney Bass + Green PA, Manchester 603 627 8167
mdrooff@sheehan.com
Recommended in Corporate/M&A
Practice Areas: Private company finance, including negotiated venture capital financing and private syndications; public offerings of equity and debt securities; public company governance and compliance; design and implementation of equity benefit plans. Corporate mergers and acquisitions, including negotiated asset and stock purchases and mergers among private companies, and mergers and tender offers involving public companies.
Prof. Memberships: Admitted to New York Bar, 1988; New Hampshire Bar, 1992.
Career: 'Best Lawyers in America': Corporate, Mergers and Acquisitions and Securities Law categories.
Publications: Contributor: 'Selling the Private Business'.
Personal: Working knowledge of Spanish. JD, University of Chicago; BA, Dartmouth College.

DYLESKI-NAJJAR, Debra
Hinckley, Allen & Snyder LLP, Concord
603 225 4334
Recommended in Employment

ELLISON, Scott
Devine Millimet & Branch PA, North Hampton 603 964 4990
Recommended in Corporate/M&A

FELMLY, Bruce W
McLane, Graf, Raulerson & Middleton Professional Association, Manchester
603 628 1448
bruce.felmly@mclane.com
Recommended in Litigation

Practice Areas: Co-Chair, McLane's Litigation Department. Concentrates in complex commercial defense and plaintiff trial practice, including products liability, environmental, insurance recovery, employment, and contract claims. Recent representation of clients has included Microsoft Corporation, Abbott Labs, Hyundai Motor Company, Bayer Corporation, Carpet One, Dartmouth College, Irving Oil Corporation, and KeySpan.

Prof. Memberships: Fellow of the American College of Trial Lawyers (former State Chairman), American and New Hampshire Trial Lawyer's Associations, American Law Institute, and a Fellow of the American and New Hampshire Bar Foundations.

Career: Shareholder and Director since 1979. President of the New Hampshire Bar Association (1995-96). In 2002, he received the New Hampshire Bar Association's Distinctive Service to the Legal Profession Award. Listed in a leading US Legal Publication. Appointed by the New Hampshire Supreme Court to chair its long range planning committee for the New Hampshire justice system.

Personal: JD, Cornell Law School, 1972.

FITZGERALD, Kevin M
Nixon Peabody LLP, Manchester
603 628 4016
kfitzgerald@nixonpeabody.com
Recommended in Litigation

Practice Areas: Litigation practice leader; Manchester office Managing Partner. Commercial litigation, focusing on complicated business disputes. Successful multimillion-dollar litigation: mergers/acquisitions, corporate fiduciary duty, directors/officers liability, insurance coverage, ERISA, employment law involving corporate executives. Healthcare, including managed care contract disputes, quality assurance and credentialing matters. Secured defendants' verdict in defense of multimillion-dollar breach of fiduciary duty claims by minority shareholders against directors and majority shareholders.

Prof. Memberships: Admitted to practice in NH, US District Courts for the Districts of NH and Northern NY, First Circuit Court of Appeals, US Supreme Court.

Personal: Suffolk University, JD; University of New Hampshire, BA.

FLYGARE, Thomas
Flygare Schwarz & Closson PLLC, Exeter 603 778 7300
Recommended in Employment

FORD, Debra
Devine Millimet & Branch PA, Manchester 603 669 1000
Recommended in Employment

FRIBERG Sr, John
Wadleigh, Starr & Peters PLLC, Manchester 603 669 4140
Recommended in Litigation

GARTRELL, Donald E
Gallagher, Callahan and Gartrell, PA, Concord 603 228-1181
gartrell@gcglaw.com
Recommended in Real Estate

Practice Areas: Counsel to buyers, sellers, developers, investors and lenders in all aspects of real estate ownership and development, including municipal, State and federal regulation, property taxation and business organizations.

Prof. Memberships: American, New Hampshire (former Chair, Real Property Probate and Trust Law Section; former member, Board of Governors) and Merrimack County Bar Associations; Fellow, NH Bar Foundation.

Publications: Frequent author and speaker on real estate development, municipal zoning and land use regulation, property taxation and earth excavation.

Personal: Vanderbilt University School of Law, LLB, 1965; Ohio Wesleyan University, BA, 1962.

GLAHN III, Wilbur A
McLane, Graf, Raulerson & Middleton Professional Association, Manchester
603 628 1469
bill.glahn@mclane.com
Recommended in Litigation

Practice Areas: Business and commercial litigation, including issues of corporate governance and control, breaches of fiduciary duty and dissenters' rights, contract disputes, securities law, and taxation. Constitutional litigation.

Prof. Memberships: New Hampshire and American Bar Associations, New Hampshire Trial Lawyers Association.

Career: Admitted to practice in the state and federal courts in New Hampshire (1976) and Massachusetts (1972); First Circuit Court of Appeals (1976); Supreme Court of the United States (1978). Former Assistant Attorney General and Head of the Civil Division of the Office of the Attorney General (New Hampshire).

Personal: Trinity College, BA with honors 1969 (Phi Beta Kappa); University of Chicago Law School, JD 1972.

HARVELL, Michael
Sheehan Phinney Bass + Green PA, Manchester 603 627 8133
mharvell@sheehan.com
Recommended in Litigation

Practice Areas: Practice areas: corporate law, corporate litigation, tax and probate litigation. He has litigated shareholder and partnership disputes, employment matters, intellectual property disputes, commercial and fiduciary disputes, state tax appeals.

Prof. Memberships: New Hampshire Bar; Bar of the United States Supreme Court; Bar of the United States First Circuit Court of Appeals.

Career: US Navy (nuclear submarines) 1968-72.

Personal: BA, Yale University; JD, Boston University. Chair, Board of Trustees, Strawbery Banke Museum; Chair, Board of Directors, NH Preservation Alliance; Former President and Director, Child & Family Services of NH; Former Trustee, NH Society for the Protection of NH Forests.

HIGGINS, James E
Sheehan Phinney Bass + Green PA, Manchester 603 627 8136
jhiggins@sheehan.com
Recommended in Litigation

Practice Areas: Civil litigation including personal injury, commercial, business, shareholder disputes, products liability, professional malpractice, eminent domain, employment law, domestic law, and labor law. Mediated, arbitrated, and tried many cases. Served as arbitrator and mediator as part of the New Hampshire Superior Court Alternative Dispute Resolution Program.

Prof. Memberships: Bar of the State of New Hampshire; New Hampshire Bar Association; American Bar Association; Court of Military Appeals; US District Court of New Hampshire; First Circuit Court of Appeals; United States Tax Court; US Supreme Court.

Personal: LLB Yale University; LLM Boston University; AB Dartmouth College.

HILL, Douglas
Nungesser & Hill, Meredith
603 279 8182
Recommended in Real Estate

HILLIARD, Russell
Upton and Hatfield LLP, Concord
603 224 7791
Recommended in Litigation

HOOD, James
Nixon Peabody LLP, Manchester
603 628 4051
jchood@nixonpeabody.com
Recommended in Corporate/M&A

Practice Areas: Corporate governance, restructuring, acquisitions, mergers, debt/equity financing, shareholder dispute resolution, joint venture/LLC formation and distribution arrangements (domestically, internationally), strategic partnerships. Serialized mortgage-backed, leased-backed securitizations. Water, gas utilities in rate matters before public utilities commission. Bank holding company on expansion, bank-regulatory issues.

Prof. Memberships: Admitted to practice in NH, US District Court for the District of NH, First Circuit Court of Appeals. Chairman, New Hampshire's Statutory International Trade Advisory Committee to the Governor and Department of Resources and Economic Development.

Personal: Georgetown University, JD; University of New Hampshire, BA, magna cum laude.

IMSE, Peter
Sulloway & Hollis PLLC, Concord
603 224 2341
Recommended in Real Estate

JOHNSON, Linda S
McLane, Graf, Raulerson & Middleton Professional Association, Manchester
603 628 1267
linda.johnson@mclane.com
Recommended in Employment

Practice Areas: Chair, Employment Practice. Concentrates on corporate risk management and employment defense. Formulates employment policies and handbooks, advises on discipline, termination, discrimination claims, wage and hour compliance, and other personnel matters. Conducts harassment and workplace training. Defends companies in State and Federal Courts and before Administrative Agencies.

Prof. Memberships: Past President, Manchester Area Human Resources Association; member, National Society for Human Resource Management; Employment Law Sections of New Hampshire and American Bar Associations; Human Resource Committee of the New Hampshire Business and Industry Association.

Career: Shareholder and Director. Awards: 2002 Marilla Ricker Award from New Hampshire Women's Bar Association, and the 2002 New Hampshire Civil Liberties Union award. Listed in leading US legal publication.

Personal: JD, Boston University, 1984.

JOHNSTONE, Andrea
Gallagher, Callahan and Gartrell, PA, Concord 603 228 1181
johnstone@gcglaw.com
Recommended in Employment

Practice Areas: Chair of the Firm's Labor and Employment Law and Litigation Departments. Advises management in the development and administration of personnel policies and strategies for handling workplace issues. Represents management in all aspects of labor and employment law, including employment agreements, state and federal employment law compliance, union organizing campaigns, labor negotiations and arbitration and employment litigation.

Career: Judicial Law Clerk, NH Superior Court 1989-90; joined firm of Gallagher, Callahan & Gartrell in 1990; Partner since 1994.

Publications: Author of numerous articles on human resource and employment law topics. Co-Author of Labor and Employment in New Hampshire (Lexis 2004).

Personal: JD, Hofstra University School of Law (1989); BA, Wheaton College (1985). Listed in 'Best Lawyers in America'.

KAPLAN, Edward
Sulloway & Hollis PLLC, Concord
603 224 2341
Recommended in Employment

LAW, David
Cleveland, Waters and Bass, P.A.,
Concord
603 224 7761
Recommended in Tax

LEHMAN, Michael
Sulloway & Hollis PLLC, Concord
603 224 2341
Recommended in Litigation

LITTLE Jr, Curtis
Cook, Little, Rosenblatt & Manson
PLLC, Manchester
603 621 7100
Recommended in Corporate/M&A

MANCHESTER, Susan A
Sheehan Phinney Bass + Green PA,
Manchester
603 627 8245
smanchester@sheehan.com
Recommended in Real Estate
Practice Areas: Member and Director
of the firm and is the Head of the Real
Estate and Lending Practice Group. Her
practice is in the areas of zoing and land
use, commercial leasing, conveyancing,
condominium, construction and commercial lending.
Prof. Memberships: New Hampshire Bar
Association. American Bar Association.
Personal: BA, magna cum laude, Brown
University 1977. JD, Boston University
1980. Heritage United Way, Board Chair
2002; Amherst Congregationalist Church,
Clerk 2005, Board of Trustees 2002-04;
active member Manchester Rotary Club.

MANSON, Tom
Cook, Little, Rosenblatt & Manson
PLLC, Manchester 603 621 7100
Recommended in Corporate/M&A

MCCUE, Mark S
Sheehan Phinney Bass + Green PA,
Manchester
603 627 8155
mmccue@sheehan.com
Recommended in Corporate/M&A
Practice Areas: Mergers and acquisitions, including tax-deferred reorganizations, stock and asset purchases and
sales, intellectual property transfers, and
multinational transactions in various
industries; healthcare, including hospital
affiliations, physician practice acquisitions, tax-exempt bond financings, regulatory compliance and representation
of state high risk insurance pool; corporate, including entity formation, governance issues, and contractual relationships.
Prof. Memberships: New Hampshire
Bar Association.
Career: Partner, Orr & Reno, PA 1990-
2002; Of Counsel, Sheehan Phinney
Bass + Green, PA since 2003.
Publications: Frequently lectures on
transactional, healthcare and employment matters.

Personal: Brown University, AB (1981);
Boston University School of Law, JD
(1985), LLM Taxation (1991).

MIDDLETON, Jack B
McLane, Graf, Raulerson & Middleton
Professional Association, Manchester
603 628 1446
jack.middleton@mclane.com
Recommended in Litigation
Practice Areas: Concentrates on arbi-
tration and mediation, utilizing 48 years
trial experience as a trial lawyer and 24
years as a New Hampshire District
Court Judge. Jack has a strong trial prac-
tice in commercial litigation.
Prof. Memberships: Former Secretary,
member, Board of Governors, American
Bar Association (ABA); member, ABA
House of Delegates; Fellow, American
College of Trial Lawyers; former presi-
dent, New Hampshire and New England
Bar Associations, the National Conference
of Bar Foundations and National Confer-
ence of Bar Presidents; former Chairman,
New Hampshire Bar Foundation.
Career: Shareholder and Director
(1962). New Hampshire District Court
Judge (1964-87). New Hampshire Busi-
ness Leader of the Year, 2002. Named
"New Hampshire's Lawyers' Lawyer".
Listed in leading US legal publication.
Personal: JD, Boston University, 1956.

MOECKEL, Jennifer
Devine Millimet & Branch PA, North
Hampton 603 964 4990
Recommended in Employment

MOORE, George
Devine Millimet & Branch PA,
Manchester 603 669 1000
Recommended in Litigation

MOSSEAU, Peter
Nelson Kinder Mosseau & Saturley PC,
Manchester 603 647 1800
Recommended in Litigation

PIGNATELLI, Michael
Rath, Young and Pignatelli, Professional Association, Concord
603 226 2600
Recommended in Litigation

POULOS, Denise
Donahue, Tucker & Ciandella, Exeter
603 778 0686
Recommended in Real Estate

RATH, Thomas
Rath, Young and Pignatelli, Profession-
al Association, Concord
603 226 2600
*Recommended in Government
Relations*

RAYMOND, James
Upton and Hatfield LLP, Concord
603 224 7791
Recommended in Real Estate

REIDY, James P
Sheehan Phinney Bass + Green PA,
Manchester 603 627 8217
jreidy@sheehan.com
Recommended in Employment

Practice Areas: Practice Group Coordinator; employment law, focusing on
assisting employers avoid or defend
against employment disputes. Represents management for all types and sizes
of organizations. Extensive experience
handling matters before state and federal agencies: wage claims/audits; hand-
books/policies; discrimination claims;
hiring practices; contracts and
covenants.
Prof. Memberships: Admitted to practice
in New Hampshire and Massachusetts.
Career: Extensive experience before
New Hampshire Department of Labor,
New Hampshire Commission for
Human Rights, US Equal Employment
Opportunity Commission and US
Department of Labor.
Publications: Please see
www.sheehan.com.
Personal: JD, cum laude, New England
School of Law; MPA, Northeastern Uni-
versity; BA, Assumption College.

REISCHE, Alan L
Sheehan Phinney Bass + Green PA,
Manchester 603 627 8225
areische@sheehan.com
Recommended in Corporate/M&A
Practice Areas: Corporate finance and
acquisitions; business succession; inter-
national law. Negotiated Danish limited
liability company for US company's
European joint venture; US counsel for
UK-based laboratory equipment manu-
facturer's global acquisitions; assisted US
client in joint venture with Chilean
company for Jamaican operations.
Prof. Memberships: Director, NH
International Trade Association; mem-
ber, Governor's Advisory Committee on
Capital Formation; Vice-Chairman, NH
Workforce Opportunity Council; mem-
ber, Venture for Growth Committee,
NH Community Loan Fund.
Career: Admitted, NH Bar; United
States District Court, District of NH; US
Tax Court .
Personal: Harvard College (BA), Uni-
versity Pennsylvania Law School (LLB),
Boston University Law School (LLM, tax).

RICE, Emily
Orr & Reno PA, Concord
603 224 2381
*Recommended in Employment,
Litigation*

ROSENBLATT, Arnold
Cook, Little, Rosenblatt & Manson
PLLC, Manchester 603 621 7100
Recommended in Litigation

ROTCH, Peter B
McLane, Graf, Raulerson & Middleton
Professional Association, Manchester
603 628 1305
peter.rotch@mclane.com
Recommended in Real Estate
Practice Areas: Chair of McLane's Real
Estate Department. His practice is
focused on commercial property devel-
opment and financing. He works with

investors and corporate clients who wish
to develop and finance real estate. He is
an agent for all of the major title insurance companies. Recent projects include
obtaining property and easements for a
major gas powered electric generating
facility.
Prof. Memberships: Fellow of the
American College of Real Estate
Lawyers, New Hampshire and American
Bar Associations.
Career: Admitted in New Hampshire,
1966; shareholder and Partner, 1974.
Listed in a leading US legal publication.
Personal: Dartmouth College (1963-
AB), University of Chicago Law School
(1966-JD).

SAMUELS, Richard A
McLane, Graf, Raulerson & Middleton
Professional Association, Manchester
603 628 1470
richard.samuels@mclane.com
Recommended in Corporate/M&A
Practice Areas: Concentrates practice
in corporate and commercial transactions, securities law, banking, and utilities regulatory matters. Advises on
merger and acquisition transactions and
securities matters, including public and
private offerings of equity securities,
entity formation, governance, and commercial matters. An author of New
Hampshire's Business Corporation Act
and Limited Liability Company Act.
Prof. Memberships: Co-Chair for Fiscal
Policy of the Fiscal Policy and Economic
Development Committee of the Business & Industry Association of New
Hampshire. New Hampshire liaison to
the American Bar Associations Business
Law Section's Committee on State Regulation of Securities.
Personal: BA, Union College, 1974;
MA, Duke University, 1976; JD, Cornell
University, 1980. Listed in a leading US
legal publication.

SKLAR, Daniel W
Nixon Peabody LLP, Manchester
603 628 4008
dsklar@nixonpeabody.com
Recommended in Corporate/M&A
Practice Areas: Lending transactions,
loan workouts/liquidations, bankruptcy
reorganizations, lender liability. More
than 20 years experience in corporate
law, commercial transactions. Represented debtors, trustees, secured creditors, committees, stockholders, lessors,
senior executives in large Chapter 11
cases, several international insolvencies.
Prof. Memberships: Admitted to practice before NH state courts, District
Court of NH, First Circuit Court of
Appeals, US Supreme Court. Certification, business bankruptcy law, American
Bankruptcy Certification Board. American Bankruptcy Institute. NH and
American Bar Associations. Fellow,
American College of Bankruptcy.
Career: Adjunct professor, Franklin
Pierce Law Center.

Personal: Boston University, LLM; Boston College, JD cum laude; University of Pennsylvania, BA.

SNOW, Ronald
Orr & Reno PA, Concord
603 224 2381
Recommended in Litigation

SPARKMAN, Jon
Devine Millimet & Branch PA, North Hampton 603 964 4990
Recommended in Tax

TAUB, Philip B
Nixon Peabody LLP, Manchester
603 628 4038
ptaub@nixonpeabody.com
Recommended in Corporate/M&A

Practice Areas: Partner and deputy practice group leader of the firm's Business Group. Mr Taub focuses his practice primarily in the area of corporate transactional work, including mergers, acquisitions, leveraged buy-outs, startups, shareholder disputes and venture capital financing. He has extensive experience in commercial financing having served as counsel to a number of lending institutions.

Prof. Memberships: Admitted to practice in New Hampshire, Massachusetts, and the District of Columbia and before the US District Court for the District of New Hampshire. Member of the American, New Hampshire and Manchester Bar Associations.

Personal: George Washington University, JD; Boston University, BS.

TUCKER, William
Wadleigh, Starr & Peters PLLC, Manchester 603 669 4140
Recommended in Real Estate

UPTON II, Robert
Upton and Hatfield LLP, Concord
603 224 7791
Recommended in Real Estate

VAN OOT, Martha
Orr & Reno PA, Concord
603 224 2381
Recommended in Litigation

VICINANZO, David
Nixon Peabody LLP, Boston
617 345 1177
dvicinanzo@nixonpeabody.com
Recommended in Litigation

Practice Areas: Practices primarily in the area of government investigations and the representation of organizations and individuals in complex civil and criminal matters.

Prof. Memberships: Admitted to practice in New York and New Hampshire; the United States Courts of Appeals (First, Second, and District of Columbia circuits); numerous federal district courts.

Career: He served as a federal prosecutor in Washington, DC, and New England for 13 years; was as an advisor to the US attorney general, and a chief prosecutor in the campaign finance investigation of the 1996 presidential election.

Personal: Fordham University, JD; Harvard University, BA, with honors.

WESTGATE, Bradford
Winer & Bennett LLP, Nashua
603 882 5157
Recommended in Real Estate

WHEAT, James
Wadleigh, Starr & Peters PLLC, Manchester 603 669 4140
Recommended in Litigation

WOLOWITZ, David
McLane, Graf, Raulerson & Middleton Professional Association, Portsmouth
603 436 2818
david.wolowitz@mclane.com
Recommended in Litigation

Practice Areas: Concentrates in risk management and litigation on behalf of corporations relating to all aspects of employment law, with a particular focus on mental health issues and difficult employees in the workplace. Recent representation of clients includes BAE Systems, Inc.; Nike, Inc.; Universal Instruments Corp.; as well as healthcare and educational organizations, including St. Paul's School.

Prof. Memberships: Admitted to practice before the state and federal courts in New Hampshire and Massachusetts. Member of the New Hampshire, Massachusetts, and American Bar Associations.

Career: Shareholder and Director since 1991; Guest faculty Harvard Law School, Trial Advocacy Workshop (1984-present). Listed in a leading US legal publication.

Personal: 1968, AB, Washington University; 1971, MA, Harvard University; 1975, JD, University of Michigan.

GALLAGHER, CALLAHAN & GARTRELL, PROFESSIONAL ASSOCIATION

THE FIRM

Founding Members: Christopher C Gallagher, Michael R Callahan, Donald E Gartrell
Managing Director & President: Michael D Ruedig
Number of shareholders: 18
Number of other professionals: 19

FIRM OVERVIEW: Gallagher, Callahan & Gartrell is a multidisciplinary law firm with offices in the capital cities of Augusta, Maine, Boston, Massachusetts and Concord, New Hampshire, from which it serves clients with markets in New England and beyond. The multidisciplinary team approach integrates the skills and experience of firm lawyers with that of firm economics, human resource, banking, accounting, communications and legislative professionals.

MAIN AREAS OF PRACTICE:

Financial Services: Gallagher, Callahan & Gartrell is a recognized leader in serving the special needs of financial institutions, insurance companies and securities firms in local, state and federal matters.

Employment/Labor & Benefits: The firm works with employers throughout the region developing strategies for limiting workplace liability. It provides comprehensive state and federal law services concerning the employment relationship from employee recruitment through termination. The firm also defends a wide range of employment-related litigation.

Land Use/Real Estate Development: Gallagher, Callahan & Gartrell represents buyers, sellers, developers, investors, and lenders in a wide range of real estate and environmental matters, including large scale residential, commercial and industrial developments, condominiums, subdivisions, vacation ownership and resort properties. The firm also represents a number of entities in the sand, gravel and aggregate industry.

Government & Regulatory: The firm is a regionally-recognized leader in the provision of governmental law and regulatory services to a broad range of industries including financial institutions, insurance companies, healthcare companies, public utilities, telecommunications companies, hospitals, energy companies and other businesses. The firm's Chief Economist and other non-lawyer professionals are intimately involved in the provision of these services.

Business, Capital & Technology: Gallagher, Callahan & Gartrell provides a broad range of corporate, business, finance, securities, information and technology law services to various institutional and business clients.

Estates & Taxation: The firm's professionals are experienced in estate planning and federal and state taxation.

Litigation/Appellate Practice: Gallagher, Callahan & Gartrell litigators practice in state and federal trial and appellate courts. The firm's trial lawyers handle various complex commercial, construction, employment, environmental and other cases.

Project & Infrastructure: The firm is experienced with the design, environmental permitting, financing, construction and operation of large scale infrastructure developments. Representative projects include an international natural gas pipeline, 525 MW power plant, intermodal transportation center and shopping centers.

INTERNATIONAL WORK: The firm represents a number of international clients in a broad range of legal matters.

HEAD OFFICE

NEW HAMPSHIRE
214 N Main Street, P.O. Box 1415, **Concord**, NH 03302-1415
Tel: 800 528 1181
Website: www.gcglaw.com

BRANCH OFFICES

MAINE
168 Capitol Street, P.O. Box 5010, **Augusta**, ME 04332-5010
Tel: 207 626 0395

MASSACHUSETTS
112 South Street, **Boston**, MA 02111
Tel: 800 528 1181

CONTACTS

Financial Services	W John Funk
Employment/Labor & Benefits	Andrea K Johnstone
Land Use/Real Estate Development	Donald E Gartrell
Government & Regulatory	Christopher C Gallagher
Business Capital & Technology	Denis J Maloney
Estate & Taxation	Donald R Saxon
Litigation/Appellate Practice	David A Garfunkel
Project & Infrastructure	Donald J Pfundstein

MCLANE GRAF RAULERSON & MIDDLETON, PA

THE FIRM

Managing Partner: Thomas J Donovan
Senior Partner: Jack B Middleton
Number of partners: 33
Number of other lawyers: 38

AREAS OF PRACTICE:

Corporate	25%
Commercial Litigation	22%
Environmental	10%
Real Estate	10%
Employment	6%
Utilities	5%
Tax	5%
Intellectual Property	3%

FIRM OVERVIEW: Over 70 lawyers and more than 25 legal assistants advise a wide range of domestic and international corporate clients with their legal needs in the greater New England area. The firm is based in New Hampshire, with locations near the Massachusetts and Maine borders, and is the State's largest full service law firm. The firm counts amongst its lawyers Fellows of the American Colleges of Trial Lawyers, Real Estate Lawyers, Tax Counsel, and Trust & Estates Counsel. The 2004-2005 edition of The Best Lawyers in America recognizes 26 of the firm's lawyers. Firm members have drafted legislation, including the Business Corporation and Limited Liability Company Acts of New Hampshire, and are the authors of the State of New Hampshire's Environmental Law Handbook. McLane's lawyers are licensed in all of the New England states, including Connecticut, as well as in New York, Pennsylvania, Washington, DC, Georgia, Arizona, Missouri, and Nebraska. The firm's lawyers actively participate in service to the public and to the profession. Current members of the firm have served as Attorney General in New Hampshire, as Presidents of the New Hampshire and New England Bar Associations and as Secretary of the American Bar Association. The McLane Law Firm is a member of TerraLex, the premier international and interstate association of independent law firms.

MAIN AREAS OF PRACTICE:

Corporate: The firm's Corporate Department advises clients on merger and acquisition transactions and securities matters, including public and private offerings of equity securities, as well as entity formation, governance, commercial matters and all aspects of corporate finance. The department has industry focus areas in the energy, manufacturing, technology and financial services industries. Recent transaction includes the representation of a publicly traded energy company in connection with the sale of their interests in the Seabrook Nuclear Power Plant, representing 17% of an $800 million transaction.

Environmental: The Environmental Practice covers administrative law and litigation under all the major federal environmental laws and their State program analogues. The firm's lawyers have extensive experience in Superfund and State hazardous waste cases, Clean Air Act, Clean Water Act, wetlands, TSCA, EPCRA, NEPA, energy facility siting, and natural resource law, in both permitting and enforcement cases. The firm has handled cases throughout New England, New York, Georgia, South Carolina, and California.

Commercial Litigation: The firm's Litigation Department possesses trial experience covering a wide range of cases including: computer software antitrust litigation; disputes over development of software for international businesses; reinsurance contract disputes over asbestos claims; patent infringement litigation; environmental insurance coverage disputes; securities arbitration and litigation; product liability; trademark opposition proceedings; and trade secret and non-competition agreement litigation. A recent case example includes representation of EnergyNorth (ENGI) in EnergyNorth Natural Gas, Inc. v Lloyd's, Underwriters at London in the USDC for the District of New Hampshire, concerning insurance coverage for environmental liabilities at a former manufactured gas plant. Energy-

HEAD OFFICE

NEW HAMPSHIRE
City Hall Plaza, 900 Elm Street, **Manchester**, NH 03101
Tel: 603 625 6464 **Fax:** 603 625 5650
Email: law@mclane.com **Website:** www.mclane.com

BRANCH OFFICES

NEW HAMPSHIRE
Bicentennial Square, 15 North Main Street, **Concord**, NH 03301
Tel: 603 226 0400 **Fax:** 603 230 4448

100 Market Street, Suite 301, **Portsmouth**, NH 03801
Tel: 603 436 2818 **Fax:** 603 436 5672

CONTACTS

Corporate	Richard A Samuels
Environmental	Gregory H Smith
Commercial Litigation	Bruce W Felmly
Utility Law	Steven V Camerino
Employment	Linda S Johnson
Tax	Steven M Burke
Real Estate	Peter B Rotch
Intellectual Property	Mark A Wright

North successfully demonstrated that the damage was the result of unintentional leaks and spills that continued for an extended period of time.

Utility Law: The firm represent gas, telephone, and water utilities; competitive energy suppliers; small power producers and other wholesale electric generators; wireless communications companies; utility holding companies; municipalities and industrial and commercial customers of electric utilities. Recent work includes extensive work on restructuring of the electric and gas industries, electric and water municipalization litigation, gas, electric and water rate proceedings and numerous financings.

Employment: Representation includes defending and prosecuting claims, workplace audits, managerial and workforce training programs, development of personnel policies and practices, and consultation and advice on the day to day challenges employers face, including internal employee complaints, responding to government investigations, or resolving disability, compensation, benefits, misconduct and termination issues.

Real Estate: The firm's Real Estate Practice advises clients on general commercial and construction financing, land use matters, leasing, and other aspects of real estate and business ownership. The firm recently obtained on behalf of a client all permits for an electric generating station producing competitive-cost power. Representation included the acquisition of all real estate, easements for the transmission lines and all environmental and regulatory work for the new 16-mile, interstate gas transmission pipeline.

Tax: The firm's Tax Department, the largest in the state of New Hampshire, represents individuals and businesses, buyers and sellers, in a variety of tax-related transactions, planning and issues. McLane's tax lawyers represent clients in every phase of contact with the IRS and state revenue agencies, including audit, collection, appeals, abatement requests and dispute resolution. When necessary, litigation lawyers experienced in tax matters assist in tax matters that require litigation.

Intellectual Property: The firm's IP lawyers represent clients on a wide range of US and international intellectual property matters and transactions. In litigated matters, it has helped large software companies, such as Microsoft Corporation, protect their copyright ownership in software against piracy and counterfeiting. The IP Group handles all aspects of IP protection, including patent, trademark, copyright, trade secret, licensing and e-commerce law.

CLIENTS: Abbott Laboratories; Algonquin Power Fund; BAUER Nike Hockey U.S.A., Inc.; BayCorp Holdings; El Paso Energy; Hitchiner Manufacturing Co., Inc.; Hyundai Motor Company; Irving Oil, Microsoft Corporation; Synagro Technologies, Inc; and Verizon Communications.

SHEEHAN PHINNEY BASS + GREEN

THE FIRM

Managing Partner: William J Donovan

Number of partners: 39
Number of associates: 9
Number of counsel: 7

AREAS OF PRACTICE:
Corporate & Finance 41%
Litigation 36%
Real Estate/Environmental 8%
Labor & ERISA 9%
Trusts & Estates 6%

FIRM OVERVIEW: Sheehan Phinney Bass + Green has been serving clients throughout New England for over 50 years. While the firm's core clients remain businesses, institutions and municipalities based in New England, the firm also regularly represents the interests of national and international concerns throughout the region and the United States. Sheehan Phinney is known for professional excellence, practical counsel, and commitment to both its clients and the communities it serves. To enhance the services provided to its clients, the firm has expanded beyond its offices in Manchester and Concord by opening an office in the heart of Boston's financial district, and establishing a presence in New Hampshire's technology-rich Upper Valley. The firm's geographic expansion springs from the regional growth and diversity of its clients and their needs, including access to major capital and international markets. These service-oriented developments complement the firm's expansion of its government relations and tax advisory services through its affiliates, the Sheehan Phinney Capitol Group and the Sheehan Phinney Tax Group. The firm is the exclusive member firm for New Hampshire of Lex Mundi, the world's leading association of independent law firms.

MAIN AREAS OF PRACTICE:

Corporate: The firm has particular expertise in mergers and acquisitions, corporate finance, healthcare, real estate, and labor law as well as corporate governance. Areas of practice also include tax matters, public and private securities, bankruptcy and insolvency, business formation, education, the environment and energy, governmental affairs, intellectual property and technology, import/export control and trust and estate planning.

Litigation: The firm's Business Litigation Practice is one of the most well respected in Northern New England. Its personal injury litigation practice includes representation of both plaintiffs and defendants. The firm has recently litigated to a successful conclusion or settlement cases involving employment discrimination, securities, class action involving state taxes, contractual disputes, non-competition, stockholder and partnership disputes, and tax matters.

Banking & Finance: In addition to its frequent representation of borrowers and lenders in numerous transactions, the firm has served as counsel in more than a billion dollars of tax-exempt financings in New Hampshire and Massachusetts over the past 18 months. The firm's clients in public finance transactions include New Hampshire's largest issuer of tax-exempt bonds, as well as borrowers, underwriters and corporate trustees.

Labor: Increasing governmental regulation of the workplace and ever-expanding rights of employees have made 'proactive prevention' the soundest method for avoiding significant liability in employment law. Legal services offered in this area include: developing effective anti-discrimination policies, proper employee screening and verifying procedures, wage and salary administration strategies (FLSA), executive employment agreements, employee handbooks and policies, noncompetition and nondisclosure covenants, employment applications and performance evaluation policies, severance agreements, early retirement programs, reduction in force procedures, substance abuse policies, workplace privacy policies, workplace violence prevention or response plans, leave of absence programs (including FMLA, maternity, military and jury duty), and personnel file record-keeping procedures.

Real Estate: The firm works with clients in all areas of commercial real estate financing and construction matters, advising and representing developers, lenders and users of commercial properties: office buildings, shopping centers, condominiums, affordable housing projects, corporate headquarters and airports. Representation includes negotiation of purchase, construction and financing documentation (including IRC Section 42 financing), appearance before land use boards and registration of condominiums with State Department of Justice (Consumer Protection Division). Agent for major title insurance companies.

CLIENTS: The firm's clients represent a diverse range of industries including: healthcare, education, manufacturing, insurance, import/export, technology, communications, banking and finance, not-for-profit, pension and mutual funds, government relations, religious institutions, commercial lenders and public finance.

HEAD OFFICE

NEW HAMPSHIRE
1000 Elm Street, PO Box 3701, **Manchester**, NH 03105-3701
Tel: 603 668 0300 **Fax:** 603 627 8121
Website: www.sheehan.com

BRANCH OFFICES

MASSACHUSETTS
260 Franklin Street, **Boston**, MA 02110
Tel: 617 897 5600 **Fax:** 617 439 9363

NEW HAMPSHIRE
143 North Main Street, **Concord**, NH 03301
Tel: 603 223 2020 **Fax:** 603 224 8899

46 Centerra Parkway, **Lebanon**, NH 03766
Tel: 603 627 8140 **Fax:** 603 641 8750

CONTACTS

Corporate Finance .... Michael J Drooff
Corporate .... Alan L Reische
Healthcare .... Matthew J Lapointe
Labor .... James P Reidy
Litigation .... Peter S Cowan
Real Estate .... Susan A Manchester
Banking .... Kenneth A Viscarello

SPBG
ATTORNEYS AT LAW

CONTENTS: Corporate/M&A p.1123; Employment p.1126; Environment p.1128; Litigation: p.1130; Real Estate p.1134; Individuals' Profiles p.1137; Firm's Profiles p.1147.

How lawyers are ranked

The opinions we gather from clients — mainly from in-house lawyers but also from other purchasers of legal services — are balanced by opinions from colleagues and competitors. Together, they provide two different perspectives — an all-round view — and biased viewpoints cancel each other out.

CORPORATE/M&A

New Jersey
Leading firms (Corporate/M&A)

[1] LOWENSTEIN SANDLER PC *Roseland*

[2] DRINKER BIDDLE & REATH LLP *Florham Park*
MCCARTER & ENGLISH, LLP *Newark*
MORGAN, LEWIS & BOCKIUS LLP *Princeton*
PITNEY HARDIN LLP *Morristown*
SILLS CUMMIS EPSTEIN & GROSS PC *Newark*

[3] GIORDANO HALLERAN & CIESLA PC *Middletown*
GREENBAUM, ROWE, SMITH *Woodbridge*
NORRIS, MCLAUGHLIN & MARCUS *Bridgewater*
ORLOFF, LOWENBACH, STIFELMAN *Roseland*
RIKER DANZIG SCHERER HYLAND *Morristown*
SONNENSCHEIN NATH & ROSENTHAL *Short Hills*
WILENTZ GOLDMAN & SPITZER, PC *Woodbridge*

Leading individuals (Corporate/M&A)

[1] AIELLO John *Giordano Halleran*, Middletown
BOYAJIAN Victor *Sonnenschein Nath*, Short Hills
EHRENBERG Peter *Lowenstein Sandler*, Roseland
SORIN David *Morgan Lewis*, Princeton

[2] COHEN Steven *Morgan Lewis*, Princeton
DAVIS Alan *Greenbaum Rowe*, Woodbridge
JANIS Ronald *Pitney Hardin*, Morristown
MINION Robert *Lowenstein Sandler*, Roseland
THOMPSON Kenneth *McCarter & English*, Newark
WOVSANIKER Alan *Lowenstein Sandler*, Roseland
ZIMMERMAN Edward *Lowenstein Sandler*, Roseland

[3] CASEY Warren *Pitney Hardin*, Morristown
FELTON Raymond *Greenbaum Rowe*, Woodbridge
GROSS STEVEN *Sills Cummis*, Newark
GUARIGLIA Michael *McCarter & English*, Newark
HUTCHEON Peter *Norris McLaughlin*, Bridgewater
KNEE Stephen *Greenbaum Rowe*, Roseland
KORNSTEIN Alan *Orloff Lowenbach*, Roseland
LAVEY Stewart *Drinker Biddle*, Florham Park
STAMELMAN Andrew *Riker Danzig*, Morristown
STODDARD III John *Drinker Biddle*, Princeton

Firms and individuals are listed alphabetically in each band.

Band 1

Lowenstein Sandler PC
See firm details p.1150
The Firm: Respected throughout New Jersey and beyond, the corporate department at this full-service firm has strengthened its hold on the market. Clients and peers recommend "*without hesitation*" the army of high-quality attorneys the firm has raised. In the past year the group has been heavily engaged in securities issuance, venture capital work, restructuring and M&A. Peers agree that the firm is one of the "*biggest and best*" in being able to provide a full corporate service to clients on a national basis. For example, it acted for ITXC in its sale to Teleglobe, and Lucent Technologies in its acquisition of Telica. Both these transactions highlight the challenge posed by Lowenstein to the traditional bastion of New York City law firms, as well as the appeal the firm has in attracting technology clients in a more cautious economic climate. In the words of one client, the firm has "*some of the hardest working, smartest lawyers I know of*," and "*they are the only firm I have worked with that actually kept me on schedule (as opposed to the other way around)*." This element of reliability seems destined to keep the firm highly attractive for future clients.
The Lawyers: Peter Ehrenberg (see p.1139) has attracted universal praise for his expertise in corporate law and his sheer dedication to the practice. Chair of the corporate department, he was a main figure in the Lucent and ITXC transactions, and has advised on several PIPE agreements. He is a "*deal junkie*," and impressed peers say "*his demeanor is toward getting things done*." Clients say they would "*hire him in a second*," as he is "*one of the hardest working and brightest lawyers around*." Alan Wovsaniker (see p.1146) impresses clients with the depth and breadth of his corporate experience and the "*high standards*" of his work. His practice encompasses securities issues as well as restructuring and banking and finance. The ascent of **Edward**

Zimmerman's (see p.1146) practice continues to attract attention, and he is firmly established as a prime mover in New Jersey's venture capital community. Clients find him "*outstanding on high-level deal work*" as his practice expands from its original hi-tech base – although he has also consolidated his hi-tech practice with his appointment to the board of the New Jersey Technology Council. **Bobby Minion** (see p.1143) enters the table for his experience and national profile in investment management. Encompassing major M&A work that challenges practitioners in New York for size and depth, his client base is extensive.
The Clients: Lucent Technologies; Cerberus Capital Management; CD&L; dynamicsoft; Inter-Atlantic Group and St Joseph's Medical Center.

Band 2

Drinker Biddle & Reath LLP
See firm details p.1549
The Firm: The Florham Park and Princeton offices at this firm can draw upon the full expertise of approximately 60 corporate attorneys spread across several states. Peers assert that the firm has a "*strong presence*" in New Jersey and beyond and this view is backed up by the extensive range of transactions it has been involved in. The practice has busied itself on acquisitions and dispositions for clients such as Chubb Group and BISYS Group, and the New Jersey team frequently joins forces with the Philadelphia headquarters on large multistate transactions. From M&A to corporate governance, emerging growth to securities, this practice provides the full range of transactional advice to clients.
The Lawyers: Stewart Lavey (see p.1142) is celebrated in the market as a very experienced corporate deal-doer. With a good grasp of the regional M&A market, he has also been busy with the growth of post-Enron corporate governance advice. **John Stoddard** (see p.1145) shines brightest in the emerging-growth field,

and his profile is particularly high in New Jersey's hi-tech and biotech industries, where he has extensive IPO experience.

The Clients: The firm's corporate clients include BISYS Group, Selective Insurance Group and Chubb Group.

McCarter & English, LLP

See firm details p.1152

The Firm: Sources agree that this firm is one of the "*distinguished*" practices in New Jersey, and that it has maintained its strength as a regional heavyweight. Via a network of East Coast offices, the firm excels in securities and finance issues for corporate clients in a variety of industry sectors, from financial services to manufacturing. Over the past year, the firm has strengthened its reputation as "*one of the top corporate firms*" for banks and financial services companies through its involvement in the $680 million consolidation of United National Bancorp and PNC Financial Services Group, one of the largest New Jersey transactions of its kind that year.

The Lawyers: The recommendations for **Ken Thompson** (see p.1146) as a "*deal-oriented*" lawyer fit in with his reputation as a determined and experienced transactional lawyer. Noted for his expertise in M&A and corporate finance (he "*absolutely will get the deal done,*" according to impressed peers), he is also sought after for his in-depth corporate governance advice. **Michael Guariglia** (see p.1140) is lauded for his tax expertise, both at the local and federal level. Working in conjunction with the other corporate lawyers he assists on strategic tax planning and the tax consequences of M&A and restructurings. He also serves as an adjunct professor at Rutgers School of Law.

Morgan, Lewis & Bockius LLP

See firm details p.1556

The Firm: The Princeton office of this international firm has continued to drive ahead by focusing on its core strengths in the New Jersey emerging growth field. Devoting considerable resources to the hi-tech and life sciences industries, the firm adapts with the New Jersey market to changes in these lucrative, if volatile, markets. "*A firm with more than enough depth,*" according to clients, it has benefited from notable lateral hires. It can also draw on the resources of offices across the USA and overseas for transactions with a cross-border element.

The Lawyers: The arrival of **David Sorin** (see p.1145) from Wilmer Cutler Pickering Hale and Dorr has ensured the firm greater prominence in the venture capital market. Peers say he "*laid a great foundation for his career*" in the emerging markets and his specialist expertise has won him a loyal client following. **Steve Cohen** (see p.1138) is the firm's life sciences expert, and he has built a sterling reputation in emerging growth work. Also noted in hi-tech matters, he

has strong New Jersey and Philadelphia contacts in the technology venture capital arena, and loyal clients proclaim him the "*right partner for any type of deal.*"

The Clients: Adolor; Aventis; Barrier Therapeutics; Bio-Imaging; FT Ventures; Schering-Plough; US Maintenance and Voxware.

Pitney Hardin LLP

See firm details p.1153

The Firm: The transactional lawyers at this firm are praised for their "*sophisticated*" approach to the deal table, with peers agreeing that the practice is "*a real player and primarily counsel for Fortune 500 clients.*" In addition to transactional work, the firm also boasts a focused financial services practice, with an extensive client base that features a number of international financial institutions. The economic climate in conjunction with the firm's sterling reputation has meant that the bankruptcy and loan workout practitioners have also been kept busy by a stream of regional work, including the acquisition and disposition of distressed assets.

The Lawyers: **Ronald Janis** (see p.1141) has been gaining increasing prominence in the market as a top-flight deal lawyer. He is a "*very effective and tough negotiator,*" according to peers, and he has been singled out in acknowledgment of his excellent transactional and securities work for banking clients. **Warren Casey** (see p.1137) serves as general counsel to a wide variety of corporate clients. "*Excellent corporate counsel,*" according to peers, the breadth of his client base establishes him as a very respected practitioner. The firm also fields Peter Forgosh, whose practice focuses on financial services and bankruptcy. His client base includes major banks and other creditors.

The Clients: Bank of America, JPMorgan Chase; Ford Motor Credit Company; Talbots; Hudson United Bank; Wyeth; Agfa Film and Linens 'n Things.

Sills Cummis Epstein & Gross PC

The Firm: An extensive range of commentators see this full-service practice as "*large and sophisticated and one of the most respected in the market.*" In recent years the firm has ridden the wave of the emerging growth industries and the corporate department now boasts over 40 attorneys. Sources endorsed the group's skill and business focus in general M&A, as well as in venture capital, bankruptcy and corporate governance. Featuring industry-focused practice groups such as life sciences and healthcare and hospitals, the firm's mature capabilities serve a variety of private and public clients, often in multistate or cross-border transactions.

The Lawyers: Since the departure of noted venture capital and private equity specialist, Victor Boyajian, the market has sought for a comparably distinctive figure at the firm. The one

name that is prominent is that of the firm's managing partner, **Steven Gross**. He is noted for his loan structuring work, but is also a player in securities transactions and corporate governance advice.

The Clients: The firm counsels and acts for a range of public and private corporate clients, encompassing traditional industries as well as hi-tech and pharmaceuticals.

Band 3

Giordano Halleran & Ciesla PC

The Firm: Increasing in market profile, the corporate and securities department at this firm has attracted praise from clients, who have been more than satisfied by the "*reputation, expertise and understanding*" provided by these attorneys. Long-standing relationships with good, accessible partner contact make this firm a stalwart for a range of corporate and finance issues including securities and loan agreements. Peers also describe the firm as a good port of call for referrals.

The Lawyers: **John Aiello** impresses many with his "*vast knowledge,*" while his "*loyalty and sound judgment*" stand him in good stead with clients. Aiello formed the corporate & securities department of the firm some quarter of a century ago, and the success of the department has been intrinsically tied to his ongoing commitment to the market.

The Clients: The firm acts for a range of clients in mid-level M&A and finance transactions. It represented a privately held professional services company in a leveraged recapitalization transaction involving over $50 million and complex concerns over fiduciary responsibilities. The firm also acts for banks, supermarket operators, consumer products companies and public companies based in New Jersey.

Greenbaum, Rowe, Smith & Davis LLP

See firm details p.1148

The Firm: From its Woodbridge and Roseland offices, this "*meaningful, well-regarded*" firm has been busy on a variety of corporate issues for a client base that consists of a good cross-section of the New Jersey business community. The client base ranges from family-owned companies to New York Stock Exchange-listed entities, as well as national companies headquartered in or with significant operations in New Jersey. Highlights have included a partner buyout for a surgical orthopaedic practice, and the negotiation and financing of a joint venture relating to the sale of part of a 40-story building in Jersey City. The firm's proven strength in real estate is beyond question, and the healthy market in New Jersey keeps the corporate department busy. "*Professional, positive and communicative,*" the team is seen by clients as easy to work with and proficient in combining legal and business skills. The team is widely regarded for its responsive and accessible service and this has resulted in a loyal client base, for instance, in the retail sector.

The Lawyers: Alan Davis (see p.1138) chairs the firm's corporate department with poise and authority. He oversees the direction of the corporate work, achieving a balanced and steady flow of mandates from small to medium enterprises, as well as significant joint venture and tax issues arising out of the real estate sector. Long-standing clients agree that he is *"conscientious and efficient,"* and peers see him as one of the community's stalwart leading practitioners and appreciate his strategic approach tremendously. Chairing the technology practice group, **Raymond Felton** (see p.1139) is the firm's linchpin for New Jersey's lucrative hi-tech market. Counseling both emerging and mature companies, Felton also has an in-depth securities practice beyond the hi-tech arena, acting for issuers and underwriters. Clients describe him as *"the partner who is not afraid of the heavy lifting,"* and peers concur that *"he is fantastically hard-working."* Recently arrived from Saiber Schlesinger Satz & Goldstein, **Stephen Knee** (see p.1142) has brought with him an impressive expertise as *"a terrific M&A lawyer – very knowledgeable."* He is an established figure for his work in M&A, financial services, and securities and professional liability litigation.

The Clients: Russell-Stanley; Pharmagistics; A.P. Deauville; Tropical Cheese Industries; Oriental Aromatics; Russell Reid; Kalian Company and iTouchpoint Technologies.

Norris, McLaughlin & Marcus, PA, A Professional Corporation

The Firm: Having secured a *"fine reputation through its good people,"* this practice provides a full transactional service for clients. Aside from traditional M&A and corporate governance, the dedicated team of almost 20 lawyers is well equipped to assist clients on any issues, from related tax concerns to environmental liabilities. This flexibility is appreciated by market sources and helps the firm fight off bigger rivals for day-to-day work beyond individual, one-off transactions.

The Lawyers: Enjoying a good reputation among peers, **Peter Hutcheon** has extensive experience in corporate and business law. He has also been active in advising on legislative reform and has been prominent in the securities arena.

The Clients: The firm's clients range from startup businesses to Fortune 500 companies with operations in many states and overseas.

Orloff, Lowenbach, Stifelman & Siegel

The Firm: This Roseland practice has captured the respect of other practitioners who view it as a *"strong middle market tax and corporate boutique."* The firm uses its smaller size to its advantage by providing clients with attorney continuity and a personalized approach. Peers agree that the firm is sophisticated in its business law approach, yet it provides a breadth of service to its clients. The caseload comprises traditional corporate fields, from M&A to corporate governance, while also encompassing ancillary issues such as employee contracts and stock options.

The Lawyers: The market continues to praise **Alan Kornstein** for his tax strength. Practitioners agree that he is of a high caliber in his field. The eponymous Ralph Lowenbach is also a main contact.

Riker Danzig Scherer Hyland & Perretti LLP
See firm details p.1154

The Firm: Making headway in the market, the corporate department at this full-service firm has worked hard to match the profile held by the firm's litigators. Peers agree that the firm has a fine corporate practice, which has honed itself over the years. With the growing prominence of its New York office, the firm is also moving to gain a greater foothold in the New York spillover market. Recent highlights have included advising a Fortune 100 company on the development of a transportation subsidiary, as well as acting as lead counsel on midmarket private equity-backed LBOs in New Jersey. Clients say *"the cost is perfect, and the size is fine too,"* and the practice is capturing a growing segment of the New Jersey market, as well as attracting international mandates.

The Lawyers: The head of Riker's tax and corporate group, **Andrew Stamelman** (see p.1145), coordinates this forward-facing group. Looking for the sweet spot of providing market-leading services at New Jersey rates, his team is praised as *"business-oriented,"* and clients also say *"there is no question: the lawyers we used had extensive expertise."*

The Clients: With a large core of privately held clients, the firm also possesses Fortune 250 public clients in a variety of industries, as well as clients based overseas. The firm acts for: Aeon; Ahold; Ecko Complex; Porky Products; PSE&G; Sumitomo Pharmaceuticals America; ZenithOptimedia; Tibbett & Britten Group Americas and Carbone Lorraine North America.

Sonnenschein Nath & Rosenthal
See firm details p.779

The Firm: This national firm made moves into the New Jersey market by acquiring one of the state's most highly regarded and dynamic corporate lawyers, Victor Boyajian. The emerging growth company group focuses on New Jersey's ever developing startup market, and impresses sources as a hungry team striving for growth itself. Clients say they are *"particularly impressed by the reputation and expertise"* of both the firm network as a whole, as well as the core practitioners. The position of the New Jersey office capitalizes on the outsourcing of New York work beyond the Wall Street firms, where clients still want to see a familiar brand and expect uniform quality. The firm acted for leading global bath products manufacturer, Jacuzzi, in sales of its water systems and pool equipment businesses. Attorneys also assisted in the $360 million sale of medical devices company Spinecore to Stryker Corporation.

The Lawyers: With the arrival of **Victor Boyajian**, (see p.1137) the firm can rely on a practitioner who is fêted across the state as a leader in the emerging growth market. His experience and foresight is valued by clients, who say *"he understands how we think,"* while peers say his practice is notable not just in New Jersey but also on the West Coast.

The Clients: The firm has recently acted for: Jacuzzi Brands, Spinecore, Teldata Control and many other companies, both emerging growth and more established companies, as well as New York investment banks and private equity firms.

Wilentz Goldman & Spitzer, PC

The Firm: Providing responsiveness and reliability, this firm is lauded by clients as *"a practice of high caliber."* The corporate group's main office is in Woodbridge with another supporting office in Eatontown, as well as two offices outside of New Jersey. Such geographic spread and the ability to call on over 100 attorneys has helped the firm establish its prominence in the market. The firm advises on corporate matters from everyday business law advice to M&A.

The Lawyers: The firm fields over a dozen partners and associates in corporate law. Michael Schaff chairs the department, and Stuart Hoberman is a further key contact.

The Clients: The group acts for a variety of clients, mainly on the East Coast. Sectors served include healthcare and technology, as well as many traditional industries.

EMPLOYMENT

MAINLY DEFENDANT

New Jersey
Leading firms
(Employment: Mainly Defendant)

[1] MCELROY, DEUTSCH, MULVANEY *Newark*
   OGLETREE, DEAKINS, NASH, SMOAK *Morristown*

[2] BALLARD SPAHR ANDREWS *Voorhees*
   GROTTA, GLASSMAN & HOFFMAN *Roseland*
   LUM, DANZIS, DRASCO & POSITAN *Roseland*
   PITNEY HARDIN LLP *Morristown*
   PROSKAUER ROSE *Newark*

[3] COLLIER, JACOB & MILLS *Somerset*
   GENOVA, BURNS & VERNOIA *Livingston*
   KIRKPATRICK & LOCKHART NICHOLSON *Newark*
   LOWENSTEIN SANDLER PC *Roseland*
   MCCARTER & ENGLISH LLP *Newark*
   RIKER DANZIG SCHERER HYLAND *Morristown*
   SILLS CUMMIS EPSTEIN & GROSS PC *Newark*

Leading individuals
(Employment: Mainly Defendant)

[1] ALITO Rosemary *Kirkpatrick & Lockhart*, Newark
   CARMAGNOLA Domenick *Lum Danzis*, Roseland
   DEE Francis *McElroy Deutsch*, Newark
   JACOB Cynthia *Collier Jacob*, Somerset
   POSITAN Wayne *Lum Danzis*, Roseland
   STANTON Patrick *Ogletree Deakins*, Morristown
   SUFLAS Steven *Ballard Spahr*, Voorhees

[2] FUREY Michael *Riker Danzig*, Morristown
   GARLAND David *Sills Cummis*, Newark
   GENOVA Angelo *Genova Burns*, Livingston
   KEYSER Denise *Ballard Spahr*, Voorhees
   MARIANI Richard *Ogletree Deakins*, Morristown
   PARLIMAN Gregory *Pitney Hardin*, Morristown
   RIDLEY John *Drinker Biddle*, Florham Park

[3] GOLDSTEIN Marvin *Proskauer Rose*, Newark
   OHNEGIAN Scott *Riker Danzig*, Morristown
   PEIRANO John *McElroy Deutsch*, Morristown
   SANDAK Lawrence *Proskauer Rose*, Newark
   SNEIRSON Marilyn *Kirkpatrick & Lockhart*, Newark

Up-and-coming individuals
   CERASIA Edward *Proskauer Rose*, Newark

Firms and individuals are listed alphabetically in each band.

Band 1

McElroy, Deutsch, Mulvaney & Carpenter, LLP

The Firm: The market sat up and took notice in May 2004 when Carpenter, Bennett & Morrissey, one of New Jersey's oldest law firms, joined forces with the fast-growing firm of McElroy, Deutsch & Mulvaney. One of New Jersey's most highly respected employment and labor firms, it has chosen to consolidate its strengths through high-profile mergers. Tracking the results, market sources agree that the firm remains a "*strong player packed with top-flight lawyers.*" Furthermore, the firm has not rested on its laurels, and in October 2004 it announced a merger with Morristown firm, Del Mauro, DiGiaimo & Knepper to add a further expertise in ERISA litigation. Through all these changes peers still distinguish the core strengths of this deep and long-standing firm – making it a practice they "*would be happy to refer work to.*" Employment discrimination claims, wage and hour issues and union-related work are all found on this group's agenda.

The Lawyers: Frank Dee is "*the best,*" according to peers. He has extensive experience in the labor field, having been a trial attorney for the NLRB. Currently, he is handling nationwide cases and class actions before the Court of Appeals and the New Jersey Supreme Court, as well as OSHA-related cases. A highly experienced trial lawyer, he continues to be a prized leader in negotiating labor agreements. Commentators also highlighted **John Peirano** as a "*very bright adviser and great courtroom performer.*" Clients see him as one of the elemental building blocks of the firm's "*great reputation.*"

The Clients: The firm has built on its impressive range of local and national clients, which include: Johnson & Johnson; Schering-Plough; Telcordia Technologies; Rutgers University and Merck.

Ogletree, Deakins, Nash, Smoak & Stewart, PC

See firm details p.638

The Firm: Since Stanton, Hughes, Diana, Mariani & Margello became part of Ogletree Deakins, one of America's largest labor and employment firms, this practice has remained in the public eye. "*Bright people – they know their stuff,*" according to peers, the 12 New Jersey lawyers have succeeded in attracting clients from a variety of industry sectors, such as construction and hotels, as well as general retail and manufacturing. The New York and Pennsylvania markets also provide ripe ground for the Ogletree practitioners to share expertise, and the firm is adept at dealing with the major employment litigation trends, such as whistle-blower claims and retaliation claims under antidiscrimination laws.

The Lawyers: Patrick Stanton (see p.1145) was made chair of the New Jersey State Bar Association's labor and employment section in May 2003, and his profile as "*the mover and shaker*" combines with acknowledgement of his "*first-rate advice.*" His "*great reputation*" is also prevalent in union negotiations and other labor law issues. **Richard Mariani** (see p.1142) is classed as one of the clear market leaders for his heavy focus on employment litigation.

The Clients: Automatic Data Processing; BAE Systems; GE; KPMG; Hewlett-Packard; Nissan Manufacturing; UnitedTrust Bancorp; Wakefern Food; Hertz; Honeywell International; Dollar Rent-A-Car Systems and New Jersey Natural Gas.

Band 2

Ballard Spahr Andrews & Ingersoll LLP

See firm details p.1541

The Firm: This excellent practice has made inroads into the New Jersey market. With the full back-up of their Philadelphia headquarters, the 12 attorneys here represent a wide variety of clients in litigation and counseling. Recently, the firm has acted on discrimination issues and accusations of wrongful discharge, as well as areas such as ERISA and wage and hour disputes. Clients include chemical manufacturers, hotels and casinos, and as a result, the practice's labor law strengths are undeniable. Clients seem especially pleased by the firm: "*I have found the work to be first rate and the responsiveness to be excellent.*"

The Lawyers: Market sources recognize **Steven Suflas** (see p.1145) for his leading role in employment litigation and his superb collective bargaining and labor practice. With notable appearances before the NLRB, peers agree that his "*significant experience*" is one of his strongest points. His forward-facing work has resulted in a string of leading clients being attracted to his ever-growing practice. **Denise Keyser** (see p.1142) is another of the firm's spearheading attorneys. She covers both employment litigation and labor issues, while also providing training for clients in all potential discrimination issues. She is also a strong force for counseling on the intricacies of ERISA and OSHA issues, and commentators agree that she is "*terrific*" in her approach and presentation.

The Clients: Sears; DuPont; Sands Casino Hotel; ConocoPhillips; Gannett Company and Mitsubishi Fuso Truck of America.

Grotta, Glassman & Hoffman

The Firm: The "*very proactive*" team is held in high esteem by satisfied clients, who note that its good lineage has produced several of the leading labor and employment lawyers that now populate the New Jersey market. "*Top of the game for traditional labor,*" according to peers, the firm maintains a good grip on this important part of the market both in New Jersey and neighboring states. The practice is involved in high-profile labor negotiations and collective bargaining, and its client base comprehensively covers service industries and manufacturing as well as many other sectors. In employment litigation the firm faces stiff competition from its market rivals, but it is praised as a "*real presence*" in discrimination claims and issues of wrongful termination. Highlights from the past 12 months include the dismissal of ERISA claims relating to liability for benefit plan withdrawal, and many successful NLRB appearances.

The Lawyers: Peers and clients see a plethora of lawyers who take a "*very practical approach*" in giving labor and employment support. Clients value the "*very relevant*" advice they receive from lawyers at all levels. The firm's managing principal, Theodore Eisenberg, is skilled in wage and hour disputes and the team can draw on the support of New York-based Craig Benson.

The Clients: The firm counsels a range of clients in industries such as manufacturing, electronics, hotels, retail chains, financial institutions, education and healthcare.

Lum, Danzis, Drasco & Positan, LLC

See firm details p.1151

The Firm: One of New Jersey's oldest practices, this is a firm with a well-established name in the market. A "*talented group of highly professional attorneys*," has netted a good market share, especially in New Jersey, where they are perceived to have useful contacts and extensive experience. The firm has litigated major noncompete issues, and the flexibility of the practice means that it is equally capable acting for companies or defending individuals in these cases. The trend towards whistle-blower claims has spurred on the firm's litigation work, but this is not at the expense of its labor law strengths.

The Lawyers: **Wayne Positan** (see p.1144) is a "*terrific lawyer*," who mixes trial experience with a deep background in union negotiations and labor issues. Peers say he is prepared to take on difficult cases. He is also a respected negotiator with a deep profile in collective bargaining. This winning formula enables him to straddle a broad range of industry sectors. **Domenick Carmagnola** (see p.1137) is a "*wonderful adviser and litigator*" both in traditional labor law and employment litigation. An emeritus editor of the NJSBA's Labor and Employment Law Quarterly publication, his mixture of knowledge and practicality helps maintain his reputation as a "*strong market leader.*"

The Clients: The firm has acted for the University of Medicine and Dentistry of New Jersey, Pepsi Bottling Group as well as a major gas distribution company and many other Fortune 500 companies.

Pitney Hardin LLP

See firm details p.1153

The Firm: In the eyes of the market, this "*classy*" practice is a force for labor and employment law. A team of 30 attorneys covers discrimination claims, collective bargaining and labor negotiations. "*They have the clients – and are talented lawyers.*" The practice has found its place in the New Jersey market, building up a wealth of "*respect over the years*," while its leading practitioners keep up with all the growing market

trends, such as whistle-blower claims, white-collar crime and sexual orientation discrimination. Attorneys are also well versed in areas such as ERISA and OSHA. A strong corporate base provides the employment and labor attorneys with a constant stream of work.

The Lawyers: An assortment of lawyers at this firm are recognized by the market, but the highest profile belongs to "*respected employment specialist,*" **Gregory Parliman** (see p.1143). His key strength is his litigation skills, and whistle-blower claims have formed a major part of his practice this year, particularly in relation to white-collar crime issues – and this ties in well with the obligations facing companies under the Sarbanes-Oxley Act.

The Clients: AT&T; Pfizer; BASF; Computer Sciences Corporation; Dassault Falcon Jet; BOC; Sony and Volvo.

Proskauer Rose

See firm details p.1365

The Firm: This practice's profile has undeniably been on the rise. From its Newark office, the firm fields 40 attorneys who work on labor, employment and employee benefits issues as well as immigration law. The firm's superb backup across these sectors pleases clients, who say its attorneys "*have come up with great results and have been extremely successful on our behalf.*" The firm is experienced not just in individual suits but also class actions facing its broad range of clients drawn from, among others, the manufacturing, retail, transport and financial services sectors. This "*personable and responsive*" practice has won the hearts of clients as well as proving itself capable of assertive market expansion.

The Lawyers: **Marvin Goldstein** (see p.1140) has been an instrumental factor in the firm's profile in New Jersey. Many major clients have followed his practice (he was a Grotta Glassman attorney several years ago), and he has been able to leverage Proskauer's national brand name for quality employment law advice. Head of the Newark office, he is respected as a "*practical*" attorney with excellent experience. With more than 20 years of experience in the sector, **Lawrence Sandak** (see p.1145) is praised for his superb control of the "*nuts and bolts of litigation.*" His trial experience, particularly in discrimination actions, is highly valued by his broad client base, which includes media corporations, financial services companies and educational institutions. "*Experienced, smart and reliable,*" he is one of the firm's key practitioners. **Edward Cerasia** (see p.1137) is an up-and-coming attorney who is an expert on employment and benefits issues, providing an "*extremely responsive*" client service.

Band 3

Collier, Jacob & Mills

The Firm: This boutique is a firm favorite of those seeking focused advice from a core of bright stalwarts. Counseling and employment litigation form the backbone of work and attorneys are also widely recognized for their arbitration and mediation expertise. Its leading lights are appropriately "*aggressive defense counsel,*" and the philosophy of the firm is to focus the energy of its experienced practitioners on to a core base of corporate clients throughout and around New Jersey. Size is less important in a practice such as this than quality, and the firm's credentials are based on its ability to serve its clients responsively and comprehensively – which it continues to do with success.

The Lawyers: **Cynthia Jacob** has received plaudits for her commitment, knowledge and ability in employment litigation. A former president of the New Jersey State Bar Association, Jacob is "*a high-quality attorney*" with a depth of experience in court. Clients concur that she is extremely intelligent and provides "*excellent results.*"

The Clients: The firm acts for Fortune 500 and medium to large companies in and around New Jersey.

Genova, Burns & Vernoia

The Firm: This practice has witnessed growth over the past year and there are now 30 employment and labor attorneys who specialize in a broad variety of issues. Sources also attested to the firm's deep public sector presence. It is particularly well known for its ability to factor in political considerations – all-important in both labor issues and employment litigation. Recently, attorneys acted for a major communications company on issues stemming from state unemployment benefit issues. Also the firm is extensively involved in labor negotiations affecting thousands of public employees.

The Lawyers: "*Highly active and reputed,*" **Angelo Genova** is the main contact for employment and labor issues. The market views him as "*a very savvy attorney,*" particularly where complex and sensitive situations are at stake. He has a client base covering public sector entities as well as prominent private sector companies.

The Clients: The firm represents clients in the public sector, including the State of New Jersey. Also the firm has represented major companies such as Time Warner.

Kirkpatrick & Lockhart Nicholson Graham LLP

See firm details p.291

The Firm: This practice is undeniably "*building up and making its mark,*" according to sources. The firm received a palpable boost with the arrival of respected employment expert

Rosemary Alito from McCarter & English. As well as very prominent corporate clients, the firm has also acted for fellow New Jersey firm, Lowenstein Sandler in a high-profile employment case. Clients say that the current mixture of attorneys provides the firm with a broad base of talents and the capacity to handle national employment issues confidently.

The Lawyers: The most notable addition to the team is **Rosemary Alito** (see p.1137). A former McCarter & English attorney, she is now one of the spearheading figures behind Kirkpatrick & Lockhart's New Jersey push. Peers respect her knowledgeable writings and courtroom skills. She is also a first port of call for advice beyond pure litigation, such as when difficult downsizing questions are at stake. **Marilyn Sneirson** (see p.1145) has worked long and hard on building up the firm's New Jersey reputation. Her practice also covers employment litigation and counseling for a diverse client base among pharmaceuticals, vehicle manufacturers and the entertainment industries. She was recently engaged to act for Lowenstein Sandler's management committee in a high-profile case.

The Clients: BMW; Goodyear; The Actors' Fund of America; ET Brown Drug Company; Allstates World Cargo and Deutsche Post Global Mail.

Lowenstein Sandler PC
See firm details p.1150

The Firm: There is "*a culture at the firm focused on delivering high-quality service,*" said market commentators. This firm has also used its excellent reputation as a top corporate law firm to attract leading clients to its employment practice. Clients who use this practice find it "*strong in each department,*" both for everyday employment litigation issues and the more complex cases. Litigation specialists are also on hand to help when further firepower is required.

The Lawyers: This firm's employment litigation profile is something of a group effort, and uniformity is part of the attraction for clients. Chair of the employment practice group, Martha Lester is also a corporate attorney, and she is very experienced in litigation and counseling.

The Clients: The firm's employment clients closely mirror the profile of the firm's corporate clients and cover a broad range of industries, including those in the Fortune 500.

McCarter & English, LLP
See firm details p.1152

The Firm: The departure of Rosemary Alito has made an impact on this well-regarded practice. However, peers can attest that the "*institutional reputation*" of the firm is strong enough for it to weather the storm. With the evolution of employment into a heavily litigation-focused practice area, the firm can capitalize on the strength of its general litigators. The firm's regional presence ensures that clients not only have access to skilled New Jersey lawyers, but also labor and employment specialists in states beyond.

The Lawyers: The practice area is covered by attorneys across disciplines, and the firm's litigation specialists are always at hand to tend to the most complex issues.

Riker Danzig Scherer Hyland & Perretti LLP
See firm details p.1154

The Firm: Clients praise this practice as "*providing a balanced commentary*" which helps guide people through the intricacies and development of employment law. As this firm is one of the premier litigation outfits in the state, backup for large-scale litigation is a major advantage here. Peers particularly rate the range of litigation specialists fielded by the firm. However, with minimal work in the labor and collective bargaining fields, this firm's focus is firmly in providing strong litigation support. Recently, whistle-blower claims have added flavor to the practice, and potential class actions have kept the firm on its collective feet.

The Lawyers: The "*outstanding*" **Michael Furey** (see p.1139) is lauded for his strong litigation experience and commercial outlook. Head of the employment group, he has litigated and advised on partnership disputes and is well versed in the defense of class actions. An "*experienced and sharp guy,*" his excellent trial skills are certainly a main attraction for clients. **Scott Ohnegian**'s (see p.1143) career has been tracked by peers and clients since his associate days, and he is clearly respected as "*the rare attorney who will give objective advice, and can express firm opinions.*" His employee manual and OSHA experience is particularly valuable to his clients.

The Clients: IBM; CIGNA; AM Best; Dow Jones; Sun Chemical; Carrier Clinic; Northeast Great Dane and Siemens Building Technologies.

Sills Cummis Epstein & Gross PC

The Firm: This firm's 20 labor and employment attorneys have had a busy year, particularly within employment discrimination litigation. Clients commend this firm's effective approach, and the fact that the partners "*do not overwork a case or staff it with unnecessary associates.*" The bulk of the firm's work is focused on the metropolitan area with some overlap with New York (where the firm's New York outpost also provides further depth). A portion of the firm's practice is in counseling, and attorneys provide a steady stream of employee handbook work and labor and union advice.

The Lawyers: **David Garland** is at the forefront of the firm's New Jersey employment presence. He is fêted by clients who profess that they are "*impressed by his good combination of employment knowledge and trial experience.*" His practice is active beyond New Jersey too, with recent cases tried in California. The all-important growth industry of retaliation actions such as whistle-blower claims has kept his practice constantly evolving. The firm also recently recruited former Associate Justice of the New Jersey Supreme Court, Peter Verniero. He has been central to some of the court's recent employment decisions.

The Clients: The firm has acted for many major corporations including Citigroup, Caesar's Entertainment and Matsushita Electrical Corporation of America.

Other Notable Practitioners

John Ridley (see p.1144) of Drinker Biddle & Reath LLP is praised by market commentators as an "*outstanding and client-savvy attorney.*" His forte is employment litigation, such as the defense of class actions and discrimination claims.

ENVIRONMENT

Band 1

Lowenstein Sandler PC
See firm details p.1150

The Firm: This major New Jersey firm has a deep history in environmental law, and observers agree that the firm is "*out there with its extensive practice and deep resources.*" Litigation on environmental issues is of major importance to this practice, and it has represented clients on a national scale. In the environmental counseling sphere, the range of work is broad and often stems from the firm's respected corporate practice. With many New Jersey transactions requiring in-depth analysis of environmental liabilities – often having a substantial effect on deal value – the market trusts this practice to get things right. And with attorneys who are perfectly able to take on work from New York City and beyond, this firm's environmental practice is set to soar. Over the years, the firm has built up a market-leading profile acting for companies such as ExxonMobil and the BOC Group.

The Lawyers: Industry experts confidently recommended **Michael Rodburg** (see p.1144) as the top environmental contact at the firm. Sharing his practice area responsibilities with his

New Jersey
Leading firms (Environment)

1 LOWENSTEIN SANDLER PC *Roseland*
 PORZIO, BROMBERG & NEWMAN *Morristown*
 RIKER DANZIG SCHERER HYLAND *Morristown*

2 BALLARD SPAHR ANDREWS *Voorhees*
 FARER FERSKO *Westfield*
 GIORDANO HALLERAN & CIESLA PC *Middletown*
 GREENBAUM, ROWE, SMITH & DAVIS *Woodbridge*
 KIRKPATRICK & LOCKHART NICHOLSON *Newark*
 MCCARTER & ENGLISH, LLP *Newark*

Leading individuals (Environment)

1 GROSS Michael *Giordano Halleran, Middletown*
 HLUCHAN Richard *Ballard Spahr, Voorhees*
 HYATT William *Kirkpatrick & Lockhart, Newark*
 KRUMHOLZ Dennis *Riker Danzig, Morristown*
 RODBURG Michael *Lowenstein Sandler, Roseland*

2 BROMBERG Lisa *Porzio Bromberg, Morristown*
 DORE Michael *Lowenstein Sandler, Roseland*
 FARER David *Farer Fersko, Westfield*
 GREENBERG Marilynn *Riker Danzig, Morristown*
 HERZBERG, Peter *Pitney Hardin, Morristown*
 HOGAN Edward *Norris McLaughlin, Bridgewater*
 MCTIERNAN Edward *Gibbons Del Deo, Newark*
 MOULTHROP Samuel *Riker Danzig, Morristown*
 TUBMAN Lloyd *Greenbaum Rowe, Woodbridge*
 WAGENBACH Jeffrey *Riker Danzig, Morristown*

Firms and individuals are listed alphabetically in each band.

position as managing director of the firm, he nevertheless attracts recognition as an "*outstanding*" practitioner and "*the big name*" for environmental law. Clients benefit from his superb litigation experience of issues ranging from Superfund to toxic torts. He is also a prolific writer and commentator on all aspects of environmental law. Environmental specialist **Michael Dore** (see p.1138) is also widely recognized. His toxic torts expertise gives him an edge in acting for clients with industrial facilities.
The Clients: The BOC Group; Georgia-Pacific; Napp Technologies; Hoechst Celanese; Exxon-Mobil and GE.

Porzio, Bromberg & Newman, A Professional Corporation

The Firm: This practice has gained a name as a firm that devotes a clear portion of its resources to top-level environmental work. Three partners and one associate form this standalone environmental practice and clients appreciate their dedication to this market. Peers agree that the practice has a "*serious approach and reputation*," and recognize that several of the leading attorneys are renowned throughout the state. Litigation, encompassing toxic torts, forms the bulk of this firm's environmental caseload, and attorneys are also called upon for advice in real estate transactions where complex environmental issues play a key role. The client base at this firm includes real estate developers and Fortune 100 companies.

The Lawyers: Lisa Bromberg steers the group and is credited with much of its success. Her workload continues to grow apace and she has cultivated has a litigation-oriented experience. But the land use and transactional backup provided by Bromberg and her team is also welcomed by clients.
The Clients: The firm's clients include real estate developers, a cosmetics company and many other manufacturers.

Riker Danzig Scherer Hyland & Perretti LLP

See firm details p.1154
The Firm: Clients have always asserted that this firm is a top litigation shop, because it fields "*first-rate*" specialist attorneys. Clients say that on the whole this practice has "*a lead in the state*" for its full-service approach and depth of resources. This "*outstanding law firm*" can handle complex permitting and land use issues as well as all the inevitable complexities of environmental litigation. Water, air and solid waste issues are all on the agenda here and practitioners are acutely aware that the State of New Jersey stands at the forefront of national environmental policy. These attorneys are equipped to handle such cutting-edge matters. Clients were also keen to impart that "*reasonable billing rates*" made the firm a cost-effective solution.
The Lawyers: Leader of the group **Dennis Krumholz** (see p.1142) is spoken of as a "*founding father*" of environmental law in the state and someone who "*really knows his stuff.*" Those who have used him say he is "*incredibly thorough,*" yet his litigation approach is practical, focused and above all effective. A former deputy attorney general at the New Jersey Department of Environmental Protection, he works on site remediation issues and toxic tort litigation. **Marilynn Greenberg** (see p.1140) is "*extremely knowledgeable and very bright,*" especially on complex brownfields issues. Her highly respected expertise is also called upon in vital transactional support, and furthermore she has a niche in mold litigation. A transactional and regulatory expert, **Jeffrey Wagenbach** (see p.1146) has just been "*excellent in dealing with the most complex issue*" reported clients. ISRA (Industrial Site Recovery Act) issues have a particular habit of catching clients unawares, and Wagenbach's support is appreciated by clients who call him a "*nationally recognized leader.*" **Samuel Moulthrop** (see p.1143) is lauded as a "*wonderful lawyer and skilled negotiator.*" He is one of the team's busiest litigators, covering issues ranging from contamination and toxic torts cases to insurance and cost recovery. A former chief of the Environmental Protection Unit at the Attorney's Office in the District of New Jersey, he has ample experience in civil litigation and environmental criminal defense.
The Clients: Bristol-Myers Squibb; First Ener-

gy; JPMorgan Chase; Lucent Technologies; Newport Associates Development Company and Wyeth.

Band 2

Ballard Spahr Andrews & Ingersoll LLP

See firm details p.1541
The Firm: This Philadelphia-headquartered firm has several high-profile attorneys who earn the respect of the market for their deep environmental expertise. The firm's caseload encompasses areas especially important for the property development market, such as brownfield redevelopments and in-depth planning and permitting. The eight specialist attorneys are also well equipped to provide a full service in other areas too, such as clean air, water and hazardous waste. The firm's base of influence covers the whole of New Jersey, with particular emphasis on the south. Attorneys display excellent familiarity with the New Jersey Department of Environmental Protection (NJDEP) as well as experience with several other bodies relevant to state environmental issues.
The Lawyers: Richard Hluchan (see p.1141) is "*a great choice for environmental advice and definitely one of the leaders,*" say sources. His excellent reputation is augmented by significant experience with the Pinelands Commission, where he was formerly a chief counsel. Many commentators were impressed by his wetlands expertise, although he is also busy on other land use and development issues and combines his environmental practice with his real estate work.

Farer Fersko

The Firm: This boutique garners great praise for its expertise in environmental law and related real estate matters. "*Excellent breadth of knowledge,*" say commentators who note that the interface between real estate and environment law is where this firm shows its mettle. This is particularly important in a state that is at the forefront for environmental land use issues; and it takes a forward-thinking firm to make an impact such as Farer Fersko has. Commentators gave praise to the firm's attorneys, who are "*prolific advisers and writers,*" able to give fresh comment on environmental issues. This translates into practical advice, for example, via the publication of a comprehensive ISRA manual. The firm has also branched out to cover clean air and water issues, as well as federal environmental law.
The Lawyers: "*One of the best environmental lawyers I've worked with,*" according to one client, **David Farer** (see p.1139) impresses with his sound advisory work. Although he is less visible on litigation, it is hard to ignore his influence on the sector. He is active in continuing legal education, and his writings have included a manual on ISRA and the complexities of rede-

velopment in New Jersey. Working "*hand in glove*" with him, clients happily report that he is their first port of call for complex matters.

The Clients: The firm's real estate clients also seek environmental advice from the firm. Clients include: K Hovnanian and Pulte Homes.

Giordano Halleran & Ciesla PC

The Firm: This full-service firm deploys significant resources to provide advice across a variety of environmental issues. Much of the firm's experience relates to the real estate sector, although that is not to say that the practice has limitations. Far from it, hard regulatory and wetlands issues are amply covered by this practice too. The firm serves as general counsel to the New Jersey Builders Association, and its leading attorneys also have a busy court schedule. Recently they secured a victory at the New Jersey Supreme Court, invalidating two rules adopted by the NJDEP.

The Lawyers: "*The environmental guy,*" **Michael Gross** is an influential lawyer with a long track record in this sector. A registered lobbyist, he was previously a deputy attorney general and has NJDEP experience. Peers are happy to report that they "*have and would refer work to him,*" as they can trust his fantastic sense of judgment. As well as showing expertise in general environmental issues related to real estate, he is also one of the foremost advisers on wetlands law.

The Clients: New Jersey Builders Association; Wesley Lake Associates; Paramount Properties; K Hovnanian and the New Jersey Shore Builders Association.

Greenbaum, Rowe, Smith & Davis LLP

See firm details p.1148

The Firm: Recognized as a standout firm for real estate, it was perhaps more than inevitable that this leading practice would also field significant environmental expertise. What is most impressive is that the firm not only pleases its existing core real estate client base but also attracts a wider set of clients. With a broad expertise, ranging from ISRA to wetlands, this practice has dedicated specialist resources in the field and has excellent integration with the real estate department.

The Lawyers: Mixing environmental law with real estate savvy, **Lloyd Tubman** (see p.1146) works closely with the zoning and land use experts at the firm. She is "*very talented and has excellent NJDEP contacts,*" according to interviewees. As well as having a very active practice on zoning applications, she is also an expert on environmental compliance, wetlands and water quality.

The Clients: The firm's environment clients overlap with its real estate clients. As such, the firm acts for a broad range of real estate developers.

Kirkpatrick & Lockhart Nicholson Graham LLP

See firm details p.291

The Firm: As one of the more litigation-oriented environmental groups, this firm has secured its prominence through a sterling Superfund practice. This practice retains its top-line reputation by focusing on the complex issues that require in-depth analysis. The firm fields 16 attorneys, who tend to matters all over the East Coast, while the "*respected environmental litigation*" profile of this practice continues to go from strength to strength.

The Lawyers: "*The first one to go to for environmental litigation,*" **William Hyatt** (see p.1141) is one of the grand masters of this highly involved Superfund discipline. He has followed Superfund through all its trends and developments, and advises on regulatory issues and litigation, including natural resources damages and toxic torts.

The Clients: The firm's clients include major manufacturers in the chemicals industry and mining companies.

McCarter & English, LLP

See firm details p.1152

The Firm: In combination with the Connecticut office, this group provides a broad transactional support and litigation service to its clients. New Jersey has always been at the forefront of cutting-edge environmental issues, and this firm can pool its assets whenever significant challenges are faced. Its caseload includes Superfund and natural resources damages, a field in which the cream of this firm's environmental litigators can show their strength.

The Lawyers: In New Jersey, Lanny Kurzweil guides the practice. An experienced litigator at state and federal level, he is very active on cost recovery and Superfund, with spills and contamination being a prominent feature of his practice.

Other Notable Practitioners

Peter Herzberg (see p.1141) of Pitney Hardin LLP is a former deputy attorney general and peers respect his broad practice. Site remediation features highly on his workload, and his land use practice goes from strength to strength. The "*learned and detail-oriented*" **Edward Hogan** of Norris, McLaughlin & Marcus, garners the "*high opinion*" of the market for his transactional and regulatory expertise. He is widely regarded for his state-specific advice such as ISRA. **Edward McTiernan** (see p.1142) of Gibbons, Del Deo, Dolan, Griffinger & Vecchione attracted high praise from peers, who are "*thrilled to see him on the other side of the deal.*" He is particularly notable in counseling owners of industrial sites and facilities on issues such as ISRA obligations.

LITIGATION

GENERAL COMMERCIAL

Band 1

Drinker Biddle & Reath LLP

See firm details p.1549

The Firm: "*A top-flight litigation firm,*" according to the market commentators. This practice has secured a name as a most accomplished litigation practice, not just in terms of trial strength but also pretrial litigation and negotiation. There is a deep vein of expertise running right through the firm: "*I see them as a terrific firm for any type of dispute – they are talented at all levels.*" Alongside its experience in general commercial contract disputes, the group has excellent insurance coverage litigation strength. It has also been highly prominent on national mass tort claims litigation involving thousands of claimants. In this regard the attorneys have displayed the necessary sensitive and thoughtful approach, and the market praises this firm for its effectiveness in complex issues.

The Lawyers: The "*top-notch*" **Thomas Campion** (see p.1137) adopts an exceptionally thorough approach to litigation. The co-head of the professional liability claims and senior member of the products liability practice groups, he has a deep trial expertise and is also a skilled settlement negotiator.

The Clients: The firm acts for a broad range of clients, including Pfizer, Merck and Johnson & Johnson.

Lowenstein Sandler PC

See firm details p.1150

The Firm: Clients praise this firm for providing "*very strong dispute resolution in each department.*" What this translates into is a practice that can assure clients of its broad reach and deep resources. Already a favorite in the state for its top-line corporate practice, the firm can also call on some of the market's leading litigators. Commercial litigation and corporate securities dis-

1130   All quotes in the text are from interviews with clients and competitors.

CHAMBERS USA 2005

New Jersey
Leading firms
(Litigation: General Commercial)

[1] DRINKER BIDDLE & REATH LLP *Florham Park*
LOWENSTEIN SANDLER PC *Roseland*
MCCARTER & ENGLISH, LLP *Newark*
RIKER DANZIG SCHERER HYLAND *Morristown*

[2] GIBBONS, DEL DEO, DOLAN, GRIFFINGER *Newark*
PITNEY HARDIN LLP *Morristown*

[3] GREENBAUM, ROWE, SMITH & DAVIS *Woodbridge*
LATHAM & WATKINS LLP *Newark*
MCELROY, DEUTSCH, MULVANEY *Morristown*
ORLOFF, LOWENBACH, STIFELMAN *Roseland*
SILLS CUMMIS EPSTEIN & GROSS PC *Newark*

Leading individuals
(Litigation: General Commercial)

Senior Statesman
GIBBONS John *Gibbons Del Deo*, Newark

[1] BERRY Andrew *McCarter & English*, Newark
CAMPION Thomas *Drinker Biddle*, Florham Park
GRIFFINGER Mike *Gibbons Del Deo*, Newark
HARRIS David *Lowenstein Sandler*, Roseland
ORLOFF Laurence *Orloff Lowenbach*, Roseland
ROLNICK Lawrence *Lowenstein Sandler*, Roseland
ROWE Paul *Greenbaum Rowe*, Woodbridge

[2] CLARK Glenn *Riker Danzig*, Morristown
GOLDSTEIN Bruce *Saiber Schlesinger*, Newark
KRAUS Alan *Latham & Watkins*, Newark
LILOIA Gerald *Riker Danzig*, Morristown
REILLY Gregory *Lowenstein Sandler*, Roseland

[3] DEUTSCH Edward *McElroy Deutsch*, Newark
DRASCO Dennis *Lum Danzis*, Roseland
EAKELEY Douglas *Lowenstein Sandler*, Roseland
MARCHETTA Anthony *Pitney Hardin*, Morristown
PATTERSON Anne *Riker Danzig*, Morristown
ROTHSCHILD Gita *McCarter & English*, Newark
VAN DEVENTER Kenneth *Riker Danzig*, Morristown

Firms and individuals are listed alphabetically in each band.

putes are areas of strength, and ones in which the firm is securing something of a national profile. For example, attorneys recently acted for the plaintiffs in claims arising out of the Adelphia Communications securities scandal. The firm is also acting for Dr Leo Kirch of Kirch Group in a multibillion-dollar action against Deutche Bank and Liberty Media.

The Lawyers: Clients are "*absolutely impressed*" by the service and ability of **David Harris** (see p.1140). Chair of the litigation department, he shines as an attorney with technical skills "*second to none*," which are also accompanied by the all-important "*street smarts*," say clients. He comes into the frame for complex commercial litigation, and he has a particularly well-developed IP ability. **Lawrence Rolnick** (see p.1144) is a securities litigation expert who is renowned nationally for his work in some of the largest securities cases of recent years. An "*outstanding and creative*" litigator, he possesses the ability to

"*think outside of the box.*" He is acting for Dr Leo Kirch in allegations that Deutsche Bank and Liberty Media conspired to dismantle Kirch's media group. **Gregory Reilly** (see p.1144) is recommended for his excellent range of skills. New Jersey's prominent universities form a key feature of his practice – with clients of the caliber of Rutgers University – as well as working with leading financial institutions. Sources described him as "*knowledgeable, ethical and very smart.*" **Douglas Eakeley** (see p.1138) is a talented litigator, who has experience in a broad spectrum of commercial issues as well as appellate level cases. His recent highlights have included acting for financial institutions and universities. In the white-collar crime sphere, the firm scored a coup in recruiting **Michael Himmel** (see p.1141) from Greenbaum, Rowe, Smith & Davis. "*One of the best,*" according to his peers, he is not only a skilled trial lawyer, but also a "*good behind-the-scenes worker.*" He has advised corporate officials in white-collar crime issues, including a CEO at a major bank. Also praised for his white-collar crime expertise is **Robert Kipnees** (see p.1142). He has experience with the US attorney's office, where he assisted on special prosecutions alleging political corruption. Much of his practice focuses on disputes arising out of the banking and financial services sector.

The Clients: The firm's clients include: Rutgers University; Kirch Media; WR Huff Asset Management; Appaloosa Management and ITXC.

McCarter & English, LLP
See firm details p.1152

The Firm: This practice has growing presence on the East Coast, particularly for its expertise in products liability. The group also enjoys a strong profile in insurance coverage cases and financial institutions litigation. According to sources: "*The firm fields some great litigators,*" who have recently been engaged in major pharmaceuticals cases. The leading lawyers at the firm boast very fine reputations for their smooth handling of commercial disputes, for instance in international arbitration, and overall the group is the model of a well-balanced and thriving practice.

The Lawyers: With an "*excellent products liability reputation,*" **Andrew Berry** (see p.1137) is guiding the firm in his role as chairman of the executive committee. He is credited with the group's strategic and sensible growth, and continues to be a popular choice for insurance litigation and products liability claims. Berry also makes regular appearances in important international arbitration. **William Heller** (see p.1140) has been singled out by sources as a key contact for IP issues. His "*first rate*" practice covers both transactional IP as well as contentious issues, and he heads a team of more than 30 attorneys dedicated to the field. His team has

secured a good profile for hi-tech-related issues and trademarks matters. **Gita Rothschild** (see p.1144) has attracted "*a high level of respect and trust*" for her growing commercial practice. A heavy-hitting trial lawyer, she has been on the ground on some of the market's major products liability cases. Peers endorse her as a flexible and knowledgeable general commercial litigator.

The Clients: The firm acts for a broad range of clients including pharmaceuticals companies and manufacturers.

Riker Danzig Scherer Hyland & Perretti LLP
See firm details p.1154

The Firm: Featuring some of the most active litigators in the state, clients endorsed the powerful technical skills of these litigators and their "*innovative thinking.*" The "*savvy fighters*" of the practice are, in the opinions of clients, a serious asset in the courtroom. Recently, the practice has litigated partnership breakup issues, securities fraud, IP and real estate disputes. Attorneys are acting for Reliance Electric in defending against a class action in relation to product stickers. A series of large reinsurance coverage actions at the state and federal level have also kept this practice busy.

The Lawyers: **Gerald Liloia** (see p.1142) is an imposing figure: a "*focused*" litigator, who "*understands business*" and is creative in his strategies. Litigation for banks and corporate governance issues have featured highly in his practice, and he is also a prominent reinsurance arbitrator. With his wealth of experience, it is no wonder that clients "*trust his judgment.*" **Glenn Clark** (see p.1138) is described as "*the touchstone of quality*" by clients. An experienced litigator, he has been successful in partnership disputes and claims of breach of fiduciary duty, and he is also heavily involved in significant employment and trade secrets cases. The "*outstanding*" **Anne Patterson** (see p.1143) has attracted a substantial caseload in products liability, representing more than a dozen pharmaceutical companies. **Kenneth van Deventer** (see p.1146) is respected as a highly capable attorney, who is best known for handling difficult cases. Clients say: "*He doesn't let ego or emotion get in the way, and he is very, very effective.*" **Robert Schoenberg** (see p.1145) is one of the firm's IP experts. His practice covers both the transactional side as well as complex patent litigation. Clients spoke of his credentials and his understanding of their business, based in part on his engineering degree.

The Clients: The firm's clients include: Reliance Electric; Conectiv; AT&T; Bank of America; CIGNA; Hertz; Lucent Technologies; Johnson & Johnson; Merrill Lynch; Prudential; Schering-Plough and UBS.

Band 2

Gibbons, Del Deo, Dolan, Griffinger & Vecchione

See firm details p.1147

The Firm: This practice houses some of the state's most highly regarded attorneys, and is built on a deep reputation of never shying away from challenging litigation. One of the main partners, John Gibbons, has been extremely prominent in a case challenging the extra-judicial detention of inmates at the Guantanamo Bay naval base. Beyond these important issues, the firm is also well equipped to handle toxic torts litigation, including asbestos cases with bankruptcy complications, corporate governance issues, and major contract disputes. Sources described the attorneys as "*strong litigators, not flashy in court*" and praised their handling of large, complex disputes. A "*worthy adversary*" with expertise in a broad range of areas, the practice encompasses all forms of dispute resolutions from trial to arbitration.

The Lawyers: The market was absolutely certain of the continuing prominence of **John Gibbons** (see p.1139), a senior figure in the market. He is a former chief judge of the Third Circuit Court of Appeals; "*a talented and hugely respected attorney*," who takes on some of the most prominent and important cases, such as challenging the Guantanamo Bay detentions. **Mike Griffinger** (see p.1140) is "*just a terrific lawyer.*" Peers praise him for his ability to "*try cases rather than just push paper*," making him a real force in the courtroom. Strong on contract disputes and also IP issues, he has been involved in a case involving the ouster of the CEO and chairman of a very large private company. "*A great name for white-collar crime litigation,*" **Lawrence Lustberg** (see p.1142) has attracted close attention for his excellent breadth of practice and strong technical understanding. He chairs the firm's white-collar crime defense department and is also prominent for his pro bono work on constitutional issues.

The Clients: The firm's clients include Sanofi-Synthelabo, LandAmerica and Deloitte & Touche.

Pitney Hardin LLP

See firm details p.1153

The Firm: Alongside the group's broad experience of commercial disputes, "*they produce a lot of value in terms of creativity and responsiveness,*" said clients. Asbestos litigation and insurance claims have remained key strengths of this practice, which has built up a reputation for its good trial skills and commercial outlook. In the past year, leading attorneys have been involved in class actions and complex commercial litigation for automobile manufacturers, real estate companies and hotel operators. The group is well staffed with attorneys who are experienced

across a range of disciplines, including white-collar crime, IP and employment disputes.

The Lawyers: **Anthony Marchetta** (see p.1142) is "*properly regarded as a leading light for litigation,*" reported interviewees. Well-versed in areas as diverse as trademarks and toxic torts, he is also experienced in securities litigation and has participated in appellate opinions in relation to allegations of securities fraud. **Dennis Kearney** (see p.1141) is respected for his trial skills. His practice has focused more on white-collar crime of late, and he continues to be respected as an effective civil fraud lawyer.

The Clients: The firm acts for: Coca-Cola; Hunter Douglas; Cendant; Ford; WR Grace; Alpharma and The Interpublic Group.

Band 3

Greenbaum, Rowe, Smith & Davis LLP

See firm details p.1148

The Firm: This full-service practice has impressed with its clear focus in litigation. More than half of the firm's 100-plus attorneys are litigators, and clients agree that its "*substantial resources*" are a major attraction. Although the firm has recently seen the loss of Michael Himmel's white-collar crime practice, it continues to field some of the most respected attorneys in the state. Other than complex commercial litigation for large regional and national companies, the attorneys of this firm have been engaged in IP and real estate disputes.

The Lawyers: **Paul Rowe** (see p.1145) is a first-rate litigator, whose broad practice encompasses a range of commercial issues. His superb general trial skills have been illustrated by his recent success in securing a $35 million ruling for Adele Ciasulli in Ciasulli v Ciasulli, the largest divorce award in New Jersey legal history.

The Clients: The firm acts for a broad base of clients, including Fortune 500 companies and real estate organizations.

Latham & Watkins LLP

The Firm: This international law firm committed resources to its New Jersey practice, focusing on major pieces of litigation such as toxic torts, securities fraud and consumer fraud class actions. Peers praised the group's "*classy*" leading practitioners, and envied its access to a wealth of resources, particularly from the New York office. The group is making its mark with work on class actions played out on a national canvas, such as the representation of Monsanto in Agent Orange-related litigation.

The Lawyers: A "*very able and tenacious commercial litigator,*" **Alan Kraus** has found his platform with Latham & Watkins. He is acting in major class actions in securities fraud as well as toxic torts. Peers "*hold him in high regard*" not only for his knowledge of the law, but also for

the thorough and extremely hard-working approach he takes to his cases.

The Clients: The firm acts for: Monsanto; Toshiba; Hertz; Campbell Soup and Swiss Army Brands.

McElroy, Deutsch, Mulvaney & Carpenter LLP

The Firm: This firm attracts market plaudits for its high-profile merger, which now combines respected employment abilities with deep resources in general commercial litigation. Clients endorsed the breadth of the practice and its ability to handle large disputes, while peers described its attorneys as "*formidable*" in court. The group's attorneys are experienced in litigation at all levels, right up to the US Supreme Court. Example of its areas of experience include partnership disputes, insurance claims and general commercial disputes.

The Lawyers: The eponymous **Edward Deutsch** is a "*strong adversary*" and managing partner at the firm. His deep experience is reflected in widespread commendations and the respect he has in the marketplace.

The Clients: The firm acts for many large clients, including oil companies, on national cases. The firm also acts for other law firms, motor manufacturers and pharmaceutical companies.

Orloff, Lowenbach, Stifelman & Siegel

The Firm: "*Very busy and highly competent,*" say peers of this flourishing litigation practice. The firm has made a particular name for itself in recent years in legal malpractice defense work. The talented attorneys here are also highly capable in handling general business litigation, including partnership issues and loan disputes. Whether on paper, or in the courtroom, this firm maintains a good presence in the market.

The Lawyers: A "*fine fellow and one of the deans of the Bar.*" **Laurence Orloff** has been engaged in an 11-week legal malpractice trial for one of the state's major firms. He has also been active in financial regulation issues and fiduciary duties litigation. He is "*excellent in court and on paper.*"

The Clients: The firm's clients include law firms, manufacturers, financial institutions, and individuals acting as fiduciaries or in the position of beneficiaries.

Sills Cummis Epstein & Gross PC

The Firm: This firm has consolidated its reputation as a stalwart, full-service practice. Its "*very business-savvy*" approach impresses the market, and it is seen as a player in areas as diverse as construction disputes and litigation related to bankruptcies. Clients also report that the group is "*excellent for evaluating the issues.*" Attorneys here have successfully defended a New York

1132   All quotes in the text are from interviews with clients and competitors.

CHAMBERS USA 2005

bank in an antitrust action, and acted nationally for a pharmaceutical company defending a class action. Further cases for the group relate to disputes centering on power stations and complex construction projects.

The Lawyers: Marc Friedman is a highly experienced and skilled attorney for IP and IT issues. Aside from an excellent litigation reputation, which spans federal and state courts, he is also a useful contact for transactional matters. His confident approach to the courtroom inspires clients; they say: "*His ability to soak up the sub-*

ject matter is remarkable." The litigation group is headed by Barry Epstein, who has more than 30 years of experience in civil and criminal trials and appeals.

The Clients: The firm has an impressive client base, and it has acted for international manufacturers, pharmaceutical companies and financial institutions.

Other Notable Practitioners

Bruce Goldstein of Saiber Schlesinger Satz & Goldstein LLC is "*a name which stands with the*

best," according to peers. He is skilled in a range of commercial issues such as insurance law and has represented law firms in malpractice suits. "*He is very good at recognizing the most important issues in a case,*" making him a skilled strategist. The eponymous **Dennis Drasco** (see p.1138) of Lum, Danzis, Drasco & Positan LLC is a popular figure in the legal community. Recently, he was crucial in several major construction defect cases, including one involving two 32-story buildings in Atlantic City.

LITIGATION   IP

New Jersey
Leading firms (Litigation: IP)
[1] LERNER DAVID LITTENBERG *Westfield*

Leading individuals (Litigation: IP)
[1] HELLER William *McCarter & English*, Newark
LITTENBERG Joseph *Lerner David*, Westfield
MENTLIK William *Lerner David*, Westfield
[2] FRIEDMAN Marc *Sills Cummis*, Newark
HARRIS David *Lowenstein Sandler*, Roseland
SALES Bruce *Lerner David*, Westfield
SCHOENBERG Robert *Riker Danzig*, Morristown
Firms and individuals are listed alphabetically in each band.

Band 1

Lerner David Littenberg Krumholz & Mentlik, LLP

The Firm: This firm is devoted to the IP field, and peers are happy to call them "*the only true IP competition.*" Although the group competes against accomplished IP departments at full-service firms, the devotion with which this firm has pursued this area is widely recognized. Enthusiastic clients are very happy about the level of service and expertise offered by the attorneys: "*They couldn't be better!*" An established boutique, it has a long-standing reputation and a considerable base of legal knowledge and market understanding. All facets of IP are covered, and the group displays a particular expertise for in-depth patent litigation. Clients attest to the "*excellent quality*"

work, and it is clear that for involved IP issues, this firm is very much in demand.

The Lawyers: The practice boasts many noted IP attorneys, among whom **Joseph Littenberg** has an excellent profile. Sources singled him out as one of the market's most experienced IP experts, pointing to his 30-plus years of practice and success in patents. Peers agree that he is an "*outstanding IP lawyer.*" Of a similar caliber is **William Mentlik.** A former DOJ trial attorney, he mixes trial skills with commercially focused transactional practice. Peers described him as a valued "*mentor*" in this practice area. **Bruce Sales** is "*an extremely smart lawyer,*" who impresses with his broad practice. He is active on patent, trademark and copyright issues not just in the USA, but also further afield.

LITIGATION   WHITE-COLLAR CRIME & GOVERNMENT INVESTIGATIONS

New Jersey
Leading firms (Litigation: White-Collar Crime & Government Investigations)
[1] WALDER, HAYDEN & BROGAN PA *Roseland*
[2] KROVATIN & ASSOCIATES LLC *Newark*
MICHAEL CRITCHLEY & ASSOCIATES *West Orange*

Leading individuals (Litigation: White-Collar Crime & Government Investigations)
[1] CRITCHLEY Michael *Michael Critchley*, West Orange
HAYDEN Joe *Walder Hayden*, Roseland
HIMMEL Michael *Lowenstein Sandler*, Roseland
KROVATIN Gerald *Krovatin & Associates*, Newark
LUSTBERG Lawrence *Gibbons Del Deo*, Newark
WALDER Justin *Walder Hayden*, Roseland
[2] KEARNEY, Dennis *Pitney Hardin*, Morristown
KIPNEES Robert *Lowenstein Sandler*, Roseland
MARINO Kevin *Marino & Associates*, Newark
Firms and individuals are listed alphabetically in each band.

Band 1

Walder, Hayden & Brogan PA

The Firm: This firm's reputation in white-collar crime is indisputable, and it was praised for its effectiveness in other criminal defense cases too, particularly for high-profile individuals. Able to take on the toughest cases, these attorneys are trusted to do their utmost to protect the clients' interests. Securities fraud litigation forms the bulk of this practice, as well as the representation of high-profile officials and media celebrities.

The Lawyers: **Joe Hayden** is "*top notch for white-collar crime,*" say market commentators. "*He is tenacious and won't leave any stone unturned.*" He is knowledgeable on all developments in the law, as well as highly effective in court. **Justin Walder** shines as another top-notch criminal defense lawyer. He has "*great judgment*" and trial skills to match.

Band 2

Krovatin & Associates LLC

The Firm: This four-lawyer litigation boutique came into existence in 1999 and since then has carved out a wonderful niche in complex commercial litigation and white-collar criminal defense. It is primarily recognized for the "*preeminence*" of its top attorneys, and is a clear leader for white-collar crime issues. Described as a cost-effective solution to white-collar crime disputes by clients and peers, the firm is also a popular port of call for advice on civil rights issues among the Sikh community.

The Lawyers: **Gerald Krovatin** is "*one of the top white-collar crime attorneys in the state*" with his deep legal knowledge and strong courtroom presence.

Michael Critchley & Associates

The Firm: This firm revolves around its lead practitioner Michael Critchley, whose reputation in white-collar crime litigation is superb.

The firm was founded in 1974, and since then it has gone from strength to strength. Aside from criminal defense, the firm also covers civil litigation in personal injury, wrongful death and employment cases.

The Lawyers: Michael Critchley has continued to fly high in the estimation of his peers. He is an *"excellent trial lawyer – he understands how* *to present facts to the jury and the judges – and he is effective at the emotional level too."* He also undertakes civil litigation, however, it is in the field of criminal defense – including expertise in jury perception and opinion – that his reputation lies.

Other Notable Practitioners

Kevin Marino of Marino & Associates PC has steered his boutique practice to greater prominence in the field of white-collar crime. He is particularly visible on issues involving attorney general of New Jersey, Peter Harvey.

REAL ESTATE

New Jersey
Leading firms (Real Estate)

[1]	**GREENBAUM, ROWE, SMITH & DAVIS** *Woodbridge*
	SILLS CUMMIS EPSTEIN & GROSS PC *Newark*
[2]	**DRINKER BIDDLE & REATH LLP** *Florham Park*
	MCCARTER & ENGLISH LLP *Cherry Hill*
[3]	**COLE, SCHOTZ, MEISEL, FORMAN** *Hackensack*
	FARER FERSKO *Westfield*
	GIORDANO HALLERAN & CIESLA PC *Middletown*
	HILL WALLACK *Princeton*
	KELLEY DRYE & WARREN *Florham Park*
	LOWENSTEIN SANDLER PC *Roseland*
	PITNEY HARDIN LLP *Morristown*
	REED SMITH LLP *Princeton*
	RIKER DANZIG SCHERER HYLAND *Morristown*
	WILENTZ GOLDMAN & SPITZER, PC *Woodbridge*

Leading individuals (Real Estate)

[1]	**DOLLINGER Martin** *Greenbaum Rowe*, Woodbridge
	HULL Gerald *Drinker Biddle*, Florham Park
[2]	**DOWD Martin** *McCarter & English*, Newark
	MORRISON Victoria *Riker Danzig*, Morristown
	NEWMAN Jeffrey *Sills Cummis*, Newark
	RADZELY Edward *Giordano Halleran*, Middletown
	SCHACHTER Robert *Greenbaum Rowe*, Woodbridge
[3]	**ABRAMSON Richard** *Cole Schotz*, Hackensack
	BLACK Margaret *Sills Cummis*, Newark
	DIVITA Robert *Sills Cummis*, Newark
	GORDON David *Reed Smith*, Princeton
	KAHN Richard *Winne Banta*, Hackensack
	O'DONNELL Matthew *Lum Danzis*, Roseland
	RABINOWITZ David *Sills Cummis*, Newark
	RACIOPPI Nicholas *Riker Danzig*, Morristown
	ROTHPLETZ Michael *Drinker Biddle*, Florham Park
	TOLCHINSKY Harold *Cole Schotz*, Hackensack
	ZANGARI Ted *Sills Cummis*, Newark

Firms and individuals are listed alphabetically in each band.

Band 1

Greenbaum, Rowe, Smith & Davis LLP

See firm details p.1148

The Firm: This is one of the firm's flagship practice groups, and market sources agree that it *"attracts the best"* when it comes to lawyers, clients, and the caliber of work. The firm has a premier reputation acting for real estate devel-opers across a range of commercial and residential projects, particularly condominium properties. The market opinion of this firm has, if anything, strengthened over the past year: *"Greenbaum Rowe is clearly the top in the state."* The firm has keenly followed the ebbs and flows of New Jersey's substantial real estate sector, and the practice is also highly sought after for land use issues vital for its developer clients. Among its recent highlights, the firm represented Amboy Plaza Holding in the acquisition of a 75,000-sq-ft shopping center for over $19.5 million.

The Lawyers: The profile of **Martin Dollinger** (see p.1138) has remained high throughout the market. He impresses clients with his easy handling of complex real estate transactions and responsive, commercial service. **Robert Schachter** (see p.1145) heads the real estate department, and has overseen its current strong form. He has been involved in several large sales and leasings, including the sale of a 514,000-sq-ft office complex located in Mount Laurel for $44 million. Those who have worked with and alongside him confirmed that his *"highly impressive"* negotiation skills are a serious asset to the firm. **Meryl Gonchar** (see p.1140) chairs the firm's land use practice group, taking over from Peter Buchsbaum, who has become a judge. She has worked on land use and condemnation issues in connection with residential and commercial property. Sources recognize her in-depth knowledge of the sector and point to her role as past chair of the land use section of the New Jersey State Bar Association as underlining her position in the market. **Marc Policastro** (see p.1143) has made an impact with his accomplished land use and zoning practice. Perceived by peers as *"talented young blood,"* he brings a thoughtful demeanor, which has proven reliable for approvals issues as well as advice on general real estate matters.

The Clients: This firm acts for a broad mix of clients, including Fortune 500 companies, construction companies, developers and real estate partnerships.

Sills Cummis Epstein & Gross PC

The Firm: This practice has carved out a reputation as one of the state's leading real estate outfits. *"I would go to Sills for the biggest and most* *complex matters,"* say clients. The firm has a reputation for its deal-making style, which leaves a good impression on the market: *"It is making a big push,"* said one peer. *"I think it is a clear leader."* The firm has continued its significant work in the retail sector, with shopping centers providing a constant stream of mandates. Retail leasing is an area where this firm already dominates, but the firm has made definite moves to cover all areas such as complex financing and land use. For example, it has been involved in the $800 million Mountain Creek resort development project by Intrawest in Vernon.

The Lawyers: The profile of **Jeffrey Newman** continues to flourish. As head of the group he *"is a knowledgeable and experienced leasing attorney, as well as being a key rainmaker for the firm."* **Margaret Black** has captured a share of market appreciation, and her fans say, *"she's just a great adviser."* She is an expert on commercial real estate transactions and combines this with experience of site recovery environmental issues. Clients described **David Rabinowitz** as *"a dean of real estate."* He has a nationwide reputation for his work with retail chains, and condominium developments are also a strong point of his practice. **Ted Zangari** has also developed a practice that is national in nature. This *"excellent attorney"* is skilled in commercial real estate development and leasing. An influential commentator not just on real estate matters but for New Jersey business affairs in general, he remains a key client relationship winner. **Robert DiVita** is a former associate real estate counsel at Toys 'R' Us. He has won the favor of both clients and peers for his transactional experience and strong commercial outlook. **Thomas Hall** is widely respected for his land use and zoning expertise. He has attracted a deep base of developer clients, with particular emphasis on medium-sized entrepreneurial developers working across New Jersey.

Band 2

Drinker Biddle & Reath LLP

See firm details p.1549

The Firm: This multistate practice fields a strong base of real estate lawyers in New Jersey from its offices in Princeton and Florham Park.

New Jersey

Leading individuals

(Real Estate: Zoning/Land Use)

1. **FERSKO Jack** *Farer Fersko*, Westfield
   GEIGER Glenn *Pitney Hardin*, Morristown
   PANTEL Glenn *Drinker Biddle*, Florham Park
2. **BERKLEY Peter** *Riker Danzig*, Morristown
   CARROLL Tom *Hill Wallack*, Princeton
   EISDORFER Stephen *Hill Wallack*, Princeton
   GIUNCO John *Giordano Halleran*, Middletown
   GONCHAR Meryl *Greenbaum Rowe*, Woodbridge
   HALL Thomas *Sills Cummis*, Newark
   HILL Henry *Hill Wallack*, Princeton
   MEISER Kenneth *Hill Wallack*, Princeton

Up-and-coming individuals

POLICASTRO Marc *Greenbaum Rowe*, Woodbridge

Individuals are listed alphabetically in each band.

Both sites can pool considerable resources into staffing large real estate transactions. Peers agree that this "*strong firm for real estate*" has continued a good run this year. It acts for some of the largest residential real estate developers in the country, as well as developers and owners of shopping malls and hotels. The firm's strong litigation capacity also stands it in good stead when disputes arise. Attorneys are also well versed in land use issues.

The Lawyers: The buzz generated by **Gerald Hull**'s (see p.1141) impressive practice places him as one of the leaders in the state. A "*marvelous lawyer,*" he possesses extensive experience in real estate leasing, financings, title insurance and land use. He is a "*good negotiator,*" and is so experienced that peers say: "*You know you will learn in a deal when he's involved.*" **Glenn Pantel** (see p.1143) is the firm's foremost land use attorney. His focus includes environmental issues such as wetlands and ISRA (Industrial Site Recovery Act) issues and his busy practice combines his land use skills with a very commercial outlook in transactions. **Michael Rothpletz** (see p.1144) is making his mark in real estate development, transactions and financing issues. His recent caseload has included advice to Matrix Realty.

The Clients: The firm's clients include: Matrix Development Group; Trammell Crow Company; IKEA and Matrix Realty.

McCarter & English LLP

See firm details p.1152

The Firm: With a significant regional presence, this long-standing firm brings a level of quality to all its real estate work. Peers agree that the firm's name alone is a main draw for clients who want a good mix of experience and leadership. The leading attorneys add value by their understanding of how businesses run, particularly where complex corporate and finance issues have been crucial to the real estate sector. The firm's real estate leasing practice attracts plaudits for its office and retail work throughout the USA.

The Lawyers: Sources were keen to endorse the accessibility of the "*experienced and friendly*" **Martin Dowd** (see p.1138). He leads the firm's real estate leasing practice, and his "*knowledgeable and confident*" manner is an asset in all his negotiations. Managing partner of the firm, Lois Van Deusen, holds the responsibility for steering the practice. Prior to managing the firm, she was highly respected for her real estate expertise, and she remains a key contact for this field.

The Clients: SJP Properties; Prudential; Crum&Forster; D&B; New York Giants and Phelps Dodge.

Band 3

Cole, Schotz, Meisel, Forman & Leonard PA

The Firm: This firm provides a consistently good service with 25 dedicated attorneys servicing the real estate sector. Peers closely follow the developments at this firm, and say "*it is good competition, especially with its leasing and retail expertise.*" In the retail sector, the firm has consolidated its experience through complex financing and development projects.

The Lawyers: **Richard Abramson** attracts the admiration of the market for his sterling retail leasing experience. As well as his legal qualifications, he is a CPA, and his client base includes major REITs. He is well placed to cover financial issues ancillary to transactional real estate. **Harold Tolchinsky** is also a highly respected figure in transactional issues for retail properties. He is a member of the International Council of Shopping Centers, and his "*very knowledgeable*" mind continues to be an asset to his clients.

The Clients: The firm acts for a range of landlords, tenants, investors, REITs and developers.

Farer Fersko

The Firm: This practice has made a name for itself as a boutique that combines real estate transactional work with a serious expertise in land use, zoning and environmental issues. These areas are of vital concern to the New Jersey property market, as the state is frequently seen at the forefront of developments in environmental policy. For the interface of real estate and land use, this "*first choice*" practice impresses peers with its bedrock of strong lawyers.

The Lawyers: **Jack Fersko** (see p.1139) is "*an excellent leading practitioner*" when it comes to any issues relating to land use. Peers feel confident that they would refer to him in the event of a conflict. He has 20 years of experience in complex transactions, and is adept at balancing environmental concerns with commerciality.

The Clients: Avi Don Management; Mack-Cali Realty; Matrix Development Group; K Hovnanian and Federal Business Centers.

Giordano Halleran & Ciesla PC

The Firm: This practice boasts a range of strengths in real estate, including work beyond the office and retail axis populated by many other firms. For example, the attorneys here have helped Sandy Hook Partners in a rare lease of National Park land at Fort Hancock. This project involves extensive rehabilitation of historic property, and shows the firm's flexibility. The firm also acted for sellers of historic buildings in Yonkers, New York. The land use practice is also worthy of praise, with market sources describing the "*phenomenal*" expertise on offer. The firm has acted for Paramount Homes in relation to development and planning issues for leisure and specialist residential properties.

The Lawyers: For the depth of his transactional knowledge, the highly reputed **Edward Radzely** wins the market's seal of approval. He has a strong leasing practice that also encompasses borrower side representation. His practice has matched the trend towards activity in the shopping centers and other retail outlets sectors. Clients are also impressed with his "*wide experience of development issues.*" **John Giunco** chairs the firm's land use and development department. His "*extensive experience*" comes in for high praise, and he has had a prominent role in contentious work for major retail outlets such as Home Depot.

The Clients: Paramount Homes; Orion Enterprises; Preit; Home Depot and Centex Homes.

Hill Wallack

The Firm: This full-service practice is well placed to serve clients in a broad range of fields. The firm has earned its place by demonstrating a broad knowledge of real estate and zoning issues, while its litigation prowess gives this firm its edge. Attorneys here are unflinching in their handling of contentious real estate matters, including disputes arising out of land use issues. The firm's "*talented specialists*" receive praise from market commentators, not least for their "*hard-edged*" litigation ability.

The Lawyers: **Henry Hill** has earned plaudits for his excellent land use practice. Peers praise the effectiveness of his style: "*He has a 'take no prisoners' approach when fighting his clients' corner.*" He heads the firm's land use division and represents landowners and developers. Chair of the land use section of the New Jersey State Bar Association, **Tom Carroll** has proven to be a popular contact for advice on the intricacies of land use. The emphasis of his practice on trial and appellate work ties in with his excellent reputation for advocacy. **Stephen Eisdorfer** also contributes to the firm's excellent reputation with his respected advice on civil rights issues relating to affordable housing. **Kenneth Meiser** is a ground-breaking litigator, whose practice covers all aspects of the land use permitting and application process.

The Clients: The firm acts for developers, municipalities and landowners.

Kelley Drye & Warren

The Firm: The Parsippany office of this national practice has continued to gain praise for its strong transactional real estate experience. "*They really know what they're doing,*" say market sources about the knowledgeable attorneys at this practice. The real estate development and financing practice spans the state and can draw on the support of a network of national offices. The firm's workload includes sales and purchases, management and financing.

The Lawyers: The Parsippany office's managing partner is Joseph Boyle.

The Clients: The firm's clients include developers, corporations, finance companies and real estate funds.

Lowenstein Sandler PC

See firm details p.1150

The Firm: The high-profile credentials of this firm's major corporate practice have translated into one of the most impressive client lists in the state and a strong spillover of work in the real estate sector. Clients appreciate the level of connectivity this firm provides between commercial real estate and corporate issues, particularly in the area of tax structuring. The group also advises clients on leasing agreements, the acquisition and disposition of property and development projects.

The Lawyers: Cochair of the department, Gary Wingens, is well equipped to advise on real estate finance issues, especially complex structured lending. Barry Stiger is also experienced in industrial real estate, financing and land use. His client base includes companies in the food service industry.

The Clients: The firm represents a diverse range of clients including telecommunications companies, hotel and casino operators, retail chains, educational institutions, hospitals and realty companies.

Pitney Hardin LLP

See firm details p.1153

The Firm: "*Strong across the board,*" agree sources, this firm provides a well-rounded service that covers a range of real estate transactions, leasing and financing issues. The firm has "*knowledgeable, practical and realistic*" attorneys who deliver their advice in an effective manner. The firm has been keen to follow the growth of real estate and development around New Jersey, and peers report on the successful appearance of this firm in key leasing issues across the state. In the land use sphere, the firm has kept up its profile by involving itself in NJ Department of Environmental Protection matters – crucial for the redevelopment sector. In a recent highlight, the

group acted for the monks running the Delbarton School, Morristown, on a prominent zoning dispute.

The Lawyers: The "*very capable*" **Glenn Geiger** (see p.1139) is one of the market's leading land use practitioners. A partner of the firm for 20 years, he generates confidence with his "*strong set of skills.*" Peers agree that his detailed understanding of environmental issues is an attractive proposition to clients and recognize his experience with state, municipal and county authorities: "*He understands what clients want to achieve and knows what the local and municipal levels require.*" His land use and site remediation work is widely respected.

The Clients: The firm has acted for St Mary's Abbey, The Gale Company, as well as other realty and financial organizations.

Reed Smith LLP

See firm details p.1560

The Firm: This major international practice has made inroads into the New Jersey market. The office is staffed with six attorneys, who cover finance, real estate development and land use. "*I see Reed Smith as having a significant presence, particularly with its national resources,*" say impressed peers. The group works on transactional issues at all stages, extending to a respected zoning and land use ability. The firm can boast an extensive national developer client list that ensures a place for the firm on property issues in New York, Pennsylvania and beyond.

The Lawyers: Peers describe **David Gordon** (see p.1140) as a prime figure in the firm's real estate practice. A "*very smart attorney and great deal-doer,*" he frequently appears on land use approvals too. Manufacturing leasing has proven a rich seam of work for him, as has mixed purpose redevelopment and landlord and tenant issues.

The Clients: Frank A Greek & Son; Toll Brothers; Mellon Financial Corporation and Bloomberg.

Riker Danzig Scherer Hyland & Perretti LLP

See firm details p.1154

The Firm: This firm shows a strong hand in not just transactional issues, but any issue which is potentially contentious in nature and where the firm's litigation reputation proves helpful. As well as the Morristown office, the real estate group has the advantage of a Trenton office, ensuring a broad geographic coverage. Clients say the "*extremely knowledgeable*" attorneys here are especially valued for their thorough advice and comprehensive attention to detail. The firm has acted for the Rockefeller Group on several large purchases and sales, including a New Jersey office park.

The Lawyers: "*An excellent and pragmatic*

lawyer," **Victoria Morrison** (see p.1143) is cochair of the real estate department, and has been busy with headline lease, and sale and leaseback work. She has attracted a following among lending institutions and is known for her work outside of the state. **Peter Berkeley** (see p.1137) possesses a flourishing land use practice. His experience, coupled with his management skills as the firm's lead partner over the past 11 years, has provided him with a strong base of commerciality. **Nicholas Racioppi** (see p.1144) has deep transactional real estate and zoning experience. He also specializes in real estate litigation, and the interface between real estate and environmental law always provides him with plenty of interesting work. His workload has featured litigation relating to the rezoning of an oil company's plant following an explosion.

The Clients: Lucent Technologies; Johnson & Johnson; Bed Bath & Beyond; Chicago Title Insurance Company; Vornado Realty Trust; The Rockefeller Group; The Schultz Organization; Independence Bank; Atlantic Mutual Insurance Company; JPMorgan Chase and Ginsburg Development Companies.

Wilentz Goldman & Spitzer, PC

The Firm: The lawyers at this firm "*have established themselves as a real presence,*" say market commentators. The firm fields 11 attorneys across its offices specializing in real estate, with a further nine who are expert in land use. The depth of advice on offer here is impressive as is the level of contacts and market understanding possessed by the attorneys. When it comes to factoring in the complexities of political issues, this firm is a "*powerhouse.*"

The Lawyers: Steve Barcan is the cochair of the environmental group. A partner of the firm for 30 years, he continues to steer the practice group towards lucrative work.

The Clients: The group's client base consists of regional malls, petroleum companies, religious institutions and development companies.

Other Notable Practitioners

The move of **Richard Kahn** to Winne Banta Hetherington Basralian & Kahn, PC has injected that firm with strong real estate muscle. Formerly of Cole Schotz, he has brought along his excellent reputation, especially in office and retail leasing and development. **Matthew O'Donnell** is a real estate and tax expert who is praised by clients for the "*great results*" achieved through his advice on tax-efficient structuring. In the field of real estate tax, clients say: "I have recommended him a lot." He built up a great profile at Lum, Danzis, Drasco & Positan, although at the time of press he was in the process of moving to O'Donnell McCord & DeMarzo.

Leaders in New Jersey

ABRAMSON, Richard
Cole, Schotz, Meisel, Forman &
Leonard PA, Hackensack
201 489 3000
Recommended in Real Estate

AIELLO, John
Giordano Halleran & Ciesla PC,
Middletown 732 714 3900
Recommended in Corporate/M&A

ALITO, Rosemary
Kirkpatrick & Lockhart Nicholson Graham LLP, Newark 973 639 2027
Recommended in Employment
Practice Areas: US federal and state
employment law matters, including
advice and litigation in federal and state
courts and administrative agencies. Discrimination, harassment, whistleblowing, wage and hour and ERISA litigation. Trials and appeals in matters ranging from single plaintiff cases to class
actions and EEOC pattern and practice
cases.
Prof. Memberships: Association of the
Federal Bar of the State of New Jersey
(Past President); American College of
Employment Lawyers (Fellow); American Bar Foundation (Fellow); International Society of Barristers (Fellow).
Publications: Has lectured and written
extensively on employment law issues,
including a treatise, New Jersey Employment Law. Chairman, Editorial Board,
'New Jersey Law Journal'.
Personal: Smith College (BA 1974);
Rutgers University School of Law
Newark (JD 1978); Law Review.

BERKLEY, Peter L
Riker Danzig Scherer Hyland & Perretti
LLP, Morristown 973 451 8403
pberkley@riker.com
Recommended in Real Estate
Practice Areas: Of counsel to Real
Estate Practice Group. Specializes in
conveyancing, leasing, financing, and
zoning and planning matters. Performs
work for major national corporations,
local businesses, real estate developers
and lenders. Featured four times in 'The
Best Lawyers in America' (Woodward/
White, Inc.).
Prof. Memberships: Member of American College of Real Estate Lawyers; Real
Property Section of the New Jersey State
Bar Association; Real Property, Probate
and Trust Law Section of the American
Bar Association; Past President of the
Harvard Law School Association of New
Jersey.
Personal: Harvard University, JD;
Williams College, BA.

BERRY, Andrew T
McCarter & English, LLP, Newark
973 639 2097
aberry@mccarter.com
Recommended in Litigation
Practice Areas: Mr Berry is Chairman
of McCarter & English, LLP. His career
has involved trial and appellate litigation, including domestic and international arbitration.
Career: Mr Berry has tried cases to verdict in a number of states and argued
appeals before four federal circuits and
the highest courts of New York, New Jersey and Maryland; some of those cases
have involved insurance coverage, product liability, franchise practices, UCC
and punitive damages issues. He was
recently recognized as one of New Jersey's business leaders; named in Who's
Who Legal, The International Who's
Who of Business Lawyers, and Best
Lawyers in America.

BLACK, Margaret
Sills Cummis Epstein & Gross PC,
Newark 973 643 7000
Recommended in Real Estate

BOYAJIAN, Victor
Sonnenschein Nath & Rosenthal, Short
Hills 973 912 7171
vboyajian@sonnenschein.com
Recommended in Corporate/M&A
Practice Areas: Venture
Capital/Emerging Growth Company
Practice Chair, focusing on emerging
growth and Fortune 500 companies in
transactions, including venture capital
and other strategic matters. Represents
portfolio companies and investment
banking and venture capital firms' interests. Counsels on business strategy,
finance, M&A, executive compensation,
board governance and intellectual property and litigation strategy.
Prof. Memberships: NY, NJ and District of Columbia Bar Associations;
Council of Economic Advisors, New Jersey; Founder, Venture Connection
Roundtable (CA and NY); Board of
Directors, New Jersey Technology
Council; The Churchill Club.
Personal: University of Pennsylvania
School of Law, JD; University of
Rochester, BA, magna cum laude.

BROMBERG, Lisa
Porzio, Bromberg & Newman, A Professional Corporation, Morristown
973 538 4006
Recommended in Environment

CAMPION, Thomas
Drinker Biddle & Reath LLP,
Florham Park 973 549 7300
Thomas.Campion@dbr.com
Recommended in Litigation
Practice Areas: Partner, Co-Head of
Professional Liability Claims Practice
and senior member of Products Liability
Practice. Focuses on civil litigation,
including professional liability, products
liability, business litigation and employment law.
Prof. Memberships: Admissions: New
Jersey, District of Columbia and New
York. Fellow, American College of Trial
Lawyers, American Bar Foundation and
the International Academy of Trial
Lawyers; Vice-Chair, New Jersey
Supreme Court Commission on the
Rules of Professional Conduct; past
Chairman, of the New Jersey Supreme
Court Board of Trial Attorney Certification.
Career: Joined Drinker Biddle in 1999.
Publications: Numerous.
Personal: LLB, Cornell University, 1961;
AB, Fordham University, 1957.

CARMAGNOLA, Domenick
Lum, Danzis, Drasco & Positan, LLC,
Roseland 973 228 6735
carmagnola@umlaw.com
Recommended in Employment
Practice Areas: Extensive experience in
labor and employment matters representing management and defendants
including: state/federal court litigation;
non-compete matters; appellate practice; traditional labor practice: NLRB,
collective bargaining, arbitration, organizing campaigns; DOL, EEOC, OSHA,
DCR; wage and hour matters; employee
benefit litigation; HR counseling; corporate investigations, ADR and mediation;
NJ Court Approved Mediator; NJ Certified Civil Trial Attorney.
Prof. Memberships: Admitted in New
Jersey, DNJ, Third Circuit Court of
Appeals and US Supreme Court. Secretary, New Jersey State Bar Association,
Labor and Employment Law Section;
President, NJSBA Sidney Reitman Labor
and Employment Law American Inn of
Court; President, Essex County Bar
Association (2002-03); editor in chief,
NJSBA Labor and Employment Law
Quarterly (1997-99); ABA, Section on
Litigation, Employment and Labor
Relations Law Committee; Member:
DRI; Recognition, 'Top Lawyers' and
'Superlawyers' New Jersey Monthly
Magazine; Top 40 Under 40, 'New Jersey
Law Journal' (2002); NJSBA Young
Lawyer of the Year Professional Achievement Award (1998); Civil Trial Attorney
Award, ECBA (2005).
Career: Lum, Danzis, Drasco & Positan,
LLC and its predecessors since 1988;
Partner/Member since 1995.
Publications: Editor/chapter author,
NJSBA-ICLE Book, 'New Jersey Labor
and Employment Law' (NJICLE); co-author, Special Evidentiary Concerns
Chapter, 'Employment Litigation Handbook' (ABA); co-author, Employment
Torts Chapter, 'Business Torts Litigation'
(ABA); Editor, 'With Honor and Dignity: 100 Years of the Practice of Law in
Essex County' (ECBA); special editor,
New Jersey Lawyer, The Magazine,
Employment Law (April 1999).
Personal: JD, Seton Hall University
School of Law, Cum Laude, 1988; BA in
Political Science, Seton Hall University
1985.

CARROLL, Tom
Hill Wallack, Princeton
609 924 0808
Recommended in Real Estate

CASEY, ESQ, Warren J
Pitney Hardin LLP, Morristown
973 966 8025
wcasey@pitneyhardin.com
Recommended in Corporate/M&A
Practice Areas: Chair of the Corporate
Group. Serves as outside general corporate and securities counsel to companies
in various sectors, including retail, technology and computer services. Successfully argued Alessi v Raybestos-Manhattan before the United States Supreme
Court.
Career: Partner since 1982.
Publications: Numerous articles
including most recently, 'Back To Basics:
Some Common Sense Principles For
Public Company Financial Disclosure
Metropolitan Corporate Counsel', January 2005.
Personal: Notre Dame Law School, JD,
cum laude, 1975, Editor, Law Review;
University of Notre Dame, BA, magna
cum laude, 1972. Finished the 2004
'Ironman Wisconsin' triathlon (2.4 mile
swim, 112 mile bike, 26.2 mile run).

CERASIA, Edward
Proskauer Rose, Newark
973 274 3224
ecerasia@proskauer.com
Recommended in Employment
Practice Areas: A Partner in Proskauer
Rose LLP's Labor and Employment Law
Department, he has significant experience handling labor, employment and
employee benefits law matters in the
financial services, transportation, media,
pharmaceutical, telecommunications
and retail industries. He regularly represents employers in labor arbitration,
handles unfair labor practice charges
and representation matters before the
NLRB and negotiates collective bargaining agreements. He also spends a substantial amount of his time counseling
clients on how to avoid litigation.
Publications: In 2004, he was a contributing author on the amicus brief
that Proskauer submitted to the US
Supreme Court on behalf of the Society
of Human Resource Management in
Pennsylvania State Police v Suders, 124
S. Ct. 2342 (2004). He also co-authored
the amicus brief that Proskauer submitted to the New Jersey Supreme Court on
behalf of the Employers Association of
New Jersey in Gerety v Atlantic City
Hilton Casino Resort (2005).
Personal: University of Bridgeport
School of Law (N/K/A Quinnipiac University School of Law), JD, summa cum
laude, 1991 editor, University of Bridgeport Law Review, 1990-91. Syracuse
University, BS, 1987.

CLARK, Glenn A

Riker Danzig Scherer Hyland & Perretti LLP, Morristown 973 451 8400
gclark@riker.com
Recommended in Litigation

Practice Areas: Managing Partner and member of Executive Committee. Senior litigator, practicing in employment, healthcare, commercial, construction matters, intellectual property and insurance coverage disputes. Extensive experience in arbitration, administrative hearings, jury and non-jury trials and appeals to the US Supreme Court and New Jersey Supreme Court. Has numerous reported decisions in state and federal courts. Successfully argued in the New Jersey Courts to adopt the 'inevitability doctrine' governing disclosure and use of trade secrets.

Personal: University of Notre Dame, JD, magna cum laude, Executive Editor, Notre Dame Law Review, MBA, highest honors; Seton Hall University, BA, summa cum laude.

COHEN, Steven

Morgan, Lewis & Bockius LLP, Princeton 609 919 6604
scohen@morganlewis.com
Recommended in Corporate/M&A

Practice Areas: Mr Cohen is a Partner in the Business and Finance Practice. Mr Cohen's practice focuses on advising mid-Atlantic emerging growth companies and the financial institutions that invest in them. He represents companies and investors in venture capital financings, representing issuers in IPOs and secondary public offerings, acquisitions, divestitures and mergers, joint ventures and strategic partnerships, and providing general corporate and securities advice to companies. Mr Cohen has significant experience assisting biotechnology, information technology and other companies in planning for and implementing growth strategies.

Prof. Memberships: New Jersey Technology Council (Board of Directors); New Jersey Entrepreneurs Network.

CRITCHLEY, Michael

Michael Critchley & Associates, West Orange 973 731 9831
Recommended in Litigation

DAVIS, Alan E

Greenbaum, Rowe, Smith & Davis LLP, Woodbridge 732 549 5600
adavis@greenbaumlaw.com
Recommended in Corporate/M&A

Practice Areas: Chair, Corporate Department. Represents both publicly and closely held business enterprises in areas including manufacturing, retailing, distribution and service. Advises clients in financing, supplier relations, customers and non-union staff, securities, business planning, and the purchase and sale of businesses and related business assets. Experience handling franchise, distribution and trade regulation matters, and problems associated with the dissolution of business entities.

Prof. Memberships: Chair, Board of Trustees, Monmouth Medical Center; member, Board of Trustees, Monmouth Medical Center Foundation; member, Board of Trustees, Monmouth University; member, Board of Trustees, Saint Barnabas Corporation.

Personal: Columbia Law School (1965), Rutgers College (1962).

DEE, Francis

McElroy, Deutsch, Mulvaney & Carpenter, LLP, Newark 973 622 7711
Recommended in Employment

DEUTSCH, Edward

McElroy, Deutsch, Mulvaney & Carpenter, LLP, Newark 973 622 7711
Recommended in Litigation

DIVITA, Robert

Sills Cummis Epstein & Gross PC, Newark 973 643 7000
Recommended in Real Estate

DOLLINGER, Martin E

Greenbaum, Rowe, Smith & Davis LLP, Woodbridge 732 549 5600
mdollinger@greenbaumlaw.com
Recommended in Real Estate

Practice Areas: Complex transactional real estate with an emphasis on office, industrial and retail leasing, and corporate matters throughout the United States.

Prof. Memberships: Member, American College of Real Estate Lawyers and the American Bar Association and its section on Real Property, Probate and Trust Law. Serves on the Board of Governors of the Ramapo College Foundation.

Publications: Author, 'New Jersey Real Estate Leasing Forms: Practice' (Michie 1991, Lexis Law Publishing).

Personal: Cornell University (1963), Cornell University Law School (1966), Master of Laws, Georgetown University (1970).

DORE, Michael

Lowenstein Sandler PC, Roseland 973 597 2344
mdore@lowenstein.com
Recommended in Environment

Practice Areas: Has more than 25 years of experience representing corporate clients in complex toxic tort and environmental litigation, and counseling. In addition, his experience in handling industrial accidents, fires, explosions and other critical incidents has given him a special understanding of dealing with catastrophe response and crisis management situations. Mr Dore is former counsel for BOC Group, Inc., a Fortune 500 company, where he was responsible for its environmental affairs.

Prof. Memberships: Rutgers University Law School, Adjunct Professor of Environmental Law, (1984 - present); Association of Defense Trial Attorneys; Defense Research Institute, Founding Chairman - Environmental Law Committee; International Association of Defense Counsel.

Career: Pennsylvania Bar (1975); New York Bar (1976); New Jersey Bar (1980).

Publications: 'Law of Toxic Torts: Litigation, Defense, Insurance,' four volume treatise published by the West Group; 'Consolidating the Crowd of Cases,' 'New Jersey Law Journal'; 'Reforming Mass Tort Coordination Procedures,' 'New Jersey Law Journal'; 'Reforming the New Jersey Supreme Courts Procedures for Consolidating Mass Tort Litigation: A Proposal for Disclosing the Rules of the Game,' Rutgers Law Review; 'Dealing with Business Emergencies: A Crisis Management Guidebook,' Lowenstein Sandler Crisis Management Practice ebook; 'Conducting Internal Corporate Investigations,' 'New Jersey Law Journal'; 'Protecting Individual Corporate Executives From Liability - Ten Cardinal Rules For Risk Managers,' NJRIMSNews; 'Dealing With Public Relations Concerns in Products Liability and Toxic Tort Litigation,' New Jersey Lawyer the Magazine.

Personal: Rutgers University School of Law (JD, 1975, Editor, 'Rutgers Law Review', National Moot Court Team); Amherst College (BA, 1972, cum laude).

DOWD, Martin F

McCarter & English, LLP, Newark 973 639 2013
mdowd@mccarter.com
Recommended in Real Estate

Practice Areas: Mr Dowd's practice involves all aspects of real estate law, with particular experience in the areas of the acquisition and disposition of commercial real estate and commercial leasing transactions.

Career: Mr Dowd heads the Real Estate Department's Leasing Practice, representing landlords and tenants in preparing and negotiating office, industrial and retail leases for properties throughout the United States. He represents institutional investors, national developers and corporate users in the structuring and implementation of complex real estate transactions; development of major real estate projects; and acquisition and disposition of real estate investments and portfolios.

DRASCO, Dennis J

Lum, Danzis, Drasco & Positan, LLC, Roseland 973 228 6770
ddrasco@lumlaw.com
Recommended in Litigation

Practice Areas: Over 30 years experience in State and Federal litigation in New Jersey and New York. Business litigation, Chancery litigation, Shareholder disputes, debtor/creditor litigation, condemnation, construction disputes, condominium association litigation, estate litigation, land use litigation, appellate practice, arbitration and mediation, environmental litigation, insurance coverage litigation, professional negligence litigation, NJ court-approved mediator.

Prof. Memberships: Admitted to practice in New Jersey and New York; Federal Courts in New Jersey, Southern and Eastern Districts of New York; Second and Third Circuit and US Supreme Court. US Tax Court; ABA House of Delegates (2003-present); Chair ABA Section of Litigation (2004-05); Secretary, Association of the Federal Bar of New Jersey; Fellow, American Bar Foundation; Master, Seton Hall Law School Inn of Court; Civil Trial Attorney Achievement Award; Essex County Bar Association (2000); Co-Chair, American Jury Project (2004-05); listed in 'Best Lawyers In America', 'Superlawyers of New Jersey' and 'Who's Who in American Law'.

Career: Lum, Danzis, Drasco & Positan, LLC and its predecessors since 1973; Partner/Member since 1980; Chair, Litigation Practice Group.

Publications: 'How To Get From The War Room To The Court Room: The Basics For Civil Trial Arguments', 15 New Jersey Lawyer 32 (1993) 'Construction Contracts: Arbitration as a Means of Dispute Resolution in New Jersey', New Jersey Lawyer, February 2003, No. 219, 'Bad Faith Condemnation', ABA Trial Notebook, 1992.

Personal: BA Political Science, Fordham College, 1970; JD Rutgers School of Law, Newark, NJ 1973; Board of Trustees, Essex County Legal Services Foundation; Board of Trustees, United Way of North Essex.

EAKELEY, Douglas S

Lowenstein Sandler PC, Roseland 973 597 2348
deakeley@lowenstein.com
Recommended in Litigation

Practice Areas: Mr Eakeley has extensive trial and appellate experience in complex commercial litigation, including securities fraud, antitrust, consumer fraud, class actions, and derivatives. A former Rhodes Scholar and graduate of Yale Law School, he served as First Assistant Attorney General of the State of New Jersey. In 1993 he was appointed by President Clinton to the Board of Directors of the Legal Services Corporation, which he chaired until April 2003. In 1997, he received the John Minor Wisdom Public Service and Professionalism Award from the American Bar Association Section of Litigation.

Prof. Memberships: American Bar Foundation, Fellow; Practising Law Institute, Trustee; New Jersey Institute for Social Justice, Trustee; Legal Services Corporation, Chairman (1993-2003); Legal Services of New Jersey, Trustee, Chairman (1982-90), Member (2003-present); 'New Jersey Law Journal', Editorial Board, Chair (1986-90), Member (1992-96); Association of the Federal Bar of the State of New Jersey, Vice President (1983-90); American Bar Association, Antitrust and Litigation Sections; New Jersey State Bar Association; NJN Public Television and Radio Foundation, Vice Chair.

Career: New York Bar (1973); New Jersey Bar (1979); Admitted to practice before US Supreme Court, US Courts of Appeals for the Second and Third Circuits, US District Courts for New Jersey, Southern and Eastern Districts of New York.

Publications: 'The Successful Practitioner of Antitrust Law', in Aspatore Books, The Art & Science of Antitrust Law; 'Defense of Consumer Fraud Class Actions', New Jersey Institute for Continuing Legal Education'; 'Defense of Private Treble-Damage Actions', in Hills, ed., Antitrust Adviser, Shepards/McGraw-Hill; 'Recent Developments in Franchise Litigation', New Jersey Institute for Continuing Legal Education'; 'Role of the Legal Services Corporation in Preserving Our National Commitment to Equal Access to Justice', Annual Survey of American Law, New York University School of Law; 'Common Ground', syndicated biweekly column in newspapers published by The Recorder Publishing Company.

Personal: Yale Law School (JD, 1972); Oxford University (BA and MA, 1970, in Jurisprudence); Yale University (BA, 1968, summa cum laude, with highest honors in economics, Rhodes Scholar, Phi Beta Kappa).

EHRENBERG, Peter H
Lowenstein Sandler PC, Roseland
973 597 2350
pehrenberg@lowenstein.com
Recommended in Corporate/M&A

Practice Areas: Chair of the Corporate Department and Corporate Finance Practice Group, has extensive experience in securities, mergers and acquisitions, and business law. He represents issuers and investment firms in the private and public offering of debt and equity securities, and participates in complex merger and acquisition transactions, recapitalizations, employee benefit matters, secured and unsecured borrowings and securities offerings. He counsels public companies regarding compliance and public reporting responsibilities, including duties under the Sarbanes-Oxley Act and other corporate governance reforms.

Prof. Memberships: New Jersey State Bar Association (Director, Corporate and Business Law Section; Past Chair, Securities Law Committee); American Bar Association.

Career: 'All-Star Lawyer Deal Makers' by NJBIZ; New Jersey Bar and Federal Courts (1973).

Publications: 'Corporate Governance ebook', provides advice regarding Sarbanes-Oxley regulations; 'What to Tell the SEC: The Intricate World of Schedule 13E-3', 'The M&A Journal'; 'SOX and Related Reforms: Where Are We?', 'The Metropolitan Corporate Counsel'; 'LLCs as the New Corporate Order', 'New Jersey Lawyer'; 'Corporate Governance

Self-Audits: Policing Yourself Before You Get Policed', 'Metropolitan Corporate Counsel'; 'Structuring the Transaction When the Tax Advisors Leave the Room', 'New Jersey Lawyer'; 'Why Private Companies Should Not Ignore the Sarbanes-Oxley Act', 'Wall Street Lawyer'; 'The Unintended Victim: Ramifications of the Sarbanes-Oxley Act for Private Companies', 'Metropolitan Corporate Counsel'.

Personal: Yale University (JD, 1973, Editor, Yale Law Journal); Trinity College (BA, 1969, Phi Beta Kappa).

EISDORFER, Stephen
Hill Wallack, Princeton 609 924 0808
Recommended in Real Estate

FARER, David
Farer Fersko, Westfield 908 789 8550
dfarer@farerlaw.com
Recommended in Environment

Practice Areas: David B Farer established the firm's Environmental Practice and chairs the firm's Environmental Law and Brownfield Redevelopment Department. A nationally-renowned environmental lawyer, he has over 20 years of experience in counseling clients on the impact of environmental laws on transactions in New Jersey and around the nation, cleanup and redevelopment of contaminated properties including brownfields, environmental compliance and insurance issues, and litigation arising from those issues. He advises clients on environmental contractual protection techniques, due diligence, transaction-triggered environmental laws, funding options for brownfields redevelopment, and environmental disclosures. Mr Farer lectures throughout the country on environmental issues. He developed and chairs two annual American Law Institute - American Bar Association ('ALI-ABA') national courses of study: 'The Impact of Environmental Law on Real Estate and Business Transactions: Brownfields and Beyond' (presented annually since 1987), and 'Environmental Insurance.' Since the mid-1980's, he has developed and presented numerous seminars for the New Jersey Institute for Continuing Legal Education, including his longstanding series of lectures and associated manuals on New Jersey's Industrial Site Recovery Act ('ISRA') and New Jersey's Brownfield Law.

Publications: Among Mr Farer's many books and articles are: 'ISRA Compliance: Environmental Issues in Transactions and Brownfields Redevelopment, 5th Ed.' (ICLE 2003), 'Contractual Allocation of Environmental Risks in Transactions' (ALI-ABA Course of Study Materials, October 2004), 'Brownfield Redevelopment Initiatives: Federal and Selected State Developments' (ALI-ABA, October 2004) and 'Transaction Triggered Environmental Laws, Transfer Notice Laws and Super Liens: Latest Developments' (ALI-ABA, October 2004).

FELTON, W Raymond
Greenbaum, Rowe, Smith & Davis LLP, Woodbridge 732 549 5600
rfelton@greenbaumlaw.com
Recommended in Corporate/M&A

Practice Areas: Chair, Technology Practice Group. Transactional practice includes mergers and acquisitions, institutional debt and equity financing, private and public offerings, joint ventures and corporate reorganizations. Counseling includes securities law compliance and corporate governance.

Prof. Memberships: Member, NJ State Bar Association and American Bar Association. Member, Board of Directors, Business Law Section of the NJ State Bar Association, Chair from 2002-04.

Publications: Author, 'Organization and Sale of Small Businesses' and numerous articles.

Personal: Rutgers Law School, Newark (1981), Research Editor, Rutgers Law Review; Rutgers College, (1978).

FERSKO, Jack
Farer Fersko, Westfield 908 789 8550
jfersko@farerlaw.com
Recommended in Real Estate

Practice Areas: Jack Fersko chairs the firm's Real Estate and Business Department. He has over 20 years' experience in the real estate field. His legal services emphasize industrial and commercial real estate activities, urban redevelopment, and the impact of environmental laws on real estate and business transactions.

Prof. Memberships: Mr Fersko has chaired and participated on numerous committees on behalf of the National Association of Industrial and Office Properties (NAIOP) and the New Jersey Home Builders Association, providing comments to proposed legislation and regulations. He is a member of the American College of Real Estate Lawyers (Chair, Land Use and Environmental Committee), the Board of Trustees of NAIOP (Chair, National Environmental and Infrastructure Committee), the Industrial and Office Real Estate Brokers Association, the American Bar Association (Chair, Industrial Leasing Committee of the Real Property, Probate and Trust Law Section) and the New Jersey State Bar Association.

Publications: Mr Fersko is editor of and contributor to 'Commercial Real Estate Transactions in New Jersey,' a two-volume treatise published by the NJ Institute for Continuing Legal Education. He has also written chapters for 'Brownfields - A Comprehensive Guide to Redeveloping Contaminated Property,' A.B.A. 2d ed. ('Environmental Insurance in Brownfield Transactions'), and 'Commercial Real Estate Transactions Handbook,' Aspen Press 3d ed. ('Environmental Issues in Commercial Real Estate Sales and Leases'), and has written numerous articles and is a frequent lecturer on real estate, redevelopment and environmental issues.

FRIEDMAN, Marc
Sills Cummis Epstein & Gross PC, Newark 973 643 7000
Recommended in Litigation

FUREY, Michael K
Riker Danzig Scherer Hyland & Perretti LLP, Morristown 973 451 8433
mfurey@riker.com
Recommended in Employment

Practice Areas: Chair of Labor and Employment Group. Experience in employment and commercial litigation in federal, state courts and before various agencies. Extensive trial experience and certified as a Civil Trial Attorney. Substantial experience arguing before New Jersey Supreme Court and US Third Circuit Court of Appeals.

Prof. Memberships: Chairman of the Board of Trustees of the New Jersey Ballet; Trustee of Legal Services of New Jersey and of the Supreme Court Committee on Disciplinary Oversight; Delegate to ABA House; Fellow of ABA Foundation; Member of Litigation Section of ABA.

Personal: University of Pennsylvania, JD; Dartmouth College, BA.

GARLAND, David
Sills Cummis Epstein & Gross PC, Newark 973 643 7000
Recommended in Employment

GEIGER, Glenn C
Pitney Hardin LLP, Morristown
973 966 8149
ggeiger@pitneyhardin.com
Recommended in Real Estate

Practice Areas: Land use and transactional real estate matters. Practice focuses on real estate development matters, including applications for land use and environmental permits and approvals, and on transactional real estate matters including acquisitions, sales, financing and leasing.

Prof. Memberships: New Jersey State Bar Association (Chairman of Board of Directors, Land Use Law Section); District of Columbia Bar Association; New Jersey Community Builders Association; National Association of Industrial and Office Properties (NAIOP).

Career: Partner since 1985.

Personal: Seton Hall University Law Center, JD, 1976; Georgetown University, BS, 1973.

GENOVA, Angelo
Genova, Burns & Vernoia, Livingston
973 533 0777
Recommended in Employment

GIBBONS, John J
Gibbons, Del Deo, Dolan, Griffinger & Vecchione, Newark 973 596 4733
jgibbons@gibbonslaw.com
Recommended in Litigation

Practice Areas: Arbitrator and mediator for commercial disputes. Founded firm's Fellowship in Public Interest and Constitutional Law. Decision in favor of Guantanamo Bay detainees in Rasul v Bush, before US Supreme Court.

Prof. Memberships: NJ State Bar Association (Past President), American Law Institute (Life Member), American Arbitration Association, National Law Journal Editorial Board.
Career: Chief Judge, US Court of Appeals Third Circuit. Professor, Seton Hall University School of Law. 'New Jersey Law Journal' Lawyer of the Year. 'The Best Lawyers in America' - First Amendment Rights Law. Harvard University (LLB), Harvard Law Review; College of the Holy Cross (BS).

GIUNCO Jr, John
Giordano Halleran & Ciesla PC, Middletown 732 714 3900
Recommended in Real Estate

GOLDSTEIN, Bruce
Saiber Schlesinger Satz & Goldstein, LLC, Newark 973 622 3333
Recommended in Litigation

GOLDSTEIN, Marvin M
Proskauer Rose, Newark
973 274 3210
mmgoldstein@proskauer.com
Recommended in Employment
Practice Areas: A Partner in the Labor and Employment Law Department and Head of the firm's Newark office, he has a nationwide practice where he represents employers in all aspects of labor and employee relations in both state and federal courts. He also represents employers in labor arbitration and before administrative boards such as the NLRB and various civil rights agencies. In addition, he represents employers in the securities industry where he regularly arbitrates employment matters before the NASD and the New York Stock Exchange.
Career: He has been recognized as one of the 'Best Lawyers in America' for the past 25 years and was ranked among the top five percent of the lawyers in the state of New Jersey by 'New Jersey Monthly' magazine.
Publications: An active speaker and writer on labor and employment law issues, he is also co-editor of West Publishing's New Jersey Practice treatise entitled 'Employment Law', which was published in 1998 and is updated annually.
Personal: Boston University School of Law, JD, 1969. Cornell University, BA, 1966.

GONCHAR, Meryl A G
Greenbaum, Rowe, Smith & Davis LLP, Woodbridge 732 549 5600
mgonchar@greenbaumlaw.com
Recommended in Real Estate
Practice Areas: Chair, Land Use Practice Group. Land use, zoning and land use litigation. Represention of developer clients for residential, commercial and industrial projects before planning and zoning boards. Represents clients in land use, condemnation and related litigation before the Superior Court of New Jersey.
Prof. Memberships: Immediate past Chair, Board of Directors-Land Use Law

Section, NJ State Bar Association, member, Legislative Committee. Member, American Bar Association, Middlesex County Bar Association. Member/Past President, Industrial/Commercial Real Estate Women-NJ.
Publications: Co-author, 'Zoning and Land Use Litigation,' Chapter 12, New Jersey Land Use and Environmental Law, 1993.
Personal: Rutgers School of Law, Newark (1981).

GORDON, David S
Reed Smith LLP, Princeton
609 514 5982
dgordan@reedsmith.com
Recommended in Real Estate
Practice Areas: Represents developers, owners, users and other clients in all aspects of real estate transactions, emphasizing land acquisition and disposition, development approvals, financing, leasing, construction contracts, and structuring business entities.
Prof. Memberships: Board of Governors of American College of Real Estate Lawyers, and Chairman of Membership Development Committee; member of faculty and Advisory Board, Georgetown University Law Center Advanced Commercial Leasing Institute.
Publications: Co-author of 'New Jersey Real Estate Forms-Practice,' and numerous other publications.
Personal: Columbia University School of Law (JD, 1971), editorial board of 'Journal of Law and Social Problems'; Bucknell University (BA, 1967).

GREENBERG, Marilynn R
Riker Danzig Scherer Hyland & Perretti LLP, Morristown 973 451 8437
mgreenberg@riker.com
Recommended in Environment
Practice Areas: Partner in Environmental Group. Extensive experience in environmental law, including litigation, transactional matters, permitting, solid waste, indoor air quality (asbestos and mold), defense of enforcement actions, and USEPA Superfund matters. Counsels clients regarding regulatory compliance with state and federal environmental statutes and regulations, with emphasis on site remediation and brownfields redevelopment.
Prof. Memberships: Member of New Jersey State Chamber of Commerces Environmental Committee; Chairs the Township of Livingstons Environmental Commission.
Career: Appointed to former Governor James McGreeveys transition team on the environment.
Personal: Rutgers University School of Law-Newark, JD, with high honors; University of Wisconsin, BA.

GRIFFINGER, Michael R
Gibbons, Del Deo, Dolan, Griffinger & Vecchione, Newark 973 596 4701
griffinger@gibbonslaw.com
Recommended in Litigation

Practice Areas: Federal and state court litigator for over 35 years, focusing on corporate disputes, securities litigation and antitrust matters. Represented major US and foreign corporations in a wide variety of industries.
Prof. Memberships: American College of Trial Lawyers (Fellow), International Academy of Trial Lawyers (Fellow), Association of the Federal Bar of New Jersey (former Vice President), New Jersey State Bar Association Business and Commercial Litigation Committee (past Chairman), Brennan Inn of Court (Master).
Career: 'The Best Lawyers in America' - business litigation, antitrust, and bankruptcy. Columbia University School of Law (JD); Cornell University (BA); Columbia School of Business (MBA).

GROSS, Michael
Giordano Halleran & Ciesla PC, Middletown 732 714 3900
Recommended in Environment

GROSS, Steven
Sills Cummis Epstein & Gross PC, Newark 973 643 7000
Recommended in Corporate/M&A

GUARIGLIA, Michael A
McCarter & English, LLP, Newark
973 639 2016
mguariglia@mccarter.com
Recommended in Corporate/M&A
Practice Areas: Mr Guariglia's practice concentrates in federal, multistate and local tax law. He frequently represents clients in tax controversies before the Internal Revenue Service, the New Jersey Division of Taxation and other state administrative bodies, and in federal courts and the Tax Court of New Jersey.
Career: Mr Guariglia also has extensive experience advising clients regarding multistate tax planning strategies, the state tax effects of mergers, acquisitions and restructurings and the state tax implications of ongoing business operations. His practice also includes various tax, business and estate planning services to medium and small businesses and their owners.

HALL, Thomas
Sills Cummis Epstein & Gross PC, Newark 973 643 7000
Recommended in Real Estate

HARRIS, David L
Lowenstein Sandler PC, Roseland
973 597 2378
dharris@lowenstein.com
Recommended in Litigation
Practice Areas: Chair of the firms 110-lawyer Litigation Department. He has over 25 years of trial and appellate experience in several jurisdictions, emphasizing intellectual property, trade secrets, antitrust, and other business litigation, insurance coverage for catastrophic events, complex criminal defense, and civil rights cases.
Prof. Memberships: American Civil Liberties Union; President 1995-99, Trial

Lawyers of New Jersey; Editorial Board 1990-94, 'New Jersey Law Journal'; Commissioner, New Jersey Commission on Racism and Racial and Religious Violence; Rutgers University Law School Alumni Association; President 1989-90, American Bar Association, Intellectual Property Committee, Chair, Subcommittee Trade Secret Damages and Other Remedies; New Jersey State Bar Association; Garden State Bar Association; National Bar Association; Presidents Advisory Council, Essex County Bar Association; President 1998-2001, Volunteer Lawyers For Justice.
Career: Business Litigation; 'Top Ten Litigators in New Jersey,' The National Law Journal; NJ Supreme Court (1979), US District Court, District of New Jersey (1979), Pennsylvania Supreme Court (1979), US Court of Appeals, Third Circuit (1982), US District Court, Eastern District of NY (1987), US Court of Appeals, Fourth Circuit (1987), US Court of Appeals, Sixth Circuit (1993), US District Court, Southern District of NY (2001). Rutgers University School of Law, adjunct Professor-Antitrust 1995-99.
Publications: 'Preparing Experts with Kumho in Mind,' 'The Practical Litigator'; 'The Absolute Pollution Exclusion: Subterfuge, Confusion and Fair Resolution,' 'ABA Monograph'; 'Meet Legal Needs of the Poor Through Organization, Not Mandatory Pro Bono,' 'New Jersey Law Journal'; 'Protecting Trade Secrets: Steps to Take When Information is Firmly Lodged in Employees Heads,' 'NJ Lawyer'.
Personal: Rutgers University School of Law, (JD, 1979); Pennsylvania State University, (MEd, 1972),(BA, 1970).

HAYDEN, Joe
Walder, Hayden & Brogan P.A., Roseland 973 992 5300
Recommended in Litigation

HELLER, William J
McCarter & English, LLP, Newark
973 639 6973
wheller@mccarter.com
Recommended in Litigation
Practice Areas: Mr Heller chairs the Intellectual Property and Information Technology Practice and regularly litigates IP and IT disputes in federal and state courts throughout the country. Some recent cases of note are a trade secrets case tried to jury verdict and a copyright infringement case against a worldwide china manufacturer. Mr Heller represents clients in transactional internet, e-commerce, computer and IP matters.
Career: He was part of a team that defended an international camera company against patent infringement claims. He frequently acts as local counsel to major New York, Chicago and other patent specialty firms litigating in New Jersey.

HERZBERG, ESQ, Peter J
Pitney Hardin LLP, Morristown
973 966 8058
pherzberg@pitneyhardin.com
Recommended in Environment

Practice Areas: Complex federal and state litigation related to government agencies and commercial and toxic tort litigation. Expertise in environmental litigation, including natural resource damages, insurance litigation, private contribution actions, and toxic tort. Former Deputy Attorney General, State of New Jersey, and Acting Assistant Counsel to New Jersey Governor Byrne.
Prof. Memberships: ABA; New Jersey State Bar Association (Past Chair, Environmental Section).
Career: Partner since 1992.
Publications: Numerous articles. Most recently, 'OPRA: Music to A Litigator's Ear' 'New Jersey Law Journal', scheduled April, 2005.
Personal: University of Pennsylvania, JD, 1975; Haverford College, BA, 1972.

HILL, Henry
Hill Wallack, Princeton 609 924 0808
Recommended in Real Estate

HIMMEL, Michael B
Lowenstein Sandler PC, Roseland
973 597 6172
mhimmel@lowenstein.com
Recommended in Litigation

Practice Areas: Chair of the firms White Collar Criminal Defense Practice Group. He has developed a national practice in white collar criminal defense including areas such as tax fraud, securities fraud, political corruption, antitrust, bank fraud, and environmental matters. His clients have included private and public corporations, officers and directors of private and public corporations, professionals and state and federal officials. He also assists corporate clients with internal investigations. A former Assistant US Attorney for the District of New Jersey, Mr Himmel is well known for his work in complex business litigation. He currently represents the State of New Jersey in the prosecution of two multi-billion dollar class action securities fraud cases.
Prof. Memberships: American Bar Association, Fellow; New Jersey State Bar Association; New York State Bar Association; Association of the Federal Bar of the State of New Jersey, President 1998-2000; Federal Bar Council; National Association of Criminal Defense Lawyers; New Jersey Association of Criminal Defense Lawyers.
Career: New York Bar (1975); US District Court, Southern and Eastern Districts of New York (1975); US Court of Appeals, Second Circuit (1975); US Supreme Court (1980); New Jersey Bar (1981); US District Court, District of New Jersey (1981); US Court of Appeals, Third Circuit (1983).
Publications: 'What Lawyers Need to Know About Accepting Cash from Clients,' 'New Jersey Law Journal'; 'When an Employee Invokes the Fifth Amendment, the Corporate Employer May Suffer the Consequences,' 'The Metropolitan Corporate Counsel'; 'Did You Say Pre-Subpoena Obstruction of Justice?', 'The Metropolitan Corporate Counsel'; 'Victims May Collude To Contest Dumping,' 'The National Law Journal'; 'The Defense of Criminal Antitrust Prosecutions: Sometimes Half The Battle is Knowing Where To Fight,' 'The Metropolitan Corporate Counsel'; 'When the White Collar Criminal Investigation Hits, No Longer Business as Usual,' 'The Metropolitan Corporate Counsel'; 'The Parallel Proceedings Pickle: Making the Best of Concurrent Civil and Criminal Federal Cases,' Complex Crimes Journal ABA, Section of Litigation; 'Grand Jury Practice,' 'The New Jersey Lawyer'.
Personal: St Louis University (JD, 1974, Member, St Louis University Law Review); Boston University; New York University (BS, 1971).

HLUCHAN, Richard M
Ballard Spahr Andrews & Ingersoll LLP, Voorhees 856 761 3420
hluchan@ballardspahr.com
Recommended in Environment

Practice Areas: For over 25 years, he has practiced environmental and land use law, including zoning and regulatory matters. He counsels clients in areas subject to regulation by the New Jersey Department of Environmental Protection and the US Environmental Protection Agency, including hazardous waste clean-ups, wetlands, and land development permits. He assists clients in land use matters, including CAFRA permitting, waterfront development, and riparian matters, as well as rezonings, variances, subdivisions, and site plans. He also represents clients in regulatory takings litigation (inverse condemnation).
Prof. Memberships: He was appointed to the Supreme Court of New Jersey's Committee on Environmental Litigation, and also has served as a member of the Supreme Court's Committee on Character. An active member of the New Jersey State Bar Association, he is currently director of the Land Use Section, having served as Chair in 2001-02, and previously serving as a director of the Environmental Section. He has taught environmental law at Rutgers University School of Law - Camden. In 1994, he was selected as a Leadership New Jersey Fellow. Since 2002, he has been a member of the American College of Real Estate Lawyers. He is a Master in the Delaware Valley Environmental American Inn of Court. He has spoken and served as a panelist at a wide array of seminars and conferences sponsored by the NJ Institute for Continuing Legal Education, the New Jersey Builders Association, and other organizations. He is a member of the editorial board of the 'New Jersey Law Journal'. In 2003, he was elected to the Board of Governors of the Georgetown University Alumni Association.
Career: Admitted to the California Bar (1975); admitted to the New Jersey Bar (1975); joined as Partner (1999). Following graduation from law school, he served as a law clerk to the Honorable John F Gerry, United States District Court, Camden, NJ. Prior to entering into private practice, he was a Deputy Attorney General in Trenton where he served as Assistant Chief of the Attorney General's Environmental Section and Chief Counsel to the Pinelands Commission. While in this capacity, he successfully litigated numerous environmental cases involving matters such as air pollution regulations, non-degradation water quality standards, and defense of the Pinelands Comprehensive Management Plan.
Personal: JD, magna cum laude, Santa Clara University School of Law (1974); BSFS, Georgetown University (1971).

HOGAN, Edward
Norris, McLaughlin & Marcus, P.A., A Professional Corporation, Bridgewater
908 722 0700
Recommended in Environment

HULL Jr, Gerald
Drinker Biddle & Reath LLP, Florham Park 973 549 7000
Gerald.Hull@dbr.com
Recommended in Real Estate

Practice Areas: Co-Head of the firm's Real Estate Practice Group. Senior real estate Partner with extensive experience including land use, zoning, construction, permanent and other types of financing transactions, leasing, sale leaseback transactions and title insurance. Practice has involved transactions throughout the United States.
Prof. Memberships: Admitted to practice in New Jersey (1965).
Career: Joined Drinker Biddle in 1999.
Personal: JD, Rutgers University, 1965; BBA, University of Miami, 1962.

HUTCHEON, Peter
Norris, McLaughlin & Marcus, P.A., A Professional Corporation, Bridgewater
908 722 0700
Recommended in Corporate/M&A

HYATT, William
Kirkpatrick & Lockhart Nicholson Graham LLP, Newark 973.848.4045
whyatt@klng.com
Recommended in Environment

Practice Areas: Served as counsel at over 25 Superfund sites in New Jersey and at Superfund sites in 10 other states. Negotiated landmark settlements with the USEPA and the USDOJ, and mediated complex allocation disputes. Practice includes products liability, building construction, environmental insurance coverage and toxic tort litigation. Firmwide practice group coordinator.
Prof. Memberships: Director, Environmental Law Institute. Member, ABA and NJSBA sections on environmental law.
Publications: Frequent speaker and writer on issues relating to natural resource damages and Superfund issues.
Personal: LLM, Boston University School of Law (1967), LLB, Columbia University School of Law (1964), BA, Middlebury College (1961).

JACOB, Cynthia
Collier, Jacob & Mills, Somerset
732 560 7100
Recommended in Employment

JANIS, Ronald H
Pitney Hardin LLP, Morristown
212 297 5813
rjanis@pitneyhardin.com
Recommended in Corporate/M&A

Practice Areas: Managing Partner of the New York office. Practice encompasses representing targets, acquirers and investment banks in mergers and acquisitions; advising banks, broker-dealers and other financial institutions with respect to regulatory issues; and counseling companies with respect to corporate governance issues.
Prof. Memberships: ABA; Association of the Bar of the City of New York, Banking Law Committee; Financial Services Roundtable; Institute for International Bankers; Securities Industry Association, Compliance and Legal Division.
Career: Partner since 1994.
Publications: Numerous articles in American Banker, Bank Director and other publications.
Personal: New York University School of Law, JD, 1975; Harvard College, BA, 1970.

KAHN, Richard
Winne Banta Hetherington Basralian & Kahn, P.C., Hackensack
201 487 3800
Recommended in Real Estate

KEARNEY, ESQ, Dennis T
Pitney Hardin LLP, Morristown
973 966 8039
dkearney@pitneyhardin.com
Recommended in Litigation

Practice Areas: Civil and criminal litigation. Recent trial successes include the prosecution of civil fraud against the most litigious plaintiff in New Jersey history, the defense of a bank against a multi-million dollar class action, and the defense of a bank against a $20 million claim involving RICO, bribery and fraud.
Prof. Memberships: ABA; New Jersey State Bar Association; New Jersey Supreme Court District X Ethics Committee (Committee Investigator, 1990-94; Hearing Panel Chairman, 1991-94), American Health Lawyers Association; I.C.L.E. Panelist Health Care Fraud.
Career: Partner since 1988.
Personal: University of Notre Dame, JD, 1980; University of Notre Dame, BA, 1976.

KEYSER, Denise M
Ballard Spahr Andrews & Ingersoll LLP,
Voorhees 856 761 3442
keyserd@ballardspahr.com
Recommended in Employment
Practice Areas: Her practice includes
representation of management in all
phases of labor and employment matters, including collective bargaining,
arbitrations, OSHA, ERISA, wage and
hour, employment-at-will, wrongful
discharge, discrimination, management
training, and affirmative action.
Prof. Memberships: Member of the
Executive Committee and a coordinator
on the Disability Discrimination Subcommittee for the Labor and Employment Law Section of the New Jersey
State Bar Association. She is also a former Co-Chair of the Section's Disability
Discrimination Committee and a former Chair of the Alternate Dispute Resolution Committee. She is a member of
both the New Jersey State Bar Association and the American Bar Association.
Career: Admitted to the New Jersey Bar
(1983); admitted to the Pennsylvania
Bar (1983); joined as Partner (2002).
Publications: She is a contributing
author to the ICLE/New Jersey State Bar
Association compendium of New Jersey
employment law, entitled New Jersey
Workplace Law.
Personal: JD, University of Pennsylvania Law School, (1983); BA, with high
honors, State University of New York at
Stony Brook (1980).

KIPNEES, Robert J
Lowenstein Sandler PC, Roseland
973 597 6220
rkipnees@lowenstein.com
Recommended in Litigation
Practice Areas: Concentrates his practice in complex white collar criminal
cases, including securities fraud, tax
fraud, antitrust and environmental
crimes and political corruption cases.
He brings to bear in defending firm
clients many years of experience, including significant trial experience in both
prosecution and defense work. Mr Kipnees also handles complex civil securities fraud cases, criminal and civil RICO
cases, class actions and complex civil
fraud and antitrust cases.
Prof. Memberships: American Bar
Association, sections of Litigation and
Criminal Justice; Association of the Bar
of the State of New York; New York State
Bar Association; New Jersey State Bar
Association; National Association of
Criminal Defense Lawyers.
Career: New Jersey Bar (1981); New
York Bar (1981); US District Court, Dis-
trict of New Jersey (1981); US District
Court, Eastern and Southern Districts of
New York (1981); US Court of Appeals,
Third Circuit (1985); US Supreme
Court (1992); US District Court, East-
ern District of Wisconsin (1995); US Tax
Court (2000).
Publications: Criminal Trial Prepara-

tion, New Jersey Institute of Continuing
Legal Education.
Personal: Harvard Law School (JD,
1980, cum laude); Cornell University
College of Arts and Sciences (BA, 1977,
cum laude, with distinction).

KNEE, Stephen H
Greenbaum, Rowe, Smith & Davis LLP,
Roseland 973 535 1600
sknee@greenbaumlaw.com
Recommended in Corporate/M&A
Practice Areas: Mergers and acquisi-
tions; corporate law and business counseling; financial services; professional
liability counseling and litigation; secu-
rities regulation and litigation; e-com-
merce and internet law.
Prof. Memberships: Director, Corporate
and Business Law Section, member,
Banking Law Section and the Bankrupt-
cy Law Section, NJ State Bar Association.
Member, Section of Business Law, American Bar Association, Committee on
Negotiated Acquisitions; Co-Chair, ABA
Task Force on Acquisitions of Public
Companies. Member, American College
of Investment Counsel; Essex County
Bar Association; founding member, the
Inn of Transactional Counsel.
Personal: New York University School
of Law (1965), Duke University (1962).

KORNSTEIN, Alan
Orloff, Lowenbach, Stifelman & Siegel,
Roseland 973 622 6200
Recommended in Corporate/M&A

KRAUS, Alan
Latham & Watkins LLP, Newark
973 639 1234
Recommended in Litigation

KROVATIN, Gerald
Krovatin & Associates LLC, Newark
973 424 9777
Recommended in Litigation

KRUMHOLZ, Dennis J
Riker Danzig Scherer Hyland & Perretti
LLP, Morristown 973 451 8454
dkrumholz@riker.com
Recommended in Environment
Practice Areas: Chair of Environmen-
tal Group. Extensive experience in cost
recovery litigation, brownfields, ISRA
compliance, and consultant malpractice.
Prof. Memberships: Held offices in the
Environmental Law Section of New Jer-
sey State Bar Association, including
Chair of the Section; Past Chair of
INFORM, environmental research
group; Founding Master of the Stewart
G Pollock Environmental American Inn
of Court; Founding Chair of Essex
County Bar Associations Environmental
Law Committee.
Career: Served as Deputy Attorney
General for the State of New Jersey; Fea-
tured in the 1996-2006 editions of 'The
Best Lawyers in America' (Wood-
ward/White, Inc.).
Personal: Boston College, JD; Oberlin
College, BA.

LAVEY, Stewart
Drinker Biddle & Reath LLP,
Florham Park 973 549 7130
Stewart.Lavey@dbr.com
Recommended in Corporate/M&A
Practice Areas: Partner, Business and
Finance Department; Associate Head,
Corporate and Securities Practice. Expe-
rienced in M&A, corporate securities,
joint ventures, and corporate governance.
Prof. Memberships: Admitted in New
York, New Jersey, Pennsylvania, District
of Columbia. Member, New York, New
Jersey, Pennsylvania, District of Colum-
bia and American Bar Associations;
Subcommittee on the Securities Act of
1933 of the Section of Business Law of
the American Bar Association. Past
adjunct faculty member, Fordham University School of Law.
Career: Joined Shanley & Fisher PC
1985 and Drinker Biddle in 1999.
Personal: JD, Fordham University
School of Law, 1970; AB, Syracuse University, 1967.

LILOIA, Gerald A
Riker Danzig Scherer Hyland & Perretti
LLP, Morristown 973 451 8500
gliloia@riker.com
Recommended in Litigation
Practice Areas: Head of Litigation
Group and Chair of Executive Committee. Focuses on a variety of commercial
litigation matters, representing banks
and other financial institutions. Has
served as lead counsel in many major
banking, insurance, reinsurance, consumer and securities class action and
professional liability suits and arbitrations. Represented major New Jersey
and money center banks in connection
with some of their largest real estate and
commercial loan workouts and restructurings. Represented US and international banks in renegotiating and
restructuring sovereign and private sector debt in Mexico, Central America and
other international venues.
Personal: Rutgers University, LLB;
Seton Hall University, BA.

LITTENBERG, Joseph
Lerner David Littenberg Krumholz &
Mentlik, LLP, Westfield 908 654 5000
Recommended in Litigation

LUSTBERG, Lawrence S
Gibbons, Del Deo, Dolan, Griffinger &
Vecchione, Newark 973 596 4731
llustberg@gibbonslaw.com
Recommended in Litigation
Practice Areas: Chair of the Criminal
Law Department and Director of the
firm's Fellowship in Public Interest and
Constitutional Law. Focuses practice in
white collar criminal defense and busi-
ness fraud litigation.
Prof. Memberships: American Bar
Association (Fellow), Lawyers Commit-
tee for Civil Rights Under Law (Trustee),
Compulsive Gambling Council of New
Jersey Advisory Board.
Career: 'The Best Lawyers in America' -

criminal defense. The American Civil
Liberties Union Roger N Baldwin
Award. Professor at Seton Hall Universi-
ty School of Law and Rutgers University
School of Law. Harvard University Law
School (JD); Harvard University (BA);
International Graduate School, Univer-
sity of Stockholm, Sweden.

MARCHETTA, Anthony J
Pitney Hardin LLP, Morristown
973 966 8032
amarchetta@pitneyhardin.com
Recommended in Litigation
Practice Areas: Certified Civil Trial
Attorney of the State of New Jersey. Trial
and appellate practice encompasses
patent and trademark jury trials, com-
mercial litigation, products liability
including medical, mass torts and other.
Prof. Memberships: ABA; New Jersey
State Bar Association; Supreme Court of
New Jersey; New York Intellectual Property Law Association.
Career: Partner since 1993; previously,
Partner with Hannock Weisman 1979-93.
Publications: Most recent of numerous
articles is 'Electronic Data Production -
Courts Begin to Set Parameters' in Metropolitan Corporate Counsel, January
and February 2004.
Personal: Rutgers College, BA, cum
laude, 1970; American University, Wash-
ington College of Law, JD, 1973.

MARIANI, Richard C
Ogletree, Deakins, Nash, Smoak &
Stewart, PC, Morristown 973 656 1600
richard.mariani@ogletreedeakins.com
Recommended in Employment
Practice Areas: Extensive experience
representing management in all types of
employment cases before state and federal trial and appellate courts and
administrative agencies, conducting
internal corporate investigations and
developing/presenting employment
training programs.
Prof. Memberships: American Bar
Association (Equal Employment Opportunity Committee), New Jersey State Bar
Association (Labor and Employment
Law Section, Trial Practices Subcommittee) and the American Employment Law
Council. Fellow of The College of Labor
and Employment Lawyers.
Publications: Has lectured extensively
and has authored numerous articles on
employment-related issues.
Personal: Boston College (AB, 1968),
Villanova University School of Law (JD,
1973). Listed in 'The Best Lawyers in
America'.

MARINO, Kevin
Marino & Associates PC, Newark
973 824 9300
Recommended in Litigation

MCTIERNAN, Edward F
Gibbons, Del Deo, Dolan, Griffinger & Vecchione, Newark 973 596 4739
emctiernan@gibbonslaw.com
Recommended in Environment

Practice Areas: Represents clients before administrative agencies in all aspects of environmental matters. Transactional and counseling experience includes environmental audits, negotiation of acquisitions/dispositions and management of complex enforcement matters. Assisted with the successful cleanup and redevelopment of numerous Brownfield properties.
Prof. Memberships: New Jersey State Bar Association Wetlands and Land-Use Committee (Board of Directors); New Jersey State Bar Association Environmental Law Section (former Chair); Environmental Law Institute.
Career: Seton Hall University School of Law (JD); Fordham University (BS); State University of New York (MS).
Publications: Numerous articles on New Jersey's Natural Resource Damage Program, most recently in 'Business Week'.

MEISER, Kenneth
Hill Wallack, Princeton 609 924 0808
Recommended in Real Estate

MENTLIK, William
Lerner David Littenberg Krumholz & Mentlik, LLP, Westfield
908 654 5000
Recommended in Litigation

MINION, Robert G
Lowenstein Sandler PC, Roseland
973 597 2424
rminion@lowenstein.com
Recommended in Corporate/M&A

Practice Areas: Co-Chair of Lowenstein Sandlers Investment Management Group. He has 19 years of experience in all aspects of corporate and business law, with an emphasis in securities law, investment partnerships, mergers and acquisitions and related corporate transactions. He represents clients throughout the United States and internationally in a wide variety of investment, investment fund, capital formation and corporate finance transactions (including fund formations, mergers and acquisitions, venture capital, and public and private securities offerings).
Prof. Memberships: Mr Minion has served as an Adjunct Professor at Rutgers University School of Law, teaching Securities Law and Regulation. He has also served as the Chairperson of the Corporate Law Committee of the Essex County Bar Association. He chaired the National Business Institute Seminar on Negotiating and Drafting Acquisition Agreements, co-chaired The New Jersey Institute for Continuing Legal Education Sale of Businesses Program, and the Summit Series on Unlocking Shareholder Value. He chairs the Annual Lowenstein Sandler Investment Management

Forum and is a frequent speaker at investment industry programs, including the 2005 New York Annual Hedge Fund Regulation and Compliance Forum, the Bank of America Fund Manager Conference and the Emerald Asset Management Investor Conference. Mr Minion also serves on the Legal Committee of The Wall Street Hedge Fund Forum and many other professional associations.
Career: New Jersey and Federal Bar (1986); New York Bar (1987).
Publications: Mr Minion is a noted author and lecturer in corporate law, securities transactions and investment management. Many of his transactions have been published in, and/or he has been quoted in or provided commentary for, among others, The Wall Street Journal, The Deal, The Deal.com, The PIPEs Report, The American Lawyer, the 'New Jersey Law Journal', and the New Jersey Lawyer. He is the editor of the Lowenstein Sandler Investment Management Alert, a quarterly newsletter of legal issues for the investment management community.
Personal: Stanford University (JD, 1986); Cornell University (AB, 1983, with distinction in all subjects).

MORRISON, Victoria A
Riker Danzig Scherer Hyland & Perretti LLP, Morristown 973 451 8470
vmorrison@riker.com
Recommended in Real Estate

Practice Areas: Partner in Real Estate and Financial Institutions Groups. Commercial real estate experience in acquisition, development, leasing and sale of commercial, retail, and industrial properties. Represents national and regional landlords and tenants in leasing transactions. Represents buyers and sellers in complex commercial transactions, including sale-leasebacks and build-to-suits. Represents lenders in real estate financings. Extensive experience in real estate partnerships and joint ventures, federal tax aspects of commercial real estate transactions and workouts and foreclosures including bankruptcy.
Prof. Memberships: Member of International Council of Shopping Centers; National Association of Industrial and Office Parks.
Personal: Case Western Reserve University, JD; BA.

MOULTHROP, Samuel P
Riker Danzig Scherer Hyland & Perretti LLP, Morristown 973 451 8471
smoulthrop@riker.com
Recommended in Environment

Practice Areas: Partner in Environmental Group. Focuses on environmental litigation, permitting, transactional, and regulatory/compliance, as well as white collar criminal defense and corporate investigations.
Career: Served in US Attorney's Office for District of New Jersey as Assistant US Attorney, Chief of Criminal Divi-

sion, Chief of the Appeals Division, Deputy Chief of Fraud and Public Protection Division and Chief of Environmental Section; Served as Acting Branch Chief and as Enforcement Attorney with US Environmental Protection Agency; Featured in the 1996-2006 editions of 'The Best Lawyers in America' (Woodward/White, Inc.).
Personal: Boston University School of Law, JD; Eckerd College, BA, with honors.

NEWMAN, Jeffrey
Sills Cummis Epstein & Gross PC, Newark 973 643 7000
Recommended in Real Estate

O'DONNELL, Matthew
In Limbo, Unionville
Recommended in Real Estate

OHNEGIAN, Scott A
Riker Danzig Scherer Hyland & Perretti LLP, Morristown 973 451 8551
sohnegian@riker.com
Recommended in Employment

Practice Areas: Partner in Labor and Employment Group. Represents clients in hearings, arbitrations and trials before federal and state courts, the American Arbitration Association, and federal and state agencies in employment-related and commercial litigation matters. Counsels clients on a variety of labor and employment issues.
Career: Served as a law clerk to Hon. John C Lifland, US District Judge, District of New Jersey; Published employment law articles in state and national publications as well as given seminars on various employment law issues.
Personal: Rutgers University School of Law, JD; Amherst College, BA.

ORLOFF, Laurence
Orloff, Lowenbach, Stifelman & Siegel, Roseland 973 622 6200
Recommended in Litigation

PANTEL, Glenn S
Drinker Biddle & Reath LLP, Florham Park 973 549 7020
Glenn.Pantel@dbr.com
Recommended in Real Estate

Practice Areas: Partner, Real Estate Practice. Experienced in land development, commercial real estate transactions, and regulatory matters, including wetlands issues, ISRA compliance, waterfront development and local zoning and planning approvals. Represents major developers and corporate users in large scale development plans and acquisitions.
Prof. Memberships: Admitted in New Jersey (1978), New York (1978), Florida (1980), the US District Court for the District of New Jersey and US Court of Appeals for the Third Circuit. Member, New Jersey, Pennsylvania and Florida Bar Associations.
Career: Joined Drinker Biddle in 1979.
Personal: BA, Johns Hopkins University, 1975; JD, University of Pennsylvania, 1978.

PARLIMAN, Gregory C
Pitney Hardin LLP, Morristown
973 966 8015
gparliman@pitneyhardin.com
Recommended in Employment

Practice Areas: Member of the firm's Executive Committee. Substantial litigation experience defending employers against discrimination, whistleblower, and wrongful discharge litigation. Advises employers in best practices, for example, with respect to employee discipline and discharge, employment and severance agreements, family and medical leave issues, and ADA compliance.
Prof. Memberships: ABA; New Jersey State Bar Association; College of Labor and Employment Lawyers; Association of the Federal Bar of the State of New Jersey (Trustee).
Career: Partner since 1980.
Publications: Editorial Board, 'Employee Relations Law Journal.'
Personal: Georgetown University Law Center, JD, 1973; Rutgers University, Rutgers College, BA, summa cum laude, 1969.

PATTERSON, Anne M
Riker Danzig Scherer Hyland & Perretti LLP, Morristown 973 451 8482
apatterson@riker.com
Recommended in Litigation

Practice Areas: Partner in Litigation Group. Experience in product liability, including pharmaceutical, tobacco and chemical litigation, and commercial litigation.
Prof. Memberships: Member of New Jersey Supreme Court Committee on Character; Vice-Chair of Product Liability and Toxic Tort Section of the New Jersey State Bar Association; Trustee of the Association of the Federal Bar of the State of New Jersey; Trustee of Trial Attorneys of New Jersey and Chair of its Education Committee.
Career: Served as Special Assistant to the Attorney General and Deputy Attorney General of New Jersey.
Personal: Cornell Law School, JD; Dartmouth College, AB, Phi Beta Kappa.

PEIRANO, John
McElroy, Deutsch, Mulvaney & Carpenter, LLP, Morristown 973 993 8100
Recommended in Employment

POLICASTRO, Marc D
Greenbaum, Rowe, Smith & Davis LLP, Woodbridge 732 549 5600
mpolicastro@greenbaumlaw.com
Recommended in Real Estate

Practice Areas: Partner of the firm. Concentrates his practice in complex environmental real estate and business transactions, environmental regulatory and redevelopment/zoning matters. Represents developers, lenders, businesses and borrowers in myriad land use contexts, including commercial and residential development.
Prof. Memberships: Member, Land Use and Environmental Law Sections, NJ

State Bar Association. Member, NJ Builders Association, Mortgage Bankers Association.

Career: Selected by the 'New Jersey Law Journal' for inclusion in its top '40 Under 40' list, citing top 40 attorneys under the age of 40.

Personal: Seton Hall University School of Law (1990), University of Richmond (1987).

POSITAN, Wayne J
Lum, Danzis, Drasco & Positan, LLC, Roseland 973 228 6730
wpositan@lumlaw.com
Recommended in Employment

Practice Areas: 30 years experience in state/federal litigation of labor and employment matters representing management and defendants; non-compete matters; appellate practice, with over 20 reported cases; traditional labor practice: NRLB, collective bargaining, arbitration; DOL, OSHA, EEOC, DCR; HR counseling; ADR and mediation; NJ Court approved mediator.

Prof. Memberships: Admitted in New Jersey and New York, DNJ, SDNY, EDNY, Third Circuit Court of Appeals, and US Supreme Court. Member, ABA House of Delegates; President-Elect, New Jersey State Bar Association; Chair, ABA Commission on MJP (2000-02); ABA Section of Litigation: Council (1997-2000) and Director of Divisions (2001-02); Council, ABA Center for Professional Responsibility (2000-02); Chair, NJSBA Labor and Employment Section (1995-97); Member: DRI. Fellow: College of Labor and Employment Lawyers (1996); American Bar Foundation; ABA Section of Litigation. Professional Lawyer of the Year Award (2002), New Jersey Commission on Professionalism; Professional Achievement Award (2001), Essex County Bar Association; 'Top Lawyers' and 'Super-lawyers', New Jersey Monthly Magazine.

Career: Lum, Danzis, Drasco & Positan, LLC and its predecessors since 1974; Partner/member, Chair of Labor and Employment Group since 1982; Managing Director since 1990.

Publications: Editor in chief, 'New Jersey Labor and Employment Law' (NJICLE); Board of Editors, 'Jury Instructions in Employment Litigation' (ABA); co-author, Employment Torts chapter, 'Business Torts Litigation' (ABA); co-author, Special Evidentiary Concerns chapter, 'Employment Litigation Desk Reference' (ABA); ABA website 'CLE Now-Practical Tips for Employment Litigators'.

Personal: BA, Government, magna cum laude, Boston University 1970; JD, NYU 1974; Board of Trustees: Montclair State University; Chaine des Rotisseurs (Saddle River).

RABINOWITZ, David
Sills Cummis Epstein & Gross PC, Newark 973 643 7000
Recommended in Real Estate

RACIOPPI Jr, Nicholas
Riker Danzig Scherer Hyland & Perretti LLP, Morristown 973 451 8492
nracioppi@riker.com
Recommended in Real Estate

Practice Areas: Partner in Real Estate and Financial Institutions Practice Groups. Considerable commercial real estate experience, particularly in the acquisition, development, zoning and planning, leasing and sale of commercial and industrial properties. Represents lenders in real estate financings and has extensive experience in complex real estate workouts and foreclosures. Experience in the formation and structuring of real estate partnerships and joint ventures.

Prof. Memberships: Member of New Jersey State and American Bar Associations; Member of National Association of Industrial and Office Parks.

Personal: New York University, JD; Rutgers University, BA, with high honors, Phi Beta Kappa.

RADZELY, Edward
Giordano Halleran & Ciesla PC, Middletown 732 714 3900
Recommended in Real Estate

REILLY, Gregory B
Lowenstein Sandler PC, Roseland 973 597 2460
greilly@lowenstein.com
Recommended in Litigation

Practice Areas: Has 30 years of first chair litigation experience representing United States and foreign companies as well as public and private universities. Practice concentrates in federal and state court injunctions and damage actions in such areas as business torts, contract actions, corporate governance, constitutional law, securities, and employment law. He has represented clients at bench trials, jury trials, arbitrations, mediations, administrative proceedings and appeals. He has advised public and private corporations and universities concerning compliance with state and federal legislation and regulations.

Prof. Memberships: National Association of College and University Attorneys; American, New Jersey State and Essex County Bar associations.

Career: New Jersey and Federal courts (1973), the US Court of Appeals, Third Circuit and US Tax Court (1975).

Publications: 'A Practical Guide to New Jersey Employment Law: The Employer's Resource', 'Managing the Workforce: Private Employees' Right to Organize and the New Jersey Anti-Injunction Act.'

Personal: Rutgers University School of Law (JD, 1973); Princeton University (BA,1967).

RIDLEY, John
Drinker Biddle & Reath LLP, Florham Park 973 549 7030
John.Ridley@dbr.com
Recommended in Employment

Practice Areas: Partner and Co-Chair, Labor and Employment Practice. Practice focuses on labor and employment law, litigation, and employment and labor disputes.

Prof. Memberships: Admitted in New Jersey. Member, Defense Research Institute; Essex County, New Jersey State and American Bar Associations, the Equal Employment Opportunity Committee of the American Bar Association's Section on Labor and Employment Law. Appointments: Executive Committee of the Labor and Employment Section of the New Jersey State Bar Association; past Board Member of the Trial Attorneys of New Jersey.

Career: Joined Drinker Biddle in 2002.

Personal: JD, University of Virginia, 1968; AB, St Peters College, 1965.

RODBURG, Michael L
Lowenstein Sandler PC, Roseland 973 597 2466
mrodburg@lowenstein.com
Recommended in Environment

Practice Areas: Michael L Rodburg is the firm's Managing Director. He has more than 30 years' experience in complex litigation and has practiced exclusively in environmental law for more than 25 years. Mr Rodburg represents business and industry in connection with significant business transactions, civil litigation and administrative agency proceedings arising out of a wide variety of environmental problems. He concentrates in hazardous waste and substances litigation, mass tort defense, and acquisition counseling.

Prof. Memberships: Chemical Waste Litigation Reporter, Editorial Board; The Environmental Claims Journal, Editorial Advisory Board; Environmental Insurance Litigation Institute, Board of Advisors; Hazardous Wastes and Toxic Torts: Law & Strategy, Contributing Editor; New Jersey State Bar Association, First Chair, Environmental Law Section (1984-85); American Bar Association, Section of Environment, Energy, and Resources; National Conference for Community and Justice, New Jersey Region, Vice-Chairman.

Career: New Jersey Bar (1971).

Publications: 'New Mexico v. General Electric: A Cautionary Tale', 'New Jersey Law Journal'; 'Groundwater Damages In New Jersey', 'Superfund and Natural Resource Damages Litigation Committee Newsletter'; 'Top Ten Reasons Why New Jersey Businesses Should Be Concerned About Natural Resource Damages', 'The Metropolitan Corporate Counsel'; 'Traps Set for the Unwary - California Supreme Court Invalidates Policy Rights in Corporate Restructuring', 'Environmental Compliance & Litigation Strategy'; 'New Jersey Environmental Law Handbook', (6th Edition), 'Government Institutes'; 'The Large Company with a Small Law Department', co-authored chapter in 'Successful Partnering Between Inside and Outside Counsel'.

Personal: Harvard University (JD, 1971,

magna cum laude, Editor, Harvard Law Review); Massachusetts Institute of Technology (BS, 1968).

ROLNICK, Lawrence M
Lowenstein Sandler PC, Roseland 973 597 2468
lrolnick@lowenstein.com
Recommended in Litigation

Practice Areas: Chair of the Securities Litigation Practice. Has extensive experience in complex commercial litigation, with emphasis in securities and class action litigation. Has represented public companies in class action litigation, institutional investors in securities litigation and directors and officers in defense of alleged breach of fiduciary duty claims. Successfully argued before the New Jersey Supreme Court on questions of first impression on securities law issues and defended clients in actions brought by the SEC, NASD and NYSE. Currently representing the Kirch Group in its suit against Deutsche Bank and Liberty Media.

Prof. Memberships: NJ State Bar Association's Securities Litigation and Regulatory Enforcement Committee (Co-founder and Chair); New Jersey and American Bar associations; Trustee of the Federal Bar Association, District of NJ.

Career: New York Bar (1985); US District Court, Southern and Eastern Districts of NY (1991); NJ Bar and US District Court, District of NJ (1992); US Court of Appeals, First and Second Circuit (1999); US Court of Appeals, Fifth Circuit (2001).

Publications: 'Complex Litigation: Defending Consumer Fraud Class Actions', 'New Jersey Law Journal'.

Personal: Rutgers University School of Law (JD, 1984, cum laude) and Officer, Rutgers Law Review; Rutgers University (BA, 1981, with high honors) and Henry Rutgers Scholar.

ROTHPLETZ Jr, Michael E
Drinker Biddle & Reath LLP, Florham Park 973 549 7284
Michael.Rothpletz@dbr.com
Recommended in Real Estate

Practice Areas: Partner in the firm's Business and Finance Department. Concentrates in real estate law, including purchase and sale transactions, leasing, financing, construction related matters and development approvals.

Prof. Memberships: Admitted to practice in New Jersey and Pennsylvania. Member of the New Jersey Bar Association, Land Use Law Section.

Career: Joined Drinker Biddle in 1999.

Publications: Co-author, Conveyance of Commercial Real Estate Chapter, 'Commercial Real Estate Transactions in New Jersey', published by New Jersey Institute of Continuing Legal Education (2003).

Personal: JD, Rutgers University School of Law (Newark), 1993; BA, University of Pennsylvania, 1987.

ROTHSCHILD, Gita F
McCarter & English, LLP, Newark
973 639 5959
grothschild@mccarter.com
Recommended in Litigation

Practice Areas: Ms Rothschild practices in the areas of litigation, including insurance coverage, class actions, products liability, toxic torts, commercial contracts and business torts.
Career: She has litigated cases in New Jersey, New York, Pennsylvania, Georgia, Texas, Connecticut, Florida, Virginia and the Virgin Islands. She has nearly 50 reported opinions, including five cases involving significant novel products liability issues in the New Jersey Supreme Court. She defends research-based pharmaceutical companies in litigation involving their medicines, and has represented corporate policyholders for more than 20 years, litigating and resolving coverage disputes issues, principally for Fortune 500 companies.

ROWE, Paul A
Greenbaum, Rowe, Smith & Davis LLP, Woodbridge 732 549 5600
prowe@greenbaumlaw.com
Recommended in Litigation

Practice Areas: Managing Partner; Chair, Litigation Department specializing in complex business and related litigations including construction, partnership and corporate disputes, anti-trust, stock fraud and all forms of chancery litigation.
Prof. Memberships: Past President, Essex County Bar Association. Fellow, American College of Trial Lawyers, International Academy of Trial Lawyers and American Bar Foundation.
Career: 1993 recipient Trial Bar Award, Trial Attorneys of NJ. Admitted New York (1961), New Jersey (1962). Best Lawyers in America, Business Litigation and Family Law.
Publications: Author, 'New Jersey Business Litigation.' Co-author, 'Guidebook to Chancery Practice in New Jersey.'
Personal: Columbia Law School (1961), Tufts College (1958).

SALES, Bruce
Lerner David Littenberg Krumholz & Mentlik, LLP, Westfield
908 654 5000
Recommended in Litigation

SANDAK, Lawrence
Proskauer Rose, Newark
973 274 3256
lsandak@proskauer.com
Recommended in Employment

Practice Areas: A Partner in Proskauer Rose LLP's Labor and Employment Law Department, he has more than 20 years of employment law experience. As a trial lawyer and civil litigator, he defends employers accused of discrimination, retaliation, sexual harassment, breach of contract, and wage and hour violations before courts and government agencies. He also has substantial experience in arbitrating, mediating and negotiating

the settlement of employment disputes. He advises his clients on all aspects of the employer-employee relationship, including the creation of sensible personnel and benefit policies and the preparation of employment contracts, policy manuals and employee handbooks. He is frequently called upon to conduct or supervise internal investigations of alleged employee misconduct, including sexual harassment, and to recommend appropriate responses. He has guided his clients through significant reductions-in-force and business closures.
Publications: He has been a commentator for Court TV, CNN and CNBC, discussing employment discrimination, sexual harassment and personnel management issues, and for the CBS News coverage of the Clarence Thomas confirmation hearings.
Personal: Brooklyn College of the City University of New York (BA, 1975) and Brooklyn Law School (JD 1978), where he served as an editor of the Brooklyn Law Review.

SCHACHTER, Robert C
Greenbaum, Rowe, Smith & Davis LLP, Woodbridge 732 549 5600
rschachter@greenbaumlaw.com
Recommended in Real Estate

Practice Areas: Chair, Real Estate Department. Real estate law specializing in commercial leasing, commercial mortgage financing, real estate brokerage, acquisitions, land use planning and zoning.
Prof. Memberships: Elected to the American College of Real Estate Lawyers. Listed in the International Who's Who of Real Estate Lawyers. Member. Real Property, Probate and Trust Section, NJ Bar Association. Past vice chair, Literature and Publications Committee, Real Property Division of the American Bar Association.
Publications: Co-author, 'New Jersey Real Estate Forms: Practice' (Michie 1992, Lexis Law Publishing), Leasing Chapter in Commercial Real Estate Transactions in New Jersey.
Personal: Rutgers Law School, Newark (1972), Rutgers College (1967).

SCHOENBERG, Robert J
Riker Danzig Scherer Hyland & Perretti LLP, Morristown 973 451 8511
rschoenberg@riker.com
Recommended in Litigation

Practice Areas: Partner in Trademark, Copyright and Computer Law Group. Represents numerous companies in patent, copyright and trademark infringement matters, including a leading software company, a major pharmaceutical company and a company which produces sporting goods and exercise equipment. Represents clients in the entertainment industry. Expertise in computer industry matters and assists clients with protecting contract and property rights arising from the development, licensing, and distribution of

computer hardware and software.
Prof. Memberships: Member of the Litigation Section and Patent, Trademark and Copyright Law Section of the American Bar Association.
Personal: Cornell University, JD, cum laude; Polytechnic University, BS.

SNEIRSON, Marilyn
Kirkpatrick & Lockhart Nicholson Graham LLP, Newark 973 848 4000
msneirson@klng.com
Recommended in Employment

Practice Areas: Employment litigation, representing management before federal and state courts and administrative agencies on employment issues, including wrongful termination, workplace harassment, whistleblower, wages and hours, and discrimination claims. Also counsels on the legal aspects of employee handbooks, compensation and training matters.
Prof. Memberships: Appointed a Master in the Justice Morris Pashman American Inns of Court.
Publications: Lectures and writes frequently on workplace issues such as employee training, sexual harassment, privacy and discipline, and employer workplace monitoring. Appeared as expert commentator on COURT TV.
Personal: Rutgers School of Law at Newark (JD, 1981); Brandeis University (BA, 1968).

SORIN, David
Morgan, Lewis & Bockius LLP, Princeton 609 919 6602
dsorin@morganlewis.com
Recommended in Corporate/M&A

Practice Areas: Mr Sorin is a Partner in the Business and Finance Practice. His practice focuses primarily on corporate transactions, securities law, mergers and acquisitions, and technology. His clients include leading software, information technology, e-commerce, communications and life sciences companies.
Prof. Memberships: Director, Co-Founder, Vice-Chair, New Jersey Technology Council.
Personal: Top 100 New Jersey Business People (NJBIZ).

STAMELMAN, Andrew J
Riker Danzig Scherer Hyland & Perretti LLP, Morristown 973 451 8515
astamelman@riker.com
Recommended in Corporate/M&A

Practice Areas: Head of Tax and Corporate Practice Groups. Serves as general counsel for many middle market companies on issues such as tax strategies, mergers and acquisitions, structuring of joint ventures, partnerships and limited liability companies, and developing executive compensation plans. Represents corporations, partnerships and other entities in many corporate transactions including mergers, acquisitions and divestitures. Assists family-owned businesses in succession planning or orchestrating exit strategies, and

plan implementation.
Prof. Memberships: Member of the New Jersey Bar Associations taxation and corporate law sections.
Personal: New York University, LLM, Taxation; Cornell University, JD; University of Virginia, BA, with honors.

STANTON, Patrick M
Ogletree, Deakins, Nash, Smoak & Stewart, PC, Morristown 973 656 1600
patrick.stanton@ogletreedeakins.com
Recommended in Employment

Practice Areas: Labor and Employment.
Prof. Memberships: New Jersey State Bar Association (Chair, Labor and Employment Law Section); NLRB Region 22 Practice and Procedure Committee; Sidney Reitman Employment Law American Inn of Court (Chair, Organizing Committee; President, 1997-2001).
Career: Admitted: New Jersey, New York, Ohio (inactive), US Supreme Court, US District Courts (DNJ; SDNY; EDNY; SDOH), US Court of Appeals (Third Circuit, and DC Circuit).
Publications: 'New Jersey Employment Laws and Regulations: A Practical Guide For Employers.'
Personal: St Joseph's (Pa.) University (BS, 1969), University of Virginia School of Law (JD, 1972), Fairleigh Dickinson University (Executive MBA Program, 1984).

STODDARD III, John E
Drinker Biddle & Reath LLP, Princeton
609 716 6504
John.Stoddard@dbr.com
Recommended in Corporate/M&A

Practice Areas: Partner, Business and Finance Department and Chair, Emerging Company and Venture Capital Practice. Over 20 years' experience advising businesses on legal and business matters, with emphasis on transactional work such as mergers and acquisitions, private placements, venture capital financings, public securities offerings, leveraged recapitalizations and joint ventures. Clients throughout the US in life sciences, software, publishing, manufacturing, education and other industries.
Prof. Memberships: Admitted in New York (1984) and New Jersey (1988). Member, New Jersey, New York, and American Bar Associations.
Career: Joined Drinker Biddle in 1987.
Personal: BS, University of Virginia, 1981; JD, Boston College, 1984.

SUFLAS, Steven W
Ballard Spahr Andrews & Ingersoll LLP, Voorhees 856 761 3466
suflas@ballardspahr.com
Recommended in Employment

Practice Areas: He concentrates his practice in the representation of management in all phases of labor and employment matters, including collective bargaining and traditional labor law issues, employment litigation, appearances before administrative agencies, ERISA, and wage and hour law.
Prof. Memberships: A past Chair of the

Labor and Employment Law Section of the New Jersey State Bar Association (1999-2001). Fellow of The College of Labor and Employment Lawyers (1996). **Career:** Admitted to the New Jersey Bar (1976); admitted to the Pennsylvania Bar (1978); joined as Partner (2002). **Publications:** Paralegals Are Eligible for Overtime Pay, 'New Jersey Law Journal', Vol. CLXXIX-No. 11, March 14, 2005; Scorecard Redux: Plaintiffs are Still Winners in Employment Cases, 'New Jersey Law Journal', Vol. CLXXIX-No. 7, Index 579 (February 7, 2005); Editor: 'New Jersey Workplace Law', published by The New Jersey Institute for Continuing Education and The NJSBA Labor and Employment Law Section; The New Jersey Labor Letter, Editorial Review Board (1999-2001); Basic Principles for Awarding Attorney's Fees in Discrimination Cases, 'New Jersey Labor and Employment Law Quarterly', Vol. 26, No. 1 (2002); And the Cy Young Award Goes to ... Plaintiff's Lawyers, 'The New Jersey Law Journal', Vol. CLXVI, No. 11, Index 903 (December 10, 2001); Rise, Fall and Rise Again of CEPA Interpretations, 'New Jersey Lawyer', Vol. 9, No. 47 (November 20, 2000); Expanding Insurance Coverage - Golden Goose or Poisoned Apple?, 'The New Jersey Labor Letter', Vol.1, No. 8 (August 2000); Are Your Workplace E-Mail Polices Ready for Y2K?, 'The New Jersey Labor Letter', Vol. 1, No.1 (January 2000); Vizcaino v Microsoft Corporation, 'New Jersey Labor and Employment Law Quarterly', Vol. 22, No. 1 (1998); It Pays To Know The Law When A Worker Is Injured Or Disabled, 'New Jersey Law Journal', Vol. CLIV, No. 2, Index 125 (October 12, 1998). **Personal:** JD, with honors, University of North Carolina School of Law (1976); BA, Davidson College (1973).

THOMPSON, Kenneth E
McCarter & English, LLP, Newark
973 639 7902
kthompson@mccarter.com
Recommended in Corporate/M&A
Practice Areas: Mr Thompson concentrates his practice in mergers and acquisitions, corporate finance and other transactions as well as general corporate counseling. He has handled transactions ranging from the traditional, outright acquisition of companies to structuring joint ventures, acquisitions of divisions and discrete business segments, and licensing both developmental and commercially distributed pharmaceutical products. Often, transactions are handled for clients with whom Mr Thompson has long-term relationships and his involvement begins at the early planning stages. For clients wishing to remain independent, Mr Thompson has advised on the implementation of various anti-takeover defensive strategies.

TOLCHINSKY, Harold
Cole, Schotz, Meisel, Forman & Leonard PA, Hackensack 201 489 3000
Recommended in Real Estate

TUBMAN, Lloyd H
Greenbaum, Rowe, Smith & Davis LLP, Woodbridge 732 549 5600
ltubman@greenbaumlaw.com
Recommended in Environment
Practice Areas: Chair, Environmental Law Practice Group. Land use and environmental law specializing in zoning approvals, federal and state environmental compliance, with broad development planning and regulatory enforcement, as well as particular wetlands, water quality, flood hazard area and utility experience.
Prof. Memberships: Member, Board of Directors, Land Use Law Section of the NJ Bar Association; member, New Jersey Tidelands Resource Council.
Career: Author, New Jersey Freshwater Wetlands Protection Act. Counsel to the New Jersey Chapter of the National Association of Industrial and Office.
Personal: University of Minnesota Law School(1982), University of Minnesota (1979).

VAN DEVENTER, Kenneth M
Riker Danzig Scherer Hyland & Perretti LLP, Morristown 973 451 8523
kvandeventer@riker.com
Recommended in Litigation
Practice Areas: Partner in Litigation Group. Represents businesses in complex commercial litigations, arbitrations and appeals. Substantial experience before Federal Courts for District of New Jersey, Southern District of New York, Western District of Virginia, Central District of California, Third Circuit Court of Appeals and US Supreme Court. Appeared before Law and Chancery Divisions of New Jersey Superior Court, New Jersey Appellate Divisions and State Supreme Court. Managed class action litigation for defense and plaintiffs and handled temporary restraining orders and preliminary injunction applications in federal and state courts.
Personal: Seton Hall University, JD, Law Review; University of Notre Dame, BA.

WAGENBACH, Jeffrey B
Riker Danzig Scherer Hyland & Perretti LLP, Morristown 974 451 8524
jwagenbach@riker.com
Recommended in Environment
Practice Areas: Partner in Environmental Group. Extensive experience in regulatory and compliance matters, litigation and transactional matters, and ECRA/ISRA compliance issues.
Prof. Memberships: Member of the New Jersey State Bar Association (Environmental Law Section) and the American Bar Association (Natural Resources Section).
Career: Frequent speaker and author on environmental topics, including underground storage tanks, water and wetlands compliance and permitting, site remediation procedures and requirements, and ISRA; Named one of 'The Best Lawyers in America' for New Jersey environmental law (Woodward/White, 2003-06 editions).

Personal: Syracuse University, College of Law, JD; Dartmouth College, BA, with honors.

WALDER, Justin
Walder, Hayden & Brogan P.A., Roseland 973 992 5300
Recommended in Litigation

WOVSANIKER, Alan
Lowenstein Sandler PC, Roseland
973 597 2564
awovsaniker@lowenstein.com
Recommended in Corporate/M&A
Practice Areas: Co-Chair of the Closely Held Business Practice, has 25 years of experience in mergers and acquisitions, business planning, securities regulation and corporate finance. He counsels clients on the funding and structuring of business organizations, and the structuring of employment relationships and equity-based compensation plans. In addition, Mr Wovsaniker represents issuers and underwriters in public securities offerings, venture capital and other private securities offerings and periodic reporting requirements.
Prof. Memberships: District V-C Ethics Committee, Supreme Court (1994-98) and Chair (1997-98); Trustee of the Essex County Bar Association (1996-99); Chair of the Essex County Bar District V-C Ethics Committee, Supreme Court (1994-98) and Chair (1997-98); Trustee of the Essex County Bar Associations Corporate Law Committee (1999-2002) and Chair of the Essex County Bar Associations Banking Law Committee (1994-97); New Jersey State and American Bar associations; former Adjunct Faculty of Rutgers University Law School and Seton Hall University of Law.
Career: New Jersey Bar (1977).
Publications: Corporate Governance e-book, provides Sarbanes-Oxley regulations including corporate governance proposals and compliance recommendations; SOX and Related Reforms: Where Are We?, Metropolitan Corporate Counsel; A New Years Resolution for Corporate Governance Reform, Metropolitan Corporate Counsel; Ten Ways to Succeed and Prosper When Selling Your Business, Commerce Magazine; Equity Compensation: Cash-Poor Employers Have Options, The National Law Journal.
Personal: Harvard University (JD, 1977, magna cum laude); Brown University (AB, 1974, magna cum laude, Phi Beta Kappa).

ZANGARI, Ted
Sills Cummis Epstein & Gross PC, Newark 973 643 7000
Recommended in Real Estate

ZIMMERMAN, Edward M
Lowenstein Sandler PC, Roseland
973 597 2568
ezimmerman@lowenstein.com
Recommended in Corporate/M&A
Practice Areas: Chairs Lowenstein Sandlers Tech Group and has extensive experience representing venture funds

and tech-based businesses in their most critical business transactions (venture capital/private equity financings, M&A, securities offerings, going private transactions, strategic alliances, management buyouts, shareholder disputes). He also represents research institutions in tech transfer/spin-offs. Representative clients include: JPMorganChase, Sandoz, Larsen & Toubro, Rutgers University, Princeton University, Stevens Institute of Technology, Datran Media, Edison Venture Fund, Updata Capital, Millenium 3 Capital, Inter-Atlantic Fund, NJTC Venture Fund, RK Ventures, Aperture Venture Partners, AppIntelligence (sold to ISO), Archive Systems, Hotspot FX, dynamicsoft (sold to Cisco Systems), Lamina Ceramics, Hydroglobe (sold to Graver Technology, a Marmon Group company), and many high-net worth individual angel investors.
Prof. Memberships: Founder and Co-Chair, Jersey Angel Network; Adjunct Professor of Venture Capital, Rutgers Law School; Member, NVCA Working Group on Model Legal Documents for Venture Capital; Board Member (and Chair, Government Affairs Committee), New Jersey Technology Council; Member, Rutgers University Equity Portfolio Committee; Founder and Chair, Hoop-A-Paluza, Inc.; Founder and Co-Chair, Rutgers Venture Advisory Council; Advisory Board Member (past Board Member), Bill T. Jones/Arnie Zane Dance Company.
Career: 40 Under 40, 'New Jersey Law Journal' (2004 and 2003); 40 Under 40, NJBiz (2001, one of two lawyers on the list.); lead counsel in venture capital deal/strategic alliance, which Future Banker Magazine listed as one of the Top 10 Technology Deals of 2000; New Jersey Bar (1992).
Publications: By Ed Zimmerman: Are Finders Also Broker Dealers?, The National Law Journal; The Trouble With Patent Shop Rights (in M&A and Venture Capital Context), The National Law Journal; Shareholder Disputes and Corporate Divorce, New Jersey CPA; Five Ways to Ruin Your B Round While Doing Youre A Round, NJ Tech News, with Scott Perricelli, LLR Partners; Angel Financing: What Entrepreneurs Need to Know, NJ Tech News, with Anthony Marino, Venrock Associates; Bridge Financing, National Law Journal; Mergers and Acquisitions in Practice, 'New Jersey Law Journal'. About Ed Zimmerman: Hoop Dream Nets Thousands for Childrens Charity,' The Star Ledger, Where Angels Tread NJBIZ; Financially Speaking With Ed Zimmerman & Steve Skolnick,' Corporate Finance Weekly; VCs Talk Candidly About Raising Money,' NJBIZ.
Personal: University of Pennsylvania (JD, 1992); Haverford College (BA, Phi Beta Kappa, 1989).

GIBBONS, DEL DEO, DOLAN, GRIFFINGER & VECCHIONE, P.C.

THE FIRM

Chairman: David J Sheehan
Managing Director: Patrick C Dunican, Jr

Number of directors: 68
Number of other lawyers: 100

FIRM OVERVIEW: Gibbons is one of the region's premier law firms established in 1926, and ranked among the nation's top 250 firms by *The National Law Journal*. The firm provides transactional, litigation and counseling services to leading businesses throughout the Metropolitan New York region and nationally. The firm's attorneys are recognized among the nation's leading business attorneys in both *Chambers USA Guide to America's Leading Business Lawyers* and *The Best Lawyers in America*.

MAIN AREAS OF PRACTICE:

Business & Commercial Litigation: Handling sophisticated and complex commercial litigation including securities class actions, regulatory and administrative law, Lanham Act and unfair competition, restrictive covenants and all manner of contractual disputes.

Corporate: Advising leading corporations and financial institutions on corporate law matters, including mergers, acquisitions, divestitures, restructurings, joint ventures, licensing, corporate finance, commercial lending, capital raising, regulatory compliance, corporate governance and tax planning, as well as serving as outside general counsel.

Criminal Defense: Investigating and defending against allegations of business, accounting, securities, bank, insurance, tax, healthcare and government contract fraud. The department attorneys have been involved in many high-profile investigations and prosecutions of alleged political corruption and business crime, particularly in the pharmaceutical and communications industries.

Employment Law: Representing employers in Federal and state court, in litigation involving discrimination, harassment, retaliation, wage and hour, employment contract, restrictive covenant, wrongful discharge, employee benefits and ERISA claims. Providing the full range of preventive and compliance counseling and training with an emphasis on discipline and discharge, harassment, disability-related leaves and accommodations, work-force restructurings, restrictive covenants and executive compensation; as well as workplace investigations and audits of employment practices.

Financial Restructuring & Creditors' Rights: Representing creditors, debtors and various fiduciaries in all aspects of complex business insolvency issues and proceedings, including federal bankruptcy proceedings, state court litigation involving receiverships, attachments, replevins and foreclosures, out of court 'workouts' and related debtor and creditor relations counseling to resolve insolvency issues and disputes outside a formal proceeding.

Government Affairs: Comprehensive State and Federal government relations counseling for entities in the public, private and nonprofit sectors including legislative lobbying, regulatory counseling and interaction with state agencies.

Intellectual Property: Full range of patent, trademark, copyright, unfair competition, e-commerce, trade secret, and computer and internet law experience in the areas of litigation, strategic licensing and transactional work, patent prosecution, trademark and copyright registrations, corporate due diligence, intellectual property audits and general intellectual property counseling.

HEAD OFFICE

NEW JERSEY
One Riverfront Plaza, **Newark**, NJ 07102
Tel: 973 596 4500 **Fax:** 973 596 0545
Email: firm@gibbonslaw.com
Website: www.gibbonslaw.com

BRANCH OFFICES

NEW JERSEY
224 West State Street, **Trenton**, NJ 08608
Tel: 609 394 5300 **Fax:** 609 394 5301

NEW YORK
One Pennsylvania Plaza, **New York**, NY 10119
Tel: 212 649 4700 **Fax:** 212 333 5980

CONTACTS

Business & Commercial Litigation	Brian J McMahon
Corporate	Frank T Cannone
Criminal Defense	Lawrence S Lustberg
Employment Law	Christine A Amalfe
Financial Restructuring & Creditors' Rights	Karen A Giannelli
Government Affairs	David J Pascrell
Intellectual Property	David E De Lorenzi
Products Liability	Kim M Catullo
Real Property & Environmental	Russell B Bershad

Products Liability: Defending and advising manufacturers of ethical pharmaceuticals and medical/surgical devices, as well as diagnostic laboratories, in complex matters involving issues such as purported adverse effects, design, warnings and/or manufacturing defects, and results of laboratory analyses. A team of attorneys is also dedicated to the defense of manufacturers of a diverse array of products such as industrial equipment, automotives and consumer products.

Real Property & Environmental: Extensive Real Property Practice handling sales, purchases and development of all types of properties, including office buildings, industrial and flex buildings, retail centers, apartment buildings and hotels. Environmental Team is comprised of attorneys with both public and private sector experience who are capable of supporting clients' litigation, regulatory and transactional needs.

INTERNATIONAL WORK: Gibbons is the North American law firm member of the Geneva Group International/Lawspan, a network of independent professional service firms offering a full range of legal, accounting and other services worldwide.

GREENBAUM ROWE SMITH & DAVIS LLP

THE FIRM

Managing Partner: Paul A Rowe

Number of partners: 50
Number of other lawyers: 47

FIRM OVERVIEW: Greenbaum, Rowe, Smith & Davis LLP is recognized throughout New Jersey as one of its most respected and distinguished law firms. Established in 1914, the firm's tradition and reputation have been based upon an unfailing commitment to the highest professional standards and a keen personal interest in its clients. The firm's approach to practicing law is cutting edge with its talented attorneys possessing the knowledge and skills necessary to meet the sophisticated demands and challenges that the modern world places upon its clients.

MAIN AREAS OF PRACTICE:

Litigation: The firm's Litigation Department is one of the largest and most comprehensive in New Jersey, providing a full complement of commercial and civil litigation services in a broad range of practice areas. The firm is distinguished in its ability to handle complex matters and manages some of the largest and most sophisticated business litigation in the State. The firm has a notable reputation for handling 'sensitive', high profile matters that include the defense of white collar criminal charges, matrimonial matters and professional malpractice.

Corporate: The firm's Corporate Department provides a broad range of general business representation necessary to respond to the diverse needs of today's demanding business climate. Its Corporate Practice encompasses all aspects of acquisitions, mergers and sales, initial formation of the business entity, business dissolutions, contract preparation and negotiation, state and federal securities law, general counseling and business planning, sophisticated estate and tax planning and dispute resolution.

Real Estate: The firm's Real Estate Department has been prominently associated with New Jersey's real estate development, financing and brokerage industries for many decades, and is one of the largest practices within the State. Representation includes all aspects of New Jersey real property law including acquisition and sales of residential and commercial real estate, registration of planned real estate developments, condominium and community association law, commercial leasing, construction and permanent financing, land use approvals, prerogative writ actions, environmental matters, condemnation and tax appeals.

Tax, Trusts & Estates: The firm's Tax, Trusts and Estates Department renders complete tax services for its commercial clients, which encompasses all phases of federal and state tax matters. The firm's attorneys practice in the areas of audits, appeals, tax planning and structuring for all business formats and transactions. The attorneys practice before all courts, including the New Jersey and United Sates Tax Courts. The firm also provides counseling in the areas of employee benefits and executive compensation. In addition to counseling corporate clients in their tax matters, its attorneys also provide services to individuals in their personal tax, trust and estate planning, estate administration, elder law concerns and business succession goals.

CLIENTS: The firm represents clients from major public corporations and Fortune 500 companies to established medium and small publicly- and privately-held businesses, as well as general and limited partnerships on both large and modest scales.

HEAD OFFICE

NEW JERSEY
P.O. Box 5600, **Woodbridge**, NJ 07095
Tel: 732 549 5600   **Fax:** 732 549 1881
Email: info@greenbaumlaw.com
Website: www.greenbaumlaw.com

BRANCH OFFICE

NEW JERSEY
6 Becker Farm Rd., **Roseland**, NJ 07068
Tel: 973 535 1600   **Fax:** 973 535 1698

CONTACTS

Litigation ....Paul A Rowe
Corporate, M&A, Securities ....Alan E Davis
Real Estate ....Robert C Schachter
Tax, Trusts & Estates ....Michael A Backer, Martin L Lepelstat

KIRKPATRICK & LOCKHART NICHOLSON GRAHAM LLP

THE FIRM

Chairman of the Management Committee &
Managing Partner: Peter J Kalis
Number of partners: 323
Number of other lawyers: 627

Website: www.klng.com

FIRM OVERVIEW: Kirkpatrick & Lockhart Nicholson Graham LLP (K&LNG) – the product of one of the largest Anglo-American legal combinations in history on January 1, 2005 – comprises 950 lawyers who practice from offices throughout the US and in London, England. K&LNG represents entrepreneurs, growth and middle-market companies and leading global corporations in every major industry group. The firm practices across all legal disciplines within the corporate, litigation and regulatory fields. K&LNG's extensive knowledge about the business sectors in which our clients operate enables the practice to be at once regional, national and international in scope, cutting edge, complex, and dynamic. K&LNG was the only law firm in the world to receive the CIO Magazine CIO 100 Award for three consecutive years, while the official publication of the Minority Corporate Counsel Association selected K&LNG as one of only four American law firms to feature for their innovative diversity initiatives.

MAIN AREAS OF PRACTICE:

Corporate: K&LNG practices law on an integrated and firm-wide basis. The multi-office, international corporate and transactional practice is one of the most substantial in the profession. The firm closed over 100 M&A transactions last year, and is perennially a leader as issuer's counsel in equities issued by corporate clients, both in terms of number of transactions and proceeds. K&LNG has completed hundreds of public debt and equity offerings over the last decade.

Litigation: K&LNG's litigation engagements including, among other substantive areas, insurance coverage, intellectual property, real estate, white-collar criminal, construction, professional liability, environmental, toxic tort, products liability, franchise, tax, bankruptcy and insolvency, antitrust and competition, employment, benefits, and securities fraud are among the largest and most attractive enjoyed by any law firm. The firm has been rated a leading practice in the representation of corporate policyholders in the insurance coverage area, and as a leading litigation firm for the financial sector. It is active in jurisdictions around the US and in the UK as well as in various international arbitration forums.

Regulatory: K&LNG's Regulatory Practice cuts across the many disciplines that require highly specialized knowledge and experience to address governmental regulation of the private markets. The firm's lawyers regularly represent clients before regulatory bodies in both the US and the UK. Its premier regulatory practice is in the diversified financial services area. K&LNG represents a large majority of the major financial institutions and securities firms in a variety of disciplines, and the Investment Management Practice is a perennial leader. Many of the firm's practice leaders as well as more junior lawyers have governmental experience that enhances their ability to serve K&LNG's clients in regulatory fields, while others have held prominent positions in regulated industries.

Emerging Practices: The firm continuously allocates resources so that its capabilities reach to the forefront of emerging disciplines. K&LNG's intellectual property practice, with approximately 100 practicing lawyers, and its Technology Practice, serving growth companies in disciplines such as biotechnology, internet services, medical devices, and information systems, are examples of how this investment has borne fruit. Most frequently, the firm continues to recruit lateral partners in such disparate fields as structured finance, bankruptcy, real estate, food and drug, ERISA litigation, Small Business Administration financing, telecommunications, project finance, intellectual property, private equity, trademarks, employment and public sector technology to address the evolving needs of its

OFFICES

CALIFORNIA
10100 Santa Monica Boulevard, 7th Floor, **Los Angeles**, CA 90067
Tel: 310 552 5000   **Fax:** 310 552 5001

Four Embarcadero Center, 10th Floor, **San Francisco**, CA 94111
Tel: 415 249 1000   **Fax:** 415 249 1001

DISTRICT OF COLUMBIA
1800 Massachusetts Avenue, NW, 2nd Floor, **Washington**, DC 20036-1221
Tel: 202 778 9000   **Fax:** 202 778 9100

FLORIDA
Miami Center, 201 South Biscayne Boulevard, 20th Floor,
Miami, FL 33131-2399
Tel: 305 539 3300   **Fax:** 305 358 7095

MASSACHUSETTS
75 State Street, **Boston**, MA 02109
Tel: 617 261 3100   **Fax:** 617 261 3175

NEW JERSEY
One Newark Center, 10th Floor, **Newark**, NJ 07102-5252
Tel: 973 848 4000   **Fax:** 973 848 4001

NEW YORK
599 Lexington Avenue, **New York**, NY 10022-6030
Tel: 212 536 3900   **Fax:** 212 536 3901

PENNSYLVANIA
Payne Shoemaker Building, 240 North Third Street, **Harrisburg**, PA 17101-1507
Tel: 717 231 4500   **Fax:** 717 231 4501

Henry W. Oliver Building, 535 Smithfield Street, **Pittsburgh**, PA 15222-2312
Tel: 412 355 6500   **Fax:** 412 355 6501

TEXAS
2828 North Harwood Street, Suite 1800, **Dallas**, TX 75201-6966
Tel: 214 939 4900   **Fax:** 214 939 4949

INTERNATIONAL OFFICES

The firm also has an office in London, UK

clientele. The firm strives to maintain a creative, interdisciplinary approach to the practice, as evidenced by the extraordinary convergence of disciplines that permitted its K&LNG colleague, former US Attorney General Dick Thornburgh, to act as the court appointed Examiner in the WorldCom bankruptcy proceeding – the largest bankruptcy in US history – and the firm itself to act as his counsel.

CLIENTS: K&LNG currently represents or recently has performed projects for over half of the FORTUNE 100; 21 of the 25 largest mutual fund complexes or their investment managers; and 18 of the 20 largest US bank holding companies or their affiliates. Representative clients include Alcoa, Bank of America, DuPont, Fidelity, Halliburton, Mellon, PPG, United Technologies, Wachovia, and World Wrestling Entertainment. The firm is a multiple winner of DuPont's Meeting the Challenge Award for its 'remarkable and extraordinary accomplishments' for that client, and is the only law firm on which PPG Industries has conferred its Excellent Supplier Award.

INTERNATIONAL WORK: With offices throughout the US and in London, K&LNG represents clients across North America and the United Kingdom on matters that span the globe. K&LNG's primary working language is English, but the firm has attorneys fluent in Afrikaans, Chinese (Mandarin), Farsi, French, German, Greek, Hebrew, Hindi, Italian, Japanese, Korean, Polish, Portuguese, Russian and Spanish. Various members of the firm have foreign degrees, which enable them to take into account legal and cultural differences in representing the firm's clients in international transaction and litigation matters worldwide.

LOWENSTEIN SANDLER PC

THE FIRM

Managing Partner: Michael L Rodburg

Number of partners: 71
Number of other lawyers: 153

FIRM OVERVIEW: Lowenstein Sandler is a nationally recognized law firm with more than 220 attorneys who provide a full range of legal services to the corporate, financial, industrial and governmental communities. Ranked among the *Am Law* 200 largest law firms in the nation, the firm assists clients ranging from small public and privately held companies to *Fortune* 500 corporations in a variety of sophisticated business and legal issues. Lowenstein Sandler is also ranked among the top 100 law firms in the United States by *The American Lawyer* and is well-known for its commitment to pro bono service, as well as for its use of technology. The firm's main areas of practice include corporate, business litigation, bankruptcy, employment, environmental, insurance, real estate, technology, trusts and estates, and white collar criminal defense. One of Lowenstein Sandler's recent achievements was its successful bid to represent the creditors' committee in the $1.3 billion bankruptcy filing of a major baked goods manufacturer, one of the nation's largest bankruptcy filings in 2004. Lowenstein Sandler's subsidiary, Issues Management, is consistently ranked as the number one lawyer-lobbying consulting firm in New Jersey.

MAIN AREAS OF PRACTICE:

Corporate: Lowenstein Sandler has extensive experience in corporate counseling and transactional work, as well as business reorganizations. The Corporate Department provides a full range of services to clients in connection with: organization and structuring of business entities; initial public offerings and subsequent offerings; general business counseling; mergers and acquisitions; financing transactions; and investment management. Lowenstein Sandler also provides a full range of tax services to the business community, as well as tax and estate planning for individuals.

Business Litigation: The firm's Litigation Department represents clients in all stages of litigation (both trial and appellate) in both state and federal courts, as well as before administrative and governmental agencies. Lowenstein Sandler is the law firm of choice for out-of-state clients embroiled in complex litigation in New Jersey and has developed several prominent, nationally recognized niche practices in areas such as environmental litigation and toxic tort defense, insurance coverage litigation, securities litigation, and white collar criminal defense.

Bankruptcy, Financial Reorganization and Creditors' Rights: Lowenstein Sandler's Bankruptcy, Financial Reorganization and Creditors' Rights Practice Group has extensive experience representing debtors, trustees, secured and unsecured creditors, and investors in high-profile Chapter 11 reorganizations, out-of-court workouts, financial restructurings, and litigation. The group also frequently provides bankruptcy advice on corporate and structured finance matters, and on the acquisition of assets out of bankruptcy.

Employment: With attorneys drawn from the corporate, securities, litigation, tax, insurance, and environmental practices, Lowenstein Sandler's Employment Law Practice Group counsels clients on a wide range of matters including managing workplace risks, compliance and documentation, and corporate transactions. The firm's ability to assist in strategic planning and follow-through affords clients the benefit of dealing with human resource and benefits issues as part of their overall integrated business plans.

Environmental: Lowenstein Sandler's Environmental Department assists clients with virtually every type of lawsuit involving environmental matters in federal and state courts throughout the country. The firm counsels clients on a variety of matters including compliance and auditing; acquisitions and divestitures; site remediation; natural resource damages; toxic tort cases; occupational health and safety; and insurance coverage.

HEAD OFFICE

NEW JERSEY
65 Livingston Avenue, **Roseland** NJ 07068
Tel: 973 597 2500   **Fax:** 973 597 2400
Website: www.lowenstein.com

BRANCH OFFICES

NEW YORK
1251 Avenue of the Americas, **New York** NY 10020
Tel: 212 262 6700 **Fax:** 212 262 7402

NEW JERSEY
Post Office Plaza, Suite 504, 50 Division Street, **Somerville** NJ 08876
Tel: 908 526 3300 **Fax:** 908 725 5124

Insurance: Lowenstein Sandler is one of a handful of nationally known firms who pioneered the development of insurance coverage litigation. The Insurance Law Practice Group has litigated coverage cases in more than 20 states, has appeared for the policyholder in more than 30 reported decisions, and has collected more than $500 million in settlements and judgments.

Real Estate & Real Estate Finance: Lowenstein Sandler's Real Estate and Real Estate Finance Group assists a wide range of clients in all phases of real estate transactions, including acquisitions, financings, leasing, construction, land use planning and environmental issues, as well as tax counseling and litigation. The firm also boasts an experienced mortgage banking practice that represents various participants in the primary and secondary mortgage markets in all aspects of the acquisition, disposition, financing and securitization of loans secured by real property.

Technology, IP & Venture Capital: The Tech Group at Lowenstein Sandler counsels technology-driven businesses and their investors at all stages of growth and has earned a reputation for excellence in venture capital and other financing transactions. The group has closed hundreds of private company financing transactions including angel rounds, complex venture financings, bridge fundings and IPOs. Members of the Tech Group also include intellectual property attorneys, registered patent lawyers and practitioners who counsel clients on matters pertaining to intellectual property, technology and privacy law.

Trusts & Estates: Lowenstein Sandler's Trusts & Estates Practice Group helps clients preserve and pass on their families' wealth, while minimizing taxes and assisting fiduciaries in fulfilling their duties. The group's attorneys are skilled in fiduciary litigation, business counseling, and domestic and international business tax planning, all of which enhance both its planning and administration practices.

White Collar Criminal Defense: Lowenstein Sandler's White Collar Criminal Defense Practice Group has decades of experience defending corporate and individual clients in state and federal prosecutions, as well as conducting internal investigations for private and public corporations. The group regularly defends clients in all phases of criminal proceedings, including grand jury investigations, trials and appeals.

LOWENSTEIN SANDLER PC

Attorneys at Law

www.lowenstein.com

LUM, DANZIS, DRASCO & POSITAN LLC

THE FIRM

Managing Director: Wayne J Positan

Number of attorneys: 40
Number of firm members: 20

FIRM OVERVIEW: The firm traces its roots back to 1870. Throughout its history, the firm has remained focused on the dynamic needs of the business community in New Jersey, and those doing business or engaged in litigation in New Jersey. The firm is regularly employed by corporate counsel or through national and international law firms to represent businesses and individuals in labor and employment, litigation, and general business counseling matters.

MAIN AREAS OF PRACTICE:

Labor & Employment: The firm represents management and defendants in employment litigation; discrimination litigation; non-competition disputes; traditional labor law, including collective bargaining negotiations, arbitration and NLRB practice, administrative law; appellate practice; human resources counseling and training; and ADR/mediation processes.

Litigation: The firm represents a broad range of clients in the areas of commercial litigation, construction law, condemnation, life and health insurance law, professional liability litigation, environmental and toxic tort law, personal injury litigation, arbitration, mediation, and appellate practice.

Business Law: The firm assists clients in the areas of finance, taxation, mergers and acquisitions, banking, estate planning, estate and trust administration, real property, zoning, loan workouts, and other commercial transactions.

Mediation: The firm has 10 members who are New Jersey Court Approved Mediators. It has successfully mediated matters in a variety of areas, including employment matters, commercial disputes and internal entity disputes. For example, Wayne Positan successfully mediated a discrimination matter which had resulted in a seven-million dollar award against a UK company through voluntary mediation while the matter was on appeal.

CLIENTS: The firm represents a variety of clients from closely held corporations to Fortune 500 companies, as well as public entities, such as the State of New Jersey, various county governments, and the University of Medicine and Dentistry of NJ, and individuals. Recent matters have included settlement of the largest wage and hour case in the history of the NJ Department of Labor representing Pepsi Bottling Group; resolution of two major design defect cases involving condominium construction in Atlantic City and Jersey City; NJ Supreme Court decisions on anti-harassment law and administrative law; handling condemnation aspects of redevelopment projects, and direct representation of the New Jersey Attorney General in employment discrimination litigation. The firm has also negotiated collective bargaining agreements in the areas of compressed gas and dry ice distribution, warehousing, moving, manufacturing, and car processing at the port, among others. The firm was also involved in a number of major non-competition litigated matters involving payroll/software; pharmaceuticals; placement/temporary staffing; and telecommunications businesses.

HEAD OFFICE

NEW JERSEY
103 Eisenhower Parkway, **Roseland** NJ 07068-1049
Tel: 973 403 9000   **Fax:** 973 403 9021
Email: wpositan@lumlaw.com
Website: www.lumlaw.com

BRANCH OFFICE

NEW YORK
325 Broadway, **New York** NY 10007
Tel: 212 775 9002

CONTACTS

Administrative Law	Richard A West
Banking Law	Edward R McMahon
Business Law	Colin M Danzis
Condemnation Law	Dennis J Drasco
Commercial Litigation	Dennis J Drasco
Construction Litigation	Paul A Sandars
Employment Law	Wayne J Positan
	Domenick Carmagnola
	Steven F Ritardi
	Richard A West
Estate Planning	Kevin F Murphy
HR Counseling/Training	Christina Silva Lee
Labor Law	Wayne J Positan
	Domenick Carmagnola
Life & Health Insurance Law	Kevin J O'Connor
Mediation	Wayne J Positan
	Dennis J Drasco
	Paul A Sandars
	Edward R McMahon
	Domenick Carmagnola
	Steven F Ritardi
Non-Compete Disputes	Wayne J Positan
	Domenick Carmagnola
Professional Liability	Jane S Kelsey
Tax Appeals	Matthew O'Donnell

McCARTER & ENGLISH, LLP

THE FIRM

Managing Partner: Lois M VanDeusen
Number of partners in US offices: 122

FIRM OVERVIEW: Established 160 years ago, McCarter & English, LLP is a premier regional firm with its headquarters in Newark, New Jersey. The firm's 350 attorneys are resident in seven locations along the eastern seaboard. The firm represents Fortune 500 and mid-cap companies in their national, regional and local litigation and provide a multi-disciplinary range of legal services to many of the country's leading financial, industrial and commercial enterprises, as well as governments, institutions and individuals.

MAIN AREAS OF PRACTICE:

Corporate, Securities & Financial Institutions: The Group serves as general counsel and special counsel to public and private companies. The group's work includes M&A, public and private offerings of securities, going-private transactions, leveraged buyouts, SEC compliance, and SBICs. The group also acts as principal counsel to lenders and borrowers in secured and unsecured public and private financings, and as counsel in corporate finance matters involving venture capital and SBICs.

Products Liability: The Group tries to verdict a significant number of cases each year. The Group handles products liability appeals in State and Federal appellate courts. M&E is counsel of record in over 120 reported decisions and regularly plays a lead role litigating class action and multi-district litigation issues.

Securities Litigation & White Collar Criminal Defense: McCarter & English's Group represents corporations and individuals in securities-related litigation, disputes over investments, regulatory investigations, shareholder disputes, and all types of criminal investigations and proceedings.

Business Litigation: The Group litigates matters such as unfair competition, patent infringement fraud, commercial torts, and real estate tax appeals. Lawyers in the group look to find non-litigation methods to resolve client matters such as contractual disputes, regulatory audits, and government agency inquiries.

Commercial Litigation: The Commercial Litigation Group has special skills in handling complex class actions. Its work ranges from national sales practices representation of one of the country's largest insurance companies to regional and local representation of life, health and disability insurers; financial institutions; and other corporations.

Healthcare: The Group provides legal, transactional and regulatory counsel to hospitals and healthcare providers. The group is involved in a spectrum of legal issues confronting management, including contracts, employee relations, insurance, liability and government matters.

Intellectual Property: The firm's Intellectual Property Group represents companies and individuals in leveraging their intellectual property assets for increased profitability. The group's lawyers work with clients from the invention of ideas and products to the marketing and maturing of those products in the marketplace.

Insurance Coverage: McCarter & English's Insurance Coverage Group represents major industrial and financial companies seeking recoveries under liability and other insurance policies. The group's practice is national and has involved litigation against virtually every US, London market, and Bermuda insurer

Real Estate: The Real Estate Group represents mortgage lenders, off shore banks, national life insurance companies, investors and developers in connection with the sale, financing, and development of real estate. The group also handles conveyances, leasing, and land use planning and zoning, including appearances before municipal bodies in zoning and subdivision matters.

Employment Law: The firm's Labor and Employment Group represents employers in litigation ranging from single plaintiff cases to class actions. Lawyers also appear before administrative agencies in cases relating to dis-

crimination, sexual harassment, wrongful discharge, unfair labor practices, and breach of contract among others.

Creditors' Rights: The Creditors' Rights Group is well-versed in general contract law, the Uniform Commercial Code, commercial transactions, creditor committee issues, fraud, foreclosure, shareholder disputes, lender liability, collection, corporate and bankruptcy aspects of commercial entities, as well as all facets of debtor-creditor relations.

Environmental Law: The Environmental Group represents clients in all aspects of environmental law such as permit applications and enforcement proceedings relating to hazardous and solid waste regulations, air pollution control regulations, and water pollution control regulations among others. The group also counsels clients with the intricacies of New Jersey's Industrial Site Recovery Act.

Tax: The Tax Group's work includes tax controversies, multistate tax advice regarding business operations and acquisitions, and business tax planning. The Tax Group also assists clients in maximizing and structuring state and federal tax credit opportunities ranging from research and development incentives to low-income housing tax credits.

Employee Benefits: The group counsels clients on plan qualification rules under the Internal Revenue Code, plan administration and related ERISA fiduciary issues, and executive compensation. It also designs employee pension and welfare benefit plans, including tax qualified pension, profit-sharing, 401(k) and employee stock ownership plans; health, life, disability, severance, fringe benefit and cafeteria plans; and VEBAs.

Private Clients: The firm's Private Client Group advises individuals on innovative strategies to minimize their income, estate, gift and generation-skipping tax exposure. The group's mix of estate, retirement, charitable gift and business planning experience makes it uniquely qualified to accomplish clients' personal and financial goals.

Public Finance: The Public Finance Group has participated in numerous public financing transaction such as general, moral and special obligation bonds, bond and tax anticipation notes, certificates of participation (lease purchase financings), variable and fixed rate obligations, demand bonds, pooled bonds, stripped municipal securities, credit-enhanced obligations, and current and advanced refundings.

HEAD OFFICE

NEW JERSEY
Four Gateway Center, 100 Mulberry Street, **Newark** NJ 07102-4056
Tel: 973 622 4444   **Fax:** 973 624 7070
Website: www.mccarter.com

BRANCH OFFICE

CONNECTICUT
Tel: 860 275 6700   **Fax:** 860 724 3397
Email: tfisher@mccarter.com

Tel: 203 324 1800   **Fax:** 203 323 6513
Email: tfisher@mccarter.com

DELAWARE
Tel: 302 984 6300   **Fax:** 302 984 6399
Email: mkelly@mccarter.com

MARYLAND
Tel: 410 659 8500   **Fax:** 410 659 8550
Email: dmeringer@mccarter.com

NEW YORK
Tel: 212 609 6800   **Fax:** 212 609 6921
Email: roleary@mccarter.com

PENNSYLVANIA
Tel: 215 979 3800   **Fax:** 215 979 3899
Email: akerr@mccarter.com

PITNEY HARDIN LLP

THE FIRM

Managing Partner: Dennis R LaFiura, Esq

Number of partners: 59
Number of other lawyers: 118

FIRM OVERVIEW: The attorneys of Pitney Hardin LLP, founded in 1902, demonstrate client-focused thinking in nine departments and 10 industry groups.

MAIN AREAS OF PRACTICE:

Criminal Law: The White Collar Crime, Corporate Governance, and Compliance Practice Group has extensive experience successfully representing corporations and individuals in complex federal and state criminal investigations and cases, and in corporate compliance matters.

Environmental Law: One of the nation's first, the Environmental Law Practice Group provides counseling and representation for industrial activities, acquisitions, and dispositions of property or corporations.

Financial Services: Some 25 attorneys provide expertise in regulatory and compliance matters, asset-based, economic development and commecial loan transactions, mergers and acquisitions, tax, disposition of businesses and asset portfolio, project finance, real estate financing, corporate restructuring, creditor's rights, bankruptcy, collection, and litigation.

Intellectual Property & Technology: The Trademark/Copyright/Internet Group represents major entertainment, leisure, retail, real estate, and travel clients, with clearance, registration, maintenance, and international filing services, as well as licensing and transactional support. The attorneys in the Patent Group have broad expertise in customized prosecution and patent protection strategies.

Labor & Employment: Some 30 attorneys deliver comprehensive labor and employment services in employer counseling, employee benefits, labor relations, employment litigation, and immigration.

Litigation: Nearly 60 litigators conduct jury and bench trials in virtually every major federal and state venue. Pitney Hardin attorneys also represent clients before administrative and arbitral forums, and actively pursue alternate dispute resolution whenever appropriate.

Real Estate: Pitney Hardin attorneys provides legal and business solutions with a special emphasis on: commercial, industrial, and retail leasing; representing developers before municipal land use boards; purchasers and sellers of corporate headquarters, golf courses, healthcare facilities, and environmentally distressed real estate; environmental due diligence; and redevelopment projects.

Transactions: Pitney Hardin attorneys advise Fortune 500 to emerging growth companies on the full range of financial matters, including corporate finance, corporate governance and compliance, private and public equity, mergers and acquisitions, and tax.

Trusts & Estates: Pitney Hardin assists families, business owners, executives, fiduciaries, and charitable organizations in conserving, increasing, managing, and transferring wealth.

Industry Groups: Advertising and promotions, chemicals, financial services, health, manufacturing, pharmaceuticals, real estate development, retail, technology and e-commerce, telecom and Internet services.

HEAD OFFICE

NEW JERSEY
PO Box 1945, **Morristown**, NJ 07962-1945
Tel: 973 966 6300 **Fax:** 973 966 1015
Email: info@pitneyhardin.com
Website: www.pitneyhardin.com

BRANCH OFFICE

NEW YORK
7 Times Square, **New York**, NY 10036-7311
Tel: 212 297 5800 **Fax:** 212 916 2940

INTERNATIONAL OFFICE

The firm also has an office in Brussels, Belgium

CONTACTS

Criminal Law	Dennis T Kearny, Esq
Environmental Law	Peter J Herzberg, Esq
Financial Services	Peter A Forgosh, Esq
IP & Technology	Gerald Levy, Esq
Labor & Employment	Patrick J McCarthy, Esq
Litigation	Elizabeth J Sher, Esq
Real Estate	Colleen R Donovan, Esq
Transactions	Warren J Casey, Esq
Trusts & Estates	Richard Kahn, Esq

CLIENTS: Pitney Hardin attorneys have built lasting relationships with clients in a cross-section of industries, including Agfa Corporation, AT&T Corp., BASF Corporation, The BOC Group, Caesars Entertainment Inc., The Coca-Cola Company, Dendrite International, Inc., Ford Motor Company, General Electric, Linens 'n Things, Inc., New Jersey-American Water Company, Novartis Corporation, Pfizer Inc., PLIVA Inc., PNC Bank, N.A., Sony Electronics Inc., The Talbots Inc., United Parcel Service of America, Inc., Verizon Communications, Inc., and Volvo Cars of North America LLC.

INTERNATIONAL WORK: Pitney Hardin's Brussels office advises major multinational clients on a full range of business law matters, including corporate and transactional law, European Union antitrust law, international trade law, and technology law. The Brussels office assists clients with organizing their corporate presence in Europe, drafting joint venture agreements, negotiating contracts and providing legislative and regulatory counseling.

RIKER DANZIG SCHERER HYLAND & PERRETTI LLP

THE FIRM

Managing Partner: Glenn A Clark
Number of partners: 48
Number of other attorneys: 120

FIRM OVERVIEW: Riker Danzig Scherer Hyland and Perretti LLP is proud to have served the New Jersey business community for over 120 years. Riker Danzig has earned a national reputation as being the firm to go to in New Jersey for practical, innovative and cost-effective legal solutions. The reputation of the firm and its lawyers provides inherent credibility in the capital markets, courts, and government hallways of New Jersey. Among the firm's attorneys are many distinguished New Jersey leaders, including former US Congressman and Ambassador to Panama William J Hughes, former New Jersey Attorneys General William F Hyland and Peter N Perretti, Jr, former New Jersey Supreme Court Justices Sidney M Schreiber and Stewart G Pollock, former New Jersey Commissioner of Transportation John P Sheridan, Jr, and former Chairman of the New Jersey State Bar Examiners Edward A Zunz. Prior to becoming the current Attorney General of New Jersey, Peter C Harvey was a partner at the firm.

MAIN AREAS OF PRACTICE:

Litigation: Riker Danzig's seasoned trial and appellate attorneys, numbering over 95 strong, have earned the firm a national reputation as zealous courtroom advocates. The group litigates complex civil cases, and is a leader in banking, securities arbitrations, fraud claims and class actions, insurance, reinsurance (national and international), product liability, construction and intellectual property litigation. The firm also has active school law and family law practices.

Real Estate: Riker Danzig's Real Estate Practice includes all aspects of real estate law, transactions and litigation, including substantial property acquisitions, complex sales and exchanges, sale-leasebacks and build-to-suits, commercial, retail and industrial leasing, joint-venture projects, zoning and planning, mortgage lending and financing, construction contracts, title litigation and real property tax appeals.

Employment: The employment law attorneys at Riker Danzig counsel clients on various issues, including employee relations, wage and hour and contract issues. They also defend management in federal and state courts in New Jersey and elsewhere on all employment related claims, including discrimination, wrongful termination, whistleblower, restrictive covenants, unfair competition and employee fidelity bonds. They also conduct internal investigations.

Corporate: A diverse client base seeks counsel and solutions from Riker Danzig's corporate attorneys, from start-up entrepreneurial enterprises to established public companies. The group counsels clients in the full spectrum of corporate matters, including mergers, acquisitions and divestitures, corporate finance, technology licensing, international transactions, regulatory matters, and logistics and distribution, as well as the issues unique to non-profit and tax-exempt corporations.

Environmental: In a state noted for its strict and pace-setting environmental legislation, Riker Danzig's Environmental Group is among the largest and most diverse practices of its kind. The experienced environmental lawyers have in-depth knowledge of federal, state and local law. The firm handles litigation, regulatory, permitting and counseling, and real estate development matters addressing all environmental areas, including hazardous substances, air, water and noise pollution, and solid waste.

Bankruptcy: Riker Danzig is unique among prominent New Jersey law firms for its expertise in bankruptcy litigation. The Bankruptcy Group has earned a nationwide reputation for its representation of debtors, secured creditors, landlords, equipment lessors, indenture trustees, creditors' committees, trustees, as well as third party plan proponents (ie, takeovers) in all aspects of litigation under the Bankruptcy Code.

HEAD OFFICE

NEW JERSEY
Headquarters Plaza, One Speedwell Avenue, **Morristown**, NJ 07962-1981
Tel: 973 538 0800   **Fax:** 973 538 1984
Email: info@riker.com
Website: www.riker.com

BRANCH OFFICES

NEW JERSEY
50 West State Street, Suite 1010, **Trenton**, NJ 08608-1220
Tel: 609 396 2121   **Fax:** 609 396 4578

NEW YORK
500 Fifth Avenue, Suite 4920, **New York**, NY 10110
Tel: 212 302 6574   **Fax:** 212 302 6628

CONTACTS

Litigation	Gerald A Liloia
Real Estate	Victoria A Morrison
Employment	Michael K Furey
Corporate	Andrew J Stamelman
Insurance	Shawn L Kelly
Bankruptcy	Dennis J O'Grady
Environmental	Dennis J Krumholz

CLIENTS: American Centennial Insurance Co., AT&T, AXA Versicherungs AG, Bank of America, Carrier Clinic, Central Garden & Pet Co., CIGNA Corp., Crum & Forster Corp., Ecko.Complex, L.L.C., Gerling Global Reinsurance Corporation of America, Harleysville Insurance Co., The Hertz Corp., Hoechst Corp., IBM, Johnson & Johnson, JPMorgan Chase, Lucent Technologies, Inc., McNeil Pharmaceuticals, Merrill Lynch, National Starch and Chemical Co., New Jersey Bankers Association, Prudential Insurance Company of America, R.J. Reynolds Tobacco Co., Schering-Plough, UBS, Unilever Ltd., Wachovia Bank, N.A., Wakefern Food Corp., Wal-Mart Stores, Inc.

INTERNATIONAL WORK: Riker Danzig handles the needs of its clients around the world. In the area of reinsurance, for example, Riker Danzig has been successful in arbitrating and litigating reinsurance claims worldwide. In one case in which the firm represented Gerling Global Reinsurance Corporation of America and other insurance companies, the United States Supreme Court struck down a California law intended to force European insurers to disclose detailed information regarding all policies sold in Europe before and during the Second World War.

RIKER
DANZIG
SCHERER
HYLAND
PERRETTI LLP

CONTENTS: Corporate/M&A p.1155; Employment p.1156; Environment, Natural Resources and Regulated Industries p.1157; Litigation: p.1159; Real Estate p.1161; Individuals' Profiles p.1162; Firms' Profiles p.1165.

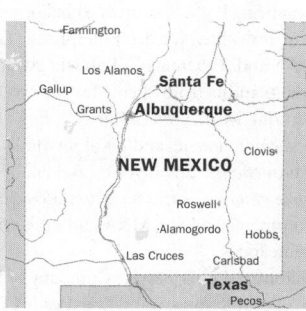

How lawyers are ranked

The opinions we gather from clients — mainly from in-house lawyers but also from other purchasers of legal services — are balanced by opinions from colleagues and competitors. Together, they provide two different perspectives — an all-round view — and biased viewpoints cancel each other out.

CORPORATE/M&A

New Mexico
Leading firms (Corporate/M&A)

1. **MODRALL, SPERLING, ROEHL PA** *Albuquerque*
2. **BROWNSTEIN HYATT & FARBER PC** *Albuquerque*
   KELEHER & MCLEOD PA *Albuquerque*
   RODEY, DICKASON, SLOAN, AKIN *Albuquerque*
   SUTIN, THAYER & BROWNE *Albuquerque*
3. **FOSTER JOHNSON MCDONALD** *Albuquerque*
   LEWIS AND ROCA JONTZ DAWE *Albuquerque*

Leading individuals (Corporate/M&A)

1. **BUCHHOLTZ David** *Brownstein Hyatt, Albuquerque*
   MOORE Charles *Keleher & McLeod, Albuquerque*
2. **BENDICKSEN Perry** *Brownstein Hyatt, Albuquerque*
   BROWN Duane *Modrall Sperling, Albuquerque*
   HALL Alan *Rodey Dickason, Albuquerque*
   HEYMAN Robert *Sutin Thayer, Albuquerque*
   PAISLEY Bonnie *Brownstein Hyatt, Albuquerque*
   ROSENBLUM Jay *Sutin Thayer, Albuquerque*
3. **APODACA Patrick** *Keleher & McLeod, Albuquerque*
   BARLOW Richard *Barlow & Wilcox, Albuquerque*
   BETZER Stan *Betzer Roybal, Albuquerque*
   JONTZ Dennis *Lewis and Roca, Albuquerque*
   MCDONALD Randall *Foster Johnson, Albuquerque*
   MONNHEIMER Donald *Rodey Dickason, Albuquerque*
   PARKER James *Modrall Sperling, Albuquerque*
   SCHULER Alison *Schuler Messersmith, Albuquerque*

Firms and individuals are listed alphabetically in each band.

Band 1

Modrall, Sperling, Roehl, Harris & Sisk PA

The Firm: Although weakened by the departure of Bonnie Paisley to the Brownstein firm – its clear lead on other firms somewhat narrowed as a result – Modrall Sperling remains the largest for corporate and finance work in New Mexico. Valued by clients for its strong political connections, it has an impressive bench of quality attorneys with particular expertise in public finance. Its attorneys have recently worked on a $1.1 billion transaction for the New Mexico Finance Authority, raising funds for new roads. The firm also advises on M&A and employment matters, as well as federal, state and local taxation issues.
The Lawyers: Vice president of the firm, *"can-do lawyer"* **Duane Brown** focuses on municipal bond issues. Clients describe him as *"accommodating"* and *"very capable of merging complex strategies into New Mexico process."* Brown's clients include the New Mexico Hospital Equipment Loan Council and the New Mexico State University. He recently worked on the $200 million dollar financing of a new hospital wing for the University of New Mexico. **James Parker** was praised by peers for his federal taxation and employee benefits expertise, as well as his *"low-key, non confrontational"* style. They described him as *"really smart"* and commented that he *"does a terrific job for his clients."*
The Clients: New Mexico Finance Authority; New Mexico Hospital Equipment Loan Council; New Mexico State University and Bank of America.

Band 2

Brownstein Hyatt & Farber PC
See firm details p.324
The Firm: The Albuquerque office of this Denver-based firm continues to grow in stature in the corporate arena. Its municipal finance practice remains particularly strong, and its expertise in high-end financial transactions led clients to describe Brownstein as *"the go-to firm for private equity work."* The firm was recently involved in the financing of the $1.1 billion New Mexico state highway project, alongside Modrall Sperling. Now numbering seven lawyers, the team has enhanced its capability in the corporate/securities area and is judged by peers to have cornered the market in the technology company/venture capital area.
The Lawyers: Bond counsel for the City of Albuquerque, **David Buchholtz** (see p.1163) elicited praise from clients and peers alike for his experience, straightforward style and ability to focus on the core issues. His practice concentrates on public finance issues, as well as economic development and state tax law. Rated as *"one of the very top lawyers in bond work,"* he has recently handled the finance for an extension of Albuquerque airport. **Bonnie Paisley** (see p.1163), recruited last year from Modrall Sperling, has added considerable weight to Brownstein's corporate team. She is *"seasoned and very down-to-earth,"* and sources regard her as *"a big loss to Modrall."* With significant experience in hi-tech and startup matters, her clients include software developers, IT companies and venture capital firms. Since joining Brownstein she has also added a municipal finance string to her bow. Another attorney with expertise in startup and venture capital work is *"savvy"* **Perry Bendicksen** (see p.1162). Clients appreciate his understanding of business goals, *"responsive"* style and efficiency. As for his knowledge base, *"when you speak to him, he knows the answer."* Private equity fund work constitutes a large proportion of his practice, although he also handles a variety of general corporate, securities and M&A transactions.
The Clients: Clients include Intel, City of Albuquerque and New Mexico Finance Authority.

Keleher & McLeod PA
The Firm: This well-established firm is regarded by some as *"top in New Mexico for breadth of practice and level of competency."* A *"fantastic"* team of attorneys undertakes a variety of general corporate, acquisitions, tax, securities and transactional work, but it is the firm's utilities practice that most impresses competitors. It does a considerable amount of work for the Public Service Company of New Mexico, the state's largest utility, and maintains strong and worthwhile relationships both within and beyond the business community.
The Lawyers: Peers consider **Charles Moore** to be *"a very fine lawyer,"* his enormous experience making him *"the man to go to for utilities."* Moore's practice centers on corporate finance,

securities and acquisitions; one highlight of the past year being PNM Resources' $1 billion acquisition of Texas-New Mexico Enterprises. *"Level-headed"* and *"thorough"* **Patrick Apodaca** received plaudits from clients for his excellent acquisitions work, *"good understanding of the business environment"* and his ability to *"facilitate transactions."* The diverse caseload of this *"resource gatherer"* includes general corporate and commercial advice, M&A and deals with a real estate focus.

The Clients: Public Service Company of New Mexico, PNM Resources and Ever-Ready Oil are among the firm's top clients.

Rodey, Dickason, Sloan, Akin & Robb, PA

The Firm: This corporate practice enjoys a *"stellar reputation"* among clients, who view them as imbued with *"the highest integrity."* Boasting a particularly well-respected bonds and securities group, the firm can call on 20 lawyers with a diversity of experience. This strength in numbers is mirrored in the quantity and scale of work undertaken for clients that include banks, utilities, healthcare providers and insurers.

The Lawyers: **Alan Hall**'s practice is primarily focused on industrial revenue bonds, municipal bonds and securities. A *"very thorough and competent"* lawyer, clients described him as *"a forceful negotiator"* who can extract unprecedented concessions for his clients. Hall recently closed a $1.8 billion industrial revenue bond for Louisiana Energy Services. **Donald Monnheimer** leads the bonds and securities practice group, working largely in economic development and industrial revenue bond transactions. Clients testify to the high level of confidence he inspires; like Hall, *"he doesn't miss a thing."* Monnheimer is currently bond counsel to the Burlington Northern and Santa Fe Railway yard redevelopment project in Albuquerque, which is expected to be worth $250-$300 million.

The Clients: Tri-State Generation and Transmission Association; Sierra Electric Cooperative; Presbyterian Healthcare Services; San Juan Regional Medical Center; Bank of America and Bank of the West.

Sutin, Thayer & Browne

See firm details p.1168

The Firm: This *"highly-qualified"* 40-lawyer firm was said to have *"across-the-board experience in business."* Clients valued the breadth of expertise it can bring to bear in M&A, its attorneys recently handling the $150 million sale of Memorial Medical Center in Las Cruces to Province Healthcare. The firm also advises on matters related to corporate and municipal finance, securities and employee benefits.

The Lawyers: *"A credit to the legal profession,"* **Jay Rosenblum** (see p.1164) has earned a reputation as an *"incredible problem solver"* who *"doesn't beat transactions to death."* Clients spoke enthusiastically about his *"sharp legal mind"* and *"strong negotiating skills."* He handles M&A, tax and employee benefits, and has recently been lead counsel on the $100 million dollar sale of a government contracting business. **Robert Heyman** is a lawyer with *"a tremendous institutional knowledge of the whys and wherefores of state law, constitutional amendments and the Attorney General's office."* He is described as *"pleasant, competent and low-key,"* and is *"good on the detailed side of things – he asks all the hard questions."*

The Clients: Clients include New Mexico State Board of Finance, City of Albuquerque and University of New Mexico Hospital.

Band 3

Foster Johnson McDonald Lucero Koinis LLP

The Firm: New to the table, this five-partner firm has been heavily involved in nonprofit economic development-related activities, through which the state government has been promoting economic and technological growth in New Mexico. Two partners specialize in corporate and commercial matters, displaying a *"sensible and intellectual, yet practical"* approach.

The Lawyers: *"Thoughtful"* **Randall McDonald** was singled out by peers as a lawyer who *"gets the job done for the client in a way that makes sense."* McDonald is best-known for his representation of technology companies.

The Clients: New Mexico Small Business Investment; Technology Ventures; Science &

Technology Corporation at the University of New Mexico and National Center for Genome Resources.

Lewis and Roca Jontz Dawe

The Firm: Another new entrant to the table is the progeny of a merger between large Arizona and Las Vegas firm Lewis and Roca and Albuquerque-based Jontz Dawe Gulley & Crown. Its four New Mexico corporate specialists now benefit from access to resources out-of-state, and impress clients with their ability to manage complex transactions including formations, M&A and securities. They also have a niche in representing federal contractors in their relationships with government.

The Lawyers: *"Probably one of the finest people I've ever met,"* enthused one client of **Dennis Jontz**. He brings a wealth of experience to acquisitions and federal procurement work (both in the state and nationwide) for clients such as Sandia National Laboratories and Phillips National. Maintaining excellent connections throughout the state, he was described by commentators as *"honest, well-read, civic-minded, well-respected and with a good business background."*

The Clients: The Bell Group; Compass Bank; Sandia National Laboratories; New Jersey Maintenance and Phillips National.

Other Notable Practitioners

Peers rated **Richard Barlow** of Barlow & Wilcox PA for his *"thoughtful and methodical"* approach. Working on corporate, taxation and estate planning matters, he is *"focused on getting the deal done."* **Stan Betzer** of Betzer Roybal & Eisenberg PC was said to combine *"good intellectual work with an understanding of the practical side of things."* Respected for his M&A experience, he also undertakes a significant quantity of work for the Santa Fe Natural Tobacco Company. With a practice focused on securities and private placements, **Alison Schuler** of Schuler, Messersmith, Daly & Lansdowne is regarded by observers as a *"bright and very experienced attorney."*

EMPLOYMENT

MAINLY DEFENDANT

Band 1

Gilkey & Stephenson PA

See firm details p.1165

The Firm: This *"excellent"* five-lawyer boutique is renowned as the premier employment practice in New Mexico. Clients held it up as the equal of any firm worldwide for

quality of service, adding that attorneys were *"sensitive to client needs on sticking to budgets."* The team handles all types of labor and employment law, and received particular praise for its smooth handling of messy discrimination cases. Long-standing clients of the firm include credit unions and several airlines.

The Lawyers: Clients valued the *"incredibly authentic"* **Duane Gilkey** (see p.1163) for his trial experience, thoroughness and his honest advice. A *"smart, skillful negotiator,"* he *"always gets the best deal for the client."* He is also a very likable person, a quality that serves clients well with both judges and opposing parties: *"He puts them at ease while setting up a motion for sum-*

New Mexico
Leading firms
(Employment: Mainly Defendant)

1 GILKEY & STEPHENSON PA *Albuquerque*
2 KELEHER & MCLEOD PA *Albuquerque*
MOODY & WARNER PC *Albuquerque*
RODEY, DICKASON, SLOAN, AKIN *Albuquerque*
TINNIN LAW FIRM *Albuquerque*

Leading individuals
(Employment: Mainly Defendant)

1 CONKLIN Robert *Keleher & McLeod, Albuquerque*
GILKEY Duane *Gilkey & Stephenson, Albuquerque*
2 GORDON Scott *Rodey Dickason, Albuquerque*
MOODY Christopher *Moody & Warner, Albuquerque*
PARKER James *Modrall Sperling, Albuquerque*
STEPHENSON Barbara *Gilkey, Albuquerque*
TINNIN Robert *Tinnin Law Firm, Albuquerque*
WARNER Whitney *Moody & Warner, Albuquerque*

Firms and individuals are listed alphabetically in each band.

mary judgment." "*Effective and knowledgeable*" **Barbara Stephenson** (see p.1164) divides her time between litigation and preventive counseling work. She maintains a strong profile through her defense of sexual discrimination claims, and numbers CUNA Mutual, Delta Airlines and Dillard's among her clients.

The Clients: Intel; CUNA Mutual Group; Southwest Airlines; Delta Airlines; Citicorp; Blue Cross Blue Shield and Dillard's.

Band 2

Keleher & McLeod, PA

The Firm: This Albuquerque firm has secured a reputation for doing quality employment work for large clients. Describing it as a "*responsive*" and "*effective, well-rounded firm*," clients were pleased to report that attorneys are "*easy to reach and prompt in returning phone calls.*" The employment team undoubtedly benefits from the full-service nature of the firm and handles all types of litigation as well as day-to-day employment counseling.

The Lawyers: "*A tough lawyer but a real gentleman,*" **Robert Conklin** is primarily an employment litigator. Regarded by some as the best lawyer in the state, he impresses clients with his ability to handle truly complex cases. "*He brings calm wisdom and wise counsel to the table... and he really knows the law.*" Conklin is handling increasing numbers of age discrimination claims.

The Clients: Public Service Company of New Mexico; Presbyterian Healthcare Services; University of New Mexico; New Mexico Mutual Casualty Group; New Mexico Lottery Authority; Wells Fargo and St. Paul.

Moody & Warner PC

The Firm: This small but highly regarded boutique covers all aspects of labor and employment work. Its attorneys have a reputation for "*zealously*" representing their clients, though at the same time they are respected in the marketplace for being "*ethical*" lawyers. Recent work includes the negotiation of a long-term labor contract for Central New Mexico Electric Cooperative containing caps on the employer portion of group health insurance contributions.

The Lawyers: Sources commended the quality of **Chris Moody**'s work. Peers describe him as a "*knowledgeable, aggressive guy,*" who "*prepares very well and minimizes risk.*" His broad practice encompasses labor relations and collective bargaining, employment counseling plus all types of employment litigation. Although less experienced than Moody, "*terrific*" **Whitney Warner** received plaudits for her "*keen intellect*" and speed in getting to the bottom of an issue. A former HR manager, she is said to have an especially good understanding of the client's perspective.

The Clients: Southwest Cheese; Coca-Cola Enterprises; Otero County Electric Cooperative; Central New Mexico Electric Cooperative and Comcast.

Rodey, Dickason, Sloan, Akin & Robb, PA

The Firm: One of New Mexico's largest full-service firms, the Rodey law firm boasts an employment practice "*able to handle everything thrown at them, from settlement conferences to motions to trials.*" The seven-strong department is in the process of expanding and its work is increasingly regional; the firm recently represented retail grocery chain Albertsons in an employment lawsuit in Arizona.

The Lawyers: Chairman of the litigation department **Scott Gordon** "*thinks of all the angles.*" A specialist in civil trials and employment law, he comes highly recommended by clients, who think of him as a "*precise, well-prepared and thoughtful*" attorney. His practice covers all aspects of employment law, and he has recently defended Los Alamos National Laboratory in a class action claim. Head of the employment practice Tom Stahl was praised for his thoughtful style and client focus.

The Clients: IBM; Santa Fe Natural Tobacco; Smiths Food and Drug Centers, and Albertsons.

Tinnin Law Firm

The Firm: Founded by a former mainstay of Hinkle, Hensley, Shanor & Martin's employment practice, this Albuquerque boutique is well-connected within the state. Its three lawyers handle a range of work, including discrimination, harassment and retaliation litigation, employment contract claims, labor relations and preventive counseling.

The Lawyers: The firm draws much of its strength from the vast experience of **Robert Tinnin**. Prominent within the state and respected by peers, his collective bargaining, unfair labor practice and union relations expertise is unparalleled. Tinnin is the editor of the New Mexico Employment Law Letter.

The Clients: The firm represents a broad range of clients including City of Albuquerque; Lockheed Martin; Halliburton Energy Services; First National Bank of Santa Fe; Bueno Foods; Sandia National Laboratories; James Healthcare; University of New Mexico; Continental Divide Electric Cooperative and Yates Petroleum.

Other Notable Practitioners

James Parker of Modrall, Sperling, Roehl, Harris & Sisk, PA was noted for his employee benefits and healthcare experience. Peers described him as "*really smart*" and commented that he "*does a terrific job for his clients.*"

ENVIRONMENT, NATURAL RESOURCES AND REGULATED INDUSTRIES

Band 1

Modrall, Sperling, Roehl, Harris & Sisk PA

The Firm: New Mexico's largest full-service firm is equipped with an impressive environment and natural resources team. Clients report "*great depth of experience*" to be the hallmark of a department staffed by "*really sharp people,*" capable of "*turning things around quickly on big projects.*" General environmental work figures strongly, but this is also one of the few firms to represent business interests in Indian law matters. The team handles all phases of natural resource development work, from site acquisition through to regulatory compliance and litigation, and has particular expertise where such issues overlap with federal Indian law. A strong client base includes BP Amoco, El Paso Natural Gas Company and Oklahoma Department of Environmental Quality.

The Lawyers: Clients regard department head **Larry Ausherman** as "*keenly diligent and conscientious.*" He is "*attentive to their needs, professional and responsive.*" His primary focus is mining and environmental law, in which field he represents BHP Billiton and Burlington

New Mexico
Leading firms
(Environment, Natural Resources and Regulated Industries)

1. **MODRALL, SPERLING, ROEHL PA** Albuquerque
2. **HINKLE HENSLEY SHANOR** Roswell
   MONTGOMERY & ANDREWS, PA Santa Fe
   RODEY, DICKASON, SLOAN AKIN Albuquerque
3. **GALLEGOS LAW FIRM PC** Santa Fe
   HOLLAND & HART LLP Santa Fe

Leading individuals
(Environment, Natural Resources and Regulated Industries)

1. **AUSHERMAN Larry** Modrall Sperling, Albuquerque
   CAMPBELL Michael Holland & Hart, Santa Fe
   COONEY John Modrall Sperling, Albuquerque
   GALLEGOS J E Gallegos Law Firm, Santa Fe
   KENDRICK Edmund Montgomery & Andrews, Santa Fe
   NIBERT Gregory Hinkle Hensley, Roswell
   SCOTT William Modrall Sperling, Albuquerque
   SINGLETON Sarah Montgomery & Andrews, Santa Fe
   SLADE Lynn Modrall Sperling, Albuquerque
   STERN III Walter Modrall Sperling, Albuquerque

Leading individuals
(Litigation: Water Supply)

★ **DRAPER John** Montgomery & Andrews, Santa Fe
1. **ADAMS Mark** Rodey Dickason, Santa Fe

Leading firms (Native American Law)
1. **MODRALL, SPERLING, ROEHL, PA** Albuquerque
2. **RODEY, DICKASON, SLOAN, AKIN** Albuquerque

Leading individuals
(Native American Law)

1. **APPLEBY Nancy** Rodey Dickason, Albuquerque
   SCOTT William Modrall Sperling, Albuquerque
   SLADE Lynn Modrall Sperling, Albuquerque
   STERN III Walter Modrall Sperling, Albuquerque

Firms and individuals are listed alphabetically in each band.

Northern Santa Fe Corporation. An "*articulate*" attorney, Ausherman is said to enjoy a good reputation with the regulators. With nearly 40 years of experience, **John Cooney** has a "*very thorough knowledge of the principles of oil and gas law.*" A natural resources specialist, he concentrates on complex litigation and arbitration. **Bill Scott** is active in environmental law, including air and hazardous waste permitting issues. "*Astute*" with regard to the scientific side of regulatory compliance, he also has significant expertise in Indian law matters. Clients value the effective arguments that result from his detail-oriented approach. **Lynn Slade** is widely regarded as one of the state's foremost Indian law experts. Respected by peers for his solid grasp of legal issues, he is also esteemed by clients for his innovative approaches: "*If he sees a window of opportunity for crafting an argument, he's not afraid to do it.*" His practice also encompasses utilities and energy work, and he has recently counseled Transwestern Pipeline Company on right-of-way acquisitions and permitting for their San Juan lateral pipeline expansion. A "*thorough litigator,*" **Walter Stern** was praised by peers and clients for his expertise in matters related to public lands and Indian lands. Sources commended his willingness to "*work something out to advance the causes of both parties,*" and were impressed by his professionalism and diligence. He typically advises on land use, environmental regulatory and administrative matters.

The Clients: BP Amoco; BHP Billiton; Transwestern Pipeline; ConocoPhillips; El Paso Natural Gas; Navajo Refining and Oklahoma Department of Environmental Quality.

Band 2

Hinkle Hensley Shanor & Martin LLP
See firm details p.1166

The Firm: Oil and gas work is the forte of this regional firm. With ten lawyers serving a clientele of major and independent producers, the team is well-placed in the market. Peers highlighted the competence and experience of the firm's lawyers who, despite losing Harold Hensley to Hinkle's office in Midland, Texas, still enjoy an excellent reputation for litigation and transactional work in New Mexico. The firm is also involved in mining, water law and environmental law, handling a range of titular, contractual and litigious matters.

The Lawyers: A new addition to the tables, **Greg Nibert** (see p.1163) is the firm's standout lawyer for natural resources work. Regarded by market commentators as a "*reliable, thoughtful oil and gas lawyer,*" he focuses particularly on transactional work related to title and ranching issues. Nibert's clients include Pogo Producing Company, Energen Resources and Yates Petroleum.

The Clients: ExxonMobil; BP Amoco; ConocoPhillips; Pogo Producing Company; Energen Resources and Yates Petroleum.

Montgomery & Andrews. PA
See firm details p.1167

The Firm: Based in Santa Fe, this general practice firm can field ten lawyers with natural resources expertise. With notable strength in water law and natural gas royalty litigation, the team also covers oil and gas, the environment and mining law. Satisfied clients commended the quality of its attorneys, whose caseload includes work for Burlington Resources and Marathon Oil.

The Lawyers: "*Bright and articulate*" **John Draper** has a nationally renowned water law practice. He has argued cases in front of the US Supreme Court, most notably representing Kansas in a dispute with Colorado over the Arkansas River. Peers admired the breadth and depth of his expertise, reporting him to be "*scholarly and very knowledgeable.*" **Sarah Singleton** is a former state Bar president, with a practice concentrated on extractive litigation. "*Intelligent, thorough and very responsive,*" she got top marks from clients and competitors for her fine judgment and solid litigating skills. They also appreciated her efficient manner, saying, "*She doesn't talk unless she knows the facts.*" El Paso Natural Gas and Devon Energy are among her clients. **Edmund Kendrick** was rated highly for his natural resources practice. Particularly well-versed in natural resource development work, he has additional expertise in Indian law matters.

The Clients: Burlington Resources; Marathon Oil; State of Kansas; El Paso Natural Gas and Devon Energy.

Rodey, Dickason, Sloan, Akin & Robb. PA

The Firm: A thriving Indian law department complements this firm's vibrant natural resources practice. Although the nine-lawyer natural resources team handles a diverse range of work, including oil, gas and mining, its principal emphasis is on water law. Matters relating to permits and contracts are handled by the firm, which also brings its considerable litigation skills to bear on water rights adjudications. With a dedicated branch office in DC, the Indian law department has special expertise in economic development and land acquisition.

The Lawyers: A broad base of natural resources expertise underpins **Mark Adams'** practice. Although now concentrating on water law, he is esteemed by peers for his "*good overall experience and perspective.*" Among others, he represents Intrepid Mining, Louisiana Energy Services and the City of Santa Fe. Peers testified that **Nancy Appleby** "*certainly knows her way around Indian law.*" A real estate lawyer with a national practice, she has garnered a reputation among clients for being "*extremely meticulous and thoroughly trustworthy.*" Her major focus is the representation of business interests in commercial and development projects on Indian lands. One client enthused that "*very few lawyers know finance as well as she does, very few know real estate as well as she does, and very few know anything about Native American law at all. She really is the top of the top!*" At time of press, she announced her intention to move to Washington, DC.

The Clients: Palm Desert National Bank; Wells Fargo Bank; Lafarge North America; Intrepid Mining; Louisiana Energy Services; City of Santa Fe; Tri-State Generation and Transmission Association and Peabody Engineering.

Band 3

Gallegos Law Firm PC

The Firm: A leading oil and gas boutique, this firm has a great deal of experience representing producers. The four-strong ensemble of litigators is especially expert on royalty, contract, regulatory and antitrust issues.

The Lawyers: J E Gallegos is regarded by peers as the foremost oil and gas plaintiff lawyer in New Mexico. Fêted for his trial skills, he is viewed as a "*tenacious litigator*" with a wealth of experience in his specialty.

The Clients: Whiting Petroleum; BNP Paribas; Doyle Hartman Oil Operator; Maralex Resources and Ramah Navajo Chapter.

Holland & Hart LLP

See firm details p.325

The Firm: The Santa Fe branch of this large regional firm boasts a robust natural resources practice. Oil and gas litigation features prominently in its caseload, which also includes environment work.

The Lawyers: Michael Campbell (see p.1163) received strong recommendations for his work for oil and gas companies. He acts on royalty and surface use disputes, as well as antitrust and tort claims. An "*aggressive litigator,*" he is revered as knowledgeable and experienced. William Carr was admired for his work in the oil and gas regulatory field.

LITIGATION

GENERAL COMMERCIAL

New Mexico
Leading firms (Litigation: General Commercial)

[1]	MODRALL, SPERLING, ROEHL PA *Albuquerque*
	RODEY, DICKASON, SLOAN AKIN *Albuquerque*
[2]	EAVES BARDACKE BAUGH KIERST *Albuquerque*
	FREEDMAN BOYD DANIELS *Albuquerque*
	HINKLE HENSLEY SHANOR & MARTIN LLP *Roswell*
	KELEHER & MCLEOD PA *Albuquerque*
[3]	GALLEGOS LAW FIRM PC *Santa Fe*
	MADISON HARBOUR MROZ *Albuquerque*
	MILLER STRATVERT PA *Albuquerque*
	PEIFER, HANSON & MULLINS PA *Albuquerque*

Leading individuals
(Litigation: General Commercial)

Senior Statesman

CARPENTER Bill *Carpenter & Stout,* Albuquerque

[1]	BARDACKE Paul *Eaves Bardacke,* Albuquerque
	HALL Bruce *Rodey Dickason,* Albuquerque
	HARRIGAN Kenneth *Modrall Sperling,* Albuquerque
[2]	FRANSE Nelson *Rodey Dickason,* Albuquerque
	SCHULTZ Andrew *Rodey Dickason,* Albuquerque
	SHANOR Stuart *Hinkle Hensley,* Roswell
[3]	BETTINGER Carl *Shapiro and Bettinger,* Albuquerque
	GALLEGOS J E *Gallegos Law Firm,* Santa Fe
	GOLDBERG Joseph *Freedman Boyd,* Albuquerque
	PEIFER Charles *Peifer Hanson,* Albuquerque
	SCHNEEBECK Douglas *Modrall Sperling,* Albuquerque
	WOLF Wayne *Wolf Taylor,* Albuquerque
	WORD Terry *Word & Bogardus,* Albuquerque
[4]	BAKER Douglas *Modrall Sperling,* Albuquerque
	EAVES John *Eaves Bardacke,* Albuquerque
	MADISON William *Madison Harbour,* Albuquerque
	MONTGOMERY Andrew *Montgomery,* Santa Fe
	PHARRIS Charles *Keleher & McLeod,* Albuquerque
	REID Spencer *Keleher & McLeod,* Albuquerque
	THROCKMORTON Rex *Rodey Dickason,* Albuquerque

Up-and-coming individuals

SULLIVAN Patrick *Salazar & Sullivan,* Albuquerque

Firms and individuals are listed alphabetically in each band.

Band 1

Modrall, Sperling, Roehl, Harris & Sisk, PA

The Firm: Commercial litigation is a particular strength of New Mexico's largest firm. Competitors affirmed that "*you can't go wrong*" with the 24 lawyers in Modrall Sperling's litigation team which, on account of its size and reputation, is involved in a large proportion of major lawsuits filed in the state. New Mexico's is one of the leading jurisdictions for national class actions, and the firm is active in this regard. It is also fully occupied in the defense of complex commercial litigation, products liability and medical malpractice cases, and has developed special expertise in the fields of natural resource and environmental litigation.

The Lawyers: Clients report a high level of satisfaction with the attorneys. "*Tremendously skilled on his feet in the courtroom,*" **Ken Harrigan**"*masters every aspect of the case.*" Peers characterize Harrigan as "*tough as hell.*" Clients likewise describe him as "*very thorough in anticipating attacks on a particular defense*" and admire his attention to detail. He takes on a wide range of cases, from products liability to legal malpractice and commercial litigation, and his strong reputation and unquestioned ability ensure a steady stream of high-profile work. He has recently represented U-Haul, BP and Burlington Resources. Heading Modrall Sperling's litigation department is **Doug Schneebeck**, whose practice includes medical device and drug liability; however, it is for class actions that he is particularly well-known. Bright, well-prepared and hard-working, he has a "*top-notch*" client base. Schneebeck's excellent judgment elicited the comment that "*he knows when to hold em and when to fold em.*" President of the firm **Douglas Baker** is a "*hands-on litigator.*" Known for his products liability work, he also takes on more general commercial cases. This "*top-flight attorney*" was praised by peers for his versatility and skill in "*squeezing information out of witnesses.*"

His clients include Takata and Hobart Corporation.

The Clients: Others include Johnson & Johnson; GlaxoSmithKline; 3M; Progressive Insurance; New York Life and Walgreen.

Rodey, Dickason, Sloan, Akin & Robb PA

The Firm: Alongside Modrall Sperling, this firm was considered to have the strongest complement of commercial litigators in the state. Respected by peers, clients and judges, the team has "*skills to match the national firms, but with good local contacts and knowledge.*" Attorneys cover all kinds of disputes, including commercial, employment, insurance defense, drug liability and class actions. Its lawyers have recently represented Wyatt and Pfizer in drug liability cases, and have handled a number of insurance-related class actions.

The Lawyers: Peers and clients alike waxed lyrical about the experience and good judgment of "*gentleman lawyer*" **Bruce Hall**. "*He reminds you of Jimmy Stewart in the courtroom.*" Considered by many to be "*at the top of the heap,*" his "*low-key and likable*" style reaps rich rewards: "*Before you know it he's won the case with some insightful questions that you didn't see coming.*" Much of his caseload is composed of legal malpractice and drug liability litigation, as well as mediation and arbitration work. He has recently been involved in the defense of cases arising from the withdrawal of the Fen-Phen diet drug combination. Highly thought of for his courtroom skills, "*delightful*" **Nelson Franse** was also lauded by market sources for his ability to "*cut through nonsense and get to a resolution.*" Exalted by commentators as "*the dean of professional liability lawyers in New Mexico,*" his caseload also includes products liability and personal injury defense. Clients were unreserved in their admiration for his "*tenacity*" and "*formidable intellect.*" "*Incredibly bright, genuine and honest as the day is long,*" **Andrew Schultz** "*is what a lawyer should be like,*" according to peers. Recently appointed managing director of the firm, he specializes in civil rights and class action defense, representing insurance companies, among others. His clients reported him to be *"one of those rare attorneys who can combine exquisite analytical skills with a temperament that is humane and pleasant"* and valued his ability to convey complex principles simply. Having stepped down as managing director, **Rex Throckmorton** now has more time to litigate. His broad practice takes in all types of commercial disputes, from oil and gas work to class actions involving life insurance companies. A *"results-oriented"* attorney, he is viewed by clients as practical, professional and very easy to work with. *"He's the whole package,"* reported one. Throckmorton has recently acted for the Fidelity National Title Insurance Company, and continues to represent The Williams Companies. Fêted by clients for his *"tremendous experience in malpractice,"* **Robert Lasater** is also respected for his knowledge of products liability matters.

The Clients: Allsops; Northrop Grumman; Fidelity National Title Insurance; The Williams Companies; Los Alamos National Laboratory; Pfizer; Wyatt; Ardent Health Services; General Motors; Chrysler and Farmers Insurance.

Band 2

Eaves Bardacke Baugh Kierst & Kiernan PA

The Firm: This firm is regarded as one of New Mexico's strongest litigation boutiques. Covering all types of complex commercial, oil and gas royalty, professional liability, antitrust and tobacco litigation, its lawyers were said to *"push the envelope for their clients."* The team handles both plaintiff and defense work, and has developed *"quite a track record of successfully resolving big cases in New Mexico."*

The Lawyers: **Paul Bardacke**, a former Attorney General of New Mexico, is politically well-connected and was chairman of Bill Richardson's successful gubernatorial campaign. Sources described him as a *"smooth and effective"* litigator, and praised him for his tenacity: *"He knows how to keep hammering at issues until he gets to the point he wants to make with the witness."* Mediation and arbitration constitutes an increasingly large part of his practice these days, though he is still sighted in court, especially in complex commercial and environmental cases.

With a background in transactional work, **John Eaves** has a practice centering on antitrust, oil and gas royalty and tobacco litigation. Competitors consider him to be *"remarkably astute,"* and were impressed by the *"great judgment"* he displays in managing large cases. *"Very determined,"* he is an *"inventive and aggressive litigator."*

Freedman Boyd Daniels Hollander Goldberg & Cline PA

The Firm: This boutique is particularly strong on negligence, securities and complex commercial litigation. The eight-lawyer team also has a strong appellate practice and experience in class actions.

The Lawyers: *"Incredibly intelligent and a tireless advocate,"* **Joseph Goldberg** earned recognition for his antitrust practice, as well as his commercial and class action litigation. Regarded by some as being *"among the best in the country"* for plaintiffs on securities cases, he *"doesn't waste time but aggressively presses the points."*

Hinkle Hensley Shanor & Martin LLP

See firm details p.1166

The Firm: Widely regarded as an oil and gas powerhouse, this Roswell firm also has offices in Santa Fe, and Midland and Austin in Texas. Although natural resources work constitutes a significant proportion of the team's caseload, Hinkle Hensley litigators have expertise in commercial, tax, insurance and employment matters. The firm has an impressive number of multinational giants among its energy clientele.

The Lawyers: Head of the Roswell office and *"one of the deans of the defense Bar,"* **Stuart Shanor** (see p.1164) is widely regarded as *"top-drawer."* He was described to researchers as *"a real gentleman - the kind that tears you apart but at the end of the case you still love 'em."* With a practice that focuses on banking and commercial litigation, he is valued for his professional manner and great courtroom skills.

The Clients: Liberty Mutual Insurance; National General Insurance; New Mexico Self Insurers' Fund; ExxonMobil; ConocoPhillips; BP Amoco; Texaco; Devon Energy; Chevron USA; EOG Resources and Pogo Producing Co.

Keleher & McLeod PA

The Firm: This full-service firm can call on 21 attorneys with litigation expertise. Particularly respected in commercial litigation, the team has also carved out an excellent reputation for utilities, employment and products liability litigation. The firm recently represented former Albuquerque mayoral candidate Rick Homans in his successful challenge to spending caps on campaign contributions.

The Lawyers: *"Very smart"* and *"utterly capable,"* **Charles Pharris** is known for his *"terrific breadth of experience"* and his integrity. His main fields of expertise are products liability, medical malpractice and personal injury defense. **Spencer Reid** is well-versed in insurance and complex commercial litigation and was applauded by clients for his intelligence and thoroughness. He represents a number of insurance companies and has recently defended Wells Fargo in a class action over banking practices.

The Clients: Public Service Company of New Mexico; Home Insurance; First American Title Insurance; Albuquerque Public Schools; Presbyterian Healthcare Services; Wells Fargo; Bridgestone; University of New Mexico and the Archdiocese of Santa Fe.

Band 3

Gallegos Law Firm PC

The Firm: For oil and gas matters, this Santa Fe boutique is viewed as among the best. With masses of experience representing producers, its quartet of litigators is particularly knowledgeable on royalty, contract, regulatory and antitrust issues.

The Lawyers: The team is spearheaded by the *"charismatic"* **J E Gallegos**, who peers regard as a tough and knowledgeable opponent with a wealth of experience in his specialty.

The Clients: Whiting Petroleum; Doyle Hartman Oil Operator; Maralex Resources; Ramah Navajo Chapter and BNP Paribas.

Madison Harbour Mroz & Brennan PA

The Firm: Peers expressed admiration for the crop of *"top litigators"* at this Albuquerque boutique. The firm's 16 lawyers handle all types of civil litigation, but their forte is insurance defense, bad faith insurance and medical malpractice cases. The team is also very well regarded for products liability matters.

The Lawyers: **Bill Madison** is respected as the firm's standout litigator. Particularly admired for his insurance work, in which he is regarded as *"incredibly knowledgeable,"* he is also a strong performer in the courtroom; peers commended his cross-examination skills and characterized him as *"a street fighter,"* adding that *"if you want to clamp a pit bull on somebody's leg, he's your man!"*

The Clients: American National Insurance; Bank of America; Baxter Healthcare; Fireman's Fund Insurance; Houston General Insurance; Pfizer and Trinity Universal Insurance.

Miller Stratvert PA

The Firm: With more than two-thirds of Miller Stratvert's 50-lawyer complement engaged in this work, litigation is the key activity of the firm. It handles all types of litigation, from antitrust and banking to products liability and tort matters, though it is for medical malpractice and insurance defense that the firm garners

1160

All quotes in the text are from interviews with clients and competitors.

CHAMBERS USA 2005

most praise. Peers commended the quality of the firm's work, and commented on the respect the judiciary have for its lawyers.

The Lawyers: Now managing director of the firm, **Ranne Miller** has long been viewed as "*the master of medical malpractice defense - he knows everything required to get a jury to forgive a doctor.*" He oversees a strong team of civil litigators, of which products liability and medical malpractice specialist Gary Gordon attracted most attention from interviewees.

Peifer, Hanson & Mullins PA

The Firm: Numbering nine attorneys, this civil litigation boutique handles securities, employment, commercial and tax disputes. Class actions are a particular specialty, with attorneys recently involved in cases related to insurance and oil and gas royalty issues. The firm continues to represent the State of New Mexico in oil and gas matters and recently undertook a defamation case for a film director.

The Lawyers: Senior partner **Charles Peifer**

has collected a strong fan base among his peers; they have warmed to his "*brilliant*" intellect and "*nonchalant*" style. Observers admitted he could usually be found "*two or three steps ahead of everybody else...which can be embarrassing!*" Peifer has considerable experience in commercial litigation, with a more specific focus on class actions.

The Clients: A superb client roster includes New Mexico Tax and Revenue Department and Wal-Mart.

Other Notable Practitioners

Carl Bettinger of Shapiro and Bettinger LLP was recommended to researchers as a "*dogged competitor*" who "*knows medical malpractice from the inside.*" A former doctor, his caseload involves a large number of nursing home matters. "*Awesome lawyer*" **Wayne Wolf** of Wolf Taylor & McCaleb is highly regarded for his enormous trial experience. His "*humble, self-deprecating*" manner belies the skills of a "*superb*" litigator, and he was particularly com-

mended for his work on bad faith insurance cases. "*Grandfather of the Bar*" **Bill Carpenter** of Carpenter & Stout Ltd excels in products liability disputes. "*Folksy, energetic, and pretty aggressive,*" he can call on over 35 years of experience in the courtroom and is considered "*one of the premier plaintiff's lawyers in the state.*" Clients view **Andrew Montgomery** of Montgomery & Andrews, PA as an "*extremely bright appellate advocate.*" He handles a broad array of cases including antitrust, tort and contract disputes. A rising talent on the medical malpractice scene, **Patrick Sullivan** of Salazar & Sullivan is "*honest*", "*low-key*" and "*forthright.*" His "*engaging style*" was widely acknowledged by peers to be popular with juries. Peers also recognized the quality of the "*very ethical*" **Terry Word** of Word & Bogardus, who is regarded as one of New Mexico's leading medical malpractice attorneys. His caseload includes doctor and hospital negligence as well as personal injury work.

REAL ESTATE

New Mexico
Leading firms (Real Estate)

1 MYERS OLIVER & PRICE *Albuquerque*

2 HURLEY TOEVS STYLES HAMBLIN *Albuquerque*
MODRALL, SPERLING, ROEHL PA *Albuquerque*
RODEY, DICKASON, SLOAN, AKIN *Albuquerque*

3 KELEHER & MCLEOD PA *Albuquerque*
SCHEUER YOST & PATTERSON PC *Santa Fe*
SOMMER, UDALL, HARDWICK *Santa Fe*
VOGEL CAMPBELL BLUEHER *Albuquerque*

Leading individuals (Real Estate)

1 HURLEY Patrick *Hurley Toevs, Albuquerque*
MYERS John *Myers Oliver, Albuquerque*
PRICE Charles *Myers Oliver, Albuquerque*

2 EK Dale *Modrall Sperling, Albuquerque*
GOLDBERG Catherine *Rodey Dickason, Albuquerque*
PATTERSON John *Scheuer Yost, Santa Fe*
SALAZAR John *Rodey Dickason, Albuquerque*
STYLES Mark *Hurley Toevs, Albuquerque*

3 AHERN Janice *Sommer Udall, Santa Fe*
KELEHER William *Keleher & McLeod, Albuquerque*
SCHIFANI Ruth *Modrall Sperling, Albuquerque*
WELLS Lawrence *Campbell and Wells, Albuquerque*

Up-and-coming individuals
MEISTER Margaret *Modrall Sperling, Albuquerque*

Leading individuals
(Real Estate: Zoning/Land Use)

1 CAMPBELL David *Vogel Campbell, Albuquerque*
SALAZAR John *Rodey Dickason, Albuquerque*

Firms and individuals are listed alphabetically in each band.

Band 1

Myers Oliver & Price

The Firm: The five-strong squad of lawyers at this specialist boutique covers all aspects of real estate work, though the attorneys have carved out an unparalleled reputation for development and transactional work. "*Strong draftsmen and negotiators,*" they have been engaged for High Desert Investment's Mariposa project, a large mixed-use development on the west side of Albuquerque. The development is one of the first to be carried out under new state laws relating to Public Improvement Districts, according to which a developer is compensated for the extension of public infrastructure through an end user property tax.

The Lawyers: Sources commended **John Myers**' problem-solving style, reporting that he is "*the man for zoning and land use issues.*" He is involved in many of the most important deals in the state and has recently done work for Forest City Enterprises on the Mesa del Sol project, a 9000-acre planned community development south of Albuquerque. A skilled negotiator, Myers was described as "*persistent and persuasive.*" Preeminent among transactional real estate lawyers in New Mexico, **Charles Price** is revered for his knowledge, experience and efficiency. "*Accessible and responsive,*" he "*knows how to do a deal*" and does an excellent job for his clients. He has recently worked on the redevelopment of downtown Albuquerque by the Historic District Improvement Company.

The Clients: Historic District Improvement Company; Forest City Enterprises; Hunt Building and High Desert Investment.

Band 2

Hurley Toevs Styles Hamblin & Panter PA

The Firm: This boutique firm of five lawyers is distinguished by its real estate work. Commercial developers, lenders and property owners constitute an increasingly active client base in a market buoyed by low interest rates and the availability of capital.

The Lawyers: **Patrick Hurley**'s broad transactional practice utilizes his diverse capabilities in the representation of large landowners and developers. Peers admired his commitment to clients, his conscientious approach and his sense of what is important in a deal. "*He's a deal-maker not a deal-obfuscator.*" A technically-oriented attorney with a fine eye for detail, **Mark Styles** has a wealth of experience representing real estate lenders and borrowers. This "*knowledgeable and thoughtful*" attorney works across the state on matters related to financing, sales and acquisitions.

Modrall, Sperling, Roehl, Harris & Sisk, PA

The Firm: New Mexico's largest full-service firm can flex considerable muscle in its real estate team. Its eight "*reliable*" attorneys represent buyers and sellers of commercial property and developers and investors. A highlight from the past year, the team handled the financing, acquisition and leases of a wind-powered electricity generation facility.

The Lawyers: **Dale Ek**, who concentrates on high-end transactions and financings, is considered by market sources to be *"very much a force in New Mexico real estate."* His studious and methodical approach inspires confidence in clients. Another attorney with considerable expertise in financing is **Ruth Schifani**. Her rigorous work ethic and commitment to clients has earned her the admiration of peers, who also respect her judgment. Schifani has recently handled the financing of a large hotel project, and is representing a group engaged in the acquisition of four apartment complexes. Head of Modrall Sperling's transactions department, **Meg Meister**, garnered praise for her solutions-oriented approach. Her practice takes in finance, acquisitions and lease work. She has recently been involved in Province Healthcare's acquisition of the Memorial Medical Center in Las Cruces, and has worked on the new arena in Rio Rancho.

Rodey, Dickason, Sloan, Akin & Robb, PA

The Firm: Attorneys at this full-service firm bring a diversity of experience to their real estate work. The large size of the firm works to clients' advantage: *"They have the bench strength – when they need to delegate, the work is done quickly and well."* Attorneys recently secured an $11 million verdict in a water utility condemnation case for El Dorado Utilities, having rejected an initial offer of $6 million for the asset.

The Lawyers: Regarded by some as the leading land use lawyer in the state, **John Salazar** is a *"hands-on attorney"* and well-thought of by clients and competitors. Recent work includes representation of the University of New Mexico in its complex sale of 9000 acres of land to Forest City Enterprises for the Mesa del Sol development. Described as *"meticulous, practical, polished and persuasive,"* he was also admired for his business acumen and sensitivity to client needs. The former campaign manager to Senator Jeff Bingaman, Salazar is well-connected, both locally and in Washington. Clients acclaimed the competence and integrity of *"tireless workaholic"* **Catherine Goldberg**. She undertakes a mixture of acquisitions, sales and real estate financings for clients such as Valor Telecommunications, The Williams Companies and SNK Realty Group.

The Clients: Prudential Insurance; University of New Mexico; Louisiana Energy Systems; Valor Telecommunications; The Williams Companies and SNK Realty Group.

Band 3

Keleher & McLeod, PA

The Firm: Keleher's eight real estate attorneys handle everything from sales, acquisitions and exchanges to financing and development work. The Albuquerque firm was rated by clients for its *"responsive"* bench and useful contacts throughout the state.

The Lawyers: *"Very sharp"* **Bill Keleher** was singled out by market sources for his experience and knowledge. He has recently handled a real estate annexation for the City of Rio Rancho.

Scheuer Yost & Patterson PC

The Firm: This well-established Santa Fe firm handles real estate transactions and litigation for a diverse client base including banks, insurance companies and public bodies. Its nine attorneys are distinguished by their smooth negotiating style.

The Lawyers: The firm's profile in the real estate market is maintained by the excellent reputation of **John Patterson**. A *"professorial attorney"* with excellent knowledge of all aspects of real estate law, he is regarded as *"the New Mexi-*

co expert on condominiums." Ralph Scheuer was also commended for his attention to detail and negotiating skills.

The Clients: Commonwealth Land Title Insurance; Tri-State Generation & Transmission; General Electric Capital; The County of Los Alamos and Union Carbide.

Sommer, Udall, Hardwick, Ahern & Hyatt LLP

The Firm: Based in Santa Fe, this 12-lawyer firm houses a strong real estate practice with adroitness in subdivision, development and zoning, as well as transactions and exchanges. Sources identified **Janice Ahern** as the firm's strongest practitioner; her caseload includes condominium, land use and litigation work.

Vogel Campbell Blueher & Castle

The Firm: This small Albuquerque firm of six partners is highly regarded for its real estate work. Former city attorney **David Campbell** is seen as the standout lawyer on account of his zoning and land use expertise. An articulate spokesman for his clients, he excels at public presentation of land use issues. Kevin Peterman was applauded for the steady hand he displays in complex transactions, and was recommended on title matters.

Other Notable Practitioners

Lawrence Wells of commercial real estate boutique Campbell and Wells PA was recommended to researchers as *"very thorough, very thoughtful and very careful."* Although his practice is primarily concentrated on transactional work, he is a *"versatile"* attorney who also undertakes litigation. With experience in the acquisition and disposition of retail and industrial property, he also handles leasing work and *"always goes the extra mile"* for his clients.

Leaders in New Mexico

ADAMS, Mark
Rodey, Dickason, Sloan, Akin & Robb, PA, Santa Fe 505 984 0100
Recommended in Litigation, Natural Resources

AHERN, Janice
Sommer, Udall, Hardwick, Ahern & Hyatt LLP, Santa Fe 505 982 4676
Recommended in Real Estate

APODACA, Patrick
Keleher & McLeod, PA, Albuquerque 505 346 4646
Recommended in Corporate/M&A

APPLEBY, Nancy
Rodey, Dickason, Sloan, Akin & Robb, PA, Albuquerque 505 765 5900
Recommended in Native Law

AUSHERMAN, Larry
Modrall, Sperling, Roehl, Harris & Sisk, PA, Albuquerque 505 848 1800
Recommended in Environment, Natural Resources

BAKER, Douglas
Modrall, Sperling, Roehl, Harris & Sisk, PA, Albuquerque 505 848 1800
Recommended in Litigation

BARDACKE, Paul
Eaves Bardacke Baugh Kierst & Kiernan PA, Albuquerque 505 888 4300
Recommended in Litigation

BARLOW, Richard
Barlow & Wilcox PA, Albuquerque 505 248 1300
Recommended in Corporate/M&A

BENDICKSEN, Perry
Brownstein Hyatt & Farber, PC, Albuquerque 505 724 9564
pbendicksen@bhf-law.com
Recommended in Corporate/M&A
Practice Areas: Shareholder in Brownstein Hyatt & Farber's Corporate

Finance Group. Focuses on private equity, venture capital, corporate finance, and mergers and acquisitions. Clients include private equity and venture capital funds and their investors, investment banking firms, and emerging technology companies.
Prof. Memberships: American Bar Association; New Mexico Bar Association; National Association of Bond Lawyers.
Personal: Harvard Law School (JD, 1982); Amherst College (BA, 1978).

BETTINGER, Carl
Shapiro and Bettinger LLP, Albuquerque 505 888 6463
Recommended in Litigation

BETZER, Stan
Betzer Roybal & Eisenberg PC, Albuquerque 505 797 0105
Recommended in Corporate/M&A

BROWN, Duane
Modrall, Sperling, Roehl, Harris & Sisk, PA, Albuquerque 505 848 1800
Recommended in Corporate/M&A

BUCHHOLTZ, David
Brownstein Hyatt & Farber, PC, Albuquerque 505 724 9565
dbuchholtz@bhf-law.com
Recommended in Corporate/M&A
Practice Areas: Shareholder in Brownstein Hyatt & Farber's Corporate and Securities, Corporate Finance, Mergers and Acquisitions, and Public Finance Groups. Focuses on government finance law, economic development and state tax incentive law, financial institutions law, securities law, and corporate matters. Additionally, he represents issuers, underwriters, and trustees in connection with the issuance of government securities.
Prof. Memberships: American Bar Association; Albuquerque Bar Association; National Association of Bond Lawyers.
Personal: Georgetown University Law Center (JD, 1976); State University of New York at Binghamton (BA, 1973).

CAMPBELL, David
Vogel Campbell Blueher & Castle, Albuquerque 505 884 8444
Recommended in Real Estate

CAMPBELL, Michael
Holland & Hart LLP, Santa Fe
505 954 7282
mcampbell@hollandhart.com
Recommended in Environment, Natural Resources
Practice Areas: Mr Campbell's practice concentrates on oil and gas, antitrust and environmental litigation, with over 25 years of litigation experience in the state and federal courts of New Mexico. He has represented large, integrated oil and gas companies, as well as independent operators, in a wide variety of oil and gas disputes, several of which were putative class actions. His jury experience has included take-or-pay litigation, surface use disputes, tort claims, and royalty controversies with both private and governmental entities. He has tried to verdict antitrust claims in the oil and gas arena, including a price fixing claim brought pursuant to Section 1 of the Sherman Act.
Prof. Memberships: Member, State Bar of New Mexico; American Bar Association; and the Oliver Seth American Inn of Court.
Career: Admitted to State Bar of New Mexico (1975); US District Court, District of New Mexico; US Court of Appeals, Tenth Circuit; and the US Supreme Court.

Personal: Received a JD (1975) and a BA (1971) from the University of New Mexico.

CARPENTER, Bill
Carpenter & Stout Ltd, Albuquerque 505 243 1336
Recommended in Litigation

CONKLIN, Robert
Keleher & McLeod, PA, Albuquerque 505 346 4646
Recommended in Employment

COONEY, John
Modrall, Sperling, Roehl, Harris & Sisk, PA, Albuquerque 505 848 1800
Recommended in Environment, Natural Resources

DRAPER, John
Montgomery & Andrews, PA, Santa Fe 505 982 3873
Recommended in Litigation, Natural Resources

EAVES, John
Eaves Bardacke Baugh Kierst & Kiernan PA, Albuquerque 505 888 4300
Recommended in Litigation

EK, Dale
Modrall, Sperling, Roehl, Harris & Sisk, PA, Albuquerque 505 848 1800
Recommended in Real Estate

FRANSE, R Nelson
Rodey, Dickason, Sloan, Akin & Robb, PA, Albuquerque
505 765 5900
Recommended in Litigation

GALLEGOS, J E
Gallegos Law Firm PC, Santa Fe
505 983 6686
Recommended in Environment, Litigation, Natural Resources
Career: Partner since 1963.
Personal: University of Texas (LLB 1960), Rice Institute (BBA, 1956).

GILKEY, Duane C
Gilkey & Stephenson PA, Albuquerque 505 242 4466
duane@gilkeylaw.com
Recommended in Employment
Practice Areas: Employment and labor; litigation; civil rights.
Prof. Memberships: State Bar of New Mexico (Member, Employment and Labor Law Section); New Mexico Board of Legal Specialization Recognized Specialist in Employment and Labor Law; Fellow, College of Labor and Employment Lawyers; Albuquerque and American Bar Associations.
Career: Managing Director, Gilkey & Stephenson, P.A., 1995-present; Rodey Law Firm, 1963-95 (Managing Director, 1980-93); Chairman, City of Albuquerque Personnel and Labor Relations Board, 1978-83.
Publications: Various.
Personal: Born Melrose, Minnesota, 21 January 1936; JD, Harvard University, 1963; BS (summa cum laude), University of Montana, 1958.

GOLDBERG, Catherine
Rodey, Dickason, Sloan, Akin & Robb, PA, Albuquerque 505 765 5900
Recommended in Real Estate

GOLDBERG, Joseph
Freedman Boyd Daniels Hollander Goldberg & Cline PA, Albuquerque 505 842 9960
Recommended in Litigation

GORDON, Scott
Rodey, Dickason, Sloan, Akin & Robb, PA, Albuquerque 505 765 5900
Recommended in Employment

HALL, Alan
Rodey, Dickason, Sloan, Akin & Robb, PA, Albuquerque 505 765 5900
Recommended in Corporate/M&A

HALL, Bruce
Rodey, Dickason, Sloan, Akin & Robb, PA, Albuquerque 505 765 5900
Recommended in Litigation

HARRIGAN, Kenneth
Modrall, Sperling, Roehl, Harris & Sisk, PA, Albuquerque 505 848 1800
Recommended in Litigation

HENSLEY Jr, Harold
Hinkle Hensley Shanor & Martin LLP, Midland 432 683 4691
hhensley@hinklelawfirm.com
Recommended in Natural Resources
Practice Areas: Complex litigation primarily in the fields of oil and gas, commercial law and condemnation. He has been involved in extended litigation in many states including New Mexico, Texas, Oklahoma, Kansas and Wyoming.
Prof. Memberships: American College of Trial Lawyers, Roehl Circle of Honor for New Mexico Trial Lawyers.
Career: Partner since 1963.
Personal: University of Texas (LLB 1960), Rice Institute (BBA, 1956).

HEYMAN, Robert
Sutin, Thayer & Browne, Albuquerque 505 883 2500
Recommended in Corporate/M&A

HURLEY, Patrick
Hurley Toevs Styles Hamblin & Panter PA, Albuquerque 505 888 1188
Recommended in Real Estate

JONTZ, Dennis
Lewis and Roca Jontz Dawe, Albuquerque 505 764 5400
Recommended in Corporate/M&A

KELEHER, William
Keleher & McLeod, PA, Albuquerque 505 346 4646
Recommended in Real Estate

KENDRICK, Edmund
Montgomery & Andrews, PA, Santa Fe 505 982 3873
Recommended in Environment

LASATER Jr, W Robert
Rodey, Dickason, Sloan, Akin & Robb, PA, Albuquerque 505 765 5900
Recommended in Litigation

MADISON, William
Madison Harbour Mroz & Brennan PA, Albuquerque 505 242 2177
Recommended in Litigation

MCDONALD, Randall
Foster Johnson McDonald Lucero Koinis LLP, Albuquerque 505 243 3000
Recommended in Corporate/M&A

MEISTER, Margaret
Modrall, Sperling, Roehl, Harris & Sisk, PA, Albuquerque 505 848 1800
Recommended in Real Estate

MILLER, Ranne
Miller Stratvert PA, Albuquerque
505 842 1950
Recommended in Litigation

MONNHEIMER, Donald
Rodey, Dickason, Sloan, Akin & Robb, PA, Albuquerque 505 765 5900
Recommended in Corporate/M&A

MONTGOMERY, Andrew
Montgomery & Andrews, PA, Santa Fe 505 982 3873
Recommended in Litigation

MOODY, Christopher
Moody & Warner PC, Albuquerque
505 944 0033
Recommended in Employment

MOORE, Charles
Keleher & McLeod, PA, Albuquerque 505 346 4646
Recommended in Corporate/M&A

MYERS, John
Myers Oliver & Price, Albuquerque
505 247 9080
Recommended in Real Estate

NIBERT, Gregory J
Hinkle Hensley Shanor & Martin LLP, Roswell 505 622 6510
gnibert@hinklelawfirm.com
Recommended in Environment, Natural Resources
Practice Areas: Oil and gas law, including title examination, financing, contract preparation, acquisitions and divestitures, division orders, oil and gas administrative agency matters.
Prof. Memberships: State Bar of New Mexico (Member: Natural Resources, Energy and Environmental Law; Board Member, 1985-. Chair, 1990-91).
Career: Partner since 1989.
Personal: Pepperdine University School of Law, JD, cum laude, 1983, Recognized by the NM Board of specialization as a specialist in oil and gas natural resources law.

PAISLEY, Bonnie
Brownstein Hyatt & Farber, PC, Albuquerque 505 724 9573
bpaisley@bhf-law.com
Recommended in Corporate/M&A
Practice Areas: Senior Counsel in Brownstein Hyatt & Farber's Public Finance and Corporate & Securities Groups. Concentrates on corporate and securities law, general business transac-

tions, and municipal finance. Represents small businesses, primarily technology companies, in various stages of development. Works with clients on many aspects of their businesses, including choice of entity, securities matters, contracts, and various types of transactions, including acquisitions and mergers. Also represents issuers, underwriters, and trustees in connection with the issuance of government securities.

Personal: Harvard Law School (JD, 1985); Salem State College (BA, 1983).

PARKER, James
Modrall, Sperling, Roehl, Harris & Sisk, PA, Albuquerque 505 848 1800
Recommended in Corporate/M&A, Employment

PATTERSON, John
Scheuer Yost & Patterson PC, Santa Fe 505 982 9911
Recommended in Real Estate

PEIFER, Charles
Peifer, Hanson & Mullins PA, Albuquerque 505 247 4800
Recommended in Litigation

PHARRIS, Charles
Keleher & McLeod, PA, Albuquerque 505 346 4646
Recommended in Litigation

PRICE, Charles
Myers Oliver & Price, Albuquerque 505 247 9080
Recommended in Real Estate

REID, Spencer
Keleher & McLeod, PA, Albuquerque 505 346 4646
Recommended in Litigation

ROSENBLUM, Jay
Sutin, Thayer & Browne, Albuquerque
505 883 3428
JDR@sutinfirm.com
Recommended in Corporate/M&A
Practice Areas: Mr Rosenblum concentrates his practice in the areas of mergers and acquisitions, corporate and business, benefits, tax and real estate.
Prof. Memberships: Mr Rosenblum is on the Board of Directors of Albuquerque Economic Development, Inc. and is a graduate of the Leadership Albuquerque and New Mexico programs.
Career: Mr Rosenblum serves as President and CEO of the Sutin, Thayer & Browne law firm.
Personal: Mr Rosenblum plays electric and acoustic bass in the Curio Cowboys, New Mexico's own western swing band.

SALAZAR, John
Rodey, Dickason, Sloan, Akin & Robb, PA, Albuquerque 505 765 5900
Recommended in Real Estate

SCHIFANI, Ruth
Modrall, Sperling, Roehl, Harris & Sisk, PA, Albuquerque 505 848 1800
Recommended in Real Estate

SCHNEEBECK, Douglas
Modrall, Sperling, Roehl, Harris & Sisk, PA, Albuquerque 505 848 1800
Recommended in Litigation

SCHULER, Alison
Schuler, Messersmith, Daly & Lansdowne, Albuquerque 505 872 0800
Recommended in Corporate/M&A

SCHULTZ, Andrew
Rodey, Dickason, Sloan, Akin & Robb, PA, Albuquerque 505 765 5900
Recommended in Litigation

SCOTT, William
Modrall, Sperling, Roehl, Harris & Sisk, PA, Albuquerque 505 848 1800
Recommended in Environment, Native Law, Natural Resources

SHANOR, Stuart D
Hinkle Hensley Shanor & Martin LLP, Roswell 505 622 6510
sshanor@hinklelawfirm.com
Recommended in Litigation
Practice Areas: Complex commercial litigation.
Prof. Memberships: American College of Trial Lawyers (President 2001-02), American Bar Foundation, Recipient - New Mexico Bar Professionalism Award, ABA, American Judicure Society, American Inns of Court, Chavez County Bar Association.
Career: Partner since 1969.
Personal: University of Michigan (LLB 1962), Wittenberg College (AB 1959).

SINGLETON, Sarah
Montgomery & Andrews, PA, Santa Fe 505 982 3873
Recommended in Environment, Natural Resources

SLADE, Lynn
Modrall, Sperling, Roehl, Harris & Sisk, PA, Albuquerque
505 848 1800
Recommended in Environment, Native Law, Natural Resources

STEPHENSON, Barbara G
Gilkey & Stephenson PA, Albuquerque 505 242 4466
barbara@gilkeylaw.com
Recommended in Employment
Practice Areas: Employment and labor; litigation; civil rights; university law.
Prof. Memberships: State Bar of New Mexico (Member, Employment and Labor Law Section); New Mexico Board of Legal Specialization Recognized Specialist in Employment and Labor Law; Albuquerque and American Bar Associations.
Career: Shareholder, Gilkey & Stephenson, P.A., 1995-present; Rodey Law Firm, 1990-95 (Director, 1994); governmental legal positions at the federal, state, and local levels, 1980-90.
Personal: Born Eureka, Montana, 6 June 1951; JD, University of New Mexico, 1979, BA 1974.

STERN III, Walter
Modrall, Sperling, Roehl, Harris & Sisk, PA, Albuquerque 505 848 1800
Recommended in Environment, Native Law, Natural Resources

STYLES, Mark
Hurley Toevs Styles Hamblin & Panter PA, Albuquerque
505 888 1188
Recommended in Real Estate

SULLIVAN, Patrick
Salazar & Sullivan, Albuquerque 505 314 1414
Recommended in Litigation

THROCKMORTON, Rex
Rodey, Dickason, Sloan, Akin & Robb, PA, Albuquerque 505 765 5900
Recommended in Litigation

TINNIN Jr, Robert
Tinnin Law Firm, Albuquerque 505 768 1500
Recommended in Employment

WARNER, Whitney
Moody & Warner PC, Albuquerque 505 944 0033
Recommended in Employment

WELLS, Lawrence
Campbell and Wells PA, Albuquerque 505 830 9213
Recommended in Real Estate

WOLF, Wayne
Wolf Taylor & McCaleb, Albuquerque 505 888 6600
Recommended in Litigation

WORD, Terry
Word & Bogardus, Albuquerque 505 842 1905
Recommended in Litigation

GILKEY & STEPHENSON, P.A.

THE FIRM

Managing Partner: Duane C Gilkey
Senior Partners: Duane C Gilkey, Barbara G Stephenson

Number of partners: 4
Number of other lawyers: 1

AREAS OF PRACTICE:
Employment & Labor Litigation 90%
Employment & Labor Counseling 10%

HEAD OFFICE

NEW MEXICO
500 Marquette Avenue NW, Suite 505, **Albuquerque**, NM 87102
Tel: 505 242 4466   **Fax:** 505 242 3145
Website: www.gilkeylaw.com

FIRM OVERVIEW: Gilkey & Stephenson, P.A. offers employers specialized representation in employment and labor law matters. From its founding in 1995, the firm's mission has been to offer the high-quality representation of a big firm with the personalized and cost-effective touch of a small firm. More than 90% of the firm's work is defending lawsuits brought against national and local clients. The firm's litigation practice is enhanced by the firm's active practice in counseling and training employers to prevent disputes from turning into administrative charges or litigation.

MAIN AREAS OF PRACTICE: The firm provides effective representation in the following areas:

Employment/Discrimination Matters: Race, sex, disability, and age discrimination; sexual harassment and hostile work environment claims; whistleblower claims; and retaliation claims, under state and federal law.

Employment Contracts: Confidentiality agreements; non-compete agreements; compensation agreements; executive compensation; and state common law claims.

Employee Benefits: ERISA litigation; FLSA litigation; FMLA litigation; workplace safety (and violence claims); employee privacy; and contract claims.

Labor Law: Claims under the NLRA; union organization, union certification, union elections, and related litigation; administration of labor contracts, including grievance procedures; renegotiation of collective bargaining agreements; strikes, picketing, lockouts, and injunctions; and federal court litigation and appeals.

Employment Law Counseling: Wage and hour issues; leaves of absence; trade secrets; wrongful termination; sexual harassment investigations; principal independent contractor relationships; litigation avoidance; policy audits; policy manual development; employee training.

Alternative Dispute Resolution: Mediation and arbitration.

Reported Cases: Some reported cases handled by the firm's attorneys include: Brillhart v Philips Electronics North America Corp., 179 F.3d 1271 (10th Cir. 1999) (reinstating jury verdict in favor of employer in retaliation claim); Armijo v Prudential Ins. Co. of America, 72 F.3d 793 (10th Cir. 1995) (decision compelling arbitration); Carr v Stryker Corp., 28 F.3d 112 (10th Cir. 1994) (affirming summary judgment for employer in breach of contract case); Jackson v City of Bloomfield, 731 F.2d 652 (10th Cir. 1984) (wrongful termination claim under 42 U.S.C. § 1983); Sheet Metal Workers Intern. Ass'n Local Union No. 49, AFL-CIO v. Los Alamos Constructors, Inc., 550 F.2d 1258 (10th Cir. 1977) (holding in favor of contractor on forum selection clause); Chicano Police Officer's Ass'n v Stover, 552 F.2d 918 (10th Cir. 1977) (suit challenging allegedly race-motivated hiring procedures); Salazar v Furr's Inc., 629 F. Supp. 1403 (D.N.M. 1986) (dismissing pregnancy discrimination and related claims); Zuniga v Sears, Roebuck & Co., 671 P.2d 662 (N.M. App. 1983) (affirming summary judgment for employer in wrongful discharge and slander action).

CLIENTS: Gilkey & Stephenson, P.A. represents a variety of employers ranging from local to international, as well as local and state-wide public entities. Some of the clients the firm has represented include: Intel Corporation; Washington TRU Solutions LLC; Philips Semiconductors; Southwest Airlines Co.; Raley's of New Mexico; Business Environments; Citigroup Inc.; CUNA Mutual Insurance Group; Dillard Store Services, Inc.; Risk Management Division, State of New Mexico; New Mexico Association of Counties; the University of New Mexico; American Gypsum Company; Lovelace Respiratory Research Institute; Bowlin Travel Centers, Inc.; and Delta Air Lines.

INTERNATIONAL WORK: The firm has represented a number of non-US clients in litigation within the United States.

HINKLE, HENSLEY, SHANOR & MARTIN L.L.P.

THE FIRM

Managing Partner: C D Martin, Midland, TX office

Number of partners: 26
Number of other lawyers: 11

FIRM OVERVIEW: Hinkle, Hensley, Shanor & Martin, L.L.P. is one of the oldest and largest law firms in New Mexico and West Texas. Tracing its history to 1888 when its founder, Granville A Richardson, opened the first law office in Roswell in the Territory of New Mexico, the firm now has offices in Roswell and Santa Fe, New Mexico, and in Midland and Austin, Texas. The firm's geographical diversity has contributed to its growth and stability. The Roswell and Midland offices are located on or adjacent to large on-shore oil and gas reserves. The Santa Fe office is located at the commercial, financial, and governmental centers of New Mexico. Offices and lawyers communicate and work together as if they were in a single location. The educational and specialty diversities of the firm's lawyers provide the highest quality of services.

MAIN AREAS OF PRACTICE:

Natural Resources: The Hinkle law firm's natural resources practice area represents the largest area of expertise in the firm. The group conducts all types of title examinations in NM and Texas including fee, state, federal and Indian lands, and land grants. The firm's attorneys also have an extensive practice in all areas of natural resources contract law, including purchase and sale agreements, oil and gas leases, oil field accidents, exploration and joint venture agreements, and Indian development contracts. An extensive litigation practice relating to natural resources also has developed within the firm. Litigators have considerable experience in specific areas of natural resources such as titles, contracts, royalty issues, operations, and taxation, as well as general knowledge and expertise in oil, gas and other natural resources and environmental operations. Oil, gas and other natural resources attorneys are continually involved in matters relating to due diligence and the preparation of instruments necessary to finance natural resources transactions, such as mortgages, deeds of trust, loan agreements, financing opinions and documentation in both Texas and New Mexico. They also practice regularly before various federal and state agencies relating to industry matters. These agencies include the New Mexico Oil Conservation Division, the Texas Railroad Commission, the Bureau of Land Management, the Forest Service, the Interior Board of Land Appeals, the Bureau of Indian Affairs, FERC, the Minerals Management Service, the New Mexico State Engineer, and various Texas, New Mexico and federal environmental agencies.

Water Law: The firm's attorneys have extensive experience in the area of water law and represent clients before state administrative agencies and state and federal courts concerning all aspects of water rights law, including permitting, acquisitions, transfers, adjudications and other litigation.

Environmental Law: Environmental attorneys have broad expertise in environmental compliance and litigation. They regularly assist with the performance of environmental audits and assessments in real estate transactions. They also analyze natural resource business activities to ensure compliance with state and federal environmental regulations, including the New Mexico Oil and Gas Act, the New Mexico Hazardous Water Act and Clean Water Act, Texas Clean Water Act, Texas Solid Waste Disposal Act, CECLA, RCRA, NEPA, and a variety of other environmental laws.

Litigation: In addition to its natural resources litigation practice the firm also has extensive litigation experience in other litigation including bankruptcy, banking, contracts, construction, corporations, environmental, general commercial, government contracts, insurance, employment, land use and zoning, personal injury and wrongful death, products liability, professional negligence, public utility, real estate, tax and torts.

HEAD OFFICE

NEW MEXICO
400 Penn Plaza, Suite 700, **Roswell**, NM 88201
Tel: 505 622 6510   **Fax:** 505 623 9332
Website: www.hinklelawfirm.com

BRANCH OFFICES

NEW MEXICO
218 Montezuma Ave, **Santa Fe**, NM 87501
Tel: 505 982 4554   **Fax:** 505 982 8623

TEXAS
550 W Texas Ave, Sute 1200, **Midland**, TX 79701
Tel: 432 683 4691   **Fax:** 432 683 6518

919 Congress Ave, Suite 1150, **Austin**, TX 78701
Tel: 512 476 7137   **Fax:** 512 476 7146

CONTACTS

Natural Resources Litigation ....Harold Hensley, Midland
Natural Resources other ....Douglas Lunsford, Roswell
General Litigation ....Stuart D Shanor, Roswell
Environmental ....Tom Hnasko, Santa Fe
Public Utilities ....Richard Wilfong, Austin

Public Utilities: Hinkle, Hensley, Shanor & Martin's longtime representation of a large electric utility operating in Texas, New Mexico, Oklahoma, and Kansas has enabled the firm to acquire the skills and experience needed for effective representation of clients before the various regulatory commissions in the four states including the Public Utility Commission of Texas and the New Mexico Public Regulation Commission.

General Business Practice: The firm maintains a broad general business practice including bankruptcy, federal and state taxation, estate planning, probate, contract, employment law, banking, real estate, and general corporate counsel.

CLIENTS: Hinkle, Hensley, Shanor & Martin, L.L.P. represents a broad range of regional and national clients including ExxonMobil, Chevron-Texaco, ConocoPhillips, Pogo Producing, Bass Enterprises, Devon Energy, The Goodyear Tire and Rubber Company, Wells Fargo Bank, Southwestern Public Service Company, and Xcel Energy.

MONTGOMERY & ANDREWS, PA

THE FIRM

Managing Shareholders: Gary Kilpatric, Thomas W Olson, Sarah M Singleton

Senior Shareholder: Victor R Ortega

Number of shareholders: 14
Number of other lawyers: 6

FIRM OVERVIEW: Montgomery & Andrews, PA, is a full-service law firm in Santa Fe, New Mexico. Founded in 1937, M&A is known for the breadth and depth of its experience in legal and regulatory matters and its familiarity with how the executive and legislative branches of the New Mexico state government function. Firm members have served as state legislators during the firm's history, and former members have gone on to serve as a Chief Judge of the United States Court of Appeals for the Tenth Circuit, as Chief Justices of the New Mexico Supreme Court, and as Chief United States District Judge for the District of New Mexico. William R Federici, who is now of counsel to the firm, is a former Chief Justice of the New Mexico Supreme Court. The firm also has a strong background in natural resources, employment, utility regulation, insurance defense and commercial and real estate transactions.

MAIN AREAS OF PRACTICE:

Environmental Law: Regulatory compliance and legislative services for mining, oil and gas, municipal and other clients.

Insurance Defense & Regulation & Commercial Litigation: General commercial litigation and litigation on behalf of insurance companies and their policyholders against all types of claims in federal and state courts and in regulatory matters before the Insurance Division of the Public Regulation Commission.

Legislative Services: Lobbying and legislation drafting for a great many corporate, business, and trade association clients.

Oil & Gas, Mining & Employment Litigation: Complex commercial litigation.

Utility Regulation & Commercial Transactions: Administrative and litigation services in a wide range of utility areas, and contractual and other business and real estate transactions.

Water Law: Litigation, legislative, administrative and transactional services in interstate water disputes, water right acquisition and transfer, and water right adjudication and administration.

CLIENTS: Representative clients include Allstate Insurance Co.; American Express; American Insurance Association; Anheuser-Busch Companies, Inc.; Bayer Corporation; Burlington Resources Oil and Gas Co.; City of Santa Fe; Community Bank; DaimlerChrysler Corporation; Delta Dental Plan of New Mexico; Devon Energy Corporation; Duke Energy Field Services, L.P.; El Paso Corporation; Giant Industries, Inc.; Harland Financial Solutions; Home Depot U.S.A., Inc.; Intel Corporation; LAC Minerals (USA), Inc.; Marathon Oil Company; Massachusetts Mutual Life Insurance Co.; Molycorp, Inc.; New Mexico Oil and Gas Association; New Mexico-American Water Co.; New Mexico Association of Counties; New Mexico Lodging Association; New Mexico Restaurant Association; New Mexico Utilities, Inc.; Oglebay-Norton, Inc.; Pfizer Inc.; Phelps-Dodge Corporation; Protection Technology Los Alamos, Inc.; Qwest Corporation; Realtors Association of New Mexico; Regents of University of California (Los Alamos National Laboratory); Schlumberger, Ltd.; St. Vincent Hospital; State of Kansas; State of New Mexico; The New Mexican; St. Paul/Travelers Insurance Co.; University of New Mexico; Wyeth-Ayerst Laboratories Company; XTO Energy.

HEAD OFFICE

NEW MEXICO
325 Paseo de Peralta, **Santa Fe**, NM 87501
Tel: 505 982 3873   **Fax:** 505 982 4289
Website: www.montand.com

CONTACTS

Environmental Law	Louis W Rose
Insurance Defense & Regulation & Commercial Litigation	Walter J Melendres
Legislative Services	Gary Kilpatric
Oil & Gas, Mining & Employment Litigation	Sarah M Singleton
Utility Regulation & Commercial Transactions	Thomas W Olson
Water Law	John B Draper

SUTIN, THAYER & BROWNE A PROFESSIONAL CORPORATION

THE FIRM

President & CEO: Jay D Rosenblum

Number of shareholders: 14
Number of other lawyers: 24

Website: www.sutinfirm.com

FIRM OVERVIEW: Sutin, Thayer & Browne is a full service law firm, with particular expertise in litigation, commercial transactions and public finance, and is committed to finding solutions to complex legal problems. The firm strives to provide clients with aggressive and innovative representation. Sutin, Thayer & Browne has established a reputation for well developed and executed legal strategies for businesses and individuals.

MAIN AREAS OF PRACTICE:

Litigation: Sutin attorneys provide a broad range of litigation services to all type of clients. The firm represents plaintiffs and defendants in matters involving contract disputes, creditor rights and collections, securities fraud, environmental, lender liability, employment, foreclosure, bankruptcy, real estate, intellectual property and bid protest litigation related to construction and government contracts. The firm also brings and defends personal injury and wrongful death claims, including strict liability and traditional negligence, and claims for damages for a variety of non-physical injuries, including claims in medical malpractice, premises liability, recreational injury, dangerous and defective products and automobile accidents. The Sutin firm also provides comprehensive family law and divorce services.

Commercial Transactions: Sutin attorneys advise all types of clients as to entity planning and operations, financing, mergers and acquisitions, securities, state and federal taxation, due diligence and employees and benefits. The firm also represents clients in real estate, including structuring, development, construction, sales, purchases, leasing, borrowing and joint venture transactions on behalf of developers, contractors, owners, lessees, institutional lenders and private capital sources.

Administrative Law: The Sutin firm is bond counsel to the State of New Mexico and is experienced in all types of public finance matters, and has served as bond, tax, issuer's, underwriter's, disclosure, trustee's and company counsel on essentially every type of municipal obligation authorized in New Mexico, including as counsel for tax-exempt issues for housing, educational and hospital facilities, issues for local government units such as sewer, road and airport construction. The firm also has an extensive university and college practice, advising and representing clients on matters of tort liability, staff evaluation, employee discipline and termination, public bidding, open meeting requirements, student rights and responsibilities and constitutional law issues. The administrative practice involves representation of clients to various regulatory agencies, including the Alcohol and Beverage Control Department and the Department of Taxation and Revenue. It also represent clients in water, environmental and oil and gas matters.

CLIENTS: Sutin, Thayer & Browne represents all types of individual, business and institutional clients, including family-owned businesses, real estate developers, banks and other financial institutions mortgage lenders and brokers public and private corporations, Native American tribes, trade associations, and city, county and state government agencies.

OFFICES

NEW MEXICO
6565 Americas Parkway NE, Suite 1000, **Albuquerque**, NM 87110
Postal Address: Post Office Box 1945, **Albuquerque**, NM 87103
Tel: 505 883 2500   **Fax:** 505 888 6565

317 Paseo de Peralta, **Santa Fe**, NM 87504
Postal Address: Post Office Box 2187, **Santa Fe**, NM 87504
Tel: 505 988 5521   **Fax:** 505 982 5297

4010 East 30th Street, **Farmington**, NM 87402
Tel: 505 327 3867   **Fax:** 505 326 0963

CONTACTS

Litigation ....Andrew J Simons
....Ronald J Segel
Commercial Transactions ....Cristy Carbon-Gaul
....Anne P Browne
Administrative ....Julia L Peters
....Robert G Heyman

SUTIN THAYER ▼ BROWNE
A PROFESSIONAL CORPORATION
LAWYERS

CONTENTS: Antitrust p.1169; Banking p.1173; Bankruptcy p.1177; Construction p.1185; Corporate/M&A p.1187; Employee Benefits p.1196; Employment p.1199; Energy p.1201; Environment p.1205; Healthcare p.1209; Insurance p.1211; IP p.1216; Litigation p.1220; Media p.1231; Private Equity p.1237; Projects p.1243; Real Estate p.1247; Tax p.1254; Technology p.1259; Individuals' Profiles p.1261. Firms' Profiles p.1335.

How lawyers are ranked

The opinions we gather from clients — mainly from in-house lawyers but also from other purchasers of legal services — are balanced by opinions from colleagues and competitors. Together, they provide two different perspectives — an all-round view — and biased viewpoints cancel each other out.

ANTITRUST

New York
Leading firms (Antitrust)

1 CRAVATH, SWAINE & MOORE LLP *New York*
DAVIS POLK & WARDWELL *New York*
SIMPSON THACHER & BARTLETT LLP *New York*
SKADDEN, ARPS, SLATE, MEAGHER *New York*
WEIL, GOTSHAL & MANGES LLP *New York*

2 SHEARMAN & STERLING LLP *New York*
SULLIVAN & CROMWELL LLP *New York*
WACHTELL, LIPTON, ROSEN & KATZ *New York*

3 BOIES, SCHILLER & FLEXNER LLP *Armonk*
DEBEVOISE & PLIMPTON LLP *New York*
FRIED, FRANK, HARRIS, SHRIVER *New York*
PAUL, WEISS, RIFKIND, WHARTON *New York*

4 AXINN VELTROP & HARKRIDER LLP *New York*
DEWEY BALLANTINE LLP *New York*
KAYE SCHOLER LLP *New York*
MAYER, BROWN, ROWE & MAW LLP *New York*
WHITE & CASE LLP *New York*
WILLKIE FARR & GALLAGHER LLP *New York*

Firms are listed alphabetically in each band.

Band 1

Cravath, Swaine & Moore LLP

See firm details p.1344

The Firm: "*Always ready to go to war and capable of it,*" this group "*could roll out a terrific team tomorrow for a major antitrust case.*" Clients emphasize a powerful fuse between M&A and antitrust, adding: "*At the end of the day, when our company faces high risk and needs to defend itself, Cravath is the firm we turn to.*" The team acted for BAT and Brown & Williamson Tobacco in handling the FTC investigation into the combination of RJ Reynolds' cigarette business with Brown & Williamson's US tobacco business. The transaction was unanimously approved. Other successful representations include defending IBM against antitrust claims alleging attempted monopolization of the market for low-end S/390 computers. Clients deem this an outfit that is "*always on duty.*"
The Lawyers: Clients dubbed **Robert Joffe** (see

p.1291) an "*intelligent and credible*" advocate who is "*rightly viewed as one of the most able of the senior practitioners in this town.*" He is most highly regarded for his litigation practice, where he has a particularly long-standing reputation. He successfully acted for Netscape in prosecuting an action against Microsoft. **Evan Chesler** (see p.1272) is also lauded for his courtroom abilities, and he heads the litigation practice at the firm. He led the Netscape case, and also defended Bristol-Myers Squibb in antitrust litigation alleging patent misuse to exclude generic competitors; two products – BuSpar, an anti-anxiety drug, and Taxol, an anticancer drug – were targeted in those disputes. Antitrust is "*the forte*" of **Ronald Rolfe** (see p.1313), who has "*terrific judgment,*" according to clients. Another strong player in the litigation arena, he handled the BAT and Brown & Williamson merger. **Katherine Forrest** (see p.1280) "*is developing into a superb litigator and transactional lawyer,*" say clients. She represented Time Warner in its $2.6 billion sale of Warner Music Group's recorded music business and music publishing business to an investor group.
The Clients: Bristol-Myers Squibb; BAT; IBM; Sprint and Time Warner.

Davis Polk & Wardwell

See firm details p.1345
The Firm: Clients have confidence in this team's strategic ability, describing its lawyers as "*experts*" who "*deal with issues on their merits – they don't play a lot of games.*" The group's workload elicits particular commendation, and it is considered "*a wonderful platform*" for the deep pool of M&A talent on offer. The team is active in litigation matters as well, representing Roche in a number of federal antitrust cases, a DOJ investigation, state court indirect purchaser litigation and a related case before the US Supreme Court concerning the extraterritorial reach of the US antitrust laws. On the transactional side, one of its most notable assignments is Comcast's $66 billion unsolicited offer for Disney.

The Lawyers: **Ronan Harty**'s (see p.1287) impressive understanding of M&A wins respect, further bolstered by his credibility before government agencies, commentators said. **Arthur Golden** (see p.1283) leads the competition and antitrust group. He has been involved in numerous M&A. He represented AstraZeneca in re pharmaceutical industry average wholesale price litigation. Clients consider him "*an expert*" in general corporate advice and legal strategy. They also appreciate his international perspective. "*Understated but capable*" **Paul Bartel** (see p.1264) is involved in litigation, agency investigations and various M&A proceedings involving US and EU competition law. "*Savvy*" **Joel Cohen** (see p.1273) wins market approval for his judgment and knowledgeable style. He represented AstraZeneca in obtaining the dismissal of a multidistrict class action suit, in which plaintiffs alleged the 1993 settlement of patent litigation concerning the cancer drug tamoxifen had violated federal and state antitrust and consumer protection laws.
The Clients: Emerson Electric; Freeport Copper & Gold; Marsh & McLennan; AstraZeneca; Roche and Syngenta.

Simpson Thacher & Bartlett LLP

See firm details p.1370
The Firm: This group "*fires on all cylinders,*" impressing clients with its work ethic, professionalism and deep bench of support. "*Everything runs like clockwork*" to produce "*a top-quality legal product.*" A wide-ranging practice, it's also admired for its ability to "*cross both sides of the street,*" evinced by its success in both transactional and litigious matters. The team represented ITT Industries in its acquisition of the Remote Sensing Systems business of Eastman Kodak, cleared by the DOJ following a full-scale investigation. In litigation, highlights have included representing Weyerhaeuser in five federal monopolization cases challenging its purchases of logs in the Pacific Northwest.
The Lawyers: "*Clearly a national player,*"

New York
Leading individuals (Antitrust)

Senior Statesman
HAWK Barry *Skadden Arps*, New York

★ ARQUIT Kevin *Simpson Thacher*, New York

[1] GOTTS Ilene *Wachtell Lipton*, New York
HARTY Ronan *Davis Polk*, New York
JOFFE Robert *Cravath Swaine*, New York

[2] AXINN Stephen *Axinn Veltrop*, New York
BOIES David *Boies Schiller*, Armonk
COLLINS W Dale *Shearman & Sterling*, New York
CONSTANTINE Lloyd *Constantine*, New York
LOGAN Kenneth *Simpson Thacher*, New York
SCHER Irving *Weil Gotshal*, New York

[3] BARTEL II Paul *Davis Polk*, New York
BOAST Molly *Debevoise & Plimpton*, New York
BYOWITZ Michael *Wachtell Lipton*, New York
GOLDEN Arthur *Davis Polk*, New York
GOLDFEIN Shepard *Skadden Arps*, New York
KOOB Charles *Simpson Thacher*, New York
ROONEY William *Willkie Farr*, New York
STOLL Neal *Skadden Arps*, New York
WARDEN John *Sullivan & Cromwell*, New York
WEINER Michael *Skadden Arps*, New York

[4] ABUHOFF Daniel *Debevoise & Plimpton*, New York
ANGLAND Joseph *Dewey Ballantine*, New York
ARONSON Clifford *Skadden Arps*, New York
BLUMKIN Linda *Fried Frank*, New York
CHESLER Evan *Cravath Swaine*, New York
COHEN Joel *Davis Polk*, New York
FASTOW Jay *Weil Gotshal*, New York
FORREST Katherine *Cravath Swaine*, New York
JAFFE Helene *Weil Gotshal*, New York
JOHNSTON M Elaine *White & Case*, New York
KESSLER Jeffrey *Dewey Ballantine*, New York
KRAMER Kenneth *Shearman & Sterling*, New York
MORGENSTERN Saul *Kaye Scholer*, New York
NEILL David *Wachtell Lipton*, New York
ORR Dennis *Mayer Brown*, New York
PEARLSTEIN Debra *Weil Gotshal*, New York
PRINCE Kenneth *Shearman & Sterling*, New York
QUINN Yvonne *Sullivan & Cromwell*, New York
ROLFE Ronald *Cravath Swaine*, New York
STEUER Richard *Mayer Brown*, New York
SYNNOTT Aidan *Paul Weiss*, New York
TRINGALI Joseph *Simpson Thacher*, New York
UROWSKY Richard *Sullivan & Cromwell*, New York
VICTOR A Paul *Weil Gotshal*, New York

Up-and-coming individuals
HARKRIDER John *Axinn Veltrop*, New York
LARSON Joseph *Weil Gotshal*, New York
SCHAEFFER Fiona *Weil Gotshal*, New York

Individuals are listed alphabetically in each band.

Kevin Arquit (see p.1263) is at the center of "*the real hot antitrust issues.*" Clients characterize him as "*the face you put in front of your board,*" acknowledging his role as "*the consummate client-focused partner.*" His expertise before agencies is renowned, and he is equally skilled in the courtroom. Arquit is defending MasterCard

in a suit brought against it and Visa by the DOJ. Regulatory officials find him "*a force to be reckoned with.*" "*Not just a nice guy,*" **Kenneth Logan** (see p.1298) is also "*a versatile antitrust lawyer*" whose practice straddles both litigation and antitrust. He is experienced in matters for the music and entertainment industry, and successfully acted for Viacom in defeating a preliminary injunction motion concerning the link between CBS retransmission rights and EchoStar's carriage of affiliated cable programming. **Charles Koob** (see p.1294) impresses peers who consider him "*a fine lawyer.*" He successfully acted as trial counsel for Appleton Papers in a criminal action alleging a price-fixing conspiracy; the case also involved Japanese paper companies. "*Thoughtful*" **Joseph Tringali** (see p.1328) enjoys a reputation built on his "*realistic understanding of business issues,*" clients said. As well as being involved in the Weyerhaeuser matter, he represented Segal in connection with a DOJ investigation linked to alleged anticompetitive practices in the actuarial industry.

The Clients: DreamWorks; MGM; Universal; Elite Models; M-real; Lehman Brothers; JPMorgan Chase; Virgin Atlantic; UPMC Health System; Bell Atlantic; Nine West Group; Reckitt & Colman; WellPoint Health Networks; Owens-Illinois; Smithfield Foods; DHL; L-3 Communications; Seagram and American Home Products.

Skadden, Arps, Slate, Meagher & Flom LLP & Affiliates
See firm details p.1372

The Firm: This "*world-class*" group is praised for its "*deep bench*" of "*practical, business-oriented and realistic practitioners.*" The group's substantial New York-based M&A practice provides a useful resource for the antitrust group, which is credited with "*a long history of merger clearance.*" To this end the team represented JPMorgan Chase in connection with the antitrust, insurance and regulatory aspects of its acquisition of Bank One. The team also has "*good insight into litigation,*" according to sources. It acted for the New York Mercantile Exchange in litigation against Intercontinental Exchange. The team is also active in cartel investigations and other criminal antitrust matters. Sports-related antitrust counseling is also on offer. Furthermore its international reach is becoming more crucial in an increasingly global business environment.

The Lawyers: "*An ambassador*" for the practice, **Barry Hawk** (see p.1287) has "*a great feel for the international landscape.*" His transatlantic practice encompasses national and EU antitrust issues, and he is a presence in both the New York and Brussels offices of the firm. A "*true expert in the field,*" he is a popular figure among clients, who appreciate his ability to blend "*academic stature*" with a "*great personality.*" His workload

spans M&A, cartel matters and non-cartel litigation in the domestic and international spheres. He successfully acted for Rock of Ages with respect to US and EU proceedings. **Shepard Goldfein**'s (see p.1284) litigation practice is much admired. Credited as a key player in the team's success in antitrust litigation, he also has expertise in sports-related antitrust matters. He counseled the National Hockey League in a labor dispute with the National Hockey League Players' Association. The antitrust practice group leader, **Neal Stoll** (see p.1325), is "*someone who helps the non-antitrust expert understand the issues very well,*" clients say. He is involved in both transactional and litigation matters, including government investigations, trial and appellate work. Known for his merger-related practice, **Michael Weiner** (see p.1331) acted for Genzyme as special antitrust counsel in connection with its acquisition of ILEX Oncology. **Clifford Aronson** (see p.1263) further enhanced his M&A antitrust practice with UnitedHealth Group's acquisition of Oxford Health Plans.

The Clients: ABN AMRO; CIBC World Markets; SG Cowen Securities; American Stock Exchange; BHP Billiton; Chase Manhattan Bank; GlaxoSmithKline; Hexcel; Honeywell; National Basketball Association; National Football League; New York-Presbyterian Hospital; PGA Tour; The BIG EAST Conference; News Corporation and Yahoo!

Weil, Gotshal & Manges LLP
See firm details p.1378

The Firm: Interviewees agree: "*It would be hard to make a list without mentioning Weil Gotshal.*" The group boasts an array of respected partners who "*leave no stone unturned.*" Though the team is perfectly capable of handling transactional proceedings, it is more often seen in antitrust litigation. The "*tremendous bench strength of this freestanding group*" draws distinction as "*the finest defense practice for antitrust in the USA.*" With its powers of endurance, the group often wields influence on "*extremely important work.*" Antitrust counseling is another area of strength, where peers count the practice among the "*broadest and deepest.*" The group also has expertise in IP-related antitrust matters.

The Lawyers: "*Distinguished*" **Irving Scher** (see p.1318) "*has prodigious knowledge of cases,*" say sources, who consider him "*one of the most knowledgeable Robinson-Patman lawyers.*" **Paul Victor** (see p.1329) remains a popular figure in the market for his antitrust and international trade practice. His workload includes criminal and civil international cartel cases. "*First-rate*" **Debra Pearlstein** (see p.1308) is experienced in complex private antitrust litigation, FTC lawsuits and merger investigations. Counseling in joint ventures, Hart-Scott-Rodino regulations, and distributor and customer relations also form a

1170   All quotes in the text are from interviews with clients and competitors.

CHAMBERS USA 2005

substantial portion of her workload. She defended American Airlines against DOJ allegations of a violation of Section 2 of the Sherman Act. "*Wonderful mentor*" **Jay Fastow** "*has tremendous insight*," according to clients, who acclaim his ability to "*deal effectively with the myriad ramifications of decisions.*" Antitrust litigation tinged with financial services issues is a significant part of the practice, as are multidefendant disputes. Global co-chair **Helene Jaffe** is "*outstanding*" in her full-service capability, offering advice on merger reviews, litigation and consumer protection law. Interviewees "*think the world of*" **Fiona Schaeffer** (see p.1317), who has proven particularly adept in healthcare-related antitrust matters, as well as in the media and financial services sectors. Multinational merger clearance is another area where she is active.

The Clients: American Airlines; UnitedHealthcare; GlaxoSmithKline; Santa Fe and Aventas.

Band 2

Shearman & Sterling LLP
See firm details p.1369
The Firm: The team's merger defense practice attracted particular recommendation from market sources. In this arena highlights have included representing Novartis in its acquisition of Mead Johnson and separately advising Syngenta in its acquisition of Advanta Seeds. Clients praise the stable of "*sharp*" attorneys, whose "*keen grasp of the law and helpful insights into the process*" have helped win loyalty. The team's profile is largely hinged to merger work, but the group is also active in litigation, including disputes related to cartels.
The Lawyers: **Dale Collins** (see p.1273) is noted for his "*in-depth knowledge of economics and economic analysis.*" A specialist in antitrust defense of M&A transactions, he has been active on behalf of Thompson in its acquisitions of Primark, Carson Group, West Publishing and Elite Information Group among a bevy of other transactions. **Kenneth Prince** (see p.1310) translates pragmatism, merger expertise and "*excellent transactional skills*" into successful results, clients said. **Kenneth Kramer** (see p.1295) enjoys a commercial litigation practice with a proclivity toward the antitrust arena, where he is considered "*bright and strategically skilled*" in his approach.
The Clients: BASF; BOC Group; Cadbury-Schweppes; Georgia-Pacific and SGL Carbon Group.

Sullivan & Cromwell LLP
See firm details p.1373
The Firm: This "*terrific*" antitrust firm is a competitor on the national stage, say peers, who acknowledge its effectiveness in both merger clearance and antitrust litigation. Its "*outstanding client service*" contributes to "*the overall luster*" of the group.

The Lawyers: "*Superb trial lawyer*" **John Warden** (see p.1330) is acknowledged for his antitrust litigation and appellate skills. His "*impressive courtroom voice*" and work on behalf of Microsoft have made him an established name in the practice area. Antitrust coordinator **Yvonne Quinn** (see p.1311) is also visible in merger clearances in the financial services and media sectors. She recently completed an antitrust arbitration on behalf of Cablevision. "*Exceptionally bright*" **Richard Urowsky** (see p.1328) "*has terrific acumen, both procedurally and strategically.*" He applies his "*skill and accomplishment*" in all areas of antitrust counseling and merger clearance. He counts as one of his anchor clients Microsoft.
The Clients: Microsoft; Royal Philips Electronics; Cablevision; Goldman Sachs and British Airways.

Wachtell, Lipton, Rosen & Katz
See firm details p.1375
The Firm: This merger-focused antitrust group is privy to "*some of the finest corporate lawyers in America,*" making it a "*first-rate*" operation for M&A transactions and related counseling. Clients appreciate its timely judgment delivered with strategic acumen. Its experience before government agencies is among the most respected in the city. Because of the firm's overall dominance in high-profile M&A, the antitrust team inevitably puts its stamp on enviable transactions. Among them is Sanofi-Synthelabo's $68 billion offer for Aventis. On behalf of AT&T Wireless, it helped marshal the proposed $42 billion acquisition by Cingular, reportedly among the largest public cash deals in history.
The Lawyers: "*Exceptional*" **Ilene Gotts**' (see p.1284) "*prodigious output of work*" has not gone unnoticed among commentators. Clients respect her as "*a partner you can rely upon in a pinch.*" Her reputation is further enhanced by her familiarity with the nuts and bolts of merger clearance. "*A no-stone-unturned approach*" has helped to garner "*real credibility with the regulators.*" She acted on the AT&T Wireless and Sanofi-Synthelabo matters, as well as representing a consortium of private equity firms in its acquisition of Intelsat. Practice head **Michael Byowitz** (see p.1269) attracts praise on the basis of his talent for strategic maneuvers, particularly in matters with an international element. He acted for Cardinal in various acquisitions, including that of Alaris Medical Systems, Intercare Group and Geodax. One client counted **David Neill** (see p.1304) as "*one of the best I've ever come across on antitrust issues.*" His practice centers on M&A matters pertaining to financial institutions and the representation of buyers and sellers in related mergers. He has participated in the Fleet Bank/Bank of America and BankOne/JPMorgan Chase transactions. "*High-caliber*" **Joseph Larson** "*cuts to the chase*

and has a lot of endurance,*" say clients. Also an expert in cross-border transactions, he has experience extending to the Canadian, European, Asian and South American markets. He has advised the FTC on policy standards that would streamline the antitrust review process.
The Clients: ConocoPhillips; AT&T; PPG Industries and Cardinal.

Band 3

Boies, Schiller & Flexner LLP
See firm details p.1337
The Firm: A litigation specialist recognized for its involvement in cutting-edge antitrust cases, this firm's New York presence is best known for plaintiff trial work although members are equally capable on the defense side. Complex high-stakes litigation and counseling is the bedrock of the practice, and examples include representing American Express in its suit against Visa and MasterCard. The dispute involved alleged anticompetitive practices that have locked the company out of the bank-issued card business in the USA.
The Lawyers: "*All-purpose litigator*" **David Boies** is a nationally renowned and "*versatile*" trial lawyer, highly regarded as "*a quick study*" and the first choice for many on the basis of his courtroom performances. With a string of headline cases to his name – involving antitrust and others issues – he has expertise in the Sherman, Clayton and Robinson-Patman acts.
The Clients: Philip Morris; DuPont; FEMSA Cerveza; SBC Communications and Tyco International.

Debevoise & Plimpton LLP
See firm details p.1346
The Firm: This group of "*talented antitrust lawyers*" is especially noteworthy in terms of "*its strategy in bringing a litigation case to the table.*" Clients also appreciate team members' candor: "*They will always tell you their true opinion without holding anything back.*" Offering a full-service, the workload has a large litigation component, spanning civil and criminal investigations and related counseling in the domestic and international spheres. The group defended Tex-Shield in an antitrust action in Puerto Rico involving a chemically protective fabric used to make clothing for the armed forces. The team prevailed at arbitration, where most of the claims were dismissed, and obtained dismissal with regards to the price discrimination aspects during trial.
The Lawyers: Former director of the FTC's Bureau of Competition **Molly Boast** is a "*lawyer of considerable renown*" who regularly gets involved in a range of antitrust matters. Clients consider her a "*powerful ally.*" Another "*first-rate*" attorney is **Daniel Abuhoff**, who combines technical acumen with a "*great sense of humor,*" which helps put clients at ease in difficult

www.ChambersandPartners.com
All quotes in the text are from interviews with clients and competitors.
1171

situations. Together, they represented Swedish Match in its lawsuit against US Smokeless Tobacco concerning the moist snuff industry. The firm obtained a $200 million settlement on behalf of its client.

The Clients: Columbian Chemicals; Pernod Ricard; SIRVA; Waste Management; Swedish Match and Clayton, Dubilier & Rice.

Fried, Frank, Harris, Shriver & Jacobson LLP

See firm details p.1349

The Firm: The group's reputation in the transactional arena dominates, prompting clients to comment on its *"pretty keen insight into how deals work."* It also boasts significant litigation capability, enhanced by an IP group that undertakes some related antitrust work. Highlights have included continued representation of the Canadian Automobile Dealers Association in class action litigation.

The Lawyers: *"Strategic thinker"* **Linda Blumkin** (see p.1268) *"lives and breathes your problems"* until she *"finds good solutions,"* according to clients. M&A is her forte, underpinned by her strength in negotiation, clients said. Litigation also forms a significant portion of her caseload, however, and she is active in private antitrust cases and international arbitrations. On behalf of El Paso, Blumkin served as antitrust counsel in the sale of its Eagle Point refinery.

The Clients: Scotts; Bear Stearns; BellSouth; Burlington Northern and Santa Fe Railway; CIGNA; Columbia TriStar Motion Picture Group; El Paso; Forstmann Little; GKN; Hilti; Loews Cineplex Entertainment; McKesson; National Service Industries; Reader's Digest Association and Rio Tinto.

Paul, Weiss, Rifkind, Wharton & Garrison LLP

See firm details p.1362

The Firm: The firm's antitrust capability enjoys a spillover effect from its established reputation as a New York litigation powerhouse, interviewees said. Clients, who *"have a great deal of confidence in both the group's legal skills and its judgment,"* credited the team with *"coming out with the right results."* Highlights have included the representation of ACNielsen in a monopolization case.

The Lawyers: Talented litigator **Aidan Synnott** (see p.1326) impresses both peers and clients in the antitrust field, where he is acknowledged for his ability to manage complex matters. His antitrust ability is part of a wider remit, which includes IP and general commercial disputes. He has defended a chemical company embroiled in the vitamins price-fixing litigation.

The Clients: Dunn & Bradstreet; VNU; Sumitomo Chemical Company; ACNielsen and Automatic Data Processing.

Axinn Veltrop & Harkrider LLP

The Firm: Clients say they are happy to put their lives in this team's hands. They point to the exceptional quality of this 20-attorney boutique, which includes 12 members who devote the bulk of their time to antitrust matters. With expertise in the economic and econometric issues, the team thrives on mergers facing government challenges. It offers *"nice work in the substantive analysis of a deal,"* clients said. The team proved skilled in the telecom and software industries. For example, it represented Cingular Wireless (through its parent company, BellSouth) in its $41 billion acquisition of AT&T Wireless. Litigation is also a significant fixture of the team. In this realm, successes included defending Yeshiva University in the resident physicians antitrust litigation. For quality and quantity, this is an *"exceptional"* team that *"works larger than its size,"* market analysts said.

The Lawyers: *"As smart as they come,"* **Stephen Axinn** is *"a super lawyer in all respects."* His instinctive understanding of government investigations and nose for potential trouble spots mean that he is able to *"give it to clients straight,"* while his *"enthusiasm for the law"* has translated into an *"amazing"* ability to *"immerse himself in the details of a business and become quite an expert."* On behalf of Reading International, the operator of the Village East movie theater, he successfully defeated the defendants' motion to dismiss a lawsuit against major film distributors and exhibitors. *"Terrific trial lawyer"* **John Harkrider** stands out to clients for his combination of antitrust and economics knowledge, aided by his expertise as an econometrician. He acted for Candle Corporation and its chairman, CEO and sole stockholder Aubrey Chernick in connection with Chernick's 2004 sale of the company to IBM.

The Clients: BellSouth; Carnival Cruise Lines; Reading International and SunGard Data Systems.

Dewey Ballantine LLP

See firm details p.1347

The Firm: Credited with a stellar reputation in its mainstay of private antitrust litigation, this group is conversant in price fixing, monopolization and the Robinson-Patman Act. Another blossoming area is its sports-related antitrust practice. The group is defending Daimler-Chrysler against allegations concerning auto parts data used by the plaintiff to operate an Internet portal permitting automobile dealers to locate the same parts at other dealerships. The team is also acting for MedImmune in a claim that its settlement of a patent property dispute effectively creates 29 years of patent monopoly in violation of the Sherman Act and state law.

The Lawyers: Co-head of the litigation practice **Jeffrey Kessler** (see p.1293) *"gets the attention of his adversaries,"* say rivals, who added: *"Don't*

underestimate him – he provides a good intellectual challenge."* A recent arrival from Weil Gotshal, he has particular expertise in sports-related antitrust issues, an area where he is considered *"one of the best in the country."* He acted for the National Football League Players Association in a dispute over rules requiring that a player wait at least three football seasons following high-school graduation before becoming eligible for the National Football League draft. *"One of the smartest people on the planet,"* **Joseph Angland** (see p.1263) is *"a ferociously good lawyer."* Clients appreciate his ability to know *"the case inside out and upside down."* The bulk of his practice involves private litigation and he acts for the likes of SEMATECH in an alleged monopolization of the market for semiconductor test wafers.

The Clients: Matsushita Electric Industrial; Matsushita Avionics Systems; Unocal; Union Oil Company of California; Feesers; Zimmer Holdings; Omnicare; Metropolitan Intercollegiate Basketball Association and Arena Football League.

Kaye Scholer LLP

See firm details p.1354

The Firm: Clients approve of this *"hands-on"* team for its *"scholarly antitrust evaluation"* and *"creative solutions to problems."* Litigation is a focus for the group, although it is also active in merger work. The team is defending Pfizer in an antitrust class action brought by pharmacies and ultimate consumers. The plaintiffs claim that multinational brand-name pharmaceuticals companies violated antitrust laws by price-fixing price discrimination. On the merger side, the team assisted RJ Reynolds in obtaining crucial FTC approval of the combination between its US cigarette business and the US cigarette business of BAT. The matter pertained to the second and third largest cigarette businesses in the USA.

The Lawyers: Clients value **Saul Morgenstern**'s (see p.1303) *"good judgment and knowledge of not just the law, but what goes on behind the scenes."* His *"levelheaded"* approach means he is adept at *"building the consensus among a disparate group of people."* A litigator, he has tried a significant number of class actions and other matters involving indirect purchasers. The nexus between antitrust and IP matters is another key area for him and he regularly advises pharmaceutical and chemical companies.

The Clients: Infineon Technologies; Union Oil Company of California; Beth Israel Medical Center; Onex; Loews Cineplex Entertainment and Estée Lauder.

Mayer, Brown, Rowe & Maw LLP

See firm details p.771

The Firm: Clients value this *"terrific"* team for its ability to *"protect the clients' best interests."* A willingness to go the extra mile has won client confidence with regards to litigation, counseling and merger work. Its New York presence is boosted

1172   All quotes in the text are from interviews with clients and competitors.

CHAMBERS USA 2005

by seasoned practices in DC, Chicago, California, London, Brussels and Frankfurt. The team acted for Lonza in the high-profile vitamins antitrust litigation. It also successfully shielded Sony against certain antitrust conspiracy claims.

The Lawyers: Peers have "*enormous respect*" for **Richard Steuer**'s (see p.1324) powers of analysis, which led clients to "*have great confidence,*" in his work. He is acting for Pepsi Bottling Group in litigation pertaining to the Robinson-Patman Act. Though litigation has occupied a significant portion of his caseload, he also offers transactional and related counseling. "*Preeminent trial litigator*" **Dennis Orr** (see p.1306) wins recommendations from clients for his sound advice. Among them is Novartis, which he is advising with regards to the Canadian reimportation antitrust litigation.

The Clients: Clients include Novartis and Pepsi Bottling Group.

White & Case LLP
See firm details p.1379

The Firm: The firm's "*absolutely superb trial lawyers and antitrust litigators*" are skilled at handling international and cross-border issues and have been involved in cartel matters in several jurisdictions. Further bolstered by its DC strength and international network, the group has participated in some notable matters. Representing First American, it shepherded the acquisition of the tax services and flood certification of a major competitor, Transamerica. The group also acted for Takeda Chemical Industries in a series of civil antitrust class actions relating to alleged global price-fixing of vitamins and food flavor enhancers. The matter also involved related criminal regulatory investigations by US and international authorities.

The Lawyers: **Elaine Johnston** (see p.1291) is commended for her understanding of business and economic issues connected to a substantial M&A-oriented practice. This includes non-merger investigations and counseling issues related to joint ventures. She acted for Agfa-Gevaert in its pending acquisition of Italian company Lastra; the deal gained clearance from the FTC following an investigation.

The Clients: Agfa-Gevaert; First American; Saudi Refining; Takeda Chemical Industries and Williams.

Willkie Farr & Gallagher LLP
See firm details p.1380

The Firm: Clients pitch this group, operating from its DC and Brussels offices as well as its New York base, as "*a truly trusted adviser*" for a range of antitrust matters. On the menu is a full range of antitrust services, including complex antitrust litigation, civil and criminal US and EU investigations, and enforcement actions. As with its competitors, M&A reviews and proceedings related to joint ventures also feature. Recent successes include participation in the Teva/Sicor merger. Litigation highlights have involved an action in the healthcare field that resulted in a favorable settlement for Teva.

The Lawyers: "*Thorough*" **William Rooney** (see p.1313) is "*polished*" in his technical expertise, and impresses peers as an attorney who "*invests a lot of time in being on top of the law.*" His practice comprises litigation, investigations and M&A transactions, as well as related counseling activity.

The Clients: Mattel; Bloomberg; Agusta; Mueller Industries; Santa Fe; Topps; Philadelphia Stock Exchange; ExxonMobil and Sappi.

Other Notable Practitioners

Lloyd Constantine of Constantine & Partners (C&P) tackles antitrust litigation "*like a dog on a bone.*" He wins loyal clients with his instinct for the jugular on behalf of both plaintiffs and defendants. He has maintained high visibility through work on behalf of Sears Roebuck, Circuit City, Safeway, News Corporation and Morgan Stanley.

BANKING & FINANCE

New York
Leading firms (Banking & Finance)

1. **CRAVATH, SWAINE & MOORE LLP** *New York*
   DAVIS POLK & WARDWELL *New York*
   SIMPSON THACHER & BARTLETT LLP *New York*
2. **MILBANK, TWEED, HADLEY & MCCLOY** *New York*
   SHEARMAN & STERLING LLP *New York*
   SKADDEN, ARPS, SLATE, MEAGHER *New York*
   WEIL, GOTSHAL & MANGES LLP *New York*
   WHITE & CASE LLP *New York*
3. **CLEARY GOTTLIEB STEEN & HAMILTON** *New York*
   LATHAM & WATKINS LLP *New York*
   MAYER, BROWN, ROWE & MAW LLP *New York*
   SULLIVAN & CROMWELL LLP *New York*

Firms are listed alphabetically in each band.

Band 1

Cravath, Swaine & Moore LLP
See firm details p.1344

The Firm: The "*incredible quality of legal advice*" on offer here continues to secure this impressive group widespread admiration from the market. It is renowned for its close ties to blue-chip clients such as JPMorgan Chase and CSFB but also represents many other leading investment and foreign banks. The group is an ideal choice for some of the market's largest and most complex transactions. In particular, it has an outstanding reputation for highly leveraged acquisitions and complex syndicated lending transactions. Key deals include acting for CSFB as agent on the $1.3 billion senior secured credit facilities used by a subsidiary of KKR to finance its acquisition of a controlling stake in Jostens and Von Hoffmann. The group also acted for JPMorgan Chase in relation to $1.2 billion in credit facilities made available to Blockbuster to finance its leveraged split-off from Viacom.

The Lawyers: Clients appreciate the personalized service provided and value the relationships they have built up with this partner-led team. They have confidence in the group's deal savvy and business-oriented lawyers, describing them as being "*always totally on top of the issues.*" The team is spearheaded by some outstanding individuals that includes **Jim Cooper** (see p.1273). Competitors admire him as a fiercely intelligent lawyer and believe, "*as a client, you can't go wrong with him.*" His portfolio of deals includes acting for JPMorgan Chase on a secured $680 million synthetic revolving loan and letter of credit facility for Goodyear. **Rob Kiessling** (see p.1293) maintains a broad practice that includes syndicated bank financings, capital markets and M&A deals and bank regulatory matters. He represented JPMorgan Chase, Deutsche Bank and CSFB as agents on the $1.9 billion multicurrency credit facilities used to finance Invista's acquisition of the worldwide textiles and interiors business of EI du Pont de Nemours. Clients value **Allen Parker**'s (see p.1307) excellent negotiating skills and appreciate that he is "*very active, even on the business side of the deals.*" DreamWorks and DreamWorks Animation recently instructed him on $1 billion of secured credit facilities, arising out of the DreamWorks Animation IPO. Clients praised **James Vardell** (see p.1329) as an "*extraordinarily smart and competent*" adviser. He is a practical and creative attorney, who "*understands that both parties are trying to work together to get the deal done.*" In one of his headline deals, he acted for JPMorgan Chase and Lehman Brothers in the $2.95 billion senior secured credit facilities to finance an acquisition by Boise Cascade and Boise Land & Timber. **Michael Goldman** (see p.1284) is "*one of the next generation around.*" His recent work includes acting for CSFB and Citigroup on the $780 million senior secured credit facilities used by an affiliate of Bain Capital for the acquisition of Loews Cineplex Entertainment.

The Clients: JPMorgan Chase Bank; CSFB; Lehman Brothers; Deutsche Bank; Citigroup and Goldman Sachs.

New York
Leading individuals (Banking & Finance)

1 COOPER James *Cravath Swaine*, New York
HIRSCHBERG William *Shearman & Sterling*, New York
HUCK L Francis *Simpson Thacher*, New York
KIESSLING B Robbins *Cravath Swaine*, New York
PARKER C Allen *Cravath Swaine*, New York
SMITH Bradley *Davis Polk*, New York

2 BERG Eric *White & Case*, New York
DOUGLAS James *Skadden Arps*, New York
HANRAHAN Marc *Latham & Watkins*, New York
KNIGHT James *Simpson Thacher*, New York
LEVIN Peter *Davis Polk*, New York
VARDELL James *Cravath Swaine*, New York
WIEMAN Lawrence *Davis Polk*, New York

3 DOKOS Daniel *Weil Gotshal*, New York
GEARY Sean *White & Case*, New York
GOLDMAN Michael *Cravath Swaine*, New York
HYLTON Hartwell *Simpson Thacher*, New York
LINDAUER Erik *Sullivan & Cromwell*, New York
MATTEI Andrew *Mayer Brown*, New York

4 BILKIS David *White & Case*, New York
BUHLE Warren *Weil Gotshal*, New York
BURESH James *Simpson Thacher*, New York
CROSS James *Simpson Thacher*, New York
FLORACK James *Davis Polk*, New York
HALLIDAY Joseph *Skadden Arps*, New York
KOSCHIK David *White & Case*, New York
MILLARD John *Shearman & Sterling*, New York
NECKLES Peter *Skadden Arps*, New York
SIMMS Marsha *Weil Gotshal*, New York
WEISS Gregory *Simpson Thacher*, New York
WESELY Marissa *Simpson Thacher*, New York
WIGHT Richard *Milbank Tweed*, New York
WOJCIECHOWSKI Mark *Mayer Brown*, New York

Leading individuals
(Banking & Finance: Mainly Regulatory)

1 COHEN H Rodgin *Sullivan & Cromwell*, New York
TORTORIELLO Robert *Cleary Gottlieb*, New York

2 BARNARD Kevin *White & Case*, New York
PULEO Frank *Milbank Tweed*, New York
SABEL Bradley *Shearman & Sterling*, New York
SWEET William *Skadden Arps*, Washington, DC
WEBSTER Robert *Pillsbury Winthrop*, New York

3 GUYNN Randall *Davis Polk*, New York
RICE Gary *Simpson Thacher*, New York
WALKER John *Simpson Thacher*, New York
WISEMAN Michael *Sullivan & Cromwell*, New York

Individuals are listed alphabetically in each band.

Davis Polk & Wardwell
See firm details p.1345
The Firm: "*A great firm with a great approach,*" it is famed for the high caliber of its advice and counts many of the market's largest financial institutions among its clients. Foremost among these is JPMorgan Chase, which it advised as lead arranger on a $9 billion credit agreement for BellSouth, as part of the acquisition of AT&T Wireless Services by Cingular Wireless. The group is also active on behalf of borrower clients. For example, attorneys advised Limited Brands on a $1 billion unsecured five-year revolving credit agreement and a $500 million unsecured term loan agreement. This is a broad practice that has the scope to advise clients on a raft of other banking and finance transactions. Securitizations, derivatives and other structured finance products can all be found in the group's caseload. It also maintains close ties with the firm's renowned restructuring lawyers.

The Lawyers: Clients appreciate the dedication that these attorneys show to their cause and the high level of service they provide. **Brad Smith** (see p.1322) is "*a person of gravitas,*" who impresses peers as "*first rate in every way.*" Clients characterized him as an extremely knowledgeable lawyer who "*cuts through things very quickly and who focuses on what's important.*" His deal portfolio includes acting for JPMorgan Chase as lead arranger on a $2 billion amended five-year credit agreement for HJ Heinz. **Peter Levin** (see p.1297) coordinates the firm's credit group. He advised on the $9 billion credit agreement for BellSouth but also has extensive experience in the field of derivatives. **Larry Wieman** (see p.1332) is a "*terrific*" lawyer, who continues to grow in prominence. He "*fights hard for his clients but you can still cut a deal with him.*" **James Florack** (see p.1280) is respected for his work in both the domestic and international markets. Clients call on him for his expertise on leveraged lending, high-yield debt offerings and structured financings. **Randall Guynn** (see p.1286) is the group's leading bank regulatory lawyer. He advises on a wide range of issues, including the regulations governing securities settlement and payment systems.

The Clients: JPMorgan Chase Bank; Wachovia; Citibank; Bank of America and Banc of America Securities.

Simpson Thacher & Bartlett LLP
See firm details p.1370
The Firm: Market observers repeatedly rated this firm as a top banking practice and spoke admiringly of its "*tremendous depth and consistency.*" It has forged enduring ties to leading financial institutions and commands a huge market share. Complex syndicated lending transactions are at the heart of the practice. Recent examples of the group's work include acting for JPMorgan Chase and Royal Bank of Scotland on a total of $6.9 billion facilities for Countrywide Home Loans. It also has a claim to the loyalty of a glittering roster of borrower clients including private equity houses such as KKR and The Blackstone Group. Work here includes acting for the borrower on a $2.7 billion facility for PanAmSat. Clients also rely on the team for its insight into the interpretation and application of the federal and state laws governing financial institutions.

The Lawyers: Competitors praised the team for the caliber of its individuals and the sheer number of partners here who have carved substantial reputations in the field. The key individual is **Frank Huck** (see p.1289); a wonderful attorney, "*he's one of the best all-round people in what we do. He's wise, thoughtful and creative.*" He routinely handles mega-deals and recently advised the arrangers, including JPMorgan Chase, on a $19.5 billion facility for GE Capital and certain of its subsidiaries. **James Knight** (see p.1294) won plaudits for his "*refreshing insights*" which stem from his work on behalf of both arrangers and borrowers. He advised the borrowers on a $1.5 billion facility for Warner Music Group. **Hartwell Hylton** (see p.1331) is a "*practical and easy to deal with*" lawyer, who advised JPMorgan and Citicorp as arrangers on a $4.2 billion facility for CIT Group. **Jim Buresh** (see p.1269) has forged links with clients such as JPMorgan Chase and Citigroup, represented them as arrangers in a $10 billion facility for IBM. **James Cross** (see p.1273) won recognition for his diverse practice and his ability to "*cut through the deals.*" Much of his work is on behalf of private equity houses although he also advises financial institutions on acquisition finance deals and restructurings. Clients appreciate **Greg Weiss'** (see p.1331) responsiveness and ability to solve complex problems. In one of his key deals, he represented JPMorgan as arranger in $7.5 billion of loan facilities for American Express. **Marissa Wesely** (see p.1332) is a high-quality adviser, who brings to the table a pragmatic and deal-oriented approach. She advised JPMorgan and Citigroup on a $3 billion facility for Delphi. She also continues to advise a range of clients on overseas financings. The firm also fields talented individuals on the bank regulatory side. **Gary Rice** (see p.1312) advises on a spectrum of bank regulatory issues and also counsels clients on the laws surrounding bank M&A and securities offerings. His colleague **John Walker** (see p.1330) is a respected figure who acts for a host of foreign banks. His practice includes advising on securitizations and insolvencies.

The Clients: JPMorgan Chase; Lehman Brothers; CIBC; Bear Stearns; Citigroup; Bank of America; Citibank; Royal Bank of Scotland; CSFB; Wachovia and UBS Warburg.

Band 2

Milbank, Tweed, Hadley & McCloy
The Firm: Although the group is busy in the domestic market, it wins most support for its well-documented international capabilities. It is particularly active in Latin America where it continues to be most closely associated with its blue-ribbon practice areas such as project finance and financial restructuring. Attorneys here benefit from a heavyweight client list that includes JPMorgan Chase and Citigroup. They also regularly counsel other entities, such as

1174

All quotes in the text are from interviews with clients and competitors.

CHAMBERS USA 2005

institutional lenders, investment funds and export and multilateral agencies in a broad caseload that encompasses LBOs, syndicated packages and structured products.

The Lawyers: Clients described this as a "*top-flight team*" that provides a "*really high-quality*" service. On the transactional side, **Richard Wight** is an "*extremely smart and creative*" lawyer who is best known for his work in the media and telecom sectors. He advises his clients, including banks and institutional lenders, on complex financings, letters of credit and corporate restructurings. **Frank Puleo** is another of the group's key individuals. Clients recommended him as a talented business lawyer who "*understands the legal side and balances this well with his commercial judgment.*" He possesses a deep insight into bank regulatory law, although he is becoming increasingly active on the transaction side. Work here includes advice to clients on a range of securitization tools.

The Clients: The group acts for commercial and investment banks, investment funds and corporate borrowers. Some of its key clients include: JPMorgan Securities; SSSB; CSFB and Deutsche Bank.

Shearman & Sterling LLP
See firm details p.1369

The Firm: Clients view this as an excellent one-stop shop that has the scope to advise on the most demanding banking transactions. It is firmly rooted in the New York market but also has an established international capability thanks to its dense coverage of overseas offices. The group has well-known ties to powerhouses such as Citigroup, but also received plaudits for broadening its client base and for advising a wide range of financial institutions. Bank lending lies at the core of the practice and key deals here include advising Morgan Stanley Senior Funding and JPMorgan Securities as joint lead arrangers, joint book runners and lenders for $865 million of secured credit facilities for Headwaters. Clients also have confidence in the group's ability to handle high-yield bond transactions where the group demonstrates legal intelligence and "*a user-friendly attitude coupled with an ability to negotiate the middle ground.*"

The Lawyers: Although one of the team's most celebrated practitioners, Vladimir Rossman, left the practice at the end of 2004, the group is still home to a number of talented individuals. Sources regard **Bill Hirschberg** (see p.1288) as "*one of the pioneers of the industry*" and respect him for the wealth of experience he brings to the negotiating table. He tops many clients' lists and is someone who "*both sides enjoy working with because he's eminently fair.*" **John Millard** (see p.1301) has an international slant to his practice and is especially active in the Latin American market. He has experience in the oil and gas sphere and advises clients on public and private

finance deals, bank investment transactions and LBOs. **Brad Sabel** (see p.1315) is "*one of the most creative bank regulatory lawyers out there.*" Clients find him personable and conscientious and believe that his time spent at the Federal Reserve Bank of New York has lent him unique insights into the workings of the regulators.

The Clients: In one of the group's leading deals it represented Banc of America Securities and Citigroup Global Markets as joint lead arrangers and joint book running managers on a $800 million leveraged acquisition financing for the acquisition of the Sweetheart Cup entities by Solo Cup. The team also acted for Bank of America and Citicorp North America on various facets of the same deal. Other clients include Morgan Stanley, Citibank and JPMorgan Chase.

Skadden, Arps, Slate, Meagher & Flom LLP & Affiliates
See firm details p.1372

The Firm: Clients of this group benefit not only from the expertise of its banking and finance specialists but from the support of lawyers from ancillary practice areas. It is well placed to advise on complex deals and "*brings all the disciplines to the table that we need to complete the deal,*" said clients. The firm's strength on the corporate side means that it receives most accolades for its work on behalf of borrowers. Here it advises on acquisition financings and restructurings. However, it also serves a deep pool of domestic and international financial institutions. Recent matters include advising on SunTrust Banks' $6 billion merger with National Commerce Financial. Its portfolio of deals also includes advising clients on unsecured syndicated loan facilities, high-yield securities offerings, private placements and asset-backed securities transactions. It also remains a potent force in project finance and is able to serve clients on a global basis thanks to its overseas network of offices.

The Lawyers: Although the practice was dealt a blow when a group of lawyers, including Marc Hanrahan, left for Latham & Watkins, the team still numbers several highly respected practitioners. It also has a reputation for responsiveness and an ability to "*provide everything you want from outside counsel.*" **Jim Douglas** (see p.1276) is co-head of the firm's banking and institutional investment group. He is well versed in acquisition financings and restructurings, and also counsels clients on the Federal Reserve Board regulations. **Joe Halliday** (see p.1286) is a senior attorney and of counsel to the group. His clients include leading commercial and investment banks and they value his years of experience in the industry and the big-picture perspective he provides. **Peter Neckles** (see p.1303) is a thorough and personable lawyer who "*takes time to make sure the client understands the issues.*" He wins most recognition for his work on behalf of borrowers although he also serves a number of banking clients. **Bill Sweet** (see p.1326) is a bank

regulatory lawyer who is "*clearly at the top of his game.*" Clients praised him for his skill in providing an excellent technical assessment together with "*a practical response of how to achieve our goals from a business point of view.*"

The Clients: The group is renowned for its glittering stable of corporate clients. However, it also acts for leading financial institutions such as CSFB; Citibank; Goldman Sachs; Merrill Lynch and JPMorgan Chase.

Weil, Gotshal & Manges LLP
See firm details p.1378

The Firm: An increasingly important player in bank lending transactions, the firm has established itself as a prime destination for leading financial institutions such as Citibank and Lehman Brothers. An impressive platform of private equity clients has also ensured the group its market prominence. Its headline deals include acting for Citigroup on a $960 million financing for Revlon. It also acted for the same client, together with JPMorgan and Goldman Sachs as joint arrangers on a $1.2 billion spin-off financing for Medco Health. On the borrower side, the team advised United Rentals on a $2.9 billion refinancing that included issuing new debt and obtaining new credit facilities. In keeping with current market trends, the team has also been busy advising various entities on second lien financings. Clients report that the group provides an excellent level of service and excels not merely from a legal standpoint but from a business perspective. Lawyers from this practice group also work closely with the firm's legendary business finance and restructuring team.

The Lawyers: Interviewees described the group's practice leader, **Daniel Dokos** (see p.1276), as a "*polished*" attorney who is making great strides in developing the practice. He acted for one of his key clients, Citigroup, alongside Bank of America on the $505 million financing of GTCR's acquisition of Prestige Brands. He also acted for CSFB on a $355 million refinancing for HealthSouth. Clients described **Warren Buhle** (see p.1269) as a "*spectacular*" lawyer, who has a keen sense of business principles. He acts for both lenders and borrowers on leveraged leases, restructurings and acquisition financings. **Marsha Simms** (see p.1321) is a practical and seasoned attorney, who is "*phenomenally well versed in lending law.*" She also has experience in restructurings and frequently acts for major lenders in debtor-in-possession financings.

The Clients: Citibank; Lehman Brothers; GE Capital and Goldman Sachs.

White & Case LLP
See firm details p.1379

The Firm: This is an important player in the domestic market that has amassed a loyal following of clients. It also fares particularly well in cross-border transactions, thanks to the resources and synergies that it enjoys with its overseas offices. Acquisition and leveraged finance remain key pillars of the practice. Its headline deals include acting for Deutsche Bank Securities and Morgan Stanley Senior Funding as joint lead arrangers in the financing provided to BCP Crystal Acquisition, a company formed by the Blackstone Group. The proceeds of the financing were then used in a voluntary public tender offer for all the outstanding registered ordinary shares of Celanese. Lawyers also acted for Nordea Bank Finland in a $225 million term loan and $600 million revolving credit facility for General Maritime.

The Lawyers: Clients value the strong relationships that they have established with the group and appreciate the lengths to which lawyers will go to understand the workings of their business. The leading individual here is **Eric Berg** (see p.1266). He is well known for his technically detailed work but also attracted praise from competitors who commented: "*He's a good-deal lawyer who doesn't create issues out of nothing.*" He advised Deutsche Bank Securities and CSFB in the provision of $500 million of debtor-in-possession senior secured credit facilities to Exide Technologies. **Sean Geary** (see p.1282) is one of the deans of leveraged finance. He is a seasoned member of the team and popular with clients for his responsive and matter-of-fact style. Clients recommended **David Bilkis** (see p.1267) as "*straightforward, smart and very precise.*" **David Koschik** (see p.1294) is another talented member of the team, who has particular experience advising on financings in the insurance and satellite industries. On the bank regulatory side, **Kevin Barnard** (see p.1264) emerged as the group's leading light. Clients benefit from his sound judgment and describe him as "*a person of the highest integrity.*" He advises on new product development, the structuring of deals and obtaining regulatory approvals. The team has been bolstered by the recent arrival of Scott Zemser, previous head of the Paul Hastings bank finance group.

The Clients: Bank of America; BNP Paribas; Citibank; Crédit Lyonnais; CSFB; Deutsche Bank; Gleacher Partners; Goldman Sachs; JPMorgan Chase; Metzler; Morgan Stanley; Newmont Mining; Nordea Bank Finland; Royal Bank of Canada; Société Générale; State Street and UBS.

Band 3

Cleary Gottlieb Steen & Hamilton LLP
See firm details p.1342

The Firm: This is an impressive group that stands out first and foremost for its bank regulatory prowess. It has a large footprint in the domestic market but also maintains a strong international profile thanks to an established network of overseas offices. It advises domestic and foreign finan-

cial institutions on laws governing their expansion overseas and at home, and on corporate governance issues such as the Sarbanes-Oxley Act. Clients also call on the lawyers here for their skill in compliance issues and for representation in enforcement proceedings and civil litigation. The group is also active in bank M&A transactions and has been involved in some of the largest deals in the market of late. Examples include advising Abbey on its $15 billion acquisition by Banco Santander. Lawyers also acted for Laredo National Bancshares on the sale of its common stock to BBVA for $850 million.

The Lawyers: Clients view bank regulatory specialist **Bob Tortoriello** (see p.1327) as "*top of his class*" for advice on new products and foreign and domestic bank expansions. He also has a strong track record representing various entities in compliance proceedings. A portion of his practice is also devoted to advising on financial institution M&A, derivative transactions and securities offerings. Clients said he has an intellectually powerful mind that guarantees highly sophisticated advice.

The Clients: Bank of America; CSFB; Commerzbank; Deutsche Bank; HSBC; BNP Paribas; BBVA; Royal Bank of Scotland and Wells Fargo.

Latham & Watkins LLP

The Firm: Interviewees traditionally associate this group with its outstanding high-yield securities practice. However, 2004 heralded the arrival of several high-profile individuals from a rival firm, who are expected to greatly enhance the team's banking profile. The group is also well placed to build on the firm's project finance expertise and an impressive client roster that includes the likes of Goldman Sachs and CSFB. One of its recent headline deals includes acting for a syndicate of lenders, including Citigroup Global Markets, JPMorgan Chase and Lehman Commercial Paper on a $3 billion term loan for Cox Communications. The group also advised Goldman Sachs Credit Partners on first lien term loans and revolving credit and base letter facilities for Texas Genco, worth in excess of $2.4 billion. The team has also been active in the field of asset-based financings and provides clients with a broad array of regulatory services. Lawyers in New York work closely with colleagues across the domestic network and have forged strong working relationships with colleagues in Europe and the Far East in order to effectively advise on cross-border deals. Clients appreciate the level of service they receive here and believe that the group has access to a deeper pool of resources than some of its competitors.

The Lawyers: The arrival of **Marc Hanrahan** (see p.1286) and a team of lawyers from Skadden Arps has been an undoubted coup for the firm and has given the team a timely boost. Hanrahan is a popular choice among high-profile clients, who appreciate his user-friendly advice and in-depth knowledge of the field. He

typically advises lenders in acquisition financings, LBOs and take-private transactions. Although he is the dominant figure here, lawyers from his group won endorsements for their enthusiasm and willingness to "*always go the extra mile for a client.*"

The Clients: The group's portfolio includes acting for Morgan Stanley and The Bank of Nova Scotia on a $900 million secured revolving credit facility and secured term loans for Calpine Generating Company. The team also acts for: Goldman Sachs; CSFB; UBS; Lehman Brothers; CIBC; JPMorgan; The Royal Bank of Scotland and Bear Stearns.

Mayer, Brown, Rowe & Maw LLP
See firm details p.771

The Firm: Competitors regard this as an important player in the market and admire the diverse client base it serves. It has developed a broad based practice over the years encompassing expertise in such areas as acquisition finance, syndicated lending and capital markets. True to the firm's reputation, it also lays claim to an impressive securitization group. A number of the group's recent deals have involved entities from the energy industry where lawyers have acted for the banks in the provision of letters of credit and in refinancings. Its portfolio also includes cross-border deals including matters concerning Canadian and Mexican entities. The team has also developed close synergies with its offices in leading financial centers such as London and Frankfurt.

The Lawyers: A sizable team in New York works closely with its finance teams throughout the USA and with other offices from the firm's international network. Clients report that **Andrew Mattei** (see p.1299) is a flexible and deal-savvy practitioner who brings "*business practicality to the negotiating table.*" They also appreciate his "*profound knowledge of the market*" and believe that he is "*far more available and involved than some partners at other firms.*" This talented team also includes **Mark Wojciechowski** (see p.1332) who is one of the global co-heads of the firm's finance practice. This practical attorney acts for both domestic and foreign commercial and investment banks in acquisition financings and first and second lien financings. He also has experience in leveraged finance and the regulatory arena.

The Clients: Bank of America; Deutsche Bank; Goldman Sachs; Barclays; CIBC; Dresdner Bank; CSFB; Morgan Stanley; Fortis Investments; Société Générale and the Bank of Nova Scotia.

Sullivan & Cromwell LLP
See firm details p.1373

The Firm: Interviewees think of this group first and foremost for its reputation in the bank M&A and regulatory fields where it is home to the market's preeminent players. Clients have "*immense respect*" for its abilities before agen-

1176   All quotes in the text are from interviews with clients and competitors.

CHAMBERS USA 2005

cies and regulators such as the Federal Reserve System, the DOJ and other state banking authorities. It advises clients on day-to-day regulatory compliance but is also on hand to represent them in investigations concerning a broad spectrum of bank law. In particular, it enjoys a stellar reputation for its regulatory advice in relation to financing and M&A transactions. Attorneys recently advised JPMorgan Chase's board of directors on the bank's $58 billion merger with Bank One. It also counseled Wachovia on its $14 billion bid for SouthTrust. Although the team is less well known for its financing work, including bank lending, this nonetheless remains an important facet of the practice. Its lawyers also advise on the securitization of receivables, derivatives products and e-trading initiatives.

The Lawyers: Sources recommend **Rodgin Cohen** (see p.1273) as *"clearly one of the most*

outstanding bank regulatory and M&A lawyers in the market." Clients call on this superb lawyer for his deep insights into the regulatory regime including the Bank Secrecy Act, money laundering issues and regulations governing new financial products. He is also a preeminent figure in bank M&A transactions where he provides *"creative ideas on how to structure complex deals."* His portfolio includes acting on the JPMorgan Chase/Bank One deal. **Michael Wiseman** (see p.1332) is also active in the regulatory sphere where his clients include domestic and foreign commercial and investment banks. He advises on derivatives, payment system issues and enforcement proceedings. **Erik Lindauer** (see p.1297) is the group's most prominent practitioner on the transactional banking and syndicated lending side. He is also well equipped to advise on restructuring law and project financings.

The Clients: The group is active in the domestic and international markets. For example, it recently advised on the proposed merger of Japanese banks, Mitsubishi Tokyo Financial Group and UFJ. It also acts for Wachovia, New York Clearing House, Barclays and UBS Warburg.

Other Notable Practitioners

Leading bank regulatory experts cited **Robert Webster** (see p.1331) of Pillsbury Winthrop LLP as one of the first people they would refer work to in conflict situations. He is also a firm favorite among clients who described him as a client-oriented practitioner who *"keeps you informed and who knows how to talk to lawyers and internal bank clients. He's someone people can easily work with."* He advises a range of financial institutions on various regulations including those governing their transactional activities and the development of new financial products.

BANKRUPTCY/RESTRUCTURING

New York
Leading firms
(Bankruptcy/Restructuring)

1	WEIL, GOTSHAL & MANGES LLP *New York*
2	AKIN GUMP STRAUSS HAUER & FELD *New York*
	DAVIS POLK & WARDWELL *New York*
	MILBANK, TWEED, HADLEY & MCCLOY *New York*
	SKADDEN, ARPS, SLATE, MEAGHER *New York*
	WACHTELL, LIPTON, ROSEN & KATZ *New York*
	WILLKIE FARR & GALLAGHER LLP *New York*
3	PAUL, WEISS, RIFKIND, WHARTON *New York*
	SHEARMAN & STERLING LLP *New York*
	SIMPSON THACHER & BARTLETT LLP *New York*
4	BINGHAM MCCUTCHEN LLP *New York*
	DEBEVOISE & PLIMPTON LLP *New York*
	FRIED, FRANK, HARRIS, SHRIVER *New York*
	JONES DAY *New York*
	KASOWITZ BENSON TORRES *New York*
	KIRKLAND & ELLIS LLP *New York*
	KRAMER LEVIN NAFTALIS & FRANKEL *New York*
	MORGAN, LEWIS & BOCKIUS LLP *New York*
	STROOCK & STROOCK & LAVAN LLP *New York*
5	BROWN RUDNICK BERLACK ISRAELS *New York*
	CADWALADER, WICKERSHAM & TAFT *New York*
	CLEARY GOTTLIEB STEEN & HAMILTON *New York*
	CLIFFORD CHANCE US LLP *New York*
	GIBSON, DUNN & CRUTCHER LLP *New York*
	KAYE SCHOLER LLP *New York*
	LATHAM & WATKINS LLP *New York*
	LUSKIN, STERN & EISLER LLP *New York*
	OTTERBOURG, STEINDLER, HOUSTON *New York*
	PROSKAUER ROSE LLP *New York*
	SCHULTE ROTH & ZABEL LLP *New York*
	WHITE & CASE LLP *New York*

Firms are listed alphabetically in each band.

Band 1

Weil, Gotshal & Manges LLP

See firm details p.1378

The Firm: Competitors freely concede that this is *"the gold standard that the others aspire to."* The firm was among the first to invest resources in this area and, as such, has a depth of experience that few can match. It lays claim to one of the largest bankruptcy groups in the country with around 80 lawyers devoted to the practice in addition to another sizable team focused primarily on bankruptcy litigation. However, it is not merely the group's *"tremendous bench strength"* that impresses interviewees – clients spoke of the caliber of its lawyers and its commitment to *"consistent high quality and results."* Commentators regard the team first and foremost as *"a debtor powerhouse,"* a claim that is supported by a glittering portfolio of cases. In 2004, the group successfully confirmed Enron's plan of reorganization, which allowed approximately $12 billion of value to be distributed to creditors. Over 25,000 claims, totaling over $900 billion, were originally filed by the creditors – Weil Gotshal succeeded in reducing those numbers to around 14,000 and $134 billion. In another headline matter, the team also helped MCI to emerge successfully from bankruptcy protection. New instructions on the debtor side include acting as US debtor's counsel to Parmalat, which it advised on the sale of Milk Products of Alabama to Dean Foods. The group also attracts its fair share of creditor representations. It enjoys especially close ties to GE Capital and has acted for the group in relation to several insolvencies and restructurings in the airline industry.

The Lawyers: Interviewees were impressed with the group's *"deep reservoir of talent at partner level"* and believe that Weil Gotshal is *"in a class by itself in terms of experience and resources."* One of its leading lights is **Martin Bienenstock** (see p.1267), who was repeatedly dubbed a *"genius"* by competitors. Clients describe him as a *"brilliant strategist"* and appreciate the *"tremendous amount of clout"* he wields in the sector. He famously led the firm's representation of Enron. **Marcia Goldstein** (see p.1284) co-heads the team with Bienenstock and is another highly esteemed lawyer. She won particular praise for her *"masterful handling of the MCI case"* and is a popular choice in tricky negotiations because of her skills as a *"terrific consensus builder who can effectively move forward protracted proceedings."* Clients also consider her a talented courtroom performer. Researchers were told that **Stephen Karotkin** (see p.1291) is a *"spectacular lawyer who understands what's important and what's not."* He has been busy of late representing Loral Space & Communications in its Chapter 11. **Lori Fife** (see p.1279) enters the table this year following vocal support from clients. Interviewees characterized her as an extremely smart attorney who can *"slog it out with the best of them."* One client also tipped her as *"one of the best people I've worked with in terms of understanding the business and the deals."* **Alan Miller** (see p.1301) is a more senior member of the group who also attracts high-profile deals and strong market support. Clients draw comfort from his experience (*"there's not much he hasn't seen"*) and some sources consider him a hidden gem (*"he deserves more kudos than he receives"*). His current workload includes advising the Institute for Cancer Prevention in its Chapter 11 proceedings.

New York
Leading individuals
(Bankruptcy/Restructuring)

[1]
- **BAKER D J** *Skadden Arps*, New York
- **BIENENSTOCK Martin** *Weil Gotshal*, New York
- **DESPINS Luc** *Milbank Tweed*, New York
- **GOLDSTEIN Marcia** *Weil Gotshal*, New York
- **NOVIKOFF Harold** *Wachtell Lipton*, New York
- **TREPPER Myron** *Willkie Farr*, New York

- **BERNSTEIN Donald** *Davis Polk*, New York
- **CIERI Richard** *Kirkland & Ellis*, New York
- **GOLDEN Daniel** *Akin Gump*, New York
- **MILMOE J Gregory** *Skadden Arps*, New York
- **PANTALEO Peter** *Simpson Thacher*, New York

[2]
- **ABRAMS Marc** *Willkie Farr*, New York
- **BARTNER Douglas** *Shearman & Sterling*, New York
- **KAROTKIN Stephen** *Weil Gotshal*, New York
- **ROSENBERG Robert** *Latham & Watkins*, New York
- **SCHONHOLTZ Margot** *Kaye Scholer*, New York

- **BALL Corinne** *Jones Day*, New York
- **DUNNE Dennis** *Milbank Tweed*, New York
- **KORNBERG Alan** *Paul Weiss*, New York
- **SCHELER Brad** *Fried Frank*, New York
- **TODER Richard** *Morgan Lewis*, New York

[3]
- **BECKERMAN Lisa** *Akin Gump*, New York
- **CANTOR Matthew** *Kirkland & Ellis*, New York
- **FELDMAN Matthew** *Willkie Farr*, New York
- **FRIEDMAN David** *Kasowitz Benson*, New York
- **GROSS Steven** *Debevoise & Plimpton*, New York
- **HANDELSMAN Lawrence** *Stroock & Stroock*, New York
- **HODARA Fred** *Akin Gump*, New York
- **HYMAN Alan** *Proskauer Rose*, New York
- **MASON Richard** *Wachtell Lipton*, New York
- **MILLER Alan** *Weil Gotshal*, New York
- **SHIMSHAK Stephen** *Paul Weiss*, New York

- **BOROWITZ Peter** *Debevoise & Plimpton*, New York
- **ECKSTEIN Kenneth** *Kramer Levin*, New York
- **FIFE Lori** *Weil Gotshal*, New York
- **FUHRMAN Steven** *Simpson Thacher*, New York
- **HAHN Richard** *Debevoise & Plimpton*, New York
- **HAZAN Scott** *Otterbourg Steindler*, New York
- **HUEBNER Marshall** *Davis Polk*, New York
- **KIRPALANI Susheel** *Milbank Tweed*, New York
- **MAYER Thomas** *Kramer Levin*, New York
- **SAGE Michael** *Stroock & Stroock*, New York
- **ZIRINSKY Bruce** *Cadwalader Wickersham*, New York

[4]
- **BELTZER Howard** *White & Case*, New York
- **BROUDE Mark** *Latham & Watkins*, New York
- **CHARLES Scott** *Wachtell Lipton*, New York
- **FRATIANNI Constance** *Shearman & Sterling*, New York
- **GRANFIELD Lindsee** *Cleary Gottlieb*, New York
- **KELLY Michael** *Willkie Farr*, New York
- **LEAKE Paul** *Jones Day*, New York
- **LUSKIN Michael** *Luskin Stern*, New York
- **RAPISARDI John** *Weil Gotshal*, New York
- **ROSNER David** *Kasowitz Benson*, New York
- **SCHEIBE Robert** *Morgan Lewis*, New York
- **STERN Richard** *Luskin Stern*, New York
- **THOMPSON Mark** *Simpson Thacher*, New York
- **WEISFELNER Edward** *Brown Rudnick*, New York

- **BROMLEY James** *Cleary Gottlieb*, New York
- **BROZMAN Tina** *Bingham McCutchen*, New York
- **COOK Michael** *Schulte Roth*, New York
- **GARRITY James** *Shearman & Sterling*, New York
- **HARRIS Adam** *O'Melveny & Myers*, New York
- **KRASNOW Richard** *Weil Gotshal*, New York
- **LISCIO Mark** *Kaye Scholer*, New York
- **MINDLIN Philip** *Wachtell Lipton*, New York
- **RICE Glenn** *Otterbourg Steindler*, New York
- **SAFERSTEIN Jeffrey** *Paul Weiss*, New York
- **SOSNICK Fredric** *Shearman & Sterling*, New York
- **TANENBAUM Jeffrey** *Weil Gotshal*, New York
- **WALSH Michael** *Weil Gotshal*, New York
- **ZIMAN Kenneth** *Simpson Thacher*, New York

Up-and-coming individuals
- **DAVIS George** *Weil Gotshal*, New York
- **SHIFF Adam** *Kasowitz Benson*, New York

- **MELWANI Vivek** *Fried Frank*, New York

Individuals are listed alphabetically in each band.

Sources also recommended **Richard Krasnow** (see p.1295) as a seasoned and technically astute practitioner. He has been busy advising GE Capital on the Midway, Southern Air Cargo and Air Canada bankruptcies. He also acted for Wells Fargo Bank in connection with the first Galey & Lord Chapter 11 case. Clients hold **John Rapisardi** (see p.1311) in high esteem for his detail-oriented and problem-solving approach. They characterized him as a "*thoughtful and low-key personality who gets on well with other people.*" **Jeff Tanenbaum** (see p.1326) also won recognition for his excellent people skills and total focus on his clients' needs. **Michael Walsh** (see p.1330) specializes in restructurings in the healthcare and telecoms industries. Clients portrayed him as a dependable counselor who is committed to achieving their goals. Interviewees described

George Davis (see p.1274) as "*a star in the making.*" He won particular praise for his work in the steel and airline industries. His recent workload includes acting for Bethlehem Steel in its Chapter 11 case and advising Citigroup in the WCI bankruptcy.

The Clients: Enron; MCI; Global Crossing; Bethlehem Steel; CSFB; BNP Paribas; Deutsche Bank; GE Capital; Bank of Montreal and JPMorgan Chase.

Band 2

Akin Gump Strauss Hauer & Feld LLP
See firm details p.477

The Firm: Researchers were left in no doubt as to the caliber of this outstanding team. Intervie-

wees recommended it as one of the leading groups for creditor committee work and pointed in particular to its skill in representing bondholders. Although it is renowned for its assertive handling of cases, the team has nonetheless also earned a reputation as a constructive force in negotiations. It boasts a strong track record in the communications industry, where it acted for the official committee of unsecured creditors in both the WorldCom and Loral Space & Communications bankruptcies. It also advised the official bondholder committee in the LTV Steel bankruptcy, while distressed M&A transactions are a further feature of the workload. The group's lawyers frequently team up with colleagues from the firm's other domestic offices and have considerable experience in multijurisdictional cases.

The Lawyers: Danny Golden (see p.1283) is without doubt the group's preeminent practitioner. Sources rate him as one of the leading bondholder lawyers in the country. He is well known for his "*vigorous representation of clients*" and wins universal praise for the "*tremendous practice*" he has built up. **Lisa Beckerman** (see p.1265) joins him on the list for the first time this year following strong market feedback. Interviewees described her as a "*smart and careful lawyer who works hard to get the right results for her clients.*" **Fred Hodara** (see p.1288) is a low-key adviser who is gradually becoming more and more prominent. He won particular renown for his expert handling of the Exide case, where he represented the official committee of unsecured creditors.

The Clients: The group is most closely associated with work on behalf of bondholder committees, where it enjoys a reputation as one of the premier firms. It also takes on a wider range of creditor committee work and acts for purchasers in distressed M&A deals. As well as its domestic clientele, the team acts for a wider international client base including entities from Europe and the Far East.

Davis Polk & Wardwell
See firm details p.1345

The Firm: "*I'd give them the highest possible rating; they are just outstanding lawyers,*" said one satisfied client of the group. Peers also rate the team as one of the strongest in the market and praised it in particular for its excellent track record in creditor representation. Interviewees spoke of the depth of work undertaken here and noted the sure touch with which the group handles both the litigious and transactional aspects of bankruptcy work. One competitor even commented, "*I'd rank them first for very complex, novel deals that require real intellect.*" The group enjoys close ties to the banking community and recently acted for Citigroup and JPMorgan Chase as co-arrangers of a $1.5 billion debtor-in-possession credit facility for Adelphia Communications. It also advised JPMorgan Chase,

Citigroup, CSFB and Deutsche Bank on an $8.8 billion exit financing package for Adelphia. The team is also adept at committee work and acts for the official committee of commercial creditors of Dow Corning. Although less well known for its debtor work, it has secured a number of high-profile instructions in this area. Foremost among them is its representation of Delta Air Lines in its reorganization. Headline international work includes acting for Telecom Argentina in the restructuring of its outstanding bank loans and debt securities.

The Lawyers: Although the legendary Stephen Case has now retired from the practice, the group still numbers several outstanding individuals. **Don Bernstein** (see p.1266) is the group's standout lawyer. He was characterized by market sources as a calm and level-headed attorney, skilled in creating consensus between the disparate parties to negotiations. Researchers also heard that he is a *"fantastic big-picture strategist"* who is *"remarkably adaptable and creative."* **Marshall Huebner** (see p.1289) is a more junior member of the group who is blazing a trail in the market. He impressed a number of important commentators, who described him as a *"terrific technical lawyer who has good deal sense."*

The Clients: The group is best known for its ties to the banking community and regularly acts for the likes of JPMorgan Chase, CSFB, Citigroup and Deutsche Bank. It is also acting for Bank of America as agent for two lender groups in connection with the Loral Space & Communications Chapter 11. The firm also represents both domestic and foreign debtors on occasion.

Milbank, Tweed, Hadley & McCloy

The Firm: This group enjoys a formidable reputation in the field and wins plaudits for its profile in both the domestic and international markets. Interviewees were particularly impressed by the strength of its creditor committee work and rated the team most highly for its bondholder representation. A key recent matter here was acting for an ad hoc committee of noteholders in the Delta Air Lines restructuring. It also attracts instructions from a number of leading financial institutions and advised Citigroup and JPMorgan Chase as agents in the Adelphia bankruptcy. The large and deep group also represents debtors and has been particularly active in Latin America, where it assisted such companies as Satmex, Alestra and TMM on their restructurings. Its work in the distressed M&A field includes acting for a bidder in relation to the sale of Enron's Cross Country Energy.

The Lawyers: This group is noted for its talented lawyers and robust representation of clients. Much of its success is attributed to **Luc Despins** who has *"done a tremendous job of putting the team on the map."* An aggressive and energetic attorney, interviewees also note his considerable intellectual gifts and his track record of success in a succession of high-profile cases. For example, he acts for the official creditors' committee in the Enron bankruptcy. **Dennis Dunne** is gaining in profile and won resounding support from market sources. As one interviewee commented, *"He's world class and is coming into his own – he has judgment, focus and talent."* He represented the committee of noteholders in the Delta Air Lines restructuring. **Susheel Kirpalani** is a younger member of the group. Observers predict that this *"cool, calm and collected"* character can look forward to a *"tremendous future."* He is popular with both clients and opposing counsel, who recommended him for his even-tempered and creative approach to deals. His recent highlights include advising the official creditors' committee on the RCN bankruptcy.

The Clients: The group is particularly well known for its work on behalf of creditors. It acted for the official creditors' committee in the Enron bankruptcy. It also acts for banks, such as Citigroup and JPMorgan Chase, and various institutional investors, such as Deutsche Bank Securities, Goldman Sachs, Satellite Asset Management and Q Investments. It also has a debtor practice, acting for a range of debtors in bankruptcy proceedings and out-of-court restructurings.

Skadden, Arps, Slate, Meagher & Flom LLP & Affiliates

See firm details p.1372

The Firm: This group is *"among the elite on the troubled company side,"* according to interviewees. It is ideally placed to advise on the market's largest and most complex cases thanks to its bench strength, the array of resources at its disposal and its tremendous geographical reach. Key recent examples include completing the Chapter 11 reorganizations of GenTek and Safety-Kleen Services. The team has also been instructed on a number of new filings such as the Interstate Bakeries Chapter 11 and the RCN reorganization. It is skilled in out-of-court restructurings, examples of which include its current representation of HealthSouth. The firm's outstanding abilities on the corporate side make it a force to be reckoned with on distressed M&A deals, such as assisting Genuity in the sale of assets to Level 3 Communications. On the creditor side, the team has been building up an impressive portfolio of work, and is especially connected with institutions like CSFB, Deutsche Bank and Goldman Sachs. Clients call on the group for assistance with the management of portfolios of troubled credit and for advice on DIP financings and investments in, and acquisitions of, distressed companies.

The Lawyers: This sizable group is spread throughout the firm's US offices, with the largest concentrations of experts in Chicago and New York. Not only is it able to field large teams to deal with multiple complex cases, it also benefits from the support of other departments within the firm. One of the key individuals in the bankruptcy group is **Jan Baker** (see p.1264). Competitors hail him as *"a prince of a guy"* who is always a pleasure to work with: *"Everyone trusts him – you always take him at his word."* His tremendous handling of the HealthSouth case drew particular praise. **Greg Milmoe** (see p.1302) is another *"phenomenal lawyer."* Clients raved about his ability to build consensus, something that was confirmed by peers, who reported: *"He has a good sense of the negotiating room and doesn't add fuel to the fire."* His strong background in corporate law is believed to make him a particularly potent force in out-of-court restructurings.

The Clients: The team is known first and foremost for its representation of debtors such as: GenTek; Hayes Lemmerz International; Kmart; ntl; Safety-Kleen and US Airways. It has also acted as special counsel to Enron, Genuity, Global Crossing and National Steel Corporation. Its roster of creditor clients includes CSFB, Deutsche Bank and Goldman Sachs.

Wachtell, Lipton, Rosen & Katz

See firm details p.1375

The Firm: Interviewees rated the firm's creditors' rights practice one of the market leaders, with one commentator even declaring it *"the premier firm on the bank side."* Several competitors held up the group as the model they aspired to, pointing to the caliber of this partner-led operation. It typically represents creditors' committees, bank groups and other major creditors, and enjoys close ties with many of the market's leading financial institutions. Examples include JPMorgan Chase, which it represented as agent bank in the restructurings of Independent Wireless One, World Kitchen and Looking Glass Networks. The group also has a strong track record in bankruptcy litigation, where its specialists can count on the support of the firm's esteemed contentious team. Headline work here includes acting for CSFB in the National Century Financial Enterprises Chapter 11 case and the related preference litigation. It also defended Campbell Soup Company in a case brought by the litigation trust created under the Vlasic Foods International Chapter 11 plan. The firm's towering reputation for corporate and transactional work positions it strongly for distressed M&A deals. It recently advised ESL Investments on the acquisition of Kmart from Chapter 11 and has advised Synergy Group on its proposed acquisition of Avianca.

The Lawyers: Although this is a relatively modest group in terms of size, its ability to pick up leading instructions places it firmly on the map. And, despite the retirement of Richard Feintuch in December 2004, the team still offers a roster of high-powered attorneys. Foremost among them is the *"fabulous"* **Hal Novikoff** (see p.1305) who won huge support from both clients and competitors. He was consistently recommended as one of the best bankruptcy lawyers in the market, with one client stating, *"There's no better lawyer than him – he's as good as they come."* He stood out, not only for his profound knowledge of bankruptcy law but for his creativity and consensus-building abilities: *"He's completely unflappable and a delight to work with."* **Richard Mason** (see p.1299) also attracted praise from interviewees, who appreciated his low key and constructive approach to deal making. His recent work includes acting for ScotiaBank as agent for the bank group in the Intermet Chapter 11 case. Interviewees admired **Scott Charles** (see p.1271) for his inventiveness and sharp business sense. He advises on distressed M&A transactions but also acted for Kimco, a major secured lender, in the Frank's Nursery & Crafts Chapter 11. **Philip Mindlin** (see p.1302) enters the table this year. Competitors consider him an ideal choice to *"represent important players in complex cases."* Examples include acting for the Cable & Wireless parent company in relation to its subsidiaries' Chapter 11 cases.

The Clients: JPMorgan Chase; Bank of America; ESL Investments; ScotiaBank; Kimco and CSFB.

Willkie Farr & Gallagher LLP

See firm details p.1380

The Firm: This team was at the top of many people's lists for debtor representation. It is respected by competitors, who report that its lawyers are good to deal with but still able to cut a hard deal. As one commented, *"They take the ego out of the negotiations and do what's best for the client."* The team has advised on a number of high-profile bankruptcies and wins market recognition for its knowledge of specialist industries, including the communications, healthcare and retail sectors. A recent highlight was representing Adelphia Communications in its Chapter 11, which included securing an $8.8 billion financing commitment from a consortium of leading financial institutions. It has also acted for the debtors in a number of international bankruptcies. For example, the group was restructuring counsel to Air Canada and advised it in its Section 304 proceedings in the USA. Also high on the agenda has been the group's advice to various entities on distressed acquisitions. It acted for Teléfonos de México on its $400 million acquisition of a majority of the voting interests in Embratel Participações, a Brazilian telecom company, from subsidiaries of MCI and advised the same company on its acquisition of substantially all the assets of bankrupt AT&T Latin American.

The Lawyers: Clients extolled the group for the depth of talent on offer. **Myron Trepper** (see p.1328) spearheads the practice and is respected in the market as a *"tremendous lawyer"* with a *"commanding presence."* He won particular praise for his performance in negotiations: *"He's easy to deal with and advances his clients' interests by simply being very straightforward,"* say peers. He led

the work for Adelphia and around 240 of its subsidiaries on its sale and reorganization process. Interviewees hailed **Marc Abrams** (see p.1261) as another outstanding member of the group. Researchers heard that *"he tries to build consensus and put things on a good footing but is not afraid to litigate."* Clients also reported that *"he knows how to lead groups of business people."* He advised ATX Communications in its restructuring and advised Monsanto as a creditor in the Solutia bankruptcy. **Matt Feldman** (see p.1278) acted for Verestar in its Chapter 11 filing, and assisted National Energy & Gas Transmission on its restructuring, including the $1.7 billion sale of its Canadian pipeline unit to TransCanada. Sources enjoy working with him because *"he's not a table-pounder and tries to build consensus – it's difficult to wind him up."* **Michael Kelly** (see p.1292) is a tough negotiator who wins plaudits from clients for his understanding of business considerations and knack of securing favorable results.

The Clients: The group is best known for its work on behalf of debtors in high-profile bankruptcy proceedings. Clients include: Adelphia Communications; 360networks; XO Communications; Maxxim Medical; NEGT and Global Crossing. Part of the workload is also devoted to representing a range of creditors in insolvencies and restructurings. Private equity houses, vulture funds and other financial institutions are clients of the practice.

Band 3

Paul, Weiss, Rifkind, Wharton & Garrison LLP

See firm details p.1362

The Firm: This quality operation wins staunch support for its wide-ranging bankruptcy practice. Interviewees view it as a strong player in an array of work, noting that the team is *"coming on strongly."* A raft of instructions on the debtors' side includes acting for Cone Mills, Penn Traffic and Garden Ridge in their Chapter 11 cases. However, it is its reputation as a *"very fine creditor shop"* that impressed commentators the most. Here, many of its cases have been in the communications field. For example, it acted for the official creditors' committee in the United Pan-European Communications Chapter 11 case and represented the noteholders in the American Cellular out-of-court restructuring. Energy-related work also remains prominent. The headline matter here was the group's successful representation of the California Public Utilities Commission in various regulatory disputes with Pacific Gas and Electric arising from its bankruptcy. The group also has a knack of securing roles in high-profile distressed M&A transactions. It is currently acting for Time Warner in its proposed joint bid with Comcast for Adelphia Communications.

The Lawyers: Interviewees were full of praise

for the technical expertise and business acumen of this talented team. The marquee name here is **Alan Kornberg** (see p.1294). One client credited him with *"really helping to bring the group to the fore,"* while other interviewees described him as *"a thoroughly impressive individual who knows how to cut a deal."* His expert handling of the Pacific Gas and Electricity case on behalf of his client, the California Public Utilities Commission, won him particular praise. He also represented the official creditors' committee in the NorthWestern Chapter 11 and is acting for Time Warner in its proposed bid for Adelphia. **Stephen Shimshak** (see p.1320) attracted plaudits for his diverse practice. He regularly advised debtors and secured creditors in out-of-court restructurings, workouts and Chapter 11 cases. His portfolio of work for investors includes advising SES Americom on its acquisition of substantially all of the assets of satellite communications company Verestar. **Jeff Saferstein** (see p.1316) is a pragmatic younger partner who *"knows the score and gets things done efficiently."* *"He's not a pushover,"* admit competitors. He recently represented a group of noteholders in the WorldCom Chapter 11.

The Clients: The group is renowned for the diversity of its practice and wins tributes for its work on behalf of debtors, investors and a range of creditors. Clients include: Top Flite Golf; Penn Traffic; Garden Ridge; California Public Utilities Commission and Time Warner.

Shearman & Sterling LLP

See firm details p.1369

The Firm: A deep bench in New York, coupled with wide-ranging international capabilities, has established this group as one of the market's leading players. It maintains close ties to several leading financial institutions and is a popular choice with a range of creditors. Key instructions on this side of the table include acting for the bank lenders in the Choice One Communications Chapter 11. Lawyers also assisted the official committee of unsecured lenders in the Mirant bankruptcy. However, the group is increasingly winning recognition for its debtors' practice. Headline deals include acting for Oneida, a manufacturer of tableware, in its out-of-court restructuring, and representing Spiegel in its Chapter 11 case. Distressed M&A is another important feature of the group's workload. Examples include acting for Savvis on the acquisition of assets from Cable & Wireless.

The Lawyers: Clients commended the firm for the depth of its bankruptcy practice and its ability to draw on experienced lawyers from other departments within its international network. **Doug Bartner** (see p.1265) is popular with clients, who rate him for his expeditious handling of cases and his sophisticated negotiation skills. He has a strong following among bankers, who pointed to his finely tuned business sense and *"excellent understand-*

ing of what drives the transaction." **Constance Fratianni**'s (see p.1280) admirers describe her as a talented all-around lawyer. One client summed up her abilities by saying, *"she's strong on all the facets – the legal issues, the business strategy and the client skills."* She acted recently for Spiegel on its debtor-in-possession financing. **Jim Garrity** (see p.1282) is a former bankruptcy judge whose experience is invaluable for clients. *"He is great at helping us work out what to expect in court and in figuring out how the judge will react,"* said one. He acted for the joint provisional liquidators of Global Crossing in its Chapter 11, as well as those of its US and Bermudan subsidiaries. **Fred Sosnick** (see p.1323) is another core member of the team. A *"great behind-the-scenes guy, who comes up with inventive strategies,"* his practice spans a range of areas. Much of his time of late has been devoted to representing the official committee of unsecured lenders in the Mirant case.

The Clients: JPMorgan Chase; Citibank; CSFB; Bank of America; Insilco Technologies; AET; Spiegel and Oneida.

Simpson Thacher & Bartlett LLP

See firm details p.1370

The Firm: This blue-chip offering emerged as a leading contender for creditor representations. Buoyed by referrals from the firm's enviable banking and finance department, the bankruptcy group is also increasingly carving out a stand-alone presence in the market. It enjoys an impressive reputation for the quality of its lawyers and the focus of the practice. JPMorgan Chase remains one of its most important names in its client roster, and the team acted for it recently as agent bank in the Interstate Bakery and RCN bankruptcies. Other highlights include advising Wachovia as agent in the Centennial Healthcare bankruptcy and representing JLL Partners in the New World Pasta Chapter 11. The group also has acknowledged strength in the distressed M&A field. Leading recent examples of this include advising the acquirer of Boston Generating and assisting the banks in acquiring the assets of Liberty Electric in an out-of-court transfer.

The Lawyers: A group of around 16 lawyers includes a number of headline individuals. Foremost among these is **Peter Pantaleo** (see p.1307), regarded by some rivals as *"by far the best bank practitioner in the country."* This claim was reinforced by one client, who stated that, *"he's one of the strongest bankruptcy lawyers I've ever worked with."* His strengths lie in a high level of practicality and an ability to devise inventive problem-solving strategies. Clients also appreciate the fact that *"he tells you the truth, rather than what you want to hear."* Commentators also roundly applauded **Steven Fuhrman** (see p.1281). Clients particularly value his role as a broader business adviser, while appreciating his meticulous approach. One remarked that, *"if I had to sign a document without reading it, it*

would be one from him – there are never even any commas out of place."* The market views **Mark Thompson** (see p.1327) as an intelligent adviser who ably supports his clients. His wide-ranging practice includes a range of restructurings, especially asbestos-driven bankruptcies, as well as acting for buyers and sellers in acquisitions of distressed companies. **Ken Ziman** (see p.1334) is popular among his peers. They report: *"If you do a deal with him, you know you've got a deal – you don't have to sign it in blood."* He recently acted for the senior secured lenders in the Centennial Healthcare Chapter 11.

The Clients: JPMorgan Chase; Wachovia Securities; Deutsche Bank; ABN AMRO; Blackstone Group; CSFB; JLL Partners and Citibank.

Band 4

Bingham McCutchen LLP

The Firm: This group is steadily increasing its market profile. It wins praise from interviewees for its work on behalf of creditors and, in particular, bondholders. The New York office works closely with its esteemed Hartford bankruptcy group, although it also benefits from support provided by the firm's other domestic offices. However, it was the group's profile in the international arena that impressed interviewees most. As one peer commented, *"What they've done with the international practice is absolutely fantastic. If you'd have told me four years ago that Bingham would become one of the leading international bondholder practices, I wouldn't have believed you."* Of late, the group has been focusing on boosting the profile of the Japanese practice, but it also operates in Latin America and enjoys strong ties to Europe through its London base. Its most important cases include acting for one of the largest groups of bondholders in the Parmalat insolvency, and the team also acted for the official committee of unsecured creditors in the NRG Energy bankruptcy.

The Lawyers: The firm can call on over 100 bankruptcy specialists worldwide. In New York, the team is led by former bankruptcy judge **Tina Brozman**. She brings a wealth of experience to the table and has recently acted for a number of agent banks and foreign investors in distressed debt deals.

The Clients: Much of the group's reputation in this area rests on its stellar reputation for bondholder work. This creditor-focused practice also acts for leading financial institutions, institutional investors, high-yield debt investors, mutual and hedge funds and insurance companies.

Debevoise & Plimpton LLP

See firm details p.1346

The Firm: This diverse bankruptcy group attracts a broad array of clients. It has recently appeared for debtors, creditors and investors and it continues to be well known for its work on behalf of insurance companies. Although the

group is smaller than many of its competitors, the close inter-departmental ties that it has forged with other teams within the firm benefit clients. It also offers a seamless cross-border service thanks to the firm's extensive international network. Recent highlights for the group on the debtor side include acting for Delta Air Lines in its out-of-court restructuring. It is also acting for Pegasus Communications in relation to the pending bankruptcy of its subsidiary, Pegasus Satellite Communications. Work on the other side of the table, meanwhile, includes advising creditors of Parmalat Canada who held $300 million of notes in the company.

The Lawyers: Interviewees rate this group highly for its consistent quality of service. Clients reported: *"It feels like they bring a lot to the table. The partners give you a lot of attention and the associates are great."* Sources described **Peter Borowitz** as a lucid and intellectually powerful attorney, endorsing him as a *"good strategist who knows the legal landscape and is aware of the political implications."* He focuses on representing institutional lenders and other creditors in bankruptcy and restructuring proceedings. **Steven Gross** was also popular with clients who portrayed him as a thoughtful practitioner who will *"give you an objective answer to a problem."* He acted for the official committee of creditors in Aurora Food's pre-arranged Chapter 11. Clients appreciate **Richard Hahn**'s strong legal skills and excellent bedside manner, describing him as *"a very accessible guy who is always available."* He represents Pillowtex in its Chapter 11 proceedings and also advised Wheeling Pittsburgh Steel on its bankruptcy.

The Clients: John Hancock Life Insurance; Oaktree Capital Management; The Prudential Insurance Company of America; Teachers Insurance and Annuity Association and XL Capital Assurance.

Fried, Frank, Harris, Shriver & Jacobson LLP

See firm details p.1349

The Firm: This group has the talent and resources to undertake restructuring work for a range of clients, but it is best known for representing creditors. Its reputation for tenacity and aggression doesn't put off clients, who hail this as a *"tremendous"* team that fares well in litigated proceedings. Recent highlights include acting for the official committee of unsecured creditors in the New World Pasta Chapter 11 case. Communications deals have also been high on the agenda this year, with the group assisting the official committee of bondholders in ntl's Chapter 11, involving $17 billion of bank and bond debt. It also acted for Telewest Global on the £5.8 billion restructuring of Telewest Communications. The team enjoys strong relationships with private equity houses and hedge funds and is well placed to advise on the sale and acquisition of assets and businesses of distressed entities. Its close cooper-

www.ChambersandPartners.com

All quotes in the text are from interviews with clients and competitors.

1181

ation with the firm's European offices also assures it a profile in international deals.

The Lawyers: The dominant figure here is **Brad Scheler** (see p.1317). This larger-than-life personality can ruffle feathers with his aggressive stance, but his clients love him. "*He's one of my favorites,*" commented one, "*he's very theatrical, very smart and very practical.*" Another described him as "*an unbelievably tough negotiator who can get results in complicated cases.*" **Vivek Melwani** (see p.1301) emerges as one of the group's most talented younger lawyers. The team also includes the respected Alan Resnick, a professor at Hofstra University School of Law who is of counsel at the firm.

The Clients: The group wins most applause for its work on behalf of creditor and bondholder committees. Examples include acting for the unofficial committee of bondholders in the out-of-court restructuring of Oxford Automotive. It also acts for trustees, financial institutions and investors in distressed securities and assets.

Jones Day
See firm details p.485

The Firm: A hit with clients for large and complex work, the team is buoyed by the "*tremendous litigation skills*" on offer at this international powerhouse. Commentators traditionally rate the group most highly for its debtor practice and it continues to attract high-profile instructions here. A recent example was acting for Globalstar, a satellite communications company, in its Chapter 11. However, the group's workload has diversified in recent years and it is now acting for a broader cross section of clients. For example, it advised the largest bondholder in the Telewest restructuring and assisted the bank group in the Trico Marine Services restructuring. The firm's well-documented skill in corporate matters also makes it a popular choice for entities looking to invest in distressed assets or companies. Examples here include acting for NuCoastal in its bid to acquire CrossCountry Pipeline Energy from Enron. The team is also assisting Continental Airlines in its bid for Avianca.

The Lawyers: Although the team in New York numbers only ten attorneys, it benefits from the comprehensive support provided by this global giant's international network and its other domestic offices. The co-leaders of the practice in New York are **Corinne Ball** (see p.1264) and **Paul Leake** (see p.1296). Clients consider Ball a first-rate practitioner with the ability to "*get things done.*" They also praised her success in helping to build up Jones Day's bankruptcy practice on the domestic and international stages. She recently represented GM in connection with its investment in Fiat. Leake is an impressive lawyer who, according to clients, is "*tough as steel.*" He is also popular among opponents. "*I'd certainly hire him and that's the highest compliment I can give him,*" said one.

The Clients: WL Ross; Citigroup; Continental Airlines; Globalstar; Wachovia Bank; IBM; Lehman Brothers; Levitz Home Furnishings; GM and American National Power.

Kasowitz Benson Torres & Friedman

The Firm: This "*phenomenal group*" won plaudits from interviewees and commands a growing market reputation. It is well known for its aggressive yet effective approach to cases. "*It is not incapable of being reasonable but tends to attract clients that are looking for a street fighter,*" said interviewees. Sources highlighted the group's particular skill in representing creditor and bondholder groups and pointed to a raft of high-profile instructions. The most prominent of these has been its work on the Adelphia Communications bankruptcy. Largely free from the conflicts that can restrict other law firms, the group sued over 400 banks on behalf of the unsecured creditors' committee. It is also a popular choice among investors, particularly hedge funds, which call on the team for its expertise in handling acquisitions of securities from distressed companies. A varied portfolio of work also sees the team act for troubled companies on occasion.

The Lawyers: The standout figure here is **David Friedman**, who spearheads the firm's bankruptcy practice. Peers respect him as "*an intelligent and practical lawyer who focuses on the main issues – he's not distracted by sideshows or irrelevancies.*" He typically acts for creditors' committees and equity security holders. **David Rosner** also won staunch market support. Interviewees described him as a "*dynamo lawyer*" who "*cuts through a lot of the chaff.*" Interviewees also singled out **Adam Shiff** as one of the group's emerging younger talents. He represents a range of clients and is well known for his skill in litigation.

The Clients: Clients include creditors' and bondholder committees, DIP, hedge funds, vulture funds and other investors in distressed companies and assets.

Kirkland & Ellis LLP
See firm details p.770

The Firm: Although this bankruptcy and restructuring powerhouse is better known for its Chicago practice, the New York office nonetheless wins considerable market recognition. In keeping with the practice's overall reputation, it is the group's expertise in representing debtors that has attracted most notice. Headline matters include acting for NRG and several related entities, as debtors in both out-of-court and Chapter 11 cases, in a bid to restructure over $11 billion in debt. Allegiance Telecom also called upon the team to represent it in its $1.4 billion debt restructuring. The caliber of the firm's private equity department stands in good stead in the distressed M&A arena. Deals here include advising Perry Capital on its acquisition of Republic Engineered Products, and Sun Capital on its purchase of Horsehead Industries.

The group also boasts considerable skill in litigated proceedings and benefits from the ability to draw on the expertise of other practice groups at the firm.

The Lawyers: The team has been boosted by the arrival of **Rick Cieri** (see p.1272) from Gibson, Dunn & Crutcher. This "*spectacular*" lawyer is a popular figure who "*has the perfect balance of good judgment, advocacy skill and business instincts. He has lots of credibility and his word can be relied on.*" Clients also believe that he appeals to CEOs because "*they find his approach comforting – he's hands-on and gets things done.*" He is best known for representing debtors and is a skilled adviser in both domestic and international restructurings. The group also includes "*impressive younger lawyer*" **Matt Cantor** (see p.1270). Clients warmly recommended him as "*a thoughtful, low-key, hard-working guy – he's one of those people who just gets things done.*" The team in New York comprises around 18 lawyers who work closely with high-profile teams in Los Angeles and Chicago.

The Clients: The group is best known for representing debtors, such as NRG Energy, Allegiance Telecom and Cornerstone Propane. It is also active on behalf of creditors and advised the statutory committee of unsecured creditors in the AT&T Latin America Chapter 11 cases.

Kramer Levin Naftalis & Frankel LLP
See firm details p.1357

The Firm: Interviewees recognize this as a deep and talented bankruptcy team that stands out in particular for its work on behalf of creditor groups. Recent high-profile examples include representing the bank group in the Owens Corning Chapter 11 case. It also enjoys a strong reputation for representing bondholder groups. Key instructions here include advising the secured noteholders in WCI Steel on its contested plan of reorganization and representing the subordinated noteholders in the NorthWestern Chapter 11 case. Although it wins less recognition for debtor work, this nonetheless remains an active part of the practice. Debtor clients include Cross Media Marketing and Micro Warehouse, both of which confirmed their plans of reorganization in 2004. A further marked strength of the group is its involvement in a range of second lien and rescue financings on behalf of investors in troubled companies.

The Lawyers: **Ken Eckstein** (see p.1277) leads a 20-lawyer team. Rivals consider him an accomplished lawyer and praise his work in the Owens Corning case in particular. As one interviewee commented: "*I found him to be very practical and level-headed.*" **Tom Mayer** (see p.1300) is renowned among industry insiders for his acute academic insight into bankruptcy law and his strategic skill. According to commentators, "*He has an amazingly broad range of knowledge and employs an incredibly creative approach,*"

1182   All quotes in the text are from interviews with clients and competitors.

CHAMBERS USA 2005

while some even regard him as "*one of the best out there.*"

The Clients: Work on behalf of various creditors remains the hallmark of this practice and it frequently represents creditors' and bondholder committees in bankruptcies and restructurings. Other clients include debtors, landlords and investors.

Morgan, Lewis & Bockius LLP

See firm details p.1556

The Firm: A loyal roster of leading financial institution clients assures this group a prominent platform in the market. Its ties to JPMorgan Chase are particularly well known, and it advised the bank as post-petition agent in a multi million- dollar DIP facility and as pre-petition agent in a syndicated secured loan in American Commercial Lines' Chapter 11 case. It also acted for the same client as agent for the bank syndicates in the PG&E National Energy Group and USGen New England bankruptcies. The team of "*effective lawyers who can get their client's will across*" also wins plaudits for its almost unrivaled expertise in debtor-in-possession financings. It has captured roles in a number of the year's most prominent cases. For example it acted for Wells Fargo Bank as a creditor in the WorldCom case and the steering committee of lenders to Loral SpaceCom in its Chapter 11. Although a lesser-known part of the practice, the team also has experience in debtor cases and in representing acquirers of assets from bankruptcy. Lawyers acted as bankruptcy counsel to Century/ML Cable Venture, a joint venture between Merrill Lynch and Adelphia Communications.

The Lawyers: Researchers were impressed with the level and warmth of recommendations received by **Richard Toder** (see p.1327). Interviewees rate him as a leading performer in the DIP finance world and admire his strong following among financial institutions. He is known as a talented courtroom performer. As one source commented: "*His courtroom persona is something else. He's very personable and judges like him. It's like listening to a conversation by the fireplace in your living room, even though it's very complex stuff.*" The market also views his colleague, **Robert Scheibe** (see p.1317) as a "*real expert in DIP financing.*" His strengths lie in his understanding of the technical aspects of deals. The firm's lawyers in New York also work closely with their counterparts in Philadelphia and the West Coast.

The Clients: The group is best known for its work on behalf of financial institutions, such as: JPMorgan Chase; Wachovia; Wells Fargo; CSFB; Mellon Bank and Bank of New York. It also receives instructions from committees of creditors and bondholders as well as debtors and investors.

Stroock & Stroock & Lavan LLP

The Firm: Interviewees identified the team's work for bondholder groups as one of the core strengths of the practice. Recent highlights here include acting for an ad hoc committee of bondholders in the International Wire case. However, the group's scope is broader than this and it is well equipped to serve a range of clients. For example, it also acts for individual creditor clients as well as committees in Chapter 11 bankruptcies, and is representing the official creditors' committee in the Texas Petrochemical insolvency. A further feature of the practice is the group's representation of domestic and overseas investors in distressed companies and assets. Here its experience spans a range of industries, and its close interaction with other departments within the firm helps it to provide a comprehensive service.

The Lawyers: Clients spoke of the group's lawyers as "*top-notch people who produce good-quality work.*" **Larry Handelsman** is a respected senior figure of the bankruptcy Bar and is held in high esteem by peers. They characterized him as a positive force in transactions: "*He's a credible lawyer who is focused on doing the deals rather than endlessly litigating.*" **Michael Sage** commands an "*impressive following*" among clients. He is best known for representing financial institutions that have acquired strategic positions in debt securities of distressed companies. Clients praised his "*excellent commercial judgment which he mixes with a strong understanding of the legal ramifications.*"

The Clients: The group regularly acts for bondholder committees, creditors' committees, debtors, banks and investors.

Band 5

Brown Rudnick Berlack Israels

The Firm: This tenacious group is renowned for its zealous representation of clients. The bulk of the group's portfolio comprises work for a variety of creditors, including instructions in a range of headline bankruptcy proceedings. Foremost among these is its role acting for an ad hoc committee of trade creditors in the Adelphia case. Other prominent matters include assisting the official equity committee in the Mirant restructuring and representing the official creditors' committee in the Budget Rent a Car Chapter 11. Another growing facet of the group's work is advising distressed debt investors, such as hedge and mutual funds and insurers. The team's close coordination with groups in the firm's other offices throughout New England is said to position it well in multistate litigation.

The Lawyers: **Ed Weisfelner** provokes strong reactions. While some peers didn't always warm to his dogged line of attack, others recommended him as a "*tough adversary who's creative, energetic and totally committed to his clients.*" He

heads the bankruptcy and corporate restructuring group and is in charge of a team of around 40 lawyers operating from New York and the firm's other offices on the East Coast.

The Clients: The group wins most recognition for its success in representing creditors' committees in bankruptcy proceedings and out-of-court restructurings. A recent highlight was acting for the official committee of unsecured creditors in the Global Crossing Chapter 11.

Cadwalader, Wickersham & Taft LLP

See firm details p.1339

The Firm: According to market sources this is a diverse practice acting for a range of clients. It continues to draw praise for its work on behalf of bondholders, but also boasts extensive experience of acting for other creditors, as well as debtors. It is well versed in the litigious aspects of cases but attracted most applause for its transactional prowess. Typical matters involve negotiating new credit facilities and advising on the sale or acquisition of distressed companies and assets. Recent assignments include acting for two investors in a successful private investment in preferred equity and debt of Milacron. It also acted for an ad hoc committee of senior secured noteholders of American Restaurant Group in an out-of-court restructuring. On the debtor side, lawyers acted for Renco Group in the Chapter 11 case of one of its subsidiaries, WCI Steel, and assisted Pharmacia in connection with the Solutia bankruptcy.

The Lawyers: A six-partner team in New York combines with colleagues in London to provide clients with cross-border bankruptcy and restructuring advice. In New York, **Bruce Zirinsky** (see p.1334) continued to impress sources as a "*talented lawyer and significant market player.*" His stable of clients includes secured and unsecured lenders, creditor committees, bondholders and debtors.

The Clients: The group represented BNP Paribas as administrative agent in a $160 million out-of-court restructuring. It also acts for investment management funds, insurance companies and Fortune 500 debtors.

Cleary Gottlieb Steen & Hamilton LLP

See firm details p.1342

The Firm: Clients told researchers that they were "*completely satisfied*" with the service they receive from this team, praising in particular the depth of restructuring experience across a range of industries. Competitors, meanwhile, acknowledged the "*fantastic*" quality of its lawyers. A large component of the group's portfolio is international work and it has been especially active in the Latin American market of late. For example, it represents Multicanal, an Argentine cable company, in its $520 million debt restructuring, and has acted for a host of other foreign clients in Chapter 11 and Section 304 proceedings. Demonstrating the firm's global reach, a team composed of lawyers from several of the firm's offices act for Close Brothers as financial adviser in the Parmalat insolvency. Other important matters include helping Covanta to emerge from Chapter 11. The firm's lawyers routinely advise on transactions arising from bankruptcies and recently acted for Texas Pacific Group in its proposed acquisition of Portland Gas & Electric.

The Lawyers: A New York team of around 15 lawyers includes **Jim Bromley** (see p.1269). According to clients he is a practical business lawyer who "*doesn't employ a lot of theatrics.*" His practice has been focused recently on representing US and international debtors and acting for clients in distressed M&A transactions. Clients also praised "*first-class professional*" **Lindsee Granfield** (see p.1285) for the breadth of her practice and her involvement in high-profile cases.

The Clients: The group acts for debtors from a range of industries and also has experience acting for creditors and creditor groups. It represents investment banks in their roles as potential funders, DIP lenders and acquirers of assets from distressed estates.

Clifford Chance US LLP

See firm details p.1343

The Firm: The group was dealt a major blow in 2005 when its team of five partners defected to Kaye Scholer. At the time of going to press it was unclear how the group would weather this storm but commentators believed it would continue to benefit from the firm's strong institutional ties to major banks and financial establishments. For example, in 2004 the team represented Bank of America in the Enron bankruptcy. This involved advising the client on several structured finance transactions in which it had acted as agent bank. The group also picked up overseas instructions, such as advising a number of banks on the restructuring of $1.2 billion of debt of Globo Participações, Brazil's largest media group. A team of lawyers from a number of the firm's offices is also acting for a major financial institution in several jurisdictions in connection with the Parmalat insolvency.

The Lawyers: The departure of five partners, including the likes of Margot Schonholtz and Mark Liscio, and a group of associates is a huge loss for the team. At this stage it is uncertain what steps the firm will take to redevelop the practice.

The Clients: ABN AMRO; Bank of America; Bank of Tokyo-Mitsubishi; CIBC; Citigroup; JPMorgan Chase and Wachovia.

Gibson, Dunn & Crutcher LLP

See firm details p.285

The Firm: The group has gradually been building its profile in the market but has been hit by the departure of one of its key partners early in

2005. Although it is too early to gauge what impact this will have, the team continues to win recognition for its debtor practice. It has secured a number of notable instructions, particularly in the energy sector. For example, the team acted for Xcel Energy on the restructuring of its wholly-owned subsidiary NRG, and assisted Allegheny Energy on the out-of-court restructuring and refinancing of $10 billion of bank, bond and other debts. Other recent highlights include acting for Solutia in a Chapter 11 that will restructure $3 billion of funded debt and other obligations. The group is increasingly visible in cross-border matters, and recently represented the Belgian subsidiary of Solutia on its out-of-court restructuring of a $200 million bond issue.

The Lawyers: The team was dealt an undoubted blow when Rick Cieri moved to Kirkland & Ellis in February 2005. A group of around 12 lawyers in New York continues to work closely with colleagues in California and Texas.

The Clients: Interviewees recognize this group first and foremost for its representation of debtors, which are drawn from a wide variety of industries. It also has experience of acting for creditors' committees and individual creditors, bondholders, lenders, potential acquirers and trustees.

Kaye Scholer LLP

See firm details p.1354

The Firm: Although this group has lacked the profile of some of its competitors in recent years, it was given a timely boost by the arrival of a crack team of bankruptcy specialists from Clifford Chance early in 2005. The group has traditionally picked up most recommendations for its debtor practice where it serves clients from a range of fields such as the healthcare and retail industries. Here, its lawyers are seasoned advisers in Chapter 11 proceedings and out of court restructurings. However, the arrival of the new team, best known for its representation of banks and financial institutions, has further enhanced the group's creditors' rights practice. It acts for individual creditors and creditors' committees and has a strong track record in representing bondholder groups. The team advises on domestic insolvency matters but also offers clients support in cross-border bankruptcies.

The Lawyers: Interviewees agree that the arrival of a team of five partners and a number of associates has really put the group on the map. They identified **Margot Schonholtz** (see p.1318) as one of the key figures. Clients believe "*she has everything you look for in a bank lawyer – she's extremely bright, experienced and has excellent negotiation skills.*" Sources also pointed to her success in representing disparate groups of creditors and her skill in working towards a solution to suit them all. **Mark Liscio** (see p.1298) is another accomplished team member who has impressed clients with his knowledge and experience.

The Clients: The group acts for a wide range of clients including debtors, creditors' committees and bondholder groups.

Latham & Watkins LLP

The Firm: The national and international scope of the firm leaves it well placed to advise on complex bankruptcies and out-of-court restructurings. It enjoys strong ties to many of the market's leading financial institutions and in recent months has advised on a diverse range of deals. These include acting for Deutsche Bank in both the Dan River and Breuners bankruptcies, and representing CSFB on a $2.75 billion exit financing for NRG. Its lawyers also assisted Lehman Brothers in recovering $1 billion that it was owed in relation to the Conseco Chapter 11. The group also won recognition for its work on behalf of debtors. Here, in one of its largest cases, it acted for Spring Air Partners in its confirmed plan of reorganization. Distressed M&A forms another component of the practice, and is an area in which the team benefits from its cross-departmental resources.

The Lawyers: **Bob Rosenberg** emerged from research as the key figure of this 12-strong New York team. Interviewees consider him "*a dean of the Bar*" who brings a wealth of experience to his cases. He has advised on numerous workouts for financial institutions and regularly acts for creditors' committees. **Mark Broude** is a younger member of the team who is making a name for himself in the market. He advised Spring Air on its restructuring.

The Clients: Calyon; Bear Stearns; Wells Fargo; General Electric Credit; Carlyle Group; Lehman Brothers and Ernst & Young.

Luskin, Stern & Eisler LLP

The Firm: A new entry to the tables this year, this boutique-style firm was a popular choice with interviewees. Bankruptcy and restructuring law is said to be the "*heart and soul*" of the practice, and the group is renowned among peers for the quality of its work. Clients also raved about the team, declaring that "*the lawyers are top caliber and are devoted to us.*" Although this is a smaller offering that cannot match the size and depth of some of its competitors, it has built up a reputation as a premier destination for bank creditors. Here the group suffers fewer of the conflicts that sometimes hamper other firms and stood out for its ability to provide pragmatic and "*meaningful advice*" to clients.

The Lawyers: Although the team numbers only around ten lawyers, clients remain confident in its ability to handle substantial bankruptcy matters. **Michael Luskin** was singled out as a "*top-flight litigator,*" while competitors praised his "*wonderful business sense.*" His colleague **Richard Stern** also caught the attention of sources, who described him as a "*fabulous bank lawyer.*"

The Clients: The group stands out for representing banks. Its client roster includes several leading financial institutions.

Otterbourg, Steindler, Houston & Rosen

The Firm: Interviewees extolled this talented group as being among the leading creditor committee practices in the market. Its niche expertise lies in its representation of trade committees, where it is said to have built up *"tremendous connections"* with the trade community. However, the team's portfolio of recent deals confirms that its work covers a broader spectrum than this. Recent highlights include acting for the official creditors' committee in the AMPAM and Geo Chemical restructurings. The airline industry has also provided the group with several high-profile instructions. For example, its lawyers represented the creditors' committees in the new US Airways Chapter 11 and the Hawaiian Airlines restructuring. Although a smaller group, the team is well versed in other complex cases and regularly appears in bankruptcy courts throughout the country.

The Lawyers: Sources nominated **Scott Hazan** as the group's *"number-one lawyer."* They described him as a talented negotiator who has *"got the skills to keep a committee group together and reconciled."* **Glenn Rice** is another gifted member of the team. *"He won me over,"* said one client. *"He's hard working, high on integrity and straight-shooting."* Their group acted for the creditors' committee in the Frank's Nursery & Crafts bankruptcy.

The Clients: The team represents creditors' committees, major financial institutions, commercial banks, insurance companies and asset-based lenders.

Proskauer Rose LLP

See firm details p.1365

The Firm: According to interviewees, this group's strength lies in its debtor practice. Here it has acted for clients from a range of industries, and handled such high-profile mandates as acting as bankruptcy counsel to Advanced Glassfiber

Yarns. The team also guided Frank's Nursery & Crafts through its Chapter 11 bankruptcy and consequent sale of assets, and has advised on a number of workouts in the retail and telecom sectors. It frequently works in tandem with the firm's corporate group to handle distressed M&A transactions. Work on behalf of creditors is also a feature of the workload. Of late, this has included international deals, such as representing major bondholders of an Argentine cable company in a Section 304 proceeding and related litigation.

The Lawyers: A *"tremendous talent,"* **Alan Hyman** (see p.1290) impresses clients as someone who is *"unbelievably easy to deal with"* and who brings a keen sense of humor to the negotiating table. He is also popular with peers, who note that *"he can fashion a deal at any time."*

The Clients: Debtors account for the largest component of the group's client base, although it also acts for creditors and commercial landlords.

Schulte Roth & Zabel LLP

See firm details p.1367

The Firm: This vibrant group has a happy knack of picking up important instructions. It is well known for an aggressive approach to cases and is closely associated with such high-profile clients as Cerberus. Interviewees praised the team in particular for its work on behalf of creditor and financing clients. For example, it represented the secured lenders in the Solutia case, and acted for Ableco as one of the senior lenders in the AMPAM plan of reorganization. The team is also active in the distressed M&A arena and advised Cerberus (as part of a trio of private equity funds) in its acquisition of Mervyn's department store. Although it does not generally take on debtor cases, the firm acted as bankruptcy counsel to Quigley in its reorganization.

The Lawyers: **Michael Cook** (see p.1273) is the most prominent name in this 20-strong group. Commentators view him as an experienced practitioner, notably in big-ticket matters.

The Clients: The group acts for secured and unsecured creditors, DIP, lenders and acquirers. Important clients include Cerberus, CIT and Ableco.

White & Case LLP

See firm details p.1379

The Firm: The firm's relationship with many major financial institutions is a key asset to a group best known for its creditor work. Here, the team has earned a reputation among clients for being solution-oriented and able to deliver results. Its headline cases include acting for Bank of America as agent to the Century Cable lenders in the Adelphia bankruptcy. The group is working with its litigation department to defend the client in proceedings brought, on behalf of the debtors, by the unsecured creditors' committee. Other matters include advising Deutsche Bank Trust Company Americas and JPMorgan Chase in relation to $609 million of pre-petition debt of the Fleming Companies. It also has a track record in debtor representations and can advise clients on a cross-border basis, thanks to the firm's considerable international spread.

The Lawyers: Although a fairly modest group, comprising around ten individuals in New York, it draws much strength from the firm's considerable network of domestic and international offices. The leader of the New York group is **Howard Beltzer** (see p.1266), who was dubbed a *"smart, thorough and surprisingly tough"* practitioner by his clients. He acted for Bank of America in the Adelphia Communications case.

The Clients: Bank of America; Bank of New York; Deutsche Bank; GE Capital; JPMorgan Chase; Royal Bank of Canada; Société Générale; United Pan-European Communications and Wilmington Trust.

Other Notable Practitioners

Adam Harris of O'Melveny & Myers LLP continues to impress with the quality of his creditor-led practice. He frequently advises his loyal financial-institution client base on the restructuring of loans, debt for equity swaps and new extensions of credit. He works closely with the firm's West Coast offices.

CONSTRUCTION

Band 1

Peckar & Abramson PC

See firm details p.1363

The Firm: Despite its headquarters being situated just across the Hudson, this firm has a perennial presence on the New York construction scene. It is without doubt one of the *"largest and most visible"* construction practices in the area with 14 core construction attorneys, complemented by lawyers with significant experi-

ence in labor issues within the industry. Clients also maintain that it has *"a level of experience, which is difficult to duplicate"* and a long history of *"producing great work."* The team provides a broad service to contractors and construction managers, including advice on contractual matters, risk management and dispute resolution. It also bolsters its presence in the sector through its work on seminars and legislative issues for leading industrial bodies.

The Lawyers: Founding partner **Robert**

Peckar (see p.1308) is at the *"top level"* of the industry. He is undoubtedly one of the sector's super-lawyers, and hugely respected by peers and key clients alike. He is considered a top choice for dispute resolution. **Steven Charney** (see p.1271) has undertaken high-profile work for contractors, including negotiating with the US government to create $1 billion of insurance coverage to aid the cleanup following 9/11. **Richard Abramson** (see p.1261) is a specialist for the energy industry and can count GE and

New York
Leading firms (Construction)

1 PECKAR & ABRAMSON PC *New York*
POSTNER & RUBIN *New York*

2 ROSS & COHEN, LLP *New York*
SACKS MONTGOMERY PC *New York*
THELEN REID & PRIEST LLP *New York*
ZETLIN & DE CHIARA LLP *New York*

3 GOETZ FITZPATRICK MOST *New York*
LEPATNER & ASSOCIATES LLP *New York*
MAZUR, CARP & RUBIN PC *New York*

Leading individuals (Construction)

1 PECKAR Robert *Peckar & Abramson, New York*
RUBIN Robert *Postner & Rubin, New York*

2 FODOR Susanna *Jones Day, New York*
GROVE Barry *Thelen Reid, New York*
MAZUR Sayward *Mazur Carp, New York*
POSTNER William *Postner & Rubin, New York*
ROSS Allen *Ross & Cohen, New York*

3 CHARNEY Steven *Peckar & Abramson, New York*
GOETZ Peter *Goetz Fitzpatrick, New York*
MONTGOMERY David *Sacks Montgomery, New York*
ZETLIN Michael *Zetlin & De Chiara, New York*

4 ABRAMSON Richard *Peckar & Abramson, New York*
DE CHIARA Michael *Zetlin & De Chiara, New York*
DYER Richard *Thelen Reid, New York*
LEPATNER Barry *LePatner & Associates, New York*
MACPHERSON Robert *Postner & Rubin, New York*
PIERSON George *Peckar & Abramson, New York*
ROHN Frederick *Sacks Montgomery, New York*

Firms and individuals are listed alphabetically in each band.

Bechtel among his key clients. Over the past year, he has advised on the construction of two power plants. Enthusiastic clients praised **George Pierson** (see p.1309) to the skies. Some valued his *"long years in industry, which give him a sound commercial edge,"* while others emphasized, *"the technical know-how that comes from being a qualified engineer."* He is also popular because he is a *"witty and entertaining"* person to work with.

The Clients: The practice specializes in representing large construction management companies and contractors. It is very active with industry bodies and works for the general contractors of New York Building Congress and the Building Trades Employers Association.

Postner & Rubin

The Firm: This specialized construction firm is home to a number of *"absolutely excellent"* lawyers, and has a broad practice engaged on an impressive range of interesting projects. For example, the current portfolio includes advising on a $600 million light rail project, representing New York City Housing in cleanup work, and acting for the contractor in a dispute related to the Memorial Pier in New Jersey. One of the firm's strengths and key selling points is that it represents all parties involved in the construction process, and so has a very well-rounded perspective on all issues. Active in alternative dispute resolution practice, the lawyers here are highly experienced mediators and arbitrators. The group has recently been advising a large Episcopalian Church on a construction project and a separate claim relating to damage to the church organ. It is also busy working on a case relating to a bridge that collapsed during construction in upstate New York, killing one and injuring seven.

The Lawyers: Robert Rubin (see p.1315) has an engineering degree, which gives him a real feel for the technical knowledge that is so essential in this sector. He is highly regarded by peers as an *"incredibly smart"* practitioner, and specializes in high-value and complex dispute resolution. **William Postner** also has a stellar reputation and is named by many as *"one of the pillars of the industry."* **Robert Macpherson** has successfully negotiated several large contracts in New York, including a $22 million nursing home, and a $40 million assisted living development.

The Clients: This firm has one of the widest client bases in the business. The list includes public owners, private owners, private developers, contractors, construction managers and surety companies.

Band 2

Ross & Cohen, LLP
See firm details p.1366

The Firm: This firm is *"a well-known and well-established"* practice that has real transactional strength and expertise in effectively representing owners. For example, it has recently been appointed as construction counsel in the $500 million redevelopment of the Mayflower Hotel site on Central Park West into a residential complex. However, the group is also named as a *"go-to firm for conflicts"* and has considerable experience in arbitrations and mediations. A highlight here was representing a large media company as plaintiff in a $500 million claim against the design-builders of its printing plant.

The Lawyers: Allen Ross is *"particularly successful in resolving matters through mediation."* Clients praised him highly, stating: *"Unlike most lawyers, he tries to find a business solution to legal issues."*

The Clients: The firm has built its reputation on its effective representation of owners, but it also counts a fair number of managers and contractors among its clientele.

Sacks Montgomery PC
The Firm: Despite its relatively small size, this practice is really punching above its weight and handling some major cases. In fact, sources consider the team to be a *"formidable and dominant force in the industry."* The lawyers are experienced in litigation, mediation and arbitration and can handle every type of dispute with ease. Recent cases vary from a claim involving a paper mill in East Texas, to a steel claim in Long Island. It also has considerable experience in contract drafting and has worked on many such matters for New York University.

The Lawyers: David Montgomery has been working in the construction sector for many years and is an *"all-around, highly effective"* practitioner. Clients also say **Frederick Rohn** *"really knows his stuff"* and he is, therefore, highly regarded as a *"very good advocate for contractors."*

The Clients: The client base is split between owners and contractors.

Thelen Reid & Priest LLP
See firm details p.300

The Firm: The New York office is a key branch of this *"tremendous national practice"* and works on projects throughout the USA. It also has an esteemed and highly active international practice, and has recently formed a joint venture with top British construction firm Pinsent Masons. This alliance means that it is better placed to work on the large international infrastructure projects that are the firm's forte The office handles a large amount of transactional work, including sophisticated financial deals, and clients report the quality of work there is *"outstandingly good."*

The Lawyers: Barry Grove has an *"eminent presence"* in the industry and is highly regarded for his international experience and skill in dispute resolution. Meanwhile, **Richard Dyer** has been getting stuck into prominent domestic transactions. For example, he has been working with the Lincoln Center for the Performing Arts on its substantial revitalization program, and is advising the developer of the first residential skyscraper in Times Square.

The Clients: The firm represents both owners and contractors.

Zetlin & De Chiara LLP
The Firm: This *"extremely experienced"* firm has the most significant practice in town for representing the design community. It is a one-stop-shop for architects and engineers and can advise them on everything from organizing the structure of the company, to employment issues and dispute resolution. It has been involved in a number of high-profile cases recently: it represented world-famous architect Richard Meier in claims relating to the construction of the Islip courthouse. Another highlight was advising the Metropolitan Transport Authority (MTA) on all aspects of the development of the Queens Midtown tunnel. This included negotiating the construction contracts, successfully litigating the cost overruns, and then acting for the authority over the allegations of improprieties.

The Lawyers: Michael Zetlin is a *"very effective"* litigator, and is also highly adept at mediation. Clients are impressed with his *"clarity of thought and rational approach"* as well as his *"dedication to serving his clients."* **Michael De Chiara** (see p.1275) is *"very passionate about the design profession and really dedicated to defending architects and their interests."* Clients stress that he is *"a zealous advocate who uses tremendous initiative and outside-the-box thinking."* As a testament to his skill, he is only the second person ever to be appointed as outside counsel to the General Services Administration for construction litigation.

The Clients: The client list reads like a who's who for the architecture world. Preeminent clients include Richard Meier, the Polshek Partnership and Kohn Pederson Fox. The firm is also outside counsel to a number of leading industry bodies, including the New York State American Institute of Architects, the New York State Association of Consulting Engineers and the New York Building Congress. The practice also counts a number of owners among its clientele.

Band 3

Goetz Fitzpatrick Most & Bruckman LLP

The Firm: This boutique construction firm has a strong reputation in the market as a home to *"a good number of capable attorneys."* It provides a wide array of services on top of the tradition-al expertise in construction contracts and litigation, including corporate transactions, real estate, and environmental and banking advice. A highlight case recently was advising Tishman Construction in its successful prosecution of a case against Rockefeller University.

The Lawyers: Founding partner **Peter Goetz** is an experienced litigator and negotiator, and has developed an impressive reputation as an arbitrator.

The Clients: The firm represents all facets of the construction industry, including owners, developers, design professionals, construction managers, general contractors, subcontractors and insurance companies.

LePatner & Associates LLP

See firm details p.1359

The Firm: This firm has been representing architects and engineers for more than 20 years now, and is moving into representing an increasing number of owners and developers. High-profile appointments include advising architects Gehry Partners on the development of its New York office, and acting as construction counsel for the design and construction of The Core Club, an exclusive private club in midtown New York.

The Lawyers: **Barry LePatner** (see p.1296) is a prominent figure in the sector, and a well-known speaker at industry events.

The Clients: The firm mainly represents design professionals.

Mazur, Carp & Rubin PC

The Firm: This firm has a uniquely knowledgeable place in the market, as its founding partner is the author of the chapter on construction law in 'Commercial Litigation in New York State Courts', the reference book that is used by every judge in the state. It also handles a number of noteworthy litigations, including the ongoing tenant build-out dispute between the Metropolitan Transport Authority and the owners of 2 Broadway.

The Lawyers: **Sayward Mazur** is one of the most experienced attorneys in the sector, and has been working on a large number of mediations of late.

The Clients: The firm traditionally represents contractors, although it has been taking more and more instructions from developers over the last few years.

Other Notable Practitioners

Susanna Fodor (see p.1280) from Jones Day specializes in representing owners, and has an invaluable combination of experience in both construction and real estate law. She has a reputation as a *"detailed, aggressive and fair"* advocate and clients really appreciate her *"responsiveness and leadership qualities."* She is especially skilled at leasing transactions.

CORPORATE/M&A

New York		
Leading firms (Corporate/M&A)		
[1] SKADDEN, ARPS, SLATE, MEAGHER *New York*		
WACHTELL, LIPTON, ROSEN & KATZ *New York*		
[2] CRAVATH, SWAINE & MOORE LLP *New York*		
DAVIS POLK & WARDWELL *New York*		
SIMPSON THACHER & BARTLETT LLP *New York*		
SULLIVAN & CROMWELL LLP *New York*		
[3] CLEARY GOTTLIEB STEEN & HAMILTON *New York*		
DEBEVOISE & PLIMPTON LLP *New York*		
FRIED, FRANK, HARRIS, SHRIVER *New York*		
SHEARMAN & STERLING LLP *New York*		
WEIL, GOTSHAL & MANGES LLP *New York*		
[4] CADWALADER, WICKERSHAM & TAFT *New York*		
DEWEY BALLANTINE LLP *New York*		
LATHAM & WATKINS LLP *New York*		
WILLKIE FARR & GALLAGHER LLP *New York*		
[5] GIBSON, DUNN & CRUTCHER LLP *New York*		
JONES DAY *New York*		
KIRKLAND & ELLIS LLP *New York*		
MAYER, BROWN, ROWE & MAW LLP *New York*		
PAUL, WEISS, RIFKIND, WHARTON *New York*		
WHITE & CASE LLP *New York*		
Firms are listed alphabetically in each band.		

Band 1

Skadden, Arps, Slate, Meagher & Flom LLP & Affiliates

See firm details p.1372

The Firm: *"Impressive throughout the USA,"* this is a firm with the manpower and cross-border capability to ensure it can *"do any deal there is."* Clients choose the firm not only because *"attorneys intrinsically understand the law,"* but also because they are *"creative and responsive"* in their dealings. This is a corporate machine consistently ranked among the leaders in worldwide M&A transactions. In 2004 it reclaimed top position in the US M&A tables, advising on 91 announced deals worth $186.3 billion, a 133% increase compared to 2003. Highlight deals included Cendant's $1.25 billion acquisition of Orbitz and Caesars Entertainment's $9.44 billion sale to Harrah's Entertainment. Bankruptcy, litigation and private equity were key drivers for growth while other strengths include antitrust, capital markets, energy and real estate. With nine offices across the country and international capability, the firm was repeatedly praised by clients, one of whom said: *"Its depth of expertise is unmatched in the marketplace."* Its strategic agility adds value to complex cross-border transactions, though the firm's diverse profile is the key to its success; it not only acts on the blockbuster deals, but also for smaller players such as emerging companies. Another highlight was representing CEMEX as US counsel in its proposed acquisition of RMC Group. The deal is reportedly valued at $5.8 billion. It is also acting for Providence Equity Partners, Texas Pacific Group and DLJ Merchant Banking Partners as equity partners in a consortium with Sony Corporation of America to acquire MGM in a deal valued at about $4.8 billion. Advising Fisher Scientific International, the group helped orchestrate the takeover of Apogent Technologies for $2.6 billion in stock plus the assumption of $1.1 billion in debt.

The Lawyers: Housing a broad range of talent, the M&A group is headed by **Kenneth Bialkin** (see p.1267), who won respect principally for his key role on behalf of anchor client Citicorp. He is also heavily involved in SEC and related government investigations. *"Icon"* **Joe Flom** (see p.1280) is credited with leading the firm to where

New York
Leading individuals (Corporate/M&A)

Senior Statesman

BEATTIE Richard *Simpson Thacher*, New York	**BIALKIN Kenneth** *Skadden Arps*, New York
FLEISCHER JR Arthur *Fried Frank*, New York	**FLOM Joseph** *Skadden Arps*, New York
HELENIAK David *Shearman & Sterling*, New York	**LIPTON Martin** *Wachtell Lipton*, New York
NUSBAUM Jack *Willkie Farr*, New York	

[1]

AARON Roger *Skadden Arps*, New York	**ATKINS Peter** *Skadden Arps*, New York
BLOCK Dennis *Cadwalader Wickersham*, New York	**COGUT Charles** *Simpson Thacher*, New York
COHEN H Rodgin *Sullivan & Cromwell*, New York	**CONDON Creighton** *Shearman & Sterling*, New York
FINKELSON Allen *Cravath Swaine*, New York	**HERLIHY Edward** *Wachtell Lipton*, New York
HERSCH Dennis *Davis Polk*, New York	**KATCHER Richard** *Wachtell Lipton*, New York
KRAMER Morris *Skadden Arps*, New York	**LEWKOW Victor** *Cleary Gottlieb*, New York
MORPHY James *Sullivan & Cromwell*, New York	

[2]

AQUILA Francis *Sullivan & Cromwell*, New York	**BROWNSTEIN Andrew** *Wachtell Lipton*, New York
FINLEY John *Simpson Thacher*, New York	**KATZ David** *Wachtell Lipton*, New York
KLING Lou *Skadden Arps*, New York	**LYONS Peter** *Shearman & Sterling*, New York
MADDEN John *Shearman & Sterling*, New York	**SPATT Robert** *Simpson Thacher*, New York
STAPLETON Benjamin *Sullivan & Cromwell*, New York	**STEPHENSON Alan** *Cravath Swaine*, New York
WASSERMAN Craig *Wachtell Lipton*, New York	

[3]

BARSHAY Scott *Cravath Swaine*, New York	**BASON George** *Davis Polk*, New York
BIRD Paul *Debevoise & Plimpton*, New York	**FRAIDIN Stephen** *Kirkland & Ellis*, New York
GELSTON Philip *Cravath Swaine*, New York	**GITTES Franklin** *Skadden Arps*, New York
HALL Richard *Cravath Swaine*, New York	**KENNEDY Thomas** *Skadden Arps*, New York
NATHAN Charles *Latham & Watkins*, New York	**NEFF Daniel** *Wachtell Lipton*, New York
O'BRIEN Clare *Shearman & Sterling*, New York	**PIERCE Morton** *Dewey Ballantine*, New York
PROFUSEK Robert *Jones Day*, New York	**ROSEN Jeffrey** *Debevoise & Plimpton*, New York
RUEGGER Philip *Simpson Thacher*, New York	**RYAN Michael** *Cleary Gottlieb*, New York
SAEED Faiza *Cravath Swaine*, New York	**SCHELL J Michael** *Skadden Arps*, New York
SCHUMER Robert *Paul Weiss*, New York	**SEYMON Pamela** *Wachtell Lipton*, New York

[4]

BEVILACQUA Louis *Cadwalader Wickersham*, New York	**CAPLAN David** *Davis Polk*, New York
CERABINO Thomas *Willkie Farr*, New York	**CHATZINOFF Howard** *Weil Gotshal*, New York
COCHRAN Eric *Skadden Arps*, New York	**EMMERICH Adam** *Wachtell Lipton*, New York
FOX David *Skadden Arps*, New York	**FRIEDMAN Dennis** *Gibson Dunn*, New York
FRIEDMAN Eric *Skadden Arps*, New York	**FRUMKIN Joseph** *Sullivan & Cromwell*, New York
GREEN Frederick *Weil Gotshal*, New York	**GREENBERG Joel** *Kaye Scholer*, New York
JEWELL Ronald *Dechert*, New York	**LEFKOWITZ Ken** *Hughes Hubbard*, New York
MEYERSON Lee *Simpson Thacher*, New York	**MILLS Phillip** *Davis Polk*, New York
PALEY Alan *Debevoise & Plimpton*, New York	**REISS John** *White & Case*, New York
ROBERTS Thomas *Weil Gotshal*, New York	**ROSENBLUM Steve** *Wachtell Lipton*, New York
SCHNELL Paul *Skadden Arps*, New York	**SEIDMAN Steven** *Willkie Farr*, New York
SHIM Paul *Cleary Gottlieb*, New York	**SORKIN David** *Simpson Thacher*, New York
STERNBERG Daniel *Cleary Gottlieb*, New York	**SUYDAM John** *O'Melveny & Myers*, New York
THOYER Judith *Paul Weiss*, New York	**TOWNSEND Robert** *Cravath Swaine*, New York
VLAHAKIS Patricia *Wachtell Lipton*, New York	**WOJCIECHOWSKI Mark** *Mayer Brown*, New York

Up-and-coming individuals

AIELLO Michael *Dewey Ballantine*, New York	**DE WIED Warren** *Fried Frank*, New York
KOTRAN Stephen *Sullivan & Cromwell*, New York	**LOBO Glyndwr** *Dechert*, New York
SHOEMATE Steven *Gibson Dunn*, New York	

Individuals are listed alphabetically in each band.

---

it is today. He is currently acting for The May Department Stores Company on its $3.24 billion acquisition of Marshall Field's and nine Mervyn's stores. **Franklin Gittes** (see p.1283) boasts an enviable client roster that includes McAndrew & Forbes, Ron Pearlman and BlackRock. He also gained peer confidence as "*a good adversary and ally.*" The "*top notch*" **Peter Allan Atkins** (see p.1263) won peer acclaim as a "*hands-on, polished straight shooter*" who fights zealously for his clients. The result is a "*good track record at convincing clients on the other side what is the best thing to do for a deal.*" Atkins's broad-based experience enables him to counsel on matters ranging from corporate governance, crisis management to straight M&A. His impressive clientele includes Warner-Lambert, Bell Atlantic and Honeywell. "*Top of the heap,*" **Roger Aaron** (see p.1261) is in charge of the firm's corporate practice. Clients praise his ability to "*walk into a*

negotiating room and have immediate presence.*" Possessed of "*terrific judgment,*" he "*instinctively understands a client's needs and desires,*" they said. His colleague, the "*insightful and talented*" **Morris Kramer** (see p.1295), is nominated as "*just about the best around.*" He is involved in the proposed $4.8 billion acquisition of MGM. When it comes to **Lou Kling** (see p.1294), clients said they get "*the whole package.*" He delivers "*strength and confidence*" in addition to a knack for serving clients' interests with a "*cheerful, thorough and pragmatic*" approach. He is representing Nortek Holdings in its $1.8 billion takeover by Thomas H. Lee Partners and the management of Nortek Holdings. **Thomas Kennedy** (see p.1293) emerged as another popular choice among clients and peers. Boasting a wide practice, he is representing Verizon Communications and Verizon Wireless in the acquisition of PCS spectrum licenses from NextWave Telecom for $3 billion. Colleague **Michael Schell** (see p.1317) "*pulls in the work on his own merits,*" for example acting for May in its acquisition of Marshall Field's and several Mervyn's stores. **David Fox** (see p.1280) enjoys a consistent deal flow that includes Cendant's $1.25 billion acquisition of Orbitz from AMR Corporation, UAL Corporation, Norwest Airlines and Delta Air Lines. "*Star in the making,*" **Eric Cochran** (see p.1272) was admired by clients as "*terrific and sharp,*" while **Paul Schnell** (see p.1318) is a new addition to the tables after receiving plaudits from clients as someone who can "*separate the big issues from the small.*" Acting on a mix of domestic and cross-border work, his repertoire includes Advance PCS's $14 billion merger with Caremark Rx and UnitedHealth Group's $4.9 billion takeover of Oxford Health Plans. "*Straightforward*" **Eric Friedman** (see p.1281) garnered respect for his adroit capabilities on behalf of Citigroup, for whom he advised in its $1.26 billion acquisition of Principal Residential Mortgage from Principal Financial Group.

The Clients: Citigroup; TRW; Verizon; The May Department Stores Company; Nortek Holdings; CEMEX; Providence Equity Partners; Texas Pacific Group; DLJ Merchant Banking Partners; Warner-Lambert; Bell Atlantic; Honeywell; Gucci; US Airways and Kmart.

Wachtell, Lipton, Rosen & Katz
See firm details p.1375

The Firm: Giants in the field, this "*high-end*" M&A powerhouse adopts a unique business model – it is particularly selective in the types of matters it advises and staffs them leanly with a band of "*incredibly skilled*" attorneys who provide "*a whole package of quality services in key areas.*" The classic New York firm led one client to comment: "*You can guarantee it will do a fabulous job.*" Quality comes at a price, however, and expense is a significant concern for clients, one of whom said: "*If you don't care about price, they are* the ones to go to." Though they also added that it's worth the money for its "*deeper, more targeted and consistent bench.*" About a quarter of the size of some of its competitors, the team of less than 200 lawyers has a partners-to-associates ratio of about one-to-one. This structure consistently pays off for the firm, which was involved in three of the largest deals of 2004. It represented, among others, AT&T Wireless in its $40.7 billion acquisition by Cingular in the largest cash acquisition to date in US history. It acted for Bank One in its $58 billion merger with JPMorgan Chase and separately helped orchestrate FleetBoston's $47 billion takeover by Bank of America. The firm, considered a pioneer of the so-called 'poison-pill defense,' is described by clients as "*extremely fit for hostile situations.*" Advising Disney, it successfully resisted Comcast's $54.1 billion hostile offer and in a separate transaction, acted for Sanofi in its $60.2 billion hostile exchange offer for Aventis. The team also advised Taubman Centers in its successful defense against a hostile bid by Simon Property and Westfield. The multijurisdictional demands of clients are catered via relationships with some of the world's most prestigious independent firms. The group additionally boasts "*a strong franchise for representing banks,*" with a handful of practitioners renowned for banking M&A. For example, it has represented GreenPoint Financial in its acquisition by North Fork Bancorporation for $6.3 billion.

The Lawyers: "*Leader of the pack,*" **Marty Lipton** (see p.1298) was acknowledged as "*a legend in the M&A arena – when he talks, you listen.*" His reputation as the top go-to practitioner for strategic and troubleshooting advice was illustrated by his involvement in such matters as Disney's defense to Comcast's $66 billion hostile takeover bid. Lipton also advised AT&T Wireless on its sale to Cingular and Bank One on its merger with JPMorgan Chase. Considered one of "*the best M&A leaders on the planet,*" **Edward Herlihy** (see p.1287) specializes in complex M&A involving banks and financial institutions. He acted for Charter One Financial in its takeover bid by Citizens Financial Group for about $10.5 billion. "*Still one of the absolute best,*" **Richard Katcher** (see p.1292) was praised by the marketplace as a "*mature and sophisticated lawyer who knows what to focus on.*" He acted for AT&T Wireless Services on its acquisition by Cingular Wireless – a joint venture between SBC Communications and BellSouth. Katcher is said to possess "*the experience and wisdom that boards of directors tend to rely on,*" while colleague **David Katz** (see p.1292) was pitched as "*the star in the younger generation,*" according to clients. Katz acted for Cardinal Health on its acquisition of Alaris Medical Systems for about $2 billion. Praise for **Andrew Brownstein** (see p.1269) centers on his "*user-friendly*" style, and his "*practical and problem-solving mind.*" His "*quick command of facts and issues*" helps to land him in headline trans-

actions, including Marsh & McLennan's acquisition of Kroll for $1.9 billion in cash. **Craig Wasserman** (see p.1331) focuses on M&A transactions related to the financial services sector. Clients said "*his breadth of experience is unsurpassed,*" and praised his "*top-notch legal advice.*" He acted for National Commerce Financial in its $7 billion merger with SunTrust Banks in a cash and stock transaction. Also recommended is **Pamela Seymon** (see p.1320), whose renown in the media and entertainment sector won favor among loyal clients. Her "*sharp and experienced*" profile led to such involvement as Comcast's failed hostile bid for Disney. Managing partner **Daniel Neff** (see p.1304) earned applause as "*tremendously smart and highly experienced.*" He acted for Western Wireless on its $6 billion acquisition by Alltel. The "*straightforward dealmaker*" **Adam Emmerich** (see p.1277) is often retained on important strategic M&A. He acted for Metropolitan Life Insurance Company on the $375 million acquisition of SSRM Holdings by BlackRock. **Patricia Vlahakis** (see p.1329) commands market respect for her ability to smoothly execute a deal while remaining "*a steady influence in times of crisis.*" **Steven Rosenblum** (see p.1314) is said by clients to be "*skilled in the larger issues and the minutiae of making a transaction happen.*" Peers added: "*He does not posture and will come out with a deal that will suit both sides.*" He was involved in AT&T Wireless's takeover by Cingular.

The Clients: Bank One; AT&T Wireless; Disney; Sanofi; Charter One Financial; Cardinal Health; Marsh & McLennan and National Commerce Financial.

Band 2

Cravath, Swaine & Moore LLP
See firm details p.1344

The Firm: "*Knowledgeable and responsive, with excellent service levels,*" this firm provides "*quality people across all categories without exception,*" clients said. Global spread combined with its access to top-notch, in-house expertise in the banking, antitrust and capital markets arenas help distinguish the firm as an ideal choice. The group landed almost $100 billion worth of M&A deals in December 2004 alone, resulting in a five-fold increase in deal value compared to the same period last year. For example, it represented Sprint in its merger with Nextel for $35 billion and separately acted for Johnson & Johnson in its acquisition of Guidant for $25 billion. It also advised on the $3 billion IPO of DreamWorks Animation, underlining a track record in the media and entertainment sector. A lockstep compensation system encourages a more concerted effort in terms of overall client services, resulting in added efficiency, analysts said. In addition, a noticeable ability to field a "*strong younger tier*" at both partner and associate level helps boost the firm's profile.

The Lawyers: In terms of seniority and respect, "*top-drawer*" **Allen Finkelson** (see p.1279) takes the laurels at the firm. He acted for Patina Oil & Gas in its acquisition of Noble Energy for about $3 billion. He also represented Jones Apparel Group in its takeover of Barneys New York. **Alan Stephenson** (see p.1324) earns marks as a "*high-quality and talented lawyer,*" while **Faiza Saeed** (see p.1316) is pitched as "*one of those people you love to see on the other side.*" She is "*cool under pressure and does an excellent job for her clients.*" She represented Associated British Foods in its acquisitions of the yeast and spice businesses of Burns Philp for $1.35 billion. The "*multifaceted*" **Richard Hall** (see p.1286) was praised as a "*smart, thoughtful and good negotiator.*" He acted for Bessemer Holdings in connection with its sale of Paint Sundry Brands to Sherwin-Williams. Colleague **Philip Gelston** (see p.1282) is said to be "*smart, serious and hard working.*" He acted for White Mountains Insurance Group on its acquisition – with Berkshire Hathaway – of Safeco's life and investments operations for $1.35 billion. The "*terrific*" **Scott Barshay** (see p.1264) is a new entry to the tables following strong commendation from clients for his "*thorough knowledge of the playing field*" combined with "*practicality and business sense.*" Barshay acted for Mandalay in its $7.9 billion takeover by MGM Mirage. He also represented King Pharmaceuticals in its acquisition by Mylan Laboratories for $4 billion. **Robert Townsend** (see p.1328) has acted on several high-profile transactions, including the Johnson & Johnson acquisition of Guidant. He also represented Citigroup as financial adviser to Varco International in connection with its $3.1 billion acquisition by National Oilwell.

The Clients: IBM; Time Warner; Johnson & Johnson; Bristol Myers Squibb; Royal Dutch; Unilever; Nestlé; Sprint; Associated British Foods and Citigroup.

Davis Polk & Wardwell
See firm details p.1345

The Firm: Thanks to its fielding of some of the most experienced senior partners in the business, this firm has the "*ability to deal with judgment issues that surround pure legal advice.*" The firm's practice is split between public M&A and merchant banking transactions, and interlocks with a top-quality general commercial litigation team, further enhanced by banking and tax expertise. Clients' multijurisdictional needs are met by a network of offices in such cities as New York, DC, Frankfurt, London and Tokyo. The firm has acted on a raft of international transactions, for instance advising Banco Santander Central Hispano on its proposed acquisition of Abbey National for $15.6 billion. Though clients are usually pleased with the end results, some said they were concerned about its time management. The firm is also acting for VF

Corporation in connection with its acquisition of substantially all of the assets of Kipling Belgium. Representing Charles River Laboratories International, it is helping to administer the proposed acquisition of Inveresk Research Group in a transaction worth $1.5 billion. Another highlight was CVS Corporation's $2.15 billion acquisition of 1,260 Eckerd drugstores located mainly in the southern USA, as well as Eckerd Health Services and three distribution centers.

The Lawyers: The *"first-rate"* **Dennis Hersch** (see p.1288) dominates the team as an agile operator who's *"senior enough to have the ears of the top people among clients."* With a commanding presence and years of experience, he is said to be *"a deal-doer who cuts through complicated transactions."* Hersch acted for Comcast in its tender offer for Disney. His able colleagues include **Gar Bason** (see p.1265), a *"seasoned lawyer with a broad-based perspective"* on sophisticated matters. As a *"first-rate conscientious lawyer from whom you would seek business advice,"* commentators consider him a rare commodity. With his *"incisive mind"* **Phillip Mills** (see p.1302) delivers a level of seniority and deal experience highly prized by clients, who also mentioned his *"reasonable, balanced and smart"* approach. He is advising JPMorgan Securities and UBS Securities in connection with National Commerce Financial's $7 billion merger with SunTrust Banks. **David Caplan** (see p.1270) is said to have a *"laid-back manner,"* which camouflages his *"super-efficient"* ability to close a deal. This *"bright"* attorney is valued for his tendency to *"cut to the chase."* He is advising Sterling Entertainment Enterprises in relation to a New York-based regional sports network joint venture formed with Comcast and Time Warner Cable.

The Clients: VF Corporation; Comcast; CVS Corporation; Charles River Laboratories International; Banc of America Strategic Solutions; Banco Santander Central Hispano and Edward H. Meyer, chairman and controlling stockholder of Grey Global Group.

Simpson Thacher & Bartlett LLP

See firm details p.1370

The Firm: A synthesis of brand recognition and fortitude mark this firm out as *"superb in every way,"* according to clients, who added that they often rely on the team for its *"first-grade strategy"* advice. The firm is so respected in the marketplace that even clients on the other side of the table are impressed: *"It's a pleasure to work with such smart, civilized and professional people."* Although the firm's reputation is inextricably linked with its preeminent private equity practice, it has nevertheless *"had a terrific run recently"* with blockbuster M&A deals. For example, the firm represented JPMorgan Chase in its $58 billion merger with Bank One. Equally distinguished is its involvement in capital markets, lit-

igation and employee benefits matters. Outside of the private equity arena, the *"absolutely terrific"* team acts for such Fortune 100 luminaries as Wyeth and Aramark, in addition to regularly appearing as counsel to financial advisers such as Lehman Brothers. Clients paid tribute to the firm's ability to supply legal services *"in all quarters,"* staffed by a *"whole slew of people for the big deals."* The firm also acted for the Adolph Coors Company in its $6 billion merger with Molson. Another highlight involved a consortium that included The Blackstone Group, Hellman & Friedman, KKR and Texas Pacific Group in the $3.6 billion acquisition of Texas Genco Holdings. International demand is serviced by offices in cities such as Hong Kong, London and Tokyo. Further enhancing its profile is its *"next generation"* of corporate attorneys.

The Lawyers: Dick Beattie (see p.1265) is a potent force whose presence brings *"an immediate impact on the boardroom,"* according to peers. Often credited as a key player in building the firm's reputation and name, he is the principal contact for JPMorgan Chase, for whom he counseled on the acquisition of Bank One in a stock-for-stock deal valued at $58 billion. *"Tough"* negotiator **Casey Cogut** (see p.1272) attracts loyalty by taking a *"practical and down-to-earth"* approach, with *"fantastic"* results according to clients. Cogut oversees relationships with the likes of KKR, Silverlake Partners and Ripplewood among others. Highlights include acting for Forest City Ratner on its acquisition of New Jersey Nets, and separately representing the Adolph Coors Company in its merger agreement with Molson. Colleague **Robert Spatt** (see p.1323) is a confident attorney who *"understands the objectives of clients on all sides of the table."* He is said to be a *"smart, creative thinker"* with a *"great sense of humor."* Spatt acted for new client CSL Limited on the acquisition of Aventis Behring's worldwide plasma business for $900 million. Benefiting from strong relationships with investment bankers, he also plays a key role in advising important clients such as HJ Heinz, Moody's and Smithfield Foods. **John Finley** (see p.1279) maintains a *"low-key and efficient"* profile and is valued for delivering *"a good deal for his client."* An ample amount of *"great technical knowledge"* ensures his participation in significant matters. He represented Kmart in its $11 billion merger with Sears Roebuck to form a new retail company named Sears Holdings Corporation. Another feather in his cap is the proposed $6.6 billion sale of the Toys 'R' Us chain to Bain Capital, KKR and Vornado Realty Trust. Head of corporate and firm chairman **Philip 'Pete' Ruegger** (see p.1315) spends about 50% of his time on transactional matters while also leading the firm's relationship with The Blackstone Group. Highlights include representing Travelers in its merger with St. Paul and separately acting for new client Vodafone in its bid for AT&T Wireless. Banking

and M&A rainmaker **Lee Meyerson** (see p.1301) focuses on the financial institutions sector. Clients paid tribute to a *"smart lawyer with good business sense."* He acted for Silver Acquisition Corporation on its acquisition of Gold Banc for $672 million in cash. **David Sorkin** (see p.1323), a new entry to the tables, won confidence with his *"self-effacing"* but effective approach. He acted for KKR in its takeover of Sealy Corporation for $1.5 billion in a secondary buyout from a private investment group. He also represented a consortium that acquired Texas Genco Holdings for $3.6 billion.

The Clients: JPMorgan Chase; Wyeth; Aramark; Adolph Coors Company; The Blackstone Group; KKR; Ripplewood; Silverlake Partners; Texas Pacific Group; CSL Limited; HJ Heinz; Moody's and Smithfield Foods.

Sullivan & Cromwell LLP

See firm details p.1373

The Firm: *"One of the premier groups in the world for complex matters,"* the band of corporate attorneys *"understands business rationale,"* clients said. This is a firm that captured market share with a revenue increase of well over 50% within five years. One of the first firms to focus on international expansion, nearly a fifth of its lawyers are stationed outside its home jurisdiction. Global expansion is reaping dividends with the recruitment of Dominique Bompoint to its Paris office and further integration of its M&A practice with the private equity group across offices in Frankfurt, London and Paris. This has led to increased visibility on the European front. Business acumen and practicality draw clients, who also value its *"straightforward guidance that gets you from A to B in a sensible way."* The firm also *"delivers what it promises,"* mainly due to abundant technical regulatory expertise combined with the ability to *"quickly know the clients' idiosyncrasies."* The firm's dominance in the financial institutions sector also helped to sustain its success. It benefits from a tight relationship with Goldman Sachs in addition to acting for Manulife following its acquisition by John Hancock. Major highlights include representing Anthem on its $16.5 billion merger with Wellpoint Health Networks, and separately advising Oxford Health Plans in its $5 billion merger with United Healthcare. The firm also garnered tribute for its participation in PeopleSoft's hostile takeover attempt by Oracle.

The Lawyers: The inevitable administrative constraints placed on chairman **Rodgin Cohen** (see p.1273) have done little to sap his strength as a corporate heavyweight. Often dubbed the *"banking guru,"* he acted for Regions Financial on its acquisition of Union Planters in an all-stock transaction valued at $5.8 billion. **James Morphy** (see p.1303), head of the M&A group, represents such principals as Computer Associates, Kodak and Lincoln National. The *"down-to-*

earth" operator won client praise across a wide spectrum of domestic and cross-border transactions. "*Go-to, wonderful guy*" **Ben Stapleton** (see p.1323) is deemed key to the firm's Goldman Sachs relationship. **Francis Aquila** (see p.1263) "*zeros in on getting a deal done.*" The client relationship partner for Diageo, he is respected for his "*service-oriented, energetic and tenacious*" approach. Aquila also acted for J Sainsbury on the sale of Albertsons for about $2.5 billion. New entry to the tables, **Stephen Kotran** (see p.1294) "*would cancel his birthday party to talk about a deal for the first time,*" commentators said. Renowned for his prodigious work in M&A transactions in the financial services arena, he is a legal intellect who also has "*a good grasp*" of the business ramifications of a deal. **Joe Frumkin** (see p.1281) impresses with his easygoing manner while remaining "*a straight shooter with a lot of integrity.*" Clients also appreciated his ability to "*put a very complicated issue into simple terms.*"
The Clients: Goldman Sachs; Anthem; Oxford Health Plans; Regions Financial; Kodak; Diageo; J Sainsbury and the JPMorgan Chase board.

Band 3

Cleary Gottlieb Steen & Hamilton LLP
See firm details p.1342
The Firm: An international player whose cross-border expertise benefits from a "*high degree of coordination within the firm,*" resulting in a fluidity between international offices that is sometimes lacking in rivals, clients said. The team is further bolstered by the addition of Italian senior partner Roberto Casati while a thriving Latin American practice has led to deals such as Laredo National Bancshares's $850 million takeover by Banco Bilbao Vizcaya Argentaria. The firm also boasts outstanding capital markets, tax and financial products experience. Clients commend its "*familiarity with our business and ability to put its fingertips on the applicable provisions.*" The firm has demonstrated that it is possible to attract blue-chip clients by leveraging off a lender-driven finance practice. It enjoys good relationships with investment banks in addition to a bevy of customers from the advertising, PR and technology sectors. The firm acted for Véolia Environnement in the $993 million divestiture of the worldwide systems and services businesses of USFilter Corporation to Siemens.
The Lawyers: **Vic Lewkow** (see p.1297) earned laurels for "*getting things done with the minimum of histrionics,*" sources said. He is "*brainy and intellectual but remains results oriented.*" He acted for Kroll in its $1.9 billion acquisition by Marsh & McLennan in addition to nurturing the firm's relationship with HSBC regarding its North American acquisitions. Alongside Lewkow is

Michael Ryan (see p.1315), a new entrant to the tables. Clients recommend his "*excellence and professionalism.*" Said to be well-connected in business and legal circles, he "*helps us out of trouble and makes us money,*" said clients, who also "*trust his judgment implicitly.*" Colleague **Paul Shim** (see p.1320) is "*one of the best in terms of technical legal knowledge.*" A player who "*can go toe-to-toe with anyone,*" Shim is pitched as a rising star at the firm. A majority of his mandates are for Texas Pacific Group, including advising an investor group led by Texas Pacific Group on its $1.4 billion acquisition of a majority stake in Iasis Healthcare from JLL Partners. **Daniel Sternberg** (see p.1324) is another whose profile is on the ascendant. He acted for New Skies Satellite on its $956 million acquisition by The Blackstone Group.
The Clients: Kroll; Texas Pacific Group; Bank of America; Citigroup Global Markets; Véolia Environnement and New Skies Satellite.

Debevoise & Plimpton LLP
See firm details p.1346
The Firm: This firm houses a "*high level of expertise and professionalism from the junior ranks right up to the most senior*" practitioners, clients said. The profile of the M&A team has rocketed following last year's representation of GE on its $14 billion agreement with Vivendi Universal to form NBC Universal. The firm has made enormous progress in the M&A arena, with escalating profits to illustrate a strong transactional year. A recognized leader in the fields of insurance, property, and casualty and asset management, it also draws clients for its private equity expertise. Clients paid tribute to "*sophisticated guys who understand the economics and financial side of a deal.*" A firm which has embraced global expansion, its network of offices now stretches across Europe and Asia, reflecting in a steady flow of cross-border work. Its ability to "*handle complex and difficult transactions*" has resulted in such deals as Kabel Deutschland's acquisition of regional cable network operators ish, iesy Hessen and Kabel Baden-Württemberg for a combined consideration of approximately €2.7 billion. The team also acted for Clayton Dubilier & Rice on its $1.68 billion purchase of VWR International from Merck KGaA. Another highlight includes acting for Verizon in the sale of its Hawaiian operations to The Carlyle Group for $1.65 billion.
The Lawyers: Former cochair of the firm's M&A group Meredith Brown retired in 2004. Renowned as a "*classy corporate counselor,*" Brown was credited as a key player in helping build the firm's practice. He is replaced as cochair by **Paul Bird**, who delivers "*practical, efficient and flexible*" advice. Clients also paid tribute to "*an absolutely tireless worker who is confrontational when he needs to be.*" He participated in FedEx's

$2.4 billion acquisition of Kinko's from Clayton Dubilier & Rice and other shareholders. "*Smart*" fellow co-head **Jeff Rosen** "*has a broad understanding of technical areas and tax issues,*" combined with an ability to translate these qualities into a transaction, analysts said. This "*extremely useful integrator*" is ably supported by securities expert **Alan Paley**, a new entrant to the tables. He earned commendation as a "*practical, efficient and flexible*" operator.
The Clients: AT&T Wireless Services; American Airlines; AXA Financial; DaimlerChrysler; GlobeNet Communications; Goldman Sachs; Hasbro; The Jim Henson Company; JPMorgan; Lever Brothers; MetLife; NFL; Oxygen Media; PwC; Prudential and Waste Management.

Fried, Frank, Harris, Shriver & Jacobson LLP
See firm details p.1349
The Firm: "*Top notch in terms of public company M&A,*" the firm has leapt up deal tables in 2004 with an almost four-fold increase in deal value. Offering the strength and depth to "*get things done,*" its enviable list of transactions includes Cingular's $47 billion acquisition of AT&T Wireless Services and The Rouse Company's $11.9 billion merger with General Growth Properties. Acting for Kirk Kerkorian and Tracinda Corporation, which controls 73% of MGM shares, the practice also helped marshal the $5 billion sale of MGM to a consortium led by Sony. Relationships with investment banks such as Merrill Lynch and Goldman Sachs continue to prosper, and the team often acts in the financial adviser role. For example, it represented Goldman Sachs in relation to Oxford Health Plans' $4.9 billion merger with UnitedHealth Group. The firm also acted for WPP Group in its acquisition of Grey Global Group for $1.52 billion.
The Lawyers: Leader of the firm's M&A practice for the about 30 years, "*grand patriarch*" **Arthur Fleischer** (see p.1280) commands industry respect as "*one of the top boardroom lawyers for pure gravitas.*" He acted for BellSouth, which jointly owns Cingular with SBC Communications, in the acquisition of AT&T Wireless. He also advised The Rouse Company in its merger with General Growth Properties. "*He is not easing off the throttle,*" commentators said. "*He does what many leave their partners or senior associates to do.*" A new entrant to the tables, the "*laid back and always very effective*" **Warren de Wied** (see p.1275) was praised for his industry experience. Clients said he brings a business-minded view to bear on proceedings. He advised Tracinda Corporation and Kirk Kerkorian in the sale of MGM.
The Clients: Merrill Lynch; Goldman Sachs; WPP Group; BellSouth; The Rouse Company; Burlington Resources; El Paso; Martha Stewart Living; Omnimedia and Merck.

Shearman & Sterling LLP

See firm details p.1369

The Firm: A firm commended by clients for providing "*one-stop shopping advice*" from a team of attorneys whose experience in the M&A arena is said to resonate a broad understanding of the complexities involved in cross-border transactions. "*For the big deals, they are fabulous.*" The approachability and user-friendly manner of the team drew widespread praise, although some commentators raised concerns that there appears to be a distinct lack of younger practitioners rising from its ranks. With a highly developed practice spanning 19 offices, the firm reaps dividends with deals such as Ispat International's acquisitions of LNM Holdings and International Steel Group through a simultaneous merger for $17.8 billion. The firm is traditionally known for its strength in complex finance transactions, which is reflected by strong profiles in banking and finance, and investment management. One commentator who would have liked to retain the practice added: "*It is the best firm we have never done a transaction with – it is always conflicted.*" The firm acted for Merrill Lynch as financial adviser to WPP on its $1.3 billion acquisition of Grey Global. Highlights involving other sectors include Siemens' $993 million acquisition of the worldwide systems and services businesses of USFilter Corporation from its parent company, Véolia Environnement. Representing Extended Stay America (ESA), it advised on the lodging chain's takeover by The Blackstone Group for about $3.1 billion.

The Lawyers: Clients enjoy a "*beautiful relationship*" with **David Heleniak** (see p.1287), who gained respect for his work in the capital markets arena as well as his involvement in major M&A transactions. He was part of a team representing the Molson board of directors' independent committee in the company's merger with the Adolph Coors Company. "*Superstar*" **Creighton Condon** (see p.1273) acted for the minority shareholders of NYCE on a $610 million acquisition by Metavante, a subsidiary of Marshall & Ilsley Corporation; the deal also involved majority shareholder First Data Corporation and other investors. "*Practical and full of energy*" **Peter Lyons** (see p.1298) is a "*result-oriented lawyer who is able to negotiate difficult transactions well.*" He is responsible for developing client relations with the likes of Siemens, Boston Scientific, BASF and Deutsche Bank. "*Drawing on a wealth of experience,*" his repertoire includes acting for Lehman Brothers as financial advisers in relation to The Blackstone Group's €3.1 billion acquisition of Celanese. "*As close to a banker mentality within a law firm as you can get,*" **John Madden** (see p.1299) won client confidence as a "*commercial and savvy*" operator. "*His judgment is absolutely world class,*" a client said. Madden acted for the bankers on the AT&T Wireless sale to Cin-

gular and separately advised Boca Resorts in its $1.23 billion acquisition by The Blackstone Group. Rising star **Clare O'Brien** (see p.1306) is "*clear, firm and charming – a pretty unique combination,*" clients said. This "*tough negotiator*" acted for The Thomson Corporation on the acquisition of TradeWeb Group from a consortium of eight investment banks. She is also counseling SunGard in the spin-off of its disaster recovery business, Availability Services. John Marzulli is on hand to advise on telecom transactions.

The Clients: CSFB; Merrill Lynch; Morgan Stanley; GlaxoSmithKline; Viacom; NBC; GE; Siemens; Boston Scientific; BASF; Deutsche Bank; The Thompson Corporation; Extended Stay America and Citigroup.

Weil, Gotshal & Manges LLP

See firm details p.1378

The Firm: Pitched as "*business people's lawyers,*" the firm comprises "*smart, assiduous and top-drawer attorneys,*" clients said. Repeatedly praised for its business-oriented approach, the group's dominance in the corporate arena is reflected by its expansion in Europe and other parts of the world while maintaining a sure grip on the domestic market. Key hires in London and Paris help enhance its international stature, which has paid off handsomely in such deals as the largest M&A transaction to come out of China; here the firm represented Lenovo Group on its agreement to acquire IBM's global PC business and form a strategic alliance with IBM for about $1.2 billion. Another highlight involved seller Vivendi Universal in its $14 billion transaction with NBC. The group also represented DIRECTV on its $4.3 billion sale of PanAmSat to KKR and separately acted for Molson on its $6 billion merger with Adolph Coors Company. On behalf of NextWave Telecom, it helped usher the company's sale of PCS spectrum licenses in 23 markets around the country to Verizon Wireless for about $3 billion. Tax, private equity and bankruptcy form a triumvirate of additional strengths for the firm.

The Lawyers: "*Top-notch*" **Frederick Green** (see p.1285) chairs the firm's M&A and Latin American practice. He acted for DIRECTV Group on its sale of PanAmSat to KKR, while colleague **Thomas Roberts** (see p.1313) is renowned in the market for his private equity expertise. The chairman of the firm's corporate department acted for UnitedHealth Group on its $2.9 billion acquisition of Mid Atlantic Medical Services. Alongside Roberts, **Howard Chatzinoff** (see p.1271) offers a sharp intelligence and negotiating style combined with a problem-solving approach to deals. His portfolio includes representing GE in relation to GE Infrastructure's $900 million acquisition of InVision Technologies.

The Clients: Hicks Muse Tate & Furst; Capital Z; CSFB Merchant Bank; Vivendi Universal; GE

Capital; Molson; Matsushita; United Healthcare; Lehman Brohers; Texas Instruments and MCI.

Band 4

Cadwalader, Wickersham & Taft LLP

See firm details p.1339

The Firm: A firm that "*knows the business inside out,*" according to clients, it has gained market confidence in a flurry of significant deals. One of its most notable achievements is helping to orchestrate Procter & Gamble's $57 billion bid for Gillette; the transaction – one of the year's largest – would create a consumer-products powerhouse. The practice also participated in BT Group's $965 million acquisition of Infonet Services from a consortium. The firm's phenomenal reputation in capital markets means that related cross references benefit its M&A practice, which has a clientele forged from the likes of major investment banks and Fortune 500 corporations.

The Lawyers: This firm's fortunes owe a great deal to the reputation of **Dennis Block** (see p.1268). A "*force of nature,*" who engenders great personal loyalty from a client list which "*reads like a who's who of corporate America,*" and for whom he "*works tirelessly – he is a dedicated, driven person.*" He acted for Banc of America Securities as financial adviser in EGL Holding's $2.3 billion acquisition of Select Medical Corporation. **Lou Bevilacqua** (see p.1267) is said to be "*diligent, knowledgeable and a pleasure to deal with.*" He acted for Group 1 Software in relation to Pitney Bowes' acquisition of all of Group 1 Software's outstanding shares for approximately $321 million.

The Clients: The firm has represented Banc of America Securities, Group 1 Software and Infonet Services.

Dewey Ballantine LLP

See firm details p.1347

The Firm: This is a firm offering "*balanced, measured and practical advice,*" clients said. It is a partner-driven firm spread across six US offices, further bolstered by an international network of offices in cities such as London, Frankfurt, Milan and Rome. The firm's traditional strengths in project finance, capital markets and insurance helped to contribute to a boon in its M&A activity of late, acting on headliners such as the $4.84 billion acquisition of MGM by a consortium that included Sony. The firm also advised on Comcast's $66 billion tender offer for Disney. Another highlight involved Omnicare in relation to the acquisition of the outstanding shares of NeighborCare for about $1.5 billion. On behalf of the financial advisers, it also participated in Sanofi-Synthelabo's €48.5 billion takeover of Aventis.

The Lawyers: With years of "*great experience,*"

Morton Pierce (see p.1308) has "*never lost the passion for what he does,*" sources said. As a result he continues to play leading roles in high-profile transactions such as LifePoint Hospitals' $1.7 billion acquisition of Province Healthcare Company. He "*is a lawyer of choice for investment banks and manages to parlay relationships into a central role.*" He is also acting for Burns Philp in the proposed sale to Associated British Foods of its Yeast and Bakery Ingredients Group and its Tones Bros herbs and spices business for $1.35 billion. Right-hand man **Michael Aiello** (see p.1262) is said to join a "*comprehensive service with good commercial advice.*" He acted for Sumitomo Corporation of America in connection with the $388 million acquisition of JWC Hartz Holdings and separately counseled The MONY Group in connection with its $2.3 billion takeover by AXA Financial.

The Clients: LifePoint Hospitals; Sumitomo Corporation of America; Sony; Omnicare and The MONY Group.

Latham & Watkins LLP

The Firm: The nine-partner practice is pitched as an example of how to crack a market using core finance expertise. Its strength in the high-yield finance market has helped enhance its efforts in "*building a real powerhouse*" within the competitive New York market. Evidence of its success can be related to the firm's turnover, which has more than doubled in the past five years. The team was part of a multi-office team that acted for Harrah's Entertainment in a $1.24 billion takeover of four casinos by Colony Capital; the deal also involved Caesars Entertainment. The team also acted for Dresser in a $575 million IPO. Among financial sponsors, "*they have become a much bigger presence,*" one client said.

The Lawyers: **Charles Nathan** leverages a wealth of respect among the investment banker community to establish "*a leg-up*" on M&A. One client added: "*We would go wherever Chuck goes,*" indicating the level of loyalty he commands. Though the sentiment also suggests how dependent the practice is on Nathan. In 2004, he led for MGM in its $4.84 billion takeover by a Sony-led consortium amongst other prominent transactions.

The Clients: Harrah's Entertainment; Dresser; MGM; Goldman Sachs; The Carlyle Group and Bear Stearns.

Willkie Farr & Gallagher LLP

See firm details p.1380

The Firm: Clients value the firm's "*holistic attitude toward a company,*" which ensures that "*all parties are working for the company's best interests.*" This practice has "*taken off in the M&A business*" after a period of transformation that has resulted in its involvement in more prominent deals. Its strong relationship with buyout fund Warburg Pincus has resulted in a steady flow of transac-

tions. For example, it acted for the buyout fund in connection with the $1.35 billion acquisition of Telcordia Technologies from Science Applications International. Other interests include bankruptcy, real estate and litigation, while an already thriving private equity practice culminates in cross references to the M&A team. The firm's foray into the international arena includes a successful Paris office among others in Frankfurt and Rome. Highlights include acting for Select Medical Corporation on its merger with a new company formed by an investment group led by private equity houses Welsh, Carson, Anderson & Stowe and Thoma Cressey Equity Partners in a deal valued at $2.3 billion. The team also represented K&F Industries on its acquisition by Aurora Capital Group in a secondary buyout for $1.06 billion. Advising Warburg Pincus, it was also involved in Electronic Data Systems' $2.05 billion divestiture of its UGS PLM Solutions unit. "*Well grounded in the law yet able to think strategically,*" the group also earned plaudits for anticipating problems before they develop, clients said.

The Lawyers: New to the senior statesman ranks, the firm's chairman **Jack Nusbaum** (see p.1305) combines "*wonderful business and legal judgment.*" A practical thinker, he has advised several boards of directors in addition to playing a strategic role on major M&A transactions. "*He has the ability to distill and reach a conclusion way ahead of most people.*" He advised Neuberger Berman in its $2.63 billion acquisition by Lehman Brothers. Colleague **Tom Cerabino** (see p.1271) acts for key clients such as Zurich Financial Services and Carlos Slim while maintaining strong gaming industry experience. He advised Colony Capital in relation to an acquisition of four casinos by one of its affiliates. The deal also involved Harrah's Entertainment and Caesars Entertainment. He is also counsel to Donald J. Trump in the proposed financial restructuring of Trump Hotels & Casino Resorts. Part of the firm's next generation, **Steve Seidman** (see p.1319) "*has made immeasurable impact on the success and well-being of our company,*" said one client. "*His responsiveness is instantaneous, the speed of his performance is lightning-like, and his thoroughness is on a par with any major M&A player in New York City.*" He acted for Matlin Patterson Global Advisers on its acquisition of Southeast Generation Portfolio from Duke Energy.

The Clients: Morgan Stanley; Warburg Pincus; Merrill Lynch; DrKW; Simon Property Group; The Feedroom and GovPX.

Band 5

Gibson, Dunn & Crutcher LLP

See firm details p.285

The Firm: The California-based firm has been making waves in New York, with clients referring to its flexibility and "*great network*" as reasons why they retain the group. They add that its lawyers

can "*work on their own and know our standards,*" often delivering fantastic results on high-end M&A. An expanding private equity team also enhances the overall corporate profile. The firm's wealth of resources – including antitrust, employment and litigation expertise – combined with its global spread distinguishes this operation as an ideal choice. The team acted for Exult when it was acquired by Hewitt Associates for approximately $798 million in stock and assumed debt. It was also involved in Unilever's sale of four home care brands to Lehman Brothers Merchant Banking. Another drawing card is its experience advising financial advisers. For example, the firm has counseled Lazard Freres in connection with Hollinger International's $1.2 billion sale of The Telegraph Group to Press Holdings.

The Lawyers: A strong presence in the marketplace, **Dennis Friedman** (see p.1281) spearheads the team. He acted for PanAmSat in its $4.1 billion takeover by KKR, Carlyle Group and Providence Equity Partners. Friedman also acted for the Maxwell Shoe Company in a $375 million unsolicited offer by Jones Apparel Group. A new addition to the tables, **Steven Shoemate** (see p.1320) advised on the $2 billion purchase of the Commercial Financial Services business from Boeing Capital.

The Clients: GE Capital; PanAmSat; Lazard Freres; Exult; Lehman Brothers Merchant Banking; ArvinMeritor and Goldman Sachs.

Jones Day

See firm details p.485

The Firm: Known as an international corporate and litigation giant with more than 2,000 lawyers in 29 locations, the firm has acted on a raft of high-profile matters. A jewel in its crown is advising Nextel Communications in a $35 billion merger with Sprint. One client stated: "*It doesn't matter what area of the law you need, they have some of the most capable people you can find.*" Advising RJ Reynolds Tobacco, it helped orchestrate the combination of the company's US tobacco business with that of BAT to form Reynolds American in a transaction valued at about $10 billion. The firm also advised RH Donnelley in its $1.42 billion acquisition of SBC Communications' directory publishing businesses in Illinois and Indiana. Its lawyers "*return calls quickly, provide adequate staffing for projects and bring expertise to the table,*" clients said. The firm also participated in Procter & Gamble's sale of Sunny Delight and Punica juice-based drink businesses to JW Childs Associates.

The Lawyers: Coordinator of Jones Day's corporate group, **Robert Profusek** (see p.1310) gathered accolades for his judgment and practicality. Peers appreciated this "*classic, well-developed central lawyer with practical business sense;*" while clients lauded his "*impeccable judgment on top-level strategy type decisions.*" Profusek acted for International Steel Group in Ispat International's $17.8 billion simultaneous acquisition of LNM Holdings and International Steel Group. He also represented International Management Group (IMG) in its takeover by Forstmann Little for an undisclosed amount.

The Clients: GenCorp; RJ Reynolds Tobacco; RH Donnelley; Nextel Communications.

Kirkland & Ellis LLP

See firm details p.770

The Firm: The Chicago-based firm is making inroads into the New York M&A market, and is further bolstered by traditional strong suits in private equity, bankruptcy and antitrust. Clients described it to be "*deep enough so that at fairly short notice they can be in touch with experts across countries and across legal boundaries.*" A team of at least seven M&A partners enjoys steady growth in the M&A arena with highlight matters such as the $723 million acquisition by ABRY Partners of Language Line Services from Providence Equity Partners. The team also acted for the selling shareholders when KKR agreed to acquire Sealy for $1.5 billion in a secondary buyout from a private investment group. Utilizing the strengths of its international operations, the firm advised on the US aspects of Bain Capital's €1.4 billion acquisition of Brenntag AG and Interfer Stahl from Deutsche Bahn.

The Lawyers: Star player **Stephen Fraidin** (see p.1280) "*has to be on anyone's list,*" commentators said. He is acting for Forstmann Little on the acquisition of International Management Group (IMG) for an undisclosed amount.

The Clients: Bain Capital; Forstmann Little; Dow Chemical; DuPont and Centurion Wireless Technologies.

Mayer, Brown, Rowe & Maw LLP

See firm details p.771

The Firm: One of the ten largest practices in the world, this firm offers M&A expertise across 13 international offices, subsequently possessing what client's praise as an ability to marshal "*the*

appropriate people across the globe.*" Clients also laud the team's consistent performance: "*When you give them an issue, they give you a solution.*" The added value of "*a strong network of the necessary experts*" further boosts its profile, which thrives on such strengths as the financial services sector and Latin America. Clients additionally paid tribute to the firm's "*great experience in the credit markets.*" Highlights include advising BellSouth in the $5.85 billion sale of its Latin American wireless interest to Telefónica.

The Lawyers: **Mark Wojciechowski** (see p.1332) is lauded for his "*ability to pick up the finer details,*" resulting in an ability to delineate between business interests and legal issues.

The Clients: The firm has advised BellSouth, Invensys and Therma-Tru among others.

Paul, Weiss, Rifkind, Wharton & Garrison LLP

See firm details p.1362

The Firm: The practice, which originally attracted clients because of its "*second-to-none*" litigation group, has developed into a significant M&A group that draws standalone work on its own merits. One client said they retain the team "*because we only deal with outstanding attorneys.*" Highlights include acting for Safeco Corporation on the $1.35 billion sale of its life and investments operations to a group of investors led by White Mountains Insurance Group and Berkshire Hathaway. The team also represented Pitney Bowes in its $321 million acquisition of the outstanding shares of Group 1 Software.

The Lawyers: Market commentators attributed much of the firm's success in the M&A arena to **Bob Schumer** (see p.1318), a "*fair-minded gentleman*" who helps nurture some of the firm's most important client relationships, including Time Warner. He advised the media giant in relation to Comcast's bid for Adelphia. Also hailed as a "*smart, even-tempered attorney who handles difficult situations well,*" Schumer also acted for EnCana Corporation in its $2.7 billion acquisition of the outstanding shares of Tom Brown Inc.

Colleague **Judith Thoyer** (see p.1327) joins him in the rankings this year following recommendations for her participation in such transactions as Hollinger International's $1.3 billion sale of the Telegraph Group to Press Acquisitions Limited, a company controlled by Sir David and Sir Frederick Barclay. Clients noted that she is "*great from the client relationship perspective.*"

The Clients: Safeco Corporation; Pitney Bowes; EnCana Corporation; Time Warner and Hollinger International.

White & Case LLP

See firm details p.1379

The Firm: A firm combining global perspective with local knowledge, it offers a 37-office international network with core strengths in areas such as project finance and banking. The New York M&A group is enjoying an ascending profile, with clients applauding the team for "*staying on top of issues and being proactive with client communication.*" Also inspiring client loyalty is the group of "*excellent negotiators,*" who have proficiently tackled such transactions as First Atlantic Capital's purchase of a majority stake in Prestolite Electric Holding from Genstar Capital. Other highlights include acting for Consorcio Comex on its acquisition of Professional Paint from Jordan. The firm is also acting for Anthem on its $16.4 billion acquisition of WellPoint Health Networks in a deal that will create the nation's leading health benefits company.

The Lawyers: **John Reiss** (see p.1312), who spearheads the team, earned client acclaim as an outstanding figure to "*lead people through difficult situations while dealing with the whole gamut of corporate matters.*" He acted for NUI Corporation in its $827 million sale to AGL Resources, and separately advised Harvest Partners and Lightyear Capital on their acquisition of New Flyer Industries.

The Clients: Echostar; Tyco; Verizon; Royal Ahold; Novartis; Deutsche Bank; Anthem; Warner Chilcott; Pitney Bowes and Mirant.

CORPORATE/M&A: MID-TIER FIRMS

Band 1

Bryan Cave LLP

The Firm: Clients gave this firm a high rating for its broad range combined with an "*ability to support the whole spectrum of deals from $10 to $100 million.*" Offering a seamless service across a broad range of expertise, the St Louis-based firm further benefits from its national and international network. It has had a phenomenal year with turnover growing 13.9% to $384 million. Bankruptcy and litigation are particularly strong suits for the firm although transactional work

has also come to the fore. This is partly due to a 2002 merger with 180-lawyer New York firm Robinson Silverman, commentators said.

The Lawyers: Co-leader of the firm's corporate finance and securities group is Ken Henderson. He and the team are "*technically competent*" attorneys, who "*bring a businessman's perspective to a deal.*"

The Clients: Deal highlights include acting on the IMN sale to Euromoney and separately advising on a $50 million stock purchase involving Infocrossing, which acquired a segment of Verizon Information Technologies. The firm

also acted on a portfolio company acquisition for Lincolnshire Equity Fund.

Dechert

See firm details p.1547

The Firm: This group of attorneys are "*responsive, sensitive to the issues and can evaluate risk,*" commentators said. Its network encompasses 17 offices across the USA and Europe, while expansion continues apace with the openings of the Palo Alto, Charlotte and Munich offices. Clients also attested to the ability of the international network to "*get in touch with experts across various*

New York
Leading firms
(Corporate/M&A: Mid-Tier Firms)

1
BRYAN CAVE LLP *New York*
DECHERT *New York*
HUGHES HUBBARD & REED LLP *New York*
KING & SPALDING LLP *New York*
MORGAN, LEWIS & BOCKIUS LLP *New York*
ROPES & GRAY *New York*

2
AKIN GUMP STRAUSS HAUER & FELD LLP *New York*
CLIFFORD CHANCE US LLP *New York*
KAYE SCHOLER LLP *New York*
KRAMER LEVIN NAFTALIS & FRANKEL LLP *New York*
MCDERMOTT WILL & EMERY *New York*
O'MELVENY & MYERS LLP *New York*
PROSKAUER ROSE LLP *New York*

Firms are listed alphabetically in each band.

legal arenas and countries at short notice." Although the firm's Philadelphia office traditionally gleans the lion's share of praise for transactional work, New York is making inroads with respected practitioners fielding matters for the firm's international client base. The recent recruitment of 57 lawyers from the New York office of Swidler Berlin Shereff Friedman will also be a boon to the team.

The Lawyers: Clients concurred that **Ron Jewell** (see p.1291) is "*usually the first person you call for a read on something, even if it isn't his specialty.*" They also feel "*comfortable putting him on the spot with both business people and legal people on the other side of the table – he is even-keeled.*" He represents clients such as VF Corporation, often in structuring its joint ventures and acquisitions in Latin America. Colleague **Glyn Lobo** (see p.1298) maintains his position as "*one of the finer, young, core finance and M&A lawyers,*" clients said. "*You get a good bench for your buck – he is efficient, knows the business and everyone loves him.*"

The Clients: Wyeth; Pfizer; B&G Foods; Campbell Soup; Merrill Lynch; Bruckmann, Rosser, Sherrill & Co. and One Equity Partners.

Hughes Hubbard & Reed LLP
See firm details p.1353

The Firm: The New York-based firm attracts a wide array of clients, particularly those more interested in the package than the packaging. "*You may not get the recognizable names,*" they said, "*but you will get quality lawyers.*" A network of offices includes satellites in Los Angeles, Miami, Jersey City, Paris and Tokyo. Clients praised a group who "*will get into the trenches and work with you,*" acting in an "*attentive, responsive, and quick*" manner on transactions. Clients noted an ability to handle the "*intricate middle-sized deals*" while additionally possessing "*good business judgment.*" This is said to set it apart from larger rivals who "*just explain the hypothetical rather than giving practical business*

advice." The firm acted for the shareholders when Cendant agreed to acquire Orbitz from AMR, UAL, Norwest Airlines and Delta Air Lines for $1.25 billion.

The Lawyers: Clients were fulsome in their praise for **Ken Lefkowitz** (see p.1296), who "*takes business interests to heart.*" Others declare him "*smart, accessible and dedicated to the process*" while being a "*persistent and determined negotiator.*" Acting for an impressive roster of airlines, Lefkowitz also advises underwriters such as Merrill Lynch and JPMorgan. He is representing Robert Burton and a Canadian fund in connection with a proxy fight relating to a Canadian company called Creo.

The Clients: A new client of the firm is Cyprus Partners. Others include: PwC; Continental Airlines; Merck; ALSTOM; Viacom and Nautica.

King & Spalding LLP
See firm details p.635

The Firm: Traditionally renowned as a blue-blooded Atlanta practice, this firm has undergone dramatic growth in the past ten years. Packed to the rafters with attorneys said to be both practical and business savvy, the team garnered applause for its "*customer service, responsiveness and a direct, efficient manner.*" Several clients additionally paid tribute to the firm's ability to "*work side-by-side*" with in-house attorneys to attain "*consistent*" results. The firm's Atlanta and New York offices advised Sprint on its $35 billion merger with Nextel. The group also represented the financial advisers on Prologic's $1.6 billion acquisition of Keystone Property and separately advised on National Senior Care's $1 billion purchase of Mariner Health Care.

The Lawyers: William Bates is a key M&A partner in the firm's New York office. He acted on Jefferson Pilot's purchase of Canada Life and on the MIM Corporation purchase of Chronimed. In addition, the team's ranks have swelled with the addition of the respected energy transactional lawyer Tia Barancik from LeBoeuf Lamb Greene & MacRae.

The Clients: The team acted for GE in the $260 million acquisition of BHA Group Holdings. The team also acted for TXU on the sale of its TXU Communications subsidiary to Consolidated Communications for $527 million. Other clients stem from the Fortune 500 ranks, including an ascending profile among investment banks and financial institutions.

Morgan, Lewis & Bockius LLP
See firm details p.1556

The Firm: With 19 offices across the USA and globe – including a recently opened Paris office, it is considered a sweet spot for mid-market transactions. Clients praise the resources available to tackle a host of transactions, ranging in value from a few million dollars up to a billion. Matters are dealt with along integrated teams

that involve such specialist areas as energy, media, life sciences, securities and private equity.

The Lawyers: Charles Engros, managing partner of the New York office and co-head of the firm's M&A practice, has advised foreign-based companies on acquisitions and financings in the USA.

The Clients: The firm's clientele is derived from an array of Fortune 500 companies, including investment banks. It has also represented a number of media clients such as the Time Out Group, The Economist and Pearson.

Ropes & Gray
See firm details p.985

The Firm: A practice straddling both the New York and Boston markets, the corporate team profits from the successful 2003 merger with Reboul, MacMurray, Hewitt & Maynard. Teams from both offices acted for Thomas H Lee Partners, in partnership with members of Nortek's management, in the $1.75 billion acquisition of Nortek Holdings. Much of the firm's transactional work has a private equity bent. It is also renowned for its work within the healthcare sector, including acting for Welsh Carson Anderson & Stowe (WCAS) on its $1.7 billion purchase of the 85.5% stake in US Oncology that it did not already own. The firm also acted for EGL Holding on the acquisition of Select Medical Corporation for a total consideration of $2.3 billion. The recent merger with IP specialists Fish & Neave has more than doubled the firm's numbers to 200, bolstering its core capabilities.

The Lawyers: Othon Prounis is the key contact for the firm's New York office while Newcomb Stillwell is the key contact in Boston.

The Clients: Bain Capital; Gillette; Thomas H Lee Partners; Berkshire Partners; EMC and Fenway Partners.

Band 2

Akin Gump Strauss Hauer & Feld LLP
See firm details p.477

The Firm: One of the largest in the world, this firm is able to draw on the resources of about 1,000 lawyers in ten offices across the USA and international branches in cities such as London and Moscow, and an affiliate office in Saudi Arabia. An impressive array of niche strengths that support its M&A capability include corporate governance and private equity among others such as a burgeoning energy practice. The firm also has a highly regarded bankruptcy practice with many corporate transactions arising from this, together with relationships with investment banks and others. The team adopts a cross-disciplinary approach exemplified when it advised Westport Resources on its $3.4 billion merger with Kerr McGee.

The Lawyers: Patrick Dooley and Susan Cohen spearhead the team.

The Clients: Other highlights include the acquisition by Getty of 800 gas stations and separately representing Sandler as one of the principal investors in MobiTel.

Clifford Chance US LLP
See firm details p.1343
The Firm: The "*top-notch*" firm is able to deliver "*huge capacity with a small-firm feel*," and can draw enviable clients who have largely remained loyal despite a series of high-profile departures over the past two years. Peers are concerned about some "*internal issues*," referring to the well-publicized problems that have arisen since its trans Atlantic merger with Rogers & Wells. Despite such woes, "*it has good lawyers and a good client roster*," peers conceded, and it still remains what many analysts believe to be the only UK magic circle firm to have made a significant impact in the USA. The team acts for a clientele that is a mix of traditional Rogers & Wells clients and instructions from its London base. "*Offices across the world are an added bonus*," clients said.
The Lawyers: John Healy is the chairman and co-head of the M&A team.
The Clients: The firm is representing The Hearst Corporation in its acquisition of White Directory Publishers. It also represented The Rubenstein Company in a takeover by Brandywine Realty Trust valued at more than $600 million. Other clients include public and private corporations, investment banks and financial institutions, private equity firms such as Colony Capital and government entities.

Kaye Scholer LLP
See firm details p.1354
The Firm: An international law firm with a corporate grouping of 85 lawyers across nine offices, the team represents public and private companies in connection with M&A, corporate control issues, stock purchases and asset acquisitions. The firm advised JW Childs Associates on the sale of The Hartz Mountain Corporation to Sumitomo of America for $388 million. The firm also acted as primary legal counsel for Sidney Frank Importing on the acquisition by Bacardi of Grey Goose Vodka.
The Lawyers: **Joel Greenberg** (see p.1285) has

acted on a series of transactions for Onex, including the $101 million purchase of its equity investment in Magellan Health Services through Onex Partners. He also advised on Onex and Oaktree Capital Management's $2 billion sale of their interests in the Loews Cineplex Entertainment Corporation.
The Clients: M&A, with a private equity bent, is a mainstay of the firm, which has represented clients such as JW Childs Associates, Onex, UBS Capital and American Securities.

Kramer Levin Naftalis & Frankel LLP
See firm details p.1357
The Firm: This firm acts across all industry sectors from startups to Fortune 500 companies. The reputation of its phenomenal litigation department helps provide a steady stream of work in the corporate sphere, and the firm also boasts an office in Paris and an affiliation with Berwin Leighton Paisner in the UK. It acted for Kroll in its $1.9 billion takeover by the Marsh & McLennan Companies (MMC).
The Lawyers: Scott Rosenblum spearheads the team.
The Clients: Bear Stearns; ATMI; Vishay Technology; Kroll; AIG; Deloitte Touche Tohmatsu and Scientific Games.

McDermott Will & Emery
See firm details p.773
The Firm: The firm has nine offices across the USA and overseas offices in Milan, Munich and Rome, representing clients in both friendly and contested public company acquisitions, divestitures and joint ventures. A highlight involved The Jean Coutu Group (PJC) in its $2.38 billion acquisition of more than 1,500 drugstores comprising Eckerd's Northern and Mid-Atlantic drugstore business from JC Penney.
The Lawyers: Grant Bagan spearheads the team.
The Clients: The firm acted for DaVita Inc. in its $3.05 billion pending acquisition of Gambro's US kidney dialysis business. A further highlight was the representation of JW Childs Associates in its acquisition of Sunny Delight and Punica from Procter & Gamble. The group also represented Merrill Lynch in its acquisition of the energy trading business of Entergy-Koch.

O'Melveny & Myers LLP
See firm details p.294
The Firm: A firm with approximately 900 attorneys in 14 offices across the world, its strong suits include private equity and litigation. Its M&A profile is somewhat less luminous, though it inevitably benefits from cross references from other departments. A burgeoning South American practice also saw the firm advising Telecom Italia Mobile in its $450 million sale of Corporacion Digitel to Compañia Anónima Nacional Teléfonos de Venezuela. A further highlight involved acting for Ask Jeeves on its acquisition of Interactive Search Holdings for about $360 million. The firm also acted for JPMorgan on its acquisition of Warner Chilcott.
The Lawyers: Peers note a talented M&A lawyer in **John Suydam**, who represented Apollo Management in the acquisition of leading chemical supplier Borden Chemical.
The Clients: Apollo Management; JPMorgan Partners; CSFB; Deutsche Bank: Dynergy; Verizon and DHL.

Proskauer Rose LLP
See firm details p.1365
The Firm: Clients declared they are "*proud*" of this cadre of "*responsive and efficient*" attorneys, who also provide the added bonus of being "*reasonable in terms of cost*." One of the largest traditional New York firms, it is able to draw on the resources provided by four other offices, including one in Paris. International work provides a strong backbone to the firm's M&A profile, for example it co-counseled Votorantim Metais on its acquisition of 99% of Sociedad Minera Refineria de Zinc de Cajamarquilla for $210 million. The firm also advised The Laird Group on its acquisition of Centurion Wireless Technologies for a total cash and stock consideration of £106.8 million.
The Lawyers: Arnold Jacobs and Steven Kirshenbaum cochair the team.
The Clients: Other highlights include acting for DNE Systems – previously a subsidiary of The Alpine Group – in a $40 million takeover by Ultra Electronics Holdings. Other clients include Charterhouse Group International, National Basketball Association, Alcatel and Gray Television.

EMPLOYEE BENEFITS & EXECUTIVE COMPENSATION

Band 1

Cleary Gottlieb Steen & Hamilton LLP
See firm details p.1342
The Firm: This talented team harnesses its "*wealth of industry knowledge*" to deliver "*superior breadth and depth*" within the employee benefits arena, analysts said. Highly regarded

especially for ERISA fiduciary matters and executive compensation, it plays a significant role in an environment where corporate investigations continue to dominate the landscape. M&A activity has also risen in the past year, providing a steady flow of work pertaining to benefit and compensation issues. Examples include advising PeopleSoft in connection with Oracle's hostile takeover. In the investment banking communi-

ty, the firm is recognized for its expertise on equity and other incentive plans such as transferable option products and co-investment plans.
The Lawyers: Commercially minded **Brick Susko** (see p.1325) is regarded as among the best in the fiduciary field. An acknowledged ERISA expert, he is "*the only person who can explain it in an easy-to-understand way without*

1196   All quotes in the text are from interviews with clients and competitors.

CHAMBERS USA 2005

New York
Leading firms (Employee Benefits & Executive Compensation)

1 CLEARY GOTTLIEB STEEN & HAMILTON *New York*
PILLSBURY WINTHROP LLP *New York*
SIMPSON THACHER & BARTLETT LLP *New York*
WACHTELL, LIPTON, ROSEN & KATZ *New York*

2 DAVIS POLK & WARDWELL *New York*
DEBEVOISE & PLIMPTON LLP *New York*
SHEARMAN & STERLING LLP *New York*
SULLIVAN & CROMWELL LLP *New York*

3 FRIED, FRANK, HARRIS, SHRIVER *New York*
PAUL, WEISS, RIFKIND, WHARTON *New York*
PROSKAUER ROSE LLP *New York*
SKADDEN, ARPS, SLATE, MEAGHER *New York*
WHITE & CASE LLP *New York*

Leading individuals (Employee Benefits & Executive Compensation)

★ SUSKO A Richard *Cleary Gottlieb*, New York

1 EDGAR Kenneth *Simpson Thacher*, New York
KRUEGER Karen *Wachtell Lipton*, New York
SCHWARTZ Max *Sullivan & Cromwell*, New York
SEROTA Susan *Pillsbury Winthrop*, New York

2 CAGNEY Lawrence *Debevoise & Plimpton*, New York
CARLEEN Donald *Fried Frank*, New York
CHINN Adam *Wachtell Lipton*, New York
GILBERT Richard *Orrick Herrington*, San Francisco
GRALA Bronislaw *Cadwalader Wickersham*, New York
KNEIP Frederick *Milbank Tweed*, New York
RAPPAPORT Linda *Shearman & Sterling*, New York
SIRKIN Michael *Proskauer Rose*, New York

3 ALPERIN Stuart *Skadden Arps*, New York
FITZGERALD Edmond *Davis Polk*, New York
FLEDER Robert *Paul Weiss*, New York
KATZKE Michael *Wachtell Lipton*, New York
KOHN Arthur *Cleary Gottlieb*, New York
LEFF Neil *Skadden Arps*, New York
MASON David *Debevoise & Plimpton*, New York
NIMS Barbara *Davis Polk*, New York
ORINGER Andrew *Clifford Chance*, New York
PAGEL SEREBRANSKY *Debevoise & Plimpton*, New York
RASKIN Kenneth *White & Case*, New York
RAYMOND Robert *Cleary Gottlieb*, New York
ROTHENBERG Laraine *Fried Frank*, New York
SEGAL Michael *Paul Weiss*, New York

Firms and individuals are listed alphabetically in each band.

dumbing things down," one client said. Another stated: "*He is the one lawyer I trust the most for his judgment.*" He represented Freddie Mac in key hirings and separately advised prominent executives such as Bob Singer, president of Abercrombie & Fitch. **Arthur Kohn** (see p.1294), who was described by one client as "*a perfect fit,*" is instrumental in non-cash compensation matters such as stock options. He is often retained when the situation requires "*exercise of judgment and an understanding of higher technical things.*" **Bob Raymond** (see p.1311) won plaudits for his handling of the employment benefits aspect of

M&A, garnering particular compliments in the area of ERISA exemption. A "*good rapport with the Department of Labor*" further bolstered his profile, clients said.
The Clients: Goldman Sachs; Morgan Stanley; TPG; Freddie Mac and PeopleSoft.

Pillsbury Winthrop LLP
See firm details p.1364
The Firm: "*Business-oriented, practical and responsive,*" the executive compensation/employee benefits group (ECEB) finds favor with clients for its depth of expertise and ability to keep apace of the market. The New York team focuses on compensation committees relating to equity compensation and pension plans, an area that's increasingly under SEC scrutiny. It also handles ERISA-based and fiduciary litigation brought against committees, often pertaining to disclosure issues. The firm continues to counsel Bristol-Myers Squibb in connection with allegations affecting qualified plans. Other projects include advising Sony BMG on the implementation of new employee benefit plans. At time of press the firm announced its merger with Shaw Pittman LLP to form Pillsbury Winthrop Shaw Pittman.
The Lawyers: "*Outstanding*" adviser **Susan Serota** (see p.1320) is particularly known for her work in the benefits arena. An attorney who understands trends, clients say: "*She knows the industry and can always provide a benchmark to frame her advice.*"
The Clients: The firm has a varied client base and is valued for its institutional knowledge in sectors such as pharmaceuticals, finance and utilities. Examples include General Re Corporation, Praxair, Sony BMG and Bristol-Myers Squibb.

Simpson Thacher & Bartlett LLP
See firm details p.1370
The Firm: The firm's prominence in the ECEB market is directly linked to its emphasis on M&A. For example, the team advised Kmart on share options relating to its $11 billion merger with Sears to create the third largest retailer in the USA. The transaction involved a top-hat structure to allocate shares. The firm navigates clients through various stages, including the negotiation, planning and compliance of executive compensation agreements in addition to all types of business plans. The firm also advises on a variety of complex issues relating to the private equity arena. For example, it represented The Blackstone Group in its $1.25 billion acquisition of Boca Resorts. Further bolstering the firm's national reach is a sizable team on the West Coast.
The Lawyers: One of the more talented and visible lawyers in the arena, **Kenneth Edgar** (see p.1277) heads the group, bringing years of experience to the fore. Areas of expertise include advice to compensation boards on corporate governance issues. Advising the Conference Board Commission on Public Trust and Private

Enterprise, he assisted on a prominent report examining executive compensation.
The Clients: Accenture; ARAMARK; JPMorgan; Wachovia and Kmart.

Wachtell, Lipton, Rosen & Katz
See firm details p.1375
The Firm: Clients are confident in allocating this firm "*the lion's share*" of its employee benefits work, ranging from "*the small concerns that arise to major strategic issues.*" The group also plays a key role in assisting the corporate department in its M&A activity. Recent transactions include MetLife's sale of State Street to BlackRock, which involved significant ERISA issues. The firm also represented Ameren in its efforts to acquire a regulated energy segment from Dynegy. In that deal, the team was instrumental in negotiating pension liabilities.
The Lawyers: The "*phenomenal*" **Karen Krueger** (see p.1295) has proven to be an agile force on governance matters, as well as handling some ERISA-based litigation. An "*exceedingly practical*" attorney with "*a high degree of integrity,*" she is often viewed by clients as a "*true business partner.*" She represents both individuals and corporations in top-level appointments. Cited as "*a most businesslike and results-oriented benefits lawyer,*" **Adam Chinn** (see p.1272) is dominant in the financial institutions arena, where he usually handles the tax side of ERISA. **Michael Katzke** (see p.1292) also has cultivated a significant reputation in the field. He handled the benefits aspects of the $3 billion acquisition of Intelsat by client Zeus Holdings, a consortium of four private equity firms.
The Clients: Mattel; Maytag; McDonald's; MeadWestvaco; Monsanto; New York Stock Exchange and Schering-Plough.

Band 2

Davis Polk & Wardwell
See firm details p.1345
The Firm: A team that can be relied on for "*extremely sound judgment,*" it is fully integrated with the firm's various departments. There is significant overlap with the estate and trusts unit on executive compensation issues, and the group coordinates with the capital markets group on designing viable financial instruments for pension plan investors. In addition, it also contributes to M&A and LBO transactions. Its prominence in the public and private sphere is illustrated in such transactions as FedEx's $2.4 billion acquisition of Kinko's in 2004.
The Lawyers: **Barbara Nims** (see p.1305) successfully combines a sophisticated securities law background with in-depth understanding of the tax implications of benefits and compensation arrangements. She also advises on investment management issues, including extensive experience in pension plans. Promoted to partner in

2000, **Edmond Fitzgerald** (see p.1279) is destined to be a key player in the market, commentators said. He is versed in all aspects of equity compensation and performance incentives, as well as handling ERISA financial products.

The Clients: Clients include boutique investment firms such as: Welsh, Carson, Anderson, & Stowe; Francisco Partners; Thomas Weisel Partners and Lindsay Goldberg & Bessemer. Others involve funds offered by the world's leading financial institutions, including CSFB, Morgan Stanley and JPMorgan Chase.

Debevoise & Plimpton LLP
See firm details p.1346

The Firm: Armed with a "*deep bench of intelligent and hard-working attorneys,*" the practice won client confidence as a strong contender across a range of matters. The ECEB team delivers a "*personal and thoughtful service*" in relation to tax, securities, compensation and benefits. Recent examples include representing AXA Financial in its $1.5 billion acquisition of the MONY Group, a deal that involved key negotiations concerning golden parachute arrangements. Other projects include the representation of Clayton, Dubilier & Rice in the sale of Kinko's to FedEx, a transaction that involved complicated compensation issues. The firm also advises fiduciaries on market timing issues, a heightened concern in the light of increased litigation surrounding 401(k) plans.

The Lawyers: The "*go-to guy*" for technical ERISA or ESOP queries, **Lawrence Cagney** is "*exceptionally knowledgeable and full of practical advice.*" The "*truly awesome*" department head also assists corporations with their IDS (income deposit security) transactions and advises executives on their compensation arrangements. Shouldering a broad practice, **David Mason** "*cuts to the chase.*" Recent work includes representing GE/NBC on pension negotiations and senior compensation issues in connection with the acquisition of Universal to form NBC Universal. Clients are equally complimentary of **Beth Pagel Serebransky**, who is "*open minded*" in terms of finding solutions. She handles the US compensation work for UBS and works with other financial services companies in relation to employee benefits.

The Clients: AXA Financial; Clayton, Dubilier & Rice; GE; NBC and UBS.

Shearman & Sterling LLP
See firm details p.1369

The Firm: Clients note that this "*technically impressive*" team has a strong practice both in the USA and Europe. Further enhancing its international reach, last year saw the addition of a London office partner. Meanwhile in New York, the team has witnessed a rise in private equity business; for example, it has assisted clients such as Citigroup in structuring alternative investment vehicles. The firm continues to

counsel boards and compensation committees on corporate governance issues pertaining to Sarbanes-Oxley. It is equally well experienced in the design and implementation of equity-based ownership schemes. It further benefits from particular strengths in financial services and entertainment, including advising Universal Music on its equity programs.

The Lawyers: The impressive **Linda Rappaport** (see p.1311) is regarded as a "*tough negotiator,*" frequently acting on executive succession issues. She has represented both companies and individuals in such matters.

The Clients: CSFB; Deutsche Bank; Merrill Lynch; Morgan Stanley and Citigroup.

Sullivan & Cromwell LLP
See firm details p.1373

The Firm: This "*top-notch*" practice is active on high-level transactional work, as well as advisory matters across the board. Last year the team represented Anthem in its acquisition of WellPoint, a deal that hit regulatory hurdles in California. Anthem resolved matters partly by pledging $265 million to state health programs. The group often provides compensation consultancy and advice on corporate governance requirements. Other features include the development and implementation of new plans, for example, retirement plans.

The Lawyers: Popular practice head **Max Schwartz** (see p.1319) is admired for his great judgment. Clients say he has "*invaluable insight into what's going on in Washington (DC) related to executive compensation, qualified plan work and insider trading.*" A significant addition to the team is of counsel Mark Iwry, who was benefits tax counsel at the US Treasury prior to joining the firm.

The Clients: CSFB; UBS; NYSE and Anthem.

Band 3

Fried, Frank, Harris, Shriver & Jacobson LLP
See firm details p.1349

The Firm: A "*service-oriented team that understands the business,*" the group won plaudits on a broad range of executive compensation, employee benefits and ERISA advice. It is especially rated for its hedge fund ERISA work, reflecting a trend in pension funds looking to alternative investment vehicles. The group tackles issues relating to traditional M&A, a flourishing area for the firm overall. For example, it is advising on executive compensation, employment and benefit arrangement issues in WPP's acquisition of Grey Global. The deal is strategically important because it gives WPP access to a raft of high-profile advertisers in the Grey group such as Procter & Gamble, 3M, Adobe, JPMorgan Chase, Mars and Warner Bros. Elsewhere the firm has also experienced a dynamic year in

the private equity arena.

The Lawyers: A "*trustworthy*" adviser with "*fair instincts and good judgment,*" **Donald Carleen** (see p.1270) is skilled in asset management. Chairman of the executive compensation and employee benefits department, he also represents clients in connection with extensive equity compensation plans. **Laraine Rothenberg** (see p.1315) heads the employee benefits and plans, executive compensation and exempt organizations group. A tax lawyer by training, she regularly advises on 'change in control' payments made to corporate executives.

The Clients: BellSouth; Wendy's; Goldman Sachs; WPP and Permira.

Paul, Weiss, Rifkind, Wharton & Garrison LLP
See firm details p.1362

The Firm: This well-rounded practice encompasses a host of ERISA, executive compensation and employee benefit matters. It debuts in *Chambers'* rankings following strong recommendations from market sources, highlighting the group's savvy business sense and technical ability. The team is experienced in the design and implementation of equity-based compensation, deferred compensation and retirement plans among other products. It regularly assists the firm's funds group in connection with ERISA requirements and exemptions.

The Lawyers: Recognized for his "*breadth of knowledge, amazing business sense and high ethics,*" **Michael Segal** (see p.1319) co-heads the practice. He is experienced in the design of stock-based plans and is an authority on ERISA investment products. Considered by experts to have a "*brilliant mind,*" **Robert Fleder** (see p.1279) often acts on ERISA fiduciary claims as well as providing M&A support to an array of clients.

The Clients: Clients include Clarion Capital Partners, Ralph Lauren Polo and Malaysia International Shipping Corporation.

Proskauer Rose LLP
See firm details p.1365

The Firm: The ECEB team operates in conjunction with the firm's leading tax and labor groups. In a notable development, the firm has opened a New Orleans office specializing in ERISA litigation, arbitration and mediation under the command of seasoned attorney Howard Shapiro. It also fields attorneys experienced in troubled plans under government investigation for major fraud, a practice area headed by New York partner Rory Albert. Other expertise lies in employee benefits advice to tax-exempt organizations such as hospitals, universities and museums. The team also handles pension plan investments, for example, representing Verizon Retirement Plan in more than $1 billion worth of alternative investments.

The Lawyers: Renowned as a "*tough negotia-*

tor" **Michael Sirkin** (see p.1322) earns peer respect for his traditional executive compensation, employee benefits and pension practice. He frequently represents management teams in IPOs and M&A. In addition, he is considered an authority in the nonprofit arena.

The Clients: Alliance Capital Management; Amerada Hess; American Standard; Bear Stearns; Foot Locker; Mount Sinai Medical Center; Smith Barney Division of Citigroup and The Metropolitan Museum of Art.

Skadden, Arps, Slate, Meagher & Flom LLP & Affiliates
See firm details p.1372

The Firm: The team won client acclaim for its exceptional ability to grasp the economic ramifications of the law, often committing a significant amount of resources to *"understanding the business."* Market sources also highlighted the group's professionalism and high quality of work. Paramount to its clients is the firm's expertise on compliance with Sarbanes-Oxley and other corporate governance issues. Inevitably, its undisputed dominance in the M&A arena culminates in key transactional-related activity as related to employee benefits and executive compensation.

The Lawyers: A top choice for cutting-edge transactional work, **Stuart Alperin** (see p.1262) has handled numerous ESOP-related projects for an array of Fortune 500 companies. Another force at the firm is **Neil Leff** (see p.1296), whose practice involves M&A, public offerings and various corporate restructurings. He has helped structure ESOPs and executive compensation techniques such as golden parachutes.

The Clients: Clients include Dana Corporation, Boise Cascade and Stanley Works.

White & Case LLP
See firm details p.1379

The Firm: The ECEB group has an impressive footprint with more than 90 lawyers practicing in 23 offices worldwide. In New York the team won recommendations from clients for its excellent delivery of advice concerning such issues as welfare benefit plan design and 401(k) products, often advising fiduciary committees. In addition, it also helps clients navigate through the difficulties of litigation involving such matters. The firm also represents top-level executives and companies in compensation negotiations, including golden parachute arrangements.

The Lawyers: **Kenneth Raskin** (see p.1311) – head of the firm's worldwide ECEB group – draws strength from his expertise on such matters as tax-qualified plans, welfare benefit structures and non-qualified products of deferred compensation. These may include top-hat and ERISA-excess plans. Additional work includes a project to introduce Western-style employee benefits to China.

The Clients: Alchemy Partners; ASCAP; The Blackstone Group; Doughty Hanson & Co; John and Mary R. Markle Foundation; Mohawk Paper; Starwood Capital Group; Stolt-Nielsen and UBS.

Other Notable Practitioners
Richard Gilbert (see p.1282) of Orrick, Herrington & Sutcliffe LLP *"will never let you get in trouble,"* one prominent client said. His sure grasp of municipal plans is a particular drawing card for clients, as is his *"sharp"* mind. On behalf of some of the country's top financial services, he has advised on various aspects of investment transactions, including 401(k) plan management. At Cadwalader, Wickersham & Taft LLP, **Broni Grala** (see p.1284) won client respect for his legal agility in *"getting you where you want to be without risk."* An adviser who will *"go the extra mile,"* his emphasis on ERISA attracts a loyal following among clients, one of whom said: *"He knows what the regulators are thinking and what direction they're heading in."* In addition, **Frederick Kneip** of Milbank, Tweed, Hadley & McCloy combines *"exceptionally good professional judgment"* with experience in the ERISA aspects of structured finance transactions. Similarly, **Andrew Oringer** (see p.1306) of Clifford Chance US LLP gained market confidence for his participation in major transactions *"in which the ERISA structure is important."* This *"smart and thoughtful ERISA lawyer"* supports a raft of important players in the investment funds market.

EMPLOYMENT

New York
Leading firms
(Employment: Mainly Defendant)

1	**PROSKAUER ROSE LLP** *New York*
2	**MORGAN, LEWIS & BOCKIUS LLP** *New York*
3	**BOND, SCHOENECK & KING, LLP** *New York*
	KAYE SCHOLER LLP *New York*
	O'MELVENY & MYERS LLP *New York*
	ORRICK, HERRINGTON & SUTCLIFFE *New York*
	SULLIVAN & CROMWELL LLP *New York*
4	**EPSTEIN BECKER & GREEN PC** *New York*
	JACKSON LEWIS *New York*
	NIXON PEABODY LLP *New York*
	PAUL, HASTINGS, JANOFSKY *New York*
	WEIL, GOTSHAL & MANGES LLP *New York*

Firms are listed alphabetically in each band.

Band 1

Proskauer Rose LLP
See firm details p.1365

The Firm: Safeguarding its position as the *"big daddy in town,"* it scores highly for its broad-based practice, quality clients and considerable market share. The firm houses the largest group of dedicated labor and employment attorneys in New York and as a long-established outfit, boasts a stellar track record. Interviewees were quick to praise its ranks of exceptional lawyers not simply for their legal application, but also for *"understanding the practical needs of the client."* As well as tackling the full gamut of employment counseling and disputes, the firm has a healthy traditional labor practice, handling high-profile bargaining negotiations with trade unions.

The Lawyers: Clients value the *"first-rate"* **Allen Fagin** (see p.1278) for his *"practical advice – designed to meet the needs of the business."* An experienced litigator he serves as nationwide coordinating counsel for all the firm's employment litigation. In the past year he acted on numerous whistle-blowing cases brought under Sarbanes-Oxley, major wage and hour class actions and nationwide gender discrimination suits. Similarly *"outstanding"* for her *"practical, thoughtful and responsive"* approach, **Betsy Plevan** (see p.1309) typically acts on key discrimination cases for high-profile clients concerning age, national origin and sex. In the employee benefits arena, she handles major class actions and recently acted for the American Federation of Television and Radio Artists (AFTRA) in the settlement of its ten-year-old case. Both Fagin and Plevan represent a deep pool of financial services clients. *"Street-smart and savvy"* **Howard Ganz** (see p.1282) cochairs the department and counsels an impressive rostrum of illustrious sports clients, including the NBA, the WNBA and MLB. Commentators praise his *"sound judgment"* and *"brilliant advocacy skills,"* noting that he brings years of experience in collective bargaining and employment litigation to the table. *"Results-focused"* **Paul Salvatore** (see p.1316) is highly regarded by clients as a *"problem solver who is passionate about his cases."* Recent work includes successfully resolving collective bargaining negotiations on behalf of the Realty Advisory Board on Labor Relations, concerning a health plan covering 40,000 employees in the real estate industry. **Bernard Plum** (see p.1309) is also active in bargaining negotiations for numerous high-profile clients including the New York Times, Dow Jones and the League of

New York

Leading individuals

(Employment: Mainly Defendant)

[1] **CURLEY Michael** *Morgan Lewis*, New York

DELIKAT Michael *Orrick Herrington*, New York

FAGIN Allen *Proskauer Rose*, New York

PLEVAN Bettina *Proskauer Rose*, New York

ROGERS Theodore *Sullivan & Cromwell*, New York

WAKS Jay *Kaye Scholer*, New York

[2] **BERNSTEIN Michael** *Bond Schoeneck*, New York

GANZ Howard *Proskauer Rose*, New York

SALVATORE Paul *Proskauer Rose*, New York

SCHAFFRAN Andrew *Morgan Lewis*, New York

[3] **CANONI John** *Nixon Peabody*, New York

DILORENZO Louis *Bond Schoeneck*, New York

FASMAN Zachary *Paul Hastings*, New York

FRIEDMAN Gary *Mayer Brown*, New York

GREEN Ronald *Epstein Becker*, New York

KLEIN Jeffrey *Weil Gotshal*, New York

KOHN Jeffrey *O'Melveny & Myers*, New York

O'NEIL Terry *Bond Schoeneck*, New York

PLUM Bernard *Proskauer Rose*, New York

REYNOLDS Christopher *Morgan Lewis*, New York

STARR Michael *Hogan & Hartson*, New York

TURNBULL Kenneth *Morgan Lewis*, New York

Individuals are listed alphabetically in each band.

American Theatres and Producers. "*Adept at reading the other side,*" clients say, he is "*creative in fashioning solutions.*"

The Clients: MetLife; Bear Stearns; Coca-Cola Enterprises; AIG; Goldman Sachs; Bristol-Myers Squibb; Citigroup and Ernst & Young.

Band 2

Morgan, Lewis & Bockius LLP

See firm details p.1556

The Firm: Fielding a "*pragmatic and solutions-oriented team,*" the firm is perceived to have "*tremendous breadth and depth*" in employment and labor law matters. It has elevated its profile in the financial services industry, advising high-caliber clients such as Morgan Stanley on its $54 million settlement of a sex discrimination lawsuit filed by the EEOC. The entertainment industry is another sector in which it excels. This national practice warrants attention for its expertise in handling overtime and wage and hour class actions. The department also runs initiatives such as Morgan Lewis Resources, which places emphasis on training employers. **The Lawyers:** "*Phenomenally responsive,*" **Michael Curley** (see p.1274) is a favorite with interviewees who say: "*He makes you feel as though you are the only client – he is perfectly in synch with our goals and objectives.*" The successful dismissal of a long-running, whistle-blowing case for Knight Trading Group in 2004 is a recent highlight for the head of department. "*Hands-on*" **Andrew Schaffran** (see p.1317) continues to represent Morgan Stanley in nego-

tiating settlements with high-profile class members of a major sex discrimination suit bought by the EEOC. Clients appreciate the "*quick thinking*" and "*deep experience*" he brings to his cases. Praised as an excellent litigator and negotiator, **Christopher Reynolds** (see p.1312) is regarded by sources as "*a great trial lawyer who is good in front of a jury.*" As well as litigating on behalf of clients, his practice focuses on implementing prevention strategies. Fortifying its position in the financial services industry, the firm recently recruited **Ken Turnbull** (see p.1328) from O'Melveny & Myers. Clients describe him as "*professional and responsive.*" As a result of his move Turnbull is reunited with his former colleague Michael Curley.

The Clients: Merrill Lynch; NBC; Home Depot; American Airlines; Cablevision; Colgate-Palmolive; Career Education Corporation; JPMorgan Chase; UBS Financial Services and H&R Block.

Band 3

Bond, Schoeneck & King, LLP

The Firm: This "*top-notch*" firm upped its game last year by opening a New York City office and boosting its numbers with experienced employment lawyers from the defunct Benetar Bernstein Schair & Stein and Rain & Pogrebin. The firm's extensive statewide network means the practice can draw on resources in Florida and Kansas as required. Its lawyers are well practiced in both traditional labor and employment law. Recent work includes advising a large manufacturing client relocating a portion of its business to Asia, a matter that included proceedings before the NLRB. On the employment side, the team is active in both litigation and counseling. Sources speak of the "*outstanding quality*" of the firm, which is particularly active in the education sector.

The Lawyers: "*One of the most ethical and hard working,*" sources say of **Michael Bernstein** (see p.1266), "*the dean of the labor and employment practice in New York.*" Traditional labor lawyer **Terry O'Neil** (see p.1306) is a "*terrific guy*" who joined from the Rain & Pogrebin firm. Completing a "*perfect trio*" in the eyes of some commentators, **Lou DiLorenzo** (see p.1275) is said to "*cement and integrate the practice.*" He is charged with establishing the New York outfit.

The Clients: Bechtel Construction Company; Otis Elevator; United Technologies; Sikorsky (Helicopter Company); Syracuse University; Pace University; Clarkson University and Hamilton College.

Kaye Scholer LLP

See firm details p.1354

The Firm: Traditionally thought of as a "*powerhouse*" in employment litigation, the firm has seen a rise in traditional labor work and counseling. It serves a raft of foreign clients with

interests in the USA, advising on union organization and compliance matters. It maintains a reputation for "*high-quality*" work.

The Lawyers: Chair of employment and labor law **Jay Waks** (see p.1330) is a highly regarded name about town. He was retained on a major collective action, involving overtime issues under the FLSA and an age discrimination claim. The case is in private arbitration – Waks also chairs the firm's alternative dispute resolution group.

The Clients: Celestica; Ameriquest Mortgage Company; Bear Stearns; RIM; JP Morgan; Anheuser-Busch; Metallgesellschaft; Miramax and Sidney Frank Importing Co.

O'Melveny & Myers LLP

See firm details p.294

The Firm: Interviewees consider this the most respected practice for airline labor work, where its remit includes collective bargaining and pension plan issues. Clients endorse the labor and employment team as "*highly responsive and professional*" whilst peers point to its active presence in the market. Other labor matters include advising on a nationwide corporate campaign for a large US employer concerning union representation. This "*high-quality outfit*" also wins national recognition for its capabilities in employment litigation, and has acted in notable wage and hour class actions.

The Lawyers: With Ken Turnbull's departure to Morgan Lewis, the department's leadership is left in the hands of **Jeff Kohn**. "*Highly regarded as a thoughtful, knowledgeable and responsive*" adviser, he is experienced in handling NLRB matters as well as discrimination disputes.

The Clients: ATLAS; UBS; Bear Stearns; CIBC; Deutsche Bank; Ford; Sony; Sotheby's; Univision and US Airways.

Orrick, Herrington & Sutcliffe

See firm details p.295

The Firm: The employment unit attracts "*serious clients*" especially within the financial services sector. Sources highlight the group's expertise in whistle-blowing cases, noting it "*gets the job done efficiently and intelligently, without creating fanfare and panic.*" Besides an active presence in New York the employment department has a national reputation, with a particularly firm foothold in California. It is also developing an international reach, with capabilities in Tokyo, Paris and Rome.

The Lawyers: Chair of the employment law group, **Michael Delikat** (see p.1275) is a "*phenomenal lawyer*" highly respected for his wealth of experience in whistle-blowing matters. He is currently acting in Livingston v Wyeth Pharmaceuticals, a case set to influence the boundaries of Sarbanes-Oxley.

The Clients: Citigroup; JPMorgan Chase; CSFB; UBS; Morgan Stanley; Lehman Brothers; Bear Stearns; Wachovia and Merrill Lynch.

1200   All quotes in the text are from interviews with clients and competitors.

CHAMBERS USA 2005

Sullivan & Cromwell LLP

See firm details p.1373

The Firm: Headed by two partners, this compact team serves an enviable client base, especially in financial services and securities sectors. Clients emphasize that the group is "*highly responsive to business needs*" and takes a thorough approach – "*they always do their homework.*" It has seen a rise in whistle-blowing claims under Sarbanes-Oxley and handled numerous discrimination suits in the past year, including stress and mental disability claims. An increase in challenges to corporate compensation plans further defined the workload.

The Lawyers: The "*exemplary*" **Ted Rogers** (see p.1313) is a popular figure with clients and peers alike. An accomplished player familiar with high-stakes litigation, he displays "*extremely good judgment*" whether in court or the boardroom. The "*outstanding*" head of employment is also renowned for his mediation practice.

The Clients: Barclays; Microsoft; Nomura and UBS Warburg.

Band 4

Epstein Becker & Green PC

The Firm: Fielding among the largest labor and employment teams worldwide, the firm has a broad-based practice targeting the mass market. It has focused its energies on the employment and benefits sphere, handling a variety of issues including major litigation. Cost effectiveness was repeatedly listed as the operation's most attractive attribute.

The Lawyers: The firm owes much of its reputation in New York to **Ronald Green**, who heads the practice. A bright and forceful lawyer he is reportedly "*great at wooing clients.*"

The Clients: Aetna, Morgan Stanley and Pfizer are among the clients.

Jackson Lewis

The Firm: This boutique firm is experienced in all aspects of workplace law, including discrimination, immigration, OSHA and union avoidance. With 20 offices in North America, the firm has a strong national presence and produces a high turnover of work at competitive rates.

Clients point to the depth of resources on offer and note that the firm boasts some excellent lawyers nationwide.

The Lawyers: William Krupman is an experienced lawyer in the New York office, whilst Bruce Schwartz was singled out in White Plains.

The Clients: Clients include Concurrent Versions System, Sears Roebuck and Target.

Nixon Peabody LLP

See firm details p.1361

The Firm: A "*practical and responsive*" firm, this outfit is known primarily for its solid upstate practice. It is building up the New York City office, recently adding Philip Berkowitz from Seyfarth Shaw to handle cross-border matters. The group has a national reach and is split into specialist teams designed to tackle hot areas including class actions, ERISA, OSHA and wage and hour issues. As well as acting frequently on union-organizing drives, the firm tackles significant class actions for clients such as Xerox.

The Lawyers: "*One of the intellectual elite at the Bar,*" practice head **John Canoni** (see p.1270) was singled out for his integrity. Regarded as an "*incredibly smart*" generalist who can turn his hand to anything, he is particularly experienced in traditional labor law.

The Clients: Xerox; Kodak; John Hancock; Tiffany & Co and Corning.

Paul, Hastings, Janofsky & Walker LLP

See firm details p.297

The Firm: Commentators paid tribute to this "*outstanding practice,*" describing it as "*one of the finest in the USA.*" Though the nucleus of the practice is on the West Coast, the New York team is viewed as "*diverse even within the context of always operating at the high end,*" handling a range of counseling, litigation and traditional labor work. The firm has a reputation for handling major class actions and the New York team is working on topical cases concerning working-time regulations.

The Lawyers: "*First-rate*" traditional labor lawyer, **Zachary Fasman** (see p.1278) is a "*responsive and thoughtful practitioner.*" Recent work includes advising a major trade group on

its national and international negotiations with an influential union. He also has a race and national origin discrimination case pending in the federal court.

The Clients: The team acts for a broad range of clients, especially in the media, hospitality, financial institutions and transport sectors.

Weil, Gotshal & Manges LLP

See firm details p.1378

The Firm: Viewed by market commentators as something of a "*boutique firm*" in terms of employment law, its three-partner team wins glowing reports from clients who describe it as "*nothing less than spectacular.*" The group supports significant standalone clients, such as UnitedHealth Group and MasterCard on big-ticket litigation, arbitration and high-level counseling work. Major cases include Rowe Entertainment v William Morris Agency, concerning race discrimination and antitrust issues. Clients can capitalize on the firm's national network. The team provided ongoing advice to Reader's Digest in several states on team-poaching attempts by competitors.

The Lawyers: "*Extremely smart and incredibly responsive,*" clients see **Jeff Klein** (see p.1293) as "*an incredible advocate who doesn't miss a beat.*" He heads the employment litigation and employee benefits units and has led on some significant ERISA class actions.

The Clients: Clients include Avon Products, Brooks Brothers and Creative Artist Agency.

Other Notable Practitioners

The leading light of Mayer, Brown, Rowe & Maw LLP's employment practice, **Gary Friedman** (see p.1281) is increasingly recognized as a leader in the field. His experience extends to weighty class actions concerning overtime and wage and hour issues. A "*personable and hard-working*" lawyer, clients say, he empathizes with their needs. His "*consistently firm but reasonable stance*" when dealing with opposing counsel also won Friedman commendation. "*Knowledgeable and creative,*" **Michael Starr** (see p.1323) of Hogan & Hartson LLP is a confident advocate equally comfortable in both litigation and arbitration contexts.

ENERGY

Band 1

LeBoeuf, Lamb, Greene & MacRae, LLP

See firm details p.1358

The Firm: The regulatory and transactional capabilities of this firm are closely intertwined, creating an all-round energy practice that is steeped in experience and industry expertise.

Clients agree that the firm is "*really plugged in and working on a myriad of deals within the energy sector; that means they can offer an insightful overview of what's going on in the industry.*" The New York office offers a strong Public Utility Holding Company Act and state regulatory service and clients go to the firm for "*experienced and seasoned regulatory lawyers to see us through the whole process.*" This expertise was harnessed

by Enron to help see it through the regulatory aspects of its bankruptcy proceedings, including the sale of Portland General. The team has also worked on several high-profile mergers and asset acquisitions this year. It represented Energy East in the sale of its Ginna nuclear plant for $900 million, the highest price paid for a nuclear plant in US history at the time. A further highlight was acting for the Macquarie Group as

New York
Leading firms (Energy: Transactional)

1 LEBOEUF, LAMB, GREENE & MACRAE *New York*
SKADDEN, ARPS, SLATE, MEAGHER *New York*

2 JONES DAY *New York*
PILLSBURY WINTHROP LLP *New York*
SIMPSON THACHER & BARTLETT LLP *New York*
SULLIVAN & CROMWELL LLP *New York*

3 CRAVATH, SWAINE & MOORE LLP *New York*
DEBEVOISE & PLIMPTON LLP *New York*
DEWEY BALLANTINE LLP *New York*
MILBANK, TWEED, HADLEY & MCCLOY *New York*
THELEN REID & PRIEST LLP *New York*
VINSON & ELKINS LLP *New York*

4 CHADBOURNE & PARKE LLP *New York*
DAVIS POLK & WARDWELL *New York*
KING & SPALDING LLP *New York*
LATHAM & WATKINS LLP *New York*
WACHTELL, LIPTON, ROSEN & KATZ *New York*

Leading firms (Energy: Regulatory)

1 LEBOEUF, LAMB, GREENE & MACRAE *New York*
THELEN REID & PRIEST LLP *New York*

2 PILLSBURY WINTHROP LLP *New York*

Leading individuals
(Energy: Transactional)

1 ADLER Sheldon *Skadden Arps*, New York
DUNN M Douglas *Milbank Tweed*, New York
FALCK David *Pillsbury Winthrop*, New York
LAMB William *LeBoeuf Lamb*, New York

2 BARANCIK Tia *King & Spalding*, New York
DAVIS Steven *LeBoeuf Lamb*, New York
ELLIS Emmett *Dewey Ballantine*, New York
FRUMKIN Joseph *Sullivan & Cromwell*, New York
HENZE II William *Jones Day*, New York
REGER Robert *Thelen Reid*, New York

3 CUSICK Michael *Jones Day*, New York
ROSENWASSER Michael *Vinson & Elkins*, New York
TERRELL Anthony *Dewey Ballantine*, New York

Leading individuals (Energy: Regulatory)

1 BAKER William *Thelen Reid*, New York
LAMB William *LeBoeuf Lamb*, New York

2 FALCK David *Pillsbury Winthrop*, New York
TONERY Lisa *King & Spalding*, New York

Firms and individuals are listed alphabetically in each band.

underwriter in AltaLink's C$850 million purchase of the TransAlta Utilities Corporation in Canada.

The Lawyers: Bill Lamb (see p.1295) is a well-known energy M&A lawyer and Public Utility Holding Company Act expert. Clients appreciate his "*experience and insight into the industry.*" He is "*even keeled and amenable – he does not get aggressive to the point where it's creating unnecessary issues.*" **Steven Davis** (see p.1275) is another "*key name*" in energy M&A. Sources observe that he is "*a professional and gentlemanly lawyer.*" He is currently chairman of the firm and about

half his time is taken up with management duties.

The Clients: Energy East; United American Energy; EDF; Hellman & Friedman; JPMorgan; UBS; Merrill Lynch; Macquarie Group; Aquila; AGL Resources; Constellation; Central Vermont; Consolidated Edison; Amera; Enron; IDACORP; PPL; Western Resources; Eon and CSFB.

Skadden, Arps, Slate, Meagher & Flom LLP & Affiliates
See firm details p.1372

The Firm: This large "*nameplate*" firm has focused on the energy sector for years, and has used its huge resources to become one of the "*undoubted energy leaders.*" The New York office represents utilities in a range of transactional work, including restructurings, mergers and sales and the purchase of energy assets. Its corporate attorneys are backed up by the DC regulatory practice, which has one of the strongest FERC teams in the country. The highlight deal this year was representing Teco Energy, a utility based in Tampa, Florida, on the transfer of two large power plants to certain banks as part of a financial restructuring to consolidate the holding company. Market observers agree it deserves its place at "*the top of the tree.*"

The Lawyers: Sheldon Adler (see p.1261) is "*a top-tier lawyer*" in the world of utility M&A. Clients admire his "*problem-solving skills*" and his "*effectively aggressive*" approach to the negotiating table. According to some sources, his "*name recognition opens doors within the industry.*"

The Clients: Clients include Teco Energy, Northeast Utilities and CMS Energy.

Band 2

Jones Day
See firm details p.485

The Firm: Jones Day climbs up the *Chambers'* ranks following a successful year in what has been a slow market. Its transactional capabilities stretch to every corner of the energy industry, including the power sector, oil pipelines, and even the coal industry. Clients enthuse that the firm can boast "*a wide range of energy experts who can handle every aspect of a deal.*" The New York lawyers work on M&A, restructuring, financing and also field FERC expertise. This year, the team has been representing American Electric Power in the largest single generating asset divestiture in the energy sector – the $1 billion disposition of AEP Texas Central. The firm also advised both FirstEnergy and Aquila in the purchase and subsequent sale of GPU subsidiary Midlands Energy. Clients rave about their "*very positive experiences*" with the practice.

The Lawyers: Fritz Henze (see p.1287) is recommended as a highly experienced lawyer for complex energy transactions. He is "*a strong negotiator, has great attention to detail, and has*

the ability to cut right down to the pertinent issues." Clients also report that he has "*an incisive perspective on what's going on in the sector and is at the forefront of the industry.*" **Michael Cusick** (see p.1274) is named as "*clearly one of the best*" for large electric utility mergers and work of an international flavor.

The Clients: Entergy; American Electric Power; JPMorgan Partners; WL Ross & Company; International Coal Group; Williams; CenterPoint; SCANA; OG&E Energy; FirstEnergy; Aquila; Burlington Resources; Entergy-Koch and BP.

Pillsbury Winthrop LLP
See firm details p.1364

The Firm: Clients firmly believe that Pillsbury Winthrop is "*one of the premier firms for power work*" and point to its experience of capital markets financings. Clients enjoy working with the Pillsbury lawyers, praising them for their "*very solutions-oriented approach when problems emerge.*" The group has worked on a number of private placements this year, and represented the placement agents in the financing for the Ravenswood gas-fired power plant in Queens, New York. While advice to underwriters in stock and bond transactions lies at the core of this practice, the team also works for the energy companies and has a flourishing M&A practice. For example, it is currently acting for PNM Resources in its acquisition of TNP Enterprises. This is one of the largest deals in the energy sector at the moment, and involves a mixed payment of stock and cash and the assumption of $835 million of debt. The firm also has a well-established reputation for Public Utility Holding Company Act regulatory advice. At time of press the firm announced its merger with Shaw Pittman LLP to form Pillsbury Winthrop LLP.

The Lawyers: David Falck (see p.1278) is a real energy generalist and has a strong reputation for M&A, capital markets and Public Utility Holding Company Act expertise. He is "*a truly outstanding lawyer in the power sector*" and possesses "*a tremendous sense of what needs to be overcome in the regulatory world.*"

The Clients: PNM Resources; Morgan Stanley; RBS Securities; Lehman Brothers; Tenaska Virginia Partners; Citigroup Global Markets and Scotia Capital (USA).

Simpson Thacher & Bartlett LLP
See firm details p.1370

The Firm: Simpson Thacher is highly renowned for its first-rate capital markets and M&A practices. It uses its vast expertise and resources to good effect in the energy sector. A generalist background ensures it has its finger on the pulse for developments in these areas, but the firm also has specialists in the energy sector, who can add the specific industry knowledge to any transaction. Observers constantly commented on the firm's "*effective representation of its clients.*" It advises a

1202   All quotes in the text are from interviews with clients and competitors.

CHAMBERS USA 2005

number of private equity groups and hedge funds that are investing in the sector and has worked on some massive deals recently. For instance, it worked on behalf of KKR, Blackstone and Texas Pacific Group in the $3.65 billion acquisition of the Texas Genco assets. It also advised KKR and JPMorgan in the $3 billion acquisition of Unisource. It occasionally works for the energy companies too. Recently it represented British Energy in the sale of its 50% interest in AmerGen. **The Clients:** KKR; Blackstone; Texas Pacific Group; JP Morgan; British Energy; Duke Energy; KeySpan; PPL and GE.

Sullivan & Cromwell LLP
See firm details p.1373
The Firm: Peers highly recommended Sullivan & Cromwell for its deep knowledge of utilities and public M&A arising out of the energy sector. As a gold-standard corporate practice, it has a leading market share in public company transactions and can bring to the deal table its broader market experience. The firm is widely respected as BP's go-to firm for major acquisitions. Among the group's recent highlights are advice to a hedge fund consortium bidding for the Texas Genco portfolio of generating assets, and representation of Allegheny Energy in the sale of its gas distribution business, Mountaineer Gas. On the capital markets side, the firm has advised Constellation Energy.
The Lawyers: Although **Joseph Frumkin** (see p.1281) is not a dedicated energy specialist, everyone agrees, "*He's smart enough to know the energy issues and does these transactions really well.*"
The Clients: Allegheny Energy; TXU; BP; Constellation Energy; Sempra and Eon.

Band 3

Cravath, Swaine & Moore LLP
See firm details p.1344
The Firm: While the firm may not house a specialist energy group, it continues to impress with its high caliber advice on energy M&A. This is because the generalist M&A lawyers have a number of prominent energy clients, ensuring a place on major deals for oil and gas companies and utilities. The firm's prime clients have been quiet of late, but it recently represented Patina Oil & Gas in its acquisition by Noble Energy for $3 billion. It is also advising Ashland in the $3 billion corporate restructuring of its refinery business. On the utilities side, it is currently acting for Florida Power & Light and WPS Resources in a number of M&A transactions.
The Lawyers: Since the departure of George Bilicic to join investment bank Merrill Lynch, the firm does not have a dedicated energy specialist. However, a team of M&A lawyers, led by respected Richard Hall, successfully advises on matters in the energy sector.

The Clients: Royal Dutch/Shell; Ashland; Patina Oil and Gas; ConocoPhillips; EnCana; Arko; Florida Power & Light; WPS Resources; RWE AG; Crown Castle International; American Securities Capital Partners and SSSB.

Debevoise & Plimpton LLP
See firm details p.1346
The Firm: Market observers say that the firm has "*good energy experience across the board.*" True to form, the firm's bankruptcy, litigation and project finance groups are all currently undertaking high-profile work in the sector. For example, the firm is representing the lenders to the 600MW Bear Swamp hydroelectric project in litigation against its parent company as part of PG&E's bankruptcy proceedings. It is also advising Sithe Energy on the sale of its international assets to Marubeni. In another high-profile appointment, it is acting for Royal Dutch/Shell in investigations by the Securities and Exchange Commission and the federal prosecutor on alleged misreporting of reserves.
The Lawyers: The team has a wide range of expertise, covering M&A, capital markets, litigation and bankruptcy.
The Clients: Drax; Kelso & Company; Oscar Wyatt consortium NuCoastal; Sithe Energy; Cogentrix; Clayton Dubilier & Rice; Royal Dutch/Shell and Mitsui & Co.

Dewey Ballantine LLP
See firm details p.1347
The Firm: This capital markets-focused group has cultivated a successful practice acting as designated underwriter for utilities. It has been working on various prominent deals. Over the past year, attorneys have acted as counsel to GE in the issue of $3.8 billion in common stock. This is a high-profile transaction because it is the first issuance of common equity by the company in 40 years and one of the largest follow-on equity offerings of all time.
The Lawyers: **Bud Ellis** (see p.1277) is the designated underwriter practice's most visible face and, according to clients, is a "*tremendously seasoned pro.*" A recent recruit from Thelen Reid & Priest, **Anthony Terrell** (see p.1327) is also rated as a leading player in the sector.
The Clients: Southern California Edison; American Electric Power; TXU; CenterPoint Energy; Consolidated Edison; Banc of America Securities LLC; Barclays Capital; Citigroup Global Markets; Goldman Sachs; Unisource; DQE and GE.

Milbank, Tweed, Hadley & McCloy
The Firm: The firm has developed a global power and energy group, which draws on energy specialists from project finance, capital markets, and the general corporate group. It has a very strong reputation in the sector for representing the sources of capital. Clients cite a number of reasons for using the firm, including "*its energy*

expertise, the strength and depth of the team, its commercial acumen and the reputation of a Wall Street brand.*" No wonder then that it has been appointed to act for the creditors' committee in the Enron bankruptcy, one of the highest profile deals in the energy sector. It has also been doing considerable work for private equity groups as they continue to enter the energy market. A highlight here was advising the purchase group in the $2.8 billion acquisition of Unisource.
The Lawyers: **Douglas Dunn** (see p.1276) is an energy specialist based in the corporate group. Clients agree that he is "*proactive, energetic, innovative and creative*" and possesses deep knowledge of the regulatory issues.
The Clients: Arcadia Realty Trust and RiverStone Group; KKR; Trimaran Capital Partners; JPMorgan Partners; Wachovia Capital and the Enron creditors' committee.

Thelen Reid & Priest LLP
See firm details p.300
The Firm: Named by many observers as the "*classic energy firm in New York,*" Thelen Reid has represented utilities since the earliest days of the market. Such experience means that the firm is renowned for "*really knowing its stuff.*" Its deep Public Utility Holding Company Act expertise is clearly evident, but its transactional capability has also come to the fore of late through the firm's involvement in high-profile deals. This year, the team has advised Unisource in its $2.8 billion acquisition by a private venture capital group. This is a controversial pathfinder project and the firm has been kept busy convincing the regulatory bodies that venture capital groups should be allowed to own public companies.
The Lawyers: Sources identified **Robert Reger** as a leading light for his representation of utilities in corporate matters. **William Baker** is revered as "*the dean of the Public Utility Holding Company Act bar.*"
The Clients: Entergy; NiSource; Ameren; Unisource and TKR.

Vinson & Elkins LLP
See firm details p.1724
The Firm: It may not be as visible as the Texas headquarters, but the group of 30 lawyers in the New York office has completed deals worth $5.5 billion in the energy sector over the past year. These have included M&A, capital markets and project finance work. As part of a firm that has "*probably the greatest depth of expertise in energy in the USA,*" the New York office is "*at the cutting edge of developments in the energy field.*" It also has a unique angle among New York firms in that it specializes in oil and gas work. It has developed a particular niche because of its expertise in general partnership work. Recently the firm represented Carlyle/Riverstone in a $1 billion acquisition of a general partnership interest in Williams Energy Partners, thereby

creating a new entity called Magellan. Capital markets work has also dominated, and the firm has worked on a number of IPOs this year.

The Lawyers: Michael Rosenwasser heads the general partnership practice. Sources say he does "*top-notch*" work in this niche area.

The Clients: Buckeye Partners; Goldman Sachs; Citigroup; CSFB; AG Edwards; Pacific Energy Partners; Forest Oil; Penn Virginia Resource Partners and US Shipping.

Band 4

Chadbourne & Parke LLP

See firm details p.1341

The Firm: The firm's reputation in the energy sector in a large part rests on its impressive project finance capability. However, the New York office has also been busy working on M&A and restructuring transactions. The market particularly endorses its work in domestic power projects. Its most prominent role recently has been representing El Paso in a series of dispositions of power plants throughout the country.

The Lawyers: The energy practice is dominated by project finance stars such as Chaim Wachsberger and Richard Sonkin.

The Clients: The firm works for both banks and energy companies. Clients include: Dexia Credit; AES Eastern Energy; EIF; El Paso; AES; CFSB; Citibank; Union Bank of California; Duke Energy and Tractebel.

Davis Polk & Wardwell

See firm details p.1345

The Firm: Davis Polk has a long-standing reputation in the oil and gas sector because of its involvement in some of the big-ticket M&A deals, such as representing Texaco in its merger with Chevron. Despite not having a specialized energy

practice, the corporate group continues to gain interesting appointments, including ones with a capital markets element. For example, it has advised KeyBanc Capital Markets as book runner in the issuance of debentures by Union Light Heat & Power. It is also acting for Cantera Resources Holdings on the sale of its natural gas midstream business to Penn Virginia Resource Partners.

The Lawyers: Many of the firm's corporate lawyers dip their toes into the energy sector, including M&A star Dennis Hersch.

The Clients: ExxonMobil; Emerson Electric; Consolidated Edison; Constellation Energy; KeyBanc Capital Markets and Cantera Resources Holdings.

King & Spalding LLP

See firm details p.635

The Firm: This firm enters the *Chambers'* tables this year in recognition of its significant presence and expanding office that, with the recent recruitment of Tia Barancik, has added an electric utilities practice to its deep oil and gas base. The group has impressive upstream capabilities, a broad M&A practice, and banking specialists who work in the energy sector. These combine to make this one of the market's most promising practices. The New York office is also home to the regulatory branch of the firm's renowned LNG practice.

The Lawyers: Tia Barancik (see p.1264) combines transactional knowledge with regulatory expertise and is a well-known name for regulated utilities work. Peers and clients comment on her "*efficient and high-quality*" work. **Lisa Tonery** (see p.1327) is a FERC practitioner and "*a major name in the LNG field.*" She has recently obtained permits for four new LNG terminals within the USA.

The Clients: Clients include CSFB, Lehman Brothers and Citigroup.

Latham & Watkins LLP

The Firm: As a top-ranking project finance firm, Latham is naturally involved in many energy transactions. Additionally, as project finance is becoming more and more intertwined with leverage financings and M&A, the firm is gaining wider expertise in the energy sector. Indeed, clients emphasize the firm's "*real energy expertise*" as much as its project finance skills. It is very active on the domestic power scene and has recently represented Goldman Sachs in the acquisition of a large portfolio of assets from ING. International oil and gas projects are a forte of the practice and it is also currently working on petrochemicals, LNG and oil field expansion projects throughout the world.

The Lawyers: The firm's project finance lawyers are all experienced in the energy sector. Stars include William Voge, Dave Gordon and Andy Singer.

The Clients: Lehman Brothers; ABN AMRO; Morgan Stanley; Société Générale; Nigerian National Petroleum and ExxonMobil.

Wachtell, Lipton, Rosen & Katz

See firm details p.1375

The Firm: Market observers recommend Wachtell, Lipton for its huge transactional capability: it can be trusted to take on high-end M&A work and offer "*brilliant corporate solutions.*" It should be noted, however, that the firm has recently lost its utility specialist Seth Kaplan.

The Lawyers: The departure of Seth Kaplan has hit the utilities practice, but sources report that M&A specialist Andrew Brownstein's forays into the energy world help to maintain the firm's presence in the sector.

The Clients: The firm represents financial institutions and energy companies.

ENERGY

UPSTATE NEW YORK

New York
Leading firms
(Energy: Upstate New York)

1	LEBOEUF, LAMB, GREENE & MACRAE *Albany*
	NIXON PEABODY LLP *Albany*
2	COUCH WHITE, LLP *Albany*
	READ AND LANIADO *Albany*

Leading individuals
(Energy: Upstate New York)

1	DAX John *Cohen Dax*, Albany
	FITZGERALD Brian *LeBoeuf Lamb*, Albany
	GANSBERG Andrew *Nixon Peabody*, Hartford
	LANIADO Sam *Read and Laniado*, Albany
	SINGER Leonard *Couch White*, Albany
	WHITE Algird *Couch White*, Albany

Firms and individuals are listed alphabetically in each band.

Band 1

LeBoeuf, Lamb, Greene & MacRae, LLP

See firm details p.1358

The Firm: As a branch of a renowned global energy practice, the Albany office has access to resources that could make local competitors weep with envy. The office specializes in state regulatory and legislative work, and has a great reputation for representing utilities at the New York Public Service Commission. It has a varied caseload, including rate cases, transmission issues, and gas production issues. The firm has a particular strength in acting for developers of wind farms, and has also devoted much of the past year to advising utilities on the development of a competitive market.

The Lawyers: Brian FitzGerald (see p.1279) has a general Public Service Commission practice, representing both energy utilities and telecom companies. Clients stress his responsiveness: "*He always calls back ASAP and produces clear advice very quickly.*" Clients comment that he is "*thorough*" but "*doesn't kill a project.*"

The Clients: Clients include Energy East subsidiaries, AES and Fortuna Energy.

Nixon Peabody LLP

See firm details p.1361

The Firm: The Albany office of this national firm has seven lawyers working in its energy and environment department. It mainly works on state regulatory issues, and is especially well known for its expertise in facilities siting. Among its highlights are advice to the Athens

1204   All quotes in the text are from interviews with clients and competitors.

CHAMBERS USA 2005

generating facility on gaining permits for the construction and operation of this gas-fired power plant in upstate New York. In another high-profile case, the team also represented TransEnergy in gaining permits for the cross-sound cable under the Long Island Sound.

The Lawyers: The "highly skilled adviser" **Andrew Gansberg** (see p.1281) has a dual role as the Albany office's managing partner and its key energy lawyer.

The Clients: The firm works for developers of generation and transmission facilities. Clients include TransEnergy, PSEG and Athens Generating Company.

Band 2

Couch White LLP

The Firm: Market observers described this firm as a highly visible force on the state energy scene because of its representation of the large power users. Peers report that it does "excellent work" for its clients. It can frequently be found on the

bigger projects going through the state regulatory agencies.

The Lawyers: Peers rate **Leonard Singer** for his representation of large Fortune 500 companies in their role as major power users. **Algird White** is also a very visible representative of the practice, who brings a wealth of experience to the negotiating table.

The Clients: Clients include large industrial consumers of electricity and natural gas, and developers of energy-related projects.

Read and Laniado

The Firm: Read and Laniado has cultivated a good name in the market for advising independent power producers, particularly through its representation of the Independent Power Producers of New York. Clients enthuse that the practice is "reputable, reliable and knowledgeable" and that the lawyers "have great technical experience and keep well abreast of current issues." The workload covers siting of transmission lines and development of wind energy projects as

well as matters regarding conventional power plants. A highlight this year was acting for the Independent Power Producers of New York at a Public Service Commission proceeding to set policies for the development of a renewable energy project, and achieving a successful outcome for its client.

The Lawyers: **Sam Laniado** is "very practical and technically strong" and also "a strategic thinker who does not always resort to pushing for litigation."

The Clients: Independent Power Producers of New York; TransGas Energy Systems; Municipal Electric Systems of New York; Calpine and Long Island Power Authority.

Other Notable Practitioners

John Dax of Cohen Dax & Koening PC came highly recommended for his track record in state energy proceedings. He is "a very fine and respected lawyer" who represents power marketers and developer companies.

ENVIRONMENT

New York

Leading firms (Environment)

1	SIVE PAGET & RIESEL PC *New York*
2	ARNOLD & PORTER LLP *New York*
	BRYAN CAVE ROBINSON LLP *New York*
	CARTER LEDYARD & MILBURN LLP *New York*
	NIXON PEABODY LLP *Albany, Rochester*
	WHITEMAN, OSTERMAN & HANNA *Albany*
3	BEVERIDGE & DIAMOND PC *New York*
	KIRKPATRICK & LOCKHART NICHOLSON *New York*
	PROSKAUER ROSE LLP *New York*
	YOUNG, SOMMER, WARD, RITZENBERG *Albany*

Leading individuals (Environment)

1	GERRARD Michael *Arnold & Porter,* New York
	RIESEL Daniel *Sive Paget,* New York
2	HEALY Kevin *Bryan Cave,* New York
	KAFIN Robert *Proskauer Rose,* New York
	PAGET David *Sive Paget,* New York
	RUZOW Daniel *Whiteman Osterman,* Albany
	SOMMER Dean *Young Sommer,* Albany
	STEVER Donald *Kirkpatrick & Lockhart,* New York
3	CHERTOK Mark *Sive Paget,* New York
	GREENTHAL John *Nixon Peabody,* Albany
	KARMEL Philip *Bryan Cave,* New York
	KASS Stephen *Carter Ledyard,* New York
	REISMAN Sharyl *Jones Day,* New York
	ROSENBERG Mark *Sullivan & Cromwell,* New York
	SACRIPANTI Peter *McDermott Will,* New York
	TURNER Scott *Nixon Peabody,* Rochester
	WARREN Charles *Bryan Cave,* New York
	YOUNG Kevin *Young Sommer,* Albany

Firms and individuals are listed alphabetically in each band.

Sive Paget & Riesel PC
See firm details p.1371

The Firm: Unbeaten experience and local knowledge allow this firm to claim the top spot in the table. Clients say it is "much more specialized" than the competition; even rivals are convinced of its status as New York's "leading environmental boutique." The city's real estate market has faced crucial environmental issues in the wake of 9/11, and the firm's in-depth knowledge in contamination and permitting makes it a favorite for development work. From impact statements and state-specific State Environmental Quality Review Act (SEQRA) issues to CWA litigation defense, the "superior" attorneys are lauded for their confidence and experience, while the name partners are awarded the accolade "fathers of environmental law in New York." For litigation, the firm is a leading player both at trial and appellate level, with increasing toxic torts work covering widespread issues including latent damage to buildings. The firm's profile has expanded to national proportions, and it is involved in several energy permitting and cleanup matters outside the state.

The Lawyers: No end of praise is heaped on **Daniel Riesel**. "Creative, forceful and dynamic," he is seen as an excellent counselor and a strong litigator who is experienced in enforcement defense, white-collar crime and civil litigation, including toxic torts, as well as rulemaking challenges. A noted writer, he "knows the ropes." Working closely with developers and city authorities, which makes him a top choice for permitting issues, **David Paget** impresses clients with his approach: "He is very good at cutting through

the morass of issues involved in these environmental matters and advising well." Paget's reputation is evidenced by a score sheet that records his involvement in a phenomenal number of high-profile developments. Clients confirm his input is often "critical" to a project's success. With his 25-plus years of experience in the Metropolitan area and upstate New York, **Mark Chertok** is viewed as "an excellent land use lawyer." Of late, he has worked on a number of brownfield redevelopments and is active in power plant projects. Chertok's talents additionally extend to litigation. All three attorneys are prominent figures, both in terms of their teaching engagements and contributions to professional bodies.

The Clients: Kraft; The Trump Organization; Empire State Development; Domino Sugar; The City of New York and World Kitchen.

Arnold & Porter LLP
See firm details p.478

The Firm: With client commentators professing to be "absolutely impressed and satisfied," Arnold & Porter's practice group continues to inspire confidence. As one source remarked: "One always has the sense of receiving value and the highest quality of work imaginable." There are numerous examples of the caliber of work on which the firm is engaged; recently, it advised the Metropolitan Museum of Art on a key development and the related environmental impact. It has also been active for GE, negotiating a long-awaited cleanup plan for the Hudson River following historic PCB contamination; and attorneys have been engaged by KeySpan Energy on a wide variety of issues

New York
Leading firms
(Environment: Mainly Transactional)

1	CRAVATH, SWAINE & MOORE LLP *New York*
	DAVIS POLK & WARDWELL *New York*
2	SIMPSON THACHER & BARTLETT LLP *New York*
	SULLIVAN & CROMWELL LLP *New York*
	WHITE & CASE LLP *New York*
3	CAHILL GORDON & REINDEL *New York*
	DEBEVOISE & PLIMPTON LLP *New York*
	PROSKAUER ROSE LLP *New York*
	SIDLEY AUSTIN BROWN & WOOD LLP *New York*

Leading individuals
(Environment: Mainly Transactional)

1	FLESHER Gail *Davis Polk*, New York
	SMITH Jeffrey *Cravath Swaine*, New York
2	BATTISTA Gregory *Cravath Swaine*, New York
	BRENNAN Matthew *Sullivan & Cromwell*, New York
	FADIL Adeeb *Simpson Thacher*, New York
	KAFIN Robert *Proskauer Rose*, New York
3	CROUGH Maureen *Sidley Austin*, New York
	HALLMAN Robert *Cahill Gordon*, New York
	HAMMER Stuart *Debevoise & Plimpton*, New York
	HORSCH Richard *White & Case*, New York
	MILMED Paul *White & Case*, New York
	PORT Gail *Proskauer Rose*, New York
	ROSENBERG Mark *Sullivan & Cromwell*, New York
	STEVER Donald *Kirkpatrick & Lockhart*, New York

Firms and individuals are listed alphabetically in each band.

from licensing to litigation. The group's versatility is beyond question.

The Lawyers: The *"heart and soul of the practice,"* **Michael Gerrard** (see p.1282) is the chair of the ABA's environmental law section. "*A giant in his field,*" Gerrard is noted for his prolific writings on environmental law, although his practical abilities are acknowledged equally as readily. *"There is no limit to the work he will take on, and no deadline he will not confront and defeat."* At times providing clear counsel, at others litigating, his style is summarized as *"modest and humble, yet direct."* The growth of his already extensive development and site remediation practice reflects changes in New York's brownfields legislation, and he is seen as an authoritative figure in this area. Gerrard continues to work on matters for Silverstein Properties in relation to the proposed Freedom Tower at Ground Zero.

The Clients: The firm's clients include Silverstein Properties, GE and Madison Square Garden.

Bryan Cave Robinson LLP

The Firm: Billed in the last edition of *Chambers* as one to watch, Bryan Cave has a regulatory and land use practice that continues to impress the market with its breadth of capability; clients report that they are *"extremely satisfied."* The group is one of the largest in the state and includes attorneys with former government roles.

Since Bryan Cave's merger with Robinson Silverman, many view the new firm as an ideal combination of the specialized knowledge of a boutique and the backup of a full-service practice. Although litigation and mediation are seen as real strengths, the group is by no means underpowered on the noncontentious side, and developments in New York brownfields law have spurred on this aspect of the practice. It is a stalwart in the clean air field for utilities clients and applauded for its Superfund and site remediation work.

The Lawyers: **Kevin Healy** shows *"clarity of thought,"* *"depth and ability"* and a demeanor that encourages loyalty from clients – his star is clearly in the ascendant. Healy's clean air expertise, which includes NSR issues, has proved important to manufacturing and utilities clients, while cleanup and Superfund matters have enabled him to show his well-rounded experience. Healy undertook pro bono work on Governor Pataki's regional Climate Change Task Force. **Philip Karmel** is well placed to handle regulatory advice and transactional work as well as litigation. CAA and toxic torts litigation are two of his strong suits; clients, including major names in energy, transport, chemicals and biotechnology, say he is *"a terrific air regulatory lawyer"* as well as a good litigator. *"Smart guy"* **Charles Warren** cochairs the firm's environmental practice group and is a former EPA regional administrator. His practice spans CAA, CWA, TOSCA and Superfund, plus transactional support. Clients describe him as *"even-keeled"* and emphasize the importance of his prior government experience.

The Clients: The firm represents many major companies in manufacturing, energy utilities and transport.

Carter Ledyard & Milburn LLP

See firm details p.1340

The Firm: This environmental practice group has developed extensively since its inception a decade ago, and has now matured into an established player in litigation, regulatory and transactional matters. The firm is most highly recommended for its land use advice, with the representation of municipalities a defining feature. It has been involved in several of the largest urban redevelopment projects in the country, including the World Trade Center redevelopment (acting for the Lower Manhattan Development Corporation), and the Hudson Yards project. These sizable projects involve several million sq ft of commercial space and go some way towards proving the firm's stature and the confidence its attorneys inspire. The firm performs reliable work in waste and contamination, as well as giving clean air and water advice. In the energy generation arena, it continues to advise the New York Power Authority and the Long Island Power Authority. The firm also engages in pro bono activities, such as assisting the Environmental Integrity Project and the

Natural Resources Defense Council in challenging the EPA's standards in clean air enforcement.

The Lawyers: **Stephen Kass** is a pivotal figure in land use matters and a particular favorite for redevelopment work, often acting for state authorities. *"Bright and highly reputed,"* clients praise Kass for his knowledge and well-honed advocacy skills, while peers agree that he is both *"dynamic"* and *"distinguished."*

The Clients: The Lower Manhattan Development Corporation; Metropolitan Transportation Authority; Environmental Integrity Project; New York Power Authority and Long Island Power Authority.

Nixon Peabody LLP

See firm details p.1361

The Firm: The Rochester and Albany offices of this firm combine to attain statewide recognition as a *"very respected"* upstate player with ample *"New York capacity."* When it comes to environmental regulatory issues and permitting, the firm's trump card is its excellent local profile. Clients looking at long-term strategies are rewarded with a firm in tune with the local legislative and administrative vista. SEQRA, hazardous waste, clean air and water are all covered within a comprehensive practice, and peers praise the firm's *"edge"* in making its clients' voices heard. Brownfields law reform provides a further opportunity for the firm to show its mettle. Clients span industries as diverse as computing, pharmaceuticals and cable television, with overseas work becoming more common.

The Lawyers: **John Greenthal** (see p.1285) is *"highly regarded"* for his *"thoughtful"* approach. With a background at the New York State Department of Environmental Conservation, he is perfectly placed to impress clients with his contacts and up-to-date working knowledge. His waste and brownfields profile is of a nationally respected standard and also includes work on Puerto Rico waste sites. *"A terrific air guy,"* according to clients, **Scott Turner** (see p.1328) is hot on enforcement defense and permitting issues, as well as transactional support. His primary focus is air pollution and solid waste, and more particularly the interface of these two areas. He acts for Covanta Energy (one of the leading waste-to-energy operators in the country) in relation to approximately 30 plants across the USA.

The Clients: Covanta Energy; Pfizer; NRG Energy; AstraZeneca; Pfaltzgraff; IBM; Honeywell; DuPont; Puerto Rico Electric Power Authority; KeySpan Energy and Eastman Kodak.

Whiteman, Osterman & Hanna

The Firm: The market respects this Albany firm for its *"scope of knowledge,"* especially in major development projects. Peers perceive it to be *"very strong in regulatory"* work and *"close to the state environmental bodies."* By nurturing a good upstate practice with a healthy lobbying capa-

1206   All quotes in the text are from interviews with clients and competitors.

CHAMBERS USA 2005

bility, the firm can boast involvement in all the top transportation-related environmental work. It has been highly visible for the New York State Thruway Authority in the Tappan Zee Bridge redevelopment project, which entails extensive reviews and permitting issues under SEQRA and NEPA. Fully aware that the best upstate firms have made inroads into the city market, peers report an increased number of sightings of Whiteman in Manhattan.

The Lawyers: A perennial feature on New York's legal landscape, **Daniel Ruzow** (see p.1315) commands respect as one of the Bar's environmental stalwarts. His role often extends beyond the purely legal to a more general business advisory role, with private sector clients appreciating his wealth of useful contacts. Peers say he is "*a star*," particularly on SEQRA matters. Ruzow has been central in assisting the New York State Thruway Authority on its Tappan Zee Bridge project. Sources also noted Scott Fein as an attorney of growing stature in environmental litigation, particularly toxic torts.

The Clients: Clients include the New York State Thruway Authority, K Hovnanian and the Benderson Development Company.

Beveridge & Diamond PC
See firm details p.480

The Firm: A growing profile ensures this boutique has a steady flow of work. Its Washington DC office has always earned extensive praise, but the New York arm has now developed to the point that it constitutes a strong standalone entity with its own East Coast following and international connections. Peers acknowledge the firm's business has been "*going well in the New York, New Jersey, Connecticut tristate area;*" they see the firm as a "*credible*" force in regulatory advice, with power and sewage treatment plant permitting a major source of work.

The Lawyers: The name the market looks out for is Stephen Gordon, who is seen as the figurehead of the practice.

Kirkpatrick & Lockhart
Nicholson Graham LLP
See firm details p.291

The Firm: The past year has been a good one for this firm, bringing as it did the arrival of Donald Stever from Dewey Ballantine. His recruitment has allowed the practice a foothold in the environmental market and the prospect of capturing an ever-greater share of it. The firm boasts a national profile for environmental law; it is a powerhouse of transactional advice and Superfund litigation (on which it can be "*aggressive*" in protecting its clients' interests). Work is frequently undertaken in conjunction with the firm's New Jersey practice.

The Lawyers: The market has sat up and taken notice of the arrival of **Donald Stever** (see p.1325). This "*scholarly*" practitioner is identified as "*one of the finest lawyers*" in the environmental

field. Regarded as a superb problem solver, he has cultivated a name for confident transactional support, and as a former chairman of the Environmental Law Institute, he is a major player in hazardous waste and contamination issues. It is apparent that several clients have followed him to his new firm: "*I have used him on many matters with great confidence,*" one client said. Among those seeking his counsel is Amerada Hess.

The Clients: The firm acts for many major corporations, including oil companies and multinational pharmaceutical manufacturers.

Proskauer Rose LLP
See firm details p.1365

The Firm: Market commentators paint a picture of a lively practice, endowed with strong management and a broad spread of work. As well as respect for its regulatory depth, the firm has also earned praise for its transactional prowess. In truth, much of its activities lie squarely in the transactional camp, with far lower levels of enforcement-related work carried out by attorneys. Brownfields and Superfund matters certainly have their place, with work covering New York and New Jersey, as well as California. Last year's highlight – working with GE on PCB issues in the Hudson – looks to have provided some notable follow-up work in solid waste management.

The Lawyers: "*Combining a strong intellect with tenacity,*" **Robert Kafin** (see p.1291) impresses clients with his environmental knowledge and the rigor and managerial skills essential to the job of chief operating partner at the firm. By all accounts he manages both legal and management roles with equal aplomb. Peers agree that he is an "*impressive and articulate thinker,*" who is capable of producing "*creative solutions.*" Kafin has witnessed a boom in transactional work over the last few years, though his talents as an all-rounder have ensured he remains active in litigation and regulatory matters. **Gail Port** (see p.1310) is primarily a transactional expert. "*Very energetic and intelligent,*" her work is good in all areas. A former general counsel to the New York State Urban Development Corporation and a former chair of the New York State Bar Association's Environmental Law Section, she is a long-standing and respected member of the New York Bar.

The Clients: The firm acts for many large corporations including GE. Non-transactional clients include those in heavy industries (foe example metals and chemicals) and real estate.

Young, Sommer, Ward, Ritzenberg, Wooley, Baker & Moore LLC

The Firm: A "*good bench*" of attorneys keeps this Albany practice high in the estimation of others, with clients reporting that it is an "*absolute pleasure*" doing business with them. *Chambers'* research indicates the firm has broken through the cordon erected by some of the

larger and better-established firms to take its place as a serious force in the market. From Superfund and site cleanup to zoning and permitting, Young Sommer is commonly brought in to handle certain specialist environmental aspects beyond the scope of other firms. Work for municipalities and on public interest issues enhances the firm's growing profile as an "*interesting*" alternative to larger firms.

The Lawyers: The first name on the lips of commentators was that of "*innovative*" **Dean Sommer** (see p.1323), who stands out for his "*completely refreshing*" approach. A noted litigator, his expertise is on show in Superfund, RCRA and CWA issues. A robust negotiator, too, clients say he "*gives straight opinions and tells us the unvarnished truth... which is the best way.*" Having spent time working at the state Attorney General's office, Sommer boasts a wealth of local contacts. **Kevin Young** is described by clients as "*extraordinarily bright.*" His regulatory compliance expertise covers many fields from solid waste through clean air to wetlands.

The Clients: GE; Union College; GasLand Petroleum; National Grid USA and Norlite.

Cravath, Swaine & Moore LLP
See firm details p.1344

The Firm: As might be expected of such a dominant corporate player, clients hail this firm as a market leader in environmental transactional support. "*Absolutely the tops,*" its approach is solidly commercial, which is exactly how clients like it. The attorneys "*see how material the issues are*" when assessing the risks and liabilities that can crucially, and substantially, affect deal value. The team acted for IBM on the $1.75 billion sale of its PC manufacturing business to Lenovo Group, China's largest PC manufacturer. It is its capacity to handle transactions of this magnitude, coupled with "*great experience and broad depth,*" which attracts clients. In a market where the capabilities of a firm's environmental team are increasingly becoming a factor in the selection of deal advisers, this practice group is inspiring trust.

The Lawyers: Speaking to market commentators, researchers became acutely aware of admiration for **Jeffrey Smith** (see p.1322) from all industry sectors. "*You are grateful to come across Jeff Smith – he is knowledgeable and excellent,*" said one commentator. "*Polished and smooth*" in negotiations and blessed with a "*forceful intellect,*" he is viewed as the ideal man to bring on board for the most important deals. **Gregory Battista** (see p.1265) is also highly sought after for large M&A. Peers admire the way he "*keeps abreast*" of developing issues.

The Clients: The group's clients have included IBM, RWE Dea and Bristol-Myers Squibb, as well many other major private equity institutions and investment banks.

Davis Polk & Wardwell

See firm details p.1345

The Firm: One of the "*main contenders in the New York transactional market*," Davis Polk has an environmental practice that is regarded as "*more cohesive and well oiled*" than the average. In addition to the prior experience of key advisers, a primary factor for most clients when choosing a transactional firm is the backup of specialist practice groups. Davis Polk comes up trumps in this respect as its environmental team has all the necessary experience. Recent highlights include advice to Kraft on the $1.48 billion sale of its sugar confectionery business to Wm. Wrigley Jr. The team also advised Emerson Electric on its $375 million acquisition of Marconi's outside plant and power systems business. Aside from M&A, the firm is also praised for its work in insurance – another area where clear advice on environmental liability is vital.

The Lawyers: The market holds **Gail Flesher** (see p.1280) in high esteem as "*the main person*" behind the firm's environmental workload. Her transactional record is rock solid and she provides advice on everything from M&A transactions to securities issues and loans.

The Clients: Emerson Electric; Kraft; Morgan Stanley Dean Witter; Lindsay Goldberg & Bessemer; Carl Zeiss; Canadian National Railway Company and Comcast.

Simpson Thacher & Bartlett LLP

See firm details p.1370

The Firm: Offering robust and reliable advice, this firm is a favorite with clients seeking "*smart lawyers*" to tackle issues of "*environmental complexity.*" The firm handles all levels of transaction, although it has not created a separate environmental law department. Attorneys acted for Kohlberg Kravis Roberts & Co and Rockwood Specialties Group in the latter's $2.7 billion acquisition of four of Dynamit Nobel's specialty chemicals business. The firm also represented Saguaro Utility Group in an agreement to acquire UniSource Energy for $3 billion in cash and debt. The firm's environmental experts have also provided support on deals with less obvious environmental issues – such as Coors's $6 billion merger of equals with Molson.

The Lawyers: **Adeeb Fadil** (see p.1278) nominally works out of the firm's litigation department, but his environmental litigation caseload has in large part given way to increased transactional involvement. It is his "*good results*" that have piqued the interest of market commentators, and they additionally like his methodical approach and attention to detail. One client was impressed by his ability to "*translate the consultant's data to useful legal liabilities.*"

The Clients: KKR; Lehman Brothers; Vestar Capital Partners; ITT Industries; Bear Stearns;

The Blackstone Group; Canadian Imperial Bank of Commerce and the Cypress Group.

Sullivan & Cromwell LLP

See firm details p.1373

The Firm: Bearing all the hallmarks of a top corporate practice, this firm succeeds in attracting a healthy market share of transactions with environmental ramifications. Experience in traditional risk areas, such as asbestos, is now complemented by knowledge of cutting-edge issues, such as global warming, especially where transactions concern facilities outside the USA. The firm is known to offer "*confident and knowledgeable*" counsel on deals concerning regions as diverse as Latin America and the Pacific Rim. It represented a global steel company in its acquisition of a US-based steel products manufacturer that specialized in the construction market. The transaction involved analysis and quantification of toxic torts liabilities and insurance issues. In a separate matter, the firm acted for J Sainsbury in the disposition of its US supermarkets business to Albertsons for $2.5 billion. Restructuring and insolvency is an important growth area for the practice group.

The Lawyers: Among several leading attorneys, "*responsive, hard-working*" **Matthew Brennan** (see p.1268) stands out for his synergy with client needs:– "*We find his philosophy very similar to ours – in line with how we respond.*" **Mark Rosenberg** (see p.1314) handles a mixture of litigation and regulatory work as well as offering transactional support. An expert on contamination and other environmental litigation, he is also a respected name in white-collar crime and political risk insurance.

The Clients: In addition to Hershey Foods, General Growth Properties and J Sainsbury, the group has advised investment banks and energy, steel and pharmaceutical companies on environment-specific issues.

White & Case LLP

See firm details p.1379

The Firm: For the sheer variety of expertise on offer, White & Case is perceived to be a good choice. Attorneys are said to be doing "*a fabulous job*" with "*tremendous sensitivity,*" and clients report that the presence of "*outstanding litigators*" makes the firm even more useful wherever there are major uncertainties. As well as boasting good transactional capabilities, the environmental team is in step with international treaty issues. The firm represented First Atlantic Capital in its acquisition of Prestolite Electric Holding, a multinational manufacturer of electric motors, and acted for Amerada Hess on a joint venture concerning the Weaver's Cove LNG terminal.

The Lawyers: **Richard Horsch** (see p.1288) is admired as a transactionalist and a litigator. On

complex global transactions, his understated yet professional manner endears him to others:– "*He's a favorite of mine; he's smart and reasonable.*" In transactional matters Horsch is best known for representing lenders, while on the contentious front, he has recently litigated over landfills and international clean-up obligations. "*Superb*" **Paul Milmed** (see p.1302) has an excellent local profile that stems from his background as a former Assistant US Attorney in the Southern District of New York. On a pro bono basis, he advised a South Bronx community association in the cleanup of an abandoned factory.

The Clients: Clients include Deutsche Bank, First Atlantic Capital, Amerada Hess and Starwood Capital as well as international pharmaceuticals and food companies.

Cahill Gordon & Reindel

The Firm: This firm has attained prominence for its small but focused environment group of three dedicated attorneys, backed by lawyers from the litigation department. The group is deeply involved in permitting and development work in New York City, as well as related litigation over liability and insurance issues. The firm has acted for Deutsche Bank on insurance claims (and related environmental aspects) arising from the World Trade Center attacks. On the transactional side, the group has worked on deals relating to a variety of industry sectors, including pharmaceuticals and healthcare.

The Lawyers: Practically "*an institution,*" **Robert Hallman** steers the practice group. The holder of a governmental position on three separate occasions (including serving with the Carter administration as a deputy general counsel at the Department of Energy), he has a broad ability to grasp the prevailing issues of the day. Peers praise his deep regulatory background and clarity of thought.

The Clients: The firm counts many leading investment banks, private equity houses and underwriters as clients.

Debevoise & Plimpton LLP

See firm details p.1346

The Firm: At Debevoise, environmental lawyers are to be found in both the litigation and corporate departments. Individuals in the latter group have made a name for themselves acting for a broad range of transactional clients, including sellers, purchasers, lenders, borrowers and underwriters. "*They have the necessary capabilities,*" say market sources. The firm has acted on several issues for Graphic Packaging, culminating in its recent merger with Riverwood Holding. The firm's client base ranges from private equity firms to manufacturers and multi-industry conglomerates with facilities across several continents.

1208   All quotes in the text are from interviews with clients and competitors.

CHAMBERS USA 2005

The Lawyers: Stuart Hammer is described as a "*cooperative*" transactions lawyer. He directs a core team of four attorneys, from both the transactional and litigation sides of the firm. He is praised for his sound judgment and management skills: "*He knows how to use the right consultants at the right time.*"
The Clients: Clayton, Dubilier & Rice; Kelso & Company; Graphic Packaging and Mitsui.

Sidley Austin Brown & Wood LLP
See firm details p.778
The Firm: This practice has undergone a reevaluation in the eyes of the market. Previously the firm was a favorite for regulatory and litigation issues in New York; however, since the departure of Kate Adams, regulatory work has

largely been undertaken by the firm's highly regarded Washington DC office. At the same time, there has been a resurgence of environmental transaction advice in New York. The connectivity between the firm's major offices is believed to be excellent.
The Lawyers: Maureen Crough (see p.1274) is identified as the partner to go to for environmental support on transactions. Her knowledge of corporate compliance and its interface with environmental law is viewed as particularly useful.
The Clients: Clients include Lucent Technologies, GE and Sun Capital.

Other Notable Practitioners
Sharyl Reisman (see p.1312) of Jones Day has attracted attention lately. Her work spans the mass torts field, and she has assisted clients on complex chemical torts and health and safety issues, yet she is also well respected for her regulatory advice on international chemicals regulations. Her knowledge of niche areas, such as vapor intrusion, gives her major corporate clients an expert advantage. Reisman was on the team that supported IBM in various environmental and health and safety lawsuits. **Peter Sacripanti** (see p.1315) of McDermott Will & Emery was highlighted to researchers as a strong litigator in toxic torts and contamination issues. He has "*a huge amount of depth*" and his skill in complex cases is valued greatly.

HEALTHCARE

New York
Leading firms (Healthcare)

1. **EPSTEIN BECKER & GREEN PC** *New York*
   GARFUNKEL, WILD & TRAVIS PC *Great Neck*
   MANATT PHELPS & PHILLIPS LLP *New York*
   NIXON PEABODY LLP *New York*
2. **CADWALADER, WICKERSHAM & TAFT LLP** *New York*
   KATTEN MUCHIN ZAVIS ROSENMAN *New York*
   PROSKAUER ROSE LLP *New York*
   ROPES & GRAY *New York*
3. **HODGSON RUSS LLP** *Buffalo*
   HOGAN & HARTSON LLP *New York*
   ISEMAN CUNNINGHAM RIESTER & HYDE *Albany*
   MCDERMOTT WILL & EMERY *New York*

Leading individuals (Healthcare)

1. **BECKER Jeffrey** *Epstein Becker*, New York
   BERGMANN Peter *Cadwalader Wickersham*, New York
   KALKINES George *Manatt Phelps*, New York
   NADEL Peter *Katten Muchin*, New York
   WILD Robert *Garfunkel Wild*, Great Neck
2. **BARNES Mark** *Ropes & Gray*, New York
   BERNSTEIN William *Manatt Phelps*, New York
   KORNREICH Edward *Proskauer Rose*, New York
   ROBFOGEL Susan *Nixon Peabody*, Rochester
   ROTH Andrew *McDermott Will*, New York
   SERBAROLI Francis *Cadwalader Wickersham*, New York
3. **ISEMAN Robert** *Iseman Cunningham*, Albany
   MILLOCK Peter *Nixon Peabody*, Albany
   SCHNEIDER Jeffrey *Hogan & Hartson*, New York
   TRAVIS Norton *Garfunkel Wild*, Great Neck
   WARNKE Stephen *Ropes & Gray*, New York
   WEISSMAN Ellen *Hodgson Russ*, Buffalo

Firms and individuals are listed alphabetically in each band.

Band 1

Epstein Becker & Green PC
The Firm: "*A national firm with New York presence,*" the practice has been active in relation to

healthcare-related government investigations, fraud and abuse. Its transactional profile covers various mergers and affiliations between large healthcare institutions. It has represented the foreign seller of a major preferred-provider organization, and separately acted for a major nursing home chain in connection with the sale and purchase of facilities. In addition, the practice represented major financial institutions as underwriters of various debt-and-equity transactions. A concerted effort to focus on the pharmaceutical and life sciences industries also appears to be paying dividends for the practice.
The Lawyers: Practice head **Jeff Becker** (see p.1265) is rated by clients for his "*good judgment*" and "*communication skills.*" Although best known for his managed care work, he has been increasingly busy on proceedings related to healthcare fraud and abuse. Transactional advice also features in his profile.
The Clients: The firm offers advice on healthcare investments to various private equity funds and separately acts for pharmaceutical companies in connection with joint ventures. Other clients include hospitals, health maintenance organizations, long-term care and retirement facilities, preferred-provider organizations, ambulatory care facilities, and homecare device and service supply companies.

Garfunkel, Wild & Travis PC
The Firm: A Long Island-based specialist "*geared fundamentally to healthcare,*" the team is equally adept in handling complex litigation related to healthcare as it is in tackling transactions. A significant development includes settling several large group actions against managed care companies for nonpayment or slow payment to hospital clients. The practice has also represented numerous tax-exempt providers in construction and financing transactions involving hundreds of millions of dol-

lars. It has "*good depth,*" according to peers, and the "*technical expertise*" to grasp a broad array of matters. In addition, the practice is participating in the sale of two of the remaining general acute care proprietary hospitals in New York.
The Lawyers: Firm chair and practice head **Bob Wild** is described as "*a lawyer of the highest reputation*" who "*can handle anything*" in the field, while **Norton Travis** is particularly rated by clients for his physician-related work.
The Clients: The firm has successfully represented a number of hospitals and other institutional providers in various litigation matters against disaffected medical staff members. Other clients include nursing homes and other health-related companies such as those providing insurance, pharmaceutical products and medical equipment.

Manatt Phelps & Phillips LLP
The Firm: "*Certainly prominent in the area,*" this California-based firm opened its New York City office in January 2003 by merging with boutique Kalkines, Arky, Zall & Bernstein. It thus gained the services of a "*strong group of healthcare people*" to further bolster a well-rounded California base and respected policy expertise in DC. The firm has helped clients navigate through the complexities of government investigations, and advised on a range of transactions. These include M&A, privatizations and reorganizations. Other capabilities pertain to compliance proceedings related to the operation of healthcare facilities.
The Lawyers: **George Kalkines** (see p.1291) was described as "*definitely a player*" in the field, benefiting from his "*outstanding*" expertise in areas such as corporate organization, regulatory compliance and finance matters. He also advises on physician and faculty practice arrangements. **Bill Bernstein's** (see p.1266) practice encompasses advising provider organizations,

www.ChambersandPartners.com

All quotes in the text are from interviews with clients and competitors.

1209

payer organizations, emerging companies and financial institutions with respect to strategic, transactional and regulatory matters.

The Clients: Active Health Management; Ascension Health; Catholic Healthcare West; CitiCare Family Services; HealthSouth; Kindred Healthcare; Mariner Post Acute Network; Memorial Sloan Kettering; Northshore/Long Island Jewish Health System; NYC Health and Hospitals Corporation; Peak Medical; Pfizer; ScrippsHealth; Sun Healthcare Group; Trinity Health System and William F Ryan Community Health Center.

Nixon Peabody LLP
See firm details p.1361

The Firm: With a handful of offices throughout New York, this practice comprises a team of lawyers who *"really understand the industry and the dynamics in the New York market."* Further enhanced by a national network of offices, the firm's health services practice group is often specifically retained on healthcare-related transactions and litigation. Its expertise cuts a wide swathe across the spectrum, and includes working with financially distressed healthcare providers. In addition, the team also advises on residency accreditation and reimbursement issues, and helps facilitate healthcare matters on behalf of nonprofit organizations. On the litigation front, it also works in tandem with other departments to handle such issues as employment and antitrust.

The Lawyers: Noted by peers for her expertise in both health and labor & employment law for healthcare providers, the *"pleasant and business-oriented"* **Susan Robfogel** (see p.1313) is prized as a *"tough negotiator who is focused on the client's interests, not on trying to demonstrate she's the smartest lawyer in the room."* **Peter Millock** (see p.1302) in Albany won market commendation for being *"one of the leaders of the shop."* He also gained respect as a former general counsel to the New York State Department of Health.

The Clients: The practice successfully represented Central Suffolk Hospital in an appellate case involving medical staff bylaws, and separately handled several significant Qui Tam lawsuits pertaining to the False Claims Act. Other clients include: NYU Hospitals Center; Lenox Hill Hospital; Strong Memorial Medical Center; Sound Shore Medical Center; TransCare; New York Hospital Queens; Albany Medical Center; North Shore LIJ Health Care System and NYU School of Medicine.

Band 2

Cadwalader, Wickersham & Taft LLP
See firm details p.1339

The Firm: The firm's dynamic healthcare practice was established on the strength of its transactional core, further strengthened on the litigation front due to a more recent spate of government investigations and related civil lawsuits. In this area, it has defended healthcare-related insurance fraud cases. The firm also acts for clients as plaintiffs, for example, advising 300 nursing homes in seeking about $950 million in additional government reimbursement from the State of New York. Its particular expertise in long-term care has been illustrated through its involvement in the development of a large $250 million continuing care retirement community on Long Island. Other corporate expertise involves M&A, restructuring, securities and capital markets among other transactional and regulatory matters.

The Lawyers: The *"enormously respected"* **Peter Bergmann** (see p.1266) has impressed peers with his long track record in the field and they especially rate him for his representation of nursing homes. Indeed, he is general counsel to the New York Association of Homes and Services for the Aging. In addition, he also advises the New York State Association of Counties on Medicaid reimbursement matters. Peers note that **Frank Serbaroli** (see p.1319) commands respect in the field, as evidenced by his involvement as a member of the New York Academy of Medicine's committee on public health. His clients have included teaching and community hospitals, clinical laboratories, home health agencies, health insurers and managed care organizations.

The Clients: The firm advised Visiting Nurse Service of New York on the acquisition of two home care agencies that were privately owned by different hospitals. Other clients include state and federal governmental and quasi-governmental agencies, hospitals, nursing homes, health insurers, HMOs and pharmaceutical companies.

Katten Muchin Zavis Rosenman
See firm details p.769

The Firm: Formed following the 2002 merger of Chicago-based Katten Muchin Zavis with Rosenman & Colin in New York, this firm's healthcare practice often involves complex reimbursement issues statewide. Clients describe its expertise as *"head and shoulders above anyone else"* in this category. A significant matter involved the New York City Department of Education in a federal investigation and audit to determine whether it submitted inappropriate Medicaid claims for health and related services to disabled children in special education programs.

The Lawyers: Clients praise **Peter Nadel**'s (see p.1303) *"integrity, responsiveness and experience"* in relation to reimbursement matters. His litigation profile has been nurtured through his participation in significant disputes. A recent one was advising 77 New York hospitals seeking to invalidate new federal Medicare Wage Index rules that will reduce payments to them by about $980 million over the next ten years.

The Clients: One of the firm's established clients is New York City Health and Hospitals Corporation. On its behalf, the team helped to negotiate three affiliation agreements whereby the Columbia, SUNY and New York universities medical schools will staff HHC's hospitals in contracts worth about $550 million over a period of three years. Other clients include the New York City Department of Education, Greater New York Hospital Association and Saint Vincent Catholic Medical Centers.

Proskauer Rose LLP
See firm details p.1365

The Firm: The practice is perceived to hinge on its cochair Ed Kornreich, and is bolstered by a somewhat larger DC presence, commentators said. In addition, the firm's vast resources mean that the group inevitably participates in some of the industry's most prominent healthcare matters. One of its drawing cards is its regulatory strength, for example, assisting Texas Pacific Group in compliance matters relating to its $1.4 billion purchase of a controlling interest in IASIS Healthcare, a 15-hospital system based in Nashville, Tennessee. Other expertise includes healthcare transactions and reimbursement issues. The practice has represented a major New York academic medical center with respect to a federal False Claims Act investigation involving potential overpayments totaling about $50 million.

The Lawyers: Cochair of the firm's healthcare department, **Ed Kornreich** focuses on regulatory due diligence and compliance as part of a broader practice that also includes transactional and healthcare payment issues.

The Clients: The team advised Avalon Health Care in relation to its acquisition of 23 skilled nursing facilities. Other clients include: Greater New York Hospital Association; Continuum Health Partners; Hospital for Special Surgery; Memorial Sloan-Kettering Cancer Center; Fresenius Medical Care North America; CON-MED; Lenox Hill Hospital; Celgene; ImClone Systems; Maimonides Medical Center; Mount Sinai Hospital; New York Organ Donor Network; Catholic Health Services of Long Island; Promise Healthcare; Radiology Corporation of America and Oxford Coverage.

Ropes & Gray
See firm details p.985

The Firm: This Boston-based firm undoubtedly has *"made inroads into New York,"* industry sources said, pointing to its regular participation in regulatory and litigation proceedings. In particular, the potential strength of the group is sustained by the arrivals in recent years of Mark Barnes and Steve Warnke from the New York offices of Proskauer Rose and Manatt Phelps respectively. *"It's certainly been more active since Barnes and Warnke got there,"* commentators said.

The Lawyers: Widely regarded by interviewees as the group's lead practitioner in New York,

1210   All quotes in the text are from interviews with clients and competitors.

CHAMBERS USA 2005

Mark Barnes (see p.1264) has represented hospitals, medical schools, physicians, social service agencies, and related organizations. His range is extensive, and includes regulatory, reimbursement, HIPAA compliance, and litigation matters. **Steve Warnke's** (see p.1331) practice focuses on healthcare fraud-related disputes, compliance and investigations. Other interests involve third-party reimbursement, capital financing and managed care.

The Clients: Clients include academic medical centers, community hospitals, pharmaceutical companies, managed care organizations and insurance companies.

Band 3

Hodgson Russ LLP

The Firm: This practice is particularly recommended for its work relating to healthcare providers in western New York, including structuring and counseling provider networks and integrated delivery systems. The health law practice group also assists its clientele – many of whom are regional nonprofit, public and for-profit health care organizations – on reimbursement, regulatory and compliance matters. In addition, the group helps marshal clients through the process of establishing assisted living programs, continuing care retirement communities and senior housing projects.

The Lawyers: The firm's health law practice group leader, **Ellen Weissman**, is based in Buffalo. Her work includes advising a range of clients such as hospitals and skilled nursing facilities on reimbursement and regulatory matters.

The Clients: Clients include hospitals, nursing homes, home health agencies, hospices, free-standing clinics, behavioral health providers and licensed professionals such as physicians.

Hogan & Hartson LLP

See firm details p.484

The Firm: The New York office is particularly rated for its academic medical center work, for example, advising the State University of New York (SUNY) Downstate Medical Center /Health Sciences Center. In one significant matter, the team helped renegotiate SUNY's affiliation agreement with its primary clinical affiliate, Kings County Medical Center, and its parent, the New York City Health and Hospitals Corporation. Although many interviewees viewed this practice as having been somewhat eclipsed by its higher profile DC office, nevertheless, it tends to hold its own when it comes to regulatory, reimbursement and related issues.

The Lawyers: *"Bright"* **Jeff Schneider** (see p.1318) is distinguished for his representation of a number of long-term care providers and home health agencies in relation to corporate compliance matters, general regulatory counseling, and coverage and reimbursement issues.

The Clients: Affectionate Home Health Care; AMDeC Foundation; American Board of Neurological Surgery; Associated Geriatric Information Network; Blue Cross and Blue Shield of North Carolina; Carlyle Group; Columbia University; Long Island Health Network; Lutheran Medical Center; New York University Medical Center; Patient Care Associates and the Rockefeller University.

Iseman Cunningham Riester & Hyde LLP

The Firm: A relatively *"smaller shop doing wonderful healthcare work,"* according to interviewees, the firm's Albany office earned market respect for its proficiency in areas such as reimbursements. It has represented both sides – advising integrated delivery systems in disputes with third party payers in some cases and in others, acting on behalf of third party payers. Other experience involves the formation of multi-provider systems and integrated delivery networks, regulatory and compliance proceedings, and corporate-related advice such as tax law.

The Lawyers: The practice's leading name is **Bob Iseman**, whose expertise involves managed care, integrated healthcare, risk management, provider reimbursement, vendor contracts and fraud.

The Clients: The firm acts for a wide range of institutional and individual healthcare providers as well as a number of national healthcare systems that have general counsel based outside the state. Other clients include hospitals, HMOs, healthcare insurers, nursing homes and home healthcare agencies.

McDermott Will & Emery

See firm details p.773

The Firm: The market consensus is that the New York office of this national health practice has somewhat diminished due to recent high profile departures including that of Harvey Werblowsky, who has joined real estate organization Kushner Companies. That said, the team still inspires confidence among commentators, particularly for its work on behalf of various doctor groups. Through its overall healthcare capacity elsewhere and its significant corporate profile in New York, it also invariably gets involved in a variety of transactional and regulatory matters.

The Lawyers: **Andy Roth** (see p.1314) is partner-in-charge of the firm's health practice whose expertise includes M&A, fraud and abuse, corporate compliance and medical staff bylaws. He also often advises on issues relating to long-term healthcare facilities.

The Clients: Clients include healthcare networks, integrated delivery systems, hospitals, managed care companies and physicians.

INSURANCE

Debevoise & Plimpton LLP

See firm details p.1346

The Firm: Seen as an *"awfully good institutionalized insurance practice,"* the cadre of *"highly skilled and seasoned individuals"* brings corporate, securities, M&A and tax expertise to the transaction. *"They've got all that expertise under one house, and regulatory and reinsurance too,"* commentators said. The team often appears in *"choice disputes"* and helps clients navigate through complex situations such as investigations by the New York Attorney General's Office and others. In addition, it has been representing a major directors and officers (D&O) insurer in connection with securities lawsuits against Honeywell, TXU Corporation, Sears, Schering-Plough and JDS Uniphase.

The Lawyers: The market consensus is that **Dick Dunham** is the *"dean of the profession,"* benefiting from *"tremendous experience and standing"* in the insurance transactional industry. One admiring competitor noted that *"he's done so much to advance insurance law – I want to grow up to be Dick."* Others praised his *"understated authority. He may just say a few words on an issue, but it's often the final word."* Rounding out the team is the *"smart and likable"* **Tom Kelly** and the *"hands-on"* **Nick Potter**, whose expertise in insurance regulations won particular praise. **Bob Cusumano** is recognized by competitors for his work in relation to coverage litigation in the asbestos arena.

The Clients: The firm has advised ACE in a worldwide investigation among other issues. It also represented insurers in connection with coverage claims of $100 million or more arising out of liabilities in the pharmaceutical and hospital fields, including those pertaining to latex gloves liabilities. Other clients include: Prudential; China Life; Chubb Group; The Hartford; Manulife Financial; MBIA; AXA Financial; Provident Mutual Life Insurance; St Paul Travelers Companies; Great American Insurance and GE Insurance Solutions.

LeBoeuf, Lamb, Greene & MacRae, LLP

See firm details p.1358

The Firm: The market consensus is that this practice has a *"genuine focus on the insurance industry across the board and side to side."*

New York
Leading firms
(Insurance: Transactional & Regulatory)

1. **DEBEVOISE & PLIMPTON LLP** New York
   LEBOEUF, LAMB, GREENE & MACRAE New York
   STROOCK & STROOCK & LAVAN LLP New York

2. **DEWEY BALLANTINE LLP** New York
   SIMPSON THACHER & BARTLETT LLP New York
   SKADDEN, ARPS, SLATE, MEAGHER New York
   SULLIVAN & CROMWELL LLP New York

3. **CLIFFORD CHANCE US LLP** New York
   EDWARDS & ANGELL New York
   FRIED, FRANK, HARRIS, SHRIVER New York
   MOUND COTTON WOLLAN New York
   WACHTELL, LIPTON, ROSEN & KATZ New York
   WHITE & CASE LLP New York

(Insurance: Dispute Resolution)

1. **SIMPSON THACHER & BARTLETT LLP** New York

2. **ANDERSON KILL & OLICK PC** New York
   CADWALADER, WICKERSHAM & TAFT LLP New York
   CLIFFORD CHANCE US LLP New York
   LEBOEUF, LAMB, GREENE & MACRAE New York

3. **DEBEVOISE & PLIMPTON LLP** New York
   MOUND COTTON WOLLAN & GREENGRASS New York
   PROSKAUER ROSE LLP New York
   SKADDEN, ARPS, SLATE, MEAGHER New York
   SONNENSCHEIN NATH & ROSENTHAL New York
   STROOCK & STROOCK & LAVAN LLP New York

4. **CAHILL GORDON & REINDEL** New York
   DEWEY BALLANTINE LLP New York
   EDWARDS & ANGELL New York
   MENDES & MOUNT LLP New York
   SULLIVAN & CROMWELL LLP New York
   WACHTELL, LIPTON, ROSEN & KATZ New York
   WILSON, ELSER, MOSKOWITZ, EDELMAN New York

Firms are listed alphabetically in each band.

Particular respect for its regulatory and litigation expertise is illustrated in its frequent role as Lloyd's of London's outside counsel. The group is also active in insurance M&A and capital markets; it is regular counsel to a number of frequent issuers in the insurance industry. In addition, it regularly represents underwriters in debt and equity offerings by insurers and reinsurers.

The Lawyers: Particularly rated by competitors for his work with issuers and underwriters in public and other offerings, the "*diligent*" **Alex Dye** (see p.1276) focuses on corporate transactions involving the insurance industry. He assisted in advising Hillenbrand Industries, the country's largest casket maker, in the sale of Forethought Financial Services and its subsidiaries. The transaction was valued at about $300 million. With a "*wealth of experience to draw upon*," **Don Henderson** (see p.1287) was particularly noted for his regulatory experience pertaining to "*life settlement and, recently, in convergence.*" If it's a demutualization transaction, **Cynthia Shoss** (see p.1321) delivers effective

results, clients said. "*She's got a tax background so she can handle the complexities of the tax issues involved.*" Described by competitors as "*a comprehensive lawyer,*" **John Nonna** (see p.1305) is "*low key but a talented litigator who knows the ins and outs of the insurance business.*" He won particular commendation in the reinsurance area. **Mike Groll** (see p.1285) was described by competitors as having "*a very amicable practicality about his approach, and great experience too.*" He assisted in advising Nationwide Mutual Insurance in connection with the establishment of a $400 million contingent surplus notes facility.

The Clients: The practice represented Scottish Re in its acquisition of the individual life reinsurance business from ING Re, and in the related offering of $180 million in new capital securities. Other clients include: Goldman Sachs; Morgan Stanley; Merrill Lynch; Citigroup; Banc of America Securities; Lehman Brothers; Allstate; Jackson National Life; MetLife; Travelers Life and Annuity; Nationwide Life; New York Life and Security Life of Denver.

Stroock & Stroock & Lavan LLP

The Firm: "*One of the preeminent firms on the regulatory side,*" the practice is a secure fixture in the insurance sphere. "*If you want access to any regulator in the country, you can't do better than having Stroock behind you.*" Its historical presence on the property casualty side is further bolstered by the recent arrival of Bill Rosenblatt, who adds strength to the firm's transactional profile. Recent highlight matters for the practice include representing Specialty Underwriters' Alliance in its $125 million IPO and separately advising Lehman Brothers as underwriter of the $400 million note issuance of Fusion Capital.

The Lawyers: Pitched as a "*lawyers' lawyer,*" **Bill Rosenblatt** has brought "*added corporate capability*" to the firm. Practice leader **Don Gabay** is an established operator on the regulatory side who brings valuable experience as a former First Deputy Superintendent with the New York State Insurance Department. Clients said the "*absolutely first-rate transactional lawyer*" **Bill Latza** also illustrates proficiency in "*extensive regulatory matters.*" On the litigation front, **Bob Lewin** impresses with "*the gravity of his arguments.*" He also gained market respect for his agile analysis skills, quietly gaining success "*without resorting to being a publicity hound,*" according to interviewees.

The Clients: The firm represented Atlantic Mutual in the sale of its commercial insurance business to OneBeacon and separately acted for the Massachusetts Division of Insurance in connection with the C$15 billion Manulife-John Hancock merger. Other clients include: MBIA; Radian Asset Assurance; Goldman Sachs; Chubb; Kemper; CNA; FGIC; PartnerRe and AIG.

Dewey Ballantine LLP

See firm details p.1347

The Firm: The transactional strength of this insurance team drives the practice, which delivers expertise on M&A, purchases and dispositions of divisions, and blocks of business, public and private financing. Capital markets activities as related to the insurance industry also feature prominently. Clients appreciate the group's ability to meet deadlines and budgets, "*and they're as good as anyone in the insurance legal world.*" Though perhaps less glowing than its transactional profile, the firm's litigation capabilities also won respect among commentators. Representing insurers and insureds, the team offers expertise on general liability, professional malpractice, and D&O liability policies linked to life and health, and property and casualty insurance. Other interests include environmental coverage and fidelity bonds.

The Lawyers: "*Thoughtful and analytical from a quantitative perspective,*" **Jeff Liebmann** (see p.1297) is noted for his representation of MetLife in various acquisitions. He is also qualified as an actuary as well as an attorney. **James FitzPatrick** (see p.1279) won praise as "*professional, smart and efficient,*" while **David Grais** (see p.1284) is recommended for his reinsurance expertise. "*He's intellectually very strong,*" interviewees said. "*He works very hard, and he has a lot of respect from clients.*"

The Clients: The practice represented Goldman Sachs as initial purchaser in connection with the issuance by FLAC Holdings of a $150 million offering. It also represented CNA Financial in various dispositions and separately assisted in a $400 million Rule 144A offering involving JPMorgan Securities, Merrill Lynch, Pierce, Fenner & Smith and UBS Securities. Other clients include: Alleghany Corporation; Beazley Group; Cincinnati Financial; Discover Re Manager; MetLife; Nationwide Mutual Insurance; Platinum Underwriters Holdings; Scottish Re and UBS Securities.

Simpson Thacher & Bartlett LLP

See firm details p.1370

The Firm: Portrayed as "*one of the best coverage firms on the seating company side,*" the firm is also considered a "*force on the contentious side,*" commentators said. Its "*awesome breadth and heft*" is parlayed in such heavyweight matters as the World Trade Center insurance coverage dispute, in which it successfully represented Swiss Re in the first jury trial ending in April 2004; the firm obtained a jury verdict that Swiss Re was obligated to pay one occurrence limit for the property damage at the WTC instead of the two-event liability that real estate developer Larry Silverstein was seeking. The firm's "*substantial insurance clientele*" enhances a "*gigantic*" profile in the field. Another substantial case was on behalf of St Paul Travelers in obtaining a

1212

All quotes in the text are from interviews with clients and competitors.

CHAMBERS USA 2005

Leading individuals
(Insurance: Transactional & Regulatory)

★ **DUNHAM Wolcott** *Debevoise & Plimpton*, New York
[1] **DYE Alexander** *LeBoeuf Lamb*, New York
  LIEBMANN Jeff *Dewey Ballantine*, New York
  ROSENBLATT William *Stroock & Stroock*, New York
  SULLIVAN Robert *Skadden Arps*, New York
[2] **COTTON Stuart** *Mound Cotton*, New York
  GABAY Donald *Stroock & Stroock*, New York
  HENDERSON Donald *LeBoeuf Lamb*, New York
  KELLY Thomas *Debevoise & Plimpton*, New York
  ROWEN Andrew *Sullivan & Cromwell*, New York
[3] **FITZPATRICK James** *Dewey Ballantine*, New York
  GREENGRASS Lawrence *Mound Cotton*, New York
  GROLL Michael *LeBoeuf Lamb*, New York
  LATZA William *Stroock & Stroock*, New York
  MEYER Paul *Clifford Chance*, New York
  PEARSON Nick *Edwards & Angell*, New York
  POTTER Nicholas *Debevoise & Plimpton*, New York
  SARCHIO John *White & Case*, New York
  SHOSS Cynthia *LeBoeuf Lamb*, New York
  WILLIAMS Nicholas *White & Case*, New York

(Insurance: Dispute Resolution)

Senior Statesman
  ANDERSON Eugene *Anderson Kill*, New York
[1] **OSTRAGER Barry** *Simpson Thacher*, New York
[2] **ASHINOFF Reid** *Sonnenschein Nath*, New York
  BARR Michael *Sonnenschein Nath*, New York
  BRANDES Lawrence *Cadwalader Wickersham*, New York
  CHAFFETZ Peter *Clifford Chance*, New York
  COTTON Stuart *Mound Cotton*, New York
  GROSS John *Proskauer Rose*, New York
  KRUGMAN Edward *Cahill Gordon*, New York
  NEWMAN Thomas *Duane Morris*, New York
  NONNA John *LeBoeuf Lamb*, New York
  VYSKOCIL Mary *Simpson Thacher*, New York
[3] **AMER Andrew** *Simpson Thacher*, New York
  BIRNBAUM Sheila *Skadden Arps*, New York
  CUSUMANO Robert *Debevoise & Plimpton*, New York
  GRAIS David *Dewey Ballantine*, New York
  GREENGRASS Lawrence *Mound Cotton*, New York
  FIELDS Richard *Dickstein Shapiro*, New York
  HORKOVICH Robert *Anderson Kill*, New York
  LEWIN Robert *Stroock & Stroock*, New York
  REYNOLDS Timothy *Skadden Arps*, New York
  SCHOENBERG Clifford *Cadwalader*, New York
  SCHWARTZ Steven *Clifford Chance*, New York
  VITKOWSKY Vincent *Edwards & Angell*, New York

Individuals are listed alphabetically in each band.

permanent, nationwide injunction precluding the prosecution against Travelers of any asbestos-related statutory or common law direct actions.

The Lawyers: Practice head and *"leading luminary"* **Barry Ostrager** (see p.1306) is described by competitors as *"an aggressive, hard-working lawyer with a lot of knowledge in the area,"* particularly in direct insurance. Further comment was that *"he's smart, strategic, takes the time to explain*

to the client what he's thinking; and his experience level is such that he doesn't hesitate to try something new."* He is *"well supported"* by the *"terrific"* **Mary Kay Vyskocil** (see p.1329), who *"always comes to the table very well prepared,"* according to clients. *"Ostrager and Vyskocil often come as a team and they're first-rate lawyers who've won some very important cases."* Clients also value the *"bright"* **Andy Amer** (see p.1262), who is *"steeped in reinsurance, knows the arbitrators and the process and gives very good client service."*

The Clients: The team successfully represented Travelers in a $5 billion arbitration involving AcandS; it was determined that, contrary to ACandS's assertion, ACandS had no 'non-products claims' and Travelers had exhausted all of its coverage for 'products claim.' On behalf of AIG American General, the group conducted a billion-dollar reinsurance arbitration against Superior National. Another significant victory involved IRI in an appellate affirmation of a prior decision ruling that the scope of coverage for Y2K claims is exceedingly narrow. Other clients include: ACE; Munich Re; ANI (American Nuclear Insurers); Royal Insurance Company of America and Mitsui Marine.

Skadden, Arps, Slate, Meagher & Flom LLP & Affiliates
See firm details p.1372

The Firm: The span of its corporate profile inevitably lands this firm in the transactional side of the insurance stage, while its increasingly important role in insurance litigation has resulted in far-reaching precedents. *"Whenever they do work, it's significant work,"* commentators said. *"It's an excellent multidimensional firm which draws on its high-level corporate connections and has a big presence in M&A and insurance defense work."* In addition to M&A, the group also tackles a host of other insurance-related deals such as IPOs, risk-linked securities and other corporate finance transactions. Reorganizations also feature highly in the firm's profile.

The Lawyers: Described by one appreciative client as *"probably the best M&A lawyer in the insurance business,"* **Bob Sullivan** (see p.1325) *"doesn't give it in code."* His *"commercially oriented"* attitude is further bolstered by a *"good rapport with the insurance regulators state by state."* Head of the firm's complex mass tort and insurance group, **Sheila Birnbaum** (see p.1267) is said to be *"a powerful litigator"* who *"enjoys a wonderful reputation"* in both insurance coverage litigation and products liability. **Tim Reynolds** (see p.1312) is *"on top of the case law and also knows the business side of insurance,"* according to interviewees. He garnered particular respect for his representation of the Port Authority in the World Trade Center litigation.

The Clients: Clients have included insurance and reinsurance companies as well as their financial advisers and underwriters.

Sullivan & Cromwell LLP
See firm details p.1373

The Firm: With a *"corporate department that's as good as any in the city,"* this practice has cultivated a notable transactional profile in the insurance industry that's further bolstered by its active financial institutions group. Its expertise encompasses insurance M&A, finance, reorganizations and securitizations. The scope of the practice extends across the range of areas, including property and casualty, and life and health insurance as related to the domestic and offshore markets. Prominent M&A, demutualizations and governmental investigations also feature in its repertoire.

The Lawyers: **Andy Rowen** (see p.1315), who coordinates the firm's international insurance practice group, is described as a *"fine transaction lawyer"* who *"doesn't focus too much on the minutiae but addresses the major issues."*

The Clients: The firm represented John Hancock in its takeover by Manulife and separately acted for Prudential in its purchase of CIGNA Corporation's retirement savings business. The practice also represented Anthem in its merger with Wellpoint. Other clients include: AIG; ING; Allianz; The PMI Group and CIFG.

Clifford Chance US LLP
See firm details p.1343

The Firm: This practice attracted plaudits for having acquired a number of practitioners through its recent merger, culminating in *"a meaningful practice in New York."* Significant work involved Sun Life in major arbitration and litigation arising from the collapse of the workers' compensation carve-out market. Especially noted by competitors for its work in relation to reinsurance disputes, its expertise also includes M&A, demutualizations, reorganizations, securities offerings and financings as related to the insurance marketplace. For example, the practice has represented Security Mutual Life Insurance in its ongoing sponsored demutualization, and separately advised Ambac Assurance in insurance and reinsurance asset-backed structures for its insurance structuring group.

The Lawyers: On the transactional side, competitors particularly note **Paul Meyer** (see p.1301) for his *"good relationship with the Pru,"* while on the reinsurance front, peers see the *"thoughtful and effective"* **Peter Chaffetz** (see p.1271) as a *"big name with an excellent practice."* Also rated for his reinsurance expertise, **Steve Schwartz** (see p.1319) was described by one admiring competitor as being *"a great intellect"* with a *"mind that takes in things much quicker than most people."*

The Clients: AXA; Hanover Re; Odyssey Re; SCOR US; BNP Paribas; CSFB; Farm Family Insurance Companies; John Hancock Financial Services; Monumental Life Insurance; Mutual of America Life Insurance; Prudential; Security Mutual Life Insurance and TIAA-CREF.

Edwards & Angell

The Firm: This practice's lawyers are *"aggressive marketers"* who have *"built a critical mass of active people,"* gaining ground in an increasingly competitive market. For example, it has counseled on numerous reinsurance disputes including ongoing Unicover-related matters. Its distinction partly derives from *"a concerted effort to expand their reinsurance practice"* in particular, though the team also gained credibility in various transactional and direct insurance matters. The group advised insurers in consumer class actions and various government enquiries. Representing more than 20 London and European insurers, the group handled issues relating to surplus lines and tax.

The Lawyers: **Nick Pearson** won commendation as an *"accomplished insurance industry lawyer,"* representing domestic and international clients in the formation, acquisition, sale and licensing of insurance and reinsurance companies and brokers. Viewed as *"a reinsurance arbitration expert,"* **Vince Vitkowsky** is valued as a *"well-prepared"* operator who effectively handles *"small to midsized disputes."* His work has included representing insurers and reinsurers in disputes involving Enron. Other coverage matters involved securities and ERISA class action claims against directors and officers. He has also been handling claims involving theatrical non-appearance coverage and various matters relating to 9/11.

The Clients: AIG; French Insurance Association; GE Insurance Solutions; Gerber Life Insurance; MassMutual Life Insurance; QBE International; The Phoenix Companies and various Lloyd's syndicates.

Fried, Frank, Harris, Shriver & Jacobson LLP

See firm details p.1349

The Firm: This practice has been especially active in relation to insurance-related M&A, financial advisory work and litigation, in addition to offering general corporate counseling and governance advice. Its link to anchor client Goldman Sachs has proven fruitful, for example, acting on the private placement of 12 million equity security units by UnumProvident Corporation. The group also assisted Merrill Lynch in the public offering of six million ordinary shares by Platinum Underwriters Holding. A drawing card is the team's overall *"capacity to do the whole thing"* in relation to insurance matters, commentators said. Though not as notable as its transactional strength, dispute resolution capabilities are also on offer. The firm advised Fortress Re in complex litigation and arbitration concerning aviation risks.

The Lawyers: Key members of the team include Lois Herzeca, Robert Juceam and Gregg Weiner.

The Clients: Transatlantic Holdings; Allied World Assurance Holdings; Kindred Healthcare; Merrill Lynch; Goldman Sachs; Fortress Re and CIGNA.

Mound Cotton Wollan & Greengrass

The Firm: A prominent insurance specialist that has broadened its profile, this practice has *"been around the block,"* according to interviewees. It represents insurance companies in direct insurance and reinsurance disputes, with particular emphasis on first and third party claims. It is especially noted by peers for its work in relation to the World Trade Center, and won client admiration for being *"cost effective on small to medium disputes."*

The Lawyers: **Larry Greengrass** offers proficient handling of reinsurance matters, while the *"knowledgeable and experienced"* **Stuart Cotton** is noted for his work in the World Trade Center case and his much-envied client relationship with AIG.

The Clients: The firm often advises direct writers, brokers, intermediaries, reinsurers and state insurance departments.

Wachtell, Lipton, Rosen & Katz

See firm details p.1375

The Firm: The insurance contingent of this M&A powerhouse is perceived as something of *"an intermittent player,"* albeit one that's *"good in everything it does,"* market analysts said. Viewed as *"a big dog out there for the big deals, which are sometimes in the insurance industry,"* it draws on its established corporate relationships. As with the overall character of the firm, the team makes up for what it lacks in size with concentrated forcefulness. It is especially noted for its representation of MetLife in *"big public company acquisitions."* As for litigation, one of its most high-profile cases involves Silverstein Properties, the 99-year leaseholder of the World Trade Center, in litigation against over 20 insurance companies seeking recovery for damages stemming from the 9/11 terrorist attacks.

The Clients: Silverstein Properties, MetLife, and other major corporations and financial institutions comprise the firm's distinguished clientele.

White & Case LLP

See firm details p.1379

The Firm: Particularly noted by peers for its regulatory expertise, this practice has continued to be active in insurance sector restructurings and insolvencies in addition to M&A and various financing transactions. It represented The First American Financial Corporation in its acquisition of Columbian National Title Insurance Company from McCaffree Financial Corporation. In addition, the group has been advising Anthem as issuer's counsel in connection with financing transactions for Anthem's $16.4 billion acquisition of WellPoint Health Networks.

The Lawyers: Chair of the firm's insurance industry practice group, the *"well-established"* **John Sarchio** (see p.1316) enjoys a diverse practice that includes insurance-related M&A, reinsurance transactions and insurance regulatory

matters. He assisted in ABB's $425 million sale of Sirius International Insurance, Sirius American Insurance and Scandinavian Reinsurance to White Mountains Insurance Group. Interviewees also applauded **Nick Williams** (see p.1332) for his *"positive energy level."* He has extensive experience in the regulatory sphere, having advised government entities as well as companies.

The Clients: Allianz; Amalgamated Life Insurance; AIG; Centre Reinsurance; Fireman's Fund; First American Insurance; Guardian Life Insurance; New York Life; Prudential and WellPoint.

Anderson Kill & Olick PC

See firm details p.1336

The Firm: The market consensus as to this *"zealous"* policyholder litigation practice was summed up by one practitioner's comment: *"When I see them there, I know it's serious stuff, so I have to bring out some heavy weapons."* The group often grabs headlines for its pugnacity on some of the most publicized disputes, often those involving environmental issues, products liability and other matters. Many of its cases result in groundbreaking decisions, leading one commentator to add: *"You can't talk about coverage litigation without mentioning Anderson Kill."*

The Lawyers: *"The grand old man on the policyholder side"* and *"one of the deans of the Bar,"* **Gene Anderson** was rated as *"a superb lawyer and marketer"* with *"a sharp mind"* and one of the most prominent careers in the industry. Another analyst credited him as having *"invented sophisticated insurance coverage litigation."* Chair of the firm's insurance coverage group, **Bob Horkovich** is described as the *"go-to person"* in the area of insurance recovery. He is recognized for his work in cases involving asbestos liabilities as related to bankruptcy proceedings. In a recent victory, he assisted Fuller-Austin in winning a jury verdict of about $188 million against Lloyd's and other insurance companies in an asbestos insurance coverage case.

The Clients: The firm has advised a range of corporate and industrial policyholders in addition to utilities, municipalities, non-profit organizations, private companies and individuals.

Cadwalader, Wickersham & Taft LLP

See firm details p.1339

The Firm: The practice is pitched as *"one of the broadest in high-end reinsurance litigation and arbitration,"* winning clients who seek its *"knowledgeable, calm, well-connected"* lawyers and their *"excellent problem-solving"* skills. Its expertise includes director and officer liability, errors and omissions, fidelity, and other forms of financial risk insurance. Its success is illustrated in such cases as a reinsurance arbitration on behalf of Sompo Japan Insurance Company. The matter involved seeking approximately $1 billion in damages arising from a dispute concerning

1214   All quotes in the text are from interviews with clients and competitors.

CHAMBERS USA 2005

Fortress Re's accounting and reporting practices.
The Lawyers: Described as "*one of the first successful reinsurance lawyers in the USA going back to the early 1980s,*" **Larry Brandes** (see p.1268) wins respect for his "*smart and strategic*" approach to insurance litigation. The "*prominent player in the field*" is ably supported by **Cliff Schoenberg** (see p.1318), who is "*most remarkable for his persistence and tenacity.*"

The Clients: XL Reinsurance America; Allstate; John Hancock Life Insurance; Trenwick America Reinsurance; PartnerRe; Converium Reinsurance (North America); Odyssey Reinsurance and Allianz Life Insurance.

Proskauer Rose LLP

See firm details p.1365

The Firm: Respected for its expertise on behalf of policyholders, the practice benefits from the firm's enduring profile in litigation. The group was involved in one of 2004's most prominent verdicts, acting as co-counsel for Silverstein Properties in the second trial of the World Trade Center insurance coverage litigation. The case sent ripples through the insurance industry when a federal jury determined that the 9/11 terrorist attacks at the World Trade Center should be treated as two occurrences, enabling Silverstein to recover up to an additional $1.1 billion from nine insurance companies above the limit for a single occurrence.

The Lawyers: Seen as "*smart and experienced*" on the policyholder side, **John Gross** (see p.1285) earned kudos for his involvement in the World Trade Center litigation.

The Clients: Silverstein Properties; Bear Stearns; International Paper; JPMorgan Chase; Lucent and Omnicom.

Sonnenschein Nath & Rosenthal

See firm details p.779

The Firm: This Chicago-based firm won considerable approbation for its work in relation to "*class actions on the defense side.*" Clients appreciate its coterie of "*thoughtful, careful and professional*" lawyers, whose ability to "*formulate a well-considered game plan*" often culminates in successful results on the insurance front. A recent victory involved a verdict in favor of Aon Corporation and one of its senior executives in an employment-related case involving claims of fraud, breach of contract, statutory violations and ERISA issues. In addition, the practice is

representing Prudential Financial in a nationwide putative class action in New Mexico relating to modal premium payments.

The Lawyers: **Michael Barr** (see p.1264) is an especially valuable asset on "*high-end complex cases,*" clients said. "*He's top notch: aggressive, smart, and really cares about us as a client, and I think that the combination has consistently brought us some very good results.*" He has represented Royal & SunAlliance as lead counsel in the World Trade Center trial and property appraisal proceedings. The "*dedicated*" **Reid Ashinoff** (see p.1263) won client respect for his "*uncanny ability to wade through the morass, distill the real issues and understand where the vulnerabilities and strengths are.*"

The Clients: The practice is representing Swiss Re in a major coverage/reinsurance dispute involving residual value of automobile insurance. On behalf of Royal & SunAlliance, it is handling matters pertaining to its issuance of credit risk insurance to Student Finance Corporation (student loans) and Commercial Money Centers (equipment leases), both of which collapsed amid allegations of massive fraud. Other clients include Fireman's Fund, Prudential Financial and Genworth Financial (formerly GE Capital Assurance).

Cahill Gordon & Reindel

The Firm: Especially noted by peers for its work with AIG in various domestic and international disputes, this practice also wins praise for its reinsurance expertise. The group has also been advising Prudential in trade secrets litigation involving the claimed 'invention' of the concept of securitization of music royalties; the case led to the issuance by rock star David Bowie of what became known as 'Bowie Bonds.'

The Lawyers: The "*hard-working*" **Ed Krugman** is "*one of the smartest guys in the reinsurance world,*" clients said. "*For a life-or-death dispute, go to him.*"

The Clients: Major matters include the representation of Deutsche Bank in insurance claims related to the World Trade Center stemming from the 9/11 terrorist attacks. The firm has also counseled other prominent investment banks, international insurance companies and major corporations.

Mendes & Mount LLP

The Firm: This established insurance specialist firm has been "*an active participant*" in the field,

especially in relation to its representation of Lloyd's and other prominent entities in the London market as outside coverage counsel in disputes. Areas of expertise for the practice include asbestos/health hazard matters, aviation and space, professional liability and property coverage. Other niche specialties encompass marine, political risk and pollution coverage disputes. Its reinsurance experience covers areas such as arbitration, litigation and audits.

The Lawyers: John Larkin is one of the key members of the team. His practice also includes a strong focus on D&O liability.

The Clients: Clients include domestic and overseas insureds, insurers and reinsurers.

Wilson, Elser, Moskowitz, Edelman & Dicker LLP

The Firm: The team won accolades as a cost-efficient outfit that largely handles "*basic insurance coverage defense work for domestic insurers.*" One appreciative client particularly pointed to its attributes of having "*multiple locations around the country and expertise in run-rate litigation.*" Insurance-related corporate and regulatory experience is also on offer.

The Lawyers: Thomas Wilson is chairman of the executive committee of the firm, with his expertise including the drafting of insurance and reinsurance agreements, defending claims, and providing counsel on product development and new types of insurance.

The Clients: The firm has advised insurers, insureds, brokers, agents, reinsurance intermediaries, surplus lines brokers, managing general agents and reinsurers.

Other Notable Practitioners

Tom Newman (see p.1305) at Duane Morris is an established name whose practice encompasses insurance coverage analysis, and insurance and reinsurance arbitrations. He has also acted as an expert witness on various cases, and co-authored, with Barry Ostrager, the prominent insurance treatise titled 'Handbook on Insurance Coverage Disputes'. The success of **Richard Fields** (see p.1305) may well be explained by his "*creative and charming approach.*" He focuses upon negotiation and is respected by insurers and outside counsel alike. He recently moved from Dickstein Shapiro Morin & Oshinsky LLP Washington, DC offices New York where he is a partner in the litigation & dispute resolution group.

INTELLECTUAL PROPERTY

New York
Leading firms (Intellectual Property)

1 FISH & NEAVE IP GROUP *New York*
FITZPATRICK, CELLA, HARPER *New York*
KIRKLAND & ELLIS LLP *New York*

2 CRAVATH, SWAINE & MOORE LLP *New York*
DEBEVOISE & PLIMPTON LLP *New York*
FISH & RICHARDSON *New York*
KAYE SCHOLER LLP *New York*
KENYON & KENYON *New York*
MORGAN & FINNEGAN, LLP *New York*
O'MELVENY & MYERS LLP *New York*
WEIL, GOTSHAL & MANGES LLP *New York*
WHITE & CASE LLP *New York*
WILMER CUTLER PICKERING HALE *New York*

3 BAKER BOTTS LLP *New York*
BROWN RAYSMAN MILLSTEIN FELDER *New York*
COWAN, LIEBOWITZ & LATMAN *New York*
FRIED, FRANK, HARRIS, SHRIVER *New York*
FROSS ZELNICK LEHRMAN & ZISSU PC *New York*
GOODWIN PROCTER LLP *New York*
JONES DAY *New York*
MAYER, BROWN, ROWE & MAW LLP *New York*
ORRICK, HERRINGTON & SUTCLIFFE *New York*
PATTERSON, BELKNAP, WEBB & TYLER *New York*
PAUL, HASTINGS, JANOFSKY & WALKER *New York*
SHEARMAN & STERLING LLP *New York*
SKADDEN, ARPS, SLATE, MEAGHER *New York*

Firms are listed alphabetically in each band.

Band 1

Fish & Neave IP Group of Ropes & Gray

The Firm: The recent merger of one of the city's most established IP outfits with the dominant international player has culminated in the tripling of the team's numbers. Renamed the Fish & Neave IP Group of Ropes & Gray, the phalanx of about 200 lawyers proved conversant in nearly every nook and cranny of the IP world. Litigation, rights management and licensing services all are on offer at this "*hardcore*" practice. Recent victories include a research tool patent case involving AstraZeneca. In a landmark ruling, the revered litigator Jesse Jenner prevailed in a case pertaining to a number of submarine patents filed by controversial inventor Jerome Lemelson; the dispute involved a small group of manufacturers of machine vision and bar code reading equipment.

The Lawyers: Fish Neave's **Herbert Schwartz** (see p.1318) remains a true behemoth of the IP litigation world. The "*vastly experienced*" Schwartz is known for his "*encyclopedic mind*" and has acted as lead counsel for a large number of influential clients. He is widely considered to "*belong at the top of the tree.*" **Jesse Jenner** (see p.1291) is "*absolutely first class,*" commentators said, leading a team that succeeded in overturning a landmark copyrights infringement case. **Robert Morgan**'s (see p.1302) trial practice is focused in the fields of telecom, electronics, semiconductor technology, and medical instruments and products. **James Haley** (see p.1286) concentrates in the worldwide procurement, defense and enforcement of patents in the biotech, pharmaceutical and chemical industries.
The Clients: Yale University; Coca-Cola; Motorola; PayPal; Aventis Pharmaceutical; TKT and Cognex.

Fitzpatrick, Cella, Harper & Scinto
See firm details p.1348
The Firm: This traditional boutique firm remains one of the leaders in the field of patent litigation. It boasts a prestigious clientele due to its "*extremely service-orientated*" approach and record of success "*right across the board.*" Its "*excellent pharmaceutical work deserves to be at the top,*" say observers; for example, the team advised Altana Pharma and Warner Chilcott amongst others. It has successfully represented Novartis in a patent infringement case involving its antifungal drug Lamisil. In defending its client Tanning Research Laboratories, it crushed giant Johnson & Johnson in a trademark dispute.
The Lawyers: The "*dominant force*" at the firm is **Bob Baechtold** (see p.1264), a "*patent litigator of extremely proficient ability,*" described as a "*go-to guy.*" **Joseph O'Malley** (see p.1306) receives plaudits as an "*effective litigator.*"
The Clients: Condé Nast Publications; Pfizer; Bausch & Lomb; St. John's University and Emory University.

Kirkland & Ellis LLP
See firm details p.770
The Firm: The litigation all-rounder inevitably stretches its tentacles to the IP sector, having established an "*excellent and very cost-effective*" operation anchored by its instinct for the jugular. Ascending in the ranks this year, the team has demonstrated proficiency not only as a stable of talented IP litigators but also as trial lawyers. "*Both older and younger lawyers there are extremely proficient,*" clients said. "*They are really a great bunch across the board.*" Though its high points no doubt involve dispute resolution, the firm also supports clients on the transaction front. Internet and e-commerce matters all figure prominently in its diet, and the team further benefits from a largely industrial client base globally. Overseas clients also rate the team's abilities: "*They really helped us to get a grip on US IP culture.*"
The Lawyers: **John Desmarais** (see p.1275) enjoys an outstanding reputation as a hard-nosed warrior with "*great legal acumen,*" which combines with his practicality to deliver success for his clients. "*He is the best of the best,*" they said, and added: "*He's a very effective IP lawyer.*"

His background in chemical engineering has also nurtured his practice.
The Clients: Hermes International, Honeywell Aerospace, Alcon Laboratories and Siemens.

Band 2

Cravath, Swaine & Moore LLP
See firm details p.1344
The Firm: This Wall Street powerhouse fields a "*thriving*" IP practice indicative of the overall market trend, which has witnessed an increase in the number of larger firms making significant inroads into the IP arena – a field once dominated by specialist boutiques. Packing a hefty punch with its "*incredible*" resources, the firm is noted for its efficiency and attention to detail. Its "*excellent expertise and very high trial experience*" covers a wide range of IP work, though a particular strength is its patent litigation practice. The firm has represented the Martha Graham Center of Contemporary Dance in a courtroom battle that ultimately granted ownership of all but two of Martha Graham's dances to its client. It has also successfully counseled Warner Music Group record labels in an action alleging infringement of their federal copyrights in sound recordings by an online 'cyber locker' service. Another feather in its cap is defending IBM against claims of patent infringement with respect to digital video compression technology.
The Lawyers: Generalist **Evan Chesler** (see p.1272) heads a team universally considered by clients to be "*exceptionally hard working and responsive.*" Peers describe Chesler as "*a clear thinker who gets to the heart of the matter very quickly.*" His skills also extend beyond the courtroom, with clients adding: "*He's a great person to have at board meetings; he brings a lot to the table.*" The "*mind-bogglingly focused*" **Katherine Forrest** (see p.1280) is another key member of the team, who has won significant cases in the past year for Time Warner. She is joined by the "*excellent*" **Tom Rafferty**, who is praised for his "*great courtroom presence.*"
The Clients: Qualcomm; Medinol; Glaxo-SmithKline; IBM; Time Warner and Alcoa.

Debevoise & Plimpton LLP
See firm details p.1346
The Firm: This international player is recognized for its "*highly skilled*" trademark practice as part of a broader and respected IP practice. Heavily involved in the burgeoning realm of Internet-based IP, the firm has successfully procured an injunction against a Canadian company in relation to the retransmission of US television broadcasts over the Internet. In a more conventional gear of the practice, the group sustains its impressive record with regards to industrial and pharmaceutical copyright and

New York
Leading individuals
(Intellectual Property)

Senior Statesman
SCHWARTZ Herbert *Fish & Neave*, New York
★ BAECHTOLD Robert *Fitzpatrick Cella*, New York

[1] BEN-AMI Leora *Kaye Scholer*, New York
DESMARAIS John *Kirkland & Ellis*, New York
DRIVAS Dimitrios *White & Case*, New York

[2] CENDALI Dale *O'Melveny & Myers*, New York
CHESLER Evan *Cravath Swaine*, New York
CORUZZI Laura *Jones Day*, New York
DISALVATORE William *Wilmer Cutler*, New York
FILARDI Edward *Skadden Arps*, New York
JENNER Jesse *Fish & Neave*, New York
KOENIGSBERG I Fred *White & Case*, New York
LEE Steven *Kenyon & Kenyon*, New York
SOBEL Gerald *Kaye Scholer*, New York
SWEENEY John *Morgan & Finnegan*, New York

[3] BECK Thomas *Sidley Austin*, New York
BERNSTEIN David *Debevoise & Plimpton*, New York
CREEL Thomas *Goodwin Procter*, New York
DABNEY James *Fried Frank*, New York
DELUCIA Richard *Kenyon & Kenyon*, New York
DEROSA Frank *Brown Raysman*, New York
DIMATTEO John *Willkie Farr*, New York
DISKANT Gregory *Patterson Belknap*, New York
FORREST Katherine *Cravath Swaine*, New York
FRANCESCANI David *Fish & Richardson*, New York
GILLIS Theresa *Jones Day*, New York
GLAZER Steven *Weil Gotshal*, New York
GUPTA Paul *Mayer Brown*, New York
HALEY James *Fish & Neave*, New York
HUGHES Christopher *Morgan & Finnegan*, New York
ISACKSON Robert *Orrick Herrington*, New York
KATSH Salem *Shearman & Sterling*, New York
KELLER Bruce *Debevoise & Plimpton*, New York
LOVE Jane *Wilmer Cutler*, New York
MORGAN Robert *Fish & Neave*, New York
NEUNER Robert *Baker Botts*, New York
O'MALLEY Joseph *Fitzpatrick Cella*, New York
PUGLIESE Frank *Brown Raysman*, New York
RABINOWITZ Stephen *Fried Frank*, New York
RAFFERTY Thomas *Cravath Swaine*, New York
SCHEINFELD Robert *Baker Botts*, New York
SEIDE Rochelle *Arent Fox*, New York
SHERMAN Robert *Paul Hastings*, New York
THOMASCH Daniel *Orrick Herrington*, New York

Up-and-coming individuals
WALDEN S Calvin *Wilmer Cutler*, New York

Individuals are listed alphabetically in each band.

patent proceedings. The team has twice succeeded in patent infringement challenges on behalf of Tilia. The firm also proved victorious in advising an internationally acclaimed rock band in a trademark infringement case involving a local wedding band of the same name.
The Lawyers: **Bruce Keller** supervises the firm's IP litigation practice. Keller has litigated a number of widely publicized disputes on behalf

of Howard Stern and CBS Radio amongst others. Straddling the litigation and IP departments is **David Bernstein**, whose courtroom prowess gained widespread client approval. "*He's balanced in his approach and goes far beyond taking instructions,*" one client said. "*I greatly value his judgment, which is impeccable. He really cares about doing the right things for the client.*"
The Clients: The group represents a stratified clientele including a major sports league, financial services companies, pharmaceutical companies, rock bands, automotive companies and the various media organizations.

Fish & Richardson
The Firm: This firm straddles the gap in the market between the specialist boutiques and generalist firms, integrating a traditional vein of IP work with a more recently established corporate and litigation core of expertise. "*They offer a very good service and since IP is a difficult specialty to understand, their straight-talking approach makes me feel really comfortable,*" one client said. The emphasis is on the technical – including semiconductors, optics, electronics, computer software and medical devices among other products. In this capacity "*they sure know what they are talking about,*" commentators said. The group proved "*effective as a team,*" which further enhances its broad repertoire.
The Lawyers: Heading up the New York practice is **David Francescani**, described by commentators as "*thorough and very dedicated.*" Clients are particularly quick to praise his "*hands-on*" approach and his ability to clarify difficult problems: "*He can communicate complex issues in an effective manner, which always convinces a jury.*"
The Clients: Atmel, LSI Logic and Nokia are featured in the firm's prominent clientele.

Kaye Scholer LLP
See firm details p.1354
The Firm: This international practice draws on the skills of approximately 500 lawyers in nine offices around the world. Its global transaction and litigation capability covers a multitude of practices in areas including litigation, corporate, real estate, bankruptcy and tax. The IP group is better known for its litigation prowess, and is considered a heavyweight in the biotech arena. Clients are attracted to its "*great strength*" in pharmaceuticals, recently participating in a major case involving genetic engineering of agricultural crops. One of the group's principal clients is Pfizer, for whom it has undertaken numerous patent infringement cases involving new pharmaceutical products such as Viagra. The team's expanding practice is also making inroads in the Internet sector.
The Lawyers: Cochair of the patent department **Gerald Sobel** (see p.1322) is often described as "*a wonderful intellectual talent.*" He

specializes in patent work in the fields of pharmaceutical, electronics and biotech. Formerly of Fish and Richardson, **Leora Ben-Ami** (see p.1266) is a "*highly sought-after*" new addition to the team. A prosecution specialist, she is known for her extensive trial experience and for being "*terrific on her feet.*" Clients and peers concur that she is "*extremely articulate*" and one of the "*smartest*" IP lawyers around.
The Clients: Siemens and Pfizer have sought the firm's expertise, along with a number of other pharmaceutical and manufacturing companies.

Kenyon & Kenyon
The Firm: A significant player in the IP market, this "*cost-effective*" boutique firm is recognized for its diversity. Lauded for its patent litigation work, it also provides licensing and counseling services regarding copyrights, trade secrets and trademarks. On behalf of Sony, this "*top firm*" prevailed against Soundview Technologies in a patent infringement dispute. It also assisted Teva Pharmaceutical USA in quashing a patent claim relating to human growth hormone. One client added: "*They provide a truly great business-sensitive service, absolutely.*"
The Lawyers: While his combative nature might not be to everyone's taste, there is no doubting **Richard DeLucia**'s effectiveness in battle. The patent litigator "*does an excellent job*" on a variety of complex disputes, while the "*extremely able*" **Steve Lee** is described as a "*star*" in the field of chemical and biochemical litigation.
The Clients: The team acts for a diverse range of corporations from varying industry sectors, as well as a number of academic and research institutions.

Morgan & Finnegan, LLP
See firm details p.1360
The Firm: This "*thorough and prompt*" team is viewed by interviewees as one of the "*established figures*" in the market. With particular expertise noted in the field of patent litigation, the group also offers IP expertise in the areas of biotech, e-commerce, pharmaceuticals, medical technology and antitrust among others. Clients comment that the firm has great relations with other departments, which act as "*team players*" on complicated issues.
The Lawyers: **Chris Hughes** (see p.1289) heads the firm's IP team, representing IBM in various patent litigations, including actions brought by TM Patents and Digital Development Corporation. Known to run a "*very lean ship,*" the firm "*does what needs to be done without overdoing it,*" clients said, referring to the clarity of work. The group is defending IBM against patent infringement claims relating to computer virus detection patents. Working with Hughes is first-rate lawyer **John Sweeney** (see p.1325), a technically savvy operator whose "*top-*

class" advocacy won client confidence.

The Clients: Bombardier; ChevronTexaco; DuPont; Fujitsu; Hoffmann-La Roche; IBM; Procter & Gamble; Rolex; Toyota and WL Gore & Associates.

O'Melveny & Myers LLP

See firm details p.294

The Firm: This established general practice draws on the resources of more than 14 offices worldwide, representing a diverse group of successful businesses and individuals. This includes emerging companies, national and multinational corporations, Internet ventures and investors. The team also works closely with a network of foreign counsel and agents to devise global IP strategies. Market commentators are especially impressed by the *"superb job"* on trademark issues: *"They put forth an astonishingly well-constructed case fairly rapidly."*

The Lawyers: Chair of the copyright, trademark and Internet practice group, **Dale Cendali** is portrayed as an exceptionally experienced IP litigator. One client added: *"Dale made me feel like the world was behind me."* Cendali's practice spans copyright, trademark, patent and trade secrets law. This IP core is supplemented by her familiarity in defamation, publicity rights, false advertising and related media law issues.

The Clients: The firm has represented individuals and businesses – including emerging and middle-market companies, major national and international corporations, venture capitalists, financial institutions and investment bankers.

Weil, Gotshal & Manges LLP

See firm details p.1378

The Firm: A host of high-profile, blue-chip clients and a long-standing presence in the IP arena are distinguishing features of this international powerhouse's IP practice. The group is widely reputed to be one of the leading lights in the litigation field, winning particular plaudits for its patents work. Covering a range of technical areas including electronics, biotech and genetics, the firm has also demonstrated *"excellence"* in traditional IP issues such as the media and Internet. The technically advanced team can call on the substantial patent resources of offices proliferated throughout the nation. Such firmwide integration allows clients to tap into the vast pool of more than 1,200 lawyers. Members of the 45-attorney team of specialists in the established New York office recently won a victory for Yeda Research and Development in a case involving a drug used to treat rheumatoid arthritis.

The Lawyers: As cochair of the New York patent litigation and counseling group, **Steven Glazer** (see p.1283) enjoys a reputation for deftly handling the needs of a wide-ranging client base. He is pitched as *"one of the smartest patent attorneys"* in the market, often coordinating a

team on multinational patent actions. He has handled cases for clients involved in such diverse fields as genetic engineering and satellite television, as well as significant patent work for GlaxoSmithKline.

The Clients: American Airlines; Applied Materials; BMW; Bristol-Myers Squibb; Cisco Systems; ExxonMobil; GE; Matsushita; Pfizer; Pirelli; Reuters and GlaxoSmithKline.

White & Case LLP

See firm details p.1379

The Firm: At *"the cutting edge"* of the international IP scene is this *"extremely effective"* firm, which houses more than 100 lawyers with expertise in the practice area. It also benefits from cross-generational strength that appears to be flourishing. Handling nearly every aspect of the multijurisdictional IP market, this *"outstanding staff"* counsels on trademarks, copyrights and trade secrets. Other interests involve counterfeiting, infringement, misappropriation and unfair competition. Clients particularly commend its international reach: *"This is a great firm for foreign work – it has a really broad-based practice."*

The Lawyers: Market commentators *"think the world"* of renowned litigator **Dimitrios Drivas** (see p.1276), who is also cochair of the IP section. He *"exceeds expectations"* on a number of high-profile cases linked to genetics and pharmaceutical companies. *"He's unbelievably good,"* said sources, who also described him as *"a lawyer with panache and flair."* Amongst his colleagues, **Fred Koenigsberg** (see p.1294) stands out as *"an engine firing on all its cylinders."* He made his mark in the field of music-related IP issues.

The Clients: American Society of Composers, Authors and Publishers (ASCAP); IBM; Disney; Pfizer; Bristol-Myers Squibb and AstraZeneca.

Wilmer Cutler Pickering Hale and Dorr LLP

See firm details p.497

The Firm: Hale and Dorr merged with Wilmer Cutler in May 2004. The result is a new firm *"punching at the top weight."* The amalgamation of these established outfits has sent the profile of this international firm skyrocketing. Described as *"a one-stop solution"* for IP prosecution, litigation and licensing, this firm offers deep bench resources further enhanced by an extensive support network. Areas of growth include Internet-related issues, particularly those that result in litigation. The firm has recently dealt with a number of *"big-ticket"* cases regarding Internet sales and pop-up advertisements. Clients believe the team is worth every penny, adding: *"They are unashamedly expensive, but unashamedly right."*

The Lawyers: Clients rave about the *"thoughtful and careful"* **Jane Love** (see p.1298). *"She's pretty much my textbook on the prosecution side,"*

one said. The indefatigable **William DiSalvatore** (see p.1276), who heads the practice, tends to a range of high-profile clients. *"He has the ability to read the complex nuances of situations,"* one said. *"I can fully understand why he wins most of his litigation cases. I wouldn't like to be on the other side."* Credited for his tenacity and attention to detail is **Calvin Walden** (see p.1330). *"He's the man"* for patent litigation and licensing disputes, clients said. He also advises clients concerning IP-related asset management, new products and licensing issues.

The Clients: Pfizer; Syngenta; Taro Pharmaceuticals and Creo.

Band 3

Baker Botts LLP

See firm details p.1708

The Firm: A *"strong, energetic"* team sustains the New York IP profile, though the group is ably supported by more than 600 attorneys firmwide serving a global client base. Representing an impressive client list, many of which are Fortune 100 companies, the team is fluent in biotech and electronics technology. With a number of its lawyers boasting degrees in such areas as medicine, chemistry and engineering, its range of expertise has proven a versatile asset for clients.

The Lawyers: The *"legendary"* advocacy skills of **Bob Neuner** (see p.1304) were successfully illustrated in the defense of Northern Telecom in a billion-dollar patent infringement trial in the Northern District of California. Head of the department in the New York office, **Robert Scheinfeld** (see p.1317) sees right to the heart of thorny IP matters, commentators said. A main contact for patent issues, his representations involve electronics, telecom, smart cards and flash memory matters among others.

The Clients: Infineon Technologies, Northern Technologies and Columbia University are among some of the companies and academic institutions that the firm represents.

Brown Raysman Millstein Felder & Steiner LLP

See firm details p.1338

The Firm: Praised for its *"excellent expertise"* in matters relating to the media, the team's scope extends from technology and IP to include matters related to corporate finance, securities, M&A and litigation. Real estate, bankruptcy, healthcare and employment law also feature in its portfolio. The *"knowledgeable"* team has litigated patent matters pertaining to computer software and biomedical devices among others. Commanding a substantial network of international contacts, it delivers quality at competitive prices. Clients appreciate its *"timely, efficient and responsive"* approach as well as the team's *"genuine interest in our business."*

The Lawyers: Frank Pugliese (see p.1310) has advised clients on IP issues related to software contract work and licensing. He is also fluent in software and hardware licensing, outsourcing, computer systems and e-commerce. One significant deal involved a major healthcare institution in the acquisition of clinical and financial systems. The *"knowledgeable and professional"* cochair of the IP group, **Frank DeRosa** (see p.1275), concentrates in patent law with an emphasis on counseling on infringement issues both domestically and internationally. He is also an expert on what can be patented.

The Clients: The team looks after the interests of a diverse clientele including investment banks, venture capital firms, software developers, financial services, insurance companies and Internet businesses. Others involve the securities trading, television, music, telecom, healthcare and gaming sectors.

Cowan, Liebowitz & Latman

The Firm: Lauded for its copyright work, this well-respected IP specialist boosted its profile in August 2004 by merging with Robin, Blecker & Daley. Described by clients as *"primarily a go-to firm for trademarks,"* it also delivers expertise in other major practice areas including litigation and commercial transactions. It is best known for its work in the fashion and media sectors, for example, obtaining permanent injunctions and monetary settlements on behalf of Calvin Klein's fragrance licensee; the civil action was against manufacturers, distributors and retailers of counterfeit Calvin Klein Eternity For Men fragrance. The firm has also successfully obtained a summary judgment on behalf of its client in a case involving SQWISH fish-shaped gummy candy.

The Lawyers: The recent merger with Robin, Blecker & Daley has increased the numbers of the respected group, whose *"top-notch"* lawyers prepare and prosecute patent and trademark applications for international and domestic clients. Arthur Greenbaum heads this team.

The Clients: Donna Karan; The Metropolitan Museum of Art; Sotheby's; Clear Channel; Estée Lauder and TriStar Pictures.

Fried, Frank, Harris, Shriver & Jacobson LLP

See firm details p.1349

The Firm: The established team amalgamates its IP and technology teams, delivering a full service that includes transactional and litigation expertise oriented toward the complex side of the spectrum. Further enhancing its strength are patent attorneys who recently joined the firm from Pennie & Edmonds. Remaining *"very active"* in the financial services sector, the team has participated in disputes that examine the notion of business method patents. In another case, the team is representing ICAP in a patent

controversy against Cantor Fitzgerald. The group also serves as US trademark agent for Virgin, which has involved a cybersquatting claim against a company that registered under 'virgin cars.'

The Lawyers: Stephen Rabinowitz (see p.1311) and **James Dabney** (see p.1274) represent opposite ends of the IP spectrum, the former taking on specialized cases with a particular focus on the pharmaceuticals industry. Formerly of Pennie & Edmonds, Dabney has a broader-based IP practice that encompasses a range of issues – including questions of validity, enforceability and infringement of US patents. His practice also features copyrights, trade secrets, trademarks and related commercial disputes.

The Clients: MCI; Apple; USinternetworking; Lucent Technologies; SRA International; Silicon Graphics and Deloitte Touche Tohmatsu.

Fross Zelnick Lehrman & Zissu PC

The Firm: One of the largest IP specialists, the team's remit is exclusively focused on such matters as trademark, copyright and related unfair competition law. Consistently involved in high-level international copyright work, the New York operation offers *"expert and dogged"* advice. Clients value the group's *"persistence"* and add that the firm is simply *"a pleasure to work with."*

The Lawyers: Ron Lehrman and Roger Zissu are key players for the team.

The Clients: Esprit International; Forbes; Fairmont Hotel Management; Honeywell; Larry Harmon Pictures; The Jim Henson Company; Guerlain and Four Seasons Hotels (Barbados).

Goodwin Procter LLP

See firm details p.980

The Firm: With a growing number of specialists joining the ranks, this practice combines the depth of expertise of a boutique IP firm with the corporate and litigation resources of one of the nation's largest law firms. The team won a summary judgment involving an antidepressant drug, and separately acted on a case linked to the rights of the film 'Dawn of the Dead'. Peers note the team is showing significant dynamism, with some success, as illustrated by its ascending profile in New York.

The Lawyers: Head of the firm's IP litigation practice, **Thomas Creel** (see p.1273) specializes in patents. He has represented clients in such industries as microprocessor manufacturing, chemical engineering and biotech.

The Clients: Wang Laboratories; Xerox; Teva Pharmaceuticals USA are among the diverse clientele that the firm serves.

Jones Day

See firm details p.485

The Firm: Firmwide cross-references helped boost this practice's standing. Deemed a *"very professional, very responsive"* IP team, its lawyers

adhere to the firm's litigious focus, though patent prosecution, trademark applications and related issues figure prominently. Also on offer is its expertise in technology transfers and licensing. Peers and clients agree the firm always *"puts together very good patent prosecution teams"* and excels in litigation.

The Lawyers: Laura Coruzzi (see p.1273) continues to wow market commentators since her move from Pennie & Edmonds. With her robust knowledge of the biotech field, she is considered *"a top-class lawyer,"* clients said. The *"competent and capable"* **Theresa Gillis** (see p.1283) is recognized for her vast experience in IP law. She has had extensive involvement in litigation relating to patent infringement, enforceability, misuse and related matters. Copyright and trademark law also feature in her portfolio.

The Clients: The firm represents national and international clients from the biotech and pharmaceutical, chemical, electrical, and mechanical industries amongst others.

Mayer, Brown, Rowe & Maw LLP

See firm details p.771

The Firm: As one of the ten largest legal outfits in the world, this Goliath of a firm's IP capability straddles the corporate and litigation departments. In the dispute resolution realm, the firm often delivers its dose of copyright, trademark and patent advocacy with exceptional skill, commentators said. Its strength overseas, particularly in the London office, further strengthens the group.

The Lawyers: An expert in cyber security, **Paul Gupta**'s (see p.1286) clients describe him as *"a tireless worker."* His tenacity is visible in a range of IP matters as part of a broader practice that also includes antitrust, IT and other commercial disputes.

The Clients: Honeywell, Fabio Perini and Ensyn Petroleum are notable clients of the practice.

Orrick, Herrington & Sutcliffe

See firm details p.295

The Firm: Gunning for a prime position in the market with a stable of high-stake clients, the team's vigorous push into the IP realm has met some success in New York. An *"accomplished"* global practice further shapes the group, which is defined by a *"competitive, business-focused approach."* The team is known to be particularly strong in patent law, counting Boston Scientific as one of its anchor clients. A proclivity toward healthcare results in expertise related to medical imaging systems, ultrasound equipment, drug delivery and angioplasty systems among others. In the field of Internet liability, the firm was immersed in a considerable cybersquatting case over the rights to use a 'delta.com' web site in Delta Funding Corporation v Delta Air Lines. The case settled with the domain name transferring to the firm's client – Delta Air Lines.

The Lawyers: Chair of the firm's nationwide litigation practice, **Dan Thomasch** (see p.1327) is especially well known for his work on patent cases. His practice focuses on complex product liability and patent infringement actions. This *"tremendous litigator"* is joined by the *"thorough"* **Robert Isackson** (see p.1290), who is considered to be an *"exceptionally dedicated"* advocate. He is involved in a patent infringement dispute concerning copper foil laminate technology used in the manufacturing of multi-layered printed circuit boards.

The Clients: Alcon Laboratories; American Express; Bayer; Delta Air Lines; Dow Agro-Sciences; Genentech; Nikko Material USA; SonoSite; Universal Instruments and Xerox.

Patterson, Belknap, Webb & Tyler LLP

The Firm: This *"top litigation shop"* exerts influence on the IP marketplace mainly through its dealings in copyright, licensing, patents, trademarks and trade secrets. The litigation department has made waves with its significant wins in the media arena. It represented a major radio network in a copyright infringement concerning the use of the Rolling Stones' song 'Satisfaction' in a network promotion. On the transaction front, the team lures clients with its high-quality, cost-efficient approach. The *"one-on-one"* attention also proved valuable to clients.

The Lawyers: The *"effective"* **Gregory Diskant** participates in IP litigation as part of a more general practice, which also comprises securities and contract disputes.

The Clients: The group acts for an array of both large corporations and small emerging companies in a diverse array of industries.

Paul, Hastings, Janofsky & Walker LLP
See firm details p.297

The Firm: The firm's strength in IP is by way of its litigation prowess, which reigns *"supreme,"* according to observers. Clients rate their *"absolutely confident, up-to-date"* approach, also noting that its lawyers *"recognize the important synergies between IP law and business goals."* Drawing on an international team of over 80 top-caliber IP attorneys in 15 offices worldwide, the *"courteous, knowledgeable and prompt"* team has attracted attention with its *"exceptional competence."*

The Lawyers: The *"insightful"* **Robert Sherman** (see p.1320) concentrates on litigating matters involving trademarks, copyrights, unfair competition and false advertising. A broad practice also takes in direct marketing, advertising and promotion law. Described by peers as *"a very skilled and capable attorney,"* he won client respect for his ability to *"assess problems on the spot."*

The Clients: Masco Corporation; Toni & Guy; Jones Apparel Group; Nine West Group; L'Oréal USA; Colgate-Palmolive and Yahoo! USA.

Shearman & Sterling LLP
See firm details p.1369

The Firm: A truly global concern, this firm's vast international presence provides deep bench resources to the team of ten patent lawyers in New York. The group works closely with the M&A department, which is a centrepiece of its transactional practice. In litigation, the team has argued complex trade secrets litigation in addition to a raft of other significant disputes.

The Lawyers: Head of the firm's IP group, **Salem Katsh** (see p.1292) is respected for his work concerning patents, trademarks, trade secrets and other related matters. He also turns a deft hand to business torts, copyrights and Internet-related matters. An ability to *"grab the essence of a point"* is blended with business acumen, clients said.

The Clients: The group acts for large Fortune 500 corporations as well as a number of smaller entrepreneurial outfits and individuals.

Skadden, Arps, Slate, Meagher & Flom LLP & Affiliates
See firm details p.1372

The Firm: With enormous influence in both the corporate and litigation arenas, it is not surprising that Skadden would also be a contender in IP. It excels in *"big-ticket"* litigation, proving so skilled in the field that one commentator dubbed its approach a *"state-of-the-art"* affair. When it comes to complex corporate deals, the firm also fields a strong team that is equally versed in antitrust law. This is a *"go-to"* firm for cross-border transactions, observers added.

The Lawyers: **Edward Filardi** (see p.1279) displays *"unequivocal talent"* across a host of complex IP matters, but particularly when they are tinged with antitrust law. He also wins plaudits for his sharp thinking and legal clarity.

The Clients: The team serves a global stable of clients from a range of industry sectors.

Other Notable Practitioners
The *"truly excellent"* **John DiMatteo** (see p.1276) of Willkie Farr & Gallagher LLP is a renowned authority on patents, trade secrets, trademarks and IP licensing issues. Chair of the IP department, he successfully defended a major European manufacturer in a case before the ITC concerning three patents relating to methods and apparatuses for mechanically locking floor panels. Formerly of Baker Botts, the *"straight-talking"* **Rochelle Seide** is perceived as a boost to the IP capabilities at Arent Fox PLLC. Her clients regard her to be extremely responsive, and value her understanding of budgetary constraints. Lauded for her appreciation of the corporate side of the biomedical industry, Siede is described as *"a real-world lawyer".* At Sidley Austin Brown & Wood LLP, **Thomas Beck** (see p.1265) focuses on complex chemical and pharmaceutical litigation matters. He has played significant roles in chemical and pharmaceutical litigation at both the trial and appellate levels. His clientele includes pharmaceutical, chemical and biotech companies.

LITIGATION

Cravath, Swaine & Moore LLP
See firm details p.1344

The Firm: This blue-blooded New York classic fields a team that *"commands tremendous respect"* from the market, winning marks for its ability to slug it out with the best of them while sustaining a certain brand of steely composure. It demonstrates particular agility in tough, thorny problems with wide-ranging repercussions. For example, it won a groundbreaking case in favor of its client Warner Music Group involving record companies' rights to distribute music over the Internet. As a reflection of its prestigious corporate and securities practices, the team is also a potent force with regards to the related litigation. In the antitrust arena, the cadre of *"tremendous strategists"* is paid homage not only by its clients, but also by government officials. On the securities side, it is defending Deloitte & Touche against a securities class action and stockholder derivative cases pertaining to Adelphia Communications. An unrelenting dedication to M&A also means that it often participates in the intricacies of corporate governance law and gets lured into subsequent bankruptcy litigation when businesses fail. Clients instinctively trust the team *"to navigate its way around difficulties."* A more recent resolution to pursue a larger role in international arbitration is also paying dividends, and the team has successfully represented Fiat in arbitration against Ford concerning a certain business acquisition.

The Lawyers: Legal all-rounder **Evan Chesler** (see p.1272) takes his cue from a stable of top-flight clients who depend on his combination of

New York
Leading firms
(Litigation: General Commercial)

1 CRAVATH, SWAINE & MOORE LLP *New York*
DAVIS POLK & WARDWELL *New York*
PAUL, WEISS, RIFKIND, WHARTON *New York*
SIMPSON THACHER & BARTLETT LLP *New York*
SKADDEN, ARPS, SLATE, MEAGHER *New York*
SULLIVAN & CROMWELL LLP *New York*
WACHTELL, LIPTON, ROSEN & KATZ *New York*

2 BOIES, SCHILLER & FLEXNER LLP *Armonk*
CAHILL GORDON & REINDEL *New York*
CLEARY GOTTLIEB STEEN & HAMILTON *New York*
DEBEVOISE & PLIMPTON LLP *New York*
WEIL, GOTSHAL & MANGES LLP *New York*

3 CADWALADER, WICKERSHAM & TAFT *New York*
GIBSON, DUNN & CRUTCHER LLP *New York*
KIRKLAND & ELLIS LLP *New York*
KRAMER LEVIN NAFTALIS & FRANKEL *New York*
SHEARMAN & STERLING LLP *New York*

4 CLIFFORD CHANCE US LLP *New York*
CURTIS, MALLET-PREVOST, COLT *New York*
DEWEY BALLANTINE LLP *New York*
FRIED, FRANK, HARRIS, SHRIVER *New York*
JONES DAY *New York*
KAYE SCHOLER LLP *New York*
LATHAM & WATKINS LLP *New York*
MORRISON & FOERSTER LLP *New York*
WHITE & CASE LLP *New York*
WILLKIE FARR & GALLAGHER LLP *New York*
WILMER CUTLER PICKERING HALE *New York*

Firms are listed alphabetically in each band.

"*fearless determination and reasonable nature*" to guide them through legal labyrinths. The leader of the firm's litigation department has partaken in some of the nation's juiciest cases, most recently defending IBM in a headline matter in Detroit. The case alleges that IBM illegally obtained information from Compuware to develop its own software and then undercut its competition by offering deep discounts. Compuware is seeking millions of dollars in lost profits. **Paul Saunders** (see p.1264) gained client confidence with his heady mixture of "*courage and adaptability*." He is participating in significant securities litigation on behalf of a French company and advising the Republic of Surinam in an international arbitration matter concerning a maritime boundary dispute. "*Often, he has to tell us what we don't want to hear or embrace a particular strategy we don't want to,*" a client said. "*He's very convincing.*" Another pillar in the international arbitration realm is **Richard Clary** (see p.1264), though he is better known throughout the marketplace as "*a consensus builder*" with regards to a prominent securities litigation practice. Also enhancing the firm's securities profile is **Robert Baron** (see p.1264), who has been involved in high-profile litigation on behalf of issuers embroiled in disputes linked to securities offerings, M&A and similar transactions.

The Clients: Westinghouse; Alcoa; BAE Systems; Deloitte & Touche; Fiat; Lucent Technologies; Republic of Surinam; PwC and IBM.

Davis Polk & Wardwell
See firm details p.1345
The Firm: "*One of the biggest and most imposing litigation animals in the jungle,*" Davis Polk has always prided itself on its success in this area. Whether it be straight commercial litigation, securities matters or white collar – where the firm really distinguishes itself, it "*has the team to delight its clients and petrify its opponents.*" As an informally constituted unit rather than a discrete department, it can call on about 150 litigators, giving it a depth few of its competitors can rival. Commentators admired the international reach of the practice, noting the existence of clients around the world "*who trust the attorneys implicitly.*" Such a combination of size and quality ensures participation in matters of the greatest standing. Thus, the firm has recently been representing Oracle in litigation arising from its $7.4 billion unsolicited offer for PeopleSoft. On behalf of Royal Dutch/Shell's audit committee, it is helping the company navigate through an investigation concerning the recategorization of almost 4 billion barrels of oil from proved reserves to other reserve categories.

The Lawyers: The firm's standing is immeasurably enhanced by the fact that it houses **Robert Fiske** (see p.1279). "*A man of unimpeachable reputation,*" he is a considerable factor in explaining why the firm is viewed as one of the very best white-collar operations in the country. Formerly a US Attorney, he has enjoyed a seat in the upper echelons of the New York litigation world and remains a huge influence. "*Steeped in gravitas,*" he recently represented Sanjay Kumar, former CEO of Computer Associates, in investigations into the company's accounting practices. Further enhancing the firm's white-collar criminal defense profile is **Denis McInerney** (see p.1300), who has used his experience as an Assistant US Attorney in the Southern District of New York to build up a strong following in private practice. Heavily involved in the Enron saga defending Arthur Andersen, he is "*both a profound thinker and a man of decisive action*" whose talents extend from white-collar to complex commercial litigation generally. Similarly blessed with a gift for adaptability is **Carey Dunne** (see p.1276) who is best known for tackling cases that involve parallel proceedings in different forums simultaneously. Accordingly, he has recently been advising insurance brokers Marsh & McLennan on investigations relating to the payment of contingency fees by insurers, handling matters with "*sensitivity and openness of mind.*" He has also been involved in the mutual fund industry investigations alongside colleague **Dennis Glazer** (see p.1283). Glazer has represented JPMorgan Chase in connection with these inquiries and is complemented by a suc-

cessful securities litigation practice with a strong showing in bankruptcy and M&A-related disputes. Completing a strong lineup, **Daniel Kolb** (see p.1294) also won favor for his work on Enron and for his polished performances in securities litigation. He is joined in our tables by **Michael Carroll** (see p.1270), "*a man for the complex deal*" whose work on the PeopleSoft litigation did not go unnoticed by clearly impressed observers.

The Clients: Altria; AstraZeneca; Bank of America; Citibank; CSFB; Deloitte & Touche; Ernst & Young; JPMorgan Chase; KPMG and Pfizer.

Paul, Weiss, Rifkind, Wharton & Garrison LLP
See firm details p.1362
The Firm: This "*tough and smart firm*" may now have almost as many corporate as litigation attorneys, but is still most readily celebrated for its disputes work. "*An outfit that never fields a bad team,*" it has always placed litigation at the heart of its endeavors, a policy that has brought its own rewards over time. The strategy has afforded a robustness that has allowed it to shake off setbacks such as the loss of some of its leading players to the federal bench. As a consequence, it is often presented as "*a bastion of securities litigation, never more than a step away from involvement in the legal consequences of the largest Wall Street scandals.*" Securities litigation remains its trump card but commentators also applaud an effective white-collar capability. The firm successfully represented Senator Robert Torricelli in a DOJ investigation into his finances and separately acted for Samuel Waksal, the former CEO of ImClone Systems, in defending various criminal charges concerning the sale of stocks by his family. Antitrust, IP, insurance, bankruptcy and real estate litigation also feature heavily for a team that caters to a truly multinational client base.

The Lawyers: The attorneys here are "*never likely to be fazed by any matter, however complex,*" having had involvement in such headliners as the Enron litigation, in which the team acted for Citigroup in resisting a number of potential class actions. Prominent among a stable of respected legal combatants is **Martin London** (see p.1298), a general litigator with a strong securities bent, who is known for his "*thoroughness of preparation.*" "*Aggressive when he needs to be but never less than respectful,*" his many impressive performances include the successful defense of a $28 million Sohio claim involving the Panama Pipeline. Displaying a similar level of flexibility, **Daniel Beller** (see p.1265) takes a broad-brush approach that encompasses antitrust, securities and government enforcement matters to name but a few. His "*acutely lively mind causes opponents untold problems*" and has been effectively applied in matters such as Black v Sumitomo. **Leslie Fagen** (see p.1278) can be as protean but

New York
Leading individuals
(Litigation: General Commercial)

1 BOIES David *Boies Schiller*, Armonk
FISKE Robert *Davis Polk*, New York
LONDON Martin *Paul Weiss*, New York
NUSSBAUM Bernard *Wachtell Lipton*, New York
OSTRAGER Barry *Simpson Thacher*, New York
REARDON Roy *Simpson Thacher*, New York
WACHTELL Herbert *Wachtell Lipton*, New York

2 CHESLER Evan *Cravath Swaine*, New York
CLARY Richard *Cravath Swaine*, New York
JOSEPH Gregory *Sole Practitioner*, New York
KAVALER Thomas *Cahill Gordon*, New York
KOOB Charles *Simpson Thacher*, New York
LERNER Jonathan *Skadden Arps*, New York
NAFTALIS Gary *Kramer Levin*, New York
WELLS Theodore *Paul Weiss*, New York
WHITE Mary *Debevoise & Plimpton*, New York

3 BELLER Daniel *Paul Weiss*, New York
CARROLL Michael *Davis Polk*, New York
DAVIS Fred *Shearman & Sterling*, New York
FAGEN Leslie *Paul Weiss*, New York
GITTER Max *Cleary Gottlieb*, New York
GLAZER Dennis *Davis Polk*, New York
KIERNAN John *Debevoise & Plimpton*, New York
KURZWEIL Harvey *Dewey Ballantine*, New York
LAUER Eliot *Curtis Mallet-Prevost*, New York
LEVINE Alan *Kronish Lieb*, New York
QUINN James *Weil Gotshal*, New York
SAUNDERS Paul *Cravath Swaine*, New York
SHUSTER Michael *White & Case*, New York

Individuals are listed alphabetically in each band.

is most regularly seen on products liability issues, where he is "*something of a demon in the class action world.*" By court appointment, he is representing all future claimants who fall victim to asbestos-related disease in connection with a class action to restructure the Manville Personal Injury Settlement Trust. Much of the firm's estimable reputation in white-collar work derives from the contribution of former federal prosecutor **Mark Pomerantz** (see p.1310). He worked on the Torricelli case and, according to observers, always demonstrates "*an unbelievably bright mind*" allied to "*a clear ability*" to anticipate his client's needs. Equally respected for this type of work is **Theodore Wells** (see p.1331), whose "*trial experience and business understanding are tough to beat.*" "*If you're on the brink of ruin he might just pull you back.*" For securities work, the firm offers some of the very best names in the field. Many of the leading financial institutions turn to **Brad Karp** (see p.1292) who despite his relative youth has appeared in some serious litigation. The likes of Morgan Stanley, Merrill Lynch and Citigroup depend on the attorney, who is "*never afraid to take a position even on the thorniest of issues.*" Also popular with such clients is **Richard Rosen** (see p.1314), whose knowledge of his subject has led him to file amicus briefs in

the Supreme Court. He has appeared in the WorldCom litigation and shares with **Daniel Kramer** (see p.1295) a reputation for "*steadfastness and calm in the roughest of seas.*" Kramer handles his securities and enforcement practice with "*a cool head and great sophistication, employing wit and good sense to defuse potentially explosive situations.*"

The Clients: Citigroup; Gillette; Philip Morris; Time Warner; Hollinger; Merck; AIG; JPMorgan Chase/Bank One; Morgan Stanley; Johnson & Johnson; Schering-Plough; MasterCard; Viacom; Chubb; Lehman Brothers; MacAndrews & Forbes; National Football League; Bear Stearns; CSFB and Goldman Sachs.

Simpson Thacher & Bartlett LLP
See firm details p.1370

The Firm: "*Well integrated cross-departmentally and committed to a high level of partner contact,*" this firm is hard for clients to resist and one of the largest and widest ranging litigation powerhouses in New York. Principal outside litigation counsel to the very best, it is a "*financial services stronghold of bewildering quality.*" The firm's 200-lawyer litigation team is perceived to have participated in more trials than many of its rivals, boasting a role in nearly every one of the major investigations initiated by New York Attorney General Eliot Spitzer. Securities matters are where the firm really earns it spurs. "*A whole clutch of securities attorneys really on their game*" has represented JPMorgan in litigation arising out of the collapse of Enron. However, the range of talents on offer here extends much beyond that. The firm's credentials in the insurance world have been emphasized with its work on behalf of Swiss Re on the question of whether the Twin Towers disaster was one occurrence or two. The firm's attorneys successfully represented Viacom in an action brought by EchoStar Communications alleging that Viacom was illegally tying CBS retransmission rights to EchoStar's carriage of affiliated cable programming. The team is also unusual in New York for having a particularly strong products liability capability, having represented BAT in tobacco litigation for a number of years and separately defended Heineken against a number of class actions. Always looking to expand its horizons, it has now obtained a further strong foothold in IP litigation as evinced by its representation of Daiichi Pharmaceutical in cases involving the anti-infective drug Levaquin.

The Lawyers: Roy Reardon (see p.1312) has been "*a true figurehead for the firm for countless years now.*" Over that time he has proved to be "*a real rock*" to clients of the distinction of Ford and BAT, delivering "*unerring judgment*" across a gamut of disciplines. More skeptical commentators express concerns about the possible succession problems when he departs, but most are satisfied with the talent on offer. Principally, they

laud **Barry Ostrager** (see p.1306), a man who has garnered widespread praise. Described as "*an astringent character quite happy to make enemies in his client's cause,*" he demonstrated his effectiveness in the successful representation of Swiss Re in the Twin Towers insurance case. He also won respect for advising Travelers in a $5-billion arbitration with ACandS. Ostrager coheads the firm's litigation department with **Charles Koob** (see p.1294), "*an attorney of the finest scruples*" who is the fount of much of the team's antitrust work. High-level securities litigation is left to a band of superior individuals led by **Michael Chepiga** (see p.1271). Also an expert on litigation arising out of M&A, Chepiga is pitched as "*the toast of many Wall Street boardrooms.*" He is hailed by clients as "*efficient, accessible and the most wonderful sounding board.*" Cochairing the group is **Bruce Angiolillo** (see p.1262), "*a fine, thoughtful and levelheaded performer who approaches his cases with great circumspection.*" Their cohorts include **Paul Curnin** (see p.1274), "*a diligent, painstaking lawyer who is expert at marshaling large legal teams,*" and **David Ichel** (see p.1290), "*a substantial performer on the defense side who combines caution with tenacity.*" Together these gifted attorneys have represented WorldCom (now MCI) before the SEC and advised Kmart in connection with several potential shareholder class actions challenging its $11 billion merger agreement with Sears Roebuck. Joining Simpson Thacher from Fried Frank Harris Shriver & Jacobson, **Mark Stein** (see p.1262) proves "*a staunch defender of his client's position.*" As an alumnus of the Attorney's Office, he handles all types of criminal investigations and their parallel proceedings. He is also pitched as "*a real staff in times of trouble.*"

The Clients: The Blackstone Group; JPMorgan Chase; Viacom; Swiss Re; American Electric Power; BAT; Teleglobe and Appleton.

Skadden, Arps, Slate, Meagher & Flom LLP & Affiliates
See firm details p.1372

The Firm: Perhaps somewhat overshadowed by Skadden's legendary transactional practice, the litigation team is progressing well in putting the firm's litigation reputation on a broadly similar footing. The firm continues to be "*inextricably associated with a fantastic corporate client base*" that has always fed through work to the litigation department. However, the band of about 25 partners is now increasingly attracting work through its own merits. Inevitably, its major strength remains corporate takeover litigation and related securities litigation. But a nationally recognized products liability capability and a discrete but effective white-collar arm lend credence to claims of diversity. Large enough to throw huge resources at any case and backed by 12 offices nationwide, the firm has "*the standing*

New York
Leading firms (Litigation: Securities)

[1]	CRAVATH, SWAINE & MOORE LLP *New York*
	DAVIS POLK & WARDWELL *New York*
	PAUL, WEISS, RIFKIND, WHARTON *New York*
	SIMPSON THACHER & BARTLETT LLP *New York*
	SKADDEN, ARPS, SLATE, MEAGHER *New York*
	SULLIVAN & CROMWELL LLP *New York*
	WACHTELL, LIPTON, ROSEN & KATZ *New York*
	WILLKIE FARR & GALLAGHER LLP *New York*
[2]	CADWALADER, WICKERSHAM & TAFT *New York*
	CAHILL GORDON & REINDEL *New York*
	CLEARY GOTTLIEB STEEN & HAMILTON *New York*
	CLIFFORD CHANCE US LLP *New York*
	DEBEVOISE & PLIMPTON LLP *New York*
	GIBSON, DUNN & CRUTCHER LLP *New York*
	LATHAM & WATKINS LLP *New York*
	MORRISON & FOERSTER LLP *New York*
	SHEARMAN & STERLING LLP *New York*
	WEIL, GOTSHAL & MANGES LLP *New York*
	WILMER CUTLER PICKERING HALE *New York*

Leading individuals
(Litigation: Securities)

[1]	CHEPIGA Michael *Simpson Thacher*, New York
	DIBLASI Gandolfo *Sullivan & Cromwell*, New York
	KASNER Jay *Skadden Arps*, New York
[2]	ANGIOLILLO Bruce *Simpson Thacher*, New York
	BASKIN Stuart *Shearman & Sterling*, New York
	BENEDICT James *Milbank Tweed*, New York
	CURNIN Paul *Simpson Thacher*, New York
	KARP Brad *Paul Weiss*, New York
	KOLB Daniel *Davis Polk*, New York
	LERNER Jonathan *Skadden Arps*, New York
	MARKEL Gregory *Cadwalader Wickersham*, New York
	MCCAW Robert *Wilmer Cutler*, New York
	MIRVIS Theodore *Wachtell Lipton*, New York
	ROSEN Richard *Paul Weiss*, New York
	VIZCARRONDO Paul *Wachtell Lipton*, New York
	YOUNG Michael *Willkie Farr*, New York
[3]	ALLERHAND Joseph *Weil Gotshal*, New York
	AUSPITZ Jack *Morrison & Foerster*, New York
	BARON Robert *Cravath Swaine*, New York
	BRODSKY David *Latham & Watkins*, New York
	GIUFFRA Robert *Sullivan & Cromwell*, New York
	HARDIMAN John *Sullivan & Cromwell*, New York
	HOLLAND Mark *Clifford Chance*, New York
	ICHEL David *Simpson Thacher*, New York
	KADET Samuel *Skadden Arps*, New York
	KRAMER Daniel *Paul Weiss*, New York
	LOWENTHAL Mitchell *Cleary Gottlieb*, New York
	MASTRO Randy *Gibson Dunn*, New York
	MITCHELL Michael *Skadden Arps*, New York
	PIETRZAK Robert *Sidley Austin*, New York
	POSEN Richard *Willkie Farr*, New York
	SHAPIRO Stuart *Shapiro Forman*, New York
	SMITH Jeffrey *King & Spalding*, New York
	YODOWITZ Edward *Skadden Arps*, New York

Firms and individuals are listed alphabetically in each band.

and ability to tackle anything the traditional leaders in the field can throw at it." Confidence is boosted by the perception that the firm's core attorneys are now all very much in their prime. By way of example, its team has represented CTF Holdings against Marriott International in one of the largest arbitrations in the world and has had a key role in Cendant's multibillion-dollar securities litigation. White-collar highlights have included defending a former senior executive at Computer Associates and separately advising Putnam Investments in the mutual fund market timing investigation. A strong products liability team served as trial counsel to Copley Pharmaceutical in multidistrict litigation involving the asthma medication albuterol.

The Lawyers: Jay Kasner's (see p.1292) "*ebullient and forthright nature*" has been supremely well harnessed to create a fantastic securities litigation practice. Now widely regarded as "*enjoying the salad days of his career*," he has represented the underwriters in the WorldCom saga and defended Merrill Lynch over the analyst reports litigation. His delighted customers revel in a performer with "*charisma, absolute command, and behind the scenes tactical mastery.*" Like many of his colleagues, he is noted for the vigor with which he promotes a case, a quality he shares with **Samuel Kadet** (see p.1291), a "*feisty*" legal pugilist at the fore of the Cendant litigation. This last piece of litigation was also a fine showcase for **Jonathan Lerner** (see p.1296), a general litigator whose practice is anchored in securities. His other successes include representing McKesson in its $960 million settlement of securities class actions relating to alleged accounting fraud at HBOC. Interviewees hailed him as "*an attorney who delivers exceptional results. He is particularly adept at digesting large volumes of complex material and quickly synthesizing it into excellent pleadings.*" **Ed Yodowitz** (see p.1333), another "*robust and thoroughly well-informed*" player, completes a quartet of recommended securities lawyers. The firm's reputation in white-collar criminal defense is somewhat less dazzling, though **David Zornow** (see p.1334) is credited with "*fashioning a good little unit made up of a number of former federal prosecutors.*" He wins personal praise for his "*accomplished handling of some very knotty legal problems.*" **Michael Mitchell** (see p.1291) of counsel has returned to the firm where he did much of his best work in the past. He is recommended as a securities lawyer of some stature.

The Clients: Merrill Lynch; CIBC World Markets; JPMorgan Chase; Cendant; Honeywell; Nextel; Thomson and Anheuser-Busch.

Sullivan & Cromwell LLP
See firm details p.1373

The Firm: Clients have to pay top dollar for this classic New York litigation firm, but all are adamant that it is worth every penny. As one put it: "*For a good old-fashioned restrained service that gets results and makes you feel comfortable every step of the way, you can't beat them.*" Although the firm is less vocal than some of its rivals, it has the pedigree and inherent talent to succeed with subdued confidence. At heart, securities work constitutes the engine of the practice. Many a financial institution views this as a go-to operation; Goldman Sachs, in particular, continues to provide a glut of work, including work relating to the government's investigation into research analyst conflicts of interest. Another highlight involved a securities fraud class action brought on behalf of purchasers of stock in Covad Communications. The team has further advised the Bank of New York in shareholder derivative litigation. Auxiliary to this specialty, the firm is a big player in other fields. Antitrust prowess is on offer, particularly in the area merger clearance. The firm also caught the public eye with its involvement in France Telecom v Compaq Computer – dubbed as possibly the largest IP case ever filed, involving the infringement of 26 patents. Products liability, too, is featured, with the firm acting for the likes of CSR in national asbestos litigation. When one adds into the pot an undoubted forte in international arbitration, it becomes clear why this firm continues to thrive.

The Lawyers: A kingpin when it comes to civil and criminal investigations involving the financial services industry, **Vince DiBlasi** (see p.1275) was described as "*Goldman Sachs' secret weapon.*" His appearances include acting as liaison counsel for the underwriters in the IPO allocation case, a task he undertook with his customary relish and gusto. Observers describe "*a tough-minded pragmatist, never one to waste time on ridiculous arguments.*" **Robert Giuffra** (see p.1275) is cut from similar cloth. He has increased his profile immeasurably in recent times through the representation of major companies in criminal and regulatory investigations and related securities class actions. His brand of "*limitless self-confidence*" played a key role in his successful defense of Computer Associates in relation to a DOJ investigation. Another highlight involved Van der Moolen, a large stock exchange specialist firm, in a separate government inquiry. **John Hardiman** (see p.1275) relies on "*tremendous sagacity and an impressive dignity of bearing, getting his point over with the minimum of fuss.*" His remit takes in M&A litigation with securities, class actions and regulatory matters adding extra flavor. One of the younger players in the field, he shares with white-collar and regulatory expert **Samuel Seymour** (see p.1275) the accolade of being "*a natural heir to the gilded throne at Sullivan & Cromwell.*" Seymour has participated in internal investigations for Computer Associates and Riggs National and other public companies under scrutiny.

The Clients: CSFB; Bank of New York; Bankers Trust; Barclays; Microsoft; Mattel; Vodafone; CSR; BP; Diageo and Glaxo Wellcome.

New York
Leading firms
(Litigation: White-Collar Crime
& Government Investigations)

[1] **DAVIS POLK & WARDWELL** *New York*
DEBEVOISE & PLIMPTON LLP *New York*
FRIED, FRANK, HARRIS, SHRIVER *New York*
PAUL, WEISS, RIFKIND, WHARTON *New York*
SKADDEN, ARPS, SLATE, MEAGHER *New York*
SULLIVAN & CROMWELL LLP *New York*
WACHTELL, LIPTON, ROSEN & KATZ *New York*

(Litigation: Specialist Firms in
White-Collar Crime & Government
Investigations)

[1] **MORVILLO, ABRAMOWITZ, GRAND** *New York*
[2] **LANKLER SIFFERT & WOHL** *New York*
STILLMAN & FRIEDMAN *New York*

Leading individuals
(Litigation: White-Collar Crime &
Government Investigations)

★ **FISKE Robert** *Davis Polk*, New York
MORVILLO Robert *Morvillo Abramowitz*, New York

[1] **MCINERNEY Denis** *Davis Polk*, New York
PEDOWITZ Lawrence *Wachtell Lipton*, New York
POMERANTZ Mark *Paul Weiss*, New York
STILLMAN Charles *Stillman & Friedman*, New York
STRAUSS Audrey *Fried Frank*, New York
WELLS Theodore *Paul Weiss*, New York
WHITE Mary *Debevoise & Plimpton*, New York

[2] **ABRAMOWITZ Elkan** *Morvillo Abramowitz*, New York
CARROLL John *Clifford Chance*, New York
DUNNE Carey *Davis Polk*, New York
FLEMING Peter *Curtis Mallet-Prevost*, New York
KAUFMAN Stephen *Sole Practitioner*, New York
NAFTALIS Gary *Kramer Levin*, New York
SAVARESE John *Wachtell Lipton*, New York
WING John *Weil Gotshal*, New York
ZORNOW David *Skadden Arps*, New York

[3] **BRODSKY David** *Latham & Watkins*, New York
EDELMAN Scott *Milbank Tweed*, New York
FISHBEIN Matthew *Debevoise & Plimpton*, New York
GIUFFRA Robert *Sullivan & Cromwell*, New York
HAFETZ Fred *Hafetz & Necheles*, New York
HEISS Howard *O'Melveny & Myers*, New York
LAWLER Andrew *Sole Practitioner*, New York
LEVANDER Andrew *Dechert*, New York
LEVINE Alan *Kronish Lieb*, New York
LIMAN Lewis *Cleary Gottlieb*, New York
MARCU Aaron *Covington & Burling*, New York
RICHARDS III Lee *Richards Spears*, New York
SCHECHTMAN Paul *Stillman & Friedman*, New York
SCHWARTZ William *Kronish Lieb*, New York
SEYMOUR Samuel *Sullivan & Cromwell*, New York
SIFFERT John *Lankler Siffert*, New York
STEIN Mark *Simpson Thacher*, New York
STRASSBERG Richard *Goodwin Procter*, New York
WOHL Frank *Lankler Siffert*, New York

Firms and individuals are listed alphabetically in each band.

Wachtell, Lipton, Rosen & Katz
See firm details p.1375

The Firm: This "*timeless classic*" of a firm has been created upon the foundations of a thriving M&A practice and its efforts, particularly on hostile takeovers, continue to stand out. The litigation emphasis has, however, subtly shifted with time; the firm now offers equally substantive expertise in complex commercial disputes, serious securities litigation, white-collar matters and general class actions. Where it is distinguished primarily from its competitors is on size. Smaller than most, it concentrates on efficiency and strategy in addition to affording clients the boon of a virtual one to one partner to client ratio. Commentators express some concern about what is seen as an aging practice and stress that its relatively small size puts a premium on accurate selection of the best lawyers available. They are united, however, in accepting that this is "*a team drawn to the larger cases like bees to honey*" and one "*capable of offering the most withering insights into a matter.*" The team has enjoyed signal success representing Silverstein Properties, the leaseholder of the World Trade Center, in insurance litigation arising out of 9/11. On behalf of Bank of America, it has played major roles in securities class actions arising out of the mutual fund investigations. Its evident strength in securities matters has further been underscored through its advice to Sears Roebuck in class actions arising out its proposed merger with Kmart and its separate representation of Interactive Corporation in its dispute with Vivendi.

The Lawyers: A cornerstone of the firm from its inception, **Herb Wachtell**'s (see p.1330) reputation precedes him. Tempered in the fire of the juiciest and furthest reaching litigation of the past few decades, he is "*a friend of the largest financial institutions who nobody can afford to take lightly.*" He demonstrates an "*ability to take unusual and creative stances*" that ensures his participation in headline matters. He was at the helm in the Silverstein/World Trade Center litigation, alongside **Bernard Nussbaum** (see p.1306), whose substantial contribution in that matter earned widespread attention. Very much a driving force, this corporate and securities litigator is presented as "*an outstanding trial lawyer with a very shrewd strength of strategy.*" The white-collar team is built around two renowned big hitters. **Lawrence Pedowitz** (see p.1308) is "*a true gentlemen with marvelous poise and bearing.*" His various engagements have molded him into an "*attorney with a detached and balanced approach*" whose "*superlative judgment and malice-free approach*" make him a popular figure all around. Colleague **John Savarese** (see p.1316) is similarly feted as "*a man with whom businesses entrust their future.*" His talent has attracted the eye of the likes of Martha Stewart and Sandy Weill, former chief executive of Citigroup. **Paul Vizcarrondo** (see p.1329) shares an ability to

tackle this type of work but tends to apply his brand of "*astute, practical and sophisticated lawyering*" to civil securities-related litigation. **Theodore Mirvis** (see p.1302), meanwhile, reflects the firm's traditional strength in corporate governance and M&A litigation. "*An absolute genius on corporate control with a fine wit to match,*" he has had a hand in much of the landmark corporate governance litigation in Delaware Chancery Court. Matters handled by the firm as a whole include the Revlon, Time Warner and Paramount cases.

The Clients: Citigroup; Lazard Freres; Silverstein; Schering-Plough; Bank of America; PNC Financial; Interactive Corporation; Sears Roebuck; Disney and Comerica.

Boies, Schiller & Flexner LLP
See firm details p.1337

The Firm: Merely eight years after its formation, the firm has secured enough respect to be spoken of in the same breath as some of the most venerated operations in town. This achievement is largely due to the presence of founder member David Boies, commentators said. On the back of his stellar reputation, the firm has attracted significant business from some of America's largest companies to become "*one of the country's foremost litigation boutiques.*" This has allowed it to expand at such a rapid pace that it now consists of 175 lawyers in ten offices, all of which tackle a rich diet of antitrust, securities and class action cases. Doubts persist as to the evenness of quality but most accept that there is sufficient talent at the top to ensure a strong service. After all, the firm's partners have enjoyed more than 300 jury and bench trials between them. Proof of the talent on offer comes from such work as the World Trade Center insurance litigation on behalf of Lloyd's of London. Boies Schiller lawyers managed to convince the court that Silverstein parties were entitled to one payout, not two, as a result of 9/11. The firm has also been flexing its antitrust muscles, advising American Express in its action to recover billions of dollars from Visa and MasterCard among others. Always in the news, this practice has further gained widespread publicity through representing Bob and Harvey Weinstein in negotiations with Disney over the distribution rights of the Michael Moore film 'Fahrenheit 9/11'. Its activities in securities class actions have involved Qwest, Tyco International and Adelphia Communications.

The Lawyers: A star in 1997 when he resigned his commission at Cravath, Swaine & Moore, **David Boies** continues to shine brightly while steering his own ship. The caliber of this lawyer is best illustrated through his portfolio of headline-grabbing cases: the World Trade Center insurance litigation, Continental Airlines v United Airlines, United States v Microsoft and the Gore electoral litigation all have his fingerprints on them. His success is ascribed to "*a lightning quick mind*" combined with "*an ability to communicate with juries in plain English.*"

The Clients: Adelphia Communications; Aetna; American Express; DuPont; Lloyd's of London; Monsanto; Northwest Airlines; Tyco International; New York Yankees; Unisys and Viacom.

Cahill Gordon & Reindel

The Firm: Cahill Gordon has nurtured "*a reputation for toughness in a tough world,*" placing litigation firmly at the heart of its efforts and rarely deviating from this "*no-nonsense, sharpshooting style.*" Its "*strong-jawed*" lawyers offer a generalist practice that peers into almost every nook and cranny of the law. Partnership dissolution and defamation disputes are therefore just as likely to be handled as the commonplace regimen of securities, antitrust and corporate governance. Those clients interviewed felt the firm delivers "*a service collaborative in nature and marked by great intelligence and expertise.*" Especially strong on First Amendment cases, the team has represented Senator Mitch McConnell in a challenge to the constitutionality of the McCain-Feingold Campaign Finance Reform Act. "*For any difficult, ugly case, they must be one of the first ports of call,*" one client said. Representing Time, the team successfully appealed an $11 million libel judgment against Sports Illustrated. Other key highlights have included acting for Deutsche Bank in the World Trade Center insurance litigation and separately advising Time Warner on a purported nationwide class action relating to alleged violations of the privacy provisions of the Cable Act. The firm's evident competency in IP was also illustrated by its advisory role to the daughter of the late Sir Arthur Conan Doyle in a US copyright dispute contingent on her father's work.

The Lawyers: "*A big personality,*" **Thomas Kavaler** is championed by clients as "*a man who goes into the courtroom with all four limbs swinging.*" "*Fast paced, and fluid in delivery,*" he offers much more than aggression, building his cases from the foundations of "*brilliant analysis.*" His recent efforts have involved Prudential Securities in matters relating to the company's employee compensation scheme and separately acting for the American Institute of Certified Public Accountants in a case challenging certain disciplinary procedures.

The Clients: Sony Music; Deutsche Bank; Time Warner; American International Group; CBS; CNN and Standard & Poor's.

Cleary Gottlieb Steen & Hamilton LLP

See firm details p.1342

The Firm: The firm appears to be fulfilling its litigation ambitions, inching back into the courtroom clutching a positive verdict. Admittedly, some commentators argue that it is still early days in the firm's bid to transform its superb international corporate practice into a litigation capability of similar renown, but the omens are good. Through the shrewd acquisition of partners from other firms and a focus on "*complete professionalism in its dealings,*" it has fostered an impressive increase in terms of volume and quality. Much of its effort has concentrated on securities litigation and related government investigations – areas in which it has picked up some choice cases. For example, it has represented UBS on a variety of matters including the IPO allocation saga and separately defended a number of financial institutions in relation to the underwriting of securities issued by Adelphia. The practice is also thriving in other respects; the burgeoning team has ramped up its capability on general contract, IP litigation and international arbitration. It acted for Newbridge in securing a $200 million arbitration award against Korea First Bank and represented Fleet National Bank in resisting claims brought by a contingent of its Argentine customers. The jewel in its crown, however, is the firm's performance as lead litigator for PeopleSoft in its hostile takeover battle with Oracle. This, above all, has done a lot to allay the fears of skeptics concerned about the lack of a marquee name.

The Lawyers: Max Gitter (see p.1283) has proved to be one of the team's most versatile advocates – a generalist who can turn an adroit hand to a wide range of disputes. A litigator with an instinct for the jugular, he has been retained on some important arbitrations as well as complex securities matters. "*One of the top courtroom litigators in the USA,*" he is respected by clients for his fluency in bet-the-company battles. More of a specialist, **Mitchell Lowenthal**'s (see p.1283) inclination is toward the securities side. He has been embroiled in headline litigation including the research analysts, derivatives and IPO allocation disputes. His "*pragmatic, solution-oriented*" determination is blended with a "*judicious*" approach to render successful results. Former Assistant US Attorney **Lewis Liman** (see p.1283) gained approval for his authority in white-collar criminal defense practice, having navigated a number of prominent clients through SEC investigations and related proceedings. He has also shepherded high-level executives embroiled in securities-related criminal actions.

The Clients: Fleet National Bank; PeopleSoft; UBS; Newbridge Capital; Crédit Lyonnais; Fitch and Freddie Mac.

Debevoise & Plimpton LLP

See firm details p.1346

The Firm: White-collar criminal defense and its accompaniments have proved fertile ground for a practice seen to be "*enhancing its profile year on year.*" Aware of the increased possibilities in this area, the firm made some astute hires a couple of years ago, bringing in one big name – Mary Jo White – and a selection of talented acolytes straight from the government. So enriched, the team has gone on to enjoy a boom in business, particularly in various proceedings concerning the insurance industry, market timing in mutual funds and securities fraud to name but a few. Now firmly affixed as a guiding light in the field, it trades on this reputation while continuing to offer a sound all-round service. Arbitration remains a central strut as illustrated by the firm's successful effort to secure a $355 million award against the Czech Republic. Securities litigation is always forthcoming, for example acting for Shell Oil in class action litigation regarding its accountancy practices and for Global Crossing in securities and ERISA class actions against current and former company leaders. Ever willing to take on litigation of every hue, the firm is also active in IP and products liability. Its defense of a chemical manufacturer in a class action brought by Vietnamese nationals claiming damages for injuries brought on by Agent Orange is an indication of the interesting nature of this caseload. Little wonder then that clients often commend its "*thoroughness, personal touch and talent for seeing which way the wind is blowing.*"

The Lawyers: Mary Jo White accounts for much of the luster attached to Debevoise's litigation practice. She came to the firm in 2002 after nine years as the US Attorney for the Southern District with a sublime reputation that has only been added to since. She "*devotes a great deal of personal attention to a case whilst seemingly spinning a thousand plates.*" Such is her experience that one interviewee added: "*It's hard to imagine a single issue in litigation that she hasn't addressed.*" Her recent forays have included acting on the DOJ investigation of Artemis relating to its acquisition of Executive Life. The legal all-rounder would be the first to admit, however, that she is just part of a good team that includes a wealth of former federal prosecutors. Prominent among them is **Matt Fishbein**, another white-collar expert noted for his "*experience, personable nature and facility for moving things along in meetings.*" **John Kiernan** affords further scope to the firm on general commercial matters and arbitrations. "*A great client handler and a man of considerable financial knowledge,*" he recently obtained the dismissal of a $1.8 billion creditors' claim against the directors of a failed telecom company. He has further represented the retail leaseholder of the World Trade Center in disputes pertaining to the reconstruction of Ground Zero.

The Clients: Merck; Ace Limited; Alcon Laboratories; American Airlines; American Express; Sony Music Entertainment and Allen Telecom.

Weil, Gotshal & Manges LLP

See firm details p.1378

The Firm: Weil Gotshal's litigation efforts are generally perceived in the marketplace as revolving entirely around bankruptcy, but, as clients made all too clear: "*The firm is a first-class outfit that can try almost any type of case and win at every stage of the litigation process.*" Perhaps years of stout work in bankruptcy and attention-grabbing appearances such as leading for Enron in related proceedings have made it difficult for the firm to break away from that mold. Yet, arranging itself in groups by areas of expertise, it has negotiated a packed caseload heavy on antitrust, IP, securities litigation, corporate governance and products liability, as well as the inevitable bankruptcy matters. Interviewees talked of "*a team studded with excellent partners and eager associates,*" all of whom display "*excellent business knowledge and a steely determination to take matters to trial where necessary.*" These "*savvy operators*" attract interest from top companies in the land, promoting their interests with assuredness. Indicative of the firm's manifest abilities, it successfully defended Procter & Gamble against an $80 million claim by Colgate-Palmolive alleging impropriety over its advertising of tooth-whitening products. The team also successfully defended Baazee.com, dubbed the 'eBay of India,' against a breach of contract lawsuit. Evincing its ability to devote resources to the heftiest of matters, it also won one of the largest defense verdicts in the USA in 2004 on behalf of ESPN in a $231 million lawsuit brought by Modi Entertainment Network. Other matters saw the firm's antitrust skills highlighted in a victory for American Airlines against DOJ claims of predatory pricing.

The Lawyers: Something of a Renaissance man, **James Quinn** (see p.1310) can turn his hand to IP, insurance, antitrust, products liability and sports matters among others. As head of the firm's global litigation and regulatory practice, he often participates in much of the practice's best work; for example, he appeared in both the ESPN and Procter & Gamble matters. "*Determined and tireless in hunting down his objectives,*" he has also represented Andersen Worldwide member firms in the largest ICC arbitration to date. His team contains **Joseph Allerhand** (see p.1262), who provides securities and bankruptcy advice while also cochairing the firm's business and securities section. "*A knockout in the courtroom as well as a deft performer behind the scenes,*" he was lead litigation counsel for WorldCom during its bankruptcy proceedings and also acted for AK Steel in defeating class certification in a securities fraud action. White-collar crime is the province of **John Wing** (see p.1332). Formerly chief of the fraud unit at the US Attorney's Office for the Southern District of New York, he is "*a man companies turn to when things seem to have irretrievably broken down.*" Indeed fellow attorneys are more than happy to repose their faith in his talents. For example, a former partner of Dickstein Shapiro indicted on major fraud charges turned to him in his darkest hour and obtained an acquittal. Together these three lawyers anchor a practice that has recently lost, through retirement, the respected Otto Obermaier, an attorney formerly featured in *Chambers*.

The Clients: UnitedHealth; Bertelsmann; Procter & Gamble; GE; Vivendi Universal; American Airlines; ExxonMobil; Heinz; Citigroup; MasterCard; CSFB; Enron and Merrill Lynch.

Cadwalader, Wickersham & Taft LLP

See firm details p.1339

The Firm: Dennis Block's arrival from Weil Gotshal in 1998 prompted a distinct upturn in the fortunes of a firm hitherto not over-celebrated for litigation. His subsequent decision to eschew day-to-day litigation in favor of corporate work put a heavy burden on his colleagues, but most commentators believe it has been a challenge they have risen too. The practice itself is one of the more sharply focused, revolving around tangible strengths in the insurance and securities sectors. More than 80 litigators have been involved in extremely high-profile matters in these fields. Examples include representing ABN AMRO in connection with WorldCom and separately advising four of the directors of Tyco in its protracted litigation. The team also assisted 40 issuers of securities in connection with the IPO allocation investigation. The firm has further garnered publicity for its representation of Bank of America in the Enron scandal. On behalf of Bear Stearns, it helped navigate through the regulatory investigations arising out of alleged conflicts of interest between investment banking and research functions. What primarily seems to attract business is the team's "*strategic know-how and the fact that they are as good as, if not better than, anyone else, at listening to what the client is really saying.*" Its legion of satisfied customers also welcome the provision of expertise in antitrust and IP.

The Lawyers: The market views this practice with optimism, largely because of the presence of **Gregory Markel** (see p.1299). He has been the wellspring for much of the securities work generated by the firm and is viewed as a player on the national stage. Formerly a managing partner at Brobeck, Phleger & Harrison's New York office, he now chairs the litigation department at Cadwalader, embracing his duties with aplomb. "*Knowledgeable and tactically sound,*" his approach is fairly low key in comparison with some of his more stentorian rivals. This approach, however, does mean he can "*quickly establish a dialogue with the other side that leads to real progress.*" His fashioning of an exit strategy for the Bank of America from the tangled skein of Enron was particularly applauded by our interviewees.

The Clients: Bank of New York; Bank of America; Bear Stearns; ABN AMRO; HSBC USA; Lehman Brothers; Merrill Lynch; Morgan Stanley; GM; Park Place Entertainment and Pfizer.

Gibson, Dunn & Crutcher LLP

See firm details p.285

The Firm: Strong nationally, Gibson Dunn has sharpened the profile of its New York office. The litigation arm, which now comprises 15 partners, has enjoyed recent success and can claim to have grown by about 50% in the past six years. It has done this through pursuing a policy of hiring legal intellects who have in due course crafted "*a tight, well-honed practice.*" Key strengths include insurance coverage – where the firm acts for many of the major players such as AIG and Empire BlueCross. Another feature is accountant liability, an area in which it has been linked to Deloitte & Touche and PwC. Historically, the team has also participated in a good deal of bankruptcy litigation. It handled the personal bankruptcy of Peter Kalikow, the Head of the Metropolitan Transport Authority, and assisted Merrill Lynch with bankruptcy litigation arising from the collapse of Enron. Increasingly, however, the firm is flexing its muscles on the securities and white-collar defense fronts, dipping into the mire of numerous Wall Street controversies. The IPO allocation, mutual fund, WorldCom and Tyco litigations have all seen input from "*a rising force that is causing some established teams to look over their shoulders.*"

The Lawyers: As New York City's Deputy Mayor for Operations in the Giuliani era, **Randy Mastro** (see p.1299) was responsible for cleaning up a good proportion of the organized crime in the city. On his return to private practice, he has put the lessons learned to good use in a practice strong on white-collar defense but liberally seasoned with a good dose of general litigation. "*Accessible and with a charming personality,*" he "*goes about his business with calm efficiency and a tough exterior when required.*" He acted for Bear Stearns in the IPO allocation litigation and took a major role in the Brooklyn political corruption investigation. He is currently lead litigator in New York City's West Side Jets Stadium project.

The Clients: Merrill Lynch; Empire Blue Cross and Blue Shield; Bear Stearns; Madison Square Garden; Cablevision; Dow Jones; UBS Financial Services; AIG and Unilever.

Kirkland & Ellis LLP

See firm details p.770

The Firm: With its "*lawyers of dominating character,*" the team is well known for its willingness to tackle difficult matters with pugnacity. Although by no means intractable in approach, it delivers "*a resolution and fixed purpose that make this a fighting force very difficult to cow.*" Such determination has led to a national reputation that the New York office has admirably gained, despite being run on a smaller scale than the firm's Chicago headquarters. The practice is broad in scope but succeeds best in certain signal areas. Antitrust work is prominent, as illustrated by the firm's involvement in the Discover Card litigation. The group successfully represented AOL and Netscape in a private suit alleging monopolization misconduct. Products liability also figures highly. Here, the firm has been involved in many a matter on behalf of the tobacco industry and has defended key client GM in cases involving rollover protection and seat belts. IP and insurance litigation are also to the fore for a group whose securities expertise did not go unnoticed. Examples of its prowess in this last regard include a $30 million victory for NL Industries in securities fraud claims relating to the Lockheed ESOP.

The Lawyers: William Pratt has been an ever-present in the firm's New York office, forging strong links with the business community in his 15-year stint. A regular presence before both jury and bench, he has a multifaceted practice that takes in everything from securities and IP litigation to antitrust and tort.

The Clients: Dow Corning; Motorola; NL Industries; Verizon Communications; Honeywell; GM; BP America; Alcon Laboratories and Bayer.

Kramer Levin Naftalis & Frankel LLP
See firm details p.1357

The Firm: "*New York lawyers through and through*," this compact unit of "*hard-ball litigators*" contains over 20 partners in its 60-strong ranks. Interviewees admired the "*dedication and unbridled energy*" on show, doffing their caps to a team capable of generating the majority of its caseload through its reputation alone rather than relying on extant corporate clients. The practice takes in employment, real estate, ERISA and bankruptcy disputes, but makes its biggest waves in white-collar criminal defense and securities litigation. In this respect it "*tends to appear in cases that people are talking about*," as confirmed by involvement in proceedings or investigations relating to Enron, Cendant and Global Crossing among others. The team successfully represented Liz Claiborne in class actions concerning earnings projections and separately acted for Bear Stearns in the NASDAQ market maker securities litigation. This last case also touched on antitrust questions, another field in which the firm scores well, as evinced by its recent appearance for a pharmaceutical client regarding patent claims. Further cause for cheer is provided by a recognized Lanham Act false advertising practice. One of the true national leaders in this field, the firm has acted for major household names such as Procter & Gamble and Johnson & Johnson.

The Lawyers: Gary Naftalis (see p.1303), head of the litigation department, provides the bulk

of the impetus for the team. Noted for his "*ease of manner and direct style*," he has effectively secured some fantastic mandates. White-collar criminal defense and securities lie at the heart of a caseload that has ministered to many high-profile individuals and corporations. Both a director of Tyco and the former CEO of Arthur Andersen have in recent times come under his auspices. Naftalis is also advising Michael Eisner, the CEO of Disney, in a shareholders derivative lawsuit and is separately representing Kenneth Langone in litigation relating to NYSE chairman Richard Grasso.

The Clients: AstraZeneca; L'Oréal; Johnson & Johnson; Procter & Gamble; Bear Stearns; CIBC World Markets; Daiwa Securities America; Lehman Brothers and GT Interactive Software.

Shearman & Sterling LLP
See firm details p.1369

The Firm: One of the dominant international operators, Shearman & Sterling has sought to place more emphasis on its litigation arm in recent years. The upshot has been that as a business area, disputes now form its fastest growing sector, with the New York office alone housing 90 litigators, including 25 partners. The firm's traditional forte has always been the financial and capital markets, and it is no surprise to see it thriving acting on related disputes for the likes of key clients Citigroup and Merrill Lynch. The enforcement and class action field is showing more signs of expansion. The team has seven former DOJ prosecutors and is appearing in about ten grand jury investigations and two dozen SEC investigations. It has been acting for a number of clients including Pilgrim Baxter in the mutual fund investigation and has had a similarly strong showing in the insurance industry investigations. Other fruitful areas include antitrust, in which the group has appeared in the vast majority of the headline international cartel cases such as those involving vitamins and magazine paper. International arbitration is another forte, bolstered by its global network of offices and strong track record. Key clients drawn by its "*top-drawer services*" include Ford, which the firm represented on the Firestone tire crisis.

The Lawyers: Stuart Baskin (see p.1265) is "*a seasoned attorney who always brings a considered, balanced and thoughtful tinge to proceedings.*" He is best known for securities litigation, having appeared as the principal litigator in class action representations for Ford, Nortel, KPMG and Elan among others. Also a strong enforcement lawyer, he is currently involved in seven SEC investigations and three grand jury investigations. His other activities have seen him appearing for Consolidated Edison, the New York City utility, in a matter relating to the failed merger with Northeast Utilities. Colleague **Fred Davis**'s (see p.1274) international expertise makes him "*a sure bet for anything*

across the water." Hugely proficient at international arbitration, he has sat as an arbitrator in the ICC and advised major concerns including GE and Citibank in matters worldwide. He melds this global expertise with a general litigation practice that has resulted in prominent matters such as the major RICO trial of John Hancock Leasing v Frank, a matter in which he obtained a $28 million award.

The Clients: BASF; Citigroup; Merrill Lynch; Morgan Stanley; UBS; Ford; Nortel and Elan.

Clifford Chance US LLP
See firm details p.1343

The Firm: Considered by many to be the only UK magic circle law firm to have made a significant impact across the Atlantic, the group is driven by its powerful allegiances to some of the world's most prestigious companies. Clients turn to the firm for "*incredible presence with the jury and the courts.*" In recent years, the firm has suffered from a number of high-profile departures that threatened its status in the USA, but its steadfastness in turbulent times has continued to shine through. One of its strongest suits is white-collar criminal defense and parallel securities litigation. It has steered the likes of Merrill Lynch through the Enron debacle and is defending the same client against claims related to the IPO securities disputes and the research reports litigation. Its "*history*" with Merrill Lynch has been sustained despite internal pressures, illustrating the firm's overall determination to hold its position in the marketplace, commentators said. A broader scope of practice takes in a considerable range, and the firm can call on its expansive worldwide network of expertise. The geographic spread of the firm is "*truly extraordinary,*" one client said. "*I cannot imagine another firm to be as good as Clifford Chance in this case.*"

The Lawyers: Mark Holland (see p.1270) gained distinction in the securities world for his defense of Merrill Lynch in disputes relating to analysts' research reports on technology companies. He has also proved "*extraordinarily effective*" on matters pertaining to the Investment Company Act of 1940 on behalf of investment advisers and mutual funds. **John Carroll** (see p.1270) lends authority in the area of white-collar criminal defense, thriving in the recent spate of corporate scandals. As head of the white-collar group, he has helped individuals and companies navigate through the murky waters of government investigations and beyond. A recent coup is the hiring of Elaine Laurence, former Goldman Sachs legal director who will focus on IP and technology disputes, particularly as related to financial institutions.

The Clients: ABN AMRO; Alliance Capital; Instinet; Merck; Merrill Lynch; Sakura Global Capital and Citigroup.

Curtis, Mallet-Prevost, Colt & Mosle LLP

The Firm: Interviewees noticed "*real pockets of excellence*" in a firm celebrated for the richness of its history. For 175 years it has performed on the global stage and, not surprisingly, its litigation endeavors are tinged with a cosmopolitan feel. Accordingly, it is complemented by a strong international arbitration practice. As an indicator of the multinational nature of its work, the team has recently represented a Swiss trading company in a dispute with an Italian shipping line over a joint venture involving multiple oil tankers. Closer to home, it really earns its stripes on white-collar and securities litigation. "*Fully up to speed on all issues,*" its attorneys acted for John Rigas – founder of Adelphia Communications – in an SEC action and separately advised Drexel Burnham Lambert in proceedings relating to securities and RICO claims. The group has a strong client in Arthur Andersen, representing the troubled accountancy firm in dealings with Enron. Also active for a number of issuers in the IPO allocation cases, this vintage name was endorsed as "*a reliable guarantee of quality.*"

The Lawyers: To consistently run a high-quality white-collar practice takes "*great stamina as well as great skill.*" These are qualities **Peter Fleming** (see p.1280) has in abundance. "*Supercharged with energy,*" he continues to be a powerful force in the field. His colleague **Eliot Lauer** (see p.1296) is no less exalted. "*Extraordinarily difficult to shake off once he's got the bit between his teeth,*" he is admired by rivals for his persistence in pursuing a practice heavily freighted with securities, professional liability and false advertising matters.

The Clients: Glencore International; Arthur Andersen; SEI Investments; Tyco Toys and MSE Direct Lenders.

Dewey Ballantine LLP

See firm details p.1347

The Firm: The firm's most celebrated appearance in recent times has been its representation of Travelers and its subsidiary Gulf in the World Trade Center insurance litigation. The practice's core strengths lie in IP and patent litigation, antitrust, securities and corporate fraud. By way of illustration, the firm acted for Victor Company of Japan and JVC in the USA in defending a patent infringement action brought by Honeywell. It also appeared for MedImmune in another patent infringement suit brought by Celltech. In both cases the firm acted for the defense, a role that allowed it to bring its "*renowned fighting spirit to the fore.*" Clients value this along with "*the high degree of partner contact and timely analysis on offer.*" Such virtues were illustrated in litigation arising from MONY Group's recent merger with AXA Financial.

The Lawyers: Litigation department cochairman **Harvey Kurzweil** (see p.1295) is behind many of the team's best and brightest efforts. Integral to both the World Trade Center and the MONY Group litigation, he is a central reason why his department can attract a substantial amount of work through its reputation alone. Known as "*a man who staffs cases in a lean but comprehensive manner,*" his diffuse practice takes in IP, antitrust, securities, defamation and complex commercial disputes.

The Clients: Travelers; DaimlerChrysler; Intel; Microsoft; PG&E; Deutsche Bank; CSFB and UBS.

Fried, Frank, Harris, Shriver & Jacobson LLP

See firm details p.1349

The Firm: Although seemingly destined to be better known for its influential corporate and M&A work, Fried Frank leverages off this well to secure involvement in some meaty pieces of litigation. "*Real pros,*" its attorneys tend to function best in the larger financial cases, nimbly moving from business area to business area as the market dictates. As a consequence, the firm has built up real adaptability and can count securities litigation, corporate governance and general commercial litigation among the feathers in its cap. Examples of this diversity include acting for Grupo Televisa in a $1 billion breach of contract claim by Comsat, representing the New York Stock Exchange in connection with the SEC's review of its floor broker surveillance and advising Bear Stearns in multifaceted litigation arising out of the 1994 collapse of the collateralized mortgage obligation markets. Its undoubted trump card, however, remains white-collar criminal defense. In this regard, the team plays host to "*some of the best attorneys in the business*" and proves invaluable in defending both corporations and individuals under criminal and regulatory investigation.

The Lawyers: In a male-dominated world, **Audrey Strauss** (see p.1325) is one of the few women to stand out as "*a white-collar player of great distinction.*" Exuding a confidence born of an extended stretch with the US Attorney's Office, she is a "*smart, ethical and hard-working lawyer with terrific judgment*" whose "*organization and immense tenacity see her through time after time.*" In March 2005, Mark Stein departed the firm to join Simpson Thacher & Bartlett's government investigations and business crimes group.

The Clients: Bear Stearns; Perrigo; Society and Corporation of Lloyd's; New York Stock Exchange; Merrill Lynch; American Institute of Certified Public Accountants; Reader's Digest and EMI Group.

Jones Day

See firm details p.485

The Firm: Interviewees applauded a team that is seen to have "*made strides and turned itself into a credible, big-ticket operation.*" It has tackled all manner of litigation both here and on a national basis. Areas of special importance include IP, securities fraud, general corporate criminal investigations and products liability. The firm represented Bridgestone/Firestone in more than 100 class actions relating to its tire litigation and defended Colt in 25 lawsuits alleging the improper design and marketing of guns. Both these matters highlighted a very real talent on the pretrial side although commentators were less convinced about the group's eagerness to take matters to trial.

The Lawyers: David Carden leads the line, negotiating a personal practice heavy on securities, derivatives and commodities work.

The Clients: AOL (now Time Warner); Bridgestone/Firestone; Citicorp; Dow Corning; GE; GM; Gillette; IBM; International Paper; Napster and Procter & Gamble.

Kaye Scholer LLP

See firm details p.1354

The Firm: This "*old and venerable firm*" may not dominate the litigation skyline in the way it once did but nevertheless remains a force in the city. Litigation is its lifeblood as it devotes some 185 attorneys to the cause in New York alone. These lawyers offer an impressive variety of skills, approaching the work in a "*hard-driven and fully committed style,*" offering everything from white-collar to employment litigation. Amidst this talent, certain areas stand out. Firstly, the firm impresses in products liability and mass tort cases, where it often acts as national coordinating counsel. In this role it has represented Pfizer in all its litigations relating to Rezulin and advised Novartis on all suits relating to phenylpropanolamine. Secondly, the team excels in patent litigation, acting for many of the biggest names in the pharmaceutical, electronics and biotechnology fields. Here, the firm acted for Pfizer against the University of Rochester in a matter relating to the product Celebrex and further counseled ABC and Granada Entertainment USA in the 'I'm A Celebrity Get Me Out Of Here' survivor litigation. Antitrust litigation is further to the fore as illustrated by recent successful sorties on behalf of Estée Lauder and Metallgesellschaft AG while derivatives and securities litigation is far from neglected. By way of example, the firm acted in a decade-long derivatives matter for China's state-owned metals trading firm, Minmetals, against Lehman Brothers.

The Lawyers: Securities and derivatives expert Aaron Rubinstein heads the department. He is currently representing Pappas Telecasting Companies in connection with litigations and disputes against TV Azteca.

The Clients: Pfizer; Novartis; Boston Scientific; Aventis; RJ Reynolds; Sony and Minmetals.

Latham & Watkins LLP

The Firm: The New York office of Latham & Watkins is but one limb of a vast national organism that generates large amounts of litigation, much of it going to trial. Its litigators cover most bases but do their best work, here at least, on classic securities litigation, white collar and corporate governance. Able to draw in top clients, the firm acts regularly for CIBC, which it recently defended on a securities class action alleging negligence in its due diligence investigations into certain securities of InterBank Funding. The firm also successfully represented John Cassese, the former CEO of Computer Horizons, in a criminal insider trading case brought by the US Attorney's Office. Demonstrating the firm's skills beyond these core disciplines, its lawyers further tackled a patent infringement case on behalf of QinetiQ against Samsung and demonstrated its First Amendment credentials in ACLU's successful challenge to the Child Online Protection Act. Clients fully endorsed a team that is *"organized, fully au fait with the law and receptive to cost containment."* As one interviewee put it: *"This is a firm that won't string you along."*

The Lawyers: There has been a discernible attempt to boost the profile of this team over the past few years, a campaign that was abetted in no little way by the arrival of **David Brodsky** in 2002. Brodsky had been general counsel at CSFB and is felt to have brought another level of *"brisk, good business sense"* to the group here. Essentially a securities litigator, he is at the forefront of much of the caseload, employing *"professionalism and personability in equal measure."* He represented Société Générale in a securities action concerning allegations that Transkaryotic Therapies had engaged in a scheme to inflate the market price of its securities through misrepresentation and nondisclosure. Société Générale had acted as Transkaryotic Therapies' underwriters.

The Clients: Société Générale; CIBC; Goldman Sachs; AOL; Lucent Technologies; SG Cowen Securities and Ernst & Young.

Morrison & Foerster LLP

See firm details p.293

The Firm: Interviewees were keen to stress the intellectual acumen on offer at *"a firm populated with some great legal minds."* As one remarked: *"The attorneys I have seen have been uniformly brilliant and creative, splicing high-quality work with tremendous responsiveness."* Many of these satisfied clients come from the technology sector but other significant names come from the banking and financial services and entertainment areas. All enjoy a service that is particularly strong on securities, antitrust and IP and

which boasts a defined capability in products liability to boot. For example, the firm has represented GM in more than 150 cases relating to alleged manufacturing defects such as faulty seat belts and air bags. The greatest feather in the litigation group's cap of late has certainly been its involvement in the sprawling IPO litigation where it took a central role. This should not detract, however, from the solid mass of top-class litigation the firm handles year in, year out, including its efforts on behalf of Bank of America, which it is representing in an antitrust suit brought by American Express against Visa, MasterCard and several major card-issuing banks.

The Lawyers: Jack Auspitz (see p.1263) continues to bask in the glory of his role as liaison counsel in the IPO securities litigation. That he should have done such *"a good job in a potentially difficult role"* came as no surprise to some of our interviewees. A man who *"always gets to the heart of a case,"* Auspitz is *"excellent at speaking on the client's level"* while *"always having enough about him to keep ahead of the game."* He has assumed an even greater role within his group since the defection of former New York managing partner Howard Heiss to O'Melveny & Myers.

The Clients: 3M; GM; Barnes & Noble and Bank of America.

White & Case LLP

See firm details p.1379

The Firm: These are fecund times for White & Case as it attempts, with some success, to increase its share of the market. In a concerted effort to raise its profile, it has invested considerably in the litigation area, principally through the recruitment of figures such as Vincent Fitzpatrick from Dewey Ballantine and Lawrence Byrne from Squadron, Ellenoff, Plesent & Sheinfeld. Such newcomers have helped to bolster a firm with an already strong local and international reputation in its key areas of arbitration, securities, banking and antitrust. The group's growth has led to improvement in other areas such as IP and corporate governance and, more importantly, to the attraction of new clients. One such client, Comcast, it recently represented in a $125 million dispute with CSG Systems arising from the purchase of AT&T Broadband. The team has also represented Deutsche Bank in various matters arising from the collapse of Enron and been involved in the successful defense of a large price-fixing case brought against client Syngenta Seeds. On the investigatory front the team is representing Royal Ahold in enforcement action brought by the SEC. Clients marveled at the written skills of a group that has *"the rare gift of being able to work as well with other firms as it does with its own clients."*

The Lawyers: Michael Shuster (see p.1321), chair of the commercial litigation group, leads manfully on both securities and general commercial matters. A fine courtroom performer, he

worked on the Comcast matter and also succeeded in getting securities action and shareholders derivative litigation dismissed against Amerada Hess.

The Clients: Pfizer; Novartis; Northrop Grumman; Mirant; Amerada Hess; Deutsche Bank and Comcast.

Willkie Farr & Gallagher LLP

See firm details p.1380

The Firm: The post-Sarbanes growth in litigation has proved especially fruitful for this firm. Already an outfit that focused heavily on SEC enforcement issues, it has prospered yet more in the area as its all too evident skills have become more and more in demand. At present, a large proportion of its more than 100 litigators are requisitioned to tackle major SEC investigations and these attorneys display skill both in the general and in the particular. Strong all round, the group has fashioned an excellent reputation for itself in specialized sectors with accounting irregularities being the most obvious of these. The practice also embraces vitality elsewhere. Insurance litigation forms a large part of the whole and attorneys have been busily engaged on behalf of Marsh & McLennan on the regulatory aspects of its difficulties. A real capacity on the IP side has bloomed, too, in the past couple of years with the appointment of John DiMatteo. He has masterminded a growth in litigation that has included a large amount of patent litigation for the likes of Philips and Johnson & Johnson. Little wonder then that interviewees spoke of an *"increased self-confidence all round."* This has been expressed in appearances for the likes of H&R Block in securities litigation and for Cablevision in relation to government investigations. The team has further shown up in the Merck drama acting for the independent director of the company and has represented some of the underwriters (Goldman Sachs, Lehman Brothers, UBS and CSFB) in the WorldCom saga.

The Lawyers: It is very rare that the accountants are not dragged into the biggest disputes and investigations. When they are, many of them call upon **Michael Young** (see p.1333). *"Indubitably one of the most experienced defenders of accountants' interests,"* he is a good part of the reason why his firm is held in such very high esteem for its accounting regularities work. Young is *"never less than busy"* and has recently acted for KPMG in litigation concerning Elan and Footstar, while also advising BDO Seidman on tax shelter fraud matters. He handles his accountancy-related work in the context of a general securities practice not dissimilar to that of his colleague **Richard Posen** (see p.1310). The *"intelligent and thoughtful"* Posen undertakes the full gamut of securities matters including investigations while also possessing great M&A knowledge. He represented Simon Property Group in its

www.ChambersandPartners.com

All quotes in the text are from interviews with clients and competitors.

1229

$4.8 billion acquisition of Chelsea Property Group and provided the impetus for the successful dismissal of consolidated class actions in White v H&R Block.

The Clients: American Institute of Certified Public Accountants; Deloitte & Touche; KPMG; BDO Seidman; Philips and Johnson & Johnson.

Wilmer Cutler Pickering Hale and Dorr LLP

See firm details p.497

The Firm: Not even a presence in New York a decade ago, Wilmer Cutler has now fully entered the consciousness of the biggest financial players in the city. Since the office's inception in 1999, it has grown to over 100 lawyers and successfully transported those qualities that have made its sister arm in DC so very lionized. Aping its illustrious forebear, it has a practice that revolves around securities regulation and enforcement. Thus, the firm has interested itself in the majority of the most important SEC investigations and their parallel proceedings, including investigations into IPO allocation practices, research analyst independence, mutual fund market timing, and revenue sharing and broker-dealer mark-ups. Such work has always been something of a forte of the firm in Washington and although the NY office may not have quite hit the heights of its illustrious forebear, it is "*clearly becoming one of the best in town for this type of work.*" Allied to this evident capability the practice takes in IP, bankruptcy and general litigation, all of which is approached in "*a practical way that really runs an issue to its full conclusion.*" The firm's recent merger is widely seen as a positive one having further boosted the IP skills on offer while also ramping up the practice's trial capability.

The Lawyers: **Robert McCaw** (see p.1300) stands out as the leading light in a disciplined team of 15 partners. He has proved himself a close confidant to a number of major brokerage firms, corporations and accounting firms through negotiating a regulatory and enforcement practice that wins the benison of many. "*A bigger star than many give him credit for,*" he is a veteran of the IPO allocation and research analyst imbroglios. To both he brought an "*understated but hugely intelligent approach which got to the nub of the problem*" and clients eulogize one of "*the grand old men of securities who has nothing to prove and everything to be proud of.*"

The Clients: Merrill Lynch; UBS; Bear Stearns; Nortel; Fannie Mae; Bank of America; Deutsche Bank and American Express.

Morvillo, Abramowitz, Grand, Iason & Silberberg, PC

The Firm: This "*unbeatable white-collar boutique*" is built on modest lines, though it has been thrust to the fore through deploying "*only the very best attorneys in its compact team.*" Its

size is such that it is unlikely to represent big companies on criminal matters, but it more than makes up for this through its representation of individuals of substance. Consequently, it has offered its services to the likes of Martha Stewart, whom it represented in various matters including a shareholder derivative suit, and litigation relating to the sale of shares in ImClone. In a case of some complexity and with the media's glare upon it, the firm was said to have done "*a highly proficient job in trying circumstances.*" Such polish doesn't come cheap but those prepared to pay for it, such as Adelphi Communications' CEO John Rigas, do so because they know that "*representation of this quality comes along rarely.*" Indeed, such is the standing of the firm that many of the massive Wall Street legal juggernauts pronounced themselves more than happy to refer work here.

The Lawyers: Something of a pioneer, **Robert Morvillo** was one of the first to see that white-collar crime was a rapidly burgeoning area of the law. The boutique that he set up as a result now has 36 attorneys but of these, he remains the best known. His qualities take in "*great discretion, brilliant tactical acumen and a self-belief that drives him time and again to glory in the courtroom.*" "*Never afraid to let both client and tribunal know exactly what he is thinking,*" Morvillo is "*a man of dominating character who is not going to blow in the wind.*" Clients rave about him whilst also reserving special praise for **Elkan Abramowitz**. Another "*stout-hearted performer,*" he matches his distinguished colleague for "*courtroom wizardry and mental agility.*"

The Clients: The firm generally acts for high-profile individuals and corporate clients.

Lankler Siffert & Wohl

The Firm: Interviewees admired the six-partner boutique that is "*devoid of weak links.*" All the partners have excellent academic backgrounds and substantial experience, and four of them are former prosecutors. Such solid legal grounding opens the way to "*quality, cost-effective representation*" in the context of a practice rich in civil, regulatory and white-collar matters. Much of the 21-lawyer team's work is for corporate entities, but it is more often seen offering "*an intense and personal service*" to individuals such as the CEOs of major companies. This brings it into contact with many of the city's leading firms either through referral or in opposition, and they were quick to testify to the group's merits. "*Tough opponents never to be taken lightly,*" these attorneys particularly focus on matters tinged with securities, banking and antitrust law.

The Lawyers: **John Siffert**'s tours of duty in the US Attorney's Office and as the cochair of the litigation department of a national law firm gave him a head start when he decided to set up on smaller lines. "*He has flourished since, shepherding any number of individuals along the rocky*

path of civil and criminal investigation." Combining "*steeliness*" with charming bedside manners on behalf of clients, he impresses foes with his "*command of a situation.*" His partner, **Frank Wohl**, excites the same sort of admiration as "*a man one reposes one's utmost faith in.*" Also a former prosecutor, his is "*a personality that makes any dealings with him as painless as possible.*"

The Clients: The firm acts for individuals and other entities in civil, regulatory and white-collar criminal matters.

Stillman & Friedman

The Firm: In its 28-year history this firm has drawn deeply from the twin wells of the US Attorney's Office and major New York law firms to assemble "*a crack team of white-collar litigators.*" The unit handles complex litigation, both civil and criminal, at all levels for businesses, partnerships and individuals including prominent political figures. It trumps many of its rivals in its breadth with a caseload comprising of matters that touch on the real estate, telecom and financial services industries to name a few. The willingness of fellow lawyers to hire the firm's services in times of delicacy goes some way to indicate its standing in the field. "*Never less than professional,*" this team has represented a former New York City mayor over allegations of election campaign irregularities contingent upon certain financial transactions. It has also acted for the chief judge of the New York State Court of Appeals on extortion charges. Recently it garnered much publicity for agreeing a final settlement for Jack Waksal with the SEC. Waksal, the father of ImClone Systems CEO Sam Waksal, had been charged with insider trading regarding shares in the firm.

The Lawyers: The great, the good and the not so good all flock to the door of **Charles Stillman** in times of trouble. With more than 40 years of experience – first as a prosecutor and then in private practice – he is pitched as "*one of the most revered denizens of the white-collar world.*" Still very much at the top of his game, he has been representing Mark Swartz, former finance chief of Tyco International, in one of the largest corruption cases in US history. Also present is **Paul Schechtman**, an alumnus of the US Attorney's Office and the Office of the Governor of New York State. "*Able to master anything that's thrown at him,*" he was appellate counsel to the Governor of New York State in a challenge by the State Legislature as to the governor's authority over the budgeting process. He has also represented the New York City Department of Environmental Protection in an investigation of the city's water treatment facilities.

The Clients: The firm represents corporations, partnerships and individuals from across the wider business community.

1230

All quotes in the text are from interviews with clients and competitors.

CHAMBERS USA 2005

Other Notable Practitioners

Tired of toiling under the constraints of life in a big city firm, **Gregory P Joseph** set up his own shop, Gregory P Joseph Law Offices LLC. From these environs he has nurtured an already healthy reputation as a financial and corporate litigator of the most complex cases. Clients and adversaries alike favor his *"measured, thoughtful and above all meticulous"* approach to his cases, praising him as *"one of the those attorneys utterly steeped in the law."* He leads a team that successfully represented a Fortune 50 company in litigation turning on a $6.9 billion foreign tender offer and acted for a major West Coast utility in securing a $65 million judgment against a foreign bank. Another to have successfully set up on his own is **Stephen Kaufman**, a sole practitioner whose *"reputation as a white-collar supremo precedes him."* Acting alone, he is limited in the amount of work he can undertake, but he is often to the fore on behalf of major individuals caught up in corporate scandals. One of these, the former chief executive of Tyco, Dennis Kozlowski, has been taking up much of his time of late. **Alan Levine** of Kronish Lieb Weiner & Hellman LLP is a general litigator with a pronounced bias towards white-collar criminal litigation. *"A lawyer business people of great stature and influence turn to,"* he acts for Sumitomo in all manner of litigation and has gained much credit for his representation of a collection of insurance companies against JPMorgan Chase in a fraud case involving $1 billion in Enron surety bonds. His colleague **William Schwartz** chairs the litigation group and is *"increasingly becoming recognized as a force in white-collar circles."* Clifford Chance's loss has been Milbank, Tweed, Hadley & McCloy LLP's gain as the latter has inveigled **James Benedict** into joining its ranks. Benedict was very much the prop of the securities practice at his old firm and is expected to provide a real shot in the arm for his new paymasters. His *"irresistible affability, relaxed approach and sound judgment"* are just a few of the qualities that have proved so attractive to his new employers. They welcome an attorney who has acted for companies such as Salomon Smith Barney and Fidelity and who appeared in Gartenberg v Merrill Lynch Asset Management, the leading case regarding the Investment Company Act of 1940. He takes his place at his new firm alongside **Scott Edelman**, *"a dynamic attorney with limitless reserves of energy,"* which he devotes to a practice that seamlessly melds big-ticket civil and criminal litigation. Edelman's notable representations include representing leading insurance brokerage firm Jardines Lloyd Thomson in litigation arising out of the demise of Bennett Funding. He also advised Ashanti Goldfields in the defense of a securities class action. At Shapiro Forman Allen Miller & McPherson LLP, **Stuart Shapiro** stands out. He crafted a respected career at Skadden Arps before transferring his talents to this, his own boutique. Very much the *"Caesar of his own fortune,"* he is felt to have brought his practice along through sheer talent. His caseload embraces many forms of complex litigation, although a distinct proliferation of securities and white-collar defense work shines through. Shapiro's career demonstrates the fluid nature of a New York legal scene that witnesses cross-firm movement continually. There has been no better recent example of this than **Howard Heiss**. Formerly of Morrison & Foerster LLP, he has now taken residence at O'Melveny & Myers LLP, where he handles a regimen of white-collar, SEC and other regulatory proceedings. *"Sagacious and unflappable,"* he dominates many commentators' thoughts with his manful exertions on behalf of investment banker Frank Quattrone in regulatory proceedings brought by the NASD. Also on the move, **Andrew Levander** was one of the contingent of 57 attorneys from Swidler Berlin LLP's New York office who trooped over to Dechert LLP earlier in 2005. The market congratulated the Philadelphia firm on snaring such an *"intelligent, knowledgeable and effective lawyer"* for their New York office, feeling his strength in the areas of securities and white-collar defense to be hugely beneficial in the promotion of its profile. **Fred Hafetz** of Hafetz and Necheles can match Levander for white-collar expertise and won support for his *"robust defense of individuals under investigation,"* while **Lee Richards** of Richards Spears Kibbe & Orbe impressed our interviewees as *"Argos eyed in detecting all the angles of a case."* Coordinator of Covington & Burling's white-collar criminal defense practice, **Aaron Marcu** (see p.1299) has marshaled institutions and individuals through various government investigations and related civil actions. Another alumnus from the US Attorney's Office, he has been involved in disputes related to Tyco, Enron, mutual funds and other corporate scandals. Similarly, **Richard Strassberg** (see p.1325) of Goodwin Procter LLP brings to bear his experience as a former chief of the Major Crimes Unit of the US Attorney's Office for the Southern District of New York. Like many others in his position, Strassberg often delivers preventative measures such as advising on corporate internal investigations. Sole practitioner **Andrew Lawler** has his hands full cradling a practice that caters to some very big shots in the business world. So persuasive is he that he *"can occasionally turn a tribunal into his sport and toy."* Finally, on the securities front, the *"forthright yet constructive"* **Jeffrey Smith** of King & Spalding LLP and **Robert Pietrzak** of Sidley Austin Brown & Wood LLP are both recommended. Interviewees admired Pietrzak's *"learned, almost professorial arguments"* on behalf of the many financial institutions he counts as clients.

MEDIA & ENTERTAINMENT   LITIGATION

Band 1

Cahill Gordon & Reindel

The Firm: *"The New York Yankees of First Amendment law,"* this firm continues to be the gold standard in contentious media work. Clients say it is *"a magnificent firm with the skills to match its reputation,"* and applaud both its litigation and regulatory expertise. Cahill Gordon boasts a truly excellent client roster with several TV and newspaper companies on board. Such clients acknowledge the part attorneys play in the training of young journalists on First Amendment issues.

The Lawyers: **Floyd Abrams** is undoubtedly the star of the practice; *"He has handled some of the most significant cases in the country and is on a different level of capability when compared to other trial lawyers."* No stranger to the limelight, he recently represented the National Association of Broadcasters and Senator Mitch McConnell in the McCain Feingold campaign finance case, eventually arguing the matter before the Supreme Court. Another of his headline-grabbing matters was Penguin Group's dispute with Fox News over Al Franken's book 'Lies and the Lying Liars Who Tell Them – A Fair and Balanced Look at the Right.' The case, which Penguin won, involved Fox News' claim that the title impinged their trademarked slogan 'Fair & Balanced.' **Dean Ringel**, who also worked on the Penguin Group case, is described as *"a knowledgeable and sharp lawyer;"* he is *"astute enough to only go to the courts when it is absolutely needed."*

The Clients: The New York Times; NBC; ABC; CBS; Time Warner; Court TV; The New Yorker; CNN and King-World Productions.

Davis Wright Tremaine LLP

See firm details p.1796

The Firm: Located on both the East and West coasts, Davis Wright is thought to have more of

New York
Leading firms
(Media & Entertainment: Litigation)

[1] **CAHILL GORDON & REINDEL** New York
DAVIS WRIGHT TREMAINE LLP New York

[2] **DEBEVOISE & PLIMPTON LLP** New York
GIBSON, DUNN & CRUTCHER LLP New York
LEVINE SULLIVAN KOCH & SCHULZ LLP New York
PROSKAUER ROSE LLP New York
WEIL, GOTSHAL & MANGES LLP New York

[3] **COWAN, LIEBOWITZ & LATMAN** New York
CRAVATH, SWAINE & MOORE LLP New York
HOGAN & HARTSON LLP New York
O'MELVENY & MYERS LLP New York
PAUL, WEISS, RIFKIND, WHARTON New York

[4] **COUDERT BROTHERS** New York
FROSS ZELNICK LEHRMAN & ZISSU PC New York
LOEB & LOEB LLP New York
WHITE & CASE LLP New York

Leading individuals
(Media & Entertainment: Litigation)

[1] **ABRAMS Floyd** Cahill Gordon, New York
KOVNER Victor Davis Wright, New York

[2] **CENDALI Dale** O'Melveny & Myers, New York
GOERING Kevin Coudert Brothers, New York
KELLER Bruce Debevoise & Plimpton, New York
METCALF Slade Hogan & Hartson, New York
SCHULZ David Levine Sullivan, New York
SIMS Charles Proskauer Rose, New York
WEISS Jack Gibson Dunn, New York

[3] **DANNAY Richard** Cowan Liebowitz, New York
MCNAMARA Elizabeth Davis Wright, New York
ORTNER Charles Proskauer Rose, New York
PAUL Marcia Davis Wright, New York
RASKOPF Robert White & Case, New York
REISNER Lorin Debevoise & Plimpton, New York
RICH Bruce Weil Gotshal, New York
RINGEL Dean Cahill Gordon, New York
SLOTNICK Barry Loeb & Loeb, New York
STEINTHAL Kenneth Weil Gotshal, New York
SUGARMAN Robert Weil Gotshal, New York

Firms and individuals are listed alphabetically in each band.

a national perspective than close rivals. Clients recommend this "*savvy group of lawyers*" for its "*genuinely broad practice and epic range of experience and expertise.*" One peer claimed: "*If I couldn't hire us, I would certainly hire them – you couldn't go wrong.*" The firm represents the publishers of newspapers, magazines and books, as well as TV and radio broadcasters on defamation, invasion of privacy and First Amendment matters. It also carries out a substantial amount of work for the producers of films and TV programs and is a popular choice for leading European media organizations. In the past year the firm acted for a literary agency in a dispute concerning copyright issues and the estate of John Steinbeck. It also handled a large test case for Bloomberg News concerning cameras in court.

The Lawyers: "*Super lawyer*" **Victor Kovner** (see p.1295) has "*a fine knowledge of the substance of the law and an air of definite authority.*" His long experience marks him out as one of the godfathers of this area of law in New York. In the past year Kovner acted for Yellow Book in its dispute with Verizon, concerning market research carried out by Harris Interactive. He was also involved in a high-profile libel case and a number of matters concerning the rights of artists. **Elizabeth McNamara** (see p.1300) is rated "*a top-drawer lawyer with a sixth sense of what a judge will accept.*" She tackles a range of broadcasting and publishing work, including libel, privacy, copyright and obscenity, and is recommended for her excellent prepublication advice and knowledge of electronic publishing. **Marcia Paul** (see p.1307) is considered "*a sharp cookie*" on copyright matters. She recently acted for Lions Gate Entertainment in a dispute about the rights to produce and distribute a prequel to '9 1/2 Weeks'.

The Clients: Wenner Media; Village Voice Media; New York Daily News; BBC; The Economist; Time Warner; Random House; CNN; Reed Elsevier; McGraw-Hill; Ziff Davis Media and US publications owned by Associated Newspapers in London, such as Institutional Investor.

Band 2

Debevoise & Plimpton LLP
See firm details p.1346

The Firm: A "*heavyweight*" practice recognized for its abilities in general media, copyright and trademark disputes, publicity rights and First Amendment issues. Said one appreciative client: "*There are good litigators in New York, and good copyright lawyers, but it's rare to have both combined.*" Attorneys are active right across the industry waterfront and boast expertise in TV, movies, radio, music, advertising, sports and both print and web publishing. The firm has enjoyed a number of recent successes in movie, trademark and defamation cases and was recently successful in a trademark dispute concerning a major Hollywood film.

The Lawyers: **Bruce Keller** is, in the view of clients, "*unbelievably smart and knowledgeable about media and IP issues. He is also practical (which not every smart lawyer is) and wonderful at combining the information you give him with the best business strategy.*" Keller's clientele is hugely varied, from Hollywood studios to small publishers and sporting bodies, among them the National Hockey League and the National Football League. The "*fantastic*" **Lorin Reisner** joins the table this year on the back of client recommendation. They see him as "*a smart, knowledgeable attorney who is good for succinct answers to media questions.*" He has been active in several notable commercial disputes, as well as suits involving world-famous talent.

The Clients: Amazon.com; Microsoft; NFL; NHL; Sony and Yahoo!

Gibson, Dunn & Crutcher LLP
See firm details p.285

The Firm: This New York and LA media team comes highly recommended. Well known for its representation of Dow Jones and The Wall Street Journal, it undertakes a range of print and new media litigation. Attorneys recently acted for Penguin Group imprint Plume in a $15 million libel claim brought by former New York governor Mario Cuomo relating to claims that he improperly influenced a federal judge. They also represented Internet search provider Info Space in a complex dispute with what is now a unit of Ask Jeeves.

The Lawyers: **Jack Weiss** (see p.1331) is "*a strategic thinker with a good client focus.*" Endorsing his preferred attorney, one client said: "*He is superb in discussion, superb in court and I have never received a bad set of papers from him.*" For principal client Dow Jones, he handles litigation across the USA and beyond. This has included a libel action brought by the owners of the London department store Harrods and the defense of The Washington Post in a libel case concerning the former chaplain of the New York prison system. Weiss has also acted on matters pertaining to former CIA agent Valerie Plume, whose name was leaked to the press.

The Clients: The group counts Penguin Group subsidiary Plume Books, Dow Jones and its subsidiaries and Internet search engine InfoSpace among its clients.

Levine Sullivan Koch & Schulz LLP

The Firm: Though traditionally a DC firm, Levine Sullivan is felt to have "*made a big splash in New York in recent years.*" It is primarily focused on litigation for news organizations and reporters, as well as high-stakes matters for broadcasters. One highlight from the past 12 months was the representation of Associated Press in a series of lawsuits to gain access to George W. Bush's National Guard records. The Freedom of Information Act has been used to secure the release of a number of documents. The team is strong on libel matters and has handled cases concerning The New York Times, Vanity Fair and The LA Times. It also represented a Reuters reporter who had been summonsed in a terrorism trial. The firm has media lawyers across the country, and clients comment that it is "*an efficient, cost-effective group, which is extremely well versed in the law.*"

The Lawyers: New York partner **David Schulz** is "*a younger, very capable guy, who is an expert on press access*" and "*a superb First Amendment lawyer.*" Last year he acted for CBS in a case concerning the right to have cameras film a major trial, as well as representing a consortium in its attempt to gain access to the jury selection process in Martha Stewart's trial.

The Clients: Associated Press; Hearst Corporation; New York Press Association; New York Times; Reuters; Tribune Company; Univision and Viacom/CBS.

Proskauer Rose LLP

See firm details p.1365

The Firm: Again, active on both East and West coasts, Proskauer Rose offers New York attorneys with expertise in publishing, music, theatre and film. It combines a strong First Amendment and copyright practice with capability in libel, rights of privacy and publicity, unfair competition, royalty disputes and finance. Market commentators regard it as "*a focused firm with a rich skill set.*"

The Lawyers: IP expert **Charles Sims** (see p.1321) is "*a very intelligent, but highly practical guy. He is direct and doesn't overcomplicate things.*" Adept at copyright issues and matters concerning new technologies, he represents LexisNexis in three ongoing national copyright cases. These concern claims for damages by authors whose articles have been included on the Nexis database, but which Nexis contends is authorized by rights duties transferred by newspapers and magazines. He has also defended The New York Times and The Discovery Channel in class action litigation. New to this year's guide is **Charles Ortner** (see p.1306), who is highly regarded for his litigation and IP skills. He has a particular reputation in the music business, and in the past year acted for EMI Music Publishing on a landmark licensing agreement with Sony BMG Music Entertainment for the exploitation of new technology including ring tones, the new DualDisc Format and digital video distribution.

The Clients: Corporate clients include BMG; EMI; Warner Bros. Records; Warner Chappell Music and Wind-Up Records. Charles Ortner has also represented such artists as Madonna, Michael Jackson, Shania Twain, Lauryn Hill, Whitney Houston and Jon Bon Jovi.

Weil, Gotshal & Manges LLP

See firm details p.1378

The Firm: The group is principally recommended for its copyright expertise, for which it is deemed "*a strong New York player.*" It lays claim to a cache of top-name clients in music, publishing, film and television, and is developing a reputation among new media and technological concerns. Attorneys recently represented the DVD Copy Control Association in a patent case, which involved a web posting giving directions on how to break DVD encryption.

The Lawyers: Copyright and publishing expert **Bruce Rich** (see p.1312) combines "*sharp commercial skills with a detailed industry knowledge.*" His work covers print, broadcast media and now new media, and he was recently retained by eBay in a case brought by Tiffany & Co concerning the authenticity of Tiffany prod-

ucts being sold on the auction site. He is also representing Bertelsmann in litigation arising from its links to Napster. Clients recommend **Robert Sugarman** (see p.1325) for his skills in media and entertainment litigation, in particular his copyright and trademark expertise. He has been acting for the National Geographic Society in a copyright case concerning a CD-Rom, which it had issued. The plaintiffs, all writers and photographers, claim the publisher had no right to reproduce their work electronically. "*Smooth and professional*" **Kenneth Steinthal** (see p.1324) continues to attract attention. He, too, is involved in the Napster/Bertelsmann litigation, reflecting his interest in digital and new media matters.

The Clients: National Geographic Society; Copyright Clearance Center; Association of American Publishers; Television Music Licensing Committee; McGraw-Hill; Disney/ABC and Sony Music.

Band 3

Cowan, Liebowitz & Latman

The Firm: This small practice is best known for its IP-related activities and offers services to a diverse media client base. Particular praise was reserved for the firm's film production work, an area in which it has a national and international client following. A recent success story involves the dismissal of a case against newspaper client, The Philippine Daily Inquirer. The case was the first of its kind in a New York court and concerned the publication on the web of an allegedly defamatory article, which could be accessed by New York residents.

The Lawyers: "*Sharp and shrewd litigator*" **Richard Dannay** is active for publishers and motion picture companies, and is well regarded for his copyright work. He recently acted for Penguin Putnam in a copyright dispute concerning the publication of Dorothy Parker's unpublished works. He was able to obtain the reversal of a summary judgment and the vacation of a permanent injunction on appeal.

The Clients: The firm acts for broadcasters, advertisers and publishers, as well as major names in the motion picture industry.

Cravath, Swaine & Moore LLP

See firm details p.1344

The Firm: This "*smart, responsive*" team joins the table on the back of ringing client endorsements for its "*dedicated litigation group, which is good at figuring out the complex issues.*" Attorneys are best known for their work for Time Warner, for whom they handle a range of work. In the past year the team was asked to assess antitrust issues relating to the multibillion-dollar sale of Time Warner's music group. Cravath's media lawyers have also handled copyright infringements (by way of Internet downloads) for the

company, as well as boxing-related litigation for its subsidiary HBO. It has just achieved a New York State appellate pronouncement affirming a trial court ruling in favor of Warner Music Group and other major record labels that recording contracts signed before the existence of the Internet were sufficiently broad to allow the companies to distribute the records over the Internet.

The Lawyers: Robert Joffe is the key member of the team.

The Clients: In addition to Time Warner, the group advises a major East Coast newspaper and a number of large music and media companies.

Hogan & Hartson LLP

See firm details p.484

The Firm: "*On the ball and totally focused*" is how this team was described to researchers; "*They have a great knowledge of the industry, so you can ask them a question and they don't even need to research it.*" The firm has been selected by Rupert Murdoch's News Corporation for litigation, regulatory advice and prepublication and prebroadcast advice, it continues to be active on libel matters for a number of different clients.

The Lawyers: The "*astute*" **Slade Metcalf** (see p.1301) is said to be "*a definite go-to person for media problems.*" He earns high praise for his copyright and defamation work, and is also skilled in new media matters. In the past year he acted in a Kentucky libel case brought by an associate professor at Kentucky University over an article that appeared on the Fox News Website.

The Clients: Clients include News Corporation and its subsidiaries plus others in print media.

O'Melveny & Myers LLP

See firm details p.294

The Firm: Although not as big as the firm's West Coast presence, O'Melveny & Myers' New York office boasts "*a nifty practice with a substantial client base.*" It handles a range of media and entertainment work for film and music companies, computer game manufacturers and individuals within the entertainment world. The team is well known for its copyright and trademark work.

The Lawyers: **Dale Cendali** is "*a sharp, intelligent lady who does very well in the cases in which she's involved.*" In the past 12 months she secured a dismissal for Sony Music in a case over Jennifer Lopez's 'I'm Glad' video, which was brought by a party who claimed it infringed copyrighted aspects of the film 'Flashdance'. She also defeated an injunction brought against MGA Entertainment – the maker of Bratz dolls – by a rival company, which was trying to block the sale of the dolls.

The Clients: Twentieth Century Fox; Electronic Arts; Sony Music; ScanSoft and JK Rowling.

www.ChambersandPartners.com
All quotes in the text are from interviews with clients and competitors.
1233

Paul, Weiss, Rifkind, Wharton & Garrison LLP

See firm details p.1362

The Firm: Although best known for its corporate media capabilities, the group has a growing reputation for litigation and tackles disputes in the theater, film and publishing industries. It has a particular following in the music industry, recently representing Capitol Records in a RICO class action arising out of the record company's alleged underpayment of health and retirement benefits to recording artists. The group has also represented Time Warner in antitrust matters in the state and federal court, as well as Sony Music in a class action concerning the ownership of digital distribution rights.

The Lawyers: Jay Cohen is well known in the media law sphere and rated for his work in antitrust and IP.

The Clients: The group's clients include Broadway producers, film producers and music companies.

Band 4

Coudert Brothers

The Firm: Boasting a long-standing reputation for publishing matters, Coudert is seen as a good choice for copyright, news gathering, rights of publicity and advertising issues, as well as pre-publication libel advice. The firm's New York office has a distinctly international flavor, with lawyers advising US television networks on news gathering in foreign countries, and recently even acting for a news company setting up an operation in Bosnia.

The Lawyers: Kevin Goering (see p.1283) is identified as "*a knowledgeable, persuasive, detail-oriented advocate*" who is admired for his First Amendment and libel work. He handled the copyright and other legal aspects of the documentaries 'Fahrenheit 9/11' and 'Weapons Of Mass Deception,' as well as copyright issues for a range of book and magazine publishers.

The Clients: Grove/Atlantic; Scholastic; Perseus Books and Condé Nast Publications.

Fross Zelnick Lehrman & Zissu PC

The Firm: The firm joins the table this year on the back of market recommendation for its "*focused litigation group.*" Although more active at the IP end of the media spectrum, the group is respected for its work on rights of publicity and privacy, and various aspects of Internet law.

The Lawyers: Ronald Lehrman is the firm's key media litigator.

The Clients: DC Comics; Edgar Rice Burroughs; Forbes; The Jim Henson Company; Miramax Film Corp; The Miss America Organization and Sony Music.

Loeb & Loeb LLP

The Firm: A West Coast player with a growing practice in its New York office, Loeb & Loeb represents clients in film and television litigation. Lawyers in the firm's office in Nashville assist their colleagues in New York, when acting for talent and producers on disputes within the recording industry.

The Lawyers: Barry Slotnick is active in both IP and entertainment law. He recently successfully defended Anheuser-Busch and DDB

Worldwide in a copyright infringement case concerning a Super Bowl commercial that depicted battling robots. The case was brought by BattleBots, which broadcasts a TV show featuring dueling robots.

The Clients: The firm acts for various broadcasters, film producers and talent.

White & Case LLP

See firm details p.1379

The Firm: "*A smart and responsive team, which has a wide understanding of media matters.*" White & Case boasts a client base stuffed with broadcasters, publishers and music companies, and has a niche in handling marketing and media matters for sporting bodies. The practice group has expertise relating to the Internet, and last year handled a Website misappropriation case for The Thomson Corporation.

The Lawyers: "*Savvy media lawyer*" **Robert Raskopf** (see p.1311) is viewed as "*a practical, can-do guy.*" He has represented ESPN in a number of disputes, including one in which he successfully obtained a preliminary injunction against cable television channel The X Channel, which broadcast a show with a logo similar to ESPN's own X Games trademark. The defendant agreed to change the program's name.

The Clients: American Society of Composers; Comcast; National Football League; National Hockey League; PR Newswire; Thomson Corporation and Disney.

MEDIA & ENTERTAINMENT

TRANSACTIONAL

New York
Leading firms
(Media & Entertainment: Transactional)

[1]	CRAVATH, SWAINE & MOORE LLP *New York*
	DAVIS POLK & WARDWELL *New York*
	DEBEVOISE & PLIMPTON LLP *New York*
	FRANKFURT KURNIT KLEIN & SELZ *New York*
	FRANKLIN, WEINRIB, RUDELL & VASSALLO *New York*
	GRUBMAN, INDURSKY & SCHINDLER PC *New York*
	HOGAN & HARTSON LLP *New York*
	LOEB & LOEB LLP *New York*
	PAUL, WEISS, RIFKIND, WHARTON *New York*
[2]	DAVIS & GILBERT *New York*
	DEWEY BALLANTINE LLP *New York*
	GREENBERG TRAURIG LLP *New York*
	MORGAN, LEWIS & BOCKIUS LLP *New York*
	PRYOR CASHMAN SHERMAN & FLYNN *New York*
	SHEARMAN & STERLING LLP *New York*
	SUKIN LAW GROUP *New York*
	WEIL, GOTSHAL & MANGES LLP *New York*

Firms are listed alphabetically in 0each band.

Band 1

Cravath, Swaine & Moore LLP

See firm details p.1344

The Firm: This "*phenomenal practice*" draws plaudits from across the marketplace, and is regarded as "*an absolutely wonderful media group*" that "*really does have its finger on the pulse.*" The group's work leans toward broadcasters, and it handles a range of M&A, financings, contracts and regulatory issues. Another significant element of the practice is its niche specialty relating to satellite broadcasters. It recently represented HBO in the sale of its 50% interest in Comedy Central to Viacom, a deal valued at $1.3 billion. The group is also highly active for publishers and film companies, for example representing DreamWorks Animation in its spin-off IPO from DreamWorks.

The Lawyers: The "*astute*" **John Gaffney** (see p.1281) is praised as "*an eminently sensible deal-maker.*" Commentators said, "*It's always good to

have him on the other side.*" He is picked out for his corporate skills and his knowledge of the media market. He represented Time Warner Cable in an agreement with Comcast and the owners of the New York Mets regarding a regional sports television network to be launched in 2006.

The Clients: Time Warner Cable; HBO; DreamWorks Animation; The New York Times; The Washington Post and International Herald Tribune.

Davis Polk & Wardwell

See firm details p.1345

The Firm: Although best known for its work for cable broadcasters, the group continues to impress for a wide range of media entities including publishers and institutional lenders. It earns marketplace endorsement as "*a tremendously astute and focused practice*" and earns particular praise for its skills on securities work. The firm is representing Banc of America Securities as financial adviser to Liberty Media Interna-

Leading individuals
(Media & Entertainment: Transactional)
[1] **BOHM Richard** *Debevoise & Plimpton*, New York
BREGLIO John *Paul Weiss*, New York
BROWN Elliot *Franklin Weinrib*, New York
GAFFNEY John *Cravath Swaine*, New York
GELBLUM Seth *Loeb & Loeb*, New York
GILLESPIE Michael *Debevoise & Plimpton*, New York
GRUBMAN Allen *Grubman Indursky*, New York
HELLER Richard *Frankfurt Kurnit*, New York
HERSCH Dennis *Davis Polk*, New York
KRESS Alan *Sole Practitioner*, New York
RUDELL Michael *Franklin Weinrib*, New York
SUKIN Michael *Sukin Law Group*, New York
[2] **AMES Mitchell** *Hogan & Hartson*, New York
ARAR Roger *Loeb & Loeb*, New York
GORDON Nicholas *Franklin Weinrib*, New York
GRIER Joseph *Pryor Cashman*, New York
HOFSTETTER Richard *Frankfurt Kurnit*, New York
JACOBSON Marc *Greenberg Traurig*, New York
RAMOS Carey *Paul Weiss*, New York
ROSINI Neil *Franklin Weinrib*, New York
SCHUMER Robert *Paul Weiss*, New York
Individuals are listed alphabetically in each band.

tional in its proposed merger with UnitedGlobalCom; the deal is valued at $7.4 billion.

The Lawyers: Corporate expert **Dennis Hersch** (see p.1288) is rated as " *a skilled and smart negotiator. He keeps a constant eye on the best interests of the clients.*" He is co-head of the M&A group and is best known for his work for Comcast. He has acted on numerous transactions, including the proposed merger with MediaOne Group and the subsequent agreement to acquire two million new cable subscribers from AT&T.

The Clients: The group has represented Sterling Entertainment – a media company formed by the New York Mets – in a deal with Comcast and Time Warner Cable for the creation of a new sports channel. Other clients include major cable companies and investment banks.

Debevoise & Plimpton LLP
See firm details p.1346

The Firm: This large media group enjoys the respect of its peers and clients. It is recommended for its "*great combination of experience, know-how and sheer enthusiasm for the work.*" The practice represents radio and television broadcasters, new media companies, publishers and talent across the range of corporate issues. On the menu are matters pertaining to M&A, venture capital, outsourcing and licensing agreements. A feather in its cap was GE/NBC's $14 billion acquisition of Vivendi Universal.

The Lawyers: Michael Gillespie is recommended as "*unflappable and pragmatic*" and as a "*hard-working, intelligent lawyer.*" On behalf of Henson, he marshaled its repurchase of the Jim Henson Company and the subsequent sale of

The Muppets to Disney. He remains strong on cross-border issues and continues to represent the Globo Organization – the largest Brazilian media group – on its international activities. **Richard Bohm** cochairs the firm's media and technology group with Michael Gillespie, and is also ranked for his private equity work. He is recommended as "*a great lawyer and a brilliant strategist – a man who gets results.*" He regularly represents Oxygen Media, a cable network devoted to women's programming, and EdgeTV, a network devoted to games of skill and chance. He is also representing the Associated Press in its development on enhanced online search capabilities.

The Clients: Sony; Hasbro; Globo Organization; Portugal Telecom; Oxygen Media; AT&T Latin America and the NFL.

Frankfurt Kurnit Klein & Selz

The Firm: One of the larger teams in the entertainment market, this broad-focused group is recommended as "*a sophisticated and skilled group of lawyers,*" observers said. "*It brings a sharp set of skills to the table.*" The team is recommended for its skills in publishing, where it represents a number of best selling authors in negotiating publishing deals and motion picture agreements. It has also represented writers looking to extend their brand beyond the published word. The group boasts a niche in the representation of fashion models, including in endorsements and the marketing of their own products.

The Lawyers: "*The most famous film lawyer in New York*" according to one source, **Richard Heller** (see p.1287) is praised as "*a total genius in movie-making matters. He really is someone to have on your side.*" He represents writers, producers and actors in motion picture productions related to both the big-studio and independent sectors. He also handles a significant amount of financing proceedings for independent films. He cochairs the firm's entertainment group with **Richard Hofstetter** (see p.1288), who is praised as "*a solid lawyer with a deep client base.*" He is particularly praised for his TV work and represents producers, performers, writers and talent in a range of TV projects.

The Clients: The firm's clients include film and TV production, broadcasting and financing companies, and high-profile individuals.

Franklin, Weinrib, Rudell & Vassallo

The Firm: One of the top entertainment firms in the city, the group boasts "*talent, know-how and the right contacts.*" Its "*savvy style*" also attracted a prominent clientele, which includes producers, directors and artists. Investors and other corporate entities also retain the firm on matters relating to film, television, theater, publishing and music. Cross-border activities feature in its repertoire.

The Lawyers: Michael Rudell is "*one of the top*

media lawyers." He earns endorsements for his film-making expertise. "*The dean of the theater world,*" **Elliot Brown** is praised as "*a superb lawyer with a thoroughly deserved reputation.*" He has advised on 'The Producers' since its opening in Broadway and acted on its recent transfer to the London stage and other overseas productions. **Nicholas Gordon** receives kudos as "*a solid gold music lawyer*" on behalf of artists and producers, while "*copyright expert*" **Neil Rosini** is recommended for his nuanced expertise in publishing.

The Clients: The group's media clients include a wide spectrum of actors, performers, writers, producers, publishers, financiers and corporations.

Grubman, Indursky & Schindler PC

The Firm: This midsized entertainment boutique enjoys one of the best reputations in New York. Focusing on the music industry, the group's practice encompasses both record companies and major recording artists. A "*dynamic*" group of attorneys has acted on numerous multimillion-dollar deals with flair.

The Lawyers: The "*outstanding*" **Allen Grubman** is one of the legendary figures of the New York entertainment market. A highly experienced lawyer, he began his career in the field as a talent-focused attorney before representing major record companies. His practice continues to be a mixture of both. "*He eats, breathes and sleeps the music industry.*" Market commentators watch with interest for what effect the departure of key partner Paul Schindler will have on the practice.

The Clients: The group's clients include U2 and Madonna, among others in the music industry.

Hogan & Hartson LLP
See firm details p.484

The Firm: Although best known for its media litigation expertise, this firm is said to be "*more than a match for anybody*" with its strong client base and corporate profile. The group handles tax, securities, joint ventures, venture capital and high-end corporate advice to a number of Fortune 100 and international media companies. It recently advised a public media conglomerate in relation to its bid to acquire the publishing assets of a Chapter 11 debtor.

The Lawyers: "*Transactional dynamo*" **Mitchell Ames** (see p.1262) is recommended for his "*cool head in the midst of a deal.*" He is particularly well regarded for his work in broadcasting on behalf of media giants such as Fox Television.

The Clients: Prominent publishers, broadcasters and film companies form the core of this practice's clientele.

Loeb & Loeb LLP

The Firm: A "*superb and substantial firm,*" this nationwide practice is recommended for its strengths in theater, film, television and music. The group's work involves actors, writers, directors, television and film production companies.

In addition, the team often works with broadcasters, film studios and banks, the latter in film-financing proceedings. It earns particular praise for its ability to examine issues pertaining to new and traditional media, including Internet access.
The Lawyers: The *"expert"* **Seth Gelblum** is hailed as *"absolutely one of the best lawyers in theater matters."* He represents playwrights, composers, producers, directors and designers, particularly with respect to television. **Roger Arar** is hailed for his skills in film and television finance matters. He acts on all contractual issues for a broad range of clients, including motion picture studios, model agencies and talent. One of his strongest suits is reality TV.
The Clients: The group represents talent as well as institutional media corporations, including Fortune 500 companies.

Paul, Weiss, Rifkind, Wharton & Garrison LLP
See firm details p.1362
The Firm: This entertainment-focused practice is recommended as *"one of the most versatile and knowledgeable firms on the East Coast."* Its experience incorporates financing, distribution and rights issues in publishing, television, music, theatre and film. It also represents talent in the arrangement of deals with film companies and producers. A significant highlight was Time Warner's multimillion-dollar reorganization; this involved moving IP assets from one part of the company to another and concerned millions of trademarks and copyrights. It also acted on the production 'The Frogs', starring Nathan Lane, at the Lincoln Center Plaza.
The Lawyers: *"Top-level lawyer"* **John Breglio** (see p.1268) chairs the firm's entertainment practice and is considered *"razor sharp in transactions."* **Robert Schumer** (see p.1318) is hailed for his skills on high-level corporate deals, while **Carey Ramos** (see p.1311) is praised as *"great for music publishers."*
The Clients: The group's clients include producers, production companies, studios and talent.

Band 2

Davis & Gilbert
The Firm: Although best known for its skills in advertising, the group has a substantial media presence in the New York market. It demonstrates agility in film production work and handles agreements for both studios and independent producers. The group's work in publishing and music is highly praised, as is its fluency in sponsorship matters. It also acts on distribution matters worldwide.
The Lawyers: Ronald Urbach heads the group.
The Clients: The team has a niche in advising on collective bargaining agreements related to major entertainment unions such as the Screen Actors Guild, Directors Guild of America and Writers Guild of America. It has also represented film companies, producers and talent.

Dewey Ballantine LLP
See firm details p.1347
The Firm: This *"smart, focused"* team is *"not only transactionally savvy, but shows a great understanding of the whole marketplace."* It is best known for its work for Disney and recently acted on the purchase of the assets of the Jim Henson Company. It further demonstrated its M&A prowess in defending Disney against a $66 billion hostile takeover bid by Comcast.
The Lawyers: Partner Michael Aiello is a major presence in the team.
The Clients: The group represents Disney, Sony and other major media bodies.

Greenberg Traurig LLP
See firm details p.564
The Firm: This *"excellent music firm"* is described as *"young and dynamic, with plenty of enthusiasm."* It represents a mix of recording artists, producers and songwriters, as well as publishing company and record company executives. Other expertise involves recording and publishing contracts, distribution, touring and sponsorship matters. It is also active in new media issues connected with music. The group remains active in film and television production and broadcast, and represents everyone from talent to studios.
The Lawyers: **Marc Jacobson** (see p.1290) is rated as *"a smart, enthusiastic lawyer with a lot of experience."* He is recommended for his *"great talent"* in film and theatre financing.
The Clients: The group has counseled production companies and individuals in traditional and new media.

Morgan, Lewis & Bockius LLP
See firm details p.1556
The Firm: Although a relatively smaller group, this team earns plaudits from a wide range of sources as *"an experienced and driven practice."* Primarily focused on media corporate work, it represents international publishers, film companies and banks on a range of corporate advice. It has a niche following among UK and European media companies entering the American market.
The Lawyers: Charles Engros and Howard Kenny are key partners in the team.
The Clients: The New York Times is a major client for the group, and it recently acted for it in the buyout of The Washington Post's interest in International Herald Tribune as well as its joint venture with the Discovery Channel. It handles securities and corporate governance advice for the same client. Other major clients include Pearson, JPMorgan and Daily Mail Group.

Pryor Cashman Sherman & Flynn
The Firm: This well-regarded practice is hailed for its expertise in music, television, theater and new media. One of its major drawing cards is film finance. It acts on studio financing and independent film financing, both on a picture-

by-picture basis and in multi-picture deals. The group is closely linked with its LA office, wielding its firmwide influence on international co-productions. This *"large and dedicated"* team also earns praise for its media acquisition skills.
The Lawyers: **Joseph Grier** is highly rated for his skills in music-related work, having represented such acts as Wilco, Ryan Adams and Diana Krall. He also shepherds a few corporate clients, including World Wrestling Entertainment. His focus is publishing and recording issues.
The Clients: In addition to an impressive roster of talent, the firm's clientele includes: Turner Communications; Capstar Broadcasting; Primedia Broadcasting Group; EMI Music Publishing and Cherry Lane Music Publishing.

Shearman & Sterling LLP
See firm details p.1369
The Firm: This well-regarded firm is best known for its work for Viacom, which it recently acted for on the $2 billion split-off with Blockbuster and separately advised on its merger with CBS. The group's international network gives clients with cross-border interests an edge. It has worked on a number of deals in the UK and Germany.
The Lawyers: Primarily a corporate generalist, Creighton Condon often participates in media-related M&A transactions and is considered a crucial member of this international team.
The Clients: Viacom, Expedia and NBC feature prominently on the team's client roster.

Sukin Law Group
The Firm: A music-focused specialist firm, the group sustains its market profile by way of its adroit transactional skills. With offices in Nashville and New York, the group represents artists, publishers and record companies in a broad range of issues. This includes trademark and copyright issues and bank and private capital financings, as well as high-value contract and publishing matters. The group also earns plaudits for its work in musical theater.
The Lawyers: The *"gifted"* **Michael Sukin** is rated as *"a lawyer of rare experience in music issues."* He earns plaudits from peers in the international marketplace for his corporate skills.
The Clients: The group boasts a *"fantastic client base"* which ranges from individual artists to established record companies.

Weil, Gotshal & Manges LLP
See firm details p.1378
The Firm: Although better known for its media litigation skills, the group enjoys a following for its corporate media work. It has been involved in a considerable transaction concerning a major television network. The firm's scope extends globally, and it also gathered applause for its skills in new technology and Internet law.
The Lawyers: Jeffrey Osterman splits his practice between litigation and transactional matters.

1236   All quotes in the text are from interviews with clients and competitors.

CHAMBERS USA 2005

The Clients: Clients include broadcasters, production companies and record companies.

Other Notable Practitioners

Sole practitioner **Alan Kress** (see p.1295) is rated as an "*experienced and genuinely smart lawyer who is reliably good.*" He represents music publishers and record labels, as well as corporations using music for marketing or promotion. Another niche is in production and licensing matters related to the home video market.

PRIVATE EQUITY

BUYOUTS & VENTURE CAPITAL INVESTMENT

New York

Leading firms (Private Equity: Buyouts & Venture Capital Investment)

1	DEBEVOISE & PLIMPTON LLP *New York*
	SIMPSON THACHER & BARTLETT LLP *New York*
2	DAVIS POLK & WARDWELL *New York*
	KIRKLAND & ELLIS LLP *New York*
	LATHAM & WATKINS LLP *New York*
	WEIL, GOTSHAL & MANGES LLP *New York*
3	FRIED, FRANK, HARRIS, SHRIVER *New York*
	GIBSON, DUNN & CRUTCHER LLP *New York*
	KING & SPALDING LLP *New York*
	MORGAN, LEWIS & BOCKIUS LLP *New York*
	ROPES & GRAY *New York*
	WHITE & CASE LLP *New York*
	WILLKIE FARR & GALLAGHER LLP *New York*

Leading individuals (Private Equity: Buyouts & Venture Capital Investment)

Senior Statesman

BEATTIE Richard *Simpson Thacher, New York*
ETTINGER John *Davis Polk, New York*

1
BASON JR George *Davis Polk, New York*
BLASSBERG Franci *Debevoise & Plimpton, New York*
COGUT Charles *Simpson Thacher, New York*
DAVENPORT Margaret *Debevoise, New York*
FRAIDIN Stephen *Kirkland & Ellis, New York*
RUEGGER Philip *Simpson Thacher, New York*

2
BICK John *Davis Polk, New York*
BIRD Paul *Debevoise & Plimpton, New York*
BOHM Richard *Debevoise & Plimpton, New York*
GARTNER Steven *Willkie Farr, New York*
RADKE Kirk *Kirkland & Ellis, New York*
ROBERTS Thomas *Weil Gotshal, New York*

3
GOLDBERG Louis *Davis Polk, New York*
GRAEV Lawrence *King & Spalding, New York*
HERBERT John *Gibson Dunn, New York*
HOPKINSON R Ronald *Latham & Watkins, New York*
JACOBS Paul *Fulbright & Jaworski, New York*
KENNEDY Robert *Latham & Watkins, New York*
PROUNIS Othon *Ropes & Gray, New York*
REISS John *White & Case, New York*
SCHWARTZ Alan *Simpson Thacher, New York*
SCHWED Robert *Wilmer Cutler, New York*
WARNER Douglas *Weil Gotshal, New York*
WERNER Philip *Morgan Lewis, New York*
WHITE Ira *Morgan Lewis, New York*

Up-and-coming individuals
BLITTNER David *Weil Gotshal, New York*
SCHMIDT Kevin *Debevoise & Plimpton, New York*

Firms and individuals are listed alphabetically in each band.

Band 1

Debevoise & Plimpton LLP

See firm details p.1346

The Firm: This "*powerhouse*" in the private equity arena has taken the strategic approach to develop the twin pillars of buyouts and fund formation, ensuring an overlap of expertise in its attorneys and prominence across the breadth of the marketplace. Clients paid tribute to a "*multidimensional and deep team*" which is "*tremendously strong across the board – they have the technical skills to cover the entire private equity universe.*" Private equity is one of the largest practice groups in the firm, and can boast an enviable client roster ranging from traditional LBO firms to market newcomers. US and European capability is offered, illustrated by recent advice to Providence Private Equity Partners and Soros Private Equity Partners in eircom Group's €800 million IPO on the London and Irish stock exchanges. The team is popular with peers and clients alike for its solutions-oriented approach; according to clients: "*Private equity lawyers are by nature a pushy bunch, but the people at Debevoise are modest; they know their role and do it well.*"
The Lawyers: This deeply talented team is home to **Franci Blassberg**. Co-head of the firm's private equity group, she is seen as the driving force behind much of the firm's success in this area. Renowned for her work for marquee client Clayton Dubilier & Rice (CD&R), she advised on its $1.65 billion acquisition of VWR International from Merck KGaA, and assisted in its $2.2 billion sale of Alliant Exchange to Royal Ahold. Clients appreciate **Peggy Davenport**'s ability to cut to the chase; she "*does not waste time and will always tell us the best way forward,*" while adopting a "*low-key, congenial, keep-it-moving approach.*" Although a tough negotiator when the situation demands, "*her strength is to be cooperative.*" Davenport most recently represented Kelso in the $465 million acquisition of Del Laboratories and represented the purchasers in NuCoastal's $2.3 billion bid for CrossCountry Energy. She also leads the firm's representation of Teachers' Private Capital, Solera Capital and the AIG Healthcare Fund. Like Davenport, **Richard Bohm** was applauded by clients for his "*incredible customer service.*" One stated: "*Nothing falls through the cracks with this guy.*" Bohm has built up a respected media and telecom practice over the years, and cochairs the firm's media

and technology and private equity groups. Clients value his ability to "*converse with us on our level and understand the dynamic of a business.*" He is senior relationship partner for Kelso & Company and Schroder Venture Partners. **Paul Bird** has won a following through his ability to "*get the deal done without risking the quality.*" According to peers, he is "*steady in the face of wild personalities, it is a pleasure to be on the other side with him.*" He represented CD&R in the $2.4 billion sale of Kinko's to FedEx. **Kevin Schmidt** is a rising star at the firm. "*Hard charging when it is required and more laid back when it isn't,*" Schmidt won strong client commendation for his ability to steer a deal to completion.
The Clients: Morgan Stanley Capital Partners; North Castle Partners; Merrill Lynch; Ripplewood Holdings and HarbourVest Partners.

Simpson Thacher & Bartlett LLP

See firm details p.1370

The Firm: Giants in the field for a some time now, attorneys at this firm have enjoyed a stellar year securing some of the market's largest transactions. For example, the team acted for marquee client KKR on the $4.3 billion acquisition of PanAmSat from DIRECTV Group. Clients highlighted the firm's dedication to the sector and its commitment in terms of resources. They appreciated its proactive approach to client service: "*It looks after us as a parent would a child.*" Responsiveness and commercial awareness are also key areas of strength. Attorneys in New York benefit from close working relationships with members of the firm's European offices; for example, the team acted in conjunction with its London office to represent KKR in the €2.4 billion offer by VDXK Acquisition BV for Koninklijke Vendex KBB NV. Further highlights include acting for The Blackstone Group on the $3.8 billion acquisition of Celanese AG and its acquisition of Boca Resorts for $1.23 billion.
The Lawyers: Sources proclaimed their confidence in firm chairman **Pete Ruegger** (see p.1315). He manages the firm's relationship with key client The Blackstone Group and recently advised Travelers in its merger with St Paul. **Dick Beattie** (see p.1265) acts as senior adviser on private equity transactions as well as frequently counseling boards of directors. "*As good a lawyer as there is,*" Beattie is "*a force in the development of both the M&A and private equity world.*" **Casey Cogut** (see p.1272) has cultivated a long track record in private equity that has endowed him

with "*good instincts on critical matters.*" Clients trust him to supply a "*seasoned, no-nonsense opinion.*" He acted for Ripplewood Holdings when it and its co-investors agreed to sell Japan Telecom to Softbank for a total consideration of ¥340 billion. Rising star **Alan Schwartz** (see p.1318) has attracted the loyalty of clients of the caliber of Ripplewood Holdings and Evercore Capital Partners.
The Clients: KKR; The Cypress Group; Silver Lake Partners; Ripplewood Holdings; Apax and Cinven.

Band 2

Davis Polk & Wardwell
See firm details p.1345
The Firm: A force in the private equity field, this practice derives much of its profile from the megadeal experience of its attorneys. A combined M&A and private equity grouping encourages breadth of experience and the department is home to some of the most venerated senior partners in the business. In addition, a widely respected fund formation practice ensures that clients receive one-stop shop service. The group has successfully cultivated close relationships with some of the central players in the industry. Its links to choice lawyers in many of the key financial markets (Slaughter and May in the UK and Hengeler Mueller in Germany, for instance) have combined with such strong client ties to provide these attorneys with a place on major international deals.
The Lawyers: Like many attorneys at the top of the buyout market, **Gar Bason** (see p.1265) combines this practice with high-value public company transactions. In the private equity sphere, his clients include the likes of CFSB and DLJ, and he acted for JPMorgan Securities as financial adviser in Pioneer Natural Resources' acquisition of Evergreen Resources in a cash and stock transaction valued at $2.1 billion. The seasoned **John Bick** (see p.1267) regularly represents clients such as Morgan Stanley Private Equity and Thomas Weisel Capital Partners. A recent highlight deal is the representation of Vanguard Health Systems on a $1.75 billion majority investment by The Blackstone Group. Bick joined forces with **Louis Goldberg** (see p.1283) to advise Morgan Stanley Capital Partners on the formation of Metalmark Capital, a New York-based independent private equity firm that manages the $3 billion in Morgan Stanley Capital Partner funds. **John Ettinger** (see p.1278), chairman of the firm, maintains his high standing in the private equity community. Although less seen on day-to-day transactions, he remains popular with clients, who seek his valuable strategic advice and sound judgment.
The Clients: Further highlights for the team include advising DLJ Merchant Banking Partners on the $1.84 billion sale of Noveon to Lubrizol.

Kirkland & Ellis LLP
See firm details p.770
The Firm: Clients pointed to this firm's vast national and international presence in the private equity arena, where it has developed a "*vibrant, strong practice.*" The New York-based team is especially busy and continues to go from strength to strength, taking its impetus from the firm's traditional heartland of Chicago. The presence of heavy hitters such as Kirk Radke and Stephen Fraidin attracts clients, while the resources provided by this team and the seven offices across the USA and overseas ensure their loyalty. Clients described a group that is "*extremely knowledgeable, up to date on current practices,*" and able to field "*talented, experienced, professionals.*" While some commentators felt that the firm adopts an aggressive approach to the negotiating table, other clients appreciated the responsive client-focused service on offer.
The Lawyers: Rainmaker **Stephen Fraidin** (see p.1280), renowned for his relationship with Forstmann Little, is a key player in the New York market. He recently advised this marquee client on the acquisition of International Management Group. He is a "*classic M&A lawyer*" who is equally adept in the private equity arena. **Kirk Radke** (see p.1311) is a "*terrific business adviser,*" who possesses deep LBO experience and the rare ability to also turn his hand to fund formation. He represented Bain Capital on the $550 million acquisition of the North American phosphates business of Rhodia SA.
The Clients: Bain Capital; Citigroup Venture Capital; Merrill Lynch Private Equity Group; Catterton Partners; Vestar Capital Partners; Centennial Ventures and Sun Capital Partners.

Latham & Watkins LLP
The Firm: For some, this firm has set the standards on how to manage and grow an international firm, and such strategic prowess has been translated into its development of the private equity practice. Latham & Watkins has successfully leveraged off its reputation in its core finance and corporate arenas to secure what clients describe as "*strength across the board.*" Clients also point to a good deployment of the specialty groups, as well as an "*understanding of what is important in a deal.*" Overseas, the firm has aggressively expanded its practice with approximately 50 partners in ten offices, including the recent recruitment of private equity megastar Thomas Forschbach from the Paris office of Ashurst. Illustrating its success on cross-border cooperation, the group recently joined with the Tokyo office to advise The Carlyle Group on its $2.03 billion acquisition with Kyocera of Japanese firm DDI Pocket.
The Lawyers: Chairman of the private equity practice, **Ronald Hopkinson** is a "*smart, charming guy,*" who represents clients such as merchant banks and LBO groups including Welsh,

Carson Anderson & Stowe. **Robert Kennedy** represents LBO funds such as Odyssey Partners and JPMorgan Partners. He is a deal-focused attorney who wins the respect of both clients and peers.
The Clients: Apollo Management and The Carlyle Group are key clients for the firm. Attorneys acted for the former on the acquisition of AMC by Marquee Holdings (an investment vehicle owned by JPMorganPartners and Apollo Management) for $2 billion. For The Carlyle Group, it advised on the acquisition of the Hawaiian operations of Verizon for $1.65 billion. Further highlights include representing the The Carlyle Group and Spectrum Equity Investors in the $1.5 billion acquisition, along with Bain Capital, of Loews Cineplex Entertainment Corporation.

Weil, Gotshal & Manges LLP
See firm details p.1378
The Firm: "*Lawyers who know how to do business,*" the group houses attorneys who "*think outside the box and add value by coming up with new ideas and being aggressive when necessary,*" clients said. Peers also conceded that the firm took a brave move in its merger with Boston's Hutchins, Wheeler & Dittmar, which has resulted in extra resources in the USA and strong ties to Thomas H. Lee Partners. The firm is already reaping the dividends by advising Thomas H. Lee Partners and senior management of Eye Care Centers of America in an agreement to sell the company to Moulin International Holdings and Golden Gate Capital for $450 million. Global expansion continues apace, and the firm has strengthened its London, Paris, Frankfurt and, more recently, Shanghai offices. The opening of the Paris office in 2003 (following the merger with Serra, Leavy & Cazals) has proved fruitful and the firm has recently lured Paris-based private equity luminary David Aknin from Linklaters. The already sizable private equity group in London has welcomed the arrival of rising star Mark Soundy. A further deal highlight involved representing (together with the London office) DLJ Merchant Banking Partners and JP Morgan Partners on the purchase of Warner Chilcott for approximately $2.97 billion.
The Lawyers: An "*absolutely fantastic business mind*" has ensured **Thomas Roberts** (see p.1313) a loyal following among clients and peers alike. Clients declared a "*high degree of confidence*" in his ability to "*deliver the goods every time.*" Also according to clients, **Douglas Warner** (see p.1331) "*sits head-to-head with the best*" because he provides "*practical advice and marshals a team effectively. He knows how to get a deal done and understands the bigger picture.*" Tipped by clients as one of the team's up-and-coming partners, **David Blittner** (see p.1267) has impressed many with his sound judgment. He

1238   All quotes in the text are from interviews with clients and competitors.

CHAMBERS USA 2005

is "*practical, good at prioritizing and adds value to a transaction.*" His sense of humor was also appreciated during difficult negotiations.

The Clients: Major LBO players such as Thomas H. Lee Partners and Hicks Muse Tate & Furst. Other clients include: DLJ Merchant Banking Partners; KKR; Lehman Brothers; Summit Partners and Texas Pacific Group.

Band 3

Fried, Frank, Harris, Shriver & Jacobson LLP
See firm details p.1349

The Firm: With resources stretching from the USA to London, Paris and Frankfurt, this firm has built upon its renowned corporate base in order to play a part in some of the market's largest deals. For instance, it acted for Permira Europe III in its joint acquisition with other buyout firms of IntelSat for $5 billion. Clients praised the firm's ability to field attorneys, who possess "*the expertise to get a deal done.*" Highlight matters include advising GS Capital Partners 2000 and related funds in their pending acquisition, together with Cypress Group, of Cooper-Standard Automotive from Cooper Tire & Rubber Company for over one billion dollars. The team also represented Noveon International (a joint investment of funds affiliated with AEA Investors, DLJ Merchant Banking Partners and DB Capital), in its $1.8 billion acquisition by Lubrizol.

The Lawyers: Chair of the firm's corporate department, Robert Schwenkel acts for an array of private investment funds managed by Goldman Sachs, Forstmann Little and Appaloosa Management, among others.

The Clients: AEA Investors; BC Partners; General Electric Capital Corporation; Penske Capital Partners; Permira Advisers; Shamrock Capital; Soros Private Equity Investors and Ziff Brothers Investments.

Gibson, Dunn & Crutcher LLP
See firm details p.285

The Firm: The firm can draw on teams of lawyers from its offices across the USA and Europe in order to support its growing New York private equity practice. Sources commended the firm's success in leveraging off its M&A and debt issuance expertise and acknowledged its success in building up an enviable client roster. Clients appreciated this team's ability to "*deploy the necessary know-how to get a deal done.*" Its attorneys "*display the knack of practical thinking with user-friendly legal knowledge.*"

The Lawyers: Spearheading the team is **John Herbert** (see p.1287) who "*goes the whole nine yards*" while remaining "*focused on delivering the goods for his clients.*" Herbert's "*tremendous amount of experience*" also won him many fans.

The Clients: The team acted for PanAmSat in its acquisition by KKR from DIRECTV Group

and News Corporation for a total consideration of $4.1 billion. Other clients include: Morgan Stanley Capital Partners; Metalmark Capital; Rhone Capital and Care Capital Investments.

King & Spalding LLP
See firm details p.635

The Firm: This firm is a new entrant to the tables following strong client commendation for its customer-oriented approach. Its lawyers are "*responsive, possess technical ability and give you what you want.*" This is a rapidly expanding operation that has scored a series of coups over the past year with key hires. These include the recruitment of Robert Finley, former cochair of Clifford Chance's US banking and financial restructuring group; and more lately, Dominick DeChiara from O'Melveny & Myers. Attorneys across five offices represent clients such as Hunt Capital, First Capital, GlenRock and First Atlantic, who provide a steady stream of work often in the $100 to $150 million bracket.

The Lawyers: Lawyer and businessman **Lawrence Graev** (see p.1284) remains the firm's standout name. As well as being a leading attorney, he is the chairman and president of the GlenRock Goup.

The Clients: AEA Investors; First Atlantic Capital; GlenRock Group; Warburg Pincus; Radius Venture Partners and SAIC Venture Capital Corporation.

Morgan, Lewis & Bockius LLP
See firm details p.1556

The Firm: "*When this team is on a deal, I rest better at night,*" concluded one client. Others concurred that the team "*does what needs to be done within a time frame and has the best resources to move a project along.*" This is one of the world's largest law firms with offices across the USA, Europe and Asia, and is developing a real presence in the private equity arena for its work for key clients such as Citicorp and One Equity Partners. Clients also lauded the team's "*cutting-edge advice and creativity.*" Deal value ranges from mid-market deal sponsors upward, and highlights include representation of One Equity Partners in its acquisition of Quintiles Transnational. The technology, energy and life sciences sectors are a recurring theme within the firm's caseload.

The Lawyers: Clients endorsed **Philip Werner** (see p.1332) for his negotiation skills: "*He finds a way through the deal, understands the issues and the strategy.*" He combines this with an ability to "*provide solutions as well as spotting the problems.*" **Ira White** (see p.1332) impressed many sources by being "*hands on and responsive,*" while delivering "*honest advice in an open and forthright manner.*"

The Clients: One Equity Partners; Sun Capital Partners; Wellspring Capital; Trivets; Catterton Partners and Apollo Management.

Ropes & Gray
See firm details p.985

The Firm: "*Exceptional in the private equity area,*" this firm is applauded by clients for its wealth of expertise and commitment to the sector. Operating from offices in Boston and New York, its market share continues to grow. The firm represents private equity houses in investment transactions, portfolio companies and service providers to the private equity industry. Highlight matters include acting for Thomas H. Lee Partners, in partnership with members of Nortek's management, on the acquisition of Nortek Holdings for a total consideration of $1.75 billion.

The Lawyers: A rising star at the firm, **Othon Prounis** (see p.1310) offers clients "*practical business sense*" melded with a "*user-friendly manner.*" He acted for Welsh, Carson, Anderson & Stowe on the acquisition of the 85.5% stake in US Oncology that it did not already own in a transaction valued at $1.7 billion.

The Clients: Further deal highlights include acting for EGL Holding Company (an acquisition vehicle for Welsh, Carson, Anderson & Stowe, Thoma Cressey Equity Partners and certain members of Select Medical Corporation management) on the acquisition of Select Medical Corporation for $2.3 billion. The firm also acted for Bain Capital on its $1.54 billion acquisition of Verizon Communication's directory operations in Canada, Superpages Canada. Other clients include: Deutsche Bank Securities; Fenway Partners; CSFB; DLJ Merchant Banking; New York City Investment Fund; Behrman Capital; BCI Partners and Bluefish Ventures.

White & Case LLP
See firm details p.1379

The Firm: This firm is making its presence felt by acting for an expanding client base, which includes the likes of The Blackstone Group, Harvest Partners and Lehman Brothers Merchant Banking. The firm has proved it can employ its acquisition finance expertise to expand into other areas, particularly in winning mandates from international clients such as Industri Kapital and Nordic Capital. Highlight deals include acting as counsel to Starwood Capital Group and BLB Investors in their recommended offer to acquire Wembley plc for approximately $560 million.

The Lawyers: At the helm, **John Reiss** (see p.1312) is a knowledgeable and professional adviser, who "*gets right to the point and provides value-added service.*" He acted for Harvest Partners in its acquisition of New Flyer Holdings Corp from KPS Special Situations Fund.

The Clients: The firm acted for The Blackstone Group on the sale by Great Lakes Transportation Company of its rail and shipping operations to Canadian Railway Company. The firm also acted for First Atlantic Capital in its acquisition of Prestolite Electric Holdings.

Willkie Farr & Gallagher LLP

See firm details p.1380

The Firm: The firm is pitched as "*extremely capable in everything they do, from simple investments to buyout situations,*" clients said. The firm has established large teams dedicated to the private equity arena across the USA, which work in conjunction with small but respected practices in the UK, France, Germany, Belgium and Italy. Marquee client Warburg Pincus dominates the list of deals; for example, the firm acted for affiliates of Warburg in the acquisition of Polypore from shareholders led by The InterTech Group and GTCR Golder Rauner for $1.2 billion. However, the European offices came into their own when

the firm also acted for CVC Capital Partners in the Owens-Illinois €1.16 billion acquisition of BSN Glasspack SA from Glasspack Participations.

The Lawyers: According to sources, **Steve Gartner** (see p.1282) brings "*good balance and judgment*" to a transaction, while remaining "*sensitive and knowledgeable*" to the long-term issues of client development. He led the team acting for Providence Equity Partners and Warburg Pincus in the acquisition of the telecom software and services subsidiary Telcordia Technologies from Science Applications International Corporation (SAIC) for $1.35 billion.

The Clients: Other clients include CSFB, Questor and Prudential.

Other Notable Practitioners

Paul Jacobs (see p.1290) of Fulbright & Jaworski LLP enters the tables following strong client commendation that described him as "*a lawyer who thinks like a businessman.*" Clients also appreciate that they can use him as a sounding board and value his high energy levels and commitment to their cause. **Bob Schwed** (see p.1319) of Wilmer Cutler Pickering Hale and Dorr LLP maintains the respect of the marketplace as a "*terrific all-around lawyer*" who is "*responsible, easy to work with and adept at handling difficult negotiations.*"

PRIVATE EQUITY

FUND FORMATION

<table>
<tr><td colspan="2">

New York

Leading firms

(Private Equity: Fund Formation)

</td></tr>
<tr><td>1</td><td>**DEBEVOISE & PLIMPTON LLP** New York
SIMPSON THACHER & BARTLETT LLP New York</td></tr>
<tr><td>2</td><td>**DAVIS POLK & WARDWELL** New York
ROPES & GRAY New York
WEIL, GOTSHAL & MANGES LLP New York</td></tr>
<tr><td>3</td><td>**AKIN GUMP STRAUSS HAUER & FELD** New York
KIRKLAND & ELLIS LLP New York
SCHULTE ROTH & ZABEL LLP New York</td></tr>
<tr><td>4</td><td>**CLEARY GOTTLIEB STEEN & HAMILTON** New York
DEWEY BALLANTINE LLP New York
LATHAM & WATKINS LLP New York
MAYER, BROWN, ROWE & MAW LLP New York
ORRICK, HERRINGTON & SUTCLIFFE New York
SEWARD & KISSEL New York</td></tr>
<tr><td colspan="2">Firms are listed alphabetically in each band.</td></tr>
</table>

Band 1

Debevoise & Plimpton LLP

See firm details p.1346

The Firm: "*World-class expertise*" can be found at this firm, claim clients, who went on to describe a group of "*creative problem solvers*" that handles the most complex matters with aplomb. Clients also appreciated that these attorneys "*get right to the heart of a matter and know the importance of deadlines.*" Cross-jurisdictional capability is a distinguishing feature of this practice with attorneys based in offices across the USA and Europe as well as Asia. The firm's market knowledge and, in particular, its proprietary database is "*second to none,*" allowing the group to track 50 variables in more than 1000 funds. The ability to field specialists in related areas such as tax, securities and ERISA also drew praise: "*The level of information you get from them is truly astonishing; they have tentacles in all sorts of places.*" The firm's good relationships with parties on the

other side of the negotiating table also ensure the smooth passage of a deal.

The Lawyers: Market sources credited **Michael Harrell** with the continued development of a "*jewel of a practice.*" A clear leader and expert in the field, he is "*great at getting parties to come to agreement.*" **Rebecca Silberstein** impresses as "*smart and energetic with lots of firepower.*" She is a popular choice among clients for her creative thinking and flexibility. Silberstein recently represented Kelso & Co in the formation of Kelso Investment Associates VII LP, a $2.1 billion private equity buyout fund, and assisted MMC Capital in the formation of Trident III LP, a $1.1 billion private equity fund focusing on the insurance, reinsurance and financial services industries. First time funds and real estate-focused funds are core areas of **Sherri Caplan**'s practice. According to clients, she is a "*superb negotiator who is dedicated and knowledgeable.*" She has represented fund sponsors such as Ripplewood Holdings on the formation of a buyout fund valued at $1.1 billion and assisted Cherokee Investment Partners in its $620 million buyout fund. **Jennifer Burleigh** mixes her strong skill set with a "*great demeanor in negotiations.*" She advises sponsors of LBOs and merchant banking, and other private investment funds. **Adele Karig** is a tax specialist who focuses on the private equity sector. "*Extraordinarily knowledgeable,*" she "*understands the business and the math.*" **Woodrow Campbell** remains "*a legend*" in the market and widely respected by both peers and clients. He brings a solutions-oriented mindset to a deal: "*He starts with a goal and then works backwards to the structure required to achieve the goal in a way which is both sound and practical.*" "*Avuncular, approachable and measured,*" he represents the independent directors of BlackRock closed-end funds and Fidelity funds.

The Clients: Highlights include advising Providence Equity Partners in the formation of its

new $4.25 billion private equity fund and advising HarbourVest Partners in the formation of a $4.4 billion private equity fund of funds that will invest in US venture, mezzanine and buyout partnership interests. Other clients include: AIG; Oaktree Capital; North Castle Partners; Kelso & Co; Prudential; Clayton Dubilier & Rice; Morgan Stanley and Merrill Lynch.

Simpson Thacher & Bartlett LLP

See firm details p.1370

The Firm: This practice cultivates attorneys whose core strengths are their "*great knowledge of the law, an ability to represent their clients to the highest degree and a clear understanding of the market.*" Although this cohesive group adopts a sensible, business-minded approach to negotiations, it "*has the depth to send people to the fight when needed,*" clients say. Quality not quantity is the order of the day here and the group's six partners serve a "*terrific roster of clients*" across an internationally diversified practice. Offices in New York, Palo Alto and Hong Kong house fund formation and private equity expertise and this geographic reach has allowed the firm to attract mandates from blue-chip clients such as Silver Lake Partners and, more recently, Citigroup. The team also acts for nonprofit organizations such as the Carnegie Corporation of New York in connection with the investment of endowments.

The Lawyers: **Thomas Bell** (see p.1265) commanded market respect as "*a true pioneer in the market,*" whose "*direct, precise and responsive*" advice is trusted and respected by all parties. He has recently advised on issues related to the JC Flowers I, Carlyle Europe Partners II and Evercore Capital Partners II structures. **Michael Wolitzer** (see p.1333) negotiates "*hard but fair*" and "*knows his stuff.*" Clients describe him as a "*real roll up your sleeves and close the deal type of attorney,*" whose superb technical knowledge ensures the smooth progress of any matter. Recent fund highlights include Silver Lake II, Palladium Equity

1240   All quotes in the text are from interviews with clients and competitors.

CHAMBERS USA 2005

New York
Leading individuals
(Private Equity: Fund Formation)

Senior Statesman
CAMPBELL Woodrow *Debevoise*, New York

[1] BELL Thomas *Simpson Thacher*, New York
HARRELL Michael *Debevoise & Plimpton*, New York
KAWATA Yukako *Davis Polk*, New York
WOLF Barry *Weil Gotshal*, New York
WOLITZER Michael *Simpson Thacher*, New York

[2] BRESLOW Stephanie *Schulte Roth*, New York
HEWITT William *Ropes & Gray*, New York
TABAK Jeffrey *Weil Gotshal*, New York
VINE Stephen *Akin Gump*, New York

[3] BERGTRAUM Howard *O'Melveny & Myers*, New York
BOWIE Scott *Linklaters*, New York
BURLEIGH Jennifer *Debevoise & Plimpton*, New York
CAPLAN Sherri *Debevoise & Plimpton*, New York
CULHANE Stephen *King & Spalding*, New York
GERSTENZANG Michael *Cleary Gottlieb*, New York
INSOLIA Robert *Goodwin Procter*, New York
JORDAN Nora *Davis Polk*, New York
KARIG Adele *Debevoise & Plimpton*, New York
MACMURRAY John *Ropes & Gray*, New York
MCCORMACK William *Ropes & Gray*, New York
MORHOUSE Sanford *Dewey Ballantine*, New York
SILBERSTEIN Rebecca *Debevoise*, New York
SINGER Louis *Orrick Herrington*, New York
SMITH Joseph *Dewey Ballantine*, New York
SOPHER Edward *Gibson Dunn*, New York
TAVSS John *Seward & Kissel*, New York
WALSH Kathleen *Mayer Brown*, New York

Up-and-coming individuals
GROSSMAN Shukie *Weil Gotshal*, New York
LANDA Leor *Davis Polk*, New York
SARNO Glenn *Simpson Thacher*, New York

Individuals are listed alphabetically in each band.

Partners III and the Blackstone CEO fund. **Glenn Sarno** (see p.1316) is a new entrant to our tables. Clients recommended him as a *"young aggressive lawyer,"* who *"negotiates well on behalf of his clients."* He has *"grown up in the private equity sector, and so he knows the market really well."*
The Clients: The firm has recently acted for new client Citigroup on a mezzanine financing, and assisted New Mountain Capital in establishing its second private equity fund, New Mountain Partners II, which raised $1.5 billion. Other clients include: The Carlyle Group; Evercore Partners; Fremont Partners; Ripplewood Holdings and Sterling Investment Partners.

Band 2

Davis Polk & Wardwell
See firm details p.1345
The Firm: Over the course of its many years in the industry, this firm has developed *"deeply sophisticated institutional knowledge"* that clients trust across a range of product types. Investment banking clients such as CSFB, JPMorgan Chase,

Bank of America and Goldman Sachs provide a strong foundation both with a steady workflow and with involvement on the development of the market's most exciting products. Such clients spoke of the firm's detailed expertise in the complex documentation necessary for a funds transaction, covering the rights of limited partners and leveraged employee plans. The firm's regulatory practice is also highly esteemed.
The Lawyers: *"One of the best private equity lawyers in the USA,"* **Yukako Kawata** (see p.1292) is the firm's best-known personality. Clients described her as a straight-talking attorney, who *"cuts through the nonsense and offers sound legal judgment."* The high quality of her advice is outstanding and has won her a following among both peers and clients. Interviewees also pointed to the growing prominence of a raft of attorneys housed in this group. Of these, **Nora Jordan** (see p.1291) is a *"brilliant lawyer in the regulatory arena,"* while **Leor Landa** (see p.1296) was applauded by clients for displaying knowledge beyond his years in both the structuring of funds and related regulatory issues.
The Clients: Clients include Chilton Investments, Mercantile Bankshares and Farallon Capital Management.

Ropes & Gray
See firm details p.985
The Firm: The 2003 merger of New York based Reboul, MacMurray, Hewitt Maynard & Kristol with Boston based Ropes & Gray has proved to be a successful one, enhancing the resources and the client base of the merged entity, especially in the private equity arena. The firm is now one of the most active in the funds sector and has enjoyed a further boost to its capabilities following the recent merger with IP specialists Fish & Neave. Its offices are in Boston, New York, DC and Palo Alto, although funds activity mainly emanates from the Boston and New York offices. This *"great set of business advisers and technically minded lawyers,"* is also *"fun to work with,"* say clients. The firm's work is not limited to the domestic arena, and international clients range from Cinven and Granville Private Equity, to Kleinwort Benson Mezzanine Fund and Industri Kapital.
The Lawyers: **William Hewitt** (see p.1288) *"knows what's important,"* claimed clients, who also highlighted his ability to provide *"great perspective and judgment."* He represents buyout and venture capital firms such as Welsh, Carson, Anderson & Stowe in fund formation and transactions. Cochair of the private equity group **William McCormack** (see p.1300) brings to the deal table his tax expertise. *"He never seems to be fazed by anything a client asks for and can always come up with a solution."* His international contacts, through clients and lawyer relations, also mark him out as a popular port of call for offshore matters. **John MacMurray** (see p.1298) is a corporate lawyer whose practice includes repre-

sentation of investment funds and so can bring a bigger picture perspective to the market.
The Clients: Highlights include advising ArcLight Capital Partners on its second private equity fund of $1.6 billion. Other clients include: StarVest Partners; Accolade Partners and Goldman Sachs.

Weil, Gotshal & Manges LLP
See firm details p.1378
The Firm: Attorneys at this respected international firm are *"instrumental in getting a deal done in a first-class manner"* because of the practical, business-minded approach they adopt. *"They know how to do business, they think outside the box and display a consistently strong client service ethic."* Clients also appreciated that the attorneys in this group are *"the complete fund formation package; they can advise us on all types of M&A, corporate governance and tax."* The firm is continuing its expansion through the recent opening of an office in Shanghai and the international reach of this practice is a major draw card for clients. Highlights include advising Ewing Management Group in the formation of its first fund at $750 million and advising Centre Partners Management in the formation of its $800 million fund Centre Capital Investors IV. The firm is also advising Hicks Muse Tate & Furst in connection with the formation of Hicks Muse Tate & Furst Europe Fund II.
The Lawyers: Head of the firm's global private equity practice **Barry Wolf** (see p.1333) possesses a *"superb negotiating style – he is an absolute treasure."* Clients also value his close attention to detail and his success in *"striking an excellent balance between protecting the client and being commercial in his advice."* **Jeffrey Tabak** (see p.1326) is a well-respected figure among industry players, with his *"deep market knowledge and great client service"* in the fund formation arena. He advises private equity investment funds and their sponsors, including the likes of Whippoorwill Associates, Ulysses Partners and WL Ross & Co. **Shukie Grossman** (see p.1285) is a younger member of the team and a highly commercial attorney, who, clients agree, *"understands the bigger picture and is already fully involved in our day-to-day proceedings."*
The Clients: The firm acted on Fund IV for Genstar Capital at $475 million. Other clients include: Lone Star Funds; Capital Z; Vestar Capital Partners; Oak Investment Partners; CSFB Private Equity and Thomas H Lee Partners.

Band 3

Akin Gump Strauss Hauer & Feld LLP
See firm details p.477
The Firm: A *"well-connected"* firm whose presence in the private equity sector continues to grow. The fund formation works with the transactions-focused private equity group to offer a

www.ChambersandPartners.com
All quotes in the text are from interviews with clients and competitors.
1241

broad service to clients. The combined department fields 11 partners, who act for a broad spectrum of clients on matters ranging from hedge funds to traditional private equity and distressed funds. The highly international flavor of the workload here has attracted clients requiring US and European market expertise. Such multijurisdictional needs are served through the firm's 16 offices around the world, including an increased presence in London.

The Lawyers: Clients espied a "*strong, dedicated adviser,*" in the form of **Stephen Vine** (see p.1329). A popular figure in the industry, Vine is "*personable and an intelligent lawyer who is genuinely a nice guy.*"

The Clients: The firm advises financial institutions, private equity houses and hedge fund managers.

Kirkland & Ellis LLP
See firm details p.770

The Firm: A firm notable for its "*aggressive stance in serving its clients' interests.*" This is a well-run operation proffering private equity expertise from seven offices, of which Chicago and New York are at the forefront for fund formation expertise. The team acts for major limited partners and general partners on the formation of funds, using expertise from the firm's respected tax, ERISA and securities departments. "*Economically, technically and strategically, the group's advice is watertight,*" conceded sources.

The Lawyers: The multitalented Kirk Radke is the standout name in private equity practice.

The Clients: The firm advised on the second private equity fund of funds raised by Danske Private Equity. Other clients include: Vestar Capital Partners; CVC Capital Partners; Bain Capital Partners; Merrill Lynch; Citigroup; Morgan Stanley Capital Partners and Cornerstone Partners.

Schulte Roth & Zabel LLP
See firm details p.1367

The Firm: This firm is renowned throughout the USA for its fund expertise, particularly within the burgeoning hedge fund arena. Venture capital funds and REITs also feature in its recent portfolio. The London office supports the US operation in providing assistance on cross-jurisdictional matters, particularly as sponsor's counsel in the formation of their private equity funds.

The Lawyers: **Stephanie Breslow** (see p.1268) is an "*incredibly smart attorney,*" who has made a real impact on the hedge funds market. She is investor-side counsel for Morgan Stanley, Columbia University and Weyerhaeuser Company Master Retirement Trust, while also handling sponsor-side work for Blackstone, Carl Icahn, Citigroup/Salomon Smith Barney, UBS O'Connor and Highfields among others.

The Clients: Clients the firm represents on hedge funds matters include: Cerberus Capital Management; Bear Stearns Asset Management and Merrill Lynch Asset Management. Venture capital clients include: Sprout; Oak; Wasserstein and TL Ventures.

Band 4

Cleary Gottlieb Steen & Hamilton LLP
See firm details p.1342

The Firm: Lawyers at this firm were praised for their ability to consistently provide "*practical advice on the most complex issues.*" Clients also spoke of "*the typical Cleary mode: intellectual, strong lawyering skills, responsive and calm demeanor – that's what we hire them for.*" Key client Texas Pacific Group continues to provide a steady flow of deals with the energy and healthcare sectors coming to the fore of late. The team acted for the group on the sale of Belden & Blake Corporation to Carlyle/Riverstone Global Energy & Power Fund II.

The Lawyers: Clients applauded **Michael Gerstenzang** (see p.1282) for his "*great style*" and ability to explain things in plain English: "*He is a practical lawyer, business savvy and not a screamer in negotiations.*"

The Clients: Further highlights include acting for an investor group led by longtime client Texas Pacific Group in its acquisition of IASIS Healthcare in a transaction valued at about $1.4 billion. The team also represented Hellman & Friedman and members of the management of London-based investment fund manager Mondrian Investment Partners in a management-led buyout of Mondrian from Lincoln National Corporation. Other clients include Och-Ziff Capital Management.

Dewey Ballantine LLP
See firm details p.1347

The Firm: A real favorite among clients, this firm is "*an active player, knowledgeable and up-to-date with the latest developments.*" This "*smart, practical team,*" has a full-service capability fielding tax and ERISA queries as they arise. The firm acts on traditional private equity funds as well as secondary, LBO and real estate funds, while its portfolio work is also on the increase.

The Lawyers: "*One hundred per cent terrific,*" enthused one client of **Sanford Morhouse** (see p.1303). "*A proactive, practical, businesslike lawyer,*" he also "*has the stature at the firm to marshal and deliver the necessary resources.*" Similarly **Joseph Smith** (see p.1322) impresses with his effective combination of business and legal understanding. Clients say he is endowed with "*an ability to be great not only with people in our office but also with our investors.*"

The Clients: GE is one of the firm's largest clients, while an impressive stable of institutional investor clients includes: the Du Pont Pension Fund; US Steel and US Airways.

Latham & Watkins LLP

The Firm: A team of three dedicated partners has a long track record in the LBO market and can often be found advising on fund structures that have an international element. Clients report that the group has "*risen in prominence and been incredibly successful at tackling this market.*" They also endorsed its attorneys as "*practical and easy to deal with.*" The workload here includes acting for venture capital, emerging markets, LBO and real estate funds and representing sponsors on the formation of funds.

The Lawyers: The departure of star partner Scott Bowie to Linklaters will undoubtedly be a blow to the firm, although it is still too early to see its full effect on the firm's funds practice.

The Clients: KKR; The Carlyle Group; Psilos Group; Goldman Sachs and Bear Stearns.

Mayer, Brown, Rowe & Maw LLP
See firm details p.771

The Firm: "*The most responsive firm I have ever dealt with*" was how one client described this "*detail-oriented*" practice. Attorneys here possess "*a clear knowledge of the legal requirements.*" Both sides of the table reported that the group was a pleasure to work with and a good sounding board for new ideas. Attorneys represent sponsors in fund formation as well as acting on portfolio work. They recently won a series of new engagements, such as acting for LS Power Group in the formation of its first private equity fund. Further highlights include acting for the Jordan Company in the formation of its first private equity fund, the Resolute Fund.

The Lawyers: **Kathleen Walsh** (see p.1330) was praised for her responsiveness and accessibility ("*I can always get hold of her immediately*") and her ability to go through all the implications of an issue. She represented Onex in the formation of its first private equity fund Onex Partners, which raised over $1.6 billion.

The Clients: Clients include the Jordan Company, Onex and LS Power Group.

Orrick, Herrington & Sutcliffe
See firm details p.295

The Firm: This respected practice focuses on fund formation and the representation of sponsors and investors in funds-related issues. Clients felt that this was the firm to go to when making a large investment: "*It is great at representing large institutions when investing in private equity funds; this is its bread and butter work and that means a huge amount of experience on tap.*" The firm also represents the sponsors of funds in fund formation, and can call upon dedicated specialists to assist with tax, ERISA and other regulatory matters.

1242   All quotes in the text are from interviews with clients and competitors.

CHAMBERS USA 2005

The Lawyers: Clients described **Louis Singer** (see p.1321) as a well-rounded attorney, who "*always keeps his cool,*" while peers paid tribute to his "*reasonable and practical approach.*"

The Clients: An impressive client roster includes California Public Employees' Retirement System and Princeton University. Insurance company clients include such firms as TIA Crest, Teachers Insurance and CIGNA. The firm also represents JPMorgan Fleming Asset Management and Goldman Sachs. It can count three New York pension funds on its roster: New York State Common Retirement Fund; New York State Teachers' Retirement System and New York City Retirement System.

Seward & Kissel

See firm details p.1368

The Firm: This firm impresses with its prodigious output in the hedge fund arena and can count over 200 fund managers as active clients. Clients praised the no-nonsense approach of this group, which is "*able to respond quickly to questions and give a straightforward answer.*" It has worked on a number of products that feature longer-term lock-ups and have liquidity focus, especially in the distressed debt area. The workload has also encompassed the structuring of incubator funds and fund of funds.

The Lawyers: **John Tavss** (see p.1326) is widely respected for his advisory skills; he "*thinks things through analytically and theoretically, then discusses them at a practical level.*"

The Clients: The Blackstone Group; Alda Capital Management; Kingdon Capital Management and Wellington Management Company.

Other Notable Practitioners

Howard Bergtraum of O'Melveny & Myers LLP is a highly skilled practitioner, noted for broad coverage of funds structuring and regulatory issues. **Stephen Culhane** (see p.1274), a recent arrival at King & Spalding LLP, is so good at negotiation "*you don't realize he is negotiating with you – he is so gentlemanly.*" A former Goldman Sachs counsel, he brings good industry knowledge to the deal table as well as a "*high level of respect and credibility in the field.*" **Robert Insolia** (see p.1290) of Goodwin Procter LLP possesses an understanding of the sector that "*goes beyond the law – he is not afraid to identify the business issues.*" **Edward Sopher** (see p.1323) of Gibson Dunn & Crutcher LLP is "*a good out of the box thinker,*" who mixes his drafting skills with "*good business instincts.*" **Scott Bowie** has recently left Latham & Watkins to join the New York office of major international firm Linklaters. Bowie was singled out for praise as an outstanding attorney with a "*calm, authoritative manner,*" who "*knows the whole structure package.*"

PROJECTS

New York
Leading firms (Projects)

1. **LATHAM & WATKINS LLP** *New York*
2. **MILBANK, TWEED, HADLEY & MCCLOY** *New York*
   SKADDEN, ARPS, SLATE, MEAGHER *New York*
   SULLIVAN & CROMWELL LLP *New York*
   WHITE & CASE LLP *New York*
3. **CHADBOURNE & PARKE LLP** *New York*
   DAVIS POLK & WARDWELL *New York*
   SHEARMAN & STERLING LLP *New York*
4. **DEBEVOISE & PLIMPTON LLP** *New York*
   DEWEY BALLANTINE LLP *New York*
   FRESHFIELDS BRUCKHAUS DERINGER *New York*
   SIMPSON THACHER & BARTLETT LLP *New York*
5. **CADWALADER, WICKERSHAM & TAFT** *New York*
   ORRICK, HERRINGTON & SUTCLIFFE *New York*

Firms are listed alphabetically in each band.

Band 1

Latham & Watkins LLP

The Firm: This dynamic international firm is extremely committed to its projects practice and has successfully set up a "*premier, absolutely A-list*" group that is universally admired for its depth and breadth. It is blessed with "*a large number of real top-notch partners,*" as the sheer weight of ranked lawyers clearly confirms. Clients also appreciate having access to "*a deep bench strength*" at associate level. The group enjoys a fine reputation for its work in the domestic power sector. It has considerable expertise in capital markets, leveraged finance and M&A and has been utilizing this to effectively represent financial institutions in the current wave of projects-related restructuring and transactional work. For example, it represented Morgan Stanley in the recent $2.4 billion refinancing of 15 Calpine power plants, and advised Société Générale as the agent to the bank syndicate acquiring the GenHoldings facilities from NEGT. This domestic work complements a formidable international practice with deep roots in the Middle East, and hence a prominent role in the area's megaprojects; it is representing the sponsor company in the $1.6 billion Q-Chem petrochemicals project in Qatar. Its lawyers are also active in such areas as the former Soviet Union and Africa, and acted for the Nigerian National Petroleum Corporation and Exxon-Mobil in the fast track $1.5 billion Nigerian NGL expansion project. Observers noted a consistency of style and quality: Latham lawyers are typically praised for their "*business-minded and solution-oriented approach.*"

The Lawyers: **Dave Gordon** is particularly renowned for his work in the domestic power sector. Clients praise him as "*a businessman's lawyer and a great deal facilitator,*" while peers acknowledge that his "*great interpersonal skills with both clients and opposing parties*" set him apart. **Andy Singer**'s practice is focused on domestic capital markets transactions in the projects sector. He operates from both the San Diego and New York offices and is considered "*a name-brand guy with a great reputation among the financial institutions.*" **Bill Voge** is helping to lead the practice into increasingly global waters and, according to interviewees, is "*a really big deal in the international market.*" Clients and peers report that his premier reputation stems from his ability to "*offer candid and pointed advice, ably direct a wide group of lawyers, and conduct negotiations in a practical, pragmatic and pleasant manner.*" **Jonathan Rod** comes from a securities background and is working on both domestic and international projects. Clients keep returning to him for his "*highly analytical*" mind, which enables him to "*give good advice on which points you mustn't relinquish and which you can live without.*" **Warren Lilien** is a younger partner who impressed observers with his "*deal-doing approach and focus on finding solutions,*" while **Michèle Penzer** is another younger partner who was admired for her "*technical skill.*" Both **Jeffrey Greenberg** and new entrant **Jennifer Frederick** have recently been made partners and were highlighted by market sources as rising stars.

The Clients: The firm acted for the export credit agency in the Qatargas II project. It also represented Lehman Brothers and ABN AMRO as lenders and underwriters in the $4.4 billion financing of the expansion of the Tengiz Chevron oil fields in Kazakhstan, and advised the sponsor company in the massive RasGas II LNG project in Qatar.

Band 2

Milbank, Tweed, Hadley & McCloy

The Firm: Milbank remains "*a formidable force*" in the projects market, and clients appreciate its "*considerable depth, experience, and a track record that speaks for itself.*" Peers describe a "*tough and disciplined*" negotiating stance. In

All quotes in the text are from interviews with clients and competitors.

New York
Leading individuals (Projects)

[1] **GORDON David** *Latham & Watkins*, New York
GREEN Jonathan *Milbank Tweed*, New York
MOORE Harold *Skadden Arps*, New York
RICH Frederic *Sullivan & Cromwell*, New York
SCAVONE Arthur *White & Case*, New York
SHUTRAN Richard *Dewey Ballantine*, New York
SINGER Andrew *Latham & Watkins*, San Diego
VOGE William *Latham & Watkins*, New York

[2] **ALEXANDER Troy** *White & Case*, New York
BAECHER John *Chadbourne & Parke*, New York
BURKE Ted *Freshfields Bruckhaus*, New York
GALVIS Sergio *Sullivan & Cromwell LLP*, New York
HARRIS L Douglas *Milbank Tweed*, New York
ROD Jonathan *Latham & Watkins*, New York
URDA KASSIS Cynthia *Shearman*, New York
WACHSBERGER Chaim *Chadbourne*, New York

[3] **BRACH Richard** *Milbank Tweed*, New York
HADLEY Joseph *Davis Polk*, New York
JACOBSON Martin *Simpson Thacher*, New York
MANN Christopher *Sullivan & Cromwell*, New York
SILVERMAN Eric *Milbank Tweed*, New York
WARNER E Waide *Davis Polk*, New York

[4] **BARTFELD Daniel** *Milbank Tweed*, New York
CHIDA Junaid *Dewey Ballantine*, New York
GIBBONS Robert *Debevoise & Plimpton*, New York
LIEBERMAN David *Simpson Thacher*, New York
LILIEN Warren *Latham & Watkins*, New York
MEYERS Michael *Orrick Herrington*, New York
OLIVIER Jeanne *Shearman & Sterling*, New York
PENZER Michèle *Latham & Watkins*, New York
RACITI-KNAPP Melissa *Freshfields*, New York
VITALE Robert *Cadwalader Wickersham*, New York
WARD Sarah *Skadden Arps*, New York
WYMAN Kenneth *Simpson Thacher*, New York

Up-and-coming individuals
CZARNIAK Julia *Skadden Arps*, New York
FREDERICK Jennifer *Latham & Watkins*, New York
GREENBERG Jeffrey *Latham & Watkins*, Los Angeles

Individuals are listed alphabetically in each band.

particular, the firm is considered "*a standard bearer*" when it comes to representing lenders. For example, it has been advising Enron's unsecured creditors' committee in the sale of its pipeline assets and Portland General assets, both extremely high-value deals. While this is its traditional forte, it must be noted that the firm is doing more and more work for the sponsor companies as well. In the international sphere, the group's recent marquee deals include acting for the lenders CSFB and OPIC in connection with the $1.5 billion Nigeria NGL project. International mining projects are another strength, and the team has advised lenders in a number of these throughout Latin America.

The Lawyers: **Jonathan Green** is well known for his capital markets expertise, and was described to researchers as "*a good quarterback

for a transaction.*" Clients particularly appreciate the way that he combines the attributes of a hands-on, "*user-friendly*" adviser with the fighting spirit of "*a relentlessly tough negotiator.*" Observers describe the academically strong **Douglas Harris** as "*a consummate technician*" and praise his "*brilliant legal intellect,*" while **Richard Brach** leads the "*prominent and excellent*" mining practice and worked on the Veladero gold mine project in Argentina. As head of the group, **Eric Silverman** has to spend time on management duties, but still regularly appears at the coal face and is admired for his "*experience in multiple countries and a variety of different deals.*" **Daniel Bartfeld** is a younger lawyer who focuses on oil and gas projects. He has been named by some observers as "*Milbank's next superstar.*"

The Clients: The firm advised a banking syndicate led by Citigroup, ABN AMRO and Scotia Capital as lenders in Brascan's $874 million acquisition of power-generating assets from Reliant Energy. Other financial institution clients include: ANZ; Fortis; Dexia; BayernLB; BNP Paribas; Matlin Patterson; Oak Tree Investors; CFSB; Citigroup and Japan Bank for International Cooperation (JBIC). Sponsor clients include: Mitsubishi; Diamond Energy; Cap Rock Energy; Leucadia National; Total and Tractebel.

Skadden, Arps, Slate, Meagher & Flom LLP & Affiliates
See firm details p.1372

The Firm: The "*aggressive, tough, relentless and thorough*" team at Skadden Arps has succeeded in securing itself a large share of the booming projects market in the Middle East. This has seen it representing the lenders in some of the most important projects in the world, such as the Qatargas II expansion project, a multibillion financing involving a bank tranche, an Islamic tranche and a bond offering. The New York office also acted for the underwriters in the $3 billion Ras Laffan LNG project in Qatar. Though not the largest team in New York, the group's experience of leading international projects has won it a first-class reputation among clients. As one put it: "*I can't think of anyone better to have working for you on a difficult deal; it's a real machine at getting the transactions done.*" The bulk of the team's work involves representing the lender or underwriter in these deals, but it also has some major developer work.

The Lawyers: Much of Skadden's reputation hangs on the quality of its leading name, **Hal Moore** (see p.1302). Clients rate his "*fantastic commercial judgment and foresight,*" and he was described as "*a walking legal encyclopedia.*" Peers, meanwhile, openly admit that "*no other lawyer has the presence or experience of Hal Moore.*" **Sarah Ward** (see p.1330) is a newcomer to the tables. She was recommended by

clients, who appreciate the way that she "*focuses on the big picture during complex transactions and doesn't get swamped by unimportant details.*" **Julia Czarniak** (see p.1274) is viewed as the best of the younger lawyers coming up through the ranks. Clients report that she is "*thorough and hard working*" and is "*confidently taking on a level of authority beyond her years.*"

The Clients: The firm represented an Israeli issuer in an offshore gas project in the Mediterranean Sea, and acted for the lenders in the Sasol gas-to-liquid project in Borneo. On the domestic front, the team represented the lenders in the development of the Astoria power plant in New York City, the largest independent power development in the USA in the past year. It also advised Edison Mission Energy on a number of domestic restructurings, and assisted it in a large power project in Indonesia.

Sullivan & Cromwell LLP
See firm details p.1373

The Firm: This "*premier league*" projects practice doesn't handle the same volume of projects as some other firms in this tier, concentrating instead on the biggest and most complex deals. Its success may be judged by the fact that the average value of the projects it has worked on over the past year is $1.5 billion. Benefiting from its reputation as a corporate heavyweight, the firm typically appears for big-name sponsor companies in international oil and gas projects. This year, for example, it represented the consortium developing the $3.6 billion Baku-Tbilisi -Ceyhan (BTC) pipeline, which will carry oil from Azerbaijan to Turkey. It also worked on the related $3.2 billion development of the ACG oil field in the Caspian Sea. The group's penetration into Latin America has been such that it is considered by some sources to be "*the strongest for Latin American projects.*" A recent highlight here was acting for Barrick Gold in the development of the Veladero gold mine in Argentina. This important deal saw the first new money entering Argentina since the currency crisis.

The Lawyers: The market was full of praise for the quality of the lawyers at this premier international projects outfit. Their pragmatism especially stood out: they are "*very commercial – deal-makers rather than pedants,*" said one client, echoing a wider view. **Fred Rich** (see p.1312) is undeniably "*the practice's household name,*" and sources rate him as "*one of the smartest lawyers out there.*" **Sergio Galvis** (see p.1281) is also highly rated by peers and clients. Peers consider him a formidable competitor, and he is held up in some quarters as "*the best lawyer out there for Latin American projects.*" **Chris Mann** (see p.1299) also has a good reputation in the market, particularly following the fine job he did of representing the consortium in the Camisea pipeline project in Peru.

1244   All quotes in the text are from interviews with clients and competitors.

CHAMBERS USA 2005

The Clients: The firm represented Kenmare Resources this year in connection with the development of the $366 million Moma titanium project in Mozambique. Other high-profile deals include assisting the consortium that developed the Camisea gas pipeline in Peru, and advising the Autoridad del Canal de Panamá in connection with the proposed expansion of the Panama Canal.

White & Case LLP
See firm details p.1379

The Firm: Global project finance is something that this firm does really well, and it is no surprise to see its *"technically excellent"* New York team emerging in many of the landmark international deals. It represented the lender consortium in the $11.3 billion Sakhalin LNG project in Russia, and is advising Qatar Petroleum and ExxonMobil as the sponsors in the Qatargas II project. With its network of offices throughout Asia and Latin America, the firm has a natural slant towards international work, and clients appreciate the value of this one-stop shop resource. It is chiefly known in the market for representing lenders, but as its work in the Qatargas II project illustrates, it also represents sponsors in high-value and complex projects. The firm is renowned for its work in Latin America, where it is representing the Inter-American Development Bank and Ambac Assurance Corporation in the Costanera Norte urban toll road project in Santiago, Chile. It has, however, also been developing its domestic practice and has been busy acting for lenders in wind energy projects.

The Lawyers: Market sources were full of praise for the *"really top-notch"* team of partners in the firm's New York office. *"Bright and practical"* **Art Scavone** (see p.1317) was envied by peers for his *"great touch with clients."* Clients themselves admire the way in which he can *"boil down the issues to what really matters."* They also singled out **Troy Alexander** (see p.1262) for particular mention. He is valued not just for *"understanding the project finance procedure inside out,"* but because *"he is a fine negotiator who doesn't antagonize the other side."* He is especially well known for his work in Latin American projects.

The Clients: The firm represented Saudi Aramco in the financing of four cogeneration plants in Saudi Arabia, and acted for the Abu Dhabi Water & Electricity Authority in connection with the $750 million Taweelah A2 water desalination project. Other clients include: CSFB; Lehman Brothers; Amerada Hess; Deutsche Bank; Ex-Im Bank; Inter-American Development Bank; IFC; JBIC; Mid-American Holdings; OPIC; BNP Paribas; Société Générale and Unocal.

Band 3

Chadbourne & Parke LLP
See firm details p.1341

The Firm: *"Expertise in project finance is a given"* at this growing international energy powerhouse, and its New York office is no exception. This year its expertise has been on show in a number of important projects, notably representing El Paso in the divesture of power plant assets valued at over $1 billion, and representing GE Commercial Finance in the $400 million financing of five Calpine power plants. These are both on the domestic stage, but its global reach also sees it involved in some interesting international projects. For example, it is advising a consortium on a tender to finance, build and operate the first line of the Tel Aviv Metro. The firm also has a strong Moscow office and is becoming increasingly involved in projects in Russia, such as the ongoing Shaka Neave pipeline project in the Caspian Sea.

The Lawyers: **Chaim Wachsberger** (see p.1329) is something of *"a guru"* in the projects market, and he was widely praised by peers and clients alike. Among other strengths, he impresses with *"extreme intelligence and creativity"* and *"his ability to stay under control and keep calm under pressure."* **John Baecher** (see p.1263) does a lot of work on the sponsor side and is especially active for AES. According to interviewees, he is a *"bright and practical"* attorney who *"doesn't get flustered easily."*

The Clients: El Paso; GE Commercial Finance; AES; CFSB; Citibank; Union Bank of California; Duke Energy and Tractebel.

Davis Polk & Wardwell
See firm details p.1345

The Firm: Davis Polk has a small but high-level practice that prides itself on its involvement in the most cutting-edge and complex projects. Clients are full of admiration for its cross-disciplinary offering – which includes expertise in structured finance, M&A and capital markets – while peers agree that it is *"an incredible firm."* As a smaller and more focused practice, its lawyers are more generalist than some, and can represent any party in a deal. The team has been especially active in Latin America, where this year it has been concentrating on restructuring distressed projects in countries with political and economic difficulties. It advised OPIC on setting up a guarantee structure for US companies investing in projects abroad, and has advised AES on the restructuring of a number of its Brazilian assets. Tapping into a rich vein of lender work from its top-class banking client base, the group advised the banks on the Cerro Negro and Hamaca heavy oil projects in Venezuela.

The Lawyers: *"Tenacious"* **Waide Warner** (see p.1331) is a popular choice with clients. According-

ing to some, he *"doesn't miss anything and never makes mistakes."* His colleague **Joseph Hadley** (see p.1286) was also recommended as *"a first-rate projects lawyer."*

The Clients: The firm represents the sponsor company in a number of petrochemicals projects in Latin America, notably the FertiNitro project in Venezuela, and the Profertil and Mega projects in Argentina. It has been focusing this year on restructuring existing projects, however it also worked on two new telecom projects, one in Bolivia for AES, and one in the Caribbean for Digicel. Other clients include Morgan Stanley and NatWest.

Shearman & Sterling LLP
See firm details p.1369

The Firm: This firm has one of the leading practices in the industry for projects in Latin America, where it benefits from a commitment to the sector going back over 50 years. This position was recently cemented when it opened an office in São Paulo, Brazil. Clients report that the firm *"has a good knowledge of the local legal and economic issues"* in the area. It also has strong relationships with Japanese banks, which are prolific investors in Latin American schemes. For example, the firm recently represented Mizuho Bank as lead arranger in the $210 million Tuxpan V power plant project in Mexico. Its other great strength is in restructuring projects. Shearman attorneys are renowned as *"good technical lawyers who excel at complicated technical work,"* which explains the team's success in this complex field. In the past year the firm has represented CSFB as agent in both the NRG and Mirant bankruptcies, which involved restructuring a total of $5 billion of debt. Combining its two key strengths, it also represented AES in the restructuring of its $1.5 billion Brazilian debt.

The Lawyers: According to clients, the lawyers here are skilled at finding solutions to complicated issues, and can *"mesh colliding worlds into a common viewpoint."* The team's most visible presence is *"classic projects lawyer"* **Cynthia Urda Kassis** (see p.1328). Clients appreciate the fact that she is *"all business and no posturing,"* and one satisfied client went so far as to report that she is *"one of the smartest, most thorough and competent lawyers I've ever used."* **Jeanne Olivier** (see p.1306) is recognized as one of the industry's leading experts in risk insurance. She has recently done considerable work on political risks in connection with projects in Argentina and Venezuela.

The Clients: The team represented the sponsor company, Placer Dome, in the development of the Cerro Casale gold and copper mine in Chile, one of the largest undeveloped gold deposits in Latin America. It also advised Citigroup as arranger of the $225 million financing of the San Fernando pipeline in Mexico. Other

www.ChambersandPartners.com

All quotes in the text are from interviews with clients and competitors.

1245

clients include: ABN AMRO; Barclays; Crédit Lyonnais; Central American Bank of Economic Integration; Netherlands Finance Company; Deutsche Investitions-und Entwicklungsgesellschaft MBH (DEG); BNP Paribas; PSEG Global and Allegheny.

Band 4

Debevoise & Plimpton LLP

See firm details p.1346

The Firm: The broad-based projects practice at this international firm offers strength in representing sponsors in domestic projects, and also acts for the lenders and guarantors in international projects. Clients note its impressive resources, saying that it "*offers a full service because of the deep-bench strength.*" This enables it to take part in major international schemes, including such highlight deals as representing MBIA as guarantor in the financing of the Autopista Central ring road, the Vespucio toll road and the Vespucio Norte ring road in Santiago. The firm also offers considerable experience in airport privatizations, and continues to represent JFK IAT in the $1.5 billion development of the international air terminal at JFK. Currently it is involved in restructuring part of the financing and drafting agreements with airlines.

The Lawyers: Head of department **Robert Gibbons** was recommended to researchers for his "*keen organizational skills and sound judgment.*" According to peers his relaxed and pragmatic approach make him "*one of the real delights to work with in this industry.*"

The Clients: The firm represented a consortium of lenders led by Sumitomo Mitsui Banking Corporation in the $400 million Tuban petrochemical project in Indonesia, and acted for the sponsor company, Mitsui, in connection with the $1 billion Malhas gas pipeline in Brazil. Other clients include: XL Capital; Inter-American Development Bank; Teachers Insurance; Metlife; Prudential; Aeroflot; American Airlines; Cogentrix Energy; Drax Power; John Hancock; Powerco and Sithe Energies.

Dewey Ballantine LLP

See firm details p.1347

The Firm: The profile of Dewey Ballantine's New York projects practice is founded to a large extent upon the reputation and experience of its lead lawyer, Rich Shutran. However, he does enjoy the support of a competent and energetic team, as well as being able to call upon the resources of a strong energy practice in DC. The group's domestic profile is to the fore, and the team has been busy in the past year working on the development of wind projects. However Latin America has also been a consistent focus for a number of years. Here, the highlight deal of the past 12 months was advising the sponsor

company on the Norte-Sur toll road project in Santiago, Chile. This is a particularly interesting transaction as it involved a mix of both US and Chilean funding.

The Lawyers: **Richard Shutran** (see p.1321) is one of New York's projects heavyweights, with a "*very visible and well-established*" presence in the industry. According to clients, he is "*smart and result-oriented, and has a great demeanor at the table.*" The department also numbers **Junaid Chida** (see p.1272) among its ranks. Widely rated as "*a great leasing lawyer,*" he has diversified his practice of late by moving increasingly into wind projects.

The Clients: The firm has also been representing Panda Gila River and Union Power Partners in relation to some restructuring transactions.

Freshfields Bruckhaus Deringer LLP

The Firm: The firm's global network of offices, which make it "*a key player in the international sphere,*" gives this emerging New York projects team a natural opening into the global market. This is evidenced in a wealth of high-profile transactions, such as representing the export credit agencies in the massive Baku-Tbilisi-Ceyhan (BTC) pipeline project. The New York office has been actively involved in representing the Ex-Im Bank. Meanwhile, in the USA and Latin America, the global firm has worked on a wide variety of projects. For example, it does a lot of work for ArcLight Capital Partners, and this year represented the company in the $300 million acquisition of a portfolio of domestic independent power plants from Aquila. It has also represented BNP Paribas and Rabobank on projects in Latin America.

The Lawyers: **Ted Burke** is the group's best-known personality and is "*an absolutely first-class lawyer,*" according to the market. Observers say that he is "*talented, creative and bright as hell,*" with the ability to present complex ideas in an easily comprehensible way. **Melissa Raciti-Knapp** is known for her expertise in Latin American projects. According to clients, she has "*a wealth of experience and incredible interpersonal skills.*"

The Clients: ArcLight Capital Partners; Ex-Im Bank; WestLB; BNP Paribas; IFC; Tractebel; BTU Ventures and Rabobank.

Simpson Thacher & Bartlett LLP

See firm details p.1370

The Firm: This firm has "*a cutting-edge*" projects practice that has been particularly active this year for sponsor companies, either in the realm of energy or Latin American infrastructure. For example, it advised Kerr-McGee in the complex $600 million financing of three offshore drilling platforms in the Gulf of Mexico. Peers also rate its "*good solid lease practice,*" which was on show recently when the firm represented Keyspan in connection with the $360

million lease financing of an expansion of its Ravenswood plant. Much of its recent Latin American work has involved the airport sector. In its most prominent deal, the team represented the sponsors in the privatization of six airports in the Dominican Republic. It has also worked on schemes concerning the Santiago and Montego Bay airports.

The Lawyers: "*Talented*" **Martin Jacobson** (see p.1290) is a favorite with clients and peers alike for his pragmatism and ability to "*get the deal done.*" The team also boasts **David Lieberman** (see p.1297), who is widely regarded as a talented projects lawyer. They are joined in this year's ranking by **Kenneth Wyman** (see p.1333), who concentrates on domestic projects. He was recommended to researchers as "*a gentleman and a fine lawyer,*" who "*focuses on the big issues.*"

The Clients: As well as Kerr-McGee and Keyspan, the firm was project counsel to Sithe Boston Generating Company in connection with the $1.2 billion refinancing of a portfolio of power plants.

Band 5

Cadwalader, Wickersham & Taft LLP

See firm details p.1339

The Firm: This firm specializes in providing complex structured finance advice to financial institutions involved in international projects. As project financing is becoming increasingly interrelated with other forms of infrastructure financing, clients find the wide breadth of experience here very helpful. As one reported: "*It has a deep team that covers all the areas of financing expertise that we need.*" This year the team's highlights have included an expansion financing of a water treatment plant in Panama, and a vendor financing for an Indonesian coal mine. It also represented Ambac Assurance as bond insurers for an offering by a Chilean power company.

The Lawyers: **Robert Vitale** (see p.1329) heads the project finance team here. Clients value his "*very detail-oriented*" advice and appreciate the fact that he is "*fully committed to meeting demanding deadlines.*"

The Clients: Key clients include The TCW Group, WestLB and Ambac Assurance. The firm has been demonstrating its versatility this year, representing the financiers in the acquisition of a Dominican power company, as well as acting for the acquirer of a Caribbean power utility and handling a loan workout connected with a North Sea oil rig.

Orrick, Herrington & Sutcliffe

See firm details p.295

The Firm: Clients are impressed with this projects group, which coordinates closely with colleagues in the firm's California offices to provide

1246   All quotes in the text are from interviews with clients and competitors.

CHAMBERS USA 2005

a seamless service. In the past year it has been particularly prominent in domestic infrastructure schemes, such as representing the lead lenders in the $900 million California SR 125 road project, and advising the lenders in the $1.8 billion Chicago Skyway bridge project. It is also active in the energy sector and notably assisted the sponsor company in the development of the $939 million Springerville gas-fired project, one of the few new power projects on the domestic scene. In the burgeoning renewable energy sphere, recent highlights include working with Eurus Energy on projects in the USA and in Spain, as well as advising AES on its investment in US Wind Force.

The Lawyers: **Michael Meyers** (see p.1301) is the team's most prominent lawyer. Clients describe him as "*an astute businessman who communicates effectively.*"

The Clients: The team does a considerable amount of work for Tennessee Valley Authority, and this year advised it on a $400 million leverage lease transaction on technology used for generating and transmitting electrical power. Other key clients include Eurus Energy; PG&E; AES; Aquila; Unisource; Babcock & Brown; Bank of America; Citigroup and Deutsche Bank.

REAL ESTATE

New York
Leading firms (Real Estate)

1 FRIED, FRANK, HARRIS, SHRIVER *New York*
PAUL, HASTINGS, JANOFSKY & WALKER *New York*
SKADDEN, ARPS, SLATE, MEAGHER *New York*

2 SHEARMAN & STERLING LLP *New York*
SULLIVAN & CROMWELL LLP *New York*
WEIL, GOTSHAL & MANGES LLP *New York*
WILLKIE FARR & GALLAGHER LLP *New York*

3 CLEARY GOTTLIEB STEEN & HAMILTON *New York*
PAUL, WEISS, RIFKIND, WHARTON *New York*
PROSKAUER ROSE LLP *New York*
STROOCK & STROOCK & LAVAN LLP *New York*

4 BRYAN CAVE ROBINSON LLP *New York*
CADWALADER, WICKERSHAM & TAFT *New York*
DEBEVOISE & PLIMPTON LLP *New York*
DLA PIPER RUDNICK GRAY CARY US *New York*
KRAMER LEVIN NAFTALIS & FRANKEL *New York*
LATHAM & WATKINS LLP *New York*

5 AKIN GUMP STRAUSS HAUER & FELD *New York*
BROWN RAYSMAN MILLSTEIN FELDER *New York*
DECHERT *New York*
KATTEN MUCHIN ZAVIS ROSENMAN *New York*
SIMPSON THACHER & BARTLETT LLP *New York*
WACHTELL, LIPTON, ROSEN & KATZ *New York*

Firms are listed alphabetically in each band.

Band 1

Fried, Frank, Harris, Shriver & Jacobson LLP
See firm details p.1349
The Firm: This powerhouse practice predominantly assists owners and developers on sophisticated financings. It also represents lenders, but less frequently and usually on more complicated matters. Developments and acquisitions remain a mainstay. These typically relate to financing, leasing and other proceedings. Interviewees particularly acclaim the practice's "*hard, intense, quality work*" and loyalty to clients. Illustrative work has included assistance on the recapitalization of the GM Building and advice on the acquisition of the New York Times headquarters building for Tishman Speyer. Peers speak of an "*an absolutely top-shelf practice with some of the brightest attorneys.*" Clients are no less glowing in their commenda-

tion, highlighting the practice's "*excellent customer service, attention to detail and work ethic.*" Its network of resources is another selling point for clients; the firm has a "*tremendously large team and can throw as many people as required at a deal.*"
The Lawyers: Few in the New York real estate can match **Jonathan Mechanic** (see p.1300) for his assistance to developers and institutions. An "*incredible intellectual capacity for the law*" makes him a top destination for real estate law, particularly as related to bankruptcy and tax issues. The "*uniquely multidimensional professional*" is able to blend a "*warm and engaging*" style with an ability to be "*as tough a negotiator as anyone I have met.*" He operates on high-profile acquisitions and their associated financings and also undertakes some leasing and a degree of joint venture work. In addition to participating in the New York Times headquarters building, he also advised Tishman Speyer on its purchase of the 'Lipstick Building' at 885 Third Avenue via three separate deals. **Stephen Lefkowitz** (see p.1296) is acclaimed in the market for his land use and zoning abilities. He is also proficient in representing public agencies and some developers in high-end development work, including structured and public financing. Commentators reflected on his "*experienced, sensible, intelligent*" style, which he ably deploys on such transactions as the development of the Time Warner Center at Columbus Circle. He is also working with the New York Jets in connection with the proposed New York Sports and Convention Center and stadium development on Manhattan's West Side. Another high point involved restructuring the leases from client New York City to the Port Authority of New York for the city's two airports. **Joshua Mermelstein** (see p.1301) spends a considerable degree of his time on corporate real estate and development transactions, specializing in representing publicly traded companies. Research revealed a "*pleasant and practical*" attorney who is "*extremely bright and thoughtful about dealing with the issues at hand.*" Partner **Robert Sorin** (see p.1323) acts on many large transactional matters. His versatility and conviction were flagged as his best traits. On behalf of Macklowe Properties, he worked on the GM Building's $1.7

billion recapitalization with partner Jamestown Properties; the transaction included a refinancing of more than $1 billion debt.
The Clients: The group is acting for Forest City Ratner on the development of an arena and associated retail and housing spaces in downtown Brooklyn on behalf of the New Jersey Nets basketball team. For the New York Yankees, it is participating in a new stadium involving complex transactions with public agencies, private financing and tax-exempt municipal bond financing. Other clients include: Hines; Whitehall Fund; Chera, Feil and Goldman families; Estée Lauder; Far City; Jack Resnick & Sons; New York City; New York Jets; New York Yankees; Time Warner; Tishman Speyer and Watchtower Society.

Paul, Hastings, Janofsky & Walker LLP
See firm details p.297
The Firm: The team has responded to the increasing importance of capital markets in the New York real estate scene with some success. As a result, it has witnessed an increase in transactional work, including the development of funds and hedge funds relating to landed properties. It couples its well-recommended leasing team with a wealth of respected abilities in transactional work related to lending, tax and REITs among other aspects. Observers underlined the firm's "*strong fundamentals and excellent reputation,*" as well as referring to "*a promising future*" in relation to its next generation of real estate lawyers. The New York team is easily one of the largest in the city and a key component of the firm's global real estate presence. Its overall strength in the USA has culminated in a robust national real estate footprint.
The Lawyers: Of counsel **Marty Edelman** (see p.1277) acts on a higher proportion of international matters and is one of the main architects of the firm's global real estate vision. An accomplished deal-maker, he was often described as "*a businessman with legal ability,*" seeking to negotiate advantages for his clients without unnecessarily rocking the boat. His experience and manner are considered "*absolutely outstanding.*" One observer said: "*He has both the macro and micro view of a transaction.*" He oversaw the establish-

www.ChambersandPartners.com
All quotes in the text are from interviews with clients and competitors.
1247

New York
Leading individuals (Real Estate)

Senior Statesman
BOXER Leonard *Stroock & Stroock*, New York

[1] **EDELMAN Marty** *Paul Hastings*, New York
MECHANIC Jonathan *Fried Frank*, New York
NEEDELL Benjamin *Skadden Arps*, New York
SHENKER Joseph *Sullivan & Cromwell*, New York

[2] **ADLER Arthur** *Sullivan & Cromwell*, New York
MERMELSTEIN Joshua *Fried Frank*, New York
PINOVER Eugene *Willkie Farr*, New York
SIMKIN Steven *Paul Weiss*, New York
SMITH Chris *Shearman & Sterling*, New York

[3] **FELTENSTEIN Martha** *Skadden Arps*, New York
FORTE Joseph *Dechert*, New York
HOROWITZ Steven *Cleary Gottlieb*, New York
LIPSON Lawrence *Proskauer Rose*, New York
NEVELOFF Jay *Kramer Levin*, New York
ROSEN J Philip *Weil Gotshal*, New York
STEIN Joshua *Latham & Watkins*, New York
URIS Harvey *Skadden Arps*, New York
WEINBERGER Michael *Cleary Gottlieb*, New York
WHITE W Christopher *Cadwalader*, New York

[4] **ALDEN Steven** *Debevoise & Plimpton*, New York
ALTSCHULER Fredric *Cadwalader*, New York
DIAMOND Brian *Stroock & Stroock*, New York
KLEIN Steven *Willkie Farr*, New York
LASCHER Alan *Weil Gotshal*, New York
MILLER Peter *Akin Gump*, New York
PANOVKA Robin *Wachtell Lipton*, New York
POLEVOY Martin *DLA Piper Rudnick*, New York
POMERANTZ Alan *Weil Gotshal*, New York
ROSS Barry *Bryan Cave*, New York
SHIPLEY Anne *Paul Hastings*, New York
WERTHEIMER Robert *Paul Hastings*, New York

[5] **BENNER Michael** *Wachtell Lipton*, New York
BOND W Michael *Weil Gotshal*, New York
CHADAKOFF Richard *Latham & Watkins*, New York
COLLETTA Anthony *Sullivan & Cromwell*, New York
EVANUSA Michel *Stroock & Stroock*, New York
FREIDUS Harris *Paul Weiss*, New York
IVANHOE Robert *Greenberg Traurig*, New York
KANE Meredith *Paul Weiss*, New York
KOBAK Scott *Simpson Thacher*, New York
ROCK Neil *Skadden Arps*, New York
SANSEVERINO Raymond *Brown Raysman*, New York
SERNAU Ronald *Proskauer Rose*, New York
SORIN Robert *Fried Frank*, New York
STEINER Jeffrey *Brown Raysman*, New York

Leading individuals
(Real Estate: Zoning/Land Use)

[1] **LEFKOWITZ Stephen** *Fried Frank*, New York
LINDENBAUM Samuel *Kramer Levin*, New York
SELVER Paul *Paul Hastings*, New York

Individuals are listed alphabetically in each band.

ment of the City Investment Fund, a joint venture between Fisher Brothers and Morgan Stanley for the purpose of investing in New York city real estate; the fund is supported by the city and state pensions funds. **Paul Selver** (see p.1319) heads the land use and zoning team. He is distinguished for his *"knowledge of the zoning laws and his ability to maneuver through its intricate world."* He led the team representing a group of four property owners in the complex rezoning of five square blocks within a historic district south of Midtown Manhattan. He also assists lenders on land use issues, including development rights transfers. The environmental aspects of his work should not be overlooked: he acts as land use and environmental counsel to Madison Square Garden in connection with the renovation and modernization of its facilities. Experienced transactional lawyer **Anne Shipley** (see p.1320) tends to focus on key client The Related Companies. A *"smart, resourceful and efficient"* attorney, she is touted as an asset in negotiations because of her ability to remain calm under pressure. **Robert Wertheimer** (see p.1332) is a new addition to *Chambers'* tables. His emergence as a practice leader relies on his cross-border expertise. His professional yet relaxed approach makes him *"at home with the most difficult and contentious situations,"* according to market sources. *"His ability to manage complexity, stress and acrimony is probably better than anyone's."*

The Clients: The group assisted The Related Companies and its joint venture partner Apollo Real Estate Advisors on the development of the mixed-use Time Warner Center. The work included a $2.1 billion construction and mezzanine loan with GMAC as well as the refinancing of condominium units in the complex. It acted for Lend Lease/Morgan Stanley on the conversion of a $1.5 billion real estate portfolio of 58 trophy assets from an insurance form of ownership to a REIT. The firm was retained by Bertelsmann to handle the $426.5 million sale and leaseback of its US headquarters in Times Square and on a similar $297 million transaction involving the headquarters of its subsidiary, Random House. Other clients include: Equity Office Properties; Acadia Realty Trust; Equity Office Properties and Fisher Brothers.

Skadden, Arps, Slate, Meagher & Flom LLP & Affiliates

See firm details p.1372
The Firm: Securitized finance has become the keystone of this practice, with the firm enjoying a reputation among many in the market for sophisticated transactions. Its lending abilities continue to flourish, with Deutsche Bank as its largest client in this area. Fund formation and other private equity structures are coupled with traditional development activities and leasing advice. A hard-nosed negotiating style is a distinguishing feature.
The Lawyers: A *"smart and savvy player,"* **Ben Needell** (see p.1303) gains his top ranking in the market through his blend of an *"often forceful, tough personal style"* and *"a sense of wisdom to*

know when to stop." The *"prodigious worker"* allies years of experience with a commercial outlook that has earned him *"the ability to tell his client to back off when it is appropriate,"* according to leading peers. He advises Larry Silverstein in connection with certain aspects of the development and financing of 7 World Trade Center. *"Talented and extraordinarily smart,"* **Martha Feltenstein** (see p.1278) continues to parlay an indomitable attitude into a successful practice centered on traditional, transactional work. Acting for Global Signal, she worked with a cross-departmental team on its approximately $1.2 billion acquisition of the exclusive 32-year rights to lease or operate more than 6,600 wireless communications towers and related assets from Sprint. **Harvey Uris** (see p.1328) is respected for his work on CMBS, mortgage loan originations and securitized deals. He led the team advising Deutsche Bank Securities on its refinancing of more than $1 billion of debt related to the GM Building; the deal involved a new joint venture between Harry Macklowe and Jamestown Properties. **Neil Rock** (see p.1313) represented Empire State Development in connection with the proposed new stadium for the New York Jets football team. He enters *Chambers'* tables with client commendation for his *"service-oriented"* and technical abilities on the more sophisticated deals.

The Clients: The team represented Boston Properties on various acquisitions and leasings, including the negotiation of a 15-year lease for Ann Taylor Stores' new corporate headquarters in Times Square Tower. It is also working with Bank of America on the development of its new global corporate investment headquarters at One Bryant Park. Poster Financial Group hired the firm for its $215 million acquisition of the Las Vegas and Laughlin Golden Nugget casinos from MGM Mirage. The practice is further acting for Centro Properties Group on its $1.1 billion purchase of Kramont Realty Trust. Other clients include Deutsche Bank Securities, Empire State Development and Larry Silverstein.

Band 2

Shearman & Sterling LLP

See firm details p.1369
The Firm: The practice approaches real estate broadly via M&A, leasing, borrowing and lending. It is well placed to assist the increasing amounts of investment capital in the New York real estate market through its strong mortgage loan practice. It works with real estate private equity funds chiefly on acquisitions, and maintains a fair balance between its domestic and international clients. Another feature is its role in representing a significant number of German banks and many foreign investors in the US real estate market.
The Lawyers: **Chris Smith** (see p.1322) is pitched as *"one of those people for whom you every*

box – *balanced, smart as a whip, tough as nails and easy to work with.*" His pragmatic drive and perception of the underlying business issues drew plaudits. He acted for Empire State Development on the acquisition and ground lease of the new Bank of America headquarters building on Sixth Avenue. Property group leader Lee Kuntz is also a key player. Because of the remaining talent pool, Kevin Hackett's departure to go in-house was not perceived by industry analysts to have significantly damaged the firm's real estate capability.

The Clients: The team advised Citisecurities, as facility agent, and Citicorp North America as US subagent, in connection with a $2.25 billion multicurrency syndicated bridge credit facility for subsidiaries of Westfield Group. Battery Park City Authority hired the firm in connection with the proposed ground lease of Site 26 in Battery Park city to Goldman Sachs. It represented Shorenstein on the formation of a $775 million fund to invest in large commercial properties in the USA, and separately acted for DekaBank in relation to its involvement with GM Building in New York city. Other clients include Anbau Enterprises; Archdiocese of New York; Ark Investment Partners; AXA Equitable Life Insurance; Citicorp North America; Empire State Development; Fosterlane Management; SRI Six; SSR Realty Advisors and Westdeutsche Immobilienbank.

Sullivan & Cromwell LLP
See firm details p.1373

The Firm: The team runs a full gamut of real estate work from large-scale acquisitions of real estate companies to billion-dollar developments. Located as a subgroup within the commercial practice, it takes in all aspects of real estate within the corporate side of its work. The recovery of the real estate market heralded deals of increasing sophistication, which the firm is well positioned to take advantage of. Interviewees particularly highlighted its performances in complicated deal structuring, difficult lease restructurings and certain strategic transactions. It remains heavily active in structures involving private equity funds and related securities law. With regards to REITs, the firm participated in transactions involving Los Angeles' Sunstone Hotel Properties and Chicago's Strategic Hotel Capital; the deal included a simultaneous private equity offering for an affiliated company and several complicated debt offerings aggregating over $2 billion.

The Lawyers: Joseph Shenker (see p.1320) represented General Growth Properties on its $12.6 billion acquisition of Rouse, one of the largest real estate deals to date. "*Big-picture oriented*" and able to see the businessman's side of the deal, he uses a "*hard, aggressive, yet positive, representation on behalf of his clients.*" He also impresses via an "*ability to crystallize in a short and simple way what the parties have agreed.*" In what was a particularly busy year for him,

Shenker also represented Soros Fund Management in the financing aspects of its $1.4 billion purchase of the GM Building, considered one of the most expensive single acquisitions in the USA. He is also credited with the firm's increased participation in high-end real estate transactions through his role as coordinator of the firm's global commercial real estate practice. **Arthur Adler**'s (see p.1261) prominence in the market is sustained by his traditional focus on 'dirt' real estate law as well as related capital markets matters. His strong reputation is built on such work as advising Goldman Sachs on its $2 billion Jersey city campus development – including office space, hotel, piers, an airport and parkland. He assisted the same client on the development of a new Manhattan headquarters at Site 26 in Battery Park City, to be built on government-owned land and involving significant complex multi-party negotiations, land use work, tax benefits and incentives. **Anthony Colletta** (see p.1273) enters *Chambers'* tables this year as he is pitched as "*the future of the firm's real estate practice.*" Among other matters, the "*extraordinarily bright and unflappable*" attorney acted on several major transactions related to the recovery of the hotel industry following 9/11. He represented the Whitehall Street Real Estate Funds, Zeckendorf Realty and Global Holdings in the acquisition, financing and development of a $1.2 billion mixed-use project on the site of the Mayflower Hotel in Manhattan.

The Clients: The firm counseled developers Vornado Realty Trust, as well as its affiliated REIT Alexander's, on mayor Michael Bloomberg's new $1.1 billion mixed-use development and world headquarters on the Upper East Side. The department has advised the Tisch family on the redevelopment of the New York Giants' stadium and adjacent mega-mall development proposal. On the West Coast, it is representing the investor group of Whitehall Street Real Estate Funds, Morgan Stanley and Oaktree Capital Management on the massive Playa Vista development project in Los Angeles. Other clients include: Aetos Capital; CIM Group; Crown American; General Growth Properties; Goldman Sachs; Lazard Freres Real Estate Investors; Lehman Brothers; New York Giants; Pritzker family businesses; Soros Fund Management; Strategic Hotel Capital; Sunstone Hotel Properties and Zeckendorf Realty.

Weil, Gotshal & Manges LLP
See firm details p.1378

The Firm: Mirroring a trend in the market, the department's real estate transactions and finance practice has increasingly advised on equity, mezzanine and pure debt work. As part of a more diversified practice, it is anchored in a strong bankruptcy foundation. The various aspects are so well integrated that some market observers express difficulty in distinguishing the firm's real

estate work from its corporate activity. Its traditional strengths in finance and corporate transactions have certainly bolstered the firm's capabilities in related real estate matters. The firm is also involved in the restructuring of energy and hydro fuel properties.

The Lawyers: Considered "*a great adviser and a highly respected figure,*" **Philip Rosen** (see p.1314) served as lead counsel representing bondholders including Morgan Stanley and Franklin Mutual regarding $1.3 billion of debt in the restructuring of Donald Trump's hotel and casino empire. Peers pointed to his business intelligence and familiarity with the minutiae of a deal. Clients were equally impressed. "*An absolutely world class lawyer, he has an understanding of markets*" and a good grasp of the business repercussions in addition to the legal ramifications, said one prominent client. He also worked with Euro Fund Properties on its procurement of Fisher Island Holdings' exclusive 216-acre island off the coast of Miami. A senior member of the real estate bar, **Alan Lascher** (see p.1296) enjoys a long-established pedigree in the sector and is involved in both strategic and day-to-day aspects of the firm's real estate work, including leasing work. Versatile and with thorough knowledge of the majority of issues, he has "*very little sizzle and a lot of steak.*" He acted for Reader's Digest Association on the $59 million sale and leaseback of its Pleasantville headquarters. **Alan Pomerantz** (see p.1309) continues to work on many real estate deals and is recommended for his private equity work. His business perspective and "*instructive, thoughtful and patient*" technique proved popular among interviewees. **Michael Bond** (see p.1268) enters the *Chambers* tables following his move from the DC office to New York. He works with investment banks and other financial institutions and is particularly associated with Lehman Brothers, assisting on real estate acquisitions and financing proceedings. "*A calm lawyer who doesn't get ruffled,*" he illustrates a tenacious drive while "*keeping his ego in check.*" For him, "*it is about getting the deal done,*" sources said.

The Clients: The team counseled Brascan on the purchase and financing of 73 hydroelectric power plants in New York state for about $1 billion – one of the largest private power deals of 2004. It also works with Blackstone Properties on a range of matters – including its involvement with high-end hotels such as Four Seasons, Marriott and Hyatt. Other clients include: CSFB; Euro Fund Properties; Franklin Mutual; Lehman Brothers; Milstein Brothers Capital Partners; the Morgan Stanley/Glick consortium and Reader's Digest Association.

Willkie Farr & Gallagher LLP
See firm details p.1380

The Firm: Interviewees continue to refer to the firm's collegiate atmosphere allied to a strategic approach and outlook. Expertise on real estate financings and related securitizations is married to know-how with REIT mergers, acquisitions and leasing activity, providing a comprehensive service for clients. Shopping center transactions are a key component of the firm's real estate portfolio; its attorneys assist about half of the top ten such organizations in the USA. The firm retains a visible profile in major office building transactions, leasings and developments. For example, the practice represented shopping mall giant Simon Property Group in its acquisition of outlet mall owner Chelsea Property Group for $3.5 billion in cash and stock.

The Lawyers: Considered by some to be "*the ultimate businessman's lawyer*," **Eugene Pinover** (see p.1309) continues to impress with his success record. He advised underwriter Goldman Sachs in the $246 million IPO for Strategic Hotels. He also acted for Mills on its purchase of a 50% interest in the GM Pension Trust's 9.6 million-sq-ft super-regional mall portfolio. As part of the group's active leasing development practice, the "*smart and low key*" **Steven Klein** (see p.1293) is working with Bloomberg on its lease for a new world headquarters at 731 Lexington Avenue.

The Clients: The team assisted long-time client Paramount Group on the creation of a real estate fund for German investors to acquire Class A properties in the USA. In the gaming sector, the team represents Colony Capital on its $1.24 billion acquisition of four casinos from Harrah's Entertainment and Caesars Entertainment; this follows a separate $280 million purchase of the legendary Las Vegas Hilton hotel and casino. Other clients include American Campus Communities; Apollo Real Estate Advisors; Bloomberg; Brandywine Realty Trust; CBL; Goldman Sachs; Habitat for Humanity International; Jim Wilson & Associates; Lazard Freres; Lehman Brothers; McKinsey; Mills Corporation; Simon Property Group and Tishman Hotel & Realty.

Band 3

Cleary Gottlieb Steen & Hamilton LLP

See firm details p.1342

The Firm: The team deals with strong concentrations of mortgage and mezzanine debt finance work and apportions equal resources to a broad range of other activities – including M&A and sale and leaseback transactions. Though a relatively small department, it has proved a contender on finance and securities matters. The team assisted Goldman Sachs on a $1.1 billion securitization of nine floating-rate mortgage loans secured by shopping malls, industrial properties, apartment buildings, office buildings and a hotel. One of its niche strengths is the gaming and hospitality sector. Among several significant transactions in this area is the $427 million acquisition financing of General Growth's purchase of the Grand Canal Shoppes at the Venetian casino resort in Las Vegas.

The Lawyers: **Steven Horowitz** (see p.1288) handles a mix that incorporates corporate real estate, restructuring and corporate governance. "*One of the most intellectual lawyers you will find*," he advised Sempra Energy on its acquisition of ten power generation plants in Texas among other assets. He also worked with Starwood Hotels' board members with respect to certain proposed transactions and corporate governance matters. **Michael Weinberger** (see p.1331) is most heavily involved in securitized mortgage financings. Viewed by commentators as a "*smart and pragmatic*" player, he advised Goldman Sachs on the financing for the $1.25 billion leveraged acquisition of Mervyn's from Target, as well as its complex $2.25 billion financing of the leveraged acquisition of LNR Property.

The Clients: Citigroup hired the firm on its purchase of a $1 billion portfolio of commercial mortgage loans from Emigrant. It advised in Ann Taylor Stores' successful leasing of a 300,000-sq ft property from Boston Properties to be used for its new corporate headquarters in New York's Times Square. The group additionally set up a program to establish a residential and commercial mortgage securitization scheme on behalf of the investment arm of the Government of Dubai; the transaction was structured to comply with Islamic law requirements. Other clients include: Brascan; Home Depot; Keystone; Kindred Healthcare; McDonald's; Pacific Life; Sempra Energy; Standard & Poor's; Starwood Hotels and Vornado.

Paul, Weiss, Rifkind, Wharton & Garrison LLP

See firm details p.1362

The Firm: The team is most active on complicated, high-end developments, acquisitions, financings and restructurings as part of a broader remit. It also deals with dispute resolutions concerning major commercial properties. Though its cachet in the marketplace may not match that of some of its larger competitors, the team is perceived as a "*deeper practice than many give it credit for.*" The group's next generation of real estate lawyers also appears to be making their mark in the industry, further enhancing the firm's profile in the long run.

The Lawyers: **Steven Simkin** (see p.1321) targets complex transactions. For example, he assisted GMAC on the development of the New York Times headquarters building. An "*excellent transactional attorney, he is able to cut through the small points and focus on getting the deal done for his client*," opponents said. He also represented Muss Development on the expansion to the New York Marriott at the Brooklyn Bridge. Two new names at the firm join *Chambers*' tables. **Meredith Kane** (see p.1291) undertakes development work, representing the Metropolitan Transit Authority in connection with the New York Jets new stadium.

She is recognized and much credited for her work with exempt organizations, acting on development deals for public agencies or developers. **Harris Freidus** (see p.1280) worked with the owner/developer of the Venetian – one of Las Vegas' largest hotel and casino complexes – on the financing, initial development and expansion of the ongoing $1.4 billion project. He provided similar advice for the same client regarding the development of hotel/casino resorts and convention centers in Macau.

The Clients: Hotel redevelopment is an important factor in the firm's most recent work advising property group the Goldman family in two separate transactions relating to the Gramercy Park and Stanhope Hotel. It acted on behalf of Sumitomo on both the $212 million sale of a New York property at 600 Third Avenue and the $132 million acquisition of a San Francisco property located at 123 Mission Street. It also assists Allied Partners and the Hadar family on a major dispute involving the sale of a property at One East 57th Street. Other clients include GMAC; Joseph Moinian; Metropolitan Transit Authority; Murray Hill Properties and Muss Development.

Proskauer Rose LLP

See firm details p.1365

The Firm: The practice is a recognized presence in real estate development, leasing and lending. However, it also demonstrates authority in the related securities, financing and loans, including work on private real estate funds and REITs. The team worked with Vornado Realty Trust on the lease to Citibank of a new, mixed-use development on the site of the former Alexander's department store at 731 Lexington Avenue. This followed its participation in leasing negotiations concerning a 700,000-sq-ft property to Bloomberg for its new world headquarters. A "*traditional, hard negotiating style*" is allied to long-term experience to deliver proficiency on a range of products. In another prestigious highlight, the team also represented JD Carlisle on the development, financing, leasing and sale of a cancer treatment center at New York University Hospital.

The Lawyers: **Lawrence Lipson** (see p.1298) is frequently feted for his development work and assistance on major leases. At the core of his practice are financings and the creation of private equity funds. "*A great lawyer and tougher than most*," he is widely respected for his "*encyclopedic knowledge of the law.*" He worked with DLJ Real Estate Capital Partners and JD Carlisle on several proceedings, including the joint venture developments of the Morton Square residential complex and the Cielo condominium tower. Rising star **Ronald Sernau** (see p.1319) is primarily associated with leasing on behalf of a loyal client base.

The Clients: The firm worked with both Barclays and Wachovia Bank regarding the origination of numerous mortgage and mezzanine loans, ranging from $15 million to $300 million. The team, which comprises more than 30 lawyers, also assisted Wachovia Bank on the $88 million financing of Ritz Carlton Hotel in New Orleans, Louisiana. Other clients include Bank of Scotland; Citigroup; DLJ Real Estate Capital Partners; GMAC; JD Carlisle; McDonald's; Morgan Stanley; UJA and Vornado Realty Trust.

Stroock & Stroock & Lavan LLP

The Firm: The traditional real estate practice historically targets midmarket conduit lending combined with parallel equity and condominium arms. This latter area has been key for the firm, as more condominiums are built instead of residential blocks in certain areas as a result of increasing land values. Although the firm is equally capable of advising financial institutions, its agile negotiating skills are more often deployed in association with a development practice. This may be due to its increasing involvement in more esoteric matters, such as mixed-use condominiums. The department previously orchestrated the acquisition of the leaseholds at the World Trade Center prior to 9/11 and has a continuing role regarding the redevelopment there on behalf of Silverstein Properties.
The Lawyers: "*The preeminent name at the firm,*" rainmaker **Leonard Boxer** is viewed as possessing "*that rare combination of long-standing experience in the market and excellent connections – he can get things done.*" His role is frequently strategic, although he still practices on the equity side with regional investors and remains the main contact for Larry Silverstein regarding the World Trade Center redevelopment. Two new entrants to the *Chambers* tables are the "*talented lawyer and respected counselor*" **Brian Diamond** and **Michel Evanusa**, who is deemed "*a cut above*" many in the market. Diamond was commended for his versatility in prominent cases and Evanusa won respect as a leading practitioner in the establishment of commercial and residential co-operatives and condominiums. Considered to exhibit "*the greatest knowledge of any lawyer in New York in this area, she knows all of the state regulations off the top of her head.*"
The Clients: The firm acted for Goldman Sachs on the development of the tallest office building in New Jersey and a major office building in the Battery Park complex in Lower Manhattan at Site 26. Another success story involved the new Bear Stearns world headquarters at 383 Madison Avenue. The team also advised the United Federation of Teachers on its move from the Park Avenue South area to Lower Manhattan in a complex combined acquisition and leasehold transaction. It is also working with the developer constructing the luxury condominium and retail space aspects of the new Bloomberg world headquarters.

Band 4

Bryan Cave Robinson LLP

The Firm: Hailed for its work on midsized real estate matters, the practice has won client confidence for its deep knowledge and ability on the low-income housing tax credit program. It also employs a professional and efficient manner on corporate planning, litigation, tax planning and general real estate transactions. Empire State Development retained the team in connection with the proposed acquisition of New York's James A. Farley Post Office building and the subsequent development of this site into the new Penn Station; the overall cost of development of the site will exceed $1 billion, with the purchase price for the existing property at $230 million.
The Lawyers: **Barry Ross** continues to work with Hudson Waterfront Associates on its development of the 50-acre Trump Place/Riverside South project. He also acted for Wachovia Bank National Association on the $505 million sale and leaseback of about 150 properties. "*Smart and really tenacious,*" he attracts clients with his fastidious approach: "*He clearly understands all of the legal issues but also aims to help us achieve what we are seeking.*"
The Clients: Asbury Partners continues to benefit from the group's counsel in connection with the 60-acre waterfront redevelopment in Asbury Park, New Jersey. It advised the National Consumer Cooperative Bank in relation to mortgage loans totaling more than $1.5 billion. The team also acted on behalf of AIMCO on a number of acquisitions, including a block of four apartment buildings on Columbus Avenue and 68th Street. Other clients include: Aareal Bank; Argent Ventures; Bank of New York; Colonnade Properties; Empire State Development; Hudson Waterfront Associates; Kmart; McGraw-Hill; Merrill Lynch; Metropolitan Housing Partners; Palladia and Wachovia Bank National Association.

Cadwalader, Wickersham & Taft LLP

See firm details p.1339
The Firm: The group focuses squarely on the origination, structuring and sale of high-leveraged debt and sophisticated financings, as well assisting on providing equity to transactions. On the lenders side, one of its drawing cards is CMBS, which constitute over two-thirds of its overall workload. As both debt and equity clients increase their investments in the market in reaction to a stalled leasing market, this ensures a steady stream of such work for the firm both in the USA and elsewhere, notably in London. In the main, the practice works on the financing side of transactions in preference to REITs, or the borrowers' side. Its deep knowledge in this area garnered the team industry support as "*absolutely top drawer.*"
The Lawyers: **Christopher White** (see p.1332) excels at debt and equity finance work, with one

observer dubbing it "*truly a dominant practice on the CMBS side.*" He enjoys a broad clientele and healthy respect in the market for his transactional skills and client relationships. He represented a foreign company in a joint venture with a US operator to acquire four casinos and 30 acres of land in Las Vegas; the deal made the company the largest private landowner in the downtown areas of the city. **Fredric Altschuler** (see p.1262) joins his colleague in *Chambers'* tables this year as a result of his "*flexible, collegial*" style. He "*comes up with a solution that works for everybody.*" He acted as special counsel to the lending group and loan servicers in connection with General Growth Properties' $12 billion acquisition of Rouse. He also advised Lehman Brothers regarding the $520 million acquisition financing for the State Street Bank headquarters in Boston. On behalf of the same client, he assisted on the similar $625 million acquisition financing for the John Hancock Tower and related portfolio by Beacon Properties.
The Clients: The firm represents the lending group consisting of Deutsche Bank, Goldman Sachs, Lehman Brothers and UBS on the origination of the $520 million mortgage financing of the Garden State Plaza Mall in Paramus, New Jersey. It assisted two lenders in connection with a mixed-use building on the renovated waterfront in Boston; the project's plans include an Intercontinental hotel and high-rise condominiums. It also represented one of the holders of five mezzanine loans linked to the acquisition of Bank of America Plaza in San Francisco. Other clients include: CSFB; JPMorgan Chase; Merrill Lynch and Morgan Stanley.

Debevoise & Plimpton LLP

See firm details p.1346
The Firm: The department centers on the buying and selling of real estate, especially trophy office buildings and shopping centers. For example, keystone client Westfield America retained the firm on the $520 million refinancing of Westfield Shoppingtown Garden State Plaza in northern New Jersey, one of the largest single-asset mortgage financings completed in 2004. On behalf of the same client, it assisted on a global credit facility in excess of $3 billion and representation on bids for Rouse and the GM mall portfolio. In addition to working on mortgage origination co-lending arrangements and refinancings, the group maintains a regular presence assisting on workouts and restructurings. The group's expertise on private equity and litigation assistance also garnered respect, with clients adding that they applaud its research abilities and its "*balanced view*" of matters.
The Lawyers: **Steven Alden** acts on the sale of major premises, representing Teachers' Insurance & Annuity Association on the $480 million sale of two New York city trophy office buildings that constitute an entire block in Manhattan. Peers noted that his amenable, low-key style

suits his real estate practice, which also includes loan sales, new financings and refinancings.

The Clients: The team acted for Prudential Financial in the sale by Prudential Real Estate Investors of PRICOA Property Investment Management (PPIM) to PPIM's senior management team. It works with Teachers' Insurance & Annuity Association nationwide, advising on its sale of a portfolio of ten mortgage loans to Morgan Stanley Mortgage Capital and on a separate $242 million transaction that covered office, multifamily and retail properties in seven states. It also counsels JPMorgan Investment Management on acquisitions, dispositions and joint ventures throughout the USA, including the acquisition of the Waterfront Corporate Center in Hoboken, New Jersey. Other clients include: Beacon Capital Partners; Carmel Partners; DaimlerChrysler; Equitable and Westfield America.

DLA Piper Rudnick Gray Cary US LLP

See firm details p.765

The Firm: The New York practice has expanded significantly in terms of both personnel and transactions undertaken. It runs a broad real estate practice, notably assisting on commercial real estate and high-rise residential development. The team's biggest recent coup is its representation of the Port Authority of New York and New Jersey as real estate counsel on the redevelopment of the World Trade Center site.

The Lawyers: **Martin Polevoy** (see p.1309) is an established player in the market whose authority is based on such work as representing the New York Times on the acquisition, construction loan and development of its new world headquarters on Eighth Avenue, a project totaling approximately $1 billion. He also advised Commerzbank on the acquisition of the Manhattan mall, which is valued at about $400 million.

The Clients: Cornerstone Real Estate Advisors hired the firm on a national basis for its real estate deals, including the purchase, sale and development of new properties for its pension fund clients. The group also acted for Lehman Brothers on the $160 million sale of its interest in its former world headquarters building at 3 World Financial Center. Other clients include the New York Times, Commerzbank and the Port Authority of New York and New Jersey.

Kramer Levin Naftalis & Frankel LLP

See firm details p.1357

The Firm: A high-end developer practice, it often advises on complicated condominium projects. The group acted on behalf of Muss Development on the development of a mixed-use retail and residential project in Queens, comprising approximately 750,000 sq-ft of retail space, 1200 residential units and 3000 parking spaces. Low and middle-income housing is also a burgeoning area, with the firm assisting on the privatization of various projects for property owners. Though more infrequently, it also undertakes restructuring work within the real estate sector.

The Lawyers: Counsel **Samuel Lindenbaum** (see p.1297) is considered by many to be "*the preeminent person in the land use area in New York.*" He has acted on many of the most significant transactions and is respected for his "*low-key and focused*" approach. "*He walks you through and tells you what you have to do.*" **Jay Neveloff** (see p.1304) regularly works with investors, bringing an "*intense and concentrated*" diligence to his work. Most notably, he is counseling developers The Related Companies and Apollo Real Estate on the preparation and negotiation of the condominium operational documents for the new Time Warner Center. He also prepared the residential offering plans and $1 billion sale of residential condominium units.

The Clients: The firm also represented Starwood Hotels in connection with the St. Regis Hotel in Manhattan and separately advised Trump Hotel and Casino Resorts on the sale of Trump Taj Mahal Casino in Atlantic City. Other clients include: Apollo Real Estate; BellWest; Muss Development; The Related Companies and Roosevelt Island Operating Corporation.

Latham & Watkins LLP

The Firm: Large-scale financings predominate, with regular assistance on developments and mixed-use projects. The team represents GE throughout the country on its national leasing program as well as on larger developments, including a mixed-use resort island in Florida. Clients were quick to praise the firm's "*extremely capable negotiators.*" The firm also works with Morgan Stanley as issuer, depositor and mortgage loan seller on a number of securitization deals, including an $847 million real estate mortgage investment conduit securitization.

The Lawyers: **Richard Chadakoff**, who heads the firm's global real estate practice group, is a respected player in the New York arena, where he targets the financial side of real estate. He closed a $340 million refinancing of a super mall for the Pyramid Company. On behalf of Apollo Real Estate Advisors, he concluded several mezzanine loans of both pledged equity and preferred equity. **Joshua Stein**'s high-end commercial practice demonstrates his noted abilities in complicated real estate financing and leasing, including the financing and leasing of hotel projects. He also counts acknowledged ground lease experience on his resume. He acted for German investment group Deutsche Immobilien Fonds on the purchase of a property at 140 Broadway for more than $450 million. He also negotiated on behalf of AvalonBay Communities for the largest wholefoods market supermarket lease in Manhattan at a new mixed-use project on Houston Street.

The Clients: Lawyers dealt with 80 separate loans for a large real estate portfolio financing aggregating $350 million on behalf of a joint venture between Health Care Property Investors and Strategic Ventures. Other clients include: Apollo Real Estate Advisors; AvalonBay Communities; BlackRock Financial Management; Calyon; DIFA; GE Capital; ING Real Estate; Kimco Realty and Morgan Stanley.

Band 5

Akin Gump Strauss Hauer & Feld LLP

See firm details p.477

The Firm: Better known for its tax practice and related corporate work, this department is pushing its boundaries to expand its real estate activity in New York, aiming to handle more sophisticated real estate financings. As a developing practice, it tends to focus on core transactional real estate matters such as acquisitions, developments and financings primarily from a borrower's perspective. Nevertheless, it does undertake some leasing and a fair amount of mezzanine lending work. Assistance from the firm's bankruptcy and litigation groups is also brought to bear on real estate matters.

The Lawyers: **Peter Miller** (see p.1301), formerly of Stroock & Stroock & Lavan LLP, heads the firm's New York real estate and finance group. A "*significant talent,*" he represents owners and developers, but is most readily associated with activity on behalf of lenders, including some mezzanine financing. He combines "*a good sense of humor with a good work ethic and a sense of proportion in the deals.*" His repertoire encompasses financings, purchases, developments and joint ventures.

The Clients: The team worked with an investment bank on the development and financing of its new 1.2 million-sq-ft world headquarters, including the structuring of a $700 million synthetic lease. It also acted for a major New York developer concerning the $200 million, 78-acre luxury Bacara resort and spa in Santa Barbara, California. Other clients include: Apollo Real Estate Advisors; Bear Stearns; Feil Organization; Oaktree Capital Management and Zev Wolfson.

Brown Raysman Millstein Felder & Steiner LLP

See firm details p.1338

The Firm: This practice advises on real estate finance transactions across multiple industry sectors, including hotels, office buildings and shopping centers. The scope of the practice also incorporates prominent leases, acquisitions and dispositions, including condominium conversion work both statewide and nationally. "*Smart, aggressive and thoughtful,*" the firm also operates a large affordable housing practice, primarily on behalf of New York banks and Wall Street institutions. In addition, the "*strong team of partners and a capable junior team*" assist a number of hedge funds and opportunity funds, and is considered a strong contender in structured finance and securitizations.

The Lawyers: Jeffrey Steiner (see p.1324), chairman of the business finance department, focuses on the finance side, working with large institutions that invest in various developments and properties. Clients compared his "*quality lawyering*" to that of market leaders and were quick to praise his cognizance of internal banking issues. His colleague **Raymond Sanseverino** (see p.1316) represented Mellon Bank on the lease extension of its 1.5 million-sq-ft headquarters in Pittsburgh, one of the largest leases closed in the USA in 2004.

The Clients: The Dreyfus Corporation retained the firm to handle its tenant lease for a 377,000-sq-ft property at 200 Park Avenue. The group acted for landlord Brookfield Financial Properties for the lease involving 470,000 sq ft at One World Financial Center, one of the largest leases completed in downtown Manhattan in 2004. It is working with the National Sports Museum as tenant on the proposed lease of retail and office space in lower Manhattan; the transaction involves Liberty Bond financing. The firm is separately advising Thomson Financial on its leasing of a 150,000-sq-ft expansion at 195 Broadway. Other clients include Citibank; CSFB; Mack-Cali Realty Corporation; Massachusetts Mutual Life Insurance Company; McDonald's; Mellon Financial Group; RFR Realty; Rockrose Development; Shorenstein and UBS Warburg.

Dechert

See firm details p.1547

The Firm: This growing practice engages in single, large multiple-asset loans for acquisitions and occasionally for refinancing. The team proved proficient on restructured financing, often representing lending banks as underwriters in CMBS deals. It also concentrates on the structuring of loans, including complex mezzanine loans and mortgage-backed securities. On behalf of a national bank, the firm handled multiple-asset loans linked to the $825 million acquisition financing of a major Chicago office tower. In a similar transaction of equal stature, it worked with a national bank on its multifaceted, complex $750 million financing for the purchase of a headquarters building in San Francisco.

The Lawyers: Joseph Forte (see p.1280) deals with real estate finance and workouts, including some larger securitized loans and transactions. "*Sharp and visible*" in the market, he advises foreign banks investing in the USA, either directly or as part of a syndicate. Described as the dean of capital markets securitization in real estate, he also won respect for his "*broad connections and experience*." Observers said: "*He would create a market wherever he was.*" Firmwide, the arrival of several attorneys specializing in asset and mortgage-backed securities has led to a notable increase in such work.

The Clients: The team worked with a national bank in originating loans on two of the largest retail centers in the Southwest – the $300 million Desert Passage mall and the $380 million Fashion Show mall in Las Vegas. It also represented the issuer in connection with the origination of a $500 million loan to fund the Department of Transportation's new headquarters in DC. Clients also include: Aegon USA Realty Advisors; Bank of America; Calyon Securities (USA); Gramercy Capital; JPMorgan Chase; Morgan Stanley; New York State Teachers' Retirement System; PB Capital and Zara USA.

Katten Muchin Zavis Rosenman

See firm details p.769

The Firm: The department combines advice on large and notable real estate acquisitions with capital markets-oriented mezzanine lending assistance for a client base of developers, owners and lenders. Some of its more notable achievements include Lehman Brothers' $215 million sale of the historic Park Central Hotel and a separate $142 million purchase of ground lease and improvements at the Sports Illustrated Building at 135 West 50th Street.

The Lawyers: Real estate cochair Marc Shapiro is the leading name in the department. He counsels the US Real Estate Lenders Association industry group of debt and equity providers, and assists investors and lenders in the hotel and hospitality industry.

The Clients: The firm assisted on the $77 million acquisition financing of six Summerfield Suites hotels located in five states and separately counseled Ramsfield Hospitality Finance on the $19.5 million mortgage and $6.5 million mezzanine financings of a 311-room hotel on the island of Kauai, Hawaii. Other clients include Lehman Brothers and Property Markets Group.

Simpson Thacher & Bartlett LLP

See firm details p.1370

The Firm: A strong rebound in the New York real estate market has been matched by the department's assistance on real estate M&A and finance transactions. It notably advised on the separate acquisitions of three publicly traded real estate companies. The vast majority of its work is international in flavor and the firm is particularly active in the London market. It counseled the Blackstone Group on the purchase of the $1.2 billion Deutsche Bank portfolio of 51 properties located in nine European countries, which included a $1.1 billion secured acquisition credit facility from Citibank.

The Lawyers: Scott Kobak's (see p.1294) practice includes assistance to real estate opportunity funds and financial institutions. "*Personable, smart and responsive*," he worked with the Carlyle Group on the $300 million acquisition and development of a 550-unit luxury condominium project in Times Square and its related $240 million con-

struction financing with Hypo Real Estate and HSBC. His partner Greg Ressa is the main contact for trophy client the Blackstone Group.

The Clients: The Blackstone Group remains the firm's key client. The firm's caseload for the company includes the $3.2 billion purchase of Extended Stay America, where the public company was taken private via an LBO involving $2.6 billion in securitized mortgage financing. Abroad, the team advised the Blackstone Group on the $1 billion sale of the Savoy Group and $1.25 billion acquisition of luxury resorts and golf course group Boca Resorts. Other clients include: Carlyle Group; Hypo Real Estate; JER Real Estate Partners and Prime Hospitality.

Wachtell, Lipton, Rosen & Katz

See firm details p.1375

The Firm: This relatively small practice tends not to operate in traditional real estate spheres, preferring to focus on high-end strategic real estate transactions frequently involving Wall Street investment bankers. Its mainstay is REIT M&A. For example, the group successfully represented the Taubman REIT in its defense of an attempted hostile takeover by the Simon REIT.

The Lawyers: Robin Panovka's (see p.1307) key client remains Silverstein Properties and the World Trade Center redevelopment. He acts as lead coordinating counsel with several other firms on various aspects; these include the negotiations with the landowner in connection with the ground lease and the development of the Freedom Tower and other buildings. He has been credited with having built a strong REIT practice at the firm, extending its M&A reputation into the real estate field. **Michael Benner** (see p.1266) is heavily involved in cross-border transactions on the REIT side in Australia and Singapore. The real estate practice also benefits from the firm's eminent corporate and tax lawyers.

The Clients: The firm worked with Lend Lease in a complex disposition of its US businesses and is separately acting for Apollo in the structuring of both US and European private equity opportunity funds. It also advised Hometown America on its purchase of public REIT Chateau Communities. Other clients include Taubman REIT, Security Capital Group and Silverstein Properties.

Other Notable Practitioners

Recommended for his business acumen, **Robert Ivanhoe** (see p.1290) of Greenberg Traurig LLP is the national practice leader in a real estate practice that draws from its nationwide office network. He assists on major acquisitions and financings and was the lead lawyer on the $675 million purchase and $900 million financing of the New York Plaza Hotel for Elad Properties. He also worked with Gale on its $600 purchase, joint venture and financing of an office portfolio in conjunction with SL Green Realty.

TAX

New York
Leading firms (Tax)

[1] CLEARY GOTTLIEB STEEN & HAMILTON *New York*
CRAVATH, SWAINE & MOORE LLP *New York*
DAVIS POLK & WARDWELL *New York*
SULLIVAN & CROMWELL LLP *New York*

[2] DEBEVOISE & PLIMPTON LLP *New York*
SIMPSON THACHER & BARTLETT LLP *New York*
SKADDEN, ARPS, SLATE, MEAGHER *New York*
WACHTELL, LIPTON, ROSEN & KATZ *New York*
WEIL, GOTSHAL & MANGES LLP *New York*

[3] CADWALADER, WICKERSHAM & TAFT *New York*
FRIED, FRANK, HARRIS, SHRIVER *New York*
MILBANK, TWEED, HADLEY & MCCLOY *New York*
PAUL, WEISS, RIFKIND, WHARTON *New York*
ROBERTS & HOLLAND LLP *New York*
SHEARMAN & STERLING LLP *New York*

[4] CAHILL GORDON & REINDEL *New York*
KIRKLAND & ELLIS LLP *New York*
MCDERMOTT WILL & EMERY *New York*
PAUL, HASTINGS, JANOFSKY & WALKER *New York*

Firms are listed alphabetically in each band.

Band 1

Cleary Gottlieb Steen & Hamilton LLP

See firm details p.1342

The Firm: This group of "*astonishing and unrivaled, quality practitioners*" is, according to clients, "*an ensemble of the crème de la crème of tax lawyers.*" In addition to possessing one of the largest financial products practices in the country, it is highly praised for its tax planning and associated dispute resolution expertise. With its 30-attorney team, the cadre "*is geared up to deal with the most intricate and sophisticated*" national and multinational M&A, joint venture and startup issues, among others. It provided post-acquisition tax advice to Bank of America in relation to its stock-for-stock merger with Fleet-Boston, valued at an estimated $47 billion. In another matter, it advised long-term client Texas Pacific Group in a series of acquisitions and the formation of its newest private equity fund. On behalf of the Ontario Teachers' Pension Plan, the team helped orchestrate the formation of a joint venture with AIG to acquire a portfolio of contracted power plants from El Paso. Market sources respect these "*bright lights*" immensely "*for not getting into tit-for-tat arguments.*"

The Lawyers: Clients praised "*approachable and prominent*" **Leslie Samuels** (see p.1316) who has been heavily involved in international tax planning, cross-border M&A and joint ventures for large corporate clients. He recently advised Fomento Económico Mexicano in the unwinding of its Mexican and US relationships with the Belgian brewing company InBev, formerly known as Interbrew. "*Intelligent*" **Yaron Reich**

(see p.1312) is commended for his transactional M&A, cross-border restructuring and international experience. He represented Texas Pacific Group in its $2.4 billion acquisition of Portland General Electric from Enron. He also advised long-standing German client Henkel KGaA in the exchange of its 28.8% stake in The Clorox Company. Financial products "*guru*" **Edward Kleinbard** (see p.1293) and "*deep thinker*" **James Peaslee** (see p.1308) are "*always looking ahead to see where the market is going,*" clients say. They bring "*the intellectual points that everyone will follow to the table.*" Another player in the financial area is "*trustworthy*" **Erika Nijenhuis** (see p.1305), who delivers "*extremely valued judgment calls.*"

The Clients: Bank of America; Henkel KGaA; Morgan Stanley; Citigroup; Texas Pacific Group and the Ontario Teachers' Pension Plan.

Cravath, Swaine & Moore LLP

See firm details p.1344

The Firm: Clients endorsed these "*technically outstanding*" tax specialists for their command of highly complex international and domestic transactional matters. The tax practice has advised on a range of multifaceted proceedings including securities offerings, banking and lease and project financings. As expected of such a dominant force in M&A, the tax team is able to draw on a wealth of experience with some of the industry's most high-flying deals. In 2004, it helped negotiate the tax aspects of Mandalay Resort Group's acquisition by MGM Mirage for $7.9 billion; the combination has resulted in the largest US casino company. The group also attracts a "*fabulous client roster*" by handling "*any matter thrown at them with poise and flair,*" particularly when it is associated with controversy and tax planning issues.

The Lawyers: **Michael Schler** (see p.1318) "*cuts to the chase in complex matters and works to a resolution that accomplishes everybody's goals.*" Clients said they retain this "*devoted and thoughtful adviser*" who also possesses "*deal sense and the intellect of a rocket scientist.*" **Steve Gordon** (see p.1284) has been "*working his magic*" in the tax field for almost 25 years and "*gets great results for clients.*" His practice includes public offerings, syndicated bank loans and partnership tax. Clients prize the "*soft-spoken and effective*" **William Brannan** (see p.1268) for his "*great commercial instinct.*" He is often retained on "*the largest, most demanding cases,*" especially those involving extensive experience in partnership, real estate and REIT matters. "*Unperturbed*" **Patricia Geoghegan** (see p.1282) impresses clients with her "*levelheaded and clear-cut style.*" She won respect in the areas of leasing tax, structured finance and employee benefits. In a significant loss for the firm, lead-

ing light Lewis Steinberg left to join UBS investment bank as managing director. The veteran had been at the firm for about 20 years and worked on such headline deals as the merger between Sprint and Nextel Communications. **The Clients:** DreamWorks; Bristol-Myers Squibb; Bacardi; IBM; Royal Dutch Shell; Time Warner; BAE SYSTEMS; Lucent Technologies; Nestlé and Vivendi Universal.

Davis Polk & Wardwell

See firm details p.1345

The Firm: While the department advises on a broad array of commercial tax, its role as a leader on the transactional side won most applause from clients. This "*deep bench is smashing it across the board.*" With a dozen "*dedicated and highly effective*" tax lawyers, it plays a leading role in developing CDOs for high-status clients such as CSFB, Bank of America and Citigroup. The "*top-notch*" group also gathered accolades for its tax controversy work, obtaining reversals in groundbreaking cases. Regarding state taxation matters, the firm has successfully represented international and domestic companies before the New York State Tax Commission and the Court of Appeals. Furthermore it deftly covers matters concerning investment funds, domestic and international M&A, and offshore insurance for large corporations. "*You just can't go wrong with this choice,*" one client concluded.

The Lawyers: Clients pitched **Dana Trier** (see p.1328) as not only "*a delight,*" but also a sophisticated operator who possesses "*superb wisdom on how to best deal with complicated tax issues.*" The lead financial products adviser to Citigroup and CSFB also shows flair in matters relating to investment partnerships, structured finance, cross-border M&A and derivatives. Also capturing the market's attention is **Avishai Shachar** (see p.1320), who clients rated as "*smart and extremely focused.*" He was commended for his leading role on high-profile mergers such as Comcast's combination with AT&T Broadband. Financial products expert **Samuel Dimon** (see p.1276) is "*thoughtful and shows terrific common sense,*" clients note. Hot on his heels is "*creative*" **Po Sit** (see p.1322), who is considered "*smart and reasonable.*"

The Clients: Deutsche Bank; CSFB; Bank of America; JPMorgan and Citigroup.

Sullivan & Cromwell LLP

See firm details p.1373

The Firm: A "*fine tax group run by geniuses who know how the tax market operates,*" clients say. This firm offers "*both, vast quantity and terrific quality.*" The "*bright lights of this team*" are powered by immense expertise on private equity, partnerships, real estate finance and dispute resolution. Market leaders appreciate the group's

New York
Leading individuals (Tax)

1
CANELLOS Peter *Wachtell Lipton*, New York
ROSEN Matthew *Skadden Arps*, New York
SCHLER Michael *Cravath Swaine*, New York
TRIER Dana *Davis Polk*, New York

2
BLESSING Peter *Shearman & Sterling*, New York
GORDON Stephen *Cravath Swaine*, New York
HEITNER Kenneth *Weil Gotshal*, New York
REINHOLD Richard *Willkie Farr*, New York
SCHWARTZ Jodi *Wachtell Lipton*, New York
SHACHAR Avishai *Davis Polk*, New York
SOLOMON Andrew *Sullivan & Cromwell*, New York
TAYLOR Willard *Sullivan & Cromwell*, New York
TODRYS Steven *Simpson Thacher*, New York
YOUNGWOOD Alfred *Paul Weiss*, New York

3
BERG Andrew *Debevoise & Plimpton*, New York
BLANCHARD Kimberly *Weil Gotshal*, New York
BRANNAN William *Cravath Swaine*, New York
COHEN Ben *Cahill Gordon*, New York
FRIEDMAN Gary *Debevoise & Plimpton*, New York
GALLAGHER Patrick *Kirkland & Ellis*, New York
GOLDRING Stuart *Weil Gotshal*, New York
HART John *Simpson Thacher*, New York
LEE Carolyn *Roberts & Holland*, New York
PHILLIPS IV Barnet *Skadden Arps*, New York
POLLACK Martin *Weil Gotshal*, New York
REICH Yaron *Cleary Gottlieb*, New York
SAMUELS Leslie *Cleary Gottlieb*, New York
SCHARFSTEIN Joel *Fried Frank*, New York
STAFFARONI Robert *Debevoise & Plimpton*, New York
SWARTZ Linda *Cadwalader Wickersham*, New York

4
AMDUR Martin *Weil Gotshal*, New York
ANDERSEN Richard *Arnold & Porter*, New York
CASSANOS Robert *Fried Frank*, New York
CREAMER Ronald *Sullivan & Cromwell*, New York
DREYFUS James *Fulbright & Jaworski*, New York
EINHORN David *Wachtell Lipton*, New York
GARDNER Stephen *Kronish Lieb*, New York
GEOGHEGAN Patricia *Cravath Swaine*, New York
HAIMS Bruce *Debevoise & Plimpton*, New York
INDOE William *Sullivan & Cromwell*, New York
LEVY Lisa *Fried Frank*, New York
MASON Andrew *Sullivan & Cromwell*, New York
MAYO David *Gibson Dunn*, New York
PAUL Deborah *Wachtell Lipton*, New York
PHILLIPS Greer *Kirkland & Ellis*, New York
ROSEN Arthur *McDermott Will*, New York
ROSEN Burt *Debevoise & Plimpton*, New York
ROSEN Seth *Debevoise & Plimpton*, New York
SAMUELS Jeffrey *Paul Weiss*, New York
SCHNABEL David *Debevoise & Plimpton*, New York
SHORT Andrew *Paul Hastings*, New York
SICULAR David *Paul Weiss*, New York
SILBERBERG Marc *Weil Gotshal*, New York
THURSTON Sally *Skadden Arps*, New York
WOLLMAN Diana *Sullivan & Cromwell*, New York

Up-and-coming individuals
FURCI Peter *Debevoise & Plimpton*, New York
KARIG Adele *Debevoise & Plimpton*, New York
RUSMAN Jared *Wachtell Lipton*, New York

Individuals are listed alphabetically in each band.

"*highly professional and wonderful approach*" in dealing with joint ventures and financial instrument developments. The firm's distinguished M&A expertise helps ensure a steady flow of work, though it often attracts clients who primarily seek its tax expertise. This includes non-US clients who retain the team to handle the US aspects of cross-border transactions, as well as controversy-related issues such as IRS advance pricing agreements. The team is celebrated for its overall "*insight and breadth in dealing with the most complex transactions.*"

The Lawyers: "*Terrific business lawyer*" **Andrew Solomon** (see p.1322), the managing partner of the New York tax group has "*great insight and tremendous judgment.*" Clients found his "*good-humored nature*" as valuable as his "*balance and perspective.*" A sophisticated practice that includes tax planning and dispute resolution helped bolster his profile. Other interests include cross-border acquisitions, joint ventures and spin-offs. He also frequently advises on the tax angle of complex financial products. **Willard Taylor** (see p.1327) "*has an intellect that cuts to the heart of the matter,*" clients said. This "*extremely sharp tax specialist*" is renowned for a broad array of international transactions, including M&A. He has also represented foreign and domestic corporations before the IRS and is "*always up-to-date on the latest tax legislation.*" Clients said the "*dynamic*" tax partner **Diana Wollman** (see p.1333) has truly earned her reputation as a "*diligent, accessible and energetic*" player. Her strong suit is an aptitude in planning and dealing with transactional tax matters for domestic and foreign corporations, investment companies and partnerships. Also in the running is partnership expert **Andrew Mason** (see p.1299), who "*has terrific business judgment*" and "*gets things rolling.*" **William Indoe** (see p.1290) and the "*careful, smart and hard-working*" **Ronald Creamer** (see p.1273) also won plaudits for their prolific practices, while on the financial products side, **David Hariton** (see p.1286) is recognized for his "*top-notch talent.*" He is associated with complex financial instruments and other transactions for top-flight clients such as Barclays Capital and Morgan Stanley. "*Rising star*" **Jeffrey Hochberg** (see p.1288) also impresses both rivals and clients alike.

The Clients: Allianz; Bank of New York; Philips; Barclays Capital; Morgan Stanley; Diageo; Securities Industry Association and UBS.

Band 2

Debevoise & Plimpton LLP
See firm details p.1346

The Firm: Leading market sources portrayed the team as one that offers a "*fantastic*" service without the hassle, further bolstered by a "*wonderful culture.*" It won commendation for its expertise in areas such as investment fund formation, financial products and M&A tax planning. Its aptitude in capital markets and partnership-related matters was also noted. Clients endorsed the team's "*reasonable prices,*" marking it as excellent value on a broad range of intricate matters. "*Some of its most talented members*" recently advised Air Liquide, the world's largest producer of industrial gases, in its $3.4 billion acquisition of Messer Griesheim's industrial gas business. The group also assisted private equity firm Clayton, Dubilier & Rice in the $610 million acquisition of the worldwide business of Culligan from a subsidiary of Vivendi of France.

The Lawyers: "*Thorough*" **Robert Staffaroni** continued to impress clients with "*impeccable*" work. He is highly rated for his public and private financing transactions for airlines, though his broader practice also involves derivatives for both dealers and non-dealers, generally relating to hedge funds and other nontraditional asset classes. **Gary Friedman** (see p.1281) is highlighted for his "*methodical*" approach to solving problems, clients said. "*He thinks through issues cautiously,*" to simplify complex matters. His focus is on federal income taxation with a particular emphasis on M&A and international taxation, always using "*the most advantageous alternatives.*" **Andrew Berg** has "*excellent practical judgment,*" clients say. He is "*an immensely broad-gauged*" transactional lawyer who is skilled in acquisitions, dispositions, debt restructurings and joint ventures. "*Unflappable*" leader of the tax department **Bruce Haims** is noted for his "*intelligent approach*" in dealing with M&A, partnerships, investment funds and executive compensation issues. He is also proficient in tax controversies for individuals and companies as related to the media, communications and entertainment sectors. In one interesting development, he advised on the proposed spin-off of Cablevision's VOOM satellite service and their national programming services. **Burt Rosen** "*was born a tax lawyer,*" commentators said, referring to his expert handling of the tax aspects of financings, including M&A, cross-border and public transactions. He is part of the project finance and structured finance practice group within the tax department, and regularly advises DaimlerChrysler, Rolls-Royce, GE and Protective Life. "*Loyal and good-humored*" **David Schnabel** "*speaks a language everybody can understand, not baffling legalese,*" clients said. He recently provided tax advice to NBC and GE in the $14 billion merger of NBC and Vivendi Universal Entertainment. "*Articulate*" **Seth Rosen** focuses on M&A, refinancing and restructurings with particular emphasis on the insurance industry. In this area, he has navigated through compliance and planning issues, capital-raising transactions and product development. His clients include AXA Financial, Hartford Financial Services Group and Swiss Reinsurance America Holding Corporation. "*Consistent*" **Peter Furci** advised Clayton Dubilier & Rice and Kinko's regarding its sale of

New York
Leading individuals
(Tax: Financial Products)

1. **BROWN Dickson** *Simpson Thacher*, New York
   DIMON Samuel *Davis Polk*, New York
   HARITON David *Sullivan & Cromwell*, New York
   KLEINBARD Edward *Cleary Gottlieb*, New York
   NIRENBERG David *Orrick Herrington*, New York
   PEASLEE James *Cleary Gottlieb*, New York
   SCARBOROUGH Robert *Freshfields*, New York

2. **HOOD Thomas** *Mayer Brown*, New York
   KAYLE Bruce *Milbank Tweed*, New York
   MILLER David *Cadwalader Wickersham*, New York
   MORGAN Charles *Skadden Arps*, New York
   NIJENHUIS Erika *Cleary Gottlieb*, New York
   SIT Po *Davis Polk*, New York
   WALLACE W Kirk *Skadden Arps*, New York

Up-and-coming individuals
HOCHBERG Jeffrey *Sullivan & Cromwell*, New York

Individuals are listed alphabetically in each band.

Kinko's to FedEx. **Adele Karig** is cultivating an increasingly visible profile particularly among clients, who described her as an effective operator who "*will dig in her heels and get on with things.*"

The Clients: AlpInvest Partners; Clayton, Dubilier & Rice; Kelso & Company; Oxygen Media; American Airlines; KBC Financial Products; Zurich Capital Markets; Westpac Banking and AMVESCAP.

Simpson Thacher & Bartlett LLP

See firm details p.1370

The Firm: Clients endorsed this "*extremely professional and highly responsive*" tax group for its bespoke approach to solving the most complex transactional and financial tax matters. Its wide-ranging set of clients – including major multinational companies, investment banks and wealthy individuals – feel "*this outstanding team really knows its stuff.*" The practice encompasses a broad range of matters, but is principally focused on the tax aspects of M&A transactions, complex financial instruments and others. A significant portion of its time is devoted to financial transactions, which range from stock and debt financings to multisecurity, debt-equity hybrids or innovative securitizations. It also deals with the formation of investment funds, the structuring of real estate investments, and cross-border financing and investment activity. The group played a vital role in structuring the recent formation of Wachovia Securities. It also helped marshal KKR's acquisition of Legrand SA in France and Royal Vendex in the Netherlands. **The Lawyers:** "*Superb*" **Steven Todrys** (see p.1327) is a "*clued-up and accomplished*" adviser whose recent work involved JPMorgan Chase's acquisition of Bank One. He is also the principal tax counsel to KKR on various trans-

actions. A new addition to the rankings, **John Hart** (see p.1287) is a "*true leader*" for intricate private equity work, clients say. His "*thoughtfulness and intelligent outlook*" made him "*one of the go-to guys.*" He frequently represents key private investment fund sponsors in fund formation matters, including The Blackstone Group, The Carlyle Group, CIBC, Citigroup and CSFB. On the financial products side, "*brilliant*" **Dickson Brown** (see p.1269) "*is extremely experienced and has the ability to work through problems,*" clients say. He represents both bankers and issuers in variations of convertible debt securities.

The Clients: Federal-Mogul; JPMorgan; Coors Brewing Co; KKR; GenTek; Hellman & Friedman; Ripplewood Holdings; Silver Lake Partners and Sunbeam.

Skadden, Arps, Slate, Meagher & Flom LLP & Affiliates

See firm details p.1372

The Firm: Complex work for big-ticket clients serves as evidence of this group's successful development. According to clients, the 14-partner tax department is a collection of "*professional, innovative and thorough*" specialists. The group demonstrates "*terrific team work*" and draws resources from its outstanding international network. Its formidable M&A reputation means that the team never has to look far for quality cross referrals, and a steady diet of tax controversies include representation before the IRS and other litigation. On the corporate side, the team recently advised MacAndrews & Forbes in its acquisitions of two security companies, Allied Security and Barton Protective Services. Furthermore it was involved in the reorganizations of Alamosa PCS and Fairfield Manufacturing, and separately restructured Revlon's debt through exchange offers and rights offerings.

The Lawyers: "*Formidably bright*" **Matthew Rosen** (see p.1314) is dubbed "*the spin-off king*" for his command of that area of law. Other features of his broader practice involve M&A, joint ventures, private equity and partnerships. Clients lauded "*Renaissance man*" **Barnet Phillips** (see p.1308) as a "*user-friendly and perceptive*" tax lawyer. He especially impresses in REITs but was also noted for his partnerships, restructurings, and charitable organizations work. **Sally Thurston** (see p.1327) is "*firm but fair,*" exhibiting panache in US and international M&A, joint ventures, restructurings and spin-offs. "*Gifted*" **Charles Morgan** (see p.1302), concentrates on advisory work in connection with financial products, hedge funds and private equity transactions. Also commended was the "*analytically minded*" **Kirk Wallace** (see p.1330), whose practice emphasizes securitization.

The Clients: MacAndrews & Forbes; Citibank; Dividend Capital Trust REIT; Merrill Lynch; Alamosa PCS and Fairfield Manufacturing.

Wachtell, Lipton, Rosen & Katz

See firm details p.1375

The Firm: The cadre of "*top-notch*" names delivers such quality of work that one client wondered "*do they feed their lawyers success and talent over at Wachtell Lipton?*" Its flourishing corporate practice further bolstered its "*terrific and technically excellent*" tax practice. In a recent matter it acted for Reckson Associates Realty in connection with the disposition of its industrial real estate portfolio involving redemption of partnership interests for real estate. Advising CSX Transportation, it was involved in a number of spin-offs in relation to its Conrail division. Moreover it advised Cable & Wireless on the sale of its US subsidiaries through Chapter 11 proceedings and a negotiated consensual plan. Another prominent transaction was its representation of MetLife with respect to the sale of SSRM Holdings.

The Lawyers: **Peter Canellos** (see p.1270) is, according to clients, in "*a league of his own.*" He won plaudits from rivals for being "*unassuming and exceptionally reasonable.*" With "*intelligence and terrific common sense,*" the head of the department delivers advice on the tax implications of financings, M&A and dispositions. "*Energetic*" **Jodi Schwartz** (see p.1319) devotes most of her time to the tax aspects of M&A and earned respect for dealing with "*the most complex*" transactions. Clients described her as "*hard working, efficient and always on the ball.*" **David Einhorn** (see p.1277) specializes in REIT and partnership matters and is considered "*one of the veterans*" within the team, while "*driven*" **Deborah Paul** (see p.1307) "*does a brilliant job for her clients.*" She is particularly noted for her experience in international proceedings. "*Bright*" **Jared Rusman** (see p.1315) also impresses on the transactional side.

The Clients: CSX; Hometown America; MacAndrews & Forbes; Goldman Sachs; Cable & Wireless; MetLife and Reckson Associates Realty.

Weil, Gotshal & Manges LLP

See firm details p.1378

The Firm: This team enjoys "*true eminence*" due to its extensive proficiency in key areas, including tax, cross-border M&A and bankruptcy. The group was extensively involved in tax planning and transactional work for Vivendi, Invensys, Millennium Chemicals and GE. The firm's international presence is an advantage, and often benefits clients who harmonize the international and domestic tax aspects of particular transactions. The group is also noted for doing "*an amazing job*" representing clients before the IRS and US Treasury, according to market sources. The team also counsels companies on matters such as federal and state payroll taxes.

The Lawyers: "*Wonderful counselor*" **Kenneth Heitner** (see p.1287) has been occupied with tax planning and transactional work for principal clients such as Vivendi, Invensys and GE, while the "*marvelous*" **Stuart Goldring** (see p.1284) wins kudos from clients as one of "*the best bankruptcy specialists around.*" "*Knowledgeable, sensible and sound,*" **Martin Pollack** (see p.1309) has wide-ranging capability in tax planning and transactional work, advising the likes of Great Lakes Chemical, UnitedHealthcare, Enron, Broadview Capital and GE Capital. "*Outstanding*" **Kimberly Blanchard** (see p.1267) is praised for her international transactions that often involve restructurings, M&A and joint ventures. This "*gifted*" practitioner is also valued for her knowledge of partnerships, real estate and exempt organization matters. "*Veteran*" **Martin Amdur** (see p.1262) is well versed in the formation of private venture capital partnerships and other transactions, clients say. Other interests involve international financings and real estate investments. "*M&A guru*" **Marc Silberberg** (see p.1321) gained credibility for his tax planning and transactional work for luminaries such as Thomas H. Lee Partners, Capital Z Investment Partners, Apax Partners, Hellman & Friedman and The DIRECTV Group.

The Clients: Merrill Lynch; Viacom; Millennium Chemicals; Broadview Capital; DLJ Merchant Banking Partners; Centre Partners; GE Capital; Great Lakes Chemical; Broadview Capital; UnitedHealthcare; Kroll, Zolfo Cooper and Enron.

Band 3

Cadwalader, Wickersham & Taft LLP
See firm details p.1339

The Firm: Clients applauded this immensely "*proactive, responsive and helpful*" tax team for its "*sophisticated and diverse*" practice. Market analysts perceive "*it is gaining strength and is on the up.*" The group offered tax counsel to The Renco Group in a joint venture with MacAndrews & Forbes Holdings to form a new entity that will own AM General. The "*results-oriented*" team also acted for Pfizer in its acquisition of Esperion Therapeutics and in its acquisition of Pharmacia. Other high-profile cases include TeleCorp's acquisition by AT&T Wireless.

The Lawyers: "*Brainy*" **Linda Swartz** (see p.1325) enters the tables due to her international M&A and partnership work. She also acts for public and private companies on tax matters concerning restructurings, joint ventures and spin-offs. Moreover, she regularly advises clients regarding high-yield debt offerings, derivatives and structured finance. Commentators said the "*fantastically smart*" **David Miller** (see p.1301) is a "*terrific*" financial products attorney. His work has involved derivatives and CDOs.

The Clients: Pfizer; Banc of America Securities; Bear Stearns; Barclays Bank; UBS Securities; Lehman Brothers; TIAA-CREF; Northwest Airlines; Burger King; American Home Mortgage; Skandia Insurance and Klesch & Company.

Fried, Frank, Harris, Shriver & Jacobson LLP
See firm details p.1349

The Firm: This respected firm has a "*top-drawer*" team, whose enviable national reach offers expertise on matters such as complex domestic and cross-border M&A, joint ventures, spin-offs and restructurings. It recently represented BellSouth Corporation in its $41 billion acquisition with SBC Communications of AT&T Wireless Services. In the real estate area it advised Goldman Sachs Capital Partners and the Whitehall Group in the $1.1 billion acquisition of National Golf Properties, a publicly traded REIT. The firm is "*on the ball*" concerning cross-border taxation issues, resulting in its enduring Canadian connections. It has advised Assicurazioni Generali, one of the world's largest insurance companies concerning the sale of Business Men's Assurance Company of America to subsidiaries of The Royal Bank of Canada.

The Lawyers: Clients lauded "*bright*" **Joel Scharfstein** (see p.1317) as "*a switched-on*" operator whose work has included acquisitions, divestitures, partnership transactions, investment partnerships and restructurings. "*Clued-up*" **Robert Cassanos** (see p.1270) "*knows how to combine technical expertise with getting the deal done,*" clients say. His practice embraces M&A, joint ventures and complex financial products, with particular emphasis on US and Canadian cross-border transactions. Other interests include real estate acquisitions, financings and REITs. Moving into the limelight is **Lisa Levy** (see p.1297), who received similarly warm praise as "*a smart and personable business counsel.*"

The Clients: Goldman Sachs; JPMorgan Chase; Forstmann Little; Procter & Gamble; Assicurazioni Generali; Merck; Nexfor; Rio Tinto; Televisa and TransCanada.

Milbank, Tweed, Hadley & McCloy

The Firm: The tax team is able to punch above its weight, dealing with an array of comprehensive issues despite its comparatively smaller size. Clients were also quick to applaud this "*effective and consistent*" group for its strength concerning financial products and structured transactions. It also offers wide-ranging knowledge on matters relating to US and foreign securities offerings.

The Lawyers: "*Extremely talented*" tax department chair **Bruce Kayle** is well versed in financial products, sophisticated committee work and restructurings. Clients say he "*possesses an exceptionally clear mind*" and adds strength "*to whatever the issue is.*"

The Clients: The team advises a range of domestic and foreign clients as well as wealthy individuals.

Paul, Weiss, Rifkind, Wharton & Garrison LLP
See firm details p.1362

The Firm: Interviewees paint a picture of a "*talented group*" with expertise in M&A, partnership work and private equity. This "*extremely effective and energetic*" team is able to deal with "*anything put before it,*" clients note. Others praise its resourceful investment funds practice, which comes in handy when dealing with equity-related matters. It is admired for its "*sophisticated*" work in the entertainment industry and won praise for its advice to "*top-draw clients*" Time Warner and Viacom.

The Lawyers: The "*respected and powerful*" team's success is partly due to the "*vivacious*" **Alfred Youngwood** (see p.1333), clients say. The "*leader of the pack*" is admired for his "*true business sense.*" "*Confident*" **David Sicular** (see p.1321) provides "*intricate*" transactional advice on matters involving bankruptcy, private equity and partnership law. **Jeffrey Samuels** (see p.1316) gained respect for delivering "*to-the-point*" advice on transactional and real estate matters.

The Clients: Viacom; EMI; BT; Time Warner and Citigroup.

Roberts & Holland LLP

The Firm: This 40-attorney tax group is, through sheer numbers, "*one of the principal players*" nationwide. It is considered by market sources a key player regarding state and city tax law. Another significant consideration is its experience in real estate tax issues. On the latter, the group advises on complicated issues relating to sale-leasebacks and installment sales. The team caters to an impressive client list on a range of matters including corporate, international taxation and executive compensation.

The Lawyers: "*Superb*" **Carolyn Joy Lee** benefits enormously from her federal tax background, clients say. She has extensive proficiency in state and local taxation, including real estate matters. Considered an authority in this field, she impresses clients with her "*incisive outlook*" and adroit handling of individual circumstances.

The Clients: The group has represented domestic and international corporations, affluent individuals and their families.

Shearman & Sterling LLP
See firm details p.1369

The Firm: The group's "*proactive and responsive*" tax practice is a vital part of the firm's international profile, and encompasses expertise in such areas as M&A, spin-offs and restructurings. Within the New York office, a handful of tax

www.ChambersandPartners.com
All quotes in the text are from interviews with clients and competitors.
1257

partners handle cross-border transactions, partnerships and REITs. For example, it advised Wyeth in a joint venture with Solvay Pharmaceuticals to jointly develop certain central nervous system compounds. It also represented Groupe Danone in a joint venture with Suntory for home-and-office water delivery in the USA. Its "*fantastic resources and good commercial advice*" has won the group plaudits from all quarters. In another prominent transaction, it acted for HypoVereinsbank on the US tax aspects of a spin-off of its real estate lending operations. And representing Eaton Vance, the team assisted in the joint acquisition of Keystone Property Trust, a publicly traded REIT holding industrial properties.

The Lawyers: "*Top-notch*" **Peter Blessing** (see p.1267) is hailed by rivals who regard him as the "*intellectual*" head of the firm. Clients agreed this "*tremendously talented*" player is "*one of the strongest international figures around.*" His "*confidence and flair*" and his "*technically sound*" practice is "*on everybody's lips.*"

The Clients: CSFB; HypoVereinsbank; Wyeth; Groupe Danone; Merrill Lynch and ABB.

Band 4

Cahill Gordon & Reindel

The Firm: This "*tough*" tax team received praise from clients for its "*refined*" transactional and international practice. It regularly shepherds clients through a range of tax matters, including M&A, debt and equity financings, spin-offs, bankruptcies and restructurings. The firm encourages tax generalists, resulting in a group of practitioners with specialist knowledge within a broader practice. This is particularly helpful when dealing with certain types of tax controversies, which the firm consistently handles.

The Lawyers: "*Luminary*" **Ben Cohen** has a "*wonderful reputation for being just plain brilliant,*" clients say. His enduring relationship with GE is the envy of rivals, who also respect "*his immense integrity.*"

The Clients: The group advises a range of national clients on a broad range of tax matters.

Kirkland & Ellis LLP

See firm details p.770

The Firm: "*One of the market leaders*" for complex litigation, the group's tax practice is constantly involved in prominent controversies such as challenges by the IRS, various state tax authorities and foreign entities. But its strength in litigation does not deflect from its command of transactional matters. In this arena, the firm often attracts a flurry of tax planning activity as related to domestic and international M&A, buyouts, restructurings, REIT, bankruptcy and financings. It recently advised on the $750 mil-

lion acquisition of IMG by Forstmann Little and separately handled the $1.2 billion acquisition of Stelmar Shipping by Fortress.

The Lawyers: Clients commended **Patrick Gallagher** (see p.1281) for his "*truly outstanding*" experience in M&A and bankruptcy matters. He is also respected for his involvement in the formation of US and offshore private equity funds. The "*thoughtful and careful*" **Greer Phillips** (see p.1308) effectively steers clients through complex cross-border transactions. In addition, his consistent success with regards to financial products has earned a loyal following.

The Clients: The team advises a wide range of companies from the USA, Europe, Asia and Latin America.

McDermott Will & Emery

See firm details p.773

The Firm: This "*responsive*" team "*gives sound advice*" on a broad range of tax matters involving corporate, employee benefits and other areas of law. Its reach not only covers state and local taxation, but also embraces federal and international issues. A strong crossover with the corporate department preserves a steady flow of transactional involvement. It recently advised Barclays Group and GECC on tax-related matters. The firm's overall international focus further enhances the team, while bench strength in DC further bolstered its tax controversy capabilities.

The Lawyers: "*State and local tax genius*" **Art Rosen** (see p.1314) is commended for his tax planning experience. In addition, he often helps corporations, partnerships and individuals navigate through complex tax controversy issues.

The Clients: Barclays Group; drugstore.com; Prudential; GE Capital and Bayer.

Paul, Hastings, Janofsky & Walker LLP

See firm details p.297

The Firm: The "*forward-looking team*" is often retained by clients who appreciate its knack for "*thinking outside the box.*" It represented Beazer Homes USA – one of the largest builders of single family homes nationwide – in the amendment and restatement of its credit facility whereby its borrowing capacity was increased to $750 million. On a different matter the team represented JPMorgan Securities in relation to Webzen's $97 million IPO on the NASDAQ.

The Lawyers: "*Very talented and perceptive*" **Andrew Short** (see p.1321) knows exactly "*how clients think and what they want.*" He advises an array of domestic and international clients with respect to planning, structuring, and other transactional aspects often involving foreign financings. He also offers substantial knowledge

in the areas of M&A, project finance and complex financial products.

The Clients: Walker Digital Management; Westbrook Partners; GE Structured Finance Group; SBC Communications; Bresnan Communications; FXM and Lexington Corporate Properties.

Other Notable Practitioners

"*Gifted*" **Richard Reinhold** (see p.1312) of Wilkie Farr & Gallagher LLP has "*superb*" tax experience under his belt, clients say. He advised a buyout group in relation to the purchase of the consumer finance operations of Conseco for $1.1 billion. He was also applauded for recent tax work on behalf of Donald J. Trump in debt restructuring of Trump Hotels & Casino Resorts. "*Practical*" international tax lawyer **Richard Andersen** (see p.1262) of Arnold & Porter LLP is, according to clients, "*great at coming up with solutions.*" He counseled Rabobank in connection with its acquisition of Lend Lease Agri-Business. He also advised a major overseas private real estate investor group on the tax-efficient disposition of a trophy property in New York City. Other clients include ABN AMRO. "*Reliable*" **James Dreyfus** (see p.1276) at Fulbright & Jaworski LLP has a particular emphasis on M&A but covers a substantial amount of partnership work. He was involved in tax planning on behalf of Petro-Canada regarding its cross-border $540 million acquisition of Prima Energy. Clients also admire his handling of a corporate income tax case for Prudential Overall Supply. Another facet of his practice is tax-exempt organizations. "*Fantastic*" **Stephen Gardner** of Kronish Lieb Weiner & Hellman LLP is one of the country's leading tax litigators, while the "*technically superb*" **Robert Scarborough** of Freshfields Bruckhaus Deringer LLP won client confidence for his "*extremely thoughtful, careful*" advice. He mainly focuses on complex structured finance transactions and other corporate issues of an increasingly international nature. "*Straight shooter*" **David Mayo** (see p.1300) of Gibson, Dunn & Crutcher LLP is, according to clients, "*incredibly no-nonsense.*" He focuses on M&A, restructurings and financial instruments, including those involving a cross-border flavor. **David Nirenberg** (see p.1305) of Orrick, Herrington & Sutcliffe impresses interviewees with his expertise on the financial products side. He particularly shines when dealing with structured finance. Financial expert **Thomas Hood** (see p.1288) of Mayer, Brown, Rowe & Maw LLP has "*forward-thinking*" expertise in matters relating to tax transactional experience.

TECHNOLOGY & IT OUTSOURCING

New York
Leading firms
(Technology & IT Outsourcing)

1 MILBANK, TWEED, HADLEY & MCCLOY *New York*
2 MAYER, BROWN, ROWE & MAW LLP *New York*
  SHAW PITTMAN LLP *New York*
3 BROWN RAYSMAN MILLSTEIN FELDER *New York*
  KAYE SCHOLER LLP *New York*
  MORGAN, LEWIS & BOCKIUS LLP *New York*
  MORRISON & FOERSTER LLP *New York*
  SKADDEN, ARPS, SLATE, MEAGHER *New York*
  WEIL, GOTSHAL & MANGES LLP *New York*
  WHITE & CASE LLP *New York*
  WILLKIE FARR & GALLAGHER LLP *New York*

Leading individuals
(Technology & IT Outsourcing)

1 HALVEY John *Milbank Tweed, New York*
2 DELANEY John *Morrison & Foerster, New York*
  HUDANISH David *Mayer Brown, New York*
  LEVI Stuart *Skadden Arps, New York*
  STERN Akiba *Morgan Lewis, New York*
  TANENBAUM William *Kaye Scholer, New York*
3 ADLER Kenneth *Brown Raysman, New York*
  BETENSKY Steven *White & Case, New York*
  CAPLAN Gordon *Willkie Farr, New York*
  EPSTEIN Michael *Weil Gotshal, New York*
  HANSEN Edward *Morgan Lewis, New York*
  HOWARD Nigel *Mayer Brown, New York*
  KENNEDY John *Morrison & Foerster, New York*
  MILLSTEIN Julian *Brown Raysman, New York*
  RAYSMAN Richard *Brown Raysman, New York*

Leading individuals
(Technology & IT Outsourcing: Telecom)

1 KRAUS Bruce *Willkie Farr, New York*

Leading individuals
(Space, Satellite & Technology)

1 NESGOS Peter *Milbank Tweed, New York*

Firms and individuals are listed alphabetically in each band.

Band 1

Milbank, Tweed, Hadley & McCloy

The Firm: *"Prominent"* and *"first class"* were two typical adjectives applied to this premier outsourcing and technology practice. One commentator summed up the market consensus when he claimed that *"if there's a company in New York looking to do IT or outsourcing work, then Milbank is always on the shortlist."* With John Halvey, *"a god of outsourcing,"* at the helm it is hardly surprising that the team is best known for its IT and general outsourcing expertise. However, the group has considerable breadth, which includes *"extensive knowledge"* in the satellite and space field.

The Lawyers: **John Halvey** is *"one of the great outsourcing lawyers, like the grandfather of the industry."* Lauded as *"a top-quality lawyer in a top-quality firm who's been in the business since the early days,"* his recent highlights include representing Deutsche Bank in the groundbreaking outsourcing of its worldwide corporate purchasing and accounts payable services to Accenture. He also advised General Atlantic Partners and Oak Hill Capital Partners in a considerable transaction with GE. With a stellar reputation preceding him throughout the industry, *"well-connected"* satellite and space specialist, **Peter Nesgos,** attracted enthusiastic recommendations from all sections of the industry. *"He deals with problems in a very elegant manner,"* said peers, while clients noted that *"he's good on integrity – he steers clear of conflicts; won't take chances; always makes sure we're well protected."*

The Clients: DuPont; AT&T; Cendant; PepsiCo; Deutsche Bank; BellSouth; General Motors; Alcatel; Xerox; Boeing; Bombardier; Hughes; General Atlantic and Commonwealth Bank of Australia.

Band 2

Mayer, Brown, Rowe & Maw LLP
See firm details p.771

The Firm: Two things stand out in particular about Mayer Brown: the impressive international network that allows it to handle the most global transactions, and the strength of its outsourcing practice, an area where it is one of the out-and-out national leaders. In this latter area, peers acknowledge that it remains a first port of call *"simply because there are so many people there who have been doing it for a long time."* Sources particularly noted its work for mammoth consulting firm, TPI, which *"throws them an enormous amount of business."*

The Lawyers: According to interviewees, both **David Hudanish** (see p.1289) and **Nigel Howard** (see p.1288) *"know the technology field inside out,"* especially when it comes to IT outsourcing. Hudanish was busy this year representing TXU Corporation, including its subsidiaries TXU Energy and TXU Gas, in a ten-year, $3.5 billion outsourcing transaction with Capgemini. This included not just IT but revenue management, finance and accounting, procurement, HR and customer care/call centers. Howard's practice, meanwhile, spans outsourcing, licensing, and advice on joint ventures and strategic alliances.

The Clients: TXU; Procter & Gamble; Fifth Third Bank; Aon Corporation; CNA Financial; IndyMac Bank; OneChicago and The Williams Companies.

Shaw Pittman LLP
See firm details p.490

The Firm: Like Milbank Tweed, Shaw Pittman is especially highly rated for the strength of its national and international outsourcing practice.

The New York office undoubtedly suffered a blow recently with the departure of Akiba Stern and Ed Hansen to Morgan, Lewis & Bockius, which led some peers to raise queries about the remaining depth at partner level in New York. However, the firm retains an impressive list of clients, as well as considerable expertise throughout its network, in particular in the firm's DC office. In addition, the firm's recently announced merger with Pillsbury Winthrop is also expected to have a positive effect on the New York practice.

The Lawyers: Vipul Nishawala and Joshua Konvisser both serve as counsel in the global sourcing group's New York office.

The Clients: The team advised iSi-Dentsu of America on a joint venture software development agreement, and represented American Express and The New York Times in technology transactions with various suppliers. Other clients include: Merrill Lynch; Sprint; Capital One; Telus; Solectron and McDonald's.

Band 3

Brown Raysman Millstein Felder & Steiner LLP
See firm details p.1338

The Firm: This practice is historically noted by interviewees for its work representing suppliers, in particular long-term client AT&T. However, in recent months it has been more active representing customers. Sources were full of praise for its expertise in both outsourcing – where IT outsourcing experience complements a well-respected BPO practice – and its more traditional IT work, including *"fantastic software development deals."*

The Lawyers: *"One of the giants of the outsourcing arena,"* **Julian Millstein** (see p.1302) has recently been handling a finance & accounting outsourcing for a large retailer in the USA. He represented one of the Big Four accounting firms in an outsourcing, involving financial work being done in India and has been handling an application, development and maintenance outsourcing involving a major global insurance company. *"Intellectually outstanding, but approachable with it,"* **Richard Raysman** (see p.1311) has been busy of late with a variety of major matters, including advising on the outsourcing of various processes for a healthcare provider, a data analysis company and a venture investment fund. **Ken Adler** (see p.1261) boasts expertise in technology and IP. His workload includes representing financial institutions, accounting firms and healthcare companies in large-scale technology procurement, licensing and system development and integration agreements.

The Clients: Clients include commercial and investment banks, hospitals, insurance companies and data companies. AT&T is perhaps the best known.

Kaye Scholer LLP

See firm details p.1354

The Firm: This practice is said by interviewees to have built on a base of "*fabulous IP and patent expertise,*" particularly in the pharmaceutical area, which it has successfully "*leveraged into IT work.*" It represents an impressive selection of domestic and international clients in transactional work, litigation, and IP protection matters. Over the past year, the group has been particularly active in relation to privacy matters, technology agreements and IT outsourcing.

The Lawyers: A patent lawyer by training, **Bill Tanenbaum** (see p.1326) was described by peers as having amassed "*great experience in the general technology area.*" The chair of the firm's technology, IP and outsourcing group, he is especially highly rated for his outsourcing and software licensing expertise. He focuses on representing institutional customers in search of IT solutions.

The Clients: The team recently advised Cendant in relation to offshore call centers, and assisted Kodak with privacy issues. Other clients include: First Data; AXA Financial; Lehman Brothers; United States Tennis Association; Flextronics and Edgenet.

Morgan, Lewis & Bockius LLP

See firm details p.1556

The Firm: The firm enters the rankings this year, mainly due to the recent arrival of high-profile players, Akiba Stern and Ed Hansen, from Shaw Pittman. Both partners join the firm's global outsourcing practice in its New York office. Although the dust is still settling from the move, the market consensus is that their arrival has "*undoubtedly bolstered*" the presence of the firm's New York office in the technology and outsourcing fields, and confirmed Morgan Lewis' commitment to technology and outsourcing as a global practice area.

The Lawyers: With his "*long track record*" in the outsourcing field, **Akiba Stern**'s (see p.1324) expertise also encompasses IT-enabled business transactions, technology transfers and licensing, and advice on internet matters and e-commerce. **Ed Hansen** (see p.1286) is a "*business-focused*" adviser, whose practice concentrates on representing users in technology transactions. Clients appreciate his ability to "*translate the complex and esoteric language of IT into a language that business people can understand.*"

The Clients: Clients range from startup software developers to multinational corporations contracting for global systems and services.

Morrison & Foerster LLP

See firm details p.293

The Firm: MoFo's New York technology group is particularly noted by peers for its skill in service-related agreements; its attorneys have "*a good understanding of technology and IT law,*" and are "*good at getting transactions done – they know when to say yes or no*". Recent work for the team has included a number of outsourcing and related IT agreements for clients in the financial services, technology and media and entertainment industries. It also advised a large company in the travel industry on complex data security issues. In addition, it has advised in relation to a joint venture in the entertainment industry involving digital technologies.

The Lawyers: **John Delaney** (see p.1275) and **John Kennedy** (see p.1293) cochair the firm's technology transactions practice group. Delaney's workload includes negotiating complex IT outsourcing contracts and service level agreements, as well as joint ventures and software and content licenses. Kennedy, meanwhile, is an expert on IT outsourcing and services agreements, as well as technology exchanges, Internet services and e-commerce.

The Clients: The team recently acted for a large financial services conglomerate in an IT outsourcing. Examples of clients include: A&E Television Networks; The Harry Fox Agency; Hertz; Miramax Films; Multex; Sumitomo Heavy Industries; Yahoo! and Zomba Records.

Skadden, Arps, Slate, Meagher & Flom LLP & Affiliates

See firm details p.1372

The Firm: As peers note, Skadden Arps is "*an M&A behemoth, so a lot of its outsourcing work spins off from that, and some of the best and largest companies go to it for technology work.*" But where the work comes from hardly matters: the fact is that the group has established a name for effectively handling complex IT transactions for hi-tech clients and huge global corporations. Recent examples include advising Capgemini North America on agreements with TXU Energy and ONCOR Electronic Delivery Company to form a joint venture to provide IT and other business processing outsourcing services to TXU. Clients describe its attorneys as "*extremely knowledgeable about the legal nuances when it comes to corporate-related work with a strong IT component.*"

The Lawyers: **Stu Levi** (see p.1297) heads the firm's IT and e-commerce practice. His expertise includes outsourcing transactions, technology and IP licensing, technology transfers, and advice on strategic alliances and joint ventures.

The Clients: The team advised Cendant on an agreement with United Airlines to operate United's internal airline reservation system and build an Internet booking agent for its United.com website. It also acted for FleetBoston Financial in outsourcing its payroll processing and human resource administration services to Fidelity Employers Services Company. Other clients are drawn from the financial services, transportation, manufacturing, publishing, entertainment and retail industries.

Weil, Gotshal & Manges LLP

See firm details p.1378

The Firm: Weil Gotshal's New York technology team is best known for its classy technology and IP litigation. Observers particularly note its "*real trade secrets expertise, going back 25 or 30 years, when software was protected by trade secrets.*" With the firm's growing global footprint, it is no surprise that it "*wins global business from institutional clients,*" and has represented the likes of GE and ChevronTexaco in technology transactions.

The Lawyers: **Michael Epstein** (see p.1277) chairs the firm's technology and proprietary rights practice, and is especially noted by interviewees for his expertise in technology litigation. Epstein's broad practice also spans advice on technology and IP acquisitions, technology transfer and licensing arrangements, and outsourcing transactions.

The Clients: Clients include broadcasters, Internet service providers, content distributors and other media companies. GE and ChevronTexaco are examples.

White & Case LLP

See firm details p.1379

The Firm: The attorneys here were recommended by interviewees as "*bright, commercial and client friendly.*" The sizable team offers a wide range of expertise, spanning IT development and service agreements, outsourcing, privacy and data protection. The New York office serves as the epicenter for the firm's global technology practice group, cooperating closely with teams across the world.

The Lawyers: **Steve Betensky** (see p.1266) is the global co-head of the firm's IT practice. He was described by clients as a "*personable, practical, knowledgeable and effective*" attorney with considerable experience in areas like service agreement and IT outsourcing.

The Clients: Comcast; Given Imaging; IBM; MBG and Verizon.

Willkie Farr & Gallagher LLP

See firm details p.1380

The Firm: According to interviewees, this is "*a go-to firm in the IT area.*" Market sources particularly note the strength of its work for software developers, and clients keep returning to the team for its "*creative solutions to complex problems.*" They were also impressed with the lawyers' ability to "*offer feedback on how various legal issues would ripple through to other parts of the business.*" Recent highlights include advising Warburg Pincus on its agreement with buyout firms Bain Capital and Silver Lake Partners to purchase design software business UGS PLM Solutions from EDS for $2.05 billion.

The Lawyers: **Gordon Caplan** (see p.1270) is highly rated for the depth of his transactional expertise in the technology sector, and his ability to "*think outside the box.*" Clients admire the way that he is "*responsive and enthusiastic about his work,*" and appreciate a "*strong business sense, that allows him to explain technical matters in a business context.*" He recently helped Sprint to negotiate three separate multiyear wireless services infrastructure build-out agreements. These were with, Lucent, Motorola and Nortel, and

have a total value of around $3 billion. In the telecom sphere, **Bruce Kraus** (see p.1295) was described by clients as "*top of his game for telecom expertise and practical advice.*" Peers, meanwhile, note that "*he's a good corporate lawyer with a huge market share of emerging telecom companies.*" He recently represented TechTronic Industries in its $626.6 million purchase of the

Milwaukee Electric Tool® and AEG® power tool businesses from Sweden's Atlas Copco.
The Clients: Sprint; Warburg Pincus; TechTronic Industries; UBS Warburg; XO Communications; Loral Space & Communications and Nextel Communications.

Leaders in New York

AARON, Roger S
Skadden, Arps, Slate, Meagher & Flom LLP & Affiliates, New York
212 735 3300
raaron@skadden.com
Recommended in Corporate/M&A
Practice Areas: Senior Partner in charge of all corporate practice areas, including mergers and acquisitions, finance, banking and institutional investing, tax, employee benefits, investment companies, and restructuring and bankruptcy reorganization. Is a frequent lecturer at various seminars and symposiums on M&A, corporate and securities law matters.
Career: LLB, JD, Yale Law School, 1968; MBA, Amos Tuck School of Business Administration, Dartmouth College, 1965 (with high distinction); AB, Dartmouth College, 1964 (magna cum laude).

ABRAMOWITZ, Elkan
Morvillo, Abramowitz, Grand, Iason & Silberberg, PC, New York
212 856 9600
Recommended in Litigation

ABRAMS, Floyd
Cahill Gordon & Reindel, New York
212 701 3900
Recommended in Media & Entertainment

ABRAMS, Marc
Willkie Farr & Gallagher LLP, New York
212 728 8200
mabrams@willkie.com
Recommended in Bankruptcy
Practice Areas: Partner in the Business Reorganization and Restructuring Department and a member of the firm's Executive Committee. Has been instrumental, principally on behalf of debtors, in several complex Chapter 11 cases and non-judicial restructurings. Frequently represents clients in the telecommunications, retail, construction, manufacturing, entertainment/recreation, automotive, healthcare, hospitality, and high-tech industries. International experience includes issues and matters involving the insolvency laws of Argentina, Australia, Bermuda, Canada, France, Germany, Russia, Spain, Switzerland, and the UK, among other nations. Recent significant matters include serving as debtors coun-

sel in the following complex Chapter 11 cases: Adelphia Communications Corp., AMF Bowling Worldwide, Inc., ATX Communications, Inc., Mosler Inc., Schwinn Cycling & Fitness, Inc., Sunterra Corporation, and The Multicare Companies. Actively involved on behalf of creditors in the W.R. Grace and Enron Corporation Chapter 11 cases. Extensive experience representing official and unofficial creditors' committees, hedge funds and sophisticated investors, individual creditors, landlords, DIP lenders, general partners, and other parties in interest.
Prof. Memberships: Chair of the Committee on Bankruptcy and Corporate Reorganization of the Association of the Bar of the City of New York, and has served as the head of its Subcommittee on DIP Financing guidelines. Fellow of the American College of Bankruptcy. Has also been active in a number of additional reorganization-related groups, including the American Bar Association (Business Reorganization Committee), the American Bankruptcy Institute, the International Bar Association (Committee J.) and the New York Chapter of the Turnaround Management Association. Certified mediator for the US Bankruptcy Courts for the Southern District of New York and the District of Delaware.
Career: Admitted to the Delaware Bar (1978), Pennsylvania Bar (1981), and New York Bar (1985); the United States Courts of Appeal for the Second and Third Circuits; and the US District Courts of Delaware and the Southern and Eastern Districts of New York.
Personal: Received a JD (cum laude) from Widener University in 1978 and a BA (cum laude) from Villanova University in 1975.

ABRAMSON, Richard
Peckar & Abramson PC, New York
212 382 0909
rabramson@pecklaw.com
Recommended in Construction
Practice Areas: Mr Abramson has enjoyed a distinguished career with substantial success in highly complex litigations and arbitrations, particularly in the area of major construction industry disputes. He has also resolved several com-

plex multiparty disputes through negotiation, mediation and other alternative dispute resolution mechanisms.
Prof. Memberships: Mr Abramson is admitted to practice before the United States Supreme Court, the United States Court of Appeals for the Third Circuit, the United States Court of Federal Claims, the United States District Court for the Eastern and Southern Districts of New York and the District of New Jersey as well as the courts of the State of New York and the State of New Jersey. He is a certified mediator for the United States District Court of New Jersey. Mr Abramson is a Member of the Bergen County and the New Jersey State Bar Association.
Career: Founding Partner.
Personal: He is a graduate of the University of Wisconsin at Madison and Brooklyn Law School, where he was editor of the 'Brooklyn Law Review'.

ABUHOFF, Daniel
Debevoise & Plimpton LLP, New York
212 909 6000
Recommended in Antitrust

ADLER, Arthur S
Sullivan & Cromwell LLP, New York
212 558 4000
adlera@sullcrom.com
Recommended in Real Estate
Practice Areas: Real estate-related expertise includes mortgage, mezzanine debt and preferred equity financings; securitisations and other rated public/private investment vehicles; sale-leasebacks and lease-backed financings; joint ventures and partnerships for development and investment projects; acquisitions and dispositions of improved and unimproved properties; construction contracting; insurance; and commercial office leasing. Clients include Goldman, Sachs & Co. and its affiliated Whitehall Street Real Estate Funds; Barclays Bank; Prudential Financial Group; Philips Electronics; Vornado Realty Trust; and The New York Giants.
Prof. Memberships: ABA; NYSBA; ABCNY.
Career: Partner since 1990.
Personal: Columbia University (AB, 1979); Columbia Law School (JD, 1982).

ADLER, Kenneth
Brown Raysman Millstein Felder & Steiner LLP, New York
212.895.2410
kadler@brownraysman.com
Recommended in Technology
Practice Areas: As a Partner in the Technology, Media and Communications Department, he concentrates on outsourcing and complex transactions relating to e-commerce, emerging technologies, telecommunications and computer law. His practice includes drafting and negotiating virtually all types of outsourcing agreements including those involving information technology, business process and human resource outsourcing, as well as agreements relating to the development, supply, licensing, marketing and distribution of e-commerce, computer and telecommunications products and services.
Personal: He writes regularly on outsourcing, e-commerce, intellectual property and technology-related issues. JD, The George Washington University Law School, 1986; BS, computer science, Union College 1983 (cum laude).

ADLER, Sheldon S
Skadden, Arps, Slate, Meagher & Flom LLP & Affiliates, New York
212 735 2136
sadler@skadden.com
Recommended in Energy
Practice Areas: Primarily responsible for development of the firm's utility merger and acquisition practice, a subgroup of the Corporate Practice that handles utility acquisition transactions. Represents a wide variety of clients in merger and other acquisition transactions. Involved in many recent public utility merger transactions. Has also been involved in many recent generation assets divestiture transactions. Clients include Sierra Pacific Resources, New England Electric Systems, Centrica plc., CMS Energy Corporation, and Orange & Rockland Utilities.
Career: JD, Yale Law School, 1979 (editor, Yale Law Journal); BA, City College of New York, 1976.

www.ChambersandPartners.com
All quotes in the text are from interviews with clients and competitors.
1261

AIELLO, Michael
Dewey Ballantine LLP, New York
212 259 8554
maiello@deweyballantine.com
Recommended in Corporate/M&A
Practice Areas: Mr Aiello regularly represents acquirors, targets, board of directors, special committees, investment banks, investors and shareholder groups in complex domestic and international negotiated and unsolicited transactions. Mr Aiello also regularly counsels clients on a broad range of corporate, securities and business-related matters including directors' duties and responsibilities and other aspects of corporate governance, disclosure issues and compliance matters.
Career: Partner, Dewey Ballantine LLP. Admitted to practice 1995. Clerkship, US Court of Appeals for the 3rd Circuit (1994-95).
Personal: Born June 1, 1969. BA, New York University, 1991. JD, Widener University School of Law, 1994.

ALDEN, Steven
Debevoise & Plimpton LLP, New York
212 909 6000
Recommended in Real Estate

ALEXANDER, Troy
White & Case LLP, New York
212 819 8532
talexander@whitecase.com
Recommended in Projects
Practice Areas: Co-Head of the firm's Energy, Infrastructure and Project Finance Group. Concentrates on international project finance and banking in the power, oil and gas, telecommunications and mining industries. Clients include sponsors, sovereigns, commercial banks, multilateral financial institutions and export credit agencies located around the world. In addition to project financings, he has been involved in construction projects, joint ventures, leasing, acquisitions, public securities offerings, domestic and international loan transactions, privatizations and debt restructurings.

ALLERHAND, Joseph
Weil, Gotshal & Manges LLP, New York
212 310 8725
joseph.allerhand@weil.com
Recommended in Litigation
Practice Areas: Litigation: securities; litigation: general commercial.
Career: Mr Allerhand co-heads Weil Gotshal's Securities/Corporate Governance Litigation Practice. With 25 years of experience, Mr Allerhand is a nationally recognized litigator with particularly extensive experience in securities litigation, arbitrations and bankruptcy. Because much of his practice arises from complex corporate transactions, Mr Allerhand regularly counsels boards of directors and special committees on a wide variety of corporate disputes. He also conducts internal investigations. Mr Allerhand has argued and tried numer-

ous high-profile cases in state and federal courts, and before arbitration panels. Equally adept at representing plaintiffs and defendants, his clients have included Krispy Kreme, Excite.
Personal: Georgetown University Law Center, JD; Columbia University, BA.

ALPERIN, Stuart N
Skadden, Arps, Slate, Meagher & Flom LLP & Affiliates, New York
212 735 3920
salperin@skadden.com
Recommended in Employee Benefits
Practice Areas: Emphasizes ERISA and other employee benefits and executive compensation matters, particularly the treatment of employee benefits in M&A and other corporate restructurings; the uses of employee stock ownership plans (ESOPs); executive compensation issues such as golden parachutes, deferred compensation tax rules and the nondeductibility of annual compensation in excess of $1 million; and issues arising under the short-swing profit and 8-K disclosure provisions of the Securities Exchange Act of 1934.
Career: LLM, Taxation, New York University, 1980; JD, Syracuse University, 1976 (survey editor, 1975 Survey of New York Law; Order of the Coif); AB, SUNY Binghamton, 1973.

ALTSCHULER, Fredric L
Cadwalader, Wickersham & Taft LLP, New York 212 504 6525
fredric.altschuler@cwt.com
Recommended in Real Estate
Practice Areas: Represents numerous clients with respect to the acquisition, financing, mortgage securitization, disposition and leasing of commercial real estate. Has represented institutional lenders and investment banks in connection with construction, interim and permanent financings of real estate (land assemblages, hotels, regional shopping centers, office buildings, industrial parks, mixed-use projects, residential and commercial condominiums and cooperatives), workouts of nonperforming loans, foreclosures and acceptances of deeds in lieu of foreclosure and dispositions of properties acquired in workouts and foreclosures. Has represented institutional lenders and investment banks in connection with the origination and securitization of commercial mortgage loans (both single asset and pools), including the establishment of numerous commercial conduit programs. Has represented investors acquiring performing and nonperforming loans and properties, including the financing of such purchases and restructuring and disposition of the purchased assets.
Personal: Graduate of Syracuse University in 1968 with a BA in history and political science; earned his JD in 1972 at St. John's University.

AMDUR, Martin
Weil, Gotshal & Manges LLP, New York
212 310 8224
martin.amdur@weil.com
Recommended in Tax
Practice Areas: Mr Amdur's broad-based tax practice includes structuring partnerships and tax-free reorganizations and taxable acquisitions of domestic and foreign corporations and counseling private equity entities.
Career: A Senior Partner, since 1968 Mr Amdur has regularly advised on sophisticated equity and debt instruments (such as contingent convertible debt, income deposit securities and Canadian exchangeable shares), derivatives, secured finance transactions, bankruptcies and executive compensation and represented taxpayers before the IRS. He is a Fellow of the American College of Tax Counsel.
Personal: New York University School of Law, LLM; Yale Law School, LLB; Cornell University, AB.

AMER, Andrew S
Simpson Thacher & Bartlett LLP, New York 212 455 2953
aamer@stblaw.com
Recommended in Insurance
Practice Areas: Litigation Partner at Simpson Thacher & Bartlett LLP. Represents clients in a wide range of commercial litigation, with particular emphasis on reinsurance and insurance-related coverage disputes.
Prof. Memberships: American Bar Association, AIDA-Reinsurance & Insurance Arbitration Society (ARIAS-US).
Career: Has served in the role of national coordinating counsel for various insurers with respect to insurance and reinsurance issues. Has represented insurers in a number of direct insurance coverage actions involving asbestos, pollution and other mass tort claims, as well as a number of significant reinsurance coverage arbitrations and lawsuits against domestic and foreign reinsurers, including Cigna Re (52 F.3d 1194) and Unigard (79 N.Y.2d 576; 4 F.3d 1049).
Personal: Received his undergraduate degree in engineering from Cornell University and his law degree from the University of Pennsylvania, where he was an editor of the 'Law Review'.

AMES, Mitchell
Hogan & Hartson LLP, New York
212 918 8423
msames@hhlaw.com
Recommended in Media & Entertainment
Practice Areas: International joint ventures and joint development groups, private equity and venture capital, restructurings, broadcasting, media and communications industry transactions, and private and public finance.
Prof. Memberships: Member, ABA; Member, New York State Bar Association.
Career: Mitchell has been a Partner at

Hogan & Hartson since March, 2002. Prior to joining Hogan & Hartson, he was a Partner at Squadron Ellenoff Plesent & Sheinfeld LLP (which merged with Hogan & Hartson in 2002) from 2000-02. Mitchell counsels international media companies, television and radio station group operators, theme park operators, music and book publishers, telecommunications service providers, technology companies and textile manufacturers on a wide range of merger and acquisition, joint venture, recapitalization and securities matters; private equity and recovery fund operators on fund formation, portfolio investment and management compensation matters; and financially-troubled and bankrupt retailers, real estate conglomerates and others in restructuring and disposition matters.
Publications: Co-author with Peter J Romeo, 'Management's Report on Internal Control over Financial Reporting,' SEC Update, Hogan & Hartson L.L.P. (June 2003); 'Sections 302 and 906 Certifications: Amended Rules and Forms,' SEC Update, Hogan & Hartson L.L.P. (June 2003).
Personal: New York University (JD, magna cum laude, editor of The Journal of International Law and Politics, recipient of two AmJur scholar awards); State University of New York at Buffalo (BA, magna cum laude). Admitted to the New York Bar US District Court for the Southern District of New York.

ANDERSEN, Richard
Arnold & Porter LLP, New York
212 715 1095
Richard.Andersen@aporter.com
Recommended in Tax
Practice Areas: Practices international tax law, primarily for foreign enterprises investing and doing business in the United States. He has extensive experience in cross-border acquisitions and joint ventures; foreign investment in the United States; cross-border leasing, licensing, and financial products; global investment funds; transfer pricing and tax treaties.
Prof. Memberships: He belongs to numerous professional associations, including the USA Branch Council of the International Fiscal Association.
Career: He has written numerous publications on such topics as tax treaties, withholding taxes and investment in US real estate. He is a frequent speaker at professional conferences and teaches international taxation at NYU Law School.

ANDERSON, Eugene
Anderson Kill & Olick P.C., New York
212 278 1000
Recommended in Insurance

ANGIOLILLO, Bruce
Simpson Thacher & Bartlett LLP, New York 212 455 3735
bangiolillo@stblaw.com
Recommended in Litigation
Practice Areas: Senior litigation Partner at Simpson Thacher & Bartlett LLP.

His areas of expertise are in securities litigation, including class actions, derivative actions and contests for corporate control, and complex commercial, bankruptcy and real estate litigation. Representative cases in the securities area include: Enron, Westar Energy, Sirius Satellite Radio, Winstar, DOV Pharmaceutical, Bre-X, Prison Realty/CCA, Teleglobe, Synthetic Industries, Smith's Foods, Computervision, Starter and WPPSS. Regularly represents Blackstone, KKR and Vestar in matters arising from their investment activities. 'The Best Lawyers in America' (2005/2006) awarded him its highest 'Bet-the-Company Litigation' ranking.
Prof. Memberships: American Bar Association, the New York State Bar Association, the Federal Bar Council and Association of the Bar of the City of New York. He is a member of the Mediation Panel of the US District Court for the Southern District of New York.
Career: Joined Simpson Thacher in 1980 and became Partner in 1985. Currently a member of the Board of Directors of Common Ground Community, which provides innovative solutions to homelessness in New York City.
Publications: Frequent contributor to legal publications on securities and other litigation topics. For the last five years, he has been a featured panelist at PLI's annual Securities Litigation Conference.
Personal: Received his BA magna cum laude from Amherst (1974) and his JD from Columbia Law School (1977). He was a member of the Presidential Search Committee for Amherst College in 1994, received its Medal for Eminent Service in 1996, and served as President of the College's Society of Alumni in 2004.

ANGLAND, Joseph
Dewey Ballantine LLP, New York
212 259 7090
jangland@deweyballantine.com
Recommended in Antitrust
Practice Areas: Mr Angland's principal areas of practice include antitrust litigation (civil and criminal); antitrust counseling; federal income and estate tax litigation; intellectual property litigation; and other complex commercial litigation. He has counseled and represented Firm clients in a variety of industries, including the automobile, banking, communications, computer software, medical equipment, mortgage, petroleum, pharmaceutical and semiconductor industries.
Prof. Memberships: American Bar Association, Vice-Chair of Antitrust Section (2004-present).
Career: Partner, Dewey Ballantine LLP. Admitted to practice 1977, New York and 1988, District of Columbia.
Personal: Born September 1, 1949. BS, Massachusetts Institute of Technology, 1972. JD, Harvard Law School, 1975.

AQUILA, Francis J
Sullivan & Cromwell LLP, New York
212 558 4048
aquilaf@sullcrom.com
Recommended in Corporate/M&A
Practice Areas: Focuses on M&A, takeover defense, strategic alliances and corporate governance matters. Wide range of representations includes: J. Sainsbury in sale of US businesses; Diageo in sale of Burger King and acquisition of The Chalone Wine Group; EchoStar in attempted acquisition of Hughes Electronics; Medtronic in MiniMed and Medical Research Group acquisitions; Pharmacia & Upjohn in Monsanto merger; and Newbridge Networks in acquisition by Alcatel.
Prof. Memberships: ABA; ABCNY; NYSBA.
Career: Partner since 1992.
Personal: Columbia University (AB, 1979); Brooklyn Law School (JD, 1983).

ARAR, Roger
Loeb & Loeb LLP, New York
212 407 4000
Recommended in Media & Entertainment

ARONSON, Clifford H
Skadden, Arps, Slate, Meagher & Flom LLP & Affiliates, New York
212 735 2644
caronson@skadden.com
Recommended in Antitrust
Practice Areas: Represents clients in antitrust matters relating to mergers and acquisitions. Has experience advising clients on other types of antitrust matters and representing them before federal and state antitrust agencies as well as grand juries.
Prof. Memberships: Vice-Chair, Clayton Act Committee of the Antitrust Section of the American Bar Association.
Career: JD, Georgetown University Law Center, 1980; BS, Wharton School, University of Pennsylvania, 1977 (cum laude).
Publications: Co-editor, 'Mergers and Acquisitions - Understanding the Antitrust Laws', American Bar Association.

ARQUIT, Kevin J
Simpson Thacher & Bartlett LLP, New York 212 455 2000
karquit@stblaw.com
Recommended in Antitrust
Practice Areas: Has represented clients in major antitrust class actions, involving the healthcare, telecommunications, financial service and insurance areas. has obtained merger clearance from the US Federal Trade Commission (FTC) or Department of Justice (DOJ) for dozens of transactions in the airline, pharmaceutical, computer hardware and software, chemical, health care, optics, food and various consumer product industries. Has extensive experience dealing with international antitrust issues. Represents Weyerhaeuser Co. in a Sherman Act Section 2 monopolization and

monopsonization case in the timber industry. Represents MasterCard in defense of a private antitrust enforcement action brought by American Express and Discover, which seek relief in connection with Visa and MasterCard rules and policies that allegedly impaired the ability of rival networks to compete. Represented MasterCard International in class action in which four million retailers alleged more than $10 billion in damages for antitrust violations by MasterCard and Visa. Successfully obtained clearance for The Quaker Oats Company's in its business combination with PepsiCo Inc., Volvo in its acquisition of Renault trucks and Smithfield Foods' in its acquisition of Farmland Inc. Also represented MusicNet Inc. during regulatory investigations of online music initiatives.
Prof. Memberships: Member, BNA Advisory Board on Trade Regulation; Member, Board of Advisors to 'The Antitrust Counsellor'; Member, Executive Committee of the Antitrust Law Section of the New York State Bar Association.
Career: Prior to joining private practice, was General Counsel of the Federal Trade Commission, and then Director of its Bureau of Competition, responsible for the FTC's antitrust enforcement program.
Personal: St Lawrence University (BA cum laude 1975), Cornell Law School (JD cum laude 1978).

ASHINOFF, Reid
Sonnenschein Nath & Rosenthal, New York 212 768 6730
rashinoff@sonnenschein.com
Recommended in Insurance
Practice Areas: Chair, Litigation Department, New York. Focuses on commercial crises, multi-jurisdiction matters, class actions, consumer fraud, complex commercial challenges to products and services. Counsels and represents companies, corporate boards, and executives in trial and appellate courts and before regulatory agencies throughout US. Served as National Coordinating Counsel and Chief Trial Counsel for The Prudential Insurance Company of America, 1995-2003.
Prof. Memberships: ABA; New York City Bar Association, US Supreme Court Bar; National Board of Directors, Tourette Syndrome Association.
Personal: Harvard Law School, JD, cum laude; City College of New York, BA, summa cum laude, Phi Beta Kappa.

ATKINS, Peter Allan
Skadden, Arps, Slate, Meagher & Flom LLP & Affiliates, New York
212 735 3700
patkins@skadden.com
Recommended in Corporate/M&A
Practice Areas: Involved since 1968 in Skadden's M&A, corporate, securities, restructuring and financial practices.

Represents acquirors, targets, special committees and investment banks in mergers, acquisitions, takeovers, leveraged buyouts and joint ventures. Involved in all phases, including planning, negotiating and implementing. Counsels on other corporate, securities and business related matters, including corporate governance, directors' duties and responsibilities, disclosure and investigations. Transactional involvement includes airline, defense and aerospace, energy, financial institutions, forest products, healthcare, information technology, insurance, media and telecommunications, retail and utilities industries. Member of firm's senior management.
Career: LLB, Harvard University, 1968; AB, Brooklyn College, 1965.

AUSPITZ, Jack
Morrison & Foerster LLP, New York
212 468 8046
jauspitz@mofo.com
Recommended in Litigation
Practice Areas: Commercial litigator focused on securities, banking and other complex civil litigation. Has litigated numerous private and class action securities and banking cases. Represented clients in dealing with the Securities & Exchange Commission and other regulatory authorities. Has been a court-appointed Special Counsel and Special Escrow Agent in various SEC cases.
Career: Admitted to practice in New York.
Publications: Co-author, 'Settling a Class Action', Settlement Agreements in Commercial Disputes (Aspen, 2000): 'A Litigator's View of Due Diligence' (PLI, annually); 'Dealing with Damages: Private Actions for Securities Fraud' (PLI, annually).
Personal: AB, Columbia University, 1964; JD, magna cum laude, Harvard Law School, 1968; editor, 'Harvard Law Review'; Law Clerk, Honorable Irving R Kaufman, US Court of Appeals, Second Circuit.

AXINN, Stephen
Axinn Veltrop & Harkrider LLP, New York 212 728 2200
Recommended in Antitrust

BAECHER, John
Chadbourne & Parke LLP, New York
212 408 5100
jbaecher@chadbourne.com
Recommended in Projects
Practice Areas: Partner John Baecher advises sponsors, lenders and investors on the development and financing of privately-financed independent power projects and on project restructurings, corporate financings and asset acquisitions and divestitures. He has assisted several of the largest global independent power companies in the expansion of their US holdings and in their international development and acquisition activities throughout Latin America and

the UK. He also advises sponsors and lenders on responding to RFPs relating to the acquisition or development of power plants and associated facilities, and transmission and distribution systems.

BAECHTOLD, Robert
Fitzpatrick, Cella, Harper & Scinto, New York 212 218 2213
rbaechtold@fchs.com
Recommended in Intellectual Property
Practice Areas: Lead counsel in litigation for major corporate clients, including Bristol-Myers Squibb, Warner-Lambert, Merck, Yamanouchi, Eisai, Wyeth, Altana Pharma AG, GD Searle, Novartis, AstraZeneca, Bausch & Lomb, Pharmacia, Pfizer, Hoffman La Roche, American Cyanamid, SC Johnson & Son, Hoechst Celanese, Hoechst-Roussel, American-Maize Products, EI du Pont, and Union Carbide. Recent cases include: successfully defending Pharmacia in inventorship challenges by the University of Rochester regarding it's sale of blockbuster products Celebrex® and Bextra®; successfully defending Bristol-Myers Squibb in inventorship challenges by the University of Michigan and Repligen Corporation concerning biotechnology patents related to therapeutic fusion proteins important in the regulation of the immune system, successfully asserting AstraZeneca patents against validity challenges to its $5 billion per year Prilosec® product and successfully defending a multi-billion dollar infringement claim and receiving an award of over $32 million in attorneys fees for client Bristol-Myers Squibb. Mr Baechtold was selected as one of the ten best patent lawyers in the world, in Euromoney's 'Best of the Best' survey in 2000, 2002 and 2004. Mr Baechtold was also selected as a top intellectual property law practitioner in the 2003-2004 edition of the Best Lawyers in America and for Euromoney Magazine's 'Guide to the World's Leading Patent Law Experts' and 'Guide to the World's Leading Trademark Law Practitioners'.
Prof. Memberships: Former President, Federal Circuit Bar Association; Founding Fellow, American Intellectual Property Law Association; Member of the Bars of New York, New Jersey and Pennsylvania and of several Federal District Courts and Courts of Appeal. Previously served as: Member, Advisory Committee of the Court of Appeals for the Federal Circuit; Board of Directors, American Intellectual Property Law Association and New York Intellectual Property Law Association; President, New Jersey Patent Law Association.
Career: Research Chemist, American Cyanamid Co. (1958-62); Patent Agent, M&T Chemicals (1962-65); Ward, McElhannon, Brooks and Fitzpatrick, joined 1965, Partner 1969; Fitzpatrick, Cella, Harper & Scinto, founding Partner, 1971.

Personal: Rutgers University (BS Chemistry); Seton Hall University School of Law (JD magna cum laude). Married with three children, five grandchildren. Enjoys music, golf, tennis, sailing and travel.

BAKER, D J (Jan)
Skadden, Arps, Slate, Meagher & Flom LLP & Affiliates, New York
212 735 2150
djbaker@skadden.com
Recommended in Bankruptcy
Practice Areas: Represents numerous public companies in restructurings. Advises officers and directors on duties and governance. Has had primary responsibility in numerous Chapter 11 cases and out-of-court restructurings. Has represented: American Pad & Paper (Company); CIRCLE K (Company); FirstCity Bank Corporation (Acquiror); Fiber Mark (Company); FoxMeyer Drug Company (Company); Gen-Tek (Company); Global Marine (Company); M Corp. (Company); MicroAge (Company); Owens Corning (Company); RCN (Company); Safety-Kleen (Company); Sterling Chemicals (Company); and Winn-Dixie (Company).
Career: JD, University of Houston Law School (editor in chief, Houston Law Review); AB, Harvard University (cum laude).

BAKER Jr, William
Thelen Reid & Priest LLP, New York
212 603 2000
Recommended in Energy

BALL, Corinne
Jones Day, New York
212 326 7844
cball@jonesday.com
Recommended in Bankruptcy
Practice Areas: Co-heads the New York office's Restructuring and Reorganization Practice and organizes the firm's global Restructuring Practice. Significant experience in business finance and restructuring with a focus on complex corporate reorganizations and distress acquisitions. Recognized as a leading bankruptcy attorney in publications such as 'Who's Who in International Insolvency,' 'Global Counsel 3000,' and the 'K&A Restructuring Register.'
Prof. Memberships: American College of Bankruptcy; American Bankruptcy Institute; and the ABA Business Bankruptcy Committee. Mediator for the US Bankruptcy Courts of the Southern District of New York.
Publications: Authors a column on distress M&A for the 'New York Law Journal.'

BARANCIK, Tia
King & Spalding LLP, New York
212 556 2222
tbarancik@kslaw.com
Recommended in Energy
Practice Areas: Extensive experience structuring and implementing strategic corporate and credit transactions in reg-

ulated industries with emphasis on regulated energy companies. Representation of US and foreign energy companies in connection with mergers, acquisitions, divestitures and restructurings. Substantial experience with US laws regulating electric and gas utilities; energy industry acquisitions; compliance with FERC regulation, Public Utility Holding Company Act of 1935 and other regulatory statutes; and advising companies and investors on pending energy legislation and other regulatory reform efforts.
Prof. Memberships: New York Bar Association.
Personal: BA, Princeton University,1983; JD, Vanderbilt University, 1986.

BARNARD, Kevin
White & Case LLP, New York
212 819 8483
kbarnard@whitecase.com
Recommended in Banking & Finance
Practice Areas: Heads the firm's Bank Advisory Practice. Represents leading global banking organizations concerning the application of US laws to their worldwide activities. Practice emphasizes helping clients structure acquisitions, develop new products, resolve complex regulatory matters and address internal management and organizational issues. Also represents clients negotiating and settling litigation and administrative enforcement actions brought by federal and state banking authorities.
Career: Was an attorney at the US Treasury Department, Office of the Comptroller of the Currency (1976-78) and Deputy Superintendent of Banks and General Counsel of the New York State Banking Department (1982-83). Joined White & Case in 1983.

BARNES, Mark
Ropes & Gray, New York
212 497 3635
mark.barnes@ropesgray.com
Recommended in Healthcare
Practice Areas: Has practiced and taught law and administered governmental programs in the healthcare field for the past 20 years. Recognized as a leading lawyer in research compliance, HIPAA, and other privacy regulations. Represents hospitals, medical schools, physicians, social service agencies, and related organizations in regulatory, reimbursement, research, HIPAA compliance, and litigation matters. Member of the Advisory Committee for Human Research Protections of the Secretary of the United States Department of Health and Human Services.
Career: Connecticut Bar (1985). New York Bar (1986). Partner, Ropes & Gray (2001).
Personal: LLM, Columbia Law School (1991). JD, Yale Law School (1984).

BARON, Robert
Cravath, Swaine & Moore LLP, New York 212 474 1422
rbaron@cravath.com
Recommended in Litigation
Practice Areas: Wide variety of commercial cases, including the representation of major domestic and foreign issuers and financial institutions in litigation related to securities offerings, complex structured financing transactions, mergers and acquisitions, securities and antitrust issues.
Prof. Memberships: Admitted to practice before the US Supreme Court; US Courts of Appeals for the Second, Third, Ninth and Federal Circuits; and the US District Court for the Southern District of New York.
Career: Partner since 1988.
Personal: Harvard Law School (JD, cum laude, 1981); Princeton University (AB, cum laude, 1978).

BARR, Michael H
Sonnenschein Nath & Rosenthal, New York 212 768 6788
mbarr@sonnenschein.com
Recommended in Insurance
Practice Areas: Litigation and Business Regulation Practice Vice-Chair. Concentrates on commercial, class action, insurance coverage and securities litigation and related counseling. Litigates before trial and appellate courts and administrative forums throughout the US. Experience includes securities, workers compensation, consumer fraud, environmental, insurance coverage, trade regulation, real estate, professional liability and contractual disputes.
Prof. Memberships: Committee on Legal Education; Bar of the City of New York.
Personal: Harvard University, JD, cum laude; Oberlin College, AB, with highest honors.

BARSHAY, Scott
Cravath, Swaine & Moore LLP, New York 212 474 1009
sbarshay@cravath.com
Recommended in Corporate/M&A
Practice Areas: Mergers and acquisitions, general representation of corporate clients.
Prof. Memberships: ABA; ABCNY; NYSBA.
Career: Partner since 1999.
Personal: Columbia Law School (JD, 1991; Stone Scholar; associate editor of the 'Journal of Transnational Law'); Colgate University (BA, magna cum laude, 1988; Phi Beta Kappa).

BARTEL II, Paul W
Davis Polk & Wardwell, New York
212 450 4000
paul.bartel@dpw.com
Recommended in Antitrust
Practice Areas: Member of Davis Polk & Wardwell's Litigation Department. Represents US and non-US companies in antitrust litigation and enforcement

agency investigations. Is active in domestic and cross-border acquisitions and joint ventures involving US and European Community anti-trust considerations. Representations include Royal Caribbean Cruises in its proposed combination with P&O Princess Cruises; EMI in its proposed combination with Warner Music; Bertelsmann in its acquisition of Random House; Compaq Computer in its acquisition of Digital Equipment; Texas Instruments in the sale of its defense business to Raytheon; Hudson Foods in the sale of its business to Tyson Foods; and Borg Warner in the creation of a joint venture combining the businesses of Wells Fargo and Loomis.

BARTFELD, Daniel
Milbank, Tweed, Hadley & McCloy, New York 212 530 5000
Recommended in Projects

BARTNER, Douglas
Shearman & Sterling LLP, New York 212 848 8190
dbartner@shearman.com
Recommended in Bankruptcy
Practice Areas: Head of Shearman & Sterling's Bankruptcy and Reorganization Practice. Mr Bartner represents debtors, creditors and acquirers of assets in Chapter 11 bankruptcies and out-of-court restructurings and has extensive experience in cross-border restructurings and insolvency matters.
Prof. Memberships: Member of the Committee on Commercial Bankruptcy, and the New York County Lawyers' Association. Admitted to the New York and California Bar.
Career: Joined Shearman & Sterling in 1982 and became a Partner in 1991.
Personal: BS, Lehigh University (1979); JD, George Washington University, National Law Center (1982).

BASKIN, Stuart
Shearman & Sterling LLP, New York 212 848 4974
sbaskin@shearman.com
Recommended in Litigation
Practice Areas: Head of Shearman & Sterling's Litigation Group. Experience in securities litigation, M&A litigation, class action litigation, criminal defense and antitrust matters.
Career: Assistant US Attorney in the Southern District of New York (1978-82); Special Assistant to Director, Office for Civil Rights, Department of Health, Education and Welfare (1977-78); Clerk to Justice William J Brennan, Jr of the US Supreme Court (1976-77) and to Judge Walter R. Mansfield of the US Court of Appeals (1975-76).
Publications: Articles in American Bar Association, Federal Bar Council and Practicing Law Institute publications.
Personal: BA, Stanford University (1972); JD, Stanford University (1975).

BASON Jr, George R
Davis Polk & Wardwell, New York 212 450 4000
george.bason@dpw.com
Recommended in Corporate/M&A, Private Equity
Practice Areas: Member of Davis Polk & Wardwell's Corporate Department. Concentrates primarily in mergers, acquisitions and joint ventures, with a special focus on merchant banking. Has experience in cross-border transactions, restructurings, takeover defenses and corporate governance issues, as well as in providing general corporate and securities law advice. Transactions he has worked on include Gillette's proposed acquisition by Procter & Gamble, JP Morgan's $38.6 billion merger with Chase; DLJ's acquisition by Credit Suisse First Boston; Exxon's $81 billion merger with Mobil; Ford's acquisition of Volvo Cars; Procter & Gamble's acquisition of Iams; and management's attempted leveraged buyout of RJR Nabisco.

BATTISTA, Gregory J
Cravath, Swaine & Moore LLP, New York 212 474 1948
gbattista@cravath.com
Recommended in Environment
Practice Areas: Specializes in environmental law. Acquisition, divestiture and financing transactions where environmental issues must be identified, quantified and properly managed. Industries represented include heavy manufacturing, mining, forestry, energy, pharmaceuticals, real estate and telecommunications. Counsels clients in remediation and regulatory matters, disputes over environmental claims.
Prof. Memberships: ABA (Section of Environment, Energy, and Resources).
Career: Senior Attorney since 2004. Former Partner at Hannoch Weisman P.C., New Jersey. Adjunct Professor of Environmental Law at Stevens Institute of Technology since 1992. New Jersey Department of Environmental Protection 1980-83.
Personal: Seton Hall University (JD, 1986); Rider University (MBA, 1983); Boston College (BA, 1980).

BEATTIE, Richard I
Simpson Thacher & Bartlett LLP, New York 212 455 2000
rbeattie@stblaw.com
Recommended in Corporate/M&A, Private Equity
Practice Areas: Chairman of Simpson Thacher & Bartlett LLP specialising in mergers and acquisitions, leveraged buyouts and corporate law and finance. Has participated in some of the larger and more complex transactions, including the merger of America Online with Time Warner, the merger of Wellpoint Health Networks with Anthem, Inc. and J.P. Morgan Chase & Co.'s $58 billion acquisition of Bank One Corporation.
Career: Has a long record of public ser-

vice. During the Carter Administration, served as General Counsel of the Department of Health, Education and Welfare, and in 1980, was Director of the Transition and Counsel to the Secretary of Education. During the 1980s, served on the New York City Board of Education. Has served as a special adviser to the Secretary of State and during 1996-97 was President Clinton's Emissary for Cyprus.
Personal: Chairman of the board and founder of New Visions for Public Schools, a not-for-profit organisation that develops and implements programs to affect system-wide improvements in public education in New York City. Is a member of the Board of Directors of Harley-Davidson, Inc, Heidrick & Struggles and the National Women's Law Center, as well as a member of the Council on Foreign Relations and Vice Chairman of the Boards of Overseers and Managers of Memorial Sloan-Kettering Cancer Center and Chairman of the Board of Managers of Memorial Hospital for Cancer and Allied Diseases. Has served on the Board of Directors of the Institute for International Education, the Board of Trustees of WNET/Channel Thirteen and as a trustee for the Carnegie Corporation. Joined Simpson Thacher in 1968 after graduating from the University of Pennsylvania Law School. Prior to law school, served four years in the Marine Corps as a jet pilot, after graduating from Dartmouth College in 1961.

BECK, Thomas H
Sidley Austin Brown & Wood LLP, New York 212 839 5940
tbeck@sidley.com
Recommended in Intellectual Property
Practice Areas: Thomas H Beck joined the New York office as Partner in the IP group and focuses on complex chemical and pharmaceutical litigation matters. He has played significant roles, including as lead counsel, in chemical and pharmaceutical litigation at both the trial and appellate levels for leading pharmaceutical, chemical and biotechnology companies. He has also counseled clients in connection with drug analogs, fusion proteins, recombinant DNA techniques, and analytical methods involving viral DNA mutations
Prof. Memberships: Mr Beck was a member of the Board of Directors and has served as Chairman of the Committee on Litigation Practice and Procedure for the New York Intellectual Property Law Association.
Career: Harvard Law School, JD, 1979; North Dakota State University, BS, 1975. Bar Admission: New York, 1980.

BECKER, Jeffrey
Epstein Becker & Green PC, New York 212 351 4500
Recommended in Healthcare

BECKERMAN, Lisa G
Akin Gump Strauss Hauer & Feld LLP, New York 212 872 8012
lbeckerman@akingump.com
Recommended in Bankruptcy
Practice Areas: Lisa Beckerman is a Partner in the Financial Restructuring Group, focusing on corporate insolvency. She has represented official and unofficial unsecured creditors' committees and bondholder committees, debtors, unofficial committees of secured noteholders and acquirers of distressed businesses and assets. Recent matters include Kaiser Aluminum Corporation, ATA Holdings, Inc., Weirton Steel Corporation, Hawaiian Airlines, National Steel Corporation, Florsheim Shoe and LTV Steel Corporation.
Personal: BA, University of Chicago (1984); MBA, University of Texas (1986); JD, Boston University (1989).

BELL, Thomas
Simpson Thacher & Bartlett LLP, New York 212 455 2000
tbell@stblaw.com
Recommended in Private Equity
Practice Areas: Corporate Partner at Simpson Thacher & Bartlett LLP. Specialises in investment management matters and oversees the firm's practice in the area of private investments funds, where the firm has a pre-eminent international presence. Advises clients globally on a wide range of buyout funds, real estate funds and other kinds of private equity funds, as well as hedge funds, and other kinds of funds for 'alternative asset' categories. Responsible for representative private equity clients, such as: The Carlyle Group, Evercore Partners, The J.E. Robert Companies, J.C. Flowers & Co., New Mountain Capital, Candover, Moorfield, Altor, Brait, Sterling and Fremont Partners. Representative hedge fund clients include JWM Partners (and its predecessor firm, Long-Term Capital Management), ESL Investments, Brummer & Partners and Watershed Capital Management.
Prof. Memberships: Founder and past Co-Chair of the annual International Conference on Private Investment Funds.
Career: Joined the firm 1983 and became Partner 1992. Past Chair of the Subcommittee on Specialised Investment Vehicles of the International Bar Association and member of the subcommittee on Private Investment Entities of the American Bar Association.
Personal: Dartmouth College, BA, summa cum laude, 1978; MA, with honours from New College, Oxford University,1980; JD, Yale Law School, 1983.

BELLER, Daniel
Paul, Weiss, Rifkind, Wharton & Garrison LLP, New York 212 373 3312
dbeller@paulweiss.com
Recommended in Litigation
Practice Areas: Senior Partner, litigation. Leading trial lawyer and litigator.

Lead lawyer in complex civil and criminal matters, and major trials in antitrust, securities, real estate and commercial matters. Formerly Chief of the Major Crimes Unit in the United States Attorney's Office, Mr Beller has extensive experience in internal corporate investigations and compliance, and white-collar criminal defense. Recent major trial successes include defending $300 million commodity fraud claim for Sumitomo Corporation and successful jury verdict on behalf of Gambro, S.A. in a securities fraud action. Fellow, American College of Trial Lawyers.

BELTZER, Howard S
White & Case LLP, New York
212 819 8306
hbeltzer@whitecase.com
Recommended in Bankruptcy
Practice Areas: Mr Beltzer, Co-Head of White & Case LLP's worldwide Financial Restructuring and Insolvency Practice Group and Head of its New York banking section, focuses on major Chapter 11 proceedings and multinational bankruptcy cases. Mr Beltzer represented United Pan-Europe Communications N.V., a leading European cable and telecommunications company, in connection with its debt restructuring, effected concurrently in the US and the Netherlands, involving over €4 billion of indebtedness. Mr Beltzer is currently representing Mirant Corp. in its Chapter 11 proceedings, and is co-counsel to Bank of America as agent to the Century Cable Holdings lenders in the Adelphia bankruptcy.

BEN-AMI, Leora
Kaye Scholer LLP, New York
212 836 7203
lbenami@kayescholer.com
Recommended in Intellectual Property
Practice Areas: Partner, patent litigation. Concentration in intellectual property and patent litigation. Her practice covers all areas of technology, including biotechnology, pharmaceutical and chemistry, medical devices, mechanical devices and electronics. She also has extensive appellate experience, having argued before the United States Court of Appeals for the Federal Circuit several times and having clerked there. Ms Ben-Ami has handled approximately 10 cases for Genentech in courts throughout the United States in the field of biotechnology. She also has been counsel to DuPont in several areas, including genetically modified plants, contrast agents, polymers and paints. Ms Ben-Ami has litigated approximately 10 cases for Pfizer Inc. in the medical device area. The verdict she won in Glaxo v Genentech was cited by the 'National Law Journal' as 'defense verdict of the year.'
Prof. Memberships: Admitted to practice in New York and before the Federal Circuit. Memberships include: New York State Bar Association, Federal Cir-

cuit Bar Association; New York Patent, Trademark and Copyright Law Association; American Intellectual Property Law Association.
Career: Formerly Partner and Chair of the Americas Intellectual Property Group at Clifford Chance. Ms Ben-Ami was recently named to the 'American Lawyer's 45 under 45', a selection, based on peer review, of the most accomplished members of the private bar. JD (cum laude), SUNY Buffalo; BS, SUNY Stony Brook; Law Clerk to Senior Circuit Judge Philip Nichols, Jr, US Court of Appeals for the Federal Circuit, 1984-85.
Publications: 'Incomplete DNA Sequences Patented; Action Under New Guidelines Raises Questions, Concerns', New York Law Journal, March 15, 1999 (co-author); 'Unpredictability Factor Narrows Biotech Patents', The National Law Journal, June 16, 1997 (co-author).

BENEDICT, James
Milbank, Tweed, Hadley & McCloy, New York 212 530 5000
Recommended in Litigation

BENNER, Michael B
Wachtell, Lipton, Rosen & Katz, New York 212 403 1253
mbbenner@wlrk.com
Recommended in Real Estate
Practice Areas: Specializes in real estate.
Prof. Memberships: The Association of the Bar of the City of New York; American Bar Association.
Career: Partner at Wachtell, Lipton, Rosen & Katz.
Personal: Graduated summa cum laude from Dartmouth College in 1977 (BA) and cum laude from Harvard Law School in 1980 (JD).

BERG, Andrew
Debevoise & Plimpton LLP, New York
212 909 6000
Recommended in Tax

BERG, Eric L
White & Case LLP, New York
212 819 8253
eberg@whitecase.com
Recommended in Banking & Finance
Practice Areas: Member of the firm's Global Bank Finance Practice. Represents leading commercial and investment banks in a broad range of matters, including representing lead agents and underwriters in leveraged finance transactions. His extensive experience includes hostile takeovers as well as negotiated public and private acquisitions. Numerous and varied representations of banks in Chapter 11 proceedings, restructurings of leveraged financings and other reorganization and workout matters.
Career: BA, cum laude, Muhlenberg College, 1978; JD, magna cum laude, Cornell Law School, 1981, Order of the Coif.

BERGMANN, Peter G
Cadwalader, Wickersham & Taft LLP, New York 212 504 6595
peter.bergmann@cwt.com
Recommended in Healthcare
Practice Areas: Chairman of Cadwalader's Health Care Department. General counsel to the New York Association of Homes and Services for the Aging and counsel to the New York State Association of Counties on Medicaid reimbursement matters.
Personal: JD from George Washington University Law School in 1973. Prior to joining Cadwalader, was a law clerk to the Chief Judge of the United States District Court for the Northern District of New York. Recently completed a three-year term as Chairman of the New York County Lawyer's Association Committee on Health Services. Member of the American Bar Association (Former Chairman, Regional Forum on Health Law); the New York State Bar Association; the Association of the Bar of the City of New York; the Federal Bar Council; and the New York County Lawyers' Association.

BERGTRAUM, Howard
O'Melveny & Myers LLP, New York
212 326 2000
Recommended in Private Equity

BERNSTEIN, David
Debevoise & Plimpton LLP, New York
212 909 6000
Recommended in Intellectual Property

BERNSTEIN, Donald S
Davis Polk & Wardwell, New York
212 450 4000
donald.bernstein@dpw.com
Recommended in Bankruptcy
Practice Areas: Partner, Davis Polk & Wardwell, concentrating in insolvency. Represents creditors, debtors, receivers and acquirers in major corporate restructurings and insolvencies. Recent matters include Enron, Conseco, Adelphia Communications, US Office Products, McLeod Communications, Citation Corporation and Maxxim Medical. Also advises financial institutions regarding transaction structuring, risk management, derivatives and other complex financial products.
Prof. Memberships: Chairman, National Bankruptcy Conference. Director, American College of Bankruptcy, International Insolvency Institute. Past Chairman, New York City Bar Association Committee on Corporate Reorganization. Board of Editors, 'Collier on Bankruptcy'. Member, US delegation to UNCITRAL Insolvency Working Group.
Personal: Princeton (AB) and University of Chicago (JD).

BERNSTEIN, Michael
Bond, Schoeneck & King, LLP, New York
646 253 8329
mbernstein@bsk.com
Recommended in Employment
Practice Areas: Represents management in every facet of labor and employment law; served as Chair of the Labor and Employment Law Section of New York State Bar Association, the Labor Committee of the New York City Bar Association and the Federal Labor Standards Legislation Committee of the American Bar Association; appointed to Task Forces of Governor and Lieutenant Governor of New York; elected Fellow to College of Labor and Employment Lawyers and to New York Bar Foundation; active lecturer and author.
Personal: University of Michigan (BA, Economics, 1959); Columbia University Law School (1962).

BERNSTEIN, William S
Manatt Phelps & Phillips LLP, New York
212 830 7282
wbernstein@manatt.com
Recommended in Healthcare
Practice Areas: Co-Chairman of the firm's Government and Regulatory Division and advises clients in the healthcare industry, including provider organizations, payor organizations, emerging companies and financial institutions, with respect to strategic, business, transactional and regulatory matters. Collaborating to launch State Summit Initiative, and is outside general counsel to a not-for-profit organization that assists clients in multiple jurisdictions with respect to the organization, development and financing of Regional Health Information Organizations.
Prof. Memberships: Syntiro Healthcare Services, Inc. (Director), Psilos Venture Fund (Advisor), Human Rights in China (Director), University of Haifa (Board of Governors), NYU, School of Law, Strategic Advisory Council.
Career: Partner.
Personal: NYU (JD, 1982); Brown University, (MA, 1979); Brown University, (BA, 1978).

BETENSKY, Steven
White & Case LLP, New York
212 819 8497
SBetensky@whitecase.com
Recommended in Technology
Practice Areas: Chair of the firm's global Technology Practice Group. Concentrates in patent, trademark and technology licenses, technology transfers, IT-related acquisitions, outsourcing arrangements, technology development agreements and collaborations, and technology diligence reviews, particularly in connection with cross-border transactions. Also litigates IP-related disputes. Clients include those in the pharmaceutical, electronic, computer software, petrochemical and finance industries.

Prof. Memberships: New York State Bar; US District Court for the Southern District of New York; US Courts of Appeals for the Federal Circuit; American Intellectual Property Law Association.
Personal: Oberlin College (BA, Honors, 1986); University of Chicago Law School (JD, Honors, 1989).

BEVILACQUA, Louis
Cadwalader, Wickersham & Taft LLP, New York 212 504 6057
louis.bevilacqua@cwt.com
Recommended in Corporate/M&A
Practice Areas: Chairman of the Corporate/Mergers & Acquisitions Department. Concentrates his practice in corporate transactions, securities law and mergers and acquisitions. Represents clients in public offerings, tender offers, mergers, leveraged buyouts, proxy contests, joint ventures, exchange offers, private placements of debt and equity securities. Much of his practice involves international transactions, including acquisitions and securities matters. Provides legal advice for a number of public and private companies in a variety of areas, including contractual negotiation, financial structuring, corporate governance and other general legal matters. Served as special counsel to Independent Directors Committees in complex international mergers and contested going-private transactions and leveraged buyouts. A frequent lecturer in the area of domestic and international corporate and securities law.
Publications: 'Have Corporate Reforms Gone Too Far? The Hidden Costs of Tighter Controls,' Chief Executive, June 2004; 'The New SEC Disclosure Rules,' The Corporate Board, May 1, 2004; 'Disclosure Under Sarbanes-Oxley: an Assessment and a Look Forward,' Directorship, December 1, 2003.
Personal: BA from Holy Cross College in 1970; MBA in Finance from New York University in 1977; JD from Fordham University School of Law in 1977. Admitted to practice in the State of New York (1977) and Member of the New York County Lawyers Association and the American Bar Association.

BIALKIN, Kenneth J
Skadden, Arps, Slate, Meagher & Flom LLP & Affiliates, New York
212 735 2130
kbialkin@skadden.com
Recommended in Corporate/M&A
Practice Areas: Extensive experience in representing insurance companies, broker-dealers, investment banks and other financial institutions. Has represented US and non-US companies involved in US public and private offerings, and government and regulatory investigations by such agencies as the SEC and the Department of Justice.
Prof. Memberships: Legal Advisory Committee (or subcommittees thereof) of the Board of Directors of the New

York Stock Exchange, Inc. (1981-present); Chair, Ad Hoc Committee on Insider Trading Legislation, Section on Business Law, American Bar Association (1987-present).
Career: JD, Harvard Law School, 1953; Certificate of Attendance, London School of Economics, 1952; AB, University of Michigan, 1950.

BICK, John
Davis Polk & Wardwell, New York
212 450 4000
john.bick@dpw.com
Recommended in Private Equity
Practice Areas: Member of Davis Polk & Wardwell's Corporate Department and advises clients in mergers and acquisitions, private equity transactions, joint ventures, partnerships, takeover defenses, and corporate governance issues. Also represents clients in general corporate and securities law matters. Works extensively in the area of private equity, regularly representing Morgan Stanley Capital Partners, Morgan Stanley Venture Partners, Metalmark Capital Partners and Thomas Weisel Capital Partners. Also regularly represents Morgan Stanley in their strategic private equity investments and other private equity clients of the firm.

BIENENSTOCK, Martin
Weil, Gotshal & Manges LLP, New York
212 310 8530
martin.bienenstock@weil.com
Recommended in Bankruptcy
Practice Areas: Mr Bienenstock's practice concentrates on corporate governance for healthy companies, crisis management and domestic and international restructuring, including the initial draft of what became Ireland's reorganization statute.
Career: Mr Bienenstock is Co-Chair of the Business Finance & Restructuring Department and a member of the firm's Management Committee. He teaches Advanced Reorganization at Harvard Law School and has been selected as an outstanding attorney in his field by publications including 'The Best Lawyers in America', Turnarounds & Workouts, The International Who's Who of Business Lawyers and Euromoney Legal Media Group's The Best of the Best. Mr Bienenstock led the firm's representation of Enron and is formulating risk reporting systems that will enable corporate management to reduce risk and increase share value to benefit from the compliance cost of section 404 of Sarbanes Oxley. He also leads the firm's representation of banks and other creditors in major reorganizations such as Owens Corning and Federal Mogul involving mass torts, and of debtors such as Footstar and G-1 Holdings, Inc. Mr Bienenstock has extensive experience in derivatives and structured finance, and frequently charts and implements acquisition strategies in troubled situations

such as Leucadia, Inc. and Berkadia in their acquisition of Finova Corporation. He also advises private equity firms on governance and acquisition opportunities in the distressed area. Mr Bienenstock authored 'Bankruptcy Reorganization', a 1,000-page treatise published by the Practising Law Institute.
Personal: University of Michigan Law School, JD; University of Pennsylvania, The Wharton School, BS.

BILKIS, David
White & Case LLP, New York
212 819 8413
dbilkis@whitecase.com
Recommended in Banking & Finance
Practice Areas: The New York Banking section's administrative Partner whose practice focuses on representing leading commercial and investment banks as lead agent and arranger in a variety of lending transactions, with an emphasis on acquisition and leveraged financings. His extensive experience includes negotiated public and private acquisitions as well as hostile takeovers and exit financings and other restructurings involving borrowers in an array of industries, including manufacturing, gaming, hotel, investment funds, real estate and media and communications.
Personal: BA, magna cum laude, Phi Beta Kappa, Brandeis University, 1985; JD, cum laude, with honors, Fordham University School of Law, 1988.

BIRD, Paul
Debevoise & Plimpton LLP, New York
212 909 6000
Recommended in Corporate/M&A, Private Equity

BIRNBAUM, Sheila L
Skadden, Arps, Slate, Meagher & Flom LLP & Affiliates, New York
212 735 2450
sbirnbau@skadden.com
Recommended in Insurance
Practice Areas: Head of Skadden's Products Liability Department. Practices primarily in the areas of products liability, toxic torts and insurance coverage litigation. Represents corporations in complex mass tort and insurance litigation.
Career: Associate Dean of the Graduate Division (1982-84), professor of law (1978-84) and adjunct professor of law (1984-Present), New York University School of Law; professor of law, Fordham University School of Law (1972-78).
Publications: Co-author, 'Practitioner's Guide to Litigating Insurance Coverage Actions'.
Personal: LLB, New York University School of Law, 1965; MA, Hunter College, 1962; BA, Hunter College, 1960 (cum laude; Phi Beta Kappa).

BLANCHARD, Kimberly S
Weil, Gotshal & Manges LLP, New York
212 310 8799
kim.blanchard@weil.com
Recommended in Tax

Practice Areas: Ms Blanchard's Tax Law Practice focuses on international transactions in which she advises domestic, foreign and multi-national clients on a wide variety of corporate issues.
Career: Ms Blanchard counsels clients on matters relating to corporate mergers and acquisitions, private equity acquisitions and dispositions, internal restructurings, cross-border tax planning and joint ventures. She also advises clients in connection with fund formation, partnerships, real estate, executive compensation and exempt organization issues.
Personal: New York University School of Law, JD; University of Wisconsin, MS; Dartmouth College, BA.

BLASSBERG, Franci
Debevoise & Plimpton LLP, New York
212 909 6000
Recommended in Private Equity

BLESSING, Peter H
Shearman & Sterling LLP, New York
212 848 4106
pblessing@shearman.com
Recommended in Tax
Practice Areas: Head of Shearman & Sterling's International Tax Group, focusing on international and domestic tax aspects of business transactions, as well as representing clients in transfer pricing matters, ruling requests and controversies.
Prof. Memberships: American College of Tax Counsel; ABA Tax Section's Committee on Foreign Activities of US Taxpayers (Chair); International Tax Institute (President); NY State Bar Association Tax Section (Executive Committee); International Fiscal Association.
Publications: Author of treatise on US tax treaties and numerous articles and other publications on international tax subjects.
Personal: BA, Princeton University (1973); JD, Columbia University Law School (1977); LLM in Taxation, New York University School of Law (1981)

BLITTNER, David
Weil, Gotshal & Manges LLP, New York
212 310 8329
david.blittner@weil.com
Recommended in Private Equity
Practice Areas: Corporate, private equity.
Career: David Blittner represents private equity sponsors in acquisitions, dispositions and financings. He has extensive experience with leveraged buyouts and dispositions of public and private companies, and with minority investments, public recapitalizations and restructurings. David has represented various private equity sponsors, including DLJ Merchant Banking Partners, Capital Z Partners and APAX Partners. He recently represented a consortium including DLJ Merchant Banking Partners, Thomas H. Lee Partners, Bain Capital and JP Morgan Partners in the

approximately $3.2 billion 'going private' leveraged buy-out of Warner Chilcott.
Personal: Columbia University School of Law, JD; SUNY Binghamton, BA.

BLOCK, Dennis
Cadwalader, Wickersham & Taft LLP, New York 212 504 5555
dennis.block@cwt.com
Recommended in Corporate/M&A
Practice Areas: Specializes in mergers and acquisitions and other corporate transactions, corporate governance, and securities law. Has handled numerous M&A transactions, both hostile and friendly, on behalf of acquirers and targets, joint ventures, self-tender offers, spin-offs, and other corporate restructurings. Has participated in many highly visible transactions including Proctor & Gamble's acquisition of Gillette (announced), Pfizer Inc.'s acquisition of Pharmacia, Vivendi Universal's acquisition of Houghton Mifflin Co., Pepsi-Cola's acquisition of Quaker Oats, Pfizer Inc.'s acquisition of Warner-Lambert, AT&T's acquisition of Media One, and US West's merger with Qwest, among many others. Has represented numerous Boards and Board Committees involved in corporate transactions, and public companies, investment and commercial banks and entrepreneurs in connection with major issues of public interest and debate, including the Business Roundtable regarding corporate governance issues, Texaco regarding discrimination matters, Cendant directors, and Merrill Lynch (lead negotiator on the $1 billion industry settlement regarding Nasdaq trading).
Publications: 'The Business Judgment Rule: Fiduciary Duties of Corporate Directors' (co-author), 'The Corporate Counsellor's Deskbook' (co-editor), and a monthly column in the 'New York Law Journal'. Member of the editorial boards of several legal publications.
Personal: Graduated from Brooklyn Law School, where he now serves as an adjunct professor teaching Advanced Corporate Law. Was formerly Branch Chief of Enforcement at the New York Regional Office of the Securities and Exchange Commission.

BLUMKIN, Linda R
Fried, Frank, Harris, Shriver & Jacobson LLP, New York 212 859 8085
Linda.Blumkin@FriedFrank.com
Recommended in Antitrust
Practice Areas: Antitrust Partner. Focuses practice in antitrust litigation and counseling, with special emphasis on M&A (including the premerger notification requirements of the Hart-Scott Rodino Act) compliance and litigation matters. Regularly represents clients before the FTC and in dealings with the Antitrust Division of the Department of Justice and litigates in federal court. Representative clients include El Paso Corporation, the Scotts Company and Hunter Douglas Inc.

Prof. Memberships: Former Chair, American Bar Association's Clayton Act Committee, Antitrust Section; Member of the ABA's Sections on Antitrust Law and Litigation; Member of the Association of the Bar of the City of New York, where formerly a Member of the Committee on Trade Regulation, the Committee on Women in the Profession and the Committee on Science and Law; member of the Executive Committee of the New York State Bar Association's Antitrust Law Section.
Career: Qualified in 1968 in New York. Joined firm in 1967 and rejoined as a Partner in 1979. Assistant Director for General Litigation, Bureau of Competition, Federal Trade Commission (1977-79); associate at Breed, Abbott & Morgan (1973-77); assistant professor at Boston University's School of Management (1972-73); and lecturer at Boston University's School of Law (1971).
Publications: Co-edited 'Corporate Sentencing Guidelines: Compliance and Mitigation' (Law Journal Seminars Press).
Personal: Born 1944. Achieved LLB, cum laude, in 1967, LLM in 1973 from Harvard Law School. Received AB, cum laude, in 1964 from Barnard College, where was elected to Phi Beta Kappa.

BOAST, Molly
Debevoise & Plimpton LLP, New York 212 909 6000
Recommended in Antitrust

BOHM, Richard
Debevoise & Plimpton LLP, New York 212 909 6000
Recommended in Media & Entertainment, Private Equity

BOIES, David
Boies, Schiller & Flexner LLP, Armonk 914 749 8200
Recommended in Antitrust, Litigation

BOND, W Michael
Weil, Gotshal & Manges LLP, New York 212 310 8035
michael.bond@weil.com
Recommended in Real Estate
Practice Areas: Mr Bond represents financial institutions in diverse transactional matters, helps create joint ventures and has extensive experience in restructurings, bankruptcy and related issues.
Career: Mr Bond co-heads the Property Transaction and Finance Practice, advising clients like investment banks, money center banks and insurance companies on general corporate issues, mortgage-backed securitizations, commercial lending transactions, company and asset portfolio acquisitions, and private equity and real estate transactions. He represents capital sources and providers of products or services in forming joint ventures and strategic alliances for new businesses.
Personal: University of Virginia, JD; University of South Carolina, BS (magna cum laude).

BOROWITZ, Peter
Debevoise & Plimpton LLP, New York 212 909 6000
Recommended in Bankruptcy

BOWIE, Scott
Linklaters, New York 212 424 9160
Recommended in Private Equity

BOXER, Leonard
Stroock & Stroock & Lavan LLP, New York 212 806 5400
Recommended in Real Estate

BRACH, Richard
Milbank, Tweed, Hadley & McCloy, New York 212 530 5000
Recommended in Projects

BRANDES, Lawrence
Cadwalader, Wickersham & Taft LLP, New York 212 504 6946
larry.brandes@cwt.com
Recommended in Insurance
Practice Areas: Experienced reinsurance litigator who has acted as counsel, arbitrator or umpire in more than 500 reinsurance arbitrations and litigations, a number of which have established industry precedents. A frequent lecturer on reinsurance arbitration and litigation, he has addressed the Independent Reinsurance Underwriters, the Society of CPCU, the American Bar Association, the British Commercial Bar Association, Executive Enterprises, Inc., and numerous Mealey's conferences. Served as Co-Chair of Mealey's 2003 Insurance Insolvency and Reinsurance Roundtable.
Personal: BA, with distinction, University of Virginia (1971); JD, New York University School of Law (1974) (member of the Law Review). Former Executive Vice President of APP-CAP Reinsurance Company, Ltd., Hamilton, Bermuda; former Chairman of the Board of Directors of National Consulting Services, Inc., a professional reinsurance auditing company. Member, New York State Bar Association; American Bar Association - Tort and Insurance Practice Section; Association of the Bar of the City of New York (served as a Member of the Insurance Law Committee and Chairman of the Reinsurance Subcommittee); British Commercial Bar Association (Honorary Overseas Member).

BRANNAN, William
Cravath, Swaine & Moore LLP, New York 212 474 1600
wbrannan@cravath.com
Recommended in Tax
Practice Areas: Wide variety of domestic and international transactions, including securities offerings, mergers and acquisitions, investment partnerships and real estate (including REIT) transactions.
Prof. Memberships: NYSBA (Member of Executive Committee; Co-Chair of Committee on Partnerships, Tax Section); ABA; ABCNY; NAREIT; Pension Real Estate Association; Tax Club of New York City.

Career: Joined firm in 1983, Partner since 1991.
Publications: Has written a number of tax-related papers and bar association reports and is a frequent speaker at tax-related seminars and professional programs.
Personal: Harvard Law School (JD, magna cum laude, 1983); Vanderbilt University (BS, summa cum laude, 1980; Phi Beta Kappa).

BREGLIO, John F
Paul, Weiss, Rifkind, Wharton & Garrison LLP, New York 212 373 3391
jbreglio@paulweiss.com
Recommended in Media & Entertainment
Practice Areas: Chair of the Entertainment Department. Member of the Intellectual Property Group. Represents companies and individuals involved in all aspects of the entertainment industry, including legitimate theater, motion picture, publishing and music businesses, and intellectual property matters. Has been instrumental in assisting his clients develop, finance and produce hundreds of plays, musicals and films for more than 30 years. Has extensive experience ranging from advising film, televison, and video companies develop, finance and distribute entertainment products to advising Broadway producers and theater owners produce and present plays and musicals. Selected for 2005 edition of 'The Best Lawyers in America'.

BRENNAN, Matthew J
Sullivan & Cromwell LLP, New York 212 558 4000
brennanm@sullcrom.com
Recommended in Environment
Practice Areas: Advises on environmental issues in commercial transactions for the firm's corporate, M&A, project finance, real estate, securities and finance groups. Evaluates environmental liabilities and risks, structures transactions to minimize risk and negotiates environmental risk allocation among parties in commercial transactions. 20 years' experience providing environmental advice to a diverse clientele, including corporations, lenders and governments.
Prof. Memberships: ABA; ABCNY.
Career: Special counsel since 1998.
Personal: State University of New York at New Paltz (BA, 1979); University of Pennsylvania Law School (JD, 1986).

BRESLOW, Stephanie
Schulte Roth & Zabel LLP, New York 212 756 2542
stephanie.breslow@srz.com
Recommended in Private Equity
Practice Areas: Investment management, partnerships and securities.
Prof. Memberships: Association of the Bar of the City of New York, including Corporation Law Committee (1993-96), Chair, Subcommittee on Business Trusts

(1995-96); Member, Committee on the Revised Uniform Partnership Act (1993-96); Member, Steering Committee, Wall Street Hedge Fund Forum; Founding Member and Past Chair, Private Investment Fund Forum; Committee of Hearts 2003-04, Hedge Funds Care; and Member of the Board of Trustees, The Joyce Theater, New York.

Career: Partner since 1996.

Publications: Has lectured and written extensively on matters related to investment management, partnerships and securities law.

Personal: Recognized in Who's Who Legal, The International Who's Who of Business Lawyers 2002, 2003 and 2004; Chambers Global - The World's Leading Lawyers, 2002, 2003 and 2004.

BRODSKY, David
Latham & Watkins LLP, New York
212 906 1200
Recommended in Litigation

BROMLEY, James L
Cleary Gottlieb Steen & Hamilton LLP, New York
212-225-2264
jbromley@cgsh.com
Recommended in Bankruptcy

Practice Areas: Bankruptcy, work-out and acquisition advice to debtors, creditors and strategic investors, and commercial litigation involving bankruptcy and insolvency matters. He has substantial experience in international restructurings with complex cross-border issues that have involved the US, Canada, Mexico, the EU, Japan, Korea and Hong Kong. He has particular expertise in mergers and acquisitions in the insolvency context. Notable transactions: Covanta Energy's successful reorganization, SK Networks' $7 billion debt restructuring, Daewoo Motors' sale of its Korean Automotive business to a joint venture controlled by General Motors, and Cable & Wireless' acquisition of the assets of Chapter 11 debtor Exodus Communications.

BROUDE, Mark
Latham & Watkins LLP, New York
212 906 1200
Recommended in Bankruptcy

BROWN, Dickson G
Simpson Thacher & Bartlett LLP, New York 212 455 2850
dbrown@stblaw.com
Recommended in Tax

Practice Areas: A senior member of the firm's Tax Department. Areas of concentration are federal income tax with an emphasis on financial instruments, domestic and foreign joint ventures, mergers and acquisitions and financial institutions. Advises on various financial products such as hybrid debt instruments, tracking stock, trust preferred securities and investment units, cross-border and domestic joint ventures, and structuring of foreign operations.

Prof. Memberships: Member of the Bar Association of the City of New York, the New York and American Bar Associations.

Career: Joined Simpson Thacher in 1971 and became a Partner in 1978.

Personal: Received BA (1968) from the University of Michigan and was elected Phi Beta Kappa; received JD (1971) from University of Michigan School of Law and also elected Order of the Coif. Earned an LLM in 1975 from New York University.

BROWN, Elliot
Franklin, Weinrib, Rudell & Vassallo, New York 212 935 5500
Recommended in Media & Entertainment

BROWNSTEIN, Andrew R
Wachtell, Lipton, Rosen & Katz, New York 212 403 1233
arbrownstein@wlrk.com
Recommended in Corporate/M&A

Practice Areas: Specializes in mergers and acquisitions, takeovers, leveraged buyouts, corporate governance and securities law matters. Has been a leading participant in numerous precedent setting transactions, including: the landmark takeover defenses of Household International, Inc., Phillips Petroleum Company, Revlon, Inc. and Universal Foods Corporation; the complex restructurings of W.R. Grace & Co.'s medical services and packaging divisions in successive Morris Trust transactions with Fresenius AG and Sealed Air Corporation; and the merger of Amoco with British Petroleum. More recently represented Sears, Roebuck & Co. in its merger with Kmart and in the sale of its credit card business to Citigroup Inc. and Novartis AG with respect to its acquisition of EON Labs. Advised Phillips Petroleum Company for many years on numerous matters including its merger with Conoco, Inc. and advised ConocoPhillips with respect to its investment in Russian oil company OAO Lukoil. Counseled the Special Committee of the Board of Directors of the Hertz Corporation in connection with a going private proposal from Ford Motor Company, and represented Household International in its acquisition of Beneficial Corporation and Reynolds Metals Company in its merger with Alcoa Inc. Also active in the technology area; represented Proxicom, Inc. in its merger with Dimension Data Holdings plc, Packard BioScience Company in its merger with PerkinElmer, Inc. and HotJobs.com, Ltd. in its merger with Yahoo. Represents several leading private equity investors, including Apollo Advisors, L.P. and Warburg Pincus LLC.

Prof. Memberships: Has been an adjunct professor of securities law at Rutgers University Law School; is past Chairman of the Ray Garrett Jr. Corporate and Securities Law Institute at

Northwestern University School of Law and is on the executive planning committee of that Institute; and is Co-Chairman of the Annual M&A Lawyers Institute held in New York City.

Career: Partner at Wachtell, Lipton, Rosen & Katz since 1985, member of the management committee of the firm and responsible for the day-to-day operations of the firm's Corporate Group. Clerked for the Honorable Leonard Garth of the US Court of Appeals for the Third Circuit.

Publications: Frequent author and lecturer on legal subjects.

Personal: Graduated from the University of Pennsylvania in 1975 (BA, English, BS, Economics), from the Wharton School of the University of Pennsylvania in 1976 (MBA) and from Harvard Law School in 1979 (JD), where he was Articles Editor of the 'Harvard Law Review'. Serves on the Boards of the New York City Public Art Fund and Trinity School in New York City.

BROZMAN, Tina
Bingham McCutchen LLP, New York 212 318 7700
Recommended in Bankruptcy

BUHLE, Warren
Weil, Gotshal & Manges LLP, New York 212 310 8898
warren.buhle@weil.com
Recommended in Banking & Finance

Practice Areas: Mr Buhle specializes in representing lenders and borrowers in a wide variety of financial transactions.

Career: Mr Buhle represents clients in matters relating to secured and unsecured credit facilities, leveraged leases, healthcare financings, restructurings, acquisition financings, letter of credit facilities, inventory and receivables borrowing base financings, tax-exempt revenue bond transactions and commercial paper facilities. He also has a particular concentration in aircraft and maritime finance, bank credit facilities, equipment leveraged leasing and healthcare finance.

Personal: Columbia University School of Law, JD; Johns Hopkins University, BA.

BURESH, James
Simpson Thacher & Bartlett LLP, New York 212 455 7221
jburesh@stblaw.com
Recommended in Banking & Finance

Practice Areas: Corporate Partner advising clients in banking and credit and capital markets and securities matters.

Prof. Memberships: Admitted to practice in New York (1989). Member, American Bar Association.

Career: Joined Simpson Thacher in 1987; became Partner in 1997.

Personal: Received JD, 1986, Yale Law School; notes editor, 'Yale Law Journal'. Received AB, with honors, 1983, The University of Chicago.

BURKE, Ted
Freshfields Bruckhaus Deringer LLP, New York 212 277 4000
Recommended in Projects

BURLEIGH, Jennifer
Debevoise & Plimpton LLP, New York 212 909 6000
Recommended in Private Equity

BYOWITZ, Michael H
Wachtell, Lipton, Rosen & Katz, New York 212 403 1268
mhbyowitz@wlrk.com
Recommended in Antitrust

Practice Areas: Specializes in antitrust law and policy, principally advising multinational corporations on major domestic and international mergers, acquisitions, joint ventures and corporate takeovers. Represents many clients at the Department of Justice, the Federal Trade Commission, and State Attorneys General in the United States and consults on investigations by foreign antitrust authorities in the European Union, Australia, Canada, Mexico, South America, the United Kingdom and many other jurisdictions.

Prof. Memberships: A leader of the American Bar Association's Section of International Law & Practice; Chair-Elect of the Section and the former Chair of its Business Regulation Division, its General Division, its Public International Law Division and its International Antitrust Law Committee. Served as the Chair of the Antitrust and Trade Regulation Committee of the Association of the Bar of the City of New York from 1998-2001.

Career: Partner at Wachtell, Lipton, Rosen & Katz, where he heads the Antitrust Department. Served as Senior Trial Attorney and Trial Attorney with the Department of Justice's Antitrust Division 1979-83.

Publications: Writes articles on antitrust issues and is a contributor to legal publications, including the international antitrust law chapter of the ABA's The International Lawyer's Deskbook. Frequent speaker on International Antitrust Law and Compliance in the United States and abroad.

Personal: Graduated from Columbia University in 1973 (AB) and from New York University School of Law in 1976 (JD), where he was awarded the Order of the Coif and served as an editor of the 'Law Review'.

CAGNEY, Lawrence
Debevoise & Plimpton LLP, New York 212 909 6000
Recommended in Employee Benefits

CAMPBELL Jr, Woodrow
Debevoise & Plimpton LLP, New York 212 909 6000
Recommended in Private Equity

CANELLOS, Peter C
Wachtell, Lipton, Rosen & Katz,
New York 212 403 1241
pcanellos@wlrk.com
Recommended in Tax

Practice Areas: Specializes in the tax aspects of the corporate acquisitions, dispositions and financings that constitute Wachtell, Lipton, Rosen & Katz's major practice areas, whose large and complex transactions frequently involve multinational tax considerations.
Prof. Memberships: Served as Chairman of the New York State Bar Association Tax Section.
Career: Partner at Wachtell, Lipton, Rosen & Katz. Clerked for the Honorable Judge Charles D Breitel of the New York Court of Appeals and was a Fulbright Scholar at the University of Amsterdam in the Netherlands.
Publications: Frequent writer and lecturer on tax matters. Published articles include: 'Contingency and the Debt/Equity Continuum' (with Deborah Paul, in the 'Journal of Financial Products', 2002); 'A Tax Practitioner's Perspective on Substance, Form and Business Purpose in Structuring Business Transactions and in Tax Shelters' (in 'SMU Law Review', 2001); 'Reasonable Expectations and the Taxation of Contingencies' (in 'Tax Lawyer', 1997); 'Dividend Access Shares' (49th IFA Congress, Cannes, 1995); and 'Corporate Inversions and Similar Transactions' (in the 54th NYU Annual Institute on Federal Taxation, 1995).
Personal: Graduated summa cum laude from Columbia University (BA), where he was elected to Phi Beta Kappa, and magna cum laude from Columbia Law School in 1967 (LLB), where he was editor in chief of 'Columbia Law Review'.

CANONI, John
Nixon Peabody LLP, New York
212 940 3169
jcanoni@nixonpeabody.com
Recommended in Employment

Practice Areas: Mr Canoni handles a wide range of labor and employment matters including: National Labor Relations Board matters, contract negotiations, arbitrations, employment discrimination, FMLA, ADA, wrongful discharge, and WARN. He represents major health care, transportation, commercial, not-for-profit, media, insurance, utility, and construction companies.
Prof. Memberships: Admitted to practice in New York, the US Supreme Court, and the First, Second, Third, Fourth, Fifth, Seventh, and District of Columbia Circuit Courts. Member of the CPR Institute for Dispute Resolution's specialized Employment Law Mediator Panel. Member of the NY State Bar Association.
Personal: Yale Law School, LLB; Amherst College, BA, cum laude.

CANTOR, Matthew
Kirkland & Ellis LLP, New York
212 446 4846
mcantor@kirkland.com
Recommended in Bankruptcy

Practice Areas: Mr Cantor focuses his practice on strategic counseling in financial and operational corporate reorganizations. Notable representations include NRG Energy; Allegiance Telecom; Wellman, Inc.; the ad hoc committee of the MAGI bondholders in the Mirant Corporation case; Limbach Facility Services LLC; KMC Telecom; Quality Stores, Inc.; American Commercial Lines, LLC; Ziff-Davis Media; and CornerStone Propane Partners LP. Additionally, Mr Cantor advises buyout, private equity and hedge funds in the management of investments in distressed situations and developing control acquisition strategies.
Personal: State University of New York at Binghamton, BA, 1986. New York University School of Law, JD, 1989.

CAPLAN, David L
Davis Polk & Wardwell, New York
212 450 4000
david.caplan@dpw.com
Recommended in Corporate/M&A

Practice Areas: Member of Davis Polk & Wardwell's Corporate Department. Advises corporate and investment banking clients in mergers and acquisitions, joint ventures, corporate governance issues and related matters. Has represented a number of clients, including Aetna, Canadian National Railway, Harvard University, Limited Brands, Lockheed Martin, the New York Mets and Random House, in a range of transactions and other matters in recent years. Has also represented a number of leading investment banking firms in connection with merger and acquisition transactions.

CAPLAN, Gordon
Willkie Farr & Gallagher LLP, New York
212 728 8266
gcaplan@willkie.com
Recommended in Technology

Practice Areas: Partner in the Corporate and Financial Services Department, specializing in technology and telecommunications related corporate matters, venture capital, and mergers and acquisitions. He has extensive experience representing public and private companies on a spectrum of corporate matters, including private equity financing, securities offerings, exchange offers, privatizations, mergers and acquisitions, banking, commercial contracts, licensing, and employment issues. He has also been responsible for the structuring, drafting and negotiation of significant technology licensing, procurement and outsourcing transactions for a number of major telecommunications and technology companies over the last several years. Significant matters in 2004

include representation of Sprint Corporation in three separate multiyear high speed data wireless services infrastructure build-out agreements with each of Lucent, Motorola and Nortel, with a total value of approximately $3 billion. He also represented Warburg Pincus in its acquisition of POS software developer InfoGenesis and in its $2.05 billion acquisition (with Bain Capital LLC and Silver Lake Partners LP) of the UGS PLM Solutions business from EDS. Additionally, he represented Aelita Software in its sale to Quest Software (Nasdaq. QSFT) and is currently representing Sprint Corporation in connection with numerous technology and contract integration matters related to the Sprint/Nextel merger.
Career: Admitted to the Bar of the State of New York.
Publications: Has published on the subject of high-technology transactions, has lectured on venture capital transactions at Columbia University Graduate School of Business and has lectured on representing technology and communications clients at Fordham Law School.
Personal: Received a JD from Fordham Law School in 1991, where he was an editor of the Fordham Law Review and a BA from Cornell University College of Arts and Sciences in 1988.

CAPLAN, Sherri
Debevoise & Plimpton LLP, New York
212 909 6000
Recommended in Private Equity

CARLEEN, Donald P
Fried, Frank, Harris, Shriver & Jacobson LLP, New York 212 859 8202
Donald.Carleen@friedfrank.com
Recommended in Employee Benefits

Practice Areas: Chairman of the Executive Compensation and Employee Benefits Department. Mr Carleen writes a column on employee benefits in the 'New York Law Journal'. He is a contributing author to Arthur Fleischer Jr and Alexander Sussman's treatise 'Takeover Defense' and has also written 'The Fiduciary Duty to Disclose Plan Amendments Under Serious Consideration' for the 'Journal of Compensation and Benefits', July/August 1997; 'ERISA Preemption of Unclaimed Property and Escheat Laws,' for the 'BNA Tax Management Multistate Tax Report,' December 1999.
Prof. Memberships: Mr Carleen is a Member of the American Bar Association, Section on Taxation, Employee Benefits Committee; the New York State Bar Association; and the Association of the Bar of the City of New York.
Career: Mr Carleen is admitted to practice in New York and New Jersey. Joined Fried Frank in 1983 and became a Partner in 1987.
Personal: Born 1953. Received JD, summa cum laude, in 1983 from Brooklyn Law School and BA 1977 from the College of Insurance.

CARROLL, John
Clifford Chance US LLP, New York
212 878 8596
john.carroll@cliffordchance.com
Recommended in Litigation

Practice Areas: Serves as global Head of the Regulatory and White Collar Practice. He represents both institutional and individual clients in various criminal, regulatory and complex civil disputes. In particular, he has represented clients in matters involving federal and state prosecutors, the SEC and other regulators, and the New York Attorney General's Office. He has frequently represented institutions, Boards of Directors and individuals in regulatory and criminal financial fraud and accounting fraud investigations and has represented clients in connection with the international price-fixing prosecutions. He has tried numerous criminal jury cases and argued numerous appeals.

CARROLL, Michael P
Davis Polk & Wardwell, New York
212 450 4000
michael.carroll@dpw.com
Recommended in Litigation

Practice Areas: Member of Davis Polk & Wardwell's Litigation Department. He has represented a wide range of clients in federal and state jury trials, and in government investigations and administrative trials. He also defends corporations and boards of directors in federal and state class-action litigation. His most recent trial was the Oracle vs. PeopleSoft M&A litigation in Delaware Chancery Court. His work also includes confidential internal investigations on behalf of corporations facing potential criminal and regulatory exposure.

CASSANOS, Robert
Fried, Frank, Harris, Shriver & Jacobson LLP, New York 212 859 8278
robert.cassanos@friedfrank.com
Recommended in Tax

Practice Areas: Mr Cassanos is Chair of the New York Tax Department of Fried Frank. He concentrates his practice in the areas of international taxation, real estate, mergers and acquisitions, hedge funds and investment funds, and structured finance and financial products.
Prof. Memberships: Executive Committee of the Tax Section of the New York State Bar Association; Tax Forum.
Career: Joined Fried Frank in 1981 and became a Partner in 1988. Admitted to practice in New York.
Publications: 'Single Taxation of Publicly Traded Entities', 99 Tax Notes 1663, June 16, 2003.
Personal: Born 1952. Received JD in 1981 from Rutgers University and AB 1974 from Cornell University.

CENDALI, Dale
O'Melveny & Myers LLP, New York
212 326 2000
Recommended in Intellectual Property, Media & Entertainment

CERABINO, Thomas M
Willkie Farr & Gallagher LLP, New York
212 728 8208
tcerabino@willkie.com
Recommended in Corporate/M&A

Practice Areas: Partner in the Corporate and Financial Services Department, Chair of the Mergers & Acquisitions Practice Group, and a member of the firm's Executive Committee. Specializes in mergers and acquisitions, debt restructurings, debt and equity financings, and general corporate and securities law matters. Significant matters in 2004 include representation of Colony Capital in its pending $1.24 billion acquisition of four casinos from Harrah's Entertainment, Inc. and Caesars Entertainment, Inc., and on its $280 million acquisition of the Las Vegas Hilton casino hotel from LVH Corporation. In 2003, he advised an investment consortium in its $1.2 billion acquisition of Conseco Corporation's consumer lending arm. Has represented various public and private companies, private equity funds, and investment banking firms in a wide range of domestic and cross border transactions, including business combinations, divestitures, leveraged buyouts, public and private offerings of securities, and change-of-control matters. Has advised Boards of Directors and board committees on a variety of governance and other issues.
Prof. Memberships: Serves as counsel and a Director of United Neighborhood Houses of New York, Inc., a not-for-profit organization, which is the umbrella organization for the New York City settlement house system, and is a member of the Board of Regents of Georgetown University. Member of the Association of the Bar of the City of New York, and previously served on its Committee on Securities Regulation (1990-92).
Career: Admitted to the Bar of the State of New York.
Personal: Received a JD from St. John's University School of Law (cum laude) in 1981, where he served as notes and comments editor of the 'St. John's Law Review', and a BSFS from Georgetown University in 1978.

CHADAKOFF, Richard
Latham & Watkins LLP, New York
212 906 1200
Recommended in Real Estate

CHAFFETZ, Peter
Clifford Chance US LLP, New York
212 878 4910
peter.chaffetz@cliffordchance.com
Recommended in Insurance

Practice Areas: Serves as global practice leader for litigation and dispute resolution for Clifford Chance. In nearly 20 years as a reinsurance specialist he has led a succession of prominent cases, involving such issues as finite risk covers, the collapse of the workers comp 'carve out' market, pollution and asbestos coverage disputes, disputes arising from managing general agencies, surety reinsurance, the enforceability of cut-through endorsements, insurance insolvency and the destruction of the World Trade Center. Regularly speaks and publishes in the field and has been US legal correspondent for 'Reinsurance Magazine'.

CHARLES, Scott K
Wachtell, Lipton, Rosen & Katz, New York 212 403 1202
skcharles@wlrk.com
Recommended in Bankruptcy

Practice Areas: Specializes in the areas of commercial transactions, distressed mergers and acquisitions and bankruptcy and has represented many institutional lenders, creditors committees and distressed securities investors in various troubled debt situations. His recent cases have included Kmart Corporation, Enron Corporation, NRG Corporation, Avianca Airlines, Calpine Corporation, Footstar, Inc., Frank's Nursery & Crafts, Inc., PSINet, Inc., Spalding Holdings Corporation and Exide Technologies.
Career: Partner in the Creditor's Rights Department of Wachtell, Lipton, Rosen & Katz in 1991. Frequently lectures at various seminars conducted by the Practicing Law Institute, the Commercial Finance Association, Turnaround and Management Association and the Continuing Legal Education.
Publications: Has authored and co-authored several articles and outlines involving distressed mergers and acquisitions, prepackaged plans of reorganization, debtor-in-possession financing, the rights of secured and unsecured creditors both inside and outside of bankruptcy, and various aspects of the Chapter 11 process.
Personal: Graduated from Wharton School of Business, University of Pennsylvania in 1981 (BS in Economics) and from Harvard Law School in 1984 (JD); member of Beta Alpha Psi, Beta Gamma Sigma and Phi Beta Kappa.

CHARNEY, Steven M
Peckar & Abramson PC, New York
212 382 0909
scharney@pecklaw.com
Recommended in Construction

Practice Areas: Mr Charney's practice includes ongoing representation of developers and contractors that are among the top 10 as reported by 'Engineering News Record'. Mr Charney's background couples extensive academic and hands-on experience in the construction industry with over 15 years of experience in litigating for and providing legal counsel to developers and contractors.
Prof. Memberships: Mr Charney is a Member of Associated General Contractors of America (AGC) and serves on both the Contract Documents and Risk Management Committees and served as Vice-Chairman of the Mold Litigation Task Force, of this leading national organization. He is a Member of the Association of the Bar of the City of New York and served on the Construction Law Subcommittee of that prestigious association. He is also a Member of the American Bar Association and the New York State Bar Association. He is admitted to practice in New York and New Jersey.
Career: Managing Partner of the New York office. Former Eastern Division Counsel for Turner Construction Company.
Publications: Mr Charney lectures nationally regarding matters related to construction contracting, and frequently presents private lectures and training to the nation's leading contractors. He vice chaired the AGC task force that drafted the industry's first guide to Mold entitled 'Managing the Risk of Mold in the Construction of Buildings' and has presented numerous lectures, including a three part seminar before the prestigious Association of the Bar of the City of New York entitled 'Truly Understanding Construction Contracts'. He has also presented various programs for prominent industry organizations on topics such as Subcontractor Default Insurance, Mold Risk Management, and legislative matters affecting the construction industry. He has also published commentary regarding issues applicable to the construction and development industries, including commentary in 'New York Construction News'.
Personal: Mr Charney is a graduate of Syracuse University, the School of Civil Engineering at New Jersey Institute of Technology, and Seton Hall University School of Law.

CHATZINOFF, Howard
Weil, Gotshal & Manges LLP, New York
212 874 8281
howard.chatzinoff@weil.com
Recommended in Corporate/M&A

Practice Areas: Mr Chatzinoff's practice focuses on corporate and securities law with an emphasis on public and private merger and acquisition transactions and joint ventures.
Career: Mr Chatzinoff represents clients in a broad spectrum of industries. In media and telecommunications, representations have included NBC in its acquisition of Telemundo, CBS in its acquisition of King World Productions (and prior thereto, Westinghouse in its acquisition of CBS), Infinity Broadcasting in its acquisition of Outdoor Systems and EXCEL Communications in its acquisition of Telco Communications. Other media/telecom clients have included Westwood One, SBC Communications, EXCEL Communications, Qwest Communications, NextWave Telecom, Rhythms Netconnections, Real Networks and Hollywood Media. Recent representations in other industries have included General Electric in its acquisitions of Ionics, Edwards Systems Technology, InVision Technologies, OSi Specialties and BetzDearborn, its split-off of Genworth Financial and its sale of a controlling interest in GE Capital International Services, Molson in its merger with Coors, Lending Tree in its merger with InterActive Corp., Centerpulse in its proposed sale to Smith & Nephew plc, Atkins Nutritionals in its sale to Parthenon Capital and Goldman Sachs, and Interactive Search Holdings in its sale to Ask Jeeves. He also regularly represents, among others, Six Flags and Elizabeth Arden, as well as several investment banks in their role as financial advisor in merger and acquisition transactions, including Citigroup, Lehman Brothers and Merrill Lynch.
Personal: University of Virginia, JD; Princeton University, BSE. He is active in the New York community, serving as a member of the Executive Committee of the Board of Directors of PENCIL (Public Education Needs Civic Involvement in Learning), the Executive Committee of the New York City Advisory Board of the Enterprise Foundation (an organization dedicated to seeing that low-income families have the opportunity for fit and affordable housing and to bridging the 'digital divide'), and the Lawyers Committee of NYC2012 (endeavoring to bring the 2012 Summer Olympic Games to New York).

CHEPIGA, Michael J
Simpson Thacher & Bartlett LLP, New York 212 455 2000
mchepiga@stblaw.com
Recommended in Litigation

Practice Areas: Represents clients in securities litigation, class actions, derivative actions and corporate control litigation. Representative securities cases include litigation involving Royal Ahold, Dynegy, St. Paul-Travelers, Deutsche Telekom, HealthSouth, American Electric Power, Celera Genomics, Express Scripts and KeySpan. M&A litigations include Wachovia/First Union/SunTrust Litigation, Telecorp Shareholders Litigation and many others.
Prof. Memberships: Fellow, American Bar Foundation (1998 -); The Association of the Bar of the City of New York (Federal Courts Committee, 1992-95); American Bar Association; NY State Bar Association (Federal Courts Committee, 1986-88); Federal Bar Council; Legal Aid Society of New York (Director 1986-98, President 1996-98, Presidents Council 1998-. Volunteers of Legal Services (Director, 2000-).
Career: Joined Simpson Thacher 1981 and became Partner 1986. Law Clerk to the Honorable Milton Pollack (SDNY) 1979-80 and to the Honorable Amalya Kearse (Second Circuit) 1980-81.
Publications: 'Commercial Litigation in

New York State Courts', second edition, Chapter on Mergers and Acquisitions; Play, 'Getting and Spending' (produced on Broadway, NYC, 1998). Numerous articles and lectures on federal civil litigation and federal securities law.
Personal: Yale University, JD, 1979; Fordham University, BA 1970, cum laude; New York University, PhD, 1976 (English Literature).

CHERTOK, Mark
Sive Paget & Riesel PC, New York
212 421 2150
mchertok@sprlaw.com
Recommended in Environment
Practice Areas: Mark A Chertok is a Partner in Sive, Paget & Riesel, P.C., with offices in New York City and White Plains, New York. Mark A Chertok, a graduate of Harvard Law School (JD 1970, cum laude) and the State University of New York at Buffalo (AB 1967, magna cum laude), has been active in environmental and land use counseling, permitting, enforcement and litigation for more than 25 years.
Prof. Memberships: He is a Member of the Executive Committee of the New York State Bar Association, Environmental Law Section, and Co-Chair of its Committee on Environmental Impact Assessment. He has served on the faculty of numerous institutions. He was an organizer of the March 2001 SEQRA 25th Anniversary Conference, co-chaired the October 2001 SEQRA 25th Anniversary Conference Symposium, and lectured at each.
Career: His experience spans a broad spectrum of substantive areas and his clients include state, regional and local governmental bodies, private industrial, commercial and financial entities, and national and regional environmental and civic organizations.
Publications: Mr Chertok is a contributing author in 'The Treatise on New York Environmental Law', New York State Bar Association (1992) and 'Supplement' (1995), as well as in Environmental Impact Review in New York, Gerrard, Ruzow and Weinberg (1999).
Personal: Mr Chertok was an adjunct professor at the Benjamin N. Cardozo School of Law, where he taught environmental litigation. He also formerly taught environmental litigation as an adjunct professor at the Pace University School of Law and development law as an adjunct associate professor at the Columbia University Graduate School of Architecture, Planning and Historic Preservation. Mr Chertok served, or currently serves, as principal counsel for project proponents in both governmental approval processes and litigation.

CHESLER, Evan
Cravath, Swaine & Moore LLP,
New York 212 474 1243
echesler@cravath.com
Recommended in Antitrust,

Intellectual Property, Litigation
Practice Areas: Head of Litigation Department. Antitrust, securities, intellectual property, general commercial cases.
Prof. Memberships: ABA; NYSBA; ABCNY; Institute for Judicial Administration (President); American College of Trial Lawyers (Fellow).
Career: Partner since 1982. Clerkship: Hon Inzer B Wyatt (US District Court for the Southern District of New York).
Publications: Numerous articles on legal topics. Chapter in 'Inside the Minds of Leading Litigators'. Editor, 'The Russian Jewry Reader'. Adjunct assistant professor of History, NYU.
Personal: New York University School of Law (JD, cum laude, 1975; Order of the Coif); Hunter College (MA, 1973); New York University (AB, highest honors, 1970).

CHIDA, Junaid H
Dewey Ballantine LLP, New York
212 259 6308
jchida@deweyballantine.com
Recommended in Projects
Practice Areas: Project finance and leasing. In particular, Mr Chida's practice focuses on infrastructure projects in the United States and internationally, utilizing highly structured nonrecourse vehicles and tax-advantaged financing. Current and recent transactions include several wind, geothermal and solar projects in the United States, oil and gas projects in Brazil and a metro/subway system expansion in Chile.
Prof. Memberships: California Bar Association.
Career: Admitted to practice New York, California, Wisconsin. Partner, Dewey Ballantine LLP.
Personal: Born June 23, 1956. BBA, University of Wisconsin-Eau Claire, 1978. JD, University of Wisconsin, 1983.

CHINN, Adam D
Wachtell, Lipton, Rosen & Katz,
New York 212 403 1000
adchinn@wlrk.com
Recommended in Employee Benefits
Practice Areas: Specializes in both merger and acquisition tax practice and its transaction related executive compensation practice, with a particular emphasis on transactions involving financial services institutions. Has been involved in many major financial institution mergers, both bank and non-bank, including Wells Fargo/Norwest, Fleet/BankBoston, GE/Heller Financial, Credit Suisse/DLJ and AIG/American General, FleetBoston Financial Corp./Bank of America Corporation, Dresdner/Wasserstein Perella, Household International, Inc./HSBC Holdings plc and National Golf Properties Inc/Goldman Sachs Group Inc.
Career: Partner in the New York law firm of Wachtell, Lipton, Rosen & Katz.
Publications: Has written and spoken

frequently on tax and executive compensation issues. Is the author of the chapter on Change of Control Arrangements in 'Executive Compensation' (Law Journal Seminars-Press 1996) and 'Bank Mergers: Change of Control Employment Arrangements and Employee Benefit Aspects of Merger Agreements', 15 Bank and Corporate Governance Law Reporter at 8 (Sept. 1995).
Personal: Graduated from Oxford University, England in 1982 (BA), from the College of Law, England in 1983 (CPE) and cum laude from New York University in 1987 (JD) where he was Order of the Coif and editor, 'New York University Law Review' and author: Note 'Attacking Tax Shelters 183 Leaves the Farm and Goes to the Movies', 61, 'New York University Law Review', 89, 1986. Was chosen by 'The American Lawyer' as one of the 45 highest performing members of the private bar under the age of 45.

CIERI, Richard
Kirkland & Ellis LLP, New York
212 446 4770
rcieri@kirkland.com
Recommended in Bankruptcy
Practice Areas: Mr Cieri's practice involves representing debtors, creditors' committees, and secured creditors in restructurings and bankruptcies; advising the boards of directors of financially troubled companies; providing advice in connection with tort and product liability claims facing a debtor, and technology and intellectual property issues; structuring of secured and commercial transactions (including advice related to fraudulent conveyance, corporate spin-offs, and related securities issues); and the acquisition of and lending to financially troubled companies.
Personal: State University of New York at Buffalo, BA, 1978. University of Michigan Law School, JD, 1981.

CLARY, Richard W
Cravath, Swaine & Moore LLP,
New York 212 474 1227
rclary@cravath.com
Recommended in Litigation
Practice Areas: Managing Partner, litigation. Securities, antitrust, patent, trade secret, trademark, bankruptcy and commercial litigation (trials and appeals). International and domestic arbitrations.
Prof. Memberships: ABA (Intellectual Property and Litigation sections); NYSBA; ABCNY; London Court of International Arbitration; Federal Bar Council.
Career: Partner since 1985. Clerkships: Hon. Thurgood Marshall (US Supreme Court), Hon Walter R Mansfield (US Court of Appeals for the Second Circuit).
Personal: Harvard Law School (JD, magna cum laude, 1978; Developments Officer of the Law Review; Sears Prize);

Amherst College (BA, magna cum laude, 1975; Phi Beta Kappa). Legal Aid Society: Vice-Chair, Executive Committee, Nominating Committee.

COCHRAN, Eric L
Skadden, Arps, Slate, Meagher & Flom LLP & Affiliates, New York
212 735 2596
ecochran@skadden.com
Recommended in Corporate/M&A
Practice Areas: Concentrates in mergers and acquisitions, securities law and general corporate law. Has advised clients on a wide variety of friendly and hostile transactions. Recent transactions have included negotiated acquisitions and divestitures, hostile defenses, proxy fights, restructurings, leveraged buyouts, private equity investments and minority buyouts. Also has advised clients on corporate governance matters. Has been on the faculty of Practising Law Institute seminars, speaking on corporate and securities topics.
Career: JD, New York University School of Law, 1986; MS, New York University, 1984; BA, Williams College, 1982.

COGUT, Charles 'Casey'
Simpson Thacher & Bartlett LLP,
New York 212 455 2550
ccogut@stblaw.com
Recommended in Corporate/M&A, Private Equity
Practice Areas: Head of Mergers and Acquisitions Practice, specialising in domestic and international mergers and acquisitions and transactions involving private equity firms. Currently oversees the firm's relationships with Kohlberg Kravis Roberts & Co., Silver Lake Partners, Ripplewood Holdings, JC Flowers & Co., JLL Partners, Aramark Corporation, Becton Dickinson & Company, Shinsei Bank and Wyeth. In addition, throughout his career he has advised boards of directors with respect to corporate governance matters and responsibilities of directors. Recently represented Special Committee of Fox Entertainment Group's Board in connection with transaction with parent, News Corporation.
Prof. Memberships: Active Member of The Association of the Bar of the City of New York and the International Bar Association.
Career: Joined firm in 1973; Partner since 1980. From 1990-93, served as the Senior Resident Partner in the firm's London office. In this capacity participated in many cross-border transactions.
Personal: Received JD (1973) from the University of Pennsylvania Law School, after graduating summa cum laude from Lehigh University (1969). Frequent speaker at seminars dealing with contests for corporate control and leveraged buyouts. Member, Board of Overseers of the University of Pennsylvania Law School and Board of Advisors of the University's Institute for Law and Economics.

COHEN, Ben
Cahill Gordon & Reindel, New York
212 701 3900
Recommended in Tax

COHEN, H Rodgin
Sullivan & Cromwell LLP, New York
212 558 4000
cohenhr@sullcrom.com
Recommended in Banking & Finance, Corporate/M&A
Practice Areas: Regulatory, acquisitions, corporate governance and securities laws matters for domestic and foreign financial institutions and The Clearing House. Regulatory matters include Bank Secrecy Act, powers and enforcement. Involved in most major US bank acquisitions as well as numerous major cross-border and other financial services acquisitions. Has been a member of Group of 30 Studies and participated in bank negotiations to free the Iranian hostages.
Career: Partner since 1977; Chairman since 2000.
Personal: Harvard College (AB, 1965); Harvard Law School (LLB, 1968).

COHEN, Joel M
Davis Polk & Wardwell, New York
212 450 4000
joel.cohen@dpw.com
Recommended in Antitrust
Practice Areas: Member of Davis Polk & Wardwell's Litigation Department. Represents clients in a variety of antitrust and general civil litigation and arbitration matters. Also represents clients in merger investigations, joint ventures, and/or antitrust counseling and litigation. Representations include civil litigation, international arbitration and governmental investigations in the areas of professional malpractice, M&A, securities law enforcement, commercial contracts and others. Has advised numerous clients regarding licensing strategies and the permissible uses of intellectual property, and has represented clients in patent and antitrust litigation concerning the alleged misuse of patents.

COLLETTA, Anthony J
Sullivan & Cromwell LLP, New York
212 558 4000
collettaa@sullcrom.com
Recommended in Real Estate
Practice Areas: Focuses on commercial real estate matters, structuring of senior and mezzanine financings, formation of joint ventures, and general corporate matters. Has worked on formation and fundraising of real estate-focused private equity funds and their financings and investments. Extensive experience in purchase, development and disposition of real estate assets and companies worldwide. Recent representations: Whitehall Street Real Estate Funds in fundraising, purchase, sale, financing and M&A activities; Aetos Capital and Broadreach Capital Partners in forma-

tion of their real estate opportunity funds; Strategic Hotel Capital in US$ 1.2 billion of financings; consortium of private investors in acquiring and financing US$ 1.5 billion mixed use development project on Central Park West; Goldman Sachs affiliates in acquisitions of assets in US and Puerto Rico and US$ 450 million+ leveraged recapitalizations of two Manhattan hotels; and Safeguard Self Storage in its US$ 400 million equity and debt recapitalization.
Prof. Memberships: ABA.
Career: Partner since 1997.
Personal: St. John's University Law School (JD, 1988); Fordham University (BA, 1985).

COLLINS, W Dale
Shearman & Sterling LLP, New York
212 848 4127
wcollins@shearman.com
Recommended in Antitrust
Practice Areas: Partner in Shearman & Sterling's Antitrust Group. Represents clients in merger investigations by federal and state antitrust enforcement agencies. Coordinates multi-jurisdictional antitrust defense of numerous transactions throughout the world.
Career: Joined Shearman in 1978. Resigned in 1981 to work in the Reagan Administration as White House Fellow, serving as Special Assistant to Vice President George Bush. Served as Deputy Assistant Attorney General in the Department of Justice Antitrust Division. Returned to Shearman in 1983.
Personal: BS with Honors, California Institute of Technology (1973); MS, California Institute of Technology (1974); JD, University of Chicago Law School (1978); PhD candidate, University of Minnesota (1979).

CONDON, Creighton
Shearman & Sterling LLP, New York
212 848 7628
ccondon@shearman.com
Recommended in Corporate/M&A
Practice Areas: Partner in Shearman & Sterling's M&A Group and Head of the firm's Sports Group. Member of the firm's Policy Committee. Represents United States and multinational corporations in acquisitions and sales of public and private companies and in joint ventures. Also represents the M&A groups of investment banks. Advises on issues regarding corporate governance and control.
Prof. Memberships: American Bar Association; New York State Bar Association; California State Bar Association.
Personal: BA, University of Pennsylvania (1978); JD, Columbia Law School (1982).

CONSTANTINE, Lloyd
Constantine & Partners (C&P), New York 212 350 2700
Recommended in Antitrust

COOK, Michael L
Schulte Roth & Zabel LLP, New York
212 756 2150
michael.cook@srz.com
Recommended in Bankruptcy
Practice Areas: Corporate restructuring, workouts and creditors' rights litigation.
Prof. Memberships: Fellow, American College of Bankruptcy; Practising Law Institute Bankruptcy Law Advisory Committee; Chair, Creditors' Rights Litigation Committee, American Bar Association Section of Litigation (1976-81); Bankruptcy Litigation Institute, Chairman, 1980-96; Vice President and Director, Columbia College Alumni Association; Past Chairman and Director, Lawyers Alliance for New York; Director, Goddard Riverside Community Center; Fellow, American Bar Foundation.
Career: Schulte Roth & Zabel Partner since 2000; Skadden, Arps, Slate, Meagher & Flom LLP, Partner and Corporate Restructuring Group practice leader, 1980-2000; Weil, Gotshal & Manges LLP, Partner, 1975-80; Associate, 1970-75.
Publications: Has lectured and written extensively on topics related to business reorganization, workouts and creditors' rights litigation.
Personal: Recognized in 'The Best Lawyers In America' (2003-04 rev ed); 'Who's Who in American Law' (2003-04 rev ed) and 'The K&A Restructuring Register' (5th ed 2004).

COOPER, James
Cravath, Swaine & Moore LLP, New York 212 474 1326
jcooper@cravath.com
Recommended in Banking & Finance
Practice Areas: Wide variety of domestic and international financing transactions, including financings of mergers, acquisitions, recapitalizations and spin-offs, working capital financings, restructurings and work-outs, and various special-purpose financings. Counsels corporate borrowers negotiating financing arrangements with banks and other financial institutions.
Career: Partner since 1986.
Personal: Yale Law School (JD, 1979); University of Chicago (AB, 1976).

CORUZZI, Laura
Jones Day, New York
212 326 8383
lacoruzzi@jonesday.com
Recommended in Intellectual Property
Practice Areas: Her 20+ years of practice covers all aspects of patent law relating to the biotechnology and pharmaceutical fields. Her patent procurement practice centers on strategic planning and management of patent portfolios designed to protect emerging technologies, including US prosecution and interferences and corresponding foreign proceedings. She also has an active client counseling, litigation, and appellate practice. She is a frequent invited speak-

er on patent law issues related to biologics, pharmacogenomics, and predictive medicine.
Prof. Memberships: NY State Bar Association; NYIPLA; AIPLA; AAAS.
Personal: Fordham University (JD 1985; PhD in Biology 1979).

COTTON, Stuart
Mound Cotton Wollan & Greengrass, New York 212 804 4200
Recommended in Insurance

CREAMER Jr, Ronald E
Sullivan & Cromwell LLP, New York
212 558 4000
creamerr@sullcrom.com
Recommended in Tax
Practice Areas: Tax-efficient structuring of acquisitions and dispositions, in cross-border corporate, real estate and utility M&A. Also practices and lectures in the area of tax-advantaged corporate financing techniques and advises investment banking clients in the design of new financial instruments.
Career: Partner since 2000.
Publications: Co-author (with S&C partner Emily McMahon) of the textbook 'Tax Planning for Transfers of Business Interests'.
Personal: Princeton University (AB, 1987); Yale Law School (JD, 1991); Yale School of Organization and Management (MPPM, 1991).

CREEL, Thomas
Goodwin Procter LLP, New York
212 813 8800
tcreel@goodwinprocter.com
Recommended in Intellectual Property
Practice Areas: Mr Creel's practice involves litigation and counseling in the areas of trade secrets, entertainment, trademarks and copyrights. Recognized for his capabilities in the area of patent litigation, Mr Creel has been appointed by federal district judges to serve as a mediator to attempt to resolve disputes, and as a Special Master to provide proper patent claim construction, supervise all pretrial discovery and recommend rulings on summary judgment motions.
Personal: LLB, University of Michigan Law School; BS, University of Kansas.

CROSS, James
Simpson Thacher & Bartlett LLP, New York 212 455 3386
jcross@stblaw.com
Recommended in Banking & Finance
Practice Areas: James Cross is a Partner at Simpson Thacher & Bartlett LLP where he is a member of the firm's Corporate Department. Mr Cross concentrates on bank finance, with an emphasis on senior credit and subordinated bridge facilities for leveraged acquisitions. He has extensive experience representing leading financial institutions and private equity firms such as JPMorgan Chase Bank and Kohlberg Kravis Roberts & Co. in significant financing transactions. Recent transactions in

which he has been involved include representations of Kohlberg Kravis Roberts & Co. in the acquisition of Masonite International and of a consortium of KKR, Blackstone, Hellman & Friedman and Texas Pacific Group in their acquisition of Texas Genco.
Career: Mr Cross became a Partner at Simpson Thacher in 1999.
Personal: He received his BA from Princeton University in 1986 and his JD from the University of Virginia in 1990.

CROUGH, Maureen
Sidley Austin Brown & Wood LLP, New York 212 839 7323
mcrough@sidley.com
Recommended in Environment
Practice Areas: Maureen Crough is a Partner in the New York office, representing domestic and non-US purchasers, sellers, lenders, landlords and tenants in the environmental aspects of a broad range of financial transactions. She handles environmental due diligence, evaluation of environmental insurance for use in transactions, negotiation of environmental provisions in acquisition and loan agreements and environmental counseling pertaining to financial transactions. She also represents clients in buyer/seller environmental dispute resolution, and counsels clients in the requirements of US and NY environmental regulatory compliance and the development and implementation of environmental management systems. Her practice also includes representing clients in the performance of voluntary cleanups in state programs, especially in NY.
Career: The University of Michigan Law School, JD, 1986; Princeton University, AB, 1983; Bar Admissions: Illinois, 1986 New York, 1995.

CULHANE, Stephen
King & Spalding LLP, New York
212 827 4361
sculhane@kslaw.com
Recommended in Private Equity
Practice Areas: Focuses on a wide range of private investment fund formation and investment, investment management and corporate matters. Substantial experience with alternative investment funds; US, Cayman Islands and Irish-domiciled equity long-short hedge funds; currency trading funds; multi-strategy hedge funds; exchange funds and collateralized bond obligation vehicles. Extensive experience representing the sponsors, managers and distributors of private investment funds.
Prof. Memberships: American Bar Association; Association of the Bar of the City of New York; International Bar Association; Securities Industry Association.
Personal: BA, Princeton University,1986; MPhil, Oxford University, England, 1988; JD, New York University 1993.

CURLEY, Michael
Morgan, Lewis & Bockius LLP, New York 212 309 6000
mcurley@morganlewis.com
Recommended in Employment
Practice Areas: Michael Curley is a Partner in the Labor and Employment Practice. Mr Curley has represented clients in numerous proceedings before the National Labor Relations Board, both in union representation and unfair labor practice cases. He has also had extensive experience in state and federal courts, defending clients in employment discrimination, whistleblower and wrongful discharge cases. In recent years, Mr Curley has tried and won a high-profile whistleblower arbitration in the securities trading industry and he also tried and won a high-profile case before the National Labor Relations Board in the entertainment industry.
Prof. Memberships: American Bar Association (Labor and Employment Law Section); New York State Bar Association (Labor and Employment Law Section and Committee on Alternative Dispute Resolution).

CURNIN, Paul C
Simpson Thacher & Bartlett LLP, New York 212 455 2000
pcurnin@stblaw.com
Recommended in Litigation
Practice Areas: Paul Curnin is a Partner in the firm's Litigation Department. He frequently represents clients in corporate and securities matters including class and derivative actions, takeover litigations, as well as government investigations and enforcement actions (particularly by the SEC), internal investigations and other matters. Selected representations include WorldCom Inc., JPMorgan Chase, as well as numerous directors, officers and other individuals.
Prof. Memberships: American Bar Association, Association of the Bar of the City of New York (Faculty, Effective Trial Advocacy Workshop, 1998-2000; Secretary, Committee on Criminal Law, 1992-95); Legal Aid Society (Member, Board of Directors).
Career: Joined Simpson Thacher in 1990 became a Partner in 1995. Prior to joining the firm, Mr Curnin was a Trial Attorney in the Federal Defenders Services Unit for the Southern District of New York, served as a law clerk to the Hon Roger Wollman of the Eighth Circuit Court of Appeals and to the late Hon Lloyd F MacMahon of the Southern District of New York. In 2003, he was named one of the country's top '45 Lawyers Under 45' in the United States by 'American Lawyer magazine'.
Personal: Received BA from Dartmouth College, 1983; JD from Fordham University School of Law, 1987.

CUSICK, Michael
Jones Day, New York
212 326 7830
mcusick@jonesday.com
Recommended in Energy
Practice Areas: Advises issuers and underwriters on public and private US and international offerings of securities, particularly in the public utility industry where he has gained national recognition. He also advises on restructuring and acquisition-related matters for regulated and unregulated companies. His representations have included: advising the successful bidder involved in the first contested takeover of an electric utility; the initial public offering for the Kingdom of Sweden and China Tire Holdings Ltd.; and the initial placement of debt securities in connection with the largest sale and leaseback ever completed.

CUSUMANO, Robert
Debevoise & Plimpton LLP, New York 212 909 6000
Recommended in Insurance

CZARNIAK, Julia
Skadden, Arps, Slate, Meagher & Flom LLP & Affiliates, New York 212 735 4194
jczarnia@skadden.com
Recommended in Projects
Practice Areas: Concentrates on banking and institutional investing, representing financial institutions and borrowers in various types of financing transactions with an emphasis on corporate and project finance. Has been the primary drafter and a principal negotiator in complex project financings in the United States, Asia and the Middle East. Has extensive experience in export credit and mulilateral agency financings as well as in pipeline projects, restructurings and expansions.
Career: JD, Georgetown University Law Center, 1997; MA, Yale University Graduate School, 1993; BA, Moscow State University, 1990.

DABNEY, James W
Fried, Frank, Harris, Shriver & Jacobson LLP, New York 212 859 8966
james.dabney@friedfrank.com
Recommended in Intellectual Property
Practice Areas: Handles a wide variety of litigation matters with an emphasis on patent, trademark, copyright, and related disputes involving intellectual property. Has acted as lead counsel in numerous cases involving questions of validity, enforceability, infringement, or non-infringement of US patents, copyrights, trade secrets, trademarks, rights of publicity, and neighboring rights, as well as civil RICO, antitrust, insurance, false advertising, contract, unfair competition, and other commercial disputes.
Career: Joined Fried Frank in 2004. Partner at Pennie & Edmonds LLP from 1989-2003. Previously, associate and deputy coordinator of the intellectual Property Group at Sullivan and

Cromwell LLP. Served as a law clerk to the Hon James C Hill, United States Court of Appeals for the Fifth Circuit in Atlanta. Admitted to the Bar in New York and New Jersey and to practice before the Supreme Court of the United States; the United States Courts of Appeals for the Second, Third, Fourth, Fifth, Sixth, Seventh, Eighth, Tenth, and Eleventh Circuits and the Federal Circuit; and the United States District Courts for the Southern, Eastern, Northern, and Western Districts of New York, the Districts of New Jersey and Connecticut, the Central and Northern Districts of Illinois, the Eastern District of Wisconsin, the Northern District of Indiana, the Eastern and Western Districts of Michigan, and the District of the District of Columbia. WIPO Panelist since 2000.
Personal: Received JD, magna cum laude, in 1979 from Cornell Law School, member of the Order of the Coif and of the Board of Editors of the Cornell Law Review. Received BA, magna cum laude, from Harvard College in 1976. Graduated from The Hotchkiss School in 1972.

DANNAY, Richard
Cowan, Liebowitz & Latman, New York 212 790 9200
Recommended in Media & Entertainment

DAVENPORT, Margaret
Debevoise & Plimpton LLP, New York 212 909 6000
Recommended in Private Equity

DAVIS, Fred
Shearman & Sterling LLP, New York 212 848 4675
fdavis@shearman.com
Recommended in Arbitration, Litigation
Practice Areas: Partner in Shearman & Sterling's Litigation Group. Experience in international arbitration and litigation, criminal defense and complex commercial litigation.
Prof. Memberships: US Courts of Appeals for the First, Second, Third, Fifth, and Eleventh Circuits. US Supreme Court.
Career: Joined Shearman as Partner in 1991. Assistant US Attorney in the Southern District of New York (1974-78 and Chief of Appeals, 1977-78). Law clerk to Henry J. Friendly, Chief Judge of the US Court of Appeals, Second Circuit and to Justice Potter Stewart, US Supreme Court.
Personal: BA, Harvard College (1967); JD, Columbia University School of Law (1972).

DAVIS, George A
Weil, Gotshal & Manges LLP, New York 212 310 8962
george.davis@weil.com
Recommended in Bankruptcy
Practice Areas: Complex debt restructurings/reorganizations, both in and out

of Chapter 11.

Career: At age 39, Mr Davis' recent debtor representations include IMPATH, Bethlehem Steel, Sunbeam Corporation and Carmike Cinemas. Recently represented lenders and major creditors in restructurings of US Airways, Delta Airlines, Independence Air, Tower Automotive, Kaiser Aluminum, Galey & Lord, WCI Steel, Weirton Steel, Liberty House, Purina Mills, Inc., Filene's Basement, Resorts International, Bradlees Stores and Barney's Stores. Recently represented potential acquirors of Cable and Wireless, FAO Schwarz and TLC Home Health Care.

Personal: Hofstra University School of Law, JD (with distinction); SUNY Binghamton, BS (magna cum laude).

DAVIS, Steven H
LeBoeuf, Lamb, Greene & MacRae, LLP, New York 212 424 8000
sdavis@llgm.com
Recommended in Energy

Practice Areas: His practice focuses primarily on companies active in the energy industry, including integrated electric and gas companies and independent power producers. He advises US and non-US clients in connection with mergers and acquisitions. He works in bankruptcy proceedings involving energy companies and provides restructuring advice for independent power producers.

Career: Joined LeBoeuf in 1977; Co-Chairman of LeBoeuf from 1999-2003 and Chairman since 2004.

Personal: Yale University (BA) 1977; Yale University (JD) 1977.

DAX, John
Cohen Dax and Koening, PC, Albany
518 432 1002
Recommended in Energy

DE CHIARA, Michael K
Zetlin & De Chiara LLP, New York
212 682 6800
mkd@zdlaw.com
Recommended in Construction

Practice Areas: Mr De Chiara is experienced in virtually all aspects of the law as it relates to the design and construction industry. In addition to litigating, he often advises clients on financial affairs and general business matters covering partnership law, corporate law, employment law, and professional practice matters, including ownership transition and licensing issues.

Prof. Memberships: American Institute of Architects (AIA) New York State-General Counsel; American Council of Engineering Companies (ACEC) of New York-General Counsel; AIA ñ ACEC/NY Special Advisory Committees-Chairman; New York Building Foundation-Board Member/General Counsel; Associated Owners & Developers (AOD)-Steering Committee; American Institute of Architects-Adjunct Member; New York Landmarks Conser-

vancy-Board of Directors/Treasurer; Institute for Urban Design-Fellow; New York State and American Bar Associations-Member; Society of American Military Engineers-MemberReal Estate Board of New York-Member.

Career: Founding Partner of Zetlin & De Chiara LLP, headquartered in Manhattan with offices in Westbury, NY, Newark, NJ and Stamford, CT.

Publications: Co-editor and co-author, New York Construction Law, Aspen Publishing (2003). Adjunct professor, Polytechnic Institute, New York, Construction and the Law.

Personal: Mr De Chiara received his undergraduate degree in Mechanical Engineering and his Masters of Science degree in quantitative policy analysis from SUNY at Stonybrook. He also attended the Graduate Degree Program in Architecture at Columbia University and received his Juris Doctorate from Vanderbilt University.

DE WIED, Warren
Fried, Frank, Harris, Shriver & Jacobson LLP, New York 212 859 8296
warren.de.wied@friedfrank.com
Recommended in Corporate/M&A

Practice Areas: Mergers and acquisitions, including negotiated transactions, hostile takeovers, takeover defense and proxy contests; leveraged buyouts and private equity transactions; restructurings, spinoffs and recapitalizations; joint ventures; corporate governance; and general corporate counseling.

Prof. Memberships: Member of the Editorial Advisory Board of 'The M&A Lawyer'. Author of numerous published articles and a frequent speaker on M&A topics.

Career: Joined Fried Frank in 1987 and became a Partner in 1994. Admitted to the Bar in New York.

Personal: Born 1962. Received his JD in 1987 from the Boalt Hall School of Law, University of California, Berkeley, where he was a member of the Order of the Coif. He received his BA in 1983 and his MA in 1987 from Trinity College, Cambridge University.

DELANEY, John
Morrison & Foerster LLP, New York
212 468 8040
jdelaney@mofo.com
Recommended in Technology

Practice Areas: Concentrates on high-technology and intellectual property matters. Advises clients from Fortune 500 companies to early-stage start-ups on a range of technology law issues. Represents clients on copyright, trademark, and other intellectual property disputes.

Prof. Memberships: Co-Chair, PLI Annual Conference ('The Outsourcing Revolution'); Board Member, Volunteer Lawyers for the Arts; Board Member, iMentor.

Career: Admitted to practice in Califor-

nia and New York. Co-Chair, Technology Group, New York office. Recognized in 'Lawyers for the New Economy' by American Lawyer magazine. Named to Crain's New York Business 'Technology 100' list of individuals "likely to shape the direction and growth of New York's economy for years to come."

Personal: BA, University of Notre Dame, 1986; JD, Columbia Law School, 1989.

DELIKAT, Michael
Orrick, Herrington & Sutcliffe, New York
212 506 5230
mdelikat@orrick.com
Recommended in Employment

Practice Areas: Represents a broad range of major corporations in all facets of labor and employment law, including class actions, trade secret misappropriation, and other impact cases, with a focus in the financial services industry. He has an active trial and appellate practice and handles high-visibility class action and impact cases. He counsels clients on the increasingly complex array of laws affecting the workplace, including Sarbanes-Oxley, as well as issues associated with mergers, acquisitions, restructurings, and other corporate transactions.

Prof. Memberships: Fellow, The College of Labor and Employment Lawyers; Board Member, NYU Center for Labor and Employment Law; American and New York Bar Association (various committees); Chairman of the Board, UJA/ Federation of Greenwich, CT; Former Board Member, New York Lawyers Alliance; Arbitrator, United States District Court for the Eastern District of New York.

Career: Managing Director of Orrick's Litigation Division; Chair of Orrick's Employment Law Department; Harvard Law School (JD, 1977); Cornell University (BS, 1974).

DELUCIA, Richard
Kenyon & Kenyon, New York
212 425 7200
Recommended in Intellectual Property

DEROSA, Frank J
Brown Raysman Millstein Felder & Steiner LLP, New York
212 895 2010
fderosa@brownraysman.com
Recommended in Intellectual Property

Practice Areas: Partner in and Co-Chair of the firm's Intellectual Property Practice Group of over 40 lawyers and technical specialists. Over 30 years of IP experience, concentrating on patent law with an emphasis on counseling, patent procurement, licensing and litigation in computers, software, Internet and electronics. Extensive experience in counseling on adopting and implementing strategies for protecting emerging and mature technologies, dealing with patents and portfolios of competitors and patent trolls, and establishing cor-

porate IP departments. Practiced as an electrical engineer before law school.

Personal: BSEE, Polytechnic University 1963; JD, St John's University Law School 1974 (Member of Law Review).

DESMARAIS, John M
Kirkland & Ellis LLP, New York
212 446 4739
jdesmarais@kirkland.com
Recommended in Intellectual Property

Practice Areas: Mr Desmarais served for three years as an Assistant US Attorney in the Southern District of New York, where he tried criminal jury trials, before joining Kirkland & Ellis in 1997. He specializes in intellectual property litigation and is a Member of the Bars of New York and Washington, DC, the US Supreme Court, the Federal Circuit Court of Appeals, and various other federal district courts and courts of appeal. Mr Desmarais is also registered to practice before the United States Patent and Trademark Office.

Personal: Manhattan College, BChE, 1985; New York University School of Law, JD, 1988.

DESPINS, Luc
Milbank, Tweed, Hadley & McCloy, New York 212 530 5000
Recommended in Bankruptcy

DIAMOND, Brian
Stroock & Stroock & Lavan LLP, New York 212 806 5400
Recommended in Real Estate

DIBLASI, Gandolfo V
Sullivan & Cromwell LLP, New York
212 558 4000
diblasig@sullcrom.com
Recommended in Litigation

Practice Areas: Represents clients in securities and commodities class actions in US federal courts, most recently as liaison counsel for the underwriters in the approximately 300 IPO allocation class actions, and counsel for UnumProvident, Cablevision, and directors/officers of Iridium. Active in civil/criminal investigations of the financial services industry, with clients in major federal and state investigations involving insurance industry, mutual funds, research analysts, accounting/financial reporting issues, IPOs, financial derivatives, and criminal cases alleging insider trading and market manipulation.

Prof. Memberships: ABA; ABCNY; NYSBA; Federal Bar Council.

Career: Partner since 1985.

Personal: Yale University (BA, 1975). Yale Law School (JD, 1978).

DILORENZO, Louis
Bond, Schoeneck & King, LLP, New York
Recommended in Employment

Practice Areas: Mr DiLorenzo represents management in labor and employment law matters. He is Co-Chair of the firm's Labor & Employment Law

Department; former Chair of the NYSBA's Labor & Employment Law Section; a Fellow of the American College of Labor & Employment Lawyers; adjunct professor at Syracuse University School of Management; has written several published articles and books on labor matters; and was selected as the "Great Negotiator" by Corporate Legal Times, January 2003 issue. Mr DiLorenzo also served as General Counsel to Agway, Inc. (2002-04).

Personal: Syracuse University (BA, 1973); University of Buffalo Law School (JD, 1976).

DIMATTEO, John
Willkie Farr & Gallagher LLP, New York
212 728 8299
jdimatteo@willkie.com
Recommended in Intellectual Property
Practice Areas: Chair of the Intellectual Property Department and a Partner in the Litigation Department, specializing in patent litigation, trade secret litigation, patent prosecution, trademarks, and IP licensing. He is currently representing a leading manufacturer of Automatic External Defibrillators in asserting its patents against an accused infringer and defending against a counter claim for infringement. He is also currently representing a leading manufacturer of high-pressure mercury-vapor lamps in asserting its patents against a Japanese company accused of infringement and is defending a leading manufacturer of electric shavers in defense of a claim for patent infringement. He recently represented a major European electronics company in federal district court in successfully asserting patents relating to fundamental integrated circuit communication protocol against eight major chip manufacturers, and successfully defended a European manufacturer in a landmark case before the International Trade Commission.
Prof. Memberships: A Member of the American Intellectual Property Law Association, the American Bar Association, the Institute of Electrical and Electronics Engineers, and the Association for Computing Machinery. He is a Registered Professional Engineer, State of New York (1989) and a Registered Patent Agent, United States Patent and Trademark Office (1987).
Career: Admitted to the Bars of New York, New Jersey, and the District of Columbia. He is also admitted to practice before the United States Supreme Court; the United States Court of Appeals for the Federal Circuit; the United States Court of Appeals for the Sixth and Seventh Circuits; the United States District Courts for the Southern and Eastern Districts of New York, the District of New Jersey, and the Eastern District of Michigan.
Personal: Received an LLM in Trial Advocacy from Temple University School of Law in 2001, an MSCS (Com-

puter Science) from the Polytechnic University of New York in 2000, a JD from St. John's University School of Law in 1988, and a BSE. (Engineering) from Polytechnic Institute of New York in 1984.

DIMON, Samuel
Davis Polk & Wardwell, New York
212 450 4000
samuel.dimon@dpw.com
Recommended in Tax
Practice Areas: Member of Davis Polk & Wardwell's Tax Department. Advises clients on federal income tax matters in a variety of contexts, domestic and international, including financial product development and use of derivatives, tax planning for financial institutions, merchant banking and hedge fund organisation and investments, securities offerings, mergers and acquisitions, joint ventures, bankruptcy reorganizations, workouts and tax audits.

DISALVATORE, William P
Wilmer Cutler Pickering Hale and Dorr LLP, New York 212 937 7202
William.DiSalvatore@wilmerhale.com
Recommended in Intellectual Property
Practice Areas: Practice is directed to patent, trade secret and commercial litigation, technology disputes and client counseling. Represents a variety of technology-related industries, including biotech, pharmaceutical, software and digital prepress.
Prof. Memberships: American Bar Association; New York State Bar Association; New York City Bar Association; Connecticut Bar Association; Federal Circuit Bar Association; and American Intellectual Property Law Association.
Publications: 'Practical Advice on Litigating a Patent Case in the U.S.' Journal of Biolaw and Business, Special Supplement - Intellectual Property (2004). 'Filing Considerations in Patent Litigation.' Practising Law Institute Patents, Copyrights, Trademarks, and Literary Property Course Handbook Series, PLI Order No. G0-00P7.
Personal: Pace University School of Law (JD 1991); Hofstra University (BS 1987).

DISKANT, Gregory
Patterson, Belknap, Webb & Tyler LLP, New York 212 336 2000
Recommended in Intellectual Property

DOKOS, Daniel S
Weil, Gotshal & Manges LLP, New York
212 310 8576
daniel.dokos@weil.com
Recommended in Banking & Finance
Practice Areas: Mr Dokos practices in all areas of bank financing, with a particular focus on leveraged lending and cross-border finance. He represents financial institutions and corporate borrowers in connection with leveraged acquisition and recapitalization transactions, syndicated lending, investment-grade lending, cash-flow lending, asset-based lending, restructurings, debtor-in-

possession financings and exit financings.
Career: Mr Dokos is the Chair of the Banking & Finance Practice. Recent lead representations include advising lead arrangers in senior secured debt financings for Novelis (in connection with its spin-off from Alcan), Jarden Corporation (in connection with its acquisition of American Household), Revlon, Prestige Brands, Johnson Wax Professional, Amkor Solutions, Swift & Company and Premcor Refining. Mr Dokos also has represented the lead agents in the restructuring of Oxford Automotive, Paragon Trade Brands, Safelite Auto-Glass, Key Plastics and The IT Group, and in high-grade financings for Phelps Dodge, Hydro Quebec and FMC Corporation, and in debtor-in-possession financings for Service Merchandise, Winstar Communications, Warnaco Group and Babcock & Wilcox.
Personal: University of Virginia, JD (Order of the Coif); Dartmouth College, BA.

DOUGLAS, James M
Skadden, Arps, Slate, Meagher & Flom LLP & Affiliates, New York
212 735 2868
jdouglas@skadden.com
Recommended in Banking & Finance
Practice Areas: Head of Skadden's Banking and Institutional Investing Group. Represents numerous financial institutions, sponsors and corporate clients in all areas of private financings. Concentrates in the areas of acquisition financings, bridge financings and restructurings. Listed in several leading US and international legal publications.
Career: JD, Fordham University, 1981 (cum laude); Member, Fordham Law Review); BA, State University of New York at Binghamton, 1978.

DREYFUS, James K
Fulbright & Jaworski L.L.P., New York
212 318 3248
jdreyfus@fulbright.com
Recommended in Tax
Practice Areas: Tax.
Prof. Memberships: Mr Dreyfus is a Member of the Tax Sections of both the New York State and American Bar Associations.
Career: Jim Dreyfus has been a Partner in the New York office since 1981. Mr Dreyfus' practice involves a broad range of transactional matters, including mergers, acquisitions, recapitalizations, buy-outs and venture capital transactions. He has also been involved in the formation of private equity funds and hedge funds. Mr Dreyfus' practice is both domestic and international in scope. In addition to his transactional work, Mr Dreyfus has significant experience in tax controversy matters. He also represents various charitable and non-profit organizations.
Personal: BA, magna cum laude, Wesleyan University (1969); JD, Harvard Law School (1973).

DRIVAS, Dimitrios
White & Case LLP, New York
212 819 8286
ddrivas@whitecase.com
Recommended in Intellectual Property
Practice Areas: Co-Chair of firm's global Intellectual Property Practice Group. Practice focuses upon patent infringement litigation for clients including pharmaceutical majors, agribusiness conglomerates, and technology firms. Practice also encompasses counseling and technology transfer, including acquisition, licensing of IP rights, joint development agreements, and strategic alliances. Registered US patent attorney.
Prof. Memberships: New York State Bar; US District Courts for the Southern and Eastern Districts of New York; US Court of Appeals for the Federal Circuit; US Patent and Trademark Office.
Personal: City College of the City University of New York (BS, Biochemistry, 1977); Fordham University School of Law (JD, 1984).

DUNHAM Jr, Wolcott
Debevoise & Plimpton LLP, New York
212 909 6000
Recommended in Insurance

DUNN, M Douglas
Milbank, Tweed, Hadley & McCloy, New York 212 530 5000
Recommended in Energy

DUNNE, Carey R
Davis Polk & Wardwell, New York
212 450 4000
carey.dunne@dpw.com
Recommended in Litigation
Practice Areas: Member of Davis Polk & Wardwell's Litigation Department. Represents clients in a wide variety of criminal, civil and regulatory matters, including grand jury inquiries, internal investigations, enforcement actions by state and federal agencies, and complex commercial disputes. Most of the cases that he handles involve 'parallel proceedings': competing actions and investigations that must be defended simultaneously in multiple forums. Recent clients include March & McLennan, Credit Suisse First Boston, ImClone Systems, Federated Investors, Bank of America, Emerson Electric, Deutsche Bank, RTL Television and Consolidated Edison.

DUNNE, Dennis
Milbank, Tweed, Hadley & McCloy, New York 212 530 5000
Recommended in Bankruptcy

DYE, Alexander M
LeBoeuf, Lamb, Greene & MacRae, LLP, New York 212 424 8642
adye@llgm.com
Recommended in Insurance
Practice Areas: Specializes in corporate transactions involving the insurance industry. He advises buyers and sellers in hostile and negotiated mergers and acquisitions transactions as well as asset

purchases structured as reinsurance. He also advises issuers and underwriters in offerings of equity, debt and hybrid securities by US and non-US insurers. In addition, Mr Dye has considerable experience in restructuring troubled insurers and demutualizing life, health and property-casualty insurers.

Career: Joined LeBoeuf in 1981.
Personal: Brown University (AB magna cum laude) 1978; University of Michigan (JD) 1981.

DYER, Richard
Thelen Reid & Priest LLP, New York 212 603 2000
Recommended in Construction

ECKSTEIN, Kenneth H
Kramer Levin Naftalis & Frankel LLP, New York 212 715 9229
keckstein@kramerlevin.com
Recommended in Bankruptcy
Practice Areas: Partner and Chairman of Kramer Levin Naftalis & Frankel LLP Creditors' Rights and Bankruptcy Department. He has practiced in the area of corporate reorganization and bankruptcy since 1979. Practice includes both in and out-of-court restructurings of financially distressed businesses on behalf of debtors, creditors' committees, major secured and unsecured creditors, bondholders, trustees, examiners, and third parties seeking to acquire the assets or businesses of financially troubled companies.
Prof. Memberships: A frequent lecturer and author in the areas of bankruptcy and corporate reorganization. He is a Member of the Section on Corporation, Banking and Business Law of the American Bar Association. He is also a former Member of the Committee on Bankruptcy and Corporate Reorganization of the Association of the Bar of the City of New York.
Career: Chairs a department of seven partners, three special counsel and 18 associates and has played a prominent role in many of the largest and most complex Chapter 11 reorganization cases and out of court workouts over the past 25 years. Representations include the Owens Corning Bank Group, the Dow Corning Claimants Committee and the Official Creditor Committees for Leap Wireless, Big V, SGL Carbon Corp., Cityscape Financial, Olympia & York, Integrated Resources, SLM International, Financial News Network, PSNH, Eastern Airlines and Texaco. Mr Eckstein also has represented the debtors in the bankruptcy of MicroWarehouse, Elite Models, Cross Media, and The Wiz, Inc. and has represented bank groups, bondholders, acquirors and other major creditors in Enron, Warnaco, NTL, Twin Lab, Amerco, Mediq, PacCoin, Big City Radio, Jitney Jungle, LTV, New Valley, Herman's Sporting Goods, Tucson Electric and Farley Industries. He has led his firm's

representation of the Examiner in Bruno's Inc. and the Independent Restructuring Advisor in Coram Healthcare. He has also represented the Trustee in Island Mortgage and in Sharp International. He regularly represents a wide range of lending and other financial institutions and distressed investors in Chapter 11 cases, workouts and out of court restructurings. These institutions include JP Morgan Chase, CSFB, BNP-Paribas, Goldman Sachs, Alliance Capital, Barclays, Elliott Associates, Angelo Gordon, Farrallon and others.
Personal: Received a JD degree from New York University in 1979 and a BA degree cum laude from the University of Pennsylvania in 1976.

EDELMAN, Marty
Paul, Hastings, Janofsky & Walker LLP, New York 212 856 7100
martyedelman@paulhastings.com
Recommended in Real Estate
Practice Areas: Concentrates his practice on large, complex real estate and corporate transactions. He has been involved in all stages of legal development of pioneering financial structures, including participating mortgages, institutional joint ventures in real estate, and joint ventures between US investors and developers in Mexico, England, France, Japan, China and the Middle East.
Prof. Memberships: Board of Directors - Cendant Incorporated, Ashford Hospitality and Capital Trust. Advisory Board - Columbia University Law School and Business School. Advisor - Fisher Brothers, Grove Real Estates Investors Millennium Partners and The Related Companies.

EDELMAN, Scott
Milbank, Tweed, Hadley & McCloy, New York 212 530 5000
Recommended in Litigation

EDGAR, Kenneth C
Simpson Thacher & Bartlett LLP, New York 212 455 2560
kedgar@stblaw.com
Recommended in Employee Benefits
Practice Areas: Ken Edgar is a Partner and Head of the firm's Executive Compensation and Employee Benefits Practice. With over 30 years experience in this area, he has advised clients on a wide variety of employee compensation and benefits issues, with emphasis on key executive programs and employment contracts, and compliance with the complex tax and other regulatory provisions associated therewith, as well as compensation and benefits issues raised in connection with complicated merger transactions and leveraged buyouts.
Prof. Memberships: Member: New York State Bar Association (Co-Chairman, Employee Benefits Committee, Tax Section, 1988-98); American Bar Association (Employee Benefits Committee, 1987-present); Association of the Bar of the City of New York.

Career: Joined Simpson Thacher in 1976 and was elected Partner in 1980.
Personal: Mr Edgar received his JD from New York University School of Law in 1973, where he also received an LLM in taxation in 1978. He received his BA from Haverford College, with honors in English, in 1969.

EINHORN, David M
Wachtell, Lipton, Rosen & Katz, New York 212 403 1213
dmeinhorn@wlrk.com
Recommended in Tax
Practice Areas: Specializes in the tax aspects of the joint ventures, corporate reorganizations, acquisitions, dispositions, financings, and restructurings that constitute Wachtell, Lipton, Rosen & Katz's primary practice, which transactions frequently involve multinational businesses and raise complex multinational tax issues.
Prof. Memberships: Tax Sections of the New York State Bar Association; Association of the Bar of the City of New York.
Career: Partner at Wachtell, Lipton, Rosen & Katz since 1982. Often lectures on tax matters at professional seminars.
Personal: Graduated from Fordham Law School in 1976 (JD) and from New York University Law School in 1979 (LLM).

ELLIS, Emmett N
Dewey Ballantine LLP, New York 212 259 6150
eellis@deweyballantine.com
Recommended in Energy
Practice Areas: Bud Ellis works with both regulated and non-regulated entities in the global power markets. Mr Ellis represents energy companies and investment banks in public and private capital markets transactions. Mr Ellis has represented corporate clients in the acquisition and divestiture of energy companies and energy assets in the United States and the United Kingdom.
Prof. Memberships: American Bar Association, Vice-Chairman, Infrastructure Finance, Mergers and Acquisitions Committee of the Section of Public Utility, Communications and Transportation Law.
Career: Partner, Dewey Ballantine LLP.
Personal: Born August 27, 1953. BA, University of Oklahoma, 1975. JD, Yale Law School, 1978.

EMMERICH, Adam O
Wachtell, Lipton, Rosen & Katz, New York 212 403 1234
aoemmerich@wlrk.com
Recommended in Corporate/M&A
Practice Areas: Mergers and acquisitions and securities law matters. Practice includes a broad and varied representation of public and private corporations and other entities in a variety of industries throughout the United States and abroad, in connection with mergers and acquisitions, divestitures, spin-offs, joint ventures, and financing transactions.

Also has extensive experience in takeover defense and corporate governance issues.
Prof. Memberships: Association of the Bar of the City of New York; New York State and American Bar Association; New York County Lawyers Association; Securities Law Committee of the American Society of Corporate Secretaries; and the Corporate Academic Bridge Group of the NYU Center for Law and Business. Member, Board of Directors of the American Friends of the Israel Museum and of the Ramaz School, President of the American Friends of the Israel Antiquities Authority. Previously served on the Visiting Committee of the University of Chicago Law School and currently a Co-Chair of its capital campaign, and as Chair of the Young Lawyers Division of the UJA-Federation in New York. Member of the board of directors of the Lawyers Alliance for New York.
Career: Joined Wachtell, Lipton, Rosen & Katz in 1986 and named a Partner in 1991. BA, Swarthmore College and JD with honors, University of Chicago. Topics and comments editor of the University of Chicago Law Review; Order of the Coif; Olin Fellow in law and economics. Law clerk to Hon Abner J Mikva, United States Court of Appeals for the District of Columbia Circuit. A frequent speaker at bar and professional conferences on topics relating to mergers and acquisitions.
Personal: Born 15 December 1960. Married with three children.

EPSTEIN, Michael
Weil, Gotshal & Manges LLP, New York 212 310 8432
michael.epstein@weil.com
Recommended in Technology
Practice Areas: Intellectual property and media, IT and IT outsourcing, litigation/regulatory.
Career: Mr Epstein has extensive experience litigating and counseling corporations worldwide on intellectual property issues. He has litigated, negotiated and resolved some of the largest and most complex intellectual property disputes. His practice involves substantial transactional work, including structuring and negotiating technology and intellectual property acquisitions, technology transfer and licensing arrangements, outsourcing transactions and joint ventures and other targeted alliances. Mr Epstein is responsible for Weil Gotshal's approximately 500-lawyer Litigation/Regulatory Department and 75-lawyer Intellectual Property/Media Practice Group. He is a member of the firm's Management Committee. He is the author of treatises 'Epstein on Intellectual Property' and 'Modern Intellectual Property', co-author of 'Online - Internet Law', 'International Intellectual Property' and a co-editor of

'Drafting License Agreements,' 'The Corporate Counsellor's Deskbook,' 'The Departing Employee,' 'Doing Business in Eastern Europe,' 'Biotechnology Law,' 'The Trademark Law Revision Act,' 'Joint Ventures and Other Cooperative Business Arrangements' and 'Trade Secrets, Restrictive Covenants and Other Safeguards.' He is also the author of numerous articles on intellectual property and has lectured worldwide on the topic. Mr Epstein is a founder and co-editor of Intellectual Property & Technology Law Journal and a member of the editorial boards of Computer Lawyer, Intellectual Property Strategist and Cyberspace Lawyer. He has served on advisory panels to the US Congress and to the National Academy of Sciences, Institute of Medicine on intellectual property matters.

Personal: New York University School of Law, JD; Lehigh University, BA.

ETTINGER, John R
Davis Polk & Wardwell, New York
212 450 4000
john.ettinger@dpw.com
Recommended in Private Equity

Practice Areas: Managing Partner of Davis Polk & Wardwell. In his own practice, he represents clients in mergers and acquisitions, joint ventures, restructuring, takeover defenses, and corporate governance issues. He represents a number of private equity funds on both transactional and fund management matters.

EVANUSA, Michel
Stroock & Stroock & Lavan LLP, New York 212 806 5400
Recommended in Real Estate

FADIL, Adeeb
Simpson Thacher & Bartlett LLP, New York 212 455 7070
afadil@stblaw.com
Recommended in Environment

Practice Areas: Counsel at Simpson Thacher in the Litigation Department. Specializes in environmental law. Experience includes: advising clients about environmental aspects of transactions, including acquisitions, divestitures, loans, securities offerings, and bankruptcies and restructurings, involving entities with domestic and multinational operations (activities ranging from exploration and extraction of oil, coal and other natural resources, to steel, chemical and paper manufacturing, to electrical generation, transmission and distribution, to commercial real estate and retail businesses); counseling clients in the management of, and in the resolution of disputes over, contractual, statutory and common law environmental liabilities; and litigating environmental matters.

Prof. Memberships: American Bar Association, Association of the Bar of the City of New York.

Career: Joined the firm in 1989, Counsel since 1994.

Publications: New EPA Policies: Reforming CERCLA by Administrative Guidance, 10 Toxics Law Reporter 611 (1995).

Personal: BA (with highest honors), University of Virginia (1980); JD, Yale Law School (1984). Clerk to the Hon Robert R Merhige, Jr, US District Judge, Eastern District of Virginia (1984-85). Admitted New York (1986).

FAGEN, Leslie
Paul, Weiss, Rifkind, Wharton & Garrison LLP, New York 212 373 3231
lfagen@paulweiss.com
Recommended in Litigation

Practice Areas: Co-Chair of Litigation Department. Member of firm's Management Committee. Has extensive experience encompassing product liability, IP, insurance, antitrust, environmental and securities law. Litigated on behalf of plaintiffs and defendants at trial and appellate level in federal and state courts. Secured a victory on behalf of AC Nielsen and other defendants dismissing a nine-year antitrust litigation on motion. Also, achieved a victory for client Polo Ralph Lauren in its trademark dispute with the US Polo Association. Fellow of the American College of Trial Lawyers. Selected for 2005 edition of 'The Best Lawyers in America'.

FAGIN, Allen
Proskauer Rose LLP, New York
212 969 3030
afagin@proskauer.com
Recommended in Employment

Practice Areas: Chairman of Proskauer Rose LLP, and the former Co-Chair of Proskauer's Labor and Employment Law Department. He represents employers in all types of employment litigation. His clients are as diverse as his practice, representing fields such as telecommunications, transportation, healthcare, insurance, legal services, utilities, financial services, entertainment and manufacturing.

Prof. Memberships: A member of the American College of Labor and Employment Lawyers. Was chosen by New York Magazine as one of the hundred best lawyers in New York, and was profiled by the National Law Journal as one of the top employment litigators in the country. Was also selected as one of 118 US attorneys in the International Who's Who of Management Labor & Employment Lawyers.

Publications: Publishes regularly in the labor and employment field, is a frequent lecturer on employment discrimination matters.

Personal: A summa cum laude graduate of Columbia College, graduated with honors from Harvard Law School, holds a masters degree in Public Policy from Harvard University's John F Kennedy School of Government.

FALCK, David
Pillsbury Winthrop LLP, New York
212 858 1438
dfalck@pillsburywinthrop.com
Recommended in Energy

Practice Areas: Mr Falck's practice involves the legal aspects of securities offerings, mergers, acquisitions and restructurings, and private equity investments. Transactions involving energy and telecommunications companies are a particular focus. Representative assignments have included: providing advice to issuers, their boards of directors and underwriters in connection with mergers, asset and stock acquisitions, restructurings and disaggregation transactions; initial public offerings for wireless telecom providers, new energy technology companies and independent power producers; Rule 144A offerings in the capital markets for issuers of high-yield and project debt; and representing private investors in the acquisition of existing businesses from major industrial companies and in the organization and financing of start-up ventures.

Career: Admitted to practice: State of New York.

Personal: JD, Washington & Lee University School of Law, 1978 (summa cum laude, Member, Washington & Lee Law Review, Member, Order of the Coif); BA, Colgate University, 1975 (magna cum laude, Phi Beta Kappa).

FASMAN, Zachary D
Paul, Hastings, Janofsky & Walker LLP, New York 212 318 6315
zacharyfasman@paulhastings.com
Recommended in Employment

Practice Areas: Chair, Employment Law Department, New York Office. Employment Law and Litigation: Labor Law Litigation and Advice.

Prof. Memberships: American Bar Association; Advisory Board, New York University Law School Center for Labor and Employment Law, National Employment Law Institute; Labor Law Committee, United States Chamber of Commerce.

Career: Paul, Hastings, Janofsky & Walker, Washington, DC 1988-2000; New York, 2000-; Crowell & Moring, Washington, DC 1983-88; Seyfarth, Shaw, Fairweather & Geraldson, Washington DC and Chicago, 1972-83.

Personal: BA Northwestern University, 1969; JD University of Michigan, 1972, with Honors, Order of the Coif. Born Chicago, Illinois, 1948.

FASTOW, Jay N
Weil, Gotshal & Manges LLP, New York
212 310 8644
jay.fastow@weil.com
Recommended in Antitrust

Practice Areas: Mr Fastow heads the firm's Consumer Financial Services Practice, is an active member of its Antitrust Practice, and has been lead counsel in litigations from New York to Guam.

Career: In the financial services area, he has litigated numerous payment card cases, and been involved in suits involving auto finance and leasing, consumer credit counseling, and other financial services activities. Mr Fastow has litigated antitrust cases in a variety of other industries, played a leading role in coordinating multi-defendant litigations, and argued appeals in courts around the country.

Personal: Yale Law School (JD, 1977); Brandeis University (BA, 1974).

FELDMAN, Matthew A
Willkie Farr & Gallagher LLP, New York
212 728 8651
mfeldman@willkie.com
Recommended in Bankruptcy

Practice Areas: Partner in the Business Reorganization and Restructuring Department. Clients include debtors, creditors, lenders, landlords, governmental agencies, and bank committees. Has been significantly involved in numerous complex Chapter 11 cases and non-judicial restructurings, including recent representation of PG&E National Energy Group, Verestar, Inc., XO Communications, Inc., Global Crossing, Ltd., Big V Supermarkets, Inc. and Golden Books Entertainment. Represented several debtors in cross-border insolvency cases and foreign restructurings including Petroleum Geo-Services ASA, Millicom Cellular SA, ish GmbH & Co. KG and Kabel Baden-Württemberg GmbH & Co. KG, two of the largest German cable television companies, Livent Inc., Teleglobe, Inc., Converse Corporation, Alliance Entertainment Corp. and AIOC Corporation. Regularly represents investors seeking to acquire assets or businesses from companies operating in Chapter 11. Recently represented investor groups that bid on or were considering bidding on assets in the Chapter 11 cases of The Darby Cycle Corporation, Harnischfager Corporation, Crimi Mae and Colt Manufacturing.

Prof. Memberships: Member of the Connecticut Bar Association, the American Bar Association, and the American Bankruptcy Institute.

Career: Admitted to the Bars of New York, Connecticut, and Massachusetts as well as the Southern and Northern Districts of New York and the District of Massachusetts.

Personal: Received a JD from New York University School of Law in 1988 and a BA (magna cum laude) from Tufts University in 1985.

FELTENSTEIN, Martha
Skadden, Arps, Slate, Meagher & Flom LLP & Affiliates, New York
212 735 2272
mfeltens@skadden.com
Recommended in Real Estate

Practice Areas: Active in all aspects of Skadden's real estate practice, including bank lending and financial products, real estate development, acquisitions,

leasing, joint ventures, financing, public and private offerings of real estate securities, and commercial mortgage securitization. Also represents US and non-US clients in their acquisition and development of hotels, shopping centers, office buildings and residential properties in the United States and abroad.
Career: JD, Columbia University, 1981; M Phil, School of Oriental and African Studies, University of London, 1977; BA, Princeton University, 1975.

FIELDS, Richard W
Dickstein Shapiro Morin & Oshinsky LLP, New York 212 896 5444
FieldsR@dsmo.com
Recommended in Insurance
Practice Areas: State and federal litigation and international arbitration, emphasis on insurance coverage, complex dispute resolution, terrorist financing, and human rights. Resolved some of the largest insurance claims in history involving professional negligence, securities fraud, pollution, asbestos, products liability, directors and officers, and mass torts for Fortune 100 clients in the oil, chemical, utility, banking, and manufacturing sectors.
Prof. Memberships: ABA; International Bar Association.
Career: Partner, Dickstein Shapiro; Partner, Director, Swidler Berlin; Associate, Arnold & Porter.
Publications: Published numerous articles on insurance and legal profession.
Personal: Indiana University (BA, Phi Beta Kappa, 1977; JD, 1982); Rose-Hulman Institute of Technology (1974-75).

FIFE, Lori R
Weil, Gotshal & Manges LLP, New York 212 310 8318
lori.fife@weil.com
Recommended in Bankruptcy
Practice Areas: Business finance and restructuring.
Career: Ms Fife's practice covers domestic and international debt restructurings, crisis management and corporate governance. She represents companies, banks, secured and unsecured creditors and committees in Chapter 11 cases and out of court restructurings. Ms Fife co-led the firm's representation of MCI / WorldCom in Chapter 11 and is representing Loral Space & Communications in Chapter 11. She has represented Sunbeam, Texaco, Bruno's, Factory Card Outlet, Best Products, R. H Macy, Premium Standard Farms, Edison Brothers Stores and CHI Energy.
Personal: Benjamin N Cardozo School of Law (JD, 1983); University of Pennsylvania (BA, 1980).

FILARDI, Edward V
Skadden, Arps, Slate, Meagher & Flom LLP & Affiliates, New York
212 735 3060
efilardi@skadden.com
Recommended in Intellectual Property

Practice Areas: Has extensive experience in patent, trade secret, unfair competition and antitrust-related matters, specifically regarding litigation and dispute resolution. Registered US patent attorney with extensive jury trial and appellate experience; has litigated patent and trademark cases for both plaintiffs and defendants. Has served as lead trial counsel in matters involving various technologies, including medical devices, chemicals, pharmaceuticals, computers, telecommunications, and mechanics in federal and state courts as well as before the International Trade Commission. Also has significant experience in international litigation related to pharmaceutical, chemical and fabricated materials industries, and has served as advisory lead counsel in coordinating litigation in France, Germany, the Netherlands, the UK, Japan, Denmark and Sweden. Has been an arbitrator and a court-appointed neutral evaluator in intellectual property rights infringement matters.
Career: JD, New York Law School, 1968 (articles editor, Law Review); BS, Iona College, 1965.

FINKELSON, Allen
Cravath, Swaine & Moore LLP, New York 212 474 1262
afinkelson@cravath.com
Recommended in Corporate/M&A
Practice Areas: Mergers and acquisitions.
Prof. Memberships: ABCNY.
Career: Partner, 1977-83. Managing Director, Mergers and Acquisitions Group, Lehman Brothers, 1983-85. Partner since 1985.
Personal: Columbia Law School (JD, 1971; editor of 'Columbia Law Review'); St. Lawrence University (BA, magna cum laude, 1968).

FINLEY, John G
Simpson Thacher & Bartlett LLP, New York 212 455 2000
jfinley@stblaw.com
Recommended in Corporate/M&A
Practice Areas: Senior Member of the Mergers and Acquisitions Group and Chairman of the firm's Corporate Governance Practice Group. Recent transactions include the announced sale of Toys R Us to a consortium including Kohlberg Kravis Roberts & Co. (2005), the business combination of Kmart with Sears (2005), the sale of Grey Global to the WPP Group (2005), the announced sale of VNU's Yellow Pages directories to Apax and Cinven (2004), the acquisition of Time Warner's Warner Music Group by a consortium led by Thomas H Lee Partners and Edgar Bronfman, Jr (2004), the acquisition of Neuberger Berman by Lehman Brothers (2003) and the sale of Osmonics to General Electric (2003). Also represents financial advisors in connection with M&A matters, including Goldman Sachs, J.P. Morgan Chase and Lehman Brothers.
Prof. Memberships: New York State Bar

Association (served on Committee on Securities Regulation); International Bar Association (currently Co-Chairman of Committee on Business Organizations).
Career: Joined firm 1981; became Partner 1989.
Publications: Author and speaker at conferences on mergers and acquisitions sponsored by the Tulane Corporate Law Institure, the UCLA Law First Annual Institute on Corporate, Securities and Related Aspects of Mergers and Acquisitions, the Centre for the Study of Mergers and Acquisitions of the University of Miami School of Law and the International Bar Association.
Personal: University of Pennsylvania (BA, College of Arts & Sciences, BS, Wharton School), summa cum laude, 1978); Harvard Law School (JD, cum laude, 1981). Trustee of the Jewish Board of Family and Children's Services.

FISHBEIN, Matthew
Debevoise & Plimpton LLP, New York 212 909 6000
Recommended in Litigation

FISKE, Robert
Davis Polk & Wardwell, New York 212 450 4000
robert.fiske@dpw.com
Recommended in Litigation
Practice Areas: Senior Member of Davis Polk & Wardwell's Litigation Department. Among his practice specialties are professional liability, securities, products liability and white collar crime. Has tried many cases concerning a wide variety of industries and areas of the law in courts across the country. Financial and securities experience includes representation of General Electric, Exxon, Bankers Trust, and other clients in securities actions. Also has significant products liability experience. Experience as a government prosecutor and lawyer is extensive, including as a former US Attorney and Whitewater Independent Counsel.

FITZGERALD, Brian T
LeBoeuf, Lamb, Greene & MacRae, LLP, Albany 518 626 9311
bfitzger@llgm.com
Recommended in Energy
Practice Areas: Representation of energy and telecommunications clients in federal and state regulatory proceedings and resulting litigation, including financings and asset transfers. Mr FitzGerald also represents PCS, VOIP, cable and utility clients in nationwide site acquisition, pole attachment, rights-of-way, franchising, rate and interconnection matters.
Prof. Memberships: New York Bar; Connecticut Bar; District of Columbia Bar, Rhode Island Bar.
Career: Joined LeBoeuf in 1990.
Personal: University of Virginia (JD) 1990; Siena College (BA) 1987.

FITZGERALD, Edmond
Davis Polk & Wardwell, New York 212 450 4000
edmond.fitzgerald@dpw.com
Recommended in Employee Benefits
Practice Areas: As a member of Davis Polk & Wardwell's Executive Compensation and Employee Benefits Practice Group, he works closely with the firm's Corporate Department on matters involving executive compensation and employee benefits, both in the ordinary course of clients' business and in the context of mergers and acquisitions, new ventures, and restructurings. He has extensive experience in structuring employment agreements, equity compensation, performance incentives, deferred compensation, change in control protections, and management participation in buyouts and new ventures. He has considerable experience in domestic and international M&A across a variety of sectors. He also works extensively with the firm's Investment Management Group and Derivatives Group in structuring financial products and investment funds to include participation by management personnel and pension plans.

FITZPATRICK Jr, James A
Dewey Ballantine LLP, New York 212 259 6220
jfitzpatrick@deweyballantine.com
Recommended in Insurance
Practice Areas: Mr FitzPatrick represents public and private insurance and other companies and their boards of directors in transactional matters such as the formation of new business ventures, public and private capital raising, purchase and sale of assets, reinsurance transactions, mergers and acquisitions, insolvencies and reorganizations and restructurings as well as general corporate, insurance regulatory and corporate governance matters.
Prof. Memberships: American Bar Association, Torts and Insurance Practice Section.
Career: Partner, Dewey Ballantine LLP.
Personal: Born July 1, 1949. BA, Dartmouth College, 1971. JD, Albany Law School, Union University, 1974.

FLEDER, Robert
Paul, Weiss, Rifkind, Wharton & Garrison LLP, New York 212 373 3107
rfleder@paulweiss.com
Recommended in Employee Benefits
Practice Areas: Partner in Employee Benefits and Executive Compensation Department. Extensive experience in legal, accounting, actuarial and human resource issues connected with implementation and operation of ERISA employee benefit plans (including ESOPs) and executive compensation arrangements. Extensive experience in M&A transactions, including dealing with stock options, underfunded pensions, retiree health, employment and

severance contracts, golden parachutes, and crafting management equity incentives. Helped defend and resolve serious ERISA fiduciary claims. Significant expertise dealing with PBGC. Member of Taxation Section of New York State Bar Association; past Co-Chair of it's Employee Benefits Committee. Selected for 2005 edition "The Best Lawyers in America".

FLEISCHER Jr, Arthur
Fried, Frank, Harris, Shriver & Jacobson LLP, New York 212 859 8120
Arthur.Fleischer@FriedFrank.com
Recommended in Corporate/M&A
Practice Areas: Senior Partner. Has led the firm's M&A Practice for more than 30 years. Represents corporate clients as acquirers and targets and many of the leading investment banks. Practice encompasses negotiated and contested transactions. Advises special committees formed to review buyout proposal and corporate restructurings.
Prof. Memberships: Member of the American Bar Association, Section of Corporation, Banking and Business Law, Committee on Federal Regulation of Securities; American Law Institute; Advisory Committee of the Securities Regulation Institute of the University of California; Association of the Bar of the City of New York.
Career: Qualified in 1959. Associated with Fried Frank in 1958 and became a Partner in 1967.
Personal: Born 1933. Achieved LLB in 1958 and BA 1953 from Yale University.

FLEMING Jr, Peter
Curtis, Mallet-Prevost, Colt & Mosle LLP, New York 212 696 6008
PFleming@CM-P.COM
Recommended in Litigation
Practice Areas: Peter Fleming Jr, Chair of the Litigation Department at the international law firm Curtis, Mallet-Prevost, Colt & Mosle LLP, has an extensive barrister practice in both civil and criminal areas. He has been lead counsel for the defense of several major white-collar criminal prosecutions of individuals and corporations. His experience also includes serving as an Assistant US Attorney (SDNY) and as Special Counsel for the Select Committee on Crime of the House of Representatives. In 1970 he was appointed Temporary Special Independent Counsel to Senators Mitchell and Dole.

FLESHER, Gail
Davis Polk & Wardwell, New York
212 450 4000
gail.flesher@dpw.com
Recommended in Environment
Practice Areas: Member of Davis Polk & Wardwell's Corporate Department. Represents companies and financial institutions on environmental matters in the context of transactions, including mergers and acquisitions, real estate investments, bankruptcies and restruc-

turings and securities offerings. She is the coordinator of the firm's Environmental Practice Group and the Chair of the Recruiting Committee.

FLOM, Joseph H
Skadden, Arps, Slate, Meagher & Flom LLP & Affiliates, New York
212 735 3100
jflom@skadden.com
Recommended in Corporate/M&A
Practice Areas: Leading attorney in M&A area. Credited with pioneering many of the strategies used by bidders, targets and investment bankers. Practice includes all forms of corporate transactions.
Prof. Memberships: Director, UrbanAmerica, LLC (1998-present); Advisory Board, RRE Investors, LLC (1999-present); and Trustee, Petrie Stores Liquidating Trust (1996-present).
Career: LLB, Harvard Law School, 1948 (cum laude; editor, 'Harvard Law Review'); College of the City of NY; LHD, Honorary Doctorate in Humane Letters, Queens College, 1984; LLD, Honorary Doctorate of Law, Fordham University, 1990; Chairman, Woodrow Wilson International Center for Scholars (1994-98).

FLORACK, James A
Davis Polk & Wardwell, New York
212 450 4000
james.florack@dpw.com
Recommended in Banking & Finance
Practice Areas: Member of Davis Polk & Wardwell's Corporate Department. Advises clients in a range of corporate finance transactions, including acquisition financings and other leveraged lending transactions, high-yield debt offerings, exchange offers and other capital markets transactions, structured finance transactions and restructurings. Practice includes transactions both in the US and in international markets, particularly Latin America. Clients include a number of financial institutions, including JPMorgan Chase, Morgan Stanley and Credit Suisse First Boston, as well as a number of corporate clients.

FODOR, Susanna
Jones Day, New York
212 326 3476
ssfodor@jonesday.com
Recommended in Construction
Practice Areas: Experienced in all transactional aspects of real property. She is among a handful of attorneys who combines a broad-based real estate practice with an equally strong specialty practice in design and construction law. Her writings and lectures on real estate law, construction law, and related topics have earned her such honors as 'Outstanding Presentation' on many occasions. Recognized globally as a leading real estate lawyer.
Prof. Memberships: American College of Real Estate Lawyers; Fellow of the American College of Construction

Lawyers; CoreNet Global; founding member of the editorial board of the Journal of Corporate Real Estate.

FORREST, Katherine B
Cravath, Swaine & Moore LLP, New York 212 474 1155
kforrest@cravath.com
Recommended in Antitrust, Intellectual Property
Practice Areas: Commercial litigation, including antitrust, competition, copyright, trademark, contract, SEC, accounting fraud issues. Obtaining regulatory clearance from FTC and DOJ in large transactions.
Prof. Memberships: ABA; NYSBA. Admitted to practice before US Supreme Court; US Courts of Appeals for Second, Third and Seventh Circuits; US District Courts for the Northern, Southern and Western Districts of New York and District of Columbia; Courts of the State of New York.
Career: Partner since 1998.
Publications: Frequent lecturer on topics in the areas of intellectual property, antitrust and competition law.
Personal: New York University (JD, 1990); Wesleyan University (BA, with honors, 1986).

FORTE, Joseph Philip
Dechert, New York
212 698 3579
joseph.forte@dechert.com
Recommended in Real Estate
Practice Areas: Mr Forte, a Partner, focuses on real estate finance, workouts, capital markets, lending, and alternative financing.
Prof. Memberships: Member, Former Chair, Vice-Chair, and Board Member, Mortgage Bankers Association of America; past president, Commercial Mortgage Securities Association.
Career: Developed program documents for first commercial mortgage loan conduit; principal draftsman of Capital Markets Mortgage form published by Capital Consortium; lead draftsman of 'New York' creditor's rights endorsement by American Land Title Association; former real estate Chair, Thacher Proffitt & Wood.
Personal: St. Francis College (BA, honors, 1969); St. John's University School of Law (JD, 1973), Managing Editor of 'Law Review'.

FOX, David
Skadden, Arps, Slate, Meagher & Flom LLP & Affiliates, New York
212 735 2534
dfox@skadden.com
Recommended in Corporate/M&A
Practice Areas: Advises leading US and international corporations in planning and structuring complex transactions involving acquisitions, divestitures, restructurings and associated corporate finance matters. Counsels clients in corporate governance matters and in connection with crisis situations (eg,

accounting restatements and corporate control contests).
Career: LLB, Hebrew University, Jerusalem, 1982 (Class Valedictorian; Member of the editorial board of 'Law Review').

FRAIDIN, Stephen
Kirkland & Ellis LLP, New York
212 446 4840
sfraidin@kirkland.com
Recommended in Corporate/M&A, Private Equity
Practice Areas: Practice includes the general representation of major companies and investment groups, acquisitions and proxy contests. Advised Forstmann Little & Co. in the creation of its leveraged buyout funds and in a series of negotiated acquisitions, dispositions and restructurings involving over $40 billion; Procter & Gamble Co. in a number of multibillion-dollar acquisitions, including its $4.95 billion acquisition of Bristol Myers Squibb Company's Clairol business and the combination of its Jif/Crisco business with JM Smucker Company in a Morris Trust transaction for $1 billion on a pretax basis.
Personal: Tufts University, BA, 1961; Yale University, LLB, 1964.

FRANCESCANI, David
Fish & Richardson, New York
212 765 5070
Recommended in Intellectual Property

FRATIANNI, Constance A
Shearman & Sterling LLP, New York
212 848 8560
cfratianni@shearman.com
Recommended in Bankruptcy
Practice Areas: Partner in Shearman & Sterling's Bankruptcy & Reorganization Group. Represents debtors and creditors in out-of-court loan workouts and Chapter 11 bankruptcies. Also represents lenders and borrowers in various financings, particularly acquisition financings.
Prof. Memberships: Admitted to the New York Bar and the Southern District of New York Bar.
Career: Joined Shearman in 1985 and became a Partner in 2000.
Personal: BA, Hofstra University (1982); JD, University of Michigan School of Law (1985)

FREDERICK, Jennifer
Latham & Watkins LLP, New York
212 906 1200
Recommended in Projects

FREIDUS, Harris B
Paul, Weiss, Rifkind, Wharton & Garrison LLP, New York
212 373 3064
hfreidus@paulweiss.com
Recommended in Real Estate
Practice Areas: Partner in the Real Estate Department. Advises developers, entrepreneurial and institutional investors and lenders in all areas of commercial real estate, including develop-

ments, mortgage and mezzanine financings, partnerships and joint ventures, sales and acquisitions, construction and leasing. Has significant experience with all real estate asset classes and significant international experience. Major transactions include Time Warner Center, New York Times headquarters building and hotel and gaming developments and financings in Las Vegas and Macau, and representative clients include Las Vegas Sands Corp., Apollo Real Estate Advisors and GMAC Commercial Mortgage Corporation.

FRIEDMAN, David
Kasowitz Benson Torres & Friedman, New York 212 506 1700
Recommended in Bankruptcy

FRIEDMAN, Dennis J
Gibson, Dunn & Crutcher LLP, New York 212 351 3900
dfriedman@gibsondunn.com
Recommended in Corporate/M&A
Practice Areas: Co-Chair of the firm's Corporate Transactions Practice, a member of the Executive Committee and the International Management Committee. Widely recognized corporate lawyer with over 30 years in the mergers and acquisitions and capital markets areas.
Career: In addition to a 30-year legal career, Mr Friedman was an investment banker at several major Wall Street firms where he was a senior M&A banker and also the head of a merchant banking group.
Personal: JD, Georgetown University Law Center, 1969, Articles Editor of the 'Georgetown Law Journal'. BS, economics, University of Pennsylvania, Wharton School of Finance, 1966.

FRIEDMAN, Eric J
Skadden, Arps, Slate, Meagher & Flom LLP & Affiliates, New York 212 735 2204
efriedma@skadden.com
Recommended in Corporate/M&A
Practice Areas: Concentrates in mergers and acquisitions, corporate finance and general corporate law. Has been involved in a number of significant transactions in the financial services industry and technology-related transactions. With respect to general corporate matters, has advised many companies on SEC-reporting obligations, board governance and stockholder affairs, and other corporate and securities law matters.
Career: JD, University of Pennsylvania, 1989; BBA, University of Michigan, 1986 (High Distinction).

FRIEDMAN, Gary
Mayer, Brown, Rowe & Maw LLP, New York 212 506 2574
gfriedman@mayerbrown.com
Recommended in Employment
Practice Areas: Practice includes all areas of employment law, with particular expertise in defending class actions, collective actions and mass actions. Has tried and argued appeals in numerous employment-related cases in federal and state courts. Has defended numerous employment discrimination and wage and hour class and collective actions nationwide. Has extensive arbitration experience in various arbitral forums, including the New York Stock Exchange, National Association of Securities Dealers, the New York Mercantile Exchange, the American Arbitration Association and JAMS/Endispute. Has Prosecuted and defended numerous actions involving restrictive covenants and protection of trade secrets, and has handled such matters in more than 30 different states within the United States.
Career: Mayer, Brown, Rowe & Maw LLP, New York, 1991 to date; Partner, 1997. Simpson Thacher & Bartlett, New York, 1988-91. Judicial Law Clerk to The Honorable Stanley S. Brotman, United States District Court for the District of New Jersey, 1987-88.
Publications: Writes and speaks extensively on employment-related topics.
Personal: JD, Georgetown University Law Center, 1987; Dean's List; American Jurisprudence Award - Evidence; Associate Editor, The Tax Lawyer. Duke University, BA magna cum laude, 1983.

FRIEDMAN, Gary
Debevoise & Plimpton LLP, New York 212 909 6000
Recommended in Tax

FRUMKIN, Joseph B
Sullivan & Cromwell LLP, New York 212 558 4000
frumkinj@sullcrom.com
Recommended in Corporate/M&A, Energy
Practice Areas: Advises clients, including utilities, on hostile and negotiated transactions, proxy fights and defensive preparedness. Energy transactions include representing: TXU in energy trading joint venture with CSFB (abandoned), Allegheny Energy in acquisition of Merrill Lynch energy trading business and sales of Western USA trading book and Mountaineer Gas Company (pending); UBS in acquisition of Enron energy trading business; Centrica in acquisition of NewPower; and Powergen in acquisition by E.ON and earlier acquisition of LG&E Energy. Non-utility clients include: USF in acquisition by Yellow Roadway, General Growth in acquisition of The Rouse Company; SBC and Cingular in acquisition of AT&T Wireless; Moore Wallace in combination with R.R. Donnelley; and Prudential Financial in acquisitions of American Skandia and CIGNA retirement business.
Prof. Memberships: ABA.
Career: Partner since 1994. Previously was an investment banker in the M&A group of Merrill Lynch & Co. (1989-90) and a senior aide to US Senator John Heinz.

Personal: Georgetown University (BA, 1980); University of Pennsylvania Law School (JD, 1985).

FUHRMAN, Steven M
Simpson Thacher & Bartlett LLP, New York 212 455 7235
sfuhrman@stblaw.com
Recommended in Bankruptcy
Practice Areas: Steven Fuhrman is a Partner at Simpson Thacher & Bartlett LLP in the firm's Bankruptcy Department. Mr Fuhrman regularly advises clients in connection with Chapter 11 restructurings, out-of-court workouts, acquisitions of troubled companies and the structuring of corporate and credit transaction. Mr Fuhrman's principal focus since 1985 has been the representation of banks and other financial institutions in the restructuring of large syndicated credit facilities extended to borrowers in a wide variety of businesses and industries. Such work has involved complex out-of-court consensual restructurings and representation prior to, during and after Chapter 11 proceedings, including 'pre-packaged' cases, cases involving the sale of substantially all of the Debtors' assets, and cases in which his lender clients became the majority owners and holders of restructured debt obligations of reorganized businesses.
Prof. Memberships: Association of the Bar of the City of New York and the New York State Bar Association.
Personal: BA summa cum laude, from Tufts University in 1982; JD with Honors from New York University School of Law in 1985.

FURCI, Peter
Debevoise & Plimpton LLP, New York 212 909 6000
Recommended in Tax

GABAY, Donald
Stroock & Stroock & Lavan LLP, New York 212 806 5400
Recommended in Insurance

GAFFNEY, John
Cravath, Swaine & Moore LLP, New York 212 474 1122
jgaffney@cravath.com
Recommended in Media & Entertainment
Practice Areas: Mergers and acquisitions, including joint ventures, principally in the media and entertainment industries. Clients include major US and non-US media and entertainment companies. Also represents underwriters in all types of capital markets transactions and general corporate representation for a variety of corporate clients.
Prof. Memberships: NYSBA; ABCNY.
Career: Partner since 1993.
Personal: New York University (JD, MBA, 1986); George Washington University (BA, 1982; Phi Beta Kappa).

GALLAGHER, Patrick C
Kirkland & Ellis LLP, New York 212 446 4998
pgallagher@kirkland.com
Recommended in Tax
Practice Areas: Mr Gallagher focuses his practice on Federal income tax aspects of complex domestic and cross-border transactions, including mergers, acquisitions, leveraged buyouts, and recapitalizations; formation of domestic and offshore private equity investment partnerships, REITs and other pooled investment vehicles; workouts and bankruptcy restructurings; private equity transactions, and public offerings and other financings (including asset-backed securities and sale-leasebacks).
Personal: Pomona College, BA, 1974. University of Chicago, MA, 1977. Harvard Law School, JD, 1985.

GALVIS, Sergio J
Sullivan & Cromwell LLP, New York 212 558 4000
galviss@sullcrom.com
Recommended in Projects
Practice Areas: Coordinates S&C's Latin American practice. Expertise in emerging markets project finance, joint venture, M&A, restructuring, and corporate and sovereign finance transactions. Represents project sponsors and lenders in major Latin American project financings, including path-breaking mining and oil and gas deals. Current assignments include advising the Autoridad del Canal de Panamá on the proposed expansion of the Panama Canal and the International Managing Banks retained by Argentina to assist in the restructuring of more than US$ 100 billion of its external debt.
Prof. Memberships: ABA; ABCNY; IBA.
Career: Partner since 1991.
Publications: Author of numerous articles in professional journals and publications of general interest on a range of topics, including sovereign debt issues, project financing, and general US-Latin American relations. 2004 Law Firm Winner of The Burton Awards for Legal Achievement. Part of group of eminent practitioners convened by G-10 Working Group to assist in the development of collective action clauses for sovereign debt financings.
Personal: College of William and Mary (BA, 1980); Harvard Law School (JD, 1983). Director, Council of the Americas. Member, Council on Foreign Relations.

GANSBERG, Andrew
Nixon Peabody LLP, Albany 518 427 2657
agansberg@nixonpeabody.com
Recommended in Energy
Practice Areas: Practice concentrates on public utility matters; has tried proceedings and negotiated settlements involving electric, gas, and water rates and regulation before several utility commissions. Mr Gansberg has repre-

sented New York utilities in connection with mergers, restructuring, asset sales, and generation and transmission facility siting proceedings. He has advised several utilities in litigation involving the protection of trade secrets and commercially sensitive information.
Prof. Memberships: Admitted to practice in New York, the Second Circuit Court of Appeals, and the US District Courts for the Southern and Eastern Districts of New York.
Personal: New York University, JD; Bucknell University, BA.

GANZ, Howard
Proskauer Rose LLP, New York
212 969 3035
hganz@proskauer.com
Recommended in Employment, Sport
Practice Areas: Co-Chair of Proskauer's Labor and Employment Law Department, as well as Co-Chair of the firm's Sports Law Group. When not practicing sports law for clients such as the NBA and MLB, he has represented a number of the nation's best-known companies with respect to a wide variety of labor and employment matters, such as employment discrimination, sexual harassment, wrongful discharge, defamation, breach of contract, and large-scale reductions-in-force. His litigation experience has run the gamut from single plaintiff lawsuits to major class actions in federal and state courts in New York and elsewhere. He has been named one of the 'World's Leading Labor and Employment Lawyers' and one of the '100 Best Lawyers in New York.'
Prof. Memberships: Currently the Chair of the Sports Law Committee of the Association of the Bar of the City of New York.
Publications: He has lectured widely on sports law and employment law matters.
Personal: A graduate of Colgate University and Columbia Law School, where he was articles editor of the 'Columbia Law Review,' spent two years as a law clerk for a federal district judge in New York before joining Proskauer Rose LLP.

GARDNER, Stephen
Kronish Lieb Weiner & Hellman LLP, New York 212 479 6000
Recommended in Tax

GARRITY, James
Shearman & Sterling LLP, New York
212 848 4879
jgarrity@shearman.com
Recommended in Bankruptcy
Practice Areas: Partner in Shearman & Sterling's Bankruptcy and Reorganization Group.
Prof. Memberships: Institute International Insolvency; Adjunct Professor, St. John's University and New York Law School; New York State Bar Association; American Bar Association; American Bankruptcy Institute.
Career: Joined firm as Partner in 1999. Served as a Judge in the US Bankruptcy Court for the Southern District of New

York and as Assistant US Attorney in the Civil Division of the US Attorney's Office for SDNY.
Personal: BA, College of the Holy Cross (1977); JD, St. John's University School of Law (1980); LLM in Taxation, New York University School of Law (1986)

GARTNER, Steven
Willkie Farr & Gallagher LLP, New York
212 728 8222
sgartner@willkie.com
Recommended in Private Equity
Practice Areas: Partner in the Corporate and Financial Services Department, Chair of the Private Equity Group and a member of the firm's Executive Committee. Specializes in private equity (buyout and venture capital) transactions, as well as mergers and acquisitions and public offerings. Actively involved in Willkie's extensive private equity practice, representing funds controlled by Warburg Pincus and others. Has been involved in over 100 private equity transactions, ranging from $1 million to well over $1 billion. Significant matters in 2004 include representation of Providence Equity Partners and Warburg Pincus in their $1.35 billion acquisition of Telcordia Technologies, Inc., representation of Warburg affiliates in the $1.2 billion acquisition of Polypore, Inc., and the sale of Information Holdings Inc. (NYSE) to the Thomson Corporation for $550 million. Has represented clients in Brazil, Hong Kong, Italy, Sweden, Switzerland, and the United Kingdom. Mergers and acquisitions experience includes going-private transactions, stock and asset sales, and privately negotiated and hostile transactions. Represents both issuers and underwriters in public offerings and private placements.
Prof. Memberships: Member of the American Bar Association (Section on Business Law), the New York State Bar Association, New York City Bar Association, and the New Jersey Bar Association. A Director of The International Center in New York, a not-for-profit organization.
Career: Admitted to the Bars of the State of New York and New Jersey.
Publications: Author of 'Corporate Minutes' (BNA 2004); co-author of 'Doing Business in Europe: Before and After 1992' (New York State Bar Association 1991).
Personal: Received a JD (magna cum laude) from St. John's University School of Law in 1984, where he served as a member of the St. John's Law Review, and a BSBA from Georgetown University in 1981.

GEARY, Sean
White & Case LLP, New York
212 819 8300
sgeary@whitecase.com
Recommended in Banking & Finance
Practice Areas: Represents commercial and investment banks in acquisition and

highly leveraged financings and in other lending transactions. Lead counsel on a number of the pioneer highly leveraged acquisitions of public companies financed principally by a syndicated bank credit facility and has subsequently served as lead counsel for the senior lenders in some of the largest of these, including the RJR-Nabisco leveraged buyout and the Time-Warner combination.
Personal: BA, Manhattan College, 1964; Captain, US Air Force assigned to the National Security Agency, 1966-71; JD, cum laude, New York University School of Law, 1974, 'Law Review', Order of the Coif.

GELBLUM, Seth
Loeb & Loeb LLP, New York
212 407 4000
Recommended in Media & Entertainment

GELSTON, Philip
Cravath, Swaine & Moore LLP, New York 212 474 1548
pgelston@cravath.com
Recommended in Corporate/M&A
Practice Areas: Mergers and acquisitions, joint ventures and general corporate counseling. His practice encompasses hostile transactions (both offense and defense), complicated negotiated transactions, cross-border transactions and advising boards and senior executives.
Prof. Memberships: International Bar Association.
Career: Partner since 1984. Clerkship: Hon. John M Wisdom (US Court of Appeals for the Fifth Circuit).
Personal: Harvard Law School (JD, magna cum laude, 1977; Supreme Court Note Editor of the 'Law Review'; Sears Prize); Harvard College (AB, cum laude, 1974).

GEOGHEGAN, Patricia
Cravath, Swaine & Moore LLP, New York 212 474 1584
pgeoghegan@cravath.com
Recommended in Tax
Practice Areas: Co-Head of Tax Department. Head of Employee Benefits Practice. Also practices in the area of equipment finance representing lessees and lessors of aircraft, satellite transponders, vessels, power plants, and manufacturing facilities and equipment.
Prof. Memberships: ABA; NYSBA; ABCNY.
Career: Partner since 1982.
Personal: New York University (LLM, 1982); Yale Law School (JD, 1974); Yale University (MA, 1972); Michigan State University (BA, with highest honor, 1969; Phi Beta Kappa). YWCA of the City of New York: Chair. Academy of the Holy Angels: Chair. Michigan State University: President's Capital Campaign Cabinet.

GERRARD, Michael
Arnold & Porter LLP, New York
212 715 1190
Michael.Gerrard@aporter.com
Recommended in Environment
Practice Areas: Heads the firm's New

York Environmental Practice.
Prof. Memberships: He is now the Chair of the American Bar Association's Section of Environment, Energy, and Resources and has chaired the Executive Committee of the Association of the Bar of the City of New York, and the Environmental Law Section of the New York State Bar Association.
Career: He has practiced environmental law in New York since 1979. He has been an Adjunct Professor at Columbia Law School and the Yale School of Forestry and Environmental Studies.
Publications: He has written or edited five books, two of which were named Best Law Book of the Year by the Association of American Publishers: the ten-volume 'Environmental Law Practice Guide' (Matthew Bender 1992) and the four-volume 'Brownfields Law and Practice: The Cleanup and Redevelopment of Contaminated Land' (Matthew Bender 1998). His other books concern environmental impact assessment, environmental justice, and facility siting.

GERSTENZANG, Michael A
Cleary Gottlieb Steen & Hamilton LLP, New York 212 225 2096
mgerstenzang@cgsh.com
Recommended in Private Equity
Practice Areas: Forming and advising private investment funds including buyout, international and hedge funds, and other 'alternative asset' investment vehicles. Regularly represents Texas Pacific Group, Newbridge Asia, CSFB, and Och-Ziff.
Prof. Memberships: Admitted in New York. Member of the Private Investment Fund Forum and the Committee on Private Investment Funds of the Bar Association of the City of New York.
Career: JD, Columbia University (Stone Scholar) (1989); BSFS, magna cum laude, Georgetown University (1986).

GIBBONS, Robert
Debevoise & Plimpton LLP, New York
212 909 6000
Recommended in Projects

GILBERT, Richard
Orrick, Herrington & Sutcliffe LLP, San Francisco 415 773 5424
rag@orrick.com
Recommended in Employee Benefits
Practice Areas: Mr Gilbert has practiced exclusively in the field of employee benefits law for 25 years, advising financial institutions, public pension funds, trustees, and employers as to the fiduciary responsibility provisions of ERISA and public pension law, and the design and implementation of numerous types of 401(k), retirement and executive benefit plans. Mr Gilbert has vast knowledge in the ERISA aspects of a wide variety of financial transactions, investment funds and new investment instruments.
Prof. Memberships: Mr Gilbert is a Charter Fellow of the American College of Employee Benefits Counsel (2000).

American Bar Association: Section of Taxation, Committee on Employee Benefits, Chair of Fiduciary Responsibility Sub-Committee, 1991-94; California State Bar; New York Bar. Mr Gilbert often lectures and serves as a panelist on employee benefits-related topics for programs and organizations such as the ALI-ABA Video Program, the American Bar Association's Section of Taxation, the Practising Law Institute, the NYU Institute on Federal Taxation, the International Foundation of Employee Benefit Plans, and the Institute for Fiduciary Education.
Career: Mr Gilbert has practiced at Orrick since 1981. He earned his JD, cum laude, with honors, University of Wisconsin School of Law, 1974, and a BA, cum laude, Yale University, 1968.

GILLESPIE, Michael
Debevoise & Plimpton LLP, New York
212 909 6000
Recommended in Media & Entertainment

GILLIS, Theresa
Jones Day, New York 212 326 3679
tmgillis@jonesday.com
Recommended in Intellectual Property
Practice Areas: Involved in all aspects of intellectual property law, with extensive litigation experience, including jury trials, relating to patents, copyrights, trademarks, unfair competition, and trade secrets. She has practiced in federal courts, the International Trade Commission, and in the US Patent and Trademark Office and argued appeals in the federal courts of appeals. She is also experienced in US and non-US trademark and patent prosecution. She has drafted and negotiated intellectual property agreements and provided advice concerning intellectual property issues in the context of mergers, acquisitions, and IPOs. Furthermore, she has counseled clients on intellectual property strategy and acquisitions.

GITTER, Max
Cleary Gottlieb Steen & Hamilton LLP, New York 212 225 2610
mgitter@cgsh.com
Recommended in Litigation
Practice Areas: Corporate and commercial litigation/arbitration, especially involving securities, M&A, intellectual property, governance issues and contracts. Clients have included Goldman Sachs, PeopleSoft, Triarc, Bank of America, Time Warner, GAF Corporation, NY State Comptroller, Governance Committee of Starwood Hotels, Texas Pacific Group.
Prof. Memberships: Member of the City of New York Bar Association and NYSBA. Admitted to practice before US Supreme Court, US Courts of Appeals for the Second, Third, Fourth, District of Columbia, Sixth and Ninth Circuits, and US District Courts for Southern and Eastern Districts of New York.

Career: Joined firm as Partner, 1999. Previously Partner at Paul, Weiss, Rifkind, Wharton & Garrison. Taught at Yale Law School (1985-86) and University of Chicago Law School (1968-69). LLB, Yale Law School (1968); BA, cum laude, Harvard College (1965).

GITTES, Franklin M
Skadden, Arps, Slate, Meagher & Flom LLP & Affiliates, New York
212 735 3760
fgittes@skadden.com
Recommended in Corporate/M&A
Practice Areas: Representations include: Johns Manville in its US$3 billion acquisition by Berkshire Hathaway Inc. and MacMillan Bloedel Limited in its US$2.45 billion acquisition by Weyerhaeuser Company.
Prof. Memberships: American Bar Association; New York State Bar Association; Association of the Bar of the City of New York.
Career: JD, Georgetown University, 1973; BSChE, Lehigh University, 1969.

GIUFFRA, Robert J
Sullivan & Cromwell LLP, New York
212 558 3121
giuffrar@sullcrom.com
Recommended in Litigation
Practice Areas: Complex civil, regulatory, and white-collar litigation (securities, banking and tax), including trials and appeals. Has represented Bank of New York, Computer Associates, Exxon, Goldman Sachs, ING, Oxford Health Plans, Philips Electronics, UBS, Vornado, David Duncan (former lead Arthur Andersen auditor for Enron), and Armand D'Amato (brother of then US Senator Alfonse D'Amato). Present matters include class action litigation and government investigations concerning Enron, HealthSouth, and NYSE specialists.
Career: Partner since 1998. Commissioner, NY State Ethics Commission, since 1998. Chief Counsel, US Senate Committee on Banking, Housing, and Urban Affairs, 1995-96. Law clerk to Chief Justice William H Rehnquist (US Supreme Court, 1988-99) and Judge Ralph K Winter (US Court of Appeals, Second Circuit, 1987-88).
Personal: Princeton University (AB, 1983); Yale Law School (JD, 1987).

GLAZER, Dennis
Davis Polk & Wardwell, New York
212 450 4000
dennis.glazer@dpw.com
Recommended in Litigation
Practice Areas: Member of Davis Polk & Wardwell's Litigation Department. Represents clients in securities litigation, mergers and acquisitions and related litigation, and major commercial litigation. Mr Glazer litigates cases throughout the country relating to significant merger and acquisition transactions (both friendly and hostile).

GLAZER, Steven D
Weil, Gotshal & Manges LLP, New York
212 310 8806
steven.glazer@weil.com
Recommended in Intellectual Property
Practice Areas: Patent litigation.
Career: Mr Glazer is Co-Chair of the Patent Litigation and Counseling Practice in the New York office. He has over 25 years experience litigating complex patent cases in diverse technologies including digital electronics, computer architecture and networking, financial systems, the internet, encryption, genetic engineering, sweetener chemistry, semiconductors, petrochemicals, satellite television, computer and medical software, and photonics. Mr Glazer is on the faculty of Rutgers Law School and retired from the US Army Reserve.
Personal: Rutgers University School of Law (JD, with honors, 1979); Fairleigh Dickinson University (MS, 1975); Rutgers University (BSEE, 1971); Rutgers University (BA, 1971).

GOERING, Kevin
Coudert Brothers, New York
212 626 4512
goeringk@coudert.com
Recommended in Media & Entertainment
Practice Areas: Media, publishing, first amendment, litigation and arbitration, intellectual property. Mr Goering's practice focuses on advising media interests, including publishers, broadcasters, authors, internet service providers and journalists, on a wide variety of First Amendment, intellectual property and dispute resolution issues. These include defamation, privacy, copyright, trademark, rights of publicity, anti-dilution and licensing matters. He also has extensive trial and appellate commercial litigation experience in state and federal courts and chairs Coudert Brothers' New York litigation practice. He is a frequent speaker and commentator on media law issues. Mr Goering is fluent in French.
Prof. Memberships: NYSBA (former Chair, Committee on Media Law); ABA (Forum on Communications Law); ABCNY (Committee on Communications and Media Law); Copyright Society of the USA; Volunteer Lawyers for the Arts (Director); Media Law Resource Defense Center (former Chair, International Law Committee).
Career: Coudert Brothers LLP, 1986 to present (Partner since 1990). Law clerk to Judge Richard J Cardamone, US Court of Appeals, Second Circuit, 1983-84. Cornell University, JD cum laude, 1981. Managing editor, Cornell International Law Journal, 1980-81. University of Kansas, BA, 1977. Phi Beta Kappa. Also studied at University of Strasbourg and University of Bordeaux.

GOETZ, Peter
Goetz Fitzpatrick Most & Bruckman LLP, New York 212 695 8100
Recommended in Construction

GOLDBERG, Louis L
Davis Polk & Wardwell, New York
212 450 4000
louis.goldberg@dpw.com
Recommended in Private Equity
Practice Areas: Member of Davis Polk & Wardwell's Corporate Department, practicing in the Mergers and Acquisitions Group. Practice focuses on mergers and acquisitions, corporate governance advice, joint ventures, spinoffs, and restructurings and recapitalizations. Also has extensive experience in securities offerings and in the formation and structuring of investment and joint venture vehicles.

GOLDEN, Arthur F
Davis Polk & Wardwell, New York
212 450 4000
arthur.golden@dpw.com
Recommended in Antitrust
Practice Areas: Partner in Davis Polk & Wardwell's Litigation Department and a member of the Management Committee. Leads the firm's practice in competition and antitrust matters, which include domestic and international mergers and acquisitions, antitrust counselling and litigation. Regularly represents large multinational companies with respect to negotiated and contested acquisition-related transactions, criminal antitrust investigations and litigation. Is currently lead counsel for Gillette in its acquisition by Procter & Gamble, represented Comcast in its acquisition of AT&T Broadband and acted as one of the two lead negotiators for the US tobacco industry in the effort to resolve, through legislation and settlements, the legal issues facing that industry. Is currently representing Freeport in the criminal investigation of the copper concentrate industry and Hoffmann-LaRoche in the vitamin cartel litigation and was counsel of record for the defense group in the Supreme Court. Is currently a Director of Emerson Electric and has been on the board of several other NYSE companies.

GOLDEN, Daniel H
Akin Gump Strauss Hauer & Feld LLP, New York 212 872 8010
dgolden@akingump.com
Recommended in Bankruptcy
Practice Areas: For more than 25 years Daniel Golden has represented creditors' committees and bondholder committees in large, complex out-of-court restructurings and Chapter 11 cases. He served as lead committee counsel in numerous high-profile restructurings and Chapter 11 cases, including WorldCom, Tower Automotive, XO Communications, Hayes Lemmerz International, Globalstar, Fruit of the Loom, Lernout & Hauspie Speech Products, Loral Space &

Communications and Solutia Inc. Additionally, Mr Golden has represented corporate debtors and acquirors of financial distressed businesses and assets. He is also a frequent lecturer on bankruptcy/restructuring issues.
Personal: BA, University of Wisconsin-Madison; JD, SUNY Buffalo.

GOLDFEIN, Shepard
Skadden, Arps, Slate, Meagher & Flom LLP & Affiliates, New York
212 735 3610
sgoldfei@skadden.com
Recommended in Antitrust, Sport
Practice Areas: Practice leader, Antitrust Group. Handles a variety of cases from antitrust litigation to white collar criminal investigations and mass disaster litigation. Advises on antitrust and sports-related issues (general compliance programs to antitrust patent licensing issues), and professional sports league issues (team ownership, collective bargaining, team location, intellectual property).
Prof. Memberships: Chairman, Sports Law Committee, Association of the Bar of the City of NY (1996-99).
Career: JD, Rutgers University, 1975 (editor, Rutgers Law Review); MA, Political Science, University of Chicago, 1977; AB, Rutgers University, 1970 (Phi Beta Kappa).
Publications: Co-author, monthly trade regulation column, 'New York Law Journal' (1983-present).

GOLDMAN, Michael
Cravath, Swaine & Moore LLP, New York 212 474 1929
mgoldman@cravath.com
Recommended in Banking & Finance
Practice Areas: Banking and finance, including complex, multicurrency and multijurisdictional syndicated loan transactions, acquisition and leveraged finance and securities offerings for US and international clients.
Prof. Memberships: ABA; NYSBA; ABCNY.
Career: Partner since 1995.
Personal: Fordham University School of Law (JD, cum laude, 1987); University of Pennsylvania (BA, cum laude, 1984).

GOLDRING, Stuart
Weil, Gotshal & Manges LLP, New York 212 310 8312
stuart.goldring@weil.com
Recommended in Tax
Practice Areas: Mr Goldring's practice focuses on tax.
Career: He has nationally recognized experience in federal income tax matters involving financial troubled companies. He has extensive experience advising debtors, creditors and potential acquirers and investors in troubled companies (both within and outside the bankruptcy context). He regularly advises on the structuring of acquisitions, dispositions and other transactions involving corporations and multi-corporate groups. He is co-author of a tax treatise on troubled

corporations and adjunct professor at NYU law school.
Personal: New York University School of Law (LLM, 1983); University of Michigan Law School (JD, 1982); University of Michigan (BBA, 1979).

GOLDSTEIN, Marcia
Weil, Gotshal & Manges LLP, New York 212 310 8000
marcia.goldstein@weil.com
Recommended in Bankruptcy
Practice Areas: Ms Goldstein's practice covers all aspects of domestic and international debt restructurings, as well as crisis management and corporate governance.
Career: Ms Goldstein is Co-Chair of the Business Finance and Restructuring Practice and is a Managing Partner of Weil, Gotshal & Manges, where she has practiced for nearly 30 years. She currently leads the firm's representation of MCI, Inc. (formerly WorldCom, Inc.) and Parmalat s.p.a., and is special restructuring counsel to Eurotunnel. She has represented debtors, bank groups, secured and unsecured creditors, statutory creditors' committees, trustees and other parties in major debt restructurings and Chapter 11 cases for clients including Regal Cinemas, Inc., Washington Group International, Inc., AMF Bowling Worldwide, Inc., Exide, Inc., Oxford Automotive, Inc., United Companies Financial Corp., Warnaco, Inc., CRIIME MAE, Inc., Babcock & Wilcox, Inc., Purina Mills, Inc., SGL Carbon Corp. and Marvel Entertainment. Ms Goldstein is a member of the National Bankruptcy Conference, the American College of Bankruptcy, and the International Insolvency Institute. She has been recognized in numerous publications as one of the 'best lawyers' in restructuring and bankruptcy and is on the Advisory Board of Colliers Bankruptcy, 15th Ed. Ms Goldstein has been a visiting lecturer in bankruptcy at Yale Law School and is a member of the National Bankruptcy Conference, American College of Bankruptcy and the International Insolvency Institute. She has been chair of the Committee on Bankruptcy and Corporate Reorganization of the Association of the Bar of the City of New York. Ms Goldstein is a certified mediator in the Southern District of New York and has served as a mediator in many Chapter 11 cases. She also has served as a Chapter 11 trustee.
Personal: Cornell Law School, JD (cum laude); Cornell University, AB (magna cum laude).

GORDON, David
Latham & Watkins LLP, New York 212 906 1200
Recommended in Projects

GORDON, Nicholas
Franklin, Weinrib, Rudell & Vassallo, New York 212 935 5500
Recommended in Media & Entertainment

GORDON, Stephen
Cravath, Swaine & Moore LLP, New York 212 474 1704
gordon@cravath.com
Recommended in Tax
Practice Areas: Co-Head of Tax Department. Advises on tax aspects of mergers and acquisitions, spin-offs and other restructurings, and corporate joint ventures. Also advises on issues related to corporate finance and domestic and international taxation. Has served as the firm's Hiring Partner and Managing Partner for Administration.
Prof. Memberships: ABA; NYSBA; ABCNY; International Fiscal Association; Tax Forum.
Career: Associate 1981-87, Partner since 1987.
Personal: Harvard Law School (JD, cum laude, 1981; editor of the 'Harvard Law Review'); Cornell University (AB, cum laude, 1978).

GOTTS, Ilene Knable
Wachtell, Lipton, Rosen & Katz, New York 212 403 1247
ikgotts@wlrk.com
Recommended in Antitrust
Practice Areas: Specializes in antitrust matters, particularly relating to mergers and acquisitions. International transactions in which she has served as antitrust counsel include Nestlé S.A./Dreyers Ice Cream Co., Diageo plc/General Mills, Inc., Deutsche Telekom AG/VoiceStream Wireless Corporation, Comcast/AT&T Corp./Time Warner Entertainment, Phillips Petroleum Company/Conoco Inc and Phillips Petroleum Company/Tosco Corporation, Fort James Corp./Georgia-Pacific Corp., and Morton International Inc./Rohm & Haas Co.
Prof. Memberships: Has long been an active participant in the Antitrust Section of the American Bar Association and is currently the Program Officer; previously served as the Chair of the Antitrust Section's Task Force on the Merger Review Process, and as a member of the International Task Force, as well as the Chair on the Antitrust Section's Mergers Committee, and Vice Chair of the Intellectual Property Committee.
Career: Partner at Wachtell, Lipton, Rosen & Katz. Previously worked as a staff attorney in the Bureau of Competition of the Federal Trade Commission in conduct and merger investigations, and in the FTC Bureau of Consumer Protection. In 1995, served as the President of the Washington Council of Lawyers. Chair of the Antitrust and Trade Regulation Section of the Federal Bar Association from 1995 to 1997. Currently a member of the American Law Institute, and the New York State Bar Association's Antitrust Section Executive Committees.
Publications: Frequent guest speaker; published over 95 articles on antitrust related topics; editor of the second edition of the ABA Merger Review Process Handbook; a member of the advisory

board of the Antitrust & Trade Regulation Report; and the editorial board of 'The Antitrust Counselor' and 'The Practical Lawyer' publications.
Personal: Graduated magna cum laude from the University of Maryland (BA), where she was elected to membership in Phi Beta Kappa; and cum laude from Georgetown University Law Center in 1984 (JD). Member of Board of Trustees, University of Maryland Foundation.

GRAEV, Lawrence
King & Spalding LLP, New York 212 556 2167
lgraev@kslaw.com
Recommended in Private Equity
Practice Areas: Private equity investment funds, including fund formation, structuring, negotiation and execution of leveraged acquisitions and venture capital and growth financings and divestitures, public offerings and recapitalizations. Represents investment and merchant banking organizations in their various corporate finance transactions and numerous high technology, e-commerce, telecommunications, healthcare and industrial and service businesses in their day-to-day operations, merger and acquisition, corporate finance transactions and strategic relationships.
Prof. Memberships: American Bar Association; New York State Bar Association.
Personal: BS, Cornell University, 1966; JD, The George Washington University, 1969.

GRAIS, David J
Dewey Ballantine LLP, New York 212 259 7860
dgrais@deweybalalntine.com
Recommended in Insurance
Practice Areas: In addition to his practice in general commercial litigation, Mr Grais has concentrated his practice in litigation and arbitration in the two areas of reinsurance and information technology. In reinsurance, Mr Grais's matters have involved virtually all of the principal issues of reinsurance law and many aspects of arbitration law and procedure under the Federal Arbitration Act.
Career: Partner, Dewey Ballantine LLP. Admitted to practice 1979, New York.
Personal: Born April 9, 1952. AB, magna cum laude, Princeton University, 1973. MA, Philosophy, Balliol College, University of Oxford, 1975. JD, Yale Law School, 1978.

GRALA, Bronislaw
Cadwalader, Wickersham & Taft LLP, New York 212 504 6466
bronislaw.grala@cwt.com
Recommended in Employee Benefits
Practice Areas: Focuses on ERISA and employee benefit matters, including ERISA fiduciary responsibilities and obligations, and the tax and ERISA implications of various plan investments and investment formats. Represents plan sponsors and advises the indi-

viduals at such sponsors who administer plans, and serves as ERISA counsel to plan asset managers, broker-dealers, and investment bankers who provide services or investment products to employee benefit plans. Has extensive experience in dealings with the Employee Benefits Security Administration in the US Department of Labor.

Personal: Cum laude graduate of Fordham College (1968); JD, cum laude, from New York University School of Law (1972), an editor of the 'NYU Law Review', a Member of the Order of the Coif, and a Founder's Day Scholar. Selected as Charter Fellow in the American College of Employee Benefits Counsel. Member of the New York State Bar Association (section on Taxation) and the Association of the Bar of the City of New York.

GRANFIELD, Lindsee P
Cleary Gottlieb Steen & Hamilton LLP, New York 212 225 2738
lgranfield@cgsh.com
Recommended in Bankruptcy

Practice Areas: Restructuring, insolvency, bankruptcy, and commercial litigation. She represents debtors, creditors committees, individual creditors and equity holders in major bankruptcy and insolvency cases throughout the United States and in international cross-border restructurings involving many industries including healthcare, financial services, heavy equipment manufacturing, telecommunications, broadcasting, retail, mining, energy generation, oil services and steel production. Clients include Citigroup; Goldman Sachs & Co.; Morgan Stanley; Multicanal, S.A.; Kindred Healthcare, Inc.

Career: Joined firm, 1985; became Partner, 1998. Admitted to practice: NY, CA., SDNY, EDNY, Second Circuit, Third Circuit. JD, University of California, Berkeley School of Law (Boalt Hall) (1985), AB, UCLA (1982).

GREEN, Frederick
Weil, Gotshal & Manges LLP, New York 212 310 8524
frederick.green@weil.com
Recommended in Corporate/M&A

Practice Areas: Mr Green's practice focuses on business combinations, including mergers, acquisitions, joint ventures and corporate spin-offs. He also advises on corporate governance matters and restructurings, and provides general corporate counseling across a broad range of commercial affairs.

Career: Mr Green joined Weil Gotshal in 1979 and is the Chairman of the firm's Mergers and Acquisitions Practice. Prominent transactions he has handled include the proposed acquisition of Sprint's US cell tower operations by Macquarie Bank, the acquisition of the direct broadcast satellite operations of Pegasus Communications, the acquisition of PanAmSat by Kolberg Kravis Roberts & Co., the sale of control of

Embratel (Brazil's national telephone company) to TelMex, the acquisition of a controlling interest in DIRECTV by NewsCorp. and concurrent spin-off of DIRECTV by General Motors, the proposed acquisition of TRW by General Dynamics Corporation, the sale to Boeing of the Hughes Satellite Manufacturing Company, the sale by BMW of the Land Rover business to Ford, the acquisitions of US Satellite Broadcasting and Primestar, the acquisition of Xircom by Intel, the internet and media-based strategic alliance between DIRECTV and America Online, the tender offer by Duke Energy for Endesa Chile, the acquisition by General Dynamics of Gulfstream Aerospace Corporation, the spin-off of the Hughes Aircraft defense business by General Motors and related merger of that business with Raytheon, and the mergers of Excel Communications with Telco Communications and with Teleglobe Inc. Mr Green also Chairs the firm's Latin American Practice, and has handled numerous debt restructurings, joint ventures, financings and commercial transactions on behalf of clients in the region.

Personal: Fordham University, JD (with honors); University of Pennsylvania, The Wharton School, BS (magna cum laude). Mr Green serves on the Advisory Board of the Council of the Americas and on Weil Gotshal's Pro Bono Committee.

GREEN, Jonathan
Milbank, Tweed, Hadley & McCloy, New York 212 530 5000
Recommended in Projects

GREEN, Ronald
Epstein Becker & Green PC, New York 212 351 4500
Recommended in Employment

GREENBERG, Jeffrey
Latham & Watkins LLP, Los Angeles 213 485 1234
Recommended in Projects

GREENBERG, Joel
Kaye Scholer LLP, New York 212 836 8201
jigreenberg@kayescholer.com
Recommended in Corporate/M&A

Practice Areas: Partner in New York City office and Co-Chair of the firm-wide Corporate and Finance Department. Concentrates in domestic and cross-border mergers and acquisitions of public and private companies, representation of financial sponsors, joint ventures, and public and private securities offerings. Also advises publicly held and private companies on a wide variety of general corporate governance and corporate matters, as well as transactional matters.

Prof. Memberships: Member, American Bar Association (Vice-Chair of Committee on Negotiated Acquisitions and Member of the Federal Regulation of Securities and Legal Opinion Com-

mittees); Association of the Bar of the City of New York (Member of the Committee on Corporation Law, 1983-87); Tribar Opinion Committee, 1987-91; Admissions: New York.

Career: JD, Yale University, 1974; BS, New York University, 1967.

Publications: 'The Impact of Sarbanes-Oxley on Merger & Acquisition Practices' (The M&A Lawyer, June 2003) (with Leigh Walton); 'Negotiating Acquisitions of Public Companies' (University of Miami Business Law Review, Winter/Spring 2002) (with Richard E Climan, Lou R Kling and the Honorable E Norman Veasey); 'The Material Adverse Change Clause' (New York Law Journal, April 23, 2001) (with A Julia Haddad); 'Forward-Looking Statements; Safe Harbor Provisions of Federal Act Create Controversy' (New York Law Journal, October 17, 1997) (with Nancy E Fuchs and Anne M Lane); 'Third Party Legal Opinions Under ABA Accord' (New York Law Journal, August 16, 1993). Frequent lecturer on mergers and acquisitions topics, including at programs sponsored by the American Bar Association, the Association of Corporate Counsel, the Association of the Bar of the City of New York, the Center for International Legal Studies, Law Journal Seminars, Stanford Law School, UCLA School of Law, the University of Miami Law School and the University of Texas Law School.

GREENGRASS, Lawrence
Mound Cotton Wollan & Greengrass, New York 212 804 4200
Recommended in Insurance

GREENTHAL, John
Nixon Peabody LLP, Albany 518 427 2670
jgreenthal@nixonpeabody.com
Recommended in Environment

Practice Areas: Environmental enforcement, hazardous waste, state/federal Superfund matters. Judicial/administrative proceedings brought by governmental authorities, private cost-recovery actions; negotiating with regulatory agencies regarding noncompliance.

Prof. Memberships: Admitted to practice in NY. NY State Bar Association (Former Chair, Environmental Law Section); Business Council of NY State; NY League of Conservation Voters (Board of Directors).

Career: Through 1987: Regional Counsel, NY State Department of Environmental Conservation (DEC); Compliance Counsel in DEC's General Counsel's Office; Director of DEC's Division of Environmental Enforcement. Chair, 11-State Northeast Hazardous Waste Project.

Personal: Harvard University, JD; Amherst College, BA, cum laude.

GRIER, Joseph
Pryor Cashman Sherman & Flynn, New York 212 421 4100
Recommended in Media & Entertainment

GROLL, Michael
LeBoeuf, Lamb, Greene & MacRae, LLP, New York 212 424 8616
mgroll@llgm.com
Recommended in Insurance

Practice Areas: He has expertise in the area of corporate and securities law, specifically public and private securities offerings, merger and acquisitions, and other transactions in the insurance industry. He has represented underwriters, insurance companies and lenders in such transactions. He has also represented investors, companies and investment banks in the formation, private financing and acquisition of insurance companies as well as many insurers and investment banks in connection with structured financial product transactions and credit derivative transactions involving both domestic and off-shore insurance and reinsurance companies.

Personal: Columbia University (JD) 1978; Boston University (BA) 1975.

GROSS, John
Proskauer Rose LLP, New York 212 969 3145
jgross@proskauer.com
Recommended in Insurance

Practice Areas: Has been lead counsel in civil litigations for many major US corporations including the holders of The World Trade Center leases in their litigation involving their insurance claims for property damage and business interruption resulting from the September 11, 2001 terrorist attacks. He also advising the City of New York on legal issues arising from the September 11 events.

Career: Served as an Assistant United States Attorney for the Southern District of New York, where he was assistant Chief of the Criminal Division. He also taught Trial Advocacy as an Adjunct Associate Professor at New York University Law School and has been a faculty Member on trial advocacy programs sponsored by the United States Department of Justice, the Association of the Bar of the City of New York, and Harvard Law School.

Personal: A graduate of The Wharton School of Finance and Commerce, of the University of Pennsylvania and George Washington University Law School, where he was a Member of the 'Law Review'.

GROSS, Steven
Debevoise & Plimpton LLP, New York 212 909 6000
Recommended in Bankruptcy

GROSSMAN, Shukie
Weil, Gotshal & Manges LLP, New York 212 310 8655
shukie.grossman@weil.com
Recommended in Private Equity

Practice Areas: Private equity fund formation.

Career: Grossman represents private equity fund sponsors in structuring and marketing domestic and offshore private investment vehicles; negotiates

employment/economic sharing agreements among private equity fund sponsors and investments in prominent private equity funds and operating companies on behalf of certain institutional investors and advises asset managers generally regarding federal securities laws. He spent several years at the Division of Investment Management at the US Securities and Exchange Commission and is a Member of the Private Investment Fund Forum and the Industry Committee on Real Estate Secondary Transfers.
Personal: Fordham University, JD; Yeshiva University, BA.

GROVE, Barry
Thelen Reid & Priest LLP, New York
212 603 2000
Recommended in Construction

GRUBMAN, Allen
Grubman, Indursky & Schindler P.C.,
New York 212 554 0400
Recommended in Media & Entertainment

GUPTA, Paul
Mayer, Brown, Rowe & Maw LLP,
New York 212 506 2670
pgupta@mayerbrownrowe.com
Recommended in Intellectual Property
Practice Areas: Intellectual property. information technology. Antitrust. Other complex litigation. Represents Fortune 500 and other clients in the following industries: computer, e-commerce, and outsourcing; telecommunications; financial services, including banking, insurance and securities; scientific, photographic and control equipment; chemicals; medical products; and energy.
Prof. Memberships: Advisory Boards of four technology law publications; 'BNA's Computer Technology Law Report', 'Electronic Commerce & Law Report', 'E-Commerce Law and Strategy', and the 'Electronic Banking Law and Commerce Report'; Special Committee on Cyberspace Law of the New York State Bar Association.
Career: Mayer, Brown, Rowe & Maw LLP, LeBoeuf, Lamb, Greene & MacRae, LLP, Sullivan & Worcester LLP., Cravath, Swaine & Moore
Publications: Writings: 'Implementing the Recent Developments in Information Security, Business Continuity and Corporate Governance,' Electronic Banking Law and Commerce Report. 'Strategic Alliances,' The Deal. 'The Festo Opinion,' European Intellectual Property Review (London). 'Lessons Learned from Three Generations of Technology Contracts,' Electronic Banking Law and Commerce Report. Frequent speaker on IP issues before Practicing Law Institute (New York and San Francisco), Association of the Bar of the City of New York, Georgetown University Law Center Annual Advanced E-Commerce Institute, and other major groups.
Personal: JD, Harvard Law School; BA, Yale College, Phi Beta Kappa.

GUYNN, Randall
Davis Polk & Wardwell, New York
212 450 4000
randall.guynn@dpw.com
Recommended in Banking & Finance
Practice Areas: Head of Davis Polk & Wardwell's Financial Institutions Group. Focuses on bank regulatory, M&A and capital markets transactions by banks, insurance companies, and other financial institutions. Has also been active in advising the firm's clients on cross-border collateral transactions, securities settlement and payment systems.

HADLEY, Joseph P
Davis Polk & Wardwell, New York
212 450 4000
joseph.hadley@dpw.com
Recommended in Projects
Practice Areas: Member of Davis Polk & Wardwell's Corporate Department. Advises corporations, financial institutions and governmental agencies on a wide variety of corporate and financing matters, with special emphasis on international joint venture and project and leveraged financings. Has extensive experience advising clients raising financing in the telecommunications, power and oil and gas sectors from the debt capital markets, syndicated loan market and governmental and multilateral financing sources.

HAFETZ, Fred
Hafetz & Necheles, New York
212 997 7595
Recommended in Litigation

HAHN, Richard
Debevoise & Plimpton LLP, New York
212 909 6000
Recommended in Bankruptcy

HAIMS, Bruce
Debevoise & Plimpton LLP, New York
212 909 6000
Recommended in Tax

HALEY, James F
Fish & Neave IP Group of Ropes & Gray, New York 212 596 9034
james.haley@ropesgray.com
Recommended in Intellectual Property
Practice Areas: Focuses on worldwide procurement, defense, and enforcement of patents in the biotechnology, pharmaceutical, and chemical industries. Drafted and prosecuted some of the basic patents in rDNA technology. Handles numerous US and foreign patent litigations, European and other oppositions. Secured more than $2.5 billion in royalties for clients.
Career: Massachusetts Bar (1975). New York Bar (1977). USPTO. Partner, Fish & Neave (1983). Partner, Ropes & Gray (2005). Co-Head, Fish & Neave IP Group of Ropes & Gray.
Personal: JD, magna cum laude, Suffolk University Law School (1975). PhD, Brandeis University (1975).

HALL, Richard
Cravath, Swaine & Moore LLP,
New York 212 474 1293
rhall@cravath.com
Recommended in Corporate/M&A
Practice Areas: Mergers and acquisitions (particularly in the media and natural resources sectors), cross-border transactions, hostile takeovers; corporate governance and general corporate advice.
Prof. Memberships: ABA; International Bar Association.
Career: Partner since 1996.
Publications: Frequent speaker and author on the topics of mergers and acquisitions and corporate governance.
Personal: Harvard University (LLM, 1988); University of Melbourne (LLB, with honors, 1986; BComm, with honors, 1984).

HALLIDAY, Joseph W
Skadden, Arps, Slate, Meagher & Flom LLP & Affiliates, New York
212 735 3260
jhallida@skadden.com
Recommended in Banking & Finance
Practice Areas: Founder, Skadden's Banking and Institutional Investing Group, represents commercial banks, investment banks, insurance companies, finance companies and leveraged buy-out funds, as well as borrowers from, and equity participants with, such institutions. Practice involves international banking and financing, project financing, aircraft financing, equipment leasing, workouts and restructurings, creditors' rights, leveraged buyouts, oil and gas transactions and public utility financings.
Prof. Memberships: Member, Banking Law Committee, NY State Bar Association; Member, TriBar Legal Opinion Committee.
Career: LLB, Fordham University, 1963 (cum laude; editor in chief, 'Fordham Law Review'); AB, Fordham University, 1960 (egregia cum laude).

HALLMAN, Robert
Cahill Gordon & Reindel, New York
212 701 3900
Recommended in Environment

HALVEY, John
Milbank, Tweed, Hadley & McCloy,
New York 212 530 5000
Recommended in Business Process Outsourcing: National, Technology

HAMMER, Stuart
Debevoise & Plimpton LLP, New York
212 909 6000
Recommended in Environment

HANDELSMAN, Lawrence
Stroock & Stroock & Lavan LLP,
New York 212 806 5400
Recommended in Bankruptcy

HANRAHAN, Marc
Latham & Watkins LLP,
New York 212 906 1200
Recommended in Banking & Finance

HANSEN, Edward J
Morgan, Lewis & Bockius LLP,
New York 212 309 6035
ehansen@morganlewis.com
Recommended in Technology
Practice Areas: Edward Hansen is a Partner in the Outsourcing Practice. Mr Hansen's practice is devoted solely to representing clients in technology transactions, with an emphasis in representing clients in complex information technology and business process outsourcing transactions. Mr Hansen frequently works with clients from the initial stages of a transaction, working from the project definition phase and assisting clients apply a 'best practices' approach to the business and legal negotiation process.
Prof. Memberships: Member, Computer Law Association; Member, American Bar Association.

HARDIMAN, John L
Sullivan & Cromwell LLP, New York
212 558 4000
hardimanj@sullcrom.com
Recommended in Litigation
Practice Areas: Focuses on complex litigation matters, including litigation related to contests for corporate control. Recent representations include First Union in its successful defeat of Suntrust's challenge to the merger with Wachovia and Dime Bancorp in its successful defense against unsolicited takeover efforts by North Fork Bancorporation. Also handles securities litigation and regulatory investigations.
Prof. Memberships: ABA; ABCNY.
Career: Partner since 1990.
Personal: Fairfield University (BA, 1979); Duke University Law School (JD, 1982).

HARITON, David P
Sullivan & Cromwell LLP, New York
212 558 4000
haritond@sullcrom.com
Recommended in Tax
Practice Areas: Focuses on the US federal income taxation of financial instruments and transactions and on cross-border financing and investment. Represents the securities industry on federal income tax matters and chairs the Tax Section of the New York State Bar Association.
Career: Partner since 1994.
Publications: Has published more than 50 articles on the taxation of financial instruments and transactions.
Personal: Stanford University (BA, 1981); Stanford Law School (JD, 1985; Order of the Coif).

HARKRIDER, John
Axinn Veltrop & Harkrider LLP,
New York 212 728 2200
Recommended in Antitrust

HARRELL, Michael
Debevoise & Plimpton LLP, New York
212 909 6000
Recommended in Private Equity

HARRIS, Adam
O'Melveny & Myers LLP, New York
212 326 2000
Recommended in Bankruptcy

HARRIS, L Douglas
Milbank, Tweed, Hadley & McCloy,
New York 212 530 5000
Recommended in Projects

HART, John
Simpson Thacher & Bartlett LLP,
New York 212 455 2830
jhart@stblaw.com
Recommended in Tax

Practice Areas: Tax Partner at Simpson Thacher & Bartlett LLP. Represents clients on a wide variety of tax matters, with an emphasis on formation of private investment funds; real estate transactions, including real estate company mergers and acquisitions; bankruptcy and insolvency matters and international matters. Has extensive experience regarding tax aspects of forming private investment funds, including real estate opportunity funds, private equity funds, mezzanine funds and other asset categories. Regularly represents leading sponsors in fund formation matters, including Blackstone, Carlyle, Hellman & Friedman, Joseph E Robert, KKR, Leeds Weld, Platinum, Ripplewood and Silver Lake. Also represents major institutional investors in private funds, such as the Howard Hughes Medical Institute.
Prof. Memberships: Member, New York City Tax Club (President, 2003-04). Member, Private Investment Fund Forum, an independent industry group of New York-based practitioners specializing in private funds. Member, International Fiscal Association and the New York State Bar Association, where he serves on the Tax Section's Committee on Partnerships and Committee on US Activities of Foreigners.
Publications: 'Restructuring the Bankrupt Corporation', 2004 Annual Survey of Bankruptcy Law (West Services, Inc.) also in PLI Course Handbook 'Tax Strategies for Corporate Acquisitions, Dispositions, Spin-Offs, Joint Ventures, Reorganizations & Restructurings 2004.'
Personal: JD, cum laude, Harvard Law School,1979; AB with High Distinction and Highest Honors in English Literature, University of Michigan, 1976, elected to Phi Beta Kappa.

HARTY, Ronan P
Davis Polk & Wardwell, New York
212 450 4000
ronan.harty@dpw.com
Recommended in Antitrust

Practice Areas: Member of Davis Polk & Wardwell's Litigation Department, provides general antitrust counseling to US and non-US companies and represents clients in enforcement agency investigations, domestic and cross-border acquisitions and joint ventures, and litigations. Recent matters include representation of parties in antitrust lawsuits and before the US federal antitrust enforcement agencies in a variety of transactions, including mergers, joint ventures and other matters in the telecommunications, electronics, paper, agricultural biotechnology, chemicals, pharmaceutical, publishing and banking industries.

HAWK, Barry E
Skadden, Arps, Slate, Meagher & Flom LLP & Affiliates, New York
212 735 3892
bhawk@skadden.com
Recommended in Antitrust

Practice Areas: Partner, New York and Brussels. Advises clients primarily in the areas of European Union and national antitrust laws and merger controls, European Union regulatory law, US antitrust law and merger control laws throughout the world. Has advised on EU and European Law in connection with M&A, joint ventures, privatizations, distribution and licensing, enforcement actions and litigation, public procurement, project financing, state aids or government subsidies, and various regulatory matters.
Career: LLB, University of Virginia School of Law, 1965; AB, Fordham College, 1962.

HAZAN, Scott
Otterbourg, Steindler, Houston & Rosen, New York
212 661 9100
Recommended in Bankruptcy

HEALY, Kevin
Bryan Cave Robinson LLP, New York
212 541 2000
Recommended in Environment

HEISS, Howard
O'Melveny & Myers LLP, New York
212 326 2000
Recommended in Litigation

HEITNER, Kenneth H
Weil, Gotshal & Manges LLP, New York
212 310 8288
kenneth.heitner@weil.com
Recommended in Tax

Practice Areas: Mr Heitner is Co-Head of the firm's Tax Practice.
Career: He is a Member of the American Bar Association, Tax Section, Association of the Bar of the City of New York, and was formerly an Executive Committee member of the New York State Bar Association, Tax Section and chairman of committees on reorganizations, corporations, practice and procedure and net operating losses. He is the past President of the Tax Club and is an Adjunct Professor at New York University School of Law.
Personal: New York University School of Law (LLM, 1977, and JD, 1973); Rutgers University (BA, 1969).

HELENIAK, David
Shearman & Sterling LLP, New York
212 848 7049
dheleniak@shearman.com
Recommended in Corporate/M&A

Practice Areas: Senior Partner at Shearman & Sterling and a Partner in the firm's Mergers and Acquisitions Group. Regularly represents the M&A groups of the leading investment banks, as well as multinational and private corporations.
Prof. Memberships: Member, The American Bar Association; Member, Bar Association of the City of New York; Committee on Securities Regulation; Committee to Enhance Diversity in the Profession.
Career: Served in the US Department of the Treasury as Executive Assistant to the Deputy Secretary and subsequently as Assistant General Counsel (1977-79).
Personal: AB, University of Michigan (1967); MSc (Economics) London School of Economics (1969); JD, Columbia University Law School (1974)

HELLER, Richard B
Frankfurt Kurnit Klein & Selz, New York
212 826 5533
rheller@fkks.com
Recommended in Media & Entertainment

Practice Areas: Co-Head of the firm's Entertainment and Sports Group. Practice focuses on motion pictures and television, new media, publishing, celebrity branding and intellectual property. Clients include actors, writers, individual producers, directors, production companies and distributors in the motion picture and television fields. Handles film clients from acquisition of rights through financing, production and exploitation of project. Actively counsels prominent best-selling authors, fashion models, designers and other celebrity clients in managing their valuable intellectual property rights and implementing fully coordinated branding strategies for exploiting motion picture, television, print, audio, electronic new media, merchandising/licensing and other rights.

HENDERSON Jr, Donald B
LeBoeuf, Lamb, Greene & MacRae, LLP, New York 212 424 8694
dhenders@llgm.com
Recommended in Insurance

Practice Areas: A corporate lawyer with extensive experience in insurance mergers and acquisitions, public and private financing and related insurance regulatory matters. His experience includes purchases and sales of businesses, including both stock and asset transactions, and purchases and sales of specific blocks of business.
Publications: A frequent public speaker, he has also written on insurance and corporate issues for numerous publications, including 'Best's Review', 'Business Insurance', 'The National Underwriter', 'International Insurance Law Review', 'Reactions and Reinsurance'.
Personal: University of Alabama (BS) 1971; University of Alabama Law Center (JD) 1974; New York University (LLM) 1976.

HENZE II, William F
Jones Day, New York
212 326 3603
wfhenze@jonesday.com
Recommended in Energy

Practice Areas: He represents energy sector clients, including integrated oil and gas companies, pipelines, local distribution companies, electric utilities, nonregulated electricity producers, and lenders to and investors in energy-related businesses and assets. Recognized for his capability to provide superior client service by BTI Consulting Group. A frequent speaker and author of numerous published articles, he is listed in 'Who's Who in America' and 'Who's Who in American Law'.
Prof. Memberships: Member of the drafting committee for the EEI Master Power Purchase & Sale Agreement. Member of the Institute for Energy Law's advisory board and the Energy Bar Association.

HERBERT, John
Gibson, Dunn & Crutcher LLP, New York
212 351 2424
jherbert@gibsondunn.com
Recommended in Private Equity

Practice Areas: Mr Herbert has over 25 years of experience in representing US and international financial buyers in the private equity, leveraged buyout and venture capital areas and a wide variety of other clients in complex M&A transactions. He advises funds in connection with their portfolio investments, including initial acquisitions or startups, divestitures, add-on acquisitions, bank financings and high-yield offerings, and various exit transactions, including dispositions, initial public offerings and recapitalizations.
Personal: JD, magna cum laude, George Washington University Law School, 1978, Order of the Coif. MBA, Harvard Business School, 1976. BA, University of Pennsylvania, 1970.

HERLIHY, Edward D
Wachtell, Lipton, Rosen & Katz, New York 212 403 1207
edherlihy@wlrk.com
Recommended in Corporate/M&A

Practice Areas: Specializes in the largest and most complex bank and financial institution mergers and acquisitions and recapitalizations throughout the United States and is often called upon to represent companies involved in takeover battles and proxy contests, including investment banking firms in connection with a wide variety of financial institution matters.
Career: Partner at Wachtell, Lipton,

Rosen & Katz.

Publications: Writes and lectures regularly on issues involving banking and financial matters.

HERSCH, Dennis S
Davis Polk & Wardwell, New York
212 450 4000
dennis.hersch@dpw.com
Recommended in Corporate/M&A, Media & Entertainment
Practice Areas: Heads Davis Polk & Wardwell's Mergers and Acquisitions Practice. Advises clients on all aspects of takeovers, restructurings and corporate governance. Has been the legal adviser to Comcast in many transactions, including the acquisition of AT&T Broadband. Represented Texaco in its merger with Chevron and Qwest Communications in its merger with US West. Acted as counsel to CVS in its merger with Revco Drug Stores and its acquisition of Arbor Drugs; to Burlington Northern in its merger with the Santa Fe Pacific Railroad; and to General Electric in the sale of Kidder, Peabody and the sale of its aerospace business.

HEWITT, William J
Ropes & Gray, New York
212 841 5709
william.hewitt@ropesgray.com
Recommended in Private Equity
Practice Areas: Specializes in private equity and mergers and acquisitions. Represents several buyout and venture capital firms, including Welsh, Carson, Anderson & Stowe, in fund formation and transactions by the funds and their portfolio companies. Member of the American Bar Association, Association of the Bar of the City of New York, and the New York State Bar Association.
Career: New York Bar (1965). Partner, Ropes & Gray (2003).
Personal: LLB, Harvard Law School (1964). AB, Harvard College (1961).

HIRSCHBERG, William E
Shearman & Sterling LLP, New York
212 848 7097
whirschberg@shearman.com
Recommended in Banking & Finance
Practice Areas: Co-Head of Shearman & Sterling's Banking Practice with extensive experience in all areas of bank financing, including acquisition and leveraged buyout financing, workouts, restructurings, structured financing, project financing and inter-creditor issues.
Prof. Memberships: Member, American Bar Association Commercial Financial Services Committee; Chairman, Acquisition Financing Subcommittee (1987-91).
Career: Attorney in the Office of the General Counsel of the Federal Deposit Insurance Corporation in Washington, D.C., 1972-76. Joined Shearman in 1976 and became a Partner in 1981.
Personal: AB, Indiana University (1969); JD, Loyola University of Chicago School of Law (1972)

HOCHBERG, Jeffrey D
Sullivan & Cromwell LLP, New York
212 558 4000
hochbergj@sullcrom.com
Recommended in Tax
Practice Areas: Primarily focused on the taxation of financial instruments and products, private equity and real estate transactions, partnership transactions, tax structured investments and structured finance transactions. Also has extensive experience advising clients on the tax consequences of domestic and cross-border mergers, acquisitions and restructurings and has worked on numerous debt exchanges and refinancings.
Prof. Memberships: NYSBA (Member, Executive Committee, Tax Section; Co-Chair, Tax Accounting Committee).
Career: Partner since 2004.
Personal: Yeshiva University (BA, 1992); Columbia Law School (JD, 1995).

HODARA, Fred S
Akin Gump Strauss Hauer & Feld LLP, New York 212 872 8040
fhodara@akingump.com
Recommended in Bankruptcy
Practice Areas: Chair, firmwide Financial Restructuring Practice Group. Represents creditors' committees in Chapter 11 cases and out-of-court and cross-border restructurings, with emphasis on committees comprised of diverse creditor constituencies. Represents insurance companies and other institutional investors, high-yield and distressed investors, trade creditors and committees of creditors, and corporate debtors. Cross-border insolvency work has included companies based in the United Kingdom, France, Germany, Norway, Canada, Korea and Australia.
Prof. Memberships: INSOL International; American College of Investment Counsel; Turnaround Management Association; 'K&A Restructuring Register': America's Top 100 Restructuring Professionals.
Personal: BA, State University of New York at Binghamton; JD, New York University.

HOFSTETTER, Richard
Frankfurt Kurnit Klein & Selz, New York
212 826 5537
Rhofstetter@fkks.com
Recommended in Media & Entertainment
Practice Areas: Co-Head of firm's Entertainment and Sports Group. Particular emphasis in all forms of television development, production and ancillary platforms, including licensing, merchandising and advertiser supported and branded entertainment. Represents performers, producers, writers and production companies for scripted and dramatic programs; news and reality-based programming; distribution companies and television networks; programming/distribution for network, syndication, cable, public television, children's programming, international production/distribution and format sales; advertising sponsorships. Counsels international producers in licensing formats, producing and distributing their programming in the US.
Prof. Memberships: Voting Member, Academy of Television Arts and Sciences; International Television Academy; BAFTA; Board of Advisors, New York Television Festival.

HOLLAND, Mark
Clifford Chance US LLP, New York
212 878 8432
mark.holland@cliffordchance.com
Recommended in Litigation
Practice Areas: Represents financial services institutions in securities class actions and shareholder derivative suits in US federal courts. Currently representing Merrill Lynch in the IPO Allocation market manipulation class actions, Citigroup in the Parmalat litigation, and Alliance Capital in the market timing MDL actions. Has extensive experience representing investment advisers and mutual funds in litigation under the Investment Company Act of 1940, including Merrill Lynch, Alliance, Fidelity, Citigroup, American Century, Dreyfus, and Prudential. Has published several articles on mutual fund litigation and has lectured on securities litigation at industry conferences and continuing legal education seminars throughout the country.

HOOD, Thomas R
Mayer, Brown, Rowe & Maw LLP, New York 212 506 2595
thood@mayerbrown.com
Recommended in Tax
Practice Areas: Tax law, with emphasis on domestic corporate matters and multi-jurisdictional corporate planning; mergers, acquisitions, and spinoffs; partnerships; domestic and international transactions, and structured finance (including securitization and financial products); IRS letter rulings.
Prof. Memberships: Admitted to practice: New York, District of Columbia, Minnesota, and Nebraska. American Bar Association Tax Section: Corporate-Shareholder Relations Committee, Financial Transactions Committee, and Committee on Legislative Recommendations.
Career: Mayer, Brown, Rowe & Maw LLP, New York, Partner, 1993. Counselor to the IRS Commissioner, Washington, DC, 1990-93. Kutak Rock & Campbell, Partner, Omaha and New York, pre-1990.
Publications: Note, 'Federal Income Tax Treatment of Business and Employment Investigatory Expenses,' 56 Minn. L. Rev. 1157.
Personal: Born August 27, 1947, Omaha, Nebraska. BA, Yale University, 1969; JD (cum laude), University of Minnesota School of Law, 1973; Primary Editor, 'Minnesota Law Review', 1972-3; LLM in Taxation, New York University School of Law, 1974.

HOPKINSON, Ronald
Latham & Watkins LLP, New York
212 906 1200
Recommended in Private Equity

HORKOVICH, Robert
Anderson Kill & Olick P.C., New York
212 278 1000
Recommended in Insurance

HOROWITZ, Steven G
Cleary Gottlieb Steen & Hamilton LLP, New York 212 225 2580
shorowitz@cgsh.com
Recommended in Real Estate
Practice Areas: Real estate finance, joint ventures, capital markets, sale-leasebacks and mortgage finance. Clients include McDonald's, The Home Depot, Starwood Hotels, Citigroup, Goldman Sachs, Genting Group, Texas Pacific Group, Kindred Healthcare.
Prof. Memberships: American College of Real Estate Lawyers; Anglo-American Real Property Institute; Legal Aid Society, Director.
Career: Joined firm, 1987; became Partner, 1989. Lecturer in Law, Columbia Law School, (2003 - present). JD, cum laude, Harvard Law School (1978); MPP, cum laude, Kennedy School of Government, Harvard University (1978); BA, magna cum laude, Yale University (1972).
Publications: Frequent lecturer and author for continuing legal education seminars.

HORSCH, Richard
White & Case LLP, New York
212 819 8866
rhorsch@whitecase.com
Recommended in Environment
Practice Areas: Chairs firm's International Environmental Practice. Advises on all aspects of environmental law. Counsels clients on environmental issues in all types of transactions across a broad range of industries, domestically and internationally. Represents clients in environmental and toxic tort litigation. Has represented chemical company, multinational oil company, multilateral development bank, and homeowner class in major environmental disputes in US and internationally.
Prof. Memberships: NY Bar; New Jersey Bar; ABA.
Personal: University of New Hampshire (BA, magna cum laude, Phi Beta Kappa, 1974), New York University School of Law (JD, 1980), NYU 'Journal of International Law and Politics' (Managing Editor).

HOWARD, Nigel
Mayer, Brown, Rowe & Maw LLP, New York 212 506 2121
nhoward@mayerbrownrowe.com
Recommended in Business Process Outsourcing: National, Technology
Practice Areas: Represents clients in complex and mission-critical technology transactions: outsourcing, licensing, joint venture, and strategic alliance

transactions; intellectual property purchases and sales and in reviews of IP portfolios in relation to corporate financing and M&A transactions; cross-border technology transfer; development and testing arrangements, distribution channels, technology deployment and electronic commerce and internet strategies. Expert on privacy laws regarding electronic databases and online services.

Prof. Memberships: Admitted in England and Wales, 1990, and New York, 1993.
Career: Joined Mayer, Brown, Rowe & Maw LLP, New York, as Partner, 2003. Brobeck, Phleger & Harrison LLP, New York, 1993-2003; Partner, 1998; Head of Technology Group, 2000. Boodle Hatfield, London, 1988-92.
Publications: Recent writings: 'Exploring the 'virtual' company strategy through outsourcing in the Biotech industry', SRI, 2003; 'Living with the FTC Safeguard Rules: Industry Tips ad Experiences' The Investment Lawyer, October, 2003; 'Outsourcing and ASP Arrangements', PLI Publications, 2002; 'New Developments in Outsourced Manufacturing Arrangements', University of Texas, 2002; 'Comparison of US and European Patent Law on the protection of software', Patent World 2002.
Personal: London University, masters degree in intellectual property law (pass with merit), 1991. Lancaster University, bachelors degree in law (with honours), 1987; Veronica Cowan prize for law.

HUCK, L Francis
Simpson Thacher & Bartlett LLP, New York 212 455 2000
lfhuck@stblaw.com
Recommended in Banking & Finance
Practice Areas: Frank Huck is a Partner in the firm's Corporate Department where he specializes in syndicated commercial lending. Over the past 20 years, Mr Huck has represented domestic and foreign banks in a variety of bank financing transactions. In recent years, he has been especially active in financing of acquisitions by private equity groups and public companies and in restructuring financings. Typical recent matters include the representation of the arranging bank in financings for Lucent Technologies, GE Capital, AT&T/Comcast, Time Warner and Standard Aero. He has also represented the bank lenders to the former Yugoslavia through four debt restructurings beginning in 1998 and the division of the external bank indebtedness among the five successor republics in 1996 through 1998.
Prof. Memberships: An active Member of the American Bar Association and the Bar Association of the City of New York.
Career: Joined Simpson Thacher in 1972 and became a Partner in 1980.
Personal: Received an AB in 1969 from Harvard University and a JD in 1972 from Stanford Law School.

HUDANISH, David
Mayer, Brown, Rowe & Maw LLP, New York 212 506 2524
dhudanish@mayerbrownrowe.com
Recommended in Business Process Outsourcing: National, Technology
Practice Areas: Partner in Outsourcing Practice and Technology Practice. Represents companies in structuring and negotiating information technology and business process outsourcing agreements, development agreements, licensing agreements, royalty agreements and strategic alliance and joint venture agreements. Advises companies in connection with all aspects of their technology development, procurement, licensing and protection. Advises clients on a variety of internet and e-commerce initiatives. Frequent author and speaker on outsourcing topics.
Prof. Memberships: Admitted: New York, New Jersey, and District of Columbia.
Career: Mayer, Brown, Rowe & Maw LLP, 2003-present. Previously, Head of Outsourcing Practice at Brobeck, Phleger & Harrison LLP.
Publications: 'Disaster Recovery and Business Continuity Update' (PLI, October 2003); 'Legally Speaking: HRO Effects on Privacy, Ethics and Security' (HRO World 2003 Conference, July, 2003); 'Influencing the Outsourcing Influencers: Who They Are And How Service Providers Can Wow Them', Ross Research (December 2002); 'Disaster Recovery and Business Continuity in the Aftermath of 9/11' (PLI, October 2002); 'Many Opportunities. Many Challenges. Outsourcing and ASP Arrangements in 2002' (PLI, January 2002); 'New Environment for IT Outsourcing: Managed Security Services' (Law Seminars International, January 2002).
Personal: Georgetown University Law Center, JD cum laude, 1991; Georgetown University, BA magna cum laude, 1987.

HUEBNER, Marshall S
Davis Polk & Wardwell, New York 212 450 4000
marshall.huebner@dpw.com
Recommended in Bankruptcy
Practice Areas: Member of Davis Polk & Wardwell's Corporate Department, concentrating in corporate restructuring and insolvency. Represents financial institutions, preeminent corporations and agent banks in large and complex domestic and international restructurings and bankruptcies, including major roles in Enron, Adelphia, Loral, Polaroid and Magellan. Currently lead restructuring counsel to Delta Air Lines. Also provides advice on insolvency issues relating to complex financial products and on M&A transactions involving troubled companies.
Personal: Attended Princeton University (awarded Fulbright Scholarship) and Yale Law School (awarded Ford Foundation Fellowship), publishes and lectures frequently on insolvency topics, including DIP lending, silent second liens, and pension and ERISA issues in bankruptcy.

HUGHES, Christopher
Morgan & Finnegan, LLP, New York 212 415 8524
chughes@morganfinnegan.com
Recommended in Intellectual Property
Practice Areas: Domestic litigation: for over 30 years, Mr Hughes has focused on complex intellectual property litigation, counseling, and licensing in major patent, trade secret and trademark matters, in such fields as computer hardware/software, telecommunications, medical devices, semi-conductor fabrication technology and business-methods/financial services. He has had notable successes in achieving favorable summary judgments, both in defending infringement charges following Markman hearings and in obtaining a relatively rare affirmative summary judgment for the patentee. Since the early 1990s, Mr Hughes has headed the Morgan & Finnegan teams representing IBM in several patent litigations involving complex computer hardware and software technologies, both in asserting patents and in defending infringement charges. These actions have been in the Southern District of New York, the District of Massachusetts, the Eastern District of Michigan, and the District of Utah. He also represented Priceline.com in litigations in the District of Connecticut and in the Northern District of California involving the famous 'Priceline Patent'. He has represented Heidelberger Druckmaschinen in printing technology (SDNY) and Robert Bosch GMBH in silicon plasma etching technology (D. Del.). He also litigated medical device patents, including orthopedic hip devices for Stryker Corporation (D. NJ and EDNY) and patent infringement actions in the District of Delaware and the Southern District of New York dealing with cardiovascular stent technologies on behalf of Medinol Ltd. International litigation: Mr Hughes has spent several years directing patent infringement trials and hearings throughout Europe (including trials seeking preliminary relief and cross-border injunctions), as well as nullity, cancellation and opposition proceedings on important patent rights in European Courts and Patent Offices. In these matters, he has coordinated the corresponding activities in the US with respect to the US counterpart patent litigations. Special Master: Mr Hughes has been appointed Special Master by the US District Court for the District of Rhode Island for the purpose of assisting the Court in Arendi U.S.A., Inc. v Microsoft Corporation, Civil Action No. 02-CV-343 (ECT). As Special Master, he dealt with several complex discovery issues and motions in limine for the Court.

Prof. Memberships: New York Intellectual Property Law Association (Board of Directors, 2001-04; Second Vice-President, 2004-to date); District of Delaware Intellectual Property Advisory Committee (2004-to date); the American Intellectual Property Law Association; the Licensing Executives Society; the American Judicature Society; the Intellectual Property Owners; the New York State Bar Association (Litigation and Intellectual Property Sections); and the American Bar Association (Litigation and Intellectual Property Sections). He is also a founding Board Member of the New York University Lawyer Alumni Mentoring Program (LAMP), where he serves on the Executive Advisory Board (1998-to date).
Career: New York University School of Engineering and Science (BS, cum laude, 1970); Tau Beta Pi and Sigma Gamma Tau Honor Societies; Founder's Day Award; National Fraternity Hall of Fame. New York University School of Law (JD, 1973); Donald Brown Fellowship in Patent Law; Moot Court Executive Board; co-author: Patent Law, Annual Survey of American Law (NYU 1972-73); Adjunct Instructor, New York Law School (1980-82). Morgan & Finnegan - Associate (1973-82), Partner (1983-to date).
Publications: Mr Hughes has lectured extensively throughout the United States, Japan and Korea on such topics as attorney-client privilege, contributory and induced infringement, means-plus-function claim elements, various aspects of Markman claim construction proceedings, the doctrine of equivalents including the impact of the Federal Circuit and Supreme Court decisions in the 'Festo' case, and US trade secret law. In addition, he has had several articles published on those topics. Mr Hughes was featured in several Lawcast presentations discussing 'New Patent Litigation Tactics for the Post-Festo World'. He also discussed 'Strategies For Litigating Against Patent Holding Companies', at the AIPLA 2004 Spring Meeting in Dallas, and participated on two panels, 'Securing Ownership of Employee Innovations', and 'Protecting and Embracing Your IP', at the 2004 IP Strategies in Deals Conference, sponsored by Findlaw Corporate Counsel Center.

HYLTON, Hartwell
Simpson Thacher & Bartlett LLP, New York 212 455 2000
hhylton@stblaw.com
Recommended in Banking & Finance
Practice Areas: A Partner at Simpson Thacher & Bartlett LLP and a Member of the firm's Corporate Department. Concentrates on banking law, corporate and international finance transactions. Represents financial institutions, including Lehman Brothers Inc. and J.P. Morgan Chase, and borrowers in credit transactions.

Career: Joined the firm in 1975 and became a Partner in 1982.
Personal: Received an AB from the College of William and Mary in 1972 and a JD from the University of Virginia in 1975.

HYMAN, Alan
Proskauer Rose LLP, New York
212 969 3275
ahyman@proskauer.com
Recommended in Bankruptcy
Practice Areas: A leading Member of the Bankruptcy and Corporate Reorganization Bar, heads Proskauer's Bankruptcy and Reorganization Practice Group. For 30 years he has been actively involved in a wide spectrum of the nation's largest corporate reorganization proceedings.
Prof. Memberships: A Member of the American College of Bankruptcy Lawyers.
Publications: Has lectured extensively in the bankruptcy and reorganization field. Has been a guest lecturer at the Turnaround Industry Conference, the United States Trustee Symposium and at programs sponsored by the American Bankruptcy Institute and the Institute for International Research.
Personal: A graduate of New York University and New York University Law School.

ICHEL, David
Simpson Thacher & Bartlett LLP, New York 212 455 2000
dichel@stb.com
Recommended in Litigation
Practice Areas: Partner at Simpson Thacher & Bartlett LLP in the Litigation Department. Specializes in complex litigation, including product liability, securities, distributor termination, intellectual property, insurance, banking, and mergers and acquisitions disputes.
Prof. Memberships: American Law Institute, Product Liability Advisory Council, Duke Law School Board of Visitors, Federal Bar Council.
Career: Joined the firm in 1978 and elected Partner in 1985.
Publications: Author of numerous publications on litigation and commercial insurance issues.
Personal: Duke University, BA 1975 (summa cum laude, phi beta kappa), and JD 1978 (Duke Law Journal). Admitted in NY, NJ, DC District, US Supreme Court and numerous federal Circuit Courts of Appeals and district courts.

INDOE, William F
Sullivan & Cromwell LLP, New York
212 558 4000
indoew@sullcrom.com
Recommended in Tax
Practice Areas: Focuses on tax structuring of complex financial transactions, particularly M&A, divestitures and spin-offs. Has represented investment banks and principals in hundreds of complex

transactions, including: tax-free mergers; cross-border acquisitions; conversions of 'C corps' into REITs; privately owned business sales; divestitures via joint ventures; and transactions involving asset managers. Renders tax advice in securities offerings; participates in preparation and negotiation of employment/severance arrangements, stock option and other incentive compensation plans, and resolution of employee benefit issues in the ordinary course and in change of control situations.
Prof. Memberships: ABA; ABCNY; NYSBA.
Career: Partner since 1976.
Personal: Lehigh University (BA, 1964); University of Virginia Law School (LLB, 1968).

INSOLIA, Robert
Goodwin Procter LLP, New York
212 813 8800
rinsolia@goodwinprocter.com
Recommended in Private Equity
Practice Areas: Mr Insolia represents and advises a wide range of clients involved in the capitalization of real estate through public and private capital markets. Mr Insolia has assisted clients with complex real estate financings (including senior and subordinate debt structures), and preferred equity and mezzanine financings; portfolio acquisitions and dispositions of real estate and loans secured by real estate; REIT IPOs and follow-on public equity and debt offerings; and mergers and acquisitions of real estate operating companies.
Personal: JD, Fordham University School of Law, 1984; BA, New York State University College at New Paltz, 1979.

ISACKSON, Robert M
Orrick, Herrington & Sutcliffe, New York
212 506 5280
rmisackson@orrick.com
Recommended in Intellectual Property
Practice Areas: Represents both plaintiffs and defendants in patent litigation. He has worked in many technical disciplines including biotechnology, electronics, financial services, medical devices, microprocessor-controlled devices, pharmaceuticals, and software systems and simulations. He also has experience in trade secret matters and commercial litigation involving technology and software, and counsels clients in procuring, protecting, and enforcing patent, trademark, copyright, and trade secret rights.
Career: Leader, Orrick's East Coast IP Practice; Partner, Orrick (1992-present); University of Michigan Law School (JD, 1982); University of Michigan College of Engineering, magna cum laude, (BSE, Electrical Engineering, 1978).

ISEMAN, Robert
Iseman Cunningham Riester & Hyde LLP, Albany 518 462 3000
Recommended in Healthcare

IVANHOE, Robert
Greenberg Traurig LLP, New York
212 801 9333
ivanhoer@gtlaw.com
Recommended in Real Estate
Practice Areas: Real estate.
Prof. Memberships: Executive Committee, Albert Einstein College of Medicine; Executive Committee, Real Estate Lawyers Division of the UJA Federation; Member, Real Estate Division and Hotel Division of Israel Bonds.
Personal: American University Washington College of Law (JD, 1978); Johns Hopkins University (BA, 1975).

JACOBS, Paul
Fulbright & Jaworski L.L.P., New York
212 318 3348
pjacobs@fulbright.com
Recommended in Private Equity
Practice Areas: Private equity; business, commercial, corporate, international, and securities law; and mergers and acquisitions.
Prof. Memberships: Mr Jacobs is a member of the American Bar Association, the Association of the Bar of the City of New York, and the New York State Bar Association.
Career: Partner in Fulbright's New York office since 1978, Mr Jacobs is Co-Head of the firm's Corporation, Business and Banking Section and a member of the firm's Policy Committee. He has been recognized by 'Who's Who in American Law', 'Who's Who in America', and 'Who's Who in the World'.
Personal: BA, Colgate University (1967); JD, Columbia University Law School (1971). Admitted to practice in New York in 1971.

JACOBSON, Marc
Greenberg Traurig LLP, New York
212 801 9200
jacobsonm@gtlaw.com
Recommended in Media & Entertainment
Practice Areas: Entertainment; technology, media and telecommunications.
Prof. Memberships: Founding Chairman, New York State Bar Association Section on Entertainment, Arts and Sports Law; Member, Board of Directors, Long Island Film and Television Foundation; Chairman of the Board of Advisors, The Internet Alliance; Advisory Board Member, New York e-Commerce Group, Business Development Network; Former member of the Board of Directors, The Direct Marketing Association.
Publications: Adjunct Professor, Fordham University Law School, Entertainment Law; Adjunct Professor, Law School of The City University of New York, Entertainment Law (2001-2002).

JACOBSON, Martin D
Simpson Thacher & Bartlett LLP, New York 212 455 7023
mjacobson@stblaw.com
Recommended in Aviation, Projects

Practice Areas: A Partner at Simpson Thacher & Bartlett LLP and a Member of the Corporate Department. Advises clients in project and infrastructure financing as well as structured equipment financing. Has represented sponsors, lenders, underwriters and other credit providers. Has a broad range of experience involving the financing of infrastructure, industrial property, aircraft and other transportation equipment.
Prof. Memberships: American Bar Association and Association of the Bar of the City of New York and founding Chair of its committee on project finance.
Career: Joined Simpson Thacher in 1979 and became a Partner in 1984. Received BS summa cum laude from the University of Pennsylvania in 1969. MBA from New York University Stern School of Business in 1973 and a JD from the University of Chicago Law School in 1976.

JAFFE, Helene D
Weil, Gotshal & Manges LLP, New York
212 310 8572
helene.jaffe@weil.com
Recommended in Antitrust
Practice Areas: Antitrust/competition; litigation/regulatory.
Career: Ms Jaffe's practice centers on the transactional, counseling and litigation aspects of advertising, marketing and antitrust issues, particularly regarding mergers, acquisitions and Hart-Scott-Rodino matters. She also has been involved in numerous Lanham Act advertising, trademark and trade dress cases for injunctions and judge/jury trials. She is global Co-Head of the Antitrust/Competition Practice and appears regularly before international, federal and state antitrust enforcement agencies, as well as the federal judiciary, representing clients buying or selling companies in the US or abroad, or whose pricing, promotional or marketing practices are under investigation. Among the mergers/joint ventures she has handled are: American Airlines' purchase of TWA, United HealthCare's purchase of Mid-Atlantic Medical Services, Inc. (MAMSI), Halliburton's purchase of Dresser Industries, CBS' purchase of Outdoor Systems, Inc., Solo Cup's acquisition of Sweetheart, Genmar's acquisition of Brunswick and GAF's joint venture with Johns Manville. Ms Jaffe has been lead trial counsel for some of the largest antitrust cases for American Airlines, for US Airways' antitrust conspiracy challenge to the American/British Airways alliance and for American's lawsuit against United Airlines' acquisition of Air Wisconsin. She also has done extensive work for leading pharmaceutical companies. She has been recognized in 'The International Who's Who of Competition Lawyers and Economists' and 'The Euromoney Expert's Guide', is a member of Global

Competition Review's Top 100 Women lawyers in the world, and teaches a graduate course in Federal Trade Commission Law as an Adjunct Associate Professor at New York University School of Law.
Personal: Columbia University School of Law, JD (Harlan Fiske Stone Scholar); Barnard College, BA.

JENNER, Jesse J
Fish & Neave IP Group of Ropes & Gray, New York
212 596 9019
jesse.jenner@ropesgray.com
Recommended in Intellectual Property
Practice Areas: IP litigator in the Fish & Neave IP Group of Ropes & Gray. Broad experience in technology litigation, with emphasis on electronics, semiconductors, manufacturing, medical products, telecommunications and the Internet. Has argued numerous appeals before the Court of Appeals for the Federal Circuit. Best known for successful decision holding 16 Lemelson patents not infringed, invalid and unenforceable.
Career: New York Bar (1973). USPTO. Partner, Ropes & Gray (2005). Partner, Fish & Neave (1981). Fellow, American College of Trial Lawyers.
Personal: JD, Harvard Law School (1972). BSEE, Cornell University (1969). Rotary Foundation Fellow, University of Warwick, UK (1972-73).

JEWELL, Ronald R
Dechert, New York 212 698 3589
ronald.jewell@dechert.com
Recommended in Corporate/M&A
Practice Areas: Partner in Mergers and Acquisitions, Private Equity, and Corporate Finance and Securities Groups. Experienced in acquisitions and dispositions; joint venture transactions; corporate debt restructurings and secured financings; and public offerings and private placements.
Prof. Memberships: Member, New York and Maryland Bars.
Career: Attorney, US Department of Treasury (Office of General Counsel, Office of Foreign Assets Control); attorney, US Securities and Exchange Commission (Division of Corporation Finance).
Personal: Loyola College (BA, 1971); University of Baltimore School of Law (JD, cum laude, 1975), articles editor of University of Baltimore Law Review; Georgetown University Law Center (LLM in Taxation, 1977).

JOFFE, Robert
Cravath, Swaine & Moore LLP, New York 212 474 1448
rjoffe@cravath.com
Recommended in Antitrust
Practice Areas: Presiding Partner. Extensive litigation and counseling experience in the areas of antitrust, securities and corporate governance.
Prof. Memberships: ABA (Litigation and Antitrust Practice Sections); NYSBA

(Antitrust Section); ABCNY (previously Trade Regulation including Chair; Vice President 2003-04).
Career: Partner since 1975. Ministry of Justice, Government of Malawi, 1967-69.
Publications: Author of numerous articles on antitrust issues.
Personal: Harvard Law School (JD, cum laude, 1967); Harvard College (AB, cum laude, 1964). Human Rights First: Board of Directors. Board of Directors, Franklin Resources and Fiduciary Trust. Learned Hand Award, American Jewish Committee, 2004.

JOHNSTON, M Elaine
White & Case LLP, New York
212 819 8736
mejohnston@whitecase.com
Recommended in Antitrust
Practice Areas: Antitrust, including antitrust aspects of mergers, acquisitions, joint ventures. Co-ordinating US, European, other antitrust clearances on complex cross-border deals. Handling government non-merger investigations. Advising on distribution, licensing, other business conduct, trade association activities.
Prof. Memberships: New York State Bar; United States District Court for the Southern District of New York; United States District Court for the Eastern District of New York; American Bar Association (Antitrust Section); New York State Bar Association (Antitrust Section, Executive Committee); 'Antitrust Law Journal' (former associate editor).
Personal: Cambridge University (BA (hons), 1980, MA, 1984); University of Michigan Law School (LLM, 1987), Fulbright Scholar.

JORDAN, Nora
Davis Polk & Wardwell, New York
212 450 4000
nora.jordan@dpw.com
Recommended in Private Equity
Practice Areas: Member of Davis Polk & Wardwell's Corporate Department. Advises clients on collective investment vehicles, including mutual funds, closed-end funds, hedge funds and private equity funds. Acts as counsel to the adviser, the fund or the independent directors, depending on the client. Many of her matters involve advising clients concerning compliance with the Investment Company Act and Investment Advisers Act. Also provides exemptive advice concerning the Investment Company Act for industrial holding companies and non-US trading companies, banks, insurance companies and other financial institutions. Has worked on a number of acquisitions, reorganizations and structurings of asset managers.

JOSEPH, Gregory
Gregory P Joseph Law Offices LLC, New York 212 407 1200
Recommended in Litigation

KADET, Samuel
Skadden, Arps, Slate, Meagher & Flom LLP & Affiliates, New York
212 735 2570
skadet@skadden.com
Recommended in Litigation
Practice Areas: Represents corporations and individuals in complex litigation, including securities, takeover and other commercial matters. Represented Cendant Corporation in proceedings arising out of the widely reported accounting irregularities at CUC International Inc., one of the companies that merged to form Cendant.
Career: JD, St John's University, 1977 (cum laude; editor, 'St John's Law Review'); BA, State University of New York at Binghamton, 1971 (magna cum laude, Phi Beta Kappa).

KAFIN, Robert
Proskauer Rose LLP, New York
212 969 3280
rkafin@proskauer.com
Recommended in Environment
Practice Areas: He is Proskauer's Chief Operating Partner responsible for the day to day management of the professional practice of the firm. Concentrates his practice in the area of environmental law where he regularly provides compliance counselling advice to businesses facing regulations under all of the major federal environmental laws and state analogues. In recent years, he has been called upon in major transactions involving almost every type of industry to review and evaluate environmental compliance and liabilities.
Prof. Memberships: He is the past Chair of the Environmental Law Section of the New York State Bar Association. He also served as Chair of the New York Parks and Conservation Association and as a Vice-Chair of the Preservation League of New York State on whose boards he currently sits.
Personal: Harvard Law School, JD, Magna Cum Laude, 1966. Franklin & Marshall College, AB, Magna Cum Laude, 1963 Phi Beta Kappa.

KALKINES, George
Manatt Phelps & Phillips LLP, New York
212 830 7233
gkalkines@manatt.com
Recommended in Healthcare
Practice Areas: Focus on healthcare law, including corporate organization, regulatory compliance, finance/reimbursement matters, physician/faculty practice arrangements, capital financing, labor relations, collective bargaining, and medical/legal issues. Represents financially distressed institutions, assisting in the planning, financing and construction of healthcare facilities. Specializes in financial turnarounds, and the planning and implementation of pre- and post-bankruptcy restructurings. Special counsel to voluntary, public and proprietary healthcare providers,

including academic medical centers, acute and specialty care hospitals, nursing homes, faculty practice plans and ambulatory care organizations.
Prof. Memberships: Member, NYC Bar, ABA, American Hospital Association, Healthcare Financial Management Association.
Career: Partner.
Personal: St. John's University, (LLB, 1965); Long Island University, (BS, 1961).

KANE, Meredith
Paul, Weiss, Rifkind, Wharton & Garrison LLP, New York 212 373 3065
mjkane@paulweiss.com
Recommended in Real Estate
Practice Areas: Partner in the Real Estate Department. Represents developers, equity investors, institutional and entrepreneurial owners and government agencies in all aspects of development, finance, acquisitions and sales, leasing and securitization of real estate. Experienced in complex joint ventures, large-scale mixed-use and multi-investor development projects. Named one of the Top 50 Women in Real Estate and one of 25 Current Leaders in the 'Industry by Real Estate Weekly' and 'The Association of Real Estate Women'; one of Top 10 Women in Real Estate Development by 'Grid Magazine'. Mayoral and gubernatorial appointee to several NY City and State boards and commissions.

KARIG, Adele
Debevoise & Plimpton LLP, New York
212 909 6000
Recommended in Private Equity, Tax

KARMEL, Philip
Bryan Cave Robinson LLP, New York
212 541 2000
Recommended in Environment

KAROTKIN, Stephen
Weil, Gotshal & Manges LLP, New York
212 310 8350
stephen.karotkin@weil.com
Recommended in Bankruptcy
Practice Areas: Business finance and restructuring: Chapter 11 reorganizations, debt restructurings, debtor/creditors' rights and financing transactions.
Career: Extensive Chapter 11 representation experience, including: Texaco, Armstrong World Industries, Loral Space & Communications, Formica Corporation, Eagle-Picher Industries (obtained first asbestos channeling injunction under §524(g) of Bankruptcy Code), Integrated Health Services, Magellan Health Services. Represented institutional lending syndicates in two major debt restructurings in Argentina, and has represented both lenders and borrowers in connection with several out of court restructuring transactions. Fellow, American College of Bankruptcy; faculty, New York University Workshop on Bankruptcy and Reorganization.
Personal: New York University, JD; Union College, BS.

KARP, Brad
Paul, Weiss, Rifkind, Wharton & Garrison LLP, New York 212 373 3316
bkarp@paulweiss.com
Recommended in Litigation
Practice Areas: Co-Chair of the Securities, Futures and Derivatives Practice Group. Member of the Management Committee. Profiled in 'The American Lawyer' (2003) as one of the 45 leading lawyers in the US under the age of 45. Achieved national prominence as a trial lawyer and corporate adviser. In 2005, named one of the leading lawyers in the US handling 'Bet The Company' litigations by "The Best Lawyers in America". Has extensive experience handling and trying a broad range of matters, with particular emphasis defending complex securities and commercial matters and representing financial institutions and other clients before regulatory authorities.

KASNER, Jay B
Skadden, Arps, Slate, Meagher & Flom LLP & Affiliates, New York
212 735 2628
jkasner@skadden.com
Recommended in Litigation
Practice Areas: Experience in federal and state court litigation, including securities, corporate and takeover litigation and general commercial matters. Represents numerous public companies in their defense of actions arising under federal and state securities and corporate laws. Handles litigation arising from corporate control contests, which traditionally require expedited litigation.
Prof. Memberships: Co-Chair, Practising Law Institute Securities Litigation Conference (1996-present).
Career: JD, Boston University, 1980 (cum laude; editor, 'Boston University Law Review'; author, 'Minimizing Minimization: Scott v United States', 'Boston University Law Review'); BA, Union College, 1977 (magna cum laude).

KASS, Stephen
Carter Ledyard & Milburn LLP,
New York 212 732 3200
Recommended in Environment

KATCHER, Richard D
Wachtell, Lipton, Rosen & Katz,
New York 212 403 1222
rdkatcher@wlrk.com
Recommended in Corporate/M&A
Practice Areas: Specializes in mergers and acquisitions and corporate and securities law and governance. Has participated in numerous mergers and acquisitions and related matters, representing both acquirers and targets as well as investment bankers. Transactions include Monsanto's merger with Pharmacia, Warner Lambert's merger with Pfizer, AT&T Corp's acquisitions of MediaOne Group and Tele-Communications, Inc, the break-up of AT&T Corp, including the AT&T Broadband/Comcast transaction, Lilly

Industries, Inc's sale to The Valspar Corporation, Hussmann International, Inc's sale to Ingersoll-Rand Company, American Stores' sale to Albertson's, Browning Ferris' sale to Allied Waste Industries, AT&T Corp's acquisition of McCaw Cellular, AT&T's disposition of Lucent Technologies and NCR Corp, and Monsanto's disposition of Solutia Inc. Cross-border transactions include the sale of Pet Incorporated to Grand Metropolitan and the sale of a greater than majority interest in Genentech Inc to Hoffman-LaRoche. Also represented clients in joint ventures and recapitalizations and has counseled boards and non-management directors on governance issues and investigations and on other crisis situations.
Prof. Memberships: Member of the Board of Trustees of New York University; former Chairman of the Special Committee on Mergers, Acquisitions and Corporate Control Contests of the Association of the Bar of the City of New York; Member of the Securities Regulation Committee of the New York State Bar Association and the Association of the Bar of the City of New York.
Career: Partner at Wachtell, Lipton, Rosen & Katz since 1971; Chairman of Wachtell Lipton's management committee from 1997-2003.
Publications: Frequent lecturer on continuing legal education programs.
Personal: Graduated from Lafayette College in 1963 (BA) and from New York University School of Law in 1966 (LLB). A Member of the 'New York University Law Review', a Member of the Order of the Coif and a John Norton Pomeroy Scholar.

KATSH, Salem
Shearman & Sterling LLP, New York
212 848 4328
skatsh@shearman.com
Recommended in Intellectual Property
Practice Areas: Founder and Head of Shearman & Sterling's 30-lawyer Intellectual Property Group. He is a nationally acclaimed trial lawyer and is responsible for litigation, transactional, counseling and other phases of the Group's work in all areas of Intellectual Property law.
Prof. Memberships: Member, Intellectual Property Owners Association.
Career: Joined Shearman as Partner in 1997. Formerly with Weil, Gotshal & Manges (1972-97).
Publications: Mr Katsh is co-author of a leading treatise on corporate governance, 'The Limits of Corporate Power' (Macmillan 1981) (reprinted by Beard Press in 2002).
Personal: BA, New York University (1969); JD, New York University School of Law (1972)

KATZ, David A
Wachtell, Lipton, Rosen & Katz,
New York 212 403 1309
Recommended in Corporate/M&A

Practice Areas: Specializes in the areas of mergers and acquisitions, complex securities transactions, corporate governance matters and crisis management, and has been involved in many major international and domestic corporate transactions.
Prof. Memberships: Member of the American Bar Association (Section on Business Law); Member of the Committee on Negotiated Acquisitions Task Force on Public Company Acquisitions and Chair of the Committee on Negotiated Acquisitions Task Force on the Dictionary of M&A Terms; Member of the Federal Securities Laws Committee; the New York State Bar Association (Section on Business Law); and the Association of the Bar of the City of New York. (Admitted to New York Bar).
Career: Partner at Wachtell, Lipton, Rosen & Katz since 1996 and joined the Firm in 1988. Adjunct professor at New York University School of Law, Senior Professional Fellow at New York University Center for Law and Business and adjunct professor at the Owens Graduate School of Management at Vanderbilt University.
Publications: Has written extensively.
Personal: Graduated from Brandeis University and from New York University School of Law.

KATZKE, Michael S
Wachtell, Lipton, Rosen & Katz,
New York 212 403 1345
mskatzke@wlrk.com
Recommended in Employee Benefits
Practice Areas: Specializes in executive compensation and employee benefits.
Career: Partner at Wachtell, Lipton, Rosen & Katz.
Publications: Author: 'Change-of-Control Employment Arrangements - What Directors Are Asking Today', The M&A Lawyer (2004); 'Post-Merger Employment Changes Insufficient to Trigger "Chute" Benefits', The M&A Lawyer (2003); 'Importance of Administration Provisions in Change in Control Severance Plans', The M&A Lawyer (2003); 'Employee Benefit Change of Control Protections: Recent Trends and Development', The M&A Lawyer, Vol. 2, No. 3, June 1998; 'Executive Compensation Practices May Inadvertently Limit Change of Control Severance Benefits', Insights, Vol. 12, No. 2, February 1998; 'Shareholder Approval of Equity Plans', INSIGHTS, Vol. 11, No. 2, February 1997; '1995 Developments in Change in Control Related Employee Benefits', INSIGHTS, Vol. 10, No. 3, March 1996.
Personal: Graduated from State University of New York at Stony Brook in 1980 (BA); from New York University School of Law (JD, 1984; LLM, 1988).

KAUFMAN, Stephen
Stephen E Kaufman, PC, New York
212 826 0820
Recommended in Litigation

KAVALER, Thomas
Cahill Gordon & Reindel, New York
212 701 3900
Recommended in Litigation

KAWATA, Yukako
Davis Polk & Wardwell, New York
212 450 4000
yukako.kawata@dpw.com
Recommended in Private Equity
Practice Areas: Member of Davis Polk & Wardwell's Investment Management Group. Advises clients on the formation and operation of private investment funds and other investment vehicles exempt under the US Investment Company Act, including private equity funds, venture capital funds, hedge funds, fund of funds and funds investing in particular sectors or countries. Also advises clients on the formation and operation of various types of carried interest plans and employee investment arrangements. Advises funds and fund sponsors on the regulatory aspects implicated by their operations, including considerations under the US Investment Advisers Act and other US securities laws.

KAYLE, Bruce
Milbank, Tweed, Hadley & McCloy,
New York 212 530 5000
Recommended in Tax

KELLER, Bruce
Debevoise & Plimpton LLP, New York
212 909 6000
Recommended in Intellectual Property, Media & Entertainment

KELLY, Michael J
Willkie Farr & Gallagher LLP, New York
212 728 8686
mkelly@willkie.com
Recommended in Bankruptcy
Practice Areas: Partner in the Business Reorganization and Restructuring Department, representing debtors in large, complex, Chapter 11 cases. Clients in this area have included AMF Bowling Worldwide, Maxxim Medical, Classic Communications, Converse, G&G Shops, The Grand Union Company, Integrated Resources, Petrie Retail, Inc., Starter Corporation, Sunterra Corp. and Winkelman. He has also represented creditors in Chapter 11 cases, including Foodtown (Twin County Chapter 11 cases), Warburg Pincus (Centennial, Phycor, Alliant and Evolve Chapter 11 cases), Crown Management (Gruntal), Ventas, Inc. (Vencor, Sun, Integrated Health, Lenox, and Texas Health Chapter 11 cases). He also represented financial and other consultants in Chapter 11 cases, including KPMG, NERA and FTI Consulting, and has represented the Trustee in the Granite cases and the examiner in the Caribbean Petroleum cases. His practice also includes representing debtors, creditors, investors and board members in out of court restructurings.
Prof. Memberships: A member of the New York State Bar Association.

Career: Admitted to the Bar of the State of New York. He is also admitted to the United States Court of Appeals for the Third Circuit and the United States District Courts for the Eastern and Southern Districts of New York.

Personal: Received a JD from New York University in 1988, where he was elected to the Order of the Coif, and a BA from the State University of New York at Albany in 1985. Serves as a lecturer at the New York University School of Continuing and Professional Studies, Center for Finance, Law and Taxation, where he teaches the Bankruptcy, Workouts and Reorganization course.

KELLY, Thomas
Debevoise & Plimpton LLP, New York
212 909 6000
Recommended in Insurance

KENNEDY, John B
Morrison & Foerster LLP, New York
212 468 8066
jkennedy@mofo.com
Recommended in Technology

Practice Areas: Transactions and counseling in technology transfer, sourcing (including information technology and business process outsourcing), licensing, technology and intellectual property-intensive M&A, joint ventures and asset-based lending, software and technology development and transfer agreements, general intellectual property counseling and strategy, electronic commerce, privacy and data protection. Substantive law experience in copyright, trademark, patent licensing, trade secret, publicity rights and privacy, data protection, unfair competition, and the law of e-commerce. Clients include Fortune 500 companies as well as emerging companies in the financial services and insurance, technology, media and entertainment, consumer product, communications, life sciences, and professional services industries. Has negotiated large, cross-border and domestic outsourcing and licensing transactions, plus settlements of contested licensing and services agreements.

Career: Prior to joining Morrison & Foerster, practiced at Skadden, Arps, Slate, Meagher & Flom, where he was Group Counsel for Intellectual Property Group.

Personal: BA, magna cum laude, Carleton College, 1970; MA, with honors, University of Chicago, 1976; JD, Columbia University School of Law, 1985.

KENNEDY, Robert
Latham & Watkins LLP, New York
212 906 1200
Recommended in Private Equity

KENNEDY, Thomas H
Skadden, Arps, Slate, Meagher & Flom LLP & Affiliates, New York
212 735 2526
tkennedy@skadden.com
Recommended in Corporate/M&A

Practice Areas: Focuses on M&A, corporate finance, and other transactions with an emphasis on the telecommunications and information technology industries. Coordinator of the firm's Corporate Technology Practice. Experience in many hostile transactions, leveraged buyouts, proxy fights and other governance matters.

Career: JD, Georgetown University Law Center, 1981; BA, University of Virginia, 1978.

KESSLER, Jeffrey L
Dewey Ballantine LLP, New York
212 259 8050
jkessler@deweyballantine.com
Recommended in Antitrust, Sport

Practice Areas: Mr Kessler has extensive experience in all aspects of antitrust law, sports law, intellectual property and other complex litigation. He has been lead counsel in some of the most complex antitrust, sports law and IP law cases in the country including major jury trials and has represented a number of US and international companies in criminal and civil investigations in the antitrust and trade areas.

Career: Partner, Dewey Ballantine LLP. Co-Chair, Litigation Department. Member of the firm's Executive Committee.

Personal: Born February 19, 1954. BA, summa cum laude, Columbia University, 1975. JD, Kent Scholar, Columbia Law School, 1977.

KIERNAN, John
Debevoise & Plimpton LLP, New York
212 909 6000
Recommended in Litigation

KIESSLING, B Robbins
Cravath, Swaine & Moore LLP, New York 212 474 1500
bkiessling@cravath.com
Recommended in Banking & Finance

Practice Areas: Broad range of finance, banking, financial institution and related matters, including syndicated bank financings, structured finance, capital markets transactions and mergers and acquisitions.

Prof. Memberships: NYSBA; ABCNY; TriBar Opinions Committee.

Career: Partner since 1983. Clerkship: Hon. Edward Weinfeld (US District Court for the Southern District of New York).

Personal: New York University School of Law (JD, cum laude, 1976; John Norton Pomeroy Prize; articles editor, 'Law Review'; Order of the Coif); Yale University (BA, cum laude, 1973).

KIRPALANI, Susheel
Milbank, Tweed, Hadley & McCloy, New York 212 530 5000
Recommended in Bankruptcy

KLEIN, Jeffrey
Weil, Gotshal & Manges LLP, New York
212 310 8790
jeffrey.klein@weil.com
Recommended in Employment

Practice Areas: Employment, litigation/regulatory, sports.

Career: Mr Klein chairs Weil Gotshal's Workplace Practices Group and heads the firm's Employment Litigation Practice. He represents employers in all aspects of labor and employment relations law, with particular emphasis on employment discrimination, healthcare benefits and trade secrets litigation. Mr Klein also is a recognized authority on sports law matters. He has litigated employment matters in all areas, with significant experience in class actions, arbitrations and mediation. Mr Klein is lead counsel for UnitedHealth Group in a series of ERISA and RICO class actions pending in several jurisdictions. He regularly serves as outside employment counsel for MasterCard International, Reader's Digest and Avon Products, among others. He recently won a complete victory for Creative Artists Agency in a multi-plaintiff suit alleging race discrimination in the concert promotion business. Mr Klein frequently is quoted in the media on employment, sports and healthcare litigation issues, including in Reuters, Bloomberg, New York Times, Wall Street Journal, Los Angeles Times, Houston Chronicle, Atlanta Constitution, Miami Herald and Financial Post (Toronto). He authors a bi-monthly column in The New York Law Journal on current developments in employment law and co-authored 'The Corporate Counsellor's Deskbook' and the treatise 'Managing Contingent Workers'. Mr Klein's sports law practice includes extensive experience in contract negotiations, litigation, licensing and endorsement agreements on behalf of numerous professional athletes, sports broadcasters, entertainers, players associations and sports entities. He has done work for Jeff Kent, Dave Winfield, Joe Torre, Al Leiter, Tommy John, Yankees Entertainment and Sports (YES) Network, National Football League Players' Association, Major League Baseball Players' Association and National Basketball Players' Association.

Personal: Columbia University Law School, JD; Amherst College, BA (magna cum laude).

KLEIN, Steven D
Willkie Farr & Gallagher LLP, New York
212 728 8221
sklein@willkie.com
Recommended in Real Estate

Practice Areas: Partner in the Real Estate Department, specializing in REITs, joint ventures, acquisition and disposition, financing, and leasing transactions. Represents clients in all types of estate transactions, and drafting and negotiating agreements in connection therewith, including REIT and securitized financing agreements, construction and permanent loan agreements and mortgages, loan restructuring agreements, partnership and limited liability company agreements, property management agreements, construction and development agreements, contracts of sale, retail and office leases, and regional shopping center agreements. Represented Bloomberg L.P. in the lease for its 700,000 square-foot new world headquarters in New York City, and in numerous other acquisitions and leases, nationally and internationally, including in California, New Jersey, Washington, DC, London, Prague, São Paulo, Rome and Tokyo. Has also represented Lehman Brothers, McKinsey & Company and Apollo Real Estate in leasing transactions, and CBL Properties, The Mills Corporation and Simon Property Group in numerous acquisitions, joint ventures and financings with respect to regional mall centers and portfolios.

Prof. Memberships: Member of the Commercial Leasing Committee of the American Bar Association, the Real Estate Development Committee of the New York State Bar Association, the Real Property Law Committee of the New York City Bar Association, the International Council of Shopping Centers and the Advisory Board of Commonwealth Land Title Insurance Company.

Career: Admitted to the Bar of the State of New York.

Publications: Has published and spoken on a variety of real estate topics for the New York Law Journal, the Practising Law Institute, the Association of the Bar of the City of New York and the International Council of Shopping Centers, among others.

Personal: Received a JD from Rutgers University in 1986 and a BA from Queens College in 1983.

KLEINBARD, Edward D
Cleary Gottlieb Steen & Hamilton LLP, New York 212 225 2480
ekleinbard@cgsh.com
Recommended in Tax

Practice Areas: Federal income tax matters, including taxation of new financial products, financial institutions, and international mergers and acquisitions.

Prof. Memberships: Member of the American College of Tax Counsel, International Fiscal Association.

Career: Joined firm, 1977; became Partner, 1984. JD, Yale Law School (1976); MA and BA, magna cum laude, Brown University (1973).

Publications: 'The Business Enterprise Income Tax: A Prospectus,' Tax Notes. 'Competitive Convergence in the Financial Services Markets,' Taxes. 'Taxing Convertible Debt: A Layman's Perspective,' SMU Law Review. 'Contingent Interest Convertible Bonds and the Economic Accrual Regime' (co-author), Tax Notes. 'Disclosing Book - Tax Differences' (co-author), Tax Notes. 'The US Taxation of Equity Derivative Instruments,' Handbook of Equity Derivatives.

'Corporate Tax Shelters and Corporate Tax Management,' The Tax Executive. 'Risky and Riskless Positions in Securities,' Taxes.

KLING, Lou R

Skadden, Arps, Slate, Meagher & Flom LLP & Affiliates, New York
212 735 2770
lkling@skadden.com
Recommended in Corporate/M&A

Practice Areas: Has extensive experience in mergers and acquisitions of public and private companies, subsidiaries and divisions, including negotiated and contested acquisitions, leveraged buyouts and recapitalizations. Represents borrowers, issuers and underwriters in a broad spectrum of financing transactions. Served on firm's Policy Committee, its top governing committee. Currently Co-Chairman of the firm's Opinion Committee, and Chairman of the Financial Oversight Audit Committee.
Career: JD, New York University, 1977 (Order of the Coif; New York University Law Review); MA, Mathematics, University of Illinois, 1974; BA, New York University, 1973 (magna cum laude; Phi Beta Kappa).

KNEIP, Frederick

Milbank, Tweed, Hadley & McCloy, New York 212 530 5000
Recommended in Employee Benefits

KNIGHT, James T

Simpson Thacher & Bartlett LLP, New York 212 455 2000
jknight@stblaw.com
Recommended in Banking & Finance

Practice Areas: James T Knight is a Partner in the firm's Corporate Department. Mr Knight's practice focuses on banking matters and the representation of lenders and borrowers in acquisitions and other leveraged transactions. His principal clients include J.P.Morgan Securities Inc., J.P. MorganChase Bank, N.A. and The Blackstone Group and its portfolio companies.
Career: Joined Simpson Thacher in 1979 and became a Partner in 1986.
Personal: He received his BA summa cum laude from Dartmouth College in 1976 where he was a member of Phi Beta Kappa and earned his JD cum laude from Harvard Law School in 1979.

KOBAK, Scott M

Simpson Thacher & Bartlett LLP, New York 212 455 7210
skobak@stblaw.com
Recommended in Real Estate

Practice Areas: Partner in the Real Estate Department at Simpson Thacher & Bartlett LLP. Main area of concentration has been representing institutional investors in complex domestic and international commercial real estate and real estate company acquisitions and developments, joint ventures and financings, including active involvement with many of the most prominent real

estate private equity funds. Recent transactions completed by Mr Kobak include Blackstone Real Estate Fund's acquisition and financing of Extended Stay America, a publicly traded hotel company (including representing Blackstone on the largest CMBS loan executed to date and multiple layers of mezzanine financing); Hovnanian Enterprises and Blackstone's joint acquisition of Town & Country Homes in the largest private home-builder acquisition to date, and Carlyle Real Estate Fund's acquisition and development of a 500-unit luxury condominium project in the Times Square area of New York City.
Career: Joined Simpson Thacher & Bartlett LLP in 1993. He was elected to become a member of the firm in November 2000.
Personal: Received JD from Boston University Law School, magna cum laude, where he was an Associate Editor of the Boston University Law Review.

KOENIGSBERG, I Fred

White & Case LLP, New York
212 819 8806
fkoenigsberg@whitecase.com
Recommended in Intellectual Property

Practice Areas: Copyright law, including counseling, litigation. Negotiates, drafts license agreements. Counsels on copyright issues. Litigates infringement claims. Conducts administrative proceedings before the US Copyright Office and Copyright Royalty Judges. Participates in legislative efforts in US Congress.
Prof. Memberships: New York State Bar, admitted 1973; United States Supreme Court; various Federal Courts of Appeal and District Courts; American Bar Association Section of Intellectual Property Law (past Chair); American Intellectual Property Law Association (past President); Columbia University (adjunct professor).
Personal: Cornell University (BA, 1967); Annenberg School of Communications, University of Pennsylvania (MA, 1969); Columbia University School of Law (JD, 1972).

KOHN, Arthur H

Cleary Gottlieb Steen & Hamilton LLP, New York 212 225 2920
akohn@cgsh.com
Recommended in Employee Benefits

Practice Areas: Compensation and benefit matters, including executive compensation, pension compliance and investment, employment law and related matters.
Prof. Memberships: Member of the Bar of New York
Career: Joined firm, 1986, became Partner, 1995. JD, Columbia University School of Law (1986); BA, Columbia University, (1986).

KOHN, Jeffrey

O'Melveny & Myers LLP, New York
212 326 2000
Recommended in Employment

KOLB, Daniel

Davis Polk & Wardwell, New York
212 450 4000
daniel.kolb@dpw.com
Recommended in Litigation

Practice Areas: Member of Davis Polk's Litigation Department. A practicing litigator and trial lawyer in both federal and state trial and appellate courts throughout the United States for more than 35 years. His practice has included a wide range of professional liability, securities litigation, general litigation, and antitrust matters for various clients, including major accounting firms, industrial corporations, and financial institutions.

KOOB, Charles E

Simpson Thacher & Bartlett LLP, New York 212 455 2000
ckoob@stblaw.com
Recommended in Antitrust, Litigation

Practice Areas: Partner at the firm and Co-Head of the Litigation Department. Specialises in competition and antitrust law. Experience includes counselling clients on antitrust issues affecting mergers, acquisitions, joint ventures and distribution practices. Has represented clients before the Federal Trade Commission, the Antitrust Division of the Department of Justice and state and foreign competition authorities; defended corporate clients in both criminal and civil anti-trust litigation; represented individuals in grand jury investigations and corporate plaintiffs in major private antitrust litigation. Recent experience includes: the successful defense of Appleton Papers Inc. in a criminal price fixing trial; the representation of Virgin Atlantic Airways in a private treble action against British Airways; and the representation of the special committee of the Board of Directors of Archer Daniels Midland in a federal grand jury investigation of price-fixing. Has also tried both large commercial and product liability actions to verdict.
Prof. Memberships: Trustee of the Natural Resources Defense Council; Chairman of Stanford Law School's Board of Visitors.
Career: Joined the firm 1969; became Partner 1977.
Publications: Co-author, 'Private Antitrust Remedies Under US Law', PLC Competition Law Handbook, 2003-04.
Personal: BA, 1966, Rockhurst College and JD, 1969, Stanford Law School.

KORNBERG, Alan

Paul, Weiss, Rifkind, Wharton & Garrison LLP, New York
212 373 3209
akornberg@paulweiss.com
Recommended in Bankruptcy

Practice Areas: Chair of the Bankruptcy Department. Handles out-of-court restructurings, Chapter 11 cases, transnational insolvency matters, bankruptcy-related acquisitions, bankruptcy-

related litigation and insolvency-sensitive transactions. Clients include debtors, official and unofficial creditors committees, equity holders, court-appointed fiduciaries and investors focusing on distressed situations. Represented California Public Utilities Commission in the Pacific Gas & Electric Company Chapter 11 case. Selected for the 2005 edition of ''The Best Lawyers in America''.

KORNREICH, Edward

Proskauer Rose LLP, New York
212 969 3000
Recommended in Healthcare

KOSCHIK, David N

White & Case LLP, New York
212 819 8241
dkoschik@whitecase.com
Recommended in Banking & Finance

Practice Areas: The firm's New York Executive Partner whose practice focuses on representing major commercial and investment banks in lending transactions, particularly in acquisition and highly leveraged financings, and in various types of financings for insurance companies. Served as senior bank lenders' counsel in connection with many notable such matters, including RJR-Nabisco, Primedia Inc., DirecTV and Intelsat. Also represents institutions in other types of financings, including letter of credit facilities and commercial paper back-up facilities.
Personal: BA, cum laude, Miami University, 1979; MSFS, Georgetown University, 1984; JD, magna cum laude, Georgetown University Law Center, 1984.

KOTRAN, Stephen M

Sullivan & Cromwell LLP, New York
212 558 4000
kotrans@sullcrom.com
Recommended in Corporate/M&A

Practice Areas: Partner, M&A and Financial Institutions Groups. Recent representations include: Anthem in acquisitions of WellPoint and Trigon; Prudential Financial in acquisitions of retirement investment services businesses of Skandia and CIGNA; Cytec in acquisition of UCB's chemicals businesses; Eastman Kodak in Creo acquisition; and Goldman, Sachs & Co. in sale of Spear, Leeds & Kellogg's fixed income business.
Prof. Memberships: ABA (Member, Committee on Negotiated Acquisitions and Committee on Federal Regulation of Securities); ABCNY (Member, Special Committee on Mergers, Acquisitions & Corporate Control Contests).
Career: Partner since 1999.
Publications: Frequent speaker for the Practising Law Institute and ABCNY.
Personal: Harvard University (AB, 1985); University of Virginia Law School (JD, 1990; Law Review, Order of the Coif).

KOVNER, Victor A
Davis Wright Tremaine LLP, New York
212 489 8230
victorkovner@dwt.com
Recommended in Media & Entertainment

Practice Areas: Partner, media/communications, IP and commercial litigation. Represents public/private companies, national broadcast/print media in all aspects of communications law: defamation, privacy, copyright, press access, reporter's privilege, First Amendment issues. Clients: McGraw-Hill, Cantor Fitzgerald, Random House, HarperCollins, Ziff Davis Media, Village Voice Media, Wenner Media (Rolling Stone, US Weekly), Yellow Book.
Prof. Memberships: Member, NY State Bar. Chair, Legal Affairs Committee, Magazine Publishers of America. Co-founder, Media Defense Resource Center.
Career: Joined firm via merger, 1998. Partner, Lankenau Kovner, 1966-98. Corporation Counsel, City of New York, 1990-91. Member (and later Chair) NY State Commission on Judicial Conduct, 1976-89.
Publications: Author/lecturer at Practicing Law Institute on recent developments in invasion of privacy/newsgathering laws (1977-present).
Personal: JD, Columbia, 1961. BA, Yale, 1958.

KRAMER, Daniel
Paul, Weiss, Rifkind, Wharton & Garrison LLP, New York 212 373 3020
dkramer@paulweiss.com
Recommended in Litigation

Practice Areas: Leading trial lawyer and litigator, with extensive experience in securities litigation matters and internal investigations. Has handled complex litigations for some of the largest companies in the United States and has significant experience representing boards of directors on corporate governance issues and special committees in internal investigations. Recent matters include representation of AIG, Bank One, Hollinger International and Merck in securities matters and special committees of Adecco and Fannie Mae in internal investigations. Lectures and writes extensively on securities litigation and regulatory issues, including issues arising out of the Sarbanes-Oxley Act and the insider trading laws, and on ethical issues for securities lawyers. Author of 'Federal Securities Litigation: A Deskbook for the Practitioner and of Regulation of Market Manipulation'. Identified as one of the nation's leading litigators in the 2005 edition of 'The Best Lawyers in America'.

KRAMER, Kenneth M
Shearman & Sterling LLP, New York
212 848 4172
kkramer@shearman.com
Recommended in Antitrust
Practice Areas: Senior Partner and for-

mer chair of the Litigation Group at Shearman & Sterling. Represents a wide range of domestic and international clients in complex commercial litigation and specializes in antitrust, securities law and corporate governance litigations.
Prof. Memberships: Director, International House; New York Lawyers for the Public Interest; Episcopal Social Services; Juvenile Diabetes Research Foundation International
Career: Clerk for Orrin G Judd, United States District Court for the Eastern District of New York, 1972 -73.
Personal: AB, Colgate University (1965); JD, Albany Law School/Union University, editor-in-chief of the 'Law Review' (1972)

KRAMER, Morris J
Skadden, Arps, Slate, Meagher & Flom LLP & Affiliates, New York
212 735 2700
mkramer@skadden.com
Recommended in Corporate/M&A
Practice Areas: Practice includes friendly and hostile transactions and has involved many of the largest and most publicised deals. Counsels bidders, targets and their financial advisors in non-negotiated acquisition situations. Extensive experience in strategic and negotiation issues involving public and private company mergers, acquisitions and dispositions. Advises shareholders, boards of directors and managements in leveraged and management buyouts, proxy fights and other corporate control transactions. Represents parties from around the globe in transactions into and from North America, as well as cross-border intra-European deals.
Career: LLB, Harvard University, 1966; AB, Dartmouth College, 1963.

KRASNOW, Richard P
Weil, Gotshal & Manges LLP, New York
212 310 8493
richard.krasnow@weil.com
Recommended in Bankruptcy
Practice Areas: Business finance and restructuring: represents borrowers, creditors, asset purchasers in domestic/foreign debt restructurings, creditors' committees, and trustees.
Career: Industry experience: retailing, real estate, offshore oil servicing, steel companies/coal production, financial services, music industry, telecommunications, transportation. Representative matters: Edison Brothers Stores, Macy's, Factory Card Outlet, W.T. Grant Company, John Muir & Co., Drexel Burnham Lambert, Thompson Mckinnon Securities, Daewoo Motor, National Steel, Lion Capital, Johns-Manville, U.S. Home, Singer, Fruit of the Loom, DirecTV Latin America. Extensive work in aviation industry: Eastern, Pan Am, U.S. Airways, United, ATA, Aloha, among others.
Personal: New York University, JD; University of Chicago, AB.

KRAUS, Bruce R
Willkie Farr & Gallagher LLP, New York
212 728 8237
bkraus@willkie.com
Recommended in Technology
Practice Areas: Partner in both the Corporate and Financial Services and Telecommunications Departments, specializing in corporate finance, mergers and acquisitions and general corporate advice for telecommunications and other corporate clients. Mergers and acquisitions experience includes public company takeovers and proxy battles, private company and subsidiary acquisitions, spin-offs, domestic and international joint ventures, and strategic equity investments. Has considerable experience in the area of corporate finance, particularly with registered public offerings and 144A placements of debt securities and preferred stock. Represents clients in venture capital financings, initial and subsequent offerings of common stock, placements of partnership and LLC interests. Significant transactions in 2004 include the representation of Hong Kong's Techtronic Industries Co. Ltd. in its acquisition of the Milwaukee Electric Tool® and AEG® power tool businesses from Sweden's Atlas Copco AB for $626.6 million in cash. Telecom industry experience includes representing undersea cable companies, competitive local exchange carriers (CLECs), long distance and Internet backbone networks, fixed and mobile wireless networks (LMDS, PCS, SMR), paging companies, and geosynchronous telecommunications satellites and low-earth orbit satellite constellation companies.
Career: Admitted to the Bar of the State of New York.
Publications: Authored 'Structuring Global Satellite Systems,' 'Space Finance', 1998 and 'Pyrrhic Victory in Spectrum Auction,' The National Law Journal, August 25, 1997 among others.
Personal: Received a JD from Yale Law School in 1979, where he was the Editor of the Yale Law Journal and the winner of the 1979 Harlan Fiske Stone Moot Court Competition, and a BA (magna cum laude) in economics from Harvard College in 1975.

KRESS, Alan
Alan H Kress, New York
(212) 944 6622
Kresslaw@att.net
Recommended in Media & Entertainment
Practice Areas: Entertainment law matters with a specialization in music, recorded music, music publishing, home video and intellectual property matters. Particular expertise in licensing and international matters and complex music clearance issues.
Career: Mr Kress is a former Vice-President of Legal and Business Affairs for RCA Records, BMG International, BMG Classics and Warner Home Video.

Publications: Is Editor of the two Music volumes of Donald Farber's 10 volume treatise of 'Entertainment Industry Contracts', published by the Matthew Bender & Co division of LexisNexis.
Personal: NYU Law School (LLM); George Washington Law School (JD with Honors); New York University (BA)

KRUEGER, Karen G
Wachtell, Lipton, Rosen & Katz, New York 212 403 1242
kgkrueger@wlrk.com
Recommended in Employee Benefits
Practice Areas: Specializes in executive compensation and employee benefits. Her practice is focused on mergers and acquisitions, and she has advised on a wide variety of such transactions.
Prof. Memberships: New York State Bar Association (Section on Tax, Co-Chair of Employee Benefits Committee).
Career: Partner at Wachtell, Lipton, Rosen & Katz. Served as a law clerk for the Hon. Wilfred Feinberg, then chief judge of the US Court of Appeals for the Second Circuit, during 1982-83.
Personal: Graduated from Princeton University (BA); and from Columbia Law School (JD), where she was articles and book reviews editor of the Columbia Law Review for 1981-82.

KRUGMAN, Edward
Cahill Gordon & Reindel, New York
212 701 3900
Recommended in Insurance

KURZWEIL, Harvey
Dewey Ballantine LLP, New York
212 259 8300
hkurzweil@deweyballantine.com
Recommended in Litigation
Practice Areas: Antitrust and trade regulation, complex commercial litigation, intellectual property.
Prof. Memberships: International Academy of Trial Lawyers, American Bar Foundation, Federal Bar Council, New York State Bar Association, American Bar Association - Section of Antitrust and Litigation, Association of the Bar of the City of New York - Committee on Trade Regulation (1982-85).
Career: Partner, Dewey Ballantine LLP. Co-Chair, Litigation Department.
Personal: Born March 23, 1945. AB, Columbia College, 1966. JD, Columbia University School of Law, 1969.

LAMB, William S
LeBoeuf, Lamb, Greene & MacRae, LLP, New York 212 424 8170
blamb@llgm.com
Recommended in Energy
Practice Areas: Advises energy companies on a wide variety of structural and corporate matters. He has represented clients in a broad range of corporate transactions, including bidders and targets in both negotiated and unsolicited mergers and acquisitions and underwriters and issuers in financing and corporate governance matters. His practice

also involves providing advice relating to the Public Utility Holding Company Act of 1935.

Prof. Memberships: Committee on Business Law, American Bar Association; AICPA.

Career: Joined LeBoeuf in 1983, Partner in 1991.

Personal: New York University (BS magna cum laude) 1978; New York University (JD, Law Review Executive Editor) 1983.

LANDA, Leor
Davis Polk & Wardwell, New York
212 450 4000
leor.landa@dpw.com
Recommended in Private Equity

Practice Areas: Associate in Davis Polk & Wardwell's Investment Management Group. Advises clients on structuring, marketing and operating private investment funds, including private equity funds, hedge funds, real estate funds and funds of funds. Advises private fund managers in connection with their formation and operation and in connection with employee compensation and investment arrangements. Represents clients in structuring and executing private equity investments and in acquisitions of investment advisers. Advises private fund clients on various regulatory and compliance matters arising under the US Investment Advisers Act, US Investment Company Act and other US securities laws. Also represents clients investing in private funds.

LANIADO, Sam
Read and Laniado, Albany
518 465 9313
Recommended in Energy

LASCHER, Alan
Weil, Gotshal & Manges LLP, New York
212 310 8144
alan.lascher@weil.com
Recommended in Real Estate

Practice Areas: Corporate, real estate transactions and finance.

Career: Developed national real estate acquisition/finance practice; nationally-recognized for closing first 'auction sale' of portfolio of assets by RTC, first third-party financing of portfolio of assets, first 'blind pool' arrangement for acquisition of portfolios of assets. Excels in development/tax-oriented transactions, including tax-oriented joint venture involving a major Boston office building, made possible by innovative structuring. Also handles leasing transactions, including department store, specialty retail store and multi-floor office space leases. Handled largest leasing transactions in New York City three of the last four years.

Personal: Brooklyn Law School, JD/BLL; Union College, BA.

LATZA, William
Stroock & Stroock & Lavan LLP, New York 212 806 5400
Recommended in Insurance

LAUER, Eliot
Curtis, Mallet-Prevost, Colt & Mosle LLP, New York 212 696 6192
elauer@cm-p.com
Recommended in Litigation

Practice Areas: Eliot Lauer, Senior Partner in the Litigation Department at Curtis, Mallet-Prevost, Colt & Mosle LLP, has extensive experience representing clients in complex civil and criminal matters and is an experienced appellate advocate. He has tried criminal and civil cases involving mail and wire fraud, tax fraud, false statements to state and federal agencies, commodities fraud, transactions in government securities and commodity futures, market manipulation, accountant's liability, and diverse commercial transactions. He has substantial experience advising audit and special board committees in connection with investigations of internal corporate affairs. He is Co-Head of the firm's Accountants Liability and Securities Litigation Practice Group.

LAWLER, Andrew
Andrew M Lawler PC, New York
212 832 3160
Recommended in Litigation

LEAKE, Paul
Jones Day, New York
212 326 3482
pdleake@jonesday.com
Recommended in Bankruptcy

Practice Areas: Co-Head of the firmwide Business Restructuring and Reorganization practice and Co-Head of the Business Practice Group in the New York Office. His practice is focused on US and transnational business reorganizations, including Chapter 11 reorganizations and liquidations, out-of-court restructurings, secured financings, distressed acquisitions, and investments in troubled companies. He has represented all of the major constituencies in restructurings, including debtors, commercial banks and bank groups, bondholder committees, official creditors' committees, and unsecured creditors. He has published and lectured on US and transnational insolvency matters and is recognized as a leading lawyer in insolvency and restructuring.

LEE, Carolyn
Roberts & Holland LLP, New York
212 903 8700
Recommended in Tax

LEE, Steven
Kenyon & Kenyon, New York
212 425 7200
Recommended in Intellectual Property

LEFF, Neil M
Skadden, Arps, Slate, Meagher & Flom LLP & Affiliates, New York
212 735 3269
nleff@skadden.com
Recommended in Employee Benefits

Practice Areas: Emphasizes ERISA and other employee benefits and executive compensations matters, particularly in the context of mergers and acquisitions, public offerings, bankruptcy reorganizations and other corporate restructurings, the various uses of employee stock ownership plans (ESOPs), and executive compensation techniques such as golden parachutes.

Career: JD, New York University, 1980 (Member, Annual Survey of American Law); BA, Brooklyn College of the City University of New York, 1977.

LEFKOWITZ, Ken
Hughes Hubbard & Reed LLP, New York
212 837 6557
lefkowit@hugheshubbard.com
Recommended in Corporate/M&A

Practice Areas: Partner, New York since 1993. Concentrates on mergers and acquisitions, joint ventures, public and private financings, corporate governance, proxy contests, venture capital and private equity.

Career: Hughes Hubbard & Reed since 1983. Member of firm's Executive Committee and Co-Chair of its Mergers, Acquisitions and Joint Ventures Practice Group.

Personal: Born February 4, 1958. Tufts University BA 1980 (summa cum laude, Phi Beta Kappa); Cornell Law School JD (cum laude) 1983.

LEFKOWITZ, Stephen
Fried, Frank, Harris, Shriver & Jacobson LLP, New York 212 859 8780
Stephen.Lefkowitz@FriedFrank.com
Recommended in Real Estate

Practice Areas: Real estate. Primary practice is real estate development, with emphasis on financing arrangements, planning, land use and zoning and large-scale, complex projects involving public/private development arrangements. Has represented Avalon Bay Communities, Durst Organization, 42nd Street Development Project, Forest City Ratner Companies, MetroTech Center, New York City Economic Development Corporation, New York Mercantile Exchange, New York Jets Development, New York Stock Exchange, NYU Downtown Hospital, Time Warner, Tishman Speyer Properties.

Prof. Memberships: Secretary, Member of Board of Directors and Member of Executive Committee of Alliance for Downtown New York.

Career: Qualified in New York in 1962. Joined Fried Frank in 2003. Formerly, senior Partner at Pillsbury Winthrop LLP. Counsel to New York State Senate Committee on Housing and Urban Development (1976). General counsel to New York State Urban Development Corporation (1971-75). Associate professor at Columbia University School of Law (1976-82).

Personal: Born 1937. Achieved LLB, magna cum laude, in 1962 from Harvard Law School, where he was member of Law Review. Received BA from Yale College, summa cum laude, in 1959; elected to Phi Beta Kappa.

LEPATNER, Barry
LePatner & Associates LLP, New York
212 935 4400
blepatner@lepatner.com
Recommended in Construction

Publications: Mr LePatner has written extensively on the subject of construction law for various real estate, design and legal publications. He is the co-author of 'Structural and Foundation Failures: A Casebook for Architects, Engineers and Lawyers'.

Personal: Barry B LePatner, Esq is the founder of Barry B. LePatner & Associates LLP, attorneys at law. For nearly three decades, he has been a prominent figure in the business and legal community on issues affecting the real estate, design, and construction industries. His firm has grown to become widely recognized as one of the nation's leading advisors to corporate and institutional clients, real estate owners, and design professionals. A nationally recognized speaker, Mr LePatner has addressed audiences on topics central to design and construction trends. In May 2002, he was elected by the American Institute of Architects to receive an Honorary AIA Membership, one of the highest honors the organization can bestow upon an individual who is not an architect.

LERNER, Jonathan J
Skadden, Arps, Slate, Meagher & Flom LLP & Affiliates, New York
212 735 2550
jlerner@skadden.com
Recommended in Litigation

Practice Areas: Federal litigation, emphasizing securities, corporate and commercial litigation, and commercial arbitration. Represented Daimler-Chrysler, AG as lead trial counsel against Kirk Kerkorian's securities action; Cendant Corporation in defending its multi-billion dollar securities litigation; McKesson HBOC's Audit Committee in its internal investigation and the Company in related class action securities litigation; and CTF Hotels & Resorts, Inc. in highly-publicized arbitration and litigation against Marriott International, Inc.

Career: JD, St John's University, 1973 (magna cum laude); BA, Binghamton University, 1970. Adjunct Professor, Brooklyn Law School.

LEVANDER, Andrew J
Dechert, New York
212 698 3683
andrew.levander@dechert.com
Recommended in Litigation

Practice Areas: Partner in Litigation Department. Concentrates practice in commercial and securities litigation and white collar defense. Extensive appellate practice in state and federal courts.

Prof. Memberships: Member, New York and District of Columbia Bars; admitted to practice before numerous federal

courts; former chair, American Bar Association Committee on Securities Litigation Professional Issues Subcommittee.
Career: Assistant to Solicitor General; Assistant US Attorney, Southern District of New York (Securities and Commodities Fraud Unit); Associate Independent Counsel in Michael Deaver investigation.
Personal: Tufts University (BA, summa cum laude, 1973); Columbia University Law School (JD, 1977), Notes and Comments Editor, 'Columbia Law Review'.

LEVI, Stuart D
Skadden, Arps, Slate, Meagher & Flom LLP & Affiliates, New York
212 735 2750
slevi@skadden.com
Recommended in Technology
Practice Areas: Head of Skadden's Information Technology and E-Commerce Practice. Represents a broad spectrum of clients, ranging from early stage start-ups to global corporations seeking to use information technologies to enhance current business models and create new opportunities. Counsels on a variety of issues, including outsourcing agreements, software licensing, joint ventures, strategic alliances web site policies, IP matters, privacy issues, and mergers and acquisitions.
Career: JD, Harvard Law School, 1986 (cum laude); BA, Computer Science, Columbia University, Columbia College, 1983 (magna cum laude).

LEVIN, Peter
Davis Polk & Wardwell, New York
212 450 4000
peter.levin@dpw.com
Recommended in Banking & Finance
Practice Areas: Practice coordinator of Davis Polk & Wardwell's Credit Group. Has broad experience in secured financing and debt restructuring transactions, including complex international syndicated lending transactions. Also advises both dealers and end users of derivatives on management controls and management and board responsibilities, documentation, issues relating to new products and new kinds of counterparties, and problems arising from the bankruptcy or insolvency of counterparties.

LEVINE, Alan
Kronish Lieb Weiner & Hellman LLP, New York 212 479 6000
Recommended in Litigation

LEVY, Lisa
Fried, Frank, Harris, Shriver & Jacobson LLP, New York 212 859 8228
lisa.levy@friedfrank.com
Recommended in Tax
Practice Areas: Tax Partner. Specializes in the taxation of mergers and acquisitions, international and cross-border transactions and financial instruments, including debt and equity offerings, asset securitizations and derivatives.
Prof. Memberships: Member, Tax Sec-

tion of the New York State Bar Association, and, in 1999-2002, served on its Executive Committee.
Career: Joined Fried Frank in 1993 and became a Partner in 1998. Admitted to the bar in New York.
Personal: Born 1963. Received JD in 1990 from Columbia Law School, where she was a Kent Scholar, a Stone Scholar and a member of the Journal of Law & Social Problems. Received LLM in taxation from New York University in 1994. Received BS, with distinction, in 1985 from the McIntire School of Commerce at the University of Virginia, where she received the Virginia Society of CPAs' Award of Achievement and was elected to the honor societies Beta Gamma Sigma and Beta Alpha Psi.

LEWIN, Robert
Stroock & Stroock & Lavan LLP, New York 212 806 5400
Recommended in Insurance

LEWKOW, Victor I
Cleary Gottlieb Steen & Hamilton LLP, New York 212 225 2370
vlewkow@cgsh.com
Recommended in Corporate/M&A
Practice Areas: Domestic and international merger and acquisitions, including public and private acquisitions, negotiated and hostile bids, proxy contests, leverage buyouts and advising Boards and Special Committees. Represented PeopleSoft (takeover defense resulting in sale to Oracle at 65% price increase), HSBC (Household International acquisition), Kroll (sale to Marsh & McLennan), South African Breweries (Miller Brewing acquisition to form SABMiller), Synopsys (Avant! acquisition), Deutsche Bank (Bankers Trust acquisition), Nortel Networks (various acquisitions).
Career: BA, State University of New York at Binghamton, (1970); JD, magna cum laude, University of Pennsylvania Law School (1973). Adjunct Professor, NYU Law School.

LIEBERMAN, David
Simpson Thacher & Bartlett LLP, New York 212 455 2000
dlieberman@stblaw.com
Recommended in Projects
Practice Areas: Corporate Partner specializing in international and domestic transactions involving energy, infrastructure and transportation assets. Advised Blackstone and First Reserve Corp. in their $1 billion acquisition of Foundation Coal Corporation; Virgin America in its purchase and lease acquisition of up to 105 Airbus A319 and A320 aircraft; CSFB in its $760 million construction/lease financing of Tri-State Generation's Springerville coal-fired power project; the underwriters in the $1.8 billion, 1,884 MW Homer City bond financing of EME; the lenders in the $730 million, 1,048 MW La Paloma project lease financing of PG&E Gener-

ating; the lenders in the $8 billion turbine and project development financing of PG&E Generating; and Elektrizitäts der Stadt Zürich as a lessee in a $1.2 billion leveraged lease financing of hydroelectric facilities in Switzerland.Representative clients include Lehman Brothers, Blackstone, Credit Suisse First Boston, Virgin America, Elektrizitäts der Stadt Zürich, HypoVereinsbank and The State of Berlin.
Prof. Memberships: New York State Bar Association.
Career: Joined the firm in 1989 and became a Partner in 1998.
Personal: BA, Columbia University, magna cum laude, Phi Beta Kappa (1986). JD with High Honors, Duke Law School, Order of the Coif (1989).

LIEBMANN, Jeff S
Dewey Ballantine LLP, New York
212 259 6230
jliebmann@deweyballantine.com
Recommended in Insurance
Practice Areas: Mr Liebmann has 25 years experience in the corporate and insurance areas. He is an Associate Member of the Society of Actuaries. He has served as counsel to Nationwide Mutual in its deaffiliation from Employers of Wausau, to New England Mutual in its merger with Metropolitan Life, to Metropolitan Life in its acquisition of GenAmerica Corporation, to MONY Group in its closed block securitization, and to Winterthur Swiss in the sale of Republic.
Prof. Memberships: New York State Bar Association; American Bar Association; Society of Actuaries.
Personal: Born April 23, 1950. JD, Harvard University, 1978; AB, Princeton University, 1971.

LILIEN, Warren
Latham & Watkins LLP, New York
212 906 1200
Recommended in Projects

LIMAN, Lewis J
Cleary Gottlieb Steen & Hamilton LLP, New York 212 225 2550
lliman@cgsh.com
Recommended in Litigation
Practice Areas: Securities, class action lawsuits, investigations, regulatory and criminal defense. Clients include Citigroup, Credit Suisse First Boston and Bear Stearns & Co.
Prof. Memberships: Trustee, Federal Bar Council; Member of the Board, NY Council of Defense Lawyers; Association of the Bar of the City of New York.
Career: Joined firm as Partner, 2003. Assistant US Attorney, Southern District of New York, (Deputy Chief Appellate Attorney) (1994-99). Clerk for US District Court, Southern District of New York (1987-88) and US Supreme Court (1989-90). JD, Yale Law School (1987), MSc, Economics with distinction, London School of Economics (1984), AB, Harvard University (1983).

Publications: Mr Liman has published articles and materials on internal investigations, the sentencing guidelines, and securities class actions.

LINDAUER, Erik D
Sullivan & Cromwell LLP, New York
212 558 4000
lindauere@sullcrom.com
Recommended in Banking & Finance
Practice Areas: Transactional banking, secured lending, commercial law (UCC), corporate reorganisations and bankruptcy. Advises on commercial lending in the US and abroad. Complex secured and unsecured financings experience. Represented General Growth Properties, Inc. in negotiation of bank lines for its acquisition of the Rouse companies; Allegheny Energy in renegotiating and securing unsecured bank lines; Intelsat, Ltd. in Loral satellites acquisition; and AIG Financial Products in various structured investments.
Prof. Memberships: ABA; ABCNY; NYSBA.
Career: Partner since 1989.
Personal: SUNY Albany (BA, 1978); SUNY Buffalo Law School (JD, 1981).

LINDENBAUM, Samuel H
Kramer Levin Naftalis & Frankel LLP, New York 212 715 7840
slindenbaum@kramerlevin.com
Recommended in Real Estate
Practice Areas: Is of Counsel to Kramer Levin Naftalis & Frankel LLP and a Member of the Land Use Department. For more than 30 years, his extensive experience in land use and zoning has been utilized in handling special permits, zoning changes, variances, landmark proceedings, air rights transfers, tax abatements and economic development incentives for many of the city's most prominent commercial and residential developments and for the expansion programs of many of the city's leading non-profit institutions.
Prof. Memberships: He is an Honorary Trustee of the Metropolitan Museum of Art, Chairman of the Executive Committee of the Board of Directors of the American Friends of the Israel Museum, a Member of the Board of Overseers of the Albert Einstein College of Medicine, Chair of the Executive Committee of the Jewish Association for Services for the Aged, a Member of the Board of Trustees of the Real Estate Institute of Baruch College, and a Member of the Board of the Real Estate Committee of UJA-Federation. He is Vice-President and a Member of the Executive Committee of the Board of Governors of the Real Estate Board of New York, and a Member of the Advisory Board of the Peggy Guggenheim Collection in Venice. He is a founder, Director and Vice-President of the Association for a Better New York, and a former Member of the New York State Council on the Arts (1976-86 and 1994-99).

Career: Represents non-profit organizations, major corporations, financial institutions and commercial and residential developers such as Carnegie Hall, The Whitney Museum, Columbia University, the Guggenheim Museum, the Archdiocese of New York, Yeshiva University, Weill Cornell Medical College, Bear Stearns, Tishman Speyer Properties, Vornado Realty Trust, Glenwood Management, Millennium Partners, and the Resnick, Silverstein and Solow Organizations. Current projects for which he acts as counsel include the expansion of the Museum of Modern Art, a new tower atop the Hearst headquarters building on Eighth Avenue, redevelopment of the former Alexander's site on Lexington Avenue and East 59th Street by Vornado, redevelopment of the Con Edison properties at First Avenue and East 40th Street, Sheldon Solow's new residential towers on York Avenue and 60th Street, and renovation of the General Motors Building. Recent approvals include renovations of Rockefeller Center and the Chrysler Building, and the new Penn Center Special Signage District. Other major approvals in recent years include Trump's Riverside South development and New York Hospital's expansion over the FDR Drive.
Personal: Earned a BA degree cum laude from Harvard College in 1956 and a JD degree cum laude from Harvard Law School in 1959. After graduating from law school, he was awarded a Fulbright Fellowship.

LIPSON, Lawrence
Proskauer Rose LLP, New York
212 969 3760
llipson@proskauer.com
Recommended in Real Estate
Practice Areas: Chair of Proskauer Rose LLP's Real Estate Department and a Member of Proskauer's nationally recognized Hospitality Practice Group. He has three decades of diverse experience crafting major real estate deals and representing all sides to the real estate transaction including lenders and borrowers, landlords and tenants, and investors and developers. His clients include a cross section of the many types of investors in and users of real estate, including individual developer entrepreneurs, large corporate tenants, equity investors, real estate investment trusts and real estate opportunity funds. He is also a key and influential player in Proskauer's Hospitality Practice Group and has closed on a substantial number of major domestic and international hotel and resort chain acquisitions.
Career: He was involved in the design of the first major office building real estate investment trust (REIT) in New York, which has become the model for future office building REIT transactions in the New York metropolitan area.
Personal: Columbia University School of Law, JD, Magna Cum Laude, 1970.

Scholar: Harlan Fiske Stone Scholar. Brooklyn College of the City University of New York, BA, Magna Cum Laude, 1967.

LIPTON, Martin
Wachtell, Lipton, Rosen & Katz, New York 212 403 1200
mlipton@wlrk.com
Recommended in Corporate/M&A
Practice Areas: Specializes in corporate law, corporate governance and mergers and acquisitions.

LISCIO, Mark F
Kaye Scholer LLP, New York
212 836 7550
mliscio@kayescholer.com
Recommended in Bankruptcy
Practice Areas: Partner, business reorganization and creditors' rights. Represents syndicate agents and major financial institutions in debt restructurings and insolvency proceedings. Mr Liscio has practiced creditors' rights and insolvency law on behalf of lenders for more than 21 years. Mr Liscio has structured and negotiated a wide variety of complex insolvency financings throughout his career, for which he has developed a reputation as a firm and fair advocate and pragmatic deal maker.
Prof. Memberships: American Bankruptcy Institute, American Bar Association.
Career: JD, Pace University School of Law, Editor of the Law Review. BBA, Pace University.

LOBO, Glyndwr P
Dechert, New York
212 698 3567
glyndwr.lobo@dechert.com
Recommended in Corporate/M&A
Practice Areas: Partner in Corporate Finance, Private Equity, and Mergers and Acquisitions Groups. Concentrates on cross-border and domestic business transactions and corporate finance, including mergers, acquisitions, capital markets transactions, venture capital transactions, and international joint venture and collaboration transactions. Also has significant experience in life sciences and pharmaceutical transactions.
Prof. Memberships: Member, New York Bar; Member, Board of Advisers of the Corporate Counsel Institute of Georgetown University Law Center and the Association of Corporate Counsel; member, Georgetown University National Law Alumni Board.
Personal: The Wharton School of the University of Pennsylvania (BS, 1985); Georgetown University Law Center (JD, 1988).

LOGAN, Kenneth
Simpson Thacher & Bartlett LLP, New York 212 455 2000
klogan@stblaw.com
Recommended in Antitrust
Practice Areas: Kenneth R Logan has been a litigator and antitrust practitioner for over 32 years at Simpson Thacher & Bartlett. He has tried jury and non-

jury antitrust cases to judgment and handled merger and non-merger proceedings before the US enforcement agencies and the European Commission. Mr Logan has also conducted a range of antitrust and other complex matters for Viacom, Paramount, MTV Networks, NBC Universal, Seagram, American Electric Power, General Motors, ITT Industries, Kohlberg Kravis & Roberts, Wyeth, Express Scripts and others. He has developed substantial background in issues affecting, among other industries, healthcare, financial services, entertainment, telecommunications and pharmaceuticals. He frequently writes and speaks on US and international antitrust issues.
Personal: Mr Logan graduated from Princeton University in 1967 and from the University of Pennsylvania Law School in 1972.

LONDON, Martin
Paul, Weiss, Rifkind, Wharton & Garrison LLP, New York 212 373 3197
mlondon@paulweiss.com
Recommended in Litigation
Practice Areas: Litigation Partner with extensive experience encompassing broad litigation issues both domestically and internationally, involving both criminal and civil matters. Civil experience includes trials and litigation of commercial cases involving antitrust, breach of contract, tortious interference, real estate, product liability, securities, environmental laws, insurance, administrative law and miscellaneous torts. Fellow of the American College of Trial Lawyers. Received the Award for Outstanding Oral Advocacy, presented by the Office of the Appellate Defender. Appointed Special Trial Counsel twice by special New York judicial tribunals to prosecute judicial misconduct cases. Selected for the 2005 edition of 'The Best Lawyers in America'.

LOVE, Jane M
Wilmer Cutler Pickering Hale and Dorr LLP, New York 212 937 7233
jane.love@wilmerhale.com
Recommended in Intellectual Property
Practice Areas: Practice focuses on patent prosecution and patent strategy, and counseling related to contentious patent issues. Advises companies and universities in the life sciences (biotechnology, molecular biology, biology, biochemistry, immunology and chemistry).
Prof. Memberships: American and New York Bar Associations; American Intellectual Property Law Association; Association for University Technology Managers; American Association for the Advancement of Science; New York Intellectual Property Law Association; and Society for Women in Science.
Publications: 'Advanced Claim Drafting and Amendment Writing', Practicing Law Institute, Chemical Inventions Patent Prosecution Workshop (1999).

Personal: Fordham University School of Law (JD); University of Pennsylvania (BA 1987).

LOWENTHAL, Mitchell A
Cleary Gottlieb Steen & Hamilton LLP, New York 212 225 2760
mlowenthal@cgsh.com
Recommended in Litigation
Practice Areas: Corporate and securities litigation. Has represented issuers, directors and officers, underwriters, lending institutions and professional advisors in complex civil litigation primarily involving the capital formation process, mergers and acquisitions, and derivative and shareholder disputes.
Prof. Memberships: Member of the Bar in New York. Admitted to practice before the US Supreme Court, US District Courts (Southern and Eastern Districts of New York and Eastern District of Wisconsin) and US Court of Appeals (Second and Ninth Circuits).
Career: Cornell University (JD, 1981; AB, 1978). Law Clerk, Hon. Edward Weinfeld (SDNY, 1982-83). Chair, Urban Justice Center.

LUSKIN, Michael
Luskin, Stern & Eisler LLP, New York
212 293 2700
Recommended in Bankruptcy

LYONS, Peter D
Shearman & Sterling LLP, New York
212 848 7666
plyons@shearman.com
Recommended in Corporate/M&A
Practice Areas: Co-Head of Shearman & Sterling's M&A Group, represents clients in acquisitions and sales of public and private companies, asset acquisition and disposition transactions and joint ventures. Regularly represents the mergers and acquisitions group of the firm's investment banking clients, and provides general securities law advice.
Prof. Memberships: Member of the Board of Editors of The M&A Lawyer.
Career: Joined Shearman in 1980, practiced in the firm's Bay Area office from 1983 to 1985, and became a Partner in 1989. Mr Lyons headed the firm's Bay Area offices during 2000 and 2001.
Personal: BA, University of Virginia (1977); JD, Georgetown University Law Center (1980).

MACMURRAY, John C
Ropes & Gray, New York
212 841 5711
john.macmurray@ropesgray.com
Recommended in Private Equity
Practice Areas: Corporate law with a practice that principally includes representation of domestic and international private investment funds. Client responsibilities principally involve representation of private equity sponsor groups in their fundraising projects and investment programs.
Career: New York Bar (1965). Partner, Ropes & Gray (2003).

1298

Personal: LLB, Columbia Law School (1965). AB, Princeton University (1961).

MACPHERSON, Robert
Postner & Rubin, New York
212 269 2510
Recommended in Construction

MADDEN, John J
Shearman & Sterling LLP, New York
212 848 7055
jmadden@shearman.com
Recommended in Corporate/M&A
Practice Areas: Co-Managing Partner of Shearman & Sterling and a Partner in the Mergers & Acquisitions Group. His practice involves assisting corporate and other clients with various M&A transactions, both negotiated and unsolicited, including tender and exchange offers, leveraged buyouts, takeover defense strategies, joint ventures, divestitures and cross-border transactions. Also advises corporate clients on other matters, including corporate governance issues.
Career: Head of the firm's M&A Group from 1995-2001; Co-Head of the group from 1987-91; Managing Partner of the firm's European offices 1991-95.
Personal: BA, University of Pennsylvania (1968); JD, Fordham Law School (1975)

MANN, Christopher L
Sullivan & Cromwell LLP, New York
212 558 4000
mannc@sullcrom.com
Recommended in Projects
Practice Areas: Oil and gas and mining. Represented borrower, sponsors or lenders in Camisea gas pipeline project (Peru), Sincor heavy oil project (Venezuela), Port Arthur refinery project (US), Kutubu oil development project (Papua New Guinea), numerous Latin American mining projects, and pending Mariscal Sucre LNG project (Venezuela) and Coega LNG regasification/power project (South Africa).
Prof. Memberships: ABCNY (former Chair, Project Finance Committee); ABA.
Career: Partner since 1998. Judicial Clerk, Hon. Ralph K. Winter, US Court of Appeals, 2nd Circuit, 1989-90.
Personal: Harvard College (AB, 1985); Cambridge University (M Phil, 1987); Harvard Law School (JD, 1989).

MARCU, Aaron R
Covington & Burling, New York
212 841 1078
amarcu@cov.com
Recommended in Litigation
Practice Areas: Chair of Covington's White-Collar Practice Group. Experienced trial and appellate lawyer focusing on the defense of white-collar criminal and SEC enforcement cases and parallel civil litigation. Handles grand jury and SEC investigations for institutions and executives, including Pfizer, Philip Morris, Goodyear, CBS, NBC, and Société

Générale, and key players in the Enron, Tyco, research analyst, mutual fund, Prudential Securities, Daiwa Bank, Bankers Trust, Salomon, and Lloyd's of London investigations, as well as for other pharmaceutical companies and financial institutions.
Career: United States Attorney's Office for the Southern District of New York (1983-89): Associate US Attorney (1989), Chief, Major Crimes Unit (1988-89); Chief Appellate Attorney (1987-88). Commissioner, New York Civilian Complaint Review Board (1995-98). Trustee, Federal Bar Council. Director, New York Council of Defense Lawyers. International Who's Who of Business Crime Lawyers. Best Lawyers in America.
Publications: 'The Evolution of RICO's Pattern-of-Racketeering Element: From Sedima to H.J. Inc. and its Progeny,' in Civil RICO, Practising Law Institute, 1990; "Internal Corporate Investigations: Promptness Pays Off," Corporate Legal Times, January 1996.
Personal: Harvard University (JD 1980, cum laude); Northwestern University (BSJ 1977, with highest distinction). Law clerk to Hon. Richard Owen, United States District Judge, Southern District of New York (1980-82).

MARKEL, Gregory
Cadwalader, Wickersham & Taft LLP, New York 212 504 6112
gregory.markel@cwt.com
Recommended in Litigation
Practice Areas: Chairman of Cadwalader's Litigation Department. Focuses on securities, antitrust and other complex commercial and financial litigation. Has extensive experience and expertise in securities litigation, including class action defense, derivative actions, and private securities litigation; antitrust; accountants defense, banking, and financial products litigation.
Publications: Mr Markel frequently speaks and writes on the following subjects: Securities Law, Class Actions, Director's and Officer's Liability, Director and Officer Market Trends, Financial Institution's Liability Developments and Litigation against Financial Institutions, as follows: 2005 D&O Market Trends Seminar Series, February 2005; Pleading Loss Causation in Securities Litigation, October 18, 2004; Author of Chapter on Derivative Litigation in Treatise on Litigation in New York Courts, 2004; Commentary and Instruction to Various Banks and Investment Banks on the Interagency Statement on Sound Practices Concerning Complex Structured Finance Activities, July and August 2004; Financial Institution's Liability Developments, June 2004; D&O Liability Developments, June 2004; The New Era of Litigation Against Financial Institutions, June 2004; A Sarbanes-Oxley Update, June 2004; The Financial Institutions Crises: An Indepth Look," February

2004; Litigating a Class Action Case, What Every Litigator Needs to Know, January 2004; Litigating the Financial Fraud Case, January 2003; Litigation and Resolution of Complex Class Actions, December 2002; 31st-36th Annual Institute on Securities Regulation - Securities Litigation Panel; Internet Litigation and How to Avoid it, May 1999; The PSLRA After Silicon Graphics, The Review of Securities & Commodities Regulation, November 1999; IPO Allocation Cases, September 2001; OnLine Securities Trading Litigation, November 2000; Directors Duties and Responsibility; Liability of Accountants for Fraud; How to Settle a Class Action, July 1998. Mr Markel also is a commentator on legal issues for CNBC, Bloomberg TV, Bloomberg Radio, New York Times, Time, Newsweek and Associated Press.
Personal: JD, Yale Law School (1972); MBA, Finance and Accounting, University of Michigan (1968); BA, Economics, Columbia College (1967). American Bar Association: Litigation Section; Antitrust Section; Federal Bar Council.

MASON, Andrew S
Sullivan & Cromwell LLP, New York
212 558 4000
masona@sullcrom.com
Recommended in Tax
Practice Areas: Provides tax advice for a wide range of transactions, including real estate, project finance, leveraged lease, mergers, acquisitions and international transactions, and matters involving the firm's individual clients.
Prof. Memberships: American Bar Association; Association of the Bar of the City of New York (former Chair, Committee on Taxation of Partnerships and Other Pass-Throughs); New York State Bar Association.
Career: Partner since 1989.
Publications: Has lectured at a number of tax conferences.
Personal: Yale College (BA, 1978); Yale Law School (JD, 1981).

MASON, David
Debevoise & Plimpton LLP, New York
212 909 6000
Recommended in Employee Benefits

MASON, Richard G
Wachtell, Lipton, Rosen & Katz, New York 212 403 1252
rgmason@wlrk.com
Recommended in Bankruptcy
Practice Areas: Specializes in Wachtell, Lipton, Rosen & Katz's insolvency practice, representing bank and bondholder groups and creditors' committees in many large Chapter 11 cases and out-of-court restructurings, including the Intermet Corporation, Cone Mills, Pacific Gas & Electric Company, Rand McNally & Company, Allegheny Energy Supply, Inc., Viatel, Integrated Health and LTV Corp. matters, and borrowers in leveraged buyouts, mergers and other

complex financing transactions.
Prof. Memberships: Active member of the Association of the Bar of the City of New York (recently serving on its Committee on Bankruptcy & Corporate Reorganization), the New York State Bar and the American Bar Association. Recently became a Fellow in the American College of Bankruptcy.
Career: Partner at Wachtell, Lipton, Rosen & Katz since 1994. Recently named one of the 'Outstanding Young Bankruptcy Lawyers of the Year' by the 'Turnarounds & Workouts' magazine. Has given numerous seminars on bankruptcy subjects for the Practicing Law Institute and other prominent organizations.
Publications: Co-author of 'Collier's Bankruptcy Practice Guide'.
Personal: Graduated magna cum laude from Virginia Commonwealth University in 1983 (BS, Economics) where he was inducted into the Phi Kappa Phi honor fraternity; and cum laude from New York University in 1987 (JD) where became a Member of the Order of the Coif and was on the staff of the 'Annual Survey of American Law'.

MASTRO, Randy
Gibson, Dunn & Crutcher LLP, New York
212 351 3825
rmastro@gibsondunn.com
Recommended in Litigation
Practice Areas: Executive Committee, Co-Chair of firm's Litigation Practice, former Co-Partner-in-Charge of New York office. Prominent litigator who handles complex civil cases, securities litigation and white collar criminal matters.
Career: Before returning to Gibson Dunn in 1998, Mr Mastro served as New York City's Deputy Mayor for Operations. During his years in the Giuliani administration from 1994-98, Mr Mastro spearheaded the City's initiatives to remove organized crime from the Fulton Fish Market, the private carting industry, and the San Gennaro Festival.
Personal: JD, University of Pennsylvania Law School, 1981, Moot Court Champion. BA, cum laude, Yale, 1978.

MATTEI, Andrew
Mayer, Brown, Rowe & Maw LLP, New York 212 506 2572
amattei@mayerbrownrowe.com
Recommended in Banking & Finance
Practice Areas: Corporate finance. Represents both domestic and foreign banks, other financial institutions. Areas of expertise: highly leveraged, syndicated lending transactions, with emphasis on acquisition financing (including tender offer financings) and corporate recapitalizations. Focuses on senior, secured financings and subordinated financings (including bridge financings). Many cross-border transactions - for example, representing the Agents (Scotia Capital, Canadian Imperial Bank of Commerce and National Bank of Canada) in 2003 Cdn. $1.1 billion

acquisition of Circle K Stores in the US (from ConocoPhillips) by Couche-Tard, one of Canada's largest convenience store operations. Routinely represents lenders in workouts and restructurings of troubled credits.

Prof. Memberships: Admitted in New York, 1988.

Career: Joined Mayer, Brown, Rowe & Maw LLP, New York, 1987; became Partner, 1996.

Publications: Contributing author: 'How to Buy a U.S. Business: A Guide to Negotiated and Hostile Acquisitions'. Chapter 5: 'Senior and Subordinated Acquisition Financing'. 'Advising Illinois Financial Institutions', Chapter 11, Multi-Bank Credit Facilities, 1997 and 2001.

Personal: JD, Fordham University School of Law, 1987; 'Fordham Urban Law Journal'. BS (honors), State University of New York, Cortland, 1979.

MAYER, Thomas Moers
Kramer Levin Naftalis & Frankel LLP, New York 212 715 9169
tmayer@kramerlevin.com
Recommended in Bankruptcy

Practice Areas: Is Partner in the Kramer Levin Naftalis & Frankel LLP Creditors' Rights and Bankruptcy Department, where he specializes in representing investors in claims against, and interests in, financially distressed businesses.

Prof. Memberships: Is a Member of the Association of the Bar of the City of New York. He is also a Fellow of The American College of Bankruptcy.

Career: Mr Mayer's recent cases include: WCI Steel, Inc. ($300 million secured noteholders seeking control of debtor); W.R. Grace (official equity committee); Venture Holdings (largest secured bank creditor) WestPoint Stevens ($165mm 2nd Lien Facility); NorthWestern Corporation ($320 million in subordinated notes; largest shareholder of reorganized debtor); Bethlehem Steel (creditors' committee) and Wheeling-Pittsburgh Corporation (parent company). Mr Mayer has represented investors who purchased claims as a way to acquire controlling or substantial equity interests in, among other reorganizations, Wheeling-Pittsburgh Steel Corporation (first Chapter 11), General Chemicals, Pinnacle Towers and Key 3 Media, and also represented investors who have bought claims against or securities issued by distressed companies to take profits in cash and debt instead of equity, such as 2nd lien lenders to Solutia, Jitney Jungle, Levitz Industries, Grand Union (2nd Chapter 11) and Reeves Industries, the majority holders of $970 million Choctaw/Zephyrus bank debt in Enron, the holders of $750 million in MCI Qualified Income Debt Securities, Washington Group and Iridium bank debt, Finova Trust Offered Preferred Certificates, and bonds and bank debt

issued by Macy's, Woodward & Lothrop, Insilco, Revco, National Gypsum and Todd Shipyards.

Publications: Mr Mayer is the leading scholar on the law of trading claims and taking control of corporations in Chapter 11, having authored or co-authored five published articles and the the Collier Bankruptcy Practice Manual chapter on that topic. In addition to his articles on trading claims, Mr Mayer's publications include Mayer, Liquidity, Disclosure and Their Enemies: Securities Issues and Trading Freezes in Chapter 11 (ABI Winter Meeting December 2004); Will the Lawyers Pay? Ethical, Civil and Criminal Exposure of Counsel in Setting Up Offshore Asset Protection Trusts (ACTEC February 2003); Mayer, Distressed Property, Workouts and Bankruptcy, Powell On Real Estate, Practice Guide 7 (1999); Fortgang & Mayer, Adventures in Subordinated Debt (N.Y.U. Workshop on Business Reorganization and Bankruptcy 1992), Fortgang & Mayer, Prepackaged Plans in Chapter 11 (N.Y.U. Workshop on Business Reorganization and Bankruptcy 1991), Mayer, Investing in Publicly Traded Debt Securities during Restructurings and Chapter 11 Reorganizations: A Comparison of Opportunities, Chapter 13 of Investing In Bankruptcies And Turnarounds (S. Levine, ed. 1991), and Fortgang & Mayer, Valuation in Bankruptcy, 32 U.C.L.A. L. Rev. 1061 (1985).

Personal: Received a JD degree magna cum laude from Harvard University in 1981, where he was on the Harvard Law Review, and an AB degree summa cum laude, Phi Beta Kappa from Dartmouth College in 1977.

MAYO, David
Gibson, Dunn & Crutcher LLP, New York 212 351 3875
dmayo@gibsondunn.com
Recommended in Tax

Practice Areas: Corporate and partnership taxation, taxable and tax-free mergers and acquisitions, cross-border transactions, financings and restructurings.

Prof. Memberships: Member of the Executive Committee of the Tax Section of the New York State Bar Association; Co-Chair of the Committee on Tax Accounting.

Career: Law clerk to the Honorable Theodore Tannenwald Jr, of the United States Tax Court from 1987-88.

Publications: Restricted Stock Notes, 57 Tax Lawyer 61 (2003); numerous Bar Reports.

Personal: JD, Harvard Law School, cum laude, 1987, editor in chief of the Harvard Journal of Law & Public Policy.

MAZUR, Sayward
Mazur, Carp & Rubin PC, New York 212 686 7700
Recommended in Construction

MCCAW, Robert M
Wilmer Cutler Pickering Hale and Dorr LLP, New York 212 230 8810
robert.mccaw@wilmerhale.com
Recommended in Litigation

Practice Areas: Senior Partner in firm's New York office and Co-Chair of firm's Securities Department, with over 30 years' experience in representing and counseling brokerage firms, investment advisers, corporations, accounting firms, lawyers and law firms, and individuals in criminal proceedings, regulatory investigations, enforcement proceedings, and litigation, including complex and multidistrict litigation involving securities fraud, insider trading, manipulation, improper sales practices, trading irregularities, failure to supervise, financial misconduct, breach of fiduciary duty, negligent misrepresentation, malpractice, rule violations, and other allegations.

Prof. Memberships: Served as part-time professional lecturer in Law (Securities Regulation) at The George Washington University School of Law from 1980-83. Has written and spoken on the topics of multidistrict litigation, insider trading, international securities crimes, and corporate confidentiality.

Personal: Georgetown University (BS 1965); University of Virginia (JD 1970). Clerked for Justice Hugo L Black of the US Supreme Court (1970-71).

MCCORMACK, William F
Ropes & Gray, New York 212 841 0627
william.mccormack@ropesgray.com
Recommended in Private Equity

Practice Areas: Practice includes representation of numerous domestic and international private investment funds, including buy-out, venture capital, mezzanine funds and fund of funds. Concentrates on tax planning for corporations, partnerships and joint ventures, focusing on mergers and acquisitions, public and private financings, international transactions, and executive compensation matters. Focuses on tax matters in connection with the formation, operation and investment activities of both domestic and offshore private equity investment funds.

Career: Virginia Bar (1971). New York Bar (1973). Partner, Ropes & Gray (2003). Co-Chairman, Ropes & Gray Private Equity Group.

Personal: LLM, University of Virginia (1972). JD, Catholic University (1971).

MCINERNEY, Denis
Davis Polk & Wardwell, New York 212 450 4000
denis.mcinerney@dpw.com
Recommended in Litigation

Practice Areas: Member of Davis Polk & Wardwell's Litigation Department. Represents corporate and individual clients in grand jury and regulatory investigations, criminal trials, internal

investigations, and civil litigation.

Career: From 1989-94, was an Assistant US Attorney in the Southern District of New York, serving as a Deputy Chief of the Criminal Division from 1993-94. In 1994, worked with Robert B Fiske Jr as an Associate Independent Counsel in the Whitewater Investigation.

MCNAMARA, Elizabeth A
Davis Wright Tremaine LLP, New York 212 603 6437
lizmcnamara@dwt.com
Recommended in Media & Entertainment

Practice Areas: Partner, communications/media and IP law. Represents broadcast/print publishers in libel, privacy, and litigation; prepublication review; advice on IP rights acquisition and licensing. Representative clients: Random House, Viacom, MTV Networks, CBS, Simon & Schuster, Warner Television, Rolling Stone, Castle Rock Entertainment.

Prof. Memberships: Member, New York State Bar. Association of the Bar of the City of New York. Board, ABA Forum on Communications Law.

Career: Joined firm via merger, 1998. Partner, Lankenau Kovner, 1990-98. Senior counsel, Simon & Schuster, 1985-90.

Publications: Author/lecturer in privacy and electronic publishing.

Personal: JD, University of North Carolina, 1981. BA, University of Wisconsin, 1975.

MECHANIC, Jonathan
Fried, Frank, Harris, Shriver & Jacobson LLP, New York 212 859 8222
Jonathan.Mechanic@FriedFrank.com
Recommended in Real Estate

Practice Areas: Chairman of the Real Estate Department. Practice includes acquisitions, dispositions, financings, joint ventures, restructurings, REIT specific transactions and commercial leasing. Representations have included Conde Nast Publications Inc., Jack Resnick & Sons, Lehman Brothers, RFR Holdings, Tishman Hotel & Realty, Tishman Speyer Properties, UBS, Vornado Realty.

Prof. Memberships: Association of the Bar of the City of New York; New York State Bar Association; American Bar Association; Board of Governors of the Real Estate Board of New York; American College of Real Estate Lawyers; New York University Real Estate Institute Advisory Board; and Chicago Title Insurance Company Advisory Board.

Career: Qualified in New York in 1978. Joined firm in 1987 as Partner. General counsel and Managing Director of HRO International (1983-87).

Personal: Born 1952. JD in 1977 from New York University, Member Law Review, and Order of the Coif, and BA, magna cum laude, from Brandeis University in 1974.

MELWANI, Vivek
Fried, Frank, Harris, Shriver & Jacobson LLP, New York 212 859 8208
melwavi@friedfrank.com
Recommended in Bankruptcy

Practice Areas: Bankruptcy Partner. Practice involves all aspects of in, and out-of-court restructurings of financially distressed businesses. Active in the representation of corporate debtors, official and unofficial creditors' committees, asset based lenders and purchasers of distressed businesses.
Career: Joined Fried Frank in 1995 and became a Partner in 2003. Admitted to practice in New York and before the United States District Court for the Southern District of New York.
Personal: Born 1971. Received JD, with distinction, in 1995 and his BBA in 1992 from Hofstra University. Member of the Law Review and the Labor Law Journal.

MERMELSTEIN, Joshua
Fried, Frank, Harris, Shriver & Jacobson LLP, New York 212 859 8137
Joshua.Mermelstein@FriedFrank.com
Recommended in Real Estate

Practice Areas: Real estate Partner. Practice includes representation of financial institutions, owners, developers, opportunity funds and offshore investors. Clients include Millenium & Copthorne Hotels plc; Brookfield Financial Properties, Inc; Reckson Associates Realty Corp.; Lazard Freres & Co's Real Estate Funds; and Credit Suisse First Boston Corporation.
Prof. Memberships: New York State Bar Association; Association of the Bar of the City of New York; Member of Board of Directors of United Help, Inc.
Career: Qualified in 1981. Joined Fried Frank in 1980 and became a Partner in 1986.
Personal: Born 1955. Received JD in 1980 from Columbia University Law School, where he was Harlan Fiske Stone Scholar, and AB from Columbia in 1977.

METCALF, Slade R
Hogan & Hartson LLP, New York 212 918 3637
srmetcalf@hhlaw.com
Recommended in Media & Entertainment

Practice Areas: Media law and litigation for various media and entertainment companies. Counsels newspapers, television stations, magazines and book publishers on pre-publication and pre-broadcast issues; assists motion picture studios on issues relating to film production; represents media companies, reporters, authors, and photographers in litigations regarding issues of libel, invasion of privacy, copyright, and trademark.
Prof. Memberships: Member, Forum on Communications Law of the ABA; Member and current Chair, Committee on Media Law of the New York State Bar Association; Member, Association of the Bar of the City of New York.

Career: Slade has been a Partner at Hogan & Hartson since March, 2002. Prior to joining Hogan & Hartson, he was a Partner at Squadron Ellenoff Plesent & Sheinfeld LLP (which merged with Hogan & Hartson in 2002) from 1981-2002. Slade is a former Chairman of the Legal Affairs Committee of the Magazine Publishers of America, Inc., and has participated in numerous bar association committees regarding media, communications, art, copyright, and literary property. He has lectured extensively on media law at forums including conferences of the Media Law Resource Center, Practicing Law Institute, the Magazine Publishers of America, Inc., and the American Society of Magazine Editors.
Publications: 'Rights and Liabilities of Publishers, Broadcasters and Reporters,' a leading media law resource book since 1981; 'Media Law Update', Hogan & Hartson L.L.P. (quarterly).
Personal: New York University School of Law (JD); Princeton University (AB). Admitted to the New York Bar.

MEYER, Paul
Clifford Chance US LLP, New York 212 878 8176
paul.meyer@cliffordchance.com
Recommended in Insurance

Practice Areas: Has over 25 years experience in insurance industry mergers, acquisitions, reorganizations, joint ventures, financings, product development and regulatory matters. Experience includes the first merger of large mutual life insurance companies in the US, the largest US leveraged buyout of a reinsurance company, several life insurance company demutualizations, and the then largest sale of a block of variable life insurance business through coinsurance and modified coinsurance converting into assumption reinsurance. He is the author of chapters on 'Investments by Insurers' and 'Holding Companies; Controlled Insurers' in the Matthew Bender New York Insurance Law Treatise.

MEYERS, Michael
Orrick, Herrington & Sutcliffe, New York 212 506 5270
mmeyers@orrick.com
Recommended in Projects

Practice Areas: Expert in infrastructure project development and finance, representing developers, lenders, and equity investors in power, telecommunications, industrial, and other US and international infrastructure projects. Recent projects: representation of participants in US and international electric industry workouts; a multinational corporation in restructuring power generation business worldwide; sellers of power projects in Latin America; insolvency workouts of failed telecommunications and power projects; and development of power projects in Spain and Greece.

Career: Chair, Orrick's Global Finance Group; Partner, Orrick (1993-present); Associate and Partner, Graham & James (1979-93); Stanford Law School (JD, 1979); Florida State University, summa cum laude (BS, 1976).

MEYERSON, Lee
Simpson Thacher & Bartlett LLP, New York 212 455 2000
lmeyerson@stblaw.com
Recommended in Corporate/M&A

Practice Areas: Senior member of the Mergers and Acquisitions Group, specialising in M&A as well as capital markets transactions for financial institutions. Has participated in many of the largest deal bank mergers of the past decade, including representing J.P. Morgan Chase & Co. in its $58 billion merger with Bank One Corporation (the third largest US bank acquisition ever announced), and representing The Toronto-Dominion Bank in its $3.8 billion acquisition of a 51% interest in Banknorth. Other M&A representations include Washington Mutual in the sale of its consumer finance business to Citigroup ($1.25 billion), Wachovia Corporation in its innovative brokerage joint venture with Prudential ($1 billion) and legacy Wachovia's merger with First Union Corporation ($14.7 billion) and concurrent defense against the hostile takeover bid by SunTrust Banks. Capital markets practice includes IPOs and a broad range of debt, equity and innovative capital securities offerings for financial institutions.
Career: Joined Simpson Thacher in 1981 and became a Partner in 1989.
Personal: Received a BA from Duke University, magna cum laude in 1977 and JD from NYU Law School in 1981, where he was an editor of 'The Law Review'.

MILLARD, John A
Shearman & Sterling LLP, New York 212 848 7028
jmillard@shearman.com
Recommended in Banking & Finance

Practice Areas: Partner in the Project Development and Finance Group at Shearman & Sterling. His broad practice includes oil and gas, public and private finance, debt and equity offerings of South American corporations, bank investment transactions and leveraged buyouts.
Prof. Memberships: Admitted to the New York Bar.
Career: Joined Shearman in 1967 and became a Partner in 1976.
Personal: AB, Harvard University (1963); LLB, Harvard Law School (1967). Mr Millard is a native Spanish speaker.

MILLER, Alan B
Weil, Gotshal & Manges LLP, New York 212 310 8272
alan.miller@weil.com
Recommended in Bankruptcy

Practice Areas: Business restructuring: Chapter 11 and out-of-court restructures.

Career: Representations include American Airlines' purchase of TWA, Rockefeller Center Properties, debtors Drexel Burnham, Texaco, MCorp, Thermadyne, Viasystems, International Wire, Formica, New World Pasta, KasperAnne Klein, Leslie Fay, Maidenform; institutional lenders Goldman Sachs, Wells Fargo Foothill in Coram Healthcare, Charter Companies, Citibank, GECC. Lecturer, New York University Law School on bankruptcy reorganization, creditors' rights, seminars nationwide. Present/past Member: American College of Bankruptcy; Committees on Bankruptcy and Reorganization, Association of Bar of City of New York; Federal Bar Council; regularly in 'Best Lawyers In America.'
Personal: Boston College JD; Trinity College, BA.

MILLER, David S
Cadwalader, Wickersham & Taft LLP, New York 212 504 6318
david.miller@cwt.com
Recommended in Tax

Practice Areas: Practice includes matters relating to the taxation of financial instruments and derivatives, cross-border lending transactions and other financings, international and domestic mergers and acquisitions, multinational corporate groups and partnerships, bankruptcy and workouts, high net worth individuals and families, and public charities and private foundations. Speaks regularly at conferences and universities. Author of numerous articles for legal publications.
Personal: BA, University of Pennsylvania (summa cum laude, 1986); JD, Columbia Law School (1989; notes and comments editor, Columbia Law Review); LLM, New York University School of Law (1994); clerk to the Honorable Mary M Schroeder of the Ninth Circuit Court of Appeals (1989-90). Awarded Burton Award for Legal Achievement (recognizing exceptional legal writing). Member, New York State Bar Association, Tax Section (Secretary); American Bar Association; Tax Forum.

MILLER, Peter A
Akin Gump Strauss Hauer & Feld LLP, New York 212 872 1004
pamiller@akingump.com
Recommended in Real Estate

Practice Areas: Heads the New York Real Estate and Finance Practice Group. Experienced in real estate finance, with an emphasis on acquisitions, development, joint ventures and financings. Represents owners and developers of investment properties, including private equity funds and other emerging titleholders in the real estate market.
Prof. Memberships: New York State Bar Association.
Career: Prior to joining Akin Gump, was a Partner at Stroock & Stroock & Lavan LLP.

Personal: BS, accounting and finance, University of Pennsylvania's Wharton School of Business (1980); JD, New York University School of Law (1984).

MILLOCK, Peter J
Nixon Peabody LLP, Albany
518 427 2651
pmillock@nixonpeabody.com
Recommended in Healthcare
Practice Areas: Affiliations and networks of physicians, hospitals and other health and mental health providers, regulatory and enforcement matters before state agencies, legislative lobbying on health care issues.
Prof. Memberships: Admitted to practice in New York; New York City Bar Association.
Career: Between 1980 and 1995 served as General Counsel, New York State Department of Health. He was chief legal advisor to the Commissioner of Health and provided advice to state policy makers on all health related matters.
Personal: Harvard University, JD cum laude; Harvard College, BA, Economics, magna cum laude.

MILLS, Phillip R
Davis Polk & Wardwell, New York
212 450 4000
phillip.mills@dpw.com
Recommended in Corporate/M&A
Practice Areas: Member of Davis Polk & Wardwell's Mergers and Acquisitions Group. Advises companies on US and cross-border strategic transactions. Advised MCI on its acquisition by Verizon; EMI on its proposed business combination with AOL Time Warner; Alliance Capital on its acquisition of Sanford Bernstein; Imclone on its strategic relationship with Bristol-Myers; Emerson Electric on a variety of M&A transactions; Roche on its acquisition of Tastemaker; Tycom on its going private with Tyco; Keebler Foods' acquisition by Kellogg; and Kawasaki Steel on its proposed merger with NKK.

MILLSTEIN, Julian
Brown Raysman Millstein Felder & Steiner LLP, New York
212 895 2420
jmillstein@brownraysman.com
Recommended in Business Process Outsourcing: National, Technology
Practice Areas: Julian Millstein concentrates on negotiating and litigating complex outsourcing and computer-related, e-commerce, and intellectual property matters. Before entering the practice of law, he had an extensive career as a computer programmer, systems analyst and information technology consultant. He is co-author of the book 'Doing Business on the Internet: Forms and Analysis.' Mr Millstein Co-Chairs the firm's Outsourcing Practice and has been a thought leader on outsourcing, presenting since 1993 at the Sourcing Interests Group, Outsourcing Institute, Conference Board, Outsourc-

ing World Summit and the Gartner Outsourcing Summit.
Personal: BA, Brandeis University 1965; JD, Fordham University Law School 1978.

MILMED, Paul K
White & Case LLP, New York
212 819 8751
pmilmed@whitecase.com
Recommended in Environment
Practice Areas: Environmental law including litigation, domestic/international M&A transactions.
Prof. Memberships: New York State Bar, 1976; New Jersey State Bar, 1975; US Court of Appeals for the Second Circuit; US District Courts for the Southern and Eastern Districts of New York and the District of New Jersey; ABCNY.
Career: Assistant US Attorney, SDNY (1983-93), Chief, Environmental Protection Unit (1990-93); US District Court for the Southern District of New York appointed mediator.
Personal: Amherst College (AB, 1966); London School of Economics and Political Science, University of London (MSc, 1968); Harvard University (EdM, 1969); New York University School of Law (JD, 1975).

MILMOE, J Gregory
Skadden, Arps, Slate, Meagher & Flom LLP & Affiliates, New York
212 735 3770
jmilmoe@skadden.com
Recommended in Bankruptcy
Practice Areas: Co-Head, Corporate Restructuring Group. Experience includes in-court and out-of-court restructurings, hostile and negotiated mergers and acquisitions, leveraged buyouts, and corporate financings (including IPOs). Draws on experience from various legal disciplines to develop pragmatic, sometimes novel solutions to complex problems.
Career: JD, Fordham University, 1975 (articles editor, Fordham Law Review); AB, Cornell University, 1970.

MINDLIN, Philip
Wachtell, Lipton, Rosen & Katz, New York 212 403 1217
pmindlin@wlrk.com
Recommended in Bankruptcy
Practice Areas: Specializes in bankruptcy and finance law.
Career: Partner at Wachtell, Lipton, Rosen & Katz since 1991. Since joining the firm in 1985, has been involved with all aspects of the firm's financing and insolvency practice, representing creditor groups and debtors in Chapter 11 cases and out-of-court workouts, buyers in purchasing assets out of bankruptcy cases and lenders and borrowers in leveraged acquisitions and other mergers and acquisitions matters. Experience includes representation of key parties in the restructurings of Cable and Wireless plc's US subsidiaries, Olympia & York, FINOVA Capital, Adelphia Communi-

cations, At Home Corp, National Golf Properties, Safelite Glass, NorthPoint Communications, American Commercial Lines, Kingston Square Associates and PA Bergner & Co. Frequent lecturer on insolvency law and is listed in the K&A Restructuring Register of America's top 100 bankruptcy lawyers and financial advisers.
Personal: Graduated from the University of Pennsylvania (BA) and magna cum laude from Fordham University (JD), where he was a member of the Fordham Law Review and was a recipient of the Stillman Memorial Prize, the Chapin Prize and the Constitutional Law Medal.

MIRVIS, Theodore N
Wachtell, Lipton, Rosen & Katz, New York 212 403 1204
tnmirvis@wlrk.com
Recommended in Litigation
Practice Areas: Specializes in litigation involving corporate governance and complex securities matters, directors' fiduciary duties in mergers and acquisitions.
Prof. Memberships: American Law Institute and Planning Committee, Tulane Corporate Law Institute.
Career: Partner at Wachtell, Lipton, Rosen & Katz since 1982; Law Clerk, Honorable Henry J Friendly, United States Court of Appeals for the Second Circuit, 1976 term.
Publications: Author of numerous articles on corporate governance; and co-author, Wachtell & Mirvis, New York Practice under the CPLR.
Personal: Graduated summa cum laude from Yeshiva College in 1973 (BA) and magna cum laude from Harvard Law School in 1976 (JD). While at Harvard Law School, he was editor of 'Harvard Law Review', vol 88, and case editor of 'Harvard Law Review', vol 89.

MITCHELL, Michael
Skadden, Arps, Slate, Meagher & Flom LLP & Affiliates, New York
212 735 2515
mmitchel@skadden.com
Recommended in Litigation
Practice Areas: Litigation experience includes defense of significant shareholder derivative and class action matters. Maintains significant white collar practice. Finally, works closely with the firm's corporate partners in advising boards of directors and special committees.
Career: LLM, Georgetown University Law Center, 1963; LLB, Columbia University School of Law, 1962; AB, Brown University, 1959.

MONTGOMERY, David
Sacks Montgomery PC, New York
212 355 4660
Recommended in Construction

MOORE, Harold F
Skadden, Arps, Slate, Meagher & Flom LLP & Affiliates, New York
212 735 3252
hmoore@skadden.com
Recommended in Projects

Practice Areas: General corporate and bank finance lawyer with a concentration in project finance. Has been the lead lawyer in over 110 domestic and international project financings, representing underwriters, banks and issuers in some of the most complex projects financed in recent years.
Career: JD, Notre Dame, 1980 (summa cum laude; articles editor, Notre Dame Law Review; Thomas J White Scholarship; Peters Scholarship; Farabaugh Prize for High Scholarship in Law); PhD, Fordham University, 1971; MA, Fordham University, 1970; BS, Fordham University, 1968.

MORGAN, Charles
Skadden, Arps, Slate, Meagher & Flom LLP & Affiliates, New York
212 735 2470
cmorgan@skadden.com
Recommended in Tax
Practice Areas: Practice emphasizes tax law relating to financial products, hedge funds, private equity and international matters. Advises clients in connection with design, operation and/or tax consequences associated with financial products and transactions; establishment of hedge fund and private equity fund structures and tax consequences associated with international transactions and legal structures.
Prof. Memberships: Executive Committee Member, NY State Bar Association Tax Section (1986-present).
Career: LLM, New York University, 1981; JD, Pepperdine University, 1977; BS, Wharton School, University of Pennsylvania, 1972.

MORGAN, Robert C
Fish & Neave IP Group of Ropes & Gray, New York
212 596 9133
robert.morgan@ropesgray.com
Recommended in Intellectual Property
Practice Areas: Intellectual property litigation in the fields of telecommunications, electronics, semiconductor technology, medical instruments and products. In addition, specializes in IP asset management, licensing, patent validity and infringement issues. Lead counsel or co-counsel in the Fish & Neave IP Group of Ropes & Gray in more than 25 trials and has argued numerous appeals before the Court of Appeals for the Federal circuit.
Career: Fellow in the American College of Trial Lawyers. California Bar (1970). New York Bar (1970). United States Patent and Trademark Office (1981). Partner, Ropes & Gray (2005; Fish & Neave 1978).
Personal: JD, Harvard Law School (1969), MSEE, California Institute of Technology (1966), BS, University of California at Los Angeles (1965).

MORGENSTERN, Saul P
Kaye Scholer LLP, New York
212 836 7210
smorgenstern@kayescholer.com
Recommended in Antitrust

Practice Areas: Partner, litigation. Practice focuses on the preparation and trial of complex cases, principally in the areas of antitrust (civil and criminal) and trade regulation, intellectual property and technology, as well as the representation of companies and individuals in connection with Department of Justice and Federal Trade Commission investigations. Mr Morgenstern has litigated jury and non-jury cases before federal and state courts throughout the United States, the Federal Trade Commission, the US International Trade Commission, and international and domestic arbitral tribunals. Has particular experience in defending multi-jurisdictional antitrust class actions in federal and state courts, in cases involving the alleged abuse of intellectual property rights and in price and promotional discrimination cases. He has counseled and represented clients in a variety of industries, including the computer hardware and software, energy, entertainment, insurance, investment banking, leasing, leisure, real estate, pharmaceutical, publishing, telecommunications and toy industries.
Prof. Memberships: American Bar Association: Section of Antitrust; Internet Committee, Trade Associations Committee, Vice-Chair 2002-present; Section of Intellectual Property; Section of Litigation. New York State Bar Association: Antitrust Law Section; Secretary 2005, Executive Committee 2001-present. Federal Bar Council: Public Service Committee 2002-present. Association of the Bar of the City of New York.
Career: JD with Distinction, Hofstra University School of Law, 1981; BS, Boston University, 1974.
Publications: 'Antitrust Enforcement in High Technology Industries: Keeping Cyberspace Safe for Innovators or Just Another Speed Trap on the Information Superhighway', with Eamon O'Kelly, 19th Annual Institute on Computer Law (Practising Law Institute (547) 1999); 'Antitrust Issues Affecting the Publishing Industry', Print and Electronic Publishing (Practising Law Institute (516) 1998 and (480) 1997).

MORHOUSE, Sanford W
Dewey Ballantine LLP, New York
212 259 8400
smorhouse@deweyballantine.com
Recommended in Private Equity

Practice Areas: Mr Morhouse focuses his practice primarily in the areas of corporate and real estate finance. His principal clients include major pension funds, investment advisors and fund sponsors, and his practice involves the creation of, and investments in, private and public investment vehicles and the representation of portfolio companies and properties acquired thereby.
Career: Partner, Dewey Ballantine LLP. Member of the Management Committee. Former Co-Chairman of the firm's Management and Executive Committees. Former Chairman of the firm's Real Estate Department, and former Co-Chairman of the firm's Corporate Department. Admitted to practice 1969, New York.
Personal: Born December 13, 1944. BA, Williams College, 1966. JD, Columbia Law School, 1969.

MORPHY, James C
Sullivan & Cromwell LLP, New York
212 558 4000
morphyj@sullcrom.com
Recommended in Corporate/M&A

Practice Areas: Managing Partner, M&A Group. M&A advice for a wide variety of friendly mergers and hostile acquisitions. Recent transactions include: Computer Associates in its acquisition of Netegrity; Masonite acquisition by KKR; Special Committee of Abercrombie & Fitch; John Hancock/Manulife merger; various Hershey Foods acquisitions; Kodak restructuring; Hewlett-Packard/Compaq merger; Special Committee of Aames Financial: split-up and sale of Carter Wallace; Reader's Digest recapitalisation; Goldman Sachs/Spear, Leeds & Kellogg; UBS/PaineWebber; and Alliance Capital/Sanford Bernstein.
Career: Partner since 1986.
Publications: Contributing author, New York and Delaware Business Entities: Choice, Formation, Operation, Financing and Acquisitions (West Publishing) and Transactional Lawyer's Deskbook (West Publishing).
Personal: Harvard College (BA, Phi Beta Kappa, 1976); Harvard Law School (JD, 1979).

MORVILLO, Robert
Morvillo, Abramowitz, Grand, Iason & Silberberg, PC, New York
212 856 9600
Recommended in Litigation

NADEL, Peter F
Katten Muchin Zavis Rosenman, New York 212 940 7010
peter.nadel@kmzr.com
Recommended in Healthcare

Practice Areas: Partner, represents a wide variety of local and national healthcare providers and hospital associations in both transactional and contested matters. Has negotiated dozens of contracts, each in excess of $100 million, and has recovered more than $1 billion in reimbursement litigations against federal and state governments for clients in New York and nationally.
Career: Joined Katten Muchin Zavis Rosenman in 1964 and became Partner in 1972.
Personal: Columbia University (LLB 1964); Columbia Law Review; Harlan Fiske Stone Scholar; Cornell University (BA 1961) With Distinction.

NAFTALIS, Gary P
Kramer Levin Naftalis & Frankel LLP, New York 212 715 9253
gnaftalis@kramerlevin.com
Recommended in Litigation

Practice Areas: One of the nation's leading trial lawyers, Co-Chair of Kramer Levin Naftalis and Frankel LLP and Head of the firm's Litigation Practice. For more than 30 years, he has represented individuals and corporations in all phases of complex civil, criminal, and regulatory matters including those involving allegations of insider trading, market manipulation, accounting irregularities and other financial fraud.
Prof. Memberships: He is a Fellow of the American College of Trial Lawyers and a member of the White Collar Crime Committee and Council Member of the Criminal Justice Section of the American Bar Association. He is also a Member of the Federal Bar Council, the New York State Bar Association, The Association of the Bar of the City of New York and the International Bar Association.
Career: During his 30+ year career, he has successfully represented numerous securities industry clients, including Salomon Brothers in the federal criminal and SEC investigations of US Treasury auction bidding practices, and Kidder, Peabody in connection with the Wall Street insider trading scandal. He currently represents Michael Eisner, the CEO of The Walt Disney Company, in the shareholders derivative lawsuit relating to the hiring and termination of Michael Ovitz. He is also counsel to Kenneth Langone in the litigation relating to the compensation of New York Stock Exchange Chairman Richard Grasso. He also represents Canary Capital Partners in the ongoing mutual fund investigations and related civil litigations. Mr Naftalis is also actively involved in representing significant figures and entities in the government's current inquiries and related civil litigation concerning corporate accounting irregularities. For example, he represents the Chairman of Global Crossing; the former CEO of WorldCom; the Chief Financial Officers of Cendant and Oxford Health Systems; the General Counsel of Rite Aid; and the investment banking firm CIBC in the Enron investigation. He also represents a Director and Senior Officer of Tyco in securities class action and ERISA litigation and the former CEO of Arthur Andersen in the Enron civil litigation. He also serves as counsel to audit and special committees of a number of major public companies in connection with regulatory inquiries. Previously, he successfully defended the general counsel and chief financial officer of the Southland Corporation against proxy fraud charges and the former Head of the New York City Transit Authority on conflict of interest charges. He also successfully represented a prominent Saudi Arabian banker against state criminal charges and in proceedings before the Federal Reserve Board relating to the disposition of his interest in the Bank of Credit and Commerce International, as well as complex civil litigation brought against him by the liquidators of BCCI seeking $10 billion in damages. All US civil, criminal and regulatory charges were ultimately dismissed. He formerly served as an Assistant US Attorney in the Southern District of New York (1968-74), holding the title of Deputy Chief of the Criminal Division. He also served as special counsel to the US Senate Subcommittee investigating abuses in the nursing home industry (1975). He was a lecturer in law at Columbia Law School from 1976-88 and was a member of the faculty of Harvard Law School in 1979. In 1993, he was selected by the American Bar Association to be lead defense counsel for Ethel Rosenberg in its Trial of the Century program: United States v Julius and Ethel Rosenberg. Ethel Rosenberg was found not guilty by the jury.
Personal: Received his AB degree from Rutgers University in 1963, his MA from Brown University in 1965, and his LLB from Columbia Law School in 1967.

NATHAN, Charles
Latham & Watkins LLP, New York
212 906 1200
Recommended in Corporate/M&A

NECKLES, Peter J
Skadden, Arps, Slate, Meagher & Flom LLP & Affiliates, New York
212 735 2466
pneckles@skadden.com
Recommended in Banking & Finance

Practice Areas: Represents corporate borrowers and institutional lenders in bank loan transactions, with an emphasis on corporate restructurings, workouts, debtor-in-possession loans, bankruptcy reorganizations, acquisition financings and other highly leveraged financings.
Career: JD, Fordham University School of Law, (cum laude; editor, Fordham Law Review); BS, Rensselaer Polytechnic Institute.

NEEDELL, Benjamin F
Skadden, Arps, Slate, Meagher & Flom LLP & Affiliates, New York
212 735 2600
bneedell@skadden.com
Recommended in Real Estate

Practice Areas: Head of Skadden's Real Estate Department. Practice emphasizes purchase and sale transactions, financings, securitized real estate loans, real estate development, partnership law, real estate investment trusts, syndications, major headquarters leases, hotel operation, development and financing, and matters relating to pension fund investments in real estate.

Prof. Memberships: Member, Board of Directors, Rock and Roll Hall of Fame (1986-present); Wenner Media, Inc. (1978-present); Stratton Mountain School (1980-present); New York Restoration Project (2002-present), Chairman (2002-present); Westchester Land Trust (2001-present).

Career: LLB, St John's University, 1966 (Editorial Board, St John's Law Review); BA, Rutgers University, 1963.

NEFF, Daniel A

Wachtell, Lipton, Rosen & Katz,
New York 212 403 1218
daneff@wlrk.com
Recommended in Corporate/M&A

Practice Areas: Specializes in mergers and acquisitions. During more than 25 years of practice has been extensively involved in negotiated as well as hostile acquisitions, and has represented bidders and targets, public and private companies, private equity firms and special committees of directors. Has represented companies in divestitures, cross-border transactions and proxy contests and has counselled managements and Boards of Directors concerning acquisition matters, conflict transactions and other significant issues. Among other matters, he has represented Goldman Sachs Capital Partners and Apollo Advisors LP in their acquisition of Nalco Chemical Company; Apollo Advisors LP in its acquisition of AMC Entertainment Inc; Western Wireless Corporation in its merger with ALLTEL Corporation; VoiceStream Wireless Corporation in its merger with Deutsche Telekom AG; Kellogg Company in its acquisition of Keebler Foods Company; Litton Industries Inc in its merger with Northrop Grumman Corporation; Orion Power Holdings Inc in its sale to Reliant Resources, Inc; Mirage Resorts Incorporated in its merger with MGM Grand Inc; Anadarko Petroleum Corporation in its acquisition of Union Pacific Resources Group Inc; Vivendi Universal SA in its acquisitions of United States Filter Corporation and Cendant Software Corporation; Transamerica Corporation in its merger with Aegon NV and its acquisition of Whirlpool Financial Corporation.; Newmont Mining Corporation in its acquisitions of Franco-Nevada Mining Corporation Limited, Normandy Mining Limited and Santa Fe Pacific Gold Corporation; Western Atlas Inc. in its merger with Baker Hughes Incorporated; and Vons Companies in its merger with Safeway Inc; and has represented special board committees of Wausau Insurance, Hayes Wheels International and Enron Oil & Gas Company (now EOG Resources Inc).

Prof. Memberships: Member of the 'Law Review' at Columbia University School of Law.

Career: Partner at Wachtell, Lipton,

Rosen & Katz since 1984. Serves as firm's Managing Partner.

Personal: Graduated magna cum laude from Brown University and from the Columbia University School of Law.

NEILL, David S

Wachtell, Lipton, Rosen & Katz,
New York 212 403 1263
dsneill@wlrk.com
Recommended in Antitrust

Practice Areas: Specializes in antitrust. Has handled the antitrust aspects of mergers affecting a broad variety of industries and has represented the buyer or the seller in most of the largest bank mergers in US history.

Prof. Memberships: The Association of the Bar of the City of New York (Antitrust and Trade Regulation Committee, 1997-98); New York State and American (section on Antitrust, Vice-Chairman of Financial Market and Institutions Committee, 1997-2001) Bar Associations.

Career: Partner at Wachtell, Lipton, Rosen & Katz.

Publications: Co-author: 'Antitrust Standards for Bank Holding Company Mergers and Acquisitions', Bank and Corporate Governance Law Reporter, Vol VIII, Nos 4 & 5, p 812 (June/July 1992); 'Justice's Review of Bank Acquisitions Continues to Reflect Uncertainty', Banking Policy Report, Vol 11, No 23, p 3 (December 7, 1992); 'FDICIA Taxes Justice Department's Antitrust Analysis of Bank Mergers', Banking Policy Report, Vol 12, No 1, p 1 (January 4, 1993); 'Relevant Product and Geographic Markets in Bank Mergers: A Comparison of the Methodologies Used by the Justice Department and the Federal Reserve Board', Special Report published by BNA (1994); 'Bank Merger Impact on Small Business Services Is Changing', Banking Policy Report, Vol 15, No 8 (April 15, 1996); 'Documentary Evidence and Antitrust Merger Enforcement', ALI-ABA's Practice Checklist Manual on Advising Business Clients, p21 (1997); 'Proposed 'Streamlining' of Bank Merger Antitrust Review by House Banking Bill May Have Unintended Consequences', BNA's Banking Report, Vol 69, No 2, p93 (July 14, 1997); 'Antitrust Considerations in Mergers and Acquisitions of Financial Institution', Bank and Corporate Governance Law Reporter, Vol 19, No 5, p762 (January 1998); 'Acquisitions of Non-Bank Operations in Financial Holding Company Mergers', The Review of Banking and Financial Services, Vol 20, No 3 (March 2004). Co-editor: Bank Merger Practice Manual, American Bar Association (forthcoming). Author: 'Lending to Small and Medium-Sized Businesses and the Antitrust Analysis of Bank Mergers', BNA's Banking Report, Vol 60, p 814 (May 31, 1993); 'Fed Antitrust Change Could Boost Thrift Acquisitions by Banks', Banking Policy Report, Vol 12,

No 17, p 1 (September 6, 1993); 'Antitrust Divestiture Policies Can Impact Bank Merger Planning', Banking Policy Report, Vol 14, No 23, p1 (December 4, 1995); 'New Antitrust Policies Add Complexity and Uncertainty to Bank Mergers', Bank and Corporate Governance Law Reporter, Vol 17, No 2, p 196 (Oct. 1996); 'New Safe Harbor or Not? Fed Clarifies Antitrust Thresholds for Bank Deals', Banking Policy Report, Vol. 16, No 13, p1 (July 7, 1997); 'M & A Review Role for the FTC on Banking Deals: A Flawed Idea', Banking Policy Report, Vol 16, No 18, p1 (Sept 15, 1997); 'The ATM Surcharge Debate: Logical Fallacies and Antitrust Reality', BNA's Banking Report, Vol 71, No 5, p233 (August 3, 1998); 'Antitrust Lessons from Recent Bank Megamergers', Banking Policy Report, Vol 17, No 21, p1 (November 2, 1998); 'U.S. Antitrust Considerations in Mergers and Acquisitions of Bank Holding Companies', Antitrust Report, p4 (February 1999). 'Antitrust Merger Review Will be More Complicated After Financial Modernization', Banking Policy Report, Vol 18, No 17, p 1 (September 7, 1999); 'New Banking Act Complicates Merger Review', International Financial Law Review, p 13 (February 2000); 'A Guide to the Policies and Procedures Affecting Antitrust Divestitures in Bank Mergers', The Banking Law Journal, Vol. 118, No 7, p 603 (July/August 2001).

Personal: Graduated cum laude from Yale University in 1979 (BA); from Goldman School of Public Policy, University of California, Berkeley in 1983 (MPP); and from Columbia Law School in 1984 (JD).

NESGOS, Peter

Milbank, Tweed, Hadley & McCloy,
New York 212 530 5000
Recommended in Space, Satellite & Technology

NEUNER, Robert

Baker Botts LLP, New York
212 408 2552
robert.neuner@bakerbotts.com
Recommended in Intellectual Property

Practice Areas: The trial of complex cases with emphasis on intellectual property. Cases tried nationwide, mostly to juries, have involved all important areas of technology. Has also functioned as a court-appointed special master.

Prof. Memberships: American Intellectual Property Law Association; Federal Bar Council; New York Intellectual Property Law Association, past President.

Career: New York State Bar (1965); USPTO (1968).

Publications: Written and lectured on trial and appeal of intellectual property cases, including a regular column in the New York Law Journal.

Personal: JD, Fordham University School of Law, 1965; BS, electrical engineering, Manhattan College, 1960.

NEVELOFF, Jay A

Kramer Levin Naftalis & Frankel LLP,
New York 212 715 9290
jneveloff@kramerlevin.com
Recommended in Real Estate

Practice Areas: Is a Partner at Kramer Levin Naftalis & Frankel LLP where he concentrates on real estate and other commercial transactions. He represents numerous nationally recognized real estate developers and owners, as well as major international lending and financial institutions, in commercial lending transactions, loan restructurings and workouts.

Prof. Memberships: Served for several years as the Vice-Chair of the American Bar Association Committee on Partnerships, Joint Ventures and Other Investment Vehicles. He is an active Member of both The American College of Real Estate Lawyers and American Law Institute, and is a Member of the Practicing Law Institute Real Estate Advisory Committee. He also served as the Vice-Chair of the International Health Network Society and has throughout his career represented owners, developers and lenders in connection with senior citizen assisted living facilities.

Career: Has represented developers of numerous mixed-use, commercial, retail and residential projects including Time Warner Center (a joint venture of The Related Companies and Apollo Investment Fund), Trump Tower (a joint venture between Donald Trump and Equitable Life), The Galleria (developed by Morgan Guaranty Trust Company), 500 Park Avenue (developed by Equitable Life) and Trump International Hotel and Tower, the former Gulf + Western Building (a joint venture of General Electric Investment Trust, Donald Trump and The Galbreath Organization); numerous regional and local shopping centers as well as other commercial projects throughout the country. He also represents a number of real estate funds in their acquisition of properties including those managed by Credit Suisse First Boston. He regularly represents numerous lending and other financial institutions in restructuring loans and other business relationships as well as in the development of new and innovative financing products. These institutions include BNP-Paribas. Additionally, he regularly assists clients actively involved in numerous hotel transactions including the acquisition of numerous hotels, the development of hotels (including a Westin Hotel on behalf of its owner, CSX Transportation) in Savannah, Georgia as well as Trump International Hotel, and loan restructurings relating to numerous hotels including The Plaza Hotel in New York.

Personal: Received a JD degree from New York University in 1974 and a BA degree from Brooklyn College in 1971.

NEWMAN, Lawrence W

Baker & McKenzie, New York
212 891 3970
lawrence.w.newman@bakernet.com
Recommended in Arbitration

Practice Areas: Partner in Litigation Department of New York office. Areas of work are litigation in the United States of transnational commercial disputes and international commercial arbitration, to a great extent in matters involving foreign languages (French, Spanish, Portuguese) and law. Lead attorney for BellSouth International in an arbitration (1994-99) that resulted in an award of $19.5 million against a French telecommunications company on the basis of fraudulent concealment of information in the sale of shares in a cellular telephone company. Was also lead attorney in arbitration between US and Mexican companies in which client obtained an award based on breach of contract and fraud.

Prof. Memberships: Member of various bar organizations including the American Law Institute; former Chairman of the United States Iranian Claimants Committee (USICC), the national organisation of US businesses with claims arising out of the Iranian revolution.

Career: Member of the Bar since 1961. Attorney, US Securities & Exchange Commission's Special Study of Securities Markets, 1961-63; Assistant US Attorney, Southern District of New York, 1964-69. Associate and partner, Baker & McKenzie New York office 1969 to present.

Publications: Co-author of 'Litigating International Disputes' (West Group 1996) 'The Practice of International Litigation' (Juris Publishing, 2d Ed 1999); general editor of a series of books on international litigation, including 'Enforcement of Foreign Judgments' and 'Attachment of Assets'. Since 1982 the author of column in the New York Law Journal 'International Litigation'.

Personal: Born July 1935. Harvard College 1957; Harvard Law School 1960. Leisure interests include writing, publishing, travel and golf.

NEWMAN, Thomas R

Duane Morris LLP, New York
212 692 1028
trnewman@duanemorris.com
Recommended in Insurance

Practice Areas: Thomas R Newman practices in the areas of insurance and reinsurance law, including coverage, claims handling, contract drafting and arbitration and litigation. He has served as lead counsel in more than 50 reinsurance arbitrations, representing both cedents and reinsurers. He has handled hundreds of appeals in both state and federal courts, including 80 in the New York Court of Appeals and 30 in the US Court of Appeals for the Second Circuit.

Prof. Memberships: American Bar Association; New York State Bar Association; The Association of the Bar of the City of New York; American Law Insti-

tute; Federation of Insurance and Corporate Counsel; American Academy of Appellate Lawyers; AIDA Reinsurance and Insurance Arbitration Society.

Career: Duane Morris LLP, Of Counsel, 2003-present; Luce, Forward, Hamilton & Scripps LLP, Of Counsel, 1999-2003; Newman & Company, PC - President, 1991-99; Bower & Gardner - Partner, 1971-91; Siff & Newman - Partner, 1971-87; Sabin, Bermant & Blau - Associate/Partner, 1963-70. Admitted to practice in New York, Supreme Court of the United States, United States Court of Appeals for the Second Circuit, United States District Courts for the Southern and Eastern Districts of New York.

Personal: New York University School of Law, LLB, 1960.

NIJENHUIS, Erika W

Cleary Gottlieb Steen & Hamilton LLP, New York 212 225 2980
enijenhuis@cgsh.com
Recommended in Tax

Practice Areas: US income tax, especially financial products and international tax planning. Clients include Citigroup, Goldman Sachs, Lehman, Merrill Lynch, Morgan Stanley.

Prof. Memberships: NYSBA Tax Section Executive Committee; Co-Chair of financial products subcommittee.

Career: Joined firm, 1990; became Partner, 1997. LLM in taxation, NYU (1996). JD, cum laude, Order of the Coif, Law Review executive editor (1987), BA, summa cum laude (1982), University of Pennsylvania.

Publications: Articles on wash sales, tax shelter disclosure and listing rules, contingent interest convertible bonds, securities futures, off-shore 'trading in securities', global dealing operations, mandatory convertible debt instruments, swaps and other derivative financial instruments.

NIMS, Barbara

Davis Polk & Wardwell, New York
212 450 4591
barbara.nims@dpw.com
Recommended in Employee Benefits

Practice Areas: Member of Davis Polk & Wardwell's Corporate Department. Advises clients on executive compensation, stock-based incentive, deferred compensation and pension plans and other employee benefit arrangements, with particular emphasis on issues arising in the contexts of merger, acquisition, corporate reorganization and bankruptcy and workout transactions. Also advises on pension investment and fiduciary considerations, employment and consulting arrangements, the applicability of federal securities and tax laws to executives and employees, and on general employment-related matters.

NIRENBERG, David Z

Orrick, Herrington & Sutcliffe, New York
212 506 5085
dnirenberg@orrick.com
Recommended in Tax

Practice Areas: Nationally recognized for his tax work in the areas of securitization and derivative products. He has played a significant role in the structuring of a wide variety of innovative, domestic and cross border financial products in both the structured finance and derivative products markets.

Career: Leader, Orrick's New York Corporate Tax Group; Columbia University School of Law (JD, 1985); Harlan Fiske Stone Scholar; Boston University Graduate School of Management, with honors, (MBA, 1985); Cornell University (BS, 1981).

Publications: Co-author, Federal Income Taxation Of Securitization Transactions (2001) and Federal Income Taxation of Mortgage-Backed Securities (Probus Publishing, 1989, revised 1994).

NONNA, John M

LeBoeuf, Lamb, Greene & MacRae, LLP, New York 212 424 8311
jnonna@llgm.com
Recommended in Insurance

Practice Areas: His practice in commercial litigation and arbitration includes insurance and reinsurance disputes. He has conducted arbitrations and bench and jury trials on a variety of claims including accounting malpractice, breach of fiduciary duty, fraud, sales and distributorship contracts, insurance and reinsurance coverage and, employment discrimination. He has lectured at numerous conferences on trial practice, arbitration, mediation, and insurance and reinsurance coverage.

Publications: Co-editor of the New York State Bar Association treatise, Insurance Law Practice.

Personal: Has served as Mayor of Pleasantville, New York. He was a member of the 1972 and 1980 United States Olympic Teams.

NOVIKOFF, Harold S

Wachtell, Lipton, Rosen & Katz, New York 212 403 1249
hsnovikoff@wlrk.com
Recommended in Bankruptcy

Practice Areas: Specializes in creditors' rights, bankruptcy, debt restructurings, and derivative and financial markets transactions. During the past year, has represented major creditors of HealthSouth, 360networks, Independent Wireless One, Looking Glass Networks, American Business Financial Services, World Kitchen, National Century Financial Enterprises, and Navigator Gas.

Prof. Memberships: Former Chair of the Committee on Bankruptcy and Corporate Reorganization of the Association of the Bar of the City of New York; and is a member of the National Bankruptcy Conference (Executive Commit-

tee; Vice-Chair of Chapter 11 and Capital Markets Committees), the American College of Bankruptcy and The Association of Commercial Finance Attorneys (Board of Directors).

Career: Partner at Wachtell, Lipton, Rosen & Katz since 1981.

Publications: Contributing author to 'Collier on Bankruptcy'.

Personal: Graduated with distinction from Cornell University in 1972 (BS) and from Columbia University Law School in 1975 (JD) (member of Law Review); Board of Visitors of the Columbia Law School; Board of Advisors of the Mailman School of Public Health at Columbia University.

NUSBAUM, Jack H

Willkie Farr & Gallagher LLP, New York
212 728 8060
jnusbaum@willkie.com
Recommended in Corporate/M&A

Practice Areas: Chairman of the firm, specializing in mergers and acquisitions, corporate governance and fiduciary duties, and internal investigations. Regularly advises Boards of Directors of public companies on issues of fiduciary duty and corporate governance, particularly in the context of change in control transactions. Continues to be involved in many of the most notable US and cross-border transactions. In 2004, advised the Management Team of PanAmSat Corp. in its $4.3 billion acquisition by Kohlberg Kravis Roberts & Co. from DirecTV Group Inc. and advised Neuberger Berman Inc. in its 2003 $2.63 billion acquisition by Lehman Brothers Holdings, Inc. Noted for his significant involvement in: the historic merger of NASDAQ with the American Stock Exchange, the leveraged buyout of R.J.R. Nabisco, the acquisition of McCaw Cellular Communications by AT&T, the acquisition of Magma Copper by Broken Hill Proprietary Limited, and various going-private transactions and restructurings on behalf of Donald Trump and his related entities. Headed the team responsible for the 1998 Cendant Report, the internal investigation of Cendant Corporation on behalf of its Audit Committee, which The New York Times called a definitive case study for accountants in the area of accounting irregularities and fraud.

Prof. Memberships: Member of the New York State and American Bar Associations. Serves as a Director of publicly held corporations including W.R. Berkley Corporation, Strategic Distribution, Inc. and The Topps Company, Inc. Serves on the Board of Visitors of Columbia University Law School and is a trustee of Prep for Prep and The Joseph Collins Foundation. Serves as a member of the Legal Advisory Committee to the Board of Directors of the New York Stock Exchange and is a member of the Board of Advisors of the New York

University Center for Law & Business.
Career: Admitted to the Bar of the State of New York.
Personal: Received a JD from Columbia Law School in 1965 and a BS from the Wharton School of the University of Pennsylvania in 1962.

NUSSBAUM, Bernard W
Wachtell, Lipton, Rosen & Katz,
New York 212 403 1266
bwnussbaum@wlrk.com
Recommended in Litigation
Practice Areas: Specializes in corporate and securities litigation.
Prof. Memberships: Admitted to practice in the United States District Courts for the Southern and Eastern Districts of New York, the United States Court of Appeals for the Second Circuit, and the United States Supreme Court; and Member of the Association of the Bar of the City of New York (Vice President from 1984-85), the New York State Bar Association, the American Bar Association, and the Federal Bar Council (President from 1990-92).
Career: Partner at Wachtell, Lipton, Rosen & Katz since 1968. Has served in both the public and private sectors throughout career, working as an assistant attorney in the United States Attorney's Office for the Southern District of New York after graduating from law school, as Senior Associate Counsel to the United States House of Representatives Judiciary Committee's impeachment inquiry in 1974 regarding President Richard Nixon and as Counsel to the President during the Clinton Administration in 1993 and 1994. Has been a lecturer at Columbia University Law School.
Personal: Graduated from Columbia University in 1958 (BA), where he was a member of Phi Beta Kappa, from Harvard Law School in 1961 (LLB), where he was notes editor of 'Harvard Law Review', and awarded a Harvard University Sheldon Travelling Fellowship, and was awarded an honorary LLD from George Washington University National Law Center in 1993.

O'BRIEN, Clare
Shearman & Sterling LLP, New York
212 848 8966
cobrien@shearman.com
Recommended in Corporate/M&A
Practice Areas: Partner at Shearman & Sterling specializing in mergers and acquisitions. Advises on a large variety of public and private transactions, including public company restructurings, joint ventures and large public transactions.
Prof. Memberships: Member of the New York Bar; Member of the Irish Roll of Solicitors.
Career: Joined Shearman in 1988 and became Partner in 1995.
Personal: Educated at the Incorporated Law Society of Ireland, and Trinity College (Dublin), BA Legal Science; Member of the Board of Directors of the American Association of the International Commission of Jurists.

OLIVIER, Jeanne
Shearman & Sterling LLP, New York
212 848 8593
jolivier@shearman.com
Recommended in Projects
Practice Areas: Partner in Shearman & Sterling's Project Development and Finance Group. Has broad experience in both international and domestic financings, including acquisition financings, asset-based financings, lease financings, project financings, privatisations and sovereign and corporate restructurings. Advises sponsors and lenders in complex political risk insurance matters. Also has extensive experience in financings and restructurings in Latin America.
Prof. Memberships: Bars of the State of New York and the State of Louisiana.
Career: Joined Shearman in 1980 and became a Partner in 1988.
Personal: BA, Newcomb College of Tulane University (1975); JD, University of Pennsylvania Law School (1979)

O'MALLEY Jr, Joseph M
Fitzpatrick, Cella, Harper & Scinto,
New York 212 218 2260
jomalley@fchs.com
Recommended in Intellectual Property
Practice Areas: Lead counsel for various clients, including Pfizer, Bristol-Myers Squibb and Kos Pharmaceuticals, through all phases of patent litigation, and has briefed and argued appeals before the Court of Appeals for the Federal Circuit. Recently, Mr O'Malley served as lead trial counsel for plaintiffs Pfizer and Warner-Lambert in a successful patent litigation involving their $700 million per year cardiovascular drug Accupril®. Mr O'Malley is also a winner of the 2004 Burton Award for Legal Achievement.
Prof. Memberships: American Bar Association; New York Intellectual Property Law Association; New Jersey Intellectual Property Law Association (Litigation Committee).
Career: Chemical Engineer, DuPont. Supervised the design and construction of new chemical and pharmaceutical processing facilities.
Personal: Rutgers College of Engineering (BS chemical engineering, highest honors); Rutgers-Camden School of Law (JD, honors). Father of three children. Enjoys sports, travel and reading.

O'NEIL, Terry
Bond, Schoeneck & King, LLP,
New York 516 267 6310
toneil@bsk.com
Recommended in Employment
Practice Areas: Mr O'Neil's practice includes collective bargaining, arbitration, employment discrimination and litigation, wage-hour matters, ERISA, and OSHA. He has represented some of the largest municipalities in New York. He has represented numerous school districts, and regularly handles 'high profile' disciplinary proceedings, including an Education Law §3020-a case with the highest fine ($100,000) in the history of the State. He has represented private sector clients in negotiations and litigation throughout the US, and has extensive experience in the printing, service and restaurant industries.
Personal: St John's University (BA, cum laude, 1967) and St John's University School of Law (JD, 1970).

ORINGER, Andrew
Clifford Chance US LLP, New York
212 878 8171
andrew.oringer@cliffordchance.com
Recommended in Employee Benefits
Practice Areas: Serves as Head of the US ERISA and Executive Compensation Practice. He counsels clients regarding their employee benefit plans and programs and regarding fiduciary issues arising in connection with the investment of employee benefit plan assets. He works closely with the Corporate Group to advise clients on employee benefits strategies in the context of corporate transactions. He has published numerous articles on such topics as executive compensation, ERISA implications of structuring investment funds, tax-qualification issues, the treatment of benefits in bankruptcy and ESOPs. He also lectures regularly and is quoted frequently in various major newspapers and other publications.

ORR, Dennis P
Mayer, Brown, Rowe & Maw LLP,
New York 212 506 2690
dorr@mayerbrownrowe.com
Recommended in Antitrust
Practice Areas: Litigation: Primary focus on antitrust; securities; products liability; environmental; general commercial litigation; insurance litigation. Notable cases: In re Vitamins Antitrust Litigation; Great Northern Nekoosa v Georgia-Pacific; In re IPO Allocation Litigation; In re Phenylpropanolamine Litigation; In re Beverly Hills Supperclub Fire Litigation; Orthofix S.r.l., et al. v EBI Medical Systems, Inc.; In re: Pay 'N Pak: The Official Unsecured Creditors Committee v Court Square Capital, Ltd.; Alesayi Beverage Corporation v Canada Dry Corporation; President Enterprises Corporation v Wyndham Foods; Arthur D. Little v Ernst & Young.
Career: Mayer, Brown, Rowe & Maw LLP, New York, 1997 to date; Partner, 1997. Shearman & Sterling, 1978-97; Partner, 1986.
Publications: Several articles on securities and commercial litigation.
Personal: JD, St. John's University (editor of law review), 1978. BA, Boston College, 1975. Nation's Top Ten Trial Lawyers 1997 (National Law Journal).

Who's Who in American Law. Faculty member in the 'Business Litigation' video series produced by the American Bar Association, Practising Law Institute and the National Institute of Trial Advocacy. Faculty member in numerous seminars and programs sponsored by the Practising Law Institute on trial practice and procedures and negotiation techniques.

ORTNER, Charles
Proskauer Rose LLP, New York
212 969 3990
cortner@proskauer.com
Recommended in Media & Entertainment
Practice Areas: Represents many of the leading institutions and creative and business leaders of the music industry in virtually every area, including copyright, trademark, enforcement of personal services contracts, rights of privacy and publicity, libel, unfair competition, personal matters, employment disputes, contract and royalty disputes and general corporate and commercial matters. He also serves as advisor on business and strategic planning for owners and senior executives of leading music industry institutions. Among the recording artists, record producers and songwriters he has represented in litigation and related matters are Madonna, Michael Jackson, Shania Twain, Lauryn Hill, Whitney Houston, Jon Bon Jovi, Kenny "Babyface" Edmonds, Sean "P. Diddy" Combs, Trent Reznor and Nine Inch Nails, Sting, Cyndi Lauper, Collective Soul, Bonnie Raitt, Matchbox 20, Rob Thomas, Phil Ramone and Rick Rubin. Among the music industry entrepreneurs Mr Ortner has represented are Chris Blackwell, Clive Calder, Jimmy Iovine, and Antonio "L.A." Reid. He represents many music companies and labels, including BMG, EMI, Warner Bros. Records, Warner/Chappell Music and Wind-Up Records.
Career: He also represents The National Academy of Recording Arts and Sciences (the GRAMMY® organization), and serves as its National Legal Counsel.
Personal: Brooklyn Law School, JD, 1971. Washington University, AB, 1967.

OSTRAGER, Barry R
Simpson Thacher & Bartlett LLP,
New York 212 455 2655
bostrager@stblaw.com
Recommended in Insurance, Litigation
Practice Areas: Barry R Ostrager is a senior litigation Partner and Co-Head of the Litigation Department. He has tried dozens of cases and argued scores of appeals throughout the country and has been prominently involved in many high-profile cases. He successfully represented Travelers in a $5 billion arbitration with ACandS, J.P. Morgan Chase in a breach of guarantee contract action against Motorola in which J.P. Morgan

Chase obtained a $370 million verdict against Motorola, and Andersen Consulting against a $14 billion claim by Arthur Andersen in connection with Andersen Consulting's successful bid to win a separation without cost from the Andersen Worldwide organization in the largest ICC arbitration in history. He was lead trial counsel for Swiss Re in the highly publicized insurance coverage dispute involving the World Trade Center tragedy, which resulted in a unanimous jury verdict in favor of Swiss Re.

Prof. Memberships: Association of the Bar of the City of New York, American Bar Association, American Law Institute.

Career: Member of the firm since 1979. He is a member of the firm's Executive Committee.

Publications: Co-author: 'Handbook on Insurance Coverage Disputes' (Aspen Publications, 12th ed 2004); co-author: 'Modern Reinsurance Law and Practice' (Glasser Publications, 2nd ed, 2000).

Personal: BA (1968) and MA (1973), City College of the City University of New York. JD (1972) New York University School of Law.

PAGEL SEREBRANSKY, Elizabeth
Debevoise & Plimpton LLP, New York
212 909 6000
Recommended in Employee Benefits

PAGET, David
Sive Paget & Riesel PC, New York
212 421 2150
dpaget@sprlaw.com
Recommended in Environment

Practice Areas: David Paget is a 1964 honors graduate of New York University Law School and editor of the Law Review. He has extensive experience in environmental law and related litigation, particularly in preparing and processing environmental impact statements and permits pursuant to the Clear Air Act, the Clean Water Act, the National Environmental Policy Act, and the Natural Historic Preservation Act. David began litigating environmental cases in the early 1970s, following his service as an Assistant United States Attorney for the Southern District of New York.

Career: Among the many projects for which David has been a central participant in the preparation of environmental impact statements and in obtaining related permits and approvals, and for which he has successfully defended legal challenges, are: the Hudson River Park, the expansion of the United States Tennis Association facilities in New York City; major residential and mixed use developments, including Battery Park City, Donald Trump's Riverside South, the Davids Island project, and the Tuxedo Reserve project. Currently, he is working on the expansion of the Javits Convention Center, a new stadium for the New York Yankees, a new basketball arena and mixed-use development for

Forest City Ratner, and major waterfront park and development projects.

PALEY, Alan
Debevoise & Plimpton LLP, New York
212 909 6000
Recommended in Corporate/M&A

PANOVKA, Robin
Wachtell, Lipton, Rosen & Katz, New York 212 403 1352
rpanovka@wlrk.com
Recommended in Real Estate

Practice Areas: Specializes in real estate M&A, including mergers and acquisitions of REITs and other real estate operating and service companies, the formation and investment activity of real estate opportunity funds, strategic joint ventures and other significant transactions, both in the United States and in cross-border transactions. Examples of recent or ongoing representations include representation of the Silverstein Properties group in connection with the redevelopment of the World Trade Center; representation of Taubman Centers, Inc. in connection with Simon Property Group's unsolicited offer; representation of Lend Lease in the sale of its US businesses; representation of Hometown in the acquisition of the Chateau REIT, and representation of Apollo Real Estate Advisors in connection with the structuring of various investment vehicles.

Prof. Memberships: Co-Chair, Advisory Board, The REIT Center for the Study of Public Real Estate Operating Companies, New York University; Member of the Board of Visitors, Duke University School of Law, 2001; Member, Advisory Board: New York University Real Estate Institute; Member of the State Bar of Georgia, New York State and American Bar Associations.

Career: Partner at Wachtell, Lipton, Rosen & Katz.

Publications: Author or Co-author, 'REIT Takeovers and Governance', Real Estate Securities Weekly, December 1, 2003; 'Taking REITs Private: A potential win-win for all parties', Real Estate Securities Daily, December 2, 2003; 'Criticism of REITs goes too far - Selling Out or Merging Isn't Always Best for Shareholders', 'Real Estate Issues', Winter 2000/01; 'Taking REITs Private', 'Real Estate Issues', Summer 2000; and 'Public Real Estate Companies Advantages Will Overpower the REIT Bear Market', 'Real Estate Issues', Winter 1999. Co-author, 'REIT M&A Transactions - Peculiarities and Complications', 'The Business Lawyer', February 2000; 'REITs and Rights Plans', 'Property', Winter 2000; 'The 'up' Factor in UPREIT Change of Control Transactions', 'The REIT Report', Spring 1998; 'REIT Takeovers — Novel Issues Raised by Excess Share Provisions and UPREIT Structures', 'The M&A Lawyer', October 1997; 'Will REIT Takeovers Take Off?', 'CPN's Real Estate

Financial Review', Summer 1997; 'REIT Mergers and Acquisitions and Takeover Preparedness: Poison Pills and Excess Shares', 'The REIT Report', Autumn 1995; and 'REIT Mergers and Acquisitions: Structuring Transactions, Protecting Deals and Responding to Unsolicited Offers', 'The REIT Report', Spring 1996; senior editor, 'Alaska Law Review' 1984-86; Member, Duke Moot Court Board, 1984-86.

Personal: Graduated cum laude from Cornell University (bachelor's degree) and with honors from Duke University (JD).

PANTALEO, Peter
Simpson Thacher & Bartlett LLP, New York 212 455 2000
ppantaleo@stblaw.com
Recommended in Bankruptcy

Practice Areas: Partner at Simpson Thacher & Bartlett LLP specialising in bankruptcy and restructuring. Has been lead lawyer on behalf of bank syndicates and other major investors in some of the largest most complex bankruptcies, including NRG Energy, Inc., Adelphia Communications Inc., Sunbeam, Inc., Dade Behring, Inc., LTV Corporation, Lomas Financial Corporation, Mariner Health Group, Burlington Industries, and in and out of court workouts in a variety of industries, including telecommunication, energy, textile and retail. Clients include most major financial institutions in the restructuring community, including JP Morgan Chase, Deutsche Bank, Wachovia Securities, Credit Suiss First Boston and ABN Amro.

Career: Joined Simpson Thacher as a Partner in October, 2001. Formerly a member of O'Melveny & Myers LLP (Head of its Restructuring Practice and Co-Head of its Finance Practice).

Publications: Recent articles include 'Unexpired Real and Personal Property Leases in Bankruptcy', Practising Law Institute (2001); 'Reorganization Value', The Business Lawyer, Vol. 51, No.2 (1996); 'Rethinking the Role of Recourse in the Sale of Financial Assets', The Business Lawyer, Vol. 52, No.1 (1996). Guest lecturer on Bankrupty Topics at Duke Law School and Cornell Business School.

Personal: BA, Columbia College, 1978; JD, NYU School of Law, 1982.

PARKER, C Allen
Cravath, Swaine & Moore LLP, New York 212 474 1765
aparker@cravath.com
Recommended in Banking & Finance

Practice Areas: Extensive experience in syndicated loan transactions, primarily in the context of acquisition financings and leveraged recapitalizations. Has served as the firm's Managing Partner, corporate.

Prof. Memberships: NYSBA; ABCNY.

Clerkship: Hon. Amalya Kearse (US Court of Appeals for the Second Circuit).

Career: Partner since 1990.

Personal: Columbia Law School (JD, magna cum laude, 1983); University of Chicago (MA, 1980); Duke University (BA, magna cum laude, 1977).

PAUL, Deborah L
Wachtell, Lipton, Rosen & Katz, New York 212 403 1300
dlpaul@wlrk.com
Recommended in Tax

Practice Areas: Specializes in the tax aspects of corporate transactions, including mergers and acquisitions, joint ventures, spinoffs and financial instruments; has been the principal tax lawyer on numerous domestic and cross-border transactions in a wide array of industries, including telecommunications, oil and gas, food, defense and energy.

Prof. Memberships: Active Member of the Executive Committee of the Tax Section of the New York State Bar Association (principal co-author of 2005 Circular 230 report and principal author of 2004 continuity of proprietary interest reports).

Career: Partner at Wachtell, Lipton, Rosen & Katz since 2001. Prior to joining the firm in 1997, was an Assistant Professor at the Benjamin N. Cardozo School of Law (1995-97) and an Acting Assistant Professor at New York University School of Law (1994-95). Clerked for Chancellor William T Allen of the Court of Chancery of the State of Delaware (1989-90).

Publications: The Use of Disregarded Entities and Pass-Throughs in Corporate Transactions (with Richard Gipstein) (in USC 56th Institute on Federal Taxation 2004); Tax-Free M&A Transactions (with Lewis Steinberg) (in NYU 62nd Institute on Federal Taxation 2004); Triple Taxation (in The Tax Lawyer 2003); Contingency and the Debt/Equity Continuum (with Peter Canellos) (in the Journal of Taxation of Financial Products 2002); United Dominion: Implications for Attribute Reduction (in Tax Notes 2002); The Sources of Tax Complexity: How Much Simplicity Can Fundamental Tax Reform Achieve? (in the North Carolina Law Review 1997).

Personal: Graduated from Harvard University in 1986 (AB), from Harvard Law School in 1989 (JD) and from New York University School of Law in 1994 (LLM in taxation).

PAUL, Marcia B
Davis Wright Tremaine LLP, New York
212 603 6427
marciapaul@dwt.com
Recommended in Media & Entertainment

Practice Areas: Partner, media and IP litigation. Representative experience includes litigation and counseling clients in copyright, trademark, libel, advertising and related intellectual property matters. Representative clients include

Paramount Pictures, Atari Inc., Simon & Schuster, PRIMEDIA Inc., Estate of J.R.R. Tolkien, Miramax Films, British Broadcasting Corporation, Lions Gate Entertainment, MTV Networks and Village Voice Media.
Prof. Memberships: Federal Bar Council; Association of the Bar of the City of New York.
Career: Joined firm via merger, 2003. Partner, Kay & Boose, 1984-2003. Greenbaum, Wolff & Ernst, 1977-82. Recipient, Professionalism Award (Second Circuit), 2002.
Personal: JD, Columbia University, 1972. BA, Barnard College, 1969.

PEARLSTEIN, Debra J
Weil, Gotshal & Manges LLP, New York
212 310 8686
debra.pearlstein@weil.com
Recommended in Antitrust
Practice Areas: Antitrust/competition; litigation/regulatory.
Career: Extensive experience in complex private antitrust litigation (including concurrent federal/state class actions), lawsuits brought by federal antitrust agencies, and merger and other counseling. Litigated on behalf of clients including American Airlines, United HealthCare, MasterCard, Applera, Cree, and Matsushita. Provided merger and other counseling to GE Capital, Texas Instruments, Reader's Digest, Sotheby's, Home Depot, Applied Biosystems, Hicks, Muse, Tate & Furst (and its portfolio companies), Fiserv. Representative cases: Applera Corp. v MJ Research, United States v AMR Corp., and Reyn's Pasta Bella v MasterCard International.
Personal: Princeton University, MPAFF; New York University, JD; Williams College, BA.

PEARSON, Nick
Edwards & Angell, New York
212 308 4411
Recommended in Insurance

PEASLEE, James M
Cleary Gottlieb Steen & Hamilton LLP, New York 212 225 2440
jpeaslee@cgsh.com
Recommended in Tax
Practice Areas: US tax matters, with an emphasis on financial products and structured finance.
Prof. Memberships: Member of the Executive Committee of the New York State Bar Association's Tax Section and Chair of the Tax Section from 1991-92.
Career: Joined firm, 1976; became Partner, 1984. LLM, New York University School of Law (1979); JD, cum laude, Harvard Law School (1976); MA, BA economics, magna cum laude, Yale University (1973).
Publications: Co-author of 'Federal Income Taxation of Securitization Transactions' (third edition - www.securitizationtax.com) and author of many articles on tax subjects.

PECKAR, Robert S
Peckar & Abramson PC, New York
212 382 0909
rpeckar@pecklaw.com
Recommended in Construction
Practice Areas: Is a recognized leader among the Construction Bar. While he has obtained very substantial recoveries in litigation and arbitration, he has gained recognition for formulating creative, multimillion dollar settlements in the litigation of complex multiparty construction disputes and the implementation of alternative dispute resolution mechanisms to achieve expeditious solutions to complicated construction disputes. Is one of the nation's leading advocates for the appropriate use of Alternative Dispute Resolution (ADR) procedures and serves as an arbitrator in complex international arbitrations.
Prof. Memberships: Is a Fellow of the American College of Construction Lawyers; Member of the New Jersey State Bar Association (Chairman, Public Contract Law Section, 1979-81; Chairman, Effective Dispute Resolution Committee, 1990-91; Member, New Jersey Supreme Court Committee on Dispute Resolution, 1991-95) as well as a Member of the American Bar Association (New Jersey State Chairman, Section on Public Contract Law, Litigation Section, 1979-83; Region II Chairman 1984-88). Admitted to practice in New York and New Jersey.
Career: Founding Partner. Serves as General Counsel Emeritus to the New York Building Congress, where he was general counsel for over 15 years. He also serves as General Counsel to the Building Contractors Association of New Jersey, the New York City Building Trades Employers Association and the National Construction Financial Management Association (CFMA).
Publications: Throughout his career in construction law, has participated as a guest lecturer to local and national construction industry groups as well as in continuing legal education programs and has otherwise devoted substantial time and effort in service to the construction industry. An author of many articles on construction law topics, he is also a contributing author in several construction law textbooks and the author of 'New Jersey Practice: Construction Law'. National publications such as ENR, cite him frequently.
Personal: Is a graduate of Rutgers University in New Jersey and Columbia University Law School in New York.

PEDOWITZ, Lawrence B
Wachtell, Lipton, Rosen & Katz, New York 212 403 1231
lbpedowitz@wlrk.com
Recommended in Litigation
Practice Areas: Specializes in corporate litigation, regulatory and white collar criminal matters.

Prof. Memberships: Has served on several committees of the Association of the Bar of the City of New York, including: the Criminal Law, Federal Legislation and Federal Courts Committees. In addition, is a Vice Chairman and Director of the Legal Aid Society, a Director and Executive Committee Member of the Brennan Center at New York University Law School, and a Co-Founder of New York Law Firms for the Homeless, which is the financial support organization for the New York Coalition for the Homeless.
Career: Partner at Wachtell, Lipton, Rosen & Katz for over 20 years. Prior to joining the firm, had significant experience as law clerk to Second Circuit Court of Appeals Chief Judge Henry J Friendly (1972-73) and to United States Supreme Court Justice William J Brennan (1973-74). Also served as Chief Appellate Attorney (1976-78) and Chief of the Criminal Division (1982-84) in the United States Attorney's Office for the Southern District of New York.
Publications: Has lectured for numerous continuing education programs, including programs sponsored by the American Bar Association, 'New York Law Journal', Practicing Law Institute, Federal Bar Council, Securities Industry Association and Hofstra Trial Advocacy Program. Has also taught Trial Practice at New York University Law School.
Personal: Graduated summa cum laude from Union College in 1969 (BA) and from New York University Law School in 1972 (JD), where he served as editor in chief of the 'Law Review' and was a Root-Tilden Scholar for the Second Circuit.

PENZER, Michèle
Latham & Watkins LLP, New York
212 906 1200
Recommended in Projects

PHILLIPS, Greer L
Kirkland & Ellis LLP, New York
212 446 4955
gphillips@kirkland.com
Recommended in Tax
Practice Areas: Mr Phillips plans and structures the tax aspects of complex domestic and cross-border transactions, including mergers, acquisitions and buyouts, joint ventures, bankruptcy and workout transactions and financial instruments. He also plans and structures a wide variety of domestic and cross-border acquisitions and recapitalizations involving strategic and financial buyers for European, Asian, and Latin American clients and for United States clients in cross-border or other complex transactions. He has structured domestic and cross-border joint ventures in the communications, entertainment, aerospace, transportation, chemical, and securities industries.
Personal: Princeton University, AB, 1979. Harvard Law School, JD, 1982.

PHILLIPS IV, Barnet
Skadden, Arps, Slate, Meagher & Flom LLP & Affiliates, New York
212 735 2220
bphillip@skadden.com
Recommended in Tax
Practice Areas: Specialises in tax aspects of corporate mergers, acquisitions, divestitures, leveraged buyouts, restructuring and recapitalisations and the structuring of business organisations and investment vehicles, including REITs, Regulated Investment Companies, investment partnerships and exchange funds.
Career: LLM, New York University, 1977 (graduate editor, Tax Law Review); JD, Fordham Law School, 1973 (associate editor, Fordham Law Review); BA, Yale University 1970.
Publications: Co-author, 'Structuring Corporate Acquisitions-Tax Aspects', Tax Management Inc., (1999).

PIERCE, Morton A
Dewey Ballantine LLP, New York
212 259 6640
mpierce@deweyballantine.com
Recommended in Corporate/M&A
Practice Areas: Morton Pierce is Co-Chairman of the firm's Management and Executive Committees, global Chairman of the firm's Corporate Department and has been Chairman of the firm's Mergers and Acquisitions Group since 1991. The group consists of more than 60 lawyers based in New York, Washington DC, Los Angeles, East Palo Alto, Houston, Austin, London, Frankfurt, Milan, Rome and Central Europe. Mr Pierce has participated in numerous merger and acquisition matters and related financings. He has represented acquirers, targets, investment bankers and investors in numerous acquisitions, including the Omnicare acquisition of NCS Healthcare, the Fortis acquisition of American Bankers, the Starwood acquisition of ITT, The Walt Disney Company acquisition of Capital Cities/ABC, the Wells Fargo acquisition of First Interstate Bank and the HCA acquisition of Healthtrust. Mr Pierce also has extensive experience in cross-border merger and acquisition transactions. These include the Zimmer Holdings acquisition of Centerpulse AG, the Burns Philp acquisition of Goodman Fielder, the Guinness/GrandMet merger, the Luxottica Group S.p.A. acquisition of The United States Shoe Corporation, the Eridania Beghin-Say S.A. acquisition of American Maize-Products Company and the Cable & Wireless acquisition of NYNEX CableComms.
Prof. Memberships: American Bar Association; Association of the Bar of the City of New York.
Career: Partner, Dewey Ballantine since 1986. Co-Chairman of the firm's Management and Executive Committees since 2002, global Chairman of the firm's Corporate Department since 1998

and Chairman of the firm's Mergers and Acquisitions Group since 1991.

Personal: Born June 25, 1948. Oxford University, 1974-75; JD, University of Pennsylvania Law School, 1974; BA, Yale University, 1970.

PIERSON, George J
Peckar & Abramson PC, New York
212 382 0909
gpierson@pecklaw.com
Recommended in Construction

Practice Areas: Mr Pierson's practice focuses primarily on the resolution of significant international construction disputes. His experience spans many construction sectors including projects in the energy, oil and gas, petrochemical, infrastructure, mining, commercial and pharmaceutical industries. He has been engaged on projects on six continents where his expertise has led to multi-million dollar recoveries for his clients. He is an accomplished trial lawyer and regularly acts for clients on international arbitrations matters. He also has extensive experience in construction transactions, construction project structuring and contract drafting and negotiation.

Prof. Memberships: Admitted to practice before federal and state courts in and is a Member of the Bars of New York, California, Pennsylvania and New Jersey. Mr Pierson is also a Member of the Steering Committee for the International Contracting Division of the American Bar Association's Forum on the Construction Industry and is the editor of publications for the International Bar Association, International Construction Projects Committee.

Career: Formerly practiced as an engineer obtaining his Professional Engineers License, Mr Pierson was also Executive Vice President/Legal Director of Kvaerner E&C, a global engineering and construction company. He is now Partner and Director of Peckar & Abramson's International Construction Practice Group.

Publications: Mr Pierson is a regular speaker at national contruction conferences and industry forums and lectures to private groups regularly on dispute resolution techniques. He has also been a contributing author to Construction.com's 'Ask the Expert' column.

Personal: Mr Pierson received his Bachelor of Sciences summa cum laude in Civil Engineering from Bucknell University. He earned a Master of Sciences from the University of California at Berkeley in Civil Engineering, Department of Structural Engineering and Structural Mechanics. He graduated cum laude from Harvard Law School and received his MBA with Honors from St Mary's College of California.

PIETRZAK, Robert
Sidley Austin Brown & Wood LLP,
New York 212 839 5537
rpietrzak@sidley.com
Recommended in Litigation

Practice Areas: Robert Pietrzak is a member of the firm's Executive Committee and Co-Head of the NY Litigation Practice. He focuses on the litigation of commercial disputes for domestic and overseas financial institutions, including the defense of securities industry practices in multi-defendant class actions, the handling of litigation relating to mergers and acquisitions, and in appeals on behalf of the Securities Industry Association. He has been counsel in regulatory proceedings and civil actions involving commercial contracts, public offerings, investment companies, investment partnerships, takeovers, bond validations, employment, antitrust, probate, energy and other major commercial disputes.

Career: Harvard Law School (LLB, 1965) University of Washington (BS, 1962) Bar Admission: New York, 1966.

PINOVER, Eugene
Willkie Farr & Gallagher LLP, New York
212 728 8254
epinover@willkie.com
Recommended in Real Estate

Practice Areas: Partner and Chair of the Real Estate Department, specializing in representing domestic and foreign real estate developers and institutional clients in acquisitions, sales, restructuring and sophisticated financings and development projects throughout the United States. Practice also includes representing public real investment trusts, underwriters and investors in equity offerings and debt securitizations. Significant matters in 2004 include representation of Simon Property Group in its $3.5 billion acquisition of Chelsea Property Group, Paramount Group in its $355 million sale of New York's 180 Maiden Lane to the Moinian Group, and The Mill's Corporation in its $1.03 billion acquisition of a 50% interest in General Motors Asset Management's regional nine-mall property portfolio. Also in 2004, Mr Pinover advised Paramount Group on its $426.5 million acquisition of 1540 Broadway and the sellers in the $430.8 million acquisition of the Mall of Louisiana and Riverchase Mall by General Growth Properties.

Prof. Memberships: Member of the Real Estate Advisory Board of Dartmouth College and associate member of the Association of Foreign Investors in Real Estate (AFIRE). Member of the Association of the Bar of the City of New York, the American Bar Association, the International Council of Shopping Centers, and the New York Advisory Board of Chicago Title Insurance Company. Serves as a Director of Trinity School, Cardigan Mountain School, Ballet Hispanico and was elected Fellow of the American College of Real Estate Lawyers.

Career: Admitted to the Bar of the State of New York.

Publications: Writings have been published extensively in the New York Law Journal, the Real Estate Finance Journal, and AFIRE News.

Personal: Received a JD (cum laude) from New York University School of Law in 1973 and a BA (cum laude) from Dartmouth College in 1969.

PLEVAN, Bettina
Proskauer Rose LLP, New York
212 969 3065
bplevan@proskauer.com
Recommended in Employment

Practice Areas: Represents a wide range of industries handling both single plaintiff and class action lawsuits involving issues of discrimination, harassment, employee benefits, alleged breaches of Fiduciary duty, COBRA violations, and termination of retiree benefits. She has extensive experience counseling employers on litigation avoidance and sexual harassment investigations and training management employees in these areas. Has successfully tried many jury and non-jury cases in New York and elsewhere in the US.

Prof. Memberships: President of the Association of the Bar of the City of New York and recently completed a two-year term as President of the Federal Bar Council. She is also a Member of the American Law Institute, and serves as Chair of the Second Circuit Judicial Conference.

Career: A Fellow of the American College of Trial Lawyers. Has argued more than 50 appeals in state and federal courts and is a member of the American Academy of Appellate Lawyers.

Personal: Graduated from Wellesley College and is a magna cum laude graduate of Boston University Law School where she was an editor of the 'Law Review'.

PLUM, Bernard
Proskauer Rose LLP, New York
212 969 3070
bplum@proskauer.com
Recommended in Employment

Practice Areas: A Partner in Proskauer's Labor and Employment Law Department, his practice concentrates on collective bargaining, arbitration, and labor and employment litigation in the newspaper, entertainment, utilities, financial services, and airline industries. He has served as chief spokesperson in a wide variety of collective bargaining situations, and has litigated in the state and federal courts of New York, New Jersey, Connecticut, Illinois and California.

Career: Among the employers he represents are The New York Times Co., Dow Jones, The League of American Theaters & Producers, The New York City Ballet, PPL, Inc., TWA, and HSBC. Bernie represented Metro-North and the Long Island Railroad in their precedent-setting suit to enjoin sympathy strikes by

railroad workers in support of striking Eastern Airlines Machinists. He has also represented many other employers faced with unlawful work stoppages.

Personal: Columbia University School of Law, JD, 1979; notes editor, 'Columbia Law Review', 1978-79; Columbia University, MPHIL, 1976; Columbia University, MA, 1974; New York University, BA, cum laude, 1973.

POLEVOY, Martin D
DLA Piper Rudnick Gray Cary US LLP,
New York 212 835 6100
martin.polevoy@dlapiper.com
Recommended in Real Estate

Practice Areas: Real estate; acquisitions, development, leasing, financing, joint ventures.

Career: Practice includes representation of well known New York, national and international owners, developers, investors and institutions. Currently acting as counsel in many high profile transactions, including redevelopment of the World Trade Center site in New York. A frequent participant as program chair and speaker, in continuing legal education programs and has written extensively on various aspects of real estate law. He is a past governor of the American College of Real Estate Lawyers and member of the Anglo-American Real Property Institute.

Personal: LLB, University of Pennsylvania; AB, Colgate University.

POLLACK, Martin
Weil, Gotshal & Manges LLP, New York
212 310 8461
martin.pollack@weil.com
Recommended in Tax

Practice Areas: Tax: nationally-recognized federal income tax advisor.

Career: Pollack advises extensively regarding the tax aspects of private equity and merger and acquisition transactions, the formation and operation of private equity funds and other ventures, bankruptcy and insolvency, leasing transactions, and technology intensive enterprises. Pollack lectures frequently at tax seminars, chairs an ABA Tax Section subcommittee, is co-author of a Little, Brown treatise on the tax considerations pertaining to partnership buy/sell agreements, and has served as an adjunct faculty member at New York University School of Law.

Personal: New York University, LLM; University of Pennsylvania, JD; Johns Hopkins University, BA.

POMERANTZ, Alan J
Weil, Gotshal & Manges LLP, New York
212 310 8402
alan.pomerantz@weil.com
Recommended in Real Estate

Practice Areas: Corporate, private equity, real estate transactions/finance.

Career: Pomerantz counsels and supervises some of the most complex private equity joint ventures, project developments, acquisitions, public and private

financings, and restructurings. Has been selected by the 'International Financial Law Review' for inclusion in its 'Guide to the World's Leading Lawyers'; 'Law Business Research' in its 'International Who's Who of Business Lawyers'; and 'Chambers Global' publication 'The World's Leading Lawyers.' Served on National Realty Committee's Commercial Capital Consortium and Capital Policy Advisory Committees; counsel to the Real Estate Lenders Association.
Personal: New York University, JD; City College of New York, BA.

POMERANTZ, Mark
Paul, Weiss, Rifkind, Wharton & Garrison LLP, New York 212 373 3010
mpomerantz@paulweiss.com
Recommended in Litigation
Practice Areas: Partner in the Litigation Department. Nationally known trial lawyer and senior litigator, with extensive public and private experience in criminal and regulatory matters. Has tried cases on behalf of individuals before juries and arbitration panels. Has substantial appellate experience, arguing dozens of appeals before courts throughout the country. Has represented some of the largest companies in the US in investigations undertaken by the US Department of Justice, the Securities and Exchange Commission, and various state and local prosecutors. Fellow of the American College of Trial Lawyers. Selected for 2005 edition of 'The Best Lawyers in America'.

PORT, Gail
Proskauer Rose LLP, New York
212 969 3243
gport@proskauer.com
Recommended in Environment
Practice Areas: Manages Proskauer Rose LLP's Environmental Practice Group, based in the New York office. She has been practicing environmental law and litigation for over 25 years. Her practice at Proskauer is concentrated in counseling clients respecting environmental risks in mergers and acquisitions and real estate transactions and financings, environmental compliance and remediation, environmental litigation and administrative proceedings and land use.
Prof. Memberships: A past Chair of the New York State Bar Association's Environmental Law Section, the former Chair of the Environmental Law Committee of the Association of the Bar of the City of New York, and a member of the Boards of Directors of the prestigious not-for-profit organizations Environmental Advocates and the New York League of Conservation Voters Education Fund.
Career: Prior to joining the firm she served as Deputy General Counsel (and Acting General Counsel) and the chief environmental advisor to the New York State Urban Development Corporation, where she was involved in the environ-

mental law aspects of high visibility large-scale land use and development projects and related financing transactions.
Personal: New York Law School, JD, magna cum laude, 1976 articles editor, New York Law School Law Review, 1974-76. State University of New York at Cortland, BS, 1973.

POSEN, Richard
Willkie Farr & Gallagher LLP, New York
212 728 8255
rposen@willkie.com
Recommended in Litigation
Practice Areas: Partner in the Litigation Department and a member of the firm's Executive Committee. Specializes in securities litigation and mergers and acquisitions. Has significant experience representing Boards of Directors on corporate governance issues and special committees in internal investigations. Significant matters in 2004 include representation of Simon Property Group Inc., the nation's largest owner of shopping malls, in its acquisition of Chelsea Property Group Inc., the nation's largest owner of outlet malls, for $3.5 billion in cash and stock. Recently represented Lehman Brothers, Goldman Sachs, UBS and CSFB in the settlement of the Worldcom securities litigation. In 2003, he represented Simon in its tender offer for Taubman Centers, Inc. and in its $5.8 billion acquisition of Rodamco North America.
Prof. Memberships: Member of the Association of the Bar of the City of New York and the Federal Bar Council. Former Director of Ralphs Supermarkets and Ralphs Grocery Company (1992-94).
Career: Admitted to the New York State Bar; various district courts including the United States District Court for the Southern District of New York; the United States Courts of Appeal for the First, Second, Third, Fifth, Ninth, and Eleventh Circuits; and the United States Supreme Court. Currently serves as Mediator in the US District Court for the Southern District of New York Mediation Program (since 1993).
Personal: Received a JD from New York University School of Law in 1975 and a BA from Johns Hopkins University in 1972.

POSTNER, William
Postner & Rubin, New York
212 269 2510
Recommended in Construction

POTTER, Nicholas
Debevoise & Plimpton LLP, New York
212 909 6000
Recommended in Insurance

PRINCE, Kenneth S
Shearman & Sterling LLP, New York
212 848 4139
kprince@shearman.com
Recommended in Antitrust

Practice Areas: Practice Group Leader of Shearman & Sterling's global Antitrust Group. Advises clients on the antitrust implications of mergers and acquisitions, joint ventures, horizontal arrangements among competitors, dominant firm conduct, intellectual property licensing agreements and pricing arrangements. Maintains an active criminal grand jury defense practice. Regularly appears before the United States Department of Justice and the Federal Trade Commission.
Career: Joined Shearman in 1975 and became Partner in 1983. Antitrust Practice Leader 1992-2003 and 2005-present.
Personal: AB, Order of the Coif, University of Pennsylvania (1972); JD, magna cum laude, Boston College Law School (1975); editor, Boston College Law Review.

PROFUSEK, Robert A
Jones Day, New York 212 326 3800
raprofusek@jonesday.com
Recommended in Corporate/M&A
Practice Areas: He is an advisor to substantial businesses, focusing on M&A/takeovers, restructurings, and corporate governance matters, including compensation. He is a frequent speaker regarding corporate takeovers and corporate governance, has authored or co-authored numerous articles, and has testified before Congress and the SEC about takeover and compensation-related matters. Recognized globally as a leading M&A lawyer, he has been featured in national legal publications and listed in Who's Who in America and Who's Who in American Law, among others.

PROUNIS, Othon
Ropes & Gray, New York
212 841 5785
othon.prounis@ropesgray.com
Recommended in Private Equity
Practice Areas: Concentrates in mergers and acquisitions, securities and transactional work, primarily for private equity funds and their portfolio companies. Has extensive experience working in the healthcare, life sciences, and technology sectors, and has represented underwriters, issuers and investors in public and private securities offerings.
Career: New York Bar (1987). Partner, Ropes & Gray (2003). Co-Head, Private Equity Transactions Group of Ropes & Gray.
Personal: JD, Columbia Law School (1986). AB, Columbia College (1983).

PUGLIESE, Frank A
Brown Raysman Millstein Felder & Steiner LLP, New York 212 895 2470
fpugliese@brownraysman.com
Recommended in Intellectual Property
Practice Areas: Mr Pugliese is a Partner in the Technology, Media and Communications Group. His practice involves representing clients in complex technology and intellectual property

related transactions, licensing, e-commerce, outsourcing, technology transfer, and other business transactions. He also counsels clients on IT and IP strategy, acquisitions and disputes. Mr Pugliese represents clients in a wide range of industries, including, technology, financial services, telecommunications, insurance, healthcare, consulting, publishing and media.
Prof. Memberships: Admitted to practice in New York and Connecticut.
Personal: Born 8 March 1966. JD, Fordham University School of Law, 1991; BA (cum laude), New York University, 1988.

PULEO, Frank
Milbank, Tweed, Hadley & McCloy, New York 212 530 5000
Recommended in Banking & Finance

QUINN, James W
Weil, Gotshal & Manges LLP, New York
212 310 8385
james.quinn@weil.com
Recommended in Litigation, Sport
Practice Areas: Litigation; general commercial, sports, arbitration
Career: Mr Quinn chairs Weil Gotshal's global Litigation/Regulatory Practice. An accomplished trial lawyer, Mr Quinn specializes in high stakes commercial disputes. He has practiced in all areas of complex litigation and alternative dispute resolution, with particular emphasis on antitrust, products liability, insurance, sports, entertainment, patent and complex related intellectual property law. Clients call upon him in matters that are high-profile, high-stakes and often international in scope. In his most recent trial victory, Mr Quinn won a complete defense verdict for Procter & Gamble Co. on an $80 million false advertising claim. A few months earlier, he secured a complete defense verdict for ESPN in a $231 million lawsuit brought by Modi Entertainment Network ñ believed to be the largest defense verdict to date in 2004. Mr Quinn also recently led the Weil Gotshal team that secured on appeal a judgment for ExxonMobil exceeding $470 million, believed to be the largest commercial case jury award in Delaware history. General Electric, Disney/ABC and UnitedHealth Group also are among his many complex litigation clients. Among many honors and awards in 2004 and 1993, National Law Journal selected Mr Quinn as one of the 10 top trial lawyers in the US in its annual feature Winning: Successful Strategies from 10 of the Nation's Top Litigators. He was ranked as highly recommended in the 2004/05 edition of the 'Global Counsel Dispute Resolution Handbook', was included in Euromoney's 2004 'Guide to the World's Leading Experts in Commercial Arbitration' and in 'The International Who's Who of Commercial Litigators 2004.'
Personal: Fordham University, LLB; University of Notre Dame, AB (cum laude).

QUINN, Yvonne S
Sullivan & Cromwell LLP, New York
212 558 4000
quinny@sullcrom.com
Recommended in Antitrust

Practice Areas: Coordinates S&C's
Antitrust Practice. Handles a variety of
antitrust and commercial litigation and
advisory work. Regularly counsels entities in connection with proposed acquisitions. Has provided antitrust counsel
in Cerberus's acquisition of Bayer's
blood plasma business, Medco's acquisition of Accredo, John Hancock's acquisition by Manulife and various acquisitions by Goldman Sachs, among others.
Prof. Memberships: ABA; ABCNY (former Chair, Antitrust and Trade Regulation Committee); Federal Bar Council;
NYSBA (Executive Committee,
Antitrust Section).
Career: Partner since 1984.
Personal: University of Illinois (BA,
1973); University of Michigan Law
School (JD, 1976); University of Michigan (MA, economics, 1977).

RABINOWITZ, Stephen S
Fried, Frank, Harris, Shriver & Jacobson
LLP, New York 212 859 8973
stephen.rabinowitz@friedfrank.com
Recommended in Intellectual Property

Practice Areas: Litigation Partner.
Concentrates practice in the field of
patent litigation with an emphasis on
biotechnology patent law. Litigated
patent cases pertaining to recombinant
DNA technology, nucleic acid amplifica-
tion technology, biochemical reagents
such as enzymes and medical diagnostics. Client counseling includes validity,
infringement, patentability and free-
dom-to-operate opinions. Has represented clients in a variety of prosecution
matters before the United States Patent
and Trademark Office.
Prof. Memberships: Member of the
British Society for Immunology, the
American Bar Association, the New York
Intellectual Property Law Association,
the New York State Bar Association and
the Association of the Bar of the City of
New York.
Career: Joined Fried Frank in 2004.
Partner from 2001-03 at Pennie &
Edmonds LLP, and before that an associate at the firm from 1994-2001. Previ-
ously, a pathology resident at the
Brigham and Women's Hospital in
Boston. Prior to residency, performed
research in immunology at the Sir
William Dunn School of Pathology and
Balliol College, University of Oxford.
Completed medical training and intern-
ship at Groote Schuur Hospital in Cape
Town, South Africa. Admitted to the Bar
in New York and to practice before Unit-
ed States District Court for the Eastern
and Southern Districts of New York and
the Northern District of California, the
United States Court of Appeals for the
Federal Circuit and the United States
Patent and Trademark Office.

Personal: Received JD, cum laude, in
1994 from Harvard Law School. Received
MB, ChB, with honours, in 1981 from
the University of Cape Town in South
Africa and DPhil in Immunology from
the University of Oxford in 1990.

RACITI-KNAPP, Melissa
Freshfields Bruckhaus Deringer LLP,
New York 212 277 4000
Recommended in Projects

RADKE, Kirk
Kirkland & Ellis LLP, New York
212 446 4940
kradke@kirkland.com
Recommended in Private Equity

Practice Areas: Primarily involved in
structuring, negotiating and documenting legal aspects of complex business
transactions, including leveraged buyouts, mergers and acquisitions involving
private and public companies, corporate
divestitures, recapitalizations, private
placements and management compensation arrangements. Extensive experience in the formation of leveraged buyout funds.
Personal: Stanford University, BA, 1980,
Phi Beta Kappa awarded 1979. University of Virginia, JD/MBA, 1984, Editorial
Board, Virginia Law Review, Order of
the Coif; William Michael Shermet
Award (MBA).

RAFFERTY, Thomas
Cravath, Swaine & Moore LLP,
New York 212 474 1000
Recommended in Intellectual Property

RAMOS, Carey R
Paul, Weiss, Rifkind, Wharton & Garri-
son LLP, New York 212 373 3240
cramos@paulweiss.com
*Recommended in Media &
Entertainment*

Practice Areas: Partner in the Litigation Department. Co-Chair of the Communications and Technology Group
and the Intellectual Property/Litigation
Group. Has a broad practice that concentrates on intellectual property and
technology matters including litigation,
transactions and counseling. Has represented prominent clients in widely publicized patent, copyright and trademark
actions involving music, motion pictures, computer technology, telecommunications and the fashion industry.
With extensive experience in transactions involving intellectual property
rights in technology and entertainment
media, serves as outside general counsel
to the DVD Forum, the international
association of companies developing
standard formats for digital versatile disc
equipment and media.

RAPISARDI, John
Weil, Gotshal & Manges LLP, New York
212 310 8840
john.rapisardi@weil.com
Recommended in Bankruptcy

Practice Areas: Business finance and
restructuring: represents debtors, credi-

tors' and bondholders' committees,
secured creditors, financial institutions,
investment bankers, and distressed
investment funds, in restructurings/
bankruptcies.
Career: Over 20 years bankruptcy experience, including clerkship for chief
bankruptcy judge of SDNY. Representative cases: Trump Atlantic City Casinos
(Committee); Owens Corning (Financial Institution); Solutia (Committee);
WestPoint Stevens (Debtor); Aladdin
Casino and Hotel (Investor); Stage
Stores (Committee); Mattress Discounters (Committee); Herald Square Center
(Financial Institution); Olympia & York
(Debtor); Drexel Burnham (Debtor);
Ritz Carlton (NY) (Debtor).
Personal: New York University School
of Law, (LLM) (corporate/commercial
law); Pace University, JD; Fordham Uni-
versity, BS.

RAPPAPORT, Linda E
Shearman & Sterling LLP, New York
212 848 7004
lrappaport@shearman.com
Recommended in Employee Benefits

Practice Areas: Partner and Head of
Shearman & Sterling's Global Executive
Compensation and Employee Benefits
Group. Specializes in all aspects of exec-
utive compensation and benefits,
including corporate, securities, employ-
ment and tax laws, and ERISA.
Prof. Memberships: Elected Member,
Shearman Policy Committee; Director
and Advisory Director, New York
Women's Foundation; Member, Adviso-
ry Committee, Practicing Law Institute;
Fellow, American College of Employee
Benefits Counsel, Inc., Member of the
Board of Governors of Mannes College
of Music.
Career: Joined Shearman in 1979 and
became Partner in 1986.
Personal: BA, magna cum laude, Wes-
leyan University (1974); JD, New York
University School of Law (1977).

RASKIN, Kenneth A
White & Case LLP, New York
212 819 8508
kraskin@whitecase.com
Recommended in Employee Benefits

Practice Areas: Executive compensation, benefits and employment law.
Prof. Memberships: New York State Bar
Association, American Bar Association.
Career: Heads the firm's Executive
Compensation, Benefits and Employment Law Practice; provides counsel to
corporations and individuals on the
entire spectrum of employee benefit
concerns, concentrating on executive
compensation and employment law.
Publications: Author of numerous articles and frequent lecturer on executive
compensation and benefits related topics.
Personal: JD, St. John's University
School of Law; MBA, SUNY Binghamton; BA, University of Vermont.

RASKOPF, Robert
White & Case LLP, New York
212 819 8200
rraskopf@whitecase.com
*Recommended in Media &
Entertainment*

Practice Areas: An experienced trial
lawyer across many subject areas, his
regular clients include media, sports,
entertainment and consumer products
companies. His practice combines the
complete range of IP and media subject
areas, and includes long time representation of sports giants such as NFL and
ESPN. He also has an extensive
libel/First Amendment and privacy
practice. Raskopf has been lead counsel
of record in over 60 reported decisions
and is Co-Chair of the firm's NY Litiga-
tion/IP Group and its worldwide IP and
Privacy Practice Groups.
Personal: Boston College (BS '73,
magna cum laude; JD '76, Law Review).

RAYMOND, Robert J
Cleary Gottlieb Steen & Hamilton LLP,
New York 212 225 2994
rraymond@cgsh.com
Recommended in Employee Benefits

Practice Areas: Executive compensation and employee benefits related matters, including executive employment
agreements, equity and non-equity
based compensation, carried interest
and coinvestment plans, particularly in
M&A and private equity and investment
fund contexts, general advice regarding
federal and state statutes and regulations
governing certain fiduciary relationships, tax and securities laws and the
terms and conditions of employment.
He advises financial institutions, private
equity and investment funds and corporate clients on executive compensation
matters and executive hiring and terminations, and Boards of Directors and
individual directors on corporate governance matters.
Career: JD, summa cum laude, New
York Law School (1994).

RAYSMAN, Richard
Brown Raysman Millstein Felder &
Steiner LLP, New York
212 895 2360
rraysman@brownraysman.com
*Recommended in Business Process
Outsourcing: National, Technology*

Practice Areas: Focuses on computer
law, outsourcing and intellectual property issues, including the structuring of
technology transactions. He has also litigated reported cases for the New York
State and federal courts and he has had
over one dozen trials.
Publications: Co-author: 'Emerging
Technologies and the Law: Forms and
Analysis', 'Computer Law: Drafting and
Negotiating Forms and Agreements' and
'Intellectual Property Licensing: Forms
and Analysis'. He also writes a monthly
computer law column for the New York
Law Journal.

Personal: BS, Massachusetts Institute of Technology 1968; JD, Brooklyn Law School 1973; Systems engineer for IBM Corporation for six years.

REARDON, Roy
Simpson Thacher & Bartlett LLP, New York 212 455 2000
rreardon@stblaw.com
Recommended in Litigation
Practice Areas: Roy L Reardon is a member of the firm's Litigation Department. His trial and litigation experience covers a wide gamut of areas, including conducting many jury trials in state and federal trial courts around the country and arguing numerous appeals, including arguments in the US Supreme Court. His areas of particular specialty include commercial law, antitrust, product liability, professional responsibility, and securities law.
Prof. Memberships: Fellow, American College of Trial Lawyers; Association of the Bar of the City of New York; New York State Bar Association; American Bar Association; Nassau County Bar Association; First Department, Disciplinary Committee, Appellate Division, Special Counsel.
Career: Mr Reardon joined Simpson Thacher in 1954. He has been a member of the firm's Executive Committee for many years, as well as Chairman of the Litigation Department.
Personal: Received his JD in 1954 from St John's University Law School, and his BA in 1951 from St Francis College.

REGER, Robert
Thelen Reid & Priest LLP, New York 212 603 2000
Recommended in Energy

REICH, Yaron Z
Cleary Gottlieb Steen & Hamilton LLP, New York 212 225 2540
yreich@cgsh.com
Recommended in Tax
Practice Areas: Taxation including tax controversies and tax aspects of corporate acquisitions, restructurings, financings and international transactions.
Prof. Memberships: Member of the Bar in New York. Admitted to practice before US District Court (SDNY), US Claims Court and Tax Court.
Career: Joined firm, 1979; became Partner, 1986. LLM in taxation, New York University School of Law (1984); JD, special issue editor of 'Columbia Law Review', Columbia University School of Law (1978); BA, summa cum laude, Columbia College (1975).
Publications: Mr Reich has published several significant articles on international tax issues.

REINHOLD, Richard L
Willkie Farr & Gallagher LLP, New York 212 728 8292
rreinhold@willkie.com
Recommended in Tax
Practice Areas: Partner and Chair of

the Tax Department, specializing in domestic and international business tax matters relative to mergers and acquisitions, joint ventures, new financial products, corporate restructurings, and financing transactions.
Prof. Memberships: Former Chair of the New York State Bar Association (Tax Section) and has been a member of its Executive Committee since 1985. Fellow of the American College of Tax Counsel, a Member of the American Bar Association (Corporate Tax Committee), a member of the New York University Tax LLM Advisory Group, and Member of the Tax Forum and Tax Club.
Career: Admitted to the New York and Florida Bars.
Publications: Has lectured and written widely on federal income tax matters.
Personal: Received a JD from the State University of New York at Buffalo School of Law in 1976 and an AB from Cornell University in 1973.

REISMAN, Sharyl
Jones Day, New York
212 326 3405
sareisman@jonesday.com
Recommended in Environment
Practice Areas: She has represented and counseled clients on virtually all aspects of environmental law, with particular emphasis on occupational safety and health counseling and toxic tort litigation. She has significant experience, during pretrial and trial phases, in cases involving reproductive issues, birth defects, and cancer, and specifically in working with experts on the clinical, epidemiology and toxicology aspects of those cases. She also has substantial experience in counseling clients on environmental regulatory matters, as well as safety and health-related issues, including media relations, employee communications, medical monitoring programs, and document retention requirements.

REISNER, Lorin
Debevoise & Plimpton LLP, New York 212 909 6000
Recommended in Media & Entertainment

REISS, John
White & Case LLP, New York
212 819 8200
jreiss@whitecase.com
Recommended in Corporate/M&A, Private Equity
Practice Areas: Global Co-Head of M&A Practice Group. Represents parties in mergers and acquisitions, private equity transactions, restructurings, and Boards of Directors in corporate governance matters. Recent representations: Management Team of Warner Chilcott PLC in its $2.9 billion going private transaction; Dr. Dennis Gillings and Pharma Services Holding in the $1.8 billion acquisition of Quintiles Transnational Corp.; NUI Corp. in its $827 million sale to AGL Resources; and Royal

Ahold in its $660 million sale of BI-LO and Bruno's.
Prof. Memberships: New York State Bar Association.
Career: Partner since 1992. Co-Head of Global M&A Practice Group since 2000. Has been recognized by American Lawyer magazine as 'Dealmaker of the Month' for his representation of Royal Ahold, and was profiled in Corporate Finance magazine in an article entitled, 'Legal Flair Can Make a Difference.'
Publications: Recipient of the Burton Award for Legal Achievement. Regularly contributes to, and is often quoted in, leading business and legal publications covering the M&A and Private Equity markets.
Personal: JD, University of Pennsylvania Law School, 1984; MBA, University of Pennsylvania (Wharton School), 1984; BS, summa cum laude, University of Pennsylvania (Wharton School), 1981.

REYNOLDS, Christopher
Morgan, Lewis & Bockius LLP, New York 212 309 6807
creynolds@morganlewis.com
Recommended in Employment
Practice Areas: Christopher Reynolds is a Partner in the Labor and Employment Law Practice Group. Mr Reynolds's practice includes the litigation of single plaintiff, multi-plaintiff and class action employment matters in federal, state and administrative fora. His practice also involves the counseling of employers in a broad range of matters, including those involving issues of discrimination, equal employment opportunity, global workforce diversity, regulatory compliance and workforce restructuring.
Prof. Memberships: National Employment Law Council; American Employment Law Council; American Bar Association (Labor and Employment Law and Litigation Sections); Association of the Bar of the City of New York.

REYNOLDS, Timothy G
Skadden, Arps, Slate, Meagher & Flom LLP & Affiliates, New York
212 735 2316
treynold@skadden.com
Recommended in Insurance
Practice Areas: Concentrates in matters involving insurance and reinsurance as well as insurance coverage litigation and arbitration. Represents clients in matters involving innovative alternative risk transfer and finite risk insurance products. Extensively represents directors and officers of various corporations with respect to obtaining D&O insurance coverage for a variety of alleged security class actions, and consults frequently with firm clients with respect to D&O placements and renewals and property insurance issues.
Career: JD, Fordham University School of Law, 1980; BA, Fordham College, 1976.

RICE, Gary
Simpson Thacher & Bartlett LLP, New York 212 455 7345
grice@stblaw.com
Recommended in Banking & Finance
Practice Areas: Gary Rice is a Partner in the firm's Corporate Department, regularly advising clients on bank regulation, bank mergers and acquisitions, and bank securities offerings.
Prof. Memberships: Association of the Bar of the City of New York, the Business Law Section of the American Bar Association and the Foreign Banking Lawyers Association.
Career: Mr Rice joined Simpson Thacher in 1985 and became a Partner in 1992. Prior to joining the firm, he served in the legal department of the Federal Reserve of New York from 1982-85.
Publications: 'Federal Deposit Insurance Reform', Banking and Financial Services Report, June 2002; 'U.S. Banking Regulation and the Internet', The Review of Banking and Financial Services, March 2000.
Personal: He received his BA summa cum laude in 1977 from Northeastern University and his JD from Harvard Law School in 1982.

RICE, Glenn
Otterbourg, Steindler, Houston & Rosen, New York
212 661 9100
Recommended in Bankruptcy

RICH, Frederic C
Sullivan & Cromwell LLP, New York 212 558 4000
richf@sullcrom.com
Recommended in Projects
Practice Areas: Head, global Project Finance Practice; Co-Head, Corporate Practice. Focus on natural resource/energy projects, political risk management and capital markets. Oil and gas work: Tengizchevroil expansion financing, BTC pipeline, ACG upstream financing, Mariscal Sucre LNG project (Venezuela) and Kutubu project (Papua New Guinea). Mining projects: Veladero and Alumbrera (Argentina), Bulyanhulu (Tanzania), Batu Hijau (Indonesia), Kumtor (Kyrgyz Republic), and Lihir (Papua New Guinea). Representative clients: BP, ExxonMobil, Panama Canal Authority, Rio Tinto, Sumitomo.
Prof. Memberships: ABA (former Chair, Committee on Privatization); ASIL; IBA.
Career: Partner since 1989.
Personal: Princeton University (AB, 1977); King's College, Cambridge (Keasby Fellow, 1978); University of Virginia Law School (JD, 1981).

RICH, R Bruce
Weil, Gotshal & Manges LLP, New York 212 310 8170
r.bruce.rich@weil.com
Recommended in Media & Entertainment
Practice Areas: Mr Rich's Intellectual

Property Law Practice focuses on the traditional and new media problems of communications industry clients such as book, magazine and newspaper publishers, broadcasters, cable television entities and related trade associations, as well as problems of other significant creators, users and market facilitators of commerce in intellectual property. Mr Rich's specialization spans copyright, music licensing, First Amendment, trademark and antitrust matters. He counsels and litigates cases in these areas.

Career: Mr Rich is a Senior Partner and serves on the firm's Management Committee. He co-chairs the IP & Media Practice, representing, in the world's leading music licensing practice, clients including major broadcast television networks, the Television Music License Committee (representing local television stations), cable television networks such as USA Networks and Lifetime Television, and background music services such as Muzak and DMX. Other significant ongoing IP litigation engagements include representations of Standard & Poor's, eBay and the Copyright Clearance Center. Mr Rich has been lead trial counsel in significant copyright, music licensing, trademark, antitrust and libel cases for clients including Random House, McGraw-Hill, The Walt Disney Company, ABC, CBS, The New York Daily News, The New York Post and Reuters. He has provided expert testimony in court cases and before the US Congress, and is co-author of 'The Business & Legal Guide to Online-Internet Law'.

Personal: University of Pennsylvania Law School, JD (cum laude); Dartmouth College, BA (magna cum laude, Phi Beta Kappa).

RICHARDS, Lee
Richards Spears Kibbe & Orbe,
New York 212 530 1840
Recommended in Litigation

RIESEL, Daniel
Sive Paget & Riesel PC, New York
212 421 2150
driesel@sprlaw.com
Recommended in Environment

Practice Areas: Daniel Riesel is a member of Sive, Paget & Riesel, P.C., a firm with offices in New York City and White Plains, New York. The firm maintains a national practice concentrating on environmental law and litigation.

Prof. Memberships: He is a Lecturer in Law at the Columbia University School of Law, and has been an Adjunct Professor at the Benjamin Cardoza School of Law. For the Annual American Law Institute-American Bar Association, Mr Riesel chairs the Annual Environmental Litigation Course, and is Co-Chair of the annual course in Environmental Law. He served as Chair of the Committee on Environmental Law for the Bar of the City of New York from 1984 to 1987, and chaired the Section on Environ-

mental Law for the New York Bar Association in 1999-2000.

Career: Although Mr Riesel's practice involves all aspects of environmental law, he specializes in litigating environmental issues before State and Federal courts and representing clients before administrative agencies in enforcement, permitting and siting matters. His work includes defense of toxic tort cases, litigation over failed commercial transactions, CERCLA cost recovery matters, and the defense of alleged environmental criminal defendants. Mr Riesel has also been engaged in numerous contested developmental projects assisting developers in land use and environmental matters.

Publications: He has authored numerous articles on litigation and environmental law, including his recent book: Environmental Enforcement: Civil and Criminal.

Personal: Mr Riesel is a 1961 graduate of Columbia Law School and has been engaged in litigation and environmental law since 1970. He served as an Assistant United States Attorney in the Southern District of New York, where he was a founder of the first Environmental Protection Unit in any US Attorney's office. Mr Riesel's clients include numerous Fortune 500 corporations as well as governmental entities that have ranged from the City of New York to the Commonwealth of Puerto Rico.

RINGEL, Dean
Cahill Gordon & Reindel, New York
212 701 3900
Recommended in Media & Entertainment

ROBERTS, Thomas A
Weil, Gotshal & Manges LLP, New York
212 310 8479
thomas.roberts@weil.com
Recommended in Corporate/M&A, Private Equity

Practice Areas: Mr Roberts' practice focuses on domestic and cross-border mergers, acquisitions, divestitures, contested takeovers and private equity matters, while advising Boards of Directors generally and on strategic issues.

Career: Mr Roberts is Chairman of the firm's more than 500-member Corporate Department and is active in representing major foreign and domestic public and private companies, leading domestic private equity funds and investment banks. Mr Roberts' clients include AMR Corporation, Brascan, Capital Z Partners, CSFB Merchant Bank, General Electric Company, Great Lakes Chemical Corporation, Hicks, Muse, Tate & Furst, Lehman Brothers, TH Lee Company, United Health and Vivendi. Recent significant transactions include representing CSFB in its acquisition of Nycomed, representing General Electric with respect to various corporate matters and in numerous acquisition

and divestiture situations (most recently in its $9.5 billion acquisition of Amersham and its offering of Genworth securities), representing UnitedHealth in its $2.7 billion merger with MAMSI and representing Great Lakes Chemical in its $1.75 billion merger with Crompton.

Personal: Mr Roberts has a BA and JD from Georgetown University, where he served on the Georgetown Law Journal. He is a frequent speaker and author on the topics of disclosure and securities issues, mergers and acquisitions, and corporate governance matters. Mr Roberts is a member of the Executive Committee, chairman of the Finance Committee and a member of the Board of Directors of Make-A-Wish Foundation of America. He is also a member of the Executive Committee and Board of Directors of Make-A-Wish Foundation of Metro New York. He is also a member of the Board of Directors of the Memorial Sloan Kettering Cancer Center Prostate Cancer Research Fund, and of the Board of Visitors of the Georgetown Law Center.

ROBFOGEL, Susan S
Nixon Peabody LLP, New York
212 940 3116
srobfogel@nixonpeabody.com
Recommended in Healthcare

Practice Areas: Practice includes extensive experience in preventive labor relations, labor negotiations, employee/executive recruitment and retention policies, substance abuse, supervisory training and human rights matters. Has wide and varied corporate experience in the healthcare industry in general. Has lectured widely on employment/healthcare topics across the country.

Prof. Memberships: Mrs Robfogel has handled cases before all New York State courts, in various federal district courts, the Second Circuit Court of Appeals and the US Supreme Court. Fellow of the College of Labor and Employment Lawyers.

Personal: Cornell Law School, JD; Smith College, BA, cum laude.

ROCK, Neil L
Skadden, Arps, Slate, Meagher & Flom LLP & Affiliates, New York
212 735 3787
nrock@skadden.com
Recommended in Real Estate

Practice Areas: Active in all areas of Skadden's real estate practice, including acquisitions, developments, shopping centers and hotels, leasings, financings, securitized real estate loans, partnerships and joint ventures, workouts and corporate retention projects.

Career: JD, Fordham University School of Law, 1988 (cum laude, Member, Fordham Law Review); BA, Brandeis University, 1985 (cum laude).

ROD, Jonathan
Latham & Watkins LLP, New York
212 906 1200
Recommended in Projects

ROGERS Jr, Theodore O
Sullivan & Cromwell LLP, New York
212 558 4000
rogerst@sullcrom.com
Recommended in Employment

Practice Areas: Manager, Labor and Employment Law Group. Represents employers on wide array of labor and employment issues. Lead counsel in one of the two consolidated cases in which New York State's highest court upheld arbitrability of employment discrimination claims. Also focuses on estates litigation, including will contests, trust accountings, issues of fiduciary responsibility.

Prof. Memberships: Fellow, College of Labor and Employment Lawyers; New York State Bar Association; Association of the Bar of the City of New York; District of Columbia Bar Association.

Career: Partner since 1987.

Publications: Co-author, Employment Litigation in New York (West Group, 1996) and Employment Law Deskbook for Human Resources Professionals (West Group, 2001).

Personal: Harvard University (AB, 1976); Harvard Law School (JD, 1979).

ROHN, Frederick
Sacks Montgomery PC, New York
212 355 4660
Recommended in Construction

ROLFE, Ronald
Cravath, Swaine & Moore LLP,
New York 212 474 1714
rrolfe@cravath.com
Recommended in Antitrust

Practice Areas: Major antitrust and securities cases, SEC and grand jury investigations and a wide range of commercial litigation and arbitrations for US and international clients.

Prof. Memberships: ABA; NYSBA; ABCNY; American Law Institute; Federal Bar Council.

Career: Partner since 1977. Clerkship: Hon. Marvin E. Frankel (US District Court, Southern District of New York).

Personal: Columbia Law School (JD, magna cum laude, 1969; editor, 'Columbia Law Review'); Harvard College (BA, cum laude, 1966). Columbia Law School Dean's Council. President, The Allen-Stevenson School Board of Trustees. Vice President, Lawrenceville School Board of Trustees. De La Salle Academy, Board of Trustees.

ROONEY, William H
Willkie Farr & Gallagher LLP, New York
212 728 8259
wrooney@willkie.com
Recommended in Antitrust

Practice Areas: Partner in the Litigation Department, specializing in complex antitrust litigation, mergers and acquisitions, and civil and criminal antitrust investigations. Antitrust experience includes litigation and counseling in matters under the Sherman Act (contracts in restraint of trade and monopolization), the Clayton Act (mergers and acquisitions), and the Robinson-Patman Act (price discrimination). Appears regularly in federal courts and before the Antitrust Division of the Department of Justice and the Federal Trade Commission.Selected significant matters include: American Express v Visa U.S.A. Inc., et al.; In Re Copper Tubing Litigation; Teva v FDA; In Re Nabumetone Antitrust Litigation; Stock Exchange Antitrust Litigation; Coalition for Level Playing Robinson-Patman litigation; Toys "R" Us antitrust litigation; Teva/Sicor; Teva/Novopharm; CompUSA/Computer City; Mattel/The Pleasant Co.; Loral/Orion; Loral/Skynet; Loral/Lockheed Martin; Mattel/Tyco; Mattel/Fisher Price.

Prof. Memberships: Association of the Bar of the City of New York (immediate past Chair, Committee on Antitrust and Trade Regulation) and the American Bar Association (Section on Antitrust Law).
Career: Admitted to the New York, New Jersey and the District of Columbia Bars.
Personal: Received a postgraduate Diploma in Law from Oxford University (Magdalen College) in 1987; a JD from Yale Law School in 1983, where he was a senior editor of the Yale Law Journal; and a BA (summa cum laude) from the University of Notre Dame in 1980, where he was elected to Phi Beta Kappa.

ROSEN, Arthur R
McDermott Will & Emery, New York
212 547 5596
arosen@mwe.com
Recommended in Tax
Practice Areas: Focuses on tax planning and litigation relating to state and local tax matters for corporations, partnerships and individuals. Chairs firm's state and local Tax Practice.
Career: Formerly Deputy Counsel of New York State Department of Taxation and Finance, and Counsel to the Governor's Temporary Sales Tax Commission and Tax Counsel to the New York State Senate Tax Committee. Has held executive tax management positions at Xerox Corporation and AT&T.
Publications: Editor of monthly newsletter Inside New York Taxes, co-editor of the semi-monthly newsletters, New York Tax Highlights and New York Tax Cases. Original editor-in-chief of CCH's E-Commerce Tax Alert and was monthly tax columnist for the E-Commerce Law Journal. Has written numerous articles that have appeared in publications such as the Journal of Taxation, the Journal of State Taxation, the Journal of Bank Taxation, the State and Local Tax Lawyer, Multistate Tax Analyst, Inc. Magazine, the Assessment Digest, the Journal of New York Taxation, and The Tax Executive.
Personal: Earned JD in 1974 from St. John's University School of Law, and MBA in 1977 from Rensselaer Polytechnic Institute. Earned APC in 1975 and BA in 1971 from New York University.

ROSEN, Burt
Debevoise & Plimpton LLP, New York
212 909 6000
Recommended in Tax

ROSEN, J Philip
Weil, Gotshal & Manges LLP, New York
212 310 8604
philip.rosen@weil.com
Recommended in Real Estate
Practice Areas: Corporate, real estate transactions and finance.
Career: Leading authority in restructuring of property debt. Considered one of the top private equity lawyers in the domestic/international property arena; considered a leading specialist in finance, joint ventures, mergers and acquisitions, real estate investment trusts, and property and debt portfolio acquisitions. Heads the firm's renowned Hospitality and Gaming Practices and co-heads its Middle East practice. Representative clients: Brascan, Starwood Hotels and Resorts, Lehman Brothers, CSFB, Reader's Digest, Comverse Technology, Fortress Investments, Loews/CNA, Estee Lauder, Morgan Stanley, Hypo Bank, Clarity Partners, Milstein Properties, Yeshiva University.
Personal: Georgetown University, JD; Yeshiva University, BA.

ROSEN, Jeffrey
Debevoise & Plimpton LLP, New York
212 909 6000
Recommended in Corporate/M&A

ROSEN, Matthew A
Skadden, Arps, Slate, Meagher & Flom LLP & Affiliates, New York
212 735 2230
mrosen@skadden.com
Recommended in Tax
Practice Areas: Co-Head, Skadden's Tax Group. Represents clients in every aspect of tax work, with particular emphasis on acquisitions, divestitures and restructurings, both domestic and cross-border. Also handles matters involving partnerships of every type, joint ventures and executive compensation. In addition, practice includes the development of financial instruments and financial products. Clients include many significant public and private companies, investment banks and investment funds. Regularly highly placed in professional rankings. Frequent lecturer on a broad variety of topics.
Career: LLM, New York University, 1979 (Memorial Award for Distinction); JD, Boston University, 1976 (cum laude); BA, Swarthmore College, 1973.

ROSEN, Richard
Paul, Weiss, Rifkind, Wharton & Garrison LLP, New York
212 373 3305
rrosen@paulweiss.com
Recommended in Litigation
Practice Areas: Litigation Partner and Co-Chair of Securities, Futures and Derivatives Practice Group. Has exten-

sive experience in civil litgation in the state and federal courts, particularly involving securities, derivatives, M&A and other complex business disputes. Has represented public companies, underwriting syndicates, open and closed-end investment funds and limited partnerships in securities fraud class actions. Defended clients in the two most significant commodity futures manipulation class actions of recent decades. Has authored numerous articles on corporate and securities law issues and frequently speaks at bar association and securities industry conferences. Selected for 2005 edition of 'The Best Lawyers in America'.

ROSEN, Seth
Debevoise & Plimpton LLP, New York
212 909 6000
Recommended in Tax

ROSENBERG, Mark F
Sullivan & Cromwell LLP, New York
212 558 4000
rosenbergm@sullcrom.com
Recommended in Environment
Practice Areas: Coordinator of Environmental Law and Insurance Groups. Extensive litigation/transactional experience in insurance, reinsurance, asbestos, environmental and toxic tort matters, including alter ego, successor liability, fraudulent conveyance, insolvency and bankruptcy issues that often arise in connection therewith. Also has extensive experience in spearheading recoveries of foreign sovereign debt. Has acted as international lead counsel in debt recovery and political risk insurance litigation, and as national counsel in domestic asbestos, environmental and other toxic tort matters.
Prof. Memberships: American Bar Association; New York State Bar Association (Chair, Environmental Committee of the International Section).
Career: Partner since 1993.
Publications: Author of several articles on environmental and related insurance and derivative liability issues.
Personal: Michigan State University (BA, 1977); George Washington Law School (JD, 1980).

ROSENBERG, Robert
Latham & Watkins LLP, New York
212 906 1200
Recommended in Bankruptcy

ROSENBLATT, William
Stroock & Stroock & Lavan LLP, New York 212 806 5400
Recommended in Insurance

ROSENBLUM, Steve A
Wachtell, Lipton, Rosen & Katz, New York 212 403 1221
sarosenblum@wlrk.com
Recommended in Corporate/M&A
Practice Areas: Specializes in mergers and acquisitions, buyouts, joint ventures, restructurings, corporate governance and securities law.

Prof. Memberships: The Association of the Bar of the City of New York; New York State and American Bar Associations.
Career: Partner at Wachtell, Lipton, Rosen & Katz since 1989. Prior to joining the firm in 1983, was a Law Clerk to the Honorable Joseph L Tauro, United States District Court Judge for the District of Massachusetts. Has extensive experience representing major telecommunications companies from creation and initial public offerings, through spin-offs, mergers and acquisitions. His clients include high profile companies in the communications, media, packaging, consumer foods, insurance and hospitality industries. Has also written and participated in panels on a number of topics, including mergers and acquisitions, corporate disclosure, proxy reform and corporate governance.
Personal: Graduated magna cum laude from Harvard College in 1978 (BA) and from Yale Law School in 1982 (JD). While at Harvard, he was a Member of Phi Beta Kappa.

ROSENWASSER, Michael
Vinson & Elkins LLP, New York
212 237 0000
Recommended in Energy

ROSINI, Neil
Franklin, Weinrib, Rudell & Vassallo, New York 212 935 5500
Recommended in Media & Entertainment

ROSNER, David
Kasowitz Benson Torres & Friedman, New York 212 506 1700
Recommended in Bankruptcy

ROSS, Allen
Ross & Cohen, LLP, New York
212 370 1200
Recommended in Construction

ROSS, Barry
Bryan Cave Robinson LLP, New York
212 541 2000
Recommended in Real Estate

ROTH, Andrew B
McDermott Will & Emery, New York
212 547 5543
aroth@mwe.com
Recommended in Healthcare
Practice Areas: Represents health clients on transactional and regulatory matters, including healthcare networks, integrated delivery systems, hospitals, managed care companies and physicians. Practice includes M&As, fraud and abuse, corporate compliance, corporate and medical staff bylaws, and long term healthcare facility representation. Has national practice involving accreditation of graduate medical education programs in academic medical centers and teaching hospitals and Accreditation Council for Graduate Medical Education (ACGME), and accreditation of medical schools by Liai-

son Committee on Medical Education (LCME). Counsels institutions and teaching programs as to compliance with ACGME and Residency Review Committee (RRC) requirements, and medical schools as to compliance with LCME requirements.

Publications: Has been published in legal and health industry journals, including New York Law Journal, Topics in Health Care Financing, and Medical Staff Overview. Author of chapters in following reference works: A Guide to Complying with Stark Physician Self-Referral Rules, and Legal Manual for New York Physicians.

Personal: JD, 1975, Hofstra University School of Law (Member, Hofstra Law Review); BA,1972, State University of New York-Stony Brook (cum laude). Admitted to practice before courts of New York and District of Columbia, US District Courts for Southern and Eastern Districts of New York, and US Supreme Court.

ROTHENBERG, Laraine S
Fried, Frank, Harris, Shriver & Jacobson LLP, New York 212 859 8745
laraine.rothenberg@friedfrank.com
Recommended in Employee Benefits

Practice Areas: Head of the Employee Benefits and Plans, Executive Compensation and Exempt Organizations Department and tax Partner. Ms Rothenberg advises compensation committees, corporations and chief executive officers and other senior management on employment agreements, governance issues, severance protection agreements, stock options, other compensatory equity participation arrangements and benefit plans and the related requirements of the securities and tax laws. She also advises clients in connection with corporate transactions and investment vehicles used by ERISA plans in collaboration with the firm's mergers and acquisitions and asset management practices.

Prof. Memberships: Ms Rothenberg is a Member of the New York State Bar Association's Tax Section and was a Member of its Executive Committee from 1981-89. She was Co-Chair of the following Tax Section committees: Committee on Continuing Legal Education; Subcommittee on Problems of the Profession; and Employee Benefits Committee. She was also Chair of the Tax Section's Exempt Organizations Committee. In addition, Ms Rothenberg was Chair of the Special Committee on Employee Benefits and a Member of the Committee on Taxation of the Association of the Bar of the City of New York. Ms Rothenberg is also a Member of the International Fiscal Association and the International Bar Association. Ms Rothenberg is on the Board of Directors of The Wallace Foundation and the Pig Iron Theatre Company. She is also a

member of the Columbia Law School Board of Visitors and a Founding Member of the Alumnae of Columbia Law School.

Career: Ms Rothenberg is admitted to practice in New York. Joined Fried Frank as a Partner in 1994.

Personal: Born 1947. Received JD in 1971 from Columbia University and BA 1967 from University of Pennsylvania.

ROWEN, Andrew S
Sullivan & Cromwell LLP, New York 212 558 4000
rowena@sullcrom.com
Recommended in Insurance

Practice Areas: Coordinator of S&C's Insurance Group. Focuses on acquisition, finance and corporate matters involving insurance companies. Practice includes: acquisitions/divestitures and other change of control transactions, including insurance regulatory approvals; securities offerings and advice as to SEC disclosure issues and investigations; demutualizations; offshore companies; securitization of insurance risks; and regulatory matters.

Prof. Memberships: American Bar Association; New York State Bar Association.

Career: Partner since 1987.

Publications: Speaker at various industry conferences.

Personal: University of California, Berkeley (AB, 1976); Harvard Law School, (JD, 1979).

RUBIN, Robert
Postner & Rubin, New York 212 269 2510
Recommended in Construction

RUDELL, Michael
Franklin, Weinrib, Rudell & Vassallo, New York 212 935 5500
Recommended in Media & Entertainment

RUEGGER, Philip T
Simpson Thacher & Bartlett LLP, New York 212 455 3220
pruegger@stblaw.com
Recommended in Corporate/M&A, Private Equity

Practice Areas: Partner at Simpson Thacher & Bartlett LLP, Chairman of the Executive Committee and head of the firm's Corporate Department. Advises clients on mergers and acquisitions, leveraged buyouts, corporate governance, corporate finance, and general corporate and securities law matters. Represented Travelers in its merger with St Paul and AOL in its merger with Time Warner. Regular clients include Blackstone, St. Paul, Travelers, Accenture, Vodafone and Vestar. Recently advised the Conference Board's Commission on Public Trust and Private Enterprise.

Career: Joined Simpson Thacher in 1974 and became a Partner in 1981. Became Head of the Corporate Depart-

ment in 2002, has been a member of the firm's Executive Committee since 1993 and became Chairman of the Executive Committee in 2004.

Publications: Articles and presentations include 'M&A of High Technology Companies', Stanford Law School Directors' College 2000; 'Structuring International Acquisition Transactions', for the Third Annual Institute on Mergers and Acquisitions in February 1999; and 'Going Global, How to Do an International Deal', The M&A Journal, Vl 1, No 6.

Personal: Received AB from Dartmouth College, magna cum laude in 1971 and was elected to Phi Beta Kappa. Received JD from the University of Virginia School of Law in 1974.

RUSMAN, Jared M
Wachtell, Lipton, Rosen & Katz, New York 212 403 1322
JMRusman@wlrk.com
Recommended in Tax

Practice Areas: Specializes in United States federal income taxation with emphasis on mergers, acquisitions and spin-offs.

Career: Partner at Wachtell, Lipton, Rosen & Katz since 2002.

Publications: Author: 'Equity Swaps and Post-Transaction Continuity of Interest,' 72 Tax Notes 113. Contributing author: Financial Institutions Mergers and Acquisitions, An Annual Review of Leading Developments.

Personal: Graduated from Georgetown University in 1991 (BSBA), summa cum laude, and from New York University School of Law in 1994 (JD), where he was notes and comment editor of the New York University Law Review and Order of the Coif.

RUZOW, Daniel
Whiteman Osterman & Hanna LLP, Albany 518 487 7619
druzow@woh.com
Recommended in Environment

Practice Areas: New York and US federal environmental and land use matters. He appears on behalf of private and governmental project sponsors throughout New York State. He served as lead environmental counsel for the development of over 10 million sf of commercial space and several NYS agency projects. From 1991-99 he served as lead counsel representing 60 municipalities in negotiation of the historic New York City Watershed Memorandum of Agreement.

Prof. Memberships: ABA, NYSBA (former Chairman, Environmental Law Section and Administrative Law Committee); NY Planning Federation (Bd of Dir.)

Career: Partner since 1986 (Managing Partner 1993-2003). Former Assistant Commissioner, NYS Department of Environmental Conservation.

Publications: He has lectured and written extensively on environmental

impact review and land use in New York State and is the co-author, of 'Environmental Impact Review in New York', Matthew Bender & Co. (1990-2005).

Personal: Fordham Law School (JD, 1976); Franklin & Marshall College (BA, 1973).

RYAN, Michael L
Cleary Gottlieb Steen & Hamilton LLP, New York 212 225 2520
mryan@cgsh.com
Recommended in Corporate/M&A

Practice Areas: Involved since 1968 in Cleary Gottlieb's corporate, M&A, Capital Markets and Restructuring Practices. Represents acquirors, targets and corporate boards. Early in his career, he had broad experience in the development of financial products (including the first collateralized mortgage obligation) and financial institution restructuring. In recent years, he has had particular focus on private equity (as longtime counsel to Texas Pacific Group) and counseling senior executives and corporate boards.

Career: JD, New York University School of Law, (1978); BA, Harvard College (1973).

SABEL, Bradley K
Shearman & Sterling LLP, New York 212 848 8410
bsabel@shearman.com
Recommended in Banking & Finance

Practice Areas: Partner of Shearman & Sterling specializing in bank and financial regulation.

Prof. Memberships: Member of the New York Bar; Chair, Banking Law Committee, Association of the Bar of the City of New York.

Career: Federal Reserve Bank of New York, 1975-94; Shearman & Sterling, 1994-present.

Publications: Author, 'Federal Reserve's Reserve Requirements', and co-author, 'Securities Activities of Foreign Banks in the U.S.', in Regulation of Foreign Banks (Gruson & Reisner, eds., 4th ed. 2003).

Personal: BA, cum laude, Vanderbilt University (1970); JD, Cornell Law School (1975); MSBP, Columbia Business School (1984).

SACRIPANTI, Peter
McDermott Will & Emery, New York 212 547 5583
psacripanti@mwe.com
Recommended in Environment

Practice Areas: Member of Trial Department. Concentrates on complex business disputes, including class action litigations and multi-party mass tort matters. Serves as Head of New York office, and sits on firm's Executive and Management Committees. Has experience defending corporations and industries in complex commercial, toxic tort and products liability litigation matters. Clients include a multinational petroleum company for whom he serves as national trial counsel in more than 100 environmental and product liability litigation matters. Recently served as liaison counsel to petroleum industry and successfully defeated class certification in In re Methyl Tertiary Butyl Ether Products Liability Litigation, a multi-district putative class action in Southern District of New York. Continues to serve as liaison counsel to industry in related environmental and product liability matters. Currently represents Fortune 500 company in management and defense of its nationwide asbestos docket. Serving as lead counsel, was instrumental in developing unprecedented legal strategy which utilized the Bankruptcy Code to restrain prosecution of an additional 200,000 asbestos-related claims against client.

Career: Began career as federal prosecutor with US Department of Justice. Recruited as part of prestigious Attorney General's Honors Program.
Personal: Fordham University, BA, summa cum laude, and Pace University School of Law, JD.

SAEED, Faiza
Cravath, Swaine & Moore LLP, New York 212 474 1454
fsaeed@cravath.com
Recommended in Corporate/M&A
Practice Areas: Mergers and acquisitions, both domestic and cross-border.
Prof. Memberships: ABA; NYSBA.
Career: Partner since 1999.
Publications: Editorial Board Member, 'M&A Lawyer'.
Personal: Harvard Law School (JD, magna cum laude, 1991); University of California at Berkeley (BA, with Highest Distinction, 1987; Phi Beta Kappa). Named a Dealmaker of the Year, 'The American Lawyer', 2005.

SAFERSTEIN, Jeffrey D
Paul, Weiss, Rifkind, Wharton & Garrison LLP, New York 212 373 3347
jsaferstein@paulweiss.com
Recommended in Bankruptcy
Practice Areas: Partner in the Bankruptcy Department. Practices exclusively in the areas of corporate restructurings and workouts, bankruptcy and specialized financings. Has been involved in major domestic and international restructurings and bankruptcies, including Worldcom, Adelphia Communications, Maxwell Communication Corporation plc., Macmillan, Inc., Drexel Burham Lambert, Canadian Airlines, The Penn Traffic Company, Loehmann's Inc., United Pan-Europe Communications N.V. and Asia Global Crossing Ltd. Has written and lectured on numerous bankruptcy topics.

SAGE, Michael
Stroock & Stroock & Lavan LLP, New York 212 806 5400
Recommended in Bankruptcy

SALVATORE, Paul
Proskauer Rose LLP, New York 212 969 3022
psalvatore@proskauer.com
Recommended in Employment
Practice Areas: Represents employers in employment law and litigation, as well as union/management relations and collective bargaining. Handles all types of employment litigation, arbitration and mediation. He also provides advice and guidance to clients, counseling employers on how to avoid litigation and achieve their employee relations objectives through such techniques as proactive human resources policies and alternative dispute resolution. Also negotiates major collective bargaining agreements in several industries, including real estate and construction. He tries arbitrations and litigations arising from the collective bargaining relationship.
Publications: An active speaker and writer on labor and employment law issues. He has been quoted in, among other publications, The New York Times, The Wall Street Journal, USA Today and The National Law Journal, and he has appeared on CNN, Fox News and other business television news programs. Among other groups he works with, he serves as a speaker for the Society for Human Resource Management (SHRM), and on its National Labor Relations Panel.
Personal: An honors graduate of Cornell University's School of Industrial and Labor Relations (ILR) and The Cornell Law School.

SAMUELS, Jeffrey B
Paul, Weiss, Rifkind, Wharton & Garrison LLP, New York 212 373 3112
jsamuels@paulweiss.com
Recommended in Tax
Practice Areas: Tax Partner whose practice covers a broad range of international and domestic transactions, including public and private M&A, the organization of investment funds, partnership and joint venture transactions, and structuring of complex real estate transactions, including the formation of public and private REITs. Clients include leading entertainment and communications companies, major investment banks and other financial institutions, major hotel owners and operators, and a number of private equity funds. Member of the New York State and City Bar Associations. Selected for the 2005 edition of 'The Best Lawyers in America' and Guide to The World's Leading Tax Advisors.

SAMUELS, Leslie B
Cleary Gottlieb Steen & Hamilton LLP, New York 212 225 2250
lsamuels@cgsh.com
Recommended in Tax
Practice Areas: International and domestic taxation, including mergers and acquisitions, joint ventures, spin-offs, for-

eign investment in the US, financial products and capital markets activities.
Prof. Memberships: Association of the Bar of the City of New York and the NYSBA.
Career: Joined firm, 1968; became Partner, 1975. Assistant Secretary for Tax Policy of the US Treasury Department (1993-96). Vice-Chair, Committee of Fiscal Affairs, OECD (1994-96). LLB, magna cum laude, Harvard Law School (1966); BS, Economics, Wharton School of Finance and Commerce, University of Pennsylvania (1963). Fulbright Scholar, London School of Economics and Political Science (1967-68). Certified public accountant.

SANSEVERINO, Raymond
Brown Raysman Millstein Felder & Steiner LLP, New York 212 895 2910
rsanseverino@brownraysman.com
Recommended in Real Estate
Practice Areas: Raymond A Sanseverino is Chair of the firm's Commercial Real Estate Leasing Group. Mr Sanseverino concentrates on commercial real estate law, with an emphasis in leasing, brokerage and conveyancing transactions. He represents both landlords and tenants in the leasing of all types of commercial real estate, including office, industrial and retail space. He also represents sellers and purchasers of real estate, real estate brokers, and owners and tenants in connection with real estate brokerage commission and agency agreements and commission claims.
Personal: AB, Franklin & Marshall College 1968; JD, cum laude, Fordham University School of Law 1972.

SARCHIO, John J
White & Case LLP, New York 212 819 8696
jsarchio@whitecase.com
Recommended in Insurance
Practice Areas: Head of Insurance Industry Practice Group. Experience in domestic and cross-border property/casualty and life mergers, acquisitions, demutualizations, financings and regulatory matters; insurer reorganizations and insolvencies; reinsurance transactions; securitizations; captive insurance; bank-insurer affiliations.
Prof. Memberships: Admitted New York (1980). Member: American Bar Association; New York State Bar Association; New York City Bar Association; International Bar Association.
Publications: Contributing author: 'New York Insurance Law & Practice' (Matthew Bender treatise); numerous speeches, seminars and trade publication articles.
Personal: Born 2 February 1954. JD, University of Pennsylvania, 1979; BS, Bucknell University, 1976; LLM (international law), London School of Economics, 1986.

SARNO, Glenn
Simpson Thacher & Bartlett LLP, New York 212 455 2000
gsarno@stblaw.com
Recommended in Private Equity
Practice Areas: Corporate Partner, focusing on private investment funds and other facets of 'alternative asset management'. Represents sponsors of domestic and international private funds, such as The Carlyle Group, Lehman Brothers, The Cypress Group, Leeds Weld & Co. and Cherokee Investment Partners, in a variety of asset classes including merchant banking, real estate, venture capital, healthcare, CDO, mezzanine debt, education, telecommunications and fund-of-funds. Advises on the creation of employee securities companies, represents various hedge fund sponsors, including Credit Suisse Asset Management, Endeavour, Pendragon and Horizon, and reviews private fund investments on behalf investors.
Prof. Memberships: Private Investment Fund Forum; Advisory Board of the Private Equity CFO Association.
Career: Joined firm in 1993, practiced in London from 1996-98, became a Partner in 2001; Judicial Clerk, Supreme Court of the State of New Jersey 1992-93 term.
Publications: 'Fund Formation - United States' in Getting the Deal Through - Private Equity, Law Business Research Limited, 2005.
Personal: University of Connecticut, BA, summa cum laude, 1989 (University Scholar; Phi Beta Kappa); Duke Law School, JD, with honors, 1992 (winner Hardt Cup Moot Court Competition; Best Judge Award Dean's Cup Competition).

SAUNDERS, Paul
Cravath, Swaine & Moore LLP, New York 212 474 1404
psaunders@cravath.com
Recommended in Litigation
Practice Areas: Trial work and international arbitration, primarily in the areas of antitrust, securities, intellectual property and employment discrimination.
Prof. Memberships: ABA; NYSBA; ABCNY; American College of Trial Lawyers (Fellow). New York State Judicial Institute on Professionalism in the Law.
Career: Partner since 1977.
Publications: Frequent speaker on topics in litigation.
Personal: Georgetown University Law Center (JD, 1966; notes editor, Law Journal); Fordham College (AB, egregia cum laude, 1963; Phi Beta Kappa). Captain, US Army JAGC, 1967-71. Fordham University: Board of Trustees. Distinguished Visitor from Practice, Georgetown University Law Center.

SAVARESE, John F
Wachtell, Lipton, Rosen & Katz, New York 212 403 1235
jfsavarese@wlrk.com
Recommended in Litigation

Practice Areas: Specializes in the representation of investment banking and financial service firms, as well as Fortune 500 companies, in connection with the defense of regulatory, white-collar criminal and complex civil litigation. Also advises clients on the design of compliance policies and systems, and on the conduct of internal investigations.
Prof. Memberships: The Association of the Bar of the City of New York (Secretary-Treasurer, Criminal Law Committee, 1989-92); American Bar Association.
Career: Joined Wachtell, Lipton, Rosen & Katz in 1988, after working for the United States Attorney's Office for the Southern District of New York for four years. Received the Attorney General's John Marshall Award for Outstanding Legal Achievement in connection with his work on United States v Salerno, in which the heads of New York's La Cosa Nostra families were prosecuted. Also served as the Chief Appellate Attorney in the US Attorney's Office. Prior to his work with the US Attorney's Office, served as a Law Clerk to the Honorable Louis H Pollak of the United States District Court for the Eastern District of Pennsylvania and to Justice William J Brennan of the United States Supreme Court. Frequent lecturer and panelist for the American Bar Association, the Practicing Law Institute, the Securities Industry Association, and Stanford Law School's Director's College program. He also has been a lecturer at Harvard Law School, teaching a course on advanced criminal procedure.
Personal: Graduated magna cum laude from Harvard University in 1977 (AB) and cum laude from Harvard Law School in 1981 (JD), where he served as articles editor of the 'Harvard Law Review' and as a Teaching Fellow in European Intellectual History.

SCARBOROUGH, Robert
Freshfields Bruckhaus Deringer LLP, New York 212 277 4000
Recommended in Tax

SCAVONE, Arthur
White & Case LLP, New York
212 819 8710
ascavone@whitecase.com
Recommended in Projects
Practice Areas: Mr Scavone is a project finance lawyer with extensive experience involving international and domestic projects, and is Co-Head of the firm's Energy, Infrastructure and Project Finance Group. He represents sponsors, commercial banks, underwriters and export credit agencies in projects involving power plants, pipelines, LNG and petrochemical facilities, and other infrastructure and industrial projects. He has worked on some of the world's most innovative and high-profile transactions, including the US$2 billion Chad-Cameroon pipeline project and the US$380 million FPL Energy American

Wind project involving the Rule 144A bond financing of a 'pool' of seven wind farms throughout the US.

SCHAEFFER, Fiona A
Weil, Gotshal & Manges LLP, New York
212 310 8919
fiona.schaeffer@weil.com
Recommended in Antitrust
Practice Areas: Antitrust/competition, litigation/regulatory.
Career: Advises leading companies in many industries; particular expertise in healthcare, financial services and consumer goods sectors. Represents major corporations in complex antitrust litigation, including multi-district treble damages class actions, and private suits in federal and state courts. Expertise in EU competition law; appeared before the European Courts, European Commission and national regulators. Advises private equity and industrial clients on antitrust-related aspects of mergers, acquisitions and other combinations. Secures approvals for transactions in the US, EU, and other jurisdictions. Principal client relationships include: United-Health Group, MasterCard.
Personal: University of Oxford, BCL; University of Adelaide, BEc, LLB.

SCHAFFRAN, Andrew
Morgan, Lewis & Bockius LLP, New York 212 309 6380
aschaffran@morganlewis.com
Recommended in Employment
Practice Areas: Andrew Schaffran is a Partner in the Labor and Employment Practice and is nationally recognized in the employment law field, particularly in the financial securities industry. Mr Schaffran regularly counsels and represents securities firms and other financial services companies in all aspects of employment law, including complex as well as single plaintiff employment litigation, arbitration before NASD and NYSE panels, Sarbanes-Oxley whistleblower complaints and corporate diversity and ADR programs.
Prof. Memberships: American Bar Association (Labor and Employment Law Section and Co-Chair of Litigation Section, Securities Employment Litigation Subcommittee); SIA Compliance and Legal Division; New York State Bar Association (Labor and Employment Law Section).

SCHARFSTEIN, Joel
Fried, Frank, Harris, Shriver & Jacobson LLP, New York 212 859 8172
Joel.Scharfstein@FriedFrank.com
Recommended in Tax
Practice Areas: Tax Partner. Practice focuses on corporate acquisitions and divestitures, partnership transactions, investment partnerships and restructurings.
Prof. Memberships: Member of the Executive Committee of the Tax Section of the New York State Bar Association (1992-2001) and Co-Chair of its committees on partnerships (1992-94),

bankruptcy (1994-96), consolidated returns (1996-98), basis and cost recovery (1999-2001), and reorganizations (current).
Career: Qualified in New York in 1978. Joined Fried Frank in 1977, and became a Partner in 1984.
Personal: Born 1947. Received JD from the University of Michigan Law School in 1977, AB from Columbia College in 1969 and AM from Harvard University in 1972.

SCHECHTMAN, Paul
Stillman & Friedman, New York
212 223 0200
Recommended in Litigation

SCHEIBE, Robert H
Morgan, Lewis & Bockius LLP, New York 212 309 6083
rscheibe@morganlewis.com
Recommended in Bankruptcy
Practice Areas: Robert Scheibe is a Partner in the Business and Finance Practice. Mr Scheibe has represented financial institutions in restructuring and bankruptcy matters for more than 30 years and has frequently acted as counsel for major financial institutions as debtor-in-possession lender (including in the Chapter 11 cases of major airlines, retailers, manufacturers, technology firms and entertainment industry companies).
Prof. Memberships: American College of Bankruptcy (Fellow).

SCHEINFELD, Robert
Baker Botts LLP, New York
212 408 2512
robert.scheinfeld@bakerbotts.com
Recommended in Intellectual Property
Practice Areas: Head of New York office's Intellectual Property Department. For 20 years, practiced IP law and litigation, representing companies in patent, copyright, and trade secret misappropriation disputes and lawsuits, resulting in favorable district court and Federal Circuit decisions. Technical expertise is diverse and representations involve a broad range of fields in the high technology industry, including electronics, data processing and management software, telecommunications, smart cards, electronic commerce, and flash memory.
Career: Bimonthly 'New York Law Journal' patent and trademark columnist (1995-present). Adjunct professor, Patent Law (1991-97). NYIPLA, Patent Law and Practice Committee, Chair (present), Trade Secret Practice Chair (1996-2003).

SCHELER, Brad Eric
Fried, Frank, Harris, Shriver & Jacobson LLP, New York 212 859 8019
Brad.Scheler@FriedFrank.com
Recommended in Bankruptcy
Practice Areas: Chairman of the Bankruptcy and Restructuring Department. Practice includes both in and out-of-

court restructurings and the rehabilitation of financially distressed businesses. Represents companies experiencing complex financial difficulties, creditors' committees, bondholders' committees, major secured and unsecured creditors, trustees, debtor-in-possession lenders, investment partnerships that buy and sell distressed securities and businesses, and third parties seeking to invest in and/or acquire the assets and businesses of financially troubled companies. Also acts as outside general counsel and strategic adviser to financially strong corporate and institutional clients in connection with financings, mergers and acquisitions, joint ventures and securities transactions.
Prof. Memberships: Fellow of the American College of Bankruptcy; American Bar Association and its Business Bankruptcy Committee, Business Law Section; New York State Bar Association; Association of the Bar of the City of New York; Delaware Bankruptcy Rule and Practice Committee.
Career: Qualified in New York in 1978. Joined Fried Frank in 1981, became Partner in 1984, became Chairman of the Bankruptcy and Restructuring Department in 1986. Began career as an associate at Weil, Gotshal & Manges (1977-81).
Publications: Contributing author, 'Collier on Bankruptcy'. Co-authors regular column for the 'Uniform Commercial Code Law Journal'; Speaker at professional seminars on bankruptcy and restructuring issues; delivered the Benjamin Weintraub Distinguished lecture on bankruptcy law at Hofstra University School of Law, 1994.
Personal: JD in 1977 from Hofstra University School of Law; BA, with high honors, from Lehigh University in 1974.

SCHELL, J Michael
Skadden, Arps, Slate, Meagher & Flom LLP & Affiliates, New York
212 735 3150
mschell@skadden.com
Recommended in Corporate/M&A
Practice Areas: Concentrates in mergers and acquisitions, corporate investments and general corporate counseling. Has extensive experience in domestic and cross-border transactions - negotiated and contested.
Prof. Memberships: Member, Board of Trustees, Boston University; Member, Board of Trustees, American Institute for Contemporary German Studies (Johns Hopkins University); Member, Board of Visitors, Boston University Law School; Member, Board of Directors, National Down Syndrome Society; Member, Board of Trustees, Lake Forest Academy; Senior Professional Fellow, Center for Law and Business, New York University.
Career: JD, Boston University School of Law, 1976; AB, Columbia University, 1969.

SCHER, Irving
Weil, Gotshal & Manges LLP, New York
212 310 8120
irving.scher@weil.com
Recommended in Antitrust

Practice Areas: Antitrust/competition, litigation/regulatory.
Career: Scher is admitted to practice in the New York State and District Courts, the US Supreme Court, and US Courts of Appeals for the First, Second, Sixth, Ninth and DC Circuits. Scher has extensive antitrust experience. Representative cases include: In Re Compact Disc Minimum Price Advertised Price Litig.; Williamson Oil Co. v Philip Morris et al. Scher is an adjunct professor at New York University Law School, teaching an advanced antitrust course, and a former Chair of the ABA and NY Sections of Antitrust Law.
Personal: Columbia University, JD; City University of New York, BA.

SCHLER, Michael
Cravath, Swaine & Moore LLP, New York 212 474 1588
mschler@cravath.com
Recommended in Tax

Practice Areas: Corporate tax, corporate finance (including structured finance and securitizations), international transactions.
Prof. Memberships: ABA (Section of Taxation); NYSBA (former Chair, Tax Section; Member of Tax Section Executive Committee); American College of Tax Counsel; New York Tax Forum (Chair); American Tax Policy Institute (Trustee); American Law Institute (Consultant).
Career: Partner since 1982. Clerkship: Hon. Max Rosenn (US Court of Appeals, Third Circuit).
Publications: Author of numerous articles on taxation. Frequent speaker at tax conferences.
Personal: New York University (LLM in Taxation, 1979); Yale Law School (JD, 1973); Harvard University (BA, magna cum laude, 1970).

SCHMIDT, Kevin
Debevoise & Plimpton LLP, New York 212 909 6000
Recommended in Private Equity

SCHNABEL, David
Debevoise & Plimpton LLP, New York 212 909 6000
Recommended in Tax

SCHNEIDER, Jeffrey G
Hogan & Hartson LLP, New York 212 918 3503
jgschneider@hhlaw.com
Recommended in Healthcare

Practice Areas: Regulatory compliance, transactions, litigation and general counseling for healthcare organizations.
Prof. Memberships: Officer and Director, Board of Directors, Hospice Care of D.C., 1992-97; Member, American Health Lawyers Association.

Career: Jeff joined Hogan & Hartson following law school in 1986. His practice focuses on healthcare provider entities, including hospitals, academic medical centers, nursing homes, home health agencies, hospices, physician groups, and mental health practitioners. He provides assistance to these clients in the areas of regulatory compliance and counseling, joint ventures, mergers, acquisitions and other transactions, and reimbursement and other litigation. He also represents a number of professional and trade associations.
Publications: 'Dispelling Myths About Employer Health Plans Under The HIPAA Privacy Rules', HIPAA Update, Hogan & Hartson L.L.P. (1/30/2003); numerous legal updates published through the National Register of Health Service Providers in Psychology, including 'Legal Issues Involving Repressed Memory of Child Sexual Abuse' (August 1994); 'Joining Battle With Your State Over Medicaid', Nursing Homes Long Term Management (August 1992).
Personal: Stanford Law School (JD); University of Michigan (BA, with highest honors). Admitted to the Bars of New York, the District of Columbia and Illinois.

SCHNELL, Paul T
Skadden, Arps, Slate, Meagher & Flom LLP & Affiliates, New York
212 735 2322
pschnell@skadden.com
Recommended in Corporate/M&A

Practice Areas: Represents many of the world's leading companies and financial firms in some of the most significant corporate transactions. Practices in M&A, governance, private equity, finance and restructuring. In last year, advised on 18 major M&A and financing transactions, including six deals valued at over $1 billion, in US, Latin America, Asia and Europe. Active in broad range of industries. Coordinates Skadden's worldwide Healthcare Practice Group. Co-heads firm's practice in Latin America. Chairs leading M&A publication; chairs leading annual program on negotiating acquisitions; and lectures and writes frequently on governance, M&A, finance and other topics. Active in firm management.

SCHOENBERG, Clifford H
Cadwalader, Wickersham & Taft LLP, New York 212 504 6992
cliff.schoenberg@cwt.com
Recommended in Insurance

Practice Areas: Has handled scores of multi-million dollar reinsurance arbitrations and litigations, and a variety of disputes between insurance companies and their agents. Primary responsibility for arbitration against Fortress Re in which Sompo Japan obtained $1 billion compensatory damage and $100 million punitive damage award. Has litigated direct insurance coverage actions, been

retained as arbitrator and expert in reinsurance arbitrations, and represented insurance companies in regulatory matters before NY State Insurance Department. Acted as co-ordinating and supervising counsel for federal and state class action lawsuits against insurers, including a large number in Alabama involving significant punitive damage claims. In addition to litigation and regulatory experience, has served as lead counsel on insurance company mergers, acquisitions and divestitures totalling over $1 billion. Written numerous articles, lectured extensively on reinsurance topics. Served on the board of directors of Zurich Life Insurance Company of New York; formerly Assistant General Counsel of The Home Insurance Company.
Personal: BA, Dickinson College (summa cum laude, 1972); JD, Boston University School of Law (magna cum laude, 1975).

SCHONHOLTZ, Margot
Kaye Scholer LLP, New York
212 836 7064
mschonholtz@kayescholer.com
Recommended in Bankruptcy

Practice Areas: Partner and Co-Chair, Business Reorganization and Creditors' Rights. Focuses her practice on bankruptcy and restructuring matters. She has more than 25 years experience representing leading institutional creditors, agents to syndicated lending groups, large lender groups, official and unofficial creditors' committees and commercial lenders in out-of-court debt restructurings, loan workouts, creditors' rights litigation, asset sale transactions and bankruptcy matters. She also has extensive cross-border experience in restructuring and insolvency proceedings in the UK, Europe, Latin America, Canada and Asia.
Prof. Memberships: Member of the Bars of the State of New York, Southern and Eastern Districts of New York and admitted to practice before the Second Circuit Court of Appeals and the US Supreme Court.
Career: JD (magna cum laude), American University Washington College of Law; Law Review, Honor Society, International Academy of Trial Lawyers' Award for Distinguished Advocacy; BA, Smith College.

SCHULZ, David
Levine Sullivan Koch & Schulz LLP, New York 212 850 6100
Recommended in Media & Entertainment

SCHUMER, Robert B
Paul, Weiss, Rifkind, Wharton & Garrison LLP, New York 212 373 3097
rschumer@paulweiss.com
Recommended in Corporate/M&A, Media & Entertainment

Practice Areas: Co-Head of M&A Group focusing on mergers and acquisitions and joint ventures. Has represent-

ed clients in significant merger and acquisition transactions, many involving multibillion-dollar acquisitions or dispositions, including contested takeovers. Representative transactions include Time Warner Cable Inc.'s bid to acquire the cable properties of Adelphia Communications for approximately $17.4 billion, King World Productions $2.5 billion merger with CBS, Time Warner's $58 billion bid for AT&T Broadband and $9 billion restructuring of Time Warner Entertainment with Comcast and AT&T, and Telemundo's $2.7 billion merger with NBC. Has been involved in numerous international and domestic multibillion-dollar joint ventures including Time Warner Inc.'s creation of Time Warner Entertainment, a $20 billion joint venture with Itochu and Toshiba. Also represents special committees of boards of directors and leading investment banking firms in mergers and acquisitions context. Selected for 2005 edition of 'The Best Lawyers in America', Law Business Research's Who's Who of Merger and Acquisitions Lawyers, and The American Lawyer's '45 Under 45' (1995). Client's include Time Warner Inc., AIG, Liz Claiborne, Inc., Lazard Freres and Airgas, Inc.

SCHWARTZ, Alan
Simpson Thacher & Bartlett LLP, New York 212 455 3629
aschwartz@stblaw.com
Recommended in Private Equity

Practice Areas: Partner in the firm's Corporate Department, where he concentrates primarily in mergers and acquisitions and leveraged buyouts. Mr Schwartz maintains strong ties with many of the firm's private equity clients, including Kohlberg Kravis Roberts & Co., Ripplewood Holdings L.L.C. and Evercore Capital Partners. Represented Ripplewood in its disposition of Kraton Polymers to the Texas Pacific Group and Evercore in restructuring its investment in a Belgium cable venture. Also recently represented Evercore in its investment in Fidelity National Information Services, Inc.
Career: Mr Schwartz has been a member of the firm since 1998.
Personal: He received his BS from the University of New Hampshire in 1983 and his JD from Fordham Law School in 1989.

SCHWARTZ, Herbert
Fish & Neave IP Group of Ropes & Gray, New York 212 596 9010
herbert.schwartz@ropesgray.com
Recommended in Intellectual Property

Practice Areas: IP litigator in the Fish & Neave IP Group of Ropes & Gray, best known for work on behalf of Polaroid Corporation in its landmark patent infringement action against Eastman Kodak Company relating to instant photography. Represents numerous clients in the pharmaceutical, technology, and consumer product sectors in patent, trademark, copyright, trade

secret, licensing litigation/appeals.
Career: New York Bar (1964). United States Patent and Trademark Office. Partner, Ropes & Gray (2005). Member, American College of Trial Lawyers.
Personal: LLB, University of Pennsylvania Law School (1964). MA, University of Pennsylvania, Wharton School (1964). BSEE, Massachusetts Institute of Technology (1957).

SCHWARTZ, Jodi J
Wachtell, Lipton, Rosen & Katz, New York 212 403 1212
jjschwartz@wlrk.com
Recommended in Tax

Practice Areas: Specializes in United States federal income taxation with emphasis on mergers, acquisitions and spin-offs.
Prof. Memberships: Member of the New York State Bar Association Tax Section Executive Committee.
Career: Partner at Wachtell, Lipton, Rosen & Katz since 1991.
Personal: Graduated magna cum laude from the University of Pennsylvania in 1981 (BS, economics), from the University of Pennsylvania (Wharton School) in 1984 (MBA), magna cum laude from the University of Pennsylvania Law School in 1984 (JD), and from New York University Law School in 1987 (LLM, taxation).

SCHWARTZ, Max
Sullivan & Cromwell LLP, New York 212 558 4000
schwartzma@sullcrom.com
Recommended in Employee Benefits

Practice Areas: Head, Executive Compensation and Benefits Practice Group. Has broad-based experience in executive compensation and employee benefit matters, provides advice on these matters both on a regular basis and in the context of corporate transactions and initial public offerings.
Prof. Memberships: American Bar Association (Tax and Business Law Sections); New York State Bar Association (Executive Committee of the Tax Section and Co-Chair of Employee Benefits Committee).
Career: Joined firm in 1998 as Of Counsel. Partner since 2000.
Publications: Writes and lectures extensively on benefits matters. Member of the Employee Benefits Advisory Committee of the Practising Law Institute and the Editorial Advisory Board for the Journal of Pension Planning and Compliance.
Personal: Institut d'Etudes Politiques (BA, 1970); University of Michigan Law School (JD, 1973).

SCHWARTZ, Steven
Clifford Chance US LLP, New York 212 878 4920
steve.schwartz@cliffordchance.com
Recommended in Insurance

Practice Areas: Specializing in reinsurance litigation and arbitration, Mr Schwartz has represented prominent companies in disputes worth hundreds of millions of dollars. His cases have involved both property/casualty and life/health insurance, as well as insurance insolvency and alternative risk transfer. His experience includes representation of a US ceding company in several arbitrations regarding asbestos and other losses, representation of insurers and reinsurers in disputes relating to pools and managing general agents, disputes relating to workers' compensation carve-out and personal accident reinsurance, and disputes relating to September 11 losses. He frequently writes and lectures on reinsurance issues.

SCHWARTZ, William
Kronish Lieb Weiner & Hellman LLP, New York 212 479 6000
Recommended in Litigation

SCHWED, Robert
Wilmer Cutler Pickering Hale and Dorr LLP, New York 212 841 0614
robert.schwed@wilmerhale.com
Recommended in Private Equity

Practice Areas: Represents private equity firms and their portfolio companies in corporate finance transactions and venture capital and buyout firms and other institutional investors in equity and subordinated debt investments, public and private buyout transactions and workouts, recapitalizations and other restructurings. Leveraged buyout experience includes the acquisition of divisions or business units from major industrial, financial services, healthcare, retailing, media and communications companies, and the acquisition of public companies in the computer, data processing, healthcare and communications industries.
Prof. Memberships: Board of Directors at Project Reach Youth (Brooklyn, NY).
Personal: Harvard Law School (JD 1974); Williams College (BA 1971).

SEGAL, Michael
Paul, Weiss, Rifkind, Wharton & Garrison LLP, New York 212 373 3364
msegal@paulweiss.com
Recommended in Employee Benefits

Practice Areas: Co-Chair of the Executive Compensation and Employee Benefits Group. Represents executives and private and public companies in the structuring and implementation of complex employment and compensation arrangements, particularly equity-related compensation. Has expertise advising corporations, trustees, lenders and advisors in the establishment and termination of employee stock ownership plans, and has advised clients on the ERISA aspects of establishing and operating venture capital funds, group trusts and other pooled investment vehicles. Regularly speaks and writes on benefits and compensation topics. Selected for the 2005 edition of 'The Best Lawyers in America'.

SEIDE, Rochelle
Arent Fox PLLC, New York 212 484 3900
Recommended in Intellectual Property

SEIDMAN, Steven
Willkie Farr & Gallagher LLP, New York 212 728 8763
sseidman@willkie.com
Recommended in Corporate/M&A

Practice Areas: Partner in the Corporate and Financial Services Department, specializing in mergers and acquisitions in both friendly and contested situations, advice to Boards of Directors, private equity and venture capital investments, public offerings, and general corporate and securities law. Clients include Eon Labs, Inc., MatlinPatterson Global Advisors, LLC, General Investment & Development Co., Warburg Pincus LLC, Merrill Lynch & Co., Credit Suisse First Boston, Simon Property Group, Inc. and The Feedroom, Inc. Recent transactions include the acquisition of Eon Labs, Inc. and Hexal AG by Novartis AG; the investment into Fortunoff by Trimaran Capital Partners/K Group; the acquisition of GovPX, Inc. by ICAP plc; MatlinPatterson's acquisition of Southeast Generation Portfolio from Duke Energy; Simon Property Group's proposed acquisition of Taubman Centers, Inc.; and the repurchase of Warburg Pincus' stake in Price Enterprises, Inc. Mr Seidman also represents a number of financial advisors in transactions, including in connection with ALLTEL's acquisition of Western Wireless and the sale of Intelsat, Ltd.
Career: Judicial Clerk, Delaware Court of Chancery (1990-91).
Personal: Yale University (BA, 1987); University of Virginia Law School (JD, 1990).

SELVER, Paul D
Paul, Hastings, Janofsky & Walker LLP, New York 212 318 6869
paulselver@paulhastings.com
Recommended in Real Estate

Practice Areas: Practice encompasses all aspects of land use and development law, with a special emphasis on environmental, zoning and historic preservation. Over the past 15 years, he has successfully co-ordinated the public approval and environmental review process for more than 8,000,000 square feet of office space, more than 7,500 apartments, hundreds of thousands of square feet of retail and entertainment space, hundreds of hotel rooms, and numerous institutional buildings.
Publications: Co-author, New York Practice Guide: Real Estate, Volume II: Land Use Regulation (1986).
Personal: JD, Harvard University Law School, 1972; BA (magna cum laude) Harvard College 1969.

SERBAROLI, Francis J
Cadwalader, Wickersham & Taft LLP, New York 212 504 6001
francis.serbaroli@cwt.com
Recommended in Healthcare

Practice Areas: Clients have included numerous teaching and community hospitals, ambulatory care centers and clinics; clinical laboratories; home health agencies; imaging service providers; individual physicians and group practices; and numerous other healthcare-related entities, as well as health insurers and managed care organizations. Served as counsel to and represented hospital governing boards, administrators and medical staffs.
Personal: BA from Fordham University in 1973; JD from Fordham University School of Law in 1977. Previously an Assistant Attorney General of New York and general counsel at two prominent teaching hospitals. Appointed by Governor Pataki to N.Y. State Public Health Council 1995, reappointed 2001, presently serve as Vice Chairman. Member of the Governor's NYPHRM task force. Chaired a special task force of the Public Health Council on the confidentiality of medical information. Authors Health Law column for the New York Law Journal; author of 'The Corporate Practice of Medicine Prohibition in the Modern Era of Health Care,' (BNA). Numerous articles published in health, pharmaceutical and insurance publications.

SERNAU, Ronald D
Proskauer Rose LLP, New York 212 969 3785
rsernau@proskauer.com
Recommended in Real Estate

Practice Areas: A Partner in the Real Estate Department, he has significant experience in real estate law, representing sophisticated real estate developers and investors in virtually all areas of real estate practice in New York City. He draws on his experience to address legitimate interests that the opposing party must protect, and to minimize negotiation of issues that the opposing party can compromise. He has represented clients in some of the most substantial real estate transactions occurring in New York City. For example, he has represented a publicly held real estate investment trust in a variety of acquisitions and lease transactions involving several hundred million dollars. He has represented a major private real estate developer in complex equity restructuring transactions for properties in the New York area. He has represented a major New York City lender in restructuring non-recourse debt on important New York City properties. He serves as the principal leasing lawyer for several major New York City landlords, addressing the variety of financial and technical issues that arise in sophisticated lease transactions.
Personal: Cornell Law School, JD, magna cum laude, 1986; Order of the Coif; editor, Cornell Law Review, 1985-86. Ithaca College, BS, summa cum laude, 1981.

SEROTA, Susan P
Pillsbury Winthrop LLP, New York
212 858 1125
sserota@pillsburywinthrop.com
Recommended in Employee Benefits
Practice Areas: Ms Serota is Chair of Pillsbury Winthrops Executive Compensation & Benefits Practice and has experience in all areas of pensions, employee benefits (health, life and severance plans), executive compensation and stock options. She has significant experience in fiduciary matters relating to ERISA. Ms Serota advises both foreign and domestic governments regarding pensions and privatization. Recent assignments include: drafting pension, profit sharing plans and executive compensation arrangements including taxation issues of nonqualified plans, stock and other equity plans, golden parachutes and anti-takeover devices; ESOP structuring; advising US and non-US companies on tax and securities issues in equity-based plans; serving as company compensation committee counsel; and advising on ERISA fiduciary litigation.
Prof. Memberships: Regent, Second Circuit, 2000- and Fellow, American College of Tax Counsel, 1996- ; President 2004- and Charter Member, American College of Employee Benefits Counsel, 2000-.
Career: Admitted to practice in New York, Illinois, and District of Columbia.
Publications: Editor, ERISA Fiduciary Law, BNA Books 1995, Supp. 2003; Employee Benefit Issues in Joint Ventures, 54 Tax Lawyer 477 (2001); Sarbanes-Oxley: Insider Trading Restrictions and Advance Notice to Participants of Blackout Periods, 2003 (PLI).
Personal: JD, New York University School of Law, 1971; AB, University of Michigan, 1967.

SEYMON, Pamela S
Wachtell, Lipton, Rosen & Katz, New York 212 403 1205
psseymon@wlrk.com
Recommended in Corporate/M&A
Practice Areas: Specializes in corporate law; mergers and acquisitions; securities; corporate governance. Has represented corporations on offense as well as defense, in both friendly and unsolicited transactions; and clients engaged in some of the most notable transactions over the years, including MCA INC. in its sale to Matsushita Electric Industrial Co., Ltd., QVC Inc. in its unsolicited bid for Paramount Communications Inc., HSN, Inc. (which then became USA Networks, Inc.) in the acquisition of USA Networks and the domestic television business of Universal Studios and, thereafter, USA Networks, Inc. (which then became USA Interactive) in the contribution of its entertainment assets to Vivendi Universal Entertain-ment; also represented CSX Corporation in its acquisition of Conrail, the Special Committee of the Board of Directors of Del-

haize America in the sale to Delhaize Group and, most recently, USA Interactive in its purchases of Ticketmaster, Expedia and Hotels.com.
Prof. Memberships: Has served on the Committee on Securities Regulation of the New York City Bar Association and as a member of the Board of Trustees for New York University School of Law.
Career: Partner at Wachtell, Lipton, Rosen & Katz, where she has practiced since 1982.
Personal: Graduated as a Wellesley Scholar from Wellesley College in 1977 (AB) and from New York University School of Law in 1982 (JD).

SEYMOUR, Samuel W
Sullivan & Cromwell LLP, New York
212 558 3156
seymours@sullcrom.com
Recommended in Litigation
Practice Areas: Head, Criminal Defense and Investigations Group. Focuses on white collar criminal defense, regulatory enforcement matters and internal investigations. Has represented clients in numerous high-profile investigations involving allegations of securities fraud, price-fixing, money laundering and obstruction of justice.
Prof. Memberships: American Bar Association; Association of the Bar of the City of New York (former Vice-President and Chair of the Executive Committee); New York Council of Defense Lawyers.
Career: Partner since 1994. Assistant US Attorney in the Southern District of New York, 1988-91.
Publications: Lecturer, Columbia Law School.
Personal: Dartmouth College (AB, 1979); Columbia Law School (JD, 1982).

SHACHAR, Avishai
Davis Polk & Wardwell, New York
212 450 4000
avishai.shachar@dpw.com
Recommended in Tax
Practice Areas: Member of Davis Polk & Wardwell's Tax Department. Advises clients primarily in the areas of US and cross-border mergers and acquisitions, leveraged buyouts, spinoffs and financial products. Designed the capital structure of SmithKline Beecham and played a leading role in the merger of SmithKline with Beecham and Comcast with AT&T Broadband, the spinoffs of YUM! Brands from Pepsi, of Visteon from Ford, and the split-off by way of an exchange offer of Abercrombie & Fitch from The Limited. Also advised Burlington Northern on tax matters relating to its acquisition of Santa Fee Pacific, Texaco on tax matters relating to its merger with Chevron, as well as Comcast on a variety of matters including the sale of its stake in QVC, the restructuring of Time Warner Entertainment and numerous cable systems acquisitions.

SHAPIRO, Stuart
Shapiro Forman Allen Miller & McPherson LLP, New York 212 972 4900
Recommended in Litigation

SHENKER, Joseph C
Sullivan & Cromwell LLP, New York
212 558 4000
shenkerj@sullcrom.com
Recommended in Real Estate
Practice Areas: Coordinator of the firm's global commercial real estate practice. Has broad ranging experience in: securitized offerings; negotiated mergers and acquisitions; cross-border joint ventures; and representation of private equity investors and family investment offices in the Americas, Europe and Asia. Has acted as counsel to a number of large real estate operating companies (Vornado; Alexander's; General Growth; Rockefeller Center Properties; Canary Wharf Holdings; Cadillac Fairview; the GS Whitehall Real Estate Funds (worldwide); and various Pritzker Family entities) and has represented issuers and underwriters in many public debt and equity offerings.
Prof. Memberships: American Bar Association; New York State Bar Association; Association of the Bar of the City of New York.
Career: Partner since 1986. Management Committee since 1996.
Personal: CUNY (BS, 1977); Columbia University (JD, 1980).

SHERMAN, Robert L
Paul, Hastings, Janofsky & Walker LLP, New York 212 318 6037
robertsherman@paulhastings.com
Recommended in Intellectual Property
Practice Areas: Has advised clients on trademark protection and risk avoidance. Has litigated cases for trademark infringement, trade dress, false advertising, dilution, counterfeiting, cybersquatting and under ICANN. Has represented clients in trademark prosecution, opposition and cancellation proceedings.
Prof. Memberships: INTA; NYSBA.
Career: Came to firm as Partner in 1992.
Publications: Adjunct professor, Medill (graduate school), Northwestern University, Evanston, IL; teaches seminar on the Law of Direct and Ineractive Marketing; frequent industry speaker on direct marketing.
Personal: American University Law School (JD 1971), member of Law Review; George Wahiongton University Law School; University of Rhode Island (BSIE 1967).

SHIFF, Adam L
Kasowitz Benson Torres & Friedman, New York 212 506 1700
Recommended in Bankruptcy

SHIM, Paul J
Cleary Gottlieb Steen & Hamilton LLP, New York 212 225 2930
pshim@cgsh.com
Recommended in Corporate/M&A

Practice Areas: Mergers, acquisitions and leveraged buyouts. Clients include American Express, Bank of America, Texas Pacific Group, HSBC, Citigroup, J. Crew, ON Semiconductor, Suntory Limited and Standard Microsystems Corporation.
Career: Joined firm, 1987; became Partner, 1996. JD, cum laude, NYU (1987). BS, MS (Chem. E.), MIT (1984).
Publications: 'You Don't Say: Information Disclaimers in M&A Contracts,' by P. Shim and D. Leinwand, The New York Law Journal, July 23, 2003. 'IBP v Tyson Foods - Acquiror Must Consummate Merger When Court Finds No "Material Adverse Effect," by v Lewkow and P. Shim, The M&A Lawyer, June 2001.

SHIMSHAK, Stephen
Paul, Weiss, Rifkind, Wharton & Garrison LLP, New York 212 373 3133
sshimshak@paulweiss.com
Recommended in Bankruptcy
Practice Areas: Partner in the Bankruptcy Department, handling restructurings, workouts, and insolvency-related matters in a wide range of Chapter 11 cases and international insolvency proceedings, involving debtors, secured creditors (including banks and other lenders), trustees, foreign administrators, asset purchasers and investors. Has written on various bankruptcy issues. Member of the Bar of the State of New York and admitted to various federal courts throughout the country. Selected for the 2005 edition of 'The Best Lawyers in America'.

SHIPLEY, Ann
Paul, Hastings, Janofsky & Walker LLP, New York 212 318 6870
annshipley@paulhastings.com
Recommended in Real Estate
Practice Areas: All areas of real estate development and finance, with a speciality in representing developers in acquisition and development of complex multi-use projects as well as borrowers in so-called '80-20' and other bond financings. She represented the developers of the new Time Warner Center in New York City from inception to completion of the project.
Prof. Memberships: New York City Bar Association—Real Property Committee.
Career: Partner since 2000; prior thereto, Partner at Battle, Fowler LLP from 1987 - 2000.
Personal: Columbia Law School (LLB, 1966); University of Illinois (BA 1963).

SHOEMATE, Steven R
Gibson, Dunn & Crutcher LLP, New York
212 351 3879
sshoemate@gibsondunn.com
Recommended in Corporate/M&A
Practice Areas: Public and private mergers and acquisitions with an emphasis on private equity, joint ventures, venture capital financings and general corporate counseling. He has extensive experience in the various types

of public and private mergers and acquisitions transactions including private company stock and asset sales, public mergers, tender offers, exchange offers stock and cash tenders and cross-border transactions.

Career: Co-Partner-in-charge of the New York office.

Personal: JD, Duke University, 1988, Member of the Duke Law Journal and the Duke chapter of the Order of the Coif.

SHORT, Andrew
Paul, Hastings, Janofsky & Walker LLP, New York 212 318 6018
andrewshort@paulhastings.com
Recommended in Tax

Practice Areas: Partner in tax whose practice includes a broad range of domestic and international transactions, including mergers and acquisitions, joint ventures, equipment and project finance, real estate, funds and capital markets.

Career: Partner since 1993.

Personal: The Johns Hopkins University (BA with honors, 1982). Cornell Law School (JD, cum laude, 1985).

SHOSS, Cynthia R
LeBoeuf, Lamb, Greene & MacRae, LLP, New York 212 424 8129
cshoss@llgm.com
Recommended in Insurance

Practice Areas: Senior insurance regulatory attorney, concentrating in demutualizations and mutual holding company conversions, complex restructurings, mergers and acquisitions, and debt and equity offerings. Advises life, health and property/casualty insurers and state insurance regulators on same and on policy, strategy, legislation and regulations. Provides insurance regulatory counsel on product launches, corporate governance, examinations and internal investigations. Certified IMSA assessor.

Career: Joined LeBoeuf in 1982; Managing Partner, London Office 1987-89. Admitted to practice in New York, Illinois, Missouri and Louisiana.

Personal: Newcomb College (BA, cum laude) 1971; Tulane University (JD) 1974; New York University (LLM) 1980, Taxation.

SHUSTER, Michael
White & Case LLP, New York 212 819 8528
mshuster@whitecase.com
Recommended in Litigation

Practice Areas: Head of firm's worldwide Commercial Litigation Practice Group. Particular experience in complex financial matters, antitrust matters, class actions. Has tried cross-border arbitration matters under rules of ICC and other arbitral bodies, and matters in US Federal Courts and New York State Courts. Extensive alternative dispute/mediation proceedings experience. Clients include major financial

institutions, insurers, multinational conglomerates.

Prof. Memberships: New York State Bar, 1987; US District Courts for the Southern and Eastern Districts; ABA (Litigation, Antitrust, Entertainment and Sports Law Sections).

Personal: York University (BA, 1982); McGill University Law School (LLB, BCL, 1986); McGill Law Journal (Senior Editorial Board).

SHUTRAN, Richard
Dewey Ballantine LLP, New York 212 259 6710
rshutran@deweyballantine.com
Recommended in Projects

Practice Areas: Richard Shutran is the Vice-Chairman of Dewey Ballantine LLP's Corporate Department and the Chairman of the Project Finance Group. Mr Shutran's practice involves the representation of developers, investors and lenders in relation to the development, financing, construction and operation of a wide range of capital-intensive projects in the energy, industrial, mining and public infrastructure sectors both in the United States and abroad. Mr Shutran has counseled clients in all phases of projects, including structuring, contract negotiation, regulatory compliance, financing and post-financing matters, including restructuring and acquisitions. Mr Shutran has extensive experience in the use of both 144A and registered capital markets offerings to finance domestic US and international projects. Mr Shutran is fluent in Spanish and has participated extensively in transactions in Latin America.

Career: Partner, Dewey Ballantine LLP.

Personal: Born March 27, 1952. JD, New York University, 1978; BA, Trinity College, 1974.

SICULAR, David
Paul, Weiss, Rifkind, Wharton & Garrison LLP, New York 212 373 3082
dsicular@paulweiss.com
Recommended in Tax

Practice Areas: Tax Partner with broad practice in corporate, partnership and international transactions, including public and private mergers and acquisitions (both domestic and cross-border), private equity and investment funds, spinoffs, financings, bankruptcy and insolvency restructurings, financial products and general tax planning. Clients include public and private companies in the United States and abroad, private equity and other investment funds, private investors and individual entrepreneurs. Member of Executive Committee, New York State Bar Association Tax Section and Tax Forum.

SIFFERT, John
Lankler Siffert & Wohl, New York 212 921 8399
Recommended in Litigation

SILBERBERG, Marc L
Weil, Gotshal & Manges LLP, New York 212 310 8261
marc.silberberg@weil.com
Recommended in Tax

Practice Areas: Tax: structuring and negotiation of mergers, acquisitions and restructurings, representation of private equity funds and their portfolio companies on domestic and cross-border transactions. Mr Silberberg's practice also includes advising on securities offerings, transactions involving REITs and executive compensation.

Career: Recent representative transactions include acquisitions of Warner Chilcott plc and Grohe AG by private equity funds, the split-off of Hughes Electronics from GM, and the sale of PanAmSat Corporation. Member, Executive Committee, NY State Bar Association Tax Section; has served as Co-Chair of Committees on Pass-Through Entities and Tax Accounting.

Personal: New York University, JD, LLM; Northwestern University, BA.

SILBERSTEIN, Rebecca
Debevoise & Plimpton LLP, New York 212 909 6000
Recommended in Private Equity

SILVERMAN, Eric
Milbank, Tweed, Hadley & McCloy, New York 212 530 5000
Recommended in Projects

SIMKIN, Steven
Paul, Weiss, Rifkind, Wharton & Garrison LLP, New York 212 373 3073
ssimkin@paulweiss.com
Recommended in Real Estate

Practice Areas: Chair of Real Estate Department. Maintains an active practice in major financings, acquisitions and development projects, representing both lenders and developers. Has been involved in multi-state mortgage financings, real estate-related litigations and disputes, and complex joint ventures and partnership agreements. Has extensive shopping centre experience, having been involved in the purchase, sale or financing of several hundred regional malls. Has represented many major tenants in New York City and elsewhere. Has broad experience in the area of commercial office leasing. Major transactions include, World Trade Center, Citicorp Centre and Time Warner Center.

SIMMS, Marsha E
Weil, Gotshal & Manges LLP, New York 212 310 8116
marsha.simms@weil.com
Recommended in Banking & Finance

Practice Areas: Banking and finance, corporate.

Career: Extensive experience in debt financing and restructuring in numerous industries, including retail, telecommunications, energy and manufacturing; represented major lenders providing debtor-in-possession financing and

exit financing to newly-reorganized companies. Simms lectures in legal areas related to asset-based lending and debt financing for the Practising Law Institute and ALI/ABA, in Africa for ABA technical legal assistance projects. Named one of the 'World's Leading Lawyers' in banking and finance by 'Chambers Global' for the years 2001-04; one of 'America's Top Black Lawyers' by 'Black Enterprise Magazine' in 2003.

Personal: Stanford Law School, JD; Barnard College, BS.

SIMS, Charles
Proskauer Rose LLP, New York 212 969 3950
csims@proskauer.com
Recommended in Media & Entertainment

Practice Areas: Concentrates on copyright, First Amendment, and defamation law.

Career: He has represented the motion picture studios in their ground-breaking and successful litigation, under the Digital Millenium Copyright Act, against hackers who were publicly providing illegal software for decrypting DVDs, and Lexis-Nexis in its victory against an internet start-up which had attempted to steal the entire Lexis database for uploading onto the Web. He has also represented the League of American Theatres and Producers in an arbitration over the ownership of the Tony Award '99 programs, and England's Royal Court Theatre in connection with a copyright infringement lawsuit based on David Hare's play Via Dolorosa. In the First Amendment field, he has litigated challenges to content-based federal restrictions of cable television programming, which the Supreme Court largely invalidated in Denver Area Educational Television Consortium v FCC, and joined in handling, a facial First Amendment challenge to New York's Son of Sam law for Simon & Schuster, which the Supreme Court unanimously invalidated.

Personal: Yale Law School, JD, 1976; Amherst College, BA, Magna Cum Laude, 1971 Phi Beta Kappa.

SINGER, Andrew
Latham & Watkins LLP, San Diego 619 236 1234
Recommended in Projects

SINGER, Leonard
Couch White, LLP, Albany 518 426 4600
Recommended in Energy

SINGER, Louis
Orrick, Herrington & Sutcliffe, New York 212 506 5055
lsinger@orrick.com
Recommended in Private Equity

Practice Areas: Chair, Orrick's Private Investment Funds Group. He advises clients regarding virtually every type of private investment fund, including buyout, venture capital, real estate opportunity, distressed assets, mezzanine and hedge funds. He has broad experience in the formation of funds-of-funds and co-investment funds and in their investment activities. He also represents investors in direct debt and equity transactions, including the purchase of senior and subordinated notes and mezzanine investments.

Prof. Memberships: President and Trustee, American College of Investment Counsel; Committee on Private Investment Funds, the Association of the Bar of the City of New York; Board of Governors, the Association of Life Insurance Counsel; Private Investment Funds Forum; National Association of Public Pension Attorneys.

Career: Associate and Partner, LeBoef, Lamb, Greene & MacRae (1979-87); Partner, Orrick, Herrington & Sutcliffe LLP (1987-present).

Publications: Various articles on corporate law and private equity funds; papers presented to the International Bar Association, the Institute for Private Investors, the American College of Investment Counsel, the Association of Life Insurance Counsel and several private equity industry conferences.

Personal: University of Pennsylvania, BA, magna cum laude, Phi Beta Kappa, 1973; Cambridge University, LLB, First Class, 1975; Stanford University Law School (JD, 1977), Stanford Law Review.

SIRKIN, Michael
Proskauer Rose LLP, New York
212 969 3840
msirkin@proskauer.com
Recommended in Employee Benefits

Practice Areas: A member of Proskauer Rose's Tax Department, he practices primarily in the areas of employee benefits and executive compensation. In addition, he frequently represents companies and senior executives in connection with executive employment and severance agreements and other compensation and equity arrangements. In the executive compensation area, he advises in connection with nonqualified arrangements, such as Supplemental Executive Retirement Plans and other deferred-compensation plans, incentive plans, rabbi trusts and other funding vehicles. He also advises corporations on the design and implementation of stock option, restricted stock and similar plans.

Career: He has represented corporations and executives in a diverse assortment of businesses, including Fortune 500 industrial companies, financial-service companies, high tech start-ups, dot.coms, REITs, tax-exempt organizations and privately held companies.

Publications: He is co-editor and co-lead author of the treatise Executive Compensation published by Law Journal Seminar-Press, and the co-author of the Chapter on ERISA in the 403(b) Answer Book. He is a contributing editor

to The Philanthropy Monthly, writing a bimonthly column on compensation and benefits for tax-exempt organizations, and on the Board of Advisors of The Journal of Taxation of Employee Benefits.

Personal: Columbia University School of Law, JD, 1972. Rutgers University, New Brunswick, BS, 1969.

SIT, Po
Davis Polk & Wardwell, New York
212 450 4000
po.sit@dpw.com
Recommended in Tax

Practice Areas: Member of Davis Polk & Wardwell's Tax Department. Works principally in the areas of derivative products, partnerships, mergers and acquisitions. Has been representing financial institutions primarily in the areas of financial products and derivatives for years.

SLOTNICK, Barry
Loeb & Loeb LLP, New York
212 407 4000
Recommended in Media & Entertainment

SMITH, Bradley Y
Davis Polk & Wardwell, New York
212 450 4000
bradley.smith@dpw.com
Recommended in Banking & Finance

Practice Areas: Senior Partner in Davis Polk & Wardwell's Credit Group and advises senior and subordinated lenders, as well as borrowers, in corporate finance transactions. Areas of concentration include secured financing; structured finance; receivables and lease purchase transactions; oil, gas and other mineral-based financing; project and other limited-recourse financing; and acquisition and other leveraged financing transactions. Has been a principal adviser to JP Morgan for many years, and has represented the Morgan interests in many US and international financing transactions, as well as in restructurings and recapitalizations.

SMITH, Chris M
Shearman & Sterling LLP, New York
212 848 8238
csmith@shearman.com
Recommended in Real Estate

Practice Areas: Partner in Shearman & Sterling's Real Estate Group. Represents clients on developments, financings, investment funds, acquisitions, dispositions, real estate workouts, foreclosures and bankruptcies.

Prof. Memberships: Member, Association of the Bar of the City of New York and New York State Bar Association; Member, Association of Foreign Investors in Real Estate; Member, Real Estate Board of New York.

Career: Joined Shearman in 1976 and became a Partner in 1984.

Personal: BS, Rutgers University (1973); JD, Columbia University School of Law (1976).

SMITH, Jeffrey
Cravath, Swaine & Moore LLP,
New York 212 474 1514
jsmith@cravath.com
Recommended in Environment

Practice Areas: Environmental matters relating to financings, underwritings and mergers and acquisitions. Counseling on environmental regulatory and compliance issues and advice on complex environmental litigation, including mass toxic torts, asbestos and insurance issues. Assessing and allocating environmental risks and liabilities.

Prof. Memberships: ABA (Co-Chair, Committee for Environmental Disclosure).

Career: Massachusetts Executive Office of Environmental Affairs, 1976-78. Private practice, Philadelphia, 1981-91. Joined Cravath 1992, Partner since 1998. Managing Partner, Administration, since 2000.

Publications: 'Environmental Disclosure Requirements under Securities Laws' (ABA).

Personal: University of Pennsylvania (JD, 1981; Legal Writing Instructor; president, Environmental Law Society); Harvard University (AB, 1974). Urban Assembly: Advisory Board.

SMITH, Jeffrey Q
King & Spalding LLP, New York
212 556 2283
jqsmith@kslaw.com
Recommended in Litigation

Practice Areas: National litigation practice with particular concentration in antitrust/trade regulation, securities, and other complex commercial cases. Experienced in the supervision and management of large cases. Well versed in various forms of alternative dispute resolution, including arbitration and mediation, and maintains an active counseling practice designed to help clients avoid and/or minimize litigation risks.

Prof. Memberships: American Bar Association (Member, Sections on: Antitrust and Litigation).

Personal: Yale University; JD, New York University, Order of the Coif, 1977.

SMITH, Joseph A
Dewey Ballantine LLP, New York
212 259 7268
jsmith@deweyballantine.com
Recommended in Private Equity

Practice Areas: Mr Smith represents fund sponsors, asset managers, pension funds and endowments in connection with fund formation, the acquisition of portfolio investments and the implementation of exit strategies. In this capacity, Mr Smith advises clients on securities, governance, ERISA, Investment Advisers Act and structural issues. Mr Smith has extensive experience with all classes of alternative assets, including international investments, secondary investments and Real Estate Investment Trusts.

Career: Partner, Dewey Ballantine LLP. Admitted to practice, 1990, New York.

Personal: Born October 14, 1960. AB, Columbia College, 1983. JD, New York University School of Law, 1988.

SOBEL, Gerald
Kaye Scholer LLP, New York
212 836 8515
gsobel@kayescholer.com
Recommended in Intellectual Property

Practice Areas: Partner, Senior Litigation Partner and Chair, Patent Group. Focuses on patent, antitrust, trade secret and licensing cases, including appeals. By way of illustration, he recently prevailed against the University of Rochester in the Celebrex patent infringement case for Pfizer on appeal at the Federal Circuit and earlier on summary judgment at the District Court level. His trials include two landmark jury wins. He represented Xerox in its win in the patent-antitrust litigation involving office copier and electromechanical technology in the District of Connecticut, the longest federal civil jury trial. He was lead counsel for Xoma in its win on patent infringement against Centocor before a San Francisco jury in the longest biotech trial to date.

Prof. Memberships: Member of the New York Bar and admitted to practice before the US District Courts for the Southern, Eastern and Northern Districts of New York, the US Courts of Appeals for the Second, Third and Federal Circuits, the United States Supreme Court and the US Patent Office. He is on the Advisory Committee for Patent Litigation of the District Court in Delaware. Teaching and Lecturing: Mr Sobel is a member of the Advisory Committee of the Engelberg Intellectual Property Institute at the New York University School of Law and taught as an adjunct associate professor there. He recently testified at the Innovation and Competition hearings conducted by the Federal Trade Commission and has delivered lectures at Columbia, Stanford, Cardozo, Washington University, Case Western and Brooklyn Law Schools. Mr Sobel has delivered over 100 lectures at CLE programs.

Career: JD, New York University School of Law, 1963, Law Review, Hays Fellow; BEE, Electrical Engineering, City College of New York, 1960; Law Clerk to Hon. Richard H Levet (SDNY) (1964-65).

Publications: Mr Sobel has also published widely. A recent publication is 'Competition Policy in Patent Cases and Antitrust' in Perspectives on Properties of The Human Genome Project (Elsevier, 2003).

SOLOMON, Andrew P
Sullivan & Cromwell LLP, New York
212 558 4000
solomona@sullcrom.com
Recommended in Tax

Practice Areas: Managing Partner, Tax

Group. Broad-based practice involving both tax planning and dispute resolution. Regularly advises on structuring acquisitions, divestitures, spin-offs and joint ventures, including cross-border transactions, and on taxation of complex financial products. Recent clients include financial institutions (including insurance companies), private equity funds and their managers, high-technology and natural resources companies. Extensive experience in domestic/international M&A, as well as the organisation, operation, acquisition and/or taking public of offshore insurers, reinsurers and insurance securitisation vehicles.
Prof. Memberships: ABA; NYSBA (Executive Committee, Tax Section).
Career: Partner since 1992.
Publications: Writes and speaks frequently on taxation of financial products/institutions and international taxation. Contributing author, 'Taxation of Financial Products', a Clark Boardman treatise.
Personal: Brown University (AB, 1975); Harvard Law School (JD, 1984; Editor, Harvard Law Review).

SOMMER, Dean
Young, Sommer, Ward, Ritzenberg, Wooley, Baker & Moore LLC, Albany
518 438 9907
dsommer@youngsommer.com
Recommended in Environment
Practice Areas: Mr Sommer is one of the founding partners of a 14-attorney law firm located in Albany, New York representing corporations, institutions, municipalities and individuals. Young, Sommer LLC was named one of the top ten environmental firms in New York State. Principal practice areas of law are environmental, municipal, land use, power and energy, insurance, labor and general litigation. Mr Sommer is primarily involved in CERCLA, RCRA and CWA litigation and brownfield development.
Prof. Memberships: Mr Sommer is Co-Chair of the Enforcement and Compliance committee of the Environmental Law Section of the NYS State Bar.
Career: Mr Sommer is a former State Assistant Attorney General (1983-86) and served as the Section Chief of the Toxics Enforcement Unit in the State Attorney General's Office (1986-95). He served on the transition team of Attorney General Eliot Spitzer (1995). Firm partners also include former government officials, law professors and experienced private practitioners.
Publications: The partners in the firm, including Mr Sommer, have published a wide variety of articles on environmental and energy law related topics.
Personal: Mr Sommer graduated from Georgetown Law Center (1978). Firm partners graduated from law schools such as Harvard, Cornell, NYU, Rutgers, Syracuse and Wisconsin.

SOPHER, Edward
Gibson, Dunn & Crutcher LLP, New York
212 351 3918
esopher@gibsondunn.com
Recommended in Private Equity
Practice Areas: Establishment and operation of private investment funds, including private equity, hedge, real estate and distressed investment funds, and funds of funds. Represents investment managers and sponsors of these funds, institutional and seed investors, placement agents and joint venture partners. Also involved in acquisition, investment and financing transactions involving investment management firms, fund clients and portfolio companies.
Prof. Memberships: New York Bar; Solicitor, England & Wales; Association of the Bar of the City of New York; New York Private Investment Funds Forum.
Personal: Cambridge University, BA 1982, MA 1985.

SORIN, Robert J
Fried, Frank, Harris, Shriver & Jacobson LLP, New York 212 859 8487
robert.sorin@friedfrank.com
Recommended in Real Estate
Practice Areas: Real Estate Partner. Practice covers a broad range of commercial real estate transactions, including the development of mixed-use buildings, commercial mortgage, construction and mezzanine financing, complex multi-asset-based lending, leasing, the sale and acquisition of office, shopping center and industrial properties, joint ventures and debt restructurings. Principal clients include: Brown Harris Stevens, LP; Emmes & Company; Intell Management and Investment Company; JPMorgan Chase & Co.; Macklowe Properties, Inc.; the Moinian Group; New York-Presyterian Hospital; the Related Companies; Swig Burris Equities LLC; and Zeckendorf Realty, LP.
Career: Joined Fried Frank as Partner in 1997. Prior to Fried Frank practiced at Reavis & McGrath (now Fulbright & Jaworski) from 1983-85, practiced for 12 years at Robinson Silverman Pearce Aronsohn & Berman LLP, becoming a Partner there in 1990. Admitted to the Bar in New York.
Personal: Born 1957. Received JD from Georgetown University, cum laude, in 1982 and BA from Washington University, magna cum laude, in 1979.

SORKIN, David
Simpson Thacher & Bartlett LLP, New York 212 455 2000
dsorkin@stblaw.com
Recommended in Corporate/M&A
Practice Areas: A Partner at Simpson Thacher & Bartlett practising in the firm's Corporate Department. Advises clients in merger and acquisition transactions, securities law matters, corporate governance and other corporate law matters. Regularly advises the investment firm Kohlberg Kravis Roberts &

Co and its portfolio companies, as well as other major private equity firms. Among other clients, provides on-going corporate advice to Time Warner Inc., and represented America Online Inc. in connection with its US$165 billion merger with Time Warner. Represented Associates First Capital Corporation in connection with its initial public offering, its spinoff by the Ford Motor Company and its US$31 billion merger with Citigroup Inc and Ford Motor Company in connection with numerous acquisitions, divestitures, joint ventures and securities law matters.
Career: Joined the firm in 1985 and became a Partner in 1993. From 1984-85 clerked for Hon Charles M Merrill of the US Court of Appeals for the Ninth Circuit in San Francisco.
Personal: Received a BA, summa cum laude in 1981 from Williams College and a JD, cum laude in 1984 from Harvard University.

SOSNICK, Fredric
Shearman & Sterling LLP, New York
212 848 8571
fsosnick@shearman.com
Recommended in Bankruptcy
Practice Areas: Partner in the Bankruptcy and Reorganization Group at Shearman & Sterling. Has extensive experience representing debtors, official creditors' committees, lender groups, creditors and acquirors of assets in large and complex domestic and international out-of-court restructurings and US Chapter 11 cases.
Prof. Memberships: Member, New York State Bar Association; Admitted in US District Courts, Southern District of New York and Eastern District of New York.
Career: Joined Shearman as a Partner in 1997.
Personal: BS, cum laude, State University of New York at Albany (1987); JD, magna cum laude, American University, Washington College of Law (1990).

SPATT, Robert E
Simpson Thacher & Bartlett LLP, New York 212 455 2000
rspatt@stblaw.com
Recommended in Corporate/M&A
Practice Areas: Partner specializing in corporate and corporate governance advice to boards of directors, and mergers, acquisitions and restructurings for buying and selling companies, their financial advisors, control stockholders, LBO firms and special committees of boards of directors.
Prof. Memberships: Co-Chairman of the Tulane Corporate Law Institute, a leading US M&A institute; Professional Fellow of the NYU Centre for Law and Business.
Career: Recent transactions include representing the Special Committee of the Board of Directors of Eon Labs in its pending acquisition by Novartis, UFJ in

its pending merger with MTFG, Harmony Gold in its bid for Gold Fields, Citizens Communications in its evaluation and execution of financial and strategic alternatives, CSL Limited in its acquisition of Aventis' blood plasma business, H.J. Heinz in its spin/merge transaction with Del Monte Foods, the controlling stockholder of Panamco in its acquisition by Coca Cola FEMSA, Moody's in its acquisition of KMV and the Special Committee of AXA Financial in its buyout by AXA. Mr Spatt also represents financial advisors in M&A transactions, including recently for MCI in its pending acquisition by Verizon, for Gillette in its pending acquisition by P&G, for Nextel in its pending merger with Sprint, for Mandalay in its merger with MGM Mirage and for Comcast in its bid for Disney and its acquisition of ATT Broadband.
Personal: Graduated from Brown University (AB, 1977), University of Michigan Law School (JD, magna cum laude 1980, Order of the Coif).

STAFFARONI, Robert
Debevoise & Plimpton LLP, New York
212 909 6000
Recommended in Tax

STAPLETON, Benjamin F
Sullivan & Cromwell LLP, New York
212 558 4000
stapletonb@sullcrom.com
Recommended in Corporate/M&A
Practice Areas: Senior Partner of M&A Group. Has participated in hundreds of transactions, representing bidders, targets and financial advisors in both friendly and contested situations. Major transactions include BP's acquisitions of Amoco and Atlantic Richfield Company, Glaxo-Wellcome's merger with SmithKline Beecham, Vodafone's acquisitions of AirTouch and Mannesmann, and SBC Communications' acquisitions of PacTel, SNET and Ameritech. Recently represented SBC in its proposed acquisition of AT&T and Medco Health Solutions in its agreement to acquire Accredo Health.
Prof. Memberships: ABA; ABCNY; NYSBA.
Career: Partner since 1977.
Personal: Harvard College (AB, 1965); Yale Law School (JD, 1969).

STARR, Michael
Hogan & Hartson LLP, New York
212 918 3638
mstarr@hhlaw.com
Recommended in Employment
Practice Areas: Employment and labor relations law, focusing on employment discrimination; employee non-competition; theft of trade secrets and disloyalty litigation; executive employment; class-action litigation; labor-management relations and collective-bargaining; mediation and arbitration of both employment and labor disputes; and international employment law.

Prof. Memberships: Member, Labor and Employment Section and International Employment Law Committee, American Bar Association; Member, Association of the Bar of the City of New York; Member, Federal Bar Council; Member, International Society for Labor Law; Founding Board Member and Member, Board of Directors of the Court Appointed Special Advocates (CASA) (1983-2000); Member, Human Resources Committee for the New York City Partnership and Chamber of Commerce (1990-98).

Career: In his 25-year career as labor and employment lawyer, Michael has represented clients in matters before the National Labor Relations Board, the Equal Employment Opportunity Commission and other administrative agencies and arbitration tribunals; defended employers in discrimination, employment contract, executive compensation, wage-hour and other matters, and represented management in injunction and other litigation against labor unions. He regularly advises global companies on preventive employment-law practices, and currently serves as a court-appointed mediator for the federal district court in New York.

Publications: 'Non-competition By Employee Choice', The National Law Journal, (1/5/2004). 'Deconstructing 'Constructive Discharge', The National Law Journal, (4/19/2004); 'Mental Disabilities', The National Law Journal (11/1/2004); 'Harassment by Consensual Sex', The National Law Journal (8/1/2004); 'The New Law of Continuing Violations', The National Law Journal (1/25/2003); 'Spoilation by Oversight', The National Law Journal (11/12/2001); 'Restrictive Covenants', The National Law Journal (9/6/1999); 'Investigating Harassment', The National Law Journal (6/21/1999); 'A Witness-Friendly Guide to Surviving a Deposition', ALI-ABA's Practice Checklist Manual on Trial Preparation II (1999); 'Hands Across the Water: Sexual Harassment and the Global Company', The Corporate Counselor (1/1997); 'Who's the Boss? The Globalization of United States Employment Law', Business Lawyer (5/1996); 'Deja Vu All Over Again: Automatic Renewal of Employment Contracts', Corporate Counselor (11/1/1996); 'Americans With Disabilities Act of 1990: Employer Responsibilities', Employment Law Handbook 44 (1993); 'The 'Sexual Shakedown' in Perspective: Sexual Harassment in Its Social and Legal Context', Employment Relations Law Journal (1982); 'Accommodation and Accountability: A Strategy for Judicial Enforcement of Institutional Reform Decrees', Alabama Law Review (1981); 'The Mental Hospitalization of Children and the Limits of Parental Authority', Yale Law Journal (1979).

Personal: JD, Yale Law School, editor of the Yale Law Journal; Woodrow Wilson Fellow, PhD (Philosophy), University of Michigan; BA, summa cum laude, State University of New York, Binghamton University. Michael served as law clerk to The Honorable Abner J Mikva, Circuit Judge for the US Court of Appeals in Washington, DC. Admitted in NY and the United States Supreme Court and several other federal trial and appellate courts.

STEIN, Joshua
Latham & Watkins LLP, New York
212 906 1200
Recommended in Real Estate

STEIN, Mark
Simpson Thacher & Bartlett LLP, New York 212 455 2310
mstein@stblaw.com
Recommended in Litigation
Practice Areas: Litigation Partner at Simpson Thacher & Bartlett LLP. Mr Stein's represents institutions and individuals in governmental and internal investigations in matters concerning securities laws and regulations, banking, antitrust, money laundering, the Foreign Corrupt Practices Act, tax evasion and commercial bribery. He regularly handles investigations by the United States Department of Justice, the SEC, securities self-regulatory organizations, the New York State Attorney General's Office and various District Attorney offices. Mr Stein also advises and reports to Boards of Directors and their committees on appropriate steps in response to possible violations applicable laws and regulations by company personnel. As a member of the Criminal Justice Act panel, Mr Stein regularly represents criminal defendants on trial in federal district court and has achieved a high rate of acquittals. Finally, Mr Stein is engaged in representing clients named as defendants in civil securties actions.
Personal: Born 1959. Received JD in 1983 from University of Michigan and BA 1980 from State University of New York at Albany.

STEINER, Jeffrey
Brown Raysman Millstein Felder & Steiner LLP, New York
212 895 2260
jsteiner@brownraysman.com
Recommended in Real Estate
Practice Areas: Jeffrey B Steiner is Chairman of the firm's Business and Finance Department and also heads the firm's Real Estate Finance Group. He regularly represents Wall Street investment banks and institutional lenders in complex structured finance transactions, including construction; conduit, floating and fixed rate financings; forward loan commitments; mezzanine loans; loan participations; low-income housing tax credit; preferred equity and mortgage-backed securities transactions. Mr Steiner has written extensively on real estate, banking and structured finance issues. He co-authors the Real Estate Finance column of the New York Law Journal.
Personal: BA, McGill University 1977; JD, Fordham University 1980.

STEINTHAL, Kenneth
Weil, Gotshal & Manges LLP, New York
650 802 3081
kenneth.steinthal@weil.com
Recommended in Media & Entertainment
Practice Areas: Mr Steinthal specializes in handling litigation and complex industry-wide licensing proceedings in the music and broader media industries, domestically and abroad; he has substantial trial experience in these and other areas, in jury and bench trial settings, in both US federal and state courts and before copyright tribunals and other arbitral bodies worldwide.
Career: Mr Steinthal Co-Heads Weil Gotshal's IP/Media Practice, and recently relocated to the firm's Silicon Valley office to build a litigation and media practice for Weil Gotshal on the West Coast. The IP/Media Practice Group has developed the world's pre-eminent music rights litigation and licensing practice, representing entities engaged in wide-scale distribution of music and other content (AOL, Yahoo!, MTV Networks, RealNetworks, MusicNet, Disney/ABC, Viacom's cable and satellite services and others). Mr Steinthal frequently has managed complex industry-wide trials in copyright/rate-setting and antitrust cases on behalf of the broadcast/cable television and online 'webcasting' industries against copyright collecting societies and other groups of copyright owners; and he and others in this practice area also specialize in developing innovative licensing solutions for traditional and new media worldwide.
Personal: Fordham University, JD; Williams College, BA (cum laude).

STEPHENSON, Alan
Cravath, Swaine & Moore LLP, New York 212 474 1400
astephenson@cravath.com
Recommended in Corporate/M&A
Practice Areas: Mergers and acquisitions, joint ventures.
Prof. Memberships: NYSBA; ABCNY.
Career: Partner, 1978-88. Managing Director, Wasserstein Perella & Co., Inc., 1988-92. Partner since 1992.
Personal: University of Virginia School of Law (JD, 1970); University of North Carolina at Chapel Hill (AB, 1967; Phi Beta Kappa). University of North Carolina at Chapel Hill: External Advisory Board, Undergraduate Honors Program.

STERN, Akiba
Morgan, Lewis & Bockius LLP, New York 212 309 6037
astern@morganlewis.com
Recommended in Business Process Outsourcing: National, Technology
Practice Areas: Akiba Stern concen-

trates his practice on complex, long-term sourcing and services arrangements including outsourcing transactions, information technology-enabled business transactions, electronic commerce, technology transfers, licensing, intellectual property, joint ventures, and strategic alliances. Mr Stern helps his clients structure, negotiate, and implement commercial strategies, alliance structures, pricing models, governance arrangements, change management protocols, contract administration, and supplier compliance strategies. In the Chambers USA and Chambers Global Leading Lawyers Guides Mr Stern was cited as "the one to go to" for information technology and corporate transactions, and for "his facility for closing enormous deals". Mr Stern lectures widely and publishes frequently.
Prof. Memberships: Member, Computer Law Association; Member, Licensing Executives Society; Member, American Bar Association.

STERN, Richard
Luskin, Stern & Eisler LLP, New York
212 293 2700
Recommended in Bankruptcy

STERNBERG, Daniel S
Cleary Gottlieb Steen & Hamilton LLP, New York 212 225 2630
dsternberg@cgsh.com
Recommended in Corporate/M&A
Practice Areas: M&A transactions, with a particular focus on cross-border transactions and the representation of international clients. Counseling on corporate governance matters, including fiduciary duties of officers and directors to corporations and their boards and representation of institutional shareholders in their relationships with public issuers.
Prof. Memberships: Member of the New York City Bar Association's Special Committee on Mergers, Acquisitions and Corporate Control Contests; ABA Negotiated Acquisition Committee Task Force.
Career: Joined firm,1980, became Partner, 1988. Resident Partner, firm's Paris office, 1991-96. JD, Columbia University Law School (1979), Kent Scholar, editor - Law Review. BA, cum laude, Yale University (1976).

STEUER, Richard M
Mayer, Brown, Rowe & Maw LLP, New York 212 506 2530
rsteuer@mayerbrownrowe.com
Recommended in Antitrust
Practice Areas: Litigates at all levels of federal and state courts, on behalf of defendants and plaintiffs, in private suits and against government entities. Represents clients in government investigations, both civil and criminal, including agency review of mergers, acquisitions and joint ventures. Regularly advises leading companies on structuring their business practices, including distribution arrangements and licensing programs.

Career: Joined Mayer, Brown, Rowe & Maw LLP, New York, as Partner, 2002. Kaye Scholer LLP, 1973-2002 (Chair, Antitrust Practice Group).

Publications: Recent writings: 'Dysfunctional Discounts', Antitrust, Vol. 19 No. 2 (2005). [With Peter A Barile III] 'Antitrust in Wartime', Antitrust, Vol. 16 No. 2 (2002).'Customer-Instigated Exclusive Dealing', 68 Antitrust Law Journal 239 (2000).

Personal: Columbia Law School, JD, 1973. Hofstra University, BA, 1970. Adjunct Associate Professor, New York University School of Law, 1985. Adjunct Professor, St John's University School of Law, 2003.Chair, Antitrust Committee, Association of the Bar of the City of New York 1995-98. Secretary and Communications Officer, ABA Section of Antitrust Law, 2004-05.

STEVER, Donald W
Kirkpatrick & Lockhart Nicholson Graham LLP, New York 212 536 4861
dstever@klng.com
Recommended in Environment

Practice Areas: Civil and criminal environmental litigation and counseling experience (all areas); transactional environmental law, domestic and international.

Prof. Memberships: Bars of NY, CT, NH, DC, US Supreme Court, numerous federal courts, Environmental Law Institute, ABA, NYS Bar Association.

Career: Kirkpatrick & Lockhart Nicholson Graham LLP (Partner); Dewey Ballantine LLP (Partner); Sidley & Austin (Partner); Pace University School of Law (Professor of Law); Day, Berry & Howard (Special Counsel); United States Department of Justice (Section Chief, Pollution Control & Environmental Defense Sections); Dartmouth College (Visitng Professor); State of New Hampshire Office of Attorney General, Environmental Protection Divison Aetna Life and Casualty, Hartford, CT.

Publications: The Law of Chemical Regulation and Hazardous Waste, West Group Environmental Law & Practice - Compliance Litigation Forms, West Group (co-author) Seabrook and the Nuclear Regulatory Commission: The Licensing of a Nuclear Power Plant, University Press of New England Several Treatise Chapters and Numerous Articles and Lectures.

Personal: JD, University of Pennsylvania Law School BA, Lehigh University.

STILLMAN, Charles
Stillman & Friedman, New York
212 223 0200
Recommended in Litigation

STOLL, Neal R
Skadden, Arps, Slate, Meagher & Flom LLP & Affiliates, New York
212 735 3660
nstoll@skadden.com
Recommended in Antitrust

Practice Areas: Represents clients

involved in investigations conducted by the staff of the Department of Justice, Antitrust Division; Part 2 investigations conducted by the staffs of the Federal Trade Commission's Bureau of Competition and Bureau of Consumer Protection; Part 3 administrative proceedings and appeals; and Federal trial and appellate experience in cases involving monopolization, distribution practices, the Robinson-Patman Act and acquisitions. Counsels clients on antitrust issues regarding mergers and acquisitions, as well as antitrust and consumer protection matters, including compliance programs and proposed business plans.

Career: JD, Fordham University, 1973 (Member, Fordham Law Review); BA, Pennsylvania State University, 1970.

STRASSBERG, Richard
Goodwin Procter LLP, New York
212 813 8800
rstrassberg@goodwinprocter.com
Recommended in Litigation

Practice Areas: Mr Strassberg specializes in white collar criminal defense, corporate internal investigations, corporate regulatory practice, and complex business and financial litigation. In addition to his work in the white collar and regulatory arenas, Mr Strassberg represents clients in complex civil litigation, including representations involving securities class action defense, minority shareholder rights, ERISA class action defense, healthcare and insurance litigation, and employment issues.

Prof. Memberships: Federal Bar Council: Member.

Personal: JD, Harvard Law School, 1988 (cum laude); BS, Cornell University, 1985 (with distinction).

STRAUSS, Audrey
Fried, Frank, Harris, Shriver & Jacobson LLP, New York 212 859 8544
audrey.strauss@friedfrank.com
Recommended in Litigation

Practice Areas: Litigation Partner. Ms Strauss represents institutions and individuals in white-collar criminal defense and regulatory matters. She also handles internal investigations and a broad range of civil litigation, including matters that run parallel to grand jury and United States Securities and Exchange Commission matters.

Prof. Memberships: Ms Strauss has spoken and written for the Practising Law Institute, the New York State Bar Association and the American Bar Association. She writes a regular column on corporate criminal issues for the 'New York Law Journal'. She is a Fellow of the American College of Trial Lawyers and a director of the Legal Aid Society and the Office of Appellate Defender. She was named in December 2001 by 'The National Law Journal' as one of the country's top 50 women litigators. She received in March 2002 the New York

Council of Defense Lawyers' Norman Ostrow Award.

Career: Ms Strauss is admitted to the Bar in New York and to practice before the US District Courts for the Southern and Eastern Districts of New York and the US Court of Appeals for the Second Circuit. Joined Fried Frank as Partner in 1990. Prior to Fried Frank she served in the US Attorney's Office for the Southern District of New York from 1975-82.

Personal: Born 1947. Received JD in 1971 from Columbia University and BA 1968 from Barnard College.

SUGARMAN, Robert
Weil, Gotshal & Manges LLP, New York
212 310 8184
robert.sugarman@weil.com
Recommended in Media & Entertainment

Practice Areas: Intellectual property and media, litigation/regulatory: specializes in intellectual property and First Amendment matters.

Career: Consistently listed in 'Best Lawyers in America' and 'America's Leading Business Lawyers;' long-term fellow, American College of Trial Lawyers. Sugarman has litigated significant cases in libel, privacy, copyright, trademark, trade dress, unfair competition and false advertising; was lead counsel to licensor of the technology used to encrypt copyrighted motion pictures on DVD in a trade secret case. Representative clients: American Eagle Outfitters, CBS, Julio Iglesias, Sony Music, Sony Pictures, Warner Chappell, National Geographic Society, DVD Copy Control Association.

Personal: Yale University, BA, JD.

SUKIN, Michael
Sukin Law Group, New York
212 302 5800
Recommended in Media & Entertainment

SULLIVAN, Robert J
Skadden, Arps, Slate, Meagher & Flom LLP & Affiliates, New York
212 735 2930
rsulliva@skadden.com
Recommended in Insurance

Practice Areas: Over 30 years of experience representing insurance and reinsurance companies and extensive experience with corporate transactions, insurance regulatory matters, reinsurance and complex restructurings.

Career: JD, New York Law School, 1974 (Research Editor, New York Law Review); BA, Fordham University, 1971.

SUSKO, A Richard
Cleary Gottlieb Steen & Hamilton LLP, New York 212 225 2410
bsusko@cgsh.com
Recommended in Employee Benefits

Practice Areas: Employee benefits and executive compensation, including fiduciary and tax aspects of pension fund investments, golden parachutes, stock

options, and other executive incentive compensation plans. Extensive experience in benefits aspect of mergers and acquisitions, ESOPs, plan terminations, and bankruptcy. He is an Adjunct Professor of Executive Compensation at New York University School of Law.

Prof. Memberships: Member of the Bar in New York; Charter Member, American College of Employee Benefits Counsel.

Career: Joined firm, 1974; became Partner, 1982. LLM in taxation, New York University School of Law (1980); JD and MBA, Stanford University (1974); BS (Mathematics), Union College (1969).

SUYDAM, John
O'Melveny & Myers LLP, New York
212 326 2000
Recommended in Corporate/M&A

SWARTZ, Linda Z
Cadwalader, Wickersham & Taft LLP, New York 212 504 6062
linda.swartz@cwt.com
Recommended in Tax

Practice Areas: Co-Chair of Cadwalader's Tax Department. Advises public and private companies and their investment advisors on the tax and business issues of global mergers and acquisitions, spin-offs, joint ventures, restructurings and bankruptcies. Routinely advises clients with respect to derivatives, structured financial products, and other financing transactions. Frequent speaker and writer on a wide range of transactional tax issues.

Personal: A Phi Beta Kappa graduate from Bucknell University, holds a JD from the University of Pennsylvania Law School. Member, New York State Bar Association Tax Section (Executive Committee); American Bar Association, New York City Tax Club. Authors the chapters on Securities Lending Transactions in Taxation of Financial Institutions (Clark Boardman Callaghan) and Debt Exchanges in Collier on Bankruptcy Taxation (Matthew Bender). Other significant recent publications include: Global Tax-Free Deals: Mergers, Acquisitions and Spins at Home and Abroad; Circular 230 and Tax Shelters in 2005; ABCs of Cross-Border Derivatives.

SWEENEY, John
Morgan & Finnegan, LLP, New York
212 415 8525
JFSweeney@morganfinnegan.com
Recommended in Intellectual Property

Practice Areas: Trials and appeals, alternative dispute resolution, interference practice, patent, licensing, antitrust, trademark and trade dress in the consumer product, medical device, pharmaceutical and computer technology industries.

Prof. Memberships: The American Bar Association, New York County Lawyers Association, Association of the Bar of the City of New York, American Intellectual Property Law Association and The New York Intellectual Property Law

Association, President of The New York Intellectual Property Law Association in 2000.

Career: Has been involved in patent, trade secret and trademark litigation since 1973. His litigation experience includes patent, antitrust, trademark and trade dress bench and jury trials and appeals. He has acted as lead trial counsel for The Procter & Gamble Company, Boehringer Ingelheim Corporation, Sankyo, Bombardier, Inc., C.R. Bard, Inc., Dot Hill Systems Corporation, Finisar Corporation, Tile Council of America and Arthur D. Little, Inc. in numerous cases. He acted as co-counsel for Digital Equipment Corporation in the Digital/Intel litigation involving microprocessor technology. He has had extensive jury trial practice and has argued many times in the United States Court of Appeals for the Federal Circuit. Before entering legal practice, Mr Sweeney worked as a mathematician and computer analyst for the US Army Strategy and Tactics Analysis Group. His work involved mathematical modeling, including war games.

Publications: John F Sweeney, author of Chapter 10, Injunctions in 'Patent Litigation', edited by Laurence H Pretty, published 2001 by The Practising Law Institute. John F Sweeney, 'What Is the Zurko Case And What Does It Mean?', American Conference Institute Seminar on Tactical Considerations And Strategies For Success In Litigating Patent Disputes, March 9-10, 2000, Washington, DC. John F Sweeney, Trying A Patent Case To a Jury And the Federal Circuit At the Same Time, 'The IP Litigator', 2000. John F Sweeney and James F Bush, 'The Doctrines of Equivalents And Prosecution History Estoppel: What Has Warner-Jenkinson Changed?', The Practising Law Institute, 1999. John F Sweeney and Charles H Sanders, 'The On-Sale Bar To Patentability: Understanding The Doctrine's Past, Present, And Future', The Practising Law Institute, 1998. John F Sweeney and Brenda Pomerance, Significant Developments In Patent Litigation In 1995, 'The IP Litigator', March 28, 1996. John F Sweeney and Elaine J Kaman, 'Inequitable Conduct Developments', The Practising Law Institute, 1995. John F Sweeney, Midge M Hyman, Scott D Greenberg and Margaret A Bitler, 'Using U.S. Courts And International Treaties To Protect Against Infringement Abroad And At Home', The Practising Law Institute, 1994. John F Sweeney and Kim D Connolly, 'The Rocky Road To Harmonization: Complications Raised By The Impending United States Transition To A First-To-File Patent System', 1993. John F Sweeney, Scott D Greenberg and Margaret A Bitler, Heading Them Off At The Pass — Can Counterfeit Goods Of Foreign Origin Be Stopped At The Counterfeiter's Border? 'The Trademark Reporter', 1993. John F Sweeney and Alexandra T Manbeck, Antitrust Law: The Year In Review, '1993 NYIPLA Intellectual Property Annual', 1993.

SWEET, William J
Skadden, Arps, Slate, Meagher & Flom LLP & Affiliates, Washington, DC
202 371 7030
wsweet@skadden.com
Recommended in Banking & Finance
Practice Areas: Focuses on financial institution merger and acquisition, regulatory and enforcement matters. Represents US and non-US banks, thrifts, insurance, securities and investment companies in connection with the acquisition of banks, savings and loan associations, savings banks, investment managers, securities firms, mutual funds, credit card issuers and other financial institutions. Counseled numerous non-US banking and investment banking clients engaged in various joint ventures with US financial institutions, especially in the securities, investment management, derivatives and leasing fields.
Career: JD, Georgetown University Law Center, 1978; BA, Bucknell University, 1974.

SYNNOTT, Aidan
Paul, Weiss, Rifkind, Wharton & Garrison LLP, New York 212 373 3213
asynnott@paulweiss.com
Recommended in Antitrust
Practice Areas: Partner in the Litigation Department. Focuses on antitrust litigation and compliance, intellectual property litigation and complex commercial litigation. Has extensive trial experience in state and federal courts as well as in alternative dispute resolution forums such as the American Arbitration Association. Frequently represents clients in antitrust investigations by the governmental agencies of the United States and the European Union. Has published in the areas of antitrust, trade regulation and intellectual property law, and serves as an associate editor of the Antitrust Law Journal. Member of the Leadership of the Antitrust Section of the American Bar Association.

TABAK, Jeffrey E
Weil, Gotshal & Manges LLP, New York 212 310 8343
jeffrey.tabak@weil.com
Recommended in Private Equity
Practice Areas: Mr Tabak's wide-ranging Corporate and Securities Law Practice focuses on representing and counseling private investment funds, institutional investors and money management firms. He also advises clients on the formation of basic business structures - particularly limited and general partnerships and limited liability companies.
Career: Mr Tabak is Co-Head of the New York Private Equity Practice and regularly represents private investment funds and their sponsors in connection with their organization and the acquisition and disposition of their investments. He counsels institutional investors, represents several money management firms and has been involved with many acquisitions of money managers. He is a member of the ABA Federal Securities Subcommittee on Private Investment Entities. Mr Tabak is also a Member of the Private Investment Fund Forum, a group of New York City attorneys who practice extensively in the private fund area.
Personal: Duke University, JD; Duke University, BA (magna cum laude, Phi Beta Kappa).

TANENBAUM, Jeffrey L
Weil, Gotshal & Manges LLP, New York 212 310 8276
jeff.tanenbaum@weil.com
Recommended in Bankruptcy
Practice Areas: Bankruptcy, business finance and restructuring.
Career: Tanenbaum represents borrowers, lenders and investors in out-of-court restructurings/Chapter 11 cases throughout the US. He has represented General Electric Capital Corporation in the Chapter 11 cases of Channel Home Centers, Plymouth Lamston Stores, Sage-Dey & Company, Duckwall-Alco Stores, Rickel Home Centers, Inc. and Superior Air Parts. His debtor representations include: Ritz Carlton (NY/DC), Placid Oil, Penrod Drilling Co., The Grand Union Company, McCulloch Corporation, Bethlehem Steel Corporation, Choice One Communications and IWO Holdings (Sprint Affiliate). Tanenbaum has extensive experience in real estate-related workouts and bankruptcies.
Personal: SUNY Buffalo, JD; SUNY Binghamton, BA.

TANENBAUM, William A
Kaye Scholer LLP, New York
212 836 7661
wtanenbaum@kayescholer.com
Recommended in Technology
Practice Areas: Chair, Technology, Intellectual Property and Outsourcing Group. Mr Tanenbaum is an internationally recognized intellectual property, technology and outsourcing lawyer. He represents clients in transactional, litigation and intellectual property matters. He advises companies in the US and around the world in the development, acquisition, licensing, protection, use, sale, marketing and litigation of technology products and services. He has longstanding experience in outsourcing and in complex computer and technology agreements. Chambers noted that he "commands the respect of his peers for his ability and success, and of clients for his efficiency and responsiveness." He is frequently retained to represent technology and non-technology companies in resolving competing patent rights in technology and outsourcing arrangements, and to obtain, enforce, defend and license intellectual property rights generally. He handles patent and technology litigations for clients in a wide range of industries. Mr Tanenbaum is a past President of the Computer Law Association and the founder and Co-Chair of a leading annual outsourcing conference. His expertise and leadership in technology law was also recognized when he was selected to serve as the neutral arbitrator in a $30 million outsourcing dispute. His speeches in a series entitled 'Tanenbaum on Technology Law' are sponsored by Westlaw and Celesq. He has advised NASA and the New York County Lawyers' Association on IP matters and is the only lawyer to have received the annual award of achievement from the New York Society of Architects (for his work on the intellectual property protection of functional works). Other areas of his practice include assisting companies in establishing privacy and data protection policies and practices; establishing technology infrastructures; developing corporate policies for the use of open source software; information technology agreements for healthcare businesses e-commerce; and the information technology and intellectual property aspects of Homeland Security legislation. Mr Tanenbaum has been selected as Outside Technology Counsel by members of the Fortune 500 and leading technology companies.
Prof. Memberships: Admitted to practice in New York. Memberships include: Past President and current advisory Board Member, The Computer Law Association; Past Chair, Internet and Electronic Commerce Task Force of the Computer Law Association; Board of Editors, Journal of Internet Law, Multimedia Law Strategist and Multimedia Law Report; Chair of annual legal conferences.
Career: JD, Cornell Law School, 1979; BA, Brown University (highest honors and Phi Beta Kappa), 1976.
Publications: 'A Guide to the European Data Protection and Privacy Laws for U.S. Companies' (co-author); a chapter on 'Intellectual Property Aspects of Outsourcing' in Technology and Offshore Outsourcing Strategies; 'Revisiting Key Provision in Software and Outsourcing Agreements' Vol. 6 No. 9 Journal of Internal Law; and 'Land Mines and Gold Mines in Intellectual Property Aspects of Outsourcing Agreements'.

TAVSS, John
Seward & Kissel, New York
212 574 1261
tavss@sewkis.com
Recommended in Private Equity
Practice Areas: Investment management.
Prof. Memberships: New York State Bar Association (Tax Division).

Career: Mr Tavss advises clients on a wide variety of securities, tax and business law matters, relating to the investment management business. He has significant expertise in the investment management area including the representation of 'hedge funds', other private investment vehicles (both onshore and offshore) and private equity funds. Seward & Kissel is one of the leading law firms in the hedge fund area dating back to the early 1950s, having represented A.W. Jones & Company, which purports to be the first 'hedge fund'. The Investment Management Group represents both registered and unregistered funds, as well as investment advisers, underwriters, sponsors and directors to those funds. Seward & Kissel, with offices in both New York and in Washington DC, offers sophisticated legal advice emphasizing business, financial and commercial law and related litigation. **Personal:** Mr Tavss received a BA degree (with honors) from University of Virginia in 1976, a JD degree from Vanderbilt University School of Law in 1979, and a LLM degree in Taxation from New York University School of Law. He has practiced at Seward & Kissel since 1979, and has been a Partner since 1988.

TAYLOR, Willard B
Sullivan & Cromwell LLP, New York
212 558 4000
taylorw@sullcrom.com
Recommended in Tax

Practice Areas: US federal/state tax matters, including advice regarding taxation of foreign operations of US corporations, US operations of foreign corporations, mergers, acquisitions and international transactions of all kinds. Represents domestic and foreign corporations before the IRS and in tax litigation; has worked with the Treasury Department and Congressional staffs on tax legislation. **Prof. Memberships:** ABA; ABCNY; NYSBA (former Chairman, Tax Section); American Law Institute (Tax Advisory Group, Federal Income Tax Project); ASIL; IBA; IFA (US Council); Adjunct Faculty, NYU Law School. **Career:** Partner since 1973. **Publications:** Extensive writings on US tax matters; regular speaker for PLI, IFA, and IBA. **Personal:** Yale Law School (LLB, 1965); Yale University (BA, 1962).

TERRELL, Anthony
Dewey Ballantine LLP, New York
212 259 7070
jterrell@deweyballantine.com
Recommended in Energy

Practice Areas: Mr Terrell represents issuers and underwriters in a wide range of capital markets transactions, both public and private, involving substantially all types of equity and equity-linked securities and debt securities (taxable and tax-exempt, secured and unsecured). Mr Terrell has extensive experience drafting bond indentures, secured and unsecured. He has also worked on lease transactions involving a variety of assets such as generating stations (including nuclear), turbines, fuel handling facilities, unit trains and office buildings. **Career:** Partner, Dewey Ballantine LLP. **Personal:** BA, New York University, 1965. JD, Villanova University, 1968. LLM, Taxation, New York University, 1975.

THOMASCH, Daniel J
Orrick, Herrington & Sutcliffe, New York
212 506 3755
dthomasch@orrick.com
Recommended in Intellectual Property

Practice Areas: Represents companies in the pharmaceutical, biotechnology, chemical, and medical device industries in the defense of patent infringement and complex product liability actions. He has substantial experience in litigating and trying cases involving organic chemistry, recombinant DNA technology, microbiology, immunology, statistics and epidemiology, and the design of drugs, vaccines, and medical devices. His appellate experience includes numerous oral arguments before the US Courts of Appeal for the Second, Third, Sixth, Eleventh, and Federal Circuits, the Court of Appeals of the State of New York, and the New York and New Jersey Appellate Divisions. **Prof. Memberships:** American Bar Association; The Association of the Bar of the City of New York, Young Lawyers Committee: Chair 1987-89. Defense Research Institute: Drug and Medical Device Litigation Steering Committee, 1996-present. American Intellectual Property Law Association. **Career:** Member of Orrick's Executive Committee; Former Managing Director of the firm's Litigation Division (2002-04); Columbia University (JD, 1981); Northwestern University (BA, 1978); Clerk, Honorable Thomas P Griesa, US District Judge, SDNY (1981-82); Partner, Orrick, Herrington & Sutcliffe LLP (1998-present); Associate and Partner, Donovan Leisure Newton & Irvine LLP (1982-98).

THOMPSON, Mark
Simpson Thacher & Bartlett LLP, New York 212 455 7355
mthompson@stblaw.com
Recommended in Bankruptcy

Practice Areas: Mark Thompson is a Partner in the firm's Bankruptcy Practice, where he concentrates on business reorganizations, acquisitions of troubled companies, creditors' rights and structured financing. **Prof. Memberships:** American Bankruptcy Institute. **Career:** Mr Thompson joined Simpson Thacher in 1982 and became Partner in 1991. He has practiced in the Bankrupt-

cy Department since 1986. **Personal:** He received his BA summa cum laude from Columbia University in 1979 and JD cum laude from Harvard Law School in 1982.

THOYER, Judith R
Paul, Weiss, Rifkind, Wharton & Garrison LLP, New York
212 373 3002
jthoyer@paulweiss.com
Recommended in Corporate/M&A

Practice Areas: Co-Head of the Mergers and Acquisitions Group of the firm's Corporate Department. Member of the firm's Management Committee. Has extensive experience in the area of acquisitions and dispositions of public and private companies, covering negotiated transactions, contested takeovers and acquisitions, and dispositions of companies in connection with Chapter 11 proceedings. Provides general representation of public companies. Advises public company Boards of Directors. Member of the Committee on Mergers, Acquisitions and Corporate Control Contests of the Association of the Bar of the City of New York. Selected for the 2005 edition of 'The Best Lawyers in America'.

THURSTON, Sally A
Skadden, Arps, Slate, Meagher & Flom LLP & Affiliates, New York
212 735 4140
sthursto@skadden.com
Recommended in Tax

Practice Areas: Advises US and international clients on a wide range of tax matters, including tax aspects of mergers and acquisitions, joint ventures, restructurings, divestitures and spin-offs. Advises multinational clients regarding the US tax aspects of cross-border merger and acquisition transactions and tax minimization structures. The former includes utilization of dual-listed company and exchangeable share structures. In US, regularly advises clients on taxable and tax-free acquisitions and divestitures and has significant experience in the partnership taxation area. **Career:** JD, Harvard Law School, 1986 (cum laude); BS, Chemical Engineering, Cornell University, 1983 (with distinction).

TODER, Richard
Morgan, Lewis & Bockius LLP, New York 212 309 6052
rtoder@morganlewis.com
Recommended in Bankruptcy

Practice Areas: Richard Toder is a Partner in the Business and Finance Practice and leader of its Finance and Restructuring Practice. Mr Toder represents major institutional creditors and committees in bankruptcy and restructuring cases throughout the nation and in cross-border situations. Mr Toder is a certified mediator in the Southern District of New York Bankruptcy Court and

is often appointed by the Court and parties to serve in that capacity. **Prof. Memberships:** American College of Bankruptcy (Vice President and Fellow); National Bankruptcy Conference (Conferee). **Career:** Mr Toder served as Assistant United States Attorney in the Southern District of New York.

TODRYS, Steven C
Simpson Thacher & Bartlett LLP, New York 212 455 2000
stodrys@stblaw.com
Recommended in Tax

Practice Areas: A Partner at Simpson Thacher & Bartlett LLP and the Head of the firm's Tax Department. Specialises in federal income taxation, with a particular emphasis on corporate mergers and acquisitions, joint ventures and restructurings. Recent experience includes the mergers of Kmart and Sears Roebuck, Travelers and The St Paul Companies and Manulife and John Hancock, the acquisition by Warner Music Group and the numerous buyout transactions of Kohlberg Kravis Roberts & Co. **Career:** Served as Chair of the Tax Section of the New York State Bar Association in 1998 and also served as a Co-Chair of the Committee on Corporations and Committee on Foreign Activities of US Taxpayers. Admitted to practice in New York, the US Tax Court and the US Supreme Court. **Personal:** Graduated from the University of Rochester in 1975 and obtained a JD, in 1978 with honors from the University of Chicago.

TONERY, Lisa
King & Spalding LLP, New York
212 556 2307
ltonery@kslaw.com
Recommended in Energy

Practice Areas: Federal and state regulatory law, litigation and transactions involving the energy industry focusing on gas, electric, oil and transactional matters on behalf of natural gas and liquefied natural gas companies, natural gas marketers and end-users, oil pipelines and shippers, independent power producers and power marketers. Regulatory advice and strategy on a transactional basis and representation in proceedings before the Federal Energy Regulatory Commission and state regulatory agencies. **Prof. Memberships:** District of Columbia Bar; New York Bar; Energy Bar Association. **Personal:** BA, Catholic University, 1984; JD, Catholic University, 1989.

TORTORIELLO, Robert L
Cleary Gottlieb Steen & Hamilton LLP, New York 212 225 2390
rtortoriello@cgsh.com
Recommended in Banking & Finance

Practice Areas: Bank capital markets and regulatory, securities and compliance matters, financial institution merg-

ers, acquisitions, joint ventures and restructurings, derivative products, activity expansion, and securities offerings. Regulatory counseling concerning the Gramm-Leach-Bliley Act, the Bank Holding Company Act, the Glass-Steagall Act and the International Banking Act.
Career: Joined firm, 1974; became Partner, 1982. JD, magna cum laude, Harvard Law School (1974); BA, summa cum laude, St. Peters College, New Jersey (1971).
Publications: 'Guide to Bank Underwriting, Dealing and Brokerage Activities' (Glasser LegalWorks, Ninth edition, 2004). 'The Federal Reserve Board's Proposed Interpretation of the Anti-tying Provisions of the Bank Holding Company Act Amendments of 1970' (Banking Law Journal, 2003). 'Financial Modernization in the United States: the Gramm-Leach-Bliley Act' (Journal of International Financial Markets, 2000). Other scholarly and professional journals.

TOWNSEND, Robert
Cravath, Swaine & Moore LLP,
New York 212 474 1964
rtownsend@cravath.com
Recommended in Corporate/M&A
Practice Areas: Mergers and acquisitions, including public and private negotiated transactions; corporate governance and general corporate advice. Managing Partner, Corporate.
Prof. Memberships: ABA; NYSBA; ABCNY (Special Committee on Mergers, Acquisitions and Corporate Control Contests).
Career: Partner since 1998.
Personal: Harvard Law School (JD, magna cum laude, 1990; Executive Editor, 'Harvard Law Review'); Harvard College (AB, magna cum laude, 1987).

TRAVIS, Norton
Garfunkel, Wild & Travis PC,
Great Neck 516 393 2200
Recommended in Healthcare

TREPPER, Myron
Willkie Farr & Gallagher LLP, New York
212 728 8276
mtrepper@willkie.com
Recommended in Bankruptcy
Practice Areas: Partner and Chair of the Business Reorganization and Restructuring Department and serves as Co-Chairman of the firm. Specializes in all areas of debtor and creditor representation and in the transactional aspects of business reorganizations. Recent significant matters include representation of Adelphia Communications Corp. and Maxxim Medical Group in complex Chapter 11 proceedings, and Teléfonos de México SA de CV in its $206.7 million acquisition of bankrupt AT&T Latin America Corp. and in its $400 million acquisition of Embratel Participacoes Ltda from MCI. He is also representing the interests of Monsanto Company in the pending Chapter 11 case of

Solutia Inc. Has practiced continuously in this area for more than 30 years and has been counsel to Petrie Retail, Inc., Heilig Meyers Company, Livent, Inc., Paragon Trade Brands, Inc., Alliance Entertainment, Corp., Harvard Industries, Inc., Woodward & Lothrop Holdings, Inc., The Grand Union Company, Orion Pictures, and Maxwell Communications, among others.
Prof. Memberships: Member of the Association of the Bar of the City of New York and the American Bankruptcy Institute; Fellow of the American College of Bankruptcy.
Career: Admitted to the Bar of the State of New York.
Publications: Has authored numerous articles and materials for legal and other publications, including: the American Bankruptcy Institute, Protecting Foreign Assets in a United States Bankruptcy Filing (Commentator); New York University School of Law, Annual Survey of American Law (Contributing Author); and Turnarounds and Workouts, Richard D. Irwin, Inc., 1991, 'The Lawyer's Role in Representing the Distressed Company.'
Personal: Received a JD from Brooklyn Law School in 1968 and a BA from Hunter College in 1965. Lectures on bankruptcy-related matters for seminars and panels sponsored by the ALI-ABA, the American Bankruptcy Institute, New York University School of Law, University of Pennsylvania Institute for Law and Economics, and other professional organizations.

TRIER, Dana L
Davis Polk & Wardwell, New York
212 450 4000
dana.trier@dpw.com
Recommended in Tax
Practice Areas: Member of Davis Polk & Wardwell's Tax Department. Principal expertise is in business taxation, including particularly domestic and international tax planning for corporate mergers, acquisitions, joint ventures, spinoffs and other major corporate transactions. Also has extensive experience in structured finance, investment partnerships and derivatives, and has done a significant amount of work involving novel executive compensation and employee benefits arrangements. In addition to his tax planning practice, has represented clients on ruling and legislative matters and in tax controversies.

TRINGALI, Joseph
Simpson Thacher & Bartlett LLP,
New York 212 455 2000
jtringali@stblaw.com
Recommended in Antitrust
Practice Areas: A Partner at Simpson Thacher & Bartlett LLP and a member of the firm's Litigation Department representing clients on antitrust and general commercial litigation. Has handled jury and bench trials and argued appeals

in diverse areas, including anti-trust, breach of contract, copyright and patent infringement and employment discrimination. Primarily, has litigated civil antitrust actions on behalf of both plaintiffs and defendants and counsels clients under the Sherman, Clayton, Robinson-Patman and Hart-Scott-Rodino Acts. Has handled merger transactions before the Department of Justice, the Federal Trade Commission and various state antitrust enforcement agencies as well as coordinating competition law filings on a global basis. Work includes acting for Master-Card, J.P. Morgan Chase, Lehman Brothers, Kohlberg Kravis Roberts, The Blackstone Group, KMart, Owens-Illinois, Veritas, Viacom, Weyerhaeuser and Wyeth.
Career: Joined the firm in 1983 and became a Partner in 1989.
Personal: Received a BA from Wesleyan University in 1977 and a JD from the New York University School of Law in 1980.

TURNBULL, Kenneth J
Morgan, Lewis & Bockius LLP,
New York 212 309 6055
kturnbull@morganlewis.com
Recommended in Employment
Practice Areas: Kenneth J Turnbull is a Partner in the Labor and Employment Law Practice Group. Mr Turnbull represents employers in a wide range of employment litigation matters before state and federal courts in cases involving discrimination and wrongful discharge, restrictive covenants and trade secrets, corporate planning and restructuring, and wage and hour issues. Mr Turnbull also works extensively in traditional labor matters and represents clients before the National Labor Relations Board in collective bargaining, union representation elections, labor arbitrations and unfair labor practice charges.
Prof. Memberships: American Bar Association.

TURNER, Scott M
Nixon Peabody LLP, Rochester
585 263 1612
sturner@nixonpeabody.com
Recommended in Environment
Practice Areas: Permitting/regulation of electric generating and other industrial facilities throughout the US. Air/water pollution permit, enforcement, rulemaking proceedings regarding power plants, waste-to-energy facilities, and landfills. Clean Air Act citizen suit defense. Prevention of significant deterioration and nonattainment new source review regulations. Clean Water Act permitting issues.
Prof. Memberships: Admitted to practice in NY, DC, US District Court (Western District of NY), US Courts of Appeals (Second, Third Circuits). Air/Waste Management Association; American Society of Mechanical Engineers.

Career: Chaired Environmental Practice Group for 14 years.
Personal: Washington & Lee University, JD, magna cum laude; Colgate University, BA, with honors.

URDA KASSIS, Cynthia
Shearman & Sterling LLP, New York
212 848 7969
curdakassis@shearman.com
Recommended in Projects
Practice Areas: Partner and Co-Head of Shearman & Sterling's Project Development and Finance Group. Represents sponsors and lenders in project finance and development transactions worldwide. Represents US and foreign corporations and financial institutions in their general private financing activities, joint ventures and letter of credit activities. Has also represented US and foreign corporations on general corporate matters.
Career: Admitted to the Bar in New York. Joined Shearman in 1984 and became a Partner in 1992.
Personal: BA, University of Virginia (1980); MA, University of Notre Dame (1981); JD, American University, Washington College of Law (1984).

URIS, Harvey R
Skadden, Arps, Slate, Meagher & Flom LLP & Affiliates, New York
212 735 2212
huris@skadden.com
Recommended in Real Estate
Practice Areas: Specializes in capital markets-related real estate transactions; commercial mortgage-backed loan origination and securitization transactions; private equity funds and private placements; bondable and other credit tenant lease transactions; sale-leasebacks; off balance sheet synthetic lease transactions; the acquisition, financing, sale, exchange and other disposition of office buildings, shopping centers, hotels, multi-family and other property types; multi-property and multi-state mortgage financing; mezzanine, preferred equity and so-called bifurcated secured financing transactions; partnerships; limited liability companies; and US and non-US joint ventures.
Career: Boston University: JD, 1979 (cum laude); BA, 1976 (cum laude).

UROWSKY, Richard J
Sullivan & Cromwell LLP, New York
212 558 5000
urowskyr@sullcrom.com
Recommended in Antitrust
Practice Areas: Focuses on antitrust, securities and tax litigation, as well as other forms of complex litigation. Extensive experience in advising clients on competition issues, including mergers, acquisitions, joint ventures and pricing policy. Representative clients: Goldman, Sachs & Co., Microsoft, Avon Products, British Petroleum, RR Donnelley & Sons.
Prof. Memberships: ABA; ABCNY; FBC; NYCLA.

Career: Partner since 1980. Law clerk to Hon. Stanley F Reed (US Supreme Court, 1972-73).
Personal: Yale University (BA, 1967); Oxford (BPhil, 1970); Yale Law School (JD, 1972).

VARDELL, James C
Cravath, Swaine & Moore LLP,
New York 212 474 1900
jvardell@cravath.com
Recommended in Banking & Finance
Practice Areas: Broad range of corporate finance transactions; primarily representing banks in complex syndicated financings, both domestic and international. Extensive experience in acquisition financings and other leveraged financings. Also experienced in equipment financings, project financings, leveraged-lease financings and vendor financings.
Career: Partner since 1987.
Personal: Yale Law School (JD, 1980); Washington and Lee University (BA, 1977).

VICTOR, A Paul
Weil, Gotshal & Manges LLP, New York
212 310 8110
paul.victor@weil.com
Recommended in Antitrust
Practice Areas: Antitrust/competition, litigation/regulatory, international trade.
Career: Ranked in world's top 20 competition/antitrust lawyers by Euromoney's, 'Best of the Best: 2000;' US top nine by Legal Media Group's 'Best of the Best: 2004.' Over 40 years experience: almost three years in Justice Department's Antitrust Division, 38 years in private practice working on biggest antitrust and international trade cases ever. Victor represents corporations in major criminal and civil international cartel cases and represented Matsushita Electric in the famous Matsushita case (Japanese Electronic Products Antitrust Litigation), decided favorably for client by the Supreme Court.
Personal: University of Michigan, BBA, JD, with distinction.

VINE, Stephen M
Akin Gump Strauss Hauer & Feld LLP,
New York 212 872 1030
svine@akingump.com
Recommended in Private Equity
Practice Areas: For the past 25 years, Steve Vine has advised some of the largest and most prominent private investment funds and fund managers in connection with their fund formation and capital raising activities in investment disciplines including global macro, distressed investments, private equity, domestic and foreign real estate, arbitrage, financial services and country funds. In addition, he provides advice on planning and execution of investment and financing transactions, and on formation and operation of investment management firms and related service companies, including broker-dealers. He

also assists fund managers in registration and regulatory compliance.
Personal: AB, JD, Harvard University.

VITALE, Robert L
Cadwalader, Wickersham & Taft LLP,
New York 212 504 6464
robert.vitale@cwt.com
Recommended in Projects
Practice Areas: Head of the firm's US and Latin American Project Finance and Privatization Practice. Sector expertise includes energy, telecommunications, water, oil and gas, pipelines, transportation and industrial facilities. Mandated for work in more than 20 countries. Privitization practice includes counseling governments and private parties on bid and tender programs, BOT contracts, management contracts, construction contracts, and asset sales. Advises clients on private/public M&A transactions in indicated sectors. Clients include private equity funds, monoline insurers, institutional investors, commercial and investment banks, governments, and industrial companies.
Personal: JD from Georgetown University Law Center, cum laude, 1984; BA from Tufts University, magna cum laude, 1981. Member, New York Bar Association's Committee on Project Finance.

VITKOWSKY, Vincent
Edwards & Angell, New York
212 308 4411
Recommended in Insurance

VIZCARRONDO Jr, Paul
Wachtell, Lipton, Rosen & Katz,
New York 212 403 1208
pvizcarrondo@wlrk.com
Recommended in Litigation
Practice Areas: Specializes in corporate and securities litigation and regulatory and white collar criminal matters.
Prof. Memberships: Served on several committees of the Association of the Bar of the City of New York, including the Criminal Law Committee and the Federal Courts Committee, has been a Master of the Federal Bar Council's Inn of Court and is a member of the Columbia Law School Board of Visitors.
Career: Partner at Wachtell, Lipton, Rosen & Katz since 1981. Has tried significant cases in courts throughout the United States. Worked as Law Clerk to the Honorable Edward Weinfeld, United States District Judge for the Southern District of New York (1973-74) and as an Assistant United States Attorney in the Southern District of New York (1974-78). Awarded the Department of Justice's Special Achievement Award for his work in the Securities and Commodities Fraud Unit of the United States Attorney's Office. Has taught Trial Practice as an Adjunct Assistant Professor of Law at New York University School of Law and as a faculty member at the National Institute for Trial Advocacy; has lectured on United States federal

securities laws for the Practicing Law Institute; and has lectured on litigation issues as a member of numerous continuing legal education panels.
Publications: Wrote the chapter on 'RICO' in Obermaier & Morvillo's 'White Collar Crime; Business and Regulatory Offenses'.
Personal: Graduated from Cornell University in 1970 (BS) and from Columbia University School of Law in 1973 (JD) where he was a Harlan Fiske Stone Scholar and Articles and Book Reviews Editor of 'Columbia Law Review'.

VLAHAKIS, Patricia A
Wachtell, Lipton, Rosen & Katz,
New York 212 403 1206
pavlahakis@wlrk.com
Recommended in Corporate/M&A
Practice Areas: Specializes in corporate and securities law, concentrating on transactional matters, mergers and acquisitions, hostile takeovers, cross-border transactions and private equity investments, as well as corporate governance. Represented Hellman & Friedman and Warburg Pincus in their investment in Arch Capital, Computer Associates in its proxy fight with Ranger Governance, Fort James in its merger with Georgia-Pacific, Young & Rubicam in its merger with WPP Group, Polygram in its acquisition by Seagrams and Motorola in a number of acquisitions, investments and divestitures.
Prof. Memberships: Member of the American Bar Association; served for five years as Co-Chair of the Practicing Law Institute's Annual Institute on Securities Regulation; is a member of the Advisory Board for the Annual Securities Regulation Institute; is a member of the Board of Directors of Phoenix House Foundation, Inc, a not for profit organization for the treatment and prevention of drug addiction.
Career: Partner at Wachtell, Lipton, Rosen & Katz.
Publications: Lectured extensively and published numerous articles in the areas of mergers and acquisitions and securities law.
Personal: Graduated summa cum laude from Bryn Mawr College in 1978 (BA) and from Columbia University School of Law in 1981 (JD).

VOGE, William
Latham & Watkins LLP, New York
212 906 1200
Recommended in Projects

VYSKOCIL, Mary Kay
Simpson Thacher & Bartlett LLP,
New York 212 455 3093
mvyskocil@stblaw.com
Recommended in Insurance
Practice Areas: Litigation Partner handling complex commercial cases, concentrated in the insurance, reinsurance, securities and financial services sectors. Represents major domestic and foreign insurers in complex coverage litigations

(including numerous jury trials) throughout the US in a wide variety of contexts, including environmental, asbestos, breast implants and other mass tort claims. Currently representing the lead property insurer in connection with coverage issues arising out of the September 11 World Trade Center attack, including the successful jury trial in the Silverstein case on one versus two occurences. Active in the representation of ceding insurers in reinsurance litigations and arbitrations in the US, the UK and Bermuda. Outside the insurance area, she was involved in a bench trial which resulted in a $365 million verdict on behalf of the firm's client, JPMorgan-Chase, against Motorola. Also involved in the representation of Paramount Communications in the Paramount-Viacom-QVC takeover litigation and represented Matsushita Electrical Industries in MCA v Epstein, which was successfully argued in the US Supreme Court. Has served as outside counsel to the Archdiocese of New York.
Career: Joined firm 1983; elected Partner 1990. Cited in the National Law Journal's '40 Under 40' (November 1995), and Euromoney's Guide to World Leading Insurance and Reinsurance Lawyers (International Financial L Rev 2003). Named one of 'America's Top 50 Women Litigators' by the National Law Journal (Dec. 2001). Currently serves on the firm's New Partners and Personnel Committees.
Publications: B Ostrager and M Vyskocil, Modern Reinsurance Law & Practice, 2d ed (Glasser LegalWorks, 2000). Frequent lecturer on insurance, reinsurance and trial skills.
Personal: JD, 1983, St. John's University School of Law (Member, National Moot Court Team).

WACHSBERGER, Chaim
Chadbourne & Parke LLP, New York
212 408 5100
cwachsberger@chadbourne.com
Recommended in Projects
Practice Areas: Heads Chadbourne's Project Finance Practice. Work includes acquisitions and divestitures, portfolio financings and development and project financing of greenfield power-industry assets, and development and financing of other major infrastructure projects, such as pipelines, transportation facilities, industrial facilities, etc. Represent sponsors and lenders (commercial banks and agencies) and underwritings. Representations involve complex structures, various type of debt and equity, multilateral or export credit agency involvement, and political risk and insurance products.
Prof. Memberships: New York State Bar Association; American Bar Association (Section on Corporation, Banking and Business Law).

WACHTELL, Herbert M
Wachtell, Lipton, Rosen & Katz,
New York 212 403 1216
hmwachtell@wlrk.com
Recommended in Litigation
Practice Areas: Specializes in major,
complex case litigation.
Prof. Memberships: Fellow, American
College of Trial Lawyers, American Bar
Association; Member, American Law
Institute, American Bar Association,
Association of the Bar of the City of
New York, New York County Lawyers.

WAKS, Jay W
Kaye Scholer LLP, New York
212 836 8558
jwaks@kayescholer.com
Recommended in Employment
Practice Areas: Partner, Litigation
Department and Chair, Employment
and Labor Law Practice. Mr Waks has
over 30 years' experience representing
major US and international companies
in employment and labor relations litigations (especially class and collective
actions) and related matters. He concentrates on litigation of fair labor standards, employment rights, discrimination and benefits claims, formulation of
employment policies and dispute resolution procedures (including sexual
harassment avoidance and Glass Ceiling, family leave, ADA, substance abuse,
workplace surveillance and privacy matters), executive employment, termination, restrictive covenant and forfeiture
matters, resolution of employment law
and benefits problems arising from corporate reorganizations and workforce
reductions, alternatives to litigation of
employment and other business disputes, preventive employee relations
programs, matters before the NLRB,
EEOC and securities exchanges, and
international labor and employment
matters. His US and overseas clients
span virtually every industrial sector.
Prof. Memberships: Mr Waks is admitted to practice in New York State, and
before the US Supreme Court, US Court
of Appeals for Second, Third and DC
Circuits, and US District Courts in
Northern, Southern and Eastern Districts of New York. He is past Chair of
the Work in America Institute and the
former Chair of the Committee on
Labor & Employment Law of the Association of the Bar of the City of New
York. He is a member of the Board of
Directors of and serves as General
Counsel to Legal Momentum (new
name of the NOW Legal Defense and
Education Fund) and is a member of
the Executive Committee of the CPR
Institute for Dispute Resolution. He is
long-time Chair of CPR's Employment
Disputes Committee. He also is a sus-
taining Member of the Federal Bar
Council, where he serves on the Execu-
tive Committee and on the board of the
Federal Bar Council Foundation. He is a
Member of the ABA and the Bar Associ-

ations of New York State and City and
California (assoc. member). He is a fre-
quent speaker at ABA and other national
CLE programs, a member of the Cornell
University Council and its Admin. Board
and the Advisory Council of Cornell's ILR
School. Mr Waks is Chair of the Advisory
Council of the Cornell Law School and
past National Chair, CLS Annual Fund.
He has authored numerous articles on
employment law subjects published in
various professional journals.
Career: JD, 1971, Cornell Law School,
editor and officer of Cornell Law
Review; BS, 1968, Cornell University
(School of Industrial & Labor Rela-
tions), co-editor in chief of ILR Forum;
Law Clerk to Hon. Inzer B Wyatt, USDJ,
SDNY 1971-72.

WALDEN, S Calvin
Wilmer Cutler Pickering Hale and Dorr
LLP, New York 212 937 7215
calvin.walden@wilmerhale.com
Recommended in Intellectual Property
Practice Areas: Practice focuses on
intellectual property advice and litigation, with an emphasis on patent litigation and licensing disputes, and on
advising clients concerning intellectual
property asset management, new products and licensing issues. Counsel for a
broad range of clients, including public
companies, private high technology and
medical technology companies, and
companies in the graphic arts.
Prof. Memberships: American Bar
Association, New York State Bar Association, and New York City Bar Association.
Personal: Yeshiva University, Benjamin
N Cardozo School of Law (JD 1996);
State University of New York at Stony
Brook (MA 1994); University of North
Carolina (BA 1989).

WALKER, John
Simpson Thacher & Bartlett LLP,
New York 212 455 2000
jwalker@stblaw.com
Recommended in Banking & Finance
Practice Areas: Simpson Thacher Partner practicing banking and corporate
law. Represents domestic and foreign
commercial banks, investment banks
and private equity firms, including JP
Morgan Chase, Toronto-Dominion
Bank, Mizuho Financial Group, Greenwich Capital Markets and Shinsei Bank.
Practice also focuses on the convergence
of commercial banking and investment
banking businesses and the consolidation of financial institutions. Advises
financial institutions regarding banking
law and regulatory matters, including
with respect to merchant banking, capital, securitization and insolvency issues.
Prof. Memberships: Association of the
Bar of the City of New York (past Chairman, Banking Law Committee); Committee of Counsel of The Clearing
House; Institute of International
Bankers. Member, Council on Foreign
Relations. Director and President of

Financial Services Volunteer Corps, a
not-for-profit organization that channels expertise of financial sector professionals to assist in strengthening the
financial infrastructure in transition and
developing countries.
Career: Joined Firm in 1979 and
became Partner in 1984. Early in career,
attorney at the Board of Governors of
the Federal Reserve System.
Publications: Include 'Guiding Principles and Core Requirements for a Legal
System in a Market Economy' (Aspen
Institute).
Personal: JD, Duke Law School, 1977.

WALLACE, W Kirk
Skadden, Arps, Slate, Meagher & Flom
LLP & Affiliates, New York
212 735 2933
kwallace@skadden.com
Recommended in Tax
Practice Areas: Practice covers a broad
range of federal income tax matters -
including M&A transactions, international financings and investment fund
offerings - with a particular focus on
financial product development and
structured finance transactions. Represents underwriters and issuers in the
development of a variety of publicly and
privately offered debt and equity derivatives and other financial products, as
well as underwriters and issuers in connection with a variety of asset-backed
securitization transactions.
Career: LLM, New York University
School of Law, 1991; JD, The University
of Chicago Law School, 1986; BA, Yale
University, 1983.

WALSH, Kathleen
Mayer, Brown, Rowe & Maw LLP,
New York 212 506 2553
kwalsh@mayerbrown.com
Recommended in Private Equity
Practice Areas: Corporate and Securities Department practice leader, New
York. Focuses on representation of private equity funds and their sponsors.
Regularly advises private equity fund
sponsors in connection with fund structuring and formation, including the representation of buyout funds, industry
focused funds and venture capital funds,
as well as the secondary purchase of private equity portfolios and the spin out of
private equity managers from financial
institution private equity funds. Advises
private equity funds and their portfolio
companies in connection with mergers,
acquisitions, leveraged buy-outs and
early- and late-stage equity and mezzanine financings, as well as dispositions
and spin-offs.
Career: Mayer, Brown, Rowe & Maw
LLP, New York, 1991 to date; Partner,
1998. Willkie Farr & Gallagher, New
York, 1989-91.
Personal: JD, Fordham University
School of Law, 1989; Dean's List; Fordham Law Review. BA, Fordham University, 1984.

WALSH, Michael F
Weil, Gotshal & Manges LLP, New York
212 310 8197
michael.walsh@weil.com
Recommended in Bankruptcy
Practice Areas: Business finance and
restructuring: represents creditors
/debtors, boards of directors, in business
reorganizations, corporate finance,
bankruptcies, secured transactions.
Career: Founded firm's Telecommunications and Technology Restructuring
Practice and Healthcare Restructuring
Practice Groups. Representative
clients: Global Crossing, Nextwave
Telcom, TAC Noteholder Committee
in the Trump Atlantic City casino
Chapter 11 cases, WestPoint Stevens,
Genesis Health Ventures, Sun Healthcare Group, Empire Blue Cross Blue
Shield, Creditors Committee for JWP,
Inc. (Emcore), Creditors Committee
for E-II Holdings, Inc. (Samsonite),
and secured creditors in El Paso Elec-
tric.
Personal: New York University, LLM;
University of San Diego, JD; Hamilton
College, BA.

WARD, Sarah M
Skadden, Arps, Slate, Meagher & Flom
LLP & Affiliates, New York
212 735 2126
sward@skadden.com
Recommended in Projects
Practice Areas: Practice focuses primarily on project finance. Represents
commercial banks, investment banks,
institutional investors and corporate
borrowers in some of the most complex
power, oil and gas, telecommunications
and infrastructure project financings in
recent years. Has extensive experience in
export credit and multilateral agency
financings. Has handled major transactions in the US as well as Asia, Europe
and Latin America.
Career: JD, Fordham University School
of Law, 1986; AB, Princeton University,
1981.

WARDEN, John L
Sullivan & Cromwell LLP, New York
212 558 4000
wardenj@sullcrom.com
Recommended in Antitrust
Practice Areas: General Commercial
Litigation Practice (antitrust, banking,
contract, corporate governance and
securities). Represented British Airways
in Virgin Atlantic antitrust case and
Microsoft in government antitrust case.
Other major litigation representations:
Amax, Bank of New York, BP, Eastman
Kodak, First Boston, Goldman Sachs,
Gulf Oil, Kennecott, TW Services and
Union Carbide. Extensive appellate
experience, including constitutional
cases. Amicus curiae for The New York
Clearing House in numerous cases in
courts of appeals and the Supreme
Court.
Prof. Memberships: United States

Antitrust Modernization Commission; American College of Trial Lawyers; American Law Institute.
Career: Partner since 1973.
Personal: Harvard College (AB, 1962); University of Virginia Law School (LLB, 1965; editor in chief, 'Virginia Law Review').

WARNER, Douglas
Weil, Gotshal & Manges LLP, New York
212 310 8751
doug.warner@weil.com
Recommended in Private Equity
Practice Areas: Mr Warner represents private equity sponsors in acquisitions, dispositions and financings with extensive experience in leveraged buyouts, dispositions of public and private domestic and European companies, minority investments and restructurings. He also has significant experience in going-private transactions, acquisitions and dispositions of bankrupt companies and corporate governance matters.
Career: Mr Warner is a member of the firm's Private Equity Practice and he recently represented DLJ Merchant Banking Partners in several transactions including its $1.2 billion public to private acquisition of Jostens, its $2.3 billion merger of their Jostens, Von Hoffmann and Arcade portfolio companies and the related recapitalization by Kohlberg Kravis Roberts & Co., and its equity participation in the $4.8 billion acquisition of Metro-Goldwyn-Mayer. Mr Warner represented Lindsay Goldberg & Bessemer in its $120 million acquisition of the wholesale liquor distribution business from the State of Maine, Capital Z Partners in acquiring a hedge fund business from Zurich Financial Services and Global Crossing in its sale of a controlling equity interest to Singapore Technologies Telemedia. He has extensive experience in both US and European transaction and was one of the group of partners that founded the firm's London office in 1996. He remained in London until 2001, during which time the London office grew from eight to 130 lawyers.
Personal: Boston University School of Law, JD (magna cum laude); University of Puget Sound, BA.

WARNER Jr, E Waide
Davis Polk & Wardwell, New York
212 450 4000
waide.warner@dpw.com
Recommended in Projects
Practice Areas: Member of Davis Polk & Wardwell's Corporate Department, heads the firm's Project Finance Group and is active in biotechnology and healthcare practice. Has been involved for more than 25 years in a wide range of US and international financings, debt and equity capital markets transactions and joint ventures, including biotechnology research and development financings and a number of project

financings in the oil and gas, petro-chemical, mining, power and telecommunications sectors.

WARNKE, Stephen A
Ropes & Gray, New York
212 841 0681
stephen.warnke@ropesgray.com
Recommended in Healthcare
Practice Areas: Healthcare fraud and abuse counseling, compliance and investigations. Specializes in third-party reimbursement, capital financing, and managed care representations, with extensive experience representing a wide range of healthcare clients before the New York State Legislature and state and federal regulatory agencies. Regularly counsels healthcare providers, managed care organizations, and pharmaceutical companies on Medicaid drug formulary and drug rebate questions, and state supplemental rebate initiatives.
Career: California Bar (1985). New York Bar (1988). District of Columbia Bar (1990). Partner, Ropes & Gray (2003).
Personal: JD, Yale Law School (1985). BA, magna cum laude, Harvard University (1981).

WARREN, Charles
Bryan Cave Robinson LLP, New York
212 541 2000
Recommended in Environment

WASSERMAN, Craig M
Wachtell, Lipton, Rosen & Katz, New York 212 403 1232
cmwasserman@wlrk.com
Recommended in Corporate/M&A
Practice Areas: Specializes in mergers and acquisitions, banking and securities law matters.
Prof. Memberships: Member of the New York State Bar and various bar associations.
Career: Partner at Wachtell, Lipton, Rosen & Katz. Law Clerk to Chief Judge Wilfred Feinberg, United States Court of Appeals, Second Circuit.
Publications: Frequent speaker and author on corporate, banking, mergers and acquisitions and securities law topics.
Personal: Graduated summa cum laude from Yale University in 1982 (BA/MA, economics) and from Yale Law School in 1986 (JD) where Editor, 'Yale Law Journal', Editor and Senior Articles Editor, 1985-86, 'Yale Journal in Regulation'.

WEBSTER, Robert
Pillsbury Winthrop LLP, New York
212 858 1303
rwebster@pillsburywinthrop.com
Recommended in Banking & Finance
Practice Areas: He represents financial institutions with particular emphasis on the effect of governmental regulation on both the ordinary conduct of their business and their acquisition and new product development activities. He also advises clients on such diverse governmental actions as capital adequacy directives, restrictions on geographic

and functional expansion, anti money laundering initiatives and sanctions in response to international crises, and represents clients subject to supervisory examinations and compliance proceedings. Mr Webster's assignments have included representation of a US bank resisting a hostile takeover by another US bank, US banks and financial holding companies with respect to the acquisition or disposition of interests in banking and non-banking companies in the US and abroad, European and Asian financial institutions with respect to acquisitions, loans and investments in the US, the US branches and subsidiaries of banks headquartered in Europe, Asia and Latin America with respect to regulatory matters and enforcement proceedings and Central Banks with respect to matters unique to those institutions.
Career: Admitted to practice: State of New York.
Personal: LLB, Harvard Law School, 1962 (cum laude); AB, Colgate University, 1959 (magna cum laude; Phi Beta Kappa).

WEINBERGER, Michael
Cleary Gottlieb Steen & Hamilton LLP, New York 212 225 2092
mweinberger@cgsh.com
Recommended in Real Estate
Practice Areas: Real estate finance, commercial mortgage securitizations. Recent transactions include $1.2 billion financing of tender offer to acquire a public REIT and subsequent refinancing through securitization; $1 billion securitization of floating rate mortgage loans; and $450 million construction loan to expand a regional mall.
Career: Joined firm, 1992; became Partner, 2000. Law clerk to the Honorable Leonard Garth, US Court of Appeals, Third Circuit (1991-92). JD, magna cum laude, Law Review, Harvard Law School (1991), BA, summa cum laude, Phi Beta Kappa, Yale University (1988).
Publications: Articles in 'The Bankruptcy Strategist' and 'Norton Bankruptcy Law Advisor'.

WEINER, Michael L
Skadden, Arps, Slate, Meagher & Flom LLP & Affiliates, New York
212 735 2632
mweiner@skadden.com
Recommended in Antitrust
Practice Areas: Represents clients in antitrust investigations of merger and acquisition transactions, and in antitrust class action and other complex litigations.
Career: JD, Georgetown University Law Center, 1980 (magna cum laude); BA, University of Pennsylvania, 1976 (cum laude).

WEISFELNER, Edward
Brown Rudnick Berlack Israels, New York 212 704 0100
Recommended in Bankruptcy

WEISS, Gregory A
Simpson Thacher & Bartlett LLP, New York 212 455 7080
gweiss@stblaw.com
Recommended in Banking & Finance
Practice Areas: A Partner at Simpson Thacher & Bartlett LLP and a member of the firm's Corporate Department where for over 30 years he has represented banks and other financial institutions and borrowers in syndicated lending transactions, including senior secured and subordinated bridge financings. In the past several years, he has represented numerous financial institutions in connection with senior secured financings including Canadian Imperial Bank of Commerce, JP Morgan Chase Bank, Barclays Bank, Merrill Lynch and The Bank of Nova Scotia.
Career: Joined Simpson Thacher in 1970 and became a Partner in 1977.
Personal: Received an AB from Yale in 1966 and a LLB, cum laude, in 1969 from the University of Pennsylvania, and was an Editor of the Law Review and elected to the Order of the Coif. Clerked for the Honourable William Gray, US District Court, Central District of California from 1969-70.

WEISS, Jack
Gibson, Dunn & Crutcher LLP, New York
212 351 3890
jmweiss@gibsondunn.com
Recommended in Media & Entertainment
Practice Areas: Co-Chair, Media Law Practice Group. Serves as principal outside publication counsel to Dow Jones & Company. Has more than 25 years hands-on courtroom experience defending the rights of the nation's leading media. Has defended many high-profile libel cases, including (currently) Umar v Dow Jones and Cuomo v Plume.
Prof. Memberships: Lecturer-in-law, Columbia Law School (media law).
Career: Law clerk, Judge John Minor Wisdom and Chief Justice Warren Burger.
Publications: 'It Depends on the Meaning of "Ex Parte,"' Litigation Magazine, Winter 2003.
Personal: JD, Harvard LS, 1971, magna cum laude; Treasurer and Managing Editor, Harvard Law Review.

WEISSMAN, Ellen
Hodgson Russ LLP, Buffalo
716 856 4000
Recommended in Healthcare

WELLS, Theodore
Paul, Weiss, Rifkind, Wharton & Garrison LLP, New York 212 373 3089
twells@paulweiss.com
Recommended in Litigation
Practice Areas: Co-Chair of the Litigation Department. Has over 25 years of experience in white-collar criminal defense and complex civil and corporate litigation, including SEC regulatory work and class action litigation. Selected

repeatedly by The National Law Journal as one of the 100 most influential lawyers in America and as one of America's top white-collar criminal defense lawyers. Has extensive experience in corporate governance issues. Fellow of the American College of Trial Lawyers. Served as Co-Chair of the White-Collar Criminal Section of the National Association of Criminal Defense Lawyers.

WERNER, Philip
Morgan, Lewis & Bockius LLP,
New York 212 309 6080
pwerner@morganlewis.com
Recommended in Private Equity
Practice Areas: Mr Werner is a Partner in the Business and Finance Practice. His practice focuses on mergers and acquisitions and corporate finance. Mr Werner is involved in a wide range of acquisition and corporate finance transactions representing private equity funds, institutional investors and strategic acquirers. He is a leader in the areas of leveraged acquisitions, strategic equity and corporate partnering investments, recapitalizations and restructurings involving various industries.
Prof. Memberships: Member, American Bar Association, International Section.

WERTHEIMER, Robert J
Paul, Hastings, Janofsky & Walker LLP,
New York 212 318 6550
robertwertheimer@paulhastings.com
Recommended in Real Estate
Practice Areas: Co-Vice Chair of firm's Real Estate Practice Group. Commercial real estate purchase/sale transactions, joint ventures, development and finance matters. Represents entrepreneurial investors, prominent real estate individuals/families, institutional/investment fund clients, not-for-profits and public agencies. Has international/domestic experience.
Prof. Memberships: New York State and American Bar Associations; active in Association of the Bar of the City of New York (served on Committee on Corrections).
Career: Donovan Leisure Newton & Irvine (1979-82); Battle Fowler (1982-2000); Paul, Hastings, Janofsky & Walker LLP (2000 to date).
Personal: Columbia University School of Law (JD, 1979); Cornell University (BA, with distinction, 1976).

WESELY, Marissa C
Simpson Thacher & Bartlett LLP,
New York 212 455 7173
mwesely@stblaw.com
Recommended in Banking & Finance
Practice Areas: Partner in the firm's Corporate Department. Specialises in domestic and international bank finance transactions, with an emphasis on leveraged acquisition finance, advising equity sponsors, corporate borrowers and lenders in connection with senior lending facilities and bridge loans. Recent experience includes: representation of

Blackstone in the financing and refinancing of its acquisition of TRW Automotive, Cypress in its acquisition of Cooper Standard and Affinia, CB Richard Ellis in its acquisition of Insignia Financial Group and representation of L-3 Communications, St. John Knits and Peabody Coal in recent refinancings of their senior debt. Also active in financing transactions in Latin America, including the representation of JPMorgan and other bank lenders in the restructuring of the debt of Sanluis Corporacion, the Mexican autoparts manufacturer, and of Banco Hipotecario, the Argentine bank, in the restructuring of its bank debt.
Prof. Memberships: International Bar Association, New York State and New York City Bar Associations, Women's Bar Association.
Career: Member of the firm since 1989.
Publications: 'Securitization Techniques in International Trade and Project Financing', The Review of Banking and Financial Services, Vol. 12, No. 7, 1996.
Personal: Williams College, BA 1976, magna cum laude, Harvard Law School, JD 1980, cum laude.

WHITE, Algird
Couch White, LLP, Albany
518 426 4600
Recommended in Energy

WHITE, Ira
Morgan, Lewis & Bockius LLP,
New York 212 309 6115
iwhite@morganlewis.com
Recommended in Private Equity
Practice Areas: Mr White is a Partner in the Business and Finance Practice and Co-Chair of the firm's Private Equity Practice. Mr White's practice focuses on mergers and acquisitions, private equity and venture capital matters. Mr White has been involved in a wide range of transactions representing private equity funds; venture capital funds; corporations, limited liability companies and partnerships; and management.

WHITE, Mary Jo
Debevoise & Plimpton LLP, New York
212 909 6000
Recommended in Litigation

WHITE, W Christopher
Cadwalader, Wickersham & Taft LLP,
New York 212 504 6633
christopher.white@cwt.com
Recommended in Real Estate
Practice Areas: Chairman of Cadwalader's Real Estate Department. Specializes in commercial real estate with emphasis on debt and equity financing. Represents many of the largest US and foreign institutional investors in the full spectrum of their real estate investment activity. Spearheads Cadwalader's representation of investment banks and institutional lenders in public and private securitizations and other secondary market transactions. Structured acquisi-

tion and financing for commercial properties in Europe and Latin America. Represented institutional investors in joint ventures and other investment vehicles for the acquisition and development of hotels, office buildings, shopping centers and internet datacenters. Experienced with hotel and property management agreements and leasing agreements. Structured acquisitions of interests in companies owning and operating hotels, shopping centers, entertainment complexes and office buildings. Experienced in the workout of troubled assets, including restructurings, foreclosures and bankruptcies. Devised procedures for foreclosure by power of sale in New York.
Personal: BA, University of Notre Dame (1973), JD University of Michigan Law School (1977).

WIEMAN, Lawrence E
Davis Polk & Wardwell, New York
212 450 4000
lawrence.wieman@dpw.com
Recommended in Banking & Finance
Practice Areas: Member of Davis Polk & Wardwell's Credit Group. Represents borrowers and lenders in secured and unsecured financings for US and non-US transactions. Advises lenders and financially distressed borrowers on workouts and debt restructurings, various clients on senior and subordinated financing for contested and friendly acquisitions, and financial institutions and other clients regarding credit risks involved in cross-border securities and derivatives transactions and related collateral arrangements. Also has worked with securities and derivative product custody, trading and execution operations at other financial institutions.

WIGHT, Richard
Milbank, Tweed, Hadley & McCloy,
New York 212 530 5000
Recommended in Banking & Finance

WILD, Robert
Garfunkel, Wild & Travis PC,
Great Neck 516 393 2200
Recommended in Healthcare

WILLIAMS, Nicholas R
White & Case LLP, New York
212 819 8200
nwilliams@whitecase.com
Recommended in Insurance
Practice Areas: Mr Williams' practice focuses on mergers, acquisitions and capital markets transactions in both the property and casualty and life and health insurance industries. He also has extensive experience in all aspects of insurance regulatory matters, including licensings, investments, reinsurance, demutualizations, insolvencies, captive insurer formations and coverage issues.
Personal: AB, magna cum laude, Brown University, 1984, Phi Beta Kappa; JD, Columbia Law School, 1988, Harlan Fiske Stone Scholar.

WILLIAMS Jr, William
Sullivan & Cromwell LLP, New York
212 558 4000
Recommended in Capital Markets

WING, John
Weil, Gotshal & Manges LLP, New York
212 310 8364
john.wing@weil.com
Recommended in Litigation
Practice Areas: Criminal defense: investigations, trial, appellate.
Career: A nationally recognized trial lawyer who has been engaged in criminal trial and appellate work for over 25 years; former Chief of Fraud Unit, US Attorney's Office, S.D.N.Y. Wing represents individuals/corporations in complex criminal matters; many grand jury investigations resolved without criminal charges; published and lectured extensively on jury trial work and criminal law topics. Fellow, American College of Trial Lawyers; past President, New York Council of Defense Lawyers; recipient, Ostrow Award for Excellence in Criminal Defense; regularly listed, 'The Best Lawyers In America.'
Personal: University of Chicago, JD; Yale University, BA.

WISEMAN, Michael M
Sullivan & Cromwell LLP, New York
212 558 4000
wisemanm@sullcrom.com
Recommended in Banking & Finance
Practice Areas: Represents domestic and foreign commercial banks, investment banks and insurance companies on regulatory issues, enforcement matters, capital markets, new products initiatives, derivative products, payment system issues, corporate governance and joint ventures.
Prof. Memberships: ABA; ABCNY (former Chair, Banking Law Committee); NYSBA (Banking Law Committee); ABF; ALI.
Career: Partner since 1985. Managing Partner, Financial Institutions Group.
Publications: 'Money Management Issues - OTC Markets' (Futures & Derivatives Law Report, February 1997); Procter & Gamble Company vs. Bankers Trust (Securities Industry Association, 1996, co-author); 'The Evolution of Banking in the United States: Comments on Present Trends' (Korea Institute of Finance, International Symposium on Universal Banking, 1996).
Personal: Harvard College (AB, 1975); Harvard Law School (JD, 1978; Editor, Harvard Law Review).

WOHL, Frank
Lankler Siffert & Wohl, New York
212 921 8399
Recommended in Litigation

WOJCIECHOWSKI, Mark S
Mayer, Brown, Rowe & Maw LLP,
New York 212 506 2525
mwojciechowski@mayerbrownrowe.com
Recommended in Banking & Finance, Corporate/M&A

Practice Areas: Firm Practice Leader in Finance. Corporate, corporate finance, and private equity. Has extensive experience not only in banking and finance but also mergers and acquisitions, joint ventures (domestic and international), and private equity investment.

Prof. Memberships: Admitted to practice in New York (1982). Member of International Law Advisory Committee of the Practising Law Institute; American Bar Association, Section on Corporation, Banking, and Business Law; the New York State Bar Association, Section of International Law and Practice; and the Association of the Bar of the City of New York. Appointments: Chairman, Corporation Law Committee, Association of the Bar of the City of New York.

Career: Joined Mayer, Brown, Rowe & Maw LLP, 1986; became Partner, 1988. Member, Mayer, Brown, Rowe & Maw Executive Committee (Policy and Planning Committee).

Publications: Co-author, 'How to Buy a US Business: A Guide to Negotiated and Hostile Acquisitions' (1999).

Personal: Born 4 May 1954. JD (cum laude), Indiana University (Bloomington), 1981; AB, Columbia College, 1976.

WOLF, Barry M
Weil, Gotshal & Manges LLP, New York
212 310 8209
barry.wolf@weil.com
Recommended in Private Equity

Practice Areas: Mr Wolf has extensive experience representing private equity funds in their organizational and operational matters and institutional investors with respect to private equity fund investments and provides advice on both commercial and tax matters.

Career: Mr Wolf is Global Head of the Private Equity Practice and a member of the Management Committee. He regularly represents a number of private investment funds and their sponsors in organizational and operational matters. He has been recognized as a leading private equity lawyer by Practical Law Company in Global Counsel and has received a '1' ranking from Chambers USA. Mr Wolf's clients include Capital Z Partners, Lindsay Goldberg & Bessemer, American Securities Partners, Genstar Capital Partners, Centre Partners, Gores Technology Group and Crow Holdings.

Personal: New York University School of Law, LLM; University of Michigan Law School, JD; SUNY Albany, BS.

WOLITZER, Michael
Simpson Thacher & Bartlett LLP,
New York 212 455 2000
mwolitzer@stblaw.com
Recommended in Private Equity

Practice Areas: Corporate Partner at Simpson Thacher & Bartlett LLP. His practice focuses on private investing and other facets of 'alternative asset management'. Represents some of the largest and well known sponsors of private

equity funds, such as Blackstone, Citigroup, Lexington Partners, Quadrangle and Silver Lake Partners. Involved in many acquisitions of, and investments in, private investment firms.

Prof. Memberships: Former Chairman and member of the Executive Committee of the 'Private Investment Fund Forum', member of the City Bar Association's Subcommittee on Private Investment Funds and Vice-Chairman of the Specialized Investment Funds Subcommittee of the International Bar Association. Member of the Advisory Boards of the Private Equity Analyst's Survey of Fund Terms and Conditions, and and the Private Equity Investment Guidelines Group. Served on many panels at private equity industry conferences.

Career: A Partner at the firm since 1998.

Personal: JD, 1989, Columbia University School of Law (James Kent Scholar and a Harlan Fiske Stone Scholar).

WOLLMAN, Diana L
Sullivan & Cromwell LLP, New York
212 558 4000
wollmand@sullcrom.com
Recommended in Tax

Practice Areas: US federal tax matters, including a broad spectrum of planning and transactional matters for domestic and foreign corporations, partnerships and investment companies. Has represented clients in tax litigation, as a lobbyist and before the IRS in controversies and requests for private rulings.

Prof. Memberships: the Tax Club; NYSBA (Member of Tax Section's Executive Committee and Co-Chair of Tax Section's Committee on 'Inbound' US Activities of Foreign Taxpayers); ABA (Tax Section).

Career: Partner since 2000. Adjunct Professor, Columbia University School of Law, since Spring 2004.

Publications: Has published numerous articles on a variety of topics. Speaking engagements include meetings of NYSBA Tax Section; ABA Tax Section; UCLA M&A Institute; USC Major Tax Planning Institute; NYU Tax Planning Institute; International Tax Institute; and PLI.

Personal: Harvard University (AB, 1986); University of California Los Angeles Law School (JD, 1991).

WYMAN, Kenneth
Simpson Thacher & Bartlett LLP,
New York 212 455 7435
kwyman@stblaw.com
Recommended in Projects

Practice Areas: Corporate Partner at Simpson Thacher & Bartlett LLP. Specializes in international and domestic finance with an emphasis on project finance and leasing. Recent transactions include representation of KeySpan Energy Corp. and subsidiaries as lessee in connection with the leveraged lease financing of its 250 MW expansion to the Ravenswood generating facility located in New York City; representation

of Credit Suisse First Boston as sole underwriter in connection with the $940 million construction and leveraged lease project financing of the 400 MW Springville Unit 3 coal-fired electric generating facility leased by Tri-State Generation and Transmission Association, awarded Euromoney's Asset Finance International/US Power Deal of the Year 2003; representation of Credit Lyonnais, BNP Paribas, Bank of America, Australia and New Zealand Bank and other project finance lenders in connection with numerous project financings of electric generating facilities sponsored by Cogentrix Energy, Inc., including its Southaven, Green Country, Rathdrum, Ouachita, Richmond and Indiantown facilities.

Prof. Memberships: Member, American Bar Association; New York State Bar Association.

Career: Joined the firm in 1987 and became a Partner in 1997.

Personal: Received BS, Wharton School of the University of Pennsylvania, 1984; JD, University of Pennsylvania School of Law, 1987.

YODOWITZ, Edward J
Skadden, Arps, Slate, Meagher & Flom LLP & Affiliates, New York
212 735 3450
eyodowit@skadden.com
Recommended in Litigation

Practice Areas: Focuses on complex securities and financial fraud investigations and related litigation, including appeals. Handles accounting litigation and securities litigation relating to the 1933 and 1934 Acts, including class and derivative actions. Represented clients in SEC enforcement actions as well as banking, professional malpractice and insurance litigation. Experienced in the management of long-term, complex and document-intensive cases. Frequent lecturer on securities litigation for the Practising Law Institute and the Securities Industry Association.

Career: JD, University of Baltimore, 1969; BS, Long Island University, 1965.

YOUNG, Kevin
Young, Sommer, Ward, Ritzenberg, Wooley, Baker & Moore LLC, Albany
518 438 9907
Recommended in Environment

YOUNG, Michael
Willkie Farr & Gallagher LLP, New York
212 728 8280
Myoung@willkie.com
Recommended in Litigation

Practice Areas: Litigation Partner specializing in securities and financial reporting. Experience includes the representation of issuers, officers, directors, audit committees, accounting firms, investment banks, brokerage firms, outside professionals, and others in securities class actions or special investigations with a particular emphasis on accounting irregularities. Trial work includes

matters in federal, state, and bankruptcy courts, including the first class action tried to a jury pursuant to the Private Securities Litigation Reform Act of 1995. Has served for more than a decade as counsel to the American Institute of Certified Public Accountants, and has accordingly assisted in such matters as the formulation of the federal securities tort reform legislation of the mid-1990s, the drafting of Generally Accepted Auditing Standards, the enactment of the Uniform Accountancy Act, and the submission to the United States Supreme Court and Courts of Appeal of amicus curiae briefs on matters of importance to financial reporting. Is also a member of the New York Mayor's Committee on the Judiciary.

Prof. Memberships: Member of the American Bar Association's Committee on Law and Accounting, and member of the Financial Accounting Standards Advisory Council to the Financial Accounting Standards Board.

Career: Admitted to the New York State Bar; the US District Courts for the Eastern and Southern Districts of New York; the United States Courts of Appeal for the Second, Ninth, and Eleventh Circuits; and the United States Supreme Court. Has submitted testimony at the request of both the SEC and the Public Oversight Board on financial reporting and corporate governance issues, and has testified before the United States Senate Banking Committee on important developments in financial reporting.

Publications: Writes and lectures frequently on financial reporting and liability issues. Publications include 'Accounting Irregularities and Financial Fraud' and 'The Financial Reporting Handbook'.

Personal: Received a JD from Duke University School of Law in 1981, where he served as Research and Managing Editor of the 'Duke Law Journal', and a BA (magna cum laude) from Allegheny College in 1978, where he was elected to Phi Beta Kappa.

YOUNGWOOD, Alfred D
Paul, Weiss, Rifkind, Wharton & Garrison LLP, New York 212 373 3080
ayoungwood@paulweiss.com
Recommended in Tax

Practice Areas: Chair of the firm and its Management Committee. Tax Partner who concentrates on acquisitions, reorganizations and financings involving American and foreign businesses through use of corporate and partnership structures. Tax representations include advising clients in the creation of major joint ventures in media and cable television for significant multimedia company, the spin-off of cable television business of one of the world's largest entertainment companies and the sale of its publishing entity, and the sale of a major beverage company. Selected for the 2005 edition of 'The Best Lawyers in America'.

ZETLIN, Michael S
Zetlin & De Chiara LLP, New York
212 682 6800
mzetlin@zdlaw.com
Recommended in Construction

Practice Areas: Practice leader in construction litigation and transactions. He has extensive experience representing owners, developers, design professionals, contractors, construction managers and other parties in the construction industry. A graduate civil engineer as well as an attorney, Mr Zetlin represents national and multinational firms in a wide range of construction matters, including litigation, general business matters, construction contracting and risk management.

Prof. Memberships: New York Building Congress-General Counsel/Board of Directors; American Institute of Architects (AIA), New York City/Long Island Chapters-General Counsel; ABA Forum on the Construction Industry-Past Chair, Design Division; Civil Engineering Research Foundation-Corporate Advisory Board/Executive Committee; The Council on Transportation-Council Member; Pratt Institute-Board of Trustees; Global Design Alliance-Board Member.

Career: Founding Partner of Zetlin & De Chiara LLP, headquartered in Manhattan with offices in Westbury, NY, Newark, NJ and Stamford, CT.

Publications: Co-editor and co-author, *New York Construction Law*, Aspen Publishing (2003); co-author, 'Liability Exposure after September 11, 2001,' Building Security: Handbook for Architectural Planning and Design, McGraw Hill Companies (2003). Adjunct Professor, Polytechnic Institute, New York, Construction and the Law.

Personal: Mr Zetlin is a graduate civil engineer from Columbia University and received his Juris Doctorate from Fordham University.

ZIMAN, Kenneth S
Simpson Thacher & Bartlett LLP, New York 212 455 2000
kziman@stblaw.com
Recommended in Bankruptcy

Practice Areas: Ken Ziman is a Partner in the Bankruptcy and Restructuring Practice Group of the firm's Corporate Department. He regularly represents clients in connection with out-of-court restructurings and Chapter 11 cases. His work has focused primarily on advising financial institutions in connection with their loans to troubled companies through all stages of the restructuring process. He also represents acquirers of financially distressed companies and significant individual creditors in Chapter 11 cases and provides advice regarding the structuring of corporate transactions.

Prof. Memberships: American Bar Association, Business Section; The Bar Association of the City of New York, Bankruptcy and Reorganization Committee.

Personal: He received his BA magna cum laude from Colgate University in 1987 and his JD from the University of Pennsylvania in 1990.

ZIRINSKY, Bruce
Cadwalader, Wickersham & Taft LLP, New York 212 504 6404
bruce.zirinsky@cwt.com
Recommended in Bankruptcy

Practice Areas: Partner and Chairman of the firm's Financial Restructuring Department. For over 30 years has counselled debtors, secured and unsecured lenders, creditor committees, public bondholders, shareholders, and investors involved in many of the largest and most complex US and international reorganizations and restructurings, mass tort reorganizations, financial transactions, mergers and acquisitions, and litigations across a multitude of industries including telecommunications, energy, airline, healthcare, manufacturing, retail, food services, financial services, real estate, rail car, shipping, forest products, petroleum, computer, media, casino gaming, and hospitality. Has represented clients in many high-profile reorganization cases, including Adelphia, Arch Wireless, Cadillac Fairview, Chase REIT, Continental Airlines, Dictaphone Corporation, Dow Corning, Eurotunnel, Flag Telecom, Florida Coast Paper, FNN, Glencore Nickel, Harrah's Jazz, Huntsman Corp., Mirant Americas Generation LLC, Olympia & York, Owens Corning, Parmalat (Notehlders), Pathmark Stores, Resorts International, RSL Communications, Solutia Inc., Quigley Company, Tucson Electric, US Air, USG, and Winstar Communications.

Career: Graduated from the New York University School of Law in 1972 and received undergraduate degree from Cornell University. Became a Partner and Chair of Financial Restructuring Department at Cadwalader in 1998.

ZORNOW, David M
Skadden, Arps, Slate, Meagher & Flom LLP & Affiliates, New York
212 735 2890
dzornow@skadden.com
Recommended in Litigation

Practice Areas: Head of firm's New York office White Collar Crime Practice. Represents corporations and individuals in connection with federal and state grand jury investigations and at trial. Also works on civil enforcement actions, including matters before the Securities and Exchange Commission, as well as internal investigations on behalf of corporate boards of directors.

Career: JD, Yale Law School, 1980; BA, Harvard College, 1976 (summa cum laude; Phi Beta Kappa).

ALLEN & OVERY

THE FIRM

Managing Partner: Mark Welling
Senior Partner: Daniel P Cunningham

Number of partners: 25

FIRM OVERVIEW: Allen & Overy is a premier international legal practice comprising Allen & Overy LLP and its affiliated undertakings (collectively described in this profile as 'Allen & Overy'). It has over 4,800 staff including some 440 partners working in 25 major cities worldwide.

MAIN AREAS OF PRACTICE:

Banking & Finance: Allen & Overy has a leading International Finance Practice acting for banks, financial houses and corporates. The practice advises on complex cross-border transactions, as well as domestic transactions, in all major financial centers worldwide. Specialist business areas include asset finance, capital markets, derivatives, financial services regulation, global loans, leveraged finance, project finance, real estate, restructuring, securitization, telecom finance and trade finance.

Corporate/M&A: The Corporate Department is the single largest practice at Allen & Overy. In addition to its mainstream mergers and acquisitions capability, the department's expertise encompasses private equity, equity capital markets, antitrust, environment and IP/IT. The department focuses increasingly on industry sector groupings in key global markets including communications, media and technology, energy, financial institutions and bioscience. Each group numbers many of these sectors' leading players among its client base and is supported by cross-practice specialists.

Litigation: Allen & Overy's global Litigation Practice has a track record of dealing with many of the world's major financial and commercial crises and disputes. Dedicated and experienced litigators in New York and around the world include arbitrators, negotiators and mediators who draw on the integrated and specialist support of all of Allen & Overy's business sectors. The department is supported by cutting edge of technology in the form of Allen & Overy's caseroom2, a total online case management system.

CLIENTS: Allen & Overy provides a comprehensive legal service to corporations, financial institutions, governments and multilateral agencies in the United States and around the world.

HEAD OFFICE

NEW YORK
Allen & Overy LLP
1221 Avenue of the Americas, **New York**, NY 10020
Tel: 212 610 6300 **Fax:** 212 610 6399
Email: info@allenovery.com
Website: www.allenovery.com

INTERNATIONAL OFFICES

Allen & Overy LLP or an affiliated undertaking has an office in each of the following: Amsterdam, Antwerp, Bangkok, Beijing, Bratislava, Brussels, Budapest, Dubai, Frankfurt, Hamburg, Hong Kong, London, Luxembourg, Madrid, Milan, Moscow, Paris, Prague, Rome, Shanghai, Singapore, Tokyo, Turin and Warsaw.

CONTACTS

Antitrust	Michael Jahnke
Asset Finance	Ian Shrank/Barry Biggar
Banking	Carl Sheldon
Corporate/M&A	Eric S Shube, A Peter Harwich
Derivatives	Daniel P Cunningham, Joshua Cohn
European Desk	Helena Sprenger
Employee Benefits & Executive Compensation	Henry Morgenbesser
Environmental Law	Kenneth Rivlin
International Capital Markets	Cathleen McLaughlin, David Wainer
Latin America Practice	Cathleen McLaughlin, Robert Kartheiser
Leveraged Finance	Tom Abbondante
Litigation	Michael Feldberg, Pamela Rogers Chepiga
Project Finance	David Slade, Ernest Chung
Real Estate	Kevin O'Shea
Restructuring	Ken Coleman, Hugh McDonald
Tax	Jack Heinberg

ALLEN & OVERY

ANDERSON KILL & OLICK P.C.

THE FIRM

Managing Partner: Jeffrey L Glatzer
Number of lawyers: 120-150

FIRM OVERVIEW: US Anderson Kill & Olick, P.C., founded in 1969, has offices in New York, Philadelphia, Newark, Washington DC, Chicago, and Connecticut. Anderson Kill has a reputation for combining corporate polish with pugnacity. This reputation is built upon the firm's central philosophy of aggressively representing clients in all areas of the firm's practice. Too often law firms forget that clients come to law firms to find solutions to their problems. Anderson Kill attorneys are problem solvers. The firm takes advantage of the wealth of knowledge and experience of Anderson Kill's attorneys and avoids 'reinventing the wheel.' This approach results in creative and cost-effective resolutions of client problems. Anderson Kill's talent is exceptional and varied. Many of Anderson Kill's attorneys are recognized experts in their practice areas, leaders and are active participants in professional associations, and frequently invited to speak at business organizations. Anderson Kill attracts and retains smart, personable and well rounded attorneys. This produces an environment reflecting a passion for the work, collegiality and a high level of job satisfaction. The effect of Anderson Kill's experience, background, and unique approach to practice is better results for clients. That is the Anderson Kill difference.

MAIN AREAS OF PRACTICE: Anderson Kill's practice areas include:
Bankruptcy & Restructuring: Anderson Kill has handled countless bankruptcy cases in courts throughout the country and has represented every constituency in major Chapter 11 cases as well as trustees in bankruptcy involving large liquidations. Anderson Kill has a premiere reputation in the representation of creditors, with engagements on behalf of committees, lending groups and holders of control positions.
Business Law: Anderson Kill's practice areas include: mergers and acquisitions in the public and private sector; financial services principally involving commercial and institutional lenders; venture capital transactions; securities law; distressed securities and claims trading; representation of general and limited partnerships and limited liability companies; restructurings and reorganizations; and general corporate representation and counseling.
Business Litigation: Anderson Kill has a diversified, transactional, corporate and securities practice that provide representation to a wide range of institutional and entrepreneurial clients covering all types of transactions both domestically and internationally. Anderson Kill has broad experience in corporate and commercial litigation representing companies, partnerships, their officers, directors and management; and individuals in a diverse mix of litigation and counseling.
Employment & Labor Law: Anderson Kill counsels and represents management in every phase of employment and labor law while focusing on two primary goals: (1) to provide accurate and practical advice on a full range of issues which may arise, and (2) if litigation ensues, to provide cost-effective, and result-oriented representation. In fact, Anderson Kill has guided many employers in successful efforts to maintain a union free workplace.
Insurance Recovery: Anderson Kill attorneys are recognized as the most prominent insurance recovery attorneys in the country, successfully representing policyholders in a variety of disputes with insurance companies. Anderson Kill has recovered billions of dollars for policyholders and has years of trial experience and a reputation in securing favorable settlements. With an unparalleled wealth of resources, including an unrivaled computerized bank of insurance materials, discovery, and advertisements, Anderson Kill makes a difference where it counts. Anderson Kill gets favorable results whether by settlement or judgment.

HEAD OFFICE

NEW YORK
1251 Avenue of the Americas, **New York**, NY 10020
Tel: 212 278 1000   **Fax:** 212 278 1733
Website: www.andersonkill.com

BRANCH OFFICES

CONNECTICUT
Two Sound View Drive, Suite 100, **Greenwich**, CT 06830
Tel: 203 622 7668   **Fax:** 203 622 0321

DISTRICT OF COLUMBIA
2100 M Street NW, Suite 650, **Washington**, DC 20037
Tel: 202 218 0040   **Fax:** 202 218 0055

ILLINOIS
1821 Walden Office Square, Suite 400, **Schaumburg**, IL 60173
Tel: 847 925 5430   **Fax:** 847 925 5431

NEW JERSEY
One Gateway Center, Suite 901, **Newark**, NJ 07102
Tel: 973 642 5858   **Fax:** 973 621 6361

PENNSYLVANIA
1600 Market Street, **Philadelphia**, PA 19103
Tel: 215 568 4202   **Fax:** 215 568 4573

CONTACTS

Insurance Recovery	Robert M Horkovich
Bankruptcy & Restructuring	J Andrew Rahl Jr
Business Law	Arnold L Bartfeld
Business Litigation	Steven Cooper
Employment & Labor Law	Bennett Pine
Products Liability	Judith A Yavitz
Intellectual Property	David A Einhorn
Trusts & Estates	James G Clements

Intellectual Property: Anderson Kill regularly works with the full range of intellectual property issues and problems for a broad cross-section of domestic and international clients. Its expertise includes all aspects of intellectual property law relating to patents, trademarks, copyrights and mask works, and unfair competition.
Products Liability: Anderson Kill is well known for its supervisory expertise as national defense counsel in product of liability actions, which includes thousands of asbestos and hundreds of DES personal injury. Having tried cases involving complex design, trade, and manufacturing issues, Anderson Kill coordinates the settlement of claims, provides analysis of verdict trends, and assesses group settlements.
Trusts & Estates: Anderson Kill regards giving advice to individuals concerning personal tax, financial planning, and trusts and estates as a significant aspect of its practice. Anderson Kill advises clients on methods of accumulating, managing, and preserving wealth, as well as its disposition during life and upon death. Specifically, Anderson Kill assists clients in building their estates and planning for the transfer of property to family members and other beneficiaries in ways that minimize income, gift, and estate taxes.

CLIENTS: Anderson Kill clients include the nation's largest corporate and industrial companies as well as utilities, municipalities, state governments, charities, major religious and not-for-profit organizations, small companies and individuals.

BOIES, SCHILLER & FLEXNER LLP

THE FIRM

Managing Partners: David Boies, Jonathan D Schiller, Donald L Flexner

Number of partners: 71
Number of other lawyers: 125

FIRM OVERVIEW: Founded in 1997 by David Boies and Jonathan Schiller, BSF now has 196 lawyers in 10 offices located in New York, Washington, DC, California, Florida, New Hampshire and New Jersey. The firm's partners, who have tried more than 300 cases before juries and judges in federal and state courts throughout the United States, include the former lead trial attorney for the United States in United States v Microsoft, a former Deputy Assistant Attorney General in charge of the Antitrust Division, a former lead attorney for the United States in United States v AT&T, and the former US Attorney who created the securities fraud branch of that office in San Francisco. The Wall Street Journal describes the firm as a 'litigation powerhouse,' (April 6, 2000), and the National Law Journal as 'unafraid to venture into controversial' and 'high risk' matters. (February 12, 2001).

MAIN AREAS OF PRACTICE:

Complex commercial trials and litigation, including antitrust, securities and class actions, and international arbitration are the centerpieces of the firm's practice. The firm also represents corporate clients and financial institutions in significant merger and acquisition and project financing transactions. Boies, Schiller & Flexner enjoys one of the most selective and successful class action practices in the country. It represents both plaintiffs and defendants, and the disputes cover the widest range of subject matters, including securities, antitrust and corporate control matters.

CLIENTS: In 2004, the firm's partners have been involved in (i) significant antitrust matters, including the prosecution of American Express' multi billion dollar claims against Visa and MasterCard, (ii) securities defense of Qwest Communications International, Tyco International, Adelphia Communications, 3Com and Unisys and (iii) most recently, the World Trade Center jury trial in New York Federal Court, and other defenses of insurance and reinsurance companies in the US and Bermuda. The firm's clients include some of the largest and most sophisticated companies in the world: Adelphia Communications, Aetna, American Express, CBS, Columbia University, DuPont, Ernst & Young, FPL Group, Goldman Sachs, Guardsmark, Monsanto, Northwest Airlines, Philip Morris, Public Broadcasting System, Qwest Communications, SBC Communications, Siemens, The New York Yankees, The Republic of France, Tyco International, Unisys, Viacom, Inc., Yankees Entertainment & Sports Network and Zurich Capital Markets Inc.

INTERNATIONAL WORK: Partners at Boies, Schiller & Flexner have practiced arbitration and international arbitration for more than 25 years, including ICC, LCIA, UNCITRAL, ICSID, AAA, NASD and ad hoc arbitration. The firm's partners have represented client's in arbitral proceedings before tribunals in Paris, Geneva, London, Zurich, Stockholm, and Hong Kong, and throughout the United States. The practice is headed by Managing Partner Jonathan Schiller, who is a member of the Milan Chamber of National and International Arbitration Club of Arbitrators, and has served both as an advocate and arbitrator in international arbitration.

HEAD OFFICE

NEW YORK
333 Main Street, **Armonk**, NY 10504
Tel: 914 749 8200 **Fax:** 914 749 8300
Website: www.bsfllp.com

BRANCH OFFICES

CALIFORNIA
1999 Harrison Street, Suite 900, **Oakland**, CA 94612
Tel: 510 874 1000 **Fax:** 510 874 1460

DISTRICT OF COLUMBIA
5301 Wisconsin Avenue, NW, **Washington**, DC 20015
Tel: 202 237 2727 **Fax:** 202 237 6131

FLORIDA
100 Southeast 2nd St, Suite 2800, **Miami**, FL 33131
Tel: 305 539 8400 **Fax:** 305 539 1307

401 East Las Olas Blvd, Suite 200, **Fort Lauderdale**, FL 33301
Tel: 954 356 0011 **Fax:** 954 356 0022

255 South Orange Avenue, Suite 905, **Orlando**, FL 32801
Tel: 407 425 7118 **Fax:** 407 425 7047

6450 Belvedere Road, **West Palm Beach**, FL 33413
Tel: 561 471 3111 **Fax:** 561 471 4644

NEW HAMPSHIRE
26 South Main Street, **Hanover**, NH 03755
Tel: 603 643 9090 **Fax:** 603 643 9009

NEW JERSEY
150 JFK Parkway, Suite 100, **Short Hills**, NJ 07078
Tel: 973 218 1111 **Fax:** 973 218 1106

NEW YORK
570 Lexington Avenue, 16th Fl, **New York**, NY 10022
Tel: 212 446 2300 **Fax:** 212 446 2350

10 North Pearl Street, 4th Floor, **Albany**, NY 12207
Tel: 518 434 0600 **Fax:** 518 434 0665

BROWN RAYSMAN MILLSTEIN FELDER & STEINER LLP

THE FIRM

Managing Partners: Peter Brown, Richard Raysman and Julian Millstein
Number of partners: 88
Number of other lawyers: 160

FIRM OVERVIEW: Brown Raysman Millstein Felder & Steiner LLP has built on its international reputation as a leader in the area of technology and intellectual property law to emerge in the new millennium as a renowned general practice law firm. Today, the focus of the firm extends from technology and intellectual property law to real estate finance and leasing and corporate transactional work, as well as securities, mergers and acquisitions, commercial and IP litigation, construction, bankruptcy, media, life sciences, healthcare, trusts and estates, tax, and employment law.

MAIN AREAS OF PRACTICE:

Technology, Media & Communications: As a leader in technology, media and communications law for over 25 years, Brown Raysman is uniquely qualified to handle transactions and disputes for its clients and does so on a regular basis in areas such as voice and data communications, cable (including interactive and other enhanced services) and broadcast television, internet and mass media, enterprise solutions, privacy and security, licensing, mobile and wireless, networking infrastructure and management, video conferencing, technology transfers and new media.

Intellectual Property: As a pioneer of technology law, Brown Raysman offers unparalleled services in the global clearance, acquisition, maintenance and enforcement of patents, trademarks, service marks, copyrights, trade secrets and related intellectual property such as internet domain names. In particular, Brown Raysman has a premier high-technology and life sciences patent prosecution and litigation practice. Many of the firm's patent attorneys are former electrical or bio-medical engineers, with prior experience in their respective fields, a number of whom have PhDs in various areas of life sciences.

Outsourcing: Brown Raysman is one of a handful of law firms internationally known for its outsourcing practice and has negotiated complex IT and BPO deals on both the vendor and customer sides of a transaction. The firm has also negotiated numerous offshore outsourcing deals with companies based in India, Europe, Asia and the Caribbean.

Real Estate & Commercial Finance: The firm's Real Estate Finance Practice is nationally recognized for its representation of both lenders and borrowers in complex real estate financing transactions, including construction, conduit, interim and permanent financings, forward loan commitments, lines of credit, mezzanine loans, low-income housing tax credit transactions, loan participations and mortgage-backed bond credit enhancement transactions. The firm's commercial finance attorneys have comprehensive expertise in equipment finance, commercial and asset-based lending, factoring, franchise finance and other corporate and transactional matters. Brown Raysman provides counsel to a wide range of financial institutions and other lenders and borrowers on business issues including capital equipment acquisitions and sales, asset-based finance transactions, and tax-advantaged leasing activities. In addition, the firm has represented issuers, servicers, credit enhancers and investors in the mortgage-backed and asset-backed securities markets.

Commercial Leasing: Brown Raysman is nationally recognized as one of the premier law firms in commercial leasing transactions. The firm's attorneys regularly represent both landlords and tenants in complex leasing transactions, including net leasing, ground leasing and subleasing, commercial office leasing, and retail leasing. They also have extensive experience with a myriad of real estate brokerage issues and regularly have served as counsel to real estate brokerage companies.

Corporate & Securities: Brown Raysman's corporate attorneys have extensive experience counseling issuers, underwriters, placement agents and selling shareholders in private placements, initial and secondary public offerings of equity and debt securities, Rule 144A offerings and other financings for domestic and foreign companies. Brown Raysman renders general securities law and regulatory compliance advice to its public company clients

regarding such matters as proxy solicitations, executive compensation disclosure, Section 16 planning and reporting, and exchange listing rules. The firm advises funds and other private equity investors in their portfolio investments, from the term sheet through due diligence and closing, and in connection with the management of their assets. The firm is experienced in organizing both domestic and offshore private equity funds.

Labor & Employment: Brown Raysman has assembled a group of skilled and experienced labor and employment attorneys capable of expertly handling any employment-related issue. The firm has a proven track record of successfully representing Fortune 100 s and smaller companies in connection with virtually every type of labor and employment controversy, and has counseled senior management of firm clients on the most sensitive and complex employee relations topics.

Commercial & IP Litigation & Arbitration: Brown Raysman's diverse and international litigation and arbitration practice encompasses both established and emerging areas of the law and is closely aligned with the firm's core expertise in the areas of intellectual property, high-technology and the internet, as well as the more traditional areas of employment, banking, bankruptcy, real estate, construction, securities (including NASD and NYSE arbitrations), antitrust and finance.

Creditors' Rights & Bankruptcy: The firm regularly represents a broad range of debtors, creditors and other stakeholders in a wide range of business restructuring and insolvency matters, including bankruptcy cases, creditors' rights, litigations, and out-of-court restructurings.

Construction & Surety & Fidelity: The firm counsels owners, developers, lenders, contractors and others on building technology, bidding, construction agreements and complex litigation matters. On surety and fidelity matters, the firm assists clients with underwriting claims investigations and issues involving all manner of bonds vehicles.

Trusts & Estates & Tax: Brown Raysman's Trusts and Estates Group advises clients in a broad range of estate planning and related tax matters, including gifts, wealth transfers, valuation issues and planning for generational transfers of interests in closely-held businesses. Brown Raysman's tax attorneys also provide sophisticated and strategic tax planning and advice regarding a wide range of complex domestic and international corporate and non-corporate commercial, real estate and other business transactions.

CLIENTS: Brown Raysman has a wide range of domestic and international clients represented in numerous industries, including: technology, real estate, internet, financial services, media and entertainment, sports, communications, satellite, direct marketing, life sciences, healthcare, timeshare finance, construction, automotive, insurance, manufacturing, government entities and public utilities.

HEAD OFFICE

NEW YORK

900 Third Avenue, **New York**, NY 10022
Tel: 212 895 2000   **Fax:** 212 895 2900
Email: info@brownraysman.com
Website: www.brownraysman.com

BRANCH OFFICES

CALIFORNIA

1880 Century Park East, **Los Angeles**, CA 90067
Tel: 310 712 8300   **Fax:** 310 712 8383

CONNECTICUT

Cityplace II, 185 Asylum Street, **Hartford**, CT 06103
Tel: 860 275 6400   **Fax:** 860 275 6410

NEW JERSEY

163 Madison Avenue, PO Box 1989, **Morristown**, NJ 07962-1989
Tel: 973 775 8900   **Fax:** 973 775 8901

BROWNRAYSMAN

BROWN RAYSMAN MILLSTEIN FELDER & STEINER LLP

CADWALADER, WICKERSHAM & TAFT LLP

THE FIRM

Managing Partner: Robert O Link Jr
Number of partners worldwide: 105
Number of other lawyers worldwide: 422

FIRM OVERVIEW: Established in New York in 1792, Cadwalader, Wickersham & Taft LLP, a premier international law firm with over 500 attorneys in four offices, offers legal advice in banking, capital markets, corporate finance, environmental, healthcare, insolvency, insurance and reinsurance, litigation, mergers and acquisitions, private client, project finance, real estate, securitization, structured finance, and tax matters.

MAIN AREAS OF PRACTICE:

Banking & Project Finance: This department advises in all aspects of banking and finance, including commercial lending, special bank regulatory needs, mortgage banking, warehouse lending and domestic and cross-border leasing. The projects group handles all aspects of project finance, infrastructure, equipment and trade finance, privatization, and energy trading transactions in more than 50 jurisdictions worldwide.

Capital Markets: This pre-eminent practice includes traditional fixed-income and equity capital markets, structured finance, synthetic products, hybrid products, and derivatives. In recognition of the firm's excellence in securitization, Cadwalader perennially ranks at or near the top of annual rankings in issuer and underwriter representations in both commercial mortgage-backed and asset-backed securitization transactions. The firm also has a broad asset-backed commercial paper practice counseling sponsors and placement agents regarding asset-backed commercial paper conduits.

Corporate/Mergers & Acquisitions: Representing issuers, purchasers and underwriters of securities in the domestic and foreign public and private capital markets, the firm's corporate attorneys participate in the full range of securities transactions, including initial public offerings, exchange and secondary offerings, private placements and workouts of senior and subordinated debt, convertible debt and equity securities, venture capital and start-up financing and commercial paper in the US and Eurodollar markets. Lawyers in the firm have represented US and multinational clients in many of the most complex and noteworthy mergers, acquisitions, recapitalizations, spin-offs, and split-offs in recent years.

Financial Restructuring: Possessing significant cross-border expertise, this department represents secured and unsecured lenders, bondholders, creditors' committees, borrowers, asset purchasers, and other entities involved in financial restructuring transactions or reorganization cases. The firm's attorneys have been at the forefront of many of the largest and most complex recent US and international insolvencies and routinely advise clients with interests in Europe, Asia, Latin America, and Africa.

Healthcare/Not-for-Profit: Cadwalader is a leader in healthcare law, with considerable resources and talented practitioners in the diverse areas affecting the industry - corporate governance, corporate finance, government regulation, Medicare and Medicaid, insolvency and restructuring, labor relations, litigation, risk management, securities, capital markets, and tax.

Litigation: Cadwalader's renowned litigators handle significant disputes for a broad spectrum of financial institutions, major commercial, industrial and service corporations, and high net worth individuals in state and federal courts throughout the US and in England, as well as proceedings before administrative and regulatory agencies and international tribunals. The practice focuses on business, corporate and securities litigation; derivatives, complex financial products and commodities; employment; environmental and 'toxic tort' liability; insurance and reinsurance; international litigation; real estate; trade regulation and antitrust; and business fraud.

HEAD OFFICE

NEW YORK
One World Financial Center, **New York**, NY 10281
Tel: 212 504 6000 **Fax:** 212 504 6666
Email: cwtinfo@cwt.com
Website: www.cadwalader.com

BRANCH OFFICES

DISTRICT OF COLUMBIA
1201 F Street, NW, **Washington**, DC 20004
Tel: 202 862 2200 **Fax:** 202 862 2400

NORTH CAROLINA
227 West Trade Street, **Charlotte**, NC 28202
Tel: 704 348 5100 **Fax:** 704 348 5200

INTERNATIONAL OFFICE

The firm also has an office in the United Kingdom

Private Client: Providing effective and creative personal, financial, charitable, and tax planning to individual clients and closely-held family companies, this department places particular emphasis on the preservation of wealth and the minimization of wealth transfer and income taxation.

Real Estate: This premier practice handles property transactions throughout the US and the world, including financings, acquisitions, sales and exchanges, development, construction, joint ventures, real estate investment funds, loan syndications, management, leasing, workouts, land use, government-assisted projects, and environmental matters. Real estate finance is of particular importance - the firm's lawyers pioneered many of the legal structures for securitized products that are now the standard worldwide - and the department is an industry leader in single-asset/single-borrower commercial mortgage securitizations.

Tax: While playing a crucial role in the firm's leading securitization, mergers and acquisitions, insolvency, structured products, and corporate finance practices, this sophisticated and diverse department also pioneers innovative tax structures that drive complex transactions, many of which involve cross-border components. The firm also maintains a significant tax controversy practice for US and non-US corporations and financial institutions.

INTERNATIONAL WORK: With strategically placed offices in New York, London, Charlotte and Washington, DC , Cadwalader is superbly positioned to offer top-flight legal services to internationally-based clients conducting transactions all over the world. The firm has built a strong and diverse international practice that can dispatch the most demanding, time-critical and resource-intensive transactions across a wide range of complementary practice areas. Fully integrated into the firm's Wall Street practice, Cadwalader's London office provides a powerful presence in Europe.

CLIENTS: The firm provides prestigious financial institutions, corporations, government entities, charitable and healthcare organizations, and private clients with innovative solutions to key legal and financial issues.

CADWALADER

CARTER LEDYARD & MILBURN LLP

THE FIRM

Managing Partner: Judith A Lockhart

Number of partners: 46
Number of other lawyers: 78

FIRM OVERVIEW: Founded in 1854, Carter Ledyard & Milburn LLP is a full service law firm serving corporations, financial institutions, government agencies and individuals. The Corporate Practice focuses on international mergers and acquisitions, joint ventures, IPOs and other public offerings, private equity, asset management and investment funds, antitrust, telecommunications and other government regulation. The Litigation and Arbitration Practice concentrates on commercial, securities, employment, environmental, intellectual property, criminal defense, maritime, insurance defense and reinsurance disputes. Other practice areas include intellectual property, bankruptcy and reorganization, real estate, trusts and estates, corporate investigations, employment, tax, employee benefits, tax exempt organizations and immigration.

MAIN AREAS OF PRACTICE:

Corporate/M&A/Securities: Mergers and acquisitions, joint ventures and strategic alliances, public and private securities offerings, venture capital and private equity investments, bank lending, securitizations, antitrust, telecommunications, broker-dealer and other regulatory compliance and investigations.

Litigation/Arbitration: Complex litigations, arbitrations and alternative dispute resolution proceedings to resolve commercial contract, securities, employment, environmental, intellectual property, insurance defense, reinsurance, criminal, first amendment and construction disputes.

Investment Management: Advice on the formation, registration, operation and regulation of exchange-traded funds, mutual funds, unit investment trusts, hedge funds, private equity funds, investment advisors, broker-dealers and other financial institutions.

Media & Technology: Representing technology-based business in media, e-commerce, telecommunications, software and biotechnology industries based in the US and overseas in financing, mergers and acquisitions, licensing transactions and general representation. The firm has helped more than 50 Israeli technology clients start and develop operations in the US.

Telecommunications: Representing television cable and radio broadcasters, programming companies, telephone system operators and telecom equipment manufacturers in all regulatory and licensing matters, mergers and acquisitions, carriage and distribution agreements and related litigation.

Real Estate: Representing property owners, lenders, tenants and government agencies in commercial and residential property sales, leases, financings, and development contracts.

Intellectual Property: Advice on protecting and commercialising technology and intellectual property assets. Filing and prosecution of patents, trademarks, copyrights and domain names, protection of trade secrets, software and technology licensing, e-commerce contracts and handling of litigation and administrative proceedings.

Maritime/Shipping: Ship finance transactions, charter parties, cross-border leasing, regulatory advice, environmental advice, bankruptcy and workouts, attachments and arrests, insurance coverage and claims, capital markets transactions, maritime litigation and arbitration.

Personal Representation: Representing US and offshore individuals in all aspects of their personal affairs requiring legal counsel, including estate and income tax planning and structuring, will and trust instrument drafting and estate administration, real estate, criminal defense and immigration work.

Bankruptcy/Reorganization: Representing creditors, debtors and asset acquirers in Chapter 11 and other bankruptcy cases and in non-bankruptcy workouts and enforcement actions.

Environmental: Environmental regulatory advice, litigation and administrative proceedings, land use planning, environmental impact assessment and disclosure, compliance and environmental audits.

Employment: Counseling concerning employment and immigration laws, regulations and claims. Litigation and arbitration of employment termination, discrimination, harassment and employee non-competition, confidentiality and trade secret claims.

Tax/Employee Benefits: Tax planning advice, transaction structuring advice, and IRS representation. Planning, documentation, IRS qualification and regulation of employee benefit and incentive plans, executive compensation plans, stock option plans, and other benefits.

CLIENTS: Clients include American Stock Exchange, Bank of New York, Bristol-Myers Squibb, Costco, Danisco A/S, Deutsche Bank, Empire State Development Corporation, Fox Sportsnet, Goldman Sachs, Globus-Gateway Tours Ltd., Honeywell, Kaneka Ltd., Liberty Media, Liberty Mutual, Lower Manhattan Development Corporation, Marvel Characters Inc., Metropolitan Transportation Authority, Pall Corporation, Playtex Products, Trinity Biotech plc, Tullett & Tokyo Liberty plc.

INTERNATIONAL WORK: Recent cross-border transactions include representing Orient-Express Hotels Ltd. (Bermuda) in its IPO and NYSE listing; United Business Media plc (UK) in US acquisitions including CMP Media Inc. and Allison-Fisher International Inc. and the sales of Visual Communications Group and United Advertising Publications; Cultor Corporation (Finland) in its acquisition of the food science group of Pfizer Inc. and in its merger with Danisco A/S (Denmark) and Danisco in connection with its pending tender offer to acquire Genencor (US); Sea Containers Ltd. (Bermuda) in its joint venture with GE Capital (US) to form shipping container lessor GE SeaCo SRL (Barbados); Bowater Incorporated (US) in its acquisition of Alliance Forest Products Inc. (Canada); Garban plc (UK) and Intercapital plc (UK) in their merger to create Garban-Intercapital plc (now ICAP plc); ICAP plc (UK) in its acquisitions of APB Energy, Inc. and First Brokers Securities, Inc.; and Pengrowth Energy Trust (Canada) in its acquisition of Calpine Corporation and in its U.S. public securities offering and New York Stock Exchange Listing.

HEAD OFFICE

NEW YORK
Two Wall Street, **New York**, NY 10005
Tel: 212 732 3200   **Fax:** 212 732 3232
Email: info@clm.com
Website: www.clm.com

BRANCH OFFICES

DISTRICT OF COLUMBIA
1401 Eye Street, NW, Suite 300, **Washington**, DC 20005
Tel: 202 898 1515   **Fax:** 202 898 1521

NEW YORK
570 Lexington Avenue, 41st Floor, **New York**, NY 10022
Tel: 212 371 2720   **Fax:** 212 371 4234

CHADBOURNE & PARKE LLP

THE FIRM

Managing Partner: Charles K O'Neill
Number of partners: 118
Number of other lawyers: 313

FIRM OVERVIEW: Founded in 1902, Chadbourne & Parke LLP has evolved into an international law firm with 10 offices in key markets around the world. The firm provides an array of legal services, both in the United States and internationally. The firm's diversity of practices enables attorneys from different practices to work together to meet its clients' full range of legal needs.

MAIN AREAS OF PRACTICE: Chadbourne provides a diverse portfolio of legal services, including mergers and acquisitions, securities, project finance, corporate finance, energy, telecommunications, commercial and products liability litigation, intellectual property, antitrust, domestic and international tax, reinsurance and insurance, environmental, real estate, bankruptcy and financial restructuring, employment law and ERISA, trusts and estates and government contract matters.

CLIENTS: The firm's clients include leading international and US corporations, financial institutions, trade associations and foundations, start-up businesses, partnerships and individuals.

INTERNATIONAL WORK: With its global network of approximately 430 attorneys, the firm is positioned to analyze market, institutional and regulatory trends as they evolve, and offer its clients a full range of legal services on virtually all matters affecting them. In addition to its European work, the firm has established substantial practices in the Commonwealth of Independent States (CIS), Central Asia and Latin America. The firm's knowledge and experience is enhanced through its long-term working relationships with law firms in other key markets around the world.

HEAD OFFICE

NEW YORK

30 Rockefeller Plaza, New York, NY 10112

Number of lawyers: 274
Office Profile: As the hub of Chadbourne's international network of offices, the New York office draws on the expertise of its other offices, both within and outside the United States, to represent clients both nationally and internationally.
Main Areas of Practice: Attorneys in the New York office represent all of the firm's practice areas, including bankruptcy and financial restructuring, corporate, employment, intellectual property, commercial and products liability litigation, securities litigation and regulatory enforcement, white collar defense, project finance, reinsurance and insurance, real estate, tax, and trusts and estates.

BRANCH OFFICES

CALIFORNIA

350 South Grand Avenue, Suite 3300, Los Angeles, CA 90071

Number of lawyers: 11
Office Profile: Chadbourne attorneys in Los Angeles represent clients on a range of matters and litigation both national and international in scope.
Main Areas of Practice: Attorneys in the Los Angeles office specialize in complex business litigation, involving commercial and securities fraud and government contract matters; products liability counseling and litigation; and reinsurance/insurance.

HEAD OFFICE

NEW YORK
30 Rockefeller Plaza, **New York**, NY 10112
Tel: 212 408 5100   **Fax:** 212 541 5369
Website: www.chadbourne.com

BRANCH OFFICES

CALIFORNIA
350 South Grand Avenue, Suite 3300, **Los Angeles**, CA 90071
Tel: 213 892 1000   **Fax:** 213 622 9865

DISTRICT OF COLUMBIA
1200 New Hampshire Avenue, NW, **Washington**, DC 20036
Tel: 202 974 5600   **Fax:** 202 974 5602

TEXAS
1100 Louisiana Street, Suite 3500, **Houston**, TX 77002
Tel: 713 571 5900   **Fax:** 713 571 5970

INTERNATIONAL OFFICES

The firm also has offices in London, United Kingdom; Moscow, Russian Federation; Warsaw, Poland; Kiev, Ukraine; Tashkent, Uzbekistan; and Beijing, China.

DISTRICT OF COLUMBIA

1200 New Hampshire Avenue, NW, Washington, DC 20036

Number of lawyers: 58
Office Profile: Attorneys in the Washington office handle a wide variety of sophisticated international and domestic transactions, as well as complex litigation.
Main Areas of Practice: Attorneys in the Washington office represent the firm's project finance and energy, corporate, reinsurance/insurance, litigation, securities litigation and regulatory enforcement, white collar defense, tax, environmental law and lobbying practices.

TEXAS

1100 Louisiana Street, Suite 3500, Houston, TX 77002

Number of lawyers: 6
Office Profile: Lawyers in the Houston office advise clients on all aspects of energy transactions, including acquisitions and divestitures, general corporate transactions, restructurings and refinancings, project development and bank and capital markets financings. The Houston office is also one of the hubs of Chadbourne's liquefied natural gas (LNG) and natural gas practice, with special expertise in the structuring, development and financing of production, pipeline and marine transportation and receiving facilities, and commodity sale, purchase, storage and transportation arrangements.
Main Areas of Practice: Attorneys in the Houston office focus primarily on corporate, project finance, energy and oil and gas matters.

CHADBOURNE
& PARKE LLP

CLEARY GOTTLIEB STEEN & HAMILTON

THE FIRM

Managing Partner: Peter Karasz

Number of partners worldwide: 171
Number of lawyers worldwide: 854

FIRM OVERVIEW: Cleary Gottlieb is a leading international law firm widely recognized for its expertise in finance, mergers and acquisitions, tax, regulatory issues, employee benefits, real estate, and litigation. The firm represents corporations, banks and other financial institutions engaged in US and international business. The firm also represents sovereign governments and international organizations, as well as individuals, trusts, and nonprofit institutions. For more than 55 years, clients have relied on the firm for its vast legal expertise, quick responsiveness and business acumen, a combination providing unparalleled value. The firm's New York and Washington offices were established in 1946 and approximately two-thirds of the firm's lawyers practice in the United States. Recent accolades include US Tax Law Firm of the Year in *Chambers and Partners* (2003); Western Europe Competition/Antitrust Law Firm of the Year in *Chambers and Partners* (2004); number one in European M&A in *Thomson Financial* (US based law firms, completed January 2004); number two in US M&A in *Bloomberg* (January 2004); number one underwriters' counsel in both worldwide IPOs by US issuers and US IPOs in *Thomson Financial* (January 2003); Top Latin America Legal Advisor from 1988 – 2002 in *LatinFinance*; Largest M&A Deal of the Year in *Thomson Financial* and *Bloomberg* (January 2004); M&A Deal of the Year in *Asian Legal Business* (February 2004); counsel in 12 Deals of the Year in *LatinFinance* (February 2004); counsel in 10 Deals of the Year in *Institutional Investor* (January 2004); and Equity Deal of the Year and Restructuring Deal of the Year in *International Financial Law Review* (March 2004).

MAIN AREAS OF PRACTICE: Antitrust and competition; banking and financial institutions; bankruptcy; corporate governance; derivatives and structured products; employee benefits and ERISA; environmental; global capital markets; individual clients and charitable organizations; intellectual property and technology; international trade; Latin America; litigation and arbitration; mergers, acquisitions and joint ventures; project development and infrastructure; real estate; restructuring; sovereigns; tax; and white-collar defense.

BRANCH OFFICES

NEW YORK

One Liberty Plaza, New York, NY 10006

Office Profile: The New York office handles corporate, securities and structured finance matters; mergers, acquisitions and joint ventures; litigation; banking and financial institutions; bankruptcy and restructuring; representation of sovereign governments in financial matters; taxation; employee benefits; real estate; and work for individual clients and charitable organizations. Clients range from the top investment banking firms and corporate entities to sovereign governments throughout Latin America and high net worth individuals. The New York office has more than 400 lawyers.

HEAD OFFICE

NEW YORK
One Liberty Plaza, **New York**, NY 10006
Tel: 212 225 2000 **Fax:** 212 225 3999
Website: www.clearygottlieb.com

BRANCH OFFICE

DISTRICT OF COLUMBIA
2000 Pennsylvania Avenue, NW, **Washington**, DC 20006
Tel: 202 974 1500 **Fax:** 202 974 1999

INTERNATIONAL OFFICES

EUROPE: Brussels, Cologne, Frankfurt, London, Milan, Moscow, Paris and Rome.
ASIA: Hong Kong and Tokyo.

WASHINGTON

2000 Pennsylvania Avenue, NW, Washington, DC 20006

Office Profile: The Washington office focuses on banking and financial institutions regulations; corporate and securities law; environmental, public and administrative law; structured finance; litigation; antitrust and international trade; taxation; and legislative counseling. The office serves as the focal point for the firm's US regulatory practice and, in particular, its counsel on corporate governance issues. Clients range from government loan agencies to Fortune 500 corporations. More than 90 lawyers work in the Washington office.

INTERNATIONAL WORK: For more than 50 years, Cleary Gottlieb has been preeminent in shaping the globalization of the legal profession. The firm's worldwide practice has a proven track record for innovation and providing work of the highest quality to meet the domestic and international needs of the clients. Cleary Gottlieb's clients include multinational corporations and international financial institutions, sovereign governments and their agencies, as well as domestic corporations and financial institutions in the countries where the firm's offices are located. Although each of the 12 offices has its own practice, Cleary Gottlieb's 'one firm' approach offers clients the ability to access the full resources of all of the firm's offices and lawyers worldwide to the extent their matters so require. More than 850 lawyers work at Cleary Gottlieb worldwide.

CLEARY GOTTLIEB STEEN & HAMILTON LLP

CLIFFORD CHANCE US LLP

THE FIRM

Regional Managing Partner: John Carroll
Number of partners: 82
Number of other lawyers: 311

FIRM OVERVIEW: US and global organizations require the highest quality US legal capability coupled with seamless international service. Clifford Chance offers a comprehensive and nationally recognized practice, backed by top-ranked practices in 28 of the world's major financial and business centers. Through a single, worldwide partnership and a client-focused approach, the firm delivers consistent, commercially-oriented advice wherever its clients do business. In the US, Clifford Chance's practice is dedicated equally to complex corporate and financial transactions and high-stakes dispute resolution. The firm's clients include nearly 40% of the Fortune 500. Clifford Chance regularly advises the leading international financial institutions and US and international corporations, as well as governments and multilateral agencies.

MAIN AREAS OF PRACTICE:

M&A & Private Equity: Clifford Chance has a long history of advising in landmark US and cross-border transactions. The firm represents publicly and privately held buyers and sellers, joint venture partners, venture capitalists, fund sponsors and financial advisors. It offers a team of investment fund, tax, ERISA and regulatory specialists that act for leading private equity groups. Clifford Chance also has an interdisciplinary practice in corporate technology, bringing commercial and intellectual property expertise to the structuring of complex IT-driven ventures.

Corporate Finance: Clifford Chance leverages its industry and product knowledge to raise capital in the most strategic way for each client. The firm has a track record of successful domestic and cross-border transactions on behalf of a wide range of issuers and virtually every Wall Street underwriter. Product coverage includes: IPOs, secondary equity, ADRs, private placements, preferred equity, equity-linked products, REITs, debt and high yield offerings.

Financial Products: Clifford Chance's team has been at the forefront of developing and issuing hybrid and synthetic products and transactions, including, among others, specialized derivatives and SEC-registered cross-border securitizations. This experience has led the firm to advise regulators rating and responding to CBO, CDO, CLO, SIVs, bank solvency and other specialized regulatory matters.

Banking & Financial Restructuring: The firm's nationally-prominent Financial Restructuring and Insolvency Practice focuses on the representation of financial institutions in complex national and multinational insolvency and restructuring proceedings. In addition, sophisticated lenders and borrowers call on the firm for acquisition finance, bank lending, asset finance, equipment leasing, debt trading and financial regulatory advice. The firm is among the most active in the world in project finance, representing lenders, sponsors and developers, particularly in the oil and gas, telecom and petrochemical sectors.

Litigation: Clifford Chance offers a preeminent national Litigation Practice, combining market leading local capability in the US with a unique ability to work efficiently with firm colleagues across its global network. The firm helps clients resolve complex disputes in a manner that promotes their business objectives and develop compliance programs to assist in minimizing future risks. The firm has trial expertise in all manners of civil and criminal cases before juries and judges in multiple juristictions, and in appellate practice before national and interntional courts and tribunals. Cifford Chance offers one of the most experienced teams of securities litigators in the US, with excellence in public company defense and in underwriter and investment company representation, combined with

a prestigious white collar capability. Its Intellectual Property Team has extensive experience in complex patent litigation and also provides full IP service in the areas of patents, trademarks, copyright, design, trade secrets and unfair competition. The international Arbitration Practice has substantial experience handling cross-border, commercial and trade-investment disputes, including those under ICC, ICSID and UNCITRAL rules. The Reinsurance Team represents insurers, reinsurers, brokers and their financial advisors, offering a comprehensive range of services including reinsurance litigation and arbitration, class actions, run-off and insurance insolvency commutations, product development and policy review. Clifford Chance has a sophisticated products liability practice in the United States representing leaders in science, engineering, and high technology. The firm's Antitrust Practice has been involved in many of the most significant antitrust and fair trade cases before the courts in the US. Its employment law practice is experienced in all aspects of employment dispute resolution. Clifford Chance's approach emphasizes practical understanding of its clients' business problems with experience across every segment of the corporate and financial world.

Real Estate: Clifford Chance helps clients execute real estate dispositions, acquisitions, leasing transactions and development arrangements. The firm offers sophisticated real estate finance expertise and is a leader in both real estate securities and private equity real estate investment funds transactions.

Tax & ERISA: The firm's Tax Group provides advice on US and international taxation, covering financing, investment, corporate and commercial transactions, the design of tax-efficient structured deals, transfer pricing and the resolution of tax disputes. The firm offers an in-depth understanding of US rules, combined with the knowledge of international tax systems and how the systems interlink. It also provides ERISA and executive compensation advice.

HEAD OFFICE

NEW YORK
31 W 52nd Street, **New York**, NY 10019
Tel: 212 878 8000   **Fax:** 212 878 8375
Email: info@cliffordchance.com
Website: www.cliffordchance.com

BRANCH OFFICES

CALIFORNIA
990 Marsh Road, **Menlo Park**, CA 94025-1949
Tel: 650 566 4300   **Fax:** 650 566 4399

DISTRICT OF COLUMBIA
2001 K Street NW, **Washington**, DC 20006 1001
Tel: 202 912 5000   **Fax:** 202 912 6000

CONTACTS

New York	John Carroll
California	Daniel Harris
Washington, DC	Leiv Blad
M&A & Private Equity	John Healy, Craig Medwick
Corporate Finance	Bob King
Financial Products	Steve Kolyer
Banking & Restructuring	Margot Schonholtz
Litigation	Peter Chaffetz, Mark Kirsch
Intellectual Property	Daniel Harris
Real Estate	Alan Gosule
Tax & ERISA	David Moldenhauer

CRAVATH, SWAINE & MOORE LLP

THE FIRM

Presiding Partner: Robert D Joffe
Number of partners in US: 83
Number of other lawyers in US: 357

FIRM OVERVIEW: Cravath, Swaine & Moore LLP is widely recognized as one of the preeminent law firms in the world, with an unparalleled reputation for superior legal work. In a recent survey of partners published in Vault's 2005 Guide to the Top 100 Law Firms, the firm was voted the most prestigious law firm in the US. Each of Cravath's four departments - Corporate, Tax, Litigation and Trusts & Estates - was recognized as among the finest, both domestically and internationally, and the firm's lawyers are counted among the most distinguished and highly respected in the country. The firm was founded in 1819 and maintains offices in New York and London.

MAIN AREAS OF PRACTICE:

Corporate: Cravath is a leader in mergers and acquisitions, securities offerings, commercial banking, environmental and international transactions. Clients repeatedly choose the firm when they need the highest quality skills and experience in large and complex matters, particularly with respect to cross-border transactions involving multiple jurisdictions. Cravath's corporate lawyers serve as valued advisors to large and small businesses in a wide range of merger and acquisition transactions, including divestitures, spin-offs and joint ventures. The firm's record of success in both making hostile bids and defending against takeover attempts is attributable to the strength and depth of its Corporate and Litigation Departments. Cravath also has one of the most highly regarded US and international securities practices, with lawyers representing issuers and investment banks across all types of US and global offerings. The firm's banking lawyers are among the most prominent and accomplished in the US and the firm serves as one of the primary outside counsels for JPMorgan Chase and Credit Suisse First Boston, as well as other major financial institutions and borrowers. Cravath also has a group of environmental lawyers who work with the firm's clients on matters related to acquisition and disposition strategies, financings and regulatory compliance with respect to a broad range of environmental issues. In addition to an outstanding base of US experience, each Cravath practice area also has a strong international focus.

Tax: Clients bring their most complex tax challenges to Cravath. The firm's tax lawyers are at the center of structuring and negotiating all types of transactions, including mergers, spin-offs, joint ventures, securities offerings and intricate private equity acquisitions and financings. Cravath's Tax Department is well-known for designing efficient tax structures for complex domestic and international transactions, having pioneered the development of innovative types of financing structures in both the US and international markets. Working with tax advisors in other countries, the firm's tax lawyers capture the benefits of differences in the tax law in different countries. Further, Cravath's Benefits Group, a part of the firm's Tax Department, works on employee benefits and compensation matters, which are often central concerns in acquisitions, dispositions and other transactions.

Litigation: Few firms can match the breadth or depth of Cravath's litigation experience or record of successes in such diverse areas of the law as antitrust, securities, contracts and commercial disputes, business torts, intellectual property, mergers and acquisitions, real estate and tax. Thus, Cravath's litigators are called upon for work involving contested merger and acquisition transactions, while boards of directors and special committees depend on the firm's lawyers to guide them through the intricacies of shareholder litigation and government investigations. Cravath's antitrust experience encompasses a broad range of industries, from mining to telecommunications. Although much of the firm's litigation work

focuses on US law, many cases have an international component and draw upon Cravath's experience in international courts and tribunals. In the area of intellectual property, the firm handles a broad range of complex and challenging matters across all industries. A significant portion of the firm's litigation work relates to contracts and commercial disputes, often in the form of business torts as well as other areas of general business litigation. In the area of securities litigation, Cravath is widely recognized for its success in handling complex and often precedent-setting cases.

Trusts & Estates: Lawyers in the firm's Trusts & Estates Department have served as advisors and trustees to several generations of the families that were responsible for building many of the most important businesses in the world. Today, the firm continues to represent successful entrepreneurs, senior executives and private corporations and partnerships. The firm's lawyers work closely with private clients and their families to protect and distribute assets by creating and endowing trusts, estates and charitable foundations. The firm's discretion and good judgment have earned the respect and trust of generations of some of the most successful private clients in their trusts and estates matters.

CLIENTS: Approximately one-fifth of the firm's 100 largest clients are non-US institutions. Along with governments and multinational institutions, the firm's client roster includes some of the world's best known companies and financial institutions, including: Alcoa, Ambac Assurance, Ashland, BAE Systems, Boyd Gaming, Bristol-Myers Squibb, British American Tobacco, Citigroup, Credit Suisse First Boston, DreamWorks Animation, DuPont, FPL Group, Goldman Sachs, Hertz, IBM, Johnson & Johnson, JPMorgan Chase, Lazard Frères, Lehman Brothers, Lucent Technologies, Martha Graham Dance Center, Morgan Stanley, Nestlé, Rogers Communications, Royal Dutch Shell, RWE AG, Sprint, Thales, The Washington Post Company, Time Warner, Vitro America and Xerox.

INTERNATIONAL WORK: Cravath has had an office in the heart of London's financial district since 1973. Lawyers here work on a diverse range of matters and regularly advise corporate and financial institution clients - in Europe and other parts of the world, including India and South Africa - on a variety of capital markets, mergers and acquisitions, general corporate and SEC compliance matters. The firm's London lawyers also work closely with leading law firms in Europe and elsewhere, providing advice on complex transactions that require extensive knowledge of and experience in the laws of multiple jurisdictions.

HEAD OFFICE

NEW YORK
Worldwide Plaza, 825 Eighth Avenue, **New York**, NY 10019
Tel: 212 474 1000 **Fax:** 212 474 3700
Website: www.cravath.com

INTERNATIONAL OFFICES

The firm also has an office in London, UK

CONTACTS

Antitrust	Robert D Joffe
Commercial Banking	C Allen Parker
Corporate	Kris F Heinzelman
Environmental	Jeffrey A Smith
International (London)	William P Rogers, Jr
Litigation	Evan R Chesler
Mergers & Acquisitions	Allen Finkelson
Securities Offerings	Kris F Heinzelman, John W White
Tax	Stephen L Gordon
Trusts & Estates	Daniel L Mosley

DAVIS POLK & WARDWELL

THE FIRM

Managing Partner: John R Ettinger

Number of partners worldwide: 146
Number of other lawyers worldwide: 457

FIRM OVERVIEW: Davis Polk & Wardwell is a global law firm based in New York City. Founded in 1849, the firm maintains a preeminent practice across a wide range of areas, including corporate finance, mergers and acquisitions, credit, litigation, insolvency and restructuring, investment management and tax. With more than 600 lawyers, Davis Polk has offices in New York, Menlo Park, CA, Washington, DC, London, Paris, Frankfurt, Madrid, Hong Kong and Tokyo.

MAIN AREAS OF PRACTICE:

Corporate: Davis Polk's global Corporate Practice is comprised of more than 400 lawyers, including 97 partners, in a range of practice areas, including capital markets, mergers and acquisitions, credit, private equity, investment management, insolvency and restructuring, executive compensation and employee benefits, equipment finance, environmental and real estate. The firm maintains one of the world's leading securities practices and regularly advises all of the major underwriters and many of the largest US and global corporations on complex debt and equity issuances. For example, in 2004 Davis Polk advised on the $3.5 billion initial public offering of common stock, equity units and preferred stock of Virginia-based insurance company Genworth Financial – the largest US initial public offering to date in 2004. The firm is also at the forefront of the design and distribution of innovative debt and equity derivatives and other complex structured products. Also among the world's preeminent mergers and acquisitions advisers, Davis Polk has been involved in some of the largest and most important M&A transactions in recent history, including the $26 billion merger of equals between The St. Paul Companies and Travelers Property Casualty completed in 2004. The firm ranked 3rd among US law firms in cross-border M&A transactions announced through the first three quarters of 2004, according to Bloomberg. Davis Polk's broad credit practice is widely considered to be among the best in the world. In the first three quarters of 2004, Davis Polk ranked in the top five among US law firms in overall representation, borrower representation and lender representation in syndicated loans, according to Loan Pricing Corporation.

Litigation: Litigation has been a cornerstone of Davis Polk's practice since the firm's inception. Companies from around the world in every industry, as well as their executives and directors, retain Davis Polk lawyers for their most significant litigation matters. The firm's 177 litigators, based in its New York and Menlo Park offices, routinely represent clients in trials, criminal and regulatory investigations, congressional inquiries, arbitrations, hearings, appeals and crisis management situations. This broad-based practice encompasses matters involving securities litigation, antitrust, white collar crime, mass tort and products liability, acquisition-related litigation, banking litigation, insolvency and restructuring, directors' and officers' liability, professional liability, commercial arbitration, tax controversy and intellectual property.

HEAD OFFICE

NEW YORK
450 Lexington Avenue, **New York**, NY 10017
Tel: 212 450 4000   **Fax:** 212 450 3800
Website: www.davispolk.com

BRANCH OFFICES

CALIFORNIA
1600 El Camino Real, **Menlo Park**, CA 94025
Tel: 650 752 2000   **Fax:** 650 752 2111

DISTRICT OF COLUMBIA
1300 I Street NW, Suite 1000 East, **Washington**, DC 20005
Tel: 202 962 7000   **Fax:** 202 962 7111

INTERNATIONAL OFFICES

London, Paris, Frankfurt, Madrid, Hong Kong, Tokyo.

Tax: Davis Polk has long been a leader in US and international tax law. Today, the firm's 39 tax lawyers remain at the leading edge of innovation, working closely with clients on complex transaction and corporate structures, as well as first-of-their-kind derivatives and other financial products. Davis Polk's Tax Controversy Group has prevailed in a number of significant tax matters and is frequently sought out by companies that are not regular clients to handle their most sensitive tax disputes.

CLIENTS: The firm's clients include ABN AMRO, Aetna, Altria, AstraZeneca, Bank of America, BBVA, Bertelsmann, Citigroup, Comcast, Credit Suisse First Boston, CVS, Delta Airlines, Deutsche Bank, E*Trade, ExxonMobil, Ford, Honeywell, JPMorganChase, KPMG, Lloyds TSB, Lockheed Martin, LVMH, Morgan Stanley, Oracle, Pepsi, Pfizer, Roche, The Royal Bank of Scotland, Shell, Banco Santander Central Hispano, Siemens, Sodexho, Suez, Telefónica, Texas Instruments, Verizon Wireless and Yahoo!

DEBEVOISE & PLIMPTON LLP

THE FIRM

Presiding Partner: Martin Frederic Evans
Number of partners worldwide: 134
Number of other lawyers worldwide: 472

FIRM OVERVIEW: Debevoise & Plimpton LLP, founded in 1931, has approximately 600 lawyers practicing in key financial centers of the world, including New York, Washington DC, London, Paris, Frankfurt, Moscow, Hong Kong and Shanghai. The firm's lawyers represent clients in all principal practice areas, including complex acquisition and financing transactions, litigation and arbitration, tax, employee benefits, and trusts and estates.

MAIN AREAS OF PRACTICE:

Corporate: The Corporate Department is the firm's largest practice group. Its work spans the full range of general corporate, transactional and regulatory representations in the United States and throughout the world. Major corporate practice areas include mergers and acquisitions, private equity, capital markets, insurance industry transactions, banking, bankruptcy and restructuring, derivatives, structured finance, project finance, equipment and leveraged finance, real estate, investment fund and asset management, intellectual property, media and technology, energy, and environmental law. The firm has a proven track record of handling innovative and complex US, international and cross-border transactions. Lawyers from the firm's offices around the world cooperate to provide integrated, seamless legal services to meet the needs of the firm's clients. Debevoise represents multinational, US and non-US industrial and commercial companies, and financial institutions including insurance companies, investment companies, banks and broker-dealers, individuals and non-profit organizations in a comprehensive range of assignments.

Litigation: The Litigation Department handles a broad range of complex matters in federal and state courts nationwide, and before agencies, administrative bodies and arbitration tribunals worldwide. Mary Jo White, the former US Attorney for the Southern District of New York, heads the Litigation Practice. The firm's litigators include another former US Attorney, eight former Assistant US Attorneys, a former Director of the Federal Trade Commission's Bureau of Competition, a former Chief Assistant US Attorney in both the Southern and Eastern Districts of New York, and a former Assistant to the US Treasury for Enforcement. Areas of concentration include securities litigation and enforcement proceedings, white collar crime, investigations, antitrust, bankruptcy, general commercial litigation, international dispute resolution, insurance industry disputes, intellectual property and media, and products liability.

Tax & Employee Benefits: The Tax Department works closely with the firm's corporate lawyers in structuring complex transactions. The department also focuses on tax planning and advice for business entities, high net worth individuals and exempt organizations and includes an active executive compensation and employee benefits practice.

Trusts & Estates: The firm's diverse and highly sophisticated Trusts and Estates Practice combines a significant tax orientation with frequent interdisciplinary projects involving the litigation and corporate areas.

CLIENTS: Clients include: Aeroflot; ACE Limited; Air Liquide; American Airlines, Inc.; American International Group; AMVESCAP; AXA Financial, Inc.; The Blackstone Group; BNP Paribas; Bristol-Myers Squibb Co.; Bruckmann, Rosser, Sherrill & Co., LLC.; The Capital Group of Companies; Central European Media Enterprises; Centre Partners Management LLC; China Life Insurance Co.; Clayton Dubilier & Rice, Inc.; The Coca-Cola Company; DaimlerChrysler; Deloitte & Touche LLP; Delta Airlines; Deutsche Bank; Fisher Scientific; Fluor Daniel, Inc.; Genbel Securities Limited; General Electric Company; Global Crossing; Globo Cabo, S.A.; Globopar; Goldman Sachs; Harbourvest; Hartford Financial; Henson

HEAD OFFICE

NEW YORK
919 Third Avenue, **New York,** NY 10022
Tel: 212 909 6000   **Fax:** 212 909 6836
Email: mailbox@debevoise.com   **Website:** www.debevoise.com

BRANCH OFFICE

DISTRICT OF COLUMBIA
555 13th Street, NW, **Washington,** DC 20004
Tel: 202 383 8000   **Fax:** 202 383 8118
Email: mailbox@debevoise.com

INTERNATIONAL OFFICES

Debevoise has offices in London, Paris, Frankfurt, Moscow, Hong Kong and Shanghai.

CONTACTS

Corporate	Michael W Blair
Mergers & Acquisitions	Paul S Bird, Jeffrey J Rosen
Private Equity/Fund Formation	Woodrow W Campbell, Jr
	Michael P Harrell
Private Equity/M&A	Franci J Blassberg, Margaret A Davenport
Insurance Industry	Wolcott B Dunham, Jr
Capital Markets	Michael W Blair
Litigation	Mary Jo White
Media & Technology	Richard D Bohm
	Michael J Gillespie, Jeffrey P Cunard
Securities Litigation	Jonathan Tuttle
Products Liability	Roger E Podesta
Intellectual Property/Litigation	Bruce P Keller
Intellectual Property/Corporate	Jeffrey P Cunard
International Arbitration	David W Rivkin
White Collar Crime	Mary Jo White
Tax	Bruce D Haims
Trusts & Estates	Barbara Paul Robinson

Family; Ingersoll Rand Co.; Jarden Corporation; John Hancock Life Insurance Company; J.P. Morgan Chase & Co.; Kelso & Company; Kinko's, Inc.; Lehman Brothers; Marsh & McLennan Capital, Inc.; MBIA; Merrill Lynch & Co.; Metropolitan Life; NBC; Mitsui & Co., Ltd; Morgan Stanley; The National Football League; North Castle Partners, LLC; Oaktree Capital; Owens Corning; Pacific Life Insurance Company; Phelps Dodge; Providence Equity Partners; Prudential Financial, Inc.; Ramius Capital Group; Rede Globo; Rosie O'Donnell; Royal Bank of Canada; St. Paul Travelers; Swedish Match; Swiss International Airlines Ltd.; Teacher's Insurance; Unibanco; Unilever; Verizon; Westfield; Westpac Banking Corporation; XE Capital; XL Capital.

INTERNATIONAL WORK: Debevoise's global partnership combines local insight and accessibility with firm-wide skills to handle its clients' assignments seamlessly across international boundaries and time zones. The firm's highly competitive, multicultural offices and multilingual teams of lawyers have established a compelling track record in both major and emerging markets, representing US, European, Asian, and Latin American clients.

DEBEVOISE & PLIMPTON LLP

DEWEY BALLANTINE LLP

THE FIRM

Chairman: Morton A Pierce
Co-Managing Partners: Richard Shutran, Gordon E Warnke
Number of partners worldwide: 145
Number of other lawyers worldwide: 424

FIRM OVERVIEW: Dewey Ballantine LLP, founded in 1909, is an international law firm with more than 550 attorneys. Through its network of offices, the firm handles some of the largest, most complex corporate transactions, litigation and tax matters in areas such as M&A, private equity, project finance, corporate finance, corporate reorganization and bankruptcy, antitrust, intellectual property, sports law, structured finance and international trade. Industry specializations include energy and utilities, healthcare, insurance, financial services, media, consumer and industrial goods, consumer electronics, technology, telecommunications and transportation.

MAIN AREAS OF PRACTICE: Antitrust and trade regulation; arbitration and alternative dispute resolution; bank and institutional finance; banking and financial institutions litigation; bankruptcy litigation; compensation and benefits; corporate finance; corporate reorganization and bankruptcy; derivatives; emerging markets; employment law; energy; insurance; insurance/reinsurance litigation; intellectual property litigation; intellectual property transactions and technology; international litigation; international trade; Latin America; leasing and tax-advantaged financing; life sciences, litigation; mergers and acquisitions; private clients; private equity; project finance; public policy: legislative and executive branch; real estate; securities, M&A and corporate governance; sports law litigation; structured finance; tax; tax controversy and litigation; tax exempt financing; taxation of corporate acquisitions and reorganizations; taxation of financial products; taxation of international transactions; white collar crime and corporate internal investigations.

Corporate Finance: Dewey Ballantine's leading Corporate Finance Group handles transactions throughout the world. Clients include a broad range of issuers and borrowers, from major international corporations to early-stage private companies. The firm advises leading investment banks, commercial banks and other financial institutions acting as principals or intermediaries in corporate finance transactions.

Litigation: Dewey Ballantine has one of the most highly regarded litigation departments in the country - representing clients in complex litigation in federal and state trial and appellate courts, before government agencies, prosecutors and administrative bodies, and in arbitrations, mediations and other forms of alternative dispute resolution, around the world.

M&A: Dewey Ballantine's Mergers and Acquisitions Group consists of experienced attorneys around the world. The Mergers and Acquisitions Group represents acquirers, targets, financial advisors, leveraged buy-out groups, independent board committees, shareholder groups, equity investors, subordinated and senior lenders and arbitrageurs. The firm's attorneys are involved in both domestic and cross-border acquisition transactions, in negotiated transactions and in hostile takeovers. The group has been active in the full range of acquisition transactions, such as mergers, assets and stock sales, leveraged buy-outs, restructurings and work outs, tender offers, spin-offs and proxy contests.

Private Equity: Dewey Ballantine's Private Equity Group works in three primary areas: fund formation, private equity and venture capital investment and private company corporate and securities representation. The firm's fund formation work includes representation of (i) sponsors raising private equity funds (including domestic and international vehicles, funds-of-funds, buyout and venture capital funds and funds primarily focused on real estate investments) and (ii) institutional investors in connection with their potential investments in blind pooled investment vehicles. The firm's private equity/venture capital investment work includes representation of pooled investment vehicles and institutional investors in con-

HEAD OFFICE

NEW YORK
1301 Avenue of the Americas, **New York**, NY 10019-6092
Tel: 212 259 8000   **Fax:** 212 259 6333
Email: smorhouse@deweyballantine.com
Website: www.deweyballantine.com

BRANCH OFFICES

CALIFORNIA
333 South Grand Avenue, Suite 2600, **Los Angeles**, CA 90071-1530
Tel: 213 621 6000   **Fax:** 213 621 6100
Email: pwalker@deweyballantine.com

1950 University Avenue, Suite 500, **East Palo Alto**, CA 94303-2225
Tel: 650 845 7000   **Fax:** 650 845 7333
Email: jsano@deweyballantine.com

DISTRICT OF COLUMBIA
1775 Pennsylvania Avenue, NW, **Washington**, DC 20006-4605
Tel: 202 862 1000   **Fax:** 202 862 1093
Email: awolff@deweyballantine.com

TEXAS
401 Congress Avenue, Suite 3200, **Austin**, TX 78701-3788
Tel: 512 226 0300   **Fax:** 512 226 0333
Email: kkudlac@deweyballantine.com

700 Louisiana, Suite 1900, **Houston**, TX 77002-2725
Tel: 713 445 1500   **Fax:** 713 445 1533
Email: agover@deweyballantine.com

INTERNATIONAL OFFICES

Dewey Ballantine LLP also has offices in London, Warsaw, Frankfurt, Milan, Rome, and Beijing, and an associated office in Prague.

nection with their investments in portfolio companies and other investment vehicles. Private company corporate and securities work includes advice on most legal aspects of forming and running a business, including corporate, securities, tax, intellectual property, employment and benefits and real estate.

Project Finance: Dewey Ballantine's Project Finance Group is widely acknowledged as one of the leading project finance practices in the world. The firm's project finance attorneys routinely coordinate with their energy regulatory and project finance colleagues worldwide to execute global transactions. Dewey Ballantine's project finance teams represent developers, investors, underwriters, lenders, financial advisors, multilateral institutions, contractors and governments in the development, financing, construction and operation of a wide range of capital intensive projects and facilities throughout the world. Financings handled by the firm have been implemented through a variety of structures, including traditional offtaker-based project financings, so-called 'merchant' structures, traditional leveraged leases, cross-border leases, joint ventures and partnership arrangements, project leases and 'genco' financings, corporate finance offerings, and various combinations of the above.

Structured Finance: Dewey Ballantine's Structured Finance Group represents issuers, underwriters, placement agents, credit enhancers, investors, trustees, warehouse lenders and borrowers, sponsors of commercial paper conduits and swap participants in all types of structured finance transactions. These include securitizations of traditional and exotic assets in the United States; structured financial products (commercial paper programs, including cash flow and market value extendible programs) and cross-border structured financings involving assets originated in a wide variety of countries in Latin America, Europe, the Middle East and Asia.

Tax: Dewey Ballantine has one of the largest tax departments among general practice law firms; with attorneys practicing a full spectrum of corporate tax work in our global offices. The principal areas of its tax practice include transactional tax, international tax, lease financing, financial products, tax controversy and litigation, legislative and employee benefits.

FITZPATRICK, CELLA, HARPER & SCINTO

THE FIRM

Managing Partner: Dominick A Conde

Number of partners: 59
Number of other lawyers: 92

AREAS OF PRACTICE:
Intellectual Property 100%

FIRM OVERVIEW: Founded in 1971, Fitzpatrick, Cella, Harper & Scinto is one of the leading intellectual property law firms in the United States, with over 150 attorneys, and offices in New York, Washington, DC, and Costa Mesa, California. The firm's practice covers the spectrum of intellectual property services, including applying for protection, litigation, appeals, interferences, alternative dispute resolution, licensing, opinions, corporate transactions and due diligence. The firm provides these services to clients from virtually every industry, including pharmaceuticals, chemicals, automotive, energy, biotechnology, medical products, consumer products, computers, electronics, transportation, telecommunications, financial services, food products, and e-commerce. As new technologies emerge, the firm is at the forefront in developing strategies for their intellectual property protection. Over 95 percent of the firm's attorneys hold scientific or technical degrees and most have substantial industry experience in various fields of technology including chemistry, biotechnology, pharmaceuticals, electronics, physics, software, computers and the mechanical arts.

MAIN AREAS OF PRACTICE: Patent, trademark, copyright, trade secret, unfair competition, computer law, licensing, antitrust and international trade law. Trials and appeals in federal and state courts and administrative agencies.

Patent & Trademark Litigation: In the past year, the firm's clients prevailed in several major intellectual property litigations. They successfully litigated a multi-million dollar patent infringement case on behalf of their clients Pfizer concerning sales of Accupril®, where the patent was found infringed, valid and enforceable. They successfully litigated a patent infringement claim for Eli Lilly on its highly successful product Sarafem®, which is used to treat Prementrual Dysphoric Disorder, a severe form of PMS. They also successfully won summary judgment of validity on behalf of client GlaxoSmithKline's patent on its epilepsy drug, Lamictal®, and upheld verdict on behalf of their client, Bristol-Myers Squibb, in support that they were the true inventors of several Bristol technology patents concerning therapeutic fusion proteins important in the regulation of the immune system.

Patent & Trademark Prosecution: The firm has an extensive practice in the prosecution of patent and trademark applications, trademark oppositions and cancellations, due diligence studies, patent and trademark opinions, technology transfers and licensing. In addition, the firm is experienced in specialized and sophisticated areas such as patent interference procedures and prosecuting applications under the Patent Cooperation Treaty. The firm has prosecuted over 15,000 patents to issuance in the past 10 years, and is responsible for obtaining more than 1800 patents in 2004 alone.

INTERNATIONAL WORK: The firm's clients include some of the world's largest multinational corporations in the United States, Asia, Europe, Australia and South America. The firm counsels clients on global intellectual property strategies, coordinates international litigation strategies and works closely with co-counsel throughout the world. The firm also assists in worldwide filing for patent, TM and copyright protection, and maintains worldwide TM portfolios.

CLIENTS: Fitzpatrick, Cella represents the world's technology and business leaders – including: AstraZeneca, Bausch & Lomb, Bristol-Myers Squibb, Canon, Conde Nast, GlaxoSmithKline, Hughes Network Systems, IBM, Merck, Novartis, Pfizer, Prudential, Salomon Smith Barney and Takeda Chemical Industries, as well as smaller corporations and Universities from the United States and abroad.

HEAD OFFICE

NEW YORK
30 Rockefeller Plaza, **New York**, NY 10112
Tel: 212 218 2100 **Fax:** 212 218 2200
Website: www.fitzpatrickcella.com

BRANCH OFFICES

CALIFORNIA
650 Town Center Drive, Suite 1600, **Costa Mesa**, CA 92626
Tel: 714 540 8700 **Fax:** 714 540 9823

DISTRICT OF COLUMBIA
1900 K Street, NW, **Washington**, DC 20006
Tel: 202 530 1010 **Fax:** 202 530 1055

FITZPATRICK, CELLA, HARPER & SCINTO

FRIED, FRANK, HARRIS, SHRIVER & JACOBSON LLP

THE FIRM

Co-Managing Partners: Valerie Ford Jacob, Paul M Reinstein
Senior Partner: Arthur Fleischer, Jr

Number of partners in US offices: 122
Number of other lawyers in US offices: 348

AREAS OF PRACTICE:

Corporate	46%
Litigation	30%
Tax	8%
Real Estate	7%
Benefits & Compensation	3%
Antitrust	2%
Bankruptcy & Restructuring	2%
Trusts & Estates	2%

HEAD OFFICE

NEW YORK
One New York Plaza, **New York**, NY 10004
Tel: 212 859 8000 **Fax:** 212 859 4000
Website: www.friedfrank.com

BRANCH OFFICES

DISTRICT OF COLUMBIA
1001 Pennsylvania Avenue, NW, **Washington**, DC 20004
Tel: 202 639 7000 **Fax:** 202 639 7003

CALIFORNIA
350 South Grand Avenue, **Los Angeles**, CA 90071
Tel: 213 473 2000 **Fax:** 213 473 2222

FIRM OVERVIEW: Fried Frank is an international law firm with over 500 attorneys located in New York, Washington, DC, Los Angeles, London, Paris and Frankfurt. The firm's rich and distinguished traditions date back before the beginning of the 20th century, and the firm continues to provide innovative and imaginative solutions to business and legal problems in the 21st.

MAIN AREAS OF PRACTICE:

CORPORATE:

Mergers & Acquisitions, including Private Equity: Fried Frank is a pioneer in M&A and enjoys one of the nation's most prominent practices, representing major corporations, investors, special committees and investment banking firms in major domestic and cross-border transactions. The firm advises clients in the most complex negotiated and contested situations, including negotiated mergers, hostile takeovers and takeover defense, leveraged buyouts, proxy contests and restructuring transactions. Its approach combines technical excellence, creativity and commercial sophistication. Recent representations: BellSouth Corporation in the acquisition of AT&T Wireless Services, Inc. by Cingular Wireless LLC; The Rouse Company in its sale to General Growth Properties, Inc.; the Special Committee of Cox Communications Inc. in connection with the buyout of the public held shares of Cox by Cox Enterprises, Inc.; Kirk Kerkorian and Tracinda Corporation in the $5 billion sale of Metro-Goldwyn-Mayer Inc. to a consortium led by Sony Corporation of America; WPP Group plc in its acquisition of Grey Global Group Inc.; Roy Disney and Stanley Gold in their "Just Vote No" campaign against The Walt Disney Company; Merck & Co., Inc. in its acquisition of Aton Pharma Inc.; New Jersey Nets in connection with the restructuring of YankeeNets LLC and the sale of the Nets to Brooklyn Basketball; Noveon International, Inc. in its acquisition by Lubrizol Corp.; Helmut Lang Group in its acquisition by Prada Holding NV; and Goldman, Sachs & Co. as financial adviser to: AMC Entertainment Inc. in its acquisition by Marquee Holdings Inc.; Cardinal Health, Inc. in its acquisition of Alaris Medical Systems, Inc.; IASIS Healthcare Corporation in its acquisition by an investor group led by Texas Pacific Group; King Pharmaceuticals Inc. in its acquisition by Mylan Laboratories; Oxford Health Plans, Inc. in its merger with United-Health Group, Inc.; and NeighborCare, Inc. in connection with the unsolicited bid by Omnicare, Inc.

Capital Markets, including Banking & Finance, Structured Finance & Asset Management: The firm has a major presence in the capital markets, representing many Fortune 500 companies, as well as Wall Street's best-known investment banks, in a wide variety of public and private debt and equity offerings and structured finance transactions in the United States and abroad. The firm also assists its clients in Sarbanes-Oxley and related corporate governance matters. Recent representations include: Merrill Lynch & Co., Goldman, Sachs & Co., Banc of America Securities LLC and J.P. Morgan Securities Inc. as underwriters or initial purchasers in many equity and debt (including high-yield) offerings; the underwriters for The Procter & Gamble Company in its debt offerings; the underwriters, initial purchasers and lenders in financing the acquisition of the Northern Eckerd Drugstore business by The Jean Coutu Group Inc.; the initial purchasers and lenders in financing the acquisition of Duane Reade Inc. by certain private equity investors; the underwriters for an equity offering by The Estee Lauder Companies, Inc.; NTL Cable plc in its high yield debt offerings; The Rouse Company in its debt and equity offerings; the underwriters and private equity investors in an equity offering by Polo Ralph Lauren Corporation; Perry Ellis International Inc. in covenant negotiations for a high yield debt offering; Citadel Broadcasting Corp. in its initial public offering and convertible debt offering; and Tracinda Corporation in the sale of common shares of Metro-Goldwyn-Mayer Inc.

Litigation & Securities Regulation, Compliance & Enforcement: Fried Frank's Commercial Litigation Practice represents domestic and foreign companies in an extremely broad range of matters, including complex contract litigation and business tort cases of all kinds. The firm has one of the leading securities and shareholder litigation practices in the United States, serving as defense counsel to issuers and financial institutions in class and derivative actions, across the full spectrum of fiduciary duty and corporate governance issues, and it is also experienced in takeover and proxy fight litigation. For disputes best resolved outside the courtroom, Fried Frank's litigators are experienced in domestic and international arbitration and alternative dispute resolution. Fried Frank's Securities Regulation, Compliance and Enforcement Practice has an international reputation in representing corporations and individuals before state and federal regulatory bodies. The practice involves crisis management and crafting creative solutions to unprecedented problems. In a related area, the White-Collar Criminal Defense and Civil Litigation Team, led by some of the country's best former prosecutors, tackles a wide range of cases, including insider trading, securities fraud and RICO matters. The Internal Investigation, Compliance and Monitoring Practice conducts internal investigations for companies, boards of directors and audit committees involving allegations of misconduct or other improprieties. In addition, the firm has one of the country's leading practices in defense of parties accused of violating the Civil False Claims Act, including many of the most complex and unusual cases brought under its unique qui tam enforcement mechanism. The Government Contracts Practice represents clients doing business with US government agencies, as well as with state and local entities. The Intellectual Property Practice provides a full range of services associated with technology related or content oriented business activities, including patent, trademark, and copyright litigation as well as issues relating to trade secrets, advertising and unfair competition. In addition, the IP practice has a transactional focus providing services in

FRIED, FRANK, HARRIS, SHRIVER & JACOBSON LLP cont'd

connection with acquisitions, divestitures, development, exploitation, procurement, alliance, outsourcing, and similar agreements. Recent public representations: Martha Stewart Living Omnimedia, Inc., and its directors and officers (other than Martha Stewart) in securities class action and shareholder derivative lawsuits; Electrolux Home Products and subsidiary White Consolidated Industries in a patent infringement lawsuit brought by the Toro Company in the United States District Court in Minnesota; Delta and Pine Land Company in several matters; Tracinda Corporation, in a multibillion-dollar lawsuit arising out of the 1998 merger of Daimler-Benz AG and Chrysler Corporation, in which Tracinda was a substantial investor; State Bank of Long Island in several litigations pending in various state and federal courts; The Reader's Digest Association, Inc. Retirement Plan, in an ERISA lawsuit that was brought in the federal court in Detroit; CDL Hotels USA Inc. in connection with insurance claims for losses sustained by various of its hotels in and out of New York; BrokerTec USA in a patent infringement suit.

Bankruptcy & Restructuring: Fried Frank's Bankruptcy and Restructuring Practice represents both debtors, creditors, secured and unsecured lenders and other interested parties, in formal bankruptcies as well as out-of-court restructurings of financially troubled companies as well as buyers and sellers of distressed securities and businesses of financially troubled companies. The firm recently represented an unofficial committee of bondholders in connection with the out-of-court restructuring of HealthSouth Inc.; the official committee of unsecured creditors in connection with the $2.5 billion chapter 11 restructuring of Conseco, Inc. and certain of its subsidiaries; and Rand McNally & Company in connection with its chapter 11 restructuring.

Real Estate: Fried Frank's Real Estate Practice, representing developers, owners, institutional investors, tenants and lenders, encompasses a broad range of transactions involving every property type. The firm recently represented Millennium & Copthorne Hotels plc and its partner Prince Alwaleed bin Talal in the sale of New York's Plaza Hotel to El-Ad Properties; the Feil, Goldman and Chera families in a contract to purchase the Sears Tower from Metropolitan Life Insurance Company; Credit Suisse First Boston in a total of approximately $1 billion of financings covering the residential, office and retail portions of Time Warner Center; the New York Jets in relation to the proposed football stadium on the West Side of Manhattan and Forest City Ratner in relation to the proposed development of the Nets basketball arena and office and residential complex in downtown Brooklyn; McKinsey & Company in a 300,000 square foot lease for its New York headquarters at Park Avenue Plaza; and Brookfield Financial Properties in the long-term sublease to PricewaterhouseCoopers LLP of 800,000 square feet of Brookfield's newly constructed building located at 300 Madison Avenue.

Tax: Fried Frank's tax lawyers have a primarily transactional focus, working on matters involving major public and private corporations and partnerships. They counsel clients in the many US and international tax aspects of mergers and acquisitions, as well as in private equity, capital markets and real estate transactions and in bankruptcy and restructuring matters, as well as in the area of tax controversies.

Antitrust: Fried Frank's Antitrust Group provides a full range of leading-edge representation for clients such as MGM Mirage, El Paso Corporation, Pasha Group, Delta and Pine Land Company, and many others in transactions, civil investigations, criminal investigations and private class action litigation.

Benefits & Compensation: In the area of executive compensation and employee benefits, Fried Frank's attorneys have a transactional focus, working with companies of all types and individuals on matters ranging from stock options to retirement plans, which are frequently the issues that can make or break a transaction.

Trusts & Estates: Fried Frank's trusts and estates attorneys advise US and non-US individuals and families with substantial wealth in a wide variety of personal planning matters and estate administration.

OTHER PRACTICES:

Environmental: Fried Frank's Environmental Practice represents companies in Superfund and other civil and criminal enforcement proceedings, as well as in a broad range of private environmental litigation. A significant component of the practice involves the environmental aspect of corporate and bankruptcy transactions. The firm also represents clients before federal and state environmental agencies and counsels clients on compliance programs, environmental audits and site remediation.

Insurance: Fried Frank's Insurance Practice provides legal services to a broad spectrum of participants in the industry, with respect to mergers and acquisitions, private equity investments, restructurings and reorganizations (including demutualizations and mutual holding company reorganizations), public and private securities offerings, insurance and reinsurance disputes, insurance regulatory compliance, and coverage negotiations and policy wordings. Firm clients for recent matters include American International Group, Inc., Transatlantic Holdings, Goldman, Sachs & Co., Merrill Lynch, The Massachusetts Division of Insurance; Assicurazioni Generali, S.p.A., Fortress Re, Gulf Insurance Group, New York Life Insurance Company, Equitas, Allianz Risk Transfer, and Aon Corporation.

International Trade: Fried Frank's International Trade Practice responds to the growing strategic needs of international and multinational corporations for legal services, including strategic consulting, international negotiation, transnational government procurement, the protection of intellectual property, advice on foreign investment restrictions and export controls, international trade law litigation, dispute resolution, arbitration and ADR.

CLIENTS: AEA Investors, American Express, ANC Rental, Banc of America Securities, Bear Stearns, BellSouth, Brookfield Financial Properties, CDL Hotels International, Cigna, Coaxial Communications, CommScope, CS First Boston, Delta & Pine Land, Deutsche Bank, Digitalnet Holdings, Dial, El Paso, Electrolux, Equitas, Forstmann Little, Fortress Re, GE Capital, Goldman Sachs, Hiro Real Estate, Humana, Invensys, JPMorgan, Lazard Freres, Lipper, Martha Stewart Living, Merck, Merrill Lynch, MGM, Microsoft, Morgan Stanley, Northrop Grumman, NTL, Procter & Gamble, PriceWaterhouseCoopers, Rouse, Salomon Smith Barney, Science Applications International, Scotts, Shamrock Holdings, SPX, Televisa, Tishman Speyer Properties, Tellium, Thales, Tracinda, UBS PaineWebber, Urenco.

INTERNATIONAL WORK: Fried Frank has an established international practice with a concentration in cross-border mergers and acquisitions and joint ventures; private equity investments; US registered and Rule 144A securities offerings; non-US debt and equity offerings, including high yield debt; commercial financing transactions; structured and securitized financings; establishment of leveraged buyout funds; international trade and investment; and tax. Lawyers in the firm's London office practice US and English law. Lawyers in the firm's Paris office practice US and French law. Lawyers in the firm's Frankfurt office, which opened in 2004, practice German law. Also, in April 2000, Fried Frank and Canada's largest law firm, McCarthy Tétrault LLP, formalized a 20 year working relationship by creating the McCarthy/Fried Frank Alliance, a collaboration on individual matters, primarily cross-border corporate transactions, by the two law firms, which remain entirely independent.

FRIED FRANK

HEALY & BAILLIE, LLP

THE FIRM

Executive Committee: John D Kimball, Jack A Greenbaum, LeRoy Lambert

Number of partners: 15
Number of other lawyers: 17

FIRM OVERVIEW: Founded in 1948 to serve the maritime industry, Healy & Baillie continues its leading position as a provider of legal services to that industry but has also expanded into an international general commercial law firm practicing in New York, Connecticut, New Jersey and Hong Kong. The firm regularly handles complex, multi-jurisdictional and international maritime and commercial litigation matters. As of the end of 2004, they have been counsel of record in more than 620 New York arbitration awards reported by the Society of Maritime Arbitrators in New York, more than any other firm. They have a strong and active bankruptcy practice and have also represented clients in several multi-million dollar corporate veil piercing and fraud cases. They have handled more than 200 personal injury jury trials over the years. The firm has also been involved in large insurance and reinsurance matters, both maritime and non-maritime in nature. The firm has an oil-spill response team ready to respond to a major casualty, and are well equipped to handle not only the civil consequences of such an incident but also the potential criminal implications that are more and more a fact of life in such matters.

Complementing the firm's strength in litigation and arbitration is a robust ship finance and corporate law practice. In 2005, the firm added public securites law to its practice areas and increased its ability to handle private equity transactions and mergers and acquisitions. The firm regularly handles corporate transactions such as ship mortgage loan financing; leasing of vessels, oil rigs and other equipment; debt and equity placements; joint ventures; commercial and residential real estate transactions; and other similar matters.

The firm's pool of talent encompasses a wide variety of backgrounds and experience. John Kimball, Chairman of the firm, is consistently ranked as the leading shipping lawyer in the United States and is referenced as "an outstanding name in the marketplace". Other attorneys include former naval and coast guard officers as well as a naval architect and marine engineer who is also a licensed professional engineer. Some have served as law clerks to state or federal judges before joining the firm. Mr Kimball teaches admiralty law at New York University School of Law, and several of the firm's partners are authors or editors of leading maritime treatises and textbooks, including *Time Charters, Voyage Charters, The Law Of Marine Collision,* the *Benedict on Admiralty* volumes relating to Salvage, Carriage of Goods by Sea, Charter Parties, and Marinas and Recreational Boating, and the law school case book *Admiralty.* Over the years, the firm's partners have served terms as president of the United States Maritime Law Association and the Connecticut Maritime Association. They have also served as Titulary Members of the Comite Maritime International. One partner recently concluded a term as MLA delegate to the BIMCO documentary committee, and another served as part of the United States delegation to the UNESCO meetings relating to the development of the Convention on the Protection of Underwater Cultural Heritage. Members of the firm have often been called upon to serve as arbitrators, and its partners have also served as expert witnesses in foreign litigation on numerous occasions, testifying in foreign courts on issues of American law. One recent case involved a major reinsurance dispute before the High Court of Justice in London arising out of the 1989 *Exxon Valdez* oil spill.

HEAD OFFICE

NEW YORK/NEW JERSEY
61 Broadway, **New York**, NY 10006-2834
Tel: 212 943 3980 **Fax:** 212 425 0131
Email: reception@healy.com
Website: www.healy.com

BRANCH OFFICES

CONNECTICUT
The Lock Building, 20 Marshall Street, Suite 104,
South Norwalk, CT 06854
Tel: 203 354 1360 **Fax:** 203 354 1363

INTERNATIONAL OFFICES

The firm also has an office in Hong Kong.

MAIN AREAS OF PRACTICE: Maritime, shipping and transportation law; commercial and general litigation; corporate/finance including ship and asset financing, private equity and M&A, public securities law; bankruptcy and debtor/creditor law; personal injury; insurance and reinsurance; environmental; criminal defense; employment; real estate.

CLIENTS: Since its inception, the firm has represented clients in all areas of the shipping industry, including: shipowners, operators and charterers; governments and government-owned carriers; marine insurers and reinsurers including P&I insurers, FD&D associations, hull and machinery underwriters and war risk insurers; NVOCC's, freight forwarders and other shipping agents; cargo interests; lending banks and other financing institutions; and debtors and creditors in bankruptcy proceedings.
Performance: Maritime casualties (Kariba, APL China, Barge Texas, Amphion, Achille Lauro hijacking, Atlantic Empress/Aegean Captain and Seiryu/Stena Freighter collisions, Estonia and Scandinavian Star ferry disasters, Marine Electric sinking, Amoco Cadiz and Torrey Canyon pollution incidents); hundreds of maritime arbitrations; over 200 personal injury trials; Norwegian Guarantee Institute v. Hambros Bank, Lexmar, Premier Products Tankers and Westbond litigations; US Lines, Hellenic Lines, Regency Lines, Premier Cruise Lines and Millenuim bankruptcies; and the Marathon Ashland Petroleum charterparty dispute.

INTERNATIONAL WORK: Healy & Baillie has a long history of representing international clients in the United States and in assisting domestic clients in protecting their interests abroad. The firm is well equipped to support its clients in the global arena. Many of the firm's attorneys are fluent or conversant in other languages, including Greek, Norwegian, Spanish, French, German, Persian, Mandarin, and Cantonese. The firm has a partner admitted to practice in Greece and two who are authorized to practice law in England and provide advice on English law. The firm's Hong Kong office, which celebrated its 10th Anniversary in 2004, offers a full service maritime practice in that jurisdiction. Healy & Baillie is the only US-based maritime law firm with a local license to practice Hong Kong law, and the firm regularly appears before the Hong Kong courts. That office is also well positioned to assist clients in China and throughout Asia and Oceania.

HOLLAND & KNIGHT LLP

THE FIRM

Managing Partner: Howell W Melton, Jr

Number of partners: 715
Number of other lawyers: 550

FIRM OVERVIEW: At Holland & Knight the talents and resources of the entire firm are leveraged to deliver effective advocacy and comprehensive, integrated solutions in virtually all areas of the law, across the US, and around the world. To address clients' needs as effectively and efficiently as possible, the firm works collaboratively, drawing upon its depth and breadth of legal experience and industry knowledge. Holland & Knight's clients' businesses range in scope from local to global and span a wide range of industries. Their 'one-firm' structure positions them to support the most complex matters at all levels, with comprehensive and integrated service. The firm is organized into five Practice Sections – Litigation, Government, Business, Real Estate and Private Wealth Services. Through integrated practice groups and industry-based teams, the firm provides efficient and responsive legal representation anywhere in the world. The firm serves clients on the basis of need, not merely location. Their interdisciplinary approach assures that clients have access to the lawyers with the most appropriate experience.

MAIN AREAS OF PRACTICE:

Litigation: Holland & Knight's Litigation Group is one of the nation's largest and most powerful with more than 500 lawyers. This highly regarded group includes more than 20 former federal prosecutors, and several former federal and state regulatory officials. Sophisticated investigative and forensic services provided by experienced former federal investigators enhance the representation of the firm's clients. Their clients include many Fortune 500 companies, regional corporations, government entities and nonprofit organizations in a broad range of venues. Holland & Knight's lawyers appear in state and federal courts across the US and in tribunals around the world. The firm's infrastructure and resources support large, complex cases and the docket includes numerous multimillion-dollar class actions, securities litigation, intellectual property, product liability and mass tort cases.

Business: Holland & Knight's Corporate Practice Group consists of more than 250 attorneys who regularly advise clients in a wide variety of corporate transactions, corporate financings, and securities law compliance matters. From complex public company acquisitions to early stage business considerations, the firm takes a proactive approach to identify key issues, develop sophisticated solutions, and adhere to clients' objectives as they help guide the matter to a successful conclusion consistent with clients' business strategy. Holland & Knight represents businesses and financial institutions of every size in all matters relating to banking and finance; syndication; mergers and acquisitions; corporate and securities law and corporate governance.

Government: Holland & Knight's Government Section is one of the most experienced and respected in the US. They have extensive knowledge of local, tribal, state and federal issues and a thorough understanding of the legislative and regulatory processes affecting business and governmental entities. They draw on the experience of their lawyers, lobbyists and public relations advisors to achieve clients' goals. Holland & Knight's bipartisan team of professionals, some of whom are former members of Congress and the executive branch, have relationships in the state capitals, the White House and Congress. They are on-site in many state capitals in major cities across the US. The firm's Government Section provides a broad range of legal and professional services, from analyzing the impact of legislation to drafting legislation and amendments, preparing testimo-

HEAD OFFICE

NEW YORK
195 Broadway, 24th Floor, **New York**, NY 10007
Tel: 212 513 3200
Email: hal.melton@hklaw.com
Website: www.hklaw.com

US OFFICES

The firm's United States offices are located in California, Florida, Georgia, Illinois, Maryland, Massachusetts, New York, Oregon, Rhode Island, Texas, Virginia, Washington state and Washington DC.

INTERNATIONAL OFFICES

Internationally, the firm's offices are located in Mexico City, Tokyo and Beijing, with representative offices in Helsinki, Caracas and Tel Aviv, and strategic alliance relations in Rio de Janeiro and São Paulo, Brazil.

ny, meeting with members of Congress, state legislators, regulators and other decision-makers, and providing strategic and communications counseling.

Real Estate: Holland & Knight's Real Estate Section represents one of the most accomplished legal resources in the United States. The firm's practice and geographic diversity are completely integrated, giving its lawyers and business professionals the industry knowledge and ability to structure sophisticated transactions. Clients rely on the lawyer's abilities in the acquisition, development, disposition, leasing and financing of commercial, retail, residential, resort, industrial, mixed-use, and public housing projects. Clients include regional and national developers, builders, investors, lenders, asset and property managers, syndicators, pension funds, tax-exempt organizations, broker-dealers, municipalities, real estate investment trusts and life insurance companies.

Private Wealth Services: Holland & Knight offers the services of the country's largest group of trusts and estates lawyers. They are nationally recognized in fields as diverse as estate, gift and generation-skipping transfer tax planning, probate litigation, IRS litigation, life insurance planning, business succession planning, asset protection, international taxation, charitable foundations and matrimonial law.

Holland+Knight

HUGHES HUBBARD & REED LLP

THE FIRM

Chair: Candace Krugman Beinecke
Managing Director: Charles Scherer

Number of partners and counsel: 95
Number of attorneys: 327

FIRM OVERVIEW: Founded over 100 years ago, Hughes Hubbard & Reed is among 20 law firms designated the best in the United States by *The American Lawyer* in its September 2004 issue. The firm takes pride in the fact that it has retained many of its clients for more than half a century. Hughes Hubbard has also been a leader in promoting diversity. This year it scored in the top four in *The American Lawyer's* Diversity assessment of law firms and has the highest percentage of female partners in the Amlaw 200.

MAIN AREAS OF PRACTICE:

LITIGATION: In a survey by *International Commercial Litigation*, Hughes Hubbard was recognized as a leading US firm for litigation. A substantial portion of the firm's practice is devoted to litigation. A number of the firm's litigators are members of the American College of Trial Lawyers and many are particularly skilled in handling complex and transnational litigation, as well as hard-to-try scientific, technical and engineering cases.
Product Liability & Toxic Tort: More than 75 attorneys in all offices have extensive product liability experience. The firm has successfully defended major product liability litigation in pharmaceuticals, aircraft, trains and automobiles, specialty chemicals, fire and other disasters, large machinery, blood and biologics, and toxic workplace exposure.
Insurance Coverage Litigation: The firm was lead counsel in large and complex insurance coverage and mass tort cases including those involving breast implants, tainted blood, dental implants, asbestos, and alleged radio frequency radiation from cellular phones.
Securities Litigation: The firm has an extensive practice in representing issuers, accounting firms, and corporate directors and executives in securities class actions and regulatory and white collar criminal investigations relating to alleged securities fraud or other business misconduct. The team includes lawyers with prosecutorial and agency backgrounds and has experience in all phases of the work, from internal investigations to civil and criminal trials and appeals.
International Arbitration: More than 50 Hughes Hubbard lawyers, located in all offices, are engaged in arbitration. Many are multi-lingual and qualified to practice in both common and civil law jurisdictions. The firm is consistently ranked among the top firms for International Arbitration and *International Commercial Litigation* ranks it 1st among US law firms and 2nd among all firms worldwide in the number of industries covered by the practice.
CORPORATE: Hughes Hubbard's corporate clients include some of the world's largest multinational companies. The firm has a strong M&A practice which includes hostile takeovers and proxy fights as well as joint ventures and other strategic alliances, including those involving multi-country cross border transactions. Attorneys involved in capital markets transactions represent issuers and underwriters in public and private equity and debt offerings, private equity transactions, initial public offerings and equipment financings.
OTHER:
Antitrust: This group advises on mergers, acquisitions, joint ventures and other business combinations, alliances and patent pools, and pricing, distribution and licensing strategies.
Corporate Reorganization: This practice is international and multidisciplinary integrating traditional bankruptcy expertise with banking, litigation, corporate and other specialties to provide maximum return for the client.
Environmental: Attorneys regularly counsel clients about the laws governing air pollution, water quality, soil contamination, and indoor environmental quality, including criminal as well as civil matters.

Financial Services: Attorneys represent banks, credit card companies and insurance companies, in matters as diverse as syndicated lending, regulatory matters, derivatives, commercial paper programs and asset dispositions.
Intellectual Property: The firm's global practice includes trademarks, patents, licenses, copyrights, technology and, increasingly, trade secrets and unfair competition.
Labor: Attorneys are well-versed in the full range of employment law issues, including collective bargaining, discrimination, harassment, wrongful discharge, and non-competition agreements.
Real Estate: Global practice covers every aspect of real estate across a wide variety of industries including construction and hospitality.
Tax & Employee Benefits: Attorneys in this area provide solutions that both comply with the labyrinth of governmental rules and regulations and achieve their clients' business objectives. Employee Benefits attorneys handle all aspects of employee pensions, executive compensation and ERISA work.

CLIENTS: ALSTOM in the disposition of its worldwide electrical contracting sector; Delta, Northwest, American, Continental and United in the $1.25 billion sale of Orbitz; Viacom in its acquisition of Sportsline.com; Merck in litigation coming out of the withdrawal of Vioxx; American Bureau of Shipping in a suit brought by the Kingdom of Spain arising out of the sinking of the oil tanker Prestige.

INTERNATIONAL WORK: With lawyers from over 20 countries who speak more than two dozen languages, Hughes Hubbard has a truly international perspective. The firm's Paris office has conducted an extensive practice throughout Europe since 1968. Hughes Hubbard also has a significant Pacific Basin practice with an office in Tokyo and a Latin America practice, located in the firm's Miami and New York offices, that is bi-lingual and bicultural. In addition, Hughes Hubbard's Washington DC office provides international trade and customs representation.

Hughes Hubbard & Reed LLP

HEAD OFFICE

NEW YORK
One Battery Park Plaza, **New York**, NY 10004-1482
Tel: 212 837 6000   **Fax:** 212 422 4726
Website: www.hugheshubbard.com

BRANCH OFFICES

DISTRICT OF COLUMBIA
1775 I Street NW, **Washington**, DC 20006-2401
Tel: 202 721 4600   **Fax:** 202 721 4646

CALIFORNIA
350 South Grand Avenue, **Los Angeles**, CA 90071-3442
Tel: 213 613 2800   **Fax:** 213 613 2950

FLORIDA
201 South Biscayne Boulevard, **Miami**, FL 33131-4332
Tel: 305 358 1666   **Fax:** 305 371 8759

NEW JERSEY
101 Hudson Street, **Jersey City**, NJ 07302
Tel: 201 536 9220   **Fax:** 201 536 0799

INTERNATIONAL OFFICES

The firm also has offices in Paris and Tokyo.

KAYE SCHOLER LLP

THE FIRM

Chairman: David Klingsberg
Managing Partner: Barry Willner
Number of partners: 140
Number of other lawyers: 334

FIRM OVERVIEW: Kaye Scholer has represented many of the world's largest corporations in some of their most significant business transactions and difficult and complex litigations. The firm's ability to handle sophisticated representation has consistently attracted clients who depend on the highest standard of legal counsel. Founded in 1917 in New York City, today the firm counts some 500 lawyers in nine offices: New York, Chicago, Los Angeles, Washington, DC, West Palm Beach, Frankfurt, Hong Kong, London and Shanghai.

MAIN AREAS OF PRACTICE:

Litigation: Kaye Scholer is widely recognized as one of the leading litigation firms in the United States. With more than 220 lawyers in its Litigation Department nationwide, it handles some of the highest-profile cases in the country. The firm's breadth of experience makes it a preferred resource for clients that seek effective and efficient representation in their most difficult and complex matters including advertising and marketing, alternative dispute resolution, antitrust, class actions, e-commerce, employment and labor, environmental, equal rights litigation and compliance, government contracts, intellectual property, international trade, legislative and regulatory, complex commercial litigation, nuclear power, patent litigation, patent prosecution, privacy and data protection, product liability litigation and counseling, securities and derivatives litigation, technology, intellectual property, outsourcing, and white collar criminal defense.

Corporate: Kaye Scholer offers talent, experience and exceptional service to its corporate and finance clients. Their lawyers are based in business centers around the world, enabling them to provide clients with an understanding of the markets and trends that affect their businesses and to extend the web of legal communication globally. They regularly handle matters involving, Asia Pacific, aviation finance and leasing, banking and commercial finance, general corporate matters, corporate governance and compliance, e-commerce, energy, entertainment and media, finance, information technology, international, mergers and acquisitions, national security/Exon-Florio, outsourcing, patent prosecution, privacy and data protection, private equity/venture capital, project finance, securities transactions, structured finance and asset securitization, technology transations and telecommunications.

Real Estate: Kaye Scholer regularly represents clients in purchase and sale disputes, construction claims, high stakes landlord-tenant disputes, site development and environmental litigation, land and real property appraisals and arbitrations, brokerage commission disputes, and co-op/condominium disputes among sponsors, investors and tenants and in real property tax reduction. The firm has also handled significant litigations concerning REITs and related securitization transactions, including proxy fights and tender offers for major limited partnerships and large REITs.

Bankruptcy: Kaye Scholer's Business Reorganization Department draws upon the expertise of its lawyers in the areas of both corporate insolvency and capital markets to help their clients identify issues, set priorities and allocate resources. The firm serves clients in virtually every industry and with every type of problem - and opportunity - that the insolvency process presents. Its innovative and disciplined approach to insolvency problem-solving maximizes their clients' position effectively and efficiently. As a result, Kaye Scholer has been extensively involved, from both debtor and creditor perspectives, in some of the largest and most complex domestic and multinational insolvencies of all time.

HEAD OFFICE

NEW YORK
Kaye Scholer LLP, 425 Park Avenue, **New York**, NY10022-3598
Tel: 212 836 8000 **Fax:** 212 836 8689
Website: www.kayescholer.com
Email: webmaster@kayescholer.com

BRANCH OFFICES

CALIFORNIA
1999 Avenue of the Stars, Suite 1700, **Los Angeles**, CA 90067-6048
Tel: 310 788 1000 **Fax:** 310 788 1200

DISTRICT OF COLUMBIA
The McPherson Building, 901 Fifteenth Street, N.W., Suite 1100,
Washington, DC 20005-2327
Tel: 202 682 3500 **Fax:** 202 682 3580

FLORIDA
Phillips Point, West Tower, Suite 900, 777 South Flagler Drive,
West Palm Beach, FL 33401-6163
Tel: 561 802 3230 **Fax:** 561 802 3217

ILLINOIS
3 First National Plaza, Suite 4100, 70 West Madison Street,
Chicago, IL 60602-4231
Tel: 312 583 2300 **Fax:** 312 583 2360

INTERNATIONAL OFFICES
The firm has offices in Frankfurt, Germany; Hong Kong; Shanghai, People's Republic of China; and London, United Kingdom.

Tax: Kaye Scholer's tax lawyers represent clients in a wide range of transactions. Their lawyers work to ensure that the tax implications of their clients' business and investment transactions are addressed in the most practical and efficient manner. The Tax Department also has a significant practice in counseling clients in tax controversies with federal, state and local tax attorneys.

Wills & Estates: Kaye Scholer's Wills and Estates lawyers service clients in all related tax and legal matters, but are also involved with the very human and personal side of wills and estates law, helping clients make sound decisions about important family matters and providing comfort and reassurance to individuals in trying times.

CLIENTS: The firm's client base includes national, foreign and multinational corporations, as well as private equity funds and government entities.

INTERNATIONAL WORK: Kaye Scholer represents public and private companies, governmental entities, financial institutions and other organizations in matters around the world. The languages spoken across Kaye Scholer's nine offices include: Cebuano, Chinese, Farsi, Filipino, Finnish, French, German, Greek, Hebrew, Hindi, Italian, Japanese, Latvian, Mandarin Chinese, Moldavian, Portuguese, Romanian, Russian, Spanish, Swedish, Tagalog, Taiwanese, Tamil, Turkish, Ukranian, Urdu, Yiddish.

KENYON & KENYON

THE FIRM

Executive Committee: Richard L DeLucia, Richard L Mayer, James E Rosini, Stuart J Sinder, Robert T Tobin and William K Wells, Jr

Number of partners: 59
Number of other lawyers: 141

AREAS OF PRACTICE:
Intellectual Property 100%

FIRM OVERVIEW: Kenyon & Kenyon is one of the largest and most diversified law firms in the country concentrating on the practice of intellectual property. Founded in 1879 and with offices in New York, Washington DC, and Silicon Valley, the firm provides litigation, prosecution, licensing and counseling services relating to patents, trademarks, copyrights, trade secrets and related matters, such as unfair business and unfair trade practices. The firm is equipped with the most preeminent intellectual property litigation group in the country. It has some of the nation's best litigators who possess very deep and first-chair trial experience. This is largely unmatched by other law firms practicing in the firm's field of expertise.

Some recent survey rankings include: *IP Law & Business* as one of the top three firms to represent defendants in patent cases brought in 2001, 2002, and 2003; consistently ranked one of the top three firms to bring patent cases for plaintiffs as well; by *Managing Intellectual Property* as one of the top firms for IP in both contentious and non-contentious patent and trademark work - survey of in-house counsel and peers; and ranked in the top 15 for number of trademarks issued in 2003 and 2004 in *IP Today*'s Top Trademark survey.

The firm strives to provide the best client representation through its experience, technological expertise, anticipation of client needs, clear and open communication, and an understanding of the vital role played by a comprehensive intellectual property protection and enforcement strategy. The firm is committed to comprehending its clients' products, processes and services in the context of their industries. It achieves this end in part through the unmatched educational backgrounds of its attorneys – 95 percent have technology and/or science degrees (many with advanced degrees) in such fields as electrical engineering, physics, computer science, mechanical engineering, chemistry, chemical engineering, and life sciences. In addition, the legal ability, training and experience of the firm's lawyers enables us to design and implement legal strategies to protect innovation essential to the health of those businesses. It helps clients identify the appropriate form or forms of protection for their assets, whether it be patents, copyrights, trademarks, trade secrets, licenses, or a combination of these. The firm protects the value of these assets in court and at the United States International Trade Commission, and defends clients against claims by others.

HEAD OFFICE

NEW YORK
One Broadway, **New York**, NY 10004
Tel: 212 425 7200   **Fax:** 212 425 5288
Email: info@kenyon.com
Website: www.kenyon.com

BRANCH OFFICES

DISTRICT OF COLUMBIA
1500 K Street, NW, **Washington**, DC 20005
Tel: 202 220 4200   **Fax:** 202 220 4201

CALIFORNIA
333 W. San Carlos Street, Suite 600, **San Jose**, CA 95110
Tel: 408 975 7500   **Fax:** 408 975 7501

CLIENTS: The firm's experience spans the business spectrum. It has represented clients in such technological areas as computers (both hardware and software), biotechnology products and processes, machinery, pharmaceuticals, and plastics. Additionally, the firm has provided services to clients in aerospace, photography, medical devices, metallurgy, basic chemicals and petrochemicals, environmental processes, food and beverages, transportation vehicles, agribio products, robotics, and telecommunications. It has also represented clients in entertainment and the arts, toys, publishing, travel, sports, marketing, and advertising.

INTERNATIONAL WORK: Kenyon & Kenyon has a worldwide clientele. The firm represents not only American companies, but also European, Japanese and multinational firms. It has coordinated multinational disputes in a number of instances, both to ensure that the US litigation, which is its primary responsibility, is not compromised by events in other countries and to assist counsel in those countries to present the most effective claims and defenses. The firm has also developed and maintained international IP portfolios for its worldwide clients and has garnered great relationships with foreign associates in virtually every major industrial country.

KIRKPATRICK & LOCKHART NICHOLSON GRAHAM LLP

THE FIRM

**Chairman of the Management Committee &
Managing Partner:** Peter J Kalis
Number of partners: 323
Number of other lawyers: 627

Website: www.klng.com

FIRM OVERVIEW: Kirkpatrick & Lockhart Nicholson Graham LLP (K&LNG) – the product of one of the largest Anglo-American legal combinations in history on January 1, 2005 – comprises 950 lawyers who practice from offices throughout the US and in London, England. K&LNG represents entrepreneurs, growth and middle-market companies and leading global corporations in every major industry group. The firm practices across all legal disciplines within the corporate, litigation and regulatory fields. K&LNG's extensive knowledge about the business sectors in which our clients operate enables the practice to be at once regional, national and international in scope, cutting edge, complex, and dynamic. K&LNG was the only law firm in the world to receive the CIO Magazine CIO 100 Award for three consecutive years, while the official publication of the Minority Corporate Counsel Association selected K&LNG as one of only four American law firms to feature for their innovative diversity initiatives.

MAIN AREAS OF PRACTICE:

Corporate: K&LNG practices law on an integrated and firm-wide basis. The multi-office, International Corporate and Transactional Practice is one of the most substantial in the profession. The firm closed over 100 M&A transactions last year, and is perennially a leader as issuer's counsel in equities issued by corporate clients, both in terms of number of transactions and proceeds. K&LNG has completed hundreds of public debt and equity offerings over the last decade.

Litigation: K&LNG's litigation engagements including, among other substantive areas, insurance coverage, intellectual property, real estate, white-collar criminal, construction, professional liability, environmental, toxic tort, products liability, franchise, tax, bankruptcy and insolvency, antitrust and competition, employment, benefits, and securities fraud are among the largest and most attractive enjoyed by any law firm. The firm has been rated a leading practice in the representation of corporate policyholders in the insurance coverage area, and as a leading litigation firm for the financial sector. It is active in jurisdictions around the US and in the UK as well as in various international arbitration forums.

Regulatory: K&LNG's Regulatory Practice cuts across the many disciplines that require highly specialized knowledge and experience to address governmental regulation of the private markets. The firm's lawyers regularly represent clients before regulatory bodies in both the US and the UK. Its premier regulatory practice is in the diversified financial services area. K&LNG represents a large majority of the major financial institutions and securities firms in a variety of disciplines, and the investment management practice is a perennial leader. Many of the firm's practice leaders as well as more junior lawyers have governmental experience that enhances their ability to serve K&LNG's clients in regulatory fields, while others have held prominent positions in regulated industries.

Emerging Practices: The firm continuously allocates resources so that its capabilities reach to the forefront of emerging disciplines. K&LNG's Intellectual Property Practice, with approximately 100 practicing lawyers, and its Technology Practice, serving growth companies in disciplines such as biotechnology, internet services, medical devices, and information systems, are examples of how this investment has borne fruit. Most frequently, the firm continues to recruit lateral partners in such disparate fields as structured finance, bankruptcy, real estate, food and drug, ERISA litigation, Small Business Administration financing, telecommunications, project finance, intellectual property, private equity, trademarks, employment and public sector technology to address the evolving needs of its clientele. The firm strives to maintain a creative, interdisciplinary approach to the practice, as evidenced by the extraordinary convergence of disciplines that permitted our K&LNG colleague, former US Attorney General Dick Thornburgh, to act as the court appointed Examiner in the WorldCom bankruptcy proceeding – the largest bankruptcy in US history – and the firm itself to act as his counsel.

CLIENTS: K&LNG currently represents or recently has performed projects for over half of the FORTUNE 100; 21 of the 25 largest mutual fund complexes or their investment managers; and 18 of the 20 largest US bank holding companies or their affiliates. Representative clients include Alcoa, Bank of America, DuPont, Fidelity, Halliburton, Mellon, PPG, United Technologies, Wachovia, and World Wrestling Entertainment. The firm is a multiple winner of DuPont's Meeting the Challenge Award for its 'remarkable and extraordinary accomplishments' for that client, and is the only law firm on which PPG Industries has conferred its Excellent Supplier Award.

INTERNATIONAL WORK: With offices throughout the US and in London, K&LNG represents clients across North America and the United Kingdom on matters that span the globe. K&LNG's primary working language is English, but the firm has attorneys fluent in Afrikaans, Chinese (Mandarin), Farsi, French, German, Greek, Hebrew, Hindi, Italian, Japanese, Korean, Polish, Portuguese, Russian and Spanish. Various members of the firm have foreign degrees, which enable them to take into account legal and cultural differences in representing the firm's clients in international transaction and litigation matters worldwide.

OFFICES

CALIFORNIA
10100 Santa Monica Boulevard, 7th Floor, **Los Angeles**, CA 90067
Tel: 310 552 5000 **Fax:** 310 552 5001

Four Embarcadero Center, 10th Floor, **San Francisco**, CA 94111
Tel: 415 249 1000 **Fax:** 415 249 1001

DISTRICT OF COLUMBIA
1800 Massachusetts Avenue, NW, 2nd Floor, **Washington**, DC 20036-1221
Tel: 202 778 9000 **Fax:** 202 778 9100

FLORIDA
Miami Center, 201 South Biscayne Boulevard, 20th Floor,
Miami, FL 33131-2399
Tel: 305 539 3300 **Fax:** 305 358 7095

MASSACHUSETTS
75 State Street, **Boston**, MA 02109
Tel: 617 261 3100 **Fax:** 617 261 3175

NEW JERSEY
One Newark Center, 10th Floor, **Newark**, NJ 07102-5252
Tel: 973 848 4000 **Fax:** 973 848 4001

NEW YORK
599 Lexington Avenue, **New York**, NY 10022-6030
Tel: 212 536 3900 **Fax:** 212 536 3901

PENNSYLVANIA
Payne Shoemaker Building, 240 North Third Street,
Harrisburg, PA 17101-1507
Tel: 717 231 4500 **Fax:** 717 231 4501

Henry W. Oliver Building, 535 Smithfield Street, **Pittsburgh**, PA 15222-2312
Tel: 412 355 6500 **Fax:** 412 355 6501

TEXAS
2828 North Harwood Street, Suite 1800, **Dallas**, TX 75201-6966
Tel: 214 939 4900 **Fax:** 214 939 4949

INTERNATIONAL OFFICES

The firm also has an office in London, UK

KRAMER LEVIN NAFTALIS & FRANKEL LLP

THE FIRM

Managing Partner: Paul S Pearlman

Number of partners: 83
Number of other lawyers: 197

FIRM OVERVIEW: Kramer Levin Naftalis & Frankel LLP is a world-class, full-service law firm with offices in New York and Paris and an alliance with UK-based Berwin Leighton Paisner. The firm's strong focus on client service has helped it to build long-term relationships with major corporations, institutions and individuals who look to it for innovative and practical solutions. Kramer Levin's counsel has guided entrepreneurs and growing businesses across a range of industries to fully realize their goals. As a leading practitioner in its fields, Kramer Levin applies its broad expertise and experience to help its clients get the results they need. With approximately 300 attorneys in 20-plus practice areas, Kramer Levin has the deep knowledge and expertise to provide a full range of innovative legal solutions. As the firm grows, it continues to draw on the qualities that have fueled its earliest successes: a single-minded commitment to excellence, an entrepreneurial spirit and a dynamic yet practical approach to achieving superior results for its clients.

HEAD OFFICE

NEW YORK
1177 Avenue of the Americas, **New York**, NY 10036
Tel: 212 715 9100 **Fax:** 212 715 8000
Website: www.kramerlevin.com

CONTACTS

Corporate	Scott S Rosenblum
Creditors' Rights & Bankruptcy	Kenneth H Eckstein
Employee Benefits	Michael J Nassau
Employment & Labor	Kevin B Leblang
Environmental	Richard G Leland
Individual Clients	John C Novogrod
Intellectual Property & Technology	Nicholas L Coch
Land Use	Samuel H Lindenbaum
Litigation	Gary P Naftalis
Paris Office	Alexander Marquardt
Real Estate	Jay A Neveloff
Tax	Howard J Rothman

MAIN AREAS OF PRACTICE:

Corporate: Handles virtually every type of complex corporate and securities transaction from public offerings and private placements to mergers, acquisitions, dispositions and joint ventures, while also providing the full range of general corporate law services from contract preparation to strategic counseling. The department regularly represents companies large and small, domestic and foreign, public and private, mature and entrepreneurial in cutting-edge as well as conventional transactions.

Creditors' Rights & Bankruptcy: The Creditors' Rights and Bankruptcy Practice, one of the nation's foremost, has played a central role in many of the country's largest and most complex reorganizations. Working closely with the firm's other departments, this diverse practice includes representation of creditors' committees, debtors, banks, bondholders, trade creditors, landlords, investors, debtor-in-possession lenders and acquirors as well as investors in the purchase and sale of securities and assets of troubled companies.

Intellectual Property & Technology Law: Handles all aspects of intellectual property law - patents, trademarks, copyrights, trade secrets, technology transfer, unfair competition and false advertising, Internet and new media. Attorneys in this full-service department provide litigation, prosecution and registration, counseling and transactional services to their clients to help them acquire, value, maintain, protect and exploit all forms of intellectual property.

Litigation: From the its start in 1968, Kramer Levin has specialized in the litigation of high-profile, high-stakes commercial cases. The firm's White Collar Criminal Defense and SEC Regulatory Group is one of the nation's most prominent. The Litigation Department is chaired by Gary P Naftalis, one of the country's leading trial lawyers, and numbers over 70 lawyers. Litigation department attorneys work in virtually every area of commercial litigation. Such expertise spans the following practice areas: antitrust; appellate and constitutional litigation; bankruptcy litigation; commercial litigation; employment and labor; ERISA litigation; false advertising litigation; insurance litigation; international dispute resolution; patent litigation; real estate litigation; securities and shareholder litigation; trademark, copyright and white collar criminal defense.

Real Estate: The Real Estate Department's attorneys have extensive experience analyzing and applying all the relevant law - real estate, corporate, environmental, land use, restructuring and tax - to deliver creative, cost-effective and practical legal and business solutions. The department has the size, knowledge, experience and dedication to assist on the full array of real property matters including office, residential, industrial, hotel and retail property development, acquisitions and sales; financings and refinancings; workouts and restructuring transactions for lenders, borrowers, and equity participants; retail and office and industrial leasing; joint ventures; structured finance sales/leasebacks; the conversion of new and existing commercial and residential properties to condominium and cooperatives uses; and zoning.

CLIENTS: Today, many of Kramer Levin's clients are Fortune 500 companies that look to the firm for creative solutions for their rapidly changing needs. KL has also played key roles in developing entrepreneurial successes in industries as diverse as fashion and cosmetics, telecommunications and financial services.

INTERNATIONAL WORK: Through its Paris office, Kramer Levin offers clients the benefits of a full-service legal practice based in Europe. The firm's Paris-based attorneys assist domestic and foreign clients with a wide variety of corporate matters, including mergers and acquisitions, corporate securities and finance, banking law, structured financings and securitizations, reorganizations and bankruptcies, complex real estate matters, employment law and foreign investment. The firm also represents clients in all types of business litigation before French courts and in international arbitrations. Kramer Levin's alliance with UK-based Berwin Leighton Paisner, further strengthens its ability to provide truly superior global representation. The UK-based alliance focuses on cross-border corporate and finance matters, and on some of the firm's other highly regarded practice areas including: real estate, litigation, intellectual property and technology, bankruptcy and tax.

LEBOEUF, LAMB, GREENE & MACRAE, L.L.P.

THE FIRM

Chairman: Steven H Davis
Number of partners: 174
Number of other lawyers: 384

FIRM OVERVIEW: LeBoeuf, Lamb, Greene & MacRae, L.L.P. has lawyers practicing in 13 US offices and in nine other cities around the globe. Well known as one of the preeminent legal services providers to the insurance/financial services and energy and utilities industries, the firm has built upon these strengths to gain prominence in corporate, litigation, bankruptcy, international, environmental, taxation, information technology/intellectual property, real estate, trust and estates, anti-trust, corporate governance and compliance, and white collar criminal defense practice. LeBoeuf's multinational network of strategically located offices and broad range practice areas serves clients' local interests as well as ensures clients' access to, and ease of doing business in, major international markets.

MAIN AREAS OF PRACTICE:

Insurance: LeBoeuf has been widely recognized as a leading legal advisor to the insurance industry for the past four decades. Its practice covers every segment of the insurance industry, with an impressive depth of resources and experience. This depth has enabled the firm to develop strong working relationships with major insurers, brokers, investment bankers, commercial bankers, regulators, legislators, actuaries and other service providers to the insurance industry.

Energy: LeBoeuf represents energy and utility suppliers in all aspects of their business. More than 100 LeBoeuf attorneys devote the bulk of their time to providing services that touch upon the energy, telecommunications and water industries, making LeBoeuf a recognized leader in the energy and utilities legal practice worldwide.

Corporate: LeBoeuf's Corporate Practice consists primarily of mergers and acquisitions, public and private securities offerings, private equity and venture capital transactions, securitizations and derivatives.

Litigation: Litigation is one of the firm's largest practice groups, with more than 150 litigators worldwide. Clients most often call upon the firm to litigate matters that are complex, high-profile and time sensitive. LeBoeuf regularly appears before courts of original and appellate jurisdiction throughout the world on the local, state/provincial and national levels, as well as in multijurisdictional disputes. It prosecutes and defends civil claims, and defends against criminal allegations.

Bankruptcy & Restructuring: LeBoeuf has one of the largest and most accomplished Bankruptcy and Restructuring Practices in the United States. With more than 20 highly experienced lawyers the firm offers top-quality service in this specialized field of law.

Technology & Intellectual Property: LeBoeuf combines its expertise in intellectual property law with a multidisciplinary approach and to devise creative and efficient methods of acquiring, protecting and exploiting intellectual property rights on a global basis.

Tax: LeBoeuf's Tax Practice is broad-based, reflecting the diversified nature of the firm's practice and experience in many subspecialty areas. The firm counsels clients on a variety of sophisticated tax issues.

Executive Compensation, Employee Benefits & ERISA: LeBoeuf has developed a comprehensive practice in employee benefits and executive compensation, reaching a clientele with the same broad scope and range as that of the firm as a whole.

Environmental, Health & Safety: LeBoeuf has developed a substantial Environmental, Health and Safety Practice to counsel regulated business operations and support merger, acquisition and divestiture strategies.

Telecommunications: Since the 1970s, LeBoeuf has been engaged in representing clients in the telecommunications field. Its telecommunications

work is truly national and international in character, often crossing borders as its clients expand and their legal needs grow, to combine its telecommunications expertise with local insight in numerous markets. The firm also has significant practices in project finance, international, real estate, trusts and estates, anti-trust, corporate governance and compliance, and white collar criminal defense. For additional information, please visit the firm online at www.llgm.com.

HEAD OFFICE

NEW YORK
125 West 55th Street, **New York**, NY 10019
Tel: 212 424 8000   **Fax:** 212 424 8500
Email: info@llgm.com   **Website:** www.llgm.com

BRANCH OFFICES

CALIFORNIA
725 South Figueroa Street, Suite 3100, **Los Angeles**, CA 90017-5404
Tel: 213 955 7300   **Fax:** 213 955 7399

One Embarcadero Center, Suite 400, **San Francisco**, CA 94111-3619
Tel: 415 951 1100   **Fax:** 415 951 1180

CONNECTICUT
Goodwin Square, 225 Asylum Street, 13th Floor, **Hartford**, CT 06103
Tel: 860 293 3500   **Fax:** 860 293 3555

DISTRICT OF COLUMBIA
1875 Connecticut Ave., N.W., Suite 1200, **Washington**, DC 20009-5728
Tel: 202 986 8000   **Fax:** 202 986 8102

FLORIDA
50 North Laura Street, Suite 2800, **Jacksonville**, FL 32202-3650
Tel: 904 354 8000   **Fax:** 904 353 1673

ILLINOIS
Two Prudential Plaza, 180 North Stetson Avenue, Suite 1175, **Chicago**, 60601
Tel: 312 794 8000   **Fax:** 312 794 8100

MASSACHUSETTS
260 Franklin Street, **Boston**, MA 02110-3173
Tel: 617 748 6800   **Fax:** 617 439 0341

NEW JERSEY
One Riverfront Plaza, **Newark**, NJ 07102-5490
Tel: 973 643 8000   **Fax:** 973 643 6111

NEW YORK
One Commerce Plaza, 99 Washington Avenue, Suite 2020
Albany, NY 12210-2820
Tel: 518 626 9000   **Fax:** 518 626 9010

PENNSYLVANIA
200 North Third Street, Suite 300, PO Box 12105
Harrisburg, PA 17108-2105
Tel: 717 232 8199   **Fax:** 717 232 8720

One Gateway Center, 420 Fort Duquesne Boulevard, Suite 1600
Pittsburgh, PA 15222-1437
Tel: 412 594 2300   **Fax:** 412 594 5237

TEXAS
Reliant Energy Plaza, 1000 Main Street, Suite 2550,
Houston, TX 77002
Tel: 713 287 2000   **Fax:** 713 287 2100

INTERNATIONAL OFFICES

The firm also has offices in Almaty, Beijing, Bishkek, Brussels, Johannesburg, London, Moscow, Paris and Riyadh.

LePATNER & ASSOCIATES LLP

THE FIRM

Managing Partner: Barry B LePatner

Number of partners: 6
Number of other lawyers: 3
Number of design consultants: 1

AREAS OF PRACTICE:

Commercial Litigation & Claims Representation 35%
Construction Contracts 35%
Business Advisory Services 30%

FIRM OVERVIEW: Founded by Barry LePatner in 1980, LePatner & Associates LLP is widely recognized as one of the nation's leading law firms providing business and legal advice affecting the real estate, design and construction industries. On behalf of its many corporate and institutional and commercial real estate clients, the firm provides sophisticated project planning, state of the art contracts and respected advisory services at all levels of today's complex real estate projects.

MAIN AREAS OF PRACTICE:

Construction Contracts: For more than 20 years, the firm has been instrumental in protecting owners' capital investments from pre-construction to lease negotiations and through post-construction claims handling. Seamlessly coordinated construction agreements are specifically tailored to address the business imperatives of each project. The firm's dedicated contract law team provides negotiation services including due diligence of all team members, structuring agreements, contract negotiation with project teams, insurance and bonding compliance and coordination of design/construction scheduling. In the area of coordinated construction contracts, the firm has outstanding expertise.

Business Advisory Services: The firm offers business advisory and consulting services for the design and construction industry from site selection, due diligence and selection of the construction team, project management, applicability of industry laws, regulations and codes, through claims management and handling of warranty issues.

Commercial Litigation & Claims: The firm is widely recognised for its expertise in litigation and arbitration, dispute resolution alternatives, claims analysis and negotiation and claims avoidance strategies.

HEAD OFFICE

NEW YORK
600 Lexington Ave, 21st Floor, **New York**, NY 10022
Tel: 212 935 4400   **Fax:** 212 935 4404
Email: blepatner@lepatner.com
Website: www.lepatner.com

CONTACTS

Contracts & Business Advisory Services . . . . .Barry B LePatner

CLIENTS: The firm's clients represent a spectrum of major commercial and residential property owners, corporations, institutions of higher education, and real estate developers, and includes: Starwood Resorts and Hotels, the Government of Spain, Thirteen.wnet, United Nations Mission in Kosovo, Rosewood Hotels and Resorts, Barnard College, Daimler-Chrysler, the Osborn Retirement Community, Asprey Ltd.

INTERNATIONAL WORK: The firm has advised international corporations and foreign government entities operating within the US with regard to their construction projects. In addition to protecting their construction investment, LePatner & Associates guides these clients through the complex maze of government building codes and regulations.

MORGAN & FINNEGAN, LLP

THE FIRM

Number of partners: 41
Number of other lawyers: 64

AREAS OF PRACTICE:

Intellectual Property 100%

FIRM OVERVIEW: Morgan & Finnegan is one of the largest and most experienced law firms specializing in litigating, protecting and securing intellectual property rights. For more than a century, the firm has represented a wide variety of clients in all aspects of intellectual property law including patents, trademarks, copyrights, trade secrets, unfair competition and antitrust matters. Morgan & Finnegan has compiled a distinguished record in patent and other complex intellectual property litigation. Several of the patent cases litigated by the firm have achieved landmark status. In addition, two inventions based on patents prosecuted by Morgan & Finnegan attorneys, one for a portable computer navigational system and the other for synthetic diamonds, are part of the permanent collection of the Smithsonian Institution in Washington. Morgan & Finnegan has amassed an impressive record of successful Markman determinations based on its intimate familiarity with the claim construction issues of patent law. In cases in which Morgan & Finnegan has defended against an infringement claim, it has used these Markman results to great advantage in obtaining successful summary judgment dispositions, avoiding the expense and uncertainty of trial for clients. Today, in an era of increasingly complex science and technology, the necessity for protecting innovation is more important than ever. As boundaries expand, and as new industries grow, the vision of the firm's founders is reflected in the high standards of service and value that the firm provides and in the spectrum of clients that it represents.

MAIN AREAS OF PRACTICE: The firm has more than 110 partners, counsel, associates and PhD scientific advisors in six primary practice groups. These are: biotechnology; chemicals and pharmaceuticals; computers and electronics; e-commerce and financial systems; medical and mechanical; and trademark, copyright and unfair competition. All the attorneys are devoted entirely to intellectual property and related unfair competition and antitrust matters.

INTERNATIONAL WORK: Morgan & Finnegan is at the forefront of international intellectual property developments. The firm's expertise enables it to understand more precisely the problems and concerns of Asian and European companies doing business both in the United States and abroad, and brings benefits to its multinational clients. The firm also has first-hand, in-depth experience directing counter-part activities in Europe, including directing patent infringement actions (such as requests for preliminary relief and cross-border relief) as well as nullity actions and patent office oppositions.

HEAD OFFICE

NEW YORK
3 World Financial Center, **New York**, NY 10281-2101
Tel: 212 415 8700   **Fax:** 212 415 8701
Website: www.morganfinnegan.com

BRANCH OFFICES

DISTRICT OF COLUMBIA
1775 Eye Street, NW, Suite 400, **Washington**, DC 20006
Tel: 202 857 7887   **Fax:** 202 857 7929

SAN FRANCISCO
44 Montgomery Street, Suite 2550, **San Francisco**, CA 94104
Tel: 415 318 8800   **Fax:** 415 676 5816

NIXON PEABODY LLP

THE FIRM

Chairman, CEO & Co-Managing Partner: Harry P Trueheart, III
Co-managing Partner: Nestor M Nicholas
Number of lawyers: 633

FIRM OVERVIEW: Nixon Peabody attorneys practice in virtually all areas of business. They provide comprehensive legal services for a range of businesses, from major US and international companies to entrepreneurs, institutions, privately held businesses and non-profit organizations. A fully integrated organizational structure along with state-of-the art technology provides clients with superior service and access through any Nixon Peabody office.

MAIN AREAS OF PRACTICE

Business: The firm serves a broad range of business clients in the areas of securities, private equity and venture capital, mergers and acquisitions, tax, bank regulatory and M&A, international trade and many other matters. While clients represent a range of technologies and services, the firm possesses specific experience in aviation, media and telecommunications, life sciences, energy, beverage and alcohol, pharmaceutical, higher education, software and digital imaging industries.

Business Litigation: More than a third of the firm's attorneys litigate a wide array of business matters concerning: antitrust, government investigations, international disputes, franchise, pharmaceutical litigation, professional relations, real estate, and financial services and securities litigation. The firm's litigators appear in courts throughout the US and abroad.

Financial Services & Specialty Finance: Services include: corporate trust, cash-flow-based lending, loan syndication, securitization and structured finance, equipment leasing and other aspects of business finance. The group structures, negotiates, documents, and manages to completion all types of financial transactions.

Technology & Intellectual Property: The practice offers a full range of patent prosecution, litigation and interference services, as well as trademark, licensing, copyright, brand management and trade secret services. Clients range from Fortune 500 companies to entrepreneurs, start-ups, universities and mature companies with significant patent portfolios.

Real Estate: The firm serves institutional owners and investors, developers, landlords, tenants, lenders, and others concerning a variety of commercial, industrial and multi-family real estate projects.

Public Finance: Nixon Peabody has one of the largest public finance practices in the US, regularly ranked among the 10 most active bond and underwriter counsels nationally in dollar value of bonds issued. The firm's experience extends from the financing of arenas and stadiums to power generation facilities and housing projects.

Labor & Employment: Experience includes counsel to large corporations, partnerships, and entrepreneurs regarding public and private employment matters, as well as multi-plaintiff and class action litigation.

Products Liability: Nixon Peabody attorneys have repeatedly proven their abilities in high stakes cases involving products liability and complex tort litigation across many industries and sectors including: aviation, automotive, medical devices and life sciences, pharmaceutical and environmental.

Energy & Environment: The firm, with an in-house staff of engineers and scientists, has an international reputation with large-scale energy and infrastructure projects, and an array of environmental regulatory and litigation issues.

Health Services: Service to healthcare providers including: corporate, regulatory, licensing and certificates of need, reimbursement counseling, development and financing of capital projects, strategic planning, graduate medical education and residency training accreditation matters, physician/ hospital and medical staff issues, patient care issues, physician practice issues and managed care contracting.

Insurance: Comprehensive services to the insurance industry with an

US OFFICES

CALIFORNIA
2040 Main Street, Suite 850, **Irvine**, CA 92614
Tel: 949 475 6900
Website: www.nixonpeabody.com

Two Embarcadero Center, **San Francisco**, CA 94111
Tel: 415 984 8200

CONNECTICUT
185 Asylum Street, **Hartford**, CT 06103
Tel: 860 275 6820

DISTRICT OF COLUMBIA
401 9th Street, N.W., Ste. 900 **Washington**, DC 20004
Tel: 202 585 8000

MASSACHUSETTS
100 Summer Street, **Boston**, MA 02110
Tel: 617 345 1000

NEW HAMPSHIRE
889 Elm Street, **Manchester**, NH 03101
Tel: 603 628 4000

NEW YORK
30 South Pearl Street, **Albany**, NY 12207
Tel: 518 427 2650

1600 Main Place Tower, **Buffalo**, NY 14202
Tel: 716 853 8100

437 Madison Avenue, **New York**, NY 10022
Tel: 212 940 30000

Clinton Square, PO Box 31051, **Rochester**, NY 14603
Tel: 585 263 1000

990 Stewart Avenue, **Garden City**, NY 11530
Tel: 516 832 7500

PENNSYLVANIA
1818 Market Street, 11th floor, **Philadelphia**, PA 19103
Tel: 215 246 3520

RHODE ISLAND
One Citizens Plaza, **Providence**, RI 02903
Tel: 401 454 1000

emphasis on international reinsurance, corporate, regulatory, litigation and pre-litigation strategic counseling. The group tries coverage disputes throughout the US in all major industries.

Bankruptcy: Nixon Peabody is skilled in addressing a wide spectrum of insolvency issues, from debt restructuring and negotiating reorganization plans to asset liquidation.

Private Clients: Services include income, estate and gift tax planning and compliance, financial planning, estate administration, retirement planning and asset protection.

Affordable Housing: With years of government and private sector experience, the firm assists clients in the numerous legal aspects of building, managing, buying, and selling federally assisted housing.

Syndication: The firm's syndication attorneys have more than 30 years of experience in matters involving equity investing for housing and other forms of real estate.

INTERNATIONAL WORK: Nixon Peabody clients include international banks and multinational and foreign-based corporations in a wide range of industries. The firm acts as general counsel to large industrial corporations, banks, media companies, developers, leasing companies, and public utilities. Its experience also includes handling major international transactions. Languages include Afrikaans, Chinese, Danish, Dutch, French, German, Italian, Norwegian, Portuguese, Russian, Spanish and Swedish.

PAUL, WEISS, RIFKIND, WHARTON & GARRISON LLP

THE FIRM

Managing Partner: Alfred D Youngwood
Number of partners: 107
Number of other lawyers: 475

FIRM OVERVIEW: Paul, Weiss, Rifkind, Wharton & Garrison LLP is a world-class law firm whose influence spans the globe and whose lawyers have left their imprint on the landscape of modern jurisprudence. Few firms can match the breadth and depth of skill provided by their leading corporate and litigation practices. The firm is equally recognized for its capabilities in the areas of bankruptcy and corporate reorganization, employee benefits and executive compensation, intellectual property, personal representation, real estate and tax law. Its lawyers serve as counsel to many of the largest publicly and privately held corporations and financial institutions in the US and throughout the world. The firm also serves numerous entrepreneurs and start-up companies, and over the years has nurtured many through their growth into industry players. The firm receives particular accolades for its work on behalf of clients in the financial services, communications, technology, media and entertainment fields.

MAIN AREAS OF PRACTICE:

Antitrust: Paul, Weiss lawyers have played an important part in shaping antitrust law in the United States. The firm has represented many of the world's largest companies in resolving antitrust issues and has handled the full range of antitrust matters, from large corporate transactions investigated by the Federal Trade Commission and Department of Justice to private litigation, involving monopolization, vertical restraints and price fixing, in federal and state courts.

Bankruptcy & Corporate Reorganization: Paul, Weiss has played key roles in many of the major cases that have grabbed the headlines over the past few years. Its Bankruptcy Department represents debtors, official and unofficial committees of creditors and shareholders, secured and unsecured creditors, and shareholders in chapter 11 cases, corporate reorganizations and work-outs, non-bankruptcy insolvency proceedings, and other matters involving litigation or transactional advice relating to financially distressed companies. The firm also has extensive experience representing purchasers of the assets, debt and securities of distressed companies, and has wide experience in transnational and cross-border insolvency matters.

Communications & Technology: Paul, Weiss has one of the world's leading practices in communications and technology. Its Communications and Technology Group lawyers are knowledgeable about US and international regulation of communications and broadcasting, and are active in matters before the FCC, other administrative agencies and the Congress, as well as non-US regulatory bodies. They advise clients about the complex interplay between the regulatory environment and the high-technology, fast-changing business of communications.

Corporate: Paul, Weiss provides to its clients comprehensive global corporate services that helps them complete sophisticated transactions in a rapidly changing competitive environment. The Corporate Department consists of lawyers who operate in five practice areas - mergers and acquisitions, capital markets and securities, finance, private equity transactions, and investment fund management, in addition to providing counsel to clients on corporate governance.

Employee Benefits & Executive Compensation: The Paul, Weiss Employee Benefits Department is comprised of lawyers who work full time on all types of ERISA, executive compensation and employee benefit matters. It has the experience and resources to handle special projects involving complex and financially important ERISA and related tax and securities laws issues. One of the department's greatest strengths is its deep knowledge of the more technical aspects of benefit plan administration.

HEAD OFFICE

NEW YORK
1285 Avenue of the Americas, **New York** NY 10019-6064
Tel: 212 373 3000   **Fax:** 212 757 3990
Email: mailbox@paulweiss.com   **Website:** www.paulweiss.com

BRANCH OFFICES

DISTRICT OF COLUMBIA
1615 L Street, NW, Suite 1300, **Washington** DC 20036-5694
Tel: 202 223 7300   **Fax:** 202 223 7420

INTERNATIONAL OFFICES

The firm also has offices in London, Tokyo, Hong Kong and Beijing.

Entertainment: The lawyers in the Paul, Weiss Entertainment Department handle an extensive range of corporate and litigation matters, on behalf of clients engaged in legitimate theater, motion pictures, music, radio and television broadcasting, and book and magazine publishing. The firm is active in counseling many of its corporate and individual entertainment clients on a broad range of copyright, trademark, and related intellectual property issues.

Environmental: The Paul, Weiss Environmental Law Group provides representation to its financial, industrial and natural resources clients in corporate transactions, litigation and regulatory disputes arising under federal and state environmental laws. The firm has played an important role in some of the most complex and influential cases of recent times.

Intellectual Property: Paul, Weiss has one of the leading intellectual property practices in the United States. Its lawyers have the qualifications and experience required to address the complex issues attending matters of dispute that span the full range of intellectual property today, including patent, trade secret, trademark, copyright, unfair competition, and advertising matters. And, members of their Intellectual Property Group specialize in handling a diverse range of intellectual property transactions, involving counseling, licensing, corporate support, due diligence, distribution and acquisitions regarding all types of intellectual property.

Litigation: The Paul, Weiss Litigation Department is involved in nearly every high-profile US litigation today. Their lawyers focus on a number of areas including antitrust, arbitration, commercial litigation, criminal and regulatory enforcement, intellectual property litigation, patent and scientific litigation, securities litigation, and tax litigation among others. They handle disputes in every forum, from traditional court cases to domestic and international arbitrations, and from alternative dispute resolution processes to administrative tribunals of all kinds. To each, they bring a sure grasp of the underlying substantive issues and the forensic skills and strategic insights necessary to produce a successful result.

Personal Representation: Attorneys in the Paul, Weiss Personal Representation Department provide services to clients ranging from estate planning and administration and representation of private foundations and public charitable organizations, to matrimonial matters, litigated Surrogate's Court cases and the tax issues affecting such matters.

Real Estate: The Paul, Weiss Real Estate Department is a recognized leader in the New York and national real estate bars. It provides clients with a full range of services, from organizing and structuring the largest, most complex transactions throughout the country and around the globe, to advising clients on their daily portfolio management issues.

Tax: Paul, Weiss fields one of the most prominent teams of tax attorneys in the country, comprised of accomplished business lawyers with tax expertise who represent clients across the globe. One of the most valued aspects of the practice continues to be the firm's dedication adding value by discovering innovative approaches to reduce the client's tax burden, thereby increasing the overall economic benefits of the deal and often providing the key to a successful transaction.

PECKAR & ABRAMSON, P.C.

THE FIRM

Managing Partner: Robert S Peckar

Number of partners: 27
Number of other lawyers: 40

FIRM OVERVIEW: Peckar & Abramson recently celebrated 25 years serving the construction industry. The firm has achieved national recognition for its successes in the representation of members of the construction industry, both domestically and internationally. The firm combines its unique problem-solving expertise and litigation/arbitration experience with its substantial experience counseling clients regarding the management of transactional risks inherent in the industry. Having represented clients in every category of construction, Peckar & Abramson has successfully resolved disputes at all levels of complexity arising from a wide range of construction projects, from moderately sized projects to mega-projects in both the public and private sectors. The firm has particular expertise in projects such as airports, government buildings, highways and bridges, power generation facilities, environmental clean-ups, sports arenas, manufacturing facilities, hotels and other hospitality industry projects and residential communities. In addition to and complementing its construction industry practice, the firm offers the full services of its employment and labor law group, as well as its business and real estate transactional practice.

INTERNATIONAL WORK: The firm focuses its practice on the representation of general contractors and construction managers, but also represents other construction industry participants with matters throughout the US, Asia, the Middle East, the Caribbean, Latin and South America and Europe.

CLIENTS: Peckar & Abramson serves the needs of its clients from its offices in New York, New Jersey, Florida and California and offers its international clients the benefits of its relationship with allied international firms through its membership in the International Construction Law Alliance (ICLA), including members in the Americas, Europe and Asia.

HEAD OFFICE

NEW YORK
546 Fifth Avenue, 17th Floor, **New York**, NY 10036
Tel: 212 382 0909   **Fax:** 212 382 3456
Email: rpeckar@pecklaw.com
Website: www.pecklaw.com

BRANCH OFFICES

CALIFORNIA
555 West 5th Street, Suite 3000, **Los Angeles**, CA 90013
Tel: 213 489 9220   **Fax:** 213 489 9215

250 Montgomery Street, 16th Floor, **San Francisco**, CA 94104
Tel: 415 8371968   **Fax:** 415 837 1320

FLORIDA
One Southeast Third Avenue, Suite 3050, **Miami**, FL 33131
Tel: 305 358 2600   **Fax:** 305 375 0328

401 East Las Olas Boulevard, Suite 1600, **Fort Lauderdale**, FL 33301
Tel: 954 764 5222   **Fax:** 954 764 5228

NEW JERSEY
70 Grand Avenue, **River Edge**, NJ 07661
Tel: 201 343 3434   **Fax:** 201 343 6306

PILLSBURY WINTHROP

THE FIRM

Chair: Mary Cranston
Executive Vice Chair: Dave Snyder
Managing Partner: Marina Park

Number of partners in US offices: 293
Number of other lawyers in US offices: 398

AREAS OF PRACTICE:

Capital Markets, Finance, Restructuring .34%
Litigation 28%
Technology/Intellectual Property 18%
Global Energy 10%
Other 10%

FIRM OVERVIEW: Pillsbury Winthrop LLP provides a tradition of excellence and service to its clients, communities and profession that taps its 135 years of experience. With offices in the major capital markets and technology centers of the world, the firm offers its clients the strength of this reach, the power of financial innovation and technical expertise and a commitment to cross-border service and responsiveness. Using a team-based client service model, the firm counsels clients on all aspects of global business, corporate governance, technology transactions, intellectual property protection, energy, real estate and complex litigation. At press time, the planned merger between Pillsbury Winthrop LLP and Shaw Pittman LLP had not yet been finalized.

MAIN AREAS OF PRACTICE:

Capital Markets & Finance: The firm provides counsel in all areas of capital markets and finance, centered on sophisticated capital formation strategies, mergers and acquisitions and structured financial solutions. It comprises one of the largest bankruptcy and creditors' rights groups in the country.
Litigation: The firm has litigation, trial and arbitration experience across a wide range of industries and areas of law, including international disputes involving joint ventures, intellectual property rights, antitrust, environmental issues and securities laws. The firm's 250 plus litigators have resolved many high profile cases in forums around the world.
Technology/Intellectual Property: The firm's understanding of both the law and the unique industry segments makes the firm's legal services unique and invaluable in dealing with this ever changing landscape. Pillsbury Winthrop attorneys have been involved in more than 300 significant intellectual property litigation cases tried in US courts over the last 10 years. The firm's IP Practice ranks among the top 10 in the US.
Global Energy: The firm is recognized as an international law firm at the center of all sectors of the energy and utility industry. The firm's Energy and Utilities Industry Practice is interdisciplinary, encompassing every practice area required by its broad client base in this industry, and advises oil and gas producers, transporters, distributors and managers, electric and gas utilities, utility holding companies and affiliates, independent power producers, and underwriters, lenders and investors.

CLIENTS: The firm's clients include global companies in banking and financial services, insurance, trading, energy, manufacturing, transportation, technology, biotech and pharmaceuticals.

INTERNATIONAL WORK: A strong emphasis on corporate and finance matters, the firm also represents clients in Europe, Asia and Australia in matters involving global energy, technology, biotech and pharmaceutical industries, intellectual property, real estate, insolvency and employment law.

HEAD OFFICES

CALIFORNIA
50 Fremont Street, **San Francisco**, CA 94105
Tel: 415 983 1000 **Fax:** 415 983 1200

NEW YORK
1540 Broadway, **New York**, NY 10036
Tel: 212 858 1000 **Fax:** 212 858 1500
Email: info@pillsburywinthrop.com
Website: www.pillsburywinthrop.com

BRANCH OFFICES

CALIFORNIA
MGM Tower, 10250 Constellation Boulevard, 21st Floor,
Los Angeles, CA 90067
Tel: 310 203 1100 **Fax:** 310 286 6672

725 South Figueroa Street, Suite 2800, **Los Angeles**, CA 90017
Tel: 213 488 7100 **Fax:** 213 629 1033

650 Town Center Drive, 7th Floor, **Costa Mesa**, CA 92626
Tel: 714 436 6800 **Fax:** 714 436 2800

400 Capitol Mall, Suite 1700, **Sacramento**, CA 95814
Tel: 916 329 4700 **Fax:** 916 441 3583

SBC Building, 101 West Broadway, Suite 1800, **San Diego**, CA 92101
Tel: 619 234 5000 **Fax:** 619 236 1995

11682 El Camino Real, Suite 200, **San Diego**, CA 92130
Tel: 858 509 4000 **Fax:** 858 509 4010

2475 Hanover Street, **Palo Alto**, CA 94304
Tel: 650 233 4500 **Fax:** 650 233 4545

CONNECTICUT
Financial Centre, 695 East Main Street, PO Box 6760,
Stamford, CT 06904
Tel: 203 348 2300 **Fax:** 203 965 8226

TEXAS
2 Houston Center, 909 Fannin, 22nd Floor, **Houston**, TX 77010
Tel: 713 425 7300 **Fax:** 713 425 7373

VIRGINIA
1600 Tysons Boulevard, **McLean**, VA 22102
Tel: 703 905 2000 **Fax:** 703 905 2500

DISTRICT OF COLUMBIA
1133 Connecticut Avenue, NW, **Washington, DC** 20036
Tel: 202 775 9800 **Fax:** 202 833 8491

INTERNATIONAL OFFICES

Pillsbury Winthrop has international offices in London, Sydney and Tokyo.

CONTACTS

Capital Markets . . . . .Dave Snyder
Finance . . . . .Michael Schumaecker
Mergers & Acquisitions . . . . .Donald Kilpatrick
Litigation . . . . .John Pritchard
Technology/Intellectual Property . . . . .Jorge del Calvo
Global Energy . . . . .Robert James

PILLSBURY WINTHROPLLP

PROSKAUER ROSE LLP

THE FIRM

Chairman: Allen I Fagin

Number of partners: 170

FIRM OVERVIEW: Proskauer Rose LLP is one of the nation's largest law firms, providing a wide variety of legal services to major corporations and other clients throughout the United States and around the world. Headquartered in New York City since 1875, the firm also has offices in Los Angeles, Washington DC, Boston, Boca Raton, Newark, New Orleans and Paris. During its history Proskauer has been distinguished by its dedication to client service, technical excellence and high integrity. It also has adapted rapidly to changes in the needs of businesses, whether it be for expertise in emerging areas of law, employing new methods of communicating, or deploying the latest information technology.

MAIN AREAS OF PRACTICE: The firm's practice areas provide traditional services to corporations and other business entities such as corporate finance and securities, tax, litigation, real estate, and labor and employment advice. It also has leading practices in the areas of arbitration and other forms of alternative dispute resolution, bankruptcy and reorganizations, broker-dealer regulation, employee benefits and executive compensation, entertainment, environmental law, healthcare and pharmaceuticals, high technology and the internet, intellectual property, private equity financing, sports, trade secrets and non-competition, and white-collar crime. Representing the publishing, motion picture and recording industries as they confront new challenges, Proskauer recently has been at the leading edge of the law, as the dramatic emergence of a freer flow of information and knowledge over the global networks of servers and computers tests and strains established principles protecting intellectual property. As its litigators handle disputes arising in this arena, Proskauer's corporate and tax lawyers have been working on the business and financial structures and contractual licensing needs of the entrepreneurs building new companies, established corporations adjusting to new technologies, and financial services firms developing new financing products. Trained at leading law schools, Proskauer lawyers are civic and philanthropic leaders as well as highly skilled practitioners. In addition to service in the wider community, lawyers in the firm have recently held the presidencies of legal organizations such as the Association of the Bar of the City of New York, the New York State Bar Association, New York Woman's Bar Association, the American College of Trial Lawyers, the Federal Bar Council, the Fund for Modern Courts, the New York County Lawyers Association and the American Judicature Society.

INTERNATIONAL WORK: Proskauer's international practice has its roots in the representation early last century of various French industrialists. Since that time the firm has developed a recognized stature in international transactions and an understanding of and commitment to the global markets and the transnational needs of its clients. The firm's international practice includes the representation of foreign clients doing business in the United States and American clients abroad. It is also called on by foreign clients for transactions based abroad to which the firm brings its particular skill and experience in international transactions. The representation of international clients encompasses all aspects of the practice and involves lawyers in each of the firm's six departments: corporate, tax, labor, real estate, litigation and dispute resolution and personal planning. The firm regularly assists its international clients in mergers and acquisitions, joint ventures, licensing, international aspects of litigation, arbitration, tax planning, labor relations, antitrust, intellectual property and immigration.

HEAD OFFICE

NEW YORK
1585 Broadway, **New York**, NY 10036-8299
Tel: 212 969 3000

BRANCH OFFICES

CALIFORNIA
2049 Century Park East, 32nd Floor, **Los Angeles**, CA 90067-3206
Tel: 310 557 2900

DISTRICT OF COLUMBIA
1233 20th Street, NW, Suite 800, **Washington**, DC 20036-2396
Tel: 202 416 6800

MASSACHUSETTS
One International Place, **Boston**, MA 02110-2600
Tel: 617 526 9600

FLORIDA
One Boca Place, 2255 Glades Road, Suite 340 West, **Boca Raton**, FL 33431-7383
Tel: 561 241 7400

NEW JERSEY
One Newark Center, 18th Floor, **Newark**, NJ 07102
Tel: 973 274 3200

LOUISIANA
909 Poydras Street, **New Orleans**, LA 70112-4017
Tel: 617 526 9600

INTERNATIONAL OFFICES

The firm also has an international office in Paris.

ROSS & COHEN, LLP

THE FIRM

Managing & Senior Partners: Allen Ross, Frederick Cohen

Number of partners: 8
Number of other lawyers: 8

AREAS OF PRACTICE:
Construction Industry Services 80%
Real Estate Services 20%

FIRM OVERVIEW: Established in 1978 by Allen Ross and Frederick Cohen, Ross & Cohen, LLP enjoys and unparalleled reputation for personal service and technical expertise in the highly specialized world of construction and real estate law. Ross & Cohen, LLP retains some of the most experienced and technically proficient specialists in these areas of law. The firm is committed to finding the most appropriate and cost-effective solutions to its clients' legal problems and provide advice and counsel that enables them to achieve their business objectives.

MAIN AREAS OF PRACTICE:
Construction Industry Services: The construction-related legal services Ross & Cohen, LLP provides encompass the complete life cycle of a project, from the earliest planning stage to occupancy and beyond including project advice; planning and counseling; construction lending; contract negotiation; preparation and review for all types of construction and development ventures; suretyship and guarantees; prosecution and defense of claims related to breach of contract, defective work, payment, delay and mechanics' liens; administrative law hearings; bid contracts and construction-related labor law matters. The additional areas of Ross & Cohen, LLP's practice related to construction of special interest to its clients are mediation and arbitration and compliance audits.
Real Estate Services: The real estate services Ross & Cohen, LLP provides to its clients are the transactional services they need to support real estate activities in both commercial and residential setting. The firm's attorneys are experts in acquisition and sales; commercial and retail leasing; construction financing and real estate secured loan transactions; workout, restructuring and foreclosure; representing co-operative corporations; and real estate taxation and tax certiorari proceedings.

CLIENTS: Ross & Cohen, LLP serves a diverse group of clients including publicly-held corporations, developers, landlords, property managers, general contractors, subcontractors, material and equipment suppliers, design and construction professionals, financial institutions, governmental agencies and municipalities on a broad range of construction and real estate issues. The firm regularly represents clients involved in such diverse projects as hotels, healthcare facilities, shopping centers, warehouses, manufacturing plants, mixed-use development, office buildings, restaurants, co-operative and condominium residences and a whole range of public projects including building and civil construction.

HEAD OFFICE

NEW YORK
711 Third Avenue, **New York**, NY 10017
Tel: 212 370 1200 **Fax:** 212 370 0334
Email: law@rosscohen.com
Website: www.rosscohen.com

SCHULTE ROTH & ZABEL LLP

THE FIRM

Firm Management: Executive Commitee
Senior Partner: Paul N Roth

Number of partners: 71
Number of other lawyers: 302

FIRM OVERVIEW: Founded in 1969, Schulte Roth & Zabel has grown to more than 370 attorneys practicing a broad variety of disciplines. The firm focuses on client service and has a deep appreciation of the importance of building and maintaining long-term relationships. Its clients include major corporations, institutional and individual clients.

MAIN AREAS OF PRACTICE:

Investment Management: SRZ has occupied the fund formation space for over 30 years and has a premier practice in the area. The firm represents over 400 investment management firms with equity capital estimated in excess of $300 billion. These include global investment banking and advisory firms, hedge fund firms, mutual fund complexes and private equity firms.

Business Transactions: SRZ is one of the preeminent law firms in the areas of mergers and acquisitions, special opportunity investments, proxy fights, leveraged buyouts and venture capital funds, initial public offerings, high-yield debt and PIPEs transactions.

Business Reorganization: The firm provides counsel to key participants in debt restructurings (workouts and reorganizations) acquisition of troubled companies, financing (debtor-in possession and reorganization plans), and bankruptcy litigation (including fraudulent transfers, preferences and contract disputes).

Finance: SRZ's Finance Group represents clients in the asset-based lending community, including asset-based loans, leveraged acquisitions, financing and restructurings, debtor-in-possession and exit financings, unsecured corporate borrowings, and private placements by investment-grade companies.

Structured Products: SRZ's Structured Products Practice has been involved in some of the most innovative structured finance transactions, including CDOs, CLOs, and CFOs, asset and mortgage securitizations and asset-backed commercial paper programs.

Litigation: More than 100 litigators counsel clients in matters including securities litigation, defense of white collar criminal cases, anti-money laundering, antitrust, defense of derivative actions, general commercial litigation and arbitrations.

Employment & Employee Benefits: SRZ's Employment Practice includes litigation and ongoing guidance, counsel and prevention of employment disputes. The firm represents employers in all aspects of labor relations and collective bargaining. The Employee Benefits Practice encompasses every aspect of benefits law and ERISA.

Intellectual Property: SRZ has expertise in all aspects of intellectual property and information technology law, including patents, trademarks, copyrights, unfair competition, trade secrets and information technology licensing, development and outsourcing.

HEAD OFFICE

NEW YORK
919 Third Avenue, **New York**, NY 10022
Tel: 212 756 2000   **Fax:** 212 593 5955

Website: www.srz.com

INTERNATIONAL OFFICES

The firm also has an office in London.

CONTACTS

Investment Management	Stephanie R Breslow
Business Transactions	Marc Weingarten
Business Reorganization	Michael L Cook
Finance	Frederic L Ragucci
Structured Products	Paul N Watterson
Litigation	Robert M Abrahams
Employment	Mark E Brossman
Intellectual Property	Joel E Lutzker
Real Estate	Jeffrey A Lenobel
Environmental Law	Howard B Epstein
Tax	Alan S Waldenberg
Individual Clients	William D Zabel

Real Estate: The firm represents a diverse group of clients in the sale and acquisition of commercial property, securitized mortgage loans and mezzanine financings, leasing of commercial property, construction and architectural agreements, all aspects of the development process and real estate equity funds.

Environmental: SRZ counsels major institutions and Fortune 500 companies on a wide range of national and international environmental issues. The firm advises on preventive methods, offering the technical knowledge and legal experience to provide the best advocacy. The firm represents clients before local, state and federal agencies and in the courtroom.

Tax: The SRZ Tax Group provides tax planning for mergers, sales and other dispositions, acquisitions and leveraged buyout arrangements, including analysis of cross-border financing and transfer pricing issues. The group structures sophisticated financing transactions, advises on special tax issues confronting foreign investors making corporate, portfolio securities and real estate investments in the US. SRZ also provides tax advice to managers of domestic and foreign private investment, private equity and mutual funds.

Individual Clients: SRZ's Client Services Department is one of the most sophisticated, extensive and diverse of any major law firm. The firm represents many of the wealthiest individuals in the country on tax planning, successor planning, charitable giving, will contests and family law matters, including mediation of large divorce matters.

SCHULTE ROTH & ZABEL LLP

SEWARD & KISSEL LLP

THE FIRM

Managing Partner: John E Tavss

Number of partners: 33
Number of other lawyers: 101

AREAS OF PRACTICE:
Investment Management 25%
Corporate Finance & Capital Markets 20%
Litigation 20%
Structured Finance & Asset Securitization 15%
Maritime 10%
Real Estate 5%
Tax, Employee Benefits, Trusts & Estates 5%

FIRM OVERVIEW: Seward & Kissel is a New York based law firm (with an office in Washington, DC) that offers sophisticated legal advice in the areas of business, financial and commercial law and litigation, as well as a number of specialized fields of law. Originally established in 1890, the firm combines its tradition of superior service with innovative and creative approaches that help clients achieve their goals.

MAIN AREAS OF PRACTICE:

Investment Management: Regularly cited as one of the leading legal advisers to the private investment fund industry, Seward & Kissel is recognized both nationally and internationally for its work in the hedge fund area. The firm also is well known for its work representing a wide range of registered investment companies and their advisers.

Corporate Finance & Capital Markets: Attorneys in Seward & Kissel's Corporate Finance and Capital Markets Group combine their skills as transactional lawyers with a comprehensive knowledge of relevant regulatory and business issues affecting clients to address a broad range of matters, including: equity and debt offerings; workouts, restructurings and distressed debt transactions; mergers and acquisitions; and new product and financial derivative transactions.

Structured Finance & Asset Securitization: The firm's Corporate Finance and Securitization Group has considerable experience representing clients in connection with a full range of financings, including both secured and unsecured, committed and discretionary commercial credit facilities, and asset-based and cash flow transactions. The firm represents many types of financial institutions, including domestic and international banks, trust companies, insurance companies, broker-dealers and investment banks.

Maritime: Internationally recognized as the leading legal advisors to the shipping industry, the firm advises many of the world's most prominent ship finance institutions, including international commercial banks, investment banks, and providers of subordinated and equity financing. The firm is involved in all aspects of the financing of ships, offshore oil rigs, barges, shipping containers and other marine equipment. In addition, the firm offers guidance in secured lending, equipment leasing, public and private debt and equity offerings, acquisition financing, debt for equity swaps and the issuance of securities backed by maritime assets representing major public and private shipping companies, lenders and investors.

Litigation: The firm represents major domestic and foreign financial institutions (including banks, broker-dealers and investment management firms) and individual clients in courts, administrative tribunals and arbitrations throughout the world, specializing in the following areas: securities related litigation; commercial disputes; employment matters; insurance; maritime; trademark; and bankruptcy and workout matters. The firm is particularly well known for its work advising clients on employment related matters and securities related litigation.

HEAD OFFICE

NEW YORK
One Battery Park Plaza, **New York**, NY 10004
Tel: 212 574 1200   **Fax:** 212 480 8421
Email: sknyc@sewkis.com
Website: www.sewkis.com

BRANCH OFFICE

DISTRICT OF COLUMBIA
1200 G Street, N.W., Suite 350, **Washington,** DC 20005
Tel: 202 737 8833   **Fax:** 202 737 5184
Email: sknyc@sewkis.com

CONTACTS

Corporate Finance & Capital Markets	James H Hancock
Employee Benefits	S John Ryan
Investment Management	John E Tavss
Structured Finance & Asset Securitization	Kalyan Das
Litigation	M.William Munno
Maritime	Lawrence Rutkowski, Gary Wolfe
Real Estate	Mark A Brody
Tax & Employee Benefits	Peter E Pront
Trusts & Estates	Hume R Steyer
Washington DC Office	Paul T Clark

Real Estate: Seward & Kissel advises real estate owners, developers, lenders and institutional investors involved with commercial and residential facilities and mixed-use projects throughout the United States. Helping major public pension funds and other institutions to structure and implement their real estate investments is a particular strength for the Real Estate Group.

Tax, Employee Benefits, & Trusts & Estates: The firm's Tax and Employee Benefit Group counsels clients from a broad range of industries on a variety of issues including tax and employee considerations relevant to structuring complex securities and financing transactions, issues relating to financial products including pooled investment funds and with regard to real estate matters. The firm also advises individual clients with planning to preserve and build wealth for future generations and achieve philanthropic objectives.

SEWARD & KISSEL LLP

SHEARMAN & STERLING LLP

THE FIRM

Senior Partner: David Heleniak
Co-Managing Partners: John Madden and Georg Thoma
Numbers of partners worldwide: 226
Number of lawyers worldwide: 1,053

FIRM OVERVIEW: Shearman & Sterling is a global elite law firm with more than 1,000 attorneys in 19 offices around the world. More than one-third of Shearman's attorneys practice outside the United States, and its lawyers are fluent in over 30 languages. Founded in 1873, Shearman is one of the few genuinely integrated global firms that provides seamless legal expertise across jurisdictions, industries and practice areas. The firm's lawyers practice US, English, French, German and EU law.

MAIN AREAS OF PRACTICE: Antitrust/competition, bank finance, bankruptcy and reorganization, capital markets, corporate governance, environmental, executive compensation and employee benefits, intellectual property, international arbitration, international trade and government relations, investment funds and asset management, litigation, mergers and acquisitions, outsourcing, privatization, project development and finance, property and tax.

Antitrust/Competition: The global strength of Shearman's Antitrust Practice is exemplified by the firm's recent representation of Eurex US in its successful application for recognition as an overseas investment exchange – the first of its kind under the Financial Services and Markets Act 2000. Shearman advises clients on a broad spectrum of antitrust issues, including US jurisdiction over activities abroad.

Bank Finance: The complex refinancing of Levi Strauss' $1.15 billion in outstanding debt is illustrative of Shearman's capabilities in global bank finance. The firm represents a wide range of clients in leveraged buyouts and recapitalizations; 'jumbo' acquisition, high-yield bridge, mezzanine, letter of credit and debtor-in-possession financings; complex debt restructurings; and secured lending and investment grade loans.

Bankruptcy/Restructuring: Shearman has a long history of involvement in US and international restructurings and bankruptcies, advising many of the world's leading financial institutions, corporations and individuals. The firm has played a prominent role in restructurings and insolvencies in both the traditional and emerging commercial centers around the world.

Capital Markets: Shearman has a formidable Global Capital Markets Practice, which includes former directors and other senior officials of the SEC's Division of Corporation Finance. The firm has extensive experience in representing issuers and underwriters in a wide range of transactions, including public and private securities offerings, liability management transactions, structured products and hybrid securities, and securities law and corporate governance.

Executive Compensation & Employee Benefits: Shearman regularly advises clients in employee-related aspects of domestic and cross-border merger and acquisition transactions. The firm's expertise in corporate, tax, securities, employment law and ERISA issues affecting ECEB is supplemented by top-tier attorneys who negotiate and implement sophisticated equity-based incentive plans, advise on issues raised in initial public offerings and design investment partnerships and co-investment vehicles for venture capital and other entities.

Investment Funds & Asset Management: Acting as regular counsel to some of the world's largest fund complexes and investment advisory organizations, Shearman represents investment companies and advisors, private domestic funds, offshore investment funds, broker-dealers, commodity pool operators, commodity trading advisors and futures commission merchants.

Litigation/International Arbitration: Shearman represents clients in major commercial, regulatory and enforcement disputes and in sensitive internal and external investigations. Shearman is a global leader in international arbitration, where it has represented clients in proceedings throughout the world and under more than 45 governing laws. The firm has also expanded its intellectual property practice to assist clients in protecting their IP assets.

Mergers & Acquisitions: Shearman is consistently ranked as a global leader in M&A in an array of transactions, including financial advisories, acquisitions, divestitures, joint ventures, strategic alliances and minority investments. The firm recently represented Ispat International NV in two major M&A transactions valued at over $24 billion. The company formed as a result of these mergers, Mittal Steel, will be the largest steel company in the world.

Project Development & Finance: With attorneys located throughout the firm's worldwide network, Shearman's PD&F Group offers US, English, French and German law capabilities in project transactions and is recognized as one of the world's leading practices. The firm's project attorneys have solid backgrounds in sovereign and project restructurings, political risk insurance and other novel split-risk arrangements, as well as experience with export credit agencies and multilateral lending institutions.

Property: Shearman's Property Group includes one of the most experienced full-service real estate practices in the world and a multinational group of attorneys dedicated to environmental counseling and litigation. The firm is active in areas such as financings, acquisitions, dispositions, development, joint ventures and leasing representing lenders, borrowers, sellers, buyers, developers, investors, general partners and limited partners.

Tax: Shearman's Tax Group plays an integral role in the firm's cross-border practice. The firm provides international strategic tax planning advice and representation on a diverse variety of complex transactions including cross-border mergers and acquisitions, spin-offs and mergers, equity and debt financings of domestic and foreign issuers, restructurings and public and private real estate transactions.

US OFFICES

NEW YORK
599 Lexington Avenue, **New York**, NY 10022-6069
Tel: 212 848 4000 **Fax:** 212 848 7179

CALIFORNIA
1080 Marsh Road, **Menlo Park**, CA 94025-1022
Tel: 650 838 3600 **Fax:** 650 838 3699

525 Market Street, Suite 2000, **San Francisco**, CA 94104-1522
Tel: 415 616 1100 **Fax:** 415 616 1199

DISTRICT OF COLUMBIA
801 Pennsylvania Avenue, N.W., **Washington**, DC 20004-2604
Tel: 202 508 8000 **Fax:** 202 508 8100

INTERNATIONAL OFFICES

Abu Dhabi, Beijing, Brussels, Düsseldorf, Frankfurt, Hong Kong, London, Mannheim, Munich, Paris, Rome, São Paulo, Singapore, Tokyo and Toronto.

SIMPSON THACHER & BARTLETT LLP

THE FIRM

Chairman, Executive Committee: Phillip T Ruegger
Administrative Partners: George R Krouse, Gary I Horowitz

Number of partners in US: 144
Number of other lawyers in US: 500

FIRM OVERVIEW: The firm was established in 1884 and currently has approximately 700 lawyers worldwide, including 157 partners. Through its New York City headquarters, the firm provides coordinated legal advice and transactional capability in the world's principal international financial centers, including London, Hong Kong and Tokyo. The firm also maintains offices in Los Angeles and Palo Alto, CA.

MAIN AREAS OF PRACTICE:

Banking & Finance: The practice has particular experience in syndicated lending and acquisition finance, with JPMorgan and its affiliates among its principal clients. The practice is increasingly representing borrowers throughout Europe, Latin America and Asia. The firm is involved in financial institution mergers and acquisitions, as well as in the interpretation and application of laws and regulations governing consolidation and convergence in the financial sector.

M&A: The firm acts for purchasers, sellers, lenders and financial advisors and is experienced in LBOs, stock and asset purchases, mergers, restructurings, spin-offs, joint ventures and contested transactions. Recent notable work includes: representation of J.P. Morgan Chase in its $58 billion merger with Bank One Corporation; Kmart Corporation in its $11 billion merger with Sears Roebuck & Co.; Adolph Coors in its $6 billion acquisition of Molson Inc.; Kohlberg Kravis Roberts in its acquisition of PanAmSat and The Blackstone Group in its acquisitions of Celanese AG.

Capital Markets & Securities: The firm advises issuers and underwriters in IPOs, high yield debt offerings and derivative and complex instruments for both domestic and international clients, with Lehman Brothers among its principal clients. In 2004, the firm represented Assurant, Inc. in one of the largest IPOs of the year. The firm also represented the underwriters in the Google and Dreamworks IPOs, two of the most high profile deals of the year. STB has represented borrowers and lenders in many of the largest multi-billion dollar syndicated credit facilities and high-yield offerings, including in connection with the Celanese and Sealy private equity backed transactions. The firm has also recently acted as underwriters' counsel in major offerings by Invensys, KfW, Owens-Brockway Glass and Wal-Mart.

Litigation: The Litigation Practice encompasses every type of complex litigation - trials and appeals - including antitrust, insurance and reinsurance, intellectual property matters, product liability, securities, mergers and acquisitions, labor and employment, and other commercial litigation for US and non-US clients. Most recently, the firm successfully represented Swiss Re in a three month jury trial concerning an insurance company dispute arising out of the September 11 World Trade Center attack.

Real Estate: The firm has one of the most sophisticated real estate practices among major US law firms. STB's practice is international in scope and spans all areas of the real estate industry, including real estate finance, sales and acquisitions, mergers and acquisitions, real estate development, leasing, synthetic leasing, joint ventures and partnerships.

Tax: The firm's Tax Practice is expert and diverse; principal tax clients are corporations and financial services institutions. STB's tax lawyers play a major role in the structuring and tax planning aspects of mergers and acquisitions, financing and capital markets transactions.

HEAD OFFICE

NEW YORK
425 Lexington Avenue, **New York**, NY 10017
Tel: 212 455 2000 **Fax:** 212 455 2502
Website: www.simpsonthacher.com

BRANCH OFFICES

CALIFORNIA
1999 Avenue of the Stars, 29th Floor, **Los Angeles**, CA 90067
Tel: 310 407 7500 **Fax:** 310 407 7502

3330 Hillview Avenue, **Palo Alto**, CA 94304-1204
Tel: 650 251 5000 **Fax:** 650 251 5002

INTERNATIONAL OFFICES

The firm also has offices in London, Hong Kong and Tokyo.

CONTACTS

Corporate	Philip T Ruegger
Banking	L Francis Huck
Capital Markets	George R Krouse, Vince Pagano, John Tehan
M&A	Charles I Cogut
Litigation	Barry R Ostrager, Charles E Koob
Insurance	Barry R Ostrager, MaryKay Vyskocil
Intellectual Property	Hank Gutman
Tax	Steven C Todrys
Executive Compensation	Kenneth C Edgar
Real Estate	Gregory J Ressa
Exempt Organizations	Victoria B Bjorklund
Personal Planning	Mildred Kalik

Executive Compensation: This practice group specializes in the planning, drafting, negotiation and compliance aspects of compensation of employees at all income levels, with emphasis on handling complex executive compensation plans and employment contracts; and all types of employee benefit plans, including retirement, profit-sharing, medical, severance and disability arrangements.

Personal Planning: The firm counsels clients regarding gift, estate, and generation-skipping transfer taxes; complex estate and trust planning and administration; wealth preservation across generations.

CLIENTS: Accenture, ACE, American Electric Power, AIG, The Blackstone Group, B.A.T. Industries plc, Doctors Without Borders, Deutsche Bank, Duke Energy, GE Capital, H.J. Heinz, JPMorgan Chase & Co. and its affiliates, Kmart Corporation, Kohlberg Kravis Roberts & Co., Lehman Brothers, Northwest Airlines, Ripplewood Holdings, St. Paul Travelers, Swiss Re, Virgin, Wachovia, Warner Music Group, Wyeth.

INTERNATIONAL WORK: International finance and capital markets, mergers and acquisitions, banking, sovereign finance and privatization, asset based and specialized financing, litigation and arbitration, tax and real estate are important aspects of the firm's international practice. The firm's three foreign offices coordinate with one another to provide a truly global capability for local clients as well as clients of the firm based elsewhere in the world.

SIMPSON THACHER & BARTLETT LLP

SIVE, PAGET & RIESEL, P.C.

THE FIRM

Founding Partner: David Sive

Number of partners: 8
Number of other lawyers: 11

FIRM OVERVIEW: Since its inception in 1962, Sive, Paget & Riesel, P.C. has focused on environmental law and litigation. It has been instrumental in the formulation of many important precedents now comprising the body of environmental law. Today, the firm's extensive experience allows it to bring comprehensive cost effective solutions to emerging development, business, real estate, and litigation problems that involve almost all aspects of environmental law.

Environmental Law Network: The firm is a member of the Environmental Law Network, consisting of 18 affiliated environmental law firms throughout the United States.

MAIN AREAS OF PRACTICE:

General Environmental: Sive, Paget & Riesel, P.C. solves environmental problems in a broad array of different economic and enforcement situations. Its professional work ranges from advice on future development to the defense of criminal enforcement actions. A significant aspect of the firm's practice involves facilitating, financial, and real estate transactions including the performance of due diligence, negotiations of environmental provisions in contractual documents, and obtaining appropriate insurance coverage. The firm is also engaged in Superfund and Brownfield remediations, development of housing, electrical generating facilities, shopping centers and public infrastructure. The firm also represents industrial facilities seeking to obtain or renew air, water and hazardous waste permits. The firm provides advice to its institutional clients on their environmental compliance programs, analysing the company's ability to meet present and ongoing environmental regulations. The firm's Environmental Litigation Practice involves all of the above described aspects of environmental law.

Development & Land Use: Large-scale development now faces a myriad of regulatory hurdles, which range from complex environmental impact studies to the remediation of hazardous waste. Often these issues become enmeshed in political disputes that further obstruct development. The firm evaluates the requirements for development and guides clients through this process by utilizing its knowledge to plot a time sensitive course of action insuring that the project successfully emerges from the process in the minimum period of time with a record that will withstand litigation.

Environmental Litigation: The firm is engaged in extensive environmental litigation, which ranges from cost recovery actions under CERCLA to the defense of Toxic Tort actions. The firm is often called upon to litigate contract disputes involving environmental liabilities. The firm has been active in litigating decisions made by state and federal regulatory agencies. The firm is also frequently called upon to defend local governments' land use and environmental actions. Usually, the attorney handling the administrative process is the attorney that is fully prepared to litigate any judicial challenge.

HEAD OFFICE

NEW YORK
460 Park Avenue, 10th Floor, **New York**, NY 10022
Tel: 212 421 2150   **Fax:** 212 421 1891
Email: sprlaw@sprlaw.com
Website: www.sprlaw.com

CONTACTS

Project Development	David Paget
Environmental Enforcement & Litigation	Daniel Riesel
Brownfield Remeidation	Mark Chertok

Hazardous & Solid Waste: The firm's practice involves development and enforcement problems arising from hazardous and solid waste. The firm has developed approaches and techniques to minimize the costs and time involved in the remediation of hazardous waste sites. It has also been active in the reduction, transfer and treatment of solid waste, often representing municipalities as well as private parties.

General Litigation: The firm has a robust Civil Litigation Practice and represents matters ranging from employment issues to construction disputes. It has also developed a speciality in representing not for profit organizations, and academic institutions.

CLIENTS: Paget & Riesel, P.C. represents a unique range of clients. In addition to a broad array of corporate development and manufacturing clients, it has and continues to represent government agencies ranging from small townships to state agencies and the Commonwealth of Puerto Rico. It represents domestic and international clients in environmental litigation, and in administrative matters involving large-scale development within the Metropolitan area.

INTERNATIONAL WORK: Sive, Paget & Riesel, P.C.'s extensive experience in representing the interest of the regulated community allows the firm to represent both domestic and international clients with respect to existing and major environmental problems in the United States.

SKADDEN, ARPS, SLATE, MEAGHER & FLOM LLP & AFFILIATES

THE FIRM

Executive Partner: Robert C Sheehan
Senior Partner: Joseph H Flom

Number of US partners: 341
Number of other US lawyers: 1,200

FIRM OVERVIEW: With approximately 1,700 attorneys in 22 offices, Skadden, Arps, Slate, Meagher & Flom LLP and Affiliates is one of the largest and most highly respected law firms in the world. The firm provides a wide array of legal services globally to the corporate, financial, industrial and governmental communities.

MAIN AREAS OF PRACTICE

Corporate/M&A: Skadden has consistently ranked first among law firms in the US for handling the greatest number of the largest M&A transactions announced annually, and has been involved in many of the largest transactions ever. The firm's clients range from start-ups and middle-market companies, to the largest of the *Fortune* 250. Transactions include recapitalizations and restructurings, including spin-offs, divestitures and other techniques for maximizing value for the client.

Corporate Restructuring: The firm's Corporate Restructuring Group serves corporations and their principal creditors and investors by providing upper margin, value-added legal solutions to troubled company merger and acquisition, financial and restructuring situations. The firm has advised on some of the most widely publicized corporate restructurings recently announced or pending, including several of the largest Chapter 11 cases in US history. The firm also has a substantial practice in advising clients on non-judicial restructurings.

Litigation: Skadden represents clients in federal and state trial and appellate courts nationwide, and has developed a premier securities class action defense practice. The firm's work on antitrust matters includes counseling and litigating for clients in connection with mergers, acquisitions and joint ventures. The firm assists clients in resolving disputes without litigation by using various alternative dispute resolution procedures, including arbitration, mediation, conciliation, and mini-trials, and has represented US and non-US clients in arbitrations under all major rules systems and before every major arbitral institution worldwide.

Banking & Finance: Skadden advises underwriters, issuers and purchasers in public and private financings. It advises on all types of debt and equity instruments; structured finance; public finance; lease and project financings; commodities and futures and derivative products. The firm's clients include investment companies; advisors and broker-dealers; and private investment funds.

Industry-related Practices: The firm has a number of industry-related practice areas, including banking and financial services, communications, energy, healthcare, information technology, insurance, real estate and utilities.

HEAD OFFICE

NEW YORK
Four Times Square, **New York**, NY 10036
Tel: 212 735 3000   **Fax:** 212 735 2000
Website: www.skadden.com

BRANCH OFFICES

CALIFORNIA
300 South Grand Avenue, **Los Angeles**, CA 90071
Tel: 213 687 5000   **Fax:** 213 687 5600

525 University Avenue, Suite 1100, **Palo Alto**, CA 94301
Tel: 650 470 4500   **Fax:** 650 470 4570

Four Embarcadero Center, **San Francisco**, CA 94111
Tel: 415 984 6400   **Fax:** 415 984 2698

DELAWARE
One Rodney Square, **Wilmington**, DE 19801
Tel: 302 651 3000   **Fax:** 302 651 3001

DISTRICT OF COLUMBIA
1440 New York Avenue, NW, **Washington**, DC 20005
Tel: 202 371 7000   **Fax:** 202 393 5760

ILLINOIS
333 West Wacker Drive, **Chicago**, IL 60606
Tel: 312 407 0700   **Fax:** 312 407 0411

MASSACHUSETTS
One Beacon Street, **Boston**, MA 02108
Tel: 617 573 4800   **Fax:** 617 573 4822

TEXAS
1600 Smith Street, Suite 4400, **Houston**, TX 77002
Tel: 713 655 5100   **Fax:** 713 655 5200

CLIENTS: The firm represents a broad spectrum of clients, from small high-technology start-up companies to nearly half of the *Fortune* 250 industrial and service corporations in the US.

INTERNATIONAL WORK: Skadden's offices in Beijing, Brussels, Frankfurt, Hong Kong, London, Moscow, Munich, Paris, Singapore, Sydney, Tokyo, Toronto and Vienna, in addition to substantial practices in Latin America, the Middle East and Africa, enable the firm to offer clients an integrated cross-border service. Main international practices include corporate transactions such as mergers and acquisitions, privatizations, joint ventures, project financings, international trade matters, litigation, capital markets, banking and finance transactions, and tax matters. The firm also has an alliance with Chiomenti Studio Legale, one of the premier corporate firms in Italy.

Skadden, Arps, Slate, Meagher & Flom LLP
& Affiliates

SULLIVAN & CROMWELL LLP

THE FIRM

Chairman: H Rodgin Cohen

Number of partners worldwide: 156
Number of other lawyers worldwide: 483

FIRM OVERVIEW: Founded in 1879, Sullivan & Cromwell comprises approximately 650 lawyers conducting a global practice through a network of 12 offices on four continents. The firm's organization as a single, unified partnership worldwide, combined with its reliance primarily on internally generated growth, has contributed to its reputation for providing consistently high quality legal services.

MAIN AREAS OF PRACTICE:

Capital Markets: Each year, Sullivan & Cromwell advises principals or their financial advisors in hundreds of securities transactions by a variety of issuers: large and first-time, US and international, commercial and governmental. The firm is a leader in SEC-registered and exempt offerings by both US and non-US issuers and is known for innovative work on the largest and most complex offerings worldwide, including offerings in the high-yield market.

Litigation: Sullivan & Cromwell's Litigation Group regularly represents industrial corporations, financial institutions and individual clients before state and federal courts throughout the US. Anti-trust, EC competition and international commercial arbitration matters comprise a significant component of the overall litigation practice.

M&A: Sullivan & Cromwell has advised on some of the largest US mergers and acquisitions as well as on cross-border and domestic transactions in major domestic markets in Europe and Asia.

Financial Institutions: The firm's Financial Institutions Practice encompasses M&A, the development of new products and services, regulatory matters, credit activities and litigation and enforcement matters for US and international banks, insurance companies and investment management firms.

E-business & Technology: Sullivan & Cromwell has established itself as a major player in advising e-business and technology enterprises, at all stages of their development and growth. Its e-business and Technology Group focuses on the strategic opportunities and issues that challenge clients in this sector.

Estates & Personal: The firm has an extremely active national and international Private Clients Practice. The scope of services provided includes estate planning, tax planning, litigation, the creation and administration of small businesses, charitable activities and a broad range of personal matters.

Real Estate: The firm advises on the purchase, sale, construction, financing, and securitisation of real estate assets worldwide. Clients include investors, developers, lenders and investment bankers.

Project Finance: Sullivan & Cromwell is counsel to sponsors of, and lenders to, world-class projects in developed and emerging markets. The practice is well diversified by industry, including oil and gas, mining, infrastructure development, telecommunications and power.

Tax: The firm's Tax Group plays a leading role in structuring new, tax-advantaged financial instruments and complex M&A transactions, and represents prominent industrial and commercial enterprises worldwide in both US and cross-border tax matters.

Private Equity: Drawing on the strength of its leading finance and M&A practices, Sullivan & Cromwell's private equity group advises on private equity M&A and strategic investments, capital markets exits from those investments, and the organisation and structure of private equity funds.

HEAD OFFICE

NEW YORK
125 Broad Street, **New York** NY 10004-2498
Tel: 212 558 4000   **Fax:** 212 558 3588
Email: osbornc@sullcrom.com
Website: www.sullcrom.com

BRANCH OFFICES

CALIFORNIA
1888 Century Park East, **Los Angeles** CA 90067-1725
Tel: 310 712 6600   **Fax:** 310 712 8800
Email: sacksr@sullcrom.com

1870 Embarcadero Road, **Palo Alto** CA 94303-3308
Tel: 650 461 5600   **Fax:** 650 461 5700
Email: millersc@sullcrom.com

DISTRICT OF COLUMBIA
1701 Pennsylvania Avenue, NW, **Washington** DC 20006-5805
Tel: 202 956 7500 **Fax:** 202 293 6330
Email: craftr@sullcrom.com

INTERNATIONAL OFFICES

London, Paris, Frankfurt am Main, Tokyo, Hong Kong, Beijing, Melbourne, Sydney.

CLIENTS: Sullivan & Cromwell serves it clients by providing the highest quality legal advice and representation. For well over a century, the hallmarks of the firm's approach to practice have been the single-minded pursuit of the client's best interests, highly responsive client service, and legal advice grounded in a sophisticated understanding of the relevant business context or market. Dedication to these principles, together with a long track record of successfully completed cases and transactions, has allowed the firm to maintain close and longstanding relationships with some of the world's most important enterprises.

Geographically, approximately half of the firm's clients are US-based; non-US clients come from Canada, Europe, Asia, Australasia, Latin America, Africa and the Middle East. The firm provides legal advice and services to industrial and commercial clients; financial institutions, including commercial banks, insurance companies, investment banks and investment companies; governments and governmental bodies; individuals; and estates and trusts.

INTERNATIONAL WORK: Sullivan & Cromwell has long played a leading role in global privatisation transactions; the expanding access by non-US enterprises to US capital markets; cross-border mergers and acquisitions; the integration of financial services; cross-border litigation and cross-border competition law matters; the evolution of the e-business and technology industry; and project and structured finance for developed and emerging markets.

SULLIVAN & CROMWELL LLP

THACHER PROFFITT & WOOD LLP

THE FIRM

Managing Partner: Paul D Tvetenstrand
Executive Committee: Thomas M Leslie, Robert E McCarthy, Douglas J McClintock, Stephen T Whelan, Anthony S Cassino (Executive Director)

Number of US partners: 56
Number of other US lawyers: 159

FIRM OVERVIEW: For more than 150 years, Thacher Proffitt has led the way in creating and implementing innovative, workable solutions that bring finance and business together. The firm's strong focus and deep experience, combined with its relationships with major financial institutions help investors and principals worldwide put capital to work.
Thacher Proffitt represents financial institutions, investors and corporations throughout the US, Latin America and Europe. While it has experience in numerous industries, the firm is known for its strength and particular expertise in financial services, structured finance, banking, insurance, maritime, automotive, aviation, construction, consumer products, energy and utilities, food and beverage, government, manufacturing, media, pharmaceutical, professional services, real estate, retail, technology, telecommunications, and transportation.

MAIN AREAS OF PRACTICE:

Corporate & Financial Institutions: Banking, corporate finance, securities, regulatory compliance, mergers and acquisitions, employment, compensation and benefits, and ERISA.
Litigation & Dispute Resolution: Alternative dispute resolution, arbitration, bankruptcy and creditors' rights, complex commercial litigation, insurance and reinsurance, maritime and admiralty, real estate litigation, and technology and intellectual property.
Real Estate: Commercial real estate finance/asset backed finance; federal and state regulation of real estate; leasing; loan sales, syndication and servicing; mezzanine financing; and mortgage securitization.
Structured Finance: Asset backed securitization; financing of financial assets; global securitization and finance; leasing and lease securitization; purchase, sale and servicing of financial assets; regulatory compliance; and residential and commercial mortgage securitization.
Tax: Public and private offerings of debt and equity, including financial instruments issued by REMICs, FASITs, REITs, qualified REIT subsidiaries, domestic special purpose entities and offshore special purpose entities; mergers and acquisitions; partnerships and limited liability companies, real estate transactions, bankruptcy and creditors' rights, cross-border leasing, equipment finance, state, local and international taxation.
Trusts & Estates: Estate planning and administration, charitable giving planning, gift and estate tax, trust administration, and will and trust preparation.
Technology & Intellectual Property: Intellectual property registration, licensing and protection; internet domain names; trademark and service mark registration, licensing and protection.

HEAD OFFICE

NEW YORK
Two World financial Center, **New York** NY 10281
Tel: 212 912 7400   **Fax:** 212 912 7751
Website: www.tpw.com

BRANCH OFFICES

NEW JERSEY
25 DeForest Avenue, **Summitt**, NJ 07901
Tel: 908 598 5700   **Fax:** 908 598 5710

NEW YORK
50 Main Street, **White Plains**, NY 10606
Tel: 914 421 4100   **Fax:** 914 421 4150

DISTRICT OF COLUMBIA
1700 Pennsylvania Avenue, NW, Suite 800 **Washington** DC 20006
Tel: 202 347 8400   **Fax:** 202 626 1930

INTERNATIONAL OFFICES

The firm also has an office in Mexico

INTERNATIONAL WORK: The firm's International Practice Group, comprised of lawyers from all offices, has assisted clients in virtually every business center worldwide. From Brazil to The Netherlands, Germany to Australia, China to Mexico, and Japan to Kazakhstan, the firm completes the most complex deals and resolves the most difficult commercial disputes. International clients call upon them to handle the structural, regulatory and tax aspects of their transactions, as well as to negotiate and implement joint ventures, mergers and acquisitions, equity and debt offerings, securitized financings, project finance, government procurement bid processes, privatizations, commercial real estate financings, cross-border financing, leasing transactions and shipping matters. Thacher Proffitt & Wood LLP lawyers also manage precedent-setting commercial arbitration and litigation throughout the world. They are known for their ability to offer practical and creative business solutions no matter where an issue arises.

Latin America: Bankruptcy and workouts; corporate and securities; energy; labor and employment; litigation and arbitration; and securitization.

Thacher Proffitt & Wood LLP

WACHTELL, LIPTON, ROSEN & KATZ

THE FIRM

Managing Partner: Daniel A Neff
Number of partners worldwide: 75
Number of other lawyers worldwide: 120

HEAD OFFICE

NEW YORK
51 West 52nd Street, **New York**, NY 10019
Tel: 212 403 1000 **Fax:** 212 403 2000
Email: info@wlrk.com **Website:** www.wlrk.com

FIRM OVERVIEW: Founded in 1965, Wachtell, Lipton, Rosen & Katz is one of the most prominent business law firms in the US. The firm specializes in merger and acquisition transactions, sensitive litigation matters, advice on corporate governance and related matters, and corporate restructurings. Comprising 195 lawyers, the leanly staffed firm handles demanding, high profile transactions and advisory matters on an extremely personalized basis. The relatively concentrated nature of the practice, together with and in addition to the absence of repetitive, standardized transactions, means that the firm's lawyers each have a broad range of skills and experience. Clients include enterprises of virtually every nature, including industrial firms, financial institutions, securities firms, healthcare providers, technology companies, and news and information systems companies, including many Fortune 500 companies and other leading enterprises.

MAIN AREAS OF PRACTICE:

Corporate: The firm has handled some of the largest and most complex US and international transactions. It advises on a range of corporate matters including mergers and acquisitions, public offerings, financial products, and financing transactions. Wachtell Lipton also counsels companies, and their boards of directors, on corporate disclosure, governance and policy issues, and served as counsel to the New York Stock Exchange in connection with the revision of the New York Stock Exchange's listing standards. Wachtell Lipton is consistently in the very top rank of legal advisors by transaction dollar volume. Since the beginning of the year 2000, Wachtell Lipton has been the legal advisor on six of the top 10 transactions in the United States, and five of the top 10 transactions globally, as well as numerous other acquisition and restructuring transactions across many industries and of virtually every description. The firm has represented many of the world's leading companies in important transactions, including Wal-Mart, AT&T, Cardinal Health, and ConocoPhillips. Recent transactions handled by Wachtell Lipton include AT&T Wireless in its sale to Cingular; Constellation Brands in its acquisition of Robert Mondavi; AT&T in its pending sale to SBC; Sanofi in its merger with Aventis; Cole National in its sale to Luxottica; Vulcan Materials Company in the sale of its chemicals division to Occidental Petroleum; Valero in its purchase of Kaneb Partners; and Cardinal Health in its acquisitions of Syncor International and The Intercare Group. In addition, Wachtell Lipton has represented the buyer or the seller in most of the largest bank mergers in US history, including FleetBoston Financial Corporation in its merger with Bank of America and Bank One in its merger with J.P. Morgan Chase.

Litigation: Wachtell Lipton handles a wide variety of high profile, complex litigation for major corporations and leading financial institutions. Work undertaken includes precedent-setting securities and corporate governance litigation, representation of corporations in highly sensitive criminal and regulatory investigations, and libel and First Amendment cases. The firm has been involved in landmark corporate governance litigation cases in Delaware, including the Household, Revlon, Newmont Mining, Macmillan, Interco, Time Warner, Paramount cases and Omnicare. The firm is representing Silverstein Properties, the 99-year lessee of the World Trade Center, in connection with the September 11, 2001 collapses of the Twin Towers and with the redevelopment of the World Trade Center. Following a jury trial in 2004, the firm obtained a verdict in Silverstein's favor that what happened on September 11 constituted two 'occurrences' for property insurance purposes with respect to $1.1 billion of Silverstein's coverage. The firm is representing Bank of America and subsidiaries in connection with regulatory investigations and civil litigation arising out of alleged market timing in mutual funds. The firm represents The Walt Disney Company in litigation brought by Roy E Disney arising from the latter's solicitation of 'withhold' votes at the 2004 annual meeting; and IAC/InterActiveCorp in its effort to recover tax distributions in connection with the 2002 transaction that created Vivendi Universal Entertainment, LLLP. The firm represents insurance companies and other defendants faced with asbestos and other mass tort liabilities. The firm has defended major securities firms, financial institutions, retailers, software manufacturers, healthcare providers, news and information systems companies, and a variety of other companies in enforcement proceedings and class actions. These matters typically involve questions of corporate governance, complex accounting issues, sensitive public and investor relations problems, and significant interaction with senior state and federal law enforcement officials.

Bankruptcy & Creditors' Rights: The firm's bankruptcy and creditors' rights practice represents buyers, investors, lenders, and creditors in national and multinational bankruptcy cases and out-of-court debt restructurings. Its lawyers regularly work with the firm's corporate group in handling complicated acquisitions and divestitures of businesses in financial distress, highly leveraged transactions, and major transactions involving significant creditors' rights issues. Recent restructuring work has included representing AT&T and Cable and Wireless in connection with troubled subsidiaries; representing the acquirer of bankrupt retailer Kmart and the Colombian-based airline Avianca; representing the official creditors committee of PSINet; and representing bank and bondholder groups (or other significant creditors) in the restructurings of Intermet Corporation, Calpine Corporation, Footstar, Inc., HealthSouth, Rand McNally, Trump Hotels & Casino Resorts, Inc., Spalding/Top-Flite, Allegheny Energy, Pacific Gas and Electric, Budget Rent-a-Car, World Kitchen, National Century Financial Enterprises, Independent Wireless One, Sunbeam, Exide Technologies, 360networks, Fruit of the Loom, Regal Cinemas, and many other companies. The group's lawyers also have significant expertise in asbestos matters, D&O liability issues and in the defense of bankruptcy-related litigation, such as fraudulent transfer litigation and litigation against control persons of bankrupt entities.

Antitrust: Wachtell Lipton's antitrust practice focuses on mergers and acquisitions, government investigations, international antitrust, and banking antitrust issues. Wachtell Lipton analyzes transactions to determine whether they raise antitrust issues, develops strategies to address those issues, and represents clients before enforcement officials in the United States, including the US Department of Justice, the Federal Trade Commission, the Board of Governors of the Federal Reserve System and state attorneys general, and in antitrust litigation challenging transactions. Wachtell Lipton is active on matters involving foreign antitrust enforcement authorities, frequently serving as worldwide lead antitrust counsel and participating with local counsel in proceedings and investigations in the European Union, Canada, Australia, Mexico, and many other jurisdictions.

Tax: The firm's tax practice centers around US and international tax and structural aspects of complex merger and acquisition transactions, divestitures, restructurings, and spin-offs. The firm's tax group is also involved in structuring complicated financing arrangements and financial instruments.

Employment & Benefits: The firm's executive compensation and employee benefits practice focuses primarily on compensation and benefit issues in connection with mergers and acquisitions and other

WACHTELL, LIPTON, ROSEN & KATZ cont'd

corporate transactions, and for executive officers of major corporations and financial institutions. Wachtell Lipton also advises clients about a wide variety of ongoing executive compensation issues, including key executive employment contracts, equity compensation plans, deferred compensation arrangements and compliance with evolving corporate governance standards.

Real Estate: Wachtell Lipton has a preeminent real estate M&A practice, focusing on strategic real estate transactions, mergers and acquisitions of REITs and other real estate companies, major development projects and joint ventures, structuring real estate opportunity funds, acquisitions and dispositions of significant assets and asset portfolios, innovative capital markets transactions, and restructurings. Recent or ongoing matters include the representation of Silverstein Properties, the 99-year lessee of the World Trade Center, in connection with the redevelopment of the World Trade Center; Tishman Speyer in an Australian LPT initial public offering and a related acquisition and restructuring of a major US office portfolio; Taubman Centers in its successful defense against Simon Property Group's unsolicited offer; Lend Lease in the sale of many of its US businesses; Hometown America in its acquisition of the Chateau Communities REIT; Tishman Speyer in the acquisition and/or recapitalization of the Chrysler Building, 666 Third Avenue, 300 Park Avenue, MGM Plaza, 1301 Avenue of the Americas, 666 Fifth Avenue, and various other trophy properties; the Seymour Milstein Family in the restructuring of the Milstein Family portfolio of office, residential, and hotel properties; Reckson Associates Realty in the disposition of its industrial portfolio; National Golf Properties in its sale to a Goldman Sachs/Starwood Capital Group joint venture; and Security Capital Group in its sale to General Electric Capital. The firm has also been involved in real estate merger and acquisition transactions involving AvalonBay Communities, New Plan Excel Realty Trust, First Union Real Estate Equity and Mortgage Investments, Boston Properties, and various hotel companies, among others; significant hotel and resort developments for Universal Studios and various financial institutions; and the formation or strategic representation of the Apollo Real Estate Advisors, UBS PaineWebber, and Lazard real estate opportunity funds.

INTERNATIONAL WORK: Wachtell Lipton represented Sanofi-Synthélabo in its successful US$60.2 billion hostile exchange offer for Aventis; Bank One in its US$58.0 billion merger with J.P. Morgan Chase; FleetBoston in its US$47.0 billion acquisition by Bank of America; AT&T Wireless in its US$40.7 billion acquisition by Cingular (the largest cash acquisition in history); the Walt Disney Company in its response to Comcast's now-withdrawn US$66.7 billion hostile offer; and the Special Committee of non-executive directors of News Corporation in connection with News Corporation's US$50.0 billion recapitalization and reincorporation from Australia to the United States and certain related-party acquisitions from the Murdoch family. In addition, the firm's representations include the following:

Cross-Border Strategic Combinations & Acquisitions: Household International in its US$14.2 billion transaction with HSBC Holdings; USA Networks in its US$11.7 billion joint venture with Vivendi Universal; Newmont Mining in its US$4.4 billion acquisitions of Normandy Mining of Australia and Franco-Nevada Mining of Canada, and its US$986.0 million equity offering; Jefferson Smurfit Group in its US$3.5 billion acquisition by Madison Dearborn Partners; Publicis Groupe in its US$3.3 billion transaction with Bcom3Group; Wal-Mart in its US$1.9 billion acquisition of The Seiyu, Ltd., and its US$225.0 million acquisition of Supermercados Amigo; VoiceStream Wireless in its US$55.0 billion transaction with Deutsche Telekom; AT&T Wireless Services in the US$9.8 billion investment by NTT DoCoMo; The Furukawa Electric Co. in its US$2.3 billion acquisition of Lucent Technologies' optical fibre business; Pinault-Printemps-Redoute in its strategic investment in and acquisition of majority control of Gucci Group, including the settlement among Pin-

ault-Printemps-Redoute, Gucci Group and LVMH Moët Hennessy Louis Vuitton, as well as in a number of other group acquisitions and dispositions; Colgate in its US$841.0 million acquisition of GABA Holding; Cole National in its US$495.0 million merger with Luxottica Group; and Cardinal Health in its US$530.0 million acquisition of The Intercare Group.

Other Strategic Combinations & Acquisitions: AT&T (AT&T Broadband & Internet Services) in its US$72.0 billion transaction with Comcast and the split-up of the US$9.0 billion Time Warner Entertainment partnership; Sears in its $13 billion merger with Kmart; Phillips Petroleum in its US$35.0 billion combination with Conoco and its US$9.4 billion acquisition of Tosco; Western Wireless Corporation in its US$6 billion sale to ALLTEL Corporation; Constellation Brands, Inc. in its successful US$1.3 billion hostile acquisition of The Robert Mondavi Corporation; American International Group in its US$24.6 billion acquisition of American General; Wachovia in its US$13.6 billion transaction with First Union; General Mills in its US$10.5 billion acquisition of The Pillsbury Company; IBP in its US$6.0 billion transaction with Tyson Foods; Heller Financial in its US$6.0 billion transaction with General Electric Capital; InterActiveCorp (formerly USA Interactive) in its US$734.0 million acquisition of LendingTree, its US$1.1 billion acquisition of Hotels.com, its US$3.3 billion acquisition of Expedia, and its US$684.0 million acquisition of Ticketmaster; Kellogg in its US$4.5 billion acquisition of Keebler Foods; Litton Industries in its US$5.2 billion transaction with Northrop Grumman; Cardinal Health in its US$802.0 million acquisition of Syncor International; Goodrich in its US$1.5 billion acquisition of TRW Aeronautics Systems; State Street Bank & Trust in its US$1.5 billion acquisition of Deutsche Bank's worldwide custody business; Unocal in its US$456.0 million acquisition of Pure Resources; HotJobs.com in its US$436.0 million acquisition by Yahoo!; and Trigon Healthcare in its US$4.0 billion transaction with Anthem.

Divestitures & Sales: Sears Roebuck in the US$31.8 billion sale of its credit card portfolio to Citigroup; Altria (formerly Philip Morris Companies) in its US$5.6 billion sale of Miller Brewing to South African Breweries; Hercules in its US$1.8 billion sale of its BetzDearborn water treatment business to General Electric Capital; and Allied Irish Banks in the US$3.1 billion sale of Allfirst Financial to M&T Bank.

Takeover Defenses: Taubman Centers in responding to the US$1.1 billion hostile tender offer by Simon Property Group, which was withdrawn; Dana in responding to the US$4.4 billion hostile tender offer by Arvin-Meritor, which also was withdrawn; and Hercules in its successful proxy fight with Sam Heyman.

Private Equity Transactions: A consortium of leading private equity firms including Apax, Apollo, Goldman Sachs and Permira in their US$5 billion acquisition of Intelsat. Apollo Management and Goldman Sachs Capital Partners in their US$4.2 billion acquisition (with the Blackstone Group) of Ondeo Nalco. Apollo in its US$1.5 billion acquisition (with Goldman Sachs and Soros) of Cablecom of Switzerland.

IPOs & Spinoffs: FMC Technologies in its initial public offerings; the issuer in the US$10.6 billion initial public offering of AT&T Wireless (the largest U.S. IPO in history), and in its subsequent US$26.8 billion exchange offers and spin-off to AT&T shareholders; Piper Jaffray in its US$804.0 million spin-off to shareholders; and Motorola in its US$5.0 billion spin-off of its semiconductor business to shareholders.

The firm is representing a number of major corporations, such as Citigroup, in connection with corporate governance and related matters, and has advised special committees of boards of directors, including PNC Financial Service Group and National Australia Bank, in connection with various corporate governance investigations and related matters. Wachtell Lipton originated the so-called 'poison pill'; structured the first cross-border 'Morris Trust' transaction, between W.R. Grace and Fresenius; and has been involved in the transactions giving rise to most of the landmark corporate governance decisions in Delaware, including the Household, Revlon, Newmont Mining, Macmillan, Interco, Time Warner, Paramount and Omnicare cases.

WATSON, FARLEY & WILLIAMS

THE FIRM

Chairman: Frank Dunne
Managing Partner: Michael Greville
New York Office Head: Alfred Yudes

Number of partners worldwide: 63
Number of other lawyers worldwide: 220

FIRM OVERVIEW: Opened in 1990, the New York office originally serviced ship finance, tax and litigation markets, but quickly expanded to include asset finance and leasing and bank finance. The firm's presence in New York acknowledges the significance of New York and US federal law to international financial and corporate transactions and the significance of New York as a global business centre. The New York office advises on US federal law and New York law. The firm works aggressively to find innovative, quality answers to meet the rapidly changing needs of clients. By using its resource of international lawyers, the firm can deliver global solutions. Particular expertise includes: asset finance and leasing; ship finance, shipping, oil and gas; litigation and arbitration; bank finance and regulation; bankruptcy and workouts; and taxation.

MAIN AREAS OF PRACTICE:

Asset Finance & Leasing: Watson, Farley & Williams has a substantial International Equipment Finance and Leasing Practice. Specialists have extensive experience with aircraft, satellites, vessels, rail equipment, real estate and power generation facilities and other industrial equipment. The practice complements the firm's international ship finance practice. In addition to straightforward secured asset-based financings, the firm has successfully developed and completed innovative transactions involving domestic and cross-border tax leasing, off-balance sheet 'synthetic' leasing, securitization, credit enhancement, Eximbank and European ECA guaranteed financing, political risk insurance and the restructuring of transactions under the US bankruptcy laws.

Ship Finance, Shipping & Oil & Gas: Watson, Farley & Williams has one of the largest shipping practices in the world. The firm acts for owners seeking finance and for banks and other financial institutions providing it. The firm advises on all legal aspects of the shipping business in all its offices. Watson, Farley & Williams experience encompasses newbuilding and secondhand ship acquisitions and financings, cross-border leasing, bareboat charters, operating leases and other off-balance sheet financings, credit enhancement structures, syndication and securitization and advice on environmental laws and all major ship registries.

Litigation & Arbitration: The Litigation Group handles all varieties of commercial litigation in US and UK courts and before all major international arbitration tribunals. The firm's litigators are admitted to practice before all state and federal courts in New York and have appeared in courts and tribunals throughout the country. Several have been appointed as commercial arbitrators in recognition of their expertise in matters relating to international finance and trade, transportation, insurance, securities and EC law. In New York, the firm advises shipping and energy clients on US environmental laws, including the Oil Pollution Act 1990.

HEAD OFFICE

NEW YORK
Watson, Farley & Williams (New York) LLP
100 Park Avenue, **New York**, NY 10017
Tel: 212 922 2200   **Fax:** 212 922 1512
Email: ayudes@wfw.com
Website: www.wfw.com

INTERNATIONAL OFFICES

Watson, Farley & Williams (New York) LLP or an affiliated undertaking also has offices in Paris, Piraeus, Rome, Singapore, Bangkok and London.

Bankruptcy & Workouts: The Bankruptcy and Workout Practice in New York has developed in conjunction with the firm's general asset finance practice with particular expertise in shipping, aviation, offshore drilling and other cross-border transactions. The firm represents various banking interests as secured creditors in Chapter 11 bankruptcy proceedings. The firm's lawyers have represented secured creditors and major trade creditors in every major shipping related bankruptcy in the US, recently including The Holt Group, Global Ocean and Golden Ocean. The firm represents secured and unsecured creditors in major cases involving US bankruptcy proceedings and has also represented creditors in tandem with its London, Paris and Singapore partners in cross-border administration proceedings.

Taxation: The tax specialists both advise clients directly and work closely with the firm's banking, asset finance, shipping and corporate teams. The firm has particular expertise in the US taxation of international financings and corporate transactions. The firm represents taxpayers in controversies with the Internal Revenue Service and state and local taxing authorities. The firm's international offices and contacts allow us to address the worldwide tax issues that arise in cross-border financings and other international business transactions. Watson, Farley & Williams tax lawyers are frequently involved in developing tax efficient structures for their clients.

WEIL, GOTSHAL & MANGES LLP

THE FIRM

Chairman: Stephen J Dannhauser
Number of partners worldwide: 305
Number of other lawyers worldwide: 854

FIRM OVERVIEW: Weil, Gotshal & Manges is a leader in the marketplace for sophisticated international legal services. With more than 1,200 lawyers across the US, Europe and Asia, the firm serves many of the most successful companies in the world in their high-stakes matters and transactions. Weil Gotshal's clients say they come to the firm for its strength in delivering good judgment. Clients seek - and receive - straightforward answers from the firm's lawyers, not just a redefinition of the problem. Weil Gotshal's lawyers collaborate successfully on a global basis in helping clients achieve their wide-ranging goals.

MAIN AREAS OF PRACTICE:

Corporate: Weil Gotshal's Corporate Practice is regularly involved in the largest and most complex transactions in the world. Its lawyers handle mergers and acquisitions, private equity transactions, joint ventures, securities offerings, financings, debt restructurings, real estate transactions and other commercial transactions. The firm's general corporate representations also include SEC and regulatory compliance, corporate governance, executive benefits and compensation plans, proxy solicitations, new business ventures and technology, and trademark licensing. Weil Gotshal's Corporate Practice has been widely recognized for high quality work, having been named US Law Firm of the Year at *The Lawyer* Awards 2004 and Law Firm of the Year for US Private Equity at the *Chambers Global* Awards 2004. The firm also is consistently ranked in the top-tier in US and global mergers and acquisitions league tables by *Bloomberg* and *Thomson Financial*.

Litigation/Regulatory: Weil Gotshal's Litigation/Regulatory Practice has earned a reputation for representing clients facing complex legal issues - efficiently and successfully. The firm has an impressive track record for winning extremely large and difficult cases. Weil Gotshal helps clients worldwide solve their toughest problems in any forum - from jury trials to appeals before the United States Supreme Court to complex international arbitrations. The firm's Litigation/Regulatory Practice is distinguished by its quality and depth of experience in virtually every major substantive area in which complex cases occur; ability to mobilize quickly a team of first-class attorneys cutting across disciplines and geography; impressive record in conducting high-stakes jury trials; and vast experience in multi-district litigation and crisis situations. Weil Gotshal is a recognized leader in a wide variety of litigation/regulatory practice areas including antitrust/competition, appellate, bankruptcy, complex commercial, consumer financial services, employment, global dispute resolution, intellectual property and media, international trade, patent, product liability/mass tort/environmental and securities/corporate governance. Weil Gotshal was a finalist for *American Lawyer*'s 2003 Litigation Department of the Year Award - the only New York-based firm named.

Business Finance & Restructuring: Weil Gotshal's Business Financing & Restructuring Practice is world-renowned. The firm has been involved in virtually every major Chapter 11 reorganization case in the US and in major international out-of-court debt restructurings. Weil Gotshal has been at the center of the massive and historic Enron and WorldCom restructurings. The firm represents boards of directors, companies, lenders, investors and court-appointed officers. Other clients include both creditors and debtors, acquirers, trustees and other-parties-in-interest in troubled situations in nearly every industry.

Intellectual Property & Media: Weil Gotshal is a leader in these fields advising on cutting-edge litigations and complex IP transactions. The scope of the practice is unrivaled, spanning traditional media issues including copyrights, First Amendment, trademarks, unfair competition/misappropriation of trade secrets, advertising, and music, broadcast and motion picture matters. In new media Weil Gotshal advises on internet/on-line litigation and licensing, e-commerce, content protection/digital rights, and, software and technology transfer/outsourcing. The Patent Practice, one of the world's most respected, provides deep technical and procedural knowledge, extensive experience to develop the right strategy, and substantial trial experience, making Weil Gotshal the 'go-to' firm for patent litigation. The firm regularly handles patent litigation for key companies in the automotive, biotechnology, semiconductor, computer hardware and software, consumer, energy, media and entertainment, financial services, medical device, pharmaceutical, publishing, and telecommunications sectors, among others.

Taxation: Weil Gotshal's Tax lawyers engage in a sophisticated practice that mirrors the breadth of the firm's transactional practices. The firm's team approach to multidisciplinary representations enables us to devise innovative solutions to problems that present a multitude of competing considerations. Weil Gotshal lawyers are well-versed in the tax and employee benefit laws of the US, the UK, France, Germany and Poland. The firm brings a combined experience together to deliver coordinated tax advice in all types of regional and cross-border transactions.

HEAD OFFICE

NEW YORK
767 Fifth Avenue, **New York** NY 10153, USA
Tel: 212 310 8000   **Fax:** 212 310 8007
Website: www.weil.com

BRANCH OFFICES

CALIFORNIA
201 Redwood Shores Parkway, Silicon Valley, **Redwood Shores** CA 94065
Tel: 650 802 3000   **Fax:** 650 802 3100

DELAWARE
1201 N Market Street, 14th Floor, **Wilmington** DE 19801
Tel: 302 656 1410   **Fax:** 302 656 1405

DISTRICT OF COLUMBIA
1501 K Street NW, Suite 100, **Washington** DC 20005
Tel: 202 682 7000   **Fax:** 202 857 0940

FLORIDA
1395 Brickell Avenue, Suite 1200, **Miami** FL 33131
Tel: 305 577 3100   **Fax:** 305 374 7159

MASSACHUSETTS
100 Federal Street, 34th Floor, **Boston** MA 02110
Tel: 617 772 8300   **Fax:** 617 772 8333

TEXAS
8911 Capital of Texas Highway, Suite 4140, **Austin** TX 78759
Tel: 512 349 1930   **Fax:** 512 527 0798

200 Crescent Court, Suite 300, **Dallas** TX 75201-6950
Tel: 214 746 7700   **Fax:** 214 746 7777

700 Louisiana, Suite 1600, **Houston** TX 77002
Tel: 713 546 5000   **Fax:** 713 224 9511

INTERNATIONAL OFFICES

The firm has offices in Brussels, Budapest, Frankfurt, London, Munich, Paris, Prague, Shanghai, Singapore and Warsaw.

WEIL, GOTSHAL & MANGES LLP

WHITE & CASE LLP

THE FIRM

Managing Partner: Duane D Wall

Number of US partners: 167
Number of other US lawyers: 588

FIRM OVERVIEW: A firm of nearly 1,900 lawyers located in 25 countries, White & Case is known for its top-tier legal services and business savvy. Among the first US-based law firms to establish a truly international presence, the firm provides counsel and representation in virtually every area of law and continues to grow to meet clients' needs. In the past few years alone, various publications have recognized White & Case as Global Law Firm of the Year, US Firm with the Best European Presence, Best US Law Firm in London and Eastern Europe Law Firm of the Year.

MAIN AREAS OF PRACTICE: Antitrust, appellate, arbitration, banking, bankruptcy and workouts, capital markets, construction and engineering, corporate, corporate defense and special litigation, employee benefits and compensation, environmental, European Union, global equity-based compensation, insurance, intellectual property, international trade, internet, media and technology, investment funds, labor and employment, leasing and equipment finance, legislative/law reform, litigation, mergers and acquisitions, private clients, private equity, privatization, project and infrastructure finance, public finance, public international law, real estate, securities, securitization, sovereign, tax, telecommunications, trade and commodity finance.

CLIENTS: The firm's clients are public and privately held commercial businesses and financial institutions, as well as governments and state-owned entities, involved in sophisticated corporate and financial transactions and complex dispute resolution proceedings.

INTERNATIONAL WORK: International practice is the foundation of the firm, which has been involved in complex transactions in virtually every corner of the world. The firm's international network of offices enables it to service clients in a wide array of jurisdictions, including all of the major financial markets around the world. The firm's lawyers understand the legal and political structure, as well as the business market and practices, in their jurisdictions, and how they relate to international markets, greatly facilitating the successful completion of complex international transactions for its clients.

US OFFICES

NEW YORK
1155 Avenue of the Americas, **New York**, NY 10036-2787
Tel: 212 819 8200 **Fax:** 212 354 8113
Website: www.whitecase.com

CALIFORNIA
633 West Fifth Street, Suite 1900, **Los Angeles**, CA 90071-2007
Tel: 213 620 7700   **Fax:** 213 687 0758

Five Palo Alto Square, 10th Floor, 3000 El Camino Real,
Palo Alto, CA 94306
Tel: 650 213 0300   **Fax:** 650 213 8158

Three Embarcadero Center, 22nd Floor, **San Francisco**, CA 94111-3162
Tel: 415 544 1100   **Fax:** 415 544 0202

DISTRICT OF COLUMBIA
701 Thirteenth Street, NW, **Washington**, DC 20005-3807
Tel: 202 626 3600   **Fax:** 202 639 9355

FLORIDA
Wachovia Financial Center, Suite 4900, 200 South Biscayne Boulevard,
Miami, FL 33131-2352
Tel: 305 371 2700   **Fax:** 305 358 5744

INTERNATIONAL OFFICES

The firm also has offices in Almaty, Ankara, Bangkok, Beijing, Berlin, Bratislava, Brussels, Budapest, Dresden, Düsseldorf, Frankfurt, Hamburg, Helsinki, Ho Chi Minh City, Hong Kong, Istanbul, Johannesburg, London, Mexico City, Milan, Moscow, Mumbai, Paris, Prague, Riyadh, Rome, São Paulo, Shanghai, Singapore, Stockholm, Tokyo and Warsaw.

CONTACTS

Los Angeles	Richard K Smith, Jr
Miami	Victor M Alvarez
New York	David N Koschik
Palo Alto	Steven D Hemminger
San Francisco	Kevin B Fisher
Washington, DC	Victor J DeSantis

WHITE & CASE LLP

WILLKIE FARR & GALLAGHER LLP

THE FIRM

Chairman, Executive Committee: Jack H Nusbaum
Co-Chairman: Myron Trepper, Richard DeScherer
Partners in US offices: 120
Number of other lawyers in US: 353

FIRM OVERVIEW: Established in 1888, Willkie Farr & Gallagher LLP is a full-service international law firm renowned for its expertise in corporate and securities law, litigation, business reorganization and restructuring, real estate and a number of specialized fields of law, including telecommunications, IT/internet, media and entertainment, tax, international trade, government relations and intellectual property. With approximately 600 attorneys in offices in New York, Washington, Paris, London, Milan, Rome, Frankfurt, and Brussels, the firm's clients rely on it for its creativity and skill in structuring and implementing complex transactions and providing counsel on critical business and legal issues in virtually all areas of business law.

MAIN AREAS OF PRACTICE: Corporate and financial services, insurance, litigation, real estate, business reorganization and restructuring, telecommunications, tax, intellectual property, private clients, international trade, government relations, environmental, executive compensation and employee benefits, compliance and enforcement, other.

Corporate & Financial Services: The firm's Corporate and Financial Services Department offers corporations and financial institutions broad expertise in all types of commercial transactions and regulatory matters. Its extensive corporate practice includes mergers and acquisitions, private equity/venture capital, investment management, public finance, insurance, broker-dealer regulation, private placement and banking, institutional lending, structured finance, and 144A offerings. The firm is a national leader in the area of public offerings of all types of equity securities by both US and foreign issuers, and is internationally renowned for handling complex, cross-border M&A transactions.

Litigation: The firm represents clients in every type of forum, including federal and state court actions, government regulatory and administrative proceedings, and arbitration, mediation and other alternative dispute resolution proceedings. It is well known for its expertise in all of the major areas of business and corporate litigation, including securities and transactional litigation, class-action lawsuits, battles for corporate control, antitrust issues, white collar crime and compliance and enforcement, First Amendment and media litigation, intellectual property, accountants' and other professional liability actions, insurance brokerage and coverage actions, environmental litigation, and employee benefits and employment litigation.

Business Reorganization & Restructuring: The firm represents debtors, lenders, secured and unsecured creditors, creditors' and shareholders' committees, shareholders, governmental units, investment advisors, investors, landlords and tenants, and entities seeking investment opportunities in Chapter 11 cases. The practice also includes deal structuring with respect to potential insolvency and bankruptcy issues.

Real Estate: The firm is regularly involved in major domestic and international real estate transactions, including REIT mergers and debt and equity offerings, pooled and stand-alone securitized financings, development projects, commercial leases, sales and acquisitions, construction and permanent financings, restructurings, joint ventures, private placements of domestic and foreign real estate funds, and real estate aspects of corporate and bankruptcy transactions. It has significant experience in all aspects of the real estate capital markets and all property types, including retail, office, healthcare, lodging and gaming, storage, and residential.

HEAD OFFICE

NEW YORK
787 Seventh Ave, **New York** NY 10019-6099
Tel: 212 728 8000   **Fax:** 212 728 8111
Website: www.willkie.com

BRANCH OFFICES

DISTRICT OF COLUMBIA
1875 K Street, NW, **Washington** DC 20006-1238
Tel: 202 303 1000   **Fax:** 202 303 2000

INTERNATIONAL OFFICES

The firm also has offices in Paris, London, Milan, Rome, Frankfurt and Brussels.

CONTACTS

Business Reorganization & Restructuring	Myron Trepper
Corporate & Financial Services	Jack H Nusbaum
Environmental	E Donald Elliott
Executive Compensation & Employee Benefits	Stephen Lindo
Government Relations	Russell L Smith
Insurance	John D'Alimonte
	Mitchell Auslander
Intellectual Property	John DiMatteo
International Trade	William H Barringer
Litigation	Richard Posen
Real Estate	Eugene Pinover
Tax	Richard L Reinhold
Telecommunications	Philip L Verveer, Bruce Kraus
Private Clients Group	David J McCabe

CLIENTS: The firm represents a roster of significant corporate clients on a wide variety of legal matters across many borders.

INTERNATIONAL WORK:

M&A: The firm regularly represents clients that buy and sell companies in complex cross-border transactions. It also represents a large number of issuers and underwriters in relation to debt and equity offerings in the United States.

Private Equity: The firm represents a number of private equity and venture capital funds and venture banking firms that provide seed money to start-up companies and make private equity investments in established enterprises. The firm has advised these clients in connection with successful investments in such areas as healthcare, biotechnology, e-commerce, computers, consumer products, electronics, publishing, telecommunications, and environmental cleanup and control.

International Trade: The firm advises many foreign manufacturers and foreign governmental bodies on issues arising from regulations governing the importation of goods from the United States.

Business & Finance: The firm handles matters such as corporate law, private equity, litigation, securitization/structured finance, taxation, environmental, and international trade.

Telecommunications & IT/Internet Media: The firm has significant expertise advising on regulatory issues and commercial transactions involving all types of telecommunications, information technology and outsourcing, e-commerce, media and entertainment matters.

WILLKIE FARR & GALLAGHER LLP

CONTENTS: Banking p.1381; Bankruptcy p.1382; Corporate/M&A p.1383; Employment p.1385; Environment p.1387; Litigation: p.1389; Real Estate p.1392; Individuals' Profiles p.1394; Firms' Profiles p.1400.

How lawyers are ranked

The opinions we gather from clients — mainly from in-house lawyers but also from other purchasers of legal services — are balanced by opinions from colleagues and competitors. Together, they provide two different perspectives — an all-round view — and biased viewpoints cancel each other out.

BANKING & FINANCE

North Carolina
Leading firms (Banking & Finance)

1	**MOORE & VAN ALLEN PLLC** *Charlotte*
2	**HELMS MULLISS & WICKER PLLC** *Charlotte*
	KENNEDY COVINGTON LOBDELL *Charlotte*
	ROBINSON, BRADSHAW & HINSON PA *Charlotte*
	WOMBLE CARLYLE SANDRIDGE *Winston-Salem*
3	**CARRUTHERS & ROTH PA** *Greensboro*
	PARKER, POE, ADAMS & BERNSTEIN *Charlotte*

Leading individuals (Banking & Finance)

1	**HAZLETT Richard** *Helms Mulliss,* Charlotte
	HOVIS James *Moore & Van Allen,* Charlotte
	KUPEC Christopher *Moore & Van Allen,* Charlotte
2	**BUCK Peter** *Robinson Bradshaw,* Charlotte
	FLINT Henry *Kennedy Covington,* Charlotte
	GREENE Kenneth *Carruthers & Roth,* Greensboro
	UBELL Donald *Parker Poe,* Charlotte
3	**CALDWELL Stokely** *Robinson Bradshaw,* Charlotte
	CAMPBELL Boyd *Helms Mulliss,* Charlotte
	DUNN J Thomas *Moore & Van Allen,* Charlotte
	FULLER III William *Moore & Van Allen,* Charlotte
	KLUTTZ Joseph *Kennedy Covington,* Charlotte
	LASSITER Donnell *Kennedy Covington,* Charlotte
	LEON Christopher *Womble Carlyle,* Winston-Salem
	LUCAS Edwin *Robinson Bradshaw,* Charlotte
	MOSER Kenneth *Womble Carlyle,* Winston-Salem
	ROBERTSON Allen *Robinson Bradshaw,* Charlotte

Firms and individuals are listed alphabetically in each band.

Band 1

Moore & Van Allen PLLC
The Firm: This is *"absolutely the number-one banking team"* in the state according to clients, who rate it as a top-notch, sophisticated group that simply *"gets things done."* It represents lenders in the full range of financings, including bond issuance, multiple lending transactions and other secured and unsecured transactions. It is particularly rated for the *"clarity and expertise of its work"* and interviewees told us: *"It can't be beaten on paper; the documentation is superb."* The group's practice is primarily focused on representing large North Carolina financial institutions, but it also acts for national banks, as well as offering lending advice to large corporations.
The Lawyers: Finance head **James Hovis** earns kudos as *"one hell of a negotiator. He's a true expert on banking."* He doubles as managing partner of the Charlotte office and is particularly rated for his skills in complex debt restructurings. **Chris Kupec** leads the private equity group, and is admired as *"an incredibly smart lawyer."* He impressed interviewees with the depth of his experience and is highly regarded for his work for venture capital, mezzanine, and other investment funds. Our sources hailed **Thomas Dunn** as *"a strong, experienced banking lawyer."* He won admiration for his insight into both banking and bankruptcy issues. **William Fuller** is *"the man to go to for complex lending transactions,"* according to sources. He primarily focuses on representing banks and financial institutions in a range of complex financings, and is particularly experienced in healthcare and telecom-related deals.
The Clients: The group acts for Bank of America and Wachovia and a number of other major financial institutions.

Band 2

Helms Mulliss & Wicker PLLC
The Firm: Clients rate this group as *"a highly focused, professional and business-savvy outfit."* It is *"a full and rounded practice,"* which offers banking law expertise as well as skills in corporate lending and syndicated transactions. The group enjoys a great following among the North Carolina banks and also continues to be bond counsel to the State of North Carolina. Its recent deals include advising BB&T in a series of tax-exempt bond offerings and credit-enhanced bond offerings worth, in total, more than $500 million.
The Lawyers: *"Effortlessly good banking lawyer"* **Rick Hazlett** received great client endorsements. According to our sources, *"he passes all the tests you could ask of a lawyer. He's responsive, understanding and highly astute."* He maintains a varied practice, which focuses heavily on corporate lending transactions and letters of credit. One of his most substantial deals was representing a large company in a $325 million syndicated loan. He has also developed a niche in handling tax-exempt financings for hospitals, retirement homes and municipalities. Interviewees admire **Boyd Campbell** as *"an experienced and highly sensible attorney."* He is highly rated for his skills in securitizations, but also advises on debt securities transactions and the sale of equity-linked notes under MTN programs.
The Clients: Bank of America; BB&T; Sun Trust; First Charter Bank; Wachovia; Merrill Lynch and The State of North Carolina.

Kennedy Covington Lobdell & Hickman LLP
The Firm: The group is recommended as *"a polished firm, which really understands the industry and does superb work."* It enjoys a strong following among the North Carolina institutional lenders, and advises on private equity transactions, structured finance deals and cross-border financings. It maintains a high profile in the syndicated lending market, and has advised banking clients on a number of high-value, nationwide deals.
The Lawyers: The *"excellent"* **Hank Flint** continues to split his time between corporate and banking matters. Market commentators believe he is *"a great client interface lawyer"* and someone who *"really listens and tries to solve problems."* He has deep experience in the field but is felt to be particularly skilled in equity financings. **Donnell Lassiter** is rated as *"a genuine expert who understands financings from top to bottom."* He stood out for his work in the debt finance arena where recent work included advising on multibank syndicated credit transactions. **Joseph Kluttz** is included in the tables for the first time. He is *"a top-class attorney who is practical, commercial and responsive."* He chairs the

firm's financial services department and focuses on the structuring and restructuring of large banking transactions. He also has an in-depth knowledge of bankruptcy law.

The Clients: The group acts on financings in the technology, telecom, fuel, manufacturing, healthcare and entertainment industries. Clients include: Academy Funds; Bank of America; Capital Investment Companies; Wachovia and Wells Fargo.

Robinson, Bradshaw & Hinson PA

The Firm: Clients hail this practice as *"a top-notch group of genteel professionals."* Interviewees appreciate the team's sensible and straightforward approach to deals saying: *"They won't take a position in negotiations unless it's logical and they can support it with facts. They are great communicators who understand their clients."* The group has enjoyed a long relationship with the local banks and handles the range of complex financing matters including leveraged transactions, private equity and mezzanine financings. It recently acted for Wachovia in the arrangement of a $250 million letter of credit for the subsidiary of a global financial services company. The group has also developed a niche representing civic bodies in healthcare financings.

The Lawyers: **Peter Buck** continues to enjoy plaudits for both his corporate and banking and finance expertise. Interviewees believe he is *"an attorney with a full vault of experience. He has seen and done everything, and can still do it better than most."* He rates highly for his skills in high-level financings and recently acted for a bank equity fund on its investments in a large utility. The *"diligent"* **Edwin Lucas** earns praise for his bond and public finance skills, and won recognition as a *"smart and resourceful"* attorney. **Allen Robertson**'s strengths lie in public finance deals. Interviewees told us that he is *"incredibly sharp on bond matters. He really understands the market."* **Stokely Caldwell** is *"an extremely accessible, personable lawyer"* who is included in the tables for the first time. He earns particular plaudits in capital markets and commercial lending work. He represented Wachovia on $135 million revolving credit and term loan

facilities, to support the leveraged acquisitions of a ceramic fiber manufacturer.

The Clients: The group's clients include Allied Capital, BB&T and Wachovia.

Womble Carlyle Sandridge & Rice, PLLC

See firm details p.1402

The Firm: This *"highly commercial"* firm won praise for its expertise in securities law and a range of high-end financings. It is particularly well regarded for its public finance skills where it has *"a solid governmental practice and is really at the top of its game in healthcare-related deals."* It also won recognition for its tax-exempt financing work in the education sector. The bulk of the group's client base remains North Carolina's large institutional banks although it also acts for other entities such as colleges, universities and hospitals. In one of its major deals it represented BB&T Capital Partners in a $70 million secured revolving credit facility for American Capital Strategies.

The Lawyers: **Chris Leon** (see p.1397) is a popular figure among clients. One satisfied customer commented: *"I like dealing with him as he knows everything that needs to be known and is a great manager of the process."* He primarily represents lenders and credit providers and is active on structured finance and syndicated lending transactions. He recently represented Wachovia on a $150 million senior credit facility for Outback Steakhouse. **Ken Moser** (see p.1397) is best known for his skill in real estate finance. Researchers heard that he is *"a smart and sensible lawyer – the kind of guy you can always trust."* He is also an experienced litigator who assists a number of banks and financial institutions in dispute resolution.

The Clients: The group's clients include BB&T Capital Partners, Reynolds America and Wachovia.

Band 3

Carruthers & Roth PA

The Firm: Although this team cannot match some of its competitors in terms of size, it

nonetheless continues to be seen as a *"highly impressive"* group. One client reported that the firm houses *"the best banking team buck for buck of any firm I've ever used."* It wins recognition for a varied practice that includes work in asset-based lending, high-value commercial loans, restructuring and real estate lending. Lawyers have been busy in the emerging market of junior secured loans and have represented a number of private funds in these transactions.

The Lawyers: Clients praised **Kenneth Greene** as *"an absolute top-class, asset-based lending attorney."* He earned plaudits for his skill in asset securitizations and has recently advised on a number of big-ticket deals.

The Clients: The group represents local, regional and national financial institutions including several large national banks. These include: Bank of America; BB&T; Capital Factors; Central Carolina Bank; CIT Group and Royal & SunAlliance.

Parker, Poe, Adams & Bernstein LLP

The Firm: This is a modestly sized team but one that commentators are confident *"punches well above its weight."* It attracted praise for its work in public finance transactions and tax-exempt financings, where it represents a range of clients including civic bodies from the education and healthcare sectors. Capital markets work is another area of activity. The group's financial institution clients also call on the team for assistance in syndicated financings, asset backed loans, structured finance transactions and restructurings.

The Lawyers: **Donald Ubell** heads the firm's public finance practice group and was recommended as *"definitely one of the best bond lawyers in North Carolina."* He is renowned for his work in the education system and has acted for The University of North Carolina at Chapel Hill on a range of financings for several years. He also serves as bond counsel to a number of the region's universities and cities.

The Clients: The group represents local, regional and national banks and lenders.

BANKRUPTCY

Band 1

Helms Mulliss & Wicker PLLC

The Firm: Clients *"cannot say enough positive things"* about this team. With over 100 lawyers spanning three offices, it houses a group of responsive attorneys who provide *"added value"* in negotiations. Clients applauded the team's ability to *"bring business sense, as well as legal*

sense, to the table." A sophisticated practice handles restructurings, Chapter 11 cases and DIP financings for clients including commercial banking and asset-based lenders drawn from states such as Tennessee, Illinois and New York. The group also advises clients on risk management and is well placed to represent them in all phases of insolvency proceedings.

The Lawyers: The excellent **Robert Pryor** is a

senior figure in the marketplace who brings a wealth of experience to the table. His practice includes bankruptcy law, workouts and commercial litigation. His colleague **Scott Vaughn** is a bankruptcy litigation specialist who was commended for his astute handling of clients' issues. He represents financial institutions in workouts, refinancings and bankruptcy proceedings.

The Clients: Bank of America, BB&T;

North Carolina
Leading firms (Bankruptcy)

[1] **HELMS MULLISS & WICKER PLLC** *Charlotte*
KENNEDY COVINGTON LOBDELL *Charlotte*
MOORE & VAN ALLEN, PLLC *Charlotte*
ROBINSON, BRADSHAW & HINSON PA *Charlotte*

Leading individuals (Bankruptcy)

[1] **BOOE Mike** *Kennedy Covington, Charlotte*
EADES David *Moore & Van Allen, Charlotte*
KLUTTZ Joseph *Kennedy Covington, Charlotte*
PRYOR Robert *Helms Mulliss, Charlotte*
SCHILLI David *Robinson Bradshaw, Charlotte*
VAUGHN Scott *Helms Mulliss, Charlotte*

Firms and individuals are listed alphabetically in each band.

Citibank; First Charter; Wachovia and Central Carolina Bank.

Kennedy Covington Lobdell & Hickman LLP

The Firm: Commentators warmly endorsed this firm's *"large, sophisticated bankruptcy practice."* They believe it is packed to the rafters with *"experienced lawyers who enjoy a good following among the banks."* The financial restructuring practice group combines the twin pillars of the firm's banking and finance and commercial litigation groups to act for lenders, private equity groups and equipment lessors. Its lawyers advise on all phases of the financial restructuring process and support clients in litigation and Chapter 11 cases.

The Lawyers: **Mike Booe** is the chair of the financial restructuring practice group. He is a certified business bankruptcy specialist who won praise from interviewees for his practicality. He advises on single lender and syndicated commercial financing transactions and has experience in the workout and recovery of non-performing credit facilities. **Joseph Kluttz** joins the rankings this year following strong peer recommendations. He advises on the structuring and restructuring of large banking transactions in order to help clients manage and avoid insolvency risk.

The Clients: The firm advises banks and private equity companies.

Moore & Van Allen, PLLC

The Firm: Clients view this group, comprising around 18 lawyers, as a *"cost-effective and responsive"* team. Its lawyers operate primarily out of the firm's Charlotte office and won praise for the quality of their service and for their knack of producing excellent results. The bankruptcy and restructuring team typically represents agents and syndicated lenders in relation to distressed companies and corporate credit facilities. The group also has experience acting as debtor's counsel where it assists in workouts and reorganizations. Recent highlight matters include advising a lender in the US Airways bankruptcy on issues concerning a billion-dollar loan facility. The team is also advising a lender on the provision of a nine-figure loan to a bankrupt furniture company.

The Lawyers: **David Eades** spearheads a team that produces *"outstanding work,"* and that benefits from the support of a *"superb finance practice."* He represents financial institutions in corporate workouts and bankruptcy proceedings.

The Clients: The group advises institutional lenders, investment funds and corporate entities.

Robinson, Bradshaw & Hinson PA

The Firm: Clients endorsed this team for its responsiveness and depth of knowledge. One client commented, *"I can give them nothing but praise and I'm a real tough grader."* The group's portfolio includes representing financial institutions in corporate workouts and Chapter 11 cases. It has particular experience in asbestos-related bankruptcies and frequently works alongside the firm's corporate and litigation departments in bankruptcy and restructuring matters. Lawyers are involved in insolvency work on a regional level and regularly appear in bankruptcy courts in the other judicial districts, including Delaware, Illinois, New York, South Carolina and Texas.

The Lawyers: The lion's share of praise went to **David Schilli**. This outstanding individual won praise from clients for doing a *"phenomenal job,"* and for his responsiveness and understanding of the legal and business issues.

The Clients: American Bankers Insurance Company of Florida; Caraustar Industries; CommScope; Crescent Resources; Faison & Associates and LaSalle Bank.

CORPORATE/M&A

North Carolina
Leading firms (Corporate/M&A)

[1] **KENNEDY COVINGTON LOBDELL** *Charlotte*
ROBINSON, BRADSHAW & HINSON PA *Charlotte*

[2] **HELMS MULLISS & WICKER PLLC** *Charlotte*
MOORE & VAN ALLEN, PLLC *Charlotte*
SMITH, ANDERSON, BLOUNT, DORSETT *Raleigh*

[3] **BROOKS, PIERCE, MCLENDON** *Greensboro*
HUNTON & WILLIAMS *Charlotte*
KILPATRICK STOCKTON LLP *Charlotte*
WOMBLE CARLYLE SANDRIDGE *Winston-Salem*

Firms are listed alphabetically in each band.

Band 1

Kennedy Covington Lobdell & Hickman LLP

The Firm: This *"first-rate, trustworthy"* firm continues to draw plaudits from across the market. Interviewees praised it as *"a great transactional practice, which acts in some of the biggest M&A deals in the state."* The rounded team, which works closely with the firm's financing group, is particularly recommended for its expertise in joint ventures, private equity deals and corporate governance. In a recent highlight the team represented a special committee of the independent directors of SciQuest, a NASDAQ-traded public company, in its acquisition by Trinity Ventures.

The Lawyers: *"Corporate guru"* **Norfleet Pruden** earns market praise as *"a top-level professional."* Clients rate him as *"the kind of guy you want in a deal - he's knowledgeable, resourceful, and above all, sensible. He's a good man to have by your side when it all gets complex."* He continues to cochair the firm's securities section and stood out for his work in public offerings. **Ace Walker** is renowned as *"a diligent, hard-working and incredibly smart attorney."* He is a highly experienced practitioner who is not only skilled in transactional and securities matters, but also in alternative dispute resolution. He has also developed a niche area of expertise in acting for utilities. **Hank Flint** wins high praise for his banking and finance work, but also earns renown as *"a sharp and astute corporate lawyer."*

The Clients: The group's client base includes large regional, national and international entities. It also enjoys a sizable following amongst the traditional Carolina industries. Clients include: Beacon Industrial Group; Charlotte Pipe and Foundry; Coca-Cola; Glenayre Technologies; Lance; McRae Industries; SELEE and Soliant.

Robinson, Bradshaw & Hinson PA

The Firm: Interviewees portrayed this as *"a top-class operation with a depth of experience and class, and a client base you'd die for."* It earns high praise for a broad spectrum of work including venture capital and private equity transactions, M&A deals and securities offerings. It acts for a client base comprising large international corporates as well as traditional North Carolina

North Carolina
Leading individuals (Corporate/M&A)

1 BUCK Peter *Robinson, Bradshaw & Hinson*, Charlotte
JERNIGAN John *Smith, Anderson, Blount*, Raleigh
PRUDEN III J Norfleet *Kennedy Covington*, Charlotte
ROBINSON II Russell *Robinson, Bradshaw*, Charlotte

2 BALDWIN III Garza *Womble Carlyle Sandridge*, Charlotte
HINSON Robin *Robinson. Bradshaw*, Charlotte
KIRKLAND Byron *Smith, Anderson, Blount*, Raleigh
ROACH Gerald *Smith, Anderson, Blount*, Raleigh
WALKER Clarence *Kennedy Covington*, Charlotte

3 CAMPBELL JR Boyd *Helms Mulliss*, Charlotte
DAGENHART Larry *Helms Mulliss*, Charlotte
FLINT Henry *Kennedy Covington*, Charlotte
HAZLETT Richard *Helms Mulliss*, Charlotte
HOPE Stephen *Moore & Van Allen*, Charlotte
LYNCH Stephen *Robinson Bradshaw*, Charlotte
SINGER Robert *Brooks Pierce*, Greensboro
WINSLOW III Edward *Brooks Pierce*, Greensboro
WREN Elizabeth *Kilpatrick Stockton*, Charlotte

Individuals are listed alphabetically in each band.

industries. It also has a following in the hi-tech market. Highlight deals include representing CorrFlex Graphics in its acquisition by Sonoco for approximately $250 million.

The Lawyers: Interviewees described **Russell Robinson** as "*one of the pillars of the North Carolina business Bar.*" He has "*an in-depth knowledge of securities work, and really has his finger on the pulse.*" He wins particular praise for his work with charities and nonprofit organizations. Clients rate **Peter Buck** as an outstanding lawyer who "*combines top-class skill, high-level experience and a great sense of what the client wants.*" His practice covers corporate and banking law, with a niche specialization in energy-related deals. His portfolio of deals includes advising Venturi Partners on a $108 million deal involving the sale of one of its divisions and on the merger of its remaining business with COMSYS Holding. The "*astute*" **Robin Hinson** is "*a great lawyer to have on your side in a tough deal.*" He excels in corporate banking deals. "*Securities expert*" **Stephen Lynch** has a strong following among public companies and is particularly well regarded for his skills in corporate governance issues and SEC investigations.

The Clients: The Cato Corporation; Duke Energy; EnPro Industries; Goodrich; Martin Marietta Materials; National Gypsum; SPX and Wachovia.

Band 2

Helms Mulliss & Wicker PLLC

The Firm: Market sources regard this as a solid corporate practice that is "*user-friendly and responsive across the board.*" A regional player, it offers M&A and private equity advice to a range of companies, and is particularly well regarded for its securities, joint venture and corporate governance skills. It recently acted for the purchaser of a public company in a $100 million deal. It has also carried out sizable transactions in the healthcare, textile, banking, transportation and franchising industries.

The Lawyers: The "*highly experienced*" **Larry Dagenhart** is an expert on federal and state securities laws. Our sources rate him as "*a surefooted lawyer with lots of ideas,*" and point, in particular, to his activities in the venture capital field. Although he is best known for his financing skills, clients praise **Boyd Campbell** as "*an excellent corporate lawyer who has an immediate grasp of what you're trying to do.*" He represents a range of public and private companies, and is particularly renowned for his work in debt financings. **Richard Hazlett** combines financing and corporate skills to great effect and is recommended as "*a sharp, immensely sensible lawyer.*"

The Clients: Bank of America, BB&T and Compass Group are among the firm's clients.

Moore & Van Allen PLLC

The Firm: The group earns market praise as a strong transactional practice that is particularly powerful on the financing front. This sizable team won admiration for its M&A work, but also picked up plaudits for its skill in joint ventures, securities law and corporate governance issues. Interviewees highlighted the international scope of the group's work, and it recently acted for Rexam on its acquisition of a Mexican company, Vitro-American National Can, from its joint venture partner. It also earns plaudits for its cross-border telecom work. The group has a deep bench on the financing side where it acts for a range of public and private bodies.

The Lawyers: The "*impeccable*" **Stephen Hope** heads up the firm's business law section and is admired by clients as "*a resourceful attorney with a great range of knowledge.*" He is a strong player in mergers and financings and proffers particular expertise in public finance. He recently represented the shareholders of TriPoint Global Communications on the sale of certain assets. He also acted for Alcatel on the American law aspects of the sale of its US fiber optics manufacturing business to a Dutch concern.

The Clients: Alcatel; Clariant; Cogentrix Energy; Loews; MedCath and Watson.

Smith, Anderson, Blount, Dorsett, Mitchell & Jernigan LLP
See firm details p.1401

The Firm: According to clients this is "*an excellent, experienced and versatile practice.*" Interviewees believe the group has "*a great approach to transactions*" and praised it for its skill in marrying legal and business concerns. They commented: "*The lawyers here really understand the practicality of the marketplace.*" The group is highly regarded for its transactional prowess and skill in securities law. It also handles the gamut of financing matters, as well as joint ventures and corporate governance issues.

The Lawyers: The outstanding **John Jernigan** (see p.1396) was a popular choice among interviewees, who recommended him as "*an expert on the nuance of the law.*" Clients appreciate his knowledge of the region and report that, "*he knows all the key individuals in business and law.*" He recently acted for Pepsi Bottling Ventures in a $100 million acquisition of a bottling company. Clients rate **Gerald Roach** (see p.1398) as a "*phenomenal*" attorney. They described him as a "*smart, responsive guy who has a great understanding of what a businessperson wants.*" He leads the corporate group but was also recommended for his finance work where he acts for public and private companies as well as venture capital funds. Acting as North Carolina counsel to Brown & Williamson Tobacco, he advised on aspects of its $2.6 billion merger with RJ Reynolds. **Byron Kirkland** (see p.1397) is a talented and articulate attorney. Clients value him as a "*solid gold problem solver*" who provides "*advice worth listening to.*" His deal highlights include advising on a $115 million public offering for The Pantry.

The Clients: Quintiles Transnational; Pharma Services Intermediate Holding; Bioglan Pharmaceuticals; Triangle Pharmaceuticals; Brown & Williamson Tobacco; Cree and The Pantry.

Band 3

Brooks, Pierce, McLendon, Humphrey & Leonard LLP

The Firm: This well-regarded transactional team earns market endorsement for its skills in M&A and financing matters. It operates from its base in Greensboro and has its finger on the pulse of the technology and development work in that area. It also advises on a broader range of regional corporate and M&A transactions.

The Lawyers: Opposing counsel warmly recommended **Robert Singer** as "*a great deal lawyer.*" They characterize him as an intelligent and commercial individual who has "*a good presence on the other side of the deal.*" He represents corporates and banks and continues to offer advice on securities litigation. His recent workload has included a number of deals in China. Managing partner **Edward Winslow** was recommended to researchers as "*a solid, experienced attorney who gives clients value for money.*" He is particularly strong in the financial services field and he represents a number of banks and banking associations across the region.

The Clients: The group represents public companies, as well as medium to large private companies. It undertakes substantial work for banks, hi-tech companies, broker-dealers, investment advisers and venture capital funds.

Hunton & Williams

See firm details p.1775

The Firm: Interviewees agree that this group – split between the firm's Raleigh and Charlotte offices – is making an impact on the marketplace. The team continues to benefit from referrals from the Hunton & Williams network but is increasingly generating its own deal flow. The transactional team handles both regional and national matters and is particularly recommended for its skills in complex financings. Highlight deals include acting for KMG America on its IPO and on its multimillion-dollar acquisition of a large insurance company.

The Lawyers: Timothy Goettel is a respected member of the team.

The Clients: The group represents entities from a broad range of industries and benefits from the firm's strong national and international client base.

Kilpatrick Stockton LLP

See firm details p.634

The Firm: This large team wins client praise as "*a business-savvy group that always impresses.*" The practice covers a range of disciplines including M&A deals, joint ventures, venture capital transactions and securities matters. It boasts an impressive client base of midsized North Carolina concerns as well as Fortune 500 companies, and is active both regionally and nationally. A highlight of 2004 was acting for Burlen on its acquisition by an Israeli company, Delta Galil Industries, which is listed on the Tel Aviv Stock Exchange.

The Lawyers: Our sources recommended securities expert **Elizabeth Wren** (see p.1399) as "*a sensible, levelheaded and quick-thinking attorney.*" She advises on corporate transactions as well as IPOs and secondary offerings.

The Clients: The client base includes midsized North Carolina businesses and large, international companies.

Womble Carlyle Sandridge & Rice, PLLC

See firm details p.1402

The Firm: Although it is best known for its litigation expertise, clients feel that this group is "*a definite regional player.*" It fields a team of "*good, business-minded people*" and is becoming an increasingly respected player in the market. The group represents a range of clients including issuers and underwriters in securities offerings. It also earns praise for its skill in M&A transactions, joint ventures and corporate governance issues.

The Lawyers: The experienced **Garza Baldwin** (see p.1394) wins industry kudos as "*a smart and charming lawyer of the old school.*" He is highly regarded for his securities work and frequently advises companies on the implications of the Sarbanes-Oxley Act.

The Clients: The firm advises clients in the financial services, telecom, IT, manufacturing and healthcare sectors.

EMPLOYMENT

MAINLY DEFENDANT

North Carolina
Leading firms
(Employment: Mainly Defendant)

1	CONSTANGY, BROOKS & SMITH *Winston-Salem*
	OGLETREE, DEAKINS, NASH, SMOAK *Cary*
	SMITH MOORE LLP *Raleigh*
2	BROOKS, PIERCE, MCLENDON *Greensboro*
	VAN HOY REUTLINGER ADAMS & DUNN *Charlotte*
3	HUNTON & WILLIAMS *Raleigh*
	KILPATRICK STOCKTON LLP *Charlotte*
	MAUPIN TAYLOR PA *Raleigh*
	PARKER, POE, ADAMS & BERNSTEIN *Charlotte*
	ROBINSON, BRADSHAW & HINSON PA *Charlotte*
	SMITH, ANDERSON, BLOUNT, DORSETT *Raleigh*
	WOMBLE CARLYLE SANDRIDGE *Winston-Salem*

Firms are listed alphabetically in each band.

Band 1

Constangy, Brooks & Smith LLC

The Firm: A specialist labor and employment law practice, with almost 100 attorneys across 13 offices. Market sources deem this firm to house "*highly skilled, specialized and focused*" attorneys whom clients applaud as "*fantastic.*" The group handles matters ranging from litigation and labor relations, to affirmative action and class action litigation. Wage and hour compliance is also dealt with. Clients range from small companies to Fortune 500 corporations, with a his-

torical emphasis on the textile industry. The service and health sectors are also rich veins of instructions. Highlight matters include defending class actions and Fair Labor Standards Act collective action lawsuits involving alleged wage and hour violations. The firm has also represented companies in over 40 compliance reviews conducted by the Office of Federal Contract Compliance Programs.

The Lawyers: "*One of the deans of the state's employment Bar,*" **John Doyle** focuses on assisting management clients with all aspects of labor and employment law. Highly respected colleague **Randolph Loftis** heads the firm's litigation practice group. A senior litigator, he has defended class action claims and cases involving, *inter alia*, sexual and racial harassment. The firm has consolidated its position with the acquisition of **Penni Pearson Bradshaw**. "*The first choice in conflicts*" for many, she focuses on immigration, counseling and litigation.

The Clients: Branch Banking & Trust; Chubb; Duke Energy; GE; Hertz; High Point Regional Hospital; RJ Reynolds; Randolph Hospital and Sara Lee.

Ogletree, Deakins, Nash, Smoak & Stewart PC

See firm details p.638

The Firm: One of the nation's largest firms specializing in labor and employment, the Raleigh

operation benefits from being able to draw upon the resources of 22 offices nationwide. Market commentators pointed to an "*excellent*" grouping boasting a "*strong pure labor practice.*" Peers conceded that the team has "*a great model for engaging in client development.*" The firm has the critical mass and scope of expertise to deal with any employment issue, including union-related issues. Age discrimination has come to the fore of late. The employment group is complemented by practice groups in business immigration, environmental law and occupational health and safety. Its depth of experience in dealing with union-organizing campaigns and running management training programs make this firm a popular choice among clients, many of whom derive from Fortune 50 companies.

The Lawyers: Focusing on workplace law, **Thomas Farr** (see p.1395) is a diligent lawyer commanding the respect of peers. Colleague **Matthew Keen** (see p.1396) is a new entrant to the table following market commendation for his litigation prowess.

The Clients: BASF; GE; IBM; Duke Energy and GlaxoSmithKline.

Smith Moore LLP

See firm details p.1400

The Firm: Clients endorsed the firm as an "*efficient and effective*" operation where attorneys are said to "*roll their sleeves up and get on with it.*"

North Carolina
Leading individuals
(Employment: Mainly Defendant)

[1]
| DOYLE John *Constangy Brooks*, Winston-Salem |
| ERWIN Martin *Smith Moore*, Greensboro |
| LOFTIS W Randolph *Constangy*, Winston-Salem |
| MCGINN Daniel *Brooks Pierce*, Greensboro |
| VAN HOY Philip *Van Hoy*, Charlotte |

[2]
| BELL Albert *Ward and Smith*, New Bern |
| BRADSHAW Penni *Constangy*, Winston-Salem |
| CARY William *Brooks Pierce*, Greensboro |
| FARR Thomas *Ogletree Deakins*, Cary |
| KEEN C Matthew *Ogletree Deakins*, Raleigh |
| RAINEY Richard *Womble Carlyle*, Charlotte |
| WARD Frank *Maupin Taylor*, Raleigh |

[3]
| JOHNSON Charles *Robinson Bradshaw*, Charlotte |
| KORANDO Kimberly *Smith Anderson*, Raleigh |
| WEDDINGTON Keith *Parker Poe*, Charlotte |
| WESTER John *Robinson Bradshaw*, Charlotte |

Individuals are listed alphabetically in each band.

Labor and employment is a core practice area with much of this firm's work centered on defending against union campaigns and unfair labor charges, alongside negotiating collective bargaining agreements. Over 20 attorneys practice in the areas of employment litigation, labor relations, human resources counseling and training, employee benefits, immigration, workers' compensation and OSHA.

The Lawyers: Proffering a wealth of experience in labor and employment matters, **Martin Erwin** (see p.1395) is a trial lawyer used by clients *"because he is like a bulldog: he won't let go of a problem until he gets a resolution."* He was also applauded as an *"excellent communicator able to create a rapport with those around him."*
The Clients: The firm represents companies from the Fortune 500 down to smaller companies across all industries.

Band 2

Brooks, Pierce, McLendon, Humphrey & Leonard LLP

The Firm: Sources acknowledge this full-service firm with offices in Greensboro and Raleigh as a force to be reckoned with in the field. Its labor and employment team defends clients against a wide variety of discriminatory actions involving age, sex, sexual harassment, race and religion. The firm also counsels on matters relating to assault, battery, defamation and wrongful death, in addition to providing advice on FLSA litigation.
The Lawyers: **Daniel McGinn** drew market praise as *"one of the state's best defense lawyers."* A seasoned employment lawyer, he is perceived as an expert negotiator in collective bargaining contexts and has represented management in over 150 arbitration hearings. Colleague **William Cary** counsels management in labor

and employment law matters, and advises clients on policy design and implementation to avoid litigation.
The Clients: AT&T; Battleground Restaurants; Citicorp; Crown Motors; Guilford County Schools; LaSalle Bank; Lorillard Tobacco; Moses Cone Health System and Wachovia.

Van Hoy Reutlinger Adams & Dunn

The Firm: This compact offering enjoys an enviable reputation in the Charlotte area for acting on the whole gamut of employment matters. It is for defending employment discrimination cases, on behalf of both government and private companies, that the firm attracts particular acclaim. For example, it defended a law firm against a claim from a former employee who alleged sexual discrimination. It also defended the Fayette Police Department against an allegation of racial harassment. Occupational health and safety, wage and hour cases and contractual disputes also contribute to the workload.
The Lawyers: *"If I could not hire myself, I'd have no hesitation in hiring him,"* conceded one peer of **Philip Van Hoy**. Credited with much of the firm's success in the field, he spearheads a team focusing on pure employment matters.
The Clients: Cape Fear Valley Medical Center; City of Charlotte; Corporate Health International; The Employers Association; Pfeiffer University; The Sanger Clinic; Mecklenburg County.

Band 3

Hunton & Williams

See firm details p.1775
The Firm: This Virginia-based firm has a broad reach across the USA and beyond. Two partners in the Raleigh office focus on labor and employment, often with a nationwide flavor. The caseload continues to be geared toward advising management on union matters, collective bargaining issues and strategic policy implementation. Highlights include acting on Dean v Philip Morris, involving Americans with Disabilities Act, discrimination, harassment and retaliation issues, and Birch v Philip Morris, a wrongful termination case. A further highlight was Rigo v Westvaco, an ERISA breach of fiduciary duty case.
The Lawyers: Thomas Manley spearheads the team.
The Clients: Dayton Power & Light; National Postal Mail Handlers Union; PacifiCorp; Public Service Company of New Mexico and United Airlines.

Kilpatrick Stockton LLP

See firm details p.634
The Firm: It is said to benefit from being able to draw on the resources of eight offices across the USA and Europe. As well as counseling employers on National Labor Relations Act matters, the team proffers experience in defending a wide

variety of employment-related lawsuits, including cases alleging employment discrimination, federal and state wage violations and wrongful discharge. Its attorneys have defended numerous multiplaintiff and class action cases under Title VII, ERISA and the Americans with Disabilities Act. The operation also gains from a firm-wide employee benefits practice.
The Lawyers: Lou Doherty is a key contact here.
The Clients: The firm acts for the likes of Sara Lee and Krispy Kreme.

Maupin Taylor, PA

The Firm: A major competitor in the marketplace, this full-service firm treats labor and employment as one of three core practice areas alongside corporate and litigation. Three offices across the state handle the full roster of employment law issues, from affirmative action to employee benefits, and employment relations to unemployment compensation defense. Nonlitigious matters are also covered, such as personnel manuals and employment relations.
The Lawyers: *"Totally first-rate lawyer"* **Frank Ward** was applauded by peers for being *"gentlemanly, low-key and effective."* He defends employers faced with allegations of discrimination. This involves representing clients before various governmental agencies, including the US Equal Employment Opportunity Commission and the North Carolina and US Departments of Labor.
The Clients: Alcoa; Blue Cross and Blue Shield of North Carolina; Caterpillar; City of Raleigh; DaimlerChrysler; Kerr Drug; SpectraSite and Waste Industries USA.

Parker, Poe, Adams & Bernstein LLP

The Firm: Esteemed by peers as a *"full-service firm with good attorneys and a strong litigation section,"* it attracts work from across the state and nationwide. Offices in North and South Carolina give it regional strength. Being part of the Employment Law Alliance, a national and international network of employment lawyers dedicated to advising employers, enhances its reach beyond the Southeast states. Its global connections are bolstered through the firm's membership of TerraLex, a network of independent law firms in 93 countries. Class actions, employment discrimination and dispute resolution all feature in the workload.
The Lawyers: Team head **Keith Weddington** attracted praise as *"a friendly competitor and a good presence in the marketplace."* Weddington benefits from extensive civil litigation experience, especially when it comes to representing employers in disputes with employees and former employees.
The Clients: Wachovia; Freightliner; Rack Room Shoes and Kernodle Clinic.

Robinson, Bradshaw & Hinson PA

The Firm: A new entrant to the table, this firm focuses primarily on nonunionized employers as well as general advice and litigation matters. Clients described a team that is *"responsive"* and *"gets the work straight to the lawyer with the appropriate expertise."* The employee benefits practice was also espied as especially talented. Highlights include acting in Mosely v Bojangles Restaurants, a case involving race discrimination where the firm's client was awarded summary judgment. The firm also enjoyed successful involvement in Clark v BASF Salaried Employees' Pension Plan.

The Lawyers: **Charles Johnson** was commended as a *"top litigator,"* while **John Wester** was also applauded by several market commentators for his expert civil litigation skills.

The Clients: Fast-food restaurants, healthcare and financial services industry players feature in the firm's clientele.

Smith, Anderson, Blount, Dorsett, Mitchell & Jernigan LLP

See firm details p.1401

The Firm: Researchers were inundated with client praise for this firm. It was acclaimed as *"just the right size, extremely responsive and cost-efficient."* One interviewee concluded, *"It does a phenomenal job for us."* Organized along the lines of an employment boutique, the team comprises approximately six partners, three with in-house experience. The firm offers specialist expertise in niche areas. Clients noted particularly proactive advice on workplace practices, personnel matters and dispute avoidance and resolution. The firm is involved in a class action lawsuit for a public company and assisted a pharmaceutical corporation on a downsizing exercise. It also assists subsidiaries of overseas entities on integration of rules within the workplace. Litigious activity includes defending clients against discrimination claims.

The Lawyers: *"Simply outstanding on employment law"* said clients of employment law practice group head **Kimberly Korando** (see p.1397). She has extensive experience assisting employers with federal and state employment law compliance and prevention of employee lawsuits.

The Clients: The firm has represented a range of clients from large multinationals to smaller local companies.

Womble Carlyle Sandridge & Rice PLLC

See firm details p.1402

The Firm: Clients praised the firm's ability to *"help us in multiple areas and be responsive to our needs,"* and appreciated the final product: *"qual-ity work at good prices."* Labor and employment attorneys reside in Charlotte, Raleigh, Durham, Greensboro and Winston-Salem. The firm has acted on a number of high-profile cases over the past year, such as the settlement of a class action in an employee benefits case. The firm was also successful in resolving a class action against the City of Wilmington and obtained summary judgment on behalf of Microsoft in a disability case.

The Lawyers: *"One of the state's best employment lawyers,"* **Richard Rainey** (see p.1398) litigates disputes on behalf of employers in the courtroom and before administrative agencies as well as giving proactive dispute avoidance advice.

The Clients: RF Micro Devices; Enterprise Rent-a-Car; Wal-Mart; Microsoft; Freightliner; Tyco Electronics; ALLTEL; INVISTA; Republic Mortgage Insurance; VF; AT&T and Patterson Dental.

Other Notable Practitioners

Albert Bell of Ward and Smith, PA attracts the admiration of peers as *"a man you would trust"* to produce *"first-rate work."* Practice head, Bell handles federal and state court litigation and advises clients on a wide range of regulatory and legislative issues.

ENVIRONMENT

North Carolina
Leading firms (Environment)

1	HUNTON & WILLIAMS *Raleigh*
2	BROOKS, PIERCE, MCLENDON *Greensboro*
	HAMILTON GASKINS FAY & MOON *Charlotte*
	HELMS MULLISS & WICKER PLLC *Charlotte*
	KENNEDY COVINGTON LOBDELL *Charlotte*
	KILPATRICK STOCKTON LLP *Raleigh*
	MAUPIN TAYLOR PA *Raleigh*
	PARKER, POE, ADAMS & BERNSTEIN *Charlotte*
	POYNER & SPRUILL LLP *Raleigh*
	ROBINSON, BRADSHAW & HINSON PA *Charlotte*
	SMITH MOORE LLP *Greensboro*
	WOMBLE CARLYLE SANDRIDGE *Charlotte*

Firms are listed alphabetically in each band.

Band 1

Hunton & Williams

See firm details p.1775

The Firm: This regionally based practice is part of a natural resources, regulatory and environmental law practice that ranks among the largest in the USA. It boasts a national reputation for its environmental work, and fields a team of 80 environment attorneys across the firm. The office in Raleigh handles both regulatory and transactional matters with the work including waste, water and air matters and brownfield redevelopments. Recent highlights for the team include securing a decision from the state Supreme Court that established that general permits for water can be appealed by industry groups. The team has also advised on water capacity programs and handled matters for the largest swine-processing center in the world.

The Lawyers: **Charles Case** (see p.1394) is the dean of the group, which peers believe has the *"premier practice in North Carolina."* He focuses on state and federal environmental, health and safety regulation. Interviewees praised him for his following among large national and international clients and for his legislative work.

The Clients: The group acts for utilities and entities from the developer and timber industries. Key clients include: Ingersoll-Rand; North Carolina Forestry Association; North Carolina Pork Council; Piedmont Triad Regional Water Authority; Raleigh-Durham Airport Authority and Waste Management.

Band 2

Brooks, Pierce, McLendon, Humphrey & Leonard LLP

The Firm: This is a group *"you can always count on for high-quality work,"* concluded clients. The firm is home to a wide-ranging environmental practice, encompassing federal and state wetland permitting and mitigation, surface and ground water pollution control and toxic torts litigation, *inter alia.* Clients benefit from the group's specialist expertise in the air, water/wetlands and hazardous waste areas; and attorneys here are well known for their strong relationships with the regulatory agencies. Highlight matters include defending an airport expansion project in Greensboro. The group succeeded in dismissing several suits filed to prevent the airport's construction and is handling a number of other related matters on appeal. The team also won a major mining litigation case where it was awarded a wetlands permit.

The Lawyers: **George House** attracted the lion's share of the praise. He is a *"first-rate litigator,"* who handles a broad range of environmental cases. One peer even commented, *"He's an excellent practitioner and might be the brightest*

North Carolina
Leading individuals (Environment)

1	**CASE Charles** *Hunton & Williams*, Raleigh
2	**BERLIN Stephen** *Kilpatrick Stockton*, Charlotte
	DAWSON Amos *Maupin Taylor*, Raleigh
	DE VORE Bradford *Womble Carlyle*, Charlotte
	DUNN Glenn *Poyner & Spruill*, Charlotte
	EARP Stephen *Smith Moore*, Greensboro
	FAY Richard *Hamilton Gaskins*, Charlotte
	FRANCHINA David *Kennedy Covington*, Charlotte
	GASKINS Richard *Hamilton Gaskins*, Charlotte
	GRIFFIN III Thomas *Parker Poe*, Charlotte
	GRUBBS R Howard *Womble Carlyle*, Winston-Salem
	HOUSE George *Brooks Pierce*, Greensboro
	HUTSON Benne *Helms Mulliss*, Charlotte
	JONES VAN BUREN Carolyn *Kennedy*, Charlotte
	LEVITAS Steven *Kilpatrick Stockton*, Raleigh
	MCCONNELL Alan *Kilpatrick Stockton*, Raleigh
	TOOLE William *Robinson Bradshaw*, Charlotte

Individuals are listed alphabetically in each band.

person I know. He will come up with new angles that nobody else has thought of."

The Clients: Caldwell County; City of Salisbury; ECOFLO; Guilford Mills; PCS Phosphate; Piedmont Triad Airport Authority; Primwest Holding and Village of Bald Head Island.

Hamilton Gaskins Fay & Moon

The Firm: Clients hailed this team as a *"highly organized, efficient operation."* Environmental litigation is a key element of this renowned niche practice group. The team's recent work includes advising on the settlement of multiparty toxic torts litigation and counseling on air pollution matters including permitting issues. Its client base has a number of national entities including ones from the oil, petroleum and chemical industries. This *"responsive"* team, comprising four partners, is well known for its prowess in litigated proceedings but also devotes much of its time to counseling clients on avoiding environmental liability and regulatory conflicts.

The Lawyers: According to peers, **Richard Gaskins** is *"a superb courtroom specialist"* who focuses on air and water permitting issues as well as other regulatory matters. Market commentators also applauded his ability to *"juggle complex litigations."* Clients also paid tribute to **Richard Fay**. He has particular experience defending companies in toxic torts litigation.

The Clients: The group represents oil companies, petroleum marketers and chemical companies.

Helms Mulliss & Wicker PLLC

The Firm: Clients endorsed this group for its *"business-minded approach to the law,"* and its responsive and *"extremely cost-effective"* attorneys. This is a national practice that comprises a team of three attorneys in the Charlotte office. They won special praise for their work on the

redevelopment of contaminated properties and brownfield sites. Recent highlights include advising on the first brownfield agreement for a public school on behalf of the Charlotte-Mecklenburg school authority and advising on a further brownfield agreement for the Johnson & Wales University. The group also successfully defended the issuance of a permit for a major municipal solid waste landfill for Allied Waste. Other facets of the workload include advising a local trade association on a legislative battle concerning the regulation of ozone from polluters. Lawyers are also busy advising on the development of compliance programs for a variety of companies.

The Lawyers: **Benne Hutson** is the key figure of this team, which is well known for its *"hard work on behalf of its clients."*

The Clients: The group acts for real estate developers, manufacturing companies and local governments. It also acts for: Rexam; Ruddick; Radiator Specialty and Siemens Westinghouse.

Kennedy Covington Lobdell & Hickman LLP

The Firm: This is one of the largest firms in the Southeast, with six offices across North and South Carolina. The environment practice is housed within the real estate department and attorneys here advise on the full gamut of environmental matters. These include acting for clients in hazardous waste litigation, defense of toxic torts suits and insurance coverage disputes. The group also provides support on all aspects of regulatory compliance and assists with permit transfers and environmental remediation in connection with transactions. The firm continues to act for Washington and Beaufort counties on one of North Carolina's highest-profile environmental cases. The team recently filed a motion with a US District Court requesting that an injunction be issued to permanently prohibit the US Navy from constructing an Outlying Landing Field in the two counties, raising issues relating to the NEPA.

The Lawyers: **Carolyn Jones Van Buren** focuses on environmental issues and risk in real estate and corporate transactions. She also won praise from peers for her strong reputation in litigation and permitting matters. Interviewees applauded chair of the environmental law practice group **David Franchina** for his *"candid, thorough, efficient"* manner. They believe that he boasts *"more experience than anyone in town in dealing with wetlands issues."*

The Clients: The group represents real estate developers, large banks, manufacturers and biotech and specialty chemical companies.

Kilpatrick Stockton LLP

See firm details p.634

The Firm: This group drew highest praise for work in the air arena where it offers clients specialist expertise in the guise of the indoor air

quality group. Preventive counseling and management of environmental permit processes form part of the firm's repertoire. Highlight matters include successfully challenging EPA's ambient air quality standards at the DC Circuit Court of Appeals. The team has also assisted in developing compliance strategies for the new ozone regulations and advises on National Ambient Air Quality Standards.

The Lawyers: Environmental law specialist **Stephen Berlin** (see p.1394) boasts a strong litigation practice. Interviewees believe his close ties with key movers and shakers in the North Carolina market ensure that matters are handled with efficiency and tact. **Steven Levitas** (see p.1397) is a talented lawyer who represents a wide range of clients on environmental regulatory matters. He focuses on wastewater permitting and compliance and waste remediation. Clients view **Alan McConnell** (see p.1397) as an *"unbeatable"* attorney, while peers admire him as a good business developer. McConnell provides environmental counseling and litigation services, with a particular emphasis on the CAA.

The Clients: The group represents southeastern and nationwide companies including textile manufacturers, food companies and hi-tech companies.

Maupin Taylor, PA

The Firm: The group handles a spectrum of environmental work including litigation, regulatory and transactional work. The team assists clients in regulatory permitting and compliance, including air emissions, water discharges, hazardous wastes and toxic substances; it also represents them in administrative and civil environmental litigation. The group's contentious work includes Superfund cost recovery actions. It has also handled a number of cases concerning federal wetlands regulations and involving negotiations with the US Army Corps of Engineers. Other cases include advising on the environmental aspects of a major expansion of a shopping center and the development of a large golf course in Southern Pines.

The Lawyers: **Amos Dawson** is *"great at dealing with the authorities"* and was heralded as an *"excellent litigator"* by numerous peers. He is currently counsel to a group of 350 companies in relation to the cleanup of an environmental waste facility that went bankrupt at Jamestown.

The Clients: The group acts for municipalities, large and midsized companies and a host of property clients.

Parker, Poe, Adams & Bernstein LLP

The Firm: Advising clients in the Southeast and beyond, this group maintains its strong litigation focus. It handles complex federal and state environmental litigation, including Superfund litigation and the defense of toxic torts actions.

1388   All quotes in the text are from interviews with clients and competitors.

CHAMBERS USA 2005

The team's noncontentious work ranges from providing regulatory compliance advice to preparing corporate procedures and policies. Brownfield work has dominated of late, with many of the group's clients hailing from the manufacturing sector.

The Lawyers: Market sources sang the praises of **Thomas Griffin**. Interviewees report that he is a good person to work with and recommended him for both his transactional and his litigation skills. He is also on hand to advise clients on compliance programs and environmental audits.

The Clients: The group acts for real estate developers, agricultural businesses, counties and municipalities.

Poyner & Spruill LLP

The Firm: This is a well-respected and broad practice that is renowned for its work on behalf of developers. The team advises on the whole gamut of environmental law including litigious matters such as permit disputes and citizen suits. Its workload also includes advising on the redevelopment of contaminated property and on wetlands-related issues. It also advises on CAA compliance and matters relating to the Coastal Area Management Act.

The Lawyers: **Glenn Dunn** continues to receive warm market acclaim. He advised a major lender on the environmental due diligence requirements and analyzed the environmental risks relating to its $50 million refinancing of convenience stores.

The Clients: Developers and municipalities are among its clientele.

Robinson, Bradshaw & Hinson PA

The Firm: Clients report that this firm offers "*excellent turnaround time and partner attention.*" It handles matters across the Southeast but its workload also has an international flavor, including advising on cross-jurisdictional matters in the Far East. The group offers clients a transactional service and advises on environmental liabilities in acquisitions and disposals of businesses. Compliance matters and litigation also form part of the practice. Recent highlights include obtaining a brownfield agreement on a complex site.

The Lawyers: Popular attorney **William Toole** was commended by clients as a "*well-rounded*" lawyer who is able to think outside the box. His practice includes a broad swath of environmental counseling and litigation work.

The Clients: CommScope; Ecusta Business Development Center; National Gypsum; Caraustar Industries and May Department Stores.

Smith Moore LLP

See firm details p.1400

The Firm: This group comprises around four lawyers, who are experienced practitioners in environmental transactional and litigation matters. Recent highlights for the team include assisting in the termination of a post-closure care permit for Avery Dennison that was originally issued under the Hazardous Waste Act. The team is also handling a number of brownfield site acquisitions.

The Lawyers: Researchers were impressed by the weight of feedback for the chair of the firm's management committee, **Stephen Earp** (see p.1395). Interviewees deemed him a key player on the North Carolina legal scene and pointed to his broad environmental practice. He advises

companies on transactional matters but also handles environmental disputes throughout the Southeast as well as regulatory matters.

The Clients: The group acts for a range of entities including municipalities and manufacturers.

Womble Carlyle Sandridge & Rice PLLC

See firm details p.1402

The Firm: Clients hailed this responsive team for its ability to meet their needs. They told us, "*The attorneys will not only use their initiative to get things done, but also work hard and go the extra mile to make sure that we are entirely satisfied.*" A new entrant to our tables, the group handles litigation and transactional matters for a number of Fortune 500 companies. It acts for several key players in the oil industry, and recent highlights include defending a number of these companies against allegations of environmental damage. Further high profile matters include acting for Bayer CropScience in a suit brought in 2002 under the CERCLA in relation to a large hazardous waste site in Henderson, Nevada. They provided regulatory and litigation counseling concerning the placement and construction of a large egg production facility in Hyde County. The issues arising are guidelines under the CWA, CAA, NEPA and equivalent North Carolina state laws.

The Lawyers: **Howard Grubbs** (see p.1396) and **Bradford De Vore** (see p.1395) form an "*excellent*" team according to clients. Their group advises on the CAA, the CWA and other state environmental regulations.

The Clients: The group acts for a number of Fortune 500 companies and several entities from the oil and gas industries.

LITIGATION

GENERAL COMMERCIAL

Band 1

Robinson, Bradshaw & Hinson PA

The Firm: This "*high-quality*" litigation department boasts expertise in a wide range of complex business disputes, including white-collar crime, fraud, antitrust and employment discrimination cases. Clients were delighted with the responsiveness and client-oriented service of the group stating that it "*shines in comparison with other firms.*" They also appreciated its commitment to "*understanding the needs of the client.*" Interviewees also pointed to the sheer effectiveness of the team, saying, "*It's just extremely good at what it does.*" The group is well known for assembling tailor-made teams to suit each case and has a knack of conjuring up inno-

vative solutions. Its headline cases include successfully arguing for 17 class actions alleging insider trading to be dismissed. It also successfully defended a national company against claims of unfair trading. Peers report that the firm also lays claim to an "*excellent*" antitrust department.

The Lawyers: The practice consists of a strong team of 40 litigators, including some highly renowned individuals. **John Wester** is a talented trial and appellate lawyer who clients report is "*very creative, diligent and thorough.*" **Ward McKeithen** is a senior member of the team and one of the most experienced commercial litigators in the region. Clients were particularly enthusiastic about **Mark Merritt**. He handles a varied caseload including antitrust and corpo-

rate securities disputes where part of his time is devoted to representing corporations in SEC investigations. The popular **Everett Bowman** is an antitrust litigation specialist who "*knows the law backwards.*" Clients report that he is "*an effective writer who gets to the crux of the issue.*"

The Clients: The firm represents clients in a wide range of industries including energy, banking, textiles, healthcare and retail. High-profile clients include: Carolina Panthers; Charlotte-Mecklenburg Hospital Authority; Duke Energy; McDevitt Street Bovis; Wachovia; Duke Endowment; Belk; National Gypsum; CommScope; Carolinas Medical Center; Mission Hospitals and Springs Industries.

North Carolina
Leading firms
(Litigation: General Commercial)

1 ROBINSON, BRADSHAW & HINSON PA *Charlotte*
WOMBLE CARLYLE SANDRIDGE *Winston-Salem*

2 BROOKS, PIERCE, MCLENDON *Greensboro*
SMITH MOORE LLP *Greensboro*

3 ELLIS & WINTERS LLP *Cary*
HELMS MULLISS & WICKER PLLC *Charlotte*
HUNTON & WILLIAMS *Charlotte*
KENNEDY COVINGTON LOBDELL LLP *Charlotte*
KILPATRICK STOCKTON LLP *Winston-Salem*
MOORE & VAN ALLEN PLLC *Charlotte*
PARKER, POE, ADAMS & BERNSTEIN LLP *Raleigh*
SMITH, ANDERSON, BLOUNT *Raleigh*

Leading individuals
(Litigation: General Commercial)

1 COWAN J Donald *Smith Moore, Greensboro*
DAVIS William *Bell Davis, Winston-Salem*
MCKEITHEN Ward *Robinson Bradshaw, Charlotte*
VAUGHAN Keith *Womble Carlyle, Winston-Salem*
WESTER John *Robinson Bradshaw, Charlotte*
WILLIAMS Jim *Brooks Pierce, Greensboro*

2 COONEY James *Womble Carlyle, Charlotte*
COVINGTON George *Kennedy Covington, Charlotte*
COVINGTON Peter *Helms Mulliss, Charlotte*
DAVIS Jeffrey *Moore & Van Allen, Charlotte*
MERRITT Mark *Robinson Bradshaw, Charlotte*
MILLEN Pressly *Womble Carlyle, Raleigh*
PATTERSON Carl *Smith Anderson, Raleigh*
RAPER William *Womble Carlyle, Charlotte*
SITTON Larry *Smith Moore, Greensboro*
TAYLOR Daniel *Kilpatrick Stockton, Winston-Salem*

3 BARBER Timothy *Womble Carlyle, Charlotte*
COPENHAVER W Andrew *Womble, Winston-Salem*
ELLIS Richard *Ellis & Winters, Cary*
EY Douglas *Helms Mulliss, Charlotte*
FURR Jeffrey *Womble Carlyle, Winston-Salem*
HANNA III George *Moore & Van Allen, Charlotte*
OLEYNIK Jeffrey *Brooks Pierce, Greensboro*
PHILLIPS Jim *Brooks Pierce, Greensboro*
RIKARD William *Parker Poe, Charlotte*
SPEARMAN Robert *Parker Poe, Raleigh*

Leading individuals (Antitrust)

1 BARNHARDT III John *Alston & Bird, Charlotte*
BOWMAN Everett *Robinson Bradshaw, Charlotte*
COPENHAVER W Andrew *Womble, Winston-Salem*
ENNS Rodrick *Enns & Archer, Winston-Salem*
HOROSCHAK Mark *Womble Carlyle, Charlotte*
KENYON Douglas *Hunton & Williams, Raleigh*
MURCHISON John *Kennedy Covington, Charlotte*
OLEYNIK Jeffrey *Brooks Pierce, Greensboro*
SAWCHAK Matthew *Ellis & Winters, Cary*
SITTON Larry *Smith Moore, Greensboro*

Firms and individuals are listed alphabetically in each band.

Womble Carlyle Sandridge & Rice PLLC

See firm details p.1402

The Firm: Clients confidently claim that this is an *"extremely high-caliber nationwide litigation practice that you could put up against anyone."* They also believe it is *"as good as a New York firm but much more cost-effective."* It covers a wide range of commercial disputes, but is particularly well known for its products liability and antitrust work. A recent highlight included securing a favorable settlement for defendant RJ Reynolds in the high profile DeLoach v Philip Morris antitrust case. This concerned claims by US tobacco growers that US cigarette manufacturers engaged in price-fixing activities at tobacco auctions.

The Lawyers: The *"thorough, thoughtful and determined"* **Keith Vaughan** (see p.1399) is the managing partner of the department and one of its most high-profile litigators. Our sources agree that **William Raper** (see p.1398) is a *"very fine choice"* for complex business disputes, while **James Cooney** (see p.1395) was also named as *"an extraordinary litigator."* **Pressly Millen** (see p.1397) excels in trade regulation, antitrust and commercial litigation and *"blends superb counseling ability with expert litigation skills."* Clients report that he listens to their concerns and involves them in all stages of the process. **Jeffrey Furr** (see p.1396) has *"an agile mind"* and clients are *"fully confident"* in his ability to handle major cases. **Timothy Barber** (see p.1394) was highly rated by peers, who also recommended **Andrew Copenhaver** (see p.1395) as *"superb"* for both general commercial and antitrust litigation. **Mark Horoschak** (see p.1396) is *"a true antitrust specialist"* who has *"extremely advanced knowledge in the healthcare field."* He also has considerable experience in government investigations.

The Clients: The group represents regional, national and international corporations and law firms.

Band 2

Brooks, Pierce, McLendon, Humphrey & Leonard LLP

The Firm: Competitors respect this team as *"a major force in the field."* Observers attribute the group's success to the quality of its lawyers and the way in which they work together so well as a team. It undertakes a broad swath of complex litigation such as antitrust, torts, professional malpractice and stockholder disputes. It also has a strong track record in unfair and deceptive trade practices and breach of contract claims.

The Lawyers: **Jim Williams** is *"a real heavyweight litigator"* who represents a long list of corporations. Clients appreciate his *"excellent analytical mind"* and peers particularly commend his vast experience in tort cases. Research

confirmed **Jim Phillips** as an excellent attorney in complex business disputes. **Jeffrey Oleynik** is a general litigator who also turns his hand successfully to antitrust matters. He currently chairs the Antitrust and Trade Regulation Law Section of the North Carolina Bar Association.

The Clients: The firm represents a wide variety of clients including financial institutions, nationwide companies, trade associations and healthcare organizations.

Smith Moore LLP

See firm details p.1400

The Firm: This courtroom-focused firm works on the full gamut of business litigation and is active on a national scale. Satisfied clients report that *"everything it files is very well prepared, targeted and relevant."* A varied caseload has seen the group defend Krispy Kreme in 12 cases brought by various groups of stockholders alleging improper financing. Lawyers also represented Honeywell in 70 toxic tort exposure cases. Additionally, the group is acting for Philip Morris in a class action suit brought by tobacco growers alleging that cigarette manufacturers rigged tobacco auctions.

The Lawyers: **Donald Cowan** (see p.1395) is *"a big hitter"* on the litigation front. He is a true generalist whom clients rate for the breadth of his expertise. They told us, *"You'd want him in any case you were working on."* **Larry Sitton** (see p.1398) is another senior member of the team and excels at both general commercial and antitrust cases.

The Clients: The client list varies between smaller local entities and Fortune 500 companies. These include: Atlantic Coast Conference; Eli Lilly; GE; Miller Brewing Company; Solutia; Stockhausen; Procter & Gamble; Philip Morris; Krispy Kreme; Tradewinds Airlines and Honeywell.

Band 3

Ellis & Winters LLP

The Firm: This is a smaller group that nonetheless attracted recommendations from peers as *"a very focused practice producing superb quality work."* Clients enjoy working with the team because *"it's responsive and the lawyers speak in layman's terms."* It is particularly noted for its work in pharmaceutical/medical device cases and antitrust litigation. Its lawyers have been involved in some major class action cases in recent times. These include acting for a number of major defendants against allegations of price-fixing in both raw polyester and cotton yarn.

The Lawyers: **Richard Ellis** is a skilled litigator who clients believe can try any kind of commercial litigation case. He is especially experienced in toxic torts and pharmaceutical cases. **Matthew Sawchak** is *"top of the list"* for antitrust cases because he is *"very sharp, and an excellent communicator who clearly explains all*

1390   All quotes in the text are from interviews with clients and competitors.

CHAMBERS USA 2005

the options."

The Clients: The firm represents a mix of regional and national players active in North Carolina.

Helms Mulliss & Wicker PLLC

The Firm: This group provides its strong financial services industry client base with a premier banking and insurance litigation practice. It also has considerable experience in IP litigation, and is leading the way in defending major class action lawsuits. It earns strong client endorsement as "*a sensible and well-rounded team*" and is particularly picked out for its skills in media and First Amendment matters.

The Lawyers: **Peter Covington** is an active member of the Bar with "*a strong reputation.*" He is an expert in financial services litigation where he regularly represents broker dealer clients in arbitrations, litigations and regulatory issues. **Douglas Ey** heads the litigation department and is another visible player in the sector. He has a wide general commercial litigation and products liability practice, and earns client respect as "*an astute advocate who thinks outside the box.*"

The Clients: The firm represents a wide array of financial institutions, insurance companies, brokers and dealers.

Hunton & Williams

See firm details p.1775

The Firm: This general commercial litigation group is popular with clients because of its "*prompt, efficient and high-quality*" service. The practice has an emphasis on technology and toxic tort cases, which includes software licensing and products liability disputes and significant antitrust cases. It also works on wrongful death cases and recently represented Duke University Health System in a case concerning a teenage girl who was given transplant organs that were incompatible.

The Lawyers: **Douglas Kenyon** (see p.1396) is the firm's most active antitrust lawyer and is rated by peers as a "*very knowledgeable*" practitioner. He represents a range of multinationals on antitrust issues in the USA and Canada, and is particularly praised for his work in merger control matters. He was also picked out as "*a go-to guy*" in contentious IP cases.

The Clients: The firm works for a variety of national entities including medical companies and large manufacturers.

Kennedy Covington Lobdell & Hickman LLP

The Firm: This firm offers a full-service commercial litigation department, but it is particularly well known for its strong performance in financial services litigation. Its work in real estate and securities litigation also garners praise, and it has "*a first-class arbitration team.*" Clients

revealed that this is an "*extremely responsive*" team, whose talented partners "*compare favorably with the big city firms.*"

The Lawyers: **George Covington** is a highly rated banking litigator who is also well versed in employment issues. Market sources say, "*He is a lawyer who has genuinely been there and done everything.*" He has been particularly active in securities cases of late. **John Murchison** is a senior member of the team whom interviewees described as an "*excellent*" antitrust lawyer. He picks up praise for his work in trade regulations, and advises international companies on various aspects of international product distribution.

The Clients: Clients include: AAC Real Estate Services; Bank of America; Coca-Cola and Duke Energy and various of its subsidiaries.

Kilpatrick Stockton LLP

See firm details p.634

The Firm: This "*business-oriented*" litigation practice handles a varied caseload for big-name clients all along the East Coast. Highlights include representing RJ Reynolds in a major products liability case, and advising Deloitte Touche Tohmatsu in a reinsurance dispute. Clients are very happy with the service they receive here, stating that the group provides "*high-caliber lawyers who are responsive and sensitive to clients' needs.*"

The Lawyers: **Daniel Taylor** (see p.1398) is a "*top-level litigator*" whom clients rate as "*one of the best lawyers out there.*" He recently acted for RJ Reynolds in the successful dismissal of an ERISA class action. The case arose out of the spin-off of RJ Reynolds Tobacco Co. from RJR Nabisco in 1999.

The Clients: The client list includes RJ Reynolds, Sara Lee and Deloitte Touche Tohmatsu.

Moore & Van Allen PLLC

The Firm: This renowned banking firm fields a talented litigation team that naturally focuses much of its practice on the representation of financial institutions. It handles a spectrum of disputes including contract-related matters, bankruptcy, lender liability and securities litigation. However, the practice extends beyond these and lawyers here have experience in a range of industries. Their portfolio of cases also includes construction and energy industry disputes and products liability litigation.

The Lawyers: **Jeffrey Davis** is a "*splendid*" litigator who has also developed deep experience in mediations and arbitrations. Peers also recommended his colleague, **George Hanna** as a "*marvelous*" attorney.

The Clients: The firm predominantly represents banks and financial institutions, but also works for telecom companies, healthcare providers and heavy industry manufacturers.

Parker, Poe, Adams & Bernstein LLP

The Firm: Widely respected by its peers, this experienced and high-quality litigation practice has expertise in a broad array of matters. The group's caseload includes antitrust, trade regulation and business torts litigation. Clients also call on the group for its support in other litigated proceedings including professional malpractice cases and IP disputes, including pharmaceutical patent cases.

The Lawyers: **Robert Spearman** leads the antitrust and business torts practice. He has a broad caseload and is respected by peers as an "*excellent*" practitioner. He successfully represented a group of school districts in a case which they brought against the State of North Carolina over education funding. The state Supreme Court recently ruled that the state had indeed neglected some of its duties and ordered it to provide better resources for education. The chair of the litigation department, **William Rikard**, has also had a very successful year and was recommended to researchers as one of the state's leading litigators.

The Clients: The group acts for a diverse client base that includes national corporations and school district authorities.

Smith, Anderson, Blount, Dorsett, Mitchell & Jernigan LLP

See firm details p.1401

The Firm: Clients enthused about this broad-based practice that specializes in serving the needs of large companies. Many highlighted the "*cost-efficient*" service, with one client stating, "*You really get your money's worth.*" Clients also raved about the "*phenomenal work*" and "*effective representation*" that you get from the firm. Highlights include acting for EDS in a dispute regarding the nonrenewal of its contract for processing North Carolina's Medicaid claims. It also recently defended a major financial institution in a New York federal court in a $300 million claim brought by another high-profile financial institution.

The Lawyers: The "*extremely talented*" **Carl Patterson** (see p.1398) specializes in high risk and high value cases, and has a great reputation among peers and clients alike.

The Clients: The client base predominantly consists of large, publicly listed companies, including financial institutions and international corporations.

Other Notable Practitioners

William Davis of Bell, Davis & Pitt, PA is a senior member of the Bar and a renowned expert in securities litigation. **John Barnhardt** (see p.1394) of Alston & Bird LLP works on both antitrust and IP disputes, where peers regard him as "*the state expert*" on the interconnection between the two areas. **Rodrick Enns** of

Enns & Archer LLP is an outstanding practitioner in the antitrust field. His practice includes defending clients against allegations of price-fixing although he also advises on employment cases.

REAL ESTATE

North Carolina
Leading firms (Real Estate)

[1] KENNEDY COVINGTON LOBDELL *Charlotte*
ROBINSON, BRADSHAW & HINSON PA *Charlotte*
WOMBLE CARLYLE SANDRIDGE *Winston-Salem*

[2] MANNING FULTON & SKINNER PA *Raleigh*
MOORE & VAN ALLEN PLLC *Charlotte*

[3] HELMS MULLISS & WICKER PLLC *Charlotte*
MAUPIN TAYLOR PA *Raleigh*
PARKER, POE, ADAMS & BERNSTEIN *Charlotte*
SMITH MOORE LLP *Greensboro*
SMITH, ANDERSON, BLOUNT, DORSETT *Raleigh*

Leading individuals (Real Estate)

Senior Statesman
FULTON Charles *Manning Fulton, Raleigh*

[1] ADAMS Alfred *Womble Carlyle, Winston-Salem*
OLIVER JR Samuel *Manning Fulton, Raleigh*
PRICHARD Allen *Kennedy Covington, Charlotte*
TORSTRICK Brent *Robinson Bradshaw, Charlotte*

[2] DONADIO Donald *Womble Carlyle, Raleigh*
OATES J Christopher *Moore & Van Allen, Charlotte*

[3] CLARK Reuben *Maupin Taylor, Raleigh*
DORTON David *Maupin Taylor, Raleigh*
EVANS Brian *Kennedy Covington, Charlotte*
HARDYMON Glen *Kennedy Covington, Charlotte*
LOEB Christopher *Robinson Bradshaw, Charlotte*
MASON C Steven *Smith Anderson, Raleigh*
TIPPS Maynard *Kennedy Covington, Charlotte*

Firms and individuals are listed alphabetically in each band.

Band 1

Kennedy Covington Lobdell & Hickman LLP

The Firm: As one of the oldest firms in the Southeast it has strong roots throughout North and South Carolina. Several clients described a *"fully integrated"* real estate practice that can be relied upon for *"seamless service in an efficient and timely manner."* It comprises 40 lawyers, said to enjoy nothing more than sinking their teeth into complex real estate issues. Located in Charlotte and Raleigh, the team is split into specialist sets responsible for land use, environment, and general commercial and real estate work. Mixed-use development and environmental matters, financing and leasing are also covered, while its zoning and land use practice was singled out as *"the best in the Southeast."* Recent highlights include representing the City of Charlotte in a $41 million hotel project.

The Lawyers: All of the following lawyers came highly recommended. **Allen Prichard** focuses on commercial real estate development and lending. He has acted on numerous retail, office, apartment and mixed-use developments. **Brian Evans** is cochair of the mixed-use/planned development practice group and a popular choice among clients who noted his excellent work in the development sector. Real estate department chair **Glen Hardymon** assists a broad range of clients with complex real estate matters. Meanwhile **Maynard Tipps** generally represents real estate developers, investors, managers and landlords on complex commercial real estate transactions.

The Clients: Clients range from municipalities involved in public-private matters to entrepreneurial developers. Other clients include: Mills Corporation; Spectrum Properties; City of Charlotte and Summit Properties.

Robinson, Bradshaw & Hinson PA

The Firm: *"Unfailingly responsive and professional,"* this firm *"gets the work done for a reasonable cost,"* concluded clients. Interviewees were also drawn to a team of attorneys who *"do what they say they are going to."* The team has ten partners who are said to *"work well together."* Primarily a developer-oriented practice, it also handles a portion of lender work. It is regularly involved in pre-development issues such as negotiating and structuring ownership entities, tax planning, property due diligence and land use planning and regulation. Recent highlights for the firm include representing Faison affiliates in the portfolio sale and leasing of an office building project in Fairfax County. It acted for the same client in negotiating a joint venture with a national private equity firm, and closing a multimillion-dollar credit facility for the development of mixed-use condominium project. Assisting Collett affiliates with the development of power centers in Asheville and Charlotte was another significant work highlight.

The Lawyers: **Brent Torstrick** received plaudits for his *"unmatched intellect"* and personable approach in dealings with peers. Clients described him as a *"wonderfully efficient person who is quick to get to the inner workings of a deal and the heart of the matter."* **Christopher Loeb** was praised by clients for his responsiveness. He specializes in environmental, commercial real estate and commercial lending matters.

The Clients: Two of the largest clients for the firm are Faison Enterprises and Crescent Resources.

Womble Carlyle Sandridge & Rice PLLC

See firm details p.1402

The Firm: A *"megafirm which does everything"* and one of the largest in North Carolina. Peers said it boasts a *"cracking real estate team"* with special expertise in the debt finance sector. The outfit is well regarded for its work in the retail sector, where it acts for a raft of clients including the likes of Lowe's Home Centers. It also advises developers on several projects, currently including a biomedical research park. Further highlights include assisting Wake Forest University Health Sciences with creating the largest downtown research park in the USA, requiring a 180-acre site.

The Lawyers: **Alfred Adams** (see p.1394) is *"a lawyer from the old school and a gentleman to deal with,"* not to mention *"always impressive."* **Donald Donadio** (see p.1395) also maintains his reputation in the marketplace.

The Clients: Thomasville Furniture Industries and Natuzzi Americas are both notable clients. They are complemented by developers in retail, office and residential sectors and large lenders.

Band 2

Manning Fulton & Skinner PA

The Firm: It proffers a large and specialized practice with an emphasis on representing developers and leaseholders. It is renowned as a *"great firm,"* handling a large volume of commercial real estate matters, particularly within the retail sector. Financings and complex multi-asset transactions involving several jurisdictions are also dealt with. Team members are experienced in residential, hotel and leisure, office, shopping center and shopping mall projects as well as mixed use developments.

The Lawyers: **Samuel Oliver** was acclaimed for his commercial acumen and as a *"resourceful lawyer who understands the business side as well as the technical aspects of a deal."* He was also applauded by peers for being *"a superbly patient straight shooter."* One of the first lawyers in the region to specialize in real estate, **Charles Fulton** is recognized by peers as having been *"the dean of the real estate Bar for years now."* The aura of success associated with the operation is largely perceived to stem from his prodigious efforts. Fulton continues to represent developers on a broad range of projects.

The Clients: Clients include real estate brokers and property management firms as well as major owners and developers of commercial and industrial properties. Others featuring in the list are: Carolantic Realty; Craig Davis Properties; Fonville Morisey Realty; Prestage Farms and Southern Equipment Company.

Moore & Van Allen PLLC

The Firm: Clients endorsed this firm for providing *"true quality above quantity"* and *"articulating the overall picture very well."* Its specialist real estate tax expertise drew special praise. Developers form the bulk of the firm's client base, though the team is equally adept at handling tenant work. A specialist financing group handles lending work. One of the fastest growing law firms in the Southeast, it acts on a variety of matters, including retail and mixed-use projects. Other work includes permanent financing, loan restructuring, workouts, collateral lease issues and environmental reviews.

The Lawyers: Charlotte commercial real estate team leader **Christopher Oates** is said to possess *"superb judgment,"* while maintaining good relationships with his peers. He focuses on commercial real estate and land use law.

The Clients: Local and regional developers, institutional investors, insurance companies and financial institutions.

Band 3

Helms Mulliss & Wicker PLLC

The Firm: This firm is primarily known for providing a real estate service to an impressive roster of corporate and banking clients. With over 100 lawyers spread across three offices, the full-service real estate practice advises a wide range of clients. These include real estate developers, brokers, contractors, managers and other real estate professionals as well as owners and corporate tenants.

The Lawyers: Notable practitioner Robert Brinkley has retired from the practice, which is now headed by Robert Simmons.

The Clients: Lenders, developers, investors and owners.

Maupin Taylor, PA

The Firm: This is a busy practice housing highly respected practitioners. It is considered especially adroit at handling the needs of clients working on complex projects involving multiple sites. The firm boasts extensive experience in the financing, acquisition and development of numerous high-value ventures, including commercial parks, mixed-use developments, apartment complexes, shopping centers and agricultural and industrial facilities. Highlights include assisting a subsidiary of a Fortune 500 company with the acquisition and leasing of photo finishing facilities across the USA. Further highlights that are national in scope include assisting a shopping center developer with sites across the country. It also acted for a regional drugstore chain on site acquisitions across North and South Carolina. Other areas of expertise include environmental as well as foreclosures and workouts for distressed real estate development and lender representation.

The Lawyers: **David Dorton** is said to be a personable and pragmatic attorney. One interviewee summed him up as being *"astute in determining cost-effective and efficient solutions."* He has represented estate clients in the acquisition, development, financing and leasing of real estate. Colleague **Reuben Clark** practices in the firm's business section and handles complex commercial real estate matters.

The Clients: Developers, lenders and businesses with property portfolios.

Parker, Poe, Adams & Bernstein LLP

The Firm: A firm enjoying a good reputation, it assists clients in structuring, negotiating and closing commercial real estate transactions. The development and financing of new projects is also a feature. Recent highlights include acting on several shopping center, office and hotel acquisitions. The sale of apartment projects to REITs and private investors also contributed to the workload. Recent development work has involved land acquisition, construction financing and takeout joint ventures for apartment projects across the USA.

The Lawyers: Samuel Woodward spearheads the team.

The Clients: Developers, lenders and owners.

Smith Moore LLP

See firm details p.1400

The Firm: A Greensboro-based firm servicing clients in North Carolina, Georgia and the Southeast in general. It has offices in Raleigh, North Carolina as well as Atlanta, Georgia. This practice boasts a long history of acting for, *inter alia*, developers of residential properties and shopping centers. Highlights include acting for Citicorp in the sale of a call center built for 2000 employees. Finance, fund formation and tax structuring are additional specialist areas handled by the team.

The Lawyers: Charles Melvin is the key contact here.

The Clients: Bonset America; Jefferson Pilot Financial; Liberty Property Trust and R Twining.

Smith, Anderson, Blount, Dorsett, Mitchell & Jernigan LLP

See firm details p.1401

The Firm: Clients claim this firm benefits from a stable of lawyers that includes *"some of the best around."* They also applaud a *"well-integrated team"* on whom they can rely for *"attorneys with the right expertise."* Primarily a real estate finance practice, it acts for the likes of Bank of America and Wachovia. Mixed-use projects have also come to the fore of late, including mixed-use and office developments. The team has additionally acted on ground lease financing and sale and leaseback transactions. Real estate work is also conducted for corporate clients and developers, focusing on retail, commercial and residential sectors.

The Lawyers: *"One of the best lawyers around,"* **Steve Mason** (see p.1397) continues to attract the lion's share of praise as a real estate attorney who *"knows the law inside out."*

The Clients: Among numerous others, the firm acts for Progress Energy.

Leaders in North Carolina

ADAMS, Alfred G
Womble Carlyle Sandridge & Rice,
PLLC, Winston-Salem 336 721 3642
aadams@wcsr.com
Recommended in Real Estate
Practice Areas: Mr Adams practices in
the areas of commercial real estate trans-
actions and real estate lending.
Prof. Memberships: North Carolina
Bar Association, Board of Governors and
Chair, Real Property Section; American
College of Mortgage Attorneys; Ameri-
can College of Real Estate Attorneys.
Certified Specialist, North Carolina State
Bar Board of Legal Specialization in Real
Property Transactions: Business, Com-
mercial, Industrial and Residential.
Career: Adjunct Professor of Law, 1995-
present, Wake Forest University School
of Law; JD, 1973, Wake Forest University
School of Law, associate editor, Wake
Forest Law Review, Moot Court Board;
BA, 1968, Wake Forest University.

BALDWIN III, Garza
Womble Carlyle Sandridge & Rice
PLLC, Charlotte 704 331 4907
gbaldwin@wcsr.com
Recommended in Corporate/M&A
Practice Areas: Garza Baldwin has 25
years of experience advising public and
private companies and their affiliates
regarding their securities law obligations. Garza helps his clients raise capital, structure, negotiate and complete
M&A transactions, and comply on an
ongoing basis with the federal securities
laws and regulations. He also advises
special committees of boards of directors and their financial advisers regarding change in control transactions.
Prof. Memberships: American Bar
Association and North Carolina Bar
Association, Business Law Sections.
Personal: JD, 1978, Wake Forest University School of Law, managing editor,
'Law Review'; AB, 1973, University of
North Carolina at Chapel Hill.

BARBER, Timothy G
Womble Carlyle Sandridge & Rice
PLLC, Charlotte 704 331 4937
tbarber@wcsr.com
Recommended in Litigation
Practice Areas: Mr Barber has a broad-
based business litigation practice, with
emphasis on securities issues and technology.
Prof. Memberships: North Carolina
Bar Association and American Bar Association, Litigation Sections. Admitted to
practice before the US Supreme Court;
US District Courts for the Eastern, Middle and Western Districts of North Carolina; US Court of Appeals for the Federal Circuit; US Court of Appeals for the
Fourth Circuit.
Career: Practice Group Leader, business
litigation, 1998-present. JD, 1985, Wake
Forest University School of Law, cum
laude, editor in chief, 'Law Review'; BA,
1977, Kenyon College.

BARNHARDT III, John J
Alston & Bird LLP, Charlotte
704 444 1009
jbarnhardt@alston.com
Recommended in Antitrust
Practice Areas: Intellectual property
litigation, antitrust claims, counter-
claims.
Prof. Memberships: State Bar of North
Carolina; U.S. Patent and Trademark
Office; American Intellectual Property
Law Association (former Chair,
Antitrust Committee)
Career: Former Co-Chair, Alston &
Bird IP Litigation Group. Practice has
included several complex, multidistrict
IP and antitrust litigation cases in feder-
al court, as well as unfair trade litigation
before the International Trade Commis-
sion. Listed in two leading legal publica-
tions for his litigation expertise.
Personal: BS, Davidson College (1967);
JD, University of Virginia (1972).

BELL, Albert
Ward and Smith, PA, New Bern
252 672 5400
Recommended in Employment

BERLIN, Stephen R
Kilpatrick Stockton LLP, Charlotte
336 607 7304
SBerlin@KilpatrickStockton.com
Recommended in Environment
Practice Areas: Environmental law,
including environmental litigation,
business transactions involving environmental issues (including Brownfields)
and environmental compliance matters,
private environmental costs recovery
actions and representations of potentially responsible parties at Superfund sites
and RCRA issues.
Prof. Memberships: Forsyth County
Bar Association (President), North Carolina Bar Association, Master of Bench,
Joseph Branch Inn of Court.
Career: Head of the firm's Environmental Group; Adjunct Professor Wake Forest University.
Publications: Has published papers and
made presentations on various environmental topics.
Personal: BA, Wake Forest University,
magna cum laude; JD, Wake Forest University cum laude, 1984; law clerk to
Chief Judge Hiram H Ward.

BOOE, Mike
Kennedy Covington Lobdell & Hickman
LLP, Charlotte 704 331 7400
Recommended in Bankruptcy

BOWMAN, Everett
Robinson, Bradshaw & Hinson PA,
Charlotte 704 377 2536
Recommended in Antitrust

BRADSHAW, Penni
Constangy, Brooks & Smith, LLC,
Winston-Salem 336 721 1001
Recommended in Employment

BRADY, Christopher J
Mayer, Brown, Rowe & Maw LLP,
Charlotte 704 444 3511
cbrady@mayerbrownrowe.com
Recommended in Capital Markets
Practice Areas: Specializes in securitization and other structured finance
products. Represents issuers, underwriters, placement agents, servicers and
trustees in private and public executions
in term securitizations of a range of
asset types, including commercial mortgages, residential mortgages, auto loans,
aircraft loans and student loans. Also
represent two of the largest servicers of
commercial mortgage-backed securities,
including in connection with acquisitions of servicing rights. Represent program sponsor in connection with the
establishment of commercial paper program and mortgage originator in connection with warehouse facility.
Career: Mayer, Brown, Rowe & Maw
LLP, Charlotte, 1999 to date; Partner,
2002. Kilpatrick Stockton LLP, 1993-99.
Personal: JD, University of North Carolina School of Law, 1993; Order of the
Coif, Dean's List; North Carolina Law
Review. BS, (cum laude) University of
North Carolina at Charlotte, 1983.

BUCK, Peter
Robinson, Bradshaw & Hinson PA,
Charlotte 704 377 2536
*Recommended in Banking & Finance,
Corporate/M&A*

CALDWELL, Stokely
Robinson, Bradshaw & Hinson PA,
Charlotte 704 377 2536
Recommended in Banking & Finance

CAMPBELL, Boyd
Helms Mulliss & Wicker PLLC, Charlotte
704 343 2000
*Recommended in Banking & Finance,
Corporate/M&A*

CARROLL, James P
Cadwalader, Wickersham & Taft LLP,
Charlotte 704 348 5116
james.carroll@cwt.com
Recommended in Capital Markets
Practice Areas: Managing Partner of
Cadwalader's Charlotte office and a
member of the firm's Management
Committee. Concentrates in the areas of
real estate finance and securitization.
Represents national, international, and
regional financial institutions, investment banks, pension funds, and
investors in the financing, acquisition,
disposition and leasing of commercial
office buildings, shopping centers,
hotels, industrial warehouses, merchandise marts, multifamily housing, residential and planned unit developments,
including golf course developments. Has
an active capital markets practice in
mortgage loan conduit programs, mortgage pool purchases and sales as well as
multiple property and single asset real
estate securitizations.

Personal: Served from 1985-96 as
adjunct Professor of Law at George
Washington University, where he lec-
tured in the area of real estate finance.
Serves as Chairman of the Real Estate
Securitization Section of the American
Bar Association's Real Property Divi-
sion. Received his BA, with honors, from
Georgetown University, and his JD, with
honors, from The Catholic University of
America. Chairman of ABA Section on
Real Estate Securitization (2001-pre-
sent).

CARY, William
Brooks, Pierce, McLendon, Humphrey
& Leonard LLP, Greensboro
336 373 8850
Recommended in Employment

CASE, Charles D
Hunton & Williams, Raleigh
919 899 3045
ccase@hunton.com
Recommended in Environment
Practice Areas: Charles Case's practice
focuses on state and federal environmental, health and safety regulation, as
well as administrative law and lobbying,
with particular emphasis on the regulation of air quality, toxic and hazardous
materials and wastes, land and water
resource usage, and contaminated site
remediation. He was named in 2004 by
Business North Carolina to the Legal
Elite Hall of Fame (ranked as the state's
top practitioner in environmental law
for the first three years of the Legal Elite
ranking).

CLARK, Reuben
Maupin Taylor, P.A., Raleigh
919 981 4000
Recommended in Real Estate

COHEN, Steven N
Cadwalader, Wickersham & Taft LLP,
Charlotte 704 348 5176
steven.cohen@cwt.com
Recommended in Capital Markets
Practice Areas: Partner resident in
Cadwalader's New York, NY and Charlotte, NC offices. Represents domestic
and foreign commercial banks, investment banks and other financial institutions in a wide variety of financing
transactions, including leveraged
finance and other syndicated bank loan
transactions, the financing of financial
assets, structured finance transactions,
cross-border financings, commodity
finance transactions, hedge fund financings, credit enhancement transactions,
workouts and debtor-in-possession
financings, the trading of distressed debt,
and various innovative financing transactions. Serves as a member of Cadwalader's Legal Opinions Committee.
Personal: Law clerk to the Honorable
Max Rosenn, Senior Circuit Judge, United States Court of Appeals for the Third
Circuit. Graduated magna cum laude in
1976 from Wesleyan University and

received his JD degree in 1981 from New York University School of Law, where he was note and comment editor of the New York University Law Review. Also attended the Lycée Classique Mixte, in Saintes, France, from which he received a baccalauréat with high honors (mention bien) in 1971. Member of the American Bar Association (including the Section of Business Law).

COONEY, James
Womble Carlyle Sandridge & Rice PLLC, Charlotte 704 331 4980
jcooney@wcsr.com
Recommended in Litigation
Practice Areas: Mr Cooney practices in the areas of business litigation, medical malpractice defense, criminal defense, commercial litigation, catastrophic torts and appellate law.
Prof. Memberships: Mecklenburg County Bar Association and North Carolina Bar Association; Permanent Member, Fourth Circuit Judicial Conference; American College of Trial Lawyers.
Career: Associate and Member, 1983-2000, Kennedy Covington Lobdell & Hickman, LLP, Charlotte, NC. Law clerk, the Honorable John D Butzer, Jr, US Court of Appeals, Fourth Circuit. JD, 1982, University of Virginia School of Law, Order of the Coif, Virginia Law Review. AB, 1979, Duke University, summa cum laude, Phi Beta Kappa.

COPENHAVER, W Andrew
Womble Carlyle Sandridge & Rice, PLLC, Winston-Salem
336 721 3633
acopenhaver@wcsr.com
Recommended in Antitrust, Litigation
Practice Areas: Andy Copenhaver's diverse litigation practice includes a range of antitrust, trade regulation and business litigation matters in state and federal courts throughout the United States.
Prof. Memberships: Forsyth County Bar Association; North Carolina Bar Association, Antitrust (Member, Executive Council), Litigation and Intellectual Property Sections; American Bar Association, Antitrust and Litigation Sections; Member, Fourth Circuit Judicial Conference; Member and Chairman, North Carolina Federal Bar Advisory Council.
Career: JD, 1972, University of North Carolina School of Law; City College, 1971, University of London Certificate in International Law, with honors; AB, 1969, Duke University.

COVINGTON, George
Kennedy Covington Lobdell & Hickman LLP, Charlotte 704 331 7400
Recommended in Litigation

COVINGTON, Peter
Helms Mulliss & Wicker PLLC, Charlotte 704 343 2000
Recommended in Litigation

COWAN, J Donald
Smith Moore LLP, Greensboro
336 378 5329
don.cowan@smithmoorelaw.com
Recommended in Litigation
Practice Areas: Litigation, product liability, antitrust, appellate, intellectual property litigation, class action.
Prof. Memberships: Fellow, American College of Trial Lawyers; Product Liability Advisory Council; American Law Institute; CPR Institute for Dispute Resolution; ABA's House of Delegates; Fellow, American Academy of Appellate Lawyers; American Board of Trial Advocates; permanent Member, Fourth Circuit Judicial Conference.
Career: 1968-73: US Army JAGC. 1973-present: Smith Moore LLP.
Personal: JD, Wake Forest University, 1968; BA, 1965. Business North Carolina's Legal Elite: patents, 2003; litigation, 2003-05; antitrust, 2004-05. Best Lawyers in America: antitrust law, personal injury litigation. Adjunct professor, Duke University School of Law, Trial Practice.

DAGENHART, Larry
Helms Mulliss & Wicker PLLC, Charlotte
704 343 2000
Recommended in Corporate/M&A

DAVIS, Jeffrey
Moore & Van Allen, PLLC, Charlotte
704 331 1000
Recommended in Litigation

DAVIS, William
Bell, Davis & Pitt, P.A., Winston-Salem
336 722 3700
Recommended in Litigation

DAWSON, Amos
Maupin Taylor, P.A., Raleigh
919 981 4000
Recommended in Environment

DE VORE, Bradford A
Womble Carlyle Sandridge & Rice PLLC, Charlotte
704 331 4941
bdevore@wcsr.com
Recommended in Environment
Practice Areas: For nearly 20 years, Brad De Vore has represented energy, chemical, pharmaceutical and manufacturing companies in environmental and toxic tort litigation throughout the United States. His experience with the fate and transport of chemicals and their impact on human health and the environment has allowed for successful results in various complicated environmental and toxic tort litigation matters.
Personal: JD, 1986, University of South Carolina School of Law.

DONADIO, Donald
Womble Carlyle Sandridge & Rice PLLC, Raleigh 919 755 2102
ddonadio@wcsr.com
Recommended in Real Estate
Practice Areas: Don Donadio represents issuers, owners, lenders and under-

writers in taxable and tax exempt financing of capital projects. He also represents companies in site selection and incentives negotiations.
Prof. Memberships: North Carolina Bar Association and American Bar Association, Business Sections; National Association of Bond Lawyers; listed in the Directory of Municipal Bond Attorneys of the US; American College of Real Estate Lawyers.
Career: Raleigh Office Managing Member, 1982-present; Captain, Judge Advocate Generals Corps, 1967-72, US Army; JD, 1967, Wake Forest University, cum laude; BA, 1965, Wake Forest University, cum laude.

DORTON, David
Maupin Taylor, P.A., Raleigh
919 981 4000
Recommended in Real Estate

DOYLE, John
Constangy, Brooks & Smith, LLC, Winston-Salem 336 721 1001
Recommended in Employment

DUNN, Glenn
Poyner & Spruill L.L.P., Charlotte
704 342 5250
Recommended in Environment

DUNN, J Thomas
Moore & Van Allen, PLLC, Charlotte
704 331 1000
Recommended in Banking & Finance

EADES, David
Moore & Van Allen, PLLC, Charlotte
704 331 1000
Recommended in Bankruptcy

EARP, Stephen W
Smith Moore LLP, Greensboro
336 378 5314
steve.earp@smithmoorelaw.com
Recommended in Environment
Practice Areas: Environmental and OSHA, commercial litigation, toxic tort litigation.
Prof. Memberships: Past Chair, North Carolina Bar Association's Environmental Law Section; President, North Carolina Beautiful.
Career: Has practiced law with Smith Moore LLP for his entire career. Currently serves as Chair of the firm's Management Committee.
Personal: JD, University of Virginia, 1977; BA, cum laude, Davidson College, 1974. Business North Carolina's Legal Elite: Environmental Law, 2003-05. Best Lawyers in America: Environmental Law.

ELLIS, Richard
Ellis & Winters LLP, Cary
919 865 7000
Recommended in Litigation

ENNS, Rodrick
Enns & Archer LLP, Winston-Salem
336 723 5180
Recommended in Antitrust

ERWIN, Martin
Smith Moore LLP, Greensboro
336 378 5327
martin.erwin@smithmoorelaw.com
Recommended in Employment
Practice Areas: Labor and employment.
Prof. Memberships: American Bar Association; North Carolina Bar Association; Greensboro Bar Association.
Career: 1967-68: clerk, Hon J Braxton Craven, Jr, US Court of Appeals for the Fourth Circuit. 1968-present: Smith Moore LLP.
Personal: JD, University of North Carolina, 1967; MA, University of North Carolina, 1965; BA, Wake Forest University, 1959. Business North Carolina's Legal Elite: Labor and Employment, 2003. Best Lawyers in America: employment law.

EVANS, Brian
Kennedy Covington Lobdell & Hickman LLP, Charlotte 704 331 7400
Recommended in Real Estate

EY, Douglas
Helms Mulliss & Wicker PLLC, Charlotte
910 254 3800
Recommended in Litigation

FARR, Thomas A
Ogletree, Deakins, Nash, Smoak & Stewart, PC, Cary 919 787 9700
thomas.farr@ogletreedeakins.com
Recommended in Employment
Practice Areas: Class action defense, complex litigation/non-competes, constitutional law.
Prof. Memberships: North Carolina Bar Association, American Bar Association, Fourth Circuit Judicial Conference, Campbell University (Adjunct Professor of Employment Law, 1990-95).
Career: Admitted in North Carolina, Virginia and Georgia. Named in The Best Lawyers in America and the 2002-05 editions of Business North Carolina's Legal Elite.
Publications: Mr Farr is the co-author of the 'NCCBI Employment Law Guide' and has written articles for the 'Campbell Law Observer' and the 'Triangle Business Journal'.
Personal: Hillsdale College (BLS, summa cum laude, 1976), Emory University (JD, 1979), Georgetown University (LLM, labor law, 1983).

FAY, Richard
Hamilton Gaskins Fay & Moon, Charlotte 704 344 1117
Recommended in Environment

FLINT, Henry
Kennedy Covington Lobdell & Hickman LLP, Charlotte 704 331 7400
Recommended in Banking & Finance, Corporate/M&A

FRANCHINA, David
Kennedy Covington Lobdell & Hickman LLP, Charlotte 704 331 7400
Recommended in Environment

FULLER, William
Moore & Van Allen, PLLC, Charlotte
704 331 1000
Recommended in Banking & Finance

FULTON, Charles
Manning Fulton & Skinner PA, Raleigh
919 787 8880
Recommended in Real Estate

FURR, Jeffrey
Womble Carlyle Sandridge & Rice,
PLLC, Winston-Salem
336 721 3532
jfurr@wcsr.com
Recommended in Litigation
Practice Areas: Jeff Furr has been liti-
gating toxic tort and product liability
cases for over 15 years. He has tried high
profile cases, including class actions in
West Virginia, Mississippi, California,
Florida, Missouri, Indiana and North
Carolina. Jeff serves as national coordi-
nating counsel for the R. J. Reynolds
Tobacco Company.
Prof. Memberships: Bar Associations:
Forsyth County Bar Association; North
Carolina Bar Association, Litigation Sec-
tion; American Bar Association.
Personal: BS Pharmacy, 1981, West Vir-
ginia University, cum laude; Residency
in Clinical Pharmacy, 1981-82, Rush-
Presbyterian-St. Luke's Medical Center;
JD, 1987, Wake Forest University School
of Law, cum laude, editor-in-chief, Wake
Forest Law Review.

GASKINS, Richard
Hamilton Gaskins Fay & Moon,
Charlotte 704 344 1117
Recommended in Environment

GOLDSTEIN, Stuart N
Cadwalader, Wickersham & Taft LLP,
Charlotte
704 348 5258
stuart.goldstein@cwt.com
Recommended in Capital Markets
Practice Areas: Partner in the Capital
Markets Department, resident in Cadwalader's Charlotte and New York
offices. Concentrates on structured
finance, structured products and the
federal securities laws. Practices primarily in the areas of commercial mortgage
and asset securitization, representing
issuers, underwriters, institutional
investors, servicers and trustees in both
public and private transactions. Has
extensive experience analyzing and
structuring securities, collateralized debt
obligations and other instruments and
products, as well as structuring transactions involving interest rate swaps, caps,
floors and other derivative instruments.
Also represents clients in the purchase
and sale of commercial and multifamily
mortgage loans, mezzanine debt, subordinate debt and residential first and second mortgage loans (including FHA,
VA, conventional and manufactured
housing) in whole loan and participation structures. Has additional extensive
experience in secured lending and repre-

sents lenders in structuring and negoti-
ating finance facilities.
Personal: Received a BS from Cornell
University and his JD from Boalt Hall
School of Law at the University of Cali-
fornia at Berkeley. Member of the New
York State Bar Association.

GREENE, Kenneth
Carruthers & Roth PA, Greensboro
336 273 8651
Recommended in Banking & Finance

GRIFFIN, Thomas
Parker, Poe, Adams & Bernstein LLP,
Charlotte 704 372 9000
Recommended in Environment

GRUBBS, R Howard
Womble Carlyle Sandridge & Rice,
PLLC, Winston-Salem 864 255 5413
hgrubbs@wcsr.com
Recommended in Environment
Practice Areas: Howard Grubbs represents industry in complex multi-party
CERCLA and RCRA litigation and
counseling matters nationwide. He also
counsels both buyers and sellers of cont-
aminated real estate on issues ranging
from Brownfields to underground stor-
age tanks.
Prof. Memberships: North Carolina
and South Carolina Bar Association;
Woodward and White's 'Best Lawyers in
America', 1994-2005; Business North
Carolina's 'Legal Elite' for Environmental Law, 2004.
Career: Practice Group Leader, Envi-
ronmental/Toxic Tort, 1992-present; JD,
1977, University of South Carolina
School of Law, with honors; BA, 1968,
Dennison University.

HAHN, Robert J
Hunton & Williams, Charlotte
704 378 4764
rhahn@hunton.com
Recommended in Capital Markets
Practice Areas: Practice focuses on
asset securitization, primarily in non-
mortgage assets, including synthetic
securitizations. Represents financial
institutions, issuers, underwriters, credit
enhancers, liquidity providers, asset-
backed commercial paper conduits and
other securitization participants in issuing, administering, servicing and underwriting asset-backed securities. Extensive experience in structuring securitizations, including public and 144A/Reg S
offerings, asset-backed commercial
paper conduits and synthetic structures.
Active in structuring transactions
involving a wide variety of financial
assets, including vehicle loans, credit
card receivables, trade receivables,
HELOCs, home equity loans,
iquipement leases, aircraft and charged-
off loans and receivables. Member of
Hunton & Williams' pro bono committee.

HANNA, George
Moore & Van Allen, PLLC, Charlotte
704 331 1000
Recommended in Litigation

HARDYMON, Glen
Kennedy Covington Lobdell & Hickman
LLP, Charlotte 704 331 7400
Recommended in Real Estate

HAZLETT, Richard
Helms Mulliss & Wicker PLLC, Charlotte
704 343 2000
*Recommended in Banking & Finance,
Corporate/M&A*

HINSON, Robin
Robinson, Bradshaw & Hinson PA,
Charlotte 704 377 2536
Recommended in Corporate/M&A

HOPE, Stephen
Moore & Van Allen, PLLC, Charlotte
704 331 1000
Recommended in Corporate/M&A

HOROSCHAK, Mark J
Womble Carlyle Sandridge & Rice
PLLC, Charlotte 704 331 4928
mhoroschak@wcsr.com
Recommended in Antitrust
Practice Areas: Mr Horoschak has a
national antitrust practice, with empha-
sis on the healthcare industry. He repre-
sents business clients before federal and
state antitrust agencies, and has a broad-
based litigation practice.
Prof. Memberships: American Bar
Association and North Carolina Bar
Association, Antitrust sections; North
Carolina State Bar; South Carolina Bar.
Career: From 1989-95, Mr Horoschak
served as Assistant Director of the
Bureau of Competition of the Federal
Trade Commission. He currently serves
as the Antitrust Practice Group Leader.
JD, 1976, College of William & Mary,
articles editor for Law Review; BA, 1973,
American University, cum laude.

HOUSE, George
Brooks, Pierce, McLendon, Humphrey
& Leonard LLP, Greensboro
336 373 8850
Recommended in Environment

HOVIS, James
Moore & Van Allen, PLLC, Charlotte
704 331 1000
Recommended in Banking & Finance

HUTSON, Benne
Helms Mulliss & Wicker PLLC, Charlotte
704 343 2000
Recommended in Environment

JERNIGAN, John L
Smith, Anderson, Blount, Dorsett,
Mitchell & Jernigan, LLP, Raleigh
919 821 6611
jjernigan@smithlaw.com
Recommended in Corporate/M&A
Practice Areas: Managing Partner of
Smith, Anderson, Blount, Dorsett,
Mitchell & Jernigan, LLP. Practices in the
areas of mergers and acquisitions, bank-
ing, and corporate law. Has over 25 years

experience structuring, negotiating, and
closing mergers and acquisitions involv-
ing public companies and large private-
ly-owned companies.
Prof. Memberships: Admitted to North
Carolina Bar (1967). Past President of
the North Carolina Bar Association.
Served as a Member of the Board of
Governors of the North Carolina Bar
Association from 1989-92, and two
terms as Chair of the North Carolina
Bar Association's Business Law Section.
Member of the Wake County Bar Asso-
ciation, North Carolina Bar Association,
and American Bar Association, the
American Judicature Society, American
College of Mortgage Attorneys, and
American Counsel Association. Fellow
of the American Bar Foundation.
Career: He is listed in a leading legal US
publication, and the Business North
Carolina Legal Elite.
Personal: JD, University of North Car-
olina, 1967; AB, Davidson College, 1964.

JOHNSON, Charles
Robinson, Bradshaw & Hinson PA,
Charlotte
704 377 2536
Recommended in Employment

JONES VAN BUREN, Carolyn
Kennedy Covington Lobdell & Hickman
LLP, Charlotte 704 331 7400
Recommended in Environment

KEEN, C Matthew
Ogletree, Deakins, Nash, Smoak &
Stewart, PC, Raleigh 919 789 3162
matt.keen@ogletreedeakins.com
Recommended in Employment
Practice Areas: Labor and employ-
ment. Represents employers in state and
federal court in employment litigation.
Advises companies on a national basis
on employment law compliance.
Prof. Memberships: American Bar
Association (Committee on WARN
Act), North Carolina Bar Association
(Member - Labor and Employment Law
Section, Litigation Section), and Ameri-
can Employment Law Council. Selected
by Business North Carolina in The Legal
Elite for employment law (2003 and
2004).
Career: Practiced with Ogletree Deakins
since 1987; Partner since 1994.
Publications: North Carolina Employ-
ers' Desk Manual (editor).
Personal: North Carolina State Univer-
sity (BS, 1983), University of North Car-
olina at Chapel Hill (JD, 1987).

KENYON, Douglas W
Hunton & Williams, Raleigh
919 899 3076
dkenyon@hunton.com
Recommended in Antitrust
Practice Areas: Doug Kenyon's practice focuses on antitrust, trade regulation and intellectual property law. Partner, Litigation, Intellectual Property and
Antitrust Group. Administration Head,
Raleigh Litigation Practice Group.

KIRKLAND, Byron B
Smith, Anderson, Blount, Dorsett, Mitchell & Jernigan, LLP, Raleigh
919 821 6682
bkirkland@smithlaw.com
Recommended in Corporate/M&A

Practice Areas: Practices in the areas of securities law, corporate law, venture capital, mergers and acquisitions, and technology law. Extensive experience in public offerings; venture capital transactions; and structuring, negotiating and closing mergers and acquisitions for both public and private companies.
Prof. Memberships: Admitted to practice in North Carolina (1987). Member of the American Bar Association, Section of Business Law, North Carolina Bar Association, Wake County Bar Association and American Counsel Association; Member of the Board of Directors of the Council for Entrepreneurial Development; past Chair of the North Carolina Bar Association Young Lawyers Division.
Career: Smith, Anderson, Blount, Dorsett, Mitchell & Jernigan, LLP, 1987 - present.
Personal: JD (with honors), University of North Carolina, 1987; MBA, University of North Carolina, 1987; BA, University of North Carolina, 1983.

KLUTTZ, Joseph
Kennedy Covington Lobdell & Hickman LLP, Charlotte 704 331 7400
Recommended in Banking & Finance, Bankruptcy

KORANDO, Kimberly J
Smith, Anderson, Blount, Dorsett, Mitchell & Jernigan, LLP, Raleigh
919 821 6671
kkorando@smithlaw.com
Recommended in Employment

Practice Areas: Heads Employment, Labor and Human Resources Practice Group. Has extensive experience with federal and state employment law compliance, HR best practices and prevention of employee lawsuits; conducting internal harassment and employee misconduct investigations; representing employers in federal and state compliance audits and investigations; and defending employers in state and federal civil actions, including multi-plaintiff and class actions.
Prof. Memberships: Admitted to practice in North Carolina (1986); US Court of Appeals, Fourth Circuit (1989), US Supreme Court (1991). ABA EEO Committee.
Career: Partner since 1993. Co-founder, Institute for Human Resources Training.
Publications: Chapter editor, 'Litigation Procedure' (2002 Cum. Supp.), 'Sexual Orientation' (4th edition in progress), 'BNA Employment Discrimination Law'. Author, 'Model Employee Policies & Forms for North Carolina Employers' (NCCBI 2002).
Personal: JD (with honors), University of Oklahoma, 1986; BS, in Psychology, University of Oklahoma, 1980.

KUPEC, Christopher
Moore & Van Allen, PLLC, Charlotte
704 331 1000
Recommended in Banking & Finance

LASSITER, Donnell
Kennedy Covington Lobdell & Hickman LLP, Charlotte 704 331 7400
Recommended in Banking & Finance

LEON, Christopher
Womble Carlyle Sandridge & Rice, PLLC, Winston-Salem 336 721 3518
cleon@wcsr.com
Recommended in Banking & Finance

Practice Areas: Chris Leon practices primarily in corporate and real estate finance and mergers and acquisitions. He has extensive experience advising public and private businesses in connection with structuring, negotiating and documenting all aspects of acquisitions, divestitures, complex financings and third party credit arrangements.
Prof. Memberships: North Carolina Bar Association; Georgia Bar Association, Corporate and Banking Law Section; Member, Loan Syndications and Trading Association, Inc.
Career: JD, 1983, Wake Forest University School of Law, cum laude, editorial staff, 'Wake Forest Law Review'; American Society of International Law Proceedings; Moot Court Board; BS Industrial Engineering, 1980, Northwestern University, with distinction.

LEVITAS, Steven J
Kilpatrick Stockton LLP, Raleigh
919 420 1707
SLevitas@KilpatrickStockton.com
Recommended in Environment

Practice Areas: Represents a wide range of corporate and governmental clients on environmental regulatory matters, with an emphasis on wastewater permitting and compliance, waste remediation, and real estate development.
Prof. Memberships: American and North Carolina Bar Associations (Environmental Law Sections); ABA Standing Committee on Environmental Law.
Career: Deputy Secretary, North Carolina Department of Environment, Health and Natural Resources (1993-96); Director and Senior Attorney, North Carolina Environmental Defense Fund (1987-92); Law clerk to Hon James B McMillan (WDNC).
Personal: BA, University of North Carolina at Chapel Hill, Phi Beta Kappa, 1976; JD, Harvard Law School, cum laude, 1982.

LOEB, Christopher
Robinson, Bradshaw & Hinson PA, Charlotte 704 377 2536
Recommended in Real Estate

LOFTIS, W Randolph
Constangy, Brooks & Smith, LLC, Winston-Salem 336 721 1001
Recommended in Employment

LUCAS, Edwin
Robinson, Bradshaw & Hinson PA, Charlotte 704 377 2536
Recommended in Banking & Finance

LYNCH, Stephen
Robinson, Bradshaw & Hinson PA, Charlotte 704 377 2536
Recommended in Corporate/M&A

MASON, C Steven
Smith, Anderson, Blount, Dorsett, Mitchell & Jernigan, LLP, Raleigh
919 821 6642
smason@smithlaw.com
Recommended in Real Estate

Practice Areas: Practices in the areas of commercial real estate, lending transactions, and corporate law.
Prof. Memberships: Admitted to practice in North Carolina (1981). Member of Wake County Bar Association, North Carolina Bar Association and American Bar Association.
Career: Joined Smith, Anderson, Blount, Dorsett, Mitchell & Jernigan, LLP, 1999. Moore & Van Allen PLLC, 1981-99.
Personal: JD, University of Virginia, 1981; BA, University of North Carolina, 1978.

MCCONNELL, Alan
Kilpatrick Stockton LLP, Raleigh
919 420 1798
AMcConnell@KilpatrickStockton.com
Recommended in Environment

Practice Areas: Provides environmental representation, counseling and litigation services on a wide range of legislative, administrative and regulatory matters, with a particular emphasis on federal and state implementation of the Clean Air Act. Other areas of experience include solid and hazardous waste regulation, the Federal Insecticide, Fungicide and Rodenticide Act, the Clean Water Act, occupational safety and health issues, land use issues, and environmental liabilities attendant to corporate transactions.
Prof. Memberships: Carolinas Air Pollution Control Association. Admitted in North Carolina, Virginia and the District of Columbia.
Personal: BS Forest Resources, University of Georgia, 1982; JD, George Washington University, 1988.

MCGINN, Daniel
Brooks, Pierce, McLendon, Humphrey & Leonard LLP, Greensboro
336 373 8850
Recommended in Employment

MCKEITHEN, Ward
Robinson, Bradshaw & Hinson PA, Charlotte 704 377 2536
Recommended in Litigation

MERRITT, Mark
Robinson, Bradshaw & Hinson PA, Charlotte 704 377 2536
Recommended in Litigation

MILLEN, Pressly M
Womble Carlyle Sandridge & Rice PLLC, Raleigh 919 755 2135
pmillen@wcsr.com
Recommended in Litigation

Practice Areas: Press Millen is a trial attorney who has litigated a wide variety of antitrust and other complex business cases, including class actions, in federal and state courts throughout the United States. Press has represented both defendants and plaintiffs in antitrust cases tried to verdict in federal courts. Press has also litigated a wide variety of other business disputes including civil RICO, securities fraud and tax.
Prof. Memberships: ABA, Antitrust and Litigation Sections; NC Bar Association.
Career: JD, 1985, Duke University School of Law, with high honors, note editor, 'Duke Law Review'; AB 1982, Yale University, magna cum laude.

MOSER, Kenneth A
Womble Carlyle Sandridge & Rice, PLLC, Winston-Salem 336 721 3504
kmoser@wcsr.com
Recommended in Banking & Finance

Practice Areas: Ken Moser has structured, documented, negotiated and closed numerous commercial real estate transactions and commercial, corporate, asset-based and real estate finance transactions. He advises banks, other financial institutions and corporations on all forms of financing and commercial real estate transactions.
Prof. Memberships: American College of Real Estate Lawyers; American College of Mortgage Attorneys; American, North Carolina and Forsyth County Bar Associations; American Counsel Association.
Career: JD, 1968, Wake Forest University School of Law, cum laude, associate editor, 'Law Review'; Phi Delta Phi Magister (President); BA, 1965, Wake Forest University; President, Senior Class; Omicron Delta Kappa Honorary Leadership Fraternity.

MURCHISON, John
Kennedy Covington Lobdell & Hickman LLP, Charlotte
704 331 7400
Recommended in Antitrust

MURPHY, Paul
Moore & Van Allen, PLLC, Charlotte
704 331 1000
Recommended in Capital Markets

NEDZBALA, Michael
Hunton & Williams, Charlotte
704 378 4703
mnedzbala@hunton.com
Recommended in Capital Markets

Practice Areas: Mr Nedzbala's practice focuses on structured finance, securitization and other capital markets transactions. He is Co-Head of the firm's Asset Securitization Group and a member of the Global Capital Markets Team.

OATES, J Christopher
Moore & Van Allen, PLLC, Charlotte
704 331 1000
Recommended in Real Estate

OBERKFELL, Keith F
Mayer, Brown, Rowe & Maw LLP,
Charlotte 704 444 3549
koberkfell@mayerbrownrowe.com
Recommended in Capital Markets
Practice Areas: Specializes in securitization and other structured finance products, including CDOs, CLOs and derivatives. Advises foreign and domestic financial institutions, underwriters, placement agents, liquidity providers and issuers in private, public and Rule 144A/Regulation S executions in securitizations of a wide range of asset types, including trade receivables; aircraft, container and other equipment loan and lease portfolios; student loans; credit card receivables; automobile loans and other financial assets. Represents program sponsors with respect to the development of novel multi-seller commercial paper and medium term note conduit structures.
Prof. Memberships: Admitted: North Carolina, 2000; Illinois, 1993.
Career: Mayer, Brown, Rowe & Maw LLP, Charlotte, 1999 to date; Chicago, 1996-99; Partner, 2002. Vedder Price Kaufman and Kammholz, Chicago, 1994-96. Chapman and Cutler, Chicago, 1993-94.
Personal: Harvard Law School, JD cum laude, 1993. University of Virginia, BA with highest distinction, 1990; Phi Beta Kappa, Dean's List.

OLEYNIK, Jeffrey
Brooks, Pierce, McLendon, Humphrey & Leonard LLP, Greensboro
336 373 8850
Recommended in Antitrust, Litigation

OLIVER, Samuel
Manning Fulton & Skinner PA, Raleigh
919 787 8880
Recommended in Real Estate

PATTERSON, Carl N
Smith, Anderson, Blount, Dorsett, Mitchell & Jernigan, LLP, Raleigh
919 821 6647
cpatterson@smithlaw.com
Recommended in Litigation
Practice Areas: Firm Practice Group Leader in commercial litigation. Practices in the areas of contract disputes and commercial litigation and corporate and securities litigation.
Prof. Memberships: Admitted to practice in North Carolina (1976). Member of the Wake County Bar Association; North Carolina Bar Association, Litigation, Business Law and Law Practice Management Sections; American Bar Association; and the American Judicature Society. Past Chairman of the Young Lawyers Division of the North Carolina Bar Association.
Career: Became partner Smith, Ander-

son, Blount, Dorsett, Mitchell & Jernigan, LLP, 1981. Member, Smith, Anderson, Blount, Dorsett, Mitchell & Jernigan Policy, Planning and Compensation Committees.
Personal: JD (with honors), University of North Carolina, 1976; BA, Davidson College, 1973.

PHILLIPS, Jim
Brooks, Pierce, McLendon, Humphrey & Leonard LLP, Greensboro
336 373 8850
Recommended in Litigation

PRICHARD, Allen
Kennedy Covington Lobdell & Hickman LLP, Charlotte 704 331 7400
Recommended in Real Estate

PRUDEN, J Norfleet
Kennedy Covington Lobdell & Hickman LLP, Charlotte 704 331 7400
Recommended in Corporate/M&A

PRYOR, Robert H
Helms Mulliss & Wicker PLLC, Charlotte
704 343 2000
Recommended in Bankruptcy

RAINEY, Richard L
Womble Carlyle Sandridge & Rice PLLC, Charlotte
704 331 4967
rrainey@wcsr.com
Recommended in Employment
Practice Areas: Richard Rainey has extensive experience litigating employment disputes on behalf of employers. He also advises clients on preventing exposure to liability.
Prof. Memberships: Mecklenburg Country Bar Association; North Carolina Bar Association, Labor and Employment Law Section. Admitted to practice before the North Carolina Supreme Court, the Fourth Circuit Court of Appeals and the US District Court for the Eastern, Middle and Western Districts of North Carolina, the District of Colorado and the Eastern District of Michigan.
Career: JD, 1987, University of North Carolina School of Law, Order of the Coif, American Jurisprudence Award.

RAPER, William
Womble Carlyle Sandridge & Rice PLLC, Charlotte
704 331 4935
braper@wcsr.com
Recommended in Litigation
Practice Areas: Bill Raper's litigation practice involves commercial, corporate and shareholder transactions and professional negligence defense.
Prof. Memberships: North Carolina and American Bar Associations, Litigation Sections; CPR Institute for Dispute Resolution; North Carolina Association of Defense Attorneys; loss prevention partner for all North Carolina and South Carolina Member law firms of Attorneys Liability Assurance Society; Fellow, American College of Trial

Lawyers.
Career: Judicial Clerk, Judge J Braxton Craven, US Court of Appeals for the Fourth Circuit, 1972-73; JD, 1972, Vanderbilt University School of Law, editor, 'Law Review'; legal assistant to Senator Sam Ervin, 1970; AB, 1968, University of North Carolina.

RIKARD, William
Parker, Poe, Adams & Bernstein LLP, Charlotte 704 372 9000
Recommended in Litigation

ROACH, Gerald F
Smith, Anderson, Blount, Dorsett, Mitchell & Jernigan, LLP, Raleigh
919 821 6668
groach@smithlaw.com
Recommended in Corporate/M&A
Practice Areas: Head of firm Corporate Team. Firm Practice Leader in Securities Practice Group. Has extensive experience with public offerings, domestic and international mergers and acquisitions, joint ventures, general corporate matters, private financings, technology law, and advising boards of directors and special committees.
Prof. Memberships: Admitted to practice in North Carolina (1982). Member of the American Bar Association, North Carolina Bar Association, Wake County Bar Association, American Counsel Association and the North Carolina Commission on Business Laws and the Economy. Past Chair of the Business Law Section of the North Carolina Bar.
Career: Joined Smith, Anderson, Blount, Dorsett, Mitchell & Jernigan, LLP, 1982. Chairman, Smith, Anderson, Blount, Mitchell & Jernigan Policy and Planning Committee. Included in a leading US legal publication. Also, he has been named one of 'Ten to Watch: Attorneys that have an impact on North Carolina business' by the Triangle Business Journal and as a member of the 'Legal Elite' in two categories by Business North Carolina.
Personal: JD (cum laude), Wake Forest University School of Law, 1982; BA (cum laude), Wake Forest University, 1980.

ROBERTSON, Allen
Robinson, Bradshaw & Hinson PA, Charlotte 704 377 2536
Recommended in Banking & Finance

ROBINSON, Russell
Robinson, Bradshaw & Hinson PA, Charlotte 704 377 2536
Recommended in Corporate/M&A

SAWCHAK, Matthew
Ellis & Winters LLP, Cary
919 865 7000
Recommended in Antitrust

SCHILLI, David
Robinson, Bradshaw & Hinson PA, Charlotte 704 377 2536
Recommended in Bankruptcy

SINGER, Robert
Brooks, Pierce, McLendon, Humphrey & Leonard LLP, Greensboro
336 373 8850
Recommended in Corporate/M&A

SITTON, Larry
Smith Moore LLP, Greensboro
336 378 5208
larry.sitton@smithmoorelaw.com
Recommended in Antitrust, Litigation
Practice Areas: Litigation, construction, land use and development, financial services litigation, antitrust, class action.
Prof. Memberships: Past President, NC Bar Association; permanent Member, Judicial Conference for the Fourth Circuit Court of Appeals; Fellow, American College of Trial Lawyers; Master of the Bench, Chief Justice Joseph Branch Inn of Court.
Career: 1964-67: Clerk, Hon Eugene A Gordon, US District Court for Middle District of NC. 1967-present: Smith Moore LLP.
Personal: LLB, cum laude, Wake Forest University, 1964; BA, cum laude, Wake Forest University, 1961. Business North Carolina's Legal Elite: antitrust 2003-05; Litigation 2004-05. Best Lawyers in America: business litigation, antitrust law.

SPEARMAN, Robert
Parker, Poe, Adams & Bernstein LLP, Raleigh 919 828 0564
Recommended in Litigation

TAYLOR, Daniel
Kilpatrick Stockton LLP, Winston-Salem
336 607 7330
DanTaylor@KilpatrickStockton.com
Recommended in Litigation
Practice Areas: Trial, appellate and arbitration experience representing plaintiffs and defendants in a broad range of business litigation matters involving corporate governance, corporate dissolution, securities, business tort, shareholder rights, intellectual property, and complex contracts.
Prof. Memberships: Fourth Circuit Judicial Conference; Chief Justice Joseph Branch Inn of Court (barrister).
Career: Army Airborne and Ranger School graduate, Vietnam veteran, resigned Commission, Captain, 1973.
Personal: BS Engineering, United States Military Academy, 1968; George Washington University, 1973 (Graduate School of Government and Business Administration); JD, Wake Forest University, cum laude, 1976; Law Clerk for Judge Hiram H Ward, USDC, MDNC; instrument rated private pilot.

TIPPS, Maynard
Kennedy Covington Lobdell & Hickman LLP, Charlotte 704 331 7400
Recommended in Real Estate

TOOLE, William
Robinson, Bradshaw & Hinson PA,
Charlotte 704 377 2536
Recommended in Environment

TORSTRICK, Brent
Robinson, Bradshaw & Hinson PA,
Charlotte 704 377 2536
Recommended in Real Estate

UBELL, Donald P
Parker, Poe, Adams & Bernstein LLP,
Charlotte 704 372 9000
Recommended in Banking & Finance

VAN HOY, Philip
Van Hoy Reutlinger Adams & Dunn,
Charlotte 704 375 6022
Recommended in Employment

VAUGHAN, Keith W
Womble Carlyle Sandridge & Rice,
PLLC, Winston-Salem
336 721 3540
kvaughan@wcsr.com
Recommended in Litigation
Practice Areas: Keith Vaughan has
extensive litigation experience involving
business, products liability, toxic tort
and environmental issues. During his 30
year career, he has tried jury and bench
trials, handled administrative proceedings and argued a wide range of matters
in appellate courts.
Prof. Memberships: Georgia Bar Association; North Carolina Bar Association
and American Bar Association, Litigation Sections; Master of the Bench,
Chief Justice Joseph Branch Chapter,
American Inns of Court.
Career: Chair of the firm Management
Committee and firm Managing Member, 2002-present; JD, 1975, University
of Georgia, cum laude, editor-in-chief,
'Georgia Law Review'; BA, 1972, Wake
Forest University, cum laude.

VAUGHN, Scott
Helms Mulliss & Wicker PLLC, Charlotte
704 343 2000
Recommended in Bankruptcy

WALKER, Clarence
Kennedy Covington Lobdell & Hickman
LLP, Charlotte 704 331 7400
Recommended in Corporate/M&A

WARD, Frank
Maupin Taylor, P.A., Raleigh
919 981 4000
Recommended in Employment

WEDDINGTON, Keith
Parker, Poe, Adams & Bernstein LLP,
Charlotte 704 372 9000
Recommended in Employment

WESTER, John
Robinson, Bradshaw & Hinson PA,
Charlotte 704 377 2536
*Recommended in Employment,
Litigation*

WILLIAMS, Jim
Brooks, Pierce, McLendon, Humphrey
& Leonard LLP, Greensboro
336 373 8850
Recommended in Litigation

WINSLOW, Edward
Brooks, Pierce, McLendon, Humphrey
& Leonard LLP, Greensboro
336 373 8850
Recommended in Corporate/M&A

WREN, Elizabeth
Kilpatrick Stockton LLP, Charlotte
704 338 5123
BWren@KilpatrickStockton.com
Recommended in Corporate/M&A
Practice Areas: Securities matters and
corporate finance transactions in connection with initial and secondary public offerings, Rule 144A offerings and
shelf offerings. Transactions have related
to investment grade and high grade
debt, trust preferred securities and
medium term note programs, as well as
common and preferred equity. Public
and private merger and acquisition
transactions, including tender and
exchange offers, corporate governance
issues and SEC reporting and compliance issues.
Personal: BA English, Emory University; JD, with honors, University of North
Carolina School of Law, 1980.

SMITH MOORE LLP

THE FIRM

Managing Partner: Stephen W Earp

Number of partners: 56
Number of other lawyers: 53

AREAS OF PRACTICE:

Litigation	53%
Business Law	27%
Healthcare	12%
Labor & Employment	8%

FIRM OVERVIEW: Smith Moore LLP serves clients in North Carolina, Georgia, the Southeast, the nation, and abroad through attorneys who are committed to excellence, teamwork, and innovation. Each attorney is personally invested in solving the firm's clients' complex legal issues. This commitment to client success has distinguished the firm since Julius C Smith began his practice in 1919.

Smith Moore's offices are located in Atlanta, Georgia, and in Greensboro and Raleigh, North Carolina. The firm has nearly 120 attorneys who concentrate in a wide range of substantive areas. The attorneys of Smith Moore have earned reputations for excellence in four core areas: litigation, business, healthcare, and labor and employment. The firm serves its clients throughout the Southeast, the United States, and abroad. Smith Moore uses its knowledge and experience to develop creative legal solutions to complicated problems.

MAIN AREAS OF PRACTICE

Litigation: Smith Moore's Litigation Group tries and litigates cases in state and federal trial courts throughout the United States. The firm regularly serves as both trial counsel and coordinating counsel in complex litigation matters. The firm's Appellate Team also has handled appeals of sophisticated matters throughout the Southeast. Smith Moore's litigation practice and trial experience cover a broad range, including: antitrust; commercial and business torts; product liability; toxic tort; financial services; construction, and catastrophic injuries. To best serve its clients, the firm is also very experienced in alternative dispute resolution methods, which are often more efficient and cost-effective. Smith Moore's Litigation Group takes pride in teamwork and on understanding its' clients' businesses, working with them to achieve their goals in complex legal situations. Smith Moore exemplifies confidence through experience.

Business: Smith Moore boasts one of the most active business law practices in the Southeast. The Business Group is comprised of experienced attorneys who handle a wide variety of issues on a daily basis for businesses ranging from small, entrepreneurial startups to large, publicly-owned companies. The firm's experience covers all forms of business enterprises, including corporations, limited liability companies, partnerships, and professional corporations. Smith Moore's Business Group is skilled in representing buyers, sellers, and equity investors with mergers, acquisitions, and other transactions involving business combinations. The firm offers tax services, advice on start-up issues and regulatory compliance, and regularly assist with contract issues involving corporate documents such as shareholder agreements, employment contracts, licensing agreements, supply contracts, consulting agreements, purchase and sale forms, and warranty agreements.

Healthcare: The firm's Healthcare Group is one of the largest in the Southeast and has helped healthcare providers in over 21 states. The firm is currently the counsel of record for more than 50 hospitals and hospital systems and 50 long term care facilities, as well as a number of physician groups. The Healthcare Group focuses on the following areas: Certificate of Need and licensure, corporate compliance, bioethical issues, financial

HEAD OFFICE

NORTH CAROLINA
300 N. Greene Street, Suite 1400, **Greensboro**, NC 27401
Tel: 336 378 5200 **Fax:** 336 378 5400
Website: www.smithmoorelaw.com

BRANCH OFFICES

NORTH CAROLINA
2800 Two Hannover Square, **Raleigh**, NC 27601
Tel: 919 755 8700 **Fax:** 919 755 8800

GEORGIA
One Atlantic Center, Suite 3700, 1201 W. Peachtree St.,
Atlanta, GA 30309
Tel: 404 962 1000 **Fax:** 404 962 1200

and business transactions, fraud and abuse, HIPAA, managed care, management counselling, medical staff matters, provider defense litigation, regulatory compliance, and risk management.

Labor & Employment: Smith Moore's Labor and Employment Group is one of the most experienced in the region, counselling and advising employers on a full range of employment issues and litigating in state and federal courts, in arbitration and before governmental agencies. The group restricts its practice exclusively to the representation of management. The Labor and Employment Group emphasizes the following areas: employee benefits, employment litigation, human resource counselling and training, immigration, labor relations, as well as workers' compensation.

CLIENTS: Smith Moore serves clients in the Southeast, the nation, and abroad. The firm represents insurance carriers, financial institutions, consumer products companies, manufacturing companies, educational institutions, hospitals, pharmaceutical companies, trade associations, and real estate developers, among many others.

INTERNATIONAL WORK: The firm's international practice includes a wide range of services sought by entities involved in international business. The firm's attorneys and staff integrate a thorough understanding of foreign cultures, high-quality legal skills, and ability to work effectively in such languages as German, French, and Spanish. Many of the attorneys have lived in the countries where the firm represents international clients. The firm has extensive international experience with both foreign and domestic companies and the legal issues that concern them.

SMITH MOORE LLP
ATTORNEYS AT LAW

SMITH, ANDERSON, BLOUNT, DORSETT, MITCHELL & JERNIGAN, LLP

THE FIRM

Managing Partner: John L Jernigan

Number of partners: 53
Number of other lawyers: 45

FIRM OVERVIEW: Since the firm's founding in 1912, it has grown to be the largest law firm in Raleigh and the Research Triangle region of North Carolina, and one of the largest in the state. The firm provides a full range of legal services and is dedicated to the principles of professionalism, excellence, and service to its clients and the community. The firm has a broad business practice representing large and medium size public and private companies and venture funds nationally and internationally in sectors that include financial services, pharmaceuticals, energy, healthcare, manufacturing, technology, service and retail, and government. The firm represents clients in litigation at every level of the judicial system, including the state and federal trial and appellate courts. It also appears regularly before state and federal agencies and in other forums to advance the interests of its clients and is experienced in all forms of alternative dispute resolution.

MAIN AREAS OF PRACTICE:

Commercial Transactions: The firm has been a leader in assisting North Carolina businesses and individuals with commercial transactions, and has the legal and business skills needed for dynamic businesses today, including bank and other private finance, access to capital markets, mergers and acquisitions, environmental compliance, commercial real estate, bankruptcy, and international transactions. The firm has significant experience in secured and unsecured bank lending, joint ventures and strategic alliances, venture and mezzanine investments, leveraged buyouts and acquisition financing, letters of credit, mergers and acquisitions, commercial paper, derivatives, workouts and reorganizations, commercial real estate, employment, environmental compliance, conduit financing, securitizations and other asset-based financings, divestitures, licensing, international trade and transactions, and franchising. The firm has an extensive tax practice providing planning and advice, as well as representation of clients in tax controversies.

Commercial Litigation: The firm's Commercial Litigation Practice Group has substantial trial experience, and is adept at handling complex, document-intensive cases. The firm offers expertise in all forms of alternative dispute resolution. Some members of the Commercial Litigation Practice Group are certified mediators or arbitrators. The Commercial Litigation Practice Group includes members of the American College of Trial Lawyers, the International Society of Barristers, the International Association of Defense Counsel, the American Board of Trial Advocates, the American Judicature Society, and the Judicial Conference of the Fourth Circuit Court of Appeals. The firm has extensive experience in counseling and representing clients in banking litigation, disputes between buyers and sellers of goods and services, commercial real estate disputes, insurance matters and shareholder actions.

Corporate, Securities & Technology: The firm has one of the state's leading public company practices as measured by number and size of transactions and public company clients. The firm provides a broad range of general corporate, mergers and acquisitions, corporate finance, securities, joint venture, venture capital, employee benefits, intellectual property and technology advice to clients ranging from established public companies to venture capital backed start-ups and venture funds, many involving technology fields. The firm also regularly advises boards of directors or committees, including special committees.

Regulatory - Government Relations, Healthcare, Public Utilities: The firm has a long history of working on behalf of its business clients with

HEAD OFFICE

NORTH CAROLINA
2500 Wachovia Capitol Center, **Raleigh**, NC 27601
Tel: 919 821 1220   **Fax:** 919 821 6800
Website: www.smithlaw.com

CONTACTS

Commercial	John L Jernigan
Corporate/Securities	Gerald F Roach
Commercial Litigation	Carl N Patterson
General Litigation	Samuel G Thompson
Regulatory	Julian D Bobbitt, Jr

local, state and federal government and represents a broad array of clients before the North Carolina General Assembly. The firm's Healthcare Practice provides business and regulatory counsel to a wide variety of healthcare clients across the Southeast, from physicians and physician organizations to other providers to informatics companies and e-health entities. Primary services and typical transactions include antitrust, business/contract disputes, certificate of need, covenants not to compete, employment agreements, HIPAA and other federal and state confidentiality and privacy laws, fraud and abuse, including Stark, healthcare financing, licensing board issues, managed care, medical staff issues, Medicare compliance, mergers and acquisitions/joint ventures, negotiations with insurers, physician organizations, PSOs and insurance, and quality assurance. The firm regularly represents clients engaged in the energy and telecommunications industries. Services include negotiation with and litigation before state regulatory agencies and drafting, management and representation of clients in connection with energy and telecommunications issues before the North Carolina General Assembly.

General Litigation: The firm's Medical Malpractice Practice Group defends physicians, hospitals, and other healthcare providers with a philosophy that combines an aggressive and efficient approach to litigation with an in-depth understanding of relevant medical issues. It is experienced in assisting health care providers through every stage of malpractice actions, including risk management prelitigation claims, discovery, depositions, trial, and appellate advocacy. The firm's products liability group regularly represents large manufacturers in the automotive, chemical and other industries providing services ranging from risk management advice to litigation defense.

CLIENTS: The firm's clients include some of the largest financial institutions, insurance companies, public utilities, retailers, manufacturing, pharmaceutical, and biotechnology companies in its region and the nation, as well as emerging growth and technology companies. The firm also represents smaller businesses and individuals, as well as trade and professional associations and their members.

INTERNATIONAL WORK: The firm represents a number of international companies that have ongoing business interests in its market, including companies based in the United Kingdom, France, Japan, Germany, Holland, and Israel, as well as numerous companies located in the United States with foreign subsidiaries or interests.

WOMBLE CARLYLE SANDRIDGE & RICE, PLLC

THE FIRM

Managing Member: Keith W Vaughan

Number of partners: 215
Number of other lawyers: 268

FIRM OVERVIEW: Womble Carlyle Sandridge & Rice, PLLC, which traces its history to 1876, is one of the largest law firms in the Southeast and mid-Atlantic, with nearly 500 lawyers in nine offices from Atlanta to Washington, DC. Womble Carlyle is a full-service business law firm providing legal advice to a wide spectrum of regional, national and international clients in sectors that include financial services, manufacturing, transportation, telecommunications, energy, health care, life sciences, government, education and technology.

MAIN AREAS OF PRACTICE

Capital Markets: The firm provides legal services – including regulatory compliance and the structuring, negotiating and closing of capital markets transactions – to participants in the capital markets, including capital providers (such as commercial banks, investment banks and investment funds), entities accessing the capital markets to obtain capital (from startups to *Fortune* 500 companies) and intermediaries acting in the capital markets to mitigate risk related to movement in the values of currencies, commodities, equities and interest rate indices.

Corporate & Securities: Lawyers in the Corporate and Securities Practice provide representation in the areas of general corporate law, mergers and acquisitions, venture capital, securities offerings and securities regulation, fiduciary obligations and rights of directors and officers, partnership and limited liability company formation and syndication and business contract negotiations.

Tax: The firm provides creative tax planning and advice on mergers and acquisitions, corporate reorganizations, real estate development, tax controversies before the Internal Revenue Service and state taxing authorities, and tax-sensitive and tax-enhanced financings.

Real Estate Development: Members of the group represent clients in the acquisition, financing, development, and sale of all types of unimproved land and improved properties for residential and commercial use, including large land assemblages, major office buildings and office parks, shopping malls and centers, luxury hotels and resorts, condominiums and multifamily housing projects throughout the region.

Intellectual Property: Representation includes all aspects of domestic and foreign intellectual property law, including patent investigations and analyses, procurement of US and foreign patents and general client counseling regarding license agreements, corporate-sponsored research contracts, development agreements, technology transfer agreements and software protection.

Litigation & Arbitration: The firm has a litigation practice of national scope, encompassing business litigation; intellectual property litigation; environmental and toxic tort litigation; insurance, governmental and tort litigation; and product liability litigation. Attorneys have handled matters from trials of national class actions, to coordination of litigation nationally, to defense of clients in mediation and arbitration in many states throughout the country, including potentially high verdict jurisdictions.

Employee Benefits: Lawyers in this group provide all facets of employee benefits representation, including design, drafting and implementation of tax-qualified retirement and welfare benefit plans, non-qualified retirement arrangements, and executive compensation programs. The group also counsels clients regarding ERISA compliance and related federal and state legislation affecting employee benefit programs.

Government Relations: Womble Carlyle bridges the gap between law practice and public policy by delivering expert advice and assistance in dealing effectively with all levels and branches of government – local, state and federal. Members of this group combine years of on-the-job experience in government with legal training and the resources of an established law firm to

HEAD OFFICE

NORTH CAROLINA
One West Fourth Street, **Winston-Salem** NC 27101
Tel: 336 721 3600 **Fax:** 336 721 3660
Email: kmoser@wcsr.com
Website: www.wcsr.com

BRANCH OFFICES

The firm has offices in Atlanta, Georgia; Charlotte, Durham, Greensboro and Raleigh in North Carolina; Greenville, South Carolina; Tysons Corner, Virginia; and Washington, DC. Please see firm's website for further details.

CONTACTS

Bankruptcy & Creditor's Rights	William B Sullivan
Business Litigation	Timothy G Barber
Capital Markets	James E Lilly
Corporate & Securities	Jeffrey C Howland
Employee Benefits	Michael D Gunter
Environmental	R Howard Grubbs
Government Relations	Burley B Mitchell, Jr
Insurance, Governmental & Tort Litigation	Reid C Adams, Jr
Labor & Employment	Charles A Edwards
Product Liability Litigation	Keith A Clinard
Real Estate Development	Bobby D Hinson
Tax	Howard N Solodky
Technology & Commerce	Mark N Poovey
Trust & Estates	George A Ragland

engage the legislative and regulatory system expertly and persistently.

Labor & Employment: The firm represents management in every aspect of the employer-employee relationship, including employment-related litigation before federal and state courts, agencies and arbitration panels, as well as providing advice on how to avoid litigation and minimize legal liabilities.

CLIENTS: Representative clients include: ALLTEL Carolina, Inc.; American International Group, Inc.; Armstrong World Industries, Inc.; BB&T Corporation; Bank of America; Centex Homes; Collins & Aikman Floorcoverings, Inc.; GlaxoSmithKline; INVISTA; LifeStyle Furnishings International, Ltd.; Lowes Companies, Inc.; Medigital, Inc.; NCR Corporation; Novartis Pharmaceuticals Corporation; R.J. Reynolds Tobacco Company; Remington Arms Corporation, Inc.; Sealy Corp.; Thomas Built Buses, Inc.; Thomasville Furniture Industries, Inc.; The Travelers; Unicomp, Inc.; Universal Tax Systems, Inc.; UnumProvident Corporation; Wachovia Bank and Wake Forest University.

INTERNATIONAL WORK: The firm's lawyers advise on business acquisitions, joint ventures, the protection and licensing of intellectual property, commercial leasing, sales and distribution arrangements, US export controls, customs and immigration in the context of inbound and outbound international transactions and operations. The firm defends the interests of its clients, including patent and trademark rights, in dispute resolution involving litigation, mediation and international arbitration throughout the world.

WOMBLE CARLYLE
OUR LAWYERS
MEAN BUSINESS

NORTH DAKOTA

CONTENTS: Corporate/M&A p.1403; Employment p.1405; Litigation p.1406; Real Estate p.1408; Individuals' Profiles p.1410.

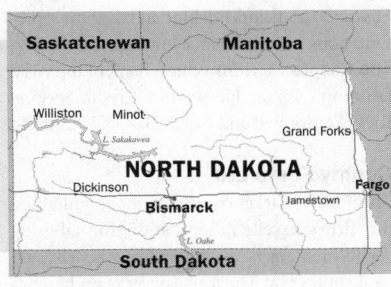

How lawyers are ranked

The opinions we gather from clients — mainly from in-house lawyers but also from other purchasers of legal services — are balanced by opinions from colleagues and competitors. Together, they provide two different perspectives — an all-round view — and biased viewpoints cancel each other out.

CORPORATE/M&A

North Dakota
Leading firms (Corporate/M&A)

1   SERKLAND LAW FIRM, PC *Fargo*
    VOGEL LAW FIRM *Fargo*

2   ANDERSON & BOTTRELL *Fargo*
    CONMY FESTE LTD *Fargo*
    DORSEY & WHITNEY LLP *Fargo*
    ZIMNEY, FOSTER, JOHNSON, DITTUS *Grand Forks*

3   DEMARS & TURMAN LTD *Fargo*
    MCNAIR, LARSON & CARLSON LTD *Fargo*
    NILLES, HANSEN & DAVIES LTD *Fargo*
    OLSON BURNS LEE PC *Minot*
    PEARSON CHRISTENSEN LLP *Grand Forks*
    TSCHIDER & SMITH *Bismarck*

Leading individuals (Corporate/M&A)

1   OLSON Richard *Olson Burns*, Minot
    SMITH Sean *Tschider & Smith*, Bismarck

2   BOTTRELL Lowell *Anderson & Bottrell*, Fargo
    JOHNSON David *McNair, Larson*, Fargo
    JOHNSON Steven *Vogel Law Firm*, Fargo
    SCHLOSSMAN William *Vogel Law Firm*, Fargo
    STRINDEN Jon *Dorsey & Whitney*, Fargo
    THOMAS Michael *Conmy Feste*, Fargo

3   CHRISTENSEN Douglas *Pearson*, Grand Forks
    FOSS Marilyn *Sole Practitioner*, Bismarck
    SELBO Gregory *Nilles, Hansen*, Fargo

Leading individuals (Bankruptcy)

1   BRAKKE Jon *Vogel Law Firm*, Fargo
    FOSTER John *Zimney, Foster*, Grand Forks
    MINCH Roger *Serkland Law Firm*, Fargo

2   DEMARS David *Demars & Turman*, Fargo

Firms and individuals are listed alphabetically in each band.

Band 1

Serkland Law Firm PC

The Firm: Peers praised this five-lawyer corporate team for attracting quality work and providing *"assertive business advice"* to clients. The group's particular forte lies in advising banks and private lenders on creditors' rights in bankruptcy and restructuring proceedings. Its impressive workload includes handling collection claims, foreclosure documentation, workout agreements and representing banks before regulatory bodies. Other matters include advising a number of banks on the development of conflict of interest policies.

The Lawyers: Clients seek out *"well-spoken and bright"* **Roger Minch** for his *"true expertise in bankruptcy and bank lending law"* and praise him for his *"detailed and solutions-oriented"* approach. His workload includes acting for a steady stream of secured creditor groups although he is also currently representing minority shareholders in an appeal case against the controlling shareholders of a private company. In this case his clients are claiming misappropriation of corporate opportunities and breaches of fiduciary responsibility.

The Clients: American Federal Bank; Bremer Bank; State Bank & Trust; First State Bank of LaMoure; CoBank; ACB; Citizens State Bank; Citizens State Bank of Finley and Union State Bank Fargo.

Vogel Law Firm

The Firm: Described as North Dakota's *"top dog,"* the firm elicited praise for its 11-member team, which is well versed in the full gamut of corporate law matters. The recent merger with Gunhus, Grinnell, Klinger, Swenson & Guy has further bolstered the firm's healthy stock of clients and cemented its profile in securities and cooperative work. The group services clients from offices in Fargo, Bismarck, and Moorhead. It advises local and regional businesses on all aspects of corporate law, including tax issues, public offerings and the creation and dissolution of corporate entities. The workload also encompasses advice on midrange mergers and acquisitions, particularly for clients in the healthcare industry. A significant portion of the practice is dedicated to the representation of creditors, especially agricultural lenders in collection claims.

The Lawyers: Market commentators recommended *"smart and tough"* **Jon Brakke** for his expertise in debtor/creditor work, and especially his advice to lending clients in the agricultural sector. Clients happily place *"full trust in his prompt and precise advice."* **Steven Johnson** also attracted widespread plaudits for his busy practice in business organization and shareholder disputes. One client said of him, *"I enjoy working with him and he is always quick to respond to my queries."* His peers also rate him as *"a fair lawyer who represents his clients well."* The solid and professional **William Schlossman** impressed interviewees with his expertise in family business matters. Clients described him as a careful lawyer who *"gives strong advice you can be confident in."*

The Clients: Acceptance Corporation; Forum Communications; Agribank; Ag Services of America; First International Bank & Trust; MeritCare Health System; State Bank of Fargo; Western State Bank and Westacre.

Band 2

Anderson & Bottrell

The Firm: Clients applauded the department's *"top-rate corporate knowledge and client care."* Its eight members undertake a diverse workload on behalf of clients such as large machinery dealerships, farming organizations and smaller local businesses. The team handles loan collections for banks and agricultural lenders and provides extensive business advice on the structuring and management of companies. Other engagements include representing North Dakota University and a number of seed companies in the licensing and enforcement of patents under the Plant Variety Protection Act. The firm has a strong practice defending farmers in crop insurance claims where it has successfully obtained various arbitration awards and settlements of over $7 million.

The Lawyers: Banking clients commended **Lowell Bottrell** as a successful leader in his field,

while peers acknowledged that he is a "*tough negotiator, who nonetheless is always reasonable.*" His caseload includes debtor and creditor representations and commercial transactional work.
The Clients: AgriPro Wheat; Bank of the West; Domino's Pizza; Household Credit Service; RDO Equipment and North Dakota University.

Conmy Feste Ltd

The Firm: Market commentators highlighted the firm's excellent reputation for advising clients on mergers and acquisitions as well as on bankruptcy law. The four-lawyer team handles a steady stream of midsized deals and is able to draw upon its store of loyal clients, particularly in the banking sector.
The Lawyers: "*Hard-working and detail-oriented*" **Michael Thomas** devotes much of his time to a busy banking and creditor bankruptcy practice, although he also advises on corporate transactions. He impressed interviewees as a "*real gentleman, who is firm but never unreasonable.*"
The Clients: Wells Fargo and Bremer Bank are among the clients of the firm.

Dorsey & Whitney LLP

The Firm: This national firm joins the table this year following the success of its three-lawyer corporate team in Fargo. The group's workload involves advising private and public companies on the full gamut of commercial law. This includes a significant M&A caseload as well as advising emerging companies on venture capital deals and structuring alternative finance. Recent highlights include representing Otter Tail in a $25 million transaction, involving the sale of Midwest Information Systems. The past year has also seen the team advising on the merger of a 120-physician multi-specialty clinic into a hospital as well as involvement in the formation and financing of a bank holding company valued at $40 million.
The Lawyers: Peers recommend **Jon Strinden** as "*a lawyer of good character*" and admire him as the corporate practice's rainmaker. Clients value his "*excellent ability to work through complex securities and tax issues,*" where his experience as a qualified accountant is thought to be invaluable.
The Clients: Otter Tail; AgCountry Financial Services; Renaissance Ventures; Flint Communications and Packet Digital.

Zimney, Foster, Johnson, Dittus & Flaten, Chartered

The Firm: This "*top-notch*" corporate and commercial team consists of seven attorneys who are proficient in banking and corporate transactional law and who have strong foundations in the debtor-creditor arena. The workload includes advising banks and financial institutions on the arrangement of finance packages for commercial and agricultural ventures.

Recent work includes advising a consortium of banks on a series of loans, guaranteed by the Bureau for Indian Affairs, to finance Native American casinos, hotels and entertainment complexes on an Indian reservation. The firm is also corporate counsel to AGSCO, a cluster of agricultural chemical supply companies.
The Lawyers: Market commentators told us that **John Foster** "*is the whole package. He is extremely smart, relates well with people and looks after his clients' best interests.*" Foster is a leading advisor to financial institutions and is presently counseling several banks on finance packages and liquidations. He has recently been involved in the financing of a number of development projects, including a sports center for the University of North Dakota, a medical clinic, shopping malls and restaurants.
The Clients: Wells Fargo; Bremer Bank; Farm Credit Services and US Bancorp.

Band 3

Demars & Turman Ltd

The Firm: Although this is a smaller two-attorney practice, interviewees acknowledged that it punches well above its weight and is "*successful in representing high-profile clients.*" They particularly recognized its long-established expertise in providing advice on bankruptcy law and debtor-creditor work.
The Lawyers: Interviewees praised **David DeMars** and singled him out as a "*top lawyer for bankruptcy,*" an area to which he devotes much of his practice. Clients benefit from his "*good judgment*" and report that he can employ a "*hardnosed approach*" when necessary.
The Clients: Alerus Financial; Bremer Bank; Community First National Bank and Ramsey National Bank & Trust Company.

McNair, Larson & Carlson Ltd

The Firm: This practice is widely admired for its quality bankruptcy and corporate work. Its client base includes banks, agricultural lenders and commercial clients.
The Lawyers: Peers praised **David Johnson** for his "*dedication to crafting a practical and reasonable solution.*" He is often seen advising on many corporate bankruptcies.
The Clients: First State Bank of Munich; Security State Bank of Wishek and Union State Bank of Hazen.

Nilles, Hansen & Davies Ltd

The Firm: This five-attorney corporate team advises on the creation of various business organizations, as well as providing advice on acquisitions and divestitures and ongoing contractual matters. The firm's varied client base includes medical groups, automobile dealerships, finance companies and numerous other businesses.
The Lawyers: Clients characterized **Gregory**

Selbo as a "*straight-shooter*" while peers applauded him as an "*extremely thorough and efficient*" operator. His practice focuses on commercial contracts and business organizational law.
The Clients: Burlington Northern and Santa Fe Railway are among the firm's clients.

Olson Burns Lee PC

The Firm: A corporate team of four lawyers in Minot handles a steady diet of work for several high-profile financial institutions and banks. Recent highlights include representing Securities State Bank in Bison Cooperative's bankruptcy case, involving $3 million debt. The group is also representing a party involved in the sale of a North Dakota bank with assets of over $60 million.
The Lawyers: "*Sharp and tenacious,*" **Richard Olson** won plaudits from clients as a skilled lawyer who, "*uses his intelligence and good people skills to represent clients well.*" He advises on many facets of corporate law, including M&A transactions. He also maintains a noteworthy bankruptcy practice and was praised for his banking law expertise.
The Clients: Securities State Bank of North Dakota, Farm Credit Services of North Dakota and First International Bank & Trust are among the banks the firm represents.

Pearson Christensen LLP

The Firm: The corporate practice impressed interviewees with its expertise in a range of commercial transactions and was applauded by clients as "*responsive and quick to accomplish our goals.*" The team regularly advises on the sale and acquisition of businesses and on the financing of projects for clients in North Dakota and out of state. The group recently assisted in the formation of 11 companies to enable the acquisition of recreational property for development in the southern states.
The Lawyers: **Douglas Christensen** is the bedrock of the corporate practice. Market commentators hailed him as an expert in both business formations and succession planning. He is a popular figure, known for his use of "*smart techniques and aggressive representation of clients.*"
The Clients: Rydell; Acme Electrical Tool Crib of the North; Alerus Financial and Milestone Investments.

Tschider & Smith

The Firm: A three-attorney corporate team advises clients on the full gamut of commercial law. The workload encompasses advice on banking, transactional and taxation matters.
The Lawyers: **Sean Smith** received widespread plaudits for his "*articulacy, intelligence and excellent people skills.*" His practice focuses on corporate transactions where he is "*particularly skilled at appreciating the complexities of issues that*

arise." Smith has a notable standing in health-care law, and is corporate counsel to St. Alexius Medical Center.

The Clients: AgriBank; FCB; Farm Credit Service of Mandan and St. Alexius Medical Center.

Other Notable Practitioners

Interviewees praised sole practitioner **Marilyn Foss** for her expertise in bank regulatory issues. The cornerstone of her practice is her role as general counsel to the North Dakota Bankers Association. This involves lobbying and provid-ing day-to-day operational advice to its members. She is also busy advising individual banks and financial institutions such as Frontier Trust Company and First International Bank & Trust.

EMPLOYMENT

North Dakota
Leading firms
(Employment: Mainly Defendant)

1	DORSEY & WHITNEY LLP *Fargo*
2	ANDERSON & BOTTRELL *Fargo*
	VOGEL LAW FIRM *Fargo*
3	CONMY FESTE LTD *Fargo*
	WOLD JOHNSON PC *Fargo*
	ZUGER KIRMIS & SMITH *Bismarck*

Leading individuals
(Employment: Mainly Defendant)

1	HERMAN Sarah *Dorsey & Whitney*, Fargo
2	DONARSKI Michelle *Anderson & Bottrell*, Fargo
	EDISON-SMITH Lisa *Vogel Law Firm*, Fargo
	PAGE Adele *Page Law Firm*, Fargo
	THOMAS Benjamin *Wold Johnson*, Fargo
	WARD Patrick *Zuger Kirmis*, Bismarck
3	ALBRECHT Kristy *Dorsey & Whitney*, Fargo
	SCHULTZ Robert *Conmy Feste*, Fargo

Firms and individuals are listed alphabetically in each band.

Band 1

Dorsey & Whitney LLP

The Firm: The Fargo office boasts a top-notch four-lawyer employment practice that is well-versed in the full gamut of labor and employment issues. Local and national clients pointed to its "*excellent resources and international reach,*" thanks to the firm's strong presence across the country. Work undertaken includes defending employers in discrimination and workers' compensation claims and negotiating collective bargaining agreements. The past year has seen the team representing a number of high-profile clients such as Nodak Mutual Insurance and Case New Holland.

The Lawyers: Clients praised "*terrific*" **Sarah Herman** for her "*resilience, and ability to translate complicated legal issues into layman's terms.*" She handles a busy roster of employment discrimination cases and classic labor arbitrations. **Kristy Albrecht** received accolades as an "*extremely bright and always scrupulously prepared*" lawyer. She is building an impressive reputation for her work in this area.

The Clients: Blue Cross Blue Shield of North Dakota; Dakota Medical Foundation; Microsoft Business Solutions; MDU Resources and Otter Tail.

Band 2

Anderson & Bottrell

The Firm: This is an impressive employment practice comprising ten lawyers. The team acts for local and national clients and provides them with ongoing employment law advice, responds to EEOC claims and defends clients against a myriad of employment litigation. In recent times the group has been particularly busy representing numerous employers from the computer industry. Following the government's recent revision of overtime regulations, the team has handled an increasing number of wage and hour claims.

The Lawyers: Clients singled out **Michelle Donarski** for her "*go-getting style*". They value her "*straight-shooting*" approach and her expertise in wrongful termination claims and severance agreements. She also assists employers in the development of employee handbooks.

The Clients: Global Electric MotorCars; Advantage Credit Bureau; Triad Broadcasting; SYSCO Food Services of North Dakota and PRACS Institute.

Vogel Law Firm

The Firm: This employment practice makes its debut in the *Chambers'* ranking tables this year. It draws on the strengths of the firm's top-rated commercial litigation practice and benefits from a high-profile client base. It has the ability to act for both large businesses and smaller enterprises, tailoring its service to suit each. The team advises employers on the full spectrum of employment law matters, including day-to-day counseling and OSHA compliance, defending discrimination claims and handling NLRB matters.

The Lawyers: "*No-nonsense*" **Lisa Edison-Smith** is at the forefront of the firm's employment practice. Clients say she possesses an "*abundance of common sense and knowledge,*" which she uses to represent clients facing litigation. She also offers clients regular training seminars.

The Clients: Dakota Clinic; Cass County Electric Co-operative; Prairie at St John's; Swanson Health Products; Forum Communications and MeritCare Health System.

MAINLY DEFENDANT

Band 3

Conmy Feste Ltd

The Firm: This eight-attorney practice impressed interviewees with its prominent employment practice. It handles a busy caseload of employment discrimination and workers' compensation claims.

The Lawyers: **Robert Schultz** is the bedrock of the employment practice. He received widespread endorsements for his employment defense work, and won particular praise for his expertise in workers' compensation.

The Clients: The firm represents numerous local and national businesses.

Wold Johnson PC

The Firm: The firm impressed market commentators with its expert handling of employment litigation, encompassing issues such as wrongful termination and workers' compensation. The team acts for both plaintiffs and defendants.

The Lawyers: Peers spoke of **Benjamin Thomas'** remarkable courtroom presence and pointed to his "*superb cross-examination skills.*" Clients look to him for his "*well-rounded*" employment law knowledge and his ability to find practical business solutions.

The Clients: Gate City Bank; Moorhead Public Service; Community First Bank; Union State Bank and US Bancorp.

Zuger Kirmis & Smith

The Firm: Interviewees praised this Bismarck-based firm for the quality of its employment work. The group defends employers in discrimination claims concerning age, sex, race, disability and retaliation. It is also well-versed in labor law and is noted for its expertise in negotiating contracts with the unions.

The Lawyers: Clients and peers applauded **Patrick Ward'**s firm understanding of employment law issues and "*succinct writing style.*" He has particular expertise in defending unions against members' claims. Ward also handles a busy caseload of antitrust, insurance defense and class action litigation.

The Clients: Montana Dakota Utilities; BNI Coal; Bridgestone-Firestone; Microsoft; Coventry Health Care and City of Medora.

Other Notable Practitioners

Adele Page left Dorsey & Whitney to set up her own boutique employment practice, Page Law Firm LLC, in August 2004. She impressed clients as a "*tough, aggressive litigator with exceptional talent.*" Her workload includes employment defense litigation as well as day-to-day consulting and training. She advises a loyal client base from the banking, manufacturing and healthcare industries.

LITIGATION

GENERAL COMMERCIAL

North Dakota
Leading firms
(Litigation: General Commercial)

1	**NILLES, HANSEN & DAVIES LTD** *Fargo*
	VOGEL LAW FIRM *Fargo*
	ZUGER KIRMIS & SMITH *Bismarck*
2	**MARING WILLIAMS LAW OFFICE PC** *Fargo*
	PEARCE & DURICK *Bismarck*
	SERKLAND LAW FIRM, PC *Fargo*
3	**DORSEY & WHITNEY LLP** *Fargo*
	FLECK, MATHER & STRUTZ LTD *Bismarck*
	MCGEE HANKLA BACKES & DOBROVOLNY PC *Minot*
	MCNAIR, LARSON & CARLSON LTD *Fargo*
	PEARSON CHRISTENSEN LLP *Grand Forks*
	SMITH BAKKE OPPEGARD PORSBORG *Bismarck*

Leading individuals
(Litigation: General Commercial)

1	**CAMPBELL Craig** *Vogel Law Firm*, Fargo
	CARLSON Bruce *McNair, Larson*, Fargo
	DURICK Patrick *Pearce & Durick*, Bismarck
	FISCHER Ronald *Pearson Christensen*, Grand Forks
	HILL James *Zuger Kirmis*, Bismarck
	MARING David *Maring Williams*, Fargo
	MCLEAN Ronald *Serkland Law Firm*, Fargo
	STORSLEE Steven *Storslee Law Firm*, Bismarck
	THIEM Rebecca *Zuger Kirmis*, Bismarck
2	**BAKKE Randall** *Smith Bakke*, Bismarck
	DUNN Daniel *Maring Williams*, Fargo
	HENDERSON Richard *Nilles, Hansen*, Fargo
	ILVEDSON Duane *Nilles, Hansen*, Fargo
	KIRMIS Lyle *Zuger Kirmis*, Bismarck
	KLINGER Edward *Vogel Law Firm*, Fargo
	MCGEE II Richard *McGee Hankla*, Minot
	MORLEY Patrick *Morley Law Firm*, Grand Forks
	PLAMBECK Stephen *Nilles, Hansen*, Fargo
	SINCLAIR Brad *Serkland Law Firm*, Fargo
	ZIMMERMAN Todd *Dorsey & Whitney*, Fargo

Firms and individuals are listed alphabetically in each band.

Band 1

Nilles, Hansen & Davies Ltd

The Firm: Interviewees concurred that this 16-lawyer litigation team has a "*first-class*" presence in the market. This respect is founded upon the team's resources and broad expertise, which give clients their "*full money's worth.*" Spanning the full range of commercial litigation, the group's caseload includes insurance defense, products liability and construction litigation. The firm's alternative dispute resolution practice continues to evolve, particularly in the form of arbitration and mediation. Experienced in advising on cases at both federal and state level, the group represents a client base that includes insurers and various local and regional commercial entities. Recent highlights include advising a lumber dealer in a copyright infringement claim concerning the design of a luxury residence.

The Lawyers: Clients singled out **Duane Ilvedson** as "*North Dakota's premier insurance defense lawyer,*" and particularly praised his "*complete thoroughness and integrity.*" Interviewees lauded him as "*a true student of the law who is a real joy at trial,*" and observed that he is frequently involved in mediations and arbitrations in the insurance industry. Market commentators praised **Richard Henderson** as a "*consummate professional*" and pointed to his "*zealous advocacy and impressive trial demeanor.*" He devotes a significant portion of his practice to the construction industry where "*he really knows his way around.*" "*Talented*" **Stephen Plambeck** handles a steady stream of professional liability cases and is especially busy in the representation of engineers. However, he sustains a broad litigation practice, having recently been involved in two antitrust class actions as well as a case concerning a motel in Minot. Clients praised his no-nonsense approach and "*confident advocacy in the courtroom,*" where he is known to fight his client's corner fervently.

The Clients: Farmers Insurance Group; State Farm Insurance; St. Paul Travelers; AutoOwner Insurance; EMC; CNA; Nodak Mutual Insurance; Burlington Northern Santa Fe Railway and Canadian Pacific Railway.

Vogel Law Firm

The Firm: The past year has seen an expansion for the state's largest firm as a result of its merger with Gunhus, Grinnell, Klinger, Swenson & Guy. This has resulted in a 20-lawyer litigation powerhouse providing expertise on a wide spectrum of commercial matters. The workload includes contractual disputes, products liability, construction and lenders' liability cases. The firm represents a broad client base ranging from small businesses to multinational corporations, as well as several insurance companies, local banks and healthcare institutions. The group boasts a strong medical malpractice team of six attorneys which is currently involved in a number of cases concerning severe birth injuries to babies. These concern questions of pre-natal care and resuscitation attempts after birth. Other highlights for the firm include obtaining a judgment for over $3 million on behalf of AgGrow Oils in a defective design and construction case that is currently on appeal. In recent years the team has also increasingly assisted clients in alternative dispute resolution.

The Lawyers: **Craig Campbell** was praised as an excellent tactical thinker whom clients value for his ability to keep them out of litigation. They also applauded him as a "*multifaceted lawyer who is pleasant and personable to work with, yet who can also be a bulldog in litigation.*" "*Dean of litigation*" **Patrick Weir** operates from the firm's Bismarck office. He is ably supported by a strong team of attorneys who were praised by clients for "*keeping the ultimate goal in mind at all times.*" Clients benefit from Weir's "*excellent manner with juries*" and "*sharp intelligence.*" He handles a number of cases for banks and financial institutions, but is best-known for his expertise in medical malpractice defense work. "*Bright and hard-working*" **Wayne Carlson** was also applauded for his medical malpractice defense practice and his ability to see the bigger picture. He is currently defending clients in 25 medical malpractice cases, but also devotes time to representing physicians before the state licensing board. **Edward Klinger** attracted widespread admiration as an "*aggressive and experienced litigator.*" His workload features bankruptcy litigation and contractual disputes, as well as legal malpractice and data privacy cases. In a recent Supreme Court case he successfully demonstrated that the State of Minnesota had violated his client's right to data privacy.

The Clients: Butler Machinery; Concordia College; Simonson Lumber; Northwestern State Bank of Ulen; MeritCare Medical Group; Dakota Clinic; North Dakota Long Term Care Association; Health Insurance Association of America; Med Center One Health Systems; West River Health Services; American Family Insurance Group and Altru Health System.

Zuger Kirmis & Smith

The Firm: This Bismarck firm houses a "*top-drawer*" team of 15 litigators who advise on the full gamut of commercial litigation. The past year has seen the group handle an increasing

1406   All quotes in the text are from interviews with clients and competitors.

CHAMBERS USA 2005

North Dakota

Leading individuals

(Litigation: Medical Malpractice Defense)

1 WEIR H Patrick *Vogel Law Firm*, Fargo

2 CARLSON Wayne *Vogel Law Firm*, Fargo

   MARCIL Jack *Serkland Law Firm*, Fargo

Leading individuals

(Energy & Natural Resources: Dispute Resolution)

1 BENDER Lawrence *Pearce & Durick*, Bismarck

   MORRISON John *Fleck Mather*, Bismarck

Individuals are listed alphabetically in each band.

number of commercial tort actions while sustaining its involvement in contract-based suits. The firm recently defended a client in a contamination case concerning a diesel oil spill. The plaintiffs were claiming damages of up to $150 million, yet the actual award paid by the firm's client was only $2 million. The team is currently defending MDU Resources in a case brought by an Oklahoma contractor for withholding payment, following the allegedly deficient construction of a pipeline. Other recent highlights include defending a claim alleging misappropriation of trade secrets. The group is prosecuting a counterclaim against majority shareholders for breach of fiduciary duty.

The Lawyers: Market commentators acknowledged that "*top-flight attorney*" **James Hill** is an "*aggressive and tenacious litigator.*" His practice focuses on the defense of personal injury claims and professional negligence cases for both attorneys and physicians. "*A-plus attorney*" **Rebecca Thiem** is "*as smart as they come.*" Clients asserted that she is "*very quick to grasp the essence of the problem and find reasonable solutions.*" Her practice encompasses complex litigation in the form of insurance and professional malpractice defense as well as a growing number of employment defense cases. Clients applauded **Lyle Kirmis**, as "*candid, honest and direct – he doesn't just tell you whatever you want to hear.*" He handles an even mixture of transactional and litigation matters that include construction and personal injury defense cases. Clients noted that his thorough analysis means he "*knows when to hold and when to fold. He provides a case evaluation you can really count on.*"

The Clients: Burlington Northern Santa Fe Railway; MDU Resources; Dan's Supermarket; North Dakota Insurance Reserve Fund; Marley Cooling Technologies; Dakota Community Bank and Great West Casualty.

Band 2

Maring Williams Law Office PC

The Firm: This "*highly respected*" group handles a steady diet of personal injury, contractual and employment disputes, insurance defense and professional liability cases. The firm recently represented GATX, a railroad car manufacturer, in a number of cases including one concerning the derailment of a cargo train that led to the spill of toxic chemicals. Other particularly notable cases include obtaining an award of over $3 million on behalf of a woman burned in an apartment building. The North Dakota supreme court recently denied the defendant's requests for appeal.

The Lawyers: Clients applauded **David Maring** as an "*aggressive and analytical litigation machine*" who understands the inner workings of business and who offers laudable trial skills. His caseload consists of an even balance of personal injury and commercial litigation, as well as a sprinkling of professional malpractice defense work. He recently represented Cenex Harvest States in a six-day trial concerning feed that allegedly damaged a dairy herd. Market commentators noted that he has a "*complete set of skills*", with some rating him as "*the most effective litigator in the state.*" "*Rising star*" **Daniel Dunn** joins the *Chambers'* ranking following market recommendations for his "*fantastic trial skills and charming jury appeal.*" He devotes the majority of his time to personal injury cases, usually representing plaintiffs, but also handles commercial and insurance defense litigation. He won praise for his client-handling skills and always has a "*roadmap of exactly how to win a case. He goes right to the heart of the issue.*"

The Clients: Attorney's Liability Protection Society; The Arc of North Dakota; Pioneer Plastics; Roers Construction; National Chiropractic Mutual Insurance; Reddaway Manufacturing; GATX; West Central; Whirlpool and Lincoln Mutual Life Insurance.

Pearce & Durick

The Firm: Interviewees expressed a high regard for this five-lawyer litigation team that is well versed in insurance defense, products liability and natural resources work. Its client base includes local businesses as well as several high-profile out-of-state companies. Recent highlights include defending an oil transport company in a case concerning a truck involved in a motor vehicle accident. It also reached a settlement in a case concerning a fire in a house on behalf of Emerson Electric in mediation in Canada.

The Lawyers: "*Charming*" **Patrick Durick** "*cuts to the chase*" and "*exudes credibility to the end of the earth*," said interviewees. His practice has a strong emphasis on products liability and insurance defense litigation. Recent work includes defending a ladder company in a products liability case. Market observers pointed to "*gentlemanly*" **Lawrence Bender** for his "*zealous representation and excellent judgment*" in numerous oil and gas matters. He is frequently seen defending natural resources companies before industrial commissions and other administrative bodies. Recent cases have involved property-related disputes and defending against allegations of negligent drilling operations.

The Clients: Ford; GM; Kawasaki Motor; Zurich North America; Emerson Electric; MDU Resources; Sinclair Oil & Gas and Midcontinent Communications

Serkland Law Firm PC

The Firm: This "*dynamic*" practice of six lawyers impressed clients with its "*excellent value*" and its rounded expertise in commercial litigation. Its work includes stockholder disputes, medical malpractice defense, and insurance defense and coverage cases. The firm represents a broad client base including several banks, insurers, pharmaceutical companies, manufacturers and oil and gas companies. Recent highlights include defending a pharmaceutical company in litigation concerning a diet drug. It also succeeded in having a class action certified on behalf of plaintiffs in litigation valued at over $50 million.

The Lawyers: "*Passionate*" **Ronald McLean** was praised for his "*colorful and creative*" advocacy. Clients described him as a "*truly outstanding attorney, impeccably prepared and extremely well versed in all aspects of insurance law and liability.*" **Jack Marcil** won praise for his "*remarkable tenacity and fair judgment,*" particularly in the area of medical malpractice defense. Recent cases include defending a doctor against allegations made by the parents of a deceased 14-year-old that they were not adequately warned of the risks of a hospital procedure. Interviewees also concurred that he is the "*best mediator in the state,*" an area to which he devotes a good portion of his time. **Brad Sinclair** impressed clients as a "*hard working, zealous advocate*" with impeccable ethical standards. His areas of expertise include debtor-creditor and transportation law. Sinclair also recently represented First Savings Bank in a case concerning bank identification numbers. Peers reported that, "*he is always well-prepared and understands his cases well. He resolves issues efficiently.*"

The Clients: Liberty Mutual; Prudential Insurance; New York Life Insurance; Cenex Harvest States; MeritCare Health Systems; Fargo School Board; Attorneys Liability Protection Society and Wyeth Laboratories.

Band 3

Dorsey & Whitney LLP

The Firm: Market commentators concurred that this firm is "*building a strong practice*" in the state, particularly in its Fargo office. The four-lawyer team handles the full spectrum of commercial claims, including shareholder disputes, breaches of contract, securities claims and employment matters. The team is currently representing a group of minority shareholders of Otter Tail in a case concerning a possible squeeze-out. The department's workload also regularly entails representing lenders in the litigation following loan defaults. Key clients here include US Bank and AgCountry.

The Lawyers: *"Talented"* **Todd Zimmerman** is a *"well-spoken and confident"* litigator who has a knack for *"getting to the heart of the issue."* He makes full use of his experience as a certified accountant and has a busy caseload defending accounting firms, including Eide Bailly, against malpractice claims.

The Clients: US Bank; AgCountry Farm Credit Services; Stutsman County Bank; Otter Tail and Dakota Medical Foundation.

Fleck, Mather & Strutz Ltd

The Firm: The full effects of Charles Miller's recent departure from the firm remain to be seen, but interviewees agreed that this ten-member litigation team retains a high profile in the market. Based in Bismarck, the group's expertise lies in insurance defense, medical and dental malpractice and natural resources work. Recent highlights include representing Petrol-Hunt in a class action concerning natural gas royalties. It also defended Koch Industries against a class action concerning the measurement of oil in crude oil pipelines.

The Lawyers: Peers observed that *"premier oil and gas lawyer"* **John Morrison** *"vigorously represents his clients and really believes in their cause."* His energy-related workload includes cases involving regulatory and tax issues. Clients endorsed him as the *"leading attorney for NDIC (North Dakota Industrial Commission) matters."*

The Clients: Basin Electric Power Co-operative; Koch Industries; Exxon; North Dakota Insurance Reserve Fund; The North American Coal and Burlington Resources Oil & Gas.

McGee Hankla Backes & Dobrovolny PC

The Firm: Based in Minot, this firm houses *"country gentlemen with city-slick brains."* Its lawyers are well versed in professional negligence, insurance defense, products liability and

construction law. They represent clients including insurance companies and several local businesses. The practice also boasts a flourishing appellate arm.

The Lawyers: **Richard McGee** impressed interviewees with his *"superlative forensic skills and no-nonsense approach"* which have led to many successes in the courtroom. His workload includes products liability and medical defense work. He is also nurturing a growing plaintiffs' practice. Clients valued his ability to *"explain things in layman's terms and apply logic to complex technicalities."*

The Clients: Attorneys Liability Protection Society; CIGNA; Dakota Fire Insurance; State Farm Mutual Insurance; Horace Mann Insurance and CNA.

McNair, Larson & Carlson Ltd

The Firm: This three-member litigation team shines for its *"remarkable responsiveness"* and for providing tailor-made solutions to suit individual client's needs. The practice is highly regarded for business litigation in which it advises insurance and finance companies, as well as local businesses. The workload includes advising on insurance defense and shareholder and contractual disputes. The firm is also frequently involved in agricultural disputes, with recent work including defending a claim concerning allegedly defective plant seed.

The Lawyers: **Bruce Carlson** impressed market commentators with his *"insightful business acumen,"* which he couples with *"thorough analysis and zealous advocacy skills."* His practice encompasses a steady stream of insurance defense and business disputes.

The Clients: The team represents numerous insurance companies, local businesses and financial institutions.

Pearson Christensen LLP

The Firm: Handling the full gamut of litigation matters, this Grand Forks firm earned plaudits for its expert handling of complex cases. The team is especially noted for advising government bodies on insurance, employment and real estate disputes.

The Lawyers: Interviewees praised **Ronald**

Fischer as a *"tough litigation machine."* He focuses almost exclusively on the representation of municipalities, school and park districts and water boards. His diverse workload includes contractual disputes, civil rights and discrimination claims and personal injury actions.

The Clients: Clients include cities, townships and water districts.

Smith Bakke Oppegard Porsborg & Wolf

The Firm: This widely admired ten-attorney group handles a broad spectrum of litigation. Its work includes advising clients on insurance defense, professional malpractice, products liability and employment litigation. The firm's client base consists of insurance companies, large corporations and smaller businesses.

The Lawyers: **Randall Bakke** is a talented attorney noted by interviewees for his tenacious style. He handles a diverse caseload including insurance coverage, construction, personal injury and tort litigation and undertakes both defense and plaintiff's work. Peers applauded his shrewd courtroom demeanor and knack of devising subtle and effective arguments.

The Clients: Cincinnati Insurance; Commercial Union; Liberty Mutual; Yasuda Fire and Marine; American International Group; CNA; Acuity; Alpha Property and Casualty and Chubb Group.

Other Notable Practitioners

At the Storslee Law Firm, *"top-flight"* **Steven Storslee** was praised as a highly ethical lawyer. His expertise lies in insurance defense and coverage work, although he is also highly regarded for products and professional liability cases. Clients benefit from his logical approach and praise him for his ability to command the respect of judges and juries. His clients include State Farm Fire & Casualty and National Farmers Union. **Patrick Morley** of Morley Law Firm Ltd elicited praise as an *"extremely smart and thorough trial lawyer."* He handles a busy caseload that includes toxic tort defense, insurance claims, construction and professional malpractice defense cases.

REAL ESTATE

Band 1

Conmy Feste Ltd

The Firm: Market observers heartily praised this two-lawyer team for its expertise in a wide spectrum of real estate matters. In particular, researchers were told that the firm is *"the first to grasp market trends before they even reach Fargo."* Its workload consists of commercial foreclosures

and transactions as well as title insurance advice. The team regularly assists in large-scale development projects such as shopping malls and handles issues such as loan documentation and the creation of legal entities.

The Lawyers: **Paul Hubbard** was singled out for his *"wealth of experience"* in real estate law. He has a stock of loyal banking and financial institution clients, including Wells Fargo and

Western State Bank. Clients recommended him for his *"attention to detail and expertise in handling complex, multistate transactions."*

The Clients: The group's client base includes banks, financial institutions and developers. Key clients include Bank of the West; Bremer Bank; Wells Fargo; Western Finance & Leasing and Western State Bank.

North Dakota
Leading firms (Real Estate)

[1] **CONMY FESTE LTD** *Fargo*
NILLES, HANSEN & DAVIES LTD *Fargo*
VOGEL LAW FIRM *Fargo*

[2] **MCCONN & RINDY** *Fargo*
OHNSTAD TWICHELL PC *Fargo*
SHAFT, REIS & SHAFT LTD *Grand Forks*
WOLD JOHNSON PC *Fargo*

Leading individuals (Real Estate)

[1] **HUBBARD Paul** *Conmy Feste, Fargo*
STROUP Robert *Nilles, Hansen, Fargo*

[2] **BUEIDE Daniel** *Vogel Law Firm, Fargo*
SHAFT Grant *Shaft Reis, Grand Forks*

[3] **JOHNSON Philip** *Wold Johnson, Fargo*
RINDY Dean *McConn & Rindy, Fargo*
WANNER David *Ohnstad Twichell, Fargo*

Firms and individuals are listed alphabetically in each band.

Nilles, Hansen & Davies Ltd

The Firm: Praised for its proficiency in the full gamut of real estate law, the department advises on both residential and commercial transactions. The work it undertakes includes advising on purchase and sale agreements, leases, document preparation, title correction and loan foreclosures. Clients also benefit from the firm's Northern Title sister division, which is dedicated to providing a range of real estate services to commercial lenders, individuals and companies.
The Lawyers: "*The dean of real estate*" **Robert Stroup** was commended for his "*excellent understanding of complex legal technicalities.*" He handles a busy caseload, advising clients on title insurance and commercial real estate projects.
The Clients: Travellers-Aetna; Prudential Insurance; Continental National Insurance Group; Bank of America; US Bancorp and Olaf Anderson & Son Construction.

Vogel Law Firm

The Firm: The past year has seen this four-lawyer department advising on numerous commercial real estate projects involving leases, purchases and land use planning. The team also works closely with the firm's highly esteemed corporate transactional department. The firm's strong bank of developer and commercial clients has been further bolstered by its recent merger with Gunhus, Grinnell, Klinger, Swenson & Guy.
The Lawyers: Clients applauded **Daniel Bueide** as "*incredibly attentive and detail-oriented.*" He is a leading figure in the firm's real estate practice and advises clients on financings, leases and development projects.
The Clients: MeritCare Medical Group; Northern Improvement; Dakota Clinic; Forum Communications; Borg Properties; Matrix Properties; Harwood Investments and Concordia College.

Band 2

McConn & Rindy

The Firm: This fledgling two-member practice, which was established in 2003, impressed interviewees with its quality advice on commercial and residential real estate transactions and financings. It boasts a high-profile client base of banks and financial institutions.
The Lawyers: Interviewees rated **Dean Rindy** for his expertise in commercial real estate matters and for his practical approach. His practice often sees him guiding clients through development projects, including planning, sales and title work.
The Clients: Alerus Financial; Union State Bank; American Federal Bank; Midwest Bank; Lifetime Financial and Community First National Bank.

Ohnstad Twichell PC

The Firm: Representing corporate entities and individuals, this widely admired practice handles the full spectrum of real estate matters. The workload encompasses advice on the sale and purchase of land, mortgage foreclosures, zoning and title work.
The Lawyers: **Dave Wanner** won plaudits from peers as a "*damn good real estate litigator*" with an "*excellent eye for detail.*"
The Clients: Developers and corporate entities make up the group's client base.

Shaft, Reis & Shaft Ltd

The Firm: This two-attorney practice provides quality advice to residential and commercial clients on issues such as real estate closings and title insurance. Recent highlights include its involvement in the development of University Village in Grand Forks, a complex containing residential town houses and a shopping center. The firm advised its client on title insurance, purchase agreements, the formation of a holding company and leasehold matters.
The Lawyers: **Grant Shaft** is a leading real estate lawyer in the Grand Forks market. Clients rate his "*exceptional grasp of title insurance issues,*" and described his advice as "*always reliable and prompt.*"
The Clients: Alerus Financial; Choice Financial; First State Bank; Gate City Bank and Wells Fargo.

Wold Johnson PC

The Firm: A team comprising two attorneys handles a steady stream of title work and development projects. The group also frequently acts as local counsel for multistate property transactions and financings.
The Lawyers: Interviewees look to **Philip Johnson** for his "*seasoned proficiency and skilled advice*" on a wide range of real estate matters. His caseload consists of commercial real estate, probate and banking work.
The Clients: Gate City Bank; Bank of America; Bank One; Red River Commodities; CIGNA; IDS Financial and Union State Bank.

Leaders in North Dakota

ALBRECHT, Kristy
Dorsey & Whitney LLP, Fargo
701 235 6000
Recommended in Employment

BAKKE, Randall
Smith Bakke Oppegard Porsborg &
Wolf, Bismarck 701 258 0630
Recommended in Litigation

BENDER, Lawrence
Pearce & Durick, Bismarck
701 223 2890
Recommended in Energy

BOTTRELL, Lowell
Anderson & Bottrell, Fargo
701 235 3300
Recommended in Corporate/M&A

BRAKKE, Jon
Vogel Law Firm, Fargo 701 237 6983
Recommended in Bankruptcy

BUEIDE, Daniel
Vogel Law Firm, Fargo 701 237 6983
Recommended in Real Estate

CAMPBELL, Craig
Vogel Law Firm, Fargo 701 237 6983
Recommended in Litigation

CARLSON, Bruce
McNair, Larson & Carlson Ltd, Fargo
701 293 9190
Recommended in Litigation

CARLSON, Wayne
Vogel Law Firm, Fargo 701 237 6983
Recommended in Litigation

CHRISTENSEN, Douglas
Pearson Christensen LLP, Grand Forks
701 775 0521
Recommended in Corporate/M&A

DEMARS, David
Demars & Turman Ltd, Fargo
701 293 5592
Recommended in Bankruptcy

DONARSKI, Michelle
Anderson & Bottrell, Fargo
701 235 3300
Recommended in Employment

DUNN, Daniel
Maring Williams Law Office PC, Fargo
701 241 4141
Recommended in Litigation

DURICK, Patrick
Pearce & Durick, Bismarck
701 223 2890
Recommended in Litigation

EDISON-SMITH, Lisa
Vogel Law Firm, Fargo 701 237 6983
Recommended in Employment

FISCHER, Ronald
Pearson Christensen LLP, Grand Forks
701 775 0521
Recommended in Litigation

FOSS, Marilyn
Marilyn Foss - Sole Practitioner,
Bismarck 701 355 4538
Recommended in Corporate/M&A

FOSTER, John
Zimney, Foster, Johnson, Dittus & Flat-
en, Chartered, Grand Forks
701 772 8111
Recommended in Bankruptcy

HENDERSON, Richard
Nilles, Hansen & Davies Ltd, Fargo
701 237 5544
Recommended in Litigation

HERMAN, Sarah
Dorsey & Whitney LLP, Fargo
701 235 6000
Recommended in Employment

HILL, James
Zuger Kirmis & Smith, Bismarck
701 223 2711
Recommended in Litigation

HUBBARD, Paul
Conmy Feste Ltd, Fargo 701 293 9911
Recommended in Real Estate

ILVEDSON, Duane
Nilles, Hansen & Davies Ltd, Fargo
701 237 5544
Recommended in Litigation

JOHNSON, David
McNair, Larson & Carlson Ltd, Fargo
701 293 9190
Recommended in Corporate/M&A

JOHNSON, Philip
Wold Johnson PC, Fargo
701 235 5515
Recommended in Real Estate

JOHNSON, Steven
Vogel Law Firm, Fargo 701 237 6983
Recommended in Corporate/M&A

KIRMIS, Lyle
Zuger Kirmis & Smith, Bismarck
701 223 2711
Recommended in Litigation

KLINGER, Edward
Vogel Law Firm, Fargo 701 237 6983
Recommended in Litigation

MARCIL, Jack
Serkland Law Firm, PC, Fargo
701 232 8957
Recommended in Litigation

MARING, David
Maring Williams Law Office PC, Fargo
701 241 4141
Recommended in Litigation

MCGEE II, Richard
McGee Hankla Backes & Dobrovolny
P.C., Minot
701 852 2544
Recommended in Litigation

MCLEAN, Ronald
Serkland Law Firm, PC, Fargo
701 232 8957
Recommended in Litigation

MINCH, Roger
Serkland Law Firm, PC, Fargo
701 232 8957
Recommended in Bankruptcy

MORLEY, Patrick
Morley Law Firm Ltd, Grand Forks
701 772 7266
Recommended in Litigation

MORRISON, John
Fleck, Mather & Strutz, Ltd., Bismarck
701 223 6585
Recommended in Energy

OLSON, Richard
Olson Burns Lee PC, Minot
701 839 1740
Recommended in Corporate/M&A

PAGE, Adele
Page Law Firm LLC, Fargo
701 237 3423
Recommended in Employment

PLAMBECK, Stephen
Nilles, Hansen & Davies Ltd, Fargo
701 237 5544
Recommended in Litigation

RINDY, Dean
McConn & Rindy, Fargo 701 271 8500
Recommended in Real Estate

SCHLOSSMAN, William
Vogel Law Firm, Fargo 701 237 6983
Recommended in Corporate/M&A

SCHULTZ, Robert
Conmy Feste Ltd, Fargo
701 293 9911
Recommended in Employment

SELBO, Gregory
Nilles, Hansen & Davies Ltd, Fargo
701 237 5544
Recommended in Corporate/M&A

SHAFT, Grant
Shaft, Reis & Shaft Ltd, Grand Forks
701 772 8156
Recommended in Real Estate

SINCLAIR, Brad
Serkland Law Firm, PC, Fargo
701 232 8957
Recommended in Litigation

SMITH, Sean
Tschider & Smith, Bismarck
701 258 4000
Recommended in Corporate/M&A

STORSLEE, Steven
Storslee Law Firm, Bismarck
701 222 1315
Recommended in Litigation

STRINDEN, Jon
Dorsey & Whitney LLP, Fargo
701 235 6000
Recommended in Corporate/M&A

STROUP, Robert
Nilles, Hansen & Davies Ltd, Fargo
701 237 5544
Recommended in Real Estate

THIEM, Rebecca
Zuger Kirmis & Smith, Bismarck
701 223 2711
Recommended in Litigation

THOMAS, Benjamin
Wold Johnson PC, Fargo
701 235 5515
Recommended in Employment

THOMAS, Michael
Conmy Feste Ltd, Fargo
701 293 9911
Recommended in Corporate/M&A

WANNER, David
Ohnstad Twichell PC, Fargo
701 282 3249
Recommended in Real Estate

WARD, Patrick
Zuger Kirmis & Smith, Bismarck
701 223 2711
Recommended in Employment

WEIR, H Patrick
Vogel Law Firm, Fargo 701 237 6983
Recommended in Litigation

ZIMMERMAN, Todd
Dorsey & Whitney LLP, Fargo
701 235 6000
Recommended in Litigation

CONTENTS: Banking & Finance p.1411; Bankruptcy p.1413; Construction p.1416; Corporate/M&A p.1419; Employment p.1421; Environment p.1424; Intellectual Property p.1427; Litigation p.1430; Real Estate p.1434; Individuals' Profiles p.1437; Firms' Profiles p.1451.

How lawyers are ranked

The opinions we gather from clients — mainly from in-house lawyers but also from other purchasers of legal services — are balanced by opinions from colleagues and competitors. Together, they provide two different perspectives — an all-round view — and biased viewpoints cancel each other out.

BANKING & FINANCE

Ohio
Leading firms (Banking & Finance)

1. JONES DAY *Cleveland*
2. CALFEE, HALTER & GRISWOLD LLP *Cleveland*
   SQUIRE, SANDERS & DEMPSEY LLP *Cleveland*
   THOMPSON HINE LLP *Cleveland*
3. FROST BROWN TODD LLC *Cincinnati*
   MCDONALD HOPKINS CO *Cleveland*
   PORTER WRIGHT MORRIS & ARTHUR *Columbus*
   TAFT, STETTINIUS & HOLLISTER LLP *Cincinnati*
   VORYS, SATER, SEYMOUR & PEASE *Columbus*
4. BENESCH, FRIEDLANDER, COPLAN *Cleveland*
   DINSMORE & SHOHL LLP *Cincinnati*

Leading individuals (Banking & Finance)

1. GUINN Guy *Calfee Halter*, Cleveland
   MILLS Osborne *Squire Sanders*, Cleveland
   RAWSON Rachel *Jones Day*, Cleveland
2. BEDREE Melvin *Vorys Sater*, Cincinnati
   CICARELLA Thomas *Calfee Halter*, Cleveland
   GATES Martin *Buchanan Ingersoll*, Cleveland
   GRADY Timothy *Porter Wright*, Columbus
   KALLAS Hani *Vorys Sater*, Cincinnati
   MIRALDI Leslee *Thompson Hine*, Cleveland
   RUSH Jeffery *Frost Brown*, Cincinnati
   SCHLOEMER Jeffrey *Taft Stettinius*, Cincinnati

Up-and-coming individuals
BARRAGATE Brett *Jones Day*, Cleveland

Firms and individuals are listed alphabetically in each band.

Band 1

Jones Day
See firm details p.485

The Firm: Banking teams don't come much slicker, or more potent, than this one, which gets "*top marks all round.*" Cleveland lies at the heart of a global network of "*superbly integrated and managed*" offices. The team acts regularly for both borrowers and lenders. These include banks from Ohio and around the USA, but the team is particularly noted for its great stable of top-drawer corporate clients. A number of banking clients declare this their "*first port of call, for sheer breadth and quality,*" noting that the firm's one-stop shop approach makes it easy to use. They add: "*Though the rates seem expensive, the bills turn out to be lower because the team is so efficient.*" A good deal of the workflow is connected with the firm's national bankruptcy practice, and the team is adept at securing credit for its clients.

The Lawyers: The "*absolutely wonderful*" **Rachel Rawson** (see p.1447) heads the department in Cleveland and is celebrated for her business acumen. Peers report: "*She doesn't get bogged down in minutiae and gets a deal done right.*" Clients, meanwhile, declare her "*a class act all the way, especially for debt negotiations.*" She led the team negotiating a $4 billion revolving credit facility on behalf of Nextel Communications. Market sources are also persuaded that associate **Brett Barragate** (see p.1437) is "*destined for great things.*" Clients are enthusiastic about this "*worthy business advocate and attorney,*" praising his "*careful forethought.*"

The Clients: National City Bank; KeyBank; The Riverside Company; Bank One; Nextel Communications; WL Ross and JM Smucker.

Band 2

Calfee, Halter & Griswold LLP
See firm details p.1451

The Firm: The large transactional practice here yields a healthy flow of finance work for a "*good-sized, experienced and professional*" team that is "*studded with fine lawyers.*" It also enjoys a considerable volume of stand-alone work. The lawyers do not, as a rule, act in bank-on-bank acquisitions, but regularly appear for bank and insurance syndicates, and the occasional borrower, in syndicated loans and highly leveraged transactions. The group advises on loans throughout their life cycle, and can work closely with its bankruptcy colleagues should difficulties arise down the line.

The Lawyers: "*Exceptionally smart, superb*" **Guy Guinn** (see p.1441) is held to be one of the most experienced lawyers in the state. Clients flagged up his extraordinary attention to detail. In addition to standing out as a brilliant adviser, he "*trains his people well,*" ensuring that he can count on top-class support. **Tom Cicarella**'s (see p.1439) reputation lies principally in the field of bankruptcy, but those in the know also respect his substantial banking and finance expertise, especially for borrowers and in work-out situations.

The Clients: Bank One; Bank of America; Key Bank; LaSalle Bank; National City Bank; Pittsburgh National Bank and US Bank.

Squire, Sanders & Dempsey LLP

The Firm: The team boasts a strong lending practice spread across Cleveland and Cincinnati. The latter office, in particular, is home to a concentration of capital markets expertise that includes cutting-edge derivatives transactions. Though Columbus is perhaps less prominent in these fields, it also plays a role in the firm's celebrated international network. The firm's lawyers act for a number of major financial institutions, but also have a healthy borrower practice advising corporate and municipal clients. Commentators particularly acknowledge the firm's "*preeminent position in public finance.*"

The Lawyers: **Osborne Mills** (see p.1445) is a "*focused and pleasant*" banking lawyer, a legacy partner from a boutique acquired by Squires some years ago to complement its existing public finance lawyers. With what clients describe as "*a real aptitude for business,*" he is billed as "*one of the top bank-side guys in town*" and boasts "*a flair for drafting.*" His team recently represented KeyBank as agent in a $250 million syndicated revolving credit facility for an insurance holding company. It also advised US Bank on restructuring an $18 million construction loan, and assisted National City Bank as agent, with a complex $300 million deal involving a syndicated and multicurrency revolving credit and term loan facility.

The Clients: KeyBank; US Bank; National City Bank; Bank One; National City Business Credit; Bank of Ireland; LaSalle Bank; Provident Bank; Huntington National Bank; Sky Financial Group; First Citizens Banc and ComBanc.

Thompson Hine LLP
See firm details p.1457

The Firm: This sizable team offers broad finance expertise combined with considerable international experience. Commentators portray it as a skilled and *"well-led"* group, often seen in large transactions. Staples of its diet include the usual loans, letters of credit and swap transactions, and the firm's name is often connected with that of major client KeyBank. It also boasts a credible public finance practice, which acts mostly for issuers but also occasionally for banks. The team's game plan is felt to hinge on close ties to the DC and New York offices, particularly in areas like project finance, where it acts for utilities and major players in the energy industry. For example, it was involved in advising Lubrizol on a $2.45 billion, 364-day revolving credit facility established to acquire Noveon International, which was spearheaded by New York group head Kathie Brandt. The firm later acted for the corporation in obtaining more than $1 billion in take-out financing.

The Lawyers: Many of the lawyers here boast considerable experience in-house at banks. For example, *"extremely smart and superb quality"* **Leslee Miraldi** (see p.1445) was formerly with KeyBank, an important client of the firm. She now assists a number of the firm's fiercely loyal lender clients, and is a whirlwind in syndicated credit transactions, clocking up innumerable high-value deals during 2004. Many of these were cross-border transactions, often involving intercreditor and subordinated debt elements.

The Clients: PolyOne; Goodyear; KeyBank; National City Bank; Bank One; JPMorgan Chase; Charter One; Verizon; Avery Dennison; Eaton; Omnicare and MeadWestvaco.

Band 3

Frost Brown Todd LLC
See firm details p.849

The Firm: This *"capable and respectable"* outfit holds its own as Southern Ohio's largest banking and finance group. The firm has a total of more than 40 attorneys in this field, spread throughout strategic offices across the region. Commentators acknowledge a sophisticated practice that serves many of the principal lenders in the state. Its lawyers will also act for their corporate clients borrowing from the financial markets. The group is no stranger to structured finance and securitizations, and work ranges from small bilateral loans to large syndicated transactions, often with an international element.

The Lawyers: *"Practical and accomplished"*

Jeffery Rush (see p.1447) represents an impressive stable of financial institutions on all aspects of commercial and consumer lending. He also has considerable experience of advising in the context of bankruptcy and workouts, and on real estate finance. He acted for US Bank National Association as lender on a $44 million agented construction loan for a shopping center in Florida, a $22 million construction loan and $6 million tax allocation bonds for a shopping center in Georgia.

The Clients: Cheviot Building & Loan; Cincinnati Bell; Convergys; First Clermont Bank; First Financial Bancorp; Huntington National Bank; KeyBank National Association; LaSalle Bank; Midland Atlantic Properties; National City Bank; PNC Bank National Association; Rookwood Properties and US Bank National Association.

McDonald Hopkins Co

The Firm: This *"highly competitive"* team has positioned itself well midmarket, growing a creditable practice, principally for lenders with a Cleveland presence. Commentators agree that it has *"earned its spurs,"* and a place within the tables, for consistently delivering polished performances in transactions, both simple and sophisticated, ranging from $5 - $500 million. The bulk of the team's workflow is secured and unsecured commercial lending, typically on behalf of lenders.

The Lawyers: Carl Grassi is the contact partner here.

The Clients: JPMorgan Chase; US Bank; National City Bank; KeyBank; Fifth Third Bank; Provident Bank; PNC Business Credit; Huntington National Bank; Charter One Bank and Roynat Capital.

Porter Wright Morris & Arthur LLP
See firm details p.1455

The Firm: This *"hugely experienced"* group acts for most of the major Ohio-based banks. It operates out of four offices, notably Columbus, handling loan transactions, leases and bonds. The team's lawyers are experienced in the origination, structuring and documentation of loans, and guide the loan through workout procedures if necessary. The firm's considerable litigation capacity is felt to be extremely useful in this respect.

The Lawyers: Clients appreciate **Timothy Grady**'s (see p.1441) *"calm manner and authority."* His personable style and ability to form good relationships with all parties to a deal are credited as the keys to his considerable success as a negotiator. Seen as something of a dean, he remains active and regularly appears in larger syndicated loans.

The Clients: The team is well known for its work for the Huntingdon National Bank across the full range of legal services. It also acts for credit unions, such as Corporate One, and for

the Community Bankers' Association, guarding the interests of small community players.

Taft, Stettinius & Hollister LLP

The Firm: This *"well-balanced"* team is the *"first port of call"* for a number of clients, thanks to a happy combination of *"technical excellence and astute business sense."* Clients also highlighted its considerable strength in a number of sophisticated areas of finance. This Cincinnati-centered group handles a wide range of work, with clients particularly beating a path to its door for international corporate finance advice and foreign exchange agreements, as well as a volume of more straightforward domestic matters.

The Lawyers: Clients commented admiringly on the deep bench here, particularly complimenting the *"first-rate support staff."* Chief among the partners is the *"brilliant"* **Jeffrey Schloemer**, whom clients declare *"extraordinarily capable and superb under pressure."* He generally acts for lenders, and is credited with great communications skills that can be invaluable in smoothing deals along.

The Clients: The team acted recently for a privately held business in a $100 million syndicated secured financing. It has also advised the Fifth Third, US, and Provident banks on multiple commercial, structured capital and equipment financings.

Vorys, Sater, Seymour & Pease LLP
See firm details p.1458

The Firm: This Columbus-centered outfit has offices throughout the state. The message from clients is that these offices are *"so well integrated that they use their resources with real efficiency."* Indeed, the two lawyers ranked in the tables are based in Cincinnati, a fact that failed to deter even Columbus-based clients. Indeed several interviewees expressly preferred Vorys to firms with all their eggs in the Columbus basket, so to speak. The team services some of the state's most important financial institutions, and clients are particularly complimentary about its skills in structuring new loan transactions, especially in asset deals. The high level of partner contact was also popular with sources.

The Lawyers: Commentators highlighted a good strong bench here packed with attorneys of *"consistent quality, and the highest integrity and intelligence."* **Melvin Bedree**'s (see p.1437) *"exceptional thoroughness"* and communication skills impress clients, as does his ability to separate the wheat from the chaff in a transaction. They particularly appreciate his firm leadership and hands-on approach in deals. He is joined in the tables by *"meticulous and business-savvy"* **Hani Kallas** (see p.1443), a younger partner who works with lenders in loans and workouts, particularly in the context of real estate and construction. The two partners are considered something of a class double act.

The Clients: The team serves an impressive range of state and national institutions, as well as loan associations and savings banks.

Band 4

Benesch, Friedlander, Coplan & Aronoff LLP

The Firm: This team has a credible presence in Ohio, especially in the northeast of the state. It typically represents banks and other financial institutions in a range of loan and financing matters, from origination to restructurings. The team is also experienced in advising on workouts.

The Lawyers: The loan transactions practice group is chaired by Ronald Teplitzky, who has experience in securitization and mezzanine financings as well as the usual raft of loan work and workouts.

The Clients: Clients are typically drawn from the state's banking and financial institution community.

Dinsmore & Shohl LLP

See firm details p.1452

The Firm: This firm has a particularly fine reputation for litigation in a range of areas, but has also developed a considerable niche at the smaller and midsized end of the finance world. The practice is focused on serving a number of community banks, handling regulatory issues, loans and strategic advice. Clients were particularly enthusiastic about the firm's familiarity with state and federal laws regulating the formation and activities of banks and other financial institutions.

The Lawyers: The heart of the practice is Susan Zaunbrecher. She acted for Wayne Bancorp in

its sale to National City.

The Clients: Best known for its wealth of small community bank clients, the team acts for Fifth Third Bancorp; Wayne Bancorp; United Bancshares; Ripley National Bank; Columbia Savings Bank; Citizens Bank and First National Bank of New Holland.

Other Notable Practitioners

Martin Gates (see p.1440) recently left McDonald Hopkins Co to join Buchanan Ingersoll PC. His *"smart loan work"* elicits enthusiastic praise from the market. He recently acted for Bank One, as agent and lead lender, in negotiating a $185 million syndicated, multicurrency asset-based revolving credit facility for Park-Ohio Industries. He also advised the same client on a $105 million syndicated, asset-based credit facility extended to Brush Engineered Materials.

BANKRUPTCY

Ohio	
Leading firms (Bankruptcy)	
[1] JONES DAY *Cleveland*	
[2] SQUIRE, SANDERS & DEMPSEY LLP *Cleveland*	
[3] DINSMORE & SHOHL LLP *Cincinnati*	
HAHN LOESER & PARKS LLP *Cleveland*	
MCDONALD HOPKINS CO *Cleveland*	
THOMPSON HINE LLP *Cleveland*	
VORYS, SATER, SEYMOUR & PEASE *Columbus*	
[4] BAILEY CAVALIERI *Columbus*	
FROST BROWN TODD LLC *Cincinnati*	
TAFT, STETTINIUS & HOLLISTER LLP *Cincinnati*	
[5] BAKER & HOSTETLER LLP *Cleveland*	
BENESCH, FRIEDLANDER, COPLAN *Cleveland*	
CALFEE, HALTER & GRISWOLD LLP *Cleveland*	
KEATING, MUETHING & KLEKAMP, PLL *Cincinnati*	
PORTER WRIGHT MORRIS & ARTHUR *Columbus*	
SCHOTTENSTEIN, ZOX & DUNN *Columbus*	
Firms are listed alphabetically in each band.	

Band 1

Jones Day

See firm details p.485

The Firm: In the opinion of many commentators this is *"an outstanding team-unbeatable for scope, scale and visibility."* It has a premier reputation for bankruptcy cases in Ohio and beyond. As one source put it: *"No other firm in the state is on the same plane"* when it comes to breadth and reach. In practice, this means that it can offer clients a blend of litigation and corporate expertise provided by teams of *"consistently competent lawyers at every level, throughout the world."* The *"powerful and aggres-*

sive" group in the firm's home jurisdiction handles a wide range of complex megacases, most of which originate outside the state. Traditionally a debtors' practice, particularly in manufacturing and retailing, it has evolved to include Ohio and Midwest creditors' group representation and secured lender counseling. However, the lawyers remain famed for their involvement in complex debtor cases, where they bring a broad and potent mix of skills to the table.

The Lawyers: *"Brilliant and elegant"* **David Heiman** (see p.1442) *"commands instant respect when he walks into a room,"* according to clients. Though he has been handling fewer of the huge debtor cases he became so well known for, he is active as secured lenders' counsel and is particularly associated with Wilbur Ross. He moves in the world of high-level, strategic advice, where his clients appreciate a style that is *"like a corporate lawyer: smooth and assured."* He recently led the team representing Wilbur Ross' Newcoal LLC in its $786 million cash and credit bid acquisition of the bulk of Horizon Natural Resources. **Heather Lennox** (see p.1444) enters the table on the strength of enthusiastic endorsement from clients, one of whom described her as *"the best bankruptcy lawyer I've ever met."* They also praised her talent for litigation and ability to command a court. She worked with Heiman to represent Oglebay Norton in $560 million worth of Chapter 11 cases.

The Clients: LTV Corporation; Oglebay Norton; USG; Wachovia Bank; WL Ross & Co; National Century Financial Enterprises; HQ Global Holdings; Federated Department Stores and Alderwoods.

Band 2

Squire, Sanders & Dempsey LLP

The Firm: This *"responsive and knowledgeable"* team is a power across the state and, indeed, the country. It won its fame on the strength of *"subtle and sophisticated"* work for a stable of financial institution clients. The practice is, therefore, particularly identified with creditors' work and has acquired considerable cachet in megacases such as the Enron bankruptcy. Clients were full of enthusiasm for a cost-effective and proficient team whose *"service is truly excellent."* They also value the depth and skill of a bench *"deep in talent"* at every level, with *"industrious and timely"* lawyers and *"an exemplary work ethic."* The firm's global expansion has seen it establish branches around the world, but local interest has been aroused in recent months by its confident expansion in Columbus and push into Cincinnati.

The Lawyers: *"Absolutely top-shelf"* attorney **Stephen Lerner** is an *"incredibly smart and upstanding"* feature of the creditors' landscape. Clients pay tribute to his goal-oriented approach, business sense and *"thoughtful analysis,"* declaring that, *"if he moves, we move."* The *"exceptional and resourceful"* **Chris Meyer** is seen by market sources as *"one of the brightest and best"* in the state. Commenting on his ethical approach, approving commentators report that he *"holds himself and others to a very high standard."* Working closely with Lerner in Cincinnati, of counsel **Jeff Marks** won warm praise from interviewees, who see him as *"gifted, calm, and a pleasure to work with."* His is a diverse practice that covers creditors and

Ohio
Leading individuals (Bankruptcy)

1
HEIMAN David *Jones Day*, Cleveland
LEPENE Alan *Thompson Hine*, Cleveland
LERNER Stephen *Squire Sanders*, Cincinnati
MEYER G Christopher *Squire Sanders*, Cleveland

2
CAVALIERI Nick *Bailey Cavalieri*, Columbus
LEWIS Kim *Dinsmore & Shohl*, Cincinnati
PIGMAN Jack *Porter Wright*, Columbus
RILEY Shawn *McDonald Hopkins*, Cleveland
SCHWARTZ Jeffrey *Benesch Friedlander*, Cleveland
SIDMAN Robert *Vorys Sater*, Columbus

3
DEMARCO Daniel *Hahn Loeser*, Cleveland
GOLD Ronald *Frost Brown*, Cincinnati
GOLDMAN Matthew *Baker & Hostetler*, Cleveland
HURLEY Timothy *Taft Stettinius*, Cincinnati
IRWIN Kevin *Keating Muething*, Cincinnati
JACKSON Reginald *Vorys Sater*, Columbus
LAWNICZAK James *Calfee Halter*, Cleveland
LENNOX Heather *Jones Day*, Cleveland
PAROBEK Drew *Vorys Sater*, Cleveland
POWAR Lee *Hahn Loeser*, Cleveland
POWERS Victoria *Schottenstein Zox*, Columbus
SANKER Robert *Keating Muething*, Cincinnati

4
BASH Brian *Baker & Hostetler*, Cleveland
HUTCHINSON Joseph *Brouse McDowell*, Cleveland
LATOUR Randall *Vorys Sater*, Columbus
MARKS Jeffrey *Squire Sanders*, Cincinnati
OSCAR Lawrence *Hahn Loeser*, Cleveland
ROBERTSON Jean *McDonald Hopkins*, Cleveland

Individuals are listed alphabetically in each band.

debtors, on both transactional work and litigation.

The Clients: The team represented the creditors' committee of Top Flight at a national level, and is counsel to WCI Steel in northern Ohio.

Band 3

Dinsmore & Shohl LLP
See firm details p.1452

The Firm: This "*super-responsive and professional*" Cincinnati-based outfit has a good-quality reputation for work within the state, but has also earned considerable credibility on the national stage. According to clients, the lawyers here "*work like hell*" to provide a proactive and business-focused service. They are experienced on both the creditor and debtor side and have acted in a number of high-profile matters. These arise within a number of different sectors, though the firm has a particularly good reputation for work within the food and retail industries.

The Lawyers: Clients laud this "*creative, energetic and thorough*" team. "*Seasoned, expert and fair,*" **Kim Martin Lewis** chairs the group and is known for her fine nationwide debtors' practice. Her clients praise her as a "*smart-as-hell lawyer*" who is pragmatic and "*always gives her best.*" She recently acted for Ormet as general bankruptcy

counsel, filing in January 2004, and for Huffy, filing in October. She also undertakes creditor work, and is closely associated with Procter & Gamble.

The Clients: High-profile debtors and creditors nationwide have included: Ormet; Huffy; Rue21; Chiquita and Wallace's Bookstores.

Hahn Loeser & Parks LLP

The Firm: This diverse group acts for clients from all sides and has something of a niche in the equipment-financing arena. Its lawyers regularly represent vendors and unsecured creditors, as well as advising clients seeking to acquire distressed businesses. Clients from around the country beat a path to the team's door, sometimes choosing it over their regular counsel because, as one put it, "*they are the best for managing complex cases with diverse elements.*" A recent highlight was its work for Cleveland-Cliffs, which sought out the team to handle over $2 billion exposure in insolvencies among its steel industry customers.

The Lawyers: Peers praise the "*superb lawyers*" here, while clients express their complete confidence in a team that is "*well set up and able to manage just about everything.*" "*Smart, seasoned and articulate*" **Lee Powar** is among the state's most experienced bankruptcy lawyers. He enjoys powerful connections with some of the biggest financial institutions in the field, and also boasts a reputation for banking work. In a deal that nicely exhibited the team's flair in complex matters, he led a group brought in to close the sale of Deaconess Hospital's assets to The MetroHealth System of Cuyahoga County, in one of the first and most notorious healthcare bankruptcy cases in the USA. **Dan DeMarco** is widely seen as Powar's number two, complementing him with great skill. Interviewees also salute the versatile **Lawrence Oscar** as "*a fine lawyer, marked for greatness.*" He acts for some of the firm's most prestigious clients.

The Clients: Deaconess Hospital; Hi-Rise Recycling Company; Corrpro Companies; Fleet Bank; ICX Corporation; The CIT Group; US Bank; Cleveland-Cliffs; Amedisys; Crown Castle USA; DeVlieg Bullard II and PHD.

McDonald Hopkins Co

The Firm: The considerable team here provides a range of services, particularly aimed at mid-market entities across the Great Lakes region, to a clientele that it is said to "*pursue relentlessly*" and to great effect. Peers acknowledge that the firm has "*done a great job to build a strong practice across the state,*" and is a favored port for referrals. Clients, meanwhile, were enthusiastic about a consistently high-quality practice that is "*genuine value for money.*"

The Lawyers: "*Super-fine and aggressive but fair*" **Shawn Riley** is credited with developing the practice's fortunes. He has built up and

heads a "*great group of core professionals,*" say commentators. His caseload includes a volume of debtor work, though he also represents lenders and creditors. The "*capable and adroit*" **Jean Robertson** is also considered "*a real asset to the team.*" Like Riley, she is experienced in both creditor and debtor representation. Significant recent matters for the team include the representation of Republic Engineered Products and Bush Leasing in their respective Chapter 11 bankruptcies.

The Clients: The clientele is largely drawn from the region's midsized businesses, and also includes the buyers of distressed businesses.

Thompson Hine LLP
See firm details p.1457

The Firm: A gilt-edged favorite of the business community, Thompson Hine boasts a long and honorable tradition of acting for lenders. It also handles a more modest, though increasing volume of debtor work. "*Capable and efficient*" teams in New York and DC complement offices throughout the state, and there is a good fit with the firm's public finance group. The group's caseload is a diverse one, but is characterized by volumes of workouts for secured lenders and representing agent banks in syndicated deals. Important clients such as KeyBank, JPMorgan Chase and National City Bank drive the practice along at a healthy pace, while winning highly acquisitive Summit Investment bodes well for instructions in Ohio and beyond. Clients are impressed by the quality of the work and the fact that "*they always manage to pull exactly the right people to the table.*"

The Lawyers: Team head **Alan Lepene** (see p.1444) "*has great instincts,*" and was described by one client as "*my second set of eyes.*" Observers are in awe of this "*exceedingly bright and aggressive*" attorney and his "*peerless craft.*" His links to the banks run deep and he is principally a lenders' man. One such client told researchers that "*walking into a room with him on your side is like going in with a big gun – it's comforting having so much power behind you – you should see the other side's faces fall!*" He recently represented KeyBank as agent and pre-petition lender under a $28 million pre-petition credit agreement, and as DIP lender in the ABDick bankruptcy pending in the District of Delaware. On the debtor side, he acted for GEO Specialty Chemicals in the US Bankruptcy Court for the District of New Jersey.

The Clients: A core of banking clients includes KeyBank and JPMorgan Chase, as well as National City Bank and Ohio Savings Bank. Other important clients include: Nationwide Life Insurance Company; GEO Specialty Chemicals; Amcast Industrial Corporation and Duke Realty.

Vorys, Sater, Seymour & Pease LLP

See firm details p.1458

The Firm: Vorys Sater is billed as *"Columbus's finest,"* and enjoys a particularly strong reputation in that part of the state. The key to the group's success is perceived to be its ability to function fluidly as a team. Its lawyers advise a considerable cross-section of Ohio's businesses, on both the creditor and lender sides, and handle the gamut of bankruptcy, restructuring and workout matters.

The Lawyers: This *"expert and aggressive"* team *"abides by the highest standards,"* say market sources. It includes the redoubtable, *"no-nonsense"* former bankruptcy judge **Robert Sidman** (see p.1448). He *"gets straight to the meat of a matter,"* and is acknowledged by peers as *"a tough adversary across any table or courtroom."* *"Results-focused"* **Reggie Jackson**'s (see p.1443) broad practice covers work for debtors and, especially, creditors. His constructive approach has won him a reputation as *"a great lawyer and the utmost gentleman."* Interviewees also described **Drew Parobek** (see p.1446) as *"an extraordinarily fine man and a great lawyer."* His track record of representing creditors speaks for itself and he has acted in some of the most notable bankruptcies in the state. *"Able and forthright"* **Randall LaTour** (see p.1443) was also recommended to researchers. He has written about and acted in numerous complex collection cases. Typically he acts for the creditors and, occasionally, the trustees.

The Clients: Clients are typically drawn from the local business community, and include both debtors and creditors.

Band 4

Bailey Cavalieri

The Firm: The backbone of this *"fine and accomplished"* team's practice is debtor and creditors' committee matters. The team of about ten professionals also handles a considerable workload of bank and lender matters, and was co-counsel to the DIP lender in the Huffy case. Its lawyers are also experienced in workouts and restructurings and in this area recently advised PNC and Provident Bank.

The Lawyers: The linchpin of the practice is said to be *"man of action"* **Nick Cavalieri**, who *"epitomizes the practical lawyer."* Aggressive and proactive, *"he doesn't rely on outsmarting people, though he can,"* say sources. A former Arter & Hadden lawyer, he is seen by peers as a particularly *"smart choice"* for creditor work within the state.

The Clients: Clients include Bank One, PNC Bank and Provident Bank.

Frost Brown Todd LLC

See firm details p.849

The Firm: The bulk of this regional heavyweight's bankruptcy practice lies in acting for large corporate debtors in Chapter 11 cases, which can range from a few million dollars up to billions. The firm has both a definite regional focus and credible depth, making it a popular choice with local clients. As commentators report, it *"knows the market and serves it well."* The team acted for Lightyear Communications and its parent and affiliates in cases brought in the Western District of Kentucky. Other highlights include advising developers CBL & Associates Properties and Glimcher Properties in a number of retail Chapter 11s.

The Lawyers: *"Aggressive but honorable"* **Ronald Gold**'s (see p.1441) reputation continues to grow, and he is seen by many as *"one of the next generation's highfliers."* Commentators are also reassured that when he's on a case a good job will be done with the least possible pain on all sides. His team was chief bankruptcy and restructuring counsel to Horizon Natural Resources and 78 of its affiliates in the enormous Chapter 11 cases filed in the US Bankruptcy Court for the Eastern District of Kentucky.

The Clients: Horizon Natural Resources; Lightyear Communications; Glimcher Properties; CBL & Associates Management and Carl Marks Consulting Group.

Taft, Stettinius & Hollister LLP

The Firm: The growth in debtor work continues apace for this high-class group, and is now a considerable component of a traditionally strong, *"100% solid"* creditors' practice. Lawyers have been ever more deeply involved in asbestos-related cases and, like many Ohio firms, inundated with steel industry work thanks to high steel prices. The team is versatile. In steel work, for example, it is as likely to be acting for the producer as for distressed customers, handling formal arrangements or informally consulting on loan restructurings and workouts. Though based in Cincinnati, the team is active across Ohio and has recently moved to strengthen the Cleveland practice. Clients praised a group that can *"guide us through the murkiest waters,"* recommending it for work nationally as well as within the state.

The Lawyers: At the root of the firm's success in this field is practice head **Tim Hurley**. According to clients, he is *"unbelievably knowledgeable,"* and has the ability to smooth tricky negotiations with his *"winning style."* His practice includes a great deal of asbestos-related work, generally acting for insurers. He also acted as debtor's counsel in the Baldwin Piano case, and was prominent in a plethora of steel company reorganizations.

The Clients: Key clients include The Cincinnati Insurance Companies and United States Steel Corporation, and the firm has also worked for the likes of Baldwin Piano, Intranet, The Hamilton Foundry & Machine Co and the Healthcare Industries Corporation.

Band 5

Baker & Hostetler LLP

The Firm: Clients value the firm for, among other things, its impressive national spread, *"substantial resources and excellent service."* These have helped it to win roles in some important cases. For example, the team represented the post-insolvency administrative claimants' committee in the LTV Steel case. The Ohio office is considered to be well connected to the national network. Its lawyers are concentrated in Cleveland and, to a lesser extent, Columbus and divide their time fairly evenly between work for creditors and debtors.

The Lawyers: **Matthew Goldman** co-manages the group and has considerable experience in advising on restructurings for both debtors and creditors. Commentators also applauded the *"exceptional"* **Brian Bash**, who was described by one of his clients as *"a guru"* in the bankruptcy field.

The Clients: The team assists both creditors and debtors. It recently acted for First Energy as the largest creditor against NRG.

Benesch, Friedlander, Coplan & Aronoff LLP

The Firm: This group offers a good-quality, stand-alone practice, but also benefits from the big firms' conflicts. In recent years it has been carving itself a particular niche as a debtors' shop. Clients tell of a *"professional and polished"* outfit that brings together *"exceedingly competent individuals"* from various disciplines into a smooth team.

The Lawyers: **Jeff Schwartz** boasts a smart national practice and, according to his clients, *"has the ability to go beyond the traditional lawyer."* His team recently counseled ABDick Company et al in their Chapter 11 cases, and represented Park Place et al in theirs. As creditors' committee counsel, it also acted for Bunting Bearings.

The Clients: Paragon Corporate Holdings; ABDick; DE Shaw Laminar Portfolios; Park Place Companies; Level Propane and the Official Committee of Physician Creditors of Dow Corning.

Calfee, Halter & Griswold LLP

See firm details p.1451

The Firm: This all-purpose corporate bankruptcy team acts mostly for debtors, despite being situated within the firm's finance group and also representing a string of major banks.

Recent examples include acting as local counsel in the LTV Steel case. The group's lawyers also handle a stream of creditor work, some of it for individuals.

The Lawyers: The bankruptcy team here sits within Tom Cicarella's finance group. **James Lawniczak** (see p.1443) is its standout attorney. He has a solid local profile and a reputation for being "*good with the academic niceties.*" Recent highlights for the team include acting for the debtor in the Wheeling Pittsburgh Steel case, and for the creditors' committee in the Gliatech case.

The Clients: Major banking clients include: Bank One; Bank of America; KeyBank; LaSalle Bank; National City Bank; Pittsburgh National Bank and US Bank.

Keating, Muething & Klekamp, PLL

The Firm: There are two strings to the bow here: a strong creditors' rights practice acting for Cincinnati banks and acquiring companies, and a thriving national mass tort practice representing trusts from across the country in asbestos cases. Clients report that this is a team that is "*really excellent at all times*" and fields a number of lawyers who "*know the area inside out.*"

The Lawyers: Clients value **Robert Sanker**'s "*sound, practical business sense.*" He heads the creditors' rights practice, which represented Curtis Papers in a $23 million out-of-court workout. It also assisted the Great American Life Insurance Company with regard to its $22 million secured debt in the Stearns Technical Textiles' Chapter 11 in the US Bankruptcy Court for the Southern District of Ohio. **Kevin Irwin** heads a team that is more narrowly focused on mass torts. He has a niche asbestos practice these

days, and more than one commentator said: "*If I needed to know everything about asbestos, I'd ask him.*" New engagements this year include representing the Armstrong World Industries Asbestos Personal Injury Settlement Trust, A-Best Asbestos Settlement Trust and the DII Industries Silica PI Trust.

The Clients: Armstrong World Industries Asbestos Personal Injury Settlement Trust; A-Best Asbestos Settlement Trust; DII Industries Silica PI Trust; Celotex Asbestos Settlement Trust; UNR Asbestos Disease Claims Trust; Curtis Papers and Great American Life Insurance Company.

Porter Wright Morris & Arthur LLP
See firm details p.1455

The Firm: This considerable regional outfit offers a stable and credible business reorganizations practice, generally acting for creditors, creditors' committees, and some secured lenders and syndicates. It is particularly associated with Huntington National Bank, with which the firm has a long history. The team is also frequently consulted by the potential purchasers of distressed assets and carries out the day-to-day business of preference defense. About a tenth of the practice is for debtors. Clients consider the team "*superb*" for large, complex matters, and find it good value for money.

The Lawyers: "*Analytical and even-tempered*" **Jack Pigman** (see p.1446) is widely seen as the secret to the firm's success in this area. "*A gentleman at all times, enormously able and unimpeachably professional,*" he is a valuable resource not just for clients but for colleagues in other areas. As well as being local counsel to Horizon PCS, he has acted for the creditors' committees

in a couple of smaller reorganizations during the past year. He also enjoys a sterling reputation as a mediator.

The Clients: The firm's client roster includes Huntington National Bank, Horizon PCS and JPMorgan Chase.

Schottenstein, Zox & Dunn
See firm details p.1456

The Firm: The team here enjoys a particularly good reputation for business reorganizations, typically in the domestic midmarket. A solid team acts for banks, trust companies and other institutions.

The Lawyers: **Victoria Powers** (see p.1447) was recommended as a "*smart and practical lawyer who crops up on all the major cases.*" Peers report seeing her more frequently over the past year, and praise her "*ethical, straightforward manner.*" She represents the official committee of unsecured creditors in the Cooker Restaurant and Genesis Worldwide bankruptcies.

The Clients: Clients are typically drawn from the state's banks, trust companies, creditors' committees and corporations.

Other Notable Practitioners

Joseph Hutchinson (see p.1442) heads the Cleveland office of Brouse McDowell and is regarded as "*a super lawyer with a robust local practice.*" Most of his work involves representing trustees, creditors' committees, asset purchasers, and separate debtors on a case-by-case basis. Much of this is generated through referrals, taking advantage of conflicts at other firms, especially those acting for banks. Key client First Energy also generates a significant volume of work.

CONSTRUCTION

Band 1

Thompson Hine LLP
See firm details p.1457

The Firm: "*Easily the outstanding practice in Ohio,*" this "*vastly experienced*" group has a national reputation and, alongside colleagues from across the firm, is increasingly looking towards a national, even international, marketplace. Its national profile is particularly strong in the field of large stadium work, where it recently landed the $350 million Florida Marlins stadium deal. All the same, Ohio-based work continues to constitute a major part of the team's caseload and there are no signs of it leaving local clients in the lurch. "*The finest team in the state*" serves a broad client base that spans all phases of the industry from owners to design professionals, though contractors undoubtedly dominate. It is visible in notable court cases,

and, on the transactional side, the firm pulls in large and unusual projects, pioneering project delivery systems through its innovative consultancy business, which handles all aspects of a project, including the nonlegal. The team also enjoys a particularly fine reputation for mediation, and is providing all the mediation for the ten-year Ohio schools' redevelopment project. Other highlights include acting as partnering facilitator, project evaluator and owners' counsel in a raft of recent projects, including a $90 million matter for Medina City Schools and a $95 million matter for Dayton Daily News.

The Lawyers: The team of "*extraordinarily talented lawyers*" here maintains "*a commanding lead*" over other firms. "*Masterful*" **Jeffrey Appelbaum** (see p.1437) does "*a great front-end job*" in every aspect of the group's practice, but is particularly linked to work for owners. His reputation as an "*incredibly committed mediator*"

grows apace, and he is widely respected for his 'partnering' work as a neutral facilitator, "*realizing projects and defusing issues before they arise.*" "*Fair-minded and diplomatic*" **Peter Welin** (see p.1450) has "*an indescribable but effective*" style, say commentators. His strong engineering background is an undeniable draw, while his "*refreshingly pragmatic*" approach wins him the praise of clients and peers. He recently represented the prime general trades contractor in connection with a complex construction project at Ohio State University. "*Tough-nosed litigator*" **Michael Currie** (see p.1439) acts aggressively for prestigious contractor clients. He is considered the perfect complement to Welin, with whom he recently led a team in a case involving $23 million in claims related to the erection of four heat recovery steam generators at a private co-generation plant project in Indiana. "*Incredibly smart and capable*" **James Robenalt** (see p.1447) is "*a*

Ohio
Leading firms (Construction)

[1] **THOMPSON HINE LLP** Cleveland

[2] **BRICKER & ECKLER LLP** Columbus
FRANTZ WARD LLP Cleveland
SCHOTTENSTEIN, ZOX & DUNN Columbus

[3] **BENESCH, FRIEDLANDER, COPLAN** Cleveland
BUCKINGHAM DOOLITTLE Columbus
FROST BROWN TODD LLC Cincinnati
KEGLER, BROWN, HILL & RITTER Columbus
SQUIRE, SANDERS & DEMPSEY LLP Columbus
ULMER & BERNE LLP Columbus

Leading individuals (Construction)

[1] **APPELBAUM Jeffrey** Thompson Hine, Cleveland
PETRO John Williams & Petro, Columbus

[2] **CURRIE Michael** Thompson Hine, Columbus
GREGORY Donald Kegler Brown, Columbus
HOLMAN Michael Bricker & Eckler, Columbus
MILLER Barry Benesch Friedlander, Cleveland
NATALE Andrew Frantz Ward, Cleveland
ROSATI Jack Bricker & Eckler, Columbus
TARULLO Michael Schottenstein Zox, Columbus
WELIN Peter Thompson Hine, Columbus

[3] **LEACH Donald** Buckingham Doolittle, Columbus
REMINGTON Royce Hahn Loeser, Cleveland
ROSENBERG Thomas Ulmer & Berne, Columbus
SABO Roger Schottenstein Zox, Columbus

[4] **FRIEDMAN Steven** Squire Sanders, Cleveland
GURNEY Scott Frost Brown, Cincinnati
LIGGETT Luther Bricker & Eckler, Columbus
ROBENALT James Thompson Hine, Cleveland
VICKERS F Thomas Ulmer & Berne, Cleveland
WAMPLER Samuel Bricker & Eckler, Columbus

Firms and individuals are listed alphabetically in each band.

neys' skills and attracting individuals from across the industry who are looking to step sideways into the law.

The Lawyers: Department head **Michael Holman** was described to researchers as a "*bulldog*" who "*charges straight ahead to take the hill.*" He was also warmly praised for bringing a deep knowledge of both the law and the industry to the table. "*Smart and thorough*" trial lawyer **Jack Rosati** is "*a gentleman litigator*" say peers. He is appreciated for his personable and pragmatic approach, and sources say that he can always be relied upon to "*try to work things out,*" but "*never doubt that he will do what he needs to do.*" **Luther Liggett** has a high profile as a lobbyist, generally acting for trade association clients. A comparatively recent arrival from Canada, **Sam Wampler** is a "*clever and hard-working*" lawyer who is "*easy to get along with*" and inspires respect in peers and clients alike. The team represented the school district in Monarch Construction Company v Ohio School Facilities Commission, et al. It also represented a public school district in resolving contractors' claims of more than $4 million. On the transactional side, lawyers acted for a large urban school district in the public procurement of program manager services for its $985 million building program.

The Clients: Public owners and, especially, school districts dominate the owner-heavy client base, which includes: City of Grove City; City of Upper Arlington; Clark County Board of Commissioners; Dayton Public Schools; Heath-Newark-Licking Port Authority; Medina City School District; Memorial Hospital of Union County; Miller Brothers Construction; Sandusky Library; Turner Construction and Westerville City School District.

Frantz Ward LLP

The Firm: The firm has carved an impressive niche for itself managing construction claims through both alternative dispute resolution and litigation. Its work is, at present, mostly in Ohio, but the team's national profile has been consistently growing of late. Its lawyers pride themselves on their cost-effectiveness, and their clients have no quarrel with that. Collaborating well with the firm's successful insurance practice, the group is particularly accomplished in the field of construction insurance claims. The sophisticated clientele consists mostly of general contractors and specialty trades, and includes some of the market's major players.

The Lawyers: Ever since his arrival from Thompson Hine, where he was Appelbaum's right-hand litigator, contractors' counsel **Andrew Natale** ("*ready to rumble and extremely capable*") has been busy pulling together an industrious and accomplished group. Natale remains the group's standout name, and commentators observe that "*he is always ready to get down and dirty with the best of them.*" Over the

past year the team arbitrated a multimillion-dollar delay and differing conditions case, obtaining a favorable result for its contractor client. It also litigated a large claim involving the interplay of Ohio's anti-indemnification statute and contractual insurance requirements.

The Clients: Great Lakes Construction; GEM Industrial; Hensel Phelps Construction; Independence Excavating; Whitacre Engineering; Precision Environmental; Mole Constructors; The Cleveland Marble Mosaic Company; Shelly Companies; Tremco and Havens Steel.

Schottenstein, Zox & Dunn
See firm details p.1456

The Firm: This sizable outfit enjoys a particularly good reputation for serving the needs of its core general contractor client base. However, the dynamic team also regularly appears for certain large developers. The group is rich in industry expertise and boasts experience of handling complex construction matters from start to finish. It has a healthy transactional bent, but also has the capacity to tackle major litigation and alternative dispute resolution as needed.

The Lawyers: **Michael Tarullo** (see p.1449) was described to researchers as a capable trial lawyer who is "*realistic and quick on the uptake.*" He enjoys a genuinely national practice and has a wealth of experience in the industry, both of which are considerable draws for clients. "*Aggressive*" **Roger Sabo** (see p.1448) can be "*pretty hard-nosed*" when he wants to be, which wins him many admirers. His practice has a labor twist and he is particularly associated with highways work. The team represented a large highway contractor in the development and certification of a $1.4 million claim on a federal highway project. It also acted for a notable developer in the negotiation of various design-build agreements for developments valued at more than $750 million.

The Clients: The team is best known for representing general contractors and their association, the AGC. A representative list would include: Nielsons Skanska; Corna/Kokosing Construction Company; Steiner & Associates; Performance Site Management; Continental Building Systems; Sauer Industries; Miles-McClellan Construction & Development; HR Gray & Associates; Pro-Terra Environmental Contracting Co and Robertson Construction Services.

Band 3

Benesch, Friedlander, Coplan & Aronoff LLP

The Firm: The construction team at this major regional firm represents a wide sweep of clients, from owners to contractors. It offers a broad service, spanning all aspects of the field, from transactional advice and contractual negotia-

truly excellent litigator" with a reputation for being "*a gentleman in any situation.*"

The Clients: Kokosing Construction; URS Corporation; Gilbane Building Company; St. Louis Cardinals; Pittsburgh Pirates; Florida Marlins; Ohio School Facilities Commission; Dugan & Meyers Construction; Rudolph/Libbe Companies; Boykin Lodging Company; XL Design Professional and The Musical Arts Association.

Band 2

Bricker & Eckler LLP

The Firm: The construction group here has "*deep market penetration and expertise,*" say commentators. It is particularly focused on owners, especially public ones, and dominates that part of the market thanks to work for large and prestigious public clients like school districts. The Columbus office houses a team studded with experienced engineers and able to lead on matters from inception to finish. Its success is due in part to an active talent development program that is dedicated to nurturing attor-

tions to complex dispute resolution. This gives lawyers a well-rounded perspective that is employed to good effect in litigation and mediations.

The Lawyers: The firm's reputation in this field sits squarely on the capable shoulders of "*diligent and formidable*" **Barry Miller** (see p.1445). A "*superb documenter and dispute resolver,*" Miller offers extensive experience in trials, mediations and arbitrations. As well as being a lawyer, he has a background as an architect, which has perhaps helped him to win an unusually diverse range of instructions.

The Clients: The team assists general and specialty contractors, owners, surety houses and design professionals.

Buckingham Doolittle & Burroughs

The Firm: This all-round team represents a mixed bag of clients from all areas of the industry, serving it in all aspects of construction law, from contract negotiations to dispute resolution. The firm's construction lawyers sit in the same group as their real estate colleagues, which helps them to "*know their way around a deal*" from all angles, and some of them boast a mixed practice. The group was also recommended for its particular niche in mechanics' liens.

The Lawyers: By all accounts it is the "*truly skilled*" **Donald Leach** who "*puts the firm on the map.*" The managing partner of the Columbus office, Leach is acknowledged by peers as a "*worthy adversary, quick and sharp,*" with considerable experience in the sector. He has a respected contractors' practice with a real estate streak. The team acted for the contractor in the negotiation of a $130 million engineering, procurement and construction contract for the construction of two hydroelectric power plants. In litigation, it represented a general contractor in a matter involving the construction of a state prison.

The Clients: Columbus Regional Airport Authority; The Smoot Construction Company; Danis Building Construction; Columbus Public Schools and Miller Pavement Maintenance.

Frost Brown Todd LLC

See firm details p.849

The Firm: The construction group at this regional heavyweight enjoys a growing profile, with commentators reporting that "*things are really coming together for them now.*" The greater part of this large, multistate practice is devoted to work for general contractors, large managers, and the odd surety. Turner Construction stands out as the keystone of a clientele that is drawn to this firm for its full-service offering. Lawyers from other departments, including labor health and safety, are ready to provide backup on complex projects. Cincinnati is the center of operations for the team in Ohio.

The Lawyers: The "*congenial*" **Scott Gurney**

(see p.1441) is considered "*one of Cincinnati's finest*" when it comes to construction advice, and is well connected in the industry. His team's work for contractors includes representing a national player in multimillion-dollar claims arising out of the collapse of a building on a construction site, and successfully resolving a multimillion-dollar bid protest on behalf of a plumbing contractor.

The Clients: Turner Construction; BBL Construction Services; The Nelson Stark Company; Ben Hur Construction; Kelchner and Allied Construction Industries.

Kegler, Brown, Hill & Ritter

The Firm: This team is known across the country as subcontractors' counsel, and is particularly renowned for its staunch advocacy on behalf of industry associations and their members. The versatile lawyers offer services in a variety of areas, and also act for owners and design professionals.

The Lawyers: Donald Gregory's (see p.1441) aggressive representation of his contractor and public clients' interests is "*tempered with pragmatism*" say commentators, who also allow that he is "*an outstanding litigator.*" His team acted recently for the Subcontractors Legal Defense Fund of the American Subcontractors Association, filing an amicus brief before the Nevada Supreme Court, which adopted ASA's position that there should be exceptions to the 'no damage for delay' clause under Nevada law.

The Clients: The team acts for several national trade associations, including the American Subcontractors Association, the Ceilings and Interior Systems Construction Association, and the National Ground Water Association. Among institutional owners, the team acts for the Butler County Transportation Improvement District, the Hamilton County Transportation Improvement District, the Catholic Diocese of Columbus, Montgomery County and school districts around the state. It counts Igel, Fishel, and Jess Howard Electric among its subcontractor and supplier clients.

Squire, Sanders & Dempsey LLP

The Firm: The firm almost exclusively serves owner clients, particularly public entities like city authorities and school districts, and the construction team is also active for the Cleveland Clinic Foundation. Inevitably its work is closely linked here with the firm's impressive public bond practice. Lawyers advise on all aspects of a project, from selecting service professionals through the construction process itself, to assisting in disputes. The team can draw upon extensive resources from across this international firm to provide a first-class, all-round commercial service.

The Lawyers: Steven Friedman is the standout name in this talented team. His reputation as a litigator, capable of handling complex, multi-

state construction disputes of all flavors, continues to grow. His team settled multiple contractor claims on a $25 million middle school project during construction for the Bay Village City School District. It also acted as claims counsel to the City of Cleveland on its $1.6 billion multiyear school construction and renovation program.

The Clients: The team's client base is dominated by public owners, and includes: Perrysburg Village Exempted School District; Garfield Heights City School District; Solon City School District; Avon Lake City School District and Nordonia Hills City School District.

Ulmer & Berne LLP

The Firm: This is considered "*the best regional firm in its niche,*" the niche in question being claims defense advocacy. It offers "*damn fine litigation*" to a range of clients, but is especially associated with work for design professionals. Lawyers also act for the occasional contractor. The varied workload in the past year has included advising the architect of a regional hospital in Burlington, assisting the engineer on a project at the Cleveland Clinic, and acting for the architect of a police facility. NBBJ remains an important and prestigious client, and lawyers also do a lot for insurers, representing their insured architects and engineers.

The Lawyers: According to the market, **Thomas Rosenberg** is "*a strong lawyer, capable and always impressive.*" He has a good track record of resolving construction disputes, and was recently successful in representing a concrete subcontractor in arbitration against a contractor concerning the construction of a multistory parking garage in Akron. Rosenberg is also advising an internationally renowned architect being sued over the design of a regional hospital in Iowa. "*Honorable*" **Tom Vickers** defends architects and engineers in insurance claims, and is respected as "*a good, careful lawyer.*"

The Clients: XL Insurance; NBBJ; Industrial Construction Company; Firestone, Jaros & Mullin; City Architecture; Architects Associated; Danbert Contractors; Orion Painting & Contracting; Horne & King Architects and Global Construction Company.

Other Notable Practitioners

"*Mr. bond law*" **John Petro**'s practice at Williams & Petro Co. LLC is almost entirely focused on the surety industry, of which he is known as variously "*the godfather*" and "*the king.*" Since his practice takes him into every aspect of the industry, he is "*100% immersed in construction law*" and widely touted as "*the finest construction lawyer in the state.*" His is a national profile and "*there's simply nothing he doesn't know.*" He represents surety companies in contract defaults, claims against a bond, and occasional litigation. At Hahn Loeser & Parks LLP,

Royce Remington "*neither overdoes nor underdoes his litigation,*" and "*proves that you don't need to be an aggressive hard-ass to get results.*"

This respected general commercial litigator's depth and skill in construction are legendary and, according to interviewees, it is "*rewarding*

to see him in action."

CORPORATE/M&A

Ohio
Leading firms (Corporate/M&A)

1	**JONES DAY** *Cleveland*
2	**BAKER & HOSTETLER LLP** *Cleveland*
	SQUIRE, SANDERS & DEMPSEY LLP *Cleveland*
	THOMPSON HINE LLP *Cleveland*
3	**CALFEE, HALTER & GRISWOLD LLP** *Cleveland*
	DINSMORE & SHOHL LLP *Cincinnati*
	FROST BROWN TODD LLC *Cincinnati*
	KATZ, TELLER, BRANT & HILD *Cincinnati*
	KEATING, MUETHING & KLEKAMP, PLL *Cincinnati*
	TAFT, STETTINIUS & HOLLISTER LLP *Cincinnati*
	VORYS, SATER, SEYMOUR & PEASE *Columbus*

Leading individuals (Corporate/M&A)

	Senior Statesman
	KREIDER Gary *Keating Muething*, Cincinnati
1	**GANSKE Lyle** *Jones Day*, Cleveland
	PORTER David *Jones Day*, Cleveland
2	**CARLSON James** *Thompson Hine*, Cleveland
	HOBERG Timothy *Taft Stettinius*, Cincinnati
	JORGENSON Mary Ann *Squire Sanders*, Cleveland
	KAISER Gordon *Squire Sanders*, Cleveland
	STEINER Edward *Keating Muething*, Cincinnati
	VINCENT George *Dinsmore & Shohl*, Cincinnati
3	**ADAMS Albert** *Baker & Hostetler*, Cleveland
	ALDRICH Thomas *Thompson Hine*, Cleveland
	GHERLEIN John *Baker & Hostetler*, Cleveland
	GROSSER Theodore *Porter Wright*, Cincinnati
	HIRSCHFELD Michael *Graydon Head*, Cincinnati
	JAHNKE Mark *Katz Teller*, Cincinnati
	KELLY Christopher *Jones Day*, Cleveland
	KESTNER Steven *Baker & Hostetler*, Cleveland
	LAPORTE Dale *Calfee Halter*, Cleveland
	RIGOT Joseph *Thompson Hine*, Dayton
	ROE Clifford *Dinsmore & Shohl*, Cincinnati
	WEIBLE Robert *Baker & Hostetler*, Cleveland
	ZAGORE David *Squire Sanders*, Cleveland
	Up-and-coming individuals
	BOISE April *Thompson Hine*, Cleveland
	WEISS Mark *Keating Muething*, Cincinnati

Firms and individuals are listed alphabetically in each band.

Band 1

Jones Day

See firm details p.485

The Firm: This "*cutting-edge,*" well-oiled commercial machine has a "*truly world-class*" bench of attorneys and a global footprint in the form of a network of offices that enables it to service the largest and most demanding clients. It boasts that most desirable of things: "*a massive brand with true boardroom recognition.*" The firm's Cleveland office hosts a formidable array of specialist lawyers who are plugged into the wider network in such a way that, wherever or whatever the deal, work is always steered to the right people. The "*fantastically strong*" clientele is largely made up of muscular industrials (many linked to oil and gas) and is evolving so as to include technology and life sciences companies as well as financial services groups. These clients praise a team that is "*top-notch all the way, and perfectly responsive;*" the in-house counsel at one major international organization declared: "*They do it all for me – they are my M&A team.*" The group advised National City in the sale to Bank of America of its 83% owned subsidiary National Processing.

The Lawyers: "*Dynamic*" **Lyle Ganske** (see p.1440) heads the global corporate/M&A group and is "*a real presence and fantastic in negotiations.*" Clients showered him with tributes, one typical respondent enthusing: "*He's my go-to man, my point man; he handles it all and I can just relax.*" Ganske advised National City in its $2.1 billion acquisition of Provident Financial Group as part of its push into the Midwest, and Ohio in particular. "*Smart and proficient*" **David Porter** (see p.1446) is well regarded for securities work. He is a "*lawyer's lawyer*" in whose advice clients have every confidence. **Christopher Kelly** (see p.1443) chairs the firm's corporate finance practice, and offers expertise in technology and life sciences work. A man who is pervasive in the marketplace, commentators applauded his "*ability to combine really good technical capability with sound, practical business judgment.*" They were also at pains to praise the "*first-rate crew*" across the board, including those at associate level.

The Clients: National City; JM Smucker; Federated Department Stores; Timken; Diebold; Riverside Company; PolyOne; Albertson's and Cooper Tire & Rubber.

Band 2

Baker & Hostetler LLP

The Firm: This "*reasonably priced*" team has an excellent profile in the midmarket. "*Their best people are absolutely the equal of anybody*" and have "*all the abilities and resources to practice effectively at a national level;*" indeed, the group is regularly seen on deals ranging all the way up to $1-2 billion. The transactions on which the firm works are both public and private, though they are generally negotiated rather than hostile. Nonetheless, lawyers do on occasion act as local counsel in national hostile takeovers managed out of the firm's New York office. Other branches on a healthy tree include private equity work for buyout groups, REITs ("*they totally dominate in this*") and the representation of a number of public clients in routine securities work. The team is "*committed to its enviable client base:*" mostly robust midsized entities (anything up to Fortune 20) and large public entities.

The Lawyers: Executive partner **Steve Kestner** is a seasoned business lawyer whose "*acumen and devotion*" are valued by clients. Locally prominent **Albert Adams** is regarded as something of "*an influential rainmaker*" and is particularly associated with the structuring and financing of transactions and REITs. "*Creative*" **John Gherlein** coordinates the Cleveland office's business group and "*innovates great solutions*" for reporting companies and public clients. "*Rational and courteous*" **Robert Weible** gets the thumbs-up as a "*simply first-rate lawyer, even by New York or DC standards.*" His practice covers M&A, securities and corporate governance issues, and he has excellent form in going-private transactions.

The Clients: The team acts for household-name corporations, ten of which are in the Fortune 25, including GE and Cardinal Health.

Squire, Sanders & Dempsey LLP

The Firm: Researchers heard plenty about this "*top-flight*" team and its delivery of transactional and corporate governance advice through an impressive network of offices reaching across many jurisdictions in the USA and around the world. Commentators also spoke of a deep synergy with the firm's bankruptcy practice. The team acts for corporations and financial institutions, many of them global, some of them Ohio giants. Key on the client list are the Eaton and Goodrich corporations. Generally speaking, work is focused more on the corporate side than on finance, though given the firm's public finance expertise, it is no surprise to find a flourishing practice in public sector bonds and underwriters' representation. Lawyers also receive a healthy flow of inbound deals from Europe and Asia.

The Lawyers: The "*quite wonderful*" **Mary Ann Jorgenson** has a glittering reputation for securities, M&A and corporate governance

www.ChambersandPartners.com

All quotes in the text are from interviews with clients and competitors.

1419

issues. Brought in at the highest levels for strategic advice, she is the brains behind more than one client's growth blueprint. **Gordon Kaiser** has a long and honorable track record in the corporate field, having acted on some of the most prestigious deals around. Clients declare him "*a proper gentleman*" and happily place their interests in his "*capable hands.*" He has extensive international experience and has made a name for himself in the world of US and European utilities. Researchers were advised to "*keep an eye on* " **David Zagore**, a "*thoughtful and impressive*" lawyer who commentators believe is "*heading for the top.*"

The Clients: The client base includes some of the world's largest corporations, such as: Eaton; Ferro; Reed Elsevier; OM Group; Furukawa Electric and Starwood Hotels.

Thompson Hine LLP
See firm details p.1457

The Firm: Clients are attracted to this "*refocused and newly invigorated*" regional firm by a "*talented and accessible*" team of lawyers who provide "*more bang for your buck.*" These ambitious attorneys are experienced in M&A, both large and small, and, professionally, the team is said to be "*aiming for the moon.*" In the absence of its own international network, the firm puts together bespoke international coalitions whenever a deal has foreign elements. Cleveland is the seat of power and the lawyers service a notable selection of Midwest clients who value their reasonable prices and "*prompt turnaround.*" The group represented Solvay Pharmaceuticals in agreements with Wyeth Pharmaceuticals to co-develop and co-commercialize several central nervous system (CNS) compounds, and to co-promote Wyeth's marketed product Effexor(r).

The Lawyers: "*Wonderful, decent*" **James Carlson** (see p.1438) has built an exemplary reputation advising predators and prey in hostile takeovers. With colleagues from the finance, tax and real estate groups, he led the team that represented Lubrizol in its $1.84 billion acquisition of Noveon International. Securities expert **Thomas Aldrich** (see p.1437) has experience of international transactions and such a long acquaintance with his clients' organizations that they "*depend on him from a heritage point of view.*" **Joseph Rigot** (see p.1447) handles corporate securities work out of the firm's Dayton office and is certainly well thought of in the region. "*He inspires real confidence*" thanks to his clear writing and "*wise counsel.*" "*Punctilious and professional*" **April Boise** (see p.1438) has made a deep and positive impression on clients who praise her "*spot-on understanding of the issues and ability to marshal the firm's assets in a timely way.*" She is an experienced transactional attorney who is well acquainted with Sarbanes-Oxley issues.

The Clients: Lubrizol; Solvay Pharmaceuticals; STERIS; Luxottica Retail Group; Eaton; Robbins

& Myers; Lexis-Nexis; TBC; Convergys; Standard Textile; Lion Apparel; Senco Products; Michelman and MeadWestvaco.

Band 3

Calfee, Halter & Griswold LLP
See firm details p.1451

The Firm: Chiefly active within Ohio and the region, this team is connected by long and deep roots to clients that range from small, aspiring enterprises to large, sophisticated corporations. It is admired for its almost paternal representation of family-owned businesses. The front line consists of a brigade of generalists, backed by specialists as needed. Commentators singled out strengths in IP and venture capital, on which the lawyers act for private individuals and buyout funds as well as companies. They additionally manage a healthy flow of M&A transactions.

The Lawyers: **Dale LaPorte** (see p.1443) is experienced in venture capital and corporate governance issues. His team frequently acts for the acquisitive RPM in transactions up to $250 million, and recently acted for TravelCenters of America in the $120 million acquisition of another travel center operator.

The Clients: Midsized public and private companies and Midwestern financial institutions feature on the client roster. These include: RPM International; Invacare; Linsalata Capital; TravelCenters of America and Agilysys.

Dinsmore & Shohl LLP
See firm details p.1452

The Firm: The team holds a commanding position in Cincinnati, largely through the representation of jewel-in-the-crown client Procter & Gamble. Another key client is Huffy, whose bankruptcy the team is managing, as well as the spin-off of its opportunity business. The group has also sewn up the market for the representation of Ohio's community banks. Peers declare their "*absolute respect*" for the team, which has "*worked hard and well to move beyond litigation into credible transactions.*" Clients stated explicitly that they seek the firm out "*for the consistent quality, high skill levels and access to the marketplace.*" Lawyers undertake a fair amount of real estate M&A, especially for developers, and are in their element when plunged into the thick of deal negotiations.

The Lawyers: Peers love to cross swords with "*extremely sharp*" **George Vincent**, whose affable manner and connections place him "*head and shoulders above others.*" Clients appreciate his big-picture thinking and ability to get "*into the chemistry*" of their organization. Vincent acted for National Underwriter in its merger with Highline Media. Managing partner **Clifford Roe** is a respected figure in the community. His general corporate practice has a healthcare twist; he led the team representing a

publicly traded corporation in its planned acquisition of a five-state privately held healthcare and services company.

The Clients: Procter & Gamble; Huffy; Standard Register; Castellini; Burke; Chiquita Brands; Xanodyne Pharmaceuticals and the Community Bank Association.

Frost Brown Todd LLC
See firm details p.849

The Firm: Prominent in the south of the state, this firm serves a long-standing and worthy clientele across the region. Of Cincinnati's largest ten public companies, the firm is general counsel to two and the corporate team provides bespoke transactional services to a further five. A thriving private clientele ranges from small mom-and-pop outfits to big success stories. The practice is said to have the character of a group of GPs, standing ready to advise and care for clients in any number of situations. The team acted for AK Steel in the $260 million divestiture of Douglas Dynamics to DDL Acquisition.

The Lawyers: Clients describe a "*diverse and business-oriented*" team, singling out support staff for special mention. Tom Anthony is vice chair of the corporate business group, and his practice has a noticeable healthcare flavor. The loss of Ted Grosser to Porter Wright was duly noted in the marketplace.

The Clients: Small and large regional companies feature on a client list that includes AK Steel, Cincinnati Bell and Convergys.

Katz, Teller, Brant & Hild

The Firm: The "*bright and resourceful*" attorneys here offer a smooth and "*creative*" service to appreciative regional clients on matters ranging from straightforward M&A to personal estate planning. The practice additionally has particular strength in tax-heavy matters. Clients like the "*close-knit, almost family-like*" team's ability to "*bring alignment and consensus*" to a deal. Researchers were made aware of the impressive professionalism of a team that, while not large, "*consists entirely of top-quality lawyers.*" It was recently appointed counsel to the Greater Cincinnati Chamber of Commerce, which sent a positive signal to the marketplace.

The Lawyers: "*Absolutely first-rate,*" **Mark Jahnke** has a healthy practice advising private companies on their mergers, disposals and acquisitions. His work is mostly sell side. The team represented Lion Apparel in the sale of its uniform division to G & K Services, and Data Storage Centers in the sale of its Cincinnati-based records storage business to Cintas. For Ampac, the team handled the acquisitions of Kapak, Longview Fibre's Bag Division and Flexicon.

The Clients: Ampac Packaging; Fisher Investment Group; Lion Apparel and Jeff Wyler Automotive Family.

Keating, Muething & Klekamp, PLL

The Firm: This relatively young Cincinnati-centered practice serves local and national clients, generally acting for acquirers in M&A deals. While the founders are still on the scene, and the spirit of the firm remains entrepreneurial, the group is transitioning into an altogether larger, more established and harder hitting entity. The market is clear in its recognition of the team's *"terrific expertise"* in securities work and it is additionally known for its *"strong and effective"* representation of public companies, in part thanks to its association with Carl Lindner. The firm enjoys a growing reputation for private company work. Clients praise the excellence of both the advice and the service, wishing only for slightly greater depth on the antitrust side.

The Lawyers: *"Sharp as a tack,"* **Gary Kreider** is respected as the *"dean of federal securities"* work and is active on an array of boards and as an expert witness in the courts. Much of the day-to-day work has passed into the hands of younger lawyers, notably the *"gentlemanly"* M&A specialist **Edward Steiner**. Clients admire his *"ability to keep abreast of every development,"* and at least one respondent enthused that *"he's probably the best corporate lawyer I've ever worked with."* On the federal securities law side **Mark Weiss** has caught the eye of peers and clients as a *"fine young lawyer who stays on top of things."*

The Clients: The firm acts for an exciting blend of companies and financial institutions from the local area and beyond.

Taft, Stettinius & Hollister LLP

The Firm: Cincinnati is the chief of four offices throughout Ohio dealing with local commercial work. The firm enjoys *"a tremendous reputation,"* with its team traditionally associated with venture capital groups such as Blue Chip Venture, and with the IPOs of ambitious young issuers. It has guided a host of startups to the marketplace and was among the first to involve itself with Internet companies; it still maintains an incubator company. There has also been a recent surge in instructions from underwriters. Strands of the practice are intertwined with the firm's national labor and employment law offering, although the corporate practice itself does not extend so widely. Cincinnati also has the distinction of acting for several Japanese clients on inbound deals. Attorneys act frequently in fairness matters, such as representing the audit committee of the board of the Dayton Power & Light Company.

The Lawyers: *"Straight shooter"* **Tim Hoberg** is a *"gifted, meticulous"* securities lawyer whose *"word is his bond."* Clients spoke of *"an experienced and practical problem solver"* who is present on many boards and committees. Hoberg acted for Cornerstone Brands in its 2004 tender offer and recently won LCA-Vision as a client.

The Clients: Blue Chip Venture; Chiquita Brands International; Federal Home Loan Bank of Cincinnati; LCA-Vision and Cornerstone Brands.

Vorys, Sater, Seymour & Pease LLP

See firm details p.1458

The Firm: This Columbus outfit is *"exactly what you'd expect from a good provincial firm."* It acts for an excellent midmarket clientele on the range of corporate matters, using strong ties to the state government to great effect.

The Lawyers: The bulk of the team is based in Columbus. M&A expert **George Jenkins** is a key contact; his practice focuses on commercial real estate and the development and sale of emerging businesses.

The Clients: Clients range from individual entrepreneurs to Fortune 500 companies and financial institutions.

Other Notable Practitioners

Porter Wright Morris & Arthur LLP's **Ted Grosser** received accolades for his representation of public and private entities and his experience in M&A. He is well known for his work with closely held businesses. Graydon Head & Ritchey LLP has had an active year on the venture capital and finance side, which further bolsters the reputation of key player **Michael Hirschfeld** (see p.1442). He acts mostly for closely held businesses, though his team also advises notable public entities such as Fifth Third Bank and Clear Channel.

EMPLOYMENT

MAINLY DEFENDANT

Ohio
Leading firms
(Employment: Mainly Defendant)

1	**BAKER & HOSTETLER LLP** *Cleveland*
	DUVIN, CAHN & HUTTON *Cleveland*
	FRANTZ WARD LLP *Cleveland, Cincinnati*
2	**FROST BROWN TODD LLC** *Cincinnati*
	JONES DAY *Cleveland*
	MILLISOR & NOBIL CO LPA *Cleveland*
	PORTER WRIGHT MORRIS & ARTHUR *Columbus*
	SQUIRE, SANDERS & DEMPSEY L.L.P. *Cleveland*
	TAFT, STETTINIUS & HOLLISTER LLP *Cincinnati*
3	**DENLINGER, ROSENTHAL & GREENBERG** *Cincinnati*
	DINSMORE & SHOHL LLP *Cincinnati*
	KEGLER, BROWN, HILL & RITTER *Columbus*
	SPIETH BELL MCCURDY & NEWELL *Cleveland*
	ULMER & BERNE LLP *Cleveland*
	VORYS, SATER, SEYMOUR & PEASE *Columbus*

Firms are listed alphabetically in each band.

Band 1

Baker & Hostetler LLP

The Firm: The Cleveland-based team covers everything from labor negotiations and collective bargaining to cutting-edge class actions. Its lawyers are blessed with *"great analytical skills"* and were recently successful in their representation of a telecom company in an FMLA case. The team has achieved a number of key decisions in the railroad industry, one of them involving a breach of the duty of fair representation.

The Lawyers: **Greg Mersol**, the *"walking encyclopedia"* of the Baker law firm, is famous for his employment litigation. He represents employers on many issues, ranging from wage and hour disputes, race and age discrimination and employee benefits. His resume confirms that he is comfortable trying cases in the state, federal and appellate courts. His client base includes companies in retailing, manufacturing and financial services. **John Lewis** is well known for his astute handling of difficult situations. *"He is always prepared for every eventuality,"*

researchers were told. This *"careful and intellectual"* attorney spends most of his time dealing with litigation and appellate work involving federal and state employment discrimination, Civil Rights Act and wrongful discharge cases. **Elliot Azoff** spends much of his time outside Cleveland, where he represents many national newspapers including The New York Post, which he has advised on union matters and various arbitrations. With more than 25 years of experience as employers' counsel, **Richard Leukart** is skilled at union avoidance and organizational drives, employee audits and wage, salary and personnel administration matters. More than 40 years of labor and employment experience have left **Victor Strimbu** with a reputation as *"an extremely good labor lawyer."* His practice focuses on the media: he represents a number of newspapers and has been dealing with a considerable amount of union work nationwide.

The Clients: Ford; CSXT; Electronic Data Systems and Progressive.

Ohio

Leading individuals

(Employment: Mainly Defendant)

Senior Statesman

DUVIN Robert *Duvin, Cahn,* Cleveland

★ **BARNARD** Thomas *Ulmer & Berne,* Cleveland

[1] **FRANTZ** Michael *Frantz Ward,* Cleveland

MILLISOR Kenneth *Millisor & Nobil,* Cleveland

SIEGEL Bradd *Porter Wright Morris & Arthur,* Columbus

[2] **ADAMS** Deborah *Frost Brown Todd LLC,* Cincinnati

HAWKINS Michael *Dinsmore & Shohl LLP,* Cincinnati

KING G Roger *Jones Day,* Columbus

LAWRENCE James *Frost Brown Todd ,* Cincinnati

LEUKART Barbara *Jones Day,* Cleveland

LEWIS John *Baker & Hostetler,* Cleveland

MERSOL Greg *Baker & Hostetler,* Cleveland

PACE Stanley *Spieth Bell McCurdy & Newell,* Cleveland

WARD Daniel *Frantz Ward,* Cleveland

WARNER Charles *Porter Wright Morris,* Columbus

WEBER Roger *Taft Stettinius & Hollister,* Cincinnati

YUND George *Frost Brown Todd,* Cincinnati

[3] **ASHMUS** Keith *Frantz Ward,* Cleveland

AZOFF Elliot *Baker & Hostetler,* Cleveland

BUCK Frank *Duvin, Cahn & Hutton,* Cleveland

BUMPASS T Merritt *Frantz Ward,* Cleveland

DIMLING Robert *Frost Brown Todd,* Cincinnati

FEHELEY Lawrence *Kegler, Brown, Hill,* Columbus

HASTINGS Susan *Squire, Sanders,* Cleveland

HILLER David *Millisor & Nobil,* Columbus

LEUKART II Richard *Baker & Hostetler,* Cleveland

MEYER Andrew *Duvin Cahn & Hutton,* Cleveland

MILLSTONE David *Squire Sanders,* Cleveland

NOBIL Steven *Millisor & Nobil,* Cleveland

NOLAN William *Squire, Sanders,* Columbus

ROSENTHAL Daniel *Denlinger, Rosenthal,* Cincinnati

RYDZEL James *Jones Day,* Cleveland

SHEERAN Timothy *Squire, Sanders,* Cleveland

STEPANIAK Mark *Taft, Stettinius,* Cincinnati

STEPHEN John *Porter Wright,* Columbus

STRIMBU Victor *Baker & Hostetler,* Cleveland

WOLFF Robert *Duvin Cahn,* Cleveland

Up-and-coming individuals

MICHEL Lisa *Keating, Muething,* Cincinnati

MOSS Steven *Kahn Kleinman,* Cleveland

Individuals are listed alphabetically in each band.

Duvin, Cahn & Hutton

See firm details p.1453

The Firm: This 48-attorney Cleveland boutique is *"a very powerful law firm."* The team is considered *"very professional and extremely tenacious."* Employment litigation is the core area of business; recently the firm won a jury trial for Hawk (Wellman Friction Products) in an invasion of privacy and infliction of emotional distress case heard in the Ohio state court and upheld on appeal. Clients include government entities and natural resources and financial services companies.

The Lawyers: Founder of this firm **Robert Duvin** (see p.1439) is *"an outstanding labor attorney"* and *"an excellent negotiator"* with *"a great style."* He has represented many national corporations in the food and northeast Ohio supermarket industry. **Frank Buck** (see p.1438) has *"a style and approach to things that differ from other people's."* His work encompasses labor relations for private companies and public sector clients. Buck recently successfully represented Electrolux in a collective bargaining procedure. **Andrew Meyer** (see p.1445) is a *"bright and efficient"* attorney who focuses on traditional labor matters. He does a considerable amount of negotiating on behalf of employers in both the private and public sector. Chairman of the firm's management committee, **Robert Wolff** (see p.1450) supervises all the high-profile cases handled by the firm. The successful trial lawyer is often depicted as *"an extraordinary tenacious litigator"* whom *"juries love."* Clients, too, love his *"dry wit"* and note that he is *"cost-efficient."* He recently tried a case for Cole National involving claims raised by a former officer seeking to enforce indemnification/advancement rights in connection with a securities investigation. Although the action was brought by a plaintiff seeking damages, following trial the judge awarded Cole approximately $500,000 in damages against the former employee.

The Clients: City of Cleveland; Dominion East Ohio Gas; Cleveland Clinic Foundation; Electrolux and Hawk.

Frantz Ward LLP

The Firm: This *"value-for-money"* Cleveland firm is bursting with *"high-quality labor and employment people."* The practice group comprises 13 attorneys who work on union law and labor arbitration as well as employment litigation for companies in the health, transport and electronics industries.

The Lawyers: Michael Frantz *"is one of the most effective lawyers I've ever seen,"* said one rival attorney. He has wide-ranging experience in employment and labor law and has worked with various industries all over the USA and Canada. **Daniel Ward** is *"a very client-focused and thorough attorney"* who *"takes matters very seriously."* A *"solid and sharp mind"* plus 22 years in practice ensures that he excels in various spheres including employment litigation, OSHA law, labor relations and healthcare. Great technical skills cause **Keith Ashmus** to be known as a *"powerful"* lawyer. He has been working on a substantial number of high-profile discrimination and sexual harassment cases including Kimberly Miller v Denny's Restaurants. **Merritt Bumpass** has worked on matters ranging from collective bargaining agreements to sexual harassment and assault cases on behalf of various clients in healthcare, aviation and electronics.

The Clients: Among many private companies,

the firm has represented Yellow Roadway, one of the largest transportation service providers.

Band 2

Frost Brown Todd LLC

See firm details p.849

The Firm: A 50-attorney national labor and employment team has been involved in a multitude of class actions and OSHA cases for numerous private companies including Smurfit-Stone Container. The team is considered *"the best in South Ohio in the labor field."* Alongside labor negotiations and employment litigation work, the firm provides extensive training to its clients.

The Lawyers: While **Deborah Adams** (see p.1437) is seen as *"an intellectual attorney,"* she is also *"very good with juries."* Interviewees remarked on the quality of Adams' work in the fields of sex discrimination and sexual harassment. She has represented management in a considerable number of cases including Debra Black v Zaring Homes. *"Clients are in very good hands"* with **George Yund** (see p.1450). This tenacious and aggressive trial lawyer represents employers in all aspects of labor and employment law before the courts and administrative agencies. A significant amount of his time is spent on labor arbitration, in which he has acted for a major league baseball player among others. **James Lawrence**'s (see p.1444) practice is increasingly focused on negotiation, mediation and conflict resolution. He is *"a knowledgeable ADR lawyer"* and *"a fine speaker."* Although this *"seasoned and competent"* attorney has been appointed chairman of the alternative dispute resolution practice group, he is still very much involved in the labor and employment world. **Robert Dimling** (see p.1439) is a *"straightforward but detail-conscious man"* who *"always does a good job."* He represents clients from various industry sectors, among them Armco Steel and Smurfit Diamond Packaging on OSHA matters, employment discrimination and workers' compensation.

The Clients: The firm has been representing clients from a broad range of industries including construction, healthcare and financial services. In the automotive industry, it has acted for a German automobile parts manufacturer.

Jones Day

See firm details p.485

The Firm: The international player acts for many Fortune 500 companies in this area of practice, and employment law dominates over traditional labor law. Nevertheless, the team did recently represent the Cedars-Sinai Medical Centre on a union law matter. Among numerous large corporate clients, the firm acts for Thomson multimedia, PETsMART and Verizon Communications.

The Lawyers: Experienced **Roger King** (see

1422   All quotes in the text are from interviews with clients and competitors.

CHAMBERS USA 2005

p.1443) is considered "*a very talented man*" with an excellent reputation. His knowledge of NLRA matters makes him a "*top-notch*" choice and he is said to have a certain "*intensity to his practice*" that peers admire. King recently obtained a summary judgment on all counts in a breach of contract lawsuit, Richard H. Hoyt v Nationwide Mutual Insurance. **Barbara Leukart** (see p.1444) is "*a classy lawyer*" who represents employers in all areas of labor and employment law. She has a good combination of academic and litigation skills – "*she can write a summary judgment motion like no other and is also great in trial.*" "*Very competent*" **James Rydzel** (see p.1447) handles employment litigation including NLRB proceedings. He was involved for Crown Cork & Seal in ERISA class action lawsuits and arbitration involving changes made to USWA retirees' health and medical benefits. Rydzel also represents clients in the newspaper industry on union-related issues.

The Clients: Thomson Multimedia; Cedars-Sinai Medical Centre; DTR Industries; Bridgestone Americas Holding; Catholic Healthcare Partners; Forum Health; ProMedica Health System and Bon Secours Health System.

Millisor & Nobil Co LPA

The Firm: This 23-attorney Cleveland boutique has a defense-only labor and employment practice. A broad clientele ranges from employers' associations to Fortune 500 companies; the team deals with all labor and employment issues including workers' compensation and employee benefits. It has lately been negotiating with unions on behalf of Goodrich.

The Lawyers: Forty-plus years of experience have made **Kenneth Millisor** a "*fine and very competent lawyer*" in the areas of labor management, equal employment opportunity, arbitration and employee benefits. **Steven Nobil** has brought a great number of new clients to the firm and is known for his thorough approach. His practice covers matters of labor management, equal employment opportunity, OSHA and arbitration. Nobil represents both private and public sector clients. **David Hiller** has been very busy working on arbitrations. He recently represented ThyssenKrupp in the strategic planning and negotiation of a new two-tier wage structure collective bargaining agreement with UAW. Besides "*substantial expertise*" he has "*good practical judgment*" and the gift of "*creative thinking.*"

The Clients: ThyssenKrupp; May Department Stores; PolyOne; Sekely Industries and Case Farms.

Porter Wright Morris & Arthur LLP

See firm details p.1455

The Firm: The 45-attorney employment group is "*good at not letting the ball drop.*" Its employment litigation practice covers class actions and

a large number of discrimination cases. For the past decade, the team has represented SBC Communications in all manner of discrimination and harassment cases as well as some general business litigation. The firm also has a long-standing relationship with UPS. It is credited with having some of the most "*efficient*" lawyers who, "*once they are on a deal, will make it through and will keep the client happy at all costs.*"

The Lawyers: "*The best wrongful termination lawyer in the state,*" **Bradd Siegel** (see p.1448) is "*a great scholar*" with "*brilliant practical skills.*" He practices employment law with surgical precision and is "*a master of the substance of the law.*" The founding chair of the Ohio Management Lawyers Association, **Charles Warner** (see p.1449) is another "*very good technician*" who devotes a great deal of his practice to labor law. He was recently brought in as counsel to Arvin-Meritor in a wrongful discharge case. The employee filed in four different forums and, after years of proceedings, Warner prevailed in all four. Warner's peers consider him "*knowledgeable and talented,*" as well as "*well connected in labor circles.*" **John Stephen** (see p.1449) has lately been involved in collective bargaining agreements as well as sexual harassment cases for clients such as UPS. According to interviewees, this "*particularly good*" lawyer manages to impress clients every time he represents them.

The Clients: Morgan Lewis; SBC Communications; UPS; Ohio State University and Arvin-Meritor.

Squire, Sanders & Dempsey LLP

The Firm: The Cleveland office of this major international law firm has a 19-attorney labor and employment practice, which has recently been involved in FLSA class actions concerning the problem of minimum wages and allegations of improper payment of overtime. A far-reaching client base includes local, national and international businesses.

The Lawyers: Columbus-based **William Nolan** has "*a good sense of balance and knows the law inside out.*" He represents private and public companies in his broad labor and employment practice. **Timothy Sheeran** is "*an outstanding lawyer in the public sector.*" The schools sector is an important one for Sheeran; he represents the Ohio school districts in every aspect of labor and employment matters including litigation and contract negotiations. His private sector client work includes wage and hour problems, class actions and employment agreements. The practice group leader, **Susan Hastings**, represents private and public sector employers in both federal and state courts. This "*thorough and smart*" attorney has advised management throughout the country in relation to sex discrimination, sexual harassment and disability discrimination. "*A solid lawyer,*" **David Millstone** represents management in both labor

and employment matters. Most of his time is devoted to a public sector clientele that includes cities, counties and school boards.

The Clients: The broad client base embraces both public and private clients and includes Prayon and Arlington.

Taft, Stettinius & Hollister LLP

The Firm: Clients with any number of problems turn to this firm. Union contracts, tax-related employee matters and trade secrets are among the issues dealt with. For some it is the "*top labor firm in south Ohio.*" Key factors include the presence of "*lawyers with good personalities and good style*" who "*really know their stuff.*" The client base includes businesses from banking and finance, manufacturing and transportation.

The Lawyers: A "*consummate, clever and dedicated lawyer,*" **Roger Weber** is the chairman of the labor and employment department at Taft. "*He does an excellent job*" in both federal and state courts in matters such as wrongful termination and discrimination. He also counsels on labor contracts and labor relations. **Mark Stepaniak** has made a name in the negotiation of collective bargaining agreements on behalf of employers. He is considered to be "*a thoughtful and professional lawyer*" and has been representing clients in the automotive, broadcast, solar heating, dairy and paper industries as well as public sector employers such as hospitals, schools and universities.

The Clients: Clients include statewide and national private businesses as well as public bodies including the University of Cincinnati.

Band 3

Denlinger, Rosenthal & Greenberg LPA

The Firm: This eight-attorney Cincinnati-based boutique targets all aspects of labor and employment law for businesses in various industries, among them construction, retailing, healthcare, hotels and restaurants.

The Lawyers: One of the founding members of the firm, **Daniel Rosenthal** has worked on the management side for over 25 years. This "*superior lawyer*" is viewed by the market as "*intellectual, but with very good common sense.*" Researchers were told, "*He can handle almost everything.*"

The Clients: These include businesses of all sizes as well as municipalities and other governmental entities.

Dinsmore & Shohl LLP

See firm details p.1452

The Firm: This seven-office, four-state firm provides its services to the management of small businesses, Fortune 500 companies and public bodies. Its Cincinnati's labor and employment team remains busy handling litigation in state and federal court as well as representing clients in collective bargaining negotiations and contract arbitrations.

The Lawyers: Michael Hawkins is *"knowledgeable and very experienced and has good presence, both with clients and in court."* He is fluent in every aspect of labor and employment law, including representation before various state and federal agencies, and provides general advice on employer-employee relations.

The Clients: The firm's clients are mainly private employers including some Fortune 500 companies.

Kegler, Brown, Hill & Ritter

The Firm: This firm has a respected eight-attorney labor and employment team in its Columbus and Marion offices. The firm deals with a substantial number of wrongful discharge cases and collective bargaining negotiations on behalf of public and private companies.

The Lawyers: Lawrence F Feheley (see p.1440) is the chairman of the practice group. He is depicted as *"a thoughtful and articulate practitioner"* who is *"competent, careful and pragmatic."*

Spieth Bell McCurdy & Newell Co LPA

The Firm: Ten attorneys from this 26-lawyer firm work on traditional labor law, advising long-standing local and national private clients. The team has represented Parker Hannifin on labor issues for more than 50 years.

The Lawyers: Stanley Dan Pace has been with the firm for more than 15 years. He is *"a focused traditional labor lawyer"* who represents employers in labor negotiations, arbitrations, wage and hour litigation and NLRA matters.

The Clients: Parker Hannifin; Brush Engineered Materials; Rolls-Royce; Ferro; MTD Products; Crane and Goodrich.

Ulmer & Berne LLP

The Firm: Twenty specialist attorneys make up the Cleveland practice group. They are regarded as *"a very skilled team that always does a great job."* The lawyers have substantial litigation experience in areas such as discrimination, health and safety, and workers' compensation. Cases have been tried before state and federal courts including the Ohio Supreme Court, the Federal Court of Appeals and the US Supreme Court.

The Lawyers: *"Intelligent, reasonable and experienced,"* **Thomas Barnard** chairs the labor and employment group and is without doubt the star attorney in his office. This *"great trial lawyer"* is, according to some sources, *"probably the most active labor and employment attorney in Ohio."* He has undertaken OSHA investigations, traditional employment and labor law and employment-related lawsuits in both the public and private sectors for over 30 years.

The Clients: CNF, Sisters of Charity Health System and Marathon Ashland Petroleum all feature on the client roster.

Vorys, Sater, Seymour & Pease LLP
See firm details p.1458

The Firm: The team has been representing the management of various healthcare organizations, often negotiating collective bargaining agreements on behalf of hospitals. The manufacturing sector, too, is one with which the team is familiar; here it handles the gamut of labor and employment matters from wrongful discharge and employment discrimination to employee benefits and workers' compensation. The team has a substantial experience in union work and NLRB matters.

The Lawyers: Jonathan Norman heads the Columbus-based group of *"quality attorneys."*

The Clients: Clients include retailers, transportation service companies, healthcare organizations and financial institutions. Clients include: Worthington Industries; AirNet Systems; ABX Air; LiquiBox and Scotts Company.

Other Notable Practitioners

Clients admire *"ERISA expert"* **Lisa Wintersheimer Michel** of Keating, Muething & Klekamp PLL in Cincinnati for her practical approach to issues including executive compensation, plan administration, employee benefits and compensation programs. **Steven Moss** of the Cleveland firm Kahn Kleinman is an *"intelligent and dedicated"* attorney representing employers in all areas of the field, including sexual harassment, wage and hour, wrongful discharge and collective bargaining agreements.

ENVIRONMENT

Ohio
Leading firms (Environment)

1 PORTER WRIGHT MORRIS & ARTHUR *Columbus*
SQUIRE, SANDERS & DEMPSEY LLP *Cleveland*
THOMPSON HINE LLP *Cleveland*
VORYS, SATER, SEYMOUR & PEASE *Columbus*

2 FROST BROWN TODD LLC *Cincinnati*
JONES DAY *Cleveland*
MCMAHON, DEGULIS, HOFFMANN *Cleveland*
SHUMAKER LOOP & KENDRICK LLP *Toledo*

3 BAKER & HOSTETLER LLP *Columbus*
BRICKER & ECKLER LLP *Columbus*
EASTMAN & SMITH LTD *Toledo*
ROETZEL & ANDRESS PA *Akron*
SCHOTTENSTEIN, ZOX & DUNN *Columbus*
TAFT, STETTINIUS & HOLLISTER LLP *Cincinnati*

Firms are listed alphabetically in each band.

Band 1

Porter Wright Morris & Arthur LLP
See firm details p.1455

The Firm: This *"extremely professional"* environmental practice has leanings toward public utility regulation, and according to the market, the team is *"the first choice of many great clients."* As well as utilities and trade associations, the client base is replete with chemical, telecom and manufacturing companies. There is inevitably a healthy chunk of Superfund work and the team is renowned for its expertise in air pollution matters. The *"consistently excellent"* attorneys remain prominent in new source review litigation for FirstEnergy, Synergy and AEP. They have also assiduously defended the latter against claims filed by various citizens groups.

The Lawyers: Jeffrey McNealey (see p.1445) is *"one of the originals,"* something of a patriarch in this field. Long experience at the highest levels of law making and lobbying has resulted in choice government connections. While still advising clients at the strategic level, these days he devotes more of his time to real estate matters. Decades of experience have made *"first-rate"* **Robert Brubaker** (see p.1438) *"a leading authority"* on air pollution matters. He *"does a terrific job"* for his clients, notably utilities, on permitting, administrative rulemaking, litiga-

tion and appeals. Formerly of the attorney general's office, **Christopher Schraff** (see p.1448) is *"an exemplary all-rounder"* who is particularly good for water. His clients regard him as *"a superb trial lawyer,"* *"independent and effective."* *"Incredibly detailed"* **Martin Seltzer** (see p.1448) has a significant practice acting for institutional clients and a fine reputation in hazardous waste law; his *"valuable scientific knowledge"* complements a good legal toolbox. Touted as *"Brubaker's protégé,"* **Katerina Eftimoff** (see p.1440) is another *"good and reliable"* attorney; she has acknowledged expertise in CAA permitting, especially Title V matters.

The Clients: The firm acts for well-known companies and has a strong public utility practice. Clients include American Electric Power, FirstEnergy and Synergy.

Squire, Sanders & Dempsey LLP

The Firm: This firm's Cleveland office is home to one of the most respected environment teams in the state. *"Present at the creation,"* it has grown, adapted and carved out a credible national, even international, reputation. Clients

Ohio
Leading individuals (Environment)

Senior Statesman

MCNEALEY J Jeffrey *Porter Wright*, Columbus

[1] BRUBAKER Robert *Porter Wright*, Columbus

CARSON Van *Squire Sanders*, Cleveland

CASPER Paul *Frost Brown*, Cincinnati

HARDY Michael *Thompson Hine*, Cleveland

SCHRAFF Christopher *Porter Wright*, Columbus

TOSI Louis *Shumaker Loop*, Toledo

[2] BARNES Geoffrey *Squire Sanders*, Cleveland

DORAN Scott *Vorys Sater*, Columbus

FAHEY Richard *Vorys Sater*, Columbus

GUNSETT Daniel *Baker & Hostetler*, Columbus

HAYES William *Vorys Sater*, Cincinnati

HAYNAM Douglas *Shumaker Loop*, Toledo

JANKE Ronald *Jones Day*, Cleveland

MCMAHON Michael *McMahon DeGulis*, Cleveland

NASH David *Thompson Hine*, Cleveland

SELTZER Martin *Porter Wright*, Columbus

[3] BLATTNER J Wray *Thompson Hine*, Dayton

BURKE Kim *Taft Stettinius*, Cincinnati

CASCARILLA Ralph *Walter & Haverfield*, Cleveland

CYPHERT Michael *Walter & Haverfield*, Cleveland

FAROLINO Shane *Roetzel & Andress*, Akron

FAY Terrence *Frost Brown*, Columbus

HAUGHEY Stephen *Frost Brown*, Cincinnati

KOLESAR Andrew *Thompson Hine*, Cincinnati

MCMURRAY Kevin *Frost Brown*, Cincinnati

NORMAN Mark *Vorys Sater*, Cincinnati

PATBERG William *Shumaker Loop*, Toledo

PFEFFERLE Ben *Baker & Hostetler*, Columbus

REIDY Joseph *Schottenstein Zox*, Columbus

SAMUELS Stephen *Schottenstein Zox*, Columbus

SARGEANT Richard *Eastman & Smith*, Toledo

STAMP Vincent *Dinsmore & Shohl*, Cincinnati

TERP Thomas *Taft Stettinius*, Cincinnati

VAN KLEY Jack *Jones Day*, Columbus

WINTERS Karen *Squire Sanders*, Columbus

Up-and-coming individuals

EFTIMOFF Katerina *Porter Wright*, Columbus

LAVEY Wendlene *Squire Sanders*, Cleveland

MCMAHON Louis *Thompson Hine*, Cleveland

STURTZ Craig *Squire Sanders*, Columbus

Individuals are listed alphabetically in each band.

rate the "*diverse and strong*" lawyers for their Superfund, regulatory and litigation expertise, and "*gladly give them the most difficult and significant matters.*" The group acted for Cooper in a groundbreaking CERCLA case before the Supreme Court, Aviall v Cooper. The team also secured an advantageous settlement for Mead-Westvaco as a PRP at the Tennessee Products Superfund site. The firm's varied diet emphasizes three main areas: metals, paper and public sector clients. Acting for foundries, manufacturers and so on in the increasingly consolidated metals industry, it is noted for its representation of ISG and US Steel. Clients in the printing sector ensure the firm is in demand throughout the

USA for its expertise in contaminated sediments. Perhaps the team's strongest voice is in the public sector, where it acts for clients like the Association of Metropolitan Sewerage Agencies. It also represents publicly owned utilities, especially coal-fired plants.

The Lawyers: Clients praise the "*innovative and solutions-driven*" lawyers for their thorough analysis. The "*prime mover*" in the group is "*darned good*" **Van Carson**, whose loyal clients speak of his "*extraordinary experience, knowledge and contacts.*" He is "*tops for water,*" leading competitors to complain: "*We can't poach their clients as long as they have Van.*" "*Polished and frighteningly intelligent*" **Geoffrey Barnes** is "*just the guy for complex matters.*" Marrying his "*huge IQ*" to a no-nonsense practicality, he provides transactional and litigation advice to an impressive client roster. Clients choose "*terrific*" **Karen Winters** for her experience of public entities. She leads the Columbus team. **Wendlene Lavey**'s clients praise her "*tremendously good judgment and keen grasp of facts,*" declaring her "*just terrific in litigation.*" She acts for private sector steel and petroleum refining clients in site investigations and remediation. "*Sharp and knowledgeable*" **Craig Sturtz** "*is on the up*" thanks to his profile on committees and at the state bar association. He counsels corporate clients, developers, and municipalities on a broad swath of environmental issues.

The Clients: Association of Metropolitan Sewerage Agencies; Cooper Industries; Electrolux Home Products; International Steel Group; MeadWestvaco; Northeast Ohio Regional Sewer District; Republic Engineered Products; US Steel and WCI Steel.

Thompson Hine LLP

See firm details p.1457

The Firm: Despite the departure of significant figures, among them Michael Cyphert, the market endorses this "*active and excellent*" team for its broad work-base and raft of genuine specialists who "*can handle everything.*" The "*large and deep*" practice grew up servicing Ohio's heavy manufacturing community, which still forms the backbone of the clientele. For these companies lawyers handle litigation and Superfund work nationally, though Ohio and the surrounding region remain the heartland. The team acted for a Japanese client and its American subsidiaries to mediate state law nuisance and trespass claims brought by the Port of Houston. For another client and its joint venture partner, the team acted in the acquisition of an alumina facility in Gramercy, LA, and a bauxite facility in Jamaica.

The Lawyers: Universally recognized as one of Ohio's finest litigators, "*hard-working, steady and incredibly organized*" **Michael Hardy** (see p.1441) is an attorney of "*great stature.*" As well as managing the Cleveland office, he finds the

time to invest himself fully in his practice. **David Nash** (see p.1445) is best known for transactional work on brownfield sites and is making a name in sustainability issues; he is "*a go-to guy for green buildings.*" Commentators agree that "*bright and aggressive*" ex-Skadden Arps lawyer **Andrew Kolesar** (see p.1443) "*stands up well*" for his clients. He heads the group, and focuses his own practice on cleanups, permitting and litigation, including criminal defense. Some commentators say **Wray Blattner**'s (see p.1438) light is somewhat hidden under a bushel, perhaps as a result of his location in Dayton, away from the main practice. Blattner is an "*admirable*" attorney whose broad practice includes the defense of enforcement actions, permitting and environment management systems. **Louis McMahon** (see p.1444) produces "*outstanding water rights work.*" In this respect he is seen as "*something of a secret weapon*" for the firm."

The Clients: FirstEnergy; Goodrich; Mead-Westvaco and Whirlpool.

Vorys, Sater, Seymour & Pease LLP

See firm details p.1458

The Firm: This "*accomplished, substantial and credible*" practice, one of Columbus's biggest, is recognized for its deep bench and "*real diversity.*" The team is "*reliable and solid*" from top to bottom and "*acquits itself well at all times.*" Commentators were particularly keen to praise the transactional work of the "*consistently excellent*" group and the "*fabulous litigation*" capability backing it up.

The Lawyers: Among the "*heavyweight, senior players*" is "*extremely capable technician*" **Scott Doran** (see p.1439), who is "*an obvious choice*" for development and wetlands matters as well as litigation. An extensive understanding of the regulatory environment makes him "*one of the most knowledgeable lawyers in the business;*" commentators add that he is "*well connected and fun to work with.*" "*Genuine and effective*" **Richard Fahey** (see p.1440) is identified as a "*tenacious litigator;*" his "*calm demeanor*" and encyclopedic knowledge fill his clients with confidence. **William Hayes** (see p.1442) is billed as a "*star air lawyer,*" while **Mark Norman** (see p.1446) is often encountered on brownfield development projects and "*always impresses.*"

The Clients: The team is "*in deep*" with an array of impressive corporate and industrial clients, such as Honda of America.

Band 2

Frost Brown Todd LLC

See firm details p.849

The Firm: Rooted in the southwest of the state, Frost Brown Todd is "*a fine firm doing well*" across the region. It thrives in each of the transactional and litigation arenas, with lawyers experienced at both criminal and civil trials. The client base includes steel, chemicals, paper, foundry and plating companies, as well as two of the largest waste management companies in the country and a number of municipal authorities and hospitals. Clients have "*confidence in the lawyers' depth, ability and integrity*" and are happy to use them on sophisticated matters around the country. New clients seem almost surprised to discover that "*they deliver outstanding service and are good value for money.*" The team is rich in scientific and engineering expertise as it is packed with nonlegal specialist consultants.

The Lawyers: The heart of the team is "*committed and diligent*" **Paul Casper** (see p.1438), whose clients are drawn to his "*razor-sharp, creative and analytical mind.*" For a notable client, he managed to force the US EPA to rescind an imminent and substantial endangerment RCRA order for the first time in its history. Commentators respect him as a litigator; he has long represented numerous Fortune 500 companies such as AK Steel in defense against high-profile agency enforcement actions. It is no surprise that his clients call him "*an outstanding, aggressive and loyal advocate*" and declare their "*complete faith*" in him. **Terrence Fay** (see p.1440), too, is "*a persistent, worthy and tough adversary*" whose opponents "*would rather not have to go up against him.*" "*Willing and able*" **Kevin McMurray** (see p.1445) is "*a very fine generalist with a chemical engineering background.*" He has built a reputation as a transactional lawyer of "*outstanding quality,*" and his clients value his "*wonderful understanding*" of their businesses. Lastly, **Stephen Haughey** (see p.1441) is highly admired as "*a first-rate water and Superfund lawyer.*"

The Clients: AK Steel; Bay West Paper; Cincinnati Bell; Givaudan; LG&E Energy; Milacron; Ryland Homes; Smurfit-Stone Container; Titanium Metals and Waste Management.

Jones Day

See firm details p.485

The Firm: A firm delivering comprehensive services to clients throughout the USA and the world offers an environment team that is "*sleek and effective.*" Specialist attorneys are spread across the USA, defending the usual Jones Day industrial heavyweight clients in enforcement actions and promoting their interests through lobbying. The team handles a large volume of transactional work and is strong in litigation.

The Lawyers: **Ron Janke** (see p.1443) is "*the man to have by your side on a major transaction.*" His clients benefit from his "*fantastic regulatory*" experience, among them Brush Wellman, for whom he and other Jones Day attorneys are worldwide environmental, health and safety counsel, administering all regulatory advice for the manufacture and use of beryllium. He was also the primary Ohio legal adviser for Transpro

on the environmental aspects of its merger with Modine Manufacturing. "*Strong but adaptable*" **Jack Van Kley** (see p.1449) has a diverse practice that includes due diligence and transactional advice in property transfers and water rights litigation. He is the team's point man in Columbus and, having spotted an opening in the market early on, he has developed a niche advising large farms coming under increasing scrutiny and regulation by the authorities. Van Kley is the Ohio's member of the team advising Cargill on environmental issues, including compliance and permitting issues under air and water pollution laws. He recently met with success in the Cuyahoga River litigation, a suit filed against the City of Akron at the Court of Appeals in order to enforce clients' rights to use contested streams and aquifers and to force Akron to release a constant flow from its new dam.

The Clients: Brush Wellman; Cargill; Cooper Tire & Rubber; Diebold; Eramet Marietta; Gould Electronics; Ohio Farm Bureau Federation; Riverside Company; Timken; Transpro; WL Ross and Yellow Roadway.

McMahon, DeGulis, Hoffmann & Lombardi LLP

The Firm: This is perhaps the most respected environmental boutique in the state. Its client list is filled with household-name multinational companies for which the group will undertake just about any sort of environmental matter involving the EPA or courts. The "*simply excellent*" team has recently added a vigorous asbestos practice with a track record for trying cases rather than settling. This approach has been so successful that the team has been selected by John Crane to act in more than 40,000 claims. The firm's expertise in underground storage tanks is unrivaled.

The Lawyers: **Michael McMahon** (see p.1444) delivers a "*great-quality and reasonably priced*" service to his clients, and it is said "*You'd have to get up very early in the morning to catch him out.*" Having started his own firm, he immediately attracted a broad industrial clientele; the competition is still trying to work out how he did it so that they can emulate his success. His team acted for First Interstate Properties to obtain environmental insurance and perform due diligence for the $60 million development of a former steel mill.

The Clients: BP; Norfolk Southern; Sears; John Crane; KraftMaid Cabinetry; Sherwin Williams; YSI and First Interstate Properties.

Shumaker Loop & Kendrick LLP

The Firm: Easily "*the strongest practice in Toledo,*" this group boasts a number of sophisticated, premium clients for which it acts with "*great style.*" Commentators attribute a "*fun*" and "*interesting personality*" to a team that is "*professional in the true sense.*"

The Lawyers: The versatile squad is "*deep and well rounded*" and has a "*strong core of experienced attorneys*" with particular expertise in Superfund and brownfield work. "*Superb, fair and hard-nosed*" **Louis Tosi** is "*a character and a joy to be with,*" according to peers and clients. An "*artful, articulate and philosophical attorney,*" he is regarded as "*an original dean*" of the field and a virtuoso litigator. Litigator **Douglas Haynam** enjoys a sterling reputation for Superfund work and "*really understands the dynamics of negotiations.*" "*Supremely knowledgeable in CWA,*" **William Patberg** is particularly recommended for his wastewater expertise.

The Clients: The impressive client base is studded with electrical utilities and Fortune 500 companies such as GM.

Band 3

Baker & Hostetler LLP

The Firm: Clients say this "*credible and significant*" team has "*outstanding technical capabilities*" and a fine track record in hazardous waste and Superfund. It has played a prominent role in several high-profile remediation cases, negotiating on behalf of client businesses with the EPA and local communities. In keeping with the firm's transactional focus, lawyers handle plenty of due diligence in major deals, often brownfield redevelopment-driven. The team acted for a client on an Ohio Superfund site adjacent to a municipal drinking water supply, achieving recognized completion of remediation 15 years ahead of schedule. Clients particularly applaud the team's "*incredible responsiveness,*" with one saying it is "*not only good value, but value-added.*" A partner was recently seconded to a Fortune 100 client to handle environmental work and has proved effective in handling several US, European and South American issues.

The Lawyers: **Dan Gunsett**'s clients see him as "*without peer in the industry*" and pay tribute to his willingness to "*leap into action, even if on vacation.*" His practice covers both litigation and transactional advice, although he is best known for the latter. **Ben Pfefferle**'s arrival from Thompson Hine is a coup for the team. Clients are impressed by his "*thoroughness and understanding,*" declaring that "*one quick call to him is worth everything – he sorts it out.*"

The Clients: The team acts for a stable of Fortune 150 clients, including energy companies (both petroleum and utility), manufacturers and real estate developers.

Bricker & Eckler LLP

The Firm: This firm's client base consists mostly of industrial and manufacturing companies as well as waste disposal businesses. Lawyers also act for municipalities and government agencies. Its familiarity with federal and Ohio regulatory and enforcement agencies stands clients in good stead in a range of administrative and judicial cases.

The Lawyers: The two best-known characters here are group chair Chuck Waterman and litigator Randy Wiseman.

The Clients: Clients include industrial and waste disposal companies as well as municipal and governmental agencies.

Eastman & Smith Ltd

The Firm: The group here in Toledo has a distinguished history in environmental law and a healthy local practice. It is best known for its representation of municipal entities and landfills. Commentators praise the team's solid waste management strength.

The Lawyers: Group head **Richard Sargeant** is "*a real feature of the landscape*" and is commended for his experience in enforcement defense.

The Clients: Clients include county solid waste management districts, municipalities, Fortune 500 companies and two major RCRA hazardous waste treatment, storage and disposal facilities.

Roetzel & Andress PA

The Firm: Lawyers have experience of diverse work and clients, offering services in litigation, enforcement defense and compliance counseling. One also has a special interest in Sarbanes-Oxley issues. The Akron-centered team is characterized by strong agency experience and connections, and boasts "*real credibility*" with both court and administrative authorities. Clients – mostly small to midsized industrial companies – affirm that the lawyers "*really understand us.*" The practice has recently expanded in brownfield and mixed-use development and redevelopment work, especially

town center projects, almost always for the developer.

The Lawyers: Clients are staunch in their praise for "*truly excellent*" **Shane Farolino**. He leads the team that recently represented a Cleveland-based developer in its application for stream and wetland fill permits connected with the construction of a large shopping center in Central Ohio.

The Clients: Marathon Ashland Petroleum; City of Akron; Lowe's; PPG Industries; Eaton; Pentair; GenCorp; FirstEnergy; TravelCenters of America; Zaremba Group and Duke Realty.

Schottenstein, Zox & Dunn

See firm details p.1456

The Firm: The team guides its small to midsized clients through the labyrinths of environmental law, often acting for entities encountering it for the first time. Lawyers are a mix of erstwhile regulators and experienced litigators, offering compliance advice and enforcement defense.

The Lawyers: Group chair **Stephen Samuels** (see p.1448) is "*an awesomely skilled litigator,*" according to the market. His practice is a varied one: "*You name it, he can do it,*" researchers were told. Bringing "*a tremendous amount of knowledge to the table,*" **Joseph Reidy** (see p.1447) is recommended for his experience in brownfield redevelopment projects.

The Clients: Clients are a quality mix of small to large businesses from across the state.

Taft, Stettinius & Hollister LLP

The Firm: A good-sized and "*responsive*" environment team is spread over four Ohio offices. The firm has an impressive industrial client base, for which lawyers act in all aspects of environment law around the country. The team

defended Brenntag and defeated class certification in a toxic tort case in the US District Court in Billings, Montana. In another matter in the Sixth Circuit Court of Appeals, the team secured a decision reversing adverse trial court rulings in a CAA case.

The Lawyers: The team's "*best-kept secret,*" according to respondents, is **Kim Burke**. His involvement on a matter is guaranteed to seize his opponents' attention. "*Cost-effective and clever*" **Thomas Terp** is another admired litigator who spent much of the past year on a Superfund case in Montana. His clients like his "*persuasive and innovative*" style.

The Clients: Though focused on the Midwest, the firm acts for diverse businesses and wealthy individuals from across the USA and beyond. These include: Cintas; Brenntag North America; Morton International and EaglePicher.

Other Notable Practitioners

"*Highly capable and always ethical*" litigator **Michael Cyphert**'s move to join **Ralph Cascarilla** gives Walter & Haverfield LLP increased capability as a local player in Cleveland. A "*leading lion of the Bar,*" Cyphert handles a considerable volume of corporate and real estate-related work as well as criminal defense. Meanwhile, eminent litigator Cascarilla is "*involved in just about every Superfund matter in the state.*" He has recognized skill in criminal defense and is seen as "*the guy to go to in a nasty matter...where the chips are on the table.*" Dinsmore & Shohl LLP's **Vincent Stamp** is an acknowledged Superfund lawyer with a strong reputation in the Cincinnati market. Peers declare him to be a very capable litigator with "*great negotiation abilities.*"

INTELLECTUAL PROPERTY

<table>
<tr><td colspan="2">Ohio
Leading firms (Intellectual Property)</td></tr>
<tr><td>1</td><td>JONES DAY Cleveland
WOOD, HERRON & EVANS LLP Cincinnati</td></tr>
<tr><td>2</td><td>CALFEE, HALTER & GRISWOLD LLP Cleveland
DINSMORE & SHOHL LLP Dayton
FAY SHARPE FAGAN MINNICH & MCKEE Cleveland
FROST BROWN TODD LLC Cincinnati</td></tr>
<tr><td>3</td><td>GREENEBAUM DOLL & MCDONALD Cincinnati
HASSE & NESBITT Mason
TAROLLI, SUNDHEIM, COVELL Cleveland
THOMPSON HINE LLP Cleveland</td></tr>
<tr><td colspan="2">Firms are listed alphabetically in each band.</td></tr>
</table>

Band 1

Jones Day

See firm details p.485

The Firm: With the assimilation of the Pennie & Edmonds boutique into its IP division, Jones Day has boosted its ranks to a whopping 275 IP practitioners worldwide. In Ohio, the heart of this firm's practice lies in the contentious arena, with over half of the 42 Cleveland specialists dedicated to contentious matters. Seen by many as one of the heaviest hitting patent litigation practices in the country, this national firm caters for a slew of similarly substantial companies. From hi-tech computer outfits to medical device manufacturers of both domestic and international provenance, household-name clients hold the firm in extremely high esteem, praising it for the "*exemplary*" service it provides.

The Lawyers: "*Number one*" in his field is the "*very persuasive*" **Ken Adamo** (see p.1437), renowned for his august presence in the courtroom. An appreciative client reports: "*He's right on top of the facts and incredibly eloquent on all points of patent law.*" With more than 25 years' experience under his belt, the trademark specialist of the team, **Joe Dreitler** (see p.1439), enjoys a reputation for excellence. Dreitler has recently brought a trademark infringement case to court on behalf of GM concerning the Hummer H2. He has also acted for Coors Brewing Co in a trademark and unfair competition lawsuit brought by the National Collegiate Athletic Association, as well as handling all domain name issues for Dell. With a background in electrical engineering and bags of expertise in infringement and trade secrets litigation, highly respected **James Wamsley** (see p.1449) is the

www.ChambersandPartners.com

All quotes in the text are from interviews with clients and competitors.

1427

Ohio
Leading individuals
(Intellectual Property)

Senior Statesman
KILLWORTH Richard *Dinsmore & Shohl*, Dayton

1 ADAMO Ken *Jones Day*, Cleveland
GERMAIN Kenneth *Thompson Hine*, Cincinnati
GOLDSTEIN Steven *Frost Brown*, Cincinnati
LYON Charles *Calfee Halter*, Cleveland
SCHMIT David *Frost Brown*, Cincinnati

2 ALBAINY-JENEI Stephen *Frost Brown*, Cincinnati
BRINKMAN David *Wood Herron*, Cincinnati
DREITLER Joseph *Jones Day*, Columbus
EBLING Louis *Greenebaum Doll*, Cincinnati
FAGAN Christopher *Fay Sharpe*, Cleveland
SCHNAPP Karlyn *Frost Brown*, Columbus
TAROLLI Thomas *Tarolli Sundheim*, Cleveland

3 BAUMGARTNER Bruce *Baker & Hostetler*, Cleveland
FREI Donald *Wood Herron*, Cincinnati
HICKEY Nicole *Frost Brown*, Cincinnati
HOGAN Patricia *Keating Muething*, Cincinnati
LEVY Mark *Thompson Hine*, Dayton
LUNN Gregory *Wood Herron*, Cincinnati
LYMAN Beverly *Wood Herron*, Cincinnati
ROESCH Lynda *Dinsmore & Shohl*, Cincinnati
SZABO Paul *Calfee Halter*, Cleveland
WAMSLEY James *Jones Day*, Cleveland

Individuals are listed alphabetically in each band.

"*bulldog*" of the firm – "*he'll wear the opposition down; he's dogged.*"
The Clients: Procter & Gamble; Kodak; Nestlé; Tennessee Eastman; MOSAID; RAM and GE.

Wood, Herron & Evans, LLP

The Firm: Acknowledged by peers to be the "*leading*" niche firm in Cincinnati, Wood Herron & Evans has an exemplary team providing a loyal clientele with expertise in the full spectrum of IP law. Although a number of the top names in the firm are quite senior, peers note an emergent generation of dynamic young trial lawyers. Combined, both generations satisfy a truly impressive client base, which has enabled this boutique to establish itself as one of the top players in the state for national work. Home to a stable of engineering experts, this is a go-to firm for any number of complex matters faced by industrials.
The Lawyers: Venerable practitioner **David Brinkman** is in consistently high demand from clients seeking out his expertise in the areas of electronic, mechanical and electrical technologies. **Donald Frei** takes care of much of the firm's international patent and trademark work. With a "*common-sense,*" results-oriented approach, Frei is replete with interpersonal skills and easily builds a good rapport with clients. "*Well versed*" in the language of mechanics, **Gregory Lunn** has a broad base of technology know-how and "*great capacity for understanding.*" Clients concur that he is "*a truly great per-*

son to take on your business.*" **Beverly Lyman** is relatively new to the firm. This "*razor-sharp*" attorney's recognized skill in the biotechnology field wins her plaudits from peers and clients alike.
The Clients: IBM; Sony; Procter & Gamble; Cincinnati Children's Research Foundation; Tyco Healthcare/Mallinckrodt and Givaudan Schweiz.

Band 2

Calfee, Halter & Griswold LLP
See firm details p.1451
The Firm: An expanding team of IP lawyers has lately taken on a slew of high-profile cases for a client base comprising a good portion of the region's pharmaceutical companies. As a result, the firm is definitely developing a reputation for high-quality counseling and litigation in the patent field. Numbering over 20 specialists, the patent litigation team packs a hefty punch on complex matters. The IP practice is further split into bioscience and technology transfer teams. The bioscience team specializes in developing patentable inventions and discoveries for entrepreneurial private clients and private and state research universities.
The Lawyers: Known for his prowess in the courtroom, **Chuck Lyon** (see p.1444) is seen as the driving force behind this regional IP practice; market commentators agree that he has built a "*first-class patent department from scratch.*" **Paul Szabo** (see p.1449) prepares and prosecutes patent applications in diverse specialized electromechanical technologies, including occupant safety devices, medical devices, power transmissions and vehicle steering and suspension components. Peers rate his expertise highly, commenting that they would "*feel more than comfortable sending clients over to him.*"
The Clients: The firm caters for a broad stable of domestic and international clients of all sizes, including research institutions and entrepreneurial startups.

Dinsmore & Shohl LLP
See firm details p.1452
The Firm: "*A cut above the rest,*" Dinsmore & Shohl is home to a full-service IP team, whose attorneys come from a range of technical backgrounds. While it has been noted that in its current incarnation the regional practice may not have the deep bench of former times, market commentators agree that this has not affected the firm's "*really excellent*" trademark work, which is an important aspect of the group's continually expanding worldwide practice. Substantial clients seek counsel in all areas of IP law and the group is adept at working with other departments in the firm. Clients agree that this makes for a "*cost-effective and results-oriented*" service.

The Lawyers: **Lynda Roesch** has served on the board of directors of the International Trademark Association and is held in exceptionally high regard by peers locally. The past year has seen her involved for the defendant in the Nationwide v Sovereign Bank case. She has also represented the company formerly known as Chiquita in a trademark dispute. "*Smart*" **Richard Killworth** deals with complex matters related to the energy and chemical industries; he is esteemed for the quality of his opinion work. Peers regard him as "*one of the top guys in licensing*" and one of the deans of Ohio IP. Said one source: "*If I need an opinion that is both sound and well supported I go to Richard.*"
The Clients: Sovereign Bank; Procter & Gamble; Standard Register; Battelle Memorial Institute and Dow Corning Foundation.

Fay Sharpe Fagan Minnich & McKee LLP
See firm details p.1454
The Firm: This well-established player holds its own as a boutique operation offering counseling and litigation services in every aspect of IP law from copyright to trademarks and patents. A steady influx of new clients and lawyers is indicative of the current health of the practice. Renowned in the Cleveland market, the firm is deemed "*cost-effective*" and is patronized by a clientele that includes prominent national and international businesses as well as research institutes.
The Lawyers: Market commentators regard the "*immensely experienced*" **Christopher Fagan** (see p.1440) as the lead trial attorney at the firm. He provides counsel on all aspects of intellectual property including patent, trademark and copyright law. Described by clients as "*truly brilliant,*" Fagan has worked on a number of major matters in the past year, among them a case for Canadian Meter in dispute with Bennett Regulator Guards.
The Clients: Canadian Meter, Xerox and Spalding & Evenflo are among the firm's clients.

Frost Brown Todd LLC
See firm details p.849
The Firm: This firm is said to boast one of the top IP practices in the region; in the biopharm arena there are no other major players with such a large market share, and in terms of dedicated specialists the firm has about 32 practitioners in Ohio alone. Known for their "*exceptional*" attention to detail and impeccable biomedical knowledge, attorneys have made a name for their diligence and efficiency. Said one client: "*They can handle our discoveries and turn them into something really profitable.*" Successfully maintaining a balance between quality and value, the top trial lawyers are supported by an "*exceptional*" team that is "*very helpful and business-oriented.*" Market commentators also enthuse about the "*extremely good working environment,*"

1428   All quotes in the text are from interviews with clients and competitors.

CHAMBERS USA 2005

which facilitates the fostering of close client relationships. The firm is presently injecting further resources into another related growth area – advertising law. In this regard, a team of attorneys has been established to look after a growing number of consumer product clients.

The Lawyers: Formerly lead in-house patent attorney for Procter & Gamble, the "*impeccable*" **Steven Goldstein** (see p.1441) is chair of the IP department. "*Genius*" **David Schmit** (see p.1448) is held in high esteem by peers for his intellectual prowess and forceful manner. They told researchers: "*He is an extraordinarily aggressive advocate with a no-earth-unscorched, no-stone-unturned sort of attitude – he does a great job.*" **Stephen Albainy-Jenei** (see p.1437) represents a variety of institutions and biotech establishments; he is simply described as "*quite excellent.*" The past year has seen him working closely on patent applications linked to the development of chimeric therapies for Regenerex, and on various projects for a largely Midwestern clientele. The "*simply superb*" **Karlyn Schnapp** (see p.1448) undertakes patent prosecutions and is highly recommended by a large number of peers and clients. Up-and-comer **Nicole Vickroy Hickey** (see p.1442) is based in Cincinnati and has a broad IP practice; she is thought by clients to be "*exquisitely*" good at her job.

The Clients: The practice serves LexisNexis; National Association of Professional Baseball Leagues; Convergys; Regenerex. Clients also include leading universities, research hospitals and research institutes, as well as pharmaceutical companies ranging from the very largest corporations to small startups.

Band 3

Greenebaum Doll & McDonald PLLC
See firm details p.850

The Firm: With a clientele including many institutions and corporations with significant interests abroad, some peers argue that such a clear emphasis on international work leaves the firm struggling to find a niche in the local market. However, it seems apparent that the firm has indeed made inroads into the local Ohio market and is growing its IP team in the state. One of the firm's biggest clients is Hillenbrand Industries.

The Lawyers: A fresh and dynamic lawyer with over 400 US filings to his name in the past 30 months, **Louis Ebling** (see p.1439) is believed to be one of the most active domestic patent prosecutors in the Midwest. He also undertakes a significant amount of trademark matters.

The Clients: Representative clients include Tetris, Hillenbrand Industries and Batesville Casket.

Hasse & Nesbitt

The Firm: This "*unique*" group is lauded for its experience in the preparation and prosecution of patents. With a useful amount of biological expertise under its belt, the team impresses clients with its consistently high standard of work. Specialties include utility and design patents, trademarks, copyrights, computer and Internet law, trade secrets and unfair competition. The team is also capable of dealing with other legal issues faced by startup companies and technology ventures. Its patent attorneys have degree-level technical qualifications in everything from chemical engineering to metallurgy and biochemistry. Lawyers can justifiably claim to have "*extensive*" international experience.

The Lawyers: Donald Hasse has a background in metallurgical engineering and material sciences and was formerly general counsel to Procter & Gamble. He and Daniel Nesbitt are the founding partners of the firm.

The Clients: The team serves a diverse client base comprised of national and international companies.

Tarolli, Sundheim, Covell, & Tummino LLP

The Firm: This Cleveland-based firm receives particular attention for its work on patent infringement and patent validity in the USA. For a comparatively small team – 16 professionals – it has an impressive roster of clients with both national and international pedigrees.

The Lawyers: An extremely experienced patent practitioner, founding partner **Thomas Tarolli** is well respected for his patents and trademarks practice. Tarolli has been involved in a number of litigious matters over the past year and has provided appreciative clients with opinion work of "*exceptional*" quality.

The Clients: Hewlett-Packard; Lockheed Martin; TRW Automotive; Northrop Grumman and the Cleveland Clinic.

Thompson Hine LLP
See firm details p.1457

The Firm: The Ohio IP practice at this, one of the best-known corporate law firms in America, is split between offices in Cincinnati, Dayton and Cleveland. It is a compact unit of business-oriented specialists who work closely together to provide a "*top-notch*" service for a well-established and diverse business clientele. The team attracts a number of clients independent of the firm's traditional corporate stable, and with recent lateral hires into the Dayton office it is set to attract more interest in the future. Areas of particular expertise include aerospace and automotive engineering, electronics, metallurgy and pharmaceuticals.

The Lawyers: **Kenneth Germain** (see p.1440) is considered by peers to be a "*number-one player*" in the trademark field. Now well established at the Cincinnati office, he continues to grow his reputation as he deals with more complex cases for a diverse clientele. Germain is often retained as an expert witness on issues relating to trademarks and unfair competition. Recently he was a consultant to the winning counsel in the landmark US Supreme Court trademark dilution case, Moseley v. V Secret Catalogue. Manifest on the prosecution side is group leader **Mark Levy** (see p.1444) who is admired by market commentators for his diverse and high-profile client base. Based in the firm's Dayton office, Levy is universally celebrated for the "*exceptional quality*" of his work.

The Clients: KeyCorp; Delphi Technologies; Procter & Gamble; Lexmark; Dayco; Goodrich and Eaton.

Other Notable Practitioners

Bruce Baumgartner of Baker & Hostetler LLP in Cincinnati is known primarily for his distinguished work in media law. He is well regarded throughout the state as an impressive intellectual force with powerful business acumen to boot. His practice places an emphasis on copyright, trademark, patent and unfair competition litigation. Responsible for a stable of notable corporate clients from across the country, Baumgartner also deals with the needs of overseas clients, especially those with interests in the Asian markets. The "*superb*" and "*brilliantly erudite*" **Patty Hogan** of Keating, Muething & Klekamp PLL is lauded by peers for her "*excellent*" work in trademarks and patent prosecution.

LITIGATION

GENERAL COMMERCIAL

Ohio
Leading firms
(Litigation: General Commercial)

1	**JONES DAY** Cleveland
2	**SQUIRE, SANDERS & DEMPSEY LLP** Cleveland
	VORYS, SATER, SEYMOUR AND PEASE Cleveland
3	**BAKER & HOSTETLER LLP** Cleveland
	PORTER WRIGHT MORRIS & ARTHUR Columbus
	THOMPSON HINE LLP Cleveland
4	**CALFEE, HALTER & GRISWOLD LLP** Cleveland
	CARPENTER & LIPPS LLP Columbus
	CHESTER, WILLCOX & SAXBE LLP Columbus
	FARUKI IRELAND & COX PLL Dayton
	KATZ, TELLER, BRANT & HILD Cincinnati
	KEATING, MUETHING & KLEKAMP, PLL Cincinnati
	KEGLER, BROWN, HILL & RITTER Columbus
	MCLAUGHLIN & MCCAFFREY, LLP Cleveland
	SCHOTTENSTEIN, ZOX & DUNN Columbus
	TAFT, STETTINIUS & HOLLISTER LLP Cincinnati
	TUCKER ELLIS & WEST LLP Cleveland
	ULMER & BERNE LLP Cleveland
	ZEIGER, TIGGES, LITTLE & LINDSMITH Columbus

Firms are listed alphabetically in each band.

Band 1

Jones Day

See firm details p.485

The Firm: The "*excellent litigation group*" at this full-service international giant enjoys successful relationships with some of the biggest corporate clients around. Indeed, Jones Day's "*very talented lawyers*" provide legal representation to more than half the Fortune 500 companies. The group deals with all aspects of commercial litigation, though there are hot spots in securities and corporate governance. It is at present involved in the Enron shareholder and bankruptcy adversary proceedings on behalf of Royal Bank of Scotland.

The Lawyers: John Newman (see p.1446) is the Cleveland office's litigation group coordinator. He was described by one of his peers as a "*fine lawyer, very difficult to beat.*" Clearly a worthy adversary, he has "*solid experience*" in general business matters, with a focus on shareholder actions and fiduciary and corporate governance claims. **John Strauch** (see p.1449) is involved in high-profile nationwide cases such as smoking and health litigation, on which he has been national coordinator for RJ Reynolds Tobacco. He also acted for a client against Nintendo on a patent infringement case, winning a $250 million verdict. Trial lawyer **Robert Weber** (see p.1450) is "*a critical thinker, fast on his feet and very client oriented.*" Besides being heavily involved as lead counsel for RJ Reynolds, he was recently successful for IBM on a landmark toxic tort case. His success lies as much in his creativ-

ity as his determination to "*always give the best service to his clients.*" **Theodore Grossman** (see p.1441) is another "*excellent attorney.*" He has been representing Wyeth in a case involving suicides alleged to have resulted from the use of the company's antidepressant drugs. Grossman, too, has substantial experience of tobacco litigation and has built a strong reputation in that field. The managing partner of the Columbus office, **Fordham Huffman** (see p.1442), is for some commentators "*the crème de la crème.*" Bankruptcy cases feature large in his general commercial litigation practice. He was recently involved in American Electric Power v Bank of Montreal, a dispute over the termination of trading contracts governed by international rules. **Kevin Cogan** (see p.1439) has a vast amount of jury trial experience in general commercial matters, including corporate control contests and securities fraud. One peer revealed that Cogan had the perfect recipe for taming juries: he is "*low key with a nice sense of humor – that works!*" "*Historically one of the best,*" senior figure **Patrick McCartan** (see p.1444) now concentrates on appellate litigation and corporate governance matters, though his 45 years of practice have spanned antitrust, taxation, takeovers and officers and directors' liability. Another attorney with "*a very broad level of expertise*" is **Steven Sozio** (see p.1448). He represents various clients including healthcare providers, medical device manufacturers, defense contractors and financial institutions. **George Moscarino** (see p.1445) has extensive experience in white-collar crime matters on a regional, national and international scale. He deals also with a considerable number of other areas of law including civil fraud and general business and commercial litigation such as IP, products liability, tort, environmental law and government contract disputes.

The Clients: OGE Energy; FirstEnergy; GM; Toyota Motor Sales; RJ Reynolds Tobacco; Pfizer; Bridgestone/Firestone North American Tire and AZ Automotive.

Band 2

Squire, Sanders & Dempsey LLP

The Firm: This firm has expanded considerably over the past five to ten years and growth is very evident in the litigation department. Displaying "*terrific litigation capabilities,*" the Ohio team has been involved in a multitude of types of commercial litigation, representing a broad range of local, national and international clients. In 2004, the team acted for the Newark Group in a trade secret case that resulted in a $3.75 million jury verdict and a permanent injunction against any use or disclosure of the trade secret.

The Lawyers: "*An extremely knowledgeable*

man," **Thomas Kilbane** leads Squire Sanders' worldwide litigation practice. This "*superb*" trial lawyer has a great deal of experience trying very technical and complex commercial disputes, among them antitrust, construction and securities cases. With more than 45 years of trial experience to his name, **David Young** has, unquestionably, "*a great legal mind*" and remains "*one of the best lawyers in Columbus.*" Although his practice tends towards complex cases concerning the healthcare sector, he has recently been involved in matters regarding the relationships between public companies and their accounting firms. **John Gall** is the head of the Columbus litigation group and, according to commentators, benefits from "*good team support.*" His commercial caseload encompasses business contract disputes, IP matters and professional liability claims. Gall represented the mayor of Columbus when the city's chief of police sued him for defamation. Each of the three lawsuits pending at the time was resolved in court in the mayor's favor. **Damond Mace**, the "*sharp kid*" of the group, has a talent for all sorts of commercial litigation matters including contract disputes, Uniform Commercial Code litigation, construction, products liability, tort and class actions. This "*very bright and strong lawyer*" has dealt with many jury trials and appeals in state and federal courts, as well as several arbitration matters.

The Clients: Newark Group; Nationwide; Glimcher Realty Trust; Medical Mutual of Ohio; Catholic Conference of Ohio and the City of Cincinnati.

Vorys, Sater, Seymour and Pease

See firm details p.1458

The Firm: With offices in the four main cities of Ohio, this firm has "*a legitimate statewide presence.*" Spread throughout the state, the team of "*very experienced litigators*" handles commercial litigation for a large number of corporate clients in manufacturing, transportation, healthcare, technology development and insurance.

The Lawyers: David Cupps (see p.1439) is one of the "*most recognized and respected attorneys in Columbus.*" According to commentators, "*amazing analytical ability*" is what leads this "*brilliant thinker to get all the big cases.*" He has been practicing commercial litigation for over 30 years, tackling topics as diverse as antitrust, IP and securities. **Sandra Anderson** (see p.1437) is a "*very bright and successful*" litigator whose practice covers all aspects of general commercial litigation, employment law and products liability. Her peers see this "*fine lawyer*" as someone who "*gets things moving.*" Placing an emphasis on healthcare litigation, **Daniel Buckley**'s (see p.1438) Cincinnati-based prac-

1430   All quotes in the text are from interviews with clients and competitors.

CHAMBERS USA 2005

Ohio
Leading individuals
(Litigation: General Commercial)

Senior Statesman
MCCARTAN Patrick *Jones Day*, Cleveland

[1] CUPPS David *Vorys Sater*, Columbus
KILBANE Thomas *Squire Sanders*, Cleveland
NEWMAN John *Jones Day*, Cleveland
STRAUCH John *Jones Day*, Cleveland
WEBER Robert *Jones Day*, Cleveland
YOUNG David *Squire Sanders*, Columbus

[2] FARUKI Charles *Faruki Ireland*, Dayton
GROSSMAN Theodore *Jones Day*, Cleveland
HOOKER David *Thompson Hine*, Cleveland
TRAFFORD Robert *Porter Wright*, Columbus
WILKINSON William *Thompson Hine*, Columbus
ZEIGER John *Zeiger Tigges*, Columbus

[3] CRAIG L Clifford *Taft Stettinius*, Cincinnati
GALL John *Squire Sanders*, Columbus
GREER David *Bieser Greer*, Dayton
HILL Thomas *Kegler Brown*, Columbus
HUFFMAN Fordham *Jones Day*, Columbus
MCDONALD John *Schottenstein Zox*, Columbus
PITCAIRN Robert *Katz Teller*, Cincinnati
SAXBE Charles *Chester Willcox*, Columbus
SOLOMON Randall *Baker & Hostetler*, Cleveland

[4] ANDERSON Sandra *Vorys Sater*, Columbus
BLAIR Mitchell *Calfee Halter*, Cleveland
BUCKLEY Daniel *Vorys Sater*, Cincinnati
BURKE James *Keating Muething*, Cincinnati
CARPENTER Michael *Carpenter & Lipps*, Columbus
COGAN J Kevin *Jones Day*, Columbus
FITCH Stephen *Chester Willcox*, Columbus
FREUND Neil *Freund Freeze*, Dayton
FRY Roger *Rendings Fry*, Cincinnati
GORE George *Tucker Ellis*, Cleveland
IRELAND D Jeffrey *Faruki Ireland*, Dayton
KAMP David *White Getgey*, Cincinnati
KARP Marvin *Ulmer & Berne*, Cleveland
KERGER Richard *Kerger & Kerger*, Toledo
MACE Damond *Squire Sanders*, Cleveland
RIDGLEY Thomas *Vorys Sater*, Columbus
ROBENALT James *Thompson Hine*, Cleveland
STANLEY Hugh *Tucker Ellis*, Cleveland
TUCKER Robert *Tucker Ellis*, Cleveland

Up-and-coming individuals
HAGGERTY John *Ulmer & Berne*, Cleveland

Individuals are listed alphabetically in each band.

tice also encompasses most aspects of commercial litigation. He has recently represented financial institutions, venture capital firms, accounting firms and software companies. A "*terrific, organized mind*" and "*wonderful communication skills*" make **Thomas Ridgley** (see p.1447) "*a better storyteller than JK Rowling*" – juries lap up his narratives. His commercial litigation experience extends to takeovers, securities, environmental law and products liability. Ridgley was the attorney behind AT&T's successful takeover of NCR. Dealing mainly with bank and tax fraud, **James Phillips** (see p.1446)

spends 40% of his time on commercial litigation and the remainder on white-collar crime. His previous experience working as a senior assistant US attorney for Franklin county proves useful when it comes to advising corporations on criminal liability. Having previously worked for the Department of Justice for four years, **Glenn Whitaker** (see p.1450) represents individuals and corporations in complex civil litigation and his specialty area of qui tam litigation. He was recently involved on a false claims case concerning Rolls-Royce.

The Clients: A roster of private and public sector clients includes Clinton Memorial Hospital and Abercrombie & Fitch.

Band 3

Baker & Hostetler LLP

The Firm: A major national law firm with three offices in Ohio, Baker & Hostetler has a highly respected litigation team that has been evolving at a constant pace. Commentators say this is "*a genuine team of strong litigators who are committed to excellence.*"

The Lawyers: Randall Solomon is a "*patient and reasonable*" lawyer who always manages to get his point across. This skill appears to be at its most fruitful when the "*very bright*" attorney is in a courtroom. A former assistant US attorney, **James Wooley** concentrates on white-collar and corporate criminal matters and has been representing corporations, business, professionals and assorted individuals in matters including antitrust, healthcare fraud and abuse, criminal tax matters, government contractor fraud, securities fraud and criminal copyright infringement. He is depicted as "*an effective, thoughtful and skilled practitioner.*"

The Clients: A broad clientele encompasses financial services and energy companies plus other American and foreign corporations such as Northwest Airlines and KLM Royal Dutch Airlines.

Porter Wright Morris & Arthur LLP
See firm details p.1455

The Firm: This firm has four offices in Ohio (with Columbus being the largest), plus one in DC and one in Florida. The 190-attorney Columbus headquarters boasts a "*very effective*" litigation group that deals with various business, commercial and securities litigation matters. Its client-friendly approach is much appreciated; indeed, one source went so far as to say: "*They think more about the clients than about the money.*"

The Lawyers: The firm's managing partner, **Robert Trafford** (see p.1449), takes on complex litigation, including securities, RICO, lender liability, takeovers, trade secrets, officers and directors' liability and constitutional law. This "*great litigator,*" who can "*handle himself superbly in*

court," has been busy dealing with lawyer malpractice suits lately. Commentators note that he is good at all levels of litigation, especially federal court matters.

The Clients: Clients come from a broad range of industries including healthcare, automotive, pharmaceutical, defense, construction, music and entertainment, agriculture, oil and gas, software and soft drinks.

Thompson Hine LLP
See firm details p.1457

The Firm: Part of a firm-wide litigation force of nearly 100, this local group of "*intelligent, diligent, hard-working and detail-conscious*" lawyers gives this international firm a stronghold in the state. The business litigation team has lately been involved in bankruptcy proceedings for a major bank, protecting its interests as former indenture trustee for approximately $1 billion in notes issued by the bankrupt corporation.

The Lawyers: The firm's managing partner, Cleveland-based **David Hooker** (see p.1442), specializes in complex business litigation and takes care of the firm's relationships with some of its biggest clients. According to commentators, he is "*a very strategic thinker*" and "*a charismatic and successful trial lawyer.*" Combining "*amazing oral argument and stand-up skills*" with the ability to comfortably examine and cross-examine witnesses, **William Wilkinson** (see p.1450) has all the ingredients for success in the courtroom. He can be "*a hard-charging and very aggressive litigator, but he will always stay decent,*" researchers were told. Wilkinson's commercial litigation practice incorporates fraud, breach of contract, franchise, securities, IP, construction and RICO litigation. He has recently been working on a multidistrict litigation arising from the financial collapse of National Century Financial Enterprises in November 2002. According to interviewees, **James Robenalt** (see p.1447) is "*a skilled, able and seasoned lawyer*" who practices business litigation in a very pragmatic way. He represents many Fortune 500 companies in a variety of areas including economic espionage and trade secret cases, international disputes, investment tax credit cases, construction litigation and arbitrations.

The Clients: Highlands Insurance Group; Clear Channel; PolyOne; PPG Industries and American Chemistry Council.

Band 4

Calfee, Halter & Griswold LLP
See firm details p.1451

The Firm: With 45 attorneys working on commercial litigation matters, this Ohio firm has offices in the two fastest growing cities in the state, Cleveland and Columbus. Its litigation group represents a vast number of private companies as well as some large public companies. Attorneys

www.ChambersandPartners.com

All quotes in the text are from interviews with clients and competitors.

1431

Ohio
Leading individuals
(Litigation: White-Collar Crime &
Government Investigations)

Senior Statesman
MOSCARINO George *Jones Day, Cleveland*
★ MESSERMAN Gerald *Messerman & Messerman, Cleveland*
[1] MCLAUGHLIN Patrick *McLaughlin & McCaffrey, Cleveland*
MEEKS William *Sole Practitioner, Columbus*
SCHWARTZ Niki *Schwartz Kushner, Cleveland*
SOZIO Steven *Jones Day, Cleveland*
[2] CASCARILLA Ralph *Walter & Haverfield, Cleveland*
MAKLEY Roger *Coolidge Wall, Dayton*
ROTATORI Robert *Rotatori Bender, Cleveland*
WOOLEY James *Baker & Hostetler, Cleveland*
[3] MCCAFFREY John *McLaughlin & McCaffrey, Cleveland*
PHILLIPS James *Vorys Sater, Columbus*
WEINER Samuel *Samuel B Weiner, Columbus*
WHITAKER Glenn *Vorys Sater, Cincinnati*

Individuals are listed alphabetically in each band.

have a good reputation for IP matters and are considered by commentators to have *"a significant presence in Cleveland"* in complex disputes.

The Lawyers: Cochair of the litigation group **Mitchell Blair** (see p.1437) is *"a bright and tough guy who gets straight to the point."* According to one interviewee, *"he has outstanding trial skills, but also excels in his early assessment of cases,"* which gives clients a realistic perspective of their prospects in pending litigation.

The Clients: FirstEnergy; Regal Cinemas; Agilysys and Cingular Wireless.

Carpenter & Lipps LLP

The Firm: This 15-attorney Columbus-based litigation boutique places an emphasis on complex litigation in the areas of business, banking and consumer finance. The team has been representing a considerable number of private sector clients, including companies from the automobile industry.

The Lawyers: **Michael Carpenter**, cofounder of the firm and *"a smooth and polished lawyer,"* focuses on commercial litigation, products liability, class actions and multidistrict litigation.

The Clients: Daewoo Motor America; Developer Finance; American Honda Motor; Isuzu Motors America; New United Motor Manufacturing and Nissan Motor.

Chester, Willcox & Saxbe LLP

The Firm: Fourteen of the 30 attorneys based in Columbus work on litigation matters. Commentators mentioned that the firm's litigation team does *"a wonderful job"* in banking, contract, fraud, RICO violations, environmental cases, foreclosures, healthcare, construction and franchise matters. The team has recently been working on a case involving home builders and developers who brought an action against a municipality to challenge its zoning laws and

development restrictions.

The Lawyers: According to interviewees, **Charles Saxbe** is *"a really capable problem solver"* with considerable experience in the field of general civil and commercial litigation. He has recent experience of electoral issues and has earned a name as *"a great fixer with great political connections."* Saxbe has tried a multitude of cases, appearing before the Ohio Supreme Court, Ohio Courts of Appeals and the Sixth Circuit Court of Appeals. Partner **Stephen Fitch** was billed by one client as *"the best trial lawyer I have ever met."* His practice focuses on civil matters, appellate litigation, alternative dispute resolution and professional responsibility. Fitch has been representing other lawyers on matters ranging from professional misconduct to racial and sexual discrimination.

The Clients: Ohio Central Railroad and State Alarm Company are among the firm's clients.

Faruki Ireland & Cox PLL

The Firm: This specialist trial firm boasts more than 40 *"tough and bright"* attorneys in its Dayton office. It has been concentrating much more on IP matters of late and has a particular interest in patents. The firm has also acquired a media practice and is now representing newspapers and a leading radio station.

The Lawyers: *"Leading business litigator"* **Charles Faruki** (see p.1440) has *"good judgment in addition to his state-of-the-art trial skills."* His trial practice leans towards business litigation, IP and products liability defense. Sources say, *"He is smart and tough and has a great deal of experience as a trial lawyer."* **Jeffrey Ireland**'s (see p.1442) business litigation practice emphasizes antitrust and commercial and environmental litigation. Clients report *"some excellent results with him,"* while peers consider him a *"strong opponent."*

The Clients: Dayton Newspaper; Miami Valley Hospital; Procter & Gamble; NCR and the Iams Company.

Katz, Teller, Brant & Hild

The Firm: This Cincinnati-based firm has a team of seven attorneys focusing on commercial litigation, frequently contractual matters and securities fraud. Its client base ranges from small businesses to Fortune 100 players and the team has recently represented numerous physicians and lawyers in malpractice litigation.

The Lawyers: With his ability to spot the weaknesses of the other party's case, **Robert Pitcairn** is considered *"invincible"* by some of his peers. This *"highly intuitive and insightful lawyer"* has been handling a high-profile case on behalf of a famous baseball player. His previous experience has included defending various types of class actions, shareholder derivative suits, commercial disputes and employment discrimination cases.

The Clients: Among various public and private clients, one of the largest is AK Steel.

Keating, Muething & Klekamp, PLL

The Firm: Founded more than 50 years ago, this Cincinnati law firm has more than 100 lawyers and a litigation team that is considered very able in all areas of general commercial litigation, including antitrust, class actions, financial services, insurance coverage and construction.

The Lawyers: Other lawyers would feel comfortable referring work to **James Burke** because of his *"efficiency and brightness."* His complex litigation practice incorporates securities, class actions and financial services disputes. Burke has extensive experience in both trial and appellate matters before many different courts across the country.

The Clients: American Financial Group; Chiquita Brands International; Great American Financial Resources; Cincom Systems and Hal Homes.

Kegler, Brown, Hill & Ritter

The Firm: The Columbus and Marion offices of this firm boast between 20 and 30 full-time litigators. The commercial litigation group successfully defended a Fortune 500 company in a lengthy federal court jury trial where the plaintiff was seeking damages in excess of $500 million.

The Lawyers: Regarded by peers as *"the number one at this firm,"* **Thomas Hill** (see p.1442) is *"a very skilled and experienced"* attorney. One of his career highlights was his successful representation of the American Cancer Society in litigation arising out of a $7 million embezzlement of its funds. *"He takes good care of his clients and always obtains very satisfactory results."*

The Clients: Ashland, Virginia Homes and Thrifty Car Rental are three of the firm's key clients.

McLaughlin & McCaffrey, LLP

The Firm: Although this six-attorney Cleveland-based practice deals with various civil and commercial litigation matters, its forte is white-collar crime. The team advises national and international companies on a variety of matters including internal investigations, economic espionage, antitrust, money laundering, RICO, securities, mail fraud, healthcare fraud and criminal tax issues.

The Lawyers: **Patrick McLaughlin** was previously a US attorney. This *"terrific lawyer has extensive expertise at the federal level,"* an advantage which leads commentators to view him as *"a unique lawyer who commends great respect."* **John McCaffrey** is also adept at federal trials and appellate hearings. His practice spans commercial litigation and white-collar criminal defense.

The Clients: The firm represents a wide variety of clients ranging from individuals to large corporations.

Schottenstein, Zox & Dunn

See firm details p.1456

The Firm: With offices in Columbus, Cincinnati and Cleveland, this firm has 40 lawyers focusing on commercial litigation. Its broad client base includes insurance companies, chemical manufacturers and clients with significant IP interests.

The Lawyers: "*An accomplished litigator*" and "*a good technician,*" **John McDonald** (see p.1444) "*prepares a case concisely and presents it effectively.*" A good example of his recent work is the recent $10 million judgment awarded in a contract dispute over a computer equipment lease renewal between CompuServe and McDonald's client Central Funding.

The Clients: Central Funding, Welsh Ohio and the Ohio Company are all on the client roster.

Taft, Stettinius & Hollister LLP

The Firm: Of approximately 70 lawyers in Ohio, at least one-third handle litigation. The team, which "*knows when to conciliate and when to fight,*" deals mainly with general commercial and financial litigation and benefits from the presence of colleagues who specialize in antitrust, bankruptcy and other business areas.

The Lawyers: Based in Cincinnati, chairman of the litigation practice **Clifford Craig** handles federal and state securities litigation, including class actions, shareholder derivative actions and enforcement proceedings, as well as corporate takeovers.

The Clients: Cincinnati Gas & Electric; Starbank; Gibson Greeting Card and Celina Financial.

Tucker Ellis & West LLP

The Firm: With clients ranging from family businesses to Fortune 500 companies, the Cleveland-based litigation group is active on general business and commercial disputes, including contractual obligations, fiduciary duties, unfair business practices, white-collar crime, antitrust violations, securities fraud, trade secrets, non-compete covenants and RICO.

The Lawyers: With over 35 years of private practice behind him, **George Gore** has an excellent name in the defense of drugs, medical device and medical malpractice cases. This "*tough guy*" has tried cases in nearly every state as well as in Europe, Australia and Canada. Trial lawyer **Hugh Stanley** concentrates on corporate, banking, insurance and commercial litigation. His recent workload includes a law firm 'divorce', a settlement in a metals industry cartel antitrust case and various insurance litigation matters. The managing partner at TEW's Cleveland office, **Robert Tucker**, is "*a pretty damned good trial lawyer*" who specializes in products liability and medical malpractice cases, with an emphasis on the defense of pharmaceutical companies, physicians, hospitals and manufacturers of consumer products.

The Clients: Clients include PharmEd, Ohio Savings Bank and AON International Risk Management Group.

Ulmer & Berne LLP

The Firm: With over 100 in its litigation group and three offices in Ohio, the firm boasts a bench of attorneys with diverse experience in bankruptcy, contract claims, franchise and distributorship agreement disputes, securities litigation and IP. Attorneys recently represented a German merchant bank in a claim against Cyrus Eaton, Jr to recover fees owed by Eaton relating to the construction financing of a hotel in Leningrad built by a Finnish consortium. The firm obtained a $2 million judgment in favor of its client.

The Lawyers: **Marvin Karp** is a "*fine lawyer*" focusing on general commercial litigation, insurance defense, securities, bad faith claims and professional liability. He was recently representing Lloyd's of London, Ohio Edison, Duquesne Light and Pennsylvania Power in a suit against GE for supplying defective circuit breakers to a power plant. The jury awarded his clients $23 million. A "*young and energetic*" lawyer, **John Haggerty** deals mainly with products liability issues and business litigation. He has represented companies in nationwide litigation concerning tobacco, lead paint, asbestos and welding rods.

The Clients: ICI Paints; Lloyd's of London; Ohio Edison; Duquesne Light and PPL.

Zeiger, Tigges, Little & Lindsmith LLP

The Firm: With three matters resolved in the Ohio Supreme Court in the past twelve months, this litigation boutique, founded more than ten years ago, is well known in the market. It boasts a team of 11 attorneys specializing in major business disputes, securities and legal professional liability.

The Lawyers: With extensive experience defending contract, trademark, copyright, bankruptcy and class action claims, **John Zeiger** is "*brilliant at pushing a case ahead*" with his "*strategic mind*" and "*strong trial skills.*" In addition to his general commercial workload, Zeiger undertakes media litigation. This "*very effective and hard-nosed litigator*" was the lead trial counsel for Columbus community leaders in a dispute with Lamar Hunt over control of the Columbus Blue Jackets NHL franchise. According to commentators, he is "*unbeatable for short-notice stuff like preliminary injunctions.*"

Other Notable Practitioners

According to his peers, **David Greer** of Bieser, Greer, & Landis LLP in Dayton is "*very business focused and knows how to deal with people.*" His affinity for complex cases enabled him to deal easily with Mead's litigation arising out of an attempted takeover by Occidental. **Neil Freund**, a 35-year-old attorney at Freund, Freeze & Arnold, is a "*smart lawyer*" who deals with a broad range of litigation matters including commercial litigation, professional liability, employment litigation, municipal defense, civil rights, products liability and white-collar crime. **Roger Fry** of Rendigs, Fry, Kiely & Dennis LLP takes on diverse litigation matters – commercial, construction, environmental, insurance coverage and products and professional liability. **David Kamp** of White, Getgey & Meyer Co. LPA is described as "*a superb lawyer with tremendous experience*" in general commercial litigation. He takes on both civil and commercial cases: personal injury, medical malpractice, family law, securities litigation, ERISA and products liability. Cofounder of the Kerger & Kerger law firm **Richard Kerger** excels at trials and appeals as well as complex employment law issues. He is one of the main points of reference in Toledo for conflicted-out lawyers. In the area of white-collar crime, **Gerald Messerman** of Messerman & Messerman Co, LPA remains the star. Commentators say, "*He is an excellent and creative lawyer who handles all the big white-collar cases in the state.*" Interviewees chorused their approval, describing him as "*incredible and terrific.*" Sole practitioner **William Meeks** is considered "*one of the most experienced and accomplished defense attorneys in the state.*" One respected commentator said: "*If one day I am accused of robbing a bank my first and only call would go to Meeks.*" **Niki Schwartz** of Schwartz, Kushner & Rendon Co, LPA is a "*first-rate lawyer*" based in Cleveland. As well as white-collar crime, he tackles a good deal of general civil litigation. With more than 30 years of experience in federal criminal matters, **Ralph Cascarilla** of Walter & Haverfield LLP is currently working on a case involving a criminal offence arising from a construction project. Besides white-collar crime, Cascarilla is involved in general civil and commercial litigation, including environmental law and antitrust matters. **Roger Makley** of Coolidge, Wall, Womsley & Lombard is a "*terrific*" lawyer with a very active white-collar crime practice. He, too, deals with other matters of a commercial variety including securities, antitrust, tax and employment litigation. Cleveland white-collar crime attorney **Robert Rotatori** of Rotatori, Bender, Gragel, Stoper & Alexander Co., L.P.A. is "*very experienced and knowledgeable*" and "*very discreet.*" Lastly, **Samuel Weiner** of Samuel B Weiner Co. LPA deals with all manner of criminal trials and appellate work ranging from arson to white-collar crime.

REAL ESTATE

Ohio
Leading firms (Real Estate)

1 BRICKER & ECKLER LLP *Columbus*
JONES DAY *Cleveland*
THOMPSON HINE LLP *Cleveland*
VORYS, SATER, SEYMOUR & PEASE *Columbus*

2 BAKER & HOSTETLER LLP *Cleveland*
KAHN KLEINMAN *Cleveland*
PORTER WRIGHT MORRIS & ARTHUR *Columbus*
SQUIRE, SANDERS & DEMPSEY *Cleveland*

3 BENESCH, FRIEDLANDER, COPLAN *Cleveland*
CALFEE, HALTER & GRISWOLD LLP *Cleveland*
FROST BROWN TODD LLC *Cincinnati*
SCHOTTENSTEIN, ZOX & DUNN *Columbus*
ULMER & BERNE LLP *Cleveland*

Leading individuals (Real Estate)

1 BUCHENROTH Stephen *Vorys Sater, Columbus*
REPPERT Richard *Jones Day, Cleveland*
ROSNER Richard *Kahn Kleinman, Cleveland*
STRIEFSKY Linda *Thompson Hine, Cleveland*

2 ARNDT Randall *Schottenstein Zox, Columbus*
BAKER David *Bricker & Eckler, Columbus*
CONRAD David *Bricker & Eckler, Columbus*
MCCREARY Charles *Bricker & Eckler, Columbus*
PARIS Zachary *Jones Day, Cleveland*
PEARLMAN Samuel *Squire Sanders, Cleveland*
ROHYANS John *Porter Wright, Columbus*

3 ARONOFF James *Thompson Hine, Cleveland*
COYNE Thomas *Thompson Hine, Cleveland*
GAYNOR Bruce *Kahn Kleinman, Cleveland*
LINDBERG Lawrence *Baker & Hostetler, Cleveland*
O'DONNELL Patricia *Baker & Hostetler, Cleveland*
SAAD Michael *Squire Sanders, Columbus*
STEINDLER Howard *Benesch Friedlander, Cleveland*
STRAUSS David *Baker & Hostetler, Cleveland*
WEIR Bill *Porter Wright, Cleveland*

4 CADWALLADER John *Frost Brown, Columbus*
GAGLIANO Bill *Ulmer & Berne, Cleveland*
GUTMACHER Norman *Benesch Friedlander, Cleveland*
INTIHAR Steve *Bricker & Eckler, Columbus*
KUEHNLE Kenton *Roetzel & Andress, Akron*
MILLER Craig *Ulmer & Berne, Cleveland*
PHILLIPS William *Calfee Halter, Cleveland*
SMITH Ted *Vorys Sater, Columbus*
VENESY Bryan *Squire Sanders, Columbus*

Up-and-coming individuals
OWENDOFF Michael *Jones Day, Cleveland*

Firms and individuals are listed alphabetically in each band.

Band 1

Bricker & Eckler LLP

The Firm: The past year has seen some significant growth for this statewide practice; clients consider the group to be "*far ahead of anyone else*" in the real estate market. They hold this "*personable*" firm in high regard, saying, "*They bring a lot to the table and know our business inside out.*" With offices in Cleveland and Columbus, the venerable Ohio firm has a clientele comprising individuals as well as corporations, among them major retail and lifestyle center developers and nationally recognized lenders. Highlights from the past year have involved a 750-unit condominium project and the mezzanine financing of apartment projects nationwide. The "*very thorough*" team also recently worked on a mortgage refinancing deal worth $200 million. The firm is respected for providing good value for money in a competitive market.

The Lawyers: "*Service-oriented*" **Dave Baker** stands at the helm of the real estate department. Baker turns his hand to every aspect of real estate law and produces exceptional work in development and commercial matters: "*He combines great business acumen with terrific legal skills.*" Maintaining a high profile in the market is head of the firm's commercial lending group, **Dusty McCreary**. With a particular emphasis on construction and interim and permanent mortgage lending, McCreary's practice regularly sees him involved in big-money transactions and various residential, retail and development projects across the country. **David Conrad**, a member of the commercial mortgage lending and bankruptcy practice groups, works with cellular companies on the siting and construction of signal transmission towers as well as with developers in the hospitality and office leasing sectors. Making a name for himself in condo development work is rising star **Steve Intihar**. With a finger in every pie, Intihar is known by clients for his extensive knowledge base and his reputation as "*an extremely capable guy.*"

The Clients: McGraw-Hill; National City Bank; North Star Realty; US Bank; Continental Real Estate Companies; Casto; Lifestyle Communities; JPMorgan Chase; Fifth Third Bank; KeyBank and Huntington National Bank.

Jones Day

See firm details p.485

The Firm: A busy year for the real estate team in the Cleveland office has meant a cluster of successful, high-value transactions, and provoked enthusiastic responses from gratified clients. "*A pleasure to work with,*" the "*highly accomplished*" team has clinched a major deal for national client Developers Diversified involving the acquisition of some 110 shopping centers in the New York area. With this $2.2 billion transaction under their belt, the "*super-lawyers*" are now embarking on a further project for this client and working to expand its interests into the Central American market with the acquisition of a number of retail developments in Puerto Rico. While the client base has a distinctly national and international flavor, the firm's local interests have not waned and it continues to represent significant local players Stark and Fogg.

The Lawyers: The "*down-to-earth*" team comprises a number of national experts who receive the highest of accolades from the market. One of the foremost financing attorneys in the state, "*very knowledgeable*" **Dick Reppert** (see p.1447) has "*exceptional negotiating skills*" and ample experience representing clients in complex financings. The past year has seen him working out of state for a national financial institution. Experienced in most aspects of commercial and industrial real estate law, the "*result-oriented*" **Zack Paris** (see p.1446) provides a full-service package to corporations and other institutions whose core business lies beyond the immediate bounds of the real estate industry. Formerly of the Benesch firm, the "*absolutely outstanding*" **Michael Owendoff** (see p.1446) is a rising star in the group; he is praised by clients for his hands-on approach and willingness to be "*there in the trenches negotiating agreements.*"

The Clients: Clients include Forest City Enterprises, Ray Fogg Building Methods and Robert L. Stark Enterprises.

Thompson Hine LLP

See firm details p.1457

The Firm: Described by market commentators as an "*outstanding shop,*" this is one of the most prominent local players in Ohio real estate. The practice is split into four teams: development, corporate, financing and capital markets; and the firm has two offices, Columbus and Cleveland, with 28 of the firm's 30 real estate specialists working in the latter. This "*very strong*" Cleveland team provided local counsel to a Chicago developer and international hotel operator in a $60 million project, including acquisition and redevelopment of a retail arcade facility in Cleveland. Other recent transactions have included major shopping center developments and the drawing up of a number of key leases for commercial clients.

The Lawyers: **Linda Striefsky** (see p.1449) is well known throughout the state for her "*excellent*" work and is consistently praised for her efficient and practical handling of clients' interests. Widely regarded as "*one of the most technically competent attorneys in Ohio,*" her "*stellar*" practice covers financing and corporate facilities work, and additionally encompasses permitting, construction and credit tenant leases. **Thomas Coyne** (see p.1439), who leads the department, is noted for his work for nonprofit organizations. Lately he assisted on a major project for a Fortune 500 automotive company involving plant separations and the restructuring of its Brazilian operations. New to the table is "*wonderworker*" **Jim Aronoff** (see p.1437). He works closely with Coyne and enjoys a reputation as an expert deal-maker.

The Clients: BMW Financial Services; Key-Bank; DeepGreen Financial and KeyCorp.

Vorys, Sater, Seymour & Pease LLP

See firm details p.1458

The Firm: Active in all types of real estate development and lending, this niche firm commands a prime position in Columbus, where it has its main location. Attorneys can also be found in the firm's Cincinnati and Cleveland offices. Rival firms happily acknowledge the firm to be "*as good as any major firm anywhere in the city,*" adding: "*There is almost nothing they cannot do and almost nothing they haven't done at least once.*" Most are aware of its particular strengths in financing and tax-driven work, and following an upturn in the condominium development market, the team has recently been involved with a number of local high-volume construction and development companies in this regard.

The Lawyers: The extremely well-connected **Stephen Buchenroth** (see p.1438) provides both regional and national clients with a "*first-class*" service and the benefit of his close ties to the Ohio legislature. His excellent reputation is enhanced by his "*wealth of expertise*" in zoning, mortgage foreclosures and franchising, and he represents a wide range of clients from small franchisers to leading lending institutions. "*Highly skilled*" up-and-comer **Ted Smith** (see p.1448) makes an impact on the scene with his technical ability and high-quality condominium development work for an impressive local client base.

The Clients: Schottenstein Stores, Pizzuti, and M/I Homes are among the firm's clients.

Band 2

Baker & Hostetler LLP

The Firm: At the forefront in financing, and providing enthusiastic clients with a range of tax-efficient advice, this focused team represents both conventional and unconventional funding sources. A "*very solid*" team works well together, especially in relation to private placements with projects involving HUD and other government agencies. Market commentators were in agreement that the real estate practice has its place on the local map. Drawing on the resources of colleagues in seven other offices across the country, the teams in the Cleveland, Cincinnati and Columbus offices also service national and, increasingly, international clients.

The Lawyers: "*Fabulous*" **Larry Lindberg** is credited with being the driving force behind the reputation of the team. He is known for his "*exceptional*" leasing work and "*high-wattage*" commercial and residential practice. Lindberg was described by peers as "*a truly great journeyman real estate attorney*" and has recently undertaken deals in the UK for a Vermont-based

outdoor products company. The "*winsome*" **Patricia O'Donnell** engages in a great deal of Ohio-based refinancing projects, including the office's "*cottage industry*" – the rehabilitation of established downtown neighborhoods. The past year has seen her represent a large public agency and manage a steady stream of nonprofit development projects, among them the financing of a new structure for the Cleveland Botanical Garden. Her "*no-nonsense, straightforward*" attitude delights clients. "*Creative*" **David Strauss**, meanwhile, receives market accolades for his skill in the structuring of transactions – "*he can string together lots of disparate things and turn them into a masterpiece.*"

The Clients: Advanced Auto Parts; OfficeMax; Trane; Advance; Cardinal Health; Citigroup; Hyatt Hotels; Cleveland Botanical Gardens and Rhodes/Dahl.

Kahn Kleinman

The Firm: This "*great boutique firm*" is acclaimed for its "*consistently excellent*" local practice. The personal touch of the "*cost-effective*" group keeps many small to midsized clients faithful and appreciative of the responsiveness of the attorneys. Said one, "*They are so attentive; with bigger firms you become just another number.*" Dealing with the full compass of real estate issues, Kahn Kleinman is particularly known for the complex structuring of real estate syndications and financings. Viewed as "*entrepreneurial*" in its outlook, the well-respected team has "*great street presence*" and occupies a crucial spot in the market. Mixed-use developments such as the first lifestyle village in Cleveland have earned them numerous plaudits. "*They don't want to be the biggest but they are one of the best. They are my team,*" said one satisfied client.

The Lawyers: Representing national as well as local clients, "*unflappable*" **Richard Rosner** is known as the "*guru*" of the condominium market. Well-connected Rosner is the cochair of the firm's real estate and environmental practice group and has recently been involved in redeveloping an environmentally challenged urban site for future use as a residential community. Clients sing his praises: "*He's gone from A to Z for us. He's a deal-maker not a deal-breaker.*" **Bruce Gaynor** is a "*very savvy*" attorney with extensive retail and development experience. Clients warm to his "*folksy*" manner and agree that he "*works hard to get the deal done.*"

The Clients: Pulte Homes; Kimball Hill Homes; First Interstate Properties and Whitlatch.

Porter Wright Morris & Arthur LLP

See firm details p.1455

The Firm: This "*excellent*" Cleveland firm maintains a high profile in the Ohio real estate market, with areas of expertise ranging from commercial and industrial projects to the full scope of residential matters. Best known for its

"*solid*" representation of lenders, the firm also looks after developers and clients in the utility, leisure and retail industries. Last year it closed almost 30 deals for client Nationwide Life Insurance, as well as dealing with a property portfolio worth over $300 million for apartment developers DEC Investment Group.

The Lawyers: Primarily known for his lending practice, "*outstanding*" **John Rohyans** (see p.1447) advises on loan transactions throughout the Midwest and is celebrated for his "*clear thinking*" and vast experience. Also waving the flag for the real estate team in Cleveland is "*real star*" **Bill Weir**, who is known among his peers as a very fine lender's counsel. As appreciative clients put it, he has "*the hallmarks of a good lending lawyer.*"

The Clients: Among the firm's clients are DEC Investment Group, Nationwide Life Insurance and Dominion Homes.

Squire, Sanders & Dempsey LLP

The Firm: A long-standing player in the market, Squire Sanders has expertise in complex commercial transactions, both domestically and internationally. The last year has seen the dynamic local team involved in a number of public and private joint ventures between state government and private enterprise. The full-service practice caters for a diverse group of international and domestic clients, with 90% of its work based out of state. The 18-strong team is wholly devoted to real estate work and attorneys are encouraged to develop their own specific areas of expertise ranging from hospitality to tax to advantage housing and shopping villages.

The Lawyers: **Sam Pearlman** has a real eye for detail and an "*exceptionally thorough*" approach. His broad practice encompasses commercial real estate transactions, real estate lending (from the perspective of both borrower and lender), business mergers, acquisitions and divestitures and the negotiation of joint venture and limited liability company agreements. **Michael Saad** is one of the firmwide coordinators of the real estate practice. His recent experience has seen him representing equity investors and financial institutions in a variety of debt, equity and mezzanine financings as well as Islamic finance transactions. The "*very gentlemanly*" **Bryan Venesy** is principally known for his work on multifamily and affordable housing projects as well as office leasing. In recent months Venesy has represented an investment fund in affordable housing tax credit and rehabilitation projects worth more than $700 million. These elements of his work sit within a broad commercial practice.

The Clients: The firm's clients include Mid-America Management and Schottenstein Stores

www.ChambersandPartners.com

All quotes in the text are from interviews with clients and competitors.

1435

Band 3

Benesch, Friedlander, Coplan & Aronoff LLP

The Firm: Traditionally one of the strongest real estate practices in Ohio, this team is reputed to be one of the best in the retail development field. As a number of commentators remarked, the firm is "*more entrepreneurial than institutional.*" Attorneys counsel on development agreements, joint ventures, limited liability companies and partnerships, real estate tax controversies, sale and leasebacks, zoning and land use. Any crossover with environmental law is seamless, with expert attorneys providing both regulatory advice and enforcement defense in such instances.

The Lawyers: The unostentatious general real estate practitioner **Howard Steindler** makes quite an impact with his work on mixed-use, residential and retail developments. He has also been spotted on a number of significant casino projects over the past year. Among the "*top-quality*" people working alongside Steindler is the inimitable **Norman Gutmacher**. Known to be a "*tough negotiator,*" Gutmacher is praised across the board for his technical know-how; he also commits a commendable amount of time to training his colleagues and grooming the next generation of real estate stars.

The Clients: The firm acts for House of Blues, Frisch's and numerous other restaurant and commercial franchises as well as many developers.

Calfee, Halter & Griswold LLP

See firm details p.1451

The Firm: One of the largest in Ohio, this firm's real estate practice provides companies and individuals with a full range of legal representation and counsel. Clients include developers and investors not only in the conventional fields of purchases, sales, loans and leases but also in investment syndicates and complex multisite, mixed-use and multistate projects. The firm also distinguishes itself in municipal bonds and securities.

The Lawyers: Clients hold newcomer to the tables **Bill Phillips** (see p.1446) in very high esteem. Formerly a partner at Kahn Kleinman, Phillips represents a significant number of Northeast Ohio and national shopping center developers. Having also represented national and regional chain tenants, he is fully conversant in all issues relating to retail projects and major anchor tenants.

The Clients: The Richard E. Jacobs Group is among the diverse group of developers, lenders, investors and major corporations that use the firm.

Frost Brown Todd LLC

See firm details p.849

The Firm: The "*cost-effective*" team at this firm is known for its great communication skills and has clout on the Cincinnati real estate scene. It boasts evident strengths in taxation, synthetic leasing and retail development for a broad client base. The past year has brought developments and transactions relating to retail centers, strip malls, office parks, mixed-use projects and golf courses.

The Lawyers: **John Cadwallader**'s (see p.1438) commercial real estate practice includes the representation of a number of public companies operating regionally and nationally. Noted for his expertise at structuring and negotiations at both entity and asset level, Cadwallader handles everything from development deals to financing. He has recently been involved in the redevelopment refinancing and renovation of a shopping complex in Athens, Ohio. Out-of-state clients bring in some of the big-ticket work on which Cadwallader has made his mark; he has an ongoing relationship, for example, with Glimcher Realty Trust. His latest refinancing deal for this client involved a $150 million regional mall development.

The Clients: AK Steel; Anchor Properties; Bunnell Hill Development; Catholic Healthcare Partners; Convergys; Glimcher Realty Trust; Bankers Guarantee Title & Trust and US National Bank Association.

Schottenstein, Zox & Dunn

See firm details p.1456

The Firm: At this firm, one of the fastest growing in Central Ohio, the real estate group certainly keeps pace with other departments. The group provides a full service to its clients on everything from residential development to financing, leasing and commercial projects. A growing cache of practitioners is dedicated to the property market, allowing the firm to make significant inroads with local clients. However, the client base includes some major retail interests, with the group taking charge of all the real estate concerns of a fast-growing national shoe retailer, for which it has negotiated leases of 40 new stores in the past year alone.

The Lawyers: The chair of the real estate practice is the "*exceedingly effective*" **Randy Arndt** (see p.1437). He represents national, regional and local landlords and tenants, developers, buyers, sellers and others in commercial real estate, practicing extensively in retail and shopping center leasing. Arndt earns particular accolades for his supportive and responsive style of working; said one client, "*He is collaborative and good at helping me find my feet, like a mentor.*"

The Clients: Nationwide Realty Investors and Schottenstein Stores are two of the best-known clients of the firm.

Ulmer & Berne LLP

The Firm: A newcomer to the table this year, Ulmer & Berne is a regional player that splits its real estate practice among its three offices in Cleveland, Columbus and Cincinnati. The firm's client base is as much national as it is regional and includes some of the most influential retail sector developers and lenders in the country. A "*sophisticated*" team regularly punches above its weight and operates in a multidisciplinary manner by including tax, regulatory and compliance, environmental and M&A experts.

The Lawyers: "*Top of his game*" is how the market describes the head of the real estate team, **Bill Gagliano**. He works for many national clients, among them Ryan Homes, but is primarily known for his representation of such familiar names as Pizza Hut, KFC and Taco Bell in their dealings with franchisees. Gagliano is supported by the "*truly fantastic*" **Craig Miller**, who excels in zoning and land use matters. Miller's other hot area is private and public funding, and he has worked with a significant number of municipalities on the acquisition of land for public use.

The Clients: Easton Town Center; Columbus International Air Center; DSW Shoe Warehouse; Taco Bell; Pizza Hut and NVR.

Other Notable Practitioners

A highly respected practitioner in the field, **Kenton Kuehnle** has left Roetzel & Andress to form his own real estate and bankruptcy boutique with two former heads of department from Thompson Hine. The firm Allen Kuehnle & Stovall LLP specializes in the representation of regional developers and a large proportion of its work involves matters related to condominiums. The "*academic*" Kuehnle remains a distinguished name in the field.

Leaders in Ohio

ADAMO, Ken
Jones Day, Cleveland 216 586 7120
kradamo@jonesday.com
Recommended in Intellectual Property
Practice Areas: Practices intellectual property law. He has extensive lead trial counsel experience in jury and nonjury matters before state and federal courts and before the International Trade Commission, as well as ex parte and inter partes experience in the US Patent and Trademark Office and with non-US patent and trademark authorities. He also has extensive appellate experience before the US Court of Appeals for the Federal Circuit, having appeared in 30 appeals, most of which he has argued himself.
Publications: Has written and lectured extensively on intellectual property law, for US and non-US publications and organizations.

ADAMS, Albert
Baker & Hostetler LLP, Cleveland 216 621 0200
Recommended in Corporate/M&A

ADAMS, Deborah
Frost Brown Todd LLC, Cincinnati 513 651 6705
dadams@fbtlaw.com
Recommended in Employment
Practice Areas: Represents employers in areas of employment discrimination and wrongful discharge through litigation defense, as well as advice and counsel. Experienced in class and collective action defense. Developed national recognition as trainer on human-resources topics.
Prof. Memberships: Admitted to practice in Ohio (1982) and Kentucky (1983). Member of Cincinnati and Ohio Bar Associations and Ohio Management Lawyers Association.
Career: Joined Frost & Jacobs, 1982; Partner 1989.
Publications: Sexual Harassment Myths and Realities - A Kentucky Employer's Guide, 'Kentucky Labor Letter.'
Personal: Born 17 May 1955. JD, Harvard Law School (1982); MA, Harvard University (1979); BA, University of Cincinnati (1977).

ALBAINY-JENEI, Stephen R
Frost Brown Todd LLC, Cincinnati 513 651 6839
salbainyjenei@fbtlaw.com
Recommended in Intellectual Property
Practice Areas: Intellectual property law, particularly patent counseling and prosecution, licensing, infringement and validity opinions, portfolio management. As a Member of Frost Brown Todd LLC, works closely with biotechnology and emerging growth companies, as well as universities and research institutions, to develop successful business models, strategic intellectual property protection and complex technology

transactions.
Career: Prior to joining Frost Brown Todd in 2000, was Assistant General Counsel for the University of Cincinnati, ultimately serving as the Acting Director of Intellectual Property. (1995-2000).
Personal: Born 7 November 1964; JD, University of Cincinnati, 1995; MS, University of Dayton, 1988.

ALDRICH, Thomas A
Thompson Hine LLP, Cleveland 216 566 5500
Recommended in Corporate/M&A
Career: Tom is a Partner in Thompson Hine's Corporate Transactions & Securities Practice Group and was practice group leader from 1999 to 2004. He focuses on domestic and international mergers and acquisitions and joint ventures, securities law compliance and reporting (including Sarbanes-Oxley issues) and corporate governance. Education: Harvard Law School, JD, 1982, cum laude. The Ohio State University, 1978-79, University Fellow, Graduate School. Ohio University, AB, 1978, summa cum laude, Phi Beta Kappa.

ANDERSON, Sandra J
Vorys, Sater, Seymour and Pease LLP, Columbus 614 464 6405
sjanderson@vssp.com
Recommended in Litigation
Practice Areas: Partner focusing on General Litigation Practice which includes employment, commercial, business and product liability law.
Prof. Memberships: Fellow, American College of Trial Lawyers; Columbus, Ohio State, and American Bar Associations; Columbus Bar Foundation; Advisory Committee on Local Rules for the U.S. District Court for the Southern District of Ohio; Board of Commissioners on Grievances and Discipline for the Supreme Court of Ohio.
Career: Admitted Ohio Bar (1976).
Personal: Northwestern University School of Law, JD, magna cum laude, Order of the Coif, 1976; Ohio University, BSC; summa cum laude, 1973.

APPELBAUM, Jeffrey
Thompson Hine LLP, Cleveland 216 566 5500
jeff.Appelbaum@ThompsonHine.com
Recommended in Construction
Career: For over 25 years, Jeff has served the construction industry as trial and transactional attorney, project counsel, project management consultant, mediator and partnering facilitator. Jeff provides distinguished service to public and private owners, design professionals, construction managers and contractors on important projects throughout the United States and Canada. He has served as lead trial lawyer for dozens of cases involving hundreds of millions of dollars of disputed claims. He has served as

project counsel for over 50 projects involving billions of dollars of construction. Jeff has facilitated over 150 partnering sessions and has conducted dozens of complex construction mediations.

ARNDT, Randall
Schottenstein, Zox & Dunn, Columbus 614 462 2235
rarndt@szd.com
Recommended in Real Estate
Practice Areas: Mr Arndt chairs the firm's Real Estate Practice. He has broad experience in real property law, including residential, commercial, retail, mixed-use and warehouse properties. He represents national, regional and local landlords, tenants, developers, buyers, sellers and others in the commercial real estate arena in the acquisition and development of undeveloped and developed land, sales, leasing, real estate title matters, including the overlay of easements, conditions, restrictions and various frameworks for mixed-use, shopping center and real estate developments. He practices extensively in the retail and shopping center leasing and development areas.

ARONOFF, James
Thompson Hine LLP, Cleveland 216 566 5500
Recommended in Real Estate
Career: Jim is a Partner in the firm's Real Estate Group and chairs the Real Estate Capital Markets Team. He represents real estate investment trusts (REIT's) both transactionally, and in evaluating internal structures to maximize shareholder value. His practice also focuses on structuring partnerships, joint ventures, LLC's and other pass-through entities; commercial real estate financing, including representation of REMIC's and others in securitized offerings; shopping center development and construction; as well as significant acquisitions and divestitures of resort and other lodging properties. A frequent lecturer, Jim is also a member of the Board of Governors of Ohio's Real Property Bar.

ASHMUS, Keith
Frantz Ward LLP, Cleveland 216 515 1660
Recommended in Employment

AZOFF, Elliot
Baker & Hostetler LLP, Cleveland 216 621 0200
Recommended in Employment

BAKER, David
Bricker & Eckler LLP, Columbus 614 227 2300
Recommended in Real Estate

BARNARD, Thomas
Ulmer & Berne LLP, Cleveland 216 621 8400
Recommended in Employment

BARNES, Geoffrey
Squire, Sanders & Dempsey L.L.P., Cleveland 216 479 8500
Recommended in Environment

BARRAGATE, Brett
Jones Day, Cleveland 216 586 7205
bpbarragate@jonesday.com
Recommended in Banking & Finance
Practice Areas: His practice focuses on all aspects of commercial financing, including the representation of banks and other financial institutions and public and private companies in connection with senior and subordinated debt facilities. Has extensive experience with syndicated, multibank senior credit facilities; asset-based and structured finance facilities; asset securitizations; acquisition financing; letter of credit facilities; foreign currency facilities; and real estate financing. He also focuses on the representation of creditors and debtors in loan restructurings, workouts, and Chapter 11 proceedings.
Prof. Memberships: Ohio State Bar Association; Cleveland Bar Association.

BASH, Brian
Baker & Hostetler LLP, Cleveland 216 621 0200
Recommended in Bankruptcy

BAUMGARTNER, Bruce
Baker & Hostetler LLP, Cleveland 216 621 0200
Recommended in Intellectual Property

BEDREE, Melvin
Vorys, Sater, Seymour and Pease, Cincinnati 513 723 4023
mabedree@vssp.com
Recommended in Banking & Finance
Practice Areas: Partner who practices in the area of commercial finance, including asset based financing. Represented national and regional asset based and structured finance lenders. Practice includes multi-borrower, multijurisdiction transactions, acquisition financing, asset sales out of bankruptcy, multi-lender (club) deals, capital expenditure financing, negotiating subordinated debt and preferred stock arrangements with institutional providers of mezzanine capital.
Prof. Memberships: Ohio State and American Bar Associations.
Career: Admitted to Ohio Bar, 1984; and US District Court, Southern District of Ohio, 1984.
Personal: University of Cincinnati, JD, 1984; Depauw University, BA, magna cum laude, 1981.

BLAIR, Mitchell G
Calfee, Halter & Griswold LLP, Cleveland 216 622 8361
mblair@calfee.com
Recommended in Litigation
Practice Areas: Business, corporate and commercial litigation; securities litigation; intellectual property litigation;

insurance coverage litigation; probate litigation; alternative dispute; resolution proceedings.

Prof. Memberships: American, Ohio State and Cleveland Bar Associations.

Career: Co-Chair of the firm's Litigation Group, heads the Securities Litigation Practice, and is a member of the Executive Committee. He litigates and tries complex disputes, with special emphasis on securities litigation and enforcement, corporate investigations and probate court litigation.

Personal: Marshall-Wythe School of Law of the College of William and Mary, JD, 1982; Union College, BA, magna cum laude, 1979.

BLATTNER, J Wray
Thompson Hine LLP, Dayton
937 443 6539
Wray.Blattner@ThompsonHine.com
Recommended in Environment

Career: Wray Blattner is a Partner in Thompson Hine's Environmental Practice Group. His practice includes defense of federal, state and local government enforcement actions and private party environmental litigation, environmental permitting, site remediations, regulatory compliance counseling and environmental management systems, environmental audits, commenting on rulemakings, and counsel in connection with business and real estate acquisitions and sales. Wray received his undergraduate degree from Denison University and his law degree from Georgetown University Law Center.

BOISE, April V
Thompson Hine LLP, Cleveland
216 566 5785
April.Boise@ThompsonHine.com
Recommended in Corporate/M&A

Career: April is a Partner in Thompson Hine's Corporate Transactions & Securities Practice Group. She focuses her practice on corporate governance including Sarbanes-Oxley; mergers, acquisitions and joint ventures; securities offerings for public and private companies; and private equity matters including the formation of venture and buyout funds and fund of funds. Education: The University of Chicago Law School, JD, 1994. University of Michigan, BBA, 1990, magna cum laude.

BRINKMAN, David
Wood, Herron & Evans, LLP, Cincinnati
513 241 2324
Recommended in Intellectual Property

BRUBAKER, Robert
Porter Wright Morris & Arthur LLP, Columbus 614 227 2033
rbrubaker@porterwright.com
Recommended in Environment

Practice Areas: Represents manufacturers, utilities, small businesses, trade associations, and public sector clients with regard to the Clean Air Act and other environmental matters. Practice

includes permitting (especially Title V and New Source Review), administrative rulemaking and appellate and trial court litigation.

Prof. Memberships: ABA Standing Committee on Environmental Law; Environmental Committee of Public Utility, Communications, and Transportation Section; National Coal Council.

Career: Admitted in Ohio; US District Court, Southern District of Ohio; US Court of Appeals, District of Columbia, Third, Fourth, Sixth, Seventh Circuits; US Supreme Court.

Personal: JD, University of Chicago, 1972; BA, Earlham College, 1969.

BUCHENROTH, Stephen
Vorys, Sater, Seymour and Pease LLP, Columbus 614 464 6366
srbuchenroth@vssp.com
Recommended in Real Estate

Practice Areas: Real estate law; franchising.

Prof. Memberships: Columbus (Member, Board of Governors, 1986-94; President, 1992-93), Ohio State (Member: Council of Delegates, 1986-88, 1991-; Real Property Section, Board of Governors, 1990; Chair, 2003-05) and American (Member: Sections on: Antitrust Law; Business Law, Chairman, Franchising Subcommittee of Small Business Committee, 1991-92; Real Property, Probate and Trust Law; Forum Committee on Franchising) Bar Associations; American College of Real Estate Lawyers; Ohio Supreme Court Commission on Continuing Legal Education, 1994-2000, Chairman, 2000.

Career: Admitted to Ohio Bar (1974).

Personal: University of Chicago, JD, 1974; Wittenberg University, AB, cum laude, 1970.

BUCK, Frank W
Duvin, Cahn & Hutton, Cleveland
216 696 7600
fbuck@duvin.com
Recommended in Employment

Practice Areas: Practice includes labor relations for both private and public sector clients. For over 25 years, he has served as the chief negotiator for employers in their negotiations with unions. He has handled negotiations for for numerous industries including food, steel, aluminum, appliances, heavy manufacturing, wholesale distribution and public sector. He provides day-to-day counsel on problems arising under collective bargaining agreements, and matters relating to employment discrimination, wrongful termination, business restructuring, and sales and acquisitions. He regularly represents clients before the National Labor Relations Board and other state and federal agencies, and appears before all levels of federal and state courts on a variety of matters.

Prof. Memberships: Member of the Cleveland and American Bar Associations.

Career: Partner since 1987.

Publications: He has lectured on various labor law topics including effective management and discipline, wage and hour laws, employment terminations, and successorship issues.

Personal: University of Michigan (JD, 1979; BA, with distinction, 1976). Serves on the Board of Trustees of the Achievement Centers for Children. Member, 1998 Class of Leadership Cleveland.

BUCKLEY, Daniel J
Vorys, Sater, Seymour and Pease, Cincinnati 513 723 4002
djbuckley@vssp.com
Recommended in Litigation

Practice Areas: Partner in Litigation Group with extensive experience in business and healthcare litigation, representing financial institutions, venture capital firms, accounting firms, software companies, inside and outside directors, pharmaceutical companies and hospitals in complex litigation.

Prof. Memberships: American, Ohio State and Cincinnati Bar Associations.

Career: Admitted to Ohio Bar (1974), US Federal Court (1974), US Supreme Court (1982).

Personal: Fellow, American College of Trial Lawyers. Adjunct Professor, University of Cincinnati College of Law. Listed in legal publication under business litigation and personal injury. Ohio Wesleyan University, BA, Pi Sigma Alpha, 1971. University of Cincinnati College of Law, JD, 1974.

BUMPASS, T Merritt
Frantz Ward LLP, Cleveland
216 515 1660
Recommended in Employment

BURKE, James
Keating, Muething & Klekamp, PLL, Cincinnati
513 579 6400
Recommended in Litigation

BURKE, Kim
Taft, Stettinius & Hollister LLP, Cincinnati 513 381 2838
Recommended in Environment

CADWALLADER, John I
Frost Brown Todd LLC, Columbus
614 464 1211
jcadwallader@fbtlaw.com
Recommended in Real Estate

Practice Areas: Partner in Retail Development Group serving as lead counsel for developers of shopping centers, and industrial, hotel and commercial properties.

Prof. Memberships: American College of Real Estate Lawyers; International Council of Shopping Centers; American, Ohio State (Member, Real Property Section Board of Governors; Chair, Legislative Review Committee) and Columbus Bar Associations.

Career: Admitted in Ohio and Florida.

Publications: Frequent speaker and author on real estate development and

leasing topics.

Personal: JD, The Ohio State University, 1978; MA, University of Chicago, 1975 (Rockefeller Foundation Fellow); BA, Denison University, 1974 (cum laude).

CARLSON, James
Thompson Hine LLP, Cleveland
216 566 5556
Jim.Carlson@ThompsonHine.com
Recommended in Corporate/M&A

Career: Jim is a Partner in Thompson Hine's Corporate Transactions & Securities Practice Group. He focuses his practice on takeover preparedness programs, including shareholder rights plans, and takeover defense; acquisitions and dispositions, including high tech transactions; mergers, including mergers of publicly held companies; leveraged recaps and buyouts; representation of special Board committees; SEC registration statements, proxy statements, other filings, and compliance; joint ventures, including e-commerce alliances; and financing, including senior, mezzanine, and junior lending and venture capital. Personal: Harvard Law School, JD, 1975. Oberlin College, BA, 1969, magna cum laude, Phi Beta Kappa.

CARPENTER, Michael
Carpenter & Lipps LLP, Columbus
614 365 4100
Recommended in Litigation

CARSON, Van
Squire, Sanders & Dempsey L.L.P., Cleveland
216 479 8500
Recommended in Environment

CASCARILLA, Ralph
Walter & Haverfield LLP, Cleveland
216 781 1212
Recommended in Environment, Litigation

CASPER Jr, Paul W
Frost Brown Todd LLC, Cincinnati
513 651 6490
pcasper@fbtlaw.com
Recommended in Environment

Practice Areas: Chair, Environmental Department; 25 years experience in virtually all areas of environmental law, with emphasis on defense of enforcement actions brought by the United States, its state brethren and/or citizens groups such as the Sierra Club, the NRDC, and Ohio Citizen Action; longstanding representation of the steel, chemical, paper, foundry and metal finishing industries.

Publications: Co-author: 'The Art & Science of Environmental Law', Aspatore Books (2004); featured speaker, environmental law, Sky Radio (2004).

Personal: Chemical Engineer, US Steel (1968); US Army 18th Airborne Corp. (1969-72); MS Biology (emphasis in Environmental Physiology); designated Ohio Super Lawyer.

CAVALIERI, Nick
Bailey Cavalieri, Columbus
614 221 3155
Recommended in Bankruptcy

CICARELLA, Thomas
Calfee, Halter & Griswold LLP,
Cleveland 216 622 8378
tcicarella@calfee.com
Recommended in Banking & Finance
Practice Areas: Commercial business
and finance; bankruptcy and creditors'
rights.
Prof. Memberships: American and
Ohio State Bar Associations.
Career: Co-Chair of the firm's Commercial Business and Finance Group
and is a member of the Executive and
Management Committees. His over 30
years of experience includes counseling
clients through the complexities of
leveraged buyouts, and domestic and
international financing.
Personal: Indiana University, JD, magna
cum laude, 1974; Indiana University,
BA, 1971.

COGAN, J Kevin
Jones Day, Columbus
614 281 3825
jcogan@jonesday.com
Recommended in Litigation
Practice Areas: Has extensive trial and
jury trial experience in complex litigation, from corporate control contests
and securities fraud, to class actions,
insurance coverage disputes and water
rights. Co-trial counsel in Danaher Corporation v Acme Cleveland and United
Dominion Industries v Commercial
Intertech, Inc wherein Jones Day successfully defended the targets of
attempted hostile takeovers. Successfully
defended MPW Industrial Services
Group in a securities class action filed in
Ohio State Court. Lead trial counsel in a
water rights case challenging the City of
Akron's use and management of the
Cuyahoga River.

CONRAD, David
Bricker & Eckler LLP, Columbus
614 227 2300
Recommended in Real Estate

COYNE, Thomas
Thompson Hine LLP, Cleveland
216 566 5500
Thomas.Coyne@ThompsonHine.com
Recommended in Real Estate
Career: Tom is the Group Leader of the
firm's 30 member, national Real Estate
Practice Group. Tom concentrates on
commercial development, planning and
strategy on properties throughout the
United States and foreign countries.
Principal types of transactions include:
corporate and international real estate;
shopping centers and mixed use; air
rights and commercial condominiums;
complex easement agreements; acquisitions, development, leasing and financing; government incentives and tax
abatement programs; office, hotel and
industrial; arena, stadium and other special use; brownfields and conservation;
asset management; real estate entity formation; real estate tax valuation contests; and a variety of commercial real
estate disputes.

CRAIG, L Clifford
Taft, Stettinius & Hollister LLP,
Cincinnati 513 381 2838
Recommended in Litigation

CUPPS, David
Vorys, Sater, Seymour and Pease LLP,
Columbus 614 464 6318
dscupps@vssp.com
Recommended in Litigation
Practice Areas: Partner in the Litiga-
tion Group. Practices in the areas of
complex and multi-district litigation;
antitrust, intellectual property, securities
litigation, and professional malpractice
litigation.
Prof. Memberships: American, Colum-
bus, District of Columbia, and Ohio
State Bar Associations.
Career: Admitted to New York Bar
(1966), Ohio Bar (1972), District of
Columbia Bar (1979), US Supreme
Court (1971).
Personal: Harvard College, AB, 1958.
The Ohio State University, JD, summa
cum laude, 1965. Order of the Coif.
Mershon Fellowship, 1964-65. Editor,
Ohio State Law Journal, 1964-65; Fel-
low, American College of Trial Lawyers
and Regent, 1997-2001.

CURRIE, Michael
Thompson Hine LLP, Columbus
614 469 3200
Mike.Currie@ThompsonHine.com
Recommended in Construction
Career: A Partner in the Construction
Practice Group, focusing on public and
private construction law, real estate law,
complex construction and commercial
litigation. His primary practice is the
representation of contractors and owners in all aspects of construction, including project structure, finance, project
delivery and claims litigation. Mike is
involved in the negotiation of numerous
construction projects, including
Olympic and stadium construction, corporate headquarters and power/indus-
trial ventures. He litigates complex
claims ranging to 40 million dollars on
industrial, power, heavy and highway
projects. He has extensive trial and
appellate experience, including five
appearances before the Ohio and Indiana Supreme Courts.

CYPHERT, Michael
Walter & Haverfield LLP, Cleveland
216 781 1212
Recommended in Environment

DEMARCO, Daniel
Hahn Loeser & Parks LLP, Cleveland
216 621 0150
Recommended in Bankruptcy

DIMLING, Robert A
Frost Brown Todd LLC, Cincinnati
513 651 6821
rdimling@fbtlaw.com
Recommended in Employment
Practice Areas: OSHA and employ-
ment discrimination.
Prof. Memberships: Admitted to practice
in Ohio (1966). Member of Ohio State
Bar Association, Section on Labor and
Employment Law, and the Cincinnati Bar
Association, Labor Law Committee.
Career: Joined Frost & Jacobs, 1966;
became Partner, 1975. Co-Chair Labor
and Employment Department, Frost
Brown Todd, LLC.
Publications: Author, Asbestos and the
Insurer as Lender, Employer and Prop-
erty Owner, 'Tax & Insurance Law Jour-
nal', Fall 1988.
Personal: Born 14 August 1941. JD,
University of Michigan, 1966; BA, Bowl-
ing Green State University, 1963.

DORAN, Scott
Vorys, Sater, Seymour and Pease LLP,
Columbus 614 464 8248
smdoran@vssp.com
Recommended in Environment
Practice Areas: Partner and Chairman
of Environmental Law Group. Focuses
on Superfund, RCRA, toxic tort, and
variety of environmental issues raised by
industrial, commercial, and residential
real estate developments. Authority on
wetland law and regulation; regularly
appears before the Army Corps of Engineers, US and Ohio EPA on permit issues
and appeals. Participated in formation of
the Ohio Wetlands Foundation.
Prof. Memberships: Columbus and
Ohio State Bar Associations.
Career: Admitted to Ohio (1986), US
District Court, Southern District of
Ohio (1986), US Federal Court (1986).
Personal: University of Cincinnati, JD,
1986. Miami University, BA, 1979;
Miami University, MS, 1983.

DREITLER, Joseph
Jones Day, Columbus 614 281 3902
jrdreitler@jonesday.com
Recommended in Intellectual Property
Practice Areas: Extensive experience in
global trademark clearance, brand
development, prosecution and portfolio
management, advertising review, and
client counseling. Practice includes the
trademark, copyright, and domain
name aspects of global business transactions; also trademark, trade dress, unfair
competition, copyright, and domain
name litigation in the courts and Trademark Trial and Appeal Board. Recent
speaking engagements include the International Trademark Association (INTA)
2004 meeting on ethics in trademark
practice and 2005 on Fair Use; and Practicing Law Institute seminars on non-
traditional trademarks, 2004 and 2005.
Prof. Memberships: Chair, Ohio State
Bar Association Intellectual Property
Section. Served on the board of INTA.

DUVIN, Robert P
Duvin, Cahn & Hutton, Cleveland
216 696 7600
rduvin@duvinlaw.com
Recommended in Employment
Practice Areas: Represents national
corporations in the retail, food, musical
arts, healthcare, sports, industrial, and
financial industries. He also represents
many large public sector clients. He provides day-to-day advice and counsel on
questions concerning contract interpretation and problems arising from collective baegaining agreements, and matters
relating to employment discrimination,
wrongful termination, and business
restructuring. As a chief negotiator, he
has successfully produced contracts
which have included company saving
concessions. Represents clients in commercial and high-stakes litigation matters. He has appeared before all levels of
federal and state courts.
Prof. Memberships: Member of the
Ohio State Bar and Cleveland Bar Asso-
ciaitons.
Career: Founded the firm in 1972.
Publications: Frequent lecturer on
labor relations.
Personal: Columbia University (LLM,
with high honors, 1964); Indiana University (JD, with honors, 1961; BA, with
honors, 1958). He has been profiled
numerous times by national media
including The American Lawyer. Firm
has been selected as one of the top six
management labor law firms in the USA
by The American Lawyer.

EBLING, Louis K
Greenebaum Doll & McDonald PLLC,
Cincinnati 513 455 7644
lke@gdm.com
Recommended in Intellectual Property
Practice Areas: US and multinational
intellectual property transactions, trade-
mark and related indicia clearance,
counseling, prosecution and enforce-
ment; large trademark portfolio logistics
and management.
Prof. Memberships: International
Trademark Association (INTA), Chair,
US Roundtable Projects Team; Ameri-
can Bar Association.
Career: Named an Ohio 'Super Lawyers'
by 'Law & Politics' magazine and
Cincinnati magazine January 2005.
Publications: 'Dilution is Remedy for
Internet Mark Misuse', National Law
Journal, May, 1998; 'Buy 4, Get 11 Free',
June, 1996 Corporate Counsel's Interna-
tional Adviser. Recent Speeches: 'Over-
coming 2(d) and 2(e) Refusals', 2003
INTA Trademark Administrator's Con-
ference; 'Protecting International Prop-
erty Overseas', 2003 Annual Kentucky
International Trade Conference; June
2004 Forbes Radio 'World Business
Monitor' interview on American Air-
lines; 2004 INTA Famous and Well-
Known Marks Forum in Brussels.

EFTIMOFF, Katerina M
Porter Wright Morris & Arthur LLP,
Columbus 614 227 2035
keftimoff@porterwright.com
Recommended in Environment
Practice Areas: Practices environmental law, particularly Clean Air Act permitting and enforcement under Title V, major, and minor New Source Review programs. Experienced with regulation under Emergency Planning and Community Right to Know Act (EPCRA). Chairs Air Subcommittee of Environmental Litigation Committee of ABA Section of Litigation and is assistant editor of the Litigation Section's 'Litigation News' magazine. Appointed to ABA Standing Committee on Environmental Law.
Career: Admitted in Ohio; US Court of Appeals, Sixth Circuit; and US District Court, Southern District of Ohio.
Personal: JD (summa cum laude), Capital University, 1994; BS (Chemical Engineering), The Ohio State University, 1989.

FAGAN, Christopher
Fay Sharpe Fagan Minnich & McKee LLP, Cleveland 216 861 5582
cfagan@faysharpe.com
Recommended in Intellectual Property
Practice Areas: Patent, trademark and copyright litigation.
Prof. Memberships: Cleveland and Ohio Bar Associations. Cleveland and American Intellectual Property Law Associations.
Career: University of Notre Dame, BSME, 1959. Lieutenant US Navy 1959-63. Georgetown University, JD, 1965. Examiner, USPTO, 1963-65. Patent Attorney, Eaton Corporation, 1965-67. Associate, Partner & Of Counsel, Fay Sharpe, 1967-present.
Publications: 'Proprietory aspects of Names & Titles', Cleveland Bar Journal, Volume 47, No. 4.
Personal: Adjunct professor of law, Cleveland-Marshall School of Law.

FAHEY, Richard
Vorys, Sater, Seymour and Pease LLP, Columbus 614 464 5601
rpfahey@vssp.com
Recommended in Environment
Practice Areas: Partner, Environmental Group.
Prof. Memberships: Columbus, Ohio State, New Mexico State and American Bar Associations.
Career: Admitted New Mexico and US District Court, District of New Mexico (1971); US Court of Appeals, Tenth Circuit (1972); Ohio and US District Court, Northern and Southern Districts of Ohio (1973); US Supreme Court (1975).
Personal: Northwestern University, JD, 1971. San Francisco State University, BA, 1966.

FAROLINO, Shane
Roetzel & Andress PA, Akron
330 376 2700
Recommended in Environment

FARUKI, Charles
Faruki Ireland & Cox PLL, Dayton
937 227 3705
cfaruki@ficlaw.com
Recommended in Litigation
Practice Areas: Business litigation; antitrust; class actions.
Prof. Memberships: Fellow, American College of Trial Lawyers; Fellow, American Bar Foundation; Past President, Dayton Bar Association; Past President, Dayton Chapter, Federal Bar Association; member Dayton, Ohio State, Federal, American, & Federal Circuit Bar Associations.
Career: 1974-89, Smith & Schnacke (Partner, 1979-89); Founder and Managing Partner, Faruki Ireland & Cox PLL, 1989-present. One of Top Ten Lawyers in Ohio in SuperLawyers poll of all Ohio attorneys. Selected as both 'Best of the Bar' and repeatedly as one of only three lawyers in Dayton Business Journal's 'Power List: Most Influential People' in Dayton area.
Publications: Numerous publications in law journals and legal press.

FAY, Terrence M
Frost Brown Todd LLC, Columbus
614 559 7213
tfay@fbtlaw.com
Recommended in Environment
Practice Areas: Firm Practice Leader in environmental law and litigation, administrative law and public contract law. Has extensive experience in environmental law, environmental litigation, environmental permitting and compliance counseling, the management of environmental issues in corporate and real estate transactions and public contract law and litigation.
Prof. Memberships: Bar Admissions State of Ohio (1978); US District Court, ND Ohio (1980); US District of Ohio, SD Ohio (1986); US District Court, ND Indiana (1987); US Court of Appeals, Sixth Circuit (1986). Member, American Bar Association (Environment, Energy and Resources section); Ohio State Bar Association (Environmental Law Committee); Columbus Bar Association (Environmental Law Committee).
Career: Frost Brown Todd LLC (2002-present); Benesch Friedlander Coplan & Aronoff LLP (1989-2002); Smith & Schnacke (1988-89); Assistant Attorney General of Ohio (1978-88).
Personal: Born 25 February 1953. JD (cum laude) Ohio State University, 1978; BS (cum laude) Baldwin Wallace College, 1976; BA (cum laude) Baldwin Wallace College 1975.

FEHELEY, Lawrence F
Kegler, Brown, Hill & Ritter, Columbus
614 462 5432
lfeheley@keglerbrown.com
Recommended in Employment
Practice Areas: Labor and employee relations; litigation.
Prof. Memberships: Columbus Bar Association, Member; Franklin University, Legal Aspects of Human Resource Management, adjunct professor; Netcare Corporation, Board of Directors, member; Ohio State Bar Association, Member; American Bar Association, Member; Ohio Management Lawyers Association, member.
Career: Elected as a Fellow of the College of Labor and Employment Lawyers. Recognized in the Best Lawyers in America. Recognized as an Ohio Super Lawyer® by Law and Politics Magazine (only five percent of lawyers in Ohio earn the designation of Super Lawyer). Chosen by his peers as one of 'Columbus' Top Lawyers' by Business First in 2004 and 2005. Among the first attorneys to be certified as a Specialist in Labor and Employment Law by the Ohio State Bar Association. Listed as a life member in the National Registry of Who's Who.

FITCH, Stephen
Chester, Willcox & Saxbe LLP,
Columbus 614 221 4000
Recommended in Litigation

FRANTZ, Michael
Frantz Ward LLP, Cleveland
216 515 1660
Recommended in Employment

FREI, Donald
Wood, Herron & Evans, LLP, Cincinnati
513 241 2324
Recommended in Intellectual Property

FREUND, Neil
Freund, Freeze & Arnold, Dayton
937 222 2424
Recommended in Litigation

FRIEDMAN, Steven
Squire, Sanders & Dempsey L.L.P.,
Cleveland 216 479 8500
Recommended in Construction

FRY, Roger
Rendings, Fry & Dennis, LLP, Cincinnati
513 381 9200
Recommended in Litigation

GAGLIANO, Bill
Ulmer & Berne LLP, Cleveland
216 621 8400
Recommended in Real Estate

GALL, John
Squire, Sanders & Dempsey LLP,
Columbus 614 365 2700
Recommended in Litigation

GANSKE, Lyle
Jones Day, Cleveland
216 586 7264
lgganske@jonesday.com
Recommended in Corporate/M&A

Practice Areas: Chairs Jones Day's global Mergers and Acquisitions Practice. His practice focuses primarily on M&A, takeovers, takeover preparedness, corporate governance, executive compensation, and general corporate counseling. He has extensive experience in transactions involving regulated industries, including telecom and energy. He is a frequent speaker on M&A, takeover preparedness, and corporate governance issues, and has submitted comments to the SEC on various proposed rules.
Publications: Co-authored many articles that have appeared in publications such as 'The Business Lawyer,' 'Director's Monthly,' and the 'New York Law Journal.'

GATES, Martin S
Buchanan Ingersoll PC, Cleveland
216 363 0984
gatesms@bipc.com
Recommended in Banking & Finance
Practice Areas: Focuses his practice on representing lending institutions, publicly and privately held companies and private equity groups in all types of secured and unsecured financing transactions, syndications, venture financings including SBIC financings, mezzanine debt financings, term B financings, asset securitization transactions, commercial transactions, mergers, acquisitions, divestitures, leveraged buyouts, restructurings, debtor-in-possession financings, workouts, multi-currency financings and reorganizations.
Prof. Memberships: Cleveland Bar Association; Ohio State Bar Association; American Bar Association.
Personal: JD University of Pittsburgh, School of Law, 1988; AB Princeton University, 1984.

GAYNOR, Bruce
Kahn Kleinman, Cleveland
216 696 3311
Recommended in Real Estate

GERMAIN, Kenneth
Thompson Hine LLP, Cincinnati
513 352 6527
Ken.Germain@ThompsonHine.com
Recommended in Intellectual Property
Career: Ken is a Partner in the Intellectual Property Practice Group. He focuses his practice on trademark and trade dress counseling, consulting and litigation. Ken is retained as an expert witness on issues relating to trademarks and unfair competition, often working on cases involving some of the largest companies in high stakes, cutting-edge cases. As a consultant, Ken worked with winning counsel on the landmark trademark dilution case, Moseley v. V Secret Catalogue (US Supreme Court, 2003). New York University School of Law, JD, 1969, associate editor, NYU Law Review. Rutgers University, AB, 1966, magna cum laude, Phi Beta Kappa.

GHERLEIN, John
Baker & Hostetler LLP, Cleveland
216 621 0200
Recommended in Corporate/M&A

GOLD, Ronald
Frost Brown Todd LLC, Cincinnati
513 651 6156
rgold@fbtlaw.com
Recommended in Bankruptcy
Practice Areas: Co-Chair of firm's national Financial Restructuring Group. Extensive experience in Chapter 11 restructurings representing corporate debtors, debtor-in-possession lenders, secured lenders, landlords, official committees and purchasers of businesses and business segments.
Prof. Memberships: Admitted to practice in Illinois (1989) and Ohio (1993). Listed in Bankruptcy Section of recent leading leading publication.
Career: Katten Muchin & Zavis (Chicago), 1989; Frost & Jacobs LLP (Cincinnati), 1992, became Partner, 1996; Member Frost Brown Todd LLC, 2000-present.
Personal: Born Erie, Pennsylvania, 1964. The University of Michigan, AB, 1986; University of Pittsburgh School of Law, JD (magna cum laude, Order of the Coif), 1989.

GOLDMAN, Matthew
Baker & Hostetler LLP, Cleveland
216 621 0200
Recommended in Bankruptcy

GOLDSTEIN , Steven J
Frost Brown Todd LLC, Cincinnati
513 651 6131
sgoldstein@fbtlaw.com
Recommended in Intellectual Property
Practice Areas: Intellectual property law, particularly US and international patent counseling, prosecution (pharmaceutical, chemical technologies), licensing, trade secrets, infringement and validity opinions, portfolio management.
Prof. Memberships: Admitted to practice in Ohio (1975); US Patent and Trademark Office (1976). Member ñ American Intellectual Property Law Association, Cincinnati Bar Association.
Career: Chairman, Intellectual Property Department. Joined Frost Brown Todd (Frost & Jacobs) 1994 as a Partner and Department Chair. Prior was Associate General Counsel-Patents, Procter & Gamble (1975-94). Adjunct professor of law, University of Cincinnati (1986-present).
Personal: Born 1 September 1951; JD, Boston University, 1975; SB (Chemistry), Massachusetts Institute of Technology, 1972.

GORE, George
Tucker Ellis & West LLP, Cleveland
216 696 1100
Recommended in Litigation

GRADY, Timothy
Porter Wright Morris & Arthur LLP, Columbus 614 227 2105
tgrady@porterwright.com
Recommended in Banking & Finance
Practice Areas: Represents lenders and corporate borrowers in asset-based lending transactions, leveraged financings, recapitalizations, syndicated lending, acquisition financing, loan workouts and restructuring. Recently, he has led financings in such diverse industries as shoes, boots and outdoor gear, optical equipment, home building, chemicals, information storage, trucking, electric coil, water sports, 'off-price' apparel and footwear, and groceries. He has also led acquisition financings in various areas.
Career: Admitted in Ohio.
Personal: JD (cum laude), University of Illinois, 1979; MA, Northern Arizona University, 1973; BA (magna cum laude), Bradley University, 1972.

GREER, David
Bieser, Greer, & Landis LLP, Dayton
937 223 3277
Recommended in Litigation

GREGORY, Donald
Kegler, Brown, Hill & Ritter, Columbus
614 462 5416
dgregory@keglerbrown.com
Recommended in Construction
Practice Areas: Trial and appellate practice with a concentration in construction law. Representative clients include subcontractors, suppliers, architects, owners, contractors and others in the construction industry.
Prof. Memberships: American Subcontractors Association, general counsel; Ceilings & Interior Systems Construction Association, general counsel; National Ground Water Association, general counsel; American Bar Association, Construction Forum, Member.
Career: Drafted Ohio's first Prompt Payment Act, which became a model for other states. Project counsel on Ohio's largest arena, stadium and construction projects.
Publications: Retainage Reform, American Bar Association Construction Forum, San Francisco, California, presented April 18, 2002; Contract Clauses, Ceilings & Interior Systems Association, Tampa, Florida, presented April 21, 2001; Risk Transfer, American Subcontractors Association, Chicago, Illinois, presented March 13, 2001; Issues in Construction Law, Ohio Supreme Court Judicial College, Columbus, Ohio, presented February 22, 2001; Contract Clauses That Can Kill You, Association of the Wall & Ceilings Industries International, Las Vegas, Nevada, presented May 1, 2000; Covering the Design Waterfront, American Bar Association Construction Forum, San Francisco, California, presented January 27, 2000.
Personal: Juris Doctorate The Ohio State University College of Law, Columbus, Ohio, 1982. Bachelor of Arts, History Miami University, Oxford, Ohio, 1979 Cum laude; Phi Beta Kappa honor society. Summitted mountains in North and South America, including Chimborazo, Cirque of the Towers, Devil's Tower, Gannett Peak, Grand Teton and Rainier.

GROSSER, Theodore
Porter Wright Morris & Arthur LLP, Cincinnati 513 381 4700
Recommended in Corporate/M&A

GROSSMAN, Theodore
Jones Day, Cleveland 216 586 7268
tgrossman@jonesday.com
Recommended in Litigation
Practice Areas: Repeatedly cited as 'one of the nation's top litigators' by 'The National Law Journal,' and other leading publications, he has tried landmark cases and argued appeals in every section of the country. He has broad experience in product liability, commercial, constitutional, and regulatory litigation and has served as lead counsel in cases brought by or against virtually every federal department. His trials have been broadcast on Court TV and covered extensively in the national and international press. He has lectured extensively on cross-examination, deposition techniques, oral advocacy, and trial tactics.
Prof. Memberships: Fellow, American College of Trial Lawyers.

GUINN, Guy
Calfee, Halter & Griswold LLP, Cleveland 216 622 8453
gguinn@calfee.com
Recommended in Banking & Finance
Practice Areas: Commercial business and finance; bankruptcy and creditors' rights; international; real estate.
Prof. Memberships: American and Ohio State Bar Associations; former Chair of American Bar Association Business Law Section's Joint Subcommittee on Domestic and International Business Transactions, and Ohio State Bar Association's Opinion and Loan Documentation Subcommittee.
Career: Co-Chair of the Commercial Business and Finance Group. He handles all forms of commercial and real estate financings and syndications, securitizations, domestic and international commercial business arrangements, capital formation and restructurings.
Personal: University of Michigan Law School, JD, cum laude, 1975; Duke University, BA, summa cum laude, Phi Beta Kappa, 1971.

GUNSETT, Daniel
Baker & Hostetler LLP, Columbus
614 228 1541
Recommended in Environment

GURNEY, Scott
Frost Brown Todd LLC, Cincinnati
513 651 6841
sgurney@fbtlaw.com
Recommended in Construction
Practice Areas: Chairman of firm's Construction Law Group. Represents construction managers, general contractors, trade/specialty contractors, suppliers, sureties, and project owners in contract drafting, bid and contract disputes, mechanics' liens, delay, disruption, and defect claims, and mediation, arbitration, and litigation of construction disputes.
Prof. Memberships: Member ABA Forum on the Construction Industry. Member ABA Committee on Construction Litigation. Past Chairman of Cincinnati Bar Association Construction Law Committee.
Career: Admitted to practice in Ohio (1986). Elected Member of Frost & Jacobs (predecessor firm) in 1997.
Personal: Born 28 April 1961. JD Indiana University (Bloomington) 1986; BA Indiana University (Bloomington) 1983.

GUTMACHER, Norman
Benesch, Friedlander, Coplan & Aronoff LLP, Cleveland 216 363 4500
Recommended in Real Estate

HAGGERTY, John
Ulmer & Berne LLP, Cleveland
216 621 8400
Recommended in Litigation

HARDY, Michael
Thompson Hine LLP, Cleveland
216 566 5500
Mike.Hardy@ThompsonHine.com
Recommended in Environment
Career: Mike Hardy is a Partner in Thompson Hine's Environmental Practice Group. His focus on environmental law began over 30 years ago. While his primary work lies in environmental litigation, he also works extensively with clients in the development of business and strategic solutions to environmental problems arising from business transactions.
Personal: Received a JD (cum laude) from the University of Michigan, an AB (magna cum laude) from John Carroll University.

HASTINGS, Susan
Squire, Sanders & Dempsey L.L.P., Cleveland 216 479 8500
Recommended in Employment

HAUGHEY, Stephen N
Frost Brown Todd LLC, Cincinnati
513 651 6127
shaughey@fbtlaw.com
Recommended in Environment
Practice Areas: Member Environmental Department. Emphasis in public and private enforcement defense litigation with particular emphasis in wastewater enforcement, counseling, criminal and civil defense, and appellate practice.
Prof. Memberships: Ohio (1984), Northern (1999) and Southern (1984) Ohio Federal District Courts, and Federal Sixth Circuit (1994). Member Ohio and Cincinnati Bar Associations and Environmental Law Committees, Water Environment Federation, and Ohio

Water Environment Association.
Career: Member of Frost Brown Todd
since 1992.
Publications: Numerous articles and
presentations on Clean Water Act issues
and Superfund defense.
Personal: Born 8 April 1955, BS Wright
State University (1978), JD University of
Dayton (1984).

HAWKINS, Michael
Dinsmore & Shohl LLP, Cincinnati
513 977 8200
Recommended in Employment

HAYES, William
Vorys, Sater, Seymour and Pease,
Cincinnati 513 723 4024
wdhayes@vssp.com
Recommended in Environment
Practice Areas: Partner, Environmen-
tal Group with focus on air quality
issues.
Prof. Memberships: Cincinnati (Chair,
Environmental Committee) and Ohio
State (Member, Environmental Com-
mittee) Bar Associations; Air and Waste
Management Association; Cincinnati
Chamber of Commerce (Member, Air
Quality Committee); Ohio Small Busi-
ness Clean Air Act Stationary Source
Compliance Advisory Panel (appointed
Chair); Southwest Ohio Air Quality
Advisory Committee; Ohio EPA Permit
Processing Efficiency Committee (Co-
Chair); Ohio EPA Advisory Committee.
Career: Admitted to Ohio and US Dis-
trict Court, Southern District of Ohio
(1986). Managing Attorney, Air and
Water Divisions, Ohio EPA (1986-91).
Personal: Capital University, JD, 1986;
Denison University, BA, 1983.

HAYNAM, Douglas
Shumaker Loop & Kendrick LLP, Toledo
419 241 9000
Recommended in Environment

HEIMAN, David G
Jones Day, Cleveland
216 586 7175
dgheimanm@jonesday.com
Recommended in Bankruptcy
Practice Areas: Coordinator of the
firmwide Business Practice Group and
heads that Group's Business Restructuring and Reorganization Practice. He
represents debtors, financial institutions,
creditors, and other parties in restructuring matters, Chapter 11 cases, and
distressed M&A. He has played a key
role in many of the country's largest
Chapter 11 and business restructuring
matters. Named one of the 'Outstanding
Restructuring Lawyers-2004' in 'Turnarounds & Workouts,' 'America's Top
100' in 'K&A Restructuring Reporter,'
and the bankruptcy section of 'The Best
Lawyers in America.'
Prof. Memberships: Director, American
College of Bankruptcy; American College of Commercial Finance Lawyers;
The American Law Institute; ABA.

HICKEY, Nicole Vickroy
Frost Brown Todd LLC, Cincinnati
513 651 6430
nhickey@fbtlaw.com
Recommended in Intellectual Property
Practice Areas: US and international
intellectual property - trademark, copyright and domain name aspects of glob-
al business transactions, including clearance, brand development, prosecution,
counseling, enforcement, portfolio
management and advertising law.
Prof. Memberships: Admitted in Ohio,
and US District Court, Southern District of Ohio, International Trademark
Association, American Bar Association,
Ohio Bar Association, Cincinnati Bar
Association.
Publications: 'Creatives and the Law' -
Roundtable Discussion on Advertising,
Cincinnati Business Courier; 'Cheaper is
Not Always Better: The Pros and Cons
of the Madrid Protocol', Cincinnati
Business Courier.
Personal: Miami University, BA; cum
laude, 1992, Pi Beta Kappa; Case West-
ern Reserve University, JD, 1995.

HILL, Thomas
Kegler, Brown, Hill & Ritter, Columbus
614 462 5403
thill@keglerbrown.com
Recommended in Litigation
Practice Areas: Trial lawyer with over
30 years experience in complex business
litigation.
Prof. Memberships: Fellow of the American College of Trial Lawyers; American
Bar Association; Columbus Bar Association; Ohio State Bar Association.
Career: Representative cases include:
successful defense of a Fortune 100
company in a $500m fraud claim tried
to a jury in federal court in Texas; representation of a publicly-traded company
in litigation in federal court in Ohio
arising out of a hostile takeover attempt
that produced a $20m settlement for the
client; representation of the American
Cancer Society in litigation arising out
of a $7-million dollar embezzlement of
Cancer Society funds; lead trial counsel
in Donatos Pizza's successful prosecution of trademark infringement claim
involving Donato's 'Edge to Edge' trademark; successful defense of a local university in wrongful discharge litigation
brought by discharged faculty members;
successful defense of a publicly traded
company in federal court litigation
alleging defectively manufactured products; defense of a Catholic Diocese in litigation alleging sexual abuse; successful
defense of a national pension fund in
claims over rights to participate in the
fund. Profiled in leading American publications.
Publications: Federal Civil Procedure
and Evidence During Trial - 6th Circuit
- a two-volume treatise on trial practice
in the federal courts in the Sixth Circuit.
Personal: Juris Doctorate, Cornell University Law School, Ithaca, New York,

1970; Bachelor of Arts, Political Science,
Grinnell College, Grinnell, Iowa, 1967.

HILLER, David P
Millisor & Nobil Co LPA, Columbus
614 221 2234
Recommended in Employment

HIRSCHFELD, Michael
Graydon Head & Ritchey LLP,
Cincinnati 513 629 2806
mhirschfeld@graydon.com
Recommended in Corporate/M&A
Practice Areas: Corporate business
law; mergers and acquisitions; closely
held business law.
Career: Hirschfeld is Chair of the Exec-
utive Committee of Graydon Head &
Ritchey LLP. His practice concentrates
on the representation of entrepreneurial
and closely-held businesses and their
owners and operators. Since 1993,
Hirschfeld has been named one of 'The
Best Lawyers in America' for corporate
law, and in 2002 he received the Hamilton County Community Mental Health
Board's Community Friend of Mental
Health Award. In 2003, the Goering
Center for Family and Privately Owned
Business presented Hirschfeld with a
special service award in recognition of
the many roles he has played in his service to the Center. Under Hirschfeld's
leadership, the firm joined the Center
for Quality of Management in 2003,
took home the Ohio Governor's Excellence in Exporting Award in June and,
according to Corporate Board Member
Magazine, has been named by corporate
directors of publicly traded US corporations as one of Cincinnati's top five law
firms for the past three years in a row.

HOBERG, Timothy
Taft, Stettinius & Hollister LLP,
Cincinnati 513 381 2838
Recommended in Corporate/M&A

HOGAN, Patricia
Keating, Muething & Klekamp, PLL,
Cincinnati 513 579 6400
Recommended in Intellectual Property

HOLMAN, Michael
Bricker & Eckler LLP, Columbus
614 227 2300
Recommended in Construction

HOOKER, David J
Thompson Hine LLP, Cleveland
216 566 5500
David.Hooker@ThompsonHine.com
Recommended in Litigation
Career: David is the Managing Partner
of Thompson Hine LLP. He previously
served as Chair of the Litigation area
where he has practiced since joining the
firm following his law school graduation. David focuses his practice on complex business litigation. He has experience in securities litigation, cases about
corporate and partnership control,
breach of contract actions, and construction disputes. He also has defended
public accountants and consultants in

malpractice claims.
Personal: Received his JD from Stan-
ford Law School (member, 'Stanford
Law Review') and his BS (with highest
honors, Phi Beta Kappa) from Denison
University.

HUFFMAN, Fordham
Jones Day, Columbus
614 281 3934
fehuffman@jonesday.com
Recommended in Litigation
Practice Areas: Partner-in-Charge of
the Columbus office. Practices general
litigation and has extensive experience
in insurance regulation, product liability, and bankruptcy litigation. He has
represented numerous clients as creditors in insurance insolvency proceedings. He served as lead litigation counsel
to the court-appointed trustee for Cardinal Industries, whose $2 billion Chap-
ter 11 case involved complex, first
impression issues of bankruptcy and
partnership law affecting thousands of
investors and secured lenders. He regularly represents clients in commercial
and employment litigation and has
coordinated two nationwide product
liability defenses.
Prof. Memberships: State Bar of Georgia; Ohio State Bar Association; Columbus Bar Association.

HURLEY, Timothy
Taft, Stettinius & Hollister LLP,
Cincinnati 513 381 2838
Recommended in Bankruptcy

HUTCHINSON Jr, Joseph
Brouse McDowell, Cleveland
216 830 6830
jhutchinson@brouse.com
Recommended in Bankruptcy
Practice Areas: Represents debtors,
trustees, asset purchasers and creditors'
committees in significant Chapter 11
cases, as well as companies involved in
complex commercial disputes, litigation,
refinancing, 363 sales and workouts.
Also counsels clients in substantial refi-
nancing transactions, spin offs, mergers
and acquisitions.
Prof. Memberships: ABA, Ohio State
Bar Association, Cleveland and Akron
Bar Associations.
Career: Joined Brouse McDowell as
Partner in 1984; Managing Partner of
Cleveland office.
Personal: The Ohio State School of Law
(JD, 1973); University of Michigan (LSA
with honors, 1971).

INTIHAR, Steve
Bricker & Eckler LLP, Columbus
614 227 2300
Recommended in Real Estate

IRELAND, D Jeffrey
Faruki Ireland & Cox PLL, Dayton
937 227 3710
djireland@ficlaw.com
Recommended in Litigation
Practice Areas: Competitive litigation,
including false advertising, trademarks

and trade secrets; antitrust; class actions and general commercial.

Prof. Memberships: American Bar Association; Ohio State Bar Association (Board of Governors, Antitrust Section); Dayton Bar Association.

Career: 1980-89, Smith & Schnacke (Partner, 1987-89); founding Partner, Faruki Ireland & Cox P.L.L., 1989-present; selected as Ohio Super Lawyer 2004-05 in poll of all Ohio lawyers and 'Best of the Bar' in poll of Dayton lawyers.

Publications: Has lectured and written on all aspects of commercial litigation.

Personal: University of Dayton, College of Law (1980); Denison University (1976).

IRWIN, Kevin
Keating, Muething & Klekamp, PLL, Cincinnati 513 579 6400
Recommended in Bankruptcy

JACKSON, Reginald W
Vorys, Sater, Seymour and Pease LLP, Columbus 614 464 6400
rwjackson@vssp.com
Recommended in Bankruptcy

Practice Areas: Partner in the bankruptcy, workout and restructuring areas with emphasis on representing secured creditors, creditors' committees and debtors in Chapter 11 reorganization proceedings and workouts.

Prof. Memberships: Columbus (former Chair, Bankruptcy Committee), American (Chapter 11 and Executory Contracts Subcommittee, former Chair of Conference of Minority Partners in Corporate/Majority Law Firms), and Ohio State (Member, Board of Governors) Bar Associations, Ohio State Bar Foundation (former President), American Bankruptcy Institute (Member, Board of Trustees, Executive Committee and editor of the 'ABI Journal').

Career: Admitted to Ohio (1980).

Personal: Cornell University, BA, 1977; University of Pennsylvania Law School, JD, 1980.

JAHNKE, Mark
Katz, Teller, Brant & Hild, Cincinnati 513 721 4532
Recommended in Corporate/M&A

JANKE, Ronald R
Jones Day, Cleveland
216 586 7279
rrjanke@jonesday.com
Recommended in Environment

Practice Areas: Has broad experience with the application of state and federal environmental laws to numerous industries, including ferrous and non-ferrous metals, mining and chemical manufacturing. Has represented clients in environmental enforcement actions; advised clients in assessing environmental liabilities in the transfer of real estate; and advised clients regarding remediation or recovery of response costs for contaminated properties. He lectures extensively

on environmental compliance and has been named a leading lawyer in various publications.

Prof. Memberships: He served on advisory committees of the US and Ohio EPA. He is Chairman of the Ohio Water Resources Council Advisory Group.

JORGENSON, Mary
Squire, Sanders & Dempsey L.L.P., Cleveland 216 479 8500
Recommended in Corporate/M&A

KAISER Jr, Gordon
Squire, Sanders & Dempsey L.L.P., Cleveland 216 479 8500
Recommended in Corporate/M&A

KALLAS, Hani R
Vorys, Sater, Seymour and Pease, Cincinnati (513) 723-4615
hrkallas@vssp.com
Recommended in Banking & Finance

Practice Areas: Partner in the Commercial and Real Estate Group that practices in the areas of banking law, commercial law, general business law, and real estate law. Concentrates in the representation of lenders and small businesses, with an emphasis on representing lenders in loan transactions and workouts.

Career: Admitted in Ohio (1994).

Personal: University of Cincinnati College of Law, JD, Order of the Coif, 1994. Miami University, BA, cum laude, 1991.

KAMP, David
White, Getgey & Meyer Co. LPA, Cincinnati 513 241 3685
Recommended in Litigation

KARP, Marvin
Ulmer & Berne LLP, Cleveland 216 621 8400
Recommended in Litigation

KELLY, Christopher
Jones Day, Cleveland
216 586 1238
ckelly@jonesday.com
Recommended in Corporate/M&A

Practice Areas: Chairs the firm's Corporate Finance Practice and is Head of the firm's Sarbanes-Oxley Act Team. His practice is concentrated in the areas of corporate finance, securities, and corporate governance matters. He represents clients ranging from Fortune 500 companies to venture-backed companies in a variety of transactions, including public offerings, Rule 144A offerings, venture capital raisings and regulatory compliance matters. Additionally, he commonly advises on securities matters in connection with many reorganization and acquisition transactions. He also represents financial institutions, investment firms, and many New York-based institutions in a wide range of corporate finance transactions.

KERGER, Richard
Kerger & Kerger, Toledo
419 255 5990
Recommended in Litigation

KESTNER, Steven
Baker & Hostetler LLP, Cleveland
216 621 0200
Recommended in Corporate/M&A

KILBANE, Thomas
Squire, Sanders & Dempsey L.L.P., Cleveland
216 479 8500
Recommended in Litigation

KILLWORTH, Richard
Dinsmore & Shohl LLP, Dayton
937 223 2050
Recommended in Intellectual Property

KING, G Roger
Jones Day, Columbus
614 281 3874
gking@jonesday.com
Recommended in Employment

Practice Areas: Concentrates on employment relations, particularly in representing management in matters arising under the National Labor Relations Act, state and federal equal employment statutes, the Americans with Disabilities Act, and the Family and Medical Leave Act. Also represents employers in employment contract matters, collective bargaining negotiations, grievance and arbitration matters, and labor-related litigation in state and federal trial and appellate courts.

Prof. Memberships: Ohio, District of Columbia Bar Associations, Fellow, The College of Labor and Employment Lawyers, Columbus Bar Foundation, NLRB Region 9 Practice and Procedure Committee member.

Publications: Editor of 'The Developing Labor Law'; contributing editor, 'HR Advisor.'

KOLESAR, Andrew
Thompson Hine LLP, Cincinnati
513 352 6545
Andrew.Kolesar@ThompsonHine.com
Recommended in Environment

Career: Andrew Kolesar is a Partner and leader of Thompson Hine's Environmental Practice Group. His practice includes permitting, litigation and administrative practice concerning environmental, health and safety matters; assisting in all stages of cleanups under state and federal programs; counseling on environmental aspects of corporate and real estate transactions; and developing pro-active environmental compliance programs. Andrew received his law degree from Georgetown University, where he was cum laude, an Olin Fellow in law and economics and an Associate Editor of the Georgetown Law Journal. Prior to becoming a lawyer, Andrew was a Supervisor of Environmental Engineering and an engineering consultant.

KREIDER, Gary
Keating, Muething & Klekamp, PLL, Cincinnati 513 579 6400
Recommended in Corporate/M&A

KUEHNLE, Kenton
Roetzel & Andress PA, Akron
330 376 2700
Recommended in Real Estate

LAPORTE, Dale C
Calfee, Halter & Griswold LLP, Cleveland 216 622 8207
dlaporte@calfee.com
Recommended in Corporate/M&A

Practice Areas: General corporate; securities and capital markets; mergers and acquisitions.

Prof. Memberships: Chairman of the dean's advisory committee at Case Western Reserve University School of Law; member of Ohio Business Roundtable and Greater Cleveland Partnership Business Retention and Expansion Committee.

Career: Partner in the Securities and Capital Markets Group, member of the Executive Committee and past Chairman of the firm. He assists in structuring venture capital investments and counsels domestic and international clients on matters of corporate governance, corporate control and takeover issues.

Personal: Case Western Reserve University School of Law, JD, 1966; University of Notre Dame, BS, 1963.

LATOUR, Randall D
Vorys, Sater, Seymour and Pease LLP, Columbus 614 464 8290
rdlatour@vssp.com
Recommended in Bankruptcy

Practice Areas: Partner focusing on bankruptcy, debtor/creditor, collection, commercial, secured lending, real estate and commercial litigation with emphasis on bankruptcy proceedings and workouts.

Prof. Memberships: Columbus Bar Association.

Career: Admitted in Ohio (1987); US Court of Appeals 4th Circuit (1990); US Court of Appeals 6th Circuit(1994); US District Court for the Northern and Southern Districts of Ohio.

Personal: The Ohio State University College of Law, JD, with Honors, 1987; The Ohio State University, BA, with Honors, 1977.

LAVEY, Wendlene
Squire, Sanders & Dempsey L.L.P., Cleveland 216 479 8500
Recommended in Environment

LAWNICZAK, James
Calfee, Halter & Griswold LLP, Cleveland 216 622 8364
jlawniczak@calfee.com
Recommended in Bankruptcy

Practice Areas: Bankruptcy and creditors' rights; commercial business and finance.

Prof. Memberships: Member and former officer of the Cleveland Bar Association's Bankruptcy and Commercial Law Section and was its 2003-04 Chairperson; member and former trustee and committee Chairman of the Northern Ohio chapter of the Turnaround Management Association.

Career: Partner in the Commercial Business and Finance Group, he handles all aspects of corporate bankruptcy and workout proceedings. Represents secured and unsecured creditors, debtors and unsecured creditors' committees.

Personal: University of Michigan School of Law, magna cum laude, JD, 1977; University of Michigan, magna cum laude, BA, 1974.

LAWRENCE, James K L
Frost Brown Todd LLC, Cincinnati
513 651 6822
jlawrence@fbtlaw.com
Recommended in Employment

Practice Areas: Firm Practice Leader in labor, employment, and negotiation. Has extensive experience in defending employment discrimination matters and unfair labor practices before the National Labor Relations Board; collective bargaining negotiations and grievance administration and arbitration; and in negotiation and mediation of disputes.

Prof. Memberships: Admitted to practice in Ohio (1965). Member of the CPR Institute for Dispute Resolution; Fellow of the College of Labor and Employment Lawyers; Member of the Dispute Resolution Committee and the Labor and Employment Law Section of the Ohio State Bar Association; Member of the Section of Dispute Resolution of the American Bar Association.

LEACH, Donald
Buckingham Doolittle & Burroughs, Columbus 614 221 8448
Recommended in Construction

LENNOX, Heather
Jones Day, Cleveland
216 586 7111
hlennox@jonesday.com
Recommended in Bankruptcy

Practice Areas: Has represented debtors, creditors' committees, prepetition secured lenders, bank groups, DIP lenders, and others in many of the nation's largest corporate restructurings. Has counseled clients in fraudulent conveyance, illegal dividend, preferential transfer, fiduciary duty, and piercing the corporate veil issues, as well as mass tort and executory contract issues in bankruptcy. She has represented clients in the structuring and consummation of spin-offs, secured financings, and distressed sales and acquisitions. Named a 2005 Ohio Super Lawyer.

Prof. Memberships: American Bankruptcy Institute.

Publications: Co-authored bankruptcy-related articles published in 'The Business Lawyer' and the 'Journal of Bankruptcy Law and Practice.'

LEPENE, Alan
Thompson Hine LLP, Cleveland
216 566 5520
Alan.Lepene@ThompsonHine.com
Recommended in Bankruptcy

Career: Alan is the leader of the firm's Bankruptcy Practice Group and a former member of the firm's Executive Committee. Alan focuses his practice on bankruptcy (primarily Chapter 11 reorganizations), workouts and commercial litigation. Alan has had significant experience representing senior lenders in major bankruptcy cases and workouts. He also has had considerable experience in the representation of creditors' committees and debtors in numerous cases under Chapter 11 of the Bankruptcy Code.

LERNER, Stephen
Squire, Sanders & Dempsey LLP, Cincinnati 513 361 1200
Recommended in Bankruptcy

LEUKART, Barbara
Jones Day, Cleveland 216 586 7190
bjleukart@jonesday.com
Recommended in Employment

Practice Areas: Has represented management and counseled companies in all areas of labor and employment relations. She has defended numerous Title VII, age discrimination, and Americans with Disabilities Act cases at the administrative, trial, and appellate levels. She has extensive experience in managing large employment litigation dockets. Named in 'Ohio Super Lawyers' as a leading Ohio employment lawyer.

Prof. Memberships: Pursuant to an appointment by the US Court of Appeals for the Sixth Circuit, she is currently serving on that court's Advisory Committee on Rules. Mediator for the US District Court for the Northern District of Ohio.

LEUKART II, Richard
Baker & Hostetler LLP, Cleveland
216 621 0200
Recommended in Employment

LEVY, Mark P
Thompson Hine LLP, Dayton
937 443 6600
Recommended in Intellectual Property

Career: Mark is a registered patent attorney and practice group leader of Thompson Hine's Intellectual Property Practice Group. He specializes in the management, prosecution and enforcement of all aspects of intellectual property, including technology transfer licensing and joint venture agreements; patent and trademark validity and infringement opinions; intellectual property audits; patent application preparation; intellectual property litigation; foreign patents; and trade secrets. Mark is admitted to practice in Ohio, the District of Columbia and before the United States Patent and Trademark Office. Mark has negotiated pharmaceutical development and license agree-

ments and participated in significant and successful patent litigations.

LEWIS, John
Baker & Hostetler LLP, Cleveland
216 621 0200
Recommended in Employment

LEWIS, Kim
Dinsmore & Shohl LLP, Cincinnati
513 977 8200
Recommended in Bankruptcy

LIGGETT, Luther
Bricker & Eckler LLP, Columbus
614 227 2300
Recommended in Construction

LINDBERG, Lawrence
Baker & Hostetler LLP, Cleveland
216 621 0200
Recommended in Real Estate

LUNN, Gregory
Wood, Herron & Evans, LLP, Cincinnati
513 241 2324
Recommended in Intellectual Property

LYMAN, Beverly
Wood, Herron & Evans, LLP, Cincinnati
513 241 2324
Recommended in Intellectual Property

LYON, Charles
Calfee, Halter & Griswold LLP,
Cleveland 216 622 8510
clyon@calfee.com
Recommended in Intellectual Property

Practice Areas: Intellectual property; intellectual property litigation.

Prof. Memberships: Active member of Northern District of Ohio Alternative Dispute Resolution Panel; acted as a mediator or special master in many intellectual property disputes; former director of Cleveland Patent Law Association.

Career: Chair of the Intellectual Property Group. Handles patent and trademark matters and litigates intellectual property cases. Has been involved in the full scope of intellectual property practice, including negotiating employment and licensing contracts, technology transfers and lawsuit settlements.

Personal: George Washington University Law School, JD, with honors, 1970; University of Oklahoma, BS in Mechanical Engineering, 1967.

MACE, Damond
Squire, Sanders & Dempsey L.L.P.,
Cleveland 216 479 8500
Recommended in Litigation

MAKLEY, Roger
Coolidge, Wall, Womsley & Lombard,
Dayton 937 223 8177
Recommended in Litigation

MARKS, Jeffrey
Squire, Sanders & Dempsey LLP,
Cincinnati 513 361 1200
Recommended in Bankruptcy

MCCAFFREY, John
McLaughlin & McCaffrey, LLP,
Cleveland 216 623 0900
Recommended in Litigation

MCCARTAN, Patrick F
Jones Day, Cleveland
216 586 7272
pmccartan@jonesday.com
Recommended in Litigation

Practice Areas: Has extensive complex case experience in antitrust, taxation, takeovers, officer and director liability, and securities and shareholder litigation matters. Active in corporate governance, product liability, and consumer class action matters. As Managing Partner he extended the firm's geographic reach to 11 new markets throughout the world. Cited in every survey conducted by 'The National Law Journal' as one of America's most respected lawyers, he is also a subject of 'America's Top Trial Lawyers: Who They Are & Why They Win.'

Prof. Memberships: Fellow of the American College of Trial Lawyers and the International Academy of Trial Lawyers.

MCCREARY, Charles
Bricker & Eckler LLP, Columbus
614 227 2300
Recommended in Real Estate

MCDONALD, John
Schottenstein, Zox & Dunn, Columbus
614 462 2201
jmcdonald@szd.com
Recommended in Litigation

Practice Areas: Mr McDonald focuses his practice on complex litigation, patent litigation, commercial litigation and arbitration and construction law. He has tried over 160 cases in State and Federal courts throughout the United States during the past 35 years. Additionally, Mr McDonald provides alternative dispute resolution services as a consultant with SZD's ancillary service, Alternative Litigation Resources, Inc.

MCLAUGHLIN, Patrick
McLaughlin & McCaffrey, LLP,
Cleveland 216 623 0900
Recommended in Litigation

MCMAHON, Louis L
Thompson Hine LLP, Cleveland
216 566 5639
Louis.McMahon@ThompsonHine.com
Recommended in Environment

Career: Lou McMahon is a Partner in Thompson Hine's Environmental Practice Group. He focuses his practice on environmental and water rights litigation, environmental regulatory and legislative matters, Great Lakes and public trust issues and brownfields redevelopment. Lou received his law degree from Cleveland-Marshall College of Law, where he graduated summa cum laude and received the H.G. Fuerst Award for Highest First Year Average.

MCMAHON, Michael
McMahon, DeGulis, Hoffmann & Lombardi LLP, Cleveland 216 621 1312
mmcmahon@mdhl.net
Recommended in Environment

Practice Areas: Experienced in environmental compliance counseling and enforcement litigation under the major environmental statutes. Frequent speaker and author, particularly on Clean Air Act issues.

Prof. Memberships: Former Chair, Cleveland Bar Environmental Law Section. Member, Ohio State Bar Environmental Law Committee.

Career: A founder of MDHL (www.mdhl.net) in 1994, and with Partner Greg DeGulis, of the Environmental Law Network (www.elnonline.com) a network of environmental law firms across the country. Many ELN member firms were also identified as leading firms in the 2004-05 'Chambers USA America's Leading Business Lawyers'.

Personal: Received JD (Stone Scholar) from Columbia University School of Law in 1981 and BA (magna cum laude) from John Carroll University in 1978.

MCMURRAY, Kevin N
Frost Brown Todd LLC, Cincinnati
513 651 6160
kmcmurray@fbtlaw.com
Recommended in Environment

Practice Areas: Environmental litigation, defense of environmental enforcement actions, and counseling on environmental and regulatory issues arising in business and transactions (real estate, financing, and corporate acquisitions/divestitures). Significant experience in acquisition and redevelopment of 'brownfield' properties.

Prof. Memberships: Admitted to practice in Ohio (1989), Southern District of Ohio, and Sixth Circuit Court of Appeals. Member of American, Ohio State and Cincinnati Bar Associations.

Career: Joined Frost Brown Todd (Frost & Jacobs), 1989; became Partner, 1996. Chair, Client Relations Committee, Member, Executive Committee (1998-2003).

Personal: Born 7 January 1963. JD University of Cincinnati, 1989; BS ChE University of Cincinnati, 1986.

MCNEALEY, J Jeffrey
Porter Wright Morris & Arthur LLP, Columbus 614 227 2074
jmcnealey@porterwright.com
Recommended in Environment

Practice Areas: Practice areas include, business formation, business transactions, Brownfields redevelopment, environmental law including Clean Air Act and Clean Water Act, real estate acquisition and development, and zoning and land use planning.

Career: Admitted in Ohio; US Supreme Court; US Court of Appeals, District of Columbia, Fourth, Sixth, Seventh, and Eighth Circuits; US District Court, District of Columbia; US District Court, Northern and Southern Districts of Ohio; US District Court, Western District of Missouri; US District Court, Western District of North Carolina.

Personal: JD, The Ohio State University College of Law, 1969; BA, Cornell University, 1966.

MEEKS, William
R. William Meeks - Sole Practitioner, Columbus 614 228 4141
Recommended in Litigation

MERSOL, Greg
Baker & Hostetler LLP, Cleveland
216 621 0200
Recommended in Employment

MESSERMAN, Gerald
Messerman & Messerman Co, LPA, Cleveland 216 574 9990
Recommended in Litigation

MEYER, Andrew C
Duvin, Cahn & Hutton, Cleveland
216 696 7600
ameyer@duvin.com
Recommended in Employment

Practice Areas: Represents private and public sector clients in all aspects of labor relations, including counsel and advice on union avoidance issues, serving as chief negotiator in numerous collective bargaining negotiations, advocate in arbitrations, employment and discrimination matters, and handling various issues under the Fair Labor Standards Act. Represents numerous clients before the National Labor Relations Board on issues including union representation and unfair labor practices.

Career: Partner since 1981.

Publications: Frequent lecturer on labor relations topics.

Personal: Case Western Reserve University (JD 1976), Heiss Labor Award for outstanding third year student; National Championship Labor Moot Court Team member; Ohio University (AB, MA, 1973, Phi Beta Kappa); Pi Gamma Mu, Omicron Delta Epsilon.

MEYER, G Christopher
Squire, Sanders & Dempsey L.L.P., Cleveland 216 479 8500
Recommended in Bankruptcy

MICHEL, Lisa
Keating, Muething & Klekamp, PLL, Cincinnati 513 579 6400
Recommended in Employment

MILLER, Barry
Benesch, Friedlander, Coplan & Aronoff LLP, Cleveland 216 363 4454
bmiller@bfca.com
Recommended in Construction

Practice Areas: Construction law (public and private), real estate law, and commercial litigation. Has represeted owners, general contractors, subcontractors, developers, public agencies, design professionals and sureties in construction dispute-related matters. His representation includes every type of construction dispute including: bid protests, extra work disputes, delay and disruption claims, lost productivity disputes and post-acceptance building failures. He has appeared before state and federal courts, contract appeals boards and arbitration tribunals.

Career: He is the Chairman of the Con-

struction Practice Group at Benesch Friedlander Coplan & Aronoff LLP. He has served as project counsel on public and private projects with a value of approximately $800 million. He has assisted in selecting project delivery systems, negotiating design and construction agreements and resolving design and construction disputes. He has also served as an arbitrator and mediator in over 110 construction cases involving up to 15 parties.

Publications: He is a contributing author to publications by the American Bar Association, the CWRU Law Review, and an editor and author of Ohio Public Contract Law (2nd and 3rd editions). He is a frequent lecturer on construction law.

Personal: Case Western Reserve University (JD, 1983); Kent State University (Masters, 1979); Miami University (BA, 1977).

MILLER, Craig
Ulmer & Berne LLP, Cleveland
216 621 8400
Recommended in Real Estate

MILLISOR, Kenneth
Millisor & Nobil Co LPA, Cleveland
440 838 8000
Recommended in Employment

MILLS Jr, Osborne
Squire, Sanders & Dempsey L.L.P., Cleveland 216 479 8343
omills@ssd.com
Recommended in Banking & Finance

Practice Areas: Leads the Cleveland office's Commercial Lending Practice. Partner with broad experience in all aspects of commercial and real estate lending, loan workouts, debtor-creditor issues and real estate law. Represents financial institutions and borrowers in syndicated and bi-lateral loan facilities, secured/unsecured loan transactions, complex commercial debt and mortgage financings, mezzanine debt transactions, venture capital transactions, loan restructurings, workouts and bankruptcy proceedings.

Prof. Memberships: American Bar Association, Business Law Section; Ohio State Bar Association; Cleveland Bar Association, Sections on Corporation, Banking and Business Law, Bankruptcy and Commercial Law and Real Estate.

Personal: Case Western Reserve University, JD, 1975; Dartmouth College, AB, 1969.

MILLSTONE, David
Squire, Sanders & Dempsey L.L.P., Cleveland 216 479 8500
Recommended in Employment

MIRALDI, Leslee
Thompson Hine LLP, Cleveland
216 566 5500
Leslee.Miraldi@ThompsonHine.com
Recommended in Banking & Finance

Career: Leslee is a Partner in the Commercial & Public Finance Practice Group. She focuses her practice on commercial lending, representing banks and financial institutions as well as public and private companies in connection with senior and subordinated debt facilities. She has extensive experience with syndicated, multi-bank senior credit facilities, asset-based and structured finance facilities, cross-border transactions (involving foreign borrowers and foreign collateral), acquisition financing, letter of credit facilities, foreign currency transactions and real estate financing. Leslee also has extensive experience in the area of secured transactions, including both personal and real property. Her representation includes loan restructuring and workouts.

MOSCARINO, George
Jones Day, Cleveland
216 586 7203
gmoscarino@jonesday.com
Recommended in Litigation

Practice Areas: International criminal defense and white-collar practice involves complex criminal litigation and government and grand jury investigations. Has extensive experience representing corporations, their management, boards of directors, and employees in criminal matters, and has represented clients in many high-profile criminal investigations and cases. Named in the criminal litigation section of a leading legal publication.

Prof. Memberships: Fellow of the American College of Trial Lawyers.

Publications: He is an active international lecturer on civil and criminal litigation techniques and white-collar crimes and has published articles on those subjects in the US, Canada, England, and Japan.

MOSS, Steven
Kahn Kleinman, Cleveland
216 696 3311
Recommended in Employment

NASH, David
Thompson Hine LLP, Cleveland
216 566 5500
Dave.Nash@ThompsonHine.com
Recommended in Environment

Prof. Memberships: Cleveland (Chair, Environmental Law Section 1997-98) and Ohio State Bar Associations (Chair, Environmental Law Commitee, 2000-01).

Career: David Nash is a Partner in Thompson Hine's Environmental Law Practice Group. He focuses his practice on environmental issues relating to corporate sustainability, business and real estate transactions, emerging technologies that are environmentally related, regulatory matters and legislative matters, environmental litigation, and environmental enforcement actions. Dave received his law degree from Duke University School of Law, with honors. Fellow, Ohio State Bar Foundation.

NATALE, Andrew
Frantz Ward LLP, Cleveland
216 515 1660
Recommended in Construction

NEWMAN Jr, John (Jack) M
Jones Day, Cleveland
216 586 7207
jmnewman@jonesday.com
Recommended in Litigation
Practice Areas: Cleveland office co-ordinator for the Litigation Group. His practice focuses on shareholder actions and fiduciary and governance claims, and also includes banking services, employee benefits, bankruptcy, tax and accounting-related litigation, and other commercial controversies. He is admitted to practice in Ohio, Illinois and California, and before the US Tax and Supreme Courts and numerous federal district courts and courts of appeals.
Prof. Memberships: Fellow of the American College of Trial Lawyers. He is a Member of the ABA; the Los Angeles County Bar Association; the Cleveland Bar Association; and the California State Bar Association.

NOBIL, Steven
Millisor & Nobil Co LPA, Cleveland
440 838 8000
Recommended in Employment

NOLAN, William
Squire, Sanders & Dempsey LLP,
Columbus 614 365 2700
Recommended in Employment

NORMAN, Mark A
Vorys, Sater, Seymour and Pease,
Cincinnati (513) 723-4006
manorman@vssp.com
Recommended in Environment
Practice Areas: Partner. Represents business in environmental compliance, business transactions, enforcement and litigation. Prosecutes and defends private cost-recovery actions, and defends toxic tort litigation and government enforcement actions in state and federal courts. Has a substantial 'brownfields' redevelopment practice (including Ohio EPA Voluntary Action and Clean Ohio programs) and a government organizations practice. Elected by peers as an 'Ohio Super Lawyer'.
Prof. Memberships: Ohio State and Cincinnati Bar Associations.
Career: Admitted to Ohio Bar (1983).
Publications: Co-author 'RCRA and Superfund', Shepards/McGraw-Hill.
Personal: Georgetown University Law Center, JD, cum laude, 1983. George Washington University, BA, with honors 1977.

O'DONNELL, Patricia
Baker & Hostetler LLP, Cleveland
216 621 0200
Recommended in Real Estate

OSCAR, Lawrence
Hahn Loeser & Parks LLP, Cleveland
216 621 0150
Recommended in Bankruptcy

OWENDOFF, Michael
Jones Day, Cleveland
216 586 7183
msowendoff@jonesday.com
Recommended in Real Estate
Practice Areas: His practice encompasses the development, financing, leasing, exchanging, purchasing, and selling of commercial real estate. He represents national and regional developers and also provides real estate advice to non-developer clients. He represents clients in the acquisition of undeveloped land, the installation of improvements, the negotiation of financing, and the drafting of reciprocal easement and operating agreements. Additionally, he represents landlords and tenants in ground, retail, office, and industrial leases; and he has experience representing clients in tax-deferred 1031 exchange transactions. He also advises borrowers and lenders in commercial real estate loan transactions.
Prof. Memberships: ABA; Cleveland Bar Association.

PACE, Stanley Dan
Spieth Bell McCurdy & Newell Co LPA,
Cleveland 216 696 4700
Recommended in Employment

PARIS, Zachary
Jones Day, Cleveland
216 586 7275
ztparis@jonesday.com
Recommended in Real Estate
Practice Areas: Practices real estate development, corporate real estate services, and hospitality industry law. He has represented developers in most aspects of commercial and industrial ownership and development. His corporate real estate services work focuses on institutions whose core business is outside the real estate industry. Examples include corporate headquarters development projects and ground leases for large industrial properties. As co-leader of the firm's hospitality practice, he has been involved in most aspects of the hotel industry including the acquisition, sale, and/or financing of individual hotels and hotel portfolios and the negotiation of hotel management and franchise agreements.

PAROBEK, Drew
Vorys, Sater, Seymour and Pease,
Cleveland 216 479 6100
dtparobek@vssp.com
Recommended in Bankruptcy
Practice Areas: Partner in the Commercial Group with emphasis on bankruptcy, commercial law and banking.

Prof. Memberships: Cleveland (Executive Committe; Trustee; Member, Bankruptcy and Commercial Law Section; Chair, Continuing Legal Education Committee), Lorain County and Ohio State Bar Associations; Turnaround Management Association.
Career: Admitted to Ohio (1984); US District Court, Northern and Southern Districts of Ohio; US Court of Appeals, Sixth Circuit.
Personal: Vanderbilt University School of Law, JD, 1984; Vanderbilt University, BA, summa cum laude, 1980. Trustee, Cleveland Zoological Society; Contemporary Youth Orchestra; Bay Soccer Club.

PATBERG, William
Shumaker Loop & Kendrick LLP, Toledo
419 241 9000
Recommended in Environment

PEARLMAN, Samuel
Squire, Sanders & Dempsey L.L.P.,
Cleveland 216 479 8500
Recommended in Real Estate

PETRO, John
Williams & Petro Co. LLC, Columbus
614 224 0531
Recommended in Construction

PFEFFERLE, Ben
Baker & Hostetler LLP, Columbus
614 228 1541
Recommended in Environment

PHILLIPS, James E
Vorys, Sater, Seymour and Pease LLP,
Columbus
614 464 6400
jephillips@vssp.com
Recommended in Litigation
Practice Areas: Partner in the Litigation Group with emphasis on criminal defense.
Prof. Memberships: Columbus (Professional Ethics Committee, 2002-; Committee on the Judiciary, 2003-), Ohio State and American (Criminal Justice Section, White Collar Crime Committee) Bar Associations; Ohio Association of Criminal Defense Lawyers (Board of Trustees, 2000-); National Association of Criminal Defense Lawyers.
Career: Admitted to Ohio (1975); US District Court, Southern District of Ohio and US Supreme Court (1979); US Court of Appeals, Tenth Circuit and US District Court, Northern District of Ohio (1983).
Personal: Case Western Reserve University, JD, 1975; Boston University, BA, cum laude, 1971.

PHILLIPS, William M
Calfee, Halter & Griswold LLP,
Cleveland 216 622 8617
wphillips@calfee.com
Recommended in Real Estate
Practice Areas: Real estate.
Prof. Memberships: Member of International Council of Shopping Centers and National Association of Corporate

Real Estate Executives; Member of American, Ohio State and Cleveland Bar Associations.
Career: Partner in the Real Estate Group. Focuses on all aspects of real estate development and leasing, including representation of both tenants and landlords, with a particular emphasis on real estate leasing and development. Has designed form leases for national chains designed to maximize business leverage, operational flexibility and value to the tenant.
Personal: The Ohio State University Law School, JD, with honors, 1983; Miami University, BS, cum laude, 1979.

PIGMAN, Jack R
Porter Wright Morris & Arthur LLP,
Columbus 614 227 2119
jpigman@porterwright.com
Recommended in Bankruptcy
Practice Areas: Represents debtors, committees, banks and other financial institutions in significant Chapter 11 bankruptcy cases, receiverships, business reorganizations, workouts and loan restructurings. Often assists clients in the purchase and sale of businesses.
Career: Admitted in Ohio; US Court of Appeals, Sixth Circuit; US District Court, Eastern District of Michigan; US District Court, Northern and Southern Districts of Ohio.
Personal: JD (cum laude), The Ohio State University, 1969; BA, University of Notre Dame, 1966.

PITCAIRN Jr, Robert
Katz, Teller, Brant & Hild, Cincinnati
513 721 4532
Recommended in Litigation

PORTER, David
Jones Day, Cleveland
216 586 7215
dporter@jonesday.com
Recommended in Corporate/M&A
Practice Areas: Practices principally securities and corporate finance law, with extensive experience in corporate restructurings and corporate governance matters, including takeover defense. His takeover work has included the successful defense of Ohio's anti-takeover legislation.
Prof. Memberships: ABA; Ohio State Bar Association; Cleveland Bar Association. He has chaired and been a Member of subcommittees of the Ohio State Bar Association that have drafted revisions to Ohio's corporate statutes.
Publications: He has authored numerous articles on securities and takeover planning topics.

POWAR, Lee
Hahn Loeser & Parks LLP, Cleveland
216 621 0150
Recommended in Bankruptcy

POWERS, Victoria E
Schottenstein, Zox & Dunn, Columbus
614 462 5010
vpowers@szd.com
Recommended in Bankruptcy
Practice Areas: Ms Powers concentrates her practice in the areas of complex Chapter 11 reorganization, bankruptcy court litigation and out-of-court workouts, with an emphasis on creditor and indenture trustee representations.
Prof. Memberships: American Bankruptcy Institute; Commercial Law League of America; International Women's Insolvency and Restructuring Confederation, Central Ohio Chapter; listed in Bankruptcy Law Section of 'The Best Lawyers in America', 2005-06.

RAWSON, Rachel
Jones Day, Cleveland
216 586 7276
rlrawson@jonesday.com
Recommended in Banking & Finance
Practice Areas: Chairs the Lending/Structured Finance Practice in the Cleveland office. She regularly represents lenders and corporate clients in a range of financing transactions, including asset-based loans, complex leveraged buy-out financings, investment grade loans, private placements of debt securities and subordinated debt facilities. She also focuses on workouts and restructurings of troubled credits, and has represented both creditors and debtors in out-of-court restructuring transactions, debtor-in-possession financings and exit financings. She advises financial institution clients on intercreditor issues, structuring and negotiating transactions with multiple debt tranches and multiple lien priorities.
Prof. Memberships: ABA.

REIDY, Joseph M
Schottenstein, Zox & Dunn, Columbus
614 462 2207
jreidy@szd.com
Recommended in Environment
Practice Areas: Mr Reidy provides counsel and representation for environmental and natural resource permits, compliance and enforcement to agriculture, industry and state and local government. He assists buyers, sellers and developers of commercial real estate in the identification and resolution of environmental issues, including hazardous waste, lead-based paint, asbestos and wetlands. He has extensive experience in obtaining state, federal and private funding for the redevelopment of brownfields. Mr Reidy also has considerable experience in toxic tort and workers' compensation litigation, especially in the areas of occupational diseases and safety violations (VSSR).

REMINGTON, Royce
Hahn Loeser & Parks LLP, Cleveland
216 621 0150
Recommended in Construction

REPPERT, Richard L
Jones Day, Cleveland
216 586 7235
rreppert@jonesday.com
Recommended in Real Estate
Practice Areas: His practice is transaction-oriented, typically pertaining to real estate or financing matters. He represents real estate developers in land acquisition, development, construction financing, and permanent financing. He represents banks and other financial institutions making loans secured. Has experience in syndicated loans, secured credit lines, and loans that are or will be securitized. He is familiar with the requirements of the capital markets and is involved in the formation of special purpose entities required by rating agencies in securitized transactions.
Prof. Memberships: ABA; Ohio State Bar Association; Pennsylvania Bar Association; Cleveland Bar Association; American College of Real Estate Lawyers.

RIDGLEY, Thomas
Vorys, Sater, Seymour and Pease LLP, Columbus 614 464 6400
tbridgley@vssp.com
Recommended in Litigation
Practice Areas: Litigator with experience in all areas of civil litigation including commercial, business, takeover, securities, labor, insurance, environmental, and products liability litigation.
Prof. Memberships: Columbus, Cincinnati, Ohio State, and American Bar Associations.
Career: Admitted in Ohio (1968); United States District Courts for the Northern and Southern Districts of Ohio; United States Courts of Appeals, Third, Sixth and Tenth Circuits; US Supreme Court.
Personal: University of Michigan, JD, with distinction, 1965; Princeton University, AB, magna cum laude, 1962. Fellow, American College of Trial Lawyers. Listed in a leading legal publication for commercial and toxic tort litigation and product liability litigation.

RIGOT, Joseph M
Thompson Hine LLP, Dayton
937 443 6586
Joe.Rigot@ThompsonHine.com
Recommended in Corporate/M&A
Career: Joe is a member of the firm's Corporate Transactions and Securities Practice Group. He focuses his practice on the representation of public companies, with an emphasis on securities law, merger and acquisition transactions, and strategic alliances. Joe is also general counsel and secretary of Robbins & Myers, Inc. which is listed on the New York Stock Exchange. Education: Washington University, JD, 1973, Order of the Coif, Law Review. University of Cincinnati, MA, 1969. University of Dayton, BA, 1966, magna cum laude.

RILEY, Shawn
McDonald Hopkins Co, Cleveland
216 348 5400
Recommended in Bankruptcy

ROBENALT, James
Thompson Hine LLP, Cleveland
216 566 5755
Jim.Robenalt@ThompsonHine.com
Recommended in Construction, Litigation
Career: Jim is a Partner in the firm's Business Litigation Practice Group and has been a trial lawyer his entire career. He has worked on major construction disputes, including contests over the construction of major buildings in New York, Cleveland and Pittsburgh. Jim has served as counsel to a Fortune 500 company on first prosecution under the Economic Espionage Act of 1996, including services with respect to FBI investigation, criminal prosecution, related lawsuits filed in Taiwan and the People's Republic of China, and trial counsel in civil RICO case, resulting in an $80 million jury verdict with attorneys' fees.

ROBERTSON, Jean
McDonald Hopkins Co, Cleveland
216 348 5400
Recommended in Bankruptcy

ROE Jr, Clifford
Dinsmore & Shohl LLP, Cincinnati
513 977 8200
Recommended in Corporate/M&A

ROESCH, Lynda
Dinsmore & Shohl LLP, Cincinnati
513 977 8200
Recommended in Intellectual Property

ROHYANS, John
Porter Wright Morris & Arthur LLP, Columbus 614 227 2055
jrohyans@porterwright.com
Recommended in Real Estate
Practice Areas: Has worked in the areas of real estate development and finance for more than 30 years. Practice areas include finance and commerce, acquisition and development, commercial leasing, mortgages and sale/leasebacks, and title insurance. Clients include Nationwide Life Insurance Company, State Farm Life Insurance Company, and Jackson National Life Insurance Company. He is the Department Manager of the firm's Real Estate Department and currently sits on the firm's Directing Partners Committee.
Career: Admitted in Ohio and US District Court, Southern District of Ohio.
Personal: JD, The Ohio State University College of Law, 1969; BS, Miami University, 1966.

ROSATI, Jack
Bricker & Eckler LLP, Columbus
614 227 2300
Recommended in Construction

ROSENBERG, Thomas
Ulmer & Berne LLP, Columbus
Recommended in Construction

ROSENTHAL, Daniel
Denlinger, Rosenthal & Greenberg LPA, Cincinnati 513 621 3440
Recommended in Employment

ROSNER, Richard
Kahn Kleinman, Cleveland
216 696 3311
Recommended in Real Estate

ROTATORI, Robert
Rotatori, Bender, Gragel, Stoper & Alexander Co. L.P.A., Cleveland
216 928 1010
Recommended in Litigation

RUSH, Jeffery
Frost Brown Todd LLC, Cincinnati
513 651 6893
jrush@fbtlaw.com
Recommended in Banking & Finance
Practice Areas: Banking, commercial law and real estate, including workouts and restructurings.
Prof. Memberships: Admitted to practice in Ohio (1975). Member, Banking, Commercial Law and Bankruptcy Subcommittee of the Ohio State Bar Association and the Section of Business Law of the American Bar Association.
Career: Joined Frost Brown Todd, 1975; Member, 1982; former Head of Commercial Transactions and Real Estate Department; former Member of the Executive Committee.
Personal: Born 18 September 1950. JD, Vanderbilt University, 1975; BS (Economics), Wharton School of the University of Pennsylvania, 1972.

RYDZEL, James
Jones Day, Cleveland
216 586 7227
jarydzel@jonesday.com
Recommended in Employment
Practice Areas: His practice includes counseling in labor and employment matters, with special focus on employment-related litigation. This includes labor arbitrations and National Labor Relations Board proceedings. His litigation experience includes ERISA cases, particularly involving retiree medical benefits and severance pay. His counseling activities have involved all phases of labor relations, including articulation of negotiation goals and strategies, strike preparation, temporary and permanent replacement of strikers, and picket line and Boys Market injunctions.
Prof. Memberships: American Bar Association. He is also a member of the bar of several federal circuits and districts, including the Sixth Circuit.

SAAD, Michael
Squire, Sanders & Dempsey LLP, Columbus 614 365 2700
Recommended in Real Estate

SABO, Roger
Schottenstein, Zox & Dunn, Columbus
614 462 5030
rsabo@szd.com
Recommended in Construction
Practice Areas: Mr Sabo represents trade associations, owners, designers and contractors involved in procurement, bidding, selection processes, alternative dispute resolutions, construction claims that include acceleration, delays defects, changed conditions and termination, affirmative action claims, prevailing wages, labor negotiations and arbitrations, matters involving age, sex, race and disability discrimination as well as occupational safety and heath law issues. He serves as General Counsel to the Associated General Contractors of Ohio and the Ohio Contractors Association. He serves as an Arbitrator on the Construction Industry Arbitration Panel and its Fast Track roster of Neutrals of the American Arbitration Association.

SAMUELS, Stephen P
Schottenstein, Zox & Dunn, Columbus
614 462 5021
ssamuels@szd.com
Recommended in Environment
Practice Areas: Mr Samuels chairs SZD's Environmental Practice Group. His practice focuses on water and air pollution permitting and litigation; hazardous, construction and demolition debris, and solid waste regulation; mold claims; and counsel regarding environmental issues associated with mergers and acquisitions, real estate development and other business and property transactions. Previously, Mr Samuels served as Chief of the Court of Claims Defense Section (which defends all claims for money damages brought against the State of Ohio) and Litigation Supervisor of the Environmental Enforcement Section of the Ohio Attorney General's Office, and as in-house counsel at the Ohio Environmental Protection Agency.

SANKER, Robert
Keating, Muething & Klekamp, PLL, Cincinnati 513 579 6400
Recommended in Bankruptcy

SARGEANT, Richard
Eastman & Smith Ltd, Toledo
419 241 6000
Recommended in Environment

SAXBE, Charles
Chester, Willcox & Saxbe LLP, Columbus 614 221 4000
Recommended in Litigation

SCHLOEMER, Jeffrey
Taft, Stettinius & Hollister LLP, Cincinnati 513 381 2838
Recommended in Banking & Finance

SCHMIT, David E
Frost Brown Todd LLC, Cincinnati
513 651 6985
dschmit@fbtlaw.com
Recommended in Intellectual Property
Practice Areas: Intellectual property law. Extensive experience in complex patent, trademark, copyright, trade secret, and unfair competition litigation and arbitration.
Prof. Memberships: Admitted to practice in Ohio (1975), US Supreme Court, Federal Circuit and Sixth Circuit. Registered patent attorney (1976).
Career: Joined Frost & Jacobs (now Frost Brown Todd) 1976, Partner/Member since 1982. Lead trial and appellate counsel in Warner Jenkinson, Inc v Hilton Davis Chemical Co; Ethicon v Quigg; Valco Cincinnati, Inc v N&D Machining Co among others.
Personal: JD (1975), Salmon P Chase College of Law; BSEE (1969), MSEE (1976), University of Cincinnati.

SCHNAPP, Karlyn
Frost Brown Todd LLC, Columbus
513 651 6865
kschnapp@fbtlaw.com
Recommended in Intellectual Property
Practice Areas: Intellectual property law, in particular patent prosecution (chemical/pharma/bio), counseling, infringement, patentability and validity opinions and licensing.
Prof. Memberships: Admitted in Ohio, US Patent and Trademark Office, Intellectual Property Law Association, Ohio Bar Association, Cincinnati Bar Association, American Chemical Society.
Career: Joined Frost Brown Todd in 2000; Prior to joining was a professor of organic chemistry at Northern Kentucky University for nine and a half years.
Personal: BS (with honors in Chemistry), University of Cincinnati, 1984; PhD (organic chemistry) 1989, University of Cincinnati; JD 2000, Chase College of Law, Northern Kentucky University.

SCHRAFF, Christopher
Porter Wright Morris & Arthur LLP, Columbus 614 227 2097
cschraff@porterwright.com
Recommended in Environment
Practice Areas: Practices environmental law, with emphasis on the Federal Water Pollution Control Act, CERCLA and RCRA, wetlands regulation, state and local environmental statutes/regulations, and lender and fiduciary liability issues. Lead counsel in Columbus & Franklin County Metropolitan Park District v Shank, 5 Ohio St.3d 86 (1992), the leading decision in Ohio on water pollution control law.
Career: Admitted in Ohio; US Supreme Court; US Court of Appeals, Sixth Circuit; and US District Court for Northern and Southern Districts of Ohio.
Personal: JD, University of Notre Dame, 1972; AB, John Carroll University, 1969.

SCHWARTZ, Jeffrey
Benesch, Friedlander, Coplan & Aronoff LLP, Cleveland 216 363 4500
Recommended in Bankruptcy

SCHWARTZ, Niki
Schwartz, Kushner & Rendon Co, LPA, Cleveland 216 696 6700
Recommended in Litigation

SELTZER, Martin S
Porter Wright Morris & Arthur LLP, Columbus 614 227 2050
mseltzer@porterwright.com
Recommended in Environment
Practice Areas: Practices environmental law, emphasis on hazardous and solid wastes, water issues, and toxic substances. Performed numerous environmental assessments in connection with business and real estate purchases and assisted many clients in obtaining US and Ohio EPA permits. Represented various entities in successful redevelopment of brownfields properties.
Prof. Memberships: General Counsel, Ohio Chemistry Technology Council; past Co-Chair, Ohio EPA Public Advisory Group on Solid and Hazardous Waste; past Chair, Environmental Law Committee, Columbus Bar Association.
Career: Admitted in Ohio.
Personal: JD, The Ohio State University, 1977; PhD, Yale University, 1962; AB, New York University, 1958.

SHEERAN, Timothy
Squire, Sanders & Dempsey L.L.P., Cleveland 216 479 8500
Recommended in Employment

SIDMAN, Robert
Vorys, Sater, Seymour and Pease LLP, Columbus 614 464 6400
rjsidman@vssp.com
Recommended in Bankruptcy
Practice Areas: Partner in the Commercial Group focusing on bankruptcy and debtor creditor law.
Prof. Memberships: Columbus, Ohio State and American Bar Associations; Association of Former Bankruptcy Judges; National Conference of Bankruptcy Judges; American Bankruptcy Institute.
Career: Admitted to Ohio Bar (1968); US Court of Appeals, Sixth Circuit (1970); US Tax Court and US Supreme Court (1972); US Court of Appeals, Fourth Circuit (1990); US Court of Appeals, Third Circuit (1993).
Personal: University of Notre Dame, JD, 1968; Benedictine College, BA, magna cum laude, 1965.

SIEGEL, Bradd N
Porter Wright Morris & Arthur LLP, Columbus 614 227 2238
bsiegel@porterwright.com
Recommended in Employment
Practice Areas: Concentrates practice on employment litigation, including defense of individual and class action claims brought under federal and state employment discrimination and labor laws, ERISA, state contract and tort law.
Prof. Memberships: Fellow, College of Labor and Employment Lawyers; OSBA, Labor and Employment Law Section; ABA, EEO Committee, Labor and Employment Law Committee, Litigation Section.
Career: Admitted in Ohio; District of Columbia; Commonwealth of Virginia; Sixth Circuit; US District Court for Northern and Southern Districts of Ohio.
Personal: LLM, Georgetown University Law Center, 1978; JD (with honors), George Washington University, 1977; AB (with distinction), Cornell University, 1974.

SMITH, Ted
Vorys, Sater, Seymour and Pease LLP, Columbus 614 464 6232
jtsmith@vssp.com
Recommended in Real Estate
Practice Areas: Senior associate concentrating his practice on condominium law, real estate acquisition and sales, real estate development, leasing, liens, evictions and real estate secured loans.
Prof. Memberships: Columbus and Ohio State (editor, Real Property Section newsletter) Bar Associations.
Career: Admitted to Ohio Bar.
Personal: University of Illinois College of Law, JD, magna cum laude, 1998. Purdue University, BS Civil Engineering, Chi Epsilon, 1992. Frequent faculty member for condominium-related seminars.

SOLOMON, Randall
Baker & Hostetler LLP, Cleveland
216 621 0200
Recommended in Litigation

SOZIO, Steven
Jones Day, Cleveland
216 586 7201
sgsozio@jonesday.com
Recommended in Litigation
Practice Areas: Represents businesses and their employees during investigations by federal and local governmental authorities for potential criminal charges. His practice involves investigating, prosecuting, and/or defending civil actions on behalf of clients involved with fraud, false claims, and other business-related wrongdoing; and advising corporate clients regarding compliance issues to avoid governmental sanctions. He is an adjunct professor at the Cleveland-Marshall College of Law of Cleveland State University where he teaches criminal procedure.
Prof. Memberships: Member of the American, Federal, and Cleveland Bar Associations and serves as the Sixth Circuit reporter for the ABA Criminal Litigation Committee newsletter.

STAMP, Vincent
Dinsmore & Shohl LLP, Cincinnati
513 977 8200
Recommended in Environment

STANLEY, Hugh
Tucker Ellis & West LLP, Cleveland
216 696 1100
Recommended in Litigation

STEINDLER, Howard
Benesch, Friedlander, Coplan & Aronoff
LLP, Cleveland 216 363 4500
Recommended in Real Estate

STEINER, Edward
Keating, Muething & Klekamp, PLL,
Cincinnati 513 579 6400
Recommended in Corporate/M&A

STEPANIAK, Mark
Taft, Stettinius & Hollister LLP, Cincinnati
513 381 2838
Recommended in Employment

STEPHEN, John M
Porter Wright Morris & Arthur LLP,
Columbus 614 227 2193
jstephen@porterwright.com
Recommended in Employment
Practice Areas: Represents employers
in administrative, arbitration, mediation, trial and appellate proceedings in
all areas of labor and employment law,
including Title VII, NLRA, FLSA, ADA
and OFCCP. Provides training and
advice on employment policies, and litigation avoidance.
Career: Joined firm in 1979; Admitted
in Ohio; US Supreme Court; US Courts
of Appeals for Second, Third and Sixth
Circuits; and US District Courts in
Ohio, Michigan, Kentucky, Indiana, and
Illinois; Adjunct Professor at Capital
University Law and Graduate Center.
Publications: 'Ohio Employment Practices Law'.
Personal: JD, The Ohio State University,
1979; BA (cum laude), DePauw University, 1976.

STRAUCH, John L
Jones Day, Cleveland
216 586 7240
jlstrauch@jonesday.com
Recommended in Litigation
Practice Areas: Immediate past Chair
of the firm's Litigation Group, with
extensive experience in complex litigation. He has been involved in cases concerning product liability, corporate
takeovers, class actions, federal securities, government regulation, commercial
litigation, and antitrust before a variety
of state and federal courts. In connection with litigation matters, he has been
widely quoted in the print media and
has appeared on numerous national
television programs. In addition, he is
frequently mentioned as a leading
lawyer in legal publications.
Prof. Memberships: Fellow, American
College of Trial Lawyers. Life member of
the US Sixth and Ohio Eighth Circuit
Judicial Conferences.

STRAUSS, David
Baker & Hostetler LLP, Cleveland
216 621 0200
Recommended in Real Estate

STRIEFSKY, Linda
Thompson Hine LLP, Cleveland
216 566 5500
Linda.Striefsky@ThompsonHine.com
Recommended in Real Estate
Career: As Chair of the Real Estate
Finance Team, Linda focuses on real
estate financing; loan workouts; secondary loan market transactions; corporate real estate counseling (new project
development, purchases and sales of
facilities with shared services agreements, corporate facilities management,
outsourcing of real estate functions,
multi-site financing); tax abatement and
other government incentives for development; ground, credit tenant and other
leasing and subleasing; and reciprocal
and other easements for commercial
developments. Linda is a member of the
American College of Real Estate
Lawyers, American College of Mortgage
Attorneys, Urban Land Institute and
International Council of Shopping Centers.

STRIMBU Jr, Victor
Baker & Hostetler LLP, Cleveland
216 621 0200
Recommended in Employment

STURTZ, Craig
Squire, Sanders & Dempsey LLP,
Columbus 614 365 2700
Recommended in Environment

SZABO, Paul
Calfee, Halter & Griswold LLP,
Cleveland 216 622 8578
pszabo@calfee.com
Recommended in Intellectual Property
Practice Areas: Intellectual property.
Prof. Memberships: Member of the
International Trademark Association,
American Intellectual Property Law
Association, Cleveland Intellectual
Property Law Association and Cleveland
and Ohio State Bar Associations.
Career: Partner in the Intellectual Property Group. Counsels publicly and privately-held clients regarding patent,
copyright and trademark matters. Handles preparing and prosecuting patent
applications in diverse mechanical and
electro-mechanical technologies,
including occupant safety devices, medical devices, power transmissions and
vehicle steering and suspension components.
Personal: Cleveland-Marshall College
of Law, JD, 1979; St. John's College, BA,
1974.

TAROLLI, Thomas
Tarolli, Sundheim, Covell, & Tummino
LLP, Cleveland 216 621 2234
Recommended in Intellectual Property

TARULLO, Michael
Schottenstein, Zox & Dunn, Columbus
614 462 2304
mtarullo@szd.com
Recommended in Construction
Practice Areas: Both a lawyer and an
engineer, Mr Tarullo has almost 20 years
of field experience in actual construction, construction-related businesses
and field construction claims evaluation
and preparation. Mr Tarullo currently
services the construction industry
through mediation, arbitration and litigation of multiple party disputes, bid
protests, quality of work disputes, time
impact and production claims.

TERP, Thomas
Taft, Stettinius & Hollister LLP,
Cincinnati 513 381 2838
Recommended in Environment

TOSI, Louis
Shumaker Loop & Kendrick LLP, Toledo
419 241 9000
Recommended in Environment

TRAFFORD, Robert W
Porter Wright Morris & Arthur LLP,
Columbus 614 227 2149
rtrafford@porterwright.com
Recommended in Litigation
Practice Areas: Serves as Managing
Partner and concentrates practice in
complex business litigation, including
securities, attorney and accountant malpractice, takeovers, trade secrets, officer
and director, constitutional law, public
utility and other complex business litigation issues.
Career: Admitted in Ohio; US Supreme
Court; US Court of Appeals for the
Fourth, Sixth & Ninth Circuits; US District Court for Northern & Southern
Ohio; US District Court for Northern
Texas; and US District Court for the
Eastern District of MI.
Personal: JD, The Ohio State University,
1977, managing editor, 'Ohio State Law
Journal'; BA (with distinction in Economics), The Ohio State University,
1974.

TUCKER, Robert
Tucker Ellis & West LLP, Cleveland
216 696 1100
Recommended in Litigation

VAN KLEY, Jack A
Jones Day, Columbus
614 281 3875
javankley@jonesday.com
Recommended in Environment
Practice Areas: Engaged in environmental litigation, property transactions,
and counseling, including water and air
pollution, agriculture, livestock and
poultry farms, water rights, Superfund,
hazardous waste, brownfields, drinking
water, mold, and natural resources. Litigates lawsuits, handles administrative
appeals of agency permits and enforcement orders, negotiates permits, conducts environmental audits, oversees
environmental due diligence in property
transfers, and advises clients on regulatory compliance. Drafts and testifies on
legislation. Former litigator for the Ohio
Attorney General for 15 years, representing Ohio EPA and other agencies.
Former chief of that office's Environmental Enforcement Section, supervising all state litigation and background
investigations.

VENESY, Bryan
Squire, Sanders & Dempsey LLP,
Columbus 614 365 2700
Recommended in Real Estate

VICKERS, F Thomas
Ulmer & Berne LLP, Cleveland
216 621 8400
Recommended in Construction

VINCENT, George
Dinsmore & Shohl LLP, Cincinnati
513 977 8200
Recommended in Corporate/M&A

WAMPLER, Samuel
Bricker & Eckler LLP, Columbus
614 227 2300
Recommended in Construction

WAMSLEY, James
Jones Day, Cleveland
216 586 7251
jlwamsleyiii@jonesday.com
Recommended in Intellectual Property
Practice Areas: Practices patent, trademark, trade secrets, and copyright law
and has been involved in litigation,
transactional, and counseling work in
each of these areas. He has extensive
experience in litigation, having served as
a lead counsel for multi-party defendant
groups as well as for plaintiffs in patent
infringement and trade secret cases
involving computer software, networks,
semiconductors and electronics. He also
has acted as counsel in Section 337 proceedings before the US International
Trade Commission, as well as in general
business and commercial litigation. His
experience includes cases involving
European and Asian parties and discovery proceedings in those locations.

WARD, Daniel
Frantz Ward LLP, Cleveland
216 515 1660
Recommended in Employment

WARNER, Charles C
Porter Wright Morris & Arthur LLP,
Columbus 614 227 2013
cwarner@porterwright.com
Recommended in Employment
Practice Areas: Represents employers
in connection with discrimination
charges, express and implied employment contract issues, employment practices, and related tort and benefit claims.
Extensive litigation experience includes
defense of both opt-out and opt-in class
actions.
Prof. Memberships: Fellow, College of
Labor and Employment Lawyers; Management Chair, ABA EEO Committee,
2000-02; OSBA, Council of Delegates

1993-; Columbus Bar Association, President 1991-92, Founding Chair, Labor and Employment Law Committee.
Career: Admitted in Ohio; Sixth Circuit; US District Court for Northern and Southern Districts of Ohio.
Personal: JD (cum laude), The Ohio State University, 1970; BA, Yale University, 1964.

WEBER, Robert
Jones Day, Cleveland
216 586 7252
rcweber@jonesday.com
Recommended in Litigation
Practice Areas: He has tried highly visible cases and counseled corporations, individuals, and boards of directors throughout the US. He has extensive experience in complex civil litigation generally, including corporate derivative and governance litigation, federal and state enforcement actions, and consumer class actions. He has been profiled in national business and legal publications.
Prof. Memberships: Fellow of the American College of Trial Lawyers and the International Academy of Trial Lawyers. Member of The American Law Institute and the Product Liability Advisory Council. He is a life member of the Judicial Conference for the Eighth District of Ohio.

WEBER, Roger
Taft, Stettinius & Hollister LLP, Cincinnati 513 381 2838
Recommended in Employment

WEIBLE, Robert
Baker & Hostetler LLP, Cleveland
216 621 0200
Recommended in Corporate/M&A

WEINER, Samuel
Samuel B Weiner Co. LPA, Columbus
614 443 6581
Recommended in Litigation

WEIR, Bill
Porter Wright Morris & Arthur LLP, Cleveland 216 443 9000
Recommended in Real Estate

WEISS, Mark
Keating, Muething & Klekamp, PLL, Cincinnati 513 579 6400
Recommended in Corporate/M&A

WELIN, Peter
Thompson Hine LLP, Columbus
614 469 3269
Peter.Welin@ThompsonHine.com
Recommended in Construction
Career: A Partner in the Construction Practice Group, focusing on public/private construction litigation, construction contracts, and government procurement law. He participates in alternative dispute resolutions, as a mediator, arbitrator and a member of dispute resolution boards involving high profile public highway projects. A member of Project Management Consultants, a wholly owned affiliate of Thompson Hine, providing project representation, owner representation and partnering/facilitation services for construction clients and owners around the country. With a previous background in construction engineering, he understands the construction industry and the nuances of the building process that aids immeasurably in the resolution of construction related disputes.

WHITAKER, Glenn
Vorys, Sater, Seymour and Pease, Cincinnati 513 723 4608
gvwhitaker@vssp.com
Recommended in Litigation
Practice Areas: Partner focusing on complex litigation in areas of qui tam, false claims; environmental issues; construction law; toxic torts; healthcare fraud, abuse; government procurement, antitrust violations.
Prof. Memberships: American, Ohio, Cincinnati, Maryland and DC Bar Associations; Fellow, American College of Trial Lawyers; American Board of Trial Advocates; University of Cincinnati College of Law (adjunct professor); Potter Stewart American Inn of Court (Emeritus, Master of the Bench).
Career: Admitted to Maryland (1972), DC (1973), Ohio (1980).
Personal: Denison University, BA, magna cum laude, Phi Beta Kappa,

1969; George Washington University, JD, cum laude, Order of the Coif, 1972.

WILKINSON, William
Thompson Hine LLP, Columbus
614 469 3200
william.wilkinson@thompsonhine.com
Recommended in Litigation
Career: Bill is a former Partner-in-Charge and current Vice-Chair of the firm's Business Litigation Practice Group. He handles trials, appeals, agency proceedings and investigations in Ohio and around the country, often representing clients in the manufacturing and financial services industries. The subject matter of Bill's cases includes mergers and acquisitions, trade regulation, intellectual property, securities regulations, financial irregularities, election law, failed business relationships, bankruptcies, and fraud/RICO claims. Those cases have resulted in more than 50 published judicial decisions. He lectures frequently on trial practice and is named on several 'top lawyer' lists.

WINTERS, Karen
Squire, Sanders & Dempsey LLP, Columbus 614 365 2700
Recommended in Environment

WOLFF, Robert M
Duvin, Cahn & Hutton, Cleveland
216 696 7600
rwolff@duvin.com
Recommended in Employment
Practice Areas: Represents clients in general litigation, with an emphasis on employment, civil rights, public sector and commercial litigation. He maintains an active trial schedule and has successfully tried wrongful death, age, race, disability, and sex discrimination, trade secret, legal malpractice defense and major civil rights class actions in addition to numerous arbitrations, and has successfully argued many cases before the Ohio Supreme Court and the US Court of Appeals.
Career: Partner since 1992. Chairman of firm's Management Committee since 1998. Prior to joining firm, he was the Chief Labor and Employment Counsel, City of Cleveland.

Personal: Oberlin College (BA 1977); University of Illinois (JD, cum laude, 1980), editor, Law Review, Harno Scholar, Illinois Governors Fellow. Currently, Trustee and program chair, National Conference for Community and Justice. Vice-Chair and trustee, Multiple Sclerosis Society of Northeast Ohio, Visiting Committee, Cleveland Marshall College of Law and Managing Partner Forum of the Cleveland Bar Association.

WOOLEY, James
Baker & Hostetler LLP, Cleveland
216 621 0200
Recommended in Litigation

YOUNG, David
Squire, Sanders & Dempsey LLP, Columbus 614 365 2700
Recommended in Litigation

YUND, George
Frost Brown Todd LLC, Cincinnati
513 651 6824
gyund@fbtlaw.com
Recommended in Employment
Practice Areas: Labor and employment litigation in federal courts and agencies throughout the country, ERISA litigation, labor arbitrations and negotiations, claims against unions for strike-related misconduct.
Prof. Memberships: Ohio and United States Supreme Court; Courts of Appeals for the Fourth, Sixth, Ninth, Eleventh and DC Circuits.
Career: Joined Frost Brown Todd's predecessor firm, Frost & Jacobs, in 1977; Partner 1984; Member, Frost Brown Todd Compensation Committee.
Personal: Born 15 April 1952. JD (cum laude), University of Michigan School of Law, 1977; BA, The Ohio State University, 1974, (summa cum laude).

ZAGORE, David
Squire, Sanders & Dempsey L.L.P., Cleveland 216 479 8500
Recommended in Corporate/M&A

ZEIGER, John
Zeiger, Tigges, Little & Lindsmith LLP, Columbus 614 365 9900
Recommended in Litigation

CALFEE, HALTER & GRISWOLD LLP

THE FIRM

Managing Partner: Brent D Ballard
Co-Chairmen: Thomas F McKee, Thomas E Wagner

Number of partners: 89
Number of other lawyers: 110

FIRM OVERVIEW: Founded in 1903, Calfee is one of the largest law firms in Ohio and provides a full range of legal services in all substantive areas of law through the US and abroad. With over 200 professionals, services encompass the entire spectrum of general business law - from M&A and litigation, to commercial finance and international, to real estate and intellectual property. Lobbying and government relations services are provided by Thomas Green & Associates LLC, a wholly owned subsidiary of the firm. Representing many *Fortune 500* companies, Calfee has been named one of the best corporate law firms in America by *Corporate Board Member* magazine.

MAIN AREAS OF PRACTICE:

Antitrust & Trade Regulation: Represents clients on antitrust matters in every procedural context before the Federal Trade Commission, US Department of Justice, and in state and federal courts on complex civil and criminal litigation.

Bankruptcy & Creditors' Rights: Services involve all aspects of bankruptcy, corporate reorganization, workout and creditors' rights matters including complex bankruptcy proceedings, debt restructurings and purchases and sales of financially troubled businesses.

Commercial Business & Finance: Counsels financial institutions and borrowers in analyzing, structuring, documenting and negotiating all aspects of finance in private, public, syndicated, international and governmental settings.

Corporate Succession Planning: Helps privately held companies prepare for and transition to the next generation of owners and managers by offering solutions that increase survival opportunities, ensure estate liquidity, address family issues, and maximize planning flexibility.

Employee Benefits & Executive Compensation: Represents clients in all phases of designing and administering employee benefit and retirement programs including design and implementation of sophisticated executive compensation programs, ESOPs and ERISA litigation.

Environmental: Represents clients on matters of compliance, proposed rules and changes, business strategies, and objectives for dealing with environmental regulations and agencies.

Estate & Succession Planning: Assists clients in developing and implementing comprehensive estate plans, probate and trust administration, litigation services and asset protection planning counsel.

General Corporate: Services a variety of public and private businesses at all stages, investors and entrepreneurs on all aspects of entity selection, capital formation, contractual arrangements, and major transactions.

Government Relations & Legislation: Represents clients in legislative, lobbying, contract, regulatory and administrative matters before federal, state and local governmental entities in legislative, lobbying, contract, regulatory and administrative matters.

Health & Long-Term Care/HIPAA: Represents long-term care providers ranging from multi-level retirement communities, to hospital-based skilled nursing units to non-profit and proprietary nursing home operators.

Information Technology: Works with IT clients ranging from start-ups to Fortune 100 companies, vendors and buyers, and from 'bleeding edge' to more traditional enterprises.

Intellectual Property/BioScience/Technology Transfer: One of the largest IP practices within the Midwest. They have more than 30 attorneys registered to practice before the US Patent and Trademark Office and more than 10 other IP attorneys. They provide the full range of prosecution, maintenance and litigation services.

HEAD OFFICE

OHIO
1400 McDonald Investment Center, 800 Superior Avenue,
Cleveland, OH 44114
Tel: 216 622 8200 **Fax:** 216 241 0816
Website: www.calfee.com

BRANCH OFFICE

OHIO
1100 Fifth Third Center, 21 East State Street,
Columbus, OH 43215-4243
Tel: 614 621 1500 **Fax:** 614 621 0010

Labor & Employment: Besides day-to-day employment counseling, they handle administrative complaints and litigation concerning state and federal discrimination laws, National Labor Relations Act, Family & Medical Leave Act, Fair Labor Standards Act and state workers' compensation systems.

Litigation: Skilled in all areas of complex business litigation including IP litigation and other specialized areas, and works to meet client objectives by developing strategies to resolve business conflicts through the traditional legal process or alternative methods of dispute resolution.

Mergers & Acquisitions: Calfee's Mergers & Acquisitions (M&A) Practice spans the entire spectrum of taxable and non-taxable transfers of private and public companies, as well as the structuring and funding of strategic alliances and other joint ventures.

Private Investment Funds: Represents issuers and investors in every type and aspect of a transaction, whether categorized as fund formation, venture capital or other private equity investments, or leveraged-buyout transactions.

Public Law & Finance: Assists community development projects from the drawing board to completion and assists clients in developing programs that are models of public and private sector collaboration.

Real Estate: Represents a wide range of clients in connection with matters related to the acquisition, disposition, construction, development, leasing and financing of real property assets.

Securities & Capital Markets: Nationally recognized as representing issuers and underwriters in more than 75 public offerings raising more than $5 billion over the last 10 years. Assists clients with public and private offerings of securities, regulatory compliance and reporting, proxy solicitations, tender offers and securities litigation.

Tax: Provides comprehensive tax law representation and planning for publicly held companies, privately held businesses, not-for-profit corporations, trusts, partnerships, associations and individuals.

Workers' Compensation & OSHA: Represents employers facing every conceivable workers' compensation, OSHA and related employer liability concern.

INTERNATIONAL WORK: Offers a broad range of services to companies transacting business across the border or overseas and to those venturing into the United States. To enhance the firm's scope of services, Calfee is a founding member of Lex Mundi, a worldwide consortium of more than 160 independent law firms.

Calfee
Halter &
Griswold LLP
calfee.com

DINSMORE & SHOHL LLP

THE FIRM

Managing Partner: Clifford A Roe, Jr
Number of partners: 119
Total number of attorneys: 257

FIRM OVERVIEW: Dinsmore & Shohl LLP is a full-service law firm with over 250 attorneys practicing in seven offices in four states. For the past 96 years Dinsmore & Shohl has provided a broad range of integrated services to meet the needs of both large and small businesses as well as institutions, associations, governments, professional firms and individuals. The firm has been named one of the best corporate law firms in America in an annual survey conducted by Corporate Board Member magazine. Dinsmore & Shohl offers counsel in the following areas of law: business and corporate, bankruptcy, employee benefits, environmental, family wealth planning, first amendment and media, general commercial and specialty litigation, intellectual property, international, labor and employment, mass tort and medical litigation, real estate and commercial finance.

MAIN AREAS OF PRACTICE:

Corporate/Securities: Dinsmore & Shohl provides a full range of transactional, regulatory and other advisory services to the firm's regional, national and international business clients. The firm handles business formation and organization; corporate finance; federal and state securities law; federal, state and local tax law; real estate; employee and executive benefits; trust and estate planning; probate; banking; commercial law; mergers and acquisitions; venture capital; partnerships; limited liability companies and joint ventures.

General Commercial & Specialty Litigation: Dinsmore & Shohl attorneys practice on a local and regional basis at the trial, appellate and Supreme Court levels in federal and state courts as well as before a wide variety of governmental agencies. The firm also has broad experience in coordinating and defending lawsuits on a national basis. The firm has represented scores of manufacturers in cases filed in various state and federal courts throughout the United States. Attorneys are trained in medicine, nursing, pharmacy, x-ray technology, toxicology and engineering. The firm has represented manufacturers of a wide variety of products in a myriad of markets including automotive, ethical pharmaceutical, household products and appliances, manufacturing/industrial, medical/device, recreational, tobacco, and toxic.

Labor & Employment: The firm handles all phases of labor and employment issues including collective bargaining, employment discrimination, sexual harassment, OSHA inspections, workers' compensation, arbitration, alternative dispute resolution, wage and hour, immigration, and class action litigation. The firm represents clients before federal, state, and local administrative agencies, including the EEOC and the NLRB.

Intellectual Property: Dinsmore & Shohl's full-service practice group includes a diverse range of technical backgrounds and legal experience to efficiently and effectively respond to client needs. The group's continually expanding worldwide practice includes substantial experience with respect to all areas of intellectual property law including: patents, trademarks, trade names, service marks, copyrights, computer software and hardware, business method and internet-related developments, trade secrets, trade dress, anti-trust, unfair trade practices, unfair competition and franchising matters. Dinsmore & Shohl was named one of the top patent and top trademark firm by Intellectual Property Today.

CLIENTS: The firm represents clients in the following industries: banking, biotechnology, coal, communications, construction, consumer goods, education, healthcare, high tech, manufacturing, pharmaceuticals, real estate development, retail, software development, telecommunications,

HEAD OFFICE

OHIO
255 East Fifth Street, Suite 1900, **Cincinnati**, OH 45202
Tel: 513 977 8200   **Fax:** 513 977 8141
Email: info@dinslaw.com
Website: www.dinslaw.com

BRANCH OFFICES

KENTUCKY
Lexington Financial Center, 250 West Main Street, Suite 1400, **Lexington**, KY 40507
Tel: 859 425 1000   **Fax:** 859 425 1099

1400 PNC Plaza, 500 West Jefferson Street, **Louisville**, KY 40202
Tel: 502 540 2300   **Fax:** 502 585 2207

OHIO
175 South Third Street, **Columbus**, OH 43215
Tel: 614 628 6880   **Fax:** 614 628 6890

One Dayton Centre, One South Main Street, Suite 1300, **Dayton**, OH 45402
Tel: 937 449 6400   **Fax:** 937 449 6405

PENNSYLVANIA
The Grant Building, 330 Grant Street, Suite 2415, **Pittsburgh**, PA 15219
Tel: 412 281 5000   **Fax:** 412 281 50550

WEST VIRGINIA
900 Lee Street, Huntington Square, Suite 600, **Charleston**, WV 25301
Tel: 304 357 0900   **Fax:** 304 357 0919

CONTACTS

Bankruptcy	Kim Martin Lewis
Corporate/Securities	George H Vincent
Employee Benefits	Ben F Wells
Environmental	Vincent B Stamp
Family Wealth Planning	J Michael Cooney
General Commercial & Specialty Litigation	Mark A Vander Laan
Intellectual Property	James F Gottman
Labor & Employment	Charles M Roesch
Mass Tort/Medical Litigation	Frank C Woodside, III
Real Estate/Commercial Finance	Thomas J Sherman
Workers' Compensation	George B Wilkinson

transportation and utilities. Representative clients include Arch Coal, Inc.; Beverly Enterprises, Inc.; Castellini Company; Chemed Corporation; Cincinnati Children's Hospital Medical Center; Clopay Corporation; Dover Resources Division/OPW Fueling Components; General Electric; General Motors Corp.; Halma PLC; Host Communications, Inc.; Huffy Corporation; International Flavors and Fragrances, Inc.; Jeffrey R. Anderson Real Estate, Inc.; Jewish Hospital Healthcare Services, Inc.; Kentucky Technology, Inc.; Lenscrafters; Liberty Mutual Insurance Co.; Milacron, Inc.; Peabody Energy; Pressley Ridge West Virginia; Progress Energy; R. J. Tobacco Company; Sherwin Williams; The Courier-Journal; The Kroger Co.; The Procter & Gamble Co.; The Standard Register Company; The U.S. Playing Card Co.; United Dairy Farmers; US Bank.

INTERNATIONAL WORK: Dinsmore & Shohl represents public and private companies and individuals in a wide range of international transactions and efficiently solves the unique legal, tax and practical issues confronting clients in their foreign dealings. Based on years of repeated collaboration, the firm has also established and maintained close working relationships with several foreign and domestic firms. Dinsmore & Shohl is a founding member of ALFA International.

Dinsmore&Shohl LLP
ATTORNEYS

DUVIN, CAHN & HUTTON

THE FIRM

Managing Partner: Robert M Wolff
Senior Partner: Robert P Duvin

Number of partners: 23
Number of other lawyers: 24

FIRM OVERVIEW: Since the firm's founding in 1972, Duvin, Cahn & Hutton has been recognized as one of the nation's pre-eminent labor and employment law firms. The firm has a nationwide practice in labor relations, employment law and complex commercial litigation.

MAIN AREAS OF PRACTICE:

Labor Relations: The historic foundation of the firm is the Labor Relations Practice which cemented the image of Duvin, Cahn & Hutton as tenacious advocates, securing concessions in collective bargaining. In addition to negotiating major collective bargaining agreements for both private and public sector clients, the firm's attorneys are continuously consulted on the administration of collective bargaining agreements and handle contract arbitrations. The practice also includes extensive union-related litigation before state and Federal courts and administrative agencies. The firm also engages in extensive union organizing counseling and all related litigation.

Employment Law: The firm's practice is nationwide including full-service counseling and an active litigation practice in the defense of class actions, employment discrimination, employee privacy issues, wrongful discharge, employment related torts, employee benefits, wage and hour issues, OSHA and workers' compensation.

Commercial Litigation: The firm handles complex contract disputes in both private industry and government, securities litigation, anti-trust actions, defense of legal malpractice claims and unfair competition claims.

CLIENTS: Duvin, Cahn & Hutton represents both private and public sector clients in the retail, food, industrial, healthcare, musical arts, sports, and financial industries nationwide.

Representative Firm Clients: Cleveland Clinic Foundation; Alcan; City of Cleveland; Avery Dennison; Cleveland Browns; Cleveland Orchestra; Continental Airlines; Dominion East Ohio Gas; Electrolux Home Products; Forest City Enterprises; Goldschmidt Chemical; Goodyear Tire & Rubber Company; Lincoln Electric; MBNA; McDonald's; Boise Office Products/OfficeMax; SBC Communications.

HEAD OFFICE

OHIO
Erieview Tower 20th Floor, 1301 E. 9th Street, **Cleveland**, OH 44114
Tel: 216 696 7600   **Fax:** 216 696 2038
Website: www.duvinlaw.com
Email: attorneys@duvin.com

CONTACTS

Labor	Robert P Duvin
	Frank W Buck
Union Avoidance	Andrew C Meyer
	Stephen J Sferra
Employment	Lee J Hutton
	Sue Marie Douglas
Commercial Litigation	Robert M Wolff
OSHA	Kenneth B Stark
Employee Benefits	Neal B Wainblat

FAY SHARPE FAGAN MINNICH & MCKEE LLP

THE FIRM

Management Committee: James W McKee, Timothy E Nauman, Richard M Klein

Number of partners: 18
Number of other lawyers: 22
Number of registered patent agents: 42

FIRM OVERVIEW: Fay Sharpe has focused on supporting the technology advancements of its clients and safeguarding intellectual property rights since 1884. The firm is one of the largest intellectual property boutiques in the Midwest with IP attorneys, technical consultants, and a worldwide network of intellectual property resources covering biotechnology, chemistry, engineering, physics, computer science and virtually every technology in between.

MAIN AREAS OF PRACTICE: Fay Sharpe offers a complete range of IP legal services and capabilities designed to protect and enhance intellectual property. These services focus on:

Patents: To protect a patentable concept or to avoid infringement upon another's patented concept, Fay Sharpe conducts patent searches and studies; renders patentability, patent validity and patent infringement opinions; and prepares, files and prosecutes patent applications (utility and design) before the US Patent and Trademark Office (USPTO), and around the world through the firm's vast network of foreign associates.

Trademarks & Service Marks: Fay Sharpe helps its clients safeguard their trademarks and service marks through counseling on selection, design and use; rendering opinions concerning trademark infringement and registration of trademarks and service marks; preparing, filing and prosecuting applications for registration of trademarks and service marks before the USPTO, state and foreign administrative offices; and representing clients in trademark opposition and cancellation proceedings in the USPTO and foreign administrative offices.

Copyrights: Fay Sharpe counsels its clients on copyright protection for their literary, dramatic, musical, artistic works and computer software; and prepares, files and prosecutes applications to federally register copyright.

Trade Secrets: Often trade secret protection is the only viable way of protecting intellectual property, especially where patent or copyright protection is not applicable, in these cases Fay Sharpe counsels clients in protection and commercial exploitation of trade secrets and prepares confidentiality agreements.

Licensing of Intellectual Property: Fay Sharpe supports the commercial exploitation of intellectual property by counseling its clients on patent, trademark, copyright and know-how licensing agreements, contracts for high technology enterprises, software licenses, and consulting agreements; and analyzing the antitrust implications of licensing.

Litigation: Fay Sharpe's litigators represent both plaintiffs and defendants in state and federal court and before state and federal agencies. Fay Sharpe's litigation services include patent infringement and patent interferences; trademark and service mark infringement; trademark opposition and cancellation proceedings; deceptive business practices; copyright infringement; unfair competition; misappropriation of trade secrets and confidential information; intellectual property related antitrust issues; license agreement disputes; employee contract disputes and actions before the International Trade Commission.

CLIENTS: Fay Sharpe clients represent some of the top names in technology and innovation, spanning Fortune 500 and mid-level companies to emerging technology start-ups and individual pacesetters.

HEAD OFFICE

OHIO
1100 Superior Avenue, 7th Floor, **Cleveland**, OH 44114
Tel: 216 861 5582 **Fax:** 216 241 1666
Email: fs@faysharpe.com
Website: www.faysharpe.com

PATENTS & TECHNOLOGY

Some representative patents, and their root technology, prepared and prosecuted by Fay Sharpe include:

Electrical: *GELcore LLC - US6799864* - High power LED power pack for spot module illumination; *General Electric Company - US6809477* - Fluorescent lamp electrode for instant start circuits; *Koninklijke Philips Electronics, N.V. - US6804546* - Multiple contrast echo-planar imaging for contrast-enhanced imaging; *Lincoln Global, Inc. - US6717108* - Electric arc welder and method of designing waveforms therefor; *Lucent Technologies Inc. - US6538416* - Border gateway reservation protocol for tree-based aggregation of inter- domain reservations; *Xerox Corporation - US6819792* - Automatic detection of colorimetry of unknown CMYK images.

Mechanical: *Argo-Tech Corporation - US6810674* - Fuel delivery system; *Barnes Group Inc. - US6773002* - Compression spring rod; *Cloyes Gear and Products, Inc. - US6761657* - Roller chain sprocket with added chordal pitch reduction; *Henkel Consumer Adhesives, Inc. - US6579587* - Paint masking for corners; *Nu-Kote International, Inc. - US6814433* - Base aperture in ink jet cartridge with irregular edges for breaking surface tension of the ink; *Royal Appliance Mfg. Co. - US6735815* - Upright vacuum cleaner with cyclonic air flow; *Steris Inc. - US6582654* - Fluid spray system for cleaning and sterilizing medical devices supported on a rack.

Chemical/Biotech: *BioStratum, Inc. - US6576418* - Method for determining the nucleotide sequence of the gene for the $\alpha 5(IV)$ chain of human type IV collagen; *Bonne Bell, Inc. - US6723307* - Cosmetic lip product with sour flavor; *Case Western Reserve University - US6586561* - Rigid rod ion conducting copolymers; *The Clorox Company - US6825158* - Bactericidal cleaning wipe comprising a cationic biocide; *Cooper Technology Services, LLC - US6800691* - Blend of EPDM and SBR using an EPDM of different origin as a compatibilizer; *Omnova Solutions Inc. - US6793861* - Optimization of in-mold coating injection molded thermoplastic substrates; *Spalding Sports Worldwide, Inc. - US6394913* - Multi-layer golf ball; *Xerox Corporation - US6770904* - Polythiophenes and electronic devices generated therefrom.

REPORTED CASES

Antonious v Spalding & Evenflo Cos., Inc., 281 F.3d 1258 (Fed. Cir. 2002); Microsoft Corp. v Action Software, 136 F.Supp.2d 735 (N.D. Ohio 2001); Dolly, Inc. v Spalding & Evenflo Cos., 16 F.3d 394 (Fed. Cir. 1994); Vanmoor v Wal-Mart Stores, Inc., 201 F.3d 1363 (Fed. Cir 2000); Hoover Co. v Royal Appliance Manufacturing Co., 238 F.3d1357 (Fed. Cir. 2001); Sherwin-Williams Co. v Glidden Co., 49 USPQ2d 1623 (N.D. Ohio 1998).

Fay Sharpe

WE PROTECT YOUR IDEAS.

PORTER WRIGHT MORRIS & ARTHUR LLP

THE FIRM

Managing Partner: Robert W Trafford
Number of partners: 149
Number of other lawyers: 164

FIRM OVERVIEW: Porter Wright Morris & Arthur LLP is a nationally recognized law firm that traces its origins to 1846 in Ohio. With 313 lawyers, the firm brings together the knowledge, skills, and experience to represent its clients effectively and efficiently in complex legal problems and business opportunities.

MAIN AREAS OF PRACTICE

Antitrust & Trade Regulation: The firm provides analysis, counseling, litigation, and alternative dispute resolution support on complex antitrust issues.

Business & Securities: From business formation to mergers and acquisitions, the firm provides full-service counseling and advice to domestic and international enterprises.

Construction: The firm represents clients in construction-related issues ranging from labor disputes to construction contracts and claims.

Employee Benefits: Porter Wright provides legal counsel on all aspects of employee benefits, including ERISA, benefits plan design and implementation, audits, and litigation.

Environmental Law: Porter Wright works with clients on permitting, compliance, planning, and enforcement matters, including EPCRA, Superfund, and environmental assessment and remediation.

Finance & Commerce: The firm represents clients in financing and credit arrangements and related commercial transactions, including bankruptcy, creditors' rights, lease/loan financing, and workouts.

Financial Institutions: The firm works with clients on matters from federal/state regulations to M&A, trust administration, real estate acquisitions, and loan/deposit products.

Government Contracts: Porter Wright assists clients with government contract matters, including contract negotiations, DCAA audits, debarment/suspension, defective pricing, and protests/claims.

Governmental Affairs: Porter Wright represents clients in administrative and legislative matters such as legislation drafting/tracking; lobbying; and legislative, hearing, or regulatory representation.

Healthcare: The firm offers comprehensive healthcare-related legal services, including HIPAA; licensing; compliance plans/audits; physician practice groups/organizations; hospital and long-term care facilities; financing; and fraud/abuse, Stark, antikickback, and false claims.

Immigration: Porter Wright represents clients on immigration matters, including temporary employment visas, national interest waivers, priority worker immigrant visa petitions, and permanent resident applications.

Insurance & Financial Services: Porter Wright represents clients in litigation/arbitration, market conduct, M&A, reinsurance, regulatory, and investment matters.

Intellectual Property: The firm assists clients in obtaining and preserving/protecting trademark, copyright, and patent protection.

Labor & Employment: The firm represents clients in matters regarding executive contracts, OSHA/MSHA, affirmative action, arbitrations, and union contract negotiations, and provides representation in employment litigation ranging from employment discrimination class actions to proceedings before state and federal oversight agencies.

Litigation: Porter Wright represents clients at pretrial, trial, and appellate litigation in federal and state courts, before regulatory agencies and arbitration panels, and in alternative dispute resolution.

Real Estate: Porter Wright represents clients in commercial real estate, including acquisition/development, fair housing, architect/contractor agreements, and industrial revenue bonds.

HEAD OFFICE

OHIO
41 South High Street, **Columbus,** OH 43215
Tel: 614 227 2000   **Fax:** 614 227 2100
Email: columbus@porterwright.com
Website: www.porterwright.com

BRANCH OFFICES

DISTRICT OF COLUMBIA
1919 Pennsylvania Avenue N.W., Suite 500, **Washington,** DC 20006
Tel: 202 778 3000   **Fax:** 202 778 3063
Email: washington@porterwright.com

FLORIDA
5801 Pelican Bay Boulevard, Suite 300, **Naples,** FL 34108
Tel: 239 593 2900   **Fax:** 239 593 2990
Email: naples@porterwright.com

OHIO
250 East Fifth Street, Suite 2200, **Cincinnati,** OH 45202
Tel: 513 381 4700   **Fax:** 513 421 0991
Email: cincinnati@porterwright.com

925 Euclid Avenue, Suite 1700, **Cleveland,** OH 44115
Tel: 216 443 9000   **Fax:** 216 443 9011
Email: cleveland@porterwright.com

One Dayton Centre, One South Main Street, Suite 1600
Dayton, OH 45402
Tel: 937 449 6810   **Fax:** 937 449 6820
Email: dayton@porterwright.com

Tax: The firm provides services in federal, state, local, and international taxation, ranging from business/entity planning and tax disputes to tax credits.

Technology: Porter Wright assists clients with technology issues and transactions, including acquisition/licensing, security, Web contracts, and e-business.

Trusts & Estates: The firm assists clients with business enterprise transfer of management and control, as well as property interest transfers through wills, trusts, family limited partnerships and LLCs, durable powers of attorney, and charitable remainder trusts.

Utilities & Energy: Porter Wright represents utilities clients in areas ranging from competitive complaint cases to market entry or restructuring, power siting, and rulemaking proceedings.

White Collar Crime/Government Enforcement: From compliance counseling to grand jury and agency investigations, internal investigations, and victim representation/fraud recovery, Porter Wright represents clients whose operations and activities are placed under government scrutiny or are the subject of governmental enforcement actions.

INTERNATIONAL WORK: Porter Wright performs a wide range of international legal services. The firm has gained an international standing and capability before the European Union through admittance of one of its attorneys to the Paris Bar.

PORTER
WRIGHT
MORRIS &
ARTHUR LLP
**Attorneys and
Counselors at Law**

SCHOTTENSTEIN ZOX & DUNN

THE FIRM

Managing Partner: James E Davidson
Number of partners: 66
Number of associates: 43

FIRM OVERVIEW: Schottenstein Zox & Dunn prides itself on being an innovative and responsive law firm dedicated to partnering with its clients to ensure the fulfillment of each client's business objectives. An exemplary corporate citizen in the communities it serves, the firm is committed to improving the way law is practiced by leveraging its strong entrepreneurial bias, business experience, superior legal talent, and advanced technologies to enhance the growth and business success of its clients.

MAIN AREAS OF PRACTICE:

Banking & Finance: Provides representation and transaction planning advice to both lenders and borrowers in virtually all types of financing transactions.

Bankruptcy: Counsels clients through the complex matters surrounding bankruptcy, debtor/creditor relations, workouts and business reorganizations.

Construction: Serves industry clients in a broad range of matters, from bidding awards and contract disputes to labor and employment issues.

Corporate: Provides the full range of legal services required by businesses regardless of their form of entity or industry.

E-commerce: Provides strategic advice and counsel to a dynamic array of clients seeking to increase efficiencies and reach new markets through the internet.

Employee Benefits: Provides analysis, advice and documentation for all types of employee benefit programs to provide solutions that mesh with clients' overall business, financial and personal objectives.

Environmental: Provides consultation, advice and legal representation to businesses and government entities on compliance with environmental laws and regulations.

Estate Planning: Assists families with all phases of the accumulation, preservation and distribution of family wealth; assists closely-held businesses with all aspects of succession planning.

Government & Regulatory Affairs: Advises clients on a variety of matters including business regulation, economic development, government contracts, legislative advocacy, telecommunications, e-commerce and zoning to help solve business problems and create opportunities.

Health Law: Provides representation and strategic advice to the dynamic healthcare industry, serving hundreds of healthcare organizations across the full spectrum of healthcare delivery and payment systems.

Immigration: Consults businesses on strategies for employing foreign nationals and assists multi-national corporations seeking to employ or transfer international personnel to the United States.

Intellectual Property & Technology Protection: Helps clients audit, protect and derive income from their intellectual property, technology and intangible rights.

Labor & Employment: Represents clients in a diversified range of industries in all aspects of labor and employment law. Provides preventive employee relations to help reduce costly and time consuming litigation.

Litigation: Advises clients as to how to take proactive efforts to protect against claims and how to be prepared to aggressively prosecute and defend claims in a manner that advances and protects clients' interests.

Public Finance: Provides clients with practical, comprehensive counsel and solutions serving significant government needs and involving some of the region's most valuable public and private projects.

HEAD OFFICE

OHIO
250 West Street, **Columbus** OH 43215
Tel: 614 462 2700   **Fax:** 614 462 5135
Website: www.szd.com

BRANCH OFFICES

OHIO
US Bank Centre, 1350 Euclid Avenue, Suite 1400, **Cleveland** OH 44115
Tel: 216 621 6501   **Fax:** 216 621 6502

8044 Montgomery Road, Suite 630, **Cincinnati** OH 45236-2926
Tel: 513 792 0792   **Fax:** 513 792 0803

CONTACTS

Bankruptcy	Victoria E Powers
Business Law	Richard A Barnhart; Robert R Ouellette
E-Commerce, Intellectual Property & Technology Protection	Susan D Rector
Environmental	Stephen P Samuels
Government & Regulatory Affairs	David J Robinson
Health Law	Peter A Pavarini
Labor & Employment	Felix C Wade
Litigation	Kevin R McDermott
Public Law	Stephen J Smith
Tax/Wealth Preservation Planning	John Terakedis Jr; Richard Holz

For specific contact information, please visit **www.szd.com**

Public Law: Provides strategic advice and counsel for addressing legal issues involved in the day-to-day delivery of government services for municipal clients, industry clients and school districts; works to spur economic growth in response to the needs of various municipalities.

Real Estate: Represents developers, lenders, investors, tenants, landlords and others in the acquisition, development, financing, selling, leasing and management of properties in all phases of real estate transactions and other property issues.

Tax: Assists clients with a myriad of tax-related situations including specific tax issues faced by individuals, small and large closely and widely-held businesses and publicly held companies.

Workers' Compensation: Represents self insured and state fund employers in all aspects of the defense of workers' compensation claims in both the administrative and court setting.

CLIENTS: Schottenstein Zox & Dunn's clients include national and international corporations as well as regional and local companies in the following industries: manufacturing; retail; transportation; distribution; real estate; communications; banking; insurance; advertising; education; healthcare; high tech; food services; lodging; construction; public sector; professional services; and not-for-profit.

INTERNATIONAL WORK: As many of the firm's clients venture into international markets, the firm has extended its legal services to Mexico, Canada, Europe, Asia and South America, focusing on strategic planning, joint ventures, mergers and acquisitions, international financing, international manufacturing, distribution and licensing agreements, export and import, intellectual property, international arbitration and litigation, international tax and immigration matters.

THOMPSON HINE LLP

THE FIRM

Managing Partner: David J Hooker

Number of partners: 165
Number of other lawyers: 185

Website: www.ThompsonHine.com
Email: info@ThompsonHine.com

FIRM OVERVIEW: Established in 1911, Thompson Hine today is among the largest business law firms in the United States. For the last three years, the firm has been named as one of the 'Best Corporate Law Firms' in America (in an annual survey of 32,000 corporate directors conducted by Corporate Board Member magazine). With more than 360 lawyers, Thompson Hine serves some of the premier businesses in the world, including: Ford, Toyota, Goodrich, Goodyear, Alltel, Verizon, KeyCorp, Bank One, Toro and Whirlpool. The firm has offices in Atlanta, Georgia; Brussels, Belgium; Cincinnati, Cleveland, Columbus, and Dayton, Ohio; New York, New York; and Washington, DC. For more information, please visit the firm's website.

MAIN AREAS OF PRACTICE:

Admirality & Maritime: Represents more than 200 carriers and shippers before state and federal courts and agencies.
Bankruptcy: Represents lenders, creditors' committees, debtors and other parties in finance transactions, workouts and bankruptcy matters.
Biotech: Represents emerging and established biotechnology companies on matters ranging from financing to joint ventures to intellectual property.
Business Litigation: Represents clients in a wide variety of business litigation - from corporate control contests and insurance disputes, to class actions, securities fraud, and tax controversies.
Commercial & Public Finance: Handle commercial finance transactions, public finance, asset securitizations and general bank regulatory law.
Competition, Antitrust & White Collar Crime: Represents clients in trade restraint price discrimination, franchising and distribution, trade secrets, false advertising, and fraud.
Construction: Represents owners, design professionals, construction managers, contractors and sureties. Serves in the role of project counsel for billions of dollars of construction at sites across the US.
Corporate Transactions & Securities: Represents both emerging and established businesses in their most important business transactions, from startup through IPOs, joint ventures, mergers, acquisitions and beyond.
International Trade & Customs: Represents clients in penalty actions, investigations, and audits before US administrative agencies responsible for regulating imports and exports; advertises clients on issues that affect their global market share, including opportunities under trade agreements and litigation of unfair trade cases.
e-Business & Emerging Technologies: Helps businesses realize the opportunities and manage the risks of electronic and technological commerce.
Employee Benefits & Executive Compensation: Advises clients regarding benefit plans, ERISA issues, controversies with the IRS, DOL, PBGC and other agencies; incentive and equity-based compensation, and ESOPs.
Energy & Utilities: Advises traditional and new business entities participating in the evolving energy markets, with respect to both regulated (at state and federal levels) and non-regulated energy transactions for natural gas, electricity, renewable energy, water and waste energy.
Environmental: Advises clients on the environmental aspects on their business transactions, crafting methods of allocating risk and counseling them on their compliance obligations under local, federal and state laws.
Healthcare: Represents physician groups, hospitals, clinical laboratories, diagnostic service providers, pharmaceutical manufacturers, medical device manufacturers and health insurance providers.

HEAD OFFICE

OHIO
3900 Key Center, 127 Public Square, **Cleveland,** OH 44114-1291
Tel: 216 566 5500   **Fax:** 216 566 5800
Email: info@ThompsonHine.com

BRANCH OFFICES

DISTRICT OF COLUMBIA
1920 N Street, NW, Suite 800, **Washington,** DC 20036-1600
Tel: 202 331 8800   **Fax:** 202 331 8330

GEORGIA
Proscenium Center, Suite 1200; 1170 Peachtree Street,
Atlanta, GA 30309-7673
Tel: 404 541 2900   **Fax:** 404 541 2905

NEW YORK
One Chase Manhattan Plaza,58th Floor, **New York,** NY 10005-1401
Tel: 212 344 5680   **Fax:** 212 809 6890

OHIO
312 Walnut Street, 14th Floor, **Cincinnati,** OH 45202-4089
Tel: 513 352 6700   **Fax:** 513 241 4771

10 West Broad Street, Suite 700, **Columbus,** OH 43215-3435
Tel: 614 469 3200   **Fax:** 614 469 3361

2000 Courthouse Plaza, NE PO Box 8801, **Dayton,** OH 45401-8801
Tel: 937 443 6600   **Fax:** 937 443 6635

Intellectual Property: Assists clients with patents, trademarks, copyrights, trade secrets, computer software, internet-related issues, and IP litigation.
International: The firm advises US clients on matters in all regions of the world, as well as foreign clients with interests in the US.
Labor & Employment: Represents clients in employment litigation, workers' compensation, immigration, collective bargaining, proceedings before the Department of Labor, OSHA, EEOC, NLRB and various state agencies.
Life Sciences: Focuses on creating business solutions and managing critical legal and regulatory issues for companies engaged in all facets of the research, development and delivery of human and animal health products and services.
Personal & Succession Planning: Assists clients in the management and transmission of wealth, the succession of businesses and other personal and family concerns.
Product Liability: Handles thousands of product liability matters involving mechanical, chemical, electrical, medical, aerospace, automotive and other products.
Product Safety: Represents companies and industry groups before the Consumer Product Safety Commission (CPSC); advises on recalls, civil penalty matters and CPSC safety standards.
Real Estate: Represents clients in development, corporate real estate, zoning and land use; real estate investment and financing, and REITs.
Tax: Advises clients in business transactions and financings, tax controversy litigation, legislative and regulatory activities, international taxation, state and local taxation and foundation and exempt organization matters.
Telecommunications: Provides clients with wide-ranging guidance on the regulations and laws affecting telecommunications, broadcasting and other electronic communications companies.
Transportation: Represents shippers, third party logistics providers and other intermediaries, as well as other transportation interests in regulatory, commercial, policy, and litigation matters.

VORYS, SATER, SEYMOUR AND PEASE LLP

THE FIRM

Managing Partner: Robert W Werth

Number of partners: 163
Total number of attorneys: 380

FIRM OVERVIEW: Established in 1909, Vorys, Sater, Seymour and Pease LLP has grown to one of the nation's largest law firms through its focus on delivering superior legal versatility, experience and depth to its clients. The culture emphasizes self-governing, high ethical standards and a teamwork approach to managing client work. Clients range from some of the world's largest companies to individuals and small businesses. The firm represents them in Ohio, across the country and around the world in litigation, business and personal transactions involving virtually every legal subject. This client and practice diversity is matched by the diversity of the firm's lawyers who come from over 25 states and are graduates of more than 20 law schools. The firm's lawyers are also extensively involved in projects, organizations and affiliations which strengthen and support their regional communities.

MAIN AREAS OF PRACTICE:

Commercial & Real Estate: Vorys' commercial and real estate attorneys advise financial institutions and large corporate borrowers in connection with sophisticated financing transactions; provide franchising counsel to some of the largest franchisors in the world; advise clients on the full range of real estate matters including acquisitions, sales and exchanges, development, commercial leasing, syndications, equity financing, foreclosures and loan workouts; and provide the full breadth of bankruptcy counsel.

Corporate & Finance: Members of the Corporate and Finance Group are legal advisers to *Fortune* 500 and other public companies, financial institutions, established private businesses and new ventures, communication and technology companies, nonprofit organizations, investment bankers and underwriters, public utilities, individual entrepreneurs and investors.

Energy & Utilities: The Energy and Utility Group represents the oil and gas industry, telecommunications companies, broadcasters and cable television operators in a wide variety of legal areas, including contract and general litigation, bankruptcy, environmental matters, and before regulatory bodies.

Environmental: Vorys' environmental attorneys have counseled clients on environmental issues since the inception of government regulation, including: regulatory matters, compliance counseling, legislation and rule-making, PRP groups, cost recovery action, contractual indemnities, toxic tort and environmental litigation, and class action defense.

Government & Lobbying: The firm's attorneys in the government and lobbying area are constantly involved in public contracting issues and litigation in all levels of government.

Healthcare: Vorys' healthcare lawyers have successfully represented and counseled clients - from independent practitioners to multi-national management systems - on a complete range of legal matters that span from business-related issues such as real estate and insurance to specialized concerns about Medicare reimbursement and HIPAA compliance.

Intellectual Property: The firm's intellectual property attorneys have extensive experience in the acquisition, enforcement, and exploitation of patents, trademarks, copyrights, and industrial designs, as well as in unfair competition, trade secrets, computer law, and related matters.

International Law: The firm's International Law Practice includes international corporate and commercial transactions, international finance and the regulation of US exports and investment abroad.

Labor & Employment: Vorys' labor and employment attorneys represent manufacturers, retailers, transportation service companies, financial institutions, healthcare facilities, colleges and universities, and public employers, many of whom the firm represents on a national or regional basis. In addition, Vorys has unique experience in representing companies, in the area of false claims litigation, who are regulated by the US government's regulatory agencies.

Litigation: About 30% of the firm's lawyers are involved in its Litigation Practice, where it is retained in large, complex and oftentimes sensitive litigation on a regular basis.

Probate & Estate Planning: The Probate and Estate Planning Group has extensive expertise in the representation of fiduciaries and beneficiaries of estates, trusts and guardianships, with special emphasis on Ohio and Florida.

Tax: The firm's tax lawyers engage in all aspects of federal, state and local tax practice as part of the firm's general representation of clients and as special tax counsel.

Technology: Vorys' Technology Group counsels users and vendors on the development, distribution and protection of their technology assets.

Toxic Tort: The Toxic Tort Group aggressively represents defendants in matters involving asbestos, silica, mold, mycotoxin, vinyl chloride, MCEs, and radiation.

HEAD OFFICE

OHIO
52 East Gay Street, **Columbus**, OH 43215
Tel: 614 464 6400   **Fax:** 614 464 6350
Website: www.vssp.com

BRANCH OFFICES

DISTRICT OF COLUMBIA
1828 L Street NW, 11th Floor, **Washington**, DC 20036
Tel: 202 467 8800   **Fax:** 202 467 8900

OHIO
Suite 200, Atrium Two, 221 East Fourth Street, **Cincinnati**, OH 45202
Tel: 513 723 4000   **Fax:** 513 723 4056

2100 One Cleveland Center, 1375 East Ninth Street, **Cleveland**, OH 44114
Tel: 216 479 6100   **Fax:** 216 479 6060

First National Tower, 106 South Main Street, **Akron**, OH 44308
Tel: 330 208 1000   **Fax:** 330 208 1001

VIRGINIA
Suite 310, 277 South Washington Street, **Alexandria**, VA 22314
Tel: 703 837 6999   **Fax:** 703 549 4492

CONTACTS

Litigation	Suzanne Richards
Corporate/Finance	John Vorys
Energy/Utilities	Scott Doran
Labor/Employment	Jonathan Norman
Probate/Tax	George Corey
Commercial/Real Estate	John Wellner
Technology/IP	Cory Amron
Marketing Director	Maureen Conley

For specific contact information, please see **www.vssp.com**

VORYS, SATER, SEYMOUR AND PEASE LLP

CONTENTS: Corporate/M&A p.1459; Employment p.1460; Litigation p.1462; Real Estate p.1463; Individuals' Profiles p.1464; Firms' Profiles p.1467.

How lawyers are ranked

The opinions we gather from clients — mainly from in-house lawyers but also from other purchasers of legal services — are balanced by opinions from colleagues and competitors. Together, they provide two different perspectives — an all-round view — and biased viewpoints cancel each other out.

CORPORATE/M&A

Oklahoma
Leading firms (Corporate/M&A)

1. **CONNER & WINTERS, PC** *Tulsa*
   CROWE & DUNLEVY *Oklahoma City*
   MCAFEE & TAFT *Oklahoma City*
2. **COMMERCIAL LAW GROUP** *Oklahoma City*
   DERRICK & BRIGGS LLP *Oklahoma City*
   HARTZOG CONGER CASON *Oklahoma City*
   MCKINNEY & STRINGER *Oklahoma City*

Leading individuals (Corporate/M&A)

1. **ELAM Theodore** *McAfee & Taft, Oklahoma City*
   MOORE Lynnwood *Conner & Winters, Tulsa*
   STEWART Michael *Crowe & Dunlevy, Oklahoma City*
2. **COLEMAN Chris** *McAfee & Taft, Oklahoma City*
   DERRICK Gary *Derrick & Briggs, Oklahoma City*
   SELF Shannon *Commercial Law Group, Oklahoma City*
   STRINGER Martin *McKinney & Stringer, Oklahoma City*
   WARREN Jerry *McAfee & Taft, Oklahoma City*

Leading individuals (Tax)

1. **FULLER Gary** *McAfee & Taft, Oklahoma City*
   HOLLOMAN James *Crowe & Dunlevy, Oklahoma City*
2. **CASON Len** *Hartzog Conger, Oklahoma City*
   DAVIS Steven *Hartzog Conger, Oklahoma City*
   MOCK Randall *Mock Schwabe, Oklahoma City*
   RATLIFF Reeder *Crowe & Dunlevy, Oklahoma City*

Firms and individuals are listed alphabetically in each band.

Band 1

Conner & Winters, PC

The Firm: The geographic reach of this firm is one of its distinguishing features. Clients can call upon attorneys based in Washington DC, Arkansas, New Mexico, Wyoming and Texas. Closer to home, a large group in Tulsa is also supported by attorneys in Oklahoma City; this ensures that the firm has the capacity to effectively staff both larger deals, which cross the state lines, as well as smaller or more local transactions. Sources commended the high-quality advice provided by this 20-strong corporate and securities group and its breadth of coverage. It advises on a range of corporate finance issues, such as M&A, corporate governance, and broker-dealer regulation.

The Lawyers: Market commentators endorsed **Lynnwood Moore's** 30 years of experience in securities law and M&A and described him as a *"well-grounded and charming attorney, who has the intellect and the experience"* to match anyone in the state on large transactions. He advises clients on public offerings, private placements, and M&A transactions.

The Clients: The firm represents issuers, broker-dealers and public and private companies of all sizes. Clients include WilTel Communications; Vintag Petroleum; Willbros Group; Dover Resources; Parker Drilling; Jameson Inn; Black Hills; Omni Air International and Global Power Equipment.

Crowe & Dunlevy PC

See firm details p.1467

The Firm: This firm remains widely recognized as one of Oklahoma's leading advisers for business, fielding over 100 lawyers and offices in three cities. Its long-established corporate department has a deep pool of experienced attorneys and a well-deserved reputation for handling some of the biggest deals in the state. In an illustration of this firm's continued success, it recently won a beauty contest to act for The Williams Companies, a major Tulsa energy conglomerate.

The Lawyers: According to sources, **Michael Stewart** is an *"eminent general corporate lawyer with a strong securities bent"* whose *"intelligence, professionalism, and toughness inspire a lot of confidence."* Most recently, his caseload has included oil and gas transactions and general securities work for publicly listed companies. Stewart is also well-versed in M&A for financial institutions. **Jim Holloman** is the firm's leading tax expert and, for some peers, one of the best tax lawyers in Oklahoma. He handles the tax aspects of corporate securities and M&A transactions, a typical recent deal being the design and closing of a tax-exempt bond issue for a local hospital. He combines such business tax planning with his successful trusts and estates practice. Sources also singled out **Reeder Ratliff** for his expertise in corporate tax law.

The Clients: The firm advises publicly traded as well as private companies. Examples include: The Williams Companies; Duncan Regional Hospital; BancFirst; Dell; DaimlerChrysler; Nestlé; MCI; Sidco Petroleum and Conaco.

McAfee & Taft
A Professional Corporation

See firm details p.1470

The Firm: Commentators praised the *"great depth"* of this firm's transactional practice and its broad clientele, which it assists in M&A transactions, venture capital financings, securities offerings and general corporate law. The firm has the capability to advise major national clients such as Devon Energy, one of the USA's largest exploration companies, as well as family-run businesses. Partnership law and tax structuring for companies and family trusts are further areas of expertise at the firm.

The Lawyers: **Ted Elam** (see p.1465) brings to the negotiating table a wealth of experience, agreed clients and peers. He provides advice on some of the market's largest public offerings and most sophisticated financings. **Gary Fuller** (see p.1465) is commended as *"one of the most cerebral lawyers in Oklahoma City;"* his low-key approach to deals masks *"great substance within."* Fuller's business tax practice overlaps with estate planning work for private companies and wealthy individuals. Although not currently practicing at full tilt, *"really sharp"* securities lawyer **Jerry Warren** (see p.1466) enjoys the immense respect of his peers for some *"truly remarkable"* transactions and huge experience in the field, while *"no-nonsense"* up-and-comer **Chris Coleman** (see p.1465) continues to enhance his reputation in securities and private equity with some *"conscientious"* SEC and M&A work for high-profile energy clients.

The Clients: The firm's client base features public and private companies, underwriters, commercial banks, and institutional and individual investors, and includes: Devon Energy; American Fidelity; Mustang Fuel; Dobson Communications; University of Oklahoma and The Fred Jones Companies. As well as catering to the larger corporations, the firm is also well-equipped to handle growth companies and family businesses.

Band 2

Commercial Law Group

The Firm: This small business-oriented firm based in Oklahoma City handles M&A, securities issuance and private equity financings for a diverse range of clients including high-profile players in the oil and gas industry. The firm also advises venture capital houses on issues of strategic growth, financing and exits.

The Lawyers: Shannon Self is the firm's driving force. A skilled transactional lawyer, he commands respect for his *"strong negotiating skills"* on behalf of his clients, most notably Chesapeake Energy.

The Clients: The firm acts for local energy giant Chesapeake Energy, in addition to a host of midsized corporates and private equity investors.

Derrick & Briggs LLP

The Firm: A transactional boutique, this firm is recognized for its work with both public and private clients, particularly those in the energy

sector. The group also advises on securities issuance, real estate-related deals and private equity-backed transactions. Corporate reorganization and governance issues related to the Sarbanes-Oxley Act also feature in the workload. **The Lawyers:** Securities specialist **Gary Derrick** has developed a reputation as an *"outstanding business adviser,"* who deals extensively with matters relating to the SEC, as well as M&A and corporate reorganizations. Clients endorsed his *"thorough and accurate approach,"* and agreed, *"his integrity is beyond doubt."*

The Clients: Derrick & Briggs' clients are drawn from the energy sector, as well as several regional corporations and professional organizations. These include Zenex International and Murrell Hall McIntosh.

Hartzog Conger Cason & Neville PC

The Firm: With just over 30 attorneys working out of its Oklahoma City offices, this firm provides advice on all aspects of commercial law. It is, however, largely for its work on business and estate planning that the group is best-known. Its practitioners have earned a reputation as *"highly competent and responsive"* in their approach to client service.

The Lawyers: Tax specialist **Len Cason** comes recommended as an *"impressive lawyer and a workaholic for his clients,"* whose expertise also includes some securities work. Sources also appreciated **Steve Davis** for his *"innovative and pragmatic"* approach to the deal table. Like Cason, he is well-equipped to advise the firm's

major high net-worth individuals on estate and business planning, including tax issues and related corporate transactions.

The Clients: The firm acts for entities drawn from a wide variety of sectors with an emphasis on privately held companies, emerging businesses, entrepreneurs, trusts and estates.

McKinney & Stringer PC

The Firm: A transactional boutique, this firm is recognized for its work with both public and private clients, particularly those in the energy sector. The group also advises on securities issuance, real estate-related deals and private equity-backed transactions. Corporate reorganization and governance issues related to the Sarbanes-Oxley Act also feature in the workload.

The Lawyers: Leading light **Martin Stringer** represents a number of banks in the regulatory area. According to sources, he possesses the *"intellect and experience"* to advise on a broad range of corporate matters, particularly M&A and other private and public securities transactions.

The Clients: The firm represents financial institutions and regional retail, energy and commercial entities including: Stage Stores; TEPPCO Crude Oil; Advanced Academics; Oklahoma Heart Hospital; Duke Energy and First Fidelity Bank.

Other Notable Practitioners

Sources singled out **Randall Mock** of Mock, Schwabe, Waldo, Elder, Reeves & Bryant in Oklahoma City for his experience in tax and estate planning work for a range of clients.

EMPLOYMENT

MAINLY DEFENDANT

Oklahoma
Leading firms
(Employment: Mainly Defendant)
1 CONNER & WINTERS, PC *Oklahoma City*
CROWE & DUNLEVY, PC *Oklahoma City*
HALL, ESTILL, HARDWICK, GABLE *Tulsa*
MCAFEE & TAFT *Oklahoma City*
2 DOERNER, SAUNDERS, DANIEL *Oklahoma City*
ELDRIDGE COOPER STEICHEN & LEACH *Tulsa*
MCKINNEY & STRINGER, PC *Oklahoma City*
NICHOLS, WOLFE, STAMPER, NALLY *Tulsa*
STRECKER & ASSOCIATES *Tulsa*
Firms are listed alphabetically in each band.

Band 1

Conner & Winters PC

The Firm: One of the largest law firms in the region, it operates from seven offices across the USA, including groups in Tulsa and Oklahoma City. A 13-strong labor and employment team

in Oklahoma serves a base of local and Fortune 500 companies. The group advises on both traditional labor law, including collective bargaining and employment litigation such as discrimination claims and wrongful dismissal actions.

The Lawyers: The group is home to some of the market's most respected attorneys. Commentators rated **Ron Petrikin** as a *"tremendous lawyer,"* particularly noting his advice on labor law matters. His courtroom skills are *"of the highest quality"* as is his advice on general employment litigation matters. **David Cordell** has cultivated a *"well-rounded practice"* and enjoys a fine reputation as a highly skilled and *"personable"* litigator.

The Clients: The team represents a variety of unionized and non-unionized clients, from small companies to large corporations, including: American Airlines, Link America and Dynergy.

Crowe & Dunlevy PC

See firm details p.1467

The Firm: This Oklahoma firm's employment team numbers 16 attorneys and caters to a plethora of Oklahoma-based corporations as well as medium and small businesses from the region. Counting some of Oklahoma's finest employment lawyers and litigators among its partners, the firm handles a broad range of employment work including restructurings, employment discrimination claims, wage and hour cases and covenants not-to-compete. The group also advises on policy development issues. Recent successes include a hard-won victory fighting race discrimination claims before the EEOC.

The Lawyers: Leonard Court is *"an expert in the field"* with many years of experience of *"just about everything in the area of labor law,"* claim observers. A seasoned defense litigator, he also has expertise in the area of traditional labor union work, and chairs the US Chamber of

1460   All quotes in the text are from interviews with clients and competitors.

CHAMBERS USA 2005

Oklahoma
Leading individuals
(Employment: Mainly Defendant)

[1]
   COURT Leonard *Crowe & Dunlevy*, Oklahoma City
   CREMIN Pat *Hall Estill*, Tulsa
   PETRIKIN Ronald *Conner & Winters*, Tulsa
   VAN DYKE Peter *McAfee & Taft*, Oklahoma City

[2]
   BARRETT Gayle *Crowe & Dunlevy*, Oklahoma City
   CORDELL David *Conner & Winters*, Tulsa
   FULKERSON Sam *McAfee & Taft*, Oklahoma City
   NEAL Kathy *Eldridge Cooper*, Tulsa
   PLUMB Charles *Doerner Saunders*, Tulsa
   PRIEST Jim *McKinney & Stringer*, Oklahoma City
   STRECKER David *Strecker & Associates*, Tulsa
   WOLFE III Frank *Nichols Wolfe*, Tulsa

Individuals are listed alphabetically in each band.

Commerce FLSA Steering and Labor Relations Committees, as well as having been an adjunct professor of law at the University of Oklahoma. Despite all this, he manages to remain *"practical and down-to-earth."* **Gayle Barrett** also continues to act for employers in a variety of discrimination cases. Interviewees commended her wealth of knowledge on employment law and employee benefits issues.

The Clients: Crowe's clients include Goodyear; Hitachi; Baptist Medical Center; St. Anthony Hospital; Mercy Health Center; Bank One; Continental Airlines; Armstrong World Industries and Grandy's.

Hall, Estill, Hardwick, Gable, Golden & Nelson PC

The Firm: This firm has offices in Oklahoma City and Tulsa in addition to locations in Washington DC and Fayetteville, Arkansas. The hub of the labor and employment group resides in Tulsa, and its attorneys are skilled in all areas of employment discrimination, collective bargaining, individual employee rights and safety in the workplace. Its *"tremendous team"* has also litigated wrongful discharge, ERISA, and intentional infliction of emotional distress claims among others.

The Lawyers: The Tulsa team of around a dozen dedicated employment lawyers fields one of the region's preeminent labor and employment specialists in **Pat Cremin.** A *"very effective trial lawyer,"* who combines the skills of an excellent public speaker with a *"superb practical sense -he's a dean of the labor market."*

The Clients: Clients range from Fortune 500 corporations, medium-sized companies, non-profit organizations and emerging businesses.

McAfee & Taft
A Professional Corporation
See firm details p.1470

The Firm: As befits one of Oklahoma's true full-service firms, McAfee & Taft's broader commercial activities are complemented by one of the largest labor and employment departments in the Southwest. More than 20 employment specialists have cultivated a fine reputation among the firm's list of regional and national corporate employers. Naturally, they deal with all the many aspects of employment and labor law, although there is a bias towards the defense of discrimination and wrongful dismissal claims. The group also advises on issues of policy direction.

The Lawyers: According to sources, the team offers *"real depth"* and foremost among its practitioners is *"top, top employment lawyer"* **Peter Van Dyke** (see p.1466). He is described as a *"gentlemanly attorney"* whose vast knowledge in the field lies in the defense of employment litigation, NLRB proceedings, union avoidance campaigns and wage and hour issues. Covering a similarly broad area is the chair of the group **Sam Fulkerson** (see p.1465). He also won the respect of market sources for his work with international energy giant Halliburton.

The Clients: Typical clients for the group are Sysco Food Systems of Oklahoma, Dobson Communications and Halliburton.

Band 2

Doerner, Saunders, Daniel & Anderson LLP

The Firm: This midsized firm has a long history of providing advice and representation to national corporations and businesses of all sizes from around the Southwest. It is also the firm of choice for a number of public employers. The labor and employment department handles the full range of issues, representing employers before state and federal courts and agencies, and additionally extending to arbitration and negotiation in employment disputes.

The Lawyers: **Charles Plumb** comes highly recommended as a *"very well-rounded, practical and tenacious litigator"* whose practice covers employment law matters as well as labor relations and collective bargaining. His background in business litigation gives him an insight into the management perspective, while his *"incredible work rate"* and strong people skills mean that he enjoys a good relationship with his clients.

The Clients: The department acts for public and private, unionized and non-unionized employers.

Eldridge Cooper Steichen & Leach PLLC

The Firm: This small but growing firm of litigation specialists has won an exceptional reputation among the clients it has represented in Oklahoma and the region. It provides guidance and representation on the full spectrum of employment disputes, with a large number of clients described as *"very, very pleased"* with their work.

The Lawyers: Clients endorsed **Kathy Neal** as an *"extremely hard-working, aggressive, diligent, straightforward and very bright"* litigator, who is *"able to grasp technical nuances quickly."* She recently conducted the successful defense of an industrial group, and continues to represent employers across the USA.

The Clients: A significant proportion of the firm's employment clients come from the manufacturing industry, a notable example being automotive giant GM.

McKinney & Stringer, PC

The Firm: The firm has successfully attracted a diverse client base of companies that are *"leaders of their industries and markets,"* acknowledged market sources. A group of dedicated labor and employment attorneys works out of both the Tulsa and Oklahoma City offices and provides representation before both state and federal agencies as well as assisting in general counseling in order to avoid such employment disputes.

The Lawyers: **Jim Priest** has years of experience of employment litigation of all kinds. A *"knowledgeable lawyer",* he has an excellent understanding of both plaintiff and defense work, and as such, has developed a strong courtroom presence.

The Clients: The firm's clients include WH Braum; Carlisle Food Service Products; Southern Nazarene University; Mercy Health Center; Enogex and many others.

Nichols, Wolfe, Stamper, Nally, Fallis & Robertson Inc

The Firm: This well-established *"business-oriented"* Tulsa firm is widely respected for its representation of management in all aspects of labor and employment law. Market observers praised its ability to handle sensitive labor relations and negotiations as well as its effective approach to employment litigation.

The Lawyers: Sources ascribed to **Frank 'Skip' Wolfe** *"a very strong reputation"* in traditional labor law fields such as collective bargaining and union election work. With experience both in private practice and as a trial lawyer for the NLRB, he also regularly represents management before the EEOC. Wolfe has a long track record in the field, and his *"efficacy in the trenches is never in doubt."*

The Clients: The firm represents management from a range of commercial and industrial clients.

Strecker & Associates

The Firm: This Tulsa labor and employment boutique makes up for its relatively smaller size with the high quality and deep knowledge of its personnel. The firm's specialist attorneys are commended for their ability to deliver practical, business-oriented advice on all aspects of employment law and regularly represent a broad spread of clients before the various federal and state courts and agencies in the region.

The Lawyers: David Strecker, commentators confirmed, *"knows his stuff"* and is a *"really well-rounded"* employment lawyer, who handles union management issues, employment discrimination, wage and hour and OSHA issues.

The Clients: The firm's clients are drawn from the banking and finance, communications, construction, manufacturing and technology industries, as well as public agencies.

LITIGATION

Oklahoma
Leading firms
(Litigation: General Commercial)
[1] **CROWE & DUNLEVY PC** *Oklahoma City*
GABLE & GOTWALS *Oklahoma City*
MCAFEE & TAFT *Oklahoma City*
[2] **FELLERS, SNIDER, BLANKENSHIP** *Oklahoma City*
HARTZOG CONGER CASON *Oklahoma City*
MCKINNEY & STRINGER PC *Oklahoma City*
[3] **KIRK & CHANEY** *Oklahoma City*
RYAN & WHALEY *Oklahoma City*

Leading individuals
(Litigation: General Commercial)
[1] **BAILEY Burck** *Fellers Snider*, Oklahoma City
CORBYN George *Corbyn Law Firm*, Oklahoma City
HERMES John *McAfee & Taft*, Oklahoma City
NEVILLE Drew *Hartzog Conger*, Oklahoma City
RYAN Patrick *Ryan & Whaley*, Oklahoma City
STURDIVANT James *Gable & Gotwals*, Tulsa
[2] **DAVIS Gary** *Crowe & Dunlevy*, Oklahoma City
KENNEY John *McAfee & Taft*, Oklahoma City
MCKINNEY Kenneth *McKinney & Stringer*, Oklahoma City
MEYERS Kent *Crowe & Dunlevy*, Oklahoma City
MUCHMORE Clyde *Crowe & Dunlevy*, Oklahoma City
[3] **BARGHOLS Steven** *Gable & Gotwals*, Oklahoma City
BOCOCK Joseph *McAfee & Taft*, Oklahoma City
BURRAGE Michael *Burrage Law Firm*, Durant
HAMPTON Joe *Ryan & Whaley*, Oklahoma City
KIRK James *Kirk & Chaney*, Oklahoma City
MCCONNELL Laura *Hartzog Conger*, Oklahoma City
ROBISON Reid *McAfee & Taft*, Oklahoma City
RUPERT Anton *Crowe & Dunlevy*, Oklahoma City
TIPPENS Terry *Fellers Snider*, Oklahoma City
Firms and individuals are listed alphabetically in each band.

Band 1

Crowe & Dunlevy PC

See firm details p.1467

The Firm: Oklahoma's largest law firm, it has its origins as a litigation powerhouse. The depth of resources combined with the broad skill set possessed by its attorneys has helped create a powerful market profile for this team. The department of over 60 attorneys, who include members of the American College of Trial Lawyers and former presidents of the ABA, provides representation across the spectrum of business disputes, particularly class actions. In addition to their tenacity and professionalism, Crowe's litigators also won plaudits from clients for their *"hands-on"* attitude – work is not simply *"passed on to others, there is a real dedication here."*

The Lawyers: Antitrust litigator and chair of the department, **Kent Meyers** is well-established among Oklahoma's leading litigators. For many sources, he is *"the standout guy"* for his wealth of experience. He is well-versed in antitrust disputes, and has advised clients on the petition process for enacting laws. *"Terrific"* oil and gas litigator **Gary Davis** displays *"incredible energy and excellent analytical skills and trial presentation,"* reported clients. A trial attorney who can handle complex litigation, he is *"extremely comfortable in the courtroom"* and has *"made law"* in many of his cases. Another of Crowe's eminent litigators is **Clyde Muchmore**, described as *"one of the smartest trial lawyers in the state."* **Anton Rupert** has a growing reputation as a *"smart, analytical and effective"* trial lawyer. A burgeoning toxic tort practice and significant experience in construction and products liability make him a leading player in the field.

The Clients: Octagon Resources; Conoco Phillips; Chevron USA; Anadarko Petroleum; Lone Star Steakhouse & Saloon; National Western Life Insurance; Dow Chemical and Citigroup Global Markets.

Gable & Gotwals, A Professional Corporation

See firm details p.1469

The Firm: This full-service firm comprises around 60 attorneys in total, of which over half form its widely respected litigation section. A sizable team in Tulsa is supported by a significant presence in Oklahoma City, ensuring the depth of resources to handle all manner of business disputes ranging from banking and securities law to corporate governance issues. The firm is especially noted for its strength in commercial loan, energy and construction and products liability litigation.

The Lawyers: Jim Sturdivant (see p.1466) has won a following among peers and clients for his work in complex commercial litigation. With over 40 years of experience, he has combined academic brilliance and *"excellent people skills."* In the courtroom he is a *"pugnacious advocate"* on behalf of his clients. **Steven Barghols** (see p.1464) is *"professionalism personified"* and has applied his *"exceptional dedication"* to the specialized field of oil and gas mediation. Excellent judgment, an even temperament and the ability to *"figure it out real quick"* have enabled him to forge an unparalleled reputation in the field, and one for which he commands the absolute respect of his peers.

The Clients: ChevronTexaco; ConocoPhillips; El Paso; ONEOK and The Williams Companies.

McAfee & Taft
A Professional Corporation

See firm details p.1470

The Firm: McAfee's litigation practice is, as one might expect from one of Oklahoma's largest and best-known business firms, *"top-flight."* The firm is credited with expertise in *"just about everything,"* including IP and oil and gas-related disputes. The group has recently been retained by Merck to mount a defense in Oklahoma in the Vioxx mass tort litigation.

The Lawyers: John Hermes (see p.1465) has a long-standing reputation as an *"exceptional and highly professional litigator,"* whose broad business litigation practice encompasses banking, insurance coverage and healthcare disputes. His *"personable but firm"* courtroom style has helped to make him one of McAfee's – and Oklahoma's – leading litigators. An IP specialist, **John Kenney's** (see p.1465) engineering degree and products liability background have assisted him in the representation of substantial multinationals such as Eli Lilly in complex technical disputes. **Joseph Bocock** (see p.1464) chairs the firm's litigation department and has a fine reputation as a *"high-IQ, high-energy"* commercial specialist. He spends a large percentage of his time representing financial institutions *"aggressively and successfully"* in commercial litigation and arbitration. **Reid Robison** (see p.1466) has developed a broad litigation practice and is well-versed in securities, antitrust, products liability and white-collar crime litigation.

The Clients: The team has advised American Cancer Society, MidFirst Bank and First National Bank.

Band 2

Fellers, Snider, Blankenship, Bailey & Tippens, A Professional Corporation

See firm details p.1468

The Firm: One of Oklahoma's midsized law firms, it has won particular renown in the state for the quality of its trial lawyers. Teams based out of both Tulsa and Oklahoma City have

1462   All quotes in the text are from interviews with clients and competitors.

CHAMBERS USA 2005

cultivated a diverse practice, undertaking all kinds of litigation including appellate work, with the bulk of the caseload centered on commercial litigation, white-collar crime and tort.
The Lawyers: The courtroom presence of **Burck Bailey** (see p.1464) has been known to leave peers with "*goose bumps.*" A "*terrifically articulate*" litigator of complex business and white-collar crime cases, he is also renowned for his "*marvelous integrity*" and his high caliber trial experience. **Terry Tippens** (see p.1466) has also had his fair share of success in the courtroom. His broad practice takes in oil and gas, banking and other commercial matters, as well as the odd large personal injury and wrongful death case. "*Oklahoma juries love his personal courtroom style*", and interviewees confirmed he has "*got as good a touch as you can get.*"
The Clients: Aetna; American Express; Hertz; BancFirst and Wal-Mart.

Hartzog Conger Cason & Neville PC

The Firm: The litigators at this 30-lawyer Oklahoma City business firm take on a broad range of cases including antitrust, insurance, professional malpractice and products liability litigation.
The Lawyers: For its size, this firm has a high proportion of leading trial lawyers. Foremost among these is **Drew Neville**. Peers would "*trust him with just about any kind of case.*" While one of the mainstays of his practice is securities litigation, he is also able to take on complicated criminal as well as civil work, and was part of the defense team that recently represented Martha Stewart. **Laura McConnell** also has a reputation as a skilled commercial litigator, and this is combined with her respected domestic relations practice.
The Clients: WR Grace & Co; General Dynamics; The Coca-Cola Bottlers' Association; Marriott; Parker Drilling; Prudential Securities;

Koch Industries; CMI and the Oklahoma Publishing Company.

McKinney & Stringer PC

The Firm: This team is made up of around 20 business litigators, who cater to the widespread litigation needs of enterprises from growth companies to national and multinational corporations.
The Lawyers: **Ken McKinney** has a reputation as a "*shrewd, all-purpose*" civil litigator. As one commentator put it: "*You know there's a major player involved when you see his name.*" A "*solid*" commercial litigator, he is able to take on environmental law, oil and gas, securities, antitrust and white-collar criminal defense cases. In addition, he has expertise in insurance defense and personal injury work.
The Clients: AT&T; City of Tulsa; Energetix and Sisters of Mercy Health System.

Band 3

Kirk & Chaney

The Firm: This Oklahoma City litigation boutique comprises a smaller yet "*highly effective and powerful*" team of specialists. According to market commentators, they "*definitely provide quality over quantity.*" The attorneys undertake products liability, insurance, environmental, real estate and oil and gas disputes.
The Lawyers: A highly respected trial attorney, **James Kirk** combines his excellent commercial disputes skills with high-profile divorce work.
The Clients: The firm represents individuals as well as businesses of all sizes, including a number of national entities.

Ryan & Whaley

The Firm: Based in Oklahoma City, this is a small law firm with a sizable reputation in litigation, energy and environmental law, whose litigation and regulatory team includes some of the state's biggest names.
The Lawyers: **Pat Ryan** is arguably Oklahoma's highest-profile litigator. He was the US Attorney in the prosecution of Timothy McVeigh and Terry Nichols and recently secured the acquittal of a CEO in one of the largest corporate fraud cases prosecuted by the DOJ. Clients declared that "*he absorbs complex information faster than anyone I've seen in my life.*" Equally important is his "*ability to communicate his methodology across a broad spectrum of society.*" As with all of Oklahoma's top litigators, Ryan's status ensures him a wide variety of work. As such, he has been involved in a raft of high-profile white-collar crime defense cases and high-value class action securities cases. Spearheading the firm's next generation of lawyers, "*highly personable and very bright*" **Joe Hampton** is a business litigator and arbitrator, who divides his time between securities, franchise and products liability litigation.
The Clients: Capital West Securities; UBS Financial Services and Sonic are examples of the firm's client base.

Other Notable Practitioners

George Corbyn of Corbyn Law Firm is a "*tenacious*" Oklahoma City commercial trial lawyer who has carved out an excellent reputation in a wide variety of business litigations and arbitrations. Peers agreed that he is "*fearless and beautiful to watch*" in court. Another significant lawyer in Oklahoma litigation is former district judge **Mike Burrage** of Burrage Law Firm in Durant. He brings to the table over 30 years of experience and a "*super ability to communicate with juries.*"

REAL ESTATE

Oklahoma Leading firms (Real Estate)	
1	CROWE & DUNLEVY, PC *Oklahoma City*
	MCAFEE & TAFT *Oklahoma City*
2	MOCK, SCHWABE, WALDO *Oklahoma City*
	PHILLIPS MCFALL MCCAFFREY *Oklahoma City*
	SPRADLING, KENNEDY *Oklahoma City*
Firms are listed alphabetically in each band.	

BAND 1

Crowe & Dunlevy PC

See firm details p.1467
The Firm: The commercial real estate team at Crowe & Dunlevy numbers around ten attorneys, but is supplemented by the depth and diversity of resources that this full-service Oklahoma City firm is able to bring to a deal. Its national and international clients come from all areas of commercial real estate including sales, acquisitions, project development, leasing and financing. The firm also represents retail property owners and institutional lenders in lease negotiations.
The Lawyers: According to sources, the "*absolutely impressive*" **James Hartmann** is involved in a vast quantity of diverse work. He often serves as "*very responsive*" local counsel on multistate real estate deals; he is "*able to explain local issues clearly,*" while reviewing and drafting jurisdiction-sensitive documents. Hartmann

recently represented a financial institution on a $130 million real estate-related loan, and he also devotes a portion of his time to lease reviews for local retail conglomerates. **Michael Laird** has attracted a loyal following among midsized and large developers, advising on a range of matters from wind farms to industrial plants. He has cultivated a subspecialty in gaming and hospitality projects.
The Clients: The firm acts for a plethora of entities drawn from local, regional and national businesses, of which John Hancock Financial Services; Harsch Investment Group; The Williams Companies; BancFirst; Kimco Realty; Regional Hospital Authority and Homeland Stores are but a few.

Oklahoma
Leading individuals (Real Estate)

Senior Statesman

HASTIE John *Phillips McFall*, Oklahoma City

ELDER James *Mock Schwabe*, Oklahoma City

HARDIN Lloyd *Phillips McFall*, Oklahoma City

HARTMANN James *Crowe & Dunlevy*, Oklahoma City

HILL Frank *McAfee & Taft*, Oklahoma City

LAIRD Michael *Crowe & Dunlevy*, Oklahoma City

RIGGS Richard *McAfee & Taft*, Oklahoma City

SPRADLING T Scott *Spradling Kennedy*, Oklahoma City

Individuals are listed alphabetically in each band.

McAfee & Taft
A Professional Corporation

See firm details p.1470

The Firm: One of Oklahoma's largest firms, McAfee & Taft possesses the depth to take on larger projects within the state and beyond. It is rated for its breadth of expertise, as well as the high-quality advice and intelligence of its attorneys. The attorneys here devote much of their time to acquisitions, dispositions, project developments and associated tax planning issues. The group also advises on land use and zoning issues.

The Lawyers: *"Practical and aggressive"* advocate **Frank Hill** (see p.1465) is one of Oklahoma's leading real estate practitioners. He is frequently to be found working on large and challenging real estate projects including acquisitions and new developments, often advising the developers. Examples of his recent caseload include the acquisition of a manufacturing facility, the development of a $135 million Texas hotel and resort complex, and the development of a major aerospace technology center. Interviewees also commended **Richard Riggs** (see p.1466) as an *"incredibly talented and pragmatic"*

attorney, who is *"a joy to work with."* He undertakes acquisitions, sales, financing and leases as well as related credit facilities and loan transactions for financial institutions. He is experienced in the use of government incentives in real estate transaction.

The Clients: Bank of Oklahoma; MidFirst Bank; Fleming; Devon Energy; Michelin; Price Edwards & Co; University of Oklahoma and Wiggin Properties.

BAND 2

Mock, Schwabe, Waldo, Elder, Reeves & Bryant

The Firm: This nine-lawyer firm has acted as lead counsel in multistate real estate and real estate-related transactions for several national financial institutions and insurance companies. Although it does not specialize exclusively in real estate, the firm has the respect of the market for the expertise of its individuals in the field. The group's workload features a mix of financing, development issues and leasing arrangements.

The Lawyers: **James Elder** is a trusted real estate lawyer who regularly represents lenders on transactions with a real estate perspective. Market observers commended his dedication, careful approach and high level of expertise, and described him as a standout in his sphere.

The Clients: BancFirst; Bank One; Cabot Petroleum; Lincoln National Life Insurance; Local Oklahoma Bank and Pan-American Life Insurance.

Phillips McFall McCaffrey McVay & Murrah, PC

The Firm: Phillips McFall is a midsized firm with offices in Norman and Oklahoma City, whose 14-attorney real estate department provides advice on real estate developments, joint ventures and sales and dispositions. Attorneys also advise on title matters and real estate-related disputes.

The Lawyers: Sources considered **John Hastie** to be one of the key rainmakers at this firm due to his *"exceptional skill and long-standing reputation."* According to some: *"If it was an extremely complicated matter, and you wanted absolutely the best person, he'd be the one."* This talented group is also home to **Lloyd Hardin**, recommended as a fine real estate attorney, whose expertise spans commercial real estate transactions, construction and international law.

The Clients: The firm represents, among others, financial institutions, healthcare providers and industrial, municipal and energy clients.

Spradling, Kennedy & McPhail LLP

The Firm: This recently formed firm comprises the real estate department of what was Spradling, Alpern & Gum, following an amicable split. The firm has, according to market commentators, *"continued as a fine practice, just like before."* Attorneys provide commercial real estate advice and representation to Oklahoma City's real estate developers and title companies.

The Lawyers: **Scott Spradling** is a knowledgeable and capable real estate lawyer, whom commentators find *"a pleasure to work with."*

The Clients: The group has maintained a respected client base that features clients such as First American Title & Trust; Lawyers Title of Oklahoma City and American Guaranty Title.

Leaders in Oklahoma

BAILEY, Burck

Fellers, Snider, Blankenship, Bailey & Tippens, A Professional Corporation, Oklahoma City 405 232 0621
bbailey@fellerssnider.com
Recommended in Litigation

Practice Areas: Extensive experience representing broad range of clients in antitrust, securities, and commercial litigation. Has represented Oklahoma Governors of both political parties in complex litigation, as well as the Oklahoma Legislature. Conducted appellate arguments in the United States Supreme Court as well as various Federal Circuits and State appellate courts.

Prof. Memberships: Fellow, American College of Trial Lawyers, International Academy of Trial Lawyers, American Academy of Appellate Lawyers; past President, Oklahoma Bar Association

and Oklahoma County Bar Association; past Chair, Oklahoma Judicial Nominating Commission.

Personal: LLB New York University, 1961; BA Westminster College, 1958.

BARGHOLS, Steven L

Gable & Gotwals, A Professional Corporation, Oklahoma City 405 235 5500
sbarghols@gablelaw.com
Recommended in Litigation

Practice Areas: Oil and gas law (litigation and debtor-creditor relations; with transactional-practice background); arbitration and mediation: attorney-fee disputes, business and commercial, eminent domain, construction, contracts, debtor-creditor relations, employment, oil and gas, environmental/pollution, franchising, insurance (coverage and claims), legal and medical malpractice,

mold, personal injury, probate/estate administration, products liability, real estate, securities, and trusts.

Prof. Memberships: Oklahoma Bar Association; Oklahoma County Bar Association (past President); American Bar Foundation (Oklahoma Fellow); Mediation, arbitration and early-neutral evaluation program panels of the U.S.D.C. - W. D. Oklahoma.

Personal: University of Oklahoma, BA, 1973 (Phi Beta Kappa); University of Texas School of Law, JD, 1976.

BARRETT, Gayle

Crowe & Dunlevy, PC, Oklahoma City 405 235 7700
Recommended in Employment

BOCOCK, Joseph

McAfee & Taft A Professional Corporation, Oklahoma City 405 552 2256
joseph.bocock@mcafeetaft.com
Recommended in Litigation

Practice Areas: Practice concentrates in commercial litigation/arbitration advocacy with extensive experience in disputes involving real estate, energy, securities, warehousing and debtor/creditor transactions and class actions.

Prof. Memberships: American Bar Association; American Inns of Court (Master-Holloway Chapter); Oklahoma Advisory Council of the American Arbitration Association.

Career: Oklahoma Bar (1978); All state and federal courts in Oklahoma; US Tenth Circuit Court of Appeals. Chair of the firm's Litigation Practice Group 2001-04.

Personal: AB magna cum laude, Dartmouth College, 1978; JD, Order of the Coif, Law Review, University of Oklahoma College of Law, 1978.

BURRAGE, Michael
Burrage Law Firm, Durant
580 920 0700
Recommended in Litigation

CASON, Len
Hartzog Conger Cason & Neville, PC, Oklahoma City 405 235 7000
Recommended in Tax

COLEMAN, Chris
McAfee & Taft A Professional Corporation, Oklahoma City 405 552 2234
chris.coleman@mcafeetaft.com
Recommended in Corporate/M&A
Practice Areas: Practice involves the representation of businesses in a broad range of business transactions, including mergers, acquisitions and divestitures; securities offerings and public reporting; contract negotiations; public and private financing; structuring and capitalizing new entities; and reorganizing existing entities.
Prof. Memberships: Oklahoma County, Oklahoma and American Bar Associations.
Career: Oklahoma Bar (1982). Has represented businesses engaged in virtually every major industry, including real estate, energy, financial services, engineering, software, food manufacturing and distribution, communications and sales.
Personal: BA with distinction, Phi Beta Kappa, University of Oklahoma, 1979; JD, University of Oklahoma College of Law, 1982.

CORBYN, George
Corbyn Law Firm, Oklahoma City
405 239 7055
Recommended in Litigation

CORDELL, David
Conner & Winters, PC, Tulsa
918 586 5711
Recommended in Employment

COURT, Leonard
Crowe & Dunlevy, PC, Oklahoma City
405 235 7700
Recommended in Employment

CREMIN, Pat
Hall, Estill, Hardwick, Gable, Golden & Nelson, PC, Tulsa 918 594 0400
Recommended in Employment

DAVIS, Gary
Crowe & Dunlevy, PC, Oklahoma City
405 235 7700
Recommended in Litigation

DAVIS, Steven
Hartzog Conger Cason & Neville, PC, Oklahoma City 405 235 7000
Recommended in Tax

DERRICK, Gary
Derrick & Briggs LLP, Oklahoma City
405 235 1900
Recommended in Corporate/M&A

ELAM, Theodore M
McAfee & Taft A Professional Corporation, Oklahoma City 405 552 2221
ted.elam@mcafeetaft.com
Recommended in Corporate/M&A
Practice Areas: Practice concentrates in corporate and securities matters, corporate finance and mergers and acquisitions.
Prof. Memberships: Oklahoma and American Bar Associations.
Career: Oklahoma Bar (1959). Lead counsel in public and private offerings of securities, mergers and acquisitions, tender offers, and in other forms of financing, for businesses involved in telecommunications, technology, energy, mortgage banking, financing, insurance and real estate. Adjunct professor of business planning, securities regulation and corporate finance, University of Oklahoma College of Law. Frequent lecturer.
Personal: BBA-Finance, University of Oklahoma, 1957; LLB, University of Oklahoma, 1959

ELDER, James
Mock, Schwabe, Waldo, Elder, Reeves & Bryant, Oklahoma City 405 235 1110
Recommended in Real Estate

FULKERSON, Sam
McAfee & Taft A Professional Corporation, Oklahoma City 405 552 2369
sam.fulkerson@mcafeetaft.com
Recommended in Employment
Practice Areas: Represents management in all phases of employment-related matters, including litigation before federal and state courts, regulatory and administrative agencies, and in arbitration matters. Chair of the firm's Labor and Employment Practice Group. Frequent author and lecturer.
Prof. Memberships: Oklahoma Bar Association (Labor and Employment Section) and American Bar Association.
Career: Oklahoma Bar (1991); Federal district courts in Oklahoma and Texas; US Court of Appeals for the Tenth Circuit, US Supreme Court.
Personal: BA, with distinction, University of Oklahoma, 1982; MA, with honors, University of North Carolina, 1985; JD, with honors, University of Oklahoma College of Law, 1991.

FULLER, Gary
McAfee & Taft A Professional Corporation, Oklahoma City 405 552 2227
gary.fuller@mcafeetaft.com
Recommended in Tax
Practice Areas: Practice is primarily concentrated in corporate, tax and estate planning law.
Prof. Memberships: American Bar Association.
Career: Oklahoma Bar (1959); Texas Bar (1963). Judge Advocate General Corps, USAF, (1959-62). Lectured extensively to lawyer groups on tax planning subjects and has been an instructor at the University of Oklahoma College of Law.

Personal: BBA, University of Oklahoma, 1957; studied law at the Academy of International Law, The Hague, Netherlands; received LLB from the University of Oklahoma, 1959; LLM, Yale Law School, 1963.

HAMPTON, Joe
Ryan & Whaley, Oklahoma City
405 239 6040
Recommended in Litigation

HARDIN, Lloyd
Phillips McFall McCaffrey McVay & Murrah, P.C., Oklahoma City 405 235 4100
Recommended in Real Estate

HARTMANN, James
Crowe & Dunlevy, PC, Oklahoma City
405 235 7700
Recommended in Real Estate

HASTIE, John
Phillips McFall McCaffrey McVay & Murrah, P.C., Oklahoma City
405 235 4100
Recommended in Real Estate

HERMES, John N
McAfee & Taft A Professional Corporation, Oklahoma City 405 552 2258
john.hermes@mcafeetaft.com
Recommended in Litigation
Practice Areas: Practice concentrates on commercial and business litigation.
Prof. Memberships: American Bar Association; American College of Trial Lawyers; American Inn of Court CV; American Bar Foundation; Oklahoma Bar Foundation.
Career: Oklahoma Bar (1975); All state and federal district courts in Oklahoma; US Fifth, Tenth and Federal Circuit Courts of Appeals; US Tax Court; US Claims Court; US Supreme Court. Serves as the firm's Managing Director.
Personal: AB, Ripon College, 1968; JD, University of Oklahoma, 1975.

HILL, Frank
McAfee & Taft A Professional Corporation, Oklahoma City 405 552 2259
frank.hill@mcafeetaft.com
Recommended in Real Estate
Practice Areas: Commercial transactions, including real estate and finance; acquisitions, sales, exchanges and other dispositions; construction and development; tax planning; private syndications; healthcare matters; tax-exempt organizations; and debt settlement transactions.
Prof. Memberships: American Bar Association; American College of Real Estate Lawyers.
Career: Texas Bar (1966); Oklahoma Bar (1971); US Tenth Circuit Court of Appeals; US District Court for the Western District of Oklahoma; US Tax Court; US Claims Court. Judge Advocate General Corps, US Army, (1967 - 1970).
Personal: BBA, University of Oklahoma, 1963; LLB, University of Texas, 1966; LLM in Taxation, The George Washington University, 1969.

HOLLOMAN Jr, James
Crowe & Dunlevy, PC, Oklahoma City
405 235 7700
Recommended in Tax

KENNEY, John A
McAfee & Taft A Professional Corporation, Oklahoma City 405 552 2244
john.kenney@mcafeetaft.com
Recommended in Litigation
Practice Areas: Trial practice concentrates on cases involving intellectual property and other technical and scientific issues. Has tried cases, arbitrations, and administrative proceedings and hearings in the United States, U.S. Virgin Islands and several foreign countries.
Prof. Memberships: American Bar Association, American Inns of Court (Master, Ginsburg Inn), Oklahoma Bar Foundation, Federal Bar Association.
Career: Texas Bar (1975); Oklahoma Bar (1981); Numerous federal trial and appellate courts and US Supreme Court. Worked as an engineer prior to law school. Frequent speaker.
Personal: BSIE with distinction, University of Oklahoma, 1971; JD, University of Oklahoma College of Law, 1975.

KIRK, James
Kirk & Chaney, Oklahoma City
405 235 1333
Recommended in Litigation

LAIRD, Michael
Crowe & Dunlevy, PC, Oklahoma City
405 235 7700
Recommended in Real Estate

MCCONNELL, Laura
Hartzog Conger Cason & Neville, PC, Oklahoma City 405 235 7000
Recommended in Litigation

MCKINNEY, Kenneth
McKinney & Stringer, PC, Oklahoma City 405 239 6444
Recommended in Litigation

MEYERS, Kent
Crowe & Dunlevy, PC, Oklahoma City
405 235 7700
Recommended in Litigation

MOCK, Randall
Mock, Schwabe, Waldo, Elder, Reeves & Bryant, Oklahoma City
405 235 1110
Recommended in Tax

MOORE, Lynnwood
Conner & Winters, PC, Tulsa
918 586 5711
Recommended in Corporate/M&A

MUCHMORE, Clyde
Crowe & Dunlevy, PC, Oklahoma City
405 235 7700
Recommended in Litigation

NEAL, Kathy
Eldridge Cooper Steichen & Leach PLLC, Tulsa 918 388 5555
Recommended in Employment

NEVILLE, Drew
Hartzog Conger Cason & Neville, PC, Oklahoma City 405 235 7000
Recommended in Litigation

PETRIKIN, Ronald
Conner & Winters, PC, Tulsa
918 586 5711
Recommended in Employment

PLUMB, Charles
Doerner, Saunders, Daniel & Anderson, LLP, Tulsa 918 582 1211
Recommended in Employment

PRIEST, Jim
McKinney & Stringer, PC, Oklahoma City 405 239 6444
Recommended in Employment

RATLIFF, Reeder
Crowe & Dunlevy, PC, Oklahoma City 405 235 7700
Recommended in Tax

RIGGS, Richard
McAfee & Taft A Professional Corporation, Oklahoma City 405 552 2265
richard.riggs@mcafeetaft.com
Recommended in Real Estate
Practice Areas: Real estate and other commercial transactions.
Prof. Memberships: American Bar Association; ABA's Real Property, Probate and Trust Law Section; the Commercial Real Estate Council; American College of Real Estate Lawyers.
Career: Oklahoma Bar (1974). Author and frequent presenter at continuing legal education seminars on the subjects of real estate acquisition and finance, commercial real estate leasing and secured transactions. Adjunct professor at University of Oklahoma College of Law.
Personal: BA with distinction, University of Oklahoma, 1971; JD cum laude, University of Michigan, 1974.

ROBISON, Reid
McAfee & Taft A Professional Corporation, Oklahoma City 405 552 2260
reid.robison@mcafeetaft.com
Recommended in Litigation
Practice Areas: Business-related litigation, including antitrust, securities, products liability, tax, white-collar criminal cases, and multi-district and other complex litigation in courts throughout

the United States.
Prof. Memberships: American Bar Association; American Inn of Court; Oklahoma Bar Foundation; International Academy of Trial Lawyers.
Career: Oklahoma Bar (1968); Colorado Bar (1971); US Fifth, Eighth, Tenth, and Eleventh Circuit Courts of Appeals; US Tax Court; US Claims Court; US Supreme Court. Judge Advocate General Corps, USAF, (1968-72).
Personal: BA, University of Oklahoma, 1966; JD, University of Oklahoma College of Law, 1968.

RUPERT, Anton
Crowe & Dunlevy, PC, Oklahoma City 405 235 7700
Recommended in Litigation

RYAN, Patrick
Ryan & Whaley, Oklahoma City
405 239 6040
Recommended in Litigation

SELF, Shannon
Commercial Law Group, Oklahoma City 405 232 3001
Recommended in Corporate/M&A

SPRADLING, Scott
Spradling, Kennedy & McPhail LLP, Oklahoma City 405 418 2700
Recommended in Real Estate

STEWART, Mike
Crowe & Dunlevy, PC, Oklahoma City 405 235 7700
Recommended in Corporate/M&A

STRECKER, David
Strecker & Associates, Tulsa
918 582 1716
Recommended in Employment

STRINGER, Martin
McKinney & Stringer, PC, Oklahoma City 405 239 6444
Recommended in Corporate/M&A

STURDIVANT, James
Gable & Gotwals, Tulsa
918 595 4846
jsturdivant@gablelaw.com
Recommended in Litigation
Practice Areas: Engaged in private practice since 1964. Has extensive experience as lead trial attorney in complex business disputes with resolution through negotiation, alternate dispute

resolution or litigation. Has represented a full spectrum of clients.
Prof. Memberships: Member, American (Member, Board of Governors), Oklahoma and Tulsa County Bar Associations. Fellow, American College of Trial Lawyers. American and Oklahoma Bar Foundations. Past Chair, Oklahoma Judicial Nominating Commission.
Publications: Lectured and written extensively on litigation related subjects. Trustee and Research Fellow, Center for American and International Law. Adjunct Professor, University of Tulsa College of Law.
Personal: JD, University of Oklahoma, 1964, Order of the Coif, Oklahoma Law Review; BBA, University of Oklahoma, 1959.

TIPPENS, Terry
Fellers, Snider, Blankenship, Bailey & Tippens, A Professional Corporation, Oklahoma City 405 232 0621
ttippens@fellerssnider.com
Recommended in Litigation
Practice Areas: Extensive experience representing broad range of clients in business and commercial litigation involving banking, taxation, oil and gas, real property, insurance, agricultural and water law, environmental liability, intellectual property rights, corporate disputes and commercial arbitration. Has handled personal injury, wrongful death and white collar criminal cases. Has tried over 50 jury trials, with some cases involving over $100 million. Recognized in 'The Best Lawyers in America' for over 20 years.
Prof. Memberships: International Society of Barristers; American Inns of Court; American, Oklahoma and Oklahoma County Bar Associations.
Personal: JD University of Oklahoma, 1971; BS Oklahoma State University, 1968.

VAN DYKE, Peter
McAfee & Taft A Professional Corporation, Oklahoma City 405 552 2211
peter.vandyke@mcafeetaft.com
Recommended in Employment
Practice Areas: Represents management in all phases of labor and employment related matters, including litigation, arbitrations, union avoidance

issues, labor negotiations, administrative agency practice, supervisory and employee training, and regular consultation. Also serves as a mediator and arbitrator.
Prof. Memberships: Oklahoma and American Bar Associations.
Career: New York Bar (1968); Oklahoma Bar (1973); US Supreme Court; Federal courts of appeal for the Tenth and Fifth Circuits; Federal district courts in Oklahoma and Texas.
Personal: BS, University of Rhode Island, 1964; JD with honors, Albany Law School of Union University, 1968; LLM in Labor Laws, The George Washington University, 1973.

WARREN, Jerry
McAfee & Taft A Professional Corporation, Oklahoma City 405 552 2224
jerry.warren@mcafeetaft.com
Recommended in Corporate/M&A
Practice Areas: Practice encompasses all areas of corporate and securities law, including corporate financing, mergers and acquisitions, investment partnerships, going-private transactions, hostile takeovers and defenses, leveraged buyouts and securities regulation.
Prof. Memberships: Oklahoma County, Oklahoma and American Bar Associations.
Career: Oklahoma Bar (1968). Has served as principal corporate and securities counsel for some of the largest corporate acquisitions and securities offerings involving Oklahoma-based companies. Instructor of securities regulation at the Oklahoma City University College of Law.
Personal: BA in Economics, University of Oklahoma, 1965; JD, University of Oklahoma College of Law, 1968.

WOLFE Jr, Frank
Nichols, Wolfe, Stamper, Nally, Fallis & Robertson Inc, Tulsa 918 584 5182
Recommended in Employment

CROWE & DUNLEVY, A PROFESSIONAL CORPORATION

THE FIRM

President: Jimmy Goodman
Number of attorneys: 115

FIRM OVERVIEW: Crowe & Dunlevy is the largest and one of the oldest law firms in Oklahoma with offices in Oklahoma City, Tulsa and Norman. The firm was founded in 1902 and represents clients in all aspects of commercial law practice, including complex business transactions, litigation in both state and federal courts, energy law, and all types of alternative dispute resolution.

MAIN PRACTICE AREAS:

Aviation/Aircraft: Crowe & Dunlevy features a well-known practice group for commercial aviation transactions, including aircraft title examination and aircraft transfers. The attorneys routinely assist major airlines as well as corporate clients and individuals with importing and exporting aircraft, US registration of foreign-owned aircraft and escrow and documentation needs.

Commercial Real Estate: Crowe & Dunlevy represents regional, national and international clients in all areas of commercial real estate, including acquisitions, sales, project development, leasing and financing, title matters, zoning and governmental issues, construction processes, environmental concerns, and tax and organizational planning.

Corporate & Securities/M&A: The firm assists a broad and diverse group of business clients, both public and private, in matters ranging from complex transactional work to day-to-day business counseling. Representative transactions include public and private securities offerings, Sarbanes-Oxley and other securities compliance issues, asset and stock sales of large and small businesses as well as organizational consulting.

Energy Law: Crowe & Dunlevy offers a dozen attorneys with broad experience in energy law, providing a wide range of legal services to clients, which include major energy companies, oil and gas producers, purchasers, contractors and others.

Financial Institutions/Finance: The firm is well known in the representation of financial institutions in Oklahoma for specialized services such as loan negotiation and documentation, bank and bank holding company organizations, acquisitions and sales, enforcement or employment law matters, as well as compliance-related issues for financial institutions.

Healthcare: The firm has a large and diverse healthcare practice representing hospitals, physicians and physician groups, clinics, HMOs and other managed care groups, long-term care facilities, home health agencies, hospices, academic medical centers and other entities that provide or pay for healthcare services. This practice is comprised of nationally known transactional and litigation attorneys.

Intellectual Property & Technology: Crowe & Dunlevy's intellectual property and technology attorneys have experience representing national, regional and local companies in patent, trademark, trade secret, copyright and other transactional and litigation intellectual property matters.

Labor & Employment: The firm represents management in the rapidly expanding area of labor and employment law. Attorneys have expertise in all facets of labor and employment relationships, including collective bargaining, employment discrimination, wrongful discharge, workers' compensation, employee benefits and administrative practice.

Litigation & Trial Practice: Half of the firm's attorneys regularly represent clients in litigation. This includes virtually all aspects of litigation in federal, state and appellate courts, as well as all types of alternative dispute resolution. The firm's litigation clients range from individuals and small businesses, to national and international companies.

OFFICES

OKLAHOMA
20 N. Broadway, Suite 1800, **Oklahoma City,** OK 73102-8273
Tel: 405 235 7700 **Fax:** 405 239 6651
Website: www.crowedunlevy.com

500 Kennedy Building, 321 South Boston Avenue, **Tulsa,** OK 74103-3313
Tel: 918 592 9800 **Fax:** 918 592 9801
Website: www.crowedunlevy.com

The Highpoint Office Building, 2500 South McGee Avenue, Suite 140, **Norman,** OK 73072-6705
Tel: 405 321 7317 **Fax:** 405 360 4002
Website: www.crowedunlevy.com

CONTACTS

Aviation/Aircraft	Gil Gaddes
Commercial Real Estate	Michael Laird
Corporate & Securities/M&A	Mike Stewart
Energy Law	Gary Davis
Financial Institutions/Finance	Gary Betow, Mike Stewart
Healthcare	Karen Rieger
Intellectual Property & Technology	Joe Ferretti
Labor & Employment	Leonard Court
Litigation & Trial Practice	Kent Meyers

Legal Alliances: *Employment Law Alliance* is the most comprehensive network of employment and labor law attorneys in the world, comprised of 2,000 employment and labor attorneys individually selected from more than 50 nations to form an alliance dedicated to assisting employers. *State Law Resources* is a national network of independent law firms - one from each state and two from the District of Columbia - selected for their abilities in handling administrative, regulatory and government relations issues at the state and federal level, helping clients navigate the complex and time-consuming process of managing both legal issues and state government relations. The firm is the sole Oklahoma member of *Lex Mundi*, a global organization of independent law firms assisting each other in the practice of international business transactions and litigation through consultations, referrals, facility use and often the joint representation of clients. Crowe & Dunlevy is also the only Oklahoma member of the *World Services Group*, an international consortium of professional business providers, including law firms, accountants, financiers and other professional groups.

CROWE&DUNLEVY
A PROFESSIONAL CORPORATION
Attorneys and Counselors at Law
Founded 1902

FELLERS, SNIDER, BLANKENSHIP, BAILEY & TIPPENS

THE FIRM

President: Kevin R Donelson
Number of attorneys: 54

FIRM OVERVIEW: Fellers, Snider, Blankenship, Bailey & Tippens was founded in 1963 and has become one of the major Oklahoma law firms offering broad and diverse legal services to both a local and national clientele. Its founder, James D Fellers served as President of the American Bar Association and the firm has had two presidents of the Oklahoma Bar Association. Its lawyers have developed a strong reputation, both locally and nationally, for providing outstanding legal services.

MAIN PRACTICE AREAS:

Banking & Bank Regulations: Extensive experience representing all categories of banks in virtually all matters, from lender liability, Regulation Z, formation and merger, to all types of regulatory proceedings.

Bankruptcy: Active practice in bankruptcy, reorganization, creditors' rights, liquidations, pre-bankruptcy negotiations, and serving as trustees in out-of-court trade arrangements.

Business, Corporate & Securities: Comprehensive representation of clients on virtually all facets of business, corporate law, and use of limited liability companies and limited partnerships including choice of entity, financing and structuring sales, mergers and acquisitions, leveraged buyouts, proxy contests and tender offers, buy/sell agreements, asset purchases and sales, stock purchases and sales and executive compensation. It also has substantial experience in the areas of formation, operation, dissolution, liquidation and governance of corporate entities.

Employment & Labor Law: Representation of both the public and private employment sectors in all facets of employment litigation and workers' compensation claims. Representation of state, county and local government entities in employment related areas, as well as defending these entities in constitutional and civil rights litigation. Additionally, the firm does extensive pre-litigation resolution of disputes arising in the workplace and formulation of personnel policies and guidelines to address evolving issues in the employment area.

Energy, Environmental & Natural Resources: Representation in all aspects of energy transactions, energy marketing and trading, natural gas, energy litigation and administrative/regulatory matters. Negotiation and drafting of agreements in connection with all aspects of the energy industry. Advice and counseling on pre-transaction activities. Development and negotiation of intricate structured transactions. Energy, environmental and toxic tort litigation are handled for the petroleum and petrochemical industry, as well as litigating enforcement actions, natural resource damage claims, citizens suits, common law, and statutory provisions for remediation and cost recovery related to exploration and production, refining, processing, retail, transportation, storage and disposal facilities, to name but a few of the key services provided to the energy industry.

Intellectual Property: Handling of intellectual property issues for virtually all technologies. The Domestic Patent Practice is supplemented by considerable experience in procuring international patents. The highly active Trademark Practice is well versed in every element associated with procurement, prosecution and defense of trademarks. The IP Group has valuable experience in obtaining copyright registrations and patents, and structuring acquisition, development and license agreements for innovations. They also advise and counsel clients on all aspects of corporate intellectual property matters. The firm is highly proficient in enforcement of all components of IP law.

Litigation: The firm has a national reputation for the quality of its Litigation Practice with a concentration on all facets of commercial litigation on behalf of both plaintiffs and defendants. Its attorneys try cases nationwide, primarily involving complex commercial and business litigation,

OFFICES

OKLAHOMA
Bank One Center, 17th Floor, 100 N. Broadway,
Oklahoma City, OK 73102-8820
Tel: 405 232 0621 **Fax:** 405 232 9659

The Kennedy Building, 321 South Boston Avenue, Suite 800
Tulsa, OK 74103-3318
Tel: 918 599 0621 **Fax:** 918 583 9659

Website: www.fellerssnider.com

but also including personal injury and other tort and property damage litigation. In particular, the firm has many attorneys with jury trial experience in oil and gas, insurance, intellectual property, anti-trust, real estate and banking litigation. The firm also represents both individuals and corporations in a variety of criminal proceedings at all levels of the criminal process. Additionally, the firm is experienced in representing its clients before federal and state administrative agencies. The firm also has an active appellate practice, having presented oral arguments in scores of cases in appellate courts around the country, including the Supreme Court of the United States.

Real Estate & Commercial Transactions: The firm serves national and local clients ranging from the most significant real estate transactions in Oklahoma to normal business and personal transactions and mortgage foreclosures. It also represents businesses and individuals in acquiring, financing, selling and leasing real estate. This firm is frequently chosen to serve as local counsel for major national corporations in conjunction with nationwide transactions.

Regulatory Matters: The firm has attorneys which have expertise in representing telecommunication and utility companies before the Oklahoma Corporation Commission in all regulatory matters.

Tax, Trusts, Probate & Estate Planning: The firm handles numerous estate plans for clients with multi-million dollar estates involving almost every aspect of estate planning. It represents on a regular basis charitable organizations in the handling and administration of charitable gifts, trust departments on numerous matters, beneficiaries in the protection of their interests, creditors and others in estate and trust matters, and handles all aspects of major probates, will contests and other similar litigation. The firm also prepares federal and state estate and gift tax returns for large estates and successfully defends them through the audit process both by the IRS and state agencies.

CLIENTS: The unique talents and backgrounds of its lawyers enable the firm to also meet the needs of clients in areas such as aircraft title and financing, agricultural law, and workers compensation. The clients of this firm range from national retail, manufacturing and service organizations whose names are household words, to governmental agencies and entities, to local businesses and individuals. Each client's needs are met and problems solved with the integrity, creativity and dedication upon which the firm's reputation for service and quality has been built.

FELLERS SNIDER
ATTORNEYS AND COUNSELLORS AT LAW
FELLERS SNIDER BLANKENSHIP BAILEY & TIPPENS, P.C.

GABLE & GOTWALS

THE FIRM

Managing Shareholder: M Benjamin Singletary
President: John R Barker

Number of shareholders: 38
Number of other lawyers: 20

Email: info@gablelaw.com
Website: www.gablelaw.com

FIRM OVERVIEW: Gable & Gotwals is a full-service law firm representing a diversified client base in Oklahoma, the southwest and across the nation.

MAIN AREAS OF PRACTICE

Business Litigation: Gable & Gotwals' trial lawyers represent and counsel major corporations, individuals, businesses and governmental agencies in domestic and international controversies over matters ranging from the simplest to the most complex. This group offers expertise in all aspects of state and federal trial work, state and federal appeals and alternative dispute resolution processes.

Business Transactions & Securities: Attorneys in the Business Practice section represent closely held enterprises, publicly traded companies of all sizes, partnerships, limited liability companies and joint ventures in a wide array of business planning opportunities and sophisticated transactions.

Commercial Law & Bankruptcy: The firm's Commercial Practice includes business and personal property acquisitions, commercial loan and lease documentation, banking, debtor-creditor relations and consumer law. Gable & Gotwals' vast experience in collections and realization by creditors ranges from the simple replevin, garnishment or attachment to complex federal foreclosures.

Energy & Regulated Industries: Gable & Gotwals' energy section offers comprehensive legal services to a wide range of oil and gas concerns, including producers, pipelines, refineries, gas processors, crude oil purchasers, gas storage companies, gas marketers, large independents, and major energy companies. Their transactional work includes acquisitions and sales of large blocks of producing properties in multiple states, preparation of exploration and development agreements, representations of both lenders and borrowers, title examination, marketing contracts, surface damage settlements, gas gathering systems, gas storage facilities, interstate pipelines, and many other oil field, contract and fiscal matters. The firm routinely represents major and independent oil companies in defending litigation throughout the southwestern US and in regulatory matters at the Oklahoma Corporation Commission. The firm successfully prosecutes cases for energy clients and has obtained the largest jury awards, affirmed on appeal, in the states of Oklahoma and Arkansas. Additionally, Gable & Gotwals has obtained defense verdicts for oil and gas companies in cases where claimed damages exceeded $500 million.

Real Estate & Finance: The focus of this group encompasses all aspects of real estate, lending and banking law, land and property acquisitions, sales, leasing and development. In lending and banking matters, the firm has a long history of representing national and local financial institutions and insurance companies involved with permanent and construction loans, syndicated credits, project financing, structured financing, sale-leaseback transactions, synthetic leases and other complex financial arrangements.

Labor & Employment: Management groups of all sizes and industries count on the attorneys in this group. The firm emphasizes preventative measures to avoid employment-related claims and provide expertise at both the administrative and judicial levels in many specialized areas.

Environmental Concerns: Gable & Gotwals routinely handles matters pertaining to environmental concerns. The firm's trial attorneys defend both large and small companies throughout the Southwest. The firm's trial experience in oil field pollution, pipeline spills and toxic waste sites allows it to provide clients with sound evaluation, realistic approaches to case resolution, and the talent needed to present sophisticated environmental issues in state and federal courts.

Tax, Estate & Business Planning/Trusts & Estates: From wills to trusts to tax exemption and asset protection, the lawyers of this group have the depth to serve any size client. This practice encompasses business and tax advice, estate planning, employee benefit planning, tax-exempt status, probates and will contests, and guardianship matters.

Intellectual Property: Gable & Gotwals provides counsel that inventor, from individuals to corporate research departments, need to protect their ideas from concept to reality. The firm counsels clients with planning and disputes related to patents, trademarks, service marks, copyrights and other intellectual property.

CLIENTS: Gable & Gotwals provides efficient, professional and ethical representation for all clients. Featuring a wide range of practice groups, the firm assists an extensive client portfolio with business planning, litigation and arbitration, contract negotiation, and dispute resolution needs. Though Oklahoma-based, the firm's connections are global. Fortune 500 corporations, entrepreneurs, privately owned companies, foundations and individuals entrust the firm every day with the stewardship and strategic management of their legal challenges.

McAFEE & TAFT A PROFESSIONAL CORPORATION

THE FIRM

Managing Partner: John N Hermes

Number of partners: 66
Number of other lawyers: 47

FIRM OVERVIEW: Guided by a client-focused, multi-disciplinary approach, McAfee & Taft has distinguished itself by being an industry leader in developing innovative legal solutions for business. Founded in 1949, the firm has grown to become one of the largest full-service civil practice law firms in the Southwest. The firm is also the sole Oklahoma member of TerraLex®, an international network of independent law firms that serves the business and personal interests of clients whose requirements transcend their state, provincial or national borders.

MAIN AREAS OF PRACTICE:

Aviation: Located just miles from the FAA in Oklahoma City, McAfee & Taft is widely recognized as having one of the largest and most experienced FAA aviation groups in the nation. Its attorneys represent local, national and international clients of all sizes on aviation matters, including the documentation of aircraft transactions, aircraft title and registration matters, aircraft title insurance, escrow closings and closing and post-recordation opinions.

Business Law: The firm has significant depth and expertise in representing clients in all aspects of business law, including administrative law, agriculture, antitrust and trade regulations, business immigration, general business and commercial transactions, construction law, energy, environmental, franchising, Native American law and gaming and secured transactions. The firm is also widely regarded for its expertise in handling oil and gas and real estate transactions of all types and sizes.

Corporate & Securities: McAfee & Taft has extensive experience advising clients on corporate governance and general corporate matters; partnerships, joint ventures and other business entities; mergers, acquisitions and divestitures; public and private securities offerings; corporate and partnership finance; and venture and private equity capital. The firm also serves the unique legal needs of financial institutions and investment companies, advisors and broker/dealers.

Employee Benefits: McAfee & Taft's premier Employee Benefits Practice offers specialized legal solutions in all major areas, including qualified plan design and implementation, multi-employers plans, collectively bargained plans, welfare plans and flexible benefits, executive compensation, plan terminations and surplus assets, plan investments, funding and taxation, plan fiduciary counseling, mergers and acquisitions, legal compliance and ERISA litigation.

Healthcare: The firm represents physicians, hospitals and hospital systems, and other healthcare institutions and facilities with respect to managed care contracting, facilities development or expansion, peer review, medical staff issues, medical-legal-ethical issues and affiliation strategies. In its regulatory Healthcare Practice, the firm routinely counsels and advises clients on the fraud and abuse, Stark, tax and antitrust implications related to joint venture arrangements, investment and ownership arrangements, development of outpatient and ancillary facilities, physician practice mergers and acquisitions, corporate affiliations and physician compensation relationship.

Intellectual Property: McAfee & Taft represents individuals and businesses in matters involving trademarks, copyrights, patents, domain names, trade secrets, counterfeiting, rights of privacy, Internet liability, unfair competition and false advertising claims, as well as publicity and multimedia rights. The firm's transactional experience includes the registration, licensing, sale and acquisition of complex intellectual property rights and the representation of clients in the entertainment and creative industries. Its dispute practice includes trials, appeals and alternate dispute resolution proceedings.

Labor & Employment: McAfee & Taft represents management in all areas of employment-related law. Its practice includes drafting and negotiating labor agreements, resolving labor disputes through arbitration, defending unfair labor practice charges before regulatory agencies, designing and implementing preventive workplace practices, ensuring state and federal compliance, representing management before state and federal administrative agencies, and litigating employment claims in state and federal courts. The firm is actively involved in designing workplace arbitration agreements and arbitrating employment-related cases.

Litigation: At its core, this group features senior trial lawyers who have received nationwide recognition from their peers for their experience in handling complex litigation. Firm trial lawyers represent clients in all types of commercial disputes, including litigation and arbitration involving banking, corporations, partnerships and other business entities, franchises, healthcare, insurance, municipal bonds, divorce, oil and gas, products liability, real estate, securities, tax, trusts, telecommunications, trademarks and patents.

Tax & Family Wealth: The firm has long been a leader in providing complex tax advice to the business community and individuals. They provide assistance in connection with all forms of family wealth and tax planning, including commercial and private transactions, mergers and acquisitions, oil and gas operations, real estate transactions, deferred compensation arrangements, gift and estate planning, post-mortem planning, foreign transactions and state and local tax issues.

CLIENTS: Firm clients are engaged in aviation, banking, communications, construction, employment, energy, wholesale food distribution, franchising, healthcare, insurance, manufacturing, pharmaceuticals, real estate, technology, telecommunications and transportation. The firm also represents non-profit organizations, including universities and foundations, entrepreneurs and individuals.

MAIN OFFICE

OKLAHOMA
Two Leadership Square, 10th Floor, 211 North Robinson
Oklahoma City, OK 73102-7103
Tel: 405 235 9621 **Fax:** 405 235 0439
Website: www.mcafeetaft.com

CONTACTS

Aircraft	Frank Polk
Business Law	Louis Price
Corporate & Securities	David Ketelsleger
Employee Benefits	Richard Nix
Healthcare	Elizabeth Tyrrell
Intellectual Property	Michael LaBrie
Labor & Employment	Sam Fulkerson
Litigation	Henry Hoss
Tax & Family Wealth	Steven Ledgerwood

CONTENTS: Corporate/M&A p.1471; Employment p.1473; Litigation: General Commercial p.1475; Real Estate p.1478; Individuals' Profiles p.1481; Firms' Profiles p.1486.

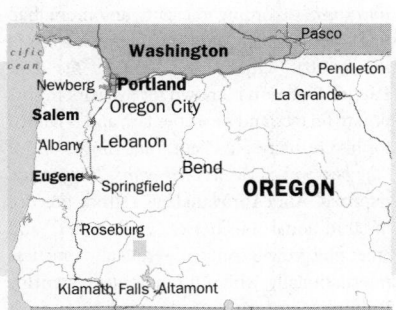

How lawyers are ranked

The opinions we gather from clients — mainly from in-house lawyers but also from other purchasers of legal services — are balanced by opinions from colleagues and competitors. Together, they provide two different perspectives — an all-round view — and biased viewpoints cancel each other out.

CORPORATE/M&A

Oregon
Leading firms (Corporate/M&A)

1. STOEL RIVES LLP *Portland*
2. PERKINS COIE LLP *Portland*
   TONKON TORP LLP *Portland*
3. ATER WYNNE LLP *Portland*
   MILLER NASH LLP *Portland*
4. DAVIS WRIGHT TREMAINE LLP *Portland*
   LANE POWELL PC *Portland*
   PRESTON GATES & ELLIS LLP *Portland*

Leading individuals (Corporate/M&A)

Senior Statesman
BOOTH Brian *Tonkon Torp, Portland*
HEWITT Henry *Stoel Rives, Portland*

1. CAMPBELL William *Ater Wynne, Portland*
   TUCKER Roy *Perkins Coie, Portland*
2. BAUMAN Todd *Stoel Rives, Portland*
   BEYER Ruth *Stoel Rives, Portland*
   GREENMAN Ronald *Tonkon Torp, Portland*
   HILL NOTO Margaret *Stoel Rives, Portland*
   MOORMAN Robert *Stoel Rives, Portland*
   SIMPSON Patrick *Perkins Coie, Portland*
   STEPHENS Kenneth *Tonkon Torp, Portland*
3. ABRAVANEL Alan *Perkins Coie, Portland*
   BACA David *Davis Wright, Portland*
   BULLOCK Brentley *Perkins Coie, Portland*
   CABLE Franklin *Miller Nash, Portland*
   CHESTLER Stuart *Stoel Rives, Portland*
   FRANTZ Mary Ann *Miller Nash, Portland*
   HIBBS Carol *Tonkon Torp, Portland*
   MCDONNELL Brendan *Preston Gates, Portland*
   PALMER Thomas *Tonkon Torp, Portland*
   STRUXNESS Gregory *Ater Wynne, Portland*
   THOMAS John *Stoel Rives, Portland*
   WOLFSTONE Jeffrey *Lane Powell, Portland*

Up-and-coming individuals
MATHESON David *Perkins Coie, Portland*

Firms and individuals are listed alphabetically in each band.

Band 1

Stoel Rives LLP

The Firm: Stoel Rives dominates the corporate/M&A market in Oregon. A group of more than 40 lawyers forms part of a 370-strong team spread across five western states, which helps to make the firm a major force throughout the region. The group serves a broad range of public and private companies in a variety of industries, with its size and prominence usually guaranteeing it a place at the table in the largest and most sophisticated transactions. Examples from the year include advising Hollywood Entertainment on a considerable amount of work, including its high-profile sale, and handling a $500 million acquisition for Tektronix. Peers envy the firm its "*unsurpassed clientele*" and acknowledge that its lawyers are "*a pleasure to work with,*" while clients keep returning to them for their "*high-quality work,*" pragmatic advice and wonderful contacts.

The Lawyers: "*Counselor extraordinaire*" **Henry Hewitt** is one of the recognized leaders in the state. Clients commend his "*outstanding advice*" and appreciate how "*well connected*" he is in Portland's legal and political circles. A veteran business lawyer and an ambassador for the firm, Hewitt remains a "*go-to guy for corporate law in Oregon.*" **Todd Bauman** chairs the firm's technology ventures group. He focuses on work for early-stage venture-backed technology companies, but is experienced in a wide range of securities and general corporate law. Peers admire his "*steadiness of focus and breadth of understanding.*" Managing partner **Ruth Beyer** still finds time for corporate counsel and M&A work, mostly with public companies. A "*deal person,*" she is valued by clients for her ability to speak with business people in a "*realistic and practical*" manner. **Robert Moorman** chairs the firm's public companies group and practices primarily in general corporate and securities law. This year saw him involved with the sale of Hollywood Entertainment. His clients consider him to be "*one of the best attorneys we have ever worked with, nationwide.*" **Margaret Hill Noto** is best known for representing publicly held companies in corporate, securities and financing transactions. Peers report that she is "*focused on the legal side of the equation, and great at nailing it down right.*" Another expert in securities law and corporate transactions, **Stuart Chestler** was described to researchers as "*efficient and technically strong.*" **John Thomas** advises on a broad range of public company work. He has a loyal following of clients who admire his quiet tenacity.

The Clients: Columbia Management Group/ Columbia Funds; Hollywood Entertainment; KinderCare Learning Centers; PacifiCorp; Stan-Corp Financial Group; Tektronix; Columbia Sportswear; Oregon Steel Mills; Pope & Talbot; Electro Scientific Industries; Schnitzer Steel Industries; Bioject Medical Technologies; Endeavour Capital and Paulson Capital.

Band 2

Perkins Coie LLP

The Firm: Although it is the Seattle office that is considered the firm's real powerhouse, the Portland team has its fair share of star players. With just under 70 lawyers in the city, the firm has a group of around 14 dedicated to corporate and M&A. They handle both public and private company work, and are renowned for their skill in finding creative solutions and managing sophisticated transactions. These include representing Movie Gallery in its bid for Hollywood Video, one of 2004's 'hot' deals. Clients say that the group's "*extreme expertise in cutting-edge law stands it apart,*" while several peers acknowledge that they would happily "*emulate the firm*" if they could.

The Lawyers: "*Top-flight lawyer*" **Roy Tucker** is highly respected for his good judgment, analytical skills, intelligence and ability to prioritize. His experience in public offerings, M&A, private placements and venture capital financings highlighted by sources. He "*leaves no stone unturned,*" according to clients, and more than one considers him "*among the better lawyers in the country.*" One of the "*lions of the Bar,*" **Patrick Simpson** is known for his work in corporate finance and securities law, and is lauded for his creativity. His clients rank him as one of "*the best we've ever worked with.*" "*Bright and respected*" **Alan Abravanel** has a strong practice in traditional businesses, midmarket, and emerging growth companies, and also practices internationally, while "*future leader*" **Brentley Bullock** focuses on growth companies, which he advises on corporate finance, securities and M&A, among other things. "*He makes you feel like you're his only client*" said one enthusiastic referee. Up-and-comer **David Matheson** is an addition to this year's tables. He is increasingly visible leading large and important transactions for the firm, often with "*outstanding results.*"

The Clients: Corillian; Teekay Shipping; Merix; Integra Telecom; Qwest, Tripwire; UPS; Wells Fargo; Weyerhaeuser; Movie Gallery and Endeavour Capital.

Tonkon Torp LLP

The Firm: This "*relationship-oriented*" firm, of some 75 lawyers, has more than 20 practicing all aspects of corporate law. An "*elite corporate practice,*" it handles a wide variety of work, advising on new corporate governance regulations as well as representing clients in M&A, financing, securities offerings and joint ventures for both large public and private entities. According to clients: "*Creativity is the hallmark of the lawyers at Tonkon Torp.*" However, their armory also includes considerable technical expertise and great contacts. As one client put it: "*Not only do they have excellent legal skills, but they have strong relationships through the Pacific Northwest and the USA, which for us has meant introductions to prospective customers and problem-solving skills that go far beyond what you'd typically see in a law firm.*"

The Lawyers: "*One of the godfathers of Oregon's securities law,*" **Brian Booth** has represented Nike for more than 20 years. This year he helped it in its acquisition of Official Starter Properties, allowing Nike to expand its portfolio of brand names. Peers hold him in extremely high regard as an "*excellent lawyer and a major contributor to the community,*" while clients praise his skill and dedication. He is an adviser to many boards and senior management. "*Sophisticated corporate practitioner*" **Ronald Greenman** has been busy over the past year working on a major European cross-border transaction for Key Technology. He specializes in securities, M&A and general business counseling. Clients described him as "*one of the top corporate finance attorneys in Oregon, and one of the finer individuals walking the earth,*" while peers commend his "*ability to drive a deal.*" **Kenneth Stephens**, one of the founding

partners, specializes in corporate and securities matters and does a lot for the financial services industry. The last year has seen him handling three important corporate takeover bids, as well as advising on two large international banking transactions. An "*exceptional detail person,*" he is the principal lawyer for The Greenbrier Companies. Peers respect him as a "*first-rate securities law practitioner.*" **Carol Hibbs** also works a lot for financial institutions, as well as advising on securities law and acquisitions of private companies. She enters the tables for the first time this year, along with **Thomas Palmer**, who chairs the firm's corporate finance group. The possessor of a broad-ranging practice, he is particularly known for his expertise in public securities work. Peers describe him as a "*strong linear thinker*" and admire his skill in "*analyzing and spotting the important legal issues.*"

The Clients: Nike; M Financial Group; The Greenbrier Companies; Endeavour Capital; Columbia Distributing; Medical Management International; Stimson Lumber; TASER International; Key Technology and DayStar Technologies.

Band 3

Ater Wynne LLP

The Firm: The firm fields some 40 lawyers in Oregon, around half of whom work in corporate/M&A. It specializes in acting for dynamically growing technology-based companies, which has won it a reputation for helping to "*build great companies.*" Some of those that it has helped become great are TriQuint Semiconductor, Pixelworks and Planar Systems, and many other prominent clients have benefited from the firm's cross-disciplinary expertise.

The Lawyers: **William Campbell** tends to focus on work for technology startups and emerging growth companies. The firm chairman, he was lauded by his clients as "*the best lawyer for business in the state*" due to his "*great legal and strategic mind*" and his ability to "*make deals happen.*" They also appreciate the benefits that accrue from being plugged into his "*incredible network of contacts.*" **Gregory Struxness** joins him in this year's tables. A "*strong technical lawyer,*" he is highly respected for his expertise in securities law, and also serves as general counsel to several of the firm's major clients.

The Clients: Pixelworks; Planar Systems; TriQuint Semiconductor; FLIR Systems; Golden Valley Electric Association; Oregon Electric Group; Northwest Pipe; Oregon Freeze Dry; Ambric and Avnera.

Miller Nash LLP

The Firm: The Portland office of this substantial regional player fields some 30 lawyers concentrating on corporate/M&A, who work closely with a further five-strong team in Seat-

tle. They represent a wide variety of clients, who range from large, household-name companies to small startups and owner-managed businesses. Peers respect the lawyers' "*professional attitude and historical strength in the state,*" while clients appreciate their empathetic approach and careful, practical advice.

The Lawyers: "*Trusted adviser*" **Franklin Cable** chairs the firm's business department, and acts as general counsel to a variety of businesses. A specialist in M&A, his recent highlights include a hotly contested takeover battle involving an AM radio station, and advice on the potential merger of a privately held organ company. According to interviewees, Cable is a technically strong "*details person*" with a meticulous approach. He is joined in this year's tables by **Mary Ann Frantz**, who handles a variety of corporate work, particularly on behalf of public companies.

The Clients: Leading names from the team's client list include: US Bancorp; RB Pamplin; Louisiana-Pacific and Pacific Financial.

Band 4

Davis Wright Tremaine LLP

See firm details p.1796

The Firm: Working closely with the firm's much larger Seattle office, this group of ten corporate lawyers focuses largely on the midmarket and a number of major national clients. These are drawn from a wide range of industries, though software technology, manufacturing, telecom and service businesses are to the fore. Clients appreciate the team's knowledge of M&A and securities law, and praise its lawyers as "*responsive and easily accessible.*"

The Lawyers: **David Baca** (see p.1481) is known for his expertise in M&A and securities, and has just closed a $27 million deal with Williams Controls. He also acts as general counsel to a number of small and midsized businesses. Clients value his "*efficiency and good understanding of business,*" and note that "*he knows lots of the answers immediately, and organizes teams effectively, so the hours are cut down.*" Peers, meanwhile, recommend him as a popular point for referrals.

The Clients: Advanced Power Technology; Clearwire; Williams Controls; Cascade Bancorp and Banner Bank.

Lane Powell PC

See firm details p.1797

The Firm: A compact but respected team of five concentrates on corporate work. Their practice covers a broad range, spanning M&A, joint ventures and investment funding, as well as commercial advice. The team is valued by clients for its hands-on, partner-led approach, strong technical capabilities and "*knowledge, expertise and responsiveness.*" Its help in strategic development was also highlighted.

The Lawyers: **Jeffrey Wolfstone** (see p.1485) cochairs the firm's business department and splits his time between deal-intensive startups, emerging and midmarket companies and work with national and international companies in the Pacific Northwest. His "*meticulous attention to detail*" wins glowing plaudits, as does his "*understanding of the whole context of an issue, not just the legal side of it, which means he can look at law from a businessman's perspective.*"

The Clients: The firm's impressive client roster of emerging and established companies includes: EthicsPoint; Norm Thompson Outfitters; Fios; Harry's Fresh Foods; Pendleton Woolen Mills; Epson Portland: Downstream and ERI Acquisition.

Preston Gates & Ellis LLP

The Firm: The firm has 430 lawyers located across five western states, as well as having international offices in China and Taiwan. Though there are only around six lawyers in Portland dedicated to corporate transactional work, they can also rely on support from the deep bench in Seattle, giving them access to considerable resources. Clients say that they "*stick with Preston Gates, for both local and out-of-state matters.*" The firm famously counts Microsoft,

T-Mobile, and Starbucks among its clients.

The Lawyers: **Brendan McDonnell** is a specialist in the venture capital and emerging growth markets, and worked with Endeavour Capital, Columbia Sportwear, Wells Fargo, and Norton Motorcyles. Clients describe him as "*approachable and a good listener,*" with one going so far as to call him "*one of the brightest lawyers*" they have worked with. He has been concentrating on building up the firm's corporate presence in the state.

The Clients: Columbia Sportswear; Quiktrak; Wells Fargo; Norton Motorcycles; Stelar Tools and Endeavour Capital.

EMPLOYMENT

MAINLY DEFENDANT

Oregon
Leading firms
(Employment: Mainly Defendant)

1 BARRAN LIEBMAN *Portland*

2 BULLARD SMITH JERNSTEDT WILSON *Portland*
STOEL RIVES LLP *Portland*

3 AMBURGEY & RUBIN PC *Portland*
PERKINS COIE LLP *Portland*
TONKON TORP LLP *Portland*
WILLIAMS, ZOGRAFOS & PECK *Lake Oswego*

4 BULLIVANT HOUSER BAILEY PC *Portland*
DAVIS WRIGHT TREMAINE LLP *Portland*
MILLER NASH LLP *Portland*
SCHWABE WILLIAMSON & WYATT PC *Portland*

Firms are listed alphabetically in each band.

Band 1

Barran Liebman
See firm details p.1486
The Firm: This leading employment boutique boasts about 17 "*consummate professionals,*" whose collective skill and experience take it firmly to "*the top of the market.*" Highly respected by peers and enthusiastically recommended by clients, the team practices labor and employment law exclusively for employers, and focuses particularly on cutting-edge employment litigation and counseling. The group also does quite a bit of training and counseling – indeed some sources suggested that it had developed quite a culture of litigation avoidance and consensual negotiation, despite fielding some of the "*most seasoned trial lawyers in the state.*"

The Lawyers: The "*queen of employment law*" in Oregon, **Paula Barran** (see p.1481) is universally recognized as "*one of the best in town.*" Clients appreciate her "*focus on preventive rather than reactive solutions.*" She was particularly admired for combining excellence in litigation with skill in senior executive training and employment counseling. She has recently been involved in First Amendment claims made by

public employers. Traditional labor lawyer **Richard Liebman** (see p.1483) is "*stunningly in touch with what seems to be all of Oregon, if not the whole Pacific Northwest business, legal, and political communities.*" He was warmly recommended by clients for his expertise in traditional labor bargaining, and recently completed successful negotiations between unions and the Portland Public Schools District. Managing partner **Edwin Harnden** (see p.1482) specializes in employment litigation, representing management from a variety of industries. He recently won a discrimination case on behalf of Home Depot. While he is described as a "*star*" by peers, his clients say that he "*works like a dog*" and is "*prepared, to the point, efficient and tough as nails.*" **Richard VanCleave** (see p.1484) focuses on traditional labor law. He recently negotiated a labor contract for a major public employer involving five different unions. His clients benefit from his "*practical experience.*" They also pay tribute to his "*skill in analyzing costs.*" **Maryann Yelnosky** (see p.1485) is known in the market as an "*aggressive, no-nonsense litigator.*" She defends employers in a variety of disputes, as well as advising on employee management and termination.

The Clients: Home Depot; Hilton; Pacific Maritime Association; Frito-Lay; Bear Creek; Safeway; Georgia-Pacific; Hollywood Entertainment; Oregonian Publishing; Hoffman Construction and Howard S Wright Construction; Samaritan Health Systems; National Electrical Contractors Association; Christie School and Port of Portland.

Band 2

Bullard Smith Jernstedt Wilson
The Firm: This boutique firm of about 21 employment and labor specialists has benefited over the past year from the addition of Tom Kramer, considerably bolstering its position in the employee benefits field. It remains best

known, however, for its expertise in traditional labor law, where the team is widely considered the "*strongest in town.*" Acting for employers, from both the public and private sectors, the "*aggressive and energetic*" team handles collective bargaining, employment regulations, and NLRB proceedings. Over the past year, it has been lead counsel in five class action suits.

The Lawyers: "*At the helm of the firm*" is **Kenneth Jernstedt**, a highly respected specialist in traditional labor law. He focuses on collective bargaining, labor contract negotiations and representing clients in NLRB proceedings and investigations. Interviewees say that they would "*go to him about any labor law matter*" for his "*well-prepared and thoughtful*" advice. **Richard Alli** has negotiated some 15 contracts over the course of the past year, including several for large regional hospitals. Clients value his "*unquestionable loyalty*" and zeal in working toward their goals while still maintaining effective working relationships with unions. "*Eager and energetic*" **Kenneth Bemis** is well respected for his considerable expertise in public sector negotiations, while "*real bright and talented*" employee benefits specialist **Tom Kramer** is of counsel to the firm and writes and speaks frequently on benefits issues. **David Wilson** was described to researchers as "*one of the best legal writers out there*" and is a "*smart and incisive thinker and analyzer.*" Up-and-comer **Jacqueline Damm** represents management in labor and employment law issues and is a "*results-oriented*" attorney.

The Clients: State of Oregon; Fred Meyer Stores; NORPAC Foods; Standard Insurance; Jesuit High School; Legacy Health System; JELD-WEN; Holy Rosary Medical Center; Portland General Electric and Rite Aid.

Stoel Rives LLP
The Firm: With its huge corporate presence, Stoel Rives commands a large share of the Oregon marketplace, which is reflected in leading

positions in areas such as labor and employment. Peers respect the young and dynamic team's "*tremendous diligence on behalf of its clients*," while clients appreciate the "*thoroughly practical advice, which helps us avoid risks.*" The firm fields about 20 attorneys in the areas of labor and employment law, including eight who focus solely on employee benefits. The past year has seen them handle a variety of substantial and cutting-edge employment disputes, as well as a volume of day-to-day counseling.

The Lawyers: Paul Buchanan chairs the firm's labor and employment group, and focuses on employment litigation and counseling on employment policies and practices. Clients admire his "*quiet tenacity*" and appreciate his ability to "*spell things out in layman's terms.*" **Chris Kitchel** was recommended to researchers as a "*superior litigator*" with extraordinary experience and ability. She focuses on employment litigation and is currently the state chair of the American College of Trial Lawyers. **Edward Reeves** specializes in advising private colleges and universities on all aspects of education and employment law. Clients rave about his attentiveness and accessibility, saying: "*He treats everyone like they're his number-one client.*" Up-and-comer **Courtney Angeli** possesses "*dogged*

determination." She is commended for her written skills as well as her energy in employment litigation and counseling.

The Clients: Columbia Sportswear; Electro Scientific Industries; Eastman Kodak; Farmers Insurance; FEI; Gunderson; Hanna Andersson; Health Net of Oregon; Holland Company; JELD-WEN; Kaiser Foundation Health Plan; Lattice Semiconductor; Legacy Health System; Leupold & Stevens; McCormick & Schmick Management Group; McDonald's; Mentor Graphics; Northwest Natural Gas; Oregon Steel Mills; Oregon Shakespeare Festival; Reed College; Sprint; T-Mobile; Tektronix; Unified Western Grocers; Verizon; Welch Allyn and Xerox.

Band 3

Amburgey & Rubin PC

The Firm: Although its client base is diverse, including a number of nationally known names, Amburgey & Rubin is particularly felt to offer "*a nice practice for smaller and midsized Oregon employers.*" The labor and employment boutique fields a team of five, acting in a wide range of matters. The firm has undeniably lost some members in recent years, but sources are in no doubt of its continuing ability to offer a combination of big-firm ability with small-firm informality and focus.

The Lawyers: "*Bright, edgy and charismatic,*" **Larry Amburgey** is commended for his flamboyant style and "*A-list*" traditional labor practice. A talented business developer and a respected teacher, he spends about a quarter of his time traveling within the USA, and is widely sought after for his skill in preventive training. "*Bright and personable*" **Howard Rubin** is "*at the cutting edge of employment law.*" He joins Amburgey in this year's tables, following enthusiastic market recommendations.

The Clients: ConAgra Foods/Lamb Weston; Port of Portland; ATT Alascom; CenturyTel; JR Simplot; Cowlitz County and Powell's Books.

Perkins Coie LLP

The Firm: This sizable regional player is much better known for its expertise in general commercial litigation. However, with its roster of major national clients, the employment and labor team has developed an impressive profile in the local market. Indeed, this "*highly respected national firm*" tends to practice more on the national than the local level. Although Perkins Coie's regional labor and employment strength is concentrated in Seattle, the five-lawyer team in Portland serves "*a silk-stocking clientele*" comprising large local and national employers.

The Lawyers: Calvin Keith heads the labor and employment practice at the firm. He was commended as a "*first-rate lawyer*" for his ability in both employment litigation and labor law. Referring to his aptitude in the courtroom, peers

describe him as a "*worthy opponent.*"

The Clients: Boeing; UPS; Longview Fiber; Boise; IBM; Starbucks; Qwest and Lowe's Companies.

Tonkon Torp LLP

The Firm: The seven-strong team at this sizable, full-service firm is dedicated to labor and employment, and includes several experts in related areas. The firm boasts a strong corporate client base, including Nike, and is increasingly leveraging this to move into a premier position in areas such as employment litigation. Its growing ability to handle complex issues is appreciated by clients, who note that the group "*does a really good job of balancing legal requirements with business necessities.*"

The Lawyers: The "*incredibly motivated*" **Victor Kisch** heads the firm's labor and employment group. Clients stress how enjoyable he is to work with, and particularly appreciate his "*extraordinary business acumen*" and the lengths he goes to in understanding their concerns. He recently litigated a highly controversial, unprecedented case regarding illegal aliens and their entitlement to back pay.

The Clients: Nike; Costco Wholesale; Key Technology; KOIN-TV; OHSU Foundation; Stimson Lumber; GemStone Systems; Marquis Companies; David Evans & Associates; Cascade General; United States Bakery; Medical Management International (The Pet Hospital) and Adecco.

Williams, Zografos & Peck

The Firm: The six attorneys at this well-respected labor and employment boutique act exclusively for management. The compact but high-quality team offers a wide range of services, ranging from cutting-edge employment litigation to traditional labor negotiations and organizing campaigns, as well as employment audits and counseling. Clients recommended the lawyers for their down-to-earth approach, business acumen and concern to deliver value for money.

The Lawyers: Kathy Peck has a broad labor and employment practice but is particularly admired for her experience in public sector work. She was described to researchers as "*just an excellent, first-rate counsel*" with an approach that is "*impressive and competent without being flamboyant.*" Clients highlighted her responsiveness and commitment to giving them personal attention.

The Clients: Allied Waste North America; City of Portland; Utility Vault/Oldcastle Precast; Salem Hospital; Kettle Foods; Clackamas Community College; West Coast Bank; Multnomah County; Alcan; Parr Lumber; Amcor; Mt Hood Beverage; Morrow Equipment; Columbia Distributing; Pacific Cast Technologies; Douglas County; PECO Manufacturing; Salem Clinic; Springfield Utility Board; Sause Bros; Oregon Hematology Oncology; First Pacific; Partnerships in Community Living and Sunshine Dairy Foods.

Band 4

Bullivant Houser Bailey PC
The Firm: This large regional outfit fields a team of eight attorneys dedicated to labor and employment, a number of whom also handle employee benefits work. The firm is also panel counsel for most of the major insurance carriers' employment practices liability insurance programs.
The Lawyers: "*Tough, aggressive*" litigator **Chrys Martin** also has a good line in manager and supervisor training. Peers are impressed by her skills as a "*problem solver*," while clients "*love how calm and sensible she is.*" In the words of one, she is a "*no-nonsense, cut-to-the-chase attorney, who seems to have laser vision to see what the real nut of the issue is.*"
The Clients: JBL&K; Salvation Army; Kinder-Care Learning Centers; Benson Industries; Paulson Investment; Standard Insurance; Tetra Pak; Fire Mountain Gems; Brink's Home Security; State Farm Insurance; Pfizer; Wieden + Kennedy; Dr. Martens AirWair USA; Sears Roebuck; Rinker Materials; FedEx; Freight West; Schwan's Sales Enterprises; Pacific Coast Restaurants and Tyco Electronics.

Davis Wright Tremaine LLP
See firm details p.1796
The Firm: This group of ten labor and employment lawyers benefits from the support of its larger Seattle office, but the Portland branch has also proved itself in the market and enters the tables this year. The team handles a broad range of employment and labor litigation and counseling, with its highest profile felt to be in the arena of employment litigation. This was emphasized last year when it won two sizable jury trials and a discrimination case in the Ninth Circuit.
The Lawyers: Boasting a tremendous win record, employment litigator **Carol Bernick** (see p.1481) also counsels and trains employers in preventive practices. "*Fabulous, smart and a good writer,*" she was acknowledged by peers for doing a great job for her clients.
The Clients: Bank of America; adidas; GE Capital and Legacy Health System.

Miller Nash LLP
The Firm: A team of 16 handles all aspects of labor and employment law, typically representing employers in collective bargaining negotiations and labor arbitrations, where the firm traditionally enjoys a strong profile. It also appears in a considerable volume of NLRB proceedings concerning alleged violations of state and federal laws. It is part of the Employment Law Alliance, a global alliance of management-focused firms.
The Lawyers: Veteran traditional labor specialist **Louis Livingston** is enormously respected by clients and peers alike. A "*powerhouse,*" he recently completed negotiations covering nurses and skilled maintenance workers at various hospitals, all without any work stoppage. He also gets involved in arbitration and grievance work as well as counseling.
The Clients: Providence Health System; Meier & Frank; Weyerhaeuser; Samaritan Health Services; Portland School District and CNF Transportation.

Schwabe Williamson & Wyatt PC
The Firm: The team comprises about 12 lawyers, who handle all aspects of labor and employment law, including litigating employment discrimination and harassment cases and providing blue-chip clients with advice, seminars and counseling for preventive practices. On the labor side, the firm does some NLRB work and assists in negotiating labor contracts.
The Lawyers: **Mike Garone** (see p.1482) handles both employment litigation and traditional labor law. A "*smart, effective lawyer,*" he enters this year's rankings following sustained recommendations from the market. Senior labor lawyer **Thomas Triplett** (see p.1484) is "*sharp and tremendously experienced*" according to his clients.
The Clients: Les Schwab; SCI; Morgan Stanley; Essilor Laboratories of America; Capgemini; Portland Trail Blazers; United Western Grocers; KeyBank National; Associated Builders and Contractors and Howard S Wright Construction.

Other Notable Practitioners
The Atlanta firm of Fisher & Phillips LLP opened in Portland through its merger with **Corbett Gordon**'s (see p.1482) firm. The office managing partner, she remains active in employment advice and litigation, with some traditional labor work. According to market sources she enjoys an "*outstanding reputation*" as one of the leaders of Oregon's employment Bar, and boasts a superb track record of wins based on an approach that is characterized as "*aggressive, inventive, practical and responsive.*"

LITIGATION

Oregon
Leading firms
(Litigation: General Commercial)
[1] MARKOWITZ, HERBOLD, GLADE Portland
PERKINS COIE LLP Portland
STOEL RIVES LLP Portland
[2] BULLIVANT HOUSER BAILEY PC Portland
DAVIS WRIGHT TREMAINE LLP Portland
STOLL STOLL BERNE LOKTING Portland
TONKON TORP LLP Portland
[3] ATER WYNNE LLP Portland
DUNN CARNEY ALLEN HIGGINS Portland
MILLER NASH LLP Portland
SCHWABE WILLIAMSON & WYATT PC Portland
Firms are listed alphabetically in each band.

Band 1

Markowitz, Herbold, Glade & Mehlhaf PC
The Firm: This boutique commercial litigation firm fields 18 lawyers exclusively focused on business litigation, including appellate law, arbitration and other methods of dispute resolution. The experienced and well-established group was enthusiastically praised for "*doing an excellent job of marshaling all of its resources to defend or prosecute a case.*" Among a number of high-profile cases from the past year, it completed the arbitration of a $50 million securities claim, representing Strategic Wealth Management.
The Lawyers: The "*phenomenal*" **David Markowitz** was described to researchers as "*an all-around exceptional litigator, first class in every way.*" Clients and peers alike rave about his skill

GENERAL COMMERCIAL

in the courtroom, and the knowledge and experience that make him a "*versatile and outstanding*" advocate. Peers were also impressed by **Peter Glade**. The possessor of a quieter and more understated style than Markowitz, he is nonetheless "*excellent*" in all types of business-related litigation. He recently won a $3 million jury verdict in an accounting malpractice case against PwC.
The Clients: adidas America; Agassi Enterprises; DR Horton; Georgia-Pacific; Hollywood Entertainment; Lewis & Clark College; Portland General Electric; Sony Pictures Entertainment; Standard Insurance; US Bank; Unified Western Grocers; The Hartford and Oregon Steel Mills.

Perkins Coie LLP
The Firm: Perkins Coie is a regional heavyweight with expertise in handling anything related to business. Although its flagship office

Oregon
Leading individuals
(Litigation: General Commercial)

Senior Statesman
MARMADUKE Don *Tonkon Torp*, Portland

★ ELLIS Barnes *Stoel Rives*, Portland
MARKOWITZ David *Markowitz Herbold*, Portland

[1] ENGLISH Stephen *Bullivant Houser*, Portland
FORTINO Paul *Perkins Coie*, Portland
HOUSER Douglas *Bullivant Houser*, Portland
SKERRITT Daniel *Tonkon Torp*, Portland
TONGUE Thomas *Dunn Carney*, Portland

[2] BERNE Gary *Stoll Stoll*, Portland
CROW William *Schwabe Williamson*, Portland
CROWE Austin *Perkins Coie*, Portland
DULCICH Thomas *Schwabe Williamson*, Portland
GIDLEY James *Perkins Coie*, Portland
GLADE Peter *Markowitz Herbold*, Portland
MOWE Gregory *Stoel Rives*, Portland
MULLIN Joel *Stoel Rives*, Portland
NEWELL Robert *Davis Wright*, Portland
RICHTER Peter *Miller Nash*, Portland
ROSENBAUM Lois *Stoel Rives*, Portland
STOLL Robert *Stoll Stoll*, Portland
WALTERS Martha *Walters Romm*, Eugene
WALTERS Stephen *Stoel Rives*, Portland

[3] ARELLANO Joseph *Kennedy Watts*, Portland
BANKS Robert *Banks Law*, Portland
BLACKHURST Steven *Ater Wynne*, Portland
ERNST David *Bullivant Houser*, Portland
HAGLUND Michael *Haglund Kelley*, Portland
HODSON Jerry *Miller Nash*, Portland
KENT Christopher *Kent Custis*, Portland
KILMER Jeffrey *Kilmer Voorhees*, Portland
KNOX Daniel *Schwabe Williamson*, Portland
MARTSON William *Tonkon Torp*, Portland
MCGRORY John *Davis Wright*, Portland
NEUPERT John *Miller Nash*, Portland
O'LEARY Daniel *Davis Wright*, Portland
RAWLINSON Dennis *Miller Nash*, Portland
SAND Thomas *Miller Nash*, Portland
SHLACHTER Robert *Stoll Stoll*, Portland
SIMON Michael *Perkins Coie*, Portland
TURNER Mark *Ater Wynne*, Portland
WHITTEMORE Richard *Bullivant Houser*, Portland

Individuals are listed alphabetically in each band.

is in Seattle, the Portland office rises to the top in this year's research following enthusiastic plaudits for its quality, capacity and experience. As clients put it, the team of over 25 lawyers boasts high-quality litigators at every level and "*has a very deep bench to support very complex litigation.*"

The Lawyers: Paul Fortino is "*extraordinarily good on his feet,*" with an "*unequaled presence in the courtroom,*" according to his clients. They particularly appreciate his ability to adjust his style to suit the case, and his realistic analysis of costs. His expertise lies in general business litigation, complex torts and products liability, and

he has had first chair responsibility in over 100 trials. Sources have the highest respect for commercial litigator **Austin Crowe**, who was also said to be excellent in front of a jury. This year has seen him involved in a highly visible environmental contamination case, concerning asbestos material affecting 400,000 homes. **James Gidley** is another "*highly competent professional*" with considerable expertise in products liability, personal injury and construction defense cases, as well as more general business disputes. Clients appreciate his "*low-key, methodical, detailed approach,*" which wins over juries. "*Thoughtful and responsive*" trial lawyer **Michael Simon** recently won a favorable settlement for Qwest in a consumer class action, and acted as first chair in two jury trials.

The Clients: The Kroger Company; Boeing; Genie Industries; Novartis; Hewlett-Packard; Brown & Williamson Tobacco; Union Pacific; Boise Cascade; UPS; Deere & Company; Altec; ACL Services; Union Carbide; Dana; Louisiana-Pacific; Abbott Laboratories; ScottishPower; PacifiCorp; Qwest and Dex Media.

Stoel Rives LLP

The Firm: Stoel Rives is renowned as "*one of the most prestigious firms in the Pacific Northwest*" with a well-earned reputation for excellence. Its size and capacity across the region, its broad experience, and its premier league roster of national and international clients, guarantee the firm's 40-strong team of "*terrific*" litigators a place at the table in many of Oregon's largest and most complex disputes. Clients stress that the quality here permeates the entire group, making it a "*strong group of lawyers at both partner and associate level.*"

The Lawyers: "*Creative and levelheaded*" **Barnes Ellis** was referred to as "*probably the best litigator in the state*" and peers "*strive to be his equal.*" An "*outstanding trial lawyer,*" Barnes has recently been involved in the Enron criminal case pending in Houston, along with other high-profile matters. "*Professional and efficient*" **Gregory Mowe**'s focuses on condemnation litigation and other real estate disputes. One client's enthusiastic recommendation speaks of his absolute confidence in Greg: "*If I were going to be hanged, I'd call him first!*" **Joel Mullin** has defended Hollywood Entertainment in connection with its highly publicized take-private transaction. Clients describe him as a "*brilliant litigator and advocate who can produce extraordinary arguments,*" and several consider him the best trial attorney they have worked with. **Lois Rosenbaum** is known for her ability in complex public company litigation. She receives high marks from peers, who regard her as a "*smart and aggressive*" securities lawyer. Clients, meanwhile, recommend her as a "*significant asset*" in their work. A "*splendid cerebral lawyer,*" **Stephen Walters** "*makes no mistakes*" according to his

clients. He has been selected by the State of Oregon to defend cases in both federal and state courts, and is involved in a major multiyear, multimillion-dollar dispute for a group of utilities that are suing over power purchase contracts.

The Clients: Farmers Insurance Group; Tektronix; PacifiCorp; NW Natural; Fred Meyer; State of Oregon; PNGC Power; Freightliner; Precision Castparts and Portland Development Commission.

Band 2

Bullivant Houser Bailey PC

The Firm: Bullivant Houser Bailey's roots are in insurance defense; however, its team of some 40 litigators is also involved in a wide variety of major business litigation. Clients described the firm to researchers as a "*powerhouse,*" particularly complimenting it on its deep bench and the talent and pragmatism of its attorneys. As well as insurance defense and general commercial litigation, typical work includes tort cases, estates work, securities litigation, environmental and real property disputes, medical and professional negligence, and there is niche expertise in food outbreak cases.

The Lawyers: "*Rising star*" **Stephen English** is the director of the firm's litigation department, and has tried more than 100 cases to verdict. Over the past year he has been involved in a number of major matters for important national and international clients. He is "*an excellent lawyer, the kind who can do the intellectual side and try the case energetically*" say his peers. Clients, meanwhile, contend that "*there's no better trial lawyer in the state.*" With "*loads of experience in the insurance arena,*" **Douglas Houser** "*remains a real signpost*" in insurance defense. As well as being a "*premier litigator,*" he is renowned as a "*true mentor*" with a reputation for helping to bring more women into the field. **David Ernst** has developed an impressive national reputation in food outbreak disputes. His "*extremely credible and sincere*" manner is said to win the trust of juries. "*First-class*" lawyer **Richard Whittemore** practices a mixture of complex business, estates and torts litigation.

The Clients: Burlington Northern Santa Fe Railway; Caterpillar; Chubb Group; Deere & Company; Dr. Martens; Eli Lilly; Kubota; Louisiana-Pacific; Medline Industries; Sears Roebuck and Standard Insurance.

Davis Wright Tremaine LLP
See firm details p.1796

The Firm: Davis Wright Tremaine has established itself as a force across the region in a variety of areas, but in Oregon itself the firm's reputation is nowhere higher than in the field of business disputes. A sizable team of more than 40 litigators handles a variety of cases for a regional and national client base that includes a number of major energy companies. In this, its expertise in real property and environmental litigation is felt to stand it in particularly good stead.

The Lawyers: Robert Newell (see p.1483) is highly respected for his activity in the community as well as for his ability in the courtroom. He handles a variety of complex corporate and commercial disputes for the firm's top-class client base. Observers admired his *"considerable experience in both our state and federal courts."* Peers and clients also praised **Daniel O'Leary** (see p.1483), a specialist in environmental and natural resources litigation, mostly connected with federal environmental statutes. His practice also includes some water rights litigation and land title disputes. **John McGrory** (see p.1483) stands out as an extremely able securities litigator; peers refer to him as *"competent and professional."*

The Clients: Clients include: Eastern Oregon Public Land Coalition; Oregon Agricultural Legal Foundation; Viacom; Bank of America; Legacy Health System; adidas America and Dryvit Systems/RPM. The team also acts for a number of energy companies.

Stoll Stoll Berne Lokting & Shlachter

The Firm: The firm fields a *"strong and honorable litigation group"* of around 15 attorneys focusing on complex business disputes. Although they boast a range of expertise, and advise both plaintiffs and defendants, there is no doubt about where their greatest strength is felt to lie: the firm is justly renowned as the *"leading plaintiff securities litigation shop in town."* Recent examples include acting as lead counsel for Digimarc and Merit in securities class action cases.

The Lawyers: Gary Berne is said by some to have *"the best plaintiffs' securities litigation practice in town."* Interviewees describe him as a *"tough, tenacious, aggressive and bright lawyer"* who consistently produces good results for clients. Senior partner **Robert Stoll** is *"one of the longtime names in class action work."* Peers acknowledge that he is *"first rate in court,"* and enjoy working with him because there is *"no nonsense, no wringing your hands and crawling in the corner to whimper, just straight talk."* Like Gary, he is also known as an excellent plaintiffs' securities litigator. **Robert Shlachter** handles complex securities cases as well as higher profile commercial cases. Peers know him as *"a bright and able advocate."*

The Clients: Oregon Public Employees Retirement System; Oregon Health & Science University; Paulson Investment; Waddell & Reed; WM Financial Services; ScanlanKemperBard Companies and Hollywood Entertainment.

Tonkon Torp LLP

The Firm: This is one of the heavyweights in the Portland market, with a strong and diverse litigation team complementing an impressive corporate group. A *"bright and hard-working"* team of over 30 dedicated litigators has built up considerable expertise in corporate governance matters and securities disputes, among other things. They are also recommended for always acting in accordance with the *"highest ethical and professional standards."*

The Lawyers: *"Recognized leader"* **Don Marmaduke** is one of the *"grandmasters of the Portland legal community."* A veteran litigator, he focuses on general commercial and antitrust disputes. Interviewees have only good things to say about **Daniel Skerritt**, who focuses on the resolution of complex commercial disputes. *"One of the top litigators in Oregon,"* he was warmly praised by clients for his talent and expertise. In the words of one, his *"years of experience have brought him a good, common-sense approach to solving disputes and an ability to connect with the judge and jury in a low-key manner."* Like Dan, many sources also regard **William Martson** as one of Oregon's leading litigators. He was described to researchers as *"intense, hard-working and effective for his clients."*

The Clients: Nike; The Greenbrier Companies; Portland General Electric; Pacific Seafood Group; PPM Energy; M Financial Group and Medical Management International.

Band 3

Ater Wynne LLP

The Firm: The team of around ten litigators at this well-respected, business-oriented firm commands a broad-based practice and a good share of local and regional clients. Along with general commercial disputes and securities litigation, the team has niche expertise in areas like construction and employment. A feature of the past year has been advising pharmaceuticals companies in connection with the claims they are permitted to make in advertisements.

The Lawyers: Steven Blackhurst is regarded by many sources as *"the main strength of the firm's litigation group."* He typically handles securities disputes and various forms of corporate governance issues, though his broad practice also encompasses a range of other corporate and commercial disputes. *"Bright and capable"* **Mark Turner** was also recommended to researchers as a force in any securities-related litigation.

The Clients: Advanced Silicon Materials; Alliance Capital Management; FLIR Systems; Golden Valley Electric Association; Metro One Telecommunications; Northwest Pipe; Oregon Health & Science University and The Schnitzer Group.

Dunn Carney Allen Higgins & Tongue LLP

See firm details p.1487

The Firm: The 20 litigators at the firm practice in a wide variety of areas, but their highest profile recent matters have fallen particularly in the fields of securities disputes and insurance defense work. Last year the team also settled two major antitrust cases against Weyerhaeuser and tried a large antitrust case for the company later in the year, obtaining a successful verdict.

The Lawyers: *"Truly one of Oregon's finest lawyers,"* **Thomas Tongue** (see p.1484) has an enthusiastic client following. One interviewee even went so far as to claim, *"He's Tom Tongue... he's perfect!"* He has a wide range of experience and considerable skill in the courtroom, all of which is said to make him a first choice for the *"more snarly"* business cases, which benefit from his calmness and piercing intellect.

The Clients: Oregon State Bar Professional Liability Fund; Northwest Physicians Mutual Insurance; Weyerhaeuser; Hollywood Entertainment; North Pacific Group; Safeco Insurance; Allstate Insurance; PacificSource Health Plans; Allied Insurance and Farmers Insurance Group.

Miller Nash LLP

The Firm: The firm might have lost William Crow to Schwabe Williamson & Wyatt, but the litigation team, which numbers around 30 lawyers, does not seem to have been badly put off its stride. With its *"solid history of excellent work,"* the firm maintains a steady commercial litigation practice, enjoying a strong reputation for doing quality, complex work on behalf of an elite group of clients. As well as handling a range of commercial trials, the team is increasingly visible in arbitrations and mediation.

The Lawyers: Peter Richter is known as *"one of the really fine trial lawyers in the state."* To date he has tried more than 200 cases spanning a broad range of legal issues. **Jerry Hodson** is considered *"smart and tenacious"* in the courtroom; he represents an assortment of clients in various forms of business litigation. **John Neupert** is another *"leading business litigation attorney"* with a practice that covers many areas of complex commercial litigation, including environmental disputes. The President-Elect of the Oregon State Bar for 2005, **Dennis Rawlinson** is also the chair of the firm's litigation department. He has a broad commercial practice and, according to interviewees, is *"experienced and professional."* Although much of his time is occupied with his duties as managing partner, **Thomas Sand** nevertheless retains a strong reputation in the market, where he is known as *"a bright advocate, a tough opponent, and a true professional."* He focuses on general trial practice and civil litigation, particularly securities and employment disputes.

The Clients: Abbott Laboratories; Glaxo-

SmithKline; 3M; Monsanto; City of Portland; Johnson & Johnson; US National Bank and Weyerhaeuser.

Schwabe Williamson & Wyatt PC

The Firm: According to interviewees, the firm is continuing to benefit from the addition in 2003 of William Crow. The litigation team consists of some 50 litigators practicing in all areas of commercial litigation. Its experience in traditional insurance defense was noted, and the team has leveraged well off the strength of its real estate group to gain a prominent position in environmental, land use and condemnation disputes.

The Lawyers: "*True gentleman*" **William Crow** (see p.1481) is consistently recommended to researchers as one of the best litigators in the state. Peers note his expertise in products liability defense, pharmaceutical defense and antitrust cases, as well as his growing reputation in alternative dispute resolution. Clients, meanwhile, are so impressed with this "*exceptional lit-*

igator" that many followed him from Miller Nash. "*Heavy hitter*" **Thomas Dulcich** (see p.1482) has recently enjoyed trial success on behalf of Morgan Stanley, YORK International, and McDonald Investments. He is heavily involved in the current Archdiocese litigation, representing the Roman Catholic Church in Portland. **Daniel Knox** (see p.1483) is known as a "*bright, forthright, no-nonsense*" attorney who specializes in the defense of maritime and construction-related claims.

The Clients: Colonial Pacific Leasing; KeyBank; AlliedSignal; Dresser Industries; Ford; Volvo Construction Equipment; Columbia Forest Products; Morgan Stanley; Wyeth; DuPont; GE and the Archdiocese of Portland.

Other Notable Practitioners

Based in Eugene, **Martha Walters**, of Walters Romm Chanti & Dickens, enjoys an outstanding reputation as a litigator. She was warmly recommended by Portland lawyers, who often refer

work to her. Another well-regarded litigator is **Joseph Arellano** of Kennedy, Watts, Arellano & Ricks LLP. He has impressed peers with his ability to "*pick his fights*" and his "*quiet, sincere manner*." Plaintiff securities litigator **Robert Banks**, of Banks Law Office, is considered an expert in his field, while **Michael Haglund** of Haglund, Kelley, Horngren & Jones LLP is also known for his strength on the plaintiff side in business cases. He represents a number of timber companies in various areas of law and was recently successful in a high-profile antitrust case involving Weyerhaeuser. **Christopher Kent**, of Kent Custis LLP, tries a wide range of litigation and has built a reputation as "*an accomplished trial lawyer in commercial cases*." Recognized for his ability in the courtroom, **Jeffrey Kilmer** of Kilmer Voorhees & Laurick PC is described as "*aggressive, confident and a pleasure to work with*." He has particular expertise in construction litigation.

REAL ESTATE

Oregon
Leading firms (Real Estate)

1	**BALL JANIK LLP** *Portland*
2	**PERKINS COIE LLP** *Portland*
	STOEL RIVES LLP *Portland*
3	**DUNN CARNEY ALLEN HIGGINS** *Portland*
	SCHWABE WILLIAMSON & WYATT *Portland*
4	**BATEMAN SEIDEL MINER BLOMGREN** *Portland*
	DAVIS WRIGHT TREMAINE LLP *Portland*
	LANDYE BENNETT BLUMSTEIN LLP *Portland*
	LANE POWELL PC *Portland*
	MCEWEN GISVOLD LLP *Portland*
	MILLER NASH LLP *Portland*
	TONKON TORP LLP *Portland*

Firms are listed alphabetically in each band.

Band 1

Ball Janik LLP

The Firm: Although Ball Janik is no longer a boutique, it remains best known for its real estate practice, which comprises over 15 lawyers dedicated to the range of real property and land use matters. Competitors acknowledge that the firm is the "*market leader*" in both of these areas, and describe it as the "*preeminent real estate firm in town – Ball Janik sets the gold standard*." Clients meanwhile value the "*energy and talent*" of the group's lawyers, as well as their impressive political connections. The firm has been closely involved this year in the development of the South Waterfront area in Portland, one of the city's most significant ongoing projects.

The Lawyers: The "*dean of real estate lawyers in Oregon*" is the "*outstanding*" **Robert Ball**. A

veteran of many years' experience, he is still involved in some of the firm's more important deals, as well as in strategic consulting work with long-standing clients. Clients themselves described him as "*the lead lawyer in the business*" and respect "*his business acumen and creative, astute thinking*." His calm, pragmatic advice has also saved many of them in a crisis: as one put it, "*if you're in big trouble, call him first.*" With his combination of understanding and experience of both real estate and land use, **Stephen Janik** has a "*unique knowledge base that sets him apart*." Add to this his "*strong political connections*" and you see why he is known as "*one of the most brilliant real estate lawyers around*." He also has a virtual monopoly in the niche specialty of stadium and public facilities development projects. Managing partner and chair of the real estate group, **Bradley Miller** focuses on leasing, acquisitions and financing. Clients say that he is "*sensitive and a good listener*." **Barbara Radler**'s practice lies principally in real estate transactional work. She is known for her strength in leasing and suburban development schemes, and represents many of the "*who's who clients in Oregon*," one of whom described her as "*as close to perfect as any attorney I've ever dealt with, and I've dealt with a lot!*" Up-and-comer **Timothy Parks** was also praised as "*the most effective and efficient attorney I've ever dealt with*" by one of the firm's major clients, and is widely seen as a future leader. He is joined in this year's tables by residential development expert **Rebecca Biermann Tom**, who is "*the condo person*" at the firm, with a specialty in planned communities. She has been busy this

year with important work on the condominium documentation in the new Pearl District in Portland. Land use specialist **Christen White** has been called Oregon's "*number-one land use lawyer*" by market sources. Clients particularly value her experience of complex, often environmentally challenged, projects, describing her as "*just as good as they come*." She recently secured approval of a new zoning code for a large area of Portland's south waterfront, and gained approval for Oregon Health & Science University's first new hospital expansion on Marquam Hill campus.

The Clients: Many of the largest developers in the community are clients, including Williams & Dame; Melvin Mark; the Goodman family; Opus Northwest and Schnitzer Northwest.

Band 2

Perkins Coie LLP

The Firm: "*They're as good as it gets*," clients say of this ten-strong team – one added that its advice is "*not cheap, but worth every penny*." The team can count on support from the firm's larger Seattle office, which helps it to win mandates in some of the region's larger and more unusual projects. As well as advising on the range of real estate development and financing matters for its blue-chip institutional and developer client base, the group is particularly strong in land use and has a specialty in environmental permitting.

The Lawyers: "*Results-driven*" and aggressive **Richard Cantlin** is recognized as one of the best real estate attorneys in the state. Interviewees described him as "*100% reliable with absolute*

Oregon
Leading individuals (Real Estate)

Senior Statesman

BALL Robert *Ball Janik*, Portland
SAMUELS Stanley *Bateman Seidel*, Portland

[1] CANTLIN Richard *Perkins Coie*, Portland
FEUERSTEIN Howard *Stoel Rives*, Portland
HAUCK Terry *Schwabe Williamson*, Portland
JANIK Stephen *Ball Janik*, Portland
PAGE Thomas *Stoel Rives*, Portland

[2] BATEMAN Randall *Bateman Seidel*, Portland
BENNETT David *Landye Bennett*, Portland
GISVOLD Dean *McEwen Gisvold*, Portland
GRANT Eugene *Davis Wright*, Portland
GREEN David *Stoel Rives*, Portland
MILLER Bradley *Ball Janik*, Portland
PARKER Gilbert *Dunn Carney*, Portland
RADLER Barbara *Ball Janik*, Portland
VOBORIL Joseph *Tonkon Torp*, Portland

[3] ANTELL Kenneth *Dunn Carney*, Portland
CARTER Don *McEwen Gisvold*, Portland
GOODLING Jonathon *Miller Nash*, Portland
GUINASSO John *Schwabe Williamson*, Portland
JOHNSON Randal *Ater Wynne*, Portland
MANULIK Mark *Schwabe Williamson*, Portland
MATTHEWS Christopher *Perkins Coie*, Portland
POWELL Bryan *Lane Powell*, Portland
RUSSELL III P Stephen *Landye Bennett*, Portland

Up-and-coming individuals

BIERMANN TOM Rebecca *Ball Janik*, Portland
GUSTAFSON Karna *Landye Bennett*, Portland
PARKS Timothy *Ball Janik*, Portland

Leading individuals
(Real Estate: Zoning/Land Use)

[1] JANIK Stephen *Ball Janik*, Portland
PFEIFFER Steven *Perkins Coie*, Portland
RAMIS Timothy *Ramis Crew*, Portland
WHITE Christen *Ball Janik*, Portland

Individuals are listed alphabetically in each band.

integrity," and noted his broad range of experience in real estate matters and his "*grasp of the big picture.*" Clients also described **Christopher Matthews** as a "*tremendous resource.*" A "*timely, practical and hard-working*" attorney, he handles a mixture of general real estate and land use work and regularly appears on behalf of agribusinesses. The firm's land use specialist is **Steven Pfeiffer**. He does a great deal of institutional and urban development permitting, as well as resort-type development outside the city. "*One of the key people in Oregon who understands land use,*" he has also served on the state land use commission.

The Clients: Specht Development; PacTrust; West Hills Development; Safeway; Albertson's; Lowe's; Providence Medical Group; Wells Fargo; Ross Island Sand & Gravel; Qwest; Three Mile Canyon Farms; PeaceHealth; Bechtel and Kaiser Foundation Hospitals.

Stoel Rives LLP

The Firm: Their "*wide variety of expertise and deep bench of players*" makes this team of 11 real estate lawyers and six land use attorneys a respected force in Oregon's real estate market. The group's "*results-oriented approach*" and "*breadth of resources*" across the region have earned it a high-quality client base. It is particularly known for its expertise in condominium work, largely thanks to the presence of leading condo expert Howard Feuerstein.

The Lawyers: "*The dean of the condo forums,*" **Howard Feuerstein** is widely recognized as the state's premier condominium specialist. Clients and peers love his "*cooperative, nonadversarial style*" and admire his skill and creativity in designing governing documents. **Thomas Page**'s expertise lies in shopping center work. One client described his virtues thus: "*He's brilliant, creative, responsive, and his ethics and integrity are unwavering.*" He recently represented Nike in leasing and purchase transactions, and advised The Oregon Clinic on the development of an office building. **David Green** is renowned in the market for his expertise in real estate development and financing. Clients were full of admiration for his deal-making skills. In the words of one: "*I've never yet had a deal that Dave's been involved in that he wasn't able to make happen.*" He has recently completed work for Consolidated Freightways and Nicol Investment, and is lead outside general counsel to Fred Meyer Stores.

The Clients: Harsch Investment Properties; Gramor Development; NW Natural; Pacific Realty Association; PPM Energy; Intel; Trendwest Resorts; Port of Portland; TriMet (Tri-County Metropolitan Transportation District of Oregon); Gerding/Edlen Development; Larkspur Hospitality and PacifiCorp.

Band 3

Dunn Carney Allen Higgins & Tongue LLP

See firm details p.1487

The Firm: With recent work on both the Brewery Blocks redevelopment project and the South Waterfront scheme, this team of eight real estate specialists has enjoyed an extremely successful twelve months. According to clients, its position has been based on doing "*a good job of providing a good-quality service at a lower price point than other big firms.*" Marquee client Gerding/Edlen Development has ensured the firm considerable prominence in current developments.

The Lawyers: With his work for the important and highly active Gerding/Edlen Development, it is hardly surprising that **Gilbert Parker** (see p.1483) is said to be "*emerging and becoming more influential.*" The year has seen him working on such major schemes as the Brewery Blocks project and the South Waterfront devel-

opment. Peers speak highly of him as an "*effective, bearish, unflappable attorney with a good sense of humor and a high level of integrity.*" "*Solid and straightforward*" **Kenneth Antell** (see p.1481) was praised for his good technical understanding of real estate law.

The Clients: Bones Construction; CalWest Industrial Holdings; Norris & Stevens; North Pacific Group; Pan Pacific Retail Properties; RREEF Management; Hollywood Entertainment; Providence Health System and Powell Development.

Schwabe Williamson & Wyatt PC

The Firm: With 17 lawyers dedicated to real estate and land use, this firm has a large and broad practice that caters to developers, owners and real estate lenders. Competitors remark on its "*solid core*" of lawyers and transactional strength, while clients consider it to be in the "*top echelon*" for quality and experience. The team enjoys the support of a strong environmental group, which is able to assist it in many matters.

The Lawyers: **Terry Hauck** (see p.1482) is clearly a favorite in the state's real estate markets. Clients and peer alike rave about his "*gruff but friendly manner and practical, get-it-done attitude.*" This year has seen him handling a number of sizable transactions in Las Vegas. "*Detail-guy*" **John Guinasso** (see p.1482) is the one to go to "*if you have a complex project – he won't be intimidated by the detail or the number of pages.*" He represents one of the larger developers in the area, Harsch Investment Properties. **Mark Manulik** (see p.1483) is another "*excellent technician.*" He has a broad-ranging practice with a focus in commercial real estate advice, and particular expertise in partnership matters and real estate lending.

The Clients: Wells Fargo; Simpson Housing; Bank One; KeyBank; Louis Dreyfus Property Group; Harsch Investment Properties; Morgan Stanley Dean Witter; United Grocers; RBC Mortgage; Bechtel; Office Depot and First Horizon.

Band 4

Bateman Seidel Miner Blomgren Chellis & Gram, PC

The Firm: The decision of the real estate practice group and the affordable housing practice group from the Portland office of Preston Gates & Ellis to split off and open this law firm early in 2005 has sent ripples through the market. Although it is too early to assess the results, the team's impressive skills and strong client base must tip the balance in favor of success. The group of ten is particularly known for its expertise in real estate financing, where it deals primarily with lenders, banks, and insurance companies. The firm also represents developers in transactional work.

www.ChambersandPartners.com

All quotes in the text are from interviews with clients and competitors.

1479

The Lawyers: "*Phenomenal*" **Stanley Samuels** has a broad-ranging real estate practice and advises an impressive list of clients. "*One of the deans of the Bar,*" he was recommended to researchers as "*a wonderful gentleman*" with years of experience and considerable integrity. **Randall Bateman** is "*one of the best in the state for real estate transactions.*" Interviewees described him as "*attentive to details and to his clients' needs.*" His work this year, while still with Preston Gates & Ellis, included the Portland Armory Building.

The Clients: Leading names from the firm's client roster include PNC Bank, Newland Communities and Homestead Capital.

Davis Wright Tremaine LLP
See firm details p.1796

The Firm: The office has a high percentage of experienced senior partners in its sizable real estate and land use practice, allowing it to provide clients with hands-on, partner-led advice. The team benefits from the support of its larger Seattle office. It handles a wide variety of real property matters, but is particularly known for its expertise in leasing matters.

The Lawyers: "*Cerebral attorney*" **Eugene Grant** (see p.1482) is known as a "*proactive deal-maker who knows the law inside-out.*" He is particularly recognized for his skill in leasing, both for private clients and for the federal government. This year saw him complete the leasing of the 1201 Lloyd Building. He also successfully represented a group of 25 of the largest downtown property owners in opposition to a city financing plan for an extension of the light rail transit line down through the central business district.

The Clients: 1201 Lloyd Associates; Louis Dreyfus Property Group; St. Paul Properties; First Technology Credit Union; XO Communications; Evergreen Industrial Park; Citibank; Manufactured Housing Communities of Oregon; PS Business Parks; ScanlanKemperBard; Oregon Rangeland Trust and Pacific Western Homes.

Landye Bennett Blumstein LLP
See firm details p.1488

The Firm: Comprising five attorneys dedicated to real estate, Landye Bennett enters the rankings this year following enthusiastic recommendations from clients and peers. The group handles a wide variety of real estate work, but was particularly recommended for its niche specialty in matters related to condominiums, planned communities and homeowners' associations.

The Lawyers: **David Bennett** (see p.1481) is renowned in the market as "*the best in the state for representing homeowners' associations.*" He

also specializes in other matters connected with planned communities and condominiums. He is joined in this year's tables by two other attorneys who do significant work for homeowners' associations. **Stephen Russell** (see p.1484) and up-and-comer **Karna Gustafson** (see p.1482) also do some land use work in conjunction with advice on transactional issues.

The Clients: The team represents a variety of clients with real estate interests, including the developers of planned communities and homeowners' associations.

Lane Powell PC
See firm details p.1797

The Firm: The team of eight here excels in projects that involve public-private partnerships, urban redevelopment and mixed-use development. It was also recommended to researchers for its experience in unique or unusual financing and tax crediting schemes. The firm fields more than 170 lawyers in total spread across the Northwest, and the real property group was particularly felt to benefit from the support of a team in Seattle.

The Lawyers: **Bryan Powell** (see p.1484) cochairs the real estate and land use group, and serves as special assistant attorney general to the Oregon DOJ, responsible for negotiating and forming complex real estate investment vehicles on behalf of the Oregon State Treasury's Investment Division. Clients appreciate his "*ability to see through a problem to its core issues and communicate options in a clear and concise matter.*" His wide-ranging practice includes leasing, private and public redevelopment projects and real estate financing for clients that include a major local developer.

The Clients: Home Depot; Sockeye Development; Oregon Public Employees Retirement System and Portland Development Commission.

McEwen Gisvold LLP

The Firm: McEwen Gisvold's real estate team represents a number of local and regional developer clients, though its greatest strength is felt to be in the field of real estate lending. With three lawyers, the team is at the smaller end of the market. However, the fact that two of them make it into the tables is an indication of the high profile of their work and the degree to which the firm has established itself in Oregon's real estate circles. Typical work includes the creation of residential, commercial and mixed-use condominiums and planned unit developments.

The Lawyers: For sensitive negotiations, **Dean Gisvold** is a name you can "*trust to handle a problem in a discreet and effective manner.*" Known for his unimpeachable integrity and intellectual strength, his real estate practice is focused on lending work. **Don Carter** also has

a lender-focused practice and is known for his "*excellent*" skills and character.

The Clients: The firm represents a base split between real estate lenders and developers.

Miller Nash LLP

The Firm: The firm's real estate and land use practice comprises ten attorneys, who advise on the spectrum of real property law. They are assisted by a number of strong attorneys who specialize in areas like construction and environmental law. Peers note an institutional bent to the team's workload, and its strength on the finance side.

The Lawyers: Real estate finance expert **Jonathon Goodling** splits his workload between lenders and project developers. A non-flamboyant practitioner, he is valued by clients for his "*common sense*" and "*fair and honest*" approach, while peers appreciate his ability to "*focus on what's important.*"

The Clients: Ashforth Pacific; McMorgan; US Bank National Association (Commercial Real Estate Division); Guardian Management and Specht Properties.

Tonkon Torp LLP

The Firm: Tonkon Torp is much better known for its strong corporate transactional and litigation practices. However, it also offers expertise in a range of real estate services. The team of seven real property specialists was recommended for handing "*a range of clients and projects.*" Obviously much of this is in support of its existing corporate clients, though it includes a share of stand-alone work.

The Lawyers: **Joseph Voboril** is the team's star, with an excellent reputation for dealing with complex transactions. He handles all forms of real estate law – "*anything that touches dirt*" – and his clients love his "*combative, no-fear, no-nonsense*" style and his "*versatility of practice.*" He has recently been involved in a complex pension funds matter involving Capital Consultants, as well as work for other large clients such as Nike.

The Clients: Holiday Retirement; Colson & Colson Construction; Costco Wholesale; Nike; Winkler Development and Staples.

Other Notable Practitioners
Randal Johnson at Ater Wynne LLP has a good name for representing developers in commercial, industrial and residential projects. He is currently involved in the $14 million sale of an office building. "*Preeminent*" land use lawyer **Timothy Ramis**, of Ramis Crew Corrigan & Bachrach LLP, was described to researchers as "*truly outstanding*" in his niche.

Leaders in Oregon

ABRAVANEL, Alan
Perkins Coie LLP, Portland
503 727 2000
Recommended in Corporate/M&A

ALLI Jr, Richard
Bullard Smith Jernstedt Wilson,
Portland 503 248 1134
Recommended in Employment

AMBURGEY, Larry
Amburgey & Rubin PC, Portland
503 221 0309
Recommended in Employment

ANGELI, Courtney
Stoel Rives LLP, Portland
503 224 3380
Recommended in Employment

ANTELL, Kenneth S
Dunn Carney Allen Higgins & Tongue
LLP, Portland 503 417 5364
ksa@dunn-carney.com
Recommended in Real Estate
Practice Areas: Practice focuses on real
estate purchase, sale, financing and leasing transactions. Extensive experience in
development, construction and envi-
ronmental issues relating to real proper-
ty transactions.
Prof. Memberships: Admitted to prac-
tice in Oregon (1986), Washington
(1993) and US District Court, District of
Oregon (1988). Member of Oregon
State Bar Association, Washington State
Bar Association, Multnomah Bar Association. Board of Directors of Building
Owners And Managers Association of
Portland (BOMA) 2001-present. International Council of Shopping Centers
(ICSC), member (1995-present).
Career: Joined Dunn Carney in 1996 as
a Partner.
Publications: 'Negligent Misrepresenta-
tion in Oregon, the Elusive Claim', Ore-
gon State Bar Litigation Journal, Vol 12
No 3, May, 1993; Numerous presenta-
tions regarding commercial leasing, real
estate purchase and sale agreements and
other real estate topics.
Personal: JD, University of Oregon
School of Law, 1986; BA, University of
Michigan, 1981.

ARELLANO, Joseph
Kennedy, Watts, Arellano & Ricks LLP,
Portland 503 228 6191
Recommended in Litigation

BACA, David C
Davis Wright Tremaine LLP, Portland
503 778 5306
davebaca@dwt.com
Recommended in Corporate/M&A
Practice Areas: Partner and Co-Chair,
Corporate Finance Practice Group.
Experience includes acting as lead counsel in public and private securities placements, mergers/acquisitions, general
counsel to small and medium-sized
businesses; works with underwriters and
placement agents in public/private securities placements; acting counsel to 34

Act reporting companies and their
boards of directors.
Prof. Memberships: Member, Oregon
State Bar Association (past Chair, Secu-
rities Regulation Section) and American
Bar Association.
Career: Admitted Oregon Bar, 1982.
Publications: Speaker at Northwest
Securities Institute and on corporate
governance matters.
Personal: JD, (magna cum laude) Har-
vard School of Law, 1981. BA, (summa
cum laude) Linfield College, 1978.

BALL, Robert
Ball Janik LLP, Portland 503 228 2525
Recommended in Real Estate

BANKS, Robert
Banks Law Office, Portland
503 222 7475
Recommended in Litigation

BARRAN, Paula
Barran Liebman, Portland
503 228 0500
pbarran@barran.com
Recommended in Employment
Practice Areas: Partner at Barran Liebman LLP. Experience in labor and
employment law since 1980.
Prof. Memberships: Listed in 'The Best
Lawyers In America' (2001-04); Ameri-
can Bar Foundation, Life Fellow; Ameri-
can Bar Association, Individual Employ-
ment Rights Section; Defense Research
Institute; Regional Drug Foundation;
Society for Human Resources Manage-
ment, Northwest Chapter, Counsel to
the Board (1998-99); Oregon State Bar,
Labor Section; Oregon Women Lawyers.
Career: Admitted to Oregon; Washington; US Court of Appeals, Ninth Circuit;
US District Court, District of Oregon;
US District Court, Eastern District of
Washington; US District Court, Western
District of Washington; and US
Supreme Court. Willamette University,
adjunct professor, Labor Law (2000-01).
Personal: Received PhD from Universi-
ty of British Columbia; MA from Cor-
nell University; LLB, with honors, from
Osgoode Hall Law School at York Uni-
versity; MBA from University of Ore-
gon, Oregon Executive MBA program.

BATEMAN, Randall
Bateman Seidel Miner Blomgren
Chellis & Gram, P.C., Portland
503 972 9920
Recommended in Real Estate

BAUMAN, Todd
Stoel Rives LLP, Portland
503 224 3380
Recommended in Corporate/M&A

BEMIS, Kenneth
Bullard Smith Jernstedt Wilson,
Portland 503 248 1134
Recommended in Employment

BENNETT, J David
Landye Bennett Blumstein LLP,
Portland 503 224 4100
dbennett@landye-bennett.com
Recommended in Real Estate
Practice Areas: All aspects of real estate
law. Represents buyers, sellers, and
developers of bare land, commercial,
industrial and retail properties, land-
lords and tenants, borrowers and
lenders. Editor of the Oregon State Bar
Continuing Legal Education Publication
'Regulation and Taxation of Real Estate.'
Sub-specialties in representing condo-
minium and planned community devel-
opers and owner associations.
Prof. Memberships: Member of the
Oregon State Bar, Real Estate and Land
Use Section; and the Washington State
Bar Association.
Personal: Law degree with honors,
Willamette University. Member, Board
of Directors, Westside Economic
Alliance. Member, Community Associa-
tion Institute College of Community
Association Lawyers.

BERNE, Gary
Stoll Stoll Berne Lokting & Shlachter,
Portland 503 227 1600
Recommended in Litigation

BERNICK, Carol
Davis Wright Tremaine LLP, Portland
503 778 5233
carolbernick@dwt.com
Recommended in Employment
Practice Areas: Partner, employment/
labor law. Representative experience:
wage and hour class action defense,
employer defense in discrimination,
wrongful discharge, preventative
employment practices training, ADA
compliance, leave policies, and sexual
harassment.
Prof. Memberships: Oregon and Washington State Bar Associations. Counsel,
Disciplinary Board, Oregon State Bar.
Board Member, Northwest EEO/Affir-
mative Action Association.
Career: 'Who's Who of Women in Portland Business', Business Journal, 2002.
Nomination, Trial Lawyer of the Year,
Trial Lawyers for Public Justice, 1999.
Publications: Chief editor, 'Oregon
Labor Letter', (1994-2001). Principal
editor/co-author, 'Oregon Employment
Law Deskbook'.
Personal: JD, University of Virginia,
1989. BA, (magna cum laude), Roanoke
College, 1985.

BEYER, Ruth
Stoel Rives LLP, Portland
503 224 3380
Recommended in Corporate/M&A

BIERMANN TOM, Rebecca
Ball Janik LLP, Portland 503 228 2525
Recommended in Real Estate

BLACKHURST, Steven
Ater Wynne LLP, Portland
503 226 1191
Recommended in Litigation

BOOTH, Brian
Tonkon Torp LLP, Portland
503 221 1440
Recommended in Corporate/M&A

BUCHANAN, Paul
Stoel Rives LLP, Portland
503 224 3380
Recommended in Employment

BULLOCK, Brentley
Perkins Coie LLP, Portland
503 727 2000
Recommended in Corporate/M&A

CABLE, Franklin
Miller Nash LLP, Portland
503 224 5858
Recommended in Corporate/M&A

CAMPBELL, William
Ater Wynne LLP, Portland
503 226 1191
Recommended in Corporate/M&A

CANTLIN, Richard
Perkins Coie LLP, Portland
503 727 2000
Recommended in Real Estate

CARTER, Don
McEwen Gisvold LLP, Portland
503 226 7321
Recommended in Real Estate

CHESTLER, Stuart
Stoel Rives LLP, Portland
503 224 3380
Recommended in Corporate/M&A

CROW, William
Schwabe Williamson & Wyatt PC,
Portland 503 796 2406
wcrow@schwabe.com
Recommended in Litigation
Practice Areas: Mr Crow's internationally recognized practice focuses on
product liability, and includes vaccine,
PPA, intrauterine device, blood contamination, heart valve, and other devices
and pharmaceuticals. Other product lia-
bility matters include general aviation,
helicopter, and airline industry trial
experience.
Prof. Memberships: American Bar
Association, Litigation Section; American College of Trial Lawyers, Co-Chair,
Access to Justice Committee; Oregon
Association of Defense Counsel; Campaign for Equal Justice, Advisory Committee; Willamette University, Board of
Trustees; Defense Research Institute.
Personal: JD, Willamette University
College of Law, 1961; MBA, New York
University, 1954; BS, University of Ore-
gon, 1953.

CROWE, Austin
Perkins Coie LLP, Portland
503 727 2000
Recommended in Litigation

DAMM, Jacqueline
Bullard Smith Jernstedt Wilson,
Portland 503 248 1134
Recommended in Employment

DULCICH, Thomas
Schwabe Williamson & Wyatt PC,
Portland 503 796 2970
tdulcich@schwabe.com
Recommended in Litigation
Practice Areas: Mr Dulcich focuses his
practice in the areas of employment and
securities litigation, defense of injury
claims and commercial litigation. He has
successfully tried numerous discrimina-
tion and harassment cases to verdict.
Prof. Memberships: Mr Dulcich is a
Fellow of the American College of Trial
Lawyers; Member, Oregon and Wash-
ington State Bar Associations (actively
practices in both OR & WA).
Personal: JD, University of Chicago Law
School, 1980; BS, University of Oregon,
Phi Beta Kappa, 1976

ELLIS, Barnes
Stoel Rives LLP, Portland
503 224 3380
Recommended in Litigation

ENGLISH, Stephen
Bullivant Houser Bailey PC, Portland
503 228 6351
Recommended in Litigation

ERNST, David
Bullivant Houser Bailey PC, Portland
503 228 6351
Recommended in Litigation

FEUERSTEIN, Howard
Stoel Rives LLP, Portland
503 224 3380
Recommended in Real Estate

FORTINO, Paul
Perkins Coie LLP, Portland
503 727 2000
Recommended in Litigation

FRANTZ, Mary Ann
Miller Nash LLP, Portland
503 224 5858
Recommended in Corporate/M&A

GARONE, Michael
Schwabe Williamson & Wyatt PC,
Portland 503 796 2401
mgarone@schwabe.com
Recommended in Employment
Practice Areas: Mr Garone has been
involved in all aspects of collective bargaining, advising clients on grievance
issues, contract negotiations and the
requirements of state and federal law. He
has also handled numerous state and
federal administrative proceedings, and
has substantial litigation experience at
both the trial and appellate levels. He
has represented management in numerous class action wage and hour claims
and has handled over 40 appeals. He has
tried over 100 labor arbitrations.
Prof. Memberships: Member, Oregon
State Bar, past Chair of Labor and
Employment Law Section; Member,
Washington State Bar.

Personal: JD, University of Oregon,
1980; BA, State University of New York,
1977.

GIDLEY, James
Perkins Coie LLP, Portland
503 727 2000
Recommended in Litigation

GISVOLD, Dean
McEwen Gisvold LLP, Portland
503 226-7321
Recommended in Real Estate

GLADE, Peter
Markowitz, Herbold, Glade & Mehlhaf
PC, Portland 503 295 3085
Recommended in Litigation

GOODLING, Jonathon
Miller Nash LLP, Portland
503 224 5858
Recommended in Real Estate

GORDON, Corbett
Fisher & Phillips LLP, Portland
503 242 4262
cgordon@laborlawyers.com
Recommended in Employment
Practice Areas: Corbett Gordon is the
Founding Partner of the Portland office
of the national law firm of Fisher &
Phillips LLP and has practiced exclusively in labor and employment law representing employers since 1982. An experienced jury trial lawyer, she has served
as an adjunct professor with Willamette
University College of Law. In 1999, Corbett argued and won a case arising
under the Americans with Disabilities
Act (ADA) before the United States
Supreme Court (Albertsons, Inc. v Kirk-
ingburg, 119 S. Ct. 2162, 527 U.S. 555
(June 22, 1999)). Corbett received her
JD from Harvard University Law School
in 1980.

GRANT, Eugene L
Davis Wright Tremaine LLP, Portland
503 778 5427
genegrant@dwt.com
Recommended in Real Estate
Practice Areas: Partner, real estate
transactions and land use work including residential, commercial and industrial. Experience includes acquisition,
permitting, CCR's, financing, construction, leasing, sale/formation of condominiums, time shares and other common interest projects. Representative
clients: St. Paul Properties, Louis Dreyfus Property Group, Pacific Landmark
Development, First Tech Credit Union.
Prof. Memberships: Ownership and
Management Committee Chair and
associate editor, 'Probate & Property',
American Bar Association. Member and
former Chair, Real Property/Land Use
section, Oregon State Bar.
Career: Joined firm as Partner, 2003.
Partner, Schwabe, Williamson & Wyatt,
1987-2003.
Personal: JD, University of Oregon,
1979. BA (honors), University of Oregon, 1976.

GREEN, David
Stoel Rives LLP, Portland
503 224 3380
Recommended in Real Estate

GREENMAN, Ronald
Tonkon Torp LLP, Portland
503 221 1440
Recommended in Corporate/M&A

GRINFAS, Dan
Stoel Rives LLP, Seattle
206 624 0900
Recommended in Employment

GUINASSO, John
Schwabe Williamson & Wyatt PC,
Portland 503 796 2971
jguinasso@schwabe.com
Recommended in Real Estate
Practice Areas: Mr Guinasso represents developers, buyers, sellers, lenders,
and borrowers on all types of commercial properties, including shopping centers, apartments, assisted living facilities,
office and industrial buildings, business
parks, and subdivisions. He also represents landlords and tenants in build-to-
suit leases, ground leases and space leases, including retail space, office space
and industrial space.
Prof. Memberships: Oregon State Bar,
Real Estate and Land Use Section; International Council of Shopping Centers;
Building Owners and Managers Association; National Association of Industrial
and Office Properties; Commercial
Association of Realtors.
Personal: JD, Stanford Law School,
Order of the Coif, 1983; BA, Lewis &
Clark College, 1979.

GUSTAFSON, Karna R
Landye Bennett Blumstein LLP,
Portland 503 224 4100
kgustaf@landye-bennett.com
Recommended in Real Estate
Practice Areas: General real estate
lawyer. Sub-specializes in representing
condominium and planned community
developers. Also represents homeowner
associations. Regularly drafts documentation to create homeowner association
projects. Advises owner associations in
the interpretation and implementation
of covenants.
Prof. Memberships: Member of the
Oregon State Bar, Real Estate and Land
Use Section; and the Washington State
Bar Association.
Personal: Law degree from Willamette
University. Member, Board of Directors,
Home Builders Association of Metropolitan Portland. Director, National Association of Home Builders Association.

HAGLUND, Michael
Haglund, Kelley, Horngren & Jones LLP,
Portland 503 225 0777
Recommended in Litigation

HARNDEN, Edwin
Barran Liebman, Portland
503 228 0500
eharnden@barran.com
Recommended in Employment
Practice Areas: Managing Partner at
Barran Liebman LLP. Experience in litigation since 1972 and labor and
employment law since 1974.
Prof. Memberships: Fellow of the College, College of Labor and Employment
Lawyers since 2003; 2001 President of
the Oregon State Bar; Federal, American, Oregon and Multnomah Bar committees; past President of the Professional Liability Fund; Life Fellow of the
American Bar Foundation; Member of
the Defense Research Institute; Member
of the Oregon Association of Defense
Counsel; Past President of the Oregon
Courts Historical Society. In addition,
he participates in numerous civic and
cultural organizations.
Career: Admitted to Oregon; Washington; Idaho; District of Columbia; US
Court of Appeals, Ninth Circuit; US
District Court, District of Oregon; US
District Court, Eastern District of Washington; US District Court, Western Dis-
trict of Washington; US District Court
of Idaho; and US Supreme Court.
Personal: Received JD from Columbia
University (1972), Harlan Fiske Stone
Scholar; BA from Columbia University
(1969.)

HAUCK, Terry
Schwabe Williamson & Wyatt PC,
Portland 503 796 2974
thauck@schwabe.com
Recommended in Real Estate
Practice Areas: Mr Hauck has devel-
oped a strong reputation for his work in
the areas of acquisition and development
of bare land, acquisition and redevelop-
ment of improved land, loan closing
documentation, land use, leasing, and
acquisition and sale agreements relating
to income-producing properties.
Prof. Memberships: Oregon State Bar,
Real Estate and Land Use section.
Personal: JD, Willamette University
College of Law, 1971; BA, Portland State
University, 1966.

HEWITT, Henry
Stoel Rives LLP, Portland
503 224 3380
Recommended in Corporate/M&A

HIBBS, Carol
Tonkon Torp LLP, Portland
503 221 1440
Recommended in Corporate/M&A

HILL NOTO, Margaret
Stoel Rives LLP, Portland
503 224 3380
Recommended in Corporate/M&A

HODSON, Jerry
Miller Nash LLP, Portland
503 224 5858
Recommended in Litigation

HOUSER, Douglas
Bullivant Houser Bailey PC, Portland
503 228 6351
Recommended in Litigation

JANIK, Stephen
Ball Janik LLP, Portland
503 228 2525
Recommended in Real Estate

JERNSTEDT, Kenneth
Bullard Smith Jernstedt Wilson,
Portland 503 248 1134
Recommended in Employment

JOHNSON, Randal
Ater Wynne LLP, Portland
503 226 1191
Recommended in Real Estate

KEITH, Calvin
Perkins Coie LLP, Portland
503 727 2000
Recommended in Employment

KENT, Christopher
Kent Custis LLP, Portland
503 220 0717
Recommended in Litigation

KILMER, Jeffrey
Kilmer Voorhees & Laurick PC,
Portland 503 224 0055
Recommended in Litigation

KISCH, Victor
Tonkon Torp LLP, Portland
503 221 1440
Recommended in Employment

KITCHEL, Chris
Stoel Rives LLP, Portland
503 224 3380
Recommended in Employment

KNOX, Daniel
Schwabe Williamson & Wyatt PC,
Portland 503 796 2908
dknox@schwabe.com
Recommended in Litigation
Practice Areas: Mr Knox focuses his practice on defense of maritime claims and claims arising out of the construction industry, particularly those involving design professionals. Mr Knox represents northwest tug and fishing interests and the west coast's leading tanker operator, along with many marine underwriters on both first- and third-party claims.
Prof. Memberships: Oregon State Bar; Member, Maritime Law Association and its Membership Committee.
Personal: JD, University of Houston, summa cum laude, 1978; BA, University of Colorado, 1970.

KRAMER, Thomas
Bullard Smith Jernstedt Wilson,
Portland 503 248 1134
Recommended in Employment

LIEBMAN, Richard
Barran Liebman, Portland
503 228 0500
rliebman@barran.com
Recommended in Employment

Practice Areas: Partner at Barran Liebman LLP. Experience in labor and employment law since 1972.
Prof. Memberships: College of Labor and Employment Lawyers, Fellow of the College, inducted 1998; instructor for EEO classes in Portland State University's Professional Development Center since 1988; Oregon State Bar Labor Law Section; Chair (1990-91); Member, Executive Board (1987-92); award for Distinguished Service 2003; Oregon State Bar Civil Rights Section; Member Executive Board since 2002; NW EEO/Affirmative Action Association, Chair (1985-87); Member of Oregon Bureau of Labor and Industries Rule-Making Task Force since 1995 and Civil Rights Advisory Committee Member (2002) Board of Directors.
Career: Admitted to Oregon; Hawaii; Washington; US Court of Appeals, Seventh Circuit; US Court of Appeals, Ninth Circuit; US District Court, District of Columbia.
Personal: Received JD from University of California at Berkeley, Boalt Hall (1972); BA from University of California at Berkeley (1969).

LIVINGSTON, Louis
Miller Nash LLP, Portland
503 224 5858
Recommended in Employment

MANULIK, Mark
Schwabe Williamson & Wyatt PC,
Portland 503 796 2990
mmanulik@schwabe.com
Recommended in Real Estate
Practice Areas: Mr Manulik represents a broad range of real estate development companies, investors and mortgage lenders, with the focus of his practice being in the areas of commercial real estate law, partnerships and real estate lending.
Prof. Memberships: Oregon State Bar and Washington State Bar Associations, Real Estate, Probate and Trust Law sections; Oregon Mortgage Bankers Association; International Council of Shopping Centers; Fellow of the American College of Mortgage Attorneys (currently serving as Treasurer).
Personal: JD, University of Houston Law Center, 1978; BA, University of Texas, 1975.

MARKOWITZ, David
Markowitz, Herbold, Glade & Mehlhaf PC, Portland 503 295 3085
Recommended in Litigation

MARMADUKE, Don
Tonkon Torp LLP, Portland
503 221 1440
Recommended in Litigation

MARTIN, Chrys
Bullivant Houser Bailey PC, Portland
503 228 6351
Recommended in Employment

MARTSON Jr, William
Tonkon Torp LLP, Portland
503 221 1440
Recommended in Litigation

MATHESON, David
Perkins Coie LLP, Portland
503 727 2000
Recommended in Corporate/M&A

MATTHEWS, Christopher
Perkins Coie LLP, Portland
503 727 2000
Recommended in Real Estate

MCDONNELL, Brendan
Preston Gates & Ellis LLP, Portland
503 228 3200
Recommended in Corporate/M&A

MCGRORY, John F
Davis Wright Tremaine LLP, Portland
503 778 5204
johnmcgrory@dwt.com
Recommended in Litigation
Practice Areas: Partner and Co-Chair, Litigation Practice Group. Representative experience includes complex litigation with an emphasis on securities litigation, antitrust litigation, antitrust counseling, representation in state and federal courts, arbitrations and administrative proceedings.
Prof. Memberships: Member, American Bar Association Antitrust Section and Oregon Association of Defense Counsel.
Career: Joined firm, 1987; became Partner, 1990.
Personal: JD, Lewis & Clark College, 1981. BA, University of Minnesota, 1978.

MILLER, Bradley
Ball Janik LLP, Portland
503 228 2525
Recommended in Real Estate

MOORMAN, Robert
Stoel Rives LLP, Portland
503 224 3380
Recommended in Corporate/M&A

MOWE, Gregory
Stoel Rives LLP, Portland
503 224 3380
Recommended in Litigation

MULLIN, Joel
Stoel Rives LLP, Portland
503 224 3380
Recommended in Litigation

NEUPERT, John
Miller Nash LLP, Portland
503 224 5858
Recommended in Litigation

NEWELL, Robert D
Davis Wright Tremaine LLP, Portland
503 778 5234
bobnewell@dwt.com
Recommended in Litigation
Practice Areas: Partner, litigation. Experience includes complex commercial litigation, securities, unfair competition, trade secrets, Uniform Commercial Code and contract litigation.
Prof. Memberships: Member, Oregon and California State Bar Associations. Past President, Multnomah Bar Association.
Career: Joined as Partner via merger, 1990. Has served as Circuit Court pro tem judge.
Publications: Contributing author, 'Federal Civil Litigation in Oregon' (Oregon State Bar). Chief editor, 'Civil Pleading and Practice' series (Oregon State Bar). Editorial Board, OSB Litigation Journal. Author/speaker on Oregon legislation, litigating UCC cases, and other litigation topics for lawyers/industry groups.
Personal: JD, University of Oregon, 1976. AB (honors), Harvard, 1969.

O'LEARY, Daniel
Davis Wright Tremaine LLP, Portland
503 778 5203
danoleary@dwt.com
Recommended in Litigation
Practice Areas: Partner, civil litigator in state/federal courts since 1963. Currently focused on environmental and natural resources issues under state and federal law.
Prof. Memberships: Fellow, American College of Trial Lawyers. Past President, American Board of Trial Advocates. Past President, Oregon Trial Lawyers Association.
Career: Admitted Oregon Bar, 1963. Joined DWT as Partner, 1994. American Board of Trial Advocates, Distinguished Trial Lawyer of Year, 1997. Multnomah County Bar Association Professionalism Award, 2001.
Publications: Author, 'Dispute Resolution in Transboundry Pollution Cases', Masters Thesis, 1993.
Personal: LLM, Lewis & Clark College, 1993. JD, Lewis & Clark College, 1963. BA, Gonzaga University, 1959.

PAGE, Thomas
Stoel Rives LLP, Portland
503 224 3380
Recommended in Real Estate

PALMER, Thomas
Tonkon Torp LLP, Portland
503 221 1440
Recommended in Corporate/M&A

PARKER, Gilbert E
Dunn Carney Allen Higgins & Tongue LLP, Portland 503 306 5315
gep@dunn-carney.com
Recommended in Real Estate
Practice Areas: Partner in the Real Estate and Land Use Section. His practice focuses on real estate development, real estate finance, business transactions, commercial lending, construction and construction liens, and secured transactions.
Prof. Memberships: Admitted to practice in Oregon (1975) and US. District Court, District of Oregon (1976). Member of Oregon State Bar Association and

Multnomah Bar Association. Member of American Bar Association Real Property, Probate and Trust Law Sections. Founding Member of Board of Directors for Meritas (formerly known as Commercial Law Affiliates). Board of Directors for Riverbend Youth Center, 1995-2004.

Career: Joined Dunn Carney in 1975 and became a Partner in 1981. Served as Managing Partner from 1991-93.

Personal: JD, University of California, Hastings College of Law (San Francisco), 1975; BA (with honors), Lewis and Clark College, 1972.

PARKS, Timothy
Ball Janik LLP, Portland 503 228 2525
Recommended in Real Estate

PECK, Kathy
Williams, Zografos & Peck, Lake Oswego 503 699 1300
Recommended in Employment

PFEIFFER, Steven
Perkins Coie LLP, Portland
503 727 2000
Recommended in Real Estate

POWELL, Bryan E
Lane Powell PC, Portland
503 778 2189
powellb@lanepowell.com
Recommended in Real Estate

Practice Areas: Partner and Co-Chair of the Real Estate and Land Use Group. His practice focuses on private/public redevelopment and mixed-use projects, acquisitions, sales, build-to-suit projects, commercial leasing, affordable housing, and complex real estate finance matters. Representative clients include the Oregon Public Employees Retirement Fund, which owns and manages an extensive nationwide real property portfolio.

Prof. Memberships: Member of Oregon, Washington and California State Bar Associations. National Association of Industrial and Office Properties (former Board Member and Chair, Public Affairs); Portland Children's Museum (former Board Member and Officer).

Career: Partner at Lane Powell since 1996. Firm's Executive Committee member 2002-04.

Publications: Has lectured on topics of real estate acquisitions, sales and due diligence, leasing, real estate finance, and mixed-used development.

Personal: University of California, Hastings College of the Law (JD, 1988); University of Washington (BA, cum laude, 1982).

RADLER, Barbara
Ball Janik LLP, Portland 503 228 2525
Recommended in Real Estate

RAMIS, Timothy
Ramis Crew Corrigan & Bachrach LLP, Portland 503 222 4402
Recommended in Real Estate

RAWLINSON, Dennis
Miller Nash LLP, Portland
503 224 5858
Recommended in Litigation

REEVES, Edward
Stoel Rives LLP, Portland
503 224 3380
Recommended in Employment

RICHTER, Peter
Miller Nash LLP, Portland
503 224 5858
Recommended in Litigation

ROSENBAUM, Lois
Stoel Rives LLP, Portland
503 224 3380
Recommended in Litigation

RUBIN, Howard
Amburgey & Rubin PC, Portland
503 221 0309
Recommended in Employment

RUSSELL III, P Stephen
Landye Bennett Blumstein LLP, Portland 503 224 4100
srussell@landye-bennett.com
Recommended in Real Estate

Practice Areas: All aspects of real estate law. Represents buyers, sellers, and developers of land, commercial, industrial and retail properties, landlords and tenants, borrowers and lenders. Has written numerous publications regarding condominiums and planned communities. Co-author of the Oregon State Bar Continuing Legal Education's article regarding homeowner associations. Sub-specializes in representing real estate multiple listing services and condominium and planned community developers.

Prof. Memberships: Oregon State Bar, Member and past Chair of the Oregon State Bar Real Estate and Land Use Section.

Personal: Law degree from Willamette University where he graduated with honors.

SAMUELS, Stanley
Bateman Seidel Miner Blomgren Chellis & Gram, P.C., Portland
503 972 9920
Recommended in Real Estate

SAND, Thomas
Miller Nash LLP, Portland
503 224 5858
Recommended in Litigation

SHLACHTER, Robert
Stoll Stoll Berne Lokting & Shlachter, Portland 503 227 1600
Recommended in Litigation

SIMON, Michael
Perkins Coie LLP, Portland
503 727 2000
Recommended in Litigation

SIMPSON, Patrick
Perkins Coie LLP, Portland
503 727 2000
Recommended in Corporate/M&A

SKERRITT, Daniel
Tonkon Torp LLP, Portland
503 221 1440
Recommended in Litigation

STEPHENS, Kenneth
Tonkon Torp LLP, Portland
503 221 1440
Recommended in Corporate/M&A

STOLL, Robert
Stoll Stoll Berne Lokting & Shlachter, Portland 503 227 1600
Recommended in Litigation

STRUXNESS, Gregory
Ater Wynne LLP, Portland
503 226 1191
Recommended in Corporate/M&A

THOMAS, John
Stoel Rives LLP, Portland
503 224 3380
Recommended in Corporate/M&A

TONGUE, Thomas H
Dunn Carney Allen Higgins & Tongue LLP, Portland 503 306 5330
tht@dunn-carney.com
Recommended in Litigation

Practice Areas: A Partner at Dunn Carney since 1973. He specializes in litigation and appeals, arbitration, mediation and healthcare law.

Prof. Memberships: Present Regent in the American College of Trial Lawyers; past President Oregon Association of Defense Counsel; American Judicature Society, Member 30+ years; Oregon State Bar, Chair of multiple committees and elected delegate; Defense Research Institute member; International Association of Insurance Counsel.

Career: Admitted to Oregon, 1968; US District Court District of Oregon, 1970; US Court of Appeals 9th Circuit, 1971; US Supreme Court, 1971.

Publications: Awards: The Multnomah County Bar Association Professionalism Award; The Oregon State Bar Litigation Section - Owen M Panner Professionalism Award in 2002.

Personal: JD, University of Wisconsin,1968; BA, University of Oregon, 1965.

TRIPLETT, Thomas M
Schwabe Williamson & Wyatt PC, Portland 503 796 2901
ttriplett@schwabe.com
Recommended in Employment

Practice Areas: Mr Triplett has developed a notable reputation for his work in the areas of antitrust and labor law. He has represented management on organizational, recognitional and unfair labor practice before the National Labor Relations Board and various federal courts, negotiated collective bargaining agreements, arbitrated disputes, and litigated Title VII and wrongful discharge cases. He has briefed and argued several cases of ERISA and MPPAA before the U.S. Supreme Court, including R.A. Gray & Co v PBGC; Patrick v Burrett;

and Pacific Northwest Chapter of the Associated Builders & Contractors v Local 701.

Prof. Memberships: Oregon State Bar Association, American Bar Association, Antitrust, and Labor and Employment Law Sections; served on Executive Committee of OSB Labor Law Section, past Chairman of OSB Antitrust Section.

Personal: LLB, Stanford Law School, 1965; BA, Yale University, 1962.

TUCKER, Roy
Perkins Coie LLP, Portland
503 727 2000
Recommended in Corporate/M&A

TURNER, Mark
Ater Wynne LLP, Portland
503 226 1191
Recommended in Litigation

VANCLEAVE, Richard
Barran Liebman, Portland
503 228 0500
rvancleave@barran.com
Recommended in Employment

Practice Areas: Partner at Barran Liebman LLP specializing in representing management in certification campaigns, collective bargaining, labor negotiations, mediations, and strike response planning.

Prof. Memberships: Oregon State Bar Labor Law and Employment Section; Industrial Relations Research Association, Oregon Chapter President (2000-01); Oregon State Bar Labor Relations and Employment Law Section; American Public Transit Association Legal Committee; Associated General Contractors Oregon-Columbia Chapter, Legal Committee; Associated Wall and Ceiling Contractors Associated Floor Covering Contractors; National Electrical Contractors Association, Oregon-Columbia Chapter; National Electrical Contractors Association, SW Washington Chapter; Associated General Contractors, Oregon-Columbia Chapter.

Career: Admitted to Oregon; US Court of Appeals, Ninth Circuit; US District Court, District of Oregon.

Personal: Received JD from Willamette University School of Law (cum laude, 1980); BS from Oregon State University (with honors, 1977).

VOBORIL, Joseph
Tonkon Torp LLP, Portland
503 221 1440
Recommended in Real Estate

WALTERS, Martha
Walters Romm Chanti & Dickens, Eugene 541 683 2506
Recommended in Litigation

WALTERS, Stephen
Stoel Rives LLP, Portland
503 224 3380
Recommended in Litigation

WHITE, Christen
Ball Janik LLP, Portland
503 228 2525
Recommended in Real Estate

WHITTEMORE, Richard
Bullivant Houser Bailey PC, Portland
503 228 6351
Recommended in Litigation

WILSON, David
Bullard Smith Jernstedt Wilson,
Portland 503 248 1134
Recommended in Employment

WOLFSTONE, Jeffrey
Lane Powell PC, Portland
503 778 2153
wolfstonej@lanepowell.com
Recommended in Corporate/M&A
Practice Areas: Corporate, securities, mergers and acquisitions and emerging companies. As Co-Chair of the firm's Business Department, his practice emphasizes the representation of deal-intensive start-ups, emerging and middle market companies, as well as national and international companies that have operations in the Pacific Northwest. Also advises on corporate and real estate finance and transactions, joint ventures and strategic partnering arrangements. Acts as counsel for investment banking firms, pension funds and investment advisors, as well as angel, VC and private equity investors.
Prof. Memberships: Oregon Entrepreneurs Forum; Software Association of Oregon (Chair of Start Team 2005); Open Technology Business Center, Advisory Board (2005); Portland Tax Forum (Board of Directors, Chair, 1996-98); Oregon Nonprofit Corporation Task Force (Chair, 1989-present).
Career: Partner since 1982.
Publications: Speaker and program organizer of CLEs covering mergers and acquisitions, corporations, partnerships and LLCs. Published in business periodicals and an author/editor on partnership and corporate matters for 'Advising Oregon Businesses,' a publication of the Oregon State Bar.
Personal: University of California at Berkeley, Boalt Hall School of Law (JD, 1977); Stanford University (AB, 1974).

YELNOSKY, Maryann
Barran Liebman, Portland
503 228 0500
myelnosky@barran.com
Recommended in Employment
Practice Areas: Partner at Barran Liebman LLP. Experience in litigation since 1986.
Prof. Memberships: Oregon State Bar, Litigation and Labor & Employment Law Sections; Portland Human Resources Management Association Counsel (2002); Washington State Bar, Litigation Section; American Bar Association; Multnomah Bar Association; Oregon Women Lawyers; Oregon Association of Defense Counsel, Chair, Employment Law Section (2004); Board of Psychologist Examiners, Public Member (2003-present); Oregon Episcopal School, Board of Trustees (1999-2004); Oregon Episcopal School Mock Trial Coach, Classroom Law Project (1999-2003); Foundation for Medical Excellence, Speaker (1998-99; 2002-03); Special Grader, Oregon Board of Bar Examiners (1993).
Career: Admitted to Oregon; Washington; US District Court, District of Oregon; US District Court, Districts of Eastern and Western Washington; US Court of Appeals for the Ninth Circuit.
Personal: Received JD from University of Oregon, College of Law (Order of the Coif, 1986); Attended University of Pennsylvania (1972-74); BS from University of Oregon (1976).

BARRAN LIEBMAN LLP

THE FIRM

Managing Partner: Edwin A Harnden

AREAS OF PRACTICE:
Litigation 50%
Labor & Employment 50%

FIRM OVERVIEW: Barran Liebman specializes in representing employers in labor relations, employment law matters such as departing employee disputes, non-competition agreements, family leave issues, and complex commercial litigation. To assist employers in preventing labor problems, the firm provides a full range of tools for employers including: breakfast seminars throughout the year, training videotapes and CD-Roms, customized on-site training programs, and Electronic AlertsSM, free email bulletins announcing important changes in labor and employment law.

MAIN AREAS OF PRACTICE:

Labor & Employment: Barran Liebman is dedicated to representing employers and finding solutions for their employment needs from day-to-day advice to complex matters. Litigation is a conscious decision that an entity may need to make in individual circumstances. Barran Liebman's goal, however, is to assist in resolving disputes as efficiently as possible. The more successful approach, however, begins with an understanding of what motivates the dispute. The firm frequently evaluates whether there is a benefit to offering counseling, retraining, retirement packages, or other unusual benefits to assist the parties to resolve a matter on mutually beneficial terms. The firm holds six 'Food for Thought' breakfast seminars as well as an annual labor and employment seminar for employers that are attended by representatives of more than 500 people. Barran Liebman also customizes seminars to meet the individual needs of employers, their area of business and level of employee. As a special service to its clients, Barran Liebman LLP provides valuable Electronic AlertsSM free of charge. The Electronic AlertsSM summarize new case law and statutes that may impact businesses and suggests methods to comply with new legal requirements.

CLIENTS: Home Depot; Hilton; Pacific Maritime Association; Frito-Lay; Bear Creek; Safeway; Georgia-Pacific; Hollywood Entertainment; The Oregonian Publishing Company; Hoffman Construction; Howard S. Wright Construction, Samaritan Health Systems, National Electrical Contractors Association.

HEAD OFFICE

OREGON
601 SW 2nd Ave, Suite 2300, **Portland**, OR 97204
Tel: 503 228 0500   **Fax:** 503 274 1212
Email: cstephens@barran.com
Website: www.barran.com

DUNN CARNEY ALLEN HIGGINS & TONGUE LLP

THE FIRM

Managing Partner: Robert L Allen

Number of partners: 21
Number of other attorneys: 25

AREAS OF PRACTICE:

Business Law & Estate Planning 44%
Litigation 41%
Real Estate & Land Use 15%

FIRM OVERVIEW: Dunn Carney is a leading client-focused law firm in the Pacific Northwest. Attorneys work with clients to develop and implement solutions designed to avoid the problems that could lead to formal proceedings. In the event of litigation, they have an experienced team of trial attorneys who provide expert counsel and representation in alternative dispute resolution and in the courtroom. Dunn Carney is Oregon's only member of Meritas, a legal service organization that offers high quality worldwide legal services through a closely integrated group of independent law firms.

MAIN AREAS OF PRACTICE:

Business Law & Estate Planning: Many of the lawyers in the firm focus on matters relating to business and corporate law. These lawyers provide counsel for the day-to-day problems and concerns of business owners - including mergers/acquisitions, succession planning, tax, employee benefits, employment law, estate planning and bankruptcy. They serve clients in many industries including manufacturing/distribution, forest products, professional services, banking and finance, auto dealerships, construction and real estate.

Litigation: Dunn Carney's litigation attorneys represent clients in a variety of legal areas, including shareholder and partnership disputes, derivative and class actions, contract and warranty issues, trademark, taxation, employment, non-competition, antitrust, securities, banking, foreclosure, construction, international transaction disputes and other types of complex litigation. Dunn Carney is widely recognized for its expertise in insurance law and insurance coverage matters. This experience includes first party claims, employment discrimination, liquor liability, products liability, professional negligence, personal injury, commercial tort and business losses, property damage cases and self-insured defense.

Real Estate & Land Use: Dunn Carney's real estate and land use attorneys are recognized as among the Northwest's best at providing efficient, effective real estate services regarding development, acquisition, sale, financing, leasing, construction, land use, environmental issues, exchanges and other real estate tax matters, litigation and dispute resolution. Their work on the nationally recognized Brewery Blocks Development with their client Gerding/Edlen Development involved many complex issues and has led to other significant real estate transactions including the South Waterfront Development on the Willamette River.

HEAD OFFICE

OREGON
851 SW Sixth Ave, Suite 1500, **Portland**, OR 97204-1357
Tel: 503 224 6440 **Fax:** 503 224 7324
Websites: www.dunncarney.com

CLIENTS: North Pacific Group, Pan Pacific Retail Properties, Weyerhaeuser Co., Eastern Western Corporation, Brewery Blocks Investors, Gerding/Edlen Development, OTAK, Inc., Hollywood Entertainment Corp., Providence Health System-Oregon, Morgan Stanley, R.J. Reynolds Tobacco Company, Microfield Group, U.S. Bancorp, Kuni Enterprises, LbL Windows, Inc., Pearl Gateway Condominiums, LLC, A.W. Chesterton Company, Professional Liability Fund, Allstate Insurance, California Casualty Insurance, Country Companies Insurance, Safeco Insurance, Allied Group Insurance, North Pacific Insurance.

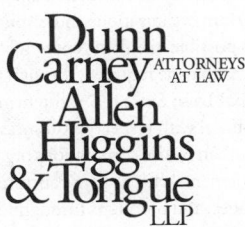

Member
MERITAS
LAW FIRMS WORLDWIDE

LANDYE BENNETT BLUMSTEIN LLP

THE FIRM

Managing Partner: David N Goulder
Number of partners: 17
Number of other attorneys: 7

AREAS OF PRACTICE:

Administrative Law	5%
Alaska Native & Tribal Law	20%
Business & Personal Injury Litigation	35%
Corporate Business & Tax	8%
Environmental Law	8%
Estate Planning, Trusts, Wills, & Probate	4%
Real Estate	20%

HEAD OFFICE

OREGON
1300 S W Fifth Avenue, Suite 3500, **Portland**, OR 97201
Tel: 503 224 4100   **Fax:** 503 224 4133
Website: www.landye-bennett.com

BRANCH OFFICES

ALASKA
701 West Eighth Avenue, Suite 1200, **Anchorage**, AK 99501
Tel: 907 276 5152   **Fax:** 907 276 8433

531 South Cobb Street, P.O. Box 4739, **Palmer**, AK 99645
Tel: 907 746 5971   **Fax:** 907 746 5972

FIRM OVERVIEW: Landye Bennett Blumstein LLP is a regional law firm, founded in 1955. With offices in Anchorage, Alaska, and Portland, Oregon, the firm serves clients throughout the Pacific Northwest. The firm's attorneys devote themselves to delivering results for their clients efficiently and effectively by remaining tuned to their clients' needs throughout the entire legal process. Landye Bennett Blumstein provides personal attention to its clients in order to deliver the best and most courteous professional service possible. The firm's close ties to the communities where it works allows it to interact effectively with businesses, government agencies, and other attorneys.

In addition to representing clients throughout the Pacific Northwest, Landye Bennett Blumstein also works with clients located in other parts of the country on specialized matters. Its clients include public and private corporations, real estate developers, condominium and community associations, municipalities, nonprofit groups, and individuals.

MAIN AREAS OF PRACTICE:

Administrative Law: The firm's Administrative Law Practice includes a broad spectrum of clients before federal, state and local government agencies, including in the areas of environmental and natural resources, tax, land use, Native American organizations and gaming. While informal resolution is not always possible, the firm represents its clients at administrative hearings and, as may be required, through the appeals processes.

Alaska Native & Tribal Law: Since 1976, the firm has acted as general counsel or special counsel with respect to business and other matters to regional, village, and urban Native corporations organized under the Alaska Native Claims Settlement Act. The firm's attorneys also represent tribal entities, municipalities, and boroughs throughout much of Alaska.

Litigation, Arbitration & Mediation: Landye Bennett Blumstein LLP's Litigation Department has successfully represented clients in a wide variety of actions in both state and federal courts throughout the region. The firm represents both plaintiffs and defendants in such practice areas as products liability and toxic torts, aviation, environmental, shareholder and partner matters, including class action, contracts, unfair competition, employment discrimination, and maritime disputes and claims.

Corporate Business & Tax: The firm helps companies manage complex business transactions and legal situations its clients may encounter, including corporate finance and securities, mergers and acquisitions, tax planning and business structuring, computer and intellectual property, employment matters, and tax controversies.

Environmental Law: The firm's Environmental Practice includes advising a wide range of commercial and industrial clients with the myriad federal, state and local laws and regulations, including compliance with hazardous waste management regulations, regulatory and compliance matters involving the Clean Air Act, the Clean Water Act, the Toxic Substance Control Act, the Resource Conservation and Recovery Act and the Endangered Species Act, among others. Environmental due diligence for lenders and real estate clients is also a key area of the practice. Representing potentially responsible parties at federal and state Superfund sites, as well as in cost recovery litigation with government agencies and private parties is another critical service provided by the firm's experienced environmental counsel.

Estate Planning, Trusts, Wills, & Probate: The firm offers services to its clients in estate planning, including the preparation of wills and trusts, post-mortem tax matters and probate.

Real Estate: The firm provides a full range of services for real estate matters. The firm's clients include more than 500 condominium and community associations and developers of more than 500 condominium and planned community projects. The firm assists its clients with acquisitions and dispositions of real estate, tax deferred exchanges, developing condominiums and planned communities, negotiating and documenting financing arrangements for both borrowers and lenders, land and building development, land use planning hearings and appeals, and commercial leases.

CLIENTS: Representative clients include A. McGill & Son; Bright Now! Dental, Inc.; Container Properties, LLC; Emerging Markets of North America, Inc.; Gould Electronics, Inc; Herbert Malarkey Roofing Company; Metro Metals Northwest; Pacific Coast Shredding, LLC; National Mortgage Co.; PPG Industries, Inc.; Sealaska Corporation; Sharp Laboratories of America, Inc., United Agri Products, Inc., Vantage Oncology, Inc.

CONTENTS: Antitrust p.1489; Banking & Finance p.1492; Bankruptcy p.1494; Corporate/M&A p.1497; Employment p.1500; Environment p.1504; Intellectual Property p.1507; Litigation p.1510; Real Estate p.1515; Individuals' Profiles p.1518; Firm Profiles p.1541.

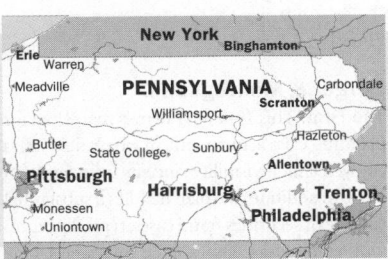

How lawyers are ranked

The opinions we gather from clients — mainly from in-house lawyers but also from other purchasers of legal services — are balanced by opinions from colleagues and competitors. Together, they provide two different perspectives — an all-round view — and biased viewpoints cancel each other out.

ANTITRUST

Pennsylvania

Leading firms (Antitrust)

1. DECHERT *Philadelphia*
2. BERGER & MONTAGUE PC *Philadelphia*
   FINE KAPLAN & BLACK *Philadelphia*
   PEPPER HAMILTON LLP *Philadelphia*
3. KOHN SWIFT & GRAF *Philadelphia*
   MONTGOMERY, MCCRACKEN, WALKER *Philadelphia*
   REED SMITH LLP *Pittsburgh*
4. DRINKER BIDDLE & REATH LLP *Philadelphia*
   DUANE MORRIS LLP *Philadelphia*
   MORGAN, LEWIS & BOCKIUS LLP *Philadelphia*
   SCHNADER HARRISON SEGAL *Philadelphia*

Leading individuals (Antitrust)

1. MATHER Barbara *Pepper Hamilton LLP, Philadelphia*
   TATE Joseph *Dechert, Philadelphia*
2. BLACK Allen *Fine Kaplan & Black, Philadelphia*
   BOOKER Daniel *Reed Smith LLP, Pittsburgh*
   GORDON George *Dechert, Philadelphia*
   KOHN Joseph *Kohn Swift & Graf, Philadelphia*
   LIEBENBERG Roberta *Fine Kaplan & Black, Philadelphia*
   MONTAGUE H Laddie *Berger, Philadelphia*
   NEWELL Francis *Montgomery McCracken, Philadelphia*
   SHIEKMAN Laurence *Pepper Hamilton, Philadelphia*
3. ARMSTRONG Stephen *Montgomery, Philadelphia*
   BIZAR Steven *Buchanan Ingersoll, Philadelphia*
   BROWN Stephen *Dechert, Philadelphia*
   CLARKE Jennifer *Dechert, Philadelphia*
   EDWARDS Mark *Morgan Lewis, Philadelphia*
   KAPLAN Arthur *Fine Kaplan, Philadelphia*
   LANGER Howard *Langer & Grogan, Philadelphia*
   LEVIN Christine *Dechert, Philadelphia*
   SAINT-ANTOINE Paul *Drinker Biddle, Philadelphia*
   SEDRAN Howard *Levin Fishbein, Philadelphia*
   SICALIDES Barbara *Pepper Hamilton, Philadelphia*
   STACK Stephen *Dechert, Philadelphia*
   SWIRSKY Sherry *Schnader Harrison, Philadelphia*

Up-and-coming individuals

CRAMER Eric *Berger & Montague, Philadelphia*
MACK Wayne *Duane Morris, Philadelphia*

Firms and individuals are listed alphabetically in each band.

Band 1

Dechert

See firm details p.1547

The Firm: When it comes to antitrust, there is no doubt that Dechert is the "*top firm in Pennsylvania, and can easily compete with the top DC and New York firms.*" The 11-partner team continues to be involved in a number of high-profile antitrust cases, such as the recent airlines class action brought by travel agencies. It also acted for GlaxoSmithKline in the Asahi Glass Company case, which involved allegations of sham patent litigation and an improper settlement with a generic ANDA filer. In this, the team from Dechert succeeded in having all the antitrust claims against its client dismissed. Clients keep returning to the firm because it is of the "*highest echelon,*" and particularly because its lawyers are "*thorough, have great depth of experience, know what we want and give high-quality advice*".

The Lawyers: The practice is headed by **Joseph Tate** (see p.1539), whom clients and peers alike portrayed as one of the "*finest antitrust lawyers in the country.*" Tate is credited by many interviewees with having built the strongest practice in the state, and, on an individual level, he is admired for his "*fine trial law instincts*" and his "*creativity in thinking complex matters through.*" He has acted as principal attorney in many of the firm's highest profile antitrust cases over the past year, and is particularly active in disputes concerning the pharmaceuticals industry, for clients such as GlaxoSmithKline, Pfizer and DuPont. He is also increasingly involved in criminal cartel work. Clients were impressed with **George Gordon** (see p.1525), who was described as being "*as smart as a whip,*" as well as "*forthright in his opinions*" and "*extremely reliable.*" He is active in the pharmaceutical sector, representing some of the industry's giants, and also spends a considerable amount of time on price fixing cases. He is currently assisting the Curtis Circulation Company, the nation's largest

distributor of magazines, in a price discrimination case in the Southern District Court of New York. Gordon also acted as lead counsel in the Naprelan antitrust litigation, in which he defended Elan Pharmaceuticals against charges of sham patent infringement litigation. **Stephen Stack** (see p.1538) was described by clients as a "*smart and creative antitrust counselor who is totally immersed in his work.*" He counsels several major pharmaceutical and chemical companies, advising on patenting strategies, licensing research and development collaborations. He was recently lead counsel, alongside Joseph Tate, in the Asahi Glass Company case, and also successfully represented GlaxoSmithKline in the Paxil antitrust litigation, which involved significant intellectual property issues. **Jennifer Clarke** (see p.1521) was described by clients as an "*extraordinarily effective writer,*" and also "*persuasive and aggressive in arguing cases.*" Her recent highlights include representing Delta Air Lines in the Sarah Futch Hall case, successfully argued in the federal court in North Carolina. **Christine Levin** (see p.1530), who is also renowned for her white-collar crime work, was highlighted for the "*true depth of experience*" she brings to antitrust matters. Alongside Joseph Tate, she successfully defended a large US chemical supplier in connection with an EU Commission investigation into an alleged cartel in the chemical sector. Additionally, she handles a large volume of patent infringement cases. **Stephen Brown** (see p.1520) enters the rankings this year following praise for his great "*leadership skills.*" He is currently representing FMC in a class action brought by three separate classes of purchasers of the product microcrystalline cellulose, and is also handling a related FTC investigation.

The Clients: The firm defended the Curtis Circulation Company against charges of monopolization, and represented Delta Air Lines in a class action in which travel agents had accused the airline, alongside 17 others, of conspiring to reduce and eliminate commissions paid to travel agents. Other clients include: Elan; FMC; GlaxoSmithKline and Pfizer.

Band 2

Berger & Montague PC

The Firm: This 19-lawyer firm is renowned for plaintiffs' class action work, in which field it has enjoyed a high visibility since its foundation in 1970. In addition, the firm handles a substantial volume of securities fraud cases, typically representing investors against large companies. One of its highlights from the past year has been its work for a class of direct purchasers of high fructose corn syrup against its manufacturers, in the High Fructose Corn Syrup antitrust litigation. This case was appealed several times and was eventually settled for a total of $531 million. Another important case was the Relafen antitrust litigation, which involved claims against a major brand pharmaceutical manufacturer accused of excluding generic competitors from the market. The case was eventually settled on behalf of a class of direct purchasers of Relafen for $175 million.

The Lawyers: Known as the "*dean of the Bar*" among his peers, the "*tremendously experienced*" **Laddie Montague** continues to act in the firm's highest profile cases. He was one of three co-lead counsel in the Corn Syrup antitrust litigation, and has enjoyed a number of recent successes against major players in the pharmaceutical industry, such as GlaxoSmithKline. Currently, he is involved in several price-fixing cases, all of them still pending. **Eric Cramer** was admired for his "*strong analytical skills*" and "*expert knowledge of the economic side of the law.*" These were on show recently in re Microcrystalline Cellulose antitrust litigation, in which the central allegation was of a worldwide conspiracy to allocate the market for microcrystalline cellulose. He has also been busy handling several class cases on behalf of direct purchasers of brand name drugs, in which pharmaceutical companies stand accused of illegally blocking the market for less expensive competitor drugs.

The Clients: The firm typically assists investors, consumers, governmental entities and employees.

Fine Kaplan & Black

The Firm: Interviewees described the boutique as being heavy with "*intellectually gifted lawyers*" who have extensive trial experience in civil and criminal antitrust cases. Although traditionally a plaintiff firm, the team has been making greater forays into defendant representation in recent years. The firm has also been particularly active in the criminal antitrust arena of late, and continues to appear in major class actions. Recent examples include its work for a class of indirect purchasers and third parties in an antitrust class action against the manufacturer of Remeron, an antidepressant. Key issues in the case – which

recently settled for $36 million – were the abuse of patent and regulatory laws to delay the entry of generic competition into the market.

The Lawyers: Allen Black (see p.1519) received ringing endorsements from interviewees, who characterized him as being "*flat out smart*" and praised his "*high integrity and credibility in court.*" His recent representative cases include Parsky v First Union, a class action brought on behalf of trust beneficiaries whose trusts were converted into shares of First Union property mutual funds. This case, brought in the Philadelphia Court of Common Pleas, was one of the first trust conversion cases to be certified as a national class action. **Roberta Liebenberg** (see p.1530) impressed market sources by combining an "*enormous amount of energy with a good dose of common sense.*" Over the past year, she has devoted a considerable amount of this energy to representing an executive in an antitrust criminal case. She is also involved in consumer litigation work, and has been acting as co-lead counsel in Roberts v Fleet Bank, which concerned representations made by Fleet in its credit card offering. **Arthur Kaplan** (see p.1528) is said by clients to be "*unusually smart*" but also "*trustworthy.*" He was co-lead counsel in the Remeron antitrust litigation. However, the main focus of his practice is on professional malpractice suits against lawyers.

The Clients: The firm represents individuals, law firms, health insurance companies, union health funds and consumers.

Pepper Hamilton LLP
See firm details p.1558

The Firm: Interviewees agree this firm is "*among the best*" in the state for antitrust advice. A team of 17 lawyers in Pennsylvania spends a considerable portion of its time counseling clients in various industries on strategies to avoid antitrust liability, as well as handling merger approvals under the Hart-Scott-Rodino Act and corollary state antitrust legislation. The group also has considerable experience of providing advice on RICO legislation and FTC litigation issues. Aside from its prominent transactional strength, the firm is also heavily involved in antitrust litigation. Here, its representative engagements include defending the glass manufacturer in re Flat Glass antitrust litigation, alongside various state and federal indirect purchasers. The firm also has a specialty in work related to patent infringement claims, and has been busy recently advising a biomedical manufacturer on such claims and expected antitrust counterclaims. Other highlights include defending a major automotive parts wholesaler in a Robinson-Patman Act class action brought by almost 200 plaintiffs.

The Lawyers: The "*effective, highly credible and intellectually strong*" **Barbara Mather** (see p.1531) is noted for her "*tremendous credibility*

with the courts." Said to be willing to take on "*high-risk*" matters, she recently represented 35 charities in a joint lawsuit against Prudential Securities, and appeared on behalf of a supplier of computer services in a multimillion-dollar claim in the Common Pleas Court. Other highlights include her lead role in the Flat Glass Antitrust Litigation, and her success in representing the ABA by obtaining summary judgment in a private action alleging price fixing in connection with law school accreditation. "*Impressive*" attorney **Laurence Shiekman** (see p.1537) was praised by clients as "*energetic and good at cutting to the chase.*" He spends a substantial amount of time on patent antitrust cases, as well as on criminal antitrust and counseling matters. His recent highlights include defending Pilkington North America against potential treble damages in a class action, and he also assisted a national pizza franchiser in a class action brought by franchisees alleging monopolization in violation of the Sherman Act. The "*straightforward and energetic*" **Barbara Sicalides** (see p.1537) is widely seen as the up-and-coming individual at the firm. She was particularly commended for her understanding of both the "*human as well as the business side of things.*" Her work is focused on merger counseling, government investigations and the effect of antitrust law on wider business issues. She was recently involved in a suit alleging conspiracy to monopolize a technology market, where she defended a French manufacturer of building materials, flat glass and abrasives.

The Clients: Important clients include Pilkington North America, Advent International and PPM America.

Band 3

Kohn Swift & Graf

The Firm: This fine firm continues to appear in, among other things, government criminal investigations, civil actions and international price-fixing cases. Founded over 25 years ago by the late Harold Kohn, its involvement in major antitrust cases is typically on the plaintiff side, though it does occasionally appear for the defense. Its recent caseload includes a number of high-profile matters, representing clients from such industries as automotives and manufacturing. The firm mixes antitrust work with a variety of other business litigation, and has recently acted in a major environmental rights case.

The Lawyers: Director of the firm **Joseph Kohn** is said to be "*extremely strong on the plaintiffs' side,*" thanks in part to his "*high integrity and leadership skills*" as well as his considerable knowledge and experience. He has been busy representing a class of purchasers of automotive refinishing paint in a case in the Eastern District Court, which turns on allegations that five major companies were colluding illegally to fix prices. The Court recently approved an additional $48 million in settlements in that case. He has recently been retained in the Plastic Additives case, where he is representing a class of purchasers of plastic additives who are alleging conspiracy among 16 companies to fix prices. **The Clients:** Manufacturers, automotive repairers, parking lot owners and employees all feature in the firm's extensive client list.

Montgomery, McCracken, Walker & Rhoads, LLP

The Firm: The firm is heavily committed to both antitrust litigation and counseling, and it fields nine antitrust partners in its Philadelphia office alone. The healthcare sector continues to be a particular area of activity for the team, and it recently assisted clients in multiparty litigation linked to the medical device industry in the District Court. The team appeared on behalf of Delta Air Lines in the District Court and the Third Circuit Court of Appeals in the Foreign Travel Agency Antitrust Class Action Litigation. Here, it succeeded in getting the claims against the client, which concerned the payment of commission to travel agencies, dismissed.
The Lawyers: According to clients, **Francis Newell** is *"thoughtful, intelligent and knowledgeable."* He has had a successful year, representing Delta Air Lines in the above-mentioned case, and also handling the Graphite Electrodes Antitrust Class Action on behalf of UCAR International in the District Court and the Third Circuit Court of Appeals. *"Leading antitrust counselor"* **Stephen Armstrong** is extremely active in both the antitrust division of the ABA and the wider market: currently he is involved in price-fixing cases, joint cooperative activities in certain healthcare and manufacturing markets and monopolization claims in the computer software industry. He also offers complementary expertise in areas of intellectual property law, having handled matters such as patent infringement litigation involving electronic surveillance systems and copyright issues concerning software operating systems.
The Clients: The firm has represented Medegen Holdings in connection with allegations of vertical resale price maintenance, a less common form of antitrust violation. It represents clients from a range of industries, including airlines, banking, manufacturing and healthcare. Examples include Wawa, Simpson Tacoma Kraft Company and Rohm and Haas.

Reed Smith LLP

See firm details p.1560
The Firm: Although more established in Pittsburgh, this well-respected international firm has a broad reach. It is renowned for its handling of high-profile cases, particularly in traditional industries, such as steel and coal. Its work for electric power generators and steel companies in

the so-called Purchased Coal Litigation has earned it considerable respect. The firm does a lot of work in price-fixing matters, and it has been extensively involved in merger enforcement, specifically relating to mergers between direct competitors. Over the past year, the team has witnessed an increase in criminal antitrust cases and class actions, complementing its diet of price fixing, acquisition agreements, securities fraud, consumer banking and deceptive advertising.
The Lawyers: Daniel Booker (see p.1520) has recently completed the US Steel case and is now busy representing a major manufacturer of textile products in connection with a price-fixing allegation. He defended Airbus in the federal court in Los Angeles against antitrust claims filed by a supplier of components for passenger aircraft, and has represented Quaker State in a class action alleging the price fixing of crude oil.
The Clients: The firm's client base includes steel manufacturers, health insurers, computer companies and aircraft manufacturers. Its attorneys have worked for Airbus, US Steel, Citadel Communications, Matthews International, PG Publishing Co and numerous other corporations in federal antitrust investigations into the acquisitions of competitors and other matters.

Band 4

Drinker Biddle & Reath LLP

See firm details p.1549
The Firm: Described by interviewees as a team of *"analytical, deep-thinking lawyers,"* it continues to be involved in a number of price-fixing cases and advises on the competition elements of mergers. It enjoys extensive dealings with the federal regulatory agencies, and has represented clients in FTC administrative proceedings, preliminary injunction proceedings and in response to second requests. Indicative of the firm's strength in antitrust matters is its work for Georgia-Pacific in the Linerboard antitrust litigation. This case, which alleged price fixing among manufacturers of corrugated sheets and corrugated boxes, received considerable national attention.
The Lawyers: The *"bright and talented"* **Paul Saint-Antoine** (see p.1536), aside from having extensive experience in dealing with federal regulatory agencies, has been on both sides of private antitrust litigation. The range of his representative cases stretches from charges of price fixing, price discrimination and group boycotts to unlawful mergers along with many other forms of anticompetitive conduct. He recently advised Cinram, a manufacturer of DVD discs, on claims arising from patent pools created by Matsushita and other owners of DVD patents. Saint-Antoine has also established a niche insurance practice and, in that regard, has appeared in some of the nation's largest cov-

erage disputes.
The Clients: Georgia-Pacific; Hewlett-Packard; Hoffmann-La Roche; Kemper Insurance Companies; Cinram International and JFC Technologies.

Duane Morris LLP

See firm details p.1550
The Firm: The firm is renowned for its expertise in the healthcare sector, and the antitrust group is no different. The team does a *"tremendous amount of detailed work"* in the area, say clients, representing major hospital associations in a range of litigation and advisory matters. Recent examples include its work for Chester County Hospital in connection with monopoly allegations against the largest health maintenance organization (HMO) in the country. In the Maine Health Alliance case, the firm represented an 11-hospital and 330-plus physician health network based in Maine before the FTC. Another highlight includes acting for the hospital in Angelico v Easton Hospital in a Sherman Act Section 1 case, which was recently decided by the Third Circuit Court of Appeals.
The Lawyers: Clients were impressed by **Wayne Mack**'s (see p.1531) *"presence in the courtroom."* His *"thorough due diligence and his opinions on how trends will unfold with the Federal Trade Commission"* were also highly valued. Like the firm, he is heavily involved in cases in the healthcare arena. However, his expertise doesn't end there: Mack was also counsel to Kreha Corporation of America as a defendant in the Plastic Additives antitrust litigation, which is currently pending in the Eastern District Court of Pennsylvania. He has also established a niche in acting on behalf of truck dealerships.
The Clients: The firm's main clients are hospitals, trade associations, trade networks, dealers and manufacturers. It recently represented Toledo Mack Sales and Services against Mack Trucks in an antitrust case involving Sherman Act Section 1 and Robinson-Patman Act claims.

Morgan, Lewis & Bockius LLP

See firm details p.1556
The Firm: The firm's particular strength lies in its antitrust counseling work, advising clients on every aspect of competition law. For example, the team has been actively engaged in advising on the antitrust aspects of mergers. This has involved it in drawing on the resources of its international network, to prepare clients for the regulatory systems of dozens of countries. The Pennsylvania branch can also count on the backing of the firm's large and impressive DC office. Over the past year, the firm has also been active defending corporations that are subject to cartel and other sensitive government investigations.
The Lawyers: With his combination of *"strong intellectual ability, thoroughness and knowledge of the law,"* **Mark Edwards** (see p.1523) has estab-

lished a reputation as *"one of the smartest guys in Philadelphia."* His two main recent highlights have been his involvement in the Anchor Health Properties case and his current work for Charming Shoppes, a leading specialty clothing retailer primarily focused on women's plus sizes. The latter is a class action brought on behalf of a class of shoppers in a state court in Illinois. He also successfully defended Hollywood Tans in an important arbitration.

The Clients: The firm recently made a foray into the healthcare arena, defending Anchor Health Properties in a matter involving the Federal Trade Commission Act, which is currently still pending in Philadelphia. Typical clients include healthcare providers, retailers and international corporations.

Schnader Harrison Segal & Lewis LLP

The Firm: The firm boasts a rich tradition of providing litigation and counseling services in the area of antitrust and trade regulation. A team of *"very fine litigators"* is strong on the plaintiff side as well as the defense side. This expertise was on show recently in the headline-making Linerboard case, in which it represented several defendant packaging companies. The accusations leveled against its clients were a combination of conspir-

acy and unreasonable restraint of trade and commerce, in violation of Sherman Act Section 1. Recently the team has been particularly busy counseling clients in the healthcare industry.

The Lawyers: The *"tremendously motivated"* **Sherry Swirsky** (see p.1538) enjoys *"a great degree of trust at the Bar,"* according to interviewees. She acted as liaison counsel in the Linerboard case, and has also been involved as co-counsel for Air France in a $14 billion lawsuit brought by plaintiff US travel agents alleging that Air France, along with 18 other airlines, had conspired to cap base commissions in violation of Section 1 of the Sherman Act. Her team was successful in winning summary judgment for its client. Increasingly she counsels clients in the healthcare industry and she has also advised a political party on election law.

The Clients: Active clients include corporations in the manufacturing, retail, insurance, technology, healthcare and telecommunications industries.

Other Notable Practitioners

The *"intellectually sound, thorough and highly knowledgeable"* **Howard Sedran** (see p.1536) of Levin Fishbein Sedran & Berman was said to be *"very good on the defense side."* His recent highlights include the Graphite Electrodes antitrust litigation and the Flat Glass antitrust litigation. The bulk of his clientele consists of small businesses, and he is increasingly prosecuting price-fixing cases. This year sees the entry of **Steven Bizar** (see p.1519) of Buchanan Ingersoll into the table. Portrayed by peers as a *"superior trial lawyer with a high level of determination,"* he recently defeated an $11 billion antitrust class action lawsuit against a pharmaceutical wholesaler, in an 11-week jury trial in the federal court in Chicago. Bizar represents clients from a diverse range of fields, spanning the chemicals to the financial services industry. The *"extraordinary"* **Howard Langer** of Langer & Grogan PC also enters the ranks this year following enthusiastic praise for his *"wonderful court style, strong work ethic and the respect he's garnered among judges."* He acted as lead counsel in the Linerboard case, which is one of the biggest antitrust cases to be heard in the Third Circuit Court of Appeals. He was instrumental in achieving a $202 million settlement for his clients, a class of direct purchasers who had bought corrugated containers from the manufacturers. His client portfolio includes the largest distributor of automobile parts in the country, and a manufacturer based in Italy.

BANKING & FINANCE

Pennsylvania
Leading firms (Banking & Finance)

1 BLANK ROME LLP *Philadelphia*
   DUANE MORRIS LLP *Philadelphia*

2 BALLARD SPAHR ANDREWS *Philadelphia*
   DRINKER BIDDLE & REATH LLP *Philadelphia*
   KLETT ROONEY LIEBER & SCHORLING *Pittsburgh*
   MORGAN, LEWIS & BOCKIUS LLP *Philadelphia*
   REED SMITH LLP *Pittsburgh*
   WOLF, BLOCK, SCHORR AND *Philadelphia*

Leading individuals (Banking & Finance)

1 BERGER Lawrence *Morgan Lewis, Philadelphia*
   FLICK II Lawrence *Blank Rome, Philadelphia*
   FRIDY Carl *Ballard Spahr, Philadelphia*

2 HERYFORD Craig *Klett Rooney, Pittsburgh*
   KLINE Eric *Morgan Lewis, Pittsburgh*
   LESSER Bruce *Wolf Block, Philadelphia*
   RABINOWITZ Mark *Blank Rome, Philadelphia*
   STERN Joan *Blank Rome, Philadelphia*

Firms and individuals are listed alphabetically in each band.

Band 1

Blank Rome LLP

See firm details p.1542

The Firm: The financial services team works closely with its top-flight bankruptcy team and also combines with the New York office to form what peers regard as *"a superlative team."* Notable niche areas of strength include public finance work and asset-based lending, to which several partners dedicate a substantial portion of their practice. The team acted for the School District of Philadelphia, the sixth largest in the country, in various debt restructurings and derivatives swap programs. These measures generated substantial savings of $792 million for the district.

The Lawyers: **Lawrence Flick** (see p.1524) is chairman of the firm's leasing and asset securitization group. He represents a comprehensive range of lenders on syndicated loans, inter-creditor arrangements, restructurings and DIP financing work. Clients praise him for being, *"first rate on the strategy and structure of deals."* **Mark Rabinowitz** (see p.1535) chairs the financial services group and specializes in healthcare business lending. He represents the likes of La Salle Business Credit and Healthcare Business

Credit and recently handled a $500 million workout. Interviewees describe him as *"a highly seasoned operator and something of a star in his area."* **Joan Stern**'s (see p.1538) practice combines transactional and legislative work in the area of public finance. She represents state and local government entities as well as underwriters and credit enhancers. Recent highlights include representing the Commonwealth of Pennsylvania in the creation of a new debt issuing body as part of the governor's economic stimulus legislation.

The Clients: Commerzbank; Wachovia; American Business Financial Services; Fleet Capital and PNC Bank.

Duane Morris LLP

See firm details p.1550

The Firm: Commentators recommend this group as *"perhaps the strongest lender-side practice in the state."* A team of 50 lawyers is particularly active in the mid-Atlantic region, but is also pursuing an organic growth strategy throughout its 17 offices nationwide. This is a multitalented team that is equally well versed in bankruptcy proceedings and restructurings as it is in the financing of business transactions.

The Lawyers: John Horstmann and Margery

1492   All quotes in the text are from interviews with clients and competitors.

CHAMBERS USA 2005

Reed are two of the firm's strongest insolvency lawyers. Both lawyers handle creditors' rights matters, workouts and complex commercial reorganizations. Horstmann is particularly active on the national stage.

The Clients: Lender clients include PNC Bank, Citizens Bank and Deutsche Bank.

Band 2

Ballard Spahr Andrews & Ingersoll LLP
See firm details p.1541

The Firm: The firm's transactional finance group represents a broad swath of commercial and investment banks, thrifts, insurance companies and private equity and venture capital businesses. Several commentators underlined the firm's traditional strength in the field of public finance, federal tax matters and the issuance of municipal bonds. The group also has expertise in real estate transactions. One rival reported that this "*high-level*" team takes a sensible approach to deal making.

The Lawyers: **Carl Fridy**'s (see p.1524) workload cuts across several practice areas and includes bankruptcy, public finance, construction, real estate and securitization deals. He is the partner in charge of the transactional finance unit where he maintains a reputation as "*a highly active and thoughtful practitioner.*"

The Clients: The client roster consists of lenders, borrowers, finance houses and governmental agencies.

Drinker Biddle & Reath LLP
See firm details p.1549

The Firm: This regional team consists of 17 lawyers in nine offices and the team is set to grow further once the integration of recently assimilated small law firms based in north New Jersey takes effect. The department has been busy counseling troubled businesses and advising on several consolidations. It has also benefited from the resurgence of deals led by private equity firms. The group has also made an impression in the New York lending market and has established a relationship with Bank of America Business Capital.

The Lawyers: Following the retirement of Bruce Shuter, managing partner Neil Haimm has emerged as a natural leader of the practice. He specializes in representing growth companies and investors in private financing and M&A activity.

The Clients: The team represents both lenders and borrowers that are drawn from the healthcare, broadcasting and media sectors.

Klett Rooney Lieber & Schorling
See firm details p.1555

The Firm: This group is highly regarded in Pittsburgh but has also enhanced its presence in Philadelphia and Wilmington. The practice has been active on several fronts, notably in venture capital-backed transactions. It has also counseled several banking groups on the creation of syndicated loan facilities and has been involved in various acquisitions.

The Lawyers: **Craig Heryford**'s broad practice encompasses financing transactions, risk assessment and counseling clients on various contractual matters. Peers praised him for being "*equally at home advising emerging businesses as he is negotiating senior credit facilities for national entities.*"

The Clients: The group's roster of lender clients includes Citizens Bank, PNC Bank, Wachovia and LaSalle Business Credit. The firm also acts for a range of borrowers, including manufacturing businesses, and steel and coal concerns.

Morgan, Lewis & Bockius LLP
See firm details p.1556

The Firm: Commentators spoke of an impressive group that "*certainly has the ear of many of the best banks in the mid-Atlantic region.*" The team recently represented Susquehanna Banc in its acquisition of Patriot Bank for $220 million. It also advised on the finance-related aspects of a strategic partnership between SI/Baker and Analytical Spectral Devices to develop new technology.

The Lawyers: One peer remarked that **Lawrence Berger** (see p.1519) "*negotiates complex corporate governance issues with the finesse of a leading diplomat.*" He recently helped secure a $200 million financing for Penn Mutual Life Insurance Company. He also counseled consumer products giant Church & Dwight in the refinancing of a $640 million syndicated credit facility in connection with an acquisition. According to interviewees, **Eric Kline** (see p.1528) is a "*well-connected and business-savvy lawyer*" who advises startup businesses on raising capital. He played a crucial role for software design business, Desantage, in securing $1.25 million in funding from the New York-based Spencer Trask Ventures.

The Clients: Church & Dwight Co; Columbia Capital; Penn Mutual Life Insurance Company; IDG Ventures; Susquehanna Banc and Blue Cross Insurance.

Reed Smith LLP
See firm details p.1560

The Firm: This Pittsburgh-based firm has been keen to expand its banking practice nationally and now represents several major banks and a significant number of Fortune 500 businesses. In addition to the firm's 14 US offices, it has also strengthened its transatlantic presence through its two offices in the UK. It wins respect for its transactional expertise but also benefits from a prominent regulatory practice that represents clients before federal and state bank regulatory agencies.

The Lawyers: Alan London advises lenders and borrowers on syndicated loans, project and acquisition financings, securitizations, restructurings and elements of capital markets transactions.

The Clients: National and international banks, thrifts, mortgage bankers and brokerages all feature on the client roster.

Wolf, Block, Schorr and Solis-Cohen LLP
See firm details p.1562

The Firm: A team comprising around 13 attorneys is divided between the firm's three offices in the state. It has enjoyed a strong deal flow and has increasingly been involved representing the borrower side in financings. Interviewees agreed that the firm's regional focus makes it the ideal choice for midmarket lenders. They praised its "*rounded and sophisticated*" knowledge of the interplay between all levels of participants on high-caliber financings. Its highly regarded asset-based lending practice continues to thrive, and it increasingly advises on acquisitions and capital raisings.

The Lawyers: Cochair of the financial services division **Bruce Lesser** (see p.1530) wins praise as "*a lawyer of integrity, energy and commitment*" among peers. His broad caseload has seen him advising on the establishment of a $500 million credit facility. He is also a "*highly accomplished*" workout and bankruptcy attorney.

The Clients: Sovereign Bank; PNC Bank; Wachovia; LaSalle Business Credit and Congress Financial.

BANKRUPTCY/RESTRUCTURING

Pennsylvania
Leading firms
(Bankruptcy/Restructuring)

1 **BLANK ROME LLP** *Philadelphia*
DUANE MORRIS LLP *Philadelphia*
REED SMITH LLP *Pittsburgh*

2 **ADELMAN LAVINE GOLD & LEVIN** *Philadelphia*
COZEN O'CONNOR *Philadelphia*
DILWORTH PAXSON LLP *Philadelphia*
HANGLEY ARONCHICK SEGAL & PUDLIN *Philadelphia*
MORGAN, LEWIS & BOCKIUS LLP *Philadelphia*

3 **KLETT ROONEY LIEBER & SCHORLING** *Pittsburgh*
PEPPER HAMILTON LLP *Philadelphia*
STEVENS & LEE, PC *Philadelphia*
WOLF, BLOCK, SCHORR *Philadelphia*

Leading individuals
(Bankruptcy/Restructuring)

Senior Statesman
SYKES David *Duane Morris*, Philadelphia
TEMIN Michael *Wolf Block*, Philadelphia

1 **DWORETZKY Joseph** *Hangley Aronchick*, Philadelphia
SHAPIRO Raymond *Blank Rome*, Philadelphia
SINGER Paul *Reed Smith*, Pittsburgh

2 **BIRON Thomas** *Blank Rome*, Philadelphia
BLOOM Myron *Hangley Aronchick*, Philadelphia
HORSTMANN III John *Duane Morris*, Philadelphia
KLEBAN Barry *Adelman Lavine*, Philadelphia
MCMICHAEL Lawrence *Dilworth Paxson*, Philadelphia
SCHAFFER Eric *Reed Smith*, Pittsburgh
SCHORLING William *Klett Rooney*, Pittsburgh
SPRINGER Claudia *Reed Smith*, Philadelphia

3 **BARSON Leon** *Adelman Lavine*, Philadelphia
BLOOM Michael *Morgan Lewis*, Philadelphia
CLARK Peter *Reed Smith*, Philadelphia
COLTON Neal *Cozen O'Connor*, Philadelphia
FATELL Bonnie *Blank Rome*, Wilmington
KASSNER Andrew *Drinker Biddle*, Philadelphia
LAPOWSKY Robert *Stevens & Lee*, Philadelphia
LAWALL Francis *Pepper Hamilton*, Philadelphia
MILLER Gregg *Pepper Hamilton*, Philadelphia
REED Margery *Duane Morris*, Philadelphia
REED Michael *Pepper Hamilton*, Philadelphia
SCHILDHORN Gary *Adelman Lavine*, Philadelphia

Firms and individuals are listed alphabetically in each band.

Band 1

Blank Rome LLP
See firm details p.1542
The Firm: This "*premier league*" bankruptcy team works closely with its New York and Delaware offices as part of a 17-partner unit, seven of whom are based in Philadelphia. One recent notable success was the firm's representation of an oil refinery that had entered into a contract to provide environmental protection from gases released by a refining process. As a result of the bankruptcy of a related processing company, the oil refinery would have been closed down, were it not for the "*sustained onslaught*" of the group's attorneys, who demonstrated a "*rare ability to turn a case everyone thought was doomed into a victory.*" Other important representations include counseling the creditors' committee in the Midway Airlines case. The team also acted for a listed financial services business, with $1 billion in assets, in pre-bankruptcy proceedings.
The Lawyers: Described by interviewees as "*one of the state's kings for debtor work,*" **Ray Shapiro** (see p.1537) maintains his high-profile role in the billion-dollar US Gen New England case. He has also had a key role acting as counsel to the liquidator of Reliance Insurance Company. One client described **Tom Biron** as an attorney who creates "*well-wrought cases and fights tooth and nail for every issue he needs to.*" He successfully represented Great American Insurance Company in the AP Green asbestos-related bankruptcy. The case settled and a protective order was issued preventing future claims against the insurance company. Biron is also respected for his work in isolating problematic assets in businesses with a history of mass torts, and for his expertise in indenture trustee work in connection with restructurings. Chair of the restructuring and bankruptcy group **Bonnie Fatell** (see p.1523) storms into this year's *Chambers'* rankings on the back of outstanding peer feedback. Though primarily acting out of Delaware, she has also been highly visible in Philadelphia where she acts for a plethora of debtors, creditors and related committees. This "*terrific*" lawyer is also an accomplished litigator.
The Clients: Philip Services; US Gen New England; LTV Steel and TWA.

Duane Morris LLP
See firm details p.1550
The Firm: The firm, and the bankruptcy team in particular, has experienced sustained growth over recent years, and the group now employs more than 50 lawyers, who are active in New York, Boston, Chicago, San Diego and Miami. Importantly, the cross-functional nature of most of the members' practices has meant that it has been less exposed to the vagaries of the economy. Since its involvement in the far-reaching bankruptcies of Enron and Adelphia, the group has also played a role in some of the market's other high-profile cases. It acted for Lucent Technologies in the bankruptcy and subsequent reorganization of Leap Wireless, where it successfully negotiated a complex settlement agreement with the debtors. The firm was also involved in the Integrated Health Services and Kmart bankruptcy cases. Peers described the team as "*a superb choice as local counsel in national, and even international cases.*"
The Lawyers: Though generally less visible on the regional stage, **John Horstmann**'s (see p.1527) involvement in three of the most high-profile Chapter 11 cases – Enron, Adelphia and Federal-Mogul – marks him out as "*a really superb practitioner, capable of cutting a route through even the densest problems.*" He represents numerous insurance businesses and financing institutions, including a major European bank, in a range of secured lending and credit enhancement deals. According to peers, **Margery Reed** (see p.1535) provides "*assured and technically superior*" advice to secured creditors, financial institutions and lenders. She also represents insurance companies acting as secured parties in bankruptcy cases such as that of Delaware Ribbon Manufacturers. She has completed numerous out-of-court restructurings, and recently represented a surety bond company in connection with the out-of-court restructuring of a building contractor. Commentators were in agreement that **David Sykes** (see p.1539) "*must be included in any review of leading bankruptcy lawyers whilst he still takes on cases: the breadth of his knowledge is staggering.*" Formerly head of the department, which he managed for almost 35 years, his forte lies in the reorganization of major businesses from across all industry sectors.
The Clients: Adelphia Communications; Oxford Finance; Delaware Ribbon Manufacturers; Allegheny Power; Federal-Mogul; Enron and Kmart.

Reed Smith LLP
See firm details p.1560
The Firm: The expansion of the firm in terms of lawyers, clients and offices has continued apace, and the merger with California-based Crosby Heafey in 2003, has enhanced the bankruptcy practice's profile considerably. One of the most significant mandates for the group in recent times was its representation of the official committee of unsecured creditors in the US Gen New England bankruptcy. This case culminated in the $1.5 billion sale and distribution of assets. Commentators praised the team for its "*healthy profile as a regional, national and even transatlantic player.*" One peer even added: "*The firm has its strategy spot on – it is true to its Pittsburgh roots while also being plugged into the New York and Delaware markets, where a lot of the really serious cases play out.*"
The Lawyers: **Paul Singer** (see p.1537) has an impressive history of counseling clients in a range of heavy industries traditionally associated with Pittsburgh, including steel, aluminum, railroad, cement, pulp and paper. This has given him extensive experience of working with labor unions and governmental agencies, such as the Pension Benefit Guaranty Corporation. "*His*

outstanding reputation translates into exceptional quality work every time," enthuse commentators. **Eric Schaffer**'s (see p.1536) "*indisputably first-rate practice*" has included advising the indenture trustees in the bankruptcy of Weirton Steel. He has also been involved in a number of matters concerning hospitals and other civic properties. Researchers were told he has an exemplary track record in representing secured and unsecured creditors in major bankruptcy cases and nonjudicial restructurings in the full range of industry sectors. Although **Claudia Springer**'s (see p.1538) focus used to be on the secured lender side, she now leans towards representing unsecured creditors, for which she earns high praise as a "*preeminent creditors' committee lawyer.*" Having represented the creditors' committees in the bankruptcies of National Steel, Rouge Steel and Slater Steel, she is, in the eyes of market observers, "*probably one of the state's leading experts on those matters.*" Her workload also includes cases involving entities from other industries, such as manufacturing and healthcare. **Peter Clark** (see p.1521) is the head of the firm's corporate restructuring and bankruptcy group and enters the table following consistently strong feedback from the market. According to commentators, he is "*as good a creditors' side lawyer as you are likely to meet.*" His client roster includes private equity and venture capital businesses, hedge funds, insurance companies and indenture trustees.

The Clients: Wachovia; Weirton Steel; Solutia; Pittsburgh Hockey Associates; National Steel; US Gen New England; US Airways; Anker Coal and Campo Electronics.

Band 2

Adelman Lavine Gold & Levin

The Firm: Like many boutiques specializing in bankruptcy and restructuring, this "*top-notch*" debtor firm has witnessed a slowing of insolvency cases as various economic factors, including lower interest rates, have enabled more and more companies to avoid bankruptcy. However, the team has offset this to a certain extent and had an extremely busy year, particularly in the Wilmington office. The group's particular expertise in asbestos-related proceedings is well documented. For example, this year it represented a manufacturer of spray-on fire resistant apparel in a Chapter 11 asbestos liability case.

The Lawyers: **Barry Kleban** played a central role in counseling the fire retardant apparel manufacturer mentioned above, and recently also acted for the creditors' committee in the restructuring of a large business specializing in bows, ribbons and packaging materials. His clientele is drawn from industries including the food and beverage, healthcare, technology, sportswear apparel and construction sectors. Peers rate him as "*one of the best debtor lawyers

you could hope to have on your side.*" Interviewees commended restructuring specialist **Leon Barson** for his "*excellent touch in sensitive or unusual proceedings.*" A new entrant to the *Chambers*' rankings, he recently worked on an especially complex business restructuring in the healthcare sector for a religious nonmedical center. He won praise from clients for his ability to "*get to grips with the issues very swiftly despite having no prior knowledge of the business.*" Commentators describe debtor specialist **Gary Schildhorn** as "*a tenacious attorney*" who "*works especially hard for his clients' interests.*"

The Clients: The team acts for a range of companies in out-of-court restructurings and insolvency proceedings. Its clients include entities from the industrial garments, healthcare, software, sportswear and construction industries, amongst others.

Cozen O'Connor

The Firm: Commentators say that the group's 12 bankruptcy attorneys "*always seem to punch above their weight.*" The team is generally more visible representing debtors in reorganizations, foreclosures and liquidations, but also acts for creditors' committees and individual investors. The firm was deeply involved in the highly contested Student Finance Corporation case in Delaware. Here the company faced allegations of participating in an illegal 'Ponzi Scheme' to mislead investors by offering an extraordinary return on investments. The group has also been involved in the reorganization of ATA Airlines following its bankruptcy filing.

The Lawyers: The "*cornerstone of the team*" **Neal Colton** has been busy representing several creditor interests in the high-profile US Airways bankruptcy. He has also been involved in an unusual case pending in the Southern District of New York. This concerns new personal injury claims arising out of the asbestos-related reorganization of a major building and specialty products manufacturer 15 years ago. Here, Colton is defending several insurers against additional lawsuits throughout the country, and is attempting to persuade the federal courts to recognize that the claims should be subject to the original bankruptcy court order.

The Clients: Adelphia Communications; Congoleum; Federal-Mogul; Hawaiian Airlines; ATA Airlines; Student Finance Corporation and US Airways.

Dilworth Paxson LLP

See firm details p.1548

The Firm: The team of around 12 partners is based principally in Philadelphia, but the firm also has offices in Delaware and Washington, DC. Commentators highlighted the group's reputation for "*doing an outstanding job in representing the underdog.*" The firm is involved in a number of sizable cases, and has been particu-

larly active in major hotel bankruptcies where it tends to represent the debtor. A recent example is the team's work for Prussia Associates, which has hotel interests in the town of King of Prussia. Interviewees also highlighted the firm's strength in litigated bankruptcy proceedings.

The Lawyers: **Larry McMichael** (see p.1532) divides his time evenly between bankruptcy work and commercial litigation. He notably represented the Rigas family in the Adelphia Communications bankruptcy in New York, and acted as special litigation counsel for a trustee in the Student Finance Corporation case in Delaware. Clients describe him as "*an exceptional guy with a good courtroom manner. He has excellent delivery and is a sharp thinker on his feet.*"

The Clients: The Dick Corporation; General Electric Credit; PNC Bank; Dow Chemical; Union Carbide; Merrill Lynch and Nomura.

Hangley Aronchick Segal & Pudlin

See firm details p.1553

The Firm: The team of three partners and as many associates may not be the largest in the market but according to commentators it has "*rapidly established itself as one of the major players in the state.*" Another interviewee remarked: "*The firm is a magnet for some of the brightest and most creative practitioners out there.*" Its strength in the litigation element of bankruptcy proceedings was on display when it represented the directors of bankrupt financing company, DVI, in the Delaware courts. In what has been generally a quieter year for insolvency lawyers, the firm has also been active advising clients on orderly asset liquidations.

The Lawyers: Described by peers as "*one of the kings of debtor work,*" **Joe Dworetzky** (see p.1522) has enjoyed another highly active year and cemented his reputation as "*one of the most active attorneys currently at work in the state.*" He has developed a forte in healthcare bankruptcy work and during the past year has worked on the complex reorganization of a group of nursing homes. He is also representing two local government agencies, the City of Philadelphia and the School District of Philadelphia, in analyzing best practices in tax collection. **Myron Bloom**'s (see p.1520) full caseload includes representing the creditors' committee of two large, jointly administered hotels at LaGuardia and JFK airports, which are $100 million in debt. He represents groups of creditors in relation to the bankruptcies of Kmart and Fleming Companies. He is also developing niche expertise in the representation of directors and officers in suits brought by bankruptcy trustees. The bankruptcy case of children's clothing manufacturer Kleinert's is one such example.

The Clients: The team has represented individual creditors, groups of creditors and debtors in the bankruptcies of Franks Nursery, Kmart and Fleming Companies. Its workload includes cases in the airline, retail, construction and healthcare sectors.

Morgan, Lewis & Bockius LLP

See firm details p.1556

The Firm: Although the firm is perhaps better known for its performance in the corporate and litigation arenas, observers described its bankruptcy practice as "*a highly capable, if understated resource.*" Lawyers here form part of the firm's network of 60 restructuring attorneys who are based in five offices on both the East and West coasts. The team especially benefits from working closely with the highly regarded New York team, which is under the direction of Richard Toder. The group in Philadelphia is active representing creditors in the provision of secured and unsecured credit. It also counsels clients on the acquisition of assets of distressed companies.

The Lawyers: **Michael Bloom** (see p.1520) has been active in several out-of-court restructurings, notably in the technology sector. He also counseled a large committee of vendors in the prepackaged bankruptcy of Tower Records, which involved the restructuring of the company's bond debt. Interviewees praised Bloom as "*an excellent quarterback in a deal. It's also reassuring to know he's been successful in national cases.*"

The Clients: Wherehouse Entertainment; Air Products and Chemicals; Sony BMG Music Entertainment and Morgan Stanley.

Band 3

Klett Rooney Lieber & Schorling

See firm details p.1555

The Firm: The firm now has offices in Washington DC, Delaware, Pennsylvania and New Jersey and is said to have its finger "*right on the pulse in midlevel bankruptcy work.*" The 13 bankruptcy practitioners here generally act for creditors and financial institutions, but are also adept at debtor representation. A recent example includes acting for the debtor in the reorganization of Voegele Mechanical, a heating and air conditioning business.

The Lawyers: **William Schorling** led the team that counseled Voegele Mechanical on its reorganization. He represents debtors, indenture trustees and secured and unsecured creditors. He is also a highly respected technical witness in bankruptcy proceedings. Clients approved of his "*willingness to roll up his sleeves,*" and added that he is "*always extremely pleasant to deal with.*"

The Clients: Wheeling Pittsburgh Steel; Oxford Finance; Allegheny International; Marvel Entertainment; USN Communications and Johnstown Corporation.

Pepper Hamilton LLP

See firm details p.1558

The Firm: A dedicated team of ten lawyers operates in Philadelphia as part of an overall group of around 30 practitioners located throughout the firm's nationwide offices. The group is skilled in representing troubled companies in out-of-court restructurings and Chapter 11 scenarios where it benefits from the depth and experience of its respected finance unit. Peers agree that the firm is "*a particularly sensible choice*" for creditors' rights work.

The Lawyers: Interviewees described **Gregg Miller** (see p.1533), head of the Philadelphia bankruptcy unit, as "*a quiet man, not given to grandstanding, but who is terrific at just getting the job done.*" His particular spheres of influence lie in healthcare and construction-related insolvencies but he is also experienced in bankruptcies arising out of toxic torts. **Francis Lawall**'s (see p.1530) representation of major oil companies in bankruptcies throughout the country earned him the admiration of peers, who describe him as "*definitely a name on the ascendancy.*" Creditors' rights and bankruptcy work relating to toxic tort liabilities feature prominently in his practice. **Michael Reed** (see p.1535) is President elect of the Pennsylvania Bar Association and won praise from sources as "*a highly active and well-connected player in the state.*"

The Clients: The group acts for commercial lending institutions, indenture trustees, equity holders, government agencies and trade associations.

Stevens & Lee, PC

The Firm: In December 2004 the firm announced its merger with Manhattan-based bankruptcy boutique Salomon Green & Ostrow. This has created a pool of about 20 bankruptcy lawyers in the mid-Atlantic region and, more crucially, enhanced the firm's capabilities in New York and Delaware. The team represented a group of seven real estate partnerships in relation to bankrupt nursing homes that were sold for $25 million. It also played a key role for Mitsubishi Imaging, the largest trade creditor of troubled printing supplier ABDick, in the $40

million sale of ABDick's assets to Presstek. Clients described the team as "*commercially very astute and probably more streetwise than some of its larger rivals.*"

The Lawyers: **Robert Lapowsky** is a popular figure among clients, one of whom described him as "*one of the best bankruptcy lawyers in town.*" He recently counseled Roxborough Memorial Hospital, on the sale of its assets to Tenet Healthcare and its Chapter 11 filing. A versatile practitioner for both debtors and creditors, he also played a key role in the ABDick case, and in the bankruptcy proceedings of Flemings Foods.

The Clients: Riddell Athletic Footwear; IBM Credit; Flemings Foods; Wachovia and Afro-Asian Satellite Communications.

Wolf, Block, Schorr and Solis-Cohen LLP

See firm details p.1562

The Firm: This group of more than ten practitioners is "*still a significant player*" and continues to enjoy its traditionally strong links to the Delaware and New York markets. The group counsels clients from most industry sectors on the acquisition and divestment of distressed assets and bankruptcy litigation. Its workload also includes Chapter 11 and Chapter 13 cases, corporate reorganizations and debt restructurings. Several commentators highlighted its representation of banks and trustees in Chapter 7 proceedings as another major area of strength.

The Lawyers: For many years **Michael Temin** (see p.1539) has been recognized as "*undoubtedly a dean of the Bar.*" Enviably well-connected to a range of civic and corporate organizations, his expertise in representing debtors, creditors and various committees in bankruptcy cases and out-of-court restructurings has been central to the group's reputation.

The Clients: New Era, Raytech and Citibank are among the clients.

Other Notable Practitioners

Andrew Kassner (see p.1528) is cochair of Drinker Biddle & Reath LLP's bankruptcy practice and boasts experience in a prodigious number of Chapter 11 cases. He acts for a complete mix of debtors, creditors and trustees and is an experienced litigator whose knowledge stretches across the healthcare, hospitality, telecommunications and real estate sectors.

CORPORATE/M&A

Pennsylvania
Leading firms (Corporate/M&A)

1 DECHERT *Philadelphia*
MORGAN, LEWIS & BOCKIUS LLP *Philadelphia*

2 BALLARD SPAHR ANDREWS *Philadelphia*
DRINKER BIDDLE & REATH LLP *Philadelphia*
KIRKPATRICK & LOCKHART NICHOLSON *Pittsburgh*
PEPPER HAMILTON LLP *Philadelphia*

3 BLANK ROME LLP *Philadelphia*
BUCHANAN INGERSOLL PC *Pittsburgh*
DUANE MORRIS LLP *Philadelphia*
REED SMITH LLP *Pittsburgh*
WOLF, BLOCK, SCHORR *Philadelphia*

4 COZEN O'CONNOR *Philadelphia*

Leading individuals (Corporate/M&A)

1 ABELSON Barry *Pepper Hamilton, Philadelphia*
GOODMAN Stephen *Morgan Lewis, Philadelphia*
WINOKUR Barton *Dechert, Philadelphia*

2 KLEIN Justin *Ballard Spahr, Philadelphia*
LAWLOR William *Dechert, Philadelphia*
MYERS Marlee *Morgan Lewis, Pittsburgh*
NASSAU Henry *Dechert, Philadelphia*
O'DONNELL G Daniel *Dechert, Philadelphia*
ROMANO Carmen *Dechert, Philadelphia*
SINGER Alan *Morgan Lewis, Philadelphia*

3 BLUME Fred *Blank Rome, Philadelphia*
FRIEDMAN Michael *Pepper Hamilton, Philadelphia*
GARRITY Vincent *Duane Morris, Philadelphia*
RAYMOND III F Douglas *Drinker Biddle, Philadelphia*

4 BRAEMER Richard *Ballard Spahr, Philadelphia*
DENINNO David *Reed Smith, Pittsburgh*
KESSLER Mark *Wolf Block, Philadelphia*
LIPMAN Frederick *Blank Rome, Philadelphia*
MCKENZIE James *Morgan Lewis, Philadelphia*
MCLEAN Michael *Kirkpatrick & Lockhart, Pittsburgh*
THOMPSON Thomas *Buchanan Ingersoll, Pittsburgh*
WEST Ronald *Kirkpatrick & Lockhart, Pittsburgh*

Up-and-coming individuals
SINATRA Geraldine *Dechert, Philadelphia*

Firms and individuals are listed alphabetically in each band.

Band 1

Dechert

See firm details p.1547

The Firm: "*A national, and nationally respected, firm which is going great guns in the public company and private equity arenas,*" is the judgment of many market commentators. The Philadelphia team must be viewed in conjunction with its highly regarded New York team, and, it is notable that the majority of its mandates take place outside of Pennsylvania. One interviewee mused that "*though the M&A team doesn't quite have the cachet of a Skadden Arps, one only has to look at the clientele to see what a very serious player Dechert is.*" The client roster lists numerous Fortune 500 businesses, such as Pfizer, Crown

Holdings and Rohm & Haas, although it is the robust links with leading private equity houses that draws the most attention. Its relationships with the likes of Bruckmann, Rosser, Sherrill & Co; One Equity Partners; Odyssey Investment Partners; Riverside Capital and Citigroup Venture Capital are the envy of most firms. The team counseled private conglomerate Berwind Capital Partners in the $400 million acquisition of adhesives business Elmer's Glue from KKR to supplement its burgeoning consumer products portfolio. The team also represented key client Citigroup Venture Capital in the $1.1 billion acquisition of airline distribution systems business Worldspan from Delta Air Lines.

The Lawyers: According to one client, chairman and chief executive of the firm **Barton Winokur** (see p.1540) is "*one of the best three or four lawyers I have ever seen in my long career*" on account of his ability "*to cut through all of the corporate finance complexities as if they simply aren't there, such that they're all cleared up the next day.*" Dividing his time between Philadelphia and New York, he represents public and private companies, LBO funds and especially venture capital firms in the full range of corporate transactions. **Bill Lawlor** (see p.1530) is widely recognized as "*something of an authority*" in public company M&A work and US federal securities law, and the majority of his cases take him outside of state boundaries. Recent trophy deals include representing key client Crown Holdings on a $5.6 billion acquisition and a $3.2 billion debt restructuring. Chair of the private equity group **Daniel O'Donnell** (see p.1534) also splits his time between New York and Philadelphia. He is perhaps best known in the market for his work with Citicorp's venture capital team. Trophy deals here include advising Citibank in the $900 million acquisition of the non-memory chip business of South Korean-based Hynix Semiconductor. He also guided the same client through the $300 million disposition of the Great Lakes Dredge & Dock Company. Chair of the business department, **Carmen Romano**'s (see p.1536) practice focuses on private and public M&A deals. In a well-publicized recent deal, he counseled Select Medical in its $2.3 billion buyout by private equity giant Welsh, Carson, Anderson & Stowe. Described by peers as "*a highly creative and insightful*" practitioner, he is developing a niche expertise in the restaurant industry, having completed a string of recent such deals. He was lately involved in the sale of the Chevy's Restaurants chain to Real Mex Restaurants, which is controlled by New York-based buyout house Bruckmann, Rosser, Sherrill & Co, for more than $90 million. Having completed his first full year back in practice, **Henry Nassau** (see p.1533) has been involved with the complex bond restructure and recapi-

talization of Internet Capital Group, thus enjoying an unbroken continuity with the business at which he was formerly a senior board executive. His recent caseload has featured several venture capital deals and securities work, in addition to regular corporate mandates. Peers mused: "*Surrounded by so many fellow stars, it is easy to lose sight of the fact that he'd be a dean of any other law firm.*" Observers singled out **Geraldine Sinatra** (see p.1537) as "*one of the most successful young private equity partners*" in Philadelphia. She won particular commendation for her work with Citigroup and its portfolio companies, and also advises on securities and public company governance matters.

The Clients: Pfizer; Crown Holdings; Select Medical; AmerisourceBergen; Rohm & Haas; Starwood Capital Group; Baxter Healthcare and One Equity Partners.

Morgan, Lewis & Bockius LLP

See firm details p.1556

The Firm: The firm's pursuit of a well-ordered growth strategy has realized the opening of new offices in California, Chicago, Dallas and Boston, and also a 20-lawyer satellite in Paris during the year. However, on balance it remains a hybrid between a super-regional brand (it has one of the highest concentrations of East Coast lawyers of any one firm) and a national firm, notwithstanding small offices in London, Paris, Brussels and Tokyo. The corporate team thrives on a diet of M&A transactions of all sizes, Sarbanes-Oxley compliance work, especially Section 404 issues, and emerging/growth company mandates. The latter forte was highlighted by numerous commentators, who were generous in their praise of a team with "*the dominant platform for servicing life science and technology businesses in the state.*" The team has acted in several award-winning transactions in this sector of late, including helping to secure $8 million in funding for Gestalt, a firm that undertakes high-level software application contracts for the US government and for various public utilities. The practice did suffer a reverse in the departure of M&A expert Jeff Klauder to an asset management business. He had returned briefly to the firm after a spell as general counsel of Safeguard Scientifics.

The Lawyers: Interviewees consistently described cochair of the firm's global technology practice **Stephen Goodman** (see p.1525) as "*the man to whom a serious entrepreneur or director of a growth business needs to be speaking.*" The list of successful companies that he has counseled and introduced to venture capital firms is an impressive one, and includes excelleRx, Fiberlink and Prophet 21, which are now acquisitive businesses in their own right. His input was important in securing $4.5 mil-

lion in financing for pre-revenue microchip testing entity DFT Microsystems. During the year **Marlee Myers** (see p.1533) has continued her work as lead outside counsel for US Steel in purchasing National Steel out of bankruptcy. As well as her work for major domestic and global businesses, she is also a highly active lawyer in venture capital-backed transactions, particularly in the technology and life sciences arenas. In addition, she played a key role in the sale of FreeMarkets to Ariba, a leading software sourcing company, for more than $400 million. One client described her as having "*a voracious appetite for keeping ahead of a deal through reading up on best practices and through her knowledge of extra-legal issues, such as business accounting.*" **Alan Singer** (see p.1537) counsels businesses in the full range of corporate governance matters required under the NYSE and NASDAQ auspices. His practice is less focused on transactions than it is on the promulgation of committee charters, guidelines and codes of conduct. During the past year, he has been especially active in assisting companies on various financial reporting matters, particularly on the exacting rules governing managements' presentation of non-GAAP financial measures. Peers agree that he possesses "*an absolutely unique, encyclopedic brain for securities and stock market disclosure laws.*" **James McKenzie** (see p.1532) is one of several attorneys in the team with relatively recent experience as general counsel in startup operations. He rejoined the practice after a spell as a senior executive at Verticalnet and, according to rivals, "*adds noticeable extra depth*" to the firm's public and private M&A capabilities. He can also boast a successful track record in guiding business through IPOs.
The Clients: Octagon Research Solutions; CDNOW; ARAMARK; Church & Dwight Co; Sandvik; CoManage and Ariba.

Band 2

Ballard Spahr Andrews & Ingersoll LLP
See firm details p.1541
The Firm: This seven-office practice is a popular recipient of referred work from New York-based firms and enjoys a particularly strong profile in the Rocky Mountain states. The team regularly acts as counsel to local businesses on Sarbanes-Oxley work and other corporate governance-related matters, and is sometimes involved as regional counsel to major national and even international entities. Recent highlights for the practice include advising specialty chemicals business Hercules on a $250 million Rule 144A securities resale. It also represented regular client Nature's Sunshine Products on a sizable issuer tender offer, another deal which highlighted the firm's preeminence in the field of securities.

The Lawyers: Head of the securities group **Justin Klein** (see p.1528) is "*an operator of the highest quality,*" according to interviewees. Although his practice spans across regular M&A work and advising growth businesses, especially technology entities, it is his "*absolutely flawless*" knowledge of securities laws that wins him the strongest market approbation. He recently represented Sinoco in two issuer tender offers, and in the simultaneous sale of securities for an aggregate value of $400 million. He also acted for insurance holding company PMA Capital Corporation in its recent strategic amendment to exchange offer of bonds for securities. Cochair of the M&A group **Richard Braemer** (see p.1520) drew praise for his "*highly impressive lateral thinking in extremely knotty transactions.*" He counsels buyers and sellers in a variety of corporate and real estate financings, restructurings and joint ventures.
The Clients: DuPont; PMA Capital Corporation; Nature's Sunshine Products; Metrologic Instruments; Janney Montgomery Scott; Toll Brothers and Sinoco.

Drinker Biddle & Reath LLP
See firm details p.1549
The Firm: The "*extraordinarily good*" team meshes with the wider corporate and securities unit, such that its lawyers are equally at home with IPOs, securitizations, and other capital markets-flavored work, as they are with joint ventures, mergers and divestitures. The team is also a respected authority on the Sarbanes-Oxley Act, other corporate governance laws and related litigation. Market sources highlighted the team's "*great culture that makes people love to work there and clients want to do business.*"
The Lawyers: Head of the firm's corporate and securities division, **Doug Raymond** (see p.1535) focuses on acquisitions, notably leveraged transactions, and securities-related mandates. One of "*Drinker Biddle's finest,*" according to several commentators, his reputation is such that "*he will speak at a securities seminar and people will go far out of their way to attend.*"
The Clients: Comcast; Chubb Group; GlaxoSmithKline and Johnson & Johnson.

Kirkpatrick & Lockhart Nicholson Graham LLP
See firm details p.291
The Firm: The firm has come a long way since its modest post-war Pittsburgh and Washington origins. The recent merger with respected UK-based firm Nicholson, Graham & Jones has capped a period of several years in which Kirkpatrick's has been successfully pursuing a national growth strategy. The united firm now operates out of 11 offices and employs almost 1000 lawyers; ensuring it is fully equipped to handle a range of transactions at an international level. This adds to the firm's already wide-

ly acknowledged strengths in litigation and insurance work, for which reason the strategic marriage has been generally very well received by market commentators. The firm's national profile does not promote state by state analysis since the teams are generally less visible at the regional level, but even a cursory glance at the client roster reveals the underlying strength of the firm. It has recently represented Allegheny Technologies, the leading US specialty steel producer, in connection with the asset acquisition of J&L Specialty Steel, one of the largest US stainless steel makers and a subsidiary of Arcelor. One interviewee noted: "*They are a great choice for uniform commercial code business transactions, and would make any seller, no matter how large, feel comfortable.*"
The Lawyers: **Michael McLean**'s (see p.1532) broad practice encompasses M&A, buyouts, notably ESOP leveraged transactions and various restructuring matters. He recently acted for Weirton Steel as DIP in its sale to International Steel Group for approximately $300 million. **Ronald West** (see p.1540) played a pivotal role in the Allegheny Technologies deal highlighted above. His practice blends corporate and securities work, particularly IPOs and private placements of debt, equity and other securities, and he is also an accomplished restructuring lawyer.
The Clients: Park Corporation; United Technologies; Weirton Steel and Education Management Corporation.

Pepper Hamilton LLP
See firm details p.1558
The Firm: Four of this firm's ever-expanding 11 offices are based in the state. The Pittsburgh team was recently strengthened by the arrival of the highly experienced Damian Georgino, formerly a partner at LeBoeuf, Lamb, Greene & MacRae. Former Dechert partner Sharon Klein also joined the department, basing her practice out of Newport Beach and Philadelphia. She brings to the group her experience of IP matters in the context of transactions. Its deal flow in terms of both public and private M&A and especially private equity-related mandates has been consistently strong over recent years. The team has lately completed a flurry of transactions on behalf of listed REIT Brandywine, culminating in the $600 million acquisition of a portfolio of 14 office properties in Philadelphia and Wilmington.
The Lawyers: **Barry Abelson** (see p.1518) and **Michael Friedman** (see p.1524) continue to receive much of the praise extended to the firm's practice. They were involved in many of the firm's most significant recent mandates, including Sungard's $584 million acquisition of SCT, and medical device-maker Animas' IPO for about $60 million. Friedman focuses his practice on corporate governance, M&A and securities matters, and he is also well versed in dealing

with REITs. Peers acknowledge: "*He may well be a future dean of the Bar.*" **Barry Abelson** is "*a tremendous lawyer and a leader of the legal community,*" according to admiring peers. His forte is counseling growth companies and smaller public entities in securities, venture capital and M&A deals.

The Clients: The team is a popular choice for businesses seeking finance or private equity funds making investments, such as Advent International. It acts for several REITs, notably Brandywine Realty Trust, and its industry clients feature medical products companies, retailers, software developers, manufacturers and automotive suppliers.

Band 3

Blank Rome LLP
See firm details p.1542
The Firm: The team now operates out of three offices in the state and 11 others concentrated on the East Coast. Recent highlights include representing Omega Financial in its acquisition of Sun Bancorp, a deal which creates one of the largest bank holding companies in central Pennsylvania by bringing together two $1 billion bank holding companies. The team also acted for TransCore Holdings in its $612 million sale to international engineering products business Roper Industries.
The Lawyers: Managing partner and chief executive **Fred Blume** (see p.1520) devotes much of his time to high-level administrative duties, but is respected by peers for his M&A work where his clients range from small businesses to major listed companies. "*He's a phenomenally busy and talented guy,*" say peers. **Frederick Lipman** (see p.1530) manages a particularly broad practice that sees him representing businesses in a range of M&A, securities, litigation and insurance matters, as well as lecturing on issues such as US IPOs in the Far East. He lately counseled a business that converted into a master LLP and went public in a $75 million IPO.
The Clients: SunGard; ARAMARK; StoneMor Partners; IKON Office Solutions; Genesis Health Ventures; Omega Financial and TransCore Holdings.

Buchanan Ingersoll PC
See firm details p.1544
The Firm: The firm's corporate and technology division comprises nearly 60 lawyers based across its 13 offices in six states. The Harrisburg office was recently strengthened by the arrival of well-regarded corporate practitioner Michael Hund from Reed Smith, and the New York and Tampa offices have benefited from the arrival of experienced M&A attorney Sanford Hausner. Commentators describe it as "*a premier Pittsburgh firm,*" and it is in this city that most of the

lawyers are located. Following its role in the highly successful IPO of Dick's Sporting Goods, the firm also acted in the retailer's acquisition of Gaylans for $800 million. The group also continues to work with health insurance giant Highmark in its major joint venture in northeastern Pennsylvania.
The Lawyers: According to peers, **Thomas Thompson**'s (see p.1539) strengths lie in his "*eye for the minutiae and, of course, spotting potential pitfalls in any deal.*" He centers his practice on M&A transactions, securities matters and special committee work, especially related to corporate governance issues. He was recently involved in the sale of a resort for more than $130 million, and the sale of a financial services company for $300 million.
The Clients: CJ Betters Enterprises; Dick's Sporting Goods; Highmark; Cendant; Gene Logic; Hershey Foods; Kennametal and McDonald's.

Duane Morris LLP
See firm details p.1550
The Firm: Described as "*a hungry, successful and growing*" firm, the corporate division now employs more than 30 lawyers in the state who integrate into a network of well over 500 lawyers in 20 US offices. Traditional strengths lie in the technology and telecom sectors, though the client base is a broad one. The team's consistently strong deal flow is supplemented by extremely highly respected finance and restructuring teams and, as in those practice areas, the attorneys are regarded as "*well rounded*" and proficient in many aspects of transactional work.
The Lawyers: Of counsel **Vincent Garrity** (see p.1524) maintains an "*excellent profile at the Bar,*" according to commentators, on account of his "*didactic knowledge of the academic aspects of the law, as well as familiarity with the realities of deal-making.*" He has been active in numerous revisions and reviews of corporate and banking transactional and regulatory laws, and has acted in numerous substantial acquisitions in recent times.
The Clients: BMW of North America; JPMorgan Chase; IKON Office Solutions; GMAC and PNC Bank.

Reed Smith LLP
See firm details p.1560
The Firm: Traditionally regarded as "*an extremely strong player*" in Pittsburgh, this international firm now employs more than 1000 lawyers in its 16 offices nationwide. Its broad client base includes businesses in the heavy industry, energy, real estate, pharmaceutical, educational and retail sectors, and it can also handle deals with a trans-atlantic element on account of its two well-established UK offices. One recent deal, which demonstrated the team's ability to handle complex and high-caliber deals,

was the representation of a major Pittsburgh-based REIT in a $1.1 billion merger with a Philadelphia-based REIT.
The Lawyers: Interviewees regard chairman of the firm's business and regulatory department **David DeNinno** (see p.1522) as "*a very accomplished lawyer and a pleasure to do business with.*" His extremely broad practice encompasses general M&A work, leveraged finance transactions, public offerings, venture capital and alternative lines of financings particularly for young and dynamic businesses.
The Clients: Mellon Financial; Wachovia; Crown American Realty Trust and Carnegie Mellon University.

Wolf, Block, Schorr and Solis-Cohen LLP
See firm details p.1562
The Firm: Now operating out of eight offices on the East Coast, market sources describe the firm as "*a sensible choice for lower/midlevel regional transactions,*" and the corporate & securities team has an impressive record in representing young e-commerce, biotech or technology companies. Other areas of strength include the team's experience in public finance transactions and corporate governance matters.
The Lawyers: Sources endorsed **Mark Kessler** as a "*well-connected and extremely personable attorney.*" His caseload leans towards M&A and public and private financing and he enjoys especially robust relationships with numerous leading private equity and venture capital houses, such as Toll Brothers, Compass Capital and Franklin Mutual.
The Clients: The AMC Group; Toll Brothers; Legg Mason Wood Walker; Comcast; Compass Capital Advisors and Osage Investments.

Band 4

Cozen O'Connor
The Firm: Now employing more than 450 lawyers in 20 US offices, the firm has long since developed a reputation beyond its traditional strengths in litigation and insurance. It also has an office in the UK that it has partnered in deals involving businesses listed on the London Stock Exchange. The business law team has had success in attracting lawyers from rival firms in the state and has emerged as a well-respected player, particularly for representing young regional businesses and entrepreneurs. Commentators also acknowledged that the department's lawyers are broad in their experiences and able to advise on areas such as tax, insurance and elements of capital markets work.
The Lawyers: Former Wolf Block lawyer, and chair of the firm's emerging companies and venture capital practice, Michael Heller advises growth businesses on their corporate transactions and business strategies.

The Clients: The client roster includes numerous venture capital and private equity houses, and growth businesses and entrepreneurs seeking such funding. Local, public and private businesses of all sizes also feature on the list.

EMPLOYMENT

Pennsylvania
Leading firms
(Employment: Mainly Defendant)

[1] **MORGAN, LEWIS & BOCKIUS LLP** *Pittsburgh*

[2] **BALLARD SPAHR ANDREWS** *Philadelphia*
BLANK ROME LLP *Philadelphia*
KLETT ROONEY LIEBER & SCHORLING *Pittsburgh*
REED SMITH LLP *Pittsburgh*

[3] **BUCHANAN INGERSOLL PC** *Pittsburgh*
COHEN & GRIGSBY PC *Pittsburgh*
DECHERT *Philadelphia*
KIRKPATRICK & LOCKHART *Pittsburgh*
LITTLER MENDELSON PC *Pittsburgh*
PEPPER HAMILTON LLP *Philadelphia*

Leading individuals
(Employment: Mainly Defendant)

[1] **DICHTER Mark** *Morgan Lewis, Philadelphia*
GIOTTO Thomas *Klett Rooney, Pittsburgh*
HARTLE MUNSCH Martha *Reed Smith, Pittsburgh*
WALL Steven *Morgan Lewis, Philadelphia*

[2] **BEVAN III William** *Reed Smith, Pittsburgh*
BROWN James *Cohen & Grigsby, Pittsburgh*
CONNORS Eugene *Reed Smith, Pittsburgh*
FELIX H Thomas *Ballard Spahr, Philadelphia*
FOLEY Mark *Klett Rooney, Philadelphia*
FRITTON Karl *Reed Smith, Philadelphia*
HORNAK Mark *Buchanan Ingersoll, Pittsburgh*
KATZ Carole *Morgan Lewis, Pittsburgh*
LADOV Donald *Cohen & Grigsby, Pittsburgh*
OLSON Stephen *Kirkpatrick & Lockhart, Pittsburgh*

[3] **BERKOWITZ Alan** *Dechert, Philadelphia*
COSTELLO Joseph *Morgan Lewis, Philadelphia*
D'ANGELO Alfred *Klett Rooney, Philadelphia*
DAVIS Doreen *Morgan Lewis, Philadelphia*
HALLER Anthony *Blank Rome, Philadelphia*
JARIN Kenneth *Ballard Spahr, Philadelphia*
KANE Jonathan *Pepper Hamilton, Berwyn*
LANGEL John *Ballard Spahr, Philadelphia*
MURPHY Terrence *Klett Rooney, Pittsburgh*
OSSIP Michael *Morgan Lewis, Philadelphia*

[4] **BISSOON Cathy** *Reed Smith, Pittsburgh*
HANLON Michael *Blank Rome, Philadelphia*
HARRIS Judith *Morgan Lewis, Philadelphia*
MALLOY Elizabeth *Klett Rooney, Philadelphia*
O'REILLY Timothy *Morgan Lewis, Philadelphia*
RICHEY P Jerome *Buchanan Ingersoll, Pittsburgh*
SULLIVAN James *Klett Rooney, Philadelphia*
ZONN Sidney *Littler Mendelson, Pittsburgh*

Individuals are listed alphabetically in each band.

Band 1

Morgan, Lewis & Bockius LLP
See firm details p.1556

The Firm: Described as a *"giant that has consistently maintained its prominence,"* the firm continues to keep an edge on its competitors on account of its *"sheer weight of numbers and caliber of lawyers."* The predominantly Philadelphia-based team is frequently involved in some of the most complex and large-scale employment litigation nationwide. In the employment litigation arena, the firm has been particularly notable for its involvement in high-profile gender discrimination cases. In keeping with the general increase in wage and hour-related disputes, the firm regularly represents companies in employee benefits class actions. The group has also been highly visible in medical benefits, representing a number of clients against charges by former employees. Additionally, the firm boasts a leading employee benefits practice, and a number of its attorneys are specialists in the ERISA area. Among the highlights for the team here has been its success in a number of class actions where plan participants challenged the prudence of 401(k) investments in company stock.

The Lawyers: Regarded by some interviewees as *"the best employment lawyer in the world,"* **Mark Dichter** (see p.1522) is said to represent the quality of the practice *"like nobody else."* Both clients and peers praised him for his *"superb interpersonal skills, his extraordinary intellect and dedication,"* which allow him to *"leave no stone unturned."* He is regularly visible in cases out of state, and is perhaps best known for his representation of Morgan Stanley against the EEOC, in which the latter brought a class action on behalf of several hundred women claiming gender and sex discrimination in compensation and promotions. This was the largest case ever brought by the EEOC and the first of its kind to go to trial before the federal district court. Dichter was instrumental in having the case settled. He is currently handling a case in Alabama and is also engaged in an employment discrimination case in Chicago. Interviewees had great praise for practice leader **Steven Wall** (see p.1539), describing him as a *"top-notch advocate who is always at ease in the boardroom and whom companies and senior employees trust."* Wall primarily oversees the strategic, day-to-day operation of the practice across each of the firm's offices, but also handles class-based discrimination and collective bargaining issues in federal and state courts and before administrative agencies. Wall has also advised clients for over 20 years in NLRA-related cases, and discrimination and preventive labor relations matters. Described as an *"exceptionally effective"* lawyer, equipped with *"great intellectual and intuitive ability,"* interviewees also observed that **Carole Katz** (see p.1528) is *"easy to sit down and talk with."* She came to prominence when she won a *"terrific"* discrimination case for one of the largest pharmaceutical companies in the world, Sanofi-Aventis. She was also extensively engaged in handling a number of Merrill Lynch arbitrations pursuant to gender discrimination class actions. Chair of the firm's ERISA litigation practice, **Joseph Costello** (see p.1522) continues to act on the *"front line"* of that area of the law. In the high-profile Unisys retiree medical benefits litigation he successfully represented the corporation in this recently decertified multi-district class action. The case centered on the retirees' challenge of Unisys' decision to replace its numerous retiree medical benefit plans with a comprehensive plan. He devotes the balance of his practice to advising senior executives in contract termination suits and in negotiating compensation packages. Interviewees praised **Doreen Davis** (see p.1522) as a *"leader in the NLRB area,"* particularly on account of her skills in collective bargaining negotiations. Davis is best known for her role in one of the largest cases ever to come out of the Philadelphia region before the National Labor Relations Board, which involved millions of dollars in potential compensation. Peers were *"mightily impressed"* with **Mike Ossip's** (see p.1534) *"very fine"* counseling skills. Clients appreciated his *"practical and pragmatic mentality,"* and relayed to researchers his extensive experience representing employers in wrongful discharge matters. Additionally, he has negotiated numerous collective bargaining agreements and regularly advises employers on union-organizing campaigns. Interviewees praised **Judith Harris** (see p.1526) as *"a joy to work with,"* and highlighted her *"tremendous credibility"* with judges. A former general counsel for the City of Philadelphia, she now represents employers in matters broadly ranging from discrimination to trade secrets and employee benefits cases. According to interviewees, **Timothy O'Reilly** (see p.1534) is one of the *"premier"* traditional labor lawyers, and he specializes in the often delicate relationships between employees and management. He frequently handles NLRB proceedings and

Pennsylvania
Leading individuals (Employee Benefits)

1 **BERNARD** John *Ballard Spahr*, Philadelphia
  LICHTENSTEIN Robert *Morgan Lewis*, Philadelphia
  RUDOLPH Andrew *Pepper Hamilton*, Philadelphia
2 **ABRAMOWITZ** Robert *Morgan Lewis*, Philadelphia
  JONES David *Dechert*, Philadelphia

Individuals are listed alphabetically in each band.

coordinates union avoidance campaigns. Described as a *"top-notch attorney who is also pragmatic, aggressive and a good negotiator,"* **Bob Lichtenstein** (see p.1530) is the managing partner of the firm's 70-strong employment benefits practice, which was the first of its type to be established in the state. The team can also exploit a team of around 12 *"sophisticated"* non-lawyers who counsel clients on such diverse matters as retirement plans, fiduciary duties and executive compensation. Lichtenstein himself also specializes in equity and incentive compensation plans, ERISA and qualified retirement plans, and frequently litigates employee benefit claims and disputes. Peers regard **Robert Abramowitz** (see p.1518) as *"the leading and best-known"* attorney in the state for his representation of clients in the healthcare arena. His large clientele also includes a number of tax-exempt organizations and NGOs that he represents in such matters as pension-sharing plans. Additional spheres of activity include the fiduciary law aspects of ERISA, executive compensation plans, welfare benefit plans and retiree health plans.

The Clients: Merrill Lynch; Unisys; CIGNA; New York Life; The Vanguard Group; The PNC Financial Services Group; Unilever; Subaru; Kimberly-Clark; Landstar; Union Pacific; Chico's Stores and Hilton Group.

Band 2

Ballard Spahr Andrews & Ingersoll LLP

See firm details p.1541

The Firm: Described as a *"very strong"* labor law firm with a *"host of leading practitioners,"* the firm maintains a prominent profile in the field. Boasting one of the largest employment practices in the state, the firm draws clients from the manufacturing and heavy industry sectors to non-governmental organizations. Representing the Commonwealth of Pennsylvania, the team negotiated a novel agreement with the police force regarding the contributions to its healthcare plans. Additionally, the firm has particular expertise in the health sector representing a number of hospitals in the state on all their employment and labor issues. The litigation team undertakes a significant amount of counseling work for clients, and handles the full range of discrimination cases.

The Lawyers: Commentators singled out senior partner **Thomas Felix** (see p.1523) for his *"effectiveness in acting as key negotiator"* in protracted collective bargaining negotiations with unions and in arbitrations. An adviser to the City of Philadelphia for over 35 years, Felix counseled the police force of the Commonwealth of Pennsylvania on significant healthcare contributions matters. Highly respected for his *"fluency with the language of unions,"* Felix is currently in negotiations regarding hospital employee contributions at the largest hospital in the state. Highly praised **Kenneth Jarin** (see p.1527) is a member of the Anti-Defamation League's national executive committee and serves as treasurer to the Democratic Governors' Association. His practice incorporates counseling clients on matters related to FLSA and FMLA legislation, and he is also chief labor negotiator for the Commonwealth of Pennsylvania and the City of Philadelphia. Interviewees complimented *"top-drawer attorney"* **John Langel** (see p.1529) on his *"considerable business acumen"* and his awareness of *"servicing clients' interests with transparency and integrity."* In recent years, Langel assumed a high-profile standing in the legal community for his representation of the US Women's Soccer Team, which he advised in relation to post-Olympic tour fees. He also acted as key negotiator for professional female soccer players in their negotiations with the soccer league, specifically on contractual matters. According to interviewees, **John Bernard** (see p.1519) is the *"dean of the benefits world."* Described as *"very accomplished and active"* in representing investment companies and mutual funds, he can draw on more than 30 years' experience in the field. His practice incorporates diverse aspects of employee benefits law, such as qualified retirement plans, stock option plans, executive and deferred compensation arrangements and healthcare benefits. This year he has worked closely with the Pension Benefit Guaranty Corporation (PBGC) on several corporate transactions, and counseled the body on its retirement plan funding for state and government entities. He is also increasingly involved in public sector work, which sees him counseling subdivisions, counties and schools.

The Clients: The Commonwealth of Pennsylvania, the US Women's Soccer Team and a range of private and state universities and banks are notable members of the firm's clientele.

Blank Rome LLP

See firm details p.1542

The Firm: Interviewees reserved particular praise for the firm's labor law team, reporting that *"they don't come any better than that."* Despite the departure of Barry Bevacqua earlier in the year, the attorneys maintain a prominent profile through work in a wide range of cases. The firm has become increasingly involved in large class actions representing large financial institutions nationwide. On the labor law side, the firm has recently represented Altec Industries in protracted negotiations and collective bargaining agreements for the southern division, and it has also handled its related litigation. The group also represented key client Moran Towing in labor and employment matters in its dealings nationwide.

The Lawyers: The *"strategic and highly professional"* **Anthony Haller** (see p.1525) is experienced in both litigation and traditional labor law matters, and is renowned for his handling of controversial matters in multiplaintiff actions. He notably represented a client accused by several parties of having discriminated against them in the workplace, on the grounds of race, whistle-blowing, retaliation and defamation. Furthermore, Haller is also heavily involved in the traditional labor law arena, and recently represented Altec Industries, among others, in the complex negotiation of a collective bargaining agreement. More recently, he handled an appeal against a several million-dollar verdict at trial on behalf of Unisys in the Sixth Circuit Court of Appeals. **Michael Hanlon** (see p.1526) is mostly involved in counseling employers confronting union-organizing efforts and spends a substantial portion of his time negotiating collective bargaining agreements and advising senior management on personnel policies. Renowned for his *"controlled aggression"* in the courtroom, he is equally at home developing and delivering training courses to management regarding personnel issues and litigation avoidance.

The Clients: Insurance, pharmaceutical companies and receivable waste management companies feature on the client roster, and its public sector clientele includes the Philadelphia School District.

Klett Rooney Lieber & Schorling

See firm details p.1555

The Firm: The Pittsburgh-based labor team of 40 lawyers won client approval as *"an extremely professional and savvy outfit."* In a market in which employers in all industries have been striving to trim costs, the firm has been particularly busy in negotiating collective bargaining agreements, most recently with several hospitals. The team has also been engaged in a substantial amount of gender discrimination issues involving high-level executives, and remains visible in cases relating to the manufacturing and heavy industry sectors.

The Lawyers: Said to be *"made for labor negotiations,"* the *"cool-headed, extremely detailed and superb negotiator"* **Tom Giotto** received overwhelming praise from both clients and peers. His strong counseling and negotiation skills have ensured him an unabated workload in the traditional labor arena. Building on his long-standing contacts with unions, he continues to negotiate collective bargaining agreements on behalf of clients in the healthcare, manufacturing and chemical industries. Most recently, he has been engaged in representing troubled companies in protracted collective bargaining negotiations. Additionally, he represents employers in suits involving race, sexual harassment, age and disability discrimination claims. "*Highly talented labor negotiator*" **Mark Foley** ascends the rankings on the back of praise for his "*sensitive handling of clients.*" He has particular experience of guiding employers through NLRA, FLSA and Title VII legislation. Praised as a "*fantastic negotiator*" at the firm, shareholder of the Philadelphia office **Alfred D'Angelo** has been a driving force in the firm for more than 30 years. In addition to advising private employers, he represents a number of public agencies in collective bargaining and employment litigation in Pennsylvania and Delaware. His area of expertise also includes the 1964 Civil Rights Act and the Age Discrimination in Employment Act. Applauded for his "*strong interpersonal skills,*" cochair of the group **Terrence Murphy** is renowned for his knowledge of civil rights issues, and regularly advises employers on their equal employment and affirmative action obligations. **Elizabeth Malloy** was singled out for her "*meticulous trial preparation*" and her skill at depositions. Boasting a long track record of successes, her practice focuses on sexual harassment, race, national origin, disability and age discrimination cases and associated litigation. Partner **James Sullivan**'s main focus is on counseling clients on both employment and labor law issues. He boasts an extensive courtroom experience, having advocated on behalf of employers in state as well as in federal courts.

The Clients: HCR Manor Care; Merit Capital Partners; Cornell-Abraxas Group and Equitable Resources.

Reed Smith LLP
See firm details p.1560

The Firm: According to interviewees, the firm "*dominates the Pittsburgh market,*" in part because of its "*wonderful historic reputation*" and partly because of its strength in niche areas, such as in ERISA litigation. The firm is also still active in traditional labor law and its lawyers frequently argue before the National Employment Board. The firm predominantly draws its clientele from the manufacturing, construction, chemicals, public utilities and financial services industries. The team recently helped Rhone Capital to obtain the agreement of all unions and employees to terms and conditions of employment, including pay structures, at a new acquisition. The firm has also been at the forefront of overtime pay disputes, notably representing a nationwide retailer in a suit filed by former employees charging that the employer had failed to pay millions of dollars in federally

required overtime pay for a sustained period of time. The attorneys were able to have the suit dismissed in its entirety, saving its client substantial legal costs and millions of dollars in potential liability. In addition, the firm has been active in the private sector where it has represented municipal governments in their dealings with union and nonunion employees. The highly regarded litigation group has handled hundreds of equal opportunity cases on both the trial and appellate levels in federal and state courts and administrative agencies locally and nationally.

The Lawyers: Described as a "*tough, responsive and highly intelligent*" lawyer, **Martha Hartle Munsch** (see p.1526) maintains a high profile in employment discrimination lawsuits. In addition to having litigated a significant number of equal opportunity cases both at trial and appellate levels, she has also represented clients in wrongful discharge, breach of contract and defamation actions. In recent years, she has become increasingly involved in college and university work, representing higher education employers on matters ranging from sexual harassment, tenure revocation and tenure denial litigation, as well as academic and scientific misconduct matters. One client credited **William Bevan** (see p.1519) as being "*one of the most intelligent people I have ever met.*" Described as a "*very methodical lawyer*" with a "*great knowledge of current federal and state law,*" Bevan remains highly active in labor law, especially in negotiations with trade unions. He is also active in representing unionized construction contractors on the requirements for an acceptable bargaining unit. Characterized as an "*outstanding all-rounder*" who "*puts an enormous amount of depth into all of his work,*" **Eugene Connors** (see p.1522) continues to represent clients in high-stakes employment litigation disputes. Highlights over the past year include representing Rhone Capital in its purchase of Alcoa's worldwide specialty chemicals business. In this matter he acted as chief negotiator of the group in obtaining union and employee consent to the wage reductions and other changes at Bauxite, Arkansas, one of the company's main facilities. Connors is presently engaged in the merger of two major hospitals, as part of which he provides strategic planning advice and recommendations, as well as bargaining advice. **Karl Fritton** (see p.1524) enjoys a healthy reputation in labor law, particularly in collective bargaining disputes, and in litigation before the NLRB, state and federal courts. He has worked with some of the largest trade unions nationwide, such as the USWA, UAW, Hospital Workers Union and the SEIU. In addition to her management duties, **Cathy Bissoon** (see p.1519) concentrates her practice on all types of employment litigation with a specific focus on sexual harassment issues.

The Clients: The firm acts for a broad range of organizations, including trade unions, nationwide retailers, hospitals, municipal governments and the Pennsylvania State System of Higher Education.

Band 3

Buchanan Ingersoll PC
See firm details p.1544

The Firm: Clients were particularly impressed with the "*spectacular job*" the firm does at handling labor contracts. Said to have an "*invaluable knowledge*" of unions, the firm is developing a reputation for its proficiency in labor contract negotiations, and lately acted for a large broadcasting company in relation to union section issues. Despite the recent departure of two partners, the nine-strong Pittsburgh team maintains a respected profile within the state and is ably supported by a six-attorney unit in Philadelphia. Reflecting a general national trend, the team is handling more class actions than ever before and is increasingly being retained to represent employers with respect to wage and hour laws. The firm also houses an active employee benefits group, which has a full workload in developing plans and programs on behalf of clients.

The Lawyers: Known as a "*marvelous*" lawyer who counsels clients "*ethically, fairly and aggressively but always with a human touch*" **Mark Hornak** (see p.1527) remains one of the firm's most familiar names, especially for his niche media and broadcasting practice. He represents a large public agency in the state and has handled employment litigation for such significant publications as The New York Times and The National Enquirer. Most recently, he has been appointed as a Special Master by federal and state courts in class actions and employment litigation. **Jerome Richey** specializes in covenants not-to-compete, another niche area of the practice. He also represents employers on trade secrets cases, handles complex commercial and construction litigation and frequently takes on professional malpractice suits.

The Clients: The team acts for a range of financial services companies, manufacturers, insurance providers, accounting firms, national broadcasters and publishers.

Cohen & Grigsby PC

The Firm: Interviewees remarked upon the firm's "*significant market presence*" in the healthcare industry and its strength in traditional labor law. The firm has lately taken on several cases alleging reverse employment discrimination of males who are suing companies for sexual harassment. Other notable cases include representing a university in a sex discrimination case filed by six female faculty members claiming to have been overlooked for promotion on account of their gender. The group also guided a hospital through an extraordinarily complicated and protracted collective bargaining agreement with the largest registered nursing unit in the state consisting of 1500 staff.

The Lawyers: Interviewees described **Donald Ladov** (see p.1529) as a *"highly practical"* lawyer who has been at the forefront of his field for many years. He is predominantly active in healthcare cases, particularly representing hospitals and institutions in collective bargaining negotiations. He is also extremely well-versed in cases brought before the NLRB and EEOC and OSHA-related. Described as a *"truly outstanding counselor,"* **James Brown**'s focus has switched to mediation and alternative dispute resolution. He regularly counsels clients on the minimization of discrimination liability and on the likelihood of litigation as a result of restructurings at all levels. He played a key role in the success of the sex discrimination suit mentioned above, which was later reaffirmed by the Federal Court of Appeals.

The Clients: The team counsels healthcare companies and providers, manufacturers, businesses in the fishing industry and restaurants.

Dechert
See firm details p.1547

The Firm: The team is perhaps best known for representing employers in class actions and in individual litigation. In keeping with the distinguished clientele serviced by the firm's marquee corporate department, the employment team also acts for a number of multinational giants, including Boeing, and Siemens, for which it handles matters ranging from sexual harassment to gender, race and disability discrimination. One of the firm's most recent successes has been a summary judgment verdict on all claims in favor of Boeing in a significant race discrimination class action, McClam-Brown v Boeing. Another highlight for the firm was its representation of Fox Television Stations of Philadelphia, defending the network against charges by a main anchor who alleged reverse racial discrimination in this high-exposure media case. The firm is also known for its extensive ERISA practice and is currently representing the principal defendants in several high-profile ERISA class actions.

The Lawyers: Described as the *"calmest person in the country"* who is *"fabulously thorough"* and *"watches your money carefully,"* **Alan Berkowitz** (see p.1519) continues to head the nine-strong team of employment lawyers. In addition to acting on behalf of the firm's most significant clients in employment law disputes, he also provides extensive labor advice involving complex union issues. In this respect, he most recently advised an international conglomerate in connection with its purchase of a large, multifacility operation from one of the Big 3 US automakers. Berkowitz also continues to handle all of GlaxoSmithKline's employment litigation

and is increasingly involved in executive contract litigation. Chair of the employee benefits team, **David Jones** (see p.1527) focuses on counseling clients on pension plans, equity and executive compensation. He also provides robust support in M&A transactions, particularly in relation to private equity mandates and contractual matters.

The Clients: Aside from such household names as GlaxoSmithKline, Boeing and Siemens, the firm also counsels water resources providers, consulting companies and universities.

Kirkpatrick & Lockhart Nicholson Graham LLP
See firm details p.291

The Firm: Headquartered in Pittsburgh, the team has 25 lawyers practicing full time, and another 23 lawyers practicing certain elements of labor and employment law. Commentators praised the firm for its ability to guide clients through cases at the more complex end of the spectrum. The team recently conducted a nationwide audit of a major listed client's payroll practices to assist the company in its obligations to comply with the state and federal wage and hour laws. Another significant success was the summary judgment it secured for the Allegheny Ludlum Corporation in a discrimination lawsuit, a verdict that was subsequently upheld on appeal to the Federal Court of Appeals. The firm is also active in counseling clients at all stages of employment disputes, and its regular training sessions on employment matters to its clients are highly respected.

The Lawyers: Clients were particularly impressed with **Stephen Olson**'s (see p.1534) ability to *"put himself in the client's shoes"* and by his *"excellent rapport with judges and juries."* Aside from handling the full range of labor and employment law matters, his niche expertise of the Railway Labor Act occupies a significant proportion of his workload. He defended a national, publicly traded corporation that was sued for violation of the FLSA in the WESCO Distribution class action, and on two occasions Olson's arguments were key in the denial of class certification.

The Clients: Allegheny Ludlum; PPG Industries; Dell and WESCO Distribution.

Littler Mendelson PC

The Firm: The firm is now home to nearly 400 attorneys in 28 offices across the United States, and is a highly regarded player in the Pennsylvania market. The team lately enhanced its profile with the addition of two Philadelphia-based partners to its team of *"pretty darn good attorneys."* The team is particularly noted for its employment litigation practice, representing employers in discrimination claims before local, state and federal agencies and courts. The firm has a vibrant labor law unit that frequently practices before the NLRB in representation pro-

ceedings and unfair labor practice cases. Another area of expertise for the team is the negotiation of collective bargaining agreements with trade unions.

The Lawyers: Described as a strong lawyer with *"an engaging personality,"* **Sidney Zonn** is involved in all aspects of the firm's labor and employment law practice. Based in Pittsburgh, he has been increasingly engaged in wage and hour investigations with the DOL. Zonn devotes a substantial portion of his practice to counseling clients on general labor relations and equal opportunity policies, and also regularly conducts training sessions with an emphasis on practical responses to employment issues in the workplace.

Pepper Hamilton LLP
See firm details p.1558

The Firm: The *"extremely responsive team"* won approval for *"always keeping clients fully abreast of how their cases are proceeding."* Although the makeup of the team has undergone some changes over the past year, it still has nine partners who dedicate themselves exclusively to labor and employment law. The firm has a particular expertise in representing clients in highly charged sexual harassment cases and in their efforts to defeat union-organizing, specifically in the manufacturing industry. In a highly controversial and protracted case, the firm represented an investment company in a sexual harassment case, and drafted in a forensic expert to successfully establish that the claims were untruthful. The firm remains highly active in the healthcare sector and scored a recent success when it represented a hospital in defeating union-organizing attempts by the maintenance workforce.

The Lawyers: Commentators described head of department **Jonathan Kane** (see p.1528) as a *"very shrewd, smart practitioner, similar in style to Jimmy Stewart,"* and he continues to handle the firm's most headline-grabbing cases. He is currently engaged in representing another major law firm in a sexual harassment suit against its partners, and lately completed contract negotiations on behalf of a small truck drivers' unit, successfully defeating several union-organizing attempts by an influential union at one of its facilities. In another high-profile case, he represented a client in defeating two separate organizing attempts by the UAW to organize different plants in several parts of Michigan. Interviewees praised **Andrew Rudolph** (see p.1536) for *"combining great technical working knowledge and skill with a creative approach and a fantastic understanding of client needs."* Rudolph is the chairman of the 14-strong unit, and his work focuses on the development of programs relating to employer securities or benefits based on the employer's performance. Recent highlights include representing a leading international pharmaceuticals business with more than 22,000 US employees on all aspects of executive compensation and employee benefits, particularly ESOP and safe harbor 401(k) plans, as well as the conversion of traditional cash balance pension plans.

The Clients: In addition to such house hold names as Comcast, GlaxoSmithKline, AmerisourceBergen and Alco Industries, the client roster features businesses in the pharmaceutical sector, public utilities entities, wholesale clothing manufacturers, real estate trusts and hospitals. Other clients include: Main Line Health; Wawa; UGI and Teleflex.

ENVIRONMENT

Pennsylvania
Leading firms (Environment)

1	**BABST, CALLAND, CLEMENTS** *Pittsburgh*
	MANKO, GOLD, KATCHER & FOX *Bala Cynwyd*
2	**BALLARD SPAHR ANDREWS** *Philadelphia*
	DRINKER BIDDLE & REATH LLP *Philadelphia*
	WOLF, BLOCK, SCHORR *Philadelphia*
3	**DECHERT** *Philadelphia*
	KIRKPATRICK & LOCKHART NICHOLSON *Pittsburgh*
	MORGAN, LEWIS & BOCKIUS LLP *Harrisburg*
	SAUL EWING LLP *Philadelphia*
4	**FOX ROTHSCHILD LLP** *Philadelphia*
	KLETT ROONEY LIEBER & SCHORLING *Pittsburgh*
	MONTGOMERY, MCCRACKEN, WALKER *Philadelphia*
	REED SMITH LLP *Pittsburgh*
5	**JONES DAY** *Pittsburgh*
	LANGSAM STEVENS & SILVER LLP *Philadelphia*
	SCHNADER HARRISON SEGAL *Philadelphia*

Firms are listed alphabetically in each band.

Band 1

Babst, Calland, Clements and Zomnir, A Professional Corporation

The Firm: This is the dominant name in the Pittsburgh environmental Bar, and market commentators across the state concur that the "*extremely experienced*" and "*cost-conscious*" professionals at the firm know environmental law "*like the back of their hands.*" With a niche in the west of the state, the firm conducts only 20% of its business in Pennsylvania. The lion's share of the work undertaken by the group sees it involved in cases on both the East and West Coasts. Occasionally it is involved in international matters in Europe. Regional cases in the past twelve months include representing a large Superfund settlement as well as various other recycling projects.

The Lawyers: Head of this flourishing practice is **Chester Babst**. The past year has seen him handle one of the largest civil penalty claims ever brought by the State of Pennsylvania. "*Ubiquitous*" on the Pittsburgh scene, the venerable Babst commands a great deal of respect from peers for his abilities in the field. Interviewees are consistently impressed by **Dean Calland**'s prowess in his specialized practice and consider him the greatest expert in brownfield redevelopment in the southwestern part of the state. He focuses on hazardous and toxic sub-

stance regulation and enforcement under RCRA, CERCLA, Toxic Substances Control Act and related federal and state legislation in the chemical, plastics, petroleum and metal industries. Up-and-comer **Kevin Garber** is described by market commentators as "*just great*" at the civil litigation and transactional elements of the practice. This "*high-quality*" lawyer has recently dealt with a substantial amount of toxic tort work and current cases have involved legislation over asbestos exposure. With a practice focused on utilities, natural gas and electrical work, **Don Bluedorn** is involved in numerous aspects of environmental law. He receives particular acclaim for his work in wastewater management, site remediation, and hazardous and non-hazardous waste issues. The "*highly experienced*" **Lindsay Howard** receives acclaim for his work in the commercial landfill arena. He is also visible in complex site remediation, solid/hazardous waste, and occupational safety and health issues. The "*extremely thorough*" **Joe Reinhart** has a background in mining and his practice focuses on areas of environmental law that concern the siting, operation and development of mines, solid waste facilities, petrochemical facilities and brownfields.

The Clients: Beazer East and Hall Corporation, national manufacturers, chemical companies and utilities entities feature on the client roster.

Manko, Gold, Katcher & Fox LLP

The Firm: A hugely busy year for this much celebrated Philadelphia firm has seen it involved once more in a large number of high-profile cases. Its "*ingrained*" market share has grown over the past twelve months with two new senior lateral hires bolstering the boutique's established stable of "*top-flight*" environmental experts. The team recently successfully represented a client in an insurance coverage dispute regarding the remediation and redevelopment of a large Superfund site, the first in the federal court system to determine the extent of an insured's coverage under a cost-cap policy. The "*seasoned environmental practitioners*" of the group enjoy a consistent flow of referrals from generalist competitors, who laud the firm for its consistent "*excellence and specialized expertise.*"

The Lawyers: Interviewees remarked on the cohesive nature of the firm's leading lights **Joe Manko** (see p.1531) and **Marc Gold** (see p.1525), who are described as "*cut from the same*

cloth." Manko is praised across the board for his remediation work as "*one of the biggest names on the field.*" A relatively new addition to the team is the "*dynamic*" **Robert Fox** (see p.1524), who is considered by market commentators to be "*a face card of the firm.*" Considered the putative heir to the team's reputation, Fox is described as "*smart and capable*" and an astute decision-maker. **Bart Cassidy**'s (see p.1521) engineering education and experience have proved a valuable asset in providing environmental regulatory counseling to satisfied clients, particularly in the highly technical realm of air quality control. He is presently involved in litigating environmental matters before federal and state courts and administrative tribunals and is particularly knowledgeable on matters of ambient and indoor air quality law. Widely respected in the market and considered on a par with Robert Fox is the "*superb*" **Mike Meloy** (see p.1532). He is able to leverage his engineering background for clients in connection with a broad spectrum of environmental litigation, regulatory and transactional issues. Experienced in dealings with numerous redevelopment and remediation projects, he is actively involved in the development and implementation of waste management programs in Pennsylvania. He has also handled health and safety matters arising under the OSHA. **Bruce Katcher**'s (see p.1528) practice addresses contaminated site assessment and remediation, solid and hazardous waste, air and water pollution control, Superfund, coastal zoning and wetlands matters. He also counsels clients on regulatory compliance, including environmental auditing and compliance management system development.

The Clients: The firm acts for a stable of clients ranging from major Fortune 500 companies to smaller local concerns.

Band 2

Ballard Spahr Andrews & Ingersoll LLP

See firm details p.1541

The Firm: Of the 25 dedicated environment lawyers across the country, more than ten are situated in Harrisburg, Pittsburgh and Philadelphia. This large, full-service firm enjoys an outstanding reputation at the environmental Bar on the strength of its highly prized political connections and well-developed practices in

Pennsylvania
Leading individuals (Environment)

[1] **BABST III Chester** *Babst Calland*, Pittsburgh
BARNETT Bonnie *Drinker Biddle*, Philadelphia
CALLAND Dean *Babst Calland*, Pittsburgh
MANDELBAUM David *Ballard Spahr*, Philadelphia
MANKO Joseph *Manko Gold*, Bala Cynwyd
WESTON Timothy *Kirkpatrick & Lockhart*, Harrisburg

[2] **BROOMAN David** *Drinker Biddle*, Berwyn
FOX Robert *Manko Gold*, Bala Cynwyd
GARBER Kevin *Babst Calland*, Pittsburgh
GOLD Marc *Manko Gold*, Bala Cynwyd
RICHMAN Hershel *Dechert*, Philadelphia
WARREN Kenneth *Wolf Block*, Philadelphia

[3] **BERGÉRE Timothy** *Montgomery*, Philadelphia
BOLSTEIN Joel *Fox Rothschild*, Atlantic City
CASSIDY Bart *Manko Gold*, Bala Cynwyd
JUDGE John *Montgomery McCracken*, Philadelphia
MELOY Michael *Manko Gold*, Bala Cynwyd
MIANO Steven *Wolf Block*, Philadelphia
MILLER Alan *Picadio Sneath*, Pittsburg
NAUGLE Louis *Reed Smith*, Pittsburgh
WEIN Howard *Klett Rooney*, Pittsburgh
WOELFLING Maxine *Morgan Lewis*, Harrisburg

[4] **BLUEDORN II Donald** *Babst Calland*, Pittsburgh
BOSSERT Terry *Post & Schell*, Harrisburg
COHEN Abbi *Dechert*, Philadelphia
COLLINGS Robert *Schnader Harrison*, Philadelphia
COLLINS Brendan *Ballard Spahr*, Philadelphia
EVERETT Carl *Saul Ewing*, Philadelphia
HINERMAN Philip *Fox Rothschild*, Philadelphia
HOWARD Lindsay *Babst Calland*, Pittsburgh
KATCHER Bruce *Manko Gold*, Bala Cynwyd
O'DEA Joseph *Saul Ewing*, Philadelphia
RADER Kermit *Wolf Block*, Philadelphia
REINHART Joe *Babst Calland*, Pittsburgh
SARACHAN Ronald *Ballard Spahr*, Philadelphia
STEVENS Mark *Langsam Stevens*, Philadelphia
STOVIAK John *Saul Ewing*, Philadelphia
STUART Glen *Morgan Lewis*, Philadelphia
TOLL Curtis *Greenberg Traurig*, Philadelphia
UBINGER John *Jones Day*, Pittsburgh

Individuals are listed alphabetically in each band.

both Pennsylvania and New Jersey. The "*total package*" offered by the group guarantees a broad range of litigation expertise on tap and a noted strength in the environmental development field. Interviewees remarked upon the team's particular strength in environmental criminal defense. The team is currently handling numerous transactional mandates and cases resulting from the problems within current environmental operations, rather than the detritus left by older cases.
The Lawyers: Dominating the environmental field is the "*technically adroit, snappy*" and "*well-connected*" **David Mandelbaum** (see p.1531). A "*top-notch*" player in the market, he is known for his "*incredible grasp*" of complex contamination matters, and clients are attracted to his "*funny and charming*" demeanor. Coordinating the

firm's petroleum products practice is **Brendan Collins** (see p.1521), who combines his experience in the disciplines of litigation, real estate and environmental law to provide clients with "*a truly exemplary service.*" He also has experience in the firm's government enforcement and white-collar crime and telecommunications practice areas. **Ron Sarachan** (see p.1536) is the "*go-to guy*" for environmental white-collar crimes. With a glittering reputation as one of the state's "*very best*" environmental specialists, he has carved a name for himself with his deft handling of investigative proceedings and his sympathetic manner: "*He inspires a lot of confidence in the clients.*" Peers and clients concur that "*he sees all the angles from where he is sitting.*"
The Clients: Sunoco; Exelon; Bechtel; BP; Glatfelter and Raytheon.

Drinker Biddle & Reath LLP
See firm details p.1549
The Firm: Respected throughout the state, this group has a name for its "*creative*" approach to environmental issues. A broad and well-respected national practice provides deep resources and bolsters the environmental practice in its provision of services. Its areas of strength include environmental and toxic tort litigation and the efficient coordination of land development approvals. The "*capable and diligent*" group works closely with the corporate, real estate and banking teams to provide a full-service product. Peers agree that they would refer clients to the group in particularly "*nettlesome*" situations. The team has dealt with environmental due diligence cases and addressed regulatory compliance for multibillion-dollar acquisitions involving multiple research and manufacturing sites.
The Lawyers: The "*energetic and bright*" **Bonnie Barnett** (see p.1519) is an expert in brownfield development and is described by peers as "*just a phenomenal personality in her field.*" She has undertaken significant redevelopment projects for the firm, one being a large new housing undertaking within the city limits of Philadelphia on formerly environmentally complicated land. She serves a broad client base that for the most part comprises sizable local and national companies in the industrial or manufacturing sectors. Thought of by peers as a "*tough competitor but always a joy to work with,*" Barnett receives accolades for her "*fantastic litigation skills*" and has a reputation for her congeniality and ability to facilitate multiparty interactions. **David Brooman** (see p.1520) is lauded for his litigation skills and expertise in the field of solid wastes.
The Clients: Pennsylvania Waste Industries Association; Merck; Millennium Chemicals and ICI Americas.

Wolf, Block, Schorr and Solis-Cohen LLP
See firm details p.1562
The Firm: This group is seen by peers to be once more enhancing its visibility on the environmental scene. Returnees to the firm Steve Miano and Ken Warren are now firmly re-established as the practice's leading lights and are helping to propel the group into a second ascendancy. Peers note its particular prowess in the water work arena. Operating out of offices in Harrisburg, Norristown and Philadelphia, the firm generates a significant presence in the southern region of the state. A noteworthy utilities clientele that has been growing steadily over the years generates much of the firm's regional business. The group comprises former attorneys for government agencies and represents a diverse group of clients including a federal interstate agency.
The Lawyers: The "*magnificent*" **Kenneth Warren** (see p.1539) enjoys a national reputation, and is renowned for his "*exemplary*" work on Superfund sites. Warren's reputation for "*logical superiority*" is noted as the driving force behind the firm's ascendancy. Cochair of the practice group, Warren has extensive experience that includes appearance as lead counsel in the prominent Superfund case USA v Atlas Minerals & Chemicals. Cochair of the practice **Steve Miano** (see p.1532) has influence in water resourcing, permits for water discharges and enforcement matters. **Kermit Rader**'s (see p.1535) practice focuses on the environmental aspects of real estate and corporate transactions. With a solid reputation for his work in the Superfund and hazardous waste arenas, Rader "*really knows his stuff.*"
The Clients: The team represents a range of industrial corporations and developers.

Band 3

Dechert
See firm details p.1547
The Firm: This "*hard-hitting*" national player is lauded for its big-ticket work for both domestic and international clients. Calling on resources of considerable depth, the firm can leverage off its substantial corporate practice. The environmental practice is unsurprisingly closely associated with M&A and transactional work, and attracts the attentions of numerous Fortune 100 companies involved in superfund matters. Much of the work the practice undertakes involves ongoing compliance issues. It also handles historic cases on behalf of the firm's stable of corporate clients and litigation and regulatory permitting work for standalone clients. The firm is gaining more work in the renewable energy sphere.
The Lawyers: The "*prominent*" **Hershel Richman** (see p.1535) works for a number of local municipalities in the litigation enforce-

ment arena. In high demand because of an upturn in the market, especially in development matters, this "*smart and capable*" attorney litigates and offers counsel to local municipalities, although the bulk of the firm's clients are to be found beyond Philadelphia. The "*simply wonderful*" **Abbi Cohen** (see p.1521) is well known for her transactional work. This leader in the field combines her practice with the firm's finance, real estate and securities groups, and her work reflects the firm's distinct business focus. A "*renowned spokesperson*," she has received particularly enthusiastic plaudits for her involvement in the negotiation of one of Pennsylvania's first prospective purchaser agreements with the state environment agency.

The Clients: Crown Cork & Seal; Pfizer; Southwest Delaware County Municipal Authority; Delco Remy International and Stepan Company.

Kirkpatrick & Lockhart Nicholson Graham LLP
See firm details p.291

The Firm: The merger of Kirkpatrick and Lockhart with London-based firm Nicholson Graham has enhanced the group's size across the firm's 11 offices to 65 lawyers, who concentrate on environmental and natural resource issues. The team has recently been selected as the convergence counsel for a significant national energy company. Considered a "*very fine practice*," the Pittsburgh group was described by peers as both large and effective and a "*perfect foil*" to the "*great*" Harrisburg office.

The Lawyers: Universally acknowledged by interviewees as the "*best water lawyer in the state*," the "*bright and knowledgeable*" **Timothy Weston**'s (see p.1540) academic reputation precedes him. He has recently represented multiple electric generation projects and is currently working for a consortium of steel, automobile and water industries in a major policy change. Known to be the "*very best of the best*" at regulatory work, this "*top-notch*" practitioner is considered "*head and shoulders*" above others in his field.

The Clients: Nestlé Waters North America; Aventis Pasteur; Allegheny Technologies; Constellation Power Source and Pennsylvania Suburban Water.

Morgan, Lewis & Bockius LLP
See firm details p.1556

The Firm: Backed by the "*first-rate hub*" of the firm's nationwide environmental practice in Washington DC, the Philadelphia team does not fail to receive praise from clients for its consistent provision of a "*truly exemplary*" service. The environmental practice's deep-seated resources reside in an efficient network of offices in the region, between which much interaction goes on. The group covers litigation, transaction and regulatory matters. The practice comprises over 100 attorneys nationwide, and its "*storming*"

team handles an increasing amount of real estate-related work in the Pennsylvania region.

The Lawyers: The litigation "*star*" resident in the firm's Philadelphia office is the "*hyper-efficient*" **Glen Stuart** (see p.1538). His consistently active practice has remained steady over the past year and has seen him doing a lot of work for AstraZeneca in a number of historic Superfund cases. Dedicated environment specialist **Maxine Woelfling** (see p.1540) is very highly regarded within the private sector and public agencies. She has been extensively involved in counseling clients regarding the remediation and reuse of former brownfields and other contaminated properties under Pennsylvania's innovative Land Recycling Act. Market commentators laud her "*practical, amiable and well-organized*" demeanor and pragmatic approach to clients' affairs.

The Clients: The firm tackles environmental issues for a comprehensive range of both public and private concerns.

Saul Ewing LLP
See firm details p.1561

The Firm: Peers say that the reputation of this mid-Atlantic focused firm "*is on the ascendant*" as its portfolio expands to embrace a growing volume of prominent brownfield work. For the most part, this workload comprises transactions involving properties that have environmental issues.

The Lawyers: **John Stoviak** (see p.1538) is the leader of the firm's trial team, and is regarded by peers as a "*fairly aggressive lawyer but a good man to go up against*." In the remediation of the number one Pennsylvania Superfund site in York County, he acted as lead lawyer and head of the industrial solvents and chemical group. Stoviak managed this case, which initially involved over 1000 potentially responsible parties. He has also successfully defeated a series of challenges to a major municipal services contract for the City of Allentown. He has been actively involved, for various clients, in at least 20 Superfund sites. **Carl Everett** (see p.1523) works in the realms of regulatory compliance and has extensive experience in tort litigation and enforcement. Also a member of the Texas bar, he undertakes a fairly substantial amount of work in the state for heavy industry clients. According to market commentators, the "*highly reputable*" **Joe O'Dea** (see p.1534) plays "*a perfect foil*" to Stoviak. He represents the nation's largest environmental services company in more than a dozen private cost recovery actions in jurisdictions throughout the Northeast.

The Clients: Piper Group; Clean Earth; Stabilus and National Realty.

Band 4

Fox Rothschild LLP
See firm details p.1552

The Firm: This well-regarded regional practice has recently bolstered its strength through the addition of environmental capabilities to the Wilmington office. The firm is known for its exemplary work in the regulatory and compliance arenas that it undertakes for a number of large national clients. It also undertakes significant work for an environmental consulting group which uses dredged mining materials in redevelopment activities. The team in Pennsylvania is also able to draw on the substantial resources of the New Jersey practice.

The Lawyers: Peers laud **Joel Bolstein** (see p.1520) as the prime partner at the firm for environmental matters. He continues to handle a significant amount of brownfield redevelopment work, in addition to his mix of regulation and litigation work. A recent project taken on by Bolstein involved the development of a former industrial site into a residential property. Peers describe him as an "*extremely proficient lawyer*." **Philip Hinerman** (see p.1527) has extensive experience in environmental regulatory litigation and receives accolades for his "*direct and focused*" approach.

The Clients: Piper Group; Clean Earth; Stabilus and National Realty.

Klett Rooney Lieber & Schorling
See firm details p.1555

The Firm: Focusing on the west of the state, the environmental lawyers at the firm are well versed in the areas of compliance, and commercial and real estate transactions.

The Lawyers: Interviewees praised the "*well-connected*" **Howard Wein** for his familiarity with the inner workings of government agencies and his "*up-to-the-minute*" knowledge of new regional environmental legislation. Wein tackles a significant workload of water quality, waste management, mining and air quality work.

The Clients: Waste management companies, developers, manufacturers and mining companies comprise a significant portion of the firm's clients.

Montgomery, McCracken, Walker & Rhoads, LLP

The Firm: This "*well-respected*" team is renowned for its compliance work and "*solid*" experience in Superfund litigation. Regularly counseling clients on all aspects of environmental law from criminal enforcement to real estate transactions, the team offers multidisciplinary solutions to a wide variety of environmental problems. Clients also comment favorably on the firm's "*savvy*" white-collar criminal defense practice.

The Lawyers: Former chair of the practice group is **Timothy Bergère**, whose areas of specialization include site remediation and environmental risk management. **John Judge** spearheads the practice group within the litigation department. He has represented clients in the gamut of environmental law issues with an emphasis on hazardous waste and clean water regulation, as well as Superfund cost recovery actions and toxic tort actions.

The Clients: IKON Office Solutions, Thyssen Krupp Budd; Cognis; Brenntag Northeast; Hercules Cement and various municipal authorities.

Reed Smith LLP
See firm details p.1560
The Firm: Representing clients in a wide range of environmental and related matters, including enforcement actions, permitting matters and state and federal rulemakings, this national player looks after the interests of major US waste management companies. A significant part of the team's current caseload involves regulatory and compliance matters, including assisting businesses in interpreting and understanding the complex maze of environmental laws and regulations. While this is not among the most frequently quoted names in the niche environment arena, the "*versatile*" team has a sizable practice in the region.
The Lawyers: Formerly of the Department of Environment Protection is the "*exceedingly professional*" **Louis Naugle** (see p.1533). He has provided environmental due diligence assistance for clients and has been involved in transactions dealing with the transfer of industrial and commercial property in more than 40 states, as well as Canada, the UK and Europe.
The Clients: Allied Waste Industries; East Penn Manufacturing; Jacuzzi Brands; Valero Energy; Milco Industries and Carmeuse North America.

Band 5

Jones Day
See firm details p.485
The Firm: This national powerhouse is best known for its dynamic Pittsburgh-based litigation team, which fields attorneys from an assort-

ment of backgrounds. Market commentators pinpointed resource management transfers as an impressive area of growth in recent months. The incredible resources that the firm's extensive network of offices affords are manifested in the weighty national and international portfolio of work. One major transaction undertaken by the team over the past year was a transfer of environmental liabilities by the Hall Corporation. The team has also been involved in a several MSOURCE transactions, one of which was valued at over $25 million.
The Lawyers: The coordinator of the environmental health and safety practice in Pittsburgh is **John Ubinger** (see p.1539). Undertaking a great deal of superfund and regulation compliance work, this "*even-handed*" litigator receives particular accolades for his work with liability issues. Handling a significant amount of national work with other lawyers at the firm, Ubinger has been embroiled in an enforcement action in Florida. He has also led on a number of cases for a leading brownfield redeveloper regarding the transfer of liability for an old aluminum mine to Pennsylvania state.
The Clients: Bayer; Kaiser Aluminum; PPG Industries and Temple - Inland Forest Products.

Langsam Stevens & Silver LLP
The Firm: Described by peers as a practice of an "*exceptional*" standard, this firm commands a niche in the insurance referral arena. Offering a number of related services such as advice on the environmental aspects of corporate and real estate transactions, the firm is primarily known for its well-respected litigation team.
The Lawyers: When questioned about the eminent lawyers in the local environmental field, commentators frequently mention **Mark Stevens**. Having formerly served as GE's environmental manager, he is well respected throughout the state as a "*sage and experienced*" practitioner.
The Clients: The firm's clientele ranges from individuals to corporations in a number of varied industries.

Schnader Harrison Segal & Lewis LLP
The Firm: Clients noted this midsized East Coast generalist firm for the emphasis it places on high-quality work at reasonable prices. Receiving particular accolades for its Superfund work, this team undertakes a wide range of projects throughout the area. The business-focused team draws on the expertise of specialists in litigation and real estate among other areas. The team plays an active part in rulemaking decisions and advises clients on environmental audits.
The Lawyers: A former enforcement attorney and manager at the US Environmental Protection Agency, **Robert Collings** (see p.1521) stands at the helm of the firm's environmental practice. His expertise encompasses air, water and solid and hazardous waste issues. He is the national coordinating counsel for environmental matters for a major international manufacturing firm.
The Clients: Manufacturing, transport and real estate clients comprise a significant proportion of the team's clientele.

Other Notable Practitioners
Alan Miller of Picadio Sneath Miller & Norton in Pittsburgh is known for his work in a variety of different technology fields. Renowned as a well-informed and experienced litigator, he "*inspires confidence*" in his clients and is lauded by peers for his "*incredibly in-depth knowledge*" and his complementary ability to translate that knowledge into lay terminology. Greenberg Traurig LLP's **Curtis Toll** (see p.1539) is an "*especially strong*" contracts and transactional lawyer, and has carved a niche for himself in environmentally focused real estate transactions. Peers agree, "*He is truly one of the leading people in the nation doing that type of work.*" Post & Schell's new partner **Terry Bossert** brings to the firm a name for "*instinctively professional and objective advice.*" Until recently a senior member of Stevens & Lee, Bossert focuses his practice on industrial permitting and brownfields work.

INTELLECTUAL PROPERTY

Band 1

Woodcock Washburn
See firm details p.1563
The Firm: Benefiting from more than 60 years of IP expertise, the reputation of this firm is founded upon its experience in patent and trademark law. One of the largest firms of its kind in the mid-Atlantic region, this "*extremely strong*" boutique serves clients on a national and

international basis. An impressive litigation team has won the group numerous plaudits and it distinguishes itself as being one of the only niche firms in the area to attract a stable of household-name international and national clients. The firm is known to be "*excellent technically*" as well as being "*totally committed to the client and thoroughly cost-effective,*" and it is one of only a handful of firms Microsoft turns to for IP counsel.

The Lawyers: Peers laud **Dale Heist** (see p.1526) for his exceptional track record in the field, and one client described him as "*a better litigator than any I've known.*" Best known for his electronics and software work, Heist is also currently involved in a complex polymer-related matter and he has been involved in some of the biggest cases in immunoassay trials. Another prominent member of the litigation group is **Dianne Elderkin** (see p.1523) whose practice

Pennsylvania
Leading firms (Intellectual Property)

1 WOODCOCK WASHBURN *Philadelphia*

2 AKIN GUMP STRAUSS HAUER *Philadelphia*
BALLARD SPAHR ANDREWS *Philadelphia*
CAESAR, RIVISE, BERNSTEIN, *Philadelphia*
DRINKER BIDDLE & REATH LLP *Philadelphia*
RATNERPRESTIA *Valley Forge*

3 BUCHANAN INGERSOLL PC *Pittsburgh*
DUANE MORRIS LLP *Philadelphia*
KIRKPATRICK & LOCKHART NICHOLSON *Pittsburgh*
REED SMITH LLP *Pittsburgh*
WEBB ZIESENHEIM LOGSDON ORKIN *Pittsburgh*

Leading individuals
(Intellectual Property)

Senior Statesman
SEIDEL Arthur *Drinker Biddle, Philadelphia*

1 JACOBS-MEADWAY Roberta *Ballard Spahr, Philadelphia*
MURRAY William *Duane Morris, Philadelphia*
PANITCH Ronald *Akin Gump, Philadelphia*
POKOTILOW Manny *Caesar Rivise, Philadelphia*
PRESTIA Paul *RatnerPrestia, Valley Forge*

2 ALSTADT Lynn *Buchanan Ingersoll, Pittsburgh*
COHEN Stanley *Caesar Rivise, Philadelphia*
COLEN Frederick *Reed Smith, Pittsburgh*
DONOHUE John *Woodcock Washburn, Philadelphia*
HEIST Dale *Woodcock Washburn, Philadelphia*
LAVORGNA Gregory *Drinker Biddle, Philadelphia*
NADEL Alan *Akin Gump, Philadelphia*

3 BERNSTEIN Alan *Caesar Rivise, Philadelphia*
BYRNE Richard *Webb Ziesenheim, Pittsburgh*
CASEY Kevin *Stradley Ronon, Philadelphia*
ELDERKIN Dianne *Woodcock Washburn, Philadelphia*
MCNICHOL William *Reed Smith, Philadelphia*

4 BECK Paul *Paul A. Beck, Pittsburgh*
BELISARIO Martin *Akin Gump, Philadelphia*
GUNDERSEN Glenn *Dechert, Philadelphia*
KOONS Robert *Buchanan Ingersoll, Philadelphia*
KRAMER J Scott *Duane Morris, Philadelphia*
KYPER James *Kirkpatrick & Lockhart, Pittsburgh*
LINDEFJELD Robert *Jones Day, Pittsburgh*
MARSHALL John *Drinker Biddle, Berwyn*
MEADWAY Jay *Ballard Spahr, Philadelphia*
MONACO Daniel *Drinker Biddle, Philadelphia*
NIGON Kenneth *RatnerPrestia, Valley Forge*
PERKINS Harriet *Drinker Biddle, Philadelphia*
ROCCI Steven *Woodcock Washburn, Philadelphia*
TABACHNICK Gene *Reed Smith, Pittsburgh*
WETTACH Thomas *Cohen & Grigsby, Pittsburgh*
YEAGER Robert *Kirkpatrick & Lockhart, Pittsburgh*

Up-and-coming individuals
LAVINE Jordan *Akin Gump, Philadelphia*
PEIRCE Richard *Ballard Spahr, Philadelphia*

Firms and individuals are listed alphabetically in each band.

centers on patent infringement cases in a wide range of industries, including the pharmaceuticals, building materials, surgical and dental products and consumer absorbent products sectors. Described by peers as "*a pioneer for women*

in the business," she enjoys robust relationships with local business, and is particularly known for having fostered a "*great relationship*" with Johnson & Johnson. Her "*up-front, straight down the line*" attitude adds to her reputation for lucidity, and is bolstered by what peers describe as her "*firm mentality*" and "*powerful*" delivery of the facts. Benefiting from a successful background in engineering, the "*awesome*" **Steven Rocci** (see p.1536) counsels a broad range of clients, particularly in the telecom, Internet and consumer products industries. His current primary focus is on patent litigation counseling and procurement. Dispersing his talents between the courts and the counseling stage is "*fine attorney*" **John Donohue** (see p.1522). One of the major rainmakers at Woodcock, his synergy of technological expertise with business acumen has clients lining up to sing his praises: "*He gets straight to the facts and speaks to us in a language we can understand.*"
The Clients: Johnson & Johnson; Philips; Crown Holdings and Bayer.

Band 2

Akin Gump Strauss Hauer & Feld LLP
See firm details p.477
The Firm: This large generalist firm commands a dominant place in the Pennsylvania IP scene, largely through the assimilation of Panitch Schwarze Jacobs & Nadel that merged with the firm in 1999. Particularly prominent in the local patent arena, the 22-member group has filed an impressive number of applications for a variety of new products including migraine treatments, aquarium equipment and embolic protection devices. An increase of activity in the litigation field has prompted the rise of a number of new names in the group. The firm also employs a significant electrical and semiconductor group of specialists whose optics work is lauded by clients as "*exceptional.*"
The Lawyers: "*Eminence grise*" **Ron Panitch** (see p.1534) chairs the transactional IP practice. Researchers were told that his forte is establishing enduring client relations, and competitors were moved to acknowledge that he is "*incredibly good at what he does.*" Panitch represents a large number of individual professionals as well as major corporations and research institutes. The "*excellent*" **Alan Nadel** (see p.1533) commands a diverse prosecution practice with a current focus on trademarks. He has recently been involved in a patent prosecution over an attic vent baffle, a device designed as a barrier for the retention of heat. Interviewees praised Nadel for his "*wonderful grasp of both chemistry and mechanics.*" Formerly a patent examiner, **Martin Belisario** (see p.1519) has a background in mechanical engineering and is known for his watertight work and forcible attitude. The

"*great*" **Jordan LaVine** (see p.1529) is extremely active in the trademark strategy field. Described by peers as solid and direct, recent successes for Lavine have seen him spearheading the firm's work in the trademark field. He is also noted for his distinguished work in matters regarding the Internet and unfair competition.
The Clients: Aquarium Pharmaceuticals; Colombia University; Universal Lighting; Fisher Price; Lutron and Osram Sylvania.

Ballard Spahr Andrews & Ingersoll LLP
See firm details p.1541
The Firm: This prominent Philadelphia firm handles the full gamut of IP both locally and nationally. The "*vigorous*" group is comprised of more than 20 specialist attorneys whose practices also overlap with related disciplines. This allows for individuals to consult with others in the group and advise clients in a wide range of IP matters. Among the foremost industry areas served by the group are financial services and hi-tech, biotech and electronic games companies. Members of the team also undertake copyright work for a local theater company. The IP group lies within the litigation section of the firm and is continually growing, but its reputation in this field is inextricably linked to its foremost trademarks lawyer, Roberta Jacobs-Meadway.
The Lawyers: According to interviewees "*no one in the city knows more about copyright*" than **Roberta Jacobs-Meadway** (see p.1527). The "*really terrific*" Meadway is the brightest star of the IP group, observers consistently reported. She is presently litigating for a dietary supplement company. She maintains enviably strong relationships with her clients, who agree that "*she really is top of the line.*" **Jay Meadway** (see p.1532) is also a prominent practitioner at the firm and works with major gaming companies and large security firms. Clients enthuse about the capabilities of the husband and wife team: "*They are great attorneys the both of them. They burn my fingers.*" Up-and-comer **Richard Peirce** (see p.1534) is the "*go-to guy*" for Internet-related litigation issues, commentators reported.
The Clients: Spencer Gifts; e-games; The Philadelphia Phillies Baseball Team and Penn National Gaming.

Caesar, Rivise, Bernstein, Cohen & Pokotilow Ltd
See firm details p.1545
The Firm: A venerable name in the Philadelphia scene, this long-standing boutique of 21 lawyers boasts an eminent name for its excellent and diverse practice. Described as "*one of the finest firms in town,*" it has a faithful clientele who remarked upon the attentive nature of the "*gentlemanly*" lawyers. The firm provides patent, trademark and copyright services and has a leaning toward biochemical and pharmaceuti-

cal expertise. The biggest name on the firm's varied client list is Canadian company Apotex, the largest manufacturer of generic drugs in the country. The growing team has recently welcomed another two partners to the fold, putting the total number of specialists at the firm at 26. They also provide counsel on all sorts of IP matters including M&A, employment policies and computer law. Undertaking a significant amount of work for research institutions and academic bodies, the firm can number among its clients the Children's Hospital of Philadelphia and numerous medical schools. Members of the team have also recently dealt with a significant case for a major national manufacturer of security systems.

The Lawyers: One of the senior partners at the firm is the renowned **Manny Pokotilow**. Renowned for his "*engaging and faintly eccentric*" personality, Pokotilow has a reputation for taking on cases that other lawyers might shy away from. He is very active on the local IP scene participating in copyright, patent and trademark litigation. **Stan Cohen**'s (see p.1521) well-regarded practice is divided more or less evenly into litigation trademark prosecution and negotiations relating to patents. Another heavyweight of the group is **Alan Bernstein** whose practice has a heavy emphasis on pharmaceutical work. He also wins praise for his prosecution experience in the hi-tech and biotech arenas.

The Clients: Apotex; Children's Hospital of Philadelphia; Drexel Universities; Wilkes University and QVC.

Drinker Biddle & Reath LLP

See firm details p.1549

The Firm: Since the 2001 merger with boutique firm Seidel, Gonda Lavorgna & Monaco, a number of notable successes in the copyright arena have helped boost this firm's outstanding reputation. One such case involved obtaining a judgment against a business alleged to have been infringing copyrights for carpet patterns. The firm also completes a lot of work in the North East region of the state, and represents a sizable stable of clients both nationally and internationally. Of the firm's 40 IP specialists more than 25 are based in Pennsylvania, and interviewees alluded to a culture of crossover at the firm, with many litigators taking on counseling work and vice versa. The patent capabilities brought in from Seidel have enhanced the firm's profile, and the team continues to expand steadily. Reflecting this trend, the firm's client base is also growing with an increasing number of sophisticated biotech and hi-tech companies coming to the group for their IP concerns.

The Lawyers: One of the best known and longest serving members of the IP Bar is the "*august*" **Arthur Seidel** (see p.1536). A patriarchal figure to many prominent local IP lawyers, Seidel is described as a fantastic resource by both

clients and market commentators and is especially well known for his outstanding and exhaustive opinion work. Long-standing clients of the "*reliable*" and "*laid-back*" **Greg Lavorgna** (see p.1530) sing his praises as their "*preferred referral attorney.*" The "*outstanding*" **John Marshall** (see p.1531) is known for his remarkable "*fight and drive*" in the courtroom. Clients are "*extraordinarily impressed*" by his capacity to rapidly disarm the opposition. Focusing his practice on patent work is **Dan Monaco** (see p.1533) who recently served as counsel in a large lawsuit in Texas that involved a claim for $200 million. He is also extremely well thought of in the biotech and chemical engineering fields. Newcomer to the tables **Harriet Perkins**' (see p.1534) practice concentrates on domestic and foreign trademark prosecution. Formerly an employee of the US patent and trademark office she has extensive experience counseling clients from a wide variety of fields including the health, publishing, insurance, technology, entertainment, banking and FMCG industries.

The Clients: Micro-coax and RetinaPharma are important clients among the small businesses, growth companies and Fortune 500 companies represented by the firm.

RatnerPrestia

See firm details p.1559

The Firm: With a well-established stable of individual lawyers committed to different areas of IP law, this firm draws on its technical breadth and depth to provide a "*top-quality*" niche practice from the suburbs of Philadelphia. Researchers were told that the practice here appears to be moving away from nonprosecution work and licensing to a narrower, more litigation-based part of the market. The past year has also seen the firm move into more progressive areas of the market such as laser physics and acoustics. During the past year, the firm notably represented a supplier of optical fiber cable in a significant patent infringement case.

The Lawyers: Interviewees were warm in their praise of **Paul Prestia** (see p.1534), a familiar figure on the Philadelphia patent scene. His practice sees him involved primarily in the due diligence and patent evaluation stages of prosecution work, and he receives particular accolades for his top-notch opinion writing and advice on matters in prospective or pending litigation. Prestia also gains recognition for his skilled alternative dispute resolution work and valuable counsel in matters pertaining to venture capital matters. **Kenneth Nigon**'s (see p.1533) primary area of expertise is in US and foreign patent procurement, with an especial focus on hi-tech concerns such as machine vision, laser physics and wireless networking. The partners at the firm have seen an increased interest in the hi-tech area of the market.

The Clients: Johnson & Johnson; Boston Sci-

entific; Temple University; Air Products; Arkema; Tate and Lyle; Kulicke & Soffa; Binney and Smith; T-Networks; V-SPAN; Continental Teves; University of Pennsylvania and University of Delaware.

Band 3

Buchanan Ingersoll PC

See firm details p.1544

The Firm: Touted as the primary "*go-to*" IP firm in the west of the state for its securities work, this respected outfit operates offices in both Pittsburgh and Philadelphia. Each site deals with a slightly different genre of clientele. The Philadelphia office handles work for significant names in the chemical industry and the Pittsburgh office has a focus on work related to mechanical and electrical patent work. More than 30 lawyers in the state deal with a range of trade secret, copyright and trademark matters.

The Lawyers: The "*brilliant and demonstrative*" **Lynn Aldstadt** (see p.1518) "*always puts on a very nice show*" for clients, say interviewees. He has coordinated foreign patent litigation on two separate sets of US and corresponding foreign patents. Through this work, he has gained a working knowledge of the structures governing IP courts in all of the major countries of the world. The low-key **Robert Koons** (see p.1528) is lauded as an "*extremely effective litigator with an outstanding understanding*" of the mechanics of litigation.

The Clients: The client roster is drawn from businesses in the medical device, energy conservation, transportation and optics industries.

Duane Morris LLP

See firm details p.1550

The Firm: One of the 100 largest law firms in the country, this firm is well versed in the principle areas of patents, trademarks, copyrights and trade secrets. The firm's lawyers have extensive experience in litigating and trying IP disputes, and represents clients in cases concerning biotech, chemical, computer, electrical and other complex technologies.

The Lawyers: Interviewees claim "*endearing and hard-grafting*" **Bill Murray** (see p.1533) is the "*anchorman*" of the department. His wide-ranging practice encompasses acquisition, evaluation, licensing and enforcement work, and he received accolades for his lucidity and broad technical expertise. Clients also frequently refer to him as an expert witness. **Scott Kramer** (see p.1529) "*gets you the verdict you want,*" interviewees enthused. He successfully represented jewelery giant Tiffany and Co in a dispute with the Morelli company.

The Clients: The firm also caters for clients in the bioscience, electronics and telecom industries.

Kirkpatrick & Lockhart Nicholson Graham LLP

See firm details p.291

The Firm: The aggregate of 950 lawyers formed by the recent merger of Kirkpatrick & Lockhart and English firm Nicholson Graham & Jones now provides the IP team with an exceedingly deep bench of resources. Splitting its practice between transactional and litigious cases, this national powerhouse harbors a stable of 35 patent lawyers and trademark prosecutors across the state. As the eighth largest registering firm of trademarks in the country, interviewees agreed that it lives up to its name as a vigorous IP group. Researchers were told that the lawyers at this "*dynamic and inventive*" outfit have a name for professionalism and taking a no-nonsense approach to their work. Clients acknowledged: "*You may pay through the nose but you certainly get value for money.*"

The Lawyers: Robert Yeager (see p.1540) is a familiar face to many on the IP scene. Over the past year he has appeared as an expert witness in a case involving the interpretation of patents for Singular Wireless. He has also been involved in a patent cover case for a company creating tissue expanders designed to be used in reconstructive breast surgery. Despite his successful and field-specific background in aerospace engineering, **James Kyper** (see p.1529) is currently involved in a number of cases for a wide range of clients, including a mixed issue case in the thermostatic mixing valve industry and a cold formed steel framing matter for Dietrich Industries. Interviewees rate him highly and concurred that "*his profile has definitely risen in recent times.*"

The Clients: Singular Wireless; Carnegie Mellon University; World Wrestling Entertainment; Archer Daniels; Home Box Office; AOL and Dietrich Industries.

Reed Smith LLP

See firm details p.1560

The Firm: The deep bench of this large, general practice, international firm enables it to counsel clients in the full spectrum: copyrights, trademarks, patents and trade secrets. The firm employs more than 30 IP specialists based predominantly in the firm's Pittsburgh and Cleveland offices. In what peers describe as an "*exceedingly good*" year, much of the workload has involved counseling clients on divestitures or company acquisitions. On the litigation side, the group has acted for a Swedish manufacturer of injectable collagen implants in a patent dispute.

The Lawyers: At the helm of the firm's IP group is the highly sought after **Frederick Colen** (see p.1521). He takes an active involvement in litigation and the licensing of proprietary technology both in the USA and abroad. Focusing on pharmaceutical and medical device matters, **William McNichol** (see p.1532) represents numerous drugs and medical device companies and has developed a name for himself as an expert in the fields of dermatology, anesthetics and optics, both at home and abroad. **Gene Tabachnick**'s (see p.1539) presence in the market is thought to be less strongly felt than in previous years, though clients praised his licensing work and his "*unrelenting*" attention to their needs.

The Clients: The group represents a diverse range of businesses, from multinational corporations to academic institutions.

Webb Ziesenheim Logsdon Orkin & Hanson, PC

The Firm: Home to a cohort of "*extremely accomplished*" patent attorneys, this small Pittsburgh firm generated positive feedback for its long-standing reputation as an "*excellent*" local practice and for its competitive rates. Comfort-ably resisting overtures from larger firms interested in assimilating the practice, the firm remains a stand-alone boutique, and has been successful in winning new clients from a diverse range of industries, such as instrumentation and safety equipment companies.

The Lawyers: Richard Byrne concentrates on engineering and technology, and wins approval for his ability to adroitly juggle work in a variety of areas of technical expertise. Aside from his transactional expertise in patent and trademark work, he is also regarded as a successful litigator.

The Clients: Clients range from Fortune 100 companies to individual inventors, notably in the chemical and mechanical engineering sectors.

Other Notable Practitioners

Kevin Casey has boosted the IP profile of Stradley Ronon Stevens & Young, LLP since his arrival in October 2004 from RatnerPrestia. **Paul Beck** of Paul A. Beck & Associates is exceedingly well regarded in Pittsburgh, and has considerable expertise in a full range of IP matters. He is a popular expert witness in patent litigation and trademark litigation cases. **Glenn Gundersen** (see p.1525) of Dechert LLP won a considerable amount of praise in spearheading the firm's geographically diverse trademark and copyright practice. He has counseled clothing manufacturer Totes and worked on a number of cases, including its acquisition by a private equity fund seeking to develop its global brands portfolio. "*Energetic*" **Robert Lindefjeld** (see p.1530) of Jones Day is known throughout the state for his work both at the firm and for a number of Bar associations. Interviewees describe him as "*the hub*" of the firm's statewide IP practice. Devoting the majority of his time to licensing work. **Thomas Wettach** chairs Cohen & Grigsby's IP group. He is known for his "*extremely deft*" handling of midlevel cases.

LITIGATION

GENERAL COMMERCIAL

Band 1

Dechert

See firm details p.1547

The Firm: According to clients, the team is "*terrific at every stage of the process, from case management to pretrial,*" and of course in court. It is acknowledged to be full of "*intelligent, strategic lawyers*" who get involved in some of the most important cases nationwide. These are drawn from a wide variety of sectors, including the media, tobacco, chemical and pharmaceutical industries. Recently, the firm has been expanding its involvement in professional malpractice suits, and has also appeared in a number of major cases in the banking sector. Media-relat-ed disputes have long represented a major source of high-profile instructions for the group, and recent years have proved no different. It notably acted for Philadelphia Newspapers against the Hon Justice James McDermott in one of the longest running libel cases in the USA. The former Pennsylvania Supreme Court judge had sued the Philadelphia Inquirer in 1983 contending that a series entitled 'Above the law' had defamed him. The Dechert team succeeded in securing a new trial, and recently managed to persuade the court to dismiss several of the justice's claims.

The Lawyers: "*Outstanding trial lawyer*" **Robert Heim** (see p.1526) is "*highly respected by peers and members of the bench for his intelligent and effective advocacy,*" agree market sources. He is particularly noted for his niche practice in tobacco litigation, which spans decades and includes work for tobacco giants like Philip Morris. In 2004 he secured a victory for that client in a major case connected with their 'light' brands, resulting in a denial of class action. Outside of tobacco litigation, he acted extensively for Philadelphia Newspapers in the defamation case outlined above. He also assisted Delta Air Lines in a high-profile antitrust lawsuit brought by a class of travel agents. **Joseph Tate** (see p.1539) is said to have "*a special talent as a trial lawyer.*" He continues to be extensively involved in criminal cartel work, and recently defended a large US chemical supplier in connection with a major

Pennsylvania
Leading firms
(Litigation: General Commercial)

1 DECHERT *Philadelphia*

2 BALLARD SPAHR ANDREWS *Philadelphia*
CONRAD O'BRIEN GELLMAN *Philadelphia*
HANGLEY ARONCHICK SEGAL *Philadelphia*
MORGAN, LEWIS & BOCKIUS LLP *Philadelphia*
PEPPER HAMILTON LLP *Philadelphia*

3 AKIN GUMP STRAUSS HAUER *Philadelphia*
BLANK ROME LLP *Philadelphia*
KIRKPATRICK & LOCKHART NICHOLSON *Pittsburgh*
MONTGOMERY, MCCRACKEN, *Philadelphia*
REED SMITH LLP *Pittsburgh*
SCHNADER HARRISON SEGAL *Philadelphia*

4 BUCHANAN INGERSOLL PC *Pittsburgh*
DRINKER BIDDLE & REATH LLP *Philadelphia*
THORP REED & ARMSTRONG *Pittsburgh*

Leading individuals
(Litigation: General Commercial)

Senior Statesman
HARKINS John *Harkins Cunningham, Philadelphia*

1 ARONCHICK Mark *Hangley Aronchick, Philadelphia*
DAVIS Alan *Ballard Spahr, Philadelphia*
HANGLEY William *Hangley Aronchick, Philadelphia*
HEIM Robert *Dechert, Philadelphia*
MATHER Barbara *Pepper Hamilton, Philadelphia*
O'BRIEN William *Conrad O'Brien, Philadelphia*
TATE Joseph *Dechert, Philadelphia*

2 BLACK Allen *Fine Kaplan, Philadelphia*
GELLMAN Nancy *Conrad O'Brien, Philadelphia*
MANNINO Edward *Akin Gump, Philadelphia*
MARION David *Montgomery McCracken, Philadelphia*
SONNENFELD Marc *Morgan Lewis, Philadelphia*
SUPLEE Dennis *Schnader Harrison, Philadelphia*
WYCOFF William *Thorp Reed, Pittsburgh*

3 FEIRSON Steve *Dechert, Philadelphia*
HICKOK Robert *Pepper Hamilton, Philadelphia*
HODGSON Clark *Stradley Ronon, Philadelphia*
KLINE Thomas *Kline & Specter, Philadelphia*
LAUPHEIMER Ann *Blank Rome, Philadelphia*
MCCLENAHAN David *Kirkpatrick, Pittsburgh*
MCGOUGH W Thomas *Reed Smith, Pittsburgh*
REICH Abraham *Fox Rothschild, Philadelphia*
SCHER Howard *Buchanan Ingersoll, Philadelphia*
SITARCHUK Eric *Ballard Spahr, Philadelphia*

Firms and individuals are listed alphabetically in each band.

EU Commission investigation. The team's defense resulted in the full acquittal of the client. This specialty in antitrust and, particularly, price-fixing cases is in addition to a heavy workload in general commercial litigation. Another much-admired lawyer is **Steve Feirson** (see p.1523). He is currently busy representing Sterling Holding Company, an affiliate of Citigroup, in Levy v Sterling Holding Company, a high-profile action brought under Section 16 (b) of the Securities and Exchange Act. The lawsuit centers on the recovery of more than $70 million in profits real-ized from an alleged 'short-swing' purchase and sale of Fairchild stock. The "*highly polished, bright and always available*" **David Howard** (see p.1527) enters the rankings this year for his extensive white-collar crime practice. Clients also praised him for involving them in "*all aspects of the decision-making process.*" Howard has repre-sented defendants in some of the nation's most talked about trials. An example is his work for Timothy J Noonan, former president and CEO of Rite Aid, in criminal and SEC investigations and in civil fraud cases arising from Rite Aid's $1.6 billion restatement of earnings. Mr. Noonan eventually pleaded guilty but was the only one of six codefendants to be sentenced to probation rather than a term in prison. Other recent high-lights include representing Michael J Kopper in connection with the investigation into Enron's securities fraud, and defending QVC, the home-shopping broadcaster, in a civil case alleging deceptive advertising claims about four different product lines. Clients claim that **Christine Levin**'s (see p.1530) "*particular forte is in white-collar criminal matters.*" She predominantly rep-resents clients in the chemical industry and continues to be active in criminal cartel pro-ceedings before the EU Commission.

The Clients: A recent highlight case was Adel-phia v Deloitte Touche. The team represented the former cable-TV provider in a major lawsuit filed in Philadelphia against the company's for-mer auditors.

Band 2

Ballard Spahr Andrews & Ingersoll LLP
See firm details p.1541

The Firm: Peers and clients attested to the firm's "*wonderful reputation*" as a litigation practice, especially noting its expertise in handling mal-practice lawsuits. With 123 attorneys in its Philadelphia office alone, the team has the capacity and expertise to represent clients in cases running from securities class actions and complex SEC proceedings to insurance coverage litigation and professional malpractice. In addi-tion, the group has handled derivatives litigation and ERISA claims and has co-counseled in DOJ proceedings. In line with its sophistication and high-profile workload, the firm is currently co-counseling in litigation relating to Adelphia Communications. Meanwhile, in the profes-sional malpractice arena, it is currently defend-ing a major California law firm against allegations of legal malpractice arising from the settlement of litigation. Another area where the firm enjoys a growing profile is health litigation. Here it has recently been acting as lead counsel in the defense of Jefferson Health System, in a putative class action alleging financial discrimi-nation against uninsured patients.

The Lawyers: Interviewees agree that **Alan Davis**' (see p.1522) "*superior intelligence and common sense*" makes him one of the best lawyers at the Pennsylvania litigation Bar. Whether, as one client claimed, he is "*one of the best lawyers ever*" is open to more doubt. However he is handling many of the state's largest securities defense cases, including representing one of the largest banks in Pennsylvania in SEC proceedings. Davis' portfo-lio also includes the civil aspects of the Adelphia litigation, and his workload encompasses bank-ruptcy, governance and malpractice lawsuits. **Donald Goldberg** (see p.1525) enjoys a reputa-tion in some quarters as the "*number-one white-collar crime attorney in Pennsylvania.*" He was especially admired for his ability to "*come up with solutions and manage to do things that no one else could,*" due to a combination of that "*tremendous experience*" and the indefinable "*magic*" that only great advocates possess. His caseload spans work for state and federal government officials to high-profile white-collar crime defense for individuals in the private sector. **Eric Sitarchuk** (see p.1537) is a new entry in this year's tables, having picked up enthusiastic commendations as an "*extraordi-nary lawyer in cases against the government.*" He is particularly active in the field of white-collar crime; he regularly handles a large volume of cases, most notably defending various corporate officers in SEC and DOJ proceedings. Sitarchuk is the partner-in-charge of the firm's government enforcement/white-collar crime group as well as being a member of the litigation and health groups.

The Clients: Clients are drawn from a variety of sections, including the financial services industry, healthcare providers, auditors and consulting firms.

Conrad O'Brien Gellman & Rohn PC
See firm details p.1546

The Firm: Interviewees were in no doubts about the firm's top reputation, especially when it comes to "*very complex litigation.*" It fields some of the state's most experienced trial lawyers, with over 30 attorneys in the Philadel-phia office alone and additional resources in two other Pennsylvania offices and one in New Jer-sey. Traditionally the firm is renowned for rep-resenting law firms in legal malpractice cases. It remains a leader in this, as demonstrated by its recent work for an international law firm of over 1000 lawyers in a case that attracted consider-able media attention. However, it is also increas-ingly focusing on alternative dispute resolution, and here its lawyers regularly act as neutrals for many state and federal courts and for private organizations like the AAA and the CPR Insti-tute for Dispute Resolution.

The Lawyers: "*Fabulous trial lawyer*" **Nancy Gellman** (see p.1524) is admired for combining "*extraordinary intelligence with natural stamina.*" Interviewees also praised her skills as an appel-late attorney. Recent highlights for her have

www.ChambersandPartners.com

All quotes in the text are from interviews with clients and competitors.

1511

Pennsylvania
Leading individuals
(Litigation: White-Collar Crime
& Government Investigations)

[1] **GOLDBERG Donald** *Ballard Spahr*, Philadelphia

[2] **BLACK Creed** *Sole Practitioner*, Philadelphia
DAVIS Alan *Ballard Spahr*, Philadelphia
HOWARD David *Dechert*, Philadelphia
MCGOUGH W Thomas *Reed Smith*, Pittsburgh
SPRAGUE Richard *Sprague & Sprague*, Philadelphia
THIEMAN Frederick *Thieman & Farrell*, Pittsburgh

[3] **LEVIN Christine** *Dechert*, Philadelphia
UNDERCOFLER J Clayton *Saul Ewing*, Philadelphia
WINNING William *Cozen O'Connor*, Philadelphia

Individuals are listed alphabetically in each band.

included a number of complex environmental insurance cases. For example, she achieved a significant victory in New Jersey, in a case clarifying the right to coverage in environmental insurance disputes. She also handles malpractice cases for a client base of legal and medical professionals. Interviewees praised the "*brilliantly street-smart*" **William O'Brien** (see p.1534) for his "*great judgment and integrity.*" Boasting extensive trial experience, he continues to handle major litigation in areas ranging from mass tort litigation to libel and slander cases, including two large defamation cases, which have both been settled. He has also served as counsel to the American Red Cross, handling its litigation matters. Additionally, he advises law firms in employment and malpractice cases, focusing particularly on high-profile employee discrimination claims. Most of O'Brien's work is conducted in the federal courts and he also has extensive experience at appellate level.

The Clients: Clients include law firms, pharmaceutical companies, charities, nongovernmental organizations and the tobacco industry. The team also acts on behalf of doctors and hospitals in medical malpractice cases, serving as counsel to the Children's Hospital in Philadelphia, among others.

Hangley Aronchick Segal & Pudlin
See firm details p.1553

The Firm: Founded as recently as 1994, the firm nonetheless boasts a core of "*wonderful litigators*" with considerable experience of large and complex class actions. It is especially known for representing clients in the healthcare, banking and insurance industries, and also acts for several public figures. Highlights from the past year include representing eight members of the West Chester University women's intercollegiate gymnastics team in a gender discrimination claim filed after the university announced it would eliminate the team in 2003. The firm conducted a four-day evidentiary hearing in the Eastern District Court of Pennsylvania, which concluded with the court granting the plaintiffs' motion

and ordering the university to reinstate the team. Other major areas of work include legal malpractice, where the firm represents a number of Philadelphia law firms.

The Lawyers: William Hangley (see p.1526) is especially respected for combining "*decency*" with "*terrific litigation skills.*" His recent representative caseload includes Northeastern Distributing Co v DG Yuengling & Son, in which he represented a large distributor of malt beverages against the territorial distributor of the Yuengling brands. The suit accused the company of having fraudulently obtained an agreement to rescind the contract between the two companies at will. Following discovery, Yuengling agreed to settle out of court. Another highlight for Hangley was his involvement in the Nise Estate case, concerning a contested will, and he was lead counsel in the West Chester University case. He also continues to be active in the healthcare sector, representing hospitals and nursing homes. **Mark Aronchick** (see p.1518) was described to researchers as an "*excellent litigator*" with an "*aggressive approach.*" He regularly assists large healthcare institutions, banks and insurance companies in class actions, as well as representing law firms and other professional partnerships in disputes with existing or departed partners. The healthcare field accounts for a major part of his work, and he advises on such issues as fraud and abuse, reimbursement, hospital privileges, affiliation and other contractual agreements between healthcare facilities and between owners and managers.

The Clients: The firm's main clients include healthcare providers, banks, insurance companies, public figures and oil companies.

Morgan, Lewis & Bockius LLP
See firm details p.1556

The Firm: According to interviewees, the litigation practice at this "*high-quality*" firm has "*taken off*" of late. The group in Philadelphia is principally known for securities litigation. However, with nearly 600 lawyers nationwide, it has the capacity to handle everything from business and corporate litigation, toxic tort cases and products liability, to insurance recovery and patent disputes. This size and significance in the market helps the group to win mandates as national coordinating counsel and national trial counsel for a number of clients, managing and trying cases on a nationwide basis. Recent highlights include several significant victories on behalf of Western MacArthur. In addition, it clawed back over $188 million in an insurance recovery win for the Fuller-Austin Insulation Company against three nonsettling insurance companies. This asbestos coverage dispute drew national attention.

The Lawyers: Marc Sonnenfeld (see p.1538) was praised for his "*excellent communication skills,*" which enable him to "*connect well with*

clients and judges alike.*" He is increasingly involved in the mutual funds field and in regulatory activities. Due to an increase in the number of SEC proceedings, he now spends a lot of time defending issuers and underwriters in securities litigation brought by government shareholders, which currently includes representing underwriters in two class actions. Aside from this, he spends a substantial portion of his time providing corporate governance counseling to boards.

The Clients: As well as representing Western MacArthur and the Fuller-Austin Insulation Company, the team obtained the dismissal of all claims against its client, the United States Gypsum Company, in a 16-year-old tort action alleging that asbestos-containing materials manufactured by the company were defective and violated the federal RICO Act.

Pepper Hamilton LLP
See firm details p.1558

The Firm: Market sources noted the firm's great reputation in litigation, attributing it to the presence of "*a deep bench of fine lawyers*" with experience in a wide range of complex commercial cases. The firm is particularly renowned for its skill in keeping cases out of court, and a substantial portion of the practice involves counseling clients in various industries. However, it is more than equal to the challenge when matters do come to trial, and enjoys a strong track record of success in representing companies and directors and officers in civil and criminal matters before a range of federal and state courts and agencies. Antitrust is considered a particular strength, and the group regularly handles matters involving the Sherman and Clayton Acts, the Robinson-Patman Act and state and federal antitrust laws, as well as civil RICO claims and consumer protection laws. Here, the team boasts involvement in such high-profile cases as the Flat Glass Antitrust Litigation. It also acted on behalf of a national franchiser in rehabilitation and insolvency proceedings in Queen City Pizza v Domino's Pizza. Another area of considerable importance to the team is representing defendants in professional malpractice claims.

The Lawyers: Barbara Mather (see p.1531) was recommended by interviewees for her "*brilliance and street smarts,*" as well as her "*fearlessness in court.*" Her broad practice mixes extensive antitrust expertise alongside considerable experience in commercial litigation. This experience recently includes representing a supplier of computer services in a multimillion-dollar contract dispute in the Common Pleas Court. She has also defended a Pennsylvania county against a challenge to its tax statute, and advised a corporation and several board members in connection with allegations that they misrepresented transactions and earnings relating to the sale and development of computer software. **Robert Hickok** (see p.1526) chairs the firm's commercial litigation group. His caseload includes antitrust, federal securities disputes, insurance litigation and class action defense. A recent highlight of his has been representing a computer company in the Apartheid Reparations Litigation – a class action seeking relief for wrongs committed by the Government of South Africa during the apartheid era.

The Clients: The group represented the Aetna Casualty & Surety Co in the Dalkon Shield litigation, which involved the bankruptcy of the AH Robins Company and the creation of a $2.75 million trust for claimants partially funded by insurance proceeds. Other clients include: ABA; Pilkington North America; Advent International and PPM America.

Band 3

Akin Gump Strauss Hauer & Feld LLP
See firm details p.477

The Firm: This well-established firm is particularly noted for its experience in the healthcare industry. Here it regularly represents plaintiffs against healthcare providers, and is extensively involved in lawsuits against national healthcare insurers. For example, the team is representing a class of physicians and medical providers against all of the Blue Cross/Blue Shield health insurance plans in the USA. In another major national class action, the firm acted for the American Dental Association against CIGNA. The plaintiffs in this are seeking a certification of a national class action on behalf of all the country's dental service providers, and triple damages under the RICO legislation. The decision is currently pending in the Southern District of Florida.

The Lawyers: Interviewees were impressed with **Ed Mannino**'s (see p.1531) "*razor-sharp mind*" and his "*thorough preparation*" before trials. Boasting extensive trial experience, Mannino was lead counsel in the class actions mentioned above. In addition, he represented Allstate in two class actions on behalf of the client's former employee agents. One of these is an independent action by the EEOC. These cases stem from a business reorganization under which the position of employee agent was eliminated and former employee agents were given the option to convert to independent contractor status. The outcome of the litigation was that one case was dismissed in its entirety and an age discrimination count was struck from the other. Mannino is also currently acting for Deloitte & Touche in two consolidated class actions touching on securities fraud and bankruptcy issues.

The Clients: Important clients include Purdue Pharma and VeriSign.

Blank Rome LLP
See firm details p.1542

The Firm: Described by clients as "*supreme*" in the field of insurance coverage litigation, the team is unusual in the state for housing no fewer than 25 attorneys specializing in insurance-related matters. An indication of the firm's strength in this area is its work for national health provider, Aetna. It is attempting to recover more than $200 million from professional liability insurers including Lloyd's Underwriters and Liberty Mutual. The amount sought is intended to settle a multidistrict class action brought against Aetna by several HMOs in the Southern District Court of Florida.

The Lawyers: Clients return to **Ann Laupheimer** (see p.1529) for her "*excellent combination of aggressiveness, thoroughness and responsiveness.*" She has acted as principal counsel to Aetna in several lawsuits against underwriters and insurance companies, and also acted for FMC in the litigation mentioned below. Currently, she is handling a case in Florida as co-counsel to the Great American Insurance Company in a dispute with the insured party. At stake is over $100 million, the amount that it is obliged to pay to settle a dispute concerning grave desecration. Laupheimer also counsels the liquidator of the Reliance Insurance Company and the Insurance Department of Pennsylvania in all aspects of the liquidation.

The Clients: The team is defending FMC in a lawsuit brought by its joint venture partner, Solutia, seeking over $300 million in damages for allegations that a particular chemical process technology failed to yield the financial benefits expected. Other active clients include Aetna and the Commonwealth of Pennsylvania.

Kirkpatrick & Lockhart Nicholson Graham LLP
See firm details p.291

The Firm: A "*fine firm in the litigation area,*" this international outfit has particular strength in handling insurance coverage disputes. Lately, it has become increasingly active in representing senior management in cases alleging fraud and mismanagement. Here, the group recently conducted special investigations into allegations of improper conduct on the part of senior management of two public companies. The alleged conduct could give rise to investigations of the companies by regulatory bodies, such as the SEC. The team continues to handle a volume of products liability cases and is currently defending two putative class actions filed in New York and Pennsylvania state courts against major automobile manufacturers alleging systematic and widespread defects. The group is active across the region, and has handled a variety of matters out of state. These include an action brought in Delaware, in which it is advising a public healthcare company against nine liability insurers, who are disputing their share of a securities class action settlement. At stake is $47 million.

The Lawyers: The "*superb*" **David McClenahan** (see p.1531) was especially lauded for his "*practical decision-making skills.*" His recent highlights include the insurance coverage case in Delaware, and the products liability cases in New York and Pennsylvania. On the plaintiff side, he has been representing an individual in a case before the Pennsylvania Superior Court against a life insurance company for breach of contract and fraud. Professional malpractice lawsuits are an important part of his caseload, and here he is representing a group of lawyers who split off from one of the largest plaintiff personal injury firms in the state taking with them a number of clients. The disputed fees in question exceed $10 million. McClenahan's caseload also encompasses white-collar criminal matters.

The Clients: Clients include public utilities, law firms, insurance companies and health maintenance companies.

Montgomery, McCracken, Walker & Rhoads LLP

The Firm: The firm's long-standing clients have nothing but praise for its attorneys, highlighting their "*great understanding of general business culture.*" They boast particular strength in First Amendment cases, having provided media clients with litigation and counseling services in areas such as trade libel, commercial disparagement and the right of access to information, among others. A recent example of the team's strength in this arena is its handling of the La Salle University case on behalf of the university and its students. This concerns the activities of a group of protesters who, as part of their opposition to the City of Philadelphia's closure of a street to two-way traffic, conduct daily demonstrations that intimidate students, faculty and employees of the university. It touches on aspects of free speech versus the right to be free from unwanted harassment and other issues. The case is currently pending and has attracted considerable media attention. The firm is also heavily involved in securities class actions, general class action defense and appellate litigation, with several of its attorneys having won cases on appeal before institutions such as the US Supreme Court.

The Lawyers: **David Marion** was described by sources as the "*glue of the firm,*" and won particular plaudits for his work in First Amendment cases. Clients were also full of praise for his "*conscientious, thorough approach,*" coupled with pragmatic decision-making ability. He is currently lead counsel in the La Salle University case, and recently handled a four-week trial for a Philadelphia TV station accused of breach of contract. In addition to media work, he is also extensively involved in securities litigation, acting, for example, for two former officials of the Loewen Group in a class securities fraud case currently pending in the Eastern District Court of Pennsylvania. The court has granted in part the firm's motion to dismiss many of the claims, and limited the plaintiffs' case to a narrower issue. Marion also has a reputation as a transactional lawyer, and recently advised AAA Mid-Atlantic in negotiating and drafting several key agreements required in connection with the relocation of its corporate headquarters to Wilmington, Delaware.

The Clients: Dun & Bradstreet; The Sherwin-Williams Company; AAA Mid-Atlantic and La Salle University.

Reed Smith LLP

See firm details p.1560

The Firm: This "*blue-blooded*" firm was roundly praised for its "*cutting-edge*" work, particularly in the field of financial services litigation. With a total of 120 attorneys operating from the Pittsburgh office alone, the firm is inevitably going to be a major player in the Pennsylvania market. Its broad workload sees it taking on cases ranging from media and defamation disputes to medical malpractice and white-collar criminal proceedings. Many of these involve matters of considerable public interest, such as its recent successful argument on behalf of the public's right to access to juvenile dependency proceedings in Pennsylvania. Another recent highlight was the firm's handling of the Varallo v Elkins Park Hospital litigation, which reversed a district court's refusal to order arbitration in an employment dispute.

The Lawyers: Thomas McGough (see p.1532) was described to researchers as a "*top-shelf*" lawyer who is "*brilliant but down-to-earth.*" His considerable trial experience is particularly marked in the area of media law, where he recently represented Paul Harvey in the defamation proceedings mentioned below. He also enjoyed success recently arguing the case for greater public access to juvenile delinquency proceedings, which is likely to have broad implications for the law beyond Pennsylvania.

The Clients: Clients include national newspapers, banks and business enterprises and high-profile individuals. In the latter area, the team recently achieved a favorable verdict in the Larkin v Harvey defamation case, on behalf of radio broadcaster Paul Harvey and ABC Radio.

Schnader Harrison Segal & Lewis LLP

The Firm: This firm is said to enjoy a long tradition in general commercial litigation, and is particularly admired for the strength of its IP practice. Reflecting this strength, the team is currently representing an advertising agency in important trademark litigation. It is also extensively involved in insurance litigation, and was

recently successful in two coverage actions, one of them in the Court of Common Pleas in Philadelphia. Though the firm lacks the network of offices of some of its competitors, branches in New York, California and DC give it a claim to be national, and much of its workload is actually international in scope. For example, it successfully assisted UPS in two cases involving international air rights, one of them between the USA and Japan, heard before the Department of Transportation.

The Lawyers: Dennis Suplee (see p.1538) was described by clients as a "*marvelously effective*" attorney, whose strengths include a combination of "*excellent litigation skills*" and "*extensive courtroom experience.*" He is renowned for his trademark work, but is also highly experienced in toxic tort cases, general commercial disputes and antitrust. A veteran trial lawyer, Suplee led in the two insurance coverage cases mentioned above, and is currently involved in trademark litigation on behalf of an advertising company. In Hall v United Airlines, he defended Air France against allegations of conspiracy to reduce travel agent commissions.

The Clients: As well as UPS and Air France, the firm has acted for clients in the advertising and chemical industries. October 2004 also saw it record successes for Wachovia in two related cases concerning losses sustained in a Ponzi scheme.

Band 4

Buchanan Ingersoll PC

See firm details p.1544

The Firm: According to clients, this is an "*impressive practice,*" which is increasingly involved in trials at the national level. More than 100 lawyers are active in the litigation practice, helping the firm to attract a range of high-profile cases. It recently obtained a successful judgment in the Fifth Circuit Court of Appeals in New Orleans for a pharmaceutical distributor, which was exonerated from any liability for breach of a contract. Subsequent to this judgment, the Federal Court in Trenton, New Jersey, ruled that fraud claims could not be brought against the same client, limiting its entitlement to contractual damages. Other highlights include successfully resolving a dispute between two lawyers regarding a substantial referral fee.

The Lawyers: Howard Scher (see p.1536) was credited by interviewees with having "*significantly enhanced the litigation practice*" here. He remains considerably involved in the firm's major cases and recently obtained a successful reversal of judgment against his pharmaceutical company client, in a contractual dispute before the Federal Appellate Court in Texas. As well as frequently representing law firms, he defends individual professionals.

The Clients: ATOFINA; Georgia-Pacific;

McDonald's and Highmark Blue Cross Blue Shield.

Drinker Biddle & Reath LLP

See firm details p.1549

The Firm: Described as having a team with "*very good brain power,*" the firm continues to be prominent in the marketplace where it has been active since the mid-1980's. With 240 attorneys in its litigation practice, the group has handled matters ranging from professional liability and environmental insurance matters to major pharmaceutical cases. Additionally, the attorneys regularly represent many of the country's leading security brokers and underwriters in class actions, regulatory matters and arbitrations. Currently, the attorneys are defending the National Collegiate Athletic Association in a class action lawsuit brought under Title VI of the Civil Rights Act.

The Lawyers: The team is headed by Kathryn Levering who has expertise in investigating and providing advice on complex questions relating to corporate governance and company policy. Additionally, she oversees the team's white-collar and corporate investigation cases across the USA.

The Clients: Pfizer, Johnson & Johnson and Comcast are among the clients.

Thorp Reed & Armstrong

The Firm: This Pittsburgh-based firm is particularly notable for its strength in securities class actions. With 45 lawyers spending most of their time on litigation, it has the capacity and expertise to represent major corporations in high-stakes cases. A recent example is its work for a major law firm in a securities class action. The client had advised a corporation whose senior executives were later found guilty of fraud. The case is of national significance as it involves unique issues relating to the liability of secondary actors, such as law firms, under securities laws. The group also recently represented a vice president of an investment advisory company whose chief investment officer lost around $400 million of public and corporate pension funds through inappropriate trading. The firm managed to resolve all civil claims and it is currently defending the client in SEC proceedings.

The Lawyers: William Wycoff (see p.1540) has achieved a record of "*big successes,*" agree commentators, especially in securities class actions. As well as leading in the securities cases mentioned above, he represented Metropolitan Life Insurance in the Metropolitan Life Sales Practice litigation, handling a total of 255 cases in the Western District of Pennsylvania, with numerous additional cases scheduled for trial over the next twelve months. He also continues to represent the second largest bank in Pittsburgh, along with a number of large manufacturers, petrochemical companies and law firms.

The Clients: Mellon Bank; MetLife; PPG Industries and Shell. It also acts for high-profile corporate executives subject to SEC investigations.

Other Notable Practitioners

Interviewees described **John Harkins** (see p.1526) of Harkins Cunningham as a "*master of his profession,*" some even nominating him among the "*leading lights in the American legal community.*" He is particularly renowned for appellate work, where he is universally acknowledged to be a "*phenomenal advocate who can present brilliant oral arguments as well as flawless written work.*" "*Witnessing Harkins in court takes your breath away,*" added one fan. He handles substantial federal law issues, representing clients in industries ranging from pharmaceuticals, through manufacturing to healthcare. Among his recent highlights is his involvement in the Diet Drugs Products Liability Litigation in the Third Circuit Court of Appeals, which related to certain orders entered in the Fen-Phen Litigation. His clients include: CIGNA; Rohm and Haas; Lafayette College and IKON Office Solutions. **Abraham Reich** (see p.1535) of Fox Rothschild LLP is an "*excellent trial lawyer*" with "*great judgment and integrity,*" according to the market. He continues to be heavily involved in class actions, especially in the healthcare field. Recent highlights include two high-profile products liability cases involving diet drugs that had been pulled out of the market. Reich also actively represents professionals, such as lawyers and doctors in malpractice suits. **Allen Black** (see

p.1519) of Fine Kaplan & Black was described as a "*fabulous lawyer,*" some peers considering him to be "*one of the leading lawyers in the country.*" Recently, Black has spent a considerable time representing a leading commercial litigator and antitrust specialist in two partnership dissolution disputes. At Stradley, Ronon, Stevens & Young LLP, **Clark Hodgson**'s "*outstanding*" reputation is based on his record of high-profile cases. In particular, his defense of the Archdiocese of Philadelphia against accusations of pedophilia has received widespread attention. In the area of white-collar crime, he successfully defended a financial institution in a lengthy jury trial in which the company stood falsely accused of money laundering. "*Highly regarded at the plaintiff's Bar,*" **Thomas Kline** of Kline & Specter PC has won a substantial number of lawsuits in the personal injury, medical malpractice and products liability arenas. Among his most notable cases is the Pier 34 litigation, in which he represented the victims, the families of three women who died and the 40 people injured by the collapse of the pier. After four years, this case was finally settled recently for $6.1 million. Interviewees were impressed by "*exceedingly bright, experienced and knowledgeable*" **Creed Black** (see p.1520), a sole practitioner, who specializes in white-collar crime. His experience spans securities fraud, political corruption, bank fraud, tax fraud, government contract fraud and money laundering. These are predominantly argued in federal court and frequently prosecuted by the DOJ. **Richard Sprague**, the senior partner of the firm Sprague

& Sprague, is engaged in general civil and white-collar criminal work at both state and federal level. He has an active antitrust and corporate litigation practice, and regularly conducts appeals. In August 2004, he was sworn in as the Judge of the Court of Judicial Discipline. **Frederick Thieman** of Thieman & Farrell combines an "*excellent style and great effectiveness as a trial lawyer*" with an "*extraordinary sensitivity in dealing with sensitive issues.*" He is particularly focused on fraud and white-collar crime. His firm recently represented an important quasi-public institution in responding to a government inquiry arising out of materials handling. It also achieved a successful jury verdict on appeal in a complex trademark infringement case, which lasted a total of three weeks. Described as a "*good, tough prosecutor,*" **Clayton Undercofler** (see p.1539) of Saul Ewing LLP in Philadelphia concentrates on internal corporate investigations. He also represents individuals and organizations that stand accused of white-collar crimes at both state and federal level. In May 2004, he achieved a significant victory for his client, a pharmaceutical company, when the Pennsylvania Superior Court and the Eastern District Court of Pennsylvania ruled in its favor in two cases related to the Fen-Phen diet drug. "*Thorough, hard-working and experienced*" **William Winning** of Cozen O'Connor, cochairs the firm's white-collar crime and complex criminal defense practice and was recommended by market sources.

REAL ESTATE

Pennsylvania
Leading firms (Real Estate)

1 BALLARD SPAHR ANDREWS *Philadelphia*
   BLANK ROME LLP *Philadelphia*
   WOLF, BLOCK, SCHORR *Philadelphia*

2 DECHERT *Philadelphia*
   MORGAN, LEWIS & BOCKIUS LLP *Philadelphia*
   SAUL EWING LLP *Philadelphia*

3 DRINKER BIDDLE & REATH LLP *Philadelphia*
   HANGLEY ARONCHICK SEGAL & PUDLIN *Philadelphia*
   REED SMITH LLP *Pittsburgh*
   SCHNADER HARRISON SEGAL *Philadelphia*

Firms are listed alphabetically in each band.

Band 1

Ballard Spahr Andrews & Ingersoll LLP

See firm details p.1541

The Firm: One of the largest real estate practices in the mid-Atlantic area south of New York, this firm maintains its uncontested position as one

of the very best "*one-stop shops*" on the Pennsylvania real estate scene. The "*extremely prominent*" team has been especially busy as a result of the upswing of condominium-related work in Philadelphia city centre. It has also acted in several projects in conjunction with regional government to promote industrial growth in the region by means of tax incentives. Working closely with its offices in Denver and Salt Lake city, the real estate team fields a substantial resort practice and has recently been developing a growing interest in the gaming sector.

The Lawyers: Renowned in the city for his accomplished land use planning work, **Michael Sklaroff** (see p.1537) is credited by interviewees for having taken the firm's real estate practice team from "*zero to the top.*" Described by one commentator as "*probably the smartest real estate lawyer around,*" he wins plaudits not only for his business-minded approach and exemplary zoning work but also for his dynamic personality and "*rainmaking*" skills. Commentators enthuse over his ability to stay "*cool, calm and collected*"

when handling complex and sophisticated projects. His extensive client base includes a number of prominent cultural institutions. The "*ubiquitous*" **Phil Korb** (see p.1529) received impressive peer feedback for his expertise in the field of state transfer taxes. He is currently involved in a number of substantial long-term projects involving the construction of both conventional and vacation homes for Blue Ridge Real Estate. Highly regarded commercial real estate and mall development practitioner **Richard Goldberg** (see p.1525) has carved a niche for himself in the hospitality sector of the real estate market. He was counsel to Loews in connection with the development and financing of the conversion of a historic office into a state-of-the-art hotel. Managing partner of the firm's Philadelphia office is the "*tough negotiator*" **Lynn Axelroth** (see p.1518). Managing a practice that spans across the healthcare, energy and projects finance sectors, Axelroth also tackles mandates in the construction arena. Recent significant building projects include counseling a

Pennsylvania
Leading individuals (Real Estate)

Senior Statesman

OMINSKY Harris *Blank Rome*, Philadelphia

1. FALA Herman *Wolf Block*, Philadelphia
GOLDBERG Richard *Ballard Spahr*, Philadelphia
KORB Philip *Ballard Spahr*, Philadelphia
MILLER Henry *Wolf Block*, Philadelphia
SKLAROFF Michael *Ballard Spahr*, Philadelphia
2. AICHELE Stephen *Saul Ewing*, Philadelphia
EBBY Stuart *Hangley Aronchick*, Philadelphia
JONES Richard *Dechert*, Philadelphia
KUTLER Marilyn *Schnader Harrison*, Philadelphia
LANE Robert *Morgan Lewis*, Philadelphia
RACKOW Julian *Blank Rome*, Philadelphia
STROBER Frederick *Saul Ewing*, Philadelphia
3. AXELROTH Lynn *Ballard Spahr*, Philadelphia
BRODERICK JJ *Morgan Lewis*, Philadelphia
EBBY David *Hangley Aronchick*, Philadelphia
FORTI David *Dechert*, Philadelphia
GIFFORD David *Ballard Spahr*, Philadelphia
GLAZER Ronald *Wolf Block*, Philadelphia
GOSFIELD Gregory *Dechert*, Philadelphia
LORD Craig *Blank Rome*, Philadelphia
ROSENBERG Kenneth *Schnader Harrison*, Philadelphia
STERN Eric *Morgan Lewis*, Philadelphia
WILLIAMS James *Wolf Block*, Philadelphia

Up-and-coming individuals

COONEY Robert *Morgan Lewis*, Philadelphia

Leading individuals
(Real Estate: Zoning/Land Use)

1. SKLAROFF Michael *Ballard Spahr*, Philadelphia
2. AICHELE Stephen *Saul Ewing*, Philadelphia
LANE Robert *Morgan Lewis*, Philadelphia
PRIMAVERA Carl *Klehr Harrison*, Philadelphia

Individuals are listed alphabetically in each band.

world-class orchestra in connection with the design and construction of a new concert hall, and the development of the largest regional visitors' centre in the country. The "*exceedingly bright*" **David Gifford** concentrates his practice on the transactional and finance elements of the firm's real estate practice. Noted for his "*charming demeanor*," Gifford received praise for his proficiency in large leasing transactions and general knowledge of the market. Peers agree that they would "*pick his brains on any particularly thorny real estate matter.*"

The Clients: Philadelphia Housing Association, Blue Ridge Real Estate and High Industries are prominent names on the client roster, which also includes state bodies and other major users of corporate real estate.

Blank Rome LLP
See firm details p.1542

The Firm: This preeminent 45-strong full-service firm is principally recognized for its expertise in the retail sector and in the rehabilitation for development of historically unsuitable sites. Serving a stratified clientele comprising REITs, developers, insurers and banks, the team leverages its traditionally robust political connections to good advantage and acts for various government bodies.

The Lawyers: Peers widely consider the "*adroit*" **Julian Rackow** (see p.1535) one of the best all-rounders in the state. His practice addresses a significant amount of retail work for major grocery chain clients, and his niche work includes advising clients on the reuse of obsolete buildings of historical significance by means of tax credits. According to market commentators, **Craig Lord** (see p.1530) "*belongs in the top echelon*" of real estate practitioners in Philadelphia. His diverse practice incorporates real estate development, financing and leasing and land use and zoning work, for which he is particularly respected. "*Scholar of the city*" **Harris Ominsky** (see p.1534) is famed for his academic credentials. Having authored a "*library's worth of books*" relating to the practice area, he receives plaudits for his impressive client base and his ability to combine his scholarly demeanor with a highly active practice.

The Clients: Important clients for the firm include a number of nationally known developers and lending institutions.

Wolf, Block, Schorr and Solis-Cohen LLP
See firm details p.1562

The Firm: Renowned for the intellectual flavor of its work, this firm caters for a mix of large, publicly traded companies and smaller, regional private interests. The team of about 50 dedicated real estate lawyers is one of the "*meat and bones*" groups at the firm, sources say, and dovetails with the well-regarded finance group for robust support in especially complex real estate transactions. Attracting a national clientele, the team has been involved in the past year in a major Michigan-based transaction for GE, as well as various large transactions with a cumulative value of over one billion dollars.

The Lawyers: The "*superb*" **Herman Fala** (see p.1523) is the chairman of the real estate department and the firm's REIT group. During the course of his outstanding career, he has been active in more than 30 states, though the past couple of years have seen him focus on clients closer to home. Described by peers as "*unflappable in the deal*," Fala represents both borrowers and developers, winning feedback for his "*gentlemanly*" demeanor. Market commentators agree that **Henry Miller** (see p.1533) matches Fala as one of the "*deans*" of the Pennsylvania Bar. "*A serious, strong-minded professional*," Miller has distinguished himself through his representation of high-profile commercial and office development companies. He also wins recommendations for his work with REITs, brokers and industrial site developers. **James Williams** (see p.1540) manages a major national practice representing pension trusts and corporate entities' major national developments and joint venture work. Peers describe him as "*simply an outstanding lawyer.*" **Ronald Glazer** (see p.1525) received accolades for his work in the growing condominium market. He has extensive experience representing permanent lenders as well as joint venture partners.

The Clients: Keystone Property Trust, Hilton Hotels and Liberty Property Trust feature prominently on the client roster, which also includes banks, mortgage lenders and shopping and conference center developers.

Band 2

Dechert
See firm details p.1547

The Firm: The major theme of market commentators' feedback was the team's national practice focus, and the deep pool of resources it can exploit. The group won praise for its "*extraordinary*" work, particularly in representing the interests of institutional lenders, for which the firm is perhaps best known.

The Lawyers: **Richard Jones**' (see p.1527) practice focuses on mortgage finance and capital markets work. Acting for large syndications and national corporations, Jones wins accolades for his in-depth grasp of highly sophisticated securities transactions for his lender-dominated portfolio of clients. The "*incredibly smart*" **Gregory Gosfield** (see p.1525) is known for his encyclopedic grasp of the real estate market and his "*extremely impressive*" academic profile. "*He is a tremendous repository for knowledge – a marvelous resource for brainstorming*," say clients. **David Forti** (see p.1524) is noted for his niche practice that focuses on all elements of the CMBS process for a number of major institutional clients. He deals with each stage of the transaction from loan origination through securitization to servicing.

The Clients: Standard & Poor's, Vantas, Commerzbank and Pacific Life Insurance are prominent among the firm's stable of clients. The group also advises businesses on development projects.

Morgan, Lewis & Bockius LLP
See firm details p.1556

The Firm: Acting for an array of high-profile local clients, this firm enjoys an excellent reputation among clients and peers alike for its outstanding transactional capacities. The Philadelphia team recently worked as part of a major firmwide collaboration that mobilized teams in Miami, New York, Irvine and San Francisco to land a huge deal for client American Financial Realty Trust. This involved the acquisition of 388 properties from the Bank of America and Wachovia for an aggregate price of over $1 billion.

The Lawyers: Robert Lane (see p.1529) represents the firm's more nationally focused clients with multijurisdictional business interests. He recently worked on the creation of a $30 million bond for the renovation and expansion of a widely known commercial development. Commentators expressed respect for Lane's busy transactional portfolio. Leader of the firmwide practice group is the "*extremely well-known*" **Eric Stern** (see p.1538). Managing much of the strategic planning work for the group, Stern has been active in raising the firm's profile in Europe, as well as expanding the practice domestically. Though less active on the day-to-day deal front, he continues to advise REITs and other corporate office portfolios. Clients were effusive in their praise of the "*dynamic*" **JJ Broderick** (see p.1520), a newcomer to the tables. Described by peers as "*combining aggression and energy in a really positive way*," he also has extensive experience with transactions in the telecommunications arena. Sources reported that up-and-comer **Robert Cooney** (see p.1522) is the firm's "*go-to guy*" for project finance work.

The Clients: American Financial Realty Trust; Brandywine Realty Trust; Tyco; Towers Perrin and Corporate Office Properties Trust.

Saul Ewing LLP

See firm details p.1561

The Firm: Lauded for its "*distinguished and effective*" style, the group at this firm enjoys established political connections and a reputation for efficiency. Despite departures over the past few years, the real estate team still packs a hefty punch and is starting to grow once more with over 40 specialists in the field practicing firm wide. Focusing on the mid-Atlantic region, the group is praised by interviewees for its extensive local knowledge and impressive responsiveness to clients needs. The team is currently working with a major construction management and development company on the acquisition of a large tract of excess state land. It is also dealing with a multimillion-dollar renovation of the Philadelphia shipyards.

The Lawyers: Warmly approved by peers as "*a super guy*," **Frederick Strober** (see p.1538) is known for his counseling work with schools and shipyards in particular. Winning plaudits for his "*broad skills and amiable manner*", the "*truly outstanding*" Strober is known to be a "*staunch advocate*" for his clients' concerns, and is adept at translating technical matters into a language that laypeople can fully understand. During the past twelve months, he has worked closely with the School District of Philadelphia on Microsoft's technologically enhanced 'School of the Future' project. He has also been dealing with the zoning and land use matters relating to the construction of a school for children with behavioral problems. Interviewees expressed

delight in working with the "*laid-back*" managing partner of the firm **Stephen Aichele** (see p.1518). His practice frequently involves him with governmental land use projects, and recent transactions have seen him working with one of the biggest healthcare providers in the region on a new hospital project.

The Clients: Philadelphia Shipyard Development, School District of Philadelphia and Thomas Jefferson University feature on the client roster, alongside a host of other public and private companies within the region.

Band 3

Drinker Biddle & Reath LLP

See firm details p.1549

The Firm: Closely allied to the firm's respected corporate and finance practices, the "*extremely skilled*" real estate group of almost 40 specialists acts for a regional clientele comprising a number of institutional investors as well as landlords, tenants and pension fund investors.

The Lawyers: Cochair of the team **Harry Cherken** counsels major retailers and specializes in commercial leasing and development work. **Ralph Rodak** provides valuable support and concentrates his practice on real estate joint ventures.

The Clients: The firm represents public sector clients, real estate brokers, REITs, cooperatives, landlords and tenants.

Hangley Aronchick Segal & Pudlin

See firm details p.1553

The Firm: Maintaining a healthy profile in the state, this midsized firm leans towards zoning and suburban development work. The team received accolades for its "*quality individuals*" and its high level of responsiveness toward clients. The firm represents a wide range of real estate concerns including insurance companies in the USA and in Canada.

The Lawyers: Long considered one of the top real estate practitioners in the city, **Stuart Ebby** (see p.1523) is described by market commentators as a "*pleasure to work with.*" A "*superb legal craftsman*," he epitomizes the practice's "*client-oriented*" approach and wins plaudits for his fair and direct style. Praised by one client as the "*most efficient attorney we have ever worked with*," the "*conscientious and knowledgeable*" **David Ebby** (see p.1523) focuses on commercial real estate work, particularly in representing American and Canadian insurance companies in permanent financing. He also counsels clients in matters relating to leasing management and the operation of high-rise office towers and retail shopping centers.

The Clients: Sunbelt Management and High Industries are key clients. The firm also serves investors, developers and construction companies.

Reed Smith LLP

See firm details p.1560

The Firm: Capable of drawing on the resources of more than 100 lawyers across the firm, the team advises clients on the full range of residential and commercial real estate development and finance mandates. The group's Pittsburgh office received particularly positive feedback and is regarded as the hub of the department.

The Lawyers: **Edward Seifert** handles sales and purchases, and his remit, like that of the team in general, is regarded as increasingly national rather than regional.

The Clients: The group acts for developers of office, residential and leisure facilities and industrial and commercial lenders.

Schnader Harrison Segal & Lewis LLP

The Firm: Enjoying a reputation for cost-effective quality, observers report that this firm houses some of the most experienced practitioners within the state's real estate community. The Philadelphia office is respected as a "*hive of activity*," and its lawyers have been at the vanguard of all the most important emerging areas of real estate law. These include such matters as construction for the telecommunications industry, multiuse and special service districts funded through joint public-private initiatives, conduit lending and tax-increment financing.

The Lawyers: The "*insightful*" **Marilyn Kutler** (see p.1529) is described by market commentators as "*highly impressive*" in her handling of real estate and government contract work. An "*effective negotiator*," she attracts praise from clients for her effective fashioning of deals. **Kenneth Rosenberg** (see p.1536) represents banks, savings and other financial institutions in all types of residential, commercial and retail development matters. He is known best for his construction lending work throughout the mid-Atlantic region and is praised by clients for his "*outstanding ability to get the deal stamped and sealed successfully*."

The Clients: The group deals with a range of clients, from large, international corporations to individual entrepreneurs.

Other Notable Practitioners

Clients regard **Carl Primavera** of Klehr Harrison Harvey Branzberg & Ellers LLP as the "*go-to guy*" at the firm for all zoning matters. As an adviser to major urban commercial and residential developers, he works closely with architects, engineers and construction professionals to help his clients navigate the often complicated issues surrounding the development of real estate in both urban areas and outlining suburban communities.

Leaders in Pennsylvania

ABELSON, Barry M
Pepper Hamilton LLP, Philadelphia
215 981 4282
abelsonb@pepperlaw.com
Recommended in Corporate/M&A

Practice Areas: Partner; Member and Chairman Executive Committee; Chairman, Corporate and Securities Practice Group. Experienced in: securities; venture capital; mergers and acquisitions of public and private companies; public and private offerings of equity and debt securities. Represents issuers, underwriters and venture capitalists. Counsels boards of directors, independent board committees and management on governance, disclosure and transactions.
Prof. Memberships: Chairman, 2005 Mid-Atlantic Venture Conference; Board of Directors, Greater Philadelphia Venture Group; Children's Crisis Treatment Center; Institute for Law and Economics, University of Pennsylvania; Crohn's & Colitis Foundation, Philadelphia Chapter.
Career: JD 1971 University of Pennsylvania Law School; BA 1968 Dartmouth College.

ABRAMOWITZ, Robert
Morgan, Lewis & Bockius LLP,
Philadelphia 215 963 4811
rabramowitz@morganlewis.com
Recommended in Employee Benefits

Practice Areas: Robert L Abramowitz is a Partner in the Employee Benefits and Executive Compensation Practice of Morgan Lewis. His practice involves counseling on all aspects of employee benefits and executive compensation. Mr Abramowitz is a frequent speaker and has published numerous articles. He was a Lecturer in Law at Villanova University Law School from 1986-2002.
Prof. Memberships: Member, ABA, Tax Section, Employee Benefits Committee. Charter Fellow, American College of Employee Benefits Counsel. Fellow, American College of Tax Counsel.

AICHELE, Stephen S
Saul Ewing LLP, Philadelphia
215 972 7797
saichele@saul.com
Recommended in Real Estate

Practice Areas: Mr Aichele has represented developers, property owners and governmental entities in all areas of land use, financing, construction and leasing.
Prof. Memberships: Member of the American College of Real Estate Lawyers. Philadelphia Chamber of Commerce's Executive Board and CEO Council for Growth; Adjunct Professor, Temple University School of Law.
Career: Managing Partner/CEO of Saul Ewing LLP.
Publications: 'The Law of Representations and Warranties in Pennsylvania', 'Summary of Zoning and Land Development Process in Pennsylvania', and 'Negotiating and Drafting an Agreement of Sale for a New Development: Allocating Risks and Rewards'.
Personal: JD, Temple University, BA, Cornell University.

ALSTADT, Lynn J
Buchanan Ingersoll PC, Pittsburgh
412 562 1632
alstadtlj@bipc.com
Recommended in Intellectual Property

Practice Areas: Experienced in all areas of patent, trademark, copyright and unfair competition law including litigation, patent solicitation, licensing, patent interference practice, trademark cancellation and opposition proceedings, International Trade Commission investigations, registration of trademarks and copyrights with the United States Customs Service and related exclusion proceedings. This work involved a wide range of technical subjects including mechanical, electrical, electronic, e-commerce, biotech, chemical, metallurgical and computer fields. He has worked extensively in the window coverings, toy and special metals industries.
Prof. Memberships: Adjunct Professor (Patent Law) University of Pittsburgh, Duquesne University; Practicing Law Institute, Patent Bar Review Course.
Personal: BS 1973; JD 1976 University of Pittsburgh.

ARMSTRONG, Stephen
Montgomery, McCracken, Walker &
Rhoads, LLP, Philadelphia
215 772 1500
Recommended in Antitrust

ARONCHICK, Mark Alan
Hangley Aronchick Segal & Pudlin,
Philadelphia
215 496 7002
maronchick@hangley.com
Recommended in Litigation

Practice Areas: Commercial, civil and/or white collar criminal matters involving intellectual property, healthcare, professional malpractice, banking, financing, accounting, tax, insurance, government fraud, civil rights, unfair trade practices, real estate, and/or regulated industries.
Prof. Memberships: Fellow, American College of Trial Lawyers. Member, Judicial Council of the Commonwealth of Pennsylvania. Philadelphia Bar Association: Chancellor, 1998; Member, Board of Governors, 1990-92; Treasurer, 1986-89; Co-Chair, Committee to Elect Qualified Judges, 1993-95; Co-Chair, Trial Advocacy Program, 1987-91; Chair and Member of numerous Bar Association Committees and Task Forces. Philadelphia Bar Foundation: President, 1996; Secretary, 1993; Trustee, 1990; Treasurer, 1986-89. Past Member, House of Delegates, Pennsylvania Bar Association. Member, The Disciplinary Board of the Supreme Court of Pennsylvania. Past Member, Bench Bar Relations Task Force, United States Court of Appeals for the Third Circuit. Judge Pro Tem, Court of Common Pleas of Philadelphia County. Mediator, United States District Court for the Eastern District of Pennsylvania. Past Chair, Hearing Committee of Disciplinary Board of Supreme Court of Pennsylvania. Member, Civil Rules Committee of Supreme Court of Pennsylvania. Member, Philadelphia Trial Lawyers Association. Member, National Association of Criminal Defense Lawyers.
Career: Founder, Shareholder and Board Member, Hangley Aronchick Segal & Pudlin, 1994-present. Shareholder, 1986-94; Executive Committee, 1992-94, Hangley Connolly Epstein Chicco Foxman & Ewing. Partner, 1983-86; Associate, 1974-79, Wolf, Block Schorr and Solis-Cohen. City Solicitor,1983; First Deputy City Solicitor, 1980-82, City of Philadelphia. University of Chicago Law School, JD with highest academic honors, 1974; University of Pennsylvania, BA, cum laude, 1971.

AXELROTH, Lynn R
Ballard Spahr Andrews & Ingersoll LLP,
Philadelphia 215 864 8707
axelroth@ballardspahr.com
Recommended in Real Estate

Practice Areas: Her practice includes representing corporate, institutional, developer, individual and public owners, public/private joint venturers, lenders, prime and trade contractors and design professionals, in all aspects of real estate development, structuring, construction, turnkey, design and design-build contracts, financing, housing assessment, sale and leasing of real estate, and alternative dispute resolution.
Prof. Memberships: Fellow of the American College of Real Estate Lawyers and the American College of Construction Lawyers. She was the first Chair and founding member of the Division of Owners and Lenders of the ABA Forum on the Construction Industry, and just completed a three year term on its Governing Committee. She was Vice Chair and then Co-Chair of the ABA Real Property Section Committee on Construction Lending (1997-2002). Current community activities include: Chair of the Board of the Independence Visitor Center Corporation, a Member of the Executive Committee of The Board of Overseers of the Annenberg Center for the Performing Arts of the University of Pennsylvania, and is a Member of the Board of the Greater Philadelphia Chamber of Commerce, the International Association of Attorneys and Executives in Corporate Real Estate, and the Women's Leadership Committee of Moore College of Art.
Career: Admitted to the Pennsylvania Bar (1983); joined firm (1985); Partner (1991); She has been Managing Partner of the firm's Philadelphia office since 1998.
Publications: She lectures extensively and is the author of numerous publications on development, construction and financing issues, including the chapter on Owner's Issues in the 2001 book published by ABA Publications entitled, 'Fundamentals of Construction Law'; and many articles such as 'The Ten Top Issues in Negotiating AIA Contracts', published by the American College of Real Estate Lawyers in 2005; 'How Construction Lawyers Can Learn to Stop Worrying and Love Public/Private Projects', published by the ABA Forum on the Construction Industry in 2005; 'Understanding the AIA Documents', published in 2000, 2001, and 2002 by the Pennsylvania Bar Institute; 'Construction Owner's Concerns in Construction Loan Agreements', published by the ABA Real Property Section in 2000; and 'The New AIA Construction Documents from Owner and Lender Perspectives', published in Probate and Property in 1999.

Personal: JD, cum laude, University of Pennsylvania (1983); editor, University of Pennsylvania Law Review; BA, summa cum laude, Temple University (1977); Phi Beta Kappa, President's Scholar.

BABST, Chester
Babst, Calland, Clements and Zomnir, A Professional Corporation, Pittsburgh
412 394 5400
Recommended in Environment

BARNETT, Bonnie Allyn
Drinker Biddle & Reath LLP, Philadelphia 215 988 2916
Bonnie.Barnett@dbr.com
Recommended in Environment
Practice Areas: Former Managing Partner, Chair of the firm's Environmental Practice. Combines an active litigation practice with general counseling on regulatory compliance issues and the environmental implications of business and real estate issues.
Prof. Memberships: Admitted in Pennsylvania (1982) and New Jersey (1996). Former Co-Chair of the Environmental Law Committee of the Philadelphia Bar Association. Helped to charter the Delaware Valley Environmental Inn of Court. Frequent lecturer on environmental law topics.
Career: Joined Drinker Biddle in 1984, after federal clerkship.
Personal: JD (summa cum laude), Temple University School of Law, 1982; BA (summa cum laude) Temple University, 1979.

BARSON, Leon
Adelman Lavine Gold & Levin, Philadelphia 215 568 7515
Recommended in Bankruptcy

BECK, Paul
Paul A. Beck & Associates, P.C., Pittsburgh 412 343 9700
Recommended in Intellectual Property

BELISARIO, Martin G
Akin Gump Strauss Hauer & Feld LLP, Philadelphia 215 965 1303
mbelisario@akingump.com
Recommended in Intellectual Property
Practice Areas: Practices intellectual property and technology law, including representation before the United States Patent and Trademark Office and foreign patent offices, technology licensing, portfolio counseling and litigation. He is the Head of the Patent Prosecution practice at Akin Gump. His practice focuses primarily on the mechanical arts. Mr Belisario's experience includes litigating patent disputes; providing opinions on patent infringement and validity; and supervising prosecution of both US and foreign patents for large high-technology portfolios.
Prof. Memberships: Pennsylvania Bar Association; Philadelphia Intellectual Property Law Association; Pennsylvania Bar.
Personal: BSME, Drexel University; JD, Widener University School of Law.

BERGER, Lawrence H
Morgan, Lewis & Bockius LLP, Philadelphia 215 963 5480
lberger@morganlewis.com
Recommended in Banking & Finance
Practice Areas: Lawrence Berger is a Partner in the Business and Finance Practice. Mr Berger's practice focuses on representing business organizations, particularly private companies, financial institutions and healthcare companies, in a variety of transactional and regulatory matters involving corporate finance, acquisitions and complex contracts. Mr Berger also frequently advises a number of nonprofit organizations, including museums and educational institutions, in connection with their business affairs and governance matters.
Prof. Memberships: Pennsylvania Bar Association (Steering Committee on Legal Opinions and member of Task Force on Business Corporation Law); American Bar Association (Model Nonprofit Corporation Act Committee); American Bar Foundation (Elected Fellow).

BERGÈRE, Timothy
Montgomery, McCracken, Walker & Rhoads, LLP, Philadelphia
215 772 1500
Recommended in Environment

BERKOWITZ, Alan D
Dechert, Philadelphia 215 994 2170
alan.berkowitz@dechert.com
Recommended in Employment
Practice Areas: Partner, Chair of Dechert's Labor and Employment Group. Represents employers in federal and state court in employment discrimination litigation and other disputes. Experienced with unfair labor practice proceedings before NLRB.
Career: Adjunct law professor, University of Pennsylvania Law School, 1982-95; instructor, The Wharton School and Rutgers University School of Law; author of treatise on Pennsylvania Employment Law; co-author, 'The Landrum-Griffin Act: Twenty Years of Federal Protection of Union Members' Rights' and 'The NLRB and Secondary Boycotts.'
Personal: Cornell University (BS, 1977); University of Pennsylvania Law School (JD, summa cum laude, 1980), first in class, Member of Law Review.

BERNARD, John M
Ballard Spahr Andrews & Ingersoll LLP, Philadelphia 215 864 8408
bernard@ballardspahr.com
Recommended in Employee Benefits
Practice Areas: He has more than 35 years of experience in all areas of employee benefits law, including qualified retirement plans, stock option plans, executive and deferred compensation arrangements, and health care, severance, and other welfare benefit plans. He also has an extensive background in tax, labor, and securities law. He has

worked closely with the US Department of Labor (DOL) and the Pension Benefit Guaranty Corporation (PBGC) to prepare training materials and conduct training programs for enforcement officers and staff of both agencies.
Prof. Memberships: He is a member of the American Bar Association, Pennsylvania Bar Association, and Philadelphia Bar Association, as well as the American Bar Association Tax Section, Committee on Employee Benefits. He has served as Chair of the Employee Benefits Committee of the Philadelphia Bar Association Tax Section. He is a member of the PENJERDEL Employee Benefits and Compensation Association, where he serves as legal counsel and a Member of the Board of Directors.
Career: He teaches and lectures throughout the country on matters relating to qualified plans, executive compensation, and welfare benefit programs. Included among the academic institutions where he has been an instructor are: University of Pennsylvania, where he has taught in both the Wharton School MBA Program and in the Aresty Institute of Executive Education; Temple University LLM Tax Program; Villanova University LLM Tax Program; the Philadelphia Academy for Employee Benefits Training; and the now defunct Institute for Employee Benefits Training. Admitted to the Pennsylvania Bar (1967); joined as Partner (1986).
Personal: BA, Swarthmore College (1963); LLB, Harvard University (1967).

BERNSTEIN, Alan
Caesar, Rivise, Bernstein, Cohen & Pokotilow Ltd, Philadelphia
215 567 2010
Recommended in Intellectual Property

BEVAN III, William
Reed Smith LLP, Pittsburgh
412 288 3184
wbevan@reedsmith.com
Recommended in Employment
Practice Areas: Practicing labor law for 33 years, a full range of general labor and employment representation on behalf of employers, emphasizing matters concerning the National Labor Relations Act and its administration by the NLRB. Provides immigration advice and counsels concerning the hiring, antidiscrimination and verification provisions of US immigration law.
Prof. Memberships: Labor and Employment Law Section, ABA.
Career: Attorney with the NLRB prior to Reed Smith.
Publications: Contributor to 'The Developing Labor Law'.
Personal: University of Kansas (JD, 1970); Kansas State University (1967); listed in 'The Best Lawyers in America'.

BIRON, Thomas
Blank Rome LLP, Philadelphia
215 569 5500
Recommended in Bankruptcy

BISSOON, Cathy
Reed Smith LLP, Pittsburgh
412 288 3268
cbissoon@reedsmith.com
Recommended in Employment
Practice Areas: Employment discrimination and harassment litigation, counseling and training clients concerning compliance with state and federal laws governing employment.
Career: Law clerk to the Honorable Gary L Lancaster, US District Court for the Western District of Pennsylvania.
Publications: Former editor of Reed Smith's 'Employment Law Review'; authored Ten Employment Law Tips for the New and Not-So-New Business, 'The Practical Lawyer'.
Personal: Harvard University (JD, 1993); Alfred University (BA, 1990); Reed Smith's Director of Diversity; in 2002, named by 'Pennsylvania Law Weekly' as one of top 50 lawyers in Pennsylvania under the age of 40.

BIZAR, Steven E
Buchanan Ingersoll, Philadelphia
215 665 3826
bizarese@bipc.com
Recommended in Antitrust
Practice Areas: Handles complex business disputes and trials in federal and state courts and before arbitration panels throughout the country. He represents clients in government antitrust and securities fraud investigations and enforcement proceedings and before administrative agencies and self-regulatory organizations, like the NASD or NYSE. He has broad experience in the defense of multi-district class actions.
Prof. Memberships: Board Member, Anti-Defamation League; Vice-Chair, Federal Courts Committee, Philadelphia Bar Association, Columbia Law School Alumni Association; Lawyers' Club of Philadelphia.
Personal: JD Columbia University, 1988; BA, 1984, summa cum laude and Phi Beta Kappa; MA, 1987 Brandeis University.

BLACK, Allen
Fine Kaplan & Black, Philadelphia
215 567 6565
ablack@finekaplan.com
Recommended in Antitrust, Litigation
Practice Areas: Commercial litigation; complex litigation; class actions; antitrust.
Prof. Memberships: The American Law Institute - elected Member, Member of Council, Member of Executive Committee, 2nd Vice President. American College of Trial Lawyers - Fellow.
Career: Founding Partner, Fine Kaplan and Black, 1975 to present. Previously Judge Advocate General's Corps, United States Navy; Trial Attorney, United States Department of Justice Civil Rights

Division; and Law Clerk to Hon John Minor Wisdom, United States Court of Appeals for the Fifth Circuit, New Orleans. He has taught at the law schools of the University of North Dakota, Rutgers University, Temple University, and the University of Pennsylvania.

Publications: 'Judge Wisdom, the Great Teacher and Careful Writer', 109 Yale LJ 1267 (2000); 'John Minor Wisdom: A Tribute and Memoir by One of His Law Clerks', 69 Miss LJ 43 (1999).

Personal: "Allen Black is quite simply one of the best and most thoughtful lawyers in the country, a highly successful litigator and important contributor to numerous law reform efforts." Burbank, Litigation in a Free Society: The Roles of Litigation, 80 Washington Univ. L.Q. 705, 719 (2002). Chairman, Bucks County Airport Authority.

BLACK, Jr, Creed C

Creed C Black Jnr - Sole Practitioner, Philadelphia 215 564 4060
ccb@creedblack.com
Recommended in Litigation

Practice Areas: White collar criminal defense - government investigations, grand jury matters, trials and appeals. Antitrust crimes, securities fraud, insider trading, tax fraud, mail and wire fraud, bank fraud, insurance fraud, healthcare fraud and abuse, RICO, money laundering, embezzlement, bid rigging, false claims, obstruction of justice, false statements, perjury, bribery and political corruption. Ancillary civil, quasi-criminal, regulatory and licensing proceedings. SEC enforcement matters.

Prof. Memberships: National Association of Criminal Defense Lawyers; Pennsylvania Association of Criminal Defense Lawyers; ABA; Philadelphia Bar Association; Federal Bar Association, Criminal Law Committee (past officer).

Career: Federal law clerk (1976-77); US Department of Justice, Criminal Division (1977-82); Ballard Spahr Andrews & Ingersoll (litigation Partner, 1985-96); sole practitioner, 1996-.

Personal: University of Pennsylvania (JD, 1976); Yale University (BA, 1973).

BLOOM, Michael

Morgan, Lewis & Bockius LLP,
Philadelphia 215 963 5032
mbloom@morganlewis.com
Recommended in Bankruptcy

Practice Areas: Michael Bloom, a Partner in the Business and Finance Practice, has handled major Chapter 11 proceedings and out-of-court restructurings throughout the United States. Mr Bloom has served as counsel to the leading five distributors of pre-packaged music in a variety of significant out-of-court restructurings of music specialty retailers and wholesalers. He also has represented the major film studio distributors of home video products in similar restructurings and Chapter 11 cases.

Prof. Memberships: The American

College of Bankruptcy (Fellow); American Bankruptcy Institute; Pennsylvania Bar Association (Chair, Judicial Evaluation Commission); Eastern District of Pennsylvania Bankruptcy Conference (former Chair).

BLOOM, Myron A

Hangley Aronchick Segal & Pudlin,
Philadelphia 215 496 7005
mbloom@hangley.com
Recommended in Bankruptcy

Practice Areas: Corporate reorganization, bankruptcy and creditors' rights. Primarily represents debtors, creditors and committees under Chapter 11 of the Bankruptcy Code. Clients include manufacturers, hospitals, nursing homes, retailers, real estate developers, mortgage originators/servicers and all levels of government. Extensive experience in workouts and out-of-court debt restructurings, including asset sales and refinancings. Founder and Chair of the firm's Bankruptcy Group.

Prof. Memberships: Board, Consumer Bankruptcy Assistance Project. Member, American Bankruptcy Institute.

Career: Founding Shareholder, Hangley Aronchick Segal & Pudlin, 1994-present. Shareholder, Hangley Connolly Epstein Chicco Foxman & Ewing, 1992-94. Partner and associate, Adelman Lavine Gold and Levin, 1981-92. Associate, Wolf, Block, Schorr and Solis-Cohen, 1978-80. Enforcement Attorney, United States Environmental Protection Agency, 1976-78. Law Clerk to the Honorable Daniel J Snyder, Jr, United States District Court, Western District of Pennsylvania, 1974-76. Research Assistant, Commission on the Bankruptcy Laws of the United States, 1972-73. JD (with honors), George Washington University, 1974. Notes and comments editor (1973) and senior editor (1974), 'The Journal of International Law and Economics'. BA, Hamilton College, 1970.

Publications: Columnist for 'The Legal Intelligencer' and frequent speaker at conferences.

BLUEDORN, Donald

Babst, Calland, Clements and Zomnir, A Professional Corporation, Pittsburgh 412 394 5400
Recommended in Environment

BLUME, Fred

Blank Rome LLP, Philadelphia
215 569 5512
blume@BlankRome.com
Recommended in Corporate/M&A

Practice Areas: Mr Blume concentrates his practice in the general corporate area, representing companies engaged in mergers, acquisitions, and divestitures. Additionally, he has extensive experience in representing publicly held, family owned, and closely held companies.

Prof. Memberships: Admitted in Pennsylvania, Florida, and New York; Member of the Philadelphia Bar Association, Pennsylvania Bar Association, Florida

Bar Association, New York Bar Association, and American Bar Association.

Career: Graduated University of Pennsylvania Law School, Member of the Order of the Coif; Managing Partner and CEO of Blank Rome LLP.

Personal: Board Member of the Greater Philadelphia Chamber of Commerce, Temple University Fox School of Business & Management, City Year, Greater Philadelphia Film Office, and the National Museum of American Jewish History.

BOLSTEIN, Joel

Fox Rothschild LLP, Warrendale
215 918 3555
jbolstein@foxrothschild.com
Recommended in Environment

Practice Areas: Environmental law and governmental affairs.

Personal: 1987 graduate of The George Washington University Law School; a Member of the Order of the Coif; a 1982 graduate of George Washington University.

BOOKER, Daniel I

Reed Smith LLP, Pittsburgh
412 288 3132
dbooker@reedsmith.com
Recommended in Antitrust

Practice Areas: Antitrust and trade regulation practice includes counseling and litigation in the fields of mergers, acquisitions, price-fixing, distributor relations, advertising, labor/antitrust, consumer banking, monopolization, and franchising. Reed Smith Managing Partner, 1991-2000.

Prof. Memberships: Pennsylvania and DC Bars.

Career: Trial attorney in the Antitrust Division of the Department of Justice, 1973-77.

Publications: Author of articles on trade regulation law, litigation.

Personal: University of Chicago Law School (JD, 1971); University of Pittsburgh (1968); listed in 'The Best Lawyers in America' for commercial litigation and corporate law; Chairman of Pittsburgh Regional Alliance.

BOSSERT, Terry

Post & Schell, P.C., Harrisburg
717 731 1970
Recommended in Environment

BRAEMER, Richard J

Ballard Spahr Andrews & Ingersoll LLP,
Philadelphia 215 864 8899
braemer@ballardspahr.com
Recommended in Corporate/M&A

Practice Areas: He practices in the areas of mergers and acquisitions, representing both sellers and buyers, corporate and real estate financings, corporate restructurings, venture capital investments, joint ventures, and executive compensation.

Prof. Memberships: Chairman of the Board of a Philadelphia-based, nonprofit healthcare network and has served as president of a childcare agency, and, in

such capacity, oversaw its merger with a family service agency. He is the Director of Toll Brothers, Inc., a NYSE-listed homebuilder, and has served on the boards of both public and private corporations.

Career: Admitted to the Pennsylvania Bar (1966); joined as Partner (1994).

Personal: LLB, cum laude, Yale University (1965); BA, magna cum laude, Amherst College (1962).

BRODERICK, JJ

Morgan, Lewis & Bockius LLP,
Philadelphia 215 963 5104
jbroderick@morganlewis.com
Recommended in Real Estate

Practice Areas: JJ Broderick is a Partner in the Real Estate Group. He has extensive experience in representing investment banks, commercial banks, insurance companies and other financial institutions in real estate capital markets, senior living real estate, real estate development and real estate workout/bankruptcy. Mr Broderick also has significant experience in representing developers, owners, operators, investors and users in all aspects of real estate including land acquisition, finance, construction, leasing and sales. He has represented real estate lenders and borrowers in complex workouts and real estate creditors and debtors in bankruptcy. Mr Broderick also has extensive experience with telecommunications transactions.

BROOMAN, David

Drinker Biddle & Reath LLP, Berwyn
610 993 2210
David.Brooman@dbr.com
Recommended in Environment

Practice Areas: Partner, Environmental Practice. Counsels clients in environmental permitting, compliance and land-use. Experienced in complex litigation and helps clients manage risk and ensure compliance in corporate, land-use and real estate transactions.

Prof. Memberships: Admitted in Pennsylvania and New Jersey. Member, American, Pennsylvania and Philadelphia Bar Associations. Past Chairman, Environmental, Mineral and Natural Resources Law Section of the Pennsylvania Bar Association; past President/current Member, Board of Directors of the Pennsylvania Resources Council. Lectures environmental and land-use topics.

Career: Joined Drinker Biddle in 1995.

Personal: JD (cum laude), Villanova Law School, 1982; BA, Rutgers University, 1979.

BROWN, James

Cohen & Grigsby PC, Pittsburgh
800 394 4904
Recommended in Employment

BROWN, Stephen D

Dechert, Philadelphia 215 994 2240
stephen.brown@dechert.com
Recommended in Antitrust

Practice Areas: Mr Brown is an

antitrust Partner and Former Chair of the White Collar Litigation Group. He has experience with internal investigations and criminal and civil antitrust, fraud, RICO, and environmental cases.
Prof. Memberships: Member, Pennsylvania Bar; Vice-Chair, American Bar Association Antitrust Section's Criminal Practice and Procedure Subcommittee (2000-02); treasurer, Villanova University School of Law Inn of Court.
Career: Law Clerk, Hon. Daniel H Huyett, III, US District Court, Eastern District of Pennsylvania.
Personal: Williams College (BA, 1971); Villanova University School of Law (JD, 1976), Member and editor-in-chief of Villanova University Law Review, Member of Order of the Coif.

BYRNE, Richard
Webb Ziesenheim Logsdon Orkin & Hanson, PC, Pittsburgh 412 471 8815
Recommended in Intellectual Property

CALLAND, Dean
Babst, Calland, Clements and Zomnir, A Professional Corporation, Pittsburgh 412 394 5400
Recommended in Environment

CASEY, Kevin
Stradley, Ronon, Stevens & Young LLP, Philadelphia 215 564 8000
Recommended in Intellectual Property

CASSIDY, Bart
Manko, Gold, Katcher & Fox LLP, Bala Cynwyd 484 430 2306
BCassidy@mgkflaw.com
Recommended in Environment
Practice Areas: A broad spectrum of environmental issues, including air and water quality control, waste management, storage tank issues, litigation, site remediation, Stormwater and business and real estate transactions.
Prof. Memberships: Member of the National Society of Professional Engineers; the Pennsylvania Society of Professional Engineers. Member of Section of Environment, Energy and Resources of the American Bar Association; the Environmental, Mineral and Natural Resources Section of the Pennsylvania Bar Association; and the Environmental Law Committee of the Philadelphia Bar Association. Admitted to the Bar in both Pennsylvania and New Jersey, as well as before the Eastern District of Pennsylvania, the District Court of New Jersey and the Court of Appeals for the DC Circuit.
Career: Attorney and licensed professional engineer; Served for approximately four years as a technical analyst to the vice president of the Grumman Corporation, where he provided technical and management expertise to the Fortune 150 company on environmental, energy and occupational safety issues.
Publications: Lectured and spoken on various aspects of environmental law, notably including ambient and indoor air quality law.

Personal: JD University of Pennsylvania Law School, summa cum laude and a Member of the Order of the Coif; Master of science in civil engineering with a concentration in environmental engineering from the Polytechnic University in New York; and a bachelor's degree in engineering from Swarthmore College.

CLARK, Peter
Reed Smith LLP, Philadelphia
215 851 8142
pclark@reedsmith.com
Recommended in Bankruptcy
Practice Areas: Head of Corporate Restructuring & Bankruptcy Group; firmwide hiring Partner. Represents lenders, private equity funds, hedge funds, mutual funds, venture capital companies, insurance companies, indenture trustees, investors, and committees of creditors in all aspects of workouts, restructurings, and reorganizations of financially distressed companies.
Prof. Memberships: Chair of the Loan Workouts Committee, Business Law Section, ABA; Editorial Advisory Board of the 'Journal of Corporate Renewal'; Turnaround Management Association; American Bankruptcy Institute.
Personal: Washington University School of Law (JD, 1982); Duke University (1979). Holds AV (highest rating level) by 'Martindale-Hubbell' for skill and integrity.

CLARKE, Jennifer R
Dechert, Philadelphia 215 994 2105
jennifer.clarke@dechert.com
Recommended in Antitrust
Practice Areas: Ms Clarke is a Partner in Dechert's Antitrust Group. She has over 20 years of experience in complex commercial litigation, including nationwide antitrust class actions, intellectual property disputes, and complex state law claims of unfair competition, breach of contract, and fraud.
Prof. Memberships: Member of the Pennsylvania Bar; admitted to practice before numerous federal courts; Member of Antitrust Section of the American Bar Association and Vice-Chair of its Transportation Committee; Member of Board of Trustees of the Women's Law Project.
Personal: Dartmouth University (BA, magna cum laude, 1977); Columbia Law School (JD, 1982), editor of Columbia Law Review.

COHEN, Abbi L
Dechert LLP, Philadelphia
215 994 2352
abbi.cohen@dechert.com
Recommended in Environment
Practice Areas: Environmental law Partner who evaluates environmental liabilities concerning corporate, real estate, and financing transactions. Advises on state and federal permitting and regulatory compliance.
Prof. Memberships: Member, Pennsylvania Bar; Chair, Mortgage Bankers

Association's 'Appropriate Inquiry' Task Force and Co-Chair of its Environmental Insurance Task Force; Member of Environmental Advisory Boards for BNA Due Diligence Guide, Real Estate Roundtable, and a national environmental consulting firm; Member of various national real estate, energy, and environmental organizations; participated in EPA's negotiated rulemaking on the 'All Appropriate Inquiry' standard.
Personal: Barnard College (BA, high honors, 1980); University of Pennsylvania Law School (JD, 1983).

COHEN, Stanley H
Caesar, Rivise, Bernstein, Cohen & Pokotilow Ltd, Philadelphia
215 567 2010
scohen@crbcp.com
Recommended in Intellectual Property
Practice Areas: Handles all areas of patent, trademark and copyright litigation, counseling, validity and opinion studies, prosecution and licensing. Has technical expertise in chemical engineering and chemistry. Has litigated over 200 cases in Federal District Courts, with more than 50 reported opinions arising from this litigation.
Prof. Memberships: Admitted to practice in 1961, Commonwealth of Pennsylvania; 1966, US Supreme Court; 1982, US Court of Appeals for the Federal Circuit; registered to practice before the US Patent and Trademark Office.
Personal: Born February 16, 1935, Drexel University (BS ChE, 1957); George Washington University (JD, with honors 1961).

COLEN, Frederick
Reed Smith LLP, Pittsburgh
412 288 4164
fcolen@reedsmith.com
Recommended in Intellectual Property
Practice Areas: Involved in patent, trademark, copyright and other IP litigation; regularly involved in licensing of proprietary technology and know-how in the United States and abroad.
Prof. Memberships: American, Pennsylvania, Allegheny Country, and Georgia Bar Associations; American Intellectual Property Law Association; International Trademark Association.
Career: Past President and Board Member of The TechLaw Group, an international network of 17 US and foreign law firms having more than 5,000 lawyers.
Publications: Author of numerous articles.
Personal: Emory University (JD, 1975); Tufts University (BS, chemical engineering, 1969); listed in 'The Best Lawyers in America'.

COLLINGS, Robert L
Schnader Harrison Segal & Lewis LLP, Philadelphia 215 751 2074
rcollings@schnader.com
Recommended in Environment
Practice Areas: Chair, Environmental Practice Group; immediate past Chair of Litigation Department. Has more than

25 years of regulatory and litigation experience in environmental law and hazardous substance issues. Also represents clients with permit needs, claims and transactional matters involving environmental or regulatory matters. Conducts environmental reviews in connection with asset transactions in many states.
Prof. Memberships: Member, Board of Directors, Pennsylvania Environmental Council; Vice-Chair, Enforcement Committee, American Bar Association (Environment, Energy and Resources Section); Secretary, Executive Committee, Water Resources Association.
Career: Member, firm Executive Committee; Former Supervising Attorney, USEPA.
Publications: Chapters on Stormwater Management, Municipal Solid Waste, and Land Recycling: Pennsylvania's Voluntary Cleanup Statute, the 'Solicitor's Handbook' (Pennsylvania Department of Community and Economic Development, 2003); PA chapter, 'Brownfields' (ABA, 2002).
Personal: Boston College, JD; Harvard University, AB (cum laude).

COLLINS, Brendan K
Ballard Spahr Andrews & Ingersoll LLP, Philadelphia 215 864 8106
collins@ballardspahr.com
Recommended in Environment
Practice Areas: Partner in Environmental Group and Litigation Department, and coordinator of the firm's petroleum products practice area. Concentrates his practice on litigation of environmental issues in state and federal courts, including actions arising from cleanup cost recovery claims, 'toxic tort' claims alleging personal injury and property damage, indemnity and other contractual claims, and civil and criminal enforcement matters. Maintains an active counseling and transactional practice, advising clients on projects involving contaminated property and operations subject to environmental regulation.
Prof. Memberships: Chair, ABA Section of Environment, Energy and Resources Environmental Litigation and Toxic Tort Committee. Former Co-Chair of the Philadelphia Bar Association's Environmental Law Committee. Member, American Bar Association (Section on Environment, Energy and Resources, Litigation Section, Tort Trial and Insurance Practice Section), Pennsylvania Bar Association, Montgomery Bar Association, and Philadelphia Bar Association. Serves on the Advisory Board of the Environmental Science Program at St. Joseph's University in Philadelphia, Pennsylvania. Governor and former President, St. Thomas More Society of Philadelphia.
Career: Partner, 1997-present, associate 1988-97. Admitted to the Pennsylvania

Bar (1988), and the Bar of the Supreme Court of the United States (1993). Has represented clients before both the United States Supreme Court and the Pennsylvania Supreme Court.

Publications: Contributing author, forthcoming 'Toxic Tort Practitioner's Handbook' (American Bar Association, 2005). Contributing author, 2005/2006 'Guidebook on Complying with Pennsylvania Environmental Laws and Regulations' (Pennsylvania Chamber of Business and Industry, 2005). Panelist, Practical Guidance for Complying with Environmental Regulations, National Assoc. of College and University Attorneys 45th Annual Conference (June, 2005). Moderator and Course Planner, The Class Action Fairness Act of 2005: Environmental and Toxic Tort Litigation (ABA Teleconference, March, 2005). Panelist and Course Planner, ABA Attorney-Client Privilege Special Task Force: Important Issues Facing Environment, Energy and Resources Lawyers (ABA Teleconference, March, 2005). Panelist and Course Planner, Environmental Risks in Real Estate Transactions, ABA Annual Meeting (August, 2003). Authored articles appearing in 'The Legal Intelligencer', 'Journal of Environmental Regulation', 'Temple Environmental Law and Technology Journal', and the 'Villanova Law Review', and was a contributing author to an 11 volume treatise on environmental law, 'Environmental Regulation Essentials', published by John Wiley & Sons, Inc.

Personal: JD, magna cum laude, Villanova University School of Law (1988), Order of the Coif, Board of Editors, Villanova Law Review; SB (Mathematics), St. Joseph's University (1985). Married to Annmarie G Collins, with six children.

COLTON, Neal
Cozen O'Connor, Philadelphia
215 665 2000
Recommended in Bankruptcy

CONNORS, Eugene
Reed Smith LLP, Pittsburgh
412 288 3375
econnors@reedsmith.com
Recommended in Employment
Practice Areas: Employment and labor law, guides national and international companies of all sizes on how to balance employer-employee needs to eliminate employment concerns, while maximizing management options.
Prof. Memberships: Labor and Employment Sections of the American, Pennsylvania, and Allegheny County Bar Associations.
Personal: Columbia University School of Law (JD); College of the Holy Cross (BA). Listed in 'America's Leading Business Lawyers,' 'Who's Who in American Law,' and 'Who's Who of Emerging Leaders in America.' Named as Pennsylvania Super Lawyer for 2004 by 'Philadelphia Magazine.' Adjunct professor in St. Francis College's Human Resources Master of Arts Program.

COONEY Jr, Robert L
Morgan, Lewis & Bockius LLP, Philadelphia 215 963 5806
rcooney@morganlewis.com
Recommended in Real Estate
Practice Areas: Bob Cooney is a Partner in the Real Estate Group. His practice includes acquisitions and dispositions, commercial leasing, build-to-suit projects, brownfields projects, joint ventures, and financings, including credit tenant and other structured finance transactions. Mr Cooney is also involved in the firm's zoning practice, principally in Philadelphia. Mr Cooney's clients include REITs, pension funds and private real estate companies, as well as Fortune 500 companies and non-profit organizations with significant real estate holdings. Mr Cooney has an active practice in Pennsylvania and New Jersey.
Prof. Memberships: Member, American Bar Association; Member, Pennsylvania Bar Association; Member, Philadelphia Bar Association.

COSTELLO, Joseph J
Morgan, Lewis & Bockius LLP, Philadelphia 215 963 5295
jcostello@morganlewis.com
Recommended in Employment
Practice Areas: Joseph Costello is a Partner in the Labor and Employment Law Practice Group. Mr Costello represents employers in a broad range of employment litigation matters and administrative agency proceedings, and provides counseling in connection with strategic and day to day human resources decisions. Mr Costello has extensive experience handling complex class actions and litigation involving multiple parties, and is Head of the firm's ERISA Litigation Practice.
Prof. Memberships: American Bar Association (Employee Benefits Committee and Committee on the Development of the Law Under the National Labor Relations Act); Philadelphia Bar Association.

CRAMER, Eric
Berger & Montague PC, Philadelphia
215 875 3000
Recommended in Antitrust

D'ANGELO, Alfred
Klett Rooney Lieber & Schorling, Philadelphia 215 567 7500
Recommended in Employment

DAVIS, Alan J
Ballard Spahr Andrews & Ingersoll LLP, Philadelphia 215 864 8230
davisa@ballardspahr.com
Recommended in Litigation
Practice Areas: Practice areas include complex and multi-district commercial litigation, securities, criminal law, municipal law and professional liability. He has served as lead counsel on behalf of major accounting firms, corporations and individual directors and officers in the defense of more than 30 securities law class actions, including associated enforcement and investigative proceedings.
Prof. Memberships: Vice-Chair of the United States Court of Appeals for the Third Circuit Lawyers Advisory Committee, past Chairman and present Member of the Executive Committee of the University of Pennsylvania Law School Inn of Court, a Fellow of the American College of Trial Lawyers, and a Fellow of the International Academy of Trial Lawyers. In January 2004, he was elected a Trustee of The Pew Charitable Trusts.
Career: Admitted to the Pennsylvania Bar (1961); joined as Partner (1991).
Personal: LLB, magna cum laude, Harvard University (1960); AB, with honors, University of Pennsylvania (1957).

DAVIS, Doreen
Morgan, Lewis & Bockius LLP, Philadelphia 215 963 5376
dsdavis@morganlewis.com
Recommended in Employment
Practice Areas: Doreen Davis is a Partner in the Labor and Employment Law Practice Group. Ms Davis practices nationwide, concentrating in NLRB advice and litigation, union organizational activities and negotiations, and employment litigation. She has served as defense counsel in EEOC nationwide charges involving sex discrimination and in a nationwide class-action lawsuit brought under the provisions of the Fair Labor Standards Act.
Prof. Memberships: College of Labor and Employment Lawyers (Fellow).

DENINNO, David L
Reed Smith LLP, Pittsburgh
412 288 3214
ddeninno@reedsmith.com
Recommended in Corporate/M&A
Practice Areas: Chairs Business and Regulatory Department. Practice is comprised of general corporate, securities, technology and financing law. Handles wide range of general corporate transactions such as mergers, acquisitions, divestitures and buyouts, and transactions involving various types of financing. Serves as principal outside counsel to a number of publicly traded and privately held business enterprises, including many technology-based businesses.
Career: Law clerk to Judge Roger Robb, US Court of Appeals for the District of Columbia.
Personal: George Washington University Law School (JD, 1981), editor of 'Law Review'; University of Virginia (BA, 1977).

DICHTER, Mark
Morgan, Lewis & Bockius LLP, Philadelphia 215 963 5291
mdichter@morganlewis.com
Recommended in Employment
Practice Areas: Mark Dichter is a Partner in the Labor and Employment Law Practice. Mr Dichter has more than 30 years of experience counseling and representing employers in the full spectrum of employment law, including age, gender and race discrimination, sexual harassment, employee benefits and ERISA litigation, employer-employee relations, and labor-management law. Mr Dichter also has extensive experience in dealing with the EEOC and OFCCP at the national and regional levels.
Prof. Memberships: American College of Employment Lawyers (Fellow); American Employment Law Council (Board of Directors); American Bar Association (past Chair and Counsel Member).

DONOHUE, John
Woodcock Washburn LLP, Philadelphia
215 568 3100
donohue@woodcock.com
Recommended in Intellectual Property
Practice Areas: Litigation and counseling involving computers and computer software, electronics, telecommunications, robotics, medical imaging and automated control systems, and Trademarks.
Prof. Memberships: Member, Pennsylvania Bar. President of the Benjamin Franklin Inn of Court, 2002-03; Co-Chair, Federal Circuit Bar Association's Jury Instruction Committee, ABA's Litigation Section and AIPLA's Federal Litigation and Electronic and Computer Law Committees.
Career: Joined Woodcock Washburn, 1987.
Publications: Recognized in Chambers Guide to the Legal Profession 2003, 2004. Named a Pennsylvania Super Lawyer.
Personal: LLM in Trial Advocacy, Temple University Law School (1997), JD, New England School of Law (1977); BEE, University of Dayton (1974).

DWORETZKY, Joseph A
Hangley Aronchick Segal & Pudlin, Philadelphia
215 568 6200
jad@hangley.com
Recommended in Bankruptcy
Practice Areas: Bankruptcy, creditors rights, commercial litigation, governmental.
Prof. Memberships: 3rd Circuit Regent, American College of Bankruptcy; Chair, Eastern District of Pennsylvania Bankruptcy Conference (2001); Board, Consumer Bankruptcy Assistance Project (2003).
Career: Board Member and Shareholder, Hangley Aronchick Segal & Pudlin, 1997-present. City Solicitor, City of Philadelphia, 1994-96. Managing Partner 1992-93; Partner 1984-93; associate 1978-84, Drinker Biddle & Reath. He served as law clerk to the Honorable Ellsworth Van Graafeiland, United States Court of Appeals for the Second Circuit,

1977-78. Villanova Law School, 1977 summa cum laude where, among other things, he won the St Ives Medal (best grades) and the Pulling Award (best Law Review Article).
Publications: Frequent speaker and writer for Professional Associations and Continuing Legal Education Seminars.
Personal: A career bankruptcy and workout lawyer, he left private practice for four years in the mid-1990s to work for the then Mayor of Philadelpia, Edward G Rendell, as City Solicitor. As Solicitor he was a member of the Mayor's cabinet and in charge of a 130-lawyer legal department handling all the legal affairs of the country's fourth largest city. He has handled numerous high profile matters both in the bankruptcy and governmental arenas, including serving as trial counsel for Liberty Mutual in JPMorganChase v Liberty Mutual (Enron-related litigation concerning circular gas sale deals); as debtor's counsel in numerous cases involving energy, hospitals, nursing homes, life care facilities and other regulated industries; and as regulatory counsel in connection with the deregulation of the electric, natural gas and local telephone industries in Pennsylvania.

EBBY, David A
Hangley Aronchick Segal & Pudlin, Philadelphia 215 496 7030
daebby@hangley.com
Recommended in Real Estate
Practice Areas: Representation of lenders in connection with construction and permanent financing for all types of real estate, including multi-state and multi-county loans on office buildings, hotels, shopping centers and apartment buildings. Has extensive experience in representing national and regional developers in office leasing and retail leasing with national chains, both in 'big box' type leases and inline and mall stores.
Prof. Memberships: Member, Executive Committee of Real Property Section of Philadelphia Bar Association, 2002-04.
Career: Shareholder, Hangley Aronchick Segal & Pudlin, 2001-present. Shareholder, Toll, Ebby, Langer and Marvin, 1994-2001. Associate, Drinker, Biddle & Reath, 1989-94. BA, Amherst College, 1985 (cum laude); JD, Villanova University, 1989 (cum laude).
Publications: 'Application Forum State's Statute of Limitations to Litigation with which State has No Significant Contacts is Unconstitutional', 'Villanova Law Review', Vol. 33, No. 3/4, page 610 (1988).

EBBY, Stuart F
Hangley Aronchick Segal & Pudlin, Philadelphia 215 496 7017
sfe@hangley.com
Recommended in Real Estate
Practice Areas: Sometimes referred to as the 'dean of the real estate bar', Mr Ebby has more than 40 years' experience

representing lending institutions, developers, investors, brokers, title insurers, and others involved in selling, buying, developing, mortgaging, leasing and managing commercial and industrial real estate. Mr Ebby frequently serves as an expert witness in cases involving Pennsylvania real estate law and practice.
Prof. Memberships: Member, American College of Real Estate Lawyers; Adjunct Professor of Law, Temple University Law School.
Career: Shareholder, Hangley Aronchick Segal & Pudlin, 2001-present. Harvard Law School, LLB, 1961; Harvard College, AB, 1958.

EDWARDS, Mark
Morgan, Lewis & Bockius LLP, Philadelphia 215 963 5769
medwards@morganlewis.com
Recommended in Antitrust
Practice Areas: Mark Edwards is a Partner in the Antitrust Practice. Mr Edwards's practice focuses on antitrust litigation, particularly Section 1 and Section 2 Sherman Act claims, price discrimination claims and state law competition claims. He also counsels corporate clients on a broad range of antitrust issues, including distribution and pricing practices, dealer terminations and the licensing of intellectual property.

ELDERKIN, Dianne
Woodcock Washburn LLP, Philadelphia 215 568 3100
elderkin@woodcock.com
Recommended in Intellectual Property
Practice Areas: Patent infringement litigation and counseling involving many technologies, including biologic therapeutics, pharmaceuticals, surgical and dental instruments, orthopedic implants, and consumer absorbent materials.
Prof. Memberships: Member, Pennsylvania Bar, American and Philadelphia Bar Associations, PIPLA, AIPLA, and the Federal Circuit Bar Association.
Career: Member, firm's Policy Committee. Joined Woodcock Washburn, 1987. Previously served nine years as DuPont's patent counsel.
Publications: Frequent lecturer and published author on IP law. Named a Pennsylvania Super Lawyer. Only Pennsylvania patent attorney named to International Who's Who of Patent Law.
Personal: George Washington University Law School, JD with high honors (1978). Bucknell University, BS (1975).

EVERETT, Carl B
Saul Ewing LLP, Philadelphia 215 972 7171
ceverett@saul.com
Recommended in Environment
Practice Areas: Mr Everett has been practicing environmental law for 30 years, focusing on CERCLA, regulatory compliance, enforcement matters brought under federal and state environmental statutes, and tort litigation.

Clients have included American Packaging Corp., Beazer East, Celanese, DuPont, Ethyl, Exelon, ChevronTexaco, W.R. Grace and CERCLA groups.
Prof. Memberships: American, Delaware, Pennsylvania and Philadelphia Bar Associations; State Bar of Texas.
Career: Joined Saul Ewing in 1987. Formerly Senior Counsel in DuPont's Legal Department. Designated a 'Pennsylvania Super Lawyer' by Philadelphia Magazine and Law and Politics Magazine.
Personal: JD University of Houston, BS, chemical engineering, Massachusetts Institute of Technology.

FALA, Herman C
Wolf, Block, Schorr and Solis-Cohen LLP, Philadelphia 215 977 2076
hfala@wolfblock.com
Recommended in Real Estate
Practice Areas: Chairman, Real Estate Department, REIT Practice Group, and Hospitality and Gaming Group. Has represented banks, pension funds, publicly traded companies, insurance companies, REITs, and real estate developers in many local and national transactions, including complex acquisitions, mergers, financings, joint venture arrangements, leases, project finance transactions, syndications, public and private debt and equity placements, and transactions involving the development and management of hotels, office buildings and other projects. Has extensive experience in the management, financing, acquisition, development and franchising of hotels.
Prof. Memberships: Member, American College of Real Estate Lawyers, and is listed in a leading American Publication. Served as Chairman of the Real Property Section of the Philadelphia Bar Association (1998) and on numerous other committees of the Philadelphia Bar Association, including the Professional Responsibility Committee and the Executive Committee of the Real Property Section.
Career: Admitted to the Pennsylvania Bar (1974). Member, Board of Directors of The Wilma Theater Company (Board Chairman from 1995-97). Member, Board of Directors of the Lawyers Club of Philadelphia and the Board of Directors of Central Philadelphia Development Corporation.
Publications: Served as editor-in-chief of The Philadelphia Lawyer, and has written numerous articles for that publication. Served as editor of the Real Property Newsletter, published by the Philadelphia Bar Association.
Personal: Received his BS, summa cum laude, in Physics from the University of Notre Dame in 1971 and JD, cum laude, from Harvard Law School in 1974.

FATELL, Bonnie Glantz
Blank Rome LLP, Wilmington 302 425 6423
fatell@blankrome.com

Recommended in Bankruptcy
Practice Areas: Chair of the firm's Business Restructuring and Bankruptcy Group and member of the firm's Partner Board. Ms Fatell has extensive experience in major bankruptcy reorganizations, out of court restructurings and other commercial matters in Delaware and nationally, representing secured and unsecured creditors, creditors' committees, debtors, plan of reorganization proponents, asset purchasers, landlords and other parties in interest. Recent representations include representing the debtors in ANC Rental Corporation, USGen New England Corporation and New Global Telecom and the creditors committees in Datatec Systems, InaCom Corporation, Bills Dollar Stores and Merry Go Round Enterprises.
Prof. Memberships: Fellow in American College of Bankruptcy, American Bankruptcy Institute, International Women's Insolvency and Restructuring Confederation, Bencher in Delaware Bankruptcy Inn of Court.
Career: Admitted to practice: Pennsylvania, 1981; Delaware, 1999; United States Supreme Court, 2002.
Publications: Contributing author, Collier Bankruptcy Forms Manual (2005), Checklist of Personal Liabilities of Corporate Fiduciaries on the Eve of Bankruptcy, Fourth Annual Business Lawyers' Institute, Pennsylvania Bar Institute (co-author) (1998), Debtors Beware: Strict Interpretation of Section 365(d)(4) Bodes Well for Landlords, American Bankruptcy Institute Journal, June (1996).
Personal: Temple University School of Law, JD, 1981; Pennsylvania State University, BS, 1973.

FEIRSON, Steven B
Dechert LLP, Philadelphia 215 994 2489
steven.feirson@dechert.com
Recommended in Litigation
Practice Areas: Mr Feirson is a litigation partner and the firm's Deputy Chair (legal resource acquisition). His practice concentrates on securities litigation. During the past 20 years, he has litigated large, complex cases and has spent a significant portion of his career handling appellate matters.
Prof. Memberships: Member, Pennsylvania Bar; admitted to practice before numerous federal courts; Master of the Inn of Court of the University of Pennsylvania Law School.
Personal: University of Pennsylvania (BA, 1972); University of Chicago Law School (JD, 1975).

FELIX II, H Thomas
Ballard Spahr Andrews & Ingersoll LLP, Philadelphia 215 864 8136
felixt@ballardspahr.com
Recommended in Employment
Practice Areas: His practice is concentrated in labor and employment law,

with emphasis on collective bargaining, arbitration, and employment discrimination issues.

Prof. Memberships: A Fellow in the College of Labor and Employment Lawyers and listed in every edition of The Best Lawyers in America and every edition of Philadelphia Magazine's Best Lawyers. Past President of the Labor Law Section of the Philadelphia and Pennsylvania Bar Associations. He has also taught labor law, collective bargaining, employment discrimination and strikes, picketing and boycotts at Temple University Law School for 12 years.

Career: Admitted to the Pennsylvania Bar (1961); joined as Partner (2002).

Publications: Co-author of two books published by John Wiley & Sons, 'Drafting and Revising Employment Contracts' and 'Drafting and Revising Employment Handbooks', and is also a Member of the Editorial Board of the 'Journal of Individual Employment Rights'.

Personal: LLB, Temple University James E Beasley School of Law (1961); BA, University of Virginia (1956).

FLICK II, Lawrence
Blank Rome LLP, Philadelphia
215 569 5556
flick@BlankRome.com
Recommended in Banking & Finance

Practice Areas: Mr Flick concentrates his practice on general business and corporate law with an emphasis on commercial lending, asset-based financing, secured transactions, securitizations, loan syndications and participations, intercreditor relationships, leasing transactions, lender liability prevention and defense, loan restructuring, debtor-in-possession financing and bankruptcy, reorganizations and workouts.

Prof. Memberships: Admitted Pennsylvania and New Jersey; American Bar Association - Section on Corporation, Banking and Business Law, Commercial Financial Services Committee - Vice-Chair, Asset Securitization and Derivatives Sub Committee, Uniform Commercial Code Committee - former Chair, Personal Property Leasing Subcommittee; College of Commercial Finance Attorneys; Association of Commercial Finance Attorneys; Equipment Leasing Association.

Publications: Structuring Insider Working Capital Advances, ABF Journal (February 2003); UCC Survey: Leases, The Business Lawyer, (1997-2004); Equipment Leasing, — Matthew Bender (1994) (co-author); Portfolio Acquisitions . . . Looking Through the Legal Lens, MA Monitor, Portfolio Supplement, September/October 1992) (co-author); The Elusive Article 9 First-Lien Security Interest: How Your Lien Position Can Be Eroded and "How to Prevent It", 20 Uniform Commercial Code Law Journal, 211 (Winter 1988) (co-author); Liability of Banks to their Borrowers: Pitfalls and Protections", Bank-

ing Law Journal (1986) (co-author).
Personal: Graduated Villanova University School of Law, cum laude.

FOLEY, Mark
Klett Rooney Lieber & Schorling, Philadelphia 215 567 7500
Recommended in Employment

FORTI, David W
Dechert LLP, Philadelphia
215 994 2647
david.forti@dechert.com
Recommended in Real Estate

Practice Areas: Mr Forti is a Partner who practices real estate finance and securitization. He represents various lenders, issuers, master servicers, and special servicers in transactions involving loan origination, mezzanine financing, CMBS securitization, CMBS/CDOs, post-closing modifications, and workouts.

Prof. Memberships: Member, Pennsylvania Bar; Member, Commercial Mortgage Securities Association (CMSA).

Personal: University of Pittsburgh (BA, cum laude, 1992; MBA and JD, magna cum laude, 1995), editor of the University of Pittsburgh Law Review and the Journal of Law and Commerce.

FOX, Robert
Manko, Gold, Katcher & Fox LLP, Bala Cynwyd 484 430 2312
Rfox@mgkflaw.com
Recommended in Environment

Practice Areas: Compliance counseling for business and industry regarding hazardous and municipal waste regulations, Superfund matters, storage tank issues and real estate transactions and real property development, including wetlands permitting, site contamination and brownfield redevelopment issues; and litigating environmental matters before federal and state courts and administrative agencies.

Prof. Memberships: Member of the Environment, Energy and Resources Section of the American Bar Association; the Environmental, Mineral and Natural Resources Section of the Pennsylvania Bar Association; the Environmental Law Committee of the Philadelphia Bar Association; and the Delaware Valley Environmental Inn of Court.

Career: JD, cum laude, Harvard Law School and Bachelor's degree, summa cum laude and Phi Beta Kappa from the University of Pennsylvania.

Publications: Mr Fox is the Thomas A. O'Boyle lecturer-in-law at the University of Pennsylvania School of Law, a Summer Lecturer at Vermont Law School, and a Lecturer-in-Law for the Temple University Master of Law program in Beijing, China.

Personal: Vice Chairperson of the Philadelphia Academies, Inc; Board Member of the Lower Merion Conservancy and the Natural Lands Trust; Member of the Lower Merion Township Planning Commission.

FRIDY, Carl H
Ballard Spahr Andrews & Ingersoll LLP, Philadelphia 215 864 8726
fridy@ballardspahr.com
Recommended in Banking & Finance

Practice Areas: He has had extensive experience in secured and unsecured commercial lending, real estate and construction finance, letter of credit-backed and other tax-exempt bond financings, and the workout and restructuring of troubled loans.

Prof. Memberships: An active Member of the Commercial Financial Services Sub-Committee of the Section of Business Law of the American Bar Association and also belongs to the Real Property Division of the Section of Real Property, Probate and Trust Law of the American Bar Association. He is also a Member of the American College of Commercial Finance Lawyers.

Career: Admitted to Pennsylvania Bar (1973); joined as Associate (1973); made Partner (1980).

Personal: JD, Duke University (1973); BA, Trinity College (1969).

FRIEDMAN, Michael H
Pepper Hamilton LLP, Philadelphia
215 981 4563
friedmanm@pepperlaw.com
Recommended in Corporate/M&A

Practice Areas: Partner, Vice-Chairman, Corporate and Securities Practice Group. Experienced in: mergers and acquisitions; corporate finance; corporate securities; joint ventures and real estate investment trusts (REITs). Counsels boards of directors and senior management of companies on governance, disclosure, regulatory compliance (Sarbanes-Oxley), transactional matters and audit committee issues.

Prof. Memberships: Member, Philadelphia Board for Corporate Governance; Board Member, The Council for Relationships. Former Board Member American Red Cross, Southeastern Pennsylvania Chapter.

Career: JD 1982 University of Virginia School of Law; MA 1979 University of Chicago; BA 1978 Hamilton College.

FRITTON, Karl
Reed Smith LLP, Philadelphia
215 241 7956
kfritton@reedsmith.com
Recommended in Employment

Practice Areas: Head of the Intellectual Property Group. Represents employers in collective bargaining, labor arbitration, and employment-related litigation before the NLRB and state and federal courts.

Publications: Frequent author on labor and employment-related matters to professional and employer organizations.

Personal: Rutgers University School of Law (JD, 1980); State University of New York at Albany (BS, 1977). Listed in 'The Best Lawyers in America.' Lecturer at Rutgers University Institute of Manage-

ment and Labor Relations; adjunct professor of labor law at Rutgers University School of Law. Member of Board of Directors of Philadelphia Volunteer Lawyers for the Arts.

GARBER, Kevin
Babst, Calland, Clements and Zomnir, A Professional Corporation, Pittsburgh
412 394 5400
Recommended in Environment

GARRITY Jr, Vincent F
Duane Morris LLP, Philadelphia
215 979 1242
garrity@duanemorris.com
Recommended in Corporate/M&A

Practice Areas: Vincent F Garrity, Jr practices in the areas of business law, mergers and acquisitions and corporate governance.

Prof. Memberships: Teaching: Adjunct Professor of Law, University of Virginia Law School, Spring Semester 2004: Selling/Acquiring a Closely Held Business; Designated as the I Grant Irey Lecturer for Academic Year 2003-04 at the University of Pennsylvania Law School; Adjunct Professor of Law, Temple University School of Law, Negotiating and Drafting Business Acquisition Documents, 1996, 1997, 1998, 1999, 2001 and 2002; Lecturer-in-Law, University of Pennsylvania Law School, The Business Acquisition Process, 2000, 2002 and 2003; Distinguished Practitioner in Residence, Cornell Law School, The Business Acquisition Process, 2001; Bar Association Activities: American Bar Association - Business Law Section, Committee on Negotiated Acquisitions, 1987-present Chair, 1995-98 Chair, Acquisition Review Subcommittee, 1991-95; Pennsylvania Bar Association - Corporation, Banking and Business Law Section, Chair, 1981-83, Vice-Chair, 1983-present.

Career: Admitted to practice in Pennsylvania, United States District Court for the Eastern District of Pennsylvania, Supreme Court of Pennsylvania; Duane Morris LLP, Director of Professional Standards, 1994-96; Partners Board, 1984-98; Co-Chairman, Corporate Section, 1984-94; Partner, 1970-present; associate, 1963-70. Judge Pro Tem Commerce Court Division of Philadelphia Court of Common Pleas.

Personal: Harvard Law School, LLB, 1962.

GELLMAN, Nancy
Conrad O'Brien Gellman & Rohn PC, Philadelphia 215 864 8065
ngellman@cogr.com
Recommended in Litigation

Practice Areas: Founding Member, Conrad O'Brien Gellman & Rohn, P.C. Practices in area of complex litigation, including commercial cases, class actions, insurance coverage, antitrust, defamation, professional liability, and employment litigation.

Prof. Memberships: Fellow, American

College of Trial Lawyers; Member, American Law Institute.
Personal: AB, Bryn Mawr College; JD, Yale Law School; Fulbright Fellowship, London School of Economics.

GIFFORD, David
Ballard Spahr Andrews & Ingersoll LLP, Philadelphia 215 665 8500
Recommended in Real Estate

GIOTTO, Thomas
Klett Rooney Lieber & Schorling, Pittsburgh 412 392 2000
Recommended in Employment

GLAZER, Ronald B
Wolf, Block, Schorr and Solis-Cohen LLP, Philadelphia 215 977 2112
rglazer@wolfblock.com
Recommended in Real Estate
Practice Areas: Partner in the firm's Real Estate Practice Group. He concentrates his practice in condominiums, homeowners' associations, cooperatives, shopping centers, office buildings, hotel and residential acquisition, sale, financing, development and operation.
Career: Mr Glazer was Chairman of Real Property Law Section of the Philadelphia Bar Association (1987) and a member of the Association's Board of Governors. Mr Glazer is a member of the American and Pennsylvania Bar Associations Sections on Real Property, Probate and Trust Law, serving on the executive committee of the latter from 1982-84. He was Chairman of subcommittees of the Pennsylvania Bar Association's Community Association Law Committee that prepared the Pennsylvania condominium, cooperative and planned community statutes. For 1995 and 1996, he chaired the Pennsylvania Bar Association Common Interest Ownership Committee. Mr Glazer serves as a member of the International Council of Shopping Centers and the Community Association Institute's College of Community Association Lawyers. Mr Glazer is a member of the American College of Real Estate lawyers.
Publications: Author of Pennsylvania Condominium Law & Practice.
Personal: Received his BA, cum laude, in Political Science from Dickinson College in 1964 and his LLB, cum laude, from the University of Pennsylvania Law School in 1967.

GOLD, Marc
Manko, Gold, Katcher & Fox LLP, Bala Cynwyd 484 430 2301
Mgold@mgkflaw.com
Recommended in Environment
Practice Areas: Environmental regulation and counseling covering solid waste, site remediation, water pollution issues including the TMDL program, corporate transactions and multi-facility environmental audits.
Prof. Memberships: Natural Resources Section of the American Bar Association and the Environmental, Mineral and

Natural Resources Section of the Pennsylvania Bar Association; the Water Pollution Control Federation; has served as Vice Chairman of the Zoning and Land Use Committee of the Pennsylvania Bar Association; and Chairman of the Philadelphia Bar Association's Environmental Law Committee.
Career: Founding Partner of Manko, Gold, Katcher & Fox, LLP. Currently serves as the firms Managing Partner. Formerly served as a Section Chief in the Legal Branch of the United States Environmental Protection Agency, Region III. Assisted in developing the Pennsylvania Land Recycling and Environmental Remediation Standards Act of 1995, the cornerstone of Pennsylvania's brownfields and site remediation program.
Publications: Frequent lecturer and author on a myriad of environmental law topics relating to site contamination and Brownfields issues, environmental auditing and due diligence processes.
Personal: JD from Villanova University School of Law and BA from The American University. Currently serves on the Board of Directors of the Clean Air Council.

GOLDBERG, Donald J
Ballard Spahr Andrews & Ingersoll LLP, Philadelphia 215 864 8345
goldbergd@ballardspahr.com
Recommended in Litigation
Practice Areas: His practice is concentrated in the 'white collar crime' area. He has represented organizations ranging from Fortune 500 companies to those more closely held. His individual representations have included, among others, lawyers, doctors, public officials, business persons, prosecutors, and other law enforcement personnel.
Prof. Memberships: He has been a Member of the American College of Trial Lawyers since 1980. In October 1999, he was appointed by Chief Justice Rehnquist to a three-year term on the Federal Judicial Conference's Advisory Committee on the Federal Rules of Criminal Procedure. In August 2003, the Chief Justice extended his membership on the Committee for an additional term that will expire on October 1, 2006.
Career: Admitted to the Pennsylvania Bar (1955); joined as Special Counsel (1993).
Personal: LLB, Harvard Law School (1954); BS, University of Pennsylvania (1951).

GOLDBERG, Richard R
Ballard Spahr Andrews & Ingersoll LLP, Philadelphia 215 864 8730
goldbergr@ballardspahr.com
Recommended in Real Estate
Practice Areas: His practice concentrates on areas of real estate including, development, financing, leasing, and acquisition.
Prof. Memberships: Past President of

the American College of Real Estate Lawyers (1991-92), past Chair of the Anglo-American Real Property Institute, past Chair of the International Council of Shopping Centers Law Conference (1986 and 1987), and a Fellow of the American College of Mortgage Attorneys. He also is a Member of the American Law Institute, the Program Advisory Committee of ALI-ABA, and the Real Estate Advisory Committees of ALI-ABA and the Practising Law Institute. He is also a Member of the American Bar Association, Section of Real Property, Trust and Probate, where he currently serves as the real property liaison to the Drafting Committee for the Revision of Articles 1, and 9 of the Uniform Commercial Code. He has served as Chair of Section Committees on Pension Funds; Management of Real Estate; and National Institutes and Satellite Programs.
Career: Admitted to the Maryland Bar (1964), New Jersey Bar (1994), Pennsylvania Bar (1994), joined as Partner (1994).
Publications: Co-author of a handbook on downtown development for Massachusetts Continuing Legal Education.
Personal: LLB University of Maryland (1964); BA Pennsylvania State University (1961).

GOODMAN, Stephen
Morgan, Lewis & Bockius LLP, Philadelphia 215 963 5086
sgoodman@morganlewis.com
Recommended in Corporate/M&A
Practice Areas: Mr Goodman is a Partner in the Business and Finance Practice and Co-Chair of the firm's Global Technology Practice. His practice focuses on representing emerging growth companies in the technology and life sciences sectors. Using the firm's vast resources, he coordinates all aspects of the representation of such companies and concentrates his practice on legal aspects of corporate finance and acquisitions.
Career: Former Law Clerk, US Supreme Court Justice William J Brennan Jr.

GORDON, George G
Dechert, Philadelphia 215 942 382
george.gordon@dechert.com
Recommended in Antitrust
Practice Areas: Mr Gordon is a Partner in Dechert's Antitrust and Commercial Litigation Groups. His experience includes antitrust class actions and litigation involving claims of monopolization, unlawful price discrimination, unlawful group boycotts, predatory pricing, and monopoly leveraging. He has also successfully represented clients in several non-public investigations by government regulatory agencies.
Prof. Memberships: Member, Pennsylvania and New Jersey Bars; admitted to practice before numerous federal courts; Co-Chair of Intellectual Property Committee of the American Bar Association Antitrust Section; Member of the American Bar Association Litigation Section.

Personal: Brandeis University (BA, 1988); University of Pennsylvania School of Law (JD, 1991).

GOSFIELD, Gregory G
Dechert, Philadelphia 215 994 2311
gregory.gosfield@dechert.com
Recommended in Real Estate
Practice Areas: Mr Gosfield is a Partner and Member of the Finance and Real Estate Group. He represents agent banks, general partners, owners, tenants, and institutional investors in matters involving senior and subordinate debt and equity; operation and maintenance of assets and entities; and workouts, insolvencies, and turnarounds.
Prof. Memberships: Member, Pennsylvania Bar.
Publications: His articles have been published in The Business Lawyer Today; The Real Property, Probate, and Trust Journal; and The Practical Real Estate Lawyer, among others.
Personal: Columbia College (BA, 1972); Temple University School of Law (JD, cum laude, 1979), Member of Temple University Law Review.

GUNDERSEN, Glenn A
Dechert, Philadelphia
215 994 2183
glenn.gundersen@dechert.com
Recommended in Intellectual Property
Practice Areas: Mr Gundersen is Co-Chair of the Intellectual Property Group. He focuses on trademark, copyright, licensing, internet, advertising, and right of publicity law. He advises on clearance, prosecution, oppositions, fair use, licensing, e-commerce, IP transactions, and infringement disputes.
Prof. Memberships: Member, Pennsylvania Bar; Meetings Board, International Trademark Association; Board of Directors, Philadelphia Volunteer Lawyers for the Arts.
Publications: Author, 'Trademark Searching' (1st & 2nd ed) and 'Intellectual Property Assets in Mergers & Acquisitions' (co-author); speaker at various industry programs; founder, Copyright Society of USA, Philadelphia Chapter.
Personal: College of William and Mary (BA, 1976); University of Virginia (JD, 1980).

HALLER, Anthony
Blank Rome LLP, Philadelphia
215 569 5690
haller@BlankRome.com
Recommended in Employment
Practice Areas: Anthony Haller's practice covers all aspects of labor and employment law including preventative counseling, complex litigation, trial and appellate work. He has represented clients in cases involving claims of race, age, sex, disability discrimination, wrongful discharge, defamation and sexual harassment. He has handled multiple plaintiff, representative, and class actions. His experience also includes liti-

gation of non-compete agreements, collective bargaining, arbitration, representation and unfair labor practice proceedings, the handling of strikes and picketing activity, federal and state law injunction proceedings, wage and hour claims, and employee benefit litigation. **Prof. Memberships:** ABA, Labor and Employment and Litigation Sections. **Career:** Master, American Temple Inn of Court; frequent lecturer on employment law issues; frequent guest on Law Journal TV, WFMZ-TV (channel 69) discussing employment law issues. **Publications:** Co-author, Chapter 8, An Introduction To The Employment Laws of The United States For The Foreign Investor, Business Opportunities In The United States (Richard D. Irwin, Inc. 1992). Co-author, Chapter 25, Labor Law In The Construction Industry, Construction Business Handbook (Aspen Pub 2003). **Personal:** BA, St. Catherine's College, Cambridge, 1977; LLM, University of Pennsylvania Law School, 1979. Barrister. Attorney.

HANGLEY, William
Hangley Aronchick Segal & Pudlin, Philadelphia 215 496 7001
whangley@hangley.com
Recommended in Litigation
Practice Areas: General business litigation; professional responsibility, legal malpractice and counseling law firms; intellectual property; First Amendment; securities; antitrust.
Prof. Memberships: Fellow, American College of Trial Lawyers, 1987- (Chair, Committee on Federal Rules of Evidence, 2001-03; Member, Outreach Committee, 2005-; Member, Communications Committee, 2002-; Member, Pennsylvania State Committee, 1998-2003; Member, Ad Hoc Committee on the Future of the Civil Trial, 2004; Member, Committee on Federal Rules of Evidence 1999-). Fellow, American Bar Foundation. Member, American Law Institute. University of Pennsylvania Fellow, Salzburg Seminar in American Studies, Law, 1975. Founding Member and Master of the Bench, University of Pennsylvania Inn of Court, 1993-. Judge Pro Tem, Philadelphia Court of Common Pleas, 1990-2000. Member, ABA Section of Litigation (Nominating Committee nominee for Council, 2005; Co-Chair, Task Force on the Judiciary, 2004-; Co-Chair, Federal Procedure Committee, 1990-95; Co-Chair, Merit Selection of Judges Task Force, 1995-97; Member, Task Force on Discovery,1997-2000; Member, Task Force on the Judiciary,2000-; Member, Task Force on Training the Trial Lawyer, 2002-03. Member, Philadelphia Bar Association (Member, Special Subcommittee on Proposed Rules of Judicial Conduct, 2005-). Public Interest Law Center of Philadelphia, Board of Advisors. Mem-

ber, Legal Club, 1993-present (President 2004-; Vice President 2002-04) Member, Junior Legal Club, 1995-.
Career: Founder, Chair, Hangley Aronchick Segal & Pudlin, 1994 - present. Founder (Chair 1983-94) Hangley Connolly Epstein Chicco Foxman & Ewing and predecessor firms, 1969-94. Associate, Schnader, Harrison, Segal & Lewis, 1966-69. University of Pennsylvania Law School, Philadelphia, Pennsylvania, 1966 (cum laude, Order of the Coif; comment editor, 'University of Pennsylvania Law Review'). State University of New York College at Fredonia, BS (Music) 1963.
Publications: 'Opinions Hidden, Citations Forbidden: Report And Recommendations Of the American College of Trial Lawyers On The Publication And Citation Of Nonbinding Federal Circuit Court Opinions', 208 F.R.D. 645 (2002); 'Teaching Through Experts: Changing the Obscure to the Obvious', Litigation, Spring, 2001; 'Direct and the Director: Writing, Staging and Telling The Story', Litigation, Fall, 1998; 'The Fourth Estate and the Second Front: Winning and Losing in the Press', Litigation, Spring, 1997; 'The Strike Zone, the Trial Judge and Other Moving Targets', California Litigation (Cal. Bar Ass'n. Section of Litigation), Spring, 1995.

HANLON, Michael J
Blank Rome LLP, Philadelphia
215 569 5652
hanlon@BlankRome.com
Recommended in Employment
Practice Areas: Firm Practice Group Leader in employment, benefits and labor. Extensive experience in traditional labor law, contract negotiations, and union avoidance as well as representing and counseling employers in employment discrimination, OSHA, and wage-hour matters and negotiating executive contracts. Clients include large publicly-traded and mid-size corporations in the manufacturing, maritime, and service sectors, as well as large government entities.
Prof. Memberships: Admitted to practice in Pennsylvania (1981). Member of the Pennsylvania and Philadelphia Bar Associations, the Industrial Relations Research Association (IRRA) and the National School Boards Association.
Personal: JD, Villanova University, 1981; BS in Economics, Wharton School, University of Pennsylvania, 1976.

HARKINS Jr, John G
Harkins Cunningham LLP, Philadelphia
215 851 6701
jharkins@harkinscunningham.com
Recommended in Litigation
Practice Areas: Throughout his career, John Harkins has been engaged in complex litigation involving issues of corporate, securities and antitrust law, contracts, intellectual property and ERISA,

frequently arguing such cases in appellate courts. Mr Harkins has also served as an advisor on a wide variety of corporate issues and transactions. He has advised directors on their fiduciary and other duties, corporate clients on disclosure issues, special committees in the investigation of alleged corporate wrongdoing, and corporations on the defenses available to them under Pennsylvania law against hostile takeover bids. He has also appeared on behalf of defendants in many derivative actions.
Prof. Memberships: Fellow, American College of Trial Laywers; Member, American Law Institute.
Career: Partner, Harkins Cunningham LLP; Member of the Bars of the Commonwealth of Pennsylvania; the Supreme Court of the United States; the United States Courts of Appeals for the Second, Third, Fourth, Fifth, Seventh, Ninth and Eleventh Circuits; and the United States District Court for the Eastern District of Pennsylvania and other Districts.
Personal: University of Pennsylvania, LLB, summa cum laude, 1958; University of Pennsylvania, BA, 1953.

HARRIS, Judith E
Morgan, Lewis & Bockius LLP, Philadelphia 215 963 5028
jeharris@morganlewis.com
Recommended in Employment
Practice Areas: Judith E Harris is a Partner in the Labor and Employment Law Practice Group. Ms Harris counsels employers in matters involving discrimination, trade secrets, non-complete agreements and employee compensation. Ms Harris represents employers in class action, collective action and single plaintiff litigation, and has successfully tried numerous complex jury and non-jury cases. She has argued in the United State Supreme Court, the United States Court of Appeals - Third, Seventh and Eleventh Circuits, Pennsylvania Supreme Court and Pennsylvania's intermediate appellate courts.
Prof. Memberships: American Bar Association, Pennsylvania Bar Association, Philadelphia Bar Association, Former President - Philadelphia Bar Foundation.

HARTLE MUNSCH, Martha
Reed Smith LLP, Pittsburgh
412 288 4118
mmunsch@reedsmith.com
Recommended in Employment
Practice Areas: General labor and employment representation for management clients in private and public sectors, including colleges and universities.
Prof. Memberships: National Association of College and University Attorneys; Labor Law Section, Allegheny County Bar Association; Labor Section's Committee on Equal Employment Opportunity Law, ABA.
Career: Joined Reed Smith in 1973;

joined the faculty of the University of Pittsburgh in 1976 to teach courses in employment discrimination, civil procedures, among others; returned to Reed Smith in 1978.
Personal: Yale Law School (JD, 1973); University of Pittsburgh (1970); listed in 'The Best Lawyers in America'.

HEIM, Robert C
Dechert, Philadelphia 215 994 2570
robert.heim@dechert.com
Recommended in Litigation
Practice Areas: Mr Heim is a nationally known trial lawyer who has represented numerous major corporations in trial and appellate matters in US state and federal courts.
Prof. Memberships: Member, Pennsylvania Bar; admitted to practice before numerous federal courts; Member, Judicial Conference Advisory Committee on Civil Rules; member, Third Judicial Circuit Advisory Committee.
Career: Former Chair, Federal Courts Committee; past Chancellor, Philadelphia Bar Association; past President of the National Conference of Bar Presidents.
Personal: University of Pennsylvania (BS, 1964); College of William and Mary (MB, 1968); University of Pennsylvania School of Law (JD, 1972).

HEIST, Dale
Woodcock Washburn LLP, Philadelphia 215 568 3100
heist@woodcock.com
Recommended in Intellectual Property
Practice Areas: Litigated more than 100 patent/IP cases in diverse fields, including robotics, polymers, medical products and computer software.
Prof. Memberships: Member, Pennsylvania and New Jersey Bars; Fellow, American College of Trial Lawyers. Member, American, Pennsylvania and Philadelphia Bar Associations; the American, Philadelphia and New York Intellectual Property Law Associations.
Career: Joined Woodcock Washburn, 1977.
Publications: Recognized in Chambers Guide to the Legal Profession 2003, 2004. Named a Pennsylvania Super Lawyer.
Personal: BS (1970) in electrical engineering and JD (1976) from Villanova University.

HERYFORD, Craig
Klett Rooney Lieber & Schorling, Pittsburgh 412 392 2000
Recommended in Banking & Finance

HICKOK, Robert L
Pepper Hamilton LLP, Philadelphia 215 981 4583
hickokr@pepperlaw.com
Recommended in Litigation
Practice Areas: Partner; Chairman, Commercial Litigation Practice Group; Executive Committee Member. Experienced in: antitrust, securities, D and O, white collar and criminal, and insurance

sales practices litigation; corporate investigations; class action defense; application of economic analysis; antitrust cases (product and market definition and product pricing); federal securities law (efficient capital market theory); commercial contract cases (measure of damages); application of technology to information/litigation management.
Prof. Memberships: Member, Executive Committee, Harvard Law School Association of Philadelphia.
Career: Former Assistant US Attorney, Eastern District of Pennsylvania (1979-83); JD 1978 Harvard Law School; AM 1978 Harvard University; BA 1974 Lehigh University.

HINERMAN, Philip L
Fox Rothschild LLP, Philadelphia
215 299 2066
phinerman@foxrothschild.com
Recommended in Environment
Practice Areas: Environmental regulatory litigation.
Personal: Level 3 Advanced Certification in Wines and Spirits from the Wine & Spirits Education Trust based in London; 1979 graduate of Washington & Lee University School of Law; 1975 graduate of Marshall University.

HODGSON, Clark
Stradley, Ronon, Stevens & Young LLP, Philadelphia 215 564 8000
Recommended in Litigation

HORNAK, Mark
Buchanan Ingersoll PC, Pittsburgh
412 562 8859
hornakmr@bipc.com
Recommended in Employment
Practice Areas: Mark represents employers in litigation, fair employment practice and employee privacy issues, and negotiates collective bargaining agreements for public and private employers. Mark advises school districts on employment and education law, and represents municipalities and government officials in constitutional and civil rights litigation. He represents national broadcasting and publishing clients in litigation and transactional matters. Mark has been appointed Special Master in complex/class action litigation in state and federal courts.
Prof. Memberships: Advisory Committee, United States District Court, Western Pennsylvania; Academy of Trial Lawyers; 'Leadership Pittsburgh' Program, American Law Institute; American Bar Foundation.
Personal: BS, 1978; JD, 1981 University of Pittsburgh.

HORSTMANN, John F
Duane Morris LLP, Philadelphia
215 979 1504
horstmann@duanemorris.com
Recommended in Bankruptcy
Practice Areas: John F Horstmann practices in the areas of bankruptcy law,

corporate reorganization, creditors' rights, out of court workouts, bank transactions, complex commercial reorganizations, international finance transactions and commercial loan documentation.
Prof. Memberships: American Bar Association - Business Law Section, Business Bankruptcy Committee, Subcommittee on International Bankruptcy; Pennsylvania Bar Association - Corporation, Banking and Business Law Section; Philadelphia Bar Association - Business Law Section, past Chairman - Subcommittee on the Uniform Commercial Code, Member - Subcommittee on Corporate Reorganization and Business Bankruptcy; Turnaround Business Management Association - Associate Member.
Career: Duane Morris LLP: Member, Partners Board; Chairman, Reorganization and Finance Section, 1994-2001; Partner, 1984-present; associate, 1976-84. Admitted to practice in Pennsylvania, the United States District Court for the Eastern District of Pennsylvania, the United States Bankruptcy Court for the Eastern District of Pennsylvania, and the Supreme Court of Pennsylvania.
Personal: Villanova University School of Law, JD, 1976.

HOWARD, David M
Dechert LLP, Philadelphia
215 994 2218
david.howard@dechert.com
Recommended in Litigation
Practice Areas: Litigation Partner and Chair of White Collar Litigation Group. Concentrates practice on white collar criminal defense, corporate investigations, enforcement proceedings, and complex civil litigation.
Prof. Memberships: Member, Pennsylvania Bar; Co-Chair, ABA White Collar Crime Committee's Subcommittee on Corporate Internal Investigations.
Career: Law Clerk, Hon. Marvin Katz (EDPA); Assistant US Attorney, Eastern District of Pennsylvania (1987-94), where he coordinated District's Securities and Commodities Fraud Task Force; Office of White House Counsel, Iran/Contra Investigations (1987).
Personal: Princeton University (AB, cum laude, 1981); University of Pennsylvania School of Law (JD, cum laude, 1984), Order of the Coif, Member of Law Review.

HOWARD, Lindsay
Babst, Calland, Clements and Zomnir, A Professional Corporation, Pittsburgh
412 394 5400
Recommended in Environment

JACOBS-MEADWAY, Roberta
Ballard Spahr Andrews & Ingersoll LLP, Philadelphia 215 864 8201
jacobsmeadwayr@ballardspahr.com
Recommended in Intellectual Property
Practice Areas: Her practice focuses on trademarks, unfair competition issues, including advertising issues, as well as

copyrights and licensing of intellectual property, and includes related litigation in the federal courts and before the Trademark Trial and Appeal Board. She has served as mediator in numerous trademark and copyright disputes.
Prof. Memberships: Member of the American Law Institute, American Bar Association, Pennsylvania Bar Association, and Philadelphia Bar Association; the Philadelphia Intellectual Property Law Association; and the International Trademark Association. She is a member of the American Bar Association's Federal Legislation Committee. Civic Activities: She serves on the Boards of the InterAct Theater Company, where she chairs the Marketing and Development Committee, and of Birthright. Lectures and seminars: She serves as the planning Co-Chair and lecturer at ALI-ABA programs on litigating trademark and unfair competition cases; on licensing of intellectual property; and on Internet law. She has also lectured on intellectual property law for PBI, the Iowa Intellectual Property law Association, the INTA and numerous other organizations.
Career: Admitted to the New Jersey Bar (1975); admitted to the Pennsylvania Bar (1975); joined as Partner (2001).
Publications: The author of numerous articles for business publications and trade periodicals, she has contributed chapters on surveys and on damages in copyright cases to Matthew Bender's treatise Intellectual Property Counseling and Litigation. She is also a contributing author to the World Copyright Law Report.
Personal: JD, with honors, Rutgers University School of Law (1975); BA, magna cum laude, Bryn Mawr College (1972).

JARIN, Kenneth M
Ballard Spahr Andrews & Ingersoll LLP, Philadelphia 215 864 8135
jarink@ballardspahr.com
Recommended in Employment
Practice Areas: Represents both public and private employers in matters relating to labor relations, contract negotiations, interest arbitration, employment discrimination litigation, and wage and hour disputes. He also counsels clients on matters related to the Fair Labor Standards Act and the Family and Medical Leave Act and has participated in administrative proceedings before the National Labor Relations Board and various state agencies. He is chief labor negotiator for the Commonwealth of Pennsylvania.
Prof. Memberships: Treasurer of the Democratic Governors Association, a Member of the ADL's National Executive Committee, and a Member of the Board of Directors of the Recreation Activities Fund for the City of Philadelphia. He also serves as Chairman of the Board of Directors of the Chamber

Orchestra of Philadelphia and is a Member of the Board of Directors for the Kimmel Center for the Performing Arts, an Executive Board Member of the Board of Directors for the Penns Landing Corporation, and a Member of the Pennsylvania Interest on Lawyers Trust Account Board (PA IOLTA).
Career: Admitted to the Pennsylvania Bar (1975); joined as Partner (2002).
Publications: Author of 'National League of Cities v. Usery Reversed: What Does It Mean For Municipal Governments?' The Reporter, Pennsylvania League of Cities, 1st Quarter, 1985, and 'Supreme Court Overturns New Cumberland Decision,' The Reporter, Pennsylvania League of Cities, 1st Quarter, 1984.
Personal: JD, Temple University James E. Beasley School of Law (1975); BA, Duke University (1972).

JONES, David F
Dechert, Philadelphia 215 994 2822
david.jones@dechert.com
Recommended in Employee Benefits
Practice Areas: Partner and Chair of the Employee Benefits and Executive Compensation Group. Practice includes all aspects of qualified and nonqualified retirement plans, equity compensation, executive compensation, and related transactional matters.
Prof. Memberships: Member, Pennsylvania Bar; Member, American Bar Association.
Publications: Lectures at seminars and conferences sponsored by the Association of Corporate Counsel, Practising Law Institute, Pennsylvania-New Jersey-Delaware Employee Benefits Association, and Strategic Research Institute.
Personal: Temple University (BBA, cum laude, 1979); Temple University School of Law (JD, cum laude, 1982), business editor of Temple Law Review; New York University School of Law (LLM in taxation, 1984).

JONES, Richard D
Dechert, Philadelphia 215 994 2501
richard.jones@dechert.com
Recommended in Real Estate
Practice Areas: Mr Jones is a Partner and Member of the Executive Committee of Dechert's Finance and Real Estate Group. His practice involves mortgage finance and capital markets.
Prof. Memberships: Member, Connecticut and Pennsylvania Bars; President, Commercial Mortgage Securities Association; founder and officer, Chartered Realty Investors Society; member and past governor, American College of Real Estate Lawyers; Member, Commercial Mortgage Board of Governors of the Mortgage Bankers Association of America; member, The Real Estate Roundtable.
Personal: Washington and Lee University (BA, 1975); University of Virginia School of Law (JD, 1978); Boston University School of Law (LLM, 1981).

JUDGE, John
Montgomery, McCracken, Walker & Rhoads, LLP, Philadelphia
215 772 1500
Recommended in Environment

KANE, Jonathan
Pepper Hamilton LLP, Berwyn
610 640 7803
kanej@pepperlaw.com
Recommended in Employment
Practice Areas: Partner, Chairman, Labor and Employment Group. Experienced in: averting union organizational campaigns, collective bargaining negotiations, labor-related litigation and arbitration; National Labor Relations Board matters; employment litigation; counseling, labor and employment aspects of corporate transactions; prevention of violence in the workplace; legal aspects of drug abuse policies and practice. Provides advice on developing and conducts comprehensive, in-house training programs. Experienced in a wide range of industries, including retail, services and healthcare.
Prof. Memberships: Fellow, College of Labor and Employment Lawyers.
Career: JD 1973 University of Virginia School of Law; BS 1967 University of Pennsylvania, The Wharton School.

KAPLAN, Arthur M
Fine Kaplan & Black, Philadelphia
215 567 6565
akaplan@finekaplan.com
Recommended in Antitrust
Practice Areas: Antitrust; complex commercial litigation; class actions.
Prof. Memberships: The American Law Institute; American Bar Association.
Career: Founding Member, Fine Kaplan and Black, 1975 to present. President, Committee to Support the Antitrust Laws, 1994-97; American Antitrust Institute, Board of Advisors, 1997 to date.
Publications: Arthur M Kaplan, Antitrust as A Public-Private Partnership: A Case Study of the NASDAQ Litigation, 52 Case W. Res. L. Review 111 (2001).
Personal: Member of the National Board of Governors of the Equality Forum, 2000 to date; Appointed Member of the Philadelphia Art Commission, 1993-2000; Member, American Civil Liberties Union of Philadelphia (Board of Directors, 1990 to date; Vice-President, 1995); American Civil Liberties Union of Pennsylvania (Board of Directors, 1993-97).

KASSNER, Andrew C
Drinker Biddle & Reath LLP, Philadelphia 215 988 2554
Andrew.Kassner@dbr.com
Recommended in Bankruptcy
Practice Areas: Managing Partner, Co-Head of the Bankruptcy and Reorganization Practice. Concentrates practice in workouts, Chapter 11 cases and bankruptcy litigation.

Prof. Memberships: Admitted: New York, Pennsylvania, Delaware. Member, New York, Pennsylvania, Philadelphia Bar Associations; Eastern District of Pennsylvania Bankruptcy Conference, Commercial Law League, American Bankruptcy Institute. Co-Chair, Bankruptcy Law Section of the Philadelphia Bar Association. Lectured at the University of Pennsylvania Wharton School of Business and on panels sponsored by the American Bankruptcy Institute and the Practicing Law Institute.
Career: Joined Drinker Biddle, 1986.
Personal: JD, (cum laude) New York School of Law, 1983, BA, University of Pennsylvania, 1980.

KATCHER, Bruce S
Manko, Gold, Katcher & Fox LLP, Bala Cynwyd 484 430 2320
BKatcher@mgkflaw.com
Recommended in Environment
Practice Areas: Contaminated site assessment and remediation, solid and hazardous waste, air and water pollution control, Superfund, underground tanks, coastal zoning and wetlands matters. He has worked with many clients in developing and implementing brownfields reuse strategies. He also counsels clients on regulatory compliance, including environmental auditing and compliance management system development.
Prof. Memberships: Member of the Environment, Energy and Resources Section of the American Bar Association; the Environmental Law Section of the New Jersey Bar Association; the Environmental Law Committee of the Camden County Bar Association; the Environmental, Mineral and Natural Resources Section of the Pennsylvania Bar Association and the Environmental Law Committee of the Philadelphia Bar Association; the Board of Directors and Executive Committee of the PEN-JERDEL Council; Chairman of the Councils Environmental Improvement Committee; Member of the Executive Committee of the Board of Directors of the Chamber of Commerce of Southern New Jersey and Chair of the Environmental Committee; member of the New Jersey Business and Industry Association; the New Jersey Builders Association; and the Builders League of South Jersey.
Career: A Founding Partner of Manko, Gold, Katcher & Fox, LLP. Previously worked for the Office of International Affairs of the US Treasury Department for two years. He is admitted to the New Jersey and Pennsylvania Bars and is the partner in charge of the firm's New Jersey office.
Publications: Lectured and written extensively on various environmental law subjects in New Jersey and Pennsylvania. Recent article topics include the New Jersey Brownfield and Contaminated Site Remediation Act and regulatory reform programs in New Jersey and

at EPA. Authored the chapter on Solid Waste Management in the Pennsylvania Bar Institute's treatise, Pennsylvania Environmental Law and Practice.
Personal: BS in economics, magna cum laude from the Wharton School of the University of Pennsylvania in 1971; JD from the University of Pennsylvania Law School, cum laude, 1976. Member of the Beta Gamma Sigma honor society. Member of the Voorhees Township (NJ) Environmental Commission and a member of the Leadership Committee for the American Heart Association's Heart Walk, Burlington and Camden Counties.

KATZ, Carole S
Morgan, Lewis & Bockius LLP, Pittsburgh 412 560 3390
ckatz@morganlewis.com
Recommended in Employment
Practice Areas: Carole Katz is a Partner in the Labor and Employment Law Practice Group. Ms Katz counsels and represents employers and tries cases in a wide variety of labor and employment law matters, including employment discrimination, harassment, and retaliation issues and cases, wrongful discharge actions, benefits litigation, restrictive covenant/trade secret matters, and all other types of employment-related litigation. Ms Katz also has extensive experience in jury, non-jury, and administrative litigation, and alternative dispute resolution such as mediation and arbitration.
Prof. Memberships: American Bar Association (Labor and Employment Law and Litigation Sections); Allegheny County Bar Association.

KESSLER, Mark
Wolf, Block, Schorr and Solis-Cohen LLP, Philadelphia 215 977 2000
Recommended in Corporate/M&A

KLEBAN, Barry
Adelman Lavine Gold & Levin, Philadelphia 215 568 7515
Recommended in Bankruptcy

KLEIN, Justin P
Ballard Spahr Andrews & Ingersoll LLP, Philadelphia 215 864 8606
kleinj@ballardspahr.com
Recommended in Corporate/M&A
Practice Areas: Concentrates on diverse securities matters, including public and private securities offerings, representing boards of directors of public and private companies, and representing parties in regulatory and enforcement proceedings before the Securities and Exchange Commission (SEC), state securities commissions, and securities industry self-regulatory organizations.
Prof. Memberships: Has chaired the Committee on Securities Regulation and the Executive Committee of the Business Law Section of the Philadelphia Bar Association. He has also served

as a Member of, and as Chair of, the National Arbitration and Mediation Committee of the National Association of Securities Dealers, Inc. He was recently appointed to the Attorney Advisory Committee of The Pennsylvania Securities Commission.
Career: Admitted to the Maryland Bar (1972); admitted to the District of Columbia Bar (1973); admitted to the Pennsylvania Bar (1983); joined as Partner (1992). He spent nine years at the Securities & Exchange Commission (SEC) in Washington DC in various positions including Assistant Director of the Division of Corporate Finance.
Publications: Extensive publications in the area of securities law.
Personal: JD, with honors, George Washington University National Law Center (1972); BA, University of Pennsylvania (1969).

KLINE, Eric
Morgan, Lewis & Bockius LLP, Pittsburgh 412 560 3363
ekline@morganlewis.com
Recommended in Banking & Finance
Practice Areas: Eric Kline is a Partner in the Business and Finance Practice. Mr Kline provides general corporate counseling to emerging growth companies from start-up through initial public offering or acquisition. In this capacity, he provides advice on the proper structuring and financing of the entity, the negotiation of key employment, licensing and partnering transactions, and business and legal strategies in liquidity event transactions. His clients are involved globally in the internet, software, and life science industries.
Career: Mr Kline was an attorney with the Securities and Exchange Commission from 1989-92.

KLINE, Thomas
Kline & Specter PC, Philadelphia
215 772 1000
Recommended in Litigation

KOHN, Joseph
Kohn Swift & Graf, Philadelphia
215 238 1700
Recommended in Antitrust

KOONS Jr, Robert A
Buchanan Ingersoll, Philadelphia
215 665 3825
koonsra@bipc.com
Recommended in Intellectual Property
Practice Areas: Registered Patent Attorney who litigates patent, trademark, and related cases. His practice includes prosecution of patents and trademarks before the United States Patent and Trademark Office and all related counseling, licensing and transactional matters. Bob has successfully prosecuted numerous applications for business method patents.
Prof. Memberships: Philadelphia Intellectual Property Law Association; American Intellectual Property Law Associa-

tion; American Society of Mechanical Engineers; Society of Automotive Engineers, Philadelphia Diversity Law Group (Director and Member of Executive Committee).

Personal: JD Temple University, 1983, magna cum laude; MBA. University of Pennsylvania, The Wharton School, 2001, with honors; BSME, 1972; Master of Engineering, 1974 University of South Carolina.

KORB, Philip
Ballard Spahr Andrews & Ingersoll LLP, Philadelphia 215 864 8709
korb@ballardspahr.com
Recommended in Real Estate

Practice Areas: His practice includes real estate acquisitions, development, leasing, taxation, and workouts.
Prof. Memberships: Past Chairman of the Real Property, Probate and Trust Section of the Pennsylvania Bar Association, and past Member of its House of Delegates. Former Chairman of the Philadelphia Bar Association's Committee on Condominiums and Cooperatives and the Pennsylvania Bar Association's Committee on Taxation of Real Estate. He is a Member of the American College of Real Estate Lawyers, in which he has served on the Board of Governors.
Career: Admitted to the Pennsylvania Bar (1975); joined as Partner (1985).
Personal: JD, magna cum laude, Temple University James E. Beasley School of Law (1975); BA, Johns Hopkins University (1969).

KRAMER, J Scott
Duane Morris LLP, Philadelphia
215 979 1122
jskramer@duanemorris.com
Recommended in Intellectual Property

Practice Areas: J Scott Kramer maintains an active trial practice in the areas of commercial litigation, copyright and trademark litigation and securities litigation, product liability and healthcare related litigation. Mr Kramer has conducted more than 40 civil jury trials and has represented clients before AAA, NASD Regulation, Inc., New York Stock Exchange, American Institute of Architects, The Securities and Exchange Commission, a variety of professional association forums and in the state and federal courts of Pennsylvania, New Jersey, New York and Maryland.
Prof. Memberships: American Bar Association; Pennsylvania Bar Association - Corporation, Banking and Business Law Section, Civil Litigation Section and Securities Law Section; Philadelphia Bar Association - Co-Chair, Medico-Legal Committee, 2003; Philadelphia Association of Defense Counsel; Defense Research Institute; Philadelphia Court of Common Pleas - Medical Malpractice Task Force.
Career: Duane Morris LLP, Partner 1988-present, Associate 1980-87. Admitted to practice in Pennsylvania, New Jer-

sey, the United States District Court for the Eastern District of Pennsylvania, and the Supreme Court of Pennsylvania.
Personal: Temple University School of Law, JD, 1980.

KUTLER, Marilyn
Schnader Harrison Segal & Lewis LLP, Philadelphia 215 751 2684
mkutler@schnader.com
Recommended in Real Estate

Practice Areas: Extensive work in real estate sales, project financing and commercial leasing. Signficant experience in real estate and government contracts with emphasis on complex public, private and institutional projects that involve governmental units and educational institutions. Major portion of practice devoted to work on large development projects that combine public and private for-profit and not-for-profit elements. Substantial experience in siting and land-use planning for developments such as sports/entertainment arenas, convention centers and energy facilities. Has drafted legislation on the state and local levels and worked extensively with federal, state and local government grant and loan programs.
Prof. Memberships: American Bar Association, Pennsylvania Bar Association, Philadelphia Bar Association.
Career: For more than a decade, served in City of Philadelphia Law Department, where she focused on public-sector business and real estate matters and supervised the City's legal work in major projects. Later joined Mayor's cabinet as city solicitor, serving as Philadelphia's chief counsel on many of the City's commercial ventures with developers utilizing mixed public-private funding.

KYPER, James R
Kirkpatrick & Lockhart Nicholson Graham LLP, Pittsburgh 412 355 6542
jkyper@klng.com
Recommended in Intellectual Property

Practice Areas: IP litigation involving patents, trademarks, trade dress, copyrights and unfair competition. Litigations involving steel framing, thermostatic mixing valves, safety equipment, automobiles, cutting tools, cellular services, medical devices, Internet business systems, software and entertainment properties. Litigates non-competes, license and distribution agreements, false advertising and insurance coverage for IP claims.
Prof. Memberships: ABA, PBA, ACBA; ABA IP Section; AIPLA, PIPLA, and IPO.
Career: K&L since 1976, Partner since 1983. Coordinated IP Litigation Group since 1993.
Publications: Presented working with experts in patent cases and discovery issues in patent and trademark cases.
Personal: JD, Duquesne University, 1976; BS, Penn State, 1967.

LADOV, Donald
Cohen & Grigsby PC, Pittsburgh
412 297 4905
dladov@cohenlaw.com
Recommended in Employment

Practice Areas: Is a labor lawyer exclusively representing management in all areas of labor/employment law both in the private and public sectors. He has regularly practiced before the National Labor Relations Board, the Equal Employment Opportunity Commission, the US Department of Labor, and many other regulatory agencies. Is also a prolific speaker on a wide variety of topics involving human resources and labor and employment law. Is listed in 'The Best Lawyers in America' for labor and employment law.
Career: BA, Labor Studies, Pennsylvania State University, 1970. JD, University of Pittsburgh School of Law, 1973. Admitted to practice in Pennsylvania, 1973.

LANE, Robert
Morgan, Lewis & Bockius LLP, Philadelphia 215 963 5174
rlane@morganlewis.com
Recommended in Real Estate

Practice Areas: Robert D Lane, Jr is the former Practice Group Leader of the firm's Real Estate Group. Mr Lane practices in all areas of commercial real estate acquisitions, development and financing. Mr Lane has represented a wide variety of Fortune 500 corporations and public entities in many industries, as well as major real estate developers, syndicators, REITs, and major lending institutions.
Prof. Memberships: Elected Fellow, American College of Real Estate Lawyers; Philadelphia Bar Foundation (Trustee and Chair of Board Development Committee); Central Philadelphia Development Corporation (President, Board of Directors); others.

LANGEL, John B
Ballard Spahr Andrews & Ingersoll LLP, Philadelphia 215 864 8227
langel@ballardspahr.com
Recommended in Employment

Practice Areas: As the Chair of the Firm's Labor, Employment and Immigration Group, he concentrates his practice in the representation of management in all phases of labor and employment matters including legal advice, training, policy development concerning labor and personnel issues, collective bargaining, employment litigation, wage and hour investigations, preparation of employment contracts and restrictive covenants, planning of early retirement and reduction in force programs, and implementation and related litigation involving the labor implications in mergers, acquisitions, and asset purchases.
Prof. Memberships: A Member and Past Chairman of the Philadelphia Bar Association Labor and Employment

Law Committee, a Member of the American Bar Association Labor and Employment Section and a Fellow of The College of Labor and Employment Lawyers.
Career: Admitted to the Pennsylvania Bar (1974); admitted to the New Jersey Bar (1978); Law Clerk for the United States Disctict Court for the Eastern District of Pennsylvania (1974); joined the firm (1975); Adjunct Professor of Law, Temple University James E Beasley School of Law.
Publications: Was a contributing editor, Schlei & Grossman, 'Employment Discrimination'.
Personal: JD, summa cum laude, Temple University James E Beasley School of Law (1974); case note editor of the Law Review and Member of the Editorial Board; Member of the Board of Visitors of Temple University James E Beasley School of Law; BA, Marietta College (1970).

LANGER, Howard
Langer & Grogan PC, Philadelphia
215 419 6536
Recommended in Antitrust

LAPOWSKY, Robert
Stevens & Lee, P. C., Philadelphia
215 575 0100
Recommended in Bankruptcy

LAUPHEIMER, Ann Blair
Blank Rome LLP, Philadelphia
215 569 5758
laupheimer@BlankRome.com
Recommended in Litigation

Practice Areas: Concentrates in insurance coverage, insurance insolvency, business litigation.
Prof. Memberships: Admitted to practice in Pennsylvania (1984), Member IAIR, Philadelphia Bar Association, past Chair of Federal Courts Committee, Advisory Committee of Local Rules of Eastern District of Pennsylvania.
Career: Joined Blank Rome, 1986, became Partner, 1994; Law Clerk Hon James Hunter III, United States Court of Appeals for the Third Circuit.
Publications: Comment, Sherman Act 'Jurisdiction' in Hospital Staff Exclusion Cases, 132 U. Pa. L. Rev. 121 (1983).
Personal: Born July 5, 1959, JD, summa cum laude, University of Pennsylvania Law School, 1984; AB, Princeton University, 1979.

LAVINE, Jordan A
Akin Gump Strauss Hauer & Feld LLP, Philadelphia 215 965 1247
jlavine@akingump.com
Recommended in Intellectual Property

Practice Areas: Practice focuses on trademark, copyright and unfair competition counseling, prosecution, licensing and litigation matters for domestic and foreign clients of all sizes, including many in the publishing industry. Frequent lecturer and author on intellectual property issues. In 2002, he was named

one of 50 on the Fast Track by 'The Legal Intelligencer' and 'Pennsylvania Law Weekly,' which featured 50 top attorneys in Pennsylvania under the age of 40.
Career: Adjunct Professor, Advanced Trademark Issues, Villanova University School of Law.
Personal: BA, 1993, Colgate University; JD, 1996, Villanova University School of Law (Member, Villanova Law Review).

LAVORGNA, Gregory J
Drinker Biddle & Reath LLP, Philadelphia 215 988 3309
Gregory.Lavorgna@dbr.com
Recommended in Intellectual Property
Practice Areas: Partner, Head of the Intellectual Property Practice. Has experience in patents, trademarks, copyrights, trade secret and employee agreements, licensing and litigation.
Prof. Memberships: Admitted in Pennsylvania, District of Columbia, and before the Court of Appeals for the Federal Circuit and US Supreme Court. Registered patent attorney with the USPTO. Member, American and Philadelphia Bar Associations; the American Intellectual Property Law Association; the Benjamin Franklin Inn of Court (Founding Member); the American Law Institute; and the Justinian Society (past secretary).
Career: Joined Drinker Biddle in 2001.
Publications: Numerous, including What the General Practitioner Should Know About Patent Law and Practice (fifth and sixth editions).
Personal: JD (cum laude), Temple University School of Law, 1981; MSEE, Drexel University, 1975; BSEE, Drexel University, 1972.

LAWALL, Francis J
Pepper Hamilton LLP, Philadelphia 215 981 4481
lawallf@pepperlaw.com
Recommended in Bankruptcy
Practice Areas: Partner, Bankruptcy and Reorganization Group. Experienced in: national bankruptcy and reorganization matters, including representation of major energy companies and creditors' committees in bankruptcy proceedings throughout the United States; also experienced in reorganization of companies with massive toxic tort liabilities. Represents companies in the petroleum, textile, automotive, clothing and construction materials industries.
Prof. Memberships: Board Member, International Energy Credit Association, Inc.
Career: JD 1985 Temple University School of Law; MA 1982 Temple University; BA 1981 Temple University.

LAWLOR, William G
Dechert LLP, Philadelphia 215 994 2823
william.lawlor@dechert.com
Recommended in Corporate/M&A
Practice Areas: Partner and Head of Mergers and Acquisitions Group. Practice areas include public and private

mergers and acquisitions, securities offerings, strategic investments, and general corporate representation, including governance and compliance. Represents corporate clients, Boards of Directors, and special committees in negotiated and contested transactions and other assignments.
Prof. Memberships: Member, Pennsylvania and New York Bars; Member of various Bar associations and DealLawyers.com Advisory Board.
Publications: Author of articles featured in publications including The Daily Deal, Mergers & Acquisitions, M&A Lawyer, Securities & Commodities Regulation, and Corporate Governance Advisor.
Personal: University of Pennsylvania (BA, 1977); Stanford Law School (JD, 1980).

LESSER, Bruce
Wolf, Block, Schorr and Solis-Cohen LLP, Philadelphia 215 977 2000
blesser@wolfblock.com
Recommended in Banking & Finance
Practice Areas: Co-Chairman of the Financial Services Department and member of the firm's Corporate/Securities Practice Group. Concentrates his practice in the representation of lenders and borrowers in the structuring and documentation of senior, subordinate, debtor in possession and mezzanine financing transactions and in related creditor's rights matters. Additional concentration in bankruptcy and business law.
Prof. Memberships: Member, Pennsylvania Bar Association, Section on Corporation, Banking and Business Law, and the American and Philadelphia Bar Associations.
Career: Admitted to the Pennsylvania Bar (1973). Graduated Villanova School of Law (1973). Member of Law review and Order of the Coif.
Personal: Received his BA from Pennsylvania State University (1969) and his JD from Villanova University (1973).

LEVIN, Christine C
Dechert, Philadelphia 215 994 2421
christine.levin@dechert.com
Recommended in Antitrust, Litigation
Practice Areas: Ms Levin is a Partner in Dechert's Antitrust and White Collar Litigation Groups. She has experience in antitrust actions involving baby food, newspapers, chemicals, and pharmaceuticals, and has been involved in class actions alleging price-fixing, false advertising, and other product liability claims.
Prof. Memberships: Member, Pennsylvania Bar; admitted to numerous federal courts.
Career: Law Clerk, Hon Clarence C Newcomer, US District Court, Eastern District of Pennsylvania.
Personal: Duke University (BA, 1976); University of Pennsylvania Law School (JD, cum laude, 1982), Order of the Coif.

LICHTENSTEIN, Robert J
Morgan, Lewis & Bockius LLP, Philadelphia 215 963 5726
rlichtenstein@morganlewis.com
Recommended in Employee Benefits
Practice Areas: Robert J Lichtenstein is the Leader of the firm's Employee Benefits and Executive Compensation Practice. He provides counseling and assists clients in designing executive employment and compensation arrangements, including equity and incentive compensation plans, and counsels clients on employee benefits issues, including qualified ESOPs, retirement, pension and profit-sharing plans. He has litigated employee benefit claims and disputes, and assists with federal tax law matters and representations before the IRS and DOL. He is an Adjunct Professor at the University of Pennsylvania School of Law and Villanova University Law School.
Prof. Memberships: Member, ABA, Tax Section, Employee Benefits Committee.

LIEBENBERG, Roberta
Fine Kaplan & Black, Philadelphia 215 567 6565
rliebenberg@finekaplan.com
Recommended in Antitrust
Practice Areas: Commercial litigation, complex litigation, anti-trust, class actions.
Prof. Memberships: The American Law Institute; American Bar Association - Board of Governors, Litigation Section, former Co-Chair Class Actions and Derivatives Suits Committee; House of Delegates; Special Advisor Commission on Women in the Profession; Pennsylvania Bar Association - Board of Governors; House of Delegates; Philadelphia Bar Association, former Chair, Anitrust Committee.
Career: 2000-present, Partner, Fine, Kaplan and Black, RPC; 1992-00, founding Partner, Mager Liebenberg & White (first female-owned litigation firm in Philadelphia); 1984-92, Partner, Wolf, Block, Schorr and Solis-Cohen; 1978-92, Associate, Wolf, Block, Schorr and Solis-Cohen; Law Clerk, United States Court of Appeals for the Fourth Circuit.
Publications: 'Communications with Absent Class Members', September 2004, Federal Trade Commission Workshop on Protecting Consumer Interests,'Anti-trust, Where Are We in 2002?'; Pennsylvania Bar Institute; Speaker, 6th Annual National Class Action Institute, 'New Strategic and Ethical Challenges for Class Counsel', May, 2001 ABA Section of Litigation, 'The Court's Application of Daubert to Proposed Expert Testimony in Anti-trust Cases'.
Personal: Married to Dr Robert Liebenberg; three children - Julie, Katie and David.

LINDEFJELD, Robert O
Jones Day, Pittsburgh 412 394 7952
rlindefjeld@jonesday.com
Recommended in Intellectual Property
Practice Areas: Practices patent, copyright, trademark, trade secrets, and unfair competition law and has been involved in litigation, transactional, opinion, counseling, or appellate work in each of these areas. He has extensive experience in infringement and trade secret litigation in state and federal courts. He has also drafted confidentiality, technology transfer, and license agreements involving intellectual property interests. He is also responsible for preparing and prosecuting patent and trademark applications before the US Patent and Trademark Office.
Prof. Memberships: Council member for the ABA Section of Intellectual Property Law. President of the Pittsburgh Intellectual Property Law Association.

LIPMAN, Frederick
Blank Rome LLP, Philadelphia 215 569 5518
lipman@BlankRome.com
Recommended in Corporate/M&A
Practice Areas: Mr Lipman has practiced corporate and securities law for over 40 years and has been the Lead Attorney on transactions of all sizes and complexities.
Career: He is the Founder and President of the Association of Audit Committee Members, Inc. (AACMI). He has taught corporate finance, accounting and securities law at the University of Pennsylvania Law School for 10 years and in the MBA program at the Wharton School of Business for five years. He has appeared on CNN, CNBC and the Bloomberg network as a national commentator on business topics.
Publications: He is the lead author of the book entitled 'Audit Committees', recently published by The Bureau of National Affairs, Inc., and distributed nationally to attorneys. He is also the author of seven other books, including: 'Going Public', 'The Complete Guide to Valuing and Selling Your Business', 'Venture Capital and Junk Bond Financing' and 'The Complete Guide to Employee Stock Options'.
Personal: LLB, Harvard Law School, 1960.

LORD, Craig
Blank Rome LLP, Philadelphia 215 569 5496
lord@BlankRome.com
Recommended in Real Estate
Practice Areas: Real estate development, real estate lending, real estate sales/acquisitions, commercial litigation, arbitration and mediation.
Prof. Memberships: Admitted to practice in Pennsylvania (1972) and Florida (1977). Appointments: Board of Directors/Executive Committee - Philadelphia Industrial Development Corporation; Board of Trustees - Friends Central

School; Member, Pennsylvania Judicial Conduct Board.
Career: Blank Rome, 1999-present, Co-Chair and Partner, Real Estate Department; Department Head, Financial Services/Real Estate Department, 2003-present. Judge, Philadelphia Court of Common Pleas, 1988-97. Raynes, McCarty, 1997-99. Blank Rome, 1972-86.
Personal: JD, magna cum laude, University of Pennsylvania Law School, 1971, BA, magna cum laude, Gettysburg College, 1968.

MACK, Wayne
Duane Morris LLP, Philadelphia
215 979 1152
wamack@duanemorris.com
Recommended in Antitrust
Practice Areas: Wayne A Mack represents clients nationally in complex commercial litigation, with particular emphasis on antitrust, franchise, healthcare and securities law and trade regulation. He is a member of the firm's Dealer Services Group, representing automobile and truck dealers in a wide range of legal matters, including contract negotiations, succession issues, regulatory and compliance matters and litigating and mediating disputes. He has represented both plaintiffs and defendants in class action litigation, including cases involving claims of securities fraud, unfair trade practices and violations of the antitrust laws.
Prof. Memberships: The American Bar Association - Antitrust Law Section, Business Law Section (Business and Corporate Litigation Committee) and Forum Committee on Franchising; the Pennsylvania Bar Association - Civil Litigation Section; Philadelphia Bar Association; and American Health Lawyers Association.
Career: Admitted to practice in Pennsylvania, the Supreme Court of the United States, the United States Court of Appeals for the Third and Fourth Circuits, the United States District Court for the Eastern District of Pennsylvania, and the Supreme Court of Pennsylvania. Duane Morris LLP, Partner 1995-present, associate 1986-94. Chair, Franchise Litigation Group; Co-Chair, Antitrust Practice Group; Chair, Professional Standards Committee.
Personal: University of Pennsylvania Law School, JD, 1986; Temple University, BS, 1982.

MALLOY, Elizabeth
Klett Rooney Lieber & Schorling, Philadelphia 215 567 7500
Recommended in Employment

MANDELBAUM, David G
Ballard Spahr Andrews & Ingersoll LLP, Philadelphia 215 864 8102
mandelbaum@ballardspahr.com
Recommended in Environment
Practice Areas: Represents clients in a full range of environmental matters including nationally significant contaminated sediment sites, commercial litigation over environmental representations

in sale of a manufacturing division, regulation of timber harvesting, regulation of shooting preserves, public trust, wetlands, and 'sprawl' regulation, and complex urban brownfields. He was appointed by the Governor to the Pennsylvania Statewide Water Resources Committee. He is an Adjunct Professor of Law and an Adjunct Associate Professor of Community and Regional Planning at Temple University.
Prof. Memberships: He serves as the Chair of the Special Committee on Smart Growth and Urban Policy of the American Bar Association Section on Environment, Energy and Resources, and he is a past Chair of the Pennsylvania Bar Association's Environmental, Mineral, and Natural Resources Law Section. He is a member of the environmental sections of the Florida Bar and Maryland State Bar Association.
Career: Admitted to the Pennsylvania Bar (1983); admitted to the Florida Bar (1984); admitted to the Maryland Bar (1993); joined the firm (1987). Wolf, Block, Schorr & Solis-Cohen (1984-87); Law Clerk to Hon Louis H Pollak (1983-84).
Publications: 'Contribution After Cooper Industries v. Aviall Services', 49 Chem. Waste Litig. Rep. 137 (Jan. 2005); 'The Timing Provisions of CERCLA for Natural Resource Damage Claims', 19 Toxics L. Rep. (BNA) 22 (Jan. 2004); 'Thoughts on the Bush Clean Air 'Strategy' So Far, and a Suggestion for What Might Work', 21 Temple Envtl. L. & Tech. J. 1 (2002); 'Does the Section 107/Section 113 Choice Affect Allocation in CERCLA Actions?', 13 Toxics L. Rep. (BNA) 979 (Jan. 6, 1999); 'Toward a Superfund Cost Allocation Principle', 3 Envtl. Lawyer 117 (1996); 'Are NOAA's Natural Resources Damages Assessment Regulations a Useful New Model?', 5 Envtl. Regul. & Permitting No. 4 at 3 (1996); 'Crossfire on Contribution: A Rejoinder to John Clewett', 28 Chem. Waste Litig. Rep. 869 (1994); 'Superfund Reform and Old Industrial Sites', 3 J. Envtl. Regul. 369 (1994); 'Professional Responsibility Issues in Pennsylvania Environmental Practice:1. Conflicts in Superfund and 2. Dealing with Former Government Lawyers', 12 Temple Envtl. L. & Tech. J. 57 (1993).
Personal: JD, magna cum laude, Harvard Law School (1983); AB, summa cum laude, Harvard College (1980).

MANKO, Joseph M
Manko, Gold, Katcher & Fox LLP, Bala Cynwyd 484 430 2310
Jmanko@mgkflaw.com
Recommended in Environment
Practice Areas: Brownfields, indoor air, ADR, land use, real estate and business transactions.
Prof. Memberships: Served as Chairman of the Pennsylvania Environmental Council from 1988 until 1999, and remains an emeritus member of their

Board of Directors where he has served for more than 25 years. Served as a Vice Chairman of the Environmental Law Committee of the American Bar Association, and a Vice Chairman of the State Water Law Committee of the Pennsylvania Bar Association, and a member of the Pennsylvania Bar Association's Environmental Hearing Board Rules Committee. Served as Chairman of the Environmental Law Committee of the Philadelphia Bar Association.
Career: Mr Manko is the founding Partner of Manko, Gold, Katcher & Fox, LLP. Previously served as Chairman of the Environmental Department at Wolf, Block, Schorr and Solis-Cohen and as the Regional Counsel of the United States Environmental Protection Agency, Middle Atlantic Region (Region 3); Served since 1988 as a lecturer-in-law at the University of Pennsylvania Law School, teaching courses on environmental law, practice and policy; Served since 1989 as a guest lecturer at Vermont Law School; Serves as a distinguished neutral for environmental issues for the CPR Institute for Dispute Resolution, ADR Options, Inc., and the Dispute Resolution Institute; Served as a Master for the Delaware Valley Environmental American Inn of Court since 1997.
Publications: Served on the CPR Commission on the Future of Arbitration which recently published Commercial Arbitration at its Best-Successful Strategies for Business Users. He has lectured on a wide variety of environmental topics including Superfund, impacts of real estate development land recycling, indoor air liability, and the financial disclosure of environmental liabilities.
Personal: Graduated cum laude from Harvard University Law School in 1964 and magna cum laude and Phi Beta Kappa from Yale University in 1961. Mr Manko is an honorary Director of the Lower Merion Conservancy and the Philadelphia Geriatric Center. He is serving his sixth four-year term as a member of the Lower Merion Township Board of Commissioners, having served in the past as its Vice-President and President.

MANNINO, Edward F
Akin Gump Strauss Hauer & Feld LLP, Philadelphia 215 965 1340
emannino@akingump.com
Recommended in Litigation
Practice Areas: Ed Mannino has tried cases nationwide for 35 years. 'The National Law Journal' named him one of the Nation's Top Litigators and one of the top 10 Pennsylvania trial lawyers, describing him as a 'stellar litigator who is known for handling high-profile cases.' He has tried to verdict business tort, securities, antitrust, accountant's liability, RICO, ERISA, healthcare, products liability, employment discrimination and intellectual property cases. In

2003 he represented a corporation at trial against its CEO, who challenged his termination for cause, seeking over $30 million before trebling. The case ended in a complete defense verdict.

MARION, David
Montgomery, McCracken, Walker & Rhoads, LLP, Philadelphia
215 772 1500
Recommended in Litigation

MARSHALL, John
Drinker Biddle & Reath LLP, Berwyn
610 993 2274
John.Marshall@dbr.com
Recommended in Intellectual Property
Practice Areas: Partner in the Intellectual Property Practice. Practice is concentrated in civil litigation involving patent, trademark and copyright infringement, representation of patent and trademark applications before domestic and foreign governments, and advice to clients on intellectual property matters.
Prof. Memberships: Admitted in Pennsylvania and before the USPTO. Member of the American Intellectual Property Association, the American Bar Association, the Philadelphia Intellectual Property Law Association and the Benjamin Franklin AIC.
Career: Joined Drinker Biddle in 2001.
Personal: JD (cum laude) Villanova University School of Law, 1979; MS, University of West Florida, 1970; BS, US Naval Academy, 1969.

MATHER, Barbara W
Pepper Hamilton LLP, Philadelphia
215 981 4895
matherb@pepperlaw.com
Recommended in Antitrust, Litigation
Practice Areas: Partner, Chair, Litigation and Dispute Resolution Department, past Executive Partner. Experienced in: antitrust, securities, professional malpractice, commercial litigation. Represented: co-counsel for plaintiff LePage's in trial and appeals in monopolization claim that awarded $65 million after trebling, defendant's petition for certiorari before US Supreme Court denied in 2004; bathroom/ kitchen fixtures and fittings manufacturer in allegations of price fixing; various entities in shareholder class actions; major law firms in malpractice allegations.
Prof. Memberships: Fellow, American College of Trial Lawyers.
Career: City Solicitor, Philadelphia, PA (1/84 - 12/85); JD 1968 University of Chicago Law School; BA 1965 Swarthmore College.

MCCLENAHAN, David
Kirkpatrick & Lockhart Nicholson Graham LLP, Pittsburgh 412 355 6484
dmcclenahan@klng.com
Recommended in Litigation
Practice Areas: Commercial litigation: antitrust, securities, healthcare, class actions, RICO, ERISA, UCC, shareholdersí litigation, restrictive covenants,

breach of fiduciary duties, real estate and general business disputes.

Prof. Memberships: American College of Trial Lawyers; Academy of Trial Lawyers of Allegheny County; Best Lawyers in America.

Career: Joined K&L 1971. Law Clerk, Honorable John L. Miller, US District Court, Western District of Pennsylvania, 1970-71; Captain, US Army, 1968-70.

Publications: Frequent lecturer, panelist on litigation process and legal aspects of healthcare.

Personal: JD, Duquesne University, 1967; BA, John Carroll University, 1964; Chairman, Board of Trustees, West Penn Allegheny Health System, 2002-present.

MCGOUGH Jr, W Thomas

Reed Smith LLP, Pittsburgh
412 288 3088
wmcgough@reedsmith.com
Recommended in Litigation

Practice Areas: Heads the Litigation Department. Represents individuals and corporations in a wide variety of civil and criminal litigation.

Prof. Memberships: Former President, Allegheny County Bar Association; American College of Trial Lawyers; American Academy of Appellate Lawyers; Academy of Trial Lawyers of Allegheny County.

Career: Law clerk to the Honorable William H Rehnquist, Chief Justice; assistant counsel to the Senate Select Committee on Secret Military Assistance to Iran and the Nicaraguan Opposition; Staff Liaison to Senator Robert Dole.

Personal: University of Virginia School of Law (JD, 1978); Princeton University (1975); listed in 'The Best Lawyers in America'.

MCKENZIE, James

Morgan, Lewis & Bockius LLP,
Philadelphia 215 963 5134
jmckenzie@morganlewis.com
Recommended in Corporate/M&A

Practice Areas: Mr McKenzie is a Partner in the Business and Finance Practice and Co-Chair of the firm's REIT Practice. He advises clients on a wide range of securities and corporate law matters, particularly public offerings and mergers and acquisitions. Mr McKenzie's practice includes a variety of transactions subject to the securities laws, principally involving acquisitions of publicly and privately held companies, public and private offerings of debt and equity securities, general counseling to corporate clients concerning obligations under the securities laws, and general corporate matters.

MCLEAN, Michael

Kirkpatrick & Lockhart Nicholson
Graham LLP, Pittsburgh 412 355 6458
mmclean@klng.com
Recommended in Corporate/M&A

Practice Areas: Corporate, securities and mergers and acquisitions, with a focus on

corporate governance, IPOs, debt and equity securities offerings and venture capital, private and public company M&A, corporate restructurings, leveraged buyouts and 'going private' transactions.

Prof. Memberships: Admitted in Pennsylvania; member of American, Pennsylvania and Allegheny County Bar Associations.

Career: Joined Kirkpatrick & Lockhart Nicholson Graham LLP in 1968, Partner since 1974.

Publications: Lectures on a variety of securities, transactional and corporate law topics.

Personal: LLB, Harvard University, 1968; MA, Yale University, 1965; BA, Lafayette College, 1964.

MCMICHAEL, Lawrence

Dilworth Paxson LLP, Philadelphia
215 575 7268
Lmcmichael@Dilworthlaw.com
Recommended in Bankruptcy

Practice Areas: Litigation, bankruptcy.

Career: Mr McMichael's practice is concentrated in commercial litigation, as well as insurance and insolvency matters. He has extensive trial experience in federal and state courts, and is a frequent lecturer on litigation practice, insurance and bankruptcy. Mr McMichael also heads the firm's Bankruptcy Practice. He has represented substantial debtors, secured lenders, bondholders and equity interests in major Chapter 11 cases on a national basis. Mr McMichael also supervises all firm insurance-related representation. He is also a member of the Board of Directors of American General Holdings, Inc., an insurance holding company, headquartered in Chicago, Illinois.

MCNICHOL Jr, William

Reed Smith LLP, Philadelphia
215 241 7950
wmcnichol@reedsmith.com
Recommended in Intellectual Property

Practice Areas: Represents technology-based enterprises in IP matters including the prosecution of patent applications, re-examination and reissues; trademark registration applications, oppositions and cancellation proceedings; and preparation of patent validity and infringement opinions in anticipation of litigation and new product introduction. Extensive background in drug, biotech, and other medical technology IP litigation. In Amgen Inc v U.S. Trade Commission, represented the amicus curiae and presented prevailing arguments in the Court of Appeals. Congress responded by enacting the Biotechnological Process Patents Act of 1995.

Personal: Villanova University (JD, 1983; MS in biochemistry, 1979; BA in biology, 1977).

MEADWAY, Jay K

Ballard Spahr Andrews & Ingersoll LLP,
Philadelphia 215 864 8101
meadwayj@ballardspahr.com
Recommended in Intellectual Property

Practice Areas: His practice focuses on foreign trademark protection. Since commencing his practice, he has been involved in all aspects of trademark protection. Fluent in German, he represents companies and law firms in trademark matters in Europe, Japan, and elsewhere.

Prof. Memberships: He is a member of the American Bar Association, Pennsylvania Bar Association, Philadelphia Bar Association, and the International Trademark Association.

Career: Admitted to Pennsylvania Bar (1981); admitted to District of Columbia Bar (1978); admitted to Virginia Bar (1979); admitted to New York Bar (1986); joined as Partner (2001). Prior to joining Ballard Spahr, he was a Partner at a large law firm, where he concentrated in international trademark practice and other areas of trademark, copyright, and unfair competition law. He has also been an in-house trademark attorney for Pfizer, Inc., with primary responsibility for the worldwide portfolio of consumer products trademarks.

Publications: 'The Community Trademark, A New Registration System For Obtaining Trademark Protection In The European Union' and 'Revised Japanese Trademark Law - An Overview Of Key Changes,' published in the Corporation, Banking and Business Law Newsletter.

Personal: JD, George Washington University (1978); BA, University of Pennsylvania (1975).

MELOY, Michael M

Manko, Gold, Katcher & Fox LLP,
Bala Cynwyd 484 430 2303
MMeloy@mgkflaw.com
Recommended in Environment

Practice Areas: Environmental litigation, regulatory, transactional issues, redevelopment and remediation projects, the development and implementation of waste management programs, environmental auditing of facilities and operations, and the development of comprehensive water planning legislation. He has also handled matters involving health and safety issues arising under the Occupational Safety and Health Act.

Prof. Memberships: Member of the Delaware Basin Regional Water Resources Committee. Chairs the Agricultural Law Committee of the Pennsylvania Bar Association and is a member of the Environment, Energy and Resources Section of the American Bar Association; the Environmental, Mineral and Natural Resources Section of the Pennsylvania Bar Association and the Environmental Law Committee of the Philadelphia Bar Association. Serves on the Pennsylvania Cleanup Standards Scientific Advisory Board's Safe Fill

Committee and the Environmental Affairs Committee for the Pennsylvania Chamber of Business and Industry; Chair of the Pennsylvania Chamber's Solid Waste Advisory Committee and serves as a member on the Pennsylvania Chamber's Water Task Force.

Career: Michael M Meloy is a Partner at Manko, Gold, Katcher & Fox, LLP. He was admitted to the Pennsylvania Bar in 1983. He is admitted to practice before the United States Courts of Appeals for the District of Columbia Circuit and the Third Circuit, and the United States District Courts for the Eastern and Middle Districts of Pennsylvania.

Publications: Authored 'An Overview of Nutrient Management Requirements in Pennsylvania', 10 Penn. State Envtl. L. Rev. 249 (2002), and also authored 'Disclosure of Environmental Liability in SEC Filings, Financial Statements, and Debt Instruments', 5 VILL. ENVTL. L.J. 315 (1994). Lecturer on a wide range of environmental matters, including presentations for the American Bar Association's Section of Environment, Energy and Resources, the Pennsylvania Bar Association; the Pennsylvania Chamber of Business and Industry; and the Pennsylvania Bar Institute.

Personal: Bachelor's degree in civil engineering, summa cum laude, from the University of Delaware, 1980. JD cum laude from Harvard Law School, 1983.

MIANO, Steven T

Wolf, Block, Schorr and Solis-Cohen
LLP, Philadelphia 215 977 2228
smiano@wolfblock.com
Recommended in Environment

Practice Areas: Partner, Environmental and Land Use Practice Group. He has been practicing environmental law since 1985, concentrating in all areas of environmental law. Served as Assistant Regional Counsel for the US Environmental Protection Agency, Region III, Hazardous Waste Branch. He is currently an Adjunct Professor at Rutgers University Law School where he teaches environmental law. Mr Miano is a frequent lecturer on national and local programs.

Prof. Memberships: Member of the American Bar Association's Section of Environment, Energy and Resources, the Pennsylvania Bar Association's Natural Resources Section and the Philadelphia Bar Association's Environmental Law Committee, where he served as Secretary in 1996. He is a former Co-Chair of the ABA Section Water Quality and Wetlands Committee and is a current member of the Section Council.

Career: Serves on the Board of Trustees for the Support Center for Child Advocates and was named Distinguished Child Advocate in 1997. He is also a graduate of the Greater Philadelphia Chamber of Commerce Arts & Business Council - Business on Board Program.

Publications: Mr Miano publishes frequently and is on the Editorial Board of the ABA Section publication, Trends. He also is the co-author of the wetlands chapter for the CWA Handbook, published in 2003.

Personal: Received his BS in Environmental Studies from George Washington University (1982) and his JD from Franklin Pierce Law Center (1985).

MILLER, Alan
Picadio Sneath Miller & Norton, Pittsburg 412 288 4000
Recommended in Environment

MILLER, Henry
Wolf, Block, Schorr and Solis-Cohen LLP, Philadelphia 215 977 2000
hmiller@wolfblock.com
Recommended in Real Estate

Practice Areas: Partner in the Real Estate Practice Group with more than 30 years experience in real estate. Areas of expertise include representing developers of shopping centers and major high-rise office buildings. Has had extensive experience in representing real estate brokers, REIT's and developers of industrial buildings and industrial parks.

Prof. Memberships: Admitted to the Pennsylvania Bar (1965). Member, American, Pennsylvania and Philadelphia Bar Associations. Served as been Chairman of the Committee on Real Estate Law of the Philadelphia Bar Association. Member, American College of Real Estate Lawyers.

Career: Joined the firm in 1964 and became a Partner in 1971. Served as a member of the firm's Executive Committee. Listed in leading US and global publications as a leading lawyer.

Personal: Received his AB, with Honors, from Lafayette College (1959) and his LLB, cum laude, from the University of Pennsylvania (1963). Law clerk to the Honorable Edwin D Steel, US District Court of Delaware (1963-65). Has been a Member of the Board and solicitor of the Association for Jewish Children of Philadelphia; former President and is a Board Member of the Jewish Family and Children's Agency of Philadelphia; a Board Member of the Philadelphia Commercial Development Corporation; and former President and is a Member of the Advisory Board of Big Brothers/Big Sisters Association of Philadelphia. He also has been a Member of the Board of Directors of Philadelphia Child Guidance Clinic.

MILLER, J Gregg
Pepper Hamilton LLP, Philadelphia
215 981 4085
millerj@pepperlaw.com
Recommended in Bankruptcy

Practice Areas: Partner, Vice-Chair Bankruptcy and Reorganization Group. Experienced in: bankruptcy and reorganization law; represents creditors, groups of creditors and debtors in workouts, mass toxic tort bankruptcies and Chapter 11 proceedings. Clients include hospitals; construction contractors, subcontractors, suppliers, sureties and lenders; asbestos products manufacturers and distributors.

Prof. Memberships: Co-Chairman, Construction, Surety and Insurance Law Subcommittee, Business Reorganization Committee, American Bankruptcy Institute. President-elect and Director, Consumer Bankruptcy Assistance Project.

Career: LLB 1969 University of Pennsylvania Law School; BA 1966 Yale University.

MONACO, Daniel A
Drinker Biddle & Reath LLP, Philadelphia 215 988 3312
Daniel.Monaco@dbr.com
Recommended in Intellectual Property

Practice Areas: Partner in the Intellectual Property Practice, with a concentration on patent practice. Has prepared and prosecuted hundreds of US and foreign patent applications, primarily in chemistry and biotechnology. Experienced representing universities in IP matters.

Prof. Memberships: Admitted in Pennsylvania (1981), New Jersey (1983) and before the USPTO. Member: Philadelphia, Pennsylvania and American Bar Associations; American Chemical Society; American Association for the Advancement of Science.

Career: Joined Drinker Biddle in 2001.

Publications: Co-author, 'What the General Practitioner Should Know About Patent Law and Practice'.

Personal: JD, Wake Forest University, 1981; BA, University of Pennsylvania, 1977.

MONTAGUE, Laddie
Berger & Montague PC, Philadelphia
215 875 3000
Recommended in Antitrust

MURPHY, Terrence
Klett Rooney Lieber & Schorling, Pittsburgh 412 392 2000
Recommended in Employment

MURRAY, William
Duane Morris LLP, Philadelphia
215 979 1264
whmurray@duanemorris.com
Recommended in Intellectual Property

Practice Areas: William H Murray has practiced in the area of intellectual property law for 30 years. His practice includes the acquisition, evaluation, licensing and enforcement of intellectual property rights including patents, trademarks and copyrights. His practice encompasses diverse areas of technology such as computer hardware and software, integrated circuits, internet, television, communication systems, medical electronics and electrical power distribution systems.

Prof. Memberships: Adjunct Professor, Villanova University School of Law, 1991-present; Certified Panelist, National Patent Board, 1999-present; American Intellectual Property Law Association - Committee on Education, 1991-present, Electronics and Computer Law Committee, 1995-present; Pennsylvania Bar Association - Member Intellectual Property Section from inception to present; Philadelphia Bar Association; Pennsylvania Bar Institute - Chair, Intellectual Property Advisory Committee; Benjamin Franklin Inn of the American Inns of Court, Executive Committee, 1997-present.

Career: Admitted to practice in New Jersey, Pennsylvania, United States Patent & Trademark Office, Supreme Court of the United States, United States Court of Appeals for the Federal Circuit, United States Court of Appeals for the Third Circuit, United States District Court for the Eastern District of Pennsylvania, United States District Court for the District of New Jersey, Supreme Court of New Jersey.

Personal: Villanova University School of Law, JD, 1973.

MYERS, Marlee
Morgan, Lewis & Bockius LLP, Pittsburgh 412 560 3310
msmyers@morganlewis.com
Recommended in Corporate/M&A

Practice Areas: Marlee Myers is a Partner in the Business and Finance Practice and is the Managing Partner of the firm's Pittsburgh office. Her practice focuses on mergers and acquisitions, initial and follow-on public offerings, corporate governance, venture finance, securities compliance, strategic alliances, international business transactions and general corporate counseling. Ms Myers represents companies in growth industries such as information technology, e-commerce, computer networking and life sciences, as well as major domestic and foreign industrial companies with subsidiaries worldwide.

Prof. Memberships: Pittsburgh Technology Council (Director).

NADEL, Alan S
Akin Gump Strauss Hauer & Feld LLP, Philadelphia 215 965 1280
anadel@akingump.com
Recommended in Intellectual Property

Practice Areas: Represents all sizes of domestic and foreign corporate clients, academic and research institutions, individual physicians and other researchers in all aspects of patent matters involving bioscience, chemical and mechanical inventions, including patent preparation, prosecution, licensing, counseling and litigation. Provides analysis and opinions concerning patent validity, infringement and due diligence. Practice includes negotiating, advising about and preparing licenses, confidentiality, technology transfer, trade secret and consulting agreements. Devises practical solutions to intellectual property problems.

Prof. Memberships: Former President, Philadelphia Intellectual Property Law Association; Director, George Washington University Alumni Association; Pennsylvania Bar.

Personal: BS (chemistry), JD (honors), The George Washington University.

NASSAU, Henry N
Dechert LLP, Philadelphia
215 994 2138
henry.nassau@dechert.com
Recommended in Corporate/M&A

Practice Areas: Partner and Co-Chair of Dechert's Corporate and Securities Group. Practice areas include mergers and acquisitions, public offerings, private equity, and venture capital. Advises on capital formation, investments, and acquisitions.

Prof. Memberships: Member, Pennsylvania Bar; Board Member of Capital Trust and ICG Commerce.

Career: Former Partner and Chair of Dechert's Business Department. Left Dechert in 1999 for Internet Capital Group to serve as Chief Operating Officer, general counsel, and secretary.

Personal: Wharton School of the University of Pennsylvania (BS, cum laude, 1976); Dickinson School of Law (JD, magna cum laude, 1979); managing editor of the Dickinson Law Review.

NAUGLE, Louis
Reed Smith LLP, Pittsburgh
412 288 8586
lnaugle@reedsmith.com
Recommended in Environment

Practice Areas: Head of the firm's Environmental Group; litigation and environmental counseling and due diligence; permitting and compliance/enforcement proceedings.

Prof. Memberships: ABA, Pennsylvania and New York Bar Associations.

Career: Formerly in the Litigation Section of the Pennsylvania Department of Environmental Resources, chief of the litigation unit in Harrisburg, 1982-84.

Publications: Author of A Practical Guide to Litigation with DER, a chapter in 'Pennsylvania Environmental Law and Practice'.

Personal: The Georgetown University Law Center (JD, 1975); Williams College (1972), Phi Beta Kappa; listed in 'The Best Lawyers in America' for natural resources and environmental law.

NEWELL, Francis
Montgomery, McCracken, Walker & Rhoads, LLP, Philadelphia
215 772 1500
Recommended in Antitrust

NIGON, Kenneth
RatnerPrestia, Valley Forge
610 993 4222
knnigon@ratnerprestia.com
Recommended in Intellectual Property

Practice Areas: Member of Management Committee; Chair of Practice Management.

Prof. Memberships: American Bar Association; American Intellectual

Property Law Association; Philadelphia Intellectual Property Law Association; Institute of Electrical and Electronics Engineers.

Career: 22 years experience in IP law, including five years as Patent Counsel for a major consumer electronics corporation. Nine years as a system programmer prior to entering legal field.

Publications: The New Written Description Requirement, 9/2002 issue of the Journal of the Patents & Trademark Office Society; Maintaining Your Competitive Advantage: A Periodic Intellectual Property Audit, 9/2002 issue of The Patent Journal; Chapters 1 and 5 of Electronic and Software Patents, Law and Practice Bureau of National Affairs, Inc. 2000.

Personal: University of Notre Dame (BSEE, cum laude, 1973); Stanford University (MSEE, Computer Engineering, 1974); Temple University (JD, 1983).

O'BRIEN, William
Conrad O'Brien Gellman & Rohn PC, Philadelphia 215 864 8073
wobrien@cogr.com
Recommended in Litigation

Practice Areas: A leading trial lawyer who has tried high profile cases in state and federal courts. Practice includes product liability and mass tort cases, class actions, defamation, employment discrimination, personal injury, medical malpractice, legal malpractice, insurance coverage, environmental, antitrust, and commercial litigation.

Prof. Memberships: Fellow, American College of Trial Lawyers; Fellow, International Academy of Trial Lawyers; Diplomate, American Board of Trial Advocacy.

Career: Founding Member, Conrad O'Brien Gellman & Rohn, P.C. Listed in legal and non-legal publications recognizing him for his accomplishments as a trial lawyer.

Personal: AB, LaSalle University; LLB, Villanova Law School.

O'DEA, Jr, Joseph F
Saul Ewing LLP, Philadelphia
215 972 7109
jodea@saul.com
Recommended in Environment

Practice Areas: Mr O'Dea represents clients ranging from privately held corporations to one of the nation's largest environmental services companies in environmental litigation matters. He handles complex commercial litigation matters, ranging from commercial contract/business disputes to governmental compliance/enforcement matters. He also represents Fortune 100 clients in the defense industry.

Prof. Memberships: Member, American, Pennsylvania, and Philadelphia Bar Associations.

Career: Designated a 'Pennsylvania Super Lawyer' by 'Philadelphia Magazine' and 'Law and Politics' Magazine.

Litigation Department, Vice Chair. Co-Chair of White Collar and Government Enforcement Practice Group, and Diversity Committee.

Personal: JD, Villanova University School of Law, BS, Civil Engineering, Princeton University.

O'DONNELL, G Daniel
Dechert, Philadelphia
215 994 2762
daniel.odonnell@dechert.com
Recommended in Corporate/M&A

Practice Areas: Partner and Chair of Dechert's Private Equity Group. Also serves on Dechert's policy committee. In addition to representing many of the firm's most active private equity clients, Dan's practice focuses on mergers and acquisitions, corporate restructurings, and venture capital transactions.

Prof. Memberships: Member, Pennsylvania Bar; Member, Board of Advisers of the Penn Wharton Institute for Law and Economics.

Career: Joined Dechert in 1976.

Personal: University of Notre Dame (BA, 1973); University of Pennsylvania School of Law (JD, 1985), Order of the Coif, recipient of McCall Prize (first in class), and Member of University of Pennsylvania Law Review.

OLSON, Stephen
Kirkpatrick & Lockhart Nicholson Graham LLP, Pittsburgh 412 355 6496
solson@klng.com
Recommended in Employment

Practice Areas: Represents employers in employment and labor matters, including counseling, training, litigation; Title VII, ADEA, ADA, FMLA, FLSA, NLRA, RLA, employment and severance agreements, force reduction programs, and performance evaluation/corrective action systems.

Prof. Memberships: Admitted in Pennsylvania; Member of American, Pennsylvania and Allegheny County Bar Associations (Labor and Employment Law Sections).

Career: Joined Kirkpatrick & Lockhart Nicholson Graham LLP in 1973, Partner since 1981. Serves as National Coordinator of the firm's Employment and Labor Practice.

Publications: Written and lectured extensively on employment and labor topics.

Personal: JD, University of Chicago, 1973; AB, Princeton University, 1970.

OMINSKY, Harris
Blank Rome LLP, Philadelphia
215 569 5668
ominsky@BlankRome.com
Recommended in Real Estate

Practice Areas: Mr Ominsky is of counsel with Blank Rome LLC. He had Co-Chaired the firm's Real Estate Department for many years. He concentrates his practice in real estate acquisitions, financing and construction.

Prof. Memberships: Admitted in Penn-

sylvania; former President, Pennsylvania Bar Institute, American College of Real Estate Lawyers; former Board Member and Vice Chair of Publications, American College of Mortgage Attorneys; Board of Directors, Apartment Association of Greater Philadelphia.

Career: Graduated University of Pennsylvania Law School, cum laude, Order of the Coif.

Publications: Authors regular weekly column, 'Ominsky's Terrain', in the Legal Intelligencer, frequent lecturer.

O'REILLY, Timothy
Morgan, Lewis & Bockius LLP, Philadelphia 215 963 5470
to'reilly@morganlewis.com
Recommended in Employment

Practice Areas: Timothy O'Reilly is a Partner in the Labor and Employment Law Practice Group. Mr O'Reilly's practice focuses on all facets of employment law with a particular emphasis on management labor relations matters. In that area, he has represented private and public sector employers in a variety of matters. He also has experience with public employment relations law, arbitration, pensions and health funds, wage and hour law issues and sports law.

Prof. Memberships: American Bar Association (Labor and Employment Law Section, Elected Council Member); College of Labor and Employment Lawyers (Fellow).

OSSIP, Michael J
Morgan, Lewis & Bockius LLP, Philadelphia 215 963 5761
mossip@morganlewis.com
Recommended in Employment

Practice Areas: Michael Ossip is a Partner in the Labor and Employment Law Practice Group. Mr Ossip's practice is devoted exclusively to the representation of management in all facets of employee relations, including the litigation of claims of employment discrimination in federal and state courts. Mr Ossip has substantial litigation experience, having tried to verdict many jury and non-jury cases.

Prof. Memberships: College of Labor and Employment Lawyers (Fellow).

PANITCH, Ronald L
Akin Gump Strauss Hauer & Feld LLP, Philadelphia 215 965 1300
rpanitch@akingump.com
Recommended in Intellectual Property

Practice Areas: Co-Chair, firmwide Intellectual Property Practice. Practice focuses on licensing and counseling in both patent and trademark matters. Has extensive experience in negotiating and designing creative settlements for issues that are difficult to resolve in contested proceedings, and is frequently asked to appear as an expert witness in such proceedings. Recognized by 'Philadelphia Magazine' as one of the Best Lawyers in that city.

Prof. Memberships: Philadelphia, Pennsylvania and American Bar Associ-

ations; Philadelphia Intellectual Property Law Association; American Intellectual Property Law Association; American Law Institute (elected); Pennsylvania Bar.

Personal: BSME, New Jersey Institute of Technology; JD, Georgetown University.

PEIRCE, Richard
Ballard Spahr Andrews & Ingersoll LLP, Philadelphia 215 864 9475
peircer@ballardspahr.com
Recommended in Intellectual Property

Practice Areas: His practice focuses in the area of trademarks, domain names and related internet issues, and unfair competition issues, including litigation in federal courts and before the Trademark Trial and Appeal Board.

Prof. Memberships: He is a member of the American Bar Association, Pennsylvania Bar Association, Philadelphia Bar Association, and New Jersey State Bar Association. He is also a member of the American Bar Association's Special Committee on Online Trademark Issues.

Career: Admitted to the Pennsylvania Bar (2000); joined as associate (2001).

Personal: JD, Syracuse University (2000); BA, Rowan University (1997).

PERKINS, Harriet
Drinker Biddle & Reath LLP, Philadelphia 215 988 3314
Harriet.Perkins@dbr.com
Recommended in Intellectual Property

Practice Areas: Counsel in the firm's Intellectual Property Practice Group. Practice focused on domestic and foreign trademark prosecution, copyright law and domain name protection, including clearance, registration, maintenance, assignments and licensing.

Prof. Memberships: Admitted to practice in Pennsylvania (1986) and the District of Columbia (1989). Member of the Intellectual Property Section of the American Bar Association, the Philadelphia Intellectual Property Association, the Philadelphia Chapter of the Copyright Society of the USA, and the International Trademark Association.

Career: Joined Drinker Biddle in 2001.

Personal: JD, Temple University School of Law, 1986; BA Temple University, 1983.

POKOTILOW, Manny
Caesar, Rivise, Bernstein, Cohen & Pokotilow Ltd, Philadelphia
215 567 2010
Recommended in Intellectual Property

PRESTIA, Paul
RatnerPrestia, Valley Forge
610 993 4204
pprestia@ratnerprestia.com
Recommended in Intellectual Property

Practice Areas: Chair of firm's Management Committee; IP business management and strategic counseling; litigation and internet disputes; alternative dispute resolution; patent procurement; trade secrets; trademarks,

Prof. Memberships: Philadelphia and American Bar Associations; American Intellectual Property Law Association; Philadelphia Intellectual Property Law Association; Benjamin Franklin Inn of Court (Founding Member; President, 1996).

Career: Began professional career as an engineer in the airmunitions and petroleum fields. He then worked as a patent agent and patent attorney for General Electric Company before entering private practice. Co-founded RatnerPrestia in 1981.

Publications: Tying and Trademark Franchising: A look at the Developing Case Law, American Intellectual Property Law Association Quarterly Journal, Vol. III, No. 4, 1975; Laches and Estoppel: Old Doctrines Finding Modern Application, 1978 Patent Law Annual, Southwestern Legal Foundation; New Era Antitrust/Licensing Issues, Selected Legal Papers, Vol. 5, No. 1 (Page H-1), July 1987, American Intellectual Property Law Association; Decision Tree: Good Tool for Analysis, Les Nouvelles, Vol. 29, No. 1, March 1994, Licensing Executive Society; Minimizing The Risk of Willfulness In U.S. Patent Infringement Litigation, 20/20 for The Twenty First Century, A Special 20th Anniversary Commemorative Issue of I. P. Japan, 1999, Shusaku Yamamoto Patent Law Offices, Osaka, Japan.

Personal: Lehigh University (BSChE, 1959); Georgetown University (JD, 1967)

PRIMAVERA, Carl
Klehr Harrison Harvey Branzberg & Ellers LLP, Philadelphia 215 568 6060
Recommended in Real Estate

RABINOWITZ, Mark I
Blank Rome LLP, Philadelphia
215 569 5629
mrabinowitz@blankrome.com
Recommended in Banking & Finance

Practice Areas: Mr Rabinowitz is Practice Group Leader of the Financial Services Group. He concentrates his practice on commercial finance including commercial lending, asset-based financing, secured transactions, personal property leasing (commercial and consumer), loan syndications and participations, and asset securitization as well as intercreditor relationships, lender liability prevention and defense and bankruptcy, reorganizations and debt restructuring.

Prof. Memberships: Equipment Leasing Association (former Board Member Equipment Leasing Association Legal Committee; former Board Member for the Eastern Regional Committee); Eastern Association of Equipment Lessors; Eastern District of Pennsylvania Bankruptcy Conference; Pennsylvania Bar Association (former Vice-Chairman - Article 2A Task Force; Business Section); American Bar Association; New Jersey Bar Association; Philadelphia Bar Asso-

ciation; Florida Bar Association.

Career: Mr Rabinowitz is a Partner and Practice Group Leader of the Financial Services Group of Blank Rome LLP. He has been with the firm since 1988.

Publications: Representative publications include: Co-author: 'Be Careful What You Look For: It Could Be an Authenticated Record' LJN's Equipment Leasing Newsletter, Volume 23, Number 7, August 2004. Contributing author: Update Chapter 23 'Regulation of Bank Leasing Activities' for Matthew Bender's Equipment Leasing Treatise, December 2003. Co-author: 'Golden Books Case Creates New 'Golden Rule' for Lessors', LJN's Equipment Leasing Newsletter, Volume XXI, Number 5, March 2002. Co-author, 'Georgia Upholds the Integrity of Hell or High Water', Equipment Leasing Today, May 1998.

Personal: Temple University School of Law (JD, Summa Cum Laude, 1988); Pennsylvania State University (BS, 1981).

RACKOW, Julian
Blank Rome LLP, Philadelphia
215 569 5671
rackow@BlankRome.com
Recommended in Real Estate

Practice Areas: Real estate and retail development and finance; emphasis on adaptive reuse of historically-certified properties and development of major mixed-use projects; served as Co-Chair of firm's Real Estate Department and Chair of innovative RetailLaw Group.

Prof. Memberships: Admitted to practice in Pennsylvania and in Federal Court for Eastern District of Pennsylvania (1966). Chair - Central Philadelphia Development Corporation; Fellow - American College of Real Estate Lawyers; Board of Directors - Avenue of the Arts, Inc.; Member - National Economic Subcommittee for International Council of Shopping Centers.

Career: Joined Blank Rome LLP in 1970; became Partner 1975.

Publications: Lectures at the Annual ALI-ABA leasing program.

Personal: Born 16 December 1941; JD, Harvard Law School, 1966; AB, Cornell University, 1963.

RADER, Kermit L
Wolf, Block, Schorr and Solis-Cohen LLP, Philadelphia 215 977 2708
krader@wolfblock.com
Recommended in Environment

Practice Areas: Partner, Environmental and Land Use Practice Group. His practice focuses on the environmental aspects of real estate and corporate transactions, regulatory compliance counseling and remediation issues. Began his legal career as an attorney in the Office of Environment at the US Environmental Protection Agency's headquarters and went on to become Assistant Regional Counsel and then Associate Regional Counsel and Chief of

the Superfund Section for the Agency's Middle Atlantic Region.

Prof. Memberships: Mr Rader is admitted to practice in Pennsylvania and the District of Columbia. He is a member of the Natural Resources Section of the American Bar Association and the Environmental Section of the Pennsylvania Bar Association. Mr Rader served as Co-Chair of the Philadelphia Bar Association's Environmental Law Committee in 1995.

Publications: Co-authored the chapter, 'A Practical Guide to Litigating with EPA Region III' for 'Pennsylvania Environmental Law & Practice'.

Personal: Mr Rader received his BA, magna cum laude, from Duke University in 1975 and his JD from George Washington Law School in 1978.

RAYMOND III, F Douglas
Drinker Biddle & Reath LLP,
Philadelphia 215 988 2548
Douglas.Raymond@dbr.com
Recommended in Corporate/M&A

Practice Areas: Partner in the firm's Business and Finance Department and Head of the firm's Corporate and Securities Practice Group. Practice focuses on mergers and acquisitions as well as joint ventures. Has extensive experience in securities offerings and compliance. In addition, counsels corporations and their Boards of Directors on corporate governance matters, including special committee assignments.

Career: Joined Drinker Biddle in 1986; became Partner in 1994, Managing Partner in 1999-2004. Previously worked as a commercial lender.

Personal: Admitted to practice in Pennsylvania, 1985; JD (magna cum laude), University of Pennsylvania, 1985; AB (cum laude), Harvard University, 1980.

REED, Margery N
Duane Morris LLP, Philadelphia
215 979 1518
mreed@duanemorris.com
Recommended in Bankruptcy

Practice Areas: Margery N Reed practices in the areas of business reorganization, bankruptcy law, corporate and commercial finance, syndicated loans, insurance insolvency and secured transactions involving securities and asset-based financing. She represents financial institutions in several capacities, including most recently as agent for a lending group as special servicer and master servicer for securitized mortgage loans and as secured lender.

Prof. Memberships: American College of Bankruptcy; American Bar Association - Chair, Business Bankruptcy-Business Transactions Subcommittee, 2002-present; Pennsylvania Bar Association; New Jersey State Bar Association; American Bankruptcy Institute; Eastern District of Pennsylvania Bankruptcy Conference - Vice Chairperson, 1998-99; Officer, 1995-98, Steering Committee,

1994-95, Co-Chairperson, Education Committee, 1993-94; Association of Commercial Finance Attorneys.

Career: Duane Morris LLP - Member, Partners Board, 2002-present; Partner, 1990-present; Associate, 1982-90. Admitted to practice in New Jersey, Pennsylvania, the United States District Court for the Eastern District of Pennsylvania, the United States District Court for the District of New Jersey, the Supreme Court of Pennsylvania, and the Supreme Court of New Jersey.

Personal: Villanova University School of Law, JD, 1982; Vassar College, BA, 1976.

REED, Michael H
Pepper Hamilton LLP, Philadelphia
215 981 4416
reedm@pepperlaw.com
Recommended in Bankruptcy

Practice Areas: Partner, Bankruptcy and Reorganization Group. Experienced in: bankruptcy, creditors' rights and insolvency law. Served as special bankruptcy counsel to Commonwealth of Pennsylvania in LTV bankruptcy and represented amici curiae in litigation that resulted in US Second Circuit landmark decision in environmental and bankruptcy law.

Prof. Memberships: President, Pennsylvania Bar Association. Fellow, American College of Bankruptcy. Member, American Law Institute. Board of Trustees, Academy of Natural Sciences. Board of Advisors, Public Interest Law Center of Philadelphia. Member, Pennsylvania Interest on Lawyers Trust Account Board.

Career: JD 1972 Yale Law School; BA 1969 Temple University.

REICH ESQ, Abraham C
Fox Rothschild LLP, Philadelphia
215 299 2090
areich@foxrothschild.com
Recommended in Litigation

Practice Areas: Commercial litigation, including antitrust, securities, trade secrets and other corporate matters.

Personal: Co-Chair of the firm and member of the firm's Executive Committee. A 1974 graduate of Temple University School of Law; 1971 Phi Beta Kappa graduate of the University of Connecticut.

REINHART, Joe
Babst, Calland, Clements and Zomnir, A Professional Corporation, Pittsburgh
412 394 5400
Recommended in Environment

RICHEY, P Jerome
Buchanan Ingersoll PC, Pittsburgh
412 562 8800
Recommended in Employment

RICHMAN, Hershel J
Dechert, Philadelphia 215 994 2571
hershel.richman@dechert.com
Recommended in Environment

Practice Areas: Special counsel and former Partner and Chair of the Environmental Litigation Group. Assists clients in all aspects of environmental law.

Prof. Memberships: Former Chair of International Association of Attorneys and Executives in Corporate Real Estate and Pennsylvania Environmental Hearing Board Rules Committee; past president of the Delaware Valley Environmental American Inn of Court.

Career: Held key positions in several governmental agencies, including Pennsylvania Department of Environmental Resources and the Bucks County Planning Commission.

Publications: Former adjunct professor of environmental law at Drexel University.

Personal: The Pennsylvania State University (BS, 1964); Villanova University School of Law (JD, 1967).

ROCCI, Steven
Woodcock Washburn LLP, Philadelphia
215 568 3100
rocci@woodcock.com
Recommended in Intellectual Property

Practice Areas: Intellectual property litigation and counseling in diverse technology areas, including electronics, computer science, telecommunications and Internet technologies, and for consumer products. Oversees substantial patent procurement program and prosecution proceedings.

Prof. Memberships: Member, Pennsylvania Bar, American, Pennsylvania and Philadelphia Bar Associations; the PIPLA and the AIPLA.

Career: Member, firm's Policy Committee. Adjunct professor, patent law, Temple University Law School. Former engineer of several Fortune 500 companies. Joined Woodcock Washburn, 1986.

Publications: Recognized in Chambers Guide to the Legal Profession 2003. Named a Pennsylvania Super Lawyer.

Personal: Temple University School of Law, JD (1981). Drexel University, BS, cum laude (1977).

ROMANO, Carmen J
Dechert LLP, Philadelphia
215 994 2971
carmen.romano@dechert.com
Recommended in Corporate/M&A

Practice Areas: Partner and Chair of the firm's Business Department and Co-Chair of the Corporate and Securities Group. Practice areas include public and private mergers and acquisitions, private equity, and restructurings.

Prof. Memberships: Member, Pennsylvania Bar.

Career: Law Clerk, Hon. Dolores K Sloviter, United States Court of Appeals for the Third Circuit; joined Dechert in 1981.

Publications: Guest lecturer in M&A courses at Columbia Law School and Temple University.

Personal: The Wharton School of the University of Pennsylvania (BS, summa cum laude, 1977); Columbia Law School (JD, Stone Scholar, 1980), note editor of

Columbia University Law Review.

ROSENBERG, Kenneth
Schnader Harrison Segal & Lewis LLP, Philadelphia 215 751 2496
krosenberg@schnader.com
Recommended in Real Estate

Practice Areas: Chairs firm's Real Estate Group. Extensive experience representing banks and financial institutions in all types of residential, commercial and retail development projects. Significant knowledge of real estate financing, particularly in construction lending in the mid-Atlantic region. Has financed numerous CBD high-rise office construction and renovation, shopping centers and 'big box' power centers, multiuse projects and new home developments. Beyond traditional financing, transactions have included use of leaseholds, commercial condominiums and tax-free bonds. Has represented agent banks in syndicated secured and unsecured real estate credit facilities, letters of credit financing and tax-free secured loans. Has negotiated complex office and retail leases for both landlords and tenants.

Prof. Memberships: American Bar Association, Pennsylvania Bar Association, Philadelphia Bar Association.

RUDOLPH, Andrew J
Pepper Hamilton LLP, Philadelphia
215 981 4749
rudolpha@pepperlaw.com
Recommended in Employee Benefits

Practice Areas: Partner, Chair, Employee Benefits Practice Group. Experienced in: employee benefits/ERISA; executive compensation, related tax and corporate law issues for public and private companies. Practice focuses on the development of programs that link compensation and benefits to the employer's performance; qualified and non-qualified retirement plans; executive employment and severance agreements; benefits and compensation aspects of corporate transactions. Represents clients before US Internal Revenue Service and Department of Labor.

Career: JD 1982 University of Pennsylvania Law School; 1978 BA University of Pennsylvania.

SAINT-ANTOINE, Paul
Drinker Biddle & Reath LLP, Philadelphia 215 988 2990
Paul.Saint-Antoine@dbr.com
Recommended in Antitrust

Practice Areas: Partner in the firm's Litigation Department and Co-Head of the firm's Antitrust Practice Group. Practice includes both antitrust litigation and counseling, with an emphasis on antitrust disputes involving intellectual property rights and high-tech industries.

Prof. Memberships: Admitted to practice in Pennsylvania (1989) and New Jersey (1989). Vice Chair of the Computer and Internet Committee of the ABA's Antitrust Section.

Career: Joined Drinker Biddle in 1989.

Publications: Editor in chief of 'Federal Antitrust Guidelines for the Licensing of Intellectual Property, Origins and Applications' (second edition).

Personal: JD, Columbia University, 1989; AB, Kenyon College, 1986.

SARACHAN, Ronald A
Ballard Spahr Andrews & Ingersoll LLP, Philadelphia 215 864 8333
sarachan@ballardspahr.com
Recommended in Environment

Practice Areas: Concentrates his practice in defending corporations and individuals facing criminal investigation and prosecution, regulatory enforcement action, and related litigation. Represents corporate clients ranging from Fortune 500 companies to closely held corporations in all aspects of complex commercial and criminal litigation, internal investigations, compliance and regulatory matters, and grand jury proceedings.

Prof. Memberships: Former Co-Chair of the Environmental Crimes Sub-Committee of the ABA White Collar Crime Section. Member of the Federal Bar Association Criminal Law Committee and the Pennsylvania Bar Association.

Career: Admitted to the Pennsylvania Bar (1990); admitted to the New York Bar (1983); joined as Partner (1997). Prior to joining Ballard Spahr, he was an Assistant United States Attorney and Chief of the Major Crimes Section in the United States Attorney's Office for the Eastern District of Pennsylvania, and served as Chief of the Environmental Crimes Section in the US Department of Justice. He served as law clerk to the Honorable Edward Weinfeld, United States District Judge for the Southern District of New York.

Publications: 'Criminal Negligence Prosecutions under the Federal Clean Water Act', Vol XXXII Environmental Law Reporter, News and Analysis (October, 2002), (co-written with Steven P Solow). Has lectured extensively on criminal and environmental law and testified before the United States Senate Judiciary Committee and the United States Sentencing Commission.

Personal: JD, magna cum laude, The University of Michigan (1981); SCB, in Chemistry, magna cum laude, Brown University (1978).

SCHAFFER, Eric A
Reed Smith LLP, Pittsburgh
412 288 4202
eschaffer@reedsmith.com
Recommended in Bankruptcy

Practice Areas: Bankruptcy and commercial litigation; served as Head of the firm's Corporate Restructuring & Bankruptcy Group, 2001-04; represents secured and unsecured creditors in major bankruptcy cases and non-judicial restructurings involving manufacturing enterprises, hospitals, retailers, utilities, airlines, real estate projects, and

other businesses.

Prof. Memberships: Fellow of the American College of Bankruptcy.

Publications: Contributing author of 'Collier Bankruptcy Practice Guide' and 'The Art of Science of Bankruptcy.'

Personal: University of Pittsburgh School of Law (JD, 1979); University of Virginia (1976); listed in 'The Best Lawyers in America'; selected as a Pennsylvania Super Lawyer.

SCHER, Howard
Buchanan Ingersoll, Philadelphia
215 665 3920
scherhd@bipc.com
Recommended in Litigation

Practice Areas: Focuses on complex litigation for business clients and the efficient resolution of complex business problems. He has achieved victories both in the prosecution and the defense of many types of complex and sophisticated business litigation, including business torts, RICO, antitrust, franchise, intellectual property, securities, fraud, tax and accounting, class action and other areas. His experience extends state and federal court actions, as well as emergency injunctions, jury trials and appeals.

Prof. Memberships: International Academy of Trial Lawyers; American College of Trial Lawyers.

Personal: JD Rutgers University, 1971; BA Brandeis University, 1967.

SCHILDHORN, Gary
Adelman Lavine Gold & Levin, Philadelphia 215 568 7515
Recommended in Bankruptcy

SCHORLING, William
Klett Rooney Lieber & Schorling, Pittsburgh 412 392 2000
Recommended in Bankruptcy

SEDRAN, Howard
Levin Fishbein Sedran & Berman, Philadelphia 215 592 1500
hsedran@lfsblaw.com
Recommended in Antitrust

Practice Areas: Antitrust.

Prof. Memberships: Pennsylvania Bar.

Career: Currently serving as co-lead counsel in: In Re Foundry Resins Antitrust Litigation; In Re EPDM Antitrust Litigation; In Re PCP Antitrust Litigation.

Personal: Born December 3, 1950.

SEIDEL, Arthur
Drinker Biddle & Reath LLP, Philadelphia 215 988 3317
Arthur.Seidel@dbr.com
Recommended in Intellectual Property

Practice Areas: Practices patents, trademarks, copyrights, unfair competition, licensing, Internet disputes, trade secrets, and rights of publicity and privacy. Represents Fortune 500 companies in major matters.

Prof. Memberships: Admitted: District of Columbia, Pennsylvania, New York, and before the USPTO. Member: Philadelphia, Pennsylvania and Ameri-

can Bar Associations; American Patent Law Association; Philadelphia Intellectual Property Association; International Trademark Association. American Law Institute; Board of Directors of the Pennsylvania Bar Institute.
Career: Joined Drinker Biddle in 2001.
Publications: 'American Law Institute - ABA Books on Patent Law Practice;' 'Trademarks and Copyrights;' and 'Trade Secrets and Employment Agreements'.
Personal: JD, George Washington University, 1949; MA, University of Michigan, 1943; BS, College of the City of New York, 1942.

SHAPIRO, Raymond
Blank Rome LLP, Philadelphia
215 569 5569
shapiro@BlankRome.com
Recommended in Bankruptcy
Practice Areas: Bankruptcy, reorganizations, workouts, banking and commercial lending, including restructurings, representing institutional lenders, lender syndicates, creditors committees, debtors, plan of reorganization proponents, asset purchasers, etc. Also served as court-appointed mediator.
Prof. Memberships: Admitted in Pennsylvania and New York; past Chair of the American College of Bankruptcy; elected Member of the National Bankruptcy Conference.
Career: Graduated Temple University School of Law with honors; Wexler, Weisman, Forman & Shapiro until 1984 when merged with Blank Rome; Member of firm's Executive Committee.
Personal: Author and lecturer on numerous subjects concerning creditors rights; active in local charities.

SHIEKMAN, Laurence Z
Pepper Hamilton LLP, Philadelphia
215 981 4347
shiekmanl@pepperlaw.com
Recommended in Antitrust
Practice Areas: Partner, past Chairman, Commercial Litigation Practice Group. Experienced in: antitrust, ERISA, securities, commercial litigation, patent and criminal antitrust. Represented: UK manufacturer in treble damage, class action; truck manufacturer in antitrust and dealer termination; national pizza franchiser in class action alleging monopolization; biomedical manufacturer in patent infringement claims, antitrust counterclaims; a major automotive wholesaler in defense of Robinson-Patman Act 'mass action' by nearly 200 competitors.
Prof. Memberships: Board of Directors, Mann Center for Performing Arts.
Career: JD 1971 University of Pennsylvania Law School; BSE 1968 University of Pennsylvania.

SICALIDES, Barbara T
Pepper Hamilton LLP, Philadelphia
215 981 4783
sicalidesb@pepperlaw.com

Recommended in Antitrust
Practice Areas: Partner, Vice-Chair Commercial Litigation Group, Head of Antitrust Section. Experienced in: antitrust counseling and litigation; Hart-Scott-Rodino filings/proceedings. Representing UK flat glass manufacturer in treble-damage class action; tobacco company in Robinson-Patman Act and distributor termination; bathroom/ kitchen fixtures/fittings manufacturer in allegations of price fixing; manufacturing companies in acquisitions.
Prof. Memberships: Philadelphia Bar Association, Co-Chair Antitrust Committee. Board of Directors and past President, Philadelphia Volunteers for the Indigent Program. Steering Committee, Philadelphia LawWorks. 2002 recipient of Philadelphia Bar Association's First Union Fidelity Award.
Career: JD 1989 Temple University School of Law; BA 1983 Barnard College, Columbia University.

SINATRA, Geraldine A
Dechert LLP, Philadelphia
215 994 2824
geraldine.sinatra@dechert.com
Recommended in Corporate/M&A
Practice Areas: Partner and Co-Chair of the hiring committee for Philadelphia office. Practice areas include private equity, mergers and acquisitions, securities offerings, debt financings, and public company governance issues. Works with financial sponsors on acquisitions of public and private companies. Advises portfolio companies on transactional matters.
Prof. Memberships: Member, Pennsylvania and New Jersey Bars.
Career: Law Clerk, Hon Norma L Shapiro, United States District Court for the Eastern District of Pennsylvania; joined Dechert in 1992.
Personal: Ohio State University (BS, 1988); Ohio State University College of Law (JD, 1991), Order of the Coif, Managing Editor of Ohio State Law Journal.

SINGER, Alan
Morgan, Lewis & Bockius LLP,
Philadelphia 215 963 5224
asinger@morganlewis.com
Recommended in Corporate/M&A
Practice Areas: Alan Singer is a Partner in the Business and Finance Practice. Mr Singer's practice focuses on sophisticated corporate and securities matters, including the representation of companies and investment banks in public and non-public offerings. He also advises companies with respect to annual and periodic Securities and Exchange Commission (SEC) filings, executive compensation disclosure, corporate governance and other corporate and SEC regulatory matters.
Career: Mr Singer worked at the SEC in a variety of positions, including Branch Chief in the Division of Enforcement in Washington, DC.

SINGER, Paul
Reed Smith LLP, Pittsburgh
412 288 3114
psinger@reedsmith.com
Recommended in Bankruptcy
Practice Areas: Founder of the firm's Bankruptcy Practice, chaired group for more than 20 years. Devotes practice to bankruptcy and workout matters, representing debtors and creditors; involved in number of industrial cases in the steel, aluminum, railroad, cement, pulp and paper, and natural resource industries.
Prof. Memberships: American, Pennsylvania, Allegheny Country Bar Associations; former Chair of the Bankruptcy and Commercial Law Section, Allegheny County Bar Association.
Personal: University of Pittsburgh Law School (JD, 1968), editor of 'Law Review'; Harvard Law School (Masters, 1970); listed in 'The Best Lawyers in America,' 'Who's Who in American Law'.

SITARCHUK, Eric W
Ballard Spahr Andrews & Ingersoll LLP, Philadelphia 215 864 8220
sitar@ballardspahr.com
Recommended in Litigation
Practice Areas: His practice is concentrated in the representation of companies and individuals under investigation for, or charged with, 'white collar crimes' and related civil and administrative litigation. He has defended individuals and institutions in criminal matters involving a variety of allegations, including, antitrust, defense contract fraud, health care fraud, federal and state tax violations, official corruption, various business frauds, and export violations.
Career: Admitted to the Pennsylvania Bar (1983); joined as Partner (1996). He was previously employed as an Assistant United States Attorney in Philadelphia. He was also a Special Assistant United States Attorney in the District of Colombia. There, he was the deputy prosecutor in charge of the criminal investigation and prosecution of the Federal Bureau of Investigation's handling of the stand-off at Ruby Ridge, Idaho.
Personal: JD, George Washington University Law School (1983); BA, Franklin & Marshall College (1979).

SKLAROFF, Michael
Ballard Spahr Andrews & Ingersoll LLP, Philadelphia 215 864 8700
sklaroff@ballardspahr.com
Recommended in Real Estate
Practice Areas: He is the Chairman of the Real Estate Department. His own practice encompasses real estate development (corporate headquarters, office buildings, industrial facilities, power centers, family entertainment centers, new town centers, condominium and other residential complexes and cultural facilities); real property tax and eminent domain (power generating stations, cor-

porate headquarters, manufacturing facilities, transportation facilities, multi-family housing and shopping centers); zoning and land use (television, radio broadcasting and telecommunications, office, retail, commercial, suburban residential, parking, industrial parks, hospitals, museums, condominiums, and urban mixed-use development); and serving as counsel to cultural institutions (orchestra, museum and medical associations). He helped bring the first civil rights action in federal court to open the suburbs to multi-family housing and enforce the landmark zoning decision in Girsh Appeal 434 Pa 237 (1970), and was part of the team that obtained site-specific relief, now a central part of Pennsylvania's land-use jurisprudence. Other cases of note: SCRUB v Keystone Outdoor Advertising, No. 131 C.D. 2001, March 15, 2002 appeal denied, Supreme Court of Pennsylvania, No. 225 EAL 2002, March 30, 2004 (approved variances for eight outdoor advertising signs in least restricted industrial zone). PECO Energy Board of Assessment Appeals, 138 Montg. Co. L.R. Part II 237 (2001) (established that taxing authorities outside the jurisdiction may not intervene in local tax appeals under Public Utility Realty Tax Act amendments); School District of Philadelphia v Tax Review Board to the Use of Realen Gateway Development Associates, L.P., 696 A.2d 906 (Pa. Cmwlth. 1997) (invalidated use and occupancy tax on public/private joint venture parking garage); DeBotton v Marple Twp., 689 F.Supp. 477 (E.D. Pa. 1988) (sustained substantive due process claim arising out of exclusionary zoning of mobile home parks under the Civil Rights Act of 1871; Ezy Parks v Larson, 499 Pa. 615 (1982) (struck down unlawful bidding of PennDOT parking lot leases); Sargo, II, Inc. City of Philadelphia, 488 F.Supp. 1045 (E.D. Pa. 1980) (challenged condominium conversion moratorium); and Resident Advisory Board v Tate, 329 F. Supp. 427 (E.D. Pa., 1971) (brought fair housing claim on behalf of public housing tenants).
Prof. Memberships: American College of Real Estate Lawyers; Counselors of Real Estate; Listed in 'The Best Lawyers in America'; former Member of the Philadelphia Planning Commission's Advisory Committee on Center City Zoning; Served as founding Chairman, Real Property Section, Philadelphia Bar Association and Chair of the Committee on Condemnation and Appraisals; Deputy Executive Director, Philadelphia Redevelopment Authority in the early 1970s; planned, chaired, and moderated the Pennsylvania Bar Institute's programs 'The Law of Historic Preservation'; and 'The Science of Land Use'. Chairs the Philadelphia Historical Commission, where he has been a member since 1996. Started the movement to save the Dream Garden, the Maxfield

Parrish/Louis C. Tiffany mural in Philadelphia's Curtis Building. He helped build the Sister Cities relationship between Philadelphia and Nizhny Novgorod, Russia; taught technology transfer, real property and corporate law in Russia under programs sponsored by USIA and USAID; and represented a Russian physics institute in the first licensing agreement to a US company of gyrotron technology used in fusion research.
Career: Admitted to the Pennsylvania Bar (1968).
Personal: AB, Columbia College (1964); LLB University of Pennsylvania Law School (magna cum laude, 1967). Served as editor of the 'Law Review' and was a member of the Order of the Coif.

SONNENFELD, Marc
Morgan, Lewis & Bockius LLP, Philadelphia 215 963 5572
msonnenfeld@morganlewis.com
Recommended in Litigation
Practice Areas: Marc Sonnenfeld is a Partner in the Litigation Practice and a Leader of the firm's Securities Litigation Practice. His practice focuses on defending securities and shareholder litigation and the defense of related regulatory enforcement proceedings, as well as counseling directors and officers on corporate governance issues. Mr Sonnenfeld has repeatedly been recognized as one of the top 10 business litigators in Philadelphia and has been named as a top business lawyer in various other publications. He is also a regular presenter on business litigation topics.
Prof. Memberships: American College of Trial Lawyers (Fellow); American Bar Association; Pennsylvania Bar Association; Philadelphia Bar Association.

SPRAGUE, Richard
Sprague & Sprague, Philadelphia 215 561 7681
Recommended in Litigation

SPRINGER, Claudia
Reed Smith LLP, Philadelphia 215 241 7946
cspringer@reedsmith.com
Recommended in Bankruptcy
Practice Areas: More than 20 years' experience in corporate workouts and bankruptcy, representing every type of constituent in a troubled company situation, including debtors, lenders, creditors' committees.
Prof. Memberships: American College of Bankruptcy; American Bankruptcy Institute; Bankruptcy Committee, Business Law Section, Pennsylvania and Philadelphia Bar Associations.
Career: Former judicial clerk to the Honorable William H McCullough, Prince George's County Circuit Court.
Publications: Court Rulings Erode Collateral Protection, 'ABA Banking Journal'.
Personal: The National Law Center of The George Washington University (JD, 1980); Trinity College (BA, 1977);

named top female bankruptcy attorney in Pennsylvania by 'Pennsylvania Law Weekly'.

STACK Jr, Stephen A
Dechert, Philadelphia 215 994 2660
stephen.stack@dechert.com
Recommended in Antitrust
Practice Areas: Stephen A Stack, Jr, is Co-Chair of Dechert's Antitrust Group. He has over 30 years of experience in antitrust litigation, preventive counseling, and practice before US courts and European enforcement agencies. He represents clients in intellectual property/antitrust matters, joint ventures, and mergers.
Prof. Memberships: Member, Pennsylvania Bar; Member, American Bar Association Antitrust Section.
Career: Mr Stack served on Department of Justice advisory committee of President George W Bush's Transition Team. He has also testified at government agency hearings.
Personal: Yale University (BA, cum laude, 1967); University of Pennsylvania School of Law (JD, cum laude, 1970).

STERN, Eric L
Morgan, Lewis & Bockius LLP, Philadelphia 215 963 5178
estern@morganlewis.com
Recommended in Real Estate
Practice Areas: Eric L Stern is the Leader of Morgan Lewis' Real Estate Practice. Mr Stern represents real estate investors and owners, including REITs, institutional lenders, retailers and other corporate end-users in the acquisition, financing, restructuring and disposition of office buildings, shopping centers, single-use properties, hotels, development parcels, residential subdivisions and mixed-used projects.
Prof. Memberships: American College of Real Estate Lawyers; National Association of Real Estate Investment Trusts; International Council of Shopping Centers; Samuel Zell and Robert Lurie Real Estate Center, The Wharton School, University of Pennsylvania; and Board of Directors, Philadelphia Region, National Association of Industrial and Office Properties.

STERN, Joan N
Blank Rome LLP, Philadelphia 215 569 5526
stern@BlankRome.com
Recommended in Banking & Finance
Practice Areas: Practices public finance law, including general government, transportation and utilities, tax and revenue anticipation financing; health care and housing finance; and refinancing and working capital. She serves as bond, underwriter's, issuer's, credit enhancement, swap and trustee's counsel. Additionally, represents clients in enforcement matters involving the SEC and IRS.
Prof. Memberships: Admitted Pennsylvania; Fellow, American Bar Founda-

tion; National Association of Bond Lawyers; Pennsylvania Association of Bond Lawyers; Committee on Public Finance, State and Local Government Section, American Bar Association.
Career: JD, Temple University School of Law; Chair, Public Finance Practice; firm's Executive Committee, Distribution Committee and Partnership Board, Co-Chair Diversity Committee.
Personal: Vice-Chair, Board of Trustees, Moore College of Art and Design; Boards of Trustees, Franklin Institute and Jewish Federation of Greater Philadelphia, Board of Directors, Police Athletic League.

STEVENS, Mark
Langsam Stevens & Silver LLP, Philadelphia 215 732 3255
Recommended in Environment

STOVIAK, John F
Saul Ewing LLP, Philadelphia 215 972 1095
jstoviak@saul.com
Recommended in Environment
Practice Areas: Chair of the Litigation Department. Handles complex commercial, fraud and environmental disputes, business valuation cases, trade secret claims and antitrust claims. Has tried cases in Federal and State courts in NY, NJ, IL, PA and DE. He has been the lead lawyer defending various public utilities in Superfund contribution claims.
Prof. Memberships: Admitted in Pennsylvania.
Career: Former Saul Ewing Managing Partner. Led Saul Ewing in eight continuous years of increasing profitability and growth. Prior to joining Saul Ewing, was a Partner at Dilworth Paxson Kalish & Kauffman.
Personal: JD, Dickinson School of Law, BA, Harvard University (cum laude).

STROBER, Frederick D
Saul Ewing LLP, Philadelphia 215 972 1985
fstrober@saul.com
Recommended in Real Estate
Practice Areas: Mr Strober is a Partner in Saul Ewing's Real Estate Department and is involved in development, construction, and leasing. Since 1997, he has been involved in the redevelopment of the former Philadelphia Naval Shipyard. He represents several universities and health systems and the School District of Philadelphia in connection with educational reform and development initiatives.
Prof. Memberships: Member, American College of Real Estate Lawyers and President, Philadelphia Volunteer Lawyers for the Arts.
Career: A former educator, he has practiced at Saul Ewing his entire legal career.
Personal: JD Temple University, MEd Temple University, BA University of Pennsylvania.

STUART, Glen R
Morgan, Lewis & Bockius LLP, Philadelphia 215 963 5883
gstuart@morganlewis.com
Recommended in Environment
Practice Areas: Glen Stuart is a Partner in the Litigation Practice and the Hiring Partner of the Philadelphia Office. Mr Stuart's complex commercial litigation practice focuses primarily on environmental law, toxic torts and energy matters. He is currently involved in the defense of more than 20 toxic tort conspiracy cases in the federal or state courts of Delaware, Florida, Illinois, Kentucky, Massachusetts, Mississippi, New Jersey, and Ohio. In a 2002 survey of more than 185 corporate officers of Fortune 1000 companies, Mr Stuart was one of only 21 lawyers in the country recognized for exceptional client service two years in a row.
Prof. Memberships: American Bar Association (Litigation Section); Philadelphia Bar Association.

SULLIVAN, James
Klett Rooney Lieber & Schorling, Philadelphia 215 567 7500
Recommended in Employment

SUPLEE, Dennis R
Schnader Harrison Segal & Lewis LLP, Philadelphia 215 751 2068
dsuplee@schnader.com
Recommended in Litigation
Practice Areas: Complex commercial litigation including antitrust, CERCLA, trademark and patent infringement, insurance and product liability matters.
Prof. Memberships: Fellow and Regent, American College of Trial Lawyers; Fellow, International Academy of Trial Lawyers.
Career: Firm Chairman, 1992-98; listed in Best Lawyers for Business Litigation; one of three Pennsylvania lawyers recognized for commercial litigation in 'The International Who's Who of Business Lawyers'; Community Legal Services, Equal Justice Award, 2003; Saint Joseph's University Francis X. McClanaghan Award, 2003.
Publications: Co-author, 'The Deposition Handbook,' Aspen Law & Business (4th ed, 2002); co-author, 'The Expert Witness: Law and Practice,' Pennsylvania Bar Institute (1993).
Personal: University of Pennsylvania Law School, JD; St. Joseph's University, BS.

SWIRSKY, Sherry A
Schnader Harrison Segal & Lewis LLP, Philadelphia 215 751 2182
sswirsky@schnader.com
Recommended in Antitrust
Practice Areas: Chair of Antitrust and Trade Regulation Practice Group. Trial and appellate litigation in antitrust, class action, corporate governance, nonprofit corporation and securities matters. Also conducts internal investigations, provides government affairs counseling and represents campaigns and PACs in cam-

paign finance law matters.
Career: Mayoral appointment to Free Library of Philadelphia Board of Trustees (2004); presidential appointment to National Skill Standards Board (2001); numerous mayoral task forces and transition teams; named one of the 50 most influential women in the legal profession in Pennsylvania; Pennsylvania's General Counsel to six presidential campaigns.
Publications: Author of a series of national and state law election manuals; Minority Voter Intimidation: The Problem That Won't Go Away, 'Temple Political & Civil Rights Law Review' (Vol. 11, No. 2 Spring 2002).
Personal: New York University School of Law, JD; Colgate University, BA (summa cum laude).

SYKES, David
Duane Morris LLP, Philadelphia
215 979 1500
sykes@duanemorris.com
Recommended in Bankruptcy
Practice Areas: David T Sykes practices in the areas of business reorganization and bankruptcy, insurance company rehabilitation, corporate and commercial finance, professional guidance, arbitration, mediation and commercial trial and appellate work. Mr Sykes directed the firm's representation of creditors and debtors in workouts and bankruptcies throughout the country for more than 34 years, and personally led the representation of US Shelter Corporation, the Unsecured Creditors' Committee of The Oxford Finance Companies, Inc., and National Railway Utilization Corporation (one of the earliest prearranged chapter 11 cases, completed within 45 days of the chapter 11 filing). He represents major financial institutions in numerous capacities, including as agent for a lending group, as secured lender and letter of credit issuer, and as indenture trustee. He also represents lawyers and law firms charged with legal malpractice and serves as an expert witness in professional liability matters.
Career: Duane Morris LLP - Vice Chairman, 1998-present, Member, Partners Board, 1981-present, of counsel, 2004-present, Partner, 1972-2004; admitted to practice in Pennsylvania, Supreme Court of the United States, US Court of Appeals for the Third Circuit, US District Court for the Eastern District of Pennsylvania, Supreme Court of Pennsylvania.
Personal: Temple University School of Law, LLB, 1965.

TABACHNICK, Gene
Reed Smith LLP, Pittsburgh
412 288 3258
gtabachnick@reedsmith.com
Recommended in Intellectual Property
Practice Areas: Intellectual Property Practice involves patents, trademarks, copyrights, and related antitrust and

unfair competition matters, emphasizing IP litigation. Counsels and represents clients in a wide variety of technologies. Presents cases to judges and juries, arbitrators and mediators, and briefs and argues appeals before the Court of Appeals for the Federal Circuit. Handles US and foreign patent prosecution in electrical and mechanical arts, and technology licensing.
Career: Worked for six years as an electrical engineer in the aerospace industry.
Personal: Rutgers Law School (JD, 1988); Fairleigh Dickinson University (MBA, 1984); University of Pittsburgh (BS, 1982).

TATE, Joseph A
Dechert LLP, Philadelphia
215 994 2350
joseph.tate@dechert.com
Recommended in Antitrust, Litigation
Practice Areas: Mr Tate is a Partner in the Antitrust and White Collar Groups. He has defended US and foreign-based corporations and executives in antitrust suits and has tried cases in US courts and before the European Commission. He has experience in civil class actions and other regulatory litigation.
Prof. Memberships: Member, Pennsylvania and Massachusetts Bars; admitted to practice before numerous federal courts; Fellow, American College of Trial Lawyers.
Career: Before entering private practice, Mr Tate was a prosecutor for the Antitrust Division of the US Department of Justice.
Personal: Villanova University (AB, 1963); Villanova University Law School (LL, 1966).

TEMIN, Michael
Wolf, Block, Schorr and Solis-Cohen LLP, Philadelphia 215 977 2000
mtemin@wolfblock.com
Recommended in Bankruptcy
Practice Areas: Partner, Business Litigation and Financial Services Practice Groups. Deals extensively with business insolvencies, representing debtors, creditors, committees and others participating in the restructuring of insolvent businesses.
Prof. Memberships: Serves as Adjunct Professor at the University of Pennsylvania Law School (10+ years). Was Chairman of the Eastern District of Pennsylvania Bankruptcy Conference; Chair of the Rules Subcommittee and Vice-Chair of the Chapter 11 Subcommittee of the Business Bankruptcy Committee of the American Bar Association; and Chairman, Bankruptcy Committee of the Section of Corporation, Banking and Business Law of Pennsylvania and Philadelphia Bar Association. Was Chairman of the Section of Corporation, Banking and Business Law of the Philadelphia Bar Association. Served as Chairman of the Professional Guidance Committee of the Philadelphia Bar Association Co-

Chair, Pennsylvania Bar Association Legal Ethics Committee. Regent, the American College of Bankruptcy.
Career: Admitted to the Pennsylvania and Delaware Bars.
Personal: Received his BA, magna cum laude, from Yale University (1954) and his LLB, cum laude, from the University of Pennsylvania (1957).

THIEMAN, Frederick
Thieman & Farrell, Pittsburgh
412 395 1245
Recommended in Litigation

THOMPSON, Thomas M
Buchanan Ingersoll PC, Pittsburgh
412 562 8855
thompsontm@bipc.com
Recommended in Corporate/M&A
Practice Areas: Tom works primarily in the areas of corporate acquisitions (both domestic and foreign publicly and privately held companies), corporate governance and private placements and public offerings of securities (representing issuers and underwriters). He has represented public companies, family businesses, venture funds, management groups, divesting companies and investors in management buyouts.
Prof. Memberships: Adjunct Professor of Law, University of Pittsburgh Law School; Chair-elect, Business Law Section of the Pennsylvania Bar Association; American Bar Association Committee on Negotiated Acquisitions and Co-Chair of its Task Force publishing a manual on the M&A process.
Personal: JD Harvard University, 1968; AB Grove City College, 1965.

TOLL, Curtis
Greenberg Traurig LLP, Philadelphia
215 988 7800
tollc@gtlaw.com
Recommended in Environment
Practice Areas: Environmental; real estate.
Career: Participated in the establishment and structuring of the of the Philadelphia Intergovernmental Cooperation Authority, the board that oversees the finances of the City of Philadelphia.
Personal: JD, The Dickinson School of Law. Member, Dickinson Law Review. Member, Appellate Moot Court Board. BS, Political Science and Communications/Rhetoric, University of Pittsburgh, 1989.

UBINGER Jr, John
Jones Day, Pittsburgh 412 394 7908
jwubinger@jonesday.com
Recommended in Environment
Practice Areas: Coordinates the Environmental Practice in the Pittsburgh Office. His experience includes the application of environmental laws to businesses; the evaluation of environmental considerations in the transfer of business assets; the assessment and remediation of contaminated property; and alternative environmental dispute

resolution strategies. He also counsels clients on strategies for the management or disposition of long-term environmental obligations at contaminated facilities. He has composed a course on environmental dispute resolution strategy that he has presented at Duquesne University since 1993. Listed by Law & Politics among the 'Top 50 Environmental/Land Use Lawyers' in Pennsylvania.

UNDERCOFLER, J Clayton
Saul Ewing LLP, Philadelphia
215 972 7799
cundercofler@saul.com
Recommended in Litigation
Practice Areas: Partner in the firm's Litigation Department. Member of the White Collar, and Antitrust and Trade Regulation Groups. Focuses his practice on complex litigation, internal corporate investigations, representation of clients accused of white collar crime.
Prof. Memberships: Admitted to practice in Pennsylvania. Member, American College of Trial Lawyers; Citizens Crime Commission of the Delaware Valley, Board of Directors; American, Pennsylvania, and Philadelphia Bar Associations.
Career: Current Chair of the firm, former Managing Partner, former Chair of the Litigation Department.
Publications: Authored chapter on defense considerations, 'Pennsylvania Grand Jury Practice'.
Personal: JD, Villanova University School of Law, BS, Drexel University.

WALL, Steven R
Morgan, Lewis & Bockius LLP, Philadelphia 215 963 4928
swall@morganlewis.com
Recommended in Employment
Practice Areas: Steven Wall is a Partner in the Labor and Employment Law Practice Group, and the national Practice Group Leader. Mr Wall's practice focuses on employment litigation matters in federal and state courts, and before several administrative agencies, with an emphasis on class-based discrimination and collective bargaining issues. He has over 20 years experience advising clients on the National Labor Relations Act, the various federal and state discrimination laws, the Fair Labor Standards Act, preventive labor relations and reductions-in-force.
Prof. Memberships: American Bar Association - Labor and Employment Law Section.

WARREN, Kenneth
Wolf, Block, Schorr and Solis-Cohen LLP, Philadelphia 215 977 2276
kwarren@wolfblock.com
Recommended in Environment
Practice Areas: Partner and Chair of the firm's Environmental and Land Use Practice Group. Principal trial and appellate counsel for General Electric Company and liaison counsel for the Third-Party Plaintiffs in United States v Atlas Minerals & Chemicals, Inc., et al., a

leading Superfund allocation case. Practice concentrates on regulatory, transactional and litigation matters involving water, waste, hazardous chemicals and compliance. Has handled numerous enforcement actions, citizen suits, environmental criminal prosecutions, insurance recovery cases, appeals of agency decisions, toxic tort actions, and other environmental cases in courts and tribunals throughout the United States. Has also represented numerous clients in a variety of environmental regulatory and transactional matters including site remediations, permitting, environmental aspects of real estate transactions, environmental management systems, and development of water quality standards and total maximum daily loads. Serves as outside general counsel to the Delaware River Basin Commission, a federal-interstate compact agency managing the water resources of the Delaware River Basin. Served as an industry stakeholder representative on the National Environmental Justice Advisory Council, a formal federal advisory commitee of the United States Environmental Protection Agency.
Prof. Memberships: Served as the Chair of the American Bar Association's Section of Environment, Energy, and Resources. Has previously served on the Section's Council and as a Section Committee Chair. Serves as Chair of the American Bar Association Section Officers Conference Task Force on Homeland Security.
Career: Admitted to the Pennsylvania Bar (1980). Joined WolfBlock in 1980 and became a Partner in 1987.
Publications: Writes a regular column for The Legal Intelligencer and is the author of numerous additional articles on environmental law published in various journals. Has written articles on water law, Superfund and other environmental topics that accompanied his presentations at continuing legal education programs. Author of a chapter in The Law of Environmental Justice.
Personal: Received his BA, magna cum laude, with honors in history, from Brown University (1975) and his JD, magna cum laude, from the University of Pennsylvania (1979). Served as an associate editor of the University of Pennsylvania Law Review. Served as a law clerk to the Honorable Joseph L McGlynn, Jr in the United States District Court for the Eastern District of Pennsylvania (1979-80).

WEIN, Howard
Klett Rooney Lieber & Schorling, Pittsburgh 412 392 2000
Recommended in Environment

WEST, Ronald
Kirkpatrick & Lockhart Nicholson Graham LLP, Pittsburgh 412 355 6500
rwest@klng.com
Recommended in Corporate/M&A
Practice Areas: Mergers and acquisitions; securities offerings; securities law compliance; joint ventures; general corporate.
Prof. Memberships: American Bar Association (Business Law Section) Pennsylvania Bar AssociationAllegheny County Bar Association.
Career: Partner since 1986.
Personal: University of Pittsburgh School of Law (JD, 1979) Mansfield State College (BA, 1974).

WESTON, Timothy
Kirkpatrick & Lockhart Nicholson Graham LLP, Harrisburg 717 231 4504
tweston@klng.com
Recommended in Environment
Practice Areas: Focuses on environmental regulatory counseling and litigation, industrial and energy development projects, environmental issues in transactions, and natural resources management. He is nationally acknowledged in the field of water resources.
Prof. Memberships: Admitted to practice in Pennsylvania, the US Supreme Court, the US Courts of Appeal for the Third and Fourth Circuits.
Career: Joined Kirkpatrick & Lockhart Nicholson Graham LLP in 1987. Previously served in Pennsylvania Department of Environmental Resources, as Assistant Attorney General (1972-79) and Associate Deputy Secretary for Resources Management (1979-87). Also previously served as Commissioner on the Delaware River Basin Commission, Susquehanna River Basin Commission, Ohio River Basin Commission, and Great Lakes Commission.
Publications: Has published numerous articles and treatise chapters in the field of brownfields development, environmental issues in transactions, and water management..
Personal: JD (cum laude), Harvard Law School, 1972; BA (cum laude) mathematics, University of California (Santa Barbara), 1969.

WETTACH, Thomas
Cohen & Grigsby PC, Pittsburgh 800 394 4904
Recommended in Intellectual Property

WILLIAMS, James
Wolf, Block, Schorr and Solis-Cohen LLP, Philadelphia 215 977 2000
jwilliams@wolfblock.com
Recommended in Real Estate
Practice Areas: Mr Williams, a Partner in the Real Estate Practice Group, represents financial institutions and developers in real estate transactions, including acquisitions, sales, leasing, development and construction. He also has been extensively involved in the negotiation of sophisticated financing transactions.
Career: Mr Williams was admitted to the Pennsylvania Bar in 1982.
Personal: Mr Williams received his BA magna cum laude from the University of Pennsylvania in 1978 and his JD from New York University School of Law in 1982.

WINNING, William
Cozen O'Connor, Philadelphia 215 665 2000
Recommended in Litigation

WINOKUR, Barton J
Dechert, Philadelphia 215 994 2505
barton.winokur@dechert.com
Recommended in Corporate/M&A
Practice Areas: Chairman and Chief Executive Officer of Dechert and a Corporate Partner since 1972. Former Chair of firm's Mergers and Acquisitions and International Law Groups. Represents public and private companies, leveraged buyout sponsor funds, and venture capital firms in complex corporate transactions including mergers, acquisitions, divestitures, joint ventures, and restructurings. Also advises boards of public companies on governance matters.
Prof. Memberships: Member of several Corporate Boards. Member and Former Chair of the Board of Trustees of Brandeis University.
Career: Joined Dechert in 1965.
Personal: Cornell University (AB, 1961); Harvard Law School (LLB, 1964), editor of the Harvard Law Review.

WOELFLING, Maxine
Morgan, Lewis & Bockius LLP, Harrisburg 717 237 4065
mwoelfling@morganlewis.com
Recommended in Environment
Practice Areas: Maxine Woelfling is of counsel in the Litigation Practice. Ms Woelfling concentrates her practice in the area of environmental law. Her practice involves regulatory compliance counseling, negotiation of permit conditions, litigation of permitting and enforcement issues before state and federal administrative and judicial tribunals, and environmental issues in business and financial transactions. She has been extensively involved in counseling clients regarding the remediation and reuse of former brownfields and other contaminated properties under Pennsylvania's innovative Land Recycling Act.
Prof. Memberships: Pennsylvania Bar Association.

WYCOFF, William
Thorp Reed & Armstrong, Pittsburgh 412 394 7782
wwycoff@thorpreed.com
Recommended in Litigation
Practice Areas: Chairman of the Commercial and Corporation Litigation Practice Group. Has extensive experience in antitrust, securities, class action, financial institution and general business litigation.
Prof. Memberships: Member, Allegheny County Academy of Trial Lawyers; Fellow, American College of Trial Lawyers; Fellow, International Academy of Trial Lawyers.
Career: Joined Thorp Reed & Armstrong, LLP in 1966; became Partner, 1974. Member, Thorp Reed & Armstrong's Executive Committee, 1990 to present.
Publications: Course Planner and Author, PBI Program, Damages in Commercial Litigation, 1997, 2003. 'Audit Committee Duties and Liabilities in the Post Enron World', Accounting Litigation after Enron, PBI, 2002. 'Recovery of Lost Profit Damages Under Pennsylvania Law', 2003. 'Daubert & Expert Economist Testimony', 2003. Course Planner and Author in Confidentiality in Civil Litigation, PBI, 1997. Course planner and author in Civil RICO Programs, PBI, 1985, 1988, 1990, 1993. Course planner and author in Product Liability Programs, PBI, 1985, 1988, 1991. Course planner and moderator in Medical Malpractice Program, PBI, 2001.
Personal: Born January 1, 1941. JD, Northwestern University School of Law, 1966; BA, Cornell University, 1963.

YEAGER, Robert
Kirkpatrick & Lockhart Nicholson Graham LLP, Pittsburgh 412 355 8605
ryeager@klng.com
Recommended in Intellectual Property
Practice Areas: Intellectual property litigation and patent infringement litigation. Served as lead counsel in dozens of trials and appeals involving a wide array of technologies and businesses. Appointed as a Special Master for claim construction purposes.
Prof. Memberships: Admitted in Pennsylvania and federal trial and appellate courts; American and Pennsylvania Intellectual Property Law Associations.
Career: Joined K&LNG in 1985, Partner since 1985.
Publications: Frequent writer and lecturer on various intellectual property litigation topics.
Personal: JD Dickinson School of Law 1966; BS, Pennsylvania State University 1958.

ZONN, Sidney
Littler Mendelson PC, Pittsburgh 412 201 7600
Recommended in Employment

BALLARD SPAHR ANDREWS & INGERSOLL, LLP

THE FIRM

Chairman: Arthur Makadon
Number of partners: 188
Number of other lawyers: 248

FIRM OVERVIEW: Ballard Spahr Andrews & Ingersoll, LLP was founded in 1886. Throughout its history, the firm has been committed to excellence in the practice of law. It has grown to be one of the 100 largest law firms in the country, with over 430 lawyers and seven offices located throughout the mid-Atlantic corridor and the western United States. As a large, multi-office, multi-regional law firm, Ballard Spahr is able to combine a national scope of practice with strong local market knowledge to represent companies, individuals, and other entities in virtually every state and around the world.

MAIN AREAS OF PRACTICE:

Business & Finance: The firm's Business and Finance Department has a regional, national, and international practice involving public and private companies and nonprofit organizations. Their clients are engaged with wide-ranging and dynamic technology, manufacturing, and service functions; pharmaceutical, energy, telecommunications, and software manufacturing companies; financial institutions; investment companies; sports and other franchises; public utilities; and hospitals and health services. They also represent issuers, underwriters, lenders, and venture capitalists in equity and debt financing for companies large and small, private and public. The firm's business and finance lawyers serve their clients on a national basis in mergers, acquisitions, and other complex transactions and provide legal counseling and compliance for investment companies and advisors, banks, broker/dealers, consumer finance companies, credit card issuers, and public companies and their boards of directors.

Financial Planning & Management: Ballard Spahr's Financial Planning and Management Department includes lawyers in the Tax Group, Employee Benefits Group, and Family Wealth Management Group. The firm's Tax Practice involves sophisticated tax planning and handling tax disputes at all levels of government – federal, state, local, and international. The Employee Benefits Group provides clients with legal advice regarding the full range of qualified and nonqualified plans. The Family Wealth Management Group provides a comprehensive range of estate planning services to individuals of means.

Litigation: The Litigation Department represents a wide range of local, national, and international clients, including large and small companies in the public, private, and nonprofit sectors. They handle all types of complex litigation and regularly represent clients in local, state, and federal courts, at both the trial and appellate levels, as well as other forums throughout the country.

Public Finance: Ballard Spahr has a nationally recognized practice in the field of public finance and federal tax matters relating to the issuance of municipal bonds. The firm has consistently been ranked as one of the leading bond and underwriter counsel firms in the country. The firm's public finance lawyers serve as bond counsel, underwriter's counsel, trustee's counsel, and borrower's counsel for state and local governments and authorities throughout the United States, and have a wide range of experience in many areas of law, including municipal, tax, securities, real estate, housing, environmental, public utilities, energy, health care, education, banking, administrative, and corporate.

Real Estate: The firm's real estate lawyers provide cutting-edge representation for national and regional clients, including corporate, institutional, entrepreneurial, and public clients in acquisition, development, financing, leasing and sales, and other flagship transactions. In order to serve their clients effectively, the department is organized into discrete service groups: acquisitions and dispositions; complex develop-

ment; construction; finance; hotel/resort/timeshare and workouts; housing; leasing; valuation; workouts; and zoning and land use.

HEAD OFFICE

PENNSYLVANIA
1735 Market Street, 51st Floor **Philadelphia**, PA 19103-7599
Tel: 215 665 8500   **Fax:** 215 864 8999
Website: www.ballardspahr.com

BRANCH OFFICES

COLORADO
1225 17th Street, Suite 2300, **Denver**, CO 80202-5596
Tel: 303 292 2400   **Fax:** 303 296 3956

DELAWARE
919 N. Market Street, 17th Floor, **Wilmington**, DE 19801
Tel: 302 252 4465   **Fax:** 302 252 4466

DISTRICT OF COLUMBIA
601 13th Street, NW, Suite 1000 South, **Washington**, DC 20005-3807
Tel: 202 661 2200   **Fax:** 202 661 2299

MARYLAND
300 East Lombard Street, 18th Floor, **Baltimore**, MD 21202-3268
Tel: 410 528 5600   **Fax:** 410 528 5650

NEW JERSEY
Plaza 1000-Suite 500, Main Street, **Voorhees**, NJ 08043-4636
Tel: 856 761 3400   **Fax:** 856 761 1020

UTAH
One Utah Center, Suite 600, 201 South Main Street, **Salt Lake City**, UT 84111-2221
Tel: 801 531 3000   **Fax:** 801 531 3001

CONTACTS

Bankruptcy	Vincent J Marriott III, William A Slaughter
Biotechnology/Life Sciences	Richard P Jaffe
Business & Finance	William H Rheiner
Construction	Lynn R Axelroth
Consumer Financial Services	Alan S Kaplinsky
Eminent Domain/Condemnation	S David Brandt, George J Kroculick
Employee Benefits	John M Bernard
Energy & Project Finance	C Baird Brown, Charles S Henck
Environmental	David G Mandelbaum
Family Wealth Management	Regina O Thomas
Financial Planning & Management	Frederic L Ballard Jr
Franchise & Distribution	Benjamin A Levin
Government Enforcement/White Collar Crime	Eric W Sitarchuk
Health Care	Jean C Hemphill
Housing	Steven P Berman
Intellectual Property	Jamie B Bischoff
Investment Management	William H Rheiner
Labor & Employment	John B Langel
Land Use	Michael Sklaroff
Litigation	Charisse R Lillie
Mergers & Acquisitions	William H Rheiner
Public Finance	Blake K Wade
Real Estate	Michael Sklaroff
Real Estate Development	Richard R Goldberg
Real Estate Finance	Beverly J Quail, Fred Wolf III
Real Estate Leasing	David L Pollack
Resorts & Hotels	W Michael Clowdus, Steven D Peterson
Securities	Justin P Klein
Securitization	Lisa M Sloan
Tax	Wayne R Strasbaugh
Technology & Emerging Companies	Raymond D Agran
Telecommunications	Jerold G Oldroyd
Transactional Finance	Carl H Fridy
Valuation	Philip B Korb

BLANK ROME LLP

THE FIRM

Chairman: David F Girard-diCarlo
Managing Partner: Fred Blume
Executive Partner: Carl M Buchholz
Finance Partner: Barry H Genkin

Partners: 236
Others: 250

FIRM OVERVIEW: Blank Rome LLP is a full-service firm of nearly 500 attorneys serving clients across the United States and abroad from its principal offices in New York, Philadelphia, Washington, DC and Wilmington, DE, and six additional locations in New Jersey, Pennsylvania, Ohio and Florida. Blank Rome's business-oriented lawyers assist companies from large multi-national corporations to start-up ventures, in a wide range of industries in virtually all aspects of their businesses. The firm has the experience and resources required to handle highly complex transactions and litigation.

Blank Rome's Washington office focuses on transactional, legislative and regulatory matters affecting the marine transportation and shipbuilding industries as well as a wide range of legislative affairs, regulatory and commercial litigation, white-collar defense and investigations, healthcare, international trade, government contracts, securities and environmental law. The Washington office is the center of the firm's extensive patent and intellectual property practices.

Blank Rome's New York office serves public and private companies in mergers and acquisitions in corporate and litigation matters. The firm's New York office represents some of the area's leading real estate, financial services and technology companies. The New York office also has one of the largest and most visible matrimonial and estates and trusts practices in the United States.

The firm's Wilmington, DE office is involved primarily in significant bankruptcy filings and intellectual property litigation in the Delaware courts and in Wilmington. It also focuses on public finance, litigation and dispute resolution and financial services.

Blank Rome Government Relations LLC: A wholly-owned subsidiary of Blank Rome LLP, Blank Rome Government Relations LLC, comprised of legal, lobbying and communications professionals, helps clients navigate the complexities of government at the federal, state and local levels. Blank Rome Government Relations LLC establishes and maintains liaisons with federal agencies, officers and elected officials, monitors legislation, pursues potential federal funding sources, arranges meetings with regulatory and congressional representatives, and coordinates lobbying efforts and strategies with government staff. The firm is actively involved in homeland security working, on behalf of clients, with federal, state and local governments on legislation in support of new laws, statutes and procedures.

MAIN AREAS OF PRACTICE: Antitrust; aviation; banking; bankruptcy and business restructuring; capital formation; commercial litigation; corporate and securities; environmental law; estate planning; public contracts; health law; insurance; intellectual property and technology; intellectual property litigation; international trade; labor and employment law; maritime law and transportation; matrimonial law; mergers and acquisitions; product liability litigation; public finance; real estate; securities litigation; tax, and white collar defense.

Pro Bono: Blank Rome attorneys devote a significant portion of their time and resources to professional and other activities in the public interest and have provided their services, without compensation, to many individuals

PRINCIPAL OFFICES

DISTRICT OF COLUMBIA
600 New Hampshire Avenue, NW, **Washington**, DC 20037
Tel: 202 772 5800   **Fax:** 202 772 5858
Email: webmaster@BlankRome.com
Website: www.BlankRome.com

NEW YORK
The Chrysler Building, 405 Lexington Avenue, **New York**, NY 10174-0208
Tel: 212 885 5000   **Fax:** 212 885 5001

PENNSYLVANIA
One Logan Square, 18th & Cherry Streets,
Philadelphia, PA 19103-6998
Tel: 215 569 5500   **Fax:** 215 569 5555

DELAWARE
Chase Manhatten Centre, 1201 Market Street, Suite 800,
Wilmington, DE 19801
Tel: 302 425 6400   **Fax:** 302 425 6464

OTHER OFFICES

FLORIDA
1200 North Federal Highway, Suite 417, **Boca Raton**, FL 33432
Tel: 561 417 8100   **Fax:** 561 417 8101

NEW JERSEY
210 Lake Drive East, Woodland Falls Corporate Park, Suite 200,
Cherry Hill, NJ 08002
Tel: 856 779 3600   **Fax:** 856 779 7647

200 West State Street, **Trenton**, NJ 08608
Tel: 609 278 2320   **Fax:** 609 278 2323

OHIO
201 East Fifth Street, 1700 PNC Center, **Cincinnati**, OH 45202
Tel: 513 362 8700   **Fax:** 513 362 8787

PENNSYLVANIA
1620 Pond Road, Suite 200, **Allentown**, PA 18104
Tel: 610 706 4300   **Fax:** 610 706 4343

Rose Tree Corporate Center, 1400 N. Providence Road, Bldg 1, Suite 301,
Media, PA 19063
Tel: 610 891 7800   **Fax:** 610 891 7804

CONTACTS

Delaware Office	Michael D DeBaecke
District of Columbia Office	Thomas M (Mike) Dyer
	Patrick O Cavanaugh
	Mark A Holman (Government Relations)
Florida Office	Michael H Leeds
New Jersey Offices	Steven D Weinstein
New York Office	Robert J Mittman
	Michael S Mullman
Ohio Office	Michael L Cioffi
Pennsylvania Offices	Fred Blume (Philadelphia)
	Bernard M Lesavoy (Allentown)
	Paul D McNichol (Media)

and causes. The firm's commitment to the local community is illustrated by a 64% increase in pro bono hours in the most recent year. In 2004, the Pennsylvania Bar Association honored partner Peggy McCausland with its Citizens Pro Bono Award for her advocacy work with children.

BLANK ROME LLP cont'd

Diversity: Blank Rome LLP and Blank Rome Government Relations LLC recognize that a diversity of ideas, backgrounds, and experiences is crucial to fulfilling its commitment to excellence. Blank Rome endeavors to recruit, hire, promote and retain, on the basis of demonstrated talent and initiative, individuals throughout the firm representing, among other things, different races, genders, ethnic groups, religions, sexual orientation and national origin. Blank Rome has established a Diversity Committee to recommend specific actions that may be taken in the firm's activities, both internal and external, to achieve these goals.

CLIENTS: Blank Rome represents businesses and organizations – from multi-billion dollar international companies to start-up entities. Blank Rome represents companies among the *Fortune 500* and the middle market. The firm represents clients in a wide variety of industries including: aviation; banking and insurance; communications; education; energy; entertainment and general services; financial services; health care; leisure; life sciences; manufacturing; professional services; real estate; retail/wholesale trade; technology; transportation, and units of state and local government.

Representative Transactions:

Represented a joint venture consisting of DRA Advisors LLC and Kimco Realty Corporation in the merger transaction with Price Legacy Corporation, a publicly traded shopping center Real Estate Investment Trust. The merger involved approximately 40 properties having a value in excess of $1 billion.

Representing USGen New England in its chapter 11 bankruptcy case in Greenbelt, Maryland including the sales of its fossil fuel and hydro electric generating assets to two separate acquirers for a combined purchase price in excess of $1.1 billion.

Served as counsel to TransCore Holdings in its $600 million acquisition by Roper Industries from an investor group.

Represented Sunoco, Inc. in lease negotiations for its new corporate-headquarters in the Mellon Bank Center, a transaction recognized as one of the Best Real Estate Deals of 2004 by the *Philadelphia Business Journal*. Acted as Bond Counsel to The School District of Philadelphia's issuance of $791 million of General Obligation Bonds.

Completed approximately $200 million of financing for Cornerstone Family Services, Inc., the fourth largest cemetery company in the United States.

Represented CapitalSource, Inc. in a $175 million financing for the acquisition of 58 nursing homes in 14 states. The financing included five separate loans secured by fee interest, leasehold interests and accounts receivable.

Reached a four-year $5 billion collective bargaining agreement with the Philadelphia Federation of Teachers on behalf of the School Reform Commission of Philadelphia.

Closed a secondary public offering for Pennsylvania Commerce Bancorp, Inc. ('PA Commerce') of 460,000 shares of its common stock raising $20.8 million. As part of the transaction, Blank Rome assisted PA Commerce in transferring its securities from the Nasdaq SmallCap Market to the Nasdaq National Market.

Closed a private placement transaction in which Commerce Bancorp, Inc. purchased 100,000 shares of PA Commerce's common stock. Commerce Bancorp, Inc. also purchased 50,000 shares of PA Commerce's common stock in the public offering.

Representative Litigation:

Represented Lyondell Chemical Company as national coordinating counsel for more than 100 lawsuits in 16 states involving the gasoline additive MTBE. Settled the City of Santa Monica case which sought over $500 million in damages for $3.55 million.

Successfully defended L-3 Communications Corp. and Northrop Grumman Corporation in an arbitration proceeding in which a scientist sought damages in excess of $175 million, contending, among other things, that L-3, the company to which he had transferred the rights to certain patents, had failed to exploit his technology, thereby reducing his royalties.

Obtained a $5.6 million judgment for Commercial Federal Bank, F.S.B., following a five-week trial, against the federal government for lost profits caused by the government's breach of contract in a case relating to United States v. Winstar Corp. This is the only Winstar case in which the US Court of Federal Claims awarded lost-profits damages to a plaintiff.

Defended Campbell Soup Company in a bench trial that concerned its 1998 spin-off of Vlasic Foods International, Inc., the transaction upon which the successor-in-interest to Vlasic Foods International, Inc., based various claims of fraud and fraudulent transfer.

Successfully prosecuted software patent infringement cases on behalf of Centillion Data Systems, Inc., reaching $25 million in favorable settlements on behalf of Centillion.

In a suit arising from the sale of numerous bank branches by Wachovia Corporation's predecessor-in-interest, caused Wachovia's adversary to abandon its claim and settled Wachovia's counterclaim on terms compelling its adversary to pay Wachovia over $8 million.

In re Genesis Health Ventures, a False Claims Act qui tam action alleging special damages of $325 million for an alleged failure to process credit to the federally-funded Medicaid program for unused and returned medications provided by a national institutional pharmacy provider. The Department of Justice declined intervention in the action. Summary judgment in favor of the pharmacy provider was obtained.

Successfully obtained a summary judgment in a consumer class action in the Superior Court of New Jersey for a national bank and its assignee, a state-licensed mortgage lender, in which the plaintiffs claimed that prepayment penalties and 'points' charged at closing violated New Jersey laws governing second mortgages.

Obtained dismissal of a nationwide consumer lending complaint challenging bankruptcy-related fees in federal bankruptcy court in San Antonio on behalf of prominent national financial institutions.

Defended a manufacturer of products used for military and aerospace applications in a qui tam lawsuit brought under the federal False Claims Act. The lawsuit alleged that the manufacturer had submitted claims to the government that falsely certified that it was in compliance with environmental, health and safety laws, and was settled on terms that were very favorable to the defendant.

Defended a shipyard that had contracted to construct ships for the United States Navy in a qui tam lawsuit brought under the federal False Claims Act. Successfully guided the company and its officials through a Senate investigation and hearing into the contract, and then obtained dismissal of various counts for failure to state a legal claim for relief, dismissal of other counts for lack of jurisdiction, and dismissal of the principal conspiracy count on summary judgment for lack of evidence.

Obtained a favorable ruling in a case of first impression for M&T Bank, holding the force majeure clause in a long-term lease did not excuse a landlord's failure to obtain governmental approvals by the date set in the lease. In so holding, the Bank was able to avoid a commitment to a long-term lease.

Obtained a $26 million award for TransCore Holdings, Inc. on its fraud and breach of contract claims in an arbitration proceeding that concerned the financial condition of a company it had acquired.

BLANK ROME LLP
COUNSELORS AT LAW

BUCHANAN INGERSOLL PC

THE FIRM

Chief Executive Officer: Thomas L VanKirk
Chief Operating Officer: Francis A Muracca, II

FIRM OVERVIEW: Buchanan Ingersoll PC is one of the 120 largest law firms in the United States, with more than 345 attorneys practicing in its offices throughout the country. The practice covers more than 65 service areas, including banking, corporate finance, government relations, tax, litigation, intellectual property and health care.

MAIN AREAS OF PRACTICE:

Corporate Finance: The Corporate Finance Section structures, negotiates, documents and concludes transactions essential to accomplishing both the operations and strategic objectives of its clients. The firm's services in this area include public and private capital formation, merger and acquisition, corporate governance and control, and regulatory issues.

Litigation: Offering broad trial and appellate experience, the Litigation Group has a long and distinguished record of successful representations that reflects the firm's commitment and determination to achieve its clients' objectives in disputed matters, whether in court of through alternative dispute resolution. The firm's attorneys litigate and provide litigation counseling on behalf of regional, national and international businesses.

Intellectual Property: The Intellectual Property Group's experience covers the full scope of intellectual property law and litigation, including patents, trademarks, copyrights, trade secrets, licensing, technology transfer and non-disclosure and non-compete agreements.

Tax: The Tax Section's more than 40 attorneys have experience in all aspects of federal tax planning, controversy, legislative and regulatory work. The group assists clients with business and international tax matters, employee benefits, estates and trusts and real estate tax issues.

Government Relations: The Government Relations Group provides clients with the strongest possible voice in the development of policies, legislation and regulations that affect their businesses. The group also provides comprehensive legislative and regulatory advocacy services.

Healthcare: The firm's Health Care Section provides a wide range of transactional and other legal services. In recent years, the firm's lawyers have been involved in a significant number of mergers, acquisitions and other transactions worth in excess of $14 billion.

Labor & Employment: The Labor and Employment Law Section provides legal services for employers on all issues that arise out of the employer-employee relationship. The group addresses workplace issues and helps clients minimize the amount of time, effort and expense required to resolve employment-related problems.

Financial Institutions: In representing lenders, the Financial Institutions Section has structured, negotiated, documented and completed hundreds of transactions worth billions of dollars. The group's experience includes syndicated credit, letter of credit, corporate and real estate transactions, as well as workout, restructuring and litigation matters.

Bankruptcy & Creditors' Rights: This group represents and counsels debtors and creditors, banks involved in workout situations, creditors' committees and corporations and individuals facing financial difficulty. The group also has experience in insurance insolvency matters.

OFFICES

PENNSYLVANIA
Founding Office
One Oxford Centre, 301 Grant Street, 20th Floor, **Pittsburgh**, PA 15219
Tel: 412 562 8800   **Fax:** 412 562 1041
Email: info@bipc.com
Website: www.buchananingersoll.com

1835 Market Street, 14th Floor, **Philadelphia**, PA 19103-2985
Tel: 215 665 8700   **Fax:** 215 665 8760

One South Market Square, 213 Market Street, 3rd Floor,
Harrisburg, PA 17101
Tel: 717 237 4800   **Fax:** 717 233 0852

NEW YORK
One Chase Manhattan Plaza, 35th Floor, **New York**, NY 10005
Tel: 212 440 4400   **Fax:** 212 440 4401

NEW JERSEY
700 Alexander Park, Suite 300, **Princeton**, NJ 08540-6347
Tel: 609 987 6800   **Fax:** 609 520 0360

DELAWARE
The Nemours Building, 1007 North Orange Street, Suite 1110,
Wilmington, DE 19801-1236
Tel: 302 428 5508   **Fax:** 302 428 3996

DISTRICT OF COLUMBIA
1776 K. Street, N.W., Suite 800, **Washington**, DC 20006-2365
Tel: 202 452 7900   **Fax:** 202 452 7989

FLORIDA
Bank of America Tower, 100 S.E. Second Street, 34th Floor,
Miami, FL 33131-2158
Tel: 305 347 4080   **Fax:** 305 347 4089

SunTrust Financial Centre, 401 East Jackson Street, Suite 2500,
Tampa, FL 33602-5236
Tel: 813 222 8180   **Fax:** 813 222 8189

CALIFORNIA
First National Bank Center, 401 West A Street, Suite 1900,
San Diego, CA 92101-7908
Tel: 619 578 5000   **Fax:** 619 578 5940

CAESAR, RIVISE, BERNSTEIN, COHEN & POKOTILOW, LTD.

THE FIRM

Managing Shareholder: Manny D Pokotilow

Number of partners: 13
Number of other lawyers: 13
Number of patent agents: 1

HEAD OFFICE

PENNSYLVANIA
1635 Market Street, 12th Floor, **Philadelphia**, PA 19103-2212
Tel: 215 567 2010   **Fax:** 215 751 1142
Email: gatekeeper@crbcp.com
Website: www.crbcp.com

FIRM OVERVIEW: Since its founding in 1926 by Abraham D Caesar and Charles Rivise, the firm has focused on patent, trademark, copyright and other intellectual property law. More recently, the firm has expanded its practice to other areas involving high technology law, such as internet, information technology and computer law, in keeping with its goal of protecting and promoting the development of creative ideas and the people who create them. The attorneys of the firm have backgrounds in the fields of chemistry, chemical engineering, pharmaceuticals, biotechnology, nuclear engineering, mechanical engineering, materials science, electrical engineering, computers, the internet and information technology. This combination of varied technical skills among the attorneys creates a synergistic energy that is maximized when fulfilling each client's needs.

MAIN AREAS OF PRACTICE:

Patents: The firm handles all aspects of patent law. This includes the evaluation of inventions for patenting, by conducting patentability searches throughout the world and drafting and prosecuting of patent applications in the United States and internationally through its foreign associates. Where appropriate, the firm conducts appeals through the relevant governmental agencies and courts.

Trademarks: The firm handles all aspects of trademark law including the evaluation of marks for registration, conducting searches throughout the world and drafting and prosecuting of trademark applications in the United States and internationally. Where appropriate, the firm conducts appeals through the relevant governmental agencies and courts.

Copyrights: The firm handles all aspects of copyright law, including drafting and prosecuting applications to register copyrights in the United States.

Litigation Matters: Where litigation is appropriate, the firm brings its considerable skills to bear - the attorneys of Caesar Rivise have considerable experience in handling ex parte and inter partes patent and trademark matters in the relevant government agencies of the United States and have been lead counsel in hundreds of cases throughout the United States involving all aspects of intellectual property law.

Client Counseling & Transactional Matters: The firm becomes deeply involved in counseling its clients on all matters involving patents, trademarks, copyrights, the internet, information technology and computer law, and in drafting and negotiating agreements for such matters, including, confidentiality agreements, consulting agreements, joint development agreements, clinical research agreements, license agreements, asset purchase and sales agreements, employment agreements and employment policy issues.

Due Diligence Matters: The firm conducts right to use and infringement studies, and is frequently involved in the evaluation of intellectual property portfolios for merger, acquisition and asset purchase matters.

Stability: Caesar Rivise has been known for its extraordinary stability. Retaining experienced attorneys and staff has resulted in an unrivaled quality of service. Training mentoring, and advancing each of its attorneys to shareholder or partners positions not only builds an extended legal family and support network, not also serves clients whose needs are ongoing. Clients seeking to obtain and maintain protection over the life of a patent or trademark can count on Caesar Rivise attorneys who know and understand their business, and who can pass that knowledge along to colleagues as necessary.

CLIENTS: The firm's client base includes individuals, small entrepreneurial organizations, *Fortune* 500 companies and foreign corporations

Caesar, Rivise, Bernstein, Cohen & Pokotilow, Ltd.

CR Intellectual Property, Computer and Information Technology Law

CONRAD O'BRIEN GELLMAN & ROHN P.C.

THE FIRM

Managing Shareholder: James J Rohn

Number of shareholders: 13
Number of other lawyers: 24

FIRM OVERVIEW: Founded over 20 years ago by three prominent litigation partners from a major Philadelphia law firm, Conrad O'Brien has established itself as one of the leading litigation practices in Pennsylvania and around the country. The firm is dedicated to one thing: providing first-rate litigation services to clients involved in complex litigation. The firm achieves that mission by drawing on the extraordinary credentials and experience of its lawyers. Widely recognized for their skills as trial lawyers, one quarter of the firm's shareholders are Fellows of the American College of Trial Lawyers. The firm's roster includes the former Chief Judge of the United States District Court for the Eastern District of Pennsylvania; the former First Assistant US Attorney for that district; a Fellow of the International Academy of Trial Lawyers; faculty members of the National Institute for Trial Advocacy; former Presidents of the Philadelphia Association of Defense Lawyers; a former Chief Assistant Solicitor for the City of Philadelphia; and numerous lawyers with decades of combined experience from practice in some of the largest law firms in the country.

MAIN AREAS OF PRACTICE: The firm's attorneys practice regularly in federal and state courts in Pennsylvania, New Jersey and around the country in matters involving commercial litigation, white collar criminal defense, professional liability, products liability, personal injury and mass torts. The firm also provides services in alternative dispute resolution proceedings.
Commercial Litigation: The firm's Commercial Litigation Practice covers a broad range of complex matters, including antitrust, unfair business practice claims, class actions, RICO, contract disputes, information technology, employment issues (including employment discrimination litigation), ERISA, defamation, directors and officers liability, copyright, trademark, construction and securities claims. The firm also represents companies in litigation with federal and state governments concerning Superfund sites and natural resource damage claims.
White Collar Criminal Defense: Conrad O'Brien attorneys conduct internal corporate investigations, represent both individuals and companies in grand jury investigations, and defend clients in any related criminal, civil, or administrative proceedings. The firm's practice includes defending against prosecutions for alleged violations of antitrust statutes, RICO, the False Claims Act, and state and federal tax and securities laws; representing clients in claims such as false statements, embezzlement, forfeiture, money laundering, insurance fraud, obstruction of justice, and public corruption; and counseling clients on Sarbanes-Oxley compliance issues.
Professional Liability: The firm's Professional Liability Practice involves the defense of malpractice claims against hospitals, physicians, law firms and other professionals. Conrad O'Brien attorneys represent physicians, hospitals, nurses, physicians' practices, and other healthcare providers in medical malpractice litigation as well as in actions involving insurance coverage, credentialing and licensing issues. Conrad O'Brien also serves as the firm to which lawyers turn when they need representation for themselves.
Products Liability, Personal Injury & Mass Torts: Conrad O'Brien lawyers represent companies in products liability, personal injury, mass tort and class action cases involving products such as pharmaceuticals, lead paint, medical devices and equipment, chemicals and tobacco.
Alternative Dispute Resolution (ADR): The firm's lawyers are routinely involved in a wide range of alternative dispute resolution procedures, from arbitrations to mediations. Their experience comes not just from being advocates in these types of cases, but also from serving as the neutrals themselves for state and federal courts and for private organizations such as the American Arbitration Association, the CPR Institute for Dispute Resolution, and the National Association of Securities Dealers.

CLIENTS: The firm's clients range from Fortune 500 companies to newer entrepreneurial businesses, who have chosen Conrad O'Brien for its cost-effective litigation, and for its dedication to client interests. Representative clients of the firm include: AEGON USA; Air Products and Chemicals; Akzo Nobel; American Red Cross; Broadband & Internet Security Task Force; Children's Hospital of Philadelphia; GE Medical Protective Company; IBM; Lorillard Tobacco Company; Motiva Enterprises; Osram Sylvania; Motion Picture Association of America; NEC America; Pennsylvania-American Water Company; Progressive Corporation; Qwest Communications; Raleigh America; Rohm and Haas Company; SLM Financial Corporation; Vanguard Group and Viacom International. The firm also represents hospitals, professional organizations, physician groups and law firms.

HEAD OFFICE

PENNSYLVANIA
1515 Market Street, Sixteenth Floor, **Philadelphia**, PA 19102-1916
Tel: 215 864 9600   **Fax:** 215 864 9620
Email: lawyers@cogr.com
Website: www.cogr.com

BRANCH OFFICES

PENNSYLVANIA
17 West Gay Street, Suite 100, **West Chester**, PA 19380-3090
Tel: 610 701 9100   **Fax:** 610 701 9195

100 Four Falls Corporate Center, Suite 300,
West Conshohocken, PA 19428-2983
Tel: 610 940 6045   **Fax:** 610 940 6046

NEW JERSEY
1000 Haddonfield-Berlin Road, Suite 202, **Voorhees**, NJ 08043-3520
Tel: 856 309 3373   **Fax:** 856 309 3375

CONRAD O'BRIEN GELLMAN & ROHN, PC

DECHERT LLP

THE FIRM

Chairman: Barton J Winokur
Number of partners: 223
Number of other lawyers: 495

Website: www.dechert.com

FIRM OVERVIEW: Dechert LLP is an international law firm providing a full range of legal services to clients in transactional, litigation, tax and regulatory matters.

MAIN AREAS OF PRACTICE: Corporate finance, mergers and acquisitions, private equity, business and technology, IP counseling & litigation, complex litigation, mass torts and product liability, financial services, finance and real estate, tax.
Corporate Finance: The firm represents issuers, sponsors, investors, underwriters, and placement agents in all types of public and private issuances of debt and equity securities.
Mergers & Acquisitions: The firm's internationally recognized M&A group represents buyers, sellers, and advisers in planning, negotiating, and executing a full range of public and private transactions.
Private Equity: The firm's dedicated Private Equity Team focuses on fund formation and capital raising, funds' investment activities, and portfolio company transactions.
Business & Technology: The firm provides strategic transactional advice to life sciences, software, IT, and other technology companies in all stages of growth, as well as the incubators, investment banks, and venture capital firms that support them.
Intellectual Property Counseling & Litigation: The firm offers the full range of services in every discipline: patent, trademark, copyright, trade secret, right of publicity, advertising, licensing, and computer law.
Complex Litigation: A national litigation team represents clients in sophisticated antitrust, securities, corporate governance, and white collar litigation. The firm also has well-established employment, commercial, environmental, and healthcare litigation practices.
Mass Torts & Product Liability: The firm's nationally recognized Mass Tort and Product Liability Defense Team represents consumer goods, chemical, and pharmaceutical companies in complex class actions and multi-district litigation.
Financial Services: The services of one of the country's largest Financial Services Practice include formation and operation of open- and closed-end investment companies as well as private, hedge, and offshore funds; mutual funds representation; regulation and compliance; and broker-dealer issues.
Finance & Real Estate: Lawyers handle mortgage finance, mezzanine lending, and debt/equity financing; structured finance and asset- and mortgage-backed securitizations and CDOs/CLOs; and investment vehicles, including REITs.
Tax: Tax lawyers advise on M&A, restructurings, real estate transactions, and investment management activities. The practice also provides employee benefits/executive compensation, private client, and state tax legal services.

CLIENTS: The firm's clients include many of the world's largest financial services companies and financial institutions; *Fortune* 500 pharmaceutical, manufacturing, and technology companies; domestic and international private equity funds and portfolio companies; hospitals and health care systems; major tax-exempt organizations; and municipal and national governments.

INTERNATIONAL WORK: With more than 700 lawyers in 17 offices in the US and Europe, Dechert LLP has the resources to deliver seamless, sophisticated legal services to clients worldwide.

USA OFFICES

CALIFORNIA
4675 MacArthur Court, Suite 1400, **Newport Beach**, CA 92660-8842
Tel: 949 442 6000 **Fax:** 949 442 6010

975 Page Mill Road, **Palo Alto**, CA 94304-1013
Tel: 650 813 4800 **Fax:** 650 813 4848

One Market, Spear Tower, Suite 1600, **San Francisco**, CA 94304-1126
Tel: 415 262 4500 **Fax:** 415 262 4555

CONNECTICUT
90 State House Square, **Hartford**, CT 06103-3702
Tel: 860 524 3999 **Fax:** 860 524 3930

DISTRICT OF COLUMBIA
1775 I Street, NW, **Washington**, DC 20006-2401
Tel: 202 261 3300 **Fax:** 202 261 3333

MASSACHUSETTS
200 Clarendon Street, 27th Floor, **Boston**, MA 02116-5021
Tel: 617 728 7100 **Fax:** 617 426 6567

NEW JERSEY
Princeton Pike Corporate Center, 997 Lenox Drive, Building 3, Suite 210, **Lawrenceville**, NJ 08648-5218
Tel: 609 620 3200 **Fax:** 609 620 3259

NEW YORK
30 Rockefeller Plaza, **New York**, NY 10112-2200
Tel: 212 698 3500 **Fax:** 212 698 3599

NORTH CAROLINA
Bank of America Corporate Center, 100 North Tryon St, Suite 400, **Charlotte**, NC 28202
Tel: 704 339 3100 **Fax:** 704 339 3101

PENNSYLVANIA
Thirty North Third Street, **Harrisburg**, PA 17101-1603
Tel: 717 237 2000 **Fax:** 717 237 2040

4000 Bell Atlantic Tower, 1717 Arch Street, **Philadelphia**, PA 19103-2793
Tel: 215 994 4000 **Fax:** 215 994 2222

INTERNATIONAL OFFICES

The firm also has offices in Brussels, Frankfurt, London, Luxembourg, Munich, and Paris. For details on these offices, please visit the firm's website.

CONTACTS

Corporate Finance ....Carl A de Brito, Henry N Nassau Carmen J Romano
Mergers & Acquisitions..William G Lawlor
Private Equity ....G Daniel O'Donnell
Business & Technology ....James A Lebovitz
IP Counseling & Litigation ..Glenn A Gundersen, John W Ryan (Counseling)
.... Martin J Black, Michael H Kalkstein (Litigation)
Complex Litigation ....Robert C Heim
Mass Torts & Product Liability ....Sean P Wajert
Financial Services...........................Joseph R Fleming, Robert W Helm
Finance & Real Estate ....Malcolm S Dorris, John J Gillies Jr,
....Richard D Jones
Tax ....Thomas E Doran

DILWORTH PAXSON LLP

THE FIRM

Chairman: Joseph H Jacovini
Managing Partner: Stephen J Harmelin
Number of partners: 63
Number of other lawyers: 46

FIRM OVERVIEW: Dilworth Paxson LLP conducts a broad and diverse regional and national practice representing clients ranging from individuals and closely held businesses to publicly held and Fortune 500 companies. The firm also acts as special counsel to numerous municipal and governmental entities as well as utilities and other institutions. Dilworth Paxson also maintains a strong and unique tradition of public service and civic involvement and, as a result, many former and present members of the firm hold a wide variety of positions at the federal, state and local levels of government and on the boards of charitable and civic institutions.

MAIN AREAS OF PRACTICE:

Corporate: The firms Corporate and Business Practice ranges from complex domestic and international transactions to guidance on day to day issues of corporate governance and business relationships including sophisticated business planning, banking and finance, securities law issues and public and private offerings, mergers and acquisitions, and general corporate matters. This department also specializes in the particular needs of small businesses, privately held companies and non-profit entities.

Litigation: The firm's Litigation Practice includes commercial contracts, lending disputes, shareholder and corporate control controversies, securities matters, healthcare related litigation, unfair competition and antitrust cases, patent and intellectual property actions, construction suits, government agency contracts and bid disputes, trust issues, environmental and real estate cases, claims involving the regulation of business (particularly in the utility and insurance industries) and white collar criminal defense.

Bankruptcy & Insolvency: Dilworth has one of the largest bankruptcy and insolvency practices in the region. The practice group is qualified to handle both litigation oriented judicial insolvency proceedings and transactional oriented out of court workouts and debt restructurings.

Employment & Labor Relations: The firm counsels management on a broad range of matters, including discipline and discharge, wage payment obligations, unemployment compensation, union avoidance, negotiations and arbitrations, work force reductions and government inspections. The practice group also advises clients in dealing with federal agencies, including EEOC, NLRB and OSHA, and their state counterparts. It also represents clients in hearings and court proceedings involving wrongful discharge, discrimination and other employment-related matters.

Healthcare: The firm offers a comprehensive approach to meeting the legal needs of the healthcare industry, including managed care, regulatory, reimbursement, transactional, employment, clinical and other issues affecting individual and institutional healthcare providers and insurers. Cases are managed by attorneys experienced in healthcare who work in concert with attorneys from other departments such as tax, labor, real estate, public finance, corporate and litigation to meet clients' needs.

Public Finance: The firm has for more than 40 years provided issuer, underwriter, trustee and borrower representation for all types of bond issues and private financings including state, city, county and school district, general obligation and revenue bonds for airport, toll road, transportation, water and sewer projects, resource recovery, healthcare and other private activity financing. Dilworth Paxson is a recognized 'Red Book' bond counsel firm.

Real Estate: The firm represents developers, investors, lending institutions, landlords, tenants, contractors and construction managers, title insurance companies, contractors, real estate brokers and agents, public entities and corporate clientele. Services include the preparation, negotiation and review of documents related to all aspects of commercial, industrial and residential property acquisition and development, leasing and

OFFICES

DELAWARE
702 North King Street, Suite 500, First Federal Plaza
Wilmington, DE 19801
Tel: 302 571 9800   **Fax:** 302 571 8875

DISTRICT OF COLUMBIA
1818 N Street NW, Suite 400, **Washington**, DC 20036
Tel: 202 452 0900   **Fax:** 202 452 0930

NEW JERSEY
Liberty View, Suite 700, 457 Haddonfield Road,
Cherry Hill, NJ 08002
Tel: 856 663 8877   **Fax:** 856 663 8855

Monmouth Shores Corporate Park, Wall Township
1305 Campus Parkway Suite 201 **Neptune**, NJ 07753
Tel: 732 751 2590   **Fax:** 732 919 1240

PENNSYLVANIA
112 Market Streer, Suite 800, **Harrisburg**, PA 17101
Tel: 717 236 4812   **Fax:** 717 236 7811

11 Campus Boulevard Suite 150, Box 1181,
Newton Square, PA 19073
Tel: 610 325 3200   **Fax:** 610 325 3293

3200 Mellon Bank Center, 1735 Market Street,
Philadelphia, PA 19103-7595
Tel: 215 575 7000   **Fax:** 215 575 7200

CONTACTS

Corporate	Roger F Wood Esq
Bankruptcy	Lawrence G McMichael Esq
Employment & Labor Relations	Randall C Schauer Esq
Healthcare	Michael D Ecker Esq
Litigation	Lawrence G McMichael Esq
Public Finance	Mark A Feller Esq
Real Estate	Joseph F Kessler Esq
Securities	Roger F Wood Esq
Tax	John W Schmehl Esq
Trusts & Estates	John R Latourette, Jr Esq

commercial lending. The firm also has particular expertise in real estate workouts, zoning and land use issues.

Securities Practice: The firm's securities attorneys address client needs from venture capital financings, to public and private offerings (both domestic and foreign), to mergers and acquisitions and SEC reporting obligations. This practice also addresses the regulatory issues facing broker-dealers, investment advisors, securities analysts and stock exchanges. The litigation and enforcement members of this group represent clients before the SEC, the NASD, and state securities commissions, and clients subject to grand jury proceedings and criminal prosecutions in securities transactions.

Tax: The firm engages in sophisticated income, gift and estate tax planning for individuals, corporations and tax-exempt organizations involving federal, state and local laws. The firm also advise clients in mergers and acquisitions, represents taxpayers before the Internal Revenue Service and state and local tax authorities, and handles civil and criminal tax litigation and real estate tax assessment appeals, as well as pension and insolvency tax planning.

Trusts & Estates: The firm offers a full range of estate planning, administration and tax services, as well as related litigation, including representation before the Internal Revenue Service. Attorneys in this group have extensive experience in the preparation of revocable and irrevocable trusts, wills, property agreements and durable powers of attorney. The group also currently counsels some of the largest trusts and foundations on operational and administrative issues.

DRINKER BIDDLE & REATH LLP

THE FIRM

Chairman: James M Sweet

Number of partners: 167
Number of other lawyers: 285

FIRM OVERVIEW: Drinker Biddle & Reath LLP is a full service law firm of more than 450 lawyers, with nine offices from coast to coast. Headquartered in Philadelphia, the firm serves clients both nationally and internationally. Founded in 1849, the firm is committed to understanding its clients, their businesses, and the competitive and regulatory environments in which they do business.

MAIN AREAS OF PRACTICE

Business & Finance: Drinker Biddle's business and finance lawyers handle difficult and complex matters within tight deadlines imposed by business transactions. The department's 190+ lawyers have extensive experience in handling securities offerings; mergers, acquisitions and joint ventures; sensitive corporate governance matters; venture capital and private equity transactions; environmental matters; real estate; intellectual property; healthcare; communications; investment management; employee benefits; domestic and international tax matters; and financings and restructurings.

Litigation: Drinker Biddle's more than 240-lawyer Litigation Department handles major litigation for some of the country's largest corporations. The firm's Litigation Practice encompasses almost every area of the law, including class actions, products liability (with emphasis on the pharmaceutical industry), antitrust, telecommunications, intellectual property, environmental and insurance coverage litigation. The firm also represents employers in an extensive array of labor and employment matters and has a significant Government Affairs Practice.

Personal & Fiduciary: Lawyers in Drinker Biddle's Personal and Fiduciary Law Department counsel individuals concerning the personal, practical and legal aspects of preserving, managing and transferring wealth. Trustees and executors are also represented in their management of fiduciary funds and operation as tax-exempt organizations.

CLIENTS: The firm represents a broad array of clients ranging from *Fortune* 500 companies, venture capitalists, private equity investors and emerging enterprises, to professional service entities, academic institutions, governmental agencies, individuals and fiduciaries.

INTERNATIONAL WORK: Internationally, Drinker Biddle counsels companies from Europe to South America to Asia, including US enterprises seeking to compete in foreign markets as well as foreign companies entering or expanding their operations in the US. The firm is uniquely able to assist clients in managing their intellectual property matters internationally through 'I-PACT', a formal alliance of the firm with the European IP firm of Murgitroyd & Company, with seven offices throughout the EU.

HEAD OFFICE

PENNSYLVANIA
One Logan Square, 18th & Cherry Streets, **Philadelphia** PA 19103-6996
Tel: 215 988 2700 **Fax:** 215 988 2757
Email: info@dbr.com
Website: www.drinkerbiddle.com

OTHER OFFICES

CALIFORNIA
Wells Fargo Building, North Tower, Suite 1700, 333 South Grand Avenue, **Los Angeles** CA 90071-1504
Tel: 213 253 2300 **Fax:** 213 253 2301

50 Fremont Street, 20th Floor, **San Francisco** CA 94105-2235
Tel: 415 591 7500 **Fax:** 415 591 7510

DELAWARE
1100 North Market Street, Suite 1000, **Wilmington** DE 19801-1254
Tel: 302 467 4200 **Fax:** 302 467 4201

NEW JERSEY
500 Campus Drive, **Florham Park** NJ 07932-1047
Tel: 973 360 1100 **Fax:** 973 360 9831

105 College Road East, Suite 300, PO Box 627, **Princeton** NJ 08542-0627
Tel: 609 716 6500 **Fax:** 609 799 7000

NEW YORK
140 Broadway, 39th Floor, **New York** NY 10005-1116
Tel: 212 248 3140 **Fax:** 212 248 3141

PENNSYLVANIA
1000 Westlakes Drive, Suite 300, **Berwyn** PA 19312-2409
Tel: 610 993 2200 **Fax:** 610 993 8585

WASHINGTON DC
1500 K Street, NW, Suite 1100, **Washington** DC 20005-1209
Tel: 202 842 8800 **Fax:** 202 842 8465 / 66

CONTACTS

Business & Finance Department ....H John Michel Jr (Philadelphia)
Litigation Department ....Kathryn H Levering (Philadelphia)
Personal & Fiduciary Law Department ....William C Bullitt (Philadelphia)

PARTNERS IN CHARGE
Los Angeles ....Thomas M Moore
San Francisco ....Charles F Preuss
Wilmington ....Andrew C Kassner
Florham Park ....Daniel F O'Connell
Princeton...Jonathan I Epstein
New York ....Matthew Farley
Berwyn ....Thomas E Wood
Washington ....Richard M Singer

DrinkerBiddle

DUANE MORRIS LLP

THE FIRM

Chairman: Sheldon M Bonovitz
Website: www.duanemorris.com

FIRM OVERVIEW: Duane Morris LLP, among the 100 largest law firms in the United States, is a full-service firm of approximately 550 lawyers. In addition, Duane Morris affiliates have approximately 50 professionals engaged in a number of non-legal service businesses. The firm represents clients across the nation and around the world through a combination of offices in major markets and relationships with international networks of independent law firms.

MAIN AREAS OF PRACTICE:

Litigation & Alternative Dispute Resolution: Duane Morris attorneys represent clients in every type of litigation, from hard fought, complex commercial disputes to more amicable solution-based mediation. The firm's attorneys have a broad range of experience, including, for example, securities, antitrust, intellectual property, real estate and construction law. All of the attorneys in its Trial Practice Group try cases; some have also devoted themselves to appellate work. Duane Morris attorneys are called upon to represent diverse clients with different needs. Its litigators work closely with the firm's corporate and bankruptcy lawyers in the representation of public and private companies, banks, insurance companies and other financial institutions. Duane Morris attorneys represent all types of business entities and their boards, as well as investors, with regard to breach of fiduciary duty claims, merger-and-acquisition litigation, and all issues involving corporate law and governance. Duane Morris lawyers represent both individuals and corporations facing federal and state allegations of criminal conduct, including fraud, environmental, securities and RICO violations, trade espionage and a variety of business-related offenses. In addition to representing clients in US forums and before international tribunals, the firm also provides counsel on settling disputes using alternative dispute resolution options and advises on methods to anticipate and avoid litigation.

Corporate, Securities, Mergers & Acquisitions: Duane Morris corporate attorneys advise early stage and mature companies on a wide variety of corporate and securities matters. The firm represents clients in all aspects of mergers and acquisitions, including negotiated acquisitions and divestitures. Its attorneys are experienced with venture capital and private equity transactions and work with entrepreneurial clients in developing and implementing creative strategies to accomplish their corporate finance and acquisition objectives. Duane Morris lawyers regularly assist closely held companies with equity incentives and succession planning. It represents clients in securities offerings and advises public companies on securities law compliance, ongoing reporting obligations and corporate governance issues.

Business Reorganization & Financial Restructuring: Lawyers in Duane Morris' Business Reorganization and Financial Restructuring Practice Group represent clients in all aspects of debt restructuring and bankruptcy proceedings. They work closely with debtors, trustees, creditors and other parties in interest to develop and implement successful strategies for achieving clients' goals. The firm has a national team of insolvency lawyers who have been actively involved in the largest and most complex bankruptcy cases in all of the major markets in the United States.

Healthcare: Healthcare providers continue to face enormous regulatory and financial pressures, while burdened by soaring costs even as demand for services increases. To meet these challenges, Duane Morris clients rely on its nationally recognized Healthcare Practice Group. Clients benefit from the collective experience of one of the nation's largest healthcare practice groups providing a full range of regulatory and transactional services in every major sector of the healthcare industry.

OFFICES

CALIFORNIA
101 West Broadway, **San Diego**, CA 92101
Tel: 619 744 2200 **Fax:** 619 744 2201

One Market, Spear Tower, **San Francisco**, CA 94105
Tel: 415 371 2200 **Fax:** 415 371 2201

DELAWARE
1100 North Market Street, **Wilmington**, DE 19801
Tel: 302 657 4900 **Fax:** 302 657 4901

DISTRICT OF COLUMBIA
1667 K Street, N W, **Washington,** DC 20006
Tel: 202 776 7800 **Fax:** 202 776 7801

FLORIDA
200 South Biscayne Boulevard, **Miami**, FL 33131
Tel: 305 960 2200 **Fax:** 305 960 2201

GEORGIA
1180 West Peachtree Street, **Atlanta**, GA 30309
Tel: 404 253 6900 **Fax:** 404 253 6901

ILLINOIS
227 West Monroe Street, **Chicago**, IL 60606
Tel: 312 499 6700 **Fax:** 312 499 6701

MASSACHUSETTS
470 Atlantic Avenue, **Boston**, MA 02210
Tel: 617 289 9200 **Fax:** 617 289 9201

NEW JERSEY
744 Broad Street, **Newark**, NJ 07102
Tel: 973 424 2000 **Fax:** 973 424 2001

PO Box 5203, **Princeton**, NJ 08543-5203
Tel: 609 631 2400 **Fax:** 609 631 2401

NEW YORK
380 Lexington Avenue, **New York**, NY 10168
Tel: 212 692 1000 **Fax:** 212 692 1020

PENNSYLVANIA
One Liberty Place, **Philadelphia**, PA 19103
Tel: 215 979 1000 **Fax:** 215 979 1020

600 Grant Street, **Pittsburgh**, PA 15219
Tel: 412 497 1000 **Fax:** 412 497 1001

TEXAS
3200 Southwest Freeway, Suite 3150, **Houston**, TX 77027-7534
Tel: 713 402 3900 **Fax:** 713 402 3901

INTERNATIONAL The firm also has an office in London.

CONTACTS

Trial	John J Soroko
Corporate	Kathleen M Shay
Business Reorganization	Rudolph J DiMassa Jr
Healthcare	Donald R Auten, David E Loder
Intellectual Property	Lewis F Gould
Employment, Benefits & Immigration	Thomas G Servodidio
Real Estate	Marc D Brookman
Finance	Barbara Adams
Energy & Resources	Stephen L Teichler
Environmental	Seth vdH Cooley
Insurance	John F McCarrick
Estates & Asset Planning	Frank G Cooper
Tax	Victor F Keen
International	Hope P Krebs, Thomas R Schmuhl

DUANE MORRIS LLP

Intellectual Property: Duane Morris' intellectual property lawyers' experience includes trademarks and copyrights, patents and brand protection. Members of the IP Practice Group include highly trained patent attorneys with backgrounds in biosciences, materials, chemicals, polymers, electronics and telecommunications. Duane Morris' IP litigators have substantial trial experience in disputes over patents, trademarks, copyrights, trade secrets and licenses involving such intangible property.

Employment, Benefits & Immigration: The Duane Morris Employment, Benefits and Immigration Practice assists clients with the complexities and challenges of the changing workplace. From advising employers on new legislative requirements, unraveling sensitive labor and employment disputes, designing benefit and executive compensation plans, to addressing cross-border employment and visa concerns, Duane Morris attorneys provide a full-range of employment-related services to help clients achieve their business goals in today's borderless global economy.

Real Estate: Duane Morris' Real Estate Practice assists clients throughout the US, Europe, Asia and South and Central America. Duane Morris attorneys draw upon their extensive experience to find solutions for complex issues in the following segments of the real estate industry: commercial, retail, hospitality, and housing. The firm represents developers, financial institutions, landowners, corporations, real estate investment trusts, architectural firms, and nonprofit institutions. Duane Morris represents leading developers on projects that range from creating world class sports stadiums, internationally renowned concert halls and high-tech medical facilities to adapting historic properties for new uses.

Complex Financial Transactions: Duane Morris has extensive experience with the financing of complex private and public projects, often representing corporations and financial institutions on a regional, national and international level. The firm's attorneys counsel clients in numerous types of transactions covering nearly every aspect of municipal, project and structured finance transactions. Duane Morris public finance attorneys represent national and regional investment banking firms underwriting tax-exempt and taxable state and local government debt, act as bond counsel and special tax counsel for issuers and represent domestic and foreign institutions providing credit enhancement for tax-exempt financing. The firm's project and structured finance attorneys represent clients in acquisition financings, securitized and syndicated loans, and other complex financial transactions. It also has a distinct group of attorneys who focus their practice on affordable housing finance.

Energy & Environment: For several decades, the firm has seen the dramatic effect of world events and climatic impacts on energy, water and natural resources. Events in recent years underscore how quickly and acutely these impacts manifest themselves. As both advisor and advocate, Duane Morris guides clients through the complex legal, financial, policy and political issues surrounding the basic necessities that power all industries and businesses. Members of Duane Morris' national Energy Practice regularly assist clients with advisory, regulatory and litigation matters involving water, natural resources and environmental issues, often counseling clients in their interactions with federal, state and municipal agencies. In addition, Duane Morris counsels clients concerning their rights and obligations under federal environmental statutes and regulations, as well as similar state and local laws, and represents clients in related enforcement proceedings and litigation.

Insurance: The changing business climate and shifting regulatory forces affect the insurance industry in unique ways. To meet these unique challenges, Duane Morris' interdisciplinary Insurance & Reinsurance Practice counsels insurer and reinsurer clients on complex litigation and business matters, as well as legislative and ethical issues. Its Insurance & Reinsurance Industry Team brings together lawyers skilled in litigation, regulatory, corporate and transactional matters, as well as lawyers with actuarial, underwriting and policy coverage experience. Duane Morris also has developed proprietary technology tools to help its clients manage their businesses, reduce risk exposure, enhance profitability and efficiently resolve costly litigation.

CONTACTS cont'd

New York	Robert J Hasday
Chicago	David B Yelin
Houston	Richard T Redano
San Diego	Christopher Celentino
San Francisco	Joseph M Burton
Boston	Martin B Shulkin
Washington, DC	Douglas Woloshin
Atlanta	Charles W Whitney
Miami	Charles C Papy, III
Pittsburgh	George M Medved
Newark	Walter J Greenhalgh
Wilmington	John L Reed
Princeton	Frank A Luchak

Life Sciences: Duane Morris clients in the life sciences industry traverse new frontiers. From pioneering lifesaving developments to exploring novel technology-sharing agreements, these businesses face a complex range of legal, business and financial challenges. The firm's Life Sciences Practice Group brings together lawyers from several of the firm's practice groups to offer clients a full panoply of legal services – including intellectual property counsel, securities counsel in connection with private and public equity funding, international trade and tax advice, labor and employment guidance, dispute resolution and litigation services – provided within the framework of their business to address each client's specific needs.

CLIENTS: Duane Morris' international client base, like its practice, is extremely diverse. Duane Morris represents clients with business and investment interests around the globe. Its clients range from established blue chip companies to start-up entrepreneurs; from publicly traded companies to family-owned businesses; from major institutional investors to governmental authorities to private clients.

INTERNATIONAL WORK: Duane Morris' dedicated International Practice Group integrates the services of its senior attorneys in nearly every legal discipline, creating a global infrastructure of international experience and enhanced sensitivity to cultural differences. Services offered by the International Practice Group range from cross-border business transactions to international dispute resolution and enforcement; from customs and international trade to international tax planning; from immigration to international wealth preservation for private clients.

DuaneMorris

FOX ROTHSCHILD LLP

THE FIRM

Co-Chairmen: Abraham C Reich, Esq, Phillip Griffin, Esq
Number of lawyers: 289

FIRM OVERVIEW: Fox Rothschild LLP is a full-service firm providing a range of legal services to public and private business entities; charitable, medical and educational institution; and individuals around the world Founded in 1907, the firm ranks among the top 200 law firms nationally (according to The American Lawyer) and has nine offices throughout the Eastern US to meet the needs of its client base. Its knowledgeable attorneys and skilled staff are supported by industry-leading technologies that link firm offices and promote rapid communication and collaboration among departments and practice groups. Clients have access to the full resources of the firm's attorney network, and to the depth of experience available firmwide. Every matter receives the individualized attention, strategic thinking and cost-effective approach that are Fox Rothschild hallmarks.

MAIN AREAS OF PRACTICE:

Civil Litigation: As the firm's largest department, litigation has effectively represented businesses and individuals in diverse and complex commercial law disputes. Its attorneys have achieved national recognition for their representation of large, publicly held corporations, family-owned businesses and individuals in a broad variety of civil and administrative matters, including contract law, corporate law, securities law, class actions, civil RICO, shareholder disputes, antitrust, banking and finance law, Uniform Commercial Code, franchise law, insurance coverage, defamation, consumer protection law, tax law and probate disputes. Firm attorneys have significant trial and appellate experience before virtually all federal and state courts and administrative agencies. Their record of success as aggressive advocates as well as skilled negotiators on behalf of clients has earned Fox Rothschild a reputation of excellence. They have a group of attorneys who regularly participate in alternate dispute resolution as arbitrators, mediators and advocates for clients.

Corporate Transactions: The firm's Corporate Department represents a diverse cross-section of public and privately owned businesses and institutions in all stages of development. Clients include small and large family-owned companies, professional practices, start-up enterprises, and large regional, national and international corporations. The Department also advises (both as attorneys and board members) a rich mix of nonprofit organizations, including public charities, hospitals and colleges. Fox Rothschild serves as general counsel to many business clients, providing advice that ranges from dealing with day-to-day employee or regulatory questions to implementing strategies for major transactions. Its transactional experience is deep and varied with a special emphasis on mergers and acquisitions, equity financing, bank and other debt financing, intellectual property, and federal and state regulatory requirements. Members of the Corporate Department work closely with members of the Tax and Estates Department in the structuring of transactions.

Labor & Employment: The firm's experience in employment law matters has involved claims of age, handicap, sex and race discrimination. Its attorneys also represent clients in cases involving wrongful discharge, employment at will, whistleblower violations, defamation, fraud, invasion of privacy, public policy employment rights, intentional infliction of emotional distress and a wide variety of other common law and statutory claims arising in the employment context. Fox Rothschild attorneys have successfully handled claims under the Americans with Disabilities Act, Family and Medical Leave Act, Family Leave Act, Older Workers Benefits Protection Act, Age Discrimination in Employment Act, and other employment protection legislation. It also counts experience in employee benefit work, including COBRA and ERISA matters, among its strengths.

Real Estate: Combing sound judgment with a practical approach, the firm's

CENTRAL OFFICE

PENNSYLVANIA
2000 Market Street, Tenth Floor, **Philadelphia**, PA 19103-3291
Tel: 215 299 2000 **Fax:** 215 299 2150
Website: www.foxrothschild.com

OTHER OFFICES

DELAWARE
Citizens Bank Center, 919 North Market Street, PO Box 2323, Suite 1300, **Wilmington**, DE 19899-2323
Tel: 302 654 7444 **Fax:** 302 656 8920

NEW JERSEY
Midtown Building, 1301 Atlantic Avenue, Suite 400, **Atlantic City**, NJ 08401-7212
Tel: 609 348 4515 **Fax:** 609 348 6834

PO Box 5231, **Princeton**, NJ 08543-5231
Tel: 609 896 3600 **Fax:** 609 896 1469
Delivery address: Princeton Pike Corporate Center, 997 Lenox Drive, Building 3, Lawrenceville, NJ 08648-2311

NEW YORK
13 East 37th Street, Suite 800, **New York**, NY 10016
Tel: 212 682 7575 **Fax:** 212 682 4218

PENNSYLVANIA
Eagleview Corporate Center, 760 Constitution Drive, PO Box 673, Suite 104, **Exton**, PA 19341-0673
Tel: 610 458 7500 **Fax:** 610 458 7337

1250 South Broad Street, PO Box 431, Suite 1000, **Lansdale**, PA 19446-0431
Tel: 215 699 6000 **Fax:** 215 699 0231

625 Liberty Avenue, 29th Floor, **Pittsburgh**, PA 15222-3115
Tel: 412 391 1334 **Fax:** 412 391 6984

2700 Kelly Road, Suite 300, **Warrington**, PA 18976-3624
Tel: 215 345 7500 **Fax:** 215 345 7507

Real Estate Department has become one of the largest in the region. Clients as diverse as developers, financial institutions, shopping center owners, retail chain operators, hoteliers, contractors and architects have benefited from its quick, decisive response to their matters involving financing, land planning, acquisition and development, commercial leasing, syndications, tax credits, condemnation, tax assessment and more. Additionally, Fox Rothschild offers real estate clients a one-stop business partnering solution that is customized to their needs. Its specialized practice groups, such as environmental, construction and finance, can be assembled quickly into a multidisciplinary team of attorneys that responds swiftly and cost-effectively as the client's circumstances require.

INTERNATIONAL WORK: Fox Rothschild serves clients in a range of legal situations across the world, including Colombia, Dominican Republic, Peru, Puerto Rico and Uruguay as well as clients in Japan, Korea, and other countries throughout Asia and Europe. Firm attorneys are versed in the intricacies and nuances of international law and are directly involved in the global business community. Services range from assisting companies seeking to establish a presence in the United States to representing corporations involved in worldwide disputes. Its international representation extends to matters of intellectual property rights, including patent, copyright and trademark cases; business litigation; taxation banking; e-commerce; corporate and contract matters; commercial transactions; casino and gaming law; immigration issues and a host of additional legal services. Additionally, as a member of the Great Lakes Law Network, Fox Rothschild is strategically aligned with 12 independent US and Canadian law firms to address the legal needs of clients – not only within their market, but beyond their respective jurisdictions. This consortium provides legal representation for Canadian and US clients, as well as for organizations within Europe and the Pacific Rim.

HANGLEY ARONCHICK SEGAL & PUDLIN

THE FIRM

FIRM OVERVIEW: Hangley Aronchick Segal & Pudlin is proud that six of its 26 members have been singled out by Chambers USA as being among the very best in the fields of commercial litigation, insolvency and real estate. Founded in 1994, the 50 lawyer firm also maintains robust practices in other areas, including corporate transactions, white collar criminal, and tax and estate planning. Readers are invited to the firm's website, www.hangley.com, for further information on those practice areas and the other outstanding lawyers at Hangley Aronchick. The sophistication of matters handled by the firm, the roster of its clients and the quality of its work belie the firm's relatively small size. In the Delaware Valley, the firm is unparalleled in its ability to attract the most highly qualified attorneys, both at the entry level and laterally. The firm includes two former Philadelphia City Solicitors, several Fellows of the American College of Trial Lawyers, the American College of Bankruptcy, and the American College of Real Estate Lawyers, a former Chancellor of the Philadelphia Bar Association, and adjunct faculty members from area law schools. Most of Hangley Aronchick's trial lawyers have clerked for federal judges: two of the partners were clerks on the United States Supreme Court; 11 of the lawyers clerked on federal circuit courts of appeals.

MAIN AREAS OF PRACTICE:

LITIGATION: Clients and referring counsel seek out Hangley Aronchick for cases that will actually have to be tried. The firm has frequently represented some of the country's largest corporations, the Commonwealth of Pennsylvania, the City of Philadelphia, the major universities and healthcare complexes in the Delaware Valley, and the Pennsylvania Bar Association. The firm also regularly represents and counsels local and national law firms when they are drawn into litigation or are seeking to avoid that fate. Lawsuits the firm is currently handling or has recently handled include the following:

Antitrust & Intellectual Property: Representing national pharmacy chains in suits against pharmaceutical manufacturers.

Finance: Representing a major writer of surety bonds in litigation with financial institutions arising out of 'circular' gas deals with Enron; defending banks and credit card companies in class and non-class litigation with card holders.

Intellectual Property: Litigating on behalf of patent holders or alleged infringers in fields ranging from securities trading protocols to coloring concrete; representing a lawyer whose book was pirated by a competing law firm and published on its web site; representing a major university in a patent royalty dispute with a former faculty member.

Public Affairs: Defending the City of Philadelphia from tort claims arising out of the arrests of demonstrators during the 2000 Republican National Convention; recovering city tax revenues from the major Philadelphia banks.

Healthcare: Representing leading health maintenance organizations, hospitals, and healthcare service providers in disputes over reimbursement and billing issues, including the defense of class actions, parallel criminal and civil actions, and complex civil disputes.

Criminal & Investigative: Representing subjects and targets in criminal investigations of commercial and financial affairs; assisting in internal investigations for publicly held companies; representing government contracted interrogator in federal Abu Ghraib investigations.

Securities & Corporate Law: Representing publicly held companies in litigation over mergers and securities offerings; representing individual officers and directors in securities fraud claims involving publicly held companies.

HEAD OFFICE

PENNSYLVANIA
One Logan Square, 18th and Cherry Streets,
Philadelphia, PA 19103-6933
Tel: 215 568 6200 **Fax:** 215 568 0300

Website: www.hangley.com

BRANCH OFFICES

NEW JERSEY
20 Brace Road, Suite 201, **Cherry Hill,** NJ 08034
Tel: 856 616 2100 **Fax:** 856 616 2170

PENNSYLVANIA
30 North Third Street, Suite 700, **Harrisburg**, PA 17101-1701
Tel: 717 364 1030 **Fax:** 717 364 1020

REAL ESTATE: The firm's Real Estate Practice covers all aspects of commercial real estate: acquisition, financing, construction, development, leasing, and management of high rise office towers, suburban corporate parks, hotels, national and regional shopping centers, industrial facilities, apartment complexes and residential subdivisions. The firm specializes in the following areas:

Finance: Representing national and regional institutional lenders and borrowers in connection with permanent and construction loans on all types of real estate.

Leasing: Representing city and suburban developers and building owners in connection with leases and management agreements.

Companies & Their Real Estate: Representing owner and tenant clients, including a national grocery chain, a cold storage company, communications companies, an owner and operator of physical rehabilitation hospitals, and other large companies in connection with their retail stores, shopping centers, headquarters and production facilities.

Development: Representing clients in the construction and development of new buildings, including development agreements, construction contracts, architect's contracts, agreements of sale and financing.

Land Use/Zoning: Representing clients before zoning and planning boards and other governmental bodies in New Jersey and Pennsylvania.

BANKRUPTCY & INSOLVENCY: The effective representation of business debtors and creditors in sensitive restructuring situations demands lawyers who are able to combine business law, negotiation, litigation and problem-solving skills, and who have the sound judgment and counseling skills to help the client navigate the difficult terrain. The firm's Insolvency Group has had significant experience in representing clients who must manage their businesses (or collect claims from other businesses) in the crisis atmosphere of insolvency, regularly handling out-of-court liquidations, restructurings and pre-packaged and pre-arranged proceedings as well as cases under Chapters 7 and 11 of the Bankruptcy Code, purchasing and selling assets in distress circumstances, advancing competing or 'hostile' reorganization plans, and prosecuting and defending bankruptcy and non-bankruptcy litigation, including lender liability claims.

HANGLEY
ARONCHICK
SEGAL
&PUDLIN

KIRKPATRICK & LOCKHART NICHOLSON GRAHAM LLP

THE FIRM

**Chairman of the Management Committee &
Managing Partner:** Peter J Kalis
Number of partners: 323
Number of other lawyers: 627

Website: www.klng.com

FIRM OVERVIEW: Kirkpatrick & Lockhart Nicholson Graham LLP (K&LNG) – the product of one of the largest Anglo-American legal combinations in history on January 1, 2005 – comprises 950 lawyers who practice from offices throughout the US and in London, England. K&LNG represents entrepreneurs, growth and middle-market companies and leading global corporations in every major industry group. The firm practices across all legal disciplines within the corporate, litigation and regulatory fields. K&LNG's extensive knowledge about the business sectors in which our clients operate enables the practice to be at once regional, national and international in scope, cutting edge, complex, and dynamic. K&LNG was the only law firm in the world to receive the CIO Magazine CIO 100 Award for three consecutive years, while the official publication of the Minority Corporate Counsel Association selected K&LNG as one of only four American law firms to feature for their innovative diversity initiatives.

MAIN AREAS OF PRACTICE:

Corporate: K&LNG practices law on an integrated and firm-wide basis. The multi-office, International Corporate and Transactional Practice is one of the most substantial in the profession. The firm closed over 100 M&A transactions last year, and is perennially a leader as issuer's counsel in equities issued by corporate clients, both in terms of number of transactions and proceeds. K&LNG has completed hundreds of public debt and equity offerings over the last decade.

Litigation: K&LNG's litigation engagements including, among other substantive areas, insurance coverage, intellectual property, real estate, white-collar criminal, construction, professional liability, environmental, toxic tort, products liability, franchise, tax, bankruptcy and insolvency, antitrust and competition, employment, benefits, and securities fraud are among the largest and most attractive enjoyed by any law firm. The firm has been rated a leading practice in the representation of corporate policyholders in the insurance coverage area, and as a leading litigation firm for the financial sector. It is active in jurisdictions around the US and in the UK as well as in various international arbitration forums.

Regulatory: K&LNG's Regulatory Practice cuts across the many disciplines that require highly specialized knowledge and experience to address governmental regulation of the private markets. The firm's lawyers regularly represent clients before regulatory bodies in both the US and the UK. Its premier regulatory practice is in the diversified financial services area. K&LNG represents a large majority of the major financial institutions and securities firms in a variety of disciplines, and the investment management practice is a perennial leader. Many of the firm's practice leaders as well as more junior lawyers have governmental experience that enhances their ability to serve K&LNG's clients in regulatory fields, while others have held prominent positions in regulated industries.

Emerging Practices: The firm continuously allocates resources so that its capabilities reach to the forefront of emerging disciplines. K&LNG's Intellectual Property Practice, with approximately 100 practicing lawyers, and its Technology Practice, serving growth companies in disciplines such as biotechnology, internet services, medical devices, and information systems, are examples of how this investment has borne fruit. Most frequently, the firm continues to recruit lateral partners in such disparate fields as structured finance, bankruptcy, real estate, food and drug, ERISA litigation, Small Business Administration financing, telecommunications, project finance, intellectual property, private equity, trademarks, employment and public sector technology to address the evolving needs of its

OFFICES

CALIFORNIA
10100 Santa Monica Boulevard, 7th Floor, **Los Angeles**, CA 90067
Tel: 310 552 5000 **Fax:** 310 552 5001

Four Embarcadero Center, 10th Floor, **San Francisco**, CA 94111
Tel: 415 249 1000 **Fax:** 415 249 1001

DISTRICT OF COLUMBIA
1800 Massachusetts Avenue, NW, 2nd Floor, **Washington**, DC 20036-1221
Tel: 202 778 9000 **Fax:** 202 778 9100

FLORIDA
Miami Center, 201 South Biscayne Boulevard, 20th Floor,
Miami, FL 33131-2399
Tel: 305 539 3300 **Fax:** 305 358 7095

MASSACHUSETTS
75 State Street, **Boston**, MA 02109
Tel: 617 261 3100 **Fax:** 617 261 3175

NEW JERSEY
One Newark Center, 10th Floor, **Newark**, NJ 07102-5252
Tel: 973 848 4000 **Fax:** 973 848 4001

NEW YORK
599 Lexington Avenue, **New York**, NY 10022-6030
Tel: 212 536 3900 **Fax:** 212 536 3901

PENNSYLVANIA
Payne Shoemaker Building, 240 North Third Street,
Harrisburg, PA 17101-1507
Tel: 717 231 4500 **Fax:** 717 231 4501

Henry W. Oliver Building, 535 Smithfield Street, **Pittsburgh**, PA 15222-2312
Tel: 412 355 6500 **Fax:** 412 355 6501

TEXAS
2828 North Harwood Street, Suite 1800, **Dallas**, TX 75201-6966
Tel: 214 939 4900 **Fax:** 214 939 4949

INTERNATIONAL OFFICES

The firm also has an office in London, UK

clientele. The firm strives to maintain a creative, interdisciplinary approach to the practice, as evidenced by the extraordinary convergence of disciplines that permitted its K&LNG colleague, former US Attorney General Dick Thornburgh, to act as the court appointed Examiner in the World-Com bankruptcy proceeding – the largest bankruptcy in US history – and the firm itself to act as his counsel.

CLIENTS: K&LNG currently represents or recently has performed projects for over half of the FORTUNE 100; 21 of the 25 largest mutual fund complexes or their investment managers; and 18 of the 20 largest US bank holding companies or their affiliates. Representative clients include Alcoa, Bank of America, DuPont, Fidelity, Halliburton, Mellon, PPG, United Technologies, Wachovia, and World Wrestling Entertainment. The firm is a multiple winner of DuPont's Meeting the Challenge Award for its 'remarkable and extraordinary accomplishments' for that client, and is the only law firm on which PPG Industries has conferred its Excellent Supplier Award.

INTERNATIONAL WORK: With offices throughout the US and in London, K&LNG represents clients across North America and the United Kingdom on matters that span the globe. K&LNG's primary working language is English, but the firm has attorneys fluent in Afrikaans, Chinese (Mandarin), Farsi, French, German, Greek, Hebrew, Hindi, Italian, Japanese, Korean, Polish, Portuguese, Russian and Spanish. Various members of the firm have foreign degrees, which enable them to take into account legal and cultural differences in representing the firm's clients in international transaction and litigation matters worldwide.

KLETT ROONEY LIEBER & SCHORLING, A PROFESSIONAL CORPORATION

THE FIRM

Managing Partner: John A Barbour
Number of partners: 64
Number of other lawyers: 68

Email: info@klettrooney.com
Website: www.klettrooney.com

FIRM OVERVIEW: Klett Rooney Lieber & Schorling is a full-service, general commercial law firm representing corporations and other business entities through interdisciplinary practice groups that allow sophisticated legal matters to be addressed comprehensively, efficiently and cost effectively.

MAIN AREAS OF PRACTICE:

Bankruptcy & Insolvency: Provides legal advice on matters covering the diversity of issues confronting financially-troubled companies. The firm also represents lending institutions, creditors' committees, secured and unsecured creditors, and other participants in the reorganization of economically-distressed businesses.

Commercial Litigation: Provides counsel in resolving commercial disputes prior to the commencement of lawsuits, through mediation and arbitration, and in the courtroom. It represents clients at all levels of the litigation process in a variety of venues, from county, state and federal jurisdictions to arbitration boards and zoning boards and commissions.

Corporate: Represents both publicly traded and privately-held business entities in a broad range of corporate and commercial transactions. Specialties include corporate and public finance; healthcare; banking; securities law; educational institutions; emerging business and venture capital; general corporate law; mergers and acquisitions; estate planning and administration; and individual, partnership and corporate taxation.

Energy & Utilities: Offers solutions to current regulatory and legislative issues facing the energy and utility industry, specializing in strategic planning and regulatory consultative services for both regulated and non-regulated utilities and suppliers of electricity, gas, water and telecommunications on a national and international basis.

Government Affairs: Assists clients in making connections with decision-makers in local, state and federal government to heighten awareness of critical issues, pursue procurement opportunities and develop government solutions to fit their unique needs. The firm has forged a network of public sector relationships with members of both major political parties across all branches of government.

Labor & Employment: Exclusively represents management in dealing with virtually every kind of workplace issue confronting employers, including collective bargaining negotiations, employee agreements, workplace restructuring, discrimination and harassment, ADA compliance, OSHA, Railway Labor Act, business immigration, employment litigation and employee benefits matters.

Real Estate: Assists developers, financial institutions and property owners in all aspects of commercial real estate transactions, including real property development, lending and leasing transactions. From the establishment of an ownership entity and the purchase of property, to the negotiation of all construction and financing-related documents, involvement continues to the development, operation and disposition of properties.

HEAD OFFICE

PENNSYLVANIA
One Oxford Centre, 40th Floor, **Pittsburgh,** PA 15219
Tel: 412 392 2000 **Fax:** 412 392 2128

BRANCH OFFICES

DELAWARE
1000 West St., Suite 1410, **Wilmington,** DE 19801
Tel: 302 552 4200 **Fax:** 302 552 4295

DISTRICT OF COLUMBIA
600 Pennsylvania Ave., SE, Suite 220, **Washington,** DC 20003
Tel: 202 544 4094 **Fax:** 202 544 9497

NEW JERSEY
550 Broad St., Suite 810, **Newark,** NJ 01702
Tel: 973 273 9800 **Fax:** 973 273 9430

PENNSYLVANIA
Two Logan Square, 12th Floor, **Philadelphia,** PA 19103
Tel: 215 567 7500 **Fax:** 215 567 2737

240 N. Third St., Suite 700, **Harrisburg,** PA 17101
Tel: 717 231 7700 **Fax:** 717 231 7712

CONTACTS

Bankruptcy & Insolvency ....William H Schorling
Commercial Litigation ....Christine L Donohue
Corporate ....Robert T Harper
Energy & Utilities...John M Quain
Government Affairs..Thomas G Paese
Labor & Employment...Terrence H Murphy
Real Estate ....Jacqui Fiske Lazo

CLIENTS: Klett Rooney's clients range from leading Fortune 500 companies and closely-held businesses to numerous colleges and universities, hospitals and other healthcare institutions, banks and other financial establishments, software and technology companies, minority businesses, charitable and community organizations, and a National Football League team.

INTERNATIONAL WORK: The firm offers a diverse range of transactional and litigation services for corporations and other entities, assisting US-based clients in overseas business operations and export of goods and services and foreign-owned businesses seeking to establish, maintain or expand operations in the US.

KLETT ROONEY LIEBER & SCHORLING
A PROFESSIONAL CORPORATION
ATTORNEYS AT LAW

www.klettrooney.com

MORGAN, LEWIS & BOCKIUS LLP

THE FIRM

Managing Partner: Francis M Milone, Chair

Number of partners: 440
Number of other lawyers: 793

FIRM OVERVIEW: With more than 1,200 lawyers and 300 other professionals (including technical specialists, patent agents, and paralegals) in offices worldwide, Morgan Lewis is the only US law firm with more than 250 lawyers in each of its New York, Washington and Philadelphia offices and more than 250 lawyers in California. They have the resources and knowledge to handle the most complex transactional and litigation needs of the world's largest corporations.

MAIN AREAS OF PRACTICE: Across practices and offices, the firm represents clients in a wide variety of issues in the energy, life sciences, media and information, securities, and technology industries.

Antitrust: The firm's Antitrust Practice offers all the personalized service and attention of a specialty law firm with the resources and global reach of a major international law firm. Their work includes counseling, litigation, representation in government cartel/criminal investigations and prosecutions. Their lawyers, many of whom have previously held senior positions in US antitrust enforcement agencies, advise clients on mergers and acquisitions, trade associations, and consumer protection matters.

Business & Finance: The firm's Business and Finance Practice is composed of nearly 300 lawyers located in more than 15 offices—more than 30 of whom are SEC alumni. Their lawyers focus on mergers and acquisitions (including joint ventures, spin-offs and strategic alliances), finance and restructuring, securities (including public and private equity and debt offerings), tax, and emerging business and technology. They service a diverse clientele ranging from Fortune 500 and FTSE 250 companies to investment banks to emerging growth companies.

Employee Benefits & Executive Compensation: The firm has more than 80 lawyers and other professionals using their skills as counselors, strategists, problem solvers and trial lawyers to assist clients in finding creative solutions to their employee benefits-related business challenges. This practice is one of the largest in the country and offers a level of substantive knowledge, industry experience and technical skills that makes us a nationwide leader in employee benefits law. It includes plan sponsor consulting, litigation, ESOPs, executive compensation and equity compensation, transactional support, and vendor consulting with regard to financial products intended for tax-favored retirement plans.

Energy: More than 60 lawyers manage a broad range of domestic and international energy matters, many of which are driven by the restructuring of the US energy industry and the expanding scope of global energy enterprises. Their energy lawyers understand the technical, legal and business needs of clients operating in the industry, and possess sophisticated knowledge and insight into each major market segment: electric, natural gas, oil, nuclear and water. Their integrated teams provide the full range of services on project and structured financing, overseas investment, mergers, acquisitions and divestitures of generation and transmission assets, and restructuring of utilities.

FDA/Healthcare Regulation: The firm's FDA/Healthcare Regulation attorneys understand the use of science to support and advance appropriate legal and regulatory positions. No other firm is better positioned to counsel life sciences clients in protecting each product through its full life cycle. Their FDA/Healthcare Practice is a key component of the firm's Life Sciences Interdisciplinary Group, which is composed of more than 200 lawyers and technical specialists and covers all regulatory issues related to research, development, testing, approval, marketing, distribution, pricing, life cycle management, and compliance activities involving pharmaceuticals, biologics, medical devices, food additives/dietary supplements, and other products regulated by the FDA and its international counterparts.

Intellectual Property: With more than 200 professionals, including lawyers, patent agents and technical specialists, and a patent litigation practice of more than 100 attorneys, we offer clients business solutions concerning all aspects of intellectual property. The firm's clients include both US and non-US enterprises, and range in size from Fortune 500 companies to small start-ups. Offering boutique-caliber services while providing the resources of a global law firm, their attorneys counsel companies throughout the life cycles of their products and services, including research and development, financing, marketing, licensing and enforcement of relevant rights.

FIRM OFFICES

CALIFORNIA
1 Ada, Suite 250, **Irvine**, CA 92618
Tel: 949 453 3000 **Fax:** 949 453 3001

300 South Grand Avenue, Twenty Second Floor, **Los Angeles**, CA 90071
Tel: 213 612 2500 **Fax:** 213 612 2501

2 Palo Alto Square, 3000 El Camino Real, Suite 900, **Palo Alto**, CA 94306
Tel: 650 843 4000 **Fax:** 650 843 4001

One Market, Spear Street Tower, **San Francisco**, CA 94105
Tel: 415 442 1000 **Fax:** 415 442 1001

DISTRICT OF COLUMBIA
1111 Pennsylvania Avenue, NW, **Washington**, DC 20004
Tel: 202 739 3000 **Fax:** 202 739 3001

FLORIDA
5300 Wachovia Financial Center, 200 South Biscayne Boulevard, **Miami**, FL 33131
Tel: 305 415 3000 **Fax:** 305 415 3001

ILLINOIS
77 West Wacker Drive, Sixth Floor, **Chicago**, IL 60601
Tel: 617 451 9700 **Fax:** 617 451 9710

MASSACHUSETTS
225 Franklin Street, Suite 1705, **Boston**, MA 02110
Tel: 617 977 2500 **Fax:** 617 977 2560

NEW JERSEY
502 Carnegie Center, **Princeton**, NJ 08540
Tel: 609 919 6600 **Fax:** 609 919 6639

NEW YORK
101 Park Avenue, **New York**, NY 10178
Tel: 212 309 6000 **Fax:** 212 309 6273

PENNSYLVANIA
One Commerce Square, 417 Walnut Street, **Harrisburg**, PA 17101
Tel: 717 237 4000 **Fax:** 717 237 4004

1701 Market Street, **Philadelphia**, PA 19103
Tel: 215 963 5000 **Fax:** 215 963 5001

One Oxford Centre, Thirty Second Floor, **Pittsburgh**, PA 15219
Tel: 412 560 3300 **Fax:** 412 560 7001

TEXAS
1717 Main Street, Suit 3400, **Dallas**, TX 75201
Tel: 214 438 1550 **Fax:** 214 438 1551

INTERNATIONAL OFFICES

The firm also has offices in Belgium, Germany, England, France and Japan.

MORGAN, LEWIS & BOCKIUS LLP cont'd

Investment Management: The Investment Management Practice is one of the most significant among US law firms, regularly ranked in industry periodicals for representing the most new mutual funds. They represent a broad array of financial services entities, including investment companies, investment advisers, broker-dealers, venture capital and hedge funds, off-shore banks and trust companies, insurance companies, pension plans, pension consultants, transfer agents and other industry participants. They provide their clients, who include many of the largest and best known financial services firms in the world, with a full range of legal services.

Labor & Employment Law: More than 225 labor and employment law and employee benefits lawyers maintain one of the premier management-side labor and employment practices in the US. Recently recognized by *The American Lawyer* magazine for its litigation prowess and traditional labor niche, our practice's scope includes employment counseling, complex employment and employee benefits litigation, labor management relations and labor disputes, employee benefits and executive compensation matters, OFCCP/Affirmative Action plans, wage and hour counseling and litigation, non-competition agreements and related obligations, and international labor and employment law counseling and advice.

Morgan Lewis Resources: A unique practice informed by the vast intellectual property and up-to-the-minute collective knowledge and skills of the entire firm, MLR provides innovative solutions that help corporate clients across industries and geographic regions meet increasingly demanding federal regulatory requirements. They help clients think and work proactively, by providing them with traditional compliance policy reviews and audits, case management and litigation technology, workplace training, and international executive travel and foreign resident worker visa processing.

Litigation: Nearly 600 lawyers throughout the firm combine the highest levels of substantive knowledge, industry experience and courtroom savvy to help meet the litigation needs of global business. They handle the entire range of issues associated with dispute resolution, with a special emphasis on coordination of national litigation, class actions and other complex business and corporate litigation. They represent many of the nation's largest and most prominent companies in high profile 'bet the company' litigation, often as national trial and coordinating counsel. They have han-dled class action and serial litigation matters in state and federal courts involving the full range of state and federal causes of action, including antitrust, securities, employment, ERISA, product liability and toxic tort/exposure.

Personal Law: The Personal Law Practice serves the legal and financial interests of individuals and family-owned businesses, particularly in traditional estate and tax planning, and the administration of estates and trusts.

Real Estate: The Real Estate Practice represents major corporations, regional and national developers, institutional lenders, investors, pension funds and advisers, real estate investment trusts, telecommunications providers, technology companies, retailers and agencies of the federal government. Their nationally recognized practice is known for handling large-volume real estate transactions in multiple jurisdictions.

INTERNATIONAL WORK: Morgan Lewis has five international offices that focus on a broad range of practice areas. The firm's lawyers work as one worldwide, integrated team, irrespective of location, and are particularly experienced in addressing complex multi-jurisdictional issues.

Morgan Lewis

C O U N S E L O R S   A T   L A W

PEPPER HAMILTON LLP

THE FIRM

Chairman: Barry M Abelson
Executive Partner: Robert E Heideck

Number of partners: 170
Number of other lawyers: 248

FIRM OVERVIEW: Pepper Hamilton LLP is a multi-practice law firm with 400 lawyers in six states and the District of Columbia providing corporate, litigation and regulatory legal services to US and international businesses, governmental entities, nonprofit organizations and individuals. Pepper was founded in 1890.

MAIN AREAS OF PRACTICE:

Bankruptcy & Reorganization: Represents creditors, debtors, trustees, commercial lenders, examiners and other parties in insolvencies.
Commercial Litigation: Represents clients in complex contract, corporate governance, securities, ERISA and antitrust litigation and alternative dispute resolution, in the single case, class action and MDL context.
Construction: Represents contractors, public and private owners, developers, subcontractors, architects, engineers and sureties in contract negotiations, arbitration, mediation and litigation.
Corporate & Securities: Represents public and private companies in M&A activities, corporate governance, disclosure, securities compliance and enforcement, and other business matters; private equity and venture funds in fund formation, investments, buy-outs and other transactions.
Employee Benefits: Benefits and executive compensation counseling, plan drafting and administration; and benefits/compensation aspects of transactions; ERISA litigation.
Environmental: Counsels and defends federal and state lawsuits and administrative proceedings.
Financial Services: Represents sophisticated institutional lenders and borrowers in leveraged transactions, secured financings, securitizations and litigation; investment advisory fund formation and regulation.
Health Effects Litigation: Risk management, regulatory counseling and litigation related to alleged adverse health effects from pharmaceuticals, medical devices, radiation, chemicals and environmental substances; product liability litigation involving consumer goods and industrial equipment; civil and criminal matters related to clinical trials.
Insurance & Reinsurance: Counsels clients on insurance and reinsurance issues and handles litigation and arbitration of complex contract and treaty-based reinsurance claims.
Intellectual Property: Procures intellectual property rights and resolves disputes, including patents, copyrights, trademarks, trade secret protection, unfair competition, false advertising, and defamation, publicity and privacy issues.
Labor & Employment: Represents employers in all aspects of labor and employment law, from management counseling to complex employment litigation.
Public Finance: Represents municipalities, agencies and other bond issuers; underwriter's and special tax counsel for investment banks.
Real Estate: Represents major developers in financing, leasing and construction of commercial and residential developments.
Tax: Structures businesses and transactions to improve local, state, national and international tax efficiency.
Trusts & Estates: Represents individuals and businesses in wealth preservation issues and family-owned businesses.

OFFICES

CALIFORNIA
895 Dove Street, Suite 300, **Newport Beach**, CA 92660-2996
Tel: 949 851 4636 **Fax:** 949 851 4637

DELAWARE
Hercules Plaza, Suite 5100, 1313 Market Street, PO Box 1709,
Wilmington, DE 19899-1709
Tel: 302 777 6500 **Fax:** 302 421 8390

DISTRICT OF COLUMBIA
Hamilton Square, 600 Fourteenth Street, NW,
Washington, DC 20005-2004
Tel: 202 220 1200 **Fax:** 202 220 1665

MICHIGAN
36th Floor, 100 Renaissance Center, **Detroit**, MI 48243-1157
Tel: 313 259 7110 **Fax:** 313 259 7926

NEW JERSEY
300 Alexander Park, CN 5276, **Princeton**, NJ 08543-5276
Tel: 609 452 0808 **Fax:** 609 452 1147

NEW YORK
14th Floor, 1180 Avenue of the Americas, **New York**, NY 10036-8401
Tel: 212 899 5090 **Fax:** 212 899 5091

PENNSYLVANIA
400 Berwyn Park, 899 Cassatt Road, **Berwyn**, PA 19312-1183
Tel: 610 640 7800 **Fax:** 610 640 7835

200 One Keystone Plaza, North Front and Market Streets, PO Box 1181,
Harrisburg, PA 17108-1181
Tel: 717 255 1155 **Fax:** 717 238 0575

3000 Two Logan Square, Eighteenth and Arch Streets,
Philadelphia, PA 19103-2799
Tel: 215 981 4000 **Fax:** 215 981 4750

50th Floor, 500 Grant Street, **Pittsburgh**, PA 15219-2502
Tel: 412 454 5000 **Fax:** 412 281 0717

CONTACTS

Bankruptcy & Reorganization	I William Cohen
Commercial Litigation	Robert L Hickok
Construction	Bruce W Ficken
Corporate & Securities	Barry M Abelson
Employee Benefits	Andrew J Rudolph
Environmental	John W Carroll
Health Care Services	Henry C Fader
Health Effects/Product Liability	Nina M Gussack
Insurance & Reinsurance	Deborah F Cohen
Intellectual Property	Vincent V Carissimi
International	James D Rosener
Investment Management	Joseph V Del Raso
Labor & Employment	Jonathan Kane
Public Finance	David W Sweet
Real Estate	Norman B Berlin, Dusty Elias Kirk
Sports	Charles M Greenberg
Tax	Joan C Arnold
Trusts & Estates	Robert J Weinberg

Pepper Hamilton LLP
Attorneys at Law

RATNER PRESTIA

THE FIRM

Chair: Paul F Prestia

Number of shareholders: 15
Number of other lawyers: 13
Number of other patent agents: 4

FIRM OVERVIEW: Practicing intellectual property law exclusively since 1981, RatnerPrestia is a progressive firm of lawyers, patent agents, paralegals and support staff. All of RatnerPrestia's attorneys, agents, and technical advisors have technical backgrounds and many have advanced degrees and industrial or research experience, enabling the firm to competently provide a wide range of services to its clients.

MAIN AREAS OF PRACTICE:

Dispute Resolution, Litigation & ADR: The firm's practice involves all types of intellectual property and domain name disputes in the federal courts and various administrative agencies, such as the Trademark Trial and Appeal Board and the Board of Patent Appeals and Interferences of the United States Patent and Trademark Office. Because RatnerPrestia takes a business approach when representing clients, alternative dispute resolution (ADR) processes are often pursued because they are less expensive and more efficient and effective than litigation. But when litigation is necessary, RatnerPrestia litigates efficiently and, when appropriate, aggressively. RatnerPrestia's litigators and ADR practitioners are a diverse group of attorneys who have long represented clients as counselors and advocates in various approaches to resolving disputes as both corporate counsel and private practitioners. They are often retained as neutrals in ADR processes not involving RatnerPrestia clients.

IP Business Management: The IP Business Management Group blends considerable IP business experience with formidable legal skills and wide ranging technical expertise (including engineering work experience) to work through IP issues and counsel clients to formulate strategies and achieve results that drive the client's business objectives.

IP Counseling: Strategic guidance, litigation planning, liability assessment (offensive and defensive) and portfolio evaluation are typical counseling objectives. Such counseling often plays a significant role in clients' business plans, due diligence studies and day-to-day risk management.

Patent Preparation & Prosecution: RatnerPrestia is well known for its strength in this area across a wide range of technologies, including software, electronics, biotechnology, biomedical devices, pharmaceutical and polymer chemistry, materials science, optics, acoustics and in non-technical areas, such as business methods and designs. Its credentials and experience in patent preparation and prosecution also translate into a strong resource for its litigation, IP business management and IP counseling activities.

Trademarks: RatnerPrestia handles a wide variety of trademark ex parte and inter parte matters and manages significant trademark portfolios.

Trade Secrets: Global competition, the immediate dissemination of information via the internet, and employee mobility -among other factors- make it more critical than ever for companies to protect their valuable trade secret assets against unauthorized disclosure and misappropriation. RatnerPrestia's trade secrets lawyers stay current on this unique area of IP practice by constantly surveying legal developments in the field.

OFFICES

PHILADELPHIA
Suite 301, One Westlakes, Berwyn,
PO Box 980, **Valley Forge**, 19482
Tel: 610 407 0700 **Fax:** 610 407 0701
Website: www.ratnerprestia.com

DELAWARE
Nemours Building, 1007 Orange Street, Suite 1100,
PO Box 1596, **Wilmington**, 19899
Tel: 302 778 2500 **Fax:** 302 778 2600

PENNSYLVANIA
Suite 265, Commerce Corporate Ctr., 5100 Tilghman St.
Allentown, PA 18104
Tel: 610 530 8100 **Fax:** 610 530 8200

CONTACTS

Litigation & ADR ....Harrie Samaras, Rex Donnelly
Electronic/Software Patents ....Kenneth Nigon, Larry Ashery
Pharma/Bio/Chem Patents ....Christopher Lewis, Jonathan Spadt
Mechanical/BioMed/Design Patents..Joshua Cohen, Jonathan Spadt
Foreign Patents ....Daniel Calder
Trademarks ....Benjamin Leace, Rex Donnelly
IP Business Transactions ....Robert Seitter
IP Counseling ....Paul Prestia, Jacques Etkowicz
Copyright ....Jacques Etkowicz

CLIENTS: RatnerPrestia's clients range from start-up companies to multi-billion dollar corporations, both domestic and international, and from private individuals to well-known institutions and universities. RatnerPrestia has also been retained, for opinions and counseling, by venture capital firms and by law firms for opinions and advice in regard to on-going litigation and for ADR processes.

Major clients: Air Products and Chemicals, Ametek, Alcan, Inc., Arkema, Binney and Smith, Boston Scientific, B. Braun, Continental Teves, InTest, ITT Industries, Johnson & Johnson, Johnson Matthey, Kulicke & Soffa, Matsushita, Morton Grove Pharmaceuticals, Multisorb Technologies, Nippon Sheet Glass, Panasonic Technologies, Sarnoff Corp, Tate & Lyle, T-Networks, Unisys, Tyco, V-Span, and various academic institutions including The University of Pennsylvania, The University of Delaware, Rensselaer Polytechnic Institute, Princeton University, Lehigh University and Drexel University.

INTERNATIONAL WORK: RatnerPrestia counsels, advises and represents numerous foreign clients in US IP matters and numerous US clients in IP matters in all other major countries and it also participates in World Intellectual Property Organization ADR Procedures.

REED SMITH LLP

THE FIRM

Managing Partner: Gregory B Jordan
Number of partners in US offices: 409
Number of other lawyers in US offices: 520
Website: www.reedsmith.com

FIRM OVERVIEW: Reed Smith is a leading international law firm with more than 1,000 lawyers in 14 offices in the United States and two in the United Kingdom. The firm's geographic and substantive breadth enables Reed Smith to form multidisciplinary teams that serve clients in nearly all types of legal matters throughout the world. Reed Smith has built exceptionally strong areas of focus in financial services and life sciences. The firm distinguishes itself through a commitment to high-quality, individual service.

MAIN AREAS OF PRACTICE:

Litigation: Reed Smith represents clients in all types of litigation. The firm is a national leader in high-stakes class-action, complex and multijurisdictional matters. Firm business trial groups are led by seasoned veterans experienced in every phase of federal and state jury and bench trials. Reed Smith has one of the oldest distinct appellate practices, and firm appellate specialists have succeeded before many of the most influential courts of appeals in the country. The firm has particularly strong substantive litigation capabilities in the areas of antitrust and competition, bankruptcy, construction, environmental law, financial services, fraud, insurance coverage, intellectual property, labor and employment, and product liability. Firm litigators also advise on risk management.

Business & Regulatory: Firm transactional lawyers represent clients in industry-leading deals that include mergers, acquisitions, divestitures, joint ventures, licensing arrangements, outsourcing and others. The firm has significant practices in the areas of project and global finance, energy and natural resources development, real estate finance and development, and venture finance. Reed Smith business lawyers assist with securities, corporate restructuring, corporate governance, executive compensation, benefits and business immigration, and provide other corporate advice and services. Firm regulatory and government relations lawyers assist clients in highly regulated sectors with compliance and advocacy in areas such as banking, communications, consumer financial services, energy, food and drug issues, healthcare fraud and abuse, healthcare reimbursement, insurance, investments and pensions.

Industry Representation: Reed Smith has multidisciplinary teams devoted to serving all the legal needs of clients operating in industry sectors such as financial services (including banking, consumer specialty finance, investment management, insurance and reinsurance) life sciences (pharmaceutical, medical device and biotechnology), advertising and marketing, construction, energy and natural resources, healthcare, media and entertainment, real estate, technology, higher education, primary and secondary education, nonprofit entities and associations.

Niche Practices: Reed Smith has significant capabilities in intellectual property, tax, public finance and government contracts. The firm has built niche practices in debt recovery; private equity; e-commerce; export, customs and trade; homeland security; information technology; infrastructure development and grants; commercial and international arbitration; international distribution; privacy; and record and data management.

CLIENTS: Reed Smith represents major corporate clients - including more than half of the Fortune 500 - as well as nonprofit and public sector entities. Firm clients include industry leaders in the financial services, life sciences, manufacturing, energy, healthcare, real estate and other sectors.

INTERNATIONAL WORK: Reed Smith serves clients in all types of legal matters throughout Europe, Asia, South America, Africa and other parts of the world. The firm has approximately 90 lawyers in two offices in the United

OFFICES

NEW YORK
599 Lexington Avenue, **New York**, NY 10022
Tel: 212 521 5400 **Fax:** 212 521 5450

CALIFORNIA
355 South Grand Avenue, Suite 2900, **Los Angeles**, LA 90071-1514
Tel: 213 457 8000 **Fax:** 213 457 8080

1901 Avenue of the Stars, Suite 700, **Los Angeles**, LA 90067-6078
Tel: 310 734 5200 **Fax:** 310 734 5299

Two Embarcadero Center, Suite 2000, **San Francisco**, LA 94111
Tel: 415 543 8700 **Fax:** 415 391 8269

1999 Harrison Street, Suite 2400, **Oakland**, LA 94612-3572
Tel: 510 763 2000 **Fax:** 510 273 8832

DISTRICT OF COLUMBIA
1301 K Street, N.W., Suite 1100 - East Tower, **Washington**, DC 20005-3317
Tel: 202 414 9200 **Fax:** 202 414 9299

PENNSYLVANIA
2500 One Liberty Place, 1650 Market Street, **Philadelphia**, PA 19103-7301
Tel: 215 851 8100 **Fax:** 215 851 1420

435 Sixth Avenue, **Pittsburgh**, 15219-1886
Tel: 412 288 3131 **Fax:** 412 288 3063

NEW JERSEY
Princeton Forrestal Village, 136 Main Street, Suite 250, **Princeton** NJ 08540
Tel: 609 987 0050 **Fax:** 609 951 0824

One Riverfront Plaza, 1st Floor, **Newark**, 07102
Tel: 973 621 3200 **Fax:** 973 621 3199

VIRGINIA
3110 Fairview Park Drive, Suite 1400, **Falls Church**, VA 22042
Tel: 703 641 4200 **Fax:** 703 641 4340

44084 Riverside Parkway, Suite 300, **Leesburg**, VA 20176
Tel: 703 729 8500 **Fax:** 703 478 8003

Riverfront Plaza - West Tower
901 East Byrd Street, Suite 1700, **Richmond**, VA 23219-4068
Tel: 804 344 3400 **Fax:** 804 344 3410

DELAWARE
1201 Market Street, Suite 1500, **Wilmington**, DE 19801
Tel: 302 778 7500 **Fax:** 302 778 7575

INTERNATIONAL OFFICES:
Reed Smith also has offices in London and the Midlands, UK.

CONTACTS

Litigation	W Thomas McGough, Jr (Pittsburgh)
Business & Regulatory	David L DeNinno (Pittsburgh)
Financial Services	Frank T Guadagnino (Pittsburgh)
Financial Services Litigation	Mary J Hackett (Los Angeles)
Life Sciences (Regulatory)	Kevin R Barry (Washington, DC)
Life Sciences (Product Liability)	Colleen T Davies (Oakland)
Life Sciences (Transactional)	Diane M Frenier (Princeton)

Kingdom, as well as multilingual French, German and Japanese teams. Reed Smith's internationally recognized global and Project Finance Team has significant experience structuring deals in India and other emerging markets.

ReedSmith LLP

It's not just business. *It's personal.*®

PENNSYLVANIA

SAUL EWING LLP

THE FIRM

Managing Partner: Stephen S Aichele
Number of partners: 134
Number of other lawyers: 111
Website: www.saul.com

FIRM OVERVIEW: Founded in 1921, Saul Ewing provides a broad array of legal services to businesses from its offices located throughout the mid-Atlantic region.

MAIN AREAS OF PRACTICE:

Bankruptcy: The firm represents companies in all aspects of cases under the bankruptcy laws, as well as in other matters relating to corporate reorganization, creditors' rights, and insolvency.

Litigation: The firm represents corporations and corporate officers and directors in all types of commercial disputes including shareholder derivative actions, securities fraud claims, and other actions to enforce or defend legal or contractual rights. The firm also defends corporations against claims by individuals including mass tort and product liability claims and claims by current or former employees.

Business: The firm provides legal services to corporations and corporate officers and directors on all issues related to the operation of their business including corporate formation, corporate governance, business transactions, corporate financings and capitalization, intellectual property rights, and other legal matters that face businesses in today's economy.

Real Estate: The firm represents owners, developers, REITs and other investors in the development and construction of new projects, in the acquisition and leasing of existing facilities, and in matters related to the ownership of land generally.

Public Finance: Saul Ewing attorneys serve as bond counsel, issuers counsel and underwriters counsel in transactions involving the issuance and sale of tax-exempt state and local government bonds.

Insurance: The firm advises corporations in the insurance industry on a wide range of issues related to the operation and regulation of companies in the insurance business including licensing, capitalization and solvency, and the marketing and sale of insurance products. The firm also represents clients in litigation related to the business of insurance including litigation concerning regulatory obligations, insurance insolvencies, agent and other producer terminations, insurance coverage and reinsurance disputes.

Telecommunications: Saul Ewing attorneys represent telecommunications clients in complex financial transactions, advise clients on implementing local competition provisions of the Telecommunications Act of 1996, and provide counsel on intellectual property rights.

Defense Contracting: The firm specializes in the representation of defense contractors, from regionally based companies to the nation's leading defense contractors, in all aspects of litigation, including federal investigations, internal compliance investigations, supplier litigation and federal enforcement litigation.

Construction: The firm provides services to commercial developers, engineers and contractors on all construction-related legal matters, including initial land acquisition, planning and design, bidding, contract negotiation, and post-construction claims resolution.

Environmental: The firm advises clients on matters related to compliance with state and federal environmental regulations and helps to structure real estate and corporate transactions to minimize environmental liability. The firm also represents corporations and corporate officers in litigation related to environmental and regulatory liabilities.

Personal Wealth, Estates & Trusts: The firm represents wealthy individuals, trusts and institutions in matters related to wealth preservation and management including tax, estate, and retirement planning, business succession and executive compensation, and charitable giving.

Labor: The firm represents clients in areas such as workplace issues, collective bargaining agreements, labor relations, procedures and protocols,

US OFFICES

DELAWARE
222 Delaware Avenue, Suite 1200, **Wilmington**, DE 19801
Tel: 302 421 6800 **Fax:** 302 421 6813

DISTRICT OF COLUMBIA
1025 Thomas Jefferson Street, NW, Suite 425W, **Washington**, DC 20007
Tel: 202 295 6600 **Fax:** 202 295 6700

MARYLAND
100 South Charles Street, **Baltimore**, MD 21201-2773
Tel: 410 332 8600 **Fax:** 410 332 8862

NEW JERSEY
750 Colllege East, **Princeton**, NJ 08540
Tel: 609 452 3100 **Fax:** 609 452 3122

PENNSYLVANIA
Penn National Insurance Tower, 2 North Second Street, 7th Floor, **Harrisburg**, PA 17101
Tel: 717 257 7500 **Fax:** 717 238 4622

Centre Square West, 1500 Market Street, 38th Floor, **Philadelphia**, PA 19102-2186
Tel: 215 972 7777 **Fax:** 215 972 7725

1200 Liberty Ridge Drive, Suite 200, **Wayne**, PA 19087
Tel: 610 251 5050 **Fax:** 610 651 5930

CONTACTS

Bankruptcy ....Norman L Pernick (Wilmington)
...........................Jeffrey Hampton (Philadelphia), Irv Walker (Baltimore)
Litigation ..John F Stoviak (Philadelphia), Charles O Monk II (Baltimore)
.............Linda Richenderfer (Wilmington), Michael Lampert (Princeton)
Michael Finio (Baltimore), Robert Gill (Washington, DC) Henry R Abrams (Baltimore) Edward J Baines (Baltimore) Dana N Pescosolido (Baltimore)
Business ....David S Antzis (Wayne), Howard Miller (Baltimore)
...................Howard Slavit (Washington, DC), Barry F Levin (Baltimore)
Real Estate..John P Pierce (Philadelphia)
...............Frederick D Strober (Philadelphia), William Gee (Wilmington)
....Wendie C Stabler (Wilmington)
Public Finance ....George T Magnatta (Philadelphia)
....Timothy Frey (Wilmington)
Insurance ....Constance B Foster (Harrisburg)
.......................Paul M Hummer (Philadelphia), Laura L Katz (Baltimore)
Telecommunications ....Nancy S Cleveland (Wayne)
....Karl Nelson (Baltimore)
Defense Contracting...........................Joseph F O'Dea (Philadelphia)
Construction ....George E Rahn, Jr (Philadelphia)
Environmental ....Pamela Goodwin (Princeton)
........................James O'Toole (Philadelphia), Joel Burcat (Harrisburg)
....Carl B Everett (Philadelphia)
Personal Wealth, Estates & Trusts..........Robert H Louis (Philadelphia)
....Sheldon S Satisky (Baltimore)
Labor ....Stephen J Cabot (Philadelphia) Gary B Eidelman (Baltimore)
....Harriet E Cooperman (Baltimore)

employment, pay practices to comply with Federal and State wage and hour laws, and affirmative action plans and programs.

CLIENTS: Saul Ewing serves a broad range of regional, national, and international clients from across the business spectrum. The firm's clients include businesses of all sizes, nonprofits, academic institutions, and governments and their agencies. Clients value Saul Ewing for the firm's industry knowledge and the responsiveness of its attorneys.

SAUL EWING LLP
Thinking ahead.
So you can move ahead.℠

WOLF, BLOCK, SCHORR AND SOLIS-COHEN LLP

THE FIRM

Chairman: Mark L Alderman

Number of partners: 142
Number of other lawyers: 167

FIRM OVERVIEW: Founded in 1903, WolfBlock is one of Philadelphia's largest law firms. With seven offices in Pennsylvania, New York, New Jersey and Delaware, the firm provides a range of commercial and private legal services to clients in the US and abroad. The firm has more than 300 lawyers working in 18 practice groups. These groups include business litigation, communications, complex liability/surety/fidelity, corporate/securities, employee benefits, employment services, environmental law, family law, financial services, government assisted/affordable housing, health law, intellectual property/information technology, private client services, real estate, real estate structured finance, tax law, utility regulation, and securitization. Complementing the firm's legal offerings are its ancillary services provided through The Wolf Institute, a division of WolfBlock, and Wolf-Block Government Relations, a wholly owned subsidiary. Employee management and executive training courses are offered at The Wolf Institute. WolfBlock Government Relations is dedicated to promoting effective government relations and lobbying services for clients.

MAIN AREAS OF PRACTICE:

Business Litigation: The firm's Business Litigation Practice covers a range of commercial disputes, including virtually every substantive area, such as: securities, antitrust, construction, malpractice, civil RICO, products liability, trademark and copyright infringement, and real estate, and First Amendment and defamation law. The firm is frequently called upon to represent many of the largest companies in both the United States and throughout the world.

Corporate/Securities: The firm has a large, diversified Corporate/Securities Practice Group. Its lawyers are noted for their work in the fields of securities, mergers and acquisitions, venture capital, and emerging business enterprises and represent public and private companies at all stages of development, including family businesses that have been firm clients for decades; start-up and emerging businesses in e-commerce, biotechnology, and other developing areas of commerce; clients going public; clients that are public; and public companies going private.

Complex Liability/Surety/Fidelity: The Complex Liability/Surety/Fidelity Group represents clients in numerous jurisdictions, including almost every major US city, and most US states, as well as Brazil, Puerto Rico, and Chile. The group has wide-ranging experience in a number of areas including: construction, directors and officers liability, errors and omissions liability, bad faith, subrogation, quia timet, indemnification, exoneration, reinsurance, bankruptcy, and policy coverage.

Real Estate: The Real Estate Group's practice is national in scope and encompasses the full range of real estate-related transactions. The group works closely with other firm lawyers skilled in other areas – including securities, tax, and environmental law – on multidisciplinary teams as needed to serve individual client segments or industries.

CLIENTS: The firm's clients include large national and international corporations in nearly every industry: banking, financial and insurance institutions, REITs, real estate developers, public utilities, venture capital and private equity investors, healthcare organizations, government entities, technology and biotechnology companies and non-profit organizations.

HEAD OFFICE

PENNSYLVANIA
1650 Arch Street, 22nd Floor, **Philadelphia**, PA 19103
Tel: 215 977 2000 **Fax:** 215 977 2334

BRANCH OFFICES

DELAWARE
Wilmington Trust Center, 1100 N. Market Street, Suite 1001, **Wilmington**, DE 19801
Tel: 302 777 5860 **Fax:** 302 777 5863

NEW JERSEY
1940 Route 70 East, Suite 200, **Cherry Hill**, NJ 08003
Tel: 856 424 8200 **Fax:** 856 424 4446

101 Eisenhower Parkway, **Roseland**, NJ 07068
Tel: 973 228 5700 **Fax:** 973 228 7852

NEW YORK
250 Park Avenue, **New York**, NY 10177
Tel: 212 986 1116 **Fax:** 212 986 0604

PENNSYLVANIA
One West Main Street, Fifth Floor, **Norristown**, PA 19401
Tel: 610 272 5555 **Fax:** 610 272 6976

212 Locust Street, Suite 300, **Harrisburg**, PA 17101
Tel: 717 237 7160 **Fax:** 717 237 7161

CONTACTS

Business Litigation	Jerome Shestack
Communications	Stuart Shorenstein
Complex Liability, Surety Fidelity	Brian Flaherty
Corporate/Securities	David Gitlin
Employee Benefits	Warren Fusfeld
Employment Services	James Redeker
Environmental Law	Kenneth Warren
Private Client Services	Clifford Schlesinger
Family Law	Lynne Gold-Bikin
Financial Services	Bruce Lesser
Government Assisted/Affordable Housing	Bernard Lee
Health Law	John Fanburg
Intellectual Property & Information Technology	Robert Zielinski
Real Estate Practice Group	Herman Fala
Real Estate Structured Finance Group	Abby Wenzel
Securitization Practice Group	Keith Krasney
Tax Law	Thomas Gallagher
Utility Regulation	Daniel Clearfield

WolfBlock
Sound Counsel. Since 1903.

WOODCOCK WASHBURN LLP

THE FIRM

FIRM OVERVIEW: As businesses grow more complex, protecting intellectual property becomes more of a challenge. As a result, the most effective intellectual property lawyers are those who specialize in the field - and who are as much at home in the laboratory as in the courtroom. For more than 60 years, Woodcock Washburn has specialized in intellectual property law. As a national firm, with offices in Philadelphia and Seattle, it has a wealth of experience in patent, trademark, and copyright law; trade secret protection; and the safeguarding of products and services from unfair competition. In addition, Woodcock Washburn offers an exceptionally wide range of general counseling services. Whether an arrangement requires a simple confidentiality agreement, a material transfer agreement, a consulting agreement, or a more complex licensing agreement, the firm's lawyers help clients negotiate transactions, structure contracts, and prepare any necessary paperwork.

HEAD OFFICE

PENNSYLVANIA
One Liberty Place, 46th Floor, **Philadelphia**, PA 19103
Tel: 215 568 3100
Website: www.woodcock.com

BRANCH OFFICES

WASHINGTON
999 Third Avenue, Suite 1606, **Seattle**, WA 98104
Tel: 206 332 1380

MAIN AREAS OF PRACTICE:

Lawyers as Scientists & Engineers: Woodcock Washburn lawyers are not just intellectual property lawyers. Most of its more than 80 lawyers are also scientists and engineers, schooled in such demanding disciplines as biotechnology, chemistry, electrical and mechanical engineering, and computer science. As technology specialists, the firm's lawyers possess a unique understanding of the issues faced by clients, and they present those issues in clear and meaningful ways to judges, juries, and government examiners around the world. Competent legal services today require more than a literal 'question asked, question answered' approach. For legal advice in the field of intellectual property law to be meaningful, lawyers must understand each client's business and the technology that affects it. Woodcock Washburn's clients include companies on the cutting edge of innovation, such as the development of new therapeutics, advanced mechanical devices, benchmarks for computer programming, and breakthrough solutions in other areas of science and technology. The firm has successfully represented clients in fields as diverse as transgenic animals, antisense DNA therapeutics, digital signal processing, and Internet/network software.

Procuring Meaningful Patent Protection: For clients seeking protection for their valuable inventions, Woodcock Washburn offers a number of singular advantages. More than 60 years of experience specializing in patent procurement has given them an in-depth understanding of the procurement process. With technical training in today's cutting-edge technologies, Woodcock Washburn lawyers also have the necessary expertise to grasp clients' ideas, speak their language, and address their concerns. This unique insight gives them the ability to guide clients through the maze of complex technological and legal requirements to obtain valid and meaningful patent protection for their inventions.

Interferences: A Specialty within a Specialty: Woodcock Washburn has extensive experience in handling patent interferences in fields as diverse as biotechnology, chemistry, computers, plastics, and high-tech metal alloys. The firm has secured a favorable outcome on behalf of a client whose pioneering patent for 'humanized' antibodies was challenged by its main competitor; for a client opposing two of the country's largest computer companies; and for a Silicon Valley start-up in an interference relating to liposomes for drug delivery. The more competitive and 'patent driven' the technology, the more likely an interference will occur. For such technologies, it is essential that patent portfolios be constructed with interferences in mind. Interference contests are much like guerilla warfare; unconventional rules apply. Moreover, knowledge of the specialized terrain surrounding interferences is vital; at Woodcock Washburn, they are the firm's specialty within a specialty.

Protecting Trademark & Copyright Assets: In a world increasingly dominated by marketing and the media, the most valuable aspect of a product or service is often the identity it has established in the marketplace. Woodcock Washburn helps clients develop a strategy for building a strong trademark portfolio that can protect the identity and reputation of the business, as well as the individual products and services it offers. Intellectual property assets also can feature prominently when it comes to buying or selling a business. Woodcock Washburn helps clients understand the legal issues that enter into the valuation of those assets so they can properly ascertain what the business is worth. In addition, the firm advises clients on the scope and validity of third-party patents and how they may or may not be legitimately avoided.

Effective Litigation Strategies: The firm aggressively pursues all aspects of litigation, carefully planning discovery and motion practice to optimize a client's position prior to trial. Woodcock Washburn's experience in patent, trademark and copyright law helps it identify the most effective litigation strategies. Woodcock Washburn lawyers have compiled an impressive record of wins before both judges and juries. On the appellate level, they have built an equally enviable chronicle of success. The firm explores alternate strategies to litigation no less aggressively. With court dockets growing more crowded and litigation expenses rising, the percentage of cases that actually make it to trial is shrinking. Often, the firm finds that productive and cost-effective outcomes for its clients are obtained through arbitration, mediation, and settlement - rather than expensively won court decisions.

CLIENTS: Please view the firm's website at www.woodcock.com to review its client list and patent portfolio.

INTERNATIONAL WORK:

A Global Reach: Woodcock Washburn's experience extends beyond the United States to other countries - an important capability in today's global economy. The firm's lawyers are familiar with the complexities of patent, trademark, copyright, trade secrets and unfair competition laws across jurisdictions worldwide. Guided by its history of practicing intellectual property law and its dedication to quality client service, Woodcock Washburn LLP protects the ideas that will shape the future.

CONTENTS: Corporate/M&A p.1564; Employment p.1565; Litigation: General Commercial p.1566; Real Estate p.1568; Individuals' Profiles p.1569; Firms' Profiles p.1571.

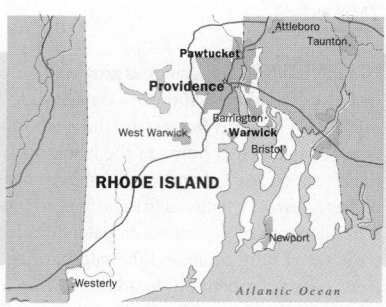

How lawyers are ranked

The opinions we gather from clients — mainly from in-house lawyers but also from other purchasers of legal services — are balanced by opinions from colleagues and competitors. Together, they provide two different perspectives — an all-round view — and biased viewpoints cancel each other out.

CORPORATE/M&A

Rhode Island
Leading firms (Corporate/M&A)

1. **EDWARDS & ANGELL, LLP** *Providence*
   HINCKLEY, ALLEN & SNYDER LLP *Providence*
2. **HOLLAND & KNIGHT LLP** *Providence*
3. **ADLER POLLOCK & SHEEHAN PC** *Providence*
   PARTRIDGE SNOW & HAHN LLP *Providence*

Leading individuals (Corporate/M&A)

1. **CARLOTTI Stephen** *Hinckley Allen, Providence*
   JOHNSON V Duncan *Edwards & Angell, Providence*
2. **DUFFELL David** *Edwards & Angell, Providence*
   FARRELL Margaret *Hinckley Allen, Providence*
   GRAHAM Christopher *Edwards & Angell, Providence*
   HAHN James *Partridge Snow, Providence*
   PANNONE Gary *Holland & Knight, Providence*
   PARTRIDGE John *Partridge Snow, Providence*
   SKEFFINGTON James *Edwards & Angell, Providence*

Firms and Individuals are listed alphabetically in each band.

Band 1

Edwards & Angell, LLP

The Firm: According to interviewees this is *"number one – the biggest by far and always very solid."* The team's size and its long-standing reputation for high-quality corporate work guarantees it a top ranking. The group handles all aspects of corporate and M&A, with private equity deals featuring particularly prominently over the past year. Here its lawyers acted for a number of major private equity houses such as Providence Equity and Nortec. Another highlight was acting for long-standing client Fleet in connection with its acquisition by Bank of America, which has now also joined the team's client base.

The Lawyers: The most famous name in the team is that of the fabulously talented **Duncan Johnson**, who continues to top our tables. He boasts a well-developed practice outside the state and acted in Bank of America's acquisition of Fleet. Clients praised **David Duffell** for his broad-ranging expertise, which spans M&A, LBOs and a variety of financing. An *"extremely efficient and user-friendly lawyer, who doesn't waste your time,"* he is particularly well versed in handing international transactions for major private equity clients such as Providence Equity. **Christopher Graham** is also *"a real expert in private equity,"* according to clients, though his practice spans a range of other transactional work. **James Skeffington**, the main point of call for CVS, is particularly prominent among private clients. An unusually broad practice also sees him involved in corporate strategy, employment and litigation management.

The Clients: Textron; CVS; G-Tech; Nortec and Wellman Dobson.

Hinckley, Allen & Snyder LLP

The Firm: This *"extremely capable and collegiate team"* boasts a number of *"terrific individuals"* and has won praise for its work on both the local and regional levels. The practice has enjoyed a busy year advising on some considerable corporate transactions. For example, it regularly represents Wembley plc in negotiations and recently acted on the $165 million privatization of a major military housing complex, as well as some large recapitalizations. Other highlights include the sale of Goldline Controls to Hayward Industries. The team also represented Bancorp Rhode Island in the issuance of an additional $5 million in securities.

The Lawyers: **Stephen Carlotti** is *"unsurpassed"* in Rhode Island's corporate circles, according to clients. His *"abundance of expertise and ability to connect with clients and ensure effective commercial conclusions"* are said to keep him firmly at the top of the tree for transactional work in the state. His colleague **Margaret Farrell** was warmly praised for her expertise in securities offerings and general corporate work. *"An extremely skilful lawyer with terrific judgment,"* she is appreciated by clients for her *"excellent business sense and responsiveness."* She recently acted for a private company in a $10 million private placement of common equity, and advised the purchaser in the acquisition of two textile printing companies and related real estate.

The Clients: The team acts for a broad selection of national and local clients.

Band 2

Holland & Knight LLP

See firm details p.1352

The Firm: This is an international firm with *"a big national footprint,"* and its aggressive push into the Providence market is giving it an increasing profile within the state. The corporate team cooperates closely with groups across its impressive network of offices, and can draw on extensive resources to service an impressive national client base. Sources were quick to point out that the firm has *"some very good people"* in Rhode Island, and an excellent reputation for leasing among other things. Typical work spans the spectrum from contract negotiations and drafting, to financing and the development of corporate structures, M&A and joint ventures.

The Lawyers: Peers described **Gary Pannone** (see p.1570) as *"a wonderful corporate lawyer and a real gentleman."* His client base ranges from startups to well-developed businesses with international scope. He is active in a wide variety of corporate work, though he has a niche in securities.

The Clients: Clients range from telecom, media, hi-tech and energy companies, to manufacturers, airlines, banks and other financial institutions.

Band 3

Adler Pollock & Sheehan PC

See firm details p.1571

The Firm: The firm is predominantly known for its market-leading litigation practice. The corporate team is smaller and less well known, but it is rising in prominence and attracts praise from clients and peers alike. The Rhode Island and Boston offices work closely together to advise on an array of matters, ranging from LBOs and recapitalizations, to asset and stock sales and the establishment of joint ventures. In recent years the firm has been adding to its client roster of family-owned businesses, entrepreneurs and domestic public companies with some significant client wins among foreign multinationals with operations in the USA. Recent highlights include a $500 million stock purchase of a global chemicals manufacturer, a $400 million merger between US and European industrial businesses and a number of disposals of US and European companies valued at over $100 million.

The Lawyers: Patricia Rocha is the contact for the corporate practice.

The Clients: Clients include US and European chemicals businesses, electronics companies, Far Eastern ceramic powder manufacturers and engineering, metallurgical and hi-tech equipment producers.

Partridge Snow & Hahn LLP

The Firm: Although smaller than the market leaders, this team wins consistent praise for its experience in corporate and commercial work. Peers were particularly impressed by the broad scope of the advice provided by a compact team. This includes advice on a range of corporate matters, such as M&A, corporate financings, public offerings, private placements, disclosure documents and regulatory reporting.

The Lawyers: **James Hahn** was warmly recommended by peers. His ability to combine corporate and securities law with a detailed knowledge of tax was felt to give him an edge. His recent highlights include advising the sellers in connection with the stock sale of a multimillion-dollar advertising business and assisting the purchaser of a 160-unit chain of convenience stores and gas stations in four New England states. **John Partridge** is the main point of call for a number of large private clients and is well known for his expertise in the insurance sector.

The Clients: Clients range from multinationals to family-run companies, as well as nonprofit enterprises.

EMPLOYMENT

MAINLY DEFENDANT

Rhode Island
Leading firms
(Employment: Mainly Defendant)

1. **ADLER POLLOCK & SHEEHAN PC** *Providence*
   HINCKLEY, ALLEN & SNYDER LLP *Providence*
   PARTRIDGE SNOW & HAHN LLP *Providence*
2. **EDWARDS & ANGELL, LLP** *Providence*
   HOLLAND & KNIGHT LLP *Providence*
   LITTLE, MEDEIROS, KINDER, BULMAN *Providence*
3. **ST PETER & KASLE** *Providence*

Leading individuals
(Employment: Mainly Defendant)

1. **BROOKS Robert** *Adler Pollock*, Providence
   GAMBOLI Michael *Partridge Snow*, Providence
   JOCELYN Richard *Hinckley Allen*, Providence
2. **KASLE Jeffrey** *St Peter & Kasle*, Providence
   KINDER Daniel *Little Medeiros*, Providence
   MCNAMARA Neal *Holland & Knight*, Providence
   POGUE Mark *Edwards & Angell*, Providence
   ST PETER Gary *St Peter & Kasle*, Providence
   WHELAN Joseph *Hinckley Allen*, Providence

Firms and Individuals are listed alphabetically in each band.

Band 1

Adler Pollock & Sheehan PC
See firm details p.1571

The Firm: As befits one of the leading litigation firms in the state, Adler Pollock retains a premier position in the employment market. Peers were particularly impressed with its lawyers' aptitude in labor matters, where they were said to be second to none. For clients, however, it is their ability to keep cases out of court, as well as their sure handling of litigation, which makes them attractive. As one noted: *"Their philosophy is the same as ours – to prevent lawsuits in the first place."* The team handles all aspects of labor and employ-

ment law for both public and private sector employers, whether unionized or union free, before state and federal courts. It often advises employers on such issues as plant closure and reduction of workforce, wage and hour disputes, OSHA proceedings and child labor matters, and is also highly experienced in discrimination and sexual harassment cases. On the noncontentious side, the firm negotiates and drafts employment, separation and noncompete agreements.

The Lawyers: **Robert Brooks** (see p.1569) won unanimous praise from clients for his professionalism, humor, responsiveness and *"good business sense – he protects you from the rift and doesn't waste your time."* His legal acumen and efforts to understand clients' businesses were particularly appreciated. As one client put it: *"I can say to him, 'Here is what I want to do; can I do it?' as opposed to him telling me what to do."*

The Clients: The client base includes large, publicly held Fortune 500 corporations, and small and medium-sized businesses, as well as public and quasi-public agencies.

Hinckley, Allen & Snyder LLP

The Firm: This top-tier team is *"first class in both employment and labor matters,"* say commentators, with *"tremendous support throughout the region."* Clients say that the services *"are not inexpensive, but they are worth every penny."* A team of four in Providence is closely supported by the Boston and Concord offices. Typical work includes collective bargaining, wage and hour disputes, and other proceedings before state and federal agencies. On the noncontentious side, it does a lot of work on contract negotiations, union consultation and advice connected with hiring and firing. Recent highlights include the successful defense of a major corporation against a union campaign organized by 500 employees. It also recently appeared for an

employer before the Rhode Island Commission for Human Rights.

The Lawyers: **Richard Jocelyn** has *"an elephantine memory and exceptional experience with frontline labor issues."* Clients appreciate his outstanding expertise, his pragmatic attitude and his work in some of the most significant labor disputes in the USA. He is, they say, *"an outstanding labor lawyer, but also anticombative – he prefers to work with everyone to try to reach a resolution."* **Joseph Whelan** enjoys a growing profile in the market. He was described by clients as *"extremely smart, thorough and confident, with resources available to him in all aspects of employment."*

The Clients: Bank Rhode Island; Brown University; The Westerly Hospital; Salter Healthcare Services and Landmark Medical Center.

Partridge Snow & Hahn LLP

The Firm: The practice maintains its excellent reputation and has enjoyed a busy year, particularly with the opening of its new Massachusetts office. The past 12 months saw an increase in discrimination claims, with the team successfully defending management and obtaining summary judgments in a number of cases. For example, the group recently represented a large banking institution in a sexual harassment and gender discrimination suit brought by former employees, and defended a large national retailer against a harassment and disability discrimination claim. It also had success for a national jewelry manufacturer and distributor in national origin, gender discrimination and breach of employment contract charges.

The Lawyers: Clients heaped praise on *"passionate and talented"* employment litigator **Michael Gamboli.** *"I use him because it's important for us to work with smart attorneys who can take a regional view of cases,"* said one, adding,

www.ChambersandPartners.com

All quotes in the text are from interviews with clients and competitors.

1565

"What I like is that he takes a practical business view of employment matters, where a lot of attorneys give me information I don't need."
The Clients: The firm represents a number of prominent local and national businesses.

Band 2

Edwards & Angell, LLP
The Firm: The market felt that the departure of Lincoln Almond for the bench has decreased the profile of this firm somewhat in the labor and employment field. The team nevertheless still features in major cases, where it works closely with the litigation and corporate/commercial teams. Recent cases of note include representing a retailer in a jury trial concerning a pregnancy discrimination claim, and handling an age discrimination claim for a major manufacturer.
The Lawyers: **Mark Pogue** is perhaps better known as a leading commercial litigator, but he is also active in labor and employment litigation. Clients were full of praise for his courtroom manner: *"He knows how best to present evidence and is great on the courtroom floor; he's forceful but never intimidates witnesses or alienates the jury."*
The Clients: Clients include major banks and insurers in Rhode Island, as well as large manufacturers and international biotech companies.

Holland & Knight LLP
See firm details p.1352
The Firm: The firm was praised for its sure handling of employment disputes on behalf of its major corporate clients. They were quick to praise the value and convenience of having the support of a large international network. *"The*

lawyers can always advise us on what measures are available nationwide, should we have a case in another state," said one. The group handles a range of labor and employment matters, recently seeing a rise in retaliation claims. Highlights from the year include an important ERISA case and a sexual discrimination claim, where the firm successfully defended a major fast food retailer. Sources were also complimentary about the team's noncontentious expertise.
The Lawyers: **Neal McNamara** (see p.1569) divides his time more or less equally between litigation and counseling. He attracted praise from clients and peers alike for his expertise in employment and general commercial litigation matters. A knowledgeable, tough and experienced attorney, he is *"one of us,"* according to clients, who say, *"He understands the idiosyncrasies and uniqueness of our business."* He is also said to benefit from the support of *"a great team."*
The Clients: New England Gas; Arch Chemicals; ExxonMobil and Hyatt.

Little, Medeiros, Kinder, Bulman & Whitney PC
The Firm: It has been less than two years since the merger between Powers, Kinder & Keeney and Little Bulman Medeiros & Whitney, and this new outfit is already a well-established force in the market. The Powers, Kinder & Keeney firm was already well known for its labor and employment expertise, which has greatly helped the new team. In particular, it is now considered one of the top addresses for traditional labor law. The team typically advises employers on matters such as equal opportunities, discrimi-

nation and harassment, wage and hour cases, union organizing and collective bargaining, as well as handling a volume of preventive counseling. Recent highlights include representing the City of North Kingston in the first instance, and Middletown in the second, in connection with the firefighters union's 30-year-long resistance to contributing to health insurance, which provoked a flood of similar cases nationwide.
The Lawyers: Peers commended **Daniel Kinder** for his extensive experience in the field, especially in labor law. His portfolio includes some of the best-known labor conflicts in the region, including the Brown and Sharpe and Women and Infants Hospital cases.
The Clients: The team advises corporate and institutional clients, such as large manufacturers, municipal governments and hospitals.

Band 3

St Peter & Kasle
The Firm: Though not as large as some of its competitors, this compact team won warm endorsement from interviewees. *"This is a small office, but it has great guys with lots of experience,"* noted peers. A popular choice for referrals, the group is active in both litigation and noncontentious work and assists clients with a range of employment and labor matters.
The Lawyers: Both name partners, **Jeffrey Kasle** and **Gary St Peter**, were recommended by peers for their knowledge and expertise.
The Clients: The firm acts for a wide selection of employers, both with and without unions, ranging from major, publicly owned companies to smaller and medium-sized private companies.

LITIGATION

Rhode Island
Leading firms
(Litigation: General Commercial)

1	**ADLER POLLOCK & SHEEHAN PC** *Providence*
	EDWARDS & ANGELL LLP *Providence*
	HINCKLEY, ALLEN & SNYDER LLP *Providence*
2	**BLISH & CAVANAGH LLP** *Providence*
	DUFFY SWEENEY & SCOTT, LTD *Providence*
	PARTRIDGE SNOW & HAHN LLP *Providence*
3	**CARROLL, KELLY & MURPHY** *Providence*
	HIGGINS, CAVANAGH & COONEY LLP *Providence*

Firms are listed alphabetically in each band.

Band 1

Adler Pollock & Sheehan PC
See firm details p.1571
The Firm: This is *"the best practice in Rhode Island, with a long-standing tradition in commercial litigation,"* according to many of our interviewees. The firm continues to rule the market with its large team of full-time litigators. Its lawyers are second to none when it comes to aggressive trial proceedings, but they are acknowledged to be equally keen on preventing lawsuits in the first place. They are well versed in pre-litigation counseling, claim evaluation and assessment, arbitration, and other dispute resolution techniques. The practice has enjoyed a successful year, which raised its profile on the national stage. Its recent record of prominent cases includes: Fraioli v Lemcke; Southern Union Company v Patrick Lynch, and Southern

GENERAL COMMERCIAL

Union Gas Co v Rhode Island Division of Public Utilities and Carriers.
The Lawyers: **John Tarantino** (see p.1570) has enjoyed a stellar year that has brought him greater national prominence. He is described by peers as an *"excellent litigator, but above all a gentlemen,"* while his clients consider him *"the number one trial lawyer and the best negotiator in this neck of the woods."* His recent work of note includes the defense of the Economic Development Corporation against a developer's claim. Tarantino frequently works in tandem with **Patricia Rocha** (see p.1570), who is said by clients to have *"tremendous ability"* and to *"provide advice on a par with leading lawyers nationwide."* Rocha boasts a national litigation practice and is one of the exclusive counsels to Dow Chemical, to which she provides a broad range of legal advice. *"You don't want to fight"* **David Wollin** (see p.1570), said clients. Valued for his

Rhode Island
Leading individuals
(Litigation: General Commercial)

[1] **CAVANAGH Joseph** *Blish & Cavanagh*, Providence
  PETROS Gerald *Hinckley Allen*, Providence
  SNOW Stephen *Partridge Snow*, Providence
  TARANTINO John *Adler Pollock*, Providence
[2] **DEMARIA Gerald** *Higgins Cavanagh*, Providence
  DUFFY Robert *Duffy Sweeney & Scott*, Providence
  FREEL Mark *Edwards & Angell*, Providence
  POGUE Mark *Edwards & Angell*, Providence
  ROCHA Patricia *Adler Pollock*, Providence
  SCOTT Craig *Duffy & Sweeney*, Providence
  WOLLIN David *Adler Pollock*, Providence
[3] **FLANDERS Robert** *Hinckley Allen*, Providence
  GRIMM William *Hinckley Allen*, Providence
  KELLY Joseph *Carroll Kelly*, Providence
  MCNAMARA Neal *Holland & Knight*, Providence
  PELCZARSKI Karen *Blish & Cavanagh*, Providence

Up-and-coming individuals
  BUSH Christine *Duffy & Sweeney*, Providence

Individuals are listed alphabetically in each band.

hard work, considerable knowledge and focus, according to one client, "*He comes down on you like a Talmudic scholar. Very honest, very fast, he seems almost timid, but knows exactly how to pull out the hammer.*" He acted recently for Atlantic Richfield in its important lead paint pigment case involving a lawsuit by the Attorney General.
The Clients: The team advises major national and international corporates, as well as publicly owned companies and governmental institutions.

Edwards & Angell, LLP

The Firm: This firm is a serious player in the market, agreed commentators, with a "*great team and great connections.*" Large corporate clients were particularly keen to take advantage of the firm's national network of offices and the group's "*outstanding hands-on experience.*" It has considerable clout in a range of commercial litigation, with IPL, shareholders' and contractual disputes, products liability and financial services litigation all identified as areas of particular strength. Recent highlights include a dispute involving a manufacturer of building products, which was related to four hotel sites in New England.
The Lawyers: **Mark Freel** continues to attract enthusiastic recommendations from clients. One client in particular keeps returning to Freel because he is "*extremely thorough in his preparation, grasps the details quickly and gets to the heart of the matter.*" He recently handled a substantial shareholders' dispute involving a large family-owned business. "*Clever and able*" **Mark Pogue** "*knows how to handle issues and he is always available – he's as good as it gets,*" according to his clients. He has acted for Janel Russell Designs in a number of copyright infringement cases.
The Clients: The team serves a range of clients,

from major national and international corporates to family-owned businesses. On the IPL front, the firm continues to represent a number of prominent jewelry businesses.

Hinckley, Allen & Snyder LLP

The Firm: One of the three big names in the market, the firm is a major competitor with a great reputation for all types of litigation. This is said to be due to the quality of the team and a "*massive scope of experience*" that stretches far beyond the more run-of-the-mill corporate and commercial litigation. Particular praise was reserved for its work in the medical, environmental and IP sectors. Other typical work includes corporate control issues, derivative claims, lender liability, and condemnation and regulatory matters. Recent highlights include the team's recent appearance in CPI v State of Rhode Island and City of Providence. The market noted the departure of Robert Corrente this year. However, it was not felt that even the loss of such a talented attorney could seriously dent the strength of this exceptional team.
The Lawyers: **Gerald Petros** has undoubtedly become the most prominent lawyer in the practice and a serious force in the market, following the departure of Robert Corrente, who leaves to become a US Attorney. A "*strong business litigator,*" he is admired for "*analyzing cases extremely well*" and "*exploiting his opponents' weaknesses well.*" Former judge **Robert Flanders** is a recent high-profile addition to the team. He is expected to make his mark quickly and, say peers, "*attract major clients to the firm.*" Sources also praised "*fine attorney*" **William Grimm**.
The Clients: The firm acts for national and local businesses, including banks and insurers, retailers, universities, and chemical and pharmaceutical companies.

Band 2

Blish & Cavanagh LLP

The Firm: According to commentators, this is "*one of the great litigation boutiques, with a number of good people.*" Although it was founded with the aim of providing first-class assistance in trial proceedings, it has since broadened and developed a great deal, and now offers its clients more comprehensive legal expertise. Litigation, however, remains its strongest suit and the team boasts lengthy experience of appearing for clients before both federal and state trial and appellate courts in Rhode Island, Massachusetts and Connecticut. It focuses on commercial and business litigation, antitrust, securities and environmental disputes, and construction and insurance law.
The Lawyers: Founding partner **Joseph Cavanagh** is "*clearly a leading name and an excellent lawyer – he deserves a top ranking,*" said interviewees. He advises on a broad range of

complex litigation, but is perhaps particularly known for representing media clients. Peers also praised **Karen Pelczarski**, who predominantly acts in business, commercial and tort disputes.
The Clients: The firm acts for individuals, partnerships, local firms and large national corporations.

Duffy Sweeney & Scott Ltd

The Firm: Clients heaped praise on the individual lawyers of this "*highly professional and sensible*" outfit. However, they were also keen to point out that the stars enjoy the support of a "*great team of people, well respected in the community, with a pretty good spread of ages and expertise.*" The team may be smaller than some of the other top addresses in Providence, but in the opinion of clients this can be an advantage as it has enabled it to develop a thorough focus and knowledge of the local market. It certainly hasn't hampered its efforts to attract a broad client base, which now includes firms with operations in South America, the UK, Continental Europe and Asia. Typical recent work has included trade regulation, broker/customer securities litigation, shareholder disputes, intellectual property, fraud and construction cases.
The Lawyers: **Robert Duffy** is "*a class act.*" "*Not only does he understand the law, but he is also a great strategist which always helps us to prevail,*" said one client. This view was echoed by a number of others, who highlighted a number of excellent qualities. He, "*always keeps a sharp eye on our bottom line and our interests and never develops his own agenda at the expense of everyone else.*" **Craig Scott** was also recommended by clients and peers alike. His practice spans general commercial, corporate and patent litigation. A newcomer to the tables, **Christine Bush** won strong endorsement from the market as "*a skilful, young and talented lawyer.*"
The Clients: The team advises companies in the TMT, manufacturing, pharmaceutical and financial services sectors, including a number from the Fortune 500.

Partridge Snow & Hahn LLP

The Firm: This is a team that does "*good-quality litigation work and represents its clients zealously,*" said observers. They also highlighted the firm's in-depth knowledge and dedication to the local market. The firm's reach does not end with Rhode Island, however, as it regularly acts for clients before the state and federal courts of Massachusetts and other states. A highly experienced team of 17 lawyers litigates practically any matter, from environmental, real estate, construction, and land use cases, to labor and employment, antitrust, unfair trade practices, and banking and securities disputes. Last year saw the team particularly busy in the IP sector, where it successfully defended an insurer against a jewelry manufacturer's claim. The group's work in medical litigation, on behalf of doctors and hospitals, also attracted praise.

The Lawyers: Stephen Snow focuses on complex federal litigation and IP. He has recently enjoyed a number of successful defenses on behalf of major mortgage banks, as well as for one of his prime clients, Blue Cross Blue Shield, in a number of class actions.

The Clients: Banks, financial institutions and insurance companies form the largest part of the team's client base. It also regularly represents colleges and universities, hospitals, insurance companies, governmental agencies and other large publicly owned businesses.

Band 3

Carroll, Kelly & Murphy

The Firm: Interviewees commended the expertise of this team in complex commercial litigation. Its experience in products liability and insurance defense, in particular, attracted praise. The group is active, however, in most aspects of business litigation and serves a wide range of

corporate clients.

The Lawyers: Joseph Kelly is still seen as the main driving force behind the firm's prominence in this field. His long-standing expertise and extensive client contacts are considered invaluable to the team.

The Clients: The firm acts for local, regional and international firms, public companies and family-owned businesses.

Higgins, Cavanagh & Cooney LLP

The Firm: This team was particularly endorsed by the market for its skill in litigation, and especially insurance defense. However, interviewees were keen to point out that "*there is a whole team there*" able to advise on complex issues. The firm has a strong focus on civil litigation and deals with a range of matters, from construction and environmental law, healthcare disputes and general corporate and commercial litigation, to products liability, PI and professional negligence. A recent success was its role in Raimbeault v Takeuchi Mfg, where the plaintiff's design expert was excluded from the proceedings.

The Lawyers: "*Good and well-established*" attorney **Gerald DeMaria** was commended by peers for his wealth of expertise. He is said to have a particular flair for insurance defense and PI cases, though he also takes on other kinds of complex commercial litigation, including products liability.

The Clients: The firm advises a broad selection of clients, including manufacturers of industrial tools, medical equipment and automobiles, owners and developers of commercial and residential property, engineers, architects, industry associations and financial and insurance companies.

Other Notable Practitioners

Neal McNamara (see p.1569) of Holland & Knight LLP was extensively praised by interviewees for his "*knowledge, competence and good rapport with clients.*" Although very active in employment law, he is seen as an "*outstanding generalist litigator.*"

REAL ESTATE

Rhode Island
Leading firms (Real Estate)
[1] HINCKLEY, ALLEN & SNYDER LLP *Providence*
HOLLAND & KNIGHT LLP *Providence*
[2] ADLER POLLOCK & SHEEHAN PC *Providence*
EDWARDS & ANGELL LLP *Providence*

Leading individuals (Real Estate)
[1] TRACY David *Holland & Knight, Providence*
[2] BATTY Jerome *Hinckley Allen, Providence*
ROGERS Charles *Edwards & Angell, Providence*
RUBIN David *Hinckley Allen, Providence*
[3] DISTEFANO Joseph *Adler Pollock, Providence*
NOONAN Elizabeth *Adler Pollock, Providence*
STOLZMAN Robert *Adler Pollock, Providence*
Firms and Individuals are listed alphabetically in each band.

Band 1

Hinckley, Allen & Snyder LLP

The Firm: This firm is one of the first ports of call in the state for major real estate developments and financings. It assists a number of developers with a variety of matters, from zoning and construction permitting to condominium creation and conversion. Financing and loan restructuring are other strong suits, and the lawyers work closely with the firm's tax and corporate teams to provide clients with all the essential services under one roof. Demonstrating its national reach, the team continues to assist a well-recognized Fortune 100 retailer in

its national real estate acquisition and development program. On the land use and permitting front, the team has acted on all matters connected with a 270,000-sq-ft mixed-use development located in Providence. Financing highlights, meanwhile, include representing the lead lender in connection with a syndicated $100 million revolving credit facility secured on 25 office, residential and industrial properties located across 12 states.

The Lawyers: Jerome Batty is a highly experienced practitioner, well versed in both transactional and regulatory matters. Interviewees also recommended **David Rubin** for his knowledge of commercial real estate and banking law.

The Clients: The firm serves major national, regional and local developers, as well as banks and insurance companies focused on construction and real estate financing. It recently represented the buyer in the $57.8 million acquisition of The Campus at Marlborough, and advised on the redevelopment and sale of the Centennial Technology Center, both in Massachusetts.

Holland & Knight LLP

See firm details p.1352

The Firm: The firm won universal praise, and was strongly recommended by clients who consider it a "*great team with excellent support throughout.*" The practice is organized on a nationwide basis, and so the group in Rhode Island can take advantage of the firm's impressive national and international resources. It handles the spectrum of real estate law, including

land use and environmental work, retail and office development, leasing and tax matters. Over the past year, it was particularly busy in the retail sector and in condominium development, areas where the team is considered especially strong. Recent highlights include negotiating an anchor tenant lease for the Woburn Mall in Woburn, Massachusetts. The team also assisted Brian Bucci with the Middletown Plaza project, which involved the creation of multilayered sandwiched ground leases.

The Lawyers: Hailed as "*the best real estate lawyer in Rhode Island,*" **David Tracy** (see p.1570) continues to top the tables. Clients could not praise him enough: as one put it, he is a "*great negotiator and a very detail-oriented person, but he also has the ability to see the bigger picture.*" Another added that "*he gets to the jugular and sees the issues immediately: you're not going to need anyone else with him.*" Tracy recently acted for Woloohojian financings in a major subsidized housing transaction.

The Clients: Order of St Benedict, Woloohojian Financing and Brian Bucci are among the firm's real estate clients.

Band 2

Adler Pollock & Sheehan PC

See firm details p.1571

The Firm: The firm has a good reputation for tenaciously representing its clients in all aspects of real estate law, including purchases and sales, development, leasing and financing. However, given the firm's top-class name for trial work, it is hardly surprising that land use and real estate litigation should also contribute towards its profile. Its dedicated team acted for Rhode Island Economic Development Corporation in the development of Rhode Island's largest industrial park, which is located on the site of a former navy base at Davisville. Other recent projects include acting for the state's major kidney dialysis group in its acquisition of properties in Tiverton, Pawtucket and Providence.

The Lawyers: According to interviewees, **Joseph Di Stefano** (see p.1569) is *"a statesman who attracts major clients."* He possesses a wealth of expertise and was closely involved in the redevelopment of downtown Providence. *"Talented"* **Beth Noonan** (see p.1569) was hailed as *"a rising star"* for land use and real estate litigation. Another of the firm's rising stars is **Robert Stolzman** (see p.1570), who was said to be gain-

ing prominence for his *"expertise in creative financing transactions involving state agencies."*
The Clients: The firm acts for individuals, family-owned businesses and large multinationals. It advises firms such as Brooks Pharmacy and Dow Chemical on commercial and retail developments and assists them with state and local regulation.

Edwards & Angell, LLP

The Firm: The firm's undisputed capacity in the corporate and commercial arena stands it in good stead in real estate, especially when it comes to transactional work. The team is experienced in sales and acquisitions, development, financings and regulatory matters. It has worked closely with the firm's nationwide network of offices to handle a number of major projects. For example, it has advised various developers on the construction and financing of neighbor-

hood shopping facilities (typically ranging from $5 million to $20 million) in Massachusetts, Rhode Island, Ohio, Florida and California. The group also assisted a developer with negotiating ground leases in the Capital Center in Providence and the subsequent development and financing of $50 million and $75 million projects.

The Lawyers: According to peers, **Charles Rogers** is a *"top real estate lawyer."* His technical knowledge was highlighted, and is said to make him *"a good choice for cutting-edge projects."*
The Clients: The team acts for individual landowners and developers, national lending institutions, Fortune 500 companies, municipalities, closely held limited liability companies and other institutional investors.

Leaders in Rhode Island

BATTY, Jerome
Hinckley, Allen & Snyder LLP, Providence 401 274 2000
Recommended in Real Estate

BROOKS, Robert
Adler Pollock & Sheehan PC, Providence 401 274 7200
rbrooks@apslaw.com
Recommended in Employment
Practice Areas: Labor and employment, alternative dispute resolution, construction, governmental and legislative.
Prof. Memberships: Rhode Island Bar Association, Labor Law Committee.
Career: Partner and Chairman of the firm's Labor and Employment Law Group, he represents management in all facets of labor relations and employment law in the public and private sectors. He has successfully represented employers in employment discrimination matters, and counsels employers on complex administrative law issues. He regularly handles collective bargaining negotiations and the defense of union organizing campaigns.
Personal: Former Deputy Chief of Staff to the Mayor of Providence.

BUSH, Christine
Duffy, Sweeney & Scott Ltd, Providence 401 455 0700
Recommended in Litigation

CARLOTTI, Stephen
Hinckley, Allen & Snyder LLP, Providence 401 274 2000
Recommended in Corporate/M&A

CAVANAGH Jr, Joseph
Blish & Cavanagh, LLP, Providence 401 831 8900
Recommended in Litigation

DEMARIA, Gerald
Higgins, Cavanagh & Cooney LLP, Providence
401 272 3500
Recommended in Litigation

DISTEFANO, Joseph R
Adler Pollock & Sheehan PC, Providence 401 274 7200
jdistefano@apslaw.com
Recommended in Real Estate
Practice Areas: Business and corporate, governmental and legislative, real estate.
Career: Partner who handles major commercial real estate transactions. He was instrumental in the redevelopment of Downtown Providence, and as one of the originators of the Capital Center Project, he spearheaded the development of several major downtown office buildings.
Personal: Previous State Senator and President of the Senate. Chair of the RI Board of Elections for over 15 years, former Chair of the RI Convention Center Authority, and current Chair of the Board of Trustees of Salve Regina University. Also serves on the New England Advisory Board of Sovereign Bank.

DUFFELL, David
Edwards & Angell, LLP, Providence 401 274 9200
Recommended in Corporate/M&A

DUFFY, Robert
Duffy, Sweeney & Scott Ltd, Providence 401 455 0700
Recommended in Litigation

FARRELL, Margaret
Hinckley, Allen & Snyder LLP, Providence 401 274 2000
Recommended in Corporate/M&A

FLANDERS Jr, Robert
Hinckley, Allen & Snyder LLP, Providence 401 274 2000
Recommended in Litigation

FREEL, Mark
Edwards & Angell, LLP, Providence 401 274 9200
Recommended in Litigation

GAMBOLI, Michael
Partridge Snow & Hahn LLP, Providence 401 861 8200
Recommended in Employment

GRAHAM, Christopher
Edwards & Angell, LLP, Providence 401 274 9200
Recommended in Corporate/M&A

GRIMM, William
Hinckley, Allen & Snyder LLP, Providence 401 274 2000
Recommended in Litigation

HAHN, James
Partridge Snow & Hahn LLP, Providence 401 861 8200
Recommended in Corporate/M&A

JOCELYN, Richard
Hinckley, Allen & Snyder LLP, Providence 401 274 2000
Recommended in Employment

JOHNSON, V Duncan
Edwards & Angell, LLP, Providence 401 274 9200
Recommended in Corporate/M&A

KASLE, Jeffrey
St Peter & Kasle, Providence 401 453 4330
Recommended in Employment

KELLY, Joseph
Carroll, Kelly & Murphy, Providence 401 331 7272
Recommended in Litigation

KINDER, Daniel
Little, Medeiros, Kinder, Bulman & Whitney PC, Providence 401 272 8080
Recommended in Employment

MCNAMARA, Neal
Holland & Knight LLP, Providence 401 751 8500
neal.mcnamara@hklaw.com
Recommended in Employment, Litigation
Practice Areas: Partner in the firm's Litigation Section, focusing on employment law and general commercial litigation. His employment law practice focuses on both litigation and counseling. He has successfully handled matters involving all major employment related statutes, including Title VII, ADEA, the ADA, FMLA, and ERISA, as well as state law employment issues and non-compete agreements. A major portion of his practice is devoted to counseling clients on a wide range of employee issues in order to prevent matters from reaching litigation. He has developed employment handbooks and policies, conducted internal investigations and regularly conducts seminars on employment law topics.

NOONAN, Elizabeth
Adler Pollock & Sheehan PC, Providence 401 274 7200
bnoonan@apslaw.com
Recommended in Real Estate
Practice Areas: Real estate, environmental, governmental and legislative, litigation.

Prof. Memberships: RI Trial Lawyers Association.

Career: Partner who represents developers of commercial and residential properties in all phases of development, from acquisition to permitting and construction. She has been involved in several significant property rights cases. She also handles commercial, tax and construction litigation, and has represented national and local clients in successfully challenging state and local tax levies. Major clients include Dow Chemical Company and Brooks Pharmacy.

Personal: Past President of RI Women's Bar Association; former delegate to the Democratic National Convention.

PANNONE, Gary R
Holland & Knight LLP, Providence
401 751 8500
gary.pannone@hklaw.com
Recommended in Corporate/M&A

Practice Areas: Mr Pannone is a Partner in the Business Law Section and also serves as the Executive Partner in the Providence office of Holland & Knight LLP. His practice concentrates in the areas of closely held business, mergers and acquisitions and healthcare matters. Pannone serves as general counsel to many of his corporate clients and during the course of his career he has acted as Solicitor to several municipalities in Rhode Island. He is experienced in representing emerging and established companies, negotiating and structuring mergers, acquisitions and joint ventures as well as providing counsel regarding corporate governance issues.

PARTRIDGE, John
Partridge Snow & Hahn LLP,
Providence 401 861 8200
Recommended in Corporate/M&A

PELCZARSKI, Karen
Blish & Cavanagh, LLP, Providence
401 831 8900
Recommended in Litigation

PETROS, Gerald
Hinckley, Allen & Snyder LLP,
Providence 401 274 2000
Recommended in Litigation

POGUE, Mark
Edwards & Angell, LLP, Providence
401 274 9200
Recommended in Employment, Litigation

ROCHA, Patricia
Adler Pollock & Sheehan PC,
Providence 401 274 7200
procha@apslaw.com
Recommended in Litigation

Practice Areas: Litigation, labor and employment, criminal/white collar defense, healthcare.

Prof. Memberships: Association of Trial Lawyers of America; RI Trial Lawyers Association.

Career: Partner and Chair of the firm's Litigation Group. She has tried and defended cases ranging from product liability and toxic tort, employment discrimination, redistricting legislation, to bribery, wire fraud, honest services and conspiracy. She has also successfully represented healthcare providers in acquiring regulatory approvals. A prolific contributor to scholarly journals, she has co-authored an important national text on trial advocacy and produced a collection of model closing arguments for defense attorneys.

ROGERS Jr, Charles
Edwards & Angell, LLP, Providence
401 274 9200
Recommended in Real Estate

RUBIN, David
Hinckley, Allen & Snyder LLP,
Providence 401 274 2000
Recommended in Real Estate

SCOTT, Craig
Duffy, Sweeney & Scott Ltd, Providence
401 455 0700
Recommended in Litigation

SKEFFINGTON, James
Edwards & Angell, LLP, Providence
401 274 9200
Recommended in Corporate/M&A

SNOW, Stephen
Partridge Snow & Hahn LLP,
Providence 401 861 8200
Recommended in Litigation

ST PETER, Gary
St Peter & Kasle, Providence
401 453 4330
Recommended in Employment

STOLZMAN, Robert
Adler Pollock & Sheehan PC,
Providence 401 274 7200
rstolzman@apslaw.com
Recommended in Real Estate

Practice Areas: Real estate, business and corporate, governmental and legislative, public finance.

Prof. Memberships: American College of Real Estate Attorneys.

Career: Partner who concentrates his practice in land use, real estate transactions, small business and governmental relations. He has shepherded projects for national and local clients through regulatory and governmental agencies. He is a registered lobbyist for trade associations and private businesses. He has drafted and assisted with the passage of a wide range of business legislation. He is counsel to the RI Economic Development Corporation and Secretary of its Board of Directors.

TARANTINO, John
Adler Pollock & Sheehan PC,
Providence 401 274 7200
jtarantino@apslaw.com
Recommended in Litigation

Practice Areas: Litigation, alternative dispute resolution, products liability/toxic tort, criminal/white collar defense, insurance, appellate.

Prof. Memberships: Defense Research Institute, American Judicature Society, National Association of Bar Presidents, American College of Trial Lawyers, International Academy of Trial Lawyers.

Career: President of the firm and Partner in the Litigation Group. He has been counsel in a number of high profile, precedent-setting cases, successfully representing local, national and international clients in sophisticated litigation matters, including matters of constitutional law for state government.

Personal: Named among top 10 attorneys in the nation in 2002 by Lawyers Weekly USA.

TRACY, David
Holland & Knight LLP, Providence
401 751 8500
david.tracy@hklaw.com
Recommended in Real Estate

Practice Areas: Partner in the firm's Real Estate Section. His practice involves all areas and aspects of commercial real estate, with particular emphasis on malls, shopping centers, office and mixed use developments, commercial real estate, commercial leasing, condominiums, construction contracts, construction and permanent financing as well as debt restructuring. He represents numerous developers in the acquisition, development and sale of various types of commercial real estate including office buildings, shopping centers and other retail projects as well as lenders in the financing of such projects. He has also represented institutional investors in various Rhode Island and national real estate transactions.

WHELAN, Joseph
Hinckley, Allen & Snyder LLP,
Providence 401 274 2000
Recommended in Employment

WOLLIN, David A
Adler Pollock & Sheehan PC,
Providence 401 274 7200
dwollin@apslaw.com
Recommended in Litigation

Practice Areas: Litigation, appellate, products liability/toxic tort, insurance, business and corporate, environmental.

Prof. Memberships: RI Bar Association, Supreme Court Bench/Bar Committee.

Career: Partner and Vice President of the firm, he handles all aspects of civil litigation, including mediations, arbitrations, trials and appellate proceedings in federal and state courts. He has successfully represented a major cigarette manufacturer in a series of cases brought by smokers seeking damages resulting from smoking-related injuries. He obtained one of the largest jury awards in RI Superior Court in 2002. A prolific writer, he recently co-authored an updated treatise on RI's civil and appellate practice.

ADLER POLLOCK & SHEEHAN P.C.

THE FIRM

Founding Partners: Walter Adler (1896-1991)
Bernard R Pollock (1926-1984)
William J Sheehan (1917-1999)
Managing Partner: Mark O Denehy

Number of attorneys: 65

FIRM OVERVIEW: For the past 45 years, Adler Pollock & Sheehan P.C. has delivered client-focused, business law services designed to achieve cost-effective solutions for today's complex challenges. AP&S successfully combines the depth and breadth of expertise of a large law firm with the advantages of responsive and direct personal service by partners found in smaller firms. Adler Pollock & Sheehan is a full service law firm featuring a sophisticated Corporate Practice and a nationally-renowned Litigation Practice. AP&S services clients in 43 jurisdictions throughout New England, across the country, and around the world.

Network: AP&S is the Rhode Island member of the State Capital Global Law Firm Group, an organization of independent law firms in every capital city and commercial center in the United States and abroad. Membership is significant since it is by invitation only to firms who have demonstrated the highest quality service and industry leadership. (Member firms practice independently and not in a relationship for the joint practice of law).

MAIN AREAS OF PRACTICE:

Litigation: Among the largest and most experienced in New England, the AP&S Litigation Department is recognized nationally for its high quality and cost effectiveness. With over 30 litigators and a dozen para-professionals, AP&S has assembled the largest litigators group in Rhode Island, which includes a diverse and broad-based civil and white-collar criminal practice. AP&S serves as national coordinating counsel in mass-tort litigation. Recent high profile cases include the landmark lead paint lawsuit brought by the State of Rhode Island Attorney General in which the firm successfully defended the paint manufacturers. Additionally, the firm defended a major tobacco company in the first New England case brought by the family of a deceased smoker. AP&S was selected as one of 18 firms internationally to be listed as Dow Chemical's selected trial firms.

Labor & Employment: The Labor & Employment Group represents and counsels public and private sector employers in connection with virtually every aspect of the employment relationship, including discrimination and wrongful discharge matters, labor-management relations and collective bargaining. AP&S has successfully represented clients before all federal and state labor and employment agencies, including the EEOC, NLRB, OSHA and the US Department of Labor.

Business & Corporate: The Business & Corporate Group is committed to understanding each client's business, offering solutions for executing business plans and proactively addressing all legal needs, including the organization and structuring of shareholder relations, securities, tax planning, bank and venture capital financing, protection and licensing of intellectual property, product distribution, employee relations, acquisitions, succession planning, execution of exit strategies and resolution of shareholder disputes.

Healthcare: The Healthcare Group serves as counsel to New England's premier hospitals and healthcare facilities, including freestanding surgi-centers and nursing homes. The firm's attorneys also represent regional and national hospital networks on interstate healthcare acquisitions as well as provide defense to healthcare providers on compliance and fraud investigations.

HEAD OFFICE

RHODE ISLAND
One Citizens Plaza, 8th Floor, **Providence**, RI 02903-1345
Tel: 401 274 7200 **Fax:** 401 751 0604
Website: www.apslaw.com

BRANCH OFFICES

MASSACHUSETTS
175 Federal Street, **Boston**, MA 02110
Tel: 617 482 0600 **Fax:** 617 482 0604

NEW HAMPSHIRE
800 Lake Street, P.O. Box 536, **Bristol**, NH 03222
Tel: 603 744 1021 **Fax:** 603 744 2799

Environmental: The Environmental Group boasts nationally-recognized lawyers who have helped define environmental standards in New England. AP&S has served as lead counsel for many cases with long-term effects on current environmental law - from the defense of multi-million dollar EPA fines and compliance actions to the initiation and management of Superfund cost recovery actions for Fortune 100 companies of over 100 parties.

Real Estate: The Real Estate Group represents developers, multi-national corporations, family-owned businesses, contractors and individuals in every aspect of industrial, commercial and residential real estate, including the permitting, financing, leasing, and development of major retail commercial centers, office building, golf courses, assisted living facilities, hotels, apartments and condominiums.

CLIENTS: The core of the AP&S approach is the personal attention each client receives. The firm's ability to create and execute winning strategies has earned AP&S national recognition and a growing roster of loyal clients, from publicly-held Fortune 500 and Fortune 100 companies to small businesses, individuals and organizations. The firm represents clients such as The Dow Chemical Company, Atlantic Richfield, Cookson America, Textron Inc., Hasbro, Inc. and Blue Cross/Blue Shield Association among others.

CONTENTS: Corporate/M&A p.1572; Employment p.1574; Litigation p.1575; Real Estate p.1577; Individuals' Profiles p.1579; Firm Profiles p.1584.

How lawyers are ranked

The opinions we gather from clients — mainly from in-house lawyers but also from other purchasers of legal services — are balanced by opinions from colleagues and competitors. Together, they provide two different perspectives — an all-round view — and biased viewpoints cancel each other out.

CORPORATE/M&A

South Carolina
Leading firms (Corporate/M&A)

1. **HAYNSWORTH SINKLER BOYD PA** *Charleston*
   MCNAIR LAW FIRM PA *Columbia*
   NELSON MULLINS RILEY *Columbia*
   NEXSEN PRUET, LLC *Columbia*
   WYCHE, BURGESS, FREEMAN *Greenville*
2. **BUIST, MOORE, SMYTHE, MCGEE PA** *Charleston*
   LEATHERWOOD WALKER TODD *Greenville*
   WARREN & SINKLER LLP *Charleston*
   WOMBLE CARLYLE SANDRIDGE *Greenville*

Leading individuals (Corporate/M&A)

1. **CURRIE John** *McNair Law Firm, Columbia*
   KING George *Haynsworth Sinkler, Charleston*
   MENZIE Edward *Nexsen Pruet, Columbia*
   WARREN III John *Warren & Sinkler, Charleston*
2. **DIXON Augustus** *Nelson Mullins, Columbia*
   HALL Cary *Wyche Burgess, Greenville*
   HOGUE P Mason *Nelson Mullins, Columbia*
   KNIGHT G Marcus *Nexsen Pruet, Columbia*
   SHOEMAKER James *Wyche Burgess, Greenville*
3. **AMSTUTZ Eric** *Wyche Burgess, Greenville*
   BLAKE Joseph *Haynsworth Sinkler, Greenville*
   BOYD William *Haynsworth Sinkler, Charleston*
   FEW Richard *Leatherwood Walker, Greenville*
   FRITZE Daniel *Nelson Mullins, Columbia*
   GRAYSON Neil *Nelson Mullins, Greenville*
   MUSSER William *McNair Law Firm, Columbia*

Firms and individuals are listed alphabetically in each band.

Band 1

Haynsworth Sinkler Boyd PA

The Firm: Market commentators heavily endorsed the group for its economic development incentive work and its traditional strength in bank formation and regulation. Taking advantage of the state's drive to expand university-based research, the firm has expanded its client base in the technology arena over the past year. Industry sources praised transactional capabilities displayed by these attorneys, and pointed to them as tough competitors for the market's most complex M&A transactions. Highlights include working on the economic incentives for the creation of the International Centre for Automotive Research and working with USC Medical School and the two main state hospitals in a $160 million health science deal.

The Lawyers: Known for his work in securities and corporate governance, **George King** is a popular attorney, respected for his professionalism. Peers praised him for his expertise in working with national and community banks. **Joseph Blake** was the lead on the collaborative health science deal involving the USC. He is widely admired for his corporate governance and financing work with businesses in the healthcare sector, while his colleague **William Boyd** continues to work on the complex transactions that arise out of his mixed corporate and real estate practice.

The Clients: The firm continues to represent Sonoco Products, Synalloy Corporation and Piggly Wiggly Carolina alongside banks, hospitals, manufacturing, healthcare and technology companies.

McNair Law Firm PA

The Firm: Clients regard the "*strong transactional capabilities*" of this firm as the main reason it remains a top player in the corporate and commercial fields. The group is renowned for its traditional strengths in bank lending and bond financing, as well as being closely identified with its government work. A further area of expertise is the technology market. Here clients have praised the lawyers for their "*willingness to work with startup firms*" and their impressive long-term commitment. As one client stated: "*They have been with us from start to finish.*" Recent highlights for the firm include advising on the sale of the Hilton Head Island resort Sea Pines. The group also benefits from its merger with Bethea, Jordan & Griffin, which adds two new offices on the coast. Increased transactional work from the now strengthened real estate practice is a further boon to this firm.

The Lawyers: **John Withers Currie** "*clearly deserves his top-tier status*" according to peers. His reputation as a top transactional lawyer and his "*engaging personality*" continue to attract clients to the firm. He was principal lawyer on the Sea Pines resort sale, and assisted on the sale of two large technology companies. Clients are impressed with his involvement and interest in their business, and praised him for being "*as much a businessman as he is a lawyer.*" Clients also commended **William Musser** for his finance work, appreciating his knowledge of the law and attention to detail. Highlights this year include a $100 million financing deal for a generating company, and representing a state agency in setting up a new hospital.

The Clients: The utility company SCANA continues to be a major client for the firm. Others include banks and other financial institutions, government agencies and businesses in the construction, healthcare and technology industries.

Nelson Mullins Riley & Scarborough LLP
See firm details p.1584

The Firm: This ambitious firm has an expanding corporate practice in the captive insurance, technology and venture capital areas. Recently the group has been involved in helping set up a state venture capital fund, and has also been assisting with the Angel Investors networks for high net-worth individuals wanting to invest in venture capital businesses. Clients point to its "*impeccable reputation,*" especially for M&A work, while peers recognize that it "*has the true securities expertise*" necessary to take on complex matters. The team's M&A work has been increasing, and ranges from $30-40 million deals to those in the vicinity of $150 million. While some interviewees point to a stronger out-of-state corporate practice, clients report that this only lends extra support to the South Carolina team. Such resources especially suit clients who want a firm that is sufficiently large to give the necessary range of legal advice or, as one client put it, "*one-stop shopping.*"

The Lawyers: Augustus Dixon (see p.1579) impresses with his wide-ranging skills in outsourcing, bankruptcies, investments and M&A. Clients praised his skills in crisis management as corporate counsel in bankruptcy proceedings where he does "*a monumental job keeping everyone happy.*" The "*extremely intelligent*" **Mason Hogue** (see p.1581) divides his time between technology and general commercial matters. Clients praise his negotiation skills and encourage others to "*bring him in whenever there is an impasse.*" **Daniel Fritze** (see p.1580) has been singled out for his work in corporate governance and M&A. He has been impressing clients, who are "*amazed with his feel for some of the more complicated financial details*" of transactions. Such clients "*rate him a ten out of ten.*" Recently relocated from the group's Atlanta banking practice, **Neil Grayson** (see p.1580) is endorsed for his finesse with public offerings and banking work. He also works in the venture capital area, where industry sources say "*he knows his field and he's easy to work with.*"

The Clients: Clients include the venture capital firm Trelys Funds and other firms in the technology industry, as well as healthcare, manufacturing, and pharmaceutical companies.

Nexsen Pruet LLC

See firm details p.1585

The Firm: Clients have said this firm has "*a commanding presence*" on the corporate scene, endorsing its advice as "*very thorough, very timely and complete.*" Recent changes in the law surrounding limited liability companies have stimulated the volume of domestications and reorganizing work, and have also contributed to an increase in M&A deals for the group. Industry sources see the practice as a "*very active representative of lenders*" and willingly refer banking work to them in instances of conflict.

The Lawyers: Edward Menzie (see p.1581) remains a very well-regarded practitioner of corporate law. He continues to excel in public/private finance transactions and the varied corporate work that arises out of his real estate practice. The "*incredibly organized*" **Marcus Knight** (see p.1581) has been active with regard to reorganizations of holding companies and complex restructurings. Peers admire his busy practice, while clients praise him for his knowledge of the law, and the swiftness of his work, describing him as "*spot on.*"

The Clients: The firm continues to represent financial institutions, manufacturers, wholesalers, and companies in the technology, transportation, and insurance industries.

Wyche, Burgess, Freeman & Parham PA

The Firm: This group moves up the table for its "*responsiveness, thoroughness and sheer intellectual horsepower.*" Though smaller than most of its direct rivals, its lawyers "*control a huge amount of capital business in Greenville,*" the strongest business center in South Carolina. The group is experienced in representing public companies in M&A, joint ventures and other corporate issues. Recent deals of note include another two major shelf registrations for financial groups, which illustrates the group's continued strength in this area. Peers appreciated the sophisticated advice provided; one noted: "*I would use them if I were picking someone to cover a complicated business case.*" Clients simply claim they are "*the premiere transaction firm in the upstate.*"

The Lawyers: Certified tax specialist **Cary Hall** continues to draw praise from peers, who say they "*think of him first*" when referring tax work in a conflict. "*Go-to lawyer*" **James Shoemaker** enjoys a high profile in banking and securities law. New to the tables this year is securities lawyer **Eric Amstutz**, recommended by clients for his intelligence and experience with public offerings.

The Clients: The group continues to represent Bowater, South Financial Group, the manufacturing company Milliken, as well as other financial institutions and development companies.

Band 2

Buist, Moore, Smythe, McGee PA

The Firm: Particularly strong in Charleston, this is a traditional South Carolina firm with a "*European feel,*" typified by its tendency to "*come at things in a different way*" from larger firms. Attorneys here apply their innovative thinking and commercial awareness to a full range of corporate services. A large part of the group's corporate work derives from the firm's thriving real estate practice in and around Charleston. This includes loan transactions and financing, where the group successfully represents both lenders and borrowers.

The Lawyers: Susan Smythe is head of the firm's business department, and also has an extensive real estate practice.

The Clients: Clients range from Fortune 500 companies to small businesses and individuals, mainly in the manufacturing, development and real estate areas.

Leatherwood Walker Todd & Mann PC

The Firm: A well-established firm, the group has cultivated a strong business presence in Greenville. A group of around 60 lawyers is well equipped to offer "*across the board*" corporate and business services to businesses in the area. This includes the formation of business entities, acquisitions and reorganizations. The group is also well versed in transactions providing economic incentives to businesses relocating or expanding in Greenville, as well as those looking to expand statewide.

The Lawyers: Regarded as the firm's leading corporate lawyer, the experienced **Richard Few** is fêted as "*an excellent transactions lawyer*" by peers.

The Clients: The firm has a well-established traditional client base in Greenville, including banks, financial institutions, manufacturing and family-owned businesses.

Warren & Sinkler LLP

The Firm: Sources agree that this firm has a presence in Charleston incommensurate with its small size. Clients who prefer more personal dealings with their lawyers found the firm impressive, enjoying the fact that they could deal with senior practitioners where there would be no danger of a conflict of interest. Clients also praised this firm for its attention to detail and communication skills; especially in its Sarbanes-Oxley Act and FCC review work.

The Lawyers: "*Clearly head and shoulders above others in the market,*" **John Warren** continues to work on large financing and tax transactions. Clients go to him for the structuring of complex deals, reporting: "*If Johnny is representing you, there is no doubt who's in charge.*"

The Clients: The group's client base includes insurance companies, property developers, small businesses, and it continues to represent major banks.

Womble Carlyle Sandridge & Rice PLLC

See firm details p.1402

The Firm: Since opening their Greenville office six years ago, this North Carolina firm has managed to establish a strong corporate practice in the area. Clients appreciated the "*great depth of skills*" within the local team, whom they praised as "*not just good lawyers but good people too.*" Backed up by the resources of a national practice, this is a firm that "*has the ability to reach out for resources as and when needed.*" The group handles M&A, financing and lending services, and was particularly noted for its transactional skills.

The Lawyers: Bankruptcy specialist Allen Grumbine is experienced in a broad range of transactions and lending work.

The Clients: Financial institutions, insurance companies, manufacturing and publishing companies are included in the client list.

EMPLOYMENT

South Carolina
Leading firms
(Employment: Mainly Defendant)

[1] FISHER & PHILLIPS LLP *Columbia*
OGLETREE, DEAKINS, NASH, SMOAK *Greenville*
[2] GIGNILLIAT, SAVITZ & BETTIS LLP *Columbia*
NELSON MULLINS RILEY *Columbia*
NEXSEN PRUET, LLC *Columbia*
[3] JACKSON LEWIS *Greenville*

Leading individuals
(Employment: Mainly Defendant)

[1] BETTIS Vance *Gignilliat Savitz, Columbia*
ELLZEY Daniel *Fisher & Phillips, Columbia*
SPETH II Charles *Ogletree Deakins, Columbia*
[2] DUBBERLY David *Nexsen Pruet, Columbia*
HARPER Sue *Nelson Mullins, Columbia*
PEARSON Jonathan *Fisher & Phillips, Columbia*
[3] CARROUTH Michael *Fisher & Phillips, Columbia*
MCWILLIAMS Susan *Nexsen Pruet, Columbia*
SATTERFIELD Andreas *Nelson Mullins, Greenville*
SAVITZ Stephen *Gignilliat Savitz, Columbia*
SMOAK Lewis *Ogletree Deakins, Greenville*
STEWART III J Hamilton *Ogletree Deakins, Greenville*
SUGGS Fred *Ogletree Deakins, Greenville*
WARREN J Steve *Jackson Lewis, Greenville*
YOUNG Kenneth *Nelson Mullins, Greenville*

Firms and individuals are listed alphabetically in each band.

Band 1

Fisher & Phillips LLP
See firm details p.630

The Firm: This national labor and employment specialist now has a strong presence in South Carolina through its acquisition of the boutique Columbia firm Ellzey & Brooks. There have been few changes to the group since the merger, and clients report it maintains its "*impeccable track record*" for both labor relation and employment discrimination litigation. Recent legal changes in the state have increased the group's preventative work on behalf of employers, and clients say that they are pleased with the "*proactive advice*." Clients also praised the lawyers' labor work, especially in arbitrations with unions and contract negotiations, while peers refer cases to them in times of conflict, as "*they are employment and labor specialists*."

The Lawyers: "*Dynamite*" lawyer **Daniel Ellzey** (see p.1580) has been praised by clients as "*a tireless worker and good strategist*" for his work on antiunion campaigns and restructurings. Industry sources identified **Jonathan Pearson**'s (see p.1582) intelligence and "*wide breadth of experience*" in all areas of labor and employment law, while clients recommended **Michael Carrouth** (see p.1579) for his skillful and sensible handling of employment disputes.

The Clients: State and local government entities, together with employers in the manufacturing, technology, banking, healthcare and insurance areas are among the clients.

Ogletree, Deakins, Nash, Smoak & Stewart PC
See firm details p.638

The Firm: The recent merger with employment firm Haynsworth Baldwin makes this the largest employment and labor firm in South Carolina. While some mid-level lawyers chose to move to other firms rather than merge, industry sources claim the group now has "*the strongest practice*" in both the labor and employment arenas in the state. Competitors recognize that the firm has "*distinguished itself because it diversified – geographically and workwise*," undertaking union avoidance, 'employment at will' briefings, employment and civil rights litigation and large class actions. Clients remain loyal to the "*business-oriented*" team because they "*have never had anything but stellar service from them*." Highlights this year include several large class action suits.

The Lawyers: Industry sources named the "*smart and ambitious*" **Ted Speth** (see p.1582) as one of the go-to people. "*If you are a Fortune 500 company and have a crisis who do you call? You call Ted.*" Clients praise labor lawyer **Lewis Smoak**'s (see p.1582) tendency to "*think outside the box and 'out-work' the other side*" along with his ability to create a legal strategy around business goals. Peers hailed **Fred Suggs** (see p.1583) as "*the premier lawyer*" for NLRB-related work. He also won plaudits from clients for his "*precise and methodical*" approach to his work. **Hamilton Stewart** (see p.1583) is "*one of the hardest-working individuals I have been around*," reported one client. He is skilled in union avoidance work and is the contact point in the firm for major clients like Michelin North America.

The Clients: Clients include GE, Milliken, Flour Construction Company, Michelin North America and others in the automotive, technology and communications industries.

Band 2

Gignilliat, Savitz & Bettis LLP
The Firm: This boutique firm represents management clients drawn from all sectors, but it is especially known for its public sector work. Sources recognize the firm has "*more of a presence in the public sector than any of us*." The small group of around ten lawyers with a "*great reputation and great clientele*" works mostly on employment law disputes. These include defending suits and class actions on the grounds of sex and age discrimination, First Amendment violations and statutory retaliation claims. The

group is currently representing a state department in a large class action suit.

The Lawyers: Peers know **Vance Bettis** as "*very experienced*" and endorse his success in building up his respected practice. Recently, he successfully defended the state in a benefits case involving federal retirees. As "*one of the stalwarts of the South Carolina scene*," **Stephen Savitz** does a lot of preventative counseling, and is experienced in proceedings before the NLRB.

The Clients: Small to large private companies, public entities and government departments are clients.

Nelson Mullins Riley & Scarborough LLP
See firm details p.1584

The Firm: This general practice firm's employment specialists combine forces with its powerful business litigation teams on employment issues, patents and trade secrets. While the group does boast expertise in the labor arena, its focus is on employment law, and in particular the litigation of class actions. The lawyers recently took on a large race discrimination class action, which was broken up into individual cases and successfully resolved. The team also represented a defense contractor in an age discrimination matter, which was won on appeal.

The Lawyers: Competitors describe **Sue Erwin Harper** (see p.1581) as "*very, very bright*," while "*clients like her a lot and respect her opinion.*" In a recent case she worked for the state legislature concerning employees' rights to display the confederate flag in the workplace. **Kenneth Young** (see p.1583) heads the firm's labor and employment practice group, and impresses with his wealth of employment law knowledge. **Andreas Satterfield** (see p.1582) recently joined the firm from Haynsworth Baldwin, bringing many clients with him. Clients followed because "*he listens and always has our best interests in mind.*" He is skilled in employment litigation, especially in harassment and wage disputes.

The Clients: These include defense contractors, restaurants and food chains, manufacturers and healthcare providers.

Nexsen Pruet LLC
See firm details p.1585

The Firm: Industry sources say this general practice firm has a good employment team to whom they will gladly refer work in instances of conflict. In the past year the team has been further strengthened by the addition of three practitioners from Ogletree Deakins. Clients praise the lawyers' "*sensible and practical*" advice on personnel policies and in employment litigation, adding that they are "*most helpful – I feel like I could go to anyone there.*" Highlights include the mediation and resolution of an unlawful

All quotes in the text are from interviews with clients and competitors.

employment suit for a large employer, and the addition of a new client, a call center with over 2,000 employees, for which the team handles all employment and employee benefit issues.

The Lawyers: The *"highly knowledgeable"* **David Dubberly** (see p.1579) splits his practice between international and employment law. Peers would gladly refer work to him in a conflict, as *"his name jumps straight to mind"* for employment issues. The *"sensible, practical and hard-working"* **Susan McWilliams** (see p.1581) is featured in recognition of her extensive employment litigation practice. Clients describe her as *"responsive and attentive to the needs of the employer as well as being focused on the employees,"* and as such would rec-

ommend her *"without hesitation; she knows her business and goes right to the bottom line."*
The Clients: Honda Cars South Carolina, statewide shopping mall and hotel chains, manufacturing and engineering companies feature on the client list.

Band 3

Jackson Lewis
The Firm: This is a national labor and employment firm making inroads into South Carolina from a small Greenville office. Peers see it as *"one of the main competitors in Greenville,"* partly because it *"has a strong national client base that*

facilitates development." Further strength came in the form of three new practitioners from Haynsworth Baldwin in August 2004.
The Lawyers: Labor lawyer **Steve Warren** is the managing partner of the Greenville office. Peers named him *"the man to remember"* in the firm.
The Clients: The practice represents a wide range of public and private businesses and non-profit institutions.

LITIGATION

	South Carolina
	Leading firms
	(Litigation: General Commercial)

[1]	HAYNSWORTH SINKLER BOYD PA *Charleston*
	NELSON MULLINS RILEY *Columbia*
	NEXSEN PRUET, LLC *Columbia*
	WYCHE, BURGESS, FREEMAN *Greenville*
[2]	BUIST, MOORE, SMYTHE, MCGEE PA *Charleston*
	LEATHERWOOD WALKER TODD *Greenville*
	MCNAIR LAW FIRM PA *Columbia*
	OGLETREE, DEAKINS, NASH, SMOAK *Greenville*
	PRATT-THOMAS EPTING AND WALKER *Charleston*
	SOWELL GRAY STEPP & LAFFITTE LLC *Columbia*
	YOUNG, CLEMENT & RIVERS LLP *Charleston*

Firms are listed alphabetically in each band.

Band 1

Haynsworth Sinkler Boyd PA
The Firm: *"Really strong on commercial litigation,"* the group moves up the tables in recognition of its ability to handle *"everything from environmental law to securities disputes to healthcare litigation."* The firm is recognized by peers as one of their main competitors and is highly visible throughout the state. The team of around 40 litigators benefits from the wisdom of older partners who are recognized as specialists in areas such as medical malpractice. Highlights this year include a number of nationwide lender liability class actions.
The Lawyers: **John Linton** is *"a formidable advocate"* and *"as good a litigator as you will find in the USA."* Interviewees were also impressed with his *"balance and excellent judgment,"* and that *"he always inspires confidence and people trust him."* The *"brilliant"* **Simmons Tate** is hugely respected for his trial skills and technical knowledge. **Dewey Oxner** is viewed as *"the most preeminent medical malpractice defense lawyer"* by peers, who claim he *"represents practically all of the doctors"* in the state.

The Clients: The client base includes financial institutions and accounting firms, manufacturing, distributing, software and cellular phone companies.

Nelson Mullins Riley & Scarborough LLP
See firm details p.1584
The Firm: *"A machine in terms of litigation,"* industry sources see this firm as being far and away the largest in South Carolina. The lawyers are credited as *"thriving on litigation,"* but clients appreciated their ability to avoid going to trial unless necessary. Traditionally big in corporate defense, the group is known for the volume of insurance defense work, products liability, employment and contract-related litigation it undertakes. Clients described the large team as *"among the most creative people I've ever encountered."* Recent highlights include multidistrict litigation relating to electrical receptacles, and continued representation of Wyeth-Ayerst Laboratories in the Norplant pharmaceuticals litigation, a case that recently settled.
The Lawyers: *"One of the best-known litigators in the state,"* **David Dukes** (see p.1579) is *"smart, extremely competent and very well thought of"* by competitors. He is recognized for his skill in products liability litigation, particularly in the pharmaceuticals industry, where he acted as national counsel for Wyeth-Ayerst. Head of the firm's litigation group is **Steven Morrison** (see p.1581). He has cultivated a national litigation practice encompassing corporate securities, and is well respected by those in the litigation scene. One to watch is **Kevin Hall** (see p.1580), who focuses primarily on commercial litigation for utilities and financial institutions. Clients appreciate his knowledge of state government, and consider him *"really brilliant – he is calm and gives the most wonderful, sound advice."*
The Clients: Clients include Fortune 500 and large South Carolina businesses, financial insti-

GENERAL COMMERCIAL

tutions, insurance companies, and pharmaceutical and chemical companies.

Nexsen Pruet, LLC
See firm details p.1585
The Firm: Industry sources rank this *"excellent firm"* as one of the top players in the litigation arena. They point to strengths in general business, healthcare and employment matters, while clients praised the team's additional trademarks and tax litigation skills. Highlights of the past year include representing KPMG in South Carolina during their national litigation over tax practices, and representing two of the directors in the Home Gold litigation.
The Lawyers: **Thomas Stephenson** (see p.1583) splits his time evenly between labor law and commercial litigation. Peers endorse him as *"bright and trustworthy,"* and wouldn't hesitate to bring him in as a mediator. Clients are impressed with his negotiating skills, and value his *"insight into human nature; he's not excitable or brash: he is discreet and effective."* Respected **Thomas Tisdale** (see p.1583) has moved to the firm from Young Clement Rivers & Tisdale, where he was one of the founding partners. He remains active in insurance, employment and general business litigation. *"Top lawyer in the employment litigation field,"* **Susan McWilliams** (see p.1581) *"knows her business and goes right to the bottom line."* Clients rate her for her thoroughness and ability to explain matters in layman's language, and point to her broader commercial practice.
The Clients: Banks and other financial institutions, insurance, accountancy and manufacturing firms comprise the client base.

Wyche, Burgess, Freeman & Parham, PA
The Firm: While some commentators point to a market trend towards larger litigation firms, this firm is successful proof against that trend.

South Carolina
Leading individuals
(Litigation: General Commercial)

Senior Statesman
OXNER Dewey *Haynsworth Sinkler*, Greenville

[1] DUKES David *Nelson Mullins*, Columbia
LINTON John *Haynsworth Sinkler*, Charleston
MORRISON Stephen *Nelson Mullins*, Columbia

[2] EPTING Andrew *Pratt-Thomas Epting*, Charleston
HOWE Gedney *Gedney M Howe III*, Charleston
LIGHTSEY Wallace *Wyche Burgess*, Greenville
SOWELL Thornwell *Sowell Gray*, Columbia
STEPHENSON Thomas *Nexsen Pruet*, Greenville

[3] CLEVELAND III William *Buist Moore*, Charleston
COCKRILL Donald *Ogletree Deakins*, Greenville
JONES Celeste *McNair Law Firm*, Columbia
MAJOR Joseph *Leatherwood Walker*, Greenville
MCWILLIAMS Susan *Nexsen Pruet*, Columbia
TATE Simmons *Haynsworth Sinkler*, Charleston
TISDALE Thomas *Nexsen Pruet*, Charleston
WALKER Trenholm *Pratt-Thomas Epting*, Charleston
YOUNG Rutledge *Young Clement*, Charleston

Up-and-coming individuals
HALL Kevin *Nelson Mullins*, Columbia
TESSIER Troy *Wyche Burgess*, Greenville

Individuals are listed alphabetically in each band.

Sources rate the group as *"extremely competent lawyers with a very sophisticated practice."* The practice is a force locally, trying high-profile cases in Greenville, and can litigate anywhere in the state. In addition to its traditional strengths, the group has expanded its practice to include plaintiff work in commercial and securities cases. Clients use these attorneys because of their *"expertise, experience and willingness to work within our fee scale."* Recently the group has been involved in several copyright infringement cases for architecture firms, in which area clients recommend it as *"the specialists."* Further highlights include First Amendment litigation involving a major motion picture company, and representing the IT firm Cisco Systems in a breach of contract matter.

The Lawyers: Wallace Lightsey is *"highly respected by both lawyers and judges"* for his intelligence and communication skills. *"When he speaks, people listen,"* say commentators. He has been lead counsel on many of the recent copyright infringement cases, where clients report he does a *"first-rate job representing us."* One to watch is the up-and-coming Troy Tessier. Peers rate him for his work in the insurance area, while clients report they are *"very impressed with him."*

The Clients: Clients include insurance, communications and IT companies, in addition to manufacturing, architecture and design firms.

Band 2

Buist, Moore, Smythe, McGee PA

The Firm: Out-of-state firms recommend this team to handle complicated contract law cases for their clients in South Carolina. In the past year, the group has undertaken several lender liability cases, representing financial institutions in cases involving employee fraud and breach of fiduciary duties. Recently, the team has resolved one such case and is in the process of discovery in another. Clients praise this smaller firm's ability to hold its own against much larger opponents, even in *"lopsided cases,"* pointing to their organizational skills and *"impeccable research"* as the keys to their successful outcomes. Other highlights include its involvement in a technical tidelands dispute with the state.

The Lawyers: William Cleveland is *"known for his intelligence, and he is meticulous in his preparation,"* say interviewees. Head of the firm's business litigation team, he represented a minority stockholder in a breach of fiduciary duty case, where the client put their success down to Cleveland's personal dedication, praising him as *"extremely organized, and so logical."*

The Clients: Banks, financial institutions, national companies, shareholders and individual stockholders are represented.

Leatherwood Walker Todd & Mann PC

The Firm: *"Still very much a player in Greenville,"* this firm continues to provide a full range of litigation expertise to businesses in the upstate. The litigation practice remains primarily defense-based, and includes loan transactions, securities and trade secrets claims and patent disputes. Clients recommend the group for all aspects of its insurance work from coverage, pre-suit investigation to the final trial. Clients placed great store in the excellent characters of all the lawyers here, citing their business ethics and fairness as one of the main reasons for using the firm.

The Lawyers: Joseph Major impresses with his *"excellent courtroom manner."* Clients use him because he is *"smart, hard-working, ethical, prepared and confident."*

The Clients: Insurance companies, corporations, partnerships, shareholders and domestic and international banks feature on the client roster.

McNair Law Firm PA

The Firm: Peers tend to see the firm as more focused on its corporate practice, yet in the past year it has been litigating some large suits in the healthcare arena, especially in the area of professional disability cover. A good portion of the practice is in the regulatory sphere, and the firm is still involved in ongoing litigation for Bayer Pharmaceuticals, which has been conducted both nationally and internationally.

The Lawyers: Industry sources praise Celeste Jones as *"colorful and aggressive,"* and recognize she handles many high-profile cases, especially in the medical community. She has attracted a lot of work in the pharmaceutical industry, and is currently involved in an Internet pharmacy case.

The Clients: Healthcare providers, hospitals, physician practice groups, medical suppliers and pharmaceuticals are among the clientele.

Ogletree, Deakins, Nash, Smoak & Stewart PC

See firm details p.638

The Firm: This firm is a huge player in the employment litigation area, and while this overshadows its general commercial litigation, it still enjoys a steady volume of such disputes, thanks largely to its sizable client following. The past year has seen an increase in products liability and patent actions, with a highlight being the recent patent litigation for Milliken, which was tried in the federal court in Greenville. The team has also recently represented the communications company Lucent Technologies and Mariner Health Care in South Carolina.

The Lawyers: Donald Cockrill (see p.1579) is a *"very fine trial attorney"* with a wide-ranging practice including products liability and wage and hour suits.

Pratt-Thomas Epting and Walker Law Firm

The Firm: This specialist litigation firm is based in Charleston, where its expertise rivals the large firms in the market. The 12 lawyers are recognized as *"creative people and excellent lawyers"* by peers, who say it takes *"the highest skills to attempt to resist them"* in the courtroom. The group undertakes both commercial and civil litigation in diverse areas including personal injury, securities arbitration, administrative criminal and environmental law, and alternative dispute resolution.

The Lawyers: *"A choreographer of litigation"* Andrew Epting is *"all the things you want your lawyer to be – very smart with lots of experience, well connected and hardworking."* His partner Trenholm Walker is known as an *"extremely gifted scholar with great peripheral vision in litigation."* Interviewees especially praised his skills as a mediator, where he is *"excellent; you won't find a better lawyer in the state."*

The Clients: Individuals, homeowners' associations, insurance companies, hospitals and healthcare organizations are all clients.

Sowell Gray Stepp & Laffitte LLC

See firm details p.1586

The Firm: This specialist litigation firm is based in the state capital and undertakes a substantial portion of government defense work along with insurance and breach of contract disputes for businesses and individuals. A particular highlight for the team was the high-profile defense of the state legislature in a case that challenged the constitutionality of education funding in South Carolina. The four-year case was recently concluded.

The Lawyers: *"Excellent trial lawyer"* **Thornwell Sowell** (see p.1582) *"brings intellectual rigor and thoroughness to a case."* Clients respect his *"nice, low-key style"* and the fact that he can *"distill a complex set of facts to an understandable message."* Recently he represented an investment banking and securities brokering firm in the HomeGold litigation, and continues to represent the Friends of the Hunley – the group who raised the Confederate submarine from the sea floor.

The Clients: South Carolina Senate and House of Representatives, investment banks and financial institutions are among the clients.

Young, Clement & Rivers LLP
The Firm: The group has undergone a name change from last year due to recent departures, although industry sources still rate it as a leading competitor, especially in Charleston. The group remains strong in its traditional areas of intellectual property disputes involving patents, trademarks and copyrights and represents clients in both the public and private sectors.
The Lawyers: The well-regarded **Rutledge Young** focuses his practice on healthcare and professional liability.

The Clients: The client base includes media, manufacturing and telecom companies, distributors, designers and wholesalers.

Other Notable Practitioners
"The leading trial lawyer in the state," **Gedney Howe** of Gedney M Howe III PA is recommended for his work with large personal injury cases. Peers have a lot of respect for him, describing him as someone who is *"gifted and talented, very well thought of by clients, and wins big cases."* Much of his work is on the plaintiff's side, but his broad trial skills can be employed to good effect by any party.

REAL ESTATE

South Carolina
Leading firms (Real Estate)

[1] **BUIST, MOORE, SMYTHE, MCGEE PA** *Charleston*
MCNAIR LAW FIRM PA *Columbia*
NEXSEN PRUET, LLC *Columbia*

[2] **GOTTLIEB & SMITH PA** *Columbia*
HAYNSWORTH SINKLER BOYD PA *Charleston*
NELSON MULLINS RILEY *Columbia*

[3] **JEFFCOAT PIKE & NAPPIER LLC** *Myrtle Beach*
LEATHERWOOD WALKER TODD *Greenville*
WARREN & SINKLER LLP *Charleston*
WOMBLE CARLYLE SANDRIDGE *Greenville*

Leading individuals (Real Estate)

★ **MENZIE Edward** *Nexsen Pruet, Columbia*

[1] **BOONE Sidney** *McNair Law Firm, Columbia*
ESTRIDGE Larry *Womble Carlyle, Greenville*
GAILLARD Foster *Buist Moore, Charleston*
GOTTLIEB Joel *Gottlieb & Smith, Columbia*
WARREN III John *Warren & Sinkler, Charleston*

[2] **BOYD William** *Haynsworth Sinkler, Charleston*
ROBINSON Neil *Nexsen Pruet, Charleston*
SWANSON David *Haynsworth Sinkler, Charleston*

[3] **BOBO William** *Nelson Mullins, Columbia*
ELLEFSON Anne *Haynsworth Sinkler, Greenville*
ELLISON Morris *Buist Moore, Charleston*
GOSSETT David *Nexsen Pruet, Greenville*
JEFFCOAT III Otis *Jeffcoat Pike, Myrtle Beach*
MCINNIS Judith *McNair Law Firm, Columbia*
QUATTLEBAUM Marvin *Leatherwood, Greenville*
SMYTHE Susan *Buist Moore, Charleston*

Firms and individuals are listed alphabetically in each band.

Band 1

Buist, Moore, Smythe, McGee PA
The Firm: This group has secured itself a reputation as an *"outstanding firm"* for real estate. This is clearly one of the strongest practice groups in the firm; peers say they would readily refer work here when faced with a conflict, as *"real estate is what they do."* In the past year, the team has been involved in large multistate transactions involving property all over the USA, along with regional hotel, office, and land development transactions. Recent highlights include continuing work with the Daniel Island Company, now in the zoning stages, and a high volume of real estate loan transactions.
The Lawyers: Sources commended **Foster Gaillard** as *"an excellent, hard-working lawyer. The kind you are always glad to see on the other side of a transaction."* He focuses on commercial lending work, and his recent transactions have involved hotels, office space, and industrial and raw land development. **Morris Ellison** has made a name for himself for his skill in dealing with mortgage closures. Peers rate him as *"definitely someone to look at"* for the future. The *"tenacious"* **Susan Smythe** is *"extremely competent and one of the smartest lawyers in the firm."* She has recently been handling condominium development plans and zoning issues for major developers.
The Clients: Banks, financial institutions, business residential and resort developers are clients.

McNair Law Firm PA
The Firm: The most significant development in the group's real estate practice has been its recent merger with boutique real estate firm Bethea Jordan. The move has strengthened the group's coastal real estate presence, adding two offices and a greater involvement in the development, public financing and high-end residential work to their already strong practice. The past year has seen an increase in zoning and annexation work, along with drafting Plan Unit Developments (PUDs) and development agreements. Clients appreciate the lawyers' skills with development projects. Highlights include assisting a national pharmaceutical company with the acquisition and zoning involved in relocating its corporate headquarters, and a $22 million deal for a hotel in the Charleston historical district, where the group did all the refinancing and architectural approvals work.
The Lawyers: *"Fabulous lawyer"* **Sidney Boone** has an extensive development practice in residential and mixed-use real estate. Peers enjoy working with him for his skill and cooperation, and rate him for his *"technical knowledge and business sense."* Clients use him because *"he's the best guy in town."* Recently, he has worked on the acquisition and development of a $30 million tract of land in Charleston. **Judith McInnis** has cultivated a broad commercial practice, and has recently acted as the lead counsel on a $50 million pharmaceutical business relocation. She is skilled in the financing aspects of real estate and impresses observers as a *"tough negotiator and a fabulous lawyer; analytical and insightful."*
The Clients: Developers, banks and other regional businesses are among those represented.

Nexsen Pruet LLC
See firm details p.1585
The Firm: This group has an extremely strong real estate practice involved in developments across the state. Traditionally leaders in both Columbia and Charleston, competitors also note that the team in Greenville is *"highly respected and getting better every year."* The team's practice encompasses commercial, industrial and resort development projects. Recently the lawyers have been involved in a 20,000-acre resort transaction at Hilton Head and a 22,000-acre mixed-use and golf course development for Duke Power in Palmetto Bluff. Peers admire the group's *"good experience in dealing with government"* on zoning issues and development plans, and would refer work to them because *"they are the leaders."*
The Lawyers: *"One of the preeminent real estate lawyers in the state,"* **Edward Menzie** (see p.1581) is *"the dean of his practice – he influences*

the market statewide." Peers and clients heap praise on this "*creative and inventive lawyer,*" and enjoy working with him on exotic and complex transactions. One interviewee stated: "*He is the person I think of first when I think of real estate.*" **Neil Robinson** (see p.1582) is renowned for his work on large development projects as he "*has the right mix of talents to do a good job on complex transactions.*" Industry sources note his influence in the area, and that he has "*so many contacts in Charleston he really brings in the business.*" **David Gossett** (see p.1580) is widely respected for his skills in real estate finance. Clients "*rely heavily on him,*" trusting his sound judgment and wealth of experience. He is currently working on the financing of a sugar processing plant in Florida, while more locally he has just completed an acquisition of commercial space for a support business in the future ICAR development.

The Clients: The group has a diverse manufacturing and automotive client base. It also represents banks, utility companies and a major grocery store chain.

Band 2

Gottlieb & Smith PA

The Firm: This small boutique firm of four lawyers has "*more clout than their numbers would make you think; they handle huge transactions.*" The group concentrates on commercial real estate, with an emphasis on retail acquisition and development, particularly shopping centers. Competitors admire the firm's strong commercial clientele, recognizing they have "*the best of all worlds; a small firm with big clients and sales all over the country.*" The lawyers have a robust base of loyal clients, who work with them because "*they have a deal-making mentality that keeps all parties to a transaction happy. It is a win-win situation.*" A recent highlight was the acquisition and development of the old Confederate printing plant in Columbia, which required lengthy negotiations to ensure the survival of the historic aspects of the site. The group is currently representing the City of Columbia in its bid to establish a cutting-edge hotel and reception centre.

The Lawyers: The "*very smart and focused*" **Joel Gottlieb** is renowned for his expertise in shopping center development, an area in which he is viewed as "*the specialist.*" Clients praise him as "*fair, open, honest and logical,*" and rate him for his "*ability to put together a consummate deal that everyone is happy with.*"

The Clients: The firm has a client base of developers like Edens & Avant and also represents municipal government.

Haynsworth Sinkler Boyd PA

The Firm: This "*business-oriented and very active firm*" has a thriving local real estate practice with a national reach. Industry sources

respect the "*experienced lawyers*" housed in the real estate practice, especially in Columbia, which can match any in the state as "*they are all very bright.*" The caseload here encompasses commercial, industrial and residential development work, and features some of the market's most complex developments. The team handles all levels of real estate transactions, and regularly represents financial institutions, including Wachovia Bank, Bank of America, and Carolina First Bank, in construction and real estate financings.

The Lawyers: **William Boyd** "*is a first-class corporate and real estate lawyer and has been so for 30 years.*" He manages large-scale acquisitions and developments, overseeing the complex corporate transactions that arise from the group's real estate practice. **David Swanson**, who heads the real estate practice in the Charleston office, is best known for his resort development work on the coast. He is a "*focused real estate lawyer with a loyal clientele.*" **Anne Ellefson**'s prowess in commercial and residential development is widely recognized by peers who commend her as a good port of call for conflict referrals.

The Clients: REITs, local and regional developers and financial institutions are clients.

Nelson Mullins Riley & Scarborough LLP

See firm details p.1584

The Firm: Although best known for its litigation practice, this full-service firm also has a good real estate practice, especially in Columbia where "*the constellation of lawyers is brightest.*" The group undertakes residential as well as commercial and industrial work, and does a high volume of lending transactions. The real estate group often work closely with the corporate and bankruptcy teams in workouts.

The Lawyers: **William Bobo** (see p.1579) moved from Young, Clement & Rivers some years ago and has been building a good practice with Nelson Mullins. He is known for his representation of commercial and residential real estate developers, and clients feel "*he is excellent in his responsive service and high-quality advice.*"

The Clients: Clients include banks, building contractors, developers, insurance and construction companies.

Band 3

Jeffcoat Pike & Nappier LLC (Myrtle Beach)

The Firm: This small firm has a flourishing coastal real estate practice. With two offices in Myrtle Beach, one in Pawleys Island, and one just across the border in Calabash, North Carolina, the group is taking advantage of the recent coastal real estate boom. The team's practice covers both commercial and residential real

estate, but distinguishes itself with the "*high volume of residential development*" it handles. The lawyers have the depth of talent to handle transactions of varying sizes, from individual home closures and mortgages to condominium and planned unit developments.

The Lawyers: The "*impressive*" **Otis Allen Jeffcoat** is described by interviewees as "*one of the best in the state*" for residential developments. "*If he puts a deal together you know it's a good one.*"

The Clients: Clients include developers, builders, realtors, lenders and homeowners' associations.

Leatherwood Walker Todd & Mann PC

The Firm: The group continues to perform a full range of real estate transactions for its established clients in the Southeast, representing both borrowers and lenders. Recently, much of the lawyers' time has been devoted to the ICAR development, as it represents the estate of a client who amassed a large amount of property in the area.

The Lawyers: **Marvin Quattlebaum** enjoys a lot of respect from peers for his smooth handling of real estate transactions and financings. He is a "*sensible negotiator, who understands how to do a deal.*"

The Clients: The group's client base includes financial institutions, developers, local manufacturers and title insurance organizations.

Warren & Sinkler LLP

The Firm: Both peers and clients agree this group "*cuts to the chase and knows how to get things done*" when working on complex transactions. Clients recommend the lawyers especially for "*the large transactions where complex tax structures are involved.*" Over the past year, attorneys have been involved in negotiating leases for shopping centers and representing a dormitory specialist in Charleston on a diverse range of business issues. The team also continues its institutional sales and development work for the Daniel Island Company.

The Lawyers: **John Warren** is well known in both the real estate and corporate circles for his skill in structuring complex deals. Clients are impressed by his "*no-nonsense business command.*" He recently worked on the acquisition and financing of 4,000 acres for the Daniel Island Company, and interviewees "*can't think of a transaction he would not be comfortable performing.*"

The Clients: Banks, developers and real estate firms are clients.

Womble Carlyle Sandridge & Rice PLLC

See firm details p.1402

The Firm: This firm has been called an anomaly

in the market by some competitors, as its real estate practice has more in common with North Carolina and Piedmont. However, it continues to successfully cater to Greenville businesses. For example, it is involved in the development of high-end residential and mixed-use projects in downtown Greenville. Further highlights for the past year include the representation of a grocery store chain in its bid to expand its business, and the group continues to represent the private element of the PPP responsible for the creation of the ICAR campus.

The Lawyers: Industry sources rate **Larry Estridge** (see p.1580) as "*a lawyer of the first order*" for his 30 years of experience and "*impeccable character.*" Known for his intelligence and meticulous attention to detail, clients view him as "*just the ultimate professional attorney.*"

The Clients: The group represents a range of developers, and commercial chains.

Leaders in South Carolina

AMSTUTZ, Eric
Wyche, Burgess, Freeman & Parham, PA, Greenville 864 242 8200
Recommended in Corporate/M&A

BETTIS, Vance
Gignilliat, Savitz & Bettis LLP, Columbia 803 799 9311
Recommended in Employment

BLAKE Jr, Joseph
Haynsworth Sinkler Boyd PA, Greenville 864 240 3200
Recommended in Corporate/M&A

BOBO Jr, William
Nelson Mullins Riley & Scarborough LLP, Columbia 843 720 4328
bill.bobo@nelsonmullins.com
Recommended in Real Estate
Practice Areas: Corporate; real estate.
Prof. Memberships: Mr Bobo is a Member of the American Bar Association, the Charleston County Bar Association, and the Real Estate Practice Section of the South Carolina Bar.
Career: William Bobo is a Partner of the firm in Charleston where he practices in the areas of commercial real estate and business law. A Member of the South Carolina Bar, Mr Bobo has extensive experience in the representation of commercial and residential real estate developers. Prior to joining Nelson Mullins, Mr Bobo practiced in real estate, banking, and corporate law with another leading South Carolina firm. He served as a lieutenant on active duty with the US Navy from 1972-77.
Publications: Mr Bobo is the author of 'Edmonds v Compagnie Generale Translantique: The Supreme Court Sets a Course in Third-Party Litigation Under the Longshoremen's and Harbor Workers Compensation Act', 31 S.C. L. REV. 1699, 1980.
Personal: In 1979, Mr Bobo earned a Juris Doctor, cum laude, from the University of South Carolina School of Law where he was a member of the Order of Wig and Robe. Mr Bobo earned a Bachelor of Science in Political Science from the US Naval Academy in 1972.

BOONE Jr, Sidney
McNair Law Firm PA, Columbia 803 799 9800
Recommended in Real Estate

BOYD, William
Haynsworth Sinkler Boyd PA, Charleston 843 722 3366
Recommended in Corporate/M&A, Real Estate

CARROUTH, Michael
Fisher & Phillips LLP, Columbia 803 255 0000
mcarrouth@laborlawyers.com
Recommended in Employment
Practice Areas: Mike Carrouth is a Partner in the Columbia office of the national law firm of Fisher & Phillips LLP, practicing exclusively in labor and employment law representing management. He frequently speaks on labor and employment and litigation matters, and he has published several articles. Mike practices before state and federal courts, the National Labor Relations Board, and state and federal administrative agencies in the areas of union avoidance, union campaigns, labor relations, employment litigation, discrimination cases, non-compete agreements, and wrongful discharge cases. He received his JD from the University of South Carolina School of Law in 1988.

CLEVELAND III, William
Buist, Moore, Smythe, McGee P.A., Charleston 843 722 3400
Recommended in Litigation

COCKRILL, Donald A
Ogletree, Deakins, Nash, Smoak & Stewart, PC, Greenville 864 271 1300
donald.cockrill@ogletreedeakins.com
Recommended in Litigation
Practice Areas: Labor and employment, civil litigation (products liability, business torts, commercial disputes, class actions), environmental and toxic tort litigation.
Prof. Memberships: District of Columbia Bar Association, South Carolina Bar Association, American Bar Association.
Career: Admitted to practice in South Carolina, District of Columbia, US Supreme Court, and US Court of Appeals (Fourth and Eleventh Circuits).
Personal: Vanderbilt University (BA, 1965), University of Virginia Law School (LLB, 1968).

CURRIE, John
McNair Law Firm PA, Columbia 803 799 9800
Recommended in Corporate/M&A

DIXON, Augustus M
Nelson Mullins Riley & Scarborough LLP, Columbia 803 255 9491
gus.dixon@nelsonmullins.com
Recommended in Corporate/M&A
Practice Areas: Corporate law; securities law; corporate finance; mergers and acquisitions; technology; outsourcing.
Prof. Memberships: Mr Dixon is a Member of numerous professional organizations, including the Columbia Technology Entrepreneurs Council, the Columbia Information Technology Council, and the Outsourcing Institute. Mr Dixon also currently serves as a Member of the Executive Council of the South Carolina Investor Network and as a Board Member of the World Affairs Council. A Member of the South Carolina Bar and the Virginia Bar, Mr Dixon served as an adjunct professor of legal writing at the University of South Carolina School of Law from 1998-2002.
Career: Mr Dixon, a Nelson Mullins Riley & Scarborough Partner, practices in Columbia, in the areas of securities law, corporate law, corporate finance, venture capital, mergers and acquisitions, outsourcing, and technology law. Mr Dixon's practice has ranged from representing publicly held companies to start ups. A Former Chairman of the Corporate, Banking and Securities Law Section of the South Carolina Bar, Mr Dixon frequently writes and lectures on significant corporate, securities and technology-related issues. Mr Dixon is a leader of the firm's South Carolina Corporate Practice.
Personal: In 1988, Mr Dixon earned a Juris Doctor, cum laude, from the University of South Carolina School of Law where he served as articles editor of the 'South Carolina Law Review' and was a Member of the Order of the Coif, and the Order of Wig and Robe. Mr Dixon earned a Bachelor of Arts in American Government, cum laude, from the University of Virginia in 1985.

DUBBERLY, David E
Nexsen Pruet, LLC, Columbia 803 253 8281
ddubberly@nexsenpruet.com
Recommended in Employment
Practice Areas: Member of Employment and International Practice Teams. Certified specialist in employment and labor law. Mr Dubberly has successfully defended companies in employment lawsuits in several federal and state courts. He has also helped clients negotiate international joint venture, distribution, and licensing agreements, and set up sales offices and distribution centers in the US and approximately 10 countries in Latin America, Europe, and Asia. Fluent in Spanish.
Prof. Memberships: Admitted in South Carolina; US Court of International Trade; US Courts of Appeals for the Fourth, Sixth, and Federal Circuits. Vice-Chair, International Employment Law Committee, ABA (2004-present); Chair, Foreign Investment in the US Committee, ABA (2001-04). Member of the SC Supreme Court's Employment and Labor Specialization Advisory Board (1995-98). Chairman of the SC Bar's Employment and Labor Law Section (1992-93) and of the International Law Committee (1998-2001).
Career: Law Clerk to the Honorable Curtis G Shaw, Associate Justice, SC Court of Appeals (1984-85).
Publications: 'Obligations to Employees on Military Leave', (2004); 'Understanding the Revised White Collar Overtime Rules', (2004); 'The New South Carolina Employee Handbook Law', (2004); 'Protecting Against Whistleblower Liability', (2003).
Personal: JD, University of South Carolina, 1984; BA, cum laude, Bob Jones University, 1981.

DUKES, David E
Nelson Mullins Riley & Scarborough LLP, Columbia 803 255 9451
david.dukes@nelsonmullins.com
Recommended in Litigation
Practice Areas: Pharmaceutical and medical device litigation; business litigation; technology law and litigation; coordination of national litigation.
Prof. Memberships: Mr Dukes is listed in The Best Lawyers in America, 2003-06 editions. He is president-elect of the Defense Research Institute (Board of Directors, 2002-present; Chairman, Drug and Device Law Committee, 1999-2001).
Career: David E Dukes is the firm Managing Partner. He practices in the areas of pharmaceutical and medical device litigation, business litigation, technology law and litigation, and coordination of

www.ChambersandPartners.com
All quotes in the text are from interviews with clients and competitors.
1579

national litigation. Mr Dukes has served as national trial counsel for companies in the pharmaceutical, computer, and consumer products industries.

Publications: Mr Dukes is the author of 'A Corporate Counsel's Guide to Discovery in the Information Age', Washington Legal Foundation, 2001; 'What You Should Know About Direct-to-Consumer Advertising of Prescription Drugs?' Defense Counsel Journal, 68, 1, January 2001; 'Consultant Liability for Year 2000 Problems', The Defense Practitioner's Guide to the Year 2000 Problem, 1998; 'Toxicology Made Easy: What Every Trial Advocate Should Know', Defense Counsel Journal, 63, 3, July 1996; 'Gaining Access to Federal Court - The Sham Defendant Doctrine in Drug and Medical Device Cases', Rx for the Defense, Spring 1994.

Personal: He is a Member of the Advisory Committee of the Law Firm Pro Bono Project, Georgetown University Law Center and a trustee of the Business Partnership Foundation, Moore School of Business, University of South Carolina. In 1984, Mr Dukes earned a Juris Doctor, cum laude, from the University of South Carolina School of Law. Mr Dukes earned a Bachelor of Science in Financial Management from Clemson University in 1981.

ELLEFSON, Anne
Haynsworth Sinkler Boyd PA, Greenville
864 240 3200
Recommended in Real Estate

ELLISON, Morris
Buist, Moore, Smythe, McGee P.A.,
Charleston 843 722 3400
Recommended in Real Estate

ELLZEY, Daniel
Fisher & Phillips LLP, Columbia
803 255 0000
dellzey@laborlawyers.com
Recommended in Employment

Practice Areas: Dan Ellzey is certified as a specialist in employment and labor law by the South Carolina Supreme Court. In the employment area, Dan counsels clients on and litigates discrimination, retaliation, wrongful discharge, non-compete, wage and hour, plant closure, OSHA, and other employment issues. In the labor area, Dan is extensively involved in preventive union avoidance work and has participated in some of the highest profile union campaigns in the United States. Co-author of the South Carolina Employers Reference Manual, Dan received his JD from the University of South Carolina and an MBA from the University of Utah.

EPTING, Andrew
Pratt-Thomas Epting and Walker Law
Firm, Charleston 843 727 2200
Recommended in Litigation

ESTRIDGE, Larry D
Womble Carlyle Sandridge & Rice
PLLC, Greenville 864 255 5401
lestridge@wcsr.com
Recommended in Real Estate

Practice Areas: Larry Estridge has 30 years of experience in all facets of real estate acquisition, finance and development, including zoning and other land use and regulation issues. He represents buyers, sellers, lenders, brokers, developers, lessors and lessees.

Prof. Memberships: South Carolina Bar Association, Pro Bono Program, Real Estate Section; Georgia Bar Association; American Bar Association.

Career: US Army, 1969-71, served in Vietnam as battalion defense counsel for courts martial, awarded Bronze Star. JD, 1969, Harvard University; BA, 1966, Furman University, cum laude, Student Body President, Blue Key, History Award, Hughes Trophy (Outstanding Army ROTC Graduate in US).

FEW, Richard
Leatherwood Walker Todd & Mann PC,
Greenville 864 242 6440
Recommended in Corporate/M&A

FRITZE, Daniel J
Nelson Mullins Riley & Scarborough
LLP, Columbia 803 255 9584
dan.fritze@nelsonmullins.com
Recommended in Corporate/M&A

Practice Areas: Corporate.

Prof. Memberships: A Member of the South Carolina Bar, Mr Fritze was named South Carolina Pro Bono Lawyer of the Year for 2001. Mr Fritze served as the chairman of the Corporate, Banking and Securities Law Section of the South Carolina Bar from 2002-03. He is a Member of the American Bar Association, the Richland County Bar Association, and the Columbia Technology Entrepreneur Council. Mr Fritze is also a Certified Public Accountant. He is a Member of the South Carolina Association of Certified Public Accountants, previously serving as Chairman of its Relations with the Bar Committee.

Career: Daniel J Fritze is a Partner of the firm who practices in Columbia in the areas of corporate and securities law. Mr Fritze has extensive experience with mergers and acquisitions, corporate formation and governance issues, private placements and general contract issues, and he represents both public and private companies with corporate and securities matters.

Publications: Author of 'Comment, Drug Testing of Government Employees and Government Regulated Industries: Expounding the Fourth Amendment,' 25 Wake Forest L Rev, 1990.

Personal: In 1991, Mr Fritze earned a Juris Doctor from Wake Forest University School of Law where he was symposium editor of the Wake Forest University Law Review and a Member of Phi Delta Phi and the Moot Court Board.

Mr Fritze earned a Bachelor of Arts in Accounting, magna cum laude, from Wofford College in 1984.

GAILLARD, Foster
Buist, Moore, Smythe, McGee P.A.,
Charleston 843 722 3400
Recommended in Real Estate

GOSSETT, David
Nexsen Pruet Jacobs & Pollard, LLC,
Greenville 864 370 2211
dgossett@nexsenpruet.com
Recommended in Real Estate

Practice Areas: Economic development, real estate and lending, and extensive experience representing a wide variety of banking and financial institutions on complex real estate, asset-based, commercial, construction and development loan transactions, as well as workouts and debt restructuring. Mr Gossett is also regularly involved in financing some of the larger agribusinesses in the country.

Prof. Memberships: Upstate Alliance, (Board of Directors); South Carolina Economic Developers Alliance; National Council of Farmer Cooperatives (Legal, Tax and Accounting Subcommittee); South Carolina Bar; North Carolina Bar Association.

Personal: University of South Carolina, JD, 1986; Columbia Bible College, BS, 1979; South Carolina Honors College.

GOTTLIEB, Joel
Gottlieb & Smith PA, Columbia
803 765 9291
Recommended in Real Estate

GRAYSON, Neil E
Nelson Mullins Riley & Scarborough
LLP, Greenville 864 250 2235
neil.grayson@nelsonmullins.com
Recommended in Corporate/M&A

Practice Areas: Corporate; financial institutions; securities.

Prof. Memberships: A Member of the South Carolina Bar, the State Bar of Georgia, and the New York State Bar, Mr Grayson is a founder and Board Member of the Entrepreneurs Foundation of the Southeast, a nonprofit organization that works closely with the venture capital community and their portfolio companies. He is a Member of the American Bar Association and its Corporate Banking and Business Law Sections.

Career: Neil E Grayson is a Partner of the firm. With offices in Greenville and Atlanta, Mr Grayson practices in the areas of corporate, securities, and banking law. Mr Grayson has handled numerous public and private securities offerings, mergers and other acquisitions, and venture capital investments, with a particular focus on companies in the financial institutions, payment systems, and electronic commerce industries. Additionally, he has handled the formation of numerous de novo community banks. Prior to joining the firm, Mr Grayson practiced securities and

corporate law in New York with Cravath, Swaine & Moore.

Personal: In 1987, Mr Grayson earned a Juris Doctor, cum laude, from the University of South Carolina School of Law where he was named to The Order of the Coif and was a member of the South Carolina Law Review, the Moot Court Bar, and the International Law Moot Court Team. He earned a Bachelor of Arts in Accounting and Economics, cum laude, from Wofford College in 1984.

HALL, Kevin A
Nelson Mullins Riley & Scarborough
LLP, Columbia 803 255 9522
kevin.hall@nelsonmullins.com
Recommended in Litigation

Practice Areas: Business litigation; securities litigation; technology law; telecommunications; utility regulation.

Prof. Memberships: A Member of the South Carolina Bar and the State Bar of Georgia, Mr Hall is admitted to practice before the 4th US Circuit Court of Appeals and the US District Court for the District of South Carolina. Mr Hall is active in civic and community affairs, serving as Trustee of the Sisters of Charity Foundation of South Carolina. He also serves on the Board of Directors for Catholic Charities for the State of South Carolina and Voices for South Carolina's Children. In 2002, he was appointed by Governor Mark Sanford as Co-Chair of the Governor's Task Force on Government Restructuring and Campaign Finance Reform, and in 2004, Governor Sanford appointed Mr Hall Chairman of the South Carolina Retirement Systems Investment Panel. Mr Hall is a Member of the American Bar Association, the Defense Research Institute, and the Richland County Bar Association. His leadership roles in the firm include chairman of the Marketing and Planning Committee, chairman of the Technology Committee, and membership on the Pro Bono Committee and numerous ad hoc committees.

Career: Kevin A Hall is a Partner of the firm practicing in Columbia in the areas of complex commercial litigation, class actions, consumer litigation, technology litigation, and utilities law. Mr Hall's practice includes representation of plaintiffs and defendants in business disputes involving claims for breach of contract, business torts, unfair trade practices, unfair competition, commercial disparagement, antitrust, and related business claims. Mr Hall has extensive experience in class action defense in both state and federal courts. Prior to joining the firm, Mr Hall served as in-house litigation and regulatory counsel for BellSouth Telecommunications, Inc. and as senior attorney for SCANA Corporation.

Personal: In 1987, Mr Hall earned a Bachelor of Arts in International Studies, magna cum laude, from the South

Carolina Honors College of the University of South Carolina. In 1990, he earned a Juris Doctor, with highest honors, from Emory University School of Law where he was inducted into The Order of the Coif. From 1990-91, Mr Hall served as law clerk to The Honorable Robert F Chapman of the US Court of Appeals for the Fourth Circuit.

HALL Jr, Cary
Wyche, Burgess, Freeman & Parham, PA, Greenville 864 242 8200
Recommended in Corporate/M&A

HARPER, Sue Erwin
Nelson Mullins Riley & Scarborough LLP, Columbia 803 255 5544
corky.harper@nelsonmullins.com
Recommended in Employment
Practice Areas: Labor and employment; business litigation; certified specialist in employment and labor law.
Prof. Memberships: Since 1994, Ms Harper has been certified by the Supreme Court of South Carolina as a Specialist in Employment and Labor Law. She is a Member of the South Carolina Bar and is admitted before the Supreme Court of the United States, the US Court of Appeals for the Fourth Circuit, and the US District Court for the District of South Carolina. Ms Harper is a permanent Member of the Fourth Circuit Judicial Conference and the John Belton O'Neall Inn of Court (president, 1990-91). She is a Member of the Board of Directors of the South Carolina Bar Foundation, a Member of the South Carolina Defense Trial Attorneys' Association, the South Carolina Supreme Court Historical Society (President, 2000-03; Vice-President, 1998-2000), and the South Carolina Women Lawyers Association (President, 1993-95).She is listed in the 2003-04 and 2004-05 editions of The Best Lawyers in America. Ms Harper has served as a Member of the South Carolina State Ethics Commission and the Supreme Court of South Carolina Board of Commissioners on Grievances and Discipline. In 2004, Ms Harper was awarded the Jean Galloway Bissell Award by the South Carolina Women Lawyers Association for advancing the status and influence of women in the profession. In 2000, she received the Tribute to Women in Industry Award from YWCA of the Midlands. In 1995, she received the Compleat Lawyer Award given by the University of South Carolina School of Law in recognition of significant contributions to the legal profession by a graduate who embraces the highest standard of professional competence, ethics and integrity.
Career: Before entering private practice, she served as a Law Clerk for US District Judge Robert F Chapman of South Carolina. A Partner of Nelson Mullins Riley & Scarborough, she leads the labor and employment practice in Columbia. Ms Harper has extensive experience in business litigation and in all aspects of employment law. She has represented and defended employers against individual and class claims of employment discrimination on the basis of age, race, national origin, disability, and sex, including sexual harassment; enforceability of covenants not to compete; breach of employment contracts (including handbook claims); retaliation; wrongful discharge; and other employment-related suits. Additionally, Ms Harper counsels employers on compliance issues and the development of strategies designed to avoid litigation.
Personal: In 1979, Ms Harper earned a Juris Doctor from the University of South Carolina School of Law where she was notes editor of South Carolina Law Review and served as a legal writing instructor. She earned a Bachelor of Arts in Political Science from Queens College in 1972.

HOGUE Jr, P Mason
Nelson Mullins Riley & Scarborough LLP, Columbia 803 255 9417
mason.hogue@nelsonmullins.com
Recommended in Corporate/M&A
Practice Areas: Corporate law; economic development; intellectual property; mergers and acquisitions; venture capital; tax incentives; strategic alliances; outsourcing and licensing.
Prof. Memberships: Mr Hogue is a Member of the South Carolina Bar and the State Bar of Georgia. Mr Hogue is a Member of the Board of Directors of EngenuitySC. Additionally, Mr Hogue is a Member of the Software Developers Association of the Midlands and the Palmetto Biotechnology Alliance and serves as the general counsel for both organizations. He also is a member of the Committee of 100 (former Board Member), the Columbia Chamber of Commerce (former Board Member), the South Carolina Economic Developers Association, the South Carolina Investor Network, the Columbia Technology Entrepreneurs Council, and the Columbia Information Technology Council.
Career: Mr Hogue, a Partner of Nelson Mullins Riley & Scarborough, is resident in Columbia where he practices in the areas of corporate law, economic development, and intellectual property law. Mr Hogue has devoted a significant part of his practice to representing entrepreneurs and other companies investing in South Carolina, with a particular focus on computer software and technology companies with respect to corporate, venture capital, strategic alliance, outsourcing and licensing matters.
Personal: In 1992, Mr Hogue was First Honor Graduate when he earned a Juris Doctor, magna cum laude, from the University of South Carolina School of Law where he served as editor-in-chief of the South Carolina Law Review. He earned a Master of International Business Studies from the University of South Carolina in 1988, and a Bachelor of Science in Chemical Engineering, magna cum laude, from the University of South Carolina in 1986.

HOWE Jr, Gedney
Gedney M Howe III PA, Charleston 843 722 8048
Recommended in Litigation

JEFFCOAT III, Otis
Jeffcoat Pike & Nappier LLC (Myrtle Beach), Myrtle Beach 843 626 9000
Recommended in Real Estate

JONES, Celeste
McNair Law Firm PA, Columbia 803 799 9800
Recommended in Litigation

KING Jr, George
Haynsworth Sinkler Boyd PA, Charleston 843 722 3366
Recommended in Corporate/M&A

KNIGHT, G Marcus
Nexsen Pruet, LLC, Columbia 803 253 8245
mknight@nexsenpruet.com
Recommended in Corporate/M&A
Practice Areas: More than 20 years experience practicing in the securities, mergers and acquisitions, corporate, LLC and partnership areas.
Prof. Memberships: A past Chairman of the SC Bar's Corporation, Banking and Securities Section, he also chaired the section's Securities, Partnership, Securities Legislative Study Committees, and continues to lead legislative activities involving limited liability company and securities laws. He is the SC liaison for the ABA Business Section's Corporate Committee.
Career: Knight was twice published in the law review as a student at the USC Law School. A frequent speaker on various M&A, securities, and corporate topics, Knight also published a leading article on limited partnerships in the USC Law Review in 1985. Two leading legal publications have named Knight among the best SC lawyers practicing in corporate, M&A and securities law. Knight served as a special hearing officer for the SC Securities Commission in 2003-04. He is a Founding Member and President-elect of the Executive Committee of the SC Investor Network and serves on the 2005 Executive Committee as Legal Chair for InnoVenture, an important Southeastern US venture capital conference.
Personal: JD, cum laude, University of South Carolina, 1981; BA, summa cum laude, Furman University, 1978.

LIGHTSEY, Wallace
Wyche, Burgess, Freeman & Parham, PA, Greenville 864 242 8200
Recommended in Litigation

LINTON, John
Haynsworth Sinkler Boyd PA, Charleston 843 722 3366
Recommended in Litigation

MAJOR, Joseph
Leatherwood Walker Todd & Mann PC, Greenville 864 242 6440
Recommended in Litigation

MCINNIS, Judith
McNair Law Firm PA, Columbia 803 799 9800
Recommended in Real Estate

MCWILLIAMS, Susan (Susi)
Nexsen Pruet, LLC, Columbia 803 771 8900
smcwilliams@nexsenpruet.com
Recommended in Employment, Litigation
Practice Areas: Products liability, employment, business litigation, malpractice defense, securities, and lender liablity.
Prof. Memberships: Fellow, American College of Trial Lawyers; American Board of Trial Advocates; South Carolina and Georgia Bars; Richland County Bar Association (President, 1998-99); American Bar Association; Federation of Defense and Corporate Counsel; Defense Research Institute; and South Carolina Defense Trial Lawyers Association.
Career: Certified Specialist in Labor and Employment Law, South Carolina Supreme Court; 2005 ed. Best Lawyers in America; Recipient, Columbia YMCA's Tribute to Women and Industry Award.
Personal: Mercer University, JD, magna cum laude, 1982; Agnes Scott College, BA, high honors, 1977.

MENZIE, Edward G
Nexsen Pruet, LLC, Columbia 803 771 8900
emenzie@nexsenpruet.com
Recommended in Corporate/M&A, Real Estate
Practice Areas: Extensive corporate, finance, real estate and securities experience in the representation of a variety of clients, including major real estate developers.
Prof. Memberships: South Carolina Bar (past Chairman, Building Committee and the Unauthorized Practice of Law Committee); American Bar Association (former SC Liaison, State Regulation of Securities Committee); listed in the Corporate Law and Real Estate Law sections of a leading US legal publication.
Career: Board of Directors, Burroughs & Chapin Company, Inc. (Myrtle Beach).
Personal: University of South Carolina, JD, magna cum laude, 1971; University of South Carolina, BS, 1968.

MORRISON, Stephen G
Nelson Mullins Riley & Scarborough LLP, Columbia 803 255 9410
steve.morrison@nelsonmullins.com
Recommended in Litigation
Practice Areas: Technology law and litigation; business litigation; product liability; securities litigation.

Prof. Memberships: Mr Morrison is a Member of the American Bar Association, the Defense Research Institute (former President), International Association of Defense Counsel, Lawyers for Civil Justice (former President), Product Liability Advisory Council, SC Bar, and SC Defense Trial Attorneys Association. **Career:** A Partner in the firm's Columbia office, Mr Morrison is Chairman of the firm's Litigation Group. He practices in technology law and litigation, business liability, product liability, and securities litigation. He has tried more than 200 cases to jury verdict and argued over 60 appeals. He is a Member of the firm's Executive Committee, a governing body of five partners who oversee firm standing committees, strategic initiatives and firm operations. Mr Morrison is experienced in litigation and negotiation with the Federal Trade Commission (FTC). He has represented businesses from the computer technology, automotive, grocery, and paper industries in FTC actions, and dealt with both the competition and enforcement branches of the FTC. He spent substantial time negotiating with the FTC on the sale of the corporate entity Mynd to CSC, a Mynd competitor, in his capacity as general counsel of Mynd. While with Mynd, Mr Morrison oversaw more than 25 domestic and international acquisitions and divestitures, involving stock acquisitions of companies, asset acquisitions, and stock sales of companies and asset sales. He has experience in class action and Attorney General litigation, litigation that often follows an FTC action. Additionally, he has extensive experience in the management of multi-million dollar commercial litigation cases in state and federal courts throughout the Southeast, and has served as lead trial counsel in over 20 states and in international chamber of commerce arbitrations in Europe. He is an adjunct professor at the University of South Carolina School of Law where he has taught courses in legal writing and trial advocacy. He has participated on seminar faculties and presented speeches in 34 states and in multiple international venues. He has published numerous articles and essays, primarily in the fields of technology, advocacy, professionalism, evidence, and damages. **Publications:** Mr Morrison is the author of 'A Fair Compliance with Regulation Defense to Tort Liability', For the Defense, Vol. 32, No.10, October 1991 and contributing author to Products Liability Pretrial Notebook, DRI, 1989. In 1986, he served as a Member of the Editorial Board for the South Carolina Appellate Practice Handbook. **Personal:** Mr Morrison earned a Juris Doctor from the University of South Carolina School of Law in 1975, and a Bachelor of Business Administration from the University of Michigan in

1971. In 1997, Mr Morrison completed the Advanced Management Program at Harvard Business School.

MUSSER, William
McNair Law Firm PA, Columbia
803 799 9800
Recommended in Corporate/M&A

OXNER, Dewey
Haynsworth Sinkler Boyd PA, Greenville
864 240 3200
Recommended in Litigation

PEARSON, Jonathan
Fisher & Phillips LLP, Columbia
803 255 0000
jpearson@laborlawyers.com
Recommended in Employment

Practice Areas: Jonathan Pearson is a Partner in the Columbia office of the national labor and employment law firm of Fisher & Phillips LLP. His practice emphasizes traditional labor law, as well as a wide range of employment litigation including Title VII, ADA, ADEA, FMLA and FLSA. He also frequently assists employers in union contract negotiations and in dealing with strike-related issues. Jon is certified as a specialist in labor and employment law by the South Carolina Supreme Court and is past Chairman of the Labor and Employment Section of the South Carolina Bar.

QUATTLEBAUM, Marvin
Leatherwood Walker Todd & Mann PC, Greenville 864 242 6440
Recommended in Real Estate

ROBINSON Jr, Neil C
Nexsen Pruet Jacobs & Pollard, LLC, Charleston 843 720 1723
nrobinson@nexsenpruet.com
Recommended in Real Estate

Practice Areas: Extensive experience: complex real estate transactions; administrative and regulatory law, including permitting, zoning and property rights; condominium, commercial and resort real estate development. **Prof. Memberships:** President, Southeastern Wildlife Exposition; President, Clemson University Advancement Foundation; President, Hibernian Society; President, Coastal Properties Institute; V-Pres., South Carolina Tourism Council; serves on Recreation Development Council, Urban Land Institute; Governor's Quality of Life Task Force; College of Charleston Advisory Board; and Charleston Education Network. (Founder and past President); South Carolina Education Oversight Committee. **Career:** 1973, Assistant Dean, USC Law School; 1974-76 judicial clerkship with Honorable Charles E Simons, Jr; Chief Judge, US District Court, District of SC; 1974, Grimball & Cabaniss in Charleston; 1980-84 Partner in Grimball Cabaniss Vaughan & Robinson; 1984 started Robinson Wall & Hastie, PA. 1991 firm merged with Nexsen Pruet, LLC. Member, Board of Direc-

tors, manager, Charleston, SC office. Awarded the Order of the Palmetto by Governor David Beasley. Recommended in various leading legal publications. **Personal:** University of South Carolina, JD, 1973; Clemson University, BS, 1966.

SATTERFIELD, Jr, Andreas N
Nelson Mullins Riley & Scarborough LLP, Greenville 864 250 2367
andy.satterfield@nelsonmullins.com
Recommended in Employment

Practice Areas: Labor and employment. **Prof. Memberships:** District of Columbia Bar; South Carolina Bar (Chairman, Employment and Labor Law Section, 1998-99). Admitted to practice before Fourth Circuit Court of Appeals; US District Court for the District of South Carolina; US Court of Federal Claims; US Court of Appeals for the Federal Circuit; US District Court for the District of Columbia; and District of Columbia Court of Appeals. **Career:** Andy Satterfield is a Partner in the firm and represents management in labor and employment matters. Mr Satterfield handles cases involving discrimination; sexual harassment; wrongful discharge; breach of contract; covenants not to compete and trade secret violations; wage and hour disputes and child labor violations under FLSA; and the Family Medical Leave Act. He has extensive experience counseling clients on compliance issues and litigation avoidance strategies; assisting employers with responses to EEOC charges and other administrative actions; drafting and implementing substance abuse policies; drafting noncompetition and nondisclosure agreements; drafting employee handbooks; and conducting supervisor training. Prior to joining the firm, Mr Satterfield was affiliated with another leading Southeastern firm. From 1987-88, he served as a Law Clerk to US Judge John L Napier of the US Court of Federal Claims. **Personal:** In 1985, Mr Satterfield earned a Juris Doctor from the University of South Carolina School of Law. He earned a Bachelor of Arts in Political Science from the University of Georgia in 1981.

SAVITZ, Stephen
Gignilliat, Savitz & Bettis LLP, Columbia
803 799 9311
Recommended in Employment

SHOEMAKER Jr, James
Wyche, Burgess, Freeman & Parham, PA, Greenville 864 242 8200
Recommended in Corporate/M&A

SMOAK, Lewis T
Ogletree, Deakins, Nash, Smoak & Stewart, PC, Greenville 864 271 1300
lewis.smoak@ogletreedeakins.com
Recommended in Employment

Practice Areas: Labor and employment, management labor law. **Prof. Memberships:** Greenville County

Bar Association, South Carolina Bar Association, District of Columbia Bar Association, American Bar Association. **Career:** Admitted to practice in South Carolina, District of Columbia and US Supreme Court. Founding Partner of Ogletree Deakins. Listed in The Best Lawyers in America and Who's Who in the World. Fellow of the College of Labor and Employment Lawyers (ABA). **Publications:** Author of a comprehensive nationwide labor relations study in the construction industry. **Personal:** Furman University (BA, 1966), University of South Carolina (JD, 1969).

SMYTHE, Susan
Buist, Moore, Smythe, McGee P.A., Charleston 843 722 3400
Recommended in Real Estate

SOWELL, Thornwell F
Sowell Gray Stepp & Laffitte LLC, Columbia 803 929 1400
bsowell@sowell.com
Recommended in Litigation

Practice Areas: Commercial litigation and corporate counseling. **Prof. Memberships:** Mr Sowell is a member of the Federation of Defense and Corporate Counsel and the American Board of Trial Advocates. He was a Member of the 'South Carolina Law Review', has served on the South Carolina Bar's House of Delegates, and is a Fellow of the South Carolina Bar Foundation. **Personal:** A native of Chesterfield, SC, Mr Sowell practices primarily in the areas of commercial litigation and corporate counseling. He graduated from Clemson University in 1973 with a BA degree and received his JD in 1976 from the University of South Carolina School of Law, where he was a Member of the 'South Carolina Law Review' and President of the Student Bar Association.

SPETH II, Charles T
Ogletree, Deakins, Nash, Smoak & Stewart, PC, Columbia
803 799 5858
ted.speth@ogletreedeakins.com
Recommended in Employment

Practice Areas: Employment, class action litigation, healthcare. **Prof. Memberships:** South Carolina Bar Association (Chair, Employment and Labor Law Section, 1990-91), Richland County Bar Association, American Bar Association, American Board of Trial Advocates (Secretary/Treasurer, South Carolina Chapter, 2005-), Greater Columbia Chamber of Commerce (General Counsel, 2004-). **Career:** Admitted to practice in South Carolina, US Supreme Court and US Court of Appeals (Fourth, Fifth and Seventh Circuits). Listed in 2003-04 edition and 2001-02 edition of The Best Lawyers in America. **Personal:** Duke University (AB, 1973), University of South Carolina School of Law (JD, 1979).

STEPHENSON, Thomas
Nexsen Pruet Jacobs & Pollard, LLC,
Greenville 864 370 2211
tstephenson@nexsenpruet.com
Recommended in Litigation
Practice Areas: Commercial litigation,
labor and employment law, employ-
ment-related litigation, mediation and
arbitration.
Prof. Memberships: Admitted before
the state and federal court of South Car-
olina, the US Court of Appeals Fourth
and Sixth Circuits.
Career: Litigator, Certified Mediator;
Certified Specialist in Labor and
Employment and Labor Law, South
Carolina Supreme Court; and former
adjunct professor in Labor Law at Clem-
son University.
Personal: University of South Carolina,
JD, 1979; University of South Carolina,
BS, 1976.

STEWART III, J Hamilton
Ogletree, Deakins, Nash, Smoak &
Stewart, PC, Greenville 864 271 1300
jimmie.stewart@ogletreedeakins.com
Recommended in Employment
Practice Areas: Representing manage-
ment in labor, employment and litiga-
tion. Advising major corporations on
positive employee relations and labor
matters, corporate campaigns, and class
action litigation. Management training.
Prof. Memberships: SCBA, TBA, DC
Bar, ABA.
Career: Founding Shareholder. Admit-
ted in South Carolina (Certified Special-
ist), Tennessee, Washington, DC, US
Supreme Court, US Courts of Appeals
(Fourth, Fifth, Eleventh, and District of
Columbia Circuits). Listed in 'The Best
Lawyers in America'. Fellow, the College
of Labor and Employment Lawyers.
Publications: Lectured extensively;
NLRB Regulations of Election Conduct
(1985-97) (Olin Institute).
Personal: Presbyterian College (AB,
1965), University of South Carolina (JD,
1969).

SUGGS Jr, Fred W
Ogletree, Deakins, Nash, Smoak &
Stewart, PC, Greenville 864 271 1300
fred.suggs@ogletreedeakins.com
Recommended in Employment
Practice Areas: Labor and employ-
ment.
Prof. Memberships: American, Alaba-
ma, Florida, and South Carolina Bar
Associations; Judicial Conference for the
Fourth Circuit, Certified Specialist in
Labor and Employment Law, and Fellow
of the College of Labor and Employ-
ment Lawyers.
Career: Admitted to practice in US
Supreme Court, the Alabama, Florida,
and South Carolina Supreme Courts,
US District Courts (various), and US
Courts of Appeal (various).
Publications: Employer Liability for
Age Discrimination, Institute of Business Law, 1992; Advising Your Corporate Client on Avoiding Charges of Sexual Harassment, Alabama Lawyer, July
1985.
Personal: Kansas State University (BS,
1970), University of Alabama (JD,
1975).

SWANSON, David
Haynsworth Sinkler Boyd PA,
Charleston 843 722 3366
Recommended in Real Estate

TATE, Simmons
Haynsworth Sinkler Boyd PA,
Charleston 843 722 3366
Recommended in Litigation

TESSIER, Troy
Wyche, Burgess, Freeman & Parham,
PA, Greenville 864 242 8200
Recommended in Litigation

TISDALE Jr, Thomas S
Nexsen Pruet Jacobs & Pollard, LLC,
Charleston 843 577 9440
ttisdale@nexsenpruet.com
Recommended in Litigation
Practice Areas: General commercial
litigation; communications law; prod-
ucts liability law; intellectual property
litigation; first amendment law.
Prof. Memberships: South Carolina Bar
(Board of Governors, 1975; Secretary,
1976; Treasurer, 1979; President-Elect,
1980; President, 1981-82); Charleston
Lawyers Club (President, 1970).
Career: Assistant Solicitor, 9th Judicial
Circuit, 1969-70; Associate Judge,
Municipal Court, City of Charleston,
1970-72; Supreme Court Commission
on Grievances and Discipline, 1977-80;
Supreme Court Commission on Con-
tinuing Lawyer Competency, 1984-87;
South Carolina Law Institute; CPR Insti-
tute for Dispute Resolution, 2002-. Mr
Tisdale was a founding Partner of
Young, Clement, Rivers and Tisdale in
Charleston, SC. He has served on the
Board of Regents of the University of the
South and the Board of Trustees of
Voorhees College; as Chairman of the
Board of Trustees of Porter-Gaud
School; and on the boards of the South
Carolina Aquarium and Spoleto Festival
USA. Mr Tisdale was also chancellor of
the Episcopal Diocese of South Carolina
from 1975-85.
Personal: University of South Carolina,
JD, 1964; University of the South, BA,
1961.

WALKER, Trenholm
Pratt-Thomas Epting and Walker Law
Firm, Charleston 843 727 2200
Recommended in Litigation

WARREN, J Steve
Jackson Lewis, Greenville
864 232 7000
Recommended in Employment

WARREN III, John
Warren & Sinkler LLP, Charleston
843 577 0660
*Recommended in Corporate/M&A,
Real Estate*

YOUNG, Kenneth E
Nelson Mullins Riley & Scarborough
LLP, Greenville 864 250 2231
ken.young@nelsonmullins.com
Recommended in Employment
Practice Areas: Business litigation;
healthcare; labor and employment; liti-
gation.
Prof. Memberships: A Member of the
South Carolina Bar, Mr Young is admit-
ted to practice before the Supreme
Court of the United States, the US Court
of Appeals for the 4th Circuit, and the
US District Court for the District of
South Carolina. He is included in The
Best Lawyers in America, 2003-04 and
2004-05, and is a Fellow of the College
of Labor and Employment Lawyers. Mr
Young is prominently affiliated with the
American Bar Association where he currently serves as the Labor and Employment Law Section's delegate to the ABA
House of Delegates. He has also served
as a Member of the ABA Board of Governors and the South Carolina Bar
Board of Governors.
Career: Kenneth E Young is a Partner in
the firm's Greenville office who practices
in the areas of employment and labor
law and business litigation. A certified
specialist in employment and labor law,
he heads the firm's Labor and Employment Practice Group, and has served as
defense counsel in several major
employment discrimination and wage-
hour class actions.

YOUNG Jr, Rutledge
Young, Clement & Rivers LLP,
Charleston 843 577 4000
Recommended in Litigation

NELSON MULLINS RILEY & SCARBOROUGH, LLP

THE FIRM

Managing Partner: David E Dukes
Marketing Partner: Kevin A Hall

Number of partners: 182
Number of other lawyers: 171

AREAS OF PRACTICE:
Corporate Finance	30%
Business Litigation	20%
Pharmaceuticals & Medical Devices	13%
Healthcare	12%
Labor & Employment	10%
Mass Tort Litigation	10%
Government Relations	5%

FIRM OVERVIEW: Founded in 1897, Nelson Mullins maintains offices in Georgia, North Carolina, South Carolina and Washington, DC. With more than 350 attorneys practicing in nine offices, the firm has more than 40 diversified practice areas and represents a wide variety of clients that range in size from start-up technology companies to Fortune 500 corporations.

MAIN AREAS OF PRACTICE:
Corporate Finance: Firm attorneys handle a broad range of securities, finance and regulatory matters for development stage private companies and large publicly held companies in a wide range of industries.
Business Litigation: Attorneys in this group provide counsel throughout the United States in the areas of business, securities and financial fraud, business torts, antitrust matters, lending liability claims, contract disputes, and other areas.
Mass Tort Litigation: Firm attorneys are equipped to handle or coordinate the defense of mass tort claims on an individual, regional or national basis, and serve as national trial and coordinating counsel for leading US companies.
Pharmaceuticals & Medical Devices: Firm attorneys have extensive knowledge in many areas of science and technology and effectively handle claims regarding clients' products and services. The attorneys have experience with mass torts and multi-district litigation, requiring coordination with attorneys from across the United States.
Healthcare: Firm attorneys are capable of providing comprehensive client services. They have experience providing services to healthcare clients in corporate transactions, regulatory and governmental affairs, litigation, finance and tax.
Labor & Employment: This diverse group of attorneys defends companies in all facets of labor and employment disputes.
Government Relations: These attorneys have extensive experience with a wide range of clients in many areas of lobbying and legislative analysis.

CLIENTS: Nelson Mullins clients include leading manufacturers, Fortune 500 companies, commercial banks and other financial institutions, public utilities, venture capital and private equity firms, industrial and service corporations, partnerships, profit and non-profit organizations, government agencies, entrepreneurs and individuals.

INTERNATIONAL WORK: The Nelson Mullins International Practice Group serves clients around the world in international business, commercial and trade matters, business immigration, and matters before federal courts, international agencies, and tribunals.

HEAD OFFICE

SOUTH CAROLINA
Meridian, Suite 1700, 1320 Main Street,
Columbia, SC 29201
Tel: 803 799 2000   **Fax:** 803 256 7500
Website: www.nelsonmullins.com

BRANCH OFFICES

DISTRICT OF COLUMBIA
101 Constitution Avenue, NW, Suite 900,
Washington, DC 20001
Tel: 202 712 2800   **Fax:** 202 712 2862

GEORGIA
999 Peachtree Street, NE, Suite 1400,
Atlanta, GA 30309-3964
Tel: 404 817 6000   **Fax:** 404 817 6050

NORTH CAROLINA
Bank of America Corporate Center, Suite 2400,
100 North Tryon Street, **Charlotte**, NC 28202-4000
Tel: 704 417 3000   **Fax:** 704 377 4814

GlenLake One, Suite 200, 4140 Parklake Avenue,
Raleigh, NC 27612
Tel: 919 877 3800   **Fax:** 919 877 3799

The Knollwood, Suite 530, 380 Knollwood Street,
Winston-Salem, NC 27103
Tel: 336 774 3300   **Fax:** 336 774 3299

SOUTH CAROLINA
Liberty Center, Suite 600, 151 Meeting Street,
Charleston, SC 29401-2239
Tel: 843 853 5200   **Fax:** 843 722 8700

Poinsett Plaza, Suite 900, 104 South Main Street,
Greenville, SC 29601-2122
Tel: 864 250 2300   **Fax:** 864 232 2925

Founders Centre, Suite 301, 2411 North Oak Street,
Myrtle Beach, SC 29577-3165
Tel: 843 448 3500   **Fax:** 843 448 3437

CONTACTS

Business Litigation	Stephen G Morrison
Corporate Finance	John T Moore
Government Relations	Edward E Poliakoff
Healthcare	Stuart M Andrews
Labor & Employment	Kenneth E Young
Mass Tort Litigation	R Bruce Shaw
Pharmaceuticals & Medical Devices	David E Dukes

NEXSEN PRUET, LLC

THE FIRM

Managing Partner: William A Pollard

Number of partners: 98
Number of other lawyers: 78

FIRM OVERVIEW: Nexsen Pruet has earned a reputation for professional, principled service. Nexsen Pruet's team of more than 170 attorneys work out of seven offices in two states: North and South Carolina. The regional locations help make Nexsen Pruet one of the Carolinas' truly comprehensive law firms, and a preferred choice for companies and individuals seeking exceptional legal representation. Nexsen Pruet has addressed the demands of an increasingly diverse client base, serving individuals, institutions, and businesses of all types and sizes by hiring attorneys whose skill and expertise covers a comprehensive range of nearly 30 areas of practice.

MAIN AREAS OF PRACTICE:

Real Estate: Nexsen Pruet's Real Estate Group represents one of the most experienced and diversified teams of real estate attorneys in the southeastern United States, with attorneys in the firm actively engaged in virtually all types of real estate investment and development. The firm's Real Estate Practice includes representation of buyers, sellers, landlords, tenants, lenders, borrowers, developers, investors, as well as all types of businesses needing real estate counseling. The Real Estate Group works closely with the firm's Corporate, Securities, Healthcare, Environmental, Tax and Bankruptcy Groups to provide seamless one-stop service.

Litigation: Nexsen Pruet's Litigation Group devotes a great deal of time to resolving its clients' legal disputes. Nexsen Pruet's attorneys combine trial advocacy with well-honed negotiating skills to aggressively seek the outcome desired by its clients. Areas of significant experience include: antitrust and unfair trade practices, aviation, civil rights defense, construction, contracts, creditor's rights and bankruptcy, environmental, health care, intellectual property, international arbitrations, labor and employment, maritime, products liability, professional malpractice, public utilities, securities, tax and worker's compensation.

Mergers & Acquisitions: Nexsen Pruet's mergers and acquisitions attorneys utilize the Corporate, Tax, Real Estate, Environmental, Labor and Employment, Securities, Finance and Litigation Practices within the firm to enhance representation, providing clients with direct access to the depth and scope of legal experience necessary to accomplish desired objectives. Along with a results-oriented philosophy, the attorneys in this practice have extensive experience in structuring complex and multi-faceted business transactions, drafting and negotiating comprehensive documents and handling the regulatory and logistical steps required to achieve closing.

Healthcare: Nexsen Pruet has an extensive Healthcare Practice which represents several hundred physicians and more than 20 hospitals on an on-going basis throughout South Carolina and North Carolina. The Healthcare Group is managed by eight full-time attorneys who have significant experience and a deep understanding of laws concerning the regulation, delivery, and financing of healthcare services.

Construction: Nexsen Pruet is involved in all areas of construction law and related activities, including planning, advice and contract review and preparation in the architectural, engineering and construction areas. The firm's practice includes multi-party and complex construction and construction-related litigation in state and federal courts, and mediation and arbitration proceedings.

HEAD OFFICE

SOUTH CAROLINA
1441 Main Street, Suite 1500, **Columbia**, SC 29201
Tel: 803 771 8900 **Fax:** 803 253 8277
Email: hmatthews@nexsenpruet.com
Website: www.nexsenpruet.com

BRANCH OFFICES

NORTH CAROLINA
201 South Tryon Street, Suite 1200, **Charlotte**, NC 28202
Tel: 704 339 0304 **Fax:** 704 338 5377

701 Green Valley Road, Suite 100 **Greensboro**, NC 27408
Tel: 336 373 1600 **Fax:** 336 273 5357

SOUTH CAROLINA
205 King Street, Suite 400, **Charleston**, SC 29401
Tel: 843 577 9440 **Fax:** 843 720 1777

201 West McBee Avenue, Suite 400, **Greenville**, SC 29601
Tel: 864 370 2211 **Fax:** 864 282 1177

400 Main Street Office Campus, Suite 100A, **Hilton Head**, SC 29926
Tel: 843 689 6277 **Fax:** 843 682 1577

2411 North Oak Street, Suite 105, **Myrtle Beach**, SC 29577
Tel: 843 445 9688 **Fax:** 843 443 8147

CONTACTS

Real Estate	Wm Leighton Lord III
Litigation	Val A Stieglitz
Mergers & Acquisitions	G Marcus Knight
Healthcare	Ralph W Barbier III
Construction	John W Davidson
Intellectual Property	William Y Klett III
Labor & Employment	David E Dubberly

Intellectual Property: Nexsen Pruet's Intellectual Property Group represents clients with a broad range of intellectual property issues. The attorneys who practice in this area include patent, trademark and copyright attorneys with a broad range of technical backgrounds and experience, intellectual property litigation attorneys and dispute resolution, and transactional attorneys experienced in licensing, technology transfer, employer/employee rights in intellectual property, due diligence and valuation issues.

Labor & Employment: Nexsen Pruet's Labor and Employment Group represents management in every area of labor and employment law. The attorneys represent both private and public sector employers in non-union and union settings. Several attorneys are Certified Specialists in Labor and Employment by the South Carolina Supreme Court.

NEXSEN|PRUET
The Carolinas Law Firm

SOWELL GRAY STEPP & LAFFITTE, LLC

THE FIRM

Managing Partner: Robert E Stepp

Number of partners: 9
Number of other lawyers: 11

HEAD OFFICE

SOUTH CAROLINA
1310 Gadsden Street, PO Box 11449, **Columbia**, SC 29211
Tel: 803 929 1400
Website: www.sowell.com

FIRM OVERVIEW: Sowell Gray Stepp & Laffitte offers a tailored approach to litigation - whether maximizing recovery, minimizing damage and legal fees, or protecting business practices. Diverse backgrounds, education, and experience promote an open exchange of knowledge and ideas. The client defines the objective; the firm analyzes the options, considers the costs and risks, and recommends approaches so that the client can choose among the alternatives. Serving clients ranging from multi-national corporations to small businesses, the firm delivers respectful service, regardless of client size.

MAIN AREAS OF PRACTICE:

Administrative & Regulatory: Attorneys represent clients before the South Carolina Public Service Commission, Department of Revenue, Department of Insurance, Manufactured Housing Board, Residential Builders Commission, the Board of Financial Institutions, the Contractor's Licensing Board, and the Administrative Law Division in South Carolina. The firm provides advice and counsel on important legal issues such as utility regulation and ratemaking, with clients ranging from utilities to consumers.

Business Litigation: The Business Litigation Team provides counsel in all areas of business disputes, litigating cases involving class actions, lender liability, premium fraud, corporate governance, business transactions, securities transactions, disputes, financial fraud, directors' liability and derivative actions. Firm attorneys have considerable experience in diverse areas of business litigation, including insurance coverage, lender liability, real estate, and title insurance.

Employment & ERISA: The Employment Law Department provides full service representation of public and private-sector management in all employment law areas. The team regularly represents clients in litigating employment-related civil rights and employment discrimination claims, including Title VII of the Civil Rights Act, the Age Discrimination in Employment Act, the Americans with Disabilities Act, and the Family and Medical Leave Act, before federal and state agencies, including the Equal Employment Opportunity Commission (EEOC) and the South Carolina Human Affairs Commission (SCHAC), as well as state and federal courts. Firm attorneys also regularly provide counseling, advice, and training to management and supervisors on employment regulations.

Medical Malpractice & Nursing Home Defense: Sowell Gray's Medical Malpractice and Nursing Home Practice defends a wide variety of claims arising from the delivery of healthcare and nursing home care. The firm represents healthcare providers in the defense of negligence and malpractice claims as well as claims brought against care facilities such as hospitals and nursing homes. Attorneys also work closely with clients to provide counseling as to methods of avoiding claims and lawsuits.

Probate Litigation: Jurisdiction frequently is placed initially in the Probate Court, and can involve complex business issues, estates and trusts, and other matters relating to the affairs of decedents and incapacitated persons. Firm lawyers represent individuals and personal representatives in litigation surrounding the estates of family members, inter vivos and testamentary trusts, and powers of attorney with sensitivity and efficacy.

Products Liability: The firm's representation has spanned local, regional and national products litigation involving diverse industries chemical, silica, asbestos, nuclear, pharmaceuticals, industrial equipment, and manufacturing, equipping firm attorneys to handle and coordinate the defense of products liability claims which attack a product or product lines of a regional or national scope. Firm attorneys also provide counseling as to methods of avoiding or minimizing potential claims, procedures which will assist in the defense of future claims, and compliance with federal, state and local regulators dealing with the manufacture and sale of potentially hazardous products.

Professional Liability: Sowell Gray provides aggressive representation at both the trial and appellate levels, with clients including directors and officers, healthcare professionals, accountants, attorneys, insurance agents and brokers, and engineers. A history of acting successfully on behalf of professionals, corporations and individuals involved in liability disputes has provided firm attorneys with in-depth knowledge and experience in this area.

SOWELL GRAY STEPP & LAFFITTE, LLC
ATTORNEYS AND COUNSELORS AT LAW

Litigation is our business

CONTENTS: Corporate/M&A p.1587; Employment p.1589; Litigation p.1589; Real Estate p.1591; Individuals' Profiles p.1592.

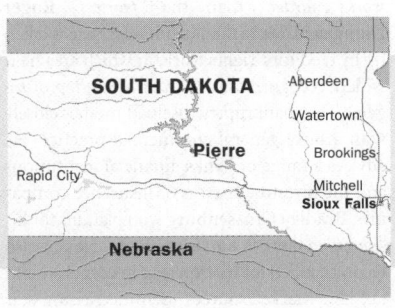

How lawyers are ranked

The opinions we gather from clients — mainly from in-house lawyers but also from other purchasers of legal services — are balanced by opinions from colleagues and competitors. Together, they provide two different perspectives — an all-round view — and biased viewpoints cancel each other out.

CORPORATE/M&A

South Dakota
Leading firms (Corporate/M&A)

1. DAVENPORT, EVANS, HURWITZ *Sioux Falls*
   WOODS, FULLER, SHULTZ & SMITH *Sioux Falls*
2. CUTLER & DONAHOE LLP *Sioux Falls*
   GUNDERSON, PALMER, GOODSELL *Rapid City*
   MURPHY, GOLDAMMER *Sioux Falls*
3. BOYCE, GREENFIELD, PASHBY & WELK *Sioux Falls*
   CADWELL SANFORD DEIBERT & GARRY *Sioux Falls*
   LYNN, JACKSON, SHULTZ & LEBRUN *Rapid City*

Leading individuals (Corporate/M&A)

1. DAMGAARD Roger *Woods Fuller,* Sioux Falls
   GOLDAMMER Vance *Murphy Goldammer,* Sioux Falls
   GROSSENBURG Bradley *Woods Fuller,* Sioux Falls
   HAYES Robert *Davenport Evans,* Sioux Falls
   KNUDSON David *Davenport Evans,* Sioux Falls
2. CUTLER Richard *Cutler & Donahoe,* Sioux Falls
   GOETZINGER Patrick *Gunderson Palmer,* Rapid City
   GULLICKSON Charles *Davenport Evans,* Sioux Falls
   HAJEK Douglas *Davenport Evans,* Sioux Falls
   WIEDERRICH James *Woods Fuller,* Sioux Falls
3. ANDERSON Scott Bradley *Davenport,* Sioux Falls
   GREENFIELD Gregg *Boyce Greenfield,* Sioux Falls
   KROON David *Woods Fuller,* Sioux Falls
   MAGNUSON Lee *Lynn Jackson,* Rapid City
   PERRENOUD Scott *Cadwell Sanford,* Sioux Falls

Up-and-coming individuals

LUST David *Gunderson Palmer,* Rapid City

Leading individuals (Bankruptcy)

1. DAMGAARD Roger *Woods Fuller,* Sioux Falls
   HAYES Robert *Davenport Evans,* Sioux Falls
2. ENTWISTLE Frederick *Woods Fuller,* Sioux Falls
   GAUER Keith *Davenport Evans,* Sioux Falls

Firms and individuals are listed alphabetically in each band.

Band 1

Davenport, Evans, Hurwitz & Smith LLP

The Firm: Sources commended this 16-lawyer corporate team for its success in developing a "*superlative practice.*" It houses a wealth of "*top-notch talent*" in corporate and financial law. Areas of expertise encompass securities law, bankruptcy and M&A for its stable of loyal clients, including local, nationwide and foreign corporations. For example, the firm often acts as corporate counsel for out-of-state lenders on commercial loans to borrowers in South Dakota or loans that are secured by collateral in the state. Recent commercial transactions include negotiating an $18 million charitable gift to a children's hospital. Other work includes advising on the financing of a student housing facility constructed by Sioux Falls School District, and advising a South Dakota organization on the attempted acquisition of a French biotechnology company. The team also provides general counsel services to the South Dakota Housing Development Authority, particularly in the financial arena.

The Lawyers: Market sources endorsed **Robert Hayes** as the "*dean of creditors' rights,*" a practice area to which he devotes a considerable amount of time. He represents institutional lenders both in South Dakota and nationwide, alongside his busy real estate practice. He recently represented a bankruptcy trustee in the liquidation of a $28 million ethanol plant. Interviewees praised him as "*incredibly articulate and creative – he achieves results with minimum fanfare.*" "*Top of his class*" **David Knudson** "*employs his creativity and succinct analysis to fashion unique results in complex matters,*" said sources. He is heavily engaged in ongoing strategic advice to high-profile clients such as Dakota, Minnesota & Eastern Railroad and Sioux Valley Hospitals & Health System. The "*tenacious*" **Keith Gauer** has cultivated a successful bankruptcy practice, in which market sources regard him as "*seasoned beyond his years.*" He works closely with Robert Hayes, and is "*excellent when thrown in at the deep end.*" **Charles Gullickson** "*thinks outside of the box,*" a skill put to great use in advising bank and financial institution clients, for whom he handles government regulatory matters. Clients commented on his "*extraordinarily high IQ and empathy with the concerns of his clients.*" **Douglas Hajek**'s finance expertise draws on his background as a banker and puts him in the perfect position to "*evaluate cases from an informed business viewpoint.*" Market sources concurred that public finance work is where his "*excellent connections and tough but gentlemanly negotiating skills*" are most effectively deployed. Furthermore, clients commended him as a good listener. Bright star **Scott Anderson** masters a demanding corporate and M&A practice, regularly advising cable television and telecommunications clients. Recent work includes handling a tax-deferred exchange transaction for a company that owns 20 radio stations. Clients look to him for "*perfect and well-thought-out results*" and his "*strong understanding of the nuts and bolts of the law.*"

The Clients: Fishback Financial; 1st Financial Bank USA; First PREMIER Bank; National Organization of Life & Health Insurance Guaranty Associations; CorTrust Bank; Midcontinent Communications; Sioux Falls School District; First National Bank in Sioux Falls; Dakota, Minnesota & Eastern Railroad; Citibank (South Dakota) and Sioux Valley Hosptals & Health System.

Woods, Fuller, Shultz & Smith PC

The Firm: According to the market, this ten-lawyer corporate team provides "*top-quality*" advice across the spectrum of corporate work. Its expertise lies in advising businesses on incorporation, financings, bankruptcies, securities and M&A matters. It acts for a diverse client base of banks, financial institutions and local and national businesses from the agriculture, ethanol and healthcare industries. In addition, the team provides general commercial and transactional advice to a number of nationwide insurance company clients operating in South Dakota. It is currently advising Thornton Capital Advisors in a multistate $100 million bankruptcy.

The Lawyers: Interviewees said that "*no one works harder*" than the "*fearless*" **Roger Damgaard**. More than half his practice is taken up by creditors' rights work, in which area he is widely recognized as "*always at the top of his game*." His bankruptcy caseload meshes closely with a busy general commercial practice. He advises a range of banks, financial institutions and the investment arms of insurance companies. **Bradley Grossenburg** won plaudits for his "*ability to stay calm under pressure*." He was also recommended for his expertise in corporate and tax law. Market sources identified rising star **Frederick Entwistle**'s talent for handling complex bankruptcy and foreclosure matters. Best known for his extensive corporate work in the ethanol industry, "*goal-driven*" **James Wiederrich** was singled out by clients for his "*shoot from the hip*" style and "*realistic evaluations leading to creative solutions*." "*Honest and straightforward*" **David Kroon** was praised for his technical expertise in a wide range of corporate matters, particularly advising healthcare clients.
The Clients: Prudential; Equitable; Great Plains Ethanol; US Bank; Broin; MetLife; Home Federal Bank and South Dakota Soybean Processors.

Band 2

Cutler & Donahoe LLP

The Firm: This team of six handles a busy workload of corporate and commercial cases, and has earned the respect of the market. It attracts a "*well-heeled*" client base of wealthy entrepreneurs and local enterprises, including distribution, manufacturing and retail businesses, telecom companies and banks. The workload encompasses advising on M&A activity, succession planning and real estate transactions.
The Lawyers: A "*man of many talents*," **Richard Cutler** is seen as the bedrock of the firm's corporate and real estate practice. Clients applauded his "*terrific long-term strategic advice*" and aggressive representation of the largest entrepreneurs in town.
The Clients: Great Western Bank; First National Bank in Sioux Falls; First American Bank & Trust; Stan Houston Equipment and Myrl & Roy's Paving.

Gunderson, Palmer, Goodsell & Nelson LLP

The Firm: This "*premier*" Rapid City commercial practice was praised by clients for the quality of its work and its "*reasonable billing*." Six attorneys of "*high integrity*" advise clients on sales and acquisitions, financings and business succession planning. The firm recently acted for Coca-Cola in its acquisition of distributorships in several states, including Utah and Colorado.
The Lawyers: "*Intelligent and quick-witted*" **Patrick Goetzinger**'s time is divided equally between corporate transactional, succession planning and real estate matters. Market sources praised his broad experience and "*knack of explaining complex legalese in layman's terms*." **David Lust** works closely with Goetzinger, assisting businesses and individuals with their legal and strategic planning needs.
The Clients: Wells Fargo; BankWest; Rapid City Telco Federal Credit Union and Credit Bureau of Rapid City.

Murphy, Goldammer & Prendergast

The Firm: Five lawyers make up the corporate team here and advise on the gamut of transactional matters. The workload regularly includes handling business organizational matters, advice on stockholder agreements and the sale and purchase of corporate entities. Clients reserved particular praise for the firm's creditor bankruptcy practice, in which its attorneys are regarded as "*technical experts*."
The Lawyers: The "*congenial and charming*" **Vance Goldammer** is always in high demand for his corporate and banking expertise. Clients report that "*he doesn't have a mean bone in his body*," and "*thrives on the challenges other attorneys would be blown away by*."
The Clients: Furniture Outlets USA, Wells Fargo and Elmen Enterprises are among the firm's clients.

Band 3

Boyce, Greenfield, Pashby & Welk LLP

The Firm: This flourishing team of five attorneys attracts a diverse clientele that ranges from small mom-and-pop businesses to large publicly traded companies. It is especially acclaimed for the representation of healthcare clients, including hospitals and surgical centers. Lawyers offer advice on incorporation, stockholder agreements, asset purchases and contractual matters. Recent highlights include acting for Sioux Falls Surgical Center in its $110 million merger with a publicly traded Canadian healthcare company.
The Lawyers: Peers and clients alike praised **Gregg Greenfield** as a "*dependable all-rounder*." In addition to his busy corporate practice he manages an environmental law caseload that includes drafting purchase agreements and indemnities, and dealing with contamination issues.
The Clients: Harms Oil, Raven Industries and First National Bank in Sioux Falls are among the firm's clients.

Cadwell Sanford Deibert & Garry LLP

The Firm: As well as acclaiming the litigation practice here, the market praised the firm's corporate and commercial capabilities. Commentators report particular expertise in transactional and bankruptcy matters, and the team draws banks, financial institutions and national businesses to its stable.
The Lawyers: Interviewees rated **Scott Perrenoud** for his "*goal-oriented and tenacious*" approach. Over the last year he successfully handled several large-scale bankruptcies and commercial transactions.
The Clients: US Bank; Security Bank; First PREMIER Bank; Security Mortgage; First Midwest Bank; Household Credit Services; Toyota Motor Credit Corporation; NationsCredit Commercial Corporation; Imperial Thrift & Loan Association and Beneficial.

Lynn, Jackson, Shultz & Lebrun PC

The Firm: This firm has a distinguished history in the state as a sound general practice with a strong trials and appeals record. It also has a maturing corporate practice with a number of high-caliber attorneys. The team advises clients on tax planning and corporate structural and transactional matters.
The Lawyers: Originally based in Rapid City, **Lee Magnuson** is the pathfinder who founded the Sioux Falls office in 1987. The market praised his expertise in corporate law. Interviewees also felt that his background as a certified public accountant supported his "*insight and understanding*" of complex business transactions.
The Clients: Black Hills Regional Eye Institute; Rushmore Electric Power Cooperative; Westhills Village; South Dakota School of Mines and Technology; US Bank of South Dakota and Montana-Dakota Utilities.

EMPLOYMENT

South Dakota
Leading firms
(Employment: Mainly Defendant)

1 BOYCE, GREENFIELD, PASHBY *Sioux Falls*
DAVENPORT, EVANS, HURWITZ *Sioux Falls*
WOODS, FULLER, SHULTZ & SMITH *Sioux Falls*

Leading individuals
(Employment: Mainly Defendant)

1 HARALDSON Comet *Woods Fuller,* Sioux Falls
MCKNIGHT Michael *Boyce Greenfield,* Sioux Falls
ORR Rick *Davenport Evans,* Sioux Falls
SIMONS Susan Brunick *Davenport Evans,* Sioux Falls

2 HOLM Kristi Geisler *Davenport Evans,* Sioux Falls
MARSO Lisa Hansen *Boyce Greenfield,* Sioux Falls
SHULTZ Jeff *Woods Fuller,* Sioux Falls
SOGN Jon *Lynn Jackson,* Rapid City

Firms and individuals are listed alphabetically in each band.

Band 1

Boyce, Greenfield, Pashby & Welk LLP

The Firm: Sources insist that this employment defense practice is "*at the forefront*" of the market. Its workload encompasses advice on a mixture of workers' compensation and employment discrimination claims. For example, the team defended a local healthcare facility against a doctor's allegations of slander, libel, defamation and interference with contract. Other recent work includes advising a college on a claim made by a student under the ADA.

The Lawyers: **Michael McKnight**'s forte lies in workers, compensation, an area in which he is widely considered to be the "*best in the state.*" One client applauded him as "*the best-prepared attorney I have worked with – he knows each case inside out,*" while several more distinguished his "*excellent courtroom demeanor.*" He advises employers and insurance companies on workers' compensation and discrimination claims. Recent work includes resolving through mediation an age and disability discrimination claim brought against a prominent healthcare facility client. New to the rankings this year, **Lisa Hansen Marso** comes warmly recommended for her employment defense and workers' compensation expertise. Peers commented that she is an "*experienced trial lawyer whose employment law practice goes from strength to strength.*"

The Clients: Acuity Insurance; Safeco; Chubb; Sentry Insurance; General Casualty Insurance; Unitrin and Western National Insurance.

Davenport, Evans, Hurwitz & Smith LLP

The Firm: Seven attorneys make up the employment team here, undertaking employee benefits, discrimination and wage and hour work. Since the recent revision of wage and hour overtime legislation, the team has been particularly busy advising clients on various changes and reclassifications affecting their businesses. It successfully represented an insurance company in a recent workers' compensation claim in which an employee's misconduct resulted in the creation of mustard gas.

The Lawyers: Market sources say that the "*aggressive*" **Susan Brunick Simons** "*puts her heart and soul into representing her clients.*" She has a noted flair for responding to claims in ways that manage to avoid litigation. Clients rate "*top-flight*" **Rick Orr** for his "*clear thinking and strong arguments.*" Peers recognize him as a "*highly principled and detail-oriented*" employment practitioner. **Kristi Holm** does a "*superb job*" for clients, who feel that she is "*always available for us and ready to help.*" She represents a number of employers and insurance companies,

MAINLY DEFENDANT

with recent highlights including acting for a national bank in a workers' compensation case on appeal.

The Clients: Gage Brothers; Citibank (South Dakota); Sioux Valley Hospitals & Health System; First PREMIER Bank; St. Paul Travelers and Liberty Mutual.

Woods, Fuller, Shultz & Smith PC

The Firm: This firm is home to an employment department of four "*top-rate*" lawyers. Clients seek out the team for its specialization in workers' compensation cases. Over the past year attorneys successfully obtained settlements for over a dozen employers. This included litigation to defend a client faced with a claim of over one quarter of a million dollars, which was eventually settled for $25,000.

The Lawyers: Respondents singled out the "*savvy*" **Comet Haraldson** for his "*aggressive representation*" of clients against workers' compensation claims. Recent highlights include obtaining a favorable ruling on an employee's back injury from the Department of Labor for a prominent retail client. **Jeff Shultz** "*really knows the law and represents his clients well.*" He was recently successful in a multiple injury case involving a truck-driving employee who had broken his doctor's restrictions following his return to work. He also represents GE in their insured losses and is state counsel for Home Depot.

The Clients: 3M; Wal-Mart; Continental Western Group; Farm Bureau and Hy-Vee.

Other Notable Practitioners

Market sources endorsed **Jon Sogn** of Lynn, Jackson, Shultz & Lebrun PC as an excellent lawyer with a busy workload of employment defense cases. He also has useful expertise in product liability and personal injury law.

LITIGATION

Band 1

Davenport, Evans, Hurwitz & Smith LLP

The Firm: This firm maintains its position as a preeminent player in the market and hosts an impressive full-service litigation team of twelve attorneys. Clients look to the firm for the variety and quality of its "*deeply specialized individuals.*" The department advises on business litigation, including contractual disputes, banking law, products liability and medical malpractice claims. Highlights of the past year include the representation of a manufacturer of baby products in the Supreme Court, achieving the reversal of a previous court's decision on a products liability claim.

The Lawyers: The "*tenacious*" **Edwin Evans** is a "*quick study, whose aggressive courtroom skills and resourcefulness make him an excellent all-rounder.*" Clients declared him "*as good as can be*" for medical malpractice defence, an area that takes up a significant proportion of his time. The "*top-flight*" **Michael Luce** possesses "*superb communication skills, particularly when dealing with juries,*" say commentators. In particular, insurance company clients spoke of his "*uncanny ability to unsettle the opposition.*" He has a varied litigation practice, advising clients on construction disputes, insurance defense and

GENERAL COMMERCIAL

products liability matters. **Mark Haigh** works closely with Edwin Evans and spends over half of his time on medical malpractice defense cases. The rest of his time is given to general commercial litigation. Peers marveled that "*he is so professionally mature that it is easy to forget he is younger than many of his rivals,*" flagging up his ability to build a good rapport with juries.

The Clients: Sioux Valley Hospitals & Health System; CNA; Citibank (South Dakota); Allied Insurance; The Doctors Company; MMIC Group; Midwest Family Mutual Insurance; AIG; St. Paul Travelers and Liberty Mutual.

South Dakota
Leading firms
(Litigation: General Commercial)

1 DAVENPORT, EVANS, HURWITZ *Sioux Falls*
WOODS, FULLER, SHULTZ & SMITH *Sioux Falls*

2 BANGS, MCCULLEN, BUTLER, FOYE *Rapid City*
BOYCE, GREENFIELD, PASHBY *Sioux Falls*
CADWELL SANFORD DEIBERT & GARRY *Sioux Falls*
GUNDERSON, PALMER, GOODSELL *Rapid City*
MAY, ADAM, GERDES & THOMPSON *Pierre*

3 COSTELLO PORTER HILL HEISTERKAMP *Rapid City*
JOHNSON, HEIDEPRIEM, MINER *Sioux Falls*
LYNN, JACKSON, SHULTZ & LEBRUN *Rapid City*
SCHAFFER LAW OFFICE *Sioux Falls*

Leading individuals
(Litigation: General Commercial)

1 ANDERSON Robert *May Adam*, Pierre
EVANS Edwin *Davenport Evans*, Sioux Falls
FULLER William *Woods Fuller*, Sioux Falls
LUCE Michael *Davenport Evans*, Sioux Falls
PALMER Crisman *Gunderson Palmer*, Rapid City
PASHBY Gary *Boyce Greenfield*, Sioux Falls
SANFORD Steven *Cadwell Sanford*, Sioux Falls
SCHAFFER Michael *Schaffer*, Sioux Falls
THIMSEN Gary *Woods Fuller*, Sioux Falls

2 CARPENTER Edward *Costello Porter*, Rapid City
FRITZ Thomas *Lynn Jackson*, Rapid City
GARRY William *Cadwell Sanford*, Sioux Falls
GOODSELL Verne *Gunderson Palmer*, Rapid City
HICKEY Michael *Bangs McCullen*, Rapid City
JOHNSON Steven *Johnson Heidepriem*, Sioux Falls
LANDON Stephen *Cadwell Sanford*, Sioux Falls
MOORE James *Woods Fuller*, Sioux Falls
WELK Thomas *Boyce Greenfield*, Sioux Falls
WILBUR Brent *May Adam*, Pierre

Leading individuals
(Litigation: Healthcare)

1 EVANS Edwin *Davenport Evans*, Sioux Falls
PALMER Crisman *Gunderson Palmer*, Rapid City

2 DUFFY Daniel *Bangs McCullen*, Rapid City
GOODSELL Verne *Gunderson Palmer*, Rapid City
HAIGH Mark *Davenport Evans*, Sioux Falls
SUDBECK Roger *Boyce Greenfield*, Sioux Falls
WELK Thomas *Boyce Greenfield*, Sioux Falls

Firms and individuals are listed alphabetically in each band.

Woods, Fuller, Shultz & Smith PC

The Firm: This team of 15 is skilled at handling litigation where antitrust regulations, insurance defense, employment law and products liability are concerned. The firm has a superior reputation in the defense of professional malpractice claims, predominantly representing lawyers and physicians. Examples of recent cases include acting for the State of South Dakota against the forest services, in a case centered on measures that could be taken to reduce fire risks in the Black Hills National Forest.

The Lawyers: **William Fuller** is a "*straight-shooter*" whom clients regard as "*extremely thorough and hard working.*" His workload is a mixed bag of products liability, professional malpractice and insurance bad faith cases. Interviewees singled out **Gary Thimsen** as an "*aggressive and charming trial lawyer with real jury appeal.*" He is active in a wide range of civil litigation and has niche expertise in aviation litigation. Over the past year he has undertaken a large volume of personal injury defense cases, as well as defending government liability claims. Rising star **James Moore** is new to the tables this year, and sources said that he "*shines in complex appellate cases.*"

The Clients: State Farm; State of South Dakota; Hy-Vee; RLI; South Dakota Public Assurance Alliance; Farmers; Associated Aviation Underwriters and Acuity Insurance.

Band 2

Bangs, McCullen, Butler, Foye & Simmons LLP

The Firm: Market sources described a quality litigation group that is an esteemed player in the South Dakota legal market. The team handles litigation of all sorts, spanning antitrust, insurance defense and coverage, professional malpractice, products liability and construction.

The Lawyers: Clients seek out **Michael Hickey**, whose "*easygoing manner and straightforward approach*" lead to "*outstanding results.*" Interviewees particularly admired his knowledge of administrative and mineral laws. His colleague **Daniel Duffy** provides "*terrific courtroom delivery*" and in-depth expertise in healthcare litigation.

The Clients: Acuity Insurance, ALPS and Fall River Water Users District are counted among the firm's clients.

Boyce, Greenfield, Pashby & Welk LLP

The Firm: Eight lawyers make up this "*result-oriented and efficient*" litigation team. The firm advises on construction disputes, automobile accidents, personal injury and professional malpractice defense, as well as complex business litigation. Highlights include representing engineers in the mutually satisfactory conclusion of mediation following the reconstruction of six miles of road near Rapid City. Other recent cases include the defense of a class action involving the government and the beef industry.

The Lawyers: Clients depicted **Gary Pashby**, president of the State Bar of South Dakota, as a "*tenacious and seasoned litigator who can be a real bulldog in the courtroom.*" He frequently represents architects and engineers in complex construction litigation, and has a creditable personal injury caseload. Interviewees acclaimed **Thomas Welk** for his "*intensely focused handling of large complex trials, where he leaves no rock*

unturned." He is active in the gamut of commercial litigation, with particular strength in healthcare law. Interviewees asserted that **Roger Sudbeck** is "*destined for the top.*" His practice is an even mix of medical malpractice defense and general civil litigation, acting in up to five jury trials a year. Recent work includes the defense of nursing staff in a case where a suicidal patient was released from a psychiatric unit. According to peers, he is "*absolutely wonderful to work with,*" and clients pointed to his "*timeliness and dexterity in handling witnesses in the courtroom.*"

The Clients: Wells Fargo; CNA; ConAgra Foods; Swift Beef; Quest; XL Design Professional; Schmitz Kalda & Associates; Schmucker, Paul, Nohr & Associates; SAFECO; St. Paul Fire & Marine; Raven Industries; Avera Health and Banner Associates.

Cadwell Sanford Deibert & Garry LLP

The Firm: This eight-lawyer litigation team offers a full service to its clients. It advises a number of banks and financial institutions in diverse litigation matters. These include organizational disputes and questions arising in the context of business relationships, such as minority stockholder issues. The team has a steady diet of insurance coverage cases, and General Casualty is an important pillar of the clientele. Recent highlights include settling a real estate case for McLeodUSA.

The Lawyers: The "*polished*" **Steven Sanford** was held up as a "*true student of the law.*" Clients rated him as "*one of the sharpest lawyers in the state, always quick on his feet.*" On top of his lively financial litigation practice he has acted on a number of toxic mold cases over the last year, as well as advising on disputes over commercial buildings. **William Garry** "*exudes credibility with juries,*" observed peers. His litigation caseload covers insurance defense and workers' compensation claims. Sources praised **Stephen Landon**'s "*quick wit and remarkable intelligence,*" extolling his expertise across a broad spectrum of law, and particularly his work in commercial disputes and personal injury cases.

The Clients: HSBC; First PREMIER Bank; Security Bank; Blue Cross & Blue Shield; Bobcat; Wellmark of South Dakota and numerous insurance companies.

Gunderson, Palmer, Goodsell & Nelson LLP

The Firm: This litigation team has a well-established footprint in the state. Its 14 lawyers manage a steady flow of banking, personal injury, products liability and insurance defense cases. The department receives special acclaim for healthcare litigation, with clients observing that attorneys "*relate well to doctors.*" Nor is medical malpractice defense work the whole story here:

the firm has acted in a wide range of matters for the medical community in South Dakota.

The Lawyers: Respondents singled out the "*charismatic and courageous*" **Crisman Palmer** for his insurance defense and medical malpractice defense work. Rivals acknowledged that he "*can see the forest despite the trees*," and praised an "*engaging and gentlemanly style*" that enables him to "*deal with delicate situations without causing offense.*" **Verne Goodsell** was admired by clients and peers alike for the "*fire in his belly*" and his ability to "*grab a courtroom.*" He divides his time equally between medical malpractice and products liability litigation.

The Clients: American State Bank; American Risk Pooling Consultants; American Underwriting Managers; Casualty Reciprocal Exchange; Austin Mutual Insurance; Center Mutual Insurance and CIGNA.

May, Adam, Gerdes & Thompson, LLP

The Firm: Commentators accorded this Pierre-based litigation practice the accolade of "*best firm in the state capital.*" The accomplished lawyers practice before courts and administrative bodies across the state, handling a rich mixture of cases. The workload spans commercial litigation, lenders liability and insurance defense claims, as well as criminal defense. Interviewees reserved special praise for the firm's expertise in governmental liability litigation.

The Lawyers: Interviewees declared themselves in awe of **Robert Anderson**'s "*photographic memory.*" They also flagged up his "*great sense of humor,*" which enables him to "*relate well to jurors.*" His practice includes personal injury cases, for either side, as well as insurance defense and general commercial litigation. Observers celebrated **Brent Wilbur** as the "*go-to guy for political issues,*" and clients were particularly "*impressed by his quick grasp of facts.*" He focuses on commercial and government liability matters.

The Clients: South Dakota Public Entity Pool

for Liability; IBM; GM; Travelers; Continental National American Group; Allstate and Employers of Wausau.

Band 3

Costello Porter Hill Heisterkamp Bushnell & Carpenter LLP

The Firm: This Rapid City group has an ancient and impressive pedigree, and comes highly recommended for litigation. The client roster includes individuals and corporations, as well as financial institutions. The team handles a varied caseload, and insurance defense, real estate litigation and healthcare law are central planks of the firm's offering.

The Lawyers: Clients informed researchers that **Edward Carpenter** is "*well tuned in to our needs and objectives.*" His forte is in construction litigation, government contracts and insurance defense litigation. Clients further commended him as a "*tenacious cross-examiner with a dry sense of humor.*"

The Clients: Clients include Ford, National Farmers Union and Clinical Laboratory of the Black Hills.

Johnson, Heidepriem, Miner, Marlow & Janklow LLP

The Firm: "*The number-one plaintiff's practice in town*" is how peers described this Sioux Falls outfit. The 14-member litigation team, however, also has an impressive track record defending clients in various forms of commercial litigation. Attorneys are adept in business litigation, personal injury, medical negligence and products liability cases, and the team is experienced in wrongful death and appellate matters.

The Lawyers: Market watchers singled out "*top dog*" **Steven Johnson** as the "*star performer*" at the firm. His reputation as a "*lawyer who cannot lose*" is complemented by his "*charming jury appeal*" and "*aggressive fidelity*" to his clients' interests. His practice is divided between per-

sonal injury and business litigation, encompassing financial disputes and securities law. The firm recently represented the family against the manufacturer following the death of an individual in a fire caused by a defective halogen lamp.

The Clients: The clientele includes First Dakota National Bank, EMC Insurance and a number of individuals.

Lynn, Jackson, Shultz & Lebrun PC

The Firm: Reports confirm that this "*credible and noteworthy*" team has a robust litigation caseload. Areas of expertise include commercial disputes, negligence, products liability and personal injury. The firm operates from offices out of Rapid City and Sioux Falls.

The Lawyers: Market sources singled out **Thomas Fritz** for his trial expertise and his "*talent in winning over juries.*" His expertise in complex litigation and his comprehensive grasp of the trial process impressed commentators.

The Clients: Allstate; American Concept Insurance; CIGNA; Design Professionals; Employers Mutual of Wausau and Equitable.

Schaffer Law Office

The Firm: This two-member civil litigation firm "*scores high marks*" for its expertise in general commercial matters. Its work covers a pretty broad spectrum, and includes product liability, personal injury and insurance defense. Attorneys are especially recommended for their trial and appeals work.

The Lawyers: According to clients **Michael Schaffer** is "*like a shrewd bulldog: he keeps his eye on the ball until he gets it.*" The two main pillars of his practice are the defense of insurance and commercial disputes, and representing plaintiffs in personal injury actions. Interviewees agreed that he "*is the best person to fight your corner – he has a lot of guts.*"

The Clients: Continental Western; American Family Insurance; State Auto Insurance and North Star Mutual Insurance.

REAL ESTATE

South Dakota	
Leading firms (Real Estate)	
1	BANGS, MCCULLEN, BUTLER, FOYE *Rapid City*
	DAVENPORT, EVANS, HURWITZ *Sioux Falls*
2	BOYCE, GREENFIELD, PASHBY *Sioux Falls*
	CUTLER & DONAHOE LLP *Sioux Falls*
	GUNDERSON, PALMER, GOODSELL *Rapid City*
Firms are listed alphabetically in each band.	

Band 1

Bangs, McCullen, Butler, Foye & Simmons LLP

The Firm: With four real estate experts "*committed to the welfare of their clients,*" this group is a power in the real estate arena. It delivers a comprehensive service to a varied clientele that includes purchasers and sellers, landlords, tenants and lenders. Attorneys' advice covers transactions, leases and development; zoning is also a prominent feature of the workload. Over the last year the team has been par-

ticularly busy with the drafting of easements for a number of community developments.

The Lawyers: Clients applauded "*seasoned and sharp*" **Thomas Foye** for his "*excellent and detailed*" real estate advice, which is bolstered by a "*formidable knowledge of tax.*" They were also warm in their praise for **Charles Riter**, who is "*as concise as can be,*" and inspires confidence with his "*practical and common-sense approach.*" He recently represented the seller of a multimillion-dollar property sold to the State of South Dakota for game hunting.

South Dakota
Leading individuals (Real Estate)

Senior Statesman
GREENFIELD Russell *Boyce Greenfield*, Sioux Falls

[1] CUTLER Richard *Cutler & Donahoe*, Sioux Falls
DONOHUE P Daniel *Davenport Evans*, Sioux Falls
FOYE Thomas *Bangs McCullen*, Rapid City
RITER Charles *Bangs McCullen*, Rapid City

[2] GOETZINGER Patrick *Gunderson Palmer*, Rapid City
HAYES Robert *Davenport Evans*, Sioux Falls
JENSEN Curtis *DeMersseman Jensen*, Rapid City

Individuals are listed alphabetically in each band.

The Clients: Crazy Horse Memorial, Corner Construction and Sutton Rodeo are typical clients of the firm.

Davenport, Evans, Hurwitz & Smith LLP

The Firm: According to market sources this capable real estate group dispenses "*consistently high-quality*" advice. Six lawyers provide services in both local and multistate transactions, riding high on the firm's stellar reputation in corporate and banking matters. Attorneys deliver "*well-rounded advice*" to an impressive stable of loyal clients. In the past year the firm has handled over one hundred foreclosures for South Dakota Housing Development Authority. A recent highlight was advising a client on a project in downtown Sioux Falls.

The Lawyers: Billed as an "*expert technician*," **Daniel Donohue** has developed a sterling reputation for complex real estate transactions, and brings considerable corporate and tax expertise to the table. He recently advised the largest commercial contractor in South Dakota on the development and leasing of an office building. **Robert Hayes** is a "*deal facilitator*" and was recommended for his extensive experience in real estate financings. Clients depict him as a "*problem solver extraordinaire*," who is "*the first to get*

a transaction done and cleaned up." Over the last year he has provided opinions on state law issues to prospective lenders in two separate multistate financings, at values of $18 million and $400 million.

The Clients: Polaris; Dakota, Minnesota & Eastern Railroad; Toronto-Dominion Bank; Prudential; South Dakota Housing Development Authority and CorTrust Bank.

Band 2

Boyce, Greenfield, Pashby & Welk LLP

The Firm: This illustrious team attracts recommendations for the scope and breadth of its real estate practice. Typical work includes advising on the acquisition, sale and leasing of commercial and residential properties. The financing, construction and development of projects is also a notable portion of the team's practice.

The Lawyers: **Russell Greenfield** is widely seen as "*one of the best*" in the state. He commands respect for his tremendous experience in the field, and his connections to Citibank boost his reputation further. His areas of expertise run to real estate development and finance, corporate, municipal bond and estate planning law.

The Clients: Citibank (South Dakota) and First American Bank & Trust.

Cutler & Donahoe LLP

The Firm: Commentators praised this Sioux Falls practice for its expert conduct of real estate acquisitions and financings. The practice is strong in family land transactions, zoning and title matters; alongside its financial institution and developer clients, the team has a tradition of acting for family businesses. Attorneys recently represented Shipley's Launderers & Dry Cleaners in a major real estate transaction.

The Lawyers: By all accounts, the cornerstone of the practice is "*top of the class*" **Richard Cutler**.

Clients admired him for "*instincts and insight*" that enable him to "*just look at a property and add value to it*." Sources characterized him as "*extremely ethical*" with a "*dogged*" commitment to his clients' needs.

The Clients: Great Western Bank; First National Bank in Sioux Falls; First American Bank & Trust; F&M Bank; Valley Bank and Fannie Mae.

Gunderson, Palmer, Goodsell & Nelson LLP

The Firm: There is general agreement in the marketplace that this firm is "*a growing force*" in real estate. The team is well versed in the gamut of transactional matters, including financings, development, zoning, sales and purchases, as well as working with landlords and tenants on leases. Recent work includes advising the owners of a Coca-Cola bottling company on the financing of a South Dakota property.

The Lawyers: Peers extolled **Patrick Goetzinger** for his knowledge and prominence in both corporate and real estate transactions. This places him ideally in the sophisticated commercial real estate transactions market. Much of his time is spent assisting developers. For example, he is involved in advising clients who own parcels of property along Highway 16 to Mount Rushmore on how to develop the land, particularly with regard to zoning requirements.

The Clients: Eagle Sales of the Black Hills; RCC Western Wear; Stoneridge Development; Rapid City Area School District; Austin Mutual Insurance; CIGNA; Casualty Reciprocal Exchange and American Underwriting Managers.

Other Notable Practitioners

Market commentators rated **Curtis Jensen** of DeMersseman Jensen Christianson Stanton & Huffman LLP highly for his adroit representation of local businesses and financial institutions in corporate, banking and estate planning matters.

Leaders in South Dakota

ANDERSON, Robert
May, Adam, Gerdes & Thompson, L.L.P., Pierre 605 224 8803
Recommended in Litigation

ANDERSON, Scott
Davenport, Evans, Hurwitz & Smith LLP, Sioux Falls 605 336 2880
Recommended in Corporate/M&A

CARPENTER, Edward
Costello Porter Hill Heisterkamp Bushnell & Carpenter LLP, Rapid City 605 343 2410
Recommended in Litigation

CUTLER, Richard
Cutler & Donahoe LLP, Sioux Falls 605 335 4950
Recommended in Corporate/M&A, Real Estate

DAMGAARD, Roger
Woods, Fuller, Shultz & Smith PC, Sioux Falls 605 336 3890
Recommended in Bankruptcy, Corporate/M&A

DONOHUE, Daniel
Davenport, Evans, Hurwitz & Smith LLP, Sioux Falls 605 336 2880
Recommended in Real Estate

DUFFY, Daniel
Bangs, McCullen, Butler, Foye & Simmons, LLP, Rapid City 605 343 1040
Recommended in Litigation

ENTWISTLE, Frederick
Woods, Fuller, Shultz & Smith PC, Sioux Falls 605 336 3890
Recommended in Bankruptcy

EVANS, Edwin
Davenport, Evans, Hurwitz & Smith LLP, Sioux Falls 605 336 2880
Recommended in Litigation

FOYE, Thomas
Bangs, McCullen, Butler, Foye & Simmons, LLP, Rapid City 605 343 1040
Recommended in Real Estate

FRITZ, Thomas
Lynn, Jackson, Shultz & Lebrun PC, Rapid City 605 342 2592
Recommended in Litigation

FULLER, William
Woods, Fuller, Shultz & Smith PC, Sioux Falls 605 336 3890
Recommended in Litigation

GARRY, William
Cadwell Sanford Deibert & Garry LLP, Sioux Falls 605 336 0828
Recommended in Litigation

GAUER, Keith
Davenport, Evans, Hurwitz & Smith LLP, Sioux Falls 605 336 2880
Recommended in Bankruptcy

1592

All quotes in the text are from interviews with clients and competitors.

CHAMBERS USA 2005

GOETZINGER, Patrick
Gunderson, Palmer, Goodsell & Nelson LLP, Rapid City 605 342 1078
Recommended in Corporate/M&A, Real Estate

GOLDAMMER, Vance
Murphy, Goldammer & Prendergast, Sioux Falls 605 331 2975
Recommended in Corporate/M&A

GOODSELL, Verne
Gunderson, Palmer, Goodsell & Nelson LLP, Rapid City 605 342 1078
Recommended in Litigation

GREENFIELD, Gregg
Boyce, Greenfield, Pashby & Welk LLP, Sioux Falls 605 336 2424
Recommended in Corporate/M&A

GREENFIELD, Russell
Boyce, Greenfield, Pashby & Welk LLP, Sioux Falls 605 336 2424
Recommended in Real Estate

GROSSENBURG, Bradley
Woods, Fuller, Shultz & Smith PC, Sioux Falls 605 336 3890
Recommended in Corporate/M&A

GULLICKSON, Charles
Davenport, Evans, Hurwitz & Smith LLP, Sioux Falls 605 336 2880
Recommended in Corporate/M&A

HAIGH, Mark
Davenport, Evans, Hurwitz & Smith LLP, Sioux Falls 605 336 2880
Recommended in Litigation

HAJEK, Douglas
Davenport, Evans, Hurwitz & Smith LLP, Sioux Falls 605 336 2880
Recommended in Corporate/M&A

HARALDSON, Comet
Woods, Fuller, Shultz & Smith PC, Sioux Falls 605 336 3890
Recommended in Employment

HAYES, Robert
Davenport, Evans, Hurwitz & Smith LLP, Sioux Falls 605 336 2880
Recommended in Bankruptcy, Corporate/M&A, Real Estate

HICKEY, Michael
Bangs, McCullen, Butler, Foye & Simmons, LLP, Rapid City 605 343 1040
Recommended in Litigation

HOLM, Kristi
Davenport, Evans, Hurwitz & Smith LLP, Sioux Falls 605 336 2880
Recommended in Employment

JENSEN, Curtis
DeMersseman Jensen Christianson Stanton & Huffman LLP, Rapid City 605 342 2814
Recommended in Real Estate

JOHNSON, Steven
Johnson, Heidepriem, Miner, Marlow & Janklow, LLP, Sioux Falls 605 338 4304
Recommended in Litigation

KNUDSON, David
Davenport, Evans, Hurwitz & Smith LLP, Sioux Falls 605 336 2880
Recommended in Corporate/M&A

KROON, David
Woods, Fuller, Shultz & Smith PC, Sioux Falls 605 336 3890
Recommended in Corporate/M&A

LANDON, Stephen
Cadwell Sanford Deibert & Garry LLP, Sioux Falls 605 336 0828
Recommended in Litigation

LUCE, Michael
Davenport, Evans, Hurwitz & Smith LLP, Sioux Falls 605 336 2880
Recommended in Litigation

LUST, David
Gunderson, Palmer, Goodsell & Nelson LLP, Rapid City 605 342 1078
Recommended in Corporate/M&A

MAGNUSON, Lee
Lynn, Jackson, Shultz & Lebrun PC, Rapid City 605 342 2592
Recommended in Corporate/M&A

MARSO, Lisa
Boyce, Greenfield, Pashby & Welk LLP, Sioux Falls 605 336 2424
Recommended in Employment

MCKNIGHT, Michael
Boyce, Greenfield, Pashby & Welk LLP, Sioux Falls 605 336 2424
Recommended in Employment

MOORE, James
Woods, Fuller, Shultz & Smith PC, Sioux Falls 605 336 3890
Recommended in Litigation

ORR, Rick
Davenport, Evans, Hurwitz & Smith LLP, Sioux Falls 605 336 2880
Recommended in Employment

PALMER, Crisman
Gunderson, Palmer, Goodsell & Nelson LLP, Rapid City 605 342 1078
Recommended in Litigation

PASHBY, Gary
Boyce, Greenfield, Pashby & Welk LLP, Sioux Falls 605 336 2424
Recommended in Litigation

PERRENOUD, Scott
Cadwell Sanford Deibert & Garry LLP, Sioux Falls 605 336 0828
Recommended in Corporate/M&A

RITER, Charles
Bangs, McCullen, Butler, Foye & Simmons, LLP, Rapid City 605 343 1040
Recommended in Real Estate

SANFORD, Steven
Cadwell Sanford Deibert & Garry LLP, Sioux Falls 605 336 0828
Recommended in Litigation

SCHAFFER, Michael
Schaffer Law Office, Sioux Falls 605 274 6760
Recommended in Litigation

SHULTZ, Jeff
Woods, Fuller, Shultz & Smith PC, Sioux Falls 605 336 3890
Recommended in Employment

SIMONS, Susan
Davenport, Evans, Hurwitz & Smith LLP, Sioux Falls 605 336 2880
Recommended in Employment

SOGN, Jon
Lynn, Jackson, Shultz & Lebrun PC, Rapid City 605 342 2592
Recommended in Employment

SUDBECK, Roger
Boyce, Greenfield, Pashby & Welk LLP, Sioux Falls 605 336 2424
Recommended in Litigation

THIMSEN, Gary
Woods, Fuller, Shultz & Smith PC, Sioux Falls 605 336 3890
Recommended in Litigation

WELK, Thomas
Boyce, Greenfield, Pashby & Welk LLP, Sioux Falls 605 336 2424
Recommended in Litigation

WIEDERRICH, James
Woods, Fuller, Shultz & Smith PC, Sioux Falls 605 336 3890
Recommended in Corporate/M&A

WILBUR, Brent
May, Adam, Gerdes & Thompson, L.L.P., Pierre 605 224 8803
Recommended in Litigation

CONTENTS: Corporate/M&A p.1594; Employment p.1596; Litigation p.1598; Media & Entertainment p.1602; Real Estate p. 1603; Individuals' Profiles p.1605; Firm Profiles p.1613.

How lawyers are ranked

The opinions we gather from clients — mainly from in-house lawyers but also from other purchasers of legal services — are balanced by opinions from colleagues and competitors. Together, they provide two different perspectives — an all-round view — and biased viewpoints cancel each other out.

CORPORATE/M&A

Tennessee
Leading firms (Corporate/M&A)

1 BASS, BERRY & SIMS PLC *Nashville*
WALLER LANSDEN DORTCH & DAVIS *Nashville*

2 BAKER, DONELSON, BEARMAN *Memphis*
BOULT, CUMMINGS, CONNERS *Nashville*
HARWELL HOWARD HYNE GABBERT *Nashville*

3 SHERRARD & ROE PLC *Nashville*
STOKES BARTHOLOMEW EVANS *Nashville*

Leading individuals (Corporate/M&A)

1 CHEEK James *Bass Berry*, Nashville
COLE J Chase *Waller Lansden*, Nashville
MANNER Mark *Harwell Howard*, Nashville
WALTON Leigh *Bass Berry*, Nashville

2 BISHOP George *Waller Lansden*, Nashville
BRAUN Stephen *Boult Cummings*, Nashville
COWART Richard *Baker Donelson*, Nashville
HILL J Reginald *Waller Lansden*, Nashville
HYNE Ernest *Harwell Howard*, Nashville
WALKER Mitchell *Bass Berry*, Nashville

3 DILWORTH Lee *Harwell Howard*, Nashville
GILBERT Paul *Waller Lansden*, Nashville
HARDCASTLE Jay *Boult Cummings*, Nashville
HOLT Berry *Boult Cummings*, Nashville
LAMAR Howard *Bass Berry*, Nashville
MCKENZIE Donald *Stokes Bartholomew*, Nashville
MITCHELL E Marlee *Waller Lansden*, Nashville
SHERRARD Thomas *Sherrard & Roe*, Nashville
THOMPSON Bob *Bass Berry*, Nashville
VOIGT John *Sherrard & Roe*, Nashville

Up-and-coming individuals
ROLAPP Todd *Bass Berry*, Nashville

Firms and individuals are listed alphabetically in each band.

Band 1

Bass, Berry & Sims PLC

See firm details p.1614

The Firm: This prominent full-service Tennessee firm drew unanimous praise from clients and peers for the *"depth and leadership of its corporate attorneys."* A long and impressive list of corporate clients includes key names in the entertainment, telecom and financial services industries. Clients particularly praised the group's handling of healthcare regulatory matters and the *"New York style-expertise"* on offer here. In complement to a busy M&A and securities practice, the firm is also seen to be *"heavily involved in policy making"* and is regularly called upon for corporate governance advice.

The Lawyers: Among this *"excellent"* group of attorneys, **Jim Cheek** (see p.1606) stands out as *"preeminent"* in securities work. Clients value his *"extreme intelligence and great judgment"* as well as his extensive connections on Wall Street. *"He is plugged into every top SEC regulator in the country,"* said one. Cheek maintains a high profile advising boards of directors on governance issues. He acted as counsel to the independent directors of the American Stock Exchange in its sale by the NASD to members of the exchange. He and his team also represented HCA in one of the largest public self-tenders ($2.5 billion) to date. *"Practical and experienced"* **Leigh Walton** (see p.1612) backs up her impressive expertise in corporate, securities and healthcare transactions with *"intelligence and thoughtfulness,"* researchers were told. In addition to handling a steady volume of M&A, Walton frequently assists early-stage healthcare companies in securing financing. In 2004, she acted for IASIS Healthcare Corporation in its $1.5 billion sale to Texas Pacific Group and also represented Spheris in its sale to Warburg Pincus and Soros Private Equity. **Mitchell Walker** (see p.1612) attracted praise for his transactional experience and securities practice. Although most of his work is for publicly traded companies, Walker also acts for a number of independent directors of mutual fund groups. After representing Gaylord Entertainment in the purchase of ResortQuest, he also completed a note financing for the same client in 2004. *"Outstanding"* **Bob Thompson** (see p.1611) has a loyal following among the boards and management of banks and mutual funds, and regularly provides corporate and securities counsel to larger financial institutions and managed care clients. He acted for Coventry Health Care in its $1.8 billion acquisition of First Health Group and represented Pinnacle Financial Partners in a $20 million common stock offering. Interviewees identified **Howard Lamar** (see p.1609) as a much-admired new talent who *"doesn't sweat the small stuff."* Lamar maintains a broad-based corporate practice, but earns highest commendation for his experience *"fathering and nurturing"* new companies. Another new entrant to the *Chambers'* tables, **Todd Rolapp** (see p.1611) was acknowledged as an *"impressive deal-doer"* with considerable industry-specific knowledge of the hi-tech sector. He represents early stage, pre-public and public companies on an ongoing basis in matters ranging from formation and financing to corporate partnering and SEC reporting.

The Clients: American Healthways; HCA; Genesco; Thomas Nelson; Gaylord Entertainment; Performance Food Group; Corrections Corporation of America and Bright Horizons Family Solutions.

Waller Lansden Dortch & Davis

See firm details p.1621

The Firm: The firm established itself as a key name in the healthcare field 40 years ago with its involvement in the creation of HCA and still retains a stellar reputation for its *"total dedication to healthcare expertise."* This, combined with *"one of the strongest M&A practices in Tennessee,"* firmly places the Nashville-based practice among the top rung of in-state corporate specialists. The firm's 170 corporate attorneys won top marks from interviewees for their *"first-rate"* experience in securities, M&A and corporate governance. An enviable base of commercial clients awarded the practice *"trusted adviser status"* and rely on the group for all their transactional needs.

The Lawyers: *"Responsive"* **Chase Cole** (see p.1606) brings a *"clear communicative style"* and *"goal-oriented approach"* to complicated securities transactions. In 2004, he acted for Braid Electric in the sale of its assets to Rexel, an international electric supply distributor based in France. Public company and corporate governance are key components of his practice, which serves a mix of healthcare and non-healthcare clients. **George Bishop** (see p.1605) enjoys a longstanding reputation as an experienced M&A lawyer who "*completes transactions quickly and efficiently.*" Thirty years' experience counseling healthcare clients is said to give him "*great insight*" into the workings of the industry. "*Fantastic*" **Reggie Hill** (see p.1608) is admired both for his work as a lead lawyer for outpatient healthcare services and for his skill in attracting new business to the firm. His practice centers around securities and M&A transactions within the healthcare industry. He handles transactional work for HealthSouth and represented Symbion in its IPO. Interviewees heaped praise on the "*experienced and patient*" **Marlee Mitchell** (see p.1610), whose recent M&A work and niche expertise in broker dealer work supplement a traditional corporate finance and securities practice. She regularly advises BancorpSouth and Nissan and filed two Form S-4 registration statements to effect a year-end acquisition by BancorpSouth of two bank holding companies. Nominated as "*one of the next generation of strong lawyers,*" **Paul Gilbert** (see p.1607) has a growing reputation for his representation of hospitals and psychiatric centers in transactional matters. He advised Deaconess Hospital, an Oklahoma-based nonprofit healthcare organization, on the negotiation of a whole-hospital joint venture with Triad Hospitals. He also represented KEYS Group Holdings in the sale of four psychiatric hospitals, located in Georgia, Nevada, Kentucky and Arkansas, to Universal Health Services.

The Clients: LifePoint Hospitals; Capstone Turbine; Psychiatric Solutions; Deaconess Hospital and KEYS Group Holdings.

Band 2

Baker, Donelson, Bearman, Caldwell & Berkowitz PC

See firm details p.1613

The Firm: The firm's strong commitment to growth and diversity was underlined by the 2004 opening of a New Orleans office, a move which further expanded its regional footprint in the South. The firm maintains five offices in Tennessee, its large Memphis practice being the most prominent. Corporate finance, securities, M&A and IP are the practice's mainstays. The Nashville team, in particular, has witnessed an increase in corporate governance and investigations work.

The Lawyers: **Dick Cowart** (see p.1606), chairman of the firm's health law department, earned approval as a "*leader in the nonprofit field.*" This "*active and hard-working*" attorney is visible advising hospital boards of directors on both regulatory and business issues. In recognition of his longstanding experience, Cowart was recently appointed president of the American Health Lawyers Association. He has represented nonprofit hospitals in acquisitions, sales and other transactions, where he is said to bring together "*knowledge of the legal minutiae, an accounting background and real policy expertise.*"

The Clients: Quorum; Wellmont Health System; Erlanger; Renal Care Group; Gaylord Entertainment; Healthcare Realty Trust and Gordon Biersch Brewing.

Boult, Cummings, Conners & Berry PLC

The Firm: Based in Nashville, this 100-lawyer firm elicited praise for its traditional strength in real estate development work and healthcare transactions in which the corporate department is able to draw upon the resources of dedicated healthcare regulatory and real estate groups. Clients consider the group a "*pleasure to work with*" and singled out a trio of "*really incredible*" attorneys for especial praise. The practice undertakes a full range of commercial finance, securities and M&A. Recent work includes representing a company in a $300 million acquisition of ten hospitals in Tulsa, OK.

The Lawyers: **Stephen Braun** was hailed as a "*hugely significant addition*" to the firm's transactional healthcare capacities. The M&A lawyer was deemed a "*top referral*" for his "*superb knowledge, vast experience and commercial pragmatism.*" Impressive industry experience, acquired as a former general counsel at HCA, contributes to his handling of acquisitions, sales and joint ventures for a loyal base of for-profit hospitals. The "*highly competent*" **Jay Hardcastle** divides his practice between transactional and regulatory work in the healthcare sector. The bulk of his workload is for nonprofit hospitals. Veteran healthcare attorney **Berry Holt** frequently acts as counsel to Saint Thomas Hospital and was recently appointed to the First Tennessee's Health Care Advisory Council. Holt handled the tender offer and repurchase of units of a specialty hospital partially owned by Baptist Hospital and the subsequent resyndication of investment units in the facility.

The Clients: American Realty Advisors; First Tennessee; Baptist Hospital and Saint Thomas Hospital.

Harwell Howard Hyne Gabbert & Manner PC

See firm details p.1616

The Firm: A small but sophisticated business law practice, highly regarded in Nashville for its ability to attract "*top-drawer talent.*" The 30-lawyer corporate practice has a heavy emphasis on hospital acquisitions, sales, M&A and securities and is seen to be increasing its market share within the biotechnology sector. Despite attorneys' "*laid-back, even-tempered*" style, the group is "*extremely effective when it comes to the crunch,*" say clients.

The Lawyers: Peers and clients enjoy working with "*personable*" **Mark Manner** (see p.1609), who, they say, is "*one of the few trusted attorneys to counsel clients on sensitive governance and board issues.*" The M&A and securities lawyer has recognized expertise in corporate healthcare transactions and capital formation. Manner counsels a variety of local healthcare companies and also regularly advises Central Parking on business transactions. "*Bright, tough and reliable*" **Ernie Hyne** (see p.1608) commands extensive experience in healthcare and M&A transactions. In addition to the sale and acquisition of hospitals, Hyne is involved in a steady volume of venture capital financing. He recently advised on the Attentus Healthcare hospital startup. **Lee Dilworth** (see p.1607), the firm's corporate chair, is a "*smart, relaxed*" practitioner with a sound reputation in healthcare, securities and M&A transactions. He is frequently seen representing physicians' and psychiatrists' practices.

The Clients: Central Parking; American HomePatient; Advocat; National HealthCare; Teleion Capital; Daymar College and FINOVA.

Band 3

Sherrard & Roe PLC

The Firm: This "*collegiate*" 23-lawyer Nashville firm may lack the numbers to compete with local rivals for large public company work, but holds its own in real estate, M&A and corporate finance transactions for medium to large privately-held clients. Interviewees considered its trust and estates expertise to be "*one of the best in town.*" A strong representation of physician clients adds to its weight in the healthcare arena.

The Lawyers: **John Voigt**, a "*mild-mannered gent and fine healthcare transactions lawyer,*" leads the firm's healthcare practice and is held in high esteem for his relationships with physician groups. He handles M&A and private finance work and recently completed the sale of a large hospital and the amalgamation of several obstetrics and gynecology facilities. "*Seasoned*" corporate lawyer **Tom Sherrard** is a founding member of the firm with a broad commercial practice spanning M&A, corporate finance and securities. He serves as general outside counsel for both public and private corporations and has acted for a key client of the firm in two leveraged buyouts.

The Clients: Bank of America; Physicians Community Health Group; State Volunteer Mutual Insurance; Vanderbilt University; Nashville Predators and Nissan.

Stokes Bartholomew Evans & Petree, PA

The Firm: Respected corporate practitioners operate from offices in Nashville and Memphis. Intellectual property is an area of considerable expertise for the group, and the firm has developed noteworthy relationships with local music and entertainment clients through its practice on Music Row.

The Lawyers: A *"sound technician"* with a long-standing reputation in the field, **Don McKenzie** inspires loyalty among clients for his deft handing of corporate and M&A matters.

The Clients: The firm advises companies across a variety of industry sectors, including manufacturing, distribution, healthcare, banking and entertainment.

EMPLOYMENT

MAINLY DEFENDANT

Tennessee
Leading firms
(Employment: Mainly Defendant)

[1] BASS, BERRY & SIMS PLC *Nashville*
   KIESEWETTER WISE KAPLAN PRATHER *Memphis*
   KING & BALLOW *Nashville*
   MILLER & MARTIN PLLC *Chattanooga*
   WALLER LANSDEN DORTCH & DAVIS *Nashville*

[2] BOULT, CUMMINGS, CONNERS & BERRY *Nashville*
   BURCH, PORTER & JOHNSON PLLC *Memphis*
   CONSTANGY, BROOKS & SMITH LLC *Nashville*
   FORD & HARRISON LLP *Memphis*
   KRAMER, RAYSON, LEAKE, RODGERS *Knoxville*
   LEWIS FISHER HENDERSON CLAXTON *Memphis*
   OGLETREE, DEAKINS, NASH, SMOAK *Nashville*

Leading individuals
(Employment: Mainly Defendant)

[1] BOSTON Robert *Waller Lansden*, Nashville
   OZIER William *Bass Berry*, Nashville

[2] BRIDGESMITH Larry *Waller Lansden*, Nashville
   ELLIS Karen *Bass Berry*, Nashville
   GARRETT Tim *Bass Berry*, Nashville
   KAPLAN Jonathan *Kiesewetter Wise*, Memphis
   KIESEWETTER Jay *Kiesewetter Wise*, Memphis
   PHILLIPS Edward *Kramer Rayson*, Knoxville
   PHILLIPS John *Miller & Martin*, Chattanooga
   PRATHER Paul *Kiesewetter Wise*, Memphis
   STEVENS C Eric *Miller & Martin*, Nashville
   WAYLAND R Eddie *King & Ballow*, Nashville

[3] BLUE William *Constangy Brooks*, Nashville
   CRENSHAW Waverly *Waller Lansden*, Nashville
   FRAZIER Keith *Ogletree Deakins*, Nashville
   GERSON Herb *Ford & Harrison*, Memphis
   KRAMER Steven *Kramer Rayson*, Knoxville
   LEWIS Frederick *Lewis Fisher*, Memphis
   LONERGAN Matthew *Boult Cummings*, Nashville
   LOWE Richard *King & Ballow*, Nashville
   SWAFFORD T Anthony *Miller & Martin*, Nashville

Up-and-coming individuals
   HATMAKER J Chadwick *Woolf, McClane*, Knoxville
   OLIVER Craig *Boult Cummings*, Nashville

Firms and individuals are listed alphabetically in each band.

Band 1

Bass, Berry & Sims PLC

See firm details p.1614

The Firm: This ten-lawyer team enjoys an *"excellent franchise in the market."* The firm's large body of corporate clients keeps the group active on a range of traditional employment matters, including discrimination cases, non-compete covenants, FLSA compliance and day-to-day employment counseling. Clients were full of praise for the team's *"business-like approach"* and the *"top-quality service"* on offer here.

The Lawyers: A *"sharp and impressive trial lawyer,"* **Bill Ozier** (see p.1610) commands *"almost unparalleled knowledge of traditional labor and employment law,"* researchers heard. His recent successes include the defense of two private universities in age discrimination claims brought by faculty members and acting in an age discrimination suit brought by a former executive of a major shoe manufacturer and retailer. Recommended for his *"sound judgment,"* **Tim Garrett** (see p.1607) undertakes labor contract negotiations and general day-to-day employment counseling. Clients appreciate his *"practical, folksy style"* and able handling of FLSA, wrongful discharge and FMLA cases. **Karen Ellis** (see p.1607), a *"highly personable and efficient"* practitioner, has experience representing unionized clients in arbitrations and contract interpretations. She was most highly rated, however, as a *"fabulous courtroom performer"* and takes on a growing number of discrimination suits and wage and hour cases.

The Clients: The firm provides employment advice to companies in sectors such as utilities, healthcare and telecom.

Kiesewetter Wise Kaplan Prather PLC

See firm details p.1617

The Firm: Voted *"one of the best firms in West Tennessee,"* the firm handles a steady stream of wage and hour and employment class actions. The 20-lawyer Memphis team holds a reputation for a *"top-flight"* traditional labor management practice and *"strong partner-client relationships,"* particularly within the healthcare, automotive and telecom sectors. In addition to litigation, the group also provides general employment and HR counseling services.

The Lawyers: **Paul Prather** (see p.1610) was praised by interviewees as an *"exceptionally smart"* employment law trial attorney. Although focused on courtroom work, Prather also offers public seminars on training. **Jonathan Kaplan**'s (see p.1608) practice has a greater emphasis on labor matters. This *"keen legal strategist"* advises companies on remaining union-free and often interfaces with the NLRB and other union entities. **Jay Kiesewetter** (see p.1609), a new entrant to the table, manages national union election campaigns and assists clients in remaining union-free.

The Clients: Johnson Controls; RR Donnelley & Sons; AT&T and Baptist Hospitals.

King & Ballow

The Firm: A highly esteemed Nashville firm, well known for its focus on management issues. Sixteen labor and employment specialists *"aggressively"* represent management rights locally and nationally in both the traditional labor and employment arenas. Interviewees highlighted the group's involvement on behalf of management in union negotiations and election campaigns as well as in EEOC, FLSA, wage and hour and noncompete cases.

The Lawyers: Twice selected as chairman of the labor section of the Tennessee Bar Association, **Eddie Wayland** was described as the *"engine"* behind this successful team. Supervisor of the firm's litigation section, Wayland acts for management in all areas of employment law and maintains a busy practice advising media clients on defamation, privacy and IP issues. He recently defended several wage and hour class action lawsuits involving millions of dollars in potential liability. This *"tough and thorough"* practitioner has also successfully defended whistle-blower and retaliatory discharge suits in both Tennessee and Florida. *"Even-tempered"* **Richard Lowe** is well respected for his considerable knowledge of traditional labor issues. He frequently handles contract negotiations and union relations for newspaper and television station clients.

The Clients: Kroger Company; Roadway; Ingram Industries; IASIS Healthcare; May Department Stores; BellSouth Mobility; Gaylord Entertainment; Post Newsweek; Lee Enterprises; O'Charley's; Thomas Nelson and Vanderbilt University.

Miller & Martin PLLC

See firm details p.1619

The Firm: This *"first-rate"* employment group retains a tight grip on the market in Chattanooga, where the majority of its 40 labor and employment law specialists are based. Observers also pointed to the team's strength in Nashville and middle Tennessee. The group takes a *"competent, controlled approach"* to a growing caseload of gender and race discrimination claims and wage and hour class actions. The practice also offers employment counseling on litigation avoidance and alternative dispute resolution programs. Attorneys have lately acted on a number of employment matters for public utility clients.

The Lawyers: Peers and clients laud **John Phillips** (see p.1610) as a *"superb"* attorney, highly visible throughout Tennessee for his public speaking and in-house seminars on employment issues. He acts for the firm's flagship client, Coca-Cola Enterprises, in connection with race and wage and hour class action suits in New York, Cincinnati and Louisiana and also advises the company on its comprehensive alternative dispute resolution program. **Eric Stevens** (see p.1611) provides counseling and litigation defense to several regional healthcare facilities, whom he also assists in OFCCP audits. He and his team recently handled a significant whistleblower case in Tennessee. **Tony Swafford** (see p.1611) enters the table following general endorsement of his *"comprehensive labor expertise."* Valued for his role as a rainmaker, Swafford advises the firm's large base of healthcare clients on union organization developments.

The Clients: Tennessee Farmers Insurance Companies; Summer Regional Medical Center; First Fleet and SMS Holdings.

Waller Lansden Dortch & Davis
See firm details p.1621

The Firm: An *"expanding client base"* in Tennessee, a depth of corporate talent, and the developing resources of its LA office all combine to make this Nashville firm a growing presence in labor and employment law, interviewees say. Twenty-three *"knowledgeable"* attorneys focus on the representation of employers and management, handling a heavy caseload of wage and hour claims and ERISA suits.

The Lawyers: *"Hugely talented"* **Bob Boston** (see p.1606) straddles the firm's labor and employment and trial and appellate practices. Concentrating on complex employment litigation, the highly respected Boston handles a large number of race discrimination cases. He has also lately brought his *"superb knowledge"* to bear in defending a major retailer, manufacturer and distributor against several nationwide opt-in wage and hour/overtime compensation challenges brought by thousands of employees. Clients admire **Larry Bridgesmith**'s (see p.1606) *"absolutely brilliant knowledge of the*

law." Well recognized as an *"old hand"* in the employment field, Bridgesmith was recently involved in two union-organizing campaigns in Tennessee and Michigan. His practice is divided between alternative dispute resolution, traditional labor matters and employment litigation. Chair of the firm's labor and employment group, **Waverly Crenshaw** (see p.1606) is a *"strong and confident"* attorney with a litigation-intensive practice. Interviewees highlighted his *"effective courtroom presentation"* and *"sensitivity to the employee's side."* He has been especially active with regards to race discrimination cases and a same-sex harassment suit.

The Clients: CVS Pharmacy; GlaxoSmithKline; Nissan North America; Gaylord Entertainment and UPS.

Band 2

Boult, Cummings, Conners & Berry PLC
The Firm: The respected corporate and healthcare practices of this Nashville firm spawn a significant volume of work for its nine-lawyer employment group. This *"well-rounded"* team handles a steady flow of FLSA and noncompete matters for local corporations and regional clients outside of Tennessee. The practice has recently witnessed a surge in employment discrimination, wrongful termination, whistleblower and retaliatory claims.

The Lawyers: *"Seasoned"* **Matt Lonergan** leads the firm's labor and employment team, acting on behalf of management in traditional labor issues and employment litigation. Interviewees lauded his *"good sense and responsiveness."* He and the team acted for a defendant in the appeal of a $1 million verdict in an employment discrimination case. **Craig Oliver** was nominated by peers as a name to watch. This *"quiet, smart"* attorney earned commendation for his well-honed legal skills. His varied practice encompasses union activity issues, Title VII and other employment discrimination litigation.

The Clients: Baptist Hospital; Doane Pet Care Enterprises; Saint Thomas Hospital and EJ Footwear.

Burch, Porter & Johnson PLLC
The Firm: Recently celebrating its 100th birthday, this much-respected Memphis firm employs *"personable and professional lawyers,"* researchers heard. Its eight-lawyer employment practice enters *Chambers'* rankings following general endorsement of its work in the employment discrimination area. The team advises management on all aspects of employment law. Attorneys recently acted for a computer con-

sulting business undergoing a merger in a significant wage and hour class action.

The Lawyers: Lisa Krupicka is a key member of the employment and labor group.

The Clients: The team advises a variety of Memphis-based and regional clients.

Constangy, Brooks & Smith LLC
The Firm: This dedicated employment firm maintains a Nashville practice of around half a dozen lawyers with *"substantive expertise"* in employment and labor law. Tennessee practitioners draw from the resources and employment law know-how of the firm's 12 other national offices. Notable areas of expertise include OSHA, ERISA, class action litigation and business immigration issues. The boutique acts for management only.

The Lawyers: **Zan Blue**, the managing member of the Nashville office, was identified by interviewees as *"the soul of the firm."* His *"bright, articulate style"* serves him well both in employment litigation and in litigation avoidance counseling. He is experienced in class action and multiplaintiff claims and spends much of his time advising on workplace audits.

The Clients: 3M; AmSouth Bank; FedEx; General Electric; HCA; NASCAR; Sony Entertainment and Wireless One.

Ford & Harrison LLP
See firm details p.631

The Firm: Headquartered in Atlanta, this *"fine, responsive"* firm devotes all its resources to labor and employment. A 17-strong Memphis team works closely with the firm's network of 140 lawyers, spread across 15 US offices. In addition to the standard range of employment and traditional labor issues, the team undertakes significant affirmative action matters and defends OFCCP investigations. The 2005 addition of offices in Dallas, Texas and the Carolinas following a merger with South Carolina boutique, Edwards Ballard, has considerably boosted the firm's capacities and market standing.

The Lawyers: Managing partner **Herb Gerson** (see p.1607) heads the Memphis practice and coordinates matters with the firm's Birmingham, Dallas, Denver and New York offices. Gerson earned praise for his experience in the field and a comprehensive practice comprising general employment counseling, litigation avoidance advice and traditional labor work. He and his team have acted for ACH Food in a number of matters, locally and in California.

The Clients: Alaska Airlines; HCA; US Security Associates; Pinnacle Airlines; ACH Food Companies; Nestlé USA and Regions.

Kramer, Rayson, Leake, Rodgers & Morgan LLP

See firm details p.1618

The Firm: Considered by many "*the best firm in Knoxville*," Kramer Rayson holds an "*excellent track record*" in employment law, researchers were told. Approximately half of the firm's 34 lawyers handle labor and employment matters, ranging from union negotiations to employment litigation. In the latter, this "*talented and formidable*" group is said to be "*highly respected by the bench*." The group has lately handled a large number of discrimination and retaliatory claims.

The Lawyers: Of counsel **Steven Kramer** (see p.1609) undertakes both traditional labor and employment work within his general corporate practice and is well respected in Tennessee for his wide-ranging experience. Managing partner **Ward Phillips** (see p.1610) heads the employment practice. Clients applauded his "*thorough compilation of evidence and data*" and his "*excellent communication skills*." Recent reported cases have included Rowan and Washington v Lockheed Martin Energy Systems, an age discrimination case brought by two employees who were laid off in a reduction in force at the Y-12 National Security Complex. Phillips also defended the president of the University of Tennessee against a reverse sex and race discrimination claim in Leadbetter v Gilley.

The Clients: UT-Battelle; Knoxville Utilities Board; National Healthcare of Oak Ridge and The University of Tennessee.

Lewis Fisher Henderson Claxton & Mulroy

The Firm: Renowned for its litigation avoidance and trial expertise, this firm enters *Chambers'* table based on strong commendations from clients and peers alike. Twenty Memphis-based attorneys boast trial experience in state and federal courts across the USA. With additional support from offices in LA and Jackson, Mississippi, the team represents clients before the EEOC, OFCCP, NLRB and other bodies and acts for defendants in employment litigation.

The Lawyers: Thirty years' experience in the field make lead partner **Fred Lewis** (see p.1609) "*the name at the firm*." He covers employment litigation and class actions, and demonstrates especial strength in wage and hour claims.

The Clients: The firm acts for a varied list of corporate employers, both locally and on a national level.

Ogletree, Deakins, Nash, Smoak & Stewart PC

See firm details p.638

The Firm: A large national labor and employment one-stop-shop, with 250 lawyers in 21 offices across the USA. The "*whip smart*" group of nine Nashville-based lawyers benefits from the firm's "*sterling reputation*" and considerable employment law resources. The practice undertakes a growing number of race, retaliatory and ERISA disputes and received particular praise from clients for its deft handling of traditional

labor matters. Nissan remains a key client for the group. In September 2004, the firm merged with southeastern labor specialists, Haynsworth Baldwin Johnson & Greaves, adding 50 lawyers to the firm's ranks.

The Lawyers: A "*competent and confident*" employment specialist, **Keith Frazier** (see p.1607) has 20 years' experience behind him. His practice focuses primarily on employment discrimination defense. He has handled a number of multiplaintiff wage and hour collection cases and routinely defends race, age and sex discrimination cases. An important case for the team was Fisher et al v GE Medical Systems, a collective action under the FLSA.

The Clients: The team counsels management in the manufacturing, construction and healthcare industries. Representative clients include Dollar General, Home Depot and HCA.

Other Notable Practitioners

Peers consider up-and-coming attorney **Chad Hatmaker** at Woolf, McClane, Bright, Allen & Carpenter PLLC to be a "*rising star*" in the employment field. In addition to his general litigation practice, Hatmaker represents clients before the EEOC, the Department of Labor and the Tennessee Human Rights Commission.

LITIGATION

GENERAL COMMERCIAL

Tennessee
Leading firms
(Litigation: General Commercial)
[1] **BOULT, CUMMINGS, CONNERS** Nashville
WALKER, BRYANT, TIPPS & MALONE Nashville
[2] **BAKER, DONELSON, BEARMAN** Nashville
BASS, BERRY & SIMS PLC Nashville
BOWEN RILEY WARNOCK & JACOBSON Nashville
HARWELL HOWARD HYNE GABBERT Nashville
NEAL & HARWELL PLC Nashville
WALLER LANSDEN DORTCH & DAVIS Nashville
[3] **ARMSTRONG ALLEN PLLC** Memphis
BURCH, PORTER & JOHNSON PLLC Memphis
GLANKLER BROWN PLLC Memphis
MILLER & MARTIN PLLC Chattanooga
SHERRARD & ROE PLC Nashville
Firms are listed alphabetically in each band.

Band 1

Boult, Cummings, Conners & Berry PLC

The Firm: The Nashville firm has relocated to new offices, and firmly retains its reputation in the market for excellence and efficiency. Thirty attorneys cover a broad spectrum of commercial litigation, with some typical specialties in areas such as plaintiff PI work. The team is seen to be on the cutting edge with regards to the increasing number of government investigations of healthcare companies. It recently handled two significant whistle-blower cases within the healthcare industry.

The Lawyers: Managing partner **Bob Patterson**'s broad experience attracts much praise and many referrals. This senior litigator's "*terrific understanding of securities law and financial statements*" stands him in good stead in high-profile securities litigation. He manages the firm's relationship with key client Central Parking and recently defended a service provider/garbage operator against allegations of mismanagement brought by a real estate com-

pany. Recognized for his "*superb*" litigation skills, **Sam Lipshie** focuses on IP and entertainment disputes. Peers describe **Paul Alexis** as a "*true New York litigator*" while clients consider him a "*go-to lawyer*" for large national antitrust and class action cases. **Thor Urness** earns an appearance in this year's tables, thanks to a growing profile in IP litigation. Client commended his "*straightforward and reasonable*" approach to contentious matters, adding that Urness "*knows how to pick his battles*." Peers regard him as a "*bright and effective trial lawyer*." "*Top-flight*" **Bill Norton** is said to be "*as good as they get*" in bankruptcy and creditor rights matters. A "*true academic*," Norton has acquired a national reputation through his seminars and writings on bankruptcy law. He typically represents major US creditors in large Chapter 11 cases. He recently acted for Briggs & Stratton as creditor and purchaser of the assets of Murray, a lawnmower manufacturer, in Chapter 11.

The Clients: Central Parking; Briggs & Stratton; Wachovia; Oaktree Capital Management and Republic Financial.

1598

All quotes in the text are from interviews with clients and competitors.

CHAMBERS USA 2005

Tennessee
Leading individuals
(Litigation: General Commercial)

[1] RILEY Steven *Bowen Riley*, Nashville
WALKER Robert *Walker Bryant*, Nashville

[2] BARFIELD Lee *Bass Berry*, Nashville
BEARMAN Leo *Baker Donelson*, Memphis
DAVIS Ames *Waller Lansden*, Nashville
DIETZ Wallace *Bass Berry*, Nashville
FARDON D Alexander *Harwell Howard*, Nashville
FEIBELMAN Jef *Burch Porter*, Memphis
GABBERT Craig *Harwell Howard*, Nashville

[3] ALEXIS Paul *Boult Cummings*, Nashville
ANDERSON Steve *Walker Bryant*, Nashville
BAHNER Maxwell *Chambliss Bahner*, Chattanooga
BOWEN Jay *Bowen Riley*, Nashville
BRYANT John *Walker Bryant*, Nashville
CAMPBELL L Webb *Sherrard & Roe*, Nashville
CHASE Lee *Glankler Brown*, Memphis
CODY W J Michael *Burch Porter*, Memphis
DICKSON Roger *Miller & Martin*, Chattanooga
GRIMES Dale *Bass Berry*, Nashville
HARBISON William *Sherrard & Roe*, Nashville
HARWELL Aubrey *Neal & Harwell*, Nashville
HICKS John *Baker Donelson*, Nashville
JACOBSON John *Bowen Riley*, Nashville
JONES Nancy *Bass Berry*, Nashville
LIPSHIE Samuel *Boult Cummings*, Nashville
MALONE Gayle *Walker Bryant*, Nashville
NEAL James *Neal & Harwell*, Nashville
NOEL Randall *Armstrong Allen*, Memphis
PATTERSON Robert *Boult Cummings*, Nashville
REID Glen *Wyatt Tarrant*, Nashville
ROSE Glenn *Harwell Howard*, Nashville
SANDERS James *Neal & Harwell*, Nashville
SWEENEY Matthew *Baker Donelson*, Nashville
THOMPSON Overton *Bass Berry*, Nashville

Up-and-coming individuals
URNESS Thor *Boult Cummings*, Nashville

Leading individuals
(Litigation: Bankruptcy)

[1] GABBERT Craig *Harwell Howard*, Nashville
NORTON Bill *Boult Cummings*, Nashville

[2] AHERN Lawrence *Greenebaum Doll*, Nashville
BUCY Rhea *Gullett Sanford*, Nashville
JENNINGS Paul *Bass Berry*, Nashville
KELLEY James *Neal & Harwell*, Nashville
MASHBURN Randal *Baker Donelson*, Nashville
ROSE Glenn *Harwell Howard*, Nashville

Leading individuals (Litigation: Medical Malpractice Defense)

[1] ANDERSON Steve *Walker Bryant*, Nashville
BARFIELD Lee *Bass Berry*, Nashville
BRYANT John *Walker Bryant*, Nashville
WISEMAN Thomas *Gideon & Wiseman*, Nashville

Individuals are listed alphabetically in each band.

Walker, Bryant, Tipps & Malone

See firm details p.1620

The Firm: This litigation boutique, founded five years ago by former Bass Berry attorneys, has established its reputation as a sophisticated outfit offering "*excellent legal analysis*" and "*client-friendly presentation.*" The growing practice now numbers 15 "*hands-on*" attorneys, commended for their "*ability to comprehend technical terminology as well as the law.*" Interviewees underlined the group's particular strength in medical, legal and other professional malpractice defense.

The Lawyers: "*Down-to-earth*" **Bob Walker** (see p.1612) possesses a "*unique combination of experience, judgment and style.*" He is "*head and shoulders above the rest*" for sophisticated business litigation, particularly securities and antitrust matters. Clients value his "*methodical and strategic*" approach to cases, which they say makes him "*instrumental in negotiating a settlement.*" Walker successfully represented Hardin Academy in a property dispute with the Metropolitan Government of Nashville and acted for Nashville Predators in a suit against Gaylord Entertainment. **Gayle Malone** (see p.1609) impresses clients as a "*measured*" attorney with experience in medical malpractice, PI and products liability suits. Malone represents several hospitals across Tennessee, but also does a significant volume of work on behalf of plaintiffs. The "*highly technical*" **John Bryant** (see p.1606) garnered admiration for his "*scientific*" handling of PI defense, medical malpractice suits and legal malpractice claims. He has recently advised professional engineers on a number of cases. "*Excellent*" **Steve Anderson** (see p.1605) is considered by clients to be "*at the top of his game*" in IP litigation and PI matters. He frequently advises Vanderbilt University on medical malpractice claims.

The Clients: Vanderbilt University; Harding Academy; HCA and Nashville Predators.

Band 2

Baker, Donelson, Bearman, Caldwell & Berkowitz PC

See firm details p.1613

The Firm: This well-respected full-service firm has branches throughout the South. Its litigation reputation is greatest in Memphis, where the largest of its five Tennessee offices is located. Clients value the "*great palate of services*" on offer here, particularly noting the team's "*ability to resolve cases in a timely manner.*" Practitioners boast "*great depth of knowledge*" in all areas of commercial litigation from antitrust and IP to product liability and white-collar crime. The firm has lately been involved in an increasing number of suits against automobile dealerships.

The Lawyers: The "*Energizer Bunny*" of trial lawyers, **Leo Bearman** (see p.1605) maintains an active and varied practice. He enjoys a superlative reputation among clients and peers, who consider him "*as good as it gets*" for complex commercial litigation. In addition to doing products liability and professional malpractice work, Bearman often represents government entities at city, county and state level. He has, for example, advised the City of Memphis and Shelby County on contentious matters. Other notable work includes acting for Union Pacific in a stockholder derivative suit involving allegations of impropriety against Union Pacific directors. Bearman also represented GM in the Supreme Court in a landmark products liability case. **John Hicks** (see p.1608) "*knows his way around the court.*" He enters *Chambers'* rankings as a well-rounded generalist with solid litigation experience. **Matt Sweeney** (see p.1611), a former Nashville circuit court judge, was noted for his expertise in mediation. He also maintains a general litigation practice and, according to observers, is "*superb in both offense and defense.*" **Randal Mashburn** (see p.1610) chairs the firm's bankruptcy and creditors' rights practice. Well known for his representation of creditors, Mashburn acted for the unsecured creditors' committee in the reorganization of Pen Holdings, involving $30 million in secured debt and $150 million in unsecured debt.

The Clients: Union Pacific; GM; City of Memphis; First Horizon; Hunter Fan; Wells Fargo Financial; Microsoft; Philip Morris and American Contract Bridge League.

Bass, Berry & Sims PLC

See firm details p.1614

The Firm: This 70-lawyer litigation group has the "*weight of experience*" behind it, as well as considerable "*name recognition*" in the field. Attorneys command "*a high degree of respect at the plaintiff bar,*" particularly for their work in medical malpractice and products liability defense. The team was retained by Wyeth to handle more than 2,300 cases in Tennessee involving individuals who opted out of the Fen-Phen class action suit.

The Lawyers: Interviewees praised **Lee Barfield** (see p.1605) as an "*effective communicator*" with a "*good mix of legal knowledge and judgment,*" especially in the areas of healthcare litigation, PI and medical malpractice. He recently represented National HealthCare Corporation, a public company that owns and operate nursing homes, in litigation arising from a fatal fire at one of its facilities. Chair of the litigation group, **Wally Dietz** (see p.1607) is an "*exceptionally talented*" attorney with notable strength in business tort litigation, trade secrets and fiduciary duty cases. Hailed as a "*strategic thinker,*" Dietz served as lead counsel to Bank One in a $151 million lender liability suit brought by Tengasco involving allegations of breach of contract, breach of fiduciary duty and other business tort allegations. He also recently represented an insurance agency on a trade secrets and breach of fiduciary duty case. Antitrust expert **Dale Grimes** (see p.1607) takes an *"intelligent and analytical"* approach to sophisticated commercial litigation and class action suits. He recently obtained the dismissal of a class action case on summary judgment for client BFI and represented Philip Morris in a patent and price discrimination case. **Nancy Jones** (see p.1608), who joined the firm from Waller Lansden in late 2004, brings both experience as a former federal prosecutor and *"attention to the minutiae of a case"* to bear in defending class actions and healthcare litigation. She obtained summary judgment for United Technologies in a recent class certification concerning an alleged fraudulent tender offer. A new entrant to the tables, the *"charming"* **Overton Thompson** (see p.1605), can be relied on to *"get it done,"* say clients. He defended London-based investment manager JO Hambro Capital Management against allegations brought by the common stockholders of World-Port Communications. *"Outstanding"* **Paul Jennings** (see p.1608) rates highly for his active bankruptcy practice and experience as debtors' counsel in large Chapter 11 cases. He was co-counsel for Capital One in a bankruptcy class action litigation and advised Regal Cinemas and Tennessee-headquartered Service Merchandise on Chapter 11 proceedings.

The Clients: HCA; National HealthCare; Wyeth; Independent Directors of Merrill Lynch; Philip Morris USA; Bank One; BellSouth; Landair; Vanderbilt University Medical Center; Insituform and Home Depot.

Bowen Riley Warnock & Jacobson, PLC

See firm details p.1615

The Firm: This Nashville litigation boutique houses 20 *"smart and hard-working"* attorneys, known for their *"aggressive and effective"* approach to significant cases. Formed by former Bass Berry attorneys, this ten-year-old firm garners admiration for its range of litigation expertise, particularly in relation to antitrust, securities and IP litigation. The team acted in a patent royalty dispute, resulting in a $650 million verdict.

The Lawyers: Corporate securities and healthcare litigation are particular strong suits for **Steven Riley** (see p.1611), an *"an incredibly bright and hard-hitting"* commercial trial lawyer involved in high-profile multiparty cases. He represented HCA in a Medicare investigation and shareholder lawsuits and served as counsel to Bridgestone in tire-related litigation. **Jay Bowen** (see p.1606) is blessed with *"an ability to aggressively protect his clients' interests without any false bravado,"* researchers were told. His business litigation practice is weighted heavily towards IP and entertainment disputes. Bowen recently handed defamation and first amend-

ment cases for a nationally known publisher in Florida. **John Jacobson** (see p.1606) received similar accolades as a capable, business-oriented attorney with a determination to *"fight his client's corner."* He provides both business litigation advice and strategic counseling to financial institutions and healthcare and entertainment clients. He handled a $15 million property dispute for New South Federal Savings Bank regarding a resort development in East Tennessee. He also acts for Morgan Stanley and American Express Financial Advisors in consumer and employment disputes.

The Clients: American Media; Coca-Cola; Gaylord Entertainment; HCA; Sony BMG Music Entertainment; Thomas Nelson; Universal Music Group; Vanderbilt University and Warner Music Group.

Harwell Howard Hyne Gabbert & Mannera PC

See firm details p.1616

The Firm: The *"lean and mean"* nine-lawyer litigation practice at this *"wonderful"* corporate law firm is highly esteemed for its strength in bankruptcy and corporate restructuring. Interviewees extolled the group's *"excellent track record"* and *"ability to deal with curve balls"* in matters ranging from trade secret and noncompete cases to securities litigation, business torts and corporate governance.

The Lawyers: Praised as a *"big-picture strategist with brilliant trial abilities,"* **Craig Gabbert** (see p.1607) maintains a comprehensive litigation practice, but is, according to market observers, *"on everyone's shortlist for bankruptcy."* He has counseled debtors in some of the largest local Chapter 11 cases. In 2004, he acted for Symphony Healthcare in four Chapter 11 filings and also advised a fast food franchisee on its reorganization. Gabbert has been instrumental as co-counsel in the bankruptcies of Regal Cinemas, Nu-Kote Holdings and Service Merchandise. Admired for his *"great integrity and work ethic,"* **Alex Fardon** (see p.1607) drew praise from clients for a *"killer intellect"* that enables him to *"boil down the complexities of a case."* He recently concluded a long-running trade secrets and non-compete case at the Tennessee Supreme Court. **Glenn Rose** (see p.1611) gained plaudits as a *"detail-oriented"* trial lawyer with significant expertise in fiduciary duty and advising corporate boards of directors.

The Clients: Select Medical; Thomas and Thorngren; Tecniflex; Universal Care and Citadel Broadcasting.

Neal & Harwell PLC

The Firm: This *"impressive"* 30-lawyer practice maintains its place in *Chambers'* rankings, thanks to a steady caseload of commercial cases and particular prominence in white-collar defense.

The Lawyers: Veteran attorney **Jim Neal** was acknowledged as a *"go-to"* individual for complex litigation questions. Observers noted that this *"first-rate"* practitioner is also *"great fun in the courtroom."* Among the most acclaimed of trial lawyers in Tennessee, Neal has acted for high-profile individuals in corruption, extortion conspiracy and racketeering charges. The firm's chief manager, **Aubrey Harwell**, enjoys a reputation as a *"sound leader"* with wide-ranging expertise in white-collar defense and general commercial litigation. **Jimmy Sanders** has an *"excellent manner with juries"* and *"effective advocacy skills."* Although recognized as a top criminal lawyer, Sanders has experience straddling civil litigation and white-collar defense work. He has served as counsel to Bridgestone/Firestone in tire litigation and acted for Ingram Industries, Morgan Stanley Dean Witter and Qwest Communications in a variety of contentious matters. **Jim Kelley**zzzz *"unique combination of bankruptcy and tax law knowledge"* makes him an ideal choice for creditors' side bankruptcy work. He acted for Grillco in the attempted purchase of the Off The Grill restaurant chain out of Chapter 11 and represented secured lenders in the American HomePatient and Murray Chapter 11 proceedings.

The Clients: The firm serves an extensive roster of Fortune 500 companies, small businesses and individuals. Clients include: Bank of America; Grillco; Bridgestone/Firestone; Ingram Industries; Morgan Stanley and Qwest Communications.

Waller Lansden Dortch & Davis

See firm details p.1621

The Firm: Headquartered in Nashville, the 100-year-old firm reinforces its profile in litigation with the considerable reputation of its corporate and healthcare transactional practice. Thirty lawyers in the trial and appellate group offer *"sound advice,"* backed by *"serious substantive knowledge."* Clients emphasized the group's commercial outlook: *"We know they won't try to reinvent the wheel."* In addition to a heavy caseload of healthcare and employment litigation, the practice handles an increasing volume of internal investigations.

The Lawyers: Interviewees singled out **Ames Davis** (see p.1606) as a *"top-notch"* attorney with a strong background in securities litigation and director and officer liability. He has recently acted in a growing number of healthcare and bankruptcy cases, including a Chapter 11 in California, in which he represented the committee of secured creditors of a non public company. The team suffered the loss of the former head of the trial and appellate group, Nancy Jones, who departed for Bass Berry in November 2004.

The Clients: The team has provided litigation counsel to companies such as UPS, Franklin Capital and Bridgestone Firestone.

Band 3

Armstrong Allen PLLC

The Firm: According to interviewees, "*ethical integrity and professionalism*" are ingrained in the culture of this "*fantastic*" regional outfit. Most of the firm's 80 attorneys work in litigation, in which the firm enjoys a historical reputation. Steady and well-respected practices in Memphis and Jackson are bolstered by the rapid growth of the firm's Mississippi and Arkansas offices.

The Lawyers: Within this talented team, CEO **Randy Noel**'s stands out as a "*top-flight*" attorney who is highly visible on an array of business and products liability disputes. Large class action cases benefit from his "*thorough preparation and confidence.*" He defended American Honda Finance in federal class action litigation involving allegations of discrimination against minorities in the financing of automobile loans. Noel also defended Tenet Healthcare against class action claims of overcharging for patient care and obtained summary judgment for Regions Bank (formerly Union Planters Bank) in lender liability litigation in Mississippi.

The Clients: Tenet Healthcare; American Honda Finance; Regions Bank; Taco Bell and DaimlerChrysler.

Burch, Porter & Johnson PLLC

The Firm: Although smaller than some of its key rivals, this 100-year-old outfit was deemed "*one of the strongest firms in Memphis*" by market sources. The team offers a variety of litigation counsel to clients, including antitrust, products liability, mass tort and white-collar crime.

The Lawyers: Former Attorney General for Tennessee, **Mike Cody** commands widespread respect as a "*go-to person for anything to do with Memphis.*" Lauded as "*fabulous and ethical,*" he is involved almost exclusively in mediation, arbitration and alternative dispute resolution. **Jeff Feibelman** is a "*low-key and well-connected*" attorney with an "*outstanding*" mediation and litigation practice. His past work includes obtaining a $100 million award for the plaintiff in Gregory et al v Chemical Waste Management.

The Clients: AutoZone; Hilton Hotels; Helena Chemical; Monsanto; BankTennessee; City of Memphis and City of Germantown.

Glankler Brown PLLC

The Firm: With two Memphis offices, the firm enjoys a "*strong local reputation*" and devotes a considerable proportion of its resources to litigation matters. A 35-strong team of "*smart, analytical trial lawyers*" is seen to be "*highly respected by Tennessee judges.*" Litigation expertise extends to such areas as aviation law, medical malpractice and directors and officers' liability. The team acted for Federal Express in a significant state tax lawsuit.

The Lawyers: Peers were impressed with "*talented*" **Lee Chase**'s varied litigation practice, which emphasizes medical malpractice and commercial disputes.

Miller & Martin PLLC

See firm details p.1619

The Firm: Approximately 37 lawyers in the firm's Nashville and Chattanooga offices practice commercial litigation. The group earned particular praise for expertise in class action litigation and mass tort products liability litigation. In addition to advising the firm's flagship client, Coca-Cola Enterprises, which, interviewees say, "*gets them everywhere,*" the team acted as national counsel for Chattem in more than 1,000 mass tort lawsuits filed by plaintiffs claiming that the Dexatrim appetite suppressant caused strokes.

The Lawyers: **Roger Dickson** (see p.1606) primarily undertakes commercial litigation, white-collar and products liability defense work for significant clients. He successfully represented Coca-Cola Enterprises in an action against Allianz Insurance to recover losses arising from a product recall in France and Belgium.

The Clients: Coca-Cola Enterprises; Chattem; Krystal; AmSouth Bank; Blue Cross & Blue Shield of Tennessee; Eastman Chemical Company and Unum Provident.

Sherrard & Roe PLC

The Firm: This small, Nashville-based business boutique is commended for its practitioners' "*sophisticated knowledge of the ins and outs of corporate and securities law.*" The firm has successfully leveraged its corporate expertise in attracting an increasing volume of commercial litigation, corporate investigations and qui tam cases. About half of the firm's 20 lawyers undertake litigation and business dispute resolution, earning praise for their handling of disputes with brokerage houses and financial advisers. Recent successes include obtaining a dismissal of a Qui Tam complaint against a healthcare company.

The Lawyers: "*Early preparation*" and a "*thoughtful trial approach*" are said to be the hallmarks of **Webb Campbell**'s litigation style. This experienced commercial litigator maintains a broad practice encompassing contract disputes, business torts, insurance liability and employment matters. **Bill Harbison** is a "*bright star*" within the practice, well known for his work for healthcare organizations and extensive litigation expertise in trust and estate matters. Described to researchers as a "*southern gent,*" Harbison has handled significant litigation for Vanderbilt University, including the settlement of a dispute between Vanderbilt and a managed care company. The team also defended a global financial firm against a class action suit filed by non-voting members of a regional brokerage firm acquired by the client.

The Clients: Clients include UBS Financial Services, State Volunteer Mutual Insurance and Scott Fetzer.

Other Notable Practitioners

Commercial Litigation:

Recognized as a "*big player in Chattanooga,*" **Max Bahner** at Chambliss, Bahner & Stophel, PC boasts an "*impressive reputation*" and long-standing experience in the field. His broad-based business litigation practice ranges from antitrust cases to professional liability suits. "*Superb*" **Glen Reid** (see p.1605) at Wyatt Tarrant & Combs LLP impressed observers with the breadth of his commercial litigation and white-collar practice.

Medical Malpractice:

Tom Wiseman at Gideon & Wiseman PLC is a "*keen and smart*" individual, widely recommended for medical malpractice defense. He and his 12-attorney team are considered specialists in the field and cater to the legal needs of a long roster of healthcare clients.

Bankruptcy:

In Nashville, the "*extremely thoughtful and well-respected*" **Rhea Bucy** of Gullett, Sanford, Robinson & Martin was noted for his representation of debtors in bankruptcy cases. **Lawrence Ahern** (see p.1605) of Greenebaum, Doll & McDonald PLLC gained respect for his "*intensely focused*" approach to bankruptcy litigation. "*He's methodical, carefully thinking through all possible solutions,*" a client said, "*and he's able to see other sides of the story that others wouldn't.*" Though his inclination is toward litigation, Ahern also offers transactional advice, including bankruptcy-related acquisitions.

MEDIA & ENTERTAINMENT

Tennessee
Leading firms (Media & Entertainment)
1 LOEB & LOEB LLP *Nashville*
2 BASS, BERRY & SIMS PLC *Memphis*
GORDON, MARTIN, JONES, HARRIS *Nashville*
RUSH LAW GROUP *Nashville*
STOKES BARTHOLOMEW EVANS *Nashville*
ZUMWALT, ALMON & HAYES *Nashville*

Leading individuals
(Media & Entertainment)
1 ALMON Orville *Zumwalt Almon*, Nashville
HOWARD Linda *Stokes Bartholomew*, Nashville
JONES Russell *Gordon Martin*, Nashville
KRAUS Kenneth *Loeb & Loeb*, Nashville
MILOM W Michael *Bass Berry*, Nashville
RUSH Stephen *Rush Law Group*, Nashville
SULLIVAN Robert *Loeb & Loeb*, Nashville
Firms and individuals are listed alphabetically in each band.

Band 1

Loeb & Loeb LLP

The Firm: The five-lawyer Nashville office is dedicated to entertainment law. Practitioners command "*impressive industry knowledge*" and can tap into the deep resources of this multiservice "*nationally respected*" law firm. The team represents music artists, songwriters, record companies and publishers in litigation and commercial agreements. The group's following is particularly strong within the country and western and contemporary Christian music circuits. Members also benefit from the considerable theater, film and television industry knowledge of attorneys at the firm's larger New York, Chicago and Los Angeles offices.

The Lawyers: Peers admired the "*high ethical standards*" of "*leading lights*" **Ken Kraus** and **Bob Sullivan**. These two "*key players*" garnered praise as "*bright and knowledgeable*" attorneys with valuable long-standing relationships on Music Row. Kraus maintains a transaction-oriented practice, primarily representing artists and smaller local record companies. Sullivan has recently handled a number of large copyright infringement sampling cases and artist-manager disputes.

The Clients: Warner; Sony; BMG and Viacom.

Band 2

Bass, Berry & Sims PLC
See firm details p.1614

The Firm: This large Tennessee corporate firm houses six entertainment law specialists, admired within the market for their "*dedication and knowledge in the music sphere.*" The team handles the negotiation of recording contracts in every genre of music, including pop, rock, rhythm and blues, country and western, and classical. IP and copyright law are integral areas of the group's practice. Collectively, the team has signed several new rock and pop artists to major record labels, renegotiated new contracts for country performers and advised on the production of an Al Green TV special.

The Lawyers: Deemed "*one of Music Row's most seasoned entertainment lawyers,*" **Mike Milom** (see p.1610) is considered a "*great source of information on specialized topics.*" Clients praised his "*personable nature and warm, communicative manner*" and his extensive knowledge of entertainment law, particularly in relation to copyright and IP.

The Clients: The firm enjoys a loyal following among individual recording artists, songwriters, record producers and entertainment industry executives.

Gordon, Martin, Jones, Harris & Shrum

The Firm: This six-attorney practice was particularly recognized for its success in representing country and western artists. Attorneys are involved in all aspects of the entertainment business and offer advice on business formations, trademark, copyright and contract negotiation.

The Lawyers: **Russell Jones** is the practice's "*key name.*" He and his team are envied for their impressive Music Row connections.

The Clients: The firm advises such well-known performers as Garth Brooks, Dixie Chicks and Tim McGraw. Other clients include Evergreen Records, Buckhorn Music Publishing and Grand Entertainment Group.

Rush Law Group

The Firm: Headquartered in Music Row, this Nashville boutique specializes in all aspects of IP, with an emphasis on music publishing. The practice also handles commercial real estate, business organizations and general business transactions for entertainment clients. The firm's market presence is enlarged by additional offices in New York and San Francisco.

The Lawyers: **Stephen Rush**, the firms founding partner, boasts more than 25 years' experience representing clients in the music publishing industry. This "*outstanding*" practitioner earned plaudits for his expertise in US and international IP law and his particular knowledge of the country and western scene.

The Clients: The firm provides transactional and due diligence advice to music publishers and purchasers of music catalogues.

Stokes Bartholomew Evans & Petree, PA

The Firm: Since opening an office on Music Row in 2001, the firm has successfully established its reputation within the local music community. Half a dozen "*excellent*" attorneys focus on IP and entertainment law. These well-respected practitioners are adept at the preparation and negotiation of contracts, the enforcement of IP law, defamation and protection of privacy issues.

The Lawyers: Chair of the firm's entertainment and new media practice group and vice chair of the firm's IP practice group **Linda Edell Howard** is a "*regular*" in the entertainment field in Nashville. This "*impressive*" attorney was commended for her "*great connections*" and transactional know-how. She has represented the copyright interests of George Gershwin, Elvis Presley and the Beatles.

The Clients: The group acts for artists, managers, songwriters, producers, record labels, authors, actors, screenwriters and software developers.

Zumwalt, Almon & Hayes

The Firm: Six lawyers offer a range of entertainment law services, including copyright, IP, trademark, unfair competition, contracts and publishing advice. While the firm's emphasis is on the music industry, practitioners also undertake matters pertaining to the video, television and motion picture sectors.

The Lawyers: The "*exceptionally talented*" **Orville Almon** was recognized as a "*star*" with close relationships with Nashville-based record labels.

The Clients: The firm counsels a variety of artists, labels and music companies.

REAL ESTATE

Tennessee
Leading firms (Real Estate)

1
BAKER, DONELSON, BEARMAN, *Memphis*
BASS, BERRY & SIMS PLC *Nashville*
BOULT, CUMMINGS, CONNERS *Nashville*
WALLER LANSDEN DORTCH & DAVIS *Nashville*

2
ARMSTRONG ALLEN PLLC *Memphis*
BURCH, PORTER & JOHNSON PLLC *Memphis*
GLANKLER BROWN PLLC *Memphis*
SHERRARD & ROE PLC *Nashville*
SHUMACKER WITT GAITHER *Chattanooga*
STOKES BARTHOLOMEW EVANS *Nashville*

Leading individuals (Real Estate)

1
LIDDON Rob *Baker Donelson, Memphis*
TRENT Tom *Boult Cummings, Nashville*

2
BERRY Dewees *Bass Berry, Nashville*
BROWN Kim *Sherrard & Roe, Nashville*
CARGILE Ann *Boult Cummings, Nashville*
CATES C Thomas *Burch Porter, Memphis*
HARKAVY Ronald *Armstrong Allen, Memphis*
HARRIS Matthew *Waller Lansden, Nashville*
HUMPHREYS Hunter *Glankler Brown, Memphis*
WEATHERSBY Woods *Stokes Bartholomew, Memphis*

3
ARONOV Mary *Baker Donelson, Memphis*
CAMPBELL Robert *Stokes Bartholomew, Nashville*
CARSON William *Burch Porter, Memphis*
DOWSLEY Felix *Bass Berry, Nashville*
EARTHMAN Douglas *Armstrong Allen, Memphis*
GUPTON John *Baker Donelson, Nashville*
HAYNES John *Boult Cummings, Nashville*
JONES Philip *Martin Tate, Memphis*
KIRKHAM Steven *Waller Lansden, Nashville*
MARSHALL COX LeeAnne *Burch Porter, Memphis*
PAPEL Laurence *Baker Donelson, Nashville*
RUTTER David *Boult Cummings, Nashville*
SCOTT W Rowlett *Armstrong Allen, Memphis*
SHEETS Mark *Bass Berry, Nashville*
STEMMLER John *Bass Berry, Memphis*
TATE James *Bass Berry, Nashville*
WOOD Robert *Boult Cummings, Nashville*

Firms and individuals are listed alphabetically in each band.

Band 1

Baker, Donelson, Bearman, Caldwell & Berkowitz PC

See firm details p.1613

The Firm: The firm's renown for "*top-quality*" real estate work "*cuts through state lines.*" The 30-lawyer practice, which operates from offices throughout the state, demonstrates a "*depth and breadth of expertise*" and a "*determination to make the deal work.*" The Memphis office was praised for its strength in financial and institutional real estate work, while the Nashville team was particularly recommended for healthcare-related real estate development and investment matters.

The Lawyers: Among this "*responsive, diligent and professional*" group of attorneys, **Rob Liddon**

(see p.1609) stands out as a "*calm and collected negotiator*" with extensive experience in the field. Liddon acts for First Horizon National and Premcor Refining Group. He has expertise in multistate lending transactions and frequently handles local leasing matters for out-of-state companies. Recognized for his "*savvy business judgment*" and "*clear, sound advice,*" **John Gupton** (see p.1608) devotes a significant portion of his practice to commercial real estate and the development of office, industrial and healthcare facilities. Gupton also handles residential development work and condominium conversions. He recently advised a large private trust with over 4,000 multifamily housing units on several acquisitions and financings in the Southeast. He also provided counsel on two apartment developments in Rutherford County. **Mary Aronov** (see p.1605), a construction and asset-based financing expert, earned praise for her "*thorough and efficient*" handling of real estate finance matters. Managing partner **Laurence Papel** (see p.1610) is a "*respected entrepreneur*" with a niche in hospitality sector work. He frequently acts for developers of shopping centers and restaurants, and recently represented a Turnberry Associates affiliate in the $40 million financing of the Hilton Nashville Downtown Hotel.

The Clients: Nestlé Waters North America; Ritzen Group; Vastland Realty Group; GBT Realty; First Horizon National; Premcor Refining Group; ADESA; Gaylord Entertainment and Renal Care Group.

Bass, Berry & Sims PLC

See firm details p.1614

The Firm: Strong practice support, combined with "*tremendous development expertise,*" keeps this 30-attorney real estate group "*at the top of the game.*" The team operates from offices in Nashville, Knoxville and Memphis, and is well known throughout the surrounding counties for its development and finance work. The firm represented Alex S. Palmer & Company in the acquisition, development, construction and permanent financing of the Burton Hills III and IV office buildings in Nashville, for a combined value of approximately $50 million. The group also advises on a number of apartment-to-condominium conversion projects and has seen a growth in real estate litigation work.

The Lawyers: With more than 25 years' experience in the field, **Dewees Berry** (see p.1605) commands an "*incredible knowledge of the law.*" Peers and clients expressed respect for his "*top-notch technical abilities*" and commitment to the real estate community. Although he still carries out transactional work, Berry devotes the greater proportion of his time to acting for title companies in title policy disputes and handling real estate litigation relating to projects and

developments. Real estate practice chair **Felix Dowsley** (see p.1607) acts for financial institutions on significant secured lending and real estate finance transactions. **John Stemmler** (see p.1611) is a "*trusted*" name for multifamily housing and hospitality industry work. Clients commend him as a "*cautious and professional*" practitioner with an "*ability to summarize the risks*" of a transaction. He represented Davidson Hotel principals in negotiating a joint venture and loan documents with a venture capital fund for the purchase of the Pasadena Hilton Hotel in California. A newcomer to the tables, **Mark Sheets** (see p.1611) was recommended as a "*smart and conscientious*" lawyer with a growing development practice. He advised American Retirement on sale and leaseback transactions with an aggregate value of $450 million. Also entering *Chambers'* tables is **Jim Tate** (see p.1611), whose finance-based practice encompasses construction loans, long-term real estate loans and real estate development projects.

The Clients: American Healthways; AmSouth Bank; Central Parking; Dialysis Clinic; First Tennessee; O'Charley's and Vanderbilt University.

Boult, Cummings, Conners & Berry PLC

The Firm: This 30-lawyer real estate team offers "*responsive*" service and "*straight to the point*" advice on real estate development and financing. Clients were particularly enthusiastic about the firm's "*competitive*" pricing structures. The firm has recently restructured its practice groups following the relocation of its Nashville headquarters and real estate attorneys look forward to increased cooperation with the firm's tax and finance specialists on large transactions. The group recently represented several German companies investing in large architectural projects in the USA.

The Lawyers: "*Easygoing*" **Tom Trent** is a "*talented and non-confrontational negotiator*" with a loyal client following. He heads the firm's newly formed real estate healthcare team and recently acted for a major Texas-based for-profit hospital system in the development and lease of a hospital facility under construction in Dublin, Ireland. Trent also represented a nonprofit hospital system in the $70 million sale of six medical office buildings and a parking garage in Nashville. Trent's "*right-hand man,*" **David Rutter**, rates highly as a "*thorough and intelligent*" development specialist, with considerable expertise in structured purchase agreements. He represented the developer in redeveloping an $8 million shopping center in Tennessee. Rutter also acted for an insurance client on an agreement to acquire the $30 million retail component of a mixed-use project currently under construction in Chicago. Other notable work includes advising an insurance company on the acquisition of a $15 million industrial facility. "*Extremely smart and technically skilful*" **Ann Cargile** is highly visible representing both landlords and tenants in retail, office and industrial leases. In 2004, she completed approximately 100 leasing transactions for regular client American Realty Advisors. She also closed a $17 million loan for Metropolitan Life Insurance on Southwind Apartments in Memphis. "*Solution-oriented*" **Bob Wood** handles a wide range of commercial real estate transactions on behalf of lenders, permanent lenders and life insurance companies, many of which are investing in office, industrial facilities and retail buildings outside Tennessee. He also advises on the acquisition, development and financing of shopping malls, golf courses and multifamily housing projects, including condominiums and apartment buildings. Clients admire **John Haynes** for his "*understanding*" demeanor and habit of "*leaving the ego out of transactions*." He has lately been visible representing German investors in connection with several high-profile developments in Washington DC, Miami, Atlanta, Chicago and Orange County. Haynes also advises on the development and financing of affordable and low-income housing.

The Clients: Lincoln National Life Insurance; Baker Storey McDonald Properties; State Farm Insurance; Willis North America; Brookside Properties and Seton.

Waller Lansden Dortch & Davis

See firm details p.1621

The Firm: The firm's stellar reputation in the healthcare field lends force to its real estate practice, much of which involves acquisition and development work for Nashville-based healthcare companies. A "*hard-working and client-friendly*" team of 18 lawyers and five paralegals also handles transactional real estate matters within the hospitality, technology and distribution sectors.

The Lawyers: Practice leader **Matthew Harris** (see p.1608) provides "*detailed, practical*" advice to clients in the telecoms, healthcare and transportation industries. His workload runs the gamut of real estate acquisitions, disposals, development work, and, increasingly, real estate finance. **Steven Kirkham** (see p.1609) is an "*impressive and driven*" attorney with a focus on site acquisition and development for shopping center and hospitality clients. He also handles the acquisition and financing of apartment complexes.

The Clients: Verizon Wireless; LifePoint Hospitals; Logan's Roadhouse; O'Charley's and Carter-Haston Holdings.

Band 2

Armstrong Allen PLLC

The Firm: This is a major real estate player in Memphis, well known for its "*quick turnaround*" in development and zoning matters. The ten-lawyer team undertakes a full range of transactional work relating to hotels, industrial and commercial developments, apartment buildings and single-family housing.

The Lawyers: Considered "*one of the finest zoning attorneys in the city*," **Ron Harkavy** enjoys a reputation as a "*pragmatic business adviser*" with noteworthy expertise in planning and zoning matters. Clients also spoke highly of his "*excellent negotiating skills*." "*Talented*" commercial real estate and municipal finance attorney **Doug Earthman** is "*easy to work with*," clients say. He advises purchasers of credit-tenant leased properties on acquisitions and financings and represents industrial companies and governmental units in connection with payment in lieu of tax agreements. Market commentators endorsed **Rowlett Scott** for his considerable transactional experience. In addition to real estate acquisitions, sales and leases, Scott frequently advises in connection with title insurance matters.

The Clients: Bank of America; Clear Channel Outdoor; Massachusetts Mutual Life Insurance and Memphis Area Association of REALTORS.

Burch, Porter & Johnson PLLC

The Firm: This old-line Memphis firm houses a well-respected team of seven "*careful and practical*" real estate attorneys. This "*professional and knowledgeable*" group handles real estate secured loans, rezoning, and conveyancing work in addition to traditional development and real estate financing matters.

The Lawyers: A "*highly qualified and skilled veteran*," **Thomas Cates** undertakes both development matters and significant lending work for a number of institutional lenders. **Bill Carson** demonstrates "*fine technical ability*" in his handling of acquisitions and disposals for Memphis-based clients. In addition to working on apartment refinancings, Carson advises the Memphis Housing Authority on low-income housing. **LeeAnne Marshall Cox** is a "*bright and well-liked*" attorney with expertise in secured lending and asset-based finance. She is most visible representing banks in real estate transactions.

The Clients: The team handles real estate matters for national clients, charitable organizations, life insurance companies and educational institutions.

Glankler Brown PLLC

The Firm: Although still more frequently associated with its historic strength in tax and litigation, the Memphis firm's 11-lawyer real estate team is seen to be growing in stature. The "*steady and solid group*" takes a "*thorough and nonconfrontational approach*" to a wide range of real estate and secured lending transactions. Typical work ranges from commercial acquisitions and sales to multifamily housing development. The group has recently advised on downtown redevelopment projects, including apartment to condominium conversions and conversions of space for retail and residential uses.

The Lawyers: A popular choice among multi-family residential and commercial developer clients, **Hunter Humphreys** (see p.1608) "*leaves no legal stone unturned*." His client roster includes Meritex Enterprises, Cooper Realty Investments and LEDIC Management, one of the largest multifamily apartment management companies in the Midsouth. In 2004, he advised on the development of a new shopping center, and on numerous multifamily housing sales and acquisitions. Interviewees also noted his expertise in secured lending and estate planning.

The Clients: The team advises a varied base of landowners, developers, borrowers and lenders.

Sherrard & Roe PLC

The Firm: The firm's real estate practice is home to "*some top-quality people*," according to market commentators. Particular expertise exists in relation to commercial lending, corporate finance and healthcare-related real estate transactions.

The Lawyers: **Kim Brown**, well respected in the market as a "*trusted and hard-working*" figure, maintains a generalist practice, handling real estate finance and development in tandem with other corporate transactions. Much of his real estate work involves commercial construction in the south and southwest of the USA. Brown acted for Tractor Supply in the purchase of around 100 units of bankrupt Quality Stores. He also advises Bank of America, US Bank and AmSouth on lending matters.

The Clients: The firm counsels Bank of America, AmSouth Bank and Tractor Supply.

Shumacker Witt Gaither & Whitaker, PC

The Firm: Formed in 2002 by members of Witt, Gaither & Whitaker and Shumacker & Thompson, this 50-lawyer Chattanooga firm devotes a fifth of its manpower to general commercial real estate work. The team enjoys a reputation as a "*collegiate and hard-working*" group with particular expertise in the acquisition, financing and development of shopping centers. The firm also handles real estate litigation, including construction contract disputes.

The Lawyers: Ron Feldman brings 30 years' transactional experience to his position as chair of the firm's real estate practice.

The Clients: CBL & Associates Properties; ABC Supply; Kenco Group and Coca-Cola Bottling.

Stokes Bartholomew Evans & Petree, PA

The Firm: This is a well-established regional firm with offices in Nashville and Memphis. Fifteen real estate and banking attorneys handle a range of commercial real estate matters, including acquisition, financing and development. The team has been involved in various local development projects in the hospitality and leisure sectors and can draw on the support of specialist construction lawyers in connection with zoning, land use and contracting issues.

The Lawyers: Vice chair of the firm's commercial real estate and banking practice, **Woods Weathersby** possesses a "*great understanding of the real estate market.*" "*Well connected*" among developers and property investment companies, Weathersby maintains a varied workload of construction, development and leasing matters. Typical matters include the development and financing of office buildings, shopping centers and apartment complexes. **Bo Campbell** commands "*a huge amount of respect*" from developer and lender clients, who consider him a figure of "*local prominence.*" A new entrant to the *Chambers* tables, he was widely praised as a hard-working attorney with a "*knack for seeing the big picture.*" Campbell chairs the firm's transactions practice group and manages the firm's commercial real estate and banking practice team. He has handled over $1 billion worth of real estate transactions and commercial credit facilities for a publicly held private prison and corrections company.

The Clients: Union Planters Bank; SunTrust Bank; Metropolitan Nashville Airport Authority; Tennessee Municipal League and Memphis City Schools Board.

Other Notable Practitioners

At Martin, Tate, Morrow & Marston PC, **Philip Jones** was commended as an attorney with long-standing experience in the market. The Memphis-based practitioner handles commercial real estate matters alongside banking and secured transactions.

Leaders in Tennessee

AHERN III, Lawrence R
Greenebaum Doll & McDonald PLLC, Nashville 615 760 7112
lra@gdm.com
Recommended in Litigation
Practice Areas: Member in Charge, Nashville; bankruptcy and commercial litigation and transactions (creditors' and debtors' interests, trustees, indenture trustees and creditors' committees); banking, lending (esp. asset-based and workout transactions, troubled institutions and debtor-in-possesion financing); corporate reorganizations and acquisitions (esp. leveraged buyouts, distressed businesses and bankruptcy transactions).
Career: Mr Ahern holds national board certification as a specialist in business bankruptcy by the American Board of Certification and has taught Secured Transactions and Banking at Vanderbilt Law School and Cumberland School of Law. Mr Ahern is author and co-author of several books and has published many articles and given numerous presentations in his concentration areas.
Personal: Vanderbilt University, BA and JD.

ALEXIS, Paul
Boult, Cummings, Conners & Berry, PLC, Nashville 615 244 2582
Recommended in Litigation

ALMON, Orville
Zumwalt, Almon & Hayes, Nashville 615 256 7200
Recommended in Media & Entertainment

ANDERSON , Steve
Walker, Bryant, Tipps & Malone, Nashville 615 313 6000
sanderson@walkerbryant.com
Recommended in Litigation
Practice Areas: Litigation including medical malpractice, commerical, intellectual property and product liability.

Prof. Memberships: Tennessee and Nashville Bar Association; Defense Research Institute; International Association of Defense Counsel.
Career: Partner.
Publications: Articles editor of the Vanderbilt Journal of Transnational Law, authored law review article 'Intrusive Border Searches: What Protection Remains for the International Traveler Entering the United States After United States v. Montoya de Hernandez and Its Progeny?'
Personal: Vanderbilt University (JD 1988); Baylor University (BA, magna cum laude 1985).

ARONOV, Mary L
Baker, Donelson, Bearman, Caldwell & Berkowitz, PC, Memphis
901 577 2223
maronov@bakerdonelson.com
Recommended in Real Estate
Practice Areas: Practice concentrated in commercial real estate and financial transactions. Extensive experience in real estate and asset-based loan transactions, purchases and sale of commercial real estate, mergers and acquisitions, multi-state lending transactions, leases, corporate finance operations, loan modifications and work-outs, foreclosures and other commercial transactions.
Prof. Memberships: Member of American Bar Association (Commercial Law, Real Estate and Probate Sections), Tennessee and Memphis Bar Associations. Member, Leo Bearman Sr. Inn of Court. Former Chairperson, Memphis and Shelby County Air Pollution Control Board. Authored articles in several legal publications.
Career: Licensed in Tennessee since 1984.

BAHNER, Maxwell
Chambliss, Bahner & Stophel, P.C., Chattanooga 423 756 3000
Recommended in Litigation

BARFIELD II, Lee
Bass, Berry & Sims PLC, Nashville
615 742 6202
lbarfield@bassberry.com
Recommended in Litigation
Practice Areas: Litigation and healthcare law. Handles broad variety of litigation, including professional liability, malpractice defense, healthcare fraud, business disputes, insurance litigation, class actions, commercial law issues, banking matters and constitutional law claims. Counsels healthcare providers on hospital operational issues, child abuse reporting, fraud and abuse and other healthcare regulatory issues.
Prof. Memberships: American, Tennessee and Nashville Bar Associations.
Career: Joined the firm in 1974. Served as President of Board of Law Examiners for the State of Tennessee, 1986-2000.
Personal: BA (1968) and JD (1974), Vanderbilt University.

BEARMAN Jr, Leo
Baker, Donelson, Bearman, Caldwell & Berkowitz, PC, Memphis
901 577 2220
lbearman@bakerdonelson
Recommended in Litigation
Practice Areas: 45 years' experience representing local, regional and national companies as well as city and county governments in class action defense, antitrust matters, insurance defense litigation, products liability defense, intellectual property litigation, professional liability and general commercial litigation.
Prof. Memberships: Fellow, American College of Trial Lawyers. Life Member, Fellows of the American Bar Foundation. Former President, Tennessee Junior Bar Association. Member, Shelby County and Memphis Bar Associations. Member, American Board of Trial Advocates. Adjunct professor of law, University of Memphis Cecil C. Humphreys School of Law.

Career: Licensed in Tennessee since 1960 and United States Supreme Court since 1973.

BERRY IV, Dewees
Bass, Berry & Sims PLC, Nashville
615 742 6215
cberry@bassberry.com
Recommended in Real Estate
Practice Areas: Litigates such real estate conflicts as eminent domain matters, mechanic's lien and construction suits, quiet title actions and contract disputes. Also advises clients concerning zoning, planning, lease disputes, boundary, easement, restrictive covenant and land use issues. Has extensive transactional experience including purchases and sales, financings, leasings and all other aspects of commercial real estate.
Prof. Memberships: Rule 31 Listed General Civil Mediator; past President, Nashville Bar Association.
Career: Joined the firm in 1981. Editor, Tennessee Real Estate Law Letter. Instructor in Real Property Law, Nashville School of Law.
Personal: BA (1973) and JD (1976), Vanderbilt University.

BISHOP III, George W
Waller Lansden Dortch & Davis, Nashville 615 244 6380
george.bishop@wallerlaw.com
Recommended in Corporate/M&A
Practice Areas: Mergers and acquisitions, particularly those involving hospitals and other healthcare facilities. Securities and offerings, especially syndications of healthcare facilities and venture capital financings. Antitrust and regulatory issues relating to healthcare. Healthcare service companies with the acquisition and disposition of healthcare facilities. Negotiation and documentation of healthcare transactions.
Prof. Memberships: Member of the Nashville Bar Association, served as the initial Chairman of the Health Law

Committee in 1989. Member of the Tennessee Bar Association, served as the Founder and initial Chairman of the Health Law Section in 1989 and 1990. Served on an Antitrust Section Task Force on Hospital Mergers for the American Bar Association and on the National Membership Committee of the National Health Lawyers Association. Member of the Tennessee Bar Association Ethics and Professional Responsibility Committee.

Career: Practiced law at Waller Lansden since 1976. Served on the firm's Executive Committee for over a decade. Past Chairman of the firm.

BLUE Jr, William
Constangy, Brooks & Smith, LLC, Nashville 615 320 5200
Recommended in Employment

BOSTON, Robert E
Waller Lansden Dortch & Davis, Nashville 615 244 6380
bob.boston@wallerlaw.com
Recommended in Employment

Practice Areas: Labor and employment and commercial litigation. Represents manufacturing, service and commercial industries in the following areas: employer/employee related issues including day-to-day management advice, labor relations, business litigation and dispute resolution.

Prof. Memberships: Member of the Nashville, Tennessee and American Bar Associations with memberships in the Labor and Employment and Litigation Sections. Fellow of the Nashville Bar Foundation.

Career: Practiced law at Waller Lansden since 1982. Serves on the firm's Board of Directors. Manages the firm's Trial and Appellate Practice Group.

BOWEN, Jay
Bowen Riley Warnock & Jacobson, PLC, Nashville 615 320 3700
jbowen@bowenriley.com
Recommended in Litigation

Practice Areas: Commercial litigation; intellectual property litigation.

Prof. Memberships: American, Tennessee and Nashville Bar Associations; past ABA Subcommittee Chairman, protection of sound and audiovisual recordings; Leadership Music.

Career: Admitted to bar 1974, Tennessee; admitted to Bars of US Supreme Court, 6th Circuit, 9th Circuit.

BRAUN, Stephen
Boult, Cummings, Conners & Berry, PLC, Nashville 615 244 2582
Recommended in Corporate/M&A

BRIDGESMITH, Larry W
Waller Lansden Dortch & Davis, Nashville 615 244 6380
larry.bridgesmith@wallerlaw.com
Recommended in Employment

Practice Areas: Employment litigation, including union relations, labor agreement negotiation, alternative dispute

resolution and strategic approaches to employee relations. Represents management in numerous industries including, automotive, manufacturing, hospitality, airport, healthcare, transportation, warehousing and distribution.

Prof. Memberships: Member of the Tennessee, Michigan and American Bar Associations. Member of the American Employment Law Council and faculty member of the National Institute of Trial Advocacy. Founder of the Human Resources Leadership Forum. Member of the Pepperdine University School of Law Board of Visitors. Member of the Tennessee Business Roundtable and member of the Tennessee Chamber of Commerce and Business.

Career: Practiced law since 1978. Prior to joining Waller Lansden in 2000, he was Managing Partner of the Nashville office of Constangy, Brooks and Smith, LLC from 1986 to 2000.

BROWN, Kim
Sherrard & Roe PLC, Nashville
615 742 4200
Recommended in Real Estate

BRYANT, John
Walker, Bryant, Tipps & Malone, Nashville 615 313 6000
jbryant@walkerbryant.com
Recommended in Litigation

Practice Areas: Litigation including professional negligence and product liability; Rule 31 listed general civil mediator.

Prof. Memberships: Nashville and Tennessee Bar Association; Lawyers-Pilot Bar Association; Defense Research Institute; Fellow American College of Trial Lawyers.

Career: Partner.

Personal: Vanderbilt University (JD 1973); Davidson College (AB 1970).

BUCY, Rhea
Gullett, Sanford, Robinson & Martin, Nashville 615 244 4994
Recommended in Bankruptcy, Litigation

CAMPBELL II, L Webb
Sherrard & Roe PLC, Nashville
615 742 4200
Recommended in Litigation

CAMPBELL Jr, Robert
Stokes Bartholomew Evans & Petree, P.A., Nashville 615 259 1450
Recommended in Real Estate

CARGILE, Ann
Boult, Cummings, Conners & Berry, PLC, Nashville 615 244 2582
Recommended in Real Estate

CARSON II, William
Burch, Porter & Johnson PLLC, Memphis 901 524 5000
Recommended in Real Estate

CATES, C Thomas
Burch, Porter & Johnson PLLC, Memphis 901 524 5000
Recommended in Real Estate

CHASE III, Lee James
Glankler Brown, PLLC, Memphis
901 525 1322
Recommended in Litigation

CHEEK III, James
Bass, Berry & Sims PLC, Nashville
615 742 6223
jcheek@bassberry.com
Recommended in Corporate/M&A

Practice Areas: Represents a number of public and private companies and investment banking firms in a wide variety of capital raising and merger and acquisition activities. Also counsels boards of directors and board committees on matters relating to corporate governance and corporate legal compliance.

Prof. Memberships: American Bar Association (past Chair, Section of Business Law and Federal Regulation of Securities Committee); National ABA Task Force on Corporate Responsibility (past Chair); Legal Advisory Committee of New York Stock Exchange (past Chair).

Career: Joined the firm in 1970.

Personal: BA, (1964), Duke University; JD, (1967), Vanderbilt University; LLM, (1968), Harvard University.

CODY, W J Michael
Burch, Porter & Johnson PLLC, Memphis 901 524 5000
Recommended in Litigation

COLE, J Chase
Waller Lansden Dortch & Davis, Nashville 615 244 6380
chase.cole@wallerlaw.com
Recommended in Corporate/M&A

Practice Areas: Corporate law and governance, securities law, public offerings, mergers and acquisitions, venture capital and financing.

Prof. Memberships: Member of the Nashville, Tennessee and American Bar Associations. Member of the American Bar Association Committees on Corporate Governance, Negotiated Acquisitions, Federal Regulation of Securities and Venture Capital. Fellow of the Nashville Bar Foundation. Member of the Dean's Council of the Vanderbilt University School of Law. Member of the Society of International Business Fellows. Member of the National Association of Corporate Directors. Co-Chair for the Host Committee, ABA Section of Business Law 2005 Spring Meeting.

Career: Practiced law at Waller Lansden since 1979. Chair of firm's Corporate Governance Task Force.

COWART, Richard
Baker, Donelson, Bearman, Caldwell & Berkowitz, PC, Nashville
615 726 5660
dcowart@bakerdonelson.com
Recommended in Corporate/M&A

Practice Areas: Chair of Baker Donelson's Health Law Department and 2004-05 President of the American Health Lawyers Association. Practice concen-

trated in advising clients regarding legal, regulatory and business issues related to health care. Mr Cowart works primarily as board counsel to health service organizations (both for-profit and not-for-profit). He is also a national columnist and frequent speaker on health law topics.

Prof. Memberships: 2004-05 President, Board of Directors/Executive Committee, American Health Lawyers Association.

Career: Licensed in Mississippi since 1978 and Tennessee since 1999.

Personal: University of Southern Mississippi, BA, 1975. University of Mississippi Law School, JD, 1978.

CRENSHAW Jr, Waverly D
Waller Lansden Dortch & Davis, Nashville 615 244 6380
waverly.crenshaw@wallerlaw.com
Recommended in Employment

Practice Areas: Labor and employment, all employer/employee-related issues and government regulatory issues.

Prof. Memberships: Fellow of the Nashville and Tennessee Bar Foundations. Life Member to the Conference of the Sixth Judicial Circuit of the United States. Served as Chair of the Tennessee Supreme Court's Advisory Committee on the Board of Professional Responsibility and Chair of the Labor & Employment Section of the Tennessee Bar Association in 2004. Charter Member of the Harry Phillips American Inns of Courts. Member of the Board of Trustees of the Napier-Looby Bar Foundation.

Career: Practiced law since 1982. Joined Waller Lansden in 1990. Manages firm's Labor and Employment Practice Group.

DAVIS, Ames
Waller Lansden Dortch & Davis, Nashville 615 244 6380
ames.davis@wallerlaw.com
Recommended in Litigation

Practice Areas: Dispute resolution with an emphasis on complex commercial disputes involving issues of federal and state securities, antitrust and healthcare regulation.

Prof. Memberships: Member of the Nashville, Tennessee and American Bar Associations. Founder and Fellow of the Tennessee Supreme Court Historical Society. Fellow of the Nashville and Tennessee Bar Foundation.

Career: Practiced law at Waller Lansden since 1971. Past Chairman of the firm.

DICKSON, Roger W
Miller & Martin PLLC, Chattanooga
423 785 8330
rdickson@millermartin.com
Recommended in Litigation

Practice Areas: Commercial litigation, white collar crime, mass tort defense. Successfully resolved over 1,000 lawsuits filed against Chattem Inc. alleging personal injuries resulting from the ingestion of the appetite suppressant, Dexatrim.

Prof. Memberships: Fellow, American College of Trial Lawyers, Fellow, American Bar Association, Fellow , Tennessee Bar Association, Member, Tennessee Commission on Continuing Legal Education and Specialization.

Career: Graduated Order of Coif: University of Tennessee Law School 1971. Private Practice in Chattanooga 1971-79. United States Magistrate, United States District Court for Eastern District of Tennessee 1979-84. Private Practice in Chattanooga 1984-present. Partner, Miller and Martin 1990-present.

Personal: Born August 14, 1945. Married, three children. Member of the Board: Chattanooga Public Education Foundation, Chattanooga Boys and Girls Club, University of Chattanooga Foundation. Member, University of Tennessee Board of Trustees, 1990-2000.

DIETZ, Wallace W
Bass, Berry & Sims PLC, Nashville
615 742 6276
wdietz@bassberry.com
Recommended in Litigation

Practice Areas: Focuses his practice on complex business and commercial litigation, including cases involving business torts, trade secrets, internal investigations, banking and commercial law, media and entertainment law, healthcare law, ERISA and mergers and acquisitions.

Prof. Memberships: Nashville Bar Association; past President and Chair, Nashville Pro Bono, Inc.

Career: Joined the firm in 1983. Legislative assistant and media aide to former US Senator Jim Sasser, 1977-81.

Personal: BA (1977), Emory University; JD (1982), cum laude, Georgetown University.

DILWORTH, Lee C
Harwell Howard Hyne Gabbert & Manner, PC, Nashville 615 256 0500
lcd@h3gm.com
Recommended in Corporate/M&A

Practice Areas: Firm corporate/M&A Practice Leader. Regularly counsels clients in mergers and acquisitions, venture capital, joint ventures and other strategic transactions. Specific expertise in healthcare arena. Over 50 hospital transactions.

Prof. Memberships: Admitted to practice in Tennessee (1986). Member of American Health Lawyers Association, American Bar Association, Tennessee and Nashville Bar Associations. Fellow, Nashville Bar Association.

Career: Joined H3GM in 1987. Former firm Managing Partner.

Personal: Born 20 January 1961. LLM in Taxation, New York University (1987); JD, University of Georgia (1986); BA, Furman University (1983).

DOWSLEY III, Felix R
Bass, Berry & Sims PLC, Nashville
615 742 6228
fdowsley@bassberry.com
Recommended in Real Estate

Practice Areas: Focuses on commercial lending, secured transactions, real estate

and general commercial law. Negotiation and documentation of a variety of financing and real estate transactions, including asset-based financings, syndicated revolving credit and term loan facilities, mezzanine and subordinated loans, construction loans and work-outs and restructures of credit facilities, as well as the sale and leasing of commerical real estate.

Prof. Memberships: Member of the Board of Directors, Mid-South Commercial Law Institute.

Career: Joined the firm in 1984.

Personal: BA (1981) and JD (1984), University of Tennessee.

EARTHMAN, Douglas
Armstrong Allen PLLC, Memphis
901 523 8211
Recommended in Real Estate

ELLIS, Karen
Bass, Berry & Sims PLC, Nashville
615 742 6226
kellis@bassberry.com
Recommended in Employment

Practice Areas: Defends discrimination lawsuits involving age, religion, gender, race, disability, FMLA and sexual harassment claims and employers and providers in denial of benefits claims under ERISA. Defends class action lawsuits involving discrimination and FLSA claims. Prepares affirmative action plans for government contractors and subcontractors.

Prof. Memberships: Fellow, American College of Labor and Employment Lawyers; Lawyers' Association for Women; Nashville Bar Association.

Career: Joined the firm in 1981.

Personal: BA (1971), with distinction, Transylvania University; MA (1978), Middle Tennessee State University; JD (1980), University of Tennessee.

FARDON, D Alexander
Harwell Howard Hyne Gabbert & Manner, PC, Nashville 615 256 0500
daf@h3gm.com
Recommended in Litigation

Practice Areas: Firm litigation Practice Leader. Concentrates exclusively on trial and appellate work in state and federal courts. Handles commercial cases and employment litigation including contract claims, business torts, employment disputes, trade secrets, securities claims and property disputes.

Prof. Memberships: Admitted to practice (1989). Member of the Nashville, Tennessee and American Bar Associations.

Career: Joined H3GM in 1989. Former Clerk to the Honorable Thomas A Wiseman, Jr, United States District Court for the Middle District of Tennessee.

Personal: Born 16 August 1963. JD, Yale Law School (1988); BA, Duke University, Summa Cum Laude, Phi Beta Kappa.

FEIBELMAN, Jef
Burch, Porter & Johnson PLLC,
Memphis 901 524 5000
Recommended in Litigation

FRAZIER, Keith D
Ogletree, Deakins, Nash, Smoak & Stewart, PC, Nashville
615 254 1900
keith.frazier@ogletreedeakins.com
Recommended in Employment

Practice Areas: Labor and employment, litigation.

Prof. Memberships: American Bar Association (Labor and Employment Section: Co-Chair of Finance, 2004 to present; Fellow of the ABA/YLD), Tennessee Bar Association (Chair, Judiciary Committee, 1999-2000; Member, Jury Reform Task Force, 1998; YLD: President, 1994-95; Fellow of the TBA/YLD), Nashville Bar Association (Federal Court Committee, 2004; Fellow, Nashville Bar Foundation).

Career: Admitted to practice in Tennessee, US Court of Appeals (Fifth, Sixth and Eleventh Circuits) and various US District Courts. Listed in The Best Lawyers in America.

Personal: University of Tennessee (BS, 1982), University of Tennessee College of Law (JD, 1985).

GABBERT Jr, Craig V
Harwell Howard Hyne Gabbert & Manner, PC, Nashville 615 256 0500
cvg@h3gm.com
Recommended in Bankruptcy, Litigation

Practice Areas: Represents debtors/creditors in commercial bankruptcies/workouts, including related litigation. Counseled trustee/debtor/committee in four largest bankruptcy cases filed in Middle District of Tennessee. Counsels businesses on dispute resolution and complex commercial litigation matters.

Prof. Memberships: Admitted to practice in (1976). Member of the Nashville (Director), Tennessee and American Bar Associations. Former Director, President Mid-South Commercial Law Institute. Fellow of the Nashville Bar Foundation.

Career: Joined firm in 1979. Captain, Judge Advocate General ('JAG'), United States Army.

Personal: Born 11 March 1949. JD, Vanderbilt University, Order of Coif, Patrick Wilson Scholar; BS, US Military Academy.

GARRETT, Tim K
Bass, Berry & Sims PLC, Nashville
615 742 6270
tgarrett@bassberry.com
Recommended in Employment

Practice Areas: Chairs the labor and employment practice area. Represents employers in all aspects of employment discrimination (both class actions and individual claims) and traditional labor law, including union avoidance, responding to unfair labor practices, grievance and arbitration matters, con-

tract interpretation, wage and hour claims (collective actions and individual claims), ERISA litigation, OSHA/TOSHA proceedings, covenants not to compete, and FMLA.

Career: Joined the firm in 1986.

Personal: BA (1983), summa cum laude, University of the South; JD (1986), Vanderbilt University.

GERSON, Herb
Ford & Harrison LLP, Memphis
901 291 1530
HGerson@fordharrison.com
Recommended in Employment

Practice Areas: Herb Gerson represents management with traditional labor and employment issues. His practice is devoted to counseling clients to avoid employment discrimination claims and to develop a positive work environment. Herb is listed in a leading legal publication, has written articles on labor and employment matters, and co-chairs the Labor and Employment Committee of the American Bar Association's Litigation Section. He is editor of the Tennessee Employers Desk Manual and the national version of the same publication. Herb earned his undergraduate and law degrees from Emory University. He is a member of the College of Labor and Employment Lawyers.

GILBERT, Paul D
Waller Lansden Dortch & Davis,
Nashville 615 244 6380
paul.gilbert@wallerlaw.com
Recommended in Corporate/M&A

Practice Areas: Securities and mergers and acquisitions, virtually always on behalf of healthcare clients.

Prof. Memberships: Member of the American Bar Association. Member of the Committee on Federal Regulation of Securities and the Subcommittee on Annual Review of Securities of the American Bar Association. Member of the Committee on Negotiated Acquisitions of the American Bar Association.

Career: Practiced law since 1991. Joined Waller Lansden in 1996. Serves on the firm's Board of Directors.

GRIMES, Dale
Bass, Berry & Sims PLC, Nashville
615 742 6244
dgrimes@bassberry.com
Recommended in Litigation

Practice Areas: Handles civil litigation matters with a special focus on antitrust, consumer fraud, complex litigation, class actions and telecommunications. Has been counsel of record for defendants in over 30 class actions. His practice includes antitrust counseling to clients on a variety of merger, distribution, pricing and joint venture issues, as well as government and internal antitrust investigations.

Prof. Memberships: Fellow, Nashville Bar Foundation; Past Chair, Civil Justice Reform Act Advisory Group of the Middle District of Tennessee.

Career: Joined the firm in 1980.
Personal: BA (1975), University of the South; JD (1978), University of Tennessee.

GUPTON, John
Baker, Donelson, Bearman , Caldwell & Berkowitz, PC, Nashville
615 726 7351
jgupton@bakerdonelson.com
Recommended in Real Estate
Practice Areas: Practice concentrated in commercial real estate and mortgage lending. Represents several life insurance companies, developers, commercial real estate owners, brokers and contractors. Extensive experience in the formation, development, financing, acquisition, disposition and leasing of commercial real estate projects and properties.
Prof. Memberships: Member, American (Real Property Section), Tennessee (Real Property Section) and Nashville Bar Associations. Fellow, American College of Mortgage Attorneys.
Career: Licensed in Tennessee since 1976.
Personal: University of Virginia, BA University of Memphis Cecil C. Humphreys School of Law, JD.

HARBISON, William
Sherrard & Roe PLC, Nashville
615 742 4200
Recommended in Litigation

HARDCASTLE, Jay
Boult, Cummings, Conners & Berry, PLC, Nashville 615 244 2582
Recommended in Corporate/M&A

HARKAVY, Ronald
Armstrong Allen PLLC, Memphis
901 523 8211
Recommended in Real Estate

HARRIS, Matthew T
Waller Lansden Dortch & Davis, Nashville 615 244 6380
matt.harris@wallerlaw.com
Recommended in Real Estate
Practice Areas: Commercial real estate, land use and zoning and real estate lending. Extensive experience in the acquisition, disposition and leasing of office, industrial and retail properties for public and private companies. Management of multi-state acquisition and financing transactions.
Prof. Memberships: Member of the Nashville, Tennessee and American Bar Associations.
Career: Practiced law since 1984. Joined Waller Lansden in 1997. Manages the firm's Real Estate Practice Group.

HARWELL Jr, Aubrey
Neal & Harwell, PLC, Nashville
615 244 1713
Recommended in Litigation

HATMAKER, J Chadwick
Woolf, McClane, Bright, Allen & Carpenter, PLLC, Knoxville 865 215 1000
Recommended in Employment

HAYNES, John
Boult, Cummings, Conners & Berry, PLC, Nashville 615 244 2582
Recommended in Real Estate

HICKS, John
Baker, Donelson, Bearman , Caldwell & Berkowitz, PC, Nashville
615 744 7337
jhicks@bakerdonelson.com
Recommended in Litigation
Practice Areas: Practice concentrated in health law litigation, medical malpractice defense, consumer fraud class action defense, ADR and commercial and banking litigation. Extensive experience in bankruptcy, creditors' rights, business reorganizations and insurance coverage litigation. Certified by the Tennessee Supreme Court as a mediator in general civil cases.
Prof. Memberships: Member, American (Litigation Section), Tennessee (Litigation, Commercial and Bankruptcy and Banking Sections) and Nashville Bar Associations. Member, American Health Lawyers Association, Tennessee Defense Lawyers Association, Defense Research Institute and American Bankruptcy Institute.
Career: Licensed in Tennessee since 1983.

HILL, J Reginald
Waller Lansden Dortch & Davis, Nashville 615 244 6380
reggie.hill@wallerlaw.com
Recommended in Corporate/M&A
Practice Areas: Extensive experience in the areas of business transaction law, mergers and acquisitions, securities, venture capital financing and health law.
Prof. Memberships: Member of the Nashville Bar Association and its Health Law Committee. Member of the Tennessee Bar Association, serving in its Health Law Section. Member of the American Bar Association and its Business Law and Health Law Sections. Member of the American Health Lawyers Association.
Career: Practiced law at Waller Lansden since 1982. Serves on the firm's Board of Directors.

HOLT III, Berry
Boult, Cummings, Conners & Berry, PLC, Nashville 615 244 2582
Recommended in Corporate/M&A

HOWARD, Linda
Stokes Bartholomew Evans & Petree, P.A., Nashville 615 259 1450
Recommended in Media & Entertainment

HUMPHREYS, Hunter
Glankler Brown, PLLC, Memphis
901 576 1744
hhumphreys@glankler.com
Recommended in Real Estate
Practice Areas: Real estate and secured lending. Mr Humphreys represents numerous investors, developers, lenders and participants in real estate, secured

lending and other business transactions.
Prof. Memberships: Admitted to practice in Tennessee. Adjunct professor, University of Memphis School of Law (Real Estate Transactions). Past President and board member of the University of Memphis Law School Alumni Association. Past Board Member of the Estate Planning Council of Memphis. Board Member of the the District Investigating Committee for the Tennessee Bar Association. Member, American Bar Association (Business Law, Real Property, Probate and Trust Sections). Member, Tennessee Bar Association (Real Estate Section). Member, Memphis Bar Association (former Member, CLE Committee, Moral Fitness for Admission to the Bar Committee; former Chairman, University of Memphis Law School Liaison Committee).
Career: Lawler, Humphreys, Dunlap & Wellford (1977-85); Glankler Brown, PLLC (1985-present), Member, Chair of Real Estate Section.
Personal: Born 24 November 1951, Memphis, TN; JD, University of Memphis, 1977; BA, University of North Carolina (Chapel Hill), 1974.

HYNE, Ernest E
Harwell Howard Hyne Gabbert & Manner, PC, Nashville 615 251 1064
eeh@h3gm.com
Recommended in Corporate/M&A
Practice Areas: Noted healthcare acquisitions expert handling over 100 hospital and numerous rehab/long-term facility transactions. Extensive securities experience, worked on variety of financing transactions for private/public companies. Represents business clients with emphasis on start-up issues, venture capital financing, joint venturing, mergers/acquisitions, contract negotiations.
Prof. Memberships: Admitted to practice in (1977). Member, Nashville and Tennessee Bar Associations. Served on Tennessee Bar Advisory Group on Blue Sky Regulations.
Career: Joined H3GM in 1977. Former Managing Partner. Speaker at numerous CLEs on M&A; guest lecturer Masters of Business Administration, Lipscomb University.
Personal: Born 3 Jan 1952. JD, Vanderbilt University; BS David Lipscomb University.

JACOBSON, John
Bowen Riley Warnock & Jacobson, PLC, Nashville 615 320 3700
Recommended in Litigation

JENNINGS, Paul G
Bass, Berry & Sims PLC, Nashville
615 742 6267
pjennings@bassberry.com
Recommended in Bankruptcy, Litigation
Practice Areas: Commercial litigation, restructuring and bankruptcy law. Represents creditors including institutional creditors in corporate bankruptcies,

counsel to state's largest corporate debtors and counsel to official unsecured creditors committees.
Prof. Memberships: American Bankruptcy Institute; Nashville Bar Association; Tennessee Bar Association (past President Section of Commercial, Bankruptcy and Banking Law); Mid-South Commercial Law Institute (Director); Tennessee Chapter Turnaround Management Association (Board Member).
Career: Joined the firm in 1990.
Personal: BS (1987), Middle Tennessee State University; JD (1990), with high honors, University of Tennessee (Order of the Coif).

JONES, Nancy S
Bass, Berry & Sims PLC, Nashville
615 742 6239
njones@bassberry.com
Recommended in Litigation
Practice Areas: Focuses on healthcare litigation, including internal investigations and qui tam defense, as well as complex federal court commercial and securities litigation.
Prof. Memberships: American, Tennessee, New York and Nashville Bar Associations; American Health Lawyers Association; Fellow, Nashville and Tennessee Bar Foundations.
Career: Joined the firm in 2004. Assistant US Attorney for the Middle District of Tennessee, 1991-93. Assistant US Attorney for the Western District of Oklahoma, 1987-91; Assistant US Attorney for the Northern District of New York, 1980-87.
Personal: BA (1971), with honors, University of Missouri; JD (1978), Syracuse University.

JONES, Philip
Martin, Tate, Morrow & Marston, P.C., Memphis 901 522 9000
Recommended in Real Estate

JONES, Russell
Gordon, Martin, Jones, Harris & Shrum, Nashville 615 321 5469
Recommended in Media & Entertainment

KAPLAN, Jonathan E
Kiesewetter Wise Kaplan Prather, PLC, Memphis 901 795 6695
jkaplan@kiesewetterwise.com
Recommended in Employment
Practice Areas: Mr Kaplan has devoted his entire career to representing management clients exclusively in all areas of labor relations, employment law, and human resource management. His practice spans litigation, training, and consulting in more than 40 states and Canada.
Prof. Memberships: Admitted, Tennessee (1982). Member, ABA Labor and Employment Law Section, Practice and Procedure Under the NLRA Committee. Past Management Co-Chair, ABA Subcommittee on Drug and Alcohol Abuse in the Workplace. Past Chair, Tennessee Bar Association, Labor and Employ-

ment Law Section. Member, Memphis Bar Association.

Career: Founding Member, Kiesewetter Wise Kaplan Prather, PLC (1996). Admitted before the US Courts of Appeals for the Fifth, Sixth, Eleventh, and DC Circuits, numerous federal district courts, and the Tennessee Supreme Court. Mr Kaplan practices extensively before the NLRB nationally, and has been admitted specially in state courts in California, Florida, Illinois, Indiana, Kentucky, Michigan, New York, and Ohio. Recognized in a leading legal publication in America.

Publications: Senior editor, 'How To Take A Case Before The NLRB' Seventh Edition (BNA, Supp. 2005). Editor in chief, 'Tennessee Labor Letter' 1992-2000.

Personal: Born 14 November, 1957. JD, University of Memphis, 1982; Research Editor, 'University of Memphis Law Review' 1981-82; BA (Cum Laude), Rhodes College, 1979.

KELLEY, James
Neal & Harwell, PLC, Nashville
615 244 1713
Recommended in Bankruptcy, Litigation

KIESEWETTER, Jay W
Kiesewetter Wise Kaplan Prather, PLC, Memphis 901 795 6695
jkiesewetter@kiesewetterwise.com
Recommended in Employment

Practice Areas: Mr Kiesewetter's practice is devoted exclusively to management-side labor relations and employment law, with a strong emphasis on maintaining non-union work environments, defending against union organizing activity, and handling related proceedings before the National Labor Relations Board and US Courts of Appeal. He has a national reputation for successfully advising companies faced with union organizing drives. He also represents employers with unions in collective bargaining, arbitrations, labor disputes, and related litigation.

Prof. Memberships: Admitted: Missouri (1974); Tennessee (1977). Member of ABA, Section of Labor and Employment Law (Committees on Development of the Law Under the NLRA; Practices and Procedures Before the NLRB; speaker at ABA's 2004 Convention); Tennessee and Missouri Bar Associations (Labor and Employment Law Sections; former officer of Tennessee Bar Labor and Employment Law Section); Memphis and Shelby County Bar Association; Federal Bar Association.

Career: Founding Member of law firm Kiesewetter Wise Kaplan Prather, PLC (1996-present); previously, private practice, management-side labor and employment law firm (1977-95; Partner 1982-95); Trial Attorney, NLRB, Region 14 (1974-77); Corporate Counsel, Brown Group, Inc. (1974).

Personal: St. Louis University School of Law (JD, cum laude, 1974); University of Missouri (AB, 1967); University of Southern California (MA, 1971). US Air Force (1968-71).

KIRKHAM, Steven
Waller Lansden Dortch & Davis, Nashville 615 244 6380
steve.kirkham@wallerlaw.com
Recommended in Real Estate

Practice Areas: Commercial real property, business and banking law. Extensive experience in representing developers and end-use retailers in shopping center and regional mall developments and has experience including work with land development companies in financing, purchasing, selling and leasing potential development sites. Represents clients in acquisition, syndication and financing of multi-family housing complexes, exerpience involves structuring and negotiating complex acquisition and financing vehicles utilizing securitized credit facilities and multi-tiered ownership structures.

Prof. Memberships: Member of the Nashville, Tennessee, Kentucky and American Bar Associations.

Career: Practiced law since 1989. Joined Waller Lansden in 2001.

KRAMER, Steven E
Kramer, Rayson, Leake, Rodgers & Morgan, LLP, Knoxville 865 525 5134
skramer@kramer-rayson.com
Recommended in Employment

Practice Areas: Mr Kramer's law practice principally involves employment and labor law, corporate law, and sports law.

Prof. Memberships: He is a Member of the Knoxville, Kingsport, Tennessee, and American Bar Associations. Mr Kramer is a member of the Regional Board of Directors for First Tennessee Bank. He serves as Chairman of the Kingsport Economic Development Board and is a Member of the Board of Directors for the Northeast State Community College Foundation and the Boys & Girls Club.

Career: The law firm of Kramer, Rayson, Leake, Rodgers & Morgan, LLP has named Steven E Kramer "Of Counsel" with the firm in 2003. Mr Kramer has been Vice-President of Human Resources and General Counsel for AFG Industries Inc. since 1990. Prior to joining AFG, Mr Kramer spent 10 years in the private practice of law as a Partner at the Hunter, Smith & Davis and Baker, Donaldson law firms. Steve has been identified as a leading employment lawyer in Tennessee by Chambers USA, The Client's Guide 2004.

Personal: Mr Kramer holds an undergraduate degree in business administration from Miami University in Oxford, Ohio. He received his MBA (finance) from the University of Southwestern Louisiana and his JD from the University Of Tennessee College Of Law. Steve

and his wife Tina have three children and reside in East Tennessee.

KRAUS, Kenneth
Loeb & Loeb LLP, Nashville
615 749 8300
Recommended in Media & Entertainment

LAMAR III, Howard H
Bass, Berry & Sims PLC, Nashville
615 742 6209
hlamar@bassberry.com
Recommended in Corporate/M&A

Practice Areas: Focuses on complex transactions, such as mergers and acquisitions for public and private companies, public and private offerings on behalf of issuers and investment banking firms and venture capital financing (equity and subordinated debt) for venture funds and issuers, including venture capital partnership formation. Counsels companies on a variety of corporate and securities matters, including corporate governance, public company disclosure matters, strategic analysis and start-up concerns.

Prof. Memberships: American and Nashville Bar Associations.

Career: Joined the firm in 1989.

Personal: BA (1983) and JD (1989), Vanderbilt University.

LEWIS, Frederick
Lewis Fisher Henderson Claxton & Mulroy, Memphis 901 767 6160
fredl@lfhc.com
Recommended in Employment

Practice Areas: Labor and employment, representing management.

Prof. Memberships: College of Labor and Employment Lawyers (Fellow); Tennessee Bar Foundation (Fellow); Federal Court Advisory Committee for the Western District of Tennessee; Federal Bar Association, Memphis Chapter (Past President).

Career: Admitted to practice in US Supreme Court, 8 Federal Courts of Appeals, 17 Federal District Courts, and State Courts of Tennessee.

Publications: A frequent speaker and author on employment law topics, and has taught Labor Legislation and Collective Bargaining as an adjunct at the Fogelman College of Business, University of Memphis. Listed in each edition of 'The Best Lawyers in America.'

LIDDON, Rob
Baker, Donelson, Bearman, Caldwell & Berkowitz, PC, Memphis
901 577 2269
rliddon@bakerdonelson.com
Recommended in Real Estate

Practice Areas: Practice concentrated in lending, financing and real estate. Experience includes multi-state lending transactions, credit and financing, bank regulatory, corporate formation, and acquisition and financing of health care facilities. Extensive experience in banking law, credit law, commercial credit,

interest and usury, shopping center law, construction contracts, asset based finance, military base closings, and commercial real estate acquisition, finance and leasing.

Prof. Memberships: Member, American, Tennessee, Mississippi and Memphis Bar Associations. Member, Phi Beta Kappa. Former adjunct professor, Real Estate Law, Memphis State University Law School and Louisiana State University.

Career: Licensed in Tennessee since 1975 and Mississippi since 1976.

LIPSHIE, Samuel
Boult, Cummings, Conners & Berry, PLC, Nashville 615 244 2582
Recommended in Litigation

LONERGAN, Matthew
Boult, Cummings, Conners & Berry, PLC, Nashville 615 244 2582
Recommended in Employment

LOWE, Richard
King & Ballow, Nashville
615 259 3456
Recommended in Employment

MALONE, Gayle
Walker, Bryant, Tipps & Malone, Nashville 615 313 6000
gmalone@walkerbryant.com
Recommended in Litigation

Practice Areas: Civil trial law; personal injury litigation including medical malpractice; products liability; premises liability and motor vehicle actions; hospital law; Rule 31 listed general civil mediator.

Prof. Memberships: American, Tennessee and Nashville Bar Associations; International Academy of Defense Counsel; Tennessee Defense Lawyers Association; Tennessee Trial Lawyers Association; American College of Trial Lawyers.

Career: Partner.

Personal: Vanderbilt University (JD 1973, BA 1970).

MANNER, Mark
Harwell Howard Hyne Gabbert & Manner, PC, Nashville 615 251 1066
jmm@h3gm.com
Recommended in Corporate/M&A

Practice Areas: Assisted clients and venture capital funds complete in excess of $1 billion in venture capital and other private transactions. Experience in structuring/negotiating mergers/acquisitions, capital formation, securities offerings, advising boards of directors of public companies. Counsels clients in healthcare, biotechnology, information technology.

Prof. Memberships: Admitted, 1978. Member, American Health Lawyers Association; Board of Directors, Tennessee Technology Development Corporation and Tennessee Biotechnology Association; Former Board Member, Nashville Healthcare Council.

Career: Current Managing Partner; Antitrust Division, US Department of Justice and Special Assistant US Attorney.

Personal: Born 11 March 1952. LLM Yale Law School; JD, University of Memphis; BA, Vanderbilt University.

MARSHALL COX, LeeAnne
Burch, Porter & Johnson PLLC, Memphis 901 524 5000
Recommended in Real Estate

MASHBURN, Randal
Baker, Donelson, Bearman , Caldwell & Berkowitz, PC, Nashville
615 726 7336
rmashburn@bakerdonelson.com
Recommended in Bankruptcy, Litigation

Practice Areas: Chair of Baker Donelson's Bankruptcy and Creditors' Rights Group. Practice concentrated in debtor-creditor issues, workouts and insolvency law. Background includes commercial litigation as well as representation of creditors, debtors, trustees, committees and examiners. Extensive experience in Chapter 11 cases, lien priority litigation and secured transaction issues.
Prof. Memberships: Member, American, Tennessee and Nashville Bar Associations. Member, American Bankruptcy Institute. Fellow, Nashville Bar Foundation. Former faculty, Southeastern Paralegal Institute.
Career: Licensed in Tennessee since 1982. Certified business bankruptcy specialist and consumer bankruptcy specialist by the American Board of Certification.

MCKENZIE, Donald
Stokes Bartholomew Evans & Petree, P.A., Nashville 615 259 1450
Recommended in Corporate/M&A

MILOM, W Michael
Bass, Berry & Sims PLC, Nashville
615 255 6161
mmilom@bassberry.com
Recommended in Media & Entertainment

Practice Areas: Has practiced entertainment and intellectual property and technology law for more than 30 years. Concentrates his practice in the areas of copyright, literary property and entertainment law.
Prof. Memberships: American Bar Association (Member, Copyright Office Committee of the Intellectual Property Section); Tennessee Bar Association (past Chair, Section on Copyright, Entertainment and Sports Law); Nashville Bar Association (past Chair, Entertainment Law Committee). Past Member, International Copyright Panel of the U.S. State Department Advisory Committee on International Intellectual Property.
Career: Joined the firm in 2001.
Personal: BS (1964), Middle Tennessee State University; JD (1971), Vanderbilt University.

MITCHELL, E Marlee
Waller Lansden Dortch & Davis, Nashville 615 244 6380
marlee.mitchell@wallerlaw.com
Recommended in Corporate/M&A

Practice Areas: Securities law, including underwritten equity and debt public offerings, private placements, joint ventures and venture capital financings, federal and state broker-dealer and investment adviser regulatory compliance matters and Tennessee Securities Division contested case issues. Corporate governance, mergers and acquisitions and intellectual property matters.
Prof. Memberships: Member of the Committees on Federal Regulation of Securities and State Regulation of Securities, Business Law Section of the American Bar Association. Member of the Tennessee Bar Association's Corporation and Business Law Section. Member of the Nashville Bar Association's Corporate and Commercial Practice Committee.
Career: Practiced law since 1983. Joined Waller Lansden in 1989. Co-manages the firm's Corporate Practice Group. Serves on the firm's Board of Directors.

NEAL, James
Neal & Harwell, PLC, Nashville
615 244 1713
Recommended in Litigation

NOEL, Randall
Armstrong Allen PLLC, Memphis
901 523 8211
Recommended in Litigation

NORTON, Bill
Boult, Cummings, Conners & Berry, PLC, Nashville 615 244 2582
Recommended in Bankruptcy, Litigation

OLIVER, Craig
Boult, Cummings, Conners & Berry, PLC, Nashville 615 244 2582
Recommended in Employment

OZIER, William
Bass, Berry & Sims PLC, Nashville
615 742 6232
bozier@bassberry.com
Recommended in Employment

Practice Areas: Represents management in all types of labor and employment matters including union avoidance, union relations, negotiation of union contracts, labor arbitration, defense of age, gender and race discrimination claims, retaliatory discharge, and enforcement and defense of non-compete agreements. Represents academic institutions in employment and student related litigation.
Prof. Memberships: Fellow, American College of Labor and Employment Lawyers; American Bar Association, Equal Employment Opportunity Law Committee; Tennessee Bar Association, Labor Law Committee; Nashville Bar Association, Federal Court Committee.

Career: Joined the firm in 1969. Served as Managing Partner, 1987-92.
Personal: BA (1966) and JD (1969), Vanderbilt University.

PAPEL, Laurence
Baker, Donelson, Bearman , Caldwell & Berkowitz, PC, Nashville
615 726 5656
lpapel@bakerdonelson.com
Recommended in Real Estate

Practice Areas: Practice concentrated primarily in the areas of real estate and related corporate transactions, including the acquisition, development and disposition of commercial, residential and industrial real estate.
Prof. Memberships: Member, American (Corporate and Real Estate Sections), Tennessee and Nashville Bar Associations.
Career: Licensed in Tennessee and US Tax Court since 1980.
Personal: Trinity College, BA, 1977. Vanderbilt University School of Law, JD, 1980.

PATTERSON, Robert
Boult, Cummings, Conners & Berry, PLC, Nashville 615 244 2582
Recommended in Litigation

PHILLIPS, Edward G
Kramer, Rayson, Leake, Rodgers & Morgan, LLP, Knoxville 865 525 5134
ephillips@kramer-rayson.com
Recommended in Employment

Practice Areas: Mr Phillips practices exclusively representing management in the areas of labor relations employment law. His practice spans litigation, prospective advice, training, and counseling from major corporations to small business, as well as public employers. He is recognized in a leading legal publication in America in employment law 2003-04.
Prof. Memberships: Admitted, Tennessee 1978. Mr Phillips is a Member of the Knox and Anderson County Bar Associations, as well as the American and Tennessee Bar Associations, where he served as Chairman of the Labor and Employment Section of the Tennessee Bar Association for 1995-96. Mr Phillips was a member of the Editorial Review Board for The Tennessee Labor Letter, a comprehensive employer information service, from its inception in 1993 through 2000.
Career: Mr Phillips is currently the Managing Partner for Kramer, Rayson, Leake, Rodgers, and Morgan, LLP, with whom he has spent all 27 years in practicing labor and employment law. Judicial clerk for the Honorable Houston Goddard, Tennessee Court of Appeals, Eastern Section (1986-87).
Personal: Born December 31, 1953, Knoxville Tennessee; JD University of Tennessee College of Law, 1978 Order of the Coif; Bachelors in Accounting, East Tennessee State University, 1975.

PHILLIPS Jr, John
Miller & Martin PLLC, Chattanooga
423 785 8325
jphillips@millermartin.com
Recommended in Employment

Practice Areas: Represent management in all areas of labor and employment law. Involved in representing Coca-Cola Enterprises Inc. in five class actions in different parts of the country.
Prof. Memberships: Chattanooga Bar Association (past Member of Board of Governors); Tennessee Bar Association (past Chair of Labor and Employment Section and a recipient of Justice Joe Henry Award for writing most outstanding article in Tennessee Bar Journal); American Bar Association (member of Labor and Employment Section).
Career: Associate at Stophel, Caldwell & Heggie from 1974-79; Partner at Caldwell, Heggie & Helton from 1979-91; Partner at Miller & Martin from 1991-2005 (Managing Partner from 1997-2002).
Publications: Editor of Tennessee Employment Law Letter (monthly newsletter) since 1986; author of Tennessee Employment Law (treatise for Tennessee attorneys); author of Employment Law Desk Book for Tennessee Employers (covering both state and federal employment law).
Personal: DOB, 01/28/47; BS from David Lipscomb College, 1969; JD from University of Tennessee, 1974; live in Chattanooga and Atlanta; married.

PRATHER, Paul E
Kiesewetter Wise Kaplan Prather, PLC, Memphis 901 795 6695
pprather@kiesewetterwise.com
Recommended in Employment

Practice Areas: Mr Prather practices exclusively in the area of labor and employment relations law. He is a nationally recognized CLE lecturer on jury trials of employment claims and also is recognized in a leading legal publication in America.
Prof. Memberships: Admitted, Tennessee (1982). Member, American Bar Association, Labor and Employment and Litigation Sections; Defense Research Institute; past Chair of the Memphis Bar Association, Labor and Employment Section; American Employment Law Counsel; past Chair of the Tennessee Bar Association, Labor and Employment Section; founding board member of the Management Labor and Employment Roundtable. Admitted before United States Supreme Court. Appointed by the Tennessee Supreme Court to the Tennessee Commission on Continuing Legal Education and Specialization.
Career: Founding Member, Kiesewetter Wise Kaplan Prather, PLC (1996). Previously Partner and Member of the Managment Committee, Armstrong Allen, PLLC. Judicial Clerk, Chief United States District Court Judge Robert M McRae, Jr of Memphis (1982-83).

Publications: Executive editor, 'Healthcare Employment Law Letter,' a national monthly publication; contributing editor, 'Workplace Privacy: Real Answers and Practical Solutions.'
Personal: Born 29 November 1957; JD, University of Memphis, 1982; editor in chief, 'University of Memphis Law Review', 1981-82.

REID, Jr, Glen
Wyatt, Tarrant & Combs, LLP, Memphis
901 537 1000
Recommended in Litigation

RILEY, Steven
Bowen Riley Warnock & Jacobson, PLC, Nashville 615 320 3700 ext 120
sriley@bowenriley.com
Recommended in Litigation
Practice Areas: Complex civil litigation, including corporate and business litigation, securities litigation, class action litigation, healthcare litigation and general commercial litigation.
Career: Admitted to practice in Tennessee and Kentucky; certified in Tennessee as civil trial specialist by Tennessee Commission on Continuing Legal Education and Specialization; adjunct professor of law at Vanderbilt Law School teaching Advanced Evidence and Trial Advocacy.
Personal: Vanderbilt University, BA 1974; Vanderbilt University, JD 1978.

ROLAPP, Todd J
Bass, Berry & Sims PLC, Nashville
615 742 6288
trolapp@bassberry.com
Recommended in Corporate/M&A
Practice Areas: Focuses on general corporate and securities law, including representation of issuers, underwriters and investors in public and private securities offerings and the representation of both public and private buyers and sellers in M&A transactions. Regularly counsels clients on matters of corporate governance and heads the firm's Executive Compensation Group.
Career: Joined the firm in 1996.
Personal: BA (1991), Brigham Young University; JD (1994), Duke University.

ROSE, Glenn B
Harwell Howard Hyne Gabbert & Manner, PC, Nashville 615 256 0500
gbr@h3gm.com
Recommended in Bankruptcy, Litigation
Practice Areas: Regularly counsels clients in complex commercial litigation and business bankruptcy/restructuring. Practice includes trials and appeals in state and federal courts including cases alleging violations of securities laws, breaches of contracts, violations of False Claims Act, breaches of fiduciary duty by officers, directors and controlling shareholders.
Prof. Memberships: Admitted, 1983. Former Director, Mid-South Commercial Law Institute; former Chair,

Nashville Bar Association Bankruptcy Committee.
Career: Joined H3GM in 1983.
Personal: Born 30 January 1958. JD (1983), University of Virginia School of Law, Order of the Coif; BA, University of Tennessee, Highest Honors.

RUSH, Stephen
Rush Law Group, Nashville
615 327 7370
Recommended in Media & Entertainment

RUTTER, David
Boult, Cummings, Conners & Berry, PLC, Nashville 615 244 2582
Recommended in Real Estate

SANDERS, James
Neal & Harwell, PLC, Nashville
615 244 1713
Recommended in Litigation

SCOTT, W Rowlett
Armstrong Allen PLLC, Memphis
901 523 8211
Recommended in Real Estate

SHEETS, Mark
Bass, Berry & Sims PLC, Nashville
615 742 6258
msheets@bassberry.com
Recommended in Real Estate
Practice Areas: Focuses on commercial real estate, commercial lending and general commercial law. Areas of representation include acquisition and development, leasing, sale - leasebacks, synthetic leases, tax-free exchanges, loss allocation vehicles, commercial financing and residential/golf course development.
Prof. Memberships: Nashville Bar Association; International Council of Shopping Centers.
Career: Joined the firm in 1990.
Personal: BA (1987), Centre College; JD (1990), with honors, University of Kentucky.

SHERRARD III, Thomas
Sherrard & Roe PLC, Nashville
615 742 4200
Recommended in Corporate/M&A

STEMMLER, John A
Bass, Berry & Sims PLC, Memphis
901 543 5908
jstemmler@bassberry.com
Recommended in Real Estate
Practice Areas: Has over 30 years of experience in commercial transactions and real estate and corporate law. Advises clients in mergers and acquisitions, commercial and residential real estate development and commercial lending. Extensive experience in the hospitality and multi-family residential industries. Represents borrowers in multi-property, multi-state hotel and apartment community financings and acquisitions.
Prof. Memberships: American, Tennessee and Memphis Bar Associations. Former Chair, Corporation and Business Law Section, Tennessee Bar Association.

Career: Joined the firm in 2000. Member of firm's Executive Committee.
Personal: BA (1968) and JD (1971), Vanderbilt University.

STEVENS, C Eric
Miller & Martin PLLC, Nashville
615 744 8423
estevens@millermartin.com
Recommended in Employment
Practice Areas: Practicing in the areas of labor and employment, representing exclusively managment/employers in a broad range of areas including union avoidance/training, labor negotiations, employment counseling, employment litigation and governmental compliance (OFCCP, EEOC, DOL, etc.).
Prof. Memberships: Member of the Tennessee and Nashville Bar Associations.
Career: Has worked his entire career with Miller & Martin and its Nashville predecessor, Trabue, Sturdivant & DeWitt. Founded the Employment Practice Group at Trabue, Sturdivant and DeWitt.
Personal: Born June 17, 1958 in Carterville, Illinois. Graduated, summa cum laude, Millikin University, 1980 (BS, Accounting). Graduated Vanderbilt University School of Law, 1983. Earned his CPA certification before entering the practice of law (not currently licensed as CPA). Married with two sons.

SULLIVAN, Robert
Loeb & Loeb LLP, Nashville
615 749 8300
Recommended in Media & Entertainment

SWAFFORD, T Anthony
Miller & Martin PLLC, Nashville
615 744 8411
tswafford@millermartin.com
Recommended in Employment
Practice Areas: Labor and employment; Vice-Chair of L&E Department; he represents national and regional clients in traditional labor and in employment-related matters and has successfully defended union organizing attempts in nine states covering all regions of the country. In 2004, successfully represented one of four private airport screening companies in the country in union organizational campaign with ramifications for entire industry.
Prof. Memberships: American Bar Association (L&E and Litigation Sections); Tennessee Bar Association; Transportation Lawyers Association; Association for Transportation Law, Logistics and Policy; Sports Lawyers Association
Career: Started L&E practice for firm in Nashville in Summer 1998; became Vice-Chair of Department in January 2005.
Publications: Frequent writer and lecturer for a number of bar association, professional associations and seminar producers including Tennessee Bar

Association, Council on Education in Management, Lorman Education and M. Lee Smith Publishers.
Personal: Born in Chattanooga, TN June 24, 1966. Graduated with High Honors from University of Tennessee in 1990 (BS in Accounting); graduated from Case Western Reserve University in 1995 (JD); married to Tara Swafford; three boys (Tyler: nine; Thomas: seven; Travis: one). Enjoys coaching youth sports.

SWEENEY, Matthew
Baker, Donelson, Bearman , Caldwell & Berkowitz, PC, Nashville
615 726 5774
msweeney@bakerdonelson.com
Recommended in Litigation
Practice Areas: Practice concentrated in commercial litigation and ADR with extensive experience in franchising, securities litigation, D&O class action litigation, fraud, RICO, antitrust and consumer protection. Former Circuit Court Judge in Nashville, Tennessee and was Presiding Judge of the district's Trial Courts.
Prof. Memberships: Fellow and former Trustee, Nashville Bar Foundation. Fellow, Tennessee Bar Foundation. Approved mediator, Tennessee Commission on Alternative Dispute Resolution. NASD Board of Arbitrators. Member, American Arbitration Association, Mediation and Arbitration Panels (Commercial, Employment, Sports Law) and CPR Panel of Neutrals (Franchise). Member, American, Tennessee and Nashville Bar Associations.
Career: Licensed in Tennessee since 1976.

TATE Jr, James S
Bass, Berry & Sims PLC, Nashville
615 742 6235
jtate@bassberry.com
Recommended in Real Estate
Practice Areas: Focuses on banking and commercial lending, secured transactions, real estate, creditors' rights and general commercial law. Represents clients in the negotiation and documentation of a variety of corporate financing, commercial lending and real estate transactions including revolving credit and term loan facilities, secured financings, construction loans, long-term real estate loans and real estate development projects.
Career: Joined the firm in 1980.
Personal: BA (1976), cum laude, and JD (1980), Order of the Coif, Vanderbilt University.

THOMPSON, Bob F
Bass, Berry & Sims PLC, Nashville
615 742 6262
bthompson@bassberry.com
Recommended in Corporate/M&A
Practice Areas: Focuses on securities regulation, mergers and acquisitions and financial institutions. Serves as principal corporate and securities counsel

for public companies in the banking, managed care, healthcare information and small business lending industries. Represents clients in going private transactions, spin-offs, initial public offerings and venture capital placements.

Prof. Memberships: Nashville, Tennessee and American (Member, Banking Law Committee; Federal Regulation of Securities Committee) Bar Associations; Tennessee Bankers Association (Member, Lawyers Committee).

Career: Joined the firm in 1975. US Navy, 1969-72.

Personal: BA (1969), Princeton University; JD (1975), Harvard.

THOMPSON III, Overton
Bass, Berry & Sims PLC, Nashville
615 742 7730
othompson@bassberry.com
Recommended in Litigation

Practice Areas: Focuses practice on complex corporate, class action and business torts litigation, including cases involving securities class action defense, officer and director liability, intellectual property, breach of contract, business and consumer fraud, corporate and partnership dissolutions, lender liability, trust and estates litigation and bad faith insurance litigation.

Prof. Memberships: Tennessee Bar Association (Chair of the Litigation Section).

Career: Joined the firm in 1999. Has practiced litigation exclusively for 20 years in Nashville.

Personal: BA (1981), University of the South; JD (1984), Vanderbilt University.

TRENT, Tom
Boult, Cummings, Conners & Berry, PLC, Nashville 615 244 2582
Recommended in Real Estate

URNESS, Thor
Boult, Cummings, Conners & Berry, PLC, Nashville 615 244 2582
Recommended in Litigation

VOIGT, John
Sherrard & Roe PLC, Nashville
615 742 4200
Recommended in Corporate/M&A

WALKER, Mitchell
Bass, Berry & Sims PLC, Nashville
615 742 6275
mwalker@bassberry.com
Recommended in Corporate/M&A

Practice Areas: Represents public companies and underwriters in public offerings and in mergers and acquisitions. Works with issuers and underwriters on public offerings of both equity and debt securities. Advises boards of directors or special committees on corporate governance issues, corporate restructurings, management led buy outs and investigations of accounting irregularities. Counsels clients on acquisitions or divestitures of operating subsidiaries or divisions and often coordinates an acquisition with raising the necessary capital to finance the purchase price.

Career: Joined the firm in 1982.

Personal: AB (1979), cum laude, Harvard University; JD (1982), Vanderbilt University.

WALKER, Robert
Walker, Bryant, Tipps & Malone, Nashville 615 313 6005
bwalker@walkerbryant.com
Recommended in Litigation

Practice Areas: General civil trial practice with significant experience in product liability, medical malpractice and aviation lawsuits; focues primarily on commercial and business litigation including securites and corporate governance lawsuits, shareholder and hostile takeover suits, antitrust, consumer protection, business fraud suits, proxy challenges and director and officer liability claims.

Prof. Memberships: Tennessee and Nashville Bar Associations; Fellow in American College of Trial Lawyers; Harry Phillips Inns of Court - Emeritus.

Career: Partner.

Personal: Vanderbilt University (JD 1968, BA 1962).

WALTON, Leigh
Bass, Berry & Sims PLC, Nashville
615 742 6201
lwalton@bassberry.com
Recommended in Corporate/M&A

Practice Areas: Concentrates her practice in corporate, securities and healthcare law matters. Represents public companies in securities, mergers and acquisitions, and corporate governance matters. Represents numerous early stage healthcare businesses in connection with securing venture capital funding.

Prof. Memberships: American, Tennessee and Nashville Bar Associations; Vice Chair, ABA Committee on Negotiat-ed Acquisitions; Member, ABA Corporate Laws and Corporate Practices Committees; American Health Lawyers Association; Fellow, Tennessee Bar Foundation.

Career: Joined the firm in 1979.

Personal: BA (1973), magna cum laude, Randolph-Macon Woman's College; JD (1979), Vanderbilt University.

WAYLAND, R Eddie
King & Ballow, Nashville
615 259 3456
Recommended in Employment

WEATHERSBY, Woods
Stokes Bartholomew Evans & Petree, P.A., Memphis 901 525 6781
Recommended in Real Estate

WISEMAN III, Thomas
Gideon & Wiseman PLC, Nashville
615 254 0400
Recommended in Litigation

WOOD, Robert
Boult, Cummings, Conners & Berry, PLC, Nashville 615 244 2582
Recommended in Real Estate

BAKER, DONELSON, BEARMAN, CALDWELL & BERKOWITZ, PC

THE FIRM

Chairman & CEO: Ben C Adams, Jr
COO: William N Reed

Shareholders: 194
Other lawyers: 213 (attorneys and public policy advisors)

FIRM OVERVIEW: Baker, Donelson, Bearman, Caldwell & Berkowitz, PC was ranked in 2004 as one of the 10 fastest growing law firms in the US and is one of the 100 largest law firms in the country. The firm has more than 400 attorneys and public policy advisors in 10 US markets, as well as a representative office in Beijing, China. Baker Donelson represents local, regional, national and international clients across numerous industries in a myriad of issues. The firm is committed to providing innovative, results-oriented solutions while placing the needs of its clients first. Baker Donelson understands the constantly evolving nature of the law, and provides the necessary continuing education to maintain the thought leadership and sophistication of its attorneys and public policy advisors.

MAIN AREAS OF PRACTICE:

Corporate/M&A: Baker Donelson represents clients in every stage of the business life cycle, including the formation of all types of business entities by negotiating commercial contracts and reorganizing and recapitalizing businesses; the purchase, sale, merger or reorganization of publicly and privately held businesses; corporate conflicts; 'going private' transactions; and public offerings. The Securities Group handles formation transactions, securities offerings and compliance matters under federal and state laws. The Mergers & Acquisitions Group guides clients through asset purchases, statutory mergers, management buy-outs and spin-offs.

Health Law: The firm delivers corporate, regulatory and financial services with an institutional knowledge of the healthcare industry. The breadth of Baker Donelson's healthcare knowledge and the diversity of its client base enable the Department to provide services in commercial and contract matters, antitrust disputes, regulatory and governmental issues, and defense of tort cases.

Labor & Employment: Much of the firm's Labor & Employment Practice focuses on litigation avoidance and works with clients to ensure compliance with employment-related laws and regulations, as well as numerous state fair employment practice acts. The firm has developed training programs for client supervisors and managers in union avoidance, workplace harassment prevention, FMLA management and drug-free workplace. When litigation is unavoidable, the firm has extensive experience in state and federal courts throughout the country, defending against a wide range of employment claims.

Litigation: Baker Donelson's Litigation Department provides aggressive representation in civil disputes of all kinds and appears in state and federal venues in every region of the country. Trial attorneys are trained to listen first and understand that clients have differing business and legal objectives, from righting a wrong to limiting financial exposure.

Real Estate: Baker Donelson's Real Estate Group has a long history in all aspects of real estate development and capital finance, including project financing, syndication and the negotiation of purchase and sale agreements. Firm lawyers have represented clients in major retail developments, office buildings, industrial and business parks and apartment projects.

Bankruptcy: Baker Donelson's Bankruptcy and Creditors' Rights Group represents clients in litigation and transaction relating to bankruptcy, insolvency, loan workouts, collections, repossessions, foreclosures, lien disputes and other matters affection debtor/creditor relationships. The group has extensive experience in both commercial and consumer issues.

HEAD OFFICE

TENNESSEE
165 Madison Avenue, Suite 2000, **Memphis**, TN 38103
Tel: 901 526 2000 **Fax:** 901 577 2303
Website: www.bakerdonelson.com

BRANCH OFFICES

ALABAMA
420 20th Street N, 1600 SouthTrust Tower, **Birmingham**, AL 35203
Tel: 205 328 0480 **Fax:** 205 322 8007

GEORGIA
Five Concourse Parkway, Suite 900, **Atlanta**, GA 30328
Tel: 678 406 8700 **Fax:** 678 406 8701

LOUISIANA
201 St. Charles Ave., Suite 3600, **New Orleans**, LA 70170
Tel: 504 566 5200 **Fax:** 504 636 4000

3 Sanctuary Blvd., Suite 201, **Mandeville**, LA 70471
Tel: 985 819 8400 **Fax:** 985 819 8484

MISSISSIPPI
4268 I-55 North, Meadowbrook Office Park, **Jackson**, MS 39211
Tel: 601 351 2400 **Fax:** 601 351 2424

TENNESSEE
633 Chestnut Street, 1800 Republic Centre, **Chattanooga**, TN 37450
Tel: 423 756 2010 **Fax:** 423 756 3447

207 Mockingbird Lane, **Johnson City**, TN 37604
Tel: 423 928 0181 **Fax:** 423 928 5694

900 South Gay Street, 2200 Riverview Tower, **Knoxville,** TN 37902
Tel: 865 549 7000 **Fax:** 865 525 8569

211 Commerce Street, Suite 1000, **Nashville**, TN 37201
Tel: 615 726 5600 **Fax:** 615 726 0464

WASHINGTON, DC
Lincoln Square 6th Floor, 555 Eleventh Street NW,
Washington, DC 20004
Tel: 202 508 3400 **Fax:** 202 508 3402

Other Areas of Practice: Antitrust; construction; ebusiness and technology; eminent domain; employee benefits and executive compensation; environmental, health and safety; equipment leasing; estate planning/probate; financial service and transactions; government investigations and litigation; immigration; intellectual property; international; state and federal public policy; taxation; transportation.

INTERNATIONAL WORK: Beijing, China, (representative office) BDBC International, LLC.

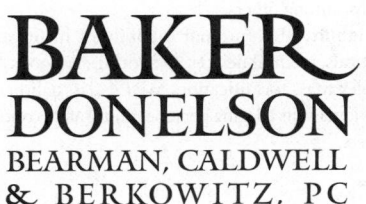

BASS, BERRY & SIMS PLC

THE FIRM

Managing Partner: Keith B Simmons

Number of partners: 91
Number of other lawyers: 85

FIRM OVERVIEW: Bass, Berry & Sims PLC has been recognized for more than 80 years as one of Tennessee's most respected law firms by offering superior client service and unsurpassed legal representation, counseling, guidance and support for its clients in the Southeast and beyond. Firm clients range from Fortune 500 companies to regional and local businesses, including representation of 40 public companies. The firm's affiliation with three legal networks includes the distinction of being a founding member of both Lex Mundi and State Capital Global Law Firm Group and also a member of Southern Law Network.

MAIN AREAS OF PRACTICE:

Bankruptcy: Offers sophisticated service in workouts, debt restructurings, reorganizations and secured financings, as well as commercial litigation matters and dispute resolution.

Corporate & Securities: Extensive experience and depth in mergers, acquisitions, public offerings, securities offerings, regulatory issues, venture capital, corporate governance and Sarbanes-Oxley compliance.

Commercial Transactions & Real Estate: Specializes in commercial lending and debt financings, real estate acquisitions, development and leasing, synthetic leases and off-balance sheet financing, equipment financing and leasing and tax-exempt and tax increment financings.

Entertainment: Extensive representation in the film, television, music, book publishing and theater industries.

Environmental: Litigation, administrative hearings, and counsel on environmental matters, including air and water pollution, hazardous and solid waste, toxic materials, Superfund and NEPA.

Government Relations: Highly skilled consulting and lobbying services in areas of administrative rules, attorney general's investigations, legislation and regulatory and administrative hearings.

Healthcare: Substantive expertise in all aspects of healthcare law such as licensing and certification, disease management, operational issues, HIPAA, physician self-referral, fraud and abuse, reimbursement, certificate of need, corporate compliance, legislative and regulatory matters and managed care contracting.

Intellectual Property & Technology: Protection of trademarks, copyrights, trade secrets and other intellectual property; intellectual property litigation and technology licensing.

Labor & Employment: Counsels on employment discrimination litigation (individual and class claims), employee relations, labor management relations, non-compete litigation, wage and hour compliance, workers' compensation and affirmative action plans.

Litigation: Specializes in complex business litigation matters such as antitrust, class actions, construction, director liability, securities liability, insurance disputes, intellectual property, professional liability and whistleblower claims, among others.

Products Liability: Exceptional capabilities in litigation involving pharmaceuticals, medical devices and consumer goods. Handles a variety of complex mass tort litigation, MDL's, class action cases, as well as serious individual suits alleging personal injury and economic loss against manufacturers.

HEAD OFFICE

TENNESSEE
AmSouth Center, 315 Deaderick Street, Suite 2700,
Nashville, TN 37238
Tel: 615 742 6200 **Fax:** 615 742 6293
Email: info@bassberry.com
Website: www.bassberry.com

BRANCH OFFICES

TENNESSEE
1700 Riverview Tower, 900 S Gay Street, **Knoxville**, TN 37902
Tel: 865 521 6200 **Fax:** 865 521 6234

The Tower at Peabody Place, 100 Peabody Place, Suite 900,
Memphis, TN 38103
Tel: 901 543 5900 **Fax:** 901 543 5999

29 Music Square East, **Nashville**, TN 37203
Tel: 615 255 6161 **Fax:** 615 254 4490

CONTACTS

Bankruptcy	Paul G Jennings
Corporate & Securities	J Page Davidson
Commercial Transactions & Real Estate	Felix R Dowsley III
Entertainment	W Michael Milom
Environmental	J Andrew Goddard
Government Relations	J Richard Lodge Jr
Healthcare	T Andrew Smith
Intellectual Property & Technology	W Michael Milom
Labor & Employment	Tim K Garrett
Litigation	Wallace W Dietz
Products Liability	Samuel L Felker
Public Finance	Charles K Wray
Tax	Michael D Sontag

Public Finance: Expertise in governmental bonds, private activity bonds, property tax abatements and pool financings. Also serves as underwriter's counsel, borrower's counsel, credit enhancer's counsel and trustee's counsel.

Tax: Comprehensive counseling in transactional tax, state and local tax, business and personal tax planning, estate planning and probate and employee benefits/ERISA.

BASS BERRY & SIMS PLC
Attorneys at Law

BOWEN RILEY WARNOCK & JACOBSON, PLC

THE FIRM

Managing Partner: John R Jacobson
Senior Partners: Jay S Bowen, Steven A Riley

Number of partners: 6
Number of other lawyers: 14

FIRM OVERVIEW: Bowen Riley Warnock & Jacobson, PLC was founded in 1995 by four experienced trial lawyers whose goal was to provide the highest quality legal services in the most responsive and cost effective means available. While the firm limits its practice to civil litigation, it defines 'litigation' broadly to encompass dispute resolution in all forums, whether state or federal courts, appellate courts, arbitration and mediation and, equally as important, resolving problems before they reach those formal processes. Bowen Riley has grown to 20 lawyers in order to provide resources necessary to deal with those complex problems which its clients face. Regardless of the circumstances, the firm's commitment is to design and execute an appropriate strategy to accomplish their clients' goals.

MAIN AREAS OF PRACTICE:

Commercial Litigation: The firm's lawyers have in-depth experience as trial lawyers in complex commercial litigation. These specific areas include antitrust, business torts and unfair competition, copyright, trademark and intellectual property, corporate and securities, employment, entertainment, healthcare, insurance, commercial and banking and shareholder derivative law.

CLIENTS: Bowen Riley Warnock & Jacobson, PLC focuses its practice on resolving complex problems for local, regional, national and international clients. The firm represents both corporate and individual clients, and plaintiffs as well as defendants. Many of the nation's major industries have a presence in Tennessee. These include the entertainment industry, healthcare businesses and financial institutions. Their experience includes litigating and resolving issues unique to those industries. Representative clients include American Express Company, Gaylord Entertainment Company, Gibson Guitar Corporation, HCA Inc., Morgan Stanley DW Inc., Sony BMG Entertainment, The Coca-Cola Company, Thomas Nelson, Inc., UnumProvident Corporation, Vanderbilt University, Warner Music Group and an array of other businesses and individuals.

HEAD OFFICE

TENNESSEE
1906 West End Avenue, **Nashville**, TN 37203
Tel: 615 320 3700 **Fax:** 615 320 3737
Website: www.bowenriley.com

HARWELL HOWARD HYNE GABBERT & MANNER PC

THE FIRM

Managing Partner: Mark Manner

Number of partners: 20
Number of other lawyers: 10

FIRM OVERVIEW: Recognized for its sophisticated clients and capabilities, 'H3GM' is a boutique business law firm in Nashville, Tennessee with a national reputation for providing superior legal services to emerging private and public growth companies. H3GM applies its experience and expertise by partnering with clients in transactions and events critical to their business success.

MAIN AREAS OF PRACTICE:

Mergers & Acquisitions: Core practice area, having closed over 300 transactions in six years with total deal value approximating $5 billion. Routine acquisitions as well as mergers of public companies, spin-offs, recapitalizations, tender offers, leveraged and management buyouts.

Commercial Bankruptcy & Reorganization: Market leader for large, complex cases. Regularly represents debtors and creditors, including official committees, and other interested parties in bankruptcy cases and related lawsuits. Full service representation of lenders with troubled loans. Special expertise acquiring assets from bankrupt entities.

Venture Capital: Regular involvement in equity transactions, including assistance with business plans, disclosure documents, stock purchase agreements, registration rights, preferences, anti-dilution provisions, voting rights, shareholders agreements, employment agreements, placement agent agreements, put and call provisions, and co-sale rights.

Securities: Extensive experience with initial and secondary public offerings, private placements and venture capital financings; tender offers and going private transactions; periodic reporting and exchange rules and regulations; proxy statements, annual reports and stockholder meetings.

Litigation & Alternative Dispute Resolution: Respected practitioners in state and federal courts and alternative dispute resolution proceedings throughout the United States. Handles disputes involving state and federal securities laws, corporate governance, debtor/creditor relations, commercial transactions, state and federal employment laws, non-competition and non-disclosure agreements, trademark and copyright law, healthcare regulations, consumer protection laws, construction issues, attorney-client relations and trusts and estates.

Healthcare: Recognized leader representing broad spectrum of healthcare clients on key industry issues. Noted expertise in transactional arena.

General Business, Corporate & Governance: Ongoing general business, corporate and governance issues, regularly advising management, boards of directors and investors.

Going Private/Related Party Transactions: Noted for representing companies and special committees in related party transactions, going private transactions, leveraged buyouts, management buyouts and tender offers.

Real Estate: Represents developers, banks, municipalities, life insurance companies, mezzanine lenders, healthcare companies, and other businesses in a broad spectrum of real estate transactions, including REIT transactions, eminent domain and condemnation disputes.

HEAD OFFICE

TENNESSEE
315 Deaderick Street, Suite 1800, **Nashville**, TN 37238
Tel: 615 256 0500 **Fax:** 615 251 1059
Website: www.h3gm.com

CONTACTS

Litigation/ADR	D Alexander Fardon
Bankruptcy/Reorganization	Glenn B Rose, Craig V Gabbert Jr
General Business, Corporate, M&A	Lee C Dilworth, David Cox
Healthcare	Michael R Hill
Healthcare Transactions	Ernest E Hyne, Lee C Dilworth
Real Estate	Jonathan Harwell, John Popham
Corporate Finance	Glen Allen Civitts, John M Brittingham
E-Commerce/Technology	Curtis Capeling
Securities	Susan V Sidwell, Mark Manner
Biotechnology/Life Sciences	Mark Manner, David Cox

Commercial Finance: Secured and unsecured transactions involving revolving credits, working capital loans, equipment financings, real estate loans, asset based loans, and high yield debt financings. Regular exposure to financial centers throughout the United States and Canada.

Information Technology: Assists in commercializing intellectual property assets and capitalizing on business opportunities, primarily in software with commercial applications.

Biotechnology & Life Sciences: The leading Tennessee firm representing companies in the biotechnology and life sciences industries.

Employment Law: Compliance with federal and state laws and regulations affecting employer-employee relations. Noncompetition disputes.

Tax: Structuring advice to transactional clients and federal and state taxation of ongoing client activities. Wealth preservation and estate planning.

For more details, visit *www.h3gm.com*.

CLIENTS: The firm has significant public company experience with NYSE, AMEX, NASDAQ and TSE listed issuers. Clients span the spectrum of commercial entities and include start-up growth ventures, private and public companies, financial institutions, insurers, healthcare providers, private equity and venture capital groups, municipalities, nonprofits and individuals. The firm's bankruptcy/reorganization practice routinely represents creditors, debtors, official committees and other participants. Visit *www.h3gm.com* for more specifics.

KIESEWETTER WISE KAPLAN PRATHER, PLC

THE FIRM

Chief Executive Member: Jay W Kiesewetter

Number of Members 9
Number of other lawyers: 10

FIRM OVERVIEW: Kiesewetter Wise is a leading labor and employment law firm representing management clients exclusively in all areas of labor relations, employment law, and human resource management. In addition to being the largest labor and employment law firm in Memphis, Kiesewetter Wise has an extensive regional and national practice. The geographically central location of the firm's offices in Memphis enables the firm's professionals to reach most business destinations across the United States within a matter of hours.

Firm Mission & Professionals: Kiesewetter Wise believes that in labor relations and employment law, it is not sufficient simply to advise clients as to the status of the law. Nor does a client benefit from receiving unengaged, detached legal advice. Rather, the firm takes great pride in partnering with its clients to assist them in addressing and resolving their labor and employment law issues, while meeting their business goals and needs. Preventive education, planning, and proactive advice are key to successful labor and employee relations in today's complex business environment. When conflict or litigation arises, Kiesewetter Wise represents its clients' interests aggressively and creatively, while seeking to resolve controversies as economically as possible. This is achieved through a combination of skill, innovation, and consistency, working together as a team with its clients. The firm's professionals are dedicated to winning, and not afraid to take reasonable risks. All of the firm's team members embody these attributes, and combine their unique talents and diverse backgrounds and experiences to bring a high-energy, team approach to meeting clients' needs.

MAIN AREAS OF PRACTICE:

Employment Law: Kiesewetter Wise represents management in proceedings before the EEOC, state equal employment opportunity and human rights commissions, as well as litigation in federal and state courts involving claims under Title VII of the 1964 Civil Rights Act, Equal Pay Act, ADEA, ADA, FMLA, Pregnancy Discrimination Act, and numerous other federal and state equal employment laws. The firm also assists in preparing and implementing Affirmative Action Plans for clients who are government contractors, and handles audits and proceedings before the OFCCP. The firm represents clients in state court litigation involving workers' compensation claims, as well as claims asserting statutory, contract, and tort theories of wrongful discharge or unjust dismissal. It represents employers in matters before the US Department of Labor, including Wage and Hour cases under the Fair Labor Standards Act, OSHA claims, and ERISA matters. Kiesewetter Wise frequently presents training initiatives in all these areas, and also assists clients in developing and implementing employee handbooks, policy and procedure manuals, substance abuse programs, employee compensation and benefit programs, etc.

HEAD OFFICE

TENNESSEE
3725 Champion Hills Drive, Suite 3000, **Memphis**, TN 38125
Tel: 901 795 6695   **Fax:** 901 795 1646
Email: info@kiesewetterwise.com
Website: www.kiesewetterwise.com

Labor Law: Kiesewetter Wise provides legal advice to employers in union organizing campaigns and representation elections, and represents clients in election proceedings before the NLRB. It also defends management in unfair labor practice charges and litigation before the NLRB. The firm's attorneys represent management in the negotiation and administration of collective bargaining agreements, as well as in the arbitration of grievances and contract disputes. As part of its strategy to strengthen the human resource environments of its clients, Kiesewetter Wise develops and conducts cutting-edge supervisory leadership training programs, labor relations seminars, and management audits and surveys of human relations issues. The firm frequently assists its clients in maintaining positive relations with their employees and any unions that may represent them.

Immigration & International Standards: Kiesewetter Wise assists clients facing global employment issues with immigration services, expatriate agreements, and the development and execution of comprehensive strategic plans designed to meet sustainable development expectations in the areas of workplace human rights and social accountability. The firm is capable of providing these sustainability services both in the US and in developing countries around the world.

CLIENTS: Kiesewetter Wise's clientele includes a broad mix of international, national, and regional companies, including many Fortune 1000 corporations. The firm's diverse client base includes both manufacturing and service companies in healthcare, oil and chemical, transportation, telecommunications, financial, technology, hospitality, automotive, retail, and pharmaceutical industries.

KRAMER, RAYSON, LEAKE, RODGERS & MORGAN, LLP

THE FIRM

Managing Partner: Edward G Phillips
Senior Partner: E H Rayson

Number of Attorneys: 34

FIRM OVERVIEW: Since its inception in Knoxville in 1948, 'Kramer Rayson' has dedicated itself to the representation of businesses and business owners in Tennessee. The firm is committed to providing superior, cost-effective legal services covering the gamut of issues its business clients face. Building on its strengths in employment law, general business counseling and litigation, Kramer Rayson has grown to over 30 attorneys. The firm is regularly employed by corporate counsel, government agencies, and public and private entities as well as individuals either doing business or involved in litigation in Tennessee.

MAIN AREAS OF PRACTICE:

Labor & Employment Law: Kramer Rayson represents management in employment discrimination litigation; unfair competition disputes; harassment and whistleblower cases; traditional labor law, including union campaign, collective bargaining, arbitration and NLRB practice; human resources counseling and training; and ADR-mediation processes. The firm has one of the largest management-side employment practices in East Tennessee and has successfully litigated through trial and appeal many high profile matters. Decisions can be reviewed on www.kramer-rayson.com.

Litigation: The firm represents a broad array of clients in commercial litigation, unfair competition, construction law, insurance defense, personal injury litigation, condemnation, worker's compensation, product liability litigation, government contract disputes, ERISA litigation, arbitration, mediation and appellate practice, as well as administrative matters including in tax and related forums.

Corporate/Business: Kramer Rayson maintains a strong practice in traditional corporate and transactional areas including corporate governance, start-up ventures, purchase, sale, merger or acquisitions, financing and credit arrangements and related commercial transactions, creditor's rights, business planning, zoning, loan workouts and other commercial transactions.

Government Relations: Kramer Rayson government relations attorneys have extensive experience representing clients' interests before federal, state and local governmental decision-makers, boards and public bodies.

Tax: Kramer Rayson's Tax Practice includes work in the areas of corporate, partnership, estate, gift, state and local tax (including sales, use and property taxes), tax exempt entities, and individuals in their personal tax planning and various other tax issues. One of the firm's partners has a highly regarded reputation representing major businesses in ad valorem, property and sales and use tax planning and litigation.

Estate/Planning/Probate: The firm provides the full range of estate planning services and advises clients with respect to succession issues and closely held businesses.

Healthcare: Kramer Rayson has successfully represented and counseled clients ranging from major hospitals and practice groups to independent practitioners on a complete range of matters spanning business-related issues, licensing, certificates of need, compliance plans/audits, Medicare reimbursement, HIPPAA compliance, fraud/abuse, Stark, anti-kickback and false claims.

HEAD OFFICE

TENNESSEE
800 S Gay Street, Suite 2500, **Knoxville**, TN 37929
Tel: 865 525 5134   **Fax:** 865 522 5723
Website: www.kramer-rayson.com

BRANCH OFFICES

TENNESSEE
105 Donner Drive, Suite B, **Oak Ridge**, TN 37830
Tel: 865 220 5134   **Fax:** 865 220 5132

CONTACTS

Labor & Employment	Edward G Phillips
Litigation	John T Johnson, Jr
Corporate/Tax/Estate	Wayne R Kramer
Healthcare/Government Relations	Warren L Gooch
Dispute Resolution	Robert P Murrian
Municipal & Local Government	Thomas M Hale

Dispute Resolution: The firm has three certified civil mediators, one of whom, Robert Murrian, is a highly regarded former US Magistrate Judge practicing alternative dispute resolution.

Municipal & Local Government: The firm has extensive experience representing local public bodies including cities, counties and public utilities in East Tennessee. One partner is attorney for the Town of Farragut, while another represents multiple utilities and public bodies in their employment-related matters.

CLIENTS: The firm represents a variety of clients from closely held corporations and start up ventures to Fortune 500 companies and multinational corporations; public entities, including cities, counties, public utilities; and individuals. The diverse client base includes manufacturing and service companies, retail establishments, utilities, banks and financial institutions, health care institutions, telecommunications, technology companies, institutions of higher learning, a national laboratory, a nuclear weapons complex, and insurance companies. Visit www.kramer-rayson.com for more specifics.

MILLER & MARTIN PLLC

THE FIRM

Chairman: Howard Levine

Number of members: 113
Number of other lawyers: 59

Website: www.millermartin.com

FIRM OVERVIEW: Miller & Martin lawyers are dedicated to knowing and understanding the industries and clients they represent. The firm's commitment is to provide quality legal services for its regional, national and international clients.

MAIN AREAS OF PRACTICE:

Labor & Employment: Miller & Martin's labor and employment attorneys represent a broad range of businesses from multi-national corporations with thousands of employees to small, family-owned businesses with only a few employees. Its lawyers have expertise in the issues that can confront today's employer, including all aspects of traditional labor, employment, wage and hour, OSHA, and employee benefits law. It has defeated various union organizing attempts in campaigns across the country including recent victories in Tennessee, Georgia, Illinois, Missouri, Maryland, Texas, Minnesota, California, and Wisconsin. The firm is representing the largest soft drink bottler in North America in opposing an application for class certification in a nationwide class action involving 12,000 potential claimants.

Corporate: Miller & Martin's corporate attorneys are knowledgeable in structuring and planning transactions, including acquisitions and divestitures of public and private companies, debt and equity investments, and public offerings. Its attorneys have handled more than $5 billion of public debt and equity offering for a corporation with operations in the US and international markets and completed domestic and international acquisitions valued in excess of $3 billion.

Financial Services: Miller & Martin's financial services attorneys serve the legal needs of financial institutions ranging from community banks to major international lenders. Services include compliance management, filing applications with state and federal regulators, forming non-bank subsidiaries, establishing complex business structures, and handling securities issues. The attorneys have represented a publicly traded bank in its sale of a merchant credit card processing portfolio valued at $206 million and represented an international bank in a $2 billion commercial loan securitization.

Litigation: Miller & Martin's litigation attorneys are able to handle any civil dispute arising in state or federal courts as well as white collar criminal matters and internal corporate investigations. Members of the department also have significant expertise in alternative dispute resolutions as advocates, arbitrators, and mediators. The firm served as national coordinating counsel for a publicly traded consumer products company in defense of pharmaceutical products liability claims in multiple jurisdictions including federal multi-district litigation.

Real Estate: Miller & Martin's real estate attorneys can handle the issues that arise in any commercial real estate transaction: tax, zoning, financing, and environmental. It represents owners, developers and/or investors in all projects, including manufacturing facilities, warehouses, office buildings, shopping centers, recreation property developments and residential developments. The firm has served as lead counsel for a $400 million mixed use project including a regional mall site, power centers, and offices and represented a publicly traded REIT which owns, manages, and redevelops properties in 29 major markets.

OFFICES

GEORGIA
Suite 800, 1170 Peachtree Street, N.E.
Atlanta, GA 30309-7649
Tel: 404 962 6100   **Fax:** 404 962 6300

TENNESSEE
Suite 1000, Volunteer Building, 832 Georgia Avenue
Chattanooga, TN 37402-2289
Tel: 423 756 6600   **Fax:** 423 785 8480

1200 One Nashville Place, 150 Fourth Avenue, North,
Nashville, TN 37219-2433
Tel: 615 244 9270   **Fax:** 615 256 8197

CONTACTS

Labor & Employment	John R Bode
Corporate	Ward W Nelson
Financial Services	Katie Edge
Litigation	Geoffrey H Cederholm
Real Estate	Terence G Clark

CLIENTS: Fast food restaurants, insurance companies, financial institutions, pharmaceutical manufacturer, soft drink bottler, and telecommunications companies.

INTERNATIONAL WORK:

Its clients benefit from the firm's membership in the World Law Group, an international network of more than 48 law firms representing 37 different countries. Its lawyers regularly secure incentives and abatements for international companies establishing operations in the US as well as assist companies seeking to do business overseas and represent clients in international litigation.

WALKER, BRYANT, TIPPS & MALONE

THE FIRM

Managing Partner: J Mark Tipps
Senior Partner: Robert J Walker

Number of lawyers: 15

AREAS OF PRACTICE:
Commercial Litigation 70%
Personal Injury/Professional Liability, Defense 20%
Personal Injury/Plaintiff 10%

FIRM OVERVIEW: Walker, Bryant, Tipps & Malone is a law firm located in Nashville, Tennessee, focusing exclusively on civil litigation. The firm was originally formed as Walker, Bryant & Tipps on January 1, 2000, by eight attorneys who formerly practiced in the litigation department of Nashville's Bass, Berry & Sims and who desired to continue their well-developed civil litigation practices in a smaller law firm, focusing exclusively on trial work. On May 1, 2002, the law firm became Walker, Bryant, Tipps & Malone when Gayle Malone, a senior partner in the litigation group of another prominent Tennessee law firm, joined the firm. WBTM represents individual, corporate, and institutional clients in Tennessee and throughout the Southeastern United States. The firm's attorneys regularly practice before federal and state courts in both jury and non-jury trials and at appellate levels. They have extensive experience in all forms of alternative dispute resolution, including arbitration and mediation. WBTM attorneys also represent clients in administrative matters before federal and state departments, agencies, boards, and commissions. The attorneys at WBTM concentrate their law practices in civil litigation and dispute resolution. Three of the firm's attorneys are Fellows in the American College of Trial Lawyers and are also listed in a leading American publication as among the top attorneys in America. WBTM attorneys have served as judicial clerks to federal district and appellate court judges and as counsel to congressional investigative committees. WBTM has grown from the initial eight attorneys to 15 and has assembled an outstanding staff of support personnel. WBTM has earned a reputation as a quality litigation boutique whose attorneys hold their clients' interest paramount while providing efficient and effective representation.

MAIN AREAS OF PRACTICE:
Commercial Litigtion: The firm's commercial litigation includes defense of class action and non-class action suits in securities, private and public corporate governance (including proxy fights and takeover litigation), products liability defense, complex commercial and business disputes, and other commercial matters.
Personal Injury: The firm is well-known for its abilities in the defense of medical malpractice litigation, but also defends personal injury suits in other areas. Additionally, WBTM has developed a plaintiff's personal injury practice in selected cases and has recovered several multi-million-dollar results for its clients.
Dispute Resolution: Two of the firm's partners are Rule 31-listed Civil Mediators.

CLIENTS: The firm's clients include individuals, teaching hospitals, commercial banks, insurance and other financial institutions, venture capital and private equity firms, industrial and service corporations, partnerships, and myriad businesses clients in the fields of health care, private prison management and ownership, accounting, and other service industries.

INTERNATIONAL WORK: The firm has represented a number of international companies engaged in civil litigation in the United States.

HEAD OFFICE

TENNESSEE
2300 One Nashville Place, **Nashville**, TN 37219
Tel: 615 313 6000 **Fax:** 615 313 6001
Email: info@walkerbryant.com

CONTACTS

Complex Business Litigation	Bob Walker, Mark Tipps, John Hayworth
Dispute Resolution	Gayle Malone, John Bryant
Financial Institutions/Insurance	Mark Tipps, Joe Welborn
Governmental Relations (federal)	Mark Tipps
Personal Injury/Defense	John Bryant, Steve Anderson
Personal Injury/Plaintiff	Gayle Malone, Joe Welborn
Product Liability	Gayle Malone, Clisby Barrow
Securities & Corporate Governance	Bob Walker, John Hayworth
Prisoner Rights Litigation	Joe Welborn

WALLER LANSDEN DORTCH & DAVIS

THE FIRM

Chairman: Ralph W Davis
Number of partners: 99
Number of other lawyers: 71

FIRM OVERVIEW: Founded in Nashville in 1905, Waller Lansden Dortch & Davis is one of the oldest law firms headquartered in Tennessee. With an unparalleled commitment to providing superior service, Waller Lansden's attorneys take pride in their ability to understand and respond to the specific needs and business goals of each of the firm's clients. The firm understands that a client wants more in its outside legal counsel than just attorneys that can solve legal problems - clients want a business partner. Waller Lansden's clients include public and private corporations, government agencies, and business enterprises both large and small throughout the United States.

MAIN AREAS OF PRACTICE:

Corporate Restructuring: Waller Lansden's corporate restructuring attorneys have served as counsel to indenture trustees, secured lenders, creditors committees, debtors-in-possession, unsecured creditors, asset purchasers, and a variety of other parties in bankruptcy and work-out proceedings nationwide.

Environmental: Waller Lansden's environmental attorneys have experience in siting, permitting, compliance and enforcement issues arising under federal and state laws regulating solid and hazardous waste, water pollution, air pollution and the use of chemical substances. The firm also is experienced in sophisticated land use issues arising under federal, state and local laws designed for the protection of sensitive environmental resources such as streams and wetlands.

Financial Services: Waller Lansden represents holding companies, banks, trust companies, securities firms, mortgage lenders, credit card and electronic payment companies, insurance underwriters and agents, consumer finance companies, and manufacturer/vendor finance companies among others. The firm also represents financial services companies in their dealings with customers. In this area, the attorneys represent secured and unsecured lenders, institutional investors, and trustees with respect to the full range of financial products and services.

Government Relations: Waller Lansden's government relations attorneys have years of experience representing the interests of clients before a broad range of state and local decision-makers. Several of the firm's attorneys have served as key governmental decision-makers themselves, enabling the practice to combine the strong advocacy skills of the firm's lawyers with the knowledge and perspective of government decision-makers. Such extensive experience has produced a government relations practice that has become a strong lobbying force.

Healthcare: Waller Lansden's clients include the largest for-profit healthcare company in the world and industry leaders engaged in non-urban hospitals, ambulatory surgical centers, psychiatric hospitals, rehabilitation hospitals and centers. The firm also represents mobile health services, dialysis centers, health management services, not-for-profit hospitals, physicians (individual and group practices), long-term care facilities, trade associations and home healthcare agencies. In addition, venture capitalists and financial institutions providing funding to healthcare companies and institutions have sought the firm's advice.

Intellectual Property: Waller Lansden has over 25 years of experience in intellectual property law. The firm provides advice and representation on a variety of matters in this rapidly growing and changing area of law. Waller Lansden regularly counsels clients on creating, securing, licensing and transferring rights in intellectual property.

Labor & Employment: The depth of this practice covers virtually every aspect of labor and employment law and related litigation, including matters arising under the Americans with Disabilities Act, the Family and Medical Leave Act, the Age Discrimination in Employment Act, Title VII of the Civil Rights Act of 1964, the Equal Pay Act, the National Labor Relations Act, the Labor Management Relations Act, the Fair Labor Standards Act, the Occupational Safety and Health Act, the Worker Adjustment and Retraining Notification Act, the Drug-Free Workplace Act, the Rehabilitation Act, the Employee Retirement Income Security Act, the Health Insurance Portability and Accountability Act, COBRA, and state workers compensation laws.

Mergers & Acquisitions: The firm represents a number of public and private clients in a wide array of industries such as real estate, manufacturing, publishing, transportation, automotive and hospitality industries. The firm has particular experience with transactions involving regulated industries, such as healthcare, financial services, information technology and telecommunications.

Real Estate: The firm's real estate attorneys have represented owners, operators, agents and developers of commercial, industrial, retail and residential properties and numerous companies which own, lease and develop real estate assets for their own use. In addition, attorneys regularly represent investors in commercial and industrial real estate projects, including REITs, pension fund group trusts and real estate investment advisors for public and private trusts.

Securities & Corporate Finance: For over 70 years, Waller Lansden has built strong relationships in the investment community. The firm has served as counsel for national and regional underwriters, venture capitalists and financing sources in public and private financings. The firm is proud to have participated in the growth of many smaller companies into large national and international corporations.

Tax: Waller Lansden's Tax Practice includes the following major areas: corporate partnership, estate, gift, state and local, tax exempt entities, deferred compensation plans, qualified and nonqualified personal tax planning, and tax controversies. The Tennessee Limited Liability Company Act was authored primarily by two of the firm's senior tax attorneys.

Trial & Appellate: From the founding of the firm nearly 100 years ago to the present, the lawyers of Waller Lansden have successfully tried hundreds of cases in courtrooms throughout the nation. The firm has former judicial clerks (state and federal), two former Assistant United States Attorneys, current and former law school faculty members, several former high ranking state and federal government officials, and lawyers who previously practiced with private firms throughout the country.

Venture Capital: Waller Lansden's attorneys counsel clients on the full range of issues confronting emerging and established businesses. From pre-organization to private capital to IPO and beyond, the firm's attorneys assist clients in charting the most efficient course to success.

HEAD OFFICE

TENNESSEE
511 Union Street, Suite 2700, **Nashville**, TN 37219
Tel: 615 244 6380   **Fax:** 615 244 6804
Website: www.wallerlaw.com

BRANCH OFFICES

CALIFORNIA
Waller Lansden Dortch & Davis LLP*
520 South Grand Avenue, Suite 800, **Los Angeles**, CA 90071
Tel: 213 362 3680   **Fax:** 213 362 3679

*Includes Waller Lansden Dortch & Davis, PLLC

TENNESSEE
809 South Main Street, **Columbia**, TN 38402
Tel: 931 388 6031   **Fax:** 931 381 7317

Waller Lansden Dortch & Davis
www.wallerlaw.com

CONTENTS: Antitrust p.1622; Banking & Finance p.1624; Bankruptcy p.1626; Construction p.1629; Corporate/M&A p.1631; Employment p.1633; Energy & Natural Resources p.1637; Environment p.1642; Healthcare p.1645; Insurance p.1647; Intellectual Property p.1649; Litigation p.1655; Projects p.1659; Real Estate p.1661; Tax p.1664; Technology p.1667; Individuals' Profiles p.1669; Firms' Profiles p.1707.

How lawyers are ranked

The opinions we gather from clients — mainly from in-house lawyers but also from other purchasers of legal services — are balanced by opinions from colleagues and competitors. Together, they provide two different perspectives — an all-round view — and biased viewpoints cancel each other out.

ANTITRUST

Texas
Leading firms (Antitrust)

1 SUSMAN GODFREY LLP *Houston*
VINSON & ELKINS LLP *Houston*

2 BAKER BOTTS LLP *Houston*
FULBRIGHT & JAWORSKI LLP *Houston*
HAYNES AND BOONE LLP *Dallas*

3 ANDREWS KURTH LLP *Dallas*
CARRINGTON, COLEMAN, SLOMAN *Dallas*
GARDERE WYNNE SEWELL LLP *Dallas*
GIBSON, DUNN & CRUTCHER LLP *Dallas*
THOMPSON & KNIGHT LLP *Dallas*

Leading individuals (Antitrust)

1 GODFREY Lee *Susman Godfrey, Houston*
MCNEIL Barry *Haynes and Boone, Dallas*
SUSMAN Stephen *Susman Godfrey, Houston*

2 BEANE Jerry *Andrews Kurth, Dallas*
CARRELL Richard *Fulbright & Jaworski, Houston*
KRUSE Layne *Fulbright & Jaworski, Houston*
OLIVER Rufus *Baker Botts, Houston*
REASONER Harry *Vinson & Elkins, Houston*
WALTERS Robert *Vinson & Elkins, Dallas*

3 BREAUX Ronald *Haynes and Boone, Dallas*
FRISBIE Curtis *Gardere Wynne Sewell, Dallas*
GAVIN Tim *Carrington Coleman, Dallas*
HUFFMAN Gregory *Thompson & Knight, Dallas*
JOHN Philip *Baker Botts, Houston*
OXFORD Terrell *Susman Godfrey, Dallas*
ROYALL Sean *Gibson, Dunn & Crutcher, Dallas*
SMITH Alison *Dewey Ballantine, Houston*
SPIVEY James *Cox Smith, San Antonio*
VAN FLEET Allan *Vinson & Elkins, Houston*

Up-and-coming individuals

HARRISON Lauren *Vinson & Elkins, Houston*
SUSMAN Harry *Susman Godfrey, Houston*

Firms and individuals are listed alphabetically in each band.

Band 1

Susman Godfrey LLP

The Firm: Sources acknowledged that this "*substantial antitrust practice*" has successfully secured a statewide and national reputation for excellence. Its "*outstanding and aggressive*" litigation group straddles both the plaintiff and defendant sides. Clients referred to the lawyers as "*extremely knowledgeable about the substantive law*" and "*wonderfully professional at courtroom presentation.*" Having built their reputation on the back of success in the Corrugated Container antitrust litigation, the firm has not looked back. It continues to make the headlines, enjoying considerable success on behalf of technology giants, pharmaceuticals and media/entertainment companies, among others.
The Lawyers: The lead antitrust attorney is the "*tremendous and flamboyant*" **Stephen Susman**, whose national reputation stems from overwhelming success and an unparallel track record. Straddling both sides of the plaintiff/defendant divide, his "*intellectual depth*" was applied to the representation of Novell in the negotiation of a settlement with Microsoft. This case concerned antitrust claims related to Novell's NetWare business, and under the terms of the settlement disclosed in November 2004, Microsoft will pay Novell $536 million in cash. The "*excellent and methodical*" trial lawyer **Lee Godfrey** was deemed a "*highly skilled advocate*" in antitrust proceedings, winning plaudits for his involvement in the high-profile Blockbuster antitrust case in San Antonio. Interviewees admired the "*very cerebral*" **Terrell Oxford** while the "*strong drive and effectiveness*" of **Harry Susman** was also widely recognized. He is developing a strong reputation in his own right, boosted by his acknowledged "*soaring academic credentials.*"
The Clients: Medtronic; Barr Laboratories; Little Caesar Enterprises; ChoiceParts; Novell and Clear Channel Communications feature strongly in an extensive client roster.

Vinson & Elkins LLP
See firm details p.1724
The Firm: "*Excellent experienced practitioners*" and a "*superb clientele*" ensure that this national litigation powerhouse remains a major player in antitrust litigation. Employing more than 50 antitrust lawyers, the team recently obtained dismissal of a $2 billion antitrust claim filed against an incumbent local exchange carrier by a competing provider. The group also secured the dismissal of price-fixing and monopolization claims brought against US and foreign cement manufacturers. Attorneys also acted for Southwest Airlines in its bid to acquire assets from bankrupt airline, ATA.
The Lawyers: This "*superb, veteran trial lawyer*" **Harry Reasoner** (see p.1698) – considered the "*father of antitrust*" – combines his considerable expertise in antitrust with a general commercial litigation practice. Employing his "*fantastic client skills*" and an "*instinctive knowledge for judge and jury presentations,*" Reasoner has acted for SBC in the federal antitrust claims brought by Premiere Network Services. Interviewees had nothing but praise for the talented **Rob Walters** (see p.1705). He is "*very good on his feet in the courtroom and cares about the results for his clients.*" The "*thoughtful and knowledgeable*" commercial litigation attorney **Allan Van Fleet** (see p.1704) is admired by clients for his "*relaxed, professional style and great communication skills.*" He handled a case for an international white-cement producer, sued by a competitor for its contract arrangements. Sources also endorsed the "*incredible intelligence and wonderful way with clients*" displayed by **Lauren Harrison** (see p.1683). She successfully defended a Norwegian refining conglomerate against plaintiffs' claims of fraud and breach of contract and obtained summary judgment for one of the nation's largest commercial air carriers in an antitrust case.
The Clients: First Nationwide Bank; Liberty Mutual; SBC and Jindal United Steel.

Band 2

Baker Botts LLP
See firm details p.1708
The Firm: "*Extreme thoroughness in fact-gathering and a legal creativity*" were among the

distinguishing features noted by interviewees of this "*highly competent*" team of around a dozen antitrust lawyers. With the resources of a large trial department behind it, the group enjoys a distinct advantage both in the Texas market and beyond the state lines. A "*supreme and inside-out knowledge of the energy sector*" also helps during antitrust cases arising out of the industry. For example, the firm was involved in the suit brought by the independent service station dealers against Shell, challenging the pricing system used by Shell and other major refiners.

The Lawyers: More than 30 years of courtroom experience and significant merger regulatory expertise ensure the continued prominence of the "*formidable, direct and highly ethical*" **Rufus Oliver** (see p.1694). Clients also appreciated the head of the antitrust group's abilities as a "*class strategist*" and noted his "*intellectual horsepower*." Recently, he has been involved in the Shell dispute and acted for Clear Channel Entertainment in allegations of a monopoly in radio broadcasts aimed at the Hispanic community. The "*outstanding*" **Philip John** (see p.1685) is considered "*very savvy on handling all the dynamics of a case.*" He has developed a diverse litigation practice, of which antitrust plays a key part. He has acted for SBC Communications in a number of class action suits.

The Clients: Among an extensive clientele, the group acts for hi-tech firms, oil companies, manufacturers, distributors, airlines banks and healthcare clients.

Fulbright & Jaworski LLP
See firm details p.1715

The Firm: "*Trial lawyers first and foremost, with antitrust expertise a close second*" noted observers about this highly respected Texas group, which cultivated its reputation in antitrust counseling and disputes on the back of a tremendous general litigation expertise. More than 40 lawyers, including half a dozen Houston partners, advise on all manner of antitrust issues, from counseling and compliance programs to price-fixing, boycotts and monopolization. International cartel work is also a major feature of the office. In 2004, the team's energy law expertise was enhanced further with the addition of Peggy Heeg, formerly in-house general counsel with one of the largest natural gas companies.

The Lawyers: **Richard Carrell** (see p.1674) possesses a wealth of experience and an "*impressive knowledge*" of the nuances to antitrust cases. Part of the broad litigation practice, his workload also comprises oil and gas and securities litigation. Lately, he has advised a London client in the DOJ investigation into the fur industry. Admired by clients for his "*high intellect and goal-driven nature,*" **Layne Kruse** (see p.1688) is a long-standing and well-known trial lawyer, who co-heads the Houston practice. His workload is split between civil antitrust litigation and

white-collar criminal and internal investigations. He is involved in an antitrust case against SBC, a local exchange carrier.

The Clients: Sony; PwC; Shell; ConocoPhillips; Duke Energy and Association of American Medical Colleges; Farmers; Coral Energy and Mitsui & Co.

Haynes and Boone LLP
The Firm: This warmly respected firm has a healthy track record of more than 25 years' experience in the defense and prosecution of competition cases. Interviewees endorsed this "*talented and aggressive*" group of more than 20 antitrust lawyers, particularly for their added expertise in criminal and grand jury investigations. The team acted for the executives of a European worldwide vitamin manufacturer against charges of forming an international pricing cartel.

The Lawyers: Leading the charge is the "*excellent*" **Barry McNeil**, considered to be a "*first-rate trial lawyer with an impressive track record.*" His enviable experience at the antitrust division at the DOJ affords him a "*strong government perspective*" on civil and criminal antitrust litigation. Retaining his place in the rankings is **Ron Breaux**, well known in Dallas, and recommended for a general commercial litigation practice and a "*tremendous capability*" in antitrust. He has defended corporate executives in DRAM cartel litigation and acted for a telecom provider in monopolization-related litigation.

The Clients: Dynegy; PepsiCo; SBC; Commercial Metals; ExxonMobil; Harley Davidson; Ryder Systems; Nortel; Tandy and Waste Management.

Band 3

Andrews Kurth LLP
See firm details p.1707

The Firm: Around a dozen antitrust attorneys earn plaudits for their counsel on distribution agreements and pricing and M&A work investigated by the FTC and DOJ. The group also handles antitrust litigation for a client base that spans the energy and mining, transportation, healthcare, technology and financial services sectors.

The Lawyers: Practice head, the "*very capable and talented*" **Jerry Beane** (see p.1671), is involved in both counseling and litigation. Of late, he has been advising clients on high-value mergers, and is a "*top referral*" for corporations under investigation across a diverse range of industries, such as energy, food, healthcare and telecom. Beane has been involved in a key dispute over promotion agreements between the manufacturers, distributors and grocery retailers affecting the soft drink industry.

The Clients: National Dairy Holdings, KoSa and Tempur-Pedic have featured in the firm's client roster.

Carrington, Coleman, Sloman & Blumenthal LLP
The Firm: This well-respected Dallas firm was considered one of the best litigation boutiques in the market. Clients appreciated the "*immediate and timely*" expertise offered and spoke of a group of lawyers, who "*don't nickel and dime you to death.*" In spite of the departure of a senior antitrust player to the West Coast, the team earned strong recommendations for its counseling and litigation expertise and resources.

The Lawyers: A broad commercial litigation practice with a strong antitrust component earns the "*responsive*" **Tim Gavin** the loyalty of clients. He has acted for EDS in a variety of litigation, including antitrust work. He also carried out a number of dealer termination claims for AT&T Wireless, after their merger with Cingular, and has counseled Realm Business Solutions on antitrust issues.

The Clients: Realm Business Solutions, EDS and AT&T Wireless feature in the team's clientele.

Gardere Wynne Sewell LLP
See firm details p.1718

The Firm: Market commentators acknowledged this firm's presence on the antitrust radar, fielding as it does around a dozen lawyers, who possess antitrust and general trial expertise. The group acted for AIG and related companies in connection with Texas attorney general's antitrust investigation of contingent commissions in the brokerage and insurance industry.

The Lawyers: The "*rational, talented and creative*" **Curtis Frisbie** (see p.1680) heads both the trial and antitrust departments at the firm and has great appeal as a trial lawyer. With a wealth of trial experience, he has lately been involved for Dynacraft in connection with a class action products liability suit filed in Birmingham, Alabama, in which the team is acting as national and supervising counsel.

The Clients: Dynacraft; AIG; Birmingham Fire Insurance; Lexington Insurance; Brook Mays Music; The Expo Group; SBC and Tyler Pipe Industries.

Gibson, Dunn & Crutcher LLP
See firm details p.285

The Firm: The firm has a historical presence in antitrust litigation and can bring to bear significant resources both from its West Coast operations and a team in Washington DC. A group of eight antitrust lawyers advise clients on antitrust cases, with litigation and complex monopolization cases among its forte. The team enjoys "*access to greater resources*" and repeated experience in complex and significant antitrust cases. In addition to key antitrust matters for Atlantic Coast Airlines, attorneys here also obtained summary judgment for American Airlines in a monopolization case raising predatory pricing issues.

The Lawyers: New to Dallas but very quickly

www.ChambersandPartners.com

All quotes in the text are from interviews with clients and competitors.

1623

recognized is the "*practical and commercial*" **Sean Royall** (see p.1699). According to interviewees, he "*knows what regulators want*" after spending two and a half years as deputy director of the Bureau of Competition at the FTC in Washington DC, where he still maintains an office. There, he was the lead FTC official responsible for the government review of several high-profile mergers, such as the Pepsi/Quaker Oats, General Mills/Pillsbury, and Chevron/Texaco mergers, as well as the proposed acquisition of online job search firm HotJobs.com by rival Monster.com.

The Clients: Atlantic Coast Airlines; American Airlines; Intel; Ticketmaster and Hewlett-Packard.

Thompson & Knight LLP

See firm details p.1722

The Firm: Around a dozen lawyers at this firm, one of the oldest in Dallas, earned market acclaim for the trial of antitrust cases in state and federal courts as well as proceedings before the FTC. Noncompetition covenants, trade secrets, and business torts feature in the services offered by the team. Dedicated antitrust attorneys are also surrounded by one of Dallas' strong trial litigation groups and can draw on their support as required. In January 2005, trial partner James Berglund was elected as the chair of the Dallas Bar Association's antitrust and trade regulation section.

The Lawyers: "*Analysis of the case's economics*" and an "*impressive theorist*" were among the compliments for **Greg Huffman** (see p.1685). He successfully represented Gruma at trial against El Aguila in federal court in Houston, where the plaintiff sued for more than $100 million. He has also been acting for North Texas Specialty Physicians before the FTC, where the FTC is seeking a precedent-setting injunction against physician groups amid claims of price-fixing.

The Clients: Chaparral Steel and Gruma feature in the group's clientele.

Other Notable Practitioners

Since her move from Vinson & Elkins to Dewey Ballantine LLP, the "*exceptionally devoted*" **Alison Smith** (see p.1701) has continued to be the subject of endorsement from industry experts. With her "*tremendous client empathy and intelligence*," she is considered a "*very good referral for an antitrust conflict.*" Her experience at the DOJ stands her in good stead. **Jim Spivey** (see p.1701) shines at Cox Smith Matthews Inc. He is one of the most significant players in San Antonio and South Texas, and is deemed an "*excellent choice*" for business litigation including antitrust matters.

BANKING & FINANCE

Texas

Leading firms (Banking & Finance)

1. **VINSON & ELKINS LLP** *Houston*
2. **BRACEWELL & GIULIANI LLP** *Houston*
3. **ANDREWS KURTH LLP** *Dallas*
   BAKER BOTTS LLP *Houston*
   DEWEY BALLANTINE LLP *Houston*
   MAYER, BROWN, ROWE & MAW LLP *Houston*
4. **JONES DAY** *Dallas*
   THOMPSON & KNIGHT LLP *Dallas, Houston*
   WEIL, GOTSHAL & MANGES LLP *Dallas*
   WINSTEAD SECHREST & MINICK PC *Dallas*

Firms are listed alphabetically in each band.

Band 1

Vinson & Elkins LLP

See firm details p.1724

The Firm: Having "*grown up with Houston,*" this firm is the clear leader in the local market and much further beyond. It has "*very deep roots*" within the energy companies and excellent market knowledge born out of its long track record of work with major finance houses. According to sources, its "*super-tenacious and commercially oriented*" attorneys are equally well equipped to advise borrowers and lenders. Over the past year, the team has been involved in various offshore platform financings, including a hybrid structured finance deal, and a leveraged operating lease. It is also representing startup companies in the midstream who are aiming to go public as master limited partnerships (MLPs). Clients praised the depth and breadth of the group as well as its "*strong attorneys who are conscientious about every aspect of client service.*"

The Lawyers: Larry Barbour (see p.1671) is a personable attorney, who is "*experienced in cutting-edge energy deals.*" He "*does not roll over and give up*" but is an "*innovative and practical*" problem solver. Interviewees also identified the "*intellectually rigorous*" **David Keyes** (see p.1687) as a "*pleasure to work with.*" His practice covers the full range of financial and commercial transactions. **Kenneth Anderson** (see p.1670) is a leader in the syndicated bank finance arena, particularly on large transactions. "*There will never be any doubt about whether he will do a good job,*" competitors agreed. **Craig Murray** (see p.1693) is one of the most senior lending lawyers in the market. He "*looks out for his clients*" and has a slightly more "*aggressive style.*" **William Young** (see p.1706) primarily represents private equity funds and lenders in the international financial markets. He represented a fund in the ¥60 billion securitized financing of 47 Japanese golf courses. A younger partner to look out for is **Robert Rabalais** (see p.1697). He is widely recognized for his high-quality work with JPMorgan Chase and BNP Paribas. One of his main strengths is his ability to defend clients' interests in negotiations.

The Clients: Wachovia Bank, National Association; JPMorgan Chase; Deutsche Bank and BNP Paribas.

Band 2

Bracewell & Giuliani LLP

See firm details p.1710

The Firm: Sources agree that this group has "*done a particularly good job cultivating a diverse set of financial institution clients.*" The impressive list includes foreign as well as domestic organizations, with a niche practice advising French banks. Over the past 12 months, it represented Citibank in a billion-dollar secured pipeline financing, and assisted JPMorgan Chase in a $600 million unsecured loan for an exploration company. It has a smaller, but equally effective borrower practice principally counseling operators in the energy field. For example, Reliant Energy turned to the team in its $4.25 billion refinancing. Clients appreciated the group's "*excellent market knowledge*" and "*superb insight into banks' needs and pressure points.*"

The Lawyers: Foremost among the "*raft of very smart, practical attorneys*" is the "*likable, fair and accessible*" **William Hayes** (see p.1683). He is an extremely talented attorney with a breadth of experience in complex financings. **Mark Evans** (see p.1678), who is key to the group's recent success, is a "*bright lawyer with excellent client skills*" and the client partner for a number of the firm's international clients. **Robin Miles** (see p.1692) was praised by clients for his "*insightful market knowledge.*"

The Clients: Citibank; JPMorgan Chase; Reliant Energy and Dynegy.

Band 3

Andrews Kurth LLP

See firm details p.1707

The Firm: This is a "*professional and capable*" group with "*profound depth*" and a striking client base that stretches across both regional and national banks. It offers a traditional lending practice and has real strength in the energy

Texas
Leading individuals (Banking & Finance)

1 BARBOUR Larry *Vinson & Elkins*, Houston
HAYES William *Bracewell & Giuliani*, Houston
NIEBRUEGGE Michael *Mayer Brown*, Houston

2 BURNS David *Dewey Ballantine*, Houston
EVANS Mark *Bracewell & Giuliani*, Houston
GOYNE Roderick *Baker Botts*, Dallas
KEYES David *Vinson & Elkins*, Houston

3 ANDERSON Kenneth *Vinson & Elkins*, Houston
FONTANA Angela *Weil Gotshal*, Dallas
HILLIARD Michael *Winstead Sechrest*, Dallas
MILES Robin *Bracewell & Giuliani*, Houston
PERICH Thomas *Andrews Kurth*, Houston

4 BARBOUR David *Andrews Kurth*, Dallas
GILLESPIE Thomas *Jones Day*, Dallas
MALONEY Marilyn *Liskow & Lewis*, Houston
MURRAY Craig *Vinson & Elkins*, Houston
RAIN John *Thompson & Knight*, Dallas
VILARDO Terry *Mayer Brown*, Houston
YOUNG William *Vinson & Elkins*, Dallas

Up-and-coming individuals

MARCUS Courtney *Weil Gotshal*, Dallas
RABALAIS Robert *Vinson & Elkins*, Houston

Individuals are listed alphabetically in each band.

arena, representing clients in oil and gas property and service loans. The keynote transaction from the past year is illustrative of the group's broadening capabilities; it represented a bank in the complex financing of a couple of nationwide automobile dealerships. It also has a *"robust"* capital markets practice and experience in mortgage and asset-backed securities as well as compliance issues.

The Lawyers: Thomas Perich (see p.1696) is an experienced banking attorney, who fosters close relations with clients such as Bank of America and JPMorgan Chase. He is *"extremely thoughtful"* and an *"excellent negotiator."* Key market players hold Dallas-based **David Barbour** (see p.1671) in high esteem for his skilled representation of issuers and underwriters in public and private offerings of equity and debt securities.

The Clients: JPMorgan Chase; Wachovia; Bank of America and Wells Fargo.

Baker Botts LLP
See firm details p.1708
The Firm: Always a *"key name in Texas,"* this group is able to draw on the firm's noted corporate and energy experience to pull together a cracking team that is active in the full range of banking and finance transactions. It represented Halliburton in a $1.2 billion letter of credit facility and Equistar in $550 million worth of accounts receivable securitzations and a $250 million revolving credit facility. On the lender side it represented a bank in a complex interest rate arbitrage arrangement. It has broad sector experience ranging across the consumer prod-

ucts, petrochemicals, IT, manufacturing and energy markets.
The Lawyers: Rick Goyne (see p.1682) has a *"remarkable memory and a wonderful mind for transactions,"* say sources. He recently led the firm's representation of Pride Offshore in two high-value credit facilities and a Rule 144A note offering.
The Clients: Encore Acquisition Company; Hines Interests; Pride Offshore; JPMorgan Chase; ConocoPhillips; Halliburton and Equistar.

Dewey Ballantine LLP
See firm details p.1347
The Firm: This is an integrated banking group, assimilating attorneys with specialist knowledge in projects, bankruptcy, structured finance and other corporate and institutional financial mechanisms. Household-name clients such as AIG and PG&E go to this group in *"sizable and sticky situations"* because they give *"top-dollar advice."* This branch of a global firm inevitably has a strong line in energy deals, this year having represented Freeport LNG Development in the $450 million initial tranche of construction financing for an LNG terminal and regasification facility. It also has experience in the real estate, hotels and IT sectors.
The Lawyers: Clients spoke of their *"huge amount of confidence in **David Burns**'* (see p.1674) *"ability to watch out for our interests."* He is the firm-wide head of bank and institutional finance and led its representation of Freeport LNG Development.
The Clients: The group represented AIG and other institutional investors in the purchase of $73.9 million of senior notes. Other clients include JPMorgan Chase, Bank of America and PG&E.

Mayer, Brown, Rowe & Maw LLP
See firm details p.771
The Firm: Picking up important deals for national and international banks, this full-service group benefits from its lack of conflicts in the Texas market. Its size and depth also means it has the resources to draw upon specialist expertise as and when necessary. Clients described this group's *"broad industry knowledge and exposure,"* and appreciated its *"willingness to staff deals with senior attorneys and responsive approach."* It recently represented the CIBC as agent bank and arranger in US Shipping's $180 million senior secured credit facilities. This transaction was run in conjunction with US Shipping converting from a private company to an MLP trading on the New York Stock Exchange.
The Lawyers: Michael Niebruegge (see p.1693) is an experienced, hands-on attorney who *"commands respect in the community."* He has a *"positive, proactive and effective style"* that

"gets deals done rather than finding roadblocks." **Terry Vilardo** (see p.1740) is a sharply intelligent attorney with a tenacious approach. Clients also appreciate her *"excellent knowledge of complex financial transactions"* and *"polished negotiation skills."*
The Clients: The group has represented the Bank of Montréal in numerous cross-border transactions including a $75 million facility to Vitrocrisa and a loan to Atlantic Power. Other clients include CIBC and Royal Bank of Scotland.

Band 4

Jones Day
See firm details p.485
The Firm: While relatively small in size, the Texas office of this global firm is not to be underestimated. Although not always the most visible player, the group undertakes large and complex deals on behalf of significant commercial and institutional clients in the private equity, lending and structured finance arenas. This year it represented Quicksilver Resources in $600 million tax secured senior multicurrency credit facilities and advised Ambac Assurance in the asset-backed securitization of a railcar leveraged lease portfolio.
The Lawyers: Joint practice head **Thomas Gillespie** (see p.1681) is an attorney respected for his attention to detail and broad-based practice. He led the firm's representation of Quicksilver Resources.
The Clients: Frost National Bank; Bank of America; SKM Growth Investors; Morgan Stanley Real Estate Funds and True Companies.

Thompson & Knight LLP
See firm details p.1722
The Firm: The group enters the *Chambers'* table this year following enthusiastic feedback from clients and competitors alike. One client claimed: *"It is my top choice for bank credit documentation,"* while peers noted its strength in midmarket secured lending and its *"depth of experience in the energy field."* With offices throughout the state, this firm has a respected track record in syndicated bank credit facilities, senior note offerings, lease financings, and project financings.
The Lawyers: John Rain (see p.1697) was recommended to researchers for his *"impressive structured finance expertise."* He has a broad practice and recently represented an issuer in the sale of $600 million of senior notes and the related tender offer for and retirement of privately placed notes.
The Clients: The firm represents pension fund managers, factoring companies, savings and loan associations, insurance companies and banks.

Weil, Gotshal & Manges LLP

See firm details p.1378

The Firm: Although it does undertake conventional lender representations, Weil Gotshal's name in this market is as a private equity powerhouse. It "*has buckets of experience*" across a "*broad array of transactions,*" and continues to act as principal adviser to Hicks, Muse, Tate & Furst. In the past year, it has counseled the group in a $207 million loan for the acquisition of Persona. It also advised on the $595 million and $875 million loans for Thomas H Lee's acquisitions of Michael Foods and Simmons Company respectively. The team "*always has its finger on the pulse,*" clients said, "*which enables us to take advantage of market nuances that others are not savvy to.*"

The Lawyers: **Angela Fontana** (see p.1679) "*can flatten other lawyers with her experience,*" declared clients. Her market profile has increased as Glenn West has turned the focus of his practice to corporate/M&A. She has a "*very effective, tough, negotiating style*" that means "*you get a better deal when she is on your side.*" High-

flying associate **Courtney Marcus** (see p.1689) is "*able to simplify legal points into business English and boil down to the heart of issues.*"

The Clients: The group represents private equity groups such as Thomas H Lee Partners; DLJ Merchant Banking Partners; Hicks, Muse, Tate & Furst and The Blackstone Group.

Winstead Sechrest & Minick PC

See firm details p.1725

The Firm: Both peers and clients hold this solid finance practice in high esteem. It has a long list of high-value transactions under its belt and is commended for its attention to client service. The group is active in the areas of mezzanine finance, syndicated credit facilities, and asset-based and energy-related lending. It is particularly "*good at highlighting structural issues and ensuring that banks' best interests are represented,*" clients noted. The attorneys are also engaged in bankruptcy proceedings and loan restructuring advice.

The Lawyers: **Michael Hilliard** (see p.1684) is the chair of the banking and credit transactions

practice. He won plaudits from interviewees for his ability to "*avoid the sword fight and deal with issues in a common-sense manner.*" He is an experienced attorney with a practice that centers around complex lending transactions, leveraged leasing, project finance, credit products and workouts.

The Clients: This group represents the interests of regional, national and international financial institutions, financial services companies and other lending organizations as well as the firm's corporate clients in establishing and maintaining credit facilities.

Other Notable Practitioners

Marilyn Maloney has recently moved to Houston to head Liskow & Lewis' first office outside of Louisiana. Currently the only banking lawyer in the office, she is well regarded by peers who "*love dealing with her*" because she is "*top notch in all that she does.*" She represents borrowers and lenders in energy, real estate and general corporate loans. Key clients include CSFB and AmSouth Bank.

BANKRUPTCY

Texas
Leading firms (Bankruptcy)
[1] HAYNES AND BOONE LLP *Dallas, Houston*
[2] FULBRIGHT & JAWORSKI LLP *Dallas*
VINSON & ELKINS LLP *Dallas*
WEIL, GOTSHAL & MANGES LLP *Dallas*
[3] AKIN GUMP STRAUSS HAUER & FELD LLP *Dallas*
ANDREWS KURTH LLP *Houston*
GARDERE WYNNE SEWELL LLP *Dallas*
NELIGAN TARPLEY ANDREWS & FOLEY LLP *Dallas*
THOMPSON & KNIGHT LLP *Dallas*
WINSTEAD SECHREST & MINICK PC *Dallas*
[4] BAKER BOTTS LLP *Dallas*
BRACEWELL & GIULIANI LLP *Houston*
COX SMITH MATTHEWS *San Antonio*
MUNSCH HARDT KOPF & HARR, PC *Dallas*
Firms are listed alphabetically in each band.

Band 1

Haynes and Boone LLP

The Firm: This firm was universally accepted to be "*right up there at the top.*" It has "*assembled a very effective group*" that frequently plays a part in the market's leading cases. In its traditional role as debtor counsel, it has advised on some of the highest-profile local and national cases, including Mirant and Schlotzky's. The group has recently broadened its base to cover more creditor and committee representations, advising one of the largest lenders in Adelphia Communications and the creditors committee in the National Benevo-

lent Association bankruptcy. Commentators find that this team is "*respected by judges*" and full of "*personalities that are easy to work with.*" Among further highlights is work on the complex American HomePatient Chapter 13 proceedings.

The Lawyers: According to sources, **Robert Albergotti** is a "*cut above all others.*" An "*exceptionally bright and pragmatic business lawyer,*" he displays the "*ability to bring disparate groups to a negotiating table,*" although there are no doubts that he will fight when necessary to protect his client's interests. It is "*hard to deny that* **Robin Phelan** *is tops,*" agreed clients. The "*extremely creative and flamboyant*" attorney has been involved in some of the biggest cases, nationally and in Texas. He is "*enormously intelligent and honest with excellent people skills.*" **Charles Beckham** is an "*easygoing attorney*" who is widely known for his depth of experience representing secured lenders. The "*tenacious and articulate*" **Stacey Jernigan** is an intelligent attorney who brings to the table his extensive negotiating skills.

The Clients: The firm has a wide network of clients including Bank of America, American Airlines and Crédit Lyonnais.

Band 2

Fulbright & Jaworski LLP

See firm details p.1715

The Firm: Market perception is that this practice is an increasingly visible and weighty force due to its "*strong individuals who always repre-

sent their clients interests skillfully.*" The full-service group has been involved in numerous high-profile cases of late. It continues to represent three of the largest creditors in the Mirant proceedings; while on the debtor side it is currently advising Yukos in its Chapter 11 proceedings. It also has experience in forward contracts and all types of insolvency litigation. The knowledgeable and experienced group "*practices at a high level in high-value cases with a high degree of professionalism,*" commentators said.

The Lawyers: **Lou Strubeck** (see p.1702) is a well-regarded attorney, who has "*the ability to drive consensus.*" He is "*smart, to the point*" and "*good at finding creative ways to solve a problem.*" Interviewees also highlighted **Evelyn Biery**'s (see p.1672) fine practice. She is an "*experienced and focused lawyer,*" who displays a "*great amount of skill*" and is a particularly accomplished negotiator. She is leading the firm's representation of Yukos. The "*fabulous*" **Toby Gerber** (see p.1681) is respected for his work with secured creditors. He is "*well versed and articulate*" in all manner of bankruptcy issues.

The Clients: The group primarily represents creditors in bankruptcy, but also counts various debtors amongst its clientele.

Vinson & Elkins LLP

See firm details p.1724

The Firm: Texas stalwart Vinson & Elkins continues to be a major force in this market. The "*capable and sophisticated*" group traditionally

Texas
Leading individuals (Bankruptcy)

★ ALBERGOTTI Robert *Haynes and Boone*, Dallas

[1] LEE John *Andrews Kurth*, Houston
PÉREZ Alfredo *Weil Gotshal*, Houston
PHELAN Robin *Haynes and Boone*, Dallas
ROBERSON Richard *Gardere Wynne*, Dallas
SOSLAND Martin *Weil Gotshal*, Dallas
STEWART Dan *Vinson & Elkins*, Dallas

[2] GIBBS Charles *Akin Gump*, Dallas
KAIM Henry *Bracewell & Giuliani*, Houston
KINZIE Jack *Baker Botts*, Dallas
LEE James *Vinson & Elkins*, Dallas
NELIGAN Patrick *Neligan Tarpley*, Dallas
RUCKMAN Deirdre *Gardere Wynne*, Dallas
STRUBECK Lou *Fulbright & Jaworski*, San Antonio
WALLANDER William *Vinson & Elkins*, Dallas

[3] BECKHAM Charles *Haynes and Boone*, Houston
BIERY Evelyn *Fulbright & Jaworski*, Houston
DANIEL Josiah *Vinson & Elkins*, Dallas
MCCONNELL Mike *Winstead Sechrest*, Fort Worth
RAY Hugh *Andrews Kurth*, Houston
REID Russell *Akin Gump*, Dallas
ROSS Judith *Baker Botts*, Houston
SPEARS Berry *Winstead Sechrest*, Austin
WILLIAMSON Deborah *Cox Smith*, San Antonio

[4] BENNETT David *Thompson & Knight*, Dallas
CAMPBELL Rhett *Thompson & Knight*, Houston
GERBER Toby *Fulbright & Jaworski*, Dallas
JERNIGAN Stacey *Haynes and Boone*, Dallas
MUNSCH Russell *Munsch Hardt*, Dallas
O'NEIL Holland *Gardere Wynne*, Dallas
ROCHELLE Michael *Rochelle Hutcheson*, Dallas
SHEINFELD Myron *Akin Gump*, Houston
STRICKLIN Samuel *Bracewell & Giuliani*, Dallas
STROUBE III H Rey *Akin Gump*, Houston
SUTHERLAND Michael *Carrington Coleman*, Dallas
WIELEBINSKI Joseph *Munsch Hardt*, Dallas

Up-and-coming individuals
BROOKNER Jason *Andrews Kurth*, Dallas

Individuals are listed alphabetically in each band.

focuses upon creditor representation – for example, advising six New York taxing authorities in a dispute with Mirant over $600 million of taxes. It also represented the public bondholders through the Tri-Union Chapter 11 proceedings. The group has also advised the debtor side of the market, recently representing VarTec in its billion-dollar international reorganization and Nucentrix Broadband Networks. In the latter case the group raised enough through auction to pay all creditors in full and returned $3 per share to stockholders. Clients are full of praise for the team, with one claiming: "*I could not have done as well as I did without Vinson & Elkins' legal and business acumen.*"

The Lawyers: Dan Stewart (see p.1701) is "*talented in every important respect.*" The "*smart and tenacious attorney*" has had a fabulous career representing "*a very long list of loyal clients.*" He is

a great manager and trainer for his team, and sources recognize that he "*appreciates the value of having well-qualified people working with him.*" **William Wallander** (see p.1704) is a tough negotiator, whose "*pre-hearing analysis and in-court strategy are right on the money.*" He led the group's involvement in VarTec. A litigator with substantial bankruptcy experience, **James Lee** (see p.1688) "*adds significant depth*" to the group. He is respected for the "*logical and concise*" approach he takes to complex matters. **Josiah Daniel** (see p.1676) is a "*magnificent practitioner*" with a strong technical background. He is "*very good at quickly figuring out what is in the client's best interests.*"

The Clients: Daisytek International; GE Commercial Finance; Lone Star Bank; Société Générale and CIBC.

Weil, Gotshal & Manges LLP
See firm details p.1378

The Firm: Having been involved in some of the largest and highest-profile local and national cases, this internationally recognized group is well respected in the Texas market as an "*outstanding competitor with a wealth of experience.*" Representing Enron, this office has been involved in the confirmation of the plan and the disposition of $6.2 billion worth of assets. It also acted for the debtor in the large out-of-court restructuring of a steel fabrication company. The group has "*considerable restructuring depth,*" and has developed niche expertise in representing clients in South America.

The Lawyers: Alfredo Pérez (see p.1696) is widely recognized as a first-rate advocate for his clients, whose "*hard-working, resourceful and practical approach*" has won many fans. Sources also find him "*easy to work with – he seeks acceptable solutions.*" The "*highly intelligent and very astute*" **Martin Sosland** (see p.1701) is an effective litigator, who wins the confidence of both clients and peers. He is a "*sophisticated thinker, good problem solver*" and possesses a wealth of experience.

The Clients: Enron; MCI; GE Capital; Lehman Brothers; Tejas Securities Group; International Wire Group; Viasystems Group; Resurgence Asset Management; Leucadia National and Omnicare.

Band 3

Akin Gump Strauss Hauer & Feld LLP
See firm details p.477

The Firm: With a reputation as a "*smaller, but extremely sophisticated*" group, Akin Gump has devoted considerable resources into building up its debtor practice of late. It represented CEI Roofing in its complex Chapter 11 proceedings and Gadzooks in its filing and subsequent efforts to sell its assets. These attorneys have

developed strong relationships with players in the bond markets, including ties that have filtered down from the New York office. Indeed, the group's efforts to work as a national practice that attracts national and international matters are wholly endorsed by clients. On the creditors' side, the team is still a significant player. It recently represented the committee of unsecured creditors in Chi Chi's.

The Lawyers: Charles Gibbs (see p.1681) impressed competitors with his "*practical approach*" that ensures "*his cases move forward in a tranquil way.*" A constructive and experienced attorney, he led the firm's representation in the Gadzooks and Chi Chi's proceedings. **Russell Reid** (see p.1698) is a skilled bankruptcy litigator with a niche expertise in default administration for corporate trustees and special servicers of commercial mortgage securitized trusts. He is "*low key, but extremely effective*" in court. With an "*unbelievable depth of experience*" **Myron Sheinfeld** (see p.1700) has made a successful career out of advising senior management and corporate boards on all aspects of financial restructuring and insolvency. With his practice still straddling London and Houston, **Rey Stroube** (see p.1702) is a "*deft practitioner with a broad base of experience*" that means he can turn his hand to a wide range of bankruptcy issues.

The Clients: This group represents large business entities across the USA including Gadzooks, Chi Chi's and CEI Roofing.

Andrews Kurth LLP
See firm details p.1707

The Firm: Primarily a creditor practice, this group has played a significant role in a number of high-end cases and is visible on the "*local and national radar.*" It continues to act as national counsel to the creditors committee in Mirant and has played a prominent role representing Deutsche Bank in the Yukos proceedings. It recently recovered $84 million from Ernst & Young on behalf of the Trustee for the Bank of New England. "*Our success was obtained through the excellent advice and guidance given by Andrews Kurth,*" acknowledged one client. In further recent highlights, the firm identified an innovative cause of action for the shareholders committee in Paragon and has represented Vlasic Foods in litigation against Campbell Soup over an alleged fraudulent conveyance in an over-leveraged spin-off.

The Lawyers: John Lee (see p.1689) is a star litigator who has the ability to "*brilliantly lay before the court, in elegant simplicity, the complex issues and facts of a case ordered to tell a compelling story,*" clients said. "*He knows exactly how long to hold and when to fold.*" **Hugh Ray** (see p.1697) has been highly visible of late, leading the firm's involvement in Yukos. He is "*great with clients,*" quick to pick up on the key points in a case and

www.ChambersandPartners.com
All quotes in the text are from interviews with clients and competitors.
1627

employs a *"smart, aggressive"* manner to serve his clients' interests. **Jason Brookner** (see p.1673) is a *"rising star,"* who has come to the fore following his involvement in Mirant. According to commentators, he has the *"sheer personality to build consensus and keep cases on track."*

The Clients: Ranging across the creditor and debtor spectrum, clients include: Deutsche Bank; Vlasic Foods; Mobile Energy Services and Crown Pacific.

Gardere Wynne Sewell LLP

See firm details p.1718

The Firm: This group's representation of the examiner in Mirant – investigating and monitoring a range of general and discrete issues – has raised its market profile recently. It is widely considered to be a *"strong team of specialists"* with commentators across the board praising the wealth of talent residing here. The practice covers restructuring outside of bankruptcy, workouts, asset purchases and creditor representation across a range of industry sectors, including retail, real estate, oil and gas and airlines. The group has also continued to act as lead debtor counsel in American Pad & Paper, with all creditors having been paid in full.

The Lawyers: Market observers believe that **Richard Roberson's** (see p.1698) *"light is shining bright."* A successful litigator who is leading the firm's involvement in Mirant, he is a *"smart, calm and professional"* attorney. **Deirdre Ruckman** (see p.1699) is a *"charismatic adversary"* and a successful problem solver, whom both peers and clients find easy to work with. The *"very capable and level-headed"* **Holland O'Neil** (see p.1694) has been supporting Roberson in the complex Mirant proceedings.

The Clients: Secured lenders; debtors; trustees and creditors committees.

Neligan Tarpley Andrews & Foley LLP

The Firm: *"One of the last remaining debtor boutiques,"* this group has established a name for itself in the market as a firm trusted to *"consistently do a magnificent job"* representing clients in mid-to-large cases. It covers all aspects of business bankruptcy and out-of-court debt restructuring. Recent debtor representations include Minorplanet Systems in its restructuring efforts and the Bag'n Baggage filing.

The Lawyers: Founding partner **Patrick Neligan** is a *"bright, savvy business person"* and a tenacious litigator, who *"knows the bankruptcy code inside out."*

Thompson & Knight LLP

See firm details p.1722

The Firm: This diverse practice covers the range of bankruptcy transactions, litigation and restructurings. It is involved in a substantial number of high-end cases, representing the agents for the bank group in Mirant; the producers and sellers of hydrocarbons in Enron and a significant counterparty in VarTec. The group is made up of *"attorneys of the highest caliber,"* peers commented. Other cases it has been involved in recently include representing the debtor in Dunhill Resources and the committee of unsecured creditors in the Texas Commercial Energy proceedings.

The Lawyers: David Bennett (see p.1672) is a *"very capable, tenacious attorney,"* best known for his particular expertise in the energy field. **Rhett Campbell** (see p.1674) is an *"exuberant and effective"* bankruptcy litigator. This experienced attorney has cultivated a broad practice.

The Clients: The firm acts on behalf of the whole spectrum of bankruptcy parties.

Winstead Sechrest & Minick PC

See firm details p.1725

The Firm: This well-regarded firm fields a team of dedicated and long-established attorneys who have successfully attracted a strong local client base. The past year has seen the team involved in a number of litigation, mediation and arbitration proceedings. The team acted as co-counsel with the bank consortium in the Phillips Services bankruptcy. Its *"highly experienced and businesslike"* attorneys are particularly active in the retail, airlines and technology sectors for clients including banks, financial institutions and oil and gas producers.

The Lawyers: Mike McConnell (see p.1691) is an *"extremely capable"* attorney who is well versed in the handling of bankruptcy disputes, often coming to conclusions that are *"right on target,"* agree sources. Austin-based **Berry Spears** (see p.1701) *"does a wonderful job at everything."* One of the market's hardest-working attorneys, he is well known for his work with leading bank groups.

The Clients: Secured and unsecured creditors committees, debtors and trustees.

Band 4

Baker Botts LLP

See firm details p.1708

The Firm: A successful Texas and national firm, this relatively small group punches above its weight in the bankruptcy market. The practice focuses on the representation of debtors and large companies in financial trouble. The team is developing significant expertise advising asbestos companies on their liabilities and has been acting as counsel for Halliburton in proceedings relating to its Dresser Industries and Kellogg Brown & Root subsidiaries. Another recent highlight was representing the debtor in possession in the bankruptcy of a telecommunications company, obtaining a significant recovery for unsecured creditors.

The Lawyers: The head of the group firmwide, **Jack Kinzie** (see p.1687) is a *"shrewd, experienced and disciplined"* lawyer who is credited with great team management skills and an ability to ensure the smooth running of complex cases. **Judith Ross** (see p.1699) is a widely respected attorney with *"very good technical and people skills."* She is *"someone you can make a deal with."*

The Clients: Primarily a debtor practice, it has recently represented Corban Communications, NextStage and Halliburton.

Bracewell & Giuliani LLP

See firm details p.1710

The Firm: A dedicated group, headed by the highly esteemed Henry Kaim, this group has broad-based expertise representing both creditors and debtors in acquisitions, workouts and Chapter 11 restructurings. It continues to represent Texas Petrochemicals following its emergence from Chapter 11 and has recently guided Cooperheat through to its sale as a going concern. It also offers counseling services to financially troubled companies prior to bankruptcy and has experience in preference actions.

The Lawyers: The head of the section, **Henry Kaim** (see p.1686), is an attorney who *"will get the deal done."* According to sources, *"He knows the code and is able to work with people to achieve results."* **Sam Stricklin** (see p.1702) is respected for his *"effective litigation skills."* The *"tenacious, pragmatic and hardworking"* attorney is an impressive figure in court.

The Clients: The firm caters for clients ranging across large secured creditors, including: bank agents in syndicated credits; unsecured creditors; institutional noteholders; purchasers of assets out of bankruptcies and debtors.

Cox Smith Matthews Incorporated

See firm details p.1713

The Firm: A strong brand name that is widely recognized and well regarded throughout the state. This San Antonio-based group offers a high-level service to clients seeking advice on all aspects of bankruptcy. The team's expertise ranges from representing clients seeking to acquire assets out of bankruptcy and advising banks and financial institutions involved in Chapter 11 proceedings alongside its more traditional debtor and creditor work. It has clients across the telecom, energy, entertainment, airline and medical devices industries.

The Lawyers: Deborah Williamson (see p.1706) leads the practice group and has extensive experience on both the debtor and creditor sides. The accomplished practitioner is *"definitely worth mentioning."*

The Clients: The clientele is drawn from debtors, trustees, committees, acquirers, secured and unsecured creditors and lenders.

Munsch Hardt Kopf & Harr, PC

The Firm: A *"local success story,"* this firm has grown from its initial group of six to 120 lawyers across Dallas, Houston and Austin. It has particular experience representing financial institutions and banks in a range of cases and is currently representing a bank client in the Yukos proceedings. It has niche expertise in power plant restructurings, having undertaken three over the past year, including representing the agent in Exelon. This is certainly a group that *"deserves to be on anyone's list,"* acknowledged market observers.

The Lawyers: Russ Munsch (see p.1693) is a highly intelligent attorney with a *"lot of common sense."* The *"creative, effective and aggressive"* lit-igator is credited with having built up this respected practice. **Joe Wielebenski** (see p.1705) is a *"feisty"* attorney, who *"brings his own kind of magic"* to the table as a successful local and national litigator, acting for clients such as the Official Committee of Franchisees in the Color Tile bankruptcy in Delaware.

The Clients: The group primarily represents financial institutions and banks. It has significant experience in the real estate and oil and gas industries.

Other Notable Practitioners

Buzz Rochelle of Rochelle, Hutcheson & McCullough LLP has *"deep roots in the Texas bankruptcy community,"* agree interviewees. With a *"high level of intelligence and integrity,"* he makes the most out of larger firms' conflicts of interest, recently representing a committee in its suit against a number of banks. **Mike Sutherland** has recently moved from Winstead Sechrest & Winick PC to Carrington, Coleman, Sloman & Blumenthal, LLP. He has spent a large proportion of his time over the past 12 months on pre-bankruptcy workouts. He is a highly esteemed local attorney with a successful and established practice.

CONSTRUCTION

Texas
Leading firms (Construction)

1 **CANTERBURY, STUBER, ELDER, GOOCH** *Dallas*

2 **ALLENSWORTH AND PORTER, LLP** *Austin*
  COATS ROSE YALE RYMAN LEE *Houston*
  COKINOS, BOSIEN AND YOUNG *Houston*
  FORD WHITE & NASSEN *Dallas*
  JONES DAY *Dallas*

3 **FISK & FIELDER** *Dallas*
  GARDERE WYNNE SEWELL LLP *Dallas*
  GOINS, UNDERKOFLER, CRAWFORD *Dallas*
  JENKENS & GILCHRIST *Houston*
  PORTER & HEDGES LLP *Houston*

Leading individuals (Construction)

1 **CANTERBURY Joe** *Canterbury Stuber, Dallas*

2 **ALLENSWORTH William** *Allensworth, Austin*
  COATS William *Coats Rose, Houston*
  COKINOS Gregory *Cokinos Bosien, Houston*
  FISK Hollye *Fisk & Fielder, Dallas*
  FORD Jeffrey *Ford White, Dallas*
  MEYERS Robert *Jones Day, Dallas*
  PEDEN David *Porter & Hedges, Houston*

3 **ALBERS Michael** *Jenkens & Gilchrist, Dallas*
  ANDREWS William *Andrews Myers, Houston*
  FLAKE Richard *Cokinos Bosien, Houston*
  GOOCH Kyle *Canterbury Stuber, Dallas*
  GRIFFITH Scott *Griffith & Nixon, Dallas*
  MERWIN Bruce *Haynes and Boone, Houston*
  PRATT Don *Pratt & Sanderford, Temple*
  SHORT William *Short How, Dallas*
  UNDERKOFLER Paul *Goins Underkofler, Dallas*
  YUNGBLUT Stephen *James Stanton, Dallas*

  Firms and individuals are listed alphabetically in each band.

Band 1

Canterbury, Stuber, Elder, Gooch & Surratt PC

See firm details p.1711

The Firm: Hailed as *"the top construction practice in Texas,"* this boutique firm can offer unrivaled experience in transactional, dispute resolution and labor relations within the construction industry. The workload here mainly consists of commercial construction, with a large chunk of multifamily residential developments, and a few industrial power plants thrown in for good measure. All of its lawyers are fully rounded construction experts and can turn their hand to both noncontentious and contentious issues. As well as being renowned for their litigation prowess, these attorneys have considerable expertise in alternative dispute resolution and mediation and they have arbitrated two large cases of late. Further recent highlights include working on the development of the new airport terminal in Dallas, and the large amount of work it is doing for the state's largest apartment builder, JPI.

The Lawyers: Market sources commended **Joe Canterbury** as *"just the best – he's the dean of the construction Bar."* Clients reported very positive experiences with him, and especially liked the fact that *"he grew up in the industry and so really understands what it's about."* He is very heavily involved in alternative dispute resolution at the moment. **Kyle Gooch** (see p.1681) has been working on some major cases recently, including the Dallas airport terminal. He impresses with his broad base of construction knowledge and is *"a very tenacious litigator."*

The Clients: The team represents mainly contractors and subcontractors, although it is increasing the volume of its representation of owners. It works on projects throughout the USA, and also has a number of international clients.

Band 2

Allensworth and Porter, LLP

The Firm: This boutique firm has the premier practice in the state for representing the design profession in construction disputes. It has gained this recognition through its experience in many high-profile litigation and arbitration proceedings. Also key is the fact that many of the lawyers have backgrounds in engineering or architecture, which ensures that they possess a very sound understanding of the industry.

The Lawyers: William Allensworth is a *"terrific"* lawyer who is especially skilled at representing engineers. Peers report that he is *"a real scholar, who does a great job for clients."*

The Clients: The firm's reputation mainly rests on its representation of architects and engineers.

Coats Rose Yale Ryman Lee

The Firm: A leading firm that has experience in every type of construction and surety matter that arises in the market. This includes advising on all stages of contract claims proceedings, bid protests, enforcement of workers' lien rights, and representing fidelity carriers and sureties on bonds and policies.

The Lawyers: William Coats is up there as *"one of the best construction lawyers in Texas."* He can boast years of experience and an excellent knowledge of the industry.

The Clients: The firm has been counsel to the Houston Chapter of Associated General Contractors for many years.

Cokinos, Bosien and Young

The Firm: This traditional construction boutique is *"a high-quality practice"* and fields a large group of 24 lawyers who are adept at both negotiating and drafting contracts, and resolving subsequent disputes. For example, it has been negotiating the construction of a series of medical centers and is involved in a swath of industrial construction disputes regarding refineries, power plants and pipelines. The firm has also devoted significant resources to its residential practice, and has been negotiating the construction of the largest condominium high-rise on the Gulf Coast of Texas.

The Lawyers: Gregory Cokinos is highly respected as a "*very skillful adversary.*" He works on a mix of litigation and transactional matters for both developers and contractors. **Richard Flake** has "*a sterling record*" as a mediator and arbitrator. Sources also commend his mastery of both transactional and litigation matters.

The Clients: The firm represents both large Fortune 500 companies and smaller local companies. It also works for both owner-developers and contractors.

Ford White & Nassen

The Firm: This small boutique firm is widely recognized as a significant presence in the sector. Its strong reputation for litigation work is complemented by considerable prowess in transactional issues. The group is well equipped to handle multijurisdictional litigation as well as international arbitrations arising out of the construction industry.

The Lawyers: Jeffrey Ford is an all-around construction specialist and is "*capable of handling a wide variety of construction clients.*"

The Clients: The firm has clients in every category of the construction industry, including public and private owners, general contractors, specialty contractors and sureties. The list includes: The Beck Group; Centex Construction; Faulkner Construction; MDI General Contractors; Santos CMI; Spring Valley Construction; Travelers; Universal Surety of America; Koll Development; Hunt Properties; United States Lime & Minerals and Collin County.

Jones Day
See firm details p.485

The Firm: Out of the large, international firms based in Texas, Jones Day stands out as the most capable construction department. It is one of the more prolific firms for representing owner-developers in both transactional issues and in dispute resolution. The caseload here spans the globe and features the construction and redevelopment of landmark buildings such as airport terminals, major office projects and transportation facilities.

The Lawyers: Robert Meyers (see p.1692) is the linchpin of the Texas branch of the international construction practice. Impressed clients say he is "*as fine a lawyer as there is on the planet and has every skill a lawyer needs.*"

The Clients: While it is renowned for representing owner-developers, the firm also does work for architects, contractors and suppliers.

Fisk & Fielder

The Firm: Many of the lawyers in this small practice are licensed architects and can offer clients a sympathetic understanding of their work as well as very fine legal advice. Attorneys here are skilled in construction litigation across a variety of disputes, but have a particular niche in professional negligence cases.

The Lawyers: Hollye Fisk is best known for his expertise displayed in the defense of architects. Clients are clearly very happy with his service as they report: he is "*quick-witted and fearless*" and "*even on his worst day he is ten out of ten.*"

The Clients: The firm represents architects and engineers.

Gardere Wynne Sewell LLP
See firm details p.1718

The Firm: Extremely well known for its work on residential developments, this group assists more than 20 large home builders with their construction projects on a national basis. It is also advising the National Association of Home Builders on shepherding through major pieces of legislation for home builders. Clients report that the firm has "*more knowledge and experience in construction defect litigation than anyone else in the state.*" They are also confident that the lawyers "*know how to attack a problem and get it resolved.*" However, the practice is also much wider than just residential work – this year's portfolio has included litigation on county court houses, malls, casinos and Terminal D at Dallas International (Dallas/Fort Worth International Airport).

The Lawyers: Steven Henry heads the construction practice group.

The Clients: National Association of Home Builders; Austin Commercial; EMJ; CF Jordan; Andres Construction and Gilbert Construction.

Goins, Underkofler, Crawford & Langdon LLP

The Firm: This well-established Dallas firm has a construction practice that specializes in dispute resolution. It is very experienced in arbitrations and mediations as well as defending claims at the federal and state courts. In addition, the group has considerable capability in construction finance and contracts for a caseload that includes residential and commercial developments such as office buildings and shopping centers.

The Lawyers: Paul Underkofler is a respected senior member of the Bar. Peers report that he is "*a highly skilled mediator*" and also excels at surety and insurance issues.

The Clients: The firm represents developers, owners, contractors and subcontractors, construction managers, design professionals and sureties.

Jenkens & Gilchrist

The Firm: This small team of construction lawyers based in Dallas has had a busy year working on new developments and various litigations and arbitrations. It has been representing developers in various multifamily condominium projects, including a 25-story condominium in Manhattan, and some in Washington DC, South Carolina and Honolulu. It has also been advising on the new Federal Reserve Bank office in Houston, which is a particularly interesting project because of heightened security considerations following 9/11.

The Lawyers: Michael Albers is "*excellent, especially at putting together construction deals,*" reported market sources.

The Clients: The firm represents large commercial and industrial clients such as: Hillwood Development; LCOR; The Hallwood Group; Champion Partners; CompUSA; Felcor Lodging Trust; Raymond Construction; Key Construction; Toyota; Federal Reserve Bank and Simmons Vedder.

Porter & Hedges, LLP

The Firm: This construction practice can boast deep bench strength as the team of six partners includes a registered architect and past chairs of the Texas Bar construction section. The group mainly works on commercial and industrial construction matters, and has recently acted for Kinder Morgan on a claim involving the construction of a pipeline in Houston. However, it also has an active residential practice and has been representing Genesis in the development of two residential tower blocks at Long Beach.

The Lawyers: The "*outstanding*" **David Peden** is popular with clients, who say "*he's very aggressive in seeking settlement and tries to resolve issues before the litigation stage wherever possible.*"

The Clients: The firm primarily represents contractors. These include Teal Construction; Phillips; Genesis and Kinder Morgan.

Other Notable Practitioners

William Andrews from Andrews Myers Coulter & Cohen PC is a noted construction litigator, who has spent this past year representing contractors and engineers in arbitrations and litigation regarding refineries and chemical plants. Widely respected **Scott Griffith** of Griffith & Nixon PC is a leading representative of subcontractors. At Haynes and Boone LLP **Bruce Merwin** is very prolific and works on multimillion-dollar projects for developers throughout the USA and the Dominican Republic. **Don Pratt** of Pratt & Sanderford is a senior member of the Bar, best known for his specialist understanding of construction-related mediation and arbitration. **William Short** of Short How Frels & Heitz is "*widely recognized as a highly skilled construction lawyer,*" while **Stephen Yungblut** from the Law Offices of James Stanton LP is a long-time member of the construction Bar and is predominantly an "*outstanding*" arbitrator these days.

CORPORATE/M&A

Texas
Leading firms (Corporate/M&A)

1 BAKER BOTTS LLP *Houston*
VINSON & ELKINS LLP *Houston*

2 ANDREWS KURTH LLP *Houston*
FULBRIGHT & JAWORSKI LLP *Houston*
WEIL, GOTSHAL & MANGES LLP *Dallas*

3 AKIN GUMP STRAUSS HAUER & FELD *Houston*
BRACEWELL & GIULIANI LLP *Houston*
GARDERE WYNNE SEWELL LLP *Dallas*
GIBSON, DUNN & CRUTCHER LLP *Dallas*
HAYNES AND BOONE LLP *Dallas*

4 HUGHES & LUCE LLP *Dallas*
KING & SPALDING LLP *Houston*

Leading individuals (Corporate/M&A)

1 JEWELL Robert *Andrews Kurth, Houston*
KELLY Mark *Vinson & Elkins, Houston*
MASSAD Stephen *Baker Botts, Houston*
O'LEARY Michael *Andrews Kurth, Houston*
SWANSON Joel *Baker Botts, Houston*
WORTLEY Michael *Vinson & Elkins, Houston*

2 BOONE Michael *Haynes and Boone, Dallas*
CONLON Michael *Fulbright & Jaworski, Houston*
KIRKLAND David *Baker Botts, Houston*
SCHOENBRUN Larry *Gardere Wynne, Dallas*
STILL Charles *Fulbright & Jaworski, Houston*
WEST Glenn *Weil Gotshal, Dallas*
WULFE Scott *Vinson & Elkins, Houston*

3 DAVIDSON Joshua *Baker Botts, Houston*
LAFOLLETTE Christine *Akin Gump, Houston*
POFF Joe *Baker Botts, Houston*
SENTILLES Irwin *Gibson Dunn, Dallas*
SZALKOWSKI Charles *Baker Botts, Houston*

4 BAKER Andrew *Baker Botts, Dallas*
BOGDANOW Alan *Vinson & Elkins, Dallas*
COHEN R Scott *Weil Gotshal, Dallas*
FINNEGAN, William *Vinson & Elkins, Houston*
HARRINGTON Michael *Vinson & Elkins, Houston*
HITT Jeffrey *Weil Gotshal, Dallas*
KORBY Mary *Weil Gotshal, Dallas*
MARSTON Edgar *Bracewell & Giuliani, Houston*
MCCORMACK William *Hughes & Luce, Dallas*
PARIS Theodore *Baker Botts, Houston*
SASLAW Michael *Weil Gotshal, Dallas*

Up-and-coming individuals

OELMAN David *Vinson & Elkins, Houston*
TABOR Jay *Weil Gotshal, Dallas*

Firms and individuals are listed alphabetically in each band.

Band 1

Baker Botts LLP

See firm details p.1708

The Firm: This firm is widely recognized as "*an outstanding purveyor of corporate legal services*" which has successfully attracted a "*good concentration of Fortune 500 clients.*" It has a breadth of expertise that covers the entire range of corporate and securities matters with the depth to fully resource niche areas. "*We get excellent results with Baker Botts,*" claimed clients, "*they are efficient, very qualified and never over-lawyer a deal.*" On the master limited partnership (MLP) front, the firm has been particularly active representing underwriters. The group recently advised on debt and equity offerings worth $3 million and on the merger of Enterprise Products and GulfTerra. It also counseled Texas Pacific in its $2.35 billion proposed acquisition of Portland General Electric, and Center-Point Energy in the sale of its subsidiary to GC Power Acquisition. The attorneys in this group are "*technicians as well as strategists*" who "*emphasize attention to detail and careful craftsmanship,*" reported clients.

The Lawyers: Stephen Massad (see p.1690) is "*truly brilliant.*" He has a "*wealth of knowledge that clients can tap into*" and the ability to "*remain calm under stress,*" finding practical solutions in the most complex deals. He recently represented Halliburton in the $129 million sale of assets to First Reserve. **Joel Swanson** (see p.1702) is a highly regarded attorney who really knows the energy industry. He is "*focused on completing the transaction – he will not get caught up in the minutiae.*" The "*creative, energetic, positive and very bright*" **David Kirkland** (see p.1687) is a great strategist who displays excellent judgment; he "*knows how to move a deal along.*" **Joshua Davidson** (see p.1676) and **Joe Poff** (see p.1697) are two of the firm's MLP specialists. They are both "*very capable and knowledgeable in this arena,*" largely representing underwriters in high-value transactions such as the billion dollar merger of Enterprise Products and GulfTerra. **Charles Szalkowski** (see p.1702) is an "*outstanding corporate adviser.*" He leads the technology and emerging growth companies practice. Chairman of the Dallas corporate department, **Andrew Baker** (see p.1670) has a broad practice that covers corporate governance, securities offerings and M&A. He is a "*successful rainmaker*" and one of the principal contacts for Halliburton. **Ted Paris** (see p.1694) is a knowledgeable securities expert and a "*superb writer and thorough in his advice.*"

The Clients: CenterPoint Energy; Halliburton; Akzo Nobel; National Energy Group; Affiliated Computer Services (ACS); Centex; Waveset Technologies; Martin Midstream Partners and Marathon Oil.

Vinson & Elkins LLP

See firm details p.1724

The Firm: This group has weathered the negative publicity surrounding the demise of key client Enron, and impressed many as still "*cream of the crop*" in this market. Peers acknowledged that "*the core lawyers there are among the best in Texas,*" while clients noted the group's "*outstanding*" sector expertise. The team has been particularly active in capital markets offerings this year. For example, it advised Enterprise Products in its $2 billion offering of senior notes and Secunda International in its cross-border offering of senior secured floating rate notes. On the M&A front, it represented Blockbuster in its split-off from Viacom and advised Tom Brown in its $2.7 billion acquisition by EnCana. Overall, sources agree that Vinson & Elkins remains an "*impressive,*" long-established practice which is "*very active on behalf of the biggest clients in the biggest deals.*"

The Lawyers: The "*creative*" and focused **Mark Kelly** (see p.1686) is an excellent source of advice on capital markets issues. He is a "*skilled executor of client goals*" and has "*successfully developed a devoted following.*" The "*crackerjack*" **Michael Wortley** (see p.1706) has the "*ability to get through issues*" and "*ensure clients are well-protected.*" Clients described his "*effective, persistent style and real mastery of the law.*" **Scott Wulfe** (see p.1706) is a personable adviser and a "*fabulous deal lawyer.*" With a particular focus on private equity, he is "*very smart, rational and calm.*" **Alan Bogdanow** (see p.1672) led the firm's representation of Blockbuster in its spin-off from Viacom. He retains a high profile as one of the Dallas market's most trusted attorneys. **Michael Harrington** (see p.1683) is "*one of the most talented debt lawyers.*" He is experienced in both the energy and airlines industries. **William Finnegan** (see p.1679) is widely respected for his "*expert understanding of MLPs.*" He impresses with both his legal skills and commercial acumen. "*Clients really love working with*" **David Oelman** (see p.1694). The talented younger lawyer, he is "*trusted to represent clients' interests effectively.*"

The Clients: Riverstone Holdings; Hicks, Muse, Tate & Furst; Plains All American Pipeline; Goldman Sachs; Pioneer Natural Resources; Hanover Compressor and Jefferies & Company.

Band 2

Andrews Kurth LLP

See firm details p.1707

The Firm: This firm is respected for its "*development of a strong and active business practice*" that encompasses MLPs, M&A and structured finance. A group of "*very fine lawyers,*" it has represented the underwriters in numerous financings by Magellan Energy and was involved in the sale of Era Aviation by Rowan. The firm provides a "*top-quality,*" highly committed service that makes clients "*feel as if they only work for us.*" The team has also been advising a large number of clients on corporate governance issues, ranging from fiduciary responsibility through to special investigations.

The Lawyers: Robert Jewell (see p.1685) is a "*calm and focused*" attorney with an "*engaging personality and a practical approach to problem solving.*" He is experienced in energy, real estate and forest products and displays expertise across a range of industries. **Michael O'Leary** (see p.1694) is a "*well-rounded and smart*" practitioner. He has a wealth of experience that makes him a "*rational, sound and reasoned negotiator.*"
The Clients: This "*polished*" group has been actively representing Cheniere Energy and El Paso over the past 12 months. Its other clients range across public and private companies, investment banks, REITs and private equity houses.

Fulbright & Jaworski LLP
See firm details p.1715
The Firm: Traditionally a strong litigation outfit, Fulbright has built a first-rate corporate practice that "*punches above its weight*" in this market. Over the past twelve months, it has been involved in numerous high-value transactions, predominantly representing publicly held companies. Keynote deals include representing PULSE EFT Association in its $311 million acquisition by Discover Financial Services and assisting Riggs National in the proposed merger with PNC National Services. These "*extremely capable attorneys*" also advised the board of directors of US Oncology as it was taken private by Welsh, Carson, Anderson & Stowe in a $1.7 billion transaction.
The Lawyers: Michael Conlon (see p.1675) represents public companies in all corporate matters. He is a "*very, very bright draftsman*" and excellent at "*finding practical solutions to difficult problems.*" According to interviewees, **Charles Still** (see p.1701) is "*as fine an M&A lawyer as there is in the country.*" He led the group in the US Oncology transaction.
The Clients: The group represented Kaneb in its $2.8 billion sale to Valero. Other clients include PULSE EFT Association and Riggs National.

Weil, Gotshal & Manges LLP
See firm details p.1378
The Firm: A globally recognized private equity powerhouse, this group is widely commended for its work with Hicks, Muse, Tate & Furst in its Texan heartland. Over the past year, the group has advised this marquee client on several transactions to develop its communications capability, including the acquisition of the Puerto Rican cable TV business of Centennial Communications. The "*resourceful and effective*" group represented Thomas H Lee in its $2.25 billion acquisition of REFCO and Millennium Chemicals in its $3.6 billion stock for stock disposition to Lyondell. Clients praised it as an "*incredibly responsive, creative*" unit with "*terrific strength and depth and associates who always move the ball forward.*"

The Lawyers: Glenn West (see p.1705) "*has the best business and legal judgment of any lawyer I have worked with,*" claimed one client. He has broad banking, corporate and private equity experience and displays great personal skills which make him an outstanding negotiator. **Scott Cohen** (see p.1675) is a dedicated practitioner with expertise in international and domestic M&As and public and private offerings. The senior M&A lawyer in the group is **Mary Korby** (see p.1687). Her practice is distinctly international, although she has recently devoted a large amount of time to representing Enron in various dispositions. "*People respect and like to work with*" **Michael Saslaw** (see p.1699). He is a "*smart and thoughtful*" attorney who is visible in some of the market's leading transactions. **Jeffrey Hitt** (see p.1684) is a respected private equity practitioner, whose responsive service and high-quality advice have won a loyal client following. **Jay Tabor** (see p.1702) is the group's rising star. He has the ability to undertake a "*sharp and meticulous analysis*" of corporate issues and has a "*personable style with the other side.*"
The Clients: GE Capital; Hicks, Muse, Tate & Furst; Thomas H Lee; Millennium Chemicals; Enron and Koch Industries.

Band 3

Akin Gump Strauss Hauer & Feld LLP
See firm details p.477
The Firm: With the recruitment of Christine LaFollette and her group from King & Spalding for its Houston office, this firm has successfully established itself as a leading player in the Texas market. The practice covers M&A and general corporate and securities matters and has been particularly active on behalf of Houston Exploration Company both in acquisitions and securities issues. It also advised an oil and gas company in its $325 million IPO. The Dallas team represented the special committee to the board of directors of Southwest Royalties in its $187.8 million acquisition by Clayton Williams.
The Lawyers: Christine LaFollette (see p.1688) is a "*knowledgeable, practical and very client-friendly*" attorney, who has broad experience. Sources credit her with providing a greater impetus to the firm's corporate department.
The Clients: The group represents issuers and underwriters and public and private companies, particularly in the energy sector. Examples include Houston Exploration Company and the board of directors of Southwest Royalties.

Bracewell & Giuliani LLP
See firm details p.1710
The Firm: Commentators agree that this is a highly credible corporate outfit that "*can bring a high degree of expertise*" to transactions. It has an enviable client roster, to which it provides

M&A, corporate governance and capital markets advice. Interviewees picked the group out as a "*known force in the energy market.*" Other industry focuses include airlines, biotech and telecom. A recent highlight for the group was its representation of Goodman Global Holdings in its $1.43 billion sale to Apollo Management.
The Lawyers: Edgar Marston (see p.1690) is an experienced corporate adviser. In addition to his duties as a key corporate partner in the Texan team, he has also supported the firm's corporate practice in Kazakhstan.
The Clients: Goodman Global Holdings; Bechtel; AKQA; Valero and Bank of America.

Gardere Wynne Sewell LLP
See firm details p.1718
The Firm: This deep-rooted corporate practice has cultivated a dynamic presence in the market, with offices throughout Texas. It has been particularly active on the corporate governance front, advising independent directors and special committees on investigations and compliance issues. Recently, this busy transactional practice has been principally counseling public companies involved in asset dispositions. It represents clients across a number of industries, including construction, energy, insurance, retail, technology and transportation.
The Lawyers: Larry Schoenbrun (see p.1700) is a client-focused lawyer, who displays his "*wonderful intellect*" across a broad range of corporate and governance issues. "*You can trust him to be rational,*" asserted both clients and peers.
The Clients: The group acts for Fortune 500 clients in matters across Texas and internationally. It advised the London-based National Express Group in a high-value credit facility.

Gibson, Dunn & Crutcher LLP
See firm details p.285
The Firm: Having recently directed its attention to building up its corporate practice in Texas, this group is making a splash in the market. It manages client relationships well, with interviewees noting, "*These attorneys know how to work with our people.*" The group can also draw on substantial resources housed in other offices across the country. Recent keynote transactions include representing Atmos Energy in its $1.9 billion acquisition of TXU Gas and advising National Petcare in its sale to VCA Antech.
The Lawyers: A bright and sensible attorney, **Irwin Sentilles** (see p.1700) "*does a great job keeping everybody informed*" and is "*aggressive but fair*" in his dealings with the other parties in a transaction.
The Clients: The firm regularly represents D.R. Horton in corporate matters. It was most recently involved in its issuances of $1.2 billion of senior notes. Other clients include Del Monte; JPMorgan Chase; Atmos Energy; National Petcare and Union Pacific.

Haynes and Boone LLP

The Firm: A corporate group with a strong reputation and an entrenched practice, Haynes and Boone is a busy domestic and international outfit. Its broad-based experience encompasses counseling boards of directors on corporate governance issues. One deal that illustrates its capacity to handle big-ticket matters is the advice to a public utility holding company in its $3.8 billion acquisition. Although market conditions mean that many deals have not come to fruition over the past twelve months, the team has substantial knowledge of going-private transactions. It is also developing an active hedge funds practice.

The Lawyers: Michael Boone is *"a great business developer,"* who understands how to bring deals to completion. An *"outstanding strategic adviser"* and cofounder of the firm, he is known for his *"tremendous work ethic."*

The Clients: Bank of America Securities; Bellwether Exploration; Kennerly Capital; Pasco Acquisition Holdings; Peerless Group; RadioShack; SunTrust Equitable Securities; Trilogy Software; Trinity Industries and United Rentals.

Band 4

Hughes & Luce LLP

The Firm: A well-respected firm packed with *"high-quality lawyers,"* Hughes & Luce is an established stable regional group offering corporate finance, M&A, securities and capital markets expertise. It represented a client in a high-value stock and cash acquisition of its primary competitor to form the largest company in its industry. The 31-strong team is particularly involved in advising clients in the healthcare and technology and Internet industries. It counseled a NASDAQ company in over $1 billion of Internet media acquisitions.

The Lawyers: William McCormack has extensive M&A expertise representing a broad range of clients. According to interviewees, his real strength lies with his *"strong negotiating skills."*

The Clients: The group advises public and privately held companies and shareholders. It has a long-standing relationship with Dean Foods, advising the company on transactions totaling over $10 billion.

King & Spalding LLP

See firm details p.635

The Firm: Although the group has this year been forced to weather the departure of Christine LaFollette to Akin Gump, it nonetheless retains key clients and a respected international and domestic M&A practice in Texas. The group's Latin American practice stands out in this market, having advised Home Depot in its acquisition of a Mexican home improvement retailer and acting as outside counsel to UPS in its general Latin American corporate matters. The firm has also represented Friedman, Billings, Ramsey in pending IPOs by Northstar Realty Finance and Feldman Mall Properties.

The Lawyers: Carlos Treistman is a key contact in the market.

The Clients: An impressive client roster includes: BHP Billiton; UPS; Home Depot; GE; Dow Chemical; Key Energy Services and Friedman, Billings, Ramsey.

EMPLOYMENT

MAINLY DEFENDANT

Texas
Leading firms
(Employment: Mainly Defendant)

[1]	**BAKER BOTTS LLP** *Dallas, Houston*
	VINSON & ELKINS LLP *Houston*
[2]	**AKIN GUMP STRAUSS HAUER** *Dallas, Houston*
	FULBRIGHT & JAWORSKI LLP *Austin, San Antonio*
	OGLETREE, DEAKINS, NASH *Austin, Houston*
[3]	**BRACEWELL & GIULIANI** *Houston, San Antonio*
	HAYNES AND BOONE LLP *Dallas*
	JENKENS & GILCHRIST PC *Dallas*
	LITTLER MENDELSON PC *Dallas, Houston*
[4]	**BAKER & HOSTETLER LLP** *Houston*
	JONES DAY *Dallas*
	KEMP SMITH LLP *El Paso*
	LOCKE LIDDELL & SAPP LLP *Dallas*
	NEEL & HOOPER, PC *Houston*

Firms are listed alphabetically in each band.

Band 1

Baker Botts LLP

See firm details p.1708

The Firm: This 30-strong national team can boast a glittering array of blue-chip clients, and a hiring policy that is widely acknowledged for developing *"dynamic, loyal and very well-rounded practitioners."* Peers agreed that this group is *"not afraid to tackle any case,"* and that *"if you pick up something they have done, it is always very persuasive."* Clients praised the firm as a *"reassuring presence"* in large class action matters where more than 2000 employees are involved. Though the team has the depth of resources to handle even the thorniest of cases, its policy focuses on litigation avoidance through periodical training and counseling, and advising on corporate actions such as separations. However, the department was successful in a number of contentious FLSA overtime collective actions recently. The group remains visible in traditional labor matters, and the Dallas office has been particularly busy in defeating several union-organizing attempts in the past 12 months.

The Lawyers: *"Keystone"* of the practice **Richard Brann** (see p.1673) has *"an encyclopedic knowledge"* of employment law, according to peers, as a result of more than 30 years' experience. An *"unassuming, unflappable"* presence, Brann has *"been there, done that, bought the t-shirt"* in his representation of employers in disputes with employees and unions. Recent work includes defeating a class certification in a race discrimination class action brought against Marathon Oil. A *"fine strategist and analyst,"* observers commend his abilities in *"setting the highest ethical standards."* **Tony Rosenstein's** (see p.1699) scientific background ensures that he is the *"top guy on evidentiary issues"* particularly in systemic class matters. He has carved a niche in the handling of expert witnesses and statistical analysis. Considered an expert on ERISA matters, Rosenstein defeated a claim by employees of third parties and independent contractors that they should be considered employees of ExxonMobil, and thus be eligible for company benefits. Litigation specialist **Teresa Valderrama** (see p.1704) earned peer praise for her *"masterful handling"* of some complex cases. For example, she successfully counseled Continental Airlines in a dispute with the International Teamsters over the enforceability of a labor arbitration award. Dallas-based **Dan Hartsfield's** (see p.1683) practice focuses on traditional labor work. He is highly experienced in hearings before the NLRB, EEOC, DOL, OFCCP, and other state and federal agencies, and is regularly instructed by clients to help combat union-organizing drives, labor contract negotiations, unfair labor practice cases and arbitrations. The *"assertive"* **Cristina Rodriguez** (see p.1699) makes her debut in the tables on the back of outstanding praise for her *"great writing, great research, effective cross-examination and swift thinking on her feet."*

The Clients: ExxonMobil; Goodyear; Sonic Automotive; Marathon Oil; Hines Interests and Omega Protein.

Vinson & Elkins LLP

See firm details p.1724

The Firm: A *"very fine law firm all round,"* some commentators opined that the employment department *"might well be the jewel in the crown."* The firm has developed a reputation for dealing with sophisticated matters such as EOC investigations, systemic discrimination matters

Texas

Leading individuals

(Employment: Mainly Defendant)

1 BRANN Richard *Baker Botts*, Houston
GREIG Brian *Fulbright & Jaworski*, Austin
HAMEL Douglas *Vinson & Elkins*, Houston
JORDAN Carl *Vinson & Elkins*, Houston
LONDA Jeffrey *Ogletree Deakins*, Houston
MELO Thomas *Ogletree Deakins*, Houston
SHEEDER Robert *Jenkens & Gilchrist*, Dallas

2 FRANZE Laura *Akin Gump*, Dallas
HARPER A J *Fulbright & Jaworski*, Houston
HEADLEY Linda *Little Mendelson*, Dallas
HIGH Charles *Kemp Smith*, El Paso
JANSONIUS John *Akin Gump*, Dallas
MASLANKA Michael *Ford & Harrison*, Dallas
MCCOWN Steven *Littler Mendelson*, Dallas
PFEIFFER Philip *Fulbright & Jaworski*, San Antonio
ROSENSTEIN Tony *Baker Botts*, Houston
STROCK William *Haynes and Boone*, Dallas

3 BARNES Hershell *The Barnes Law Firm*, Dallas
FOX Michael *Ogletree Deakins*, Austin
FRIEDMAN Edward *Locke Liddell*, Houston
HALEVY Amy *Bracewell & Giuliani*, Houston
HARTSFIELD Dan *Baker Botts*, Dallas
HOOPER Samuel *Neel & Hooper*, Houston
MANTHEY Ron *Baker & McKenzie*, Dallas
MCALPINE Fraser *Akin Gump*, Houston
MCDONALD Scott *Littler Mendelson*, Dallas
MCNAMARA Lawrence *Locke Liddell*, Dallas
MEYER Theodore *Jones Day*, Houston
NEEL James *Neel & Hooper*, Houston
PATERSON Nancy *Baker & Hostetler*, Houston
SHANK Mark *Hughes & Luce*, Dallas
VALDERRAMA Teresa *Baker Botts*, Houston
WILLIAMSON Holly *Akin Gump*, Houston

Up-and-coming individuals

CROW Carter *Fulbright & Jaworski*, Houston
O'DONNELL Laura *Haynes and Boone*, San Antonio
RODRIGUEZ Cristina *Baker Botts*, Houston

Individuals are listed alphabetically in each band.

and class actions. FLSA claims, whistle-blower protection work and corporate governance concerns raised by Sarbanes-Oxley legislation have kept the team of 25 particularly busy recently, and helped them retain their place at the head of the market. A niche area for the firm is counseling Fortune 100 companies and financial institutions on sensitive and high-profile issues such as the termination of executive contracts. **The Lawyers:** The *"playmaker"* of the team **Carl Jordan** (see p.1686) is well recognized by commentators as a *"prominent figure"* in the legal community. With the benefit of more than 20 years' experience, clients expressed *"absolute confidence"* in his skills, and he was notably one of the first practitioners to become involved in litigation arising out of the Sarbanes-Oxley act. Jordan has also handled several whistle-blower cases, discrimination cases, a large class action

concerning pay practices and the development of mandatory arbitration procedures. Clients reported that **Doug Hamel** (see p.1682) is a *"high energy"* practitioner whose *"cutting-edge"* practice and robust grasp of new developments allows him to handle class-based discrimination matters adroitly. His representation of the Houston Symphony in sensitive negotiations with the American Federation of Musicians over wage concessions was successfully concluded and created a buzz in the legal community. Other clients include businesses in the beef and pork processing industries, the Hovensa oil refinery facility in the US Virgin Islands and the US Capitol Police. **The Clients:** Notable among the firm's impressive clients are Halliburton, JPMorgan Chase and Shell.

Band 2

Akin Gump Strauss Hauer & Feld LLP

See firm details p.477

The Firm: The employment team offers all that clients would expect from an internationally renowned firm. It can boast significant depth in its offices in Houston, Dallas and San Antonio, considerable experience in handling complex matters both in and out of court, and an efficient network of offices beyond Texas that ensures the repeat business of multinational companies. Nor is the size of the department static: the market perceived the acquisition of Littler Mendelson partners in 2003 to have been *"a smart move."* Of late, the firm's time has been devoted to retaliation litigation, internal investigations concerning the recording of injuries and a large volume of work for the construction sector. ERISA cases on the determination of an acquisition as a merger to settle severance issues, wage and hour class actions also feature significantly in the workload.

The Lawyers: *"Superwoman"* **Laura Franze** (see p.1680) is a *"dynamic"* employment litigator, peers say. Blessed with *"a good manner, proven trial skills, broad-ranging knowledge and intellectual depth,"* clients agree she is an excellent deal manager. Head of the Dallas team and recognized national expert on ADA matters, Franze has vast experience in representing movie theaters and technology companies. According to interviewees, the current chair of the labor and employment section of the state bar **John Jansonius** (see p.1685) is *"a mine of information."* Jansonius handles a significant number of NLRA and ERISA-related cases, and his collective action practice has recently seen him embroiled in a dispute over benefits following the closure of an electronic component plant in Dallas. The *"dynamic duo"* of **Fraser McAlpine** (see p.1690) and **Holly Williamson** (see p.1706) also enjoyed a successful year. Regarded as *"a great addition"* to the firm,

McAlpine *"always delivers the goods."* He has recently been active in Kentucky, Louisiana, Dakota, Chicago and New York, and his forte is in handling complex cases involving benefits and executive compensation. He was also successful in two protracted ERISA trials, with a further victory in a dispute over the existence of an employment contract. Clients were eager to praise McAlpine's advising and drafting skills. The *"tough and tenacious"* Williamson was also involved in two significant trials in the past year, relating to equal pay and sexual abuse disputes. **The Clients:** Cinemark USA; Regal Entertainment; Automotive Investment Group; Fujitsu Network Transmission Systems; Pier 1 Imports and AT&T.

Fulbright & Jaworski LLP

See firm details p.1715

The Firm: The practice is now more than 80 years old, and labor law has been a key component of its repertoire throughout the firm. The current team of 25 lawyers operates out of four Texas offices, and its bench strength enables it to address the full spectrum of labor and employment mandates. The Austin unit, for example, handles a large volume of work for technology companies including both trade secrets and noncompetition covenants, and works closely with a respected IP team highly experienced in field-specific science matters. Defamation cases, affirmative action plans, FLSA class action work, employment torts and severance pay claims generated by mergers in the oil industry supplement a steady stream of discrimination cases.

The Lawyers: **Brian Greig**'s (see p.1682) *"mature judgment"* has benefited clients for more than 20 years and, according to interviewees, his work in Austin *"put the practice on the map."* As well as counseling clients on union-organizing activities, Greig advises on termination decisions, and the creation and review of employment policies. He also enjoys a strong reputation as a litigator in trade secrets theft cases and in NLRB matters, and was recently successful in defending a client against a labor union that had failed in an organizing attempt. **John Harper** (see p.1683) *"has a wealth of information at his fingertips, but is always prepared to do his homework,"* researchers were told. Clients applauded his *"calmness in the face of chaos,"* while competitors acknowledged that he is *"as good as it gets."* Harper's practice focuses on union-related matters and working in tandem with his corporate partners with due diligence on union contracts and employee options. Recent trials in which Harper has been involved include an FMLA-related matter and a major defamation case brought by a former employee against a medical school. The *"charismatic"* **Philip Pfeiffer** (see p.1696) is a *"vigorous problem solver"* who has *"a solid understanding of what works in the real world,"* say clients. A speaker who can *"light up the room,"*

Pfeiffer acts on all aspects of employment law, with an emphasis on complex civil rights and discrimination claims, and he is also experienced in both mediation and arbitration proceedings. **Carter Crow** (see p.1676) joins the tables on the back of consistent praise for his growing practice. *"Always well-received by juries,"* Crow advises on executive contract and compensation disputes, retaliation and discrimination claims, and corporate governance matters; and he has in-depth knowledge of trade secrets matters.
The Clients: The team represents a number of Fortune 500 companies.

Ogletree, Deakins, Nash, Smoak & Stewart, PC

See firm details p.638
The Firm: The third largest employment firm in the country boasts a team of 39 Texas lawyers and a reputation for being *"consistently on par with the very best firms in the country."* Moreover, its active growth strategy *"continues to create a buzz in the legal community,"* according to sources. The firm is active in many traditional labor law contexts, particularly in countering union-organizing efforts, union salting and unfair labor practice cases. The bulk of the firm's caseload, however, derives from employment law engagements, and the team addresses the full range of federal and state employment, EEOC, federal discrimination, ERISA, wage and hour, and OSHA cases throughout the country. The team has lately been advising several public transit authorities regarding labor and bonus agreements. The group recently displayed its litigation prowess with a precedent-setting victory in Pressley v Sanderson Farms; a class action case in which the claimants sought compensation under the FLSA for time spent donning and doffing safety clothing and equipment.
The Lawyers: The practice of *"fantastic negotiator"* **Jeff Londa** (see p.1689) mirrors the firm's equal focus on both labor and employment concerns. He has advised the Metropolitan Transit Authority since its foundation in 1978, and recently worked on the first labor agreement in the transit industry to contain a two-tier wage structure and performance-based bonuses. Channeling his *"innately competitive streak,"* Londa's style is to *"go for the jugular"* when litigating employment matters. He played a key role in the Sanderson case highlighted previously, and he also successfully represented The Diamond Group in a union arbitration contesting the discharge of 19 security guards at NASA. The acquisition of the *"relaxed and reassuringly calm"* **Tom Melo** (see p.1692) from Bracewell & Giuliani *"brings extra luster to the Houston office,"* say peers. A perfect foil for the *"aggressive"* Londa, Melo *"knows his case law inside out."* His practice as a top-level counselor and litigator incorporates advising management on matters varying from reductions in force to senior executive termina-

tions. **Michael Fox** (see p.1679) *"has a knack of identifying the points in the case to focus on,"* according to clients, who identified him as a *"great trial lawyer."* He was recently instrumental in securing a favorable jury verdict in a federal court in Amarillo on behalf of Allsup's Convenience Stores in a major FLSA case, which also involved age and race discrimination issues.
The Clients: Metropolitan Transit Authority; ARAMARK; American Habilitation Services; Eastman Chemical; Duke Energy; Chubb Group; TurboCare and BancTec.

Band 3

Bracewell & Giuliani LLP

See firm details p.1710
The Firm: The firm's diverse public and private sector clientele exposes the team to organizations in the chemical, energy, financial services, food, healthcare and technology sectors, as well as schools and districts. Clients were suitably swift to note that the team was *"able quickly to understand their business drivers and culture."* The group does have some niche strengths: its strong client base in the railroad, airline and related transportation sectors has generated a wealth of knowledge in compliance and litigation under the Railway Labor Act. Notable successes of late included several motions for summary judgment for Levi Strauss in cases involving claims of workers' compensation retaliation.
The Lawyers: Chair of the labor and employment department **Amy Halevy** (see p.1682) apportions her time between counseling clients on matters such as sexual harassment policies and litigating before the courts and administrative agencies, including the EOC and the Texas Commission on Human Rights. Clients appreciated the national scope of her work and ability to grasp the intricacies of corporate culture, as much as her academic expertise.
The Clients: SYSCO Corporation; Adventist Health Systems; San Antonio Spurs; Levi Strauss and Southwest Airlines.

Haynes and Boone LLP

The Firm: Commentators consistently described the team of 26 attorneys as *"good across the board,"* and highlighted *"a talented core of associates"* working alongside the established partners. Widely regarded as one of the largest remaining traditional labor practices, the team successfully defeated eight union-organizing campaigns across the USA in the past year. Equally well versed in the range of employment matters, the team was recently engaged to defend a failure to promote, retaliation and termination claim brought by the CEO of a leading communications company.
The Lawyers: The *"outstanding"* **William Strock** maintains his exceptional reputation among peers. He has guided clients through class action discrimination cases for 30 years, and

maintains an active litigation practice that focuses upon wage and hour and promotion discrimination claims. His reputation in traditional labor law ensures that he is also heavily involved in corporate restructurings, either in preparation for affirmative action audits or in the acquisition or disposal of unionized companies. **Laura O'Donnell** already has *"the total package"* despite her relative youth, according to interviewees. Focusing on employment litigation, her *"super-organized approach"* has impressed peers, clients and courts alike in sexual harassment, restrictive covenant and workers' compensation retaliation claims.
The Clients: Hanson Building Materials; America Dynegy; Bank of America and American Airlines.

Jenkens & Gilchrist PC

The Firm: Though smaller in size than some of its immediate competitors, this Dallas-based group retains the resources to represent management in every aspect of employment law. The team is active in employment counseling and litigation, and an eight-strong unit providing guidance on benefits and ERISA-related matters supplements its capabilities in union-related engagements. The team's respected litigators have experienced the statewide increase in discrimination class actions, promotion denial and harassment suits, while other attorneys have been busy with the labor and employment-related aspects of corporate transactions, especially workforce reductions. The group recently reported a victory before the NLRB in Dallas on a unit clarification issue following the relocation of a manufacturing facility.
The Lawyers: Clients stated **Bob Sheeder** is *"hands down the go-to labor and employment guy in town."* Equipped with an *"extremely deep knowledge of the law"* he also *"understands the real world application of the law, over and above textbook answers."* Researchers were also told that Sheeder conveys *"considerable appeal to both judges and jurors."* He recently defended Towers Perrin before the Fifth Circuit Court of Appeals in Milofsky v American Airlines, a class action concerning fiduciary duties relating to the transfer of an airline pilots' retirement fund.
The Clients: MCI; Vought Aircraft Industries; PwC; Belo and CompuCom Systems.

Littler Mendelson PC

The Firm: This truly national labor and employment firm operates out of offices in both Dallas and Houston, and benefits from a network of almost 30 offices throughout the country. Despite departures to both Baker & McKenzie and Akin Gump in recent times, almost 40 attorneys remain in Texas, offering comprehensive advice on everything from employment discrimination to union avoidance and elections.

The Lawyers: Managing partner of the Houston office **Linda Headley** enjoys a reputation as "*a dependable, safe pair of hands,*" with an approach to litigation and counseling that is "*tenacious without being offensive.*" Although frequently mandated by clients with union activity concerns, it is the rapport Headley has developed with clients on discrimination, harassment and workplace privacy issues that earned her the most attention. "*What* **Steven McCown** *doesn't know about OSHA isn't worth knowing,*" claimed suitably impressed commentators, keen to impress upon researchers McCown's "*national reputation for excellence*" on safety legislation. McCown's practice also incorporates traditional labor law work and he has significant experience in handling discrimination class actions. Also in Dallas, the "*extremely well-spoken*" **Scott McDonald** is "*outstanding in noncompete cases.*" His dedication to counseling and litigation on employment contracts, wrongful termination and unfair competition cases has earned him the respect of companies in the manufacturing, leisure, real estate and transportation sectors, among others.
The Clients: Clients come from a broad spread of industry sectors.

Band 4

Baker & Hostetler LLP

The Firm: The Houston-based team within this national firm predominantly advises clients in the energy sector, though its growing reputation in employment cases has also turned heads in the telecom, healthcare and transportation arenas. Its willingness to tackle virtually any employment-related matter and well-publicized run of success in discrimination class actions have put the team on the national map, researchers were told.
The Lawyers: Interviewees agreed that **Nancy Paterson** is "*a force to be reckoned with*" in employment litigation matters. Undertaking "*high-profile*" trade secrets, discrimination and ERISA cases, Paterson has also achieved distinction in the class action field where her "*tough but pleasant*" demeanor plays well to the courts.
The Clients: Bayer; Case Credit; ChevronTexaco; Fisher Scientific; Hitachi Construction Machinery and Shell.

Jones Day

See firm details p.485
The Firm: Interviewees agreed that the 15-strong team benefits from its full-service global network in terms of both kudos and depth of resources, in employment and related practice areas. Key strengths include assisting in the resolution of disputes surrounding alleged discrimination, safety standards and wrongful discharge, and the team is often called upon to conduct internal investigations and offer management counseling. Commentators reported that the Dallas team, in particular, is exerting a

growing influence in the complex work in the state.
The Lawyers: The recent acquisition of the highly regarded **Ted Meyer** (see p.1692) further enhances the reputation of the Houston office. Formerly with Seyfarth Shaw, Meyer's clients benefit from his considerable experience of multistate cases. He has advised in numerous post-Enron corporate governance matters, and also demonstrated his well-honed trial abilities recently in the resounding defeat of an ERISA claim.
The Clients: The firm represents clients of all shapes and sizes, including several Fortune 500 entities, and a number of significant players in the technology and construction sectors.

Kemp Smith LLP

The Firm: According to some sources, this "*rich practice puts other firms in the shade.*" Generally considered the best firm in the west of Texas, the team of six attorneys handles the full range of employment matters. Well-versed in addressing the concerns of both public and private entities, the team is also experienced in labor relations and provides counseling on employee benefits.
The Lawyers: "*Outstanding*" trial lawyer **Charlie High** combines his deep experience with "*great enthusiasm*" to maintain his preeminent status within the west of Texas. Clients expressed particular admiration for his ability to "*boil down legalistic issues and concentrate on the facts.*" His 30 years in practice has honed his expertise in matters before the OSHA and ADA, and all issues ranging from union contract negotiations to wage and hour issues.
The Clients: IMC Potash Carlsbad; 3M; The Toro Company; Border Steel; dmDickason Personnel Services; Western Refining and Pizza Properties.

Locke Liddell & Sapp LLP

The Firm: In addition to its recognized aptitude for the cut and thrust of union relations work, commentators viewed this team as "*a tour de force*" in employment litigation. Interviewees described the team of 20 attorneys, based out of Dallas and Houston, as "*among the very best in unfair competition matters.*" Notable recent successes include ERISA and employment contract litigation cases. The group recorded a particularly significant victory in the latter area before the Texas Supreme Court in preventing claims for emotional distress from being combined with discrimination and harassment claims.
The Lawyers: **Edward Friedman** (see p.1680) enters the tables on the back of praise as a lawyer who "*handles the pressure cooker of litigation extremely well.*" Friedman has built a national practice specializing in the resolution of noncompete and nondisclosure claims. His expertise has attracted an enviable client base that includes Guidant. Commentators endorsed **Lawrence McNamara** (see p.1691) as "*one of the most intelligent management labor lawyers in*

Texas." Primarily a litigator of discrimination and employment torts, his "*extremely focused*" practice advises clients such as Greyhound Lines on union arbitration matters.
The Clients: Neopost; Goodrich; Greyhound Lines; Sally Beauty; Mary Kay; Microsoft; Vetco Gray; Disney; Acme Brick; Wyndham International; Southern Methodist University; Capital One; Guidant; Ernst & Young and ABB Lummus Global.

Neel & Hooper, PC

See firm details p.1721
The Firm: This labor and employment boutique has provided specialist advice to construction, energy, retail and leisure entities for more than 30 years. Described as offering clients capabilities that "*amount to more than the sum of its parts,*" the five-strong team traditionally enjoys a strong reputation in the collective bargaining and NLRB sphere. Recently, however, employment matters especially noncompete clauses, wage and hour laws and retaliation claims, have tended to account for the bulk of its caseload.
The Lawyers: **Sam Hooper** (see p.1684) and **James Neel** (see p.1693) won the respect of peers for their ability to keep clients away from the courthouse using their skills in management counseling, and for their subsequent successes when matters proceed to litigation. Another busy year has seen Hooper involved in the investigation of several Sarbanes-Oxley issues, and Neel traveling the country to participate in union contract negotiations at ten plants for one of his clients.
The Clients: Amco Insurance; Houston Hotel and Motel Association; Kinko's Graphics and Texas Petrochemicals.

Other Notable Practitioners

Michael Maslanka (see p.1690), formerly of Godwin Gruber, recently opened the Dallas office of Ford & Harrison LLP. Also a widely respected columnist in the Texas Lawyer, Maslanka was instrumental in the decertification of a Mississippi union that had been in place for more than 30 years, and in defeating a national origin claim. His "*analytical and academic*" technique has been notably successful in keeping clients, especially national hotel chains, ahead of changes within the FLSA. The "*extremely effective*" **Hershell Barnes** of The Barnes Law Firm PC joins the tables following strong recommendation for his long-standing traditional labor practice. Applying "*excellent lateral thinking skills*" to union campaigns and bargaining, Barnes is said to "*field questions with aplomb.*" **Ron Manthey** (see p.1689) was another lawyer on the move in 2004. Recruited by Baker & McKenzie to head their Dallas office, his "*great analytical skills*" are complemented by a "*tenacious and tireless*" effort on behalf of clients in complex class action litigation. His success in recent FLSA cases can be attributed to a "*killer instinct in cross-examination.*" At trial recently he vindicated American Airlines in a race harassment case in Fort Worth, and obtained a zero damages award in a jury trial for BHP Billiton Investment Corp (Americas) in an age case in Houston. **Mark Shank**, described as the "*main playmaker*" of Dallas firm Hughes and Luce LLP, acts for an array of clients in the telecom and technology sectors. Highly experienced in all areas of employment litigation, Shank currently serves as legal counsel to US congressman Pete Sessions.

ENERGY & NATURAL RESOURCES

Texas
Leading firms
(Energy & Natural Resources)

1. VINSON & ELKINS LLP *Houston*
2. BAKER BOTTS LLP *Houston*
   FULBRIGHT & JAWORSKI LLP *Houston*
3. AKIN GUMP STRAUSS HAUER & FELD *Houston*
   KING & SPALDING LLP *Houston*
4. ANDREWS KURTH LLP *Houston*
   BRACEWELL & GIULIANI LLP *Houston*
   SKADDEN, ARPS, SLATE, MEAGHER *Houston*
5. LOCKE LIDDELL & SAPP LLP *Dallas*
   THOMPSON & KNIGHT LLP *Dallas*

Leading individuals
(Energy & Natural Resources)

★ DILG Joseph *Vinson & Elkins*, Houston
1. ASMUS David *Baker Botts*, Houston
   BILGER Bruce *Vinson & Elkins*, Houston
   COGAN John *Akin Gump*, Houston
2. ALE John *Skadden Arps*, Houston
   CULOTTA Ken *King & Spalding*, Houston
   GOOLSBY George *Baker Botts*, Houston
   KUTZSCHBACH George *Fulbright & Jaworski*, Houston
   WEEMS Philip *King & Spalding*, Houston
3. KELLEY Jay *Vinson & Elkins*, Houston
   TAYLOR Lyndon *Skadden Arps*, Houston
   UNGER Timothy *Andrews Kurth*, Houston
4. BACKUS Marcia *Vinson & Elkins*, Houston
   BLAND Douglas *Vinson & Elkins*, Houston
   GITOMER Deborah *Fulbright & Jaworski*, Houston
   GREMILLION L Todd *Akin Gump*, Houston
   IRVIN Michael *Fulbright & Jaworski*, Houston
   LANGLOIS Jack *Akin Gump*, Houston
   RAFTE Alan *Bracewell & Giuliani*, Houston
   THURBER Mark *Andrews Kurth*, Houston
5. CUCLIS James *Vinson & Elkins*, Houston
   DARDEN Michael *Baker Botts*, Houston
   MOORE Thomas *LeBoeuf Lamb*, Houston
   PATTON David *Locke Liddell*, Houston
   ROGERS Daniel *Chadbourne & Parke*, Houston
   THOMPSON Dahl *Andrews Kurth*, Houston

Up-and-coming individuals
STEPHENS Robert *Bracewell & Giuliani*, Houston

Firms and individuals are listed alphabetically in each band.

Band 1

Vinson & Elkins LLP
See firm details p.1724
The Firm: Vinson & Elkins retains its stand-alone position at the top of the table this year following a wealth of plaudits from impressed clients and because of the sheer diversity of the practice. Clients say it is "*without doubt the number one choice*" partly because it is a worldwide energy firm with global reach, and partly because it has "*excellent deal lawyers who know the business.*" The firm has such wide and deep experience in the energy sector that it can bring a level of expertise and creativity that is difficult to surpass. The case history speaks for itself, but clients add that they "*like working with the lawyers because they are practical and result-oriented and will just make sure that the deal gets done.*" The firm was hit by the bankruptcy of key client Enron a few years ago, but has weathered the storm well and bounced back with an increasingly diversified client base. To illustrate its continued prominence in the power sector, the firm recently advised a private equity group on the $3.6 billion acquisition of the Texas Genco assets, and also represented Entergy-Koch in the sale of its energy trading company. Its oil and gas deals are equally impressive. For example, it acted for Enterprise Products in its high-profile $14 billion merger with GulfTerra. This highlights the firm's role as the "*MLP gurus*" of the energy industry, as this merger created the second largest MLP in the sector. It also has acknowledged expertise in the robust LNG sector where it handles all BG's US work, including the procurement of LNG from Trinidad and Equatorial Guinea.
The Lawyers: Joe Dilg (see p.1677) is the firm's managing partner and "*one of the most senior practitioners around.*" He continues to advise several clients on strategic decisions. **Bruce Bilger** (see p.1672) has been keeping himself occupied with high-end M&A deals. Clients say he is "*dynamite – very sharp and resourceful;*" while peers feel "*he's the transactional lawyer with the best reputation in town.*" **Jay Kelley** (see p.1686) is heavily involved in the burgeoning LNG industry and clients report that he is a "*thorough and conscientious*" attorney who understands the complex structures of the LNG industry inside out. **Marcia Backus** (see p.1670) is one of the firm's leading M&A lawyers. Sources describe her as "*a tiger in negotiations,*" saying "*she knows how to be ruthless when she needs to be.*" **Douglas Bland** (see p.1672) is a general transactional lawyer who is very hands on and provides "*a thorough analysis and good problem-solving skills.*" **James Cuclis** (see p.1676) leads the international side of the practice. Clients enthused: "*He's a great lawyer but also has a businessman's mind and understands the commercial concerns we have.*"

The Clients: While Vinson & Elkins has historically been more prolific representing the energy companies, it has recently also seen an uptake of representation on the lender side. Representative clients include: Enterprise; The Blackstone Group; Entergy-Koch; Reliant; BG Group; Chevron Phillips Chemical; JPMorgan Chase; WestLB; AES; PSEG Global; Bank of Nova Scotia; Bonus Energy; AIG; El Paso and Shell Oil.

Band 2

Baker Botts LLP
See firm details p.1708
The Firm: For decades major energy companies have placed Baker Botts at the top of their list of go-to firms, and the group is rated as second to none for upstream work. Clients are impressed with "*the depth and bench strength*" of the energy practice and report that the lawyers are "*well educated, professional and highly competent.*" Clients also focused on the firm's management skills, stating that it is "*efficient, doesn't over-lawyer, and manages the work well.*" Brand name oil and gas companies turn to the firm for mergers and divestitures: for example, it recently represented BP in the disposition of its North American assets. It also assists US companies on sales abroad and is currently assisting a bidder in a $1 billion sale in South America. A powerful profile in upstream work has seen the firm channel much of this expertise into the LNG industry. It is currently working on two major LNG production facilities in Equatorial Guinea and Peru. Baker Botts also works on a number of financing transactions in the upstream sector, mainly for rigs and offshore vessels.
The Lawyers: **David Asmus** (see p.1670) is a clear market leader for upstream work. He is "*hard working, careful and meticulous*" and has "*a very deep knowledge base*" in the sector. **George Goolsby** (see p.1681) has a huge reputation as a pipeline lawyer as he has been involved in the Caspian Sea pipelines since the early pioneering days. Clients say he is "*very pragmatic and has good common sense,*" and they also rate his people skills. **Michael Darden** (see p.1676) has been working on some high-profile divestitures for Anadarko and is "*a very bright and aggressive attorney,*" who knows how to bring a deal to its conclusion.
The Clients: The firm mainly works for the oil majors. Representative clients include: BP; ExxonMobil; Marathon; ConocoPhillips and Anadarko.

Fulbright & Jaworski LLP

See firm details p.1715

The Firm: The firm has developed a general oil and gas practice that covers a wide range of work, but it is particularly noted as the home to "*some of the best oil and gas lawyers for upstream leases, exploration and development in the state.*" This year, it has been particularly focused on pipeline transactions. It has represented Enbridge in several bids for pipeline systems, including the $663 million acquisition of Shell's deepwater Gulf of Mexico pipeline systems. On the other side of the table, it has been acting for Anadarko in a $2.5 billion divestiture of various upstream oil and gas assets. Attorneys here also have considerable deepwater exploration experience and are currently working on the formation of a new deepwater exploration company. The firm also has an interesting downstream caseload, and has been advising Crown Central Petroleum on the divestiture of its crude oil refining and marketing business. These attorneys score well with clients because they are so user friendly and business minded. As one client put it: "*They remember that we look for oil and gas, not practice law; so they stay focused on our business aim and help us in avoiding litigation and extensive negotiation where possible.*"
The Lawyers: **George Kutzschbach** (see p.1688) is a leading name in oil and gas drilling and exploration contracts. Clients report that he is "*cost effective because he stays focused on the main issues*" and also praise him as "*an outstanding drafter of contracts.*" Recently **Deborah Gitomer** (see p.1681) has concentrated on the upstream and midstream pipeline transactions. Clients say she is "*technically superior to other M&A lawyers.*" They point to her "*effective negotiating strategies and extreme attention to detail*" and her "*willingness to work 24/7 when required.*" **Michael Irvin** (see p.1685) has a general energy transactional background. Clients enjoy working with him because he is "*bright, responsive and very experienced in multimillion-dollar transactions.*"
The Clients: Enbridge; Anadarko; BG; Blackstone Capital Partners; AEP; Calpine; Magnum Hunter Resources; Crown Central Petroleum; PetroCanada; El Paso; Sempra Energy Trading; Total SA; Forest Oil; Cabot Oil & Gas; EOG Resources and TEPPCO Partners.

Band 3

Akin Gump Strauss Hauer & Feld LLP

See firm details p.477

The Firm: This firm has a very strong international energy practice, which is currently working on projects in the Middle East, Russia, Latin America, Asia, the Caribbean and Africa. It is particularly focused on Russia and has been involved in some high-profile and interesting transactions in the region. The clear stand-out

deal here is LUKOIL's $2 billion merger with ConocoPhillips, and their joint venture to develop Russia's Timan-Pechora oil fields and the West Qurna oil field in Iraq. Following a year of intensive recruitment, the firm has also considerably built up its LNG and marine capability. Illustrative of its success is the firm's role as counsel to the Qatargas project company on all marine transportation elements. It is also an expert on floating production systems and is currently developing one in Malaysia. According to sources, this successful firm has certainly cemented its "*long-standing reputation with the upper tiers of the oil industry.*"
The Lawyers: The addition from King & Spalding of **John Cogan** (see p.1675), who is "*probably the leading lawyer in the LNG sector*", has been a huge bonus for the firm. He has "*loads of international experience and can easily handle complex deals*" and peers also comment that he is "*phenomenally bright.*" He is particularly well versed in the marine elements of the oil and gas industry. **Todd Gremillion** (see p.1682) is a "*smart and sophisticated*" energy lawyer, who operates on an international playing field. "*He stays fully up to date on different structures related to oil and gas transactions,*" reported clients. Respected **Jack Langlois** (see p.1688) successfully displayed his skill in negotiating large transactions this year as lead attorney in the massive LUKOIL deal
The Clients: ExxonMobil; Murphy Oil; FirstEnergy; PetroAlliance Services; UPS; Gaz Naturel; Burlington Resources; Anadarko; Baker Hughes; GulfTerra and Vanco Energy.

King & Spalding LLP

See firm details p.635

The Firm: Despite losing its star LNG lawyer this year, King & Spalding continues to impress as one of the leading firms for LNG work. It stands out because it has expertise in every facet of this industry. Firstly, it has experience with many production facilities abroad, including working on construction issues and offtake agreements for the Trinidad LNG project. Secondly, it also has experience in shipping LNG, and is currently advising ConocoPhillips on a fleet to transport LNG from Qatar to the USA. Finally, it is working on a substantial number of LNG receiving terminals in the USA. For example, as counsel to the Freeport LNG terminal, it negotiated all the necessary construction permits and is negotiating with multiple customers.
The Lawyers: **Ken Culotta** (see p.1676) has broad international expertise and has gradually come to specialize in energy transactions. Clients appreciate that "*he really gets to know your business and can offer customized advice.*" **Philip Weems** (see p.1705) has a wealth of experience in LNG and clients also comment that he "*really understands the in-house mentality and is a joy to work with.*"

The Clients: El Paso; Calhoun LNG; Woodside Energy; Freeport LNG; Dow Chemical; ChevronTexaco; Cheniere; Gulf LNG; BHP Billiton; ConocoPhillips; Anadarko and Point Fortin LNG Exports.

Band 4

Andrews Kurth LLP

See firm details p.1707

The Firm: Following the slowdown in the power sector, Andrews Kurth has spent the last year concentrating on oil and gas and alternative energy deals. The firm has established a key role for itself in the LNG sector and represents Cheniere in the development of domestic receiving terminals. It is working on a number of acquisitions and divestitures of oil and gas properties, and has also advised banks in pipeline and processing facilities deals. Its oil and gas capability stretches to international transactions, and the firm has been engaged on upstream projects in China. The practice has an impressive wind energy resumé, which is noteworthy for a Houston firm, and in the last year has worked on the development of three wind farms. Observers commend the firm as home to a collection of "*impressive and talented*" lawyers, whose technical understanding of the law is matched by their commercial awareness.
The Lawyers: **Tim Unger** (see p.1704) leads the team; he is a highly experienced lawyer with "*a great reputation for knowing how to get a deal done.*" His practice encompasses cogeneration and IPP matters, and, while much of his very recent practice has been domestic in its focus, he remains widely respected for his Latin American expertise. Both **Mark Thurber** (see p.1703) and **Dahl Thompson** (see p.1703) were endorsed as "*bright lawyers who attract innovative deals.*" Thurber is well versed in upstream oil and gas issues as well as project finance and related corporate M&A, while Thompson has devoted a healthy portion of his practice to LNG issues and, recently, advising on a power project in Oklahoma.
The Clients: Cheniere; DKR; Babcock & Brown; Marathon; DKRW Energy; Chase Manhattan; Wachovia; Bank One; Royal Bank of Scotland; Duke Energy; ConocoPhillips and Sitco.

Bracewell & Giuliani LLP

See firm details p.1710

The Firm: The energy practice here is particularly respected for its expertise in financings. It mainly represents financial institutions investing in the sector, and a highlight this past year was acting for the bank agents buying the Transwestern, Florida Gas and Northern Borders pipelines from Enron. An interesting market development of late has been the increased interest by financial institutions in downstream projects, and Bracewell & Giuliani has been at the forefront of this trend. It is also working on more and more restructuring transactions for large corporate clients. For example, it recently advised InterGen in a $2.5 billion restructuring of its domestic power development program. Clients say that the firm is *"very up to speed on what is going on in the industry"* and are satisfied by the *"thorough and responsive"* service provided by the lawyers.

The Lawyers: Alan Rafte (see p.1697) came highly recommended as *"a really smart energy transactional lawyer,"* while **Robert Stephens** (see p.1701) is fast making a name for himself with his high-quality advice and the thoroughness of his contract drafting.

The Clients: JPMorgan Chase; Citibank; Calyon; Bank One; Calpine; InterGen; Apache; Union Bank of California and BNP Paribas.

Skadden, Arps, Slate, Meagher & Flom LLP & Affiliates
See firm details p.1372

The Firm: This international firm has a small outpost in Houston that enjoys a forte in power and LNG work. Both these strengths were fully utilized during its representation of Sempra Energy in the development of the Mexicali power plant in Baja California. The team has recently been negotiating the energy supply contract for the plant, and is developing a 20-year contract with the Tangguh facility in Indonesia for $15 billion worth of LNG. Clients enthuse that the firm's *"technical capability is very strong"* and also appreciate the *"very efficient"* service provided by the team.

The Lawyers: John Ale (see p.1670) is *"a practical lawyer with a business-oriented outlook."* Clients particularly like working with him

because he *"finds ways around obstacles that suit all parties involved and keep the deal moving."* Observers point to the fact that **Lyndon Taylor** (see p.1703) is *"such a nice, friendly guy,"* but they are also alive to his being a *"very thorough and clever deal-maker."*

The Clients: Fortress Investment Group; Cinergy; Vulcan; Bank of Nova Scotia; Royal Bank of Scotland; Excelerate Energy; Sempra Energy; Goldman Sachs and BHP Billiton.

Band 5

Locke Liddell & Sapp LLP
The Firm: The energy group is one of the firm's largest practices, and regularly assists clients in corporate aspects of the oil, gas and energy industry. Clients are enthusiastic about the high-quality service, and point out that the lawyers are *"really skilled at walking the line between our operational needs and the legal requirements."*

The Lawyers: David Patton (see p.1695) is rated as a highly skilled oil and gas lawyer. Peers say he is *"very knowledgeable and practical. He has all the skills needed to see a deal through to the end."*

The Clients: AEP; Amerada Hess; BP America; Calpine; Centrica; ChevronTexaco; ConocoPhillips; Coral Energy; Dynegy; El Paso; Entergy; Kinder Morgan Energy Partners; Marathon; Shell and Total Exploration and Production USA.

Thompson & Knight LLP
See firm details p.1722

The Firm: This well-established Dallas energy practice has recently expanded into Houston

and is emerging as a real force in the industry. Observers say it is *"a knowledgeable practice with considerable oil and gas capability."* It is particularly well known for upstream work, and has a strong reputation among oil and gas independents both in the USA and abroad. The firm has attracted a host of lenders to its client list and its representation on this side has been recognized as *"innovative and successful,"* particularly in mezzanine debt transactions.

The Lawyers: The firm has a number of respected energy lawyers. John Rain is a useful contact as he works from both the Houston and Dallas offices.

The Clients: Clients include multinational and independent oil and gas companies, host government oil and gas companies, large utilities, private power plants, energy industry service companies, refineries, petrochemical companies, financial institutions, and multinational drilling contractors.

Other Notable Practitioners
Thomas Moore (see p.1693) is LeBoeuf, Lamb, Greene & MacRae LLP's leading energy transactional lawyer, and cochair of the energy practice. He is well known in the power sector and clients speak highly of the exceptional service that he provides. *"He has a very quick mind, is a good negotiator and is someone who can get to the heart of issues quickly."* Sources recommend **Dan Rogers** (see p.1699) from Chadbourne & Parke LLP as a lawyer who possesses a wealth of LNG knowledge. Clients particularly rate his *"understanding of the technical side of the work."* He has been representing the lenders to the Freeport LNG terminal.

ENERGY & NATURAL RESOURCES

DISPUTE RESOLUTION

Texas
Leading firms (Energy & Natural Resources: Dispute Resolution)
[1] **FULBRIGHT & JAWORSKI LLP** *Houston*
VINSON & ELKINS LLP *Dallas*
[2] **BAKER BOTTS LLP** *Houston*
GIBBS & BRUNS LLP *Houston*
[3] **BRACEWELL & GIULIANI LLP** *Houston*
JONES DAY *Houston*
KING & SPALDING LLP *Houston*
LEBOEUF, LAMB, GREENE & MACRAE LLP *Houston*
MCDADE FOGLER LLP *Houston*
SUSMAN GODFREY LLP *Houston*
Firms are listed alphabetically in each band.

Band 1

Fulbright & Jaworski LLP
See firm details p.1715

The Firm: The firm is home to a highly renowned specialist energy litigation practice

that handles every conceivable type of litigation and arbitration a client in the energy industry could face, from upstream drilling contracts to cases involving power or alternative energy. It is equally comfortable representing clients as either plaintiff or defendant; due to the sheer size of the team, it is an ideal choice for cases that require a considerable level of resources. Clients say they turn to the firm for *"the high degree of expertise"* and also commend the *"reliable and straightforward lawyers who are just very easy to deal with."* The team has worked on a number of Qui Tam cases and is appearing for multiple defendants in the Grindberg case – where the plaintiff is alleging a widespread fraud by the natural gas industry to undervalue royalties due to the federal government. It also achieved a significant victory this year in obtaining the dismissal of an antitrust case brought against AEX by Texas Commercial Energy. Fulbright also boasts a world-renowned international arbitration practice. Attorneys here have additionally worked on

a dispute over ownership of oil fields in the former Soviet Union, and a construction dispute regarding a gas pipeline in Bolivia.

The Lawyers: Jeff Dykes (see p.1678) is a general litigator but he spends the vast majority of his time on energy cases, particularly those involving pipelines. Clients report that he is an excellent trial lawyer, who is *"very good at analyzing situations."* **William Wood** (see p.1706) has been engaged in litigation arising out of the California energy crisis, and is nominated as an *"exceptional litigator who excels at getting the jury on side and is successful in settlement negotiations."* A fluent Spanish speaker, he is also commended for his work with bilingual juries. **Gerald Pecht** (see p.1695) specializes in securities litigation but has worked on a number of energy cases recently. Clients spoke of his *"good sense of the business and great customer service mentality."* **John Bowman** (see p.1673) is a world leader in the field of arbitration and a superb tactician with *"unsurpassed knowledge of*

www.ChambersandPartners.com

All quotes in the text are from interviews with clients and competitors.

1639

Texas
Leading individuals (Energy: Litigation)

1
BECK David *Beck Redden*, Houston
GIBBS Robin *Gibbs & Bruns*, Houston
GODFREY Lee *Susman Godfrey*, Houston
REASONER Harry *Vinson & Elkins*, Houston

2
BRUNS Phillip *Gibbs & Bruns*, Houston
COPELAND Gregory *Baker Botts*, Houston
DYKES Jeff *Fulbright & Jaworski*, Houston
FELDT Harrell *Vinson & Elkins*, Houston
GUNTER Clifford *Bracewell & Giuliani*, Houston
HARVIN David *Vinson & Elkins*, Houston
MCDADE Thomas *McDade Fogler*, Houston
WOOD William *Fulbright & Jaworski*, Houston

3
BAYKO Tom *Jones Day*, Houston
DYE Phillip *Vinson & Elkins*, Houston
FOGLER Murray *McDade Fogler*, Houston
LIPE Guy *Vinson & Elkins*, Houston
MCCOLLAM Andrew *Vinson & Elkins*, Houston
MEADOWS Robert *King & Spalding*, Houston
PECHT Gerald *Fulbright & Jaworski*, Houston
REYNOLDS Chris *Gibbs & Bruns*, Houston
ROBECK Mark *Baker Botts*, Houston
SCHIFFER Adam *King & Spalding*, Houston
WATT Dick *Watt Beckworth*, Houston

Individuals are listed alphabetically in each band.

the rules and schemes of various arbitration tribunals." **Mark Baker** (see p.1671) is a "*highly effective*" arbitrator who works on energy matters from a construction standpoint.

The Clients: Baker Hughes; Shell Trading Gas and Power; Coral Energy; Shell Oil; Apache Corporation; Anadarko; ExxonMobil; Arctic Slope Regional Corporation; BP Pipelines; Air Liquide America; Sitco; ConocoPhillips; Enterprise Products; Equistar Chemicals; Explorer Pipeline; Kinder Morgan; Marathon Oil; Shell Pipeline; Tepco; Valero Energy; Total SA; Repsol YPF SA; Duke Energy; El Paso Energy; EOG Resources; Enbridge; The Williams Companies and NNPC.

Vinson & Elkins LLP
See firm details p.1724

The Firm: Clients report that this practice is "*known as the best, and it certainly lives up to this reputation.*" It has succeeded in maintaining this prime position because "*it consistently hires the top law graduates and produces the most capable lawyers.*" The group specializes in representing oil companies or major natural gas producers as either plaintiff or defendant. It is frequently appointed to important market defining cases and has an especially strong reputation for royalty matters, or cases with an international dimension, for instance major international arbitrations, and the firm is also fast becoming the first choice for foreign companies being sued in US courts. For example, the team recently represented German company Ruhrgas, in a case brought by Marathon Oil in the Texas state court, alleging $1.2 billion damages arising from

a gas exploration and production project in the North Sea. Vinson & Elkins succeeded in gaining a landmark decision from the US Supreme Court, allowing the case to be dismissed for lack of personal jurisdiction. Its pipeline caseload is also impressive. Attorneys here have brought billions of dollars worth of claims against natural gas pipelines on behalf of natural gas producers in a series of take-or-pay cases, and it is also one of the most active firms in proceedings involving the Alaska oil pipelines.

The Lawyers: Harry Reasoner (see p.1698) is a litigator who deals with complex civil litigation, and has handled a wide variety of cases in the energy sector. Observers say he is "*not just one of the best litigators in Texas, but one of the best in the USA.*" **Harrell Feldt** (see p.1679) is another headline name on the Texas litigation scene, and has worked on some major energy cases throughout a long and distinguished career. He is a superb communicator, who has a highly effective courtroom presence. **David Harvin** (see p.1683) specializes in antitrust litigation, representing energy companies in some key cases. Observers remark that he is "*understated but very very effective*" in court. **Phillip Dye** (see p.1678) is "*a procedural whiz,*" who has carved out a niche as a real expert on jurisdiction cases precluding foreign companies from being sued in the US courts. **Guy Lipe** (see p.1689) works on international litigation and arbitrations. Both clients and peers praised his "*good strategic instincts,*" his attention to detail and "*ability to think on his feet in the courtroom.*" **Andrew McCollam** (see p.1691) is a premier litigator for domestic oil and gas cases. Commentators highlighted the advantages he brings to negotiations due to his background as a geologist. He is particularly skilled at royalty cases and is "*very good with juries.*" **Ben Sheppard** (see p.1700) heads the international arbitration team, and is respected for upstream work. **Platt Davis** (see p.1676) has handled a number of large-scale international arbitrations, but is also renowned as "*a major domestic regulatory attorney.*" **Henry May** (see p.1690) specializes in FERC proceedings, and has a long-standing reputation as one of the foremost regulatory lawyers in Houston. Vinson & Elkins is also home to some of the country's leading lawyers for Alaska oil pipeline work. **Bert Tabor** (see p.1702), "*the dean of the oil pipelines Bar,*" leads this team and worked alongside **Charles Caldwell** (see p.1674) on the SSFP pipeline. **John Kennedy** (see p.1687) represented the shippers using the Trans Alaska Pipeline in the Alaska quality dispute and observers say he is "*an exceptionally able oral advocate and an excellent writer.*"

The Clients: Shell Oil; BP; Amoco; Duke Energy; Forest Oil; Union Texas Petroleum; Fina Oil and Gas; Ruhrgas; China Oil and Gas Pipeline Bureau and China National Petroleum.

Band 2

Baker Botts LLP
See firm details p.1708

The Firm: This energy trial group has a broad expertise in all areas of litigation and "*a well-deserved reputation for developing bright capable lawyers.*" Clients value the culture of the firm, stating "*everyone is interested in doing a good job, is efficient, and manages the work well.*" It represents large oil companies, utilities and energy trading companies, and is particularly well regarded for defending large domestic class actions. For example, it is lead counsel for Reliant in litigation arising from the California energy crisis, which entails approximately 30 class action lawsuits. The team has succeeded in securing several appellate court decisions that were favorable to its client. The lawyers are also defending Marathon and ChevronTexaco in Qui Tam cases where it is claimed that the large oil companies with federal oil and gas leases have been defrauding the federal government out of royalties. As its successful track record suggests, clients use the firm because it is "*very well qualified and gets excellent results.*"

The Lawyers: Gregory Copeland (see p.1675) is "*at the top of the stack*" for domestic class actions. Sources say "*he is a great advocate without being obnoxious*" while clients enthuse that he is "*creative, good in front of the jury, and gets great results.*" **Mark Robeck** (see p.1698) is leading the charge for the next generation at Baker Botts. Clients say he is "*knowledgeable and well accomplished, but most importantly is also really personable and a good guy to have on your side in negotiations.*"

The Clients: BP; Burlington Resources; CenterPoint Energy; ExxonMobil; Shell; Marathon Oil; Wagner Brown and Reliant Energy.

Gibbs & Bruns, LLP
See firm details p.1719

The Firm: This litigation boutique firm is home to a group of "*absolutely terrific trial lawyers.*" Although a general commercial practice, the caseload naturally includes a high proportion of energy matters. It represents both plaintiffs and defendants and has the breadth of experience to handle a variety of issues that affect energy companies. Recent representative matters include defending a company in a wrongful death claim arising out of an explosion at a plant, and arguing for the defendant in an injunction to prevent the construction of an $800 million natural gas pipeline. The group also appeared in a claim of underpayment of royalties by an oil company.

The Lawyers: Robin Gibbs (see p.1681) is named by many as "*simply one of the best trial lawyers in the world.*" He is very good in front of a jury because "*he excels at making complex matters understandable*" and is "*an excellent story-teller.*" He has surrounded himself with a

Texas
Leading individuals (Energy: Arbitration)

1. **BISHOP Doak** *King & Spalding*, Houston
   BOWMAN John *Fulbright & Jaworski*, Houston
2. **BAKER Mark** *Fulbright & Jaworski*, Houston
   SHEPPARD Ben *Vinson & Elkins*, Houston

Leading individuals (Energy: Regulatory)

1. **DAVIS Platt** *Vinson & Elkins*, Houston
   MAY Henry *Vinson & Elkins*, Houston
   MOORE Charles *LeBoeuf Lamb*, Houston
   TABOR Bert *Vinson & Elkins*, Houston
2. **CALDWELL Charles** *Vinson & Elkins*, Houston
   KEITHLEY Brad *Jones Day*, Dallas
   KENNEDY John *Vinson & Elkins*, Houston

Individuals are listed alphabetically in each band.

supporting team of top-level litigators. **Phillip Bruns** (see p.1674) is *"really bright, a very strong analyst and highly detail oriented."* **Chris Reynolds** (see p.1698) is a younger lawyer who has succeeded in establishing a name for himself through the high caliber of his trial work.

The Clients: Boyce Engineering International; The Coastal Corporation; MW Kellogg; Stone Energy; Stone Petroleum; Sunrise Gas Marketing and Pennzoil.

Band 3

Bracewell & Giuliani LLP
See firm details p.1710

The Firm: Known as a haven for *"some really great lawyers,"* this litigation practice encompasses a broad array of energy matters including oil and gas and electricity. It has been engaged in the spate of litigation resulting from the California energy crisis and has been representing BC Hydro and Powerex throughout the refund proceedings. A real highlight this year was successfully defending Kinder Morgan in a case brought by ExxonMobil alleging fraud and breach of a gas processing contract. The team succeeded in getting all claims dismissed. International arbitrations also feature in the caseload, and the firm recently appeared for the Shell Petroleum Development Company of Nigeria in a dispute over the construction of a gas processing plant in Nigeria.

The Lawyers: **Clifford Gunter** (see p.1682) is the team's leading light. He has an excellent reputation as a general trial lawyer who has been involved in numerous oil and gas cases over the years. He is *"polished and has a lot of credibility,"* and clients endorsed him as *"smart, creative and really good for big-ticket litigation."*

The Clients: Valero Energy; El Paso; BC Hydro; Powerex; McDermott International; Kinder Morgan; Oneok; Bechtel; Shell Petroleum Development Company of Nigeria; Stone Energy and Intratex Gas.

Jones Day
See firm details p.485

The Firm: Clients praise the *"very bright and creative"* litigation team at Jones Day, citing its *"successful results"* and *"suitability for big-ticket litigation"* as prime reasons for using the firm. The lawyers are adept at both domestic litigation and international arbitration in the oil and gas field. To illustrate its breadth, the group recently represented Kellogg Brown & Root in a dispute with Shell regarding the construction of a gas processing plant in Nigeria. In another international highlight, the team successfully prosecuted the claims of Occidental Yemen Sabatain against Adair Yemen Exploration in an ICC arbitration relating to an oil and gas exploration and production project in Yemen. The domestic litigation side is also thriving and the team has been representing BP in investigations prompted by the California energy crisis.

The Lawyers: **Tom Bayko** (see p.1671) is a senior member of the energy litigation team. Clients appreciate his responsive service and noted his *"vast credibility in court with both judges and juries."* **Brad Keithley** (see p.1686) is a hybrid oil and gas lawyer, possessing expertise in litigation, regulation and transactional issues. A long-standing player in the market, he is dedicated to the sector while being *"a very effective"* advocate for his clients.

The Clients: Halliburton; BP; Occidental Petroleum; ChevronTexaco; Total; Unical and Apache Corporation.

King & Spalding LLP
See firm details p.635

The Firm: The broad practice has cultivated a considerable energy litigation expertise, particularly related to oil and gas royalty litigation. Of late, it has represented ChevronTexaco on a number of such cases in Oklahoma. The firm has also devoted resources and effort toward the development of a distinguished international arbitration practice. It recently achieved a successful result for ChevronTexaco in a complex arbitration relating to offshore properties in Asia.

The Lawyers: **Robert Meadows** (see p.1691) is *"a really good trial lawyer no matter what the subject is"* and he has dealt with a number of matters for energy companies. He is *"adept at handling difficult and sensitive litigation"* and has a strong record of success. **Adam Schiffer** (see p.1700) is a *"skilled trial lawyer"* who *"knows the industry, can relate well to people and make complex issues interesting and understandable to a jury."* **Doak Bishop** (see p.1672) is a headline name in the international arbitration sector and is hailed by commentators in the USA and overseas as a master of his trade.

The Clients: ChevronTexaco; Shell; Halliburton and ExxonMobil. It also represents a long list of midsized companies.

LeBoeuf, Lamb, Greene & MacRae LLP
See firm details p.1358

The Firm: LeBoeuf, Lamb has an integrated energy group that offers *"exceptional service"* for its clients in transactional, regulatory and litigation matters. Market observers comment on the firm's success in securing interesting electricity work, quite a feat for a Texas firm. A prime example of this is its representation of Enron in various litigation and regulatory proceedings arising out of the California energy crisis. However, the firm also has a robust natural gas practice. In a highlight case, the lawyers have been advising the consortium responsible for developing an LNG project in West Africa. In addition, the team is appearing for Aquila in natural gas litigation stemming from the California energy crisis.

The Lawyers: **Charles Moore** (see p.1692) is cochair of the energy practice. He specializes in FERC proceedings but also has litigation experience. Clients report that he is *"an incredibly well-informed energy lawyer"* and trust the depth of support around him.

The Clients: The firm's prime clients include Aquila and Enron.

McDade Fogler LLP

The Firm: This small but highly regarded litigation boutique was formed by a group of former Fulbright & Jaworski lawyers. It handles a range of general commercial litigation, but approximately half of its caseload stems from the energy industry. Oil and gas matters form a core part of its attorneys experience and they represented a major petrochemical company throughout the Enron litigation. Further highlights include prosecuting a case on behalf of Transocean against a manufacturer of an allegedly faulty pipeline.

The Lawyers: A senior figure in the market, **Thomas McDade** provides his clients with a valuable strategic understanding of complex litigation and a wealth of courtroom experience. He represents a number of major oil and gas companies and peers report that he is *"very quick thinking on his feet."* **Murray Fogler** is an excellent all-around trial lawyer, who has *"loads of energy and enthusiasm for his work."*

The Clients: Transocean; The Coastal Corporation; Duke Energy; Ocean Energy and Valero Marketing and Supply Company.

Susman Godfrey LLP

The Firm: This top litigation boutique was nominated by many peers, who have *"a huge amount of respect for the litigation talent there."* It has a strong reputation as a plaintiff's firm, but also undertakes a substantial amount of defense work. The recent caseload features a number of oil and gas royalty matters and take-or-pay gas contracts. For example, the firm recently won a summary judgment for client Southern Natural Gas Pipeline in a $100 million take-or-pay lawsuit against ExxonMobil. It is prosecuting a number of plaintiff class actions, including a suit against oil companies challenging the method of calculating royalties. It also defends clients in a variety of other disputes arising from the operation of gas and oil wells.

The Lawyers: Many observers commented on the powerful trial skills displayed by **Lee Godfrey**. He predominantly works for the plaintiff, and

sources report he "*has great charm and is very articulate.*"

The Clients: Unocal; Valence Operating Company; El Paso; Tennessee Gas Pipeline; Southern Natural Gas Pipeline; Texas General Land Office; Sonat and Tenneco.

Other Notable Practitioners

David Beck, of Beck, Redden & Secrest LLP is an outstanding general litigator, who has worked on a number of significant energy mat-

ters. Sources observe that he is "*well prepared, relates beautifully to juries, and is good on his feet.*" **Dick Watt** from Watt, Beckworth & Thompson LLP is renowned for representing plaintiffs and works exclusively in the energy sector. He has prosecuted many cases on behalf of royalty owners and he "*knows the oil and gas business inside out and does a very fine job of representing his clients,*" acknowledged sources.

ENVIRONMENT

Texas
Leading firms (Environment)

1   **BAKER BOTTS LLP** *Austin*
    VINSON & ELKINS LLP *Houston*

2   **BRACEWELL & GIULIANI LLP** *Houston*
    FULBRIGHT & JAWORSKI LLP *Houston*
    HAYNES AND BOONE LLP *Austin*

3   **AKIN GUMP STRAUSS HAUER & FELD LLP** *Austin*
    BROWN MCCARROLL LLP *Austin*
    THOMPSON & KNIGHT LLP *Dallas*

4   **GUIDA SLAVICH & FLORES PC** *Austin*
    LOCKE LIDDELL & SAPP LLP *Dallas*

5   **CONNELLY BAKER WOTRING JACKSON** *Houston*
    FRITZ, BYRNE, HEAD & HARRISON *Austin*
    KELLY, HART & HALLMAN *Austin*
    LLOYD, GOSSELINK, BLEVINS, ROCHELLE *Austin*

Firms are listed alphabetically in each band.

Band 1

Baker Botts LLP
See firm details p.1708

The Firm: This powerhouse firm for environment law advice fields a "*vibrant and dynamic practice, packed with talented people.*" Skilled in all aspects of environmental litigation and counseling, it is particularly prominent in regulatory compliance. Sources spoke of the group's ability to project manage and coordinate major, multi-jurisdictional litigation. Of late, the lawyers have been busy with an increase in LNG projects for large multinationals, and a substantial volume of permit projects. These include working with a utility company on the first coal-fired power plant to be built in Texas in the past 15 years.

The Lawyers: The prominent and experienced **Pamela Giblin** (see p.1681) focuses on strategic permitting and issues of air quality regulation. Her 30 years' experience gives her an extensive range of contacts and competitors envy her "*incredible client base.*" Most recently she has advised on a radioactive waste facility and assisted in obtaining permits for various LNG projects on behalf of ExxonMobil and ConocoPhillips. **Walter Conrad** (see p.1674) is renowned as "*an incredibly skilled*

litigator," and clients describe his excellent toxic tort practice. They also cite his intelligence and scientific understanding as the main reasons for his effectiveness. Recent lateral hire **Sara Burgin** (see p.1674) joins the firm from Brown McCarroll, adding her "*impressive experience*" as a top water quality lawyer to the team. She continues to work with industrial, commercial and municipal clients, who praise her as "*an effective lawyer who always gets results.*" The "*very thorough and well-prepared*" **Derek McDonald** (see p.1691) has been advising on the intricacies of a radioactive waste facility project and the coal-fired power plant. Up-and-comer **Matthew Kuryla** (see p.1688) has been tagged "*one of the most competent environmental lawyers in Houston.*" He has been coordinating LNG projects with a focus on air permitting, an area in which clients view him as "*a real guru.*" **Jennifer Keane** (see p.1686) was singled out by competitors for her strength with Clean Air Act issues.

The Clients: The group's clients include large multinationals such as ExxonMobil, ConocoPhillips, Halliburton, Valero and ChevronTexaco, alongside other chemical, technology and utility companies.

Vinson & Elkins LLP
See firm details p.1724

The Firm: This "*very responsive and very knowledgeable*" specialist team covers the full gamut of environmental issues. Industry sources rate it as "*a big competitor,*" while clients choose the group because it offers a full environmental service with expertise in both regulatory and litigation matters. Recent highlights include representing a private investment group in the acquisition of 17 Texas power plants. The group also provided advice to the Port of Houston Authority on a multibillion-dollar port project, in which attorneys handled all the permitting and NEPA issues.

The Lawyers: **Christopher Amandes** (see p.1670) is widely recognized for his specialist knowledge of enforcement and contaminated property issues. "*In terms of intellect, he is without peer.*" Clients praised his pragmatism and appreciation of business realities, which produce advice

"*steeped in practicality.*" He is the lead counsel in three major enforcement cases, and is representing a client in the purchase of a major Superfund site. Leading litigator **Molly Cagle** (see p.1674) is "*a warrior*" who "*has a real passion for her work.*" Known as "*tenacious and articulate in court,*" she has a diverse practice and is particularly respected for her handling of Superfund cases for manufacturing and refinery companies. **Carol Dinkins** (see p.1677) splits her time between Houston and Washington, DC, and has secured an outstanding reputation as "*a leading expert in the environmental arena.*" Noting her work with both federal and state government, peers opine that "*her experience makes her stand out – she has done it all.*" Over the past year, Dinkins has advised timber and oil exploration companies, and litigated claims related to contaminated sediments and natural resources damage. **Sharon Mattox** (see p.1690) is "*the expert on wetlands issues*" and "*the go-to person for issues before the Corps of Engineers.*" Transactional lawyer **Larry Nettles** (see p.1693) "*really excels at environmental contracts and negotiations.*" He continues to work closely with the firm's corporate lawyers and is currently advising on the pending offering for Huntsman. Austin-based **John Howard** (see p.1684), an experienced government relations attorney, was an environmental policy adviser on Governor Bush's staff. According to peers, he possesses "*more experience in government than the rest of the market combined.*"

The Clients: The firm's large client base comprises leaders in the energy sector such as Shell, as it "*very much understands the energy business.*" Added to these are chemical industry, transportation, timber and pipeline companies, as well as developers, federal agencies, government authorities and private investment groups.

Band 2

Bracewell & Giuliani LLP
See firm details p.1710

The Firm: This smaller practice group has impressed market sources with its volume of high-profile and complex matters. The group has a broad practice, but generally focuses on

Texas
Leading individuals (Environment)

Senior Statesman
GOLEMON Kinnan *Brown McCarroll*, Austin

[1] AMANDES Christopher *Vinson & Elkins*, Houston
CAGLE Molly *Vinson & Elkins*, Austin
CIVINS Jeff *Haynes and Boone*, Austin
DINKINS Carol *Vinson & Elkins*, Houston
FINN BRADDOCK Patricia *Fulbright* Austin
FROMM O'BRIEN Eva *Fulbright & Jaworski*, Houston
GIBLIN Pamela *Baker Botts*, Austin

[2] BRADDOCK James *Haynes and Boone*, Austin
BURGIN Sara *Baker Botts*, Austin
DUTTON Diana *Akin Gump*, Dallas
HESTER Tracy *Bracewell & Giuliani*, Houston
MATTOX Sharon *Vinson & Elkins*, Houston
MORRISS James *Thompson & Knight*, Austin
RAMIREZ Kenneth *Bracewell & Giuliani*, Austin
SEALS Paul *Akin Gump*, Austin
STEWART Robert *Kelly Hart*, Austin

[3] BOHANNON Paul *Andrews Kurth*, The Woodlands
HARRIS James *Thompson & Knight*, Dallas
HEAD J D *Fritz Byrne*, Austin
HOPSON Keith *Brown McCarroll*, Austin
NETTLES Larry *Vinson & Elkins*, Houston
PELS Gerald *Locke Liddell*, Houston
SLAVICH John *Guida Slavich*, Austin

[4] AXE Albert *Jenkens & Gilchrist*, Austin
BAKER Debra *Connelly Baker*, Houston
COOKE Gregg *Guida Slavich*, Austin
GOSSELINK Paul *Lloyd Gosselink*, Austin
GROTEN Eric *Bracewell & Giuliani*, Austin
HOWARD John *Vinson & Elkins*, Austin
RENBARGER Robert *Fritz Byrne*, Austin
VAY John *Kelly Hart*, Austin
WORRELL Danny *Brown McCarroll*, Austin

Up-and-coming individuals
KEANE Jennifer *Baker Botts*, Austin
KURYLA Matthew *Baker Botts*, Houston
MCDONALD Derek *Baker Botts*, Austin
MCQUAID Janet *Fulbright & Jaworski*, Austin
NASI Michael *Lloyd Gosselink*, Austin

Leading individuals
(Litigation: Environmental)

[1] CAGLE Molly *Vinson & Elkins*, Austin
CONRAD Walter *Baker Botts*, Houston
SMITH James *Beirne Maynard*, Houston

[2] CONNELLY Michael *Connelly Baker*, Houston
DEATHERAGE Scott *Thompson & Knight*, Dallas
ELDRIDGE John *Haynes and Boone*, Houston
FAULK Richard *Gardere Wynne*, Houston
FROMM O'BRIEN Eva *Fulbright & Jaworski*, Houston
HARRIS James *Thompson & Knight*, Dallas
MATTOX Sharon *Vinson & Elkins*, Houston
MORSE Robert *Crain Caton*, Houston
RENFROE Tracie *Bracewell & Giuliani*, Houston
STEWART Robert *Kelly Hart*, Austin

Individuals are listed alphabetically in each band.

regulatory compliance and corporate issues such as environmental risk management. The talented team of lawyers has seen an increase in criminal defense work, and recently assisted a local entity in an investigation on sediment management. Attorneys in the group have also been involved in the drafting of standards related to nanotechnology issues.

The Lawyers: "*Pure environmental lawyer*" **Tracy Hester** (see p.1684) earns praise for his diligent and professional representation of clients. He is currently working with emerging technologies, including renewable energy and nanomaterials, in developing strategies to deal with cutting-edge environmental issues. He represents the International Council on Nanotechnology and the American National Standards Institute's nanotechnology standards panel. Water specialist **Kenneth Ramirez** (see p.1697) is "*quick on his feet with a great knowledge of the law.*" He is an "*exceptional, hard-working lawyer,*" who advises on both federal and state regulatory issues. Ramirez continues to advise municipalities on protected water rights and water reuse issues. Head of the firm's environmental litigation practice group, **Tracie Renfroe** (see p.1682), focuses solely on litigation and trial work. She is currently representing clients in the chemical and refining industries on toxic tort and Superfund cases. **Eric Groten** (see p.1682) is a highly experienced air emissions lawyer, distinguished in the market by the sizable volume of contested air permitting work he undertakes. He is currently conducting a high-profile permit proceeding for mineral extraction and smelting operators in El Paso.

The Clients: The firm advises: local government bodies; Goodyear; Hanover Compressor; Shell; ChevronTexaco and other energy, refining, technology and chemical companies.

Fulbright & Jaworski LLP
See firm details p.1715

The Firm: According to peers, this firm has cultivated a "*very high-quality practice*" both regionally and statewide. Its "*top-notch*" lawyers have been praised as "*knowledgeable and easy to work with*" and most can boast environmental or chemical engineering degrees. Recently the team has been busy devising mechanisms to protect the interests of its clients in large M&A deals. This includes developing insurance policies against historic contamination and other past liabilities. Highlights include winning a $75 million arbitration award for a client from the former owners of a manufacturing facility over contamination of water and property.

The Lawyers: The "*fantastic*" **Patricia Finn Braddock** (see p.1679) continues to earn praise for her excellent enforcement defense work, especially on clean air issues. Clients recommend her for her insight into how the regulatory structure works, rating her "*knowledgeable, practical,*

bright and responsive." She recently assisted a processing company with an audit under the Texas Environment Health and Safety Audit Privilege Act to determine the cause of upsets to its emission levels. It was the first time the Texas Commission on Environmental Quality allowed such occurrences to be privileged under the Audit Act. The "*extremely bright*" **Eva Fromm O'Brien** (see p.1680) is the group's new environmental department head. With expertise in transactional, regulatory and litigation matters, she was described by one competitor as having "*one of the broadest skill sets I know of.*" Clients appreciated her background in chemical engineering, which they view as a "*really special added value.*" A highlight for her was advice on a criminal investigation over wastewater noncompliance for a Houston-based ship channel company. Formerly a chemical engineer for Exxon, **Janet McQuaid** (see p.1691) is a name to watch in the future, especially in environmental litigation. She is working on behalf of the Storm Water Joint Appeals Group in a high-profile appeal of EPA rules regarding storm water permits for gas and oil excavation activities.

The Clients: The group serves energy, utility and chemical companies, including Baker Hughes, Solvay America and Texas Eastern Products Pipeline Company.

Haynes and Boone LLP

The Firm: Some of the foremost environmental lawyers for regulatory and litigation matters are housed in this group. In litigation, the attorneys have drawn praise for their handling of criminal defense and toxic tort cases, where clients recommend them as "*cost conscious, efficient and decisive*" and "*extremely adroit at problem solving.*" In the regulatory area, clients are impressed with their tactical counseling on compliance matters, which they consider "*extremely skilled and practical advice.*" The group has recently advised on several high-profile Superfund cases, and assisted a major real estate company in the sale of properties, performing all the environmental due diligence work.

The Lawyers: "*Keeping the industry exciting,*" **Jeff Civins** is known for his strong and effective interaction with regulatory agencies. "*He is a very credible spokesperson for clients.*" Competitors rate him for his skill in contaminated property cases, as "*he has tenacity and plays for every single point.*" Air quality specialist **James Braddock** earns respect for his effective, low-key approach to problems. He deals with all air compliance issues for the firm's major clients, who appreciate that "*he has a better knowledge of the core air programs than anyone else in the state.*" Environmental litigator **John Eldridge** impresses with his effective representation of businesses in Superfund cases, where, according to clients "*he knows more about the laws on cost recovery than anyone.*"

The Clients: BP; El Paso Energy; Shell; Acme

Brick; Amerada Hess; Anadarko; Elk; SACAM and Seneco.

Akin Gump Strauss Hauer & Feld LLP

See firm details p.477

The Firm: The group produces *"technically able and persuasive lawyers"* whose broad knowledge sees them active on a range of environmental law issues. The past year has seen an increase in transactional work for this group, with clients buying and selling assets as a result of the consolidation within the energy industry. Traditionally strong in development issues, attorneys here have also represented clients in the purchase of pipelines and refineries such as in recent advice to a company investing in an oil project in Australia. Among the group's highlights was working with El Paso Energy in obtaining the necessary licensing for a deepwater port in the Gulf of Mexico, the first of such licenses to be granted in the USA.

The Lawyers: Diana Dutton (see p.1678) *"always brings substantive advice to the table because of her deep level of experience."* An expert in regulatory and transactional matters, she has *"a very good rapport with clients and wins a lot of respect with the agencies."* Clients are impressed with her ability to function across a broad range of areas, and endorsed her as a *"good person to seek out with an unusual problem."* The *"knowledgeable and savvy"* **Paul Seals** (see p.1700) provides first-rate litigation and regulation advice to clients. He is currently representing a pulp and paper industry client who is facing a toxic tort class action suit. He is also representing refining industry clients in the appeal against an EPA ruling on air emissions.

The Clients: The firm continues to represent its core clients in the oil and energy industry. It has recently added Waste Management, CITGO and Buckeye Pipeline to its client roster.

Brown McCarroll LLP

The Firm: This firm is *"one of the originals"* on the Texas environmental law scene. Although smaller than its direct competitors, it continues to play a prominent role in environmental legislative work. At present the group represents various industry entities, for which it is counseling on legislative efforts related to such issues as taxes and asbestos. Clients also recommended the group for its air and water permitting skills.

The Lawyers: Described as *"the dean of Texas environmental lawyers,"* senior figure **Kinnan Golemon** is active in state lobbying and federal government affairs. At present, he is representing a group of rural water suppliers on issues of drinking water standards under the Safe Drinking Water Act. **Keith Hopson** has

won a loyal following among peers and clients with his skills as a problem solver, typified by the fact that *"he doesn't see litigation as the first stance to get an issue resolved."* He is currently involved in a number of contaminated site disputes, one being the toxic waste litigation for Texas Disposal Systems. Featured this year for his strength in compliance issues and permitting is the *"very effective and experienced"* **Danny Worrell**. Peers respect his intelligence and single him out because *"he has the ability to keep up with the changes in the industry."* Among recent highlights, he has worked on the renewal of a major injection well permit, alongside advising the firm's clients in the chemical industry.

The Clients: Texas Chemical Council; Shell; Devon Energy; Serco; DuPont and Gulf Coast Waste Disposal Authority.

Thompson & Knight LLP

See firm details p.1722

The Firm: This Dallas-based firm has taken a broad approach to the development of its environmental law practice, combining experience of specialist litigation with considerable lobbying and policy work. In the regulatory arena, the lawyers are proficient in air, water and solid waste disputes, with clients especially recommending them for their skills in toxic waste and water permitting. For example, the group is advising on toxic polychlorinated biphenyl regulations for several different industries. In their lobbying capacity, attorneys are currently focused on permit processing reform.

The Lawyers: Peers are particularly impressed with the legislative and policy work of **James Morriss** (see p.1693). According to one source *"He manages to get a bill passed every session."* Clients respect his thoughtfulness and his ability to strategize, as *"he always seems to get a good result."* In the past year, he has undertaken more Superfund work, and continues compliance counseling for clients concerned with endangered species issues. **James Harris'** (see p.1683) excellent representation of clients in the areas of cost recovery, enforcement and criminal actions means peers *"always think of him for environmental litigation."* He is currently addressing industry standards on storm water issues for the building and construction industry, and advising on how contractors can best satisfy them. **Scott Deatherage's** (see p.1683) litigation expertise in air emissions, wastewater discharges and hazardous waste is widely recognized. He is currently focusing on groundwater litigation and brownfield development projects.

The Clients: The group serves industrial companies drawn from the steel, cement, petrochemicals, refining, building materials, quarrying, concrete and brick sectors.

Guida Slavich & Flores PC

The Firm: Industry sources rated this group of 13 lawyers *"the best environmental boutique firm in Dallas."* Founded in 1991, this firm *"enjoys a position that is well established and well known"* based in part on its litigation prowess. Attorneys are also well equipped to handle environmental issues as they relate to corporate and real estate transactions. One of the founding members of the Environmental Law Network, the group is able to undertake multijurisdictional litigation, as the network gives clients access to more than 200 attorneys across the country, providing services that are national in scope but locally focused.

The Lawyers: John Slavich has a broad corporate and commercial law background that makes him well suited to assist on environmental issues that relate to transactions, particularly the development of brownfield sites. Now of counsel to the firm, **Gregg Cooke** was formerly the regional administrator at the EPA for an area comprising Texas, Louisiana, Arkansas, Oklahoma, and New Mexico. His deep knowledge and strength in environmental litigation, particularly air issues, have meant that peers use him as an expert witness in their cases.

The Clients: Clients include industrial enterprises, international and local developers, commercial and retail businesses, and financial institutions.

Locke Liddell & Sapp LLP

The Firm: The environment lawyers in this large general practice firm continue to draw praise for their skills in risk management and compliance issues. Clients are *"very comfortable that once we have their blessing on things, we won't have any issues."* Recently the team has worked with David Weekley Homes on a national compliance program and on indemnity liability proceedings concerning a string of national and international sites. The lawyers are also assisting a client in the redevelopment of Buffalo Bayou and other major downtown Houston brownfield sites.

The Lawyers: Gerald Pels (see p.1695) continues to impress clients with his *"good combination of legal knowledge and business sense."* He is recommended for his broad skill set, but clients especially praise him as *"the best negotiator I've ever seen irrespective of practice areas."*

The Clients: The group serves energy, industrial and manufacturing companies including: Nabors Industries; ConocoPhillips; Smith International; MI Drilling Fluids; Riviana Foods and David Weekley Homes.

Connelly Baker Wotring Jackson LLP

The Firm: This self-proclaimed boutique firm enters the tables on the recommendation of both clients and competitors. Based in Houston, it specializes in environmental law, with a strong emphasis on litigation. Clients endorsed these lawyers for their effective representation across the board, observing, *"They're good at straight regulatory issues like cleanup, but also do all the tort litigation that arises."* The small group has represented clients on issues arising from over 200 Superfund sites throughout the country.

The Lawyers: Hailed as a *"good strategic thinker,"* **Debra Baker** is respected for her expertise in Superfund cost recovery. She has over 20 years' experience in the area and is a founding member of the firm. Managing partner **Michael Connelly**'s *"specialty is in the courtroom."* A talented torts lawyer, he focuses on mass community suits and government cost recovery actions as well as mass toxic tort cases. Interviewees report that *"for bare knuckles litigation, he's the one to have in your corner."*

The Clients: The firm serves the chemical companies ARCO/Lyondell, ChevronTexaco and Shell, Union Pacific and municipal authorities, including the City of Houston and the Port of Texas City.

Fritz, Byrne, Head & Harrison

The Firm: Based in Austin, this general practice firm has a small environmental team led by two partners that undertakes both defendant and plaintiff work. Market sources compliment these attorneys for their awareness of developing environmental issues: *"They have their ear close to the ground and know what's going on."* In the past year, they have handled a steady volume of surface and groundwater rights work and an increasing amount of enforcement work. For example, recent cases have included the defense of two large clients in the water supply and container industries.

The Lawyers: **J D Head**'s practice is geared toward water, waste, and enforcement issues. Peers respect his *"broad-based litigation skills,"* and feel that his *"good sense of humor"* ensures the support and loyalty of clients. Clients also spoke of his *"fantastic advice – I have never seen an attorney so conscientious."* Both clients and peers rate **Robert Renbarger** for his experience

and substantial contacts in the field, praising him as *"an efficient lawyer and a good communicator."*

The Clients: The firm serves a diverse range of clients, including individuals, financial institutions, insurance companies, healthcare organizations, commercial businesses and government entities.

Kelly, Hart & Hallman, A Professional Corporation

The Firm: This Texas firm has two offices, with the one in Austin devoted to environmental and regulatory issues. The group of eight dedicated attorneys provides clients with compliance counseling, regulatory assistance, environmental litigation, and business transaction support. The team handles the air permitting work for GM across 28 states. It has also acted in enforcement defense cases for large chemical companies, and represented both plaintiffs and defendants in cost recovery cases.

The Lawyers: The *"tremendous"* **Robert Stewart** recently joined the firm from Baker Botts. According to interviewees, he *"is one of the best in the state for criminal white-collar environment work."* Clients also deem him *"very effective in working with both the state agencies and the technical staff."* He is the primary contact for GM and is currently involved in several criminal liability defense cases. **John Vay** is head of practice group and was formerly general counsel to the Texas Water Commission. Interviewees value his depth of experience, describing him as *"incredibly knowledgeable – he has a strong regulatory background and can spot the nuances to a case."*

The Clients: GM; Kawasaki; Bridgestone/Firestone; Aviall; XTO Energy and other railway and manufacturing companies.

Lloyd, Gosselink, Blevins, Rochelle, Baldwin & Townsend, PC

The Firm: With two offices and 28 lawyers, this firm's practice is centered on environmental, administrative, public utilities and municipal law. The lawyers also undertake construction-related litigation. The firm has a diverse client base that ranges from municipal authorities to private businesses, which the lawyers represent

before both local and federal agencies and courts.

The Lawyers: Paul Gosselink, one of the founding partners of the firm, is well regarded for his experience in waste management and air issues. Peers respect his innovative thinking and praise his ability to *"come up with a creative approach to problems."* Market commentators are watching the rise of young partner **Michael Nasi**. He continues his diverse compliance counseling and also manages the firm's environmental enforcement defense practice. Peers agree that he *"always does a good job for his clients."*

The Clients: The firm serves municipal governments, developers, utilities and mining, waste management and manufacturing companies.

Other Notable Practitioners

"Old school environmental lawyer" **Paul Bohannon** (see p.1672) is a key environmental specialist at Andrews Kurth. Peers rate him *"a smart and tenacious lawyer"* and readily refer clients to him in a conflict. He is primarily noted for his Superfund work with chemical and pipeline companies. From the Austin office of Jenkens & Gilchrist, **Albert Axe** has *"been very prominent in recent regulatory issues on hazardous waste management and deep well disposals."* Industry sources also highlighted his technical skills and success in securing a loyal client following in the pulp, paper and forestry, electronic chemical and mining industries. **James E Smith** of the litigation boutique Beirne, Maynard & Parsons LLP is known for his *"great presence in the courtroom."* He has *"a passion for his cases,"* which mostly center on toxic torts. Interviewees identified **Richard Faulk** (see p.1695) of Gardere Wynne Sewell LLP for having *"carved out a great appellate practice."* Clients recommend him as a *"proactive and creative attorney who enables us to go in the direction we want to,"* and point to him as prime choice for their key cases. He recently represented Aviall Services in a cost recovery case that went all the way to the Supreme Court. *"One of the most senior environmental lawyers in town,"* **Robert Morse** of Crain Caton & James is a skilled litigator, who *"knows the law inside out, and is always well prepared."*

HEALTHCARE

Texas

Leading firms (Healthcare)

1	FULBRIGHT & JAWORSKI LLP *Houston*
2	VINSON & ELKINS LLP *Houston*
3	BAKER & MCKENZIE *Dallas*
	BROWN MCCARROLL LLP *Austin*
	DAVIS & WILKERSON PC *Austin*
	JENKENS & GILCHRIST *Houston*

Firms are listed alphabetically in each band.

Band 1

Fulbright & Jaworski LLP

See firm details p.1715

The Firm: Acclaimed by clients as *"the best in the business,"* this heavyweight team is based predominantly in Texas, and comes close to numbering 100 lawyers nationwide. Having established its healthcare practice in the late 1970s, the firm has built up a dominant reputa-

tion in the nonprofit sector. For instance, it represents integral bodies, such as Memorial Hermann, the largest nonprofit healthcare system in the state. This experience extends to the formation of bodies such as a nonprofit Texas healthcare provider that maintains 42-member institutions. In recent times, the firm has witnessed a rising trend in joint ventures between hospitals and physician groups, while typical projects include the formation of

www.ChambersandPartners.com

All quotes in the text are from interviews with clients and competitors.

1645

Texas
Leading individuals (Healthcare)

1. BELL Jerry *Fulbright & Jaworski*, Houston
   EILAND Gary *Vinson & Elkins*, Houston
2. DARLING William *Brown McCarroll*, Austin
   EPSTEIN J D *Vinson & Elkins*, Houston
   FOUST Lawrence *Jenkens & Gilchrist*, Houston
   GORDON Ken *Baker & McKenzie*, Dallas
   HILGERS David *Brown McCarroll*, Austin
   JOHNSTONE Debbi *Vinson & Elkins*, Houston
   PATTERSON J A *Fulbright & Jaworski*, Dallas
   PUIG Yvonne *Fulbright & Jaworski*, Austin
   REED Kevin *Davis & Wilkerson*, Austin
   STRAMA Brenda *Vinson & Elkins*, Austin

Individuals are listed alphabetically in each band.

outpatient/ambulatory centers. In the transactional arena, the firm's track record is undisputed. In 2004 it represented Ilex Oncology, a successful drug development company, in its $1 billion sale to Genzyme Corporation. The department divides into three main units: transactional, litigation and regulatory, the latter centered in Washington, DC. The firm also fields a formidable nursing home litigation and medical malpractice group out of Texas.

The Lawyers: "*Equally at ease in the corporate boardroom as in the hospital waiting room,*" **Jerry Bell** (see p.1671) is a prominent figure on the Texas healthcare scene. Valued by clients as an "*effective problem-solver,*" his practice spans transactional work, regulatory issues and medical staff matters. Bell is head of the firm's health law business and regulatory department and still finds the time to remain "*dedicated to his clients,*" enthused sources. Similarly well-regarded is the proactive **Yvonne Puig** (see p.1697), who displays a "*great breadth of experience and knowledge.*" A talented medical malpractice attorney, she is equally able when it comes to complex corporate and regulatory matters. "*She really is a rare find,*" one client said, "*she is able to work both sides of the great divide with ease and achieves fantastic results.*" Areas of expertise include antitrust, EMTALA (the federal Emergency Medical Treatment and Active Labor Act) and product work related to the healthcare industry. "*Bright, thorough and ethical,*" **Tony Patterson** (see p.1695) is one of the most highly regarded physician lawyers in the country, who handles recruitment, contracting and other operational issues. He also represents a large pool of hospital clients, for whom recent work includes outsourcing services. He is serving as chair of the health law section of the ABA (August 2004-2005.)

The Clients: Memorial Hermann Hospital System; Baylor Health Care System; Seton Medical Center; Trinity Mother Frances Health System; Scott & White Healthcare System and CHRISTUS Health.

Band 2

Vinson & Elkins LLP
See firm details p.1724

The Firm: Clients value this firm's proactive approach to healthcare law and are quick to praise a team that is both comprehensive and wellestablished. The "*fully matured practice*" is diverse, spanning a range of business transactions, litigation and regulatory work on behalf of healthcare providers. Significant engagements in 2004 include acting as interim general counsel to the Parkland Health and Hospital System, advising on business expansion and other projects. In contentious matters the firm is handling a series of class actions on behalf of three hospitals, East Texas Medical Center, Baptist Hospital of South Florida and East Houston Regional Medical Center, concerning their provision of charity or uninsured care. It is regulatory matters however that make up the bulk of the practice, including third-party reimbursement, encompassing all aspects of Medicare and Medicaid programs. The firm also houses a cutting-edge HIPAA (Health Insurance Portability and Accountability Act) unit.

The Lawyers: Described as "*the dean of health law in the nation,*" **J D Epstein** (see p.1678) is an experienced player who co-heads the firm's health unit. He has a particular expertise in reimbursement matters, and is active on cases such as Baystate Health System v Thompson, concerning Medicare payments affecting over 600 hospitals. Epstein was one of the founders of the now-dissolved Wood Lucksinger & Epstein, a firm that kick-started national interest in health industry practice groups. **Gary Eiland** (see p.1678) shares the management responsibility and is credited with running a team of consistently high-quality advisers. Clients appreciate "*his strategic approach to handling sensitive issues,*" while peers point to his record as the premier reimbursement expert in the USA, stating: "*On Medicare he is number one!*" Eiland frequently represents clients before the DOJ and Office of Inspector General. **Brenda Strama** (see p.1702) has a sophisticated regulatory practice, spanning medical staff issues, managed care contracting and AIDS issues. Another "*standout*" practitioner in this deeply talented group is **Debbi Johnstone** (see p.1678), best known for her hospital-physician contracting work.

The Clients: HCA; The Methodist Hospital System; The University of Texas; Parkland Health and Hospital System; Community Health Systems; Montefiore Medical Center and Henry Ford Health System.

Band 3

Baker & McKenzie
See firm details p.761

The Firm: The firm operates a national healthcare industry practice, drawing in lawyers from diverse areas to address healthcare matters. A smaller number of about ten practitioners focus solely on this area of law, with an emphasis on provider representation. Particular experience lies in long-term care, assisted living and hospital operational advice. Although it is building up its broader client base, the firm has long-term connections with clients such as Abbott Laboratories and is historically strong in the pharmaceutical and medical devices arena. The team keeps abreast of regulatory development and business changes arising out of the Medicare Modernization Act, the Stark Law and other regulatory developments governing the healthcare industry. The firm does take on litigation and is currently representing hospital clients in connection with numerous physician recruitment disputes.

The Lawyers: A "*smart practitioner*" who has wide experience in the field, **Ken Gordon** (see p.1682) leads the charge at Baker & McKenzie. He is currently chair of the State Bar of Texas' health law section.

The Clients: Triad Hospitals; VHA Southwest Community Health; Schering-Plough and Abbott Laboratories.

Brown McCarroll LLP

The Firm: Clients agree that this highly responsive firm provides "*well thought out and researched advice.*" A substantial healthcare team comprises "*lawyers who are willing to listen,*" and displays great commitment to representing physicians in regulatory matters and reimbursement issues. Particular experience lies in legislative and government affairs, long-term care, HIPAA (Health Insurance Portability and Accountability Act) compliance and Medicare and Medicaid reimbursement and appeals. Recent work includes joint ventures between healthcare facilities. In the past year, the firm has represented both physician groups and hospitals joining forces to create ambulatory surgery centers. Other strengths include litigation, where typical disputes touch on labor and employment issues, asset purchase agreements, practice management contracts, and real estate.

The Lawyers: A widely admired figure in the market, **David Hilgers** has an excellent track record, particularly in physician work, though he is equally well-versed in the representation of hospitals. This dual perspective adds value, according to our sources: "*He brings knowledge from both the hospital and physician side – his clients see the benefit.*" Recent engagements include representing a physician-owned hospital to ensure compliance with federal laws and to obtain contracts with local managed care companies. An excellent communicator, who "*knows what he's talking about,*" **Bill Darling** combines an "*easygoing style*" with the ability to "*get straight down to business.*" His practice encompasses litigation and he has represented clients before various state regulatory and licensing agencies as well as state and federal courts.

The Clients: Clients run the gamut from hospitals to physicians, health plan providers and imaging centers.

Davis & Wilkerson, PC

The Firm: A specialist firm that is "*truly interested in rural healthcare and rural hospitals in Texas,*" it is closely associated with the industry it serves. The practice focuses on transactional, regulatory and general advisory work, representing community and regional hospitals as well as senior housing and assisted living organizations. Clients point to the "*strong pool of experts*" on hand, who are well equipped to advise on medical staff relations, involving hearings and credentialing, and contracting matters for hospitals. Litigation, including medical malpractice, is a further area of expertise.

The Lawyers: Widely admired for his work with rural hospitals, **Kevin Reed** can "*demysti-fy all the legal aspects of a complicated industry,*" according to clients. Serving an industry that has its own unique set of issues, Reed is seen as an attorney who "*truly cares and understands all the implications.*" He is experienced in licensing and regulatory matters for healthcare facilities and practitioners, representing clients before both state and federal agencies.

The Clients: Trinity Medical Center, St. Joseph Regional Health Center and Mission Hospital in Mission, Texas, are clients.

Jenkens & Gilchrist

The Firm: Despite the departure of Ken Gordon to Baker & McKenzie in 2003, this firm retains a team of well-respected healthcare lawyers, although it lacks the prominence it once enjoyed. The practice encompasses a wide spectrum of healthcare matters, including fraud and abuse issues, Stark Law compliance and tax-exempt bond financing. Recent work includes representing Adventist Health System in a bond transaction. The firm is experienced in financing work, especially for nonprofit organizations, and works with banks in providing loans to hospitals. Other projects include representing physician groups in the formation of startup long-term care facilities. The firm also handles clinical trial cases.

The Lawyers: "*Simply excellent when it comes to the managed care industry,*" **Lawrence Foust** is a well-respected name in healthcare circles. He is experienced in all aspects of provider and managed care financing and M&A. Other areas of expertise include hospital operations and licensing.

The Clients: Clients include the East Texas Medical Center and Hendrick Medical Center.

INSURANCE

Texas
Leading firms (Insurance)

[1]	**AKIN GUMP STRAUSS HAUER & FELD LLP** *Austin*
	FULBRIGHT & JAWORSKI LLP *Houston*
	HAYNES AND BOONE LLP *Dallas*
	MARTIN, DISIERE, JEFFERSON *Houston*
	THOMPSON, COE, COUSINS & IRONS LLP *Dallas*
[2]	**COOPER & SCULLY PC** *Dallas*
	GARDERE WYNNE SEWELL LLP *Houston*
	NICKENS KEETON LAWLESS FARRELL *Austin*
	VINSON & ELKINS LLP *Houston*
	YORK, KELLER & FIELD *Austin*
[3]	**COOK & ROACH, LLP** *Houston*
	GRAVES, DOUGHERTY, HEARON *Austin*
	STRASBURGER & PRICE LLP *Dallas*

Firms are listed alphabetically in each band.

Band 1

Akin Gump Strauss Hauer & Feld LLP

See firm details p.477

The Firm: This firm fields a formidable team of insurance litigators out of its San Antonio office, which forms part of a larger, national offering. Typical matters include reinsurance arbitration, life insurance class actions and cases concerning market conduct. With high-profile investigations into insurance broking foremost on the national agenda, the firm has been instructed on several such matters, ranging from negotiations with state authorities to running internal audits of broking companies. The team is also active in life insurance settlement and financing; for example it represented organizations starting insurance operations for medical liability companies. It has also negotiated a large homeowners insurance enforcement case with industry regulators.

The Lawyers: Known as a key regulatory and transactional player in Texas, **Thomas Bond** (see p.1672) leads the charge at Akin Gump. As well as representing a wide range of holding companies, life insurance companies and trade associations, he is actively involved in bringing forward legislative changes, principally in the regulation of health maintenance organizations.

The Clients: Clients include AIG, The Hartford and Liberty Mutual.

Fulbright & Jaworski LLP

See firm details p.1715

The Firm: This broad-based practice operates out of the firm's four offices in Texas and is further bolstered in international markets work by its presence in London. The firm is an active player in coverage litigation and major class actions, according to market commentators. The experienced team has represented Pan-American Life in a long-running ERISA-related class action, as well as in numerous life insurance claims. Other strengths include regulatory and transactional matters, as well as corporate finance and capital markets work. The firm can also be called upon for its expertise in the formation of insurance holding companies.

The Lawyers: The widely respected **Reagan Brown** (see p.1674) is experienced in both trial and appellate work and is recognized in the insurance market for his representation of policyholders. Recent work includes acting for Gerling America Insurance on a commercial business policy dispute. Similarly regarded by peers as a "*highly credible*" practitioner, **Steve Pate** (see p.1695) concentrates his practice on first-party insurance and commercial coverage litigation, among other areas. With an extensive career in third-party insurance coverage and extra contractual liability defense behind him, **Arno Krebs** (see p.1687) is a name that continues to add kudos to the practice.

The Clients: AIG; Progressive Casualty Insurance; Amica Mutual Insurance; Gray Insurance; MetLife; MONY Life Insurance; National Western Life and Texas Mutual Insurance.

Haynes and Boone LLP

The Firm: Commentators endorsed litigation prowess at the core of this highly capable department, which earns a stellar reputation for corporate policyholder work. The dedicated team specializes in litigating all forms of liability policies, including life insurance products. Recent successes include securing in excess of $20 million in settlement in connection with a major trial concerning surplus lines insurance markets. As an extension of the insurance practice the team represents corporate plaintiffs in securities, antitrust and RICO matters.

The Lawyers: "*A name that's on the tip of everyone's tongue,*" commentators place **Ernest Martin** "*at the top of his game.*" Chair of the insurance practice, he is a leading advocate for corporate clients in insurance-related disputes. Recent experience includes handling mold litigation for major hotel chains. Founder of the insurance practice, **Werner Powers** has over 25 years' experience in the field. He is currently handling a broker-dealer regulation case on a national level on behalf of Michaels Stores.

The Clients: Amerada Hess; Texas Health Resources; ExxonMobil; ACE Cash Express; AMRESCO; CellStar; Craftmade International; Cybershield; Elcor and Trilogy.

Texas
Leading individuals (Insurance)

[1] BROWN Reagan *Fulbright & Jaworski*, Houston
COOPER Brent *Cooper & Scully*, Dallas
HUDDLESTON Michael *Shannon Gracey*, Dallas
MARTIN Brian *Thompson Coe*, Houston
MARTIN Christopher *Martin Disiere*, Houston
MARTIN Ernest *Haynes and Boone*, Dallas

[2] BOND Thomas *Akin Gump*, Austin
BROWN David *Vinson & Elkins*, Houston
HIGGINS Roger *Thompson Coe*, Dallas
KELLER Mary *York Keller*, Austin
LAWLESS Mark *Nickens Keeton*, Austin
MOODY James *Quilling Selander*, Dallas
YORK Larry *York Keller*, Austin

[3] BURNER Burnie *Long Burner*, Austin
CONWAY Susan *Graves Dougherty*, Austin
COOPER James *Gardere Wynne*, Houston
DAVIS Will *Heath Davis*, Austin
GEIGER Richard *Thompson Coe*, Dallas
HOYT Scott *Gibson Dunn*, Dallas
KREBS Arno *Fulbright & Jaworski*, Houston
PATE Steve *Fulbright & Jaworski*, Houston
PEARSON John *Gardere Wynne*, Houston
POWERS Werner *Haynes and Boone*, Dallas
THOMPSON Jay *Thompson Coe*, Austin

Up-and-coming individuals

SHIDLOFSKY Lee *Nickens Keeton*, Austin

Individuals are listed alphabetically in each band.

Martin, Disiere, Jefferson & Wisdom LLP

See firm details p.1720

The Firm: Commentators agree that with Christopher Martin at the helm, this is a leading coverage practice. The team has expanded to house 36 attorneys statewide, advising a host of marquee personal lines carriers, such as State Farm, USAA, The Hartford and Prudential. While the group is shaping up for an anticipated run of litigation stemming from the Marsh & McLennan v AIG case, it remains one of the state leaders in mold litigation, representing companies of the caliber of Farmers. Last year the firm fought three such cases all the way to successful trial conclusion.

The Lawyers: One of the market's outstanding figures on the coverage side, **Christopher Martin** wins plaudits as a well-respected scholar and an advocate who is *"quick on his feet in court."* He is currently embroiled in one the largest bad faith cases pending in Texas, where significant damages are at stake for client Zurich.

The Clients: ACE USA; Horace Mann Educators; USAA; State Farm; The Hartford; Fireman's Fund; Royal & SunAlliance and Zurich.

Thompson, Coe, Cousins & Irons LLP

See firm details p.1723

The Firm: As well as leveraging off its long-established reputation, the insurance team is well connected throughout the state, according

to clients. The broad remit encompasses first-party representation, defense of torts litigation and, according to competitors, a particularly impressive insurance regulatory unit. Attorneys regularly appear before arbitration panels and at court in rate hearings or disciplinary matters. A popular choice for coverage work, this strong team achieves successful results in umbrella or excess policy claims and national class actions.

The Lawyers: A favorite with clients, **Brian Martin** (see p.1690) is a *"brilliant trial lawyer, who achieves outstanding results."* Successful casework in the last year includes Ranger Insurance v Scottsdale Insurance, involving a decision on the priority of payment of specialty policies. Martin also has a reputation for environmental coverage work and has handled large asbestos claims. *"A creative and tenacious advocate,"* **Roger Higgins** (see p.1684) has seen a good deal of first-party and class action litigation. Head of the insurance litigation and coverage group, he has recently handled cases concerning credit scoring and territorial ratings. He acted for Allstate in a class action concerning insurance premiums, in keeping with the firm's dominance in automobile insurance. Another distinguished player, **Richard Geiger** (see p.1680) continues to play an active role representing insurance trade associations before the legislature and takes part in industrywide rate hearings. Singled out as a *"specialist in regulatory matters,"* **Jay Thompson** (see p.1703) is illustrative of the firm's tradition for producing quality advisers. He has recently been involved in a hotly contested hearing concerning medical insurance rates on behalf of GE Medical. This is an area that has seen a shift in regulation to the Department of Insurance, subsequent to torts reform being passed in Texas in 2003, hence it has had significant press coverage as well as precedent-setting implications. Thompson has also spent time lobbying for the Association of Fire and Casualty Companies in Texas (AFACT).

The Clients: The firm has a loyal base of clients including Texas Association of Life & Health Insurers, AFACT, ICT Insurance and TAIPA.

Band 2

Cooper & Scully PC

See firm details p.1712

The Firm: This high-quality, litigation-oriented outfit represents insureds, insurers and reinsurers in coverage disputes across the board. Experience ranges from bad faith representation, to professional liability cases, to toxic and mass torts. Since torts reform in Texas, the market has seen an influx of new insurers especially in the healthcare sector, an area in which the firm has a solid track record. The team tackles an increasing number of medical malpractice cases, representing insureds, before the Court of Appeal and the Texas Supreme Court in Austin. The 16-partner team also drafts policies and represent insurers before regulatory bodies.

The Lawyers: *"A giant in his field"* **Brent Cooper** is considered one of the best medical malpractice appellate lawyers in the state. Clients enthuse that *"he is the go-to person for the occasional miracle: he can always make a difference on a case."* With further experience in coverage work on the carrier side, Cooper was also active in paving the way for torts reform in the state.

The Clients: Zurich; AIG; Texas Medical Liability Trust; St. Paul Travelers; Unitrin; Employers Reinsurance and American Healthcare Indemnity.

Gardere Wynne Sewell LLP

See firm details p.1718

The Firm: For *"on-the-spot technical expertise"* this firm scores highly, according to clients. Pre-loss coverage advice is an area of increasing importance to the firm's clients, and the team has been called on to review policies and procedures for corporate policyholders before a loss occurs. Clients comment that the firm's insurance attorneys are *"good at alerting us to risks that are coming up"* in a manner that is both *"responsive and thorough – we never have to second guess them."* The recently expanded team totals 20 lawyers concentrating on Directors & Officers insurance, Errors & Omissions, general commercial liability, and areas as diverse as marine and oil field-related insurance.

The Lawyers: Clients look to *"efficient and customer-focused"* **John Pearson** (see p.1695) for Directors & Officers and marine insurance advice. He is experienced in major disputes, typically revolving around asbestos claims and is currently embroiled in a $40 million private equity-related case. Leading the section in Houston, **James Cooper** (see p.1675) is well practiced in commercial general liability and a high-profile figure in the market. Beverly Godbey heads up the Dallas group.

The Clients: American River Transportation; Lennar; Oil States Industries; Cooper/T. Smith Stevedoring; Schlumberger; Van Seumeren Holland and Walter Oil & Gas.

Nickens Keeton Lawless Farrell & Flack LLP

The Firm: A successful outfit that *"knows how to run complex cases,"* clients turn to the practice for insurance coverage disputes. The firm houses a team of respected civil trial attorneys, three of whom focus on insurance defense work. These specialists have secured a reputation among competitors as *"one of the best options in Texas if you need someone to fight your corner."* The small but skilled team has seen a recent influx in Directors & Officers cases and is typically engaged in high stakes litigation.

The Lawyers: A contender who is not afraid to *"take a gutsy approach,"* **Mark Lawless** wins respect from all sides. He enjoys an outstanding track record for insurance defense work and

1648   All quotes in the text are from interviews with clients and competitors.

CHAMBERS USA 2005

maintains his edge in long running environment-related, asbestos and toxic tort cases. Clients are also full of praise for "*straight shooter*," **Lee Shidlofsky**, who has recently handled insurance coverage matters related to construction defects and products liability. An "*extremely bright*" younger lawyer, he is "*instrumental in coming up with effective legal solutions*."

The Clients: Potter Concrete; S&B Engineers and Constructors; Temple-Inland; JT Thorpe & Son; Total and Tyler Technologies.

Vinson & Elkins LLP

See firm details p.1724

The Firm: This hugely respected full-service firm takes on policyholder work for a host of blue-chip clients. Its remit extends to all facets of general and professional liability policies, coverage analysis and first-party litigation. With a team of "*excellent insurance litigators*" on board, competitors say the firm maintains an active presence in the market, despite the departure of Susan Conway to Graves, Dougherty, Hearon & Moody. The firm's contentious practice includes bad faith litigation, appeals and arbitration proceedings, and cases in connection with the duty to defend.

The Lawyers: Dubbed by commentators as "*an insurance lawyer for business*," **David Brown** (see p.1674) is the standout figure here and head of the practice. He is typically called upon to advise on insurance, indemnity, and casualty loss-allocation matters.

The Clients: Clients include corporations, business policyholders, large domestic life and casualty insurers, and European and international underwriters. The firm has acted for Southwest Airlines and Reliant Resources among others.

York, Keller & Field

The Firm: In this firm, applauded for its insurance regulatory and trial work, there is a team of four lawyers, who bring over 20 years of experience in Texas state government to private practice. Particular areas of expertise include regulatory issues before the state Department of Insurance and reinsurance as well as insolvency, restructurings and a host of corporate transactions.

The Lawyers: A widely respected figure, **Mary Keller** can turn her hand to compliance and regulatory matters, as well as representing clients in antitrust investigations brought by the Attor-

ney General. She has an energetic class action practice, representing clients of the caliber of State Farm. **Larry York** is similarly well connected, with contacts in state government, which competitors own "*serves the firm well.*" Both attorneys are highlighted for their "*extensive experience*" in the insurance field.

The Clients: State Farm; CIGNA; ACE American Insurance; Lloyd's; Affiliated Computer Services and Washington Mutual.

Band 3

Cook & Roach, LLP

The Firm: Home to some excellent insurance lawyers, this five-strong outfit has significant status in commercial policyholder work, peers say. Other areas of expertise include environmental and toxic torts, premises liability and related construction matters. The team handles trial work, appeals, mediations and arbitrations in connection with insurance coverage.

The Lawyers: Founding partners, Ronald Cook and Robert Roach are the names most closely identified with insurance work. Their joint experience extends to antitrust, securities and partnership disputes as well as products liability.

The Clients: Alliance Capital Management; Skyways International; Park National Bank of Houston; GE; Michelin; BP; Chevron USA and Waste Management.

Graves, Dougherty, Hearon & Moody, PC

The Firm: This firm debuts in the tables this year, due to an increased profile in insurance regulatory and administrative work, following the arrival of Susan Conway from Vinson & Elkins in 2004. As an adjunct to the firm's litigation offering, a number of lawyers handle insurance-related work, including class actions and regulatory litigation. For example, the firm represents a major workers' compensation carrier in connection with its insurance disputes.

The Lawyers: Described as a "*top regulatory lawyer*," **Susan Conway** has devoted a substantial amount of her time over the past year to a large insurance rate case. She also handles non-contentious insurance work, such as compliance, filings and licensing matters.

Strasburger & Price LLP

The Firm: With more than 40 lawyers practicing in the field of insurance law, the firm is well positioned to cover the full gamut, from counseling to litigation. Typical matters include the design of specialty insurance programs, drafting insurance policies and complying with regulations. The team also represents insurers in a broad range of commercial litigation, where cases include market conduct, antitrust and civil RICO.

The Lawyers: Practice area leader, Michael Keeley is representing a Directors & Officers insurer and a fidelity bond insurer in connection with the HealthSouth litigation pending in Birmingham, Alabama. He often represents insurers in coverage disputes on a national level.

The Clients: St. Paul Travelers; Allianz; The Hartford and Zurich.

Other Notable Practitioners

"*Definitely a class A player*," **Michael Huddleston** is the leading light at Shannon, Gracey, Ratliff & Miller LLP. Praised by market sources for his "*wealth of knowledge*," he represents both corporate and insurance companies in coverage disputes and bad faith litigation. **James Moody** of Quilling, Selander, Cummiskey & Lownds, P.C. is a lawyer whose work on behalf of excess insurance companies earns him a reputation as an "*expert in the field*." Moody has a busy practice encompassing insurance defense, reinsurance matters and environmental insurance coverage. Described by one interviewee as "*the dean of the insurance regulatory and lobbying bar*," **Will Davis** at Heath, Davis & McCalla brings years of experience to the table; while at Long, Burner, Parks & DeLargy, **Burnie Burner** is equally well known for his regulatory and lobbying practice. A name that peers say "*pops up a lot*," Burner is seen representing mutuals, foreign mutuals and small life insurance companies. "*Bright and knowledgeable*," **Scott Hoyt** (see p.1684) of Gibson, Dunn & Crutcher LLP is an attorney, who "*knows the ins and outs of insurance law*," according to clients. Representative matters include Gruma v Zurich of Mexico, where Hoyt acted for Zurich in a jury trial over coverage for business recall. His cases often have an environmental bent and he is experienced in asbestos issues.

INTELLECTUAL PROPERTY

Band 1

Baker Botts LLP

See firm details p.1708

The Firm: Sources consistently cited this "*first-class*" practice as a "*powerhouse*" in intellectual property. Clients regard the team as "*very responsive, thorough and always willing to go the extra mile to achieve success.*" Competitors also concede: "*Baker Botts excels in all areas of IP in the state.*" A long-established presence in the practice area and a sizable team of 106 attorneys

provide the group with the resources and depth to handle the full gamut of IP matters, from day-to-day portfolio management issues to patent and trademark litigation and prosecution. The group benefits from a potent client roster of Fortune 500 companies and has been involved

Texas

Leading firms (Intellectual Property)

1 BAKER BOTTS LLP *Houston*

FULBRIGHT & JAWORSKI LLP *Houston*

VINSON & ELKINS LLP *Houston*

2 AKIN GUMP STRAUSS HAUER & FELD LLP *Houston*

HAYNES AND BOONE LLP *Dallas*

HOWREY SIMON ARNOLD & WHITE *Houston*

JONES DAY *Dallas*

MCKOOL SMITH *Dallas*

SIDLEY AUSTIN BROWN & WOOD LLP *Dallas*

3 BRACEWELL & GIULIANI LLP *Houston*

CONLEY, ROSE & TAYON *Houston*

COX SMITH MATTHEWS *San Antonio*

DAVIS MUNCK *Dallas*

DEWEY BALLANTINE LLP *Houston*

DILLON & YUDELL LLP *Austin*

FISH & RICHARDSON *Dallas*

GARDERE WYNNE SEWELL LLP *Dallas*

HUGHES & LUCE LLP *Dallas*

JENKENS & GILCHRIST PC *Dallas*

LOCKE LIDDELL & SAPP LLP *Houston*

SLUSSER, WILSON & PARTRIDGE LLP *Houston*

THOMPSON & KNIGHT LLP *Dallas*

Firms are listed alphabetically in each band.

in a number of high-profile matters this year. The team notably provides counsel to Halliburton on various patent prosecutions, litigation and risk management issues. Recent deals of note include acting for EDS in a successful patent interference matter concerning the invention of prepaid phone cards activated via an automated teller machine. The group also achieved a series of positive trial verdicts on a patents infringement case for Applica, Black & Decker's household products arm.

The Lawyers: Houston IP chair **Scott Partridge** (see p.1695) remains *"highly visible and a fair adversary who can easily relate to a jury and discern an opponent's weakness in a heartbeat."* He is famed for his patent litigation skills and was the lead counsel on the aforementioned Tilia v Applica Consumer Products, ITC hearing. *"Articulate and focused"* **Jerry Mills** (see p.1692) chairs the intellectual property department. His practice is centered on advising companies on the licensing and enforcement of patent portfolios. He assisted Texas Instruments in the preparation of their patent portfolio and licensing of their children's product 'Speak and Spell'. *"Superb communicator"* **Thomas Felger** (see p.1679) instills confidence in clients as *"a dedicated strategist"* in patents-related mandates. He is currently acting for Trinity Industries on a range of technology, licensing and distribution agreements across the globe. He also oversees the firm's IP activities in its Austin office. **Mitch Lukin** (see p.1689) applies his *"brilliant intellect"* to patent and copyright infringements on behalf of his prominent IT client base, and has lately represented Dell on patent litigation related to computer display systems. His diverse practice

additionally encompasses corporate transactions linking technology transfers and intellectual property rights. MIT graduate **Barton Showalter** (see p.1700) continues to impress interviewees with his expertise in the electronics, telecommunications and software industry spheres. Rising newcomers **Carey Jordan** (see p.1686) and **Luke Pedersen** (see p.1695) are both described by clients as *"helpful and willing to go above and beyond to win a case."* Jordan specialises in the energy industry, while Pedersen focuses on patent prosecution and litigation for emerging technology companies.

The Clients: Aventis Pharmaceuticals; Halliburton; i2 Technologies; Raytheon; Texas Instruments; Trinity Industries; Cisco Systems and Dell Computer Corporation

Fulbright & Jaworski LLP

See firm details p.1715

The Firm: A group of 78 IP lawyers works out of offices in Austin, Dallas, Houston and San Antonio, and handles some of the most significant cases across the country. *"The firm just does marvellous work,"* clients enthused. The team is renowned for its successful track record in high-level patent and trademark trials. It represented Sony and Phoenix Productions in obtaining a favorable settlement on an infringement of another party's movie manuscript of an Arnold Schwarzenegger film. Interviewees also applauded the leading, nationally recognized, trademarks practice, which acts for such prestigious names as ExxonMobil, LexisNexis and Starbucks. According to market sources, *"all of the attorneys are extremely professional, analytical and can handle any IP litigation case under the sun."* Clients especially appreciate the fact that senior partners are *"very hands-on and pay attention to the nuts and bolts of it all"* when advising on copyrights, patents, trademarks and trade secrets.

The Lawyers: Sources commended **Lou Pirkey**'s (see p.1697) *"knowledge and wealth of experience in patents and trademarks."* According to rivals, *"he stands out as one of the top patent trial attorneys in the country."* He has acted in over 300 trademark and unfair competition litigation mandates in both federal district and appellate courts across the country, and has previously served on the Trademark Public Advisory Committee of the US Patent and Trademark Office. He is also the lead counsel to 3M for all of its trademark defense work. **Paul Krieger** (see p.1687) is head of the firm's intellectual property and technology department. He is widely endorsed as *"an outstanding IP litigator,"* with more than 50 patent, trademark and copyright trials under his belt. He obtained a successful verdict for Weatherford International in a patent infringement case brought by Frank's Casing Crew & Rental Tools in the Federal Court of Appeals. Clients singled out **Brett Govett** (see p.1682) for his patent infringement litigation work. He is viewed as *"a calm and*

rational thinker with great business acumen and a fantastic legal brain." He is a member of the firm's litigation department and also undertakes instructions in general commercial matters. Head of the firm's IP and technology team in Austin, **David Parker** (see p.1695) focuses his practice on biotechnology and on the protection and licensing of patent portfolios. He also serves as a senior intellectual property executive for Introgen Therapeutics, a gene therapy company involved in clinical trials of gene-based anti-cancer therapies.

The Clients: Transocean; Schlumberger; Rohm; Aerobus; PepsiCo; Harris Corporation; Infowave Software; Hollywood Entertainment; ExxonMobil; Starbucks; Home Depot; Lexis-Nexis; Weatherford International and 3M.

Vinson & Elkins LLP

See firm details p.1724

The Firm: This practice is one of the largest full-service firms in the southwest. It employs 700 lawyers spread across ten offices in Austin, Dallas, Houston, New York and Washington, and also has satellite offices in Asia, the Middle East and Europe. Clients particularly love *"Vinson & Elkins' supreme reliability, wondrous resources and broad repertoire of expertise"* in patents, copyrights and trademarks. The 35 Texas-based IP lawyers represent a range of technology and biotechnology, pharmaceutical and energy companies in counseling and litigating patents, trademarks and trade secrets. Patent litigation is perceived as this group's forte. In a major litigation coup, the Dallas and Washington teams won a significant victory in one of the largest patent cases ever trialed in the Northern District of Texas for Lutron Electronics, regarding a lighting controls patent infringement claim by Genlyte Thomas Group.

The Lawyers: *"Plain-spoken and imbued with the best IP know-how around,"* **William LaFuze** (see p.1688) remains a prominent and highly esteemed figure in this practice area. Clients especially extol his *"enthusiasm and 24/7 availability"* in patent litigation matters, deeming him *"a resourceful problem solver."* He concentrates on representing clients in the electronics, oilfield and computer industries and is the new chair of the American Bar Association's section of intellectual property law. *"Highly incisive and superb IP litigator"* **Willem Schuurman** (see p.1700) *"can manage a budget, achieve cost-effective results and enjoys amazing trial success,"* according to clients. His caseload includes representing clients in the technology, medical device and chemical and industrial manufacturing sectors. Notable successes of late include acting for Dow Chemical on a successful $45 million patent claim, and defending Internet service provider Prodigy Communications against allegations of patent infringement by British Telecommunications. Interviewees generously praised **Clark Martin**

Texas
Leading individuals
(Intellectual Property)

[1] LAFUZE William *Vinson & Elkins*, Houston
MEDLOCK Bryan *Sidley Austin*, Dallas
PARTRIDGE Scott *Baker Botts*, Houston
PETERSON Gale *Cox Smith*, San Antonio
PIRKEY Louis *Fulbright & Jaworski*, Austin
SCHUURMAN Willem *Vinson & Elkins*, Austin
SLUSSER William *Slusser Wilson*, Houston

[2] BARZOUKAS Nicolas *Howrey Simon*, Houston
CLONTS David *Akin Gump*, Houston
DILLON Andrew *Dillon & Yudell*, Austin
HEWITT Lester *Akin Gump*, Houston
KIMBALL Albert *Bracewell & Giuliani*, Houston
KNOLL Susan *Howrey Simon*, Houston
LYNCH John *Howrey Simon*, Houston
MARTIN Clark *Vinson & Elkins*, Houston
MCAUGHAN Robert *Locke Liddell*, Houston
MCCOMBS David *Haynes and Boone*, Dallas
MILLS Jerry *Baker Botts*, Dallas
NORRIS John *Howrey Simon*, Houston
RICHARD Molly *Thompson & Knight*, Dallas
TOBOR Ben *Bracewell & Giuliani*, Houston
TURNER Robert *Jones Day*, Dallas

[3] BECKER Jeffrey *Haynes and Boone*, Dallas
BOULWARE Margaret *Baker & McKenzie*, Houston
CAWLEY Douglas *McKool Smith*, Dallas
COTROPIA Charles *Sidley Austin*, Dallas
FELGER Thomas *Baker Botts*, Austin
FLOYD Adam *Vinson & Elkins*, Austin
GALVAN Hilda *Jones Day*, Dallas
GLASER Kenneth *Gardere Wynne*, Dallas
GOVETT Brett *Fulbright & Jaworski*, Dallas
HAMMOND Herbert *Thompson & Knight*, Dallas
HEIM Mike *Conley Rose*, Plano
ISRAEL Sharon *Jenkens & Gilchrist*, Houston
KRIEGER Paul *Fulbright & Jaworski*, Houston
KUDLAC Kevin *Dewey Ballantine*, Austin
LUKIN Mitch *Baker Botts*, Houston
MCKOOL Mike *McKool Smith*, Dallas
MUNCK William *Davis Munck*, Dallas
NATION Floyd *Howrey Simon*, Houston
PARKER David *Fulbright & Jaworski*, Austin
ROSE David *Conley Rose*, Houston
SAROSDY Randall *Akin Gump*, Austin
SCHWARTZ Michele *Hughes & Luce*, Dallas
SELINGER Jerry *Morgan Lewis*, Dallas
SHOWALTER Barton *Baker Botts*, Dallas
SOSTEK Bruce *Thompson & Knight*, Dallas
TEMPLIN Donald *Haynes and Boone*, Dallas
WHITE T Gordon *McKool Smith*, Austin

Up-and-coming individuals
JORDAN Carey *Baker Botts*, Houston
PEDERSEN Luke *Baker Botts*, Dallas

Individuals are listed alphabetically in each band.

(see p.1690), who is said to provide "*stellar expertise and support*" in advising clients on patents, copyright and trademark infringements. Highlights include representing Continental Airlines in a software case against Butler Aviation, and representing Core Laboratories in two separate patent infringement actions, brought by Schlumberger and Authentix respectively. Clients brimmed with praise for younger partner, **Adam Floyd** (see p.1679). He impresses many as "*a talented protégé of Willem Schuurman.*" Floyd is building credibility for "*quick thinking on his feet*" in courtroom scenarios when handling patent and trade secret litigation matters.

The Clients: Lutron Electronics; Core Laboratories; Continental Airlines; Prodigy Communications; Dynegy; Textron, Kearney & Trecker and Dow Chemical.

Band 2

Akin Gump Strauss Hauer & Feld LLP
See firm details p.477

The Firm: This long-established Dallas firm has grown into a national and global player with offices across the USA and Europe and in the Middle East. It impresses clients and peers on the national IP scene, and was described as the new "*hot tamale*" that is "*spicing things up*" in the patents arena. The foundations for this practice were laid in 1999 when attorneys from the former Houston IP boutique of Pravel, Hewitt & Kimball joined the group. The team now numbers 18 lawyers and enjoys a diet of patent, trademark, copyright and trade secret cases in the technology and hi-tech sectors, acting in some of the most high-profile IP disputes both within and outside of state boundaries. The group has guided Samsung Electronics and medical device company Kinetic Concepts in a series of major patent infringement trials in Texas. The group is also currently acting for ArvinMeritor in Boler v ArvinMeritor, a patent infringement case involving truck suspension systems that is pending in the state of Illinois. Although its claim to fame is in patents litigation, the group additionally benefits from the resources of a larger, national network of patent attorneys and agents registered with the US Patent and Trademark Office, who specialize in advising on application prosecutions.

The Lawyers: Much of the group's preeminence in the field is linked to the litigation talents of the practice cochair and former name partner of Pravel, Hewitt & Kimball, **Lester Hewitt** (see p.1684). According to clients, "*He puts together a tremendous team and is well-versed in the law, highly experienced and is extremely helpful*" when it comes to dealing with all areas of contentious IP. His experience also encompasses IP-related antitrust issues and, prior to joining private practice, he worked as an examiner at the US Patent and Trademark Office. **David Clonts** (see p.1675) wins kudos from clients as "*a proactive and conscientious IP attorney*." His practice leans towards counseling clients in the software, electronic and computer industries in all areas of IP licensing, procurement and litigation matters. Prior to joining the firm's Austin office, **Randall Sarosdy** (see p.1699) served as head of its litigation practice in Washington, DC. His wealth of expertise in IP, technology and class action litigation earned him a steady stream of praise from competitors. He is presently representing AT&T in a patent infringement case involving MyMail and AOL (now Time Warner).

The Clients: ArvinMeritor; Bausch & Lomb; AT&T; Samsung Electronics; Lufkin Industries; Kinetic Concepts and IQ Products.

Haynes and Boone LLP

The Firm: The firm's strong intellectual property presence in Texas is accompanied by impressive depth in technology law. Its niche is in advising established and emerging hi-tech companies on patent and copyright infringements and trade secret disputes. A group of "*dedicated and first-class*" attorneys impresses clients with its "*flawless technical interpretation of the law.*" A full-service intellectual property group, its attorneys have acknowledged expertise in the management and enforcement of worldwide trademark portfolios, notably for RadioShack, coupled with experience in handling the preparation and prosecution of both US and international patents for clients such as Dell and Halliburton. The group has an impressive history of work in the telecommunications sector, recently acting for inventors in an enforcement campaign for patents covering messaging services against AT&T, Unisys and other long-distance carriers. The team also acts for inventors in patent applications involving the electronic processing of call detail records against AT&T and other service providers.

The Lawyers: **David McCombs** is regarded by clients as "*very smart and level-headed*" and "*unflappable*" when it comes to advising and litigating in patent-related matters. He is currently counsel to the DOJ in the case of Summit Technology and VISX involving the dissolution of the patent pooling arrangement for patents on LASIK eye surgery. **Jeffrey Becker** concentrates his practice on patent portfolio acquisitions and the protection of software and mechanical technology. He notably advises Dresser-Rand on the technology assets of Biphase Energy and Infobase Services on its software-related portfolio. **Donald Templin** is renowned for his successfully diverse IP litigation practice. His caseload includes matters for clients in the software, media and entertainment, and semiconductor industries, where he is often involved in trade secret, patent infringement and media defense cases.

The Clients: Acutex; Aloha Housewares; Cell-Star; Cisco Systems; Dell; Descartes Software; Halliburton; Hitachi; NEC; Nortel Networks; Novell; Tristar Products and RadioShack.

Howrey Simon Arnold & White

The Firm: This national and international firm continues to enjoy a commanding presence in the state for its litigation and antitrust expertise. Its team-working skills and international network of offices are big draws for clients, as are its *"ultra-bright and sound group of practitioners."* The past year was especially successful for the 60-lawyer IP team in Houston. The patent litigation unit continues to handle perhaps the greatest number of mandates, and it regularly acts as counsel to such Fortune 500 giants as Merck, Monsanto and Coca-Cola. The Texas-based team is actively representing these companies in some of the most significant IP disputes in the country.

The Lawyers: Robert McAughan's departure to Locke Liddell & Sapp has been one of the most talked-about moves in Houston intellectual property circles. However, commentators agree that it is too early to say to what extent this will affect the firm's excellent general profile. Newcomer to the tables **Nicolas Barzoukas** inspires confidence in clients as *"an intellectually gifted and committed"* IP lawyer, particularly in the pharmaceutical arena. It is here that he has successfully represented clients in several Hatch-Waxman Act patent infringement cases, resulting in the protection of well-known drug brands Pepcid®, Actonel®, and VIOXX®. **John Norris** is widely acknowledged as an eminent figure in the intellectual property patent litigation world. He specializes in patent, trademark and trade secret litigation, with a niche in chemical and petrochemical technologies. **John Lynch** is considered *"one of the best IP lawyers in the state,"* according to rivals. He acts for such clients as Quantum, Medtronic and Westinghouse Electric on patent litigation and prosecution matters. Clients are *"delighted"* with **Susan Knoll**'s performance in providing *"reasonable options and wonderful strategy"* on patent litigation. She handles IP patent litigation matters in the semiconductor, computer and oil field industries. **Floyd Nation** retains an excellent profile for patent litigation in the hi-tech industry, acting for clients such as Sun Microsystems. His practice specializes in advising on patents mediation, licensing and infringement matters.

The Clients: Coca-Cola; Texaco; Merck; Xerox; Caterpillar; Dana; Monsanto; Quantum and Eli Lilly.

Jones Day

See firm details p.485

The Firm: Sources agreed that this firm is *"expanding into a national and international giant"* in IP litigation. According to clients and peers, the team is *"building a pretty significant presence in patents,"* with Dallas attorneys relying upon the resources of its national network and the talents of Cleveland-based star IP trial attorney Ken Adamo. The firm also has a substantial roster of clients in the IT, electronic and pharmaceutical industries. The team successfully represented Texas Instruments in three major patent infringement suits relating to their semiconductor products in front of the federal court and the ITC. It also acted as counsel to The MathWorks in a software patent infringement dispute, and Fujitsu Network Communications in obtaining a temporary restraining order against Cisco Systems in a trade secrets matter. The group's success is also replicated in patent and trademark prosecution and transaction work, due in large measure to the fact that many of the team are US Patent and Trademark-registered lawyers with mixed IP litigation and prosecution practices.

The Lawyers: Market commentators continue to praise **Hilda Galvan**'s (see p.1680) *"superb litigation prowess"* and her skills in resolving patent, copyright and trademark infringement disputes, particularly in the technology sector. She successfully represented Nextel in a patent infringement case related to its specialized mobile radio technology (SMR). In another key case, she defended Beautone Specialties and Taiwan Hopax Chemicals in a trademark infringement action in which 3M asserted rights to the color 'canary yellow' for sticky notes. The case settled after she helped successfully to limit 3M's damages claim on summary judgment. She is also registered with the US Patent and Trademark Office and is active in counseling clients in the telecommunications sector on managing technology portfolios. The *"terrific"* **Robert Turner** (see p.1704), *"one of the leading, long-standing IP personalities"* in the state, is widely acknowledged as a key member of the IP team. His practice addresses patent and trademark prosecution, with heavy emphasis on IP dispute resolution work and handling complex copyright and trade secret cases in the courts and in front of the ITC. He is also a former chairman of the IP chapter of the Texas State Bar.

The Clients: Fujitsu Network Communications; The MathWorks; Texas Instruments; Nextel; PepsiCo and JBL.

McKool Smith

The Firm: This firm's high-caliber work in IP litigation has placed it at the forefront of this market, and interviewees praised the lawyers as being at the *"top of their game and replete with excellent knowledge of the courts."* The team has a history of high-profile national successes in commercial, civil and appellate cases in state and federal courts. Its IP litigators are actively representing Lockheed Martin and Monsanto on prominent patent litigations in the states of Delaware, California and Alabama. The firm has also reaped the benefits of having an office in Marshall, a town recognized as a hotbed for intellectual property patent trials, and here the team has represented the likes of Ericsson and Intel in some of the most significant patent disputes in the country. In addition to its strengths in patent litigation, burgeoning areas of success include trade secrets, licensing and antitrust-related IP work. Highlights include acting for Wal-Mart on a trade secret dispute and EDS on a software licensing litigation against Computer Associates.

The Lawyers: The cornerstone of the team is the practice founder **Mike McKool**, who is *"clearly one of the most accomplished"* business and IP trial specialists in the state, according to commentators. He successfully represented National Instruments against The MathWorks in a patent infringement action involving software technology. In another widely reported software technology case, he successfully acted for Excel Communications in obtaining a grant of summary judgment of invalidity before the federal court. **Douglas Cawley**'s focus is on patent and software copyright litigation. He defended Intel and subsidiary Xircom in an alleged patent infringement of Ethernet protocols, and also acted for DGI Technologies against Alcatel in complex copyright, trade secret and antitrust-related litigation. Peers singled out **Gordon White** for his *"tremendous experience"* in patent litigation. His skills were recently put to the test in Samsung Electronics v Texas Instruments, a patent infringement claim relating to the design and modes of operation of computer memory chips. He also represented Samsung against Texas Instruments, in a case regarding counterclaims of IP antitrust.

The Clients: Ericsson; Lockheed Martin; National Instruments; Hicks, Muse, Tate & Furst; EDS; Samsung Electronics; Taiwan Semiconductor; Excel Communications and Wal-Mart.

Sidley Austin Brown & Wood LLP

See firm details p.778

The Firm: Market sources endorse this firm for having had *"a very active year on the patents front,"* in which the team represented Ciba, Microsoft and other leading technology and pharmaceutical companies in high-profile disputes across the country. Its local reputation was further enhanced by the merger with the boutique of Richards, Medlock and Andrews, which notably brought on board leading IP dispute resolution specialist Bryan Medlock. Further afield, its impressive national and international network continues to offer a *"first-rate breadth of resources"* for clients. The group of 21 attorneys in Dallas has an established forte in litigating patents and prosecuting applications on behalf of a diverse array of multinationals, emerging growth and small to medium-sized companies in the software and telecommunications, and healthcare, consumer goods and biotechnology sectors. The practice additionally comes with a wealth of experience in the areas of copyright, trademark, trade secret and unfair competition litigation, and can rely upon an effective appellate practice for cases in the federal courts.

The Lawyers: Sources unequivocally take note

of **Bryan Medlock**'s (see p.1692) "*wonderful ability in a courtroom to relate to a trial jury in a fair manner while adeptly targeting an opponent's Achilles' heel.*" Peers felt that he undoubtedly deserved his top ranking due to his "*long-standing experience*" in litigating patents and trademarks. **Charles Cotropia** (see p.1675) is "*making waves,*" according to clients. His diverse IP practice encompasses clients in the restaurant, clothing apparel and building design industries in trademark, trade dress and copyright matters. His mixed practice also addresses a steady number of patent prosecutions and litigations.

The Clients: Ciba; Kimberly-Clark; Microsoft; Delphion; MicroPatent; PTO Web site; Litex Industries; TGI Friday's; Fuddruckers; Holiday Retirement Corporation and Justin Brands.

Band 3

Bracewell & Giuliani LLP
See firm details p.1710

The Firm: Market sources see the departure of Andrew Dillon and his team to form the practice of Dillon & Yudell as a potential setback to the group's profile, but acknowledge that it is too early to judge the extent of the impact. Nevertheless, this full-service practice consists of IP attorneys who are "*practical, business-minded and can actually work with non-legal staff because they keep it simple,*" according to clients. The group of 32 lawyers operating out of Austin, Houston, Dallas and San Antonio specialize in advising clients in the nanotechnology and biotechnology sectors on patent, trademark and copyright applications, and on the management of these portfolios. The IP group can also call upon the litigation department for robust support in its patent defense, enforcement and infringement caseload.

The Lawyers: The "*no-nonsense and client-friendly approach*" of **Ben Tobor** (see p.1703) wins him the consistent praise of his peers. A keynote element of his practice is advising on the direction of intellectual property assets after M&A activity. Advice on patent and trademark infringement work also represents a substantial component of his practice. He counseled Propex Fabrics on its acquisition of BP Amoco's fabrics and fibers business and, in another notable IP-driven transaction, he represented Goodman Global in its acquisition by Apollo Management. He also continues to represent Farouk Systems in a trademark infringement matter against Wal-Mart. A former founding member of IP boutique Pravel, Hewitt & Kimball, **Albert Kimball** (see p.1687) earned the commendation of clients and peers for his "*top-notch problem-solving abilities,*" particularly with respect to counseling multinational entities in IP transfer questions. He can boast extensive experience in advising on international and domestic trademarks.

The Clients: Waste Management, Goodman

Global and Farouk Systems are key names in the firm's client roster.

Conley, Rose & Tayon
The Firm: Established in 1991, this 'one-stop' IP boutique now employs 50 attorneys in Dallas and in Houston. The firm is active in all areas of IP work including patents, trademarks, copyrights and trade secrets, as well as the drafting of commercial non-competition covenants. Its "*strong reputation*" in handling patents prosecutions is viewed by observers as a key draw, while clients commended the overall "*resourcefulness, intelligence and dependability*" of its generalist IP talent pool.

The Lawyers: Clients praised **David Rose** for his "*exceptional reliability and brilliant mind*" in counseling on general IP matters. His work centers on negotiating the transfer and registration of patents and trademarks, and he is also skilled in dispute resolution. Clients expressed unequivocal approbation for the "*splendidly bright and superbly consistent*" **Mike Heim**. His multifaceted IP practice addresses technology litigation and licensing, with a niche in representing direct purchasers of pharmaceutical products in class action antitrust cases involving drug companies using IP exclusively to protect their brand name. Prior to his work in private practice, he served as a patent examiner at the US Patent and Trademark Office for three years, specializing in cases involving electrical communications and computer software and hardware.

The Clients: ATI Technologies; Centerpulse Dental; Chevron Phillips Chemical; ConocoPhillips; Cooper Cameron; Daniel Industries; E*TRADE; Halliburton; Hewlett-Packard; Nortel Networks; Rice University; Sprint and Texas Instruments.

Cox Smith Matthews Incorporated
See firm details p.1713

The Firm: Although not generally credited with the same profile as some rivals, sources nevertheless were "*most impressed*" with this San Antonio firm's national and international work in patents and trademark prosecutions and litigation. The firm is notably one of the first in southern Texas successfully to assimilate its IP team into its business and litigation department. The IP department consists of ten attorneys who specialize in domestic and international patent, trademark and copyright registration, enforcement, licensing and dispute matters. A significant highlight included advising a hospital system on a trademark development and licensing program. The group is also active in advising on alternative dispute resolutions in the IP arena. The team was recently called upon in an arbitration and mediation capacity in a multiparty patent litigation involving disposable baby diapers.

The Lawyers: **Gale Roy Peterson** (see p.1696) is widely acclaimed as "*one of the best patent prosecutors in Texas.*" He impresses interviewees with his "*super trial style, fantastic technical savoir faire and*

prodigious writing skills." Peterson devotes the majority of his practice to advising global and national clients in the IT and entertainment industry on patent, trademark and copyright issues.

The Clients: Cancer Therapy & Research Center; Clear Channel Communications; Eye Care Centers of America; Kinetic Concepts; Sirius Computer Solutions; Southwest Foundation for Biomedical Research and Trinity University.

Davis Munck
See firm details p.1714

The Firm: This small, full-service Dallas firm is acknowledged for providing quality intellectual property dispute resolution advice. It remains active in representing emerging companies on a wide array of patent, trademark and copyright, and unfair competition cases.

The Lawyers: The practice's high profile in this field is linked to the prestigious reputation of the "*entrepreneurial*" **William Munck** (see p.1693). He litigates patent and trademark cases in state and federal courts, and is registered to practice at the US Patent and Trademark Office.

The Clients: The firm represents growth companies and entrepreneurs, SME and also larger listed or public companies in a range of industry sectors.

Dewey Ballantine LLP
See firm details p.1347

The Firm: This IP team, though a relative newcomer to the Texas legal scene, benefits from its access to the resources of a major national and international law firm. Traditionally regarded as an energy and project finance legal superpower, the firm opened its Austin office in October 2002 with the strategic hire of a core group of IP lawyers from the now defunct Brobeck Phlege & Harrison. Presently home to 16 attorneys, the group is visible in numerous litigious IP matters in a range of national jurisdictions. Recent engagements include advising Intel in two significant patent infringement cases in Marshall, Texas, and in the New Jersey District Court. The unit is also counseling Microsoft in a patent infringement suit currently pending in the Federal Court of Appeals, in which software company VMware is appealing denial of preliminary injunction.

The Lawyers: At the forefront of the team is ex-Brobeck IP contentious specialist **Kevin Kudlac** (see p.1688). He played a key role in the cases mentioned above, and specializes in representing clients in the computer industry in predominantly patent-related litigation.

The Clients: Microsoft; Intel; Brother International and Edwards International.

Dillon & Yudell LLP
The Firm: Clients were "*chock-full of praise*" for this emergent patent prosecution boutique, and highlighted its "*timely, reliable and cost-effective service.*" Led by former Bracewell Patterson

www.ChambersandPartners.com
All quotes in the text are from interviews with clients and competitors.
1653

attorney Andrew Dillon, the group advises on IP procurement, portfolio capitalization and enforcement issues, and patents and trademarks defense. The team now consists of nine former Bracewell lawyers and notably advises IBM as national counsel for its acquisition maintenance and patent portfolio activities.

The Lawyers: Clients admire **Andrew Dillon** for his "*hard work and exceptional diligence*" in IP prosecution matters. According to sources, "*Dillon and his team always put our interests first.*"

The Clients: IBM, Nortel Networks and Hitachi feature prominently on the client roster.

Fish & Richardson

The Firm: The firm is considered a rising force in the Texas IP market and has been acquisitive of talent from rival firms. Despite a market perception that the team lacks a Texan rainmaker, it continues to make market inroads. The team greatly benefits from being part of a nationally renowned practice, with an established reputation in both patent prosecution and litigation work. Thomas Melsheimer is the partner contact for clients.

The Clients: Its client base consists of local and regional SME and some national and international businesses.

Gardere Wynne Sewell LLP

See firm details p.1718

The Firm: This full-service IP practice consists of 23 attorneys who advise and litigate on behalf of clients in the aviation, semiconductor and biotechnology and energy industries, with a particular emphasis on patent and unfair competition dispute resolution work. Several attorneys are equipped with field-specific technical backgrounds, adding extra depth to the general expertise in patent, copyright and trademark protection work.

The Lawyers: **Ken Glaser** (see p.1681) is the former head of Akin Gump's IP department and remains the standout figure of the group. He is especially noted for his patents and trademark work in the electronics industry.

The Clients: The team represents businesses ranging from emerging entities to multinational companies.

Hughes & Luce LLP

The Firm: This firm's intellectual property caseload is concentrated in the technology sector and it acts for marquee clients such as EDS on patent and copyright infringements and trade secret disputes. The practice blends with "*great effectiveness*" litigation, transactional and prosecution work, playing a particularly active role in Internet and domain name jurisprudence.

The Lawyers: **Michele Schwartz**'s highly regarded practice leans towards advising clients on IP-driven M&A, insolvency and unfair competition issues. She also has a strong background in advising on international trademarks and

copyright portfolios, due in no small measure to her experience of prosecution work in front of the Trademark Trial and Appeal Board.

The Clients: EDS; Perot Systems; Crane Merchandising Systems; HBK Investments; VLPS Lighting Services and CNET Networks.

Jenkens & Gilchrist PC

The Firm: Following last year's decampment of patent prosecution lawyers to Fish & Richardson and Patton Boggs, the firm was hit again this year by the departure of two highly respected experts in the shape of Jerry Selinger and Margaret Boulware, who left for Morgan, Lewis & Bockius, and Baker & McKenzie respectively. Despite this, a sizable team of lawyers maintains an active caseload in the telecommunications, biotechnology and semiconductor sectors. Of recent note, the group has increasingly become more involved in patent infringements and domain name resolution hearings, and it advised on portfolio management issues to the tune of $1.5 billion in the past year. This firm is renowned for its "*superlative*" patents, trademarks and litigation work. The losses in its New York office are unlikely to help the firm, however a robust network still includes offices throughout Texas and in the cities of Chicago, Los Angeles, Pasadena and Washington.

The Lawyers: **Sharon Israel** attracts market praise for her "*superior performance*" in litigating IP matters. She handles a steady diet of patent, trademark and copyright litigation and additionally specializes in unfair competition and infringement cases under the Plant Variety Protection Act.

The Clients: Poly-America; Ericsson; Applied Materials; KwikSYSTEM and Galt Medical.

Locke Liddell & Sapp LLP

The Firm: The arrival of Robert McAughan from Howrey Simon has confirmed Locke Liddell & Sapp's entry as "*a notable player*" in IP matters, according to interviewees. However, the firm already enjoyed a strong reputation prior to McAughan's arrival having advised established IT and technology companies on licensing, copyright and claim issues. This is reflected in a roster of illustrious clients that includes the likes of Microsoft and Hewlett-Packard. In a landmark case, the group represented Compaq in an $800 million copyright infringement claim brought by Ergonome, Brown and Mowrey. The Fifth Circuit Court of Appeals affirmed the jury verdict that no copyright infringement had taken place, resulting in the largest-ever award of attorney fees ($2.76 million) in a copyright case. Attorneys also represented Microsoft in successfully securing a claim construction brought by MIT, and also achieved positive results for Baker Hughes in a significant arbitration matter.

The Lawyers: Observers rate **Robert McAughan** (see p.1691) as "*a top-flight*" patents litigator. His varied practice undertakes instructions in other

IP areas, including trademarks, trade dress and trade secrets, on both the dispute resolution and transactional front. Of recent note, he achieved success in obtaining a preliminary injunction in Ridge Tool v Reed.

The Clients: Compaq; Microsoft; Hewlett-Packard; Baker Hughes; Emerson Electric; Acuity Brands; Varco International; Mary Kay Cosmetics; Gerber Products; BP and Technip.

Slusser, Wilson & Partridge LLP

The Firm: Founded in 1999, this Houston-based practice enjoys an excellent reputation for patent litigation, with an impressive record of achieving results for clients. The group acts for both plaintiffs and defendants on IP and commercial litigation matters. Much of the team's profile in intellectual property is linked to the success of practice cofounder, trial lawyer William Slusser. Several members of the team are also qualified engineers, and are actively involved in national patent, licensing and infringement cases.

The Lawyers: Practice leader **William Slusser** is considered a "*mighty advocate*" in a courtroom, with an "*innate aptitude for exposing an opposing counsel's weak spots in an argument.*" He is actively involved in a slew of high-profile patents infringements, notably Halliburton Energy Services v Smith International. In another major case, he is representing Shell Oil, Shell Chemical and CRI Catalyst in a patent infringement brought by Union Carbide.

The Clients: BJ Services; Smith International; Shell Oil; Shell Chemical and CRI Catalyst.

Thompson & Knight LLP

See firm details p.1722

The Firm: This long-established practice advises clients on the full range of domestic and international patents, copyrights, trade secret and unfair competition matters. With offices in Texas and also in Latin America, Europe and North Africa, it is able to exploit a substantial presence abroad, notably in energy and information technology transactions. The firm is also highly sought-after for handling all areas of trademarks, actively representing multinationals in the prosecution and negotiation of foreign and domestic applications across the globe.

The Lawyers: The "*talented and energetic*" **Molly Richard**'s (see p.1698) practice encompasses advising computer manufacturers, software and semiconductor companies on domain name disputes and trademark protection work. She also has a wealth of experience in ICANN-driven arbitration proceedings. **Herbert Hammond** (see p.1683) continues to command respect for his impressive all-around IP litigation skills. He represents clients on invention agreements, trade secrets and copyright and patent infringements. **Bruce Sostek** (see p.1701) manages a practice embracing a diverse caseload

1654   All quotes in the text are from interviews with clients and competitors.

CHAMBERS USA 2005

of intellectual property, technology and commercial litigation matters. He also advises clients on the use of IP as a tool for strategic business planning.

The Clients: The firm's impressive client roster includes Hewlett-Packard, Fossil and Greyhound.

Other Notable Practitioners

Jerry Selinger (see p.1700) caused a stir this year with his move from Jenkens & Gilchrist to the new Dallas office of international giant Morgan, Lewis & Bockius LLP. He continues to elicit praise for his "*dynamite*" patent litigation practice, and, while at Jenkens & Gilchrist, was particularly admired for his work with Ericcson and Applied Materials. His successes from the past year include a major victory for Poly-America in a patent infringement lawsuit. Also formerly with Jenkens & Gilchrist is **Margaret Boulware**, who joins the Houston office of Baker & McKenzie. She receives market commendation for her international biotechnology portfolio and trademark appeal work. Her experience also encompasses handling validity and infringement arbitrations of US patents before the International Chamber of Commerce.

LITIGATION

GENERAL COMMERCIAL

Texas
Leading firms
(Litigation: General Commercial)

1 GIBBS & BRUNS, LLP *Houston*
   SUSMAN GODFREY LLP *Houston*
   VINSON & ELKINS LLP *Houston*

2 BAKER BOTTS LLP *Houston*
   BECK, REDDEN & SECREST LLP *Houston*
   FULBRIGHT & JAWORSKI LLP *Houston*

3 CARRINGTON, COLEMAN, SLOMAN *Dallas*
   HAYNES AND BOONE LLP *Houston*
   KING & SPALDING LLP *Houston*
   MAYER, BROWN, ROWE & MAW LLP *Houston*
   MCDADE FOGLER LLP *Houston*

4 AKIN GUMP STRAUSS HAUER & FELD LLP *Houston*
   BRACEWELL & GIULIANI LLP *Houston*
   LOCKE LIDDELL & SAPP LLP *Houston*
   THOMPSON & KNIGHT LLP *Houston*
   WEIL, GOTSHAL & MANGES LLP *Dallas*

Firms are listed alphabetically in each band.

Band 1

Gibbs & Bruns, LLP

See firm details p.1719

The Firm: This "*excellent firm*" boasts a deep bench of "*absolute terrific trial lawyers,*" making it a first choice for any type of high-quality, complex commercial litigation. Clients respect the team's "*collegiate atmosphere,*" which they say helps to enhance its efficiency, while a small-firm feel makes it pleasant to deal with. The team of around 30 litigators is involved in a variety of sophisticated, bet-the-company-type cases. Securities disputes remain an area of particular expertise, however, and the group has also witnessed a notable rise in IP litigation over the past year. Highlights include successfully defending nine mutual funds managed by Merrill Lynch Asset Management, Franklin Advisers and others, against allegations of federal and state securities law violations.

The Lawyers: Robin Gibbs (see p.1681) remains "*one of the finest litigation attorneys in the country.*" He is admired for his broad experience, "*personal commitment to mastering the facts,*" "*commanding presence in court*" and skill in mentoring the firm's younger lawyers. In par-ticular, he is considered a go-to person for high-stakes securities litigation. Here, the firm has been acting for 15 former Enron directors involved in a flood of class actions initiated by investors and employees groups, alleging fraud and misrepresentation. "*Smart analyst*" **Phillip Bruns** (see p.1674) is lauded for his "*brilliant legal arguments*" and "*detail-oriented mind.*" His broad practice comprises energy disputes and high-profile patent litigation among other things. IP and energy-related litigation, along with general commercial disputes, also feature strongly in the caseload of "*impressive, intelligent and hard-working*" **Chris Reynolds** (see p.1698). He is defending Korean company, Doosan, in a dispute with ExxonMobil, seeking in excess of $40 million in damages over alleged defects in reactors built by Doosan. He is also defending New York Guangdong Finance against contractual claims made by Agricultural Bank of China, Construction Bank of China and GITC. Commentators were also full of admiration for **Jean Frizzell** (see p.1680), who is considered by many to be "*as good a younger lawyer as you will find.*" He is currently representing the former directors of a petrochemical company in a securities litigation concerning $52 million in bond losses.

The Clients: Unocal; Pennzoil; Fidelity Management; Coastal Corporation and Stone Energy.

Susman Godfrey LLP

The Firm: A tremendously impressive trial record is combined with technical skill, a national profile and an aggressive style to maintain this litigation boutique at the forefront of the market. In addition to two Texas offices, the 60+ litigators can draw on extra resources in Los Angeles and Seattle. The team collected particular praise for its "*ambition and strength,*" and its ability to handle complex, high-stakes commercial litigation. Typically this is undertaken on behalf of plaintiffs, however the firm is increasingly appearing for corporate defendants. The best-known recent example is undoubtedly its success in securing a $536 million settlement for Novell against Microsoft in a highly publicized antitrust dispute. Securities litigation, IP and products liability all also feature strongly in the group's caseload.

The Lawyers: The "*professionalism, tremendous experience and energy*" of nationally renowned **Steve Susman** were cited by interviewees as major factors behind the success of the team. He co-led the group handling Novell's NetWare antitrust claims, and negotiated a pre-filing settlement. Observers highlighted **Lee Godfrey** for his "*great jury appeal and articulate presentation*" and his "*excellent judgment,*" while **Neal Manne** was recommended as a "*superb thinker and strategist.*" He commands a broad practice, including energy litigation, breach of contract disputes, insurance coverage and asbestos litigation. Godfrey and Manne are leading a team acting for Bermuda-based insurance company, ACE, in class actions filed following a public investigation by the New York attorney general, Eliott Spitzer, into relationships between insurance companies and brokers. "*Detail-oriented*" **Mark Wawro** is said by market sources to be "*smart, tough and good on his feet.*" He has been involved of late in substantial energy-related disputes and major breach of contract litigation. **Kenneth Marks** joins his colleagues in the tables this year. "*One hell of a jury trial lawyer,*" he is said to be excellent in securities litigation, particularly following his $75 million settlement for a class of Alcatel shareholders in 2002.

The Clients: Nokia; Hertz; ConocoPhillips; Apache Corporation; Novell; Ace Insurance; Texas Instruments; Amazon.com; Equitas; Aetna; Fox Television; Universal Studios and Alaska Airlines.

Vinson & Elkins LLP

See firm details p.1724

The Firm: The Houston-based juggernaut boasts substantial resources, far-reaching trial experience, a developing international network and a strong appellate section among the weapons in its armory. All these were cited by observers as reasons for its leading position in the Texas market, as was the "*efficient and results-oriented*" style of its lawyers. The firm is acknowledged to be an ideal choice for major international disputes involving oil and gas majors, as well as other high-stakes, bet-the-company commercial litigation. It is also continuing to enhance its already respected reputation

Texas
Leading individuals
(Litigation: General Commercial)

[1] **BECK David** *Beck Redden,* Houston
BRISTOW Daryl *Baker Botts,* Houston
GIBBS Robin *Gibbs & Bruns,* Houston
GODFREY Lee *Susman Godfrey,* Houston
REASONER Harry *Vinson & Elkins,* Houston
SUSMAN Stephen *Susman Godfrey,* Houston
TERRELL Irvin *Baker Botts,* Houston

[2] **ADDISON Linda** *Fulbright & Jaworski,* Houston
BROWN Reagan *Fulbright & Jaworski,* Houston
BRUNS Phillip *Gibbs & Bruns,* Houston
CHEAVENS Joseph *Baker Botts,* Houston
COLEMAN James *Carrington Coleman,* Dallas
FOGLER Murray *McDade Fogler,* Houston
HARVIN David *Vinson & Elkins,* Houston
JONES Frank *Fulbright & Jaworski,* Houston
MANNE Neal *Susman Godfrey,* Houston
MEADOWS Robert *King & Spalding,* Houston
PHELAN Rod *Baker Botts,* Dallas
REDDEN Joe *Beck Redden,* Houston

[3] **DAWSON William** *Vinson & Elkins,* Dallas
DENNY Otway *Fulbright & Jaworski,* Houston
DILLARD Steve *Fulbright & Jaworski,* Houston
DYE Phillip *Vinson & Elkins,* Houston
FRIZZELL Jean *Gibbs & Bruns,* Houston
GOLDEN Bruce *Golden & Owens,* Houston
KNULL William *Mayer Brown,* Houston
LEAHY James *Thompson & Knight,* Houston
MARKS Kenneth *Susman Godfrey,* Houston
MCKOOL Mike *McKool Smith,* Dallas
MCNIEL D Ferguson *Vinson & Elkins,* Houston
MILLER Ralph *Weil Gotshal,* Dallas
OLDHAM Dudley *Fulbright & Jaworski,* Houston
REYNOLDS Chris *Gibbs & Bruns,* Houston
SCHICK Robert *Vinson & Elkins,* Houston
SCHIFFER Adam *King & Spalding,* Houston
VOYLES Robb *Baker Botts,* Austin
WALTON Gibson *Vinson & Elkins,* Houston
WAWRO Mark *Susman Godfrey,* Houston

Up-and-coming individuals
DAWSON Alistair *Beck Redden,* Houston

Leading individuals
(Litigation: Appellate)

[1] **FROST Claudia** *Mayer Brown,* Houston
SIMPSON Reagan *King & Spalding,* Houston
YEATES Marie *Vinson & Elkins,* Houston

[2] **BOYCE William** *Fulbright & Jaworski,* Houston
GUNN David *Beck Redden,* Houston
HATCHELL Mike *Locke Liddell,* Austin

Individuals are listed alphabetically in each band.

in growing niche specialties, including diet drug litigation and cutting-edge IP disputes.

The Lawyers: As well as being the "*godfather*" of the firm's growing antitrust group, **Harry Reasoner** (see p.1698) remains an integral part of the litigation team, with a broad practice that also includes IP disputes. He recently represent-

ed Innovative Truck Storage in a patent infringement case against Ford, GM and other automobile manufacturers and refitters. The "*professional, responsive, effective and bright*" cohead of the group, **David Harvin** (see p.1683) has particular experience in litigation relating to diet drugs, energy and securities. He is acting for Shell in a $1 billion claim against the insurers of a bankrupt manufacturer, which used Shell resin to make plastic plumbing systems that spawned widespread litigation in the 1980s and 1990s. **Gib Walton** (see p.1705) enters the tables this year. An experienced litigator, he has enjoyed considerable success in a career spanning almost 30 years, especially in major construction cases. He also offers experience in securities, professional liability and energy litigation, and recently acted for a publicly traded national engineering, procurement and construction contractor, as plaintiff, securing a $34.5 million federal court jury verdict. "*Real long-range vision*" helps the accomplished **Ferguson McNiel** (see p.1691), whose practice includes products liability, mass torts, and construction litigation. He handled a breach of contract case for Waste Management, involving the construction and operation of a transfer station at a landfill site near Fort Worth. He and the team also acted for Occidental in agricultural product toxic tort cases against 25,000 non-US workers, who filed suits in many Texas state and federal courts. Joining the tables this year is the "*underrated, but superb*" **Bill Dawson** (see p.1676). He enjoys broad experience but is especially renowned for his professional liability expertise. He secured a take-nothing verdict in 2004 for a big four accounting firm, in a case concerning the audit of a failed public company. Interviewees also admired "*procedural whiz*" and generalist litigator **Phillip Dye** (see p.1678). A "*rising star*," he has carved out a particular forte in jurisdictional challenges. On behalf of Royal Dutch/Shell Group's Argentine subsidiary, he successfully shielded the company from a $186 million securities fraud claim. Also joining the rankings is **Bob Schick** (see p.1699), whose experience in products liability, mass toxic torts and environmental litigation was highlighted by clients. He has overseen diet drug litigation and was lead Texas counsel for Wyeth in suits arising from the use of a prescription drug and an over-the-counter drug. Watching the firm's appellate star, **Marie Yeates** (see p.1706) in action is "*like watching someone conduct an orchestra*," said one client of her ability to pull together the many strands of an argument. She is currently handling an appeal for Anadarko from a $145 million judgment in an oil and gas contractual and fraud dispute, and representing Equilon (owned by Shell) in the California state court of appeals in a dispute with service station distributors.

The Clients: Waste Management; UBS Financial Services; Wyeth; Bridgestone/Firestone; Blockbuster; Shell; HCA; Continental Airlines;

Dell; Lutron Electronics; Trammell Crow and Occidental Petroleum.

Band 2

Baker Botts LLP
See firm details p.1708

The Firm: This growing international firm boasts a particularly strong institutional clientele in its Texas heartlands. Broad corporate expertise and an "*outstanding,*" and long-standing, tradition of major litigation drive the reputation of the 600-lawyer outfit. It was recommended for the breadth of expertise on offer, with areas of particular strength including IP, products liability and securities litigation. The Texan lawyers can draw on additional trial capacity from a growing New York office, which is especially valuable when it comes to securities cases.

The Lawyers: Observers were full of praise for "*one of the brightest, most experienced and astute tactical lawyers*" in Texas, **Irv Terrell** (see p.1703). He boasts a national reputation for expertise in contract, IP, securities and antitrust litigation. In June 2004, he enjoyed success in the Eleventh Circuit Court of Appeals on behalf of Univision (formerly the Hispanic Broadcast Corporation) in a long-running antitrust dispute. The "*fabulous*" **Daryl Bristow** (see p.1673) has numerous trials under his belt in a career spanning more than 35 years. Clients particularly appreciate his "*ability to boil down complex technical documents to the key issues.*" Bristow is experienced in major litigation of all types, including securities disputes, derivative class actions and environmental litigation, and was instrumental in representing Alcoa in groundwater contamination cases involving more than 1,200 plaintiffs. He is also counseling CenterPoint Energy in a class action alleging wrongful manipulation of residential gas prices. Dallas-based **Rod Phelan** (see p.1697) is known for a "*truly Texan style*" and for his considerable experience in professional negligence and malpractice cases for legal, accounting, architectural and engineering firms. He has been representing a prominent local law firm involved in tax shelter litigation. Patent infringement, trade secrets and complex business litigation have been keeping **Joe Cheavens** (see p.1674), the head of the trial department, busy this year. He successfully acted for Alcatel USA in trade secret misappropriation cases against Samsung and Chiaro Networks. **Robb Voyles** (see p.1704) boasts considerable skills as a rainmaker as well as a lawyer. The partner in charge of the Austin office, he handles professional liability and securities litigation, for clients that have included accounting giants Deloitte & Touche, Ernst & Young and KPMG. In May 2004 a summary judgment was affirmed for his client, Deloitte & Touche, after fraud allegations were brought by investors in its former audit client, Just for Feet.

The Clients: Alcoa; ExxonMobil; Dr Pepper/Seven Up; Hispanic Broadcasting Corporation; Alcatel; Deloitte & Touche and CenterPoint.

Beck, Redden & Secrest LLP

The Firm: This classy Houston litigation boutique was started 13 years ago by former Fulbright & Jaworski attorneys and now stands at around 35 attorneys. Its lawyers have earned a reputation for being more pragmatic than some of their competitors, and for being more defense-oriented than many other boutiques. Observers consistently admired the strength of its trial experience and expert handling of complex commercial disputes and mass tort litigation, including high-profile cases involving breast implants and diet drugs.

The Lawyers: *"Preparation, dedication and an attractive, polished jury presence"* are among the weapons in the armory of the *"first-rate"* **David Beck**. His widely admired commercial and business litigation practice includes a strong energy element. Considerable praise was also heaped on the shoulders of **Joe Redden**. His *"quietly effective"* style hides the fact that he is a *"talented assassin"* in the courtroom. He undertakes major products liability and complex tort cases. *"Rising star"* **Alistair Dawson** is *"able to develop large commercial cases,"* according to market sources. An increasingly established player in the market, he enjoys a broad practice spanning general commercial, antitrust and oil and gas litigation, among other things. He recently defended Compaq Computer in four consumer class actions brought in Beaumont, Texas, alleging defects in the floppy disk controller. He also counseled ExxonMobil in a suit brought by the State of Texas for unpaid royalties. Having joined the firm in April 2003 from an appellate boutique, the new appellate head, **David Gunn**, enters the rankings on the back of enthusiastic recommendations from peers and clients alike.

The Clients: 3M; Allied Waste Industries; Becton Dickinson; Central Parking; GE and Wyeth.

Fulbright & Jaworski LLP

See firm details p.1715

The Firm: A large number of *"experienced trial attorneys,"* combined with a strong historical reputation for handling complex commercial litigation, help to drive this firm up the rankings this year. Its lawyers were valued by clients for being *"comfortable in the courtroom"* and achieving *"a good turn around"* of work. The group boasts expertise in a variety of areas, including insurance defense, IP, and securities litigation. Observers also noted an up-turn in its ERISA and benefits litigation, and the firm is known to be beefing up its international arbitration prowess.

The Lawyers: The *"safe and reliable"* **Frank Jones** (see p.1685) was recommended for having *"good judgment and plenty of business sense."* His broad practice includes a range of general commercial disputes and products liability cases. He is leading a case on behalf of a computer manufacturer concerning alleged defective floppy disk controller. The *"incredibly smart"* **Reagan Brown** (see p.1674) drew widespread praise for his trial experience and expertise in insurance class actions and legal malpractice defense. **Linda Addison** (see p.1669) is a *"wonderful and tenacious"* attorney with a great reputation in the legal and business communities. She was lead counsel for GE in a suit brought by two Mexican companies claiming to be the exclusive distributors of GE medical equipment in Mexico. The plaintiffs were seeking damages of more than $35 million, but the court dismissed the case in February 2004. She has also acted as counsel for the former directed trustee of the Enron 401(k) in the consolidated Enron employee benefit plan cases, and is assisting Mars in a patent case against Heinz and Del Monte set for trial in Los Angeles in February 2005. **Otway Denny** (see p.1677) won particular plaudits for his skill in construction, mass torts, personal injury and environmental litigation. He has been busy in recent months trying an environment case in South Louisiana. **Dudley Oldham** (see p.1694) is a veteran litigator, who is approaching 40 years at the firm. Widely admired as a *"smart and appropriately aggressive"* player, he enjoys a diverse practice with a heavy emphasis on patent infringement litigation. Entering the tables this year is the *"great"* **Steve Dillard** (see p.1677), who chairs the firm's global litigation group. He earned warm commendations for his work in defense of toxic tort, mass tort and environmental litigation. Also entering the tables this year following enthusiastic recommendations is appellate specialist, **Bill Boyce** (see p.1673).

The Clients: The firm acts for a diverse clientele drawn from the telecom, IT, real estate, and oil and gas sectors, among others. GE and Mars are examples.

Band 3

Carrington, Coleman, Sloman & Blumenthal, LLP

The Firm: There is a considerable amount of respect in the local market for this *"wonderful"* Dallas law firm. Its trial lawyers earned enthusiastic commendations for their *"professionalism and effectiveness,"* and the breadth of their expertise. This spans most areas of business and commercial litigation, including antitrust and trade regulation, IP and securities disputes. In this latter area, which is seen as one of the firm's particular strengths, the group acts for investment banking houses and broker-dealers, as well as issuers of securities and directors and officers of public companies.

The Lawyers: **Jim Coleman**, a *"wise counselor and a litigation veteran,"* is the standout practitioner and a point of contact in this team of 90-plus litigators. He boasts a diverse range of expertise, but is particularly associated with breach of fiduciary duty and malpractice claims. Todd Murray joined the firm as of counsel in April 2004.

The Clients: The team acts for leading private and public companies from a variety of fields.

Haynes and Boone LLP

The Firm: This well-established firm fields an enormous force in the litigation arena. A business litigation group of more than 200 lawyers is especially well known for its prowess in insurance coverage disputes. It has acted over the past year for a number of policyholders, such as Craftmade International, Neutral Posture Ergonomics and National Spirit Group, in obtaining liability insurance coverage for the defense of trademark infringement claims. IP, securities litigation and white-collar defense are other key areas of practice for the team.

The Lawyers: This high-quality team was felt to operate in a low-profile, collegiate manner, which mitigates against the identification of stars. Ken Broughton is the administrative partner of the Houston office, which relocated in June 2004, while Lynne Liberato leads the charge in the appellate field.

The Clients: Bank of America; Blockbuster; Dynegy; Waste Management; HCA; Toshiba and Viacom.

King & Spalding LLP

See firm details p.635

The Firm: King & Spalding is *"very much on the map"* in Texas. Indeed, it has just celebrated its 10th anniversary in Houston, where a team of 40 *"proactive and intelligent"* litigators earned considerable praise for their expertise in a range of complex business and tort litigation. Appellate cases and international arbitration are also considered to be strengths, and interviewees highlighted the team's experience in oil and gas royalty disputes, where it regularly represents flagship client, ChevronTexaco. In April 2004, the team won a precedent-setting judgment for the Houston Astros against Fox Sports, affirming its right to form a team-owned regional sports network with the Houston Rockets.

The Lawyers: **Bobby Meadows** (see p.1691) is a *"phenomenal trial lawyer and excellent legal strategist,"* say clients. He is particularly admired for his *"judgment and big-picture approach"* and *"excellent courtroom skills."* Recently, he has been busy defending Shell against a number of lawsuits filed in California, which allege personal injury and property damage from exposure to a pesticide Shell manufactured in the late 1960s and early 1970s. He successfully defended Kellogg, Brown & Root after a chemical explosion in Pasadena injured four employees of Phillips Petroleum Company. Formerly with Vinson &

www.ChambersandPartners.com

All quotes in the text are from interviews with clients and competitors.

1657

Elkins, **Adam Schiffer** (see p.1700) is said to be "*really coming into his own*" at his new firm, and joins the tables this year. He also represented Shell in the above matter, and has been acting for Kellogg, Brown & Root, in pursuing a substantial delay and disruption damages claim against Pemex, the state-owned oil company of Mexico. "*Excellent appellate lawyer*" **Reagan Simpson** (see p.1700) offers clients a combination of a "*first-rate intellect*" and a "*beautiful writing style*." He acted recently for Coastal Corporation in a personal injury case arising out of a refinery explosion. He was also lead attorney for Diamond Shamrock in Diamond Shamrock Refining Co v Hall, in the Texas Supreme Court.
The Clients: ChevronTexaco; Halliburton; Shell; ExxonMobil; UPS and Home Depot.

Mayer, Brown, Rowe & Maw LLP
See firm details p.771
The Firm: Sources agree that the Houston office of this international giant is "*moving in the right direction*," having recently bulked up to around 35 commercial litigators. This gives it a level of "*consistent quality and depth*" that allows it to compete with the best in the market. The huge resources of its global network are said to make it an excellent choice for international arbitrations and litigation in the oil and gas industry. The Houston office is also known for its experience in toxic tort litigation and the strength of its appellate practice.
The Lawyers: Sources identified **Bill Knull** (see p.1687) as a "*talented, reliable and effective*" litigator with a great profile in the market. His reputation is based upon more than 25 years' experience in commercial litigation and arbitration, much of it international, and he is especially renowned for the arbitration of international disputes relating to the oil and gas industry. He has been lead counsel for elements of the Government of Turkmenistan in a series of ICC arbitrations arising out of failed oil and gas joint ventures, an enormous dispute with total claims aggregating to $3 billion. Interviewees underlined the steady growth of the firm's appellate group, which is centered on **Claudia Wilson Frost** (see p.1680). A "*professional adviser and an excellent networker*," she is said to be "*brilliant at bringing together all the issues*." She has been acting recently as lead counsel in an appeal against a billion-dollar verdict in a products liability case.
The Clients: Dow Chemical; Marathon Oil; Equistar; Agrium; Ameritrade; Apache and Government of Turkmenistan.

McDade Fogler LLP
The Firm: Corporate and commercial litigation, personal injury and white-collar defense are among the services offered by this small but well-respected Houston litigation boutique, which represents plaintiffs as well as defendants. There is an oil and energy flavor to much of the team's litiga-

tion. For example, as well as its role in the Enron proceedings, it is carrying out work for Transocean, the biggest offshore drilling company, in a products liability case against a manufacturer.
The Lawyers: **Murray Fogler** is a "*dedicated, multifaceted*" trial lawyer who is "*excellent on his feet*," and also a "*good brief writer*," according to commentators. His mixed practice includes both plaintiff and defense civil litigation, and he has been busy of late defending Andrews & Kurth in several malpractice cases related to the Enron bankruptcy, including the class action shareholder litigation. Other recent highlights include acting for Service Corporation International, a large funeral company, in two related insurance coverage cases, pending in Florida, against excess insurers.
The Clients: Coastal Corporation; Transocean; Andrews & Kurth; Service Corporation International; Duke Energy; Field Services and El Paso.

Band 4

Akin Gump Strauss Hauer & Feld LLP
See firm details p.477
The Firm: The expansion of the firm's Houston office, and in particular its litigation capacity, thrusts Akin Gump firmly into the *Chambers*' tables. The recent growth of its capabilities in employment, products liability, toxic torts and general commercial litigation are spectacular, and have come through a program of lateral recruits in both Dallas, where there are now around 40 litigators, and in Houston, with about half that total.
The Lawyers: Murry Cohen heads the firm's appellate practice in Texas. He joined the firm in August 2004 after 20 years' experience on the bench.
The Clients: The client roster includes many of the country's largest Fortune 500 companies, as well as numerous smaller business entities and individuals.

Bracewell & Giuliani LLP
See firm details p.1710
The Firm: A new addition to our litigation tables, this regional giant operates from a total of six Texas offices, and houses more than 50 "*very strong advocates*" in the Houston trial department alone. The team serves a client base drawn from a variety of sectors, including energy and natural resources, banking and financial services and technology, winning a place at the table in some of the state's most interesting work. For examples, it acted for BP entities in a lawsuit brought by three Mauritius companies, alleging breach of agreements and fraud arising out of a proposed gas liquids project in India. In July 2004, the team successfully acted for Kinder Morgan and ONEOK Bushton Processing against ExxonMobil, in relation to a disputed gas processing agreement.

The Lawyers: Cliff Gunter heads the firm's trial section, while Betsy Whitaker is managing partner of the Dallas office.
The Clients: BP; Apple; Bank of America; San Antonio Spurs; Houston Livestock Show and Rodeo and Coral Energy.

Locke Liddell & Sapp LLP
The Firm: This old-line Texas firm fields around 200 trial lawyers in its four offices, three of which are in Texas. It offers a wide range of litigation expertise, including complex class action defense, as well as a stream of more straightforward business, contract and tort disputes, and it has a strong appellate practice. Recent highlights include obtaining a successful verdict for Crown Life Insurance in state court in Austin, against a former insurance agent who was seeking damages exceeding $70 million.
The Lawyers: The "*superb*" **Mike Hatchell** (see p.1683) is the firm's head of appellate work. He boasts more than 40 years of experience in local and federal appellate cases, and is a popular choice for complex disputes requiring sophistication and intellectual weight. The firm also boasts a former attorney general and chief justice of the Texas Supreme Court, in the shape of John Hill.
The Clients: Crown Life Insurance and Houston Astros feature in a long client list.

Thompson & Knight LLP
See firm details p.1722
The Firm: Although not one of the highest profile players in the Texas litigation market, this well-respected firm enters the tables this year. Four of its 12 offices are located in the state, and more than half of the 120 lawyers in the trial department are in Dallas. These include a number of recent recruits from Porter & Hedges, who are felt to have boosted its strength in toxic tort, products liability and asbestos-related litigation.
The Lawyers: Houston-based **James Leahy** (see p.1688) joins the rankings this year, having made something of a transition to defense work. He is admired as "*one of the great cross-examiners in the courtroom*," combining penetrating intellect with a "*good ol' boy*" style that appeals to juries. A diverse practice comprises expertise in commercial, business, securities and oil and gas disputes.
The Clients: American National Petroleum; Frio Exploration; Total Minatome Corporation; Nicor Petroleum and Total Oil Marine.

Weil, Gotshal & Manges LLP
See firm details p.1378
The Firm: The firm enters this year's litigation tables following a wealth of feedback on its big-case ability and depth of resources in the state. A "*sizable Dallas team*" is complemented by around 20 attorneys in Houston, where it offers expertise in IP, mass torts and environmental litigation. Over the past year, the group has been kept busy with a

stream of general commercial disputes, securities litigation and a rising number of arbitrations.

The Lawyers: Ralph Miller (see p.1692) is in charge of the Dallas litigation team and co-heads the firm's complex commercial litigation practice. He boasts almost 30 years of experience in a wide range of cases. Recent highlights include defending ExxonMobil against allegations of defense and indemnification obligations relating to hundreds of asbestos liability lawsuits linked to a Louisiana oil refinery it had purchased.

The Clients: In addition to Dallas-based client UICI, the firm acts for ExxonMobil; MasterCard International; Prudential Securities and STMicroelectronics.

Other Notable Practitioners

The *"really smart and experienced"* Dallas-based **Mike McKool** is principal and co-founder of litigation boutique McKool Smith. He earned commendations for his trial skills, in both commercial and IP litigation. A roster of major clients includes Ericsson, who he recently defended in a patent infringement action. **Bruce Golden** of Golden & Owens gained recognition for his *"superb"* litigation skills, which is parlayed into an impressive track record encompassing a broad array of issues. He has advised on Enron-related litigation, and his remit also includes plaintiff-oriented work.

PROJECTS

Texas

Leading firms (Projects)

1. VINSON & ELKINS LLP *Houston*
2. BAKER BOTTS LLP *Houston*
3. AKIN GUMP STRAUSS HAUER & FELD LLP *Houston*
   ANDREWS KURTH LLP *Houston*
   KING & SPALDING LLP *Houston*
4. BAKER & MCKENZIE *Houston*
   BRACEWELL & GIULIANI LLP *Houston*
   SKADDEN, ARPS, SLATE, MEAGHER *Houston*

Leading individuals (Projects)

1. ASMUS David *Baker Botts,* Houston
   BILGER Bruce *Vinson & Elkins,* Houston
   COGAN John *Akin Gump,* Houston
2. ALE John *Skadden Arps,* Houston
   BLAND Douglas *Vinson & Elkins,* Houston
   CULOTTA Ken *King & Spalding,* Houston
   GOOLSBY George *Baker Botts,* Houston
   KELLEY Jay *Vinson & Elkins,* Houston
   TAYLOR Lyndon *Skadden Arps,* Houston
   UNGER Timothy *Andrews Kurth,* Houston
   WEEMS Philip *King & Spalding,* Houston
3. KREBS Stephen *Baker Botts,* Houston
   MAUEL John *Baker & McKenzie,* Houston
   PINKERTON Glenn *Vinson & Elkins,* Houston
   THURBER Mark *Andrews Kurth,* Houston
   WEIL Thomas *Skadden Arps,* Houston
4. BACKUS Marcia *Vinson & Elkins,* Houston
   CULWELL Todd *Baker & McKenzie,* Houston
   EVANS Mark *Bracewell & Giuliani,* Houston
   RAFTE Alan *Bracewell & Giuliani,* Houston
   ROGERS Daniel *Chadbourne & Parke,* Houston
   THOMPSON Dahl *Andrews Kurth,* Houston

Up-and-coming individuals

ARRINGTON Scott *Akin Gump,* Houston

Firms and individuals are listed alphabetically in each band.

Band 1

Vinson & Elkins LLP

See firm details p.1724

The Firm: This is the quintessential Texas energy law firm, and stands out from the crowd due to the sheer depth and breadth of its practice. It has, obviously, had a tough couple of years following the bankruptcy of Enron, but it appears to have weathered the worst of that now and market observers agree: *"The quality of the lawyers remains very high."* Clients stay loyal to the firm because its lawyers are *"business-oriented and can share their views of the legal issues in the context of the business world."* They also value the fact that you get *"hands-on partners who'll be with you all the way to the finish line."* The firm is handling high-profile international projects for the oil majors, including the development of two large petrochemicals projects in the Middle East, with a combined capital investment of approximately $2.5 billion, for Chevron Phillips Chemical. Another key client is British Gas, and the firm represents the company in most of its LNG projects, including in its role as buyer of LNG in the Trinidad and Equatorial Guinea projects. As well as established relationships with the giant energy companies, however, the firm has also developed a strong practice for financial institutions investing in energy projects. Here, the team recently represented JPMorgan Chase and WestLB in the $325 million financing of Cameron Highway Oil Pipeline's offshore pipeline in the Gulf of Mexico.

The Lawyers: Bruce Bilger (see p.1672) is the practice's big name and is *"at the top of the heap"* of Texas energy lawyers. According to clients, he is *"particularly skillful at getting the art of compromise right,"* while peers describe him as *"a classic old-style Texas lawyer"* with an astute tactical mind. **Doug Bland** (see p.1672) was recommended as *"a client-focused and hands-on"* lawyer who offers *"thorough analysis and great problem-solving skills."* Another of the team's high-profile lawyers is **Jay Kelley** (see p.1686). He was noted for his *"thorough understanding of the LNG industry"* and is said to be *"highly adept at putting together complicated structures."* **Glenn Pinkerton** (see p.1697) has worked recently on a variety of major deals, including representing Hunt Oil in connection with its involvement in the Camisea LNG project in Peru. **Marcia Backus** (see p.1670) is another *"top energy lawyer"* who works for Shell and Occidental Petroleum.

The Clients: BG Group; Chevron Phillips Chemical; JPMorgan Chase; WestLB; AES; PSEG Global; Bank of Nova Scotia; Shell; Occidental Petroleum and Hunt Oil.

Band 2

Baker Botts LLP

See firm details p.1708

The Firm: As one of the foremost firms in the country's oil and gas heartland, the practice naturally has *"a top-notch oil and gas projects group."* It has long-standing relationships with the major oil and gas companies, and boasts a particularly good reputation for representing them in upstream projects, including LNG export projects, pipeline schemes and offshore infrastructure developments. Understandably, as *"a major worldwide energy firm with worldwide reach,"* it has been involved in some high-profile international work. A current highlight is representing Marathon in its Equatorial Guinea LNG project. This has been one of the fastest LNG export projects to get up and running in recent years, and Baker Botts handled everything from negotiations with the host government to the sales agreements for the LNG. The group is also heavily involved in the domestic scene, and recently represented ConocoPhillips in its negotiations with the Freeport LNG terminal. Clients maintain that the practice is *"extremely well qualified and delivers excellent results,"* and express their satisfaction with the way cases are handled, stating that the firm *"is efficient and doesn't over-lawyer."*

The Lawyers: David Asmus (see p.1670) is without doubt one of the top lawyers in the country for upstream and LNG work, and is widely acknowledged to be *"a leader in the legal community."* According to sources, he is *"careful and meticulous"* and *"really understands the complicated stuff"* due to his oil industry background. Clients also like the fact that he is *"fully aware of current issues on the international energy scene."* **George Goolsby** (see p.1681) has enjoyed a long and illustrious career in the sector, and has a great reputation, particularly for his pioneering work on pipelines in the Caspian Sea area. **Stephen Krebs** (see p.1687) specializes in the financing of energy projects. He

www.ChambersandPartners.com

All quotes in the text are from interviews with clients and competitors.

1659

has a reputation for "*avidly protecting his clients' interests*."

The Clients: The firm represents a number of large oil companies that include: BP; ExxonMobil; Marathon; Hunt Oil and ConocoPhillips.

Band 3

Akin Gump Strauss Hauer & Feld LLP

See firm details p.477

The Firm: This firm enters the projects tables following a dramatic push to acquire new talent, notably luring John Cogan over from King & Spalding. The firm already has a long-established international energy practice with "*significant name recognition,*" so the new acquisitions herald an exciting new phase for its projects practice. A suitably high note for the team was the announcement of ConocoPhillips' purchase of a $1.988 billion share in Russian oil company, LUKOIL. The two companies have also formed a joint venture to develop Russia's Timan-Pechora oil and gas field, and will jointly seek the right to develop the West Qurna oil field in Iraq. Akin Gump represented LUKOIL throughout this exciting development and is involved in the high-profile Qatargas project, representing the project company in the development of a fleet of tankers to transport the LNG from Qatar.

The Lawyers: **John Cogan** (see p.1675) is "*an accomplished international lawyer*" who is "*a real step up from the run of the mill,*" according to interviewees. His recruitment is considered to be a real coup for the team. A leader in the field of LNG projects, he is noted for being "*incredibly bright and cerebral.*" **Scott Arrington**, considered "*a big star*" in the making, recently moved here from Baker & McKenzie. He recently worked on the Bahamas LNG project for Tractebel.

The Clients: As well as the major projects described above, the practice has been representing Murphy Oil in a number of projects, including a floating production storage and offloading program in Indonesia.

Andrews Kurth LLP

See firm details p.1707

The Firm: This firm is particularly well known in the market for its "*strong and robust domestic LNG capability.*" This has been on view recently in a number of headline deals. For example, it has been representing Cheniere in connection with the development of a series of proposed LNG-receiving terminals, including the $1 billion Corpus Christi project on the Gulf Coast. The team is also utilizing its expertise in this area on the international stage, and has been advising DKRW Energy on the development of an LNG terminal in Mexico. In recent years it has been steadily emerging as a prominent presence

in the wind energy industry. Here, highlights include acting for the Sweetwater partnership, owned by DKR Development and Babcock & Brown, in the development of its wind farm in Texas.

The Lawyers: **Timothy Unger** (see p.1704) is regarded as "*a classic developer's lawyer.*" His negotiating skills and ability to keep a deal moving are particularly prized by clients. Market sources are also full of praise for **Mark Thurber** (see p.1703) and, in particular, his ability to "*close innovative deals.*" The "*thoughtful and considerate*" **Dahl Thompson** (see p.1703) is cut from the same cloth, say sources, and has the rare ability to "*get a deal done even if it is breaking the mold.*"

The Clients: Wachovia; Bank One; Royal Bank of Scotland; Duke Energy; ConocoPhillips and CapRock (owned by Babcock & Brown).

King & Spalding LLP

See firm details p.635

The Firm: Satisfied clients rate this projects practice as possibly "*the strongest LNG team of any law firm out there.*" It is active as project counsel in a number of proposed domestic LNG terminals, leading one peer to comment: "*It owns the developer industry.*" A prominent example is its role as project counsel to the Freeport LNG terminal, the most advanced of the current spate of proposed new sites. It is also prolific in international LNG projects. For example, the team is handling the gas supply issues for all five participants in the Angola LNG project, and advising the Trinidad LNG project company on export sales into the USA. The recent departure of John Cogan is undoubtedly a blow to the practice. However, the remaining team is strong and experienced and clients say it still provides "*an outstanding service*" and "*can handle complex transactions with ease.*"

The Lawyers: **Ken Culotta** (see p.1676) stands out here, according to interviewees. An international lawyer through and through, he has come to specialize more and more in energy projects. Clients rate him as "*an excellent lawyer*" who is "*detail oriented and skillful,*" as well as "*responsive and client-focused.*" **Philip Weems** (see p.1705) is popular with his clients, to the point that one described him as "*probably the strongest LNG lawyer in the world.*" He is particularly renowned for his "*wealth of experience in the LNG industry.*"

The Clients: The team has been representing Cheniere in the development of the Sabine Pass LNG terminal, and advising BHP Billiton on an offshore LNG terminal in California. In the international arena, it represents Dow Chemical in the acquisition of LNG supplies all over the world. It also advised Chevron Texaco on the development of its Venezuela LNG projects, along with the related import terminals in the USA.

Band 4

Baker & McKenzie

See firm details p.761

The Firm: Clients particularly like using this firm as it grants them access to a huge network of global offices and a wide breadth of international resources. They also appreciate the "*responsive*" attitude of the lawyers here. As one testified, they "*went out of their way to help facilitate the project under great time pressures.*" Understandably, the greatest highlights for this global-facing team tend to be international in nature. The high point of the year was probably acting as lead project counsel on the $600 million Tractebel Bahamas LNG project. It has also been representing Sun Coke in the development of a $390 million coke and electricity generation plant in Brazil.

The Lawyers: **John Mauel** (see p.1690) is the most senior member of the practice. According to clients he is "*a skilled and knowledgeable attorney*" and "*a gifted draftsman with an understanding of the peculiarities of nuances.*" **Todd Culwell** (see p.1676) recently joined the firm from Andrews Kurth. Peers rate him as "*a real catch*" for the practice.

The Clients: As well as Tractebel and Sun Coke, the firm has acted for Rolls-Royce and Globeleq.

Bracewell & Giuliani LLP

See firm details p.1710

The Firm: This firm has been focusing of late on restructuring transactions in the domestic power and oil and gas sectors. Here it typically represents large financial institutions investing in the energy sector. For example, a highlight of the year involved representing the banks acting as agents in the sale of the Enron pipelines. The firm represented JPMorgan Chase and Citibank in connection with their interests in the Transwestern pipeline; assisted Calyon in the Florida gas pipeline; and acted for Bank One in connection with the Northern Borders pipelines. The firm also works on restructurings for large corporate clients, and advised InterGen on restructuring $2.5 billion of debt and equity for three power projects.

The Lawyers: **Mark Evans** (see p.1678) specializes in representing the financial institutions, while **Alan Rafte** (see p.1697) represents both lenders and project companies. As well as the InterGen deal, outlined previously, Rafte also represented Apache Corporation in the $750 million purchase of a large oil and gas package from Shell.

The Clients: InterGen; Calpine; Reliant; Plains Exploration and Production; JPMorgan Chase; Citibank; Bank One; Calyon; Société Générale; BNP Paribas; Wells Fargo and Union Bank of California.

Skadden, Arps, Slate, Meagher & Flom LLP & Affiliates
See firm details p.1372

The Firm: The Houston branch of the Skadden Arps projects empire is fairly small, but as a part of this huge worldwide network it has access to considerable resources. These help to make it, in the eyes of the market, a *"great transactional practice."* Recently, the group has been busy working for Excelerate Energy, a new LNG shipping and marketing company formed from the old El Paso LNG group. It advised on the formation of the new company, and its subsequent acquisition of the Gulf of Mexico project from El Paso, among other things. The Houston office

also does a lot of work for Sempra Energy. In recent times, this has included negotiating a $15 billion, 20-year energy supply contract for Sempra's Mexicali power plant in Baja California, with the Tangguh facility in Indonesia.

The Lawyers: According to impressed sources, **John Ale** (see p.1670) is a *"strong and experienced"* projects lawyer with *"a stellar reputation"* that extends beyond the local market. His fame is matched, however, by that of *"smart and hardworking"* **Lyndon Taylor** (see p.1703). According to clients, Taylor's pragmatic and dynamic approach makes him a popular choice: *"He ensures that things get done."* Peers, meanwhile, note: *"What stands him apart is that he is such a*

nice guy." **Thomas Weil** (see p.1705) is also well respected for his *"great international experience."* Peers described him as *"an expert energy lawyer."*
The Clients: Other clients include Goldman Sachs, Sumitomo Mitsui Banking and BHP Billiton.

Other Notable Practitioners
Daniel Rogers (see p.1699) helped establish the Chadbourne & Parke Houston office two years ago. He has recently been busy representing the Royal Bank of Scotland as lender to the Freeport LNG project. Clients described him as *"excellent and very creative; a valuable member of any team."*

REAL ESTATE

Texas
Leading firms (Real Estate)

1	**BAKER BOTTS LLP** Houston
	HAYNES AND BOONE LLP Dallas
	VINSON & ELKINS LLP Houston
	WINSTEAD SECHREST & MINICK PC Dallas
2	**AKIN GUMP STRAUSS HAUER & FELD LLP** Dallas
	ANDREWS KURTH LLP Houston
	FULBRIGHT & JAWORSKI LLP Houston
	JENKENS & GILCHRIST PC Dallas
	LOCKE LIDDELL & SAPP LLP Houston
	MAYER, BROWN, ROWE & MAW LLP Houston
3	**BRACEWELL & GIULIANI LLP** Dallas
	GARDERE WYNNE SEWELL LLP Dallas
	JACKSON WALKER LLP Houston
	THOMPSON & KNIGHT LLP Houston
	WEIL, GOTSHAL & MANGES LLP Dallas

Firms are listed alphabetically in each band.

Band 1

Baker Botts LLP
See firm details p.1708

The Firm: Commentators praised the firm's *"extremely selective"* recruitment process that is successful in securing the organic development of *"highly sophisticated lawyers"* servicing a large blue-chip client base. Considerable depths of resources allied to a *"distinctly strong work ethic"* ensure that the team has both the requisite know-how and drive to handle complicated projects in all facets of commercial real estate: from acquisitions, development, leasing, financing and debt restructuring to disposals. Clients reported a *"reassuring"* presence at all stages of the transaction, confident in the knowledge that the team *" works extremely efficiently."* In addition, the group's expertise in office development projects, both domestically and abroad, remains the envy of the market.
The Lawyers: Among the firm's *"top-flight attorneys"* **Fred Dunlop** (see p.1678) comes to

the fore as *"a statesman of the real estate Bar."* *"One of the brightest people to have walked the earth,"* according to one commentator, Dunlop has represented institutional lenders and developers, such as Hines Interests, across the country on a number of office builds. A *"logical dealmaker,"* Dunlop *"always understands the business aspects and the legal ramifications."* The *"hugely practical"* **Jon Dunlay** (see p.1678) *"doesn't put up artificial barriers to getting things done."* Dunlay has recently been involved with the formation of single-family and town home development ventures in Texas, and a golf course resort development in Colorado. He has advised lenders and joint venture investors, buyers, and developers, in all elements of property transactions. Interviewees feel that his major asset is his ability to *"collate huge amounts of information quickly and then explain it in a manner that people understand."* Clients expressed approval for **Robert Wright**'s (see p.1706) commercial acumen and foresight in avoiding *"negotiating a deal to death."* His practice blends real estate engagements with a considerable amount of environmental work, and he is particularly respected within the energy industry for his knowledge of power plant transactions. His *"ability to understand both sides' point of view"* derives from more than 25 years' working for all parties in the sector. Described by peers as *"one of the finest leasing lawyers,"* **Mark Van Kirk** (see p.1704) is skilled in the negotiation of leases with major anchor and national chain tenants on retail projects. Counseling buyers, sellers and investment funds on financing matters forms the balance of his practice. Regarded as a lawyer who *"never fails to hit the nail on the head,"* **Marley Lott**'s (see p.1689) experience in financing and development work for joint ventures and partnerships has helped her achieve national recognition.
The Clients: BP; Hines Interests; Reliant Energy and Kellogg Brown & Root.

Haynes and Boone LLP
The Firm: The market lavished praise on this *"first-rate"* firm for its ability to *"lead the charge on complex issues that touch every phase of the business."* Employing 28 attorneys in its six Texas offices, the firm is well placed geographically to offer comprehensive real estate advice to clients throughout the Southwest. While the firm prides itself on its representation of institutional clients, competitors accept that *"they bring good lawyers to everything they do, even the smaller regional deals."* Recently, the group advised Hillwood Properties in negotiating a strategic partnership with ING Clarion involving more than eight million sq ft of industrial properties. It also counseled long-standing client Crescent Real Estate Equities on an $898.5 million partnership with a pension fund investor advised by JPMorgan Fleming.
The Lawyers: *"Straight shooter"* **Robert Wilson** earns the respect of peers on account of his *"sense of where and when to push a point"* at the negotiating table. Recent transactions include the representation of a pension fund in the acquisition of 15 warehouses located in multiple states, and counseling an investor on the acquisition of publicly traded bonds secured by real estate. Interviewees also praised his commitment to legal education and Bar association activities: *"There's so much more about him than just making money from his work."* Rueful competitors reported being *"never able to get anything over"* **Ann Saegert**. Although best recognized for her extensive work in advising the hospitality and resort industry, Saegert recently advised Hillwood on an arena project, and devoted much of her time to managing the Bank of America's assets in 22 states. Interviewees agreed that she is both *"dependable"* and *"fun to work with."* The *"masterful"* **Steve Jenkins** *"always has his hand in some of the most interesting work around,"* according to sources. Credited with reinvigorating the Dallas office, his focus is on development

Texas
Leading individuals (Real Estate)

1. **DOW Melvin** *Winstead Sechrest*, Houston
   DUNLOP Fred *Baker Botts*, Houston
   KATZ M Marvin *Mayer Brown*, Houston
   WALLENSTEIN Jim *Jenkens & Gilchrist*, Dallas
   WEINER Sanford *Vinson & Elkins*, Houston
   WELLER Phillip *Vinson & Elkins*, Houston
   WILSON Robert *Haynes and Boone*, Dallas

2. **BOULDEN Michael** *Vinson & Elkins*, Dallas
   DOW T Andrew *Winstead Sechrest*, Dallas
   DUNLAY Jon *Baker Botts*, Dallas
   ERWIN Greg *Winstead Sechrest*, Houston
   FELDMAN Robert *Weil Gotshal*, Dallas
   FIELDS Jack *Andrews Kurth*, Houston
   JURGENSMEYER Randy *Vinson & Elkins*, Dallas
   NEWSOME Kent *Fulbright & Jaworski*, Houston
   ROBERTS Harry *Thompson & Knight*, Dallas
   WRIGHT Robert *Baker Botts*, Houston

3. **CAMPBELL Andrew** *Andrews Kurth*, Dallas
   HOLLYFIELD John *Fulbright & Jaworski*, Houston
   JACOBS Stephen *Locke Liddell*, Houston
   JENKINS Steve *Haynes and Boone*, Dallas
   KELLEY Kevin *Gardere Wynne*, Dallas
   KUHN Michael *Jackson Walker*, Houston
   LEE Carl *Akin Gump*, Dallas
   LOTT Marley *Baker Botts*, Houston
   NONDORF Kurt *Jackson Walker*, Dallas
   PETERSON Edward *Winstead Sechrest*, Dallas
   RATNER Randall *Akin Gump*, Dallas
   SAEGERT Ann *Haynes and Boone*, Dallas
   THOMPSON, Clark *Bracewell & Giuliani*, Houston
   VAN KIRK Mark *Baker Botts*, Dallas

Up-and-coming individuals
   MARTIN Paul *Vinson & Elkins*, Dallas
   MILLER Walter *Haynes and Boone*, Richardson

Individuals are listed alphabetically in each band.

major selling points is that it can address even the most multifaceted of real estate cases on account of its depth of resources and experience in corollary areas of law such as tax, finance, intellectual property and the environment. The group's experience of late includes acquisitions, financings, securitizations, leasing and management, construction contracting, and workouts and restructurings. It recently demonstrated its strength in depth in assisting four private equity funds in the acquisition and financing of a $3 billion Texas-based company whose assets include 12 power plants, coal mines and canals.

The Lawyers: Several interviewees opined: "*It would be hard to imagine anybody better than* **Phillip Weller** (see p.1705)." A major contributing factor to his "*tremendous talent*" is a "*desire to listen to all parties in a transaction, yet still get the best deal for his clients.*" Equally at home with the financing aspects of a deal, Weller's robust relationship with Greystar Capital Partners highlights his all-rounder status: in the past year alone he worked with the client on a loan refinancing, a restructuring/workout and the formation of several limited liability companies. President of the American College of real estate lawyers **Sanford Weiner** (see p.1705) successfully negotiated and closed two lucrative transactions with a major healthcare provider to enable Trammel Crow to become the exclusive developer of professional office buildings on two hospital campuses. His experience on sale and leaseback and other leveraged lease transactions, synthetic lease transactions and project finance issues inspires "*tremendous confidence*" in his clients. "*Quick to identify the problem and even quicker to offer a solution,*" Weiner is in particular demand among REITs keen to invest in new developments. **Michael Boulden**'s (see p.1672) broad-based practice incorporates guiding clients through construction, commercial lending, joint ventures, acquisitions and development matters. He notably represented a private equity fund in its acquisition of a listed REIT with assets of $1.7 billion, and subsequent termination of trust status. **Randy Jurgensmeyer** (see p.1686) won the approval of peers for being "*receptive and perceptive*" when at the deal table, and for being "*a creative thinker in his own right.*" He lately advised Crow Holdings on the $209 million acquisition of Industrial Properties (IPC), which manages more than 70 buildings equating to eight million sq ft. "*Technically proficient and with an excellent eye for the practical,*" **Paul Martin** (see p.1690) is quickly making a name for himself as head of the Dallas leasing practice.

The Clients: Greystar Capital Partners; Crow Holdings; Trammell Crow; Archon Group; Clarion; Triton Energy; Holly Corporation; AIG; Dell; Dow Chemical; ARCO; TEPPCO Partners; Penn Virginia and Duke Energy.

Winstead Sechrest & Minick PC
See firm details p.1725

The Firm: Viewed as the strongest department within this Dallas-based firm, commentators concurred that the group of 60, unmatched in size in the state, merits its top-tier status. The firm's commitment to real estate in the face of reductions by competitors, exemplified by the successful merger with Dow Cogburn & Friedman in 2001, has produced "*a deep bench of great lawyers who pull together efficiently as a team,*" according to clients. Equally visible acting for developers or lenders, the firm handled a large number of portfolio transactions during the past year. These include the $133 million sale of 20 medical office buildings in Texas for Baylor Health Care System, and the acquisition of a $180 million hotel portfolio for Crow Holdings. On the development side, the team are advising the Dallas Cowboys Football Club in connection with the proposed development of a new $650 million stadium in Arlington.

The Lawyers: The "*spectacular*" **Melvin Dow** (see p.1677) earned peer praise as "*one of the smartest lawyers in any discipline throughout the country.*" They also noted that his years of experience in Houston have made him "*very knowledgeable about the finance element of transactions.*" A genuine deal-maker, his principal client is Weingarten, a leading REIT, whom he counseled in around $500 million worth of acquisitions in the past twelve months, predominantly in the retail sector. He also guided Century Development through the formation of an equity partnership with hausInvest on Reliant Energy Plaza, and advised various other clients on issues as diverse as marina developments and mold in student accommodation. **Greg Erwin**'s (see p.1678) highly regarded practice addresses the acquisition, development, leasing, financing and sale of shopping centers. He was also heavily involved on behalf of Weingarten recently. His "*phenomenal attention to detail*" means that "*he doesn't miss anything,*" and competitors also acknowledged his "*constant involvement in spectacular transactions.*" According to interviewees, **Andrew Dow** (see p.1677) is able "*to play hardball or be a peace-maker, according to how circumstances demand.*" Highly regarded for his development and leasing work, Dow has had a busy year in which he advised a partnership between Champion Partners and GE Capital in connection with the acquisition of a $100 million, 2.6 million sq ft industrial property portfolio. He also counseled Omni Hotels on the development of a proposed 600-room hotel in the City of Fort Worth. **Ed Peterson** (see p.1696) enjoys a burgeoning reputation for lending and finance work. For many years he has advised several institutional clients, including life insurance companies, pension plans and banks, in their corporate real estate needs on a national basis.

projects where his expertise extends to land use regulatory issues. Commentators expressed respect for Jenkins' "*ability to attract the strong loyalty of clients.*" Commentators describe **Walter Miller**, whose clients include investment advisers, developers, opportunity funds, REITs and pension plans, as a "*rising superstar.*" Experienced in structuring, negotiating and documenting transactions, peers agree that he has "*already built a great practice.*"

The Clients: Hillwood Properties; Bank of America; Crédit Lyonnais; American Airlines; Crescent Real Estate; Ericsson; Transworld Properties; RREEF; USAA Real Estate and Wal-Mart.

Vinson & Elkins LLP
See firm details p.1724

The Firm: During the last decade, this "*dynamite*" team of 25 lawyers has blasted its way onto the national and regional scene from its bases in Houston and Dallas. "*The biggest and best*" in the eyes of some clients, other interviewees enthused that there are "*more good lawyers here than at any other firm.*" One of the firm's

Band 2

Akin Gump Strauss Hauer & Feld LLP

See firm details p.477

The Firm: As part of a firm with a growing national and even international profile, the real estate group of 40 lawyers has the *"pedigree for success,"* according to interviewees, and the bench strength to handle all aspects of real estate work, including financing, acquisition and disposals, development and joint venture mandates. Market sources reserved particular praise for the team's performance in the arranging and servicing of complex conduit loans, and for its representation of both companies and investors in the hospitality industry.

The Lawyers: Dallas-based **Randy Ratner** (see p.1697) *"has an excellent manner in executing the deal,"* according to peers. His forte is the formation of partnership, joint venture and limited liability company agreements with public companies. Ratner recently counseled Prentiss Properties Acquisition Partners in the sale and leaseback of Cityplace Center, a 1.2 million sq ft Class AA development in Dallas. Cochair of the practice group **Carl Lee** (see p.1688) advises both lenders and borrowers in a broad range of transactions, especially the acquisition or disposal of real estate portfolios. His *"highly sophisticated"* work within the hotel sector in particular impressed many interviewees.

The Clients: Prentiss Properties; Centex Destination Properties; Lumbermen's Investment; Republic Property Group and Spire Realty Group.

Andrews Kurth LLP

See firm details p.1707

The Firm: The group of 29 attorneys based out of Dallas and Houston dovetail with respected banking, construction, environment and tax teams, providing clients with deep and broad resources. Interviewees also affirmed that the team's *"global, strategic approach,"* speedy analysis and *"concise"* communications reinforce *"tried and trusted"* capabilities in such specialized areas as CMBS. Commentators also praised an oil and gas practice that is *"second to none,"* as the group plays an integral role in the acquisition, financing and development of oil and gas, pipeline, and electric generating facilities throughout the USA.

The Lawyers: According to our sources, **Jack Fields** (see p.1679) *"has a great understanding of developers' concerns."* He recently demonstrated his development expertise in guiding Wal-Mart through the purchase of property for the construction of a two million sq ft distribution facility in Baytown. Observers agreed that **Andrew Campbell** (see p.1674) *"has a sharp eye for critical points in a deal."* His forte is advising on leasing development and multistate acquisitions for a largely institutional clientele.

The Clients: GE Capital; Hilton Hotels; INVESCO; LJ Melody; Citigroup; Archon Group; Rouse Company; AEW Capital Management; Wal-Mart; Fortune Brands; Wells Fargo; ING Clarion and JPMorgan Chase.

Fulbright & Jaworski LLP

See firm details p.1715

The Firm: This national firm's real estate experience stretches back to its foundation more than 85 years ago. The team of 26 attorneys operates out of four Texas offices and a unit specifically assigned to deal with real estate litigation enhances its presence. The *"consistently excellent"* lawyers routinely advise clients about land use, zoning, platting, permitting and related matters as part of a full-service real estate package. Moreover, a recent boom in the tourist industry prompted a spate of activity including the refinancing of several extended-stay hotel facilities operated by Marriott and the development of a new convention center and hotel in San Antonio for Hyatt. The San Antonio team was also notably busy with the development of an abandoned quarry into a 500-acre multiuse community.

The Lawyers: Commentators agreed that **Kent Newsome** (see p.1693) deserved credit for *"working hard to make the firm a major player."* Supplementing his broad-based real estate practice with a keen interest in entertainment law, sources noted that Newsome's most high-profile work has been a steady stream of acquisitions and developments in the healthcare sector. Of counsel **John Hollyfield** (see p.1684) can boast 30 years of experience in leasing and lender work. Other recent engagements include acting for families with large land holdings, and for the developer of a 500,000-sq-ft freight facility at an airport.

The Clients: The team represents a mix of owners, tenants and developers in a range of matters, such as the purchase, sale and development of office, retail, apartment and hotel complexes.

Jenkens & Gilchrist PC

The Firm: Commentators described this 21-strong unit as an all-around performer. A prevailing climate of low interest rates has encouraged the firm's lender and developer clients to participate in refinancing existing facilities, enabling the team to play to its acknowledged strengths in this area.

The Lawyers: A *"huge gulf exists between* **Jim Wallenstein** *and most other real estate practitioners,"* was the enthusiastic verdict of one commentator. In addition to his landmark work with leading developers and investors within the state, Wallenstein is also highly respected for his academic interest in the law, and is frequently visible at both university and Bar association sessions. Dubbed *"the professor"* by some, his *"succinct drafting skills"* ensure that his knowledge is also conveyed at a practical level.

The Clients: The firm has extensive experience in counseling developers, government agencies, financial institutions, REITs and individual investors with their real estate assets.

Locke Liddell & Sapp LLP

The Firm: Based out of offices in Dallas, Houston and Austin, the department's successful track record in real estate engagements left interviewees in no doubt that the firm *"hires extremely talented people and trains them thoroughly."* A strategy of steady growth of late has seen the team's repertoire expand from predominantly counseling lenders to a full-service real estate operation. The recent development ledger features significant mandates in condominium, retail and sports stadium projects, while its work for institutional lenders includes acquisition financings, complex mortgages of private correctional facilities and other deals in the healthcare and retail sector.

The Lawyers: In a uniformly strong team, Houston-based **Stephen Jacobs**' (see p.1685) *"encyclopedic"* retention of information, allied to his *"commerciality and flexibility at the deal table,"* marks him out as the standout figure for many market commentators. He has had an active year representing landlords in the development of multifamily residential sites, several golf courses and a resort in Mexico. He also acted for a REIT on a $700 million joint venture with institutional investors.

The Clients: The team's client roster includes Fortune 500 companies and individual investors and entrepreneurs.

Mayer, Brown, Rowe & Maw LLP

See firm details p.771

The Firm: In keeping with its international profile, the team is currently working on several cross-border projects in the expanding markets of Costa Rica and Mexico. The team recently combined its renowned finance expertise with its real estate skills in assisting a local developer in the acquisition, by means of a joint venture, of the Fashion Square complex in Galleria. The intricate project required liaising with the city authorities to facilitate road closure, the acquisition of several adjacent properties and attendant financial arrangements. The team has also been retained to handle the leasing of the retail units.

The Lawyers: According to commentators, **Marvin Katz** (see p.1686) is not just the *"talisman"* of this group, he is *"the best in the business."* The chair of the Houston Planning Commission, Katz is an authority on land use issues, and his business acumen also allows him to *"cut through to the underlying economic issues in a deal."* Described as *"culturally attuned"* to the Latin American market, his fluency in Spanish allows him to perform to an equally high standard in these countries too. He played a central role in the Fashion Square project, and also represented a principal owner of the Reliant Energy office building in downtown

Houston in its sale to a joint venture with a foreign REIT.

The Clients: The firm's international profile and traditional strengths in finance make it an attractive choice for major institutional lenders and borrowers, banks and other leading financial houses and REITs, both domestically and abroad.

Band 3

Bracewell & Giuliani LLP
See firm details p.1710

The Firm: Commentators were highly impressed by this group's ability *"to effectively coordinate transactions with conflicting priorities."* The firm is also able to boast a comprehensive statewide coverage through its six offices. It can apply itself to sophisticated land development work, complex asset-based financing, synthetic leases and other structured finance work for a broad clientele that includes banks, insurance companies, pension funds, mortgage lenders and investors.

The Lawyers: **Clark Thompson** (see p.1703) counsels clients on the acquisition, development, finance and divestiture of commercial and industrial projects, ranging from power plants and other energy-related facilities to office and retail developments. Observers highlighted in particular the standard of his leasing work, and agreed that his straightforward style, coupled with *"strong lateral thinking skills,"* ensures that he does not become mired in the minutiae of a deal.

The Clients: Coral Energy; HNG Storage; FPL Energy and Louisiana-Pacific.

Gardere Wynne Sewell LLP
See firm details p.1718

The Firm: The department of 24 Texas attorneys is split into teams based in Dallas and Houston, and the former tends to counsel borrowers while the latter's strengths lie in acting for lenders. The group is also frequently visible in transactions outside state boundaries. It recently acted on the $250 million sale of a hotel portfolio to a large REIT in Virginia, and represented Vail Resorts on the sale of assets in Colorado. Both of these transactions highlight its acknowledged forte in the hospitality sector.

The Lawyers: New entrant to the tables **Kevin Kelley** (see p.1686) earned the praise of inter-

viewees, who agreed: *"He's as good a lawyer in the development arena as you could hope to have on your side."* Recent engagements include several multifamily projects in Florida, sale and leaseback transactions for a hotel chain and a negotiated $150 million restructuring of existing debt on a portfolio of hotels.

The Clients: Macfarlan Real Estate Investment Management; Inland Real Estate; Koll Development Company (KDC); Cisco Systems; Lehman Brothers; Gaylord Entertainment; Vail Resorts and Western International.

Jackson Walker LLP

The Firm: The firm's seven offices, 30 specialists and its dedicated land use team in Dallas provide an extremely thorough geographical coverage for real estate engagements. Clients approved of the team's style that inculcates *"a feeling of membership of a single team, rather than an external service."* Fêted for its leasing and lending work, the group has lately been involved on a number of projects for one of the country's largest REITs.

The Lawyers: **Kurt Nondorf** *"always puts his clients' interests first,"* according to sources. During the past year he has counseled clients in managing existing assets, acquiring several new office facilities and, in some cases, expanding facilities into commercial condominiums. However it is his high-profile work with large REITs that impresses commentators most. Peers admire **Michael Kuhn** for his leasing expertise. His ability to *"take tricky details off the plate"* in large transactions inspires such confidence in clients that they *"trust his negotiations implicitly."*

The Clients: The Texas Medical Center and several REITs feature on a list of clients that includes individual investors, pension funds, retailers and banks.

Thompson & Knight LLP
See firm details p.1722

The Firm: The team of more than 40 lawyers, based out of four Texas offices, advises clients in the full spectrum of real estate matters. This ranges from regular development and leasing mandates to new areas of the market such as telecom licensing, electricity services contracts, asbestos containment and removal, indoor pol-

lution, and legislative or regulatory disputes. Recent engagements include several significant loan securitizations and assisting the City of Austin in the redevelopment of an airport and various other tracts of land.

The Lawyers: The *"extremely responsive"* **Harry Roberts** (see p.1699) is adept at *"getting his clients over all of the legal hurdles,"* interviewees said. Equally attentive to the needs of developers and lenders, Roberts recently advised one of his many lender clients in securing a loan of $133 million on 81 separate properties.

The Clients: The client roster features buyers and sellers, lessors, lessees, and developers of office and industrial properties in more than half of the states in the USA.

Weil, Gotshal & Manges LLP
See firm details p.1378

The Firm: This real estate group may be small in number but focuses on deals at the higher end of the market. The team is generally much more visible in real estate financing transactions, such as the issuance of preferred shares or in negotiating mezzanine loans, than commodity work; and the recent caseload underlines the success of this strategy. The unit acted on the sale of the Enron Building in Houston and the resolution of $300 million of related debt, as well as advising a publicly traded hotel and resort developer in the restructuring and acquisition of certain assets of a major Mexican timeshare operator for $80 million.

The Lawyers: Peers agree that when **Bob Feldman** (see p.1679) is across the deal table they can expect *"a tough but fair negotiation."* Also well versed in bankruptcy proceedings, Feldman is often the first port of call for companies seeking to restructure debt or establish partnerships and limited liability companies to facilitate real estate acquisitions. Headline-grabbing work this past year included the sale of Hallwood Realty to a public REIT for more than $250 million and the representation of CitiCapital, an affiliate of Citigroup, in the restructuring of defaulted utility bonds in Kaufman County.

The Clients: The Enron estate, several REITs, developers, lenders and landowners, including several sports franchises, rank among the firm's clients.

TAX

Band 1

Vinson & Elkins LLP
See firm details p.1724

The Firm: A firm that operates at the *"cutting edge,"* market observers agree it is *"clearly top tier"* when it comes to advice on a range of tax matters. The firm has enjoyed a robust year in terms

of M&A activity, with the tax team taking on an integral role. Recent work includes representing Enterprise Product Partners in its high-profile merger with GulfTerra Energy Partners, to create a $13 billion midstream energy partnership. Additional projects include providing tax advice to Crow Holdings in its $209 million acquisition of Industrial Properties, where the benefits and

ERISA task force was also involved. The practice spans five primary areas: transactional, tax controversy, tax-exempt financing, state and federal tax and personal tax. The controversy team represents clients in various tax disputes, such as tax shelters and assists on IRS audits.

The Lawyers: A *"top name,"* **Edward Osterberg** (see p.1694) is recognized by peers as an *"all-*

1664   All quotes in the text are from interviews with clients and competitors.

CHAMBERS USA 2005

Texas
Leading firms (Tax)
1 VINSON & ELKINS LLP *Dallas*
2 BAKER BOTTS LLP *Dallas*
   BRACEWELL & GIULIANI LLP *Houston*
   FULBRIGHT & JAWORSKI LLP *Houston*
   LOCKE LIDDELL & SAPP LLP *Dallas*
   THOMPSON & KNIGHT LLP *Dallas*
3 AKIN GUMP STRAUSS HAUER & FELD LLP *Dallas*
   BAKER & MCKENZIE *Dallas*
   GARDERE WYNNE SEWELL LLP *Dallas*
   MEADOWS, OWENS, COLLIER, REED *Dallas*
   TOWNSEND & JONES *Houston*
   WINSTEAD SECHREST & MINICK PC *Dallas*

Leading individuals (Tax)
1 KALTEYER Ronald *Locke Liddell, Dallas*
   OSTERBERG Edward *Vinson & Elkins, Houston*
   WELLS Benjamin *Baker Botts, Houston*
2 ALLISON Christopher *Locke Liddell, Dallas*
   ASOFSKY Paul *Weil Gotshal, Houston*
   BOWERS William *Fulbright & Jaworski, Dallas*
   HARDIE Thornton *Thompson & Knight, Dallas*
   HELFAND Thomas *Winstead Sechrest, Dallas*
3 ALLENDER John *Fulbright & Jaworski, Houston*
   CRAIG III Allen *Gardere Wynne, Houston*
   MICCICHE Daniel *Akin Gump, Dallas*
   MILLER Barry *Vinson & Elkins, Houston*
   SALCH Steven *Fulbright & Jaworski, Houston*
   WHEAT David *Thompson & Knight, Dallas*
4 FIJOLEK Richard *Haynes and Boone, Dallas*
   HULL Robert *Bracewell & Giuliani, Houston*
   MOOREFIELD G Crawford *Akin Gump, Houston*
   SINAK David *Gibson Dunn, Dallas*
   STONE Susan *Baker & McKenzie, Houston*

Leading individuals (Litigation: Tax)
1 TAYLOR Jasper *Fulbright & Jaworski, Houston*
2 ALBRIGHT Val *Gardere Wynne, Dallas*
   GERACHIS George *Vinson & Elkins, Houston*
   LEE William *Fulbright & Jaworski, Houston*
   MEADOWS Charles *Meadows Owens, Dallas*
   TOWNSEND John *Townsend & Jones, Houston*
Firms and individuals are listed alphabetically in each band.

around fantastic lawyer," especially for transactions that have an international dimension. He chairs the international and transactional unit of the firm's tax group and concentrates on business income tax, with an emphasis on corporate and partnership taxation. He typically acts as lead tax counsel on the structuring or restructuring of worldwide operations for US-headquartered multinationals. **Barry Miller** (see p.1692) has a reputation as a leading tax lawyer for energy companies. His forte lies in the formation and taxation of publicly traded partnerships (master limited partnerships) and royalty trusts. Co-head of the tax section, **George Gerachis** (see p.1680) is an experienced player, who leads the firm's federal tax controversy and litigation practice.

The Clients: The firm advised EDS on the sale of its software unit for more than $2.05 billion to a private equity group of Bain Capital, Silver Lake Partners and Warburg Pincus, making it the largest private equity investment ever made in a technology company. Other clients include: AIG; Dow Chemical; Duke Energy; TEPPCO Partners and Dell.

Band 2

Baker Botts LLP
See firm details p.1708
The Firm: Universally renowned as an "*upper market*" player, the firm fields a team of "*fine tax lawyers*." It successfully leverages its position as a go-to firm in the energy sector to provide premier tax advice for a range of related transactions. Major clients include CentrePoint Energy, which the firm represented in its $3.65 billion sale of subsidiary, Texas Genco to GC Power Acquisition. Other significant projects include representing both parties in TODCO's $283 million secondary public offering for Transocean. In the securities sphere, the team represented K-Sea Transportation Partners in its IPO, valued at $98 million. Other areas of particular strength include income tax advice on both inbound and outbound investments, state and local tax matters, litigation and private client work. The firm also houses a dedicated employee benefits and ERISA practice.
The Lawyers: With a "*deep technical knowledge of tax law*" at his fingertips, **Benjamin Wells** (see p.1705) chairs the firm-wide tax department. He focuses on federal income tax matters and is well versed on a wide range of transactions. He recently acted for Lyondell Chemical Company in its $3.6 billion acquisition of Millennium Chemicals; the resulting company will be the third-largest, publicly traded chemical producer in North America. Wells is devoting an increasing amount of his time to cross-border work, including tax planning for American companies operating abroad, and structuring inbound investments by outside investors.
The Clients: Crosstex Energy; Link Energy; Encore Acquisition; Evergreen Resources; Enterra Energy Trust; Oceaneering International and GlobalSantaFe.

Bracewell & Giuliani LLP
See firm details p.1710
The Firm: This top-notch firm has cultivated a team of talented attorneys, who work out of the Houston office. They possess a broad experience in domestic and international transactions, benefit plans and tax controversy issues. Although well placed to advise a range of clients, the team has proved particularly successful in the banking arena, representing community banks. Other strengths include a sophisticated M&A understanding and years of experience in the energy arena. For example, the team has recent-ly been engaged by Dynegy to work on a series of partnership interest sales.
The Lawyers: A respected figure in the Texas market, **Robert Hull** (see p.1685) takes on both planning and controversy work for a range of clients. He is particularly experienced in real estate transactions and the formation and operations of business partnerships. Hull recently handled the Texas tax audit work for Cooperheat in its Chapter 11 filing.
The Clients: Dynegy; Hillenbrand; Coral Energy; Calpine; GE; Eaton; PG&E Gas Transmission-Texas; Apple and SYSCO.

Fulbright & Jaworski LLP
See firm details p.1715
The Firm: A firm that finds "*legal solutions to business problems*," clients also spoke of its "*professional and knowledgeable*" tax attorneys. Its reputation is foremost in tax controversy and litigation, an area that has witnessed an upsurge of late. Clients report that the tax group does a "*marvelous job*," from advising on state and local tax matters to more complicated multijurisdictional issues, such as trapped tax. The team's breadth of experience encompasses high-value M&A. Recent highlights include acting for Anadarko, in its sale of oil and gas assets to Apache and Morgan Stanley, for in excess of $1 billion.
The Lawyers: Clients value **William Bowers**' (see p.1673) skill in partnership tax matters, and spoke of his "*depth of knowledge and technical expertise*." An adviser who leaves "*no stone unturned*," he sets the mold for the team's "*service-oriented*" approach. Head of the firm's tax department, **John Allender** (see p.1670) impresses clients as a strong business lawyer, who is both "*creative and practical*." **Steven Salch** (see p.1699) maintains his "*superb*" reputation in tax controversy, litigation and international tax planning matters. Renowned for his leading contentious practice, **Jasper Taylor** (see p.1703) represents taxpayers at both federal and state level. A "*technically outstanding lawyer*," clients say he is well versed in his subject and combines a "*professional manner*" with "*tough negotiation skills*" in court. Another lawyer who concentrates his practice on all aspects of federal tax controversy is **Bill Lee** (see p.1689). He is widely respected for his success rate in representing clients before the IRS.
The Clients: The team represented Fiesta Mart, the largest ethnic supermarket chain in the USA, in its sale to Grocers Supply. Kaneb Services also used the firm in its $2.8 billion sale to Valero. Other clients include: American Bureau of Shipping; Bank of New York; Baker Hughes; Baylor Health Care System; El Paso; Memorial Hermann Hospital and SEMATECH.

Locke Liddell & Sapp LLP
The Firm: Clients described this as a talented team that displays good depth and "*has all the*

disciplines well covered." The tax department offers a wide range of tax planning and controversy services, providing advice on federal, state and local matters. The firm is prized for its leading REIT practice, where a team of dedicated attorneys advises on tax and regulatory complexities and plays an integral role in REIT M&A. In a recent highlight, the firm represented US Restaurant Properties in a proposed merger with CNL Restaurant Properties, a union that will create the largest restaurant REIT in the country. The firm is also acting on the announced IPO of Bois d'Arc Energy, a company controlled by Comstock Resources.

The Lawyers: A name that "*stands out from the crowd,*" **Ronald Kalteyer** (see p.1686) is a key player in the Texas tax market. Recent work includes a large restructuring program for Crescent Real Estate Equities, including a joint venture with a leading financial institution. **Christopher Allison** (see p.1670) is a "*top-notch lawyer,*" whom clients rate for his "*analytical mind*" and "*responsive and service-oriented*" approach.

The Clients: INVESCO Institutional; Service Corporation International; Crescent Real Estate Equities; JPMorgan Chase Bank; Dell; JC Penney and Sabre Holdings.

Thompson & Knight LLP

See firm details p.1722

The Firm: This "*stellar*" tax group is "*thorough, professional and smart,*" according to sources. A sizable tax group, with 47 lawyers based primarily in Dallas, advises on a broad range of tax issues. The team benefits from long-established links with the state's oil and gas companies, displaying particular aplomb in this sector. Other strengths include working with tax-exempt organizations on the formation and operation of nonprofit organizations. Further expertise lies in real estate, partnership and estate planning for high net worth individuals.

The Lawyers: Leading the charge at the firm, **Thornton Hardie** (see p.1683) is an outstanding lawyer well versed in federal income tax planning for corporations, partnerships and individuals. He is widely respected as an oil and gas taxation and energy finance specialist. Sources singled out **David Wheat** (see p.1705) for his advice on business transactions, including M&A as well as the formation and operation of partnerships and limited liability companies.

The Clients: Clients include individuals and all types of business entities and organizations.

Band 3

Akin Gump Strauss Hauer & Feld LLP

See firm details p.477

The Firm: In Texas the firm's practice has a focus on corporate, international and partnership taxation, as well as handling gift tax and estate planning matters. Attorneys here can also draw on the support of a prominent Washington DC offering, which is respected for its tax controversy expertise. Sources described its attorneys as strong advisers, who display sound business judgment.

The Lawyers: **Daniel Micciche** (see p.1692) is chair of the taxation committee of the State Bar of Texas and head of the firm's practice group. His practice strikes a balance between tax and business planning on corporate transactions and representing clients in federal and state controversies. **Crawford Moorefield** (see p.1693) joins Micciche in the table this year, following a wealth of recommendations from clients. His forte lies in partnership work, though as one source commented: "*His advice extends way beyond his stated area of expertise – you could count him as a legal or business adviser for any problem that ever came across your desk.*"

The Clients: Clear Channel Communications; Westport Resources; EEX Corporation and Cinemark.

Baker & McKenzie

See firm details p.761

The Firm: Best known for its strong international presence, the tax practice boasts 450 lawyers across 66 offices worldwide. The Texas team has vast experience in sophisticated tax planning and transactional support, as part of this global network. Particular strengths include international private banking and estate management, cross-border tax planning and advice on financial products. The firm is also known for its tax dispute resolution practice, although in Texas it has had to weather the departure of the widely respected Val Albright to Gardere Wynne Sewell.

The Lawyers: **Susan Stone** (see p.1702) typically advises clients on structuring their outbound transactions, by implementing global and regional tax minimization strategies. Recent projects include restructuring work and compliance for outbound clients moving in and out of various treaty jurisdictions.

The Clients: US and foreign multinationals feature among the firm's client base.

Gardere Wynne Sewell LLP

See firm details p.1718

The Firm: This highly competent team has a good track record for "*responsive services and sound judgment,*" according to market sources. The department is structured around various subsections: international taxation; federal, state and local tax; estate planning and employee benefits. Attorneys are also well versed in litigation, including disputes arising from international tax planning. Transfer pricing also remains a strong suit, where the team assists clients with developing comprehensive, cross-border tax planning strategies.

The Lawyers: Head of the tax section, **Allen Craig** (see p.1675) is one of the market's most attentive lawyers: "*There's not an attorney we deal with who is as responsive as Allen,*" one client said. Described as a "*thorough and efficient*" adviser, he is "*extremely knowledgeable in his subject,*" generally dealing with tax planning in a transactional context. Formerly of Baker & McKenzie, **Val Albright** (see p.1669) recently bolstered the tax litigation practice here with his established authority on various proceedings before the IRS and federal courts. His portfolio includes civil examinations, criminal investigations, protests before appeals and other tax-related disputes. He also has experience in transfer pricing matters, and often advises clients on domestic and international tax planning.

The Clients: The firm serves Fortune 500 companies, private clients and governmental entities.

Meadows, Owens, Collier, Reed, Cousins & Blau

The Firm: A "*go-to firm*" for tax litigation, peers say this specialist outfit has a fine reputation that has ensured it a position within the market. The firm's historical roots lie in tax planning and litigation although the practice has expanded to encompass other related disciplines, such as corporate/securities work and commercial litigation. The firm typically represents taxpayers in civil and criminal tax controversies at all levels. It is recognized as a leading player in the field of tax disputes with the IRS involving wealth transfer tax.

The Lawyers: **Charles Meadows** is an outstanding adviser, with over 25 years of experience in tax litigation and white-collar criminal defense. He is well versed in litigation related to income taxes, and estate and gift taxes, and has advised on the proposed application of civil and criminal penalties under the Internal Revenue Code.

The Clients: Clients include Fortune 100 corporations, private corporations, nonprofit entities, individuals, and estates and trusts.

Townsend & Jones

The Firm: This boutique firm is respected for its tax controversy and litigation skills at all levels of the legal circuit. The two-partner team focuses on representing clients in IRS audits and appeals. Other controversies before the IRS include collections, criminal tax matters, and civil and criminal litigation. The firm tends to win a substantial volume of referral work from high-level accounting or law firms.

The Lawyers: Before going in to private practice, **John Townsend** (see p.1703) was a trial attorney in the tax division of the DOJ, and he brings such expertise to his thoroughly detailed and knowledgeable advice. His principal area of expertise is in federal income tax controversy. Recently, he has seen an increase in tax crime

1666

All quotes in the text are from interviews with clients and competitors.

CHAMBERS USA 2005

litigation and is currently acting on a nationwide case concerning an investigation into tax products sold by a major accounting firm.
The Clients: Corporations and individuals are clients of this firm.

Winstead Sechrest & Minick PC
See firm details p.1725
The Firm: *"Great at understanding all tax, legal and business issues,"* this team finds favor with a myriad of clients. A significant part of the firm's practice is devoted to real estate, where attorneys advise on related tax issues. Attorneys here are experienced in advising on real estate mortgage investment conduits, while other strengths lie in oil and gas partnership work and M&A support for business transactions. The firm also fields dedicated employee compensation and tax controversy groups.

The Lawyers: Chief operating administrator, **Thomas Helfand** (see p.1684) scores points with clients for his *"unrivaled command of the technical issues,"* and his *"ability to evaluate risk."* He is master of a broad practice, with particular experience in partnership formations, transactions and roll-ups, and clients appreciate his *"responsive manner and creative advice."*
The Clients: Publicly traded and private companies operating in a range of business sectors, including banking, construction, energy, healthcare and real estate are clients.

Other Notable Practitioners
Identified as an *"outstanding"* practitioner, Houston-based **Paul Asofsky** (see p.1670) flies the tax flag at international giant Weil, Gotshal & Manges LLP. An active spokesperson for his practice area, Asofsky serves as chairman of the ABA Tax Section's special task force on the tax recommendations of the National Bankruptcy Review Commission and enjoys a national reputation as an *"extremely strong"* adviser. *"Technically one of the best in the state,"* **Richard Fijolek** of Haynes & Boone LLP advises clients on legal and tax issues from the formation to the operation of their businesses and is highly rated for his expertise in international transactions. *"Professional and responsive,"* **David Sinak** (see p.1701) carries the torch at Gibson, Dunn & Crutcher LLP, where he primarily focuses on M&A. Recent work includes providing tax advice to Atmos Energy on the acquisition of Texas' largest gas utility, TXU Gas Company. He has also provided tax and structuring advice to Papa John's Pizza in establishing a joint venture with an NFL professional football club to operate and market pizza operations in Texas.

TECHNOLOGY

Texas
Leading firms (Technology)

1	**BAKER BOTTS LLP** *Austin*
2	**FULBRIGHT & JAWORSKI LLP** *Houston*
	HUGHES & LUCE LLP *Dallas*
	JONES DAY *Dallas*
	VINSON & ELKINS LLP *Dallas*
3	**ANDREWS KURTH LLP** *Houston*
	BRACEWELL & GIULIANI LLP *Houston*
	GARDERE WYNNE SEWELL LLP *Dallas*
	HAYNES AND BOONE LLP *Houston*
	JENKENS & GILCHRIST PC *Dallas*
	LOCKE LIDDELL & SAPP LLP *Houston*
	THOMPSON & KNIGHT LLP *Dallas*
	WILSON SONSINI GOODRICH & ROSATI *Austin*

Firms are listed alphabetically in each band.

Band 1

Baker Botts LLP
See firm details p.1708
The Firm: Commentators agree that this *"juggernaut of the Texas technology arena"* continues to dominate the market. Clients reported that the group is *"so competent and skilled that it can handle any type of complex M&A-driven technology transaction and outsourcing agreement."* The firm fields a technology team of about 43 lawyers in Texas, including lawyers cross-skilled in corporate and securities matters. The group can call upon a wealth of experience in acting for telecom, media and IT purchasers and sellers in negotiating acquisitions, buyouts and spin-off transactions. It notably represented Liberty Media in its $42 million split-off divestiture from parent company AT&T. It also guided Electronic Data Systems through the $900 mil-

lion acquisition of IT services company Feld Group. The department derives key support from the highly rated national outsourcing practice, which enjoys an outstanding reputation in information and infrastructure technology and business process outsourcing transactions. Highlights include advising on a $2.2 billion global IT and business process outsourcing services agreement with an airline reservation company, and significant involvement in a $250 million design development and support agreement for an international electronic company's SAP implementation.
The Lawyers: Clients praise the *"likable and personable"* **John Martin** (see p.1690) as an *"intelligent and helpful asset who really knows how to put a team together in negotiating outsourcing transactions."* Notably he is advising Accenture on setting up venture capital investments for startup companies and Electronic Data Systems in various split-offs, mergers and acquisitions. Clients applauded **Charles Szalkowski** (see p.1702) as *"one of the state's best lawyers for technology matters during M&A activity."* He is also described as *"wonderfully astute and calm"* when advising investors on issues relating to technology businesses and growth companies. According to a leading entrepreneur *"He can communicate with both the inventors and investors and is so accomplished at the bargaining table that you feel he is 100% fighting your corner."* **Don McDermett** (see p.1691) elicits market praise for his high-profile involvement in corporate finance-related technology transactions, especially ones involving US and international outsourcing agreements.
The Clients: Accenture; Alcatel; Cisco; Dell; EDS; Morgan Stanley; Liberty Media; Nokia

Networks; Northern Telecom; Motive Communications and Sprint.

Band 2

Fulbright & Jaworski LLP
See firm details p.1715
The Firm: The firm is widely recognized for its *"fantastic IP practice"* and *"outstanding reputation"* in serving technology clients. It is also deemed to have *"first-class"* biotech expertise. In particular its Austin office is recognized as a hotbed of life sciences legal expertise. The only reservation expressed by some peers was that the team as yet lacks a strong profile in outsourcing matters. Nevertheless, its high-caliber experience in representing technology startups, established companies, underwriters and investors in venture capital financings, M&A and private placements remains *"absolutely first rate."*
The Lawyers: Following the departure at time of press of Robert Gray to Mayer, Brown, Rowe & Maw, the market awaits to see the effect on the practice. Sources identified *"highly capable"* **David Peterman** (see p.1696) as a *"tenacious grafter for clients."* He acts for telecom and technology companies on domestic and international corporate transactions.
The Clients: Houston Technology Center; Tyrell; University of Texas Health Science Center and MD Anderson Cancer Center.

Hughes & Luce LLP
The Firm: According to clients and peers, this firm is *"huge in outsourcing and has been active in the technology transactions arena for a very long time."* The team has more than 30 years'

Texas
Leading individuals (Technology: Corporate and Commercial)

1. **GRAY Robert** *Fulbright & Jaworski*, Houston
   PARKER Dallas *Thompson & Knight*, Houston
   POWELL Charles *Haynes and Boone*, Houston
   SZALKOWSKI Charles *Baker Botts*, Houston
2. **DODD Jeff** *Andrews Kurth*, Houston
   JEWELL Robert *Andrews Kurth*, Houston
   PETERMAN David *Fulbright & Jaworski*, Houston
   PUTMAN Frank *Gardere Wynne*, Houston
3. **BEARD Brian** *Wilson Sonsini*, Austin
   FOX Nixon *Vinson & Elkins*, Austin
   MANFORD Thomas *Bracewell & Giuliani*, Houston
   MCDERMETT Don *Baker Botts*, Dallas

Leading individuals (Technology & IT Outsourcing)

1. **FUNK John** *Jones Day*, Dallas
   GUEDRY David *Hughes & Luce*, Dallas
   HOWELL John *Hughes & Luce*, Dallas
   MARTIN John *Baker Botts*, Dallas
2. **BAYS Richard** *Locke Liddell & Sapp*, Houston
   HARVEY Dean *Vinson & Elkins*, Dallas
   STOCKBRIDGE Edward *Vinson & Elkins*, Houston
   VOGEL Peter *Gardere Wynne Sewell*, Dallas
3. **KING Chad** *Hughes & Luce*, Dallas
   KRIESER Jason *Jones Day*, Dallas

Individuals are listed alphabetically in each band.

experience in advising in the structuring and negotiations of outsourcing contracts in the IT, telecom, financial services and healthcare industries. It has a historic relationship with leading client EDS, dating back to former US presidential candidate Ross Perot's tenure as CEO. The group continues to represent the electronics giant in its multibillion-dollar outsourcing arrangements with Airlines, Chevron, BellSouth and GM. In a landmark transaction, the group acted for Canadian IT solutions business CGI Group in winning a $350 million US outsourcing contract to service Fireman's Fund Insurance with a ten-year IT support program. The group also acts for 3Com in the outsourcing of its IT needs.

The Lawyers: Interviewees were consistent in their praise of **John Howell** as "*probably the longest tenured outsourcing lawyer in the world.*" He advises Fortune 500 and international companies on complex technology and outsourcing agreements. Key clients include Worldspan, the IT service provider to the airline industry, which he advises on its various outsourcing arrangements with IBM, Unisys and Expedia. Interviewees endorse **David Guedry** as "*a rainmaker*" who instills confidence in clients with his "*marvelous project management skills and fantastic problem-solving abilities.*" His practice focuses on advising technology companies on business process outsourcing agreements. Head of the firm's outsourcing and technology division **Chad King** specializes in advising clients in new media and e-commerce on technology contracts, licensing, distribution, sponsorship and privacy issues. His highly regarded practice also addresses a range of IP issues, including federal trademark transactions.

The Clients: 3Com; CGI Group; EDS; Perot Systems and CNET Networks.

Jones Day
See firm details p.485

The Firm: Sources frequently referred to the team's "*potent national presence in both business process outsourcing and litigation.*" According to commentators, the team's capabilities in technology-related transactions are "*emerging as a rising force,*" and complement its excellent track record in patents, antitrust and unfair competition work. The Dallas-based team is said to have "*extensive experience and just the right synergy*" in advising on IT and business process outsourcing deals. The arrival of John Funk from the Los Angeles office of Milbank, Tweed, Hadley & McCloy has been instrumental in this respect.

The Lawyers: Commentators agreed that the firm is reaping the rewards of acquiring "*five-star business process outsourcing specialist*" and former Howell protégé **John Funk** (see p.1680). Market sources describe him as "*a class act and a seasoned player in outsourcing.*" He notably represents Eckerd, Mitsubishi, and Perot Systems on complex outsourcing work. **Jason Krieser** (see p.1688) continues to shine on technology transactions, interviewees reported. His practice focuses on IP and technology-related M&A transactions. He acts for computer companies on a wide range of technology service agreements, licenses and business alliances.

The Clients: Diebold; Eckerd; Mitsubishi; Washington Mutual; Chiron and Eastman Chemical.

Vinson & Elkins LLP
See firm details p.1724

The Firm: "*Outstanding quality of advice and a very high level of service*" are what distinguishes this firm, say peers. The broad practice is recognized for being home to partners who are "*hands on, cost effective and creative thinkers.*" The team advises an enviable client base that features numerous Fortune 500 companies on web claims solutions, procurement transactions and domain name and Internet security and privacy matters. It is also growing in strength on the corporate-related technology front, and is highly visible in acting for public and private companies and startups on technology-related M&A, joint ventures and other business transactions. The group recently represented DuPont Photomasks in its $650 million acquisition by Toppan Printing, one of the largest cross-border technology company mergers of recent times.

The Lawyers: **Nixon Fox** (see p.1679) earns the respect of clients for his "*smart, enthusiastic and ethical*" approach to technology-related transactions. He acts for startups, public companies and emerging businesses in the negotiation of portfolio investments, joint venture formations and many other technology-related issues. Software industry expert **Dean William Harvey** (see p.1683) cochairs the technology practice and specializes in counseling clients on the acquisition and development of software technology. Clients endorse **Edward Stockbridge** (see p.1702) for his "*wonderful knowledge, excellent drafting skills and ability to keep the costs down.*" He focuses on technology transactions and licensing, recently acting for a US airline carrier in a $1.5 billion outsourcing agreement.

The Clients: Perficient; Photomask; Austin Ventures; Electronic Data Systems; BearingPoint USA and Halliburton.

Band 3

Andrews Kurth LLP
See firm details p.1707

The Firm: According to sources, the firm's reputation in the technology arena is linked with its "*stellar*" corporate finance team, which advises on national and international outsourcing transactions. The group assists emerging companies in raising capital and protecting IP assets and advises on licensing agreements.

The Lawyers: The "*terrific*" **Robert Jewell** (see p.1685) commands market respect for his corporate and securities work in the energy and hi-tech industries. **Jeff Dodd** (see p.1677) manages an active practice addressing IP, IT and communications matters, and is considered by interviewees to be a "*well-known name*" in licensing issues. He counsels startups and other entities on technology acquisitions and distribution agreements.

The Clients: The group represents clients in the following industry sectors: semiconductors; telecom; computers and electronics; enterprise software; life sciences and biotech; aerospace; Internet and e-commerce.

Bracewell & Giuliani LLP
See firm details p.1710

The Firm: Market observers highlighted this firm's technical knowledge and regulatory expertise in the nanotechnolgy and biotech sectors. The team acts for investors, emerging companies and public and private entities on contracts and licenses. It is also very well respected for its IP patent, trademark and copyright portfolio work.

The Lawyers: **Thomas Manford** (see p.1689) runs a general corporate practice, with notable experience in acting for startups and venture capital funds in acquisitions, mergers and LBO transactions.

The Clients: Clients include Carbon Nanotechnologies, CardioSoft and Enersea Transport.

Gardere Wynne Sewell LLP
See firm details p.1718

The Firm: A well-known name in the IP and technology Texas circles, this group has particular expertise in acting for buyers and sellers of computer hardware and software products. Practice attorneys draft and negotiate contracts for the sourcing, licensing and protection of computer, Internet and telecom-related systems and inventions.

The Lawyers: According to market sources, **Frank Putman** (see p.1697) is considered "*one of the best technology lawyers in the state*" because of his ability to "*negotiate and communicate effectively to both investors and inventors.*" He has a niche in advising energy companies, financial institutions and manufacturing companies. **Peter Vogel**'s (see p.1704) practice focuses on advising businesses on software patents, copyrights and trade secret protection issues. He is also active in counseling on enterprise resource planning implementation projects.

The Clients: The client base encompasses software companies, banks, insurance companies and electronics companies.

Haynes and Boone LLP
The Firm: Much of the firm's kudos derives from its excellent reputation in handling outsourcing deals. The group practices across a broad spectrum of sectors, counseling businesses ranging from established listed companies to startups. Other areas of strength include venture capital-related deals and transactions requiring the maximization of patent and trademark portfolios.

The Lawyers: The "*cornerstone*" of the firm's practice is **Charles Powell**, who continues to impress peers as a "*wonderful*" corporate lawyer with an excellent reputation for serving technology clients.

The Clients: Key clients include Dell and Nortel Networks.

Jenkens & Gilchrist PC
The Firm: The small technology team operates out of the firm's Austin and Dallas offices, and is described by peers as "*more than just the sum of its parts.*" The department dovetails with respected corporate and private equity teams in particular, and so can be seen as part of the firm's overall network of nine US offices. Other areas of strength include IP protection strategies, various contract and compliance issues, shareholder arrangements, noncompete, employment and license agreements.

The Lawyers: Dallas-based John Holzgraefe is team contact partner.

The Clients: The firm counsels clients ranging from entrepreneurial entities to emerging growth companies and some Fortune 500 businesses.

Locke Liddell & Sapp LLP
The Firm: Sources agreed that the firm is growing in stature on the technology stage. It represents a prominent roster of IT clients, including Fortune 500 businesses, on such matters as licensing, alliance agreements and the implementation of business alliances and strategies.

The Lawyers: **Rick Bays** (see p.1671) is the firm's front runner for computer, Internet and information service-oriented transactions. He notably advises clients on the licensing of enterprise software packages such as SAP, Oracle and JD Edwards.

The Clients: Clients include website owners, media, financial services and electronic industry clients.

Thompson & Knight LLP
See firm details p.1722

The Firm: Supported by the firm's highly regarded corporate department, the technology team derives strength from its breadth of technical and academic experience in science disciplines such as engineering. The department advises emerging companies in the telecom and aerospace industries, as well as commercial research institutions.

The Lawyers: Interviewees recognize **Dallas Parker** (see p.1694) as one of the state's leading technology and acquisition finance lawyers. Recent practice highlights include acting for a public oil and gas exploration company in a $430 million merger. He was also involved in a major SEC filing and represented a public telecom and ISP business in its public offering and private placement.

The Clients: Clients are drawn from the biogenetics, semiconductor, electronics, pollution control and waste treatment sectors.

Wilson Sonsini Goodrich & Rosati
See firm details p.302

The Firm: This California firm is making waves in the state for its work in technology-related M&A deals. The Austin office was only established in 1999 but quickly built a strong following with various computer and other IT businesses. The group is able to exploit the resources of a respected national and international network of offices.

The Lawyers: **Brian Beard**'s (see p.1671) practice focuses on technology-driven securities and M&A transactions. He has niche expertise in advising startups on how best to raise venture capital.

The Clients: MetaSolv Software; Pervasive Software; Vignette and Ashford.com.

Other Notable Practitioners
Robert Gray recently joined Mayer, Brown, Rowe & Maw. He "*effectively combines his superb legal mind with a huge wealth of experience in dealing with transactional technology issues,*" say clients. One leading medical device company commended his "*unique practical sense, responsiveness and utterly dependable strategic advice.*" He enjoys a prominent reputation in representing emerging companies in the energy, life sciences and information technology sectors, specifically in NASA-originated technology and nanotechnology cases.

Leaders in Texas

ADDISON, Linda L
Fulbright & Jaworski L.L.P., Houston
713 651 5628
laddison@fulbright.com
Recommended in Litigation
Practice Areas: Complex commercial litigation, intellectual property litigation, international litigation, business litigation, arbitration and ADR; ERISA litigation.
Prof. Memberships: American Board of Trial Advocates (ABOTA); American Law Institute (ALI); Houston and American Bar Associations, State Bar of Texas; Life Fellow: American Bar Foundation, Texas Bar Foundation, Houston Bar Foundation; Life Member, Texas Law Review Ex-Editors' Association; Federal Judicial Evaluation Committee of United States Senators Hutchison and Cornyn.
Career: Named one of 'America's Top 50 Women Litigators' ('National Law Journal', 2001); named by 'Texas Lawyer' as one of Texas' top five lawyers to defend civil cases ('Texas Lawyer' 'Go-To' Guide 2002) and one of Texas Super Lawyers (2003-2004). Has tried over 50 cases. Admitted to practice: Texas, 1976; United States Supreme Court; United States Court of Appeals for the Fifth Circuit; United States District Court (Northern, Southern, and Eastern Districts of Texas); joined Fulbright & Jaworski in 1976; admitted to partnership, 1984 (Executive Committee, Technology Partner, heads one of firm's litigation teams).
Personal: University of Texas, 1973 (BA cum laude in Plan II Honors Program); University of Texas School of Law, JD 1976 (managing editor, 'Texas Law Review').

ALBERGOTTI, Robert
Haynes and Boone LLP, Dallas
214 651 5000
Recommended in Bankruptcy

ALBERS, Michael F
Jenkens & Gilchrist PC, Dallas
214 855 4500
Recommended in Construction

ALBRIGHT, Val
Gardere Wynne Sewell LLP, Dallas
214 999 4825
valbright@gardere.com
Recommended in Litigation
Practice Areas: Tax, tax litigation,

transfer pricing.

Career: Mr Albright has represented numerous clients in US federal tax matters before the Internal Revenue Service and in federal courts. Mr Albright's practice also includes advising clients concerning US domestic and international tax planning matters. Prior to entering private practice in early 1994, Mr Albright worked for the Office of Chief Counsel for the Internal Revenue Service of the US Treasury Department in Chicago, Illinois and Dallas, Texas. During his tenure with the Office of Chief Counsel, Mr Albright was involved in the development, settlement and trial of numerous corporate and individual federal tax cases involving diverse domestic and US international tax issues, including many transfer pricing and related issues.

Personal: LLM, Southern Methodist University School of Law, 1986; JD, University of Arkansas School of Law, 1977; BA, University of Arkansas at Monticello, 1971.

ALE, John C
Skadden, Arps, Slate, Meagher & Flom LLP & Affiliates, Houston
713 655 5263
jale@skadden.com
Recommended in Energy, Projects
Practice Areas: Concentrates in US and international energy, infrastructure, finance, and corporate matters. Represents clients in the development, financing and acquisition of energy and water infrastructure projects; privatizations; and acquisitions and divestitures. Has experience in MLPs and other equity structures.
Career: JD, University of Virginia, 1979 (Order of the Coif; Executive Director, Virginia Law Review); BA, University of Virginia, 1976.
Publications: Author, 'Partnership Law for Securities Practitioners' (The West Group).

ALLENDER, John R
Fulbright & Jaworski L.L.P., Houston
713 651 5664
jallender@fulbright.com
Recommended in Tax
Practice Areas: Taxation.
Prof. Memberships: Mr Allender is a former Chair of the Section of Taxation of the State Bar of Texas and the Houston Bar Association. Mr Allender is a Member of the State Bars of Texas (1977) and California (1976).
Career: Mr Allender joined the firm in 1976 and heads the firm's Tax Department. His practice focuses on taxation and corporate matters emphasizing federal income taxation. Mr Allender is often involved in the negotiation and planning of complex transactions, often related to the firm's substantial mergers and acquisition practice. In addition, Mr Allender is frequently involved in tax and business matters for wealthy indi-

viduals and their closely held businesses. He has been named in 'Texas Super Lawyers', 'The Best Lawyers in America' in tax law, 'Who's Who in America', and 'Top 100 Houston Region Super Lawyers'. Mr Allender is a frequent speaker on complex taxation topics.
Personal: BS, Iowa State University (1972); JD, cum laude, University of San Diego (1975); LLM, New York University School of Law. A long-term member of Ronald McDonald House-Houston's Board of Directors, he served as President from 2003-05. Mr Allender is also an Advisory Director of Catholic Charities-Galveston/Houston.

ALLENSWORTH, William
Allensworth and Porter, L.L.P, Austin
512 708 1250
Recommended in Construction

ALLISON, Christopher
Locke Liddell & Sapp LLP, Dallas
214 740 8692
callison@lockeliddell.com
Recommended in Tax
Practice Areas: Partner practicing in tax law. Section coordinator of the firm's Taxation, Trust and Estates Section. Over 20 years of experience in representing clients in the following areas: (i) corporate taxation including corporate formations, liquidations, distributions, reorganizations and recapitalizations, S corporation taxation, partnership taxation and taxation of limited liability companies; (ii) tax issues related to investments by tax exempt entities; and (iii) handling federal and state tax controversies at the audit, administrative and court levels.
Prof. Memberships: Member, American Bar Association, Section of Taxation; Member, State Bar of Texas, Section of Taxation; Member, Dallas Bar Association.
Career: Admitted to South Carolina Bar (1977); admitted to the Texas Bar (1981). A Partner in Locke Liddell & Sapp LLP since 1983; Board Certified in Area of Taxation by the Texas Board of Legal Specialization.
Personal: Received a LLM degree in Taxation from New York University in 1981; Juris Doctor degree from the University of South Carolina in 1977; Bachelor of Arts degree, cum laude, from Davidson College in 1974.

AMANDES, Christopher B
Vinson & Elkins LLP, Houston
713 758 1146
camandes@velaw.com
Recommended in Environment
Practice Areas: Principal area of practice is environmental law, with emphasis on compliance counseling, enforcement defense, transactional environmental issues, and cost-recovery litigation. Listed in a leading legal publication in America in environmental law, since 1995.
Prof. Memberships: Co-Chair: City of Houston's Brownfield Redevelopment

Committee, 1996-2000; ABA Annual Conference on Environmental Law (Keystone), 2004 - present. Air and Waste Management Association.
Career: Admitted to practice: Texas, 1985. Joined Vinson & Elkins, 1986; admitted to partnership, 1994. Registered Professional Engineer, Texas, 1983-present.
Personal: Rice University, BA, 1976; Masters of Environmental Engineering, 1978; University of California at Los Angeles, JD, 1985.

ANDERSON, Kenneth M
Vinson & Elkins LLP, Houston
713 758 2444
kanderson@velaw.com
Recommended in Banking & Finance
Practice Areas: Chair of Vinson & Elkins' Syndicated Finance Practice Group. Extensive syndicated finance experience including private equity, project, structured and energy financings. Representative clients include JPMorgan Chase Bank, Deutsche Bank AG and Hicks Muse Tate & Furst.
Prof. Memberships: Admitted to practice in Texas (1982). Member of Texas Association of Bank Counsel and American Bar Association, Business Law Section. Appointments: Chair, Syndicated Finance Subcommittee (Developments in Business Finance Committee, Business Law Section, ABA).
Career: Joined Vinson & Elkins LLP, 1982; became Partner, 1992.
Personal: JD (cum laude), BYU Law School, 1982 (associate editor, law review); BS, accounting, BYU, 1979.

ANDREWS, William
Andrews Myers Coulter & Cohen PC,
Houston 713 850 4200
Recommended in Construction

ARRINGTON, Scott
Akin Gump Strauss Hauer & Feld LLP,
Houston 713 220 5800
Recommended in Projects

ASMUS, David
Baker Botts LLP, Houston
713 229 1539
david.asmus@bakerbotts.com
Recommended in Energy, Projects
Practice Areas: Practice focuses on offshore and international oil and gas development projects (including LNG projects, FPSO and platform-based offshore developments, and integrated field development, pipeline, and processing projects); acquisitions and divestitures (including auction and negotiated sales and property exchanges); and energy-based financings (including reserve-based loans, project financings, and production payments).
Prof. Memberships: Past President of Association of International Petroleum Negotiators (AIPN); Houston Producers Forum; Houston Bar Association; State Bar of Texas; International Bar Association.

Career: Head of firm-wide Oil and Gas Practice.
Personal: JD from Harvard Law School, 1985; BS from Yale University, 1981.

ASOFSKY, Paul
Weil, Gotshal & Manges LLP, Houston
713 546 5118
paul.asofsky@weil.com
Recommended in Tax
Practice Areas: Mr Asofsky has headed the tax practice in Houston since 1990. His practice encompasses the full range of tax issues, federal and state, including mergers and acquisitions, partnerships, financing, issuance and restructuring of debt, and bankruptcy. He heads the firm's private equity tax group.
Career: Mr Asofsky has chaired many Bar Association tax committees. He is Chair of the Private Equity Subcommittee of the American Bar Association, Tax Section, Committee on Partnership, and an Adjunct Professor in the LLM tax program at New York University School of Law.
Personal: Harvard Law School (JD, 1965); Columbia University (BA, 1962).

AXE, Albert
Jenkens & Gilchrist, Austin
512 499 3800
Recommended in Environment

BACKUS, Marcia E
Vinson & Elkins LLP, Houston
713 758 1101
mbackus@velaw.com
Recommended in Energy, Projects
Practice Areas: Domestic and international acquisition, divestiture and project finance and project development transactions, corporate law, power-related transactions and other energy-related transactions. Is Co-Administrative Head of the Houston office, a member of the firm's Management Committee, the Energy Practice Group, and Chair of the partner Admissions Committee.
Prof. Memberships: Fellow: Houston Bar Association; Keeton Fellow, The University of Texas.
Career: Came to the firm in 1983 and was admitted to the partnership in 1991.
Personal: Attended Georgetown University and graduated from The University of Texas, BA in 1976 and JD in 1983 (Order of the Coif).

BAKER, Andrew M
Baker Botts LLP, Dallas
214 953 6735
andrew.baker@bakerbotts.com
Recommended in Corporate/M&A
Practice Areas: Chair: Dallas Corporate Section. Principal practice areas: general corporate, mergers, acquisitions, corporate finance/securities and technology. Practice emphasizes development of close, long-term, value-added relationships with public and private entities. Counseled with senior management/boards of directors on numerous matters, led transaction teams in com-

plex mergers and acquisitions involving businesses around the world, represented companies in varied corporate finance transactions and represented numerous companies in a variety of high technology transactions.

Personal: BA, summa cum laude, State University of New York at Albany, 1976; JD, magna cum laude, Cornell Law School, 1979.

BAKER, Debra
Connelly Baker Wotring Jackson LLP, Houston 713 980 1700
Recommended in Environment

BAKER, Mark
Fulbright & Jaworski L.L.P., Houston
713 651 7708
mbaker@fulbright.com
Recommended in Arbitration, Energy
Practice Areas: Arbitration, mediation, and litigation.
Prof. Memberships: Mr Baker has arbitrated before most of the world's arbitral bodies and has been involved in numerous alternative dispute resolution procedures. In every year since 1998, he has chaired at least eight significant arbitration cases while acting as lead counsel in dozens more on five continents. He is a Fellow of the Chartered Institute of Arbitrators; a Director and arbitrator for numerous panels of the AAA and ICDR; a court member and arbitrator for the LCIA; an arbitrator for CPR, WIPO, CAM, CAS; and a mediator for CEDR and the Texas courts. He is also a member of the ICC Commission.
Career: Mr Baker is a Co-Head of Fulbright's 11 office International Department and also Co-Head of the firm's Arbitration and ADR Practice Group. He has also represented numerous clients in international and domestic energy contracts, power purchase and sale agreements, construction contracts, joint ventures, and project finance and development agreements.
Personal: BA, summa cum laude Yale University (1981); JD, with high honors, Duke University School of Law (1984). Before joining Fulbright, Mr Baker was a law clerk to the Honorable John R Brown, Chief Judge of the US Fifth Circuit.

BARBOUR, David
Andrews Kurth LLP, Dallas
214 659 4444
dbarbour@andrewskurth.com
Recommended in Banking & Finance
Practice Areas: Expertise in various commercial transactions on a national and international basis, including the representation of issuers and underwriters in public and private offerings of equity and debt securities, with an emphasis in structured debt issuances of mortgage-backed and asset-backed securities.
Career: Received a JD with honors from The University of Texas School of Law in 1974. Was a member of Chancellors and received Order of the Coif. Received a

BBA with highest honors from The University of Texas at Austin in 1971. Admitted to the State Bar of Texas 1974. Partner with Andrews Kurth since 1994.

BARBOUR, Larry G
Vinson & Elkins LLP, Houston
713 758 2126
lbarbour@velaw.com
Recommended in Banking & Finance
Practice Areas: Business transactions, finance, including project and structured finance, and mergers and acquisitions. Has extensive experience in international transactions and complex syndicated bank transactions, representing either the lenders or the borrower. Worked on all aspects of energy finance.
Career: Came to the firm in 1977 and was admitted to the partnership in October 1985.
Personal: Graduated from Princeton University, AB in Economics with honors in 1972, New York University, MBA in Finance in 1974, and The University of Texas, JD with high honors, in 1977. (Chancellors; Order of the Coif.)

BARNES Jr, Hershell
The Barnes Law Firm PC, Dallas
214 615 7920
Recommended in Employment

BARZOUKAS, Nicolas
Howrey Simon Arnold & White, Houston
713 787 1400
Recommended in Intellectual Property

BAYKO, Tom
Jones Day, Houston 832 239 3700
tbayko@jonesday.com
Recommended in Energy
Practice Areas: He has extensive trial and international arbitration experience representing oil and gas companies, oil field service companies, equipment manufacturers, and contractors in many jurisdictions and under the applicable laws of many countries, and he was described as a "litigator-of-choice for international conflicts" by 'The Houston Business Journal.' His international litigation and arbitration experience includes successfully prosecuting and defending claims involving offshore blowouts, tortious interference with contractual and prospective contractual relationships, construction, production sharing agreements, joint operating agreements, participation agreements, area of mutual interests agreements, theft of technology and other trade secrets, and other commercial disputes.

BAYS, Richard
Locke Liddell & Sapp LLP, Houston
713 226 1458
rbays@lockeliddell.com
Recommended in Communications, Technology
Practice Areas: Technology transactions, software, alliances, application service provider, outsourcing, e-commerce, distribution, supply, real estate, finance and corporate transactions.

Prof. Memberships: Member, State Bar of Texas; Computer Law Section; Member, Houston Bar Association; Member, Computer Law Association.
Career: Partner in the law firm of Locke Liddell & Sapp LLP, 1992-Present; Associate in the law firm of Locke Liddell & Sapp LLP, 1985-91; Founder and Head of Technology & Commercial Transactions Section.

BEANE, Jerry
Andrews Kurth LLP, Dallas
214 659 4520
jerrybeane@andrewskurth.com
Recommended in Antitrust
Practice Areas: Antitrust and commercial litigation.
Prof. Memberships: The State Bar of Texas; American Bar Association; President, Baylor Law Review Ex-Editors Association; Chairman, Continuing Legal Education Committee of Dallas Bar Association; Chairman, Bar Activities Committee of Dallas Bar Association; Chairman, Client's Security Fund Committee of State Bar of Texas; Chairman, Antitrust Section of Dallas Bar Association (1998); Adjunct Professor, for Antitrust, Southern Methodist University School of Law (1989 - present). Fellow, American College of Trial Lawyers; 'Who's Who in American Law; Best Lawyers in Dallas', 'D Magazine', May 2001 and May 2003; 'Top 100 Texas Super Lawyers' Texas Monthly Magazine, November 2003.
Career: Admitted to the State Bar of Texas 1967. Partner with Andrews Kurth since 2003.
Publications: 'Antitrust: Standing and Passing On', 26 Baylor L.R. 331 (1974); 'Deceptive and Unfair Acts Under the Federal Antitrust Laws' 42 Texas Bar Journal 563 (1979), co-authored with Wilson Herndon; 'Passing-On Revived: An Antitrust Dilemma' 32 Baylor L. Rev. 347 (1980); 'The Antitrust Implications of Airline Deregulation', 45 J. of Air Law & Commerce 1001 (1980); 'Antitrust,' Fifth Circuit Survey, 19 Tex. Tech L. Rev. 339 (1988); 'Antitrust,' Fifth Circuit Survey, 20 Tex. Tech L. Rev. 303 (1989); 'Antitrust Aspects of Lender Liability' Lender Liability Law and Litigation, Matthew Bender, 1989; 'Antitrust,' Fifth Circuit Survey, 21 Tex. Tech L. Rev. 79 (1990); 'Antitrust,' Fifth Circuit Survey, 22 Tex. Tech L. Rev. 391 (1991); 'Antitrust,' Fifth Circuit Survey, 23 Tex. Tech L. Rev. 89 (1992); 'Antitrust,' Fifth Circuit Survey, 24 Tex. Tech L. Rev. 393 (1993); 'Antitrust,' Fifth Circuit Survey, 25 Tex. Tech L. Rev. 453 (1994); 'Antitrust,' Fifth Circuit Survey, 26 Tex. Tech L. Rev. 331 (1995); 'Antitrust,' Fifth Circuit Survey, 27 Tex. Tech L. Rev. 331 (1996); 'Antitrust,' Fifth Circuit Survey, 28 Tex. Tech. L. Rev. 273 (1997); 'Antitrust,' Fifth Circuit Survey, 29 Tex. Tech. L. Rev. 335 (1998).
Personal: Received a JD from Baylor University Law School in 1967. Presi-

dent, Phi Delta Legal Fraternity, and editor in chief, Baylor Law Review. Was in 'Who's Who in American Colleges and Universities', and honored as an Outstanding Mid-Law Student. Received a BA from Baylor University in 1965.

BEARD, Brian
Wilson Sonsini Goodrich & Rosati, Austin 512 338 5400
bbeard@wsgr.com
Recommended in Communications, Technology
Practice Areas: Specializes in areas of corporate and securities law with a focus on representation of start-up and growth companies, representation of issuers and underwriters involved in public offerings, and representation of companies involved in merger and acquisition transactions.
Prof. Memberships: Admitted to practice in Illinois, California and Texas.
Career: Joined WSGR as Partner, 2002. Former Partner, Austin office of Gunderson Dettmer Stough Villeneuve Franklin & Hachigian, LLP (which he co-founded in 1997).
Personal: JD, 1990, University of Iowa and BA (Economics), 1987, University of Illinois.

BECK, David
Beck, Redden & Secrest L.L.P, Houston
713 951 3700
Recommended in Energy, Litigation

BECKER, Jeffrey
Haynes and Boone LLP, Dallas
214 651 5000
Recommended in Intellectual Property

BECKHAM Jr, Charles
Haynes and Boone LLP, Houston
713 547 2000
Recommended in Bankruptcy

BELL, Jerry
Fulbright & Jaworski L.L.P., Houston
713 651 8482
jbell@fulbright.com
Recommended in Healthcare
Practice Areas: Health law.
Prof. Memberships: Board certified by the Texas Board of Legal Specialization, Health Law Examination Commission (2003-05); Chair, Managed Care and Integrated Delivery Systems Committee, American Academy of Hospital Attorneys (1993-95); Chair, Health Law Section of the State Bar of Texas (1994-95); Board of Directors, American Health Lawyers Association (1997-2001); Board of Directors, American Academy of Healthcare Attorneys (1995-97); Member, Texas Board of Legal Specialization, Health Law Examination Commission, 2003-05.
Career: Mr Bell is Head of Fulbright & Jaworski L.L.P.'s Health Law Business and Regulatory Department and practices in the Houston office. He practices exclusively in the healthcare area. Mr Bell is also an adjunct professor at the The University of Texas Law School where he teaches the course 'Business

and Regulatory Aspects of Health Law.'
Personal: BA - University of Texas (1974); JD - University of Texas School of Law (1977).

BENNETT, David
Thompson & Knight LLP, Dallas
214 969 1486
david.bennett@tklaw.com
Recommended in Bankruptcy
Practice Areas: Mr Bennett's expertise includes both transactions and litigation involving troubled and insolvent businesses. His clients include debtors, creditors, capital providers, as well as other counter-parties in reorganization and liquidation bankruptcy cases. Mr Bennett has been named as a 'Top' bankruptcy lawyers in Texas Lawyer (2002) and as a Texas 'Super Lawyer' (Texas Monthly, 2003 and 2004).
Prof. Memberships: State Bar of Texas, Dallas Bar Association, American Bankruptcy Institute, Turnaround Managers' Association.
Career: Partner since 1992.
Personal: The University of Texas School of Law (JD, with high honors, 1986); University of Texas at Austin (BA, with high honors, 1983).

BIERY, Evelyn H
Fulbright & Jaworski L.L.P., San Antonio
713 651 5544
ebiery@fulbright.com
Recommended in Bankruptcy
Practice Areas: Bankruptcy, reorganization and international insolvency matters.
Prof. Memberships: Chair of the Board of Directors, American College of Bankruptcy; President, Miller Foltz Inn of Court; past Chair, Business Law Section and Bankruptcy Law Committee, the State Bar of Texas; Past Director, Texas Association of Bank Counsel; past Texas Chair, Society of International Business Fellows; Director, International Insolvency Institute; Diplomat, World Affairs Council.
Career: As Partner with over 30 years of experience, Ms Biery heads Fulbright's Bankruptcy, Reorganization and Creditors' Rights Department.
Personal: BA- summa cum laude, Abilene Christian University (1968); JD - Southern Methodist University School of Law (1973).

BILGER, Bruce R
Vinson & Elkins LLP, Houston
713 758 2614
bbilger@velaw.com
Recommended in Energy, Projects
Practice Areas: Chair of the firm's Energy Practice Group and Co-Head of the firm's Business and International Section. Practice consists primarily of domestic and international business transactions, including mergers and acquisitions, international infrastructure development projects, project finance, and other corporate transactions, particularly in the energy industry.
Prof. Memberships: Member and For-

mer Trustee: American College of Investment Counsel.
Career: Lecturer and author: programs and articles on partnership law, corporate law, merger and acquisitions, project finance, and international law topics.
Personal: Graduated from Dartmouth College, BA in 1973, and the University of Virginia, MBA and JD in 1977.

BISHOP, Doak
King & Spalding LLP, Houston
713 751 3205
dbishop@kslaw.com
Recommended in Arbitration, Energy
Practice Areas: 28 years of experience focusing on international arbitration and litigation of oil and gas, energy, construction, environmental and foreign investment disputes. Board Certified in Civil Trial Law by the Texas Board of Legal Specialization.
Prof. Memberships: American Bar Association; Dallas Bar Association; State Bar of Texas; Vice Chairman of the Institute of Transnational Arbitration (1990-present); member of the US delegation to the NAFTA Advisory Committee on Private Commercial Disputes.
Personal: BA, Southern Methodist University, 1973; JD, University of Texas, 1976.

BLAND, Douglas S
Vinson & Elkins LLP, Houston
713 758 2498
dbland@velaw.com
Recommended in Energy, Projects
Practice Areas: Partner in Business and International Section. Has a domestic and international business transactions practice focusing on the development, acquisition, divestiture, and financing of energy-related projects. Co-Head of Project Finance and Development Practice Group and member of Merger and Acquisitions and Electric Power Practice Groups.
Prof. Memberships: Houston Bar Association.
Career: Admitted to Texas Bar in 1984. Joined Vinson & Elkins in 1984; admitted to the partnership in January 1992.
Personal: Graduated from the University of Virginia, BA with high honors, 1981 (Phi Beta Kappa), and the University of Michigan, JD cum laude, in 1984 (Order of the Coif).

BOGDANOW, Alan J
Vinson & Elkins LLP, Dallas
214 220 7857
abogdanow@velaw.com
Recommended in Corporate/M&A
Practice Areas: Primary areas of practice are mergers and acquisitions, public and private financings, and corporate control and governance matters. Represents public and private acquirers, targets, sellers, special committees, and investment bankers in a broad range of merger and acquisition transactions.
Career: Admitted to New York Bar in 1972 and Texas Bar in 1977. Came to the firm as a Partner in 2001.
Personal: Graduated cum laude from

Brown University, AB in 1968 and Columbia Law School, JD in 1971, served as editor of the 'Columbia Law Review'.

BOHANNON, Paul
Andrews Kurth LLP, The Woodlands
1 713 220 4193
pbohannon@andrewskurth.com
Recommended in Environment
Practice Areas: Emphasis is on ambient groundwater and air issues. He has tried a number of ambient groundwater contamination cases to final verdict for various oil and gas, chemical and pipeline companies. Having practiced in New Mexico for eight years, Paul is the author of the Bohannon's New Mexico Environmental Law Handbook (Butterworth's Legal Publishers, 560 pg., supplemented twice annually). He served as lead counsel for seven major oil companies in the rulemaking hearing, and the subsequent task force negotiations, for the development of the New Mexico air toxic program. He has represented a national solid waste management firm in permitting and regional landfill issues. Paul also has tried many contested environmental permitting cases before the Railroad Commission of Texas.
Prof. Memberships: State Bar of Texas, 1975; United States Supreme Court, 1987; United States District Courts for the Districts of New Mexico, 1976; Northern District of Texas, 1977; Western District of Texas, 1983; Southern District of Texas, 1993; United States Courts of Appeals for the Fifth and Tenth Circuits, 1976; American Bar Association, 1975.
Career: Partner in the Environmental Section of The Woodlands, Texas Office. Has been with Andrews Kurth since 1993.
Personal: Received his JD from Southern Methodist University, Order of the Coif in 1975. Graduated from Oklahoma State University with a BA in 1972.

BOND, Thomas J
Akin Gump Strauss Hauer & Feld LLP, Austin
512 499 6217
tbond@akingump.com
Recommended in Insurance
Practice Areas: Chair, firmwide Insurance Practice. Represents holding companies, life insurance companies, property and liability companies, trade associations, reinsurers, HMOs, e-commerce insurance ventures, title underwriters and agencies, prepaid legal entities, agents, large insureds and the insurance departments of other states. Has been involved in the rehabilitation and liquidation of troubled companies, both hostile and negotiated acquisitions and mergers, numerous regulatory approval projects, investment decisions, and design and approval of new coverages.
Prof. Memberships: Founding Board Member, Federation of Regulatory Counsel.

Career: Texas Commissioner of Insurance, 1982-85.
Personal: BA, Baylor University; MFA, Bowling Green State University; JD (honors), University of Texas.

BOONE, Michael
Haynes and Boone LLP, Dallas
214 651 5000
Recommended in Corporate/M&A

BOULDEN, Michael R
Vinson & Elkins LLP, Dallas
214 220 7840
mboulden@velaw.com
Recommended in Real Estate
Practice Areas: Experience includes construction and permanent lending on commercial real estate; joint ventures and equity participations involving the formation of partnerships and limited liability companies; participating mortgages; real estate debt and partnership workouts; representing institutional lenders and equity investors; real estate outsourcing, and US and foreign investment by private equity funds.
Prof. Memberships: American Bar Association; State Bar of Texas; Dallas Bar Association; Dallas Real Estate Council.
Career: Admitted to Texas Bar, 1977. Came to the firm as a Partner, 1994.
Personal: Graduated from Rice University, BA in 1973, and Southern Methodist University, JD in 1977.

BOULWARE, Margaret
Baker & McKenzie, Houston
713 427 5003
meg.boulware@bakernet.com
Recommended in Intellectual Property
Practice Areas: Ms Boulware's practice in intellectual property includes patent practice, with emphasis on chemistry and biotechnology; trademark, particularly for international portfolios; and domestic copyright issues.
Prof. Memberships: Patent Public Advisory Committee, First Chair; American Intellectual Property Law Association, President 1998-99; State Bar of Texas, Intellectual Property Section, past Chair; Texas Bar Foundation, Life Fellow; Houston Bar Foundation, Life Fellow; Houston Intellectual Property Law Association, past President; Intellectual Property Owners Association; National Inventors Hall of Fame Foundation; Foundation for Creative America; University of Houston Law Alumni Board, Director; Trustee, Copyright Society of the USA, 1996-98; Secretary, National Inventor's Hall of Fame, 1994-95; National Coordinator of the Bicentennial Celebration of the Patent and Copyright Laws 1990 in Washington, DC while serving as a Board Member of the Foundation for a Creative America; International Trademark Association - Panel of Neutrals.
Career: Ms Boulware has been selected as one of 'The Best Lawyers in America' for Intellectual Property in IP Law &

Business, and included in 'The International Who's Who of Business Lawyers'. She has served on the Board of the Clemson University Foundation from 1999 to present. Ms Boulware also served as an Officer and Director of the University of Houston Law Center Alumni Board from 1982-87. She was appointed by the Secretary of Commerce to serve as the inaugural Chair of the Patent Public Advisory Committee for the United States Patent and Trademark Office. Ms Boulware was the founding Chair of the Advisory Board of the University of Houston Law Center Intellectual Property Law Program.
Publications: 'A Tale of Two Roles: Functionality Analysis of Marks,' State Bar of Texas, 18th Annual Intellectual Property Law Course, Austin, Texas, March 2005; 'Patent Quality,' Intellectual Property Owner's Association, Annual Meeting, Los Angeles, California, September 2002; 'Patent Public Advisory Committee Report on Patent and Trademark Office,' Texas Technology Conference, The Woodlands, Texas, January 2001; 'Privatization of the Internet and Intellectual Property Considerations,' International Association of Defense Counsel Midyear Meeting, Palm Springs, California, January 2001; 'Non-Statutory Defenses, Inequitable Conduct and Rule 11,' Practising Law Institute Patent Litigation 2000, New York, New York, October 2000; 'E-Commerce and Privatization of the Internet,' International Paper Customer Counsel Council Meeting, Palm Harbor, Florida, March 15-17, 2000; 'Inequitable Conduct, Laches and Other Nonstatutory Defenses,' Practising Law Institute Patent Litigation 1999, New York, New York, November 1999; 'Determining the Probability of Litigation Outcome: Risk Analysis and Other Case Management Techniques,' The 11th National Conference for Women Corporate Counsel, Washington, DC, 1999; 'Use of Affidavits and Data in Patent Prosecution,' ABA Section of Intellectual Property, Arlington, Virginia, 1997; 'International Intellectual Property and Special Considerations,' State Bar of Texas Professional Development, Austin, Texas, March 1997; 'An Overview of Intellectual Property Rights Abroad,' Hou. J. Int'l. L., Vol. 16, No. 3, Spring 1994; 'Technology Transfer and Protection in Mexico - Then (1980s) and Now (1990s),' State Bar of Texas Professional Development Program, Intellectual Property Law 1992, Austin, Texas, February 1992; 'Protecting Your Client's Intellectual Properties Abroad,' State Bar of Texas Annual Meeting, Corpus Christi, Texas, 1992; 'Opinions of Counsel in Patent Litigation,' Practicing Law Institute, New York, New York, 1990; 'Foreign Patents,' ALI-ABA Securing and Enforcing Patent Rights, Washington, DC, 1990; 'Alternative Dispute Resolution,' 5th Annual

Intellectual Property Law Institute, Sponsored by the Houston Intellectual Property Law Association, Houston, Texas, 1989; 'Avoiding Inequitable Conduct in Chemical and Biotech Applications,' American Intellectual Property Law Association, Basic Chemical and Biotechnology Practice Seminar, San Francisco, California and Washington, DC, 1988; 'Issues of Fraud, Inequitable Conduct and Willful Infringement in Cases Before the Courts and the PTO,' Intellectual Property Symposia, Marco Island, Florida, 1988; 'Issues of Fraud, Inequitable Conduct and Willful Infringement in Cases Before the Courts and the PTO,' American Bar Association, Arlington, Virginia, 1987; 'Using Data and Affidavits in the PTO - Avoiding Inequitable Conduct,' Houston Intellectual Property Law Association and the State Bar of Texas, The Woodlands, Texas, 1986; 'Avoiding Inequitable Conduct: Proper Use of Data and Affidavits and a Review of Fraud Under the CAFC,' American Intellectual Property Law Association, Washington, D.C., 1986; 'Use of Affidavits and Duty of Candor,' American Intellectual Property Law Association, Chemical Practice Basics Seminar, Chicago, Illinois, 1986; 'Candor in Prosecution,' Monograph, Editor and Contributor, American Intellectual Property Law Association, 1985.
Personal: Education: BS, University of Georgia (1969); MS, Clemson University (1970); JD, University of Houston Law Center (1975). Admissions: Texas and United States Patent and Trademark Office.

BOWERS, William
Fulbright & Jaworski L.L.P., Dallas
214 855 8219
bbowers@fulbright.com
Recommended in Tax
Practice Areas: Tax.
Prof. Memberships: Mr Bowers teaches partnership tax at the University of Texas School of Law, and has taught taxation of property transactions at the Southern Methodist University School of Law. He is an officer of the Tax Section, State Bar of Texas and served as past Chair, Tax Section of the Dallas Bar Association, as well as the past Chair of the ABA Committee on Tax Accounting Problems. Mr Bowers was certified as a public accountant in Maryland in 1978.
Career: Mr Bowers joined the Dallas office of Fulbright & Jaworski L.L.P. as a Partner in 2003. A member of the Fulbright Tax Practice Group, his practice focuses on tax planning in complex transactions. His practice concentration is federal income tax planning for complex business transactions involving corporations, partnerships and real estate investment trusts.
Personal: Mr Bowers received a Bachelor of Business Administration in accounting, with honors, in 1972 from Texas A&M University; a Master of Law

Taxation in 1979 from Georgetown University Law Center and a Juris Doctor in 1975 from the Southern Methodist University School of Law.

BOWMAN, John
Fulbright & Jaworski L.L.P., Houston
713 651 3732
jbowman@fulbright.com
Recommended in Arbitration, Energy
Practice Areas: Energy and petrochemicals, arbitration and litigation.
Prof. Memberships: Fellow of the College of Commercial Arbitrators and of The Chartered Institute of Arbitrators; member of Association of International Petroleum Negotiators; International Arbitration Club, London; International Arbitration Institute, Paris; Advisory Board of the Institute for Transnational Arbitration; Panel of International Centre for Dispute Resolution; CPR Institute Oil and Gas Panel; LCIA; IBA Committee D; and Houston International Arbitration Club; Board of Directors, Houston World Affairs Council.
Career: He is engaged in an arbitration and litigation practice representing primarily energy and petrochemicals companies. His practice focuses on arbitration, domestic and international, of commercial disputes, including disputes involving state-owned oil companies and Host Governments. He regularly advises regarding dispute resolution agreements, acts as an advocate in arbitrations and judicial proceedings and sits as an arbitrator.
Publications: The Panama Convention and Its Implementation under the Federal Arbitration Act (Kluwer 2002)
Personal: Married to Katie-Pat Bowman. He received a BA in 1974 and a JD in 1980 from the University of Kansas, where he was editor in chief of the 'Kansas Law Review'. He is licensed to practice law in Texas.

BOYCE, William J
Fulbright & Jaworski L.L.P., Houston
713 651 5313
wboyce@fulbright.com
Recommended in Litigation
Practice Areas: Commercial, constitutional, and libel law; appellate practice.
Prof. Memberships: Mr Boyce is a Member of the Appellate Practice Section of both the State Bar of Texas and the Houston Bar Association. He is also a member of the State Bar Pro Bono College, a fellow of the Texas Bar Foundation, and the current chair of the Civil Appellate Law Examination Committee of the Texas Board of Legal Specialization.
Career: A board certified appellate specialist and partner, Mr Boyce joined the Houston office of Fulbright & Jaworski L.L.P. in 1989. 'Texas Monthly' recognized him as a 'Texas Super Lawyer' in 2003 and 2004; 'Texas Lawyer,' '40 Under 40' in 2001.
Personal: BS, Highest Distinction, Northwestern University (1985); JD,

cum laude, Northwestern University School of Law. He was admitted to practice law in Texas in 1989.

BRADDOCK, James
Haynes and Boone LLP, Austin
512 867 8400
Recommended in Environment

BRANN, Richard
Baker Botts LLP, Houston
713 229 1563
richard.brann@bakerbotts.com
Recommended in Employment
Practice Areas: Represents management in all aspects of labor and employment law. Defends collective actions under the Fair Labor Standards Act and class actions alleging employment discrimination, plus individual lawsuits and agency proceedings. Represents employers in disputes under the National Labor Relations Act, the Railway Labor Act, and Occupational Safety and Health Act. Counsels employers on managing workplace legal issues and lawsuit prevention.
Career: 30+ years of practice. Chairs firm's Labor and Employment Law Practice.
Personal: JD, magna cum laude, University of Texas School of Law, 1968; Order of the Coif BA, magna cum laude, Mississippi State University, 1965.

BREAUX, Ronald
Haynes and Boone LLP, Dallas
214 651 5000
Recommended in Antitrust

BRISTOW, Daryl
Baker Botts LLP, Houston
713 229 1400
d.bristow@bakerbotts.com
Recommended in Litigation
Practice Areas: Represents a sundry of civil litigation clients in federal and state courts. Provides legal counsel for major corporate clients in many industries regarding trial, appellate, and corporate governance issues. Extensive experience with a broad spectrum of civil disputes, including energy, securities, commercial real estate, environmental, trade secret, technology, will contests and general business.
Career: 35+ years of practice.
Personal: LLB, magna cum laude, Harvard Law School, 1964; BA, letters, University of Oklahoma, 1961.

BROOKNER, Jason S
Andrews Kurth LLP, Dallas
214 659 4457
jasonbrookner@andrewskurth.com
Recommended in Bankruptcy
Practice Areas: Jason's practice includes participation in a wide variety of litigation and corporate matters in Chapter 11 cases, including the representation of debtors, committees, individual creditors and purchasers of assets.
Prof. Memberships: State Bar of Texas, 2001; Wisconsin, 1996; New York, 1995; American Bankruptcy Institute.

Career: Jason is a Partner in the Bankruptcy Section of the Dallas office and has been with Andrews Kurth since 1997.
Personal: Received a JD from Hofstra University School of Law in 1994 (articles editor, Hofstra Property Law Journal, 1993-94) and a BA from State University of New York at Binghamton 1991.

BROWN, David H
Vinson & Elkins LLP, Houston
713 758 2098
dbrown@velaw.com
Recommended in Insurance
Practice Areas: Principal area of practice is the representation of policyholders in insurance coverage disputes. Has represented a variety of business enterprises, including energy and transportation companies, and healthcare providers, in insurance litigation and arbitration matters under both first party and liability policies. Represents the Port of Houston Authority in litigation matters.
Prof. Memberships: Member: Houston Bar Association; Texas Association of Defense Counsel; Texas Bar Foundation; Maritime Law Association.
Career: Admitted to practice: Texas, 1976. Joined Vinson & Elkins, 1977; admitted to partnership, 1984.
Personal: Northwestern University, BS, 1972; The University of Texas School of Law, JD with honors, 1975.

BROWN, Reagan
Fulbright & Jaworski L.L.P., Houston
713 651 5469
rbrown@fulbright.com
Recommended in Insurance, Litigation
Practice Areas: Trial and appellate litigation, insurance, legal malpractice, ERISA and products liability.
Prof. Memberships: Member of the American Board of Trial Advocates. Admitted to practice before the United States Supreme Court, the United States Court of Appeals for the Fifth Circuit.
Career: Admitted to the Texas Bar (1981). A Partner of Fulbright & Jaworski L.L.P. since 1990. Has tried over 85 cases and arbitration proceedings with over 50 jury cases to verdict. Certified by the Texas Board of Legal Specialization in Civil Trial Law, Civil Appellate Law and Personal Injury Trial Law.
Personal: Received a BS and BA, summa cum laude, (1978) from Southern Methodist University and a JD, with honors, in 1981 from the University of Texas.

BRUNS, Phillip T
Gibbs & Bruns, LLP, Houston
713 650 8805
pbruns@gibbs-bruns.com
Recommended in Energy, Litigation
Practice Areas: Full range of commercial and business litigation and arbitration, both plaintiff and defendant. Has extensive experience with intellectual property disputes, including trade secrets, patent infringement and non-

competition in construction and engineering disputes.
Prof. Memberships: Admitted to practice in Texas in 1981 and admitted to various federal district courts, as well as the Fifth Circuit Court of Appeals and the Third Circuit Court of Appeals. Member American Bar Association, Section of Litigation, Houston Bar Association and Houston Bar Foundation.
Career: Joined Wood, Campbell, Moody & Gibbs in Houston in 1981. Founding Partner in Gibbs & Ratliff, LLP in 1983, which became Gibbs & Bruns, LLP in 1994.
Personal: Born January 24, 1956 in Bartlesville, Oklahoma. JD with honors, University of Texas 1981. Chancellors and Order of Coif; BA University of Oklahoma, 1978.

BURGIN, Sara
Baker Botts LLP, Austin
512 322 2649
sara.burgin@bakerbotts.com
Recommended in Environment
Practice Areas: Practice includes all water matters and solid and hazardous waste.
Prof. Memberships: State Bar of Texas - Environmental and Natural Resources Section, American Bar Association - Environment, Energy and Resources Section; Water Quality Committee.
Career: JD, University of Houston Law Center (1982), associate editor, 'Houston Law Review', MS, Texas A&M University (1977), BS, The University of Texas (1973).
Personal: Recognized in 'The Best Lawyers in America'; 'Go-To Lawyer' in 'Environmental Law', 'Texas Lawyer'; 'Best in Bar' by the 'Austin Business Journal', 'Texas Super Lawyer' by 'Texas Monthly and Law & Politics Magazine'.

BURNER, Burnie
Long, Burner, Parks & DeLargy, Austin
512 474 1587
Recommended in Insurance

BURNS, David
Dewey Ballantine LLP, Houston
713 445 1540
dburns@deweyballantine.com
Recommended in Banking & Finance
Practice Areas: Finance, banking, reorganization, energy and real estate. Industry experience includes oil and gas, power, information technology, hotels, contracting, insurance, and banking. Clients include Pennzoil Company in the Texaco Chapter 11, Reliant Energy, Freeport LNG, JPMorganChase, AIG, and DTE.
Prof. Memberships: American, Texas, and Houston Bar Associations, American College of Investment Counsel, American Bankruptcy Institute, and Texas Association of Bank Counsel.
Career: Admitted 1971, Texas, and USDC in the Southern Districts of Alabama and Texas. Partner, Dewey Ballantine LLP.
Personal: Born November 26, 1945. AB,

University of Oklahoma, 1968. JD, Harvard Law School, 1971.

CAGLE, Molly
Vinson & Elkins LLP, Austin
512 542 8552
mcagle@velaw.com
Recommended in Environment, Litigation
Practice Areas: Administrative and environmental law.
Career: Admitted to Texas Bar in 1981. Joined Vinson & Elkins in 1981 and was admitted to the partnership in January 1989.
Personal: Attended the University of Southwestern Louisiana and graduated from Texas Tech, BS magna cum laude in 1978, and The University of Texas, JD with honors in 1981.

CALDWELL, Charles
Vinson & Elkins LLP, Houston
713 758 4518
ccaldwell@velaw.com
Recommended in Energy
Practice Areas: Partner in the firm's Energy Regulatory Practice and member of Executive Committee of Energy Practice Group. Practice consists primarily of representation of oil and gas pipelines before regulatory authorities, regulatory compliance counseling, and energy transactions involving regulatory assets.
Prof. Memberships: Member, Energy Bar Association; past President, Energy Bar Association - Houston Chapter.
Career: Regular speaker: continuing education and client compliance programs on energy regulatory law. Law clerk to Hon George P Kazen, US District Court, Southern District of Texas (1990-91).
Publications: Co-editor, Gas Regulation 2003 (Global Competition Review).
Personal: Rice University, BA 1985; University of Virginia, JD 1990.

CAMPBELL, Andrew
Andrews Kurth LLP, Dallas
214 659 4511
acampbell@andrewskurth.com
Recommended in Real Estate
Practice Areas: Representation of institutional owners in individual and portfolio acquisitions, including multi-state portfolio acquisitions for both real property and loan assets, and drafting and negotiating commercial leases, management agreements, and purchase and sale agreements; and representation of private investor funds in the acquisition, development and financing of commercial properties including multi-state portfolio acquisitions.
Prof. Memberships: The State Bar of Texas, 1990.
Career: Partner with Andrews Kurth since 1999.
Personal: Received a JD from Southern Methodist University in 1990. Received an MBA from Southern Methodist University in 1999 and a BBA from Southern Methodist University in 1985.

CAMPBELL, Rhett
Thompson & Knight LLP, Houston
713 653 8660
rhett.campbell@tklaw.com
Recommended in Bankruptcy
Practice Areas: Mr Campbell is experienced in all aspects of business bankruptcy, particularly energy bankruptcies, representing public and private companies, creditors committees, bondholders, individual working interest owners and operators, exploration, and production companies. He was selected for inclusion in Texas Monthly's 2003 and 2004 listing of Texas Super Lawyers.
Prof. Memberships: State Bar of Texas, American College of Bankruptcy, College of the State Bar of Texas, American and Houston Bar Associations.
Publications: Mr Campbell has written extensively in the area of bankruptcy.
Personal: SMU Dedman School of Law (JD, 1973); Southern Methodist University (BA, 1970).

CANTERBURY Jr, Joe
Canterbury, Stuber, Elder, Gooch & Surratt, PC, Dallas 972 239 7493
Recommended in Construction

CARRELL, Richard
Fulbright & Jaworski L.L.P., Houston
713 651 5447
rcarrell@fulbright.com
Recommended in Antitrust
Practice Areas: Antitrust, business litigation, securities litigation, contracts, and oil and gas litigation.
Prof. Memberships: The Houston and the American Bar Associations and the State Bar of Texas. Trustee of Baylor College of Medicine and the Kelsey Foundation for Research.
Career: Admitted Texas Bar (1970). A Partner of Fulbright & Jaworski L.L.P. which he joined in 1970. Served as a member of the firm's Executive and Policy Committees.
Personal: Received a BA from Washington & Lee University in 1965 and a JD from the University of Virginia in 1970.

CAWLEY, Douglas
McKool Smith, Dallas
214 978 4000
Recommended in Intellectual Property

CHEAVENS, Joseph
Baker Botts LLP, Houston
713 229 1250
joseph.cheavens@bakerbotts.com
Recommended in Litigation
Practice Areas: Represents diverse clientele within trial practice. Handles general civil, intellectual property, securities and maritime litigation. Represents cases involving misappropriation of trade secrets, patent infringement, refinery and chemical plant problems, and oil and gas exploration and production disputes, as well as securities transactions and maritime casualties. Serves as counsel and arbitrator in arbitration cases before International Chamber of

Commerce, the American Arbitration Association and the Society of Maritime Arbitration.
Career: 39 years in practice. Serves on firm's Executive and Sarbanes-Oxley Committee.
Personal: JD, cum laude, Harvard Law School, 1965; BA, magna cum laude, Baylor University, 1962.

CIVINS, Jeff
Haynes and Boone LLP, Austin
512 867 8400
Recommended in Environment

CLONTS, David
Akin Gump Strauss Hauer & Feld LLP, Houston 713 220 5886
dclonts@akingump.com
Recommended in Intellectual Property
Practice Areas: A member of Akin Gump's Patent Litigation Practice, Mr Clonts focuses on patent litigation and intellectual property counseling for large US and international companies in electronics, software, medical device and business method fields.
Personal: BSEE, Georgia Institute of Technology (1987); JD, University of Texas (1991).

COATS, William
Coats Rose Yale Ryman Lee, Houston
713 651 0111
Recommended in Construction

COGAN Jr, John
Akin Gump Strauss Hauer & Feld LLP, Houston 713 220 5885
jcogan@akingump.com
Recommended in Energy, Projects
Practice Areas: Focuses on international energy, financial, shipping and commercial transactions, particularly involving projects for international exploration, extraction, processing, transportation and sale of hydrocarbons. Named one of the top five international lawyers in Texas.
Prof. Memberships: Corresponding editor, 'International Legal Materials'; Member - Association of International Petroleum Negotiators; frequent lecturer on international energy matters.
Personal: BA, 1965, JD, 1968, University of Texas. Attended Universidad Autónoma de Guanajuato, Mexico, Escuela de Derecho, 1968; Universidad Nacional Autónoma de México, Instituto de Derecho Comparativo, 1967; Bucknell University, 1961-62. Work/study program at Université de Nantes, France, 1964.

COHEN, R Scott
Weil, Gotshal & Manges LLP, Dallas
214 746 7738
scott.cohen@weil.com
Recommended in Corporate/M&A
Practice Areas: Corporate, capital markets, mergers and acquisitions, and private equity.
Career: A Partner in the firm's Dallas office, Mr Cohen has practiced in the area of corporate and securities law for

over 25 years. Mr Cohen has led acquisition and financing transactions for such clients as Texas Instruments Incorporated, Viasystems Group, Inc., Thermadyne Holdings Corporation, Berg Electronics, Inc., International Wire Group, Inc., Dr Pepper/Seven-Up Companies, Inc., Dr Pepper/Seven-Up Bottling Group, Inc., The Morningstar Group, Inc., and Inet Technologies, Inc.
Personal: Southern Methodist University School of Law (JD, 1979); University of Texas (BBA, 1976).

COKINOS, Gregory
Cokinos, Bosien and Young, Houston
713 535 5500
Recommended in Construction

COLEMAN, James
Carrington, Coleman, Sloman & Blumenthal, LLP, Dallas 214 855 3000
Recommended in Litigation

CONLON, Michael W
Fulbright & Jaworski L.L.P., Houston
713 651 5427
mconlon@fulbright.com
Recommended in Corporate/M&A
Practice Areas: Corporation, banking and business.
Prof. Memberships: State Bar of Texas; Houston and American Bar Associations.
Career: He is Co-Partner in charge of Fulbright & Jaworski L.L.P.'s Houston office, and Co-Head of its Corporation, Business and Banking Practice. His general corporate practice primarily involves the representation of publicly held corporations in matters involving securities offerings and routine reporting, corporate governance and compliance matters, disclosure issues, secured and unsecured borrowing, mergers, acquisitions and dispositions. He has represented special committees of boards of directors connected with takeover offers and corporate restructurings.
Personal: He received a BA from Catholic University of America in 1968 and a JD from Duke University in 1971.

CONNELLY, Michael
Connelly Baker Wotring Jackson LLP, Houston 713 980 1700
Recommended in Litigation

CONRAD, Walter
Baker Botts LLP, Houston
713 229 1230
walter.conrad@bakerbotts.com
Recommended in Litigation
Practice Areas: Expert in toxic tort and environmental litigation. Represents corporations in suits brought by individual plaintiffs, groups of plaintiffs, government agencies and nonprofit organizations. Nationally recognized practice focuses on trials in both state and federal courts. Extensive experience in administrative litigation. Develops innovative group defense strategies that provide significant savings in legal fees for clients.

Career: 38 years of practice.
Personal: LLB, The University of Texas School of Law, 1964; Member, Texas Law Review Phi Alpha Delta; BA, Princeton University, 1961.

CONWAY, Susan
Graves, Dougherty, Hearon & Moody, P.C., Austin 512 480 5600
Recommended in Insurance

COOKE, Gregg
Guida Slavich & Flores PC, Austin
1 214 692 0009
Recommended in Environment

COOPER, Brent
Cooper & Scully PC, Dallas
214 712 9500
Recommended in Insurance

COOPER, James
Gardere Wynne Sewell LLP, Houston
713 276 5884
jcooper@gardere.com
Recommended in Insurance
Practice Areas: Insurance coverage, commercial litigation, class action defense, trial.
Prof. Memberships: Co-Chair, ABA Insurance Coverage Litigation Committee, Products Liability Subcommittee; Board of Directors, American Inns of Court, Houston Chapter; Proctor Member, Maritime Law Association of the United States.
Career: Jim Cooper has 20 years' experience handling a wide variety of commercial litigation and insurance matters. He is involved primarily in the resolution of multimillion-dollar insurance coverage disputes, representing policyholders, brokers and insurers in litigation and arbitration. He also handles a wide variety of commercial litigation matters, including breach of contract cases, maritime liens, and litigation arising out of damage to international shipments of cargo.
Publications: 'Maximizing Insurance Coverage for Pre-Suit Settlements of Construction Defects Claims,' 5 Journal of Texas Insurance Law 2, 2004; 'Maximizing Insurance Coverage for Pre-Suit Settlements of Construction Defect Claims,' 5 Journal of Texas Insurance Law 2, 2004 (Special Construction Coverage Issue); 'Recovery of Economic Damages for Delayed Offshore Production,' 28 J. Maritime Law & Commerce, 1997; 'Weathering the Storm: International Loss of Hire Policies and the Problem of Unchartered Rigs,' 17 University of Houston International Law Journal, 1994.
Personal: JD, Tulane University School of Law, cum laude, 1984; BA, Wabash College, 1981.

COPELAND, Gregory
Baker Botts LLP, Houston
713 229 1301
greg.copeland@bakerbotts.com
Recommended in Energy
Practice Areas: Represents clients in

the energy industry in complex litigation, covering an expansive array of matters involving the production, transmission and sale of electricity, oil, gas, lignite, coal and nuclear fuels. Represents clients in state and federal courts throughout the United States, and in arbitration proceedings, mediations and administrative hearings.
Career: 30+ years of practice. Serves on the Contributions Committee for the firm. Member of the CPR Panel of Neutrals on Energy.
Personal: JD, The University of Texas School of Law, 1972; Phi Delta Phi; BA, University of Oklahoma, 1970.

COTROPIA, Charles S
Sidley Austin Brown & Wood LLP, Dallas 214 981 3305
ccotropia@sidley.com
Recommended in Intellectual Property
Practice Areas: Charles Cotropia handles cases involving trademarks, service marks, copyrights and patents and has represented clients in diverse areas, including wearing apparel (Justin Brands, Inc.), consumer products (Litex Industries, Inc.), high-tech products (Lockheed Martin) and restaurants (T.G.I. Friday's and Fuddrucker's) and building design (Holiday Retirement Corporation). He handles infringement issues involving trademarks/service marks, copyrights, unfair competition, product trade dress and building décor. He represents Justin Brands, Inc., handling all litigation and registration of trademarks, copyrights and patents and trade dress infringement for the company. He has 30 years' experience dealing with the US Patent and Trademark Office, and has registered more than 800 trademarks and has obtained more than 600 patents.
Prof. Memberships: Served as Chairman of the Intellectual Property Law Section of the State Bar of Texas, served as a director of the Dallas Bar Association, of the Intellectual Property Law Section of the Dallas Bar Association and as an officer of the Dallas-Fort Worth Intellectual Property Law Section. He is a Fellow of the Dallas and Texas Bar Foundations.
Career: Cornell Law School, JD, 1973; University of Texas - Austin, BS in Aerospace Engineering, 1968. Bar Admissions: Texas, 1973; US Patent & Trademark Office, 1973.

CRAIG III, Allen
Gardere Wynne Sewell LLP, Houston
713 276 5570
acraig@gardere.com
Recommended in Tax
Practice Areas: Tax, tax litigation, trusts and estates.
Prof. Memberships: Board Certified, Taxation Law, Texas Board of Legal Specialization; American Bar Association; Member, State Bar of Texas (Tax Section); Current Council Member, Tax

Section of the State Bar of Texas; Houston Bar Association; Texas Representative, Internal Revenue Service Liaison Council.

Career: Allen Craig is board certified as a specialist in taxation law. His practice includes merger and acquisitions, corporate reorganizations, partnership and limited liability company planning, state tax planning, and international inbound and outbound transactions. He is additionally involved in income and estate planning for individuals and closely held businesses, in audit and compliance matters before the IRS and state taxing authorities and has experience in obtaining private letter rulings from the IRS.

Publications: 'American Jobs Creation Act of 2004', Lone Star Network, 2005; KTRH (Radio), Business Law Brief, cession Planning, 2004; 'A Guide to Potential Tax Shelter Transactions', State Bar of Texas, Corporate Committee, 2002; 'A Guide to Potential Tax Shelter Transactions', Houston Tax Roundtable, 2002.

Personal: JD, University of Texas School of Law, 1971; BS, Washington & Lee University, with special attainments, 1968.

CROW, Carter
Fulbright & Jaworski L.L.P., Houston
713 651 5218
mcrow@fulbright.com
Recommended in Employment
Practice Areas: Labor and employment, commercial litigation, oil and gas.
Prof. Memberships: Mr Crow is a member of both the Labor & Employment, and Commercial Litigation Sections of the American Bar Association. He is a past President of the Houston Management Lawyers Forum.
Career: Mr Crow joined Fulbright's Houston office in 1991. As Partner, he co-chairs the firm's Unfair Competition Practice Group. He is listed in the Best Lawyers in America and Texas Lawyer Rising Stars publications.
Personal: BS, Oklahoma State University, accounting (1988); JD, University of Oklahoma College of Law (1991). Mr Crow is a member of the Children's Fund, a charity for children's causes.

CUCLIS, James
Vinson & Elkins LLP, Houston
713 758 3415
jcuclis@velaw.com
Recommended in Energy
Practice Areas: Coordinator of the firm's International Practice. Practice consists of international mergers and acquisitions and project development and finance, primarily in the energy industry. Represented clients in over 45 countries throughout the Americas, Europe, Asia, the Middle East, and Africa.
Prof. Memberships: International Bar Association, Association of International Petroleum Negotiators.
Career: Frequent lecturer/author on

international energy topics.
Publications: 'Key Legal Issues in International M&A Transactions', 'Texas Lawyer', April 2004; 'Capitalism Behind the Iron Curtain', 'Houston Business Review', Spring 1997; 'Bringing Capitalist Ways to Russia', 'National Law Journal', August 1996.
Personal: University of Texas, JD 1981. Working knowledge of Russian.

CULOTTA, Ken
King & Spalding LLP, Houston
713 276 7374
kculotta@kslaw.com
Recommended in Energy, Projects
Practice Areas: Advises US and non-US clients in domestic and international oil, gas, LNG, power and natural resources transactions, including mergers and acquisitions, joint ventures, project development and finance, energy management services and other direct and indirect investment transactions. Experienced with industry documentation, including concession, production sharing, joint operating, power purchase, tolling, fuel supply, O&M, construction, gas and electricity transportation and distribution, marketing and other agreements. Languages: German; Spanish.
Prof. Memberships: Association of International Petroleum Negotiators; Houston Bar Association; State Bar of Texas.
Personal: BA University of Texas 1979; JD 1985; Albert Ludwigs-Universität, Freiburg, Germany (DAAD Fellow 1980-81).

CULWELL, Todd
Baker & McKenzie, Houston
713 427 5035
todd.culwell@bakernet.com
Recommended in Projects
Practice Areas: Domestic and international (Latin America, Middle East and Asia) project development and project financings for power plants, LNG facilities and petrochemical facilities; corporate financing activities; and acquisition and disposition of a variety of energy-related assets.
Prof. Memberships: State Bar of Texas, Houston Bar Association, American Bar Association(International Law Section, Business Law Section and Oil, Gas and Mineral Law Section), and Rocky Mountain Mineral Law Foundation.
Career: Admitted to practice law in Texas.
Publications: Authored several articles on energy projects.
Personal: South Texas College of Law (JD, magna cum laude, 1993, Order of Lytae). University of Texas at Austin (BA, Economics, 1990).

DANIEL, Josiah
Vinson & Elkins LLP, Dallas
214 220 7718
jdaniel@velaw.com
Recommended in Bankruptcy
Practice Areas: Represents lenders,

debtors, creditors' committees, trustees, and unsecured creditors in Chapter 11 cases, including: plan formulation and confirmation; fraudulent transfer, preference, and other bankruptcy litigation; mass torts; resolution of secured and unsecured claims; Section 363 asset acquisitions; postpetition financing and cash collateral; leases and executory contracts; bankruptcy settlements.
Prof. Memberships: Business Bankruptcy Committee, American Bar Association; Bankruptcy Law Section, State Bar of Texas; Texas Association of Bank Counsel.
Career: Admitted to Texas Bar, 1978. Came to firm as Partner, 1999.
Personal: University of the South, BA, 1973; University of Texas School of Law, JD, 1978.

DARDEN, Michael
Baker Botts LLP, Houston
713 229 1559
mike.darden@bakerbotts.com
Recommended in Energy
Practice Areas: Practice focuses on international and US oil and gas ventures, LNG projects, international and US infrastructure projects, multijurisdictional business transactions, and asset acquisitions and divestitures. Board Certified in Oil and Gas Law by the Texas Board of Legal Specialization.
Prof. Memberships: State Bar of Texas; American Association of Professional Landmen; Association of International Petroleum Negotiators (AIPN); Houston Bar Association.
Personal: MBA from Rice University in 2002; JD from the University of Houston Law Center in 1986; BBA in Petroleum Land Management from The University of Texas in 1980.

DARLING, William
Brown McCarroll LLP, Austin
512 472 5456
Recommended in Healthcare

DAVIDSON, Joshua
Baker Botts LLP, Houston
713 229 1527
joshua.davidson@bakerbotts.com
Recommended in Corporate/M&A
Practice Areas: Concentrates on a wide range of corporate and securities work; nationally recognized for expertise in master limited partnership (MLP) transactions. In the past 10 years he has participated in over 70 public offerings of MLPs, including 20 initial public offerings. Represents issuers and underwriters in public offerings of equity and debt securities, many clients in acquisitions and joint ventures, particularly in the energy industry, and numerous special committees of boards of directors on such matters as asset dropdowns, mergers and reorganizations.
Personal: JD, cum laude, Harvard Law School, 1985; BA, summa cum laude, history, Yale University, 1981.

DAVIS, Platt W
Vinson & Elkins LLP, Houston
713 758 2294
pdavis@velaw.com
Recommended in Arbitration, Energy
Practice Areas: Principal areas of practice are international arbitration, energy transactions and regulation, and construction law.
Prof. Memberships: Advisory Board: Institute for Transnational Arbitration. Member: The Chartered Institute of Arbitrators; International Bar Association; London Court of International Arbitration; Energy Bar Association; American Bar Association; and AAA National Roster of Neutrals.
Career: Admitted to practice: Texas, 1969; District of Columbia, 1973. Joined Vinson & Elkins, 1970; admitted to partnership, 1976.
Personal: The University of Texas, BA, 1966; The University of Texas School of Law, JD, 1970; George Washington University Law School, LLM, 1974.

DAVIS, Will
Heath, Davis & McCalla, Austin
512 478 5671
Recommended in Insurance

DAWSON, Alistair
Beck, Redden & Secrest L.L.P., Houston
713 951 3700
Recommended in Litigation

DAWSON, William B
Vinson & Elkins LLP, Dallas
214 220 7926
bdawson@velaw.com
Recommended in Litigation
Practice Areas: Defends professionals, lawyers and auditors, in malpractice actions (eg, tried to take nothing jury verdict August 2004 audit malpractice case filed by public company in bankruptcy). Leads trial teams in significant patent infringement cases on both sides of the docket (e.g. currently lead plaintiff's counsel in patent case against Gillette involving its Mach3 razor blades). Defends securities actions. Continues to try oil and gas cases and is expert in matters involving pipeline safety. Transplants trial techniques from one area of trial practice to others.
Prof. Memberships: Fellow, The American College of Trial Lawyers (Past-chair and member of its Science and Technology in the Courts Committee); Fifth Circuit Bar Association; American Law Institute (consultative group on Restatement of the Law Governing Lawyers).
Career: Admitted to Texas Bar in 1975.
Personal: Graduated from Texas Tech University, BBA, 1972 and JD with highest honors, 1975.

DEATHERAGE, Scott
Thompson & Knight LLP, Dallas
214 969 1206
scott.deatherage@tklaw.com
Recommended in Litigation
Practice Areas: Mr Deatherage's expe-

rience includes permitting, compliance counseling and auditing, administrative, and judicial litigation in air emissions, waste water discharges, hazardous waste, hazardous substances, and toxic substances before local, state and federal courts. He is experienced in drafting environmental disclosure statements for Securities and Exchange Commission documents and the impact of the Sarbanes-Oxley Act on such disclosures.
Prof. Memberships: Member of the State Bar of Texas, American and Dallas Bar Associations.
Publications: Mr Deatherage has written extensively on a variety of environmental and litigation matters.
Personal: Harvard Law School (JD, 1987); University of Oklahoma (BA, 1984).

DENNY, Otway
Fulbright & Jaworski L.L.P., Houston
713 651 5588
odenny@fulbright.com
Recommended in Litigation
Practice Areas: Product liability, personal injury, commercial, and professional liability litigation; mass and toxic tort litigation.
Prof. Memberships: Mr Denny is past President of the Houston Bar Association, and past Chair of the Board of Directors of both the State Bar of Texas, and the Houston Bar Foundation. Mr Denny is a Fellow of the American College of Trial Lawyers, an advocate of the American Board of Trial Advocates, and a Member of the International Association of Defense Counsel, the Defense Research Institute and the Texas Association of Defense Counsel. He has been selected for Texas Super Lawyers, the 'International Who's Who of Product Liability Defense Lawyers' and other leading legal publications.
Career: Partner in the Houston office since 1981. He has litigated numerous cases in state and federal courts, including products liability cases involving chemicals, automobiles and other vehicles and construction equipment. He has extensive experience in the defense of personal injury claims and other tort matters, and has handled matters involving plant and refinery explosions. He has also handled cases involving professional liability litigation and commercial litigation.
Personal: BA - Texas A&M University (1971); JD - cum laude, Baylor University (1973).

DILG, Joseph C
Vinson & Elkins LLP, Houston
713 758 2062
jdilg@velaw.com
Recommended in Energy
Practice Areas: Practice focuses on domestic and international business transactions, including acquisitions, divestitures, joint ventures, and financings. Well-versed in all aspects of the

domestic and international energy business.
Career: Currently serves as managing partner of Vinson & Elkins. Director: The Business Committee for the Arts, Inc.; and the Greater Houston Partnership. Trustee: The University of Texas Law School Foundation.
Personal: Graduated from Southern Methodist University, BA in economics in 1973, and The University of Texas School of Law, JD with high honors in 1976; Chancellors Society; Note Editor, 'Texas Law Review'.

DILLARD, Steve
Fulbright & Jaworski L.L.P., Houston
713 651 5507
sdillard@fulbright.com
Recommended in Litigation
Practice Areas: Mr Dillard's concentration in the litigation practice area includes environmental, mass and toxic tort, product liability, and complex civil litigation.
Prof. Memberships: Mr Dillard is a fellow of the American College of Trial Lawyers, and a life fellow of the Texas Bar Foundation. He has held leadership positions as a Member of the State Bar of Texas Pattern Jury Charge Committee, the Houston and American Bar Associations, and the State Bar of Texas. Mr Dillard is also a member of the Defense Research Institute, the International Association of Defense Counsel, and the Texas Association of Defense Counsel.
Career: Mr Dillard has been a Partner in the Houston office of Fulbright & Jaworski L.L.P. since 1978, and he currently serves as Chair of the firm's worldwide Litigation Department. He has been selected by his peers as one of 'The Best Lawyers' in America as published in 'Who's Who in American Law'. In 2003 and 2004, he was recognized as a 'Texas Super Lawyer.'
Personal: Mr Dillard received a BA in 1968 and a JD, cum laude, in 1971 from Baylor University.

DILLON, Andrew
Dillon & Yudell LLP, Austin
512 343 6116
Recommended in Intellectual Property

DINKINS, Carol
Vinson & Elkins LLP, Houston
713 758 2528
cdinkins@velaw.com
Recommended in Environment
Practice Areas: Chairs Vinson & Elkins' Administrative and Environmental Law Practice. Practice includes client counseling on business transactions and permit matters; civil litigation, mediation, and criminal defense.
Prof. Memberships: Immediate past Chair: Standing Committee on Federal Judiciary, American Bar Association.
Career: Admitted to practice: Texas, 1971. Joined Vinson & Elkins, 1973; admitted to partnership, 1980. Served

as: Assistant Attorney General in charge of the Environment and Natural Resources Division of the Department of Justice, 1981-83; Deputy Attorney General of the United States, 1984-85.
Personal: The University of Texas, BS, 1968; University of Houston, JD, 1971.

DODD, Jeff
Andrews Kurth LLP, Houston
713 225 7726
jdodd@andrewskurth.com
Recommended in Communications, Technology
Practice Areas: Intellectual property, technology, electronic commerce and communications: extensive licensing experience in a variety of domestic and international transactions; general representation of various parties in registering, enforcing and licensing intellectual property rights with respect to diverse technologies; infringement and similar analysis as to copyright and trademark matters; representation of various parties in the planning, design and implementation of electronic commerce strategies and arrangements, domestic and international (including those relating to business-to-business exchanges, co-branding, hosting, development, and other similar activities), electronic data interchange arrangements, and electronic trading transactions and activities; advising domestic and international clients on data protection and privacy laws and devising compliance strategies; representation of software developers, as well as distributors and end-users, in structuring, negotiating and documenting computer hardware and software ownership, acquisition, and distribution agreements; representation of companies acquiring software and other technology companies; representation of various communications companies and service providers.
Prof. Memberships: The State Bar of Texas; Houston Bar Association, Texas Bar Association (Business Law Section and Sub-Committee on Electronic Commerce), American Bar Association (Sections on Business Law, Taxation, Science and Technology, Forum Committee on Franchising). Member, Electronic Commerce Sub-Committee, Business Law Section of the Texas Bar Association. Chairman, Computer Contracts and Liaison to Uniform Commercial Code Article 2 Revision Committee, Computer Law Section, Texas Bar Association. Advisory Board Member, Honors College of the University of Houston. Adjunct Professor of Law, University of Houston Law Center, Intellectual Property and Information Law Program, Licensing Law (1999, 2000, 2001).
Career: Admitted to the State Bar of Texas 1979.
Publications: Presentations: 'Attack Web Sites' Fifth Annual Doing Business Online Conference (Seattle 2003); 'Attack Web Sites: Offense and Defense',

Practicing Law Institute (April 2002); 'Strategies and Structures for Commercializing Internally Developed Technologies', 4th Annual Doing Business Online Conference (Seattle 2002); 'Overview of Intellectual Property for the Business Lawyer' (Houston 2002); 'E-Procurement and E-Contracting in Government Contracts: The Impact of Electronic Contracting Legislation', eGovernment Conference (San Diego 2002); 'The Impact of the PATRIOT Act on Electronic Transactions, Surveillance, and Privacy', Practicing Law Institute (New York and San Francisco 2002).
Personal: Received a JD summa cum laude from the University of Houston in 1979. Received a BA magna cum laude from the University of Houston in 1976.

DOW, Melvin
Winstead Sechrest & Minick P.C., Houston 713 650 2724
mdow@winstead.com
Recommended in Real Estate
Practice Areas: Shareholder in Real Estate Section. Has extensive experience representing clients in transactions: purchases, sales, leases; joint venture agreements involving shopping centers, office buildings, and subdivision developments.
Prof. Memberships: American Bar Association, Houston Bar Association, and American College of Real Estate Lawyers.
Career: Admitted, State Bar of Texas. Board Certified, Commercial Real Estate Law, Texas Board of Legal Specialization. Listed in Best Lawyers in America for 20 consecutive years. Listed as a 'Super Lawyer' by 'Texas Monthly.'
Personal: Harvard Law School, JD (magna cum laude), 1951. Editor, 'Harvard Law Review.' Rice University, BA (cum laude, Phi Beta Kappa), 1948.

DOW, T Andrew
Winstead Sechrest & Minick P.C., Dallas 214 745 5387
adow@winstead.com
Recommended in Real Estate
Practice Areas: Chair, 60-lawyer Real Estate Section. Extensive experience representing clients in matters involving development, leasing, property management, acquisitions and dispositions, entity and transaction structure, finance, and corporate facilities management.
Prof. Memberships: American and Dallas Bar Associations, International Council of Shopping Centers, National Association of Industrial and Office Properties.
Career: Admitted, State Bar of Texas.
Personal: Southern Methodist University, JD, 1991. Managing editor, 'SMU Law Review.' Best Lawyers in Dallas Under 40, 'D Magazine,' 2002. Texas Rising Star, 'Texas Monthly,' 2004. Former Adjunct Professor of Business Law, Dallas Baptist University.

DUNLAY, Jon
Baker Botts LLP, Dallas
214 953 6711
jon.dunlay@bakerbotts.com
Recommended in Real Estate
Practice Areas: Practice focuses on commercial real estate transactions, with significant involvement in the restructuring of hotel ownership, management, and financing. Experience includes representation of public pension funds, insurance companies, national banks, and other lenders in their placement, workout, restructuring, and foreclosures of participating mortgages, construction loans, and permanent loans, including financings of shopping centers, hotels, office buildings, and apartments in Texas and other parts of the country.
Prof. Memberships: State Bar of Texas.
Personal: JD, with honors, from the University of Maryland School of Law, 1982; AB, cum laude, from Princeton University, 1979.

DUNLOP, Fred
Baker Botts LLP, Houston
713 229 1273
fred.dunlop@bakerbotts.com
Recommended in Real Estate
Practice Areas: Represents clients in complex commercial real estate transactions for major developers, institutional lenders and investors; Works with insurance companies and other institutional investors to structure their investments, including long-term mortgage loans for apartment, office, hotel, and shopping center projects; and represents clients in workouts, foreclosures, and a variety of restructurings.
Prof. Memberships: American College of Real Estate Lawyers; State Bar of Texas.
Personal: JD from Vanderbilt University School of Law, 1971; BA from Vanderbilt University, 1968.

DUTTON, Diana C
Akin Gump Strauss Hauer & Feld LLP, Dallas 214 969 2855
ddutton@akingump.com
Recommended in Environment
Practice Areas: Focuses on all areas of environmental law, including Comprehensive Environmental Response, Compensation and Liability Act (Superfund); Resource Conservation and Recovery Act; Clean Water Act; Clean Air Act; other state/federal environmental statutes and related legislation, eg, Deep Water Port Act.
Prof. Memberships: Former Chair, Environmental Section, State Bar of Texas, Dallas Bar Environmental Section, Greater Dallas Chamber's Environmental Committee; Board of Directors, Girls Inc. Dallas; Mental Health Association of Dallas; University of Texas Law School Dean's Roundtable.
Career: Regional Counsel and Director, Enforcement Division, US Environmental Protection Agency, Region 6 (1976-81).
Personal: BS, Georgetown University; JD, University of Texas.

DYE, Phillip
Vinson & Elkins LLP, Houston
713 758 2048
pdye@velaw.com
Recommended in Energy, Litigation
Practice Areas: Complex civil litigation and arbitration practice, with a particular expertise in representing non-US based corporations who are sued in the Courts of the United States; in the handling of matters in which foreign governments or their institutions are involved; and in the law of personal jurisdiction.
Prof. Memberships: ABA, International Bar Association, International Association of Defense Counsel, Maritime Law Association. Licensed: Texas and Louisiana.
Career: Partner since 1993.
Publications: Has lectured extensively on the law of personal jurisdiction and transnational litigation.
Personal: Louisiana State University (BS, 1982; JD with honors, 1986).

DYKES, Jeff
Fulbright & Jaworski L.L.P., Houston
713 651 5545
jdykes@fulbright.com
Recommended in Energy
Practice Areas: Energy, environmental, tort, construction, and contracts.
Prof. Memberships: Mr Dykes has been certified since 1979 as a Specialist in Civil Trial Law by the Texas Board of Legal Specialization. He holds the rank of Avocate in the American Board of Trial Advocates, and is a director and past President of The Texas Association of Civil Trial and Appellate Specialists. He is Secretary of the Federal Bar Association (South Texas Chapter) and a Member of the Houston and American Bar Associations; Bar Association of the Fifth Federal Circuit; Independent Petroleum Association of America; Rocky Mountain Mineral Law Foundation. He is a Life Fellow of the Houston, Texas, and American Bar Foundations.
Career: Jeff Dykes is a senior litigation Partner in Fulbright & Jaworski L.L.P.'s Houston office where he is Co-Chair of the firm's Energy Practice Group. His practice as a trial lawyer covers a wide range of cases, including energy, tort, contract, construction and antitrust matters. He has tried over 60 cases to jury verdict and has been named as a 'Texas Super Lawyer' by Texas Monthly magazine.
Personal: BA - Stanford University (1966); MA - Stanford University (1968); JD - University of Texas School of Law (1972).

EILAND, Gary
Vinson & Elkins LLP, Houston
713 758 3474
geiland@velaw.com
Recommended in Healthcare
Practice Areas: Co-Section Head of Health Industry Group. Represents health care providers, academic medical centers, medical group practices, and pharmaceutical and medical device manufacturers in handling fraud and abuse, Stark, and False Claims Act matters; compliance matters; business transactions; Medicare and Medicaid and other federal and state regulatory issues.
Prof. Memberships: State Bar of Texas (Former Chair, Health Law Section); Charter Member, Health Law Exam Commission, Texas Board of Legal Specialization; AHLA (Former President).
Career: Admitted to practice: Texas, 1976.
Personal: The University of Texas, BBA with honors, 1973; The University of Texas School of Law, JD with honors, 1976.

ELDRIDGE, John
Haynes and Boone LLP, Houston
713 547 2000
Recommended in Litigation

EPSTEIN, Jon David
Vinson & Elkins LLP, Houston
Recommended in Healthcare
Practice Areas: Co-Chair Health Industry Group. Represented healthcare providers throughout the country for over 30 years, including representation before administrative boards and federal courts; consulting and negotiating third-party payor contract disputes; illegal remuneration, Stark, and federal FCA matters; and structuring and contracting for integrated delivery systems.
Prof. Memberships: AAHA (Fellow and Past President); Health Law and Policy Institute, University of Houston Law Center (Board Member).
Career: Admitted to practice: Illinois, 1970; Texas, 1974; DC, 1978.
Publications: Numerous articles on subjects ranging from fraud and abuse to capital financing.
Personal: University of Illinois, BS, 1965; JD, 1967.

ERWIN, Greg
Winstead Sechrest & Minick P.C., Houston 713 650 2781
gerwin@winstead.com
Recommended in Real Estate
Practice Areas: Shareholder in Real Estate Section. Represents developers and owners in the acquisition, development, leasing, financing, and sale of all forms of commercial properties. Experienced in structuring, negotiating and documenting commercial real estate transactions.
Prof. Memberships: American Bar Association, Houston Bar Association, American College of Real Estate Lawyers.
Career: Admitted, State Bar of Texas. Board Certified, Commercial Real Estate Law and Residential Real Estate Law, Texas Board of Legal Specialization.
Personal: University of Texas at Austin, JD (cum laude), 1974. Southern Methodist University, BA (cum laude), 1970.

EVANS, Mark C
Bracewell & Giuliani LLP, Houston
713 221 1300
mark.evans@bracewellgiuliani.com
Recommended in Banking & Finance, Projects
Practice Areas: Represents domestic and international lenders in complex financing transactions, such as syndicated loans, revolving credit and term 'B' loans, leveraged transactions, structured transactions, subordinated and mezzanine investments and project finance. Heads Bracewell's Finance Team, which has been ranked among the nation's leaders for handling syndicated loans.
Career: Has practiced finance law for over 25 years and represented numerous agents in large syndicated bank credit facilities. Clients include Société Générale, Calyon, BNP Paribas, ABN AMRO and Union Bank of California.
Personal: JD, The University of Texas School of Law, 1977; BBA, The University of Texas at Austin, 1974.

FAULK, Richard
Gardere Wynne Sewell LLP, Houston
713 276 5651
rfaulk@gardere.com
Recommended in Litigation
Practice Areas: Environmental, personal injury defense, class action defense, products liability, appellate.
Prof. Memberships: Board Certified, Civil Appellate Law, Texas Board of Legal Specialization; American Bar Association; State Bar of Texas; Houston Bar Association; Texas Association of Civil Trial and Appellate Specialists.
Career: Richard Faulk has served as lead counsel for toxic tort and environmental litigation in Texas and other jurisdictions, including class actions and other 'mass tort' cases, in almost 30 years of practice. He has significant expertise in cases with international implications and comparative mass tort procedures. Mr Faulk is experienced in environmental litigation, including groundwater contamination cases, cost recovery and contribution actions under CERCLA and state environmental laws, and 'neighborhood' exposure cases alleging residential toxic exposures and property value diminution from alleged pollution released by manufacturing facilities.
Publications: 'Dispelling the Myths of Asbestos Litigation: Solutions for Common Law Courts,' South Texas Law Review, October 2003; 'Armageddon Through Aggregation: The Use and Abuse of Class and Group Actions in International Dispute Resolution,' 10 MSU-DCL International Law Journal 205, 2002.
Personal: JD, Southern Methodist University Dedman School of Law, 1977; Leading Articles Editor, Journal of Air Law and Commerce, Symposium Scholar. BA, University of North Texas, 1974.

FELDMAN, Robert C
Weil, Gotshal & Manges LLP, Dallas
214 746 7744
robert.feldman@weil.com
Recommended in Real Estate
Practice Areas: Mr Feldman's practice focuses on corporate and real estate transactions and finance.
Career: A founder of the Dallas office in 1987, he has experience in secured finance, real estate finance and business transactions involving partnerships, limited liability companies and private equity funds. Mr Feldman represents both lenders and debtors in restructuring. His representative clients include Citibank, GE Capital, Lehman Bros., Commercial Metals Company, Hicks Muse Tate & Furst, Olympus Real Estate Fund, Olympia & York, Martin Marietta Materials, Prentiss Properties, and Starwood Hotels.
Personal: University of Texas School of Law (JD, 1973); Duke University (BA, 1970).

FELDT, Harrell
Vinson & Elkins LLP, Houston
713 756 3868
hfeldt@velaw.com
Recommended in Energy
Practice Areas: Mr Harrell has tried cases in New Mexico, Oklahoma, and Louisiana, and in more than 50 Texas counties (with jury trials in more than 25 of these counties). He has also appeared before ad valorem taxing authorities, conducted Texas Water Commission hearings, and handled zoning matters before municipal authorities.
Prof. Memberships: Member: American College of Trial Lawyers; American Law Institute; International Association of Insurance Counsel; Texas Association of Defense Counsel; American Board of Trial Advocacy (ABOTA); Fellow American Bar Foundation; International Association of Defense Counsel.
Career: Partner at V&E since 1986.
Personal: The University of Texas (BBA 1961); The University of Texas School of Law (JD 1963)

FELGER, Thomas
Baker Botts LLP, Austin 512 322 2599
tom.felger@bakerbotts.com
Recommended in Intellectual Property
Practice Areas: Head of Austin office's Intellectual Property Department. 25+ years of experience in managing intellectual property portfolios, intellectual property-related transactions and patent and trademark prosecution. Clients include medical device/biotechnology companies, oil and gas service companies, computer manufacturers, and telecommunications companies. Served in over 20 arbitration proceedings involving intellectual property disputes. Worked on many technology-based strategic alliances including joint technology development agreements and patent licensing agreements.
Prof. Memberships: Texas State Bar Business Law Section, E-Commerce Committee, founder; Dallas Bar Association, Intellectual Property Law and International Law Sections; American Arbitration Association, Commercial Arbitration Panel; Registered Texas Professional Engineer.

FIELDS, Jack
Andrews Kurth LLP, Houston
713 220 4348
jfields@andrewskurth.com
Recommended in Real Estate
Practice Areas: Jack Fields is a Partner practicing in the Business Transactions Section of Andrews Kurth LLP since 1978, specializing in real estate. He is a member of the firm's Opinion Committee. He achieved Board Certification by the Texas Board of Legal Specialization in the real estate-commercial and real estate-farm and ranch areas.
Prof. Memberships: The State Bar of Texas; Council Member of the Real Estate, Probate and Trust Law Section of the State Bar of Texas, 1988-92; Chairman, Title Insurance Subcommittee, 1990-92; Houston Bar Association; Houston Real Estate Lawyer's Council. Named as a best lawyer in America (Texas Metro Area) in a leading US legal publication; as one of Texas' Top Notch Lawyers in the October 2002 'Go To Guide' of Texas Lawyer; as a 'Recommended Real Estate Lawyer' in the 2003-04 'Chambers USA - America's Leading Business Lawyers'; in the 2003-04 edition of a leading legal US publication; and as a 'Texas Super Lawyer for 2003' by Texas Monthly.
Career: Admitted to the State Bar of Texas in 1978. Partner with Andrews Kurth since 1986.
Publications: Co-authored a law review article on Texas usury laws entitled 'A Topic of Interest: An Analysis of the Status of the Usury Laws of Texas.' Speaker - real estate topics at several seminars, including the State Bar of Texas Advanced Real Estate Law Course, including a speech on Real Estate Deeds and Warranties and Granting and Reserving Easements.
Personal: Received a JD cum laude from The University of Texas School of Law in 1978. Received Order of the Coif. Received a BBA in Finance summa cum laude from the University of Houston in 1975.

FIJOLEK, Richard
Haynes and Boone LLP, Dallas
214 651 5000
Recommended in Tax

FINN BRADDOCK, Patricia
Fulbright & Jaworski L.L.P., Austin
512 536 4547
pbraddock@fulbright.com
Recommended in Environment
Practice Areas: Toxic tort; environmental law.
Prof. Memberships: Member of the American Bar Association, the Texas Bar Association and the Travis County Bar Association. Fellow of the State Bar of Texas. Member of the Air and Waste Management Association and Texas Water Pollution Control Association.
Career: Admitted to Texas Bar (1974). A Partner in Fulbright's Austin office since 1992. Prior to joining the firm, she worked for Texas' environmental regulatory agencies for almost 15 years.
Personal: Received a BA (1971) from the American University in Washington, DC and a JD (1974) from St. Mary's University College of Law in San Antonio, Texas. Certified in Administrative Law by the Texas Board of Legal Specialization.

FINNEGAN, IV, William N
Vinson & Elkins LLP, Houston
713 758 3704
bfinnegan@velaw.com
Recommended in Corporate/M&A
Practice Areas: Practice is focused on various corporate and securities transactions on both a national and international basis, including: representing issuers and underwriters in public and private offerings of equity and debt securities, including MLPs; negotiating and structuring asset and stock acquisitions; the formation and financing of joint venture and partnership transactions; and advising on general corporate and securities matters.
Prof. Memberships: American Bar Association; Houston Bar Association; Houston Bar Foundation.
Career: Admitted to Texas Bar in 1981. Joined the firm in 2000 as a Partner.
Personal: The University of Texas, BBA, 1978; University of Houston, JD, 1981.

FISK, Hollye
Fisk & Fielder, Dallas
214 638 3744
Recommended in Construction

FLAKE, Richard
Cokinos, Bosien and Young, Houston
713 535 5500
Recommended in Construction

FLOYD, Adam
Vinson & Elkins LLP, Austin
Recommended in Intellectual Property
Practice Areas: Intellectual property. Specifically patent litigation.
Prof. Memberships: Federal Circuit Bar Association, AIPLA, ABA, ATLA.
Career: Partner since 2003.
Publications: Legal Research Guide to Mechanical Patent litigation, Hein Publishing Company (1994).
Personal: Texas A&M University, BS in aerospace engineering summa cum laude, 1991 (Engineering Scholars Program; All-American Scholar; National Dean's List; Sigma Gamma Tau Honor Society); Tau Beta Pi Honor Society; Harvard Law School, JD cum laude, 1994 (Journal of Law and Technology); Recipient: National Science Foundation Fellowship; Garland Coker Endowed Scholarship; J.G. McGuire Engineering Scholarship; Admitted to practice: Texas, 1994; United States Patent and Trademark Office.

FOGLER, Murray
McDade Fogler LLP, Houston
713 654 4300
Recommended in Energy, Litigation

FONTANA, Angela
Weil, Gotshal & Manges LLP, Dallas
214 746 7895
Recommended in Banking & Finance
Practice Areas: Ms Fontana represents borrowers and financial institutions in cash-flow and asset-based lending, leveraged acquisitions, recapitalizations, bridge and mezzanine financing, and workouts and restructurings.
Career: Ms Fontana represents private equity funds including DLJ Merchant Banking, Ewing Management, Hicks, Muse, Tate & Furst, Summit Partners and Thomas H Lee Partners, and corporate clients including Greyhound Lines, Key Safety Systems and United Stationers. She recently represented the lead arrangers in financing deals for Kmart, Bon-Ton, The New York Mets and Budget Rent-a-Car.
Personal: University of Iowa College of Law (JD, with distinction, 1989); University of Iowa College of Business (BBA, 1987).

FORD, Jeffrey
Ford White & Nassen, Dallas
214 523 5100
Recommended in Construction

FOUST, Lawrence
Jenkens & Gilchrist, Houston
713 951 3300
Recommended in Healthcare

FOX, J Nixon
Vinson & Elkins LLP, Austin
Recommended in Technology
Practice Areas: Corporate and securities law, including public offerings, private placements, mergers and acquisitions, joint ventures and strategic alliances, licensing and other technology-related business transactions and international business transactions.
Prof. Memberships: Texas Bar Association; the Bar Association of the District of Columbia.
Career: Partner since joining the firm in 2001. Co-chairs the firm's Technology Practice Group. Has practiced in Austin, Washington, DC. and Hong Kong.
Personal: Southern Methodist University, BA magna cum laude, 1981; The University of Texas School of Law, JD with honors, 1984; New York University School of Law, LLM (in taxation), 1985.

FOX, Michael W
Ogletree, Deakins, Nash, Smoak & Stewart, PC, Austin
512 344 4711
michael.fox@ogletreedeakins.com
Recommended in Employment

Practice Areas: Employment litigation.
Prof. Memberships: American Bar Association, Society for Human Resource Management, Management Labor & Employment Roundtable.
Career: Admitted to practice in all state and federal courts in Texas. Listed in 'The Best Lawyers in America' and named as a Texas Monthly 'Super Lawyer' in employment litigation.
Publications: 'Being an Employer After Sarbanes-Oxley,' University of Houston Law Foundation (2002); 'Trial Tactics: What Works For Employers,' Texas Association of Business (2002); 'Whistleblowers and Retaliation,' University of Texas School of Law (2004).
Personal: Stephen F Austin State University (BA, with honors, 1972), University of Texas (JD, with high honors, 1975).

FRANZE, Laura M
Akin Gump Strauss Hauer & Feld LLP, Dallas 214 969 2779
lfranze@akingump.com
Recommended in Employment
Practice Areas: As Chair of Akin Gump's Texas and California Labor Sections, Laura Franze leads one of the region's most respected employment practices, representing leading employers including Cinemark USA, Fujitsu Network, Regal Cinemas and Wyndham Hotels. Board Certified, listed in leading legal publications, and designated a top Texas practitioner by 'Texas Lawyer,' Franze has authored numerous employment-related articles. Franze currently serves on the management committee at Akin Gump. Regal Cinemas recently chose Franze to represent the company before the US Supreme Court in Regal Cinemas v Stewmon.
Publications: Texas Employment Law (1998-2004).

FRIEDMAN, Edward
Locke Liddell & Sapp LLP, Houston 713 226 1214
efriedman@lockeliddell.com
Recommended in Employment
Practice Areas: Protection of proprietary information/trade secrets; covenants not to compete, employee raiding and unfair competition litigation; defending against claims by former executives and managers; management employment law.
Prof. Memberships: Speaker, Houston Bar Association, 'Protection of Trade Secrets and Enforcement of Non-Compete Agreements'; Member, Houston Bar Association; Member, American Bar Association; Member, State Bar of Texas.
Career: Partner in the law firm of Locke Liddell & Sapp LLP.
Personal: Cornell University, School of Industrial and Labor Relations, BS, honors, 1984; University of Michigan Law School, honors, 1987.

FRISBIE Jr, Curtis L
Gardere Wynne Sewell LLP, Dallas 214 999 4757
cfrisbie@gardere.com
Recommended in Antitrust
Practice Areas: Trial Section Chair, antitrust and trade regulation, class action defense, commercial and IP litigation.
Prof. Memberships: American Bar Association; State Bar of Texas; Past Chair, State Bar of Texas Antitrust and Business Litigation Section; Past President, Dallas Bar Association Section on Antitrust and Trade Regulation Law; Selected for 'Texas Super Lawyers' and 'Best Lawyers in Dallas'.
Career: Curt Frisbie has more than 30 years of trial experience handling major antitrust and other commercial litigation matters. He has substantial experience defending class action cases involving antitrust, RICO, usury and other claims.
Personal: JD, St. Mary's University School of Law, 1971; BS, University of Alabama, 1966. US Marine Corps (1966-69), Bronze Star with V and Purple Heart. Trial Attorney, US Department of Justice Antitrust Division (Special Achievement Award).

FRIZZELL, Jean C
Gibbs & Bruns, LLP, Houston 713 650 8805
jfrizzell@gibbs-bruns.com
Recommended in Litigation
Practice Areas: Practice is complex commercial and business litigation for both plaintiffs and defendants, including breach of contract, securities, environmental, trade secret, trademark, copyright, oil and gas, director liability, and partnership disputes in both state and federal courts.
Prof. Memberships: Admitted to practice in the State of Texas in 1990 and admitted before the United States District Courts for the Eastern, Northern, and Southern Districts of Texas, District of Colorado, and Federal District, and United States Court of Appeals for the Fifth Circuit. A member of the State Bar of Texas, American Bar Association, Texas Bar Foundation (Fellow), Houston Bar Association, Houston Bar Foundation (Fellow).
Career: Joined Gibbs & Bruns, LLP in 1990.
Personal: Born in New Jersey, October 6, 1965; Rice University (BA, 1987); University of Texas (JD, honors, 1990); member, Texas Law Review.

FROMM O'BRIEN, Eva
Fulbright & Jaworski L.L.P., Houston 713 651 5321
efrommobrien@fulbright.com
Recommended in Environment, Litigation
Practice Areas: Environmental law, crimes and litigation; enforcement controversies, mergers and acquisitions,

permits, and property damage litigation.
Prof. Memberships: Included in a leading legal publication. Past secretary, Vice-Chair and Chair of the Houston Bar Association's Environmental Law Section. Former Chair of the American Bar Association's Real Estate and Probate Section's RCRA and Underground Storage Tank Committee.
Career: Admitted to Texas Bar (1985). Partner at Fulbright & Jaworski L.L.P. joining the firm in 1986. Heads the Environmental Law Department.
Personal: Received a BS in Chemical Engineering in 1978 from Syracuse University and a JD in 1985 from the University of Houston.

FROST, Claudia Wilson
Mayer, Brown, Rowe & Maw LLP, Houston 713 547 9636
cfrost@mayerbrownrowe.com
Recommended in Litigation
Practice Areas: Specializes in appellate litigation and civil trial law. Briefed and argued cases in the Texas Supreme Court and intermediate Texas appellate courts. Significant appearances before United States Courts of Appeals including in the Fifth, Federal and DC Circuits. Merits and amicus briefs in the United States Supreme Court. Handled numerous civil trials and provided appellate and error preservation assistance in complex litigation in federal and state courts in Texas, Delaware, California, Colorado, Louisiana, and Alabama, among others. Board certified by the Texas Board of Legal Specialization in both Civil Appellate and Civil Trial law. Areas of expertise include general commercial litigation, oil and gas, products liability and torts, intellectual property, ERISA, securities law and class actions.
Prof. Memberships: Admitted: Texas, 1982; US Court of Appeals, Fifth and Federal Circuits; Texas and US District Court, Southern, Northern and Eastern Districts; US Supreme Court.
Career: Joined Mayer, Brown, Rowe & Maw LLP as Partner, 2003. Slusser & Frost, LLP, 1999-July 2003. BakerBotts, LLP, 1982-98.
Personal: JD, magna cum laude, University of Houston Law Center, 1982; editor in chief, 'Houston Law Review'; Order of the Barons and The Advocates; Teaching Assistant. MA, University of Houston, 1979. BA, University of Texas at Austin, 1975.

FUNK, John A
Jones Day, Dallas 214 969 2981
jafunk@jonesday.com
Recommended in Business Process Outsourcing: National, Technology
Practice Areas: Chairs Jones Day's global Outsourcing Practice. He has extensive experience in complex business process and information technology outsourcing transactions and also has experience in other technology transactions such as software licensing, software

development, and systems integration. His experience in business process outsourcing transactions include finance and accounting, human resource administration, item processing, logistics, mortgage loan application processing and servicing, and procurement. His outsourcing practice includes representing clients in complex multijurisdictional BPO and IT outsourcing transactions, including the first European outsourcing transaction over $1 billion.

GALVAN, Hilda
Jones Day, Dallas 214 969 4556
hcgalvan@jonesday.com
Recommended in Intellectual Property
Practice Areas: Her intellectual property law practice includes patent, trademark, copyright, trade secret, and unfair competition matters. She has extensive experience in patent litigation in various federal and appellate courts, including the International Trade Commission. These cases have dealt with a variety of technologies including simulation software, digital signal processors, specialized mobile radio technology, semiconductor processing techniques, offshore oil and gas platforms, optic lenses, and soft drink preparation systems. She has also developed a growing practice in trademark litigation, with an emphasis on domestic and foreign protection.
Prof. Memberships: ABA; State Bar of Texas; Dallas Bar Association.

GAVIN, Tim
Carrington, Coleman, Sloman & Blumenthal, LLP, Dallas 214 855 3000
Recommended in Antitrust

GEIGER, Richard S
Thompson, Coe, Cousins & Irons, LLP, Dallas 214 871 8281
rgeiger@thompsoncoe.com
Recommended in Insurance
Practice Areas: Representation of insurance companies and trade associations before the legislature, Commissioner of Insurance, and Texas Department of Insurance.
Prof. Memberships: Admitted to the State Bar of Texas, Fellow of the Texas Bar Foundation and serves as a Member of the Board of Directors with such organizations as: the Adamson Scholarship Foundation, Texas Legal Protection Plan, Inc., the Dallas Zoological Society.
Career: From 1973-77, he served in the Texas House of Representatives. During two terms in the legislature, he served as a delegate to the Texas Constitutional Convention and served on the Committees on State Affairs, Transportation, Public Health, and Elections.

GERACHIS, George Matthew
Vinson & Elkins LLP, Houston 713 758 1056
ggerachis@velaw.com
Recommended in Litigation
Practice Areas: Co-Chair of the firm's Taxation Practice and leader of the

firm's Tax Controversy and Litigation Group. Member of firm's Management Committee. Practice consists primarily of resolving complex tax disputes for individuals and business clients. Also counsels multinational companies in cross-border tax issues, including transfer pricing.

Prof. Memberships: American Bar Association, Section of Taxation; International Fiscal Association.

Career: Admitted to practice US Tax Court; frequent lecturer to professional groups on tax matters, including Tax Executives Institute.

Personal: Graduated from University of Virginia, BA 1979, JD 1983. Languages: German and Spanish.

GERBER, Toby L
Fulbright & Jaworski L.L.P., Dallas
214 855 7171
tgerber@fulbright.com
Recommended in Bankruptcy

Practice Areas: Bankruptcy and transportation.

Prof. Memberships: Mr Gerber is a Member of the Dallas and American Bar Associations, the State Bar of Texas, the Texas Association of Bank Counsel, and the American Bankruptcy Institute.

Career: Mr Gerber regularly represents financial institutions in troubled loans and insolvencies across all industries throughout the US. He also represents the International Air Transport Association and its air carrier members in insolvency matters throughout the world. Gerber has been named one of the 'Best Lawyers in Dallas' by D Magazine and was named a 'Texas Super Lawyer' and one of the 'Top 100 Dallas/Fort Worth Region Super Lawyers' by Texas Monthly and Law & Politics Magazine.

Personal: Mr Gerber received his AB, and BJ, with honors, from the University of Missouri-Columbia in 1972, and in 1975 he earned his JD from Georgetown University Law Center.

GIBBS, Charles R
Akin Gump Strauss Hauer & Feld LLP,
Dallas 214 969 4710
cgibbs@akingump.com
Recommended in Bankruptcy

Practice Areas: Represents secured and unsecured creditors in complex restructurings, frequently advising unsecured creditor committees, banks and non-bank lenders, and special servicers of commercial mortgage securitized trusts. Experienced particularly in real estate, oil and gas, textiles, retail and restaurant industries. Has represented several private investment funds that provide rescue equity and reorganization services to troubled real estate syndications and ventures, and has acted as lead debtor's counsel in several significant Chapter 11 proceedings.

Prof. Memberships: ABI; Chapter 11 and Secured Creditor Subcommittees, Business Bankruptcy Committee; Texas

Bar Foundation.

Personal: BA, Duke University; MBA and JD, Southern Methodist University.

GIBBS, Robin C
Gibbs & Bruns, LLP, Houston
713 650 8805
rgibbs@gibbs-bruns.com
Recommended in Energy, Litigation

Practice Areas: Mr Gibbs' practice include the representation of plaintiffs and defendants in significant contract, securities, trade secret, intellectual property, patent, insurance, antitrust, lender liability, oil and gas, director liability, copyright, and partnership disputes in Texas, throughout the United States, and in various courts and tribunals outside the United States.

Prof. Memberships: Fellow, American College of Trial Lawyers. Advocate, American Board of Trial Advocates. Fellow, International Academy of Trial Lawyers. Member, The American Law Institute. Member, Texas Bar Association. Fellow, Texas Bar Foundation Member, American Bar Association. Fellow, American Bar Foundation. Member, Harris County Bar Association.

Career: Upon graduation from law school in 1971, Mr Gibbs joined Vinson & Elkins as an associate in its insurance defense group. In 1974, he left to form a full-service law firm, Wood, Campbell, Moody & Gibbs, P.C., in which Mr Gibbs undertook to develop a general litigation practice and career. In 1983, Mr Gibbs and the litigation attorneys formed Gibbs & Bruns, L.L.P. (formerly known as Gibbs & Ratliff, L.L.P.), a firm which limits its practice to all forms of commercial litigation. Mr Gibbs was ranked among the top 15 commercial trial lawyers in the United States in a survey conducted by 'International Commercial Litigation magazine'. In September 1999, the 'National Law Journal' ranked Mr Gibbs as one of the top trial lawyers in Texas. Mr Gibbs was recently selected by the 'Texas Lawyer' as the 'Go To' lawyer in securities litigation in Texas and was also listed among America's leading business lawyers in 'Chambers USA - America's Leading Business Lawyers'. Mr Gibbs was recognized as one of the 'Top 100 Texas Super Lawyers' in 2003 and 2004.

GIBLIN, Pamela
Baker Botts LLP, Austin
512 322 2509
pam.giblin@bakerbotts.com
Recommended in Environment

Practice Areas: Head of firmwide Environmental Department. Practice focuses on permitting, acquisitions, and enforcement under state and federal laws dealing with air, water, and hazardous waste.

Prof. Memberships: State Bar of Texas, Environmental and Natural Resources Law Section.

Career: Admitted to Texas Bar, 1970.

Baker Botts Partner since 1994.

Personal: University of Texas, BA, with honors, 1967; JD, 1970. First woman to receive the Travis County Bar Association's Distinguished Lawyer Award, 2003.

GILLESPIE, Thomas
Jones Day, Dallas 214 969 5076
tgillespie@jonesday.com
Recommended in Banking & Finance

Practice Areas: Has practiced corporate and commercial law in New York, London and Dallas, specializing in the representation of both financial institutions and corporations in complex domestic and international financial transactions, syndicated loans, asset based lending, workouts and restructurings. He has considerable experience working in specific industry areas, including health care financings, energy financings, private equity financings, and transportation financings (aircraft, vessels, and rolling stock).

Prof. Memberships: New York and Texas Bar associations.

Publications: Co-editor and contributing author of 'The Commercial Finance Guide' and contributing author of 'NAFTA and Beyond - A New Framework for Doing Business in the Americas.'

GITOMER, Deborah
Fulbright & Jaworski L.L.P., Houston
713 651 3636
dgitomer@fulbright.com
Recommended in Energy

Practice Areas: Oil, gas and energy transactions.

Prof. Memberships: Ms Gitomer is a Member of the Houston Bar Association and the State Bar of Texas.

Career: Deborah Gitomer joined Fulbright & Jaworski L.L.P.'s Houston office in 1982, and has been a Partner since 1991. Her practice is concentrated in transactions related to the acquisition, and disposition of oil and gas reserves, pipelines, gas processing plants, refineries, petrochemical facilities and storage facilities, whether structured as asset or entity acquisitions as well as joint ventures, partnerships and other joint ownership or participation arrangements in the oil, gas and energy areas.

Personal: BA, Trinity University (1979); JD, St. Mary's University (1982). She was admitted to practice in Texas in 1982.

GLASER, Kenneth
Gardere Wynne Sewell LLP, Dallas
214 999 4352
kglaser@gardere.com
Recommended in Intellectual Property

Practice Areas: Intellectual property, intellectual property litigation.

Prof. Memberships: State Bar of Texas; President, Dallas-Fort Worth Patent Law Association; Dallas Bar Association; AIPLA; IHTA; and ABA.

Career: Mr Glaser has represented clients worldwide in patent, trademark, copyright and other intellectual property matters for more than 30 years. Dur-

ing his career, Mr Glaser has held a variety of positions, including division patent counsel for Texas Instruments, partner and founding partner of Dallas, Texas-based intellectual property firms, and chair of the Intellectual Property practices of Akin Gump Strauss Hauer & Feld and Gardere Wynne Sewell. Mr Glaser has taught intellectual property law at The University of Texas and Southern Methodist University.

Personal: JD, University of Texas School of Law, 1964, with honors; BSEE, University of Texas at Austin, 1962.

GODFREY, Lee
Susman Godfrey LLP, Houston
713 651 9366
Recommended in Antitrust, Energy, Litigation

GOLDEN, H Bruce
Golden & Owens LLP, Houston
713 223 2600
Recommended in Litigation

GOLEMON, Kinnan
Brown McCarroll LLP, Austin
512 472 5456
Recommended in Environment

GOOCH, W Kyle
Canterbury, Stuber, Elder, Gooch & Surratt, PC, Dallas
972 239 7493
kgooch@canterburylaw.com
Recommended in Construction

Practice Areas: Construction litigation and arbitration; construction insurance (builder's risk, commercial general liability, errors and omissions).

Prof. Memberships: Admitted to the Texas and Dallas Bar Associations; Construction Law Section of the Texas Bar (Chairman, past Vice Chairman, past Council Member); American Arbitration Association (arbitrator); and American College of Construction Lawyers.

Career: Following graduation from Baylor Law School, he commenced law practice in Dallas, Texas and has practiced consistently in the field of construction and insurance. He has been a member and shareholder of Canterbury, Stuber, Elder, Gooch & Surratt since 1981.

Publications: 'Builder's Risk'; 'The Forgotten Insurance, 1999' and other articles on construction and insurance issues.

Personal: Born Greenville, Texas, November 14, 1952; Bachelor of Science - Texas A & M University; JD Baylor University. Married to the former Suzy Davis, they have three children.

GOOLSBY, George
Baker Botts LLP, Houston
713 229 1416
george.goolsby@bakerbotts.com
Recommended in Energy, Projects

Practice Areas: Practice includes oil and gas ventures and pipeline projects. Regularly consults with project sponsors and lenders on LNG, cogeneration, and power projects, and has a wide range of regulatory, transactional, trial, and dispute resolution experience representing producers, marketers, transporters, and distributors of oil, gas, and refined petroleum products.

Prof. Memberships: State Bar of Texas; Energy Bar Association; Institute for Transnational Arbitration, Advisory Board; London Court of International Arbitration.

Personal: JD from The University of Texas School of Law, 1974; BA from The University of Texas, 1971.

GORDON, R Kenneth
Baker & McKenzie, Dallas
214 978 3002
kenneth.gordon@bakernet.com
Recommended in Healthcare

Practice Areas: Significant experience with a wide variety of issues facing health care providers, pharma and device companies, and others involved in the healthcare industry. Regularly work with both the laws and the practical considerations involved with strategic planning; fraud and abuse compliance and representation; hospital operations; joint ventures; HIPAA privacy and security; pharmaceutical regulation; medical staff relations; physician, hospital and other provider integration; group medical practices; DME suppliers; group purchasing; joint ventures; mergers and acquisitions; third-party reimbursement; FHA-insured financings; and managed care organizations.

Prof. Memberships: Health Law Legal Specialization Exam Commission (Founding Chair 2002 - present); State Bar of Texas (Health Law Section; Chair 2004-05); Health Industry Council of Dallas-Fort Worth (Board of Directors 2005-present).

Career: Admitted in Texas and Illinois; North America Pharma & Healthcare Industry Group Leader.

Publications: Presenter and author of 100+ live and audio presentations and articles on various health law issues.

GOSSELINK, Paul
Lloyd, Gosselink, Blevins, Rochelle, Baldwin & Townsend, PC, Austin
512 322 5800
Recommended in Environment

GOVETT, Brett C
Fulbright & Jaworski L.L.P., Dallas
214 855 8118
bgovett@fulbright.com
Recommended in Intellectual Property

Practice Areas: Commercial litigation, patent infringement litigation, personal injury defense litigation.

Prof. Memberships: American Bar Association, State Bar of Texas, Dallas Bar Association, American Chemical Society.

Career: Brett Govett, a Partner, has been with the Dallas office of Fulbright & Jaworski L.L.P. since 1991 and practices in the firm's Litigation Department. He is Board Certified in Civil Trial Law by

the Texas Board of Legal Specialization and is a registered patent attorney. In 2003, he completed his term as a Barrister in The Patrick E. Higginbotham American Inn of Court. Some of his trial wins have been featured in the 'National Law Journal', 'Texas Lawyer', 'Dallas Business Journal', 'Dallas Morning News' and numerous other daily and weekly publications. Mr Govett is also experienced in the defense and handling of mass toxic tort lawsuits representing multiple defendants in claims brought by multiple plaintiffs. His representation is responsible for over $100 million in jury verdicts and client recoveries.

Personal: Mr Govett received a BA in Chemistry, with honors, from The Citadel in 1987. He continued his education at Texas Tech University, where he received a JD, with honors, in 1990.

GOYNE, Roderick
Baker Botts LLP, Dallas
214 953 6527
rick.goyne@bakerbotts.com
Recommended in Banking & Finance

Practice Areas: Chair: Finance Section (firmwide). Concentrates on private placements, primarily on behalf of institutional purchasers, and has broad experience in transactions involving senior secured and unsecured debt, mezzanine investments, subordinated debt, acquisition and MLP financings, financing leases, and a variety of structured securities and debt restructurings. Additionally handles asset securitizations and other structured financings in the oil, gas, petrochemicals, computers, information technology and consumer products industries. Represents agent lenders/borrowers in acquisitions, margin credits, debt restructurings and other financings.

Personal: JD, cum laude, Harvard Law School, 1974; BA, with highest honors, history, The University of Texas at Arlington, 1971.

GRAY, Robert
Mayer, Brown, Rowe & Mawe LLP, Houston
713 546 0522
Recommended in Communications, Technology

GREIG, Brian
Fulbright & Jaworski L.L.P., Austin
512 536 4510
bgreig@fulbright.com
Recommended in Employment

Practice Areas: Labor and employment law, trade secrets, federal practice, commercial litigation, construction litigation, energy.

Prof. Memberships: Member of the Travis County, Federal and American Bar Associations; and the State Bar of Texas. Included in leading legal publications.

Career: Partner since 1983, practices in Fulbright & Jaworski L.L.P.'s Austin office, where he heads the office's Labor

and Employment Practice.

Personal: Received his BA in Economics from Washington & Lee University (1972) and a JD from The University of Texas School of Law (1975).

GREMILLION, L Todd
Akin Gump Strauss Hauer & Feld LLP, Houston 713 220 5875
tgremillion@akingump.com
Recommended in Energy

Practice Areas: Handles domestic and international oil and gas and related energy transactions. Is experienced in joint ventures and contractual arrangements and related economic issues regarding transportation, marketing and distribution of hydrocarbons; acquisition and sale of oil and gas properties; processing and extracting of natural gas liquids; gas-fired electric generation projects and related power distribution and marketing; and equity and debt financing. Is involved extensively with oil and gas exploration and production operations in Latin America, Eastern Europe, the Russian Federation, the Caspian Region and the Central Asian Republics of the former Soviet Union.

Personal: BA, JD, Louisiana State University.

GRIFFITH, Scott
Griffith & Nixon, P.C., Dallas
972 386 8988
Recommended in Construction

GROTEN, Eric
Bracewell & Giuliani LLP, Austin
512 494 3660
eric.groten@bracewellgiuliani.com
Recommended in Environment

Practice Areas: Serves industrial, manufacturing, utility and municipal clients in environmental matters, principally air quality, including representation in permit application proceedings, defense of enforcement actions, environmental audits and investigations, compliance counseling, transaction of emission rights, advocacy in state and federal rulemakings and related litigation. Recognized by Texas Lawyer as a leading 'legal innovator' for an air emissions project along Texas/Mexico border and by Austin Monthly among 'Best in Environmental Law.' Also named Texas Super Lawyer in 2004, 2003.

Personal: JD, The University of Texas School of Law, 1985; BA, Chemistry and Environmental Studies, Baylor University, 1981.

GUEDRY, David
Hughes & Luce LLP, Dallas
214 939 5500
Recommended in Business Process Outsourcing: National, Technology

GUNN, David
Beck, Redden & Secrest L.L.P, Houston
713 951 3700
Recommended in Litigation

GUNTER, Clifford
Bracewell & Giuliani LLP, Houston
713 221 1213
clifford.gunter@bracewellgiuliani.com
Recommended in Energy

Practice Areas: Maintains an extensive commercial litigation background with a client roster listing some of the nation's largest energy companies. Experience includes cases involving fraud, theft of trade secrets, breach of contract, construction litigation, antitrust litigation, securities fraud litigation, special matters and investigations, international dispute resolution, arbitrations of transnational gas sales contracts and take-or-pay and pricing disputes. Has tried several cases to verdict involving international corporate project finance issues. Heads firm's Trial Section of more than 100 attorneys.

Personal: LLB, The University of Texas School of Law, 1967; BA, The University of Texas at Austin, 1965.

HALEVY, Amy Karff
Bracewell & Giuliani LLP, Houston
713 221 1329
amy.halevy@bracewellgiuliani.com
Recommended in Employment

Practice Areas: Head of the firm's nationally regarded Labor and Employment Section. Represents employers in all areas of employment law, including litigation in state and federal court and complaints before the Equal Employment Opportunity Commission and the Texas Commission on Human Rights. Provides advice to employers regarding the preparation and application of employment policies, including sexual harassment policies. Board certified in labor and employment law, she is also a prolific legal writer, editor and speaker. Recognized in her practice by two other legal publications.

Personal: JD, University of Houston Law Center, 1987; BA, with honors, Wesleyan University, 1984.

HAMEL, Douglas
Vinson & Elkins LLP, Houston
713 758 2036
dhamel@velaw.com
Recommended in Employment

Practice Areas: Representing management in labor and employment law, civil rights law, ERISA litigation and related issues. Represented clients in connection with numerous class action employment discrimination lawsuits involving issues of disparate treatment and disparate impact. Also regularly appears before federal and state agencies including NLRB, EEOC, and OFCCP.

Career: Partner since 1983; Section Head, Employment Litigation and Labor, and chairs firm's Benefits and Compensation Committee.

Publications: Planning Committee and faculty, University of Texas Annual Employment Law Conference since 1996 and speaker at University of Texas

Corporate Counsel Institute.
Personal: University of Virginia, (BA, 1972; JD, 1976)

HAMMOND, Herbert
Thompson & Knight LLP, Dallas
214 969 1607
herbert.hammond@tklaw.com
Recommended in Intellectual Property
Practice Areas: Mr Hammond specializes in patent, trademark, copyright, trade secret, computer, and entertainment law, focusing on litigation, licensing, mediation, and arbitration. He is listed in Texas Monthly's Texas Super Lawyers and The Best Lawyers in America.
Prof. Memberships: State Bar of Texas; Dallas Bar Association; American Intellectual Property Law Association.
Career: Partner since 1995.
Publications: 'Texas Intellectual Property Handbook' (LexisNexis 2005) and numerous chapters and articles.
Personal: New York University (JD, 1976), University of New Mexico (BS, 1973).

HARDIE, Thornton
Thompson & Knight LLP, Dallas
214 969 1504
thornton.hardie@tklaw.com
Recommended in Tax
Practice Areas: Mr Hardie's practice includes the taxation of business transactions, oil and gas taxation, energy finance, and tax and business planning. He is experienced in structuring oil and gas debt and equity financing and representing both industry parties and institutional investors. He was selected for inclusion in Texas Monthly's 2003 and 2004 listing of Texas Super Lawyers.
Prof. Memberships: Member of the State Bar of Texas, American and Dallas Bar Associations, Texas Bar Foundation.
Career: Partner since 1981.
Personal: University of Texas School of Law (JD, 1975); Washington and Lee University (BS, 1973).

HARPER, A J
Fulbright & Jaworski L.L.P., Houston
713 651 5442
ajharper@fulbright.com
Recommended in Employment
Practice Areas: Labor and Employment law.
Prof. Memberships: Member of the State Bar of Texas, the Houston Bar Association and the American Bar Association. Fellow in the College of Labor and Employment Lawyers and is included in a leading legal publication.
Career: Admitted to the Texas Bar (1967). Admitted before the United States Court of Appeals for the First, Second, Fifth, Sixth, Eighth, Ninth, Tenth and Eleventh Circuits. Admitted to practice before the United States Supreme Court. Admitted to the US District Courts for the Eastern, Northern, Southern and Western Districts of Texas, and District of Nebraska. Partner

since 1975 and currently heads the firm's Labor and Employment Law Department. Certified by the Texas Board of Legal Specialization in Labor & Employment Law.
Personal: Received a BA (1964) from North Texas State University and an LLB, cum laude, (1967) from Southern Methodist University.

HARRINGTON, C Michael
Vinson & Elkins LLP, Houston
713 758 2148
charrington@velaw.com
Recommended in Corporate/M&A
Practice Areas: Corporate finance, mergers and acquisitions law. Corporate finance practice emphasizes high-yield debt. Industry experience includes energy companies, beer wholesalers, and airlines.
Prof. Memberships: State Bar of Texas, Houston Bar Association, and Texas Business Law Foundation.
Career: Admitted to practice: Texas, 1973. Came to V&E in 1973; admitted to partnership in 1980.
Personal: Graduated from Yale College, BA in 1969 (Phi Beta Kappa), Cambridge University, Diploma in Development Economics in 1970, and Harvard University, JD in 1973.

HARRIS, James
Thompson & Knight LLP, Dallas
214 969 1102
james.harris@tklaw.com
Recommended in Environment, Litigation
Practice Areas: Mr Harris has practiced environmental law with the firm since 1978. His practice focuses on regulatory litigation and counseling. He is experienced in environmental litigation, environmental client counseling, and environmental due diligence, land use, and zoning, property tax litigation and general regulatory work including litigation and counseling. His work involves various federal and state agencies including the Consumer Product Safety Commission, FAA, FTC, FCC, ICC, Postal Service, the Texas Worker's Compensation, and the Texas Motor Vehicles Commissions. His environmental litigation practice includes cost-recovery and enforcement actions, contested permits, claims in bankruptcy, regulatory challenges, debarment proceedings, and criminal actions.

HARRISON, Lauren
Vinson & Elkins LLP, Houston
713 758 4430
lharrison@velaw.com
Recommended in Antitrust
Practice Areas: Lauren handles complex commercial cases before judges, juries, and arbitrators. Recent cases have involved antitrust, intellectual property, breach of contract, fraud, consumer protection and fiduciary duty issues. Lauren has represented companies in the medical device manufacturing, con-

tract manufacturing, computer software, technology leasing, aviation and rail transportation industries.
Prof. Memberships: American Bar Association; Houston Bar Association.
Career: Partner since 2005.
Personal: Dartmouth College, (BA 1990); Cornell Law School (JD 1995).

HARTSFIELD, Dan
Baker Botts LLP, Dallas
214 953 6575
dan.hartsfield@bakerbotts.com
Recommended in Employment
Practice Areas: Represents management in individual and class action discrimination, wrongful discharge and other employment-related litigation and in union organizational efforts and collective bargaining. Defends clients against federal and state administrative charges and represents government contractors before the Office of Federal Contract Compliance Programs (OFCCP). Exclusive representation of management in matters brought before the NLRB, EEOC, US Department of Labor, OFCCP, and other state and federal agencies.
Career: Chairs Labor and Employment Practice Group in Dallas. Serves on firm's Client Development Committee.
Personal: JD, Southern Methodist University, 1982; Phi Delta Phi; BA, magna cum laude, The University of Texas, 1979.

HARVEY, Dean William
Vinson & Elkins LLP, Dallas
214 220 7815
dharvey@velaw.com
Recommended in Communications, Technology
Practice Areas: Practice focuses on technology and communications related business transactions such as licensing, outsourcing and joint ventures. Counsels clients on communications and technology related legal issues such as privacy and security, and assists clients in protecting, acquiring and developing technology.
Prof. Memberships: Licensing Executives Society.
Career: Admitted to Texas Bar, 1997. Came to firm, 1997. Admitted to partnership, January 2001.
Publications: Special Member HIPAA Briefing Collection: Section IV - Security Standards, 'American Health Lawyers Association,' October 2004.
Personal: Graduated from West Virginia University, BS summa cum laude, 1986 and The University of Texas, JD, Order of the Coif, 1997.

HARVIN, David
Vinson & Elkins LLP, Houston
713 758 2368
dharvin@velaw.com
Recommended in Energy, Litigation
Practice Areas: Principal areas of practice include business litigation, class actions, securities and corporate litigation, and antitrust. Fellow of the Ameri-

can College of Trial Lawyers; listed since 1987 in the area of Business Litigation in a leading legal US publication.
Career: Admitted to Texas Bar in 1970. Joined Vinson & Elkins in 1971; admitted to partnership, 1977. Elected to Management Committee, 2000; Chair, Litigation Section.
Personal: Graduated from Yale University, BA magna cum laude, 1967 (Phi Beta Kappa); The University of Texas School of Law, JD, high honors, 1970 (Chancellors; Order of the Coif; articles editor, 'Texas Law Review').

HATCHELL, Mike A
Locke Liddell & Sapp LLP, Austin
512 305 4752
mahatchell@lockeliddell.com
Recommended in Litigation
Practice Areas: Appellate law; Mr Hatchell has experience as lead counsel in over 150 appeals. He has argued more than 30 appeals in the Supreme Court of Texas, en banc to the federal Fifth Circuit Court of Appeals twice, and in all 14 courts of appeals in Texas. Mr Hatchell has specialized in appeals to all local and federal appellate courts since 1965.
Prof. Memberships: Member, Supreme Court Advisory Committee; Supreme Court Task Force on Revision of Charge Rules; Member, American Academy of Appellate Lawyers; The State Bar of Texas (Organizer, Chairman-Elect, Chairman, Immediate Past Chairman, Appellate Practice and Advocacy Section, State Bar of Texas, 1988-90); Past Member, Civil Appellate Law Specialization Commission (1988 - present).
Career: Of Counsel for the law firm Locke Liddell & Sapp LLP, Head of the firm's Appeals Section, May 2004 - present; Shareholder for the law firm Hatchell PC in Tyler, Texas, February 2001 - April 2004; Attorney, Partner, and Shareholder with Ramey & Flock, P.C. in Tyler, Texas, 1965 - January 2001; Briefing Attorney for the Senior Associate Justice, Meade F. Griffin, The Supreme Court of Texas, 1964-65.

HAYES, William
Bracewell & Giuliani LLP, Houston
713 221 1333
bill.hayes@bracewellgiuliani.com
Recommended in Banking & Finance
Practice Areas: Focuses on structuring, drafting and negotiating a wide variety of financing transactions, including secured and unsecured credit facilities, acquisition financings, borrowing base financings, insured credit facilities, subordinated debt, work-outs of troubled credits, sales of accounts receivable, letters of credit and interest rate and currency and commodity derivatives.
Career: Has practiced finance law for more than 25 years and has represented a number of agents in significant syndicated bank credit facilities. Clients include Citibank NA and JPMorgan Chase Bank.

Personal: JD, Harvard Law School, 1974; BSEE, University of Arkansas, 1970.

HEAD, J D
Fritz, Byrne, Head & Harrison, Austin
512 476 2020
Recommended in Environment

HEADLEY, Linda
Littler Mendelson PC, Dallas
214 880 8100
Recommended in Employment

HEIM, Mike
Conley, Rose & Tayon, Plano
972 731 2288
Recommended in Intellectual Property

HELFAND, Thomas
Winstead Sechrest & Minick P.C.,
Dallas 214 745 5342
thelfand@winstead.com
Recommended in Tax

Practice Areas: Former Chair, Tax Practice. Experienced tax practitioner representing clients in corporate organizations, reorganizations, mergers, acquisitions, bankruptcy reorganizations, restructurings, e-commerce, international, partnership formations, transactions and roll-ups, REITs, REMICs, real estate planning, state tax planning, and tax controversies.
Prof. Memberships: American Bar Association - Tax Section (Real Estate Committee); State Bar of Texas - Tax Section; Dallas Bar Association - Tax Section.
Career: Admitted, State Bar of Texas. Board Certified, Taxation, Texas Board of Legal Specialization.
Personal: Southern Methodist University, JD, cum laude, 1977. University of Texas, BBA, accounting, 1974. Former Adjunct Professor, real estate tax planning, SMU Law School.

HESTER, Tracy
Bracewell & Giuliani LLP, Houston
713 221 1407
tracy.hester@bracewellgiuliani.com
Recommended in Environment

Practice Areas: Counsel on environmental civil and criminal enforcement defense, permitting, cost recovery litigation, environmental aspects of corporate transactions, emergency response planning, and security assurance legal requirements. Industrial clients include petrochemicals, petroleum and natural gas pipelines, refineries, local governments, emerging technologies, renewable energy providers and financial institutions.
Career: Elected to American Law Institute; past Chair of Houston Bar Association Environmental Section; Vice-Chair, American Bar Association SEER Environmental Enforcement and Crimes Committee. Adjunct Professor, University of Houston Law Center.
Personal: JD, Stone Scholar, Columbia University, 1986; BA, Plan II Honors Program, The University of Texas at Austin, 1983.

HEWITT, Lester
Akin Gump Strauss Hauer & Feld LLP,
Houston 713 220 5800
lhewitt@akingump.com
Recommended in Intellectual Property

Practice Areas: Co-Chair, firmwide Intellectual Property Practice. Has served as lead counsel in numerous complex lawsuits, including proceedings related to patents and trademarks. Counsels clients on broad range of IP issues in antitrust law. Often involved in patent/antitrust issues in litigation, e.g., standard-setting, patent and antitrust cases.
Prof. Memberships: Past President, Houston Intellectual Property Law Association; past Secretary, board member, Houston Bar Association; former Director, State Bar of Texas and Texas Young Lawyers Association; American Intellectual Property Law Association; American Bar Association, Intellectual Property Law Section; 'Best Lawyers in America,' 2001-present.
Personal: BS (Mechanical Engineering) and JD, University of Houston.

HIGGINS, Roger
Thompson, Coe, Cousins & Irons, LLP,
Dallas 214 871 8256
rhiggins@thompsoncoe.com
Recommended in Insurance

Practice Areas: Representation on broad range of insurance related matters; regulatory, coverage and extra-contractual litigation and exposure.
Prof. Memberships: Admitted to practice in Illinois and Texas, a Member of the State Bar of Texas, the American and the Dallas Bar Associations.
Career: An experienced trial and appellate attorney, he has served as lead counsel in numerous high profile class action and regulatory matters. He is board certified in both Civil Trial and Civil Appellate Law by the Texas Board of Legal Specialization. Frequent contributor to the 'Texas Insurance Law Reporter' and speaker at seminars for both insurance representatives and attorneys.

HIGH Jr, Charles
Kemp Smith LLP, El Paso
915 533 4424
Recommended in Employment

HILGERS, David
Brown McCarroll LLP, Austin
512 472 5456
Recommended in Healthcare

HILLIARD, Michael
Winstead Sechrest & Minick P.C.,
Dallas 214 745 5843
mhilliard@winstead.com
Recommended in Banking & Finance

Practice Areas: Former Chair, Banking and Credit Transactions. His experience covers the full range of financial institution and lender representation, with emphasis on complex lending and debt placement transactions, debt restructuring, workouts, leveraged leasing, and project finance across a wide spectrum

of industries. His experience includes energy sector lending, maritime financings, asset-based lending, asset and loan portfolio sales, trust indenture matters, real estate auctions, and mezzanine financings.
Career: Licensed in Texas, New York and Missouri; Fellow, American College of Investment Counsel and American College of Commercial Finance Lawyers.
Personal: University of Notre Dame, JD, 1972. St. Louis University, BA, 1969.

HITT, Jeffrey
Weil, Gotshal & Manges LLP, Dallas
214 746 7702
jeffrey.hitt@weil.com
Recommended in Corporate/M&A

Practice Areas: Mr Hitt's practice focuses primarily on private equity, mergers and acquisitions, and securities matters.
Career: His range of corporate and transactional experience includes representation of private equity firms and their portfolio clients with public and private acquisitions, divestitures, and recapitalization transactions; representation of issuers in public and private placements of debt and equity; and representation of fund sponsors with the formation of private equity and other pooled investment vehicles. Representative clients include Hicks, Muse, Tate & Furst, Ewing Management, Activant Solutions, Southwest Sports, and Lehman Brothers.
Personal: Boston University School of Law (JD, 1988); Colgate University (BA, 1985).

HOLLYFIELD, John S
Fulbright & Jaworski L.L.P., Houston
713 651 3717
jhollyfield@fulbright.com
Recommended in Real Estate

Practice Areas: Real estate law.
Prof. Memberships: Mr Hollyfield is included in multiple leading legal US publications. He is a Member of the Houston Bar Association, where he was a past Chair of the Real Estate Law Section; the American Bar Association, where he is a past Chair of Real Property, Probate and Trust Law Section; the State Bar of Texas; a past President of the American College of Real Estate Lawyers; and past President of the Anglo-American Real Property Institute. He is a former Member of the House of Delegates of the American Bar Association.
Career: Mr Hollyfield focuses his legal practice on real estate matters, including mortgage lending, leasing (landlord and tenant), real estate development, construction (owner, contractor, lender and architect), sale and purchase of raw land, commercial and industrial properties, real estate brokerage and management, joint venture partnerships, mortgage foreclosures and loan workouts.
Personal: Mr Hollyfield received a BBA in 1961 and an LLB, with honors, in 1968 from The University of Texas.

HOOPER, Samuel E
Neel & Hooper, P.C., Houston
713 629 1800
shooper@neelhooper.com
Recommended in Employment

Practice Areas: Represents management in labor and employment law matters before administrative agencies as well as state and federal courts.
Career: Mr Hooper has defended Title VII class actions as well as individual discrimination and wrongful termination actions in the trial court and in appeals. He has also litigated administrative claims before the NLRB and DOL brought under the NLRA, OSHA, ERA and Sarbanes-Oxley Act.
Personal: JD from the University of Oklahoma College of Law, 1967; Order of Coif; contributing editor, 'Oklahoma Law Review'; BBA, University of Oklahoma, 1964; Board Certified (Labor and Employment) Texas Board of Legal Specialization, 1975-2005.

HOPSON, Keith
Brown McCarroll LLP, Austin
512 472 5456
Recommended in Environment

HOWARD, Jr, John L
Vinson & Elkins LLP, Austin
512 542 8564
jhoward@velaw.com
Recommended in Environment

Practice Areas: State and federal environmental, natural resource and energy matters, including complex public policy and legislation. Has represented major corporations, associations, and local governments.
Career: Partner since 2004; Federal Environmental Executive (appointed by President Bush, 2002-04); Senior Associate Director, White House Council on Environmental Quality (2001-02); Bush-Cheney Environmental Transition Team Director (2000-01); Environment and Natural Resources Policy Director to Governor Bush (1996-2000).
Publications: Has lectured and written extensively on environmental policy.
Personal: University of Texas School of Law (JD, 1988, Texas Law Review); Baylor University (BA, 1985, Phi Beta Kappa).

HOWELL, John
Hughes & Luce LLP, Dallas
214 939 5500
Recommended in Business Process Outsourcing: National, Communications, Technology

HOYT, Scott
Gibson, Dunn & Crutcher LLP, Dallas
214 698 3265
shoyt@gibsondunn.com
Recommended in Insurance

Practice Areas: Commercial litigation, focus on insurance, telecommunications, accounting malpractice defense, and products liability defense. Experience defending environmental, asbestos bodily injury/property damage, defective products, advertising and intellectual property coverage cases and insurance bad faith cases. Fluent in Spanish and has developed an expertise in defending Mexican companies in cases involving Mexican law.

Prof. Memberships: State Bars of Texas and California, J Reuben Clark Law Society.

Publications: Numerous articles in Mealey's Litigation, Insurance Reports, Insurance Journals.

Personal: JD, University of California Hastings College of Law, 1983, Order of the Coif and Hastings Law Review; California Supreme Court Law Clerk.

HUDDLESTON, Michael
Shannon, Gracey, Ratliff & Miller LLP, Dallas 214 245 3090
Recommended in Insurance

HUFFMAN, Gregory
Thompson & Knight LLP, Dallas
214 969 1144
gregory.huffman@tklaw.com
Recommended in Antitrust

Practice Areas: Mr Huffman is experienced in commercial and antitrust litigation. He has tried numerous cases and has been the drafter of a Congressional statute amending the Sherman Act. He was listed in Texas Lawyer's Go-To Guide as one of the state's top litigators and was selected for inclusion in the Texas Monthly's 2004 listing of the top 100 Texas Super Lawyers.

Prof. Memberships: State Bar of Texas, Dallas Bar Association, Texas and Dallas Bar Foundations.

Career: Partner since 1980.

Publications: Mr Huffman is an active author and speaker.

Personal: Harvard Law School (JD, 1973); Stanford University (BA, 1969).

HULL, Robert J
Bracewell & Giuliani LLP, Houston
713 221 1589
joe.hull@bracewellgiuliani.com
Recommended in Tax

Practice Areas: Has represented clients in diverse industries, including real estate (development and finance, syndications and REITs); oil and gas, financial, aerospace, equipment leasing, high tech and telecommunications. Expertise includes partnerships and limited liability companies; business planning and formation, acquisitions and reorganizations; and executive compensation. Has handled matters of corporate income and franchise taxes, including unitary, allocation and apportionment issues; property taxes; sales and use taxes; city taxes; utility taxes; environmental taxes; transfer taxes; and unclaimed property and escheat laws.

Personal: JD, The University of Texas School of Law, 1969; BA, The University of Texas at Austin, 1966.

IRVIN, Michael P
Fulbright & Jaworski L.L.P., Houston
713 651 3705
mirvin@fulbright.com
Recommended in Energy

Practice Areas: Oil, gas and energy transactions, project finance, real estate.

Prof. Memberships: Mr Irvin is a member of the Houston and American Bar Associations and the State Bar of Texas. While in law school, he was editor in chief of the 'Houston Law Review' and a member of Phi Delta Phi.

Career: Mr Irvin heads the firm's Energy and Real Property Department. His practice focuses on domestic and international oil, gas and energy transactions related to the acquisition and disposition of oil and gas exploration and producing properties, pipelines, gas processing plants, petrochemical facilities and oil and gas companies, whether accomplished through asset or stock acquisitions; the exploration, development, project finance, construction and operation of oil and gas properties, pipelines, gas processing plants, petrochemical and LNG facilities or projects; joint ventures, partnerships and other joint ownership or participation arrangements in the energy area; mortgage and asset based financing relating to oil, gas and petrochemical related properties, pipelines, plants and other assets; and other areas of oil and gas practice, including production sales, storage, processing and transportation agreements.

Personal: Mr Irvin received a BA in 1972 from The University of Texas and a JD in 1975 from the University of Houston.

ISRAEL, Sharon
Jenkens & Gilchrist, Houston
713 951 3300
Recommended in Intellectual Property

JACOBS, Stephen C
Locke Liddell & Sapp LLP, Houston
713 226 1382
sjacobs@lockeliddell.com
Recommended in Real Estate

Practice Areas: Partner practicing in real estate and business organizations. Experience in the representation of developers and those involved in acquisition programs, including foreign nationals; transactional experience involving all types of income producing properties including representation of owners and developers of office buildings, retail facilities, hotels, resort properties, residential developments and multi-family developments; representation of landlords and tenants in negotiation of leases and telecommunications companies in connection with roof top and raceway facilities; involvement in public/private financing of projects; representation of sports franchises in facilities leasing and development as well as related naming rights; representation of

civic facilities operating companies in facilities management contracts with governmental authorities.

Prof. Memberships: Member, State Bar of Texas.

JANSONIUS, John V
Akin Gump Strauss Hauer & Feld LLP, Dallas 214 969 4770
jjansonius@akingump.com
Recommended in Employment

Practice Areas: Board Certified in Labor and Employment Law, Texas Board of Legal Specialization. Defends employment discrimination claims, wrongful discharge claims, unfair labor practice claims under National Labor Relations Act, plan administration and denial of benefits claims under Employee Retirement Income Security Act, and collective and individual actions under Fair Labor Standards Act. Has represented the defense in jury and non-jury trials in state/federal court and presented oral arguments to US Supreme Court and several federal courts of appeals.

Prof. Memberships: Chair, Labor and Employment Law Section, State Bar of Texas, 2004-05.

Personal: BA, Drake University; JD, Southern Methodist University.

JENKINS, Steve
Haynes and Boone LLP, Dallas
214 651 5000
Recommended in Real Estate

JERNIGAN, Stacey
Haynes and Boone LLP, Dallas
214 651 5000
Recommended in Bankruptcy

JEWELL, Robert V
Andrews Kurth LLP, Houston
713 220 4358
bjewell@andrewskurth.com
Recommended in Communications, Corporate/M&A, Technology

Practice Areas: All areas of corporate and securities law, including representation of issuers and underwriters in public and private offerings of equity and debt securities in a variety of industries, mergers and acquisitions, both domestic and foreign, the negotiation and structuring of various corporate and partnership debt financings and corporate governance. Particular experience relating to energy services, real estate investment trusts, the forest products industry and special committees of boards of directors.

Prof. Memberships: The State Bar of Texas, Member, Corporation Law Committee of the Corporation, Banking and Business Law Section; Texas Business Law Foundation; Houston Bar Association.

Career: Admitted to the State Bar of Texas in 1978. Entire career with Andrews Kurth, Partner since 1986.

Personal: Received a JD from Southern Methodist University School of Law in 1978. Editor, 'Southwestern Law Journal'. Received a BBA in Finance from The University of Texas in 1975.

JOHN, Philip
Baker Botts LLP, Houston
713 229 1215
Philip.john@bakerbotts.com
Recommended in Antitrust

Practice Areas: Mr John has a diverse Commercial Litigation Practice. He has headed litigation efforts for clients involved in prosecuting or defending hostile acquisition attempts and has successfully defended a number of class action suits. He also represents clients before the Securities and Exchange Commission. He has tried a number of lawsuits to a jury verdict, including antitrust claims.

Prof. Memberships: State Bar of Texas; Houston Bar Association.

Personal: JD (with honors), The University of Texas School of Law, 1967, Order of the Coif, Chancellors, associate editor of Texas Law Review; BA (with honors), The University of Texas, 1965.

JOHNSTONE, Debbi M
Vinson & Elkins LLP, Houston
713 758 3420
djohnstone@velaw.com
Recommended in Healthcare

Practice Areas: Specializes in representation of healthcare entities on transactional and regulatory matters, and third party reimbursement, including coverage and payment under Medicare and Medicaid, anti-kickback, physician self-referral, false claims, and civil monetary penalties.

Prof. Memberships: American Health Lawyers Association; ABA, Health Law Section; Houston Bar Association, Health Law Section (Chair 2004-05); Healthcare Financial Management Association.

Career: Admitted to practice: Indiana, 1980; Texas, 1982; Board Certified in Health Law by the Texas Board of Legal Specialization.

Publications: Various articles on health law issues.

Personal: Northwestern University, BA, 1977; Indiana University School of Law, JD, cum laude, 1980.

JONES, Frank G
Fulbright & Jaworski L.L.P., Houston
713 651 5473
fjones@fulbright.com
Recommended in Litigation

Practice Areas: Mr Jones has tried over 100 jury cases and has particular experience in product liability, securities, construction, and professional liability litigation.

Prof. Memberships: Mr Jones has been certified in Civil Trial Law by the Texas Board of Legal Specialization, elected to membership in the American College of Trial Lawyers, the American Board of Trial Advocates and the International Academy of Trial Lawyers, and is a member of The Chartered Institute of Arbitrators.

Career: Mr Jones has been a Partner in

the Houston office of Fulbright & Jaworski L.L.P. since 1974, and is Co-Partner-In-Charge of the Houston office.

Personal: BS, History, Rice University (1963); LLB, The University of Texas (1966).

JORDAN, Carey
Baker Botts LLP, Houston
713 229 1233
carey.jordan@bakerbotts.com
Recommended in Intellectual Property

Practice Areas: Has particular expertise in advising clients on effectively creating and managing patent portfolios to protect valuable technology, aggressively asserting patent rights when appropriate, and recognizing competitive advantages and licensing opportunities. Often provides counsel on conducting research programs that involve competitive intelligence. Experienced with technologies including developments in the downstream energy industry and all facets of oil and gas exploration and production; chemical refining processes such as catalysis and polymerization; alternative fuel technologies such as fuel cells; and products like films, laminates, paints, carpets, diapers, and other personal care products. Also works on prosecution and litigation involving business methods.

JORDAN, Carl
Vinson & Elkins LLP, Houston
713 758 2258
cjordan@velaw.com
Recommended in Employment

Practice Areas: Practice focuses on representing management in labor, ERISA, and employment-related trial work and counseling. Certified in labor and employment law by the Texas Board of Legal Specialization.
Prof. Memberships: Member: Labor and Employment Section and Section's Committee on Equal Employment Opportunity Law, American Bar Association. General Counsel: Texas Employment Law Council. Fellow: American College of Labor and Employment Lawyers.
Career: Admitted to practice: Texas, 1974. Joined Vinson & Elkins, 1974; admitted to partnership, 1981.
Personal: Baylor University, BA, 1971; Harvard Law School, JD, 1974.

JURGENSMEYER, Randy R
Vinson & Elkins LLP, Dallas
214 220 7790
rjurgensmeyer@velaw.com
Recommended in Real Estate

Practice Areas: Practice areas include business and finance, concentrating on real estate transactions. Randy has extensive involvement representing private equity funds, investors and REITs in forming joint ventures and strategic alliances and acquiring, selling, developing, financing, restructuring and leasing shopping centers, office buildings,

hotels, industrial parks and apartment complexes.
Prof. Memberships: American Bar Association; Texas Bar Association; Dallas Bar Association.
Career: Admitted Texas Bar in 1985. Came to the firm as Partner in 1996.
Personal: Graduated from University of Missouri, BA magna cum laude, 1982; and Southern Methodist University School of Law, JD, 1985. Member of Phi Beta Kappa.

KAIM, Henry
Bracewell & Giuliani LLP, Houston
713 221 1204
henry.kaim@bracewellgiuliani.com
Recommended in Bankruptcy

Practice Areas: Heads Bankruptcy Section of Bracewell & Giuliani. Experienced in all aspects of Chapter 11 reorganizations, including negotiation of complex plans of reorganization and the litigation of contested matters and adversary proceedings. For 27 years, has represented Chapter 11 debtors in possession, creditors quote committees, secured creditors, and landlords and acquirers in bankruptcy in a variety of industries in major Chapter 11 cases nationwide.
Prof. Memberships: Fellow, American College of Bankruptcy.
Career: Teaches Chapter 11 bankruptcy at University of Houston Law Center as an Adjunct Professor.
Personal: JD, University of Houston Law Center, 1977; BA, Southern Methodist University, 1974.

KALTEYER, Ronald
Locke Liddell & Sapp LLP, Dallas
214 740 8771
rkalteyer@lockeliddell.com
Recommended in Tax

Practice Areas: Partner in the firm's Business Tax Section. Practice focuses on partnership tax planning and corporate tax planning, with a specialty in the taxation of REITs and the taxation of workouts and bankruptcies.
Prof. Memberships: American Bar Association Section of Taxation (Partnership Committee: Co-Chairman of Subcommittee on UPREIT Partnerships; former Chairman of Subcommittee on Workouts). American Bar Association Real Property, Probate and Trust Section (Vice-Chairman of the Real Estate Investment Trust Committee).
Career: Admitted to Texas Bar (1979). Law clerk to Judge Homer Thornberry of the United States Court of Appeals for the Fifth Circuit (1980). A Partner of Locke Liddell & Sapp since joining the firm in 1994.
Publications: Co-author of the treatise entitled 'Federal Tax Aspects of Cancellation of Indebtedness and Foreclosures'.
Personal: Received a JD (1979), MPA (Taxation) (1977) and BBA (Accounting) (1975) from the University of Texas.

KATZ, M Marvin
Mayer, Brown, Rowe & Maw LLP, Houston 713 546 0513
mkatz@mayerbrownrowe.com
Recommended in Real Estate

Practice Areas: Real estate, estate planning, probate, corporate.
Prof. Memberships: Admitted in Texas, 1958. US District Court for the Southern District of Texas, 1959. US Court of Appeals for the Fifth Circuit, 1961. US Supreme Court, 1972. American College of Real Estate Lawyers. Real Estate Roundtable. Board Certified, Commercial Real Estate Law, Texas Board of Legal Specialization; former Adjunct Professor of Law, University of Houston School of Law, Real Estate Transfers and Finance; City of Houston Planning Commission from 1980 to present (served as Chairman from 1991-2005 and as Vice-Chairman from 1984-91).
Career: Joined Mayer, Brown, Rowe & Maw LLP as partner, 1989. De Lange, Hudspeth, Pitman & Katz, Houston, 1959-89. United States Air Force, 1955-57.
Personal: Born 12 May 1935. University of Texas School of Law, LLB with honors, 1959; Order of the Coif; Article Editor, 'Texas Law Review'. Texas A&M University, BBA, 1954. Speaks Spanish.

KEANE, Jennifer
Baker Botts LLP, Austin
512 322 2594
jennifer.keane@bakerbotts.com
Recommended in Environment

Practice Areas: Practice focuses on the regulatory aspects of environmental law, particularly Clean Air Act issues. Counsels industrial clients throughout the United States on permitting, enforcement, and compliance matters, and participates in state and federal rulemakings aimed at establishing equitable environmental standards for industry.
Career: Admitted to Texas Bar, 1990. Baker Botts Partner since 1999.
Personal: JD (with honors), The University of Texas School of Law (1989), Order of the Coif, Phi Delta Phi; MS, BS, BA, University of South Carolina (1986, 1984).

KEITHLEY, Brad
Jones Day, Dallas
214 969 2920
bgkeithley@jonesday.com
Recommended in Energy

Practice Areas: Co-heads the firm's Oil and Gas Practice Team. His litigation and regulatory practice concentrates on matters affecting companies involved in the oil and natural gas industry. Additionally, he has been responsible for structuring a broad range of complex industry-related commercial transactions. For the past five years, he has been extensively engaged in litigation and regulatory matters related to the Alaska North Slope. He speaks frequently on industry matters and appears regularly before federal and state commissions, appeals boards, and courts.

Prof. Memberships: ABA; Virginia State Bar; Oklahoma Bar Association; District of Columbia Bar; Energy Bar Association.

KELLER, Mary
York, Keller & Field, Austin
512 867 1616
Recommended in Insurance

KELLEY, Jay D
Vinson & Elkins LLP, Houston
713 758 4838
jkelley@velaw.com
Recommended in Energy, Projects

Practice Areas: Commercial practice, with an emphasis on project development and finance in the energy sector, particularly gas fired and renewable power projects and LNG liquefication and receiving projects.
Prof. Memberships: Member: State Bar of Texas, New York State Bar Association, International Bar Association, and College of the State Bar of Texas.
Career: Admitted to practice law in Texas (1985) and New York (1995).
Personal: Graduated from The University of Texas, BBA (Accounting) in 1981, and the University of Houston, JD summa cum laude in 1985.

KELLEY, Kevin
Gardere Wynne Sewell LLP, Dallas
214 999 4503
kkelley@gardere.com
Recommended in Real Estate

Practice Areas: Diverse commercial real estate practice advising owners, investors, developers, landlords and lenders, both domestic and foreign. Types of projects include resort properties, hotels, golf courses, office and industrial buildings, and retail and multi-family projects.
Career: Heads Gardere's Real Estate Practice; member of Gardere's Partners' Board. Clients range from Fortune 500 companies, institutional lenders, equity funds and REITS, to private businesses and individuals.
Personal: JD, St. Mary's University School of Law, 1985; Articles Editor, St. Mary's Law Journal; BBA, Texas Christian University, with honors, 1981.

KELLY, Mark T
Vinson & Elkins LLP, Houston
713 758 4592
mkelly@velaw.com
Recommended in Corporate/M&A

Practice Areas: Partner and Co-Chair of the firm's Corporate Practice and a member of the firm's Management Committee. Practice focuses on mergers and acquisitions and public and private offerings. Serves as principal outside counsel to several public and private companies in the exploration and production, oilfield service, insurance and manufacturing industries, and also represents a number of major investment banks. Extensive experience in merger and acquisition transactions, representing clients in transactions totaling over

$6 billion in the last two years. Has represented clients in over 100 domestic and cross-border debt and equity offerings since 2000. Recognized as one of 12 corporate lawyers in the United States as Dealmaker of the Year for 2003 by a leading legal publication. Also listed: Texas Lawyer "Go To" Lawyer in corporate law, 2002-04; Texas Monthly's Top 100 Lawyers, 2003-04.
Career: Joined Vinson & Elkins in May 1981 and admitted to partnership in January 1989. Past Chair, Houston Bar Foundation; past President, Houston Young Lawyers Association; past Director, Texas Young Lawyers Association; past Vice-Chair, Center for Hearing and Speech.
Personal: Graduated magna cum laude from Texas A&M University in 1978 (BBA) and Southern Methodist University in 1981 (JD). Editor of SMU Law Review.

KENNEDY, John
Vinson & Elkins LLP, Houston
713 758 2550
jkennedy@velaw.com
Recommended in Energy
Practice Areas: Practice consists primarily of representing oil pipelines in proceedings before the Federal Energy Regulatory Commission and state commissions and appeals from decisions of these commissions, providing regulatory advice to oil pipelines, and providing regulatory advice in connection with acquisitions of oil pipelines.
Prof. Memberships: Member: Federal Energy Bar Association.
Personal: Graduated from Harvard College, AB cum laude in 1968; Harvard Law School, JD magna cum laude in 1971.

KEYES, David
Vinson & Elkins LLP, Houston
713 758 2418
dkeyes@velaw.com
Recommended in Banking & Finance
Practice Areas: Structured, secured and commercial finance; Uniform Commercial Code; bank-payments systems. Clients include large banks, corporations and clearing-house organizations.
Prof. Memberships: ABA, State Bar of Texas, Houston Bar Association (Fellow in each). Chairman of State Bar Business Law Section Legal Opinions Committee.
Career: Admitted to Texas Bar in 1968. Joined the firm in 1969 and admitted to Partner in 1975.
Publications: Articles on legal opinions, secured transactions, and conflicts of law.
Personal: Graduated from Princeton University, 1965 and The University of Texas Law School with high honors, 1968.

KIMBALL, Albert
Bracewell & Giuliani LLP, Houston
713 223 2900
albert.kimball@bracewellgiuliani.com
Recommended in Intellectual Property
Practice Areas: Represents US and multinational clients in IP litigation, and in acquiring and transferring rights in IP and technology. Has participated on

behalf of an international company entering US operations in the transfer of IP rights required for US operations of a petroleum refinery.
Prof. Memberships: Presently serving as elected officer of local IP Bar association; previously served as member of Council of the IP Law Section of the American Bar Association.
Personal: LLM, The George Washington University Law School, 1972; LLB, The University of Texas at Austin, 1968; BSEE, The University of Texas at Austin, 1962.

KING, Chad
Hughes & Luce LLP, Dallas
214 939 5500
Recommended in Communications, Technology

KINZIE, Jack L
Baker Botts LLP, Dallas
214 953 6727
jack.kinzie@bakerbotts.com
Recommended in Bankruptcy
Practice Areas: Partner in Charge of Dallas Office; Chair: Bankruptcy Section (firmwide). Represents a diverse range of institutional lenders, asset acquirers, creditors, debtors, officers and directors, and parent companies in virtually every aspect of complex Chapter 11 cases, as well as out-of-court workouts. He has particular experience in prepackaged mass tort bankruptcies.
Career: Prior to joining Baker Botts in 1988, he worked for an Oklahoma City law firm and previously served as Adjunct Professor of oil and gas law at Oklahoma City University.
Personal: JD, University of Oklahoma College of Law, 1975; BS, psychology, Oklahoma State University, 1971.

KIRKLAND, David
Baker Botts LLP, Houston
713 229 1101
david.kirkland@bakerbotts.com
Recommended in Corporate/M&A
Practice Areas: Chair: Corporate Department (firmwide); Member: Executive Committee. Concentrates on mergers and acquisitions, securities offerings and corporate control and governance issues. Represents parties and investment bankers in mergers and acquisitions, including negotiated acquisitions and dispositions, controlled auctions, tender offers and related financings. Involved in many of the largest mergers in the oilfield service sector and participates in numerous contested takeovers and proxy fights. Represents issuers, underwriters and shareholders in registered public offerings, Rule 144A transactions and private placements.
Personal: JD, Yale Law School, 1983; BA, summa cum laude, economics, Yale College, 1980.

KNOLL, Susan
Howrey Simon Arnold & White, Houston
713 787 1400
Recommended in Intellectual Property

KNULL III, William H
Mayer, Brown, Rowe & Maw LLP, Houston 713 546 0528
wknull@mayerbrownrowe.com
Recommended in Litigation
Practice Areas: Extensive experience in transnational disputes involving oil and gas, mergers and acquisitions, contracts, corporate, lending practices, governance; ICC, AAA, NASD, ICDR and UNCITRAL arbitrations. Lead counsel in multi-billion dollar disputes in Central Asian, domestic and Chinese oil and gas projects.
Prof. Memberships: LCIA. Advisory Board, Institute of Transnational Arbitration. Member, Chartered Institute of Arbitrators. Fellow, Center for International Legal Studies.
Career: Joined Mayer, Brown, Rowe & Maw LLP, Houston, 1986; Partner 1987. Sullivan & Cromwell, New York, 1977-86. US Navy, 1970-74.
Publications: 'Bridas v. Turkmenistan: A Case Study in Arbitration as an Instrument of Risk Management,' presented at Managing Risk - Dispute Avoidance & Resolution, London, April 2004'; Betting the Farm on International Arbitration: Is it Time to Offer an Appeal Option?' 11 Am. Rev. Int'l. Arb. 531 (2002). 'Uncertainty in the Courts: Split in US Appellate Courts on Expanded Judicial Review by Agreement of Parties' presented at Barriers to Free Movement of Civil Justice, CILS, Salzburg, Austria, November 2001.
Personal: University of Virginia, JD, 1977; Order of the Coif; Virginia Law Review, Member, 1975-77; Notes Editor, 1976-77. Yale University, BA, magna cum laude, 1970; Departmental Honors in Political Science.

KORBY, Mary
Weil, Gotshal & Manges LLP, Dallas
214 746 7864
mary.korby@weil.com
Recommended in Corporate/M&A
Practice Areas: Ms Korby focuses on mergers and acquisitions, including complex cross-border public and private transactions, and she represents private equity investors in acquisitions, dispositions and public and private debt and equity offerings. She also advises in restructurings and acquisitions relating to companies in bankruptcy.
Career: Ms Korby's mergers and acquisitions practice involves diverse industries such as offshore exploration and production, chemicals, aviation and manufacturing. She represented Millennium Chemicals in its $3.6 billion stock-for-stock disposition to Lyondell Chemicals, American Airlines in its acquisition of TWA, Enron in the $3 billion disposition of its online energy trading business and in its $300 million disposition of Mariner Energy. She acted as senior advisor to Enron in the disposition of numerous other domestic and foreign businesses in connection with its bank-

ruptcy, both through bankruptcy court procedures and in out-of-court transactions. Ms Korby is named in the 2004 'Who's Who of Corporate Governance Lawyers' and has been notified that she will be included in the 2005-2006 edition of 'The Best Lawyers in America'.
Personal: Southern Methodist University School of Law, JD; Baylor University, BA.

KREBS, Arno
Fulbright & Jaworski L.L.P., Houston
713 651 5522
akrebs@fulbright.com
Recommended in Insurance
Practice Areas: Extracontractual liability and insurance coverage.
Prof. Memberships: Listed in a leading legal US publication. Member of the Houston, State Bar of Texas, and the American Board of Trial Advocates.
Career: Admitted to Texas Bar (1967). Admitted to the United States Court of Appeals for the Fifth and Eleventh Circuits. Partner in Fulbright & Jaworski L.L.P.'s Houston office.
Personal: Received a BA (1964) from Texas A&M University and an LLB (1967) from the University of Texas.

KREBS, Stephen
Baker Botts LLP, Houston
713 229 1467
stephen.krebs@bakerbotts.com
Recommended in Projects
Practice Areas: Practice focuses on representation of sponsors and lenders in infrastructure projects and financings. He has broad expertise in capital market, bank, lease, and private placement financings involving power plants, petrochemical and LNG facilities, refineries, drilling rigs, drillships, FPSOs, pipelines, and oil and gas projects. He advises clients on risk allocation and structuring arrangements.
Prof. Memberships: State Bar of Texas, Commercial Financial Services Committee; State Bar of Georgia; American Bar Association.
Career: Head of firm's Project Finance Practice.
Personal: JD, cum laude, from the University of Georgia School of Law, 1985; BS from the Georgia Institute of Technology, 1978.

KRIEGER, Paul
Fulbright & Jaworski L.L.P., Houston
713 651 5167
pkrieger@fulbright.com
Recommended in Intellectual Property
Practice Areas: Intellectual property, litigation, and licensing.
Prof. Memberships: Mr Krieger is a Life Fellow of the American Bar Foundation, the Houston Bar Foundation, and the Texas Bar Foundation. He also serves as a Member of the American Bar Association, the American Intellectual Property Law Association, the International Association of Defense Counsel, and the State Bar of Texas.
Career: As a Partner in the Houston

office of Fulbright & Jaworski L.L.P, Mr Krieger heads the Intellectual Property and Technology Department. He also mentors students at the University of Houston Law Center where he has taught trademark and trade secret law courses for 20 years. Mr Krieger has been recognized by 'Who's Who in American Law', 'Who's Who in America', and 'Who's Who in the World'.
Personal: BS, University of Pittsburgh (1964); LLB, University of Maryland (1968); LLM, George Washington University (1971). Mr Krieger was admitted to practice law in Texas in 1980.

KRIESER, Jason D
Jones Day, Dallas 214 969 4865
jdkrieser@jonesday.com
Recommended in Communications, Technology
Practice Areas: Represents companies in technology transactions and general corporate matters. These technology transactions include information technology outsourcing, business process outsourcing, licensing, distribution arrangements for software and hardware, joint ventures, strategic alliances, and technology service arrangements. The general corporate matters include mergers and acquisitions and corporate finance matters. He also represents clients in IP asset transfers and evaluations of IP rights portfolios. He counsels clients on day-to-day operational issues relating to general corporate and technology matters, such as advice on strategic customer and supplier relationships, privacy issues, data security issues, product distribution channels, software development, and software implementation.

KRUSE, Layne
Fulbright & Jaworski L.L.P., Houston
713 651 5194
lkruse@fulbright.com
Recommended in Antitrust
Practice Areas: Antitrust, marketing and trade regulation; securities litigation; international litigation and arbitration; intellectual property litigation; class actions and government investigations; and energy.
Prof. Memberships: Board Certified in Civil Trial Law, Texas Board of Legal Specialization; Member of ABA Antitrust and Litigation Sections; Chair, ABA Antitrust Section Fuel and Energy Committee; former Chair Ethics and Professional Responsibility Committee and Exemption and Immunities Committee; Former Chair, Antitrust and Business Litigation Section, Texas State Bar; Former President, Texas Association of Civil Trial Specialists.
Career: Partner since 1986. Former judicial clerk, Chief Judge John Brown, US Court of Appeals, Fifth Circuit. Co-Chair of firm Antitrust, Marketing and Trade Regulation Practice Group; Member of Firm Policy Committee.
Personal: JD, Yale Law School (1977);

MSc, London School of Economics (1974); BA (Economics), Texas A&M University (1973).

KUDLAC, Kevin
Dewey Ballantine LLP, Austin
512 226 0600
kkudlac@deweyballantine.com
Recommended in Intellectual Property
Practice Areas: Mr Kudlac's practice is dedicated primarily to intellectual property litigation and is primarily focused on semiconductor, computer, and software technologies. He has handled such matters in the United States and around the world including London, Düsseldorf, Hong Kong, Taipei, and Beijing.
Prof. Memberships: State Bar of Georgia, State Bar of Texas, Austin Intellectual Property Law Association, American Bar Association, American Intellectual Property Law Association.
Career: Partner, Dewey Ballantine LLP.
Personal: Born November 7, 1965. BS, University of Dayton, 1987. JD, cum laude, Georgia State University College of Law, 1991.

KUHN, Michael
Jackson Walker LLP, Houston
713 752 4200
Recommended in Real Estate

KURYLA, Matthew
Baker Botts LLP, Houston
713 229 1114
matthew.kuryla@bakerbotts.com
Recommended in Environment
Practice Areas: Environmental regulatory litigation, compliance counseling, project authorization and permitting.
Prof. Memberships: State Bar of Texas, Houston Bar Association, Houston Bar Foundation (Fellow), Houston/Galveston Regional Air Quality Planning Committee, Greater Houston Partnership Environment Committee.
Career: JD, University of Virginia School of Law (1989), Executive Editor, Virginia Environmental Law Journal, BA (with highest distinction), University of Virginia (1986), Phi Beta Kappa, Named a 'Texas Rising Star' by 'Texas Monthly' and 'Law & Politics Magazine' (July 2004).
Personal: LifeHouse of Houston, Inc. (President).

KUTZSCHBACH, George
Fulbright & Jaworski L.L.P., Houston
713 651 3702
gkutzschbach@fulbright.com
Recommended in Energy
Practice Areas: Energy.
Prof. Memberships: Houston and American Bar Associations and the State Bar of Texas.
Career: He is a Partner in the firm's Houston office and Co-Chairman of the firm's Energy Practice Group. He focuses his practice on domestic and international transactions related to the exploration, acquisition, disposition, development and financing of (and joint ven-

ture, operational, transportation and marketing activities concerning) oil, gas, petrochemical and energy properties, pipelines, plants, refineries and other energy assets and companies.
Personal: He received a BBA in 1969 and a JD in 1972 from The University of Texas at Austin.

LAFOLLETTE, Christine B
Akin Gump Strauss Hauer & Feld LLP, Houston 713 220 5896
clafollette@akingump.com
Recommended in Corporate/M&A
Practice Areas: Represents issuers and underwriters in public offerings and private placements of equity and debt securities, restructurings and financings, including master limited partnerships, and federal and state securities laws matters. Represents clients in public and private M&A and disposition transactions, particularly in the energy industry. Has represented boards of directors in securities-related and corporate governance matters.
Prof. Memberships: Sustaining Fellow, Houston Bar Association and Chair, Corporate Counsel Section; Fellow, Texas Bar Foundation; Director, Houston World Affairs Council; Member, National Association of Corporate Directors (Houston Chapter).
Personal: BS (highest honors), University of Texas; JD (honors), Loyola University.

LAFUZE, William L
Vinson & Elkins LLP, Houston
713 758 2595
blafuze@velaw.com
Recommended in Intellectual Property
Practice Areas: Practices in most areas of intellectual property law, with emphasis on electronics, oilfield equipment, and computer-related patent litigation.
Prof. Memberships: Member: Patent Public Advisory Committee, United States Patent and Trademark Office. Chair: American Bar Association, Section of Intellectual Property Law. Former President: American Intellectual Property Law Association.
Career: Admitted to practice: Texas, 1973. Joined Vinson & Elkins, 1973; admitted to partnership, 1980.
Personal: The University of Texas, BS, 1969; Southern Methodist University, MS in Applied Science, 1971; The University of Texas School of Law, JD, 1973.

LANGLOIS, Jack J
Akin Gump Strauss Hauer & Feld LLP, Houston 713 220 5857
jlanglois@akingump.com
Recommended in Energy
Practice Areas: Focuses on domestic and international energy law. Is experienced in mergers, acquisitions, dispositions and privatizations of assets and stock of energy companies, joint ventures, investments in and financings of energy projects and acquisitions of exploration rights from sovereigns. Also

handles acquisitions and dispositions of interstate natural gas pipelines, gathering systems and other midstream assets, as well as power plants and other downstream assets. Is involved in North America, Russia, Latin America and Europe.
Personal: BA (honors), University of Southwestern Louisiana; JD, Louisiana State University.

LAWLESS, J Mark
Nickens Keeton Lawless Farrell & Flack LLP, Austin 512 472 3067
Recommended in Insurance

LEAHY, James R
Thompson & Knight LLP, Houston
713 951 5836
james.leahy@tklaw.com
Recommended in Litigation
Practice Areas: Mr Leahy has represented both plaintiffs and defendants in general civil litigation proceedings in both federal and state courts. He is experienced in representation of clients in all facets of the oil and gas industry, commercial and business disputes, lender liability, securities litigation, fraud, insurance, deceptive trade practices, and class actions.
Prof. Memberships: Member of the State Bar of Texas, Texas Bar Foundation, American College of Trial Lawyers, Houston Bar Association, American Bar Association, American Board of Trial Advocates.
Personal: University of Texas School of Law (JD, 1971); University of Texas at Austin (BBA, 1968).

LEE, Carl B
Akin Gump Strauss Hauer & Feld LLP, Dallas 214 969 2726
clee@akingump.com
Recommended in Real Estate
Practice Areas: Chair, firmwide Real Estate and Finance Practice and Chair, firmwide Hospitality Practice. Has extensive experience in real estate finance, including securitizations, portfolio financings, and workouts and restructurings, representing both lenders and borrowers. Has handled many significant acquisitions and dispositions of real estate, including portfolios of office buildings and hotels and sale/leasebacks.
Prof. Memberships: Texas Academy of Real Estate, Probate and Trust Lawyers; Real Estate Council; Real Estate Financial Executives Association; National Association of Real Estate Investment Trusts; Past President-Dallas Bar Association Real Property Section.
Personal: AB (cum laude), Harvard College; JD, University of Chicago (Order of the Coif).

LEE, James J
Vinson & Elkins LLP, Dallas
214 220 7744
jimlee@velaw.com
Recommended in Bankruptcy
Practice Areas: Complex commercial

and bankruptcy litigation. Board Certified in Civil Trial Law, Texas Board of Legal Specialization. Litigation experience includes creditors' rights, lender liability, securities fraud, class actions, and all forms of business torts. Has litigated a broad range of matters in large bankruptcy cases on behalf of secured lenders, debtors, creditors' committees, and trustees, including cash collateral, stay relief, lien priorities, substantive consolidation, plan confirmation, and avoidance actions.

Prof. Memberships: American Bar Association.

Career: Admitted to Texas Bar, 1976. Came to firm as Partner, 2000.

Personal: Tulane University, BA, 1973; University of Virginia School of Law, JD, 1976.

LEE, John
Andrews Kurth LLP, Houston
713 220 4260
jlee@andrewskurth.com
Recommended in Bankruptcy

Practice Areas: First chair trial litigation experience in virtually all types of state and federal court business and commercial litigation and arbitration, including energy, securities, tax, lender-liability, broker-dealer, fiduciary, partnership, oil and gas, unfair competition, trust indenture, and financial institution receiverships. He has successfully represented clients as lead counsel in contested litigation, arbitration, and bankruptcy matters involving more than $2 billion in controversy in the aggregate. First chair bankruptcy litigation practice primarily involves the representation of creditors and trustees in preference, insolvency, and fraudulent conveyance litigation, including claims against parties responsible for several recent high profile corporate failures. Rated by Martindale-Hubbell as 'AV' (highest rating for ethics and ability).

Prof. Memberships: The State Bar of Texas; licensed to practice in all Texas state courts and in the United States District Courts for the Southern, Northern, and Western Districts of Texas; Fifth Circuit Court of Appeals; Third Circuit Court of Appeals; Eleventh Circuit Court of Appeals,

Career: Admitted to the State Bar of Texas in 1985. Partner with Andrews Kurth since 1993.

Personal: Received a JD with high honors from The University of Texas School of Law in 1985. Named Grand Chancellor of the University of Texas Law School after having the highest GPA in his class. Scored the second-highest grade on the Texas Bar Examination. Received a BA with highest honors in accounting from The University of Texas in 1982.

LEE, William S
Fulbright & Jaworski L.L.P., Houston
713 651 5633
wlee@fulbright.com
Recommended in Litigation

Practice Areas: Tax, appellate courts, and settlement negotiations.

Career: Bill Lee has been a Partner since 1985 in Fulbright's Houston office. He concentrates his practice on all phases of federal tax controversy, including representation of individual taxpayers, partnerships, and corporations in a wide range of industries. Before joining Fulbright, Mr Lee practiced as a certified public accountant in the Tax Department of the Houston office of Arthur Andersen & Co.

Personal: BA - The University of Texas at Austin (1972); LLB - The University of Texas Law School (1975); LLM - Taxation, New York University School of Law (1979).

LIPE, Guy
Vinson & Elkins LLP, Houston
713 758 1109
glipe@velaw.com
Recommended in Energy

Practice Areas: Guy engages in a litigation and arbitration practice, primarily representing clients in the energy industry, with an emphasis on international litigation and arbitration. He has particular expertise in representing non-US parties sued in courts in the United States, in the handling of litigation matters involving foreign governments, and in compelling arbitration of disputes that are subject to arbitration under the Federal Arbitration Act and the Convention on the Recognition and Enforcement of Foreign Arbitral Awards.

Career: Partner since 1991.

Personal: Texas A&M University (BBA 1980); The University of Texas School of Law (JD 1983).

LONDA, Jeffrey C
Ogletree, Deakins, Nash, Smoak & Stewart, PC, Houston
713 655 5750
jeffrey.londa@ogletreedeakins.com
Recommended in Employment

Practice Areas: Labor and employment.

Prof. Memberships: Texas Association of Business (Chair, State Employment Relations Committee), American Arbitration Association (Panel of Arbitrators), American Public Transit Association Legal Affairs/13(c) Committee.

Career: Listed, 'The Best Lawyers in America'; Fellow, the College of Labor and Employment Lawyers. Adjunct professor at Thurgood Marshall School of Law, TSU.

Publications: Author, O'Connor's Texas Employment Codes Plus (Jones McClure Pub); author, O'Connor's Federal Employment Codes Plus (Jones McClure Pub); executive editor, Texas Labor Letter (1991-2000).

Personal: University of Texas at Austin (BA with honors, 1972), SMU (JD, 1975).

LOTT, Marley
Baker Botts LLP, Houston
713.229.1666
marley.lott@bakerbotts.com
Recommended in Real Estate

Practice Areas: Practice focus in commercial real estate transactions, with emphasis on structuring, development, leasing, and equity and debt financing. Ms Lott is a frequent speaker on a range of topics, including office leasing, usury, commercial leasing, and partnerships.

Prof. Memberships: Houston Bar Association; American Bar Association, Real Property, Probate and Trust Law Section; Contemporary Arts Museum of Houston, Board of Directors; Friends of Hermann Park, Executive Committee Member and Vice Chairman of Projects.

Career: Head of firm-wide Real Estate Practice.

Personal: JD (cum laude) from Harvard Law School in 1977; BA (with honors) from Hollins College in 1969.

LUKIN, Mitch
Baker Botts LLP, Houston
713 229 1733
mitch.lukin@bakerbotts.com
Recommended in Intellectual Property

Practice Areas: Primary expertise in intellectual property litigation, representing both plaintiffs and defendants. Counsels clients on intellectual property asset management, including implementation of protection programs, transaction due diligence, evaluation of intellectual property assets and minimization of litigation risks. Represents clients in licensing and other intellectual property transactions.

Personal: JD, with high honors, University of Houston Law Center, 1982; Bachelor of Electrical Engineering (1972) and MSEE (1976), Georgia Tech.

LYNCH, John
Howrey Simon Arnold & White, Houston
713 787 1400
Recommended in Intellectual Property

MALONEY, Marilyn
Liskow & Lewis, Houston
713 651 2900
Recommended in Banking & Finance

MANFORD III, Thomas D
Bracewell & Giuliani LLP, Houston
713 221 1303
tom.manford@bracewellgiuliani.com
Recommended in Communications, Technology

Practice Areas: Emphasizes acquisitions; mergers; private placements of securities; management and leveraged buy-out transactions; debt and equity financings; venture capital transactions; and negotiation and preparation of a broad variety of commercial agreements, including preparation of general and limited partnership agreements and limited liability company agreements. Has represented early-stage companies in connection with their organization,

structuring and seed and other private financings.

Career: Former Chairman, Venture Capital Committee, Business Law Section, State Bar of Texas and former Chairman, MIT Enterprise Forum of Texas.

Personal: JD, The University of Texas School of Law, 1970; BA, The University of Texas at Austin, 1966.

MANNE, Neal
Susman Godfrey LLP, Houston
713 651 9366
Recommended in Litigation

MANTHEY, Ron
Baker & McKenzie, Dallas
214 978 3030
Ron.Manthey@Bakernet.com
Recommended in Employment

Practice Areas: Employment litigation and advice and counseling on US employment laws, with special emphasis on Class Actions, Discrimination and Civil Rights, employment law torts, privacy, defamation, wage and hour disputes, and unfair competition. Represents management clients in trial and administative proceedings and has successfully argued before numerous Federal Circuit Court of Appeals.

Prof. Memberships: ABA; State Bar of Texas; ABA Subcommittee on Individual Rights and Responsibilities in the Workplace; admitted in 4th, 5th, 10th, and 11th US Circuit Court of Appeals, as well as the US Supreme Court.

Career: Principal Shareholder of Baker Mckenzie, LLP and Head of Labor Section in Dallas (2004 to present); Littler Mendelson and Chair of Class Action group (1992-2004); Jenkens and Gilchrist(1983-92); USAF JAG officer: Chief of the Labor and General Law Division for HQ. SAC (1979-83).

Publications: Numerous papers on discrimination laws, class actions, privacy, remedies for employment law claims, electronic discovery, and new common law employment torts for ABA subcommittee and other legal publications.

Personal: University of Virginia School of Law (JD; Earle K Shawe Labor Relations Award 1979); University of Southern Mississippi (BA 1976); spouse: Donna Lewis Manthey; daughters: Katharine and Alison.

MARCUS, Courtney
Weil, Gotshal & Manges LLP, Dallas
214 746 8127
courtney.marcus@weil.com
Recommended in Banking & Finance

Practice Areas: Ms Marcus focuses on a variety of corporate finance and restructuring transactions, including acquisition, working capital, debtor-in-possession and real estate financings, restructurings and workouts.

Career: Recent restructurings include Darling International Inc. and US Lec Corp. and debtor-in-possession financing for LLS Corp. and Orion Refining

Corporation. Ms Marcus has recently represented a variety of private equity sponsors in acquisition financings including Texas Pacific Group, Thomas H Lee Partners, Summit Partners and Hicks, Muse, Tate & Furst. Recent corporate lending transactions include Southwest Sports Group and Martin Group Inc.
Personal: St. Mary's University (JD, 1998); Vanderbilt University (BA, 1995).

MARKS, Kenneth
Susman Godfrey LLP, Houston
713 651 9366
Recommended in Litigation

MARSTON, Edgar
Bracewell & Giuliani LLP, Houston
713 221 1315
edgar.marston@bracewellgiuliani.com
Recommended in Corporate/M&A
Practice Areas: Expertise includes asset acquisitions, business combinations and divestitures, securities offerings and contests for corporate control. Has represented clients in various industries, including oil and gas, cement production, computer manufacturing, telecommunications, biotech, heating and air conditioning manufacturing and retail sales businesses. Has served as counsel to special committees of boards of directors and controlling stockholders in public companies.
Career: Recognized in 'Chambers Global' 2004, 2003.
Personal: LLB, The University of Texas School of Law, 1964; BA, Brown University, 1961.

MARTIN, Brian
Thompson, Coe, Cousins & Irons, LLP, Houston 713 403 8282
bmartin@thompsoncoe.com
Recommended in Insurance
Practice Areas: Representation of insurance coverage and defense matters, specializing in environmental, toxic tort, products cases and frequent author and speaker on insurance topics.
Prof. Memberships: Admitted in Texas, he is a Counsel member, State Bar of Texas, Insurance Section. Past Chairman of Reinsurance Committee of the Insurance Section, State Bar of Texas. Member of the American Bar Association; Insurance Coverage Litigation Section Subcommittees on Products Liability and Bad Faith; Texas Association of Defense Counsel; Defense Research Institute.
Publications: Columnist, Insurance Journal. 'Insurance Update', State Bar of Texas 'Reservation of Rights: The Insurance Company's Perspective', University of Houston Law Foundation.

MARTIN, Christopher
Martin, Disiere, Jefferson & Wisdom LLP, Houston 713 632 1700
Recommended in Insurance

MARTIN, Clark
Vinson & Elkins LLP, Houston
713 758 2490
cmartin@velaw.com
Recommended in Intellectual Property
Practice Areas: Clark practices in all areas of intellectual property law and has represented firm clients in litigation involving such matters as trade secret disputes; contract disputes involving technology; and patent, trademark, and copyright infringement.
Career: Partner since 1975.
Personal: Louisiana State University, BSEE, 1963; JD, 1966.

MARTIN, Ernest
Haynes and Boone LLP, Dallas
214 651 5000
Recommended in Insurance

MARTIN, John
Baker Botts LLP, Dallas
214 953 6757
john.martin@bakerbotts.com
Recommended in Business Process Outsourcing: National, Communications, Technology
Practice Areas: Mergers and acquisitions, corporate finance/securities, outsourcing, and joint ventures. Represents purchasers and sellers in complex M&A transactions, acquisitions, divestitures, leveraged buyouts, and spin-offs. Represents issuers and underwriters in public offerings. Extensive experience with venture capital and private equity fund transactions. Represents industry leaders in wide variety of technology transactions, including complex BPO/ITO outsourcings. Counsels senior management, boards of directors and special committees on corporate governance, disclosure, Sarbanes Oxley and compliance issues. Significant client concentration in technology sector.
Personal: JD, with honors, The University of Texas School of Law, 1984; BA, summa cum laude, political science, Baylor University, 1981.

MARTIN, Paul
Vinson & Elkins LLP, Dallas
214 220 7875
pmartin@velaw.com
Recommended in Real Estate
Practice Areas: Experience includes representation of a wide variety of clients engaged in many types of real estate, financing and other business transactions, as well as institutional lenders in the sale of commercial property and the restructuring of existing credit facilities. Experience in commercial leasing, lease disputes, and general corporate representation.
Prof. Memberships: American Bar Association; Real Property, Probate, and Trust Section, the Texas Bar Association and the Dallas Bar Association.
Career: Admitted to Texas Bar in 1991.
Personal: Graduated from Stanford University, BA with highest honors, 1988; and The University of Texas

School of Law, JD with honors, 1991.

MASLANKA, Michael
Ford & Harrison LLP, Dallas
214 256 4700
mmaslanka@fordharrison.com
Recommended in Employment
Practice Areas: Mike Maslanka has more than 20 years of experience in litigation and trial of employment law cases, including defending several multiparty cases under the Age Discrimination in Employment Act, the Fair Labor Standards Act and the Civil Rights Act of 1991. He has served as Adjunct Counsel to a Fortune 10 company where he provided multi-state counseling on employment matters. He has also served as a Field Attorney for the National Labor Relations Board. Mike received his JD degree, cum laude, from Tulane University.

MASSAD, Stephen A
Baker Botts LLP, Houston
713 229 1475
stephen.massad@bakerbotts.com
Recommended in Corporate/M&A
Practice Areas: Chair: Houston Corporate Department (1994-2002); Member: Executive Committee (1995-2001). Concentrates practice in general corporate, securities, mergers, acquisitions and joint ventures. Has substantial experience in M&A transactions and related financings, including negotiated acquisitions, tender offers, proxy contests and takeover defense. Much of his practice has involved representing major participants in the restructuring and consolidation of the oil and gas, power and chemicals sectors. Additional areas of emphasis include underwritten public offerings, Rule 144A transactions, and audit committee and other internal investigations.
Personal: JD, cum laude, Harvard Law School, 1975; AB, summa cum laude, Princeton University, 1972.

MATTOX, Sharon
Vinson & Elkins LLP, Houston
713 758 4598
smattox@velaw.com
Recommended in Environment, Litigation
Practice Areas: Principal areas of practice are administrative and environmental law. Is a Fellow of the Texas Bar Foundation and is listed in a leading legal US publication in environmental law.
Career: Admitted to Texas Bar in 1981. Joined Vinson & Elkins in 1981; admitted to the partnership in 1990.
Personal: Graduated from Emporia State University, BA in 1974, The University of Texas, PhD in 1978, and The University of Texas School of Law, JD in 1981 (Order of Barristers, Order of the Coif).

MAUEL, John
Baker & McKenzie, Houston
713 427 5002
john.g.mauel@bakernet.com
Recommended in Projects
Practice Areas: Practice involves domestic and international energy projects, oil and gas transactions, and project finance; including the development, financing, acquisition and sale of electric power projects, oil and gas reserves, pipelines, processing plants, and LNG receiving and regasification terminals.
Prof. Memberships: State Bar of Texas, American Bar Association, Houston Bar Association.
Career: Admitted to practice law in Texas in 1986. Partner with Baker & McKenzie since joining the firm in 2001.
Publications: Regular author and presenter on energy projects.
Personal: Received his BA (cum laude) from Harvard University in 1983 and his JD from Notre Dame University in 1986.

MAY, Jr, Henry S
Vinson & Elkins LLP, Houston
713 758 2554
hmay@velaw.com
Recommended in Energy
Practice Areas: Extensive experience in the regulatory, policy and transactional aspects of the natural gas and electric industries. Has represented clients before federal and state agencies and courts, and assisted in the development of energy policy initiatives, and participated in the structuring and negotiation of domestic and international energy transactions.
Career: Attended: The University of Texas (BA with honors, 1969); The University of Texas School of Law (JD with honors 1971); Admitted to practice (Texas, 1972; US Supreme Court; Court of Appeals of the District of Columbia; Fifth Circuit and Eleventh Circuit.

MCALPINE, Fraser A
Akin Gump Strauss Hauer & Feld LLP, Houston 713 220 8129
fmcalpine@akingump.com
Recommended in Employment
Practice Areas: Board Certified in Labor and Employment Law, Texas Board of Legal Specialization. Focuses on complex employment disputes involving class actions, collective actions, and claims by former executives and managers involving stock options and other incentive compensation arrangements. Has represented employers in state and federal cases involving employee raiding, misappropriation of trade secrets and restrictive covenants. Handles federal and state court cases alleging discrimination, retaliation and harassment, and federal court litigation alleging violations of ERISA or FLSA.
Personal: BA, Colorado College; JD, University of Toledo; Clerk, Woodrow B Seals, US District Court for the Southern District of Texas.

MCAUGHAN Jr, Robert J
Locke Liddell & Sapp LLP, Houston
713 226 1154
bmcaughan@lockeliddell.com
Recommended in Intellectual Property
Practice Areas: Partner practicing in all areas of intellectual property (patents, trademarks, trade dress, trade secrets) including litigation, transactional matters, and general counseling.
Prof. Memberships: Texas "Super Lawyer" for 2003 and 2004 (As named in Texas Monthly magazine); Selected EuroMoney as a Leading Patent Law Expert; Member, American Intellectual Property Law Association; Licensing Executive Society; Member, Houston Bar Association; Member, Houston Intellectual Property Law Association; Member, State Bar of Texas; Member, American Bar Association.
Career: Partner in the law firm of Locke Liddell & Sapp LLP; Partner in the law firm of Howrey Simon Arnold & White, LLP; Partner in the law firm of Arnold, White & Durkee, LLC; Licensed to practice in 1993; admitted to practice before the United States Patent and Trademark Office.

MCCOLLAM, Andrew
Vinson & Elkins LLP, Houston
713 758 1004
DMcCollam@velaw.com
Recommended in Energy
Practice Areas: Commercial litigation. Drew is a trial lawyer specializing in energy-related matters for plaintiffs and defendants. He has been involved in the resolution of cases and administrative proceedings in Alaska, the District of Columbia, in 10 states in the lower-48, before the US Tax Court, and in the Louisiana and Texas Supreme Courts and the Fifth, Eighth, and Tenth federal circuit courts.
Prof. Memberships: ABA; Louisiana State Bar (1983); Texas State Bar (1990).
Career: Partner since 1993; energy trial practice in New Orleans, Louisiana, 1983-90.
Personal: Louisiana State University (JD, 1983); Washington & Lee University (BA, 1980).

MCCOMBS, David
Haynes and Boone LLP, Dallas
214 651 5000
Recommended in Intellectual Property

MCCONNELL, Mike
Winstead Sechrest & Minick P.C., Fort Worth 817 420 8214
mmcconnell@winstead.com
Recommended in Bankruptcy
Practice Areas: Shareholder, Bankruptcy Section. Represents clients across all aspects of reorganization and bankruptcy-related litigation. Represents secured and unsecured creditors in business restructurings, formulation of prepackaged Chapter 11 Plans of Reorganization, and Chapter 11 Debtor and Chapter 11 Official Unsecured Creditor Committee representation. Advises

Boards of Directors on liability and fiduciary responsibility issues.
Prof. Memberships: National Conference of Bankruptcy Judges, National Foundation of American Inns of Court, American College of Bankruptcy, American Law Institute.
Career: State Bar of Texas. Former US Bankruptcy Judge, Northern District of Texas.
Personal: University of Texas School of Law, JD, 1975. Loyola University, BA, 1969.

MCCORMACK, William
Hughes & Luce LLP, Dallas
214 939 5500
Recommended in Corporate/M&A

MCCOWN, Steven
Littler Mendelson PC, Dallas
214 880 8100
Recommended in Employment

MCDADE, Thomas
McDade Fogler LLP, Houston
713 654 4300
Recommended in Energy

MCDERMETT Jr, Don J
Baker Botts LLP, Dallas
214 953 6454
don.mcdermett@bakerbotts.com
Recommended in Communications, Technology
Practice Areas: Securities, mergers and acquisitions, corporate finance, capital markets, IT/BPO outsourcing. Represents issuers and underwriters in securities offerings, private placements and venture capital financings; counsels clients in corporate governance, compliance and disclosure issues, executive compensation, negotiated acquisitions and defensive measures, strategic alliances, joint ventures, spin-offs, reorganizations and recapitalizations. Significant client concentration in the information technology and software industries.
Career: Former Senior Vice-President, General Counsel and Secretary of Sterling Software, Inc.
Personal: JD, with honors, The University of Texas School of Law, 1984 (Texas Law Review, Order of the Coif); BBA, with high honors, finance, The University of Texas, 1981.

MCDONALD, Derek
Baker Botts LLP, Austin
512 322 2667
derek.mcdonald@bakerbotts.com
Recommended in Environment
Practice Areas: Focuses practice in the areas of environmental law and litigation, concentrating on federal and state permitting and remediation projects.
Prof. Memberships: Member, State Bar of Texas; Member, Travis County Bar Association.
Career: Admitted to Texas Bar in 1993. Joined Baker Botts in 1994; admitted to partnership 2001.
Personal: University of Texas, BA, with honors, 1989; JD, with honors, 1992.

MCDONALD, Scott
Littler Mendelson PC, Dallas
214 880 8100
Recommended in Employment

MCKOOL Jr, Mike
McKool Smith, Dallas
214 978 4000
Recommended in Intellectual Property, Litigation

MCNAMARA, Lawrence J
Locke Liddell & Sapp LLP, Dallas
214 740 8567
lmcnamara@lockeliddell.com
Recommended in Employment
Practice Areas: Board Certified in Labor and Employment Law by the Texas Board of Legal Specialization (1981). Extensive experience in corporate representation, counseling, arbitration and litigation as to all facets of labor and employment law, including unionization and strike issues, FLSA, and equal employment law.
Prof. Memberships: Admitted to practice in Texas (1976) and the District of Columbia (1988). Admitted to practice before United States Supreme Court (1981); US Courts of Appeals for the Fifth, Seventh, Eighth, Ninth, Tenth, and Eleventh Circuits; US District Courts for the Northern, Southern, Eastern and Western Districts of Texas; Eastern and Western Districts of Arkansas. Member of Employee Rights and Responsibilities Committee, American Bar Association Section of Labor and Employment Law; Texas Bar Association, Labor and Employment Law Section.
Career: Associate, Baker & Botts (1976-84); Partner, Baker, Smith & Mills (1985-87); Partner, Johnson & Gibbs (1988-95); Partner, Locke Liddell & Sapp (1995-present).
Publications: 'Sexual Harassment', University of Houston Employment Law Seminar (1999-2003).
Personal: Born 10 August 1950. JD, Vanderbilt University, 1976; BA(cum laude), Illinois College, 1973; Phi Beta Kappa, 1973.

MCNEIL, Barry
Haynes and Boone LLP, Dallas
214 651 5000
Recommended in Antitrust

MCNIEL, D Ferguson
Vinson & Elkins LLP, Houston
713 758 3882
fmcniel@velaw.com
Recommended in Litigation
Practice Areas: Represents clients in various types of litigation. Practice concentrates on toxic tort, product liability, professional malpractice, construction, and commercial litigation. Certified: civil trial law and personal injury trial law by Texas Board of Legal Specialization.
Prof. Memberships: International Society of Barristers; American Board of Trial Advocates; International Association of Defense Counsel; Defense

Research Institute; American Bar Association; Texas Association of Defense Counsel; Houston Bar Association. Fellow: Texas Bar Foundation; Houston Bar Foundation.
Career: Admitted to practice: Texas, 1980. Joined Vinson & Elkins, 1980; admitted to partnership, 1990.
Personal: University of Arkansas, BSBA, 1977; University of Arkansas, JD, 1980.

MCQUAID, Janet
Fulbright & Jaworski L.L.P., Austin
512 536 2429
jmcquaid@fulbright.com
Recommended in Environment
Practice Areas: Environmental regulations, water law, contested permits, property and environmental litigation.
Prof. Memberships: Ms McQuaid is a Member of the Environmental, Real Estate, Construction, and Administrative Law Sections of the State Bar of Texas and the Travis County Bar Association. She is a member of the Section on Environment, Energy and Resources, in which she is Co-Vice-Chair of the Water Quality and Wetlands Newsletter, as well as the Construction Law Forum and the Administrative Law Section of the American Bar Association, along with the Texas Water Conservation Association and the Society of Women Engineers.
Career: Janet McQuaid, a Partner, joined Fulbright's Austin office in 1992. Prior to attending law school she worked for 11 years for a major oil company, where she designed, built, and operated oil and gas production and oil refining facilities.
Personal: BSChE, University of Pittsburgh (1978); MBA, Houston Baptist University (1989); JD, The University of Texas (1992).

MEADOWS, Charles
Meadows, Owens, Collier, Reed, Cousins & Blau, Dallas
214 744 3700
Recommended in Litigation

MEADOWS, Robert E
King & Spalding LLP, Houston
713 276 7370
rmeadows@kslaw.com
Recommended in Energy, Litigation
Practice Areas: Extensive trial experience in general commercial litigation and defense of corporations including oil/gas companies, construction/engineering companies, and product manufacturers in tort litigation. Oil/gas litigation includes lease and royalty disputes, offshore property evaluation and contract disputes arising under operating agreements. Tort litigation includes defense of corporations confronted with multi-plaintiff environmental claims.
Prof. Memberships: American Board of Trial Advocates (ABOTA); American College of Trial Lawyers; Connecticut State Bar; Houston Bar Foundation; State Bar of Texas; Texas Association of Defense Counsel; Texas Supreme Court

Advisory Committee.

Personal: BA, University of Texas, 1971; JD, University of Houston, Order of the Barons, 1977.

MEDLOCK, Bryan
Sidley Austin Brown & Wood LLP, Dallas 214 981 3302
bmedlock@sidley.com
Recommended in Intellectual Property

Practice Areas: V Bryan Medlock, Jr has 35 years of experience trying patent cases. He has served as special master, arbitrator, mediator and expert witness in numerous patent cases.

Prof. Memberships: Mr Medlock served as Chairman of the Patent, Trademark and Copyright Law Section of the Texas State Bar, and received the Chairman's Award in 1993. He also served as Chairman of the American Bar Association's Committee on Patent Litigation, Litigation Section. He is a Member of the American Intellectual Property Law Association.

Career: University of Oklahoma College of Law, LLB, 1962; University of Oklahoma, BS in Chemical Engineering, 1959. Bar Admissions: Texas, 1962; US Patent & Trademark Office, 1964.

Publications: Mr Medlock was a guest lecturer on Trade Secret Law at Southern Methodist University and has served as Chairman of the annual Southwestern Legal Foundation Institute on Patent Law.

MELO, Thomas M
Ogletree, Deakins, Nash, Smoak & Stewart, PC, Houston
713 655 5752
tom.melo@ogletreedeakins.com
Recommended in Employment

Practice Areas: Employment discrimination, employment litigation, traditional labor, workplace safety and health, unfair competition, and executive employment.

Prof. Memberships: American, Federal, Texas, and Houston Bar Associations, Houston Bar Foundation, Houston Management Lawyers' Forum, Texas Association of Business, Texas Lyceum Association, and Houston Human Resource Management Association.

Career: Listed, The Best Lawyers in America, Fellow, College of Labor & Employment Lawyers. Named as a Houston Super Lawyer in 2003 and 2004.

Publications: Texas Employment Law Handbook (editor and chapter author), BNA's Occupational Safety & Health Law (contributing author).

Personal: University of Georgia (BBA, 1974), University of Virginia Law School (JD, 1977).

MERWIN, Bruce
Haynes and Boone LLP, Houston
713 547 2000
Recommended in Construction

MEYER, Theodore D
Jones Day, Houston
832 239 3616
tdmeyer@jonesday.com
Recommended in Employment

Practice Areas: Has broad-based, multistate experience in labor and employment law and is board certified in labor and employment law by the Texas Board of Legal Specialization. He handles a wide variety of employment litigation, counseling, and training matters, including multiplaintiff cases, discrimination and contract matters, ADA/FMLA/Workers' Comp matters, ERISA litigation, wage and hour litigation, and training and counseling/advice involving all levels throughout organizations. He is a frequent speaker at labor and employment seminars and has been recognized as one of the 'Texas Super Lawyers' in labor and employment law.

MEYERS III, Robert L
Jones Day, Dallas
214 969 4829
rlmeyers@jonesday.com
Recommended in Construction

Practice Areas: His global practice is concentrated on design, construction, and related transactional areas, as well as dispute resolution including construction litigation, arbitration, and mediation. He has represented all parties in the development/design/construction process. He is a frequent speaker and panelist on the Construction Litigation Superconference and the Global Construction Superconference.

Prof. Memberships: ABA; State Bar of Texas; Dallas Bar Association. He currently serves on the board of trustees of the Center for American and International Law and is chairman of the Research Fellows. He was a founding member of the American College of Construction Lawyers.

MICCICHE, Daniel J
Akin Gump Strauss Hauer & Feld LLP, Dallas 214 969 2797
dmicciche@akingump.com
Recommended in Tax

Practice Areas: Has extensive experience in tax and business planning for acquisitions, divestitures and specialized capital structure planning, as well as in the formation and operation of corporations, partnerships and limited liability companies. Also represents clients in federal and state tax controversy matters.

Prof. Memberships: Chair, State Taxation Committee of the State Bar of Texas; Appointed by Texas Comptroller of Public Accounts, Carole Keeton Strayhorn, to the Comptroller's Tax Advisory Group; past Chair, Dallas Bar Association Tax Section (2001); past Chair, Corporate Taxation Committee of the State Bar of Texas (1998-99).

Personal: BA, SUNY Stony Brook; JD, University of Chicago.

MILES, Robin J
Bracewell & Giuliani LLP, Houston
713 221 1319
robin.miles@bracewellgiuliani.com
Recommended in Banking & Finance

Practice Areas: Extensive experience in representing lenders and borrowers in bank and capital markets debt transactions, including syndicated loans, secured notes offerings, asset securitizations, structured financings, lease financings, project and acquisition financings, tax-exempt bond financings, private debt placements, restructuring of problem credits, subordinated debt offerings, leveraged buyouts, recapitalizations and hedge arrangements. Recently, as lead counsel for Reliant Energy Inc., Miles handled numerous financings totaling multi-billions; he has also served as lead counsel for Dynegy Inc. in more than $1 billion in financings.

Personal: JD, The University of Kansas School of Law, 1986. BS, University of Colorado, 1978.

MILLER, Barry
Vinson & Elkins LLP, Houston
713 758 4438
brmiller@velaw.com
Recommended in Tax

Practice Areas: Nationally recognized authority on taxation and formation of publicly traded partnerships (MLPs) and royalty trusts. Practice includes all aspects of federal income taxation and state tax (Texas) with emphasis in asset monetization, REITs, natural resource taxation, partnership taxation, and mergers and acquisitions.

Prof. Memberships: American Bar Association; Houston Bar Association.

Career: Speaker and author: numerous conferences and publications and MLPs, royalty trusts and income taxation.

Personal: Graduated from University of Illinois School of Commerce, BS (highest honors), 1967 and University of Illinois School of Law, JD, 1970 (honors).

MILLER, Ralph I
Weil, Gotshal & Manges LLP, Dallas
214 746 7756
ralph.miller@weil.com
Recommended in Litigation

Practice Areas: Mr Miller's complex commercial litigation practice includes regular roles as lead counsel in cases and arbitrations with hundreds of millions of dollars in issue, including several with more than $1 billion at issue.

Career: Mr Miller is the Partner in charge of the firm's Dallas Litigation Section and Co-Head of the firm's Complex Commercial Litigation Practice. Mr Miller was recognized by the Dallas Business Journal in 2002 as a 'Top 10' litigator in Dallas, by 'Texas Monthly' among 100 Dallas-Ft. Worth lawyers receiving the most votes in its 2003 and 2004 'Superlawyers' surveys and by D Magazine in the business litigation category of its 2001 and 2003 Best Lawyers

in Dallas surveys. He is listed in Woodward/White, Inc.'s 'Best Lawyers in America.' In 28 years of trial experience, Mr Miller has had substantial experience in antitrust, arbitrations, business tort cases, contract disputes, insurance coverage actions, professional malpractice matters, securities class actions and general commercial litigations. His clients have included Arthur Andersen LLP, UICI, Wal-Mart Stores, Inc., Ernst & Young, the European Bank for Reconstruction and Development and Nomura. Before beginning his practice, Mr Miller served as law clerk to Justice Harry A Blackmun of the Supreme Court of the United States and as Captain in the Army Judge Advocate General's Corps.

Personal: University of Texas School of Law, JD; University of Texas, BA.

MILLER, Walter
Haynes and Boone, LLP, Richardson
972 739 6900
Recommended in Real Estate

MILLS, Jerry
Baker Botts LLP, Dallas
214 953 6665
jerry.mills@bakerbotts.com
Recommended in Intellectual Property

Practice Areas: Chairman of the Baker Botts Intellectual Property Department, which numbers over 115 attorneys. Has extensive experience preparing and prosecuting electronic and software patent applications and designing and managing corporate intellectual property protection programs. Has been involved in complex patent and trademark litigation, including the Texas Instruments DRAM litigation and conducted numerous successful licensing programs for patents involving, for example, voice mail, automated attendant PBX systems, electronic learning aids and semiconductor portfolios. Worked two years as patent examiner in the electronics arts in the USPTO in Washington, DC Practiced patent, trademark and copyright law in Dallas since 1967.

MOODY III, James
Quilling, Selander, Cummiskey & Lownds, P.C., Dallas 214 871 2100
Recommended in Insurance

MOORE, Charles A
LeBoeuf, Lamb, Greene & MacRae, LLP, Houston 713 287 2086
cmoore@llgm.com
Recommended in Energy

Practice Areas: Internationally recognized authority in the field of energy industry regulation and litigation. He has held a number of high level government positions in this field. In private practice, he has been involved in numerous international and domestic transactions in the energy sector.

Prof. Memberships: American Bar Association (Litigation Section); Energy

Bar Association; Maritime Law Association of the United States.
Career: Joined LeBoeuf in 2002. Chairman, Energy and Converging Industries, Akin, Gump, Strauss, Hauer & Feld, LLP; General Counsel, US Federal Energy Regulatory Commission (1981-83).
Personal: University of Houston (JD magna cum laude) 1975; University of Houston (BA) 1972.

MOORE, Thomas J
LeBoeuf, Lamb, Greene & MacRae, LLP, Houston 713 287 2066
tmoore@llgm.com
Recommended in Energy
Practice Areas: Lead role in national energy mergers and acquisitions practice. Representation of high profile clients in areas that include mergers and acquisitions and the sale and project financing of merchant power plants. He has a strong presence in the international arena, leading the firm's representation in client development of foreign investment initiatives and natural gas based economic expansion.
Prof. Memberships: Colorado Bar; Texas Bar.
Career: Joined LeBoeuf in 1994; Faegre & Benson 1974-77, 1979-94; University of Minnesota, Associate Professor of Law 1977-79.
Personal: University of Minnesota Law School (JD) 1974; University of California at Berkeley (AB) 1971.

MOOREFIELD, G Crawford
Akin Gump Strauss Hauer & Feld LLP, Houston 713 220 5884
cmoorefield@akingump.com
Recommended in Tax
Practice Areas: Practice encompasses all aspects of US federal income tax planning for business transactions, including acquisitions, divestitures and specialized capital structure planning, taxation of partnerships, limited liability companies, with a particular emphasis on energy and natural resource industries. Extensive experience in the area of publicly traded partnerships, as well as tax issues related to bankruptcy and troubled corporations.
Prof. Memberships: State Bar of Texas, Section of Taxation; Houston Bar Association, Taxation Section.
Personal: AB (cum laude), Woodrow Wilson School of Public and International Affairs, Princeton University (1984); JD, Harvard Law School (1987).

MORRISS, James
Thompson & Knight LLP, Austin 512 752 8611
james.morriss@tklaw.com
Recommended in Environment
Practice Areas: Mr Morriss' experience includes permitting, compliance counseling, legislative lobbying, and litigation in environmental matters. His practice includes enforcement cases, superfund litigation; policy development and counseling clients regarding solid waste,

air and water matters, risk matters, sustainable development, and endangered species. He was included in Texas Monthly's 2003 and 2004 listings of Texas Super Lawyers.
Prof. Memberships: State Bar of Texas, Austin and American Bar Associations.
Career: Partner since 1982.
Publications: Mr Morriss is an active author and speaker.
Personal: University of Texas School of Law (JD, 1976); Southern Methodist University (BS, 1973).

MORSE, Robert
Crain Caton & James, Houston 713 658 2323
Recommended in Litigation

MUNCK, William A
Davis Munck, Dallas 972 628 3630
wmunck@davismunck.com
Recommended in Intellectual Property
Practice Areas: Domestic and foreign intellectual property (IP) procurement, exploitation, enforcement and counseling. Practice focus on development of market-focused offensive and defensive IP portfolios in hardware, firmware, software, communications and medical device industries (pre- and post-FDA approval). Practice emphasis on long-range corporate strategies for the domestic and foreign enforcement and defense of IP rights, rendering legal opinions, IP licensing negotiation, prosecution of reexamination proceedings, and counseling on IP issues associated with private and public financings, mergers, acquisitions and establishing market leadership.
Prof. Memberships: State Bar of Texas, New York State Bar, USPTO, ABA, DBA, AIPLA, DFW IPLA.
Career: Chairman of Davis Munck, P.C. since 2002; Shareholder since 1987.
Publications: Frequent media source for commentary and analysis on technology-related legal issues, particularly IP issues in the fields of hardware, software, telecommunications, medical devices, motion pictures and entertainment, and global convergence of technology.
Personal: Hofstra University School of Law (JD 1992 - Highest Honors, List Distinction), and Hofstra University (MS Computer Science 1989 - Highest Honors; BS Computer Science (Electrical Engineering and Mathematics) 1987).

MUNSCH, Russell
Munsch Hardt Kopf & Harr, P. C., Dallas 214 855 7555
rmunsch@munsch.com
Recommended in Bankruptcy
Practice Areas: Reorganization and creditors' rights, bankruptcy, international insolvency and commercial litigation. Represents financial institutions, bank groups and significant creditors, debtors, and creditors committees and entities acquiring assets from troubled

organizations. Served as Bankruptcy Trustee and Examiner in both Chapter 11 and Chapter 7 cases.
Prof. Memberships: American Bankruptcy Institute; American Bar Association; State Bar of Texas (Business Bankruptcy Section); Dallas Bar Association; Travis County Bar Association.
Career: Founding Shareholder of Munsch Hardt Kopf & Harr, P.C.
Publications: Frequent speaker and writer on various bankruptcy and creditors' rights issues.
Personal: University of Houston (JD, with honors, 1980); The University of Texas (BA, with honors, 1977).

MURRAY, Craig
Vinson & Elkins LLP, Houston 713 758 2008
cmurray@velaw.com
Recommended in Banking & Finance
Practice Areas: Business transactions, finance, including structured and project finance and mergers and acquisitions. Has extensive experience in complex syndicated bank transactions, representing either the lenders or the borrower. Has worked on all aspects of energy finance and commercial finance.
Career: Came to the firm in 1976 and was admitted to the Partnership in October 1983.
Personal: Graduated from Rhodes College, BA in English, 1969 and Louisiana State University, JD with high honors in 1976. (Order of the Coif; Managing Editor, 'Louisiana Law Review'.)

NASI, Michael
Lloyd, Gosselink, Blevins, Rochelle, Baldwin & Townsend, PC, Austin 512 322 5800
Recommended in Environment

NATION, Floyd
Howrey Simon Arnold & White, Houston 713 787 1400
Recommended in Intellectual Property

NEEL, James M
Neel & Hooper, P.C., Houston 713 629 1800
jneel@neelhooper.com
Recommended in Employment
Practice Areas: Exclusively represents management in all phases of labor and employment matters including union avoidance training and election campaigns; collective bargaining; arbitration cases; unfair labor practice trials; claims of race, age, sex, disability and other types of employment discrimination under state and federal civil rights laws; wage and hour, equal pay and federal contract claims investigated by government agencies or tried in federal and state courts.
Personal: LLB with honors University of Texas School of Law, 1962; Texas Law Review; BA University of Texas,1960; Certificate of Special Competence in Field of Labor Law, 1975-2005, Texas Board of Legal Specialization.

NELIGAN Jr, Patrick
Neligan Tarpley Andrews & Foley LLP, Dallas 214 840 5300
Recommended in Bankruptcy

NETTLES, Larry
Vinson & Elkins LLP, Houston 713 758 4586
lnettles@velaw.com
Recommended in Environment
Practice Areas: Extensive experience in virtually all areas of environmental law, including site remediation, facility permitting, civil and criminal enforcement defense, land development, environmental due diligence for transactions, and dispute resolution.
Prof. Memberships: Admitted to practice before state and federal courts in Texas; Life Fellow, Texas Bar Foundation; Fellow, Houston Bar Foundation; Founder, Houston Bar Association Environmental Law Section.
Career: Joined V&E 1981; admitted to partnership, 1990.
Publications: 'Conservation and Land Use Statutes', Texas Environmental Law Handbook (West 1997).
Personal: Born 1 July 1956; BS Civil Engineering, Rice University, 1978; JD with Honors, University of Texas School of Law, 1981.

NEWSOME, J Kent
Fulbright & Jaworski L.L.P., Houston 713 651 3659
kent@fulbright.com
Recommended in Real Estate
Practice Areas: Commercial real estate, real estate development, hospital acquisitions and development, entertainment law, general business law, and internet related transactions.
Prof. Memberships: Member, Houston and American Bar Associations and the State Bar of Texas; Fellow, Houston Bar Foundation and member of the American College of Real Estate Lawyers; Voting member, National Academy of Recording Arts and Sciences.
Career: Admitted to practice in Texas (1985). Joined the firm in 1985, is a Partner in Fulbright's Houston office.
Personal: BA, cum laude, in 1982 from Wake Forest University; JD in 1985 from Vanderbilt University.

NIEBRUEGGE, Michael E
Mayer, Brown, Rowe & Maw LLP, Houston 713 546 0507
mniebruegge@mayerbrownrowe.com
Recommended in Banking & Finance
Practice Areas: Represents lenders and arrangers in negotiating and documenting secured lending and securitization agreements with corporations, general partnerships, limited partnerships, individuals, and trusts engaged in energy, mining, transportation and manufacturing. Represents creditors in negotiating and documenting debt restructurings; disputes with other creditors and debtors. Represents oil and gas producers in a variety of onshore matters. Rep-

resents corporations engaged principally in service businesses and extractive businesses on acquisitions and general corporate matters.

Prof. Memberships: State Bar of Texas. Texas Association of Bank Counsel. Admitted in Texas, 1981. Illinois, 1977. US District Court for the Southern District of Texas, 1988. US District Court for the Northern District of Illinois, 1977.
Career: Joined Mayer, Brown, Rowe & Maw LLP, 1982; became Partner, 1984. Partner-in-charge of Houston office, 1995 to date. Formerly with Gulf Coast Royalty Co., Vice President and General Counsel, Houston, 1981-82. Mayer, Brown, Rowe & Maw LLP, Chicago, 1977-81. Northwestern University, Lecturer in Business Law, Chicago, 1979-80.
Personal: Born 21 April 1952. Cornell University, JD, 1977; note and comment editor, Cornell Law Review. Harvard College, AB, cum laude, 1974.

NONDORF, Kurt
Jackson Walker LLP, Dallas
214 953 6000
Recommended in Real Estate

NORRIS, John
Howrey Simon Arnold & White, Houston
713 787 1400
Recommended in Intellectual Property

O'DONNELL, Laura
Haynes and Boone LLP, San Antonio
210 978 7000
Recommended in Employment

OELMAN, David
Vinson & Elkins LLP, Houston
713 758 3708
doelman@velaw.com
Recommended in Corporate/M&A

Practice Areas: Focuses primarily on corporate and securities transactions, including representation of public and private companies and investment banking firms; advising boards on corporate governance matters; public offerings and private placements of equity and debt; publicly traded limited partnerships; mergers, acquisitions and dispositions; venture capital and private equity investments; issuance of high yield debt securities; redemptions and exchanges of preferred equity and debt.
Personal: Graduated from Princeton University, Woodrow Wilson School of Public and International Affairs, BA (Summa Cum Laude, Phi Beta Kappa), 1987; The University of Texas School of Law, JD (Chancellors, Order of the Coif), 1990.

OLDHAM, Dudley
Fulbright & Jaworski L.L.P., Houston
713 651 5397
doldham@fulbright.com
Recommended in Litigation

Practice Areas: Complex commercial and business litigation.
Prof. Memberships: Fellow, the American College of Trial Lawyers; the American Board of Trial Advocates; Former

Chair, the American Bar Association Standing Committee on Independence of the Judiciary, the ABA Standing Committee on Federal Judicial relations; the Advisory Council of the National Judicial College; Chairman of the Board and past President, the Federation of Defense & Corporate Counsel, one of the three major defense trial organizations in the United States; Board of the Defense Research Institute; and President, Lawyers for Civil Justice, a national organization of corporations and corporate counsel.
Career: Senior Partner. Resident in the Houston office. Member firm's Executive Committee over 25 years and former Chairman, firm's Litigation Management Committee. Practice consists of complex litigation primarily in the areas of energy, intellectual property, commercial and business litigation, class actions, arbitration, securities, insurance disputes and mass torts. Certified mediator and arbitrator, member of the AAA Texas Large Complex Case Panel and CPR.
Personal: BA, the University of Texas (1964); JD, UT School of Law (1966). Admitted in Texas (1966), the US Supreme Court, all US District Courts in Texas and the US Courts of Appeals for the Third, Fifth and Eleventh Circuits.

O'LEARY, Michael
Andrews Kurth LLP, Houston
713 220 4360
moleary@andrewskurth.com
Recommended in Corporate/M&A

Practice Areas: Expertise in representing public and private companies and investment banking firms in corporate finance and M&A transactions, including: public and private company mergers, acquisitions and dispositions (by tender offer, exchange offer, private auction or otherwise), including changes of control, business combinations, divestitures of subsidiaries or operating divisions, sales of MLP general partners or undivided interests therein and public MLP combinations; public offerings and private placements of equity, debt and convertible securities; IPOs of MLPs; formations of partnerships and joint ventures and negotiation of definitive documentation; public company spin-offs and split-offs; redemptions and consent solicitations for preferred equity and debt; public and private royalty trusts and volumetric production payment financings; advise boards of directors and board committees on fiduciary duties in the context of change of control transactions and business combinations, and on Sarbanes-Oxley Act and corporate governance matters; international joint ventures and alliances. Particular expertise in energy and oilfield service companies, pipeline transportation, staff leasings, royalty trusts and forest products companies.

Prof. Memberships: The State Bar of Texas; Houston Bar Association.
Career: Admitted to the State Bar of Texas in 1980. Partner with Andrews Kurth since 1988.
Personal: Received a JD with honors from the University of Houston Law Center in 1980. Received a BS cum laude in Finance from the University of Alabama in 1977.

OLIVER III, Rufus W
Baker Botts LLP, Houston
713 229 1366
Rufus.oliver@bakerbotts.com
Recommended in Antitrust

Practice Areas: Concentrates on antitrust law, with extensive experience in class action and other complex litigation and in government review of mergers and acquisitions. Matters involving a wide variety of industries including steel; oil and gas; petrochemicals; offshore drilling and other oilfield services; automotive products; electric utilities; airlines; data processing.
Career: Chairs firm's antitrust section. Has served in leadership positions in American and Houston Bar Associations and State Bar of Texas.
Personal: JD, honors, The University of Texas School of Law, 1972; Research Editor, Texas Law Review; Phi Delta Phi; BA, high honors, Plan II, The University of Texas, 1969.

O'NEIL, Holland
Gardere Wynne Sewell LLP, Dallas
214 999 4961
honeil@gardere.com
Recommended in Bankruptcy

Practice Areas: Bankruptcy, financial services.
Prof. Memberships: State Bar of Texas; State Bar of Arizona; Texas Turnaround Management Association; Dallas Bar Association, Bankruptcy Section, Bankruptcy Liaison Committee; American Bar Association, Women Rainmakers Institute; American Bankruptcy Institute.
Career: Holly O'Neil has a comprehensive Financial Services Practice, focused on complex bankruptcies, workouts, acquisitions, and bankruptcy litigation. In her 18 years of practice, Ms O'Neil's clients have included debtors in possession, creditor's committees, secured creditors, trustees, examiners, as well as clients interested in acquiring assets from troubled companies. Ms O'Neil is currently representing the Examiner in the Mirant bankruptcy cases, multiple clients in various Enron-related litigation proceedings, as well as various creditor's committees in the retail and food industries. Ms O'Neil has been named as a 'Texas SuperLawyer' by Law & Politics Magazine for 2003 and 2004 and was recently named one of the Best Lawyers in Dallas (2005) by D Magazine.
Personal: JD, Texas Tech University School of Law, 1987; BBA-Finance, University of Texas at Austin, 1983.

OSTERBERG, Edward
Vinson & Elkins LLP, Houston
713 758 2192
eosterberg@velaw.com
Recommended in Tax

Practice Areas: Federal income taxation with emphasis on international transactions, mergers and acquisitions, and partnerships and joint ventures.
Prof. Memberships: Vice-President, International Fiscal Association USA Branch; President, International Tax Forum of Houston.
Publications: 'Using the Brown Group Regulations to Minimize Subpart F Income', 'Journal of Taxation of Global Transactions', Summer 2003; 'Basic U.S. Tax Considerations in Buying or Selling a Non-U.S. Business', 'Tax Notes', June 2, 2003; 'International Joint Ventures: Basis Tax Goals and Structures', 'Tax Notes', April 23, 2001.
Personal: BA, JD cum laude, Northwestern University; LLM in Taxation, Southern Methodist University.

OXFORD, Terrell
Susman Godfrey LLP, Dallas
214 754 1900
Recommended in Antitrust

PARIS, Theodore W
Baker Botts LLP, Houston
713 229 1838
ted.paris@bakerbotts.com
Recommended in Corporate/M&A

Practice Areas: Deputy Department Head: Corporate (Houston). Mergers, acquisitions, securities offerings, corporate control and governance issues and joint ventures. Represents parties in negotiated acquisitions and dispositions, controlled auctions, tender offers and related financings. Also represents domestic and foreign issuers, underwriters and selling shareholders in public offerings and in Rule 144A transactions and other private placements. Substantial experience in a wide variety of industries, including oil and gas, oilfield services, shipping, manufacturing, industrial services and consumer products and services.
Personal: JD with honors, The University of Texas School of Law, 1988; MBA and BBA-Accounting, Texas A&M University - Corpus Christi, 1983.

PARKER, Dallas
Thompson & Knight LLP, Houston
713 951 5800
dallas.parker@tklaw.com
Recommended in Communications, Technology

Practice Areas: Mr Parker heads the firm's Houston office. His focus areas include technology/communications and corporate and securities law. He has experience in mergers, acquisitions, takeovers, proxy contests, public and private offerings of equity and debt securities, and related matters. He was included in Texas Monthly's 2004 listing of Texas Super Lawyers and is listed in

Inside Houston's Best Lawyers in Houston issue (May 2004).

Prof. Memberships: State Bar of Texas, Houston, Texas, and American Bar Associations, Houston and Bar Foundations.

Career: Partner Since 1979.

Personal: University of Texas School of Law (JD, 1972); Vanderbilt University (BA, 1960).

PARKER, David
Fulbright & Jaworski L.L.P., Austin
512 536 3055
dparker@fulbright.com
Recommended in Intellectual Property

Practice Areas: Litigation, prosecution, licensing, and biotechnology.

Prof. Memberships: Member of the American Bar Association, the American Intellectual Property Law Association, the Austin Intellectual Property Law Association, the Travis County Bar Association and the Association of the University Technology Managers.

Career: Mr Parker is admitted to the US Court of Appeals for the Federal Circuit, the US Supreme Court, and the US Patent and Trademark Office. He also serves as VP of Intellectual Property of Introgen Therapeutics, Inc. a publicly traded (INGN) gene therapy company.

Personal: BA, The University of Texas (1976); PhD, Molecular Pharmacology and Genetic Engineering, Baylor College of Medicine (1981); JD, The University of Texas (1986).

PARTRIDGE, Scott
Baker Botts LLP, Houston
713 229 1569
scott.partridge@bakerbotts.com
Recommended in Intellectual Property

Practice Areas: Chairs Houston Office Intellectual Property Department. Expertise in litigation and counseling involving patents, trade secrets, copyrights, trademarks and unfair competition. Represented clients in bench and jury trials in federal and state courts throughout the US and before International Trade Commission.

Prof. Memberships: American Bar Association, House of Delegates; past Chair, Science and Technology Section; Section Officers Conference, Executive Committee. International Trade Commission Trial Lawyers Association, Executive Council and past President. Admitted in DC, Virginia, Texas. Frequent lecturer on IP law in US and internationally.

Personal: JD, Georgetown University, 1974; BS, electrical engineering, University of Cincinnati, 1969.

PATE, Stephen
Fulbright & Jaworski L.L.P., Houston
713 651 5132
spate@fulbright.com
Recommended in Insurance

Practice Areas: First-Party Insurance, Commercial Insurance, Coverage, Extracontractual and Bad Faith Litigation, and Construction Litigation.

Prof. Memberships: Pate is a past Chair of the Property Insurance Committee of the TIPS Section of the ABA. He is an active member of the Federation of Defense and Corporate Counsel and is Chair of that body's Property Insurance Section. Pate was awarded the prestigious 2004 John S. Appleman Award by that body. Pate is a frequent speaker at seminars on bad faith and property insurance issues and has authored several articles and books. Pate served as director of both the Texas and Houston Young Lawyers Associations. He is a fellow of the Texas and Houston Bar Foundations.

Career: Pate has been a Partner in the Houston office of Fulbright since 1994. He appears honored by 'Who's Who in America', 'Who's Who in American Law', 'Who's Who in the South and Southwest', and 'Who's Who in the World'.

Personal: Pate received his BA, magna cum laude, in 1980 from Vanderbilt University, and his JD, from Vanderbilt in 1983. He was admitted to practice law in Texas in 1984. He is a member of Phi Beta Kappa.

PATERSON, Nancy
Baker & Hostetler LLP, Houston
713 751 1600
Recommended in Employment

PATTERSON Jr, J A 'Tony'
Fulbright & Jaworski L.L.P., Dallas
214 855 8036
japatterson@fulbright.com
Recommended in Healthcare

Practice Areas: Health law and business organizations.

Prof. Memberships: Mr Patterson is an Adjunct Professor at the University of Iowa College of Law, and a former Adjunct Professor at the Southern Methodist Univeristy Law School. He is also a Member of the Health Law Section of the State Bar of Texas and American Bar Assocaiton and is the Chair of the American Bar Association Health Law Section.

Career: Having been a Partner in the Dallas office of Fulbright & Jaworski L.L.P since 1988, Tony Patterson heads the firm's Health Law Practice in Dallas. He is certified in Health Law by the Texas Board of Legal Specialization.

Personal: BA, Coe College (1970); JD, cum laude, Southern Methodist University (1973). Mr Patterson has served as a Trustee for Coe College since 1974. He is also involved with the Dallas-Fort Worth Health Industry Council.

PATTON, David
Locke Liddell & Sapp LLP, Houston
713 226 1254
dpatton@lockeliddell.com
Recommended in Energy

Practice Areas: For over 28 years has specialized in oil and gas issues. Co-chairs firm's Energy Group. Has represented clients in the acquisition and disposition of oil and gas properties, the negotiation and preparation of agreements relating to the ownership and operation of oil and gas interests. He advises clients on a daily basis concerning the practical implications of oil and gas law upon their ongoing business affairs. His representative clients include BP, Devon, Black Stone Minerals Company, Energen, El Paso, Amerada Hess, Marlin Energy, JP Morgan Chase Bank, Nabors, ONEOK, Stallion Energy, Chalker Energy, Palo Energy, MBIA and FSA.

Prof. Memberships: State Bar of Texas; Houston Bar Association; College of the State Bar of Texas; Federal Bar Association (Board of Directors South Texas Region); Rocky Mountain Mineral Law Foundation (National Trustee and Chairman, Regional Planning Committee); Center for American and International Law (Advisory Board).

Career: Admitted to State Bar of Texas 1977; Practiced with Locke Liddell & Sapp LLP entire career, named Partner in 1982.

Personal: JD University of Houston 1977, BA University of Texas 1973.

PEARSON, John R
Gardere Wynne Sewell LLP, Houston
713 276 5500
jpearson@gardere.com
Recommended in Insurance

Practice Areas: Insurance, oil and gas litigation, commerical litigation and arbitration, personal injury defense, trial.

Prof. Memberships: State Bar of Texas.

Career: John Pearson is a litigator with over 35 years' experience handling commercial disputes, including maritime and oilfield matters and insurance coverage. Mr Pearson represents policyholders and brokers in insurance litigation and arbitration. Mr Pearson represents several oil field service companies. Mr Pearson also handles a wide variety of maritime disputes, including charter party disputes, maritime liens, personal injury/death, and indemnity.

Personal: JD, University of Texas School of Law, 1968; BE, Chemical Engineering, Vanderbilt University, 1965.

PECHT, Gerald
Fulbright & Jaworski L.L.P., Houston
713 651 5243
gpecht@fulbright.com
Recommended in Energy

Practice Areas: Energy, business, and international litigation; class actions and intellectual property.

Prof. Memberships: Mr Pecht is a Member of both the Houston and the American Bar Associations, and is a Fellow of the Texas Bar Foundation and a Life Fellow of the Houston Bar Association. He is a Council Member of the Antitrust and Business Litigation Section of the State Bar of Texas.

Career: Gerry Pecht, a Partner in Fulbright & Jaworski L.L.P.'s Houston office, practices in the firm's Litigation Section. He regularly represents investment banking firms, energy companies, healthcare institutions, broker dealers, and numerous other types of companies, individuals, and institutions. Mr Pecht was named as a 'Texas Super Lawyer' in business litigation law in the November 2003 issue of 'Texas Monthly'.

Personal: Mr Pecht received a BA from Georgetown University in 1975 and a JD, with honors, from the University of Cincinnati in 1978.

PEDEN, David
Porter & Hedges, LLP, Houston
713 226 0600
Recommended in Construction

PEDERSEN, Luke
Baker Botts LLP, Dallas
214 953 6655
luke.pedersen@bakerbotts.com
Recommended in Intellectual Property

Practice Areas: Intellectual property law with an emphasis on patent prosecution, litigation, technology transfers, and licensing involving complex and emerging technologies. Develops and monitors comprehensive intellectual property protection programs that allow organizations to identify, protect, manage and exploit intellectual property assets. Significant patent prosecution experience with various technologies including telecommunications, Internet infrastructure, software, oil and gas production, and medical equipment. Counsels clients regarding priority of invention and initiation of interference proceedings. Drafts and negotiates license and technology transfer agreements. Litigation experience includes misappropriation of trade secrets, patent infringement, and breach of agreements governing intellectual property assets.

PELS, Gerald
Locke Liddell & Sapp LLP, Houston
713 226 1402
gpels@lockeliddell.com
Recommended in Environment

Practice Areas: Firm practice leader in environmental compliance and counseling. Has extensive experience in agency negotiations and hearings, defending enforcement actions, environmental permitting, Superfund and other environmental litigation, as well as due dilligence and transactional structuring related to environmental responsibility.

Prof. Memberships: Admitted to practice in Texas (1983). Member, Greater Houston Partnership Environmental Advisory Committee; American Bar Association, Natural Resources and Administrative Law Section; Association of Chemical Industry of Texas.

Career: Joined Locke Liddell & Sapp LLP in 1983, became Partner 1990; Adjunct Professor, Environmental Law and Advanced Hazardous Waste Seminar, South Texas College of Law, Houston, Texas 1991-97.

Publications: Selected publications and speeches include: editor, 'Texas Environmental Compliance Update', 1998-present; author, 'The Federal Toxicity Characteristic Regulations: Expanding the Roster of Hazardous Waste Players' (1991); author and presenter, 'Air Compliance: The Legal Consequences of Failure and an Approach for Risk Management' (Houston, Texas 1992); author, 'Additional Environmental Scrutiny for the Oil Patch: Texas Prepares to Enter the NORM Fray' (1992); author and presenter, 'Legal Implication of Abandoned Mine Clean-up' (Superfund Conference Washington DC 1993); speaker, 'Legislating Water Resource Management: Identifying Costs and Establishing a Basis for Compliance' (International Assn. of Water Quality, Budapest Hungary 1994); author and presenter, 'Environmental Mediation: Filling Data Gaps to Resolve Disputes' (American Bar Association, San Jose, Costa Rica 2001); author and presenter, 'Chevron USA, Inc. v. NRDC: The Foundation of Judicial Deference to Agency Action' (Austin, Texas 2004).
Personal: Born 30 January 1958 in Philadelphia, Pennsylvania; JD from Vanderbilt University in 1983 (Order of the Coif); AB from St. Joseph's University in 1980, (summa cum laude).

PÉREZ, Alfredo R
Weil, Gotshal & Manges LLP, Houston
713 546 5040
alfredo.perez@weil.com
Recommended in Bankruptcy
Practice Areas: Mr Pérez heads the Business Finance and Restructuring Practice in the Houston office.
Career: He represents Chapter 11 debtors and other parties, including purchasers of distressed assets, secured creditors and committees in court proceedings and out-of-court workouts. Mr Pérez played a major role in the largest bankruptcy ever filed, WorldCom. He is involved in most significant bankruptcies in the Southwest including TransAmerican and Cajun and many cross-border insolvencies including, most recently, Parmalat. Mr Pérez is a native Spanish speaker and member of the American College of Bankruptcy.
Personal: University of Chicago Law School (JD, 1980); Haverford College (BA, 1977).

PERICH, Thomas J
Andrews Kurth LLP, Houston
713 220 4268
tperich@andrewskurth.com
Recommended in Banking & Finance
Practice Areas: Practice has centered in banking and finance, including loan documentation for commercial, energy, construction and real estate development loans; leasing and project finance; monetization and structured finance including off-balance-sheet financing, production payments, prepaid forward

contracts and credit insurance; regulatory issues; workout and restructuring work with extensive experience in creditors' rights; work on lender liability and usury matters, representation of banks and bank holding companies before state and federal regulatory and administrative agencies and the acquisition and disposition of banks and bank assets.
Prof. Memberships: The State Bar of Texas; admitted to practice before all federal districts in Texas and the 5th and 11th Circuits; Texas Association of Bank Counsel; American Bankruptcy Institute; Houston Commercial Lawyers Forum; Houston Bar Association; various civic and charitable organizations.
Career: Admitted to the State Bar of Texas in 1976. Partner with Andrews Kurth since 1983.
Publications: 'Project Finance - Past, Present and Future' - Presentation to the Houston Commercial Finance Lawyer's Forum, January, 2004; 'Banking Law Overview', presentation as part of the Houston Bar Association's Continuing Legal Education Series, November 15, 2002; 'Who's the Boss' - The Dispute between FERC and the Bankruptcy Courts in IPP Chapter 11 Filings - Project Finance 2003 Supplement - Power Report, September 2003; 'State of the Art - An Analysis of Portfolio Power Project Financing'; Project Finance 2001 Supplement - Power Report, September 2001.
Personal: JD with honors from The University of Texas Law School in 1975. Order of the Coif, Texas Law Review. MA in economics from The University of Texas at Austin in 1971. BSFS from Georgetown University School of Foreign Service in 1967. Served in the US Foreign Service as assistant commercial attache, Economics and Commercial Section, US Consulate General, 1973-75. Responsible for Export Control Regulations, Foreign Trade issues and economic reporting. Former officer, United States Navy. Member of the Board of Directors of the Battleship Texas Foundation, Knights of Momus; University of Texas Medical Branch Development Board. Volunteer and legal representative, Justice for Children.

PETERMAN, David
Fulbright & Jaworski L.L.P., Houston
713 651 3635
dpeterman@fulbright.com
Recommended in Communications, Technology
Practice Areas: Corporate, securities and transactions.
Prof. Memberships: Mr Peterman is a Member of the Texas and Houston Bar Associations.
Career: Mr Peterman has successfully represented clients in numerous corporate, securities and business law matters. He joined Fulbright & Jaworski as a Partner in 2003. His experience includes

representing a broad range of domestic and international buyers, sellers, issuers, underwriters and investors in a number of substantial acquisitions and corporate finance transactions, including acquisitions and dispositions of stock, assets and business divisions, and public and private securities transactions. He has represented clients in industries including energy, telecom, automobile, technology, hospitality and staffing.
Personal: 1982 - BBA, Finance, the University of Texas-Austin; 1985 - JD, with honors, the University of Texas School of Law, Austin.

PETERSON, Edward
Winstead Sechrest & Minick P.C., Dallas 214 745 5642
epeterson@winstead.com
Recommended in Real Estate
Practice Areas: Former Chair, Real Estate Section; Chair, Condominium Practice, Co-Chair, Institutional Investment Practice and Co-Chair Insurance Industry Practice. Represents institutional clients in corporate real estate needs, real estate developers and investors in acquisition and disposition of real estate portfolios, and condominium developers in high rise, mixed-use and commercial condominium projects.
Prof. Memberships: American College of Real Estate Lawyers, American College of Mortgage Lawyers, Texas College of Real Estate Attorneys.
Career: State Bar of Texas. Listed in Best Lawyers in America. Texas Super Lawyers, 'Texas Monthly.' Former Member, Executive Committee.
Personal: Southern Methodist University, LLB, 1966. Washington University, BSBA, 1963.

PETERSON, Gale R
Cox Smith Matthews Incorporated, San Antonio 210 554 5327
grpeters@coxsmith.com
Recommended in Intellectual Property
Practice Areas: Pete provides litigation and transactional representation to emerging and established technology-based and research-oriented companies in intellectual property, information technology, e-commerce and related unfair competition law. He represents clients in obtaining and enforcing domestic and international patents, trademark/trade dress, domain name, copyright and trade secret protection, as well as defending clients charged with infringing those rights. Pete also represents clients in domestic and international technology acquisition and licensing.
Prof. Memberships: Division Head, American Bar Association, Section of Intellectual Property Law, 2000-present; Publications Committee, International Trademark Association, 1987-present; Director, Texas Business Hall of Fame, 1986-present; Past-President and Current Director, Society of International Business Fellows, 1991-present.

Career: Pete has served as a court-appointed special master, expert, court technical advisor, mediator and arbitrator, in cases involving technologies ranging from communications to pharmaceuticals.
Publications: Peterson & Pizarro, 2004 Federal Circuit Yearbook: Patent Law Developments in the Federal Circuit (Practicing Law Institute); Peterson & Pizarro, 'Recent Developments in Patent Law - Decisions by the US Court of Appeals for the Federal Circuit', Texas Intellectual Property Law Journal (Spring 2004).
Personal: Examiner - George Washington University, LLM, trade regulation law (with highest honors), 1978; University of Baltimore, JD, magna cum laude, 1975; University of Nebraska, BS, Electrical Engineering, 1970.

PFEIFFER, Philip J
Fulbright & Jaworski L.L.P., San Antonio
210 270 7117
ppfeiffer@fulbright.com
Recommended in Employment
Practice Areas: Labor and employment law.
Prof. Memberships: Mr Pfeiffer is a Member of the San Antonio Bar Association, the San Antonio Bar Foundation and the Texas Bar Foundation; and a Member of the American Bar Association's Equal Employment Opportunity Committee. He served as Co-Chair of the ABA's EEO Liaison Committee for the South Texas area. He also served as editor-in-chief of the Second Supplement to Lindemann and Grossman, Employment Discrimination Law. He has been elected by his peers to membership in the College of Labor and Employment Lawyers.
Career: Mr Pfeiffer focuses his legal practice on labor and employment matters, with particular emphasis on complex civil rights and employment discrimination cases; employment torts, including wrongful discharge and defamation; alternative dispute resolution, including arbitration programs; employment contracts, including restrictive covenants; and Employment Retirement Income Security Act litigation. In addition, Mr Pfeiffer, has with increasing frequency, served as a mediator in employment and civil rights cases, including class actions and has completed the approved mediator training program of the A.A. White Dispute Resolution Institute.
Personal: Mr Pfeiffer received a BS in 1969 from Sam Houston State University and a JD in 1972 from Southern Methodist University.

PHELAN, Robin
Haynes and Boone LLP, Dallas
214 651 5000
Recommended in Bankruptcy

PHELAN, Rod
Baker Botts LLP, Dallas
214 953 6609
rod.phelan@bakerbotts.com
Recommended in Litigation
Practice Areas: Concentrates in commercial litigation, primarily defending claims of professional malpractice (against accountants, lawyers, architects, and engineers), representing parties on both sides of cases involving oil and gas, partnerships, intellectual property, antitrust, securities, tax and corporate governance. Also handles appeals of cases tried by others. Clients are professional service firms, national and local business entities, and their principals.
Career: 30+ years of experience. Member, American College of Trial Lawyers, American Board of Trial Advocates.
Personal: JD, cum laude, Duke University School of Law, 1973; Order of the Coif Editorial Board, Duke Law Journal; BA, cum laude, Vanderbilt University, 1970.

PINKERTON, Glenn
Vinson & Elkins LLP, Houston
713 758 2701
gpinkerton@velaw.com
Recommended in Projects
Practice Areas: Member of the firm's Private Equity Practice Group, Project Finance and Development Practice Group, and International Practice Group. Has extensive experience in mergers and acquisitions, project development and finance, and international transactions.
Career: Admitted to Texas Bar, 1986. Came to the firm, 1986 and was admitted to the partnership, January 1995.
Personal: Graduated from The University of Texas at Austin, BBA in 1981, and Columbia University, JD in 1986.

PIRKEY, Louis
Fulbright & Jaworski L.L.P., Austin
512 536 3001
lpirkey@fulbright.com
Recommended in Intellectual Property
Practice Areas: Trademark litigation and counseling.
Prof. Memberships: Past President of the American Intellectual Property Law Association, past Chairman of the Intellectual Property Law Section of the State Bar of Texas, and was the charter President of the Austin Intellectual Property Law Association.
Career: Represented clients in over 300 trademark and unfair competition litigations in federal district and appellate courts across the country.
Personal: Received a BSChE (1960) from The University of Texas at Austin and a JD, with honors, (1964) from The George Washington University Law School.

POFF, Joe
Baker Botts LLP, Houston
713 229 1410
joe.poff@bakerbotts.com
Recommended in Corporate/M&A
Practice Areas: Chair: Houston Corporate Section. Corporate finance, securities, and mergers and acquisitions, especially in energy and telecommunications. Handles US and international M&As and represents US and non-US issuers, underwriters, and investment banking firms in public, private, Rule 144A, and Regulation S offerings, as well as specialized financings including offerings of American Depositary Receipts, interests in master limited partnerships and trust preferred securities. Counsels clients in financings, general corporate matters and corporate governance issues and special investigations.
Personal: JD, with high honors, The University of Texas School of Law, 1979; BS, summa cum laude, economics, Texas A&M University, 1976.

POWELL, Charles
Haynes and Boone LLP, Houston
713 547 2000
Recommended in Communications, Technology

POWERS, Werner
Haynes and Boone LLP, Dallas
214 651 5000
Recommended in Insurance

PRATT, Don
Pratt & Sanderford, Temple
254 773 8311
Recommended in Construction

PUIG, Yvonne Karen
Fulbright & Jaworski L.L.P., Austin
512 474 5201
ypuig@fulbright.com
Recommended in Healthcare
Practice Areas: Health Law.
Prof. Memberships: Ms Puig is currently a Council Member and past Chair of the Health Law Section of the State Bar of Texas. She is also a member of the American Board of Trial Advocates, the American Health Lawyers Association, and the Texas Association of Defense Counsel.
Career: Yvonne Puig joined the Austin office of Fulbright as a Partner with over 24 years of experience. She has extensive experience in a variety of health law regulatory matters, such as EMTALA, JCAHO accreditation, credentialing, and due process hearings.
Personal: BA, High Honors, University of Texas (1975); JD, University of Texas School of Law (1978). Ms Puig was admitted to practice in Texas in (1978).

PUTMAN, Frank
Gardere Wynne Sewell LLP, Houston
713 276 5777
fputman@gardere.com
Recommended in Communications, Technology
Practice Areas: Corporate, securities,

M&A, energy and energy services, global projects.
Prof. Memberships: American Bar Association; State Bar of Texas; Houston Bar Association.
Career: Over the last 30 years, Frank Putman has developed a comprehensive national and international business practice focusing on corporate and securities work and general business matters. He also offers a particular expertise in energy-related companies, financial institutions and manufacturing companies. Earlier in his career, Mr Putman pioneered the development and implementation of creative financing strategies utilizing investment tax credits in public and private partnerships to finance offshore drilling rig construction projects.
Personal: LLB, University of Texas School of Law, 1965; BS, University of Texas, 1962.

RABALAIS, Robert René
Vinson & Elkins LLP, Houston
713 758 4526
RRabalais@velaw.com
Recommended in Banking & Finance
Practice Areas: Co-Chair of the firm's Financial Institutions Practice Group; practice consists of secured and unsecured syndicated finance transactions, capital markets and privately placed debt securities.
Personal: Louisiana State University, BS, 1986; Louisiana State University, JD, 1989.

RAFTE, Alan
Bracewell & Giuliani LLP, Houston
713 221 1411
alan.rafte@bracewellgiuliani.com
Recommended in Energy, Projects
Practice Areas: Handles diverse commercial transactions involving energy industries such as electric power, oil and gas exploration and production and gas and liquid pipelines and facilities. Has represented project sponsors, equity investors and credit providers in transactions that have included acquisitions and divestitures of a variety of assets and companies, structured and commercial finance and project development and project finance. Recognized by 'Project Finance' magazine with 'Deal of the Year' honors for innovative work on a power generation project. Honored in Chambers' Global in 2004, 2003.
Personal: JD, Emory University School of Law, 1979; BA, Syracuse University, 1976.

RAIN, John W
Thompson & Knight LLP, Dallas
214 969 1644
john.rain@tklaw.com
Recommended in Banking & Finance
Practice Areas: Mr Rain's practice focuses on structuring and negotiating volumetric production payment and other energy transactions involving the combination of property or commodity sales with derivative contracts; general

representation of both lenders and borrowers in bank and mezzanine loans and private placements; transactional aspects of bankruptcies and reorganizations.
Prof. Memberships: Member of the State Bar of Texas, State Bar of New York, American College of Investment Counsel, Texas Association of Bank Counsel, Dallas Bar Association, Dallas Bar Foundation.
Personal: University of Texas Law School (JD, 1978); Gordon-Conwell Theological Seminary (graduate study, 1974-75); Amherst College (BA, 1973).

RAMIREZ, Kenneth
Bracewell & Giuliani LLP, Austin
512 494 3611
ken.ramirez@bracewellgiuliani.com
Recommended in Environment
Practice Areas: Focuses on Texas water law and assisting corporations and municipalities in acquiring, managing and planning water supplies. Also garnered expertise in early career regulatory roles, including executive positions in waste management and in legal services at the Texas Natural Resources Conservation Commission. Also served as management attorney for the EPA in San Francisco and staff attorney for the Texas Water Commission, where he authored much of Texas' Superfund policy.
Career: Recognized by 'Texas Lawyer' among the state's top administrative law attorneys.
Personal: JD, The University of Texas School of Law, 1980; BA, North Texas State University, 1977.

RATNER, Randall M
Akin Gump Strauss Hauer & Feld LLP, Dallas 214 969 2893
rratner@akingump.com
Recommended in Real Estate
Practice Areas: Extensive experience in office, hotel, industrial, apartment and retail projects development, including negotiation of partnerships, joint ventures, LLC agreements with public companies, national and regional developers, insurance companies, pension funds. Has represented clients in acquisition and disposition of real estate portfolios, including portfolios of office and industrial buildings, hotels and closed retail stores, and borrowers in all aspects of financings (securitized loans, loans secured by portfolio of buildings, construction loans, permanent loans, lines of credit financings).
Prof. Memberships: Texas Academy of Real Estate, Probate and Trust Lawyers.
Personal: BS (high distinction), Indiana University; JD (honors), University of Texas.

RAY, Hugh M
Andrews Kurth LLP, Houston
713 220 4164
hray@andrewskurth.com
Recommended in Bankruptcy
Practice Areas: Heads Andrews Kurth's national Bankruptcy Practice. Represents or has represented the Debtor in

Crown Pacific; Deutsche Bank in Yukos; the Unsecured Creditors' Committee of Flagstar Corporation (Denny's); the Trustee for the Bank of New England Corporation; the Unsecured Creditors' Committee of In re First Republic Bank Corporation; Rubus Realty (Furr's Supermarkets); Drypers Corporation; Doskocil (Wilson Foods); the Debtor in Friede Goldman Halter, Inc.; the Debtor in Physicians Resource Group; the ad hoc Bondholder's Committee of American Rice, Inc.; the Agent Bank and Bank Syndicate in In re William Herbert Hunt, Nelson Bunker Hunt Trust Estate, et al.; the Institutional Lenders for In re Storage Technology; the Institutional Creditors of In re Continental Airlines, Inc. (both cases); and the Insurance Company Lenders of In re Braniff Airlines, Inc. He has also represented the Unsecured Creditors' Committee and Petitioning Creditors for In re First City Bancorporation of Texas. He also represented the bondholders in the CalFed and GlenFed restructurings.

Prof. Memberships: The State Bar of Texas; New York State Bar; US District Court, Southern District of Texas; US District Court, Western District of Louisiana; US District Court, Western District of Texas; US District Court, Northern District of Texas; US Circuit Court of Appeals, 5th Circuit; US Circuit Court of Appeals, 11th Circuit; US Circuit Court of Appeals, 9th Circuit; US Supreme Court. Board Certified Business Bankruptcy Specialist, Texas Board of Legal Specialization and the American Board of Bankruptcy Certification. Elected American College of Bankruptcy. Selected Best Lawyers in America. Elected Member, American Law Institute. Member, Consultative Group, Transnational Law Project. Past Chair, Bankruptcy Committee, State Bar of Texas 1986-89. Council of the Business Law Section of the American Bar Association (1997-2001). Past chair of the ABA Business Law Section's Business Bankruptcy Committee; Chair of the Energy Business Committee. Past Chair of the Committee on Trust Indentures and Indenture Trustees of the Business Law Section of the American Bar Association. Past Member of the Standing Committee of the American Bar Association on Judicial Selection, Tenure and Compensation.

Career: Admitted to the State Bar of Texas in 1967 and the New York Bar in 1991. Partner with Andrews Kurth since 1977.

Publications: Lecturer at ABA satellite seminars. Co-author of 'Bankruptcy Investing' (Beard, 2004) and of 'Texas Practice Guide Rights' Vols. 1 and 2 (West Publishing - 2005). Lecturer for the Central and Eastern European Law Initiative, Vilnius, Lithuania, 1996. Has presented positions before congressional committees by testifying four times

before the House Judiciary Committee and the Senate Judiciary Committee concerning proposed amendments to the Federal Bankruptcy Code. Was invited to lead a presentation before the National Bankruptcy Review Commission.

Personal: Received an LLB from Vanderbilt University School of Law in 1967. Received a BA in English from Vanderbilt University in 1965; Governing Board, Houston Symphony; Trustee, South Texas College of Law.

REASONER, Harry
Vinson & Elkins LLP, Houston
713 758 2358
hreasoner@velaw.com
Recommended in Antitrust, Energy, Litigation

Practice Areas: Complex civil litigation. Served as lead counsel in trials, arbitrations, and appeals involving antitrust, securities, energy, insurance, contract, and tort claims.

Prof. Memberships: Fellow: American College of Trial Lawyers; International Academy of Trial Lawyers; International Society of Barristers; American Law Institute; American Board of Trial Advocates. Chair, ABA Section of Antitrust Law.

Career: Admitted: Texas; District of Columbia; New York. Law Clerk, USCA, 2d Cir. Partner, Vinson & Elkins L.L.P.

Publications: With C. A. Wright, 'Procedure: The Handmaid of Justice'.

Personal: Rice University, BA; The University of Texas Law School, JD; Rotary Foundation Fellow, University of London.

REDDEN, Joe
Beck, Redden & Secrest L.L.P, Houston
713 951 3700
Recommended in Litigation

REED, Kevin
Davis & Wilkerson, PC, Austin
512 482 0614
Recommended in Healthcare

REID Jr, Russell L
Akin Gump Strauss Hauer & Feld LLP, Dallas 214 969 4769
rreid@akingump.com
Recommended in Bankruptcy

Practice Areas: Focuses on creditors' rights, bankruptcy, and corporate reorganization and refinance, with particular emphasis on default administration for corporate trustees and servicers of commercial mortgage securitized trusts. Client representations include parties in bankruptcy proceedings, receiverships and out-of-court restructurings, and related litigation. On behalf of debtors, creditors, committees, indenture trustees, loan servicers and other parties-in-interest, has developed, negotiated and drafted disclosure materials, plans of reorganization, and related documents and pleadings and has prosecuted and defended litigation involving the automatic stay, cash collateral, claim determination, debtor-in-possession

financing and plan confirmation.
Personal: BFA, BBA, Southern Methodist University; JD, University of Texas.

RENBARGER, Robert
Fritz, Byrne, Head & Harrison, Austin
512 476 2020
Recommended in Environment

RENFROE, Tracie
Bracewell & Giuliani LLP, Houston
713 221 1404
tracie.renfroe@bracewellgiuliani.com
Recommended in Litigation

Practice Areas: Maintains national practice focusing on environmental and toxic tort litigation and product liability disputes, including federal and state class actions and multi-district litigation. Has significant experience in contaminated groundwater and drinking water cases. Serves as national coordinating counsel for several oil companies in MTBE contamination litigation. Has handled cases involving petroleum hydrocarbons, solvents, chlorinated compounds, oxygenates and radioactive materials. Has litigated actions under CERCLA, RCRA, Safe Drinking Water Act and state and local statutes. Has litigated deep injection well disputes, personal injury and chemical exposure suits.

Personal: JD, Baylor University School of Law; BA, Baylor University.

REYNOLDS, Chris
Gibbs & Bruns, LLP, Houston
713 751 5214
jreynolds@gibbs-bruns.com
Recommended in Energy, Litigation

Practice Areas: Practice consists of commercial litigation, with an emphasis on intellectual property and energy-related litigation.

Prof. Memberships: Fellow in the Texas Bar Foundation, and a Member of Tau Beta Pi and Chi Epsilon, each of which is an engineering honor society.

Career: Started with Wood, Campbell, Moody & Gibbs, P.C. (a predecessor firm), in March of 1983; joined Gibbs & Ratliff in the fall of 1983; and has been with it (the name changed to Gibbs & Bruns LLP in 1993) ever since. Became a full Partner in October of 1987.

Publications: Has written and presented seminar papers on the following topics: i) the use of statistics in litigation; ii) how lawyers can avoid liability when deals 'go bad.'

Personal: Married with two children and loves deep sea fishing and fox hunting.

RICHARD, Molly
Thompson & Knight LLP, Dallas
214 969 1677
molly.richard@tklaw.com
Recommended in Intellectual Property

Practice Areas: Ms Richard represents clients extensively in trademark clearance and registration worldwide, copyright protection and advice, and litigation in trademark and copyright mat-

ters. She has obtained numerous favorable arbitration panel decisions under the UDRP to transfer infringing domain names for a world-renowned computer company. She was selected for inclusion in Texas Monthly's 2004 listing of Texas Super Lawyers.

Prof. Memberships: State Bar of Texas, American Bar Association, Dallas Bar Association, Dallas/Ft. Worth Intellectual Property Law Association.

Publications: Ms Richard is an active author.

Personal: SMU Dedman School of Law (JD, 1981); Austin College (BA, 1977).

ROBECK, Mark
Baker Botts LLP, Houston
713 229 2071
mark.robeck@bakerbotts.com
Recommended in Energy

Practice Areas: Mr Robeck counsels oil and gas producers, regulated utilities, independent wholesale power generators, and electricity and power traders in complex litigation and regulatory matters, including commercial disputes, securities, mass tort/class actions, wrongful death claims, and criminal and administrative investigations. He represents clients before state and federal courts and regulatory agencies, including the SEC, FERC, CFTC, NRC, and PUCT.

Prof. Memberships: State Bar of Texas; American Bar Association; Houston Bar Association; Texas Bar Foundation; Houston Bar Foundation.

Personal: JD (with honors), The University of Texas School of Law, 1989; BS (cum laude), Physical Education, Texas A&M University, 1982.

ROBERSON, Richard
Gardere Wynne Sewell LLP, Dallas
214 999 4955
rroberson@gardere.com
Recommended in Bankruptcy

Practice Areas: Bankruptcy, financial services.

Prof. Memberships: American Bar Association; State Bar of Texas; Dallas Bar Association; American Bankruptcy Institute; Turnaround Management Association; Honorable John C. Ford American Inn of Court.

Career: Richard Roberson has a comprehensive Bankruptcy Practice that includes the representation of secured lenders, debtors, trustees, examiners and creditors' committees, primarily in large corporate reorganizations. Mr Roberson's practice also includes all litigation arising from his bankruptcy and creditors' rights matters. Mr Roberson's clients have included major banks, asset based lenders, trustees, creditors' committees, receivers, examiners, creditors and debtors in a variety of industries. Mr Roberson is currently the lead attorney for the Examiner in the In re Mirant Corporation, et al bankruptcy proceedings.

Personal: JD, St. Mary's University School of Law, with honors, 1978; BBA, Southern Methodist University, cum laude, 1975.

ROBERTS, Harry
Thompson & Knight LLP, Dallas
214 969 1616
harry.roberts@tklaw.com
Recommended in Real Estate

Practice Areas: Mr Roberts' practice primarily focuses on real estate transactions including permanent and construction loan work, loan servicing, purchase and sale of commercial real estate, development of real property, leasing, local counsel opinions, loan workouts, foreclosure, and usury analysis. He was selected for inclusion in Texas Monthly's 2003 and 2004 listings of Texas Super Lawyers.

Prof. Memberships: State Bar of Texas, American College of Real Estate Lawyers, Dallas Bar Association, American, Texas, and Dallas Bar Foundations.

Publications: Mr Roberts is an active author and speaker.

Personal: Harvard Law School (JD, 1963); Southern Methodist University (BBA, 1960).

ROCHELLE, Michael
Rochelle, Hutcheson & McCullough, LLP, Dallas 214 953 0182
Recommended in Bankruptcy

RODRIGUEZ, Cristina
Baker Botts LLP, Houston
713 229 1188
cristina.rodriguez@bakerbotts.com
Recommended in Employment

Practice Areas: Ms Rodriguez's practice encompasses professional malpractice and federal securities cases, including cases consolidated into multidistrict litigation (MDL), defending employers in various types of discrimination and sexual harassment, including class action suits. Fluent in Spanish, Ms Rodriguez has also represented businesses that operate or have been sued in Mexico and Central America.

Prof. Memberships: State Bar of Texas; Houston Bar Association; Houston Young Lawyers Association; Leadership Texas, 2004.

Career: Member, Attorney Development Committee - Houston; Member, Diversity Committee - Firmwide.

Personal: JD (cum laude), Harvard Law School, 1995; BA (summa cum laude), English and Sociology, University of Miami, 1992.

ROGERS, Daniel
Chadbourne & Parke LLP, Houston
713 571 5930
drogers@chadbourne.com
Recommended in Energy, Projects

Practice Areas: Represents sponsors, lenders, suppliers, transporters, operators, and marketers in all aspects of gas-related energy infrastructure projects. Extensive experience in the develop-

ment and financing of Liquefied Natural Gas production. Has written articles and spoken at several conferences on issues affecting the natural gas and LNG industries. Recently included in the International Who's Who of International Oil & Gas Lawyers, 2004.

Prof. Memberships: American Bar Association, State Bar of Texas, Houston Bar Association.

Career: Previously served as Assistant General Counsel to Enron Corp. and was Senior Attorney for VICO Services, Inc.

ROSE, David
Conley, Rose & Tayon, Houston
713 238 8000
Recommended in Intellectual Property

ROSENSTEIN, Tony P
Baker Botts LLP, Houston
713 229 1582
tony.rosenstein@bakerbotts.com
Recommended in Employment

Practice Areas: Specializes in labor and employment litigation matters in state and federal court. Represents employers before the Equal Employment Opportunity Commission, National Labor Relations Board, the Occupational Safety and Health Review Commission, the Department of Labor, and related administrative agencies. Board certified in labor and employment law, Texas Board of Legal Specialization. Represents major national oil and gas, insurance, and banking companies.

Career: 27+ years in practice.

Personal: JD, cum laude, University of Houston, 1976; MA, clinical psychology, Memphis State University, 1969; BS, Rensselaer Polytechnic Institute, 1967.

ROSS, Judith
Baker Botts LLP, Houston
214 953 6605
judith.ross@bakerbotts.com
Recommended in Bankruptcy

Practice Areas: Partner. Represents a diverse range of asset acquirers, lenders, creditors, debtors, officers and directors in virtually every aspect of complex Chapter 11 cases, as well as out-of-court workouts. She has particular experience in bankruptcy litigation.

Career: Prior to joining Baker Botts in 2004, she was a Partner at Thompson & Knight L.L.P.

Personal: JD, The University of Texas School of Law, 1985; BA, Miami University, 1979.

ROYALL, M Sean
Gibson, Dunn & Crutcher LLP, Dallas
214 698 3256
sroyall@gibsondunn.com
Recommended in Antitrust

Practice Areas: Co-Chair, Antitrust and Trade Regulation Practice. Litigates complex antitrust matters and represents firms before federal/international antitrust agencies; advises on antitrust issues in the M&A, joint venture, distribution, and IP contexts; litigates other

commercial disputes, including IP, securities, and false advertising.

Prof. Memberships: Vice Chair, FTC Committee, ABA Section of Antitrust Law.

Career: Former Deputy Director of the Bureau of Competition, Federal Trade Commission.

Publications: Editor, Von Kalinowski Antitrust Treatise. Former Editorial Chair, Antitrust Law Journal. Numerous articles on antitrust issues.

Personal: JD, University of Chicago Law School, with honors, 1990; Managing Editor, University of Chicago Law Review.

RUCKMAN, Deirdre
Gardere Wynne Sewell LLP, Dallas
214 999 4250
druckman@gardere.com
Recommended in Bankruptcy

Practice Areas: Bankruptcy, financial services.

Prof. Memberships: State Bar of Texas; Fellow, Texas Bar Association; Master, American Inns of Court.

Career: Deirdre Ruckman has 30 years of experience in the financial services sector. She specializes in representation of both debtors and creditors in business reorganizations involving private and/or public debt. She is currently the section head for Gardere's Creditors Rights and Business Reorganization Group and a member of the firm's Partners' Board. She has earned the designation of Master, in the American Inns of Court, is a fellow of the Texas Legal Foundation, a participant in the Private Attorney Project for Legal Services of North Texas and a delegate to the Fifth Circuit Judicial Conference. Mrs Ruckman was selected and recently participated in the Joint Civilian Orientation Conference, the premier civic leader program of the Secretary of the Department of Defense. As part of this conference, she visited US bases and military personnel in Hawaii, Japan, South Korea, Singapore, and Guam.

Personal: JD, Southern Methodist University Dedman School of Law, 1975; BS, Chestnut Hill College, 1970.

SAEGERT, Ann
Haynes and Boone LLP, Dallas
214 651 5000
Recommended in Real Estate

SALCH, Steven
Fulbright & Jaworski L.L.P., Houston
713 651 5433
ssalch@fulbright.com
Recommended in Tax

Practice Areas: Tax controversy, state and federal tax planning, multi-national tax and business law, mediation, arbitration, expert witness, administrative agency determinations and rulemaking, legislation, antiboycott compliance, foreign asset controls, and export administration.

Prof. Memberships: Listed in 'Who's Who in America'; Past Chair, Section of Taxation, American Bar Association;

Fifth Circuit Regent, American College of Tax Counsel; Member, American Law Institute, the International Fiscal Association, the American Bar Foundation, and the Houston Bar Foundation.

Career: Admitted to Texas Bar (1968). Partner in the Houston office of Fulbright since 1975.

Personal: BBA, Accounting (1965) and JD, (1968) from Southern Methodist University.

SAROSDY, Randall
Akin Gump Strauss Hauer & Feld LLP, Austin 512 499 6225
rsarosdy@akingump.com
Recommended in Intellectual Property

Practice Areas: Patent litigation and complex commercial litigation. Represents clients in and has tried to judgment numerous patent infringement and complex commercial litigation matters, including multi-state class actions, in federal district and appellate courts throughout the nation.

Prof. Memberships: Adjunct Professor, George Mason University School of Law, fall 2000; Member, Intellectual Property Section, State Bar of Texas; Member, Civil Litigation Section, Austin Bar Association; Life Fellow, Texas Bar Foundation.

Personal: AB (high honors), College of William and Mary (1974); JD, University of Texas School of Law (1977) (Associate Editor, Texas Law Review).

SASLAW, Michael A.
Weil, Gotshal & Manges LLP, Dallas
214 746 8117
michael.saslaw@weil.com
Recommended in Corporate/M&A

Practice Areas: Mr Saslaw's primary practice areas are mergers and acquisitions, securities offerings, financings, restructurings, real estate investment trusts and corporate counseling.

Career: He has extensive experience with businesses in a variety of industries, including media, real estate, retail, consumer products and manufacturing. Representative clients include AMX Corporation, Bear Stearns & Co., Bell Helicopter Textron, Inc., Citigroup, Citicorp Venture Capital Ltd., Covad Communications Group, Electronic Data Systems Corporation (EDS), General Electric Company, General Motors Corporation, Hollywood Casino Corporation, J.C. Penney Company, and Lone Star Funds.

Personal: University of Pennsylvania Law School (JD, 1982); Miami University (BBA, magna cum laude, 1979).

SCHICK, Robert M
Vinson & Elkins LLP, Houston
713 758 4582
rschick@velaw.com
Recommended in Litigation

Practice Areas: Over 20 years of experience in all aspects of products liability, environmental and toxic tort litigation, representing domestic and foreign corporations throughout Texas and in eight other states.

Prof. Memberships: American Board of Trial Advocates; Product Liability Advisory Council; IADC; DRI.

Career: Partner since 1989. Texas Board certified since 1987 in Civil Trial Law and Personal Injury Law. Listed, Best Lawyers in America, 2003-2005; Texas Super Lawyer, 2003-2004.

Publications: Co-author: Hampton, Schick & McGehee's Texas Civil Practice and Remedies Code Annotated, Thompson West 2002-2004.

Personal: Princeton University (AB 1976), University of Houston (JD 1981).

SCHIFFER, Adam
King & Spalding LLP, Houston
713 715 3234
aschiffer@kslaw.com
Recommended in Energy, Litigation

Practice Areas: Extensive experience representing both plaintiffs and defendants in complex business and construction litigation and arbitrations involving a wide variety of contract and tort claims. Has tried over 30 commercial cases throughout Texas (state and federal courts), Pennsylvania (federal court) and Delaware (Chancery Courts). Has arbitrated disputes in Texas, Nevada, Geneva, Switzerland and London, England under AAA, JAMS, UNCITRAL, LCIA and ICC rules.

Prof. Memberships: Texas Bar Association.

Personal: BA, Dickenson College,1983; JD, University of Houston, 1986.

SCHOENBRUN, Larry
Gardere Wynne Sewell LLP, Dallas
214 999 4703
lschoenbrun@gardere.com
Recommended in Corporate/M&A

Practice Areas: Corporate, M&A, securities.

Prof. Memberships: Dallas Bar Association; American Bar Association; Former Chairman, Securities Committee of the Council of the Business Law Section of the State Bar of Texas; Former Chairman, Texas Business Law Foundation; Former Chairman, Council of the Business Law Section of the State Bar of Texas.

Career: With more than 30 years of experience as a corporate and securities practitioner, Larry Schoenbrun has served as the coordinator of legal activities for large and medium-sized corporations. He has represented corporations in their initial public offerings, corporate reorganizations, reincorporations, roll-ups and structuring of employee benefit plans. Mr Schoenbrun has also represented underwriters in public offerings, buyers and sellers in various corporate acquisitions and dispositions and venture capitalists in their investments. He has served as counsel for special committees of boards of directors dealing with affiliate transactions and conflict situations and for audit com-

mittees dealing with various corporate governance and fiduciary issues.

Personal: LLB, University of Texas School of Law, 1965; BA, University of Texas at Austin, 1962.

SCHUURMAN, Willem
Vinson & Elkins LLP, Austin
512 542 8663
bschuurman@velaw.com
Recommended in Intellectual Property

Practice Areas: Partner, co-section head at Vinson & Elkins, Intellectual Property Section, Austin Texas. Practice is devoted to patent law with emphasis on patent litigation. Technical background in the chemical and chemical engineering fields. Also handles matters in the electrical, mechanical, biotechnology, and computer fields. Author of several journal articles.

Prof. Memberships: US Patent and Trademark Office, and the South African Patent Office; American, Federal, Travis County and Federal Circuit Bar Associations; International, American, and Austin Intellectual Property Law Associations.

Career: South Texas College of Law, JD, magna cum laude, 1981; University of Cape Town, LLB (1964) and BS (1962).

SCHWARTZ, Michele
Hughes & Luce LLP, Dallas
214 939 5500
Recommended in Intellectual Property

SEALS, Paul
Akin Gump Strauss Hauer & Feld LLP, Austin 512 499 6203
pseals@akingump.com
Recommended in Environment

Practice Areas: Paul Seals has more than 30 years of experience in environmental regulatory matters, focusing on environmental licensing and compliance matters as well as public policy issues. He provides environmental and natural resource counseling on project development issues in the energy, paper, petroleum refining and waste management industries. His experience includes both administrative and judicial litigation and appeals.

Prof. Memberships: Environmental and Natural Resources Law Section, Texas State Bar (former Chairman).

Career: Regional Counsel, US Environmental Protection Agency, Dallas (1982-86); Assistant General Counsel, Texas Department of Water Resources (1977-82).

Personal: BA, St. Edwards University; JD, University of Texas.

SELINGER, Jerry
Morgan, Lewis & Bockius LLP, Dallas
214 438 1569
jselinger@jenkens.com
Recommended in Intellectual Property

Practice Areas: Jerry R Selinger is a Partner in the Litigation Practice. Mr Selinger's practice focuses on litigation of intellectual property and related mat-

ters. He has tried cases in federal and state courts and appeared before various appellate courts and agencies, including the International Trade Commission. He has handled patent litigation in an extensive range of technical disciplines, including computer science technology, electrical devices, chemical processes and mechanical devices.

SENTILLES III, Irwin F
Gibson, Dunn & Crutcher LLP, Dallas
214 698 3119
isentilles@gibsondunn.com
Recommended in Corporate/M&A

Practice Areas: Extensive experience in corporate and securities law. Practice encompasses mergers and acquisitions, debt and equity financings, restructurings, joint ventures, securities law compliance, corporate governance and general corporate advice for both publicly and privately held companies. Industry experience includes energy, healthcare, homebuilding, manufacturing, retail, technology, transportation and utilities.

Prof. Memberships: Admitted before New York and Texas Bars.

Publications: Frequent speaker on corporate and securities law topics.

Personal: JD, Yale Law School, 1972.

SHANK, Mark
Hughes & Luce LLP, Dallas
214 939 5500
Recommended in Employment

SHEEDER, Robert
Jenkens & Gilchrist PC, Dallas
214 855 4500
Recommended in Employment

SHEINFELD, Myron M
Akin Gump Strauss Hauer & Feld LLP, Houston 713 220 5801
msheinfeld@akingump.com
Recommended in Bankruptcy

Practice Areas: Focuses on reorganization and bankruptcy law, bankruptcy tax, creditors' rights, workout matters, commercial litigation, business transactions. Has 40+ years of experience in all aspects of Chapter 11 reorganizations, including negotiation of complex plans of reorganization and litigation of contested matters and adversary proceedings. Has been involved in many of the major bankruptcy reorganizations or business problems in the United States.

Prof. Memberships: Chair, American Bar Association Standing Committee on Specialization; Member, National Bankruptcy Conference and American College of Bankruptcy; President and Director, National Association of Corporate Directors (Houston Chapter).

Personal: BA, Tulane University; JD, University of Michigan.

SHEPPARD, Ben
Vinson & Elkins LLP, Houston
713 758 2574
bsheppard@velaw.com
Recommended in Arbitration, Energy

Practice Areas: Practice concentrated

in domestic and international litigation and arbitration, both as counsel and as arbitrator, and has included disputes over gas contracts, operating agreements, marketing and storage agreements, liquefied natural gas contracts, and royalties.

Prof. Memberships: Member, The Chartered Institute of Arbitrators; AAA Commercial and Energy Panels; ICDR International Panel.

Career: Law Clerk to Honorable Homer Thornberry, US Court of Appeals for the Fifth Circuit; Partner, Vinson & Elkins, L.L.P., Houston, Texas.

Publications: Editor in chief, 'The International Arbitration News'.

Personal: University of North Texas, BA, 1965; University of Texas School of Law, LLB with High Honors, 1968.

SHIDLOFSKY, Lee
Nickens Keeton Lawless Farrell & Flack LLP, Austin 512 472 3067
Recommended in Insurance

SHORT Jr, William
Short, How, Frels & Heitz, Dallas
214 720 2220
Recommended in Construction

SHOWALTER, Barton E
Baker Botts LLP, Dallas
214 953 6509
bart.showalter@bakerbotts.com
Recommended in Intellectual Property

Practice Areas: Partner practicing patent law emphasizing patent procurement, litigation, licensing and counseling for high technology companies. Significant experience litigating and licensing patents in a variety of fields, including video conferencing, telecommunications, semiconductor fabrication, software simulation, computer architecture, and medical devices. Also provides strategic counseling to maximize research and development investments. Develops and implements innovative processes and tools for patent portfolio management, enforcement, licensing, IP risk mitigation.

Personal: BS and MS in Aerospace Engineering, MIT; teaches several IP courses at SMU School of Law; Texas State Bar, Treasurer IP Section and Conference Chair; Executive Committee, Institute of Law and Technology.

SIMPSON, Reagan
King & Spalding LLP, Houston
713 751 3229
RSimpson@kslaw.com
Recommended in Litigation

Practice Areas: Handles a wide variety of trial and appellate matters, including litigation involving personal injury, commercial torts, mass torts, media law and defamation, and products liability. Has active appellate and trial practice in both state and federal courts.

Prof. Memberships: American Board of Trial Advocates; American College of Trial Lawyers; Federation of Insurance

and Corporate Counsel; Houston Bar Association; State Bar of Texas.
Personal: BA, highest honors, University of Texas, 1974; JD, high honors, University of Texas, 1977.

SINAK, David
Gibson, Dunn & Crutcher LLP, Dallas
214 698 3100
dsinak@gibsondunn.com
Recommended in Tax
Practice Areas: Focuses on federal income taxation of corporations, partnerships, limited liability companies, investment securities, and Texas franchise taxation. Involved in tax planning for corporate and partnership M&A, financings, solvent/insolvent restructurings, tax free spin-offs, tax free corporate reorganizations, partnership structuring and reorganizations, debt/equity offerings, and foreign investments in US. Experienced in obtaining private letter rulings from IRS, handling cases through IRS administrative appeals process, and litigating tax disputes in the federal courts.
Publications: American Bar Association, State Bar of Texas, Dallas Bar Association.
Personal: JD, cum laude, Boston College Law School, 1979, Articles Editor, 'Boston College Law Review'.

SLAVICH, John
Guida Slavich & Flores PC, Austin
214 692 0009
Recommended in Environment

SLUSSER, William
Slusser, Wilson & Partridge LLP, Houston 713 860 3300
Recommended in Intellectual Property

SMITH, Alison
Dewey Ballantine LLP, Houston
713 445 1590
asmith@deweyballantine.com
Recommended in Antitrust
Practice Areas: Co-Chair of Dewey Ballantine's Antitrust & Trade Regulation Group. Practice entails complex business litigation, emphasizing antitrust, securities and commercial litigation.
Prof. Memberships: The American Law Institute; The American Bar Association (Section of Antitrust Law, Vice-Chair of the Sherman Act Section 1 Committee); State Bar of Texas; Texas Bar Foundation; Houston Bar Association.
Career: Partner, Dewey Ballantine LLP. Deputy Assistant Attorney General of the Antitrust Division of the US Department of Justice (1989-91). Vinson & Elkins (1977-89 and 1991-2004), admitted to partnership 1984.
Personal: Born September 24, 1952. BJ, 1974 and JD, 1977 University of Texas.

SMITH, James E
Beirne, Maynard & Parsons, L.L.P., Houston 713 963 7348
jsmith@bmpllp.com
Recommended in Litigation
Practice Areas: Environmental

enforcement; environmental permitting; toxic torts; natural resources (gas and electricity); patent and related intellectual property litigation.
Prof. Memberships: Texas State Bar - Litigation; Environmental and Natural Resources; Intellectual Property; American Bar Association - Litigation; Natural Resources and Environmental; Intellectual Property; Houston Bar Association - Litigation; Environmental; Intellectual Property.
Career: Admitted to Bar, 1982, Texas; also admitted to practice before US Court of Appeals, Fifth Circuit and Federal Circuit; US District Court, Northern, Southern, Eastern and Western Districts of Texas; and United States Patent and Trademark Office. Selected by a leading US legal publication for environmental litigation in Texas.
Publications: 'Fundamentals of Environmental Enforcement'; 'Suggestions on Dealing With Agency Investigations'.
Personal: BS Chemical Engineering, 1978, University of Kansas, Tau Beta Pi (Engineering Honor Society), Phi Lambda Upsilon (Chemistry Honor Society); JD, 1982, University of Texas, with Honors. Mr Smith's trial practice generally involves environmental, energy, and natural resource issues, and also intellectual property matters. He has tried civil cases in state and federal court, and before arbitration panels.

SOSLAND, Martin
Weil, Gotshal & Manges LLP, Dallas
214 746 7730
martin.sosland@weil.com
Recommended in Bankruptcy
Practice Areas: Mr Sosland concentrates in reorganizations, debtor and creditors' rights, and refinancings and acquisitions of troubled companies.
Career: He was one of the firm's principals representing Enron in Chapter 11. He also led the firm's representation of Sulzer Orthopedics to class-action settlement; of US ONE, Heartland Wireless, Verado Holdings and Hedstrom in Chapter 11; of the creditors' committee for Diagnostic Health; of creditor-acquirers of Fitz & Floyd and Trenwick America, and of major creditors of Harbor Financial, FirstPlus Financial, Mirant, Williams Communications and Covad.
Personal: University of Texas School of Law (JD, with honors, 1983); Rice University (BA, 1976).

SOSTEK, Bruce
Thompson & Knight LLP, Dallas
214 969 1237
bruce.sostek@tklaw.com
Recommended in Intellectual Property
Practice Areas: Mr Sostek heads the firm's Intellectual Property Section. His litigation practice concentrates on patents, trademarks, copyrights, trade secrets, unfair competition which includes ITC matters. He counsels clients on identification, valuation,

licensing, and strategic uses of intellectual property. Mr Sostek is listed in Texas Monthly's 2004 Texas Super Lawyers and in The Best Lawyers in America, 2005-06.
Prof. Memberships: State Bars of Texas, Massachusetts, and Washington, DC, Federal Circuit Bar Association.
Publications: Mr Sostek writes and speaks extensively regarding intellectual property.
Personal: Emory University (JD, 1981); State University of New York at Albany (MA, 1977); Union College (BA, 1975).

SPEARS, Berry
Winstead Sechrest & Minick P.C., Austin 512 370 2822
bspears@winstead.com
Recommended in Bankruptcy
Practice Areas: Chair, Bankruptcy Section. Assists clients in bankruptcy and insolvency proceedings, non-bankruptcy reorganizations and liquidations, debtor-in-possession financing arrangements, and all types of bankruptcy litigation. Advises secured and unsecured lenders, creditors and official and unofficial committees. Counsels agent and lenders/institutions in syndicated multilender credit facilities, and lead banks/participants under participation agreements.
Prof. Memberships: American Bankruptcy Institute, Turnaround Management Association, American, Austin and Houston Bar Associations.
Career: Admitted, State Bar of Texas (1982).
Personal: The University of Texas School of Law, JD, 1982. Austin College, BA, 1979. Texas Super Lawyer and Central Texas' Top 50 Lawyers, Texas Monthly (2003, 2004).

SPIVEY, James K
Cox Smith Matthews Incorporated, San Antonio 210 554 5218
jkspivey@coxsmith.com
Recommended in Antitrust
Practice Areas: Jim is a shareholder in the firm's Litigation Department. Jim has represented clients in a variety of business disputes, including disputes involving claims brought under the Texas and federal antitrust laws. He has advised clients on all aspects of business litigation and has represented clients from a number of industries.
Prof. Memberships: Jim is a former Chair of the State Bar of Texas, Antitrust and Business Litigation Section. He is also former Director of the Defense Counsel of San Antonio, and the San Antonio Young Lawyers Association. He is a Member of the San Antonio Bar Association, Fifth Circuit Bar Association, William S. Sessions American Inn of Court and American Bar Association, Litigation and Antitrust Sections and Business Torts Litigation Committee.
Career: Jim has been licensed to practice law in the State of Texas since 1995.

He is also licensed to practice before all Texas state courts, the United States Court of Appeals for the Fifth Circuit and the United States District Courts for the Northern, Southern, Eastern, and Western Districts of Texas.
Personal: University of Texas School of Law, JD, 1995; Texas A&M University, BS, Economics, magna cum laude, 1992.

STEPHENS, Robert
Bracewell & Giuliani LLP, Houston
713 221 1202
robert.stephens@bracewellgiuliani.com
Recommended in Energy
Practice Areas: Expertise in representing energy companies, financial institutions, and private investors in domestic and international energy and energy finance transactions. Has handled multi-billion dollar secured financings involving public and private secured debt, bankruptcy remote structured transactions, international project financings, long-term trading, netting, and supply contracts, and asset acquisition and disposition transactions.
Personal: JD, with honors, The University of Texas School of Law, 1990; MBA, Finance, University of Wisconsin School of Business, 1987; BBA, Marketing and Management Information Systems, University of Wisconsin School of Business, 1985.

STEWART, Dan
Vinson & Elkins LLP, Dallas
214 220 7761
dstewart@velaw.com
Recommended in Bankruptcy
Practice Areas: Practice spans all aspects of debtor/creditor relationships. Major creditor representations include agent banks, bank groups, and creditor committee representations in connection with bankruptcy proceedings for major corporations. Served as lead counsel for Borrowers in some of the largest workouts and reorganizations in Texas for over 25 years. Served as Bankruptcy Trustee in hundreds of Chapter 7 and Chapter 11 cases under the Bankruptcy Act and Code.
Prof. Memberships: Dallas Bar Association.
Career: Admitted to Texas Bar, 1972. Came to firm as Partner, 1999.
Personal: Graduated from Brown University, BA (1969), and Duke University School of Law, JD (1972).

STEWART, Robert
Kelly, Hart & Hallman, A Professional Corporation, Austin
512 495 6400
Recommended in Environment, Litigation

STILL, Charles
Fulbright & Jaworski L.L.P., Houston
713 651 5270
cstill@fulbright.com
Recommended in Corporate/M&A
Practice Areas: Corporate and securi-

ties laws.

Prof. Memberships: American Law Institute; American Bar Association; State Bar of Texas; Life Fellow, Texas and American Bar Foundations; Fellow, Houston Bar Foundation; Clark Fellow, University of Texas School of Law; and Board Member, Texas Business Law Foundation.

Career: Mr Still has been a Partner in Fulbright's Houston office since 1975. He has served as Head of the Corporate Department and as a member of the firm's Executive Committee. Among other honors, Mr Still has been recognized in An International Who's Who of Merger and Acquisition Lawyers; American's Leading Business Lawyers; The Best Lawyers in America; and Super Lawyers as published in 'Texas Monthly' magazine.

Personal: BBA - Texas Tech University (1965); JD - with honors, University of Texas (1968).

STOCKBRIDGE, Edward T
Vinson & Elkins LLP, Houston
713 758 1032
tstockbridge@velaw.com
Recommended in Technology

Practice Areas: Focus on various types of technology-related business transactions: information technology outsourcing transactions; offshore outsourcing; business process outsourcing (including human resource BPO and billing and account service BPO); technology and software licensing; e-Commerce and Internet matters; international licensing; structured purchase of royalty payments derived from licenses of IP rights and acquisition and divestitures of technology companies.

Career: Admitted to practice: Texas 1982 and Florida 1983. Attorney at V&E since 1982.

Personal: Duke University, BSE, mechanical engineering magna cum laude (1976); University of Florida, JD high honors (1982) (Phi Kappa Phi; Order of the Coif; University of Florida Law Review).

STONE, Susan
Baker & McKenzie, Houston
713 427 5008
n.susan.stone@bakernet.com
Recommended in Tax

Practice Areas: International tax and business transactions, including structuring inbound/outbound transactions for US and foreign clients, implementing global/regional tax minimization strategies, tax structuring of foreign oil, gas, energy and related infrastructure projects, transfer pricing planning and controversy, including competent authority proceedings and advance pricing agreements.

Prof. Memberships: American Bar Association, Council Director and immediate past Secretary for the Section of Taxation; State Bar of Texas; Houston

Bar Association.

Career: Admitted to Bar, Texas, 1982.

Publications: Frequent speaker; including, Using Partnerships Affirmatively in International Tax Transactions, Tax Executives Institute, November 2003.

Personal: 2003: Named in various leading US legal publications.

STRAMA, Brenda
Vinson & Elkins LLP, Austin
512 542 8544
bstrama@velaw.com
Recommended in Healthcare

Practice Areas: Healthcare. Peer review and credentialing, health information privacy, health facility licensure, and Medicare survey and certification.

Prof. Memberships: ABA; TBA; AHLA; Texas Attorney General's Task Force on HIPAA Preemption; Health Law Exam Commission, Texas Board of Legal Specialization.

Career: Partner since 1993.

Publications: Author: 'The AIDS Epidemic and Local Government Liability' (ABA); 'The National Practitioner Data Bank: Has it Accomplished its Objectives?' 'Health Lawyers News', February 2002 (AHLA); Editor: 'Vinson & Elkins Healthcare Legal Update; TBA; AHLA'.

Personal: Georgetown University School of Foreign Service, BA 1962; University of Houston Law Center, JD cum laude, 1984.

STRICKLIN, Samuel M
Bracewell & Giuliani LLP, Dallas
214 758 1095
sam.stricklin@bracewellgiuliani.com
Recommended in Bankruptcy

Practice Areas: Board certified in business bankruptcy law by the Texas Board of Legal Specialization, he has extensive trial and courtroom experience on a wide variety of commercial bankruptcy issues, including contested hearings before 37 bankruptcy judges in 17 states. Recognized in his practice by regional legal publication for the last two years.

Personal: JD, University of Houston Law Center, 1987; BA, Texas A&M University, 1984.

STROCK, William
Haynes and Boone LLP, Dallas
214 651 5000
Recommended in Employment

STROUBE III, H Rey
Akin Gump Strauss Hauer & Feld LLP,
Houston 713 220 5858
rstroube@akingump.com
Recommended in Bankruptcy

Practice Areas: For 30 years, Mr Stroube has focused on debt restructurings and business reorganizations, representing debtors, secured creditors (individually and as participant groups), unsecured creditors, official and unofficial committees of creditors, and equity interest committees. His experience includes serving as primary debtor's counsel in major national cases and

leading the representation of various formal and informal creditor committee constituencies. He also represents clients acquiring assets, debt and equity positions from financially distressed entities.

Prof. Memberships: Texas Bar Foundation.

Personal: AB, Yale University; JD, University of Texas; Clerk, Ben C Connally, US District Court for the Southern District of Texas.

STRUBECK, Lou
Fulbright & Jaworski L.L.P., San Antonio
214 855 8040
lstrubeck@fulbright.com
Recommended in Bankruptcy

Practice Areas: Bankruptcy law and debtor/creditors' rights, with emphasis on representation of financial institutions, institutional lenders, investors and creditors in complex workouts and Chapter 11 bankruptcy reorganization cases.

Prof. Memberships: Member, American Bankruptcy Institute; Inns of Court; Dallas and American Bar Associations; State Bar of Texas, Fee Dispute and Judiciary Subcommittee of the Dallas Bar Association (Officer) and the Dallas and Tarrant County Bankruptcy Bar Associations.

Career: Admitted to Texas Bar (1983). Partner in Dallas office of Fulbright since 1992. Former panel bankruptcy trustee in the Northern District of Texas.

Personal: BA, College of Charleston (1980); JD, Temple University (1983).

SUSMAN, Harry
Susman Godfrey LLP, Houston
713 651 9366
Recommended in Antitrust

SUSMAN, Stephen
Susman Godfrey LLP, Houston
713 651 9366
Recommended in Antitrust, Litigation

SUTHERLAND, Mike
Carrington, Coleman, Sloman & Blumenthal, LLP, Dallas
214 855 3000
Recommended in Bankruptcy

SWANSON, Joel
Baker Botts LLP, Houston
713 229 1330
joel.swanson@bakerbotts.com
Recommended in Corporate/M&A

Practice Areas: Partner in Corporate Department. Practice focuses on securities, mergers and acquisitions and joint ventures. In the past several years, he has participated in more than 30 public offerings of all types of securities, representing both issuers and underwriters and handled numerous acquisitions and divestitures. He has represented many energy companies, particularly those in the refining industry.

Career: Worked for Exxon as a chemical engineer prior to law school.

Personal: JD, cum laude, Harvard Law School, 1972; MBA, Harvard Business School, 1972; BS, chemical engineering, The University of Texas, 1967, highest ranking engineering graduate.

SZALKOWSKI, Charles
Baker Botts LLP, Houston
713 229 1480
charles.szalkowski@bakerbotts.com
*Recommended in Communications,
Corporate/M&A, Technology*

Practice Areas: Mergers, acquisitions, general corporate, financing for technology-focused companies, venture capital and private equity transactions. Represents emerging growth and small public companies, venture capitalists, investment bankers, and investors in, such companies, private equity funds, hedge funds, institutional investors, insurance companies, universities and endowments. Representation of software and telecommunications companies, consumer and industrial products manufacturers, oil, gas and energy service companies, consolidators in various industries and other ventures with prospects embodied in intellectual property, including biotechnology, medical devices, internet content and e-commerce.

Personal: JD, cum laude, and MBA, Harvard University, 1975; BA, cum laude, and BS Accounting, Rice University, 1971.

TABOR, Bert
Vinson & Elkins LLP, Houston
713 758 2620
btabor@velaw.com
Recommended in Energy

Practice Areas: Broad-based practice counseling clients in the energy and transportation industries mainly related to the formation, construction, acquisition, financing, sale, regulation, and operation of oil pipelines and products pipelines, and representing clients in administrative litigation before the Federal Energy Regulatory Commission and state regulatory agencies. He has represented clients in pipeline ventures throughout the United States, including extensive experience in Alaska.

Prof. Memberships: Member: Energy Bar Association (Served, Executve Committee; past Chair; Oil Pipeline Committee).

Career: Joined the firm in 1973; admitted to the partnership in January 1976.

Personal: Ohio State University, BS, 1961; JD, 1964 (Phi Delta Phi).

TABOR, Jay
Weil, Gotshal & Manges LLP, Dallas
214 746 7889
Recommended in Corporate/M&A

Practice Areas: Mr Tabor's practice focuses on complex corporate, mergers and acquisitions, and private equity transactions.

Career: Mr Tabor is representing Enron in its announced $2.35 billion sale of Portland General Electric, and Great Lakes Chemical in its $1.8 billion merger with Crompton Corporation. He also represented Thomas H Lee Partners in its acquisition of a controlling interest in Refco Group. Additional representative clients include American Airlines, Yell Group and Wal-Mart. Mr Tabor also represents a number of private equity funds, in acquisition and investment transactions.

Personal: Harvard Law School (JD, magna cum laude, 1990); Oklahoma Christian College (BS, 1986).

TAYLOR, Jasper
Fulbright & Jaworski L.L.P., Houston
713 651 5670
jtaylor@fulbright.com
Recommended in Litigation

Practice Areas: Tax litigation and tax controversies.

Prof. Memberships: Mr Taylor has been a Member of the American Bar Association's Section of Taxation for over 15 years and has served as Chair of the Section's Committee on Court Procedure. He has also served as Chair of the Texas State Bar's Section of Taxation.

Career: Jack Taylor, an attorney and certified public accountant, has an active practice in tax controversy, including representation of taxpayers in both administrative proceedings and litigation. A Partner with Fulbright & Jaworski L.L.P. since 1985, Mr Taylor has served a wide range of clients. He has actively litigated in Texas district courts, federal district courts, the US Tax Court, the US Court of Federal Claims and predecessors, and respective appeals courts. He also represented the Texas State Bar for several years as one of several practitioners attending an annual meeting with IRS regional officials. His professional background includes Big 8 accounting firm experience prior to attending law school.

Personal: Mr Taylor received a BBA in 1973 from the University of Florida and a JD in 1978 from Duke University.

TAYLOR, Lyndon C
Skadden, Arps, Slate, Meagher & Flom LLP & Affiliates, Houston
713 655 5110
ltaylor@skadden.com
Recommended in Energy, Projects

Practice Areas: Head of Skadden's Houston office Energy Practice. Concentrates on domestic and international project finance, with emphasis on the development and financing of LNG terminals and other energy infrastructure projects. Has represented project developers, commercial lenders, investment banks, construction companies, LNG sellers and purchasers and equity investors. Also represents clients in energy-related corporate matters, including a number of complex natural gas and petroleum asset and securities acquisition transactions.

Career: JD, University of Oklahoma College of Law, 1984 (With Honors, Order of the Coif, Earl Appleton Brown Award for Oil & Gas Law); BS, Industrial Engineering, Oklahoma State University, 1981.

TEMPLIN, Donald
Haynes and Boone LLP, Dallas
214 651 5000
Recommended in Intellectual Property

TERRELL, Irvin
Baker Botts LLP, Houston
713 229 1231
irv.terrell@bakerbotts.com
Recommended in Litigation

Practice Areas: Trial practice concerning business litigation in Texas, Arizona, California, Delaware, Florida, Illinois, New Mexico, Louisiana, New York, and Pennsylvania: takeover suits, contract disputes, intellectual property claims, and business torts, including such matters as tortious interference, antitrust, fiduciary duty, and securities fraud. Trial counsel for President Bush in the 2000 Florida election contest against Vice President Gore.

Career: 32 years in practice.

Personal: JD, cum laude, The University of Texas School of Law, 1972; Order of the Coif; Phi Delta Phi; BA, cum laude, The University of Texas, 1968.

THOMPSON, Dahl
Andrews Kurth LLP, Houston
713 220 4376
dahlthompson@andrewskurth.com
Recommended in Energy, Projects

Practice Areas: Extensive experience representing project developers, financial institutions and equity investors in domestic and international project finance transactions, with particular emphasis on electrical power plants and other energy infrastructure projects. Representation has included all aspects of the structuring, development, financing, acquisition and sell-down of such projects, including the negotiation and drafting of joint venture agreements, shareholder and partnership agreements, power sales contracts, tolling agreements, construction contracts, water supply and fuel supply agreements, gas and electricity interconnection agreements, operation and maintenance agreements, long-term service agreements, credit agreements, security agreements, equity subscription agreements, guaranties, letters of credit, complex funds flow agreements and stock and asset purchase and sale agreements.

Prof. Memberships: The State Bar of Texas.

Career: Admitted to the State Bar of Texas in 1990. Partner with Andrews Kurth since 2001.

Personal: Received a JD from Columbia University in 1990. Harlan Fiske Stone scholar. Received a BS summa cum laude from Utah State University in 1987.

THOMPSON, Jay
Thompson, Coe, Cousins & Irons, LLP, Austin
512 703 5060
jthompson@thompsoncoe.com
Recommended in Insurance

Practice Areas: Represents insurance companies, trade associations in legisla-

tive, regulatory, litigation matters.

Prof. Memberships: Admitted to practice in Texas, and is a member of the Texas Association of Defense Counsel; Federation of Regulatory Counsel, and Insurance Section of the State Bar.

Career: He regularly participates in regulatory proceedings involving contested case hearings, benchmark rate setting, policy form approvals, rulemaking, licensing, mergers, acquisition, dissolution of insurance companies and other regulatory matters. He has worked on numerous bills in the biennial sessions of the Texas legislature since 1977, and served in the United States Air Force Reserves as a Judge Advocate from 1972-99.

THOMPSON, Jr, Clark
Bracewell & Giuliani LLP, Houston
713 221 1477
clark.thompson@bracewellgiuliani.com
Recommended in Real Estate

Practice Areas: Expertise in the acquisition, development, finance and divestiture of commercial and industrial projects, ranging from power plants, pipelines, terminals and other energy-related facilities to office, industrial, residential and retail developments. Has also developed a particular area of expertise in large corporate relocations, having been personally involved in leasing transactions totaling in excess of 5,000,000 square feet over the past few years. Recognized in his practice by a regional legal publication for the last two years.

Personal: JD, with honors, The University of Texas at Austin, 1980; BA, magna cum laude, Washington and Lee University, 1977.

THURBER, Mark
Andrews Kurth LLP, Houston
713 220 4338
markthurber@andrewskurth.com
Recommended in Energy, Projects

Practice Areas: Focuses on energy and infrastructure transactions issues and related matters. Actively involved in energy projects in Bangladesh, Benin, Brazil, Guam, Ivory Coast, Nicaragua, Nigeria, Peru, Philippines and Tanzania. Has prepared and negotiated a wide variety of infrastructure-related agreements, including those covering construction; liquid and gas fuel supply and transportation; power purchase; and operation and maintenance. Has represented clients in negotiating electricity trading contracts in nascent trading environments and developing generating assets to support trading positions. In addition to work on behalf of developers and investors, has represented a variety of financial institutions, including lenders, investment banks, and other capital providers and arrangers, in connection with financing a variety of domestic and foreign infrastructure projects and acquisitions, both on a non-recourse and balance-sheet basis.

Has led and participated in a comprehensive range of oil and gas transactions, including stock and asset divestitures and financings, international joint venture arrangements and indigenous hydrocarbon concessions.

Prof. Memberships: The State Bar of Texas; listed in 'Chambers Global, The World's Leading Lawyers', 2001-2004; Board Member and Past President, Japan America Society of Houston.

Career: Admitted to the State Bar of Texas in 1989. Partner with Andrews Kurth since 2001.

Personal: Received a JD from Columbia University in 1989. Served as articles editor, Columbia Business Law Review. Received an MBA from Brigham Young University in 1981. Received a BS with high honors from Brigham Young University in 1980.

TOBOR, Ben D
Bracewell & Giuliani LLP, Houston
713 221 1352
ben.tobor@bracewellgiuliani.com
Recommended in Intellectual Property

Practice Areas: Recognized by 'IP Worldwide' in 2001 in 'Patent Plums' for 'the most valuable US patents and the lawyers who nurtured them' and again in 2002 among the lawyers who obtained one of the '10 Patents That Changed The World.' Experience includes acquisition of intellectual property rights, including copyrights, US and international patents and trademarks, intellectual property licensing and litigation concerning patents and trade secrets. Represents clients in many technologies including medical equipment and devices, oil and gas field equipment, air conditioning and heating equipment, waste treatment, chemicals and chemical processing, beauty care products and computer software.

TOWNSEND, John
Townsend & Jones, Houston
713 521 3249
jack@tjtaxlaw.com
Recommended in Litigation

Practice Areas: Civil and criminal federal tax controversy (audits, appeals and litigation); Representation in all federal courts and before the IRS and Department of Justice.

Prof. Memberships: ABA Tax Section; Houston Tax Roundtable; Tax Procedure Group.

Career: US Dept. of Justice, Tax Division (Trial Section 1974-77; Appellate Section 1969-74); private practice since 1977.

Publications: More recent publications include: Collateral Estoppel in Civil Cases Following Criminal Convictions, 2005 TNT 4-28 (1/6/05); Analysis of the Fastow Plea Bargains, 2004 TNT 44-46 (3/5/04); Tax Treaty Interpretation, 55 Tax Lawyer 219 (Fall 2001); Federal Tax Crimes (2005 edition), a book for Mr Townsend's Tax Fraud class at the UH Law School; Federal Tax Procedure

(2004 edition), a book for Mr Townsend's Tax Procedure class the UH Law School (these books may be viewed and downloaded from www.tjtaxlaw.com).
Personal: University of Virginia Law School, LLB 1967; New York University School Law School, LLM 1969; Adjunct Professor, University of Houston Law School (Tax Procedure and Tax Fraud and Money Laundering); Tax Law Specialist, Texas Board of Legal Specialization; Listed in 'Texas Lawyer's' 'Go-to-Guide' as being among Texas' top five tax lawyers (October 15, 2002).

TURNER, Robert
Jones Day, Dallas
214 969 2984
rwturner@jonesday.com
Recommended in Intellectual Property
Practice Areas: While his experience includes patent and trademark prosecution and transaction work, his primary emphasis has been in intellectual property litigation. He has been lead trial counsel in numerous complex patent, trade secret, trademark, and copyright matters and has tried nonjury and jury cases as well as International Trade Commission and arbitration cases. He is an Adjunct Professor of law at The University of Texas School of Law.
Prof. Memberships: ABA; State Bar of Texas; Dallas Bar Association; Dallas-Fort Worth Intellectual Property Law Association. He is a past Chairman of the IP Section of the State Bar of Texas.

UNDERKOFLER, Paul
Goins, Underkofler, Crawford & Langdon LLP, Dallas
214 969 5454
Recommended in Construction

UNGER, Timothy
Andrews Kurth LLP, Houston
713 220 4370
tunger@andrewskurth.com
Recommended in Energy, Projects
Practice Areas: Represents a variety of corporate and institutional clients. In recent years, has focused primarily on energy and petrochemical acquisitions, developments and financings including power and LNG.
Prof. Memberships: The State Bar of Texas, 1974.
Career: Partner with Andrews Kurth since 1982. Has been with the firm since 1974, and has represented a variety of corporate and institutional clients.
Personal: Received a JD with honors from The University of Texas School of Law in 1974. Received Order of the Coif; served on Texas Law Review. Received an AB magna cum laude from the University of Notre Dame in 1969.

VALDERRAMA, Teresa S
Baker Botts LLP, Houston
713 229 1860
teresa.valderrama@bakerbotts.com
Recommended in Employment

Practice Areas: Handles employment-related and commercial lawsuits and appeals, government and corporate investigations. Concentrates in defense of discrimination, collective action, labor law, workplace tort, whistleblower, contract, non-competition/trade secret disputes. Experience with SOX, NLRA, RLA, Title VII, FLSA, ADEA, ERISA, ADA, OSHA, Texas Codes, federal and state statutory and common law affecting workplace.
Career: Commissioner, Houston Police Officers' Civil Service Commission; immediate past Chair, Houston Management Lawyers Forum; Member, Houston Bar Association Employment Law Section Advisory Council. Formerly Adjunct Professor, University of Houston Law Center.
Personal: JD, summa cum laude, University of Houston Law Center, 1988; BA, Rice University, 1983.

VAN FLEET, Allan
Vinson & Elkins LLP, Houston
713 758 2006
avanfleet@velaw.com
Recommended in Antitrust
Practice Areas: Co-Chair of Vinson & Elkins' Antitrust Practice Group; practice also includes commercial and technical litigation and international arbitration.
Prof. Memberships: Delegate: American Bar Association House of Delegates; Officer: ABA Antitrust Law Section Council Member: State Bar of Texas, International Law Section. Past President, Texas-Mexico Bar Association.
Career: Admitted to practice: Texas, 1978. Joined Vinson & Elkins: 1977; admitted to partnership: 1984.
Publications: See www.velaw.com for publications.
Personal: Rice University, BA (summa cum laude),1976; Columbia University School of Law, JD (first in class), 1977.

VAN KIRK, Mark
Baker Botts LLP, Dallas
214.953.6593
mark.vankirk@bakerbotts.com
Recommended in Real Estate
Practice Areas: Practice focuses on representing developers, investors and other privately held buyers, sellers, and lenders in connection with development, acquisition, debt and equity financing, and sale of major retail, office, hotel, multifamily, industrial, resort, assisted living, and mixed-use projects; complex lease arrangements; and workouts and restructurings.
Prof. Memberships: State Bar of Texas; Dallas Bar Association.
Personal: JD from University of Chicago Law School in 1982; MBA from University of Chicago in 1982; BA (magna cum laude) from Duke University in 1978.

VAY, John
Kelly, Hart & Hallman, A Professional Corporation, Austin 512 495 6400
Recommended in Environment

VILARDO, Terry Otero
Mayer, Brown, Rowe & Maw LLP, Houston 713 546 0509
TVilardo@mayerbrown.com
Recommended in Banking & Finance
Practice Areas: Represents lenders and developers in domestic, emerging markets and cross-border and international transactions including acquisitions, cross-border investments, greenfield projects, project finance including construction and term financings, joint ventures, and privatizations; represents lenders in securitizations, including structuring of cross-border multiseller vehicles and sales of receivables resulting from the sale and transportation of oil and gas; represents lenders in structured and secured financings, including synthetic leasing, production payments, financings of oil and gas onshore and offshore properties including methane gas financings, financings of pipelines, power plants, chemical plants, airplanes, refineries and shipping financings.
Prof. Memberships: Texas, 1984 Hispanic Bar Association. American Bar Association, Section of Corporation, Business and Banking Law. Houston Bar Association.
Career: Joined Mayer, Brown, Rowe & Maw LLP, Houston, 1984; Partner, 1992.
Personal: University of Houston, JD cum laude, 1984. Georgetown University, Washington, DC, BSFS, 1979. Speaks Spanish (native); knowledge of French and Italian.

VOGEL, Peter
Gardere Wynne Sewell LLP, Dallas
214 999 4422
pvogel@gardere.com
Recommended in Communications, Technology
Practice Areas: Internet and computer technology, intellectual property, outsourcing, trial.
Prof. Memberships: Chair, Texas Supreme Court Judicial Committee on Information Technology; Founding Chair, Computer and Technology Section of the State Bar of Texas; Task Force for Uniform Electronic Transaction Act (UETA).
Career: Peter Vogel's involvement with the computer industry began in 1967. For over 27 years of legal practice, Peter has drawn on his Masters in Computer Science and his experience as a mainframe programmer, systems analyst, and management consultant. In addition to offering practical advice on technology-related business issues, Peter negotiates complex agreements and litigates disputes. Areas include ERP implementation projects, Internet security, software patents, copyrights, trade secret protection, website business management, and outsourcing. As an Adjunct Professor in the Law of the eCommerce at SMU Peter stays on the leading edge of emerging internet law. (smu-ecommerce.gardere.com) Peter is often

appointed as an Arbitrator, Court Ordered Mediator, and Special Master in Internet, intellectual property, and computer technology litigation.
Publications: 'Due Diligence and Don't Be Sorry - 7 Absolute Rules of Computer Contracts', www.watchIT.com, January 2002; 'Limiting Liability Exposure of the IT Manager', www.watchIT.com, February 2003.
Personal: MS, Computer Science, American University, 1972; JD, St. Mary's University School of Law, 1976; BBA, University of Texas at Austin, 1969.

VOYLES, Robb L
Baker Botts LLP, Austin
512 322 2500
robb.voyles@bakerbotts.com
Recommended in Litigation
Practice Areas: Mr Voyles is Chair of Baker Botts' worldwide Litigation Practice. He has represented US accounting firms regarding accountants' liability and securities actions and has counseled law firms in professional liability actions. He has also represented high-technology companies in disputes involving trade secrets, noncompetition agreements, computer software and the performance of computer systems, and other high-tech products and services.
Career: 23+ years of practice. Partner-in-Charge of the Austin office (1994-2005). Member of the firm's Executive Committee.
Personal: JD (magna cum laude), University of Michigan Law School, 1982. (summa cum laude), Business Administration in Accounting, University of Dayton, 1979.

WALLANDER, William
Vinson & Elkins LLP, Dallas
214 220 7905
bwallander@velaw.com
Recommended in Bankruptcy
Practice Areas: Experience includes representation of creditors, committees, trustees, and debtors in restructuring, exchange offers, remedies enforcement, prepackaged plans, and bankruptcy cases.
Prof. Memberships: American Bar Association; Dallas Bar Association; Dallas Bankruptcy Bar Association; Texas Banker's Association; American Bankruptcy Institute; Turnaround Management Association; Keeton Fellow, University of Texas School of Law; Dean's Roundtable, University of Texas School of Law.
Career: Admitted to Texas Bar, 1984. Came to firm as Partner, 1999.
Personal: University of Pittsburgh, BA magna cum laude, 1981; The University of Texas School of Law, JD, 1984; and University of Phoenix, MBA summa cum laude, 2001.

WALLENSTEIN, Jim
Jenkens & Gilchrist PC, Dallas
214 855 4500
Recommended in Real Estate

WALTERS, Robert
Vinson & Elkins LLP, Dallas
214 200 7704
rwalters@velaw.com
Recommended in Antitrust
Practice Areas: Antitrust, securities, technology, class action, and business controversies in federal and state courts. Counsels clients on the antitrust implications of business transactions, including mergers and acquisitions.
Prof. Memberships: Texas Bar Foundation; The Center for American and International Law; Dallas Citizens Council; The Dallas Assembly; University of Texas Plan II Alumni Board; Dallas Council on World Affairs.
Career: Admitted to Texas Bar, 1983. Admitted to partnership, 1990. Serves on firm's Management Committee.
Personal: Graduated from The University of Texas, BA with highest honors, 1980; and The University of Texas School of Law, JD with honors, 1983. 'Texas Law Review'.

WALTON, Gibson
Vinson & Elkins LLP, Houston
713 758 2026
gwalton@velaw.com
Recommended in Litigation
Practice Areas: Civil trial work; represents both plaintiffs and defendants in commercial, corporate, securities, fiduciary, construction, professional liability, product liability, probate, and energy litigation.
Prof. Memberships: International Society of Barristers; ABOTA; IADC; Houston Bar Association (former President); Houston Bar Foundation (former Chair); Fellow, American Bar Foundation; American Inn of Court; Board Certified, 1981.
Career: Partner since 1982.
Publications: Numerous papers and speeches on trial advocacy, evidence, procedure, mediation, joint defense agreements, construction law, and other litigation topics for various professional organizations.
Personal: University of Virginia (BA 1972); The University of Texas School of Law (JD 1975).

WATT, Dick
Watt, Beckworth & Thompson, Houston
713 650 8100
Recommended in Energy

WAWRO, Mark
Susman Godfrey LLP, Houston
713 651 9366
Recommended in Litigation

WEEMS, Philip
King & Spalding LLP, Houston
713 276 7373
pweems@kslaw.com
Recommended in Energy, Projects
Practice Areas: Practice includes structuring, negotiating and documenting projects involving the international exploration, production, processing,

transportation and sale of oil and gas and the acquisition and disposition of energy-related assets. Extensive energy company experience. Possesses special expertise in legal aspects of developing, marketing, constructing and operating LNG and natural gas projects.
Prof. Memberships: Association of International Petroleum Negotiators; California Bar Association; International Bar Association; Texas State Bar.
Personal: BA, Texas Tech University, 1979; JD, cum laude, Texas Tech University, 1982.

WEIL, Thomas E
Skadden, Arps, Slate, Meagher & Flom LLP & Affiliates, Houston
713 655 5120
tweil@skadden.com
Recommended in Projects
Practice Areas: Represents energy and financial institution clients in domestic and international energy project transactions involving the formation, acquisition, restructuring and sell-down of energy development companies and project corporations, partnerships and joint ventures, as well as in the development of cogeneration, alternative energy and independent power projects, including the negotiation of power purchase agreements, wheeling and transmission agreements, steam sales agreements, onshore and offshore turnkey construction contracts, operations and maintenance agreements, environmental permitting and compliance issues, and fuel supply agreements.
Career: JD, University of Virginia School of Law, 1978 (Notes Editor, Virginia Journal of International Law); BA, Yale University, 1970.

WEINER, Sanford A
Vinson & Elkins LLP, Houston
713 758 2558
sweiner@velaw.com
Recommended in Real Estate
Practice Areas: Real estate transactions and finance law. Co-head of National Real Estate Practice.
Prof. Memberships: Member: Board of Governors (President 2003), American College of Real Estate Law; Anglo-American Real Property Institute.
Career: Admitted to Texas Bar, 1971. Joined Vinson & Elkins, LLP 1971, became partner 1978.
Publications: Introduction: 'Making Choice of Law a Contact Sport: Contractual Choices of Law in Texas', 54 'Texas Bar Journal' 262 (1991).
Personal: Born August 21, 1946. Graduated The University of Texas, BA in 1968 (cum laude, Phi Beta Kappa), and Harvard University, JD in 1971 (cum laude).

WELLER, Phillip
Vinson & Elkins LLP, Houston
713 758 2242
pweller@velaw.com
Recommended in Real Estate
Practice Areas: Real estate transactions

and finance. Co-head of National Real Estate Practice Group.
Prof. Memberships: Admitted to practice in Texas (1975), District of Columbia (1999), and New York (1999). Member, American College of Real Estate Lawyers, Anglo-American Real Property Institute, American College of Mortgage Attorneys, Urban Land Institue. ICSC.
Career: Joined Vinson & Elkins 1974, became Partner 1981.
Publications: 'Industrial Leases' in 'Commercial Real Estate Transactions Handbook' (2000).
Personal: Born May 5, 1948. JD (summa cum laude) University of Houston 1975, BS (summa cum laude) Bowling Green University 1970.

WELLS, Benjamin
Baker Botts LLP, Houston
713 229 1210
benjamin.wells@bakerbotts.com
Recommended in Tax
Practice Areas: Chair: Tax Department (firmwide). Concentration: cross-border transactions, tax planning for American companies operating abroad, structuring 'inbound' investments by investors in other countries, other acquisitions and joint ventures, debt and stock offerings, and other tax planning.
Prof. Memberships: ABA Tax Section (Chair, Corporate Tax Committee, 2001-02); American College of Tax Counsel.
Career: Captain in US Army in the Judge Advocate General's Corp 1969-72.
Publications: Articles on international tax, corporate tax, and other tax subjects.
Personal: JD, cum laude, Harvard Law School, 1968; BA, magna cum laude, Latin, Amherst College, 1965.

WEST, Glenn D
Weil, Gotshal & Manges LLP, Dallas
214 746 7780
gdwest@weil.com
Recommended in Corporate/M&A
Practice Areas: Mr West's practice focuses on private equity, mergers & acquisitions, and corporate finance for domestic and international clients.
Career: Mr West has led public and private acquisition and corporate finance transactions for clients including Ewing Management Group, Hicks, Muse, Tate & Furst Incorporated, Lindsay, Goldberg & Bessemer, Koch Industries, American Airlines, Greyhound Lines, Inc., Six Flags, Inc., Home Interiors & Gifts, Inc., LIN Television Corporation, Blockbuster, Inc., NextMedia Group and Brazos Equity Partners. He also represents Southwest Sports Group, owner of the Texas Rangers Baseball Club and the Dallas Stars Hockey Club, and led the project finance for the new American Airlines Center in Dallas. Mr West was listed in Woodward/White's The Best Lawyers in America 2001-2002, recognized as a leading lawyer in his field in

'Chambers Global - The World's Leading Lawyers 2004-2005' and as one of America's leading business lawyers in 'Chambers USA 2004' in two categories: Banking & Finance and Corporate/M&A.
Personal: Mr West is a member of the Finance Committee and a member of the Board of Directors of the Vogel Alcove Childcare Center for the Homeless in Dallas, Texas, and was co-chair for the 2004 Vogel Alcove Arts Performance Event.

WHEAT, David
Thompson & Knight LLP, Dallas
214 969 1468
david.wheat@tklaw.com
Recommended in Tax
Practice Areas: Mr Wheat's practice includes transactional consultations, document preparation and tax opinions for of business transactions, including corporate mergers and acquisitions and the formation and operation of partnerships and LLCs. He also represents clients in compliance, administrative proceedings, and judicial litigation in federal and state tax matters.
Prof. Memberships: Member of the State Bar of Texas, State Bar of Louisiana, American and Dallas Bar Associations, Dallas Bar Foundation.
Career: Partner since 1995.
Publications: Mr Wheat is an active author.
Personal: New York University (Master of Laws in Taxation, 1989); Louisiana State University (JD, 1988; BS, 1985).

WHITE, T Gordon
McKool Smith, Austin
512 692 8700
Recommended in Intellectual Property

WIELEBINSKI, Joseph
Munsch Hardt Kopf & Harr, P. C., Dallas
214 855 7561
jwielebinski@munsch.com
Recommended in Bankruptcy
Practice Areas: All aspects of reorganization, creditors' rights and corporate finance. Practice includes loan workouts and restructures, bankruptcy litigation, and representation of Committees (both official and ad hoc) and Trustees. Currently serves as Federal Court Receiver.
Prof. Memberships: American Bankruptcy Institute; American Bar Association; Turnaround Management Association (past President, Dallas/Ft. Worth Chapter); and Dallas Bar Association (past President, Commercial Law Section).
Career: Shareholder (since 1987) and Chairman of the Reorganization/Corporate Finance practice group.
Publications: Frequent speaker and writer on various bankruptcy, creditors' rights and litigation issues.
Personal: Syracuse University College of Law (JD, 1983); Syracuse University Maxwell School (MBA, 1983); Temple University (BA, magna cum laude, 1980).

WILLIAMSON, Deborah

Cox Smith Matthews Incorporated, San
Antonio 210 554 5275
ddwilliamson@coxsmith.com
Recommended in Bankruptcy

Practice Areas: Deborah is a shareholder and the Department Leader for the firm's Bankruptcy Department and is Board Certified by the Texas Board of Legal Specialization in Business Bankruptcy Law and by the American Bankruptcy Board of Certification in Business Bankruptcy Law. Deborah advises clients on all aspects of business bankruptcy, including pre-bankruptcy strategic planning, fraudulent conveyances, acquisitions, lending, and complex issues in real estate and commercial transactions.
Prof. Memberships: Past President, American Bankruptcy Institute; Former Executive Editor and Author of Bench Notes Column, 'ABI Journal'; Vice Chair, State Bar of Texas, Bankruptcy Section; Chair, Examination Committee for Texas Board of Legal Specialization (Bankruptcy); Chair, San Antonio Bar Association, Bankruptcy Subcommittee of Federal Courts Committee; Director, American Board of Certification; Former Vice President, San Antonio Bankruptcy Bar Association.
Career: Deborah has testified before the United States Senate Judiciary Committee Subcommittee on Administrative Oversight and the Courts and was selected by 'Texas Monthly' as one of the Top 50 Women Lawyers in Texas and as an Outstanding National Bankruptcy Attorney in 1998.
Personal: University Of Houston Law Center, JD, cum laude, 1981. Order of the Coif; Order of the Barons; Director, Board of Advocates; Phi Delta Phi. University of Texas at El Paso, BA, Political Science, 1977.

WILLIAMSON, Holly H

Akin Gump Strauss Hauer & Feld LLP,
Houston 713 220 8136
hwilliamson@akingump.com
Recommended in Employment

Practice Areas: Represents corporations in the chemical; transportation; oil and gas production, retailing and servicing; and telecommunications industries in complex litigation and appeals involving trade secrets, unfair competition, discrimination and harassment claims, benefits, and wage and hour issues. Practice includes federal, state employment matters involving ADA,

ADEA and laws prohibiting discrimination, harassment and retaliation under Title VII of the Civil Rights Act of 1964.
Prof. Memberships: Fellow, Texas and Houston Bar Foundations.
Personal: BBA (honors), Southwest Texas State University; JD (magna cum laude), South Texas College of Law; Clerk, Edith Hollan Jones, US Court of Appeals for the 5th Circuit.

WILSON, Robert

Haynes and Boone LLP, Dallas
214 651 5000
Recommended in Real Estate

WOOD, William

Fulbright & Jaworski L.L.P., Houston
713 651 5537
wwood@fulbright.com
Recommended in Energy

Practice Areas: Litigation and arbitration, domestic and international.
Prof. Memberships: Mr Wood is a Member of the State Bar of Texas, and the Houston, American, and International Bar Associations. He is a fellow of the Houston Bar Foundation, past President of The University of Houston Law Alumni Association, and a current board member of the University of Houston Law Foundation. A skilled trial advocate, Mr Wood is an elected member of the American Board of Trial Advocates.
Career: As a Partner in the Houston office of Fulbright & Jaworski L.L.P., Mr Wood holds leadership roles in the firm's Energy, Energy Litigation, and Latin America Practice Groups and has an active Trial and Arbitration Practice. He concentrates his practice on the defense and prosecution of business litigation matters with an emphasis on energy industry controversies.
Personal: BBA (Accounting), Texas A&M, (1981); JD, University of Houston Law Center (1984), associate editor of the Houston Law Review.

WORRELL, Danny

Brown McCarroll LLP, Austin
512 472 5456
Recommended in Environment

WORTLEY, Michael

Vinson & Elkins LLP, Dallas
214 220 7732
mwortley@velaw.com
Recommended in Corporate/M&A

Practice Areas: Primary area of practice is corporate and securities law. Experience in the food, telecommunica-

tions, oil and gas, REITs, manufacturing, healthcare, biotechnology, and high technology industries. Clients include issuers, underwriters, and private equity and other investors in public and private securities and M&A transactions.
Prof. Memberships: American Bar Association and Dallas Bar Association.
Career: Admitted to Texas Bar, 1978. Came to the firm as a Partner, 1995.
Personal: Graduated from Southern Methodist University, BA with highest honors, 1970, the University of North Carolina at Chapel Hill, Masters of Regional Planning, 1973, and Southern Methodist University, JD with honors, 1978.

WRIGHT, Robert

Baker Botts LLP, Houston
713 229 1237
bob.wright@bakerbotts.com
Recommended in Real Estate

Practice Areas: Represents clients in Texas and multi-state acquisitions and divestitures, financing, workouts, development, and leasing of real estate and energy projects. Counsels clients on environmental issues including investigations, remediation, voluntary cleanup programs, public disclosure requirements, and environmental claims involving real estate projects.
Prof. Memberships: American College of Real Estate Lawyers (Board of Governors); Houston Real Estate Lawyers Council; State Bar of Texas (former section chair); Houston Bar Association (former section Chair).
Personal: JD from Columbia University School of Law, 1975 (Harlan Fiske Stone Scholar, Phi Delta Phi); AB, magna cum laude, from Princeton University, 1972.

WULFE, Scott

Vinson & Elkins LLP, Houston
713 758 2750
swulfe@velaw.com
Recommended in Corporate/M&A

Practice Areas: Concentrates on public and private mergers and acquisitions, securities offerings and corporate control and governance issues. Has extensive experience representing private equity funds and public companies.
Career: Admitted to Texas Bar, 1983; joined Vinson & Elkins, 1983; admitted to the partnership, January 1991.
Personal: Graduated from The University of Texas, Plan II BA with highest honors in 1979 (Phi Beta Kappa) and JD in 1983 with high honors (Chancellors).

YEATES, Marie

Vinson & Elkins LLP, Houston
713 758 4576
myeates@velaw.com
Recommended in Litigation

Practice Areas: Chairs V&E appellate practice; concentrates on civil appeals. Certified in civil appellate law by Texas Board of Legal Specialization. Named by 'National Law Journal' as one of top 50 women litigators in US.
Prof. Memberships: American Academy of Appellate Lawyers, American Bar Association; American Law Institute.
Career: Admitted to practice: Louisiana, 1980; Texas, 1982. Joined Vinson & Elkins: 1981; admitted to partnership: 1988.
Personal: Louisiana State University, BS, 1977 (summa cum laude); Louisiana State University School of Law, JD, 1980 (first in class); editor in chief, 'Louisiana Law Review'; clerk to US Fifth Circuit Judge Alvin Rubin, 1980-81.

YORK, Larry

York, Keller & Field, Austin
512 867 1616
Recommended in Insurance

YOUNG, William

Vinson & Elkins LLP, Dallas
214 220 7994
byoung@velaw.com
Recommended in Banking & Finance

Practice Areas: Represents US and international private investment funds, commercial banks and corporations in private debt transactions, including syndicated credits, asset based loans, real estate finance and mezzanine debt. Significant emphasis on international financings, and particularly, securitized financing of Asian and European distressed debt and real estate portfolios.
Prof. Memberships: Section on Business Law, American Bar Association, International Law Section, and Dallas Bar Association.
Career: Admitted to Texas Bar, 1985. Came to firm as Partner, 1998.
Personal: University of Mississippi BBA (1982), JD (1984); managing editor, 'Mississippi Law Journal'; married, three children.

YUNGBLUT, Stephen

Law Offices of James Stanton LP,
Dallas 214 559 3232
Recommended in Construction

ANDREWS KURTH LLP

THE FIRM

Managing Partner: Howard Ayers

Number of partners: 184
Number of other lawyers: 225

AREAS OF PRACTICE:

Litigation	21%
Business Transactions	19%
Corporate & Securities	24%
Bankruptcy	27%
Public Law	3%
Tax	1%
Environmental	2%
Labor & Employment	2%
Intellectual Property	1%
Energy Regulatory	1%

FIRM OVERVIEW: A prominent participant in the early commercial development of the Southwest region of the US, Andrews Kurth today is a nationally ranked and recognized firm that handles the vital interests of established companies and emerging businesses around the globe. Founded in 1902, the firm has an international client base and has experience in all major industries and areas of business law and litigation. The result is the consistent delivery of efficient, effective and valuable legal services. Andrews Kurth enjoys an international presence, providing legal services worldwide from offices in major corporate and government centers on two continents.

MAIN AREAS OF PRACTICE:

Corporate & Securities: Andrews Kurth is recognized as having one of the most effective corporate and securities departments, representing many of the *Fortune* 500 companies. Since the inception of the firm more than 100 years ago, Andrews Kurth has maintained the focus of practicing quality law. The firm's lawyers serve public and private corporations, partnerships, joint ventures, national and regional investment banks, merchant banks, and other financial institutions, venture capital firms, capital market groups of commercial banks and individual clients. The firm is recognized as a leading securities firm for the energy industry. Areas of practice include all types of corporate finance transactoins, joint venture transactions, mergers and acquisitions, and complex, tax-sensitive financings. In addition, the firm created the master limited partnership, and has been involved in establishing more than 80 percent of the MLPs in existence.
Business Transactions: Lawyers in this practice counsel to a far-ranging client base, with specific emphasis on transactional matters related to energy, banking, public and private financing and real estate. These involve work in project and structured finance, syndicated lending, leasing, swaps and loan workouts, and restructuring, and in the real estate area, acquisition and development and the financing of a wide array of commercial, industrial and public projects. In addition, the firm's work includes representation to all aspects of the energy industry.
Litigation: With trial lawyers in Houston, Dallas, New York, Austin, Washington, DC and Los Angeles, the firm offers coast to coast experience in jury and bench trials in state and federal courts and other tribunals. The majority of the firm's lawyers concentrate on general corporate and business litigation, handling a variety of complex cases for companies in virtually every industry.

HEAD OFFICE

TEXAS
600 Travis, Suite 4200, **Houston**, Texas 77002
Tel: 713 220 4200 **Fax:** 713 220 4285
E-mail: webmaster@andrewskurth.com
Website: www.andrewskurth.com / www.aktechlaw.com

BRANCH OFFICES

TEXAS
111 Congress Ave, Suite 1700, **Austin**, Texas 78701
Tel: 512 320 9200 **Fax:** 512 320 9292

1717 Main Street, Suite 3700, **Dallas**, Texas 75201
Tel: 214 659-4400 **Fax:** 214 659 4401

Waterway Plaza Two, 10001 Woodloch Forest Drive, Suite 200
The Woodlands, Texas 77380
Tel: 713 220 4801 **Fax:** 713 220 4815

CALIFORNIA
601 South Figueroa, Suite 1725, **Los Angeles**, California 90017
Tel: 213 896 3100 **Fax:** 213 896 3137

NEW YORK
450 Lexington Avenue, **New York**, New York 10017
Tel: 212 850 2800 **Fax:** 212 850 2929

WASHINGTON
1701 Pennsylvania Avenue, N.W., Suite 300, **Washington**, District of Columbia 20006-5805
Tel: 202 662 2700 **Fax:** 202 662 2739

INTERNATIONAL OFFICES

The firm also has an office in London, England.

CONTACTS

Corporate & Securities	Michael O'Leary
Business Transactions	Thomas J Perich
Litigation	Rosemarie Donnelly
Bankruptcy	Hugh M Ray

Bankruptcy: The firm offers a sophisticated insolvency practice, representing clients nationwide in large, complex bankruptcies under both Chapter 11 and Chapter 7. Currently, Andrews Kurth ranks among the country's seven largest bankruptcy practices. The firm enjoys a large, diverse client base, representing debtors, creditors, trustees, creditors' committees, and institutional lenders. Bankruptcy issues are handled out of all the firm's offices. Firm lawyers also handle a significant volume of out of court restructurings and workouts, and Houston and New York lawyers handle the regulatory aspects of financial institution insolvency work.

ANDREWS
ATTORNEYS KURTH LLP

BAKER BOTTS LLP

FIRM OVERVIEW

Managing Partner: Walter J Smith

Number of partners worldwide: 245
Number of other lawyers worldwide: 449

FIRM OVERVIEW: Baker Botts is a leading international law firm, recognized for its energy, intellectual property, corporate, litigation, tax and environmental practices. This depth of knowledge enables the firm to work in partnership with its clients to deliver the right solution. Founded in Houston, Texas in 1840, Baker Botts has a network of offices in the US, Europe, Russia, and the Middle East, advising clients in over 100 countries around the world. Baker Botts ranks among the largest law firms in the United States and conducts operations on a basis that is global in scope and influence. Baker Botts also has one of the largest IP practices in the US for a general service firm, with IP Law & Business recognizing Baker Botts as one of the leading firms to represent IP America.

CLIENTS: Baker Botts is legal and business counsel to many of the world's leading companies, including nearly every major oil company in the United States, as well as numerous international companies. The firm's clients include private and public companies, banks, insurance companies, investment banking and venture capital firms, nonprofit organizations, individuals, estates, partnerships and government agencies. Its lawyers work with clients in almost every area of the law, including international and domestic corporate and financial matters, corporate governance, technology, intellectual property, business litigation, appellate matters, white collar criminal defense, government contracts, federal and state legislative matters, energy and oil and gas matters, real estate, administrative and regulatory matters involving energy, environmental and international trade.

HEAD OFFICE

TEXAS
One Shell Plaza, 910 Louisiana Street, **Houston** TX 77002-4995
Tel: 713 229 1234 **Fax:** 713 229 1522
Email: greg.nelson@bakerbotts.com
Website: www.bakerbotts.com

BRANCH OFFICES

NEW YORK
30 Rockefeller Plaza, **New York** NY 10112-4498
Tel: 212 408 2500 **Fax:** 212 408 2501
Email: lee.charles@bakerbotts.com

TEXAS
1500 San Jacinto Center, 98 San Jacinto Blvd, **Austin** TX 78701-4039
Tel: 512 322 2500 **Fax:** 512 322 2501
Email: robb.voyles@bakerbotts.com

2001 Ross Avenue, **Dallas** TX 75201-2980
Tel: 214 953 6500 **Fax:** 214 953 6503
Email: jack.kinzie@bakerbotts.com

DISTRICT OF COLUMBIA
The Warner, 1299 Pennsylvania Avenue, NW,
Washington DC 20004-2400
Tel: 202 639 7700 **Fax:** 202 639 7890
Email: bruce.kiely@bakerbotts.com or james.doty@bakerbotts.com

INTERNATIONAL OFFICES

The firm also has offices in Baku, Azerbaijan; Moscow, Russia; Riyadh, Saudi Arabia; London, United Kingdom.

WORLDWIDE OFFICES

CASPIAN SEA

Regional Profile: Baker Botts has one of the most active practices of any law firm with respect to investment in the Caspian and Caucasus regions, and its Baku office has been very much involved in the re-emergence of the onshore and offshore oil and gas industry in the region. Examples of major projects include the $3bn BTC crude oil pipeline from the Caspian Sea, through Georgia to Ceyhan, Turkey, and the $3.2bn SCP "Shah Deniz" natural gas pipeline, which together are among the largest active infrastructure projects in the world.

MIDDLE EAST

Regional Profile: The firm's Riyadh office operates in association with the law office of Mohammed bin Saud Al-Rasheed. It is acknowledged as one of the leading practices it the region and advises clients in Saudi Arabia and throughout the Middle East on a broad range of commercial, banking, project finance, telecoms, oil and gas matters, as well as litigation and arbitration.

EUROPE

Regional Profile: The London office plays a pivotal role in the firm's international activity; serving clients in the UK, continental Europe, and beyond. It handles market leading energy, finance, corporate/M&A, TMT, chemicals and dispute resolution matters, and has both UK and US law capabilities.

RUSSIA

Regional Profile: Baker Botts' Moscow office, with its growing portfolio of Russian work, advises on energy, mining, corporate/M&A, intellectual property, dispute resolution, real estate, finance, and investment funds. In its most recent survey, the firm was acclaimed by the *Petroleum Economist* magazine as having 'Best Knowledge of Energy Law and Transaction in the CIS'.

BEIRNE, MAYNARD & PARSONS, L.L.P.

THE FIRM

Managing Partner: Martin D Beirne
Number of partners: 40
Number of other lawyers: 80 (include of counsels as well as associates)

AREAS OF PRACTICE:

Civil Trials, Appellate & Arbitration 100%

FIRM OVERVIEW: Founded in 1987, Beirne, Maynard & Parsons, L.L.P. has become a nationally significant force in civil trial and appellate work. The firm is now the largest firm in Texas dedicated solely to litigation. Beirne, Maynard & Parsons has pursued a growth path based on both general litigation and industry specialization. As specialists, the firm has developed one of the nation's leading life sciences and pharmaceutical litigation practices, along with prestigious national practice teams serving the energy and transportation industries. As generalists, the firm continues to serve a diverse range of Fortune 500 companies locally, nationally, and internationally. Because the firm specializes in winning trials, all its lawyers are trained to practice in court, which, in turn, has enabled Beirne, Maynard & Parsons to attract attorneys who might not otherwise obtain courtroom experience working at larger firms. The firm's arbitration specialists have vast experience before national and international tribunals. The Arbitration/Alternative Dispute Resolution Group (AADR) has successfully resolved disputes through mediation, national and international arbitration and other resolution forums. Beirne, Maynard & Parsons understands that going to court may not always be in the client's best interest. There are many avenues for dispute resolution. As such, the firm's trial lawyers are also trained to recognize when matters are best resolved through other mechanisms.

MAIN AREAS OF PRACTICE:

Civil Trials, Appeals & Arbitration: As one of the nation's leading litigation firms, Beirne, Maynard & Parsons is distinguished for both breadth and depth. As civil trial generalists, Beirne, Maynard & Parsons represents hundreds of diverse corporations and other clients. Cases have ranged from product liability defense to anti-counterfeiting to representation of sovereign states. The firm's biomedical litigation specialty is supported by a network of MDs, PhD pathologists, and nurse paralegals. In addition to energy and transportation, the firm continues its significant practices in aviation, intellectual property, coverage and mass tort litigation and computer sciences. Because Texas is a plaintiff-friendly jurisdiction, Fortune 500 companies throughout the country have retained the firm when they are sued in the state. Beirne, Maynard & Parsons' trial practice also includes substantial work in courtrooms and arbitration panels throughout the United States and globally.

CLIENTS: As generalists, the firm's client list includes AIG Companies; Chevron Phillips Chemical Company; Fireman's Fund Insurance Companies; Lloyd's of London; Marriott Corporation; Pratt & Whitney of Canada, Inc; The Travelers Insurance Companies; and United Technologies Corporation. The firm's fabled transportation client list includes: American Suzuki Motor Corporation; Associated Aviation Underwriters; Aviation Office of America; The Cessna Aircraft Company; Freightliner, LLC; Hyundai North America; Mercedes-Benz Truck Company; Mitsubishi Motor Sales of American, Inc; Subaru of America, Inc; Toyota Motor Sales, USA, Inc; Union Tank Car Company; and Volvo North American Corporation. The list also includes the People's Republic of China and the Republic of Estonia. Energy clients include Air Liquide Corporation; BP Amoco; Conoco Phillips; Marathon Oil; Schlumberger Technology Corporation, and Brazos Electric Power Cooperative, Inc. In Life Sciences, Pfizer Inc is a major client; Beirne, Maynard & Parsons represents Pfizer in major litigation matters. Among other leading life science clients: Tanox, a biopharmaceutical company with expertise in allergy, asthma and immunological diseases; and Baylor College of Medicine, an internationally respected medical institution.

HEAD OFFICE

TEXAS
1300 Post Oak Boulevard, Suite 2500, **Houston**, TX 77056
Tel: 713 623 0887 **Fax:** 713 960 1527
Email: info@bmpllp.com
Website: www.bmpllp.com

BRANCH OFFICES

TEXAS
1700 Pacific Avenue, Suite 4400, **Dallas**, TX 75201
Tel: 214 237 4300 **Fax:** 214 237 4340

CONTACTS

General Litigation/Commercial	Jeffrey R Parsons
	Roger L McCleary
	Martin D Beirne
Life Sciences & Pharmaceutical	Jack Urquhart
	Joseph S Cohen
	Thomas Sartwelle
Energy/Utilities	Martin D Beirne
	Brit T Brown
	Sawnie A McEntire
	Edward J Murphy
	David A Pluchinsky
	Wm Bruce Stanfill
Telecommunications	Joseph S Cohen
Transportation	Martin D Beirne
	Brit T Brown
Intellectual Property	William Norvell
	Scott D Marrs
Toxic Tort/Environmental	Timothy Hogan
	Blaine D Edwards
	James Smith
Aviation	William L Maynard
Appellate	Jeffery Nobles
	Terry Adams
Product Liability	Sawnie A McEntire
	Mark A Waite
	Roger L McCleary
Coverage/Reinsurance Bad Faith	Jay W Brown
	David A Clark
	Roger L McCleary
	Jeffrey R Parsons
Labor & Employment	Benjamin A Escobar

INTERNATIONAL WORK: Beirne, Maynard & Parson's has represented numerous Fortune 500 companies in foreign disputes. In addition, the firm has been retained by sovereign nations like the People's Republic of China and the Republic of Estonia to litigate on their behalf. In one major case, Beirne, Maynard & Parsons represented the Republic of Estonia in a bilateral investment treaty issue. The Arbitration of the case was conducted under the auspices of the International Center for the Settlement of Investment Disputes (ICSID). The case was arbitrated in Switzerland, the UK and Washington, DC, with a final decision rendered on behalf of the Republic of Estonia.

BEIRNE
MAYNARD
&
PARSONS
LLP

BRACEWELL & GIULIANI LLP

THE FIRM

Managing Partner: Patrick C Oxford

Number of partners: 110
Number of other lawyers: 261

FIRM OVERVIEW: Bracewell & Giuliani maintains nine offices in Texas, New York, Washington, London and Kazakhstan. The firm is one of the largest in Texas. Founded in 1945 in Houston, Bracewell & Giuliani serves a wide array of domestic and international clients and government and public entities. With 50 practice areas, Bracewell offers a balance of expertise in business transactions, litigation and government relations, including a specific focus on bank finance and securities law, tax, corporate restructuring, intellectual property, environment law, labor and employment law, energy and telecommunications regulation and federal and state legislative strategies.

MAIN AREAS OF PRACTICE

Energy: Bracewell's oil and gas expertise mirrors the worldwide expansion of the industry to serve energy clients in a diverse practice that incorporates regulatory matters of corporate financing and restructuring, federal and state, environmental, corporate governance, tax, and litigation, among others. *Texas Lawyer* recently named one of the firm's litigation partners as the 'Go-to Lawyer' for Energy Law in Texas and he has been noted for his leading work by Chambers Global.

Regulatory: As one of the largest groups of its type in the country, Bracewell's regulated and restructured industry attorneys bring extensive experience in the development of gas pipeline, electric transmission infrastructure projects and telecommunications. Lawyers have been involved in the ongoing California power crisis via related litigation and administrative proceedings. Among its veteran team are former top officials with FERC and the former chairman of the Public Utility Commission of Texas.

Bankruptcy & Corporate Restructuring: Bracewell's Debt Restructuring and Corporate Finance Group participated in nearly every recent major energy industry restructuring deal in Texas. Bankruptcy attorneys have extensive experience representing both secured and unsecured creditors, committees, debtors, and trustees in formal bankruptcy proceedings, out-of-court workouts and loan restructures.

Finance: Bracewell structures documents and negotiates a wide variety of financing arrangements, including syndicated loan transactions, bilateral financing, project finance, trade finance, specialized financing, restructuring and workouts. *Project Finance* magazine listed the firm among the top ten legal advisers in North America and recognized its finance work for a power generation facility in Mississippi as 'Deal of the Year' for 2002.

Trial: Litigation attorneys have extensive experience arguing before Texas courts and federal district courts in commercial and complex tort contingency cases. Among its premier practice areas are energy litigation, defendant securities fraud class action and shareholder derivative claims, toxic tort/environmental defense and international dispute resolution. One of Bracewell's partners was named among the best product liability lawyers in Central Texas by the *Austin Business Journal* in 2004. Another litigator was named among the Top 50 Female Texas Super Lawyers.

Corporate & Securities: The firm has represented clients involved in domestic and international transactions ranging in size from $1 million to multibillions. Chambers Global ranked one of the firm's veteran partners among the top lawyers in this practice. *Corporate Board Member* magazine recognized Bracewell among the Top 5 corporate firms in Houston and San Antonio. Lawyers' corporate expertise includes industry-leading work in biotech and nanotech, venture capital, corporate governance, LBOs and M&As.

HEAD OFFICE

TEXAS
711 Louisiana, Ste. 2300, **Houston**, TX 77002
Tel: 713 223 2300   **Fax:** 713 221 1212
Website: www.bracewellgiuliani.com

BRANCH OFFICES

Austin, Texas; New York, New York; Dallas; San Antonio, Texas; Washington, DC.

INTERNATIONAL OFFICES

Kazakhstan and London.

CONTACTS

Bankruptcy & Corporate Restructuring	Henry J Kaim
Corporate & Securities	William D Gutermuth
Environment & Natural Resources	Luis M Nido
Financial Services	William T Luedke IV
Government Relations, Advocacy & Strategy	James Chapman
	Michael L Pate
Intellectual Property	Ben D Tobor
Labor	Amy K Halevy
Public Law	Jeffrey J Horner
Real Estate, Energy & Finance	Mark C Evans
Regulated & Restructured Industries	Paul W Fox, Charles H Shoneman
Tax	Roger D Aksamit
Trial	J Clifford Gunter III

Government Relations: Staffed with a former governor, several congressmen and others with experience in high-level federal, state and local government posts, Bracewell's lobbyists maintain a strong, active presence in Washington and Texas. Bracewell created the nation's first Homeland Security Practice in September 2001, and it established in 2003 a dedicated team of strategic communications professionals to assist companies with issues messaging and crisis communications.

Banking: *American Banker* ranked Bracewell's financial services team first in the nation as the most active legal adviser for bank and thrift acquisitions in 2003, and in 2002, *Bank Director* magazine named the group among the ten most active bank legal advisers in the country.

Intellectual Property: Intellectual property work highlights Bracewell's strength in technology law. In its annual rankings, NameProtect Trademark Insider ranked Bracewell as the No. 1 Houston law firm for trademark filing for 2004 and 2003.

Environment & Natural Resources: Bracewell's team brings comprehensive know-how to environmental law, with a keen focus on water rights and clean air regulations as well as lobbying and environmental transactional work. One partner was recognized for his groundbreaking air emissions work along the Texas-Mexico border when *Texas Lawyer's De Novo* magazine named him among the state's leading legal innovators in 2003.

International: Bracewell provides counsel to companies, private investors, financial institutions and foreign governments doing business in Europe, Latin America and the Caspian Sea Region or entities in those countries working to build investments in the US. For his corporate work in Kazakhstan one partner was noted in Chambers Global.

Other: The firm has equally strong assets across the balance of its practice areas including tax, real estate, government contracting, labor and employment, and school and public law.

CANTERBURY, STUBER, ELDER, GOOCH & SURRATT

THE FIRM

Managing Committee: Robert C Elder
W Kyle Gooch
David G Surratt

Number of partners: 9
Number of other lawyers: 4

AREAS OF PRACTICE:
Construction 70%
Labor & Employment 15%
Corporate & Real Estate 10%
Personal Injury & Property Damage 5%

FIRM OVERVIEW: The firm has an emphasis on construction law and labor and employment law related to the construction industry. The firm's practice has expanded into the areas of real estate, corporate, public construction law, personal injury law and insurance law; however, the mainstay is the construction industry. Three members of the firm are also active in arbitration and mediation of construction disputes.

MAIN AREAS OF PRACTICE:
Construction: The firm has expertise and extensive experience in the construction industry. Members of the firm have represented developers, owners, contractors, subcontractors and suppliers in construction disputes and other legal problems of construction and development, including commercial, industrial, highway, power plant and pipeline projects.

Labor & Employment: The firm represents employers in labor and employment matters. Specifically, the firm handles defense of discrimination and other claims arising under the State and Federal Equal Employment Opportunity law, Occupational Safety and Health Act, and the National Labor Relations Act. The firm has extensive experience in advising clients regarding union-related matters, personnel situations, harassment situations and wage and hour claims. It will review and prepare, where appropriate, personnel manuals and handbooks on behalf of clients.

Corporate/Real Estate: The firm provides corporate services in entity organization and corporate reorganizations such as mergers and conversions by analyzing innovative business solutions that serve the firm's clients' best interest. The firm represents sellers and purchasers of asset and stock purchase transactions. The firm serves as counselors and negotiators for developers, buyers, sellers, landlords and tenants in office and industrial properties. The firm counsels borrowers in construction financing and analyzes a wide variety of construction issues for commercial developments.

Personal Injury: The firm actively represents its corporate clients and employees of its clients in the defense and prosecution of claims arising from construction sites. The firm has defended and continues to defend claims relating to asbestos exposure, construction site injuries and claims of building defects.

HEAD OFFICE

TEXAS
Occidental Tower, 5005 LBJ Freeway, Suite 1000, **Dallas**, TX 75244
Tel: 972 239 7493 **Fax:** 972 490 7739
Email: csegs@canterburylaw.com
Website: www.canterburylaw.com

CLIENTS: Clients include Carter & Burgess, Inc.; Centex Construction Co.; Charter Builders; Clark Contractors, Inc.; Dee Brown Masonry, Inc.; douglas e. barnhart, inc.; Driver Pipeline Company; Federal Reserve Bank of Dallas; Gilbane Building Company; GLF Construction Corporation; Granite Construction Co.; Haws & Tingle, Ltd., Hensel-Phelps Construction; Independent Electrical Contractors Association; JPI Companies; L.H. Lacy Company; Linbeck Construction; Lloyd Plyler Construction, Inc.; Manhattan Construction; Marek Companies; Sundt Corporation; Morgan Buildings; Prudential Insurance Company; Roy Anderson Corporation; Sunmount Corp.; TAC Americas, Inc.; Tellepsen Builders, L.P.; S&B Constructors and Engineers; Walker Engineering, Inc.; Zachry Construction Company.

The POWER OF
Experience

Canterbury,
Stuber,
Elder,
Gooch &
Surratt, P.C.

COOPER & SCULLY, P.C.

THE FIRM

Managing & Senior Partner: R Brent Cooper

Number of partners: 19
Number of other lawyers: 40

AREAS OF PRACTICE:
Healthcare & Medical Malpractice 25%
Appellate 15%
Insurance Coverage 15%
Professional Liability 15%
Bad Faith 10%
Construction 5%
Employment 5%
Governmental Entities.. 5%
Products Liability 5%

FIRM OVERVIEW: Cooper & Scully, P.C. is recognized as one of the leading firms in Texas for the handling of complex litigation. The firm is known for its expertise and ability in trial and appellate work. Areas of litigation practice include insurance coverage, professional liability, bad faith, products liability, representation of governmental entities, construction, employment, and healthcare and medical malpractice. Cooper & Scully P.C. is engaged in the representation of clients on a statewide basis and has the staffing and resources that permit it to pursue aggressively all types of cases, from the most complicated to the most basic.

MAIN AREAS OF PRACTICE:

Healthcare & Medical Malpractice: The firm has an extensive practice in the representation of physicians, hospitals, and other healthcare providers. The firm's attorneys have substantial experience and expertise in the trial of medical negligence cases. In addition, the firm provides advice to individual healthcare providers, as well as institutional healthcare providers. The firm also represents individuals and entities before state and federal agencies. The firm provides representation in administrative areas such as peer review and credentialing process. The firm also provides representation to insurers and healthcare providers in all aspects involving managed healthcare.

Appellate Practice: The firm has a statewide reputation for the handling of appeals in both state and federal courts, and as a result, receives referral appeals from numerous attorneys throughout the state. The Appellate Section is involved in the drafting of final pleadings and common jury charges, and in the handling of post-trial motions. The Appellate Section has been involved in a number of landmark cases in Texas jurisprudence, involving both Texas procedure as well as Texas substantive law.

Insurance Coverage: The firm has extensive knowledge and expertise in the analysis of insurance coverage matters. The firm represents both insurers and insureds in disputes over the coverage afforded by various policies. Additionally, the firm is among a relatively small number of firms who have the expertise to represent reinsurers.

Professional Liability: The firm has represented many professionals in both legal malpractice, agents, errors and omissions, and other professional errors and omissions. The services provided to many professionals include representation before the respective licensing boards as well as in the courtroom.

Bad Faith: The firm has been at the forefront in the development of Texas law in the area of bad faith. The firm has attorneys who have tried numerous bad faith cases to successful results. The firm's attorneys have the knowledge and expertise to analyze and evaluate the exposure presented by these cases, in addition to providing advice to its insurance clients on steps that can be taken to minimize such risks.

HEAD OFFICE

TEXAS
900 Jackson Street, Suite 900, **Dallas**, TX 75202
Tel: 214 712 9500   **Fax:** 214 712 9450
Email: brent.cooper@cooperscully.com
Website: www.cooperscully.com

BRANCH OFFICES

ARIZONA
4835 East Cactus Road, Suite 330, **Scottsdale**, AZ 85254
Tel: 602 354 8900   **Fax:** 602 354 8980
Email: amy.mcgaw@cooperscully.com

TEXAS
2700 Chase Tower, 600 Travis Street, **Houston**, TX 77002
Tel: 713 236 6800   **Fax:** 713 236 6880
Email: john.raley@cooperscully.com

200 N Travis, Suite 500, PO Box 1235, **Sherman**, TX 75090
Tel: 903 813 3900   **Fax:** 903 868 1919
Email: cyndy.goosen@cooperscully.com

Products Liability: The firm represents manufacturers directly and others through their insurance carriers. The firm provides representation and advice to various manufacturers on issues of design defects, warnings, and negligence in the manufacture of the particular product. The clients represented include designers and manufacturers of medical equipment and pharmaceutical products, as well as manufacturers of other product.

Construction: The firm provides a variety of services to its construction clients. These include the drafting and interpretation of contract documents, as well as contract negotiations. Included in these services is the analysis of risk presented by certain projects and drafting of contract provisions to minimize risk to the client. The firm is also well experienced in construction personal injury litigation, litigation involving contract claims, and construction defect litigation.

Employment: The firm also handles employment work.

CLIENTS: A.I Healthcare; AIAC; American International Group; American Modern Homes Ins. Co; American Physicians Insurance Exchange; American Safety Casualty Ins. Co; Arch Ins. Co; Baylor Hospital Group; Columbia/HCA Healthcare Corporation; Covenant Hospital Group; Discover Re Managers; Employee Reinsurance Corporation; Farmers Insurance Group of Companies; Gainsco Insurance Group; Great American Insurance Companies; Health Care Indemnity, Inc.; Joint Underwriters Association; Kaiser Foundation Health Plan; Medical Claims Management Group; Mid-Continent Group; The Medical Protective Company; Mitsui Sumitomo Ins. Group; National Union Fire Insurance Company; North American Risk, Inc.; OneBeacon Ins. Co; Republic Western Ins. Co; Steadfast Insurance Company; St. Paul Insurance Company; State Farm Insurance Company; Tenet Health Systems; Texas Health Resources; Texas Medical Liability Insurance Company; Texas Medical Liability Trust; Underwriters of Lloyds, London; Western Litigation Specialists, Inc.; Zurich Insurance Company.

COX SMITH MATTHEWS INCORPORATED

THE FIRM

FIRM OVERVIEW: Cox Smith Matthews Incorporated is the leading San Antonio commercial law firm with expertise ranging from sophisticated corporate transactions to complex litigation to personal estate planning. Headquartered in San Antonio, Texas with an office in Austin, the firm employs 120 attorneys with diverse experience in 17 primary practice areas and more than 25 areas of specialization. This depth of experience enables Cox Smith Matthews to deliver exceptional legal services and the best in client service to regional, national and international clients.

MAIN AREAS OF PRACTICE:

Appellate: The firm advises general counsel and trial lawyers to supply immediate and ongoing support relating to appellate issues. Additionally, the firm provides representation from entry of verdict through briefing and argument in federal and state appellate courts, including the Fifth Circuit and the Texas Supreme Court.

Business Litigation: The firm's Litigation Practice focuses primarily on business-related disputes and issues. Additionally, the firm provides counseling before problems arise on how best to structure business operations to avoid unnecessary risk of litigation.

Corporate & Securities: The firm provides counseling on mergers and acquisitions, public and private offerings of securities, corporate governance, partnerships, joint ventures and strategic alliances, and technology contracting.

Creditors' Rights, Corporate Restructuring & Bankruptcy: The firm advises on all aspects of business bankruptcy, including representation of debtors, trustees, committees, acquirers, secured and unsecured creditors, lenders and other parties-in-interest. The firm advises clients in connection with restructuring; lending issues and maximization of realization on extended credit; pre-bankruptcy strategic planning; issues involving preferences and fraudulent conveyances under both state and federal law; and a multiplicity of bankruptcy issues in real estate and other commercial transactions.

Employee Benefits: The firm advises on a variety of employee benefit matters, including qualified and non-qualified retirement and deferred compensation plans, health plans, executive compensation and a broad range of tax and ERISA matters.

Energy & Natural Resources: The firm's Natural Resources Department provides legal counseling, structuring of transactions and litigation services to companies involved in the development, operation and marketing of natural and mineral resources. The firm also provides legal advice to clients relating to environmental compliance and environmental issues in structuring acquisition and disposition transactions.

Estate Planning, Probate & Wealth Transfer: The firm advises on the preparation of wills, life insurance trusts, educational trusts, powers of attorney, strategies for tax advantaged charitable giving, life insurance, tax minimization and pre-marital agreements.

Healthcare: The firm's healthcare attorneys work with a full range of providers in business formation and restructuring, healthcare transactions, general healthcare law and regulatory matters, and dispute resolution.

Intellectual Property: The firm's intellectual property attorneys assist clients with domestic and international trademark prosecution and licensing; domestic and international franchising formation and evaluation; registration and enforcement of copyright prosecution; licensing and enforcements of patents; and trademark, copyright and patent litigation.

Labor & Employment: The firm advises on personnel policies, discrimination claims, employee contracts, COBRA, ERISA, ERISA litigation, class actions, alternate dispute resolution, labor/union issues, wage and hour claims and employment litigation.

HEAD OFFICE

TEXAS
112 East Pecan Street, **San Antonio**, TX 78205-1521
Tel: 210 554 5500 **Fax:** 210 226 8395
Website: www.coxsmith.com

BRANCH OFFICES

TEXAS
111 Congress, Suite 2800, **Austin**, TX 78701-4084
Tel: 512 703 6300 **Fax:** 512 703 6399

CONTACTS

Appellate	Renee F McElhaney
Business Litigation	Brett W Schouest
Corporate & Securities	Steven A Elder
Creditors' Rights, Corporate Restructuring & Bankruptcy	Deborah D Williamson
Employee Benefits	Mary M Potter
Energy & Natural Resources	John R Ray
Estate Planning, Probate & Wealth Transfer	Allan G Gilman
Healthcare	James A Gilman
Intellectual Property	Pamela B Huff
Labor & Employment	Daniel R Stern
Public Law	Howard D Bye
Public Utility	Howard D Bye
Real Estate	James M McDonough
Tax	William H Lester, Jr

Public Law: The firm counsels on matters including elections; annexation; condemnation and land use; water rights and service; depository and investment issues; and organizational and governance issues.

Public Utility: The firm advises on matters related to franchise work for public utilities; condemnations; sales tax and other taxation issues; cable television and fiber optics infrastructure; construction contracts; and public utility litigation.

Real Estate: The firm advises on matters related to real estate acquisition, development and finance, environmental and land use planning issues, lease agreements, landlord/tenant issues, workout and commercial construction.

Tax: The firm advises on matters related to tax controversies, tax planning, business succession planning, Texas franchise tax planning, international tax planning, and employee benefits.

CLIENTS: The firm provides a wide variety of services to clients ranging from entrepreneurs and family business owners to Fortune 100 public companies and represents some of the region's largest businesses, including SBC Communications, Clear Channel Communications, Valero Energy Corporation and City Public Service.

INTERNATIONAL WORK: The firm advises clients on international acquisitions and investments; the formation of offshore corporations; structuring international joint ventures; international tax planning; international patent, trademark and copyright protection; and the implications of the North American Free Trade Agreement (NAFTA).

COX SMITH MATTHEWS
INCORPORATED

DAVIS MUNCK

THE FIRM

Co-Chairman: William A Munck, James E Davis

Number of shareholders: 11
Number of other lawyers: 9

FIRM OVERVIEW: Davis Munck is a Dallas, Texas based law firm offering full-service counsel in the areas of corporate and securities matters, intellectual property, litigation, employment and business reorganization and restructuring. Technology and technology-focused business are a passion for the firm and a central component of the firm's practice.

MAIN AREAS OF PRACTICE:

Intellectual Property: In addition to trademark, copyright and patent preparation and prosecution, the firm has extensive experience in the development of comprehensive corporate IP strategies. Through technology assessment techniques and applied research, Davis Munck helps clients improve business performance and institute organizational and strategic change for competitive advantage.

IP Audits & Legal Opinions: The firm performs intellectual property audits on specific licenses, trademarks, patents or technologies to determine whether any rights are being or could be protected or infringed upon. The firm also investigates the validity of registrations, contracts, schematics and filings to be certain all avenues are explored and all proper precautions are in effect.

Commercial Litigation & Dispute Resolution: Davis Munck maintains a nationwide Commercial Litigation and Arbitration Practice. The firm's trial lawyers have expertise in matters ranging from intellectual property issues to corporate, contract and employment disputes. The Litigation Practice is focused on clients' business objectives. Through rigorous case development and pre-trial preparation, Davis Munck attorneys provide legal strategies that are most likely to yield maximum value to clients.

Employment: The firm's Employment Practice focuses on preventing disputes by ensuring that employer policies are in compliance with discrimination, safety and other laws and that the policies are consistently applied. The firm has extensive experience with policies and procedures that protect a company's intellectual property. Davis Munck attorneys also counsel businesses on employment disputes through arbitration and litigation.

Corporate/Mergers & Acquisitions/Private Equity: The firm provides counsel on entity formations, venture and other finance transactions, mergers and acquisitions, and business restructuring. Davis Munck attorneys negotiate and prepare a wide variety of technology and other agreements, including licensing, employment, development and distribution agreements.

Reorganization/Restructuring/Bankruptcy: If significant financial changes occur in a business, relationships with investors, lenders and other creditors often become more complex. Effectively managing those relationships requires experienced counsel. The firm counsels businesses on planning and structuring reorganizations or restructurings to make the process more manageable. The firm also represents both debtors and creditors in disputes that may arise in connection with proceedings under the Bankruptcy Code.

HEAD OFFICE

TEXAS
900 Three Galleria Tower, 13155 Noel Road, **Dallas**, TX 75240
Tel: 972 628 3600   **Fax:** 972 628 3616
Email: info@davismunck.com
Website: www.davismunck.com

CONTACTS

Intellectual Property	William Munck
	Robert McCutcheon
IP Audits & Legal Opinions	William Munck
	Daniel Venglarik
Commercial Litigation	James Davis
Employment	John Palter
Corporate Transactions	Vincent Slusher
Reorganization/Bankruptcy	Vincent Slusher

CLIENTS: The firm's clients range from start-ups to Fortune 50 international technology companies. The firm also works with foreign associate firms in the areas of patent preparation and prosecution.

INTERNATIONAL WORK: The firm represents a number of non-US companies in the areas of patent procurement, maintenance and enforcement of their multinational intellectual property portfolios.

FULBRIGHT & JAWORSKI L.L.P.

THE FIRM

Managing Partner: Steven B Pfeiffer

Number of partners: 344
Number of other lawyers: 570

FIRM OVERVIEW: Founded in 1919, Fulbright & Jaworski L.L.P. is a leading full-service international law firm, with approximately 900 attorneys in 11 offices in Houston, New York, Washington, DC, Austin, Dallas, Los Angeles, Minneapolis, San Antonio, Hong Kong, London and Munich. Fulbright provides a full range of legal services to both domestic and foreign clients worldwide. For the third year in a row, the 2004 BTI survey of FORTUNE 1000 general counsel ranked Fulbright in client service as a "Top 30 Best A-Team Law Firm" and in 2004, *Corporate Board Member* magazine named Fulbright among the top 20 corporate law firms in the US in their survey of board members of public companies. An international lawyers survey published in the Global Counsel 2004-2005 *Dispute Resolution Handbook* picked Fulbright as one of the best US dispute resolution firms. Additionally, the firm was named one of the American Lawyer's international 'Arbitration Elite.' *IP Worldwide* ranked Fulbright among the top US law firms for trademark counseling and litigation.

MAIN AREAS OF PRACTICE

Arbitration & ADR: Fulbright's Arbitration & ADR Practice Group move easily between traditional litigation, arbitration and ADR. They are one of the only 17 firms in the world named as the "Arbitration Elite" by *The American Lawyer*. Their peers have also named them as one of the top ten national firms in the US for dispute resolution in the *Global Counsel 2004/2005 Dispute Resolution Handbook*.

Bankruptcy, Reorganization & Creditors' Rights: Fulbright & Jaworski's Bankruptcy, Reorganization and Creditors' Rights Practice Group represents creditors and debtors in restructure, refinance and insolvency litigation, including bankruptcy. The firm also represents persons buying from, lending to and investing in Chapter 11 debtors. The group has substantial experience in restructure and refinance negotiations and documentation, and insolvency litigation, particularly valuation litigation, and takes advantage of the firm's resources and broad transaction and litigation experience.

Corporate, Securities & Transactions: Fulbright & Jaworski provides a broad array of corporate legal services to a diverse client base that ranges from start-up ventures to large multinational companies. The firm carefully guides its clients through the legal issues that affect not only their ability to obtain financing, but also to maintain their operations in today's highly competitive, high-speed business environment. As a result of its survey of more than 2,000 board members, *Corporate Board Member Magazine* recently ranked Fulbright & Jaworski as one of the top 20 corporate law firms in the United States. Fulbright's skill and commitment to service spans many industries including energy, healthcare, media, financial services, insurance software and hardware, biotechnology, telecommunications, information technology, transportation, business services, manufacturing, retail, e-commerce and consumer products.

Energy: Fulbright is recognized as a premier energy firm with a diversified practice that has more than 50 years experience serving the needs of the global energy industry. The firm's attorneys are regularly involved in both international and domestic energy matters and are highly skilled in energy litigation, transactions, regulatory matters and dispute resolution. Chambers & Partners ranked Fulbright among the top three energy law firms in the US.

Environmental: Fulbright & Jaworski's Environmental Law Practice Group represents clients in all aspects of environmental law and environmental litigation. In a nationwide survey of its peers, Fulbright was voted among the

HEAD OFFICE

TEXAS
1301 McKinney, Suite 5100, **Houston**, TX 77010-3095
Tel: 713 651 5151 **Fax:** 713 651 5246
Email: info@fulbright.com
Website: www.fulbright.com

BRANCH OFFICES

NEW YORK
666 Fifth Avenue, **New York**, NY 10103-3198
Tel: 212 318 3000 **Fax:** 212 318 3400
Email: info@fulbright.com

DISTRICT OF COLUMBIA
801 Pennsylvania Avenue, NW, Market Square,
Washington, DC 20004-2623
Tel: 202 662 0200 **Fax:** 202 662 4643
Email: info@fulbright.com

CALIFORNIA
865 South Figueroa, Twenty-Ninth Floor, **Los Angeles**, CA 90017-2571
Tel: 213 892 9200 **Fax:** 213 680 4518
Email: info@fulbright.com

MINNESOTA
2100 IDS Center, 80 South Eighth Street, **Minneapolis**, MN 55402
Tel: 612 321 2800 **Fax:** 612 321 9600
Email: info@fulbright.com

TEXAS
600 Congress Avenue, Suite 2400, **Austin**, TX 78701-3271
Tel: 512 474 5201 **Fax:** 512 536 4598
Email: info@fulbright.com

2200 Ross Avenue, Suite 2800, **Dallas**, TX 75201-2748
Tel: 214 855 8000 **Fax:** 214 855 8200
Email: info@fulbright.com

300 Convent Street, Suite 2200, **San Antonio**, TX 78205-3792
Tel: 210 224 5575 **Fax:** 210 270 7205
Email: info@fulbright.com

CONTACTS

Arbitration & ADR	Mark Baker, John Bowman
Bankruptcy	Evelyn H Biery
Corporate	Mike W Conlon, Paul Jacobs
Energy	Jeff Dykes, Poe Leggette, George Kutzschbach
Energy & Real Property	Michael P Irvin
Environmental	Eva Fromm O'Brien
Family Law	Stewart W Gagnon
Healthcare	Jerry A Bell, Robert J Swift, Terry O Tottenham
Intellectual Property & Technology	Paul Krieger
International	Mark Baker, Jeff Blount
Labor & Employment Law	AJ Harper II
Litigation	Steve Dillard
Public Finance	Fredric A Weber
Tax	John R Allender
Technology & Emerging Companies	John C Boehm
	Robert F Gray, Merrill M Kraines

10 best firms in the country for environmental law. Its attorneys have extensive experience in environmental litigation matters, government enforcement actions, regulatory interpretations and administrative civil and criminal proceedings before the United States Environmental Protection Agency (EPA), the Texas Natural Resource Conservation Commission (TNRCC) and other environmental agencies. The firm's legal services also include the evaluation of environmental impacts and liabilities associated

FULBRIGHT & JAWORSKI L.L.P. cont'd

with real estate and business transactions, including drafting indemnification and other contractual terms to protect against the impact of environmental and toxic tort liabilities.

Family Law: Fulbright & Jaworski is the only major international law firm with a practice group dedicated specifically to family law and have handled thousands of related matters. Representation includes: divorce suits, including child custody matters; child support and visitation enforcement/modifications; prenuptial/postnuptial agreements and enforcement; adoptions; custody issues related to international conventions; division of the marital estate; post-divorce partition of undivided property, paternity suits and asset protection plans. The firm also advises hospitals regarding their obligation to release medical records relating to child support, divorce matters and other family issues.

Healthcare: Fulbright's Health Law Practice Group provides multi-disciplinary solutions, drawing upon the experience of attorneys who devote their practices to healthcare operational, regulatory transactional and litigation matters, as well as other key practice groups such as antitrust, labor and employment, intellectual property and litigation.

Information Technology: Fulbright & Jaworski's Information Technology Practice Group is one of the nation's largest, and the knowledge of its attorneys is highly diverse. This practice group is dedicated to delivering timely, well-informed and practical legal advice to both vendors and users of information technology. Members of Fulbright's Information Technology Practice Group apply their knowledge not only to IT businesses, but also to the many non-technology companies that encounter problems linked to technology. In search of resolutions to these issues, companies call upon Fulbright for IT consultations and guidance. Companies the firm assists range from traditional businesses to those on the cutting edge of the most advanced technology in the world.

Intellectual Property & Technology: Fulbright & Jaworski's Intellectual Property and Technology Department encompasses one of the largest concentrations of intellectual property attorneys in the country. The firm's experienced team of attorneys, patent agents and technical advisors helps clients obtain and protect intellectual property rights in the United States and around the world. The breadth of the firm's services is extensive as it: counsels clients about copyrights, patents, trade secrets and trademarks; practices before government agencies to secure those rights; handles arbitration, mediation and other litigation alternatives; negotiates licenses to maximise the value of such property; handles technology transfers, manufacturing and supply agreements, research and development agreements, and start-up agreements; handles intellectual property audits and due diligence, either separately or as part of mergers and acquisitions.

Iraq: Fulbright & Jaworski provides legal assistance, primarily through the Houston and DC offices, and, as necessary, works with corresponding counsel in Baghdad and throughout the region, to clients involved in Iraq-related business opportunities.

Labor & Employment Law: Fulbright & Jaworski's Labor and Employment Practice Group provides extensive services that range from counseling companies (relative to the increasing number of state, federal and local laws regulating employment) to representation in state and federal jury and non-jury trials and before administrative agencies. The firm has more than 80 years of experience representing employers across the United States in virtually every industry and on subject matters as diverse as the problems that arise in the workplace. Areas the firm has advised on include: civil rights charges and litigation; management-union relations; wrongful discharge and employment tort litigation; affirmative action; employment contracts; corporate transactions and restructuring; employment benefits litigation; public sector employment issues; safety and health; wage-hour and other labor standards; miscellaneous labor and employment laws.

Litigation: Fulbright & Jaworski's Litigation Department emphasizes a hands-on philosophy tailored to a client's specific needs, covering the widest possible range of legal matters from local litigation to the most complex international disputes. The firm's attorneys frequently author legal treatises and law review articles, participate in continuing legal education programs sponsored by national, state and local organizations, and serve as elected leaders of the local, state and American Bar Associations.

Public Finance: Fulbright & Jaworski has more than 50-plus industry leading public finance attorneys, making the firm one of the nation's leading public finance resources. It was ranked 5th in the nation (1st in Texas) as bond counsel in 2004, helping raise $11.0 billion in 304 issues. The firm's attorneys also have extensive experience as underwriters counsel, disclosure counsel, bank counsel, special tax counsel and general counsel to municipal securities issuers and with interest rate hedging transactions.

Tax: Fulbright & Jaworski's Tax Group has extensive experience in all facets of tax controversy resolution, from audit to appeals to competent authority relief, including litigation when an acceptable settlement is not forthcoming from taxing authorities. In addition to advising clients, Fulbright's Tax Practice is often retained by other law firms to provide tax expertise to their clients.

Technology & Emerging Companies: Fulbright & Jaworski has a long history of representing start-up companies and mature companies alike. The TEC Department is an innovative portal for the firm's emerging-company and technology clients to access a wide spectrum of experience, including corporate finance, tax, securities compliance, real estate, labor and employment, intellectual property and technology, information technology and e-commerce, product liability and class actions and general litigation.

INTERNATIONAL WORK: Fulbright & Jaworski's international lawyers have counseled and represented US and non-US businesses with regard to their international activities in almost every part of the world. The firm's International Department comprises more than 100 attorneys from its US, European (London and Munich) and Asian (Hong Kong) offices and has considerable experience in the wide array of business and legal issues involved in cross-border financial, commercial and investment transactions. Its international clients represent a broad cross-sector of industry groups, including energy, manufacturing, mining, information and communications technologies, telecommunications, banking and financial services and insurance. To meet the diversity of clients' needs, Fulbright & Jaworski's international attorneys are drawn from throughout the firm and work closely with attorneys in all areas of practice. Many of the firm's international lawyers are multilingual, have lived and worked outside of the United States and are intimately familiar with different legal and business cultures. As a complement to its own capabilities, the firm has developed an extensive network of relationships with law firms throughout the world that provide expert assistance with respect to various 'host' nation legal issues that arise in international investments, transactions and disputes.

International Offices: Fulbright and Jaworski has offices in Hong Kong, London and Munich.

Languages: Afrikaans, Arabic, Bengali, Cantonese, Chinese, Croatian, Dutch, French, German, Hebrew, Hindu, Italian, Japanese, Korean, Mandarin Chinese, Polish, Portuguese, Romanian, Russian, Spanish, Tagalog, Taiwanese, Urdu, Vietnamese and Yugoslavian.

HEAD OFFICE

TEXAS

1301 McKinney, Suite 5100, Houston, TX 77010
Partners in charge: Michael W Conlon, Frank G Jones
Number of lawyers: 318

FULBRIGHT & JAWORSKI L.L.P. cont'd

Office Profile: Founded on October 1, 1919, Fulbright & Jaworski's Houston office is its largest. The combined creativity, commitment and experience of its attorneys produces prompt, innovative solutions to both routine and complex legal problems. Its highly trained and motivated attorneys understand the needs of the firm's clients in today's global community and are committed to playing a meaningful, efficient and effective role in their growth and success. As a full-service, international law firm at the forefront of the evolving legal marketplace, Fulbright is well positioned to assist its clients, as they move into the new millennium, in the following areas: admiralty, alternative dispute resolution, appellate, bankruptcy, reorganization and creditors' rights, corporate, securities and transactions, employee benefits, environmental, energy, family law, healthcare, intellectual property and technology, international, labor and employment, litigation, project finance, public finance, real estate, tax, technology and emerging companies, trusts and estates.

US OFFICES

NEW YORK

666 Fifth Avenue, New York, NY 10103-3198
Partner in charge: William Bush
Number of lawyers: 126
Office Profile: Formed over 65 years ago, the New York office serves a broad client base including large publicly-held corporations, investment banking and brokerage firms, venture capital and leveraged buy-out firms, investment funds, private equity and institutional investors, life science, high-technology and other emerging growth companies, privately-held companies, partnerships, individuals, estates and charitable organizations and foundations.

WASHINGTON, DC

801 Pennsylvania Avenue, NW, Market Square, Washington, DC 20004-2623
Partner in charge: Joseph T Small, Jr
Number of lawyers: 98
Office Profile: Since its founding in 1927, Fulbright & Jaworski's Washington, DC office has grown from a few lawyers providing federal agency representation in support of the firm's practice, to a full-service office of more than 90 lawyers handling litigation, business and regulatory matters for a national and international clientele.

CALIFORNIA

865 South Figueroa, Twenty-Ninth Floor, Los Angeles, CA 90017-2571
Partner in charge: Peter H Mason
Number of lawyers: 76
Office Profile: Fulbright & Jaworski's growing Los Angeles office is full-service, with a diverse litigation and sophisticated business practice that includes: appellate; corporate, securities and transactions; banking and business; bankruptcy, reorganization and creditors' rights; environmental; healthcare; intellectual property and technology; international; labor and employment law; litigation; public finance; real estate; tax; trusts and estates; venture capital.

MINNESOTA

2100 IDS Center, 80 South Eighth Street, Minneapolis, MN 55402
Partner in charge: Ronn B Kreps
Number of lawyers: 18
Office Profile: The Minneapolis office of Fulbright opened in February 2000 and has grown rapidly over the past four years to serve a broad client base both in the Midwest and throughout the United States. The Minneapolis team remains focused on the ever-changing needs of clients who face a broad range of issues involving intellectual property, commercial litigation and products liability.

TEXAS

600 Congress Avenue, Suite 2400, Austin, TX 78701-3271
Partner in charge: Terry O Tottenham
Number of lawyers: 86

Office Profile: Opened in January 1978, Fulbright & Jaworski's Austin Office is a full-service presence with more than 85 lawyers. In 2000 alone it added more than 35 patent, trademark and technology attorneys and scientific advisors in Austin, many of whom joined the firm from the IP specialty firm Arnold, White & Durkee, and several of whom have served as senior in-house counsel. Integrating that in-house experience with the firm's practice reflects Fulbright & Jaworski's commitment to deliver prompt and practical solutions to its clients.

2200 Ross Avenue, Suite 2800, Dallas, TX 75201-2748
Partner in charge: Kenneth L Stewart
Number of lawyers: 109

Office Profile: Fulbright & Jaworski's Dallas office opened in 1981 by merging with the bond firm of Dumas, Huguenin, Boothman & Morrow. For several years, the firm's Dallas attorneys focused on municipal finance transactions, then expanded to a full-service office to include: appellate; bankruptcy, reorganization and creditors' rights; corporate, securities, and transactions; healthcare; intellectual property and technology; international; labor and employment law; litigation; public finance; real estate; tax.

300 Convent Street, Suite 2200, San Antonio, TX 78205-3792
Partner in charge: George W Scofield
Number of lawyers: 63
Office Profile: Fulbright & Jaworski opened its San Antonio office in 1980, which has since grown to a full-service office with more than 60 attorneys to include: appellate; bankruptcy, reorganization and creditors' rights; corporate, securities and transactions; environmental; healthcare; labor and employment law; litigation; public finance; real estate; tax and employee benefits; trusts and estates.

GARDERE WYNNE SEWELL LLP

THE FIRM

Managing Partner: Stephen D Good
Number of partners: 166
Number of other lawyers: 125

AREAS OF PRACTICE:

Trial	33%
Corporate	26%
Financial Services	19%
Labor & Employment	7%
Environmental	6%
Tax	8%
Intellectual Property	6%

FIRM OVERVIEW: Gardere is one of the preeminent full-service law firms in the Southwest. With approximately 290 lawyers and more than 40 practice areas to serve its clients, Gardere is strong and diverse, combining the comprehensive resources of a large firm with an interdisciplinary approach to providing clients with effective counsel in terms of time, cost, and results. This approach creates a team-based professional service environment in which attorneys experienced in specific areas of law and particular industries are available to provide effective, timely counsel according to specific client and case needs. The firm provides solutions to complicated legal matters to achieve its client's goals - Gardere's primary objective.

MAIN AREAS OF PRACTICE

Corporate: Counsels companies on strategic planning, outsourcing and a full range of issues involving business operations. Attorneys are recognized for their aggressive approach to finding meaningful solutions for the companies they represent, and not only provide general counsel but specialized expertise in areas such as investment partnerships, major business transactions, partnership interests, public and private offerings, start-up ventures, and venture capital.

Environmental: Covers a breadth of issues including high-stakes complex litigation involving multiple parties, regulatory rulemaking, transactions and compliance assistance for ongoing operations. This national practice includes team members from diverse backgrounds including federal and state environmental agencies, the judiciary, Fortune 500 companies and academia.

Financial Services: Serves both public and private as well as regulated and unregulated entities and institutions in a variety of issues including regulatory matters, financing transactions, development transactions and restructurings. Attorneys have experience with virtually every form of commercial financing, both secured and unsecured, and handle transactions involving all types of assets, including real estate, mineral interests, inventory, accounts receivable, factoring and various forms of intangible properties. Attorneys are particularly experienced in the special issues involved in the financing and operation of hotels and resorts, ships, and energy assets, such as drilling rigs and production platforms.

Intellectual Property: Focuses on patent, trademark, copyright, trade secret and unfair competition law and the antitrust aspects of intellectual property law, with significant expertise in trademark and patent prosecution, licensing, IPOs, and related litigation. Clients range between individual inventors, artists and authors, universities and large multinational corporations.

Labor & Employment: Provides counsel and representation for employers in decision making and litigation involving the National Labor Relations Act, the Fair Labor Standards Act, and individual and class action employment discrimination matters. Representative matters include wrongful discharge claims, such as workers compensation retaliation, negligent hiring or retention, implied contract, acquisition-related, and those pendant to employment claims (libel, slander, infliction of emotional distress, fraud). Matters also include Executive Order 11246 affirmative action plans and

HEAD OFFICE

TEXAS
3000 Thanksgiving Tower, 1601 Elm Street, **Dallas**, TX 75201-4761
Tel: 214 999 3000   **Fax:** 214 999 4667
Website: www.gardere.com

BRANCH OFFICES

TEXAS
3000 One American Center, 600 Congress Avenue,
Austin, TX 78701-2978
Tel: 512 542 7000 **Fax:** 512 542 7100

1000 Louisiana, Suite 3400, **Houston**, Texas 77002-5011
Tel: 713 276 5500   **Fax:** 713 276 5555

DISTRICT OF COLUMBIA
1667 K Street, NW, Suite 450, **Washington**, DC 20006-1649
Tel: 202 659 3560   **Fax:** 202 659 3565

INTERNATIONAL OFFICES

Gardere, Arena y Robles, S.C. is based in **Mexico City**.

CONTACTS

Corporate	NL Stevens
Environmental	Richard Faulk
Financial Services	Clifford Risman
Intellectual Property	Kenneth Glaser
Labor & Employment	Ronald Gaswirth
Tax	Suzan Fenner
Trial	Curtis Frisbie, Jr

audits, Occupational Safety and Health Act matters, government contractor employment issues, and immigration and naturalization matters.

Tax: Consists of several practice specialties including federal income taxation, state and local taxation, international taxation, estate planning and administration, employee benefits and executive compensation.

Trial: Focuses on trials in United States District Courts and all State courts, and appellate matters in both federal and state courts of appeals and the US Supreme Court as well as representation before various state, national and international arbitration boards. Practice areas within the section include admiralty, antitrust, appellate, aviation litigation, class action, computer technology, construction, environmental/toxic tort, government contracts, medical malpractice, securities, and tort defense/insurance litigation.

INTERNATIONAL WORK: Provides a comprehensive range of legal services to both Mexican and foreign clients. The office of Gardere, Arena y Robles, S.C. (GAR) in Mexico City is a civil partnership formed by Mexican and US attorneys. GAR has developed a special focus on assisting Mexican and foreign clients in acquisitions, joint ventures, and other investments; the development of infrastructure projects with the Mexican government and private sector entities involving the privatization or operations of public assets, e.g., tollroads, potable water and water treatment facilities, airports, seaports, drilling contracts and electrical energy projects; and representing clients generally in the energy, manufacturing, technology, telecommunications, financial and environmental sectors.

GARDERE

attorneys and counselors

GIBBS & BRUNS, LLP

THE FIRM

Managing Partner: Robin C Gibbs

Number of partners: 14
Number of other lawyers: 16

AREAS OF PRACTICE:
Commercial Litigation......................................90%
Appellate..10%

FIRM OVERVIEW: Gibbs & Bruns, LLP engages exclusively in a commercial litigation practice in Texas, throughout the United States, and in various courts and tribunals outside the United States. The firm practices in a broad range of business-related complex litigation, and has been involved in much of the major litigation in the region since the firm's inception in 1983. The firm prides itself on its ability to handle difficult and novel legal problems and routinely represents plaintiffs and defendants in significant contract, securities, trade secret, intellectual property, patent, class action, antitrust, insurance, construction, lender liability, energy, director liability, copyright, and partnership disputes.

MAIN AREAS OF PRACTICE:
Commercial Litigation: The firm prides itself on its ability to handle all types of complex and high-stakes commercial litigation for both plaintiffs and defendants. They handle every aspect of the most complicated commercial disputes, from discovery through trials and on to appeal, and they are committed to winning. In each of the last two years, the National Law Journal has included Gibbs & Bruns on its short-list of 'Hot' Plaintiff's firms – signifying the top 20 go-to firms in the country; seven of its partners have been designated among the state's 'Super Lawyers', many of its lawyers were cited as 'Rising Stars', and four have made the 'Best' of Houston list.
Appellate: The firm's appellate attorneys prosecute and defend appeals in a variety of jurisdictions and at all levels of the appellate process, including the Supreme Court of the United States. Gibbs & Bruns' appellate work arises from litigation work performed by the firm as well as cases in which other counsel has handled the case in the lower courts.

CLIENTS: The firm's clients include many of the world's largest industrial companies, banks, brokerage firms, and professional firms. Representative clients are Merrill Lynch Investment Managers, Franklin Templeton Funds, Fidelity Management & Research, the outside directors of Enron Corporation, certain officers of Dynegy, Hermann Hospital, John J. Moores (owner of the San Diego Padres), Preussag AG, Saipem SpA, Zachry Construction Corporation and Unocal Corporation.

HEAD OFFICE

TEXAS
1100 Louisiana, Suite 5300, **Houston**, TX 77002
Tel: 713 650 8805   **Fax:** 713 750 0903

CONTACTS

Commercial Litigation ....Robin C Gibbs
Appellate ....Jennifer Horan Greer

INTERNATIONAL WORK: In addition to its nationwide practice, the firm has been called upon to represent parties in international courts and tribunals. The firm has handled litigation in the courts of the United Kingdom, and to arbitration panels in the United Kingdom and Kuala Lumpur. The firm is also called upon frequently to handle multi-jurisdictional litigation that involves simultaneous proceedings in the United States and other countries. Recently, the firm has handled such litigation involving disputes addressed jointly by the courts of the United States and the courts of Norway and the United Kingdom.

Not certified by the Texas Board of Legal Specialization

MARTIN, DISIERE, JEFFERSON & WISDOM LLP

THE FIRM

Senior Partner: Christopher W Martin
Managing Partner: David D Disiere

Number of partners: 11
Number of other lawyers: 26

AREAS OF PRACTICE
Insurance Coverage & Litigation............................70%
Appellate...10%
Employment & Labor 10%
Commercial Litigation 10%

FIRM OVERVIEW: Over the past decade, the firm's lawyers have literally reshaped and redefined the parameters of Texas Insurance Law. Martin, Disiere, Jefferson and Wisdom LLP is a rapidly growing Texas litigation boutique focused on solving clients' problems in first-party insurance lawsuits in Texas and particularly those lawsuits alleging extra-contractual causes of action or involving complex coverage claims. The firm's lawyers have extensive experience in handling lawsuits and disputes arising out of commercial and professional liability policies including environmental and products coverage issues, primary and excess disputes, and defense/indemnity coverage questions. The firm also has considerable experience defending lawsuits arising out of homeowner policies with particular expertise in SIU claims (arson, alleged theft, etc.), foundation and mold claims allegedly caused by plumbing leaks and other moisture sources. Additionally, the firm regularly handles liability disputes arising out of auto, homeowner, commercial and professional policies including Stowers disputes and has extensive experience in UM/UIM value disputes and auto property claims. While the vast majority of lawsuits the firm is currently handling involve personal or commercial lines insurance claims, the firm also represents life and health insurers in lawsuits arising out of life, major medical, and medicare supplement sales practices, underwriting, and claims. The matters entrusted to the firm encompass a wide range of lawsuits from large class-action insurance lawsuits and multi-party coverage disputes, to auto cases with value disputes and individual homeowner's property loss claims, from problematic life insurance claims to pre-existing health issue related claims. For some insurers, the firm also defends third-party claims against their insureds and some involving injuries to non-subscribers' employees. These third party liability cases usually involve fatalities, mass torts, severe personal injuries, or other catastrophe damage claims. In many instances, the firm is called upon to assist local and other counsel when major issues of concern for the insurance industry arise in remote parts of the state, or before the various state and federal courts of appeal. In these instances the firm is called upon to provide briefing, support and to develop a litigation strategy to either resolve the lawsuit or position the matter to enhance the possibility of bringing it to a successful conclusion. Acting as coordinating counsel, litigation support or directly on behalf of the insurance industry, insurance companies or their insureds, the firm has a proven track record as a highly successful and integral part of its clients' litigation and defense team. The firm also has considerable experience in representing employers in a wide variety of employment and labor disputes and lawsuits. With two partners Board Certified in Labor and Employment Law by the Texas Board of Legal Specialization and a vast amount of experience in the field, the labor and employment section frequently provides consultation, advice and training to employers on a wide variety of topics including drug testing, hiring and termination practices, RIFs, OSHA investigations and employment training and compliance.

HEAD OFFICE

TEXAS
808 Travis, Suite 1800, **Houston** TX 77002
Tel: 713 632 1700 **Fax:** 713 222 0101
Email: martin@mdjwlaw.com
Website: www.mdjwlaw.com

BRANCH OFFICES

TEXAS
The Littlefield Building, 106 East Sixth Street, Suite 900, **Austin** TX 78701
Tel: 512 322 5757 **Fax:** 512 322 5707
Email: farrell@mdjwlaw.com
Website: www.mdjwlaw.com

CONTACTS

Insurance Coverage & Litigation	Christopher Martin
Employment Law	Jack Wisdom
Appeals	Levon Hovnatanian
Commercial Litigation	Dale Jefferson

MAIN AREAS OF PRACTICE:

Insurance Coverage & Litigation: The firm is one of the premier first-party coverage and insurance litigation firms in Texas and its lawyers handle coverage matters, extra-contractual suits, and declaratory judgment actions in Texas and in multiple jurisdictions across the country.

Appellate: The firm routinely handles appeals before the Texas Supreme Court, the intermediate appellate courts of Texas, and the Fifth Circuit Court of Appeals. The partner in charge of the firm's appellate section is Levon G Hovnatanian who is Board Certified in Civil Appellate Law and a former Chief Staff Attorney for the First Court of Appeals. Other attorneys in the section have similar credentials and experience.

Employment & Labor: The firm has particular expertise in advising and defending employers in claims alleging discrimination, wrongful discharge, harassment, affirmative action, privacy violations, non-competition agreements, wage and hour disputes, OSHA compliance, Title VII violations, and ADEA compliance.

Commercial Litigation: The firm represents a host of public and private companies in litigation involving business torts, partnership disputes, real estate transactions, First Amendment violations, fiduciary duty claims, and indemnity obligations.

CLIENTS: The firm's clients consist of a wide array of businesses and corporations including some of the largest property, casualty, life and health insurers in the world.

NEEL & HOOPER, P.C.

THE FIRM

Founding Partners: James M Neel, Samuel E Hooper

Number of partners: 2
Number of other lawyers: 4

AREAS OF PRACTICE
Labor & Employment Law................................. 100%

FIRM OVERVIEW:
Since opening its doors in 1972, Neel & Hooper, P.C. has focused on the exclusive representation of management in all aspects of labor and employment law before both state and federal agencies and courts. Since its inception, the firm has prided itself on providing individualized, cost effective legal services. Three of the firm's attorneys are Board Certified in Labor and Employment Law by the Texas Board of Legal Specialization. The depth of knowledge and experience covers virtually every aspect of labor and employment law arising under the American with Disabilities Act, the Family and Medical Leave Act, the Age Discrimination in Employment Act, Title VII of the Civil Rights Act of 1964, the Equal Pay Act, the National Labor Relations Act, the Labor Management Relations Act, the Fair Labor Standards Act, the Occupational Safety and Health Act, the Worker Adjustment and Retraining Notification Act, the Drug-Free Workplace Act, the Rehabilitation Act, the Health Insurance Portability and Accountability Act, COBRA, as well as equivalents arising under Texas law. In addition, the firm assists employers in securing and administering government contracts in compliance with applicable regulations.

MAIN AREAS OF PRACTICE:
Traditional Labor: Neel & Hooper's traditional Labor Practice assists non-union clients in remaining union free, advises and counsels employers that are the subject of union organizing drives, and represents unionized clients in collective bargaining negotiations, arbitration proceedings and unfair labor practice cases.

Employment Litigation: Neel & Hooper has handled to conclusion, at both the trier of fact and appellate levels, cases involving alleged sex, age, race, national origin, disability and retaliation discrimination; alleged breaches of employment contracts created by oral promises and/or handbooks or other written pronouncements; alleged discriminatory treatment because of an employee's filing of a workers' compensation claim or complaining about unsafe practices; slander, libel, blacklisting; claimed breaches of covenants not-to-compete; and alleged tortious interference with contractual relationships.

Administrative Agency Representation: Neel & Hooper has considerable experience representing employers in discrimination, harassment and retaliatory charges brought before the Equal Employment Opportunity Commission and other state fair employment practices agencies. The firm also has ample experience handling claims brought before other administrative agencies such as the Department of Labor, the National Labor Relations Board, the Occupational Safety and Health Administration and the Texas Workforce Commission.

Wage & Hour: Neel & Hooper assists clients to achieve compliance with the minimum wage, overtime and record keeping requirements of all federal and state wage and hour laws. The firm also assists clients in complying with state wage payment laws involving vacation pay, deductions, commissions, etc., and reviews and designs pay plans. The firm conducts preventive audits, as well as represents clients in investigations conducted by the US Department of Labor's Wage and Hour Division and similar state agencies. It also defends wage and hour lawsuits in court, including class actions.

HEAD OFFICE

TEXAS
1700 West Loop South, Suite 1400, **Houston**, TX 77027-3008
Tel: 713 629-1800 **Fax:** 713 629-1812
Website: www.neelhooper.com

BRANCH OFFICES

Neel & Hooper is a member of the Worklaw Network. Consequently, the firm works with over 25 firms with offices throughout the US so that it may further service clients with diverse geographical needs.

Training & Counseling: Neel & Hooper's attorneys counsel employers on compliance strategies and the prevention of litigation – including issues on the hiring and termination of employees in both union and non-union settings. Similarly, the firm regularly conducts reviews of employee handbooks and personnel policies for both legal compliance and completeness. The firm also conducts training encompassing such subjects as harassment in the workplace, union avoidance, proper record keeping, and effective disciplinary counseling. Finally, the firm drafts and reviews employment-related agreements, including covenants not-to-compete and severance agreements.

INDUSTRIES SERVED: Neel & Hooper represent clients involved in the following industries: petrochemical, restaurant and food service, banking and finance, retail, construction, insurance, manufacturing, property management, healthcare, printing and publishing, telecommunications, steel erection, municipal government, auto service, consumer products, employee providers, oil and gas, engineering and parcel carriers.

THOMPSON & KNIGHT LLP

THE FIRM

Managing Partner: Peter J Riley
Number of attorneys: 380

FIRM OVERVIEW: Since 1887, Thompson & Knight attorneys have been anticipating clients' needs and striving to exceed expectations. With an emphasis on international energy, litigation, tax, and insolvency matters, the firm's attorneys provide clients with innovative, cost-effective legal and business solutions to their issues. Thompson & Knight's experience in these areas establishes it as a leading international energy law firm, with more than two-thirds of its practice relating to the energy industry.

MAIN AREAS OF PRACTICE:

Corporate & Securities: Thompson & Knight's corporate and securities attorneys serve as outside general counsel and as advisors on day-to-day operational matters for a diverse range of corporations, partnerships, limited liability companies, and other business entities. They provide similar counsel to investment banking firms, investment advisors, financial institutions, and insurance companies, and are particularly adept at public offerings and private placements of debt and equity securities.

Corporate Reorganization & Creditors' Rights: The firm's attorneys represent trade creditors, lien claimants, and large and small creditor and debtor companies in all aspects of bankruptcy litigation and take a leading role in corporate reorganizations, both in and out of court, and in bankruptcy proceedings of all types throughout the country. They often serve as special litigation counsel in extremely complex cases, and excel at conceptualizing and negotiating innovative business finance solutions.

Energy: Thompson & Knight attorneys counsel oil, gas, and energy industry clients worldwide - those who explore, develop, produce, store, market, transport, and process energy resources. The firm's client roster is a 'who's who' of the industry and includes nearly half of the largest publicly traded energy companies and a host of oil and gas exploration, production, refining, pipeline, marketing, and investment businesses.

Environmental: For nearly half a century, the firm's environmental attorneys have been assisting clients in all aspects of federal, state, and local environmental laws, from their development to their application. Thompson & Knight's practice includes permitting, environmental auditing, administrative and judicial proceedings, environmental tort litigation, and rulemaking and legislative lobbying.

Finance: Thompson & Knight's finance attorneys are experienced in all types of domestic and international private debt and equity finance transactions, as well as public offerings and commercial finance transactions. The firm's clients include banks, insurance companies, pension fund managers, savings and loan associations, factoring companies, and other lenders located around the world.

Government Relations & Public Policy: With expertise gained through years of regulatory counsel in major industries and legislative lobbying at all levels of government, Thompson & Knight attorneys guide clients' participation in the lawmaking process. The firm's attorneys assist in negotiating with governmental and quasi-governmental entities and represent clients' interests in regulatory, legislative, and administrative rulemaking and licensing matters.

Intellectual Property & Technology: Thompson & Knight attorneys counsel clients in the development, protection, licensing, valuation, and enhancement of their technology, ideas, and goodwill. The firm's core practice includes client counseling, applications and registrations, prosecution, licensing, technology transfer, corporate advisory work, and litigation in the areas of patents, trademarks, copyrights, trade dress, and common-law rights. Technology attorneys also provide comprehensive counsel to science- and technology-oriented clients.

Labor & Employment: The firm's attorneys counsel and represent private and public employers in all aspects of the employment relationship. Their practice encompasses defending employers against all types of labor- or employment-related claims, as well as counseling employers on compliance strategies and the prevention of litigation.

Real Estate: Thompson & Knight's real estate attorneys have an innovative, multi-state, and international practice. They structure and document numerous matters, including the purchase, sale, development, leasing, and financing of properties used for multi-family housing, retail shopping centers, research facilities, mixed use industrial warehouses, distribution centers, and manufacturing and office buildings.

Tax: Thompson & Knight offers comprehensive federal, state, and local tax compliance and tax planning advice to individuals and all types of business entities and organizations. With extensive experience in federal and state tax matters, the firm's tax attorneys resolve clients' tax law challenges by creatively applying current and comprehensive knowledge of tax law and best practices to their needs.

Trial & Appellate: Thompson & Knight has an extensive trial practice worldwide, combining keen analysis, careful preparation, practical skills, and comprehensive experience to represent clients effectively before judges and juries, and in alternative dispute resolution forums. The team includes more than 150 skilled trial and appellate lawyers, staff attorneys, and legal assistants who work resolutely to resolve the issues in dispute and achieve clients' objectives.

INTERNATIONAL WORK: The firm's attorneys work with clients worldwide in connection with a variety of transactions, particularly legal matters related to energy, litigation, tax, and creditors' rights. In the realm of global energy, the firm offers a full range of legal and commercial services including advice on host government contracts; joint operating, study, and bidding agreements; service contracts; regulatory matters; tax; corporate structure; arbitration; mergers and acquisitions; financings; pipeline and refinery projects; and other matters. Its attorneys are adept in all aspects of international upstream, midstream, and downstream energy matters, and negotiate and provide legal and commercial advice related to all forms of international hydrocarbon contracts. The firm is a member of Interlaw®, an association providing access to more than 5,000 lawyers worldwide.

HEAD OFFICE

TEXAS
1700 Pacific Avenue, Suite 3300, **Dallas**, TX 75201
Tel: 214 969 1700   **Fax:** 214 969 1751
Website: www.tklaw.com

BRANCH OFFICES

TEXAS
98 San Jacinto Boulevard, Suite 1900, **Austin**, TX 78701
Tel: 512 469 6100   **Fax:** 512 469 6180

801 Cherry Street, Unit 1, Burnett Plaza, Suite 1600,
Fort Worth, TX 76102
Tel: 817 347 1700   **Fax:** 817 347 1799

333 Clay Street, Suite 3300, **Houston**, TX 77002
Tel: 713 654 8111   **Fax:** 713 654 1871

INTERNATIONAL OFFICES

The firm has offices in Algiers, Algeria; Monterrey, Mexico; Rio de Janeiro, Macaé, and Vitória, Brazil.

Thompson & Knight Impact

THOMPSON, COE, COUSINS & IRONS, LLP

THE FIRM

Managing Partner: Jack M Cleaveland Jr

FIRM OVERVIEW: Founded in 1951, Thompson Coe has roots in the earliest days of the 20th century legal practice in Texas. The founding partners brought an extensive knowledge of the insurance business to the firm and quickly built a reputation unparalleled for experience in areas unique to insurance. Today the firm is recognized nationally as not only a preeminent insurance firm, but a provider of a wide range of legal services to clients in many industries. The firm spans the state of Texas with offices in Austin, Dallas and Houston, and has now expanded further, establishing an office in Saint Paul, Minnesota.

MAIN AREAS OF PRACTICE:

Insurance Law: Recognized as a national authority on insurance law, the firm's clients depend on its broad insurance background and knowledge to provide reliable and efficient legal advice and assistance for all insurance business and regulatory matters. Whether giving advice pertaining to insurance laws, representing a client before an insurance regulator, handling mergers, acquisitions or formations of insurance companies and agencies, or drafting or reviewing documents needed for insurance-related transactions, this practice group brings extensive experience to areas of law which are unfamiliar to many.

Insurance Litigation & Coverage: This practice group provides counsel to insurance companies with a broad range of insurance-related litigation, coverage disputes, bad faith and other extra-contractual liabilities litigation. Drawing upon the firm's experience in the administrative and regulatory arena, they represent carriers facing complex corporate, regulatory and class action litigation.

Casualty & Tort Litigation: The firm's casualty and tort attorneys have been recognized for their proficiency in the trial and defense of personal injury cases involving premises liability, products liability, medical malpractice, mass tort litigation, negligence and other tort-related claims. They are committed to excellence in trial advocacy and pride themselves in responding to litigation needs with practical, creative solutions.

Commercial Litgation: This practice group has handled every type of commercial dispute ranging from simple contract matters to complex international disputes. The attorneys share a commitment to do whatever it takes in terms of preparation and development of innovative strategies to ensure the best possible results for its business litigation clients and actually try cases to a conclusion with successful results.

Governmental & Legislative Advocacy: The firm's attorneys help clients achieve legislative initiatives and resolve regulatory issues. Their involvement and experience in the legislative and governmental process enables them to provide efficient and effective representation to the firm's clients to advocate their positions before the legislature or other governmental agencies.

General Litigation: This practice group represents clients in mass tort litigation, nursing home negligence cases, healthcare regulatory matters, and medical products/device litigation. These successful litigators are adept at handling high-profile clients and are experienced at devoting the necessary resources in terms of personnel, time, database management and preparation to ensure the best possible results for their clients.

Labor & Employment: The firm's attorneys counsel both private and public sector management in connection with all employment-related matters, including compliance with the FLSA, Title VII, ADEA, ADA, WARN, OHSA and other federal, state and local laws regulating employment. They have an active labor litigation practice defending management against EEO claims, wrongful termination, workers' compensation retaliation, civil rights and other employment-related claims. The firm handles employment and non-competition agreements, as well as collective bargaining, grievance-arbitrations, unfair labor practice proceedings, and other labor-management relations issues.

Professional Liability: Lawsuits involving malpractice claims against attorneys, accountants, insurance agents and brokers, corporate directors and officers and other business professionals are being asserted at an increasing rate. The attorneys draw upon years of hands-on experience in dealing with claims to provide the firm's professional clients with the finest in quality legal representation.

Business Transaction: This practice group encompasses everything from contractual relationships, including mergers and acquisitions, sales and purchases of ownership interests, shareholder agreements, management compensation arrangements, entity formation and financing, to bankruptcy, real estate transactions, estate planning and tax issues.

CLIENTS: Association of Fire and Casualty Companies in Texas (AFACT); Progressive Insurance Company; All American Life Insurance Company; Zurich; Allstate; 3M; Employers General Insurance Company and Texas Medical Liability Insurance Underwriting Association.

HEAD OFFICE

TEXAS
700 N Pearl Street, Twenty-fifth Floor, **Dallas**, TX 75201-2832
Tel: 214 871 8200 **Fax:** 214 871 8209
Website: www.thompsoncoe.com

BRANCH OFFICES

MINNESOTA
The Historic Hamm Building, 408 St. Peter Street, Suite 510
Saint Paul, MN 55102
Tel: 651 389 5000 **Fax:** 651 389 5059

TEXAS
701 Brazos, Suite 1500, **Austin**, TX 78701
Tel: 512 708 8200 **Fax:** 512 708 8777

One Riverway, Suite 1600, **Houston**, TX 77056
Tel: 713 403 8210 **Fax:** 713 403 8299

CONTACTS

Austin	Steve Wood
Dallas	Beth D Bradley
Houston	Kevin Risley
St Paul	Lynn M Meyers

THOMPSON COE

VINSON & ELKINS

THE FIRM

Managing Partner: Joseph C Dilg

Number of partners worldwide: 309
Number of other lawyers worldwide: 428

FIRM OVERVIEW: For almost a century, Vinson & Elkins lawyers have provided innovative business solutions for clients whose needs are as diverse as the entities they represent. In today's challenging environment of global markets, volatile economies and complex human and environmental issues, the firm's time-tested role as trusted advisor has become even more critical. The depth and breadth of its lawyers' experience, combined with the responsiveness and efficiencies of the firm's global reach, enable Vinson & Elkins to serve clients from start-up, to the negotiating table and boardroom, before legislative and regulatory bodies in the courtroom, and beyond.

Diversity: At Vinson & Elkins, the approach to diversity is driven by core values, which stress the firm's commitment to hiring and developing the best legal talent; providing excellence in service to their clients; and creating an environment of 'shared values of civility, compassion and respect for one another.' These core values of individuality and innovation are factors that have driven the firm's success for nearly 90 years and are the basis upon which it builds its diversity efforts. It is the firm's hope that its efforts will lead it to be not only the law firm of choice for its clients, but also the employer of choice for top lawyers.

MAIN AREAS OF PRACTICE: Core practice areas include admiralty; antitrust; bankruptcy; business transactions; capital markets; communications; contracts; e-Commerce; eminent domain; employee benefits (ERISA) and executive compensation; energy and electric power regulation; environmental; finance; financial institutions; government and international procurement; health law; intellectual property; international arbitration; international law; internet; labor and employment relations; litigation; mergers and acquisitions; oil and gas; outsourcing; private equity; project finance and development; public finance; public policy; real estate; securities; structured finance; syndicated finance; taxation; technology; trusts and estates; and white collar criminal defense. At Vinson & Elkins, their approach to diversity is driven by their core values, which stress their commitment to hiring and developing the best legal talent; providing excellence in service to the firm's clients; and creating an environment of 'shared values of civility, compassion and respect for one another.' These core values of individuality and innovation are factors that have driven the firm's success for nearly 90 years and are the basis upon which they build their diversity efforts. It is their hope that their efforts will lead them to be not only the law firm of choice for their clients, but also the employer of choice for top lawyers.

CLIENTS: Since the firm was founded in 1917, it has attracted an outstanding and diverse group of lawyers who serve an international clientele. Clients include the governments of sovereign nations and of North American states, cities and municipalities, public and private companies, domestic and international financial institutions, new entities, joint ventures, project companies, and individuals and families.

HEAD OFFICE

TEXAS
2300 First City Tower, 1001 Fannin Street, **Houston,** TX 77002-6760
Tel: 713 758 2222 **Fax:** 713 758 2346
Website: www.velaw.com

BRANCH OFFICES

DISTRICT OF COLUMBIA
The Willard Office Building, 1455 Pennsylvania Avenue NW
Washington, DC 20004-1008
Tel: 202 639 6500 **Fax:** 202 639 6604

NEW YORK
666 Fifth Ave., 26th Floor, **New York,** NY 101031-0040
Tel: 212 237 0000 **Fax:** 212 237 0100

TEXAS
The Terrace 7, 2801 Via Fortuna, Suite 100, **Austin,** TX 78746-7568
Tel: 512 542 8400 **Fax:** 512 542 8612

3700 Trammell Crow Center, 2001 Ross Avenue, **Dallas,** TX 75201-2975
Tel: 214 220 7700 **Fax:** 214 220 7716

INTERNATIONAL OFFICES

The firm also has offices in Beijing, China; Dubai, United Arab Emirates; Moscow, Russia; Tokyo, Japan; and London, United Kingdom.

INTERNATIONAL WORK: Vinson & Elkins has developed a wealth of international experience since its inception. The firm's lawyers have worked in virtually every country in the world, and many have competency in several languages. Firm lawyers work closely with lawyers in their own network of offices, as well as with local lawyers in foreign jurisdictions to accomplish clients' objectives. In addition to the firm's legal experience, the personal relationships of its lawyers with international business people and other professionals offer significant benefits to clients.

Vinson & Elkins
Vinson & Elkins L.L.P.

WINSTEAD SECHREST & MINICK P.C.

THE FIRM

Chairman, CEO: W Mike Baggett

Number of partners in US: 164
Number of other lawyers in US: 148

FIRM OVERVIEW: Winstead Sechrest & Minick P.C. has grown steadily since it was founded as a four-attorney practice in Dallas in 1973. The firm's initial period of growth was organic, but in the last few years it has expanded by merging with small firms that specialize in its traditional strengths of real estate and corporate law. In 2001, the firm bucked the industry-wide trend for downsizing by acquiring three Texas boutique firms in the space of five months, and now employs nearly 320 attorneys in seven locations across the US. The political consulting practice of Winstead Sechrest & Minick P.C., Winstead Consulting Group, LLC, provides local, state and federal government relations and strategic services throughout the United States.

MAIN AREAS OF PRACTICE:

Banking & Credit Transactions: The firm advises regional, national, and international financial institutions, financial services companies, and other lending organizations in virtually all aspects of their business activities. Attorneys represent and counsel lenders, agents, participants, and borrowers in single-lender and syndicated credit facilities of all types and complexities. Winstead also represents the firm's corporate clients in establishing and maintaining credit facilities. Attorneys have extensive experience in restructurings of troubled credits, debtor-in-possession financing, postconfirmation financing, and other workout matters. The firm regularly advises financial services clients who seek counsel on mergers and acquisitions, the development of new products and services, regulatory matters, enforcement actions, litigation, and other financial services problems.

Business Restructuring/Bankruptcy: Winstead's Business Restructuring/Bankruptcy Practice is one of the largest in Texas and the southwestern United States. This cross-sectional practice involves not only the traditional bankruptcy practice, but also attorneys from banking, corporate, securities, tax, real estate and other areas, who all have extensive experience in both operational and financial restructurings. The practice is national in scope and focuses on nonjudicial workouts and restructures, as well as the traditional bankruptcy court process. This unique focus, combined with the substantial experience of the firm's Business Restructuring Practice, provides clients with the ability to analyze all of the possible options in a workout, from the inception. The practice covers representation of debtors, creditors, committees, and other parties in interest in all aspects of financial restructurings, including out-of-court restructurings, prebankruptcy negotiation and strategy, the bankruptcy process itself, and all types of litigation arising out of, or related to, bankruptcy and insolvency matters. Given their broad diversity of experience, Winstead's business restructuring professionals are able to provide a keen understanding of the business goals of all interested parties, to any transaction, along with the ability to craft solutions that will achieve those goals in a manner that is consistent with the client's goals and expectations.

Corporate, Securities & Taxation: Winstead attorneys are experienced in corporate finance, securities regulation, tax matters related to federal, state, and local governments, insurance regulation, asset securitization, and investment management. Attorneys also provide specialized counsel and insight with respect to the successful operation of both public and private businesses. The firm represents clients in connection with the offering and sale of public and private equity, public and private debt, mortgage and asset-backed securities, and tax-exempt public bond issuances. Winstead

provides counsel to both mature and start-up businesses with respect to corporate governance, public and private financing, mergers, acquisitions and divestitures, antitrust issues, shareholder disputes and agreements, adoption of employee incentive and stock option plans, implementation of anti-takeover defenses, noncompetition agreements, and protection and exploitation of intellectual property and other proprietary information.

Government Relations: Winstead operates a local, state and federal Government Relations Practice supported by Winstead Consulting Group, LLC, the firm's wholly owned, political consulting subsidiary. Attorneys and consultants represent a wide range of corporate clients, associations and large public entities before all levels of government. Winstead's government relations practice in the Washington, DC office focuses on federal and national government relations. Each of the firm's Texas offices handles state and local government matters working with the Governor's office, the Texas Legislature and state agencies as well as municipal governments. Attorneys' and consultants' experience includes, but is not limited to, condemning authority in condemnation litigation matters, healthcare, energy, telecommunications, financial institutions, transportation including public-private partnerships, government procurement and contracting, sports authorities and facilities, international trade, high technology, land use, environment and natural resources, public finance and real estate.

Intellectual Property: The firm's IP lawyers seek to identify, exploit, and protect a client's intellectual property by a wide variety of techniques, beginning with the protection of trade secrets and know-how, to the

HEAD OFFICE

TEXAS
5400 Renaissance Tower, 1201 Elm Street, **Dallas**, TX 75270
Tel: 214 745 5400 **Fax:** 214 745 5390
Website: www.winstead.com

BRANCH OFFICES

DISTRICT OF COLUMBIA
1850 M Street NW, Suite 800, **Washington**, DC 20036
Tel: 202 572 8000 **Fax:** 202 572 8001

TEXAS
401 Congress Avenue, Suite 2100, **Austin**, TX 78701
Tel: 512 370 2800 **Fax:** 512 370 2850

2100 McKinney Avenue, Suite 1501, **Dallas**, TX 75201
Tel: 214 745 5400 **Fax:** 214 745 5883

777 Main Street, Suite 1100, **Fort Worth**, TX 76102
Tel: 817 420 8200 **Fax:** 817 420 8201

2400 Bank One Center, 910 Travis Street, **Houston**, TX 77002
Tel: 713 650 8400 **Fax:** 713 650 2400

700 North St. Mary's Street, Suite 1900, **San Antonio**, TX 78205
Tel: 210 277 6800 **Fax:** 210 277 6810

600 Town Center One, 1450 Lake Robbins Drive,
The Woodlands, TX 77380
Tel: 281 681 5900 **Fax:** 281 681 5901

CONTACTS

Banking & Credit	T Randall Matthews
Bankruptcy	Berry D Spears
Corporate	Bruce A Cheatham
Government Relations	Paul N Wageman
Intellectual Property	Kelly K Kordzik
Labor & Employment	Dan C Dargene
Litigation	Wayne W Bost
Real Estate	T Andrew Dow

WINSTEAD SECHREST & MINICK P.C.

preparation and prosecution of patents, copyrights, trademarks, to the negotiation of related technology agreements and licenses, to the enforcement and/or defense of such rights, in all forums, i.e., mediation, arbitration, various state and US District/Appellate Courts, and the International Trade Commission. Clients are drawn from diverse sciences and technologies, ranging from oilfield, display signage, highway safety, and medical devices to nanotechnology and biotechnology.

Labor & Employment: Winstead represents employers across the spectrum of the employment relationship. The firm's representation includes traditional union-management disputes before labor arbitrators and administrative law judges, as well as the needs of management in the multifaceted and complex area of employees' individual rights. Attorneys provide comprehensive advice to employers faced with restrictions on the exercise of their business judgment in dealing with employees, and counsel employers so they may act in a manner that is lawful, yet consistent with their business objectives. Winstead also offers advice and training programs aimed at preventing employment-related complaints and lawsuits. The Labor and Employment Group has substantial experience defending all forms of workplace litigation, including defense of claims under virtually every federal and state fair employment practices statute, governmental entities against whistleblower claims, substantive and procedural due process claims, and other state and federal constitutional and statutory claims unique to the public employment sector. Winstead's employment litigators are also experienced in the defense of labor arbitrations, administrative proceedings before state and federal agencies, and all forms of alternate dispute resolution.

Litigation: When it is reasonably possible and consistent with the firm's clients' objectives, Winstead initially strives to resolve a dispute without resorting to litigation. In this regard, negotiation, arbitration, and mediation are viable alternatives. When litigation is unavoidable, however, the firm provides analysis, advice, and representation that enables its clients to properly evaluate, manage, and control the risks, costs, and uncertainties associated with litigation. Attorneys enforce or defend clients' rights wherever disputes arise, in Texas or elsewhere, and whether in court (state or federal) or an arbitration organization. From massive class actions for publicly traded entities to simple commercial disputes for small businesses, Winstead represents clients from numerous industries in a wide variety of cases, and in many different venues.

Real Estate: Winstead's Real Estate Group includes over 60 full-time real estate attorneys and more than 20 paralegals. The depth and breadth of Winstead's real estate expertise gives its clients access to real estate profes-

sionals with experience in virtually every type of real estate and every transaction structure, anywhere in the US and in any stage of the real estate cycle. For example, Winstead has successfully represented Fortune 500 retailers in the rapid roll-out of new retail concepts during periods of economic expansion. Yet at the same time, Winstead enjoys, as a result of the significant size of its Real Estate Group, a national reputation in the field of real estate restructuring. Winstead's client list includes many of the largest and most active real estate development companies, institutional investors, mortgage lenders and loan servicers in the United States, as well as individual investors and entrepreneurs. The firm's attorneys achieve desired results across the full real estate spectrum, including the development of all property types in mixed-use configurations and common ownership structures, acquisition and disposition of all property types, zoning and land use, construction, environmental, corporate facilities management, development and private investment, real estate finance (including new construction, mezzanine, portfolio, and CMBS debt and structured leases), loan servicing, restructuring and workouts, REITs and REMICs, sports and public facilities, taxation issues (from TIF districts to 1031 exchanges), leasing and asset management, portfolio acquisitions and dispositions, and institutional equity and mortgage investments.

INTERNATIONAL WORK: Group attorneys have experience in over 30 foreign jurisdictions and have represented US and foreign clients engaged in international business throughout the world and in a variety of industries. The firm is particularly experienced at handling large, high-profile mergers and acquisitions, energy projects and new investments abroad. Winstead is a member of both the Interlex Group and The Bridge Group, which are associations of leading law firms serving international clients.

CONTENTS: Corporate/M&A p.1727; Employment p.1729; Litigation p.1731; Real Estate p.1733; Individuals' Profiles p.1735; Firms' Profiles p.1739.

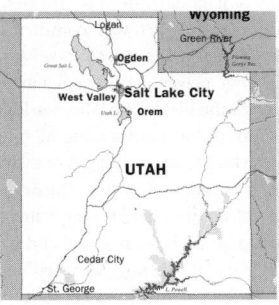

How lawyers are ranked

The opinions we gather from clients — mainly from in-house lawyers but also from other purchasers of legal services — are balanced by opinions from colleagues and competitors. Together, they provide two different perspectives — an all-round view — and biased viewpoints cancel each other out.

CORPORATE/M&A

Utah
Leading firms (Corporate/M&A)

1 STOEL RIVES LLP *Salt Lake City*
WILSON SONSINI GOODRICH *Salt Lake City*

2 HOLME ROBERTS & OWEN LLP *Salt Lake City*
JONES WALDO HOLBROOK *Salt Lake City*
PARR WADDOUPS BROWN GEE *Salt Lake City*
SNELL & WILMER LLP *Salt Lake City*

3 BALLARD SPAHR ANDREWS *Salt Lake City*
DORSEY & WHITNEY LLP *Salt Lake City*
HOLLAND & HART LLP *Salt Lake City*

4 DURHAM JONES & PINEGAR *Salt Lake City*
PARSONS BEHLE & LATIMER PC *Salt Lake City*
RAY, QUINNEY & NEBEKER PC *Salt Lake City*

Leading individuals (Corporate/M&A)

1 LLOYD Brian *Stoel Rives*, Salt Lake City
O'CONNOR Robert *Wilson Sonsini*, Salt Lake City
TAYLOR Nolan *Dorsey & Whitney*, Salt Lake City

2 ANDERSON Chris *Snell & Wilmer*, Salt Lake City
BONHAM Mark *Wilson Sonsini*, Salt Lake City
LOVELESS Scott *Parr Waddoups*, Salt Lake City
MOFFITT Ronald *Stoel Rives*, Salt Lake City
POELMAN Ronald *Jones Waldo*, Salt Lake City
RUDD David *Ballard Spahr*, Salt Lake City

3 FREDMAN Stuart *Holme Roberts*, Salt Lake City
LINDLEY Greg *Holland & Hart*, Salt Lake City
LITTLE David *Holme Roberts*, Salt Lake City
MANGUM Geoffrey *Parsons Behle*, Salt Lake City
STEVENSON Brent *Parr Waddoups*, Salt Lake City
TAYLOR Tom *Holme Roberts*, Salt Lake City
WESTON John *Snell & Wilmer*, Salt Lake City
WILSON Randon *Jones Waldo*, Salt Lake City
WINGER Gary *Ray Quinney*, Salt Lake City
YOUNG Howard *Jones Waldo*, Salt Lake City

Up-and-coming individuals

LINDQUIST Shawn *Wilson Sonsini*, Salt Lake City
TOPHAM Reed *Stoel Rives*, Salt Lake City

Firms and individuals are listed alphabetically in each band.

Band 1

Stoel Rives LLP

The Firm: This huge, Portland-headquartered regional outfit is recognized as one of the clear market leaders for corporate/M&A in the state. The 20-member team *"really hits the sweet spot for clients in Utah,"* say commentators. Their leading position is said to be based on the size and resources of the team, which allows it to handle large, interstate public and private company M&A for its national clients. The team is also rated as one of the best for securities transactions in the region.

The Lawyers: **Brian Lloyd** is *"an outstanding, technically solid lawyer who is a pleasure to work with,"* according to commentators. His portfolio of skills includes, in the words of one client, *"tenacity, responsiveness and the ability to listen to what the client needs and figure out what needs to be done."* Lloyd's practice is oriented toward serving large public and private companies in M&A. He also advises publicly traded companies on corporate governance, regulatory compliance and second-generation Sarbanes-Oxley initiatives, as well as being a strong resource for venture capital, equity venture and portfolio investment advice to early stage companies. **Ronald Moffitt** is a *"sophisticated, experienced M&A lawyer,"* who commands the respect of peers and clients. His previous incarnation as general counsel for Huntsman allowed him to develop *"a level of experience of corporate governance that few have."* In addition, he maintains a thriving M&A practice. Highlights of the year include advising on the international expansion of the Alpha Graphics franchise. He is also experienced in real estate finance, and has advised PSC Military Housing, a US Air Force contractor, on the privatization of military housing in Texas, Oklahoma and Arizona. **Reed Topham** was commended by one client as being *"as good a securities lawyer as anyone I've ever worked with on Wall Street."* Despite his relative youth, his stature is such that one industry analyst even dubbed him *"the best pure securities lawyer in the intermountain West."* He works predominantly with public companies and, in 2004 represented Precision Cash Parts in their Rule 144A debt work. Other recent work includes assisting MK Resources in negotiating a substantial credit facility.

The Clients: SkyWest Airlines; Merit Medical Systems; Alpha Graphics; EventSource Middle East; Acquired Fluid Systems; GreyWestern USA; Huntsman; Huntsman Cancer Foundation; PSC Military Housing; KF Holdings; Precision Cash Parts and MK Resources.

Wilson Sonsini Goodrich & Rosati

See firm details p.302

The Firm: The Wilson Sonsini name has long been associated with corporate and financing expertise in the hi-tech sector and the firm is a major global player for IPOs. Given that Utah has one of the largest concentrations of computer software firms outside California, the opening of a Salt Lake City office was therefore a logical step in the West Coast firm's development. The ten-attorney team has *"a wonderful, broad, neat international platform,"* and is praised by clients as being *"high caliber, responsive to our needs and attuned to our best interests."* In addition to the firm's undoubted strength in IPOs and other securities issuances, the corporate-focused team is noted for its skill in venture capital financing. Here, it acts as primary counsel for no fewer than four Utah-based venture capital funds.

The Lawyers: **Robert O'Connor** (see p.1737) was one of the founding members of the Salt Lake City practice and is the office's managing partner. Universally agreed to be *"one of the best business lawyers in Utah,"* he was recently involved in the Google IPO. Clients admire him for always being *"up to speed on all the relevant issues and for knowing what's going on in the industry."* He is the primary contact for venture capital funds and UV Partners; and also represents several Utah-based biotech companies, including Huntsman Biotechnologies, as well as a number of national hi-tech companies. **Mark Bonham** (see p.1736) was commended by clients as *"a phenomenal asset to have here in Salt Lake City."* A newer arrival in Utah, having moved from the firm's Palo Alto headquarters, he concentrates on representing high-growth and hi-tech businesses at all stages of their development. He is one of the lead attorneys in the Nu Skin restructuring, and is heavily involved in venture capital deals for regional and national clients. *"Fabulous young attorney"* **Shawn Lindquist** (see p.1737) is developing a reputation for expertise beyond his years: *"He plays a leadership role in all the transactions he's involved in,"* noted one source. In the past year Lindquist represented Morgan Stanley in connection with the $52 million public offering of Myriad Genetics. He also advised Altiris on its acquisition of Wise Solutions, and counseled the special committee of the board of directors of MOXTEK in its acquisition by Polatechno.

The Clients: UV Partners; Starbridge Systems; ProLexis; Huntsman Biotechnologies; Sonic Innovations; MyFamily.com; Nu Skin; Altiris; Semaphore-Mayfair; Morgan Stanley and MOXTEK.

Band 2

Holme Roberts & Owen LLP

See firm details p.326

The Firm: With its international presence and national resources, this Denver-based firm is a strong player in Utah's corporate/M&A market. Commentators report that members of the 40-strong team leverage their depth and expertise to *"complement every transaction in every category and industry imaginable."* Its international reach was demonstrated recently when the team assisted Canadian telecom company, Tellus, with a series of transactions. Its established international, national and local clientele also turns to the team for a range of financing and commercial advice.

The Lawyers: Considerable plaudits are heaped upon the shoulders of **Tom Taylor**. Peers describe him as *"a skilled practitioner with a solid book of clients,"* and confirm that he is a popular choice for referrals. He recently represented aircraft parts supplier, Wencor West, in its acquisition of a Seattle-based in-flight entertainment center business. Other representative deals include stock buy-backs for Benel, and the acquisition of a Coca-Cola bottler for a Midwest client. **Stuart Fredman** is another perennial favorite. Clients commend him in particular as a *"very receptive and responsive,"* attorney, and peers admire his leadership and negotiation skills. **David Little** represents leading Utah-based corporations, as well as several national clients. The past year has seen him primarily involved in financing and transactions for the

Intermountain Power Agency related to its construction of a third power generation unit in Millard County.

The Clients: Wencor West; Citigroup; Benel; Jenson; First Industrial Trust and Intermountain Power Agency.

Jones Waldo Holbrook & McDonough PC

The Firm: Jones Waldo is distinguished from many of its competitors by its *"really strong homegrown practice."* Clients are particularly impressed by the *"bright group of people, diverse skill set and reasonable fees,"* while competitors admire the *"overall reputation and high quality of work."* The group's diverse workload encompasses general M&A, corporate governance counseling, securities issues and venture capital financing, and it has an almost unique wealth of expertise in agri-business.

The Lawyers: **Ronald Poelman** was described by one source as the *"spiritual leader"* of this practice group, perhaps because his *"experience and authority makes him level-headed, calm and secure in everything he does."* Undoubtedly one of the best-known corporate lawyers in the state, he is particularly valued by clients for his *"superior service – he's very responsive."* Highlights of his year include financing, disclosure and acquisition work for prepaid mobile phone solutions company Q Comm International. He has also been busy acting for venture capital start-up Agilix Labs, and developed his long-term relationship with medical device manufacturer, Zevex International, helping to negotiate its international expansion into Europe, Oceania, Africa and the former USSR. *"Outstanding lawyer"* **Howard Young** is becoming increasingly involved in multimillion-dollar headline deals. Clients depict him as *"diligent and intelligent – a super lawyer."* Formerly in-house at Baxter, he led the team advising Bonneville International on the acquisition of Emmis Communications. The firm boasts a unique agricultural cooperatives practice area, which is the focus of **Randon Wilson**'s practice. Since 1999, he has been at the forefront of the major reorganization of the US sugar beet industry, acquiring independent sugar factories for client farmer cooperatives. According to clients, *"nobody else does what he does as well as he does it."*

The Clients: Bonneville International; Q Comm International; Agilix Labs; Zevex International; Computer Consultants; Future Smart Network Systems and Michigan Sugar.

Parr Waddoups Brown Gee & Loveless

The Firm: This substantial local firm enjoys a great reputation among Utah's corporate movers and shakers. In particular, it is considered to offer possibly the best combination of skills and value for money when it comes to rep-

resenting local companies in deals both in and out of state. As one source claimed: *"They're best at getting the deals done for Utah clients."* A team of 16 attorneys makes this one of the larger corporate groups in Salt Lake City.

The Lawyers: Name partner **Scott Loveless** is admired. *"One of the absolute leaders in M&A,"* according to his clients, he offers high-class technical skills combined with *"a tremendous amount of big-deal experience."* Recent examples of this include several major venture capital deals, and acting in a $400 million transaction for key client Huntsman Chemical. On the financing side, he has been handling a $75 million null-finance deal and a $40 million preferred stock deal. Loveless also led the teams advising on the sale of Innovative Products to K2, and the sale of SBI to Acquantive. As a former president of Huntsman, **Brent Stevenson** is a natural choice to manage the firm's relationship with that important client. Rivals describe him as *"one of the most sophisticated business and finance lawyers in Utah."*

The Clients: Innovative Products; Huntsman Chemical; SBI and the Huntsman Corporation.

Snell & Wilmer LLP

See firm details p.167

The Firm: This nine-strong corporate/M&A group is rated highly by clients and competitors alike. Clients are particularly delighted with the long-term relationships they have fostered with the firm, praising the lawyers for their responsiveness, technical expertise and business acumen. The group handles a wide variety of transactional work, including both major private and public company M&A, and a range of associated financing techniques. The past year, however, has been marked in particular by its success in capitalizing on the current resurgence in the Salt Lake City's venture capital market.

The Lawyers: Sources lavished praise on **Chris Anderson** (see p.1735), dubbing him *"a stellar guy and a pillar of corporate governance in Salt Lake City."* While corporate governance is indeed a significant component of his practice, he is also known for advising mature public and private companies on M&A, and assisting emerging growth companies with venture capital transactions. Clients also praised **John Gary Weston**'s (see p.1738) efficiency. *"He under-promises and over-delivers,"* said one, *"you know he'll get the deal done."* The past year saw him involved in substantial private company M&A deals in Utah and California. He also counseled Bank of America Securities, the underwriter in the Utah Telecommunication Open Infrastructure Agency's $85 million bond issue.

The Clients: Accuride; Oficia Group; OGIO International; TruVision; GH Peterson Holdings and SBI-USA.

Band 3

Ballard Spahr Andrews & Ingersoll LLP

See firm details p.1541

The Firm: With its wealth of resources across the country, and its *"sizable presence in the state,"* this Philadelphia-based firm commands a large and growing client following within Utah's business circles. Making the best use of its coherent network of offices, the corporate team's work certainly has more of a national and international flavor than many of its competitors. For example, it recently counseled 1-800-Contacts on its acquisition of a contact lens manufacturing plant in Plymouth, England, and its subsequent acquisition of Vision Tech.

The Lawyers: The standout partner here is **David Rudd** (see p.1738). Clients love him, and he was even described by one as *"top of the heap – he's got to be among the best business lawyers in the State of Utah."* He boasts a sophisticated cross-border M&A practice, which he combines with substantial corporate finance activity. For example, in the past year Rudd has closed several finance facilities for hi-tech companies, including venture capital financing worth around $10 million for Technoscan. He was also the lead partner in the 1-800-Contacts acquisitions.

The Clients: 1-800-Contacts; Sonosite; Zars; Technoscan and KennCott Utah Copper.

Dorsey & Whitney LLP

The Firm: This international firm's Salt Lake City outpost boasts a high proportion of public companies among its clients. While the three-partner team is smaller than some of Utah's larger players, there is no doubt that the firm's national resources and expertise are a considerable draw for clients. Competitors too acknowledge that the firm is *"great for transactional work,"* whether national or international public company M&A or, one of the team's fortes, venture capital investment.

The Lawyers: Commentators agreed that **Nolan Taylor** was *"the most experienced venture capital guy in Salt Lake City."* However, his practice is not limited to volume investment in growth companies, as evidenced by his involvement in some of the largest deals in the state. Recent examples include advising NYSE-listed Arch Coal on its $364 million acquisition of Tri-

ton Coal. Clients reinforce the view that his expertise is not confined to venture capital: *"He has a broad base of knowledge and excellent judgment."* Rivals, meanwhile, acknowledge him as *"a stellar counselor and effective advocate."*

The Clients: The firm serves both public and private companies of varying sizes, as well as private equity and venture capital funds.

Holland & Hart LLP

See firm details p.325

The Firm: This sizable firm has a notable profile throughout the West, and *"is well on the way to becoming a leader in the Utah market,"* say peers. A compact group of 12 attorneys, four of them partners, has been particularly active on the finance side of transactions. So far its profile in M&A activity has been stronger at the lower end of the market, though the firm's substantial network gives it the resources to handle large and complex transactions. There is no formal division within the team between corporate and finance work – all group members participate in both areas.

The Lawyers: **Greg Lindley** (see p.1737) was recommended by the market as particularly strong on the finance and securities side, though he also undertakes more general corporate transactions. He has devoted a considerable portion of his time over the past year to counseling smaller companies on the implications of Sarbanes-Oxley, speaking on the topic at conferences.

The Clients: The team acts for a number of larger and midsized Utah-based corporations and, through the firm's extensive national network, has access to clients of national importance in a variety of sectors.

Band 4

Durham Jones & Pinegar, A Professional Corporation

The Firm: This practice has *"really grown in the past year,"* say commentators. It was described as a *"local firm that has become much more of a significant player,"* and its name is becoming increasingly well known in the Utah corporate market. A department of 18 attorneys operates from three offices across the state, handling a variety of smaller M&A, joint ventures, corporate finance and general commercial advice.

The Lawyers: With Kevin Pinegar absent from

the firm until 2007, Paul Durham is the primary contact partner for the corporate group.

The Clients: The firm has established a particularly good reputation among Utah's midsized companies.

Parsons Behle & Latimer PC

See firm details p.1742

The Firm: This high-quality, homegrown firm fields a smaller corporate team than many of its competitors; however it wins more than its fair share of in-state deals. Its success is said to be due in large part to the impressive academic credentials of its attorneys and their deep understanding of the local market. These have served it well in deals such as the recent acquisition of Commercial Explosive by DynamoBell for $57 million.

The Lawyers: **Geoff Mangum** (see p.1737) is considered to be the leading player here for corporate finance and M&A. His recent highlights include acting in the DynamoBell deal mentioned previously, and he also advised on Rubicon Medical's acquisition by Boston Scientific for $15 million in stock. In addition to a steady stream of M&A, Mangum maintains a thriving land use practice.

The Clients: The firm represents companies, ranging from the smaller and midsized local concerns to major institutions, from a variety of industries.

Ray, Quinney & Nebeker PC

The Firm: As one of the oldest firms in the state, Ray, Quinney & Nebeker is a constant in Utah's business circles. The profile of the corporate/M&A team is not as strong as that of the firm's litigators. However, it handles a broad variety of transactional work and was widely endorsed as *"a perennially strong corporate firm with good lawyers across the board."*

The Lawyers: **Gary Winger** chairs the firm's business law section. A young and energetic lawyer, he was described as *"a highly skilled practitioner who is definitely one to watch."* He advises some substantial corporate clients on M&A and general business law.

The Clients: United Subcontractors; Set Point; Market Star; Headwaters and Mining Services International.

EMPLOYMENT

MAINLY DEFENDANT

Band 1

Jones Waldo Holbrook & McDonough PC

The Firm: The dedicated, 10-lawyer labor and employment law team at this homegrown Utah

firm is *"deservedly top tier,"* acknowledge sources. The standard to which others aspire, the already broad team was recently bolstered by the arrival of an employee benefits specialist. Its highlights from the past year include successfully enforcing a noncompete agreement on behalf

of a large insurance company, and defending a large hospital group against a discrimination claim. In the latter case, attorneys obtained summary judgment for their client. The firm also successfully concluded a civil rights case concerning the right of an employer to ban

Utah
Leading firms
(Employment: Mainly Defendant)

1 JONES WALDO HOLBROOK *Salt Lake City*
RAY, QUINNEY & NEBEKER PC *Salt Lake City*

2 JANOVE BAAR ASSOCIATES *Salt Lake City*
MANNING CURTIS BRADSHAW *Salt Lake City*

3 HOLME ROBERTS & OWEN LLP *Salt Lake City*
PARSONS BEHLE & LATIMER PC *Salt Lake City*
STOEL RIVES LLP *Salt Lake City*

Leading individuals
(Employment: Mainly Defendant)

1 O'BRIEN Michael *Jones Waldo*, Salt Lake City
SMITH Janet *Ray Quinney*, Salt Lake City

2 BAAR Lois *Janove Baar*, Salt Lake City
BEDNAR Steven *Manning Curtis*, Salt Lake City
DUNNING Elizabeth *Holme Roberts*, Salt Lake City
JANOVE Jathan *Janove Baar*, Salt Lake City

3 ANDERSON David *Parsons Behle*, Salt Lake City
CLAWSON Carol *Clawson & Falk*, Salt Lake City
DURHAM Matthew *Stoel Rives*, Salt Lake City
ZODY Michael *Parsons Behle*, Salt Lake City

Up-and-coming individuals

BENARD Bryan *Holland & Hart*, Salt Lake City
LEVIN Ali *Jones Waldo*, Salt Lake City

Firms and individuals are listed alphabetically in each band.

weapons on the premises. It submitted a brief on behalf of a number of clients, arguing that employers should retain discretion to determine their own policies, and this was affirmed by the court in an opinion issued in spring 2004.

The Lawyers: **Michael O'Brien** (see p.1737) is known throughout the state as a leading media and First Amendment lawyer, and also heads up the employment practice group. Renowned as *"omnipresent in employment law in Utah,"* sources claim that he has *"totally immersed himself into the legal and legislative voice of the community."* In addition to counseling employers on risk management, he is also skilled at representing them when disputes become lawsuits. An admired public speaker and noted author, he is also a frequent guest orator at employer association meetings. Younger attorney **Ali Levin** (see p.1737), is *"really striking out and making a name for herself,"* according to market sources. Her practice is focused on civil rights and wage and hour matters, among other things, and she has considerable experience before the NLRB.

The Clients: Utah Society for Human Resource Management (SHRM); Salt Lake Chamber of Commerce; Ogden/Weber Chamber of Commerce; Utah Restaurant Association; Utah Employer Council and Utah Hospital Association.

Ray, Quinney & Nebeker PC

The Firm: The firm fields a core employment group of nine attorneys, who are, say industry analysts, *"a very bright bunch."* Recommendations focused on the quality of the advice at partner level, with interviewees also agreeing that the firm is one of the strongest in the state for employment litigation. Its typical caseload includes wage and hour issues, discrimination and harassment claims, unfair dismissal, workers' compensation, and civil rights. It also handles some traditional labor law.

The Lawyers: *"Savvy, capable and experienced"* **Jan Smith** was enthusiastically praised by clients and competitors alike. *"I would never hesitate to recommend her,"* said one client: *"If you have to go to battle, it's extremely reassuring to have her on your side."* She is currently working on several race discrimination cases, including one with national ramifications. Other highlight matters include her involvement in disputes over state employment laws before the State Supreme Court.

The Clients: Kennecott Utah Copper; Delta Airlines; Target and Home Depot.

Band 2

Janove Baar Associates

The Firm: A local outfit with a national presence, this team was lauded as *"a fantastic firm with a terrific reputation – they never put a foot wrong."* This compact boutique promotes an ethos of early settlement, attempting to spare clients the cost and stress of litigation. However it boasts a strong litigator, in the form of name partner Lois Baar, and the team's litigation experience should not be underestimated. The three-partner firm is looking to expand in 2005.

The Lawyers: **Jathan Janove** enjoys a strong reputation in Salt Lake City, according to interviewees. He is a prolific author, with a preventative management skills book due to be published in 2005 and articles in a number of national periodicals. During the past year he has undertaken substantial amounts of litigation, including several class action lawsuits concerning workers' compensation, and a wrongful dismissal case in New York. **Lois Baar** was enthusiastically recommended for her strong litigation skills. *"A great negotiator, counselor and litigator,"* she is principally involved in whistleblower cases, sexual discrimination and harassment claims. Her experience also spans mediation and arbitration, age discrimination, and ADA and FMLA claims. Clients describe her as *"tremendously experienced, aggressive and tenacious."*

The Clients: La-Z-Boy; Ken Garff Automotive Group; BurrellesLuce; American Express; Zion Bank and Ogden Press.

Manning Curtis Bradshaw & Bednar

The Firm: According to commentators, the relatively small team at this *"high-profile, well-respected boutique"* has a good standing among Utah's major employers. Clients are extremely pleased with its services: *"We like the team's friendly and constructive approach, which is why we are still with them;"* and highlight the attention to detail and personal, partner-led service as particularly attractive traits.

The Lawyers: *"Sharp attorney"* **Steven Bednar** has a strong employment defense practice, representing primarily institutional clients. Clients acknowledge the way in which he *"grasps problems and gets his arms around them,"* and appreciate that *"you can call him whenever and it feels like he's just finished reading up on your case and knows it back to front."* The majority of Bednar's caseload is discrimination-related, including age, disability, sex, gender, national origin and race cases. He is also active defending wrongful discharge claims.

The Clients: Intermountain Health Care; Smith Food & Drugs; Sinclair Oil and RC Willey Home Furnishings.

Band 3

Holme Roberts & Owen LLP

See firm details p.326

The Firm: This firm has an international profile, with offices in London and Munich. This makes the team particularly attractive to clients expanding into Europe, as the Utah office has access to experts on European employment law. The large outfit also boasts an impressive regional footprint encompassing the intermountain West; and, as well as handling a range of workplace matters for some of Utah's leading employers, its attorneys have experience of handling out-of-state cases.

The Lawyers: Described by one client as *"the most knowledgeable employment law attorney I've ever worked with,"* **Elizabeth Dunning** regularly advises on such areas as English language proficiency, drug testing in the workplace, and minimum wage amendments. Her practice spans both counseling and complex litigation. Recent times have seen her assist a client with an EEOC audit of a chemical plant, defend an ADA claim, represent a Utah electronics manufacturer in a discrimination case, and advise a well-known nutritionist on a trade secrets issue. Clients enthuse: *"She is easy to talk to and has the ability to boil a case down to the essentials."*

The Clients: The firm is assisting Wasatch Academy in its establishment of an English language academy in China. Other clients include: Huish Detergents; Questar; Rowland Hall-St Mark's School; Huntsman and Boede & Partners.

1730

All quotes in the text are from interviews with clients and competitors.

CHAMBERS USA 2005

Parsons Behle & Latimer PC

See firm details p.1742

The Firm: This is one of the oldest Utah-based firms and is unusual in being active on both the plaintiff and defense sides. Its long-standing ties to the Salt Lake City business community, and Utah's employers in general, is said to ensure it a steady stream of interesting work, while its concentration on old-line quality ensures that team members are consistently *"top flight."*

The Lawyers: **David Anderson** (see p.1735) has made a positive impact upon the market, according to sources. Clients depict him as *"knowledgeable and confident,"* and were impressed by his skill in *"brainstorming the issues as they arose."* In the past year the team's other star, **Michael Zody** (see p.1738), has done a considerable amount of OSHA work and is diversifying his practice to include environmental whistle-blower cases. The environmental law side has dominated his workload of late, but he retains a considerable profile among colleagues

at the employment bar.

The Clients: The firm's client roster includes ClearOne Communications and McWayne.

Stoel Rives LLP

The Firm: This Portland-based firm is noted for its depth and broad geographic scope. A network of offices from Seattle to San Francisco gives it an enviable market position in the North West. The Salt Lake City employment practice group handles a wide variety of employment cases but, over the past year, it has seen a particular increase in trade secrets and proprietary information litigation.

The Lawyers: Sources note that **Matthew Durham** is *"starting to make a name for himself"* in the state, and is one of the more visible *"younger lawyers on the scene."* He *"will be a leader one day,"* predicted one interviewee. The past twelve months have seen him acting in a number of sexual harassment cases, including a same-sex case. One of these claims reached the

Tenth Circuit Court of Appeals, though many more were settled out of court on favorable terms. Durham is also working on the implementation of language proficiency tests at a Utah manufacturing firm, where he is introducing English proficiency standards.

The Clients: The firm acts for employers from a variety of industries located across the North West.

Other Notable Practitioners

Carol Clawson is described by competitors as *"a real professional – I'd refer my own clients to her,"* added one. A former solicitor-general for the state, she has now established her own three-partner firm, Clawson & Falk LLC. Up-and-comer **Bryan Benard** (see p.1735), was singled out as a *"particularly impressive"* younger lawyer. Based at Holland & Hart LLP, he regularly represents clients in wrongful termination, harassment and discrimination cases.

LITIGATION

GENERAL COMMERCIAL

Utah

Leading firms

(Litigation: General Commercial)

[1]	**BENDINGER, CROCKETT, PETERSON** *Salt Lake City*
	BURBIDGE & MITCHELL *Salt Lake City*
	HOLME ROBERTS & OWEN LLP *Salt Lake City*
	RAY, QUINNEY & NEBEKER PC *Salt Lake City*
[2]	**PARSONS BEHLE & LATIMER PC** *Salt Lake City*
	SNELL & WILMER LLP *Salt Lake City*
	STOEL RIVES LLP *Salt Lake City*
[3]	**FABIAN & CLENDENIN** *Salt Lake City*
	PARR WADDOUPS BROWN GEE *Salt Lake City*
	VAN COTT, BAGLEY, CORNWALL *Salt Lake City*

Firms are listed alphabetically in each band.

Band 1

Bendinger, Crockett, Peterson, Greenwood & Casey

See firm details p.1739

The Firm: This litigation boutique places a heavy emphasis on trial practice – a formula that has assured it a high profile in the market. *"Its reputation is well deserved,"* agreed competitors, *"its lawyers are good and aggressive."* As is often the case for dedicated trial firms, the group's work frequently takes its attorneys outside the state. It is currently involved in litigation between the owners of Utah's only two daily newspapers.

The Lawyers: Name partner **Gary Bendinger** (see p.1735) was singled out by interviewees for the high quality of his advocacy. Clients in particular were effusive in their praise for his work: *"He's not afraid to take a difficult position and he*

puts his clients' wishes before any concern about his personal reputation." In addition to general commercial disputes, Bendinger also handles investigations by government agencies, including the SEC. **David Greenwood** (see p.1736), a recent arrival at the firm, has been occupied recently with a three-month bench trial in federal district court in Idaho, where he represented a leading defense contractor.

The Clients: Allstate Insurance; Better Business Bureau of Utah; Bridgestone/Firestone; Deloitte & Touche; Farmers Insurance; Intermountain Health Care; International Union of Police Associations; KPMG; Lockheed Martin; Salt Lake Tribune Publishing and Siemens.

Burbidge & Mitchell

See firm details p.1740

The Firm: This specialist litigation firm has developed a superb name in the local market as a high-quality, dedicated and *"exclusive"* outfit, as well as a first port of call for complex litigation. The firm's trial expertise falls broadly into two categories: complex commercial disputes, including those with an antitrust or securities fraud aspect; and catastrophic injury litigation, including class actions. It is perhaps best known for its role as plaintiffs' counsel in the ongoing national tobacco litigation. The compact team is composed of just three partners and two assistants.

The Lawyers: This smaller firm's sizable reputation is founded on the name and considerable profile of **Richard Burbidge** (see p.1736), who is a popular choice among both clients and peers. *"He's experienced and aggressive, but also personable,"* said one, *"when he tries a case, he*

takes over the courtroom." "I'd always refer to him first," added a rival. Among his colleagues, younger partner **Jefferson Gross** (see p.1736) is felt to particularly stand out. Senior competitors described him as *"a bright spark – tough and practical, with a lot of potential."*

Holme Roberts & Owen LLP

See firm details p.326

The Firm: This Denver-based powerhouse remains popular with clients throughout the Midwest. Building on the firm's stellar reputation for corporate finance and M&A, the litigation team acts for a number of the region's largest companies in commercial disputes of all kinds. The group is growing steadily, and currently numbers 27 attorneys in Utah, with others based across the region.

The Lawyers: **George Haley** is particularly well regarded for his methodical approach to complex securities litigation. *"He's just extraordinary,"* enthused clients, pointing to his impressive track record in sizable cases. Recent examples include defending Questar against a $500 million claim for fraud and breach of fiduciary duty. The claim was successfully dismissed, and his client was awarded damages of $110 million on its counterclaim. Younger partner **Blaine Benard** was also warmly recommended by clients. *"He's just stupendous – his experience shines through: I really can't fault him"* said one. He is building up a substantial practice advising companies based across the USA.

The Clients: Key litigation clients include: Delta Air Lines; Questar; Qwest; Chase Manhattan Mortgage and Rolls Royce North America.

Utah

Leading individuals

(Litigation: General Commercial)

[1] BENDINGER Gary *Bendinger Crockett*, Salt Lake City
  BURBIDGE Richard *Burbidge*, Salt Lake City
  HALEY George *Holme Roberts*, Salt Lake City
  JARDINE James *Ray Quinney*, Salt Lake City
  JORDAN David *Stoel Rives*, Salt Lake City
  SULLIVAN Alan *Snell & Wilmer*, Salt Lake City

[2] BILLINGS JR Peter *Fabian & Clendenin*, Salt Lake City
  BLACK Kenneth *Stoel Rives*, Salt Lake City
  CAMPBELL JR Robert *Van Cott Bagley*, Salt Lake City
  CLARK Robert *Parr Waddoups*, Salt Lake City
  ETCHEVERRY Raymond *Parsons Behle*, Salt Lake City
  GREENWOOD David *Bendinger*, Salt Lake City
  KARRENBERG Thomas *Anderson*, Salt Lake City
  WADDOUPS Clark *Parr Waddoups*, Salt Lake City
  WIKSTROM Francis *Parsons Behle*, Salt Lake City

Up-and-coming individuals

  BENARD Blaine *Holme Roberts*, Salt Lake City
  GROSS Jefferson *Burbidge & Mitchell*, Salt Lake City
  HUNT Jeffrey *Parr Waddoups*, Salt Lake City

Individuals are listed alphabetically in each band.

Ray, Quinney & Nebeker PC

The Firm: This is a full-service firm with a substantial pedigree. Clients characterized the litigation team, the largest in the firm, as *"talented, professional and reliable – I'd recommend them to anybody,"* added one. The firm is, of course, known for its top-drawer employment litigation group, and also offers considerable expertise in antitrust and securities disputes.

The Lawyers: There is no doubt that the reputation of the firm in commercial litigation is closely bound up with that of *"real standout partner"* **James Jardine**. *"He's by far the best"* in the firm, acknowledged interviewees, as well as being among the best in the state. The diversity of his litigation practice is demonstrated by his recent caseload, which has included antitrust, SEC civil enforcement and whistle-blowing cases.

The Clients: An impressive client roster includes: CR England; Allied Waste; Huntsman; Goldman Sachs and Microsoft.

Band 2

Parsons Behle & Latimer PC

See firm details p.1742

The Firm: This substantial Salt Lake City firm enjoys a considerable profile in the commercial litigation arena, and is known in particular for its thriving environmental practice, which is anchored by key client Albertsons. The firm boasts around 50 general commercial litigators whose practice takes them all over the Midwest.

The Lawyers: *"Strong litigator"* **Ray Etcheverry** (see p.1736) is widely felt to be the key player here. The national nature of his practice is illustrated by his involvement in a recent case in Cal-

ifornia, in which his client was accused of causing toxic emissions at Los Angeles Airport. Peers also pointed to **Francis Wikstrom** (see p.1738) as a talented attorney and a popular choice for referrals.

The Clients: Albertsons is an important client in the environmental field. The firm also represents a number of major local and national companies in a variety of fields.

Snell & Wilmer LLP

See firm details p.167

The Firm: A diverse group at this old-line western firm is active in all areas of commercial litigation, including the more esoteric areas of products liability, healthcare and pharmaceuticals litigation. Also covered are professional malpractice, construction and environmental litigation. Market sources picked out the practice as being particularly strong in the field of banking litigation.

The Lawyers: **Alan Sullivan** (see p.1738) *"deserves to be at the top,"* in the opinion of many sources: *"He'd be my first choice if I were conflicted out of a case"* said peers. He boasts an unusually diverse trial practice. As an indication, his recent workload has included a First Amendment claim on behalf of the Church of Jesus Christ of Latter-Day Saints, a case for the University of Utah concerning the prohibition of guns on campus, and a number of IP and healthcare disputes.

Stoel Rives LLP

The Firm: Appropriately for a firm of its size and stature, Stoel Rives sustains a successful litigation practice. As well as a steady stream of commercial disputes, shareholder litigation, tort and negligence claims, recent times have seen the group in particular demand to assist corporate clients with internal investigations and Sarbanes-Oxley-related preemptive action. The team is perceived in the market to be solid throughout. As one source put it: *"They have a group of midlevel lawyers that create an impressive work product for the firm."*

The Lawyers: *"Fine trial lawyer"* **David Jordan** stands out here for his large and successful commercial litigation practice, which includes a considerable element of media representation. In recent months he has appeared in federal court on behalf of the Las Vegas Sun and the Desert News, leading daily newspapers in Nevada and Utah. He is joined in the tables by **Ken Black** who was enthusiastically recommended by interviewees. *"He's really one to watch,"* said one source: *"I'm constantly impressed by his output."*

Band 3

Fabian & Clendenin

The Firm: This well-established Salt Lake City firm also operates from offices in Dublin, Ohio

and Las Vegas. The sizable litigation department is competent in a wide variety of business disputes, ranging from relatively straightforward insurance coverage litigation to complex shareholder cases. However, it is perhaps best known for its skill in antitrust work.

The Lawyers: Interviewees were enthusiastic in their recommendation of **Peter Billings**. As one put it: *"He's a long-time quality lawyer,"* who is *"able to cut through the chaff and get to the heart of the matter."* His focus on class action defense frequently takes him to California and other parts of western USA. In addition to general commercial claims, Billings is also experienced in insurance coverage disputes.

Parr Waddoups Brown Gee & Loveless

The Firm: Though the litigation team at this established Utah firm is a substantial one, it has eschewed rapid growth in favor of organic development and fields a smaller group of high-quality attorneys. The firm acts across a number of areas of civil litigation, and has lately seen a surge in its intellectual property caseload.

The Lawyers: Name partner **Clark Waddoups** is probably the best-known personality in the team. He is particularly well regarded in the market for his expertise in antitrust and securities litigation. **Robert Clark** has also enjoyed a successful year. He recently represented a group of minority shareholders in a mining company that was the subject of a squeeze-out merger, obtaining $2 million in damages. **Jeffrey Hunt**, a new entry in the rankings, is a younger lawyer with a focus on First Amendment and media litigation. Commentators view him as *"a bright lawyer who is making a fine name for himself."* His clients include many of the local media networks and newspapers, and his work for them frequently involves elements of IP law.

The Clients: The firm's litigation client roster is drawn primarily from the medical, general manufacturing, hi-tech and airline sectors.

Van Cott, Bagley, Cornwall & McCarthy

The Firm: This full-service firm has a long and successful history in civil litigation within Utah. The group's particular strength is in complex commercial litigation, and its caseload encompasses elements of antitrust and fraud, as well as the more straightforward corporate, commercial tort and negligence disputes.

The Lawyers: **Robert Campbell**, the firm's standout litigator, focuses on antitrust, securities and commercial fraud disputes. These are areas that frequently involve some overlap with white-collar crime defense, a field in which he is also known and respected. While Campbell is undoubtedly an aggressive and tenacious litigator, he remains popular with peers, who consider him a top choice for referrals.

Other Notable Practitioners

Thomas Karrenberg is a name partner in civil litigation boutique Anderson & Karrenberg. He has built a substantial reputation on the strength of his *"strong and aggressive"* courtroom manner.

REAL ESTATE

Utah
Leading firms (Real Estate)

[1]	**PARR WADDOUPS BROWN GEE** *Salt Lake City*
	STOEL RIVES LLP *Salt Lake City*
[2]	**BALLARD SPAHR ANDREWS** *Salt Lake City*
	JONES WALDO HOLBROOK *Salt Lake City*
	KIRTON & MCCONKIE *Salt Lake City*
	SNELL & WILMER LLP *Salt Lake City*
[3]	**FABIAN & CLENDENIN** *Salt Lake City*
	HOLLAND & HART LLP *Salt Lake City*
	PARSONS BEHLE & LATIMER PC *Salt Lake City*
	RAY, QUINNEY & NEBEKER PC *Salt Lake City*
	VAN COTT, BAGLEY, CORNWALL *Salt Lake City*

Leading individuals (Real Estate)

Senior Statesman	
MAAK Charles *Parr Waddoups, Salt Lake City*	
[1] **ELLISON Thomas** *Stoel Rives, Salt Lake City*	
GEE David *Parr Waddoups, Salt Lake City*	
[2] **BERGGREN Tom** *Jones Waldo, Salt Lake City*	
COOK Rand *Van Cott Bagley, Salt Lake City*	
FERRIN Shawn *Parsons Behle, Salt Lake City*	
HYDE Robert *Kirton & McConkie, Salt Lake City*	
JONES Cary *Snell & Wilmer, Salt Lake City*	
KROESCHE Guy *Stoel Rives, Salt Lake City*	
ROWE Keven *Jones Waldo, Salt Lake City*	
[3] **BANKS Diane** *Fabian & Clendenin, Salt Lake City*	
BENNETT Thomas *Ballard Spahr, Salt Lake City*	
BROADBENT David *Holland & Hart, Salt Lake City*	
HELLEWELL Read *Kirton & McConkie, Salt Lake City*	
HOLMES Ervin *Stoel Rives, Salt Lake City*	
MOORE Larry *Ray Quinney, Salt Lake City*	
RUBINFELD Ira *Ray Quinney, Salt Lake City*	
WILLIAMS Gregory *Van Cott Bagley, Salt Lake City*	
Up-and-coming individuals	
BARTON Carl *Holland & Hart, Salt Lake City*	

Firms and individuals are listed alphabetically in each band.

Band 1

Parr Waddoups Brown Gee & Loveless

The Firm: This market-leading team of *"amazingly strong lawyers"* retains its position at the forefront of Utah's real estate bar. The firm serves its top-class client base of owners, developers and contractors in a wide range of fields, from contract preparation and negotiation to leasing, development and construction. It boasts a good name for handling construction disputes in state and federal courts, and has been at the forefront of developing alternative dispute resolution procedures. It has been particularly active,

however, on mixed-use developments, one of the fastest growing sectors in the Midwest.

The Lawyers: This firm is home to several of Utah's most respected real estate attorneys. **Charles Maak** is universally acknowledged as *"the founding father of real estate in Utah."* Peers emphasize that he is a great ambassador for the firm and still active in real property circles. **David Gee** is well known as the contact partner for star client The Boyer Company. As such, he is the key figure in many of the region's largest development projects. *"Clearly one of the top attorneys"* in his field, he has been particularly active of late in the growing market for privatization of housing on military bases.

The Clients: In addition to The Boyer Company, the firm acts for major retailers and developers across the region. Clients are also drawn from the healthcare industry.

Stoel Rives LLP

The Firm: Stoel Rives is among the largest firms in the North West, and its real estate practice boasts a sizable team packed with *"great attorneys from top to bottom."* Interviewees are in no doubt that *"this is one of the few firms that really controls the deals in this business."* Operating seamlessly across the region, the team is particularly well regarded for project development and construction work. Real estate finance is another major area of expertise, and the firm has been involved in the development and expansion of many of the state's resorts.

The Lawyers: **Thomas Ellison** is heavily involved in the privatization of US Air Force housing, one of the hot areas of the past year. He is currently helping to negotiate a $400 million financing package for this purpose. Development work forms the mainstay of his practice, and he frequently arranges finance for developers. He is also highly experienced in land use, to the extent that some commentators consider him *"the strongest land use and zoning attorney in the state."* **Guy Kroesche** makes his first appearance in the rankings this year, following enthusiastic recommendation from peers and clients alike. Reflecting the firm's focus, his talents lie in the development arena. He specializes in particular in advising healthcare providers, including Intermountain Health Care, on the construction and expansion of hospitals. *"Experienced and intelligent"* **Ervin Holmes**'s diverse practice has a distinct environmental slant. He recently advised on the sale of a 600-acre brown-

field site, handling both the transaction and the preliminary environmental work. He is also involved in the high-profile development of a third-generation power generating plant by the Intermountain Power Agency.

The Clients: Lender clients, including Key-Bank and Citibank, regularly turn to this firm for advice in the Midwest.

Band 2

Ballard Spahr Andrews & Ingersoll LLP
See firm details p.1541

The Firm: This large, Denver-based firm is known throughout the West for its geographical footprint and its top-class real property offering, especially in the fields of real estate finance and resort development. As part of this extensive network of offices, the Utah team enjoys access to work of national quality. It is little surprise, then, that market commentators single out the firm as, *"right up there in terms of volume, size and complexity of deals."*

The Lawyers: **Tom Bennett** (see p.1735) has spent a lot of time over the past year advising developers on the construction of a resort village comprising more than 100 units. He has built an interesting niche in the emerging area of private residence clubs – a hybrid of a timeshare and a country club.

The Clients: The firm's client list includes some of the biggest names in the worlds of development and real estate finance.

Jones Waldo Holbrook & McDonough PC

The Firm: This sizable, Salt Lake City-based firm is active in commercial property acquisitions and disposals throughout the Midwest. A real estate group of around 12 is experienced in a broad range of real property law, from acquisitions, development and construction to real estate finance, environmental and land use matters. Over the past year, despite the quiet market, the team handled the acquisition of a $40 million office development in Denver, and advised key client Wells Fargo on acquisitions totaling more than $200 million.

The Lawyers: **Keven Rowe** (see p.1737) was enthusiastically recommended to researchers. As one source put it: *"He's thorough, detail oriented and can handle the biggest deals effectively."* The leader of the real estate finance practice group, he recently advised a major resort developer on

the $40 million purchase and expansion of the Deer Valley Resort. **Tom Berggren** (see p.1736) has handled a number of multimillion-dollar sale and leaseback deals for national retail chains. He has advised Fortune 500 companies and regularly represents portfolio managers and asset managers. According to market sources: *"He's the consummate real estate lawyer, who understands everything – he's so technically proficient."*
The Clients: An impressive list includes: Wells Fargo; Lowe's; Bridge Investment Group; Albertsons and Browning.

Kirton & McConkie
See firm details p.1741
The Firm: Though a genuine full-service firm, it is the real estate practice that has really caught the imagination of the market. This is principally due to its prominent work for the Church of Jesus Christ of Latter-Day Saints. A substantial proportion of the team's caseload is for the church, the remainder being composed mainly of development and finance work for substantial local developers.
The Lawyers: **Robert Hyde** (see p.1737) is the primary contact partner for the church, and work for them occupies roughly half his time. Clients are delighted with his style, commitment and business acumen. As one put it: *"He sees the issues from our point of view and doesn't over-lawyer us."* **Read Hellewell** is a notable development specialist who *"represents clients without nitpicking."* His *"aggressive, no-nonsense manner"* makes him a popular choice with clients. The team has made several hires in recent months, including Loyal Hulme, formerly with LeBoeuf, Lamb, Greene & MacRae in New York.
The Clients: As well as the Church of Jesus Christ of Latter-Day Saints, the team represents a number of important local developers.

Snell & Wilmer LLP
See firm details p.167
The Firm: This sizable western firm, headquartered in Phoenix, is active in real estate transactions throughout the region. Competitors were full of praise for the group's professionalism: *"I've had a number of transactions with them, and I've been continually impressed."* Clients expressed their appreciation of its quality advice and practical, deal-driven approach. The team handles everything from straightforward real estate transactions and leases, to advice on every aspect of the development of huge planned communities.
The Lawyers: **Cary Jones** (see p.1737) *"totally stands out – he's an amazing lawyer, and we have a great relationship,"* noted his clients. He has recently advised on the Mission Bay mixed-use infill development, and has also handled the development of new summer amenities at the Park City Mountain Resort. He is also known for acting as general counsel for the Sundance

Institute, the nonprofit organization behind the Sundance Film Festival.
The Clients: The Salt Lake City office serves a diverse client base, including Park City Mountain Resort, Santa Fe Partners and SITLA.

Band 3

Fabian & Clendenin
The Firm: This firm's real estate group has enjoyed a bumper year, with a notable rise in the volume of commercial and retail leasing instructions. The practice commonly represents national retail chains as tenants in negotiations with their landlords. On the investor side, the team recently represented the Salt Lake City Redevelopment Agency, a long-standing client, in the acquisition of a property from the Utah Museum of Fine Arts.
The Lawyers: **Diane Banks** was singled out here as a *"strong and capable"* attorney with a good profile in the market. Clients, who include developers and retailers, characterize her as *"diligent and responsive; good at making transactions work, rather than being a roadblock."* In addition to a number of high-value acquisitions and disposals, including a 300,000-sq-ft office complex in Salt Lake City, her recent highlights include advising on a new campus development at Salt Lake Community College.
The Clients: A diverse roster includes public sector bodies such as the Salt Lake City Redevelopment Agency.

Holland & Hart LLP
See firm details p.325
The Firm: This firm is an ever-present force across the Midwest with offices in most important business centers. Its Salt Lake City office houses eight real estate attorneys and assists a number of well-known clients. The team covers all the bases, with lawyers advising on acquisitions and disposals, development and construction, real estate finance and leasing. It also has a strong hotels and resorts practice.
The Lawyers: **David Broadbent**'s (see p.1736) practice spans a wide variety of areas, but he receives particular recognition for his finance, workout and foreclosure work. In recent months he has advised on the acquisition and finance of several large multifamily projects, and the acquisition, redevelopment and sale of a substantial shopping center. Up-and-comer **Carl Barton** (see p.1735) enjoys a growing profile for his finance and development advice. Recent highlights include arranging loan facilities of $130 million and $140 million for the developers of two assisted living projects. He is also acting in the development of a luxury condo project in Hawaii.
The Clients: The firm's extensive national network allows the Salt Lake City team access to many of the largest clients in the region.

Parsons Behle & Latimer PC
See firm details p.1742
The Firm: The real estate team here has expanded successfully beyond its traditional Utah and Nevada heartlands to serve clients throughout the region. It is increasingly being mentioned in the same breath as the larger regional outfits. The group's profile is particularly strong in the areas of retail and industrial development and leasing, and it is also active in the resort sector.
The Lawyers: According to commentators, **Shawn Ferrin** (see p.1736) continues to grow in prominence: *"He's really come on in the past year."* He has primary responsibility at the firm for major client Home Depot, and advises the retailer on the development and construction of new stores in the region. Ferrin also advises investors on the finance, purchase and sale of stakes in local ski resorts.
The Clients: The firm acts for major local and regional clients, including Home Depot and Powder Ski Resort.

Ray, Quinney & Nebeker PC
The Firm: This is *"a group of decent lawyers who really know what they're doing,"* according to market sources. The firm enjoys a first-class reputation in both general civil litigation and employment cases, so it's hardly surprising to find it a leading name for real estate disputes. However, the team is also active on both the landlord and tenant side of commercial leasing transactions and manages large retail and commercial portfolios for institutional investors and pension funds.
The Lawyers: **Larry Moore** has been busy representing a major retailer, which recently filed for bankruptcy, in negotiations with its many landlords regarding obligations under its leasehold covenants. He is also a prolific real estate litigator, and is currently involved in a test case that will determine whether leasehold covenants can be waived by a long course of conduct on the landlord's part. **Ira Rubinfeld** combines work for major investors, one of which recently acquired an apartment complex in New York and an office building in New Jersey, with a more esoteric nonprofit practice. The latter entails advising charitable housing groups on new affordable housing developments in Salt Lake City. From time to time Rubinfeld, *"a really good younger lawyer,"* also handles real estate litigation.
The Clients: The team's client list includes Solitude Ski Resort, Wells Fargo and Washington Mutual.

Van Cott, Bagley, Cornwall & McCarthy
The Firm: This small but talented team has a broad-based practice, which features a considerable real estate financing and workout element, alongside a steady stream of leasing,

development and transactional work. It serves an impressive client base and received particular approval for its experience in resort development.

The Lawyers: Rand Cook combines *"a deep knowledge of the law"* with *"a cooperative working manner,"* a combination that endears him to rivals as well as clients. Much of his caseload has

a finance flavor, and clients often turn to him for advice on workouts and restructurings with a real estate element. By contrast, **Greg Williams** is heavily involved in resort development, generally representing the borrower side. Williams came to prominence as a result of his involvement in the redevelopment of the Park City resort following the Winter Olympics.

The Clients: Gastronomy; America First Credit Union; Kern River Gas Transmission; General Electric Credit; BMW Bank and Franklin Templeton Bank.

Leaders in Utah

ANDERSON, Chris
Snell & Wilmer LLP, Salt Lake City
801 257 1997
canderson@swlaw.com
Recommended in Corporate/M&A

Practice Areas: Practices primarily in the areas of business, securities and international law. Extensive background in venture capital transactions for emerging growth companies, and in the representation of high technology companies in the initial stages of development. Mr Anderson represents more mature companies in public and private financings, acquisitions, dispositions, recapitalizations, mergers, and other complex commercial transactions and agreements. He assists with matters related to corporate structuring, establishment of commercial and strategic relationships, international expansion and franchising.
Prof. Memberships: Utah State Bar, State Bar of California and American Bar Association.

ANDERSON, David A
Parsons Behle & Latimer PC, Salt Lake City 801 532 1234
DAnderson@pblutah.com
Recommended in Employment

Practice Areas: Employment law; employee benefits; collective bargaining, grievance arbitration and National Labor Relations Act matters; discrimination; wrongful discharge and employment-at-will counsel and litigation.
Prof. Memberships: Member, American Bar Association: Labor and Employment Law Section, Employee Benefits and Litigation Section.
Career: Shareholder, Chair of Employment Department. Past Chairman, Utah Bar Section, Labor and Employment Law. Adjunct professor, University of Utah College of Law, pension and employee benefits law. Frequent speaker at employer conferences and seminars on employment law topics.
Personal: JD, Cornell University, 1979. Master of Industrial and Labor Relations, Cornell University, 1980. BA, University of Utah, 1976.

BAAR, Lois
Janove Baar Associates, Salt Lake City
801 530 0404
Recommended in Employment

BANKS, Diane
Fabian & Clendenin, Salt Lake City
801 531 8900
Recommended in Real Estate

BARTON, Carl
Holland & Hart LLP, Salt Lake City
801 595 7831
cbarton@hollandhart.com
Recommended in Real Estate

Practice Areas: Mr Barton's practice focuses on real estate acquisitions, sales, leasing, options, finance, development, and 1031 tax-deferred exchanges. Projects include the development and financing of golf course and luxury condominium resorts, hotels, shopping malls and strip centers, business and industrial parks, large ranches, power plants and energy facilities, national restaurants, office buildings and condominiums, and multi-family residential ventures in all regions of the United States. He specializes in leasing, representing both landlords and tenants in retail, office, industrial, agricultural, and ground leases. His practice also involves real estate loans and other financial transactions on behalf of developers and owners, banks, insurance companies, and private lenders. Transactions include real estate and asset based loans, tenant-in-common loans, construction loans, conduit loans, lines of credit, mezzanine loans, energy project financing, and sale/leaseback financing. Mr Barton is also experienced in obtaining rights of way, in land-use planning and zoning, and in the purchase, sale, and financing of water rights.
Prof. Memberships: Real Property and Business Law Sections, Utah State Bar; Honorary French Consul, State of Utah (1988-2001).
Career: Admitted to the Utah State Bar (1986).
Personal: Received a JD (1986) and two BA degrees (1982) from the University of Utah.

BEDNAR, Steven
Manning Curtis Bradshaw & Bednar, Salt Lake City 801 363 5678
Recommended in Employment

BENARD, Blaine
Holme Roberts & Owen LLP, Salt Lake City 801 521 5800
Recommended in Litigation

BENARD, Bryan
Holland & Hart LLP, Salt Lake City
801 595 7833
bbenard@hollandhart.com
Recommended in Employment

Practice Areas: Practices in labor and employment counseling and litigation, commercial litigation, and civil appellate matters. Regularly represents both private and public clients in wrongful termination, harassment, and discrimination claims in both federal and state courts, as well as in administrative proceedings before federal and state agencies. Counsels clients regarding employee relations, employee contracts, and employee handbooks. Represents employers in matters related to the Family and Medical Leave Act, the Uniformed Services Employment and Reemployment Rights Act, the Americans with Disabilities Act, and the Fair Labor Standards Act, including administrative investigations into wage and hour complaints as well as defending against collective actions. Broad experience in natural resources and environmental disputes, intellectual property litigation, inverse condemnation, land use regulation and zoning, and constitutional law issues.
Prof. Memberships: American Bar Association; California State Bar Association; Utah State Bar Association; Salt Lake County Bar Association.
Career: Admitted to California Bar and US District Courts for Central and Southern Districts of California (1997); Utah State Bar and US District Court, District of Utah (2001); US Court of Appeals, Tenth Circuit and US Supreme Court (2004).
Personal: Received a JD (1997) from the University of Utah and a BA (1994) from Weber State University.

BENDINGER, Gary F
Bendinger, Crockett, Peterson, Greenwood & Casey, Salt Lake City
801 533 8383
gfb@bendinger-crockett.com
Recommended in Litigation

Practice Areas: Practices in complex commercial litigation in federal courts throughout the United States. His experience involves securities, antitrust and intellectual property litigation involving claims for hundreds of millions of dollars.
Prof. Memberships: Is a Fellow in the American College of Trial Lawyers and has been consistently recognized by a leading publication in the area of Commercial Litigation. Is a Member of the State Bar of Utah, the American Bar Association, and has been admitted to practice before the United States Supreme Court, The United States Court of Appeals for the Ninth and Tenth Circuits and numerous federal and state courts.
Career: Started his career by representing plaintiffs in federal antitrust litigation and has since represented both plaintiffs and defendants in complex commercial litigation involving important issues and claims for substantial monetary damages. Has tried successfully numerous cases to jury verdict. Was recently recognized by Utah Business as one of the most feared litigators in the State of Utah.

BENNETT, Thomas G
Ballard Spahr Andrews & Ingersoll LLP, Salt Lake City 801 531 3060
bennett@ballardspahr.com
Recommended in Real Estate

Practice Areas: He concentrates his practice in the development of commercial and resort properties, with an emphasis on property acquisition, community structuring, financing, zoning and entitlements, construction, state and federal regulatory compliance, and sales of planned communities, condominiums, timeshares, private residence clubs, golf courses, condominium hotels, office buildings, and shopping centers.
Prof. Memberships: An active member of the American Resort Development Association (ARDA) serving on ARDA's State Legislative Committee. He also serves as a member of the editorial

www.ChambersandPartners.com

All quotes in the text are from interviews with clients and competitors.

1735

board of the Timeshare Law Compendium being prepared as a joint effort between ARDA and the American Bar Association.
Career: Admitted to the Utah Bar (1981); joined as Of Counsel (1998).
Personal: JD, cum laude, J. Reuben Clark Law School, Brigham Young University (1981); BS, cum laude, Brigham Young University (1976).

BERGGREN, Tom
Jones Waldo Holbrook & McDonough PC, Salt Lake City 801 521 3200
tberggren@joneswaldo.com
Recommended in Real Estate
Practice Areas: Practice includes the purchase and sale, leasing, financing, development and entitlement of commercial office buildings, retail space, industrial parks, professional buildings and multi-family complexes. Has extensive experience in assisting national retailers acquire property for stores in the West, by both purchase and ground lease. Represented several Fortune 500 companies in connection with negotiating governmental incentive packages, including for regional distribution centers. Acts as local counsel for out-of-state real property lenders and borrowers.
Prof. Memberships: ICSC, NAIOP, ABA's Committee on Legal Opinions and SLC Board of Adjustment for Zoning Appeals.
Career: First four years with Morrison & Foerster (San Francisco and London). Practicing in Utah since 1983. Chair of Real Estate Department and Member of Opinion Letter Committee.
Personal: Harvard (College '74 Law '78).

BILLINGS Jr, Peter
Fabian & Clendenin, Salt Lake City 801 531 8900
Recommended in Litigation

BLACK, Kenneth
Stoel Rives LLP, Salt Lake City 801 328 3131
Recommended in Litigation

BONHAM, Mark E
Wilson Sonsini Goodrich & Rosati, Salt Lake City 801 993 6400
mbonham@wsgr.com
Recommended in Corporate/M&A
Practice Areas: Counsels technology-based companies on financing, public offerings, mergers and acquisitions, equity compensation, technology licensing, public company governance and disclosure, structuring of transactions and basic corporate and securities matters.
Prof. Memberships: Admitted to practice in California and Utah.
Career: Joined WSGR, 1987; became Partner, 1995. Co-Chair of WSGR's Knowledge Management Initiative.
Personal: JD, 1987, Harvard Law School. Recipient of the John M Olin Fellowship in Law and Economics; BA (magna cum laude), 1984, Brigham Young University.

BROADBENT, David K
Holland & Hart LLP, Salt Lake City 801 595 7806
dbroadbent@hollandhart.com
Recommended in Real Estate
Practice Areas: Mr Broadbent practices primarily in the fields of real estate and corporate law. He represents both developer and lender clients in real estate acquisition, development, leasing and tax-free exchanges, as well as conventional, tax credit, and bond financing. He has helped clients develop and finance shopping center, office building, office park, condominium, hotel, multi-family housing and residential and recreational projects.
Prof. Memberships: Member, Real Property, Corporate Counsel and Business Law sections, Utah State Bar; Member, Business Law and Real Property Sections of the American Bar Association. Mr Broadbent has served as the Chairman of the Real Property Section of the Utah State Bar. Appointments: Board of Directors, Valley Mental Health.
Career: Admitted to the Utah State Bar (1979).
Personal: Received a JD (1979, Order of the Coif) and a BA (1976, magna cum laude) from the University of Utah.

BURBIDGE, Richard D
Burbidge & Mitchell, Salt Lake City 801 355 6677
rburbidge@burbidgeandmitchell.com
Recommended in Litigation
Practice Areas: Trial practice in complex commercial litigation and prosecution of catastrophic injury. Represents a wide range of clients, including emerging and established national and local concerns, governmental entities and prominent individuals. His extensive experience includes a wide range of business claims, including contract disputes, antitrust, securities, intellectual property and national and local class action cases.
Prof. Memberships: Fellow, American College of Trial Lawyers; Fellow (State Chair), International Academy of Trial Lawyers; Fellow (State Chair), International Society of Barristers; and Member, American Board of Trial Advocacy; Trial Lawyer of the Year 2002 (ABOTA, Utah Chapter).
Career: Over 27 years of litigation and trial practice throughout the United States. Has won numerous jury verdicts for both plaintiffs and defendants in multi-million dollar cases.
Personal: Graduated with a Juris Doctor degree in 1972 from the University of Utah College of Law; Order of the Coif. Articles Editor, 'Utah Law Review'. Adjunct professor, Trial Practice, University of Utah College of Law, 1986-93. Listed in leading legal publication.

CAMPBELL JR, Robert S
Van Cott, Bagley, Cornwall & McCarthy, Salt Lake City 801 532 3333
Recommended in Litigation

CLARK, Robert
Parr Waddoups Brown Gee & Loveless, Salt Lake City 801 532 7840
Recommended in Litigation

CLAWSON, Carol
Clawson & Falk LLC, Salt Lake City 801 322 5000
Recommended in Employment

COOK, Rand
Van Cott, Bagley, Cornwall & McCarthy, Salt Lake City 801 532 3333
Recommended in Real Estate

DUNNING, Elizabeth
Holme Roberts & Owen LLP, Salt Lake City 801 521 5800
Recommended in Employment

DURHAM, Matthew
Stoel Rives LLP, Salt Lake City 801 328 3131
Recommended in Employment

ELLISON, Thomas
Stoel Rives LLP, Salt Lake City 801 328 3131
Recommended in Real Estate

ETCHEVERRY, Raymond J
Parsons Behle & Latimer PC, Salt Lake City 801 532 1234
retcheverry@pblutah.com
Recommended in Litigation
Practice Areas: Antitrust, patent, trade secret and other complex business litigation, also insurance coverage disputes.
Prof. Memberships: Fellow, American Bar Foundation. Member, American Bar Association: Litigation Section; Antitrust Section; Intellectual Property Section. Master of the Bench, American Inns of Court II.
Career: President and Chairman of the Board of Directors, Parsons Behle & Latimer, 1992 - present.
Personal: JD, Duke University, 1976. Honors BS, magna cum laude, University of Utah, 1973.

FERRIN, Shawn
Parsons Behle & Latimer PC, Salt Lake City 801 532 1234
Sferrin@pblutah.com
Recommended in Real Estate
Practice Areas: Real property development and financing transactions, with an emphasis on retail and resort development, including land use planning and zoning; and acquisition, development and construction.
Prof. Memberships: American Bar Association: Real Estate and Probate Section. Utah State Bar Association: Real Estate Section.
Career: Shareholder, Chair of the Real Estate & Finance Department, Parsons Behle & Latimer. Board of Trustees and Executive Committee, Economic Development Corporation of Utah. Advisor

to the Governor's Task Force on Economic Development and the Environment.
Personal: JD, University of Utah, 1986. BUS, University of Utah, 1982.

FREDMAN, Stuart
Holme Roberts & Owen LLP, Salt Lake City 801 521 5800
Recommended in Corporate/M&A

GEE, David
Parr Waddoups Brown Gee & Loveless, Salt Lake City 801 532 7840
Recommended in Real Estate

GREENWOOD, David
Bendinger, Crockett, Peterson, Greenwood & Casey, Salt Lake City 801 533 8383
dag@bendinger-crockett.com
Recommended in Litigation
Practice Areas: Mr Greenwood is an experienced trial lawyer who represents clients in complex cases, business disputes, condemnation, construction litigation, and arbitration. He has represented railroads, healthcare facilities, water companies, oil companies, defense contractors, bank and other financial institutions, and pipeline companies.
Prof. Memberships: Mr Greenwood is an Associate of the American Board of Trial Advocates. He is a Fellow of the American College of Trial Lawyers, and a Fellow of the American Bar Foundation.
Career: Admitted to the Utah Bar in 1973.
Personal: Mr Greenwood received his BA with honors from the University of Utah in 1970 and his JD from the University of Chicago in 1973.

GROSS, Jefferson W
Burbidge & Mitchell, Salt Lake City 801 355 6677
jwgross@burbidgeandmitchell.com
Recommended in Litigation
Practice Areas: Trial practice for both plaintiffs and defendants in complex commercial litigation and catastrophic injury. Has experience in a range of disputes, including general business litigation, patent infringement, real estate disputes, securities fraud claims and class action lawsuits.
Personal: JD, University of Southern California (1993); AB (Economics), University of California, Berkeley (1989).

HALEY, George
Holme Roberts & Owen LLP, Salt Lake City 801 521 5800
Recommended in Litigation

HELLEWELL, Read
Kirton & McConkie, Salt Lake City 801 328 3600
Recommended in Real Estate

HOLMES, Ervin
Stoel Rives LLP, Salt Lake City 801 328 3131
Recommended in Real Estate

HUNT, Jeffrey
Parr Waddoups Brown Gee & Loveless, Salt Lake City 801 532 7840
Recommended in Litigation

HYDE, Robert C
Kirton & McConkie, Salt Lake City
801 323 5915
rhyde@kmclaw.com
Recommended in Real Estate
Practice Areas: Robert Hyde specializes in real estate and land use law, as well as real estate lending. He is heavily involved in the representation of developers of commercial real estate properties. He also has a substantial practice in representing mortgage lenders and borrowers.
Career: After graduating from BYU's law school, Robert Hyde practiced from 1979 to 2000 with Parsons Behle & Latimer in Salt Lake City, Utah. After taking a three year leave of absence to serve a mission for his church, he resumed his career with Kirton & McConkie in 2003.

JANOVE, Jathan
Janove Baar Associates, Salt Lake City
801 530 0404
Recommended in Employment

JARDINE, James
Ray, Quinney & Nebeker PC,
Salt Lake City 801 532 1500
Recommended in Litigation

JONES, Cary
Snell & Wilmer LLP, Salt Lake City
801 257 1811
cjones@swlaw.com
Recommended in Real Estate
Practice Areas: Areas of concentration include real estate transactions, focusing in hotel, retail, office and resort development and disposition; office/retail leasing; zoning and land use; partnerships and joint ventures.
Prof. Memberships: Admitted Utah Supreme Court; Supreme Court of Arizona; Utah State Bar, Former Chairman, Real Property Section; American Bar Association.
Career: Representative cases include: lead counsel for Utah Transit Authority on all real estate and land use matters for $200 million acquisition of Union Pacific facilities for 75 mile Wasatch Front Commuter Rail Project.

JORDAN, David
Stoel Rives LLP, Salt Lake City
801 328 3131
Recommended in Litigation

KARRENBERG, Thomas
Anderson & Karrenberg, Salt Lake City
801 534 1700
Recommended in Litigation

KROESCHE, Guy
Stoel Rives LLP, Salt Lake City
801 328 3131
Recommended in Real Estate

LEVIN, Ali
Jones Waldo Holbrook & McDonough PC, Salt Lake City 801 521 3200
alevin@joneswaldo.com
Recommended in Employment
Practice Areas: Counsels employers in all aspects of labor and employment law and represents employers in employment litigation. Negotiates, drafts and litigates employment contracts, confidentiality and non-competition agreements, collective bargaining agreements and severance packages. Provides in-house unlawful harassment training, investigations and drafts employee policies and handbooks. Frequent speaker and contributor on employment law topics. Listed in Utah Business Legal Elite.
Prof. Memberships: Society for Human Resource Management (SHRM).
Career: Admitted to practice in Massachusetts (1997), Colorado (1991) and Utah since 2002.
Personal: University of California Santa Cruz (1992); Northeastern University School of Law (1997).

LINDLEY, Greg
Holland & Hart LLP, Salt Lake City
801 595 7829
glindley@hollandhart.com
Recommended in Corporate/M&A
Practice Areas: Corporate law, securities law, mergers and acquisitions, and franchise law. Mr Lindley has represented numerous companies with their bank financings, joint ventures and strategic alliances, distributorship and licensing agreements, and general contractual matters. He has worked on numerous public and private offerings of securities for a wide variety of clients. He also represents public companies in the compliance work required by the Securities and Exchange Act of 1934, including the preparation of Forms 10-K, 10-Q, and 8-K and proxy statements, and the Sarbanes-Oxley Act. He has represented both buyers and sellers in many mergers and acquisitions in a variety of industries, including food manufacture and distribution, banking, printing and publishing, insurance, mine drill bit manufacturing and servicing, and medical diagnostics. Mr Lindley has also counseled many companies with organizational, executive compensation, and fundraising issues.
Prof. Memberships: Utah State Bar and the State Bar of Texas.
Career: Admitted to Utah Bar (1988) and Texas Bar (1983).
Personal: Received a JD from Duke University (1983), an MBA (1981) and a BS (1978) from Utah State University.

LINDQUIST, Shawn J
Wilson Sonsini Goodrich & Rosati, Salt Lake City 801 993 6400
slindquist@wsgr.com
Recommended in Corporate/M&A
Practice Areas: Specializes in the corporate representation of growth compa-

nies, underwriters, and venture capital firms and other investors in the Intermountain West. Principal experience has been in matters such as public offerings of securities, mergers and acquisitions, and private equity and debt financings.
Prof. Memberships: Admitted to practice in California, Washington and Utah. Member, ABA (Business Law Section). Member, Utah/Silicon Valley Alliance (Legal and Banking and Venture Capital Committees).
Career: WSGR Associate. Former Vice President and General Counsel of Whizbang! Labs, Inc.
Personal: JD, 1997, and BS, 1994, Brigham Young University.

LITTLE, David
Holme Roberts & Owen LLP,
Salt Lake City 801 521 5800
Recommended in Corporate/M&A

LLOYD, Brian
Stoel Rives LLP, Salt Lake City
801 328 3131
Recommended in Corporate/M&A

LOVELESS, Scott
Parr Waddoups Brown Gee & Loveless,
Salt Lake City 801 532 7840
Recommended in Corporate/M&A

MAAK, Charles
Parr Waddoups Brown Gee & Loveless,
Salt Lake City 801 532 7840
Recommended in Real Estate

MANGUM, Geoffrey W
Parsons Behle & Latimer PC,
Salt Lake City 801 532 1234
Gmangum@pblutah.com
Recommended in Corporate/M&A
Practice Areas: Corporate and commercial real estate, with an emphasis on negotiating and structuring complex business transactions, including mergers and acquisitions, joint ventures and commercial real estate financing arrangements. Also has extensive experience on co-branding identity issues, including co-branded credit and loyalty card programs.
Prof. Memberships: Utah State Bar Association; American Bar Association.
Career: Currently, shareholder and Chair of Corporate and Tax Department, Parsons Behle & Latimer; 1996-99: Vice President of Corporate Transactions for American Stores Company; 1979-99: Associate and shareholder, Prince Yeates & Geldzahler.
Personal: JD, Georgetown University Law Center, 1979. BA, magna cum laude, University of Utah, 1976.

MOFFITT, Ronald
Stoel Rives LLP, Salt Lake City
801 328 3131
Recommended in Corporate/M&A

MOORE, Larry
Ray, Quinney & Nebeker PC,
Salt Lake City 801 532 1500
Recommended in Real Estate

O'BRIEN, Michael
Jones Waldo Holbrook & McDonough PC, Salt Lake City 801 521 3200
mobrien@joneswaldo.com
Recommended in Employment
Practice Areas: Practice includes counseling businesses and employers on how to minimize and manage risks in all aspects of labor and employment law and representing employers in employment-related litigation. Has extensive experience assisting news and publishing organizations in obtaining access to places and records, and in minimizing risks and responding to claims of defamation, invasion of privacy, tort and other matters related to publishing. Serves as an arbitrator and mediator in employment law disputes. Utah Employment Lawyer of the Year. Listed in Utah Business Legal Elite.
Prof. Memberships: Works with the local and national Society for Human Resource Management (SHRM) and serves as the legal and legislative director for Utah SHRM and Salt Lake SHRM.
Career: Practicing in Utah since 1986. Chair of Litigation Department and Employment Group.
Personal: University of Notre Dame (1983); University of Utah College of Law (1986).

O'CONNOR, Robert
Wilson Sonsini Goodrich & Rosati,
Salt Lake City 801 993 6400
roconnor@wsgr.com
Recommended in Corporate/M&A
Practice Areas: Focuses on advising technology and growth companies, organizing and capitalizing businesses, raising capital through private and public debt and equity financings, and buying/selling companies and technologies. Also represents a number of venture capital investors in connection with investments in their portfolio companies.
Prof. Memberships: Admitted to practice in California and Utah. Member, Westminster College's Technology Commercialization and Entrepreneurship Program Advisory Board. Member, Utah Information Technology Association Board of Trustees. Director, Utah Life Science Association.
Career: Managing Partner, Salt Lake City Office. Became Partner, 2002.
Personal: JD, 1993, Loyola Law School; BA, 1990, University of California (Los Angeles).

POELMAN, Ronald
Jones Waldo Holbrook & McDonough PC, Salt Lake City 801 521 3200
Recommended in Corporate/M&A

ROWE, Keven
Jones Waldo Holbrook & McDonough PC, Salt Lake City 801 521 3200
krowe@joneswaldo.com
Recommended in Real Estate
Practice Areas: Partner and Head of the firm's Real Estate Finance Group and practices in the areas of complex

real estate and asset based lending for institutional and governmental clients, including construction, permanent and securitized financings, complex real estate transactions including shopping center, apartment, residential and resort developments (including negotiation of acquisition documents, leases, development agreements and restrictive covenants), office and commercial building acquisition and leasing. Also handles business acquisitions and divestures involving real estate and non-real estate assets.
Prof. Memberships: ICSC, NAIOP.
Career: Admitted to practice in the State of Utah, Jones, Waldo, Holbrook & McDonough, P.C.; Partner, 1986-present; President, 2003; Executive Committee Member, 1996-2003.
Personal: University of Utah (JD, 1986, Order of the Coif, William H Leary Scholar), University of Utah (BA, 1983).

RUBINFELD, Ira
Ray, Quinney & Nebeker PC,
Salt Lake City 801 532 1500
Recommended in Real Estate

RUDD, David R
Ballard Spahr Andrews & Ingersoll LLP,
Salt Lake City 801 517 6829
ruddd@ballardspahr.com
Recommended in Corporate/M&A
Practice Areas: He practices exclusively in the area of complex domestic and international business transactions in a wide variety of legal fields and industrial sectors.
Prof. Memberships: Member, US Senator Orrin G. Hatch's Trade Advisory Group, advising on NAFTA and GATT; Co-Chair, International Special Interest Group, Utah Information Technology Association; Member, Utah Life Sciences Association; Chairman ex officio, board of trustees of the Mexico Utah Business Council; Member, State of Utah Securities Advisory Committee; Officer, Mountain West Venture Group; Past Chairman, Utah State Bar Business Law Section; Member, American Bar Association, Inter-American Bar Association,

Utah State Bar Association, and District of Columbia Bar Association.
Career: Admitted to the Utah Bar (1982); admitted to the District of Columbia Bar (1989); joined as Partner (2001).
Personal: JD, Pepperdine University School of Law (1982); BA, Brigham Young University (1979).

SMITH, Janet
Ray, Quinney & Nebeker PC,
Salt Lake City 801 532 1500
Recommended in Employment

STEVENSON, Brent
Parr Waddoups Brown Gee & Loveless,
Salt Lake City 801 532 7840
Recommended in Corporate/M&A

SULLIVAN, Alan
Snell & Wilmer LLP, Salt Lake City
801 257 1955
asullivan@swlaw.com
Recommended in Litigation
Practice Areas: Representation of clients in litigation relating to healthcare, intellectual property, natural resources development, manufacturing, and finance. Frequent representation of lawyers and law firms in relation to ethical issues pending before courts and disciplinary boards.
Prof. Memberships: American College of Trial Lawyers (Fellow 1996-present, State Chair 2000-02); American Bar Foundation (Fellow 1998-present); Utah Constitutional Revision Commission; Salt Lake County Bar Association (Past President).

TAYLOR, Nolan
Dorsey & Whitney LLP, Salt Lake City
801 933 7360
Recommended in Corporate/M&A

TAYLOR, Tom
Holme Roberts & Owen LLP,
Salt Lake City 801 521 5800
Recommended in Corporate/M&A

TOPHAM, Reed
Stoel Rives LLP, Salt Lake City
801 328 3131
Recommended in Corporate/M&A

WADDOUPS, Clark
Parr Waddoups Brown Gee & Loveless,
Salt Lake City 801 532 7840
Recommended in Litigation

WESTON, John
Snell & Wilmer LLP, Salt Lake City
801 257 1931
jweston@swlaw.com
Recommended in Corporate/M&A
Practice Areas: Areas of concentration include securities regulation, private placements, public offerings, mergers, acquisitions, consolidations, joint ventures and partnerships, commercial loans and other financings, venture capital financing, and general corporate law.
Prof. Memberships: Utah State Bar Association; California State Bar Association; American Bar Association.
Career: Partner, Snell & Wilmer L.L.P., Salt Lake City, Utah; Associate, Andrews and Kurth, L.L.P., Los Angeles, California (1995-96).

WIKSTROM, Francis M
Parsons Behle & Latimer PC,
Salt Lake City 801 532 1234
Fwikstrom@pblutah.com
Recommended in Litigation
Practice Areas: Complex civil litigation, white collar criminal defense, environmental and intellectual property litigation.
Prof. Memberships: Fellow, American College of Trial Lawyers. International Association of Defense Counsel. Fellow, American Bar Foundation (State Chair). National Association of Former US Attorneys. Chair, Utah Supreme Court Advisory Committee on the Rules of Civil Procedure. Utah Representative, Tenth Circuit Advisory Committee (1997-2004). Program Chair, 2004 Tenth Circuit Judicial Conference. Master of the Bench, American Inns of Court II.
Career: Shareholder, Parsons Behle & Latimer since 1981. Former US Attorney and Assistant US Attorney.
Personal: JD, Yale University, 1974. BS, Weber State College, 1971.

WILLIAMS, Gregory
Van Cott, Bagley, Cornwall & McCarthy,
Salt Lake City 801 532 3333
Recommended in Real Estate

WILSON, Randon
Jones Waldo Holbrook & McDonough
PC, Salt Lake City 801 521 3200
Recommended in Corporate/M&A

WINGER, Gary
Ray, Quinney & Nebeker PC,
Salt Lake City 801 532 1500
Recommended in Corporate/M&A

YOUNG, Howard
Jones Waldo Holbrook & McDonough
PC, Salt Lake City 801 521 3200
Recommended in Corporate/M&A

ZODY, Michael A
Parsons Behle & Latimer PC,
Salt Lake City 801 532 1234
Mzody@pblutah.com
Recommended in Employment
Practice Areas: Environmental litigation, including defense of civil and criminal enforcement actions, citizens' suits, landfill litigation, environmental disputes arising from the sale of land and CERCLA cases. Employment law, including ADA (also public accommodation/access barrier cases), ADEA, Title VII, Fair Housing, employment contracts (including non-compete clauses) and OSHA. Whistleblower/retaliation cases, including environmental and Sarbanes-Oxley whistleblower cases.
Prof. Memberships: American Bar Association: Natural Resources, Energy and Environmental Law Section; Tort Trial and Insurance Practice Section, Toxic Torts and Environmental Law Committee; Employment Law Section.
Career: Shareholder, Parsons Behle & Latimer.
Personal: JD, cum laude, Indiana University, 1990. BA, Purdue University, 1987.

BENDINGER, CROCKETT, PETERSON, GREENWOOD & CASEY

THE FIRM

Managing Partner: David A Greenwood
Number of partners: 10
Number of other lawyers: 12

HEAD OFFICE

UTAH
170 South Main Street, Suite 400, **Salt Lake City**, UT 84101
Tel: 801 533 8383   **Fax:** 801 531 1486
Website: www.bendinger-crockett.com

FIRM OVERVIEW: The firm's practice is principally in complex business litigation, where it has achieved a national reputation in the fields of securities and antitrust law, including recognition as one of the top 20 trial firms in the nation in these fields. It has litigated throughout the United States involving a wide range of issues. The firm's present practice covers a broad range of matters, including antitrust, securities fraud, patent and trademark infringement, employment discrimination, contract matters, and other complex commercial litigation. Unlike many similarly prominent firms, it does not formally segregate its attorneys according to practice area. While it does have experts in various fields of law, much of the firm's success derives from a combination of deep knowledge, litigation experience, and experience with innovative approaches taken from other disciplines.

In a world where good law firms compete for business based on the intangibles of reputation, experience, and affinity for the work, standing out is often hard to do. But not for Bendinger, Crockett, Peterson, Greenwood & Casey.

It is small by design. Bendinger, Crockett, Peterson, Greenwood & Casey's 22 trial lawyers are as gifted and motivated as they come. This focus on quality of both people and work has meant that over the last 30 years the firm's record puts it in a very small and exclusive league.

It understands both sides of litigation. The firm started in the 1970s doing plaintiff's antitrust work. By the early 1980s, its understanding of these cases meant that it was well-prepared to take on significant defense-side work. It has also developed a national practice in securities litigation in addition to its antitrust and commercial litigation. The firm remains committed to representing plaintiffs in significant litigation, including antitrust and securities matters. This combination makes it unique in Utah and among a select few firms in the United States.

It has reach. The firm's home is Utah, where it takes on major litigation. It served as counsel to the State of Utah in litigation against the major tobacco companies, and it is currently involved in two of the most significant cases in Utah: litigation between the owners of the only two daily newspapers in Utah; and an antitrust action brought against one of its clients, the largest healthcare provider in the State of Utah. The firm's practice is focused on national matters, as well. While the lawyers relish living in Utah, they work with clients in Los Angeles, New York, and throughout the country. Whether the firm is defending one of the large national accounting firms, pursuing substantial recoveries on behalf of plaintiffs, or working with major companies in the mid-west, its lawyers are on the ground and actively engaged with clients - wherever they may be.

It has talent. Aside from the usual cohort of judicial clerks, law review and journal editors, and community leaders, Bendinger Crockett has four fellows of the American College of Trial Lawyers, a Fellow of the International Society of Barristers, an Associate of the American Board of Trial Advocates, and three of its shareholders are consistently included in 'The Best Lawyers in America.' Not only does the firm recruit and hire the best talent; it seems to gravitate to them.

CLIENTS: Allstate Insurance Company; Better Business Bureau of Utah; Bridgestone Firestone; Comdata Network, Inc.; Deloitte & Touche; E & H Investments; Farmers Insurance Co.; Fedex Freight West, Inc.; Intermountain Health Care; International Union of Police Associations; Kern River Gas Transmission Company; KPMG, LLP; Lockheed Martin; Motor Cargo; Prows, Becknell & Alles; Salt Lake Tribune Publishing Company, LLC; Siemens Medical Solutions; Terrabrook; Texaco; The Bionetics Corp.; Union Pacific; Wilson Davis.

The firm has successfully represented:

Various national accounting firms in federal securities litigation in eight states; Coca Cola Company, Kraft, Intermountain Health Care (IHC) and CBS, Inc. in antitrust cases; the Polaroid Corporation in government procurement litigation; the Denver & Rio Grande Western Railroad in its effort to recover the costs of rebuilding rail lines and tunnels on its main track following a $60 million landslide; antitrust action in Florida involving alleged price fixing on infant formula, which was settled in 1993 for a publicly-reported amount exceeding $230 million; Sears/Dean Witter in a nationally significant antitrust dispute with VISA over VISA membership rights; Nestle Food Company in a major antitrust action in California federal court; major grocery chains, including Safeway, A&P, Kroger, Albertson's, The Vons, Fred Meyer, and five others in one of the largest and most complex lawsuits in the country against the major pharmaceutical drug manufacturers for violations of the Robinson-Patman Act and Sherman Act; the Plaintiffs' Class in the Commercial Explosives Antitrust Litigation that recovered more than $70 million for the class; and major corporations such as the Union Pacific Railroad in property and sales and use tax matters; pipeline companies in mass condemnations and defense contractors in major litigation.

BURBIDGE & MITCHELL

THE FIRM

Managing Partner: Richard D Burbidge
Number of partners: 3
Number of other lawyers: 3

FIRM OVERVIEW: Since its founding in 1976, Burbidge & Mitchell has emphasized excellence in litigation and trial practice. The firm's consistent success in all phases of litigation and trial practice is founded on the philosophy that the best results for its clients are achieved by thoroughly assessing and preparing each case as though it were going to be tried. The activities of the firm are strategically and purposefully directed to achieve maximum result and value for its clients. The firm has successfully applied its extensive litigation and trial experience in a wide range of complex business disputes, including contract, antitrust, securities, intellectual property and class action litigation. Small by design, the firm has the talent and flexibility to direct the considerable energies of its trial attorneys and experienced staff to quickly and efficiently respond to the needs of its clients. Although based in Utah, the firm includes attorneys licensed to practice in California and has experience in federal and state courts throughout the United States.

MAIN AREAS OF PRACTICE:

Trial Practice: Litigation and trial practice are hallmarks of the firm. Unlike some law firms devoted to commercial litigation, the firm's lawyers have extensive trial experience. This experience translates into an ability to analyze, create and employ intelligent trial strategies and assess risks and potential benefits of trial. By virtue of its reputation and experience in the trial setting, the firm has represented national and local commercial interests and individuals in a wide range of complex litigation. In addition to commercial litigation, the firm has extensive experience in the prosecution and defense of catastrophic personal injury and product liability claims.

Antitrust Litigation: Clients interested in protecting and advancing their competitive positions in the marketplace will find that the firm provides litigation support in areas such as antitrust and competition law. The firm most recently succeeded in securing dismissal of antitrust claims against an automotive industry association.

Securities & Corporate Litigation: The firm offers its corporate and individual clients representation on issues related to securities and corporate governance, including securities fraud and shareholder derivative claims.

Intellectual Property Litigation: The firm is committed to protecting its clients' intellectual property resources. The firm recently recovered $31 million for a client on a jury verdict in a patent infringement case (which was affirmed by the Federal Circuit) involving medical products. In addition to its Patent Litigation Practice, the firm also represents clients in copyright, trademark and unfair competition issues. Firm lawyers have degrees in engineering and information technology.

Class Actions & Mass Torts: The firm has extensive experience in class actions, in both state and federal courts. Corporate clients and their employees can rely on the firm's experience in prosecuting and defending national and local class actions.

Banking Litigation: The firm represents state, national and foreign commercial banks in litigation and trial practice, including protection of security assets, defense and prosecution of claims, and complex foreclosure disputes.

Real Estate Litigation: The firm has successfully represented corporate and individual clients in cases involving commercial, industrial and residential real estate disputes related to transactions, lease agreements, boundary disputes, and destruction of property.

HEAD OFFICE

UTAH
215 South State Street, Suite 920, **Salt Lake City**, UT 84111
Tel: 801 355 6677   **Fax:** 801 355 2341
Email: rburbidge@burbidgeandmitchell.com
Website: www.burbidgeandmitchell.com

CONTACTS

Antitrust Litigation ....Richard D Burbidge, Jefferson W Gross
Banking & Real Estate Litigation ....Stephen B Mitchell
General Litigation & Trial Practice ......Richard D Burbidge, Jefferson W Gross
Class Action & Mass Torts ....Richard D Burbidge
Securities & Corporate Litigation .... Jefferson W Gross
Intellectual Property Litigation ....Richard D Burbidge

CLIENTS: The firm's clients include emerging businesses and established corporations, corporate executives and directors, public and governmental entities, entrepreneurs, and individuals. Burbidge & Mitchell represents clients in a broad range of businesses and industries, including energy, healthcare, medicine and medical products, computers and information technology, telecommunications, real estate, manufacturing, banking and finance. References are available upon request.

BURBIDGE & MITCHELL
TRIAL ATTORNEYS

KIRTON & McCONKIE

THE FIRM

President: Berne S Broadbent
Vice President: Lorin C Barker
Secretary/Treasurer: William A Meaders

HEAD OFFICE

UTAH
60 East South Temple, Suite 1800, **Salt Lake City**, UT 84111
Tel: 801 328 3600   **Fax:** 801 321 4893
Website: www.kmclaw.com

FIRM OVERVIEW: Kirton & McConkie's 80 plus attorneys provide proven expertise and practical experience in a broad spectrum of legal services in essential practice areas including real estate, finance, business taxation, intellectual property, international law, business litigation, immigration, employment, bankruptcy, appellate work and healthcare. Since being founded in 1964, Kirton & McConkie's client base has permitted it to develop extensive worldwide contacts and expertise as reflected in the firm's slogan of having 'local roots' and a 'global reach'. Many of the firm's lawyers have practiced and/or lived throughout the world, including lawyers native to China, Japan, and Mexico. In addition, the lawyers of Kirton & McConkie collectively speak 21 languages. Kirton & McConkie is recognized as one of the "preeminent law firms" in the nation by the prestigious Bar Register and is the recipient of the highest rating for professional and ethical standards by Martindale-Hubbell. The experience of the attorneys permits the firm to meet the needs of its clients, whether a complex, multifaceted entity, a smaller entrepreneurial company, or an individual.

MAIN AREAS OF PRACTICE:

Real Property & Land Use Development: Kirton & McConkie's broad real estate experience includes acquisition and disposition, financing, development, commercial leasing, entitlement, zoning and land use planning and management of real property. The firm's Real Estate Section is one of the largest in the state of Utah and its client base includes the largest and second largest commercial mortgage brokers in Utah, leading real estate development and ownership firms, several life insurance companies, and the largest independent supermarket chain in the west.

Intellectual Property: Kirton & McConkie's intellectual property lawyers are all registered patent attorneys and constitute the largest intellectual property section in Utah for a general practice firm. The firm represents clients ranging from start-ups to large international entities with intellectual property interests in over one hundred countries. Clients such as The Olympic Organizing Committee, Fanny May Chocolates and other such clients owning long-established trademarks have turned to Kirton & McConkie to protect their valuable assets.

Corporate & Taxation: The firm's Corporate and Tax Section has experience in mergers and acquisitions, entity formation and governance for all types of entities. This practice group also assists clients with tax planning, tax controversies, personal tax, estate planning, wills, charitable donations, IRS representation, retirement plans, and administrative practice benefits.

Business Litigation: The firm's Business Litigation Section represents a variety of clients ranging from Fortune 100 companies to individuals with complex problems requiring alternative dispute resolution, litigation and related appeals in federal and state courts. The firm's attorneys have experience in the following types of cases: business tort, construction, shareholder derivative, lender liability, securities, healthcare, environmental, labor and employment, creditor rights, qui tam and constitutional claims.

Constitution, Appellate & Religious: With one of its largest clients being a prominent religious organization, the firm has extensive experience in First Amendment and other constitutional issues, trial and appellate litigation, amicus briefs, and legislative services.

Risk Management: The firm's services include insurance defense litigation, construction defects, tort claims, malpractice, automobile accidents, commercial liability, PIP claims, declaratory actions, and statements under oath. The firm also offers coverage opinions, coverage analysis, and alternative dispute resolution.

Construction & Surety Bonds: The firm offers expert legal assistance on every phase of construction from the initial concept and design through post-substantial completion matters. It is regularly involved with many aspects of contractor defaults, claims defense, indemnity/salvage, license and other bonds. The firm expeditiously resolves payment bond claims and successfully mediates, arbitrates, and litigates various construction disputes, including Miller Act, Little Miller Act, and claims for bad faith. The firm has drafted construction contracts for worldwide use and for many of the major buildings in downtown Salt Lake City. The firm advises clients on construction issues in all 50 states, most Canadian provinces, Europe, Asia, Latin America, and Africa.

Healthcare & Risk Management: For over three decades, Kirton & McConkie has provided a broad range of healthcare related services, including risk management, quality assurance, medical malpractice defense, corporate and financial issues, Medicare/Medicaid representation, bioethical legal issues, consent policies and procedures, death and dying, taxation and emergency medicine.

Immigration: The firm handles the full spectrum of immigration cases including employment and family based immigration, asylum, naturalization, compliance, employer sanctions, removal defense and all nonimmigrant matters, such as issuance of visas and changes of status.

Employment: The firm's Employment Section has broad experience with federal and state employment matters including compensation, liability, audits, agreements, training procedures, claims, and litigation.

CLIENTS: 3Com; Morinda, Inc.; Ogio; Cephalon, Inc.; Sharp Labs, Inc.; Xactware, Inc.; In2M Corporation; The Church of Jesus Christ of Latter-day Saints; Property Reserve, Inc.; Brigham Young University; University of Utah; General Growth Properties; Bonneville Mortgage Co.; Johanson Thackeray Real Estate Commercial Services; International Development Group/Affordable Housing Partners; Jiangsu Easthigh International Group; and Zions Securities Corp.

INTERNATIONAL WORK: The firm represents not only local clients doing business abroad, but also works for a variety of non-foreign and foreign clients with activities throughout the United States. The firm can help determine the optimal structure for international transactions, including technology transfers, licensing arrangements, joint ventures, manufacturing contracts and distribution agreements, acquisitions and joint ventures. The firm works closely with an established network of law firms and legal professionals in all 50 states and throughout the world as it represents one of the nation's largest multinational corporations. Kirton & McConkie can leverage this worldwide relationship to assist clients in selecting local counsel.

PARSONS BEHLE & LATIMER

THE FIRM

Chairman: Raymond J Etcheverry
Senior Shareholder: James B Lee
Number of shareholders: 75
Number of other lawyers: 28

AREAS OF PRACTICE:

Litigation 50%
Environmental – Natural Resources 30%
Corporate, Tax & Technology 20%

FIRM OVERVIEW: Parsons Behle & Latimer was founded in 1882 and is one of the oldest and best known law firms offering litigation and business law services in the intermountain region. The firm's first clients were in the business of mining - one of the major industries that helped fuel the growth of the area. Over time, its reputation and client base has grown with the dynamic intermountain region. The firm offers clients the resources and capabilities of a large and diverse firm, coupled with the highest levels of accessibility and responsiveness. With over 100 attorneys, it brings a depth and range of experience to six major practice areas: litigation; environmental, energy and natural resources; corporate and tax; intellectual property and technology; real estate, banking and finance; and employment. Within those practice areas, attorneys focus on selected industries, legislative or regulatory issues or specific transactional processes. Parsons Behle & Latimer are dedicated to offering a complete range of litigation and business services to all types of industries. Responsiveness to clients' needs has been the long-standing commitment of the firm. Its approach is creative and preventive; it strives to anticipate and resolve clients' legal problems as promptly and efficiently as possible.

MAIN AREAS OF PRACTICE:

Litigation: The firm has one of the largest litigation departments in the Intermountain West. Its trial lawyers take an interdisciplinary approach. They assemble appropriate teams for each client need, allowing them to address a client's concerns in the most efficient manner possible. And, it gives clients the benefits of multiple, informed viewpoints based on years of business acumen. They practice before federal and state courts, administrative agencies, and arbitration panels. Representative areas of trial practice are: commercial litigation, natural resources and environmental, intellectual property and antitrust, banking, insolvency, personal injury, products liability, mass media and white collar criminal law.

Employment: The firm's Labor and Employment Law Practice is the broadest and most extensive in Utah. Many of its attorneys practice exclusively in the labor and employment area and a number of others devote a portion of their practice to individual matters. Areas of representation include wrongful discharge and discrimination, sexual harassment, employee benefits and ERISA, workers' compensation, OSHA and MSHA, immigration and National Labor Relations Act.

Intellectual Property & Technology: The Intellectual Property and Technology Department is a team of attorneys, patent agents and paralegals who represent the firm's clients in all aspects of intellectual property, technology and computer law, including: representation before the Patent and Trademark Office and the Copyright Office; litigation in state and federal courts throughout the country; contract and other transactional matters; and international intellectual property protection and licensing.

Corporate & Tax: Members of the firm's Corporate & Tax Department regularly participate in the negotiation and documentation of complex business transactions furnishing timely advice about securities, tax, natural resources, employment law and other issues. A significant percentage of the department's work involves international transactions. The firm regularly advises clients concerning business, corporate and securities, tax, international business, regulatory and administrative, energy and government relations.

HEAD OFFICE

UTAH
201 South Main Street Suite 1800, **Salt Lake City**, UT 84111
Tel: 801 532 1234 **Fax:** 801536 6111
Email: webmaster@parsonsbehlelaw.com
Website:www.parsonsbehlelaw.com

BRANCH OFFICES

NEVADA
One East Liberty Street, Sixth Floor, **Reno**, NV 89504
Tel: 775 686 6686 **Fax:** 775 686 6066

UTAH
333 South 520 West, Suite 220, **Lindon,** UT 84042
Tel: 801 805 3920 **Fax:** 801 852 0392

CONTACTS

Chairman . . . . .Raymond J Etcheverry (SLC)
Litigation . . . . .Michael L Larsen (SLC)
Corporate & Tax . . . . .Geoffrey W Mangum (SLC)
Technology . . . . .Daniel P McCarthy (SLC)
Employment . . . . .David A Anderson (SLC)
Environmental, Energy & Natural Resources Michael J Malmquist (SLC)
Real Estate & Finance . . . . .Shawn C Ferrin (SLC)
Retail . . . . .Hal J Pos (SLC)
Mining . . . . .Michael J Malmquist (SLC)
Media . . . . .Randy Dryer (SLC)
Energy & Telecommunications .Robert Reeder (SLC)
Sports . . . . .R Craig Johnson (SLC)

Real Estate & Finance: These department members represent commercial banks, savings and loans, mortgage companies, and other financial institutions. They also handle all aspects of real estate transactions, including acquisition, finance, development, condominium and PUD documentation, and zoning and land use regulations.

Environmental, Energy & Natural Resources: Parsons Behle & Latimer has one of the largest environmental, energy and natural resources practices in the western United States. Over 20 attorneys, many with state and federal regulatory agency backgrounds, including employment with the US Environmental Protection Agency; US Department of Justice; the President's Council on Environmental Quality, and the Utah Department of Natural Resources advise corporate and individual clients on all aspects of environmental, energy and natural resources law. The practice is national and international in scope with particular emphasis on the western United States and Latin America. Areas of practice include mining, oil and gas, water rights, public lands, energy and electrical power, air and water quality, hazardous waste, Superfund and Brownfields, and occupational issues. In these and other areas we advise and assist clients with transactions and finance, project development and closure, property acquisition and title, permitting, compliance, enforcement, cost recovery, rate cases, litigation, rulemakings and legislation.

INTERNATIONAL WORK: Parsons Behle & Latimer maintains an active and varied practice internationally, in particular in Latin America. Over the years it has assembled appropriate teams of attorneys and paralegals who have worked on a wide range of legal and business matters often while working on site in Bolivia, Chile, Colombia, Peru and Venezuela.

Parsons
Behle &
Latimer®

A PROFESSIONAL
LAW CORPORATION

CONTENTS: Corporate/M&A p.1743; Employment p.1744; Litigation p.1745; Real Estate p.1747; Individuals' Profiles p.1748.

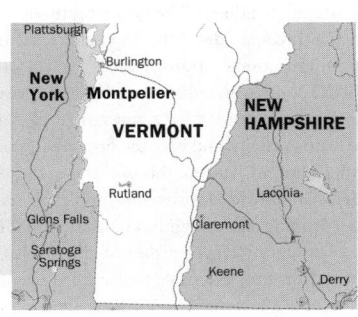

How lawyers are ranked

The opinions we gather from clients — mainly from in-house lawyers but also from other purchasers of legal services — are balanced by opinions from colleagues and competitors. Together, they provide two different perspectives — an all-round view — and biased viewpoints cancel each other out.

CORPORATE/M&A

Vermont
Leading firms (Corporate/M&A)

[1] **DINSE, KNAPP & MCANDREW PC** *Burlington*
DOWNS RACHLIN MARTIN PLLC *Burlington*
GRAVEL AND SHEA *Burlington*

[2] **EGGLESTON & CRAMER, LTD** *Burlington*
PAUL, FRANK + COLLINS *Burlington*
PRIMMER & PIPER, *Burlington*
SHEEHEY FURLONG & BEHM PC *Burlington*

Leading individuals (Corporate/M&A)

[1] **BOE Kathleen** *Eggleston & Cramer, Burlington*
FRYE B Michael *Paul Frank, Burlington*
KNAPP Spencer *Dinse Knapp, Burlington*
MCCONAUGHY Stewart *Gravel and Shea, Burlington*
ODE Paul *Downs Rachlin, Burlington*

[2] **EGGLESTON Jon** *Eggleston & Cramer, Burlington*
ERLY Peter *Gravel and Shea, Burlington*
GANNON Christopher *Sheehey Furlong, Burlington*
HAEFNER Gail *Paul Frank, Burlington*
MCMAHAN Jeffrey *Dinse Knapp, Burlington*
MONTGOMERY Margaret *Gravel and Shea, Burlington*
MOODY Thomas *Downs Rachlin, Burlington*
MURPHY Brian *Dinse Knapp, Burlington*
PORT Alan *Paul Frank, Burlington*

Firms and individuals are listed alphabetically in each band.

Band 1

Dinse, Knapp & McAndrew PC
The Firm: This firm received extensive praise from interviewees who recommended the practice for a top ranking. It is home to "*experienced and knowledgeable lawyers who are very helpful and a pleasure to work with*," clients report. The firm has a stellar reputation in the healthcare field and advised on a $350 million refinancing of a medical center in 2004. It continues to advise the well-known teaching college Fletcher Allen Health Care on all its general corporate and operational matters. Other strengths lie in the manufacturing, real estate and hi-tech sectors. The firm's corporate deal load typically includes financings, restructurings and equity agreements.

The Lawyers: "*A creative thinker and a plain gentleman,*" **Spencer Knapp** is the firm's best-known corporate adviser. Clients benefit from his ability to "*bring very complex matters to simple conclusions*" and also note his network of excellent contacts. Knapp continues to act as general counsel for Fletcher Allen Health Care. "*Detail-oriented*" **Jeffrey McMahan** was highly recommended for his work on tax-related matters. Clients describe him as a "*personable lawyer who is knowledgeable about the deal in hand.*" Making up the trio of well-regarded practitioners, **Brian Murphy** is viewed as "*creative and service-oriented — he always provides valuable advice,*" clients say.

The Clients: High-profile clients include Vermont Teddy Bear. The firm also acts for hospitals and colleges.

Downs Rachlin Martin PLLC
The Firm: The largest firm in Vermont boasts "*extremely smart and focused practitioners,*" according to interviewees. It is well equipped to handle a full range of major corporate transactions. The firm received particular praise for its IP-related work, which spans patent, trademark and licensing matters. Other typical instructions include acting for corporates on MBOs, recapitalizations and reorganizations. The team regularly assists clients with the structuring of financial proposals for presentation to bodies such as the Vermont Economic Development Authority.

The Lawyers: "*Tireless and devoted*" **Paul Ode** won praise from peers and clients alike as a player at the top of his game. Sources were particularly complimentary about his deliberate and thorough approach: "*He thinks everything through, doesn't rush things and has a nice, non-confrontational style.*" The chair of the firm's business law group, he enjoys a broad transactional practice. **Thomas Moody** also picked up recommendations as "*a younger, energetic and capable lawyer.*" Moody heads up the firm's venture capital group.

The Clients: Ridgewood Capital; Rural Cellular; Mass. Bay Brewing; Marlboro College; Vermont Gas System and Crown Castle International.

Gravel and Shea
The Firm: This well-established firm has an excellent reputation and is often seen to represent large local businesses and private investment funds. The firm's financing practice is thriving. It acts for both lenders and borrowers in matters involving limited partnerships, limited liability company interests and the issuance of equity securities. On the M&A front the firm acted on a number of transactions with tax structuring implications for a range of nationwide companies.

The Lawyers: **Stewart McConaughy** is relied upon for his "*tremendous analytical skill*" and his "*good business head.*" He is particularly experienced in bank financing work: "*When you have Stewart on your side there is no need for an educational process — he knows exactly what he is doing,*" sources said. Clients were equally quick to compliment **Peter Erly**, describing him as a "*systematic and technically strong professional.*" This plain-speaking adviser is especially well versed in the securities arena. Continuing in the firm's mold of "*bright and efficient*" advisers **Margaret Montgomery** is noted for her expertise in acquisitions and financings. Her large client base consists of Internet businesses and cable companies.

The Clients: Champlain Oil; VELCO; IBM and Merchants Bank.

Band 2

Eggleston & Cramer Ltd
The Firm: This firm advises a wide range of small to midsized clients drawn from various industry sectors including banking, healthcare, hospitality and real estate. It is increasingly

involved with the nonprofit sector and also represents public utilities. The firm recently closed a major three-part deal – the disposal of Citizens Communication's transmission assets to VELCO. Work with internationally active clients has always accounted for a substantial part of the team's activity, and here the firm advises on both inbound and outbound transactions. Clients are provided with a one-stop-shop service spanning tax, immigration, customs and IP.

The Lawyers: *"Highly dedicated and focused,"* **Kathy Boe** won extensive praise from clients who said: *"She never leaves a stone unturned."* Particular strengths include estate planning, small business planning and bank financings especially for low-income housing projects. Although he has been less visible in the past year, **Jon Eggleston** remains a major influence at the firm and one of the regions best-known corporate lawyers.

The Clients: Vermont Association of Hospitals and Health Systems; Porter Medical Center; Central Vermont Medical Center and Northeastern Vermont Regional Hospital.

Paul, Frank + Collins, A Professional Corporation

The Firm: One of the top corporate players in Vermont, the firm has developed close contacts with Canadian firms and a leading practice for foreign business formation in the state. The firm's experience includes all matters concerning the formation of new corporations, limited liability companies and partnerships. It also provides immigration advice to support its interna-

tional practice. When it comes to transactional work, the firm approaches client's projects according to their individual needs by working on a cross-departmental basis. The team has recently been involved in the sale of three companies and a merger between two regional pension funds. Other notable areas of expertise include franchising and licensing, advice on federal and state taxes and international law.

The Lawyers: The *"methodical and detail-oriented"* **Michael Frye** won client praise for his *"professional demeanor and well-tailored advice."* A top corporate lawyer, he is particularly skilled in financing issues, including financial restructurings. A strong deal-maker, **Gail Haefner** regularly acts on the firm's flagstone transactions. Clients say: *"She always meets her commitments on time and takes the right measures for the problem in hand."* Recent highlights include the complete overhaul of Systems & Software's client contracts. President of the firm, **Alan Port** is a recognized specialist in captive insurance, estate planning and corporate tax organization. He often works with insurance companies at an early establishment stage.

The Clients: HSBC; Vermont Tubbs; Vermont Information Processing; Magma Design; Bell Helicopter; Unilever; Bank North; Merchants Bank and Ben & Jerry's.

Primmer & Piper, Professional Corporation

The Firm: This firm features on the ranking tables for the first time, based on its strength as a corporate/commercial player with a flair for

regulated industry work. The firm typically acts for financial services, insurance and utility clients. The 16-strong team is composed of *"highly capable and active lawyers"* based in Montpelier, Burlington and St. Johnsbury.

The Lawyers: John Primmer and William Piper are contacts for corporate/M&A matters.

The Clients: The firm serves a selection of Fortune 500 companies, small businesses and municipalities.

Sheehey Furlong & Behm PC

The Firm: This Burlington-based practice acts for a broad range of national, regional and local clients including businesses, nonprofit organizations and individuals. The team advises on a full spectrum of corporate matters as well as debt and equity financings. The firm has a strong client base in the TMT sector where it assists clients on IP protection, website development, content licensing and commercial contracts.

The Lawyers: Interviewees singled out **Christopher Gannon** as a *"solid business lawyer with a commercial bent."* Clients particularly appreciated his ability to see the deal through: *"He is a problem solver who never causes a transaction to blow up."*

The Clients: Competitive Computing; Bruegger's Enterprises; Hill Associates; Mt. Mansfield Television; SymQuest; GS Blodgett; Green Mountain Coffee Roasters and Rowe International.

EMPLOYMENT

Vermont
Leading firms
(Employment: Mainly Defendant)
1 DINSE, KNAPP & MCANDREW PC *Burlington*
DOWNS RACHLIN MARTIN PLLC *Burlington*
GRAVEL AND SHEA *Burlington*
PAUL, FRANK + COLLINS *Burlington*
Firms are listed alphabetically in each band.

Band 1

Dinse, Knapp & McAndrew PC

The Firm: This firm is widely seen as *"the top address"* for a full array of employment law services. The team has a strong track record in dispute avoidance, and is equally adept in litigation and alternative dispute resolution when the need arises. The workflow is as impressive as ever and there has been a marked increase over the last year in cases involving union issues and disputes in the health center sector. Typical matters include retaliation cases, age and disability

discrimination, as well as disputes over contractual discrimination and tort. Colleges are among the firm's most prominent clients, and the team furnishes them with advice along a broad front: for example, faculty tenure, student governance and campus injury matters.

The Lawyers: Clients expressed their appreciation of **Karen McAndrew** as a litigator and trial attorney, and peers were swift to endorse her as a *"skilled and reputable lawyer."* Colleges and universities from across the state figure heavily in her client list. Sources also singled out group leader **Robert McKearin**, who was said to have *"a nice way about him – competent, collaborative and always open to ideas."* He is an experienced litigator and mediator, and is a member of the state's panel of early neutral evaluators.

The Clients: Vermont Teddy Bear; Hubbardton Forge; The University of Vermont; Fletcher Allen Health Center; Ryder; Middlebury College; Bombardier Capital and Verizon.

Downs Rachlin Martin PLLC

The Firm: Commentators were clear that this is *"one of the best broad service firms"* in town, with *"a large, premium employment group."* The team is established and stable, advising its exclusively employer clients on all employment and labor matters including wage and hour, discrimination and OSHA-related cases. Union issues and collective bargaining are a house specialty too. The team recently advised a national firm that was sued in connection with overtime remuneration.

The Lawyers: **Peter Robb** is *"100% devoted to labor law,"* say clients, who point to his national reputation in traditional labor matters and collective bargaining. Interviewees described **Patricia Sabalis** as a *"terrific human resources specialist – thoughtful, quick and always providing good, sound advice."*

The Clients: Otis Elevator, Dominion Resources Services and Entergy are on the client roster.

EMPLOYMENT

Vermont
Leading individuals
(Employment: Mainly Defendant)
1 ROBB Peter *Downs Rachlin*, Brattleboro
SABALIS Patricia *Downs Rachlin*, Burlington
2 BRIGGS Heather *Gravel and Shea*, Burlington
GRANT Elizabeth *Paul Frank*, Burlington
MAITLAND Johan *Gravel and Shea*, Burlington
MCANDREW Karen *Dinse Knapp*, Burlington
MCKEARIN Robert *Dinse Knapp*, Burlington
Individuals are listed alphabetically in each band.

Gravel and Shea
The Firm: The firm remains a prominent feature of the local market despite the recent departure of Chris Reiss to the bench. Sources told of a reliable and credible team that includes a number of talented young practitioners. Attorneys act on the employer side in the full range of employment law, with a particular focus on preventive strategies and defense against all varieties of claims. They also assist in dealing with unions and any union actions. Much of the team's work is transaction-related, assisting the firm's corporate and M&A clients with labor and employment issues arising in the course of a deal.

The Lawyers: Heather Briggs is active on both transactional and regulatory matters for management clients, and commentators praise her *"smart and sophisticated"* work. Clients were particularly impressed by the fact that she is *"never afraid to give her opinions,"* and her knack for putting legal jargon into plain language. Peers endorsed **Johan Maitland** for his transaction-related employment advice. He is considered a specialist in human resources issues, and serves on Vermont's Society for Human Resources Management Council.

The Clients: The team advises a broad client base that includes Merchant Bank and Geiger.

Paul, Frank + Collins, A Professional Corporation
The Firm: This group has a sterling reputation for employment litigation and advises its corporate client base on a host of matters. Attorneys are effective litigators and also experienced in alternative dispute resolution arenas. The team acted over the last year on a number of discrimination cases before the EEOC and counterpart state agencies in Michigan, Illinois and Massachusetts. Its opinion was also sought on Uniform Service Employment Act issues arising out of the engagement of reserve guards in Iraq. A decent chunk of the workload centers on age discrimination lawsuits and the team recently acted for a high-profile corporate client in a claim concerning the downsizing of its employee benefits package.

The Lawyers: Elizabeth Grant heads the group and is the driving force behind the firm's consistently good reputation. Her practice emphasizes procedural and policy advice as well as early conflict resolution.

The Clients: Green Mountain Coffee Roasters; Gap; Ben & Jerry's; Unilever and Casella Waste Systems.

LITIGATION

GENERAL COMMERCIAL

Vermont
Leading firms
(Litigation: General Commercial)
1 DINSE, KNAPP & MCANDREW PC *Burlington*
DOWNS RACHLIN MARTIN PLLC *Burlington*
GRAVEL AND SHEA *Burlington*
PAUL, FRANK + COLLINS *Burlington*
SHEEHEY FURLONG & BEHM PC *Burlington*
2 CLEARY SHAHI ASSOCIATES *Rutland*
EGGLESTON & CRAMER, LTD *Burlington*
SPINK & MILLER PLC *Burlington*
THERIAULT & JOSLIN PC *Montpelier*
Firms are listed alphabetically in each band.

Band 1

Dinse, Knapp & McAndrew PC
The Firm: This *"litigation hothouse"* fields a substantial team that is exclusively devoted to trial work. The lawyers *"have in-depth expertise"* and *"show a rare level of care for their clients."* The practice is adept in all facets of business litigation, including banking, corporate, securities and contracts disputes. Attorneys practice in state and federal courts throughout the region. In insurance defense matters it has developed a particular expertise in environmental coverage issues. Real estate and construction disputes also account for a substantial share of the team's workload.

The Lawyers: *"Dynamite trial lawyer"* **Ritchie Berger** won extensive praise from clients and peers alike. Interviewees described him as *"exceptionally bright, extra resourceful,"* and commented that he is *"hard nosed, but not to the point of being unreasonable."* Most of his workload is consumed by complex litigation, with medical malpractice featuring as an important niche. **Karen McAndrew** was commended as *"a talented and experienced lawyer."* Sources credited her with a particular flair for insurance defense, and her commercial practice meshes neatly with a thriving employment practice. *"Incisive and quick"* **John Monahan** was also endorsed for medical and insurance defense work, and is expert in malpractice and liability issues.

The Clients: Green Mountain College; Dartmouth-Hitchcock Medical Centre; Middlebury College; IBM and The University of Vermont.

Downs Rachlin Martin PLLC
The Firm: Commentators regard this prominent firm as one of Vermont's finest. Its strong business practice makes it the first point of call for an impressive list of big corporate clients seeking comprehensive legal advice. The team recently dealt with a number of class action claims brought on behalf of individual purchasers, particularly in the financial industry. For example, it acted for a large German bank in connection with overpriced loans, and for a large utility in a matter concerning Internet charges. In the health sector, which accounted for a significant share of the firm's turnover last year, attorneys acted in a number of cases centering on traumatic brain injuries. The firm has also expanded on its business and commercial fronts, and by the acquisition of lawyers from respected Burlington boutique Schoenberg & Associates it has boosted its capacity in family law considerably.

The Lawyers: Robert Rachlin is the team's kingpin, still active litigating and advising clients, who commend his ability to *"boil the case down to its essence."* His career has involved him in some of the most notorious and celebrated cases in the state, and he is a leading light in mediation. **Marc Heath**'s list of desirable qualities encompasses *"great tactics, legal posture and a willingness to listen to clients' needs."* He chairs the firm's litigation practice group and has seen over 60 jury trials through to verdict. His commercial litigation practice benefits from expertise in products liability and personal injury.

The Clients: Sopakco; Vermont Mutual Insurance; Scott Construction; Home Depot and OneSource.

Gravel and Shea
The Firm: According to interviewees the firm has *"more litigation experience than most,"* and its estimable reputation *"is due to the top-notch individuals in the team."* The attorneys serve numerous local clients that have business interests nationwide. They also act for major national and international corporates. Last year lawyers represented Eli Lilly in a lawsuit concerning veterinary pharmaceuticals, and acted for a Dutch company sued in Vermont for alleged antitrust

www.ChambersandPartners.com
All quotes in the text are from interviews with clients and competitors.
1745

Vermont
Leading individuals
(Litigation: General Commercial)

Senior Statesman
RACHLIN Robert *Downs Rachlin, Burlington*

[1] BEHM Jeffrey *Sheehey Furlong, Burlington*
BERGER Ritchie *Dinse Knapp, Burlington*
HEMLEY Robert *Gravel and Shea, Burlington*

[2] BENNETT II Crocker *Paul Frank, Burlington*
CLEARY David *Cleary Shahi, Rutland*
MCANDREW Karen *Dinse Knapp, Burlington*
O'NEILL Robert *Gravel and Shea, Burlington*
SARTORE John *Paul Frank, Burlington*

[3] HEATH Marc *Downs Rachlin, Burlington*
JOSLIN Peter *Theriault & Joslin, Montpelier*
KLINE Scot *Eggleston & Cramer, Burlington*
MANITSKY Andrew *Gravel and Shea, Burlington*
MILLER Elizabeth *Spink & Miller, Burlington*
MONAHAN JR John *Dinse Knapp, Burlington*
SPINK James *Spink & Miller, Burlington*

Individuals are listed alphabetically in each band.

violations. The team also assisted key client Middlebury College in a dispute involving a general contractor, and in a number of lawsuits arising out of the construction of projects on the college's campus. It also assisted IBM in a case involving an $8.8 million contractor's claim.
The Lawyers: **Robert Hemley** "*has the right tact and feel for every situation,*" said clients who also praised the clarity of his communication. This "*savvy trial attorney sets the tone at the firm*" and is well known for his defense work for the Vermont printed media. Praising **Robert O'Neill**'s tenacity and energy, sources said, "*He knows it is going to be a long, hard slog and never lets up.*" Commendations for **Andrew Manitsky**'s work in technology matters have propelled him into the tables this year. Commentators reported, "*He works extremely hard*" and "*always gets the business done.*"
The Clients: Bombardier; Middlebury Equity Partners; Independent Wireless One; Amtrak; Burlington Free Press; Rutland Herald and Valley News.

Paul, Frank + Collins, A Professional Corporation
The Firm: The team here is extremely well regarded because "*it can do it all.*" Quite apart from traditional corporate and commercial matters, attorneys have carved out a reputation for the successful representation of clients in white-collar crime cases. The team has had a busy year and advised on a wide range of issues including professional and medical negligence, tax appeal, contract disputes, insurance coverage and products liability. Whatever the matter at hand, said clients, "*they have a whole network of people that are great, and their stewardship and compassion is amazing.*"

The Lawyers: Market sources recommended the "*experienced and bright*" **Crocker Bennett** for his standout work in the medical malpractice area. Clients praised **John Sartore** for his "*thorough and analytical approach.*" Commenting especially on his criminal and corporate/commercial litigation, they declared, "*He's your true nuts-and-bolts lawyer – he always conducts thorough research and doesn't go overboard.*"
The Clients: St. Paul; Kemper Professional; Fletcher Allen Health Care and Medical Mutual of Maine.

Sheehey Furlong & Behm PC
The Firm: This is a firm of excellent standing in the litigation community. It acts for major local businesses, notably in the banking, manufacturing and technology sectors. Typical work covers utility litigation, insurance coverage cases and antitrust defense. Over the last year the team has been particularly prominent in the healthcare sector. It defended a local hospital when its previous management was investigated by the US Attorney General, and it acted for a medical laboratory seeking redress for billing errors allegedly committed by a state medical agency. Peers distinguished the team's commercial and antitrust expertise, observing that "*the lawyers are excellent and always know where to get expert witnesses.*"
The Lawyers: **Jeffrey Behm** enjoys a strong profile, with clients describing him as "*definitely a court lawyer.*" He is renowned for the "*impeccable preparation of his cases*" and has plenty of jury and appeals experience under his belt.
The Clients: Volkswagen of America; Mt. Mansfield Television; Green Mountain Power and Burlington Drug.

Band 2

Cleary Shahi Associates, A Professional Corporation
The Firm: This litigation boutique focuses on commercial and personal injury-related disputes. It also handles a substantial volume of medical malpractice claims, an area in which, say peers, its accomplished lawyers enjoy an admirable reputation. The firm's recreational injury practice is widely recognized, and attorneys also deal with products liability claims involving insurance companies and private clients.
The Lawyers: **David Cleary** won approbation for his trial work, and respondents commented that he is "*very good with jurors and has a flair for case presentation.*" He litigates in state and federal courts, and is particularly rated for his expertise in the medical sector.
The Clients: Dartmouth Hitchcock Medical Center and Affiliates; Washington County Mental Health Services; Acordia Resort Services; American Skiing; Okemo Mountain Resort and Cumberland Farms.

Eggleston & Cramer Ltd
The Firm: Studded with dedicated trial lawyers, this team has a thriving litigation practice across the board. Commercial, banking and bankruptcy-related disputes form the backbone of the caseload. Lawyers also advise on antitrust, professional and products liability and construction matters. The team recently defended Mansfield Heliflight against claims of misappropriation of trade secrets, unfair competition and conspiracy in Dodson International Parts, Inc v Phillip Alterndorf, et al. winning a summary judgment motion in the US District Court for Kansas.
The Lawyers: **Scot Kline** is "*a litigator through and through,*" according to peers. Over the last year he has acted in a number of trade secrets and tax appeal cases. He also lectured on advocacy skills at the National Institute of Trial Advocacy in Boston.
The Clients: The team acts for a range of local and national businesses, as well as private clients.

Spink & Miller PLC
The Firm: Peers recommended this group for complex civil litigation. Lawyers act for both plaintiffs and defendants across the range of professional negligence and malpractice cases. The team represents commercial and individual stockholders in contractual disputes and on an array of products liability matters. Companies in the transport sector account for a significant slice of the client base, and here the team recently acted for a number of carriers in matters ranging from negligence and cargo claims to disputes over technical compliance with federal Motor Carrier Safety Regulations and US Department of Transportation regulations. The firm's excellent relations with a number of insurers in Vermont and Canada are another important source of work.
The Lawyers: "*Sharp as anything*" **Elizabeth Miller** has a practice which focuses on commercial disputes, toxic torts and products liability, and elicited compliments from all quarters. Peers also commended managing partner **James Spink**, who acts as both an arbitrator and a litigator. He has developed a special focus on transportation, products liability and professional negligence matters.
The Clients: A wide range of businesses and corporates are on the client list, as well as individual professionals.

Theriault & Joslin PC
The Firm: This Montpelier team has one of the finest and longest pedigrees in the state. The well-respected trial practice is all about civil litigation, focusing on the defense of medical malpractice, products liability, personal injury and workers compensation claims. The group was particularly noted for its professional liability advice. Real estate regulatory matters also feature prominently on the team's agenda and here

it acted on a number of cases relating to land use and permitting disputes.

The Lawyers: Sources recommended the *"authoritative"* **Peter Joslin** for his trial experience. A fellow of the American College of Trial Lawyers, he acts mainly in medical malpractice, products liability and commercial cases.

The Clients: The firm advises a range of local and national clients.

REAL ESTATE

Vermont
Leading firms (Real Estate)
[1] DINSE, KNAPP & MCANDREW PC *Burlington*
GRAVEL AND SHEA *Burlington*
MURPHY SULLIVAN KRONK *Burlington*
[2] DOWNS RACHLIN MARTIN PLLC *Burlington*
LANGROCK SPERRY & WOOL LLP *Burlington*
LISMAN, WEBSTER, KIRKPATRICK *Burlington*
PAUL, FRANK + COLLINS *Burlington*
[3] EGGLESTON & CRAMER, LTD *Burlington*
KENLAN, SCHWIEBERT & FACEY, PC *Rutland*
SHEMS DUNKIEL KASSEL & SAUNDERS *Burlington*

Leading individuals (Real Estate)
[1] LEBOWITZ Molly *Dinse Knapp*, Burlington
MURPHY Liam *Murphy Sullivan*, Burlington
RUSHFORD Robert *Gravel and Shea*, Burlington
SCHROEDER William *Downs Rachlin*, Burlington
[2] CONARD David *Langrock Sperry*, Burlington
KRONK Catherine *Murphy Sullivan*, Burlington
LISMAN Carl *Lisman Webster*, Burlington
[3] FARKAS Michelle *Gravel and Shea*, Burlington
HART Austin *Dinse Knapp*, Burlington
KNUDSEN Eric *Langrock Sperry*, Burlington
WHEELWRIGHT Neil *Eggleston & Cramer*, Burlington

Leading individuals (Real Estate: Zoning/Land Use)
[1] KENLAN Jay *Kenlan Schwiebert*, Rutland
MURPHY Liam *Murphy Sullivan*, Burlington
[2] HALL Mark *Paul Frank*, Burlington
KASSEL John *Shems Dunkiel*, Burlington
PONSETTO John *Gravel and Shea*, Burlington
SULLIVAN Brian *Murphy Sullivan*, Burlington
Firms and individuals are listed alphabetically in each band.

Band 1

Dinse, Knapp & McAndrew PC

The Firm: The response from interviewees was unambiguous as they endorsed this top real estate team, particularly noting its strength in financing matters. The firm has a lively transactional practice and advises an impressive roster of private and public clients. Attorneys act on all aspects of development projects, including zoning and permitting. Recent highlights include assisting the State of Vermont in the provision of a guaranteed loan to Winooski City.

The Lawyers: Clients praised **Molly Lebowitz** for her transactional and financing work: *"She makes her point clearly, doesn't waste time and knows what she is talking about."* **Austin Hart** also won endorsement from market observers for his *"great attention to detail and confident approach."*

The Clients: The client list features Middlebury College, University of Vermont and Bank North, as well as a wide selection of real estate developers, owners and investors.

Gravel and Shea

The Firm: This team *"rules the market,"* according to sources, thanks to a stable of prominent practitioners and proven expertise on the transactional and land use fronts. It acted in the Winooski City redevelopment project, where its work drew admiring comments from peers.

The Lawyers: **Robert Rushford** is respected as a transaction-focused attorney with *"an in-depth knowledge of the law and high-profile clients,"* said respondents. **Michelle Farkas** continues to act on major projects and is still engaged on the development of Sugarbush ski resort. **John Ponsetto** is the lawyer of choice for permitting and land use. He brings considerable experience in environmental law to the table.

The Clients: O'Brien Brothers; Casella Waste Systems; The Snyder Group; Velco and Sprint.

Murphy Sullivan Kronk

The Firm: This group is something of an all-stars outfit, having been formed relatively recently out of *"highly experienced lawyers from various well-established real estate practices."* Each attorney contributed to what is now envied as one of the finest portfolios of clients in the state. The team fields professionals who are prominent in the transactional and regulatory arenas. In addition to ongoing involvement in the Winooski Community Development project, attorneys have acted in a number of contentious matters, such as the successful defense of a telecom client regarding the erecting of a mobile phone mast.

The Lawyers: **Liam Murphy** (see p.1749) is *"good at everything he does,"* is the unanimous opinion of the market. This *"absolute star"* features in all aspects of the practice and acts on the firm's most prominent transactional, zoning and permitting matters. **Catherine Kronk** (see p.1749) is *"the first choice for difficult transactions"* according to observers, who also distinguish the *"totally smart"* **Brian Sullivan** (see p.1749) for his regulatory advice to a mainly telecom client base.

The Clients: American Tower; Vermont National Golf Course; Verizon Wireless; Devon Mobile Communication and US Cellular.

Band 2

Downs Rachlin Martin PLLC

The Firm: This firm is prominent in the state for just about every area of law, though there is a general view that real estate is not in the front rank of its offering. Nevertheless the firm has fairly comprehensive commercial and contentious real estate capability to support its corporate and individual clients in their transactions. Typical work includes regulatory, construction and financing aspects of commercial and residential developments, property sales and acquisitions and the negotiation of commercial leases.

The Lawyers: **William Schroeder** received strong recommendations for his *"broad and excellent"* transaction-centered practice. He is well versed in development projects and has expertise in complementary areas of law, such as banking, corporate and environmental.

The Clients: The team acts for a wide range of clients including banks and financial institutions, developers, contractors and title insurance companies.

Langrock Sperry & Wool, LLP

The Firm: Interviewees acknowledged that the firm has managed to *"continue the good work undisturbed"* despite the departure of Liam Murphy last year. Moreover, David Conard's arrival on the team has *"strengthened them appreciably"* in the view of many. The Burlington and Middlebury offices work across a broad spectrum and enjoy particularly good relations with local lenders. Recent work includes a multimillion-dollar loan for subsidized accommodation for the elderly. The team also acted in matters related to the multiuse Maple Tree Place development project.

The Lawyers: The versatile **David Conard** *"cuts to the chase"* and market sources assert that *"he can handle any deal and always makes sure it gets through."* He is generally seen as the force that has bound the team together through recent upheavals. **Eric Knudsen** is particularly prominent in commercial leasing and also acted in the Winooski City project. Peers commend his prospering practice acting for small businesses.

The Clients: The client base comprises developers, contractors, architects, owners and lenders.

www.ChambersandPartners.com
All quotes in the text are from interviews with clients and competitors.
1747

Lisman, Webster, Kirkpatrick & Leckerling, PC

The Firm: Commentators identify this notable transactional player with its roots in the resort industry, and hence with innovative leasing and financing solutions. The clientele also includes borrowers, lenders, contractors and developers. The team is a credible size and endowed with attorneys who command the respect of the market. In a busy year, the lawyers have acted on a considerable volume of commercial leases and financings, such as the recent $7.2 million financing of an office building.

The Lawyers: Carl Lisman is a "*real estate man to the core,*" say peers, and drives relentlessly to his goal: "*For him the deal must succeed.*" He divides his time between business and real estate transactions and disputes.

The Clients: Local, regional, national and international lenders, mortgage brokers, property managers and developers.

Paul, Frank + Collins, A Professional Corporation

The Firm: This well-resourced firm has capacity on many fronts and provides comprehensive business services under one roof. The team is still an important feature of the real estate landscape, though the market impression is that it has been somewhat less visible on transactions over the past year. Typical work includes the purchase, sale, financing and development of retail, office, commercial and industrial facilities. Zoning and planning is a key plank of the practice, and lawyers are familiar with all aspects of federal, state and local permitting.

The Lawyers: Clients recommended "*capable, effective and honest*" Mark Hall for his expertise in land use litigation. His practice has an environmental and construction slant, and he has a

track record in appellate litigation.

The Clients: The team represents a broad base of developers, investors, lenders, landlords, tenants, corporations, real estate brokerage firms, construction, title insurance companies and property management companies.

Band 3

Eggleston & Cramer Ltd

The Firm: This "*polished*" team has capabilities in the development, leasing, acquisition and finance areas. It is particularly recommended for title services, which are a genuine specialty of the firm and a field in which its market strength is undisputed. Over the year attorneys have acted on a number of commercial, banking and bankruptcy-related matters, and its title search expertise was sought out by a notable utility.

The Lawyers: Neil Wheelwright's practice has a tight real estate focus, and he offers useful expertise in banking and commercial matters. Respondents recommended him strongly for his title search work.

The Clients: Chicago Title Insurance; Century 21 Jack Associates; University Wholesales and Commonwealth Land Title Insurance.

Kenlan, Schwiebert & Facey, PC

The Firm: This Rutland firm has a robust real estate practice and a fine name for land use expertise. The team advises on the range of real estate matters, including development, finance and litigation. It is well known for its work on commercial, industrial and residential projects, and close ties to ski resort developers.

The Lawyers: Jay Kenlan is a key figure in the field of ski resort development. Commentators described him as "*a great lawyer who always makes things interesting.*" His general commercial

and transactional expertise drew praise, and his knowledge of land use issues was especially noted.

The Clients: The team acts for both local and international clients whose businesses are directly or indirectly involved in the real estate sector.

Shems Dunkiel Kassel & Saunders PLLC

The Firm: This recently formed group's clearly stated ethical mission draws praise from sources that also flag up its expertise in land use and permitting matters. The emphasis here is on environmentally friendly practices, and lawyers promote social responsibility in real estate development among their conscientious clients. Affectionately dubbed "*the greens,*" this "*talented team*" will act for developers as long as they share its ethos. Attorneys are experienced in regulatory, contentious and transactional work, and peers also noted significant capability in banking and finance.

The Lawyers: The "*richly varied*" team has experience ranging from the Attorney General's Office, through representing Friends of the Earth, to assisting Howard Dean, the state governor. Respondents were particularly vocal about the "*superb, genuinely impressive*" John Kassel. He has developed a focus on energy, environmental, and regulatory law, in connection with permitting for renewable energy projects. Recent highlights for the team include the successful representation of the Residents Opposing Quarries in Neighborhoods group, resulting in the denial of a permit to Pike Industries, which had hoped to open a crushed rock quarry near a rural residential neighborhood in Williamstown.

The Clients: Businesses, nonprofit corporations, government agencies, cooperatives and individuals.

Leaders in Vermont

BEHM, Jeffrey
Sheehey Furlong & Behm PC,
Burlington 802 864 9891
Recommended in Litigation

BENNETT II, Crocker
Paul, Frank + Collins, A Professional
Corporation, Burlington 802 658 2311
Recommended in Litigation

BERGER, Ritchie
Dinse, Knapp & McAndrew PC,
Burlington 802 864 5751
Recommended in Litigation

BOE, Kathleen
Eggleston & Cramer, Ltd, Burlington
802 864 0880
Recommended in Corporate/M&A

BRIGGS, Heather
Gravel and Shea, Burlington
802 658 0220
Recommended in Employment

CLEARY, David
Cleary Shahi Associates, A Professional
Corporation, Rutland 802 775 8800
Recommended in Litigation

CONARD, David
Langrock Sperry & Wool, LLP,
Burlington 802 864 0217
Recommended in Real Estate

EGGLESTON, Jon
Eggleston & Cramer, Ltd, Burlington
802 864 0880
Recommended in Corporate/M&A

ERLY, Peter
Gravel and Shea, Burlington
802 658 0220
Recommended in Corporate/M&A

FARKAS, Michelle
Gravel and Shea, Burlington
802 658 0220
Recommended in Real Estate

FRYE, B Michael
Paul, Frank + Collins, A Professional
Corporation, Burlington 802 658 2311
Recommended in Corporate/M&A

GANNON, Christopher
Sheehey Furlong & Behm PC,
Burlington 802 864 9891
Recommended in Corporate/M&A

GRANT, Elizabeth
Paul, Frank + Collins, A Professional
Corporation, Burlington
802 658 2311
Recommended in Employment

HAEFNER, Gail
Paul, Frank + Collins, A Professional
Corporation, Burlington
802 658 2311
Recommended in Corporate/M&A

HALL, Mark
Paul, Frank + Collins, A Professional
Corporation, Burlington
802 658 2311
Recommended in Real Estate

1748   All quotes in the text are from interviews with clients and competitors.

CHAMBERS USA 2005

HART, Austin
Dinse, Knapp & McAndrew PC,
Burlington 802 864 5751
Recommended in Real Estate

HEATH, Marc
Downs Rachlin Martin PLLC, Burlington
802 863 2375
Recommended in Litigation

HEMLEY, Robert
Gravel and Shea, Burlington
802 658 0220
Recommended in Litigation

JOSLIN, Peter
Theriault & Joslin PC, Montpelier
802 223 2381
Recommended in Litigation

KASSEL, John
Shems Dunkiel Kassel & Saunders
PLLC, Burlington 802 860 1003
Recommended in Real Estate

KENLAN, Jay
Kenlan, Schwiebert & Facey, P.C.,
Rutland 802 773 3300
Recommended in Real Estate

KLINE, Scot
Eggleston & Cramer, Ltd, Burlington
802 864 0880
Recommended in Litigation

KNAPP, Spencer
Dinse, Knapp & McAndrew PC,
Burlington 802 864 5751
Recommended in Corporate/M&A

KNUDSEN, Eric
Langrock Sperry & Wool, LLP, Burlington 802 864 0217
Recommended in Real Estate

KRONK, Catherine
Murphy Sullivan Kronk, Burlington
802 861 7000
ckronk@mskvt.com
Recommended in Real Estate
Practice Areas: Real estate; business;
commercial financings and transactions.
Prof. Memberships: Admitted to the
Quebec Bar Association in 1985 and to
the Vermont Bar Association in 1989.
Currently a member of the Vermont Bar
Association, and the American Bar
Association. Chair of the Stormwater
Sub-Committee of the Property Law
and Environmental Law Committees of
the Vermont Bar Association in 2003.
Member of the Board of Directors of the
Vermont Development Credit Union,
2000-03.
Career: Attended Trent University,
Peterborough, Ontario and obtained at
BA in 1979. Attended University of
Ottawa law school and obtained a Bach-
elor of Civil Law (BCL) in 1983 and a
Bachelor of Common Law (LLB) in
1984. Legislative Assistant to The Hon-
ourable Donald J Johnston, President of
the Treasury Board, and Minister in the
Cabinet of the Honourable Pierre Elliot
Trudeau, Prime Minister of Canada,

1980-81. Associate, Mackenzie Gervais,
Montreal, Quebec 1985-88. Associate
and of Counsel to Paul, Frank & Collins
and Eggleston & Cramer, Burlington,
Vermont during the period of 1988-
2004.
Publications: Regularly present seminars on various matters concerning real
estate law in Vermont, including seminars sponsored by the Vermont Bar
Association on the issue of stormwater
regulation.
Personal: Born Montreal, Quebec July
5, 1958. Resided in Montreal until 1988,
before moving to Vermont. Fluent in
French.

LEBOWITZ, Molly
Dinse, Knapp & McAndrew PC,
Burlington 802 864 5751
Recommended in Real Estate

LISMAN, Carl
Lisman, Webster, Kirkpatrick & Lecker-
ling, P.C., Burlington 802 864 5756
Recommended in Real Estate

MAITLAND, Johan
Gravel and Shea, Burlington
802 658 0220
Recommended in Employment

MANITSKY, Andrew
Gravel and Shea, Burlington
802 658 0220
Recommended in Litigation

MCANDREW, Karen
Dinse, Knapp & McAndrew PC,
Burlington 802 864 5751
*Recommended in Employment,
Litigation*

MCCONAUGHY, Stewart
Gravel and Shea, Burlington
802 658 0220
Recommended in Corporate/M&A

MCKEARIN, Robert
Dinse, Knapp & McAndrew PC,
Burlington 802 864 5751
Recommended in Employment

MCMAHAN, Jeffrey
Dinse, Knapp & McAndrew PC,
Burlington 802 864 5751
Recommended in Corporate/M&A

MILLER, Elizabeth
Spink & Miller PLC, Burlington
802 864 1100
Recommended in Litigation

MONAHAN JR, John
Dinse, Knapp & McAndrew PC,
Burlington 802 864 5751
Recommended in Litigation

MONTGOMERY, Margaret
Gravel and Shea, Burlington
802 658 0220
Recommended in Corporate/M&A

MOODY, Thomas
Downs Rachlin Martin PLLC, Burlington
802 863 2375
Recommended in Corporate/M&A

MURPHY, Brian
Dinse, Knapp & McAndrew PC,
Burlington 802 864 5751
Recommended in Corporate/M&A

MURPHY, Liam
Murphy Sullivan Kronk, Burlington
802 861 7000
lmurphy@msk.vt.com
Recommended in Real Estate
Practice Areas: Litigation, permitting
and transactions in the areas of real
estate, land use, environmental and
commercial law.
Prof. Memberships: District of Colum-
bia Bar, 1981. Vermont Bar, 1983. Chair,
Real Property Committee, VBA, 1997-
2000. Current Member of the Environmental Law Committee, VBA.
Career: Drew University, BA 1976.
Georgetown University Law Center, JD
1981. Legislative Assistant to Senator
Patrick J Leahy 1976-78. Director, Legislative Affairs, Food Safety and Quality
Service, Department of Agriculture
1978-81. Associate, Butler, Binion, Rice,
Cook, Knapp, Washington, DC 1981-83.
Langrock, Sperry & Wool 1983-2004.
Publications: Since 1988 annually
teaches a course on 'Title to Real Estate
in Vermont' for attorneys and paralegals
and publishes a companion reference
book. Frequent lecturer on land use and
development law and related issues.
Recently presented a series of courses
regarding 'Stormwater Regulation in
Vermont'. January, 2004 presented
'Drafting Commercial Leases'. September, 2004 presented 'Land Use Development in Vermont'.
Personal: Born Wexford, Ireland, May
19, 1954. Lived in Ireland until 1960 and
in Wales until 1968. Moved to Brattleboro, Vermont in 1968.

ODE, Paul
Downs Rachlin Martin PLLC, Burlington
802 863 2375
Recommended in Corporate/M&A

O'NEILL, Robert
Gravel and Shea, Burlington
802 658 0220
Recommended in Litigation

PONSETTO, John
Gravel and Shea, Burlington
802 658 0220
Recommended in Real Estate

PORT, Alan
Paul, Frank + Collins, A Professional
Corporation, Burlington 802 658 2311
Recommended in Corporate/M&A

RACHLIN, Robert
Downs Rachlin Martin PLLC, Burlington
802 863 2375
Recommended in Litigation

ROBB, Peter
Downs Rachlin Martin PLLC,
Brattleboro 802 258 3070
Recommended in Employment

RUSHFORD, Robert
Gravel and Shea, Burlington
802 658 0220
Recommended in Real Estate

SABALIS, Patricia
Downs Rachlin Martin PLLC, Burlington
802 863 2375
Recommended in Employment

SARTORE, John
Paul, Frank + Collins, A Professional
Corporation, Burlington 802 658 2311
Recommended in Litigation

SCHROEDER, William
Downs Rachlin Martin PLLC, Burlington
802 863 2375
Recommended in Real Estate

SPINK, James
Spink & Miller PLC, Burlington
802 864 1100
Recommended in Litigation

SULLIVAN, Brian
Murphy Sullivan Kronk, Burlington
802 861 7000
bsullivan@mskvt.com
Recommended in Real Estate
Practice Areas: Land use, planning and
zoning, environmental, telecommunica-
tions law, immigration law and appellate
litigation.
Prof. Memberships: Admitted to the
Illinois Bar in 1987 and to the Vermont
Bar in 1990. Admitted to practice before
the Second Circuit Court of Appeals in
1998 and US Supreme Court in 2000.
Currently a Member of the Vermont
and American Bar Associations and the
American Immigration Lawyers Associ-
ation.
Career: University of Chicago, BA with
General and Special Honors, 1984.
Elected to Phi Beta Kappa and chosen as
a Student Marshal. Harvard Law School,
JD, Cum Laude, 1987. Associate, Sidley
& Austin, Chicago, Illinois, 1987-89.
Burak Anderson & Melloni, 1989-2003.
Publications: Writes and speaks regu-
larly on matters involving telecommuni-
cations law. Published articles include,
Effect of the Telecommunications Act
on Zoning and Planning, 16-SUM
Comm. Law 3 (1998) in the Communi-
cations Lawyer, a publication of the
American Bar Association.
Personal: Born Chicago, Illinois, Janu-
ary 6, 1962. Near fluency in French and
Spanish. Strong working knowledge of
Italian and Brazilian-Portuguese.

WHEELWRIGHT, Neil
Eggleston & Cramer, Ltd, Burlington
802 864 0880
Recommended in Real Estate

CONTENTS: Construction p.1750; Corporate/M&A p.1752; Employment p.1755; Environment p.1757; Intellectual Property: p.1758; Litigation p.1762; Real Estate p.1765; Individuals' Profiles p.1767; Firm Profiles p.1775.

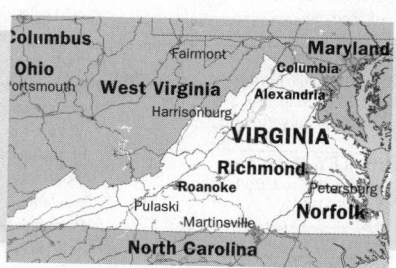

How lawyers are ranked

The opinions we gather from clients — mainly from in-house lawyers but also from other purchasers of legal services — are balanced by opinions from colleagues and competitors. Together, they provide two different perspectives — an all-round view — and biased viewpoints cancel each other out.

CONSTRUCTION

Virginia
Leading firms (Construction)

[1]	**WATT, TIEDER, HOFFAR & FITZGERALD** *McLean*
[2]	**HOLLAND & KNIGHT LLP** *McLean*
	MOORE & LEE LLP *McLean*
	SMITH PACHTER MCWHORTER & ALLEN *Vienna*
	VENABLE LLP *Vienna*
	WICKWIRE GAVIN *Vienna*
[3]	**KRAFTSON CAUDLE LLC** *McLean*
	WRIGHT ROBINSON OSTHIMER *Richmond*

Leading individuals (Construction)

[1]	**FITZGERALD Robert** *Watt Tieder, McLean*
	HOFFAR Julian *Watt Tieder, McLean*
	LALLE Wayne *Venable, Vienna*
	LANE David *Venable, Vienna*
	TIEDER John *Watt Tieder, McLean*
	WATT Robert *Watt Tieder, McLean*
	WICKWIRE Jon *Wickwire Gavin, Vienna*
[2]	**ALLEN Randall** *Smith Pachter, Vienna*
	BAKER Lewis *Watt Tieder, McLean*
	BROWNELL Thomas *Holland & Knight, McLean*
	LEE Charlie *Moore & Lee, McLean*
	LOULAKIS Michael *Wickwire Gavin, Vienna*
	MCWHORTER Val *Smith Pachter, Vienna*
	MOORE Robert *Moore & Lee, McLean*
	WRIGHT Murray *Wright Robinson, Richmond*
[3]	**COX Robert** *Watt Tieder, McLean*
	KRAFTSON Daniel *Kraftson Caudle, McLean*

Up-and-coming individuals

	VARELA Paul *Watt Tieder, McLean*

Firms and individuals are listed alphabetically in each band.

Band 1

Watt, Tieder, Hoffar & Fitzgerald LLP

The Firm: This *"formidable"* firm has a wall-to-wall presence in the construction arena and continues to grow in a competitive market. Its group of over 90 lawyers enjoys great strategic bearing with clients who are based both nationally and internationally. Competitors admire the team's continued participation on many of the most significant recent cases, matters that have included the representation of Mitsubishi on the litigation at Miller Park, home of the Milwaukee Brewers. The practice's remit is huge, encompassing industrial and power plants, highways, sports and entertainment and homeland security. Competitors add that it is *"the firm for surety representation. Deserving of the highest praise,"* this group can be measured by the talent of the people it has produced in the 27-year history of its practice.

The Lawyers: Interviewees spoke highly of **Julian Hoffar** as a man with *"a million-dollar personality and the brains to go with it."* An *"excellent trial lawyer,"* he brings his significant presence to bear when acting as mediator or arbitrator in high-profile dispute resolution cases among other matters. Similarly gifted is **John Tieder** who has developed a stellar reputation in the field of international construction arbitration. Recognized for his exceptional negotiating and litigation skills, this *"very highly rated"* attorney is also active in the power and government contract businesses. Colleague **Robert Watt**, the *"consummate surety lawyer,"* enjoys many high visibility projects: one peer rates him *"the best negotiator I have ever seen."* He has worked on the Aviano Air Force base in Italy and a courthouse and detention center in Las Vegas. The equally accomplished **Robert Fitzgerald** is the powerhouse of the heavy construction market, taking on tough cases for contractors and litigating where necessary. His *"well-respected national practice"* covers dams, canals, power plants and water treatment facilities among others. *"As an engineer as well as a lawyer,"* **Lewis Baker** *"better understands the complexities of technical issues."* Clients commended him stating: *"He understands the work and the industry and can see issues more far-reaching than may be immediately noticeable on paper."* **Robert Cox** has a wide-ranging practice and works all over the USA. He is currently largely focused on questions of upgrading security on existing structures due to the recent emphasis on homeland security. *"Excellent trial attorney"* **Paul Varela**'s reputation is building due to the heavyweight cases he takes on. Examples have included the representation of Mitsubishi Heavy Industries America.

The Clients: Zurich North America; St. Paul Travelers; Mitsubishi Heavy Industries America; The Shaw Company; HSG – Bilfinger Berger; Clark Construction and Washington Group International.

Band 2

Holland & Knight LLP

See firm details p.1352

The Firm: The depth and breadth of this quality national firm allied to its interdisciplinary approach allow it to compete across geographic borders on matters for a wide range of construction and government concerns. Commentators regard it as one of the bigger players in the state made up of *"formidable opponents"* who work out of a network of eight Florida offices. The practice focuses on a range of issues including construction claims, project finance, contract preparation and alternative dispute resolution. It also has a strong government contracts arm.

The Lawyers: **Tom Brownell** (see p.1767) was praised by peers as *"one of the brightest attorneys in his specialty."* His field is that of government contracts and construction claims and disputes where competitors note that he has *"dazzled people with his intellect"* throughout a long career.

The Clients: The team represents contractors, subcontractors, designers, engineers and owners across a range of private and public matters.

Moore & Lee LLP

The Firm: This growing firm concentrates exclusively on construction law and goes all out to *"effectively and efficiently represent its clients."* With a focus on heavy industry and complex commercial projects (including government contracts), this group has a strong presence in Virginia. Competitors have much respect for its "*ability to take on large cases and handle them effectively.*"

The Lawyers: **Charlie Lee**, previously with Watt Tieder, is "*efficient and effective*" in all areas of construction, government contracts and suretyship law. With a strong aptitude for construction litigation he has enjoyed recent successes, firstly in the case of a $120 million federal prison in Pennsylvania, and, secondly, regarding a major wastewater treatment facility in the District of Columbia. "*Articulate and experienced*" **Robert Moore** has built a thriving practice with an emphasis on the resolution of contract disputes. His representations involve a variety of projects including power plants, dams and hospitals. Practitioners who interact with him on such deals laud him as an "*excellent lawyer, very well trained and very bright.*"

The Clients: Clark Construction; Fru-Con Construction; Sunrise Assisted Living; Babcock & Wilcox and Bell Corporation.

Smith Pachter McWhorter & Allen

The Firm: This "*high-quality construction firm*" based in Vienna scores "*ten out of ten*" with clients; its in-depth understanding of the business is particularly noted, with sources saying: "*They understand construction 100%.*" The team has expertise in all aspects of the construction, contracting and dispute resolution process and enjoys long-standing relationships with a clientele that encompasses general engineering, procurement and construction (EPC) contractors, architects, engineers and manufacturers.

The Lawyers: "*Top-notch attorney*" **Randall Allen** commands a "*tremendous amount of respect*" from competitors and peers. He typically takes on large cases, often internationally, and is known for being both "*reasonable and practical.*" Clients particularly rate his work with subcontractors and on deals where there is a change in conditions saying: "*He will see that the contract is correct and if there are issues in the project he will fix them.*" Fellow attorneys admire **Val McWhorter**'s "*good reputation*" as a leading construction lawyer. He has been busy with the design/build contract for a New Jersey light rail system and tackled matters pertaining to the construction of tunnels for the Washington Metro.

The Clients: Soletanche; Washington Group International; Sundt Construction and Fru-Con Construction.

Venable LLP

The Firm: The depth of experience fielded by these lawyers makes the Vienna office of this regional giant strategically important to the firm's growing practice. Clients applaud the group for its "*top-level construction and government contracts professionals.*" These generally undertake complicated legal matters that require "*a sophisticated understanding of the applicable law and realities of the industry.*" The firm is "*consistently attentive to the many requirements of an engagement and communicates with regularity and depth.*" It handles numerous large infrastructure and environmental mediation projects relating most notably to bridges, dams and highways.

The Lawyers: **Wayne Lalle** is a "*top, go-to lawyer for serious litigation.*" Recognized as being "*affable, intelligent and responsive to the needs of his client,*" he inspires loyalty and is rapidly developing a high-status role in the market. Recent matters include advising in relation to a missile facility in California and regarding environmental mediation projects across the country. According to competitors, **David Lane** is "*as good as there is.*" He combines "*excellent communication skills*" with a comprehensive understanding of the construction industry and has a particular leaning towards dispute resolution. He is variously regarded as the "*leading man*" and the "*driving force*" at Venable.

The Clients: Gannett Co; Parsons Corporation; Dynalectric; Lockheed Martin and Zachary Construction.

Wickwire Gavin

The Firm: Identified chiefly for representation of owners, this group works both regionally and nationally taking "*a proactive approach to problem solving.*" Refining and petrochemicals form a substantial part of the practice with the firm also maintaining an active involvement in design-build in the public sector. In this last regard it recently worked on the Fairfax County Parkway Extension for the Virginia Department of Transportation. This "*substantial competitor*" has a wide-ranging complement of professionals acting from conception to completion on a host of construction projects.

The Lawyers: Dean of the firm **Jon Wickwire** has experienced a fruitful professional career and earns high respect from peers. He is "*particularly experienced in scheduling matters in construction claims*" and has recently represented the joint venture of a Fortune 50 corporation and the Malaysian government in a claim totaling more than $30 million. "*Excellent*" **Michael Loulakis** serves as special counsel for a multitude of major design-build infrastructure projects. Competitors "*like his style*" and admire his growing practice.

The Clients: Virginia Department of Transportation; El Paso; AEP; BP; Tractebel; Nevada Power and Mobil Power Company.

Band 3

Kraftson Caudle LLC

The Firm: Daniel Kraftson left the Washington office of Jenkens and Gilchrist to set up this quality construction boutique. It frequently involves itself in the arbitration of complex cases.

The Lawyers: Trusted **Daniel Kraftson** is "*chosen because both sides believe in him.*" He has over 30 years' experience in law and competitors assert that he "*operates with integrity and zeal in representing his clients.*"

The Clients: The firm represents numerous clients on a regional and national basis.

Wright Robinson Osthimer & Tatum

The Firm: Based in Richmond, the group occupies a prominent niche in the construction domain with its representation of designers and architects, often through their professional liability insurance. The firm is recognized as "*far and away the best*" in this field and has developed great bench strength with which to take on national cases.

The Lawyers: Founder **Murray Wright** has a diverse practice and wins industry recognition as a "*dynamic lawyer*" who fights hard for his clients. An excellent attorney with over three decades' experience in the field, Murray expertly handles the complexities of contractual liability in the construction industry.

The Clients: The firm advises contractors, subcontractors, suppliers and designers across the country.

CORPORATE/M&A

Virginia
Leading firms (Corporate/M&A)

1 HUNTON & WILLIAMS LLP *Richmond*
MCGUIREWOODS LLP *Richmond*

2 HOGAN & HARTSON LLP *McLean*
TROUTMAN SANDERS LLP *Richmond*
WILLIAMS MULLEN *Richmond*

3 COOLEY GODWARD LLP *Reston*
DLA PIPER RUDNICK GRAY CARY US LLP *Reston*
KAUFMAN & CANOLES *Norfolk*
SHAW PITTMAN LLP *McLean*
WILMER CUTLER PICKERING HALE AND *Reston*

4 LECLAIR RYAN, PROFESSIONAL CORP *Richmond*
VENABLE LLP *Vienna*
WILLCOX & SAVAGE *Norfolk*

Leading individuals (Corporate/M&A)

1 BUCKLEY Kevin *Hunton & Williams*, Richmond
BURRUS Robert *McGuireWoods*, Richmond
CUTCHINS IV Clifford *McGuireWoods*, Richmond
GOOLSBY Allen *Hunton & Williams*, Richmond
JOHNSTON Jay *Troutman Sanders*, Richmond

2 FRANTZ Thomas *Williams Mullen*, Richmond
GRANDIS Leslie *McGuireWoods*, Richmond
LECLAIR Gary *LeClair Ryan*, Richmond
LINCOLN Michael *Cooley Godward*, Reston
MASTRACCO Vincent *Kaufman & Canoles*, Norfolk
SMITH Julious *Williams Mullen*, Richmond

3 CHASON Craig *Shaw Pittman*, McLean
CONROY Joseph *Cooley Godward*, Reston
HORAN Richard *Hogan & Hartson*, McLean
LEWIS Jack *Shaw Pittman*, McLean
MCKEE T Braxton *Kaufman & Canoles*, Norfolk
MOORE Justin *Hunton & Williams*, Richmond
MOORE Thurston *Hunton & Williams*, Richmond
RAINEY Gordon *Hunton & Williams*, Richmond
SYLVESTER David *Wilmer Cutler*, Reston
WHEATON James *Troutman Sanders*, Virginia Beach

4 BECKER Richard *Hogan & Hartson*, McLean
FRANCE Thomas *Venable*, Vienna
INGLIMA Thomas *Willcox & Savage*, Norfolk
MELTZER Steven *Shaw Pittman*, McLean
OLD William *Williams Mullen*, Richmond
PARKS Randall *Hunton & Williams*, Richmond
PARRINO Richard *Hogan & Hartson*, McLean
SPANGLER Nancy *DLA Piper*, Reston
THOMPSON Gary *Hunton & Williams*, Richmond
VAUGHAN III C Porter *Hunton & Williams*, Richmond

Firms and individuals are listed alphabetically in each band.

Band 1

Hunton & Williams LLP
See firm details p.1775

The Firm: This *"first-class,"* all-purpose law firm is credited with having one of the state's most consummate corporate and business groups and is the first place many competing firms think of when looking to refer. The vibrant practice continues to focus on a broad client base numbering, among others, issuers, underwriters, trustees and insurers. It also acts as senior strategic adviser in the areas of tax and securitization structures. Never shying away from the complexities of major deals, the group of 50-plus attorneys has expanded its national and international representations; clients looking for broad-ranging representation benefit from lawyers working out of multiple offices. Market sources recognize that the firm has a team of *"terrific and trusted"* lawyers that understands the client's business and is *"responsive and adaptable."* Interviewees spoke of a group that is *"thoughtful, insightful and able to come up with mechanisms to get around limitations."* This is a team *"innovative, creative and capable of changing very quickly with the times."*

The Lawyers: Allen Goolsby (see p.1769) is an acknowledged dean of the Virginia corporate Bar who in recent years has authored many of the changes to the corporate code. Market sources acknowledge him to be *"a composite of high intelligence and strong judgment – if you go to him, you go to someone who really knows what he is talking about."* These sources also accorded **Kevin Buckley** (see p.1768) the highest accolades, with one client describing him as *"perhaps the best securitization lawyer I have ever worked with."* Another remarked that his *"reputation and work are recognized as stellar in the asset securitization market – not only does he have a complete mastery of the law but he also understands and is sensitive to the business requirements of any transaction. His excellent insight always brings forth the appropriate solution."* **Gordon Rainey** (see p.1772) brings a similar perceptiveness to his work advising special committees of boards of directors, negotiated joint ventures and represented institutional lenders in syndicated and direct corporate acquisition financings and leveraged buyouts. Managing partner of the firm **Thurston Moore**'s (see p.1771) interests include corporate financing and governance, venture capital and real estate investment trusts; while *"knowledgeable and professional"* **Justin Moore** (see p.1771) forges a dominant reputation in private equity and venture capital representations. He has recently worked on a prestige auction deal and the sale of public companies. Head of the US M&A group, **Gary Thompson** (see p.1773) represents Smithfield Foods in its ongoing acquisition program and handles matters for Chesapeake. In a recently rebounding tech market, he has picked up a number of noteworthy midmarket company representations. **Porter Vaughan** (see p.1773) is particularly strong in the securities area and M&A concerns. He has represented many Fortune 500 companies and advised clients on takeover matters and protective measures. **Randall Parks** (see p.1772) has done extremely well in the firm's growth area of sourcing and systems integration. In addition he has negotiated and documented multiple large-scale sourcing transactions valued at several billion dollars.

The Clients: Bank of America; Chesapeake; Smithfield Foods; Department of Veterans Affairs; Fieldstone Investment; Wells Fargo and Barclays.

McGuireWoods LLP

The Firm: Key selling points for this firm are its tremendous depth and the measure of its reach into the corporate arena. It is essentially a national and global practice enveloping every sector of the economy and dealing with every size and structure of business. A *"large inventory of quality business lawyers,"* 100 in number, works out of 15 offices throughout the USA and internationally, though the Richmond base is regarded as its structural linchpin in business law. Clients vouch for the *"outstanding work"* the firm does with nationally reputed attorneys taking on the needs of large concerns. Not much passes under the group's radar as it focuses on the whole gamut from corporate finance, technology and venture capital and intellectual matters to property, energy and utilities and government relations work. The Virginia group recently advised both Circuit City Stores and Dominion on a string of transactions.

The Lawyers: Robert Burrus (see p.1768) is chairman of McGuireWoods and oversees all significant representations handled by the firm's corporate group. Described as *"the constant in a very fine practice,"* he has been at the top of his game for a long time. He is highly regarded by peers as a strong boardroom negotiator and is the *"pre-eminent bond lawyer in the state."* **Clifford Cutchins** mainly focuses on acquisitions. With a stint in-house under his belt, he benefits from *"superior business judgment"* as well as legal skill; clients are satisfied that he understands both their needs and the mechanics of the boardroom. He is described as *"diligent, cost-effective and not one to fight over every comma."* *"Excellent corporate lawyer"* **Leslie Grandis** heads up the M&A practice and is additionally flagged up for his work in private equity where an increase in transactions has built up his workload. Sources universally attested to the benefits of using him on a transaction – *"he can make deals happen; he has a very easy disposition but is a tough negotiator."*

The Clients: Dominion; Circuit City Stores; Lockheed Martin; CSX and Peoples Energy.

Band 2

Hogan & Hartson LLP
See firm details p.484

The Firm: This *"excellent firm"* continues to flourish long after the tech boom that brought initial corporate business to the area petered out. The Northern Virginia office of the DC-headquartered group is of strategic importance to its overall dealings, with 20 attorneys working on M&A, corporate and securities. Focus areas include public and private companies in industries such as communications and media, technology, energy, pharmaceuticals and healthcare. With the ability to draw on expertise cross-state, clients know the practice to be a *"tremendous resource"* that is continually evolving. Along with servicing mature companies, the firm plays a major role in clients' financing activities, from raising startup venture capital to private and public offerings of debt and equity. Market sources claim the attorneys *"have a good sense of what is important; they protect their client."* As an example of a recent representative deal, the Northern Virginia office closed the sale of i2, a global intelligence analysis supplier, to ChoicePoint for $100 million.

The Lawyers: Although **Richard Horan** (see p.1770) works on the whole package of M&A and corporate markets activity, one of his specialties is broadcast acquisition. He has continued to represent Fox Television Stations for more than a decade, advising on purchases, dispositions and swaps. Clients recognize him as a *"tireless worker, both competent and incredibly effective."* **Richard Becker** (see p.1767) covers public and private merger transactions in the information technology, biotechnology, defense, hospitality and healthcare industries. He led the team on behalf of the DIRECTV group in connection with its $400 million sale of the set-top box manufacturing business of its subsidiary Hughes Network Systems. **Richard Parrino** (see p.1772) counsels boards of directors and their committees on corporate governance issues and advises issuers on compliance with securities laws. He impresses clients with his knowledge of historical situations and executive procedure.

The Clients: DIRECTV; Fox Television Stations; King Pharmaceuticals; Titan; Primus Telecommunications and ITC^DeltaCom.

Troutman Sanders LLP

The Firm: This *"dynamic"* firm remained at the forefront of interviewees' minds for its substantial corporate and securities practice group and its growing presence in the Virginia market. The group represents publicly traded and privately owned businesses in M&A, corporate governance and securities regulation matters recognizing the intricate concerns of these companies as they operate in a global economy. Competitors noted that the *"sound, full-service office"* has the depth to handle large transactions and also

praised the group for its expertise on the litigation side of deals. The firm emphasizes this full-service approach by bringing together experts from different practice fields to focus on individual transactions as and when required.

The Lawyers: **Jay Johnston** gives an excellent all-round showing in terms of his substance and his approach. He has a sterling reputation as *"one of the top securities lawyers in the state"* and is admired as a *"thorough, soft-spoken, thoughtful and inquisitive"* attorney. **James Wheaton** has developed a powerful presence and is seen to be particularly active with smaller corporations. He has represented underwriters and issuers in private placements of debt and equity securities.

The Clients: The group advises clients from a range of key industry areas and specializations.

Williams Mullen

The Firm: Possessing a heavily corporate and transaction-based practice and representing many Fortune 500 companies, this firm is praised as *"knowledgeable, reasonable and easy to work with."* It provides corporate services to virtually every industry in Virginia boasting significant representations in the broadcast, healthcare, real estate, retail and government contracts sectors. M&A activity has been high and the group complements its practice with related expertise in intellectual property, real estate and litigation. Interviewees claim the firm *"looks out for the client's interests and works well to get the job done"* adding that the large volume of acquisitions that the firm handles never affects the quality of its work. Attorneys here are widely held by clients to be *"responsive to our issues and willing to take the time to know the business side of, often sophisticated, transactions."*

The Lawyers: *"Top-notch"* **Thomas Frantz** works on deals across the country, primarily in M&A, a large amount of which are in the areas of broadcast, healthcare, retail and manufacturing. Competitors drew attention to his tax knowledge, which bolsters his corporate practice work, and his solid commercial expertise. **Julious Smith** displays *"good judgment and common sense"* together with leadership skills when representing clients ranging from publicly owned corporations to family businesses. Competitors see him as a smart lawyer who pays a lot of attention to his clients. He has added the representation of CarMax to his already significant list of clients. These two are joined in *Chambers'* tables by **William Old** who arrived as a result of Williams Mullen's merger with Norfolk firm Hofheimer Nusbaum in 2004. He is praised as *"detail-oriented but focused on getting deals accomplished"* and is considered by many clients to be part of their outsourced strategic leadership team.

The Clients: Max Media; AMERIGROUP; Sentara Healthcare; CarMax; Media General; Universal Corporation and LandAmerica Financial Group.

Band 3

Cooley Godward LLP

The Firm: One of the core competencies of this national firm is its technology focus. The Reston office of the Silicon Valley heavyweight is widely known to have *"created a good shop in early-stage companies"* and represents hi-tech startups, growth corporations and venture capital firms. The firm has brought its reputation to bear in the life sciences and biotech markets seeing significant growth in this field out of the Northern Virginia office. Along with venture capital transactions, this successful group is also credited with expanding its base among mature companies and has added a number of public entities to its portfolio including MCI, a Northern Virginia-based communications company.

The Lawyers: Cofounder of the Reston office **Michael Lincoln** is *"highly regarded on the venture capital side"* of corporate activity. Peers praise him as a *"real go-getter"* who tracks down a large volume of technology deals. **Joseph Conroy** is described as *"excellent in the technology field."* His practice is concerned with corporate and securities transactions and transfer matters with a focus on life science, software and telecommunications.

The Clients: MCI; GTSI; Blackboard; The Carlyle Group; Columbia Capital; Updata Ventures; Prestwick Pharmaceuticals; iDirect Technologies; mindSHIFT Technologies and Rivermine Software.

DLA Piper Rudnick Gray Cary US LLP
See firm details p.765

The Firm: Following its tie-up with DLA and Gray Cary Ware & Freidenrich, this player in the corporate market is focused on growing both nationally and internationally while remaining true to its traditional client base. The firm has a significant transactional-based practice and concentrates on middle and upper-midmarket clients for whom it provides *"diversified and long-term representation."* Observers note its *"strong technology practice"* – the group has represented telecom providers in Northern Virginia and seen increased movement in this market. Other hot industries include life sciences, healthcare, insurance and business and financial services.

The Lawyers: The highly regarded **Nancy Spangler** (see p.1773) concentrates her practice on technology companies and investors. She represents clients on venture capital transactions and is experienced in more traditional M&A work.

The Clients: The firm acts for a range of public and private clients from technology and associated industries.

Kaufman & Canoles

The Firm: Competitors praised the "*high-quality work*" of this multioffice law firm. It operates from seven bases across Virginia and can draw upon expertise from each area of the firm. The breakdown of practice areas with a corporate emphasis is highly specialized and includes particular wells of skill in M&A and healthcare. In this last regard the group was recently selected as national counsel for a Canadian health and diet clinic franchise in its US operations. The firm serves as both general and special counsel to local, regional, national and international clients. **The Lawyers:** The preeminent **Vincent Mastracco** has been a leader in the corporate market for many years. Described by peers as "*an absolute gem to deal with,*" he has extensive business sense and a developed commercial transaction background. Other leading practitioners note his "*good vision and finely honed instincts for getting deals done*" important qualities when dealing with high-level individuals and companies. Stablemate **Braxton McKee** is "*well-schooled on healthcare matters*" and takes part in sophisticated deals many of which draw on his extensive knowledge of specialized rules and regulation. His practice is wide-ranging geographically, covering more than 18 states, with a concentration in the rapidly evolving healthcare industry of Hampton Roads, Virginia. **The Clients:** The practice serves a number of regional players in healthcare and other industries and includes public, private, individual and foreign entities.

Shaw Pittman LLP

See firm details p.490
The Firm: Clients pronounced themselves well satisfied with this McLean-based firm, stating: "*you can be confident that you are getting the top people working on your issues.*" The group of over 40 lawyers has bankable experience representing large and growing enterprises in corporate transactional, securities and regulatory matters. It is described as a "*one phone number*" law firm where clients receive the power of a large operation and its multiple disciplines. The practice works with leading US venture capital funds and has solidified its base in the government contracting area. In recent representations the firm has advised Macquarie Securities, a subsidiary of Macquarie Bank, in its $220 million acquisition of Executive Air Support, and represented SIGNAL, provider of information services to the federal government, in connection with its $227 million sale to Veridian. At time of press the firm announced its merger with Pillsbury Winthrop LLP to form Pillsbury Winthrop Shaw Pittman. **The Lawyers:** **Craig Chason**'s (see p.1768) practice involves a fusion of both public and private company transactions and includes commercial and government sector clients. He

has "*terrific expertise*" in the latter area and is well versed at dealing with classified transactions and proxy boards. Clients from his many commercial deals appreciate him for being "*extremely good at taking a win-win as opposed to an adversarial perspective.*" **Jack Lewis** is praised as one of the most prominent lawyers in the Virginia corporate arena. He has more than 30 years' experience in business law dealing with firms from the startup stage to public offering. He is particularly noted for his work in IT and technology. **Steven Meltzer** (see p.1771) is widely respected as a Harvard Business School educated counselor for high-growth entrepreneurial ventures. In recent years he has widened his expertise to include healthcare and life sciences technologies while also remaining at the forefront of information technology. **The Clients:** Macquarie Securities; Dimensions International; Legg Mason Wood Walker; FC Business Systems; Current Analysis and Pharm Athene.

Wilmer Cutler Pickering Hale and Dorr LLP

See firm details p.497
The Firm: The merger in 2004 has expanded and solidified the capabilities and contacts of this "*wonderful*" Virginia firm. Historically recognized for the representation of technology and life sciences, the addition of key clients from Wilmer Cutler Pickering has increased breadth on the non-tech side of the business. The firm is seen as "*a key factor in the market*" and can boast a diverse range of clients in key industries. Of particular interest is the group's representation of emerging companies in public offerings of equity and debt securities. In addition to its quality lawyers in the Reston office, the firm can also draw on experts in the McLean and DC branches. **The Lawyers:** **David Sylvester** (see p.1773) engages in significant representations in the technology section looking after the interests of entrepreneurs and venture capitalists. "*A scarily smart operator,*" he recently represented the lead investor in the $6 million NFR Security venture financing and acted for the issuer in the PowerGrid Fitness Series A offering. **The Clients:** The team represents technology and life sciences companies including Valhalla Partners, Network Alliance, TGS Soft and NetSec.

Band 4

LeClair Ryan, A Professional Corporation

The Firm: Corporate and securities law was one of the firm's first specialties and it is an area in which it continues to have a substantial market presence. The tech boom may have subsided but the group is still known for picking up quality clients in this field many of whom are small and midsize firms. The team also represents clients

in management buyouts, sale and leasebacks, international joint ventures, business acquisitions and sales, providing a well-rounded legal service out of its Richmond office. **The Lawyers:** Competitors claim **Gary LeClair** (see p.1770) is "*the guy to go to for startup companies.*" "*Successful, hard working and entrepreneurial,*" he has developed a sterling reputation in the technology area, being as well respected as a businessman as he is as a traditional corporate lawyer. **The Clients:** A diverse client base includes a number of NASDAQ traded companies.

Venable LLP

The Firm: This "*great firm*" operates via an alliance of offices across the USA, being particularly strong in Northern Virginia, Baltimore and DC. Competitors admire the depth in the firm and the number of quality lawyers on hand. Its ability to handle complex transactions in M&A, joint ventures, corporate governance and venture capital was much commented upon. The firm recently advised SafeNet in its merger with Rainbow Technologies, a transaction that was valued at approximately $450 million. It also handles a range of smaller transactions including those for government contractors looking to consolidate. **The Lawyers:** **Thomas France** fields experience in securities law, M&A and corporate transactions often focusing on public and private offerings of equity and debt securities. He has represented SafeNet in an $84 million public stock offering and helped Intersections Inc in their acquisition of a private company for $21 million. **The Clients:** The group serves corporate, institutional, nonprofit and individual clients throughout the USA and globally.

Willcox & Savage

The Firm: The corporate, securities and finance practice group of this Norfolk-based firm has developed long-standing relationships with its clients over their business lifetimes. The result is that many of these look upon the team as their outsourced legal department. Services proffered include the structuring of business entities, corporate governance, regulatory compliance, financing and business acquisitions. As many of its matters are of some complexity, they require a mixture of skill from related practice areas. The firm addresses this by assembling the required expertise from a pool of talented attorneys. **The Lawyers:** **Thomas Inglima** is the chairman of the firm's corporate, securities and finance section. He primarily deals with M&A transactions and high technology work, providing the same to a variety of national businesses. Peers particularly admire his twin qualities of "*thoughtfulness and inquisitiveness.*"

The Clients: Privately held national communications companies, issuers, underwriters and venture capital firms form part of a diverse client base.

EMPLOYMENT

MAINLY DEFENDANT

Virginia
Leading firms
(Employment: Mainly Defendant)

1 HUNTON & WILLIAMS LLP *Richmond*
MCGUIREWOODS LLP *Richmond*
WILLIAMS MULLEN *Richmond*

2 LECLAIR RYAN, PROFESSIONAL CORP *Richmond*
TROUTMAN SANDERS LLP *Richmond*
VENABLE LLP *Vienna*

3 DLA PIPER RUDNICK GRAY CARY US LLP *Reston*
HOGAN & HARTSON LLP *McLean*
KAUFMAN & CANOLES *Norfolk*
PILLSBURY WINTHROP LLP *McLean*
RAY & ISLER PC *Vienna*

Leading individuals
(Employment: Mainly Defendant)

1 MEATH James *Williams Mullen, Richmond*
ROBERTSON Gregory *Hunton & Williams, Richmond*
WEBB Eugene *Troutman Sanders, Richmond*
WELLFORD Hill *Hunton & Williams, Richmond*

2 BREDEHOFT John *Venable, Vienna*
ISLER Edward *Ray & Isler, Vienna*
NAGLE David *LeClair Ryan, Richmond*
ROBINSON Stephen *McGuireWoods, McLean*
YOUNGER Carter *McGuireWoods, Richmond*

3 BROWN Stanley *Hogan & Hartson, McLean*
CONNOLLY Theresa *DLA Piper, Reston*
CONSTINE David *Troutman Sanders, Richmond*
DARE Mark *Reed Smith, Falls Church*
FLAHERTY Thomas *Pillsbury Winthrop, McLean*
MARSHALL Gary *McGuireWoods, Richmond*
MORSE Clinton *LeClair Ryan, Roanoke*
MURPHY Thomas *Hunton & Williams, McLean*
RUST Dana *McGuireWoods, Richmond*
SMITH David *Venable, Vienna*
SPARKS Robert *Herge Sparks, McLean*
WHITT Burt *Kaufman & Canoles, Norfolk*

Leading individuals (Employee Benefits)
1 DRAY Mark *Hunton & Williams, Richmond*
Firms and individuals are listed alphabetically in each band.

Band 1

Hunton & Williams LLP
See firm details p.1775
The Firm: This large firm *"prescribes the gold standard in employment law,"* its depth and national presence placing it at the forefront of the market. The team represents banks, brokerages and companies in the chemical industry such as Honeywell. It is also well prepared for dealing with all Sarbanes-Oxley related issues.
The Lawyers: The *"dean of employment litigation in the state,"* **Hill Wellford** (see p.1774) represents a variety of blue-chip clients. This *"superb attorney"* remains as active as ever on sex discrimination claims and further handles a number of FLSA class actions. Peers regard fellow team head **Gregory Robertson** (see p.1772) as *"the star of labor practice"* due to his frequent appearances in the Supreme Court. Sources praise him for his *"hard work, professionalism, and outstanding expertise on employment law."* According to market sources *"he deserves the highest accolades."* Colleague **Thomas Murphy** (see p.1771) is a lawyer with *"a great practical approach"* whose good all-round employment practice has a particular specialism involving discrimination cases. Market observers highlighted his *"ethical way of handling cases"* and his *"pleasant manner with clients."* **Mark Dray** (see p.1769) is highly respected for his expertise in employee benefits and executive compensation issues. He has advised three of the largest companies in the country.
The Clients: IBM; Constellation Energy Group; Honeywell and other blue-chip companies.

McGuireWoods LLP
The Firm: This *"powerhouse"* has a labor and employment team that handles everything from employee benefits and labor/management relations to wrongful discharge matters. Interviewees enthused over its international capabilities, applauding the firm for its work with clients in overseas markets. They were quick to point out, however, that it remains *"one of the big players on the local and regional scene"* as well.
The Lawyers: *"Efficient and practical"* **Carter Younger** was praised by peers for his *"technical superiority,"* and by clients for his *"high levels of responsiveness."* In addition to his expert knowledge of employment discrimination and union-management relations, he also stands out in alternative dispute resolution. **Stephen Robinson** was described as *"simply a top litigator in employment issues."* *"Persistent and bright,"* he recently acted for a large healthcare client and is currently representing approximately 40 professional athletes. **Dana Rust**, meanwhile, is a seasoned trial lawyer with extensive experience in a variety of courts. He is mainly involved in litigating in the employment discrimination area and is a *"quick-witted"* lawyer respected for his *"successful litigation practice."* Completing the picture is **Gary Marshall**. As chairman of the labor and employment team he is *"a great friend to the unions"* having counseled the Teamsters, UNITE, PACE, and the IBEW. He is widely admired for his *"excellent client base."*
The Clients: The team represents household names from a variety of sectors.

Williams Mullen
The Firm: This large concern may be *"run like a vast business"* but has an excellent feel when it comes to handling local issues. It tackles both labor and employment cases offering a high-quality service described as *"a cut above the normal."* Its recent sorties have seen it act for clients in defeating union-organizing attempts in a number of major manufacturing sectors.
The Lawyers: **James Meath** gained distinction for his *"brilliant client relation skills"* and the *"ability to give advice beyond the current matter."* This *"A-lawyer with a great perspective on matters"* represents clients including Media General Corp and Exel Mining Systems.
The Clients: Attorneys in this team have experience of serving a full range of industries such as mining, printing, steel and food and beverages.

Band 2

LeClair Ryan, A Professional Corporation
The Firm: Market sources acknowledge the *"remarkable versatility"* of this national and regional-oriented labor and employment group. The team compromises approximately 18 attorneys and offers a full range of employment litigation and counseling services. Clients praised it, in particular, for its mediation capability.
The Lawyers: **David Nagle**'s (see p.1771) practice is focused on the implementation and enforcement of arbitration programs. Interviewees endorsed the outstanding counseling and teaching skills of this *"intelligent and comprehensive"* attorney. He is joined in the tables by *"the best lawyer in Roanoke"* **Clinton Morse** (see p.1771), the cochair of the practice group. Morse specializes in the representation of unionized companies and is an acknowledged maven on union avoidance strategies.

The Clients: The team's clients include high-tech manufacturers, financial institutions, automotive suppliers, airlines, local government bodies and trade associations.

Troutman Sanders LLP

The Firm: Clients welcomed the *"affordable service"* offered by a firm looking to make strides following its merger with Mays & Valentine in 2001. *"Top of the class in the corporate employment arena,"* it is also strongly involved in collective bargaining agreements acting for clients exclusively on the management side. Interviewees were of the opinion that the group needs to expand further to reach its full potential but admired it for its *"solid, dependable approach."*
The Lawyers: **Eugene Webb** is highly regarded by competitors for his *"honest approach to employment matters."* More than one interviewee used the phrase *"knowledgeable and reliable"* to describe this excellent lawyer and litigator. Also on board is **David Constine**, a *"bright and tenacious"* pure commercial litigator whose practice encompasses contractual disputes, employee benefits and general civil rights litigation.
The Clients: The team advises clients from a variety of industries on a regional and national basis.

Venable LLP

The Firm: Commentators respect this Vienna-based *"responsive and knowledgeable"* team for its *"swiftness and straightforward approach".* The team advises management in claims of sexual harassment, wrongful discharge, employment class actions, as well as matters involving occupational safety and health and immigration.
The Lawyers: Peers endorsed **John Bredehoft** as a *"practical, academic and astute tactician."* A *"unique individual with a relaxed approach,"* he focuses on civil litigation and business counseling in the field of employment and civil rights law. The other standout in this team is **David Smith**, an *"aggressive and successful"* attorney who has extensive experience in labor law and collective bargaining negotiations. He recently participated in collective bargaining that resulted in a replacement agreement and special drug formulary for Freeman United Coal Mining Company.
The Clients: The firm represents a range of businesses on a regional and national level.

Band 3

DLA Piper Rudnick Gray Cary US LLP

See firm details p.765
The Firm: The firm has an impressive international network having 49 offices throughout Asia, Europe and the USA. Nationally it can call on 55 attorneys nationwide who come together to *"provide a comfort level to the client that is exceptional".* The Northern Virginia labor and employment team was hailed for its *"excellent advice and training"* on how to avoid litigation. Much of its work is tailored to the railway and airline industries.
The Lawyers: *"Reachable 24 hours a day,"* **Theresa Connolly** (see p.1768) is a dominant force within the team. Clients distinguished her as *"responsive"* and her legal advice as *"right on the target."* While she has made a name for her litigation skills, sources add that she is also valued for handling traditional labor relations issues including union elections, unfair labor practices, union arbitrations, and related proceedings before the NLRB.
The Clients: The team represents clients in a wide variety of fields, including agriculture, aluminum, communications, construction, electronics, food and beverages, pharmaceuticals, steel, trade associations, telecommunications and textiles.

Hogan & Hartson LLP

See firm details p.484
The Firm: This Northern Virginia office has been serving regional, national, and international clients since opening its doors in 1985. Part of a network of 21 offices across the USA, Europe and Asia, it has a labor and employment team that has recently been expanding to serve growing demand in the market. Clients confessed to researchers that its service can be expensive but stressed the benefit of being able to capitalize on the team's *"extremely deep resources and depth of manpower."*
The Lawyers: *"The truly gifted"* **Stanley Brown** (see p.1767) has represented Dana Corporation on major labor relations matters including NLRB cases involving the company's partnership agreement with the UAW. He has also advised Dana on NAFTA proceedings in Canada and the USA and handled class action work for Pepco Energy Services.
The Clients: Many clients hail from the telecommunications and technology fields but many other industries are serviced. These include the automotive, construction, broadcasting, real estate management, publishing, and healthcare sectors.

Kaufman & Canoles

The Firm: The labor and employment practice of this firm is one of the largest in Southeastern Virginia. Founded by confidentiality and non-compete expert Burt Whitt, the practice includes two consultants who work closely with the team, one a former area director of the EEOC and the other a former director of the Wage-Hour Division of the DOL.
The Lawyers: **Burt Whitt** garnered interviewees' plaudits for his general expertise in the employment field. *"A real hot ticket"* in his chosen arena, he is particularly celebrated in the Norfolk and Tidewater districts of the state.

The Clients: The firm acts for Virginia-based employers as well as for national and international companies with branches in the state.

Pillsbury Winthrop LLP

See firm details p.1364
The Firm: This excellent coast-to-coast firm brings its reputation as a *"heavyweight performer"* to North Virginia. The employment and labor team here has a wide remit advising employers in federal, state and local litigation. Its recent outings have seen it representing a healthcare client before the California Supreme Court, acting for PG&E and Chevron in class litigation and advising an Internet company on the Worker Adjustment and Retraining Notification Act. At time of press the firm announced its merger with Shaw Pittman to form Pillsbury Winthrop Shaw Pittman.
The Lawyers: Team leader **Thomas Flaherty** (see p.1769), was described as a *"very ethical, accessible and practical"* lawyer. Born of a strong litigation background, this *"thorough and tenacious lawyer"* has a reputation such that *"his word is law."*
The Clients: The team represents clients in many sectors including the grocery, medical, shipping, software, education, electronics, telecommunications, airlines, biotechnology, retail, power, chemical, finance and construction industries.

Ray & Isler PC

The Firm: One client described the six lawyers of this firm as *"brilliant strategic thinkers supremely adept at advising and negotiating in employment disputes."* The firm's practice is dedicated exclusively to the representation of management in all aspects of labor, employment and employee benefits law. Up to 70% of the practice is devoted solely to litigation.
The Lawyers: *"Sincerity, depth and breadth"* earn **Edward Isler** (see p.1770) a strong reputation in the market. According to clients he is an *"energetic, warm, humorous"* counselor who *"does wonders for the reputation of the profession."*
The Clients: DCI Publishing; Jorge Scientific Corporation; Enterprise Rent-a-Car; Cable & Wireless USA; Mid Atlantic Medical Services; Community Residences; Richmond American Homes of Virginia; The Hartford; Infonet Services and Global Printing Company.

Other Notable Practitioners

"Very skilled litigator" **Mark Dare** (see p.1768) focuses upon rendering advice to employers on litigation avoidance and defending them when they are forced to the courtroom door. Strong on wrongful discharge and discrimination claims, peers praise this Reed Smith LLP attorney for his *"ability to battle through the storm armed with dry humor and wit."* **Robert Sparks** from Herge, Sparks & Christopher LLP was also

1756   All quotes in the text are from interviews with clients and competitors.

CHAMBERS USA 2005

well received for his "*fighting spirit on behalf of his clients.*" Interviewees were particularly impressed at his commitment to pro bono work in the context of a busy practice.

ENVIRONMENT

Virginia
Leading firms (Environment)

1. **HUNTON & WILLIAMS LLP** *Richmond*
   MCGUIREWOODS LLP *Richmond*
2. **TROUTMAN SANDERS LLP** *Richmond*
3. **AQUALAW PLC** *Richmond*
   ELLIS THORP & JEWETT *Richmond*
   LECLAIR RYAN, PROFESSIONAL CORP *Richmond*
   WILLIAMS MULLEN *Richmond*

Leading individuals (Environment)

1. **EVANS David** *McGuireWoods*, Richmond
   FINTO Kevin *Hunton & Williams*, Richmond
   HAYES Timothy *Hunton & Williams*, Richmond
2. **DANIEL II John** *Troutman Sanders*, Richmond
   ELLIS William *Ellis Thorp*, Richmond
   GASCH Manning *Hunton & Williams*, Richmond
   KNAUER Thomas *McGuireWoods*, Richmond
   MARTIN Channing *Williams Mullen*, Richmond
   RYAN James *Troutman Sanders*, Richmond
   SLONE Daniel *McGuireWoods*, Richmond
3. **BUNIVA Brian** *LeClair Ryan*, Richmond
   CALAMITA Paul *Aqualaw*, Richmond
   THORNHILL James *McGuireWoods*, Richmond

Up-and-coming individuals

   SMITH Brooks *Hunton & Williams*, Richmond

Firms and individuals are listed alphabetically in each band.

Band 1

Hunton & Williams LLP
See firm details p.1775

The Firm: The firm is acknowledged by peers as "*a major player in the environmental market,*" mainly due to its team of "*multitalented and persistent*" operators. The Virginia team now consists of 12 attorneys who integrate with a wider national network of about 60 lawyers. In addition, the firm can draw upon the international resources of five offices in the Far East and Europe, highlighted by its flourishing reputation in European environmental law anchored in the Brussels office. In the USA, its established profile initially centered upon counseling electric utilities on the Clean Air Act and Clean Water Act among other matters. The department has since expanded in terms of clientele and experience – now boasting expertise in a full range of environmental issues such as audit and compliance work, environmental crimes, regulatory enforcement and mass tort litigation. Examples of recent engagements include counseling on the conversion of a 300-acre railroad facility into a mixed-use development

The Lawyers: Timothy Hayes (see p.1770) earned respect as "*a master in the field of environmental law,*" according to commentators. The head of the department impressed clients with his mastery of a wide range of environmental issues, most recently for his work involving a major management project. **Kevin Finto** (see p.1769) has been focusing on the energy, electricity generation and agriculture sectors. His ability to give "*excellent regulatory*" advice is highly appreciated by clients. **Manning Gasch** (see p.1769) is described as "*a veteran in environmental law,*" while "*rising star*" **Brooks Smith** (see p.1772) is an "*all-rounder*" with emphasis on the Clean Water Act and multimedia compliance audits.

The Clients: Smithfield Foods; American Water; Bank of America; General Dynamics; Georgia-Pacific; Nortel Networks and Wells Fargo.

McGuireWoods LLP

The Firm: The Richmond office enjoys a reputation for handling complex environmental cases, particularly taking a lead on the concept of water trading. A significant highlight this year involves the federal government in a dispute concerning a combined water and sewer system. The firm's clientele consists of a mixture of large and small domestic international businesses, trade organizations and municipalities. Clients applaud the environmental team for their "*outstanding knowledge of environmental issues,*" which encompasses such areas as the Clean Air Act, Clean Water Act and OSHA-related defense. The team's "*breadth and depth*" is also demonstrated by work in land use and zoning.

The Lawyers: Considered as "*truly one of the top water lawyers in the country,*" **David Evans** attracts praise for his "*meticulous and incredible knowledge of the environmental practice.*" **Thomas Knauer** has recently been involved in some significant enforcement actions for the EPA. Knauer has built a reputation as an outstanding lawyer in the field of air law. Clients portray him as a lawyer who "*understands their business needs.*" Described by interviewees as "*creative and decent,*" **Daniel Slone** has developed a reputable practice centered on sustainability issues and the development of new towns. He heads the environmental solutions group along with **James Thornhill**, who specializes in the environmental aspects of M&As. Armed with "*incredible legal knowledge of environmental issues,*" he also regularly advises clients on environmental, land use and zoning

matters.

The Clients: DuPont, Dominion and the City of Richmond are examples of the firm's diverse clientele.

Band 2

Troutman Sanders LLP

The Firm: The team, which draws on resources from its multiple offices in the southeast, earns high marks for its expertise on compliance and permitting matters related to water, air quality and hazardous waste. This multidisciplinary team divides its time between counseling and litigation. It also has experience of extensive involvement in regulatory negotiations work at the federal and state levels. The team has handled numerous municipal solid waste facility construction projects, including gaining various government approvals.

The Lawyers: Jim Ryan is respected for his "*vast institutional knowledge*" of environmental law, while **John Daniel** is valued by clients for delivering "*perfect counseling on complicated issues*" such as those relating to municipal solid waste facilities. His "*strategic intelligence*" is also illustrated in various air permitting proceedings.

The Clients: Akzo Nobel Chemicals; ATOFINA Chemicals; Cinergy; USFilter; General Mills; Southern Nuclear; American Home Products and Nuclear Energy Institute (NEI).

Band 3

Aqualaw PLC

The Firm: This newcomer to the environmental table has a broad water law practice, operating as general counsel to several national and statewide trade associations. It often assists clients on federal and state water-related proceedings, including those related to municipal wastewater projects. Another drawing card is the firm's expertise on legislative representation, and its litigation prowess extends to enforcement defense.

The Lawyers: Paul Calamita is an "*experienced and respected practitioner*" in water law issues. He formerly worked for McGuireWoods before setting up this "*preeminent*" environmental boutique with Chris Pomeroy.

The Clients: Maryland Association of Municipal Wastewater Agencies; South Carolina Water Quality Association; Virginia Association of Municipal Wastewater Agencies; West Virginia Municipal Water Quality Association and CSO Partnership.

Ellis Thorp & Jewett

The Firm: Although relatively smaller than some of its competitors, this Richmond-based boutique has an excellent reputation in the field. The respected environmental practice has acted for clients in different areas such as the Clean Air Act, water pollution, toxic substances and regulatory programs.

The Lawyers: The firm enters *Chambers'* rankings on the strength of some talented environmental lawyers, led by the *"outstanding"* **William Ellis.** Formerly of Hunton & Williams, he parlays more than 20 years of experience in environmental law into *"effective advocacy"* for clients. Credited with a *"formidable intellect,"* he has handled cases for and against municipalities.

The Clients: The team has advised public companies, small businesses and various government entities.

LeClair Ryan, A Professional Corporation

The Firm: This firm's debut in the table was largely due to the *"highly effective lawyer"* Brian Buniva. With ten offices statewide and in DC, it can draw on a wealth of resources to assist clients on a broad array of legal problems, including zoning and environmental permitting. Its litigation experience is equally impressive, and involves such areas as the Resource Conservation and Recovery Act and the Clean Water Act.

The Lawyers: **Brian Buniva** (see p.1768) is a key component to the firm's success in this area, boasting more than 25 years of experience. Viewed as an *"aggressive environment lawyer with a strong litigation background,"* he is also considered a commanding force in land use.

The Clients: The team has advised municipalities, developers and agricultural clients among others.

Williams Mullen

The Firm: The seven-attorney environmental team in the Richmond office is relatively smaller than some of its competitors, though its influence on the market is considerably more substantial, observers said. The group *"successfully handles a variety of issues concerning the environment,"* including core strengths in environmental permitting and related litigation.

The Lawyers: Praise for the firm often centers on **Channing Martin**, a *"top-notch lawyer"* who has a *"perfect grasp of how to present the facts to a client's advantage."* Chairman of the environmental team, he is also experienced in mediation as well.

The Clients: Manufacturers, petroleum companies, municipalities and trade associations among others feature in the firm's client list.

INTELLECTUAL PROPERTY

> **Virginia**
> **Leading firms**
> (Intellectual Property: Northern Virginia)
>
> **1** OBLON, SPIVAK, MCCLELLAND *Alexandria*
> PILLSBURY WINTHROP LLP *McLean*
>
> **2** ARNOLD & PORTER LLP *McLean*
> BIRCH, STEWART, KOLASCH & BIRCH *Falls Church*
> BURNS DOANE SWECKER & MATHIS *Alexandria*
> FINNEGAN HENDERSON FARABOW *Reston*
> HOGAN & HARTSON LLP *McLean*
> MCGUIREWOODS, *McLean*
> MORRISON & FOERSTER LLP *McLean*
> NIXON & VANDERHYE P.C. *Arlington*
> OLIFF & BERRIDGE, PLC *Alexandria*
> SHAW PITTMAN LLP *McLean*
>
> Firms are listed alphabetically in each band.

Oblon, Spivak, McClelland, Maier & Neustadt PC

The Firm: The long-standing reputation of this specialist firm leaves a *"substantial footprint on the market"* thus setting the standard for others. Something of a powerhouse organization, it covers litigation, copyright, nanotechnology and export control among others, combining its historical knowledge of procedure with up-to-date understanding of new technology. Appreciating its manifold strengths, commentators describe the firm as a *"great patent prosecution house, and probably the most prolific builder of patent practice in the state."* While the high number of patents was highlighted, sources emphasized that quality was in no way sacrificed for quantity, confirming the firm to be a bastion of efficiency and effectiveness.

The Lawyers: Venerated **Arthur Neustadt** maintains high visibility in the market. He specializes in IP litigation where he is known to get great settlements quickly due in part to the good grasp he has of the dynamics of litigation. A man who *"knows when to push forward and when to stand back,"* he is, according to competitors, *"proficient at identifying issues and working with a cost-benefit approach."* **Charles Gholz** specializes in litigation, particularly patent interferences, and is described as the *"preeminent guy in the USA in this area."* An expressive and experienced attorney, he knows how to promote himself to the best advantage and enjoys a high degree of success.

The Clients: The firm advises a range of clients including foreign and US government agencies, multinationals and universities.

Pillsbury Winthrop LLP

See firm details p.1364

The Firm: The Northern Virginia branch of this *"terrific multioffice firm"* is located in a hot spot for innovative businesses and as such is ideally placed to serve the needs of emerging growth and technology companies. In the opinion of interviewees, the group is *"thorough with a good deal of depth,"* which affords it coast-to-coast reach. The 45 lawyers in the IP section handle a large proportion of big-ticket litigation in all technological areas, demonstrating *"great control in many a high-profile case."* The firm successfully represented American Biophysics against Blue Rhino in widely publicized proceedings that resulted in the upholding of the validity of American Biophysics' pioneering insect-trap patent. At time of press the firm announced its merger with Shaw Pittman to form Pillsbury Winthrop Shaw Pittman.

The Lawyers: **Jack Barufka** (see p.1767) heads up the practice area working with clients on strategizing patent portfolios and dispute resolution. His recent outings have included constructing a large patent portfolio for Stanley Tools and leading a successful enforcement campaign to enable the company to capture a monopoly on the market. Clients described him as *"conscientious and extremely focused."* *"Successful"* attorney **William Atkins** (see p.1767) typically handles large complex commercial matters that relate to infringement, ownership and abuses of IP. He has shone in several jury trials lately, obtaining a successful defense verdict in a contentious commercial patent infringement case. Primarily focused on IP litigation, **Adam Hess** (see p.1770) also completes high-level client counseling, advising on strategies for IP portfolios. He took a leading position in the representation of American Biophysics on its patent infringement case. According to competitors, trusted lawyer **James Gatto** (see p.1769) is *"good at answering the question asked"* and *"has the ability to convince others of the validity of his answers."* Peers described him as *"polished, well practiced and well spoken."* Prior to joining the firm, he headed the IP practice of Mintz Levin's Reston and Washington offices.

The Clients: Corvis; Sharp Electronics; Home Depot; American Biophysics and further national and international clients feature on the client list.

Virginia
Leading individuals
(Intellectual Property: Northern Virginia)

1 BARUFKA Jack *Pillsbury Winthrop*, McLean
BRETSCHNEIDER Barry *Morrison & Foerster*, McLean
GHOLZ Charles *Oblon Spivak*, Alexandria
NEUSTADT Arthur *Oblon Spivak*, Alexandria

2 ANDERSON John *Troutman Sanders*, McLean
ATKINS William *Pillsbury Winthrop*, McLean
CAMPBELL Christopher *Hunton & Williams*, McLean
DOYLE Scott *Morrison & Foerster*, McLean
GATTO James *Pillsbury Winthrop*, McLean
GOTTS Lawrence *Shaw Pittman*, Washington, DC
HESS Adam *Pillsbury Winthrop*, McLean
MEYER Richard *McGuireWoods*, McLean
NIXON Larry *Nixon & Vanderhye*, Arlington
OLIFF James *Oliff & Berridge*, Alexandria
OSSOLA Charles *Arnold & Porter*, Washington, DC
PORTER Philip *Hogan & Hartson*, McLean

Individuals are listed alphabetically in each band.

Arnold & Porter LLP

See firm details p.478

The Firm: The distinguished transactional and litigation record of this established firm is such that clients in varied industries choose it as their one-stop shop for IP representation. More than able to solve multidimensional business problems through the utilization of the firm's substantial resources, the practice covers a cornucopia of technology areas from pharmaceuticals to communications systems.

The Lawyers: **Charles Ossola** (see p.27537) is "*about as smart as they come*" in the cutting-edge field of trademark and patent litigation. He is "*a quick thinker, good on his feet*" and consequently a formidable presence in federal district courts.

The Clients: The team represents cutting-edge clients in the technology, biotech and communications industries ranging from start-up companies to global firms.

Birch, Stewart, Kolasch & Birch, LLP

The Firm: This highly respected boutique has been providing a range of IP services for more than 25 years, and is described by competitors as a "*great patent prosecution house.*" Industries it covers number chemistry, medical devices, biotech, pharmaceuticals, computer science and mechanical technologies among others. The firm also handles a large amount of foreign patent prosecution work taking advantage of its "*great support and infrastructure.*" The presence of trademark and copyright and litigation practices further helps to give the firm a well-rounded perspective.

The Lawyers: Raymond Stewart acts as senior counsel in the firm and brings to bear over 45 years' experience in the IP field.

The Clients: The client base embraces pharmaceutical and chemical companies from around the world, as well as clients from the electrical, life sciences and mechanical engineering sectors.

Burns Doane Swecker & Mathis LLP

The Firm: The full spectrum of IP matters is undertaken by this Alexandria-based firm. Its group of more than 80 attorneys provides a "*good, solid service to European clients*" but is generally better known for its domestic work. Many of its representations emanate from inside the state and the opening of offices in California and North Carolina has provided further local support for its major domestic clients. Interviewees were quick to single out the firm's "*leading biotech practice,*" praising specialist attorneys who negotiate utility and plant patent prosecutions, patent litigation and patent interference matters. Members of the group have specific expertise in genetic engineering, neuroscience and immunology applications, applying to all these areas "*a strategic skill that is most impressive.*" The practice as a whole has been going through a period of reorganization but most commentators feel that it is holding its own and is set to make further progress in the future.

The Lawyers: The team includes Ibrahim Bassam who heads up the trademark/copyright practice group.

The Clients: Biotech clients feature prominently. These range from startup companies to Fortune 500 entities spread across the USA and beyond.

Finnegan Henderson Farabow Garrett & Dunner LLP

The Firm: A legion of experienced and well-regarded lawyers is at hand here to act on representations in virtually all of the familiar technology and product categories. Opened in 2002, the Reston office offers areas of expertise covering biotech, trademark law, electrical issues and computer technology. Notably, the group's experience in cutting-edge technologies gives it a great track position on cases coming from the fastest growing industries such as gene therapy and the world of Internet operating systems. When asked to single out a particular strength, competitors designated the firm "*great for litigation,*" pointing to attorneys who "*ask the right questions and shore them up with solid argument.*" Such skills prove a particular boon in the appeals area where the team has built up a fine reputation due to years of experience managing contentious cases in the US Eastern District Court.

The Lawyers: Charles Lipsey works from the Reston office concentrating on IP litigation, and in particular patent infringement, in the District, Federal and US Supreme Courts.

The Clients: The team represents clients in virtually every industry sector from cosmetics and pharmaceuticals to semiconductors and telecom.

Hogan & Hartson LLP

See firm details p.484

The Firm: The Northern Virginia office of this global firm is well versed in IP matters, being a veteran in the representation of emerging and progressive technology. It takes a holistic approach to the full gamut of IP matters and has forged strategic alliances across borders with in-house attorneys and outside clients. Competitors admire its long-standing reputation, noting that through length of experience and depth of practice it has forged seamless contacts and connections all over the world. Many attorneys in its team have prior experience of in-house positions and are accordingly rated by clients for their accumulated business knowledge and ethics: "*Prompt, responsive, available and willing to go the extra mile, these attorneys know how to keep the customer satisfied.*" In recent times the McLean office has noticed a sharpening focus on outsourcing deals and government regulation while maintaining its more traditional IP representations. Its recent efforts, many of which occur on the global stage, have included acting for King Pharmaceuticals whom the firm represented in distribution deals and strategic alliances with hospitals.

The Lawyers: **Philip Porter** (see p.1772) "*balances a sense of industry and business practice with legal knowledge*" and has "*comprehensive and up-to-date IP acumen,*" according to clients. He has a "*patient, respectful manner*" and clients appreciate his accessibility.

The Clients: King Pharmaceuticals, Textron and Martek Biosciences alongside Fortune 500 companies in the telecom arena feature on the client roster.

Morrison & Foerster LLP

See firm details p.293

The Firm: This global-reaching firm has 19 offices in total and is a solid IP presence in the market. Its interdepartmental group specializes in patent, trademark, trade secrets and unfair competition and related matters. Amidst this, the patent group is heavily involved in the preparation and prosecution of patents for domestic clients, patent applications from foreign clients and patent enforcement on both the offensive and defensive side. Its work here leans heavily toward computers and biotech. Of particular note lately has been its work on behalf of Johnson & Johnson in an interference case and its representation of Siemens as its chief counsel on company prosecutions. The Northern Virginia office has strengthened its outlook in recent years and continues to expand, reflecting its belief in the long-term strength of the region.

The Lawyers: **Barry Bretschneider** (see p.1767) is a patent interference specialist who breaks down his time into litigation, prosecution and advice on patent matters. He represents top-end US and foreign corporations and has been a

Virginia

Leading firms
(Intellectual Property: Southern Virginia)

1. **HUNTON & WILLIAMS LLP** *Richmond*
2. **KAUFMAN & CANOLES** *Norfolk*
   LECLAIR RYAN, PROFESSIONAL CORP *Richmond*
   MCGUIREWOODS LLP *Richmond*
   TROUTMAN SANDERS LLP *Richmond*
   WILLIAMS MULLEN *Richmond*

Leading individuals
(Intellectual Property: Southern Virginia)

1. **MARTINEZ DE ANDINO J Michael** *Hunton*, Richmond
   MUGEL Christopher *Kaufman & Canoles*, Richmond
   NOONA Stephen *Kaufman & Canoles*, Norfolk
   TITLEY Ian *Williams Mullen*, Richmond
2. **BROOKE Robert** *Troutman Sanders*, Richmond
   FARMER John *Leading-Edge*, Richmond
   KRIZAN Lisa *LMK*, Richmond
   MYTELKA Craig *Williams Mullen*, Richmond
   RIOPELLE Brian *McGuireWoods*, Richmond
   TATA Robert *Hunton & Williams*, Norfolk

Firms and individuals are listed alphabetically in each band.

lead player in the representation of Dyson advising the company on its US patent portfolio and securing significant protection on its washing machine technology. Colleague **Scott Doyle** (see p.1769) is active nationally and has continued to litigate on IP matters since joining the company in 1993. A broad practice also sees him handling portfolio development and licensing for a selection of national clients.

The Clients: Dyson; Nikon; Siemens; Johnson & Johnson and ACTV.

Nixon & Vanderhye P.C.

The Firm: Our interviewees highlighted the tough advocacy skills on offer at this Arlington outfit. Specializing in IP law in all its many guises, its lawyers are described as "*analytically quick*" and "*full of presence in court.*" Best known as a "*highly successful litigation firm,*" its group of more than 30 IP attorneys also excels on the paperwork front preparing and prosecuting patent applications, registering copyrights and protecting the foreign IP rights of its clients.

The Lawyers: "*Standout*" **Larry Nixon** receives due respect for helping to grow the firm from its seed. With his well-rounded skill set and technical background, clients value his "*service and responsiveness.*"

The Clients: Clients include individuals, entrepreneurial companies, midsized manufacturers, universities and multinational corporations.

Oliff & Berridge, PLC

The Firm: Described by market forces as a "*great patent prosecution house,*" this committed boutique has provided the full spectrum of IP legal services to a range of clients for more than

20 years. Characterized by "*clear, frank and prompt communication,*" the group assists multinationals, domestic entities, smaller privately owned companies and individual investors. Its standing is such that it routinely ranks in the top ten IP firms nationally in terms of the number of US patents issued and is feared for its litigation skills. Able to call upon lawyers who have experienced litigation in all its guises, the team offers representation that is both "*aggressive and efficient.*"

The Lawyers: **James Oliff** handles litigation and patent prosecution work for a range of clients cross-state and internationally. His "*teamwork skills are particularly strong,*" a fact identified by clients who praised him for "*always striving to secure the best possible outcome.*"

The Clients: The team acts for a large and diverse selection of domestic and international clients including Fortune 200 corporations.

Shaw Pittman LLP
See firm details p.490

The Firm: Termed a "*high-quality firm*" by significant competitors, Shaw Pittman takes on cases in a myriad of fields, including, but not limited to, antitrust law, products liability, international trade and government contracting. The firm's high-profile representations have included acting for Honeywell International in a Section 1498 action that alleged government infringement of patents regarding night vision technology. At the time of going to press, the firm announced its merger with Pillsbury Winthrop to form Pillsbury Winthrop Shaw Pittman.

The Lawyers: **Lawrence Gotts**' (see p.1769) "*track record is phenomenal*" according to competitors. He is regarded as an "*impressive litigator*" who has obtained recoveries for clients running into several hundred million dollars while also successfully defending against claims of a similar magnitude. He represents clients, ranging from Fortune 100s to emerging companies in all facets of IP law.

The Clients: The firm provides representation to leading corporations, government entities, emerging growth companies and privately owned organizations.

Hunton & Williams LLP
See firm details p.1775

The Firm: The success of this megafirm's IP group is founded on its representation on matters pertaining to the full panoply of IP law. Peers recognize excellence across the board from a team of "*top-notch lawyers able to handle very complex cases.*" While counseling in all aspects of patent law, the firm has significant experience in complex patent law prosecution matters, interferences, re-examinations and reissues. An increase in M&A activity has prompted a follow-on rise in due diligence leading to further

involvement in counseling and portfolio advice. Many of the cases tackled are high profile, covering areas that include Internet business, telecom and biotech issues. A lineup impressive in its depth and diversity includes lawyers who have shown themselves to be "*savvy, committed and communicative.*" One client was prompted to enthuse that it's "*the best of the firms that we have used.*"

The Lawyers: Thought by many to have the strongest patent practice in the state, **Michael Martinez de Andino** (see p.1770) impresses with his "*comprehensive knowledge and abilities.*" Clients note that he has "*pinpoint accuracy in sorting out problems with contracts: he finds the best way to file patents and is conscious of cost-effective concerns.*" One competitor sums up his superior standing by saying: "*While everyone talks a big game, he can play it.*" **Christopher Campbell** (see p.1768) focuses on a mix of litigation and counseling and is domestically oriented with the cases he chooses. Peers say he is "*instrumental in expanding patent work,*" doing so with energy and panache. A close competitor noted that "*negotiating with him was a pleasure and mutually beneficial, due to his acumen for the law and practical abilities.*" **Robert Tata** (see p.1773) is described as a "*down-to-earth and extremely smart litigator*" who clients find easy to approach. He has represented Sony Pictures in a copyright issue and also taken part in several high-profile jury trials.

The Clients: Active Communications; Electrolux; Tyco; Smithfield Foods; Pentair; Globespan Virata and General Dynamics.

Kaufman & Canoles

The Firm: The technology ventures group of this full-service law firm specializes in counseling businesses in managing their IP assets under patent, trademark, copyright and trade secrets laws. Its attorneys have combined expertise encompassing all these areas and generally contract their business for both regional and national clients. Technology firms form the bulk of this client base but general business clients of all sizes are catered for including engineering concerns and universities.

The Lawyers: **Stephen Noona** specializes in federal litigation within the rocket docket court of the Eastern District of Virginia, a forum where speedy trial skills are of the essence. A combination of "*efficiency in abundance*" and "*splendid trial skills,*" he has successfully handled innumerable cases involving trademark, copyright, patent and trade secrets law. He is now joined at the firm by **Christopher Mugel**, a lateral hire from LeClair Ryan. Mugel is known for his "*deep knowledge of IP law*" and his "*good sense regarding the practical application of the law.*" He is a counselor who is "*aware of the business ramifications and realities of deals*" and "*not one to fight over pointless issues.*"

The Clients: Software, computer and other technology developers, scientists, engineers and research firms form the bulk of the clientele.

LeClair Ryan, A Professional Corporation

The Firm: This national firm operates from three bases in Virginia projecting a "*dynamic and enterprising*" aspect to competitors. Its proactive nature has led to it growing its presence across the area, particularly from its bases in the Alexandria and Norfolk offices. In terms of specialization, while the group is broad-based in its concerns, it has a visible niche in serving the needs of emerging technology companies. As a compact firm itself, it is experienced in handling small and medium-sized clients and startups in the hi-tech, semiconductor, software, database provider and pharmaceutical sectors among others. The type of work taken on is expansive and includes complex licensing matters, trademark and copyright issues, enterprise and outsourcing arrangements and insolvency litigation.

The Lawyers: Dana Finberg heads up the firm's IP practice.

The Clients: The firm represents a mixture of emerging companies and technology-based firms across the country.

McGuireWoods LLP

The Firm: Traditionally strong, this Richmond firm has developed a definite IP presence through the cultivation of its established client base. It acts, in the main, for a "*nice stable of publicly traded clients*" and an assortment of retailers, merchandisers, financial institutions, insurance companies and telecom providers, most of its work being handled in the domestic marketplace. Acknowledged by peers for its robust registration and prosecution practice, the firm also takes on a range of work in the core areas of IP law such as trademark, unfair competition and copyright. In the patent arena, the firm files and prosecutes applications in the USA and abroad, proceeding to litigation where necessary. Commentators were swift to praise a team heralded for its "*formidable advisory skills*" and one that also tackles trademark and trade secrets litigation in abundance.

The Lawyers: Richard Meyer is head of the firm's patent practice working out of its Tysons Corner office. Described by competitors as "*a man who bows to no one*," he has been successful in building a practice based on the strategic intersection between the enforcement, defense

and development of patent and trademark rights both domestically and abroad. Brian Riopelle is, first and foremost, an established IP litigator with considerable experience in trademark, copyright, trade dress and patent litigation. Known to competitors as being "*reasonable about where to draw the line*," he is also lauded as a "*man of integrity*" with an enduring reputation.

The Clients: Circuit City; Siemens; Infineon Technologies and Dominion Power.

Troutman Sanders LLP

The Firm: With a respected presence across the state and nationwide, the firm fields a broad IP practice group that adds to its overall depth. Matters arise from an evenly spread range of trademark prosecution, maintenance work, litigation, preliminary patent advice and general licensing advice, for national and local clients. Much of the business comes through the established corporate department and conversely attorneys take on specialist IP matters in general M&A deals. The primary focus in Virginia is on litigation, where much of the firm's representations are for brick and mortar type industries, rather than startups, which were not affected by the recession.

The Lawyers: John Anderson is described as a "*great litigator who knows the game*" and understands how to lead outside firms around the depths and shallows of the Virginia system: "*On a big task he will nail it.*" Peers respect his "*personal integrity*," saying he will get to the heart of the matter fairly and honestly. Robert Brooke heads up the department and is principally known for IP and general commercial litigation, most of which takes place in the federal court. He is also credited for his work on Internet audits and is praised by competitors for his ability to "*focus and quickly identify problems*" as they arise.

The Clients: On the client list are businesses and individuals engaged in IP matters based nationally and locally.

Williams Mullen

The Firm: A long-standing landmark on the Virginia legal landscape, this firm is recognized by the market for its breadth of experience and the poise of its practitioners. The largest slice of its work comes from the computer and hi-tech industries, out of which has arisen an increased focus on trade secrets matters. In addition to working around this subject, the group brings its experience to bear on patent and trademark

prosecution, licensing and IP litigation. In particular, infringement litigation on behalf of manufacturing companies has been prevalent. The group's abilities in specialized IP law are complemented by general corporate and business knowledge. As an indication of the interdisciplinary ties forged by the firm, the IP group assists and supports the M&A practice on due diligence and works to design creative and effective strategies for meeting complex business needs.

The Lawyers: The "*fantastic*" Ian Titley rises above the average by virtue of his "*in-depth knowledge and supremely professional style.*" Able to "*explain things to people so that they don't have to do the research themselves,*" he concentrates on the commercial services side of the business tackling a substantial amount of trademark analysis, prosecution and licensing work. Internet law is something of a forte as this "*energetic and personable performer*" assists in both the prosecution and defense of infringement claims. He is also well known as an accomplished speaker and an effective negotiator. Craig Mytelka's practice has enjoyed unprecedented growth in the past year. He predominantly handles litigation where, in one matter, peers noted that his "*assistance had been outstanding and he got some outstanding results.*" He further employs his skill in strategic planning and licensing for a wide variety of small and medium-sized clients and possesses a strong trademark portfolio.

The Clients: The group serves many companies, some of them international, in a variety of industries and locations.

Other Notable Practitioners

John Farmer of Leading-Edge Law Group is a "*serious and devoted practitioner,*" whose "*straight-shooting style*" is often deployed in the e-commerce and hi-tech fields. He works with both existing businesses and startups in building strategies to protect and license IP and also acts for them on a transactional and litigation basis. Interviewees described him as "*highly articulate, intelligent and well-read.*" After establishing her own Richmond-based boutique, LMK PLC, Lisa Krizan has become increasingly well regarded by peers for assisting smaller clients creatively and efficiently. Noted for her "*care in keeping an eye on the costs,*" she was described to our interviewees as "*honest and hard-working*" in her securities work for startups.

LITIGATION:

GENERAL COMMERCIAL

Virginia
Leading firms
(Litigation: General Commercial)

1 HUNTON & WILLIAMS LLP *Richmond*
   MCGUIREWOODS LLP *Richmond*
2 KAUFMAN & CANOLES *Norfolk*
   TROUTMAN SANDERS LLP *Richmond*
   WILLCOX & SAVAGE *Norfolk*
3 CHRISTIAN & BARTON LLP *Richmond*
   HIRSCHLER FLEISCHER *Richmond*
   HOGAN & HARTSON LLP *McLean*
   LATHAM & WATKINS LLP *Reston*
   MORRIS & MORRIS PC *Richmond*
   WILLIAMS MULLEN *Richmond*
   WOODS ROGERS PLC *Roanoke*

Leading individuals
(Litigation: General Commercial)

1 ALLEN Everette *Allen & Allen, Richmond*
   KING William *McGuireWoods, Richmond*
   MORRIS James *Morris & Morris, Richmond*
   POFF William *Woods Rogers, Roanoke*
   ROBERTS James *Troutman Sanders, Richmond*
   SLATER Thomas *Hunton & Williams, Richmond*
   SMITH Michael *Christian & Barton, Richmond*
   STILLMAN Gregory *Hunton & Williams, Norfolk*
2 BROADDUS William *McGuireWoods, Richmond*
   HARLESS Warren *Christian & Barton, Richmond*
   HIXON Samuel *Williams Mullen, Richmond*
   JENNINGS James *Woods Rogers, Roanoke*
   PAGE Rosewell *McGuireWoods, Richmond*
   RUDLIN D Alan *Hunton & Williams, Richmond*
   SHUMADINE Conrad *Willcox & Savage, Norfolk*
   SIMS Hunter *Kaufman & Canoles, Norfolk*
   WHITTEMORE Anne *McGuireWoods, Richmond*
   WITTHOEFFT Charles *Hirschler Fleischer, Richmond*
3 BAYLISS William *Williams Mullen, Richmond*
   BISHOP Bruce *Willcox & Savage, Norfolk*
   BURKE John *Troutman Sanders, Richmond*
   CULLEN Richard *McGuireWoods, Richmond*
   DONOVAN David *Wilmer Cutler, McLean*
   FARNHAM James *Hunton & Williams, Richmond*
   FUHR Edward *Hunton & Williams, Richmond*
   KEARFOTT Joseph *Hunton & Williams, Richmond*
   MCCLARD Jack *Hunton & Williams, Richmond*
   NORTHUP Stephen *Troutman Sanders, Richmond*
   PEARSON John *Willcox & Savage, Norfolk*
   SMILAN Laurie *Latham & Watkins, Reston*
   WILLIAMS Steven *McGuireWoods, Richmond*

Firms and individuals are listed alphabetically in each band.

Band 1

Hunton & Williams LLP
See firm details p.1775

The Firm: This "*top-shelf firm has a great reputation for thoroughness and efficiency nationally,*" and is no less well regarded in Virginia; market sources applaud a "*wealth of resources*" that enable the litigation department to handle complex cases on behalf of major corporations. Its "*responsive and cooperative*" attorneys specialize in a range of matters, including general commercial litigation, IP, torts, environment and products and premise liability disputes. Reflecting a national growth in insurance litigation, the team's work this year has encompassed the defense of tobacco producer Philip Morris and a variety of silica and asbestos-related class actions. Further recent successes have included winning summary judgment for Texas Utilities in an antitrust case.

The Lawyers: **Thomas Slater** (see p.1772) is co-head of the litigation group. "*Top of the heap*" in antitrust and IP matters, his "*phenomenal organizational abilities*" ensure that competitors regard him as "*one of a few guys truly adept at handling big cases*" in these areas. His practice also encompasses unfair trade, white-collar defense and products liability work. **Gregory Stillman** (see p.1773) enjoys a great reputation as an "*experienced and intelligent trial litigator.*" According to one interviewee: "*If you want to know what he's up to, open a newspaper.*" Working primarily within the field of IP, he is involved in a major breach of contract claim being tried in North Carolina with damages estimated at $250 million. He is also representing Texas Utilities in a Sarbanes-Oxley securities fraud lawsuit pending in Dallas. Displaying a "*legal acumen and rapport with juries*" that makes him the envy of many of his competitors, **Alan Rudlin** (see p.1772) specializes in mass torts, pharmaceutical, environmental and defamation matters. He recently obtained a favorable settlement in a mass tort claim filed by 1200 residents, related to emissions from a nearby industrial facility. Currently, he is general counsel for the Association of American Railroads, creating a defense strategy intended to anticipate and negate toxic tort claims. **James Farnham** (see p.1769) is "*good on his feet, prepared, flexible and agile*" according to observers. He focuses on litigation of all types, and has handled hundreds of cases on behalf of Fortune 500 companies, on both sides of the aisle, including the defense of class actions, securities frauds and business torts. Peers agree that **Edward Fuhr** (see p.1769) provides "*terrific*" counsel in securities and corporate governance litigation. In addition to representing the directors of one of the country's largest home mortgage companies in a fraud investigation, he has successfully resolved a potentially damaging eavesdropping case on behalf of the Republican Party. "*Strategic thinker*" **Joseph Kearfott** (see p.1770) is also a "*first-rate guy*" in the estimation of his competitors. With almost 30 years of civil litigation experience at both state and federal level, he devotes approximately 50% of his practice to toxic tort matters. **Jack McClard** (see p.1771) is famed for "*going the extra mile*" for his clients. Those who reap the benefits of this stamina and commitment include companies involved in major security fraud claims and patent litigation. He is currently involved in two matters related to cable and direct broadcast satellite television, with potential costs exceeding $200 million.

The Clients: Union Pacific; Georgia-Pacific; IMC Global; Genworth Financial and Philip Morris.

McGuireWoods LLP

The Firm: A range of "*superstar attorneys bring the muscle to bear in big commercial cases*" guaranteeing the firm a stellar reputation for litigation in Virginia. While a strong commercial group runs the gamut of business-oriented matters, from contract actions to antitrust and professional liability, it is the "*excellent products liability team*" that prompts the majority of its accolades. Also highly active in civil rights and environmental litigation, the team uses its respected "*size and power*" to negotiate successful conclusions to a host of high-profile cases.

The Lawyers: Considered by many observers to have "*the best natural trial instincts at the firm,*" **William King** has handled products liability defense litigation throughout the USA for more than two decades. He specializes in the representation of automobile manufacturers, and counts Ford among his clients. Peers also admire the way in which he has "*cultivated a stable of talented partners around him.*" **William Broaddus** "*brings a lot to the table*" when it comes to civil rights litigation most recently settling a class action pertaining to a 1940's housing development that had been brought by 500 families against the City of Portsmouth. In a similar vein, he had a series of discrimination claims arising from the treatment of prisoners in a Richmond police cell successfully dismissed. Very few lawyers can match **Rosewell Page** for "*experience, reputation and excellence in court.*" He has tried cases for product manufacturers before state and federal courts all over the country and acts as outside counsel for several state healthcare providers in professional liability litigation. When **Anne Marie Whittemore**, a member of the firm's executive committee, goes into trial "*the court puts down its pencil and pays attention.*" An "*excellent*" counselor who peers "*would hire in a nanosecond,*" she has a wealth of expertise in complex commercial litigation issues, supplemented by an advisory role in corporate governance matters. **Richard Cullen** is in charge of the white collar and government investigations team. A "*trusted*" political adviser, he frequently acts on behalf of corporations in major commercial litigation: he recently advised Time Warner during its investigation by the security and justice department. Completing the roll call, **Steven Williams** is the firm's national coordinating counsel, developing defense strategies for major industry clients subject to tort class actions. He is also in charge of the practice subset responsible for representing automobile manufacturers in asbestos litigation matters.

The Clients: The firm's client base includes Ford and DuPont.

Band 2

Kaufman & Canoles

The Firm: This 35-attorney litigation group handles cases ranging from major federal court matters to state court family law disputes. A well-known presence in the Tidewater area, it represents its broad base of regional, national and international clients in a variety of IP, white-collar and antitrust matters. Peers describe the firm as "*particularly good on the business and commercial side of the ledger*," and it is currently involved in a number of high-profile patent cases.

The Lawyers: **Hunter Sims** earns praise from his peers for his "*excellent*" understanding of the law and "*forceful*" presentation of cases. A former assistant US attorney, he handles complex litigation and white-collar criminal defense work. His high profile is no surprise to market observers who describe him as "*good on his feet, relaxed and in control of every situation in court.*"

The Clients: The team acts on behalf of clients ranging from national and global manufacturers to technology and retail companies.

Troutman Sanders LLP

The Firm: Demonstrating a "*degree of professionalism and bench strength*" that finds favor with its competitors, the firm's complex litigation practice group represents clients drawn from a variety of industry sectors. It acts on behalf of telecom companies, banks, clothing manufacturers, media and entertainment networks and utility holdings in matters ranging from class action lawsuits to commercial fraud, antitrust, corporate governance, IP, business torts and lender liability matters.

The Lawyers: When interviewees discuss the firm's litigation practice, **James Roberts** is a name that figures prominently. "*Dean of the trial Bar,*" peers envy his ability to combine a "*tough guy approach*" with a "*courteous manner.*" He has handled countless civil and criminal cases before Virginia's state and federal courts, focusing on a spectrum of matters, including internal investigations, corporate governance and conspiracy and fraud allegations. **Stephen Northup** is "*a worthy adversary, as honest as the day is long,*" who "*successfully marries the law with the facts of a case.*" The arbitration, mediation and litigation of business disputes related to lender liability

and corporate shareholder issues form the bulk of his practice. **John Burke** won respect as a hard-nosed warrior whose generalist practice leans toward complex healthcare, environmental and real estate law. In the latter category, he has obtained significant decisions in the area of eminent domain.

The Clients: The spectrum of clients represented by the firm includes healthcare providers, banks, telecom companies and manufacturers.

Willcox & Savage

The Firm: Boasting a stable of "*really good trial lawyers*" split between two offices in Virginia, peers noted this firm's rapidly growing reputation in the asbestos defense and products liability arenas. In this context the team advises a good deal of national and global companies on a range of asbestos-related issues including the question of punitive damages. It also involves itself in aviation litigation, toxic tort personal injury defense, premises liability and issues pertaining to the Longshore and Harbor Workers' Compensation Act.

The Lawyers: In addition to giving "*excellent briefings,*" **Conrad Shumadine** is credited by many as "*the best libel and slander attorney in the south of the state.*" He brings "*huge credibility*" to an antitrust and trade regulation practice that also takes in advising health providers on M&A issues and a role as special counsel to a variety of media companies. **Bruce Bishop** is a "*first-rate lawyer with a great client base.*" Representing common carriers, manufacturers, hospitals and a range of corporations, he has a stellar reputation in asbestos defense supplemented by an expertise in aviation, trucking and environmental litigation. According to several market onlookers, **John Pearson** "*doesn't overwork cases and achieves great results.*" His resume includes representing the seller of a national hotel network in a breach of contract suit and obtaining a successful jury verdict in a multimillion-dollar products liability case on behalf of a national manufacturer of electrical transformers.

The Clients: Drawn from a variety of industries, the firm's clients include media, healthcare, energy, retail and insurance companies.

Band 3

Christian & Barton LLP

The Firm: This Richmond-based firm has developed a "*strong niche in constitutional and civil rights litigation,*" particularly in relation to matters connected to the print and broadcast media's First Amendment Rights. Its team of talented attorneys also acts on behalf of developers, contractors and project owners in construction litigation. Further representation is provided to a variety of corporate clients on tax, antitrust, business torts and ownership disputes. Environmental, insurance liability and

employment work complete the remit of this full-service practice.

The Lawyers: **Michael Smith** chairs the firm's executive committee as well as its litigation department. A "*well-liked and charming man,*" he is widely admired by competitors for his products liability defense work. The circumference of his practice extends further, covering securities, healthcare and defense of bad faith claims. Interviewees praise the advantageous way in which he applies this knowledge to courtroom situations – "*great on his feet, he has tremendous credibility in front of judges and juries.*" **Warren David Harless** also demonstrates an "*ability to establish a strong rapport with the court.*" In his role as chair of the employment group, he "*wrings every meaningful ounce*" out of a myriad of wrongful discharge, discrimination, wage and hour, and labor matters. Peers characterize him as a "*very good trial lawyer*" particularly when it comes to litigating products liability and commercial cases before state and federal courts.

The Clients: The firm counsels organizations from a diverse range of industries, including transport, banking, healthcare and communications.

Hirschler Fleischer

The Firm: While this firm may lack a little of its former glory, having suffered a number of key departures in recent years, this has not prevented it from continuing to make an impact on the market. Its litigators conduct cases at state and federal level, specializing in commercial, probate, shareholder, construction, partnership and labor disputes. Expertise extends to zoning and land use, bankruptcy, employment, securities and antitrust matters.

The Lawyers: "*Thorough and gentlemanly,*" **Charles Witthoefft** (see p.1774) is considered by admiring onlookers to be "*one of the best lawyers in the state.*" He chairs the firm's litigation section and has developed an "*aura of real credibility,*" as a result of more than 27 years of "*commanding trial experience.*" His practice runs the gamut of commercial disputes including contract, antitrust, securities, banking, trust and estate, tort and insurance liability issues. His clients in these matters range from auto manufacturers to regional banks and physician groups.

The Clients: Insurance and construction companies, manufacturers and banks make up the firm's client base.

Hogan & Hartson LLP

See firm details p.484

The Firm: Consisting of "*top-caliber lawyers,*" this firm has a "*major presence*" in the Northern Virginia litigation community. The antitrust group advises and represents manufacturing, media and entertainment clients in a wide spectrum of matters, including competition and consumer protection disputes. An additional 40 "*bright and talented*" attorneys nationwide provide patent and trademark counseling and prosecution, trade secret and copyright litigation in both state and federal courts. Capitalizing on its strong reputation, the firm bolsters its expertise in individual practice areas through its encouragement of interdepartmental collaboration and referral.

The Lawyers: The team includes Tom Connally, Bob Duncan, Bill Flanagan and Joseph Hassett.

The Clients: The firm represents a number of Fortune 500 companies and clients in the media and entertainment industries.

Latham & Watkins LLP

The Firm: Although primarily the satellite of a larger national practice, the Reston office litigation group has, according to a number of observers, successfully achieved a "*significant depth of expertise in handling large, complex cases.*" The four-strong attorney team specializes in securities litigation undertaking class actions, special committee representations, regulatory enforcement matters and internal investigations. In the past year the group's practice has been shaped by a rise in SEC investment actions.

The Lawyers: Laurie Smilan cochairs the securities litigation and professional liability practice. Lead counsel in the recent Adecco Group class action, she is representing a Tyco International director in both external and internal investigations.

The Clients: The client list includes: Dell; Boeing; Tyco International; The Carlyle Group; 3Com and Cirrus Logic in addition to a variety of pharmaceutical companies.

Morris & Morris PC

The Firm: This Richmond-based boutique has a cast-iron reputation as a premier civil litigation firm. Boasting "*excellent trial attorneys,*" it represents clients in a spectrum of matters, ranging from products liability to transportation, retail, medical malpractice, and business and construction disputes. Observers noted the firm has "*one heck of a good insurance defense practice*" that transforms it into an essential litigation resource. The team is frequently before state and federal courts throughout the mid-Atlantic region.

The Lawyers: "*Gifted on his feet,*" **James Morris** is a "*first-class civil litigator*" who has established a rapport with judges and juries that has made him the envy of his rivals. Peer assessments that he "*can hold his own in a national context*" are confirmed by his recent election as President of the American College of Trial Lawyers.

The Clients: The group represents a panoply of clients across several industry sectors.

Williams Mullen

The Firm: Displaying an aggressive growth posture that wins plaudits from market observers, this firm's "*very good*" litigation team has represented electric companies, insurers, manufacturers, retailers and national governmental agencies in a broad sweep of matters, ranging from contract litigation to antitrust, IP and professional liability disputes.

The Lawyers: Interviewees praise "*terrific*" commercial litigator **Samuel Hixon** for upholding a "*fine tradition of gentlemanly lawyering.*" His highly successful role in the settlement of a class action brought against Virginia Power – resulting in damages exceeding $13 million – has won him the respect of the litigation community. He has represented plaintiffs and defendants before state, federal and appellate courts throughout Virginia. **William Bayliss** is "*an insurance company's dream attorney.*" In addition to insurance issues, he focuses on civil litigation relating to professional liability defense, toxic torts, products liability and construction matters.

The Clients: The firm's comprehensive client list ranges from power and insurance companies to manufacturers and government agencies.

Woods Rogers PLC

The Firm: "*Historically one of the premier firms,*" this midsized outfit has "*an excellent civil litigation practice that is widely known.*" It represents businesses throughout the state in matters ranging from contractual disputes to IP and patent litigation. The 20-strong team is working on a series of railroad injury cases that have recently gone to trial and remains heavily involved in a large patent infringement matter.

The Lawyers: "*Warhorse*" **William Poff** is an appellate lawyer of some stature and "*one of the best in the state*" according to commentators. Interviewees were as one in the opinion that attorneys opposing this "*smart and diligent character*" in court "*must be on top form to compete.*" He is renowned for his work in the IP arena, but has tried a variety of cases at state and federal level, including medical malpractice and trade secrets disputes. Colleague **James Jennings** "*enjoys a fine reputation among the state federal courts of Western Virginia.*" In addition to the business interruption litigation he undertakes for numerous state manufacturers, he conducts public utility and construction disputes for clients who range from paper mills to railroads.

The Clients: Adams Construction; Allstate Insurance; Augusta Hospital; Roanoke Electric Steel; Virginia Insurance Reciprocal; GE and First Union National Bank.

Other Notable Practitioners

Market sources commend the "*tenacious*" **Everette Allen** of Allen & Allen Attorneys at Law PC for an illustrious career that has witnessed "*a series of first-rate successes.*" He specializes in commercial disputes law. Interviewees were also adamant that **David Donovan** (see p.1768) of Wilmer Cutler Pickering Hale and Dorr LLP "*definitely demands the keenest respect.*" Noted for his securities work, his practice further includes products liability, antitrust, insurance and complex commercial disputes.

REAL ESTATE

Virginia
Leading firms (Real Estate)

1 HIRSCHLER FLEISCHER *Richmond*
 HUNTON & WILLIAMS LLP *Richmond*
 MCGUIREWOODS LLP *Richmond*
 TROUTMAN SANDERS LLP *Richmond*

2 HOLLAND & KNIGHT LLP *McLean*
 REED SMITH LLP *Falls Church*
 WILLIAMS MULLEN *Richmond*

Leading individuals (Real Estate)

1 BAGLEY Philip *Troutman Sanders*, Richmond
 WALSH William *Hunton & Williams*, Richmond

2 LITTLE Nancy *McGuireWoods*, Richmond
 PULLEY III J Waverly *Hunton & Williams*, Richmond
 TERRY Mike *Hirschler Fleischer*, Richmond
 THEOBALD James *Hirschler Fleischer*, Richmond

3 BRENNAN James *Reed Smith*, Falls Church
 CAMPBELL Daniel *Hunton & Williams*, Richmond
 HARMON T Craig *McGuireWoods*, Richmond
 ROTHENBERG Charles *Hirschler Fleischer*, Richmond
 TAPSCOTT Andrew *Hunton & Williams*, Richmond

Leading individuals
(Real Estate: Zoning/Land Use)

Senior Statesman
 WEINBERG Jay *Hirschler Fleischer*, Fredericksburg

1 AXSELLE Ralph *Williams Mullen*, Richmond
 BATES John *McGuireWoods*, Richmond
 COGBILL John *McGuireWoods*, Richmond
 THEOBALD James *Hirschler Fleischer*, Richmond
 THOMAS Bill *Reed Smith*, Falls Church

Up-and-coming individuals
 CONDLIN Andrew *Williams Mullen*, Richmond

Firms and individuals are listed alphabetically in each band.

Band 1

Hirschler Fleischer

The Firm: It is a credit to the strength of the lawyers and the profile of their representative deals that this firm is as highly regarded for land use as it is for general real estate. Competitors recognize the "*great depth of experience and expertise*" running through a diverse practice which is sharply weighted towards real estate. Solidly ensconced in a growth cycle, the firm enjoys a presence on many of the largest developments and transactions in the state including high-profile mixed-use developments and residential and commercial projects. On the land use side, the firm is known to be "*well-connected politically and extremely capable*," allowing it to become associated with deals early on in the process and to swiftly obtain the necessary approvals to allow development to happen. With continued success in large portfolio financings and a niche expertise in real estate securities and tenant in common transactions,

the firm not only has the connections but, as one peer notes, a team that has "*not one lawyer it wouldn't be a pleasure to work with.*"

The Lawyers: Interviewees emphatically defined **Jay Weinberg** (see p.1773) as the "*all-time king of land use,*" with one competitor claiming to have "*never found a better lawyer than him in 20 years.*" He is greatly respected for the work he has completed over a 45-year career handling a comprehensive array of sophisticated real estate and zoning matters. Many real estate attorneys see him as a mentor and appreciate the depth of knowledge he brings to proceedings. Put simply, he is "*tremendous at what he does.*" A protégé of his, **James Theobald** (see p.1773), is furthering an already strong career in the land use arena, taking advantage of his excellent grounding in real estate fundamentals. Commentators noted his recent success on difficult, high-profile cases, singling out his work on land use approvals for one of the largest mixed-use planned unit developments (PUDs)in the Eastern Virginia market, on the James River area. A client summed up his success: "*it's a matter of strategy and presentation, leg work and background preparation; he covers a wide range of capabilities.*" Competitors say that **Mike Terry** (see p.1773) "*can do almost anything*" in the real estate sector. He has particular experience representing developers, property owners and tenants in connection with the acquisition, development and leasing of raw land for PUDs, retail projects and office complexes. He was described as "*very pragmatic, very honest and an up-front deal-maker.*" Peers noticed the rise of talented **Charles Rothenberg** (see p.1772), an attorney who negotiates and implements real estate sales and assists purchasers in all phases of the acquisition process. He represents commercial lenders, developers, builders, commercial landlords and tenants.

The Clients: Cargill; HH Hunt; Daniel Corporation and Wal-Mart.

Hunton & Williams LLP
See firm details p.1775

The Firm: This "*excellent all-round firm*" scores highly on the list of real estate players in Virginia due to its broad-based knowledge and reputation for working on complex transactions and unique finance work. Expertise is established across the board and encompasses certain niche areas in, for example, the development of healthcare facilities, student housing, hospitality and leisure, transportation infrastructure and REIT work. Transactions generally play out nationally as the team gets to grips with the complicated nationwide financings of clients, one of whom enthused about the "*professional ethics and attitude demonstrated by everyone at the firm.*" In recent years the group has acted as

bond counsel, developer's counsel and bank counsel on university and college projects totaling over $1.65 billion. On the REIT side, the firm is well known for representing underwriters and issuers and spin-off projects. In addition, the group is particularly noted for addressing transportation needs in an innovative way. In tackling all these varied deals, the team, according to one interviewee, "*always gives an honest opinion of the situation and never just tells the client what it thinks they want to hear.*"

The Lawyers: Top-rated **William Walsh** (see p.1773) was described as "*truly one of the finest lawyers; he works tirelessly for his clients and has a great mind.*" Regarded as a seasoned, across-the-board real estate lawyer, he often works on the strategic real estate planning aspects of large projects. Peers stated that he is "*smart in the sense that he knows what's important and what's not*" and praised him for being "*industrious, pleasant to deal with and a good advocate for his clients.*" He has been particularly involved in student housing transactions across the USA. Termed a fine lawyer by competitors, **Waverly Pulley** (see p.1772) has carved a niche for himself in the field of public-private infrastructure and transportation projects. He has been representing Kellogg Brown & Root, a subsidiary of Halliburton, in a proposal to improve and widen an interstate route in a $10 billion deal – challenging and politically sensitive work on which he has excelled. Sources stated: "*Not only is he professionally competent in his field but he is very astute in handling difficult situations and clients.*" Rising star **Daniel Campbell** (see p.1768) specializes in healthcare-related development and finance. He has represented hospitals in the development of new and expanding facilities and handled a number of public and private companies and healthcare facilities in the acquisition of assets nationally and internationally. **Andy Tapscott** (see p.1773) is actively making a name for himself as a "*good lawyer with good expertise.*" He focuses on commercial real estate transactions with a particular focus on the hospitality industry and troubled debt.

The Clients: Halliburton; Fluor; Virginia Commonwealth University; Norfolk State University and investment bank clients.

McGuireWoods LLP

The Firm: Competitors spoke of a "*uniformly positive experience*" when dealing with this powerhouse. A significant player in the market, it fields over 80 real estate attorneys from its offices across the country, enabling it to work on the whole gamut of traditional and nontraditional real estate transactions, many of which are cross-border in nature. Interviewees noted that it is a multifaceted firm with expertise ranging across land use and finance. It is particularly active in capital markets, project financing and synthetic leases. The firm has a significant presence in the representation of the retail real estate market and the hospitality sector and takes part in a large number of transactions involving mixed-use development and neo-traditional housing projects. This multilayered firm also represents a number of power companies, staffing its transactions with a large number of *"senior, highly experienced partners who have a great depth of expertise."*

The Lawyers: John Bates is *"one of the deans of real estate"* according to Virginia competitors. He is active in zoning, land use and major projects with local government, and demonstrates strong leadership and transactional skills. A popular figure, peers acknowledged that *"he is a pleasure to deal with. You know where you stand with him."* Stablemate **John Cogbill** was described as *"technically excellent"* with *"impeccable trust and integrity."* With his *"strong mind and leadership skills,"* he has been successful in numerous zoning cases and is also active in transportation projects. Interviewees noted that he is *"very creative and a good advocate for his clients."* As an illustration of his standing and government connections, he was recently appointed by President George W Bush to be chairman of the National Capital Planning Commission in Washington DC. *"Superb"* **Nancy Little** is respected on a national basis, and was hailed by her contemporaries as *"precise, organized and one of the finest real estate lawyers in Virginia."* According to one, she has *"become an expert in synthetic and leveraged leases"* and has an incredible intellect. **Craig Harmon** focuses on real estate finance: real estate venture representation, mezzanine debt and sale-leaseback among other matters. He handles the representation of both developers and end users on acquisitions and lease transactions, with a particular emphasis on national retailers. He is described as *"very bright and absolutely ethical, capable of working on the most complicated of transactions."*

The Clients: Dominion Resources; Circuit City; SunTrust; CarMax; Microsoft and Lockheed Martin.

Troutman Sanders LLP

The Firm: This regional, respected firm is known for *"some sophisticated real estate work"* out of its established Virginia offices. The practice represents a range of interests from national developers to entrepreneurs and investors across the full spectrum of real estate interests. Recently, the firm has become involved in regional, neighborhood and strip shopping centers and office building development. The expe-

rienced group of attorneys also has long-standing experience working for lenders active in the multifamily housing industry. The broad practice group is active across the country and internationally, with traditional real estate clients and others that have more specific property needs.

The Lawyers: Preeminent **Philip Bagley** has an enduring, visible presence at Troutman Sanders and is recognized for his top-notch practice and his ability to attract nationally important clients to the firm. He is termed a *"hard-working, bright lawyer who can handle the very complicated deals"* and *"truly a lawyer who works to get a deal done while protecting his clients."*

The Clients: Wachovia, Daniel Corporation and State Fair of Virginia are among the clients.

Band 2

Holland & Knight LLP

See firm details p.1352

The Firm: Distinct areas of expertise operate under the umbrella of this firm's prominent real estate section, thereby ensuring it remains worthy of its position as a heavyweight in the eastern states. Competing in the strong market of Northern Virginia, the *"prolific"* firm fields experts in hospitality, leasing, real estate finance and residential and planned development. With substantial transaction experience and what is often regarded as one of the deepest land use and zoning groups in the northern part of the state, the group is admired for its penetration of the market. Alongside real estate, expertise in the construction and environment fields provides comprehensive coverage, a plus point for developer clients. It is clear that for this firm regional boundaries are not set in stone; the attorneys here practice across three states to follow clients' business, which includes acquisitions and disposals, leasing, community and condominium development. A heavy amount of government contracting completes the picture for this firm.

The Lawyers: David Kahn leads the real estate practice group and is the main contact. He is based at the firm's DC office.

The Clients: The practice represents regional and national investors and developers, investment banks and housing finance agencies.

Reed Smith LLP

See firm details p.1560

The Firm: Described as a *"big player nationally,"* competitors have a high regard for this firm's sophisticated real estate practice and bank of quality attorneys. The practice deals with builders, developers and institutional and commercial lenders throughout the market, representing players in transactions as varied as

shopping centers, mixed-use developments, hotel property and entertainment venues. The real estate group works closely with attorneys across the specialties in order to access resources from the firm's other departments such as tax, corporate transactions and construction.

The Lawyers: Bill Thomas (see p.1773) brings his accomplished lobbying skills to bear on land use matters before state agencies. Competitors described him as *"good to have around if you have land use issues of a political nature."* **James Brennan** (see p.1767) concentrates his expertise on high-profile and larger deals involving commercial real estate, residential, office, retail and industrial development. He works on varied aspects of the real estate process from acquisition to financing and leasing.

The Clients: The client base includes a number of developers in the fields of leisure and hospitality, residential, office buildings and entertainment.

Williams Mullen

The Firm: An inveterate Virginia firm that shores up its reputation in the state by representing the full gamut of real estate services. The group covers land use, government approvals, transactional work and leasing. It draws on its knowledge of, and connections with, the local market to act on localized, specialist deals. Clients include retailers, office builders, public companies, REITs and lending institutions and the team has recently acted on the construction of large mixed-use projects in urban and suburban areas. Observers applauded its niche expertise on bank deals and pointed to the quality of the litigators in the firm as an indication of its stature.

The Lawyers: *"Terrific lawyer"* **Ralph Axselle** has forged a distinguished practice with an emphasis on zoning and land use issues, lobbying, regulatory issues and administrative law. A former Virginia legislator, others often turn to him in the early stages of deals due to his in-depth knowledge of local politics and laws. Peers described him as *"very much a gentleman and consensus builder,"* characteristics which stand him in good stead when working with medium to large-sized clients. As a complement to Ralph's seasoned experience, fresh-faced **Andrew Condlin**'s reputation is on the rise. He represents developers and landowners in deals relating to commercial real estate and in particular land use and zoning. He also takes part in matters pertaining to historic preservation and local government laws.

The Clients: The firm acts for a variety of clients from across the region in the public, non-profit, banking and finance and retail sectors.

Leaders in Virginia

ALLEN, Everette
Allen & Allen Attorneys at Law, PC,
Richmond 804 545 1500
Recommended in Litigation

ALLEN, Randall
Smith Pachter McWhorter & Allen,
Vienna 703 847 6300
Recommended in Construction

ANDERSON, John
Troutman Sanders LLP, McLean
703 734 4334
Recommended in Intellectual Property

ATKINS, William P
Pillsbury Winthrop LLP, McLean
703 905-2007
watkins@pillsburywinthrop.com
Recommended in Intellectual Property
Practice Areas: Mr Atkins is an intellectual property attorney and trial lawyer who focuses on handling matters that typically relate to portfolios, protection, infringement, ownership, misappropriation, and abuses of IP. He is a member of the his firm's Managing Board and Co-Chair of the Global Intellectual Property Section, and President-Elect of the Bar Association of DC. He has extensive experience in trial, arbitrations, mediations, and appellate matters involving IP and related commercial matters. He personally handles his cases using the latest trial management techniques and software with a trial team that is carefully selected for their technical and legal expertise. For example, he recently won a three week jury trial in a contentious commercial and patent infringement case, where plaintiff sought hundreds of millions of dollars.
Prof. Memberships: American Bar Association; Virginia, Maryland, and DC Bar Associations; Bar Association of DC (current President-Elect); and Federal Circuit Bar Association.
Career: Admitted to practice: DC, Virginia, and Maryland. Admitted to: US Supreme Court, US Court of Appeals for the Federal, DC, and Fourth Circuits, and numerous District Courts. Registered to practice: US Patent and Trademark Office.
Personal: LLM, George Washington University, 1996; JD/MBA, University of Baltimore, 1992; BS, University of Maryland, 1986.

AXSELLE, Ralph
Williams Mullen, Richmond
804 643 1991
Recommended in Real Estate

BAGLEY, Philip
Troutman Sanders LLP, Richmond
804 697 1200
Recommended in Real Estate

BAKER, Lewis
Watt, Tieder, Hoffar & Fitzgerald, L.L.P.,
McLean 703 749 1000
Recommended in Construction

BARUFKA, Jack S
Pillsbury Winthrop LLP, McLean
703 905 2012
jbarufka@pillsburywinthrop.com
Recommended in Intellectual Property
Practice Areas: Mr Barufka currently heads the Northern Virginia office Intellectual Property Counseling Practice. His practice includes intellectual property counseling, patent prosecution, dispute resolution, licensing and pre-litigation opinions. He represents a broad spectrum of technology companies in the areas of electronics, semiconductor manufacturing, computers, software, medical devices and mechanical technologies. He has served as an expert witness in patent infringement litigation. He has been ranked as one of the top IP attorneys in the Washington DC Metro area ('Legal Times'), and recognized by peers as one of the best IP lawyers in Virginia (poll conducted by 'Virginia Business' magazine and The Virginia Bar Association). Mr Barufka is an adjunct professor of law at George Washington University National Law Center.
Prof. Memberships: National Physics Honor Society, Sigma Pi Sigma; International Prosecution Practice Committee for Intellectual Property Owners; American Intellectual Property Law Association.
Career: Admitted to Practice: District of Columbia, Commonwealth of Virginia, States of New York and New Jersey; and US Patent and Trademark Office.
Publications: Co-founder and editor of 'Patent Strategy and Technology Management'.
Personal: JD, American University, Washington College of Law (cum laude), 1992; LLM, George Washington University National Law Center (Intellectual Property), 1996; BS Binghamton University (Physics), 1987.

BATES, John
McGuireWoods LLP, Richmond
804 775 1000
Recommended in Real Estate

BAYLISS, William
Williams Mullen, Richmond
804 643 1991
Recommended in Litigation

BECKER, Richard K A
Hogan & Hartson LLP, McLean
703 610 6123
rkbecker@hhlaw.com
Recommended in Corporate/M&A
Practice Areas: Mr Becker advises on M&A, private equity and venture capital matters in the information technology, biotechnology, defense, satellite, hospitality and healthcare industries. Recent transactions include advising The DIRECTV Group, Inc. in the sale of its set top box and VSAT businesses.
Prof. Memberships: Steering Committee, Corporation, Finance and Securities

Law Section, District of Columbia Bar Member, Virginia State Bar Member, Virginia Bar Association.
Career: Mr Becker is Administrative Partner of the firm's Northern Virginia office.
Publications: 'Focus On Venture Capital: Legal Primer for Emerging Business' (5/1/2004).
Personal: Harvard Law School (JD, 1983); Princeton University, (AB, cum laude, 1980).

BISHOP, Bruce
Willcox & Savage, Norfolk
757 628 5500
Recommended in Litigation

BREDEHOFT, John
Venable LLP, Vienna
703 760 1600
Recommended in Employment

BRENNAN, James C
Reed Smith LLP, Falls Church
703 641 4252
jbrennan@reedsmith.com
Recommended in Real Estate
Practice Areas: Commercial real estate and business transactions. Represents clients in all aspects of acquisition, development, construction, financing and leasing. Experienced in developing golf course communities, shopping centers, and air cargo facilities at airports around the country; negotiating long-term ground leases; and providing representation of complex financing transactions through conventional or bond financing.
Career: Joined Hazel & Thomas in 1997, which combined with Reed Smith in 1999.
Personal: New York Law School (JD, 1992), member of the 'Law Review'; Georgetown University Law Center (LLM, 1998); University of Richmond (1989).

BRETSCHNEIDER, Barry E
Morrison & Foerster LLP, McLean
bbretschneider 703 760 7743
Recommended in Intellectual Property
Practice Areas: Concentrates on patent infringement litigation in the district courts and before the International Trade Commission, patent interferences, patent licensing and related transactional work, patent prosecution and trademark litigation and prosecution. Represents US and foreign corporations, and clients cover a wide range of industries, including the medical devices, electronics, polymers, composite materials and consumer products industries, among many others.
Career: Admitted to practice in the District of Columbia, Virginia and Texas. Former Chair, Education and Interference Committees, American Intellectual Property Law Association.
Personal: AB, Princeton University; JD, University of Iowa College of Law; LLM, The George Washington University Law School.

BROADDUS, William
McGuireWoods LLP, Richmond
804 775 1000
Recommended in Litigation

BROOKE, Robert
Troutman Sanders LLP, Richmond
804 697 1200
Recommended in Intellectual Property

BROWN, Stanley
Hogan & Hartson LLP, McLean
703 610 6150
sjbrown@hhlaw.com
Recommended in Employment
Practice Areas: Single plaintiff and class action equal employment litigation, wrongful discharge, whistleblower, FLSA and ERISA litigation; Trade secrets and non-compete litigation, labor management relations, including collective bargaining arbitration and cases before the NLRB; Employment contracts and employment disputes relating to senior level executives.
Prof. Memberships: American Bar Association; Committee on Development of the Law under the National Labor Relations Act; Faculty, Virginia State Bar Professionalism Course; Virginia Bar Association, Labor Relations and Employment Law Section.
Career: Partner since 1994. Former Attorney, Appellate Litigation Branch, National Labor Relations Board.
Publications: 'An Ounce of Prevention Inoculating Your Company Against Sarbanes-Oxley and Whistleblower Threats', Hogan & Hartson L.L.P. Managing Your People: From Hiring to Firing and Everything in Between., Hogan & Hartson L.L.P. (5/6/2004); Has presented papers at conferences sponsored by the US Department of Labor and received a Certificate of Commendation from that agency for his contributions.
Personal: Georgetown University Law Center (JD, 1969); Columbia University (BS, 1966).

BROWNELL, Thomas
Holland & Knight LLP, McLean
703 720 8600
thomas.brownell@hklaw.com
Recommended in Construction
Practice Areas: Partner in the firm's Litigation Section practicing in the areas of intellectual property law, government contracts, construction claims and disputes and real estate and business litigation. He is experienced in the preparation and trial of complex civil cases, and in the counseling and drafting of agreements in the areas of software development, software licensing, construction and real estate. He has significant trial experience in the areas of patent infringement, trade secret, and copyright infringement in the computer software industry, commercial disputes relating to the delivery and installation

of integrated computer systems and a wide range of construction disputes.

BUCKLEY, Kevin J
Hunton & Williams LLP, Richmond
804 788 8616
kbuckley@hunton.com
Recommended in Capital Markets, Corporate/M&A

Practice Areas: Mr Buckley is Co-Head of Hunton & Williams' nationally-prominent Asset Securitization Practice. His practice focuses on mortgage and asset-backed securitizations, structured financings, and other capital markets transactions. He represents issuers, underwriters, trustees, master servicers, insurers, and other participants in securitizations and other capital markets transactions. Mr Buckley has served as issuer's counsel in connection with the design and implementation of securitization programs involving unique asset types and innovative securities structures, including and the first REMIC program backed by a full faith and credit guarantee of the US and the first public securitization of reperforming government-guaranteed loans.

BUNIVA, Brian L
LeClair Ryan, A Professional Corporation, Richmond 804 916 7130
bbuniva@leclairryan.com
Recommended in Environment

Practice Areas: Administrative law; environmental; land use and zoning; local government; and litigation. Represents public utilities, local governments, publicly traded and privately held companies, developers, healthcare providers, and manufacturing interests.
Prof. Memberships: Past Chair, Virginia State Bar's Administrative and Environmental Law Sections. Board of Governors, Virginia Bar Association's Environmental Section and Past Chair, Administrative Law Section. Past Chair, Richmond Bar's Environmental Section. Vice-Chair, Solid Waste Committee - ABA's Environmental Section. Virginia State Bar's Bench-Bar Relations Committee.
Career: Virginia Assistant Attorney General for Health and Environmental Sections (1979-83), private practice (1983 to present). Listed, Virginia's 'Legal Elite' for 'Environmental Law', 2000, 2001 (profiled), 2003, and 2004 in 'Virginia Business Magazine'; among top Environmental Lawyers, 'Richmond Magazine'.
Personal: University of Richmond Law, JD, 1979; Georgetown University, AB, 1972.

BURKE Jr, John
Troutman Sanders LLP, Richmond
804 697 1200
Recommended in Litigation

BURRUS, Robert
McGuireWoods LLP, Richmond
804 775 1000
Recommended in Corporate/M&A

CALAMITA, Paul
Aqualaw PLC, Richmond
804 716 9021
Recommended in Environment

CAMPBELL, Christopher C
Hunton & Williams, McLean
703 714 7553
ccampbell@hunton.com
Recommended in Intellectual Property

Practice Areas: Mr Campbell's practice focuses on intellectual property with emphasis on all aspects of patent law, including patent infringement litigation, client counseling, licensing and transactional matters, patent prosecution and freedom to operate opinions. He also has extensive experience in complex patent practice matters, including patent interference, reissues, reexaminations, appeals and protests, as well as claims relating to trademark and copyright matters, including infringement claims; unfair competition and deceptive trade practices; misappropriation of trade secrets, false advertising; claims relating to licensing, distribution and other contracts relating to intellectual property rights in US district court and before the International Trade Commission.

CAMPBELL, Daniel
Hunton & Williams LLP, Richmond
804 788 8503
dcampbell@hunton.com
Recommended in Real Estate

Practice Areas: Daniel Campbell focuses on land development, in particular the needs of Hunton & Williams' energy and healthcare clients in addressing the unique development, financing and related regulatory issues facing those industries. He also has substantial experience in the leasing, acquisition, disposition and securitization of real estate assets in the context of real estate investment trusts and mergers, acquisitions and other corporate restructurings.

CHASON, Craig
Shaw Pittman LLP, McLean
703 770 7947
craig.chason@shawpittman.com, craig.chason@pillsburylaw.com
Recommended in Corporate/M&A

Practice Areas: Mr Chason has extensive expertise in mergers and acquisitions, venture capital financings and public and private securities offerings. Mr Chason's practice includes advising clients on consolidation strategies, auction sales and public company acquisitions. While he represents a broad range of private and public corporations, a significant number of his clients are high-tech companies and government contractors.
Prof. Memberships: Admitted to Practice: District of Columbia, Virginia; American Bar Association Section of Business Law; Northern Virginia Technology Council; Association of Corporate Growth.
Career: Mr Chason's background

includes serving as a corporate officer and general counsel for Applied Bioscience International, Inc., a major public company headquartered in the Washington, DC, metropolitan area engaged in clinical trial management and environmental consulting. As general counsel for Applied Bioscience, he was responsible for all securities counseling and merger and acquisition related representation.
Publications: 'Web Extra! How to move from letter of intent to M&A success,' published in 'Washington Technology,' Vol. 20, No. 3. 'Pooling Transactions: Constraints on Indemnification and Other Legal Remedies,' published in 'Corporate Counsel,' October 1996.
Personal: Co-founder of the Greater Washington Government Contractors Awards and lectures extensively on merger and acquisition strategies for government contractors. Education: University of Virginia School of Law, JD, 1983; University of Virginia, BA, with High Honors, 1977 (At press time, Shaw Pittman LLP had entered into a merger agreement with Pilsbury Winthrop LLP. The merger is expected to close by April 2005. Post-closing, the name of the firm will be Pillsbury Winthrop Shaw Pittman LLP).

COGBILL III, John
McGuireWoods LLP, Richmond
804 775 1000
Recommended in Real Estate, Transport

CONDLIN, Andrew
Williams Mullen, Richmond
804 643 1991
Recommended in Real Estate

CONNOLLY, Theresa
DLA Piper Rudnick Gray Cary US LLP, Reston 703 773 4007
theresa.connolly@dlapiper.com
Recommended in Employment

Practice Areas: Labor and employment.
Career: Represents employers in all labor and employment law matters, including litigation in state and federal courts, before arbitration panels and administrative agencies, negotiating employment agreements, drafting employment policies and compliance with employment-related statutes and regulations. Performs training on human resource management and employment law issues. Handles traditional labor matters including union avoidance, elections, arbitrations and NLRB proceedings. She has written or co-authored numerous articles on employment-related topics, including investigating and resolving harassment complaints, privacy in the workplace, violence in the workplace, union organizing and union avoidance.
Personal: JD, Fordham University; BS, Cornell University.

CONROY, Joseph
Cooley Godward LLP, Reston
703 456 8000
Recommended in Corporate/M&A

CONSTINE III, David
Troutman Sanders LLP, Richmond
804 697 1200
Recommended in Employment

COX, Robert
Watt, Tieder, Hoffar & Fitzgerald, L.L.P., McLean 703 749 1000
Recommended in Construction

CULLEN, Richard
McGuireWoods LLP, Richmond
804 775 1000
Recommended in Litigation

CUTCHINS IV, Clifford
McGuireWoods LLP, Richmond
804 775 1000
Recommended in Corporate/M&A

DANIEL II, John
Troutman Sanders LLP, Richmond
804 697 1200
Recommended in Environment

DARE, Mark
Reed Smith LLP, Falls Church
703 641 4290
mdare@reedsmith.com
Recommended in Employment

Practice Areas: Employment litigation and counseling, advising and defending employers faced with employment-related claims, handling counseling and representation before local human rights commissions, the EEOC, and state and federal courts.
Prof. Memberships: American, Virginia and Fairfax Bar Associations. Former President, Fairfax Bar Association.
Publications: Editor of 'Employment Law in Virginia,' a two-volume reference work. Frequent lecturer and author of written materials on employment issues for Virginia State Bar, and Fairfax and Alexandria Chambers of Commerce, among others.
Personal: University of Virginia (JD, 1974); Princeton University (1971); named one of state's 'Legal Elite' by 'Virginia Business' magazine.

DONOVAN, David
Wilmer Cutler Pickering Hale and Dorr LLP, McLean 703 251 9760
David.Donovan@wilmerhale.com
Recommended in Litigation

Practice Areas: Has nearly 20 years of experience litigating cases involving products liability, securities, antitrust, insurance and complex commercial disputes. Has broad experience representing officers, directors and corporate defendants in multi-district class action and other litigation asserting securities and common law fraud claims.
Prof. Memberships: American Bar Association; District of Columbia Bar Association; and Defense Research Institute.
Publications: Retroactive Awards of Attorneys' Fees: Finding a Fair Interpre-

tation of the Equal Access to Justice Act (April 30, 1983).
Personal: Georgetown University Law Center (JD, magna cum laude, 1984; editor in chief, Georgetown University Law Journal); Iowa State University (BS, with Honors, 1980).

DOYLE, Scott
Morrison & Foerster LLP, McLean
703 760 7721
sdoyle@mofo.com
Recommended in Intellectual Property
Practice Areas: Focused on client counseling, intellectual property litigation and valuation, technology transfer and licensing matters, patent prosecution, opinions, and due diligence. Advises on portfolio development, strategic alliances, licensing, acquisitions, and standards body relationships. Expertise includes communications systems, electronics, computer hardware and software, internet, digital media and interactive television, semiconductor manufacturing, industrial products and advanced medical devices.
Career: Admitted to practice in Colorado, Virginia, the District of Columbia, and before the US Patent and Trademark Office.
Personal: BSEE, Virginia Tech; MSEE, George Washington University; JD, The George Mason University School of Law; LLM, The George Washington University School of Law.

DRAY, Mark S
Hunton & Williams LLP, Richmond
804 788 8408
mdray@hunton.com
Recommended in Employee Benefits
Practice Areas: Mark Dray's practice focuses on all areas of ERISA, including the design, implementation and administration of pension and welfare benefits plans for public and private taxable and exempt private sector employers and governmental entities. Mark has significant experience with all types of executive and incentive compensation arrangements, with the fiduciary provisions of Title I of ERISA, in addressing qualified plan compliance problems, and in coordinating benefits issues arising in the context of mergers and acquisitions. Mr Dray is a frequent speaker on benefits topics and has long held leadership roles in ABA related and other professional organizations.

ELLIS, William
Ellis Thorp & Jewett, Richmond
804 355 4043
Recommended in Environment

EVANS, David
McGuireWoods LLP, Richmond
804 775 1000
Recommended in Environment

FARMER, John
Leading-Edge Law Group, PLC, Richmond 804 343 3220
Recommended in Intellectual Property

FARNHAM, James
Hunton & Williams LLP, Richmond
804 788 8501
jfarnham@hunton.com
Recommended in Litigation
Practice Areas: James Farnham's practice focuses on commercial litigation and arbitration of all types, with particular emphasis in the areas of financial services, securities, mergers and acquisitions, corporate governance, business torts and class actions. He has more than 36 years of trial work in a variety of substantive areas, including more than 40 significant jury trials tried to verdict.

FINTO, Kevin J
Hunton & Williams LLP, Richmond
804 788 8568
kfinto@hunton.com
Recommended in Environment
Practice Areas: Kevin Finto's practice focuses on air and water permitting (electric generation facilities, pulp and paper mills, steel mills and specialty chemical facilities), enforcement (New Source Review) and permit challenges; wetlands; voluntary remediation; economic development; environmental aspects of business transactions; and environmental management system development. He is listed in Who's Who in Executives and Professionals and has been selected to Virginia's Legal Elite, December 2000-04.
Career: Engineer, Chevron USA; Adjunct Professor, Virginia Commonwealth University School of Engineering.

FITZGERALD, Robert
Watt, Tieder, Hoffar & Fitzgerald, L.L.P., McLean 703 749 1000
Recommended in Construction

FLAHERTY, Thomas
Pillsbury Winthrop LLP, McLean
703-905-2186
tflaherty@pillsburywinthrop.com
Recommended in Employment
Practice Areas: Mr Flaherty is Managing Partner of Pillsbury Winthrop's Northern Virginia office and leader of the local office's Employment and Labor Group. He has a national and local practice encompassing all areas of employment and labor law, including litigation and advice involving both individual and class action matters. He has litigated in many jurisdictions and is experienced in federal court class action litigation under the employment discrimination laws and the wage-hour laws, as well as in multi-plaintiff litigation in harassment and downsizing cases. He also has extensive experience representing management in all aspects of traditional labor relations, including both representation cases and unfair labor practice proceedings before the National Labor Relations Board. He has represented employers in a wide range of industries and has handled numerous arbitrations involving a broad array of disciplinary, operational and financial issues. He also

has experience in trade secret, unfair competition, whistleblower and general commercial matters.
Career: Admitted to practice: Commonwealth of Virginia, State of Maryland, Commonwealth of Massachusetts.
Publications: January 28, 2004, New Code of Ethics Requirements for All Employees of NYSE and NASDAQ Listed Companies.
Personal: JD, Boston College, 1975, BA, Yale University, 1972.

FRANCE, Thomas
Venable LLP, Vienna
703 760 1600
Recommended in Corporate/M&A

FRANTZ, Thomas
Williams Mullen, Richmond
804 643 1991
Recommended in Corporate/M&A

FUHR, Edward
Hunton & Williams LLP, Richmond
804 788 8201
efuhr@hunton.com
Recommended in Litigation
Practice Areas: Ed Fuhr's Litigation Practice focuses on corporate governance and securities litigation, mergers and acquisitions, business torts, commercial contract disputes and appellate litigation. He has received recognition in Who's Who in American Lawyers, The Best Lawyers In America - Business Litigation, and Virginia's Legal Elite.

GASCH Jr, Manning
Hunton & Williams LLP, Richmond
804 788 8342
mgasch@hunton.com
Recommended in Environment
Practice Areas: Manning Gasch's practice focuses on 'environmental disaster' cases including all phases of CERCLA, general toxics, oil spill and natural resource damages practice, from development of expert reports and testimony to negotiations with various state and federal regulatory, law enforcement and trustee entities, through state and federal litigation.

GATTO, James
Pillsbury Winthrop LLP, McLean
703-905-2054
jgatto@pillsburywinthrop.com
Recommended in Intellectual Property
Practice Areas: Mr Gatto's focuses on patent, trademark, copyright, trade secret, open source and internet law in the areas of computer software, bioinformatics, medical devices and personalized medicine, optics, semiconductors, telecommunications, financial services, business methods and internet-related. Mr Gatto regularly handles high profile IP matters, including: Won patent interference for Nobel-prize winner; Successfully sued the US Government for patent infringement; Successfully defended two internet coupon patent lawsuits; representing Plaintiff in third; Successfully defended patent lawsuit

involving OGT patents enforced DNA image array analysis software patent for same company; Developed a patent portfolio for pioneering gallium nitride-based blue LEDs/lasers, which was licensed for significant value; Prevailed in competitor-initiated patent reexamination for cellphone compatible hearing aids.
Career: Positions: Board of Trustees and Secretary, Software Patent Institute; Board of Governors, Patent and Trademark Office Society; President (and other offices), Patent Lawyers Club of Washington; Chaired Patent, Trademark and Copyright Committee of American Bar Association/YLD. Voted one of the top IP/IT attorneys, Virginia Business Journal Survey, 2001.
Personal: JD, Georgetown University, 1988; BE Manhattan College (Electrical Engineering with a Physics minor), 1984.

GHOLZ, Charles
Oblon, Spivak, McClelland, Maier & Neustadt PC, Alexandria
703 413 3000
Recommended in Intellectual Property

GOOLSBY, Allen
Hunton & Williams LLP, Richmond
804 788 8289
agoolsby@hunton.com
Recommended in Corporate/M&A
Practice Areas: Allen Goolsby's practice focuses on corporate law, including corporate governance, mergers and acquisitions, and securities and finance.
Career: Mr Goolsby has worked on a variety of merger, acquisition and financing transactions involving publicly held corporations. He specializes in advising publicly-held corporations regarding corporate governance. He also served as the princial draftsman of the Virginia Stock Corporation Act.
Publications: Goolsby on Virginia Corporations (LexisNexis); Virginia Corporation Law and Practice (Prentice Hall Law & Business).

GOTTS, Lawrence J
Shaw Pittman LLP, Washington, DC
703 770 7604
lawrence.gotts@shawpittman.com, lawrence.gotts@pillsburylaw.com
Recommended in Intellectual Property
Practice Areas: Intellectual property: patent, trademark, copyright and trade secret litigation and counseling; litigation in federal district courts throughout the United States and the ITC; appeals before the Court of Appeals for the Federal Circuit.
Prof. Memberships: American Intellectual Property Association; American Bar Association; Tau Beta Pi; Pi Tau Sigma.
Career: Awarded 'Washington's Top IP Lawyer,' 2004, Washington Business Journal; Chair: Litigation and Intellectual Property Group; Registered to Practice Before USPTO.
Personal: BSME, University of Maryland, 1980, summa cum laude; JD,

George Washington, 1985, high honors; married with two children. (At press time, Ssaw Pittman LLP had entered into a merger agreement with Pillsbury Winthrop LLP. The merger is expected to close by April 2005. Post-closing, the name of the firm will be Pillsbury Winthrop Shaw Pittman LLP).

GRANDIS, Leslie
McGuireWoods LLP, Richmond
804 775 1000
Recommended in Corporate/M&A

HARLESS, Warren
Christian & Barton LLP, Richmond
804 697 4100
Recommended in Litigation

HARMON, Craig
McGuireWoods LLP, Richmond
804 775 1000
Recommended in Real Estate

HAYES, Timothy G
Hunton & Williams LLP, Richmond
804 788 8244
thayes@hunton.com
Recommended in Environment
Practice Areas: Timothy Hayes' Environmental Practice focuses on enforcement, permitting, litigation, regulatory counseling, appellate advocacy, project development, land use and government relations.

HESS, Adam R
Pillsbury Winthrop LLP, McLean
703 905 2089
ahess@pillsburywinthrop.com
Recommended in Intellectual Property
Practice Areas: Mr Hess' practice encompasses all aspects of intellectual property litigation, including 337 cases before the United States International Trade Commission. In addition, he also has extensive experience in patent prosecution; preparation of patentability, validity and infringement opinions; licensing; and ADR. Currently the IP Litigation Group leader in Northern Virginia, he has represented US, European, and Far East clients in a wide range of chemical, mechanical and electrical technologies. He has been recognized by peers as one of the best IP lawyers in Virginia (poll conducted by 'Virginia Business' magazine and The Virginia Bar Association). Prior to joining the firm, he worked at Hercules Chemicals, Borg Warner Chemicals, and FMC Corporation.
Prof. Memberships: American Bar Association, Virginia Bar Association, Federal Circuit Bar Association, American Intellectual Property Law Association, and American Institute of Chemical Engineers.
Career: Admitted to practice: District of Columbia, Commonwealth of Virginia, State of Pennsylvania. Admitted in: United States Supreme Court, US Court of Appeals for the Federal Circuit, and numerous US District Courts. Registered to practice before the US Patent

and Trademark Office.
Personal: JD, George Washington University, 1992; BS, Lehigh University (Chemical Engineering), 1987.

HIXON III, Samuel
Williams Mullen, Richmond
804 643 1991
Recommended in Litigation

HOFFAR, Julian
Watt, Tieder, Hoffar & Fitzgerald, L.L.P., McLean 703 749 1000
Recommended in Construction

HORAN, Richard
Hogan & Hartson LLP, McLean
703 610 6111
rthoran@hhlaw.com
Recommended in Corporate/M&A
Practice Areas: Mr Horan serves as a Director of the firm's Corporate, Securities and Finance Group and is a member of the firm's Executive Committee.
Career: His practice focuses on mergers and acquisitions. Mr Horan represents public and private companies in strategic transactions in many different industries, including communications and media, technology, energy, pharmaceutical, healthcare and government contracts. He has wide-ranging experience advising clients on various acquisition matters, including public and private mergers, stock and asset purchases, divestitures, spin-offs, and auction transactions.
Personal: James Madison University (BA, summa cum laude, 1984); University of Virginia School of Law (JD, 1987).

INGLIMA, Thomas
Willcox & Savage, Norfolk
757 628 5500
Recommended in Corporate/M&A

ISLER, Edward
Ray & Isler PC, Vienna
703 748 2690
eisler@rayandisler.com
Recommended in Employment
Practice Areas: Practice dedicated exclusively to representation of management in all aspects of labor and employment law. Provides employers with ongoing assistance and advice relating to every facet of the employer-employee relationship, including advising on employee discipline/termination issues, responding to discrimination and harassment claims before the EEOC and in federal or state court, providing guidance on wage-hour issues (FLSA and SCA), and drafting and enforcing non-compete agreements.
Prof. Memberships: Member, Executive Council, VBA Labor and Employment Law Section, 2002-06; Presenter, Judicial Conference of Virginia, Employment-at-Will (September 2003) and Non-Compete Agreements and Duty of Loyalty (May 2004).
Career: Previously with Gibson, Dunn & Crutcher, 1988-95. Judicial Clerk,

USDC, WD Va., 1987-88.
Publications: Author, Virginia Employment Practices and Forms (Virginia Law Foundation, 2002); Virginia Wage & Hour Handbook (Virginia Chamber of Commerce Legal Reference Series, 2005).
Personal: JD, William & Mary, 1987 (Law Review, Order of the Coif); BA, University of Virginia, 1983.

JENNINGS Jr , James
Woods Rogers PLC, Roanoke
540 983 7600; 800 552 4529
Recommended in Litigation

JOHNSTON, Jay
Troutman Sanders LLP, Richmond
804 697 1200
Recommended in Corporate/M&A

KEARFOTT, Joseph C
Hunton & Williams LLP, Richmond
804 788 8446
jkearfott@hunton.com
Recommended in Litigation
Practice Areas: Joseph Kearfott's practice focuses on all aspects of civil litigation, both state and federal, at the trial and appellate levels, with particular focus on complex product liability and toxic tort litigation. Other areas of practice include premises liability and other personal injury litigation, commercial disputes, business torts and valuation litigation. He is listed in Who's Who in America, Who's Who in American Law, Virginia Business Magazine, 'Legal Elite' in 2001-02 (best civil litigators in Virginia), and the 2005 BTI Client Service All-Star Team for Law Firms.

KING, William
McGuireWoods LLP, Richmond
804 775 1000
Recommended in Litigation

KNAUER, Thomas
McGuireWoods LLP, Richmond
804 775 1000
Recommended in Environment

KRAFTSON, Daniel
Kraftson Caudle LLC, McLean
703 873 5500
Recommended in Construction

KRIZAN, Lisa
LMK PLC, Richmond
804 359 2964
Recommended in Intellectual Property

LALLE, Wayne
Venable LLP, Vienna
703 760 1600
Recommended in Construction

LANE, David
Venable LLP, Vienna
703 760 1600
Recommended in Construction

LECLAIR, Gary D
LeClair Ryan, A Professional Corporation, Richmond
804 783 2003
gleclair@leclairryan.com

Recommended in Corporate/M&A
Practice Areas: Represents public and privately held companies and Boards of Directors as securities and general counsel. Lead attorney in numerous private and public debt and equity financings, joint ventures, strategic alliances, mergers and acquisitions, and other major domestic and international transactions. Director of various business and civic entities including banks, trusts, civic foundations and university boards of visitors.
Prof. Memberships: Virginia Bar.
Career: Co-founder and Chairman of LeClair Ryan.
Publications: Frequent lecturer/author at CLE and industry conferences.
Personal: Georgetown University, JD, magna cum laude, 1982. Virginia Business' 'Legal Elite.' Ernst & Young Virginia Entrepreneur of the Year Award, 1997. The Leadership Award by the Greater Richmond Technology Council, 1999.

LEE, Charlie
Moore & Lee LLP, McLean
703 506 2050
Recommended in Construction

LEWIS, Jack
Shaw Pittman LLP, McLean
703 770 7900
Recommended in Corporate/M&A

LINCOLN, Michael
Cooley Godward LLP, Reston
703 456 8000
Recommended in Corporate/M&A

LITTLE, Nancy
McGuireWoods LLP, Richmond
804 775 1000
Recommended in Real Estate

LOULAKIS, Michael
Wickwire Gavin, Vienna
703 790 8750
Recommended in Construction

MARSHALL, Gary
McGuireWoods LLP, Richmond
804 775 1000
Recommended in Employment

MARTIN, Channing
Williams Mullen, Richmond
804 643 1991
Recommended in Environment

MARTINEZ DE ANDINO, J Michael
Hunton & Williams LLP, Richmond
804 788 7216
mmartinez@hunton.com
Recommended in Intellectual Property
Practice Areas: Patent law, patent litigation, prosecution, licensing, due diligence investigations, audits, and other transactional work. Counsels clients concerning intellectual property issues in structuring deals and drafting agreements.
Prof. Memberships: Virginia, Kansas, Missouri State Bars. US Court of Appeals for the Federal Circuit, US

Patent & Trademark Office; ABA, AIPLA.

Career: Partner since 1998.

Publications: 12/01/04 Careers in Intellectual Property Law, Minority Trial Lawyer; 08/01/04 Conducting an Intellectual Property Due Diligence Investigation, Intellectual Property & Technology Law Journal; 06/01/98 Strategies for Patent Protection.

Personal: University of Kansas Law School (1991), William & Mary (MBA 1986), University of Virginia (BS 1978).

MASTRACCO, Vincent
Kaufman & Canoles, Norfolk
757 624 3000
Recommended in Corporate/M&A

MCCLARD, Jack E
Hunton & Williams LLP, Richmond
804 788 8490
jmcclard@hunton.com
Recommended in Litigation

Practice Areas: Jack McClard's practice focuses on complex litigation-general, patent, securities, commercial and appellate litigation. He has received recognition in 'Who's Who in America'; 'Who's Who in American Law'; 'Who's Who in Emerging Leaders', and 'Best Lawyers in America'.

Prof. Memberships: ABA, Va Bar Assn, Richmond Bar Assn, Lewis F Powell, Jr Inn of Court (Executive Committee).

Publications: 'Discovery In The Digital Age' (chapter in Civil Discovery in Virginia); 'The Applicability of Local Securities Acts to Multi-State Securities Transaction', 20 U Rich L Rev 139 (1985); 'The Tax Man Cometh to Securities Litigation', 34 Va Bar News 15 (1986).

MCKEE, Braxton
Kaufman & Canoles, Norfolk
757 624 3000
Recommended in Corporate/M&A

MCWHORTER, Val
Smith Pachter McWhorter & Allen, Vienna 703 847 6300
Recommended in Construction

MEATH, James
Williams Mullen, Richmond
804 643 1991
Recommended in Employment

MELTZER, Steven
Shaw Pittman LLP, McLean
703 770 7950
steven.meltzer@shawpittman.com
Recommended in Corporate/M&A

Practice Areas: Corporate, technology and life sciences, with particular focus on strategic transactions such as financings, mergers and acquisitions, licences, development and distribution agreements, and joint ventures for growing public and private companies.

Prof. Memberships: Chair of Board of Trustees, New England Institute of Technology; Member of Board of Visitors, College of Life Sciences of the University

of Maryland; General Counsel and Member of Board of Directors and Executive Committee, Technology Council of Maryland; General Counsel of Maryland Angels Council, Member of Mid-Atlantic Venture Association, Northern Virginia Technology Council, Economic Club of Washington and International Bar Association.

Career: Partner since 1980, Member of Shaw Pittman Board of Directors since 2001, former Chair of Corporate/Technology Practice Group, former Chair of Finance Committee, Senior Partner in Northern Virginia Office.

Publications: Has lectured and written extensively on corporate and finance matters; has been a regular guest lecturer in entrepreneurship courses in the Georgetown University MBA program; recent publications include 'Strategies for Attracting Angel Investors' by John Holaday, Steven Meltzer and James McCormick, Journal of Commercial Biotechnology, January, 2003; and 'Intellectual Property as a Foundation for Funding' by Steven Meltzer, Michelle Marks and James McCormick, Nature Biotechnology, July, 2002.

Personal: Brown University (AB Economics, Cum Laude, 1968), Harvard Business School (MBA with High Distinction/Baker Scholar, 1973), Harvard Law School (JD,1973).

MEYER, Richard
McGuireWoods LLP, McLean
703 712 5000
Recommended in Intellectual Property

MOORE, Justin
Hunton & Williams LLP, Richmond
804 788 8464
jmoore@hunton.com
Recommended in Corporate/M&A

Practice Areas: Justin Moore's practice focuses on mergers and acquisitions, corporate finance, corporate governance and securities regulation. He is Co-Head of the firm's Global Capital Markets and Mergers and Acquisitions Team.

MOORE, Robert
Moore & Lee LLP, McLean
703 506 2050
Recommended in Construction

MOORE, Thurston R
Hunton & Williams LLP, Richmond
804 788 8295
tmoore@hunton.com
Recommended in Corporate/M&A

Practice Areas: Thurston Moore's practice focuses primarily on corporate and securities representation with emphasis on corporate financing and governance, venture capital, real estate investment trusts and partnership law. He has been Managing Partner of the firm since 1991.

Prof. Memberships: Trustee, Virginia Museum of Fine Arts; Chairman, The Nature Conservancy of Virginia.

MORRIS III, James
Morris & Morris PC, Richmond
804 344 8300
Recommended in Litigation

MORSE, Clinton S
LeClair Ryan, A Professional Corporation, Roanoke 540 510 3023
clinton.morse@leclairryan.com
Recommended in Employment

Practice Areas: Labor and employment; represents unionized companies (collective bargaining, grievance/arbitrations, NLRB matters). Counsel on union-free management issues (union avoidance strategies, management training, election campaigns).

Prof. Memberships: Roanoke, Virginia (Past Chairman, Labor Relations and Employment Law Section) and American (Development of the Law of Individual Rights and Responsibilities in the Workplace Committee) Bar Associations; State Bar of Texas (Labor Law Section); Virginia State Bar.

Career: Co-Chair, LeClair Ryan's Employment and Labor Practice.

Publications: National lecturer/author on labor and employment topics. Contributor, Virginia Employment Law Letter.

Personal: University of Texas, JD, 1970. Order of the Coif. Texas Law Review. 'The Best Lawyers in America', Virginia Business' 'Legal Elite.'

MUGEL, Christopher
Kaufman & Canoles, Richmond
804 771 5700
Recommended in Intellectual Property

MURPHY, Thomas P
Hunton & Williams, McLean
703 714 7533
tpmurphy@hunton.com
Recommended in Employment

Practice Areas: Thomas Murphy's practice focuses on all areas of labor and employment law, with particular emphasis on the trial of discrimination cases. He has been listed in 'The Best Lawyers In America' for over 10 years, and listed in 'The Legal Elite' by 'Virginia Business' magazine the last three years.

MYTELKA, Craig
Williams Mullen, Richmond
804 643 1991
Recommended in Intellectual Property

NAGLE, David E
LeClair Ryan, A Professional Corporation, Richmond 804 343 4077
dnagle@leclairryan.com
Recommended in Employment

Practice Areas: Employment and labor law (management). Representation in litigation, and counsel on personnel practices to avoid litigation. Extensive experience enforcing workplace arbitration programs. Substantial appellate practice including Circuit City v. Adams,, 532 US 105 (2002). Clients include retailers, airlines, local governments, financial institutions and service firms.

Prof. Memberships: Virginia, American

Bar Associations; American Arbitration Association, Panel of Arbitrators.

Career: Co-Chair, firm's Employment Law Practice, 1993-; practicing since 1981. AV rating (Martindale). Virginia Business 'Legal Elite' 2000-04; Richmond Magazine 'Top Lawyers'.

Publications: Editor, Virginia Employment Law Letter, 2003-; columnist, Metro Business (Richmond Times Dispatch), 1986-90; articles in law review, trade publications; 250+ presentations on employment law topics.

Personal: Georgetown, LLM (Labor Law), 1983; University of Richmond, JD, 1981; William & Mary, AB, 1976.

NEUSTADT, Arthur
Oblon, Spivak, McClelland, Maier & Neustadt PC, Alexandria
703 413 3000
Recommended in Intellectual Property

NIXON, Larry
Nixon & Vanderhye P.C., Arlington
703 816 4000
Recommended in Intellectual Property

NOONA, Stephen
Kaufman & Canoles, Norfolk
757 624 3000
Recommended in Intellectual Property

NORTHUP, Stephen
Troutman Sanders LLP, Richmond
804 697 1200
Recommended in Litigation

OLD, William
Williams Mullen, Richmond
804 643 1991
Recommended in Corporate/M&A

OLIFF, James
Oliff & Berridge, PLC, Alexandria
703 836 6400
Recommended in Intellectual Property

OSSOLA, Charles
Arnold & Porter LLP, Washington, DC
202 942 5075
Charles.Ossola@aporter.com
Recommended in Intellectual Property

Practice Areas: Charles D Ossola is a Senior Partner and Litigator in Arnold & Porter LLP's Intellectual Property and Technology Practice Group. Mr Ossola's National Intellectual Property Litigation Practice encompasses patent, trademark, copyright, trade secret, unfair competition and antitrust cases for plaintiffs and defendants. In the technology arena, Mr Ossola's patent Litigation Practice includes pharmaceutical, patent and related antitrust litigation, as well as cases involving communication systems and software. His trademark and copyright litigation practice involves novel issues in the fields of on-line advertising on search engines, print and television media, software and photography.

Career: Mr Ossola serves as lead counsel in intellectual property litigation matters and has extensive trial experience in federal courts throughout the country.

Publications: Recent Speeches: 'Navigating Internet Issues - The use of 'Keyword' Advertising in Search Engines,' The John Marshall Law School Conference on Developments in Intellectual Property Law, Change Here and Now: Navigating Among New Landmarks, February 25, 2005; 'Brand Summit: Life After Google-Geico,' Jupiter Media Search Engine Strategies 2005 Conference & Expo, March 2, 2005.

PAGE, Rosewell
McGuireWoods LLP, Richmond
804 775 1000
Recommended in Litigation

PARKS, Randall S
Hunton & Williams LLP, Richmond
804 788 7375
rparks@hunton.com
Recommended in Corporate/M&A
Practice Areas: Mr Parks' outsourcing practice focuses on large-scale business process and IT outsourcings for Global 2000 firms. Recent transactions include human resources, finance and accounting and data center outsourcings for large consumer products, defense and energy companies. His capital markets practice focuses on public and private securities offerings and mergers and acquisitions. Recent transactions include a public merger creating the world's largest supplier of an agricultural commodity, the IPO of a homebuilder and numerous offerings of REIT securities. He is author of the Virginia Business Trust Act and Vice-Chairman of the Virginia Bar Association's Section of Business Law.

PARRINO, Richard
Hogan & Hartson LLP, McLean
703 610 6174
rjparrino@hhlaw.com
Recommended in Corporate/M&A
Practice Areas: Mr Parrino represents US and international companies in public and institutional securities offerings, mergers and acquisitions, private equity investments, and other corporate transactions. He counsels extensively on corporate governance and securities regulation matters. His clients operate in telecommunications, information technology, manufacturing, consumer products, defense, and other industries.
Career: Co-editor of Hogan & Hartson's SEC Update newsletter; Chairman of Hogan & Hartson's Corporate Governance Group.
Personal: Georgetown University (BSFS, summa cum laude, 1975); University of Virginia School of Law (JD, Managing Editor, Virginia Law Review, 1978); Cambridge University (LLM, first class honors, 1980).

PEARSON Jr, John
Willcox & Savage, Norfolk
757 628 5500
Recommended in Litigation

POFF, William
Woods Rogers PLC, Roanoke
540 983 7600
Recommended in Litigation

PORTER, Philip
Hogan & Hartson LLP, McLean
703 610 6108
PDPorter@hhlaw.com
Recommended in Intellectual Property
Practice Areas: Structures and negotiates domestic and international IT, telecommunications and business process outsourcing transactions and helps companies to acquire and commercialize technology and information, including through joint ventures, strategic alliances, assignments, license grants, and consulting services. Assists with selection of outsourcing service providers and leads outsourcing negotiations. Particular experience helping companies commercialize computer hardware and software, biotechnology, data, and electronic commerce, in the US and overseas.
Prof. Memberships: Member, Computer and Telecommunications Law Section, DC Bar; Member, Computer Law Association.
Career: Adjunct professor for graduate course titled 'Commercialization of Biotechnology,' Johns Hopkins University, 2002-03 academic year. Faculty member of Advanced Computer Law Institute, Georgetown University Law Center, 1990-99.
Publications: Co-author, 'The Technology Escrow: A Critical Business Continuity Tool', IP Update, Hogan & Hartson (5/7/2004). Co-author, 'Open Source Software and Risks Associated with its Use in a Commercial Environment', IP Update, Hogan & Hartson (3/12/2004).
Personal: Awards/Rankings: Virginia Business magazine 'The 2004 Legal Elite' for Intellectual Property Law, 2004; International Who's Who of E-Commerce Lawyers, 2001.

PULLEY III, J Waverly
Hunton & Williams LLP, Richmond
804 788 8783
wpulley@hunton.com
Recommended in Real Estate, Transport
Practice Areas: Waverly Pulley's practice focuses on capital finance, public-private infrastructure projects, commercial lending and leasing.

RAINEY Jr, Gordon F
Hunton & Williams LLP, Richmond
804 788 8275
grainey@hunton.com
Recommended in Corporate/M&A
Practice Areas: Gordon Rainey's practice focuses on corporate law, corporate governance, international law, mergers and acquisitions, joint ventures and other business combinations. He is Chairman of the firm's Executive Committee. Rainey has advised corporations,

including Fortune 500 companies and their boards of directors, on issues of corporate governance, change of control, anti-takeover defenses and related matters.

RIOPELLE, Brian
McGuireWoods LLP, Richmond
804 775 1000
Recommended in Intellectual Property

ROBERTS, James
Troutman Sanders LLP, Richmond
804 697 1200
Recommended in Litigation

ROBERTSON, Gregory
Hunton & Williams LLP, Richmond
804 788 8526
grobertson@hunton.com
Recommended in Employment
Practice Areas: Greg Robertson's practice focuses on all aspects of labor and employment law including employment advice and litigation, representation elections and all labor relations matters with expertise in the service, manufacturing, food distribution, textile, meatpacking, healthcare, coal and other natural resource industries.

ROBINSON, Stephen
McGuireWoods LLP, McLean
703 712 5000
Recommended in Employment

ROTHENBERG, Charles
Hirschler Fleischer, Richmond
804 771 9503
crothenberg@hf-law.com
Recommended in Real Estate
Career: Chuck is a real estate attorney who represents commercial lenders, developers, builders, commercial landlords and tenants. Chuck routinely negotiates and closes real estate sales and acquisitions for commercial, office, residential and mixed-use projects. Additionally, he assists purchasers in all phases of feasibility studies for acquisitions; represents owners and purchasers on zoning and other matters before planning commissions, boards of supervisors, city councils, and boards of zoning appeals; negotiates, documents, and closes commercial loans, loan modifications, and loan workouts; and prepares integrated project documents for planned unit developments, including declarations of covenants, marketing agreements and form contracts for the sale of lots to builders and consumers.
Personal: JD, University of Richmond; BA, State University of New York, Oneonta.

RUDLIN, D Alan
Hunton & Williams LLP, Richmond
804 788 8459
arudlin@hunton.com
Recommended in Litigation
Practice Areas: Alan Rudlin's practice focuses on class actions, mass torts, pharmaceutical, product and toxic litigation, as well as commercial, First

Amendment, and constitutional litigation. Specialty includes national coordinating counsel role in managing complex litigation, and development of expert evidence and medical causation issues for product, pharmaceutical and environmental litigation. Co-Chair of the ABA Litigation Section's Mass Torts Litigation Committee.

RUST, Dana
McGuireWoods LLP, Richmond
804 775 1000
Recommended in Employment

RYAN Jr, James
Troutman Sanders LLP, Richmond
804 697 1200
Recommended in Environment

SHUMADINE, Conrad
Willcox & Savage, Norfolk
757 628 5500
Recommended in Litigation

SIMS, Hunter
Kaufman & Canoles, Norfolk
757 624 3000
Recommended in Litigation

SLATER, Thomas
Hunton & Williams LLP, Richmond
804 788 8475
tslater@hunton.com
Recommended in Litigation
Practice Areas: Tom Slater's practice focuses on complex litigation matters with emphasis on antitrust, intellectual property, trade secrets, unfair trade practices, product liability and white collar criminal defense.
Prof. Memberships: Fellow, American College of Trial Attorneys; Fellow, American Bar Foundation; Fellow, Virginia Law Foundation; Member, Fourth Circuit Judicial Conference; Listed in 'Best Lawyers in America' for over 10 years, antitrust and corporate litigation
Publications: Co-author, 'Communication Methods and Skills' chapter, 'Successful Partnering Between Inside and Outside Counsel', American Corporate Counsel Association, 2000; author, 'Sentence Yourself' article on Federal Sentencing Guidelines, ABA Journal.

SLONE, Daniel
McGuireWoods LLP, Richmond
804 775 1000
Recommended in Environment

SMILAN, Laurie
Latham & Watkins LLP, Reston
703 456 1000
Recommended in Litigation

SMITH, Brooks
Hunton & Williams LLP, Richmond
804 787 8086
bsmith@hunton.com
Recommended in Environment
Practice Areas: Brooks Smith concentrates on proceedings that arise under the Clean Water Act, including rule, permit, enforcement and TMDL actions. Brooks also counsels clients on a wide

range of regulatory compliance issues in voluntary environmental audit, EMS, permit and enforcement proceedings, as well as transactions.

SMITH, David
Venable LLP, Vienna
703 760 1600
Recommended in Employment

SMITH, Julious
Williams Mullen, Richmond
804 643 1991
Recommended in Corporate/M&A

SMITH, Michael
Christian & Barton LLP, Richmond
804 697 4100
Recommended in Litigation

SPANGLER, Nancy A
DLA Piper Rudnick Gray Cary US LLP, Reston 703 773 4021
nancy.spangler@dlapiper.com
Recommended in Corporate/M&A
Practice Areas: Corporate; mergers and acquisitions.
Career: Her practice is devoted to representing public and private technology companies, and investors in these companies. She represents clients in a variety of corporate finance and securities activities, including public offerings, mergers and acquisitions, corporate governance and compliance with securities laws, venture capital transactions, private placements, corporate partnering arrangements and general corporate matters.
Personal: JD, University of Virginia, Dillard Fellow; BA, Iowa State University.

SPARKS Jr, Robert
Herge, Sparks & Christopher LLP, McLean 703 848 4700
Recommended in Employment

STILLMAN, Gregory
Hunton & Williams, Norfolk
757 640 5314
gstillman@hunton.com
Recommended in Litigation
Practice Areas: Gregory Stillman's practice focuses on federal trial and appellate litigation, with emphasis on business torts, intellectual property (copyright and patent), securities and corporate governance. He is Managing Partner of the Firm's Norfolk Office.

SYLVESTER, David
Wilmer Cutler Pickering Hale and Dorr LLP, Reston 703 654 7001
david.sylvester@wilmerhale.com
Recommended in Corporate/M&A
Practice Areas: Represents public and private technology companies and other general corporate clients in the areas of venture capital, intellectual property, mergers and acquisitions, domestic and international technology licensing, and securities law.
Prof. Memberships: National and American Bar Associations; Board of Directors, Heads-Up Incorporated, a private, non-profit after school enrich-

ment program in Washington, DC; Board of Directors, Mid-Atlantic Venture Association.
Career: Serves as pro bono general counsel to the Midnight Basketball League, Inc., and to the National Association of Midnight Basketball Leagues, Inc.
Personal: University of Virginia School of Law (JD 1981); Stanford University (BA 1978).

TAPSCOTT, Andrew
Hunton & Williams LLP, Richmond
804 788 8620
atapscott@hunton.com
Recommended in Real Estate
Practice Areas: Andy Tapscott's practice focuses on commercial real estate transactions, including sophisticated finance, development, acquisitions, dispositions, joint ventures, leasing, loan workouts and foreclosures. Mr Tapscott's practice has a special emphasis on the hospitality and leisure industry.

TATA, Robert M
Hunton & Williams, Norfolk
757 640 5328
btata@hunton.com
Recommended in Intellectual Property
Practice Areas: Bob Tata's practice includes complex commercial litigation, intellectual property (copyright, trademark, trade dress, trade secret and patent) litigation, class action defense and other high stakes litigation in federal and state courts. Bob at one time held the record for the largest jury verdict in the history of Virginia. He has won and recovered seven and eight figure awards for his IP clients and defeated multi-million dollar IP claims. Bob has spoken and been quoted extensively on IP topics.

TERRY, Mike
Hirschler Fleischer, Richmond
804 771 9510
mterry@hf-law.com
Recommended in Real Estate
Career: Mike has assisted the financial restructuring of a wide range of commercial businesses and real estate development companies. He also has represented numerous lenders (inside and outside of bankruptcy) in collecting their credit and realizing upon their collateral from borrowers. Mike's experience in financial workouts / reorganizations has led to a practice consulting with business owners and negotiating on their behalves with respect to organization of assets, general business planning and division / dissolution of business organizations (business divorces). Mike also represents financial institutions and investors in the purchase and sale of loan portfolios and servicing portfolios.
Personal: JD, College of William & Mary; BS, University of Richmond.

THEOBALD, James
Hirschler Fleischer, Richmond
804 771 9513
jtheobald@hf-law.com
Recommended in Real Estate
Career: Jim has assisted some of the nation's largest developers and retailers in making their projects a reality for over two decades. From contract negotiations through rezoning, licensing and permitting, entity structuring, financing and leasing, Jim brings creative, aggressive advocacy to bear in finding a way to make a deal work. Jim has, among other things, represented one of the nation's largest discount appliance chains in acquiring sites throughout the country. He also has structured sale/lease back transactions, including those with foreign investors, and other financing related to the acquisition and development of store locations. Additionally, Jim has represented Wal-Mart Stores, Inc. and other national retailers in the acquisition, rezoning and approval process in various portions of Virginia.
Personal: JD, Cleveland Marshall College of Law; BA College of William & Mary.

THOMAS, Bill
Reed Smith LLP, Falls Church
703 641 4238
wthomas@reedsmith.com
Recommended in Real Estate
Practice Areas: Administrative practice before state agencies; legislative practice before the Virginia General Assembly; land use and administrative practice before all Northern Virginia jurisdictions and agencies; and corporate governance practice.
Prof. Memberships: American Law Institute, American College of Real Estate Lawyers, member of the Fourth Circuit Judicial Conference.
Career: Partner at Hazel & Thomas, which combined with Reed Smith in 1999.
Publications: Writes extensively in the condominium field.
Personal: University of Richmond (JD, 1963), editor of 'Richmond Law Notes'; served by Governor's appointment to the Board of Directors of The Center for Innovative Technology.

THOMPSON, Gary
Hunton & Williams LLP, Richmond
804 788 8787
gthompson@hunton.com
Recommended in Corporate/M&A
Practice Areas: Gary Thompson's practice focuses on mergers and acquisitions, hostile and friendly tender offers, public and private securities offerings, corporate governance issues and a wide range of corporate finance activities. Head of the firm's US Mergers and Acquisitions Group.

THORNHILL, James
McGuireWoods LLP, Richmond
804 775 1000
Recommended in Environment

TIEDER, John
Watt, Tieder, Hoffar & Fitzgerald, L.L.P., McLean 703 749 1000
Recommended in Construction

TITLEY, Ian
Williams Mullen, Richmond
804 643 1991
Recommended in Intellectual Property

VARELA, Paul
Watt, Tieder, Hoffar & Fitzgerald, L.L.P., McLean 703 749 1000
Recommended in Construction

VAUGHAN III, C Porter
Hunton & Williams LLP, Richmond
804 788 8200
pvaughan@hunton.com
Recommended in Corporate/M&A
Practice Areas: Mr Vaughan's practice focuses on mergers and acquisitions, corporate financings, corporate governance and securities regulation. He is Co-Head of Business Practice Group.

WALSH, William
Hunton & Williams LLP, Richmond
804 788 8378
wwalsh@hunton.com
Recommended in Real Estate
Practice Areas: Bill Walsh's practice focuses primarily on strategic real estate planning, student housing for colleges and universities, urban redevelopment and private-public ventures. He is listed in 'Best Lawyers in America,' 'Who's Who in America' and 'America's Leading Business Lawyers' and was named Best Real Estate and Construction Lawyer in Virginia by 'Virginia Business magazine'. Bill is a member of the American College of Real Estate Lawyers.

WATT, Robert
Watt, Tieder, Hoffar & Fitzgerald, L.L.P., McLean 703 749 1000
Recommended in Construction

WEBB, Eugene
Troutman Sanders LLP, Richmond
804 697 1200
Recommended in Employment

WEINBERG, Jay
Hirschler Fleischer, Fredericksburg
804 771 9533
jlweinberg@hf-law.com
Recommended in Real Estate
Career: Jay Weinberg is a founding member of the real estate section of Hirschler Fleischer. His practice focuses on sophisticated land use and zoning matters. He has practiced law for over 40 years and has handled virtually all forms of sophisticated real estate matters, including the acquisition, rezoning, financing, syndication, development, adaptive reuse and sale of major residential communities, apartment complexes, shopping centers, industrial parks and office-service buildings. He has had substantial experience in counseling real estate developers in connection with the taxation and structure of legal entities to develop, own and sell

real estate projects.

Personal: LLB (JD), University of Virginia; BA, University of Virginia.

WELLFORD, Hill

Hunton & Williams LLP, Richmond
804 788 8518
hwellford@hunton.com
Recommended in Employment

Practice Areas: Hill Wellford's practice focuses on equal opportunity law, labor relations, labor arbitrations, collective bargaining, executive employment agreements, wage-hour law, occupational safety and health law and litigation of employment claims, including class actions, under federal and state labor and employment statutes. He is listed in: 'Best Lawyers in America' for labor and employment law; 'Who's Who in America'; 'Who's Who in American Law'; and selected to Virginia's Legal Elite Virginia Business magazine, December, 2000-04.

WHEATON, James

Troutman Sanders LLP, Virginia Beach
757 687 7500
Recommended in Corporate/M&A

WHITT, Burt

Kaufman & Canoles, Norfolk
757 624 3000
Recommended in Employment

WHITTEMORE, Anne Marie

McGuireWoods LLP, Richmond
804 775 1000
Recommended in Litigation

WICKWIRE, Jon

Wickwire Gavin, Vienna
703 790 8750
Recommended in Construction

WILLIAMS, Steven

McGuireWoods LLP, Richmond
804 775 1000
Recommended in Litigation

WITTHOEFFT, Charles

Hirschler Fleischer, Richmond
804 771 9562
rwitthoefft@hf-law.com
Recommended in Litigation

Career: Rick Witthoefft is Chair of the firm's Litigation Section and has over 27 years of trial experience in handling a wide variety of commercial disputes in state and federal courts throughout Virginia. He has represented both plaintiffs and defendants in complex, frequently multiparty, commercial cases including contract, business tort, landlord-tenant, land use, professional liability, employment, utilities law, administrative law, antitrust, securities, banking, RICO, construction, trust and estate, environmental, and liability insurance issues. Additionally, Rick is a fellow of the prestigious American College of Trial Lawyers.

Personal: JD, University of Richmond; BA, Hampden-Sydney College.

WRIGHT, Murray

Wright Robinson Osthimer & Tatum, Richmond 804 783 1100
Recommended in Construction

YOUNGER, Carter

McGuireWoods LLP, Richmond
804 775 1000
Recommended in Employment

HUNTON & WILLIAMS LLP

THE FIRM

Managing Partner: Thurston R Moore
Chairman, Executive Committee: Gordon F Rainey, Jr
Number of partners worldwide: 339
Number of other lawyers worldwide: 526

FIRM OVERVIEW: Since its establishment in 1901, Hunton & Williams has grown to more than 850 attorneys who have served clients in over 100 countries from 17 offices around the world. The firm has experience in more than 60 separate practice areas.

MAIN AREAS OF PRACTICE:

Capital Markets, Mergers & Acquisitions: The capital markets attorneys at Hunton & Williams have broad experience and insight on initial public and private offerings of equity securities, the issuance of debt securities in foreign and domestic markets, the creation of open- and closed-end mutual funds, and public and private partnership offerings. The corporate attorneys counsel clients on domestic and international merger and acquisition transactions. The firm provides guidance in all aspects of contested and negotiated acquisitions, including tender offers, proxy fights, takeover defenses, leveraged buyouts, corporate spin-offs, holding company formations, corporate auctions, mergers of equals, and strategic acquisition and divestiture programs.

Energy: Hunton & Williams' Energy Practice represents clients throughout the United States and in more than 50 other countries on six continents. The firm's attorneys handle matters as diverse as convergence mergers between electric and gas utility holding companies; corporate restructurings; debt and equity finance; representation of energy marketing and trading companies; corporate and regulatory work associated with the formation and operation of independent system operators and regional transmission organizations; privatization of distribution, transmission and generating assets in Asia, Latin America, Europe and Africa; and the development and financing of energy projects around the world.

Environmental: Hunton & Williams' Environmental Practice is among the oldest and largest in the nation. Its attorneys have helped clients navigate every major federal environmental statute, and those of most states and international jurisdictions. The team advises a range of industries on innovative response to environmental compliance, represents companies in litigation and administrative proceedings, and ensures that clients have a voice in shaping policy.

Labor & Employment: Hunton & Williams' Labor and Employment Practice covers the entire spectrum of labor and employment litigation; arbitration; administrative practice before the NLRB, EEOC and the Labor Department; federal contract compliance; wage-house standards; Occupational Safety and Health Administration standards; workers' compensation; and client counseling under federal and state labor and employment laws.

Litigation: Hunton & Williams' Litigation Team is recognized as one of the premier litigation groups in the country. Its nearly 300 attorneys handle litigation in virtually every area of law including antitrust, appellate, business crimes defense, corporate governance/mergers and acquisitions, intellectual property and patent, international arbitration/dispute resolution, product liability, securities, telecommunications, toxic tort and workouts/creditors' rights.

CLIENTS: Hunton & Williams serves clients in the following industry sectors: associations, biotech and chemical, consumer products, energy, environmental services, financial services, government entities, healthcare, hospitality, international, manufacturing, professional services, real estate, technology, telecommunications and transportation.

HEAD OFFICE

VIRGINIA
Riverfront Plaza, East Tower, 951 East Byrd Street, **Richmond**, VA 23219-4074
Tel: 804 788 8200 **Fax:** 804 788 8218
Email: info@hunton.com **Website:** www.hunton.com

BRANCH OFFICES

DISTRICT OF COLUMBIA
1900 K Street, NW, **Washington**, DC 20006-1109
Tel: 202 955 1500 **Fax:** 202 778 2201

FLORIDA
1111 Brickell Avenue, Suite 2500, **Miami**, FL 33131
Tel: 305 810 2500 **Fax:** 305 810 2460

GEORGIA
Bank of America Plaza, Suite 4100, 600 Peachtree Street, NE
Atlanta, GA 30308-2216
Tel: 404 888 4000 **Fax:** 404 888 4190

NEW YORK
200 Park Avenue, 43/F, **New York**, NY 10166-0136
Tel: 212 309 1000 **Fax:** 212 309 1100

NORTH CAROLINA
Bank of America Plaza, Suite 3500, 101 South Tryon Street
Charlotte, NC 28280
Tel: 704 378 4700 **Fax:** 704 378 4890

421 Fayetteville Street Mall, Suite 1400, **Raleigh**, NC 27601
Tel: 919 899 3000 **Fax:** 919 833 6352

TENNESSEE
2000 Riverview Tower, 900 South Gay Street
Knoxville, TN 37902
Tel: 865 549 7700 **Fax:** 865 549 7704

TEXAS
Frost Bank Building, Suite 1200, 816 Congress Avenue
Austin, TX 78701
Tel: 512 480 5050 **Fax:** 512 480 5051

Energy Plaza, 30/F, 1601 Bryan Street, **Dallas**, TX 75201-3402
Tel: 214 979 3000 **Fax:** 214 880 0011

VIRGINIA
1751 Pinnacle Drive, Suite 1700, **McLean**, VA 22102
Tel: 703 714 7400 **Fax:** 703 714 7410

500 East Main Street, Suite 1000, **Norfolk**, VA 23510-3889
Tel: 757 640 5300 **Fax:** 757 625 7720

INTERNATIONAL WORK: Hunton & Williams has a significant international presence with offices in London, Brussels, Hong Kong, Singapore and Bangkok. As the firm's clients pursue international opportunities, they appreciate the support of locally experienced lawyers who know the legal and business practices of their region. Hunton & Williams' international clients include leading US and foreign corporations, governments and governmental entities, financial institutions, commercial and investment banks, multilateral and bilateral lending and guarantee agencies.

CONTENTS: Bankruptcy p.1776; Corporate/M&A p.1777; Employment p.1780; Environment p.1782; Intellectual Property p.1783; Litigation p.1785; Real Estate p.1787; Individuals' Profiles p.1790. Firms' Profiles p.1796.

How lawyers are ranked

The opinions we gather from clients — mainly from in-house lawyers but also from other purchasers of legal services — are balanced by opinions from colleagues and competitors. Together, they provide two different perspectives — an all-round view — and biased viewpoints cancel each other out.

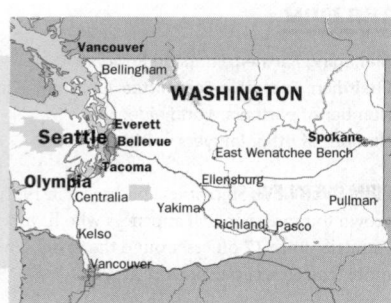

BANKRUPTCY

Washington
Leading firms (Bankruptcy)

1. BUSH, STROUT & KORNFELD *Seattle*
   DAVIS WRIGHT TREMAINE LLP *Seattle*
   FOSTER PEPPER & SHEFELMAN PLLC *Seattle*
   LANE POWELL PC *Seattle*
   PRESTON GATES & ELLIS LLP *Seattle*

Leading individuals (Bankruptcy)

1. BUSH Gayle *Bush, Strout & Kornfeld, Seattle*
   CULLEN Jack *Foster Pepper & Shefelman, Seattle*
   EKBERG Charles *Lane Powell PC, Seattle*
   OSENBAUGH Kim *Preston Gates, Seattle*

2. ALLRED Keith *Davis Wright, Seattle*
   HESTON Mary Jo *Lane Powell, Seattle*
   KORNFELD Armand *Bush Strout, Seattle*
   LEAVERTON Bruce *Lane Powell, Seattle*
   POWERS Ragan *Davis Wright, Seattle*

Firms and individuals are listed alphabetically in each band.

Band 1

Bush, Strout & Kornfeld

The Firm: According to a number of market sources, this eight-strong boutique is *"probably the best in town"* for bankruptcy advice and representation. The *"effective, pragmatic"* group is the first port of call for a range of debtors, trustees and creditors because it *"gets great results."* Its broad experience encompasses Chapter. 7, 11 and 13 proceedings, and the team was recently responsible for the reorganization of Alaska Power and Telephone Company. Other highlights from the past year include serving as counsel in Seattle's X10 bankruptcy.

The Lawyers: A *"creative and practical"* bankruptcy attorney, **Gayle Bush** has accumulated a wealth of experience in the field. Branded an *"honorable and seasoned lawyer,"* he recently represented a 25-outlet Burger King franchisee in bankruptcy proceedings. Sources say that he makes a particularly fine debtors' counsel, by reason of his *"instinct for building consensus and striving for a constructive outcome."*

Armand Kornfeld represents creditors and trustees in a broad range of matters, and has recently been involved in a major bankruptcy in the fishing industry. He is chosen by clients for his *"intelligent arguments"* and *"exceptional diligence,"* which he combines with an even-tempered approach and great responsiveness.

The Clients: Alaska Power & Telephone Company, Pacific Realty Advisors and X10 are among the clients.

Davis Wright Tremaine LLP

See firm details p.1796

The Firm: The credit recovery and bankruptcy department at this regional powerhouse is noted for its *"sheer number of quality lawyers."* Clients also turn to the firm for its depth of knowledge and *"plain good advice."* It makes regular appearances in Seattle's most important cases, as well as assisting teams across the country, and excels at representing secured and unsecured creditors in a wide range of proceedings. The team can also draw on the capabilities of its well-respected litigation group to assist in bankruptcy disputes.

The Lawyers: **Keith Allred** (see p.1790) has tried bankruptcy cases in courts across the nation. He was described as a *"knowledgeable and personable"* attorney, and particularly shines in counseling work for banks and lenders. He is also frequently involved in out-of-court restructurings. His colleague, **Ragan Powers** (see p.1794) represents debtors, creditors and trustees in a wide range of issues. These include loan workouts and the arbitration and litigation of bankruptcy-related issues. Interviewees consider him a *"practical, solution-oriented"* attorney with an *"excellent grasp of the law."*

The Clients: Bank of America, GE Capital and US Bank feature in the team's client roster.

Foster Pepper & Shefelman PLLC

The Firm: The nine Seattle-based bankruptcy and creditors' rights attorneys here were recommended by clients as *"excellent in the largest and most complicated matters."* The group is well versed in all aspects of insolvency law, from restructuring financial transactions, to liquidating assets and Chapter 11 reorganizations. It acts for debtors, creditors, trustees, committees and landlords in proceedings across the USA, and is frequently chosen by major corporations as national or regional counsel. Its national profile is complemented by a considerable breadth of technical expertise, as the firm can draw on a variety of experts in other departments.

The Lawyers: Commentators applaud *"smart, tough and practical"* **Jack Cullen** for his *"great technical know-how"* in all aspects of bankruptcy law. Having practiced in the area for 25 years, he is deservedly recognized as a *"superbly experienced"* insolvency lawyer. Over the past twelve months he has acted for a variety of clients in bankruptcies, workouts and related-litigation. These have included publicly held telephone companies, hotel chains and timber companies.

The Clients: The firm advises buyers, debtors, landlords, secured creditors and creditor and equity committees from various sectors, including manufacturing, timber, fishing, real estate and retail.

Lane Powell PC

See firm details p.1797

The Firm: The firm recognized bankruptcy as a separate practice area as early at 1972, giving it a long tradition in the field, and it now houses ten bankruptcy specialists. This *"especially broad and strong"* group was recommended by clients for its commitment to their businesses; as one put it: *"They really understand our goals."* It represents a wide range of parties, including secured creditors, trustees, debtors, creditor committees and mortgagees, while financial institutions frequently benefit from the team's robust advice. Typical work spans foreclosures, loan workouts, reorganizations and liquidations.

The Lawyers: Interviewees are impressed by **Chuck Ekberg**'s (see p.1791) *"practically* photographic memory." Moreover, his "*results-oriented and client-focused*" approach, together with his technical excellence, have won him a reputation as a "*brilliant lawyer and counselor.*" Over the past twelve months he has been busy representing Metropolitan Mortgage and Securities as debtor in one of the largest Chapter 11 filings in Washington state history. **Mary Jo Heston** (see p.1792) is a former United States Trustee, and she "*brings a breadth of experience*" to her bankruptcy practice. Currently focusing on business bankruptcies, reorganizations and workouts, she also advises creditors on various remedies. **Bruce Leaverton** (see p.1793) is known as a "*thoughtful and meticulous*" lawyer, who manages large cases well. Peers admire his "*wry sense of humor*" and his "*sharp intelligence.*"

He has recently represented Wells Fargo, KeyBank and other lenders in distressed secured loan and workout matters.

The Clients: Transamerica Commercial Finance; The Mutual Life Insurance Company of New York; GE Capital; Wells Fargo Bank; ATT Commercial Finance; Navistar Financial; Washington Mutual; West Coast Bank; Blue Cross of Washington and Alaska, and IDS Life Insurance Company.

Preston Gates & Ellis LLP

The Firm: The market reserved particular praise for the firm's "*excellent experience*" in the areas of loan workouts, restructurings, foreclosures and receiverships. However, the group assists lenders, landlords, trustees, unsecured creditors and creditor committees with the full range of insolvency issues. Reflecting the current market, the group is involved in a number of bankruptcies in the retail industry, and airport authority reorganizations.

The Lawyers: **Kim Osenbaugh** chairs the firm's bankruptcy and insolvency practice and is one of Seattle's preeminent bankruptcy lawyers. According to commentators, she is "*smart and results-oriented,*" as well as being a "*tough negotiator.*" Clients also value her "*innate ability to get disparate points of view to agree.*" Osenbaugh focuses on bankruptcy reorganization and debtor/creditor-related issues.

The Clients: Garden Botanika; Metawave Communications; Pietro's Pizza; Country Harvest and Deep Sea Fisheries.

CORPORATE/M&A

Washington
Leading firms (Corporate/M&A)

1	**PERKINS COIE LLP** *Seattle*
	PRESTON GATES & ELLIS LLP *Seattle*
2	**DAVIS WRIGHT TREMAINE LLP** *Seattle*
	DLA PIPER RUDNICK GRAY CARY US LLP *Seattle*
	LANE POWELL PC *Seattle*
3	**DORSEY & WHITNEY LLP** *Seattle*
	FOSTER PEPPER & SHEFELMAN PLLC *Seattle*
	HELLER EHRMAN WHITE & MCAULIFFE LLP *Seattle*
	STOEL RIVES LLP *Seattle*
	WILSON SONSINI GOODRICH & ROSATI *Seattle*
4	**GRAHAM & DUNN PC** *Seattle*
	ORRICK HERRINGTON & SUTCLIFFE LLP *Seattle*
	RIDDELL WILLIAMS PS *Seattle*

Firms are listed alphabetically in each band.

Band 1

Perkins Coie LLP

The Firm: Perkins Coie is widely considered to be "*the acknowledged number-one corporate adviser*" in Washington. A "*strong international firm,*" it is equipped with "*the broadest and deepest practice in the northwest,*" and a client base to match. The corporate team assists a varied roster of clients, from startups to household name Fortune 100 companies, and has particular strength in the technology sector; the team represents 32 of the 50 fastest growing technology companies in the state, as well as advising a majority of its publicly traded companies. For corporate finance, securities and M&A work, clients keep returning to the firm because of its "*critical mass*" of 80 experienced lawyers and its "*good consistent quality.*"

The Lawyers: "*Insightful, credible, responsive and pragmatic*" **Stewart Landefeld** is one of Washington's "*clear leaders.*" Clients praise his talent and intelligence, and note that he "*excels*

at business concepts and corporate governance principles.*" This corporate governance advice, which is utilized by such leading companies as Nintendo and Coinstar, lies at the core of his practice. However, he also handles M&A and private equity advice. This was on show last year when he advised Quinton Cardiology on its $35 million public equity offering, and assisted with the IPO and subsequent sale of Financial Pacific Company to Allied Capital. **Andrew Bor** is one of the leading public securities and corporate finance lawyers in the state. An "*extremely well-organized attorney,*" he was also admired by market sources for his "*perceptive, meticulous and hard-working*" nature. He typically represents public companies on financing and transactional issues, as well as advising on corporate governance and disclosure issues. Recent highlights include leading a number of large transactions, including one for Coinstar, and handling a common stock offering for another client. "*Smart and practical*" **Evelyn Cruz Sroufe** represents public companies in securities offerings and high-profile M&A transactions. It is in this field that she has recently undertaken a large equity offering for a client. Interviewees admire her tremendous credibility with boards of directors, allied with her "*high level of business acumen*" and "*great communication skills.*" **Scott Gelband** was recommended to researchers as a "*well thought of, pragmatic lawyer,*" with a "*fine technology practice.*" He represents household names of the order of Amazon.com. "*Rising star*" **Dave McShea** works primarily with emerging high-growth businesses and larger public companies. He has a good deal of venture capital experience, though his practice extends to corporate finance, securities transactions and public M&A. His technology focus involves him in work for such companies as aQuantive. **Steven Yentzer** has earned his

spurs as a "*great tax lawyer.*" In addition to this, market sources report that he also excels at company formation and financing work.

The Clients: Coinstar; Amazon.com; aQuantive; Quinton Cardiology and Nintendo.

Preston Gates & Ellis LLP

The Firm: Preston Gates & Ellis has strong roots in the northwest, where it forms part of a regional elite with the sophistication and capacity to handle the largest and most complex multimillion-dollar corporate deals. It is well recognized, of course, as Microsoft's traditional first choice counsel. However, its practice does not end with the international software giant, and indeed is considered by some to be "*exceptionally well diversified.*" As evidence for this, over the past year the firm's stable of "*high-quality attorneys*" have advised on $3 billion worth of investments for a variety of regular clients. Private equity investments and venture capital financings, securities transactions, and public and private M&A characterize the activities of the team.

The Lawyers: **Kent Carlson** is "*the dean of the corporate practice*" at Preston Gates. As a former professor of corporate law, his "*excellent grasp of the law*" and "*intellectually sound judgment*" can be taken as read, and he also enjoys an "*active and high-quality*" practice, comprising a mixture of M&A and general counseling work. Beyond this, he is also regularly involved in updating the state's corporate statutes for the Washington State Bar Committee. **Stephan Coonrod** was recommended to researchers as a "*smart*" attorney, with "*wide-ranging experience*" and "*expertise in a variety of transactions, even ones with anomalous features.*" Over the past year he has put these skills to good use, handling six venture capital financings, including one for Speakeasy. **Rick Dodd** is "*the sort of*

Washington
Leading individuals (Corporate/M&A)

1
CARLSON Kent *Preston Gates, Seattle*
LANDEFELD Stewart *Perkins Coie, Seattle*
MORGAN Michael *Lane Powell, Seattle*
SCHULTHEIS Patrick *Wilson Sonsini, Seattle*
STEEL John *DLA Piper, Seattle*

2
ADAMS Greg *Davis Wright, Seattle*
BOR Andrew *Perkins Coie, Seattle*
COONROD Stephan *Preston Gates, Seattle*
DIERCKS Robert *Foster Pepper, Seattle*
DODD Richard *Preston Gates, Seattle*
GELBAND Scott *Perkins Coie, Seattle*
GREENBURG Scott *Wilson Sonsini, Seattle*
ISRAEL Allen *Foster Pepper, Seattle*
KAPLAN Robert *Dorsey & Whitney, Seattle*
SROUFE Evelyn *Perkins Coie, Seattle*
TUNE James *Stoel Rives, Seattle*
WEINSTEIN Joseph *Davis Wright, Seattle*

3
DWYER Michael *Lane Powell, Seattle*
GRAHAM Stephen *Orrick Herrington, Seattle*
GROHMAN Thomas *Lane Powell, Seattle*
HOFFMAN Mark *DLA Piper, Seattle*
KOCHER Gary *Preston Gates, Seattle*
MCSHEA David *Perkins Coie, Seattle*
PUCKETT Laura *DLA Piper, Seattle*
SHERMAN Craig *Wilson Sonsini, Seattle*
STROTHER Jack *Graham & Dunn, Seattle*
WHITFORD Joseph *Davis Wright, Seattle*
YENTZER Steven *Perkins Coie, Seattle*

Individuals are listed alphabetically in each band.

transactions. Observers also noted the team's strength in a variety of niches, which range from healthcare to media and telecommunications. **The Lawyers:** *"Client-oriented"* **Greg Adams** (see p.1790) serves as general counsel to a number of public and larger private companies, such as The Seattle Times and Pope Resources. He recently represented Buckner News Alliance in the $44 million sale of a Pennsylvanian newspaper, and in its subsequent acquisition of another newspaper. *"Technically astute"* **Joe Weinstein** (see p.1795) impressed sources with his *"unassuming yet powerful presence"* and his *"almost uncanny ability to get to the right place on every issue."* He handles a variety of high-profile transactions, combining this with general commercial advice for long-standing clients such as John McCaw. His wealth of experience in the food sector was also noted. As a prominent venture capital attorney, **Joe Whitford** (see p.1795) focuses on advising emerging companies in technology-oriented sectors. He recently advised his client, Confirma, on its strategic alliance with GE.
The Clients: Clearwire Communications; The Seattle Times; Lanoga; Tenzing; Pacific Crest Securities; Services Group of America; The Washington Group; Orca Bay Capital and John McCaw.

DLA Piper Rudnick Gray Cary US LLP

See firm details p.765
The Firm: The 2004 union of West Coast dynamo Gray Cary with DLA and Piper Rudnick has provided the Seattle office of what is now one of the world's largest law firms with access to a vast slew of resources and expertise across North America, Asia and Europe. In Washington, clients turn to this *"thoughtful, smart and client-oriented bunch"* because of the capabilities of its M&A and corporate governance attorneys, and their wealth of knowledge of venture capital work and portfolio companies.
The Lawyers: **John Steel** (see p.1795) is a *"bright and dedicated attorney,"* with an excellent reputation for corporate transactional work. Interviewees drew particular attention to his fine public company securities practice and his corporate governance work. Clients appreciate his *"clear and quick-thinking"* advice and his *"practical and insightful"* approach. Another *"smart and diligent"* lawyer, **Laura Treadgold Puckett** (see p.1794) is known for her M&A, securities and venture capital financing work, according to interviewees. She is selected by clients for combining strong knowledge of these areas with *"commitment to clients, high energy and good business sense."* Interviewees report that **Mark Hoffman** (see p.1792) *"lives and breathes the law."* A young securities and capital markets partner, he is cited as one to watch in this field.
The Clients: The team acts for public and private companies that range from Fortune 100

giants to local startups, in such fields as banking and finance, venture capital and private equity, technology, manufacturing and insurance.

Lane Powell PC

See firm details p.1797
The Firm: This full-service, 55-strong, general corporate team operates a *"high-level, sophisticated"* transactional practice, according to market sources. It represents a range of predominantly Pacific Northwest clients, from conglomerates down to individuals. Retailing is an area of particular expertise, in which the team's work for Nordstrom is a reflection of the experience it has accrued throughout the supply chain. The team also boasts considerable strength in hi-tech and biotech matters, while natural resources work – particularly timber and fisheries – is an area of growth.
The Lawyers: The dean of the corporate securities practice, **Mike Morgan** (see p.1793), is a *"savvy and experienced"* practitioner, to whom clients turn for his *"comprehensive understanding"* and ability to focus on the most important aspects of a deal. With his broad business knowledge, he is also called upon when clients *"need more than a lawyer."* He is responsible for all securities work for Nordstrom as well as being retained by numerous retailers. A recent highlight includes representing United Online in its acquisition of classmates.com. **Tom Grohman** (see p.1792) heads the firm's corporate group. He works predominantly with private companies, serving as general and acquisition counsel to numerous foreign and US companies in Seattle. For example, as general counsel to Northwest Biotherapeutics, he recently handled a bridge loan financing, as well as working on an asset sale for Primal. Clients appreciate his *"hard-working"* style and *"excellent work product."* The *"efficient and knowledgeable"* **Mike Dwyer** (see p.1791) concentrates on private transactions. Recently he was involved in the sale of approximately 137 acres of Georgia-Pacific waterfront property to the Port of Bellingham, in exchange for its assumption of environmental obligations.
The Clients: Nordstrom; Cutter & Buck; Georgia-Pacific and the Simpson Investment Company.

Band 3

Dorsey & Whitney LLP

The Firm: The solid Seattle office of this successful global firm gets involved in international transactions, and boasts expertise in cross-border M&A and financings. The corporate team of around 20 attorneys maintains a strong profile for a range of financing work, including venture capital investment in emerging companies, as well as more general corporate transactions. Its strength in the

person you choose as team leader for large complicated projects," say interviewees. An *"excellent securities and corporate lawyer,"* he has been retained by Microsoft as counsel for transactional work, and his advice is also sought by such clients as Starbucks and Western Wireless. **Gary Kocher** chairs the firm's life sciences group, and is viewed as a *"fine younger lawyer"* with *"good technical skills."* He boasts considerable knowledge of the issues facing emerging businesses, and focuses his transactional practice on hi-tech and biotech companies, and venture capital investors.
The Clients: Microsoft; Speakeasy; Starbucks and Western Wireless.

Band 2

Davis Wright Tremaine LLP

See firm details p.1796
The Firm: The *"large and long-standing corporate practice"* in the Seattle office of this national firm is comprised of 35 skilled and dedicated attorneys. Market sources highlighted the *"good quality and breadth"* of the transactional team here. It serves a client base that includes traditional local companies, such as The Seattle Times and SGA, alongside smaller, emerging technology firms, assisting them in negotiating funding and completing public and private

biotechnology sector was noted, as was the team's experience of cross-border tax issues.

The Lawyers: *"Dorsey superstar"* and longtime Seattle attorney **Bob Kaplan** has a traditional business practice, with particular expertise in complex tax and transactional planning for a predominantly private client base. Clients value him for his deep, specialized knowledge, *"sharp brain"* and *"tough but thoughtful"* approach. He has extensive experience in Canadian cross-border issues, and is currently chair of the firm's Iraq practice group.

The Clients: The firm serves public and private companies, ranging from small owner-managed businesses to large multinationals.

Foster Pepper & Shefelman PLLC

The Firm: The 20 corporate attorneys here *"excel at sophisticated deals,"* according to interviewees. They advise a predominantly regional client base on a diverse range of corporate issues, but have particularly strong links with the hi-tech industry, courtesy of a long-standing relationship with Microsoft cofounder, Paul Allen, and his venture capital firm, Vulcan Ventures. Strong banking and real estate capabilities also inform and reinforce the firm's corporate practice.

The Lawyers: **Allen Israel** is recognized by market sources as an *"excellent captain of the team for large deals."* He has substantial experience, in real estate as well as financing and corporate transactions, drawn from industry sectors that include financial services, sports and technology. **Bob Diercks'** practice revolves around public and private securities transactions, M&A and corporate governance advice. However, it is for his broker dealer and securities work that he is considered among the *"finest in the field."*

The Clients: The firm represents a number of venture capital investors, broker dealers, technology companies and banks, primarily on a regional level. These include Vulcan Ventures, First Mutual Bank and Costco.

Heller Ehrman White & McAuliffe LLP
See firm details p.288

The Firm: This Californian firm has established a strong Seattle office and a substantial presence in Washington's corporate market, picking up local and regional work as well as incoming matters from its national and international clients. Its work for Washington Mutual particularly impressed sources. The office's *"terrific corporate practice"* attracts a variety of interesting matters, appearing at the table in some of the most notable transactions in the state. Observers also noted the firm's burgeoning expertise in venture capital funding and technology transactions.

The Lawyers: Bruce Pym is firm-wide chair of

the business practice.

The Clients: The firm represents public and private clients from a variety of industries at all stages in their development. It is particularly well known in Seattle for its work with Washington Mutual.

Stoel Rives LLP

The Firm: Stoel Rives is regarded as *"a fine Portland firm with a solid Seattle presence,"* a footprint that gives it considerable resources across the Northwest. The strengthening corporate group currently fields 29 *"terrific"* attorneys with expertise in corporate finance, M&A, venture capital investments, securities issues and governance. Unusually, the firm also boasts an energy and wind power practice group. The technology-focused team is responsible for all the securities work for Dendreon and recently completed a public offering for its long-standing computing client, Cray.

The Lawyers: *"An excellent lawyer and a long-standing presence in the market,"* **Jim Tune** is heavily involved in the sale of assets and raising of capital for software and e-commerce companies. He also possesses acknowledged expertise in corporate governance and firm management issues. Highlights from the past year including working with clients such as WestFarm Foods and Keynetics.

The Clients: Cray; Dendreon; WestFarm Foods and Keynetics.

Wilson Sonsini Goodrich & Rosati
See firm details p.302

The Firm: This national technology heavyweight boasts a *"small but sophisticated"* Seattle arm, which serves the needs of a number of public and private companies from the areas of technology, life sciences, financial services and other emerging growth industries. Typical work includes advising on corporate governance, venture capital financings, public offerings, M&A and technology transactions.

The Lawyers: *"Dynamic"* **Patrick Schultheis** (see p.1794) is the managing partner of the Seattle office. Well connected in the dot.com and technology communities, with a *"thoughtful and practical"* approach, he represents underwriters and technology, life sciences and venture capital companies in a range of corporate matters. His *"broad and impressive"* knowledge of public securities issues was also widely praised. **Scott Greenburg** (see p.1792) is prominent in private financings for companies in the retail and consumer sectors, and advises on corporate governance, M&A, corporate finance and venture capital matters. Market sources praise his *"excellent work"* on a number of recent high-profile matters, such as the Starbucks IPO and the acquisition of Seattle SuperSonics. The *"superbly knowledgeable"* **Craig Sherman** (see p.1795) was recommended to researchers as a *"future*

superstar." He specializes in corporate finance, M&A and corporate governance, and has a particularly good reputation in the emerging companies sector. Recently highlights include representing 4thpass in its sale to Motorola and Atom Corporation in its sale to Shockwave Corporation.

The Clients: The team represents public and private companies from a variety of industries, including Fortune 500 technology, venture capital and financial services companies.

Band 4

Graham & Dunn PC

The Firm: This compact but classy Seattle-based law firm was admired by market sources for fielding *"a number of excellent partners."* Its seven corporate attorneys focus on corporate finance and securities transactions for a client base that encompasses individuals, startups and publicly held companies.

The Lawyers: Peers recommend **Jack Strother** as a *"careful and practical lawyer"* who gets great results for his clients. The fact that he is *"not intimidated by anyone"* also counts in his favor. An admired general corporate attorney, he has experience in handling M&A and new venture formations in a variety of industry sectors.

The Clients: The group advises a range of public and private companies, typically on a state or regional basis.

Orrick, Herrington & Sutcliffe LLP
See firm details p.295

The Firm: Nationally, the firm is particularly known for its municipal finance practice, however it also boasts a strength in preferred stock financing and public company work, with particular experience of acting for technology and biotech companies. It is currently handling some notable transactions in the area of microbiology.

The Lawyers: **Stephen Graham** (see p.1791) divides his time between the firm's California and Washington offices. According to interviewees, he has *"substantial experience"* of transactions within the biotech industry, and he was also praised for his strength in the banking and finance sector.

The Clients: The group represents public and private companies from a broad spectrum of industries, including retail, financial services, technology and life sciences.

Riddell Williams PS

The Firm: The corporate team here merits recognition, according to market sources, because of its *"superb lawyers"* and their *"high level of skills and experience."* It advises on a range of matters, from corporate M&A to joint ventures, financing transactions and securities issues.

The Lawyers: David Buck chairs the firm's business department, while James Minorchio chairs the tax practice group.

The Clients: The firm advises a variety of clients, from small businesses to large publicly traded companies. It has recently undertaken

work for Tegic Communications; American Package Express; CLC Communications; Premera and Blue Cross of Washington and Alaska.

EMPLOYMENT

MAINLY DEFENDANT

Washington
Leading firms
(Employment: Mainly Defendant)

[1] **DAVIS WRIGHT TREMAINE LLP** *Seattle*
   PERKINS COIE LLP *Seattle*
[2] **PRESTON GATES & ELLIS LLP** *Seattle*
   SEBRIS BUSTO JAMES *Bellevue*
[3] **LANE POWELL PC** *Seattle*
   RIDDELL WILLIAMS PS *Seattle*
   STOEL RIVES LLP *Seattle*
   WINTERBAUER & DIAMOND, P.L.L.C. *Seattle*

Leading individuals
(Employment: Mainly Defendant)

Senior Statesman
ASLIN John *Perkins Coie, Seattle*

[1] **BUSTO Mark** *Sebris Busto, Bellevue*
   CAIRNS Carolyn *Stokes Lawrence, Seattle*
   HUTCHESON Mark *Davis Wright, Seattle*
   LEMLY Thomas *Davis Wright, Seattle*
   PERISHO Russell *Perkins Coie, Seattle*
   REISS Michael *Davis Wright, Seattle*
   WILLIAMS Nancy *Perkins Coie, Seattle*
[2] **BARNES Clemens** *Perkins Coie, Seattle*
   BLACKSTONE Robert *Davis Wright, Seattle*
   CROSS Bruce *Perkins Coie, Seattle*
   JONES Karen *Riddell Williams, Seattle*
   KLEIN III Otto *Summit Law Group, Seattle*
   MOONEY Douglas *Preston Gates, Seattle*
   RUBIN Jerome *Stoel Rives, Seattle*
   SEBRIS Robert *Sebris Busto, Bellevue*
   WINTERBAUER S *Winterbauer & Diamond, Seattle*
[3] **BARBIER Margaret** *Stoel Rives, Seattle*
   DIAMOND Kenneth *Winterbauer & Diamond, Seattle*
   HUMPHREY Lawton *Davis Wright, Seattle*
   MADDEN Patrick *Preston Gates, Seattle*
   O'CONNELL Timothy *Stoel Rives, Seattle*
   REILLY D Michael *Lane Powell, Seattle*

Firms and individuals are listed alphabetically in each band.

Band 1

Davis Wright Tremaine LLP
See firm details p.1796

The Firm: This firm's employment department is noted for its winning combination of "*sheer mass,*" a deep bench of "*strong lawyers*" and an enviable roster of "*big clients.*" A considerable proportion of its practice is devoted to preventative employment counseling, though it is perhaps best known for its first-class traditional labor law expertise. With the support of the

firm's successful litigation department to draw upon, the group also ably represents clients in a full range of employment litigation, from straightforward administrative cases to large, cutting-edge class actions. In all three of these areas, commentators are impressed by the "*high quality*" of this one-stop employment shop.

The Lawyers: **Thomas Lemly** (see p.1793) is the "*long-standing dean of Seattle's labor and employment law Bar.*" Able to "*relate well with juries,*" and equipped with "*an incredible communication style,*" he excels in the field of employment litigation. Within this sphere, he has recently enforced noncompete agreements and defended major discrimination and wage-hour claims for prominent clients. His "*fabulous judgment*" and "*good business sense*" also win him supporters. **Mike Reiss** (see p.1794) was formerly with the EEOC, and has drawn on this experience to establish a position as a leading employment litigator. He commands national respect for his "*terrific knowledge*" and track record in the defense of nationwide discrimination and wage-hour class actions, where he "*brings a balanced perspective*" to resolving conflicts. Sources also noted a growing profile as an "*excellent mediator.*" Clients report that **Mark Hutcheson** (see p.1792) is a "*creative, imaginative lawyer who is not afraid to pursue new ways of solving problems.*" Admired for his comprehensive knowledge of labor law and "*masterful negotiating skills,*" he is frequently involved in collective bargaining agreements. Noting his "*marvelous*" ability to secure consensus, almost before others realize, one interviewee described him as "*stealth personified.*" **Robert Blackstone** (see p.1790) is widely considered "*one of the best labor lawyers in town.*" Experienced at collective bargaining and labor arbitrations, he also provides strategic advice on union issues, and recently negotiated a labor contract for a large hotel. A "*well-rounded*" attorney, he deals with executive employment matters and employer counseling with equal skill. **Lawton Humphrey** (see p.1792) chairs the firm's employment department and divides her practice between employment litigation and preventative employment training. Interviewees consider her "*incredibly effective*" at defending companies against discrimination, wage-hour, wrongful discharge, failure to provide leave and defamation claims. Over the past year she has deftly guided a client through a major workforce reduction, as well as defending various discrim-

ination and wage-hour claims.
The Clients: Bank of America; Seattle Times; ConocoPhillips; Virginia Mason Clinic; Boeing; Calpine; adidas America; Comcast; Seattle Opera; Campbells; FedEx and Amgen.

Perkins Coie LLP
The Firm: The Seattle and Bellevue offices house a substantial team of around 30 labor and employment attorneys. This "*well-developed*" group handles a wide range of labor and employment law for an enviable client base that spans a range of public entities and private companies. Market sources report that the group's premier position in the state is founded on its "*great size and strength,*" and the "*powerful*" litigation capabilities that help to guarantee it a place at the table in many of the state's largest and most interesting matters. For example, it recently defended Boeing against a class action employment discrimination claim.
The Lawyers: Veteran employment litigator **John Aslin** "*studies and knows the law inside out,*" yet is able to "*take off his litigation hat and provide a clear, good analysis.*" Peers, meanwhile, appreciate his courtesy and "*phenomenal ability to organize large employment cases.*" **Russ Perisho** was recommended as a "*first-class employment lawyer*" who impresses with his good strategic sense and "*sharp, effective style.*" He brings a lot of experience in the fields of wrongful discharge and discrimination defense to the table, and also has a solid traditional labor practice. Clients single out a "*nice touch and great judgment*" among his many professional attributes. The head of Seattle's employment group, **Nancy Williams** engenders confidence in clients with her "*real command of the law*" and "*subtle and effective trial presentation skills.*" Concentrating on employment litigation, she was recently involved in a gender discrimination class action, and is currently working with the Alaska Pipeline Service in a case brought by the EEOC. Her advisory work, for clients such as Puget Sound and InfoSpace, is also notable for its "*sophistication, knowledge, wisdom and experience.*" **Clem Barnes** is a "*well-liked and well-rounded*" attorney and a "*tremendous trial lawyer.*" Sources enthuse that he "*handles matters with the highest degree of intellectual rigor*" and can "*articulate complex ideas in plain English.*" His skills find another outlet through his growing and highly respected mediation practice, where sources report that he ably "*convinces*

All quotes in the text are from interviews with clients and competitors.

both sides why they should compromise." According to the market, **Bruce Cross** has "ingrained familiarity with, and complete mastery of, traditional labor law." An "invaluable and crucial" part of the team, he also offers experience of OSHA and wage-hour disputes.

The Clients: Boeing; Puget Sound Energy; Amazon.com; UPS; Starbucks; Safeco Insurance; InfoSpace; KremeWorks; Swedish Hospital; Matsushita Avionics Systems and a number of school districts.

Band 2

Preston Gates & Ellis LLP

The Firm: This large, full-service firm incorporates a successful labor and employment practice, which has been bolstered in recent years by the acquisition of several former Bogle & Gates lawyers. The "able, experienced and knowledgeable" group handles the entire spectrum of labor and employment matters, from traditional labor law to cutting-edge employment litigation and preventative counseling. Particular areas of focus include wage-hour disputes, collective bargaining agreements, immigration, ERISA and employment discrimination matters.

The Lawyers: Interviewees note that **Doug Mooney** is "not only a good technical lawyer, he also has tremendous people skills." His astonishing ability to "walk into the room and sense personalities and undercurrents" greatly assists his clients. He is valued for his considerable knowledge in the range of labor and employment issues, and admired for his ability to "handle a variety of matters in an appropriate and creative way." **Patrick Madden** is rated highly by the market as a knowledgeable attorney who "aggressively represents clients, with great results." Sources report that he is "red hot" in the field of wage and hour-related litigation and counseling. Beyond this, and his well-respected general advisory practice, he is also an "excellent writer and speaker," sources say.

The Clients: The team represents management from a variety of industry sectors.

Sebris Busto James

The Firm: This "top-notch boutique" dedicates its substantial expertise to advising management on traditional labor law matters, alternative dispute resolution, employment litigation and counseling. With its focus firmly on preventative counseling and avoiding costly litigation, the strong and "uniformly good" group provides excellent value for money, according to its clients. Interviewees also commended the firm for the breadth of its practice and the quality and responsiveness of its "personable and engaging" lawyers.

The Lawyers: Applauded as a "dynamic, creative and energetic" litigator, **Mark Busto** remains "calm and steady" in his approach. Having defended management in discrimination cases across state and federal courts, he has acquired extensive legal knowledge and the "ability to make an excellent presentation." He is also well respected as a "practical and effective" employment counselor and policy adviser to management. Traditional labor expert **Robert Sebris** has written and spoken widely on labor and employment law developments. Sources affirm that he is a "real good lawyer and a delightful person," which helps to explain his popularity among interviewees. He has also acquired considerable experience of providing preventative employment counsel to management.

The Clients: The firm represents companies from a range of industries, spanning financial services, retail, healthcare, communications, technology, transportation and real estate, as well as public sector bodies. They include: State of Washington; King County; Stafford Homes; Getty Images; Alaska Airline; Ernst & Young; Central Washington Hospital and the Renaissance Seattle Hotel.

Band 3

Lane Powell PC

See firm details p.1797

The Firm: This reputable labor and employment department boasts a wide range of expertise. Important areas of focus include ERISA, noncompete agreements and wage and hour-related matters. The group also represents management in a considerable amount of complex employment-related litigation, including discrimination cases and the defense of benefits mishandling claims. With the aid of the firm's litigation department, the office was involved in the first national class action against Wal-Mart brought by employees.

The Lawyers: According to market sources, **Mike Reilly** (see p.1794) is the "cream of the crop" at Lane Powell. A "darned good" employment litigator, he handles a wide range of employment disputes, from the straightforward to the complex, touching on such issues as employee benefits, discrimination and ERISA. His approach to training is that if people laugh a little they remember the underlying ideas, which makes him a popular choice in this field. The remainder of his practice is dedicated toward preventative management counseling.

The Clients: Home Depot; Nordstrom; Cutter & Buck; Wells Fargo; Metropolitan Mortgage and JC Penney Company.

Riddell Williams PS

The Firm: This firm's seven-strong employment department represents management in the full spectrum of matters, providing advice, counseling and training on wage and hour, nondiscrimination and privacy law, among a host of other things. It also offers strong capabilities in litigation and traditional labor law. In the latter sphere, the group advises both unionized and nonunionized employers on NLRB proceedings and arbitrations, union-organizing campaigns and contract negotiations, while also ably trying a variety of employment disputes before state and federal courts.

The Lawyers: **Karen Jones** commands enormous respect from the market for her experience in employment litigation, counseling, arbitration and training practice. Clients appreciate that she is "always on track" with her "good judgment" and ability "to take the law and turn it into English." Peers, meanwhile, consider her a "good leader and role model" who "adapts her advice in line with her clients' broader goals."

The Clients: Primera Blue Cross; Philips; Allstate; Redhook Brewing; T-Mobile; AT&T Wireless; DHL Airborne and Idaho Power.

Stoel Rives LLP

The Firm: Clients praise the 10-strong labor and employment group at this office as "creative, responsive and thorough." The group's practice spans the range of labor and employment law matters, including discrimination and harassment litigation, policy development, training and counseling. It also undertakes a lot of wage and hour, OSHA and executive compensation-related advice and litigation. In the field of traditional labor law, the firm has established a particularly strong reputation and represents the labor law interests of the Swedish Hospital Catholic Health Initiative.

The Lawyers: Clients report that **Jerry Rubin** has a lot of credibility in the field of traditional labor law, and a "large body of knowledge with regard to employee relations." He also practices employment law, and has recently been working on a major wage and hour case for the Good Samaritan Hospital. He was formerly a trial attorney with the NLRB. **Margaret Barbier** is best known for her excellent counseling work and expertise in disability discrimination. Skilled at drafting executive level employment contracts and policy reviews, she is "great at providing strategic options and evaluating them," say clients. Employment litigation is another aspect of her practice, and over the past year she has defended whistle-blower, wage and hour, and discrimination lawsuits. "Bright, practical and creative" **Tim O'Connell** has an active traditional labor and employment litigation practice. He recently argued an important matter before the State Supreme Court on behalf of the Washington Association of Business, and handles all the labor work for Verizon. Interviewees admire his "intricate knowledge" and "help in shaping the law."

The Clients: Cray Supercomputers; McDonald's; London Fog; Jim Pattison Group; Verizon; MultiCare Medical Center and Good Samaritan Hospital.

Winterbauer & Diamond, P.L.L.C.

The Firm: Sources commend the *"excellent quality of work"* on offer at this litigation boutique. The employment and labor team is well versed in every aspect of employer-employee relations, and sources report that it is also *"definitely on the map"* for counseling work as well as litigation. Areas of focus include civil rights, employment contracts, wage and hour disputes, and labor relations advice. The firm is also experienced in the areas of employee benefits and OSHA.

The Lawyers: The *"collaborative and collegial"* **Steven Winterbauer** enjoys a successful labor and employment litigation practice. Interviewees were full of praise for his detail-oriented style and *"excellent and articulate presentation skills,"* which he effectively employs in a broad range of courts and agencies. He is cochair of the Washington State Bar Association's Annual Employment Law Institute. **Ken Diamond** was also warmly recommended to researchers. Interviewees drew attention to the *"level-headed and pragmatic approach"* he brings to his employment and labor litigation and counseling work. A well-rounded lawyer, his practice also includes commercial litigation and insurance law.

The Clients: Costco; Safeway; Les Schwab Tire Centers; Sheraton Seattle Hotel and Towers; Swedish Medical Center; Northwest Airlines; Volkswagen; DeVry and Lee Enterprises.

Other Notable Practitioners

Carolyn Cairns, of Stokes Lawrence, PS is a top-tier employment lawyer and *"one of the most highly regarded mediators in the Pacific Northwest."* A *"knowledgeable and bright"* counselor, she has an in-depth understanding of policy review and contract drafting. She frequently appears on mediation shortlists for her *"terrific ability to help disputing parties come together."* As well as representing private and public companies in a wide range of discrimination, wrongful termination and wage-hour lawsuits, she also acts for individuals. At the Summit Law Group, **Otto Klein** is well respected in the traditional labor law arena. Praise was especially directed at his experience in public sector collective bargaining and arbitrations. However, sources also acknowledged him as an *"all-around good lawyer"* with extensive experience in a range of employment litigation.

ENVIRONMENT

Washington
Leading firms (Environment)

1. **CASCADIA LAW GROUP** *Seattle*
   DAVIS WRIGHT TREMAINE LLP *Seattle*
   HELLER EHRMAN WHITE & MCAULIFFE *Seattle*
   PERKINS COIE LLP *Seattle*
   STOEL RIVES LLP *Seattle*
   SUMMIT LAW GROUP, PLLC *Seattle*

Leading individuals (Environment)

1. **BLUMENFELD Chuck** *Perkins Coie, Seattle*
   BROWN Rodney *Cascadia Law, Seattle*
   LEPPO Jeffery *Stoel Rives, Seattle*
   PALUMBO Ralph *Summit Law Group, Seattle*
   SCHNEIDER Mark *Perkins Coie, Seattle*
2. **CHAPMAN William** *Preston Gates, Seattle*
   COHEN Matthew *Heller Ehrman, Seattle*
   DUNN Loren *Riddell Williams, Seattle*
   ELLIOTT Richard *Davis Wright, Bellevue*
   GINSBERG Beth *Stoel Rives, Seattle*
   MANOLOPOULOS Lynn *Davis Wright, Bellevue*
   THORP Michael *Heller Ehrman, Seattle*

Firms and individuals are listed alphabetically in each band.

Band 1

Cascadia Law Group

The Firm: This boutique is highly regarded for the skill and experience of its attorneys in land use, natural resources and environmental matters. Market sources single it out in particular for doing *"an excellent job of solving complex problems in a professional manner."* Its broad-ranging practice encompasses air quality, endangered species, water rights, waste management and permitting matters. It is also admired for its work in the fields of environmental litigation, and in connection with property development and acquisitions.

The Lawyers: Commentators praise **Rodney Brown**'s expertise in clean air, water and hazardous waste cleanup cases. The principal author of one of the most authoritative texts in this area, he is viewed as a *"superb, highly talented practitioner"* who excels equally at both environmental transactions and litigation. His clients particularly appreciate his *"smart, fair and straightforward"* style and recognize him as *"effective with both state and federal regulators."*

The Clients: The firm advises an impressive array of Fortune 100 companies, government agencies, environmental groups and small businesses.

Davis Wright Tremaine LLP

See firm details p.1796

The Firm: The firm's multidisciplinary environment practice incorporates a wide spread of expertise, spanning such areas as environmental criminal defense, Superfund cleanups and national audit compliance. The team commands a high profile in litigation, and is also widely respected for its environmental counseling in the areas of permitting, water rights resources and contaminated property transactions.

The Lawyers: As a former nuclear physicist, **Richard Elliott** (see p.1791) stands out for his *"incredibly deep understanding of technical issues."* Sources also report that *"he goes all out to find creative solutions for his clients"* in the areas of federal and state Superfund cleanups, permitting, regulatory compliance and water resources. He also provides robust advice on the Endangered Species Act and contaminated properties transactions. His varied client base includes a number of petroleum industry heavyweights. **Lynn Manolopoulos** (see p.1793) was commended for both environmental litigation skills and extensive transactional experience. Interviewees consider her an *"intelligent and tenacious attorney,"* and a great resource to clients in hazardous waste, water quality, brownfields and permitting-related matters.

The Clients: Shell; Pope Resources; Seattle Art Museum; AT&T and Lanoga.

Heller Ehrman White & McAuliffe LLP

See firm details p.288

The Firm: This full-service firm has a well-organized national environmental practice, advising on litigation, permitting, regulatory proceedings and transactional work. Its group of *"fine lawyers"* is particularly noted in Washington's business community for its *"good understanding of natural resource damages."* Other substantive areas of expertise include hazardous waste, water and air pollution, land use permitting and endangered species issues.

The Lawyers: In the course of a long and distinguished career, **Matthew Cohen** has gained a particularly strong reputation in the fields of clean water and air law. Actively involved in the development of state law in these fields, he is also knowledgeable in matters related to the Endangered Species Act and general environmental regulatory compliance. Interviewees report that **Mike Thorp** is *"technically strong, smart and experienced."* His practice is focused on litigation and counseling in environmental and natural resource issues, including Superfund cases, the clean air and water acts, water rights and RCRA. His strong litigation background also makes him a *"persistent and effec-*

tive advocate for his clients" in toxic torts class actions.

The Clients: The firm's diverse client roster includes companies from the manufacturing, oil refining, mining, hazardous waste, real estate and financial sectors. It also advises municipal governments and public ports, and has been involved in the Portland Harbor Superfund site.

Perkins Coie LLP

The Firm: This regional heavyweight commands respect from the market for its strength across environmental counseling, regulatory compliance, permitting and transactional work. Around 30 lawyers have experience of advising clients from a range of industries on such issues as hazardous waste, Superfund cleanups, endangered species, water rights and clean air. When necessary, the group also represents its clients in environmental litigation. Clients particularly recommended the group for its comprehensive knowledge of the field and for guiding them through every stage of projects, from conception to completion.

The Lawyers: With his 30 years of practice in this field, **Chuck Blumenfeld** is deservedly recognized as an "extremely knowledgeable and experienced" attorney. He concentrates on regulatory compliance, clean water, clean air and hazardous waste issues, serving an impressive client base across the region. The "superb" **Mark Schneider** excels at environmental, land use and natural resources litigation at both the state and federal levels. Peers acknowledge him as an "experienced and effective advocate for his clients." These include such prominent names as Weyerhaeuser and Boeing, which involves him in some of the largest and most important matters in the state.

The Clients: Boeing; BP; Weyerhaeuser; Plum Creek Timber; Noveon and Puget Sound Energy.

Stoel Rives LLP

The Firm: The 13-strong Seattle-based environment group at this large regional firm was warmly recommended to researchers. It has built up a wealth of expertise in the fields of hydroelectric power and renewable energy, and maintains substantial strength in endangered species, permitting, clean air and water-related issues. Supported by an impressive network of offices across the region, the team is a regular in major litigation and transactions across the Northwest.

The Lawyers: **Jeff Leppo** is a "well-rounded and successful" environmental lawyer. He frequently represents oil and gas majors in state and federal environmental reviews, and also focuses on permitting and endangered species, particularly in the context of the fisheries industry. He is frequently visible working with the forestry industry on a regional basis, in Washington, Alaska and Hawaii among other places. "Talented and creative" **Beth Ginsberg** is a former senior adviser in the US Environmental Protection Agency. She was recommended for her thorough understanding of the subtleties of the law, and focuses on environmental and natural resources litigation and counseling.

The Clients: ConocoPhilips; Port of Portland; Hawaii Longline Association and Alyeska Pipeline Service.

Summit Law Group, PLLC

The Firm: This "tremendous" environmental law group handles the full spectrum of environmental matters, from regulatory advice to litigation. Areas of particular focus include permitting, hazardous waste, natural resource damages, clean water and clean air matters. Interviewees are particularly impressed with the team's dedication to providing a comprehensive and high-quality service to its blue-chip base of corporate clients in the manufacturing, environmental consulting, timber and oil sectors.

The Lawyers: "One of the original environmental lawyers in Seattle and still one of the best," **Ralph Palumbo** has been at the cutting edge of Washington environmental law for decades. He litigated the first imminent and substantial endangerment case under RCRA, and has "exceptional knowledge" of clean water, clean air, CERCLA, Oil Pollution Act and toxic substance-related issues. His wealth of experience is coupled with a "creative and innovative" approach to problem solving.

The Clients: Alyeska Pipeline Service; FMC; FMC Technologies; PACCAR; Port of Seattle; Waste Management; Weyerhaeuser and DuPont.

Other Notable Practitioners

The market recommends **William Chapman** of Preston Gates & Ellis LLP as an "extremely good and personable" lawyer. Boasting extensive experience, he focuses on, inter alia, permitting, hazardous waste and environmental compliance. **Loren Dunn** of Riddell Williams PS has also earned his spurs during 18 years of practice. He is currently working on complex multiparty cleanups, especially within the fisheries industry.

INTELLECTUAL PROPERTY

Band 1

Christensen O'Connor Johnson Kindness, PLLC

The Firm: This litigation boutique is acknowledged to be a "substantial player" in the intellectual property market. A team of around 45 "knowledgeable and detail-oriented" lawyers possess degrees in a science or engineering discipline, enabling them to understand their clients' needs and businesses, and advise on the most technical of issues. These span patent prosecution and litigation, trademark and copyright disputes and protection, trade secrets and unfair competition. It also advises international clients on the day-to-day challenges of managing international IP portfolios. The firm boasts an impressive client roster, and has recently secured 40 US patents for Amazon.com and Digeo.

The Lawyers: Market sources warmly recommend **Kevan Morgan** for his patent prosecution practice. Described as an "excellent writer and communicator," he has a background in electrical engineering and has accumulated valuable experience in the computer, electronics, telecommunications and medical instrument industries. He is also valued as a skilled patent litigator.

The Clients: Amazon.com; Digeo; Nintendo; Starbucks; Boston Scientific, Weyerhaeuser and Microsoft.

Davis Wright Tremaine LLP

See firm details p.1796

The Firm: This top-notch outfit houses a sizable, full-service IP practice group in its Seattle office. Well versed in patent prosecution, licensing and litigation, it acts for a wide range of companies, including major players from sectors like technology, food and publishing. Clients value the team because of the "knowledgeable and responsive" approach of its lawyers. Its growing international network was also cited as an important factor in choosing the firm, as it "has more than enough resources" to handle the largest disputes and to serve as a one-stop shop for firms looking to protect their interests in multiple jurisdictions. As one client put it, you get "great bang for the buck."

The Lawyers: **Brian Bodine** (see p.1790) is universally applauded as a top-tier patent and trademark infringement litigator. This skill was recently on show in the patent infringement case of Forcillo v LeMond Fitness & Brunswick. Beyond patent prosecution and litigation, he is also prominent in the fields of trade secrets and licensing litigation, and acts for both plaintiffs

Washington
Leading firms (Intellectual Property)

1 CHRISTENSEN O'CONNOR JOHNSON *Seattle*
DAVIS WRIGHT TREMAINE LLP *Seattle*
DORSEY & WHITNEY LLP *Seattle*
PERKINS COIE LLP *Seattle*

2 BLACK LOWE & GRAHAM *Seattle*
HELLER EHRMAN WHITE & MCAULIFFE *Seattle*
LANE POWELL PC *Seattle*
PRESTON GATES & ELLIS LLP *Seattle*
SEED IP LAW GROUP *Seattle*

Leading individuals
(Intellectual Property)

1 AL-SALAM Ramsey *Perkins Coie, Seattle*
BODINE Brian *Davis Wright, Seattle*
BULCHIS Ed *Dorsey & Whitney, Seattle*
MEIKLEJOHN Paul *Dorsey & Whitney, Seattle*
RIEDINGER Jerry *Perkins Coie, Seattle*

2 BATEMAN David *Preston Gates, Seattle*
DUNWOODY Stuart *Davis Wright, Seattle*
FERRON William *Seed IP Law Group, Seattle*
GRAHAM Lawrence *Black Lowe, Seattle*
MORGAN Kevan *Christensen O'Connor, Seattle*
NELSON Marshall *Davis Wright, Seattle*
RHEAUME Warren *Heller Ehrman, Seattle*
SIEFERT Richard *Merchant & Gould, Seattle*

Firms and individuals are listed alphabetically in each band.

and defendants. Clients praise his "*extremely sharp understanding*" and "*great grasp of possible defenses*." "*Intelligent and practical*" **Stuart Dunwoody** (see p.1791) boasts considerable experience of litigating patent, trademark, copyright and trade secrets cases. His "*professional courtroom style*" and excellent foresight win him the highest praise from contented clients. **Marshall Nelson** (see p.1793) has a great reputation as a copyright and trademark attorney. He particularly caters toward the media industry, and has outstanding knowledge of advanced electronic publishing issues and their associated licensing and computer law considerations.
The Clients: LeMond Fitness; adidas America; Seattle Times; Seattle Gourmet Foods; FarWorks and Trinity Glass.

Dorsey & Whitney LLP
The Firm: Peers acknowledge that the "*large and diversified IP group*" at the Washington office of this international IP leader deserves the highest respect. Its practice spans the full range of IP issues, including patent litigation and prosecution, trademark and copyright issues, and advice on general brand management. Particular praise was reserved for its extensive experience in anything related to patents or licensing. Many of the team's attorneys hold advanced degrees in technical disciplines, giving them outstanding

knowledge of the most arcane technical issues, while clients also benefit from access to the resources available at a full-service, global firm.
The Lawyers: Ed Bulchis concentrates on patent prosecution, patent litigation and counseling. His background in electrical engineering makes him a favorite with electrical technology companies. Peers, meanwhile, are impressed with his "*sheer combination of competence and experience in the field*," and point to his thorough understanding of the law and his skill in identifying the winning arguments. According to sources, **Paul Meiklejohn** "*has done more IP litigation and jury trials than anybody in this district*." His "*great judgment*" is considered to stem in part from the tremendous knowledge he has built up as a professor of patent infringement litigation at the University of Washington.
The Clients: The firm represents a range of clients from various industries, including from the technology, life sciences and food sectors.

Perkins Coie LLP
The Firm: Perkins Coie "*brings in the higher talent in town*," agree sources, and attracts "*the bigger companies with complex legal issues*." Its outstanding IP capabilities span the range from patent procurement to patent, trademark and trade secrets litigation, while the respected team also handles licensing, trademark procurement, outsourcing and trade secrets advice. The prominent and active group tops the shortlists of a number of knowledgeable interviewees, and was recommended for its full-service expertise coupled with the extensive resources housed within its network of international offices.
The Lawyers: Ramsey Al-Salam is a "*tremendously good*" IP litigator with experience in complex patent, trademark and trade secrets cases. Peers hold him in the highest regard for the volume and quality of his work, while clients appreciate that he "*not only knows the law in detail but sells well to juries too.*" **Jerry Riedinger** was described to researchers as an "*outstanding, top-tier*" patent litigator, and is valued as "*one of the few around with significant patent jury trial experience.*" As such, he tops many interviewees' lists in this field. Over the years he has acquired an in-depth knowledge of the areas of software, semiconductors and medical devices, among others. Clients admire his thorough preparation and a soft-spoken nature that "*develops a lot of jury confidence.*"
The Clients: Boeing; Intel; Microsoft; Micron; Nintendo and Semitool.

Band 2

Black Lowe & Graham
The Firm: Market sources report that this 16-strong IP boutique boasts a particularly sturdy

patent prosecution practice. Noted for its "*excellent people and substantial clients*," its lawyers have a thorough understanding of patents, copyrights, trademarks and trade secrets, combining this with expertise in unfair competition, franchising, and computer and internet law. It also advises clients on strategic portfolio development and the international protection of IP rights.
The Lawyers: Lawrence Graham is a respected patent expert with experience in patent prosecution, patent and trademark litigation, and licensing. A prolific author on IP law, he was recently involved in a case involving a motorcycle helmet patent, and defended Costco in a dispute relating to shoe patents. The past year has also seen him appear in a number of trade secrets cases.
The Clients: This "*superb, smaller shop*" serves a roster of around 2000 clients, including companies from the engineering, chemicals, biotech and software industries and individual inventors. Examples include: Costco; Alaska Airlines; AOL; Honeywell and K2.

Heller Ehrman White & McAuliffe LLP
See firm details p.288
The Firm: This large, full-service and increasingly international firm houses a widely respected patent procurement, trademark, copyright, licensing and trade secrets practice. Part of a growing global network, the Seattle group has a wealth of resources at its disposal. Clients appreciate a cross-disciplinary approach that brings together experts from a range of different practice areas as required. The team handles a range of IP litigation and advice for high profile clients drawn from various industries, including semiconductors, software, technology, telecommunications and biotechnology.
The Lawyers: "*Experienced and skilled*" litigator **Warren Rheaume** concentrates on trademark, copyright and trade secrets disputes. As well as exhibiting great courtroom presence, Rheaume is "*extremely comfortable with technology*," say sources. His "*personable*" approach also wins him fans. In recognition of his expertise, Barnes & Noble chose him as counsel in the 'one click' patent infringement case.
The Clients: The Seattle office represents a broad range of clients, including Garden Botanika, Philip Morris and the Children's Hospital & Regional Medical Center.

Lane Powell PC
See firm details p.1797
The Firm: The "*technically savvy*" and knowledgeable group at Lane Powell was admired by sources for its strong capabilities in IP litigation. Here, it skilfully represents clients in patent,

1784   All quotes in the text are from interviews with clients and competitors.

CHAMBERS USA 2005

copyright, trademark, trade secrets and domain name disputes. Beyond the realm of litigation, the group also provides robust advice to clients on the procurement, transfer, preservation and enforcement of IP rights.

The Lawyers: Steven Winters is considered a key player in the firm's IP practice, focusing primarily on contracting and licensing issues. The team also weaves dispute resolution expertise into its practice, and calls on experienced litigators inclined toward IP-related matters.

The Clients: Clients include Tektronix and Sunstream.

Preston Gates & Ellis LLP

The Firm: The *"talented and tenacious"* IP department here advises on all aspects of patent, trademark, copyright and trade secrets-related matters. The team is particularly knowledgeable and influential in the field of e-commerce, and is frequently sought out by clients for advice on this area. It efficiently litigates a range of IP cases; however sources report that its real strength lies on the prosecution, transfer, outsourcing and licensing side where it *"wins the day with its attention to detail and logic."*

The Lawyers: **David Bateman** is a member of the firm's IP practice group. Acknowledged as an authority in the law related to cyber technologies and spam, he served as lead trial law in Microsoft's highly publicized, nationwide anti-spam litigation.

The Clients: The firm's work for Microsoft is, of course, well known. However, it also represents a number of other major companies with intellectual property interests.

Seed Intellectual Property Law Group PLLC

The Firm: This strong intellectual property boutique houses a *"collection of wonderful lawyers,"* according to interviewees, and offers a broad range of expertise. Its strict IP-focus allows for a deep understanding of the varied niche areas, and many of the firm's attorneys hold advanced degrees in science or technology disciplines. As such, the group combines considerable understanding of the technical underpinnings of its clients' businesses with an intricate knowledge of the governing law. Typical work ranges from patent prosecution to licensing and litigation, and the team enjoys a

great reputation for trademark expertise and biotech work.

The Lawyers: **Bill Ferron** is a former president of the Washington State Patent Law Association, and boasts a superb reputation for his patent, trademark and copyright counseling and licensing. Market sources report that he has earned his spurs as *"one of the best trademark lawyers in the city."*

The Clients: The firm's strong client base includes a number of names, among them Red Robin International.

Other Notable Practitioners

"Well-connected and superbly experienced" patent litigator **Richard Siefert** recently moved from Lane Powell PC to Merchant & Gould PC. He has been involved in some of Seattle's most sizable and complex patent cases. His litigation capabilities extend to trademark, copyright and trade secrets disputes, and market sources also recommend him as an authority on the interface between IP and competition law. His recent highlights include represented Sunstream in a major trade secrets case brought against Boeing.

LITIGATION

GENERAL COMMERCIAL

Washington Leading firms (Litigation: General Commercial)	
1	**BYRNES & KELLER** Seattle
	PERKINS COIE LLP Seattle
2	**CORR CRONIN LLP** Seattle
	DANIELSON HARRIGAN LEYH Seattle
	DAVIS WRIGHT TREMAINE LLP Seattle
	PRESTON GATES & ELLIS LLP Seattle
	SUMMIT LAW GROUP, PLLC Seattle
3	**DORSEY & WHITNEY LLP** Seattle
	GORDON MURRAY TILDEN Seattle
	HELLER EHRMAN WHITE & MCAULIFFE Seattle
	LANE POWELL PC Seattle
	MCNAUL EBEL NAWROT HELGREN Seattle
	STOEL RIVES LLP Seattle
Firms are listed alphabetically in each band.	

Band 1

Byrnes & Keller

The Firm: A *"superior"* general commercial litigation boutique, its practice encompasses complex contractual disputes, securities litigation, products liability and IP-related proceedings. The nine lawyers at this firm also manage a strong professional liability practice. To bear testament to this latter expertise, they have advised virtually all of the major law firms in the Pacific Northwest on professional liability matters. Interviewees dubbed this group *"one of the West*

Coast's best" tobacco defense practices, and it is thereby able to attract prominent clients such as RJ Reynolds. Clients singled out its *"great tactical lawyers,"* who offer *"abundant trial experience."*

The Lawyers: Managing Partner **Brad Keller's** practice is focused on business torts, products liability and professional liability. Clients enthuse over his *"innovative"* and *"tenacious"* style, while peers admire him as *"tough as nails."* *"A hit with the juries,"* he has achieved a defense verdict for one of the nation's largest law firms, in addition to participating in several securities-oriented investment cases. **Peter Byrnes** has proven his capabilities as a *"terrific"* courtroom lawyer over the years, capable of navigating through even the most complex of cases. Interviewees consequently view him as *"the dean of Seattle trial lawyers."* His practice has more recently focused on mediation and professional liability defense.

The Clients: Abbott Laboratories; Clear Channel Communications; Hewlett-Packard; Philips and RJ Reynolds.

Perkins Coie LLP

The Firm: As the state's largest firm, its litigation practice has the all-essential *"resource of top lawyers"* to sustain its reputation as one of Washington's finest. Aided by its merger with Phoenix's Brown & Bain firm in July 2004, its network and expanse of expertise continue to

grow. Particular strengths include IP-related and technology litigation in addition to products liability and other complex commercial disputes. While its link to Microsoft reflects a strong technology litigation practice, its long-standing representation of Boeing represents its *"superlative"* expertise in aviation defense, sources say.

The Lawyers: The *"affable and bright"* **David Burman** has a practice focused on class action, antitrust, False Claims Act and soft IP-related litigation. His *"superb"* litigation skills are also illustrated in the appellate arena. A leading constitutional lawyer and a *"good strategic thinker,"* he has recently represented the state's Democratic Party in a prominent dispute concerning the governorship. He has also argued a case relating to Washington's wine regulations on behalf of Costco, in addition to separately advising Amazon.com regarding the False Claims Act. *"A brilliant strategist and an excellent courtroom lawyer,"* **Harry Schneider** is applauded for his general commercial litigation practice. The regularity of his sophisticated trial work, combined with his *"ability to see the big picture,"* distinguishes his practice, sources said. He has tried a case regarding the control of numerous thrift stores in Chicago and Cleveland.

The Clients: Boeing; Amazon.com; Nintendo; Microsoft; Costco; Semitool and Amgen.

Washington
Leading individuals
(Litigation: General Commercial)

[1] **BURMAN David** *Perkins Coie*, Seattle
BYRNES Peter *Byrnes & Keller*, Seattle
HARRIGAN Arthur *Danielson Harrigan*, Seattle
KELLER Brad *Byrnes & Keller*, Seattle

[2] **CORR Kelly** *Corr Cronin*, Seattle
CRONIN William *Corr Cronin*, Seattle
GORDON Charles *Gordon Murray*, Seattle
GRAY Marvin *Davis Wright*, Seattle
PALUMBO Ralph *Summit Law Group*, Seattle
RUMMAGE Stephen *Davis Wright*, Seattle
SCHNEIDER Harry *Perkins Coie*, Seattle

[3] **BATEMAN David** *Preston Gates*, Seattle
DUNNE Daniel *Heller Ehrman*, Seattle
ENGLUND Rudy *Lane Powell*, Seattle
GOODNIGHT David *Stoel Rives*, Seattle
GREER George *Heller Ehrman*, Seattle
KAPLAN Barry *Wilson Sonsini*, Seattle
KEEHNEL Stellman *DLA Piper*, Seattle
MCDONALD David *Preston Gates*, Seattle
MILLER Craig *Davis Wright*, Seattle
SCHWAB Evan *Dorsey & Whitney*, Seattle
SIEFERT Richard *Merchant & Gould*, Seattle
SQUIRES William *Summit Law Group*, Seattle
SULKIN Robert *McNaul Ebel*, Seattle

Individuals are listed alphabetically in each band.

Band 2

Corr Cronin LLP

The Firm: Market commentators endorse this litigation specialist's proficiency in commercial, products liability, employment, construction and IP-related litigation. It has established particular prominence in representing newspapers. For example, it has represented Hearst in litigation between its newspaper, the Seattle Post-Intelligencer, and its rival the Seattle Times. Sources consistently applaud its "*distinctive superlative product.*"

The Lawyers: **Kelly Corr** is involved in high-profile commercial and products liability litigation. In addition to handling the case for the Seattle Post-Intelligencer, he is also involved in civil litigation stemming from the DC sniper shootings on behalf of the gun manufacturer. He's a "*bulldog who fights the fight*" and is "*comfortable handling tough cases.*" His partner, **Bill Cronin**, is also viewed highly by the market for complex business, professional liability, securities and breach of contract litigation. Cronin is applauded as a "*pragmatic, experienced attorney.*"
The Clients: Microsoft; Hearst; Amazon.com; Deloitte Touche Tohmatsu; Bushmaster Firearms; Alaska Airlines; Alamo Rent A Car; National Car Rental and Georgia-Pacific.

Danielson Harrigan Leyh & Tollefson, LLP

The Firm: Although this litigation boutique is comparatively smaller than some of its competitors, it is certainly equipped with an extensive scope of practice. As a consequence, it is highly commended by the market for its "*sophistication of analysis.*" Its practice shines in the areas of professional negligence, complex commercial, aviation, admiralty, construction and securities litigation.
The Lawyers: "*A master strategist,*" **Art Harrigan** has the "*clairvoyant ability to conceptualize the case at the outset and envisage its journey.*" Interviewees report that he mixes a "*tremendous intellect*" with a genuine curiosity for the subject, which enables him to understand even the finest of details.
The Clients: AIG Aviation; Associated Aviation Underwriters; BP; AXA Global Risks; Port of Seattle; Lloyd's and Weyerhaeuser.

Davis Wright Tremaine LLP
See firm details p.1796

The Firm: The Seattle office of this national firm offers a broad portfolio of skills, though it is best known for its prowess in the financial services industry. This is coupled with expertise in general business, securities, land use, employment and healthcare litigation. Also considered a leader in First Amendment and media litigation, the team's "*experience and great judgment*" garnered tremendous respect among peers.
The Lawyers: **Monty Gray** (see p.1791) possesses a "*wonderful legal mind*" and is very adept at mastering complex subject matters. A "*senior gentleman of the Bar,*" his practice spans such areas as antitrust, employment and IP. Over the past five years, he has also appeared as an increasingly prominent figure in alternative dispute resolution. **Craig Miller**'s (see p.1793) focus lies in disputes relating to commercial real estate foreclosures, lender liability defense and other aspects of bankruptcy proceedings. Admiralty financing litigation is also a feature of his practice. Sources commend this "*flexible thinker,*" who has the insightful ability to "*zero in on the heart of a case.*" **Steve Rummage** (see p.1794) often represents banks and financial institutions in a wide variety of litigation, including consumer class actions and traditional commercial disagreements. Interviewees applaud the talented speaker as "*awesome in front of a judge.*" They also note that he is a "*smart, excellent writer*" and a highly regarded appellate attorney.
The Clients: Washington Mutual; Getty Images; Bank of America; Holland America Line; Banner Bank and Providence Healthcare Group.

Preston Gates & Ellis LLP

The Firm: Viewed as a "*litigation shop with great lawyers,*" the firm cuts a broad swath in litigation. And as a result of its long-standing association with Microsoft, it has cultivated a particular interest in IP litigation. It also maintains a good reputation for its commercial finance litigation and possesses strong antitrust, healthcare and environmental litigation capabilities.
The Lawyers: **David Bateman** has established a strong IP, technology and cyber law practice. A "*smart and personable*" attorney, he has a bright future and "*all the tools*" required of a standout Seattle attorney, sources say. Involved in a number of leading cases, **David McDonald**'s ability to understand complex matters is deemed "*impressive*" by rivals. His forte lies in technology and IP, further enhanced by expertise in constitutional and statutory law.
The Clients: Microsoft; Verizon; Seagate Technology; State of Alaska; Nike and Premera Blue Cross.

Summit Law Group, PLLC

The Firm: This firm impresses with its cadre of "*excellent lawyers and a strong supporting cast,*" comprising 16 lawyers who deftly handle complex commercial litigation. A worthy combination of "*high level of expertise and cost-effective counsel*" has led to its involvement in matters relating to environmental, antitrust, products liability and toxic torts among other areas of law. Like others on the table, it also demonstrates proficiency in the IP arena, while commercial property and insurance coverage disputes continue to be a mainstay. Its clients range from individuals to Fortune 100 companies in various industry fields, although software companies feature prominently in its client roster.
The Lawyers: "*A great, original thinker,*" **Ralph Palumbo** has a practice encompassing antitrust, products liability, IP, environmental and complex commercial litigation. His ability to "*turn his positions into winners*" is a notable trademark of his practice, sources said. He has recently represented RealNetworks in its civil antitrust lawsuit against Microsoft in the USA and related enforcement proceedings against Microsoft by the European Union. Respected for his expertise in toxic torts, **William Squires** has recently participated in disputes involving alleged exposure emitted from a weapons production facility. "*Tough but fair,*" he attracts persistent client loyalty and is well regarded as a "*smart and experienced*" attorney.
The Clients: Boeing; RealNetworks; Budget Rent a Car; Hertz; FMC; King County; Motorola and St. Paul Travelers.

Band 3

Dorsey & Whitney LLP

The Firm: With offices across North America, Europe and Asia, the Seattle branch's corporate attorneys have a wealth of resources at their disposal. Interviewees note that this outfit is "*doing a great job around town,*" demonstrating proficiency particularly in M&A and corporate finance. The group is also known for its fluency in securities advice to a vast array of public company clients.

The Lawyers: Evan Schwab of Dorsey & Whitney stands out in Washington as the "*toughest bulldog you will find*" to defend a client's position. His "*strategic and terrifically insightful*" brand of lawyering gained tremendous client confidence, sources said.

The Clients: The firm boasts an impressive client roster that incorporates individuals and Fortune 500 companies, including Western Wireless, Qwest and ConocoPhillips.

Gordon Murray Tilden

The Firm: The litigation specialist advises a range of clients, from individuals to international companies. Peers report that the group of nine attorneys has a "*wealth of commercial litigation experience.*" Its complex litigation practice is first choice for insurance coverage disputes and also spans other areas of business law such as professional negligence, products liability, real estate, employment and IP.

The Lawyers: Described as a "*terrific trial lawyer,*" **Chuck Gordon** has a broad civil litigation practice and is particularly well versed in complex insurance coverage work. Interviewees report that he deftly combines an "*extremely sincere, personal touch with judges and jurors*" with "*good instincts when handling cases.*"

The Clients: Puget Sound Energy; Weyerhaeuser; Boeing; GlaxoSmithKline; Safeway and Wells Fargo.

Heller Ehrman White & McAuliffe LLP

See firm details p.288

The Firm: The Seattle office is part of this firm's wider network of 13 offices, spanning San Francisco to New York, and also including overseas outposts in Hong Kong, Beijing and Singapore among others. Given this breadth of resources, the Seattle office is able to "*bring together the talents of many exemplary lawyers.*" The full-service capabilities feature a strong suit in securities litigation, and further encompass products liability, real estate and IP-related disputes.

The Lawyers: Cochair of the firm's litigation

group, **George Greer** has "*lots of talent and experience*" with complex securities law disputes and accountant liability litigation. The market describes him as a "*bright, strategic*" lawyer who "*understands how to deal with people effectively*" and "*gets great results.*" Chair of the Northwest litigation group **Daniel Dunne** has a notable consumer and securities litigation practice. He is described as an "*excellent*" lawyer, who "*deals with complex issues well.*"

The Clients: The firm's client base includes a range of companies, from small startups to Fortune 500 companies traversing a broad spectrum of industries.

Lane Powell PC

See firm details p.1797

The Firm: Seattle's 46-lawyer commercial litigation group is well regarded for its expert handling of complex contractual disputes, class actions, arbitrations, and IP-related litigation. It has a particularly defined reputation for its insurance coverage work on behalf of such notable clients as Lloyd's. Securities litigation and professional liability work also fall under the auspices of the practice.

The Lawyers: Rudy Englund's (see p.1791) practice has an emphasis on complex business litigation, class actions, securities and IP-related litigation. A "*smart and hard-working*" lawyer, he has recently defended Wal-Mart in a wage and hour collective action, and separately advised Prudential on securities litigation.

The Clients: Wells Fargo; Wal-Mart; Nordstrom; Prudential; ChevronTexaco and Lloyd's.

McNaul Ebel Nawrot Helgren & Vance PLLC

The Firm: Interviewees commend this Seattle-based group as a sought-after firm with a strong litigation practice and established community presence. It has recently been working on a class action against Boeing. It is also counsel to a high-profile football coach embroiled in litigation.

The Lawyers: "*Street fighter*" **Robert Sulkin** has a practice encompassing commercial, environmental, real estate and employment litigation. In addition to this, insurance coverage and professional malpractice feature heavily in his

caseload. Interviewees identify the managing partner as a "*standout*" attorney for his blend of "*thoughtful and strategic*" style and "*good instincts.*"

The Clients: Stewart Title Guaranty; Washington State Convention & Trade Center; Dragnet Fisheries; Food Services of America and Pacific Portfolio Consulting.

Stoel Rives LLP

The Firm: The 20 trial lawyers in the Seattle office of this regional firm are applauded for their general commercial and environmental litigation expertise. The firm houses "*good, strong people,*" clients said, demonstrating flair in a range of disputes. Further illustrating its prowess is its selection as national trial counsel for Qwest as well as coordinating counsel for the Harvard Drug Group.

The Lawyers: As a key player in the firm's relationship with Qwest, **David Goodnight** is viewed as a "*smart guy with a promising future.*" An "*extremely thorough attorney,*" he is willing to take charge and is further acknowledged as an "*excellent writer.*" His practice is focused on general commercial litigation and professional malpractice.

The Clients: US Bank; ConocoPhillips; Harvard Drug Group and McDonald's.

Other Notable Practitioners

Barry Kaplan (see p.1792) of Wilson Sonsini Goodrich & Rosati is also an established force within the legal community. Interviewees deem him a "*tremendous*" lawyer who excels at securities litigation, class action defense and corporate governance. He has recently litigated on behalf of Boeing. **Stellman Keehnel** (see p.1792) at DLA Piper Rudnick Gray Cary is well regarded as a securities litigator whose impressive track record won client respect. They applaud his "*great judgment*" and responsive style. An "*authority on antitrust matters,*" **Richard Siefert** also has a strong IP litigation practice. He recently moved to Merchant & Gould PC. He is viewed as a "*detail-oriented, thorough and experienced*" lawyer.

REAL ESTATE

Band 1

Buck & Gordon LLP

The Firm: The 23 attorneys at this "*top-quality*" boutique firm are perhaps best known for their undisputed strength in land use and zoning matters. However, the team also has a premier reputation for complex commercial real estate

transactions, and offers associated environmental capabilities. The transactional group deals with all aspects of large-scale retail, office and warehouse development projects, and boasts particular expertise in advising the developers of hi-tech facilities on the requisite arrangements. The "*highly sophisticated*" group is currently involved in a number of major projects, including the redevelopment for King County's housing authority.

The Lawyers: Clients look to **Bill Block** for technical understanding coupled with good business sense and reliable advice. He undertakes complex real estate transactional work for major investors and developers, who appreciate his "*active and bright*" manner and "*unquestion-*

Washington
Leading firms (Real Estate)

1 BUCK & GORDON LLP *Seattle*
FOSTER PEPPER & SHEFELMAN PLLC *Seattle*
PRESTON GATES & ELLIS LLP *Seattle*

2 ALSTON COURTNAGE & BASSETTI LLP *Seattle*
DAVIS WRIGHT TREMAINE LLP *Seattle*
MCCULLOUGH HILL FIKSO *Seattle*
PERKINS COIE LLP *Seattle*

3 LANE POWELL PC *Seattle*
REAL PROPERTY LAW GROUP PLLC *Seattle*
STOEL RIVES LLP *Seattle*

Leading individuals (Real Estate)

1 BLOCK William *Buck & Gordon, Seattle*
KUNTZ Michael *Foster Pepper, Seattle*
OSBORNE Scott *Preston Gates, Seattle*

2 BARRETT Michael *Perkins Coie, Seattle*
BASSETTI Andrew *Alston Courtnage, Seattle*
COURTNAGE Michael *Alston Courtnage, Seattle*
DIAL Ellen *Perkins Coie, Seattle*
FLUHRER Gary *Foster Pepper, Seattle*
ROCKWELL David *Stoel Rives, Seattle*
THOMAS Cynthia *Real Property Law Group, Seattle*

3 ACKERMAN Gary *Foster Pepper, Seattle*
FIKSO Robert *McCullough Hill, Seattle*
GREEN William *Perkins Coie, Seattle*
KOONS Warren *Davis Wright, Bellevue*
MCLEAN Dennis *Davis Wright, Seattle*
NELSON Jane *Lane Powell, Seattle*
NEUGEBAUER Robert *Preston Gates, Seattle*
PEPPLE Daniel *Pepple Johnson, Seattle*
RAKAY NELSON Jane *Lane Powell, Seattle*
SKINNER Shannon *Preston Gates, Seattle*
TANNER Gordon *Stoel Rives, Seattle*

Firms and individuals are listed alphabetically in each band.

able credentials." Observers described **Peter Buck** as an extremely experienced lawyer who "*knows the lay of the land*" and the intricacies of the market. An important figure in the land use arena, he has recently managed the due diligence for property acquisitions worth over $300 million, including many with multiple entitlement issues.

The Clients: Amazon.com; King County Housing Authority; Tacoma Housing Authority; Cingular Wireless; Nintendo; Puget Sound Energy; Target and Plum Creek Timber.

Foster Pepper & Shefelman PLLC

The Firm: This full-service outfit fields a substantial team, currently numbering around 39 real estate and land use attorneys. This combination of extensive resources and considerable expertise, along with a number of star names, has assisted the firm in attracting a number of clients of the size and quality of Washington Mutual. It also helps the team to win a place at the deal table in large institutional developments, such as the downtown monorail project.

Beyond this, the firm is also recognized as a leader for land use advice.

The Lawyers: Interviewees report that **Michael Kuntz** handles complex projects well and "*doesn't allow extraneous matters to get in the way.*" As "*one of the best deal-oriented lawyers in Seattle,*" he advises on many of the largest commercial and residential real estate development schemes, and also has a good name for financing work. The market also commends **Gary Fluhrer** for his "*analytical and practical*" approach teamed with his "*terrific understanding*" of the business and tax aspects of transactions. "*Extremely knowledgeable about financing,*" he also advises on real estate transactions and development issues. **Gary Ackerman** has considerable experience of advising on condominium and homeowner association law. A well-established land use attorney, **Judith Runstad** is noted for her political connections. Having achieved considerable success over her career, she brings a "*substantial stable of knowledge and experience*" to anything in which she is involved.

The Clients: The firm's real estate clients include: Washington Mutual; Costco; Safeway; Sheraton Seattle Hotel and Towers; Seattle University and Corporate Property Investors.

Preston Gates & Ellis LLP

The Firm: This sizable group has a particular name for excellence in the field of real estate finance. Its "*talented and responsive*" lawyers are experienced in handling the largest and most complex development finance and structured finance transactions. With this sort of strength, it is unsurprising that the group attracts notable banks and insurance clients, such as Nationwide. It also boasts solid transactional and land use expertise. The firm employs an interdepartmental approach to ensure clients receive the most rounded advice possible.

The Lawyers: An expert in municipal finance, **Scott Osborne** is viewed as one of the most experienced real estate lawyers in Seattle. Clients turn to him for his "*agile brain*" and ability to identify the most pertinent matters. He employs these attributes to provide superior transactional representation, and also in his writing and reports on current cases. **Robert Neugebauer** was recommended to researchers as a responsive attorney who "*really knows his stuff.*" His strengths lie in the areas of commercial real estate transactions and finance, and he advises on the construction and development of office, retail, hospital and industrial projects. **Shannon Skinner** is a "*fine attorney,*" with a "*firm but fair*" approach, say peers. Active in lender representation, she is valued for her comprehensive understanding of complex financings.

The Clients: Nationwide Mutual Insurance; Merrill Gardens; Simon Property Group and the Newland Group.

Band 2

Alston Courtnage & Bassetti LLP

The Firm: This six-strong real estate boutique skillfully handles all aspects of transactional real estate, from acquisitions and sales, to complex financings, leasing and development projects. Its strong reputation in the transactional and financing field has attracted a number of financial institutions to its client base, perhaps most notably the Bank of America. An international reach is conferred to the team through its work for European companies, such as Metzler.

The Lawyers: A "*bright, likable*" attorney, **Andrew Bassetti** is a leading force in the world of real estate lending. His recent highlights have included a series of major real estate financings, including one on a regional basis for GE Capital. Sources report that his strength is based on "*using his good sense to get a deal done.*" **Michael Courtnage**'s strong transactional practice is increasingly oriented to overseas-based clients, especially German companies. A "*tough negotiator,*" he is currently advising a foreign fund that will soon be investing a billion dollars in the USA.

The Clients: The firm acts for a number of lending institutions and local, national and international landlords and tenants. Typical clients include: Bank of America; GE Capital; SAFECO and Metzler North America.

Davis Wright Tremaine LLP
See firm details p.1796

The Firm: Housed at one of the oldest and largest full-service firms in Seattle, Davis Wright Tremaine's real estate and land use team is widely commended for its "*diversity and strength in numbers.*" It boasts a highly regarded transactional practice, which acts in real property acquisitions, dispositions, development schemes and land use planning, as well as commercial leasing for office, retail and industrial properties. The group's client roster includes the names of a number of banks and financial institutions, and it also works for timber companies.

The Lawyers: **Dennis McLean** (see p.1793) is a smart, careful lawyer who "*doesn't miss a trick,*" according to peers. Clients, meanwhile, note that he has mastered "*the art of drafting contracts with real business sense.*" His practice is centered on commercial real estate development, acquisitions and disposals. As the primary contact for Hines in the Northwest, he has represented its interests over the past few years, handling some major transactions, including in the sale of downtown Seattle's IDX Tower. "*Brilliant*" **Tom Goeltz** (see p.1791) is a great player in the land use and development arenas. A former chair of the Washington State Bar Association real property, probate and trust section, **Warren Koons** (see p.1793) is a highly regarded transactional real estate lawyer, based in the Bellevue office. Described to researchers as a "*smart and practical*"

Washington
Leading individuals
(Real Estate: Zoning/Land Use)

1 BUCK Peter *Buck & Gordon*, Seattle
MCCULLOUGH Jack *McCullough Hill*, Seattle
RUNSTAD Judith *Foster Pepper*, Seattle

2 AMSTER Glenn *Lane Powell*, Seattle
GOELTZ Thomas *Davis Wright*, Seattle
HILL Richard *McCullough Hill*, Seattle
MARCY Donald *Cairncross & Hempelmann*, Seattle

Individuals are listed alphabetically in each band.

attorney, he handles the structuring, sale and purchase of commercial property and timberland.
The Clients: Port Blakely Communities; Hines; Bank of America; Banner Bank; Grand-Glacier and Ditty Properties.

McCullough Hill Fikso Kretschmer Smith

The Firm: The nine attorneys at this boutique firm have built a strong reputation in the region, especially for land use and real estate transactional work. Four attorneys focus on land use, including permitting and entitlement-related matters. The transactional side, meanwhile, encompasses the acquisition, financing, leasing and disposition of all types of real property. The group advises owners, developers and private clients, and boasts particular expertise in work for public sector clients.
The Lawyers: Jack McCullough (see p.1793) is an esteemed land use and permitting lawyer, who typically acts for private property owners and developers. A "*politically well-connected*" attorney, he serves as general counsel to the Downtown Seattle Association, and also acts for Wal-Mart on Washington land use matters. **Rich Hill**, is another prominent land use attorney, whose clients include the Seattle School District and Housing authority. He is well regarded in the market: to quote one admiring interviewee, "*he knocked my socks off.*" Another of the firm's attorneys who was singled out by the market, is **Robert Fikso**. "*The transactional counterpart to McCullough,*" he was described to researchers as "*practical and effective in negotiations.*"
The Clients: Quadrant Homes; Downtown Seattle Association; Washington Mutual; Weyerhaeuser and Gregory Broderick Smith Real Estate.

Perkins Coie LLP

The Firm: This full-service regional giant boasts a comprehensive real estate and land use practice. The 19-strong Seattle group advises a good variety of clients, ranging from major public companies to individual developers, on the real estate acquisitions, sales, financing, development, leasing and workouts. Its strength across the region has been further strengthened in recent years by the opening of its Chicago and Phoenix offices. Highlights of the year include acting for the University of Washington on

issues relating to its extensive downtown property portfolio.
The Lawyers: Michael Barrett was recommended to researchers as a "*superb advocate for handling complex loan negotiations.*" His practice emphasizes investment, be it debt or equity, and he is involved in real property financing, acquisitions and disposals, often on behalf of pension funds. "*A peach of a guy to work with,*" he recently completed a complex synthetic lease for an international engineering company. **Ellen Dial** is a "*superb*" development attorney, who is "*incredibly perceptive about the realities of transactions.*" Her practice is a mix of leasing, project development and general real estate advice, and she is currently working with the Port of Vancouver to research how environmentally sensitive areas can coexist with sound business development. **William Green** "*gets deals done,*" say interviewees. Highly regarded for general leasing and purchase and sales transactions, he serves an impressive client list, featuring Boeing and the University of Washington, as well as school districts, and hi-tech and old industrial clients.
The Clients: Washington Mutual; University of Washington; Shurgard; Wells Fargo; Amazon.com; Evergreen Aluminum and Teachers Insurance & Annuity Association.

Band 3

Lane Powell PC

See firm details p.1797
The Firm: This firm's Seattle office houses a 20-strong real estate and land use group packed with "*good, solid lawyers.*" The group is focused on real estate acquisitions and disposals, financing and commercial leasing, and is also well known in the market for its expertise in land use, planning and development issues. An impressive client base contains several oil majors, alongside developers, investors and retailers.
The Lawyers: Glenn Amster (see p.1790) has considerable experience in land use, permitting and development matters. Clients value his ability to assess the potential for development and assist with maneuvering through governmental processes. He has recently advised Home Depot on permitting issues related to several large store developments. **Jane Nelson** (see p.1794) cochairs the firm's real estate and land use group, and commands considerable respect in the market for her "*tremendous knowledge.*" Acquisitions, sales, financing and leasing are all features of her practice.
The Clients: Home Depot; Nordstrom; Chelsea Property Group; ChevronTexaco; Shea Homes; Chaffey Homes; ExxonMobil and Sound Transit.

Real Property Law Group PLLC

The Firm: According to market sources, this classy real estate boutique is well versed in the full range of real property issues facing its

clients. Sources admire the "*fine group of experienced lawyers*" with its considerable experience in acquisitions, sales, workouts, leasing and development schemes, among other things. The group can also offer assistance in related areas, such as land use and real estate taxation.
The Lawyers: The "*absolutely superb*" **Cynthia Thomas** was praised by interviewees as an "*engaging and energetic*" client-focused attorney. She offers experience in sales and acquisitions, financing, development projects and leasing, and is particularly well known in the community for her expertise in mixed-use projects.
The Clients: The firm's wide-ranging client base includes buyers and sellers, landlords, tenants, developers, contactors and investors.

Stoel Rives LLP

The Firm: The Seattle arm of this regional powerhouse boasts a broad-based commercial real estate practice. Areas of focus include leasing, development and land use, in addition to the usual purchases, sales and exchanges. Although its client book comprises a varied range of companies, a substantial number derive from the areas of financial services, agriculture and condominiums, reflecting the team's particular strengths in these fields.
The Lawyers: David Rockwell excels at real estate financing, leasing, purchases and sales, and exchanges. Sources report that he is "*effective at analysis and structuring deals,*" and are particularly enthusiastic about his "*superb*" reputation in the field of condominium development. Over the past year he has been working on the largest mixed-use development in the USA. **Gordon Tanner** was described to researchers as "*amazingly energetic and knowledgeable.*" Especially talented at commercial real estate finance transactions, he attracts a strong client following from the agricultural industry. In recent years he has also frequently been involved in developing legislation.
The Clients: Representative clients include: AEGON USA Realty Advisors, Eddie Bauer and Del Monte Foods.

Other Notable Practitioners

The "*exceptionally well-qualified*" **Daniel Pepple**, from Pepple Johnson Cantu & Schmidt, PLLC, is held in high regard for his real estate financing and leasing expertise. He is considered by some to be "*the best lender lawyer in town,*" and clients report that his efficient and straightforward approach instills banks with the "*utmost respect for his judgment.*" **Don Marcy** of Cairncross & Hempelmann, PS is an astute and highly experienced land use lawyer. Over 25 years of practice in the field, he has acquired extensive experience of advising owners and developers of commercial, residential and industrial property.

Leaders in Washington

ACKERMAN, Gary
Foster Pepper & Shefelman PLLC,
Seattle 206 447 4400
Recommended in Real Estate

ADAMS, Greg
Davis Wright Tremaine LLP, Seattle
206 628 7610
gregadams@dwt.com
Recommended in Corporate/M&A
Practice Areas: Partner, corporate
finance/business transactions. Representative experience includes serving as
outside general counsel to public and
private companies, boards of directors
and senior management entities regarding corporate governance matters and
shareholder rights, mergers and acquisitions; creation and reorganization of
corporate and partnership entities;
counseling corporations regarding succession planning. Representative clients
include Seattle Times Company and
Pope Resources.
Prof. Memberships: Member, Washington State Bar.
Career: Joined firm, 1978; named Partner, 1984. Named 'Super Lawyer', Washington Law & Politics, 2001-04.
Personal: JD, University of Washington,
1977. BA (magna cum laude), Pomona
College, 1973.

ALLRED, C Keith
Davis Wright Tremaine LLP, Seattle
206 628 7611
keithallred@dwt.com
Recommended in Bankruptcy
Practice Areas: Partner, bankruptcy
and litigation. Representative experience
includes bankruptcy and non-bankruptcy litigation concerning secured
loans, and complex real and personal
property lien issues. Serves as active
counsel to banking and commercial
lending institutions, asset-based lenders,
and leasing companies. Representative
clients include Bank of America, GE
Capital Corporation, US Bank.
Prof. Memberships: Member, American, Washington State, and King County
Bar Associations.
Career: Joined firm, 1975; became Partner, 1981. Named 'Super Lawyer', Washington Law & Politics, 1999-2003. Visiting professor, Brigham Young Law
School, 1991.
Personal: JD, University of Chicago, 1975.

AL-SALAM, Ramsey
Perkins Coie LLP, Seattle
206 583 8888
Recommended in Intellectual Property

AMSTER, Glenn J
Lane Powell PC, Seattle
206 223 6241
amsterg@lanepowell.com
Recommended in Real Estate
Practice Areas: Land use, zoning and
subdivisions, environmental, water
rights, public and private land development.

Prof. Memberships: National Association of Industrial and Office Properties,
Washington Chapter (Chair, Governmental Affairs); WSBA Section of Environmental and Land Use Law (Member
since 1978); Law Seminars International
(Co-Chair, Annual Seminar on Washington Water Law, 1994-96); Department of Ecology Attorney Work Group,
Reclaimed Water Rights (member,
1996-97); Washington Department of
Community Development (Destination
Resort Task Force Member, February
1994); Puget Sound Water Quality
Authority (Shoreline Resources and
Development Subcommittee Member,
1986).
Career: Partner since 1994.
Publications: Has lectured and written
extensively on real estate, land use and
environmental issues.
Personal: Washington University
School of Law (JD, 1978); Syracuse University (BA, 1971). He is a member and
former Chair of the Cornish College of
the Arts Board of Trustees.

ASLIN, John
Perkins Coie LLP, Seattle
206 583 8888
Recommended in Employment

BARBIER, Margaret
Stoel Rives LLP, Seattle
206 624 0900
Recommended in Employment

BARNES, Clemens
Perkins Coie LLP, Seattle
206 583 8888
Recommended in Employment

BARRETT, Michael
Perkins Coie LLP, Seattle
206 583 8888
Recommended in Real Estate

BASSETTI, Andrew
Alston Courtnage & Bassetti LLP,
Seattle 206 623 7600
Recommended in Real Estate

BATEMAN, David
Preston Gates & Ellis LLP, Seattle
206 623 7580
*Recommended in Intellectual
Property, Litigation*

BLACKSTONE, Robert A
Davis Wright Tremaine LLP, Seattle
206 628 7624
bobblackstone@dwt.com
Recommended in Employment
Practice Areas: Partner, labor and
employment law. Regularly counsels
clients on strategic labor relations, preventive employee relations, executive
employment agreements, noncompetition and trade secret issues, protecting
intellectual property and employment
privacy. Acted as chief collective bargaining negotiator for firms in a variety
of industries.
Prof. Memberships: Washington State

and American Bar Associations. Chairman, Labor and Employment Law Section, King County Bar Association,
1996-97. Co-Chair, ABA Subcommittee
on Covenants Not to Compete.
Career: Joined firm, 1976; became Partner, 1982.
Personal: JD, Columbia University,
1976. BA (magna cum laude), Amherst
College, 1973.

BLOCK, William
Buck & Gordon LLP, Seattle
206 382 9540
Recommended in Real Estate

BLUMENFELD, Chuck
Perkins Coie LLP, Seattle
206 583 8888
Recommended in Environment

BODINE, Brian
Davis Wright Tremaine LLP, Seattle
206 628 7623
brianbodine@dwt.com
Recommended in Intellectual Property
Practice Areas: Partner, IP litigation.
Experience includes litigating mechani-
cal, electrical, biotechnology, chemical
and software patents, litigating trade-
mark infringement, trade secrets, and
complex intellectual property disputes.
Prof. Memberships: Washington State
Bar. Past President, Washington State
Patent Law Association. Adjunct Profes-
sor of Law, Patent/Trade Secret Law,
Seattle University Law School.
Career: Joined firm in 2002 as a Partner.
Clerk to Hon Carolyn R Dimmick, US
District Court and Hon Joseph F Baca,
NM Supreme Court 1991-96. Registered
Patent Attorney.
Personal: JD (magna cum laude), Uni-
versity of Puget Sound (now Seattle
University) School of Law, 1991. BS,
Montana State University, 1974.

BOR, Andrew
Perkins Coie LLP, Seattle
206 583 8888
Recommended in Corporate/M&A

BROWN, Jr, Rodney
Cascadia Law Group, Seattle
206 292 6300
Recommended in Environment

BUCK, Peter
Buck & Gordon LLP, Seattle
206 382 9540
Recommended in Real Estate

BULCHIS, Ed
Dorsey & Whitney LLP, Seattle
206 903 8800
Recommended in Intellectual Property

BURMAN, David
Perkins Coie LLP, Seattle
206 583 8888
Recommended in Litigation

BUSH, Gayle
Bush, Strout & Kornfeld, Seattle
206 292 2110
Recommended in Bankruptcy

BUSTO, Mark
Sebris Busto James, Bellevue
425 454 4233
Recommended in Employment

BYRNES, Peter
Byrnes & Keller, Seattle
206 622 2000
Recommended in Litigation

CAIRNS, Carolyn
Stokes Lawrence, PS, Seattle
206 626 6000
Recommended in Employment

CARLSON, Kent
Preston Gates & Ellis LLP, Seattle
206 623 7580
Recommended in Corporate/M&A

CHAPMAN, William
Preston Gates & Ellis LLP, Seattle
206 623 7580
Recommended in Environment

COHEN, Matthew
Heller Ehrman White & McAuliffe LLP,
Seattle 206 447 0900
Recommended in Environment

COONROD, Stephan
Preston Gates & Ellis LLP, Seattle
206 623 7580
Recommended in Corporate/M&A

CORR, Kelly
Corr Cronin LLP, Seattle
206 625 8600
Recommended in Litigation

COURTNAGE, Michael
Alston Courtnage & Bassetti LLP,
Seattle 206 623 7600
Recommended in Real Estate

CRONIN, William
Corr Cronin LLP, Seattle
206 625 8600
Recommended in Litigation

CROSS, Bruce
Perkins Coie LLP, Seattle
206 583 8888
Recommended in Employment

CULLEN, Jack
Foster Pepper & Shefelman PLLC,
Seattle 206 447 4400
Recommended in Bankruptcy

DIAL, Ellen
Perkins Coie LLP, Seattle
206 583 8888
Recommended in Real Estate

DIAMOND, Kenneth
Winterbauer & Diamond, P.L.L.C.,
Seattle 206 676 8440
Recommended in Employment

DIERCKS, Robert
Foster Pepper & Shefelman PLLC,
Seattle 206 447 4400
Recommended in Corporate/M&A

DODD, Richard
Preston Gates & Ellis LLP, Seattle
206 623 7580
Recommended in Corporate/M&A

DUNN, Loren
Riddell Williams PS, Seattle
206 624 3600
Recommended in Environment

DUNNE, Daniel
Heller Ehrman White & McAuliffe LLP,
Seattle 206 447 0900
Recommended in Litigation

DUNWOODY, Stuart R
Davis Wright Tremaine LLP, Seattle
206 628 7649
stuartdunwoody@dwt.com
Recommended in Intellectual Property
Practice Areas: Partner, intellectual
property litigation and complex civil litigation. Litigation of patent, trademark,
trade dress, copyright, and trade secret
infringement and ownership issues, and
related counseling; domain name disputes; advertising law; defense of
defamation and invasion of privacy
claims, art law.
Career: Joined firm, 1984; became Partner, 1990. Clerk to Hon Alfred T Goodwin, US Court of Appeals, Ninth Circuit, 1983-84. Named 'Super Lawyer',
Washington Law & Politics, 2002-04.
Personal: JD, Yale, 1983. BA, Oberlin
College, 1977.

DWYER, Michael
Lane Powell PC, Seattle
206 223 7000
dwyerm@lanepowell.com
Recommended in Corporate/M&A
Practice Areas: General business practice, including mergers and acquisitions,
business formation, debt and equity
financing, commercial transactions and
real estate transactions of all kinds. Has
represented both profit and non-profit
organizations on a wide range of commerical and real estate transactions for
over 32 years.
Prof. Memberships: ABA, Business Section; Washington State Bar Association,
Business and Real Property Sections;
Seattle-King County Bar Association;
U.S. Law Firm Group (former President
and current Trustee); Greater Seattle
Chamber of Commerce (former Trustee
and current Secretary and General
Counsel).
Career: Joined firm in 1973; Partner
since 1978; and has served as Co-Managing Partner of firm (1998-2002) and
Partner in Charge for Seattle (1994-
2002).
Personal: George Washington University
(JD, Order of the Coif, 1972); University
of Washington (BA, cum laude, 1969).

EKBERG, Charles
Lane Powell PC, Seattle
206 223 7012
ekbergc@lanepowell.com
Recommended in Bankruptcy
Practice Areas: Bankruptcy, creditors
rights, real estate, commercial law. As
Chair of the Litigation Department's
Banking/Financial Services/Creditors
Rights/Collections Practice Group, he is
involved in business reorganizations,
workouts, creditors remedies, real estate
financing and litigation.
Prof. Memberships: ABA Business
Bankruptcy Subcommittee (Member),
American Bankruptcy Institute, Washington State Bar Association's Credi-
tor/Debtor Section (four-term Executive
Committee Member); King County Bar
Association's Bankruptcy Section (former Chairperson); Western District
Federal Bar Association Bankruptcy
Committee (Member); American College of Bankruptcy (fellow); Ninth Circuit Judicial Conference (lawyer representative).
Career: Joined firm in 1971; Partner
since 1978.
Publications: Has lectured at various
seminars on bankruptcy practice and
authored numerous articles and papers
which have appeared in various publica-
tions relating to bankruptcy practice.
Personal: University of Washington
(JD, Order of the Coif, 1971; BA, with
honors, 1968). Served on the Board of
Editors for the University of Washington
Law Review from 1970-71, and as a
research associate under Professor
William H Rodgers, Jr. He has served on
the board of directors of the Bainbridge
Foundation, the Sigma Tau Association,
the Hamlin Robinson School, and the
University of Washington Law School
Foundation.

ELLIOTT, Richard W
Davis Wright Tremaine LLP, Bellevue
425 646 6140
richelliott@dwt.com
Recommended in Environment
Practice Areas: Partner, environmental
and natural resources, land use and litigation. Represents petroleum-industry
and other clients before federal and state
courts and in negotiations/disputes with
federal and state agencies involving
water resources, permitting and appeals
before administrative tribunals. Assists
clients in complex transactions involving contaminated properties and other
Superfund sites.
Prof. Memberships: Member, Washington State Bar Association. Admitted to
practice before various federal courts.
Career: Joined firm, 1983; became Partner, 1986. Named 'Super Lawyer', Washington Law & Politics, 2004.
Personal: JD (honors) University of
Washington, 1974. MS, University of
Washington, 1971. BA, Oregon State
University, 1964.

ENGLUND, Rudy A
Lane Powell PC, Seattle
206 223 7042
englundr@lanepowell.com
Recommended in Litigation
Practice Areas: Complex commerical
litigation, intellectual property disputes,
class action litigation, business dispute resolution. As Co-Chair of the firm's Litigation Department, his practice also includes
extensive wage and hour experience.
Prof. Memberships: Washington
Defense Trial Lawyers Association; ABA
Standing Committee on Federal Judiciary (Member, 1997-2002); ABA Section
of Litigation (council member, 1994-
97); ABA Section of Litigation - Multiple Task Forces (2003-present).
Career: Partner since 1984.
Publications: Has lectured and written
extensively on litigation issues.
Personal: University of Washington
(JD, 1975; BA, magna cum laude, 1972).
Phi Beta Kappa.

FERRON Jr, William
Seed Intellectual Property Law Group
PLLC, Seattle 206 622 4900
Recommended in Intellectual Property

FIKSO, Robert
McCullough Hill Fikso Kretschmer
Smith, Seattle 206 448 1818
Recommended in Real Estate

FLUHRER, Gary
Foster Pepper & Shefelman PLLC,
Seattle 206 447 4400
Recommended in Real Estate

GELBAND, Scott
Perkins Coie LLP, Seattle
206 583 8888
Recommended in Corporate/M&A

GINSBERG, Beth
Stoel Rives LLP, Seattle
206 624 0900
Recommended in Environment

GOELTZ, Thomas
Davis Wright Tremaine LLP, Seattle
206 628 7662
tomgoeltz@dwt.com
Recommended in Real Estate
Practice Areas: Partner, real estate law
and Chair of firm's Real Property Practice Group. Representative experience:
real estate development and joint ventures; zoning, land use and environmental, mixed use projects and master plans;
transportation agreements; property
acquisition, sales, and financing. Representative clients include Port Blakely
Tree Farms, Seattle Times Company and
Seattle Art Museum.
Prof. Memberships: Member, American College of Real Estate Lawyers,
Washington State/American Bar Associations. 'Super Lawyer', Washington Law
& Politics, since 1999.
Career: Joined firm as Partner, 1986.
Personal: JD (magna cum laude), University of Michigan, 1973. BA (high distinction), DePaul University, 1969.

GOODNIGHT, David
Stoel Rives LLP, Seattle
206 624 0900
Recommended in Litigation

GORDON, Charles
Gordon Murray Tilden, Seattle
206 467 6477
Recommended in Litigation

GRAHAM, Lawrence
Black Lowe & Graham, Seattle
206 381 3300
Recommended in Intellectual Property

GRAHAM, Stephen M
Orrick, Herrington & Sutcliffe LLP,
Seattle 206 839 4320
sgraham@orrick.com
Recommended in Corporate/M&A
Practice Areas: Stephen M Graham is
Chair of Orrick's 140-attorney Corporate Department, and is based in San
Francisco and Seattle. Steve focuses his
practice in the areas of securities law
compliance, mergers and acquisitions,
public offerings, private placements, and
general corporate matters. His diverse
practice is focused on the representation
of emerging and established technology
and life science companies, as well as
major investment banking and venture
capital firms. Representative clients
include Corixa Corporation, ICOS Corporation, Onyx Software Corporation,
SonoSite, Inc., Targeted Genetics Corporation, WatchGuard Technologies, Inc.,
and a number of private companies,
including Cardiac Dimensions, Inc.,
Corus Pharma, Inc., LipoSonix and
Sealaska Corporation. Steve has represented companies and investment banks
in numerous initial public offerings, a
wide variety of merger and acquisition
transactions, and private offerings of
debt and equity.
Prof. Memberships: Speaker, Annual
Institute on Securities Regulation, Prac-
ticing Law Institute, New York, NY,
November 2001-04. Board of Directors,
Washington Software Association;
Board of Directors, Washington
Biotechnology and Biomedical Associa-
tion.
Career: Super Lawyer, 2000-04, Wash-
ington Law & Politics. Who's Who in
America, Marquis Biographical Refer-
ence.
Personal: JD, Yale Law School, 1976; BS,
Iowa State University, 1973.

GRAY Jr, Marvin L
Davis Wright Tremaine LLP, Seattle
206 628 7665
montygray@dwt.com
Recommended in Litigation
Practice Areas: Partner, litigation. Representative experience includes complex
cases in antitrust, intellectual property,
employment, ERISA, and other business
and contract disputes, and acting as
arbitrator or mediator in alternate dispute resolution.
Prof. Memberships: Fellow, American

College of Trial Lawyers, 1992-present. Member, Washington State Bar. Member, American Law Institute. Named 'Super Lawyer', Washington Law & Politics, 2000-03.

Career: Joined firm, 1976. Became Partner, 1979. Managing Partner of firm, 1986-88. Previously worked as an Assistant United States Attorney and law clerk to Jude Henry J Friendly and Justice John M Harlan.

Personal: JD (magna cum laude), Harvard, 1969. AB, Princeton, 1966.

GREEN, William
Perkins Coie LLP, Seattle
206 583 8888
Recommended in Real Estate

GREENBURG, Scott G
Wilson Sonsini Goodrich & Rosati, Seattle 206 883 2500
sgreenburg@wsgr.com
Recommended in Corporate/M&A

Practice Areas: More than 20 years experience in venture capital, public offerings, intellectual property and technology issues, mergers and acquisitions, complex commercial transactions and international product distribution. Has completed more than 100 corporate transactions.

Prof. Memberships: Admitted to practice in Washington.

Personal: JD, 1980, Seattle University, University of Puget Sound, (cum laude). Editor in chief, University of Puget Sound Law Review, 1979-80. Law Clerk to Judge William T Beeks, US District Court, Western District of Washington, 1980-81.

GREER, George
Heller Ehrman White & McAuliffe LLP, Seattle 206 447 0900
Recommended in Litigation

GROHMAN, Thomas
Lane Powell PC, Seattle
206 223 7000
grohman@lanepowell.com
Recommended in Corporate/M&A

Practice Areas: Mergers and acquisitions, corporate finance, business, taxation. As Co-Chair of the firm's Business Department, he has extensive experience with both US and foreign companies in commercial transactions, including acquisitions, financing, joint ventures, loan transactions and other operations and the related tax consequences.

Prof. Memberships: ABA (Member of Corporation Banking and Business Law, International Law, and Taxation Sections); Washington Council on International Trade (Member); Seattle Chamber of Commerce (Member); King County Bar Association (member of Corporate Counsel Section); Washington State Bar Association (Member of Real Property, Probate and Trust, and Business and Banking Sections).

Career: Partner since 1986.

Personal: New York University (LLM in taxation, 1979); Gonzaga University (JD, magna cum laude, 1978); Seattle University (BA, summa cum laude, 1975).

HARRIGAN Jr, Arthur
Danielson Harrigan Leyh & Tollefson, LLP, Seattle 206 623 1700
Recommended in Litigation

HESTON, Mary Jo
Lane Powell PC, Seattle
206 226 7015
hestonm@lanepowell.com
Recommended in Bankruptcy

Practice Areas: Business bankruptcies, reorganizations and workouts, creditors' remedies, UCC transactions, commercial litigation, troubled business acquisitions, and international insolvency matters.

Prof. Memberships: American College of Bankruptcy Lawyers (member since 2002); Turnaround Management Association, Northwest Chapter (Board Member, 2001-present, chapter president, 2004); Debtor Creditor Resource Committee - pro bono organization (board member since 1996 and current secretary); 2003 Recipient of Sydney C. Volinn Award from Washington State Bar, Debtor Creditor Section (for contributions to debtor-creditor practice); American Bankruptcy Institute (former board member, contributing author to ABI Journal); INSOL International - international insolvency practitioners (council member, 1996-99, current member); Washington State Bar Association; Creditor Debtor Executive Committee (member, 1988-96).

Career: Partner at Lane Powell, PC. United States Bankruptcy Court, Region XVIII (trustee, 1988-93). Adjunct professor of bankruptcy law at Seattle University (1984-2004) and at the University of Washington (1997-99). Estate Administrator, USDC, WD. WA. (1981-1988). Former Law Clerk to US District Judge Walter T McGovern and to Bankruptcy Judge Robert W Skidmore.

Publications: M Heston, 'Missing Link of Bankruptcy Crime Prosecutions', 6 ABI Law Review, 359 (1989); Chapter 36, Bankruptcy, 1A Washington Practice; Methods of Practice (West Publishing, 1989); M Heston 'Bankruptcy and Dissolution: Prevention, Action and Reaction'. 13 Comm. Prop. J. 10 (1987); Norton Annual Survey of Bankruptcy Law, Sections 724-726 (1984). She is a frequent speaker at regional, national and international seminars on insolvency issues.

Personal: University of Puget Sound (JD cum laude, 1980); University of Washington (BS cum laude, 1975).

HILL, Richard
McCullough Hill Fikso Kretschmer Smith, Seattle 206 448 1818
Recommended in Real Estate

HOFFMAN, Mark F
DLA Piper Rudnick Gray Cary US LLP, Seattle 206 839 4823
mark.hoffman@dlapiper.com
Recommended in Corporate/M&A

Practice Areas: Corporate and securities; mergers and acquisitions.

Career: He specializes in corporate finance, securities and general corporate law.

Personal: JD, University of Michigan; AB, Princeton University.

HUMPHREY, Lawton
Davis Wright Tremaine LLP, Seattle
206 628 7672
lawtonhumphrey@dwt.com
Recommended in Employment

Practice Areas: Partner, employment law, Chair of firm's Employment Law Department. Representative experience includes defending discrimination claims based on race, gender, age, or disability; defending wrongful discharge cases; advising on wage and hour issues, performing audits and defending claims for unpaid wages; family and medical leave issues; accommodating disabled workers; minimizing liability with terminations; corporate diversity. Representative clients include Seattle Times Company, PACCAR Inc., Virginia Mason Medical Center, Pepsi Bottling Group.

Prof. Memberships: Member, Washington State Bar Association and American Bar Association.

Career: Joined firm, 1991. Became Partner, 1997.

Personal: JD, UCLA, 1991. BA, Stanford, 1988.

HUTCHESON, Mark A
Davis Wright Tremaine LLP, Seattle
206 628 7678
markhutcheson@dwt.com
Recommended in Employment

Practice Areas: Partner, labor and employment law. Representative experience includes labor relations counseling and extensive experience representing employers in collective bargaining. Has negotiated agreements on behalf of employers engaged in a number of industries throughout the West Coast, Alaska and Hawaii.

Prof. Memberships: Fellow, College of Labor and Employment Lawyers. Member, Washington State and American Bar Associations.

Career: Joined firm, 1968. Became Partner, 1973. Firm Chairman, 1994-present. Former Managing Partner, 1989-94.

Publications: Co-author, 'Employer's Guide to Strike Planning and Prevention', (Practicing Law Institute, 1985).

Personal: JD, University of Washington, 1967. BA, University of Puget Sound, 1964.

ISRAEL, Allen
Foster Pepper & Shefelman PLLC, Seattle 206 447 4400
Recommended in Corporate/M&A

JONES, Karen
Riddell Williams PS, Seattle
206 624 3600
Recommended in Employment

KAPLAN, Barry M
Wilson Sonsini Goodrich & Rosati, Seattle 206 883 2500
bkaplan@wsgr.com
Recommended in Litigation

Practice Areas: Securities and corporate governance litigation, class action defense, SEC and internal corporate investigations, complex commercial litigation including international disputes.

Prof. Memberships: Admitted in Washington and before the US Court of Appeals for the Ninth Circuit; US District Courts for the Western and Eastern Districts of Washington; and the US Tax Court. Member, American Bar Association, Washington Bar Association, King County Bar Association, and Federal Bar Association for the Western District of Washington.

Career: Joined WSGR as Partner, 2005. Former Partner, Seattle office of Perkins Coie LLP.

Personal: JD, (cum laude) University of Michigan, 1976; BA, Colgate University, 1973.

KAPLAN, Robert
Dorsey & Whitney LLP, Seattle
206 903 8800
Recommended in Corporate/M&A

KEEHNEL, Stellman
DLA Piper Rudnick Gray Cary US LLP, Seattle 206 839 4888
stellman.keehnel@dlapiper.com
Recommended in Litigation

Practice Areas: Securities litigation; intellectual property litigation; class action defense.

Career: His practice focuses on defense of securities class actions and shareholder derivative/fiduciary breach actions. He has a record of securing pre-discovery dismissals of securities and derivative lawsuits using Rule 12(b)(6) motions. He represents public companies and directors/officers in SEC and SRO proceedings and in corporate governance litiation. He defends and prosecutes lawsuits involving patent infringement, trademark, copyright, and trade secrets. He defends consumer class actions and high-stakes commercial and real estate lawsuits.

Personal: JD, Yale Law School; AB, Stanford University.

KELLER, Brad
Byrnes & Keller, Seattle
206 622 2000
Recommended in Litigation

KLEIN III, Otto
Summit Law Group, PLLC, Seattle
206 676 7000
Recommended in Employment

KOCHER, Gary
Preston Gates & Ellis LLP, Seattle
206 623 7580
Recommended in Corporate/M&A

KOONS, Warren
Davis Wright Tremaine LLP, Bellevue
425 646 6117
warrenkoons@dwt.com
Recommended in Real Estate
Practice Areas: Partner, real property
law. Representative experience spans a
wide range of commercial real estate
transactions, including purchase and
sale transactions, 1031 exchanges, leases
and real estate financing transactions.
Prof. Memberships: Member of Nominating Committee, Real Property, Probate & Trust Section, Washington State
Bar Association. Chair, Real Property
Section, East King County Bar Association.
Career: Joined firm, 1981; became Partner, 1987.
Personal: JD, University of California -
Berkeley, 1981. MA, University of Arizona, 1977. BA, Arizona State University,
1975.

KORNFELD, Armand
Bush, Strout & Kornfeld, Seattle
206 292 2110
Recommended in Bankruptcy

KUNTZ, Michael
Foster Pepper & Shefelman PLLC,
Seattle 206 447 4400
Recommended in Real Estate

LANDEFELD, Stewart
Perkins Coie LLP, Seattle
206 583 8888
Recommended in Corporate/M&A

LEAVERTON, Bruce
Lane Powell PC, Seattle
206 223 7000
leavertonb@lanepowell.com
Recommended in Bankruptcy
Practice Areas: Business bankruptcy,
reorganizations and workouts, commercial litigation, intellectual property litigation, real estate foreclosure.
Prof. Memberships: ABA (Member of
subcommittee on technology related
bankruptcies); Creditor/Debtor Section
of Washington State Bar Association
(member of International Insolvency
Subcommittee).
Career: Joined firm in 1985; Partner
since 1991. Began his career with the
Houston law firm of Baker and Botts.
Publications: Has lectured and written
extensively on bankruptcy, insolvency
and financial matters. Published Note:
'Workers' Compensation: Death Benefits are the Problem of Dependency,' 35
Okla. L. Rev. 182-92 (1982).
Personal: University of Oklahoma (JD,
1983); University of Kansas (BA, with
honors, 1975; MA, 1978). Served as chief
articles editor for the Oklahoma Law
Review from 1982-83. Received the
International Academy of Trial Lawyers
Award in 1983.

LEMLY, Thomas A
Davis Wright Tremaine LLP, Seattle
206 628 7716
tomlemly@dwt.com
Recommended in Employment
Practice Areas: Partner, labor and
employment law. Representative experience includes litigation and counseling
in most employment law matters,
including discrimination, wrongful discharge, enforcement of noncompetition
agreements and related contracts. Rep-
resentative clients include Bank of
America, Farmers Insurance Group,
Microsoft, FlightSafety-Boeing Interna-
tional.
Prof. Memberships: Fellow, American
College of Trial Lawyers. Member,
Washington State Bar. Chairman of
Board, Association of Washington Busi-
ness. Past Chair, AWB Human Resources
Council.
Career: Joined firm, 1973; became Part-
ner, 1979.
Publications: Editor, 'Washington, Alas-
ka, California and Oregon Employment
Law Deskbooks'. Principal Contributor,
'Employment Discrimination Law'.
Personal: JD (honors), University of
North Carolina, 1973. BA, Duke, 1970.

LEPPO, Jeffery
Stoel Rives LLP, Seattle
206 624 0900
Recommended in Environment

MADDEN, Patrick
Preston Gates & Ellis LLP, Seattle
206 623 7580
Recommended in Employment

MANOLOPOULOS, Lynn T
Davis Wright Tremaine LLP, Bellevue
425 646 6146
lynnmanolopoulos@dwt.com
Recommended in Environment
Practice Areas: Partner, Chair of firm's
Environmental Department. Representative experience focuses on environmental compliance and litigation,
including administrative proceedings
involving environmental and toxic
materials claims, cost recovery and contribution claims, purchase/sale, refinance and development of contaminated real property, ground water contami-
nation/remediation, national environmental audits, citizen suits under
EPCRA, CERCLA and Clean Water Act.
Prof. Memberships: Member, Washington State Bar. Admitted to Practice in US
District Court for the Eastern and Western Districts of Washington.
Career: Joined firm, 1991; became Partner, 1997.
Personal: JD, UCLA, 1991. MBA, California State University, 1988. BS, University of Washington, 1984.

MARCY, Donald
Cairncross & Hempelmann, A Professional Service Corporation, Seattle
206 587 0700
Recommended in Real Estate

MCCULLOUGH, Jack
McCullough Hill Fikso Kretschmer
Smith, Seattle 206 448 1818
jack@mhfks.com
Recommended in Real Estate
Practice Areas: Practice focused on real
estate development, land use permitting,
zoning entitlements and environmental
matters, typically acting on behalf of
property owners, developers and users.
Prof. Memberships: Professional mem-
berships have included: ABA; Urban
Land Institute; American Planning
Association; ICSC; Downtown Seattle
Association; Greater Seattle Chamber of
Commerce.
Career: Has practiced for over 20 years
in real estate and land use law in the
Pacific Northwest. Formerly a Partner at
Heller Ehrman White & McAuliffe and
has been General Counsel of the Downtown Seattle Association since 1989.
Recent engagements include downtown
high-rises in Seattle and Bellevue, hospital and medical office development,
urban mixed-use projects, adaptive
redevelopment of historic structures,
and major retail developments throughout the state of Washington.
Personal: JD, Harvard Law School,
1982; AB, Harvard College, 1978.

MCDONALD, David
Preston Gates & Ellis LLP, Seattle
206 623 7580
Recommended in Litigation

MCLEAN, Dennis E
Davis Wright Tremaine LLP, Seattle
206 628 7723
dennismclean@dwt.com
Recommended in Real Estate
Practice Areas: Partner, commercial
real estate. Representative experience
includes commercial property acquisitions, sales and exchanges; commercial
leasing; development and joint ventures;
financing; real estate counseling for
medical centers, research laboratory
centers, and aircraft facilities; restaurant
acquisitions, leasing and franchise transactions. Representative clients include
Hines Interests Limited Partnership,
Bank of America, Children's Hospital,
Seattle Biomedical Research Institute,
and Apple American Group.
Prof. Memberships: Member, Washington State and American Bar Associations.
Career: Joined firm, 1980. Became Partner, 1986. Named 'Super Lawyer', Washington Law & Politics, 2001-04.
Personal: JD, University of California -
Hastings, 1980. BA, University of Cali-
fornia - Berkeley, 1976.

MCSHEA, David
Perkins Coie LLP, Seattle
206 583 8888
Recommended in Corporate/M&A

MEIKLEJOHN, Paul
Dorsey & Whitney LLP, Seattle
206 903 8800
Recommended in Intellectual Property

MILLER, Craig
Davis Wright Tremaine LLP, Seattle
206 628 7724
craigmiller@dwt.com
Recommended in Litigation
Practice Areas: Partner, litigation and
bankruptcy. Representative experience
includes state and federal court trials,
mediations and arbitrations; bankruptcy and non-bankruptcy litigation concerning commercial loans; complex real
and personal property lien issues; major
arbitration before International Chamber of Commerce arbitration panel,
Paris, France. Representative clients
include Archon Group, Bank of America, Banner Bank, GE Commerical
Finance, and Westward Seafoods.
Prof. Memberships: Member, Washington and California State Bar Associations.
Career: Joined firm, 1980. Became Partner, 1985.
Personal: JD, University of Southern
California, 1976. Editor in chief, Southern California Law Review. BA, History
(with honors), Grinnell College, 1973.

MOONEY, Douglas
Preston Gates & Ellis LLP, Seattle
206 623 7580
Recommended in Employment

MORGAN, Kevan
Christensen O'Connor Johnson
Kindness, PLLC, Seattle 206 682 8100
Recommended in Intellectual Property

MORGAN, Michael
Lane Powell PC, Seattle
206 223 7013
morganm@lanepowell.com
Recommended in Corporate/M&A
Practice Areas: Mergers and acquisitions, securities, emerging growth companies, and corporate governance.
Prof. Memberships: ABA; Washington
State Bar Association.
Career: Partner since 1980. Firm's Executive Committee.
Publications: Has lectured and written
extensively on corporate and securities
law issues.
Personal: Loyola University at Los
Angeles (JD, cum laude, 1974); University of California at Berkeley (AB, with
distinction, 1971). He serves on the
board of The Kline Galland Center,
which provides senior housing and
related services.

NELSON, Marshall J
Davis Wright Tremaine LLP, Seattle
206 628 7733
marshallnelson@dwt.com
Recommended in Intellectual Property
Practice Areas: Partner, intellectual
property, First Amendment/media law.
More than 30 years representing national and regional media and other businesses in copyright, trademark, advertising, and media law. Extensive experience
with electronic publishing and related
licensing. Representative clients include

Seattle Times, Seattle Art Museum, Belo Corporation, Kaiser Permanente, Far-Works Inc., copyright management for works of Gary Larson.
Prof. Memberships: Past Chair, IP Section, Washington State Bar. American Bar Association IP Section, ABA Forum Committee on Communications Law.
Career: Joined firm, 1972. Became Partner, 1978.
Personal: JD, Northwestern University, 1972. BA, Northwestern University, 1965.

NEUGEBAUER, Robert
Preston Gates & Ellis LLP, Seattle
206 623 7580
Recommended in Real Estate

O'CONNELL, Timothy
Stoel Rives LLP, Seattle
206 624 0900
Recommended in Employment

OSBORNE, Scott
Preston Gates & Ellis LLP, Seattle
206 623 7580
Recommended in Real Estate

OSENBAUGH, Kim
Preston Gates & Ellis LLP, Seattle
206 623 7580
Recommended in Bankruptcy

PALUMBO, Ralph
Summit Law Group, PLLC, Seattle
206 676 7000
Recommended in Environment, Litigation

PEPPLE, Daniel
Pepple Johnson Cantu & Schmidt, PLLC, Seattle 206 625 1711
Recommended in Real Estate

PERISHO, Russell
Perkins Coie LLP, Seattle
206 583 8888
Recommended in Employment

POWERS, Ragan
Davis Wright Tremaine LLP, Seattle
206 628 7752
raganpowers@dwt.com
Recommended in Bankruptcy
Practice Areas: Partner, credit recovery and bankruptcy law. Representative experience includes commercial loan workouts and restructuring, representation of debtors and creditors in all aspects of commercial Chapter 7 and 11 proceedings. Representative industry experience includes aerospace, agriculture, construction, environmental remediation, retail, maritime and commercial real estate.
Prof. Memberships: Member, American Bankruptcy Institute. Member, American Bar Association. Member, Washington State Bar Association Creditor-Debtor Section.
Career: Joined firm, 1997; became Partner, 2000. Helsell Fetterman, 1981-97. Listed as 'Super Lawyer', Washington State & Politics 2001-02, 2004.
Personal: JD, University of Washington,

1981. BA (highest honors), University of California - Davis, 1978.

PUCKETT, Laura Treadgold
DLA Piper Rudnick Gray Cary US LLP, Seattle 206 839 4822
laura.puckett@dlapiper.com
Recommended in Corporate/M&A
Practice Areas: Corporate and securities; emerging growth and venture capital; mergers and acquisitions.
Career: She has extensive experience in corporate matters, venture capital financings, and mergers and acquisitions. She works with companies in diverse industries with a focus on software, internet, wireless and medical device companies.
Personal: JD, University of Washington; AB, Stanford University.

RAKAY NELSON, Jane
Lane Powell PC, Seattle
206 223 6249
nelsonj@lanepowell.com
Recommended in Real Estate
Practice Areas: Real estate law. As co-Chair of the firm's Real Estate and Land Use Group, she has handled numerous financing, lease and acquisition transactions.
Prof. Memberships: American Land Title Association Lender's Counsel (member since 1997); Executive Committee of the Real Property, Probate and Trust Section, Washington State Bar Association (member, 1997-99); Washington State Bar Association Continuing Legal Education Committee (member, 1998-99); International Conference of Shopping Centers (member).
Career: Partner since 1993.
Publications: Has lectured and written extensively on real estate transaction matters.
Personal: Duquesne University School of Law (JD, 1985); Ohio State University (BS, 1975; MA, 1980). She currently is the Co-Chair of the Fred Hutchinson Business Alliance Executive Industry Board and is a member of the Downtown Seattle Association Board of Trustees and Rotary. She also has served as a member and president of the local Boys and Girls Club.

REILLY, D Michael
Lane Powell PC, Seattle
206 223 7051
reillym@lanepowell.com
Recommended in Employment
Practice Areas: Partner and Co-Chair of firm's Employment/Labor Department. Focuses his active trial practice on employment litigation and advice, specializing in wrongful discharge, wage hour, ERISA, workplace violence, as well as race, sex, religion, whistleblower/retaliation and disability claims. Also frequently litigates trade secrets and unfair competition claims.
Prof. Memberships: ABA; Washington State Bar Association; National Employment Law Institute (NELI); Society for

Human Resource Management (SHRM); National Retail Federation.
Career: Joined firm in 1986; Partner since 1992. Served appellate court judicial clerkship before joining Lane Powell.
Publications: 'The ADEA and the U.S. Supreme Court,' Employee Litigation Reporter (February 2005); 'ERISA Fiduciary Claims: Planning, Protecting and Preparing for Class Actions,' Employee Relations Law Journal (2005); 'Handling Employment Litigation in Washington' (1998, 2001). Has spoken at numerous local and national seminars on employment law topics.
Personal: Catholic University of America, Washington, DC (JD, 1984); Gonzaga University, Spokane WA (BBA, cum laude, 1981). He is a member of the Gonzaga University Board of Regents and is a past member of the Board of Directors of the American Red Cross.

REISS, Michael
Davis Wright Tremaine LLP, Seattle
206 628 7750
mikereiss@dwt.com
Recommended in Employment
Practice Areas: Partner, employment/labor litigation. Experience includes litigating cases on behalf of large/small employers throughout the West Coast. Lead counsel in state/nationwide race discrimination, sex discrimination and wage/hour class actions. Also served as court-appointed Special Master in nationwide Title VII race discrimination class action.
Prof. Memberships: Washington and California State Bars. American Employment Law Council; National Employment Law Institute.
Career: Joined as Partner, 1986. Program Director, National Institute for Trial Advocacy, 1975-present. Law Professor, University of Southern California Law Center, 1968-79.
Publications: Principal Contributor, Lindemann & Grossman, 'Employment Discrimination Law'.
Personal: JD, Yale, 1968. BA (high honors), Harvard, 1965.

RHEAUME, Warren
Heller Ehrman White & McAuliffe LLP, Seattle 206 447 0900
Recommended in Intellectual Property

RIEDINGER, Jerry
Perkins Coie LLP, Seattle
206 583 8888
Recommended in Intellectual Property

ROCKWELL, David
Stoel Rives LLP, Seattle
206 624 0900
Recommended in Real Estate

RUBIN, Jerome
Stoel Rives LLP, Seattle
206 624 0900
Recommended in Employment

RUMMAGE, Stephen M
Davis Wright Tremaine LLP, Seattle
206 628 7755
steverummage@dwt.com
Recommended in Litigation
Practice Areas: Steve's experience in complex commercial litigation includes defense of securities, contract and unfair competition cases. He has successfully defended over a dozen consumer class actions, representing national financial services clients. Additionally, he has an active appellate practice, having argued significant cases to Washington Supreme Court addressing novel State Securities Act-related issues, environmental/land use regulation, labor law, administrative law, and commercial contracts.
Prof. Memberships: Member, Washington State and American Bar Associations.
Career: Joined firm, 1980. Became Partner, 1986. Named 'Super Lawyer', Washington Law & Politics, 1999-2004.
Personal: JD, University of California - Berkeley, 1980. BA (with distinction), Stanford, 1977.

RUNSTAD, Judith
Foster Pepper & Shefelman PLLC, Seattle 206 447 4400
Recommended in Real Estate

SCHNEIDER, Mark
Perkins Coie LLP, Seattle
206 583 8888
Recommended in Environment

SCHNEIDER Jr, Harry
Perkins Coie LLP, Seattle
206 583 8888
Recommended in Litigation

SCHULTHEIS, Patrick J
Wilson Sonsini Goodrich & Rosati, Seattle 425 576 5800
pschultheis@wsgr.com
Recommended in Corporate/M&A
Practice Areas: Specializes in the corporate representation of technology, life science and other growth companies (start-ups to large public companies) in the Pacific Northwest. Regularly represents underwriters and venture capital investors. Has extensive transactional experience in public offerings, mergers and acquisitions and private financings.
Prof. Memberships: Admitted to practice in Washington and California, USDC for the Northern District of California and US Court of Appeals for the Ninth Circuit. Member, ABA (Business Law Section).
Career: Managing Partner, Kirkland office. Joined WSGR, 1989; became Partner, 1997.
Personal: JD, 1989, University of Chicago; AB, 1986 (with distinction, departmental honors), Stanford University.

SCHWAB, Evan
Dorsey & Whitney LLP, Seattle
206 903 8800
Recommended in Litigation

SEBRIS, Robert
Sebris Busto James, Bellevue
425 454 4233
Recommended in Employment

SHERMAN, Craig E
Wilson Sonsini Goodrich & Rosati,
Seattle 206 833 2500
csherman@wsgr.com
Recommended in Corporate/M&A
Practice Areas: Focuses on corporate
and securities laws, representing companies, venture capital firms and invest-
ments banks in private placements and
public offerings. Also has extensive
experience in mergers and acquisitions,
technology licensing, and domestic and
international joint ventures.
Career: Joined WSGR as Partner, 2002.
Managing director of Venture Law
Group's Kirkland office from May 2000
- August 2002.
Personal: JD, 1989, Harvard Law School
(cum laude). Articles editor, Harvard
Human Rights Yearbook, 1988-89. AB
(with honors), and MA from Stanford
University, 1985.

SIEFERT, Richard
Merchant & Gould PC, Seattle
206 342 6200
*Recommended in Intellectual
Property, Litigation*

SKINNER, Shannon
Preston Gates & Ellis LLP, Seattle
206 623 7580
Recommended in Real Estate

SQUIRES III, William
Summit Law Group, PLLC, Seattle
206 676 7000
Recommended in Litigation

SROUFE, Evelyn
Perkins Coie LLP, Seattle
206 583 8888
Recommended in Corporate/M&A

STEEL, John M
DLA Piper Rudnick Gray Cary US LLP,
Seattle 206 839 4833
john.steel@dlapiper.com
Recommended in Corporate/M&A
Practice Areas: Corporate and securities; emerging growth and venture capital; mergers and acquisitions; public
company and corporate governance.
Career: He concentrates in structuring
and negotiating a wide range of financing transactions, acquistions, and strategic alliances. He has managed hundreds
of private equity financings for issuers
and investors and served as lead counsel
on approximately 30 public offerings.
He is experienced in a broad variety of
commercial transactions including
commercial finance, licensing, and distribution arrangements.
Personal: JD, University of Washington;
BA, Stanford University.

STROTHER, Jack
Graham & Dunn PC, Seattle
206 624 8300
Recommended in Corporate/M&A

SULKIN, Robert
McNaul Ebel Nawrot Helgren & Vance
PLLC, Seattle
206 467 1816
Recommended in Litigation

TANNER, Gordon
Stoel Rives LLP, Seattle
206 624 0900
Recommended in Real Estate

THOMAS, Cynthia
Real Property Law Group PLLC, Seattle
206 625 1717
Recommended in Real Estate

THORP, Michael
Heller Ehrman White & McAuliffe LLP,
Seattle 206 447 0900
Recommended in Environment

TUNE, James
Stoel Rives LLP, Seattle
206 624 0900
Recommended in Corporate/M&A

WEINSTEIN, Joseph D
Davis Wright Tremaine LLP, Seattle
206 628 7791
joeweinstein@dwt.com
Recommended in Corporate/M&A
Practice Areas: Partner, business transactions, mergers/acquisitions. Experience includes representing owners in the
sale of National Basketball Association
franchise; representing Tyson Foods in
multi-state sale of seafood division; representing Japanese lease companies in
structure sale of 25 Boeing aircraft; handling the purchase and finance of a
major fish processing company.
Prof. Memberships: Maritime Law
Association of the US.
Career: Joined firm, 1986; became Partner, 1991. Admitted to Washington State
Bar, 1981.
Publications: Frequent speaker on topics
concerning lawyer ethics, client representation in international transactions and
investment in the maritime industry.
Personal: JD, University of Washington,
1981. BA, Unversity of Washington,
1978.

WHITFORD, Joseph P
Davis Wright Tremaine LLP, Seattle
206 628 7794
josephwhitford@dwt.com
Recommended in Corporate/M&A
Practice Areas: Partner, business and
corporate finance. Representative experience includes capital formation and
general counsel activities, venture capital
and strategic investment transactions,
mergers and acquisitions, public securi-
ties practice, board of directors and
executive officer counseling, domestic
and international joint ventures, and
equity compensation planning.
Prof. Memberships: Member, New
York, Washington State, and American
Bar Associations.
Career: Joined firm as Partner, 2002.
Named 'Super Lawyer', Washington Law
& Politics, 2003-04. Previously worked
at Division of Corporation Finance,
Securities and Exchange Commission,
Washington DC.
Personal: JD, Syracuse University, 1975.
LLM, George Washington University,
1978. BA, Union College, 1972.

WILLIAMS, Nancy
Perkins Coie LLP, Seattle
206 583 8888
Recommended in Employment

WINTERBAUER, Steven
Winterbauer & Diamond, P.L.L.C.,
Seattle 206 676 8440
Recommended in Employment

YENTZER, Steven
Perkins Coie LLP, Seattle
206 583 8888
Recommended in Corporate/M&A

DAVIS WRIGHT TREMAINE LLP

THE FIRM

Firmwide Managing Partner: Richard D Ellingsen
Chairman: Mark A Hutcheson
Number of partners: 253
Number of other lawyers: 157

FIRM OVERVIEW: Davis Wright Tremaine LLP is one of the nation's largest full service law firms with over 400 attorneys in eight offices across the US and one office in Shanghai, China.

MAIN AREAS OF PRACTICE:

Business Transactions/Tax/Corporate Finance/Commercial Transactions: DWT has a significant general corporate and transactional practice representing every type of client. The firm's experience in M&A and commercial finance is extensive. The robust Financial Institutions Industry Practice represents banks and financial institutions in the US and foreign financial institutions doing business in the US.

Communications, Media Law & First Amendment: A leader in media and First Amendment law for decades, clients include many of the nation's most recognized print and online publishers, producers of news and entertainment programs, and national publishers and broadcasters. Telecommunications clients include international telephony carriers and online networks.

Employment/Employee Benefits/Immigration: The firm provides all services: human resources counseling, regulatory advice, labor/management relations, employee benefits plans, and complex litigation. Many immigration lawyers are bilingual.

Healthcare: The firm has an unparalleled depth and breadth of expertise in virtually every aspect of healthcare law. The firm was a pioneer in advising on the impact of technology on the healthcare industry.

Intellectual Property: DWT's fastest growing practice, the Intellectual Property Group offers the full range of services - from traditional copyright, trademark, trade secret and patent issues to the developing law of the internet and computers, with licensing and litigation experience in all areas.

Litigation: Over 70 lawyers concentrate their practices in litigation, some focusing almost exclusively in media, antitrust, securities, employment and environmental litigation. The practice embraces virtually every subject matter.

Energy: The firm assists energy producers and suppliers, project developers, energy consumers and energy industry investors to best understand markets and structures, and to take advantage of opportunities arising from the complex energy regulatory landscape.

Real Property/Environmental & Natural Resources: The Real Property Group coordinates with the Environmental and Natural Resources Law and Energy Industry Group to address the complexities of purchasing, owning, developing and using real estate.

CLIENTS: adidas America, Inc., Bank of America, N.A., The Boeing Company, British Petroleum, Calpine Corp., Discovery Communications, Equilon Enterprises LLC, GE Capital Services, Holland-America Lines, Intel Corporation, Microsoft Corp., OHSU, SesameWorkshop, Shell Oil Company, Sony Pictures Entertainment, Starbucks Coffee Co., and Virginia Mason Medical Center.

INTERNATIONAL WORK: The firm provides services to international businesses, particularly in the Pacific Rim and Canada. In 1994, DWT became the first US law firm allowed to open an office in Shanghai. The International Group represents clients establishing subsidiaries, forming international joint ventures and investing in the US and in international financing, development/ financing for energy infrastructure, international trade, mar-

itime law, international tax, technology transfers, immigration, transnational litigation, and other related matters. The firm is a member of Lex Mundi, the world's leading association of law firms in 155 countries, states and provinces, and of the Pacific Rim Advisory Council, an alliance of 30 law firms that serve major international companies across the Pacific Rim.

HEAD OFFICE

WASHINGTON
1501 Fourth Avenue, Suite 2600, **Seattle**, WA 98101-1688
Tel: 206 622 3150 **Fax:** 206 628 7699
Website: www.dwt.com **Email:** info@dwt.com

OTHER OFFICES

ALASKA
701 West Eighth Avenue, Suite 800, **Anchorage**, AK 99501-3468
Tel: 907 257 5300 **Fax:** 907 257 5399

CALIFORNIA
865 South Figueroa Street, Suite 2400, **Los Angeles**, CA 90017-2566
Tel: 213 633 6800 **Fax:** 213 633 6899

One Embarcadero Center, Suite 600, **San Francisco**, CA 94111-3611
Tel: 415 276 6500 **Fax:** 415 276 6599

DISTRICT OF COLUMBIA
1500 K Street NW, Suite 450, **Washington,** DC 20005-1272
Tel: 202 508 6600 **Fax:** 202 508 6699

NEW YORK
1633 Broadway, **New York**, NY 10019-6708
Tel: 212 489 8230 **Fax:** 212 489 8340

OREGON
1300 SW Fifth Avenue, Suite 2300, **Portland**, OR 97201-5630
Tel: 503 241 2300 **Fax:** 503 778 5299

WASHINGTON
777 108th Avenue NE, Suite 2300, **Bellevue**, WA 98004-5149
Tel: 425 646 6100 **Fax:** 425 646 6199

INTERNATIONAL OFFICES

The firm aso has an office in Shanghai, China.

CONTACTS

Business Tax	Martin Morfeld
Business Transactions/Corporate Finance	Greg Adams
	Keith Baldwin, Dave Baca
China Practice	Al Clark, Norm Page
Communications/Media	Victor Kovner, Dan Waggoner
Credit Recovery & Bankruptcy	Ragan Powers
Employee Benefits	Anne Northrup, Jim Ambrose
Employment/Labor Law	Mary Drobka
Energy	Steve Greenwald
Environmental Law & Natural Resources	Rick Glick
	Lynn Manolopoulos
Finance & Commercial Transactions	Norm Page, Bill Miller
Health Law	Bob Homchick
Immigration	Rich Rawson
Intellectual Property	Bruce Kaser, Allie Nicholson, Stuart Dunwoody
International	Rich Rawson
Life Sciences	Gerry Hinkley, Jane Potter
Litigation	Ladd Leavens, John McGrory
Real Property	Tom Goeltz
Tax Exempt Organizations	Laverne Woods
Telecommunications	Mark Trinchero
Trusts & Estates	Jim Flaggert

LANE POWELL PC

THE FIRM

President: Mark Rossi
Vice-President: Jack Walsh
Number of partners in US: 110
Number of other lawyers in US: 65

FIRM OVERVIEW: Lane Powell PC, *Your Pacific Northwest Law Firm®*, offers a broad range of legal services in business, employment and litigation. Founded more than 125 years ago, the firm provides insightful counsel to emerging and established businesses and individuals. Lane Powell has more than 170 attorneys located throughout Washington, Oregon, Alaska and London, England. The firm is a member of the US Law Firm Group and the World Law Group.

MAIN AREAS OF PRACTICE:

Business: Lane Powell provides a full range of services to emerging and established businesses and individuals on a regional, national and international level. The business services the firm provides include: administrative law, banking and financial services, construction, corporate finance, securities, mergers and acquisitions, initial public offerings, emerging companies and venture investment, environmental, franchise and dealership, healthcare, intellectual property and internet, international business and investment, international tax, natural resources and forest products, real estate, retail distribution and trade regulation, tax and estate planning, and transportation and utilities.

Labor & Employment: Lane Powell represents management in the entire range of labor and employment matters and issues. It serves clients in virtually every industry in both the private and public sectors. Lane Powell advises clients with matters relating to labor relations, employment discrimination, wrongful discharge, civil rights, employee benefits (ERISA, COBRA, etc.), immigration in state and federal courts, and before the NLRB, OFCCP, EEOC and all other state and federal agencies involved in employment matters. The firm frequently arbitrates or represents clients in employment-related jury trials. Lane Powell's attorneys have designed ERISA plans for some of America's best known companies, and many smaller companies. The firm regularly advises plan administrators and plan fiduciaries on administrative compliance with state and federal law. With many published and unpublished court opinions, Lane Powell is one of the leading firms representing clients in litigated ERISA matters involving breach of fiduciary duty, plan benefit, and many other related claims.

Litigation: The firm represents clients in all aspects of commercial litigation, including trials and appeals in all state and federal courts; federal, state and self-regulatory administrative proceedings; and arbitrations and mediations under alternative dispute resolution procedures. The broad range of litigation matters that Lane Powell handles includes complex litigation, securities, commercial cases, creditor-debtor and bankruptcy, labor and employment, antitrust, healthcare, franchise/dealership law, software licensing, intellectual property and internet.

CLIENTS: American International Companies; Aramark Corporation; AT&T Corporation; Callison Architecture, Inc.; ChevronTexaco Corp.; Coffman Engineers, Inc.; Con-Agra Inc.; CNF, Inc.; Corbis Corporation; Cutter & Buck, Inc.; Eagle River; ERA Aviation, Inc.; Ethicspoint; Exxon Mobil Corporation; Fios, Inc.; Fred Hutchinson Cancer Research Center; Frito-Lay, Inc.; General Electric Capital Corporation; Georgia-Pacific Corporation; Harry's Fresh Foods; Home Depot U.S.A., Inc.; Honda North America, Inc.; IBP, Inc.; ImageX, Inc.; Java Trading Company; Les Schwab Tire Centers; Monsanto Company; The Mony Group, Inc.; Morgan Stanley Dean Witter & Co.; Mowat Construction Company; Nike, Inc.; Nordstrom, Inc.; Norm Thompson Outfitters, Inc.; Northwest Biotherapeutics, Inc.; Novartis Consumer Health; Oregon Public Employees Retirement

HEAD OFFICE

WASHINGTON
1420 Fifth Avenue, Suite 4100, **Seattle,** WA 98101-2338
Tel: 206 223 7000   **Fax:** 206 223 7107
Email: info@lanepowell.com
Website: www.lanepowell.com

BRANCH OFFICES

ALASKA
301 West Northern Lights Boulevard, Suite 301, **Anchorage,** AK 99503-2648
Tel: 907 277 9511   **Fax:** 907 276 2631

OREGON
601 SW Second Avenue, Suite 2100, **Portland,** OR 97204-3158
Tel: 503 778 2100   **Fax:** 503 778 2200

WASHINGTON
111 Market Street, Suite 360, **Olympia,** WA 98501
Tel: 360 764 6001   **Fax:** 360 754 1605

INTERNATIONAL OFFICES

The firm also has an office in London, UK

CONTACTS

BUSINESS DEPARTMENT
Corporate, Finance & M&A ....Thomas Grohman
....Mike Morgan, Jeffrey Wolfstone
Employee Benefits & Executive Compensation ....Jack Walsh
Estate Planning ....Chuck Riley
Healthcare & Regulatory ....Jeffrey Gingold
Intellectual Property ....Anne Glazer
Real Estate ....Jane Nelson, Bryan Powell
Tax..Gary Tober

EMPLOYMENT DEPARTMENT
Labor & Employment ....Gail Mautner, Ralph Pond, Michael Reilly

LITIGATION DEPARTMENT
Banking/Financial Services/Creditor Rights/Collections..Charles Ekberg
Class Actions/Securities Litigation/Appellate ....Rudy Englund
Commercial Disputes/Complex Litigation...................Randall Beighle
Insurance Litigation/Maritime/London ....Barry Mesher
Product Liability/Catastrophic Injury..............................Bruce Hamlin
Real Estate/Land Use/Condemnation/
Environmental/Construction & Design ....Grant Degginger

System; Oremet-Wah Chang; Premera Blue Cross; Quinton Inc.; Shell Oil; Simpson Investment Company; Sound Transit; T-Mobile; The Fishing Company of Alaska; Tokai Carbon Co., Ltd.; TransAlta Corporation; Triad Hospitals, Inc.; Tri-County Metropolitan Transportation District of Oregon (TriMet); Underwriters at Lloyd's; Union Pacific Railroad Corp.; Verisign, Inc.; Wal-Mart Stores, Inc.; Wells Fargo & Company; Weyerhaeuser Company; White Consolidated Industries, Inc.

INTERNATIONAL WORK: Lane Powell's international practice includes business, insurance, maritime, aviation, and international trade. Some areas in which the firm has provided legal representation include: independent sales representative agreements; joint ventures; strategic alliances; licensing and other forms of proprietary protection; distribution arrangements; establishment, financing, and operation of foreign branches and subsidiaries; international business negotiations; structuring, acquisition and disposition of real estate investments; handling of international disputes; trade regulation; compliance with US securities and export laws; immigration matters; trademark, copyright and other intellectual property matters; and all aspects of international and domestic tax law matters.

CONTENTS: Corporate/M&A p.1798; Employment p.1800; Litigation p.1802; Real Estate p.1805; Individuals' Profiles p.1807. Firms' Profiles p.1811.

How lawyers are ranked

The opinions we gather from clients — mainly from in-house lawyers but also from other purchasers of legal services — are balanced by opinions from colleagues and competitors. Together, they provide two different perspectives — an all-round view — and biased viewpoints cancel each other out.

CORPORATE/M&A

West Virginia
Leading firms (Corporate/M&A)

1. BOWLES RICE MCDAVID GRAFF *Charleston*
   JACKSON KELLY PLLC *Charleston*
2. STEPTOE & JOHNSON PLLC *Clarksburg*
3. GOODWIN & GOODWIN, LLP *Charleston*
   HUDDLESTON BOLEN LLP *Huntington*
   KAY CASTO & CHANEY PLLC *Charleston*
   ROBINSON & MCELWEE PLLC *Charleston*
   SPILMAN THOMAS & BATTLE, PLLC *Charleston*

Leading individuals (Corporate/M&A)

1. ALBERT Michael *Jackson Kelly, Charleston*
   CAPPELLANTI Ellen *Jackson Kelly, Charleston*
   HEYWOOD Thomas *Bowles Rice, Charleston*
   SOUTHWORTH II Louis *Jackson Kelly, Charleston*
2. COLEMAN Leonard *Goodwin & Goodwin, Charleston*
   DEEM Patrick *Steptoe & Johnson, Clarksburg*
   GRAFF F Thomas *Bowles Rice, Charleston*
   KING Evans *Steptoe & Johnson, Clarksburg*
   MURRAY Thomas *Huddleston Bolen, Huntington*
3. BASILE Michael *Spilman Thomas, Charleston*
   FERRETTI David *Spilman Thomas, Charleston*
   HIGGINS David *Robinson & McElwee, Charleston*
   LORD Elizabeth *Jackson Kelly, Charleston*
   STUMP John *Steptoe & Johnson, Charleston*

Up-and-coming individuals

   KONRAD Daniel *Huddleston Bolen, Huntington*

Leading individuals (Corporate/M&A: Tax)

1. LORENSEN Charles *George & Lorensen, Charleston*
   SOUTHWORTH II Louis *Jackson Kelly, Charleston*
2. CARYL Michael *Bowles Rice, Charleston*
   KAY Craig *Kay Casto, Charleston*
   TWEEL Robert *Jackson Kelly, Charleston*

Leading individuals
(Corporate/M&A: Banking & Finance)

1. BOOKER William *Kay Casto, Charleston*
   MURPHY Sandra *Bowles Rice, Charleston*
2. DUNBAR Charles *Jackson Kelly, Charleston*
   GARDILL James *Phillips Gardill, Wheeling*

Firms and individuals are listed alphabetically in each band.

Band 1

Bowles Rice McDavid Graff & Love LLP

The Firm: One of the largest firms in West Virginia, with six offices established across the region and a seventh recently opened in Richmond, "*its greatest strength is in business representation.*" Lauded by clients and peers alike for its finance and banking practice, it represents the West Virginia Bankers' Association and a significant number of financial entities throughout the state. It has a sterling reputation in the area of economic development (public-private initiatives, new financing opportunities), working closely with state regulatory agencies. Extensive civic and administrative ties ensure it is the first port of call for many clients when it comes to governmental issues. Additionally, it enjoys close relationships with coal, oil and gas sector entities. Significant mineral industry acquisitions have punctuated the workload over the past 12 months.

The Lawyers: A "*well-recognized figure statewide,*" market sources praised politically-connected **Thomas Heywood** for being "*a pleasure to deal with and efficient.*" As well as his traditional lobbying practice, corporate finance and regulatory healthcare work, his public-private civic initiatives are indicative of his "*people-oriented, outreach approach*" to the business community. This was exemplified by his recent involvement in the improvement of Charleston waterfront. New clients for Heywood include West Virginia Physicians Mutual Insurance – a product of the recent medical malpractice reform legislation in which he played a pivotal role. **Thomas Graff**, referred to as "*the guts of the firm*" by those in the know, combines his role as managing partner with his business practice to attract many high-profile clients. A "*consummate, all-round business lawyer*" according to one peer, interviewees appreciated his thorough knowledge of state regulatory agencies, particularly in the energy market. "*Assertive, open and dependable*" banking and securities law specialist **Sandra Murphy** is heavily involved in the legislative agenda of the banking industry. Many of the state's financial institutions acknowledge her as their primary resource when it comes to compliance issues. In the past year she worked on a number of major acquisitions for United Bankshares. With a "*tremendous wealth of experience,*" former state tax commissioner **Michael Caryl** is "*trusted counsel*" for market leaders when it comes to advice on transactions and deal structures.

The Clients: Caterpillar; United Bankshares; West Virginia Physicians Mutual Insurance; West Virginia Bankers' Association; Bright Enterprises; Acordia; McJunkin; West Virginia Media Holdings and Summit Community Bank.

Jackson Kelly PLLC
See firm details p.1815

The Firm: The largest, oldest firm in West Virginia, its attorneys are "*some of the best legal minds in the business,*" according to observers. Encompassing a wide array of talents in a variety of disciplines, it comprises more than 30 attorneys and is acclaimed by industry sources for "*high-quality*" work in bankruptcy, mineral and tax matters. Its representation of West Virginia American Water Company has cemented the group's reputation in the public utility arena. Participation in the recent Cabela project in the north of the state is a prime example of the firm's commitment to large-scale, public service transaction deals. Earlier this year it acted as local counsel in JPMorgan's acquisition of Bank One.

The Lawyers: Commentators consider practice group leader **Michael Albert** (see p.1807) to be West Virginia's preeminent public service utility lawyer. In addition to handling work for two of the state's leading electric utilities, Allegheny Energy and the Potomac Edison Company, he acts as state counsel for Bluefield Gas and is currently involved in the acquisition of common

stock for buyers in the gas market. Clients expressed *"utmost respect"* for his judgment in regulatory matters. **Ellen Cappellanti**'s (see p.1808) diverse practice area buttresses her strong *"grasp of corporate niceties"* with her expertise in bankruptcy and real estate. Peers envy the *"unique perspective"* this grants her, while praising the way in which she works *"hard, effectively and aggressively"* on behalf of her clientele. During the past year she completed the sale of a large resort, conducted numerous loan refinancings and concluded two major condominium projects for one of her main clients, Snowshoe Mountain Ski Resort. **Louis Southworth** (see p.1810) is a *"deal maker"* who, in the words of one grateful client, *"manages to influence and bring parties together"* during difficult negotiations. His reputation as the *"top person in the state"* for federal tax transactions has grown to include recognition of his extensive lobbying and legislative work. Excelling in the federal securities area, **Elizabeth Osenton Lord** (see p.1809) has a strong corporate practice, overseeing SEC filings and reports for a panoply of financial organizations. Market sources drew attention to the quality of her work on behalf of state automobile associations, commending her *"good analytical abilities"* and *"approachability and availability."* **Robert Tweel** (see p.1810) specializes in federal tax, and works closely with partnerships on corporate transactional matters. Head of the banking and securities group, market sources agreed that **Charles Dunbar** (see p.1808) is *"one of the most knowledgeable in his field,"* impressing clients by *"knowing banking laws like the back of his hand."* He is renowned for working with new business enterprises. This year he was inordinately busy with the regulatory side of his practice, advising clients on the intricacies of Sarbanes-Oxley and USA Patriot Act compliance.
The Clients: West Virginia American Water Company; Cabela; Centra Bank; Allegheny Energy; Snowshoe Mountain Ski Resort; Potomac Edison; Bluefield Gas and Bright Enterprises.

Band 2

Steptoe & Johnson PLLC
The Firm: A sizable Clarksburg-based firm with an ever-increasing statewide presence and a corporate practice incorporating real estate, commercial and bankruptcy matters. Considered to be the *"dominant firm in northern West Virginia,"* the ten-partner M&A team focuses on asset stock purchasing agreements and property sales for high-profile clients like Dominion and CONSOL Energy. The firm is also strong in the area of public finance, having represented Huntington Bank and Bank One in major transactions throughout the year. In the past twelve months, the commercial group has also been

involved in the creation of a neurology faculty for West Virginia University and a retail shopping area development in Morgantown. Market sources praised the *"multidisciplinary approach"* used by the firm in its dealings with corporate clients.
The Lawyers: One of Dominion's principal lawyers, **Patrick Deem** also handles title insurance on behalf of Chicago Title, dividing his time between mineral, real estate and corporate transaction work. He oversaw the production of several gas properties and provided Wal-Mart with title advice relating to their construction of new stores in West Virginia. Chairman of the firm's business department, Deem received plenty of market endorsement: *"A well-rounded, well-schooled corporate attorney"* who is the *"leading business lawyer in the north."* According to sources in the energy industry, **Evans King** combines a *"high level of professionalism"* with a strong transactional background. *"Smart, and good on his feet,"* his work this year has encompassed acquisitions for Ogden Newspapers and loan closings for several of his firm's major financial clients, including Huntington and Bank One. **John Stump**, saluted as *"the best young bond lawyer in the state"* by one observer, excels in municipal financing and industrial development bonds. He is considered by market sources to be heir apparent at the firm in both these areas.
The Clients: Dominion Energy; CONSOL Energy; West Virginia University; Wal-Mart and Ogden Newspapers.

Band 3

Goodwin & Goodwin, LLP
See firm details p.1813
The Firm: As a midsized firm this well-respected operation covers a formidable amount of ground. The corporate and commercial group deals with public entity formation, asset purchases and dispositions, and secured transactions. Market observers acknowledge its *"terrific expertise"* in municipal bonds and public finance matters: *"the firm is involved in every bond issuance."*
The Lawyers: **Leonard Coleman** was billed *"as good a bond lawyer as any other in the state; there are very few attorneys at his level."* He has acted as bond counsel and special counsel for interstate public finance projects and participated in State Supreme Court of Appeals litigation relating to the validity of bond issues involving West Virginia's political bodies.
The Clients: The firm represents large and small businesses in all areas of corporate law.

Huddleston Bolen LLP
The Firm: Based in Huntington, this firm's commercial practice – consisting of six partners and one associate – has greatly expanded

beyond its origins in railroad representation. Its remit now includes general corporate governance, transactional work, M&A, and securities law compliance at both state and federal level; the group has spent a large part of the past year advising clients on the ramifications of the Sarbanes-Oxley Act. This focus has not limited the scope of the practice or affected the market appreciation it attracted. One client said, *"we have turned to it more than any other firm for oil and gas rights – that seems to be one of their niches."*
The Lawyers: **Thomas Murray** is one of two partners at the firm who specialize in sophisticated federal securities work. Onlookers are quick to praise him for his *"diligence"* and *"superior technical skills."* Murray has long-standing relationships with several of the state's major financial entities. Clients placed a premium on his regular communication and consultation during the drafting process, while peers granted him the epithet of *"leading business attorney in the west."* Much of his work this year has been concerned with Sarbanes-Oxley compliance. Concentrating his practice on securities, M&A and general commercial law, **Daniel Konrad** earned praise from clients for his *"familiarity with the complexities of property rights"* and *"knowledgeable approach"* to oil, gas and mineral acquisitions and divestitures.
The Clients: Bank One; Champion Industries; Premier Financial Bancorp and CSX.

Kay Casto & Chaney PLLC
The Firm: Originating in Charleston, the firm has another office in Morgantown. The midsized full-service business practice prides itself on its authority in the areas of business organization, M&A, and debt and equity financing and refinancing. Clients confirmed that the group boasts a *"great reputation"* for commercial and consumer debt collection. Peers admired its *"quality lawyers"* who assisted in the sale of several Pizza Hut units to a national company and the financing of Intrawest resorts in West Virginia and beyond.
The Lawyers: Regarded as *"one of the best banking lawyers in the state,"* by observers, much of cochairman **William Booker**'s time this year has been occupied with consumer litigation work in the residential mortgage lending market, and he is local counsel for several of the state's major financial entities. Clients were quick to praise his responsiveness, and the way in which *"he doesn't let personality get in the way of the job."* During the last twelve months he has also undertaken a significant amount of transactional and refinancing work. His rivals were no less effusive than his clients in their appreciation of a *"detail-oriented"* approach that ensures he *"doesn't miss a beat"* when it comes to commercial foreclosure matters. His partner, **Craig Kay**, is an *"outstanding"* tax lawyer who specializes in federal and state taxation, estate

planning and trust, and probate matters. While he principally represents businesses in IRS dispute resolutions, he has also branched out into inheritance law and business tax matters. Market sources compliment him on his *"practical approach"* to complex issues.

The Clients: Intrawest Corporation; Bank One; EquiFirst Corporation; First National Bank.

Robinson & McElwee PLLC

The Firm: In a year that has seen one partner, Brent Benjamin, appointed as a justice on the West Virginia Supreme Court, it has been business as usual for the corporate department. Although the firm has diminished in size in recent years, the group's six members and associate continue to focus on transactions, local tax matters, contracts, investments and divestitures. Earlier in the year they advised Southridge shopping center on lease and title issues.

The Lawyers: David Higgins has divided the past twelve months between his role in the formation of a new bank in West Virginia's Eastern Panhandle and advising clients involved in State Tax Department assessments. Although the latter has taken up considerable time, he continues to participate in the sphere of securities litigation as well as representing companies in matters relating to financing. Ancillary activities include lecturing on transactional matters. Peers deem him a *"bright and entertaining"* attorney who is highly knowledgeable about corporate developments.

The Clients: The team's client base includes Southridge Center and Columbia Natural Gas.

Spilman Thomas & Battle, PLLC

See firm details p.1816

The Firm: Historically considered a *"quality firm, with top people."* Observers noted that in spite of John Lukens's retirement, it has been *"very aggressive in the marketplace"*, displaying rapid growth in the M&A sector. The group now represents many of the state's major financial and industrial institutions in acquisitions. Recent client roster additions identify a *"particular strength"* in the group's synthesis of commercial expertise with governmental knowledge: *"if your matter falls within the arena of politics and state agencies, it is one of the best."*

The Lawyers: Appointed managing partner of the firm this year, **Michael Basile** (see p.1807) enjoys a high profile within West Virginia. He has overseen the group's expansion and advised clients on M&A, sales, purchases and dissolutions. His main areas of expertise are business, state tax, administrative and governmental matters. Commentators attributed Basile's continuing *"success at generating clients"* to his position *"at the forefront"* of the business community, combined with his capacity for *"strategic thinking."* Much of his work during the past 12 months has been transactional, with observers noting the large number of lending transactions he concluded on behalf of the state economic development authority. **David Ferretti** (see p.1808) currently chairs the M&A practice group and specializes in corporate law and pub-

lic finance. His practice encompasses tax-exempt governmental financings of public and private facilities. Commentators were impressed by his proactive approach to winning instructions. Ferretti was singled out as a *"well respected, great guy,"* particularly within the coal properties market.

The Clients: The group aids clients ranging from private entities to multimillion dollar corporations, including Bank One.

Other Notable Practitioners

"Top of a lot of lists when it comes to tax," **Charles Lorensen**'s name provokes the kind of praise that most attorneys dream about. Considered by peers to be one of the brightest individuals in the market, sources note that his primary focus is on state rather than federal tax issues. In this area, his *"brilliant legal mind"* is a force to be reckoned with. Phillips, Gardill, Kaiser & Altmeyer's managing partner **James Gardill** garners praise from all quarters of the market for his *"extremely sophisticated"* securities practice; peers include him in a *"small group"* of banking lawyers at the top of their game in the state, and praise his *"combination of thoroughness, care and technical skill."* Beyond the banking law for which he is renowned, he focuses on commercial, tax and estate planning matters. Reflecting his extensive regulatory experience, he counts Wesbanco Bank among his clients and serves as adjunct lecturer at the West Virginia University School of Law.

EMPLOYMENT

MAINLY DEFENDANT

West Virginia
Leading firms
(Employment: Mainly Defendant)

[1]	**STEPTOE & JOHNSON PLLC** *Clarksburg*
[2]	**BOWLES RICE MCDAVID GRAFF** *Charleston*
	DINSMORE & SHOHL LLP *Charleston*
	SPILMAN THOMAS & BATTLE, PLLC *Charleston*
[3]	**JACKSON KELLY PLLC** *Charleston*
	JENKINS FENSTERMAKER, PLLC *Huntington*
	ROBINSON & MCELWEE PLLC *Charleston*

Firms are listed alphabetically in each band.

Band 1

Steptoe & Johnson PLLC

The Firm: Offering *"expertise in a wide spectrum of areas"* including collective bargaining and union elections, this Clarksburg-based firm's labor and employment group comprises over 40 *"top-notch, creative and responsive"* attorneys supported by colleagues in other offices throughout the state. Clients were full of praise

for the group's employment litigation work and in particular for its members' exemplary knowledge of OSHA and FMLA issues. Representing the likes of Eastern Association Coal and American Electric, the team obtained multiple defense verdicts amid a recent surge in workers' compensation claims as well as in age discrimination cases.

The Lawyers: Bryan Cokeley runs the gamut of employment litigation work, bringing a *"mature, reasoned perspective and tremendous academic skills"* to cases ranging from sexual harassment to wrongful discharge. Enormously well-respected by competitors for being *"energetic, aggressive and knowledgeable,"* he has a reputation for *"slugging it out with the best of them."* Cokeley was responsible for much of the firm's success in representing American Electric. He also obtained a $2.3 million defense verdict for a client in an embezzlement case and continues to do a large amount of insurance defense work related to employment practices liability insurance. Beyond acting as chair of the labor depart-

ment, **David Morrison** focuses on employment litigation. *"A gentleman and great lawyer,"* he defended Waste Management in two lawsuits, and directed two charges of discrimination brought against Eastern Associated into arbitration. Clients value his legal advice for being *"well tempered with practical considerations"* while peers envy his success rate. Managing partner **Robert Steptoe** is respected throughout the state. Although his position has necessitated a cutback in his labor and employment practice, Steptoe's reputation is undiminished. One source praised him for *"good judgment in ticklish employment situations."* Clients regularly turn to him for advice on NLRB-related issues, an area in which he is considered to be a market authority. With a *"tremendous reputation for integrity,"* he is, at least for one admiring competitor, *"the lawyer everyone should aspire to be like."* As a former human resources director for a large corporation, **David Dick** impresses observers with his *"good judgment"* and *"down-to-earth familiarity with employment issues."* He divides his

West Virginia
Leading individuals
(Employment: Mainly Defendant)

[1] **BROWN Ricklin** *Bowles Rice*, Charleston
CARTER Mark *Dinsmore & Shohl*, Charleston
COKELEY Bryan *Steptoe & Johnson*, Charleston
MORRISON David *Steptoe & Johnson*, Clarksburg
ROLES Forrest *Dinsmore & Shohl*, Charleston
STEPTOE Robert *Steptoe & Johnson*, Clarksburg
WOODY Charles *Spilman Thomas*, Charleston

[2] **DAILEY Anna** *Dinsmore & Shohl*, Charleston
DICK David *Steptoe & Johnson*, Morgantown
HARTER Elizabeth *Bowles Rice*, Charleston
ISKRA Eric *Spilman Thomas*, Charleston
KRIEGER Thomas *Jenkins Fenstermaker*, Huntington
LEDBETTER Cheryl *Jackson Kelly*, Charleston
PAUL Niall *Spilman Thomas*, Charleston
PRICE Joseph *Robinson & McElwee*, Charleston
WOLFE Roger *Jackson Kelly*, Charleston

Up-and-coming individuals
BEAN Rodney *Steptoe & Johnson*, Morgantown
CARR Kevin *Spilman Thomas*, Charleston

Individuals are listed alphabetically in each band.

practice between union work and the OSHA litigation for which he is renowned. Clients express no hesitation in turning to Dick first for FMLA matters. In recent months he negotiated an important contract for Swanson Industries. Often before administrative agencies, Dick's advisory role is also preventive, extending to policy development and employee training. He is *"more than just an attorney – he is an educator,"* one source noted appreciatively. **Rodney Bean** leads the firm's appellate practice group in Morgantown, while sustaining a wide-ranging employment litigation practice. An expert on wage and hour issues, he earns industry acclaim for being *"a fine draftsman, who always keeps you up to date."*
The Clients: Eastern Associated Coal Corporation; Waste Management; Rite Aid; Pechiney Rolled Products; ISG Weirton Steel; American National Rubber; NiSource; Genesis HealthCare Corporation and Goodrich.

Band 2

Bowles Rice McDavid Graff & Love LLP

The Firm: This labor and employment practice consists of four attorneys in Charleston, supported by colleagues in Martinsburg and bolstered by a separate workers' compensation group. The team spends about a third of its time on traditional labor matters, while advising on a comprehensive range of employment issues. Applauded for its *"proactive approach to changes in government and public policy,"* it has represented a varied media, finance and industry client base in the State Supreme Court and before all significant West Virginia administra-

tive agencies. This year the group has successfully concluded several landmark compensation and discrimination cases. New clients include Allegheny Wood Products, one of the largest timber manufacturers in the eastern United States.
The Lawyers: Considered an expert in the sphere of labor law, **Ricklin Brown** *"sticks to his guns"* for his clients. Peers admire his *"wisdom and experience"* in negotiating collective bargaining agreements. Brown has provided human resources training for financial clientele and recently devoted time to cultivating links between West Virginia University and private industry in Morgantown. Further work highlights include successfully representing Verizon in a class unemployment claim. **Elizabeth Harter** divides her practice between traditional labor matters and employment litigation pertaining to disability and sexual harassment claims. She also engages in preventive work, writing employment handbooks and auditing companies. Competitors respect her *"nice blend of common sense and intellect"* and market sources acknowledge she has developed a formidable reputation in FMLA issues.
The Clients: Allegheny Wood Products; Verizon; West Virginia Media Holdings; Century Aluminium; United Bank; FMC; Petroleum Products; Community Bank of Parkersburg; Seneca Mental Health Council; Montgomery General Healthcare Systems and NGK Spark Plugs.

Dinsmore & Shohl LLP

See firm details p.1452
The Firm: Originating in Ohio, this huge firm's Charleston office has grown exponentially in recent years, with the addition of 14 attorneys to its labor and employment department since 2002. The team is a recognized authority in the area of union certification. Observers were unanimous in their praise of its arbitration work before the NLRB board. Other areas of expertise include ERISA work and advising on a variety of discrimination issues. The group's impact has not gone unnoticed by peers, who agree that this firm is *"heading upwards"* in the employment field and has become *"major competition"* in the West Virginia labor market.
The Lawyers: For **Mark Carter**, the past twelve months have been defined by work for new clients. His representation of Wal-Mart has seen the dismissal of six unfair labor practice charges, and he has acted on behalf of Right Aid and Coca-Cola before the NLRB board. His practice regularly takes him outside West Virginia and he has a national reputation in civil RICO matters. The author of several papers on the subject, he performs a *"big-picture advisory role"* in its application to union strikes that clients find indispensable. Market sources admire his *"talent for crafting an argument"* and peers praise his

ability to *"cut through big egos"* during negotiations. **Forrest Roles** is the *"shining star"* of the firm. Displaying an *"encyclopedic knowledge"* of traditional labor issues, clients value him for his *"aggressive, out-of-the-box thinking"* when it comes to union certification, collective bargaining and NLRA work. Rivals admire his *"intuitive sense of how to get to the bottom line of an issue."* He tried a case in Alaska, oversaw an election and concluded numerous NLRB-related matters throughout the region. Observers have great respect for the way in which **Anna Dailey** *"digs in and immerses herself in the issues"* surrounding labor law. Specializing in strikes, contract negotiations and unfair practices, she is the *"go-to"* attorney for union-related matters. A large proportion of her work this year involved advising union subsidiaries on how to ward off organization campaigns. Market sources deem her *"outstanding"* in this area.
The Clients: Wal-Mart Stores; Peabody Energy Corporation; Matanuska Electric Association; Foundation Coal Holdings; Coca-Cola Bottling; ResCare; Rite Aid.

Spilman Thomas & Battle, PLLC

See firm details p.1816
The Firm: This 20 lawyer-strong labor and employment practice works in cooperation with its workers' compensation group on large-scale class action litigation, as well as more traditional collective bargaining, arbitration and NLRB matters. Market sources speak admiringly of the *"great network"* the team has established outside West Virginia, a perception confirmed by its three-state representation of Kroger during recent union action. In the past 12 months the group handled an ERISA matter for Coventry Health Care, a strike for Weirton Medical Center and a discrimination case for DuPont. Clients praise its *"tough, insightful and fair"* attorneys. With a new office recently opened in Pittsburgh, its star shows no sign of diminishing.
The Lawyers: Chair of the litigation department **Charles Woody** (see p.1810) is praised by competitors for his ability to *"separate what is important from what is not and to get to the heart of the matter."* Counting several Fortune 500 businesses among his clients, he played an important role in strategy and planning during the Kroger strike. His *"great judgment"* derived from years of experience in the employment market is exemplified by Woody's pivotal involvement in Weirton Medical's recent collective bargaining negotiations. His practice also includes bad faith and products liability defense. In charge of the labor and employment group, **Niall Paul**'s (see p.1810) practice has witnessed a shift from counseling to litigation during the last couple of years. He tried an age case for Acordia, obtained a defense verdict for Juliana Coal and had a racial discrimination charge dismissed on behalf of DuPont. Peers praise Paul's

"*knowledgeable and thorough*" approach, while clients laud his "*dedication to success.*" **Kevin Carr** (see p.1808) focuses on labor and employment law as well as wage issues. Market sources identify him as a name to watch who clients turn to for union and arbitration matters. Extensively involved in the Kroger strike, he is currently working on a huge unfair practice case outside Pittsburgh. Carr frequently practices before the NLRB and other state and federal-level agencies. **Eric Iskra** (see p.1809) impresses with "*tact and diplomacy,*" particularly in negotiating difficult courses for clients. "*He has a good sense of balance to understand the legal and practical side,*" one client said. He handled a landmark ERISA case involving the preemptive effect of a wrongful death matter.

The Clients: Acordia; DuPont; Coventry Health Care and Juliana Coal Company.

Band 3

Jackson Kelly PLLC

See firm details p.1815

The Firm: Comprising eight attorneys, the firm's labor and employment group demonstrates expertise in a range of areas, from union and NLRB-related issues to equal employment opportunity discrimination. Spread across seven offices, the team advise management on the drafting of contracts, policies and handbooks. It has cultivated out-of-state connections that have raised its national profile and broadened its remit by taking on plaintiff cases for established clientele. Work highlights include obtaining summary judgments in a number of matters, including an age discrimination case on behalf of Massey Coal in a pro-union region of the state. It was also successful in negotiating the union contract that ended ABB Analytical's

labor union strike.

The Lawyers: Sexual harassment law is **Cheryl Ledbetter**'s (see p.1809) specialty, but she has firmly consolidated her position in the general sphere of employment discrimination, defending employers before the West Virginia Human Rights Commission and the EEOC. Known in industry circles as a "*great lawyer who gives good advice in difficult situations,*" peers remark on the depth of her knowledge and admire her "*poise and professionalism.*" "*Extremely smart and capable,*" **Roger Wolfe** (see p.1810) has a practice that covers the full range of traditional labor issues. He is the West Virginia representative for the Employment Law Alliance. Devoting a large percentage of his time to equal employment opportunity litigation, Wolfe obtained summary judgment for Arch Coal in a number of cases this year and prevailed in several arbitrations for West Virginia University Hospitals. In addition, he teaches labor and employment law. Peers accordingly praise his "*thoughtful and scholarly*" style.

The Clients: Massey Coal Company; ABB Analytical; Arch Coal and West Virginia University Hospitals.

Jenkins Fenstermaker, PLLC

The Firm: This 19-attorney multi-service firm is based in Huntington. The major focus is on traditional labor law. A partner specializing in workers' compensation supplements two full-time labor and employment lawyers. Competitors are "*bowled over*" by its regional dominance. The group's size is belied by its work this year on three large class certification cases.

The Lawyers: **Thomas Krieger** has a reputation as a "*well-rounded*" attorney within the labor arena. According to market onlookers, he is "*extremely good*" at union-related negotiation,

arbitration and mediation. On top of a bevy of filings dismissed before the NLRB, his work has encompassed the successful completion of contractual negotiations involving a bargaining unit of 1000 people on behalf of a major hospital. A multitude of grievance arbitrations contributed further to Krieger's workload.

The Clients: ACF Industries; Special Metals; Cabell Huntington Hospital and Steel of West Virginia.

Robinson & McElwee PLLC

The Firm: With offices in Charleston and Clarksburg, this midsized firm's labor and employment group is primarily based in West Virginia's capital. Six attorneys act for management before all state and federal agencies and have expertise in a broad range of issues, including unfair labor practices, arbitrations and union organizational campaigns. Clients were full of praise for the "*outstanding job*" the team does in these areas. In recent months, the group has begun to branch out into plaintiff representation.

The Lawyers: "*Knowledgeable in every area,*" **Joseph Price** is a "*good generalist*" who practices in a broad spectrum of matters. As well as his work before the NLRB, Price oversees labor agreement negotiations, aids clients with strike planning and litigates employment cases in both trial and appellate courts. Market sources spoke approvingly of his "*common sense and great people skills.*"

The Clients: American Electric Power; Columbia Gas Transmission; Koch Industries; Georgia-Pacific; Marathon Ashland Petroleum and West Virginia Manufacturers Association.

LITIGATION

GENERAL COMMERCIAL

Band 1

Allen Guthrie McHugh & Thomas, PLLC

The Firm: This Charleston-based boutique consists of 12 partners and eight associates. "*Discriminating in the cases it accepts,*" the group focuses on complex litigation in a variety of areas, including commercial and civil matters. Mediation forms a large part of the practice, and recent years witnessed a sharp increase in the number of pharmaceutical and industry-related torts handled by the team. Displaying the sort of "*judgment, background, contacts and experience*" that clients find attractive, it is heavily involved in ongoing personal protective equipment litigation for various state manufacturers and recently concluded a golden parachute con-

tract case for NiSource worth in excess of $7 million.

The Lawyers: "*If you end up in a foxhole*" then **Robert Allen** is, according to many in the litigation community, "*the one you'd want to be there with you.*" Venerated throughout the market, he has mediated 130 matters in the past year and conducted a substantial amount of coal-related and civil litigation. Observers praise his "*bedside manner*" and "*strong presence in the courtroom.*" **David Thomas** specializes in products liability defense and mass tort litigation for several of West Virginia's major pharmaceutical companies. A "*personable, intelligent and hard-working guy,*" he has supplemented ongoing class action defense work for DuPont with a series of out-of-state cases to be tried in Delaware. Partner **Rebecca Betts** comes highly recommended. A

former US District Attorney, she focuses her practice on appellate law and civil and criminal defense work. Betts offers additional expertise in consumer fraud.

The Clients: The team acts on behalf of a range of pharmaceutical companies including NiSource, Johnson & Johnson and DuPont.

Bowles Rice McDavid Graff & Love LLP

The Firm: Industry sources and competitors agree that for "*general breadth of practice*" this litigation group is among the most competitive in the market. Comprising over 14 lawyers, it mixes medical and legal malpractice defense work with several other types of litigation. The group won a landmark case concerning attorney liability in bad faith matters. It also prevailed in

All quotes in the text are from interviews with clients and competitors.

West Virginia
Leading firms
(Litigation: General Commercial)

1. **ALLEN GUTHRIE MCHUGH** *Charleston*
   BOWLES RICE MCDAVID GRAFF *Charleston*
   JACKSON KELLY PLLC *Charleston*
   STEPTOE & JOHNSON PLLC *Clarksburg*
2. **BAILEY & GLASSER LLP** *Charleston*
   DINSMORE & SHOHL LLP *Charleston*
   DITRAPANO, BARRETT *Charleston*
   SPILMAN THOMAS & BATTLE, PLLC *Charleston*
3. **CAREY, SCOTT & DOUGLAS, PLLC** *East Charleston*
   FARMER, CLINE & CAMPBELL PLLC *Charleston*
   FLAHERTY, SENSABAUGH *Charleston*
   GOODWIN & GOODWIN, LLP *Charleston*
   HENDRICKSON & LONG, PLLC *Charleston*
   JENKINS FENSTERMAKER, PLLC *Huntington*
   THE TINNEY LAW FIRM *Charleston*

Leading individuals
(Litigation: General Commercial)

Senior Statesman
ALLEN Robert *Allen Guthrie, Charleston*

1. **BAILEY Benjamin** *Bailey & Glasser, Charleston*
   EMCH Al *Jackson Kelly, Charleston*
   FARMER Stephen *Farmer Cline, Charleston*
   JERNIGAN W Henry *Dinsmore & Shohl, Charleston*
   LOVE III Charles *Bowles Rice, Charleston*
   THOMAS David *Allen Guthrie, Charleston*
   TINNEY John *The Tinney Law Firm, Charleston*
2. **BARRETT Joshua** *DiTrapano Barrett, Charleston*
   BETTS Rebecca *Allen Guthrie, Charleston*
   CAREY Michael *Carey Scott, East Charleston*
   GEORGE Shawn *George & Lorensen, Charleston*
   GOODWIN Thomas *Goodwin & Goodwin, Charleston*
   HENDRICKSON David *Hendrickson & Long, Charleston*
   LACAGNIN Stephen *Jackson Kelly, Morgantown*
   LONG Scott *Hendrickson & Long, Charleston*
   SCARR Thomas *Jenkins Fenstermaker, Huntington*
   STOWERS Gerard *Bowles Rice, Charleston*
   SWEENEY Robert *Jenkins Fenstermaker, Huntington*

Up-and-coming individuals
CIMINO Michael *Jackson Kelly, Charleston*
GLASSER Brian *Bailey & Glasser, Charleston*

Leading individuals
(Litigation: Healthcare)

1. **FLAHERTY Thomas** *Flaherty Sensabaugh, Charleston*
   JERNIGAN W Henry *Dinsmore, Charleston*
2. **BREWER Susan** *Steptoe & Johnson, Morgantown*
   GALEOTA William *Steptoe & Johnson, Morgantown*
   HURNEY Thomas *Jackson Kelly, Charleston*
   LUSK Neva *Spilman Thomas, Charleston*
   SENSABAUGH Don *Flaherty Sensabaugh, Charleston*

Firms and individuals are listed alphabetically in each band.

a large class action suit related to former employment contracts, and gained summary judgment on behalf of tire manufacturer Bridgestone/Firestone.

The Lawyers: One of the "*deans*" of commercial litigation, practice group leader **Charles Love** is a "*strong, steady, competent presenter of cases and positions.*" He specializes in insurance coverage issues, toxic torts and products liability. Recently elected president of the State Bar Association, competitors award Love "*high marks across the board.*" Malpractice has become a substantial part of the workload of the "*excellent*" **Gerard Stowers**, in addition to sizable commercial litigation and professional liability matters. Strongly endorsed by the market for his "*nice presence in the courtroom,*" Stowers "*knows his stuff sideways and backwards.*" During the past 12 months he defended a large law firm in a legal malpractice matter and won a significant class action case for a major client.
The Clients: Bridgestone/Firestone North American Tire, Exxon and Verizon.

Jackson Kelly PLLC
See firm details p.1815
The Firm: This "*large and sophisticated*" firm has over 25 members in its litigation department, mainly located in Charleston. With extensive experience in all forms of dispute resolution, the group has made a name for itself in the areas of products liability and complex industrial accident litigation. One client confidently identified Jackson Kelly as the "*leading natural resource firm*" in West Virginia. Competitors note the team's consummate representation of employers in the coal industry. The group received praise for its handling of mass tort litigation and, although a small part of its remit, medical malpractice work: "*The attorneys could be doctors, they know medicine so well.*"
The Lawyers: Firm CEO **Al Emch** (see p.1808) now has less time to devote to his practice, but sustains his reputation as a "*superb trial lawyer*" by taking on some of the most significant cases in the state. He and the group are currently acting as liaison counsel in a mass hearing relating to a loss matter and co-representing more than 170 coal mining companies in flood litigation. "*Personable, likable and professional,*" his "*ethical and methodical*" approach garners a huge amount of respect in the energy market. "*Tenacious litigator*" **Stephen LaCagnin** (see p.1809) is, according to one competitor, an "*incredibly powerful force in the community.*" Lead counsel in the Massey Coal discrimination case, his expertise in employee dispute situations is reflected in the volume of age, gender and sexual harassment claims that constitute his day-to-day work. Industry sources consider him "*tough enough to win every time.*" Excelling in the defense of doctors, hospitals and other healthcare providers in cases related to the Medical Professional Liability Act, **Thomas Hurney** (see p.1809) chairs the firm's group in this area. He is recognized by market sources as an "*intellectual authority*" on medical liability issues.

Michael Cimino (see p.1808) was identified as a "*capable trial lawyer,*" well-liked within the litigation community, whose practice emphasizes products and premises liability, deliberate-intent matters and medical professional liability.
The Clients: The firm conducts litigation for several of West Virginia's major energy companies, including Massey Coal, CONSOL and Consolidation Coal. It also represents healthcare providers throughout the state.

Steptoe & Johnson PLLC
The Firm: With a substantive practice spread throughout six offices, this full-service group employs 23 partners and an extensive paralegal staff on a diverse range of cases before West Virginia's trial and appellate courts. While it has no single focus, the team has established a statewide reputation for medical malpractice defense work, displaying a "*rapid growth posture*" in this area that makes them a "*major competitor*" in the north. Its profile also extends beyond state boundaries. Several attorneys served as national counsel on a case that settled in favor of the defendants. The past year have also witnessed the successful conclusion of a pharmaceutical IP matter and the end of a class action suit in which only one of 245 plaintiffs was eventually awarded damages.
The Lawyers: **William Galeota** chairs the Morgantown litigation department. An "*effective courtroom lawyer*" whom clients praise for his ability to "*interact with people at all levels,*" he devotes much time to personal injury and commercial defense matters. While Galeota manages the group's toxic tort caseload, he is best-known for his medical malpractice work: "*extremely knowledgeable in medicine,*" he represents physicians throughout the state. This year he has obtained a significant number of defense verdicts for a client base that includes the University Health Sciences Center. Similarly, "*seasoned professional*" and "*superwoman*" **Susan Slenker Brewer** centers her practice on professional liability and personal injury defense, frequently defending healthcare providers throughout the state in medical negligence cases. She and Galeota are lead counsel for West Virginia Physicians Mutual. The medical community is united in its praise of her "*excellent work.*"
The Clients: The group represents a variety of healthcare organizations, ranging from the University Health Sciences Center, St Paul Travelers Company and Mongolia Health Systems to West Virginia Physicians Mutual Insurance.

Band 2

Bailey & Glasser LLP
See firm details p.1811
The Firm: This Charleston-based "*perfect example of a litigation boutique*" covers a broad range of issues, concentrating on commercial,

environmental and white-collar criminal defense work. Market sources identify a swing in favor of plaintiff representation. Recently the group tried a case before the federal court for a bank president against an international auditing firm. Confirming competitor perceptions of its "*broad spectrum*" of clients, it has also tried an environmental case involving the dewatering of wells against a large coal company, winning a verdict that exceeded $1.4 million in damages, and prevailed in a dispute concerning the acquisition of a coal-testing laboratory.

The Lawyers: Benjamin Bailey (see p.1807) conducts most of the white-collar crime litigation and has earned a reputation as an "*effective, articulate advocate, who makes complex issues understandable*." Lead counsel on the Keystone case, his successes in 2004 include winning summary judgment in a significant fee dispute matter. "*Effective with witnesses*," liked by juries, and displaying an "*abundant, infectious enthusiasm*" for his work, **Brian Glasser** (see p.1809) specializes in trials and appeals, practicing before all state and federal courts in West Virginia.

The Clients: The firm engages in litigation work associated with a broad range of commercial and plaintiff clients.

Dinsmore & Shohl LLP
See firm details p.1452

The Firm: With three partners and four associates operating out of Charleston, this litigation group mixes products liability work with natural resource and personal injury litigation. Its size does not correspond to the magnitude of its caseload. Peers point to its representation of Purdue Pharma as a sign of its increasing profile, and it is currently involved in extensive tobacco litigation before the Supreme Court.

The Lawyers: Market sources awarded **Henry Jernigan** high marks within the ambit of complex pharmaceutical litigation. A "*tenacious and honorable adversary*" who "*does a great job for his clients*," he has had a multitude of cases dismissed on behalf of OxyContin. Observers credit him with being responsible for the firm's increase in size and professional stature since it opened its West Virginia office.

The Clients: Representing commercial and medical companies in a number of class actions, two of the group's major clients are Purdue Pharma and OxyContin.

DiTrapano, Barrett & DiPiero, PLLC
The Firm: When peers need to refer plaintiff work, this is one of the premier firms. With four members, four associates and one of counsel in total, the firm devotes half of its resources to commercial litigation. As well as dealing with personal injury, wrongful termination and sexual discrimination claims, the team (which includes a former US District Attorney) often acts as outside counsel for the state and its vari-

ous agencies. In addition to regular defamation defense work for The Charleston Gazette, the group is currently involved in class action litigation pertaining to royalty underpayments.

The Lawyers: Market observers praise **Joshua Barrett** for his "*meticulous and studied*" approach to commercial litigation. Although he still does some personal injury work, his practice has shifted towards governmental issues in recent years. In the past twelve months he has acted on behalf of the state in litigation related to pharmaceutical marketing and pricing. He has also effected partial settlements for several Keystone shareholders.

The Clients: The firm mixes its representation of oil and gas companies with its work for The Charleston Gazette.

Spilman Thomas & Battle, PLLC
See firm details p.1816

The Firm: This "*growth-oriented*" firm places a high premium on its litigation practice. More than half of its attorneys try cases in a wide variety of areas, ranging from asbestos, personal injury, products liability and business litigation to white-collar crime and appellate work. In addition, the firm represents both of the tertiary care hospitals in West Virginia. "*Thorough and knowledgeable*," its labor and employment litigation is held in high regard by others in the field.

The Lawyers: Assuming the presidency of the state Defense Trial Counsel in May 2005, **Neva Lusk** (see p.1809) is an ex-prosecuting attorney "*who is bright, and good on her feet*." She is particularly busy in the fertile toxic tort arena, having recently pursued a medical device manufacturer case to dismissal. Healthcare is her specialty, and she tries a substantial number of pharmaceutical, products liability and privilege cases on behalf of state hospitals. She synthesizes this work with her participation in federal-level investigations of various medical and energy companies.

The Clients: The team represents several state hospitals and a variety of healthcare organizations and coal-mining companies.

Band 3

Carey, Scott & Douglas, PLLC
The Firm: This small, locally prominent firm acts for both plaintiffs and defendants in civil litigation and trial practice. It emphasizes issues relating to personal injury and wrongful death, asbestos defense, business disputes and white-collar criminal defense. The firm also advises clients on internal investigations and corporate compliance.

The Lawyers: Michael Carey "*talks the talk, and walks the walk*." Possessed of "*great judgment*," his expertise is as broad as the firm's practice is varied. He casts a long shadow within the litigation community as a "*smart and capable*" trial lawyer.

The Clients: The firm's client base comprises numerous commercial entities, particularly those drawn from coal, oil and gas industries.

Farmer, Cline & Campbell PLLC
See firm details p.1812

The Firm: This litigation boutique has developed a well-respected niche in legal malpractice defense. Clients also valued its pharmaceutical sector experience. Other areas in which the group specializes include wrongful death, child injury, product liability and insurance bad faith claims.

The Lawyers: Sources credited **Stephen Farmer** with making this firm such a successful competitor for complex litigation work. An authoritative trial lawyer, his practice incorporates commercial, product liability and personal injury cases. Farmer was described as "*versatile, fearless and bright*" in his defense of clients. Rivals would not hesitate in referring work to him.

The Clients: Pharmaceutical companies and corporations throughout West Virginia.

Flaherty, Sensabaugh & Bonasso PLLC
The Firm: The "*first-class*" lawyers at this boutique prompt claims that it is "*one of the best malpractice defense firm in the whole state*." With offices in Charleston, Morgantown and Wheeling, the team is "*the best there is*" when it comes to medical malpractice. In recent years, the firm has branched out into other areas including class actions, products liability and workplace injury claims.

The Lawyers: Thomas Flaherty is an "*outstanding*" medical malpractice attorney. According to one interviewee, he is a "*guy who holds respect on all sides of a case*." This view is echoed throughout the marketplace, with a series of competitors complimenting him on his integrity, "*strong grasp of the law*" and skill in front of a jury. His partner, **Don Sensabaugh** enjoys a similar profile. Several peers named him as their "*number-one choice*" when it came to the referral of medical malpractice defense work.

The Clients: The firm acts on behalf of a number of healthcare organizations, including the West Virginia Physicians Mutual Insurance Company.

Goodwin & Goodwin, LLP
See firm details p.1813

The Firm: This "*politically well-connected*" family firm represents clients in a variety of complex and sophisticated cases, including contract disputes, insurance coverage, personal injury and wrongful death litigation and products liability.

The Lawyers: Prominent member **Thomas Goodwin** is a "*really good representative of larger commercial clients*," acting on their behalf in varied civil litigation before West Virginia's state and federal courts.

1804

All quotes in the text are from interviews with clients and competitors.

CHAMBERS USA 2005

The Clients: The attorneys represent a stable of large corporate clients.

Hendrickson & Long, PLLC
See firm details p.1814

The Firm: Although this dedicated litigation practice has made an effort in recent years to broaden its remit – encompassing defective product allegations and insurance coverage disputes – it remains best known for its asbestos and toxic tort work. Consolidating its reputation at this end of the spectrum, the group has successfully tried a solvent exposure case for a major energy sector corporation and undertaken a series of silica-related class action suits.

The Lawyers: **David Hendrickson** is applauded for his "*substantive and meaningful*" briefs, primarily concentrated in the area of products liability. From fan blade cases to faulty baby seat litigation, his practice extends well beyond market perceptions of the firm's inclination towards mass tort matters. "*Top of his class,*" **Scott Long** has also furthered his involvement in products liability, supplementing existing expertise in medical malpractice, personal injury and toxic tort defense work.

The Clients: This boutique engages in work for insurance coverage companies such as AIG, while representing major players in the energy market, most notably Exxon.

Jenkins Fenstermaker, PLLC
The Firm: Consisting of 12 attorneys, the firm's "*prestigious*" litigation practice covers insurance defense, professional liability and toxic tort class action claims. It is currently awaiting motion to dismiss in a series of medical monitoring claims, and earlier this year it won summary judgment in a single plaintiff toxic tort case with burden of proof ramifications.

The Lawyers: **Thomas Scarr** is a "*discreet, multifaceted*" commercial litigator who employs his "*tenacious personality*" to good effect in wrongful discharge cases and litigation that falls within the scope of Title VII employment discrimination law. Market sources concur that **Robert Sweeney** demonstrates a "*thoughtful and objective*" approach that pays dividends for his litigation practice, which also includes plaintiff representation. He deals in broad civil litigation, with an emphasis on asbestos, lead and toxic tort issues.

The Clients: ACF Industries; Special Metals Corporation; Cabell Huntington Hospital; Steel of West Virginia and Huntington Alloys.

The Tinney Law Firm
The Firm: With a substantial part of its practice devoted to advocacy and litigation, this Charleston-based firm receives praise for its involvement in commercial and financial dispute resolution. It also undertakes plaintiffs' cases in the fields of personal injury, wrongful death and breach of contract.

The Lawyers: **John Tinney** "*has a nice way of making complicated issues understandable.*" One of the founding members of the firm, he is "*one of the best trial lawyers in the state, bar none.*" Competitors are in awe of Tinney's "*commanding presence,*" as an "*excellent and vigorous*" litigator. He has followed through to verdict over 100 cases – many at national level.

The Clients: The firm acts on behalf of clients ranging from financial entities to railroad companies, and individual plaintiffs.

Other Notable Practitioners
Shawn P George at George & Lorenson, PLLC is a "*bright, capable and aggressive guy*" who, observers note, does important plaintiff work and "*zealously*" defends his clients.

REAL ESTATE

West Virginia
Leading firms (Real Estate)
1   **BOWLES RICE MCDAVID GRAFF** *Charleston*
JACKSON KELLY PLLC *Charleston*
STEPTOE & JOHNSON PLLC *Clarksburg*
2   **HUDDLESTON BOLEN LLP** *Huntington*
PILL & PILL *Martinsburg*
REEDER & SHUMAN *Morgantown*
ROBINSON & MCELWEE PLLC *Charleston*
SPILMAN THOMAS & BATTLE, PLLC *Charleston*
Firms are listed alphabetically in each band.

Band 1

Bowles Rice McDavid Graff & Love LLP

The Firm: It is prominent in natural resources sector real estate matters. Peers and clients alike acknowledge that few firms can compete with the 12-strong team when it comes to the relationship between real estate and oil and gas law, mining permits and land use regulations. During the past year alone, Bowles has overseen the formation of a major new coal-fired power plant, litigated many large lost coal claims and concluded several significant coal acquisitions. As a further testament to its formidable reputation it is also at the forefront of legislative change. A large and well-established firm, it has expanded well beyond its Charleston base.

The Lawyers: **Thomas Lane** is regarded by many as one of the "*premier*" energy lawyers in the eastern USA. He supplements his membership of the firm's executive committee and energy, environment and regulatory practice group with his professorship at West Virginia University College of Law, where he teaches a coal, oil and gas course. This synthesis of theoretical insight with practical application makes him the "*go-to guy*" when it comes to the interface between the energy sector on the one hand and commercial real estate, zoning and land development on the other. One satisfied client's description of Lane as "*the first attorney I will utilize in all my real estate transactions*" is typical of the high regard he inspires in all those who have worked with him. **Carl Andrews** received a similarly favorable response from interviewees. His broad-based practice encompasses both pure real estate work (land development, zoning and residential lending for construction) and title insurance. He was praised by observers for being "*more than capable and competent*" in all these areas. Based in Morgantown, "*very service-oriented attorney*" **Robert Dinsmore** counts among his clients several of West Virginia's major coal companies. He assists them with everything from acquisitions and sales of coal reserves to cemetery removal. Additionally, Dinsmore has advised governmental organizations on creating and operating sewer and water utilities. He also has extensive experience of county planning and subdivision creation. **Charles 'Chud' Dollison** heads up the firm's energy, environment & regulatory practice group. He was consistently commended by interviewees for expanding his practice beyond pure real estate law and into land planning, litigation and mineral work.

The Clients: The group's clientele includes several developers, lenders, landowners and major energy corporations such as CONSOL, Peabody Energy and Emax Oil.

Jackson Kelly PLLC
See firm details p.1815

The Firm: Dating back as far as 1822, and praised by peers for its "*terrific client base,*" this firm is one of the largest in West Virginia. Boasting more than 30 attorneys dedicated to real estate firmwide, the Charleston team divides its time between traditional commercial real estate, environmental law and development of industrial and natural resources facilities. The energy sector has seen much new activity amid a resurgence in the coal, oil and gas industries. The group conducted real estate aspects of the West Virginia portion of Foundation Coal's restructuring process and acquisitions for Massey

West Virginia
Leading individuals (Real Estate)

[1] ANDREWS Carl *Bowles Rice*, Charleston
BROGLIO Dennis *Jackson Kelly*, Charleston
DEEM Patrick *Steptoe & Johnson*, Clarksburg

[2] CAPPELLANTI Ellen *Jackson Kelly*, Charleston
DOLLISON Charles *Bowles Rice*, Charleston
GILPIN Thomas *Huddleston Bolen*, Huntington
HAMMOND David *Spilman Thomas*, Charleston
PILL Richard *Pill & Pill*, Martinsburg
PLYBON Christopher *Huddleston Bolen*, Huntington
SHUMAN Stephen *Reeder & Shuman*, Morgantown

[3] DINSMORE Robert *Bowles Rice*, Charleston
ENDERLE Louis *Steptoe & Johnson*, Clarksburg
LOEB JR Charles *Jackson Kelly*, Charleston
LONDON Eric *Jackson Kelly*, Morgantown
OFSA Joyce *Spilman Thomas*, Charleston
SHUMAN Robert *Reeder & Shuman*, Morgantown

Leading individuals
(Real Estate: Energy & Natural Resources)

[1] LANE Thomas *Bowles Rice*, Charleston

[2] DOLLISON Charles *Bowles Rice*, Charleston
FLUHARTY Robert *Jackson Kelly*, Charleston
RUSSELL James *Steptoe & Johnson*, Morgantown

[3] BOLEN Richard *Huddleston Bolen*, Charleston
MCELWEE Douglas *Robinson & McElwee*, Charleston

Firms and individuals are listed alphabetically in each band.

Energy. In a similar vein, clients noted their "*specialized knowledge*" in the area of alternative energy, particularly the title issues surrounding coal bed methane production.

The Lawyers: According to one happy customer **Dennis Broglio** (see p.1808) offers "*a superlative understanding of the intricacies of West Virginia property law.*" His practice focuses on title work and pure real estate transactions. Broglio has been a central figure in most of the firm's major deals this year. Highlights include advising on licensing and environmental issues for an ongoing alternative energy project originating in Europe. He is acclaimed by clients for his ability to handle large deals with complex financing arrangements. Peers identify him as one of the true "*quality guys*" in real estate law. For his partner **Robert Fluharty** (see p.1808), the past year has been one of the busiest periods of his career. He concluded several large coal acquisitions and has provided ongoing advice on titles to coal bed methane properties. Respected by his peers for his "*sound judgment,*" he is considered by many clients to be a preeminent authority on mineral law in the southern part of the state. Widely appreciated for her ability to work "*effectively and aggressively*" on behalf of her clients, **Ellen Cappellanti** (see p.1808) is recognized for her "*strong subject mastery*" in a diverse number of practice areas, encompassing real estate, corporate and bankruptcy matters. Much of her real estate work is located in the lucrative Eastern Panhandle. Cappellanti con-tinued her involvement with the Snowshoe Mountain Ski Resort and undertook two major commercial/residential condominium projects this year. Her recent out-of-state work paid dividends for her in-state reputation, with one interviewee confident that there was no one better qualified within West Virginia to handle projects requiring US Department of Housing and Urban Development approval. **Eric London** (see p.1809), based in Morgantown, primarily concentrates his real estate practice on leasing and property development. Acknowledged to be a "*bright fellow*" by rivals, clients praise his ability to explain the matters at stake lucidly. "*Extremely bright and hard-working,*" **Charles Loeb** (see p.1809) mixes corporate and real estate transactions for some of the state's biggest coal companies with a variety of acquisitions, banking and general commercial matters for public and financial entities throughout West Virginia.

The Clients: Foundation Coal; Bright Enterprises; Peabody Coal; Chicago Title Insurance.

Steptoe & Johnson PLLC

The Firm: An influential presence in Morgantown and Clarksburg and rapidly growing in Charleston, the firm's real estate and commercial transactions group received plentiful accolades for "*competence, timeliness and quality of product.*" Making the most of a practice consisting of around 35 attorneys, it deals with a wide variety of property transactions, often connected to the acquisition and divestiture of coal or oil and gas properties. The field of coal bed methane production has been a focus for recent activity. Many consider the firm as the leading authority on title insurance matters. One major insurance sector player praised the group's excellent work and timekeeping: "*You certainly don't have to crack the whip on them.*" The group is no stranger to deals of considerable magnitude. This year it concluded a huge financing for CONSOL Energy involving a harbor facility in Maryland and coal properties in a number of states, including Ohio, Wyoming and Kentucky.

The Lawyers: Generally viewed by all comers to be at the "*top of his game*" and to possess a "*broad spectrum of experience,*" **Patrick Deem** is a venerated presence in the firm's Clarksburg office. Principal attorney for Dominion Exploration and Production and resident agent for many of the state's major title insurance companies, he combines corporate and bankruptcy expertise with real estate know-how to great effect. Recipients of Deem's advice applaud his "*attention to detail*" while peers praise his humility and "*team approach.*" He continues to be instrumental in cultivating a well-integrated real estate group in the southern part of the state. According to research, there aren't many attorneys out there with more knowledge about the coal and gas property market than **James Russell**. One particularly impressed client observed "*he knew what I wanted before I asked it.*" At the vanguard of mineral law, this "*bottom-line oriented*" attorney has recently concluded the negotiation of a large, multimillion dollar coal-mining lease in southern West Virginia for an affiliate of CONSOL Energy. His professional reach extends to environmental matters and Russell was counsel to the Fish and Wildlife Service in its expansion of the Canaan Valley National Wildlife Refuge. He is currently closing three transactions on its behalf. **Louis Enderle**'s practice covers general commercial work and business entity formation. Recent highlights include advising on several shopping center developments. A large proportion of his time is devoted to mineral real estate transactions. During the summer of 2004 he and Deem closed a large, sophisticated production payment deal for Dominion. He is also a formidable title agent, currently working on his third large timber acquisition for Heartwood Forestland and acting for Drilling Appalachian on the leasing of oil and gas tracts. Interviewees spoke highly of his "*technical ability, accuracy, timeliness, clarity and excellent writing abilities.*"

The Clients: Dominion Energy; Penn Virginia; Huntington National Bank; Chicago Title Insurance; Columbia Gas Transmission; Heartwood Forestland Group; West Virginia University Foundation; Fish and Wildlife Service; Drilling Appalachian and Greenbrier Hotel.

Band 2

Huddleston Bolen LLP

The Firm: Characterized as "*large, multifaceted, with a great variety of expertise*" by one commentator, this firm dominates the Huntington area, with additional offices in Charleston and Ashton, Kentucky. Less rigidly compartmentalized than other market leaders, this real estate group regularly liaises with its commercial practice to advise on a range of issues. Typical work includes the purchase of industrial and natural resource properties, mineral law, acquisitions and leasings, public-private sector financing and retail development. One competitor's observation that the firm attracts "*the lion's share of interesting and complex deals in its region*" is borne out by recent representation of the Tri-State Transit Authority in the construction of a major entertainment and shopping center in downtown Huntington. The group continues to work closely with railroad clients and has been instrumental in the development of several manufacturing facilities throughout West Virginia.

The Lawyers: Managing Partner **Thomas Gilpin** is a master of real estate in several sectors, with an emphasis on mineral transactions, banking and healthcare. Clients applaud his attention to detail. This year he aided one of the more sizable groups of medical providers in West Virginia in its purchase of a large property vacated by Wal-Mart. Additionally, he continues to do a significant amount of natural resource work for the coal giant Western Pocahontas – expanding his profile well beyond state boundaries. The "*first line of interpretation*" for many of the firm's clients, **Christopher Plybon**'s practice is a mixture of acquisition leasing and financing. He is largely responsible for the West Virginia statute relating to delinquent real estate taxes. "*Thorough, patient, precise and accurate*", much of Plybon's work has recently revolved around hotel financing. His involvement in the construction of three new strip shopping centers amid a statewide rejuvenation in the property market provided a further highlight. "*Tenacious and bright*" **Richard Bolen** brings coal and oil and gas expertise to the real estate table. With years of experience and countless lectures and papers on mineral issues under his belt, many rivals would not hesitate in referring work to him.

The Clients: Tri-State Transit Authority; Bank One; Huntington Industrial and Natural Resource Partners/Western Pocahontas.

Pill & Pill

The Firm: Recurrently the subject of praise, this Martinsburg-based firm was credited with a growing profile. Specializing in residential real estate, it was reckoned by several clients to be the "*best in West Virginia at what it does.*" One major competitor happily admitted the group's "*statewide reputation is more than justified.*"

The Lawyers: Displaying a level of commitment to clients so high it prompted one peer to observe: "*he will close cases at the weekend, if circumstances demand,*" **Richard Pill** is his firm's shining light. Market sources praised his strength in all areas of residential real estate, particularly foreclosures, mortgages and loans.

Reeder & Shuman

The Firm: This Morgantown-based group enjoys a long-standing reputation in the field of mineral real estate transactions and one that transcends regional boundaries. Clients were unanimous in their praise of its "*outstanding quality.*"

The Lawyers: "*Responsive, competent and meticulous,*" **Stephen Shuman** is the undisputed king of real estate in Morgantown. Companies turn to him when they want someone who won't "*play fast and loose with underwriting,*" with a deep, authoritative knowledge of all the issues involved. His son **Robert Shuman** is certainly not content to live in his father's shadow. Previously an adjunct lecturer in real estate, his "*brilliant and academic*" approach to subjects like delinquent tax has won him plaudits from all quarters of the marketplace.

The Clients: The firm represents a variety of developers and regional owners. Insurance agents such as Chicago Title Insurance also feature in the client base.

Robinson & McElwee PLLC

The Firm: Although research suggests this firm no longer has the presence it once did in terms of size, this Clarksburg group still handles a significant amount of environmental law related to mining and mineral properties.

The Lawyers: Considered by peers to be a "*good and dependable*" practitioner, **Douglas McElwee** specializes in mineral law.

The Clients: The firm has a diverse client base, ranging from entrepreneurial enterprises to international organizations engaged in commercial, industrial and financial transactions.

Spilman Thomas & Battle, PLLC

See firm details p.1816

The Firm: Basing its operation in Charleston, this ever-growing practice represents secured lenders in multistate commercial transactions as well as handling title insurance, zoning and land development matters. Earlier in the year it participated in several transactions pertaining to West Virginia's bond issue, including the development of a private prison. The group's full-service reputation is bolstered by its continuing involvement in mineral real estate and economic development finance.

The Lawyers: **David Hammond** (see p.1809) has been instrumental in redrafting the West Virginia code related to land use planning, the culmination of which will have a huge impact on the adoption and implementation of land use legislation. When he isn't changing the face of the legal landscape, Hammond is commended by market sources for his "*thorough and detailed*" approach to loan workouts and foreclosures. During the past year he continued to represent a government entity in the development of a minor league baseball stadium, recently concluding the sale of the old ballpark. His colleague **Joyce Ofsa** (see p.1810) is the firm's real estate chairperson. She focuses on commercial and residential deals, mineral title work, landlord and tenant leases and secured financing. Interviewees describe her as "*attentive to detail,*" with a reputation for "*playing hardball*" on behalf of her clients.

The Clients: Leading names include Old Republic National Title Insurance, United Bank and University of Charleston.

Leaders in West Virginia

ALBERT, Michael
Jackson Kelly PLLC, Charleston
304 340 1287
malbert@jacksonkelly.com
Recommended in Corporate/M&A
Practice Areas: Administrative, business and commercial, corporate, insurance regulation, public utilities, securities, transportation law.
Prof. Memberships: American Bar Association; WV Bar Association; WV State Bar; WVU Alumni Association; Kanawha County Bar Association.
Career: Kanawha County Public Library (Board of Directors); former Board Member of the Charleston Regional Chamber of Commerce; former Chairman of the Board of Junior Achievement; former Chairman of the Board of National Institute for Chemical Studies; Chairman of the Board of the

Education Alliance; listed in a leading American legal publication.
Personal: BS from West Virginia University, JD from the West Virginia University School of Law.

ALLEN, Robert
Allen Guthrie McHugh & Thomas, PLLC, Charleston 304 345 7250
Recommended in Litigation

ANDREWS, Carl
Bowles Rice McDavid Graff & Love LLP, Charleston 304 347 1100
Recommended in Real Estate

BAILEY, Benjamin
Bailey & Glasser LLP, Charleston
304 345 6555
bbailey@baileyglasser.com
Recommended in Litigation
Practice Areas: Complex commercial,

coal and environmental litigation and white collar criminal defense.
Prof. Memberships: West Virginia State Bar; Fourth Circuit Judicial Conference; American Bar Association; American Inns of Court.

BARRETT, Joshua
DiTrapano, Barrett & DiPiero, PLLC, Charleston 304 342 0133
Recommended in Litigation

BASILE, Michael
Spilman Thomas & Battle, PLLC, Charleston 304 340 3854
mbasile@spilmanlaw.com
Recommended in Corporate/M&A
Practice Areas: Business, administrative law, government relations.
Prof. Memberships: WV Polymer Alliance Zone; WV Vision Shared, Co-Chair; Energy Village, Inc., Board of

Directors; Fifth Third Bank, Board of Directors (Ohio Valley); Charleston Area Alliance, Board of Directors; Governor Manchin III's Transition Member.
Career: Managing Member. Previously Associate General Counsel, General Counsel and Deputy Chief of Staff to the Office of Governor Gaston Caperton, General Counsel to the West Virginia Development Office and Assistant and Senior Assistant Attorneys General.
Personal: West Virginia University (BS in Finance, 1987), University of Pittsburgh (JD, 1991), Governor's School at Duke University's Terry Sanford Institute (1995).

BEAN, Rodney
Steptoe & Johnson PLLC, Morgantown
304 598 8000
Recommended in Employment

BETTS, Rebecca
Allen Guthrie McHugh & Thomas, PLLC, Charleston 304 345 7250
Recommended in Litigation

BOLEN, Richard
Huddleston Bolen LLP, Charleston
304 344 9869
Recommended in Real Estate

BOOKER, William
Kay Casto & Chaney PLLC, Charleston
304 345 8900
Recommended in Corporate/M&A

BREWER, Susan Slenker
Steptoe & Johnson PLLC, Morgantown
304 598 8000
Recommended in Litigation

BROGLIO, Dennis
Jackson Kelly PLLC, Charleston
304 340 1322
dbroglio@jacksonkelly.com
Recommended in Real Estate
Practice Areas: Real estate/property law; Business and Commercial Practice Group.
Prof. Memberships: West Virginia State Bar, Kanawha County Bar Association, California State Bar Association, New York State Bar Association.
Personal: JD, West Virginia University; BSCE, University of Notre Dame.

BROWN, Ricklin
Bowles Rice McDavid Graff & Love LLP, Charleston 304 347 1100
Recommended in Employment

CAPPELLANTI, Ellen
Jackson Kelly PLLC, Charleston
304 340 1277
ecappellanti@jacksonkelly.com
Recommended in Corporate/M&A, Real Estate
Practice Areas: Bankruptcy, real estate development, mergers and acquisitions, general commercial law.
Prof. Memberships: Chair of West Virginia Law Institute; American Bar Association; WV State Bar; Master, The Judge John A Field, Jr. Inn of Court; Judicial Conference of the United States Court of Appeals for Fourth Circuit.
Career: Listed in a leading American legal publication (bankruptcy law); Discover the Real West Virginia Foundation; current Co-Chair, Advantage Valley, Inc.; past Chair and Member of Board of Trustees of the Avampato Discovery Museum; past Vice-Chair and current Member of Board of Trustees of Clay Center for the Art and Sciences; Member, Board of Directors of Charleston YMCA.
Personal: JD, West Virginia University; BA, West Virginia University.

CAREY, Michael
Carey, Scott & Douglas, PLLC, East Charleston 304 345 1234
Recommended in Litigation

CARR, Kevin L
Spilman Thomas & Battle, PLLC, Charleston 304 340 3877
kcarr@spilmanlaw.com
Recommended in Employment
Practice Areas: Chair of the Labor and Employment Practice Group; traditional labor, employment litigation, wage and hour law.
Prof. Memberships: Kanawha County Bar Association; American Bar Association, Past Chairman, Technology Subcommittee of Individual Employee Rights and Developing Labor Law.
Career: Member of Spilman since 2002; union organizing, collective bargaining, union decertification, employment trial work, wage and hour audits, preventative advice and counseling; frequent author and national lecturer to human resources professionals on a myriad of traditional labor and employment issues.
Personal: West Virginia University (BA, cum laude, honors graduate, Presidential Scholar, 1992), West Virginia University (JD, 1995).

CARTER, Mark
Dinsmore & Shohl LLP, Charleston
304 357 0900
Recommended in Employment

CARYL, Michael
Bowles Rice McDavid Graff & Love LLP, Charleston 304 347 1100
Recommended in Corporate/M&A

CIMINO, Michael
Jackson Kelly PLLC, Charleston
304 340 1299
mcimino@jacksonkelly.com
Recommended in Litigation
Practice Areas: Litigation.
Prof. Memberships: Kanawha County Bar Association; West Virginia Defense Trial Counsel (Board of Governors); Adjunct Faculty, University of Charleston.
Publications: Medical and Professional Liability Issues, Workshop for the New River Family Health Center, January 1999; Criminal Prosecution of Workplace Safety Violations, 94 W.Va. Law Review 1007 (Summer 1992); Prosecutorial Discretion under the Federal Sentencing Guidelines: Is the Fox Guarding the Henhouse?, 97, W.Va. Law Review (Spring 1995); 'West Virginia Law Review' (member 1991-92; Student Works Editor 1992-93).
Personal: 1993 JD - West Virginia University; 1989 BBA - University of Notre Dame (IN) (Finance).

COKELEY, Bryan
Steptoe & Johnson PLLC, Charleston
304 353 8000
Recommended in Employment

COLEMAN, Leonard
Goodwin & Goodwin, LLP, Charleston
304 346 7000
Recommended in Corporate/M&A

DAILEY, Anna
Dinsmore & Shohl LLP, Charleston
304 357 0900
Recommended in Employment

DEEM, Patrick
Steptoe & Johnson PLLC, Clarksburg
304 624 8000
Recommended in Corporate/M&A, Real Estate

DICK, David
Steptoe & Johnson PLLC, Morgantown
304 598 8000
Recommended in Employment

DINSMORE, Robert
Bowles Rice McDavid Graff & Love LLP, Charleston 304 347 1100
Recommended in Real Estate

DOLLISON, Charles
Bowles Rice McDavid Graff & Love LLP, Charleston 304 347 1100
Recommended in Real Estate

DUNBAR, Charles
Jackson Kelly PLLC, Charleston
304 340 1196
cdunbar@jacksonkelly.com
Recommended in Corporate/M&A
Practice Areas: Banking, business and commercial, contracts, insurance, international, commercial litigation, corporate, securities, technology and computer law.
Prof. Memberships: American Bar Association, Section on Corporations; Banking and Business Law; Committees on Banking Law and Consumer Financial Services; Section on International Law; West Virginia State Bar; Kanawha County Bar.
Career: Listed in a leading American legal publication (banking law).
Publications: Interest, Inducements and the IRS, Compliance with Regulations Q and D in the New Competitive Landscape, 'American Banking Association Bank Compliance Magazine', 2001.
Personal: JD, West Virginia University; CPA; BS, West Virginia University.

EMCH, A L
Jackson Kelly PLLC, Charleston
304 340 1172
aemch@jacksonkelly.com
Recommended in Litigation
Practice Areas: Admiralty, alternative dispute resolution, aviation, class actions, contracts and business litigation, personal injury litigation, product liability, toxic, mass tort, other complex litigation.
Prof. Memberships: Fellow, American College of Trial Lawyers; American Board of Trial Advocates; International Association of Defense Counsel; Fellow, American Bar Foundation; Fellow, West Virginia Bar Foundation; Mediator, US District Courts, Northern and Southern Districts of West Virginia, state courts; Defense Trial Counsel of West Virginia, permanent Member, Fourth Circuit Judicial Conference.

Career: U.S.A.F. and WV Air National Guard, Pilot, Lt. Col. Retired; Listed in a leading American legal publication; currently CEO of Jackson Kelly PLLC.
Personal: JD University of Virginia, AB West Virginia University.

ENDERLE Jr, Louis
Steptoe & Johnson PLLC, Clarksburg
304 624 8000
Recommended in Real Estate

FARMER, Stephen
Farmer, Cline & Campbell PLLC, Charleston 304 346 5990
Recommended in Litigation

FERRETTI, David P
Spilman Thomas & Battle, PLLC, Charleston 304 340 3859
dferretti@spilmanlaw.com
Recommended in Corporate/M&A
Practice Areas: Corporate, mergers and acquisitions, public finance and healthcare law.
Prof. Memberships: National Association of Bond Lawyers; American Bar Association, Member, Business Law section; American Health Lawyers Association.
Career: Member of Spilman since 1981, Member in Charge of Lawyer Administration, Co-Chair of Recruiting.
Personal: University of Virginia (BA in Economics with high distinction, 1978); University of Virginia School of Law (JD, 1981).

FLAHERTY, Thomas
Flaherty, Sensabaugh & Bonasso PLLC, Charleston 304 345 0200
Recommended in Litigation

FLUHARTY, Robert
Jackson Kelly PLLC, Charleston
304 340 1174
rfluharty@jacksonkelly.com
Recommended in Real Estate
Practice Areas: Business and commercial law, commercial and mineral real estate law, natural resources recovery, transportation and sales.
Prof. Memberships: West Virginia State Bar; West Virginia Bar Association; Kanawha County Bar Association; American Bar Association; Eastern Mineral Law Foundation, Trustee.
Personal: LLM, Cambridge University (England); JD, Rutgers University; BA, Washington & Lee University.

GALEOTA, William
Steptoe & Johnson PLLC, Morgantown
304 598 8000
Recommended in Litigation

GARDILL, James
Phillips Gardill Kaiser & Altmeyer, Wheeling 304 232 6810
Recommended in Corporate/M&A

GEORGE, Shawn
George & Lorensen, Charleston
304 343 5555
Recommended in Litigation

GILPIN, Thomas
Huddleston Bolen LLP, Huntington
304 529 6181
Recommended in Real Estate

GLASSER, Brian
Bailey & Glasser LLP, Charleston
304 345 6555
bglasser@baileyglasser.com
Recommended in Litigation
Practice Areas: Coal, environmental and commercial litigation.
Prof. Memberships: West Virginia State Bar; American Inns of Court.

GOODWIN, Thomas
Goodwin & Goodwin, LLP, Charleston
304 346 7000
Recommended in Litigation

GRAFF Jr, F Thomas
Bowles Rice McDavid Graff & Love LLP, Charleston 304 347 1100
Recommended in Corporate/M&A

HAMMOND, David
Spilman Thomas & Battle, PLLC, Charleston 304 340 3835
dhammond@spilmanlaw.com
Recommended in Real Estate
Practice Areas: Secured lending and other commercial transactions, loan workouts and foreclosures and all aspects of real estate law, including real estate development, land use, landlord-tenant law and title insurance.
Prof. Memberships: American Bar Association, Member, Section of Real Property, Probate and Trust Law and Section of Business Law; West Virginia State Bar, past Chair, Committee on Real Estate, Zoning and Land Use; West Virginia Real Estate Lawyers Association, Charter Member; Kanawha County Bar Association.
Career: Member of Spilman since 1994.
Personal: Virginia Polytechnic Institute and State University (BS, 1984); Washington and Lee University School of Law (JD, 1987).

HARTER, Elizabeth
Bowles Rice McDavid Graff & Love LLP, Charleston 304 347 1100
Recommended in Employment

HENDRICKSON, David
Hendrickson & Long, P.L.L.C., Charleston 304 346 5500
Recommended in Litigation

HEYWOOD, Thomas
Bowles Rice McDavid Graff & Love LLP, Charleston 304 347 1100
Recommended in Corporate/M&A

HIGGINS, David
Robinson & McElwee PLLC, Charleston
304 344 5800
Recommended in Corporate/M&A

HURNEY Jr, Thomas J
Jackson Kelly PLLC, Charleston
304 340 1346
thurney@jacksonkelly.com
Recommended in Litigation
Practice Areas: Medical professional

liability, personal injury, products liability, healthcare.
Prof. Memberships: West Virginia State Bar (Board of Governors 2002-); Defense Trial Counsel of W.Va. (Board of Governors 2000-); DRI; ADTA; IADC.
Career: Member, Jackson Kelly PLLC 1983-present.
Publications: Hurney & Aliff, Medical Professional Liability in West Virginia, 105 W.Va. L. Rev 369 (2003); Hurney, Hospital Liability in W.Va. 95 W.Va. L. Rev. 943 (1993).
Personal: University of Dayton: BS Business Administration, 1980; JD, Cum Laude, 1983.

ISKRA, Eric W
Spilman Thomas & Battle, PLLC, Charleston 304 340 3875
eiskra@spilmanlaw.com
Recommended in Employment
Practice Areas: Trial work/litigation, including employment law, employee benefits/ERISA litigation, class actions, labor law, health care/disability and complex litigation matters.
Prof. Memberships: Member (one of 15), ABA Commission on Mental & Physical Disability Law (2001-present); Fellow (YLD), ABA Labor & Employment Law (2001-03).
Career: Member in Charge of Client Relations; frequent national lecturer, including speaker at ABA Annual Meeting (2000-03).
Publications: Editorial Advisory Board, Mental & Physical Disability Law Reporter ; multiple publications, including, co-author, 'Employment Law,' West Virginia Continuing Legal Publication,' 1998.
Personal: College of William and Mary (BA, 1991); Wake Forest University School of Law (JD, 1994).

JERNIGAN Jr, W Henry
Dinsmore & Shohl LLP, Charleston
304 357 0900
Recommended in Litigation

KAY, Craig
Kay Casto & Chaney PLLC, Charleston
304 345 8900
Recommended in Corporate/M&A

KING Jr, Evans
Steptoe & Johnson PLLC, Clarksburg
304 624 8000
Recommended in Corporate/M&A

KONRAD, Daniel
Huddleston Bolen LLP, Huntington
304 529 6181
Recommended in Corporate/M&A

KRIEGER, Thomas
Jenkins Fenstermaker, PLLC, Huntington 304 523 2100
Recommended in Employment

LACAGNIN, Stephen
Jackson Kelly PLLC, Morgantown
304 284 4108
slacagnin@jacksonkelly.com
Recommended in Litigation

Practice Areas: Civil litigation, employment law, products liability, insurance and professional liability.
Prof. Memberships: Admitted to practice before the West Virginia and North Carolina State Bars as well as the United States Court of appeals for the Fourth Circuit; Member of the American Bar Association; Defense Research Institute; West Virginia State Bar and North Carolina State Bar.
Career: Administrative Manager and head of the Litigation Department of the Morgantown office of Jackson Kelly PLLC.
Personal: West Virginia University, JD 1983; West Virginia University BS Journalism, 1975.

LANE, Thomas
Bowles Rice McDavid Graff & Love LLP, Charleston 304 347 1100
Recommended in Real Estate

LEDBETTER, Cheryl
Jackson Kelly PLLC, Charleston
304 340 1107
cledbetter@jacksonkelly.com
Recommended in Employment
Practice Areas: Employment discrimination with an emphasis on sexual harassment law.
Prof. Memberships: Kanawha County Bar; West Virginia Bar Association; American Bar Association (Labor Section).
Personal: JD, Washington & Lee University; BA, University of Arkansas.

LOEB JR, Charles W
Jackson Kelly PLLC, Charleston
304 340 1298
cloeb@jacksonkelly.com
Recommended in Real Estate
Practice Areas: Corporate law, banking law, mergers and acquisitions.
Prof. Memberships: American Bar Association
Career: Clerk - Honorable James M Sprouse, US Court of Appeals for the Fourth Circuit (1982-83); Charleston City Council 1995 - present (Majority Leader, 1999 - present, Chairman, Rule and Ordinance Committee, 1995 -present); Chairman of the Board of the Avampato Discovery Museum, 2005.
Personal: Yale University, BA 1979; University of Virginia Law School, JD 1982 (Member, Law Review).

LONDON, Eric
Jackson Kelly PLLC, Morgantown
304 284 4109
elondon@jacksonkelly.com
Recommended in Real Estate
Practice Areas: Banking, business/commercial, contracts, landlord/tenant, leasing, real estate/property law, trusts/estates.
Prof. Memberships: West Virginia State Bar Association; Monongalia County Bar Association.
Career: Frequent speaker on banking, business and related topics.

Personal: JD, University of Pittsburgh School of Law; BS, Pennsylvania State University.

LONG, Scott
Hendrickson & Long, P.L.L.C., Charleston 304 346 5500
Recommended in Litigation

LORD, Elizabeth Osenton
Jackson Kelly PLLC, Charleston
304 340 1390
elord@jacksonkelly.com
Recommended in Corporate/M&A
Practice Areas: Securities, corporate, homeland security, mergers and acquisitions, technology and emerging companies, white collar compliance and defense.
Prof. Memberships: West Virginia State Bar; Maryland State Bar Association; District of Columbia Bar Association; American Bar Association, US Securities and Exchange Commission Historical Society.
Career: 1990-present Jackson Kelly PLLC; 1987-90 US Securities & Exchange Commission, Division of Corporation Finance, Attorney.
Publications: 'The New Sarbanes-Oxley Attorney Responsibility Standards,' Jackson Kelly PLLC, 2003; 'Sarbanes-Oxley - Aftermath of the Perfect Storm', The West Virginia Lawyer, 2003.
Personal: JD - The American University; BS - West Virginia University (Business Administration and Accounting).

LORENSEN, Charles
George & Lorensen, Charleston
304 343 5555
Recommended in Corporate/M&A

LOVE III, Charles
Bowles Rice McDavid Graff & Love LLP, Charleston 304 347 1100
Recommended in Litigation

LUSK, Neva
Spilman Thomas & Battle, PLLC, Charleston 304 340 3866
nlusk@spilmanlaw.com
Recommended in Litigation
Practice Areas: General litigation with emphasis on product liability, including medical device and pharmaceuticals; toxic torts; and class actions.
Prof. Memberships: West Virginia State Bar, Member, Board of Governors; The Defense Trial Counsel of West Virginia, Vice President and Member, Board of Governors; International Association of Defense Counsel; Defense Research Institute, Member, Drug and Medical Device and Toxic Tort Committees.
Career: Member of Spilman since 1994; former Assistant Prosecuting Attorney for Kanawha County, West Virginia, 1981-91.
Personal: Marshall University (BA, 1977); West Virginia University (JD, 1980).

MCELWEE, Douglas
Robinson & McElwee PLLC, Charleston
304 344 5800
Recommended in Real Estate

MORRISON, David
Steptoe & Johnson PLLC, Clarksburg
304 624 8000
Recommended in Employment

MURPHY, Sandra
Bowles Rice McDavid Graff & Love LLP,
Charleston 304 347 1100
Recommended in Corporate/M&A

MURRAY, Thomas
Huddleston Bolen LLP, Huntington
304 529 6181
Recommended in Corporate/M&A

OFSA, Joyce
Spilman Thomas & Battle, PLLC,
Charleston 304 340 3847
jofsa@spilmanlaw.com
Recommended in Real Estate
Practice Areas: Commercial, mineral,
residential real estate, zoning, land use,
eminent domain, landlord/tenant, title
insurance.
Prof. Memberships: WV State Bar;
American Bar Association; American
College of Mortgage Attorneys.
Career: Member since 1979.
Publications: Contributing author,
'Challenges in Title Transfers,' PESI,
2000, 2003; 'Title Examination in West
Virginia,' Lorman, 2000, 2001;
'Advanced Principles of Title Insurance'
NBI, 1997; 'Real Estate 1995,' WVCLE,
1995; 'Survey Issues: Resolution and
Remediation,' NBI, 1995; 'Current Issues
in Commercial Real Estate Leases,' NBI,
1993; 'Boundary Law in West Virginia,'
NBI, 1993, 1991.
Personal: West Virginia University (BA,
magna cum laude, 1975); West Virginia
University (JD, 1979).

PAUL, Niall
Spilman Thomas & Battle, PLLC,
Charleston 304 340 3874
npaul@spilmanlaw.com
Recommended in Employment
Practice Areas: Trial work, complex lit-
igation and appellate practice.
Prof. Memberships: American Bar
Association, Litigation Section, Torts
and Insurance Practice Section and
Labor and Employment Law Section.
Career: Member of Spilman since 1990.
Publications: Spoken and published
internationally on Sarbanes-Oxley liti-
gation; 'Client Service in the Twenty-
First Century – Finding Profits in Part-

nering,' Texas State Bar 2003; 'The Older
Workers' Benefit Protection Act: Forcing
a New Look at Early Retirement Incen-
tives and Waivers,' Employee Relations
Law Journal, 1991.
Personal: Bridgewater College of Virginia
(BA in Philosophy and Religion, cum
laude, 1987); University of Richmond, TC
Williams School of Law (JD, 1990).

PILL, Richard
Pill & Pill, Martinsburg
304 263 4971
Recommended in Real Estate

PLYBON, Christopher
Huddleston Bolen LLP, Huntington
304 529 6181
Recommended in Real Estate

PRICE, Joseph
Robinson & McElwee PLLC, Charleston
304 344 5800
Recommended in Employment

ROLES, Forrest
Dinsmore & Shohl LLP, Charleston
304 357 0900
Recommended in Employment

RUSSELL, James
Steptoe & Johnson PLLC, Morgantown
304 598 8000
Recommended in Real Estate

SCARR, Thomas
Jenkins Fenstermaker, PLLC,
Huntington 304 523 2100
Recommended in Litigation

SENSABAUGH, Don
Flaherty, Sensabaugh & Bonasso PLLC,
Charleston 304 345 0200
Recommended in Litigation

SHUMAN, Robert
Reeder & Shuman, Morgantown
304 292 8488
Recommended in Real Estate

SHUMAN, Stephen
Reeder & Shuman, Morgantown
304 292 8488
Recommended in Real Estate

SOUTHWORTH II, Louis S
Jackson Kelly PLLC, Charleston
304 340 1231
lsouthworth@jacksonkelly.com
Recommended in Corporate/M&A
Practice Areas: Administrative, legislative services, business and commercial,
mergers and acquisitions, business planning, securities, corporate, taxation,
leases, trusts and estates.
Prof. Memberships: American Bar

Association; West Virginia Bar Associa-
tion; Kanawha County Bar Association;
American College of Tax Counsel, Fel-
low; West Virginia Tax Institute; Univer-
sity of Charleston, Trustee Emeritus;
CAMC Foundation, Trustee; Highland
Hospital Foundation, Trustee; Clay
Foundation, Board Member; West Vir-
ginia Bar Foundation, Fellow.
Career: Listed in a leading American legal
publication (corporate law and tax law).
Personal: LLM, New York University;
JD, West Virginia University; AB, Mar-
shall University.

STEPTOE Jr, Robert
Steptoe & Johnson PLLC, Clarksburg
304 624 8000
Recommended in Employment

STOWERS, Gerard
Bowles Rice McDavid Graff & Love LLP,
Charleston 304 347 1100
Recommended in Litigation

STUMP, John
Steptoe & Johnson PLLC, Charleston
304 353 8000
Recommended in Corporate/M&A

SWEENEY, Robert
Jenkins Fenstermaker, PLLC,
Huntington 304 523 2100
Recommended in Litigation

THOMAS, David
Allen Guthrie McHugh & Thomas, PLLC,
Charleston 304 345 7250
Recommended in Litigation

TINNEY, John
The Tinney Law Firm, Charleston
304 720 3310
Recommended in Litigation

TWEEL, Robert
Jackson Kelly PLLC, Charleston
304 340 1111
rtweel@jacksonkelly.com
Recommended in Corporate/M&A
Practice Areas: Federal taxation.
Prof. Memberships: American Bar
Association (Section of Taxation); West
Virginia Bar Association; Kanawha
County Bar Association.
Personal: 1994 LLM - New York Uni-
versity; 1993 JD - West Virginia Univer-
sity; 1990 BA - Southern Methodist Uni-
versity (TX) (Mathematics/English).

WOLFE, Roger
Jackson Kelly PLLC, Charleston
304 340 1105
rwolfe@jacksonkelly.com
Recommended in Employment
Practice Areas: Discrimination, labor
and employment, unemployment compensation, wrongful discharge litigation,
NLRB proceedings, collective bargaining, class actions, statistics, public sector
employment law, alternative dispute resolution.
Career: Listed in a leading American
legal publication (labor and employment law); frequent lecturer on various
employment law topics; Adjunct Professor of Employment Law for West Virginia University; Member, Governor's
Commission on Public Employment
and Employee Relations.
Personal: JD, West Virginia University;
AB, West Virginia University.

WOODY, Charles
Spilman Thomas & Battle, PLLC,
Charleston 304 340 3862
cwoody@spilmanlaw.com
Recommended in Employment
Practice Areas: Litigation,
labor/employment, appellate.
Prof. Memberships: ABA,
Labor/Employment Law, Litigation Sec-
tions; US District Court for the South-
ern District of WV, Member, Local Rules
Committee (2004).
Career: Chair, Litigation Department.
Publications: 'NLRB Alters Successor
Bar Rule,' The WV Lawyer 14 (Decem-
ber 2002); 'Clinchfield Coal Co. v. Dis-
trict 28, UMW: A New Standard for
Judicial Review of Labor Arbitration
Awards,' 88 W. Va. L. Rev. 613 (1986);
'Impact of District 29, UMW v. Royal
Coal Co. on the Sale of a Coal Facility,'
88 W. Va. L. Rev. 605 (1986).
Personal: University of Virginia (BA,
1969); Florida State University (JD,
1972).

BAILEY & GLASSER LLP

THE FIRM

Partners: Benjamin L Bailey, Brian A Glasser, John W Barrett
Number of other lawyers: 5

FIRM OVERVIEW: Bailey & Glasser LLP was formed in March of 1999, when Ben Bailey and Brian Glasser left a larger Charleston firm to start their own litigation practice. Both partners are graduates of the Harvard Law School and served as law clerks to federal judges before entering the private practice of law. The firm has grown from two lawyers, one investigator and a secretary to 26 people today. Virtually all of the firm's practice is trial work. The firm's eight lawyers are assisted by a team of in-house investigators, environmental specialists, and paralegals. The firm has made a substantial investment in the technology of trial lawyering, to enable it to compete with much larger firms. The firm occupies its own building in the center of downtown Charleston, West Virginia, the state's capitol city. For all of its clients, the firm offers either fixed, contingent or standard hourly fees, in an effort to be sure the clients' interests are best served.

MAIN AREAS OF PRACTICE: Bailey & Glasser's practice is litigation oriented. Whether aggressively pursuing a commercial claim or vigorously defending business clients, the firm plans and strategizes as if all its cases are going to trial. Though many matters are ultimately resolved through negotiation, the firm firmly believes that no case can be resolved to the maximum benefit of the client unless it is exhaustively investigated, meticulously researched and prepared for courtroom presentation.

Commercial & General Civil Litigation: A substantial portion of the firm's practice is commercial litigation, for both plaintiffs and defendants. The firm routinely handles substantial disputes involving sales or acquisitions of businesses, disputes between business clients and their insurance carriers, and disputes involving professional corporations and partnerships. Bailey & Glasser is also heavily involved in litigation involving natural resource issues. In the past five years, its lawyers have handled cases involving coal contracts and leases, natural gas pipelines, oil and gas contracts and leases, lost coal claims and coal and timber waste claims. The firm also does some serious personal injury work, for defendants and plaintiffs. The firm handles these matters in state and federal courts, as well as before arbitrators and mediators. The firm averages four to five major trials per year, and a partner serves as lead counsel in every trial.

Environmental Litigation: The firm took a lead role for the State of West Virginia in two landmark environmental cases governing the way all coal mining is conducted and permitted in West Virginia: Bragg v Robertson and OVEC v Castle. Largely as an outgrowth of these cases, the firm has undertaken environmental cases, often for business and individual plaintiffs, in the energy and manufacturing sectors of West Virginia's economy. Those cases have included NEPA, SMCRA, RCRC and CWA challenges. The firm's clients have included coal companies, small businesses, and land owners in disputes with larger coal companies or other manufacturing enterprises.

White-Collar Criminal Defense: Bailey & Glasser enjoys an active criminal defense practice. In the last five years, the firm's lawyers have been involved in some of the most high profile cases pending in West Virginia. While most criminal defense work must remain confidential, in cases of public record the firm has represented the Majority Leader of the West Virginia Senate, the Education Committee Chairman of the West Virginia House of Delegates, the Chairman of the West Virginia Republican Party, former gubernatorial candidates, prominent doctors and businessmen. In many of these cases, the firm prevailed at trial. Trials have involved clients accused of murder, attempted murder, wire fraud, mail fraud, Medicaid fraud, Medicare fraud, distribution of controlled substances, and medical billing/record keeping violations. In addition to handling the trial of cases, the firm often takes over cases that have been tried to prosecute the appeal. The firm has handled criminal defense matters in West Virginia, Virginia, North Carolina, Pennsylvania, Washington State and Washington, DC.

CLIENTS: The firm's clients have included the State of West Virginia, several governors of West Virginia, a manufacturer of railroad parts, a major West Virginia-based media holding company, several medium-sized coal companies, major national and international insurance carriers, a national labor union, a large regional insurance brokerage firm, and various smaller businesses, lawyers, doctors, commercial landlords, and politicians in West Virginia.

HEAD OFFICE

WEST VIRGINIA
227 Capitol Street, **Charleston**, WV 25301
Tel: 304 345 6555 **Fax:** 304 342 1110
Email: info@baileyglasser.com
Website: www.baileyglasser.com

FARMER, CLINE & CAMPBELL PLLC

THE FIRM

Managing Partner: Stephen B Farmer

Number of lawyers: 9

AREAS OF PRACTICE:

Commercial Litigation	40%
Products Liability Litigation	40%
Miscellaneous Litigation	20%

FIRM OVERVIEW: The firm was established in 1996. The firm provides representation for many businesses, including coal and energy companies, pharmaceutical companies, law firms and small businesses.

MAIN AREAS OF PRACTICE:

Commercial Litigation: The firm represents clients in all aspects of commercial litigation. These matters include large-scale and long-running cases, as well as special expertise in key niche areas such as coal-related transactions and employment issues.

Products Liability Litigation: The firm has experience in both the prosecution and defense of products liability actions. Specific areas include prescription drugs, asbestos, tobacco, dietary supplements and defective design cases.

Miscellaneous Litigation: The firm is often retained to represent clients in special instances on important specific projects. These include legal malpractice, deliberate intent cases and employer's rights.

CLIENTS: The firm's clients include *Fortune* 500 companies engaged in energy, healthcare, pharmaceutical, tobacco and coal. The firm also represents small companies in the banking, automobile, retail and healthcare sectors. The firm also provides counsel to professional organizations including large law firms and physician groups.

HEAD OFFICE

WEST VIRGINIA
746 Myrtle Road, **Charleston**, WV 25311
Tel: 304 346 5990

Postal Address: Post Office Box 3842, **Charleston**, WV 25338

CONTACTS

Commercial Litigation	Stephen B Farmer
Products Liability Litigation	Stephen B Farmer
Miscellaneous Litigation	Stephen B Farmer

GOODWIN & GOODWIN

THE FIRM

Managing Partner: Thomas R Goodwin

Number of lawyers: 22

FIRM OVERVIEW: Goodwin & Goodwin was founded shortly after World War II in Ripley, West Virginia by Robert B Goodwin and CE Goodwin. In 1970, Tom and Joseph R 'Joe Bob' Goodwin resumed the family practice by founding the modern-day Goodwin & Goodwin, and two years later Steve Goodwin joined his brothers in the family business. In 1995, Joe Bob was appointed a federal district judge for the Southern District of West Virginia, but the firm's family ties have remained strong. A third generation is presently represented at the firm by Tom's daughter, Carrie Goodwin Fenwick, and Steve's son, Carte Goodwin. Over the past three decades, the firm has been much more than just a family business. Maintaining between 20 to 30 diverse attorneys throughout recent years, Goodwin & Goodwin is considered one of West Virginia's finest and most respected law firms. Since its inception, Goodwin & Goodwin has grown and evolved to keep pace with developments in the law as well as business processes and technology that best meet client needs. The knowledge and experience of the firm's attorneys allow the firm to specialize in numerous areas of the law. The diverse educational backgrounds and extensive experience of the firm's members provide a foundation for legal representation of the highest professional quality.

The State Capital Global Law Firm Group: Goodwin & Goodwin is a member of The State Capital Global Law Firm Group, an association of independent law firms serving businesses in state, provincial and other capital cities and major commercial centers around the world.

MAIN AREAS OF PRACTICE:

Litigation: Goodwin & Goodwin has considerable experience in handling litigation of all types. The firm is well suited to represent clients in any litigation, particularly sophisticated and complex cases, including: commercial/contract disputes; personal injury and wrongful death; products liability/toxic tort; insurance coverage; employment law; arbitration/ADR; complex and mass litigation.

Corporate & Commercial Law: Throughout its history, the firm has represented both large and small corporations in all areas. Goodwin & Goodwin brings sophisticated knowledge and expertise to legal issues facing today's businesses, including financing, asset purchases, buying and selling businesses, real estate matters, and bankruptcies. Work handled includes: corporate formation, acquisitions, asset purchases and dispositions, financing/secured transactions, real estate transactions.

Appellate Practice: Successful representation of a variety of clients at the appellate level in both the state and federal courts has given Goodwin & Goodwin a reputation for excellence in this area. An accurate and thorough understanding of the appellate process has enabled the firm to represent clients effectively in the appeals process, before the West Virginia Supreme Court and the Fourth Circuit Court of Appeals.

Municipal Bonds/Public Finance: Recognized as one of West Virginia's and the region's leading counsel in the area of bond financing, the firm can provide invaluable assistance to any business or governmental agency in need of counsel and advice on sophisticated financing transactions.

Legislative Lobbying/Government Affairs: Since its inception, Goodwin & Goodwin has prided itself on working with and through the legislative process on behalf of its clients. Goodwin & Goodwin's excellence in this area is exemplified through its effective assessments of proposed legislation and detailed monitoring of bills through each stage of the legislative process. The firm also represents clients in the variety of ways a business interacts with governmental agencies, from licensing and permitting issues to regulatory matters and representation before administrative bodies. The firm undertakes lobbying, bill/regulation monitoring, bill drafting, representation before government agencies, licensing/permitting, and strategic planning.

Employment Law: Including litigation, compliance counselling, employee handbooks/policies.

Bankruptcy: The firm advises creditors and debtors on a range of bankruptcy issues.

Family Law: The firm handles divorce, adoption, custody and support work.

HEAD OFFICE

WEST VIRGINIA
300 Summers Street, Suite 1500, **Charleston**, WV 25301-1678
Tel: 304 346 7000 **Fax:** 304 344 9692
Website: www.goodwingoodwin.com
Email: jdf@goodwingoodwin.com

BRANCH OFFICES

WEST VIRGINIA
201 Third Street, **Parkersburg**, WV 26101
Tel: 304 485 2345

P.O. Box 349, 500 Church Street, **Ripley**, WV 25271
Tel: 304 372 2651

HENDRICKSON & LONG, P.L.L.C.

THE FIRM

Managing Partner: David K Hendrickson, R Scott Long

Number of partners: 5
Number of other lawyers: 4

AREAS OF PRACTICE:

Toxic Tort Defense 35%
Product Liability Defense 35%
Insurance Law Defense 15%
Commercial Law 15%

FIRM OVERVIEW: Hendrickson & Long, P.L.L.C. is a general litigation firm, formed in July 1994 by David K Hendrickson and R Scott Long. The firm is counsel for individuals, local West Virginia companies, national and international companies and is recognized as one of the most progressive legal establishments in the state. The law firm's attorneys are supported by paralegals and an administrative and secretarial staff who are afforded the latest state-of-the-art communications and computer technology. The firm's mission is to provide quality legal services in a manner that exceeds clients' expectations.

MAIN AREAS OF PRACTICE:

Toxic Tort Defense: The firm's toxic tort defense includes representing clients in all aspects of litigation. The firm regularly defends manufacturers, distributors, premises owners and/or employers in the glass, chemical, electronics, mining, welding, silica, rubber, automotive and utilities-related industries against individual and mass tort personal injury claims. The firm offers a group of experienced first-chair lawyers who know how to relate to both judge and jury in West Virginia. Lawyers in the firm are especially skilled at developing factual and legal defenses for complex scientific and technical issues.

Products Liability Defense: The firm's product liability defense includes representing clients in all aspects of litigation. The firm regularly defends manufacturers and distributors in the medical, chemical, and home products industries against individual and mass tort personal injury claims. The firm offers a group of experienced first-chair lawyers who know how to relate to both judge and jury in West Virginia.

Insurance Law Defense: The firm regularly handles insurance defense, including bad faith and direct actions. Lawyers in the firm regularly research, write and deliver coverage opinions. Hendrickson & Long is also adept at handling subrogation issues.

Commercial Law: Hendrickson & Long has long represented clients on creditor bankruptcies. Lawyers in this form are adept at retail and healthcare collections.

CLIENTS: Range from International conglomerates to individual West Virginia businesses. Routinely represent Fortune 100 companies. Rountinely represent clients in states outside of West Virginia.

HEAD OFFICE

WEST VIRGINIA
214 Capitol Street, **Charleston**, WV 25301
Tel: 304 346 5500   **Fax:** 304 346 5515
Email: handl@handl.com
Website: www.handl.com

Hendrickson & Long PLLC
ATTORNEYS AT LAW

JACKSON KELLY PLLC

THE FIRM

Chief Executive Officer: AL Emch
Assistant Managing Member: Michael D Foster
Number of members: 93
Number of other lawyers: 78

FIRM OVERVIEW: Jackson Kelly PLLC is historically synonymous with the practice of law. The oldest and largest law firm in West Virginia, Jackson Kelly traces its roots back to the early 1800s. In 11 offices across the country, with over 170 lawyers, Jackson Kelly combines diversity and specialization, with a strong commitment to excellence. Although meeting the legal needs of myriad corporate and individual clients effectively and efficiently is of paramount concern, the firm maintains a strong tradition of public involvement through charitable generosity and participation in the arts and education. The tradition that has become the trademark of Jackson Kelly is perhaps exemplified in these areas of support, a dedication that complements the legal services performed for employers, business and commercially-oriented clients.

MAIN AREAS OF PRACTICE:

Business/Commercial & Economic Development: The firm offers services that range from general corporate law and public and private financing to more specialized areas such as the formation of bank holding companies. Businesses of all sizes seek the firm's advice, from companies planning multimillion dollar mergers and acquisitions to small, family-owned businesses planning to incorporate.

Employee Benefits: Jackson Kelly established the Employee Benefits Group to assist with the development and administration of the firm's clients' employee benefits plans. The focus of this group includes non-qualified and qualified design plans, consultation and administration.

Energy & Natural Resources: Jackson Kelly is a national leader in all aspects of the law relating to the extraction of Federal, Native American, state, and private natural resources and the industries associated with the development, processing, refining, transportation, and marketing of those resources, including: coal, oil, natural gas, coalbed methane, metals, hard rock, synfuels, aggregates, timber, and other minerals, as well as alternate energy.

Environmental: The firm provides assistance in obtaining permits and approvals, and in defending both private and governmental environmental claims in numerous areas. Firm lawyers are nationally known as experts in the handling of claims involving hazardous waste disposal.

Federal & Workers' Compensation: A management-oriented firm, Jackson Kelly provides the nation's largest defense practice against claims arising under the Federal Black Lung Act. The firm also has one of the most extensive defense practices under the Kentucky Workers' Compensation Act and the largest defense practice in West Virginia.

Government Contracts: An important part of Jackson Kelly's service to its clients is to help government prime contractors and subcontractors meet applicable statutory and regulatory requirements in various procurement environments through a number of menus, including compliance audits and training. The firm also assists clients in initiating and defending both private and governmental contract claims, disputes and protests.

Health Law: The Health Law Group's specialized experience and expertise assists healthcare organizations in meeting the challenges offered by today's environment of keen economic competition, strict government regulation, and new business relationships.

Immigration: This practice covers all aspects of legal representation relating to immigration and naturalization, including temporary and permanent immigration visa petitions, visa application and processing abroad, and exclusion and deportation proceedings. The practice also encompasses internal reviews of company compliance with employment-related immigration rules and representations in any civil proceedings that may result from enforcement of such rules.

HEAD OFFICE

WEST VIRGINIA
1600 Laidley Tower, PO Box 553, **Charleston**, WV 25322
Tel: 304 340 1000   **Fax:** 304 340 1033
Website: www.jacksonkelly.com

BRANCH OFFICES

The firm also has offices in Morgantown, WV; Clarksburg, WV; New Martinsville, WV; Martinsburg, WV; Parkersburg, WV; Wheeling, WV; Denver, CO; Lexington, KY; Pittsburgh, PA; Washington, DC.

Intellectual Property: Services involve legal counseling regarding the various aspects of broadcasting, copyrights, patents, trademarks, or other matters concerning the many facets of intellectual property and technology law.

International Law: Whether clients are buying or selling goods internationally or considering the establishment of operations in a foreign country or the United States, Jackson Kelly's International Law Group can help.

Labor & Employment: An employer-oriented firm, Jackson Kelly is dedicated to representing management's interests in all types of employment-related matters at both the state and federal levels.

Legislative Services: In addition to considerable experience in legislative drafting, Jackson Kelly lawyers render lobbying services to clients by regularly advising about the impact of pending legislation, preparing position statements, preparing legislative amendments, and testifying at or preparing witnesses for committee appearances. Included in this field of expertise are lawyers who have served in the West Virginia Legislature or as clerks of major committees of the West Virginia Legislature and in Kentucky as members of various state commissions and study committees.

Litigation: The firm offers its clients experienced representation from advice, planning and litigation avoidance or mitigation to case development and trial representation including jury trials and, if necessary, appellate advocacy.

Medical Professional Liability: This Practice Group provides aggressive representation of hospitals, physicians and other healthcare providers. Through thorough medical and legal research, the firm's goal is to identify issues and problems and come to an early evaluation of the best defense strategy for a given case. The MPL Practice Group also offers advice and counsel on risk management, confidentiality and medical records issues.

Occupational Safety & Health: Jackson Kelly's Safety and Health Practice Group provides a broad spectrum of services to the firm's clients, emphasizing MSHA, OSHA, and DOT.

Taxes, Estates & Trusts: Clients, which include lawyers outside the firm, accountants, fiduciaries and other professionals, are advised with regard to tax planning, purchases and sales of business interests, corporate mergers, and personal estate planning.

CLIENTS: Clients include manufacturing, natural resources, business and commercial, trade associations, medical, retail, transportation, government contractions, utilities, local, state and federal agencies.

SPILMAN THOMAS & BATTLE, PLLC

THE FIRM

Managing Member: Michael J Basile
Member in Charge of Lawyer Administration: David P Ferretti
Member in Charge of Client Relations: Eric W Iskra
Number of members: 47
Number of other lawyers: 38

FIRM OVERVIEW: Spilman Thomas & Battle, PLLC was formed in 1864 - one year after West Virginia became a state - and has been serving the legal needs of its clients ever since. Today, the firm has more than 175 attorneys and professional support staff dedicated to providing outstanding legal services and helping clients achieve their business goals. As one of the region's largest law firms, Spilman Thomas & Battle, PLLC offers a full-service legal practice and is proud of the diversity of its client base - one that includes Fortune 500 companies with thousands of employees and family-owned businesses that are just around the corner. The firm's attorneys have been carefully trained to serve as an extension of its clients' management team - working with them as one to prevent problems before they occur and guiding them carefully and successfully through the legal process. That has been the firm's tradition for more than a century and continues to be its guiding force today.

MAIN AREAS OF PRACTICE:

Corporate & Business Law: The firm's business attorneys are skilled in virtually all areas of a commercial business practice and are prepared to meet the needs of multi-million dollar public corporations as well as closely held private entities. Spilman Thomas & Battle, PLLC is proficient in all aspects of corporate governance, including formation, board and shareholder issues, and liquidation and dissolution. The firm also performs work for partnerships, limited liability companies, and limited liability partnerships. In addition, the firm handles all types of corporate issues including banking and finance law, bankruptcy, business expansion and development, consumer debt regulation and collections, federal/state/local taxation, immigration and naturalization, intellectual property, mergers and acquisitions, natural resources, public finance, real estate, securities, and venture capital finance.

Litigation: Whether the case is simple or complex, the firm's goal is to manage the litigation as efficiently and effectively as possible. Spilman utilizes an early case assessment (ECA) for virtually every new litigation matter. The ECA reflects the firm's philosophy to proactively identify and quantify the risks in order to ensure that clients achieve their goals. The firm has successfully tried numerous cases to verdict in various jurisdictions and legal avenues, including almost every substantive area of the law. These include antitrust, appellate, asbestos, banking, bankruptcy, commercial and business litigation, construction, creditors' rights and foreclosures, consumer protection, environmental, federal black lung, healthcare, insurance, intellectual property, personal injury, product liability, Public Service Commission, real estate, shareholder and partnership disputes, toxic tort, white collar crime, and workers' compensation.

Labor & Employment: The firm's lawyers regularly counsel, advise, and represent clients on every legal issue arising out of the employment relationship. The firm's goal is to work with clients to avoid employment litigation. Nevertheless, the firm's lawyers are often retained to defend employers against an ever increasing array of employment litigation matters. The firm's labor and employment lawyers are trial lawyers who have developed best-in-class strategies, not only for single-plaintiff litigation, but also for class actions and administrative agency maintained actions. Spilman also provides counsel and represents management in connection with union organizing campaigns, salting attacks, collective bargaining negotiations, arbitration pursuant to collective bargaining agreements, representation in unfair labor practice proceedings before the National Labor Relations Board, injunction proceedings to halt unlawful union picketing and violence, and lawsuits in federal and state courts against labor unions based on union member misconduct and damage to the company.

Energy: The Spilman Energy Group is comprised of attorneys from varied practice areas. From acquisitions to litigation to government relations, the firm's dedication to providing outstanding legal counsel to the energy industry is founded on a commitment of furthering this growing industry. The Spilman Energy Group is well versed in issues that most impact energy clients, including regulatory issues, contract negotiations, litigation, and labor and employment. The firm's goal is to keep its clients well informed about trends and changes in the industry, and to help clients stay one step ahead of the multitude of other issues that arise in business every day.

Environmental: The goal of the firm's Environmental Practice Group is to resolve the environmental challenges that face clients in a cost-effective manner using negotiation, mediation, compliance planning, regulatory or legislative changes, and, where necessary, litigation. Attorneys provide environmental counseling to a wide range of businesses and industries, including manufacturing, mining, oil and gas development and transmission, forestry, banking and lending, and retail establishments.

Healthcare: Spilman has a large and diverse practice in the area of healthcare law. During the past 30 years, the firm has represented nearly all of the general acute care hospitals in West Virginia. The firm also represents healthcare systems, nursing homes, home health agencies, physicians, and other healthcare providers. The experienced lawyers that focus on the healthcare industry are continually contacted to serve as speakers, authors, and advisors on a multitude of healthcare issues, including certificates of need, contracts, corporate reorganizations, due diligence investigations, Health Care Quality Improvement Act, integrated delivery systems, internal investigations, Medicare and Medicaid fraud abuse, rate review, and reimbursement issues.

Government Relations: Since West Virginia was formed, Spilman has effectively represented clients before the West Virginia Legislature and within state and local government. Numerous Spilman lawyers have held elected and appointed positions within the legislature and state and local government, equipping the firm with the experience and insight to effectively assist clients. And, the firm continues to maintain strong contacts and access with government entities, which are the keys to a successful government relations practice.

HEAD OFFICE

WEST VIRGINIA
Spilman Center, 300 Kanawha Boulevard, East, **Charleston**, WV 25301
Tel: 304 340 3800   **Fax:** 304 340 3801
Email: stb@spilmanlaw.com   **Website:** www.spilmanlaw.com

BRANCH OFFICES

WEST VIRGINIA
990 Elmer Prince Drive, Suite 205, **Morgantown**, WV 26505
Tel: 304 599 8175   **Fax:** 304 599 8229

417 Grand Park Drive, Suite 203, **Vienna (Parkersburg)**, WV 26105
Tel: 304 422 6700   **Fax:** 304 422 6733

333 Penco Road, Suite A, **Weirton**, WV 26062
Tel: 304 723 6980   **Fax:** 304 723 6986

PENNSYLVANIA
One Oxford Centre, Suite 3440, 301 Grant Street, **Pittsburgh**, PA 15219
Tel: 412 325 3301   **Fax:** 412 325 3324

 SPILMAN THOMAS & BATTLE, PLLC

CONTENTS: Corporate/M&A p.1817; Employment p.1819; Litigation p.1820; Real Estate p.1822; Individuals' Profiles p.1824. Firms' Profiles p.1828.

How lawyers are ranked

The opinions we gather from clients — mainly from in-house lawyers but also from other purchasers of legal services — are balanced by opinions from colleagues and competitors. Together, they provide two different perspectives — an all-round view — and biased viewpoints cancel each other out.

CORPORATE/M&A

Wisconsin

Leading firms (Corporate/M&A)

1 FOLEY & LARDNER *Milwaukee*

2 GODFREY & KAHN, SC *Milwaukee*
  QUARLES & BRADY LLP *Milwaukee*

3 MICHAEL BEST & FRIEDRICH LLP *Milwaukee*
  REINHART, BOERNER, VAN DEUREN SC *Milwaukee*

Leading individuals (Corporate/M&A)

1 BUONO Kathryn *Quarles & Brady, Milwaukee*
  GARMER Benjamin *Foley & Lardner, Milwaukee*
  SOMMERHAUSER Peter *Godfrey & Kahn, Milwaukee*

2 BARTELL Jeff *Quarles & Brady, Madison*
  BEDORE James *Reinhart Boerner, Milwaukee*
  DAVIDSON Bruce *Quarles & Brady, Milwaukee*
  LINSTROTH Tod *Michael Best, Madison*
  RYAN Patrick *Quarles & Brady, Milwaukee*
  SIMS Luke *Foley & Lardner, Milwaukee*
  SKINDRUD Michael *LaFollette Godfrey, Madison*
  TYSON Joseph *Foley & Lardner, Milwaukee*

3 ABRAHAM Bill *Foley & Lardner, Milwaukee*
  COFFEY Peter *Michael Best, Milwaukee*
  DICKENS John *Godfrey & Kahn, Milwaukee*
  EHRMANN Mark *Quarles & Brady, Madison*
  GOODKIND Conrad *Quarles & Brady, Milwaukee*
  LUNDGREN Thor *Michael Best, Milwaukee*
  PEPKE Michael *Reinhart Boerner, Milwaukee*
  ROBISON John *Quarles & Brady, Madison*
  SEIDENSTRICKER Paul *von Briesen & Roper, Milwaukee*
  WAHL Nicholas *Godfrey & Kahn, Milwaukee*
  WALSH David *Foley & Lardner, Madison*

Up-and-coming individuals

QUICK Patrick *Foley & Lardner, Milwaukee*
ROTHMAN Jay *Foley & Lardner, Milwaukee*

Firms and individuals are listed alphabetically in each band.

Band 1

Foley & Lardner

See firm details p.1828

The Firm: In another highly successful year, the firm has once more been prominent in all aspects of corporate work. Its pursuit of a national model has convinced many market observers that it has now positioned itself as "*the leading corporate firm in Wisconsin and the firm of choice as local representative of multinational businesses.*" The firm advised Minneapolis-based Pentair in the $875 million acquisition of WICOR Industries from Wisconsin Energy Corporation, and advised the same client on the $800 million sale of its tools group to Black & Decker. The firm has also been active in various energy projects of late. Its effective and efficient handling of recent wind energy deals has aptly demonstrated the level of expertise in structured finance and complex tax credit issues that the firm can bring to bear on such matters.

The Lawyers: **Ben Garmer** (see p.1825) played a critical role in both of the recent Pentair deals and also advised key client Oshkosh Truck in a major acquisition. Sources say that he is "*very much the senior lawyer at the firm, a business man's lawyer,*" citing his "*top-notch credentials, boardroom gravitas and sound judgment.*" **Luke Sims** (see p.1826) specializes in general securities-related work, including debt and equity offerings, particularly those under Rule 144A. He notably counselled NYSE listed Extendicare Health Services in a $225 million high-yield debt offering. Interviewees agree: "*You won't find a better leveraged buyout specialist in the state.*" Chairman of the business law department **Joseph Tyson** (see p.1826) addresses the full range of corporate transactions, typically advising the department's highest caliber clients. He has completed several multibillion dollar public utility company deals in recent years. Clients report that he is "*far beyond being just a lawyer; his strategic vision is comparable to any leading corporate executive.*" Former chairman of the business law department **Bill Abraham** (see p.1824) earned praise as "*an excellent, pragmatic and well-connected attorney.*" His practice leans towards acquisition finance and he is also well versed in real estate matters. Madison-based **David Walsh** (see p.1827), a former managing partner of the firm, is the department's expert in business transactions relating to mainly private telecommunications companies. He also enjoys considerable experience in litigation and in the restructuring and reorganization of businesses. **Patrick Quick**'s (see p.1826) practice features a volume of securities law compliance, M&A, and counseling on the best practice defense to hostile takeovers. He "*inspires a high level of confidence in his clients and shows a great deal of business acumen.*" Market sources also concur that **Jay Rothman** (see p.1826), chair of the firm's national transactional and securities practice group, is "*an excellent legal mind and a future authority in securities law.*"

The Clients: Manitowoc; Extendicare Health Services; Goldman Sachs; Lehman Brothers; Charter Communications; TDS Telecom; Johnson Controls; Oshkosh Truck and Harley-Davidson.

Band 2

Godfrey & Kahn, SC

The Firm: This corporate and securities unit falls under the wider umbrella of the firm's business practice and fields attorneys across five offices. The group focuses on midmarket clients but also acts for SMEs, growth companies and Fortune 500 businesses. Prime among these is Kohl's Department Stores, which the firm has counseled from its origins into a national 450-unit entity. Recent highlights include acting for equipment asset management services business US Counseling Service in its acquisition by Thermo Electron for $80 million. It also guided Quad/Graphics through the $120 million sale of its package delivery business, Parcel Direct, to FedEx. Clients report that the team is "*a delight to work with,*" and praise the "*close attention paid to our strategy and overall vision.*"

The Lawyers: For many, **Peter Sommerhauser**'s very presence represents "*a valid enough reason in itself to choose the firm.*" One client praised his "*conciliatory style*" and "*patience in reasoning with the unreasonable when the situation* demands." He played a central role in the deals mentioned above, and counseled independent insurance agency Frank Haack & Associates in its sale to H&R Block. Sommerhauser is also experienced in helping companies pursue the real estate acquisitions of troubled entities through the bankruptcy courts. **Michael Skindrud** continues to cement his reputation as an expert in counseling growth technology companies related to the University of Wisconsin in Madison. His clientele also features healthcare businesses, physicians, and health insurance companies. **John Dickens** enters the tables due to market recognition of his "*highly visible and hugely active practice.*" His general corporate and commercial workload also encompasses buyout and private placement matters. **Nicholas Wahl** completes this trio of new entrants to the tables. Market sources agree that he is "*one of the most prominent venture capital lawyers currently active in the state.*"

The Clients: Mark Travel Corporation, Kohl's Department Stores and Mason Wells are major names on the firm's client roster.

Quarles & Brady LLP

The Firm: The sizable corporate services team features around 60 lawyers in Wisconsin alone, but can marshal considerably more resources in dovetailing with other practice areas. The group generally focuses upon deals in the midmarket arena, and has exploited the recent pickup of the economy in this sector; but it also enjoys strong relationships with some of the most prominent public companies in the state. The firm remains at the forefront of private equity and venture capital activity. It retains a close working relationship with private equity giant Mason Wells, and will benefit from its recent creation of an additional fund for investments ranging from $25 million to $250 million in speciality packaging paper, engineering and outsourced businesses. Moreover, it continues to foster robust relationships with various portfolio companies. Key deals of late include advising Mason Wells on the sale of General American to Fiserv. Commentators praised the firm's "*bench strength and excellent all-around credentials for both higher profile deals and midmarket work.*"

The Lawyers: **Kathy Buono**'s busy securities and transactional practice has seen another outstanding year, a highlight of which was her involvement in the $228 million acquisition of Simplicity Manufacturing by Briggs & Stratton. Interviewees praised her "*attentive and extremely professional demeanour*" and her "*unwavering ability to set a budget in advance of a deal and never fail to meet it.*" One client also noted, "*by the time we get to the negotiating stage, she will have already done most of the drafting herself.*" **Jeff Bartell** garners high praise from anybody

who has worked opposite or alongside him on a deal. His forte is securities work and he is also regarded as an expert in the field of insurance regulation. Chair of the corporate finance and securities team **Bruce Davidson** dedicates the majority of his practice to counseling clients in SEC regulation and Sarbanes-Oxley matters. The balance of his practice also involves financings and filings, and he is well connected with various public bodies. Managing partner **Patrick Ryan** remains a figure afforded "*tremendous respect*" by commentators for his "*full set of management tools and wealth of experience.*" He enjoys a robust relationship with Mason Wells, and is particularly valued for his knowledge of investments in the speciality packaging, paper and technology industries. **Conrad Goodkind** can draw upon his experience as a former deputy commissioner for securities in his advice to public companies and a range of mutual funds. He possesses a "*fantastic knowledge of the securities market.*" **John Robison**, according to market sources, has established "*probably the strongest healthcare-related practice in Madison.*" His caseload centres upon private entities, investment agreements, sales and distribution and taxation matters. **Mark Ehrmann** recently moved from Godfrey & Khan. His corporate finance practice addresses external financing, M&A and divestitures.

The Clients: Sybron Dental, Mason Wells, Briggs & Stratton and a range of dairy cooperatives, physician groups, retail and service businesses are prominent on the firm's client list.

Band 3

Michael Best & Friedrich LLP
See firm details p.1830

The Firm: Another particularly strong showing by the Madison team convinces market observers that "*this office is the prime choice for counseling tech businesses and startups, and for commercializing talent related to the University of Wisconsin.*" This has been formalized in the creation of Venture Best, which calls upon attorneys from the firm's Madison, Milwaukee and Chicago offices. This unit has advised market leading startups such as plant genetics entity Nutra-Park, Genomix and OpGen. The Milwaukee office also benefits from relationships with some significant public company clients that have enjoyed robust relations with the firm's leading employment and labor law practice. The firm's recent deals of note include counseling Berbee Information Systems, a $300 million technology company in Madison, on two major acquisitions. The group also counselled the state's largest biotech company, Promega Corporation, on a large share repurchase transaction.

The Lawyers: Chair of the firm's management committee **Tod Linstroth** was also the driving force behind the creation of the Venture Best unit. Commentators acknowledge his "*unparalleled experience in guiding young businesses*" and his "*unflappable presence in transactions.*" Linstroth notably represented design and build company Marshall Erdman Associates in its sale to a private equity entity. A former Harnischfeger Industries senior lawyer, **Thor Lundgren**'s forte lies in restructurings and debt and equity financings under securities and banking laws. **Peter Coffey** impresses with his "*measured and eminently sensible*" counsel in the field of corporate governance, MBOs and premerger activity, whether hostile or uncontested.

The Clients: Stratatech; Deltanoid; Mero; Genomix; Newell Industries; Seattle Systems; OpGen and Nutra-Park.

Reinhart, Boerner, Van Deuren SC
See firm details p.1831

The Firm: This "*top-notch*" firm is prominent in the midmarket arena, both within Wisconsin and beyond, particularly Chicago and its environs. While this is proving to be a fruitful area for the firm, it has also demonstrated the requisite legal muscle to handle higher caliber transactions. For example, it advised Associated Banc-Corp in its $613 million acquisition of First Federal Capital Bank Corp. It has also recently guided toy producer and distributor RC2 through a flurry of sizable company acquisitions. Market commentators concur that the department "*goes about its business with minimum fanfare and impressive efficiency.*"

The Lawyers: Peers maintain "*very high levels of respect*" for **James Bedore**'s (see p.1824) practice. He played a pivotal role in the Associated Banc-Corp deal, and has also been involved in a series of deals in the $20 million to $40 million bracket. Interviewees refer to his work in financing buyouts and knowledge of securities as key strengths. **Michael Pepke** (see p.1826) "*combines the commercial edge of an investment banker with proven technical legal expertise.*" His practice addresses corporate sales and acquisitions, corporate capital raising and strategic planning.

The Clients: Allen-Edmonds; RC2; Ruud Lighting and Emmber Foods.

Other Notable Practitioners

Interviewees commended **Paul Seidenstricker** of von Briesen & Roper SC to researchers as a skilled practitioner, who "*fully appreciates all the angles and sensitivities in a deal.*" His forte is the healthcare sector, and he has been particularly active in numerous multifaceted hospital mergers and development matters.

1818   All quotes in the text are from interviews with clients and competitors.

CHAMBERS USA 2005

EMPLOYMENT

MAINLY DEFENDANT

Wisconsin
Leading firms
(Employment: Mainly Defendant)

1 FOLEY & LARDNER *Madison*
  MICHAEL BEST & FRIEDRICH LLP *Milwaukee*
  QUARLES & BRADY LLP *Milwaukee*

2 DAVIS & KUELTHAU, SC *Milwaukee*
  LINDNER & MARSACK, SC *Milwaukee*
  MELLI WALKER PEASE & RUHLY SC *Madison*

Leading individuals
(Employment: Mainly Defendant)

1 AUEN Michael *Foley & Lardner, Madison*
  BOBBER Bernard *Foley & Lardner, Milwaukee*
  KERN David *Quarles & Brady, Milwaukee*

2 DUFFY Robert *Quarles & Brady, Milwaukee*
  LEICHTLING Ely *Quarles & Brady, Milwaukee*
  SCRIVNER Tom *Michael Best, Milwaukee*

3 CRONE Tom *Melli Walker, Madison*
  CROYSDALE David *Michael Best, Milwaukee*
  LYNCH Lawrence *Foley & Lardner, Milwaukee*
  MARSACK Gary *Lindner & Marsack, Milwaukee*
  NINNEMAN Mary *Quarles & Brady, Milwaukee*
  PENCE Thomas *Foley & Lardner, Milwaukee*
  STEVENS Charles *Michael Best, Milwaukee*
  VETTER Mark *Davis & Kuelthau, Milwaukee*

Up-and-coming individuals
  PLOOR Pamela *Quarles & Brady, Milwaukee*
  SCULLEN Sean *Quarles & Brady, Milwaukee*

Firms and individuals are listed alphabetically in each band.

Band 1

Foley & Lardner
See firm details p.1828
The Firm: The firm's Wisconsin-based labor and employment unit should be seen in the context of the wider national group of more than 75 lawyers. Several interviewees alluded to the firm's pursuit of a national model and the group certainly represents a number of national and international businesses as primary or lead local counsel. Its highly publicized and successful work in the 30-state Wal-Mart class action aptly illustrates the wider reputation of the department. The 20-strong Wisconsin group's regular caseload blends traditional labor law expertise with employment law experience, particularly in the field of discrimination litigation. Its *"high integrity"* practitioners are described as some of the state's *"toughest."*
The Lawyers: **Michael Auen**'s (see p.1824) practice focuses upon traditional labor law, though he has also been involved in discrimination issues of late. Interviewees commended his strengths in negotiations, arbitrations and grievance procedures, noting his *"absolute willingness to immerse himself in the issues for his clients in order to get the required result."* He recently rep-

resented a major automotive components manufacturer in a strike subsequent to job losses. The issue was further complicated due to resentments created by the arrival of temporary cover. Clients praised Auen's *"instant credibility to all sides and foresight in identifying potential flashpoints."* **Bud Bobber**'s (see p.1824) outstanding reputation as *"a superb strategist and a fine gentleman"* has been reinforced by his prominent role in the Wal-Mart class action. His work was critical in persuading a judge to reject successive requests for class certification which, if granted, would have potentially created a class of some 100,000 plaintiffs. The balance of his practice is consumed by labor arbitration work and non-competition trade secrets issues. **Lawrence Lynch**'s (see p.1825) highly regarded practice leans towards discrimination, contractual disputes, union relations and OSHA matters. Interviewees agree that he has been *"a stalwart of the team for many years now."* Chair of the labor and employment team **Tom Pence** (see p.1825) once again received high praise from market sources as *"an excellent director of resources as well as an experienced practitioner."* His caseload is biased towards employment law, not least ADA and FMLA matters, but he is also experienced in collective bargaining and arbitrations.
The Clients: SABMiller; Johnson Controls; Monster Worldwide and Northwestern Mutual.

Michael Best & Friedrich LLP
See firm details p.1830
The Firm: According to interviewees, the group remains *"one of the most established and comprehensive teams in the state, particularly in traditional labor matters."* The team also received praise for its capabilities across the board in collective bargaining, discrimination, wage and hour, and mediation services. Moreover, the firm has been involved in sensitive employment matters, particularly regarding large-scale relocations, relating to some of the most high-profile mergers in recent times, such as Unilever's takeover of Best Foods and Pfizer's acquisition of Warner-Lambert.
The Lawyers: Former head of the employment relations division **Tom Scrivner** has developed a diverse practice that addresses all elements of labor and employment law. His clients, who come from sectors ranging from printing to construction, appreciate his *"successful blend of experience, tact and gravitas."* **David Croysdale** is *"an immensely experienced practitioner,"* particularly in relation to issues arising from the armed services. New entrant to the table, **Charles Stevens'** workload leans towards specialist employment relations and employee benefits matters, including ERISA, employee benefits and compensation issues. Clients noted his *"excellent demeanor and willingness to roll up his sleeves."*

The Clients: Fortune Brands; Unilever Bestfoods; Procter & Gamble; JohnsonDiversey and Journal Communications.

Quarles & Brady LLP
The Firm: The firm's *"watertight grasp of traditional labor and employment matters and an impressive conversancy with recent FMLA, FLSA and EEOC laws"* continue to impress interviewees. Though the sizable team of 38 lawyers is comparable with the largest in the state, more than one commentator suggested that *"it could be double this number since their influence is very pervasive."* This influence manifests itself in highly regarded in-service coaching programs for clients, labor law audits, proactive legal digests and seminars.
The Lawyers: National department chair **David Kern** earned a plethora of commendations as a *"highly practical, calm lawyer and an adviser of great integrity."* Recent highlights include counseling Master Lock on various matters arising out of its acquisition and consolidation of a facility in Illinois. His input was also crucial in the dismissal of various discrimination allegations aimed at a global outboard engine manufacturer. Peers describe **Bob Duffy** as *"probably the busiest lawyer in the employment group."* He was recently successful in extricating Menasha Corporation from allegations of unfair labor practices in failing to bargain the issue of transferring work away from a union facility. He is also highly visible in both federal and district courts against the EEOC and other plaintiffs. **Ely Leichtling** won praise as *"an exceptionally bright counselor for even the trickiest of cases."* He has defended management in a significant number of wage and hour discrimination issues, and race and retaliation cases of late. Notable recent successes include defending an international waste management company against an investigation by government agency OFCCP into discrepancies in race and gender compensation. **Mary Pat Ninneman**'s workload is heavily accented by wrongful discharge, discrimination and sexual orientation litigation. Peers commended her *"sharp, analytical eye which never misses a trick."* *"Outstanding young talent"* **Sean Scullen** has been involved in several FSLA wage and hour compliance matters of late. He received particular praise for his knowledge of disability legislation in which he *"demonstrates a legal sensitivity beyond his years."* **Pam Ploor** counsels clients through discrimination cases and affirmative action programs. One interviewee remarked: *"She is the state expert in thorny FMLA matters,"* whilst another praised her *"extraordinarily concise briefs"* and *"skills in handling witnesses and depositions to get cases knocked out before trial."*
The Clients: Northwestern Mutual Life Insur-

www.ChambersandPartners.com
All quotes in the text are from interviews with clients and competitors.
1819

ance Company; SABMiller; Onyx Waste Services Midwest; M&I Bank; Aurora Health Care and WS Packaging Group.

Band 2

Davis & Kuelthau, SC

The Firm: The firm, now approaching its 40th anniversary, fields a labor and employment team that is home to 30 lawyers operating out of the six state offices. The department has lately been involved in several notable private sector workforce reduction strategies, discrimination matters and arbitration proceedings, but remains a "*public sector powerhouse*" in the eyes of interviewees.

The Lawyers: **Mark Vetter**'s broad client base features many school districts and municipal government entities. Commentators agree he probably has "*an unparalleled depth of experience in this area.*"

The Clients: The firm's private sector client ros-

ter features businesses ranging from startups and SMEs to listed entities. The public sector clients include nonprofit concerns, school districts and municipalities.

Lindner & Marsack, SC

The Firm: This boutique of 17 attorneys predominantly addresses traditional labor matters, for which it enjoys a reputation amongst peers as "*a very accomplished outfit.*" It also advises on the full range of employment and worker compensation matters. The firm itself is almost 100 years old and is home to some of the most experienced practitioners in the state.

The Lawyers: Firm president **Gary Marsack** combines expertise in traditional labor matters, notably collective bargaining, worker relocations and facility closures, with experience of employment issues arising from M&A and other entrepreneurial business activity. Peers regard him as "*a cornerstone of both his firm and the state Bar.*"

The Clients: Fortune Brands; Mercury Marine;

Harnischfeger Corporation and Master Lock Company.

Melli Walker Pease & Ruhly SC

The Firm: Widely regarded as the premier labor and employment boutique in Madison, the 15 lawyers are active in trial and appellate work at both the state and federal level, including the US Supreme Court. Interviewees highlighted the reputation of the team as "*doughty fighters for their clients.*"

The Lawyers: **Tom Crone**'s practice balances labor and employment, civil rights, and business-related matters, and he is highly experienced in trial and appellate proceedings and before administrative agencies.

The Clients: The primarily nonunion client base features Associated Builders & Contractors of Wisconsin and Town & Country Electric.

LITIGATION

GENERAL COMMERCIAL

Wisconsin
Leading firms
(Litigation: General Commercial)
[1] **FOLEY & LARDNER** *Milwaukee*
[2] **HELLER EHRMAN WHITE & MCAULIFFE** *Madison*
QUARLES & BRADY LLP *Milwaukee*
[3] **GODFREY & KAHN, SC** *Milwaukee*
LIEBMANN, CONWAY, OLEJNICZAK *Green Bay*
MICHAEL BEST & FRIEDRICH LLP *Milwaukee*
REINHART, BOERNER, VAN DEUREN *Milwaukee*
STAFFORD ROSENBAUM LLP *Madison*
Firms are listed alphabetically in each band.

Band 1

Foley & Lardner

See firm details p.1828

The Firm: This is the largest department in the firm by a considerable margin, and its Wisconsin-based attorneys work with over 400 litigation attorneys nationwide. Commentators praised the firm as "*extremely broad and deep by any standards.*" Another source noted, "*the firm is more national in profile; Wisconsin is where the youngsters tend to cut their teeth.*" A truly full-service offering addresses traditional commercial litigation but is also well equipped to advise on such diverse matters as sensitive Native American questions, civil rights and environmental disputes. Recent noteworthy cases include an international arbitration matter in Texas hinging on a dispute between a major petrochemical company and a service provider over the potential ramifications of a new con-

tract. In an unprecedented case, the firm represented a retired state court judge who entered into a contract to provide services to one of the Potawatomi tribes, which subsequently repudiated the contract. The judge sued the tribe in the Wisconsin state court to enforce an arbitration requirement, while the tribe sued the judge in its own tribal court for a declaration that the executive council of the tribe had not had authority to enter into the contract.

The Lawyers: In a characteristically varied year, **Tom Shriner** (see p.1826) has been involved in another precedent setting case before the Wisconsin Supreme Court, representing a judge who has asked the court to determine if it is against the state constitution to try a judge. He also represented a bank asserting the rights of handicapped individuals against various zoning issues brought by a municipality. Observers mused that "*if a company faces a catastrophe and absolute victory is required, Shriner would be the man to call.*" Dealership expert **Michael Bowen**'s (see p.1824) practice has focused upon distribution litigation, trial and appellate work. He recently successfully represented Sub-Zero, the freezer company, which was being sued in a distributor termination dispute. The case was subsequently dismissed. Clients professed "*tremendous respect for his ability to keep businesses out of potentially damaging trials by getting cases dismissed early on.*" **Jon Christiansen** (see p.1824) recorded several more notable wins during the year. He successfully counseled Freightliner in Idaho in a delicate case focusing upon the termination of an

underperforming motor vehicle dealer. He also represented Oshkosh Truck, which was sued by Miller Industries in an attempt to block the acquisition by Oshkosh of a Miller competitor. Clients describe Christiansen as "*a highly analytical trial lawyer who writes an impressive brief.*" **James Clark**'s (see p.1824) broad practice addresses a mixture of professional malpractice, real estate, environmental, products liability and antitrust defense work. He has recently been involved in investigations into price-fixing allegations stemming from investing in the foundry resin industry, and several large contractual disputes. Interviewees acknowledge that he enjoys a "*spectacularly good reputation amongst peers.*" **Nancy Sennett** (see p.1826) is managing partner of the firm's Milwaukee office. Although a significant portion of her time is devoted to high-level administrative tasks, she maintains a highly respected securities litigation practice. **Brian McGrath** (see p.1825) is the firm's distribution and franchise practice group leader, but also tries cases in other areas, notably real estate. "*Deliriously happy*" clients describe him as a "*crackerjack*" litigator with a lower profile but "*an extremely impressive manner about him.*" **Marc McSweeney**'s (see p.1825) management commitments and ongoing involvement in the firm's diversity program render him less visible than in recent years, but he maintains a reputation as a "*lion of the Bar.*" His practice addresses antitrust, professional malpractice, dealership questions and other general commercial litigation matters. A staple diet of M&A, finance, real estate and securities matters features in "*hugely*"

Wisconsin
Leading individuals
(Litigation: General Commercial)

Senior Statesman
MCSWEENEY Maurice *Foley & Lardner*, Milwaukee
PARSONS W Stuart *Quarles & Brady*, Milwaukee

[1] SHRINER Thomas *Foley & Lardner*, Milwaukee

[2] BOWEN Michael *Foley & Lardner*, Milwaukee
BUSCH John *Michael Best*, Milwaukee
BUTLER Brian *Stafford Rosenbaum*, Madison
CHRISTIANSEN Jon *Foley & Lardner*, Milwaukee
CLARK James *Foley & Lardner*, Milwaukee
HANSEN Scott *Reinhart Boerner*, Milwaukee
SKILTON John *Heller Ehrman*, Madison

[3] CARTER Eugenia *Whyte Hirschboek*, Madison
CONWAY Gregory *Liebmann Conway*, Green Bay
CURTIS Charles *Heller Ehrman*, Madison
HARTH David *Heller Ehrman*, Madison
MCGRATH Brian *Foley & Lardner*, Milwaukee
RENFERT Blaine *Foley & Lardner*, Madison
SENNETT Nancy *Foley & Lardner*, Milwaukee
TROUPIS James *Michael Best*, Madison

respected" **Blaine Renfert**'s (see p.1826) litigation practice.

The Clients: Freightliner; NCR; Oshkosh Truck; Coors Brewing Co; Aurora Health Care; Sub-Zero and Kennametal.

Band 2

Heller Ehrman White & McAuliffe LLP
See firm details p.288

The Firm: This Californian headquartered firm's four-year-old Madison office now employs 20 lawyers, and commentators believe it has *"pursued an eminently successful strategy and made some outstanding hires."* Its strength in IP is by now well documented and clients remain extremely satisfied with its ability to exploit Madison's reputation for filing patents at speed. Patent litigation remains the firm' greatest forte and it continues its leading work in the area of stem cell research related to the WARF licensing arm of the University of Wisconsin-Madison. However, the operations of the lawyers are by no means limited to state boundaries, and the firm is active in New York, Seattle, Texas and New Jersey. Several of the firm's partners are also involved in political reform programs and in questions centering upon Native American tribal rights and attendant commercial relations.

The Lawyers: Highly experienced trial lawyer **John Skilton** recently counseled endovascular therapeutics company ev3 in its dispute with the University of California over lucrative patents concerned with the repair of brain aneurysms. Skilton counter-sued the University with allegations of inappropriate and inequitable conduct

in obtaining and maintaining certain patents, and successfully rejected its claims to exemption from antitrust laws. Commentators regard him as *"an extraordinary lawyer with an outstanding ability to pick weaknesses in opposition arguments and flip a case onto its head."* **Chuck Curtis'** diverse practice continues to address Native American law, in which field he has become more involved of late, as well as campaign finance matters and high-profile antitrust cases. He recently won an unprecedented victory in representing the sponsors of the congressional reform program, in which a federal district judge struck down 15 Federal Election Commission clauses. He has also been busy with briefings around the country for Microsoft, primarily in the area of collateral estoppel. Commentators describe him as an *"incredibly smart man of impeccable integrity, able to put his hand to many areas of the law."* *"Extraordinarily talented"* patent litigator **David Harth**'s recent caseload includes representing General Electric on a dispute over the design of variable speed wind turbines. He also represented Mylan Laboratories in a dispute with the University of California over patent rights to endovascular coils aimed at tackling brain aneurysms.

The Clients: 3M; Visa; Mylan Laboratories and Microsoft.

Quarles & Brady LLP
The Firm: This highly respected team comprises more than 100 attorneys operating in Wisconsin, who all possess significant transactional expertise. This is facilitated by the structure of the group, which dovetails with all of the other practice areas and ensures that clients have access to litigators skilled in real estate, construction, professional liability, securities, insurance, IP, antitrust and white-collar crime disputes.

The Lawyers: **Stuart Parsons** has been *"a cornerstone"* of the firm's litigation team for many years, according to clients. He has represented many of the firm's major clients in an array of disputes focusing on antitrust issues, liability insurance claims, federal securities litigation, products liability and M&A matters.

The Clients: M&I Bank; Harnischfeger Industries; Wisconsin Energy; Harley-Davidson; Briggs & Stratton; Kohler Company and Mitsui.

Band 3

Godfrey & Kahn, SC
The Firm: Employing more than 40 lawyers in the five statewide offices, the litigation team is one of the firm's most significant departments. The team's experience in intellectual property disputes received particular attention, and it has even played a role in the international arena through advising on cross-continent licensing deals, distribution and European trademark

issues. The team is also politically connected and is regarded as *"a natural choice"* for First Amendment and election law issues.

The Clients: Weider Nutritional Products; L'Koral; Acme United Corporation; Manpower; Pillar Corporation and George Fischer Foundry Systems.

Liebmann, Conway, Olejniczak & Jerry, SC
See firm details p.1829

The Firm: Market commentators describe the firm as *"undoubtedly the leading legal outfit in Green Bay."* It specializes in general corporate work, commercial litigation, private client matters and the nonprofit sector. Of the firm's 21 attorneys, nine focus on litigation arising out of personal injury, commercial transactions, construction, insurance matters and professional malpractice suits.

The Lawyers: **Greg Conway** concentrates his practice in the areas of corporate law and litigation. He is experienced in matters of alternative dispute resolution and in the prosecution and defense of business, commercial, and personal injury suits. Peers applaud him as *"a superb lawyer and a highly experienced practitioner at both state and federal levels."*

Michael Best & Friedrich LLP
See firm details p.1830

The Firm: The firm's growing Wisconsin litigation practice, which now numbers over 50 attorneys, recently announced the hiring of highly experienced former state prosecutor Daniel Vaccaro. This further bolsters its capabilities in civil and criminal litigation, particularly in tort and white-collar criminal defense cases. Sources also underlined its traditional strength in patent and securities litigation matters. Recent highlights include a substantial victory for Navitas Energy in overcoming objections against the construction of an 80-megawatt wind farm in Marshfield, a case that may have significant ramifications for future projects. Clients endorsed the lawyers for a marked ability to *"think strategically on their feet."*

The Lawyers: **John Busch** enjoys a reputation as *"a strong lead counsel, and experienced manager who is at the top of his game."* He achieved a high-profile victory as the lead counsel in the reversal of a $94 million personal injury punitive damages verdict, and continues to enjoy a niche in advising clients on various privacy laws, including the Telecommunications Privacy Act. Chair of the litigation group **James Troupis** focuses on general civil trial, intellectual property and appellate litigation, in which arena he has appeared at every level. Described as *"one of, if not the best, writer of briefs in the state"* by peers, his practice addresses antitrust, securities, IP, real estate and criminal cases.

The Clients: Affinity Health System; Bayer;

Sears Roebuck; Harley-Davidson; Toys 'R' Us; Fiserv and Medtronic.

Reinhart, Boerner, Van Deuren SC
See firm details p.1831

The Firm: The department's 40 litigators practice across the full range of litigation matters and arguably boast the most diverse set of backgrounds of any comparable department in the state. Many of the lawyers previously worked as US attorneys, assistant district attorneys, and law clerks for federal, appellate and Wisconsin Supreme Court justices. Notable highlights include successfully defending JohnsonDiversey in a dispute with various dealers, which arose after a $1billion acquisition. The dealers claimed the right to control the branding in all of their territories, which amounted to approximately $200 million in sales and profits, but the case was dismissed on summary judgment. The practice is active nationally, particularly in the area of risk financing and failed healthcare insurance plans, and has also been visible in the UK in cases arising out of failed acquisitions.

The Lawyers: Scott Hansen (see p.1825) recently reported a victory in a $250 million trade secret trial, and, in another high-profile matter, defended Milwaukee County and the County Pensions Board against charges that its ordinances were not constitutionally adopted. Hansen won the $140 million case on summary judgment. He remains particularly respected for his knowledge of dealership matters. Clients highlighted his ability "*to spot quickly the weaknesses in a case and adopt an appropriate and highly pragmatic strategy.*"

The Clients: Milwaukee County, Weigel Broadcasting, Johnson Wax and Harley-Davidson are among the firm's key clients.

Stafford Rosenbaum LLP

The Firm: The 16-lawyer Madison team represents the firm's best known and most visible practice area. Clients highlighted the "*successful combination of young talent and senior experience.*" Though the group advises sizable clients in disputes arising out of bankruptcy, antitrust and dealership matters, it is also equipped to advise on day-to-day land use cases and niche areas such as motor vehicle matters and professional ethics. Recent cases include representing a drug company being sued by the State of Wisconsin for alleged fraud, acting in an accounting malpractice case and representing a grocery store chain in a dispute with a franchiser.

The Lawyers: Brian Butler is "*undoubtedly one of the most experienced lawyers in the state.*" He remains best known for his expertise in the dealership arena, though he is also acknowledged as an all-around trial lawyer and mediator. Lately, he has acted in a dispute between several fast food franchisees and the franchiser concerning an outstanding account. He also represented a financially troubled golf and country club in an ongoing dispute with a landowner who allegedly reneged on $1 million contribution to the club.

The Clients: Bank One; Swiss Valley Farms; Joseph Huber Brewing and Meridian Group.

Other Notablr Practitioners

Gina Carter recently joined Whyte Hirschboeck Dudek SC from Godfrey & Kahn, SC. Her practice encompasses patent, trademark, copyright and trade secret litigation, though she is also a highly experienced transactional lawyer, especially where IP is an important component of the assets of a business undergoing merger activity. She is also experienced in comic book character copyright matters, and has notably represented Todd McFarlane Productions in this regard. Peers describe her as a "*marvelous lawyer and a very savvy litigator.*"

REAL ESTATE

Wisconsin
Leading firms (Real Estate)

1	FOLEY & LARDNER *Milwaukee*
2	GODFREY & KAHN, SC *Milwaukee*
	QUARLES & BRADY LLP *Milwaukee*
	REINHART, BOERNER, VAN DEUREN SC *Milwaukee*
3	MICHAEL BEST & FRIEDRICH LLP *Milwaukee*
	WHYTE HIRSCHBOECK DUDEK SC *Madison*

Leading individuals (Real Estate)

1	BLOCK Bruce *Reinhart Boerner, Milwaukee*
	CHERNOF Steve *Godfrey & Kahn, Milwaukee*
	HATCH Michael *Foley & Lardner, Milwaukee*
	JOST Lawrence *Quarles & Brady, Milwaukee*
2	DALTON Larry *Whyte Hirschboeck, Milwaukee*
	DANIELS Joh *Quarles & Brady, Milwaukee*
	DWYER Michael *Godfrey & Kahn, Milwaukee*
	ISHIKAWA Jesse *Reinhart Boerner, Madison*
	LEVIN Benjamin *Foley & Lardner, Milwaukee*
	LEVIN Jim *Michael Best, Milwaukee*
	OSTERMEYER Michael *Quarles & Brady, Milwaukee*
	PUCHNER Joseph *Quarles & Brady, Milwaukee*
	TEMKIN Harvey *Reinhart Boerner, Madison*
	ZABROWSKI Patrick *Foley & Lardner, Milwaukee*

Firms and individuals are listed alphabetically in each band.

Band 1

Foley & Lardner
See firm details p.1828

The Firm: According to commentators, the group – home to more than 100 real estate practitioners – continues to build upon its "*outstanding reputation for handling deals with significant levels of sophistication.*" The firm fields an impressive depth of resources that are "*always mobilized efficiently to address multifaceted deals.*" The team has completed several complex structured projects requiring syndicated equity financings, particularly multifamily housing deals involving up to 400 units. Clients appreciate the group's technical expertise and its attention to detail: "*The thick closing document had quite clearly had some extraordinarily thoughtful care put into it.*" Highlights for the group include its pivotal role in the development of the $85 million architectural showpiece University Club Tower at 825 North Prospect Avenue in Milwaukee. The team is also engaged in the high-profile development of the Harley-Davidson Museum in downtown Milwaukee on the site of the City of Milwaukee Department of Works yard.

The Lawyers: Michael Hatch (see p.1825) has cemented his reputation as "*quite possibly the best real estate lawyer in the state, and certainly amongst the best in the Midwest.*" His broad experience in traditional real estate matters and in sophisticated financings means that "*whatever the product type, he will separate which points need to be negotiated and which do not.*" His instrumental role in the ongoing Menomonee Valley development project remains well known. He is also heavily involved in the $100 million Kenilworth project, a new mixed-use development of a condominium tower and student housing for the University of Wisconsin-Milwaukee, funded by private finance and the issue of tax-free bonds. **Benjamin Levin** (see p.1825) impressed commentators as "*an extraordinarily good, no-nonsense lawyer.*" He represents a range of businesses in land acquisition, redevelopment, loan, and tax incremental finance transactions. Levin is currently playing a key support role in the development of the Harley-Davidson Museum project. "*Results-oriented*" **Patrick Zabrowski**'s (see p.1827) practice encompasses purchase and sale transactions, construction and real estate development projects and commercial leasing matters.

The Clients: Harley-Davidson; US Bank; Johnson Controls; Milwaukee Brewers; Mandel Group; Interstate Partners and Oakbrook Corporation.

All quotes in the text are from interviews with clients and competitors.

Band 2

Godfrey & Kahn, SC

The Firm: The practice is now home to 25 lawyers operating out of the firm's five Wisconsin offices. This broad coverage of the state's major business centers convinces sources that the firm is "*a natural choice for mid-level deals,*" while its relationships with some of the major entities with a presence in the state (such as GE Healthcare), also proves its credentials for higher caliber mandates. The team is active in all aspects of industrial and residential development and it is well placed to take advantage of the upturn in retail property work. Additional areas of expertise are low-income housing credit deals and the rehabilitation of historic buildings.

The Lawyers: Steve Chernof maintains an outstanding reputation within the state as a "*thoroughly respected practitioner.*" He has recently advised on a range of low-income housing credit deals, and completed a major $100 million refinancing of 46 properties for a mobile home parks client. **Mike Dwyer** notably represented the developer in the construction of an $80 million HQ building for GE Healthcare in Wauwatosa. At 500,000 sq ft, the building is the second largest ever constructed in Wisconsin. He has also been recently involved in the development of a children's hospital and biomedical research facility. Commentators agree that he is a "*highly commercial and practical man.*"

The Clients: Gleischman Sumner Company, Gilbane Properties, Asset Development Group and a range of other developers and healthcare entities feature in the client roster.

Quarles & Brady LLP

The Firm: Observers applaud the firm for its ability to form robust client relationships at the national and local level. Clients appreciate the fact that the team "*bats right down to the last man*" and is "*thoroughly well connected to movers and shakers within the community, which is key in getting deals done.*" The group's high-profile involvement with a major PPP, the Neighborhood Schools Initiative, to develop a significant number of new facilities within the region, is ongoing. This work highlights the sort of impact the firm delivers at the local government level. On the corporate scene, the team is working closely with Ziegler-Bence on the development of a new 160,000 sq ft headquarters and distribution facility for West Bend Housewares. This major project is one example of the way the firm has focused more on urban infill and development than the use of greenfield sites.

The Lawyers: "*Compromise is often the name of the game in the real estate sector,*" reported one client, "*and* **Lawrence Jost** *has been inspirational in this respect.*" Jost continues to work closely with major developer WISPARK in its various downtown projects. He has also been involved with the Ovation Plaza project, a $100 million office, retail and parking structure that has been proposed for what is now the parking structure at the Marcus Center for the Performing Arts. Market sources believe that **John Daniels** "*must surely be one of the most well-connected real estate lawyers in the state.*" He has worked closely with the State of Wisconsin Investment Board in the disposal of several investment interests in Kmart, and remains a key figure in various major PPP deals, such as the Neighborhood Schools Initiative. **Joe Puchner** is a "*personable and talented lawyer who is carving a growing reputation for himself.*" Recent highlights include working with We Energies and its affiliates on the real estate issues relating to the 'Power The Future' project, a billion-dollar, ten-year initiative to address electricity supply and reliability issues for customers. He has also been involved in several hospital joint ventures, recently advising one client on the development of new medical and hospital office buildings, and another on the $100 million construction of a research facility in Milwaukee. **Mike Ostermeyer**'s principal sphere of influence is public development work. He has spent a considerable amount of time working on a major bond-financed project involving the expansion of many dozens of sites for various Milwaukee school districts. He also advises major public or private entities as codevelopers or as co-occupants. In other areas, a recent highlight was the purchase and sale of a brewery in Washington State for in excess of $20 million. Clients appreciate his willingness "*to cut to the chase in a deal*" and his "*straight-shooting approach.*"

The Clients: SABMiller; WISPARK; Milwaukee Children's Hospital; Marshfield Clinic; MB Realty and Hansen Storage.

Reinhart, Boerner, Van Deuren SC
See firm details p.1831

The Firm: Clients noted: "*One of the great things about working with this group is that the knowledge of a particular deal seems to reside in the heads of all the team: they are extraordinarily communicative.*" The practice employs more than 20 lawyers based in the three Wisconsin offices, and is experienced in the full range of real estate transactions. The firm recently demonstrated its impact in municipal politics during extension work for Columbia St Mary's hospital. During construction work, a helipad used in the transportation of critically ill patients had to be moved, and numerous hurdles had to be surmounted for the approval of its relocation. The team has also been involved in a number of projects that have contributed to the rejuvenation of downtown Madison. The recent construction of the $200 million Overture Center in particular fostered numerous subsequent developments in the form of new restaurants and condominiums, and the firm has lately been involved in negotiating new leases for the Madison Museum of Contemporary Art, one of the Center's anchor tenants.

The Lawyers: Commentators were effusive in their praise of **Bruce Block**'s (see p.1824) substantial experience in land use and zoning matters. He also benefits from a considerable knowledge of mixed-use projects and complex deals in which PPP development agreements are central. He was recently involved in the $60 million rework of a major shopping center in Glendale, and his ongoing involvement with the 1500-acre Pabst Farms development is well documented. Clients appreciate his "*invaluable familiarity with key city figures and his knowledge of politics and procedures.*" The focus of **Jesse Ishikawa**'s (see p.1825) practice of late has been on new residential real estate development, in keeping with the increased demand in the state capital for, in particular, luxury condominiums. He has also been busy with various issues relating to the creation of six research parks in Dane County. Clients and peers alike agree that he is "*thoroughly commercial and technically gifted.*" **Harvey Temkin** (see p.1826) enjoys a longstanding reputation as "*a dean of the Madison real estate Bar.*" His wide client base features real estate developers and lenders, business clients and healthcare providers. He is also particularly respected for his knowledge of the issues relating to stem cell research and other biotechnology spin-offs from the highly respected University of Wisconsin in Madison.

The Clients: The firm acts for an impressive range of lenders, leading developers, biotechnology businesses, healthcare institutions and public sector bodies.

Band 3

Michael Best & Friedrich LLP
See firm details p.1830

The Firm: Commentators respect the firm for its success in establishing a loyal client base and acknowledge its "*sure handedness*" in complex, multifaceted real estate transactions. The real estate division is one of the largest in the state, and peers admire the "*aggregate quality of the team, which favors the collective approach rather than showcasing individual stars.*"

The Lawyers: Jim Levin is one of Wisconsin's most seasoned real estate lawyers, and benefits from an extra dimension of top-flight business experience at Sidney Kohl Company, where he was chief executive for several years. He represents clients in the industrial, retail and office sectors, and is especially familiar with multifamily retail real estate matters. Commentators describe him as "*a brilliant lawyer and a good man, though he can become a tiger if the situation demands.*"

The Clients: The firm represents major contractors and construction entities, developers, owners and lenders, and several major finance and leasing companies.

Whyte Hirschboeck Dudek S.C.

The Firm: The department's 22 lawyers operate out of four Wisconsin offices and address the full range of real estate matters, representing tenants, landlords, municipalities, developers, contractors and lenders. The firm has a reputation as being home to some "*hard charging and astute individuals.*"

The Lawyers: Larry Dalton is perhaps the most familiar name in the team. He is regarded as a "*seasoned and highly experienced practitioner,*" and he possesses an acknowledged expertise in the field of lending and leasing. Peers regard his robust relationship with grocery store giant Roundy's with particular envy.

The Clients: Acuity Mutual Insurance Company; Alexian Village of Milwaukee; Independent Physicians Network; Pro Technical Products and Siepmann Realty.

Leaders in Wisconsin

ABRAHAM, Bill
Foley & Lardner, Milwaukee
414 297 5667
wabraham@foley.com
Recommended in Corporate/M&A
Career: A Partner in Foley & Lardner's Milwaukee office, William J Abraham Jr served as Chair of the Business Law Department and Head of its Securities Law Practice Group and is a former member of the firm's Management Committee. Mr Abraham practices in a broad range of business and real estate law matters, with an emphasis on securities, acquisitions, leveraged buyouts and finance. He has participated in more than 100 acquisition transactions and represents aggressively growing companies that finance growth through creative use of private and public markets. He graduated magna cum laude from the University of Michigan Law School.

AUEN, Michael H
Foley & Lardner, Madison
608 258 4221
mauen@foley.com
Recommended in Employment
Career: Michael H Auen is a Partner in Foley & Lardner's Madison office and a member of the Litigation Department. His practice has focused on advising and defending employers for over 25 years in labor law, employment, and litigation. His work involves collective bargaining, arbitration and organizing campaigns, as well as discrimination and wage and hour cases, assistance with individual employment issues and problems, drafting and litigating confidentiality, non-compete and trade secret issues, and ERISA litigation. Mr Auen was a field examiner with the National Labor Relations Board prior to graduating from the University of Wisconsin Law School.

BARTELL, Jeff
Quarles & Brady LLP, Madison
608 251 5000
Recommended in Corporate/M&A

BEDORE, James M
Reinhart, Boerner, Van Deuren SC, Milwaukee 414 298 8196
jbedore@reinhartlaw.com
Recommended in Corporate/M&A
Practice Areas: Business law; securities.
Prof. Memberships: State Bar of Wis-

consin; American Bar Association.
Career: Shareholder, focuses on corporate and securities issues including public securities offerings on behalf of issuers and underwriters, private placements, venture capital, bank and other financing arrangements, mergers and acquisitions, takeover defenses, proxy contests, employment matters, executive compensation, general contract matters, licensing and shareholder matters. Bedore works with corporate clients and in-house counsel to manage corporate and securities law compliance needs, including developing internal compliance programs and preparing and filing quarterly and annual reports, proxy statements and other filings required by the SEC.

BLOCK, Bruce
Reinhart, Boerner, Van Deuren SC, Milwaukee 414 298 8130
bblock@reinhartlaw.com
Recommended in Real Estate
Practice Areas: Real estate; government relations.
Prof. Memberships: State Bar of Wisconsin; American College of Real Estate Lawyers; Advisor to National Trust for Historic Preservation.
Career: Bruce Block, shareholder and Chair of the firm's Real Estate Department, focuses on land use planning, zoning, eminent domain, historic tax credits, multiple and mixed-use ownership structures, tax incremental financing, leasing and construction and design contracts. He has also played an active role in structuring complex financing schemes for public/private developments throughout Wisconsin.

BOBBER, Bernard J
Foley & Lardner, Milwaukee
414 297 5803
bbobber@foley.com
Recommended in Employment
Career: Bernard J ('Bud') Bobber is a Partner in the Labor and Employment Practice Group and a member of the Food Industry Team. He represents employers before federal and state courts and administrative agencies in all areas of employment law and labor law, including employment discrimination, trade secrets, noncompete, employee benefits and wage and hour matters, and

routinely represents clients in labor arbitration proceedings. Mr Bobber also provides both organized and union-free employers with employment law advice, and provides assistance with problem prevention. Mr Bobber has developed specific expertise in the defense of class action cases.

BOWEN, Michael A
Foley & Lardner, Milwaukee
414 297 5538 mbowen@foley.com
Recommended in Litigation
Career: Michael Bowen, a Partner in Foley & Lardner's Milwaukee office, concentrates on commercial litigation and arbitration at both the trial and appellate levels. Dealer and distributor disputes play an important role in his practice. He is co-author of The Wisconsin Fair Dealership Law (Wisconsin State Bar, 1988). Other key practice areas include lender liability, constitutional challenges to land use regulation, and original appellate work. Mr Bowen also is an accomplished novelist, having published 12 such works since 1987. He received his JD degree, cum laude, from Harvard Law School.

BUONO, Kathryn
Quarles & Brady LLP, Milwaukee
414 277 5000
Recommended in Corporate/M&A

BUSCH, John
Michael Best & Friedrich LLP, Milwaukee 414 271 6560
Recommended in Litigation

BUTLER, Brian
Stafford Rosenbaum LLP, Madison
608 256 0226
Recommended in Litigation

CARTER, Eugenia
Whyte Hirsch Boeck Dudek SC,, Madison 608 225 4440
Recommended in Litigation

CHERNOF, Steve
Godfrey & Kahn, SC, Milwaukee
414 273 3500
Recommended in Real Estate

CHRISTIANSEN, Jon P
Foley & Lardner, Milwaukee
414 297 5557
jchristiansen@foley.com
Recommended in Litigation

Career: Jon P Christiansen is a Partner in Foley & Lardner's Milwaukee office. Mr Christiansen serves as Chair of the firm's national General Commercial Litigation Group. He formerly chaired the firm's Distribution and Franchise Practice Group and practices primarily in the areas of distribution and commercial litigation. His experience includes preliminary injunctions, trials, arbitrations and appeals throughout the United States in commercial and distribution cases. He has drafted numerous national distribution agreements in diverse industries and is one of the principle authors of the Product Distribution Guide, published by CCH. He was awarded his JD degree by Vanderbilt University.

CLARK, James R
Foley & Lardner, Milwaukee
414 297 5543 jclark@foley.com
Recommended in Litigation
Career: James R Clark has over 30 years' experience in civil litigation as a Partner in Foley & Lardner's Milwaukee office. He is experienced in arbitrations and other forms of alternative dispute resolution, has tried over 40 cases and has negotiated settlements in many other major cases. His areas of trial practice include negligence and product liability matters (including drug, medical devices, and toxic torts), professional malpractice defense, construction disputes, condemnation and other real estate litigation, trade secret and non-competition agreements, antitrust, securities, general contract, and other commercial disputes. He received his JD degree from the University of Wisconsin.

COFFEY, Peter
Michael Best & Friedrich LLP, Milwaukee 414 271 6560
Recommended in Corporate/M&A

CONWAY, Gregory
Liebmann, Conway, Olejniczak & Jerry, S.C., Green Bay 920 437 0476
Recommended in Litigation

CRONE, Tom
Melli Walker Pease & Ruhly S.C., Madison 608 257 4812
Recommended in Employment

CROYSDALE, David
Michael Best & Friedrich LLP,
Milwaukee 414 271 6560
Recommended in Employment

CURTIS, Charles
Heller Ehrman White & McAuliffe LLP,
Madison 680 663 7460
Recommended in Litigation

DALTON, Larry
Whyte Hirschboeck Dudek S.C.,
Milwaukee 414 273 2100
Recommended in Real Estate

DANIELS Jr, John
Quarles & Brady LLP, Milwaukee
414 277 5000
Recommended in Real Estate

DAVIDSON, Bruce
Quarles & Brady LLP, Milwaukee
414 277 5000
Recommended in Corporate/M&A

DICKENS, John
Godfrey & Kahn, SC, Milwaukee
414 273 3500
Recommended in Corporate/M&A

DUFFY, Robert
Quarles & Brady LLP, Milwaukee
414 277 5000
Recommended in Employment

DWYER, Michael
Godfrey & Kahn, SC, Milwaukee
414 273 3500
Recommended in Real Estate

EHRMANN, Mark
Godfrey & Kahn, SC, Milwaukee
414 273 3500
Recommended in Corporate/M&A

GARMER III, Benjamin F
Foley & Lardner, Milwaukee
414 297 5675
bgarmer@foley.com
Recommended in Corporate/M&A
Career: Benjamin F Garmer III is a
Partner in the firm's Business Law
Department and Transactional & Securities Practice Group. His practice focuses on acquisitions and financings for
public and private companies and
takeover defense. He has represented
national underwriters, including CS
First Boston, Merrill Lynch, and Goldman Sachs, as well as regional underwriters, Robert W Baird, William Blair
and others, in financings and other matters. He has lectured on issues regarding
acquisitions and takeover defense. Mr
Garmer received his JD, cum laude,
from the University of Michigan Law
School and an LLM in taxation from
New York University.

GOODKIND, Conrad
Quarles & Brady LLP, Milwaukee
414 277 5000
Recommended in Corporate/M&A

HANSEN, Scott W
Reinhart, Boerner, Van Deuren SC,
Milwaukee 414 298 8123
shansen@reinhartlaw.com

Recommended in Litigation
Practice Areas: Litigation: general
commercial; product distribution and
franchise law.
Prof. Memberships: State Bar of Wisconsin; American Bar Association; Wisconsin Academy of Trial Lawyers; Milwaukee County Bench Bar Committee.
Career: Litigation Chair; competition
law: antitrust, distribution and franchising, trade secrets, unfair competition,
and complex commercial disputes.
Recent examples: defeated $200M
encroachment claim by 10 dealers;
defeated $250M trade secret claim
against motor vehicle manufacturer;
defeated $150M wrongful taking claim
by pension retirees; and defeated wrongful termination claim by exclusive Mexican cocoa distributor. Writings and seminars: antitrust; business torts; racketeering; Wisconsin Fair Dealership Law;
Expert Witnesses; Effective Depositions
and Civil Procedure. For sample reported cases, representative clients and more
information, visit Mr Hansen's biography at reinhartlaw.com.

HARTH, David
Heller Ehrman White & McAuliffe LLP,
Madison 680 663 7460
Recommended in Litigation

HATCH, Michael W
Foley & Lardner, Milwaukee
414 297 5706
mhatch@foley.com
Recommended in Real Estate
Career: Michael W Hatch chairs Foley
& Lardner's Real Estate Practice Group.
He has practiced extensively in the areas
of real estate development, finance,
restructuring and workouts, brown-
fields/urban redevelopment, public/pri-
vate partnerships, syndication, historic
rehabilitation, real estate investment
trusts, and investment analysis. He has
been lead counsel for several billion dollars of real estate transactions, including
Milwaukee Center, the largest commercial
development in Milwaukee; East Point
Commons, the largest residential development in Milwaukee; Cathedral Place,
the largest mixed-use development in
Milwaukee; and the purchase (and later
the sale) of the Firstar Center, the largest
real estate transaction in Wisconsin.

ISHIKAWA, Jesse S
Reinhart, Boerner, Van Deuren SC,
Madison 608 229 2208
jishikaw@reinhartlaw.com
Recommended in Real Estate
Practice Areas: Real estate.
Prof. Memberships: State Bar of Wisconsin;
American College of Real Estate Lawyers.
Career: Shareholder and Managing
Partner of the firm's Madison office,
represents developers, lenders and busi-
nesses in real estate purchases, sales,
commercial leasing transactions and
land development transactions. He has
represented developers in a number of
tax incremental financing projects,

including research parks, distribution
centers and downtown developments.
He was voted Madison's number one
real estate lawyer in Madison Magazine's
most recent poll of local attorneys.
Personal: Member, board of trustees of
Madison Museum of Contemporary
Art; former member, Madison Board of
Parks Commissioners.

JOST, Lawrence
Quarles & Brady LLP, Milwaukee
414 277 5000
Recommended in Real Estate

KERN, David
Quarles & Brady LLP, Milwaukee
414 277 5000
Recommended in Employment

LEICHTLING, Ely
Quarles & Brady LLP, Milwaukee
414 277 5000
Recommended in Employment

LEVIN, Benjamin D
Foley & Lardner, Milwaukee
414 297 5715
blevin@foley.com
Recommended in Real Estate
Career: Benjamin D Levin, a Partner in
the Milwaukee office and a member of
the Real Estate Practice Group, represents municipalities, underwriters, and
businesses in land acquisition, redevelopment, loan, and tax incremental
finance transactions. His practice also
encompasses annexation and financing
via community and redevelopment area
borrowing. Mr Levin graduated from
Harvard Law School, cum laude, in
1990, and Amherst College, Phi Beta
Kappa, in 1985.

LEVIN, Jim
Michael Best & Friedrich LLP,
Milwaukee 414 271 6560
Recommended in Real Estate

LINSTROTH, Tod
Michael Best & Friedrich LLP, Madison
608 257 3501
Recommended in Corporate/M&A

LUNDGREN, K Thor
Michael Best & Friedrich LLP,
Milwaukee 414 271 6560
Recommended in Corporate/M&A

LYNCH, Lawrence T
Foley & Lardner, Milwaukee
414 297 5824
llynch@foley.com
Recommended in Employment
Career: Lawrence T Lynch, a Partner in
the Milwaukee office, practices employment law, focusing on employee relations, employment discrimination,
employment contracts, public and private sector union relations, occupational
safety and health regulations, and wage
and hour laws. Admitted to practice in
Iowa and Wisconsin, Mr Lynch is also
admitted to practice before the U.S.
Court of Appeals for the Sixth and Seventh Circuits, and the US Supreme

Court. His law degree was awarded, with
high distinction, by the University of
Iowa, where he was editor in chief of the
Journal of Corporation Law.

MARSACK, Gary
Lindner & Marsack, S.C., Milwaukee
414 273 3910
Recommended in Employment

MCGRATH, Brian W
Foley & Lardner, Milwaukee
414 271 2400
Recommended in Litigation
Career: Brian W McGrath is a Partner
at Foley & Lardner, where he specializes
in the areas of real estate and dealership
litigation and is the Head of the Milwaukee office Litigation Department. Along
with several other attorneys, Mr
McGrath created a 50-state computerized database that has been trademarked
as NationLink and which the firm uses
to advise clients on a nationwide basis
regarding the law relating to dealership
terminations and related issues. He has
litigated numerous dealership cases all
over the country and speaks and writes
on dealership topics frequently. He is a
graduate of Harvard Law School.

MCSWEENEY, Maurice J
Foley & Lardner, Milwaukee
414 297 5520
mmcsweeney@foley.com
Recommended in Litigation
Career: Marc McSweeney is a Partner in
Foley & Lardner's Milwaukee office and
a member of the firm's General Commercial Litigation and Antitrust Practice
Groups. Mr McSweeney serves as Diversity Partner, a role in which he is a catalyst for and leader in carrying out the
firm's commitment to diversity. He was
formerly the Chair of the firm's Litigation Department and a member of the
Management Committee. His practice
focuses on a wide variety of commercial
litigation and counseling, including
antitrust, dealer and distributor questions, professional malpractice, securities, and takeovers. He received his JD
from the University of Chicago.

NINNEMAN, Mary
Quarles & Brady LLP, Milwaukee
414 277 5000
Recommended in Employment

OSTERMEYER, Michael
Quarles & Brady LLP, Milwaukee
414 277 5000
Recommended in Real Estate

PARSONS, W Stuart
Quarles & Brady LLP, Milwaukee
414 277 5000
Recommended in Litigation

PENCE, Thomas C
Foley & Lardner, Milwaukee
414 297 5809
tpence@foley.com
Recommended in Employment
Career: Thomas C Pence, a Partner in
Foley & Lardner's Milwaukee office and

chair of the firm's Labor & Employment Practice Group, represents employers in all aspects of employment and labor law. Mr Pence handles employment litigation, labor arbitrations, and collective bargaining. Mr Pence counsels employers concerning all aspects of employment and labor law, including the ADA, the FMLA, and workplace harassment. He works with employers to develop problem prevention processes, training programs, and alternative dispute resolution programs. Mr Pence is a frequent speaker on employment and labor law topics. He received his law degree from Indiana University.

PEPKE, Michael T
Reinhart, Boerner, Van Deuren SC, Milwaukee 414 298 8133
mpepke@reinhartlaw.com
Recommended in Corporate/M&A
Practice Areas: Business law.
Prof. Memberships: State Bars of Wisconsin and Colorado; Member of the Boards of Directors of Children's Service Society of Wisconsin, Inc., Junior Achievement of Wisconsin, Inc., Children's Hospital and Health Systems, Inc. and US Bank Championship.
Career: Michael Pepke represents businesses in all phases, from start-up/acquisition, to growth financing, to recapitalization, to exit strategies through sale or public offering. He advises clients with respect to routine legal and business matters, including banking relationships, customer and supplier relationship, manufacturing and distribution matters, employee and key executive relationships, executive compensation planning, owner relationships and strategic and succession planning.

PLOOR, Pamela
Quarles & Brady LLP, Milwaukee 414 277 5000
Recommended in Employment

PUCHNER, Joseph
Quarles & Brady LLP, Milwaukee 414 277 5000
Recommended in Real Estate

QUICK, Patrick G
Foley & Lardner, Milwaukee 414 297 5678
pgquick@foley.com
Recommended in Corporate/M&A
Career: Patrick G Quick is a Partner in Foley & Lardner's Milwaukee office and a member of the Business Law Department and the Transactional & Securities Practice Group. Mr Quick practices corporate law, with an emphasis in securities law compliance, acquisitions, and takeover defense. He counsels public companies concerning compliance requirements and governance matters and has participated in initial and other public offerings for Wisconsin corporations. He also participates in many complex acquisition transactions, representing both buying and selling parties, and

assists clients doing advance takeover preparedness planning, including those who have received unsolicited takeover proposals or similar overtures.

RENFERT, Blaine
Foley & Lardner, Madison 608 258 4220
brenfert@foley.com
Recommended in Litigation
Career: Blaine Renfert is a Partner with Foley & Lardner and heads the firm's Business Law Department in Madison. Mr Renfert counsels individuals, partnerships, businesses and national companies on corporate and commercial law, mergers and acquisitions, finance, real estate and securities matters. Mr Renfert's approach is to combine practical business sense with vigorous negotiation and precise legal craftsmanship. Mr Renfert's practice involves corporate and commercial law matters and he has represented buyers and sellers in more than 300 purchases and sales of businesses over the past 18 years. He graduated from the University of Michigan Law School.

ROBISON, John
Quarles & Brady LLP, Madison 608 251 5000
Recommended in Corporate/M&A

ROTHMAN, Jay O
Foley & Lardner, Milwaukee 414 297 5644
jrothman@foley.com
Recommended in Corporate/M&A
Career: Jay O Rothman is a Partner in Foley & Lardner's Milwaukee office and a member of the firm's Management Committee. Mr Rothman serves as Chair of the national Transactional & Securities Practice Group and practices in the areas of mergers and acquisitions, securities law, takeover defense, and general corporate and business law. He has structured and negotiated numerous acquisition transactions in various industries and has represented both underwriters and corporate issuers in various public offerings of both debt and equity securities. Mr Rothman also regularly counsels publicly held companies regarding compliance matters under federal and state securities laws.

RYAN, Patrick
Quarles & Brady LLP, Milwaukee 414 277 5000
Recommended in Corporate/M&A

SCRIVNER, Tom
Michael Best & Friedrich LLP, Milwaukee 414 271 6560
Recommended in Employment

SCULLEN, Sean
Quarles & Brady LLP, Milwaukee 414 277 5000
Recommended in Employment

SEIDENSTRICKER, Paul
von Briesen & Roper SC, Milwaukee 414 276 1122
Recommended in Corporate/M&A

SENNETT, Nancy J
Foley & Lardner, Milwaukee 414 297 5522
nsennett@foley.com
Recommended in Litigation
Career: Nancy J Sennett is Managing Partner of Foley & Lardner's Milwaukee office. Ms Sennett is a member of the Litigation Department and was founder and first Chair of the Securities Litigation, Enforcement & Regulation Practice Group. Ms Sennett's practice includes all aspects of commercial and business litigation. Her practice is focused on securities litigation representing corporations, boards of directors, broker-dealers, investment advisers, law firms and individuals in private securities litigation, including shareholder class actions and derivative suits, SEC enforcement actions, and SRO proceedings. She received her JD degree, cum laude, from Northwestern University.

SHRINER Jr, Thomas L
Foley & Lardner, Milwaukee 414 297 5601
tshriner@foley.com
Recommended in Litigation
Career: Thomas L. Shriner, Jr. is a Partner in the Milwaukee office of Foley & Lardner. He concentrates his practice in commercial and public law litigation (in judicial and arbitral forums) and has an extensive appellate practice in both state and federal courts. He has handled disputes arising from business acquisitions; the law applicable to banks and other financial institutions (including lender liability and loan participation); shareholder disputes; trade secrets and agreements not to compete; pension, insurance, and dealership disputes; and claims under the UCC, including its articles on sales, bank deposits, secured transactions, and letters of credit.

SIMS, Luke E
Foley & Lardner, Milwaukee 414 297 5680
lsims@foley.com
Recommended in Corporate/M&A
Career: Luke E Sims, a Partner in Foley & Lardner's Milwaukee office, is a corporate lawyer with concentrations in acquisitions, leveraged buyouts, and securities law matters. He has extensive experience in all aspects of mergers and acquisitions (and particularly leveraged buyouts), including structuring, negotiating and financing acquisitions and dispositions of private and publicly held companies. Mr Sims is a member of the firm's Transactional & Securities Practice Group. He is a frequent lecturer and author on acquisitions, leveraged buyouts, and public offerings, and received his JD from Georgetown University.

SKILTON, John
Heller Ehrman White & McAuliffe LLP, Madison 680 663 7460
Recommended in Litigation

SKINDRUD, Michael
LaFollette Godfrey & Kahn, SC, Madison 608 257 3911
Recommended in Corporate/M&A

SOMMERHAUSER, Peter
Godfrey & Kahn, SC, Milwaukee 414 273 3500
Recommended in Corporate/M&A

STEVENS, Charles
Michael Best & Friedrich LLP, Milwaukee 414 271 6560
Recommended in Employment

TEMKIN, Harvey L
Reinhart, Boerner, Van Deuren SC, Madison 608 229 2100
htemkin@reinhartlaw.com
Recommended in Real Estate
Practice Areas: Real estate.
Prof. Memberships: American College of Real Estate Lawyers; American Bar Association.
Career: Shareholder in the firm's Madison office, represents real estate developers and lenders, business clients and health care providers since 1978. Areas of concentration include mergers and acquisitions, sales, zoning, land division and development, real estate litigation, commercial finance, business organizations and tax deferred exchanges. Frequently named one of the top real estate lawyers in Madison Magazine's survey of Madison lawyers.

TROUPIS, James
Michael Best & Friedrich LLP, Madison 608 257 3501
Recommended in Litigation

TYSON Jr, Joseph B
Foley & Lardner, Milwaukee 414 297 5631
jtyson@foley.com
Recommended in Corporate/M&A
Career: Joseph Tyson is a Partner in Foley & Lardner's Milwaukee office and chairman of the Business Law Department. He is a member of the Transactional and Securities, Finance, and Commercial Transactions and Business Counseling Practice Groups. His practice focuses on acquisitions, financing for public and private companies, Uniform Commercial Code matters, and general corporate law. He has over 20 years experience in dealing with the legal issues involving mergers, financing transactions, and business needs, including mergers, divestitures, credit facilities, secured and unsecured commercial loans, and commercial and consumer credit. He received his JD degree from the University of Virginia.

VETTER, Mark
Davis & Kuelthau, S.C., Milwaukee 414 276 0200
Recommended in Employment

WAHL, Nicholas

Godfrey & Kahn, SC, Milwaukee
414 273 3500
Recommended in Corporate/M&A

WALSH, David G

Foley & Lardner, Madison
608 258 4269
dwalsh@foley.com
Recommended in Corporate/M&A

Career: Mr. Walsh is a Partner and member of Foley & Lardner's Regulatory Department. He has assisted communication entities in all aspects of their business, including corporate structuring, franchising, and facility siting for over 30 years. In addition, Mr Walsh counsels and represents business clients in all phases of business activity including the restructuring of reorganized entities. In addition to particular skill in cable television and telecommunications law, he has an extensive estate planning practice and counsels clients and families on business succession and wealth management and transfer. His JD degree was conferred in 1970 by Harvard Law School.

ZABROWSKI, Patrick M

Foley & Lardner, Milwaukee
414 297 5716
pzabrowski@foley.com
Recommended in Real Estate

Career: Patrick M Zabrowski, a Partner in Foley & Lardner's Milwaukee office, has experience in a broad spectrum of real estate matters, such as purchase and sale transactions, construction and development of real estate projects, mortgage loan transactions and commercial leasing matters. He has developed expertise in title insurance-related legal matters and has counseled a number of clients in the timber, nursery and Christmas tree producing industries. Prior to law school, he worked as a real estate broker in the Milwaukee area, and he continues to hold his real estate broker's license. His JD is from the University of Wisconsin.

FOLEY & LARDNER

THE FIRM

Chairman & Chief Executive Officer: Ralf-Reinhard Böer

Number of partners: 443
Number of associates: 295

Total number of attorneys: 951
Total number of support staff: 1,356

Website: www.foley.com

FIRM OVERVIEW: For over 160 years, Foley & Lardner has delivered legal services focused on meeting their clients' business objectives with integrity, insight and innovation. Foley & Lardner is a strong and reliable business partner with a culture dedicated to understanding industry issues, government policies, and client goals. This philosophy has led the firm through tremendous growth, and today they have emerged as a highly regarded firm with offices across the United States. With more than 60 practice areas encompassing the full range of corporate legal services, their attorneys understand today's most complex business issues including corporate governance, securities enforcement, litigation, mergers and acquisitions, intellectual property and IP litigation, labor and employment, and tax. The firm offers total solutions in the automotive, e-business and information technology, energy, financial services, food, golf and resort services, insurance, health care, life sciences, nanotechnology, and sports industries.

MAIN AREAS OF PRACTICE:

Business Law: The firm's Business Law department has skilled attorneys in virtually all areas of business and transactional needs. Clients range from investment banks and Fortune 100 companies to entrepreneurs and emerging growth companies, as well as the small and middle market companies in between.

Litigation: The Litigation Department applies business insight during disputes to reduce client risk. The firm's attorneys leverage multiple tools and strategies, ranging from jury trials to Alternative Dispute Resolution methods to deliver results that are favorable to its clients. To counsel is a key fundamental in the firm's approach, but to achieve their clients' business goals is the critical component in their strategy.

Intellectual Property: Foley & Lardner's Intellectual Property Department continues to be recognized as a leading provider of Intellectual Property (IP) services - in a 2003 survey by *IP Law & Business*, more global corporations named Foley & Lardner as their go-to firm for IP counsel than any other firm. In addition, according to *IP Law & Business*, the firm is sixth among 200 Top Patent Litigation Defense Firms, a testament to its experience in handling patent trials in 2002 and 2003. They are among the Top 10 patent firms for prosecution, according to *Intellectual Property Today*, with 1,893 patents prosecuted in 2002 and 1,848 in 2003. The firm's goal has been to successfully combine the breadth of a general practice firm and the depth of an intellectual property boutique. They are gratified that these rankings reflect the strides they have made toward achieving this goal.

Regulatory: The attorneys in the Regulatory Department have achieved unparalleled success addressing insurance, energy, telecommunications, environmental, and product safety issues in state capitals throughout the country, and before Congress and other federal agencies.

Tax & Individual Planning: The firm's Tax and Individual Planning attorneys have set precedents through landmark trial decisions that have laid the groundwork for many current state and federal tax procedures.

Health Law: The firm provides the largest Health Law practice in the United States, having advised industry and government on major healthcare policies for decades.

US OFFICES

Boston, Chicago, Detroit, Jacksonville, Los Angeles, Madison, Milwaukee, New York, Orlando, Sacramento, San Diego, San Diego/Del Mar, San Francisco, Silicon Valley, Tallahassee, Tampa, Washington, DC, West Palm Beach.

INTERNATIONAL OFFICES

The firm has offices in Brussels and Tokyo.

CONTACTS

Business Law	Joseph B Tyson Jr
White Collar Defense & Corporate Compliance	Thomas F Carlucci
Corporate Governance Services	Patrick G Quick
Health Law	George L (Jody) Root
Intellectual Property	Richard S Florsheim
IP Litigation	Sharon R Barner
Labor & Employment	Thomas C Pence
Litigation	Jon M Wilson
Regulatory	Allen W (Sandy) Williams Jr
Tax & Individual Planning	Richard S Gallagher
Transactional & Securities	Jay O Rothman

Industry Teams: Foley & Lardner's unique industry-focused approach enables them to blend hands-on industry experience with sophisticated legal skills to provide clients with the most significantly enhanced value-added service. The firm's industry teams include attorneys and related practitioners who have served as industry executives within corporations, associations, and regulatory agencies, among others – many of whom are viewed as industry pioneers and sought out as experts. These teams represent a range of service offerings, enabling them to take a comprehensive view of their clients' industries and bring together the right practitioners and competencies to address their needs.

Industries Represented: Automotive, e-business and information technology, energy, entertainment and media, food, golf and resort services, healthcare, insurance, life sciences, nanotechnology and sports.

Award-Winning Technology Trendsetter: The firm is exceedingly proud of its commitment to innovation and technology, which has earned it accolades from industry experts. For instance, in 2001, *InformationWeek* magazine named Foley & Lardner to its list of "25 Innovators in Collaboration" as the only law firm honored for effective use of technology in collaborating with clients. In 2001, 2002, and 2004, *CIO* magazine recognized the firm - the only law firm to be honored more than once - as one of 100 global companies demonstrating innovation in improving products, services, and relationships with clients. As well, Foley & Lardner was named to BTI Consulting Group's 2003 Tech-Savvy Team for providing "technological prowess" in serving its clients.

FOLEY & LARDNER LLP

LIEBMANN, CONWAY, OLEJNICZAK, & JERRY, S.C.

THE FIRM

Managing Partner: Gregory B Conway

Number of partners: 11
Number of other lawyers: 10

FIRM OVERVIEW: Liebmann, Conway, Olejniczak & Jerry, S.C. is committed to careful preparation, prompt service, and aggressive advocacy in providing assistance and advice to individuals and businesses alike. The firm provides a wide range of legal services in consultative non-adversarial settings and through all phases of litigation in state, federal, and bankruptcy courts, and before administrative agencies and arbitrators.

MAIN AREAS OF PRACTICE:

Litigation: Liebmann Conway's Litigation Team provides services in all areas of commercial litigation and dispute resolution including: insurance coverage disputes, breach of contract, construction, environmental, finance and banking, labor and employment, medical malpractice defense, product liability, real estate, regulatory matters, torts, trademark and copyright issues. The firm provides representation at the state and federal levels, appellate representation, and representation for arbitration and mediation.

Mergers & Acquisitions: Liebmann Conway represents buyers, sellers and investors in various transactions, including mergers and other business combinations, leveraged buy-outs and purchase/sale transactions. Their attorneys have guided clients through and closed hundreds of transactions ranging in size from thousands of dollars to hundreds of millions of dollars.

Banking & Financial: Liebmann Conway represents multiple financial institutions in all aspects of banking operations, including the preparation of loan documentation for transactions ranging from several hundred thousand to multi-million dollars. In addition, the firm provides assistance in creditor rights' replevins, work-out situations, foreclosure actions and general litigation support.

Corporate Law: Liebmann Conway provides assistance in business organization and operation and in all aspects of commercial relationships between business entities.

Environmental Issues: Liebmann Conway represents clients ranging from individuals to major corporations and municipalities in connection with environmental matters, including negotiations and litigation with the Department of Natural Resources and the Environmental Protection Agency. These matters often involve the Clean Air Act, the Clean Water Act, the Superfund Act and corresponding state regulations. Their role is frequently advisory as we guide clients through environmental complexities before they become problems. The firm also works with corporations and individuals in obtaining necessary permits for their development and operations including air permits, NPDES permits and wetland permits. The firm regularly advises engineering consulting firms in the design of landfills and other heavily regulated waste disposal activities.

HEAD OFFICE

WISCONSIN
231 South Adams Street, **Green Bay**, WI 54301
Tel: 920 437 0476 **Fax:** 920 437 2868
Website: www.lcojlaw.com

Intellectual Property: The firm's intellectual property services include counseling clients on the intricacies of intellectual property law, and in representation of clients before the United State Patent and Trademark Office, Trademark Trial and Appeal Board, Copyright Office, and state and local courts regarding intellectual property infringements, misappropriation, unfair competition, non-compete/trade secrets and related actions.

Real Estate: Liebmann Conway provides a full rage of legal services in real estate matters relating to commercial, industrial and residential properties including reviewing abstracts, title insurance commitments, negotiating and drafting limited partnership, condominium, joint venture, and other types of conveyance agreements. In addition, the firm provides assistance in evaluating financing arrangements such as industrial and developmental revenue bonds, and tax increment and government-assisted financing.

CLIENTS: Clients range from individuals requiring assistance in personal injury matters, estate planning, real estate transactions and business advice, to publicly-traded Fortune 500 corporations involved in manufacturing, banking, insurance, healthcare, financial services, communication, publishing, construction and engineering.

MICHAEL BEST & FRIEDRICH LLP

THE FIRM

Managing Partner: Thomas E Obenberger
Chair of the Management Committee: Tod B Linstroth
Number of partners: 189
Number of attorneys: 317
Website: www.michaelbest.com

FIRM OVERVIEW: Michael Best & Friedrich LLP was founded in 1848 in Milwaukee, Wisconsin. Clients range in size from one-person start-up ventures to Fortune 500 companies. As a broad-based business law firm, Michael Best is able to offer the experience needed to handle a complete range of business legal matters.

MAIN AREAS OF PRACTICE:

Corporate & Business Law: Corporate and business law is a core competency of the firm. The range of services involves individuals, partnerships, limited liability companies and corporations and includes assisting in the organization, financing and operation of business ventures, through and including mergers, acquisitions, divestitures and joint ventures. Experience in corporate finance has resulted in representation of venture capital investors through the firm's VentureBest℠ Group, mezzanine lenders, and start-up and later-phase companies in all facets of business, including distribution, manufacturing and emerging technology.

Employment Law: Michael Best's 50 labor and employment attorneys and professionals work on the leading edge of labor and employment law, representing some of the most innovative and ground breaking businesses, public sector, and non-profit organizations in the nation. The attorneys continually strive to develop close partnerships with clients, focusing on litigation prevention and the achievement of strategic objectives through human resources counseling, planning, and training in order to cultivate the client's superior labor force. The attorneys are recognized by their clients and peers as among the best and most respected management-side labor, employment, and employee benefits attorneys in the Midwest, providing legal defense in all aspects of labor and employment litigation; union organizing, collective bargaining, and grievance arbitration; wage-hour issues; safety and workers compensation; employee benefits; and immigration. They have decades of experience practicing in state and federal trial courts, appellate and Supreme courts, administrative agencies and arbitrators, and designing compensation, retirement, pension, stock, and health plans.

Healthcare: Michael Best's Healthcare Practice Group has earned a national reputation as a leading healthcare practice in a number of areas including bioethics, HIPAA compliance, and healthcare transactions. The February 2004 issue of *Modern Healthcare* ranked Michael Best & Friedrich as one of the top 20 largest health law practices in the nation. Michael Best provides counsel to a wide variety of healthcare clients, including hospitals and health systems, academic medical centers, physician group practices, clinical laboratories, skilled nursing facilities, community residential facilities, home health agencies, hospices, health maintenance organizations, health insurance carriers, and healthcare associations. Services provided for clients range from acting as general counsel for health systems, to representing healthcare providers in complex transactional matters.

Intellectual Property Law & IP Litigation: Michael Best has one of the nation's leading intellectual property practices. Nearly 100 professionals offer a complete range of services to clients throughout the nation and around the world. Michael Best offers legal and technical experience in areas such as patent, trademark and copyright prosecution and counseling; all types of intellectual property litigation; internet and e-commerce; technology transfer and joint venture agreements; computer software and system acquisition agreements; M&A due diligence; and trade secrets.

OFFICES

WISCONSIN
100 East Wisconsin Avenue, Suite 3300, **Milwaukee**, WI 53202-4108
Tel: 414 271 6560   **Fax:** 414 277 0656

One South Pinckney Street, Suite 700, **Madison**, WI 53703-4257
Tel: 608 257 3501   **Fax:** 608 283 2275

Two Riverwood Place, Suite 200, N19 W24133 Riverwood Drive, **Waukesha**, WI 53188-1174
Tel: 262 956 6560   **Fax:** 262 956 6565

1000 Maritime Drive, **Manitowoc**, WI 54220-2922
Tel: 920 686 2800   **Fax:** 920 686 2810

ILLINOIS
401 North Michigan Avenue, Suite 1900, **Chicago**, IL 60611-4274
Tel: 312 222 0800   **Fax:** 312 222 0818

PENNSYLVANIA
Stabler Corporate Center, Suite 360, 3773 Corporate Parkway, **Center Valley**, PA 18034
Tel: 610 798 2170   **Fax:** 610 798 2180

Nationally, the firm ranks 18th among the top trademark law firms, and among the top intellectual property litigation practice groups. When clients choose litigation as the right strategy for a given situation, the firm offers them a roster of experienced litigators whose practices are dedicated to intellectual property. Michael Best was recently ranked by *IP Worldwide* as one of the top IP defense firms in the nation. In addition, *IP Law & Business*, which ranks law firms by those who filed the most IP suits, placed Michael Best among the nation's top 25 law firms.

Land & Resources: The attorneys in Michael Best's Land and Resources Group practice in all areas of environmental, construction, development and real estate law, serving property owners, developers, all types of manufacturers and industrial operations, public utilities, construction and agribusiness companies.

Litigation: Michael Best's Litigation Practice Group has an unmatched depth of experience and success with more than 150 published cases at every level of State and Federal Courts in the recent years. Its members include a host of former judicial law clerks, law review editors, a former Wisconsin Supreme Court Justice and board members and officers of local, state and national bar associations. The attorneys have been consistently honored by publications as among the best counsel in their fields. More than 70 members strong, Michael Best is equipped to provide clients with first class representation in any type of litigation.

Tax & Wealth Planning Services: Michael Best provides high quality, cost effective and innovative services regarding individual and business transactional tax planning; business succession planning; financial planning and asset protection planning; risk management; retirement planning; and family counseling.

INTERNATIONAL WORK: Through various international legal alliances, Michael Best has the ability to bring global resources to clients. Michael Best is the exclusive Wisconsin member of Lex Mundi ('Law of the World'), enabling the firm to arrange effective representation for clients around the world. The China Alliance is a unique arrangement allowing the member firms to enhance their ability to serve the needs of clients in the rapidly developing China market.

REINHART BOERNER VAN DEUREN S.C.

THE FIRM

Chairman: Robert E Bellin
President & Chief Executive Officer: Richard W Graber
Number of partners: 109
Number of associates: 70
Total number of attorneys: 183
Total number of support staff: 227

FIRM OVERVIEW: Reinhart Boerner Van Deuren s.c. serves business needs with innovation, focus and commitment. The firm's attorneys are dedicated to providing service efficiently and cost-effectively throughout their offices in Milwaukee, Madison and Waukesha, Wisconsin. Founded in 1894, the firm's total commitment to clients and to innovation has allowed it to grow to nearly 200 attorneys. Reinhart serves as attorneys and business counselors to public and privately held corporations, financial institutions, family-owned businesses, retirement plans, exempt organizations and individuals.

MAIN AREAS OF PRACTICE:

Banking & Finance: Reinhart's Banking and Finance Department brings projects to life. The firm's attorneys go beyond counseling banks and financial institutions on state and federal regulatory compliance. It also brings together lenders and borrowers to meet the needs of business or help municipalities finance memorable projects.

Bankruptcy & Creditors' Rights: Reinhart's Bankruptcy Department has taken the lead role in virtually every major bankruptcy in Milwaukee and throughout Wisconsin. Representing debtors, creditors, trustees or creditors' committees, its attorneys have produced exceptional outcomes in an area where good results don't come easily.

Business Law: The firm's staff of more than 40 professionals tailors innovative solutions to the complex needs of corporate clients. Partnered with in-house counsel, they create a team with the depth and experience to tackle any issue cost-efficiently and effectively.

Employment Benefits: Highly respected, Reinhart's Employee Benefits Department is one of the largest in the country with clients in almost every state. As one of the first law firms to represent employee benefit plans more than 40 years ago, Reinhart is large enough to offer clients the advantage of working with sub-specialists in every field as employee benefits laws expand.

Environment Law: Reinhart's environmental attorneys aren't just experts in the law, they're experts in science, too. With credentials in a number of scientific and technical fields, Reinhart's Environmental Law Department provides one-stop shopping for resolution of environmental problems.

Estate Planning: Because the only certainties in life are death and taxes, Reinhart's Estate Planning Department helps clients preserve wealth when it passes to the next generation. Many of Wisconsin's most successful family-owned businesses rely on Reinhart estate planning attorneys for tax planning and estate/trust administration.

Government Relations: Reinhart's Government Relations Department is unique in its ability to get attention on both sides of the aisle. Its attorneys include the chairman of the Wisconsin Republican Party as well as a long-time activist for Wisconsin Democrats.

Healthcare: With several attorneys who have worked inside the healthcare system, Reinhart's Healthcare Department offers experience unmatched by any other law firm in Wisconsin. Its attorneys understand first-hand the intricate network of legal relationships that bind patients, physicians, hospitals, and third-party payers.

Intellectual Property: Reinhart's Intellectual Property Department understands how businesses maintain a competitive edge. The firms IP attorneys identify, establish, expand, and enforce intellectual property portfolios domestically and internationally. Often in conjunction with the litigation and business law departments, Reinhart's IP attorneys make sure clients have all the tools they need to compete.

HEAD OFFICE

WISCONSIN
1000 North Waters Street Suite 2100, **Milwaukee** WI 53202
Tel: 414 298 1000 **Fax:** 414 298 8097
Website: www.reinhartlaw.com

CONTACTS

Business Law	Michael T Pepke
Banking	William F Flynn
Bankruptcy	Peter C Blain
Employee Benefits	Steven D Huff
Government Relations	Barbara K Boxer
Healthcare	Robert J Heath
Intellectual Property	Leslie S Miller
Labor & Employment	Robert K Sholl
Litigation	Scott W Hansen
Telecommunications & Energy	Peter L Gardon
Trusts & Estates	John A Herbers
Real Estate	Bruce T Block
Environmental	Michael H Simpson
International	Daniel J Brink
Tax	Timothy P Reardon
Securities	James M Bedoe

International: Reinhart's International Law Department attorneys are not only up to date on business laws around the world, they have the connections to compete in any foreign political or economic system. Whether it's helping a US company do business away from home, or helping a foreign business succeed in the US, Reinhart's International Department has the experience needed for today's global business world.

Labor & Employment: Reinhart's labor and employment attorneys are proactive in approach minimizes employment law violations for both public and private sector employers. When litigation does occur, they are experienced at representing management before federal and state courts or administrative agencies.

Litigation: Reinhart's Litigation Department includes former assistant US attorneys, former assistant district attorneys, and several attorneys who have clerked for federal, appellate, or Wisconsin Supreme Court justices. The firm has experienced practice teams that focus on key areas including products liability, sales and distribution, intellectual property, healthcare and financial professional liability defense. Its litigation attorneys have more trial experience than their counterparts in most firms this size. Reinhart's attorneys test cases in their own state-of-the-art, high-tech courtroom.

Real Estate: With the largest Real Estate Department of any law firm in Wisconsin, Reinhart offers clients custom-tailored expertise. Attorneys form groups of subspecialties so that its broad range of expertise and depth of experience apply to every matter.

Securities: Efficiency, responsiveness, and the ability to get involved in the early stages of financing are what set apart Reinhart's Securities Department. Its attorneys do more than just structure and negotiate financial transactions. They're experienced at raising capital by locating the right source.

Tax: Attorneys in Reinhart's Tax Department are dedicated to saving clients money. The firms Tax Controversy Group is the largest in Wisconsin, enjoying a reputation for winning large reductions from tax agencies. Four of its attorneys are former IRS or Department of Revenue trial attorneys. Moreover, most of its lawyers teach or have taught other tax practitioners in the University of Wisconsin-Milwaukee Master of Tax Program.

CONTENTS: Corporate/M&A p.1832; Employment p.1833; Litigation p.1834; Real Estate p.1836; Individuals' Profiles p.1838. Firms' Profiles p.1840.

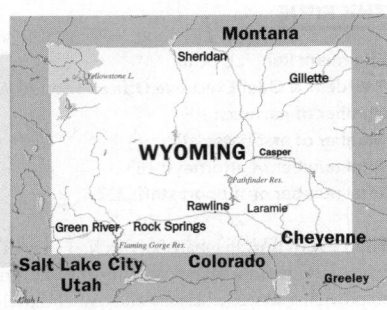

How lawyers are ranked

The opinions we gather from clients — mainly from in-house lawyers but also from other purchasers of legal services — are balanced by opinions from colleagues and competitors. Together, they provide two different perspectives — an all-round view — and biased viewpoints cancel each other out.

CORPORATE/M&A

Wyoming
Leading firms (Corporate/M&A)

① BROWN, DREW & MASSEY LLP *Casper*
  DRAY, THOMSON & DYEKMAN PC *Cheyenne*
  THOMAS N LONG PC *Cheyenne*

② HIRST & APPLEGATE, PC *Cheyenne*
  HOLLAND & HART LLP *Cheyenne*

Leading individuals (Corporate/M&A)

① DRAY W Perry *Dray Thomson, Cheyenne*
  LONG Thomas *Thomas N Long, Cheyenne*

② BARBE J Kenneth *Brown Drew, Casper*
  BELCHER James *Holland & Hart, Cheyenne*
  BUFFINGTON Teresa *Holland & Hart, Cheyenne*
  COTTAM Dale *Hirst & Applegate, Cheyenne*
  DYEKMAN Gregory *Dray Thomson, Cheyenne*
  MCCALL Donn *Brown Drew, Casper*
  METZKE John *Hirst & Applegate, Cheyenne*
  REED Randall *Dray Thomson, Cheyenne*

Firms and individuals are listed alphabetically in each band.

Band 1

Brown, Drew & Massey LLP
See firm details p.1840

The Firm: Interviewees recommended this transactional practice for its ability to *"work quickly and with precision."* The team focuses on bankruptcy and creditors' rights law as well as banking and financial services issues. Its recent highlights include working on the financial aspects of a major real estate project. Satisfied clients report that lawyers here are *"simply great."* They also appreciate the technical support provided by specialists working in ancillary practice areas such as employment.

The Lawyers: Donn McCall is one of the managing partners of this Casper-based firm. He has a banking background and represents a considerable number of lenders in the state. He was recommended to researchers as a talented bankruptcy lawyer although he also handles acquisitions, oil and gas matters and asset-based financings. **Kenneth Barbe** is a *"fine lawyer"* who advises on estate planning and commercial transactions, such as business acquisitions, lending transactions and the creation of limited liability companies. Interviewees value the experience he has accumulated as a corporate lawyer but they also point to his skill in litigation.

The Clients: Bank of the West; Greiner Ford Lincoln Mercury and White's Mountain Motors.

Dray, Thomson & Dyekman PC
See firm details p.1841

The Firm: This group provides a wide array of services to clients that range from Fortune 500 companies and international concerns to large banks. It provides expertise in areas such as estate planning, tax, insurance and administrative law. Clients who call on the firm for support in relation to a number of business transactions report that this is *"one of the sharpest corporate operations"* in Cheyenne.

The Lawyers: Perry Dray (see p.1838) is a *"first-rate lawyer"* who has wide commercial experience including advising on corporate law and civil litigation matters. He has also recently been involved in one of the biggest bankruptcy cases in Wyoming. Part of his practice is also devoted to representing physician groups and hospitals in healthcare issues. The *"client-focused and knowledgeable"* **Gregory Dyekman** (see p.1838) always *"comes up with very practical solutions."* His practice encompasses commercial law, litigation, banking and real estate law. **Randall Reed** (see p.1839) is a *"careful lawyer who will never put his clients in a risky situation."* He maintains a diverse practice which sees him advising clients on a range of matters including business organization, employment law and oil and gas acquisitions.

The Clients: The team represents international businesses, healthcare providers, lenders and real estate developers.

Thomas N Long PC
The Firm: This *"brilliant"* five-attorney team based in Cheyenne handles a broad portfolio of work including a range of business transactions and tax-related issues. It fields a team of *"highly knowledgeable lawyers"* who routinely handle issues such as corporation and partnership law, and who provide advice to charitable organizations. In a recent highlight, the team successfully acted for a client embroiled in a tax dispute where it was able to save its client $4 million.

The Lawyers: The founder of the firm, **Thomas Long** is a *"meticulous, knowledgeable and detail-focused attorney"* who is well known for his tax law capabilities. He deals with a variety of matters including trust administration, business planning and partnership law. He is also an authority on tax-exempt organizations. He recently represented a major bank on a divestment and advised a telephone company on a transaction valued at $20 million. Commentators described Long as *"one of the best attorneys you could hope to meet."*

The Clients: American National Bank of Cheyenne; Wyoming Department of Revenue; L & L Liquor; Cheyenne Radiology Group and Citicorp.

Band 2

Hirst & Applegate, PC
The Firm: This Cheyenne-based firm fields a team of three attorneys who focus on corporate matters. The group has made impressive client gains in the past year and has been especially active in business sectors such as the computer, food distribution and investment industries. It provides expertise on the formation of new business entities as well as on M&A transactions and the sale of assets. It represents national and international clients active in the Wyoming market.

The Lawyers: With more than 11 years of corporate law experience behind him, clients consider **Dale Cottam** a bright, detail-oriented

WYOMING

lawyer who is *"terrific to work with."* He recently acted on the share exchange between Liquid Cognition and Seventh Floor. He also advised on a $25 million transaction involving the Halliburton facility located near Rock Springs. Cottam is also actively involved in real estate matters. Work here includes advising on an ongoing real estate acquisition and development for Cheyenne's economic development agency, Cheyenne LEADS. **John Metzke** is a *"real perfectionist,"* who clients praised for his *"outstanding"* work. He is best known for his knowledge of estate planning, trust administration and family limited partnerships.

The Clients: Liquid Cognition; Pacific Energy Partners; AARP; Cheyenne LEADS and Wyoming Bank & Trust.

Holland & Hart LLP

See firm details p.325

The Firm: The Cheyenne office of this *"top-notch"* regional firm has two partners specializing in corporate work. The team handles all areas of financial and corporate business matters for a range of industry groups, including entities from the natural resources sector. The team's day-to-day workload includes advising on right of way acquisitions, commercial financing transactions and entity planning.

The Lawyers: Our sources told us that **James Belcher** (see p.1838) is a *"tough, talented, and hard-working"* lawyer who is *"a real expert"* in the fields of banking and bankruptcy law. He also advises clients in energy development and transmission matters, including wind energy

projects, natural gas gathering and pipelines. He uses his past experience as a commercial banker to good effect and is a *"very bright guy who leaves no stone unturned."* **Teresa Buffington** (see p.1838) is a *"meticulous attorney who is easy to work with."* She advises on a range of commercial transactions including M&A deals and financings. She is also becoming increasingly involved in real estate matters, particularly in relation to natural resources. She recently advised a client on the sale of its northeastern gas gathering system in Wyoming.

The Clients: The firm acts for public and private clients including local, national and international businesses. It also acts for a number of Fortune 500 companies

EMPLOYMENT

MAINLY DEFENDANT

Wyoming
Leading firms
(Employment: Mainly Defendant)

[1] **DAVIS & CANNON** *Cheyenne*
WILLIAMS, PORTER, DAY & NEVILLE PC *Casper*
YONKEE & TONER LLP *Sheridan*
[2] **HIRST & APPLEGATE, PC** *Cheyenne*
HOLLAND & HART LLP *Cheyenne*
MURANE & BOSTWICK LLC *Casper*
SCHWARTZ, BON, WALKER & STUDER *Casper*

Leading individuals
(Employment: Mainly Defendant)

[1] **DAVIS Michael** *Yonkee & Toner, Sheridan*
FOX Kate *Davis & Cannon, Cheyenne*
ORTIZ Scott *Williams Porter, Casper*
SCOTT Gary *Hirst & Applegate, Cheyenne*
[2] **CAVE Bradley** *Holland & Hart, Cheyenne*
SHUMATE Roger *Murane & Bostwick, Casper*
STUDER Judith *Schwartz Bon, Casper*
Firms and individuals are listed alphabetically in each band.

Band 1

Davis & Cannon

The Firm: This general practice firm has offices in Cheyenne and Sheridan and advises on a wide variety of legal issues. Its lawyers are well versed in commercial and natural resources law, but also stand out for their employment law expertise. Here the team represents a number of major corporations and local governmental organizations on a spectrum of employment issues including employment litigation.

The Lawyers: A *"smart lawyer,"* **Kate Fox** is one of the firm's standout employment practitioners. Although she is increasingly involved in general commercial litigation, she continues to advise on employment matters. Recent work

includes advising on the enforcement of a non-compete agreement, which eventually resulted in a settlement. Commentators agree that Fox is a *"superb lawyer"* who manages to *"break new ground"* whenever she is engaged in a difficult matter.

The Clients: First Interstate Bank of Commerce; Memorial Hospital of Sheridan County and Marion Merrell Dow.

Williams, Porter, Day & Neville PC

The Firm: A team comprising five partners and two associates advises a diverse stable of clients on matters including labor law management and discrimination issues. A particularly hot topic of late has been drug-related issues, where it has advised employers on how to implement drug testing in the workplace. Based in Casper, the group's broad client base includes utilities and other industrial employers.

The Lawyers: With around 16 years of labor and employment experience, **Scott Ortiz** can handle employment law matters *"like no other."* He has recently been successful in a labor law arbitration and is also active in employment litigation. Interviewees rate him as *"a real trial attorney"* who has a full skill set. They told us, *"He thinks about the big picture and has a common-sense approach to solving problems."*

The Clients: ScottishPower; PacifiCorp; City of Casper; Allstate; Bituminous Insurance and BP.

Yonkee & Toner LLP

The Firm: This Sheridan-based firm boasts a *"really dedicated team"* of six attorneys. It maintains a broad repertoire that includes advising on water rights, oil and gas law, insurance defense and environmental law, but also continues to be active in the employment arena. Its workload includes advising on civil rights law and a variety of employment litigation cases.

The Lawyers: Interviewees characterized **Michael Davis** as a *"real problem solver"* who is *"always involved in the biggest cases."* This smart and aggressive lawyer handles a diverse caseload including medical malpractice and insurance defense, personal injury and a variety of employment cases. Sources admire him as a smart and experienced litigator who *"knows how to move the process forward."*

The Clients: Ohio Hospital Insurance; Alliance Ditch; Wyeth; West Park Hospital and Sheridan County School Districts 1, 2 and 3.

Band 2

Hirst & Applegate, PC

The Firm: Although employment law accounts for a relatively small percentage of this firm's practice, it has established a respectable position in the labor and employment market in Cheyenne. It has a strong reputation in litigation and advises a range of Wyoming-based public and private entities on a spectrum of employment matters.

The Lawyers: **Gary Scott** is a *"smart and knowledgeable"* attorney who spearheads the firm's employment law work. He is popular among peers, who feel comfortable referring work to him. They report that *"he works hard for the client and won't break the bank."*

The Clients: Thunder Basin Coal; Royal Construction; Frontier Refining; Nautilus Insurance and GM.

Holland & Hart LLP

See firm details p.325

The Firm: This regional firm has a 13-attorney office in Cheyenne that deals with a range of business, litigation and natural resources matters. A team of three lawyers is dedicated to handling employment issues. These include discrimination cases, wage and hour disputes, wrongful discharge and breach of contract claims. The group is devoted to representing employers drawn from a range of sectors including the energy industry.

The Lawyers: Bradley Cave (see p.1838) focuses his practice solely on employment law and handles cases concerning alleged harassment and wrongful discharge. He has also recently acted for a client in a religious discrimination case and has taken several matters to the Tenth Circuit Court of Appeal.

The Clients: The group acts for numerous local and national clients including: Kennecott Energy; Triton Coal; ChevronTexaco and United Medical Center.

Murane & Bostwick LLC

The Firm: This is a full-service firm that has offices in Cheyenne and Casper. Its team of nine attorneys advises on a range of business transactions but is also well versed in litigation,

including employment cases. The practice handles a steady stream of instructions including wrongful termination and sexual harassment cases. It also advises on disputes concerning ADA, EEOC cases and workers' compensation.

The Lawyers: Roger Shumate concentrates his practice primarily on employment law and has niche expertise in wrongful termination cases. His competitors feel comfortable referring employment work to him because he is a *"competent and tough lawyer"* with broad market experience.

The Clients: The group's client base includes rental companies, midsized Wyoming businesses, insurance companies, hospitals and county government.

Schwartz, Bon, Walker & Studer LLC

The Firm: This seven-attorney, Casper-based firm is a general civil and trial practice that handles various legal matters. Its work includes cor-

porate, environmental and oil and gas law but it also wins recognition for its employment work. Here, its client base includes insurance companies, banks and a variety of other small, medium and large businesses.

The Lawyers: Our interviewees admire **Judith Studer** as a *"very ethical lawyer."* She is famous for her litigation skills and was described by one commentator as being *"tough as nails."* Her practice includes advising on general commercial, oil and gas and employment litigation, where she does *"a great job."*

The Clients: Union Carbide; Equitable; St. Paul; Kemper Insurance; Wyoming Association of Municipalities; Community First National Bank and The Hartford.

LITIGATION

GENERAL COMMERCIAL

Wyoming
Leading firms
(Litigation: General Commercial)

1 HICKEY&MACKEY *Cheyenne*
HIRST & APPLEGATE, PC *Cheyenne*
HOLLAND & HART LLP *Cheyenne*
WILLIAMS, PORTER, DAY & NEVILLE PC *Casper*
YONKEE & TONER LLP *Sheridan*

2 DAVIS & CANNON *Cheyenne*
LATHROP & RUTLEDGE *Cheyenne*
MASON & MASON PC *Pinedale*
SCHWARTZ, BON, WALKER & STUDER *Casper*
SUNDAHL, POWERS, KAPP & MARTIN *Cheyenne*

Firms are listed alphabetically in each band.

Band 1

Hickey&Mackey

The Firm: This full-service firm, which is the continuation of a practice started in Cheyenne more than 70 years ago, focuses on business law, administrative law and trial matters. Key areas of strength include PI, public utilities, energy, environmental, labor and employment and general private client law. It represents individuals and corporations throughout Wyoming as well as several national businesses.

The Lawyers: *"Always thoroughly prepared, an effective speaker and exuding jury appeal,"* **Paul Hickey** has *"all the qualities a good litigator should have,"* clients remarked. This *"excellent lawyer"* deals more with regulatory and administrative matters, and can boast an extensive public utility practice, both trial and appellate experience and a strong grasp of school law.

"One of the very few criminal defense lawyers in the state," **Terry Mackey** is an effective trial lawyer with an extensive statewide practice. Besides his trial practice, Mackey deals with a vast amount of commercial transactional work.

The Clients: Qwest; PacifiCorp; Kinder Morgan and Laramie County School District 2.

Hirst & Applegate, PC

The Firm: This Cheyenne practice boasts an eight-attorney litigation team that has an *"outstanding reputation"* in representing clients in all sorts of industries with an emphasis on the risk and energy-related industries. Its marquee litigation department tends to address products liability, energy litigation, medical malpractice, insurance extracontractual cases and casualty cases.

The Lawyers: Benefiting from more than 30 years of litigation experience, **Thomas Nicholas** *"is one of the smartest lawyers you'll ever run into,"* say interviewees. Able to leverage *"tremendous expertise"* in areas such as insurance litigation and defense, energy and environmental litigation, administrative hearings and appeals, he is respected by peers because *"he knows the ropes, does the homework and is great with juries."*

The Clients: AT&T; Aetna; Simon Contractors; Bank of America; Wells Fargo and Ford.

Holland & Hart LLP

See firm details p.325

The Firm: Benefiting from 12 offices in the Rocky Mountain states and Washington DC, the team of six litigators counsels its local and national clientele in matters such as lost profits,

receivership, injunctions or specific performance. The Wyoming team leans towards oil and gas-related cases.

The Lawyers: Commentators agreed that **Donald Schultz** (see p.1839) *"is extremely well prepared, efficient and is very highly competent."* His Cheyenne practice handles issues such as construction and design, oil and gas, general business and environmental litigation. Regarded as *"an obvious choice"* for large and complex litigation of any sort, recent representative cases include a statewide class action and a multibillion-dollar matter.

The Clients: EOG Resources; Burlington Resources; ExxonMobil and Questar Pipeline.

Williams, Porter, Day & Neville PC

The Firm: Composed of a majority of litigators, the firm *"has a long history of litigation excellence."* Clients use the firm for a range of matters going from bankruptcy and business litigation to torts litigation. Its client base comprises insurance companies, energy sector industries and healthcare providers.

The Lawyers: *"Distinguished and extremely client-friendly,"* **Frank Neville** is *"loved by juries,"* according to market sources. Neville focuses on personal injury, medical malpractice defense, products liability, civil rights, employment and environmental litigation. Other practitioners feel confident in referring work to him, especially for energy-related matters, because he is *"always reliable and well prepared."* *"One of the best in insurance matters,"* **Patrick Murphy** is an *"excellent, well-skilled and knowledgeable"* attorney. His practice embraces professional malpractice,

Wyoming
Leading individuals
(Litigation: General Commercial)
Senior Statesman
DAY Richard *Williams Porter*, Casper
[1] **NICHOLAS Thomas** *Hirst & Applegate*, Cheyenne
REEVES Weston *Reeves & Miller*, Casper
TONER Tom *Yonkee & Toner*, Sheridan
[2] **BRINKERHOFF Jeffrey** *Brown Drew*, Casper
CANNON Kim *Davis & Cannon*, Cheyenne
FOX Kate *Davis & Cannon*, Cheyenne
GIFFORD Mark *Mark W. Gifford*, Casper
HICKEY Paul *Hickey&Mackey*, Cheyenne
MACKEY Terry *Hickey&Mackey*, Cheyenne
MASON Gerald *Mason & Mason*, Pinedale
MURPHY Patrick *Williams Porter*, Casper
NEVILLE Frank *Williams Porter*, Casper
POWERS George *Sundahl Powers*, Cheyenne
RUTLEDGE Kent *Lathrop & Rutledge*, Cheyenne
SCHULTZ Donald *Holland & Hart*, Cheyenne
STUDER Judith *Schwartz Bon*, Casper
SUNDAHL John *Sundahl Powers*, Cheyenne
Individuals are listed alphabetically in each band.

insurance bad faith, products liability, personal injury, wrongful death and wrongful termination suits, though he focuses primarily on insurance defense and insurance extracontractual litigation. Able to exploit more than 40 years' experience in the field, **Richard Day** can rightly claim to be the most well-versed practitioner in the state. He has a successful track record in personal injury, products liability, business litigation, employment, environmental and taxation law cases.
The Clients: PacifiCorp; Wyoming Medical Center; Devon Energy and Marathon Oil.

Yonkee & Toner LLP
The Firm: This *"extremely reliable"* Sheridan-based firm addresses such matters as medical malpractice defense, environmental law and litigation, insurance defense and employment law. Its six attorneys are very active in general civil litigation on behalf of clients such as major insurance companies, healthcare providers and public entities.
The Lawyers: *"A creative man who knows how to adapt to each client,"* **Tom Toner** is *"one of the best lawyers in Wyoming, hands down,"* enthused commentators. His broad practice encompasses oil and gas, natural resources, water rights, commercial and estate planning. According to commentators *"he knows how to analyze a case and how to handle things the right way."*
The Clients: State Farm; Memorial Hospital of Sheridan County; Wyeth; Sheridan County School Districts 1, 2 and 3; MetLife and West Park Hospital.

Band 2

Davis & Cannon
The Firm: *"Outstanding in general commercial litigation,"* this firm fields a team of nine attorneys handling a wide spectrum of cases in the mining, environmental, water, natural resources, private client, insurance, professional negligence, employment and taxation sectors. According to clients, the team *"always does a great job."*
The Lawyers: Renowned for her high levels of activity, **Kate Fox** has been dealing with more and more general civil litigation lately. Regarded by peers as a *"very knowledgeable and fine lawyer,"* she was involved in the fenfluramine mass torts litigation in which the plaintiffs alleged that the diet drug caused heart damage. **Kim Cannon** has developed an *"outstanding"* general civil and commercial practice over the years, and his 30 years of experience make him one of the most respected trial lawyers in Sheridan.
The Clients: The team represents clients including insurance companies, banks, healthcare providers and natural resources and energy-related industries.

Lathrop & Rutledge
The Firm: Devoting the majority of its overall caseload to litigation matters, the seven attorneys of this Cheyenne firm represent physicians, hospitals, chiropractors, architects and engineers in all sorts of litigation including insurance coverage disputes, bad faith claims, professional negligence and licensing claims.
The Lawyers: *"A pretty active litigator with a nice profile,"* **Kent Rutledge** *"is one of the leading medical malpractice lawyers in the state,"* according to legal insiders. The balance of his practice encompasses commercial litigation, insurance and bad faith litigation, products liability defense and other civil litigation.
The Clients: Wyoming Hospital Association; Underwriters Indemnity Company; Omaha Property & Casualty; The Doctors Company; Continental General Insurance and United States Life Insurance.

Mason & Mason PC
The Firm: Focusing mainly on natural resources work, this family-run firm enjoys a healthy reputation for its litigation practice. On account of the considerable experience of its founding member, Gerald Mason, this two-attorney firm is the most prominent general litigation practice in Pinedale.
The Lawyers: **Gerald Mason** deals with a wide range of cases, particularly mineral and real estate litigation. According to interviewees, Mason is an *"outstanding gentleman"* who *"can just do anything you give him."*
The Clients: An area school district and a homeowner association are notable among the firm's clients.

Schwartz, Bon, Walker & Studer LLC
The Firm: This five-attorney Casper-based firm deals with general civil litigation matters including corporate, employment, environmental, natural resources, torts, banking and insurance law. Established less than 30 years ago, the team represents both plaintiffs and defendants, and recently represented Goodyear in a case centering upon allegations of substandard tires.
The Lawyers: Peers agree that **Judith Studer** *"has been a very solid lawyer for years."* Renowned for her specialization in insurance defense, casualty claims and labor and employment law, Struder made her name through various high-profile successes, including the Cordero Mining Company v United States Fidelity & Guarantee Insurance Company case.
The Clients: Union Carbide; Equitable; St. Paul and Community First National Bank.

Sundahl, Powers, Kapp & Martin LLC
The Firm: Specialized in civil litigation, this Cheyenne firm possesses a team of seven lawyers who have developed an expertise in the areas of torts, medical malpractice, insurance defense and administrative practice. According to commentators its litigation team is particularly recognized in the field of insurance issues. It has been representing clients from across Wyoming, in both state and federal courts.
The Lawyers: *"An outstanding litigator,"* **George Powers** has been practicing for 23 years and has developed his practice around appellate law, general civil litigation, insurance law and railroad law. **John Sundahl** is a popular choice for peer referrals and concentrates his workload on general civil litigation, taxation law, insurance law, medical malpractice and products liability.
The Clients: Insurance companies and healthcare providers feature prominently in the firm's broad clientele.

Other Notable Practitioners
"One of the brightest lawyers in the state," **Weston Reeves** of Casper-based Reeves & Miller handles both defense and plaintiff cases in areas such as complex commercial litigation, personal injury and medical malpractice. He has handled a sizable number of commercial lawsuits during his long career and has always been very well regarded in insurance-related matters. His clients include Baker Hughes, Koch Industries and Black Hills Bentonite. **Jeffrey Brinkerhoff** of Brown, Drew & Massey LLP in Casper, is the *"leading medical malpractice defense attorney in Wyoming,"* say some commentators. This *"outstanding lawyer"* has been spending most of his time of late in representing medical malpractice insurance carriers in the defense of major personal injury claims including wrongful death cases. Founder of the general practice Mark W.

Gifford based in Casper, **Mark Gifford** *"is a very bright lawyer who is the most effective mediator in the state."* Besides mediation, his practice focuses on complex commercial litigation, personal injury, employment, oil and gas litigation, medical malpractice, product and torts claims, banking and insurance law. He played a prominent role in the Capshaw v WERCS case, and according to commentators *"he is one of the most gifted lawyers in the state."*

REAL ESTATE

Wyoming
Leading firms (Real Estate)

[1] **DRAY, THOMSON & DYEKMAN PC** *Cheyenne*
   MULLIKIN, LARSON & SWIFT *Jackson*

[2] **HOLLAND & HART LLP** *Jackson*
   WILLIAMS, PORTER, DAY & NEVILLE PC *Casper*
   YONKEE & TONER LLP *Sheridan*

[3] **BROWN, DREW & MASSEY LLP** *Casper*
   DAVIS & CANNON *Sheridan*
   JORGENSON MOFFETT LLC *Jackson*
   MACPHERSON KELLY & THOMPSON *Rawlins*
   PHIBBS LAW OFFICE PC *Jackson*

Leading individuals (Real Estate)

[1] **DYEKMAN Gregory** *Dray Thomson, Cheyenne*
   LARSON David *Mullikin Larson, Jackson*
   TONER Tom *Yonkee & Toner, Sheridan*

[2] **BARBE J Kenneth** *Brown Drew, Casper*
   DAVIS Richard *Davis & Cannon, Sheridan*
   DRAY W Perry *Dray Thomson, Cheyenne*
   GALLINGER John *Holland & Hart, Jackson*
   HAWKS Christopher *Christopher Hawks, Wyoming*
   JORGENSON Larry *Jorgenson Moffett, Jackson*
   MACPHERSON John *MacPherson Kelly, Rawlins*
   PHIBBS Henry *Phibbs Law Office, Jackson*
   RICHARD Andrea *Andrea Richard, Jackson*
   SWIFT Phelps *Mullikin Larson, Jackson*

Firms and individuals are listed alphabetically in each band.

Band 1

Dray, Thomson & Dyekman PC

See firm details p.1841

The Firm: Established 30 years ago, this Cheyenne firm has three attorneys handling real estate-related issues ranging from transactional work to estate planning. The practice deals with other issues encompassing tax, commercial law, insurance, administrative law and corporation law on behalf of a variety of clients from the banking and insurance sector as well as the oil and gas and energy industries.

The Lawyers: *"A formidable adversary,"* **Gregory Dyekman** (see p.1838) represents clients in matters including commercial and banking law, estate and business planning, and litigation. Besides working on numerous commercial property transactions, he recently took care of a major ranch sale in Wyoming. Other lawyers feel comfortable referring work to this *"first-tier man"* because he is a *"very competent lawyer."* **Perry Dray** (see p.1838) *"is a well-connected lawyer"* who deals with an extensive range of matters including health care law, business and estate planning corporate law, general civil litigation and real estate law. He deals primarily with transactional work for corporate clients that also use his help on tax and corporate governance issues.

The Clients: The firm has advised insurance companies, financial institutions, healthcare companies and other small and large local and national corporations.

Mullikin, Larson & Swift

The Firm: Based in Jackson, this five-attorney firm is a general and trial practice that represents clients in both federal and state courts. Its real estate practice is very well known for its transactional work especially in the areas of land use and development. In addition to that expertise, the team deals with other issues covering insurance, products liability, banking, corporate, probate law, wills, trust and estate planning.

The Lawyers: **David Larson** *"has been practicing for 32 years and has always done an amazing job."* He is famous for being the best in land use and zoning law, particularly in Jackson. He also deals with banking, corporate and commercial law, wills, trust, estate planning, probate and municipal law. This very knowledgeable, experienced and smooth lawyer *"is able to do the heavy lifting"* when it comes to real estate matters. **Phelps Swift**'s real estate practice specializes in land use and development issues. According to commentators he is *"a very capable guy."*

The Clients: Jackson State Bank & Trust, Teton County School District and Teton Pines Resort.

Band 2

Holland & Hart LLP

See firm details p.325

The Firm: With a two-attorney real estate practice, the Jackson office of this national firm benefits from a 290-attorney backup. The *"very competent lawyers"* cover a broad range of services in branches of law including labor and employment law, natural resources and environmental law, commercial and construction litigation. Regarding real estate matters, the team handles the transactional work as well as the litigious side of land-related matters.

The Lawyers: *"Extremely detail-oriented and thorough,"* **John Gallinger** (see p.1838) is a *"sophisticated transactional lawyer"* who deals with matters including litigation, environmental compliance, mining, oil and gas and financial issues. His real estate practice focuses on both residential and commercial properties on behalf of sellers and buyers and on planning and zoning issues and land exchanges.

The Clients: The team represents such clients as real estate owners, property companies and realtors.

Williams, Porter, Day & Neville PC

The Firm: This *"highly ethical firm"* has suffered the loss of one of the most terrific real estate lawyers Wyoming has known. Nonetheless, the late Barry Williams has left an efficient team of attorneys behind him. The team is engaged in general commercial litigation in all state and federal courts throughout the state of Wyoming.

The Lawyers: The three main contacts regarding real estate issues are Nicol Thompson, Kevin Huber and Margo Harlan Sabec.

The Clients: AIG; Attorneys Liability Protection Society; Baker Hughes; Converse County School District; Devon Energy; First American Title Insurance; First Interstate Bank and ChevronTexaco.

Yonkee & Toner LLP

The Firm: Established more than 40 years ago, this six-attorney general civil and trial firm deals with various matters including water rights, corporation, oil, gas, minerals, insurance, probate and trust administration, trust and estate planning, insurance defense, environmental law and litigation, education law, local government law, personal injury, medical malpractice defense, employment law, civil rights and land use.

The Lawyers: **Tom Toner** *"belongs in the first tier."* His practice focuses on real estate, litigation, oil and gas, natural resources, water rights, commercial and estate planning. This *"great lawyer"* is famous for both his effective litigation skills and his real estate experience.

The Clients: Ohio Hospital Insurance; Lexington Insurance; Utica Mutual Insurance; Sheridan County School Districts 1, 2 and 3; Memorial Hospital of Sheridan County; North Big Horn Hospital and West Park Hospital.

Band 3

Brown, Drew & Massey LLP

See firm details p.1840

The Firm: Representing clients throughout the state, the two offices in Casper and Sheridan devote their practice to matters including banking law, bankruptcy law, business law, civil trial practice, commercial law, commercial litigation, construction law, creditors' rights and environmental law. This *"excellent firm"* has developed a good client base since it was established almost 70 years ago.

The Lawyers: **Kenneth Barbe** spends most of his time between corporate, real estate and commercial matters and on litigation arising out of those areas of law. His experience is not limited to those areas; he also deals with torts claims, either as lead counsel or assisting other attorneys in the firm, and advises insurance carriers concerning coverage issues. Highlights include representing a big client on the transformation of the biggest building owned by the city into offices.

The Clients: Wells Fargo; JPMorgan Chase; United Pacific Insurance; Crum & Forster Managers; AlliedSignal; Utah Medical Insurance Association; Marathon Oil; Benedek Broadcasting and Citation Oil & Gas.

Davis & Cannon

The Firm: The firm has always advised its clients on real estate matters since its establishment in 1948. With two offices, in Sheridan and Cheyenne, the real estate team can provide a comprehensive service throughout the state on matters such as oil, gas, coal or other mineral leasing, water, grazing, access issues, title problems, mortgages and liens.

The Lawyers: *"A very eloquent and articulate litigator,"* **Richard Davis** is a *"very competent"* real estate lawyer. He deals with other matters such as probate, estate planning, trusts, business organizations, business planning and real property transactions.

The Clients: Life Care Centers of America; Memorial Hospital of Sheridan County; Peter Kiewit Sons'; Padlock Ranch and Hawkins & Powers Aviation.

Jorgenson Moffett LLC

The Firm: This two-attorney firm handles a broad range of legal matters in which we can find real estate law, litigation, business law, land use, estate and trust law, environmental law, construction law, business litigation, taxation, bankruptcy and reorganization, corporate, insurance coverage, insurance bad faith and automobile accidents. This Jackson practice deals with various clients including individual buyers, financial institutions and conservation organizations.

The Lawyers: **Larry Jorgenson** is a *"very capable guy with a broad experience of real estate law, and is hard-working."* His *"great sense of the law"* enables him to handle legal issues like business law, land use law, environmental law, construction law and business litigation with ease, but he is also a *"confident lawyer"* when it comes to real estate issues.

The Clients: The firm represents various local and national businesses. First Interstate Bank is one of them.

MacPherson Kelly & Thompson

The Firm: Boasting a team of five partners and one associate, this Rawlins firm is a general civil trial practice that deals with issues encompassing banking, employment, insurance, real estate, ranching and agriculture, estate planning and probate, elder law and natural resource law. The firm has been busy with real estate matters during the past twelve months, closing between 75 and 100 million dollars' worth of real estate deals.

The Lawyers: The only man in charge of real estate matters, **John MacPherson** handles ranching, agricultural law, probate, water law and natural resource law. He is considered to be one of the most trustworthy real estate lawyers in Rawlins, and *"has and is doing some great work over there."*

The Clients: Silver Spur Land & Cattle, Carbon County and the State of Wyoming are clients.

Phibbs Law Office PC

The Firm: This Jackson firm has developed a good reputation in real estate and related issues including all phases of residential ranch transactions. The team has been working on some major real estate transactions throughout the Jackson area over the past year.

The Lawyers: **Hank Phibbs** has been handling real estate matters in Jackson for a very long time, which makes him one of the most knowledgeable lawyers in his field. He is *"careful, cautious, well informed with regards to statutes and well connected."* Clients like to work with him for various reasons including the fact that he is a *"competent, thorough and very smooth lawyer."*

The Clients: Hansen-Mueller is one of the many clients that include landowners, developers and purchasers.

Other Notable Practitioners

Christopher Hawks of Christopher Hawks, P.C. is the founder of a three-attorney firm that deals mainly with real estate issues together with the business side of every transaction. Someone who *"works hard and gets the results,"* Hawks has been involved in a series of multimillion deals including the Three Creek Ranch, an 18-hole golf course coupled with a 145-lot residential property and the Four Seasons resort in Jackson Hole. **Andrea Leah Richard** has recently started her practice in Jackson, Andrea Richard PC. This *"very powerful lawyer"* works on significant construction and real estate litigation matters. This *"top-notch real estate lawyer"* has the *"best oral and writing skills"* and is *"very articulate, great on her feet and good at getting to the bottom of things."* Her clients can be sure she will always *"give 99%"* to do an excellent job for a reasonable billing

Leaders in Wyoming

BARBE, J Kenneth
Brown, Drew & Massey LLP, Casper
307 234 1000
Recommended in Corporate/M&A, Real Estate

BELCHER, James
Holland & Hart LLP, Cheyenne
307 778 4200
jbelcher@hollandhart.com
Recommended in Corporate/M&A
Practice Areas: Partner practicing in all areas of financial and corporate business matters. Works with corporations, limited partnerships and limited liability companies in formation, merger, continuance into Wyoming, and transfer from Wyoming to another jurisdiction. Has also assisted clients with securities matters. Assists clients with energy development and transmission, including wind energy projects, natural gas gathering and pipelines, and electrical transmission, including project development and finance, right-of-way acquisition and condemnation and related advice. In his financial and corporate practice, has assisted both borrowers and lenders with UCC, real estate, mortgage, and loan documentation, and has extensive experience in issuing opinions for business and secured transactions.
Prof. Memberships: Wyoming Bar Association, Business Law Section (past Chairman), Wyoming Bar Foundation (Director and past President).
Career: Admitted to the Wyoming (1988) and Colorado (1989) Bar. Commercial Finance (1972-85); Attorney (1988-present).
Publications: Editor, 'The Wyoming Law of Mortgages' (2d ed 1993).
Personal: Received a JD (with honors) from the University of Wyoming (1988) and a BS from the University of Colorado (1972).

BRINKERHOFF, Jeffrey
Brown, Drew & Massey LLP, Casper
307 234 1000
Recommended in Litigation

BUFFINGTON, Teresa
Holland & Hart LLP, Cheyenne
307 778 4237
tbuffington@hollandhart.com
Recommended in Corporate/M&A
Practice Areas: A Partner practicing in all areas of commercial transactions throughout the state of Wyoming, including real estate, business, finance, and construction. Her practice includes acquisitions and sales, contract preparation and negotiation, energy project transactions, rights of way for gathering and pipelines, commercial financing, entity planning, formation and continuation, design, engineering and construction, transactional due diligence, and legal opinions. She has assisted clients in a variety of industries, projects, and businesses.

Prof. Memberships: Member of the Laramie County Bar Association; Wyoming Bar Association; Colorado Bar Association; and the American Bar Association.
Career: Admitted to the Colorado (1985) and Wyoming Bar (1991). Administrative Partner of Holland & Hart's Cheyenne Office since January 2003. Formerly Manager of the firm's Business Entities and Transactions Practice Group.
Personal: Received a JD from the University of Colorado (1985) and a BA (with highest honors) from Ohio University (1977).

CANNON, Kim
Davis & Cannon, Cheyenne
307 643 3210
Recommended in Litigation

CAVE, Bradley
Holland & Hart LLP, Cheyenne
307 778 4210
bcave@hollandhart.com
Recommended in Employment
Practice Areas: A Partner practicing employment law and litigation, he represents employers in matters involving discrimination, harassment, wage and hour disputes, defamation, wrongful discharge, breach of contract and employment-related torts. Also advises employers on issues related to employee handbooks and personnel policies, compliance with federal and state statutes and regulations and employee investigations, discipline and termination. Regularly conducts training sessions for employers, managers and supervisors in areas such as investigations, discipline and termination, harassment, discrimination, disability accommodation and supervisory responsibilities.
Prof. Memberships: Member of the American Bar Association; Wyoming Bar Association; Colorado Bar Association; Defense Lawyers Association of Wyoming; Defense Research Institute; and the Society of Human Resource Management.
Career: Admitted to the Colorado (1988) and Wyoming (1991) Bar. Editor of the Wyoming Employment Law Letter.
Personal: Received a JD (with honors) from George Washington University (1988) and a BS from the University of Wyoming (1985).

COTTAM, Dale
Hirst & Applegate, PC, Cheyenne
307 632 0541
Recommended in Corporate/M&A

DAVIS, Michael
Yonkee & Toner LLP, Sheridan
307 674 7451
Recommended in Employment

DAVIS Jr, Richard
Davis & Cannon, Sheridan
307 672 7491
Recommended in Real Estate

DAY, Richard
Williams, Porter, Day & Neville PC, Casper 307 265 0700
Recommended in Litigation

DRAY, W Perry
Dray, Thomson & Dyekman PC, Cheyenne 307 634 8891
Perry.Dray@draylaw.com
Recommended in Corporate/M&A, Real Estate
Practice Areas: Estate planning, health and hospital law, commercial litigation, business and corporate law.
Prof. Memberships: Laramie County, Wyoming State and American (Member, Section on Taxation) Bar Associations; Wyoming Trial Lawyers Association; Defense Lawyers Association of Wyoming, Inc.; Southeast Wyoming Estate Planning Council; American Health Lawyers Association.
Career: Dray, Thomson & Dyekman, P.C.'s founding Partner in 1975.
Personal: University of Wyoming (BSL, 1962; JD, 1964); George Washington University (LLM, Taxation, 1968); admitted to Bar 1965, Wyoming, 1968 US Supreme Court, US Court of Appeals, Tenth Circuit and US Tax Court; Judge Advocate, General Corp., US Army, 1965-68.

DYEKMAN, Gregory C
Dray, Thomson & Dyekman PC, Cheyenne 307 634 8891
Greg.Dyekman@draylaw.com
Recommended in Corporate/M&A, Real Estate
Practice Areas: Business and corporate law, real estate, banking, creditor's bankruptcy.
Prof. Memberships: Laramie County and American Bar Associations; Wyoming State Bar; Wyoming Trial Lawyers Association; Southeast Wyoming Estate Planning Council; Law School Liaison Committee.
Personal: University of Wyoming (BS, with honors in Accounting, 1977; JD, 1980); adjunct professor University of Wyoming College of Law; Member, 1978-80 and editor in chief, 1979-80, 'Land and Water Law Review;' editor in chief, Wyoming Trial Lawyers Association Newsletter, 1982 to present; admitted to Bar 1980, Wyoming, US District Court and US Court of Appeals, Tenth Circuit and US Tax Court; 1988, US Supreme Court.

FOX, Kate
Davis & Cannon, Cheyenne
307 643 3210
Recommended in Employment, Litigation

GALLINGER, John
Holland & Hart LLP, Jackson
307 734 4505
jgallinger@hollandhart.com
Recommended in Real Estate
Practice Areas: Substantial experience in real estate and natural resources law. Real estate practice involves both residential and commercial developments including planning and zoning issues, land exchanges, 1031 exchanges, and representation of both sellers and buyers.
Career: Admitted to the Montana (1971), Wyoming (1975), and District of Columbia Bar (1975). Prior to joining Holland & Hart, Mr Gallinger worked with the Office of Legal Counsel, US Department of Justice, and served as a special assistant to the general counsel for the Federal Trade Commission.
Publications: Mr Gallinger has published several articles about natural resources law and has given several presentations on various aspects of real estate transactions.
Personal: Received a JD (1971, with Honors) and a BA (1968) from the University of Wyoming.

GIFFORD, Mark
Mark W. Gifford, Casper
307 265 3265
Recommended in Litigation

HAWKS, Christopher.
Christopher Hawks, P.C., Wyoming
307 733 9437
Recommended in Real Estate

HICKEY, Paul
Hickey&Mackey, Cheyenne
307 634 1525
Recommended in Litigation

JORGENSON, Larry
Jorgenson Moffett LLC, Jackson
307 733 6021
Recommended in Real Estate

LARSON, David
Mullikin, Larson & Swift, Jackson
307 733 3923
Recommended in Real Estate

LONG, Thomas
Thomas N Long PC, Cheyenne
307 635 0710
Recommended in Corporate/M&A

MACKEY, Terry
Hickey&Mackey, Cheyenne
307 634 1525
Recommended in Litigation

MACPHERSON, John
MacPherson Kelly & Thompson, Rawlins 307 324 2713
Recommended in Real Estate

MASON, Gerald
Mason & Mason PC, Pinedale
307 367 2134
Recommended in Litigation

MCCALL, Donn
Brown, Drew & Massey LLP, Casper
307 234 1000
Recommended in Corporate/M&A

METZKE, John
Hirst & Applegate, PC, Cheyenne
307 632 0541
Recommended in Corporate/M&A

MURPHY, Patrick
Williams, Porter, Day & Neville PC,
Casper 307 265 0700
Recommended in Litigation

NEVILLE, Frank
Williams, Porter, Day & Neville PC,
Casper 307 265 0700
Recommended in Litigation

NICHOLAS, Thomas
Hirst & Applegate, PC, Cheyenne
307 632 0541
Recommended in Litigation

ORTIZ, Scott
Williams, Porter, Day & Neville PC,
Casper 307 265 0700
Recommended in Employment

PHIBBS, Henry
Phibbs Law Office PC, Jackson
307 733 5004
Recommended in Real Estate

POWERS Jr, George
Sundahl, Powers, Kapp & Martin LLC,
Cheyenne 307 632 6421
Recommended in Litigation

REED, Randall B
Dray, Thomson & Dyekman PC,
Cheyenne 307 634 8891
randy.reed@draylaw.com
Recommended in Corporate/M&A
Practice Areas: Real property, oil and
gas, hospital and healthcare, business
and mineral tax law. Has represented oil
and gas producers in mineral tax issues
before the State Board of Equalization
and has extensive experience represent-
ing regulated industries before the
Wyoming Public Service Commission.
Prof. Memberships: ABA, Wyoming
Bar Association, ABA Young Lawyers
Division District Representative for
Wyoming and Colorado, President of
Wyoming State Bar Young Lawyers
Division, Leadership Cheyenne Steering
Committee Chairman.
Career: Associate, 1991-95; Partner, 1996-
2002; Managing Partner 2002-present.
Personal: University of Wyoming; BS
1988; JD 1991.

REEVES, Weston
Reeves & Miller, Casper
307 265 3843
Recommended in Litigation

RICHARD, Andrea Leah
Andrea Richard PC, Jackson
307 732 6680
Recommended in Real Estate

RUTLEDGE, Kent
Lathrop & Rutledge, Cheyenne
307 632 0554
Recommended in Litigation

SCHULTZ, Donald I
Holland & Hart LLP, Cheyenne
307 778 4217
dschultz@hollandhart.com
Recommended in Litigation
Practice Areas: A Partner practicing in
commercial litigation, primarily in the
oil and gas and construction industries.
Serves as court-appointed Liaison
Counsel to coordinate among hundreds
of defendants in nearly 100 MDL-con-
solidated gas measurement and gas valuation lawsuits. Has jury trial and appellate experience in gas measurement disputes, gas contract pricing and take-or-
pay disputes, JOA disputes, and gas balancing claims. Represents owners in litigation of construction disputes involving pipelines, gas plants, refineries, coal
mines, trona mines, and resort properties. Substantial experience in defense of
class actions, False Claims Act actions,
and in gas royalty and accounting cases.
Leads firm's Oil and Gas Service Group
to enhance service to industry across
Rocky Mountain regional network of
offices.
Prof. Memberships: Member of the
American Bar Association, Forum of the
Construction Industry; Wyoming Bar
Association; and the Defense Lawyers
Association of Wyoming.
Career: Admitted to the Colorado
(1982) and Wyoming (1985) Bar.
Personal: Received a JD from Harvard
University (1982) and a BA from the
University of Wyoming (1979).

SCOTT, Gary
Hirst & Applegate, PC, Cheyenne
307 632 0541
Recommended in Employment

SHUMATE, Roger
Murane & Bostwick LLC, Casper
307 234 9345
Recommended in Employment

STUDER, Judith
Schwartz, Bon, Walker & Studer LLC,
Casper 307 235 6681
*Recommended in Employment,
Litigation*

SUNDAHL, John
Sundahl, Powers, Kapp & Martin LLC,
Cheyenne 307 632 6421
Recommended in Litigation

SWIFT, Phelps
Mullikin, Larson & Swift, Jackson
307 733 3923
Recommended in Real Estate

TONER, Tom
Yonkee & Toner LLP, Sheridan
307 674 7451
*Recommended in Litigation, Real
Estate*

BROWN, DREW & MASSEY, LLP

THE FIRM

Managing Partner: J Kenneth Barbe

Number of partners: 11
Number of other lawyers: 4

FIRM OVERVIEW: Tracing its roots back to 1936, Brown, Drew & Massey, LLP (Brown & Drew) is one of Wyoming's oldest and largest law firms. The firm's principal office is in Casper, Wyoming, and it has a branch office in Sheridan, Wyoming. Brown & Drew is Wyoming's only representative in Lex Mundi, a world-wide alliance of leading law firms, and is the reviser of the Martindale-Hubbell Wyoming Law Digest. The firm has the distinction of being listed in the Martindale-Hubbell Bar Register of Preeminent Attorneys in all of its primary practice areas. Former members of the firm have received judicial appointments to both the federal and state district courts in Wyoming, and one member was elected and served two terms as Governor of the state.

MAIN AREAS OF PRACTICE: Brown & Drew operates statewide, offering a full range of legal services that are concentrated in the areas of oil and gas, mining, energy, and natural resources; banking and finance; bankruptcy and creditor's rights; business transactions; corporations and business organizations; intellectual property; real estate; construction; healthcare; medical malpractice, products liability, tort claims, and insurance defense; employment and labor; environment; regulatory and administrative; probate and estate planning; and alternative dispute resolution. The firm specializes in civil litigation and appellate practice incidental to its main practice areas.

CLIENTS: Brown & Drew is a full legal resource for its diverse national and Wyoming-based clientele, which includes oil and gas companies, state and national banking and financial institutions, commercial, consumer, and mortgage lenders, private corporations and other business organizations, physicians and other healthcare providers, casualty and liability insurers, small businesses, construction firms, utility companies, railroads, ranchers, and professionals. The firm frequently acts as Wyoming counsel for money center banking and financial institutions and other commercial and mortgage lenders in major mult-state financing transactions. Brown & Drew is employed to represent its clients in substantial litigation matters as well as by corporate counsel or other law firms to represent corporate entities and individuals in substantial, non-recurring litigation. The firm's corporate clients include Wells Fargo Bank, JP Morgan Chase Bank, Bank of the West, ChevronTexaco Company, ConocoPhillips Company, Cabot Oil & Gas Corp., Marathon Oil Company, Bituminous Insurance Co., The Doctor's Company, ITT Hartford Insurance Company, Protective Life Insurance Co., The CIT Group, Chase Manhattan Mortgage Corp., and Wells Fargo Home Mortgage Corp., among others.

INTERNATIONAL WORK: Brown & Drew advises a number of international clients in the formation of a variety of business organizations under Wyoming's favorable business laws. The firm also has represented a number of foreign clients in litigation within the United States.

HEAD OFFICE

WYOMING
Suit 200, 159 North Wolcott Street, **Casper**, WY 82601
Tel: 307 234 1000   **Fax:** 307 265 8025
Email: bdm@browndrew.com
Website: www.browndrew.com

BRANCH OFFICES

Suite 109, 45 East Loucks Street, **Sheridan,** WY 82801
Tel: 307 673 8565   **Fax:** 307 673 6612

CONTACTS

Alternative Dispute Resolution	Rex O Arney
Appellate	Drake D Hill
Banking & Finance	Donn J McCall
Bankruptcy & Creditor's Rights	Donn J McCall
Business Transactions	Donn J McCall
Commercial Litigation	Donn J McCall
Construction	Thomas F Reese
Energy	Thomas F Reese
Environmental	Drake D Hill
Healthcare	Jeffrey C Brinkerhoff
Intellectual Property	J Kenneth Barbe
Insurance Defense	Jeffrey C Brinkerhoff
Labor & Employment	J Kenneth Barbe
Medical Malpractice & Products Liability	Jeffrey C Brinkerhoff
Mining	Harry B Durham III
Oil & Gas	Thomas F Reese
Probate & Estate Planning	J Kenneth Barbe
Regulatory & Administrative	Drake D Hill
Real Estate	J Kenneth Barbe
Torts & Insurance	Jeffrey C Brinkerhoff

BROWN, DREW & MASSEY, LLP
ATTORNEYS AT LAW

DRAY, THOMSON & DYEKMAN P.C.

THE FIRM

Senior Partners: W Perry Dray, William J Thomson, II,
Gregory C Dyekman, Randall B Reed
Junior Partner: Nicholas G J Healey

Number of partners: 5

HEAD OFFICE

WYOMING
204 East 22nd Street, **Cheyenne**, WY 82001-3799
Tel: 307 634 8891 **Fax:** 307 634 8902
Email: greg.dyekman@draylaw.com

FIRM OVERVIEW: Dray, Thomson & Dyekman, P.C. has long been recognized for its breadth and depth of experience and capabilities, which allow it to serve a very broad clientele, both locally and nationally. The firm's commitment to client service and timely quality legal work have made it one of Wyoming's most successful business law firms with highly rated attorneys in a number of practice areas. It's reputation is further enhanced by its commitment to the betterment of Wyoming through public service.

MAIN AREAS OF PRACTICE:

Corporate: The firm works with corporations and other business entities of all kinds and sizes, including non-profit organizations, in some cases as general counsel and in others as transactional counsel. The firm advises clients on governance issues as well as compliance and transactional matters. Wyoming features a form of the Revised Model Business Corporation Act which is very management friendly and easy to use for large and small companies alike. The firm's general counsel duties include a very broad array of legal subject areas. Business litigation is also conducted in all courts and administrative bodies in Wyoming. The firm has experience with Transfers and Continuances of Canadian entities to and from Wyoming.

Real Estate: The firm maintains a broad real estate practice, including representation of lenders, developers, municipalities, realtors, buyers and sellers of both urban and rural properties. Recent transactions have involved ranches, commercial property, undeveloped land, condominium projects, annexation litigation and appeals, mineral rights and interests, water rights and residential real estate.

Health: The firm advises hospitals, physicians and other healthcare providers concerning a tremendously broad range of issues facing the healthcare industry, including state and federal compliance issues, reimbursement issues, hospital-physician relationships, privileging, licensing and litigation matters. Clients include hospitals in Cheyenne and throughout Wyoming.

Governmental Relations: The firm boasts one of the most active governmental relations and lobbying practices in Wyoming, representing corporations, individuals, non-profit organizations, and trade associations before the Wyoming Legislature, administrative agencies and federal agencies.

Banking & Lending: The firm advises banks and other financial institutions in Wyoming and elsewhere on all aspects of lending and retail transactions and assists lenders with Wyoming law compliance and operational matters relating to consumer and commercial lending, retail operations, employee dishonesty, trust department matters including litigation, regulatory matters and general business matters. The firm also represents creditors of all sorts in connection with business and consumer bankruptcy case, loan collections and foreclosures.

State Tax: The firm has an active trial and appellate practice in state taxation matters, including mineral taxation, sales and use taxation, and property tax issues. The firm also has represented businesses in connection with state tax audits and negotiations and settlements with taxing authorities.

Civil Litigation & Appeals: The firm serves as lead or local counsel in state and federal courts throughout Wyoming for a broad range of commercial litigation and defense of personal injury and property injury matters. Representations are undertaken at the request of insurance companies as well as self-insured entities and individuals. The firm also features an active appellate practice, including appeals of cases tried by members of the firm, those tried by other attorneys and consultations with other counsel with respect to appellate matters.

Estate & Business Planning: The firm assists individuals with business continuation, sophisticated estate planning, charitable gift planning and pre-death disability planning, frequently working as part of a team with other estate planning professionals and client advisors. The firm also has an active probate and trust administration practice throughout Wyoming, which also includes representation of non-residents in connection with the administration of estates in Wyoming.

General Business Practice: The firm has long represented businesses of various kinds, both locally and nationally, with respect to a wide array of strategic and operational issues including choice of entity, contracts, employment matters, licensing, worker's compensation and compliance with regulatory requirements. Collaborative representations are often utilized with other professionals, both local and distant.

CLIENTS: Dray, Thomson & Dyekman. P.C. represents business entities of all types, including local, national and international companies. Among the many types of clients are manufacturers, financial institutions, trade associations, real estate developers, health care providers, transportation companies, natural resources companies, mail orders/internet retailers, non-profit organizations, private trust companies, mortgage bankers, mortgage brokers, governmental entities, contractors and individuals.

INTERNATIONAL WORK: The firm has represented international business entities, primarily in connection with mineral industry, energy transportation, governmental relations and corporate issues. The special provisions of the Wyoming Business Corporation Act have led to representation of Canadian companies, in particular, who seek to transfer their jurisdiction of incorporation to Wyoming or to continue their jurisdiction back to Canada.

Dray, Thomson & Dyekman P.C.

FIRM INDEX

A

Abrahams Kaslow & Cassman LLP
Table: Corporate/M&A p.1082

Adams & Jones Chartered
Table: Real Estate p.821

Adams and Reese LLP
Profile: p.879
Tables: Corporate/M&A p.858,
Employment: p.861

Adduci, Mastriani & Schaumberg LLP
Table: International Trade p.39

Adelman & Gettleman Ltd
Profile: p.760
Table: Bankruptcy p.668

Adelman Lavine Gold & Levin
Table: Bankruptcy/Restructuring p.1494

Adler Pollock & Sheehan PC
Profile: p.1571
Tables: Corporate/M&A p.1564,
Employment: p.1565, Litigation: General
Commercial p.1566, Real Estate p.1568

Ahlers & Cooney PC
Tables: Corporate/M&A p.802,
Employment: p.804, Litigation: General
Commercial p.806

Akerman Senterfitt
Profile: p.555
Tables: Antitrust p.498, Banking &
Finance p.500, Bankruptcy p.502,
Construction p.506, Corporate/M&A
p.509, Employment: p.511, Healthcare
p.517, Insurance p.519, Litigation:
General Commercial p.520, Real Estate
p.526, Real Estate: Zoning/Land Use
p.528, Shipping p.71, Tax p.530

Akin Gump Strauss Hauer & Feld LLP
Profile: p.477
Tables: Bankruptcy p.372,
Bankruptcy/Restructuring p.1177,
Corporate/M&A p.1631, Corporate/M&A:
Mid-Tier Firms p.1195, Employment:
p.380, Energy & Natural Resources
p.1637, Environment p.1642, Insurance
p.1647, Intellectual Property p.1508,
International Trade p.39, Litigation:
General Commercial p.1511, Media &
Entertainment: Transactional p.233,
Private Equity: Fund Formation p.1240,
Projects p.1659, Real Estate p.417, Tax
p.1665

Allen & Overy LLP
Profile: p.1335
Table: Capital Markets: Derivatives p.16

Allen Guthrie McHugh & Thomas, PLLC
Table: Litigation p.1803

Allen Law Firm
Table: Litigation p.172

Allen Matkins Leck Gamble & Mallory LLP
Profile: p.279
Table: Real Estate p.237

Allison, MacKenzie, Russell, Pavlakis, Wright & Fagan, Ltd
Tables: Environment p.1093, Real Estate
p.1098

Alschuler Grossman Stein & Kahan LLP
Profile: p.280
Tables: Bankruptcy p.190, Insurance
p.212, Litigation: General Commercial
p.223, Media & Entertainment: Litigation
p.229

Alston Hunt Floyd & Ing Attorneys At Law, A Law Corporation
Profile: p.651
Tables: Employment: p.642, Litigation:
General Commercial p.644

Alston & Bird LLP
Profile: p.626
Tables: Antitrust p.578, Banking &
Finance p.580, Banking & Finance:
Mainly Regulatory p.581, Bankruptcy
p.582, Business Process Outsourcing:
National p.9, Construction p.584,
Corporate/M&A p.587, Employment:
p.589, Energy & Natural Resources
p.591, Environment p.592, Healthcare
p.594, Intellectual Property p.595,
Litigation: ERISA p.25, Litigation:
General Commercial p.598, Real Estate
p.601, Tax p.603

Alston Courtnage & Bassetti LLP
Table: Real Estate p.1788

Amburgey & Rubin PC
Table: Employment: p.1473

Anderson & Bottrell
Tables: Corporate/M&A p.1403,
Employment: p.1405

Anderson & Kreiger LLP
Table: Environment p.943

Anderson Kill & Olick P.C.
Profile: p.1336
Table:
Insurance: Dispute Resolution p.1212

Andrews Kurth LLP
Profile: p.1707
Tables: Antitrust p.1622, Banking &
Finance p.1624, Bankruptcy p.1626,
Corporate/M&A p.1631, Energy &
Natural Resources p.1637, Energy: Oil &
Gas p.382, Projects p.1659, Real Estate
p.1661, Technology p.1667

Anthony Ostlund & Baer
Table: Litigation p.1010

Aqualaw PLC
Table: Environment p.1757

Arent Fox PLLC
Tables: Bankruptcy p.372, Construction
p.373, Healthcare p.397, Real Estate
p.417

Armstrong Teasdale LLP
Tables: Corporate/M&A p.1042,
Employment: p.1045, Litigation: General
Commercial p.1048, Real Estate p.1052

Armstrong Allen PLLC
Tables: Litigation: General Commercial
p.1598, Real Estate p.1603

Arnall Golden Gregory LLP
Profile: p.627
Table: Corporate/M&A p.587

Arnold & Porter LLP
Profile: p.478
Tables: Antitrust p.366, Bankruptcy
p.372, Business Process Outsourcing:
National p.9, Construction p.373,
Corporate/Commercial p.376,
Environment p.391, Healthcare:
Pharmaceutical/Medical Products
Regulatory p.397, Intellectual Property
p.215, Intellectual Property: Northern
Virginia p.1758, IT & IT Outsourcing
p.221, Litigation: General Commercial
p.223, Products Liability p.48, Real
Estate p.417, Telecom, Broadcast &
Satellite: Regulatory p.426, Transport:
Rail p.62

Bailey Cavalieri
Table: Bankruptcy p.1413

Tucker Ellis & West LLP
Table: Litigation p.1430

Ashburn & Mason, PC
Tables: Environment, Natural Resources
and Regulated Industries p.136,
Litigation: General Commercial p.138,
Real Estate p.140

Ashby & Geddes
Profile: p.359
Tables: Bankruptcy/Restructuring p.341,
Chancery p.344, Intellectual Property
p.348

Ashe, Rafuse & Hill, LLP
Profile: p.628
Table: Employment: p.589

Ashford & Wriston
Table: Real Estate p.646

Astigarraga Davis
Profile: p.556
Table: Arbitration (International) p.32

Ater Wynne LLP
Tables: Corporate/M&A p.1471,
Litigation: General Commercial p.1475

Atkinson, Conway & Gagnon
Tables: Litigation: General Commercial
p.138, Real Estate p.140

August, Kulunas & Dawson, PA
Table: Tax p.530

Ausley & McMullen
Table: Tax p.530

Axinn Veltrop & Harkrider LLP
Table: Antitrust p.1169

B

Baach Robinson & Lewis PLLC
Table: Insurance: Insurer Firms p.400

Babst, Calland, Clements and Zomnir, A Professional Corporation
Table: Environment p.1504

Badiak Will & Ruddy
Table: Shipping p.66

Bailey & Glasser LLP
Profile: p.1811
Table: Litigation p.1803

Bainbridge, Mims, Rogers & Smith, LLP
Table: Litigation p.115

Baird, Holm, McEachen, Pedersen, Hamann & Strasheim LLP
Tables: Corporate/M&A p.1082,
Employment: p.1084, Litigation: General
Commercial p.1085, Real Estate p.1086

Baker & Daniels
Profile: p.796
Tables: Corporate/M&A p.781,
Employment: p.783, Litigation: General
Commercial p.785, Real Estate p.788

Baker & Hostetler LLP
Tables: Bankruptcy p.1413,
Corporate/M&A p.1419, Employment:
p.511, Environment p.1424, Litigation:
General Commercial p.1430, Real Estate
p.1434

Baker Botts LLP
Profile: p.1708
Tables: Antitrust p.1622, Banking &
Finance p.1624, Bankruptcy p.1626,
Business Process Outsourcing: National
p.9, Corporate/M&A p.1631,
Employment: p.1633, Energy & Natural
Resources p.1637, Energy & Natural
Resources: Dispute Resolution p.1639,
Energy: Electricity p.385, Energy: Oil &
Gas p.382, Environment p.391,
Intellectual Property p.1216, Litigation:
General Commercial p.409, Projects
p.52, Real Estate p.1661, Tax p.1665,
Technology p.1667

Baker & McKenzie
Profile: p.761
Tables: Arbitration (International) p.32,
Banking & Finance p.665, Business
Process Outsourcing: National p.9,
Corporate/M&A & Private Equity p.674,
Healthcare p.1645, Litigation: General
Commercial p.699, Projects p.1659, Tax
p.241, Technology & IT Outsourcing
p.712

Balch & Bingham
Profile: p.127
Tables: Corporate/M&A p.111,
Employment: p.113, Litigation: General
Commercial p.115, Real Estate p.119

Ballard Spahr Andrews & Ingersoll LLP
Profile: p.1541
Tables: Banking & Finance p.1492,
Corporate/M&A p.1497, Employment:
p.1126, Environment p.1129, Intellectual
Property p.1508, Litigation: General
Commercial p.310, Real Estate p.313

Ball Janik LLP
Table: Real Estate p.1478

Bangs, McCullen, Butler, Foye & Simmons, LLP
Tables: Litigation: General Commercial
p.1590, Real Estate p.1591

Bankston, Gronning, O'Hara, PC
Table: Litigation p.138

Banner & Witcoff Ltd
Tables: Intellectual Property p.403

Barack Ferrazzano Kirschbaum Perlman & Nagelberg
Table: Real Estate p.705

Barger & Wolen
Table: Insurance p.212

Barnes & Thornburg
Tables: Corporate/M&A p.781, Employment: p.783, Litigation: General Commercial p.785, Real Estate p.788

Barnett, Bolt, Kirkwood, Long & McBride
Table: Tax p.530

Barran Liebman
Profile: p.1486
Table: Employment: p.1473

Barrasso Usdin Kupperman Freeman & Sarver LLC
Profile: p.880
Table: Litigation p.865

Barris, Sott, Denn & Driker, PLLC
Tables: Litigation: General Commercial p.993, Real Estate p.996

Bartlit Beck Herman Palenchar & Scott
Tables: Corporate/M&A p.303, Litigation: General Commercial p.310

Bass, Berry & Sims PLC
Profile: p.1614
Tables: Corporate/M&A p.1594, Employment: p.1596, Litigation: General Commercial p.1598, Media & Entertainment p.1602, Real Estate p.1603

Bassford Remele, A Professional Association
Table: Litigation p.1010

Bastianelli, Brown & Kelley
Table: Construction p.373

Bateman Seidel Miner Blomgren Chellis & Gram, P.C.
Table: Real Estate p.1478

Bates & Carey
Tables: Insurance: Coverage Litigation p.694, Insurance: Reinsurance Litigation p.693

The Bayard Firm
Profile: p.360

Bays Deaver Lung Rose Baba
Tables: Litigation: General Commercial p.644, Real Estate p.646

Beasley, Allen, Crow, Methvin, Portis & Miles, PC
Table: Litigation p.115

Beck, De Corso, Daly, Kreindler & Harris
Profile: p.281
Table: Litigation: White-Collar Crime & Government Investigations p.225

Beck, Redden & Secrest L.L.P
Table: Litigation p.1655

Becker & Poliakoff PA
Table: Construction p.506

Bedell, Dittmar, DeVault, Pillans & Coxe
Tables: Litigation: General Commercial p.520, Litigation: White-Collar Crime & Government Investigations p.522

Bedrava & Lyman
Table: Construction p.672

Beirne, Maynard & Parsons, L.L.P.
Profile: p.1709

Belin Lamson McCormick Zumbach Flynn, PC
Tables: Corporate/M&A p.802, Employment: p.804, Litigation: General Commercial p.806, Real Estate p.810

Bell, Boyd & Lloyd LLC
Tables: Antitrust p.661, Construction p.373, Corporate/M&A & Private Equity p.674, Healthcare p.690, Real Estate p.705

Belles Graham Proudfoot and Wilson
Table: Land Use p.643

Bendinger, Crockett, Peterson, Greenwood & Casey
Profile: p.1739
Table:
Litigation: General Commercial p.1731

Benesch, Friedlander, Coplan & Aronoff LLP
Tables: Banking & Finance p.1411, Bankruptcy p.1413, Construction p.1417, Real Estate p.1434

Bercow & Radell PA
Profile: p.557
Table:
Real Estate: Zoning/Land Use p.528

Berens & Tate PC
Table: Employment: p.1084

Berger & Montague PC
Table: Antitrust p.1489

Berger Singerman
Profile: p.558
Table: Bankruptcy p.502

Berkes Crane Robinson & Seal, LLP
Table: Insurance p.212

Berkowitz Stanton Brandt Williams & Shaw LLP
Table: Litigation p.1048

Baker, Donelson, Bearman, Caldwell & Berkowitz, PC
Profile: p.1613
Tables: Corporate/M&A p.111, Healthcare p.29, Litigation: General Commercial p.865, Real Estate p.119

Berman & Simmons
Table: Litigation p.893

Berman DeValerio Pease Tabacco Burt & Pucillo
Table: Antitrust p.498

Bernstein, Cushner & Kimmell PC
Table: Environment p.943

Bernstein, Shur, Sawyer & Nelson, PA
Profile: p.903
Tables: Corporate/M&A p.888, Employment: p.890, Environment p.892, Litigation: General Commercial p.893, Real Estate p.895

Beus Gilbert PLLC
Table:
Real Estate: Zoning/Land Use p.155

Beveridge & Diamond PC
Profile: p.480
Tables: Environment p.206

Bierce & Kenerson, P.C.
Table: Business Process Outsourcing: National p.9

Bilzin Sumberg Baena Price & Axelrod LLP
Profile: p.559
Tables: Bankruptcy p.502, Real Estate p.526, Real Estate: Zoning/Land Use p.528, Tax p.530

Bingham McCutchen LLP
Tables: Antitrust p.183, Banking & Finance p.187, Bankruptcy/Restructuring p.1177, Construction p.194, Corporate/M&A p.937, Environment p.206, Litigation: General Commercial p.223, Private Equity: Buyouts & Venture Capital Investment p.952, Real Estate p.333, Sports Law p.55, Tax p.959

Bingham McHale LLP
Tables: Litigation: General Commercial p.785, Real Estate p.788

Birch, Horton, Bittner & Cherot
Profile: p.145
Tables: Corporate/M&A p.134, Employment: p.135, Litigation: General Commercial p.138

Birch, Stewart, Kolasch & Birch, LLP
Table: Intellectual Property: Northern Virginia p.1758

Bird, Marella, Boxer & Wolpert PC
Table: Litigation: White-Collar Crime & Government Investigations p.225

Black Lowe & Graham
Table: Intellectual Property p.1784

Black, Srebnick, Kornspan & Stumpf PA
Table: Litigation: White-Collar Crime & Government Investigations p.522

Blackwell Sanders Peper Martin LLP
Profile: p.1062
Tables: Corporate/M&A p.816, Employment: p.1045, Litigation: General Commercial p.1048, Real Estate p.1052

Blank Rome LLP
Profile: p.1542
Tables: Banking & Finance p.1492, Bankruptcy/Restructuring p.1494, Corporate/M&A p.1497, Employment:

p.1500, Litigation: General Commercial p.1511, Real Estate p.1515, Shipping p.71

Blecher & Collins
Profile: p.282
Tables: Antitrust p.183, Litigation: General Commercial p.223

Blish & Cavanagh, LLP
Table: Litigation p.1566

Bloom, Hergott and Diemer LLP
Table: Media & Entertainment: Transactional p.233

Bodman LLP
Tables: Banking & Finance p.987, Corporate/M&A p.988, Litigation: General Commercial p.993

Boehl Stopher & Graves, LLP
Profile: p.848
Table: Litigation p.834

Boies, Schiller & Flexner LLP
Profile: p.1337
Tables: Antitrust p.366, Arbitration (International) p.32, Litigation: General Commercial p.1221

Bond, Schoeneck & King, PLLC
Table: Employment: p.1199

Bondurant, Mixson & Elmore, LLP
Profile: p.629
Tables: Antitrust p.578, Litigation: General Commercial p.598

Boone, Karlberg PC
Tables: Corporate/M&A p.1072, Litigation: General Commercial p.1074, Real Estate p.1078

Boose Casey Ciklin Lubitz Martens McBane & O'Connell
Table: Construction p.506

Bose McKinney & Evans LLP
Tables: Corporate/M&A p.781, Litigation: General Commercial p.785, Real Estate p.788

Bouchard Margules & Friedlander PA
Table: Chancery p.344

Boult, Cummings, Conners & Berry, PLC
Tables: Corporate/M&A p.1594, Employment: p.1596, Litigation: General Commercial p.1598, Real Estate p.1603

Bowditch & Dewey LLP
Table: Environment p.943

Bowen Riley Warnock & Jacobson, PLC
Profile: p.1615
Table: Litigation p.1598

Bowles Rice McDavid Graff & Love LLP
Tables: Corporate/M&A p.1798, Employment: p.1800, Litigation: General Commercial p.1803, Real Estate p.1805

B

Boyce, Greenfield, Pashby & Welk LLP
Tables: Corporate/M&A p.1587, Employment: p.1589, Litigation: General Commercial p.1590, Real Estate p.1591

Bracewell & Giuliani LLP
Profile: p.1710
Tables: Banking & Finance p.1624, Bankruptcy p.1626, Corporate/M&A p.1631, Employment: p.1633, Energy & Natural Resources p.1637, Energy & Natural Resources: Dispute Resolution p.1639, Energy: Oil & Gas p.382, Environment p.1642, Intellectual Property p.1650, Litigation: General Commercial p.1655, Projects p.1659, Real Estate p.1661, Tax p.1665, Technology p.1667

Bradley & Riley, PC
Tables: Corporate/M&A p.802, Employment: p.804, Litigation: General Commercial p.806, Real Estate p.810

Bradley Arant Rose & White LLP
Profile: p.128
Tables: Corporate/M&A p.111, Employment: p.113, Litigation: General Commercial p.115, Real Estate p.119

Bradshaw, Fowler, Proctor & Fairgrave, PC
Tables: Corporate/M&A p.802, Employment: p.804, Litigation: General Commercial p.806, Real Estate p.810

Brady Hathaway Brady & Bretz
Profile: p.1001
Table: Employment: p.991

Brault Graham Scott & Brault LLC
Table: Litigation p.914

Breazeale, Sachse & Wilson, LLP
Table: Employment: p.861

Bricker & Eckler LLP
Tables: Construction p.1417, Environment p.1424, Real Estate p.1434

Bricklemyer Smolker & Bolves PA
Table: Real Estate: Zoning/Land Use p.528

Briggs and Morgan, Professional Association
Tables: Corporate/M&A p.1005, Employment: p.1008, Litigation: General Commercial p.1010, Real Estate p.1014

Brinks Hofer Gilson & Lione
Profile: p.762
Table: Intellectual Property p.695

Broad and Cassel
Tables: Construction p.506, Healthcare p.517, Real Estate p.526, Tax p.530

Brockelman Fatica PLC
Table: Employment: p.148

Bronstein, Carlson, Gleim & Smith, PA
Table: Tax p.530

Brooks, Pierce, McLendon, Humphrey & Leonard LLP
Tables: Corporate/M&A p.1383,
Employment: p.1385, Environment p.1387, Litigation: General Commercial p.1390

Brown Clark DeMay & Froman PA
Table: Construction p.506

Brown, Drew & Massey LLP
Tables: Corporate/M&A p.1832, Real Estate p.1836

Brown, Winick, Graves, Gross, Baskerville and Schoene baum PLC
Profile: p.815
Tables: Corporate/M&A p.802, Litigation: General Commercial p.806, Real Estate p.810

Peifer, Hanson & Mullins PA
Table: Litigation p.1159

Browning, Kaleczyc, Berry & Hoven PC
Tables: Litigation: General Commercial p.1074, Natural Resources & Environment p.1077

Brown Law Firm PC
Tables: Employment: p.1073, Litigation: General Commercial p.1074

Brown McCarroll LLP
Tables:
Environment p.1642, Healthcare p.1645

Brown Raysman Millstein Felder & Steiner LLP
Profile: p.1338
Tables: Business Process Outsourcing: National p.9, Intellectual Property p.1216, Real Estate p.1247, Technology & IT Outsourcing p.1259

Brown Rudnick Berlack Israels LLP
Tables: Bankruptcy p.934, Bankruptcy/Restructuring p.1177, Environment p.943, Healthcare p.946, Real Estate p.333

Brownstein Hyatt & Farber PC
Profile: p.324
Tables: Corporate/M&A p.303, Employment: p.305, Real Estate p.313

Bruder Gentile & Marcoux LLP
Table: Energy: Electricity p.385

Brunini, Grantham, Grower & Hewes, PLLC
Profile: p.1037
Tables: Corporate/M&A p.1024, Litigation: General Commercial p.1028, Real Estate p.1031

Bryan Cave LLP
Tables: Corporate/M&A p.146, Corporate/M&A: Mid-Tier Firms p.1195, Employment: p.148, Environment p.1205, Environment (including water rights) p.150, Litigation: General Commercial p.1048, Real Estate p.153, Real Estate: Zoning/Land Use p.155

Buchalter Nemer Fields & Younger
Table: Banking & Finance p.187

Buchanan Ingersoll PC
Profile: p.1544
Tables: Corporate/M&A p.1497, Employment: p.1500, Intellectual Property p.1508, Litigation: p.1511

Buck & Gordon LLP
Table: Real Estate p.1788

Buckingham Doolittle & Burroughs
Table: Construction p.1417

Buist, Moore, Smythe, McGee P.A.
Tables: Corporate/M&A p.1572, Litigation: General Commercial p.1575, Real Estate p.1577

Bullard Smith Jernstedt Wilson
Table: Employment: p.1473

Bullivant Houser Bailey PC
Tables: Employment: p.1473, Litigation: General Commercial p.1475

Burbidge & Mitchell
Profile: p.1740
Table: Litigation p.1731

Burch & Cracchiolo
Table: Real Estate: Zoning/Land Use p.155

Burch, Porter & Johnson PLLC
Tables: Employment: p.1596, Litigation: General Commercial p.1598, Real Estate p.1603

Burke & Parsons
Table: Shipping p.66

Burns Doane Swecker & Mathis LLP
Table: Intellectual Property: Northern Virginia p.1758

Burr & Forman LLP
Profile: p.129
Tables: Corporate/M&A p.111, Employment: p.113, Real Estate p.119

Bush, Strout & Kornfeld
Table: Bankruptcy p.1776

Butler, Snow, O'Mara, Stevens & Cannada, PLLC
Profile: p.1038
Tables: Corporate/M&A p.1024, Employment: p.1026, Litigation: General Commercial p.1028, Products Liability p.48, Real Estate p.1031

Butler Burnette Pappas, LLP
Table: Insurance p.519

Butler Rubin Saltarelli & Boyd
Table:
Insurance: Reinsurance Litigation p.693

Butzel Long
Profile: p.1002
Tables: Corporate/M&A p.988, Employment: p.991, Litigation: General Commercial p.993, Real Estate p.996

Byrnes & Keller
Table: Litigation p.1785

C

Cabaniss, Johnston, Gardner, Dumas & O'Neal
Tables: Employment: p.113, Litigation: General Commercial p.115

Cades Schutte
Tables: Bankruptcy p.640, Corporate/M&A p.641, Employment: p.642, Land Use p.643, Litigation: General Commercial p.644, Real Estate p.646

Cadwalader, Wickersham & Taft LLP
Profile: p.1339
Tables: Aviation p.57, Bankruptcy/Restructuring p.1177, Capital Markets: Derivatives p.16, Capital Markets: Securitisation p.18, Corporate/M&A p.1187, Healthcare p.1209, Insurance: Dispute Resolution p.1212, Litigation: General Commercial p.1221, Litigation: Securities p.1223, Projects p.1243, Real Estate p.1247, Tax p.1254

Cadwell Sanford Deibert & Garry LLP
Tables: Corporate/M&A p.1587, Litigation: General Commercial p.1590

Caesar, Rivise, Bernstein, Cohen & Pokotilow Ltd
Profile: p.1545
Table: Intellectual Property p.1508

Cahill Gordon & Reindel
Tables: Capital Markets: Debt & Equity p.13, Environment: Mainly Transactional p.1206, Insurance: Dispute Resolution p.1212, Litigation: General Commercial p.1221, Litigation: Securities p.1223, Media & Entertainment: Litigation p.1232, Tax p.1254

Calfee, Halter & Griswold LLP
Profile: p.1451
Tables: Banking & Finance p.1411, Bankruptcy p.1413, Corporate/M&A p.1419, Intellectual Property p.1427, Litigation: General Commercial p.1430, Real Estate p.1434

Campbell & Williams
Table: Litigation p.1096

Canterbury, Stuber, Elder, Gooch & Surratt, PC
Profile: p.1711
Table: Construction p.1629

Caplin & Drysdale
Table: Tax p.422

Carey, Scott & Douglas, PLLC
Table: Litigation p.1803

Carlsmith Ball LLP
Tables: Corporate/M&A p.641, Litigation: General Commercial p.644, Real Estate p.646

Carlton Fields PA
Profile: p.560
Tables: Antitrust p.498, Bankruptcy p.502, Construction p.506, Corporate/M&A p.509, Employment: p.511, Environment p.515, Healthcare p.517, Insurance p.519, Litigation: General Commercial p.520, Real Estate p.526, Tax p.530

C

Carlton, DiSante & Freudenberger
Table: Employment: p.201

Carmody & Torrance LLP
Table: Litigation p.331

Carrington, Coleman, Sloman & Blumenthal, LLP
Tables: Antitrust p.1622, Litigation: General Commercial p.1655

Carroll, Kelly & Murphy
Table: Litigation p.1566

Carruthers & Roth PA
Table: Banking & Finance p.1381

Carter Ledyard & Milburn LLP
Profile: p.1340
Tables: Environment p.1205, Shipping p.66

Carver Darden Koretzky Tessier Finn Blossman & Areaux LLC
Table: Banking & Finance p.857

Cascadia Law Group
Table: Environment p.1782

Case Bigelow & Lombardi, A Law Corporation
Profile: p.652
Tables: Bankruptcy p.640, Corporate/M&A p.641, Litigation: General Commercial p.644, Real Estate p.646

Chadbourne & Parke LLP
Profile: p.1341
Tables: Energy: Electricity p.385, Energy: Transactional p.32, Insurance: Insurer Firms p.400, Products Liability p.48, Projects p.52

Chaffe, McCall, Phillips, Toler & Sarpy, L.L.P.
Profile: p.881
Tables: Banking & Finance p.857, Real Estate p.867

Chamberlain, Hrdlicka, White, Williams & Martin
Table: Tax p.603

Chapman and Cutler LLP
Profile: p.763
Table: Banking & Finance p.665

Chester, Willcox & Saxbe LLP
Table: Litigation p.1430

Choate Hall & Stewart
Tables: Antitrust p.930, Banking & Finance p.932, Bankruptcy p.934, Corporate/M&A p.937, Environment p.943, Healthcare p.946, Intellectual Property p.947, Private Equity: Buyouts & Venture Capital Investment p.952

Christensen, Moore, Cockrell, Cummings & Axelberg PC
Tables: Litigation: General Commercial p.1074, Natural Resources & Environment p.1077, Real Estate p.1078

Christensen, Miller, Fink, Jacobs, Glaser, Weil & Shapiro, LLP
Table: Media & Entertainment: Litigation p.229

Christensen O'Connor Johnson Kindness, PLLC
Table: Intellectual Property p.1784

Christian & Small LLP
Profile: p.130
Table: Litigation p.115

Christian & Barton LLP
Table: Litigation p.1762

Christian, Samson, Jones & Chisholm, PLLC
Table: Corporate/M&A p.1072

Christianson, Boutin & Spraker
Table: Bankruptcy p.133

Chun, Kerr, Dodd, Beaman & Wong
Table: Corporate/M&A p.641

Cichanowicz, Callan, Keane, Vengrow & Textor LLP
Table: Shipping p.66

Clarence Snell & Dyer LLP
Table: Litigation: White-Collar Crime & Government Investigations p.225

Clark, Atcheson & Reisert
Table: Shipping p.66

Clark Hill PLC
Tables: Corporate/M&A p.988, Employment: p.991, Litigation: General Commercial p.993, Real Estate p.996

Cleary Gottlieb Steen & Hamilton LLP
Profile: p.1342
Tables: Antitrust p.366, Arbitration (International) p.32, Banking & Finance p.1173, Bankruptcy/Restructuring p.1177, Capital Markets: Debt & Equity p.13, Capital Markets: Derivatives p.16, Capital Markets: Securitisation p.18, Corporate/M&A p.1187, Employee Benefits & Executive Compensation p.1197, Litigation: General Commercial p.1221, Litigation: Securities p.1223, Private Equity: Fund Formation p.1240, Real Estate p.1247, Tax p.1254

Cleary Shahi Associates, A Professional Corporation
Table: Litigation p.1745

Clifford Chance LLP
Profile: p.1343
Tables: Arbitration (International) p.32, Bankruptcy/Restructuring p.1177, Corporate/M&A: Mid-Tier Firms p.1195, Insurance: Dispute Resolution p.1212, Litigation: General Commercial p.1221, Litigation: Securities p.1223, Projects p.415

Cline, Williams, Wright, Johnson & Oldfather LLP
Tables: Corporate/M&A p.1082, Litigation: General Commercial p.1085

Coats Rose Yale Ryman Lee
Table: Construction p.1629

Coblentz, Patch, Duffy & Bass LLP
Table: Real Estate p.237

Coffman, Coleman, Andrews & Grogan
Table: Employment: p.511

Cohen & Grigsby PC
Table: Employment: p.1500

Cohn & Whitesell LLP
Table: Bankruptcy p.934

Cokinos, Bosien and Young
Table: Construction p.1629

Cole, Schotz, Meisel, Forman & Leonard PA
Table: Real Estate p.1134

Collier, Jacob & Mills
Table: Employment: p.1126

Collier Shannon Scott
Table: International Trade p.39

Colson Hicks Eidson
Profile: p.561
Tables: Litigation: General Commercial p.520, Litigation: White-Collar Crime & Government Investigations p.522

Comiter, Singer & Baseman, LLP
Table: Tax p.530

Commercial Law Group
Table: Corporate/M&A p.1459

Condon & Forsyth LLP
Table: Aviation p.57

Conley, Rose & Tayon
Table: Intellectual Property p.1650

Conmy Feste Ltd
Tables: Corporate/M&A p.1403, Employment: p.1405, Real Estate p.1409

Connelly Baker Wotring Jackson LLP
Table: Environment p.1642

Conner & Winters, PC
Tables: Corporate/M&A p.1459, Employment: p.1460

Connolly, O'Malley, Lillis, Hansen & Olson LLP
Table: Real Estate p.810

Connolly Bove Lodge & Hutz LLP
Profile: p.361
Table: Intellectual Property p.348

Conrad O'Brien Gellman & Rohn PC
Profile: p.1546
Table: Litigation p.1511

Constangy, Brooks & Smith, LLC
Tables: Employment: p.113

Conway & Mrowiec
Profile: p.764
Table: Construction p.672

Cook & Roach, L.L.P.
Table: Insurance p.1647

Cook, Little, Rosenblatt & Manson PLLC
Tables: Corporate/M&A p.1107, Litigation: General Commercial p.1111

Cooley Godward LLP
Tables: Antitrust p.183, Corporate/M&A p.303, Corporate/M&A: Northern California p.196, Intellectual Property p.215, IT & IT Outsourcing p.221, Litigation: General Commercial p.223, Tax p.241

Cooper & Scully PC
Profile: p.1712
Table: Insurance p.1647

Corr Cronin LLP
Table: Litigation p.1785

Correro Fishman Haygood Phelps Walmsley & Casteix LLP
Profile: p.882
Tables: Banking & Finance p.857, Corporate/M&A p.858, Litigation: General Commercial p.865

Corretti, Newsom & Hawkins
Table: Real Estate p.119

Cosho, Humphrey, Greener & Welsh, PA
Table: Litigation p.657

Costello Porter Hill Heisterkamp Bushnell & Carpenter LLP
Table: Litigation p.1590

Cotchett, Pitre, Simon & McCarthy
Table: Litigation p.223

Cotsirilos Tighe & Streicker Ltd
Table: Litigation p.699

Couch White, LLP
Table: Energy: Upstate New York p.1204

Coudert Brothers
Table: Media & Entertainment: Litigation p.1232

Covington & Burling
Profile: p.481
Tables: Antitrust p.366, Arbitration (International) p.32, Bankruptcy p.372, Corporate/Commercial p.376, Environment p.391, Healthcare: Pharmaceutical/Medical Products Regulatory p.397, Insurance p.212, Insurance: Policy Holder p.401, Litigation: General Commercial p.409, Real Estate p.417, Sports Law p.55, Telecom, Broadcast & Satellite: Regulatory p.426, Transport: Rail p.62

Cowan, Liebowitz & Latman
Tables: Intellectual Property p.1216, Media & Entertainment: Litigation p.1232

Cox Smith Matthews Incorporated
Profile: p.1713
Tables: Bankruptcy p.1626, Intellectual Property p.1650

Cox Castle & Nicholson LLP
Tables: Construction p.194, Real Estate p.237

Cozen O'Connor
Table: Bankruptcy/Restructuring p.1494

Cravath, Swaine & Moore LLP
Profile: p.1344
Tables: Antitrust p.1169, Banking & Finance p.1173, Capital Markets: Debt & Equity p.13, Capital Markets: Securitisation p.18, Corporate/M&A p.1187, Energy: Transactional p.1202, Environment: Mainly Transactional p.1206, Intellectual Property p.1216, Litigation: General Commercial p.1221, Litigation: Securities p.1223, Media & Entertainment: Litigation p.1232, Media & Entertainment: Transactional p.1234, Tax p.1254

Croker, Huck, Kasher, DeWitt, Anderson & Gonderinger, P.C.
Table: Real Estate p.1086

Cronin, Fried, Sekiya, Kekina & Fairbanks Attorneys At Law
Table: Litigation p.644

Cross, Gunter, Witherspoon & Galchus, PC
Profile: p.179
Table: Employment: p.169

Crowe & Dunlevy, PC
Profile: p.1467
Tables: Corporate/M&A p.1459, Employment: p.1460, Litigation: General Commercial p.1462, Real Estate p.1463

Crowell & Moring LLP
Profile: p.482
Tables: Antitrust p.366, Aviation p.57, Energy: Electricity p.385, Energy: Oil & Gas p.382, Government Contracts p.26, Insurance: Insurer Firms p.400, International Trade p.39, Investment Management p.405

Crowley, Haughey, Hanson, Toole & Dietrich, PLLP
Profile: p.474
Tables: Corporate/M&A p.1072, Employment: p.1073, Litigation: Appellate p.408, Litigation: General Commercial p.1074, Natural Resources & Environment p.1077, Real Estate p.1078

Cunningham, Bounds, Yance, Crowder & Brown, LLC
Table: Litigation p.115

Curran & Parry
Profile: p.1104
Table: Gaming & Licensing p.1094

Gilioli Alemani Bocchiola Tamburini e Partners in assoc with Curtis Mallet-Prevost Colt & Mosle LLP
Table: Litigation p.1221

Cutler & Donahoe LLP
Tables: Corporate/M&A p.1587, Real Estate p.1591

D'Amante Couser Steiner Pellerin, P.A.
Tables: Litigation: General Commercial p.1111, Real Estate p.1114

Daniels, Kashtan, Downs, Robertson & Magathan
Table: Construction p.506

Danielson Harrigan Leyh & Tollefson, LLP
Table:
Litigation: General Commercial p.1785

Dann Pecar Newman & Kleiman, PC
Table: Real Estate p.788

Davenport, Evans, Hurwitz & Smith LLP
Tables: Corporate/M&A p.1587, Employment: p.1589, Litigation: General Commercial p.1590, Real Estate p.1591

Davis & Boghigian, PC
Table: Real Estate p.1114

Davis & Cannon
Tables: Employment: p.1833, Litigation: General Commercial p.1834, Real Estate p.1836

Davis & Gilbert
Table: Media & Entertainment: Transactional p.1234

Davis & Wilkerson, PC
Table: Healthcare p.1645

Davis Munck
Profile: p.1714
Table: Intellectual Property p.1650

Davis & Kuelthau, S.C.
Table: Employment: p.1819

Davis, Brown, Koehn, Shors & Roberts, PC
Tables: Corporate/M&A p.802, Employment: p.804, Litigation: General Commercial p.806, Real Estate p.810

Davis Graham & Stubbs LLP
Tables: Corporate/M&A p.303, Employment: p.305, Environment p.307, Litigation: General Commercial p.310, Real Estate p.313

Davis Polk & Wardwell
Profile: p.1345
Tables: Antitrust p.1169, Banking & Finance p.1173, Bankruptcy/Restructuring p.1177, Capital Markets p.23, Capital Markets: Debt & Equity p.13, Corporate/M&A p.1187, Corporate/M&A: Northern California p.196, Employee Benefits & Executive Compensation p.1197, Energy: Transactional p.1202, Environment: Mainly Transactional p.1206, International Trade p.39, Litigation: General Commercial p.1221, Litigation: Securities p.1223, Litigation: White-Collar Crime & Government Investigations p.1224, Media & Entertainment: Transactional p.1234, Private Equity: Buyouts & Venture Capital Investment p.1237, Private

Equity: Fund Formation p.1240, Projects p.1243, Tax p.1254

Davis Wright Tremaine LLP
Profile: p.1796
Tables: Bankruptcy p.133, Corporate/M&A p.134, Employment: p.135, Energy & Natural Resources p.204, Environment p.1782, Healthcare p.29, Intellectual Property p.1784, Litigation: General Commercial p.1475, Media & Entertainment p.413, Media & Entertainment: Litigation p.229, Real Estate p.140

Dawda, Mann, Mulcahy & Sadler PLC
Table: Real Estate p.996

Day, Berry & Howard LLP
Tables: Corporate/M&A p.327, Employment: p.329, Litigation: General Commercial p.331, Real Estate p.333

Day Casebeer Madrid & Batchelder LLP
Table: Intellectual Property p.215

Deacy & Deacy LLP
Table: Litigation p.1048

Dean, Mead, Egerton, Bloodworth, Capouano & Bozarth PA
Tables: Litigation: General Commercial p.520, Real Estate p.526, Tax p.530

Deaner, Deaner, Scann, Malan & Larsen
Table: Real Estate p.1098

Debevoise & Plimpton LLP
Profile: p.1346
Tables: Antitrust p.1169, Arbitration (International) p.32, Bankruptcy/Restructuring p.1177, Corporate/M&A p.1187, Employee Benefits & Executive Compensation p.1197, Energy: Transactional p.1202, Environment: Mainly Transactional p.1206, Insurance: Dispute Resolution p.1212, Intellectual Property p.1216, Litigation: General Commercial p.1221, Litigation: Securities p.1223, Litigation: White-Collar Crime & Government Investigations p.1224, Media & Entertainment: Litigation p.1232, Media & Entertainment: Transactional p.1234, Private Equity: Buyouts & Venture Capital Investment p.1237, Private Equity: Fund Formation p.1240, Projects p.1243, Real Estate p.1247, Tax p.1254

Dechert LLP
Profile: p.1547
Tables: Antitrust p.1489, Corporate/M&A p.1497, Corporate/M&A: Mid-Tier Firms p.1195, Employment: p.1500, Environment p.1504, Investment Management p.405, Litigation: General Commercial p.1511, Real Estate p.333

Demars & Turman Ltd
Table: Corporate/M&A p.1403

Denlinger, Rosenthal & Greenberg LPA
Table: Employment: p.1421

Dennis, Corry, Porter & Smith LLP
Table: Transport: Road

(Carriage/Commercial) p.64

DeOrchis & Partners, LLP
Tables: Shipping p.66, Transport: Rail p.62, Transport: Road (Carriage/Commercial) p.64

Derrick & Briggs LLP
Table: Corporate/M&A p.1459

Devine Millimet & Branch PA
Tables: Corporate/M&A p.1107, Employment: p.1109, Litigation: General Commercial p.1111, Real Estate p.1114

Dewey Ballantine LLP
Profile: p.1347
Tables: Antitrust p.1169, Banking & Finance p.1624, Capital Markets: Securitisation p.18, Corporate/M&A p.1187, Energy: Electricity p.385, Energy: Oil & Gas p.382, Energy: Transactional p.1202, Insurance: Dispute Resolution p.1212, Intellectual Property p.215, International Trade p.39, Litigation: General Commercial p.1221, Media & Entertainment: Transactional p.1234, Private Equity: Fund Formation p.1240, Projects p.1243, Real Estate p.237, Sports Law p.55, Tax p.422

Dickinson, Mackaman, Tyler & Hagen, P.C.
Tables: Employment: p.804, Litigation: General Commercial p.806, Real Estate p.810

Dickinson Wright PLLC
Tables: Banking & Finance p.987, Corporate/M&A p.988, Employment: p.991, Litigation: General Commercial p.993, Real Estate p.996

Dickstein Shapiro Morin & Oshinsky LLP
Profile: p.483
Tables: Bankruptcy p.372, Corporate/Commercial p.376, Employment: p.380, Energy: Electricity p.385, Insurance: Policy Holder p.401

Dillon & Yudell LLP
Table: Intellectual Property p.1650

Dilworth Paxson LLP
Profile: p.1548
Table: Bankruptcy/Restructuring p.1494

Dinse, Knapp & McAndrew PC
Tables: Corporate/M&A p.1743, Employment: p.1744, Litigation: General Commercial p.1745, Real Estate p.1747

Dinsmore & Shohl LLP
Profile: p.1452
Tables: Banking & Finance p.1411, Bankruptcy p.1413, Corporate/M&A p.1419, Employment: p.830, Environment, Natural Resources and Regulated Industries p.832, Intellectual Property p.1427, Litigation: General Commercial p.834

DiTrapano, Barrett & DiPiero, PLLC
Table: Litigation p.1803

DLA Piper Rudnick Gray Cary US LLP
Profile: p.765
Tables: Bankruptcy p.668, Construction p.373, Corporate/M&A p.909,

D

Corporate/M&A: Northern California p.196, Employment: p.911, Energy & Natural Resources p.685, Environment p.391, Government Contracts p.26, Insurance: Coverage Litigation p.694, Insurance: Reinsurance Litigation p.693, Insurance: Transactional & Regulatory p.692, IT & IT Outsourcing p.221, Litigation: General Commercial p.914, Media & Entertainment: Litigation p.229, Products Liability p.48, Real Estate p.237, Technology & IT Outsourcing p.712

Doerner, Saunders, Daniel & Anderson, LLP
Table: Employment: p.1460

Doffermyre, Shields, Canfield, Knowles & Devine
Table: Litigation p.598

Donahue, Tucker & Ciandella
Table: Real Estate p.1114

Doney, Crowley, Bloomquist, Payne & Uda, P.C.
Table: Natural Resources & Environment p.1077

Donovan Parry McDermott & Radzik
Table: Shipping p.66

Dorsey & Whitney LLP
Tables: Corporate/M&A p.134, Employment: p.135, Environment, Natural Resources and Regulated Industries p.136, Intellectual Property p.1784, Litigation: General Commercial p.138, Real Estate p.140

Dover Dixon Horne
Table: Real Estate p.174

Dow, Lohnes & Albertson, PLLC
Table: Telecom, Broadcast & Satellite: Regulatory p.426

Downey, Brand, Seymour & Rohwer LLP
Table: Energy & Natural Resources p.204

Downs Rachlin Martin PLLC
Tables: Corporate/M&A p.1743, Employment: p.1744, Litigation: General Commercial p.1745, Real Estate p.1747

Dray, Thomson & Dyekman PC
Profile: p.1841
Tables: Corporate/M&A p.1832, Real Estate p.1836

Drinker Biddle & Reath LLP
Profile: p.1549
Tables: Antitrust p.1489, Banking & Finance p.1492, Corporate/M&A p.1123, Environment p.1504, Intellectual Property p.1508, Litigation: General Commercial p.1131, Real Estate p.1134

Drummond Woodsum & MacMahon
Profile: p.904
Tables: Corporate/M&A p.888, Employment: p.890, Real Estate p.895

Duane Morris LLP
Profile: p.1550
Tables: Antitrust p.1489, Banking & Finance p.665, Bankruptcy p.934, Bankruptcy/Restructuring p.1494,

Chancery p.344, Corporate/M&A p.1497, Intellectual Property p.1508

Duffy, Sweeney & Scott Ltd
Table: Litigation p.1566

Dunn Carney Allen Higgins & Tongue LLP
Profile: p.1487
Tables: Litigation: General Commercial p.1475, Real Estate p.1478

Durant, Nichols, Houston, Hodgson & Cortese-Costa, P.C.
Table: Employment: p.329

Durham Jones & Pinegar, A Professional Corporation
Table: Corporate/M&A p.1727

Durrell Law Group, PC
Table: Corporate/M&A p.134

Dutton, Braun, Staack & Hellman PLC
Table: Litigation p.806

Duvin, Cahn & Hutton
Profile: p.1453
Table: Employment: p.1421

Dykema Gossett PLLC
Tables: Corporate/M&A p.988, Employment: p.991, Litigation: General Commercial p.993, Real Estate p.996

E

Earl, Curley & Lagarde, P.C
Table: Real Estate: Zoning/Land Use p.155

Eastman & Smith Ltd
Table: Environment p.1424

Eaton Peabody
Tables: Corporate/M&A p.888, Employment: p.890, Environment p.892, Litigation: General Commercial p.893, Real Estate p.895

Eaves Bardacke Baugh Kierst & Kiernan PA
Table: Litigation p.1159

Eberle, Berlin, Kading, Turnbow & McKlveen, Chartered
Table: Litigation p.657

Eckert Seamans Cherin & Mellott, LLC

Edwards Frickle Anner-Hughes & Cook
Table: Litigation p.1074

Edwards & Angell, LLP
Tables: Banking & Finance p.932, Corporate/M&A p.327, Employment: p.1565, Insurance: Dispute Resolution p.1212, Litigation: General Commercial p.1566, Private Equity: Buyouts & Venture Capital Investment p.952

Eimer Stahl Klevorn & Solberg
Profile: p.766
Table: Antitrust p.661

Elam & Burke PA
Table: Litigation p.657

Elarbee, Thompson, Sapp & Wilson, LLP
Table: Employment: p.589

Elderkin & Pirnie PLC
Table: Litigation p.806

Eldridge Cooper Steichen & Leach PLLC
Table: Employment: p.1460

Ellis & Winters LLP
Table: Litigation p.1390

Ellis Thorp & Jewett
Table: Environment p.1757

Epstein Becker & Green PC
Tables: Employment: p.511, Healthcare p.29

Erickson & Sederstrom, PC
Tables: Corporate/M&A p.1082, Litigation: General Commercial p.1085

Everett Law Firm
Table: Litigation p.172

F

Fabian & Clendenin
Tables: Litigation: General Commercial p.1731, Real Estate p.1733

Fabyanske, Westra & Hart PA
Table: Real Estate p.1014

Faegre & Benson LLP
Profile: p.1022
Tables: Corporate/M&A p.303, Employment: p.305, Environment p.307, Intellectual Property p.309, Litigation: General Commercial p.310, Real Estate p.313

Farella Braun & Martel LLP
Tables: Construction p.194, Environment p.206, Insurance p.212, Intellectual Property p.215, Litigation: General Commercial p.223

Farer Fersko
Tables: Environment p.1129, Real Estate p.1134

Farmer, Cline & Campbell PLLC
Profile: p.1812
Table: Litigation p.1803

Farr & Taranto
Table: Litigation: Appellate p.407

Faruki Ireland & Cox PLL
Table: Litigation p.1430

Fay Sharpe Fagan Minnich & McKee LLP
Profile: p.1454
Table: Intellectual Property p.1427

Feldman & Orlansky
Table: Litigation p.138

Felhaber, Larson, Fenlon & Vogt, PC
Tables: Employment: p.1008, Real Estate p.1014

Fellers, Snider, Blankenship, Bailey & Tippens, A Professional Corporation
Profile: p.1468
Table: Litigation p.1462

Fennemore Craig
Profile: p.164
Tables: Corporate/M&A p.146, Employment: p.148, Environment (including water rights) p.150, Litigation: General Commercial p.151, Litigation: White-Collar Crime & Government Investigations p.153, Real Estate: Zoning/Land Use p.155

Fenwick & West LLP
Profile: p.283
Tables: Corporate/M&A: Northern California p.196, Intellectual Property p.215, Tax p.241

Ferencik, Libanoff, Brandt, Bustamante & Williams
Table: Construction p.506

Ferrell Schultz Carter & Fertel PA
Table: Bankruptcy p.502

Fine Kaplan & Black
Table: Antitrust p.1489

Finley, Alt, Smith, Scharnberg, Craig, Hilmes & Gaffney PC
Table: Litigation p.806

Finn Dixon & Herling LLP
Profile: p.339
Table: Corporate/M&A p.327

Finnegan Henderson Farabow Garrett & Dunner LLP
Tables: Intellectual Property p.215

Fish & Neave IP Group of Ropes & Gray
Tables: Intellectual Property p.215

Fish & Richardson
Tables: Intellectual Property p.215

Fisher & Phillips LLP
Profile: p.630
Tables: Employment: p.511

Fisk & Fielder
Table: Construction p.1629

Fitzpatrick, Cella, Harper & Scinto
Profile: p.1348
Table: Intellectual Property p.1216

Flaherty, Sensabaugh & Bonasso PLLC
Table: Litigation p.1803

Fleck, Mather & Strutz, Ltd.
Table: Litigation p.1406

F

Fleeson, Gooing, Coulson & Kitch, LLC
Tables: Corporate/M&A p.816, Real Estate p.821

Flygare Schwarz & Closson PLLC
Table: Employment: p.1109

Foley Hoag LLP
Tables: Antitrust p.930, Banking & Finance p.932, Corporate/M&A p.937, Employment: p.939, Environment p.943, Intellectual Property p.947, Litigation: General Commercial p.950, Private Equity: Buyouts & Venture Capital Investment p.952, Tax p.959

Foley & Lardner
Profile: p.1828
Tables: Antitrust p.498, Bankruptcy p.502, Construction p.506, Corporate/M&A p.509, Employment: p.511, Energy & Natural Resources p.685, Environment p.391, Healthcare p.29, Insurance p.519, Insurance: Transactional & Regulatory p.692, Litigation: General Commercial p.950, Media & Entertainment: Litigation p.702, Real Estate p.526, Real Estate: Zoning/Land Use p.528, Telecom, Broadcast & Satellite: Regulatory p.715

Ford & Harrison LLP
Profile: p.631
Tables: Employment: p.511

Ford White & Nassen
Table: Construction p.1629

Forizs and Dogali PL
Table: Construction p.506

Forman Perry Watkins Krutz & Tardy LLP
Profile: p.1039
Table: Litigation p.1028

Foster Johnson McDonald Lucero Koinis LLP
Table: Corporate/M&A p.1155

Foster Pepper & Shefelman PLLC
Tables: Bankruptcy p.1776, Corporate/M&A p.1777, Environment, Natural Resources and Regulated Industries p.136, Real Estate p.140

Foulston Siefkin LLP
Profile: p.826
Tables: Corporate/M&A p.816, Employment: p.818, Litigation: General Commercial p.819, Real Estate p.821

Fowler, White, Burnett PA
Table: Shipping p.71

Fowler White Boggs Banker
Tables: Employment: p.511, Healthcare p.517, Insurance p.519, Real Estate: Zoning/Land Use p.528, Tax p.530

Fox Rothschild LLP
Profile: p.1552
Table: Environment p.1504

Franczek Sullivan
Table: Employment: p.680

Frankfurt Kurnit Klein & Selz
Table: Media & Entertainment: Transactional p.1234

Franklin, Weinrib, Rudell & Vassallo
Table: Media & Entertainment: Transactional p.1234

Frantz Ward LLP
Tables: Construction p.1417, Employment: p.1421

Fraser Stryker Law Firm
Tables: Corporate/M&A p.1082, Employment: p.1084, Litigation: General Commercial p.1085, Real Estate p.1086

Fredrikson & Byron PA
Tables: Corporate/M&A p.1005, Employment: p.1008, Litigation: General Commercial p.1010, Real Estate p.1014

Freeborn & Peters
Tables: Antitrust p.661, Litigation: General Commercial p.699, Media & Entertainment: Transactional p.703

Freedman Boyd Daniels Hollander Goldberg & Cline PA
Table: Litigation p.1159

Freehill Hogan & Mahar LLP
Table: Shipping p.66

Freeman, Freeman & Salzman
Table: Antitrust p.661

Freshfields Bruckhaus Deringer
Tables: Antitrust p.366, Arbitration (International) p.32, Projects p.1243, Tax p.422

Friday, Eldredge & Clark
Tables: Corporate/M&A p.168, Employment: p.169, Litigation: General Commercial p.172, Real Estate p.174

Fried, Frank, Harris, Shriver & Jacobson LLP
Profile: p.1349
Tables: Antitrust p.366, Bankruptcy/Restructuring p.1177, Capital Markets: Debt & Equity p.13, Corporate/M&A p.1187, Employee Benefits & Executive Compensation p.1197, Government Contracts p.26, Insurance: Transactional & Regulatory p.1212, Intellectual Property p.1216, Litigation: General Commercial p.1221, Litigation: White-Collar Crime & Government Investigations p.1224, Private Equity: Buyouts & Venture Capital Investment p.1237, Real Estate p.1247, Tax p.422

Frilot, Partridge, Kohnke & Clements LC
Table: Litigation p.865

Fritz, Byrne, Head & Harrison
Table: Environment p.1642

Fross Zelnick Lehrman & Zissu PC
Tables: Intellectual Property p.1216, Media & Entertainment: Litigation p.1232

Frost Tamayo Sessums & Aranda PA
Profile: p.562

Frost Brown Todd LLC
Profile: p.849

Tables: Banking & Finance p.1411, Bankruptcy p.1413, Construction p.1417, Corporate/M&A p.827, Employment: p.830, Environment p.1424, Environment, Natural Resources and Regulated Industries p.832, Intellectual Property p.1427, Litigation: General Commercial p.834, Real Estate p.837

Fulbright & Jaworski L.L.P.
Profile: p.1715
Tables: Antitrust p.1622, Arbitration (International) p.32, Aviation p.57, Bankruptcy p.1626, Corporate/M&A p.1631, Employment: p.1633, Energy & Natural Resources p.1637, Energy & Natural Resources: Dispute Resolution p.1639, Energy: Oil & Gas p.382, Environment p.1642, Healthcare p.29, Insurance p.1647, Intellectual Property p.1650, Litigation: General Commercial p.1655, Products Liability p.48, Real Estate p.1661, Tax p.1665, Technology p.1667

Fullenkamp, Doyle & Jobeun
Table: Real Estate p.1086

Gable & Gotwals
Profile: p.1469
Table: Litigation p.1462

Gainsburgh, Benjamin, David, Meunier & Warshauer
Table: Litigation p.865

Gallagher & Kennedy PA
Tables: Environment (including water rights) p.150, Litigation: General Commercial p.151, Litigation: White-Collar Crime & Government Investigations p.153, Real Estate: Zoning/Land Use p.155

Gallagher, Callahan and Gartrell, PA
Profile: p.1120
Tables: Banking & Finance p.932, Employment: p.1109, Litigation: General Commercial p.1111, Real Estate p.1114

Gallagher, Evelius & Jones, LLP
Table: Real Estate p.916

Gallegos Law Firm PC
Tables: Environment, Natural Resources and Regulated Industries p.1158, Litigation: General Commercial p.1159

Gallop, Johnson & Neuman LC
Table: Litigation p.1048

Gammage & Burnham, P.L.C.
Table:
Real Estate: Zoning/Land Use p.155

Gang Tyre Ramer & Brown
Table: Media & Entertainment: Transactional p.233

Gardere Wynne Sewell LLP
Profile: p.1718
Tables: Antitrust p.1622, Bankruptcy p.1626, Construction p.1629, Corporate/M&A p.1631, Insurance p.1647, Intellectual Property p.1650, Real Estate p.1661, Tax p.1665, Technology p.1667

Gardner Carton & Douglas LLP
Profile: p.767
Tables: Antitrust p.661, Corporate/M&A & Private Equity p.674, Employee Benefits & Executive Compensation p.680, Environment p.687, Healthcare p.29, Technology & IT Outsourcing p.712

Garfunkel, Wild & Travis PC
Table: Healthcare p.1209

Garlington, Lohn & Robinson, PLLP
Tables: Corporate/M&A p.1072, Employment: p.1073, Litigation: General Commercial p.1074, Natural Resources & Environment p.1077, Real Estate p.1078

Garofalo Goerlich Hainbach PC
Table: Aviation p.57

Gelber, Gelber, Ingersoll & Klevansky, A Law Corporation
Tables: Bankruptcy p.640, Corporate/M&A p.641, Litigation: General Commercial p.644

Genova, Burns & Vernoia
Table: Employment: p.1126

Genovese Joblove & Battista, P.A.
Profile: p.563
Table: Bankruptcy p.502

George & Titus PA
Table: Litigation: White-Collar Crime & Government Investigations p.522

Gibbons, Del Deo, Dolan, Griffinger & Vecchione
Profile: p.1147
Table: Litigation p.1131

Gibbs & Bruns, LLP
Profile: p.1719
Tables: Energy & Natural Resources: Dispute Resolution p.1639, Litigation: General Commercial p.1655

Gibbs, Giden, Locher & Turner
Profile: p.284
Table: Construction p.194

Gibson, Dunn & Crutcher LLP
Profile: p.285
Tables: Antitrust p.183, Banking & Finance p.187, Bankruptcy p.190, Bankruptcy/Restructuring p.1177, Capital Markets p.23, Construction p.373, Corporate/Commercial p.376, Corporate/M&A p.1187, Corporate/M&A: Southern California p.196, Employee Benefits p.378, Employment: p.201, Environment p.206, Government Contracts p.26, Insurance p.212, Intellectual Property p.215, International Trade p.39, Litigation: Appellate p.407, Litigation: General Commercial p.223, Litigation: Securities p.1223, Media & Entertainment: Litigation p.229, Media & Entertainment: Transactional p.233, Private Equity: Buyouts & Venture Capital Investment p.1237, Products Liability p.48, Tax p.241

Gignilliat, Savitz & Bettis LLP
Table: Employment: p.1574

Gilbert Heintz & Randolph LLP
Table: Insurance: Policy Holder p.401

Gilker and Jones PA
Table: Employment: p.169

Gilkey & Stephenson PA
Profile: p.1165
Table: Employment: p.1157

Gilmartin, Poster & Shafto
Table: Shipping p.66

Giordano Halleran & Ciesla PC
Tables: Corporate/M&A p.1123,
Environment p.1129, Real Estate p.1134

Givens Pursley LLP
Tables: Employment: p.656, Real Estate
p.658

Glankler Brown, PLLC
Tables: Litigation: General Commercial
p.1598, Real Estate p.1603

Glenn Rasmussen Fogarty & Hooker
Tables: Bankruptcy p.502,
Corporate/M&A p.509

Godfrey & Kahn, SC
Tables: Corporate/M&A p.1817,
Litigation: General Commercial p.1820,
Real Estate p.1822

Goetz, Gallik & Baldwin, PC
Table: Litigation p.1074

Goetz Fitzpatrick Most & Bruckman LLP
Table: Construction p.1186

Goins, Underkofler, Crawford & Langdon LLP
Table: Construction p.1629

Goldberg, Kohn, Bell, Black, Rosenbloom & Moritz, Ltd
Tables: Banking & Finance p.665,
Bankruptcy p.668, Real Estate p.705

Goodell, DeVries, Leech & Dann, LLP
Profile: p.926
Table: Litigation p.914

Goodin MacBride Squeri Ritchie & Day LLP
Table: Energy & Natural Resources
p.204

Goodsill Anderson Quinn & Stifel
Tables: Corporate/M&A p.641,
Employment: p.642, Litigation: General
Commercial p.644, Real Estate p.646

Goodwin & Goodwin, LLP
Profile: p.1813
Tables: Corporate/M&A p.1798,
Litigation: General Commercial p.1803

Goodwin Procter LLP
Profile: p.980
Tables: Banking & Finance p.932,
Bankruptcy p.934, Corporate/M&A
p.937, Employment: p.939, Environment
p.391, Intellectual Property p.947,
Litigation: General Commercial p.409,
Private Equity: Buyouts & Venture
Capital Investment p.952, Private Equity:

Fund Formation p.955, Real Estate
p.956, Tax p.959

Goold Patterson Ales Roadhouse & Day
Table: Real Estate p.1098

Gordon Murray Tilden
Table: Litigation p.1785

Gordon & Glickson
Table: Technology & IT Outsourcing p.712

Gordon & Silver Ltd
Table: Gaming & Licensing p.1094

Gordon, Martin, Jones, Harris & Shrum
Table: Media & Entertainment p.1602

Gordon, Arata, McCollam, Duplantis & Eagan LLP
Tables: Energy & Natural Resources
p.862, Litigation: General Commercial
p.865

Gordon, Feinblatt, Rothman, Hoffberger & Hollander, LLC
Tables: Corporate/M&A p.909,
Employment: p.911, Litigation: General
Commercial p.914, Real Estate p.916

Gottlieb & Smith PA
Table: Real Estate p.1577

Gough, Shanahan, Johnson & Waterman
Tables: Employment: p.1073, Litigation:
General Commercial p.1074, Natural
Resources & Environment p.1077

Goulston & Storrs
Tables: Banking & Finance p.932,
Bankruptcy p.934, Environment p.943,
Litigation: General Commercial p.950,
Real Estate p.417

Graham & Dunn PC
Table: Corporate/M&A p.1777

Grant & Eisenhofer PA
Profile: p.362
Table: Chancery p.344

Gravel and Shea
Tables: Corporate/M&A p.1743,
Employment: p.1744, Litigation: General
Commercial p.1745, Real Estate p.1747

Graves, Dougherty, Hearon & Moody, P.C.
Table: Insurance p.1647

Gray Robinson PA
Tables: Construction p.506, Real Estate
p.526, Real Estate: Zoning/Land Use
p.528

Gray, Plant, Mooty, Mooty & Bennett, PA
Tables: Corporate/M&A p.1005,
Employment: p.1008, Litigation: General
Commercial p.1010, Real Estate p.1014

Greenbaum, Rowe, Smith & Davis LLP
Profile: p.1148
Tables: Corporate/M&A p.1123,
Environment p.1129, Litigation: General
Commercial p.1131, Real Estate p.1134

Greenberg Glusker Fields Claman Machtinger & Kinsella LLP
Table: Media & Entertainment: Litigation
p.229

Greenberg Traurig LLP
Profile: p.564
Tables: Antitrust p.498, Arbitration
(International) p.32, Banking & Finance
p.500, Bankruptcy p.502,
Bankruptcy/Restructuring p.341,
Chancery p.344, Construction p.506,
Corporate/M&A p.146, Employment:
p.148, Environment p.307, Healthcare
p.517, Litigation: General Commercial
p.520, Litigation: White-Collar Crime &
Government Investigations p.522, Media
& Entertainment: Transactional p.1234,
Real Estate p.526, Real Estate:
Zoning/Land Use p.528, Tax p.530

Greene Espel PLLP
Table: Litigation p.1010

Greenebaum Doll & McDonald PLLC
Profile: p.850
Tables: Corporate/M&A p.827,
Employment: p.830, Environment,
Natural Resources and Regulated
Industries p.832, Intellectual Property
p.1427, Litigation: General Commercial
p.834, Real Estate p.837

Greener Banducci Shoemaker
Table: Litigation p.657

Greensfelder, Hemker & Gale, P.C.
Tables: Employment: p.1045, Real
Estate p.1052

Greenstein Delorme & Luchs
Table: Real Estate p.417

Griffin Cochrane & Marshall
Profile: p.632
Table: Construction p.584

Gronek & Latham
Table: Bankruptcy p.502

Groom Law Group
Tables: Employee Benefits p.378,
Litigation: ERISA p.25

Gross & Welch, P.C.
Table: Real Estate p.1086

Grossberg Yochelson Fox & Beyda
Table: Real Estate p.417

Grotta, Glassman & Hoffman
Table: Employment: p.1126

Grubman, Indursky & Schindler P.C.
Table: Media & Entertainment:
Transactional p.1234

Guess & Rudd PC
Tables: Environment, Natural Resources
and Regulated Industries p.136, Native
Law p.140

Guida Slavich & Flores PC
Table: Environment p.1642

Gunderson Dettmer Stough Villeneuve Franklin & Hachigian
Table: Corporate/M&A: Northern
California p.196

Gunderson, Palmer, Goodsell & Nelson LLP
Tables: Corporate/M&A p.1587,
Litigation: General Commercial p.1590

Gunster, Yoakley & Stewart PA
Tables: Banking & Finance p.500,
Environment p.515, Real Estate p.526,
Real Estate: Zoning/Land Use p.528,
Tax p.530

H

Haddon, Morgan, Mueller, Jordan, Mackey & Foreman PC
Table: Litigation: White-Collar Crime &
Government Investigations p.310

Hahn Loeser & Parks LLP
Table: Bankruptcy p.1413

Hale Lane Peek Dennison and Howard
Tables: Corporate/M&A p.1089,
Litigation: General Commercial p.1096,
Real Estate p.1098

Hall, Estill, Hardwick, Gable, Golden & Nelson, PC
Table: Employment: p.1460

Hall, Farley, Oberrecht & Blanton, PA
Table: Employment: p.656

Hall, Render, Killian, Heath & Lyman Professional Services Corporation
Table: Healthcare p.29

Hamilton Gaskins Fay & Moon
Table: Environment p.1387

Hancock Rothert & Bunshoft LLP
Profile: p.286
Table: Insurance p.212

Hangley Aronchick Segal & Pudlin
Profile: p.1553
Tables: Bankruptcy/Restructuring
p.1494, Litigation: General Commercial
p.1511, Real Estate p.1515

Hanify & King
Profile: p.981
Table: Bankruptcy p.934

Hankins & Hicks
Table: Real Estate p.174

Hansen, McClintock & Riley
Table: Litigation p.806

Hansen Jacobson Teller Hoberman Newman, Warren, Sloane & Richman, LLP
Table: Media & Entertainment:
Transactional p.233

Hanson, Bridgett, Marcus, Vlahos & Rudy, LLP
Profile: p.287
Table: Construction p.194

Haralson, Miller, Pitt & McAnally PLC
Table: Litigation p.151

Harding Shultz & Downs
Table: Employment: p.1084

Hare, Wynn, Newell & Newton LLP
Table: Litigation p.115

Harrison, Kemp & Jones, LLP
Table: Litigation p.1096

Harris, Wiltshire & Grannis LLP
Table: Telecom, Broadcast & Satellite: Regulatory p.426

Hartig Rhodes Hoge & Lekisch PC
Table: Environment, Natural Resources and Regulated Industries p.136

Hartzog Conger Cason & Neville, PC
Tables: Corporate/M&A p.1459, Litigation: General Commercial p.1462

Harvey & Frank
Table: Litigation p.893

Harwell Howard Hyne Gabbert & Manner, PC
Profile: p.1616
Tables: Corporate/M&A p.1594, Litigation: General Commercial p.1598

Hassard Bonnington LLP
Table: Healthcare p.209

Hasse & Nesbitt
Table: Intellectual Property p.1427

Hawley Troxell Ennis & Hawley LLP
Tables: Corporate/M&A p.655, Employment: p.656, Litigation: General Commercial p.657, Real Estate p.658

Haynes and Boone LLP
Tables: Antitrust p.1622, Bankruptcy p.1626, Corporate/M&A p.1631, Employment: p.1633, Environment p.1642, Insurance p.1647, Intellectual Property p.1650, Litigation: General Commercial p.1655, Real Estate p.1661, Technology p.1667

Haynsworth Sinkler Boyd PA
Tables: Corporate/M&A p.1572, Litigation: General Commercial p.1575, Real Estate p.1577

Healy & Baillie LLP
Profile: p.1351
Table: Shipping p.66

Heard & Howard
Table: Real Estate p.1078

Heller Ehrman LLP
Profile: p.288
Tables: Antitrust p.183, Bankruptcy p.190, Corporate/M&A p.1777, Corporate/M&A: Northern California

p.196, Employment: p.201, Environment p.1782, Environment, Natural Resources and Regulated Industries p.136, Insurance p.212, Intellectual Property p.215, Litigation: General Commercial p.223, Real Estate p.237

Helmsing, Leach, Herlong, Newman & Rouse, PC
Profile: p.131
Table: Litigation p.115

Helms Mulliss & Wicker PLLC
Tables: Banking & Finance p.1381, Bankruptcy p.1383, Environment p.1387, Litigation: General Commercial p.1390, Real Estate p.1392

Henderson Daily Withrow & DeVoe
Table: Corporate/M&A p.781

Hendrick, Phillips, Salzman & Flatt P.C.
Profile: p.633
Table: Construction p.584

Hendrickson & Long, P.L.L.C.
Profile: p.1814
Table: Litigation p.1803

Hennigan, Bennett & Dorman LLP
Profile: p.289
Tables: Bankruptcy p.190, Litigation: General Commercial p.223

Henson & Efron
Table: Corporate/M&A p.1005

Herman, Herman, Katz & Cotlar LLP
Table: Litigation p.865

Hickey&Mackey
Table: Litigation p.1834

Higgins, Cavanagh & Cooney LLP
Table: Litigation p.1566

Hill Wallack
Table: Real Estate p.1134

Hill & Robbins PC
Table: Litigation p.310

Hill, Ward & Henderson, PA
Tables: Corporate/M&A p.509, Litigation: General Commercial p.520, Real Estate p.526

Hill Rivkins & Hayden LLP
Table: Shipping p.66

Hinckley, Allen & Snyder LLP
Tables: Corporate/M&A p.1107, Employment: p.1565, Litigation: General Commercial p.1111, Real Estate p.1568

Hinkle Hensley Shanor & Martin LLP
Profile: p.1166
Tables: Environment, Natural Resources and Regulated Industries p.1158, Litigation: General Commercial p.1159

Hinkle Elkouri Law Firm LLC
Table: Real Estate p.821

Hirschler Fleischer
Tables: Litigation: General Commercial p.1762, Real Estate p.1765

Hirst & Applegate, PC
Tables: Corporate/M&A p.1832, Employment: p.1833, Litigation: General Commercial p.1834

Hite, Fanning & Honeyman LLP
Table: Litigation p.819

Hodge Dwyer Zeman
Table: Environment p.687

Hodgson Russ LLP
Table: Healthcare p.1209

Hoffman Reilly Pozner & Williamson
Table: Litigation p.310

Hogan Marren
Table: Healthcare p.690

Hogan & Hartson LLP
Profile: p.484
Tables: Antitrust p.366, Arbitration (International) p.32, Aviation p.57, Bankruptcy p.372, Corporate/Commercial p.376, Corporate/M&A p.303, Employee Benefits p.378, Employment: p.305, Energy: Electricity p.385, Energy: Oil & Gas p.382, Environment p.307, Healthcare p.29, Insurance: Insurer Firms p.400, Intellectual Property p.309, Intellectual Property: Northern Virginia p.1758, International Trade p.39, Litigation: General Commercial p.409, Litigation: White-Collar Crime & Government Investigations p.310, Media & Entertainment: Litigation p.229, Media & Entertainment: Transactional p.1234, Products Liability p.48, Projects p.415, Real Estate p.417, Telecom, Broadcast & Satellite: Regulatory p.426

Holland & Hart LLP
Profile: p.325
Tables: Corporate/M&A p.303, Employment: p.305, Environment p.307, Litigation: General Commercial p.310, Real Estate p.1733

Holland & Knight LLP
Profile: p.1352
Tables: Antitrust p.498, Arbitration (International) p.32, Aviation p.57, Banking & Finance p.500, Bankruptcy p.502, Construction p.373, Corporate/M&A p.509, Employment: p.511, Environment p.515, Healthcare p.517, Insurance p.519, Litigation: General Commercial p.520, Litigation: White-Collar Crime & Government Investigations p.522, Media & Entertainment p.413, Media & Entertainment: Transactional p.703, Products Liability p.48, Real Estate p.417, Real Estate: Zoning/Land Use p.528, Shipping p.66, Tax p.530

Holme Roberts & Owen LLP
Profile: p.326
Tables: Corporate/M&A p.303, Employment: p.305, Environment p.307, Litigation: General Commercial p.1731, Real Estate p.313

Honigman Miller Schwartz and Cohn
Tables: Corporate/M&A p.988, Litigation: General Commercial p.993, Real Estate p.996

Hooper Lundy & Bookman Inc
Tables: Healthcare p.29

Hopping Green & Sams, P.A.
Profile: p.565
Tables: Environment p.515, Real Estate: Zoning/Land Use p.528, Tax p.530

Howard, Rice, Nemerovski, Canady, Falk & Rabkin
Table: Bankruptcy p.190

Howrey Simon Arnold & White
Tables: Antitrust p.183, Insurance p.212, Insurance: Policy Holder p.401, Intellectual Property p.215, Litigation: General Commercial p.223

Huddleston Bolen LLP
Tables: Corporate/M&A p.1798, Real Estate p.1805

Hughes Hubbard & Reed LLP
Profile: p.1353
Tables: Arbitration (International) p.32, Corporate/M&A: Mid-Tier Firms p.1195, Products Liability p.48

Hughes, Kellner, Sullivan & Alke
Tables: Employment: p.1073, Litigation: General Commercial p.1074

Hughes & Luce LLP
Tables: Business Process Outsourcing: National p.9, Corporate/M&A p.1631, Intellectual Property p.1650, Technology p.1667

Hughes Thorsness Powell Huddleston & Bauman LLC
Tables: Corporate/M&A p.134, Environment, Natural Resources and Regulated Industries p.136

Hunt, Ortmann, Blasco, Palffy & Rossell Inc
Table: Construction p.194

Hunter, Maclean, Exley & Dunn, PC
Table: Environment p.592

Hunton & Williams LLP
Profile: p.1775
Tables: Antitrust p.498, Banking & Finance p.580, Bankruptcy p.502, Capital Markets: Securitisation p.22, Corporate/M&A p.1383, Employment: p.589, Energy: Electricity p.385, Environment p.391, Intellectual Property p.595, Intellectual Property: Southern Virginia p.1760, Litigation: General Commercial p.520, Projects p.415, Real Estate p.1765, Transport: Road (Carriage/Commercial) p.64

Hurley Toevs Styles Hamblin & Panter PA
Table: Real Estate p.1161

Hurwitz & Sagarin LLC
Table: Litigation p.331

H

Husch & Eppenberger, LLC
Tables: Corporate/M&A p.1042,
Employment: p.1045, Litigation: General
Commercial p.1048

Hyman Phelps & McNamara
Table: Healthcare:
Pharmaceutical/Medical Products
Regulatory p.397

Ice Miller
Profile: p.797
Tables: Corporate/M&A p.781,
Employment: p.783, Litigation: General
Commercial p.785, Real Estate p.788

Imanaka Kudo & Fujimoto
Tables: Land Use p.643, Real Estate
p.646

Irell & Manella LLP
Tables: Corporate/M&A: Southern
California p.196, Intellectual Property
p.215, Litigation: General Commercial
p.223, Media & Entertainment: Litigation
p.229, Media & Entertainment:
Transactional p.233, Tax p.241

**Isaacson, Rosenbaum, Woods
& Levy, PC**
Tables: Litigation: White-Collar Crime &
Government Investigations p.310, Real
Estate p.313

**Iseman Cunningham Riester
& Hyde LLP**
Table: Healthcare p.1209

Ivins, Phillips & Barker
Table: Tax p.422

Jack, Lyon & Jones, PC
Table: Corporate/M&A p.168

Jackson Lewis LLP
Tables: Employment: p.201

Jackson Kelly PLLC
Profile: p.1815
Tables: Corporate/M&A p.1798,
Employment: p.1800, Environment,
Natural Resources and Regulated
Industries p.832, Litigation: General
Commercial p.1803, Real Estate p.1805

Jackson Walker LLP
Table: Real Estate p.1661

**Jacobs, Chase, Frick, Kleinkopf
& Kelley**
Tables: Litigation: General Commercial
p.310, Real Estate p.313

Jacobs, Grudberg, Belt & Dow PC
Table: Litigation p.331

Jaffe, Raitt, Heuer & Weiss, PC
Tables: Corporate/M&A p.988, Real
Estate p.996

Janove Baar Associates
Table: Employment: p.1730

**Jeffcoat Pike & Nappier LLC
(Myrtle Beach)**
Table: Real Estate p.1577

Jenkens & Gilchrist PC
Tables: Construction p.1629,
Employment: p.1633, Healthcare
p.1645, Intellectual Property p.1650,
Real Estate p.1661, Technology p.1667

Jenkins Fenstermaker, PLLC
Tables: Employment: p.1800, Litigation:
General Commercial p.1803

Jenner & Block LLP
Profile: p.768
Tables: Antitrust p.661, Bankruptcy
p.668, Corporate/M&A & Private Equity
p.674, Employment: p.680, Environment
p.687, Government Contracts p.26,
Insurance: Coverage Litigation p.694,
Intellectual Property p.695, Litigation:
Appellate p.407, Litigation: General
Commercial p.699, Media &
Entertainment p.413, Media &
Entertainment: Litigation p.702, Real
Estate p.705, Tax p.709, Telecom,
Broadcast & Satellite: Regulatory p.426

Jennings, Strouss & Salmon, PLC
Table: Corporate/M&A p.146

Jensen Baird Gardner & Henry
Table: Real Estate p.895

**Johnson, Heidepriem, Miner,
Marlow & Janklow, LLP**
Table: Litigation p.1590

**Johnson, Pope, Bokor, Ruppel &
Burns, PA**
Table: Tax p.530

**Johnston Barton Proctor &
Powell LLP**
Tables: Corporate/M&A p.111,
Employment: p.113

Jolley, Urga, Wirth & Woodbury
Table: Litigation p.1096

**Jones, Foster, Johnston &
Stubbs, P.A.**
Table: Litigation p.520

**Jones Walker Waechter
Poitevent Carrère &
Denègre, LLP**
Profile: p.883
Tables: Banking & Finance p.857,
Corporate/M&A p.858, Employment:
p.861, Energy & Natural Resources
p.862, Gaming & Licensing p.864,
Litigation: General Commercial p.865,
Real Estate p.867

Jones Day
Profile: p.485
Tables: Antitrust p.183, Banking &
Finance p.580, Bankruptcy p.668,
Bankruptcy/Restructuring p.1177,
Business Process Outsourcing: National
p.9, Construction p.1629,
Corporate/M&A p.587, Corporate/M&A
& Private Equity p.674, Employment:
p.380, Energy & Natural Resources
p.685, Energy & Natural Resources:
Dispute Resolution p.1639, Energy:
Electricity p.385, Energy: Oil & Gas
p.382, Energy: Transactional p.1202,
Environment p.391, Intellectual Property
p.215, Litigation: Appellate p.407,

Litigation: General Commercial p.223,
Products Liability p.48, Real Estate
p.705, Technology p.1667

Jones Vargas
Tables: Corporate/M&A p.1089,
Litigation: General Commercial p.1096,
Real Estate p.1098

**Jones Waldo Holbrook &
McDonough PC**
Tables: Corporate/M&A p.1727,
Employment: p.1730, Real Estate
p.1733

Jorgenson Moffett LLC
Table: Real Estate p.1836

Kahn Kleinman
Table: Real Estate p.1434

Kamer Zucker & Abbott
Table: Employment: p.1091

Kantrow Spaht Weaver & Blitzer
Table: Corporate/M&A p.858

Kaplan, Strangis & Kaplan
Table: Corporate/M&A p.1005

**Kaplan, Brewer, Maxey &
Haralson**
Tables: Employment: p.169, Litigation:
General Commercial p.172

Karaganis, White & Magel
Table: Environment p.687

Karp & Genauer PA
Table: Tax p.530

Karp, Heurlin & Weiss PC
Table: Litigation: White-Collar Crime &
Government Investigations p.153

**Kasowitz Benson Torres &
Friedman**
Table: Bankruptcy/Restructuring p.1177

Katten Muchin Zavis Rosenman
Profile: p.769
Tables: Antitrust p.661, Banking &
Finance p.665, Corporate/M&A &
Private Equity p.674, Healthcare p.690,
Intellectual Property p.695, Litigation:
General Commercial p.699, Media &
Entertainment: Transactional p.233, Real
Estate p.705, Tax p.709

Katz, Teller, Brant & Hild
Tables: Corporate/M&A p.1419,
Litigation: General Commercial p.1430

Kaufman & Canoles
Tables: Corporate/M&A p.1752,
Employment: p.1755, Intellectual
Property: Southern Virginia p.1760,
Litigation: General Commercial p.1762

Kay Casto & Chaney PLLC
Table: Corporate/M&A p.1798

Kaye Scholer LLP
Profile: p.1354
Tables: Antitrust p.1169, Bankruptcy
p.668, Bankruptcy/Restructuring p.1177,

Corporate/M&A: Mid-Tier Firms p.1195,
Employment: p.1199, Intellectual
Property p.1216, International Trade
p.39, Litigation: General Commercial
p.1221, Media & Entertainment:
Transactional p.233, Products Liability
p.48, Technology & IT Outsourcing
p.1259

**Kean, Miller, Hawthorne,
D'Armond, McCowan &
Jarman, LLP**
Tables: Corporate/M&A p.858,
Employment: p.861, Energy & Natural
Resources p.862, Litigation: General
Commercial p.865

**Keating, Muething &
Klekamp, PLL**
Tables: Bankruptcy p.1413,
Corporate/M&A p.1419, Litigation:
General Commercial p.1430

Keesal Young & Logan pC
Table: Shipping p.71

Kegler, Brown, Hill & Ritter
Tables: Construction p.1417,
Employment: p.1421, Litigation: General
Commercial p.1430

Keker & Van Nest LLP
Profile: p.290
Tables: Intellectual Property p.215,
Litigation: General Commercial p.223

Keleher & McLeod, PA
Tables: Corporate/M&A p.1155,
Employment: p.1157, Litigation: General
Commercial p.1159, Real Estate p.1161

Kelley Drye & Warren
Tables: Real Estate p.1134, Telecom,
Broadcast & Satellite: Regulatory p.426

**Kellogg, Huber, Hansen, Todd &
Evans PLLC**
Table: Telecom, Broadcast & Satellite:
Regulatory p.426

Kelly & Berens P.A.
Table: Litigation p.1010

**Kelly, Hart & Hallman, A
Professional Corporation**
Table: Environment p.1642

Kemp Smith LLP
Table: Employment: p.1633

Kennedy Lillis Schmidt & English
Table: Shipping p.66

**Kenlan, Schwiebert &
Facey, P.C.**
Table: Real Estate p.1747

**Kennedy Covington Lobdell &
Hickman LLP**
Tables: Banking & Finance p.1381,
Bankruptcy p.1383, Environment
p.1387, Litigation: General Commercial
p.1390, Real Estate p.1392

Kenny Nachwalter P.A.
Profile: p.566
Tables: Antitrust p.498, Litigation:
General Commercial p.520

Kenyon & Kenyon
Table: Intellectual Property p.1216

Kenyon & Kenyon
Profile: p.1355

Kerr Russell & Weber
Tables: Litigation: General Commercial p.993, Real Estate p.996

Kienbaum Opperwall Hardy & Pelton P.L.C.
Profile: p.1003
Table: Employment: p.991

Kiesewetter Wise Kaplan Prather, PLC
Profile: p.1617
Table: Employment: p.1596

Kilpatrick Stockton LLP
Profile: p.634
Tables: Antitrust p.578, Banking & Finance p.580, Banking & Finance: Mainly Regulatory p.581, Bankruptcy p.582, Construction p.584, Corporate/M&A p.587, Employee Benefits p.378, Employment: p.589, Environment p.592, Healthcare p.594, Intellectual Property p.595, Litigation: General Commercial p.598, Real Estate p.601, Tax p.603

King Hershey, A Professional Corporation
Profile: p.1063
Table: Real Estate p.1052

King & Ballow
Table: Employment: p.1596

King, Blackwell & Downs PA
Table: Litigation p.520

King & Spalding LLP
Profile: p.635
Tables: Antitrust p.366, Arbitration (International) p.32, Banking & Finance p.580, Bankruptcy p.582, Business Process Outsourcing: National p.9, Construction p.584, Corporate/M&A p.587, Corporate/M&A: Mid-Tier Firms p.1195, Employment: p.589, Energy & Natural Resources p.591, Energy & Natural Resources: Dispute Resolution p.1639, Energy: Transactional p.1202, Environment p.391, Healthcare p.594, Intellectual Property p.595, Litigation: General Commercial p.598, Private Equity: Buyouts & Venture Capital Investment p.1237, Products Liability p.48, Projects p.1659, Real Estate p.601, Tax p.422

Kirk & Chaney
Table: Litigation p.1462

Kirkland & Ellis LLP
Profile: p.770
Tables: Antitrust p.366, Arbitration (International) p.32, Banking & Finance p.665, Bankruptcy p.668, Bankruptcy/Restructuring p.1177, Business Process Outsourcing: National p.9, Capital Markets p.21, Corporate/Commercial p.376, Corporate/M&A p.1187, Corporate/M&A & Private Equity p.674, Employee Benefits & Executive Compensation p.680, Energy: Electricity p.385, Energy: Oil & Gas p.382, Environment p.391, Insurance: Coverage Litigation p.694, Intellectual Property p.215, Litigation: General Commercial p.409, Private Equity: Buyouts & Venture Capital Investment p.1237, Private Equity: Fund

Formation p.1240, Products Liability p.48, Real Estate p.705, Tax p.709, Technology & IT Outsourcing p.712

Kirkpatrick & Lockhart Nicholson Graham LLP
Profile: p.291, 1356
Tables: Corporate/M&A p.1497, Employment: p.1126, Environment p.1129, Intellectual Property p.1508, Investment Management p.405, Litigation: General Commercial p.1511

Kirschner & Legler
Table: Corporate/M&A p.509

Kirshman Harris & Rosenthal
Table: Employment: p.1091

Kirton & McConkie
Profile: p.1741
Table: Real Estate p.1733

Kirwin Norris PA
Table: Construction p.506

Klee, Tuchin, Bogdanoff & Stern LLP
Profile: p.292
Table: Bankruptcy p.190

Klett Rooney Lieber & Schorling
Profile: p.1555
Tables: Banking & Finance p.1492, Bankruptcy/Restructuring p.1494, Employment: p.1500, Environment p.1504, Real Estate p.349

Kluger, Peretz, Kaplan & Berlin P.L.
Profile: p.567
Table: Bankruptcy p.502

Knobbe Martens Olson & Bear
Table: Intellectual Property p.215

Kobayashi, Sugita & Goda
Profile: p.653
Table: Litigation p.644

Kohn Swift & Graf
Table: Antitrust p.1489

Kohn, Shands, Elbert, Gianoulakis & Giljum,LLP
Table: Litigation p.1048

Koley Jessen P.C.
Table: Corporate/M&A p.1082

Kollman & Saucier PA
Table: Employment: p.911

Kozyak Tropin & Throckmorton
Profile: p.568
Tables: Bankruptcy p.502, Litigation: General Commercial p.520

Kraftson Caudle LLC
Table: Construction p.1750

Kramer, Rayson, Leake, Rodgers & Morgan, LLP
Profile: p.1618
Table: Employment: p.1596

Kramer Levin Naftalis & Frankel LLP
Profile: p.1357
Tables: Bankruptcy/Restructuring

p.1177, Corporate/M&A: Mid-Tier Firms p.1195, Litigation: General Commercial p.1221, Real Estate p.1247

Kramon & Graham, PA
Profile: p.927
Table: Litigation p.914

Krasow, Garlick & Hadley LLC
Table: Real Estate p.333

Krieg DeVault LLP
Table: Real Estate p.788

Krovatin & Associates LLC
Table: Litigation: White-Collar Crime & Government Investigations p.1133

Kummer Kaempfer Bonner & Renshaw
Profile: p.1105
Tables: Corporate/M&A p.1089, Litigation: General Commercial p.1096, Real Estate p.1098

Kutak Rock LLP
Tables: Corporate/M&A p.168, Employment: p.818, Litigation: General Commercial p.1085, Real Estate p.174

Lamberth, Cifelli, Stokes & Stout, P.A.
Table: Bankruptcy p.582

Lamson, Dugan & Murray, LLP
Tables: Employment: p.1084, Litigation: General Commercial p.1085

Landers & Parsons
Table: Environment p.515

Landis Rath & Cobb LLP
Table: Bankruptcy/Restructuring p.341

Landye Bennett Blumstein LLP
Profile: p.1488
Tables: Corporate/M&A p.134, Native Law p.140, Real Estate p.1478

Lane & Waterman LLP
Tables: Corporate/M&A p.802, Litigation: General Commercial p.806, Real Estate p.810

Lane Powell PC
Profile: p.1797
Tables: Bankruptcy p.1776, Corporate/M&A p.1471, Employment: p.1780, Intellectual Property p.1784, Litigation: General Commercial p.1785, Real Estate p.1478

Laner, Muchin, Dombrow, Becker, Levin, Tominberg
Table: Employment: p.680

Langrock Sperry & Wool, LLP
Table: Real Estate p.1747

Langsam Stevens & Silver LLP
Table: Environment p.1504

Lanier Ford Shaver & Payne
Table: Litigation p.115

Lankler Siffert & Wohl
Table: Litigation: Specialist Firms in White-Collar Crime & Government Investigations p.1224

Latham & Burwell PLLC
Table: Litigation p.1028

Latham & Watkins LLP
Tables: Antitrust p.183, Banking & Finance p.187, Bankruptcy p.190, Bankruptcy/Restructuring p.1177, Capital Markets p.23, Capital Markets: Debt & Equity p.13, Corporate/Commercial p.376, Corporate/M&A p.1187, Corporate/M&A & Private Equity p.674, Corporate/M&A: Northern California p.196, Employment: p.201, Energy & Natural Resources p.204, Energy: Electricity p.385, Energy: Transactional p.1202, Environment p.206, Healthcare p.29, Insurance p.212, Intellectual Property p.215, IT & IT Outsourcing p.221, Litigation: General Commercial p.223, Litigation: Securities p.1223, Private Equity: Buyouts & Venture Capital Investment p.1237, Private Equity: Fund Formation p.1240, Products Liability p.48, Projects p.52, Tax p.241, Technology & IT Outsourcing p.712, Telecom, Broadcast & Satellite: Regulatory p.426

Lathrop & Rutledge
Table: Litigation p.1834

Lathrop & Gage L.C.
Profile: p.1064
Tables: Corporate/M&A p.816, Employment: p.1045, Litigation: General Commercial p.819, Real Estate p.821

Lau, Lane, Pieper, Conley & McCreadie
Table: Shipping p.71

Lavely & Singer PC
Table: Media & Entertainment: Litigation p.229

Lawler, Metzger, Milkman & Keeney, LLC
Table: Telecom, Broadcast & Satellite: Regulatory p.426

Laxalt & Nomura
Table: Litigation p.1096

Leatherwood Walker Todd & Mann PC
Tables: Corporate/M&A p.1572, Litigation: General Commercial p.1575, Real Estate p.1577

LeBoeuf, Lamb, Greene & MacRae, LLP
Profile: p.1358
Tables: Employment: p.329, Energy & Natural Resources: Dispute Resolution p.1639, Energy: Electricity p.385, Energy: Oil & Gas p.382, Energy: Regulatory p.1202, Energy: Upstate New York p.1204, Insurance: Dispute Resolution p.1212, Real Estate p.526

LeClair Ryan, A Professional Corporation
Tables: Corporate/M&A p.1752, Employment: p.1755, Environment p.1757, Intellectual Property: Southern Virginia p.1760

Lehr Middlebrooks Price & Vreeland, P.C.
Table: Employment: p.113

Leiby Stearns Linkhorst & Roberts, PA
Profile: p.569
Table: Construction p.506

Leitman, Siegal & Payne, PC
Table: Real Estate p.119

Lenrow, Kohn & Oliver
Table: Real Estate p.916

Leonard, Street and Deinard Professional Association
Tables: Corporate/M&A p.1005, Employment: p.1008, Litigation: General Commercial p.1010, Real Estate p.1014

LePatner & Associates LLP
Profile: p.1359
Table: Construction p.1186

Lerach Coughlin Stoia Geller Rudman & Robbins LLP
Table: Litigation p.223

Leventhal & Slaughter PA
Table: Litigation: White-Collar Crime & Government Investigations p.522

Leventhal Senter & Lerman PLLC
Table: Telecom, Broadcast & Satellite: Regulatory p.426

Levine, Blaszak, Block & Boothby LLP
Profile: p.488
Table: Telecom, Broadcast & Satellite: Regulatory p.426

Levine Sullivan Koch & Schulz LLP
Tables: Media & Entertainment p.413, Media & Entertainment: Litigation p.1232

Levy, Ram & Olson
Table: Media & Entertainment: Litigation p.229

Lewis & Slovak PC
Table: Litigation p.1074

Lewis Fisher Henderson Claxton & Mulroy
Table: Employment: p.1596

Lewis, Longman & Walker PA
Table: Environment p.515

Lewis, Rice & Fingersh, L.C.
Profile: p.1065
Tables: Corporate/M&A p.1042, Litigation: General Commercial p.1048, Real Estate p.1052

Lewis and Roca
Tables: Corporate/M&A p.146, Employment: p.148, Environment (including water rights) p.150, Litigation: General Commercial p.151, Litigation: White-Collar Crime & Government Investigations p.153, Real Estate: Zoning/Land Use p.155

Leydig, Voit & Mayer, Ltd
Table: Intellectual Property p.695

Lichter Grossman Nicholas Adler & Goodman
Table: Media & Entertainment: Transactional p.233

Liebert Cassidy Whitmore
Table: Employment: p.201

Liebmann, Conway, Olejniczak & Jerry, S.C.
Profile: p.1829
Table: Litigation p.1820

Lightfoot, Franklin & White, LLC
Table: Litigation p.115

Lindner & Marsack, S.C.
Table: Employment: p.1819

Lindquist & Vennum PLLP
Profile: p.1023
Tables: Corporate/M&A p.1005, Litigation: General Commercial p.1010, Real Estate p.1014

Linowes and Blocher LLP
Table: Real Estate p.916

Lionel Sawyer & Collins
Tables: Corporate/M&A p.1089, Employment: p.1091, Environment p.1093, Gaming & Licensing p.1094, Litigation: General Commercial p.1096, Real Estate p.1098

Liskow & Lewis PLC
Tables: Banking & Finance p.857, Corporate/M&A p.858, Energy & Natural Resources p.862, Gaming & Licensing p.864, Litigation: General Commercial p.865, Real Estate p.867

Lisman, Webster, Kirkpatrick & Leckerling, P.C.
Table: Real Estate p.1747

Little, Medeiros, Kinder, Bulman & Whitney PC
Table: Employment: p.1565

Littler Mendelson PC
Tables: Employment: p.201

Lloyd, Gosselink, Blevins, Rochelle, Baldwin & Townsend, PC
Table: Environment p.1642

Locke Liddell & Sapp LLP
Table: Environment p.1642

Locke Liddell & Sapp LLP
Tables: Employment: p.1633, Energy & Natural Resources p.1637, Intellectual Property p.1650, Litigation: General Commercial p.1655, Real Estate p.1661, Tax p.1665, Technology p.1667

Locke Reynolds LLP
Table: Litigation p.785

Loeb & Loeb LLP
Tables: Media & Entertainment p.1602, Media & Entertainment: Litigation p.229, Media & Entertainment: Transactional p.233, Tax p.241

Lommen, Nelson, Cole & Stageberg, P.A.
Tables: Corporate/M&A p.1005

Lord, Bissell & Brook
Tables: Insurance: Coverage Litigation p.694, Insurance: Reinsurance Litigation p.693, Insurance: Transactional & Regulatory p.692

Lottner Rubin Fishman Brown & Saul, PC
Table: Real Estate p.313

Lovells
Table: Insurance: Reinsurance Litigation p.693

Lowenstein Sandler PC
Profile: p.1150
Tables: Corporate/M&A p.1123, Employment: p.1126, Environment p.1129, Litigation: General Commercial p.1131, Real Estate p.1134

Lowndes Drosdick Doster Kantor & Reed, PA
Tables: Real Estate p.526, Real Estate: Zoning/Land Use p.528

Lueders, Robertson & Konzen
Table: Energy & Natural Resources p.685

Lum, Danzis, Drasco & Positan, LLC
Profile: p.1151
Table: Employment: p.1126

Luskin, Stern & Eisler LLP
Table: Bankruptcy/Restructuring p.1177

Lynn, Jackson, Shultz & Lebrun PC
Table: Litigation p.1590

M

MacPherson Kelly & Thompson
Table: Real Estate p.1836

Maddin, Hauser, Wartell, Roth & Heller PC
Tables: Real Estate p.996

Madison Harbour Mroz & Brennan PA
Table: Litigation p.1159

Manatt Phelps & Phillips LLP
Tables: Banking & Finance p.187, Healthcare p.209, Media & Entertainment: Transactional p.233

Mancini Welch & Geiger LLP
Table: Real Estate p.646

Manko, Gold, Katcher & Fox LLP
Table: Environment p.1504

Manning Curtis Bradshaw & Bednar
Table: Employment: p.1730

Manning Fulton & Skinner PA
Table: Real Estate p.1392

Maring Williams Law Office PC
Table: Litigation p.1406

Mariscal, Weeks, McIntyre & Friedlander PA
Tables: Litigation: General Commercial p.151, Real Estate p.153

Markowitz, Herbold, Glade & Mehlhaf PC
Table: Litigation p.1475

Marr Hipp Jones & Wang
Table: Employment: p.642

Marshall, Gerstein & Borun
Table: Intellectual Property p.695

Marshall Hill Cassas & De Lipkau
Table: Environment p.1093

Martin & Churchill Chartered
Table: Employment: p.818

Martin, Disiere, Jefferson & Wisdom LLP
Profile: p.1720
Table: Insurance p.1647

Martin, Pringle, Oliver, Wallace & Bauer, L.L.P.
Table: Employment: p.818

Maslon Edelman Borman & Brand, LLP
Table: Litigation p.1010

Mason & Mason PC
Table: Litigation p.1834

Matkov Salzman Madoff & Gunn
Table: Employment: p.680

Maupin Taylor, P.A.
Tables: Employment: p.1385, Environment p.1387, Real Estate p.1392

May, Adam, Gerdes & Thompson, L.L.P.
Table: Litigation p.1590

Mayer, Brown, Rowe & Maw LLP
Profile: p.771
Tables: Antitrust p.366, Arbitration (International) p.32, Banking & Finance p.665, Bankruptcy p.668, Business Process Outsourcing: National p.9, Capital Markets p.21, Capital Markets: Derivatives p.16, Capital Markets: Securitisation p.18, Corporate/M&A p.1187, Corporate/M&A & Private Equity p.674, Employee Benefits & Executive Compensation p.680, Energy & Natural Resources p.685, Environment p.687, Government Contracts p.26, Insurance: Coverage Litigation p.694, Intellectual Property p.403, International Trade p.39, IT & IT Outsourcing p.430, Litigation: Appellate p.407, Litigation: General Commercial p.699, Private Equity: Fund Formation p.1240, Products Liability p.48, Projects p.415, Real Estate p.237, Tax p.709, Technology & IT Outsourcing p.712, Telecom, Broadcast & Satellite: Regulatory p.715, Transport: Rail p.62, Transport: Road (Carriage/Commercial) p.64

Maynard, Cooper & Gale PC
Tables: Corporate/M&A p.111,
Employment: p.113, Litigation: General
Commercial p.115, Real Estate p.119

Mazur, Carp & Rubin PC
Tables: Construction p.1186

**McAfee & Taft A Professional
Corporation**
Profile: p.1470
Tables: Corporate/M&A p.1459,
Employment: p.1460, Litigation: General
Commercial p.1462, Real Estate p.1463

McAndrews, Held & Malloy, Ltd
Profile: p.772
Table: Intellectual Property p.695

McCarter & English, LLP
Profile: p.1152
Tables: Corporate/M&A p.1123,
Employment: p.329, Litigation: General
Commercial p.331, Real Estate p.1134

McConn & Rindy
Table: Real Estate p.1409

**McCorriston Miller Mukai
MacKinnon LLP**
Profile: p.654
Tables: Litigation: General Commercial
p.644, Real Estate p.646

**McCullough Hill Fikso
Kretschmer Smith**
Table: Real Estate p.1788

McDade Fogler LLP
Tables: Energy & Natural Resources:
Dispute Resolution p.1639, Litigation:
General Commercial p.1655

McDermott Will & Emery
Profile: p.773
Tables: Antitrust p.366, Banking &
Finance p.187, Corporate/M&A p.937,
Corporate/M&A & Private Equity p.674,
Corporate/M&A: Mid-Tier Firms p.1195,
Employee Benefits & Executive
Compensation p.680, Energy: Electricity
p.385, Environment p.943, Healthcare
p.29, Intellectual Property p.215,
International Trade p.39, Litigation:
ERISA p.25, Litigation: General
Commercial p.699, Private Equity:
Buyouts & Venture Capital Investment
p.952, Tax p.241

McDonald Hopkins Co
Tables: Banking & Finance p.1411,
Bankruptcy p.1413

**McDonald Carano Wilson
McCune Bergin Frankovich &
Hicks LLP**
Tables: Environment p.1093, Gaming &
Licensing p.1094, Litigation: General
Commercial p.1096, Real Estate p.1098

**McDonnell Boehnen Hulbert &
Berghoff LLP**
Profile: p.774
Table: Intellectual Property p.695

**McDowell Knight Roedder &
Sledge LLC**
Table: Litigation p.115

**McElroy, Deutsch, Mulvaney &
Carpenter, LLP**
Tables: Employment: p.1126, Litigation:
General Commercial p.1131

McEwen Gisvold LLP
Table: Real Estate p.1478

**McGee Hankla Backes &
Dobrovolny P.C.**
Table: Litigation p.1406

McGlinchey Stafford
Profile: p.885
Tables: Banking & Finance p.857,
Corporate/M&A p.858, Employment:
p.861, Gaming & Licensing p.864,
Litigation: General Commercial p.865

**McGrath North Mullin &
Kratz PC**
Tables: Corporate/M&A p.1082,
Employment: p.1084, Litigation: General
Commercial p.1085, Real Estate p.1086

McGuireWoods LLP
Tables: Corporate/M&A p.1752,
Employee Benefits & Executive
Compensation p.680, Environment
p.1757, Healthcare p.690, Intellectual
Property: Southern Virginia p.1760,
Litigation: General Commercial p.1762,
Real Estate p.916, Transport: Road
(Carriage/Commercial) p.64

McKee Nelson LLP
Profile: p.489
Tables: Capital Markets: Securitisation
p.18, Tax p.422

McKenna Long & Aldridge LLP
Profile: p.636
Tables: Bankruptcy p.582, Construction
p.194, Corporate/M&A p.587, Energy &
Natural Resources p.591, Environment
p.391, Government Contracts p.26, Real
Estate p.601

McKinney & Stringer, PC
Tables: Employment: p.1460, Litigation:
General Commercial p.1462

McKool Smith
Table: Intellectual Property p.1650

**McLane, Graf, Raulerson &
Middleton Professional
Association**
Profile: p.1121
Tables: Corporate/M&A p.1107,
Employment: p.1109, Litigation: General
Commercial p.1111, Real Estate p.1114

McLaughlin & McCaffrey, LLP
Table: Litigation p.1430

**McMahon Berger Hanna Linihan
Cody & McCarthy, A Professional
Corporation**
Profile: p.1066
Table: Employment: p.1045

**McMahon, DeGulis, Hoffmann &
Lombardi LLP**
Table: Environment p.1424

**McManus Schor Asmar &
Darden, L.L.P.**
Table: Construction p.373

McNair, Larson & Carlson Ltd
Tables: Corporate/M&A p.1403,
Litigation: General Commercial p.1406

McNair Law Firm PA
Tables: Corporate/M&A p.1572,
Litigation: General Commercial p.1575,
Real Estate p.1577

**McNaul Ebel Nawrot Helgren
& Vance PLLC**
Table: Litigation p.1785

McTurnan & Turner
Profile: p.798
Table: Litigation p.785

**Meadows, Owens, Collier, Reed,
Cousins & Blau**
Table: Tax p.1665

Meardon, Sueppel & Downer
Table: Real Estate p.810

Meckler, Bulger & Tilson
Table: Employment: p.680

**Meland Russin Hellinger &
Budwick**
Table: Bankruptcy p.502

Melli Walker Pease & Ruhly S.C.
Table: Employment: p.1819

Mendes & Mount LLP
Table: Insurance: Dispute Resolution
p.1212

Meuleman Miller LLP
Table: Real Estate p.658

Meyer Capel, PC
Table: Telecom, Broadcast & Satellite:
Regulatory p.715

Meyer, Hendricks & Bivens PA
Table: Litigation p.151

Michael Critchley & Associates
Table: Litigation p.1133

Michael Best & Friedrich LLP
Profile: p.1830
Tables: Corporate/M&A p.1817,
Employment: p.1819, Litigation: General
Commercial p.1820, Real Estate p.1822

Middleton Reutlinger PSC
Profile: p.851
Tables: Environment, Natural Resources
and Regulated Industries p.832,
Litigation: General Commercial p.834

**Milbank, Tweed, Hadley &
McCloy**
Tables: Banking & Finance p.187,
Bankruptcy p.190,
Bankruptcy/Restructuring p.1177,
Capital Markets p.23, Energy & Natural
Resources p.204, Energy: Transactional
p.1202, Projects p.52, Tax p.1254,
Technology & IT Outsourcing p.1259,
Transport: Road (Carriage/Commercial)
p.64

Miles & Stockbridge PC
Profile: p.928
Tables: Corporate/M&A p.909,
Employment: p.911, Litigation: General
Commercial p.914, Real Estate p.916

Miller & Martin PLLC
Profile: p.1619
Tables: Employment: p.1596, Litigation:
General Commercial p.1598

**Miller Hamilton Snider &
Odom LLC**
Table: Banking & Finance: Mainly
Regulatory p.581

**Miller, Canfield, Paddock and
Stone, P.L.C.**
Profile: p.1004
Tables: Aviation p.57, Banking & Finance
p.987, Corporate/M&A p.988,
Employment: p.991, Litigation: General
Commercial p.993, Real Estate p.996,
Sports Law p.55

Eggleston & Cramer, Ltd
Tables: Corporate/M&A p.1743,
Litigation: General Commercial p.1745,
Real Estate p.1747

**Miller, Johnson, Snell &
Cummiskey, P.L.C.**
Tables: Corporate/M&A p.988,
Employment: p.991, Litigation: General
Commercial p.993

Miller, Morton, Caillat & Nevis
Table: Construction p.194

Miller Stratvert PA
Table: Litigation p.1159

Miller, Balis & O'Neil, PC
Table: Energy: Electricity p.385

Miller & Chevalier Chartered
Tables: Government Contracts p.26,
International Trade p.39, Tax p.422

Miller Nash LLP
Tables: Corporate/M&A p.1471,
Employment: p.1473, Litigation: General
Commercial p.1475, Real Estate p.1478

Millisor & Nobil Co LPA
Table: Employment: p.1421

**Mintz Levin Cohn Ferris Glovsky
and Popeo PC**
Tables: Bankruptcy p.934,
Corporate/M&A p.937, Employment:
p.939, Environment p.943, Litigation:
General Commercial p.950, Telecom,
Broadcast & Satellite: Regulatory p.426

**Mitchell, Williams, Selig, Gates
Woodyard, PLLC**
Profile: p.180
Tables: Corporate/M&A p.168,
Employment: p.169, Litigation: General
Commercial p.172, Real Estate p.174

Mitchell, McNutt & Sams PA
Table: Litigation p.1028

Mitchell, Silberberg & Knupp LLP
Table: Media & Entertainment: Litigation
p.229

**Mock, Schwabe, Waldo, Elder,
Reeves & Bryant**
Table: Real Estate p.1463

**Modrall, Sperling, Roehl, Harris
& Sisk, PA**
Tables: Corporate/M&A p.1155,
Environment, Natural Resources and

M

Regulated Industries p.1158, Litigation: General Commercial p.1159, Real Estate p.1161

Moehrke, Mackie & Shea, P.C.
Table: Environment p.943

Moffatt Thomas Barrett Rock & Fields
Tables: Employment: p.656, Litigation: General Commercial p.657, Real Estate p.658

Monteleone & McCrory, LLP
Table: Construction p.194

Montgomery & Andrews, PA
Profile: p.1167
Table: Environment, Natural Resources and Regulated Industries p.1158

Montgomery, McCracken, Walker & Rhoads, LLP
Tables: Antitrust p.1489, Environment p.1504, Litigation: General Commercial p.1511

Moody & Warner PC
Table: Employment: p.1157

Moon, Moss & Shapiro, P.A.
Profile: p.905
Table: Employment: p.890

Moore & Lee LLP
Table: Construction p.1750

Moore & Van Allen PLLC
Tables: Banking & Finance p.1381, Bankruptcy p.1383, Litigation: General Commercial p.1390, Real Estate p.1392

Moore, O'Connell & Refling PC
Table: Real Estate p.1078

Morgan & Finnegan, LLP
Profile: p.1360
Table: Intellectual Property p.1216

Morgan, Brown and Joy LLP
Profile: p.983

Morgan, Lewis & Bockius LLP
Profile: p.1556
Tables: Antitrust p.366, Arbitration (International) p.32, Banking & Finance p.1492, Bankruptcy/Restructuring p.1177, Corporate/M&A p.1123, Corporate/M&A: Mid-Tier Firms p.1195, Corporate/M&A: Northern California p.196, Employment: p.201, Energy: Electricity p.385, Energy: Nuclear p.389, Energy: Oil & Gas p.382, Environment p.206, Insurance p.212, Insurance: Coverage Litigation p.694, Investment Management p.405, Litigation: ERISA p.25, Litigation: General Commercial p.1511, Media & Entertainment: Transactional p.1234, Private Equity: Buyouts & Venture Capital Investment p.1237, Projects p.235, Real Estate p.1515, Tax p.422, Technology & IT Outsourcing p.1259

Morris & Morris PC
Table: Litigation p.1762

Morris, James, Hitchens & Williams LLP
Tables: Bankruptcy/Restructuring p.341, Chancery p.344, Corporate/M&A p.346, Real Estate p.349

Morris, Laing, Evans, Brock & Kennedy, Chartered
Tables: Employment: p.818, Real Estate p.821

Morris, Manning & Martin, LLP
Profile: p.637
Tables: Environment p.592, Litigation: General Commercial p.598, Real Estate p.601, Tax p.603

Morris, Nichols, Arsht & Tunnell
Profile: p.364
Tables: Bankruptcy/Restructuring p.341, Chancery p.344, Corporate/M&A p.346, Intellectual Property p.348, Real Estate p.349

Morrison & Foerster LLP
Profile: p.293
Tables: Antitrust p.183, Banking & Finance p.187, Corporate/M&A: Northern California p.196, Employment: p.201, Energy & Natural Resources p.204, Environment p.206, Intellectual Property p.215, Intellectual Property: Northern Virginia p.1758, Investment Management p.405, IT & IT Outsourcing p.221, Litigation: General Commercial p.223, Litigation: Securities p.1223, Real Estate p.237, Tax p.241, Technology & IT Outsourcing p.1259, Telecom, Broadcast & Satellite: Regulatory p.426

Morris Pickering & Sanner
Table: Litigation p.1096

Morse, Barnes-Brown & Pendleton PC
Table: Private Equity: Buyouts & Venture Capital Investment p.952

Morvillo, Abramowitz, Grand, Iason & Silberberg, PC
Table: Litigation: Specialist Firms in White-Collar Crime & Government Investigations p.1224

Moscowitz, Moscowitz & Magolnick PA
Table: Litigation: White-Collar Crime & Government Investigations p.522

Moseley Warren Prichard & Parish
Table: Shipping p.71

Moulton, Bellingham, Longo & Mather, PC
Table: Real Estate p.1078

Mound Cotton Wollan & Greengrass
Tables: Insurance: Dispute Resolution p.1212

Moye, O'Brien, O'Rourke, Pickert & Martin, LLP
Profile: p.570
Table: Construction p.506

Moyer & Bergman, PLC
Table: Real Estate p.810

Moyes Storey
Table: Environment (including water rights) p.150

Much Shelist Freed Denenberg Ament & Rubenstein, P.C.
Tables: Antitrust p.661, Construction p.672

Mullikin, Larson & Swift
Table: Real Estate p.1836

Munger, Tolles & Olson LLP
Tables: Antitrust p.183, Corporate/M&A: Southern California p.196, Employment: p.201, Energy & Natural Resources p.204, Litigation: General Commercial p.223, Media & Entertainment: Litigation p.229, Real Estate p.237, Tax p.241

Munsch Hardt Kopf & Harr, P. C.
Table: Bankruptcy p.1626

Murane & Bostwick LLC
Table: Employment: p.1833

Murphy Sullivan Kronk
Table: Real Estate p.1747

Murphy & Shaffer
Table: Litigation p.914

Murphy, Goldammer & Prendergast
Table: Corporate/M&A p.1587

Murtha Cullina LLP
Tables: Corporate/M&A p.327, Employment: p.329, Litigation: General Commercial p.331

Myers Oliver & Price
Table: Real Estate p.1161

Nagin Gallop Figueredo PA
Table: Antitrust p.498

Neal & Harwell, PLC
Table: Litigation p.1598

Neal, Gerber & Eisenberg LLP
Tables: Banking & Finance p.665, Employment: p.680, Real Estate p.705

Needle & Rosenberg, P.C
Table: Intellectual Property p.595

Neel & Hooper, P.C.
Profile: p.1721
Table: Employment: p.1633

Neligan Tarpley Andrews & Foley LLP
Table: Bankruptcy p.1626

Nelson Kinder Mosseau & Saturley PC
Table: Litigation p.1111

Nelson Mullins Riley & Scarborough LLP
Profile: p.1584
Tables: Corporate/M&A p.1572, Employment: p.1574, Litigation: General Commercial p.1575, Products Liability p.48, Real Estate p.1577

Neubert, Pepe & Monteith PC
Table: Real Estate p.333

Nexsen Pruet, LLC
Profile: p.1585
Tables: Corporate/M&A p.1572, Employment: p.1574, Litigation: General Commercial p.1575, Real Estate p.1577

Nichols, Wolfe, Stamper, Nally, Fallis & Robertson Inc
Table: Employment: p.1460

Nickens Keeton Lawless Farrell & Flack LLP
Table: Insurance p.1647

Nicoletti Hornig Campise and Sweeney
Table: Shipping p.66

Nilles, Hansen & Davies Ltd
Tables: Corporate/M&A p.1403, Litigation: General Commercial p.1406, Real Estate p.1409

Niro, Scavone, Haller & Niro
Table: Intellectual Property p.695

Nixon & Vanderhye P.C.
Table: Intellectual Property: Northern Virginia p.1758

Nixon Peabody LLP
Profile: p.1361
Tables: Bankruptcy p.934, Corporate/M&A p.1107, Employment: p.1199, Energy: Upstate New York p.1204, Environment p.1205, Healthcare p.1209, Litigation: ERISA p.25, Litigation: General Commercial p.1111, Real Estate p.417

Norman, Hanson & DeTroy, LLC
Table: Litigation p.893

Norris, McLaughlin & Marcus, P.A., A Professional Corporation
Table: Corporate/M&A p.1123

Nourse & Bowles LLP
Table: Shipping p.66

Nungesser & Hill
Table: Real Estate p.1114

Nutter, McClennen & Fish, LLP
Tables: Antitrust p.930, Banking & Finance p.932, Environment p.943, Real Estate p.956

Nyemaster, Goode, West, Hansell, and O'Brien
Tables: Corporate/M&A p.802, Employment: p.804, Litigation: General Commercial p.806, Real Estate p.810

Ober Kaler Grimes & Shriver
Tables: Corporate/M&A p.909, Employment: p.911, Healthcare p.29

Oblon, Spivak, McClelland, Maier & Neustadt PC
Table: Intellectual Property: Northern Virginia p.1758

Oertel, Fernandez, Cole & Bryant, P.A.
Table: Environment p.515

Ogden Newell & Welch PLLC
Profile: p.852
Tables: Corporate/M&A p.827, Employment: p.830, Environment, Natural Resources and Regulated

Industries p.832, Litigation: General Commercial p.834

Ogletree, Deakins, Nash, Smoak & Stewart, PC
Profile: p.638
Tables: Construction p.672, Employment: p.113, Litigation: General Commercial p.1575

Ohnstad Twichell PC
Table: Real Estate p.1409

Oliff & Berridge PLC
Table: Intellectual Property: Northern Virginia p.1758

Olson Burns Lee PC
Table: Corporate/M&A p.1403

O'Melveny & Myers LLP
Profile: p.294
Tables: Antitrust p.183, Arbitration (International) p.32, Banking & Finance p.187, Bankruptcy p.190, Corporate/M&A: Mid-Tier Firms p.1195, Corporate/M&A: Northern California p.196, Employee Benefits p.378, Employment: p.201, Insurance p.212, Intellectual Property p.215, International Trade p.39, Litigation: ERISA p.25, Litigation: General Commercial p.223, Media & Entertainment: Litigation p.229, Media & Entertainment: Transactional p.233, Products Liability p.48, Tax p.241

Oppenheimer Wolff & Donnelly LLP
Tables: Corporate/M&A p.1005, Litigation: General Commercial p.1010, Real Estate p.1014

Orloff, Lowenbach, Stifelman & Siegel
Tables: Corporate/M&A p.1123, Litigation: General Commercial p.1131

Orr & Reno PA
Tables: Employment: p.1109, Litigation: General Commercial p.1111

Orrick, Herrington & Sutcliffe LLP
Profile: p.295
Tables: Antitrust p.183, Banking & Finance p.187, Bankruptcy p.190, Corporate/M&A p.1777, Employment: p.201, Energy & Natural Resources p.204, Intellectual Property p.215, Private Equity: Fund Formation p.1240, Products Liability p.48, Projects p.235, Real Estate p.237, Tax p.241, Transport: Road (Carriage/Commercial) p.64

Osborn Maledon PA
Profile: p.165
Tables: Corporate/M&A p.146, Litigation: General Commercial p.151, Litigation: White-Collar Crime & Government Investigations p.153

Oshima, Chun, Fong & Chung
Table: Real Estate p.646

Otten, Johnson, Robinson, Neff & Ragonetti, PC
Table: Real Estate p.313

Otterbourg, Steindler, Houston & Rosen
Table: Bankruptcy/Restructuring p.1177

P

Pachulski, Stang, Ziehl, Young, Jones & Weintraub P.C.
Profile: p.296
Tables: Bankruptcy p.190, Bankruptcy/Restructuring p.341

Packman, Neuwahl & Rosenberg
Table: Tax p.530

Palmer & Dodge LLP
Profile: p.984
Tables: Antitrust p.930, Banking & Finance p.932, Real Estate p.956

Pansing Hogan Ernst & Bachman LLP
Table: Real Estate p.1086

Pappas Metcalf Jenks and Miller
Table: Real Estate: Zoning/Land Use p.528

Parker, Poe, Adams & Bernstein LLP
Tables: Employment: p.1385, Environment p.1387, Litigation: General Commercial p.1390, Real Estate p.1392

Parker, Hudson, Rainer & Dobbs LLP
Tables: Banking & Finance p.580, Bankruptcy p.582, Corporate/M&A p.587, Healthcare p.594

Parr Waddoups Brown Gee & Loveless
Tables: Corporate/M&A p.1727, Litigation: General Commercial p.1731, Real Estate p.1733

Parsons Behle & Latimer PC
Profile: p.1742
Tables: Corporate/M&A p.1727, Employment: p.1730, Litigation: General Commercial p.1731, Real Estate p.1733

Partridge Snow & Hahn LLP
Tables: Corporate/M&A p.1564, Employment: p.1565, Litigation: General Commercial p.1566

Patterson, Belknap, Webb & Tyler LLP
Table: Intellectual Property p.1216

Pattishall, McAuliffe, Newbury, Hilliard & Geraldson
Table: Intellectual Property p.695

Patton Boggs LLP
Tables: Environment, Natural Resources and Regulated Industries p.136, Litigation: General Commercial p.138

Paul, Frank + Collins, A Professional Corporation
Tables: Corporate/M&A p.1743, Employment: p.1744, Litigation: General Commercial p.1745, Real Estate p.1747

Paul, Johnson, Park & Niles, Attorneys At Law, A Law Corporation
Table: Litigation p.644

Paul, Hastings, Janofsky & Walker LLP
Profile: p.297
Tables: Antitrust p.578, Banking & Finance p.187, Bankruptcy p.190, Corporate/M&A p.587, Corporate/M&A: Southern California p.196, Employment: p.201, Healthcare p.209, Intellectual Property p.215, International Trade p.39, Litigation: General Commercial p.598, Real Estate p.237, Tax p.241

Paul, Weiss, Rifkind, Wharton & Garrison LLP
Profile: p.1362
Tables: Antitrust p.366, Bankruptcy/Restructuring p.1177, Corporate/M&A p.1187, Employee Benefits & Executive Compensation p.1197, Litigation: General Commercial p.1221, Litigation: Securities p.1223, Litigation: White-Collar Crime & Government Investigations p.1224, Media & Entertainment: Litigation p.1232, Media & Entertainment: Transactional p.1234, Real Estate p.1247, Tax p.1254, Telecom, Broadcast & Satellite: Regulatory p.426

Pearce & Durick
Table: Litigation p.1406

Pearson Christensen LLP
Tables: Corporate/M&A p.1403, Litigation: General Commercial p.1406

Peckar & Abramson PC
Profile: p.1363
Tables: Construction p.506

Peitzman, Glassman, Weg & Kempinski
Table: Bankruptcy p.190

Pennington, Moore, Wilkinson, Bell & Dunbar, PA
Table: Insurance p.519

Pepper Hamilton LLP
Profile: p.1558
Tables: Antitrust p.1489, Bankruptcy/Restructuring p.341, Corporate/M&A p.1497, Litigation: General Commercial p.1511

Perkins, Thompson, Hinckley & Keddy, P.A.
Table: Real Estate p.895

Perkins Coie LLP
Tables: Aviation p.57, Corporate/M&A p.146, Employment: p.135, Environment p.1782, Environment, Natural Resources and Regulated Industries p.136, Intellectual Property p.1784, Litigation: General Commercial p.151, Real Estate p.153

Pettiette, Armand, Dunkelman, Woodley, Byrd & Cromwell LLP
Table: Banking p.857

Phelps Dunbar LLP
Profile: p.886
Tables: Banking & Finance p.857, Corporate/M&A p.858, Employment:

p.861, Energy & Natural Resources p.862, Litigation: General Commercial p.865, Real Estate p.867, Shipping p.71

Phibbs Law Office PC
Table: Real Estate p.1836

Phillips McFall McCaffrey McVay & Murrah, P.C.
Table: Real Estate p.1463

Piccarreta & Davis PC
Table: Litigation p.153

Pierce Atwood LLP
Profile: p.906
Tables: Corporate/M&A p.888, Employment: p.890, Environment p.892, Litigation: General Commercial p.893, Real Estate p.895

Pill & Pill
Table: Real Estate p.1805

Pillsbury Winthrop LLP
Profile: p.1364
Tables: Aviation p.57, Banking & Finance p.187, Corporate/M&A: Northern California p.196, Employee Benefits & Executive Compensation p.1197, Employment: p.1755, Energy & Natural Resources p.204, Energy: Regulatory p.1202, Environment p.206, Intellectual Property: Northern Virginia p.1758, Real Estate p.237

Pircher, Nichols & Meeks
Table: Real Estate p.237

Pitney Hardin LLP
Profile: p.1153
Tables: Corporate/M&A p.1123, Employment: p.1126, Litigation: General Commercial p.1131, Real Estate p.1134

Podhurst Orseck, P.A.
Tables: Litigation: General Commercial p.520, Litigation: White-Collar Crime & Government Investigations p.522

Polsinelli Shalton Welte Suelthaus (PSWS)
Tables: Corporate/M&A p.816, Litigation: General Commercial p.1048, Real Estate p.821

Poore, Roth & Robinson, P.C.
Table: Litigation p.1074

Porter & Hedges, LLP
Table: Construction p.1629

Porter Wright Morris & Arthur LLP
Profile: p.1455
Tables: Banking & Finance p.1411, Bankruptcy p.1413, Employment: p.1421, Environment p.1424, Litigation: General Commercial p.1430, Real Estate p.1434

Porzio, Bromberg & Newman, A Professional Corporation
Table: Environment p.1129

Postner & Rubin
Table: Construction p.1186

P

Potter Anderson & Corroon LLP
Tables: Bankruptcy/Restructuring p.341, Chancery p.344, Corporate/M&A p.346, Employment: p.347, Intellectual Property p.348

Powell Goldstein LLP
Tables: Antitrust p.578, Banking & Finance p.580, Banking & Finance: Mainly Regulatory p.581, Bankruptcy p.582, Corporate/M&A p.587, Litigation: General Commercial p.598, Real Estate p.601

Poyner & Spruill LLP
Table: Environment p.1387

Pratt-Thomas Epting and Walker Law Firm
Table: Litigation p.1575

Preston Gates & Ellis LLP
Tables: Bankruptcy p.1776, Corporate/M&A p.1471, Employment: p.135, Intellectual Property p.1784, Litigation: General Commercial p.1785, Real Estate p.140, Telecom, Broadcast & Satellite: Regulatory p.426

Preti Flaherty Beliveau Pachios & Haley LLC
Profile: p.907
Tables: Corporate/M&A p.888, Employment: p.890, Environment p.892, Litigation: General Commercial p.893, Real Estate p.895

Prickett, Jones & Elliott PA
Table: Corporate/M&A p.346

Primmer & Piper, Professional Corporation
Table: Corporate/M&A p.1743

Proskauer Rose LLP
Profile: p.1365
Tables: Bankruptcy/Restructuring p.1177, Corporate/M&A: Mid-Tier Firms p.1195, Employee Benefits & Executive Compensation p.1197, Employment: p.1126, Environment p.1205, Environment: Mainly Transactional p.1206, Healthcare p.1209, Insurance: Dispute Resolution p.1212, Intellectual Property p.403, Litigation: ERISA p.25, Media & Entertainment: Litigation p.1232, Private Equity: Fund Formation p.955, Real Estate p.1247

Pryor Cashman Sherman & Flynn
Table: Media & Entertainment: Transactional p.1234

Q

Quarles & Brady LLP
Tables: Corporate/M&A p.146, Employment: p.148, Environment (including water rights) p.150, Litigation: General Commercial p.151, Litigation: White-Collar Crime & Government Investigations p.153

Quattlebaum, Grooms, Tull & Burrow PLLC
Profile: p.181
Tables: Employment: p.169, Litigation: General Commercial p.172, Real Estate p.174

Quinn Emanuel Urquhart Oliver & Hedges, LLP
Profile: p.298
Tables: Intellectual Property p.215, Litigation: General Commercial p.223, Media & Entertainment: Litigation p.229

R

Radey, Thomas, Yon & Clark
Table: Insurance p.519

Ramsay, Bridgforth, Harrelson & Starling LLP
Table: Employment: p.169

Raskin & Raskin PA
Table: Litigation: White-Collar Crime & Government Investigations p.522

RatnerPrestia
Profile: p.1559
Table: Intellectual Property p.1508

Ravich Meyer Kirkman McGrath & Nauman, PA
Table: Real Estate p.1014

Ray & Isler PC
Table: Employment: p.1775

Ray, Quinney & Nebeker PC
Tables: Employment: p.1730, Litigation: General Commercial p.1731, Real Estate p.1733

Read and Laniado
Table: Energy p.1204

Real Property Law Group PLLC
Table: Real Estate p.1788

Rebein Bangerter PA
Table: Litigation p.819

Reed Weitkamp Schell & Vice PLLC
Tables: Corporate/M&A p.827, Litigation: General Commercial p.834

Reeder & Shuman
Table: Real Estate p.1805

Reed Smith LLP
Profile: p.1560
Tables: Antitrust p.1489, Banking & Finance p.1492, Bankruptcy/Restructuring p.1494, Corporate/M&A p.1497, Employment: p.1500, Environment p.1504, Healthcare

p.29, Intellectual Property p.1508, Litigation: General Commercial p.1511, Real Estate p.1134

Reges & Boone LLC
Table: Environment p.136

Reinhart, Boerner, Van Deuren SC
Profile: p.1831
Tables: Corporate/M&A p.1817, Litigation: General Commercial p.1820, Real Estate p.1822

Rice Pugatch Robinson & Schiller
Table: Bankruptcy p.502

Rice Silbey Reuther & Sullivan LLP
Table: Real Estate p.1098

Richards Layton & Finger
Tables: Bankruptcy/Restructuring p.341, Chancery p.344, Corporate/M&A p.346, Intellectual Property p.348, Real Estate p.349

Richman Greer Weil Brumbaugh Mirabito & Christensen
Profile: p.571
Table: Litigation p.520

Riddell Williams PS
Tables: Corporate/M&A p.1777, Employment: p.1780

Rider, Bennett, Egan & Arundel, LLP
Table: Employment: p.1008

Riegels Campos & Kenyon
Table: Media & Entertainment: Litigation p.229

Reimer & Braunstein LLP
Table: Banking p.932

Riker Danzig Scherer Hyland & Perretti LLP
Profile: p.1154
Tables: Corporate/M&A p.1123, Employment: p.1126, Environment p.1129, Litigation: General Commercial p.1131, Real Estate p.1134

Robbins, Russell, Englert, Orseck & Untereiner LLP
Table: Litigation: Appellate p.407

Roberts & Holland LLP
Table: Tax p.1254

Robins Kaplan Miller & Ciresi
Table: Litigation p.1010

Robinson & Cole LLP
Profile: p.340
Tables: Corporate/M&A p.327, Litigation: General Commercial p.331, Real Estate p.333

Robinson & McElwee PLLC
Tables: Corporate/M&A p.1798, Employment: p.1800, Real Estate p.1805

Robinson, Bradshaw & Hinson PA
Tables: Banking & Finance p.1381,

Corporate/M&A p.1383, Employment: p.1385, Environment p.1387, Litigation: General Commercial p.1390, Real Estate p.1392

Robison, Belaustegui, Sharp & Low
Table: Litigation p.1096

Rodey, Dickason, Sloan, Akin & Robb, PA
Tables: Corporate/M&A p.1155, Employment: p.1157, Environment, Natural Resources and Regulated Industries p.1158, Litigation: General Commercial p.1159, Real Estate p.1161

Roetzel & Andress PA
Table: Environment p.1424

Rogers Joseph O'Donnell & Phillips
Table: Government Contracts p.26

Rogers & Hardin
Profile: p.639
Tables: Antitrust p.578, Corporate/M&A p.587, Employment: p.589, Litigation: General Commercial p.598

Rogers, Towers, Bailey, Jones & Gay, PA
Tables: Real Estate p.526, Real Estate: Zoning/Land Use p.528

Allensworth and Porter, L.L.P.
Table: Construction p.1629

Ropes & Gray LLP
Profile: p.985
Tables: Banking & Finance p.932, Bankruptcy p.934, Corporate/M&A p.937, Corporate/M&A: Mid-Tier Firms p.1195, Employment: p.939, Healthcare p.29, Litigation: General Commercial p.950, Private Equity: Buyouts & Venture Capital Investment p.952, Private Equity: Fund Formation p.955, Tax p.959

Rose Law Firm
Tables: Corporate/M&A p.168, Employment: p.169

Rosenberg, Martin, Funk, Greenberg, LLP
Tables: Litigation: General Commercial p.914, Real Estate p.916

Ross Dixon & Bell LLP
Table: Insurance: Insurer Firms p.400

Ross & Cohen, LLP
Profile: p.1366
Table: Construction p.1186

Rothgerber Johnson & Lyons LLP
Tables: Litigation: General Commercial p.310

Rouse Hendricks German May PC
Table: Litigation p.1048

Ruden McClosky SC
Tables: Environment p.515, Litigation: White-Collar Crime & Government Investigations p.522, Real Estate p.526, Real Estate: Zoning/Land Use p.528

Rudman & Winchell LLC
Table: Employment: p.890

Rush Law Group
Table: Media & Entertainment p.1602

Rush Moore LLP
Tables: Bankruptcy p.640, Real Estate p.646

Rushton, Stakely, Johnston & Garrett
Table: Litigation p.115

Rusing & Lopez PLLC
Table: Litigation p.151

Ryan & Whaley
Table: Litigation p.1462

Ryley Carlock & Applewhite
Profile: p.166
Tables: Corporate/M&A p.146, Employment: p.148, Environment (including water rights) p.150, Litigation: General Commercial p.151

S

Sabo & Zahn
Table: Construction p.672

Sachnoff & Weaver LTD
Table: Corporate/M&A & Private Equity p.674

Sacks Montgomery PC
Table: Construction p.1186

Sacks Tierney PA
Table: Real Estate p.153

Sale & Kuehne PA
Table: Litigation: White-Collar Crime & Government Investigations p.522

Sandler, Travis & Rosenberg
Table: International Trade p.39

Santoro, Driggs, Walch, Kearney, Johnson & Thompson
Tables: Environment p.1093, Real Estate p.1098

Saul Ewing LLP
Profile: p.1561
Tables: Bankruptcy/Restructuring p.341, Corporate/M&A p.909, Employment: p.911, Environment p.1504, Litigation: General Commercial p.914, Real Estate p.349

Seaton, Beck, Peters, Bowen & Feuss
Table: Employment p.1008

Schaffer Law Office
Table: Litigation p.1590

Scheuer Yost & Patterson PC
Table: Real Estate p.1161

Schiff Hardin LLP
Profile: p.775
Tables: Banking & Finance p.665, Construction p.672, Corporate/M&A & Private Equity p.674, Employment: p.680, Energy & Natural Resources

p.685, Environment p.687, Insurance: Coverage Litigation p.694, Insurance: Reinsurance Litigation p.693

Schnader Harrison Segal & Lewis LLP
Table: Litigation p.1511

Schneider Tanaka Radovich Andrew & Tanaka, LLLC
Table: Real Estate p.646

Schopf & Weiss
Table: Antitrust p.661

Schottenstein, Zox & Dunn
Profile: p.1456
Tables: Bankruptcy p.1413, Construction p.1417, Environment p.1424, Litigation: General Commercial p.1430, Real Estate p.1434

Schreck Brignone
Tables: Corporate/M&A p.1089, Employment: p.1091, Gaming & Licensing p.1094, Litigation: General Commercial p.1096, Real Estate p.1098

Schully, Roberts, Slattery, Jaubert & Marino
Table: Energy & Natural Resources p.862

Schulte Roth & Zabel LLP
Profile: p.1367
Tables: Bankruptcy/Restructuring p.1177, Private Equity: Fund Formation p.1240

Schwabe Williamson & Wyatt PC
Tables: Employment: p.1473, Litigation: General Commercial p.1475, Real Estate p.1478

Schwartz, Bon, Walker & Studer LLC
Table: Litigation p.1834

Schwartz, Cooper, Greenberger & Krauss, Chartered
Profile: p.776
Tables: Banking & Finance p.665, Real Estate p.705

Sebris Busto James
Table: Employment: p.1780

Seed Intellectual Property Law Group PLLC
Table: Intellectual Property p.1784

Serkland Law Firm, PC
Tables: Corporate/M&A p.1403, Litigation: General Commercial p.1406

Serotte, Rockman & Westcott
Table: Employment: p.911

Seward & Kissel
Profile: p.1368
Tables: Private Equity: Fund Formation p.1240, Shipping p.66

Seyfarth Shaw LLP
Profile: p.777
Tables: Construction p.373, Employee Benefits & Executive Compensation p.680, Employment: p.201, Environment p.687, Media & Entertainment: Transactional p.703, Real Estate p.705

Shaft, Reis & Shaft Ltd
Table: Real Estate p.1409

Shapiro Fussell
Table: Construction p.584

Shaw Gussis Fishman Glantz Wolfson & Towbin LLC
Table: Bankruptcy p.668

Shaw Pittman LLP
Profile: p.490
Tables: Aviation p.57, Business Process Outsourcing; National p.9, Corporate/Commercial p.376, Corporate/M&A p.1752, Energy: Nuclear p.389, Environment p.391, Intellectual Property p.403, Intellectual Property: Northern Virginia p.1758, IT & IT Outsourcing p.221, Real Estate p.417, Technology & IT Outsourcing p.1259

Shawe & Rosenthal LLP
Profile: p.929
Table: Employment: p.911

Shearman & Sterling LLP
Profile: p.1369
Tables: Antitrust p.366, Arbitration (International) p.32, Aviation p.57, Banking & Finance p.187, Bankruptcy/Restructuring p.1177, Capital Markets: Debt & Equity p.13, Capital Markets: Derivatives p.16, Corporate/M&A p.1187, Employee Benefits & Executive Compensation p.1197, Intellectual Property p.1216, Investment Management p.405, Litigation: General Commercial p.1221, Litigation: Securities p.1223, Media & Entertainment: Transactional p.1234, Projects p.1243, Real Estate p.1247, Tax p.422

Sheehan Phinney Bass + Green PA
Profile: p.1122
Tables: Corporate/M&A p.1107, Employment: p.1109, Litigation: General Commercial p.1111, Real Estate p.1114

Sheehey Furlong & Behm PC
Tables: Corporate/M&A p.1743, Litigation: General Commercial p.1745

Shefsky & Froelich
Table: Real Estate p.705

Shems Dunkiel Kassel & Saunders PLLC
Table: Real Estate p.1747

Sheley & Hall
Table: Real Estate p.601

Sheppard, Mullin, Richter & Hampton LLP
Tables: Antitrust p.183, Banking & Finance p.187, Corporate/M&A: Southern California p.196, Employment: p.201, Government Contracts p.26, Media & Entertainment: Litigation p.229, Media & Entertainment: Transactional p.233, Real Estate p.237

Sher & Blackwell
Table: Shipping p.71

Sher Garner Cahill Richter Klein McAlister & Hilbert, LLC
Tables: Corporate/M&A p.858, Litigation: General Commercial p.865, Real Estate p.867

Sherin and Lodgen LLP
Table: Litigation p.950

Sherman & Howard LLC
Tables: Employment: p.305, Environment p.307, Real Estate p.313

Shernoff, Bidart & Darras LLP
Table: Insurance p.212

Sherrard & Roe PLC
Tables: Corporate/M&A p.1594, Litigation: General Commercial p.1598, Real Estate p.1603

Shipman & Goodwin LLP
Tables: Corporate/M&A p.327, Employment: p.329, Litigation: General Commercial p.331, Real Estate p.333

Shook, Hardy & Bacon LLP
Profile: p.1067
Tables: Corporate/M&A p.816, Employment: p.1045, Environment p.515, Litigation: General Commercial p.520, Products Liability p.48

Shubin & Bass
Profile: p.572
Table: Real Estate: Zoning/Land Use p.528

Shughart Thomson & Kilroy PC
Profile: p.1068
Tables: Corporate/M&A p.816, Litigation: General Commercial p.819, Real Estate p.1052

Shulman, Rogers, Gandal, Pordy & Ecker, PA
Table: Real Estate p.916

Shumacker Witt Gaither & Whitaker, P.C.
Table: Real Estate p.1603

Shumaker Loop & Kendrick LLP
Tables: Corporate/M&A p.509, Environment p.1424

Shuttleworth & Ingersoll PLC
Tables: Corporate/M&A p.802, Employment: p.804, Litigation: General Commercial p.806

Shutts & Bowen LLP
Profile: p.573
Tables: Banking & Finance p.500, Corporate/M&A p.509, Real Estate p.526

Sidley Austin Brown & Wood LLP
Profile: p.778
Tables: Antitrust p.661, Arbitration (International) p.32, Banking & Finance p.665, Bankruptcy p.190, Capital Markets p.21, Capital Markets: Debt & Equity p.13, Capital Markets: Derivatives p.16, Capital Markets: Securitisation p.18, Corporate/M&A & Private Equity p.674, Corporate/M&A: Southern California p.196, Employee Benefits & Executive Compensation p.680, Energy & Natural Resources p.685, Energy: Oil & Gas p.382, Environment p.391, Insurance: Coverage Litigation p.694, Insurance: Reinsurance Litigation p.693, Insurance: Transactional & Regulatory p.692, Intellectual Property p.403, Litigation: Appellate p.407, Litigation: General Commercial p.409, Media & Entertainment: Litigation p.702,

Products Liability p.48, Real Estate
p.705, Tax p.709, Telecom, Broadcast &
Satellite: Regulatory p.426, Transport:
Rail p.62

Siegel, O'Connor, Zangari,
O'Donnell & Beck PC
Table: Employment: p.329

Siegfried, Rivera, Lerner, De La
Torre & Sobel, PA
Table: Construction p.506

Sills Cummis Epstein & Gross PC
Tables: Corporate/M&A p.1123, Real
Estate p.1134

Simmons Perrine Albright &
Ellwood P.L.C.
Tables: Employment: p.804, Litigation:
General Commercial p.806, Real Estate
p.810

Simpson Thacher & Bartlett LLP
Profile: p.1370
Tables: Antitrust p.1169, Arbitration
(International) p.32, Banking & Finance
p.1173, Bankruptcy/Restructuring
p.1177, Capital Markets: p.23, Capital
Markets: Debt & Equity p.13, Capital
Markets: Securitisation p.18,
Corporate/M&A p.1187, Employee
Benefits & Executive Compensation
p.1197, Energy: Transactional p.1202,
Environment: Mainly Transactional
p.1206, Insurance: Dispute Resolution
p.1212, Intellectual Property p.215,
Litigation: General Commercial p.1221,
Litigation: Securities p.1223, Private
Equity: Buyouts & Venture Capital
Investment p.1237, Private Equity: Fund
Formation p.1240, Products Liability
p.48, Projects p.1243, Real Estate
p.1247, Tax p.1254

Sirote & Permutt PC
Tables: Corporate/M&A p.1817, Real
Estate p.119

Sive Paget & Riesel PC
Profile: p.1371
Table: Environment p.1205

Skadden, Arps, Slate, Meagher &
Flom LLP & Affiliates
Profile: p.1372
Tables: Antitrust p.366, Arbitration
(International) p.32, Banking & Finance
p.187, Bankruptcy p.190,
Bankruptcy/Restructuring p.341, Capital
Markets p.23, Capital Markets: Debt &
Equity p.13, Chancery p.344,
Corporate/M&A p.346, Corporate/M&A
& Private Equity p.674, Corporate/M&A:
Northern California p.196, Employee
Benefits & Executive Compensation
p.1197, Energy & Natural Resources
p.1637, Energy: Electricity p.385,
Energy: Oil & Gas p.382, Energy:
Transactional p.1202, Environment
p.391, Insurance: Dispute Resolution
p.1212, Intellectual Property p.215,
Litigation: General Commercial p.223,
Litigation: Securities p.1223, Litigation:
White-Collar Crime & Government
Investigations p.1224, Products Liability
p.48, Projects p.52, Real Estate p.1247,
Sports Law p.55, Tax p.422, Technology
& IT Outsourcing p.1259, Telecom,
Broadcast & Satellite: Regulatory p.426

Slover & Loftus
Table: Transport: Rail p.62

Slusser, Wilson & Partridge LLP
Table: Intellectual Property p.1650

Smith Bakke Oppegard
Porsborg & Wolf
Table: Litigation p.1406

Smith & Smith Attorneys
Profile: p.853
Table: Employment: p.830

Smith Hulsey & Busey
Profile: p.574
Tables: Bankruptcy p.502, Real Estate
p.526

Smith Pachter
McWhorter & Allen
Table: Construction p.1750

Smith & Kotchka Ltd
Table: Employment: p.1091

Smith, Anderson, Blount,
Dorsett, Mitchell & Jernigan, LLP
Profile: p.1401
Tables: Corporate/M&A p.1383,
Employment: p.1385

Smith, Currie & Hancock LLP
Table: Construction p.584

Smith Gambrell & Russell LLP
Tables: Antitrust p.578, Banking &
Finance: Mainly Regulatory p.581,
Construction p.584, Environment p.592,
Intellectual Property p.595, Real Estate
p.526

Smith Moore LLP
Profile: p.1400
Tables: Employment: p.1385,
Environment p.1387, Litigation: General
Commercial p.1390, Real Estate p.1392

Snell & Wilmer LLP
Profile: p.167
Tables: Corporate/M&A p.146,
Employment: p.148, Environment
(including water rights) p.150, Litigation:
General Commercial p.151, Real Estate
p.153, Real Estate: Zoning/Land Use
p.155

Sommer Barnard Attorneys PC
Profile: p.799
Tables: Corporate/M&A p.781, Litigation:
General Commercial p.785, Real Estate
p.788

Sommer, Udall, Hardwick, Ahern
& Hyatt LLP
Table: Real Estate p.1161

Sonnenschein Nath &
Rosenthal LLP
Profile: p.779
Tables: Antitrust p.661, Bankruptcy
p.668, Business Process Outsourcing:
National p.9, Corporate/M&A p.1042,
Corporate/M&A & Private Equity p.674,
Employee Benefits & Executive
Compensation p.680, Environment
p.687, Healthcare p.29, Insurance p.212,
Insurance: Dispute Resolution p.1212,
Litigation: General Commercial p.1048,
Media & Entertainment: Litigation p.702,
Real Estate p.705, Technology & IT
Outsourcing p.712

Sonosky, Chambers, Sachse,
Miller & Munson LLP
Table: Native Law p.140

Sowell Gray Stepp & Laffitte LLC
Profile: p.1586
Table: Litigation p.1575

Spencer Fane Britt
& Browne LLP
Tables: Corporate/M&A p.1042,
Employment: p.1045, Litigation: General
Commercial p.819

Sperling & Slater
Table: Antitrust p.661

Spieth Bell McCurdy &
Newell Co LPA
Table: Employment: p.1421

Spilman Thomas & Battle, PLLC
Profile: p.1816
Tables: Employment: p.1800, Litigation:
General Commercial p.1803, Real Estate
p.1805

Spink & Miller PLC
Table: Litigation p.1745

Spink Butler, LLP
Table: Real Estate p.658

Spradling, Kennedy
& McPhail LLP
Table: Real Estate p.1463

Spriggs & Hollingsworth
Profile: p.491
Table: Construction p.373

Squire, Sanders &
Dempsey L.L.P.
Tables: Banking & Finance p.1411,
Bankruptcy p.1413, Construction p.1417,
Corporate/M&A p.146, Employment:
p.1421, Environment p.1424,
Environment (including water rights)
p.150, Litigation: General Commercial
p.1430, Real Estate p.153

Stafford Rosenbaum LLP
Table: Litigation p.1820

Starnes & Atchison LLP
Profile: p.132
Table: Litigation p.115

Stearns Weaver Miller Weissler
Alhadeff & Sitterson, P.A.
Tables: Bankruptcy p.502,
Corporate/M&A p.509, Employment:
p.511, Litigation: General Commercial
p.520, Real Estate p.526, Real Estate:
Zoning/Land Use p.528

Steel Hector & Davis LLP
Profile: p.575
Tables: Corporate/M&A p.509,
Employment: p.511, Litigation: General
Commercial p.520, Tax p.530

Stein, Ray & Harris LLP
Table: Construction p.672

Steiner, Darling &
Hutchinson LLP
Table: Real Estate p.313

Steptoe & Johnson LLP
Profile: p.492
Tables: Employee Benefits p.378,
Employment: p.148, Energy: Electricity
p.385, Energy: Oil & Gas p.382,
Insurance: Insurer Firms p.400,
International Trade p.39, Litigation:
ERISA p.25, Litigation: General
Commercial p.409, Tax p.422,
Transport: Rail p.62

Steptoe & Johnson PLLC
Tables: Corporate/M&A p.1798,
Employment: p.1800, Litigation: General
Commercial p.1803, Real Estate p.1805

Sterne, Kessler, Goldstein
& Fox P.L.L.C.
Profile: p.493
Table: Intellectual Property p.403

Stetler & Duffy Ltd
Table: Litigation p.699

Stevens & Lee, P. C.
Table: Bankruptcy/Restructuring p.1494

Stevens & O'Connell LLP
Table: Litigation: White-Collar Crime &
Government Investigations p.225

Stewart & Stewart
Table: International Trade p.39

Stichter, Riedel, Blain
& Prosser PA
Profile: p.576
Table: Bankruptcy p.502

Stinson Morrison Hecker LLP
Profile: p.1069
Tables: Corporate/M&A p.816,
Employment: p.1045, Litigation: General
Commercial p.819, Real Estate p.821

Stites & Harbison PLLC
Profile: p.854
Tables: Corporate/M&A p.827,
Environment, Natural Resources and
Regulated Industries p.832, Litigation:
General Commercial p.834, Real Estate
p.837

Stoel Rives LLP
Tables: Corporate/M&A p.655,
Employment: p.656, Environment
p.1782, Litigation: General Commercial
p.657, Projects p.235, Real Estate p.658

Stokes Bartholomew Evans &
Petree, P.A.
Table: Media & Entertainment p.1602

Stoll, Keenon & Park, LLP
Tables: Corporate/M&A p.827,
Employment: p.830, Environment,
Natural Resources and Regulated
Industries p.832, Litigation: General
Commercial p.834

Stoll Stoll Berne Lokting &
Shlachter
Table: Litigation p.1475

Stone Pigman Walther
Wittmann L.L.C.
Profile: p.887
Tables: Corporate/M&A p.858, Litigation:
General Commercial p.865, Real Estate
p.867

S

Storey & Burnham PLC
Table: Real Estate p.153

St Peter & Kasle
Table: Employment: p.1565

Strasburger & Price LLP
Table: Insurance p.1647

Strecker & Associates
Table: Employment: p.1460

Stroock & Stroock & Lavan LLP
Tables: Bankruptcy/Restructuring p.1177, Capital Markets: Derivatives p.16, Insurance: Dispute Resolution p.1212, Real Estate p.1247

Stutman, Treister & Glatt Professional Corporation
Profile: p.299
Table: Bankruptcy p.190

Sukin Law Group
Table: Media & Entertainment: Transactional p.1234

Sullivan, Tabaracci and Rhoades PC
Table: Real Estate p.1078

Sullivan & Cromwell LLP
Profile: p.1373
Tables: Antitrust p.1169, Arbitration (International) p.32, Banking & Finance p.187, Capital Markets: p.23, Capital Markets: Debt & Equity p.13, Corporate/M&A p.1187, Employee Benefits & Executive Compensation p.1197, Employment: p.1199, Energy: Transactional p.1202, Environment: Mainly Transactional p.1206, Insurance: Dispute Resolution p.1212, Litigation: General Commercial p.223, Litigation: Securities p.1223, Litigation: White-Collar Crime & Government Investigations p.1224, Projects p.52, Real Estate p.1247, Tax p.1254

Sullivan & Worcester
Table: Tax p.959

Sulloway & Hollis PLLC
Tables: Litigation: General Commercial p.1111, Real Estate p.1114

Summit Law Group, PLLC
Tables: Environment p.1782, Litigation: General Commercial p.1785

Sundahl, Powers, Kapp & Martin LLC
Table: Litigation p.1834

Susman Godfrey LLP
Tables: Antitrust p.1622, Energy & Natural Resources: Dispute Resolution p.1639, Litigation: General Commercial p.1655

Sutherland Asbill & Brennan LLP
Profile: p.494
Tables: Corporate/M&A p.587, Energy & Natural Resources p.591, Intellectual Property p.595, Litigation: General Commercial p.598, Real Estate p.601, Tax p.422

Sutin, Thayer & Browne
Profile: p.1168
Table: Corporate/M&A p.1155

Swanson & McNamara LLP
Table: Litigation: White-Collar Crime & Government Investigations p.225

Swidler Berlin LLP
Profile: p.495
Tables: Bankruptcy p.372, Energy: Electricity p.385, Environment p.391, Telecom, Broadcast & Satellite: Regulatory p.426

T

Tachau Maddox Hovious & Dickens PLC
Profile: p.855
Table: Litigation p.834

Taft, Stettinius & Hollister LLP
Tables: Banking & Finance p.1411, Bankruptcy p.1413, Corporate/M&A p.1419, Employment: p.1421, Environment p.1424, Litigation: General Commercial p.1430

Lightfoot, Vandevelde, Sadowsky, Medvene & Levine
Table: Litigation: White-Collar Crime & Government Investigations p.225

Tarolli, Sundheim, Covell, & Tummino LLP
Table: Intellectual Property p.1427

Taylor, Porter, Brooks & Phillips, LLP
Table: Corporate/M&A p.858

Tescher Gutter Chaves Josepher Rubin Ruffin & Forman PA
Table: Tax p.530

Temkin Wielga & Hardt LLP
Table: Environment p.307

Tew Cardenas LLP
Table: Real Estate p.526

Thacher Proffitt & Wood LLP
Profile: p.1374
Tables: Capital Markets: Securitisation p.18, Shipping p.66

The Kullman Firm PLC
Profile: p.884
Tables: Employment: p.861

The Steeg Law Firm, LLC
Table: Real Estate p.867

The Tinney Law Firm
Table: Litigation p.1803

The Wexler Firm
Table: Antitrust p.661

Thelen Reid & Priest LLP
Profile: p.300
Tables: Construction p.194, Energy: Regulatory p.1202, Government Contracts p.26, Projects p.235

Theriault & Joslin PC
Table: Litigation p.1745

Thomas Kayden Horstemeyer & Risley LLP
Table: Intellectual Property p.595

Thomas N Long PC
Table: Corporate/M&A p.1832

Thompson, Coe, Cousins & Irons, LLP
Profile: p.1723
Table: Insurance p.1647

Thompson, Sizemore & Gonzalez
Profile: p.577
Table: Employment: p.511

Thompson Coburn LLP
Profile: p.1071
Tables: Corporate/M&A p.1042, Employment: p.1045, Litigation: General Commercial p.1048

Thompson Hine LLP
Profile: p.1457
Tables: Banking & Finance p.1411, Bankruptcy p.1413, Construction p.1417, Corporate/M&A p.1419, Environment p.1424, Intellectual Property p.1427, Litigation: General Commercial p.1430, Real Estate p.1434, Transport: Rail p.62

Thompson & Knight LLP
Profile: p.1722
Tables: Banking & Finance p.1624, Bankruptcy p.1626, Environment p.1642, Intellectual Property p.1650, Litigation: General Commercial p.1655, Real Estate p.1661, Tax p.1665, Technology p.1667

Thorp Reed & Armstrong
Table: Litigation p.1511

Tindall Bennett & Shoup PC
Tables: Employment: p.135, Real Estate p.140

Tinnin Law Firm
Table: Employment p.1157

Titus, Brueckner & Berry PC
Table: Corporate/M&A p.146

Todd & Weld LLP
Table: Litigation p.950

Tonkon Torp LLP
Tables: Corporate/M&A p.1471, Employment: p.1473, Litigation: General Commercial p.1475, Real Estate p.1478

Topel & Goodman PC
Table: Litigation: White-Collar Crime & Government Investigations p.225

Torkildson, Katz, Fonseca, Jaffe, Moore & Hetherington Attorneys At Law, A Law Corporation
Table: Employment: p.642

Townsend & Jones
Table: Tax p.1665

Townsend and Townsend and Crew LLP
Tables: Antitrust p.183, Intellectual Property p.215

Trenam, Kemker, Scharf, Barkin, Frye, O'Neill & Mullis PA
Tables: Antitrust p.498, Bankruptcy p.502, Corporate/M&A p.509, Real Estate p.526

Triplett, Woolf & Garretson LLC
Table: Real Estate p.821

Troutman Sanders LLP
Tables: Antitrust p.578, Banking & Finance p.580, Banking & Finance: Mainly Regulatory p.581, Corporate/M&A p.587, Employment: p.589, Energy & Natural Resources p.591, Energy: Electricity p.385, Energy: Oil & Gas p.382, Environment p.592, Intellectual Property p.595, Intellectual Property: Southern Virginia p.1760, Litigation: General Commercial p.598, Real Estate p.601, Shipping p.71

Tschider & Smith
Table: Corporate/M&A p.1403

Tsukazaki Yeh & Moore
Table: Land Use p.643

Tydings & Rosenberg LLP
Table: Employment: p.911

U

Ugrin, Alexander, Zadick & Higgins, PC
Table: Employment: p.1073

Ulmer & Berne LLP
Tables: Construction p.1417, Employment: p.1421, Litigation: General Commercial p.1430, Real Estate p.1434

Ungaretti & Harris
Table: Healthcare p.690

Upton and Hatfield LLP
Tables: Litigation: General Commercial p.1111, Real Estate p.1114

V

Van Hoy Reutlinger Adams & Dunn
Table: Employment: p.1385

Van Cott, Bagley, Cornwall & McCarthy
Table: Litigation p.1731

Van Ness Feldman PC
Tables: Energy: Electricity p.385, Energy: Oil & Gas p.382, Environment p.391

Varnum, Riddering, Schmidt & Howlett LLP
Tables: Banking & Finance p.987, Corporate/M&A p.988, Employment: p.991, Litigation: General Commercial p.993

Vaughan & Murphy
Table: Antitrust p.578

Vedder, Price, Kaufman & Kammholz
Tables: Aviation p.57, Bankruptcy p.668, Employee Benefits & Executive Compensation p.680, Litigation: ERISA p.25

Venable LLP
Tables: Construction p.1750,
Corporate/M&A p.909, Employment:
p.911, Environment p.391, Government
Contracts p.26, Litigation: General
Commercial p.914, Real Estate p.916

**Vercruysse Murray
& Calzone, PC**
Table: Employment: p.991

Verrill Dana, LLP
Profile: p.908
Tables: Corporate/M&A p.888, Litigation:
General Commercial p.893, Real Estate
p.895

Vezina Lawrence & Piscitelli PA
Table: Construction p.506

Vickers Madsen & Goldman
Table: Tax p.530

Vinson & Elkins LLP
Profile: p.1724
Tables: Antitrust p.1622, Arbitration
(International) p.32, Banking & Finance
p.1624, Bankruptcy p.1626,
Corporate/M&A p.1631, Employment:
p.1633, Energy & Natural Resources
p.1637, Energy & Natural Resources:
Dispute Resolution p.1639, Energy:
Electricity p.385, Energy: Oil & Gas
p.382, Energy: Transactional p.1202,
Environment p.391, Healthcare p.29,
Insurance p.1647, Intellectual Property
p.1650, Litigation: General Commercial
p.1655, Projects p.52, Real Estate
p.1661, Tax p.1665, Technology p.1667

Vogel Law Firm
Tables: Corporate/M&A p.1403,
Employment: p.1405, Litigation: General
Commercial p.1406, Real Estate p.1409

Vogel Campbell Blueher & Castle
Table: Real Estate p.1161

**Vorys, Sater, Seymour
and Pease LLP**
Profile: p.1458
Tables: Banking & Finance p.1411,
Bankruptcy p.1413, Corporate/M&A
p.1419, Employment: p.1421,
Environment p.1424, Litigation: General
Commercial p.1430, Real Estate p.1434

W

Wachtell, Lipton, Rosen & Katz
Profile: p.1375
Tables: Antitrust p.1169,
Bankruptcy/Restructuring p.1177,
Corporate/M&A p.1187, Employee
Benefits & Executive Compensation
p.1197, Insurance: Dispute Resolution
p.1212, Litigation: General Commercial
p.1221, Litigation: Securities p.1223,
Litigation: White-Collar Crime &
Government Investigations p.1224, Real
Estate p.1247, Tax p.1254

Wadleigh, Starr & Peters PLLC
Tables: Bankruptcy p.640

Wagner Choi Evers
Table: Litigation: White-Collar Crime &
Government Investigations p.1133

Walder, Hayden & Brogan P.A.
Table: Litigation: White-Collar Crime &
Government Investigations p.1133

Walker, Bryant, Tipps & Malone
Profile: p.1620
Table: Litigation p.1598

**Wallace King Domike &
Branson PLLC**
Table: Environment p.391

Wallack Somers & Haas PC
Profile: p.800
Table: Real Estate p.788

Waller Lansden Dortch & Davis
Profile: p.1621
Tables: Corporate/M&A p.1594,
Employment: p.1596, Litigation: General
Commercial p.1598, Real Estate p.1603

**Walston, Wells, Anderson
& Bains**
Table: Real Estate p.119

Warner Norcross & Judd LLP
Tables: Corporate/M&A p.988, Litigation:
General Commercial p.993

Warren & Sinkler LLP
Tables: Corporate/M&A p.1572, Real
Estate p.1577

**Watanabe Ing Kawashima
& Komeiji**
Table: Employment p.642 Land use
p.643 Litigation p.644

**Watkins Ludlam Winter &
Stennis, P.A**
Profile: p.1041
Tables: Corporate/M&A p.1024,
Employment: p.1026, Litigation: General
Commercial p.1028, Real Estate p.1031

Watkins & Eager PLLC
Profile: p.1040
Tables: Corporate/M&A p.1024,
Employment: p.1026, Litigation: General
Commercial p.1028

Watson, Farley & Williams LLP
Profile: p.1377
Table: Shipping p.66

**Watt, Tieder, Hoffar &
Fitzgerald, L.L.P.**
Table: Construction p.1750

**Webb Ziesenheim Logsdon Orkin
& Hanson, PC**
Table: Intellectual Property p.1508

Weil, Gotshal & Manges LLP
Profile: p.1378
Tables: Antitrust p.366, Arbitration
(International) p.32, Banking & Finance
p.1173, Bankruptcy p.1626,
Bankruptcy/Restructuring p.1177,
Capital Markets: Securitisation p.18,
Corporate/M&A p.937, Employment:
p.1199, Environment p.391, Intellectual
Property p.215, Litigation: General
Commercial p.1221, Litigation:
Securities p.1223, Media &
Entertainment: Litigation p.1232, Media
& Entertainment: Transactional p.1234,
Private Equity: Buyouts & Venture
Capital Investment p.952, Private Equity:
Fund Formation p.955, Real Estate
p.1247, Tax p.1254, Technology & IT
Outsourcing p.1259

Weinberg Richmond LLP
Table: Real Estate p.705

**Weinberg, Wheeler, Hudgins,
Gunn & Dial, LLC**
Table: Construction p.584

**Welbaum, Guernsey, Hingston,
Greenleaf & Gregory LLP**
Table: Construction p.506

Welsh & Katz, Ltd
Table: Intellectual Property p.695

**Weston Benshoof Rochefort
Rubalcava MacCuish LLP**
Profile: p.301
Table: Environment p.206

Wheeler Trigg Kennedy LLP
Tables: Litigation: General Commercial
p.310, Products Liability p.48

**White Goss Bowers March
Schulte & Weisenfels, A
Professional Corporation**
Table: Real Estate p.1052

**White O'Connor Curry &
Avanzado LLP**
Table: Media & Entertainment: Litigation
p.229

White & Case LLP
Profile: p.1379
Tables: Antitrust p.366, Arbitration
(International) p.32, Banking & Finance
p.187, Bankruptcy p.372,
Bankruptcy/Restructuring p.1177,
Corporate/M&A p.509, Energy & Natural
Resources p.204, Environment p.515,
Environment: Mainly Transactional
p.1206, Intellectual Property p.1216,
International Trade p.39, Litigation:
General Commercial p.1221, Private
Equity: Buyouts & Venture Capital
Investment p.1237, Projects p.52, Real
Estate p.526, Tax p.530, Technology &
IT Outsourcing p.1259

Whiteford, Taylor & Preston LLP
Tables: Employment: p.911, Real Estate
p.916

**Whiteman Osterman
& Hanna LLP**
Table: Environment p.1205

Whitfield & Eddy, P.L.C
Tables: Employment: p.804, Litigation:
General Commercial p.806

Whyte Hirschboeck Dudek S.C.
Table: Real Estate p.1822

Wickwire Gavin
Table: Construction p.1750

Wiggin & Dana LLP
Tables: Corporate/M&A p.327,
Employment: p.329, Litigation: General
Commercial p.331, Real Estate p.333

Wiggin & Nourie
Table: Litigation p.1111

Wilentz Goldman & Spitzer, P.C.
Table: Real Estate p.1134

Wiley Rein & Fielding LLP
Profile: p.496
Tables: Government Contracts p.26,
Insurance: Insurer Firms p.400,
International Trade p.39, Telecom,
Broadcast & Satellite: Regulatory p.426

Willcox & Savage
Table: Litigation p.1762

**Williams Bradbury,
Attorneys at Law**
Table: Real Estate p.658

Williams & Anderson PLC
Tables: Corporate/M&A p.168, Litigation:
General Commercial p.172

Williams & Connolly LLP
Tables: Litigation: General Commercial
p.409, Media & Entertainment p.413,
Products Liability p.48

Williams, Zografos & Peck
Table: Employment p.1473

Williams Mullen
Tables: Corporate/M&A p.1752,
Employment: p.1755, Environment
p.1757, Intellectual Property: Southern
Virginia p.1760, Litigation: General
Commercial p.1762

**Williams, Porter, Day
& Neville PC**
Tables: Employment: p.1833, Litigation:
General Commercial p.1834, Real Estate
p.1836

Willkie Farr & Gallagher LLP
Profile: p.1380
Tables: Antitrust p.1169,
Bankruptcy/Restructuring p.1177,
Corporate/M&A p.1187, Environment
p.391, Litigation: General Commercial
p.1221, Litigation: Securities p.1223,
Real Estate p.1247, Telecom, Broadcast
& Satellite: Regulatory p.426

**Wilmer Cutler Pickering Hale
and Dorr LLP**
Profile: p.497
Tables: Antitrust p.366, Arbitration
(International) p.32, Bankruptcy p.372,
Corporate/M&A p.909, Employment:
p.939, Environment p.943, Intellectual

Property p.947, Investment Management p.405, Litigation: General Commercial p.409, Private Equity: Buyouts & Venture Capital Investment p.952, Real Estate p.956, Tax p.959, Telecom, Broadcast & Satellite: Regulatory p.426

Wilson, Elser, Moskowitz, Edelman & Dicker LLP
Table:
Insurance: Dispute Resolution p.1212

Wilson Sonsini Goodrich & Rosati
Profile: p.302
Tables: Antitrust p.183, Capital Markets p.23, Corporate/M&A p.1727, Corporate/M&A: Northern California p.196, Employment: p.201, Intellectual Property p.215, IT & IT Outsourcing p.221, Litigation: General Commercial p.223, Tax p.241, Technology p.1667

Winer & Bennett LLP
Table: Real estate p.1114

Winn & Alexander LLP
Table:
Media & Entertainment: Litigation p.229

Winstead Sechrest & Minick P.C.
Profile: p.1725
Tables:
Bankruptcy p.1626, Real Estate p.1661

Winston & Strawn LLP
Profile: p.780
Tables: Antitrust p.661, Arbitration (International) p.32, Banking & Finance p.665, Bankruptcy p.190, Corporate/M&A & Private Equity p.674, Employment: p.680, Energy: Electricity p.385, Environment p.687, Litigation: General Commercial p.699, Media & Entertainment: Transactional p.703, Real Estate p.705, Tax p.709

Winterbauer & Diamond, P.L.L.C.
Table: Employment: p.1780

Winthrop & Weinstine
Table: Litigation p.1010 Real estate p.1014

Wise Carter Child & Caraway
Table: Litigation: General Commercial p.1028 Employment: p.1026 Corporate/M&A: p.1024

Withey Anderson & Morris PLC

Wold Johnson PC
Table: Employment: p.1405

Wolf, Block, Schorr and Solis-Cohen LLP
Profile: p.1562
Tables: Banking & Finance p.1492, Corporate/M&A p.1497, Environment p.1504, Real Estate p.1515

Womble Carlyle Sandridge & Rice, PLLC
Profile: p.1402
Tables: Banking & Finance p.1381, Banking & Finance: Mainly Regulatory p.581, Corporate/M&A p.1383, Employment: p.1385, Environment p.1387, Litigation: General Commercial p.1390, Real Estate p.1392

Wood, Herron & Evans, LLP
Table: Intellectual Property p.1427

Woodburn and Wedge
Profile: p.1106
Table: Environment p.1093

Woodcock Washburn LLP
Profile: p.1563
Table: Intellectual Property p.1508

Wooden & McLaughlin LLP
Profile: p.801

Woods & Aitken LLP
Table: Corporate/M&A p.1082

Woods, Fuller, Shultz & Smith PC
Tables: Corporate/M&A p.1587, Litigation: General Commercial p.1590

Woods Rogers PLC
Table: Litigation p.1762

Woodward, Hobson & Fulton LLP
Tables: Employment: p.830, Litigation: General Commercial p.834

Worden Thane PC
Tables: Employment: p.1073, Real Estate p.1078

Wright & Talisman PC
Table: Energy: Electricity p.385

Wright, Fulford, Moorhead and

Brown P.A.
Table: Construction p.506

Wright, Henson, Somers, Clark & Bake
Table: Litigation p.819

Wright, Lindsey & Jennings LLP
Profile: p.182
Tables: Employment: p.169, Litigation: General Commercial p.172

Wright Robinson Osthimer & Tatum
Table: Construction p.1750

Wyatt, Tarrant & Combs LLP
Profile: p.856
Tables: Corporate/M&A p.827, Employment: p.830, Environment, Natural Resources and Regulated Industries p.832, Litigation: General Commercial p.834, Real Estate p.837

Wyche, Burgess, Freeman & Parham, PA
Tables: Corporate/M&A p.1572, Litigation: General Commercial p.1575

Wyrsch Hobbs & Mirakian PC
Table: Litigation p.1048

Yonkee & Toner LLP
Tables: Employment: p.1833, Litigation: General Commercial p.1834, Real Estate p.1836

York, Keller & Field
Table: Insurance p.1647

Young & Susser PC Attorneys and Counselors
Table: Litigation p.993

Young, Clement & Rivers LLP
Table: Litigation p.1575

Young Conaway Stargatt & Taylor LLP
Profile: p.365
Tables: Bankruptcy/Restructuring p.341, Chancery p.344, Corporate/M&A p.346, Employment: p.347, Real Estate p.349

Z

Carpenter & Lipps LLP
Table: Litigation p.1430

Zeiger, Tigges, Little & Lindsmith LLP
Table: Litigation p.1430

Zetlin & De Chiara LLP
Table: Construction p.1186

Ziffren Brittenham Branca Fischer Gilbert-Lurie & Stiffelman LLP
Table: Media & Entertainment: Transactional p.233

Zimney, Foster, Johnson, Dittus & Flaten, Chartered
Table: Corporate/M&A p.1403

Zinober & McCrea, P.A.
Table: Employment: p.511

Zuckerman Spaeder LLP
Tables: Litigation: General Commercial p.520, Litigation: White-Collar Crime & Government Investigations p.522

Zuckert, Scoutt & Rasenberger, LLP
Table: Transport: Rail p.62

Zuger Kirmis & Smith
Table: Litigation p.1406

Zumwalt, Almon & Hayes
Table: Media & Entertainment p.1602

Z

LEADING LAWYERS INDEX

A

Aaron, Roger S (New York)
Profile: p.1261
Corporate/M&A Band 1
Table: p.1189

Aaron, William (Florida)
Profile: p.533
Litigation Band 2
Table: p.522

Abaunza, Donald R
(Louisiana)
Profile: p.869
Litigation Band 2
Table: p.865

Abbott, Michael (Georgia)
Profile: p.604
Litigation Band 1
Table: p.599

Abbott, Scott M (Nevada)
Profile: p.1101
Employment Band 3
Table: p.1091

Abel, Kenneth (Maryland)
Profile: p.919
Corporate/M&A
Up and coming
Table: p.909

Abel, Sally (California)
Profile: p.243
Intellectual Property Band 4
Table: p.216

Abell, Nancy L (California)
Profile: p.243
Employment Band 1
Table: p.202

Abelson, Barry M
(Pennsylvania)
Profile: p.1518
Corporate/M&A Band 1
Table: p.1497

Abelson, Ned
(Massachusetts)
Profile: p.961
Environment Band 2
Table: p.943

Abernathy, Thomas (Georgia)
Profile: p.604
Construction Band 2
Table: p.584

Aborn, Richard A (National)
Profile: p.74
Aviation Band 2
Table: p.58

Abraham, Bill (Wisconsin)
Profile: p.1824
Corporate/M&A Band 3
Table: p.1817

Abramowitz, Elkan
(New York)
Profile: p.1261
Litigation Band 2
Table: p.1224

Abramowitz, Robert
(Pennsylvania)
Profile: p.1518
Employee Benefits Band 2
Table: p.1501

Abrams, Donald-Bruce
(Massachusetts)
Profile: p.961

Tax Band 3
Table: p.959

Abrams, Floyd (New York)
Profile: p.1261
Media & Entertainment Band 1
Table: p.1232

Abrams, Jeffrey (Indiana)
Profile: p.790
Real Estate Band 2
Table: p.788

Abrams, Kevin (Delaware)
Profile: p.351
Chancery Band 4
Table: p.344

Abrams, Lee N (Illinois)
Profile: p.716
Antitrust Band 1
Table: p.662

Abrams, Marc (New York)
Profile: p.1261
Bankruptcy Band 2
Table: p.1179

Abramson, Gil (Maryland)
Profile: p.919
Employment Band 3
Table: p.912

Abramson, Richard
(New York)
Profile: p.1261
Construction Band 4
Table: p.1186

Abramson, Richard
(New Jersey)
Profile: p.1137
Real Estate Band 3
Table: p.1134

Abravanel, Alan (Oregon)
Profile: p.1481
Corporate/M&A Band 3
Table: p.1471

Abuhoff, Daniel M
(New York)
Profile: p.1261
Antitrust Band 4
Table: p.1170

Acker, Lawrence G
(District of Columbia)
Profile: p.430
Energy Band 2
Table: p.382
Energy Band 1
Table: p.386

Ackerman, Gary
(Washington)
Profile: p.1790
Real Estate Band 3
Table: p.1788

Ackerman, Jill Robb
(Nebraska)
Profile: p.1087
Litigation Band 1
Table: p.1085

Acord, Bobbi (Georgia)
Profile: p.604
Banking & Finance Band 2
Table: p.580

Adamo, Ken (Ohio)
Profile: p.1437
Intellectual Property Band
Table: p.1428

Adams, Albert T (Ohio)
Profile: p.1437
Corporate/M&A Band 3
Table: p.1419

Adams, Alfred G
(North Carolina)
Profile: p.1394
Real Estate Band 1
Table: p.1392

Adams, Andy (Arkansas)
Profile: p.175
Litigation Band 1
Table: p.172

Adams, Deborah (Ohio)
Profile: p.1437
Employment Band 2
Table: p.1422

Adams, Garth (Iowa)
Profile: p.812
Corporate/M&A Band 3
Table: p.802

Adams, Greg (Washington)
Profile: p.1790
Corporate/M&A Band 2
Table: p.1778

Adams, H Mark (Louisiana)
Profile: p.869
Employment Band 2
Table: p.861

Adams, Helen (Iowa)
Profile: p.812
Employment Band 1
Table: p.805

Adams, James (Michigan)
Profile: p.998
Real Estate Band 3
Table: p.996

Adams, Joseph Lee
(Mississippi)
Profile: p.1032
Employment Band 2
Table: p.1026

Adams, Mark K (New Mexico)
Profile: p.1162
Litigation Band 1
Table: p.1158

Adams, Robert (Missouri)
Profile: p.1055
Litigation Band 2
Table: p.1049

Adams, Stephen (Missouri)
Profile: p. 1055
Corporate/M&A Band 1
Table: p.816
Corporate/M&A Band 1
Table: p.1043

Adams Jr, Alfred G (Georgia)
Profile: p.604
Real Estate Band 1
Table: p.601

Addison, Linda L (Texas)
Profile: p.1669
Litigation Band 2
Table: p.1656

Adduci II, V James
(National)
Profile: p.74
International Trade Band 4
Table: p.40

Adelfio, Marco
(District of Columbia)
Profile: p.430
Investment Management
Band 2
Table: p.406

Adelman, Howard (Illinois)
Profile: p.716
Bankruptcy Band 3
Table: p.669

Adelstein, Harvey M
(Illinois)
Profile: p.716
Employment Band 3
Table: p.681

Adler, Arthur S (New York)
Profile: p.1261
Real Estate Band 2
Table: p.1248

Adler, Howard B
(District of Columbia)
Profile: p.430
Corporate/Commercial Band 1
Table: p.376

Adler, James (California)
Profile: p.243
Employment Band 4
Table: p.202

Adler, Kenneth (New York)
Profile: p.1261
Technology Band 3
Table: p.1259

Adler, Robert L (California)
Profile: p.243
Corporate/M&A Band 4
Table: p.197

Adler, Sheldon S (New York)
Profile: p.1261
Energy Band 1
Table: p.1202

Aguilar Jr, Rodolfo J
(Louisiana)
Profile: p.869
Corporate/M&A Band 4
Table: p.859

Ahearn, Dale (Kentucky)
Profile: p.839
Real Estate Band 1
Table: p.838

Ahern, Janice M (New
Mexico)
Profile: p.1162
Real Estate Band 3
Table: p.1161

Ahern III, Lawrence R
(Tennessee)
Profile: p.1605
Litigation Band 2
Table: p.1599

Ahrens, Michael (California)
Profile: p.243
Bankruptcy Band 4
Table: p.191

Ahrens, Philip FW (Maine)
Profile: p.897
Environment Band 1
Table: p.892

Aichele, Stephen S
(Pennsylvania)
Profile: p.1518
Real Estate Band 2
Table: p.1516

Aiello, Anthony (Illinois)
Profile: p.716
Real Estate Band 4
Table: p.706

Aiello, John (New Jersey)
Profile: p.1137
Corporate/M&A Band 1
Table: p.1123

Aiello, Michael (New York)
Profile: p.1262
Corporate/M&A
Up and coming
Table: p.1189

Aisenbrey, John C (Missouri)
Profile: p.1055
Litigation Band 1
Table: p.1049

Aizenstein, Neal (Illinois)
Profile: p.716
Corporate/M&A Band 4
Table: p.675

Aksen, Gerald (National)
Profile: p.74
Arbitration Band 1
Table: p.34

Albainy-Jenei, Stephen R
(Ohio)
Profile: p.1437
Intellectual Property Band 2
Table: p.1428

Albergotti, Robert (Texas)
Profile: p.1669
Bankruptcy ✪
Table: p.1627

Albers, Michael F (Texas)
Profile: p.1669
Construction Band 3
Table: p.1629

Albert, Michael
(West Virginia)
Profile: p.1807
Corporate/M&A Band 1
Table: p.1798

Alberts, Sam J
(District of Columbia)
Profile: p.430
Bankruptcy Band 3
Table: p.372

Albertson, Terry (National)
Profile: p.74
Government Contracts Band 3
Table: p.27

Albin, David I (Connecticut)
Profile: p.336
Corporate/M&A Band 2
Table: p.327

Albrecht, Kristy L
(North Dakota)
Profile: p.1410
Employment Band 3
Table: p.1405

Albrecht, Thomas W
(Illinois)
Profile: p.74
Capital Markets Band 1
Table: p.21

Albrecht, Virginia S
(District of Columbia)
Profile: p.430
Environment Band 2
Table: p.392

A

Albright, Val (Texas)
Profile: p.1669
Litigation **Band 2**
Table: p.1665

Alden, Steven M (New York)
Profile: p.1262
Real Estate **Band 4**
Table: p.1248

Aldock, John
(District of Columbia)
Profile: p.430
Litigation **Band 3**
Table: p.410

Aldrich, Marcy Levine
(Florida)
Profile: p.533
Insurance **Band 2**
Table: p.519

Aldrich, Thomas A (Ohio)
Profile: p.1437
Corporate/M&A **Band 3**
Table: p.1419

Aldridge Sr, John G
(Georgia)
Profile: p.604
Real Estate **Band 3**
Table: p.601

Ale, John C (Texas)
Profile: p.1670
Energy **Band 2**
Table: p.1637
Projects **Band 2**
Table: p.1659

Alessandra, M Nan
(Louisiana)
Profile: p.869
Employment **Band 2**
Table: p.861

Alexander, Bruce (Florida)
Profile: p.533
Construction **Band 1**
Table: p.507

Alexander, Frederick H
(Delaware)
Profile: p.351
Corporate/M&A **Band 1**
Table: p.346

Alexander, James P
(Alabama)
Profile: p.121
Employment **Band 1**
Table: p.113

Alexander, Jennifer C
(Alaska)
Profile: p.141
Employment **Up and coming**
Table: p.135

Alexander, Judith
(California)
Profile: p.243
Media & Entertainment **Band 4**
Table: p.230

Alexander, Lee
(District of Columbia)
Profile: p.431
Energy **Band 5**
Table: p.382

Alexander, Miles (Georgia)
Profile: p.605
Intellectual Property **Band 1**
Table: p.596

Alexander, Troy (New York)
Profile: p.1262
Projects **Band 2**
Table: p.52
Projects **Band 2**
Table: p.1244

Alexandrov, Stanimir A
(National)
Profile: p.74
Arbitration **Band 3**
Table: p.33

Alexis, Geraldine (California)
Profile: p.243
Antitrust **Band 3**
Table: p.184

Alexis, Paul (Tennessee)
Profile: p.1605
Litigation **Band 3**
Table: p.1599

Alford, Carolyn Zander
(Georgia)
Profile: p.605
Banking & Finance **Band 3**
Table: p.580

Alfred, Richard
(Massachusetts)
Profile: p.961
Employment **Band 1**
Table: p.940

Alhadeff, Richard (Florida)
Profile: p.533
Real Estate **Band 1**
Table: p.526

Alito, Rosemary (New Jersey)
Profile: p.1137
Employment **Band 1**
Table: p.1126

Alkalay, Peter C (National)
Profile: p.74
Sport **Band 2**
Table: p.55

Allen, Everette (Virginia)
Profile: p.1767
Litigation **Band 1**
Table: p.1763

Allen, Pinney L (Georgia)
Profile: p.605
Tax **Band 2**
Table: p.603

Allen, Rand L (National)
Profile: p.74
Government Contracts
Band 2
Table: p.27

Allen, Randall (Virginia)
Profile: p.1767
Construction **Band 2**
Table: p.1750

Allen, Randall L (Georgia)
Profile: p.605
Antitrust **Band 2**
Table: p.578

Allen, Richard A. (National)
Profile: p.74
Transport **Band 3**
Table: p.62

Allen, Robert (West Virginia)
Profile: p.1807
Litigation **Band S**
Table: p.1803

Allen, William (Arkansas)
Profile: p.175
Litigation **Band 2**
Table: p.172

Allender, John R (Texas)
Profile: p.1670
Tax **Band 3**
Table: p.1665

Allensworth, William
(Texas)
Profile: p.1670
Construction **Band 2**
Table: p.1629

Allerhand, Joseph
(New York)
Profile: p.1262
Litigation **Band 3**
Table: p.1223

Alley, John-Edward (Florida)
Profile: p.533
Employment **Band 2**
Table: p.513

Allgeyer, David (Minnesota)
Profile: p.1017
Litigation **Band 1**
Table: p.1012

Alli Jr, Richard J (Oregon)
Profile: p.1481
Employment **Band 3**
Table: p.1474

Allingham II, Thomas J
(Delaware)
Profile: p.351
Chancery **Band 2**
Table: p.344

Allison, Christopher (Texas)
Profile: p.1670
Tax **Band 2**
Table: p.1665

Allred, C Keith (Washington)
Profile: p.1790
Bankruptcy **Band 2**
Table: p.1776

Almon, Orville (Tennessee)
Profile: p.1605
Media & Entertainment **Band 1**
Table: p.1602

Alonso, Michael G (Nevada)
Profile: p.1101
Gaming & Licensing **Band 2**
Table: p.1094

Alperin, Stuart N (New York)
Profile: p.1262
Employee Benefits **Band 3**
Table: p.1197

Al-Salam, Ramsey
(Washington)
Profile: p.1790
Intellectual Property **Band 1**
Table: p.1784

Alstadt, Lynn J
(Pennsylvania)
Profile: p.1518
Intellectual Property **Band 2**
Table: p.1508

Alston, Paul (Hawaii)
Profile: p.648
Litigation **Band 1**
Table: p.644

Altman, Paul (Delaware)
Profile: p.351
Corporate/M&A **Band 3**
Table: p.346

Altman, Ross (Illinois)
Profile: p.716
Construction **Band 3**
Table: p.672

Altschuler, Fredric L
(New York)
Profile: p.1262
Real Estate **Band 4**
Table: p.1248

Alvarez, Fred (California)
Profile: p.351
Employment **Band 2**
Table: p.202

Alvarez, Pedro A (Florida)
Profile: p.533
Banking & Finance **Band 2**
Table: p.500

Alvarez, Victor M (Florida)
Profile: p.533
Banking & Finance **Band 1**
Table: p.500

Alvarez-Farré, Emilio
(Florida)
Profile: p.533
Corporate/M&A **Band 2**
Table: p.509

Amandes, Christopher B
(Texas)
Profile: p.1670
Environment **Band 1**
Table: p.1643

Ambash, Joseph
(Massachusetts)
Profile: p.961
Employment **Band 2**
Table: p.940

Ambler, Diane
(District of Columbia)
Profile: p.431
Investment Management
Band 2
Table: p.406

Amburgey, Larry (Oregon)
Profile: p.1481
Employment **Band 1**
Table: p.1474

Amdur, Martin (New York)
Profile: p.1262
Tax **Band 4**
Table: p.1255

Amend, James M (Illinois)
Profile: p.716
Intellectual Property **Band 2**
Table: p.696

Amer, Andrew S (New York)
Profile: p.1262
Insurance **Band 3**
Table: p.1213

Ames, Mitchell (New York)
Profile: p.1262
Media & Entertainment **Band 2**
Table: p.1235

Ames, Robert (Maryland)
Profile: p.919
Employment **Band 2**
Table: p.912

Ames, Stuart (Florida)
Profile: p.533
Corporate/M&A **Band 3**
Table: p.509

Ammon, Jeffrey (Michigan)
Profile: p.998
Corporate/M&A **Band 2**
Table: p.989

Amory, Daniel (Maine)
Profile: p.897
Bankruptcy **Band 1**
Table: p.888

Amster, Glenn J
(Washington)
Profile: p.1790
Real Estate **Band 2**
Table: p.1789

Amstutz, Eric B
(South Carolina)
Profile: p.1579
Corporate/M&A **Band 3**
Table: p.1572

Andersen, Richard
(New York)
Profile: p.1262
Tax **Band 4**
Table: p.1255

Andersen, Steven (Idaho)
Profile: p.659
Litigation **Band 2**
Table: p.657

Anderson, Chris (Utah)
Profile: p.1735
Corporate/M&A **Band 2**
Table: p.1727

Anderson, David A (Utah)
Profile: p.1735
Employment **Band 3**
Table: p.1730

Anderson, Eugene
(New York)
Profile: p.1262
Insurance **Band S**
Table: p.1213

Anderson, James E
(District of Columbia)
Profile: p.431
Investment Management
Up and coming
Table: p.406

Anderson, John (Virginia)
Profile: p.1767
Intellectual Property **Band 2**
Table: p.1759

Anderson, Kenneth M
(Texas)
Profile: p.1670
Banking & Finance **Band 3**
Table: p.1625

Anderson, Kimball (Illinois)
Profile: p.717
Litigation **Band 4**
Table: p.700

Anderson, M Jean
(National)
Profile: p.74
International Trade **Band 1**
Table: p.40

KEY TO RANKINGS: ✪ = STAR INDIVIDUAL   S = SENIOR STATESMAN

Anderson, Philip S
(Arkansas)
Profile: p.175
Litigation Band 2
Table: p.172

Anderson, Reuben V
(Mississippi)
Profile: p.1032
Litigation Band 2
Table: p.1028

Anderson, Richard L
(Nebraska)
Profile: p.1087
Real Estate Band 2
Table: p.1086

Anderson, Robert
(South Dakota)
Profile: p.1592
Litigation Band 1
Table: p.1590

Anderson, Robert (Arizona)
Profile: p.156
Environment Band 3
Table: p.150

Anderson, Sandra J (Ohio)
Profile: p.1437
Litigation Band 4
Table: p.1431

Anderson, Scott Bradley
(South Dakota)
Profile: p.1592
Corporate/M&A Band 3
Table: p.1587

Anderson, Stephen W
(Arizona)
Profile: p.156
Real Estate Band 2
Table: p.155

Anderson, Steve
(Tennessee)
Profile: p.1605
Litigation Band 1
Table: p.1599

Andeweg, Robert (Iowa)
Profile: p.812
Real Estate Band 3
Table: p.810

Andreozzi, Bradley J
(National)
Profile: p.74
Sport Band 2
Table: p.55

Andress, Scott (Mississippi)
Profile: p.1032
Gaming & Licensing Band 1
Table: p.1024

Andrews, Carl (West Virginia)
Profile: p.1807
Real Estate Band 1
Table: p.1806

Andrews, Walter J (Virginia)
Profile: p.431
Insurance Band 3
Table: p.400

Andrews, William (Florida)
Profile: p.533
Employment Band 3
Table: p.513

Andrews, William K (Texas)
Profile: p.1670
Construction Band 3

Table: p.1629
Andril, David T
(District of Columbia)
Profile: p.431
Energy Band 2
Table: p.382

Angeli, Courtney (Oregon)
Profile: p.1481
Employment Up and coming
Table: p.1474

Angelo, Percy L (Illinois)
Profile: p.717
Environment Band S
Table: p.687

Angiolillo, Bruce (New York)
Profile: p.1262
Litigation Band 2
Table: p.1223

Angland, Joseph (New York)
Profile: p.1263
Antitrust Band 4
Table: p.1170

Angle, Stephen
(District of Columbia)
Profile: p.431
Energy Band 3
Table: p.386

Anglehart, Donald
(Massachusetts)
Profile: p.961
Environment Band 3
Table: p.943

Ankers, Norman C.
(Michigan)
Profile: p.998
Litigation Band 3
Table: p.994

Ankney, Gordon L (Missouri)
Profile: p.1055
Litigation Band 1
Table: p.1049

Anner-Hughes, Roberta
(Montana)
Profile: p.1079
Litigation Band 3
Table: p.1075

Antalics, Michael
(District of Columbia)
Profile: p.431
Antitrust Band 4
Table: p.367

Antell, Kenneth S (Oregon)
Profile: p.1481
Real Estate Band 3
Table: p.1479

Anthony, Joseph
(Minnesota)
Profile: p.1017
Litigation Band 1
Table: p.1011

Anthony, Michael F (Illinois)
Profile: p.717
Healthcare Band 1
Table: p.690

Anthony, William (California)
Profile: p.243
Intellectual Property Band 3
Table: p.216

Apfel, David J
(Massachusetts)
Profile: p.961

Litigation Band 1
Table: p.951

Apodaca, Patrick V
(New Mexico)
Profile: p.1162
Corporate/M&A Band 3
Table: p.1155

Appel, Brent (Iowa)
Profile: p.812
Litigation Band 3
Table: p.807

Appelbaum, Jeffrey (Ohio)
Profile: p.1437
Construction Band 1
Table: p.1417

Appelbaum, Mitchel
(Massachusetts)
Profile: p.961
Bankruptcy Band 3
Table: p.935

Appicelli, Frank
(Connecticut)
Profile: p.336
Real Estate Band 2
Table: p.334

Applebaum, Harvey M
(National)
Profile: p.75
International Trade Band 4
Table: p.40

Appleby, Nancy J
(District of Columbia)
Profile: p.1162
Native Law Band 1
Table: p.1159

Aquila, Francis J (New York)
Profile: p.1263
Corporate/M&A Band 2
Table: p.1189

Arar, Roger M (New York)
Profile: p.1263
Media & Entertainment Band 2
Table: p.1235

Archibald, James (Maryland)
Profile: p.919
Litigation Band 3
Table: p.914

Archibald, Jeanne S
(National)
Profile: p.75
International Trade Band 4
Table: p.40

Ardinger, William F J
(New Hampshire)
Profile: p.1116
Tax Band 1
Table: p.1107

Arellano, Joseph C (Dorset)
Profile: p.1481
Litigation Band 3
Table: p.1477

Arfmann, Dennis (Colorado)
Profile: p.316
Environment Band 2
Table: p.307

Arguedas, Cristina C
(California)
Profile: p.243
Litigation Band 1
Table: p.225

Arkell, Betty (Colorado)
Profile: p.316
Corporate/M&A Band 3
Table: p.303

Armentrout, Randall (Iowa)
Profile: p.812
Employment Up and coming
Table: p.805

Armistead III, I Cary
(Massachusetts)
Profile: p.961
Antitrust Band 2
Table: p.930

Armstrong, Stephen
(Pennsylvania)
Profile: p.1518
Antitrust Band 3
Table: p.1489

Arndt, Randall (Ohio)
Profile: p.1437
Real Estate Band 2
Table: p.1434

Arnholz, John (National)
Profile: p.75
Capital Markets Band 3
Table: p.19

Arnold, Beth E
(Massachusetts)
Profile: p.961
Intellectual Property Band 2
Table: p.948

Arnold, Dennis (California)
Profile: p.243
Real Estate Band 3
Table: p.238

Arnold, Richard (Florida)
Profile: p.533
Antitrust Band 2
Table: p.498

Arnold, Scott (Georgia)
Profile: p.605
Real Estate Band 2
Table: p.601

Arnold III, Edward H.
(Louisiana)
Profile: p.869
Energy Band 1
Table: p.863

Aro, Edwin (Colorado)
Profile: p.316
Employment Band 2
Table: p.306

Aronchick, Mark Alan
(Pennsylvania)
Profile: p.1518
Litigation Band 1
Table: p.1511

Aronoff, James (Ohio)
Profile: p.1437
Real Estate Band 3
Table: p.1434

Aronov, Mary L (Tennessee)
Profile: p.1605
Real Estate Band 3
Table: p.1603

Aronson, Clifford H
(New York)
Profile: p.1263
Antitrust Band 4
Table: p.1170

Aronson, Daniel H (Florida)
Profile: p.533
Corporate/M&A Band 2
Table: p.509

Aronson, Seth (California)
Profile: p.243
Litigation Band 3
Table: p.224

Aronson, Virginia (Illinois)
Profile: p.717
Real Estate Band 2
Table: p.706

Aronzon, Paul S (California)
Profile: p.243
Bankruptcy Band 1
Table: p.191

Arquit, Kevin J (New York)
Profile: p.1263
Antitrust ✪
Table: p.1170

Arrajj, David (Nevada)
Profile: p.1101
Gaming & Licensing Band 1
Table: p.1094

Arrington, Scott J (Texas)
Profile: p.1670
Projects Up and coming
Table: p.1659

Asbill, Rick (Georgia)
Profile: p.605
Antitrust Band 3
Table: p.578

Aschleman, James A
(Indiana)
Profile: p.790
Corporate/M&A Band 1
Table: p.781

Ash, James (Missouri)
Profile: p.1055
Corporate/M&A Band 1
Table: p.1043

Ashburn, Mark (Alaska)
Profile: p.141
Litigation Band 1
Table: p.138

Ashby, Kimberly (Florida)
Profile: p.533
Construction Band 2
Table: p.507

Ashcraft, Howard
(California)
Profile: p.243
Construction Band 3
Table: p.194

Ashe, Lawrence (Georgia)
Profile: p.605
Employment Band 1
Table: p.589

Asher Jr, William B
(Massachusetts)
Profile: p.961
Corporate/M&A Band 1
Table: p.937

Ashford, Leon (Alabama)
Profile: p.121
Litigation Band 1
Table: p.116

Ashinoff, Reid (New York)
Profile: p.1263
Insurance Band 2
Table: p.1213

Ashmus, Keith A (Ohio)
Profile: p.1437
Employment Band 3
Table: p.1422

Askew, Anthony (Georgia)
Profile: p.605
Intellectual Property Band 1
Table: p.596

Askew, Jess (Arkansas)
Profile: p.175
Litigation Up and coming
Table: p.172

Aslin, John (Washington)
Profile: p.1790
Employment Band S
Table: p.1780

Asmar, Mark A (Connecticut)
Profile: p.336
Real Estate Band 1
Table: p.334

Asmus, David (Texas)
Profile: p:1670
Energy Band 1
Table: p.1637
Projects Band 1
Table: p.52
Projects Band 1
Table: p.1659

Asofsky, Paul (Texas)
Profile: p.1670
Tax Band 2
Table: p.1665

Asperger, James (California)
Profile: p.244
Litigation Band 2
Table: p.225

Assaf, Eugene F
(District of Columbia)
Profile: p.431
Intellectual Property Band 3
Table: p.403

Asselin, Thomas (Georgia)
Profile: p.605
Construction Band 1
Table: p.584

Astigarraga, José I
(National)
Profile: p.75
Arbitration Band 2
Table: p.33

Astle, Richard W (Illinois)
Profile: p.717
Energy Band 3
Table: p.685

Atchison, W Michael
(Alabama)
Profile: p.121
Litigation Band 2
Table: p.116

Atkins, Peter Allan
(New York)
Profile: p.1263
Corporate/M&A Band 1
Table: p.1189

Atkins, William P (Virginia)
Profile: p.1767
Intellectual Property Band 2

Attanasio, Donna
(District of Columbia)
Profile: p.431
Energy Band 5
Table: p.386

Atwood, James
(District of Columbia)
Profile: p.431
Antitrust Band 5
Table: p.367

Auen, Michael H
(Wisconsin)
Profile: p.1824
Employment Band 1
Table: p.1819

Auerbach, Reed (National)
Profile: p.75
Capital Markets Band 2
Table: p.19

Aughtry, David D (Georgia)
Profile: p.605
Tax Band 2
Table: p.603

August, Jerald (Florida)
Profile: p.533
Tax Band 2
Table: p.531

Ausherman, Larry P
(New Mexico)
Profile: p.1162
Environment Band 1
Table: p.1158

Auslander, Charles (Florida)
Profile: p.533
Litigation Band 1
Table: p.525

Auspitz, Jack (New York)
Profile: p.1263
Litigation Band 3
Table: p.1223

Austin, Brad (Iowa)
Profile: p.812
Real Estate Band 4
Table: p.810

Austin, Jesse (Georgia)
Profile: p.605
Banking & Finance Band 3
Table: p.580
Bankruptcy Band 1
Table: p.582

Avil, Richard
(District of Columbia)
Profile: p.431
Energy Band 4
Table: p.382

Avila, Alcides (Florida)
Profile: p.533
Banking & Finance Band 1
Table: p.500

Aviv, Joseph (Michigan)
Profile: p.998
Litigation Band 2
Table: p.994

Awner, Jonathan L (Florida)
Profile: p.534
Corporate/M&A Band 2
Table: p.509

Axe, Albert (Texas)
Profile: p.1670
Environment Band 4
Table: p.1643

Axelberg, Tracy (Montana)
Profile: p.1079
Litigation Band 3
Table: p.1075

Axelroth, Lynn R
(Pennsylvania)
Profile: p.1518
Real Estate Band 3
Table: p.1516

Axinn, Stephen (New York)
Profile: p.1263
Antitrust Band 2
Table: p.1170

Axselle, Ralph (Virginia)
Profile: p.1767
Real Estate Band 1
Table: p.1765

Ayers, David (Mississippi)
Profile: p.1032
Litigation Band 3
Table: p.1028

Ayres, Jeffrey (Maryland)
Profile: p.919
Employment Band 1
Table: p.912

Ayres, Margaret M
(National)
Profile: p.75
International Trade Band 2
Table: p.41

Azoff, Elliot (Ohio)
Profile: p.1437
Employment Band 3
Table: p.1422

Baach, Martin
(District of Columbia)
Profile: p.432
Insurance Band 2
Table: p.400

Baader, Michael (Maryland)
Profile: p.919
Corporate/M&A Band 3
Table: p.909

Baar, Lois (Utah)
Profile: p.1735
Employment Band 2
Table: p.1730

Babbe, David B (California)
Profile: p.244
Insurance Band 3
Table: p.212

Babcock, Kathleen
(Kansas)
Profile: p.823
Employment Band 1
Table: p.818

Baber, Bruce (Georgia)
Profile: p.605
Intellectual Property Band 2
Table: p.596

Babst III, Chester
(Pennsylvania)
Profile: p.1519
Environment Band 1
Table: p.1505

Baca, David C (Oregon)
Profile: p.1481
Corporate/M&A Band 3
Table: p.1471

Bach, Robert (Colorado)
Profile: p.316
Real Estate Band 3
Table: p.313

Bachman, Gary
(District of Columbia)
Profile: p.432
Energy Band 5
Table: p.386

Bachman, John Q
(Nebraska)
Profile: p.1087
Real Estate Band 1
Table: p.1086

Bachman, Katharine E
(Massachusetts)
Profile: p.961
Real Estate Band 3
Table: p.956

Backus, Marcia E (Texas)
Profile: p.1670
Energy Band 4
Table: p.1637
Projects Band 4
Table: p.1659

Bacon, Douglas J (Illinois)
Profile: p.717
Bankruptcy Band 3
Table: p.669

Badgerow, J Nick (Kansas)
Profile: p.823
Litigation Band 2
Table: p.819

Baecher, John (New York)
Profile: p.1263
Projects Band 2
Table: p.1244

Baechtold, Robert
(New York)
Profile: p.1264
Intellectual Property ✪
Table: p.1217

Baena, Scott L (Florida)
Profile: p.534
Bankruptcy Band 1
Table: p.503

Baer, Bill
(District of Columbia)
Profile: p.432
Antitrust Band 1
Table: p.367

Bagley, Philip (Virginia)
Profile: p.1767
Real Estate Band 1
Table: p.1765

Bagnall, Robert G
(District of Columbia)
Profile: p.432
Investment Management
Up and coming
Table: p.406

Bahner, Maxwell
(Tennessee)
Profile: p.1605
Litigation Band 3
Table: p.1599

Baier, Kelly (Iowa)
Profile: p.812
Employment Band 1
Table: p.805

Bailey, Benjamin
(West Virginia)
Profile: p.1807
Litigation Band 1
Table: p.1803

Bailey, Burck (Oklahoma)
Profile: p.1464
Litigation Band 1
Table: p.1462

Bailey, Deena (Kansas)
Profile: p.823
Employment Up and coming
Table: p.818

Baine, Kevin T
(District of Columbia)
Profile: p.432
Media & Entertainment Band 1
Table: p.413

Bains, Kay (Alabama)
Profile: p.121
Real Estate Band 2
Table: p.119

Baird, Peter (Arizona)
Profile: p.156
Litigation Band 1
Table: p.152

Baker, Andrew M (Texas)
Profile: p.1670
Corporate/M&A Band 4
Table: p.1631

Baker, D J (Jan) (New York)
Profile: p.1264
Bankruptcy Band 1
Table: p.1179

Baker, David (Ohio)
Profile: p.1437
Real Estate Band 2
Table: p.1434

Baker, Debra (Texas)
Profile: p.1671
Environment Band 4
Table: p.1643

Baker, Douglas
(New Mexico)
Profile: p.1162
Litigation Band 4
Table: p.1159

Baker, Lewis (Virginia)
Profile: p.1767
Construction Band 2
Table: p.1750

Baker, Mark (Texas)
Profile: p. 1671
Arbitration Band 3
Table: p.33
Energy Band 2
Table: p.1641

Baker, Pamela (Illinois)
Profile: p.717
Employee Benefits Band 1
Table: p.681

Baker, Tyler A (California)
Profile: p.244
Antitrust Band 3
Table: p.184

Baker III, Frank Lewis
(Connecticut)
Profile: p.336
Real Estate Band 2
Table: p.334

Baker Jr, William T
(New York)
Profile: p.1264
Energy Band 1
Table: p.1202

Bakke, Randall J
(North Dakota)
Profile: p.1410
Litigation Band 2
Table: p.1406

Balabanian, David
(California)
Profile: p.244
Litigation Band 4
Table: p.224

Baldiga, William R
(Massachusetts)
Profile: p.961
Bankruptcy Band 3
Table: p.935

Baldwin, Charles B
(Indiana)
Profile: p.790
Employment Band 3
Table: p.783

Baldwin III, Garza
(North Carolina)
Profile: p.1394
Corporate/M&A Band 2
Table: p.1384

Bales, Scott (Arizona)
Profile: p.156
Litigation Band 1
Table: p.153

Balick, Steven J (Delaware)
Profile: p.351
Intellectual Property Band 4
Table: p.348

Balis, Stanley
(District of Columbia)
Profile: p.432
Energy Band 3
Table: p.386

Ball, Corinne (New York)
Profile: p.1264
Bankruptcy Band 2
Table: p.1179

Ball, Dan H (Missouri)
Profile: p.1055
Litigation Band 3
Table: p.1049

Ball, Robert (Oregon)
Profile: p.1481
Real Estate Band S
Table: p.1479

Ballantine, Douglas C
(Kentucky)
Profile: p.839
Litigation Band 4
Table: p.835

Ballantine, Frank D (Illinois)
Profile: p.717
Private Equity Band 3
Table: p.676

Ballantine, John T
(Kentucky)
Profile: p.839
Litigation Band 4
Table: p.835

Ballard, Brian (Idaho)
Profile: p.659
Real Estate Band 2
Table: p.658

Ballati, Deborah (California)
Profile: p.244
Construction Band 2
Table: p.194

Ballis, Jon A (Illinois)
Profile: p.717
Private Equity Band 2
Table: p.676

Balotti, Franklin (Delaware)
Profile: p.351
Chancery Band 2
Table: p.344
Corporate/M&A Band 2
Table: p.346

Banducci, Thomas (Idaho)
Profile: p.659
Litigation Band 2
Table: p.657

Bangs, Frank (Arizona)
Profile: p.156
Real Estate Band 2
Table: p.155

Bankoff, Joseph (Georgia)
Profile: p.606
Intellectual Property Band 2
Table: p.596

Banks, David F E (Hawaii)
Profile: p.648
Employment Band 2
Table: p.642

Banks, Diane (Utah)
Profile: p.1735
Real Estate Band 3
Table: p.1733

Banks, Jim
(District of Columbia)
Profile: p.432
Environment Band 4
Table: p.392

Banks, Robert S (Oregon)
Profile: p.1481
Litigation Band 3
Table: p.1477

Banks Jr, Fred L
(Mississippi)
Profile: p.1032
Litigation Band 2
Table: p.1028

Bankston, William M
(Alaska)
Profile: p.141
Litigation Band 2
Table: p.138

Banner, Mark T (Illinois)
Profile: p.717
Intellectual Property Band 3
Table: p.696

Banoff, Sheldon I (Illinois)
Profile: p.717
Tax Band 2
Table: p.710

Baptista Jr, Robert C
(Illinois)
Profile: p.718
Banking & Finance Band 1
Table: p.665

Barad, Edward N (Colorado)
Profile: p.316
Real Estate Band 1
Table: p.313

Barancik, Tia (New York)
Profile: p.1264
Energy Band 2
Table: p.1202

Barbash, Barry
(District of Columbia)
Profile: p.432
Investment Management
Band 1
Table: p.406

Barbe, J Kenneth (Wyoming)
Profile: p.1838
Corporate/M&A Band 2
Table: p.1832
Real Estate Band 2
Table: p.1836

Barber, Timothy G
(North Carolina)
Profile: p.1394
Litigation Band 3
Table: p.1390

Barbier, Margaret Louise
(Washington)
Profile: p.1790
Employment Band 3
Table: p.1780

Barbin, Jeffrey M
(Louisiana)
Profile: p.869
Gaming & Licensing
Up and coming
Table: p.864

Barbour, David (Texas)
Profile: p.1671
Banking & Finance Band 4
Table: p.1625

Barbour, Larry G (Texas)
Profile: p.1671
Banking & Finance Band 1
Table: p.1625

Barbuti, Thomas (Maryland)
Profile: p.919
Real Estate Band 4
Table: p.917

Barclay , James M (Florida)
Profile: p.534
Healthcare Band 2
Table: p.518

Bardacke, Paul (New
Mexico)
Profile: p.1162
Litigation Band 1
Table: p.1159

Bardenwerper, William B
(Kentucky)
Profile: p.839
Real Estate Band 2
Table: p.838

Barfield II, Lee (Tennessee)
Profile: p.1605
Litigation Band 1
Table: p.1599
Litigation Band 2
Table: p.1599

Barford, George (Florida)
Profile: p.534
Employment Band 3
Table: p.513

Barghols, Steven L
(Oklahoma)
Profile: p.1464
Litigation Band 3
Table: p.1462

Barker, Christopher
(Massachusetts)
Profile: p.961
Real Estate Band 2
Table: p.956

Barker, James H
(District of Columbia)
Profile: p.432
Telecom, Broadcast & Satellite
Band 4
Table: p.427

Barker, John (National)
Profile: p.75
International Trade Band 2
Table: p.41

Barker, Scott (Colorado)
Profile: p.316
Litigation Band 2
Table: p.311

Barkett, John (Florida)
Profile: p.534
Environment Band 2
Table: p.516

Barliant, Ronald (Illinois)
Profile: p.718
Bankruptcy Band 2
Table: p.669

Barlow, Richard
(New Mexico)
Profile: p.1162
Corporate/M&A Band 3
Table: p.1155

Barmeyer, Patricia
(Georgia)
Profile: p.606
Environment Band 1
Table: p.593

Barnard, Gregg (Nevada)
Profile: p.1101
Corporate/M&A Band 3
Table: p.1089

Barnard, Kevin (New York)
Profile: p.1264
Banking & Finance Band 2
Table: p.1174

Barnard, Thomas (Ohio)
Profile: p.1437
Employment ✪
Table: p.1422

Barnes, Clemens H
(Washington)
Profile: p.1790
Employment Band 2
Table: p.1780

Barnes, Geoffrey K (Ohio)
Profile: p.1437
Environment Band 2
Table: p.1425

Barnes, Mark (New York)
Profile: p.1264
Healthcare Band 2
Table: p.1209

Barnes, Thomas J
(Michigan)
Profile: p.998
Employment Band 2
Table: p.991

Barnes Jr, Hershell L
(Texas)
Profile: p.1671
Employment Band 3
Table: p.1634

Barnett, Bonnie Allyn
(Pennsylvania)
Profile: p.1519
Environment Band 1
Table: p.1505

Barnett, Robert B
(District of Columbia)
Profile: p.432
Media & Entertainment Band 2
Table: p.413

Barnhardt III, John J
(North Carolina)
Profile: p.1394
Antitrust Band 1
Table: p.1390

Baron, Robert (New York)
Profile: p.1264
Litigation Band 3
Table: p.1223

Baronsky, Kenneth
(California)
Profile: p.76
Capital Markets Band 3
Table: p.23

Barr, Daniel C (Arizona)
Profile: p.156
Employment Band 4
Table: p.148

Barr, Lynne (Massachusetts)
Profile: p.962
Banking & Finance Band 1
Table: p.932

Barr, Michael H (New York)
Profile: p.1264
Insurance Band 2
Table: p.1213

Barr, Michael R (California)
Profile: p.244
Environment Band 1
Table: p.207

Barragate, Brett (Ohio)
Profile: p.1437
Banking & Finance
Up and coming
Table: p.1411

Barran, Paula (Oregon)
Profile: p.1481
Employment Band 1
Table: p.1474

Barrasso, Judy Y (Louisiana)
Profile: p.869
Litigation Band 2
Table: p.865

B

Barrett, Gayle (Oklahoma)
Profile: p.1464
Employment Band 2
Table: p.1461

Barrett, Joshua
(West Virginia)
Profile: p.1807
Litigation Band 2
Table: p.1803

Barrett, Michael A
(Washington)
Profile: p.1790
Real Estate Band 2
Table: p.1788

Barrett, Patrick (Nebraska)
Profile: p.1087
Employment Band 1
Table: p.1084

Barrier, W Christopher
(Arkansas)
Profile: p.175
Real Estate Band 1
Table: p.174

Barriere, Brent B
(Louisiana)
Profile: p.869
Corporate/M&A Band 1
Table: p.859
Litigation Band 2
Table: p.865

Barringer, William H
(National)
Profile: p.76
International Trade Band 2
Table: p.40

Barris, William (Michigan)
Profile: p.998
Real Estate Band 2
Table: p.996

Barrow, Peter (Illinois)
Profile: p.718
Banking & Finance Band 3
Table: p.665

Barry, Dennis
(District of Columbia)
Profile: p.432
Healthcare Band 1
Table: p.398

Barry, Desmond T (National)
Profile: p.76
Aviation Band 2
Table: p.58

Barshak, Edward
(Massachusetts)
Profile: p.962
Litigation Band 3
Table: p.951

Barshay, Scott (New York)
Profile: p.1264
Corporate/M&A Band 3
Table: p.1189

Barshefsky, Charlene
(National)
Profile: p.76
International Trade Band 1
Table: p.40

Barsky, Wayne (California)
Profile: p.244
Intellectual Property Band 4
Table: p.216

Barson, Leon R
(Pennsylvania)
Profile: p.1519
Bankruptcy Band 3
Table: p.1494

Bartel II, Paul W (New York)
Profile: p.1264
Antitrust Band 3
Table: p.1170

Bartell, Jeff (Wisconsin)
Profile: p.1824
Corporate/M&A Band 2
Table: p.1817

Bartelsmeyer, Fred W
(Missouri)
Profile: p.1055
Corporate/M&A Band 3
Table: p.1043

Bartfeld, Daniel D
(New York)
Profile: p.1265
Projects Band 4
Table: p.1244

Bartine, William (Iowa)
Profile: p.812
Real Estate Band 1
Table: p.810

Bartlit Jr, Fred (Colorado)
Profile: p. 718
Litigation Band 1
Table: p.311
Litigation Band 1
Table: p.700

Bartner, Douglas (New York)
Profile: p.1265
Bankruptcy Band 2
Table: p.1179

Barton, Bernard (Florida)
Profile: p.534
Tax Band 2
Table: p.531

Barton, Carl (Utah)
Profile: p.1735
Real Estate Up and coming
Table: p.1733

Barufka, Jack S (Virginia)
Profile: p.1767
Intellectual Property Band 1
Table: p.1759

Barzoukas, Nicolas G
(Texas)
Profile: p.1671
Intellectual Property Band 2
Table: p.1651

Bash, Brian (Ohio)
Profile: p.1437
Bankruptcy Band 4
Table: p.1414

Bash, Roy (Missouri)
Profile: p.1055
Litigation Band 3
Table: p.1049

Basich, Anthony M
(California)
Profile: p.244
Media & Entertainment Band 3
Table: p.230

Basile, Michael
(West Virginia)
Profile: p.1807
Corporate/M&A Band 3
Table: p.1798

Basile, Michael (Florida)
Profile: p.534
Banking & Finance Band 2
Table: p.500

Baskin, Maurice
(District of Columbia)
Profile: p.432
Employment Band 3
Table: p.380

Baskin, Stuart (New York)
Profile: p.1265
Litigation Band 2
Table: p.1223

Bason Jr, George R
(New York)
Profile: p.1265
Corporate/M&A Band 3
Table: p.1189
Private Equity Band 1
Table: p.1237

Bass, Hilarie (Florida)
Profile: p.534
Litigation Band 3
Table: p.521

Bass, Jo (Nebraska)
Profile: p.1087
Corporate/M&A Band 3
Table: p.1082

Bass Jr, Ross F (Mississippi)
Profile: p.1032
Litigation Band 2
Table: p.1028

Bassett, David
(Massachusetts)
Profile: p.962
Intellectual Property Band 2
Table: p.948

Bassett, Peter Q (Georgia)
Profile: p.606
Litigation Band 2
Table: p.598

Bassetti, Andrew B
(Washington)
Profile: p.1790
Real Estate Band 2
Table: p.1788

Bastianelli, Adrian
(District of Columbia)
Profile: p.432
Construction Band 1
Table: p.374

Bateman, David A
(Washington)
Profile: p.1790
Intellectual Property Band 2
Table: p.1784
Litigation Band 3
Table: p.1786

Bateman, Randall (Oregon)
Profile: p.1481
Real Estate Band 2
Table: p.1479

Bates, Jeffrey
(Massachusetts)
Profile: p.962
Environment Band 1
Table: p.943

Bates, John (Virginia)
Profile: p.1767
Real Estate Band 1
Table: p.1765

Bates, Robert (Arizona)
Profile: p.156
Real Estate Band 4
Table: p.154

Bates Jr, Robert J (Illinois)
Profile: p.718
Insurance Band 3
Table: p.694
Insurance Band 3
Table: p.695

Bath, Thomas J (Kansas)
Profile: p.823
Litigation Band 2
Table: p.819

Batson, R Neal (Georgia)
Profile: p.606
Bankruptcy Band 1
Table: p.582

Battcher, Frederick R
(Nevada)
Profile: p.1101
Corporate/M&A
Up and coming
Table: p.1089

Batten, Fred (Michigan)
Profile: p.998
Employment Band 3
Table: p.991

Battista, Gregory J
(New York)
Profile: p.1265
Environment Band 2
Table: p.1206

Battista, Paul J (Florida)
Profile: p.534
Bankruptcy Band 1
Table: p.503

Batty, Jerome (Rhode Island)
Profile: p.1569
Real Estate Band 2
Table: p.1568

Bauer, Steven M
(Massachusetts)
Profile: p.962
Intellectual Property Band 1
Table: p.948

Bauman, Carl (Alaska)
Profile: p.141
Environment Band 2
Table: p.137

Bauman, Todd (Oregon)
Profile: p.1481
Corporate/M&A Band 2
Table: p.1471

Baumann, Frederick J
(Colorado)
Profile: p.316
Litigation Band 1
Table: p.311
Litigation Band 3
Table: p.311

Baumbusch, Peter L
(District of Columbia)
Profile: p.432
Tax Band 4
Table: p.422

Baumgarten, Jon
(District of Columbia)
Profile: p.432
Intellectual Property Band 3
Table: p.403

Baumgartner, Bruce (Ohio)
Profile: p.1437
Intellectual Property Band 3
Table: p.1428

Bausch, James (Nebraska)
Profile: p.1087
Litigation Band 2
Table: p.1085

Baxa Jr, Edmund T (Florida)
Profile: p.534
Construction Band 3
Table: p.507

Baxley, C William (Georgia)
Profile: p.606
Corporate/M&A Band 2
Table: p.587

Baxter, Michael St Patrick (District of Columbia)
Profile: p.432
Bankruptcy Band 2
Table: p.372

Bayko, Tom (Texas)
Profile: p.1671
Energy Band 3
Table: p.1640

Bayliss, William D (Virginia)
Profile: p.1767
Litigation Band 3
Table: p.1763

Bays, Richard (Texas)
Profile: p.1671
Technology Band 2
Table: p.1668

Bayt, Phillip (Indiana)
Profile: p.790
Real Estate Band 1
Table: p.788

Beale, Walter (Alabama)
Profile: p.121
Corporate/M&A Band 2
Table: p.111

Beall, George (Maryland)
Profile: p.919
Litigation Band 1
Table: p.914

Bean, Rodney L
(West Virginia)
Profile: p.1807
Employment Up and coming
Table: p.1801

Beane, Jerry (Texas)
Profile: p.1671
Antitrust Band 2
Table: p.1622

Beard, Brian (Texas)
Profile: p.1671
Technology Band 3
Table: p.1668

Beard, James (Illinois)
Profile: p.718
Real Estate Band 3
Table: p.706

Beard III, RT (Arkansas)
Profile: p.175
Litigation Band 1

Table: p.172
Litigation **Band 3**
Table: p.172

Bearman Jr, Leo
(Tennessee)
Profile: p.1605
Litigation **Band 2**
Table: p.1599

Beasley, Jere (Alabama)
Profile: p.121
Litigation **Band 2**
Table: p.116

Beaton, Glenn (Colorado)
Profile: p.316
Intellectual Property **Band 1**
Table: p.309

Beattie, Richard I
(New York)
Profile: p.1265
Corporate/M&A **Band S**
Table: p.1189
Private Equity **Band S**
Table: p.1237

Beaudoin, Thomas A
(Massachusetts)
Profile: p.962
Private Equity **Band 2**
Table: p.955

Beaudrot Jr, Charles R
(Georgia)
Profile: p.606
Tax **Band 3**
Table: p.603

Beavers, Charles (Alabama)
Profile: p.121
Real Estate **Band 1**
Table: p.119

Becerra, Jacqueline
(Florida)
Profile: p.534
Litigation **Up and coming**
Table: p.521

Beck, David (Texas)
Profile: p.1671
Energy **Band 1**
Table: p.1640
Litigation **Band 1**
Table: p.1656

Beck, Joseph (Georgia)
Profile: p.606
Intellectual Property **Band 2**
Table: p.596

Beck, Mark (California)
Profile: p.244
Litigation **Band 1**
Table: p.225

Beck, Paul (Pennsylvania)
Profile: p.1519
Intellectual Property **Band 4**
Table: p.1508

Beck, Philip (Illinois)
Profile: p.718
Litigation **Band 1**
Table: p.700

Beck, Philip (Georgia)
Profile: p.606
Construction **Band 1**
Table: p.584

Beck, Thomas H (New York)
Profile: p.1265
Intellectual Property **Band 3**
Table: p.1217

Beck, William G (Missouri)
Profile: p.1055
Litigation **Band 3**
Table: p.1049

Beck Jr, Robert M
(Kentucky)
Profile: p.839
Corporate/M&A **Band 3**
Table: p.827

Becker, Brandon
(District of Columbia)
Profile: p.433
Investment Management
Band 2
Table: p.406

Becker, Jeffrey (Texas)
Profile: p.1671
Intellectual Property **Band 3**
Table: p.1651

Becker, Jeffrey H (New York)
Profile: p.1265
Healthcare **Band 1**
Table: p.1209

Becker, Richard K A
(Virginia)
Profile: p.1767
Corporate/M&A **Band 4**
Table: p.1752

Becker, Scott (Illinois)
Profile: p.718
Healthcare **Band 2**
Table: p.690

Becker, Wendy (Kentucky)
Profile: p.839
Employment **Band 3**
Table: p.830

Beckerman, Lisa G
(New York)
Profile: p.1265
Bankruptcy **Band 3**
Table: p.1179

Beckham Jr, Charles
(Texas)
Profile: p.1671
Bankruptcy **Band 3**
Table: p.1627

Beckman, David (Kentucky)
Profile: p.839
Corporate/M&A **Band 3**
Table: p.827

Bednar, Steven C (Utah)
Profile: p.1735
Employment **Band 2**
Table: p.1730

Bedore, James M
(Wisconsin)
Profile: p.1824
Corporate/M&A **Band 2**
Table: p.1817

Bedree, Melvin (Ohio)
Profile: p.1437
Banking & Finance **Band 2**
Table: p.1411

Beeson, Christopher
(Idaho)
Profile: p.659
Real Estate **Band 1**
Table: p.658

Behm, Jeffrey (Vermont)
Profile: p.1748
Litigation **Band 1**
Table: p.1746

Behnia, Hatef (California)
Profile: p.244
Tax **Band 3**
Table: p.241

Behrends IV, Samuel
(District of Columbia)
Profile: p.433
Energy **Band 4**
Table: p.386

Belanger, James J (Arizona)
Profile: p.156
Litigation **Band 2**
Table: p.153

Belcher, James (Wyoming)
Profile: p.1838
Corporate/M&A **Band 2**
Table: p.1832

Belisario, Martin G
(Pennsylvania)
Profile: p.1519
Intellectual Property **Band 4**
Table: p.1508

Bell, Jerry (Texas)
Profile: p.1671
Healthcare **Band 1**
Table: p.1646

Bell, Joseph C
(District of Columbia)
Profile: p.433
Energy **Band 4**
Table: p.386

Bell, Robert B
(District of Columbia)
Profile: p.433
Antitrust **Band 5**
Table: p.367

Bell, Rodney H (Florida)
Profile: p.534
Corporate/M&A **Band 3**
Table: p.509

Bell, Stephen (Illinois)
Profile: p.718
Real Estate **Band 3**
Table: p.706

Bell, Suzanne (California)
Profile: p.244
IT Outsourcing **Band 2**
Table: p.221

Bell, Thomas (New York)
Profile: p.1265
Private Equity **Band 1**
Table: p.1241

Bell Jr, Albert
(North Carolina)
Profile: p.1394
Employment **Band 2**
Table: p.1386

Bellah Maguire, Jennifer
(California)
Profile: p.244
Corporate/M&A **Band 5**
Table: p.197

Beller, Daniel (New York)
Profile: p.1265
Litigation **Band 3**
Table: p.1222

Beller, Herbert N
(District of Columbia)
Profile: p.433
Tax **Band 3**
Table: p.422

Belles, Michael J (Hawaii)
Profile: p.648
Land Use **Band 1**
Table: p.643

Belt, David L (Connecticut)
Profile: p.336
Litigation **Band 2**
Table: p.331

Beltzer, Howard S
(New York)
Profile: p.1266
Bankruptcy **Band 4**
Table: p.1179

Belzer, Irvin (Missouri)
Profile: p.1055
Litigation **Band 2**
Table: p.1049

Bemis, Kenneth E (Oregon)
Profile: p.1481
Employment **Band 3**
Table: p.1474

Ben-Ami, Leora (New York)
Profile: p.1266
Intellectual Property **Band 1**
Table: p.1217

Benard, Blaine (Utah)
Profile: p.1735
Litigation **Up and coming**
Table: p.1732

Benard, Bryan (Utah)
Profile: p.1735
Employment **Up and coming**
Table: p.1730

Bender, Jack (Kentucky)
Profile: p.839
Environment **Band 3**
Table: p.832

Bender, Jeanne Matthews
(Montana)
Profile: p.1079
Employment **Band 1**
Table: p.1073

Bender, Lawrence (North
Dakota)
Profile: p.1410
Energy **Band 1**
Table: p.1407

Bender Jr, Albert E
(Georgia)
Profile: p.606
Real Estate **Band 3**
Table: p.601

Bendicksen, Perry
(New Mexico)
Profile: p.1162
Corporate/M&A **Band 2**
Table: p.1155

Bendinger, Gary F (Utah)
Profile: p.1735
Litigation **Band 1**
Table: p.1732

Benedict, James (New York)
Profile: p.1266
Litigation **Band 2**
Table: p.1223

Benham III, Paul B
(Arkansas)
Profile: p.175
Corporate/M&A **Band 2**
Table: p.168

Benjamin, Alan (California)
Profile: p.244
Banking & Finance **Band 1**
Table: p.187

Benjamin, William
(Massachusetts)
Profile: p.962
Tax **Band 3**
Table: p.959

Benner, C. Jonathan
(National)
Profile: p.76
Shipping **Band 1**
Table: p.71

Benner, Michael B
(New York)
Profile: p.1266
Real Estate **Band 5**
Table: p.1248

Bennet, Blake (Louisiana)
Profile: p.869
Energy **Band 1**
Table: p.863
Gaming & Licensing **Band 2**
Table: p.864

Bennett, Bruce S
(California)
Profile: p.245
Bankruptcy **Band 4**
Table: p.191

Bennett, David (Texas)
Profile: p.1672
Bankruptcy **Band 4**
Table: p.1627

Bennett, Fred G (California)
Profile: p.245
Construction **Band 3**
Table: p.194

Bennett, J David (Oregon)
Profile: p.1481
Real Estate **Band 2**
Table: p.1479

Bennett, Jackie (Indiana)
Profile: p.791
Litigation **Band 3**
Table: p.785

Bennett, Mary
(District of Columbia)
Profile: p.433
Tax **Band 3**
Table: p.422

Bennett, Robert S
(District of Columbia)
Profile: p.433
Litigation **Band 1**
Table: p.410

Bennett, Thomas G (Utah)
Profile: p.1735
Real Estate **Band 3**
Table: p.1733

B

Bennett, Wilfred (Alaska)
Profile: p.141
Employment **Band 2**
Table: p.135

Bennett II, Crocker
(Vermont)
Profile: p.1748
Litigation **Band 2**
Table: p.1746

Bennett Jr, Charles R
(Massachusetts)
Profile: p.962
Bankruptcy **Band 2**
Table: p.935

Benoit, Wilfred
(Massachusetts)
Profile: p.962
Employment **Band 2**
Table: p.940

Benvenutti, Peter J
(California)
Profile: p.245
Bankruptcy **Band 3**
Table: p.191

Beranek, John R (Florida)
Profile: p.534
Litigation **Band 2**
Table: p.525

Berchild, John (California)
Profile: p.245
Banking & Finance **Band 3**
Table: p.187

Bercow, Jeffrey (Florida)
Profile: p.534
Real Estate **Band 3**
Table: p.528

Berenstein, Marvin (Iowa)
Profile: p.812
Corporate/M&A **Band 4**
Table: p.802

Berenter, Steven (Idaho)
Profile: p.659
Employment **Band 1**
Table: p.656

Berg, Andrew (New York)
Profile: p.1266
Tax **Band 3**
Table: p.1255

Berg, Eric (Illinois)
Profile: p.718
Construction **Band 3**
Table: p.672

Berg, Eric L (New York)
Profile: p.1266
Banking & Finance **Band 2**
Table: p.1174

Berg, Gracia (National)
Profile: p.76
International Trade **Band 4**
Table: p.40

Berger, Benjamin
(Delaware)
Profile: p.351
Real Estate **Band 3**
Table: p.350

Berger, Don I (California)
Profile: p.245
Real Estate **Band 3**
Table: p.238

Berger, Lawrence H
(Pennsylvania)
Profile: p.1519
Banking & Finance **Band 1**
Table: p.1493

Berger, Ritchie (Vermont)
Profile: p.1748
Litigation **Band 1**
Table: p.1746

Bergère, Timothy
(Pennsylvania)
Profile: p.1519
Environment **Band 3**
Table: p.1505

Bergeson, Donna (Georgia)
Profile: p.606
Healthcare **Band 2**
Table: p.594

Bergeson, Lynn
(District of Columbia)
Profile: p.433
Environment **Band 4**
Table: p.392

Berggren, Tom (Utah)
Profile: p.1736
Real Estate **Band 2**
Table: p.1733

Berghoff Jr, John C (Illinois)
Profile: p.718
Environment **Band 3**
Table: p.687

Bergin, Leo (Nevada)
Profile: p.1101
Real Estate **Band 3**
Table: p.1099

Bergman, Michael
(California)
Profile: p.245
Media & Entertainment **Band 4**
Table: p.230

Bergmann, Peter G
(New York)
Profile: p.1266
Healthcare **Band 1**
Table: p.1209

Bergtraum, Howard M
(New York)
Profile: p.1266
Private Equity **Band 3**
Table: p.1241

Berkeley, Jill B (Illinois)
Profile: p.718
Insurance **Band 3**
Table: p.695

Berkes, Robert H
(California)
Profile: p.245
Insurance **Band 4**
Table: p.212

Berkley, Peter L
(New Jersey)
Profile: p.1137
Real Estate **Band 2**
Table: p.1135

Berkman, Jerome
(Connecticut)
Profile: p.336
Real Estate **Band 2**
Table: p.334

Berkoff, Mark (Illinois)
Profile: p.718
Bankruptcy **Band 3**
Table: p.669

Berkowitz, Alan D
(Pennsylvania)
Profile: p.1519
Employment **Band 3**
Table: p.1500

Berkowitz, Lawrence
(Missouri)
Profile: p.1055
Litigation **Band 2**
Table: p.1049

Berlack, Evan R (National)
Profile: p.76
International Trade **Band 1**
Table: p.41

Berlin, Howard (Florida)
Profile: p.535
Bankruptcy **Band 2**
Table: p.503

Berlin, Kenneth
(District of Columbia)
Profile: p.433
Environment **Band 1**
Table: p.393

Berlin, Stephen R
(North Carolina)
Profile: p.1394
Environment **Band 2**
Table: p.1388

Berman, David
(Massachusetts)
Profile: p.962
Banking & Finance **Band 3**
Table: p.932

Berman, Mark N
(Massachusetts)
Profile: p.962
Bankruptcy **Band 3**
Table: p.935

Berman, Michael P
(Arizona)
Profile: p.156
Employment **Band 4**
Table: p.148

Bermann, George A
(National)
Profile: p.76
Arbitration **Band 1**
Table: p.34

Bernard, J Michael
(Michigan)
Profile: p.998
Corporate/M&A **Band 3**
Table: p.989

Bernard, John M
(Pennsylvania)
Profile: p.1519
Employee Benefits **Band 1**
Table: p.1501

Berne, Gary (Oregon)
Profile: p.1481
Litigation **Band 2**
Table: p.1477

Berner, Frederic
(District of Columbia)
Profile: p.434
Energy **Band 4**
Table: p.382

Bernick, Carol (Oregon)
Profile: p.1481
Employment **Band 3**
Table: p.1474

Bernick, David M (Illinois)
Profile: p.718
Litigation **Band 1**
Table: p.700

Bernius, Robert
(District of Columbia)
Profile: p.434
Media & Entertainment **Band 2**
Table: p.413

Bernstein, Alan
(Pennsylvania)
Profile: p.1519
Intellectual Property **Band 3**
Table: p.1508

Bernstein, Bruce (Illinois)
Profile: p.718
Banking & Finance **Band 1**
Table: p.665

Bernstein, David (New York)
Profile: p.1266
Intellectual Property **Band 3**
Table: p.1217

Bernstein, Donald S
(New York)
Profile: p.1266
Bankruptcy **Band 1**
Table: p.1179

Bernstein, Greg (Maryland)
Profile: p.919
Litigation **Band 2**
Table: p.914

Bernstein, Howard (Illinois)
Profile: p.718
Employment **Band 1**
Table: p.681

Bernstein, Michael
(New York)
Profile: p.1266
Employment **Band 2**
Table: p.1200

Bernstein, Michael
(District of Columbia)
Profile: p.434
Bankruptcy **Band 3**
Table: p.372

Bernstein, Stephen W
(Massachusetts)
Profile: p.963
Healthcare **Band 2**
Table: p.946

Bernstein, William S
(New York)
Profile: p.1266
Healthcare **Band 2**
Table: p.1209

Berry, Andrew T
(New Jersey)
Profile: p.1137
Litigation **Band 1**
Table: p.1131

Berry, Charles (Arizona)
Profile: p.156
Corporate/M&A **Band 4**
Table: p.146

Berry, John V (Arizona)
Profile: p.156
Real Estate **Band 1**
Table: p.155

Berry, Leo (Montana)
Profile: p.1079
Natural Resources **Band 2**
Table: p.1077

Berry IV, Dewees
(Tennessee)
Profile: p.1605
Real Estate **Band 2**
Table: p.1603

Bertelsen, Mark (California)
Profile: p.245
Corporate/M&A **Band 5**
Table: p.197

Berz, David
(District of Columbia)
Profile: p.434
Environment **Band 2**
Table: p.393

Beshar, Sarah (National)
Profile: p.76
Capital Markets **Band 4**
Table: p.14

Bessette-Smith, Suzanne
(Illinois)
Profile: p.718
Real Estate **Band 4**
Table: p.706

Best, Edward S (Illinois)
Profile: p.718
Corporate/M&A **Band 4**
Table: p.675

Betensky, Steven
(New York)
Profile: p.1266
Technology **Band 3**
Table: p.1259

Bethune, Scott S (Missouri)
Profile: p.1055
Litigation **Band 3**
Table: p.1049

Bettencourt, Mark
(Massachusetts)
Profile: p.963
Corporate/M&A
Up and coming
Table: p.937

Better, Herbert (Maryland)
Profile: p.919
Litigation **Band 2**
Table: p.914

Bettinger, Carl J
(New Mexico)
Profile: p.1163
Litigation **Band 3**
Table: p.1159
Litigation **Band 1**
Table: p.1160

Bettis, Vance J
(South Carolina)
Profile: p.1579
Employment **Band 1**
Table: p.1574

Betts, Rebecca A
(West Virginia)
Profile: p.1808
Litigation **Band 2**
Table: p.1803

Betzer, Stan (New Mexico)
Profile: p.1163
Corporate/M&A **Band 3**
Table: p.1155

Beus, Leo R (Arizona)
Profile: p.156
Litigation **Band** 4
Table: p.152

Bevan III, William
(Pennsylvania)
Profile: p.1519
Employment **Band** 2
Table: p.1500

Beveridge, Cathy (Florida)
Profile: p.535
Employment **Up** and coming
Table: p.513

Bevilacqua, Louis
(New York)
Profile: p.1267
Corporate/M&A **Band** 4
Table: p.1189

Beyda, Richard
(District of Columbia)
Profile: p.434
Real Estate **Band** 2
Table: p.418

Beyer, Ruth (Oregon)
Profile: p.1481
Corporate/M&A **Band** 2
Table: p.1471

Bialecki, Gregory
(Massachusetts)
Profile: p.963
Real Estate **Band** 1
Table: p.957

Bialkin, Kenneth J
(New York)
Profile: p.1267
Corporate/M&A **Band** S
Table: p.1189

Biasetti, Jon (Illinois)
Profile: p.719
Insurance **Band** 2
Table: p.692

Bice, Todd L (Nevada)
Profile: p.1101
Litigation **Up** and coming
Table: p.1096

Bick, John (New York)
Profile: p.1267
Private Equity **Band** 2
Table: p.1237

Bickel, John M (Iowa)
Profile: p.812
Litigation **Band** 3
Table: p.807

Bidart, Michael J
(California)
Profile: p.245
Insurance **Band** 4
Table: p.212

Bieke, James
(District of Columbia)
Profile: p.434
Environment **Band** 3
Table: p.392

Bienenstock, Martin
(New York)
Profile: p.1267
Bankruptcy **Band** 1
Table: p.1179

Bierce, William B.
(National)
Profile: p.76

Business Process
Outsourcing: National **Band** 3
Table: p.10

Bierig, Jack R (Illinois)
Profile: p.719
Antitrust **Band** 3
Table: p.662

Biermann Tom, Rebecca
(Oregon)
Profile: p.1481
Real Estate **Up** and coming
Table: p.1479

Biery, Evelyn H (Texas)
Profile: p.1672
Bankruptcy **Band** 3

Biles, Blake A
(District of Columbia)
Profile: p.434
Environment **Band** 3
Table: p.392

Bilger, Bruce R (Texas)
Profile: p. 1672
Energy **Band** 1
Table: p.1637
Projects **Band** 1
Table: p.52
Table: p.1659

Bilkis, David (New York)
Profile: p.1267
Banking & Finance **Band** 4
Table: p.1174

Billings Jr, Peter W (Utah)
Profile: p.1736
Litigation **Band** 2
Table: p.1732

Bilzin, Brian L (Florida)
Profile: p.535
Real Estate **Band** 1
Table: p.526

Binnig, Christian F (Illinois)
Profile: p.719
Telecom, Broadcast & Satellite
Band 2
Table: p.715

Birchfield, Thomas J
(Kentucky)
Profile: p.839
Employment **Band** 2
Table: p.830

Bird, Paul S (New York)
Profile: p.1267
Corporate/M&A **Band** 3
Table: p.1189
Private Equity **Band** 2
Table: p.1237

Bird, Terry (California)
Profile: p.245
Litigation **Band** 2
Table: p.225

Birge, Taggart (Indiana)
Profile: p.791
Real Estate **Up** and coming
Table: p.788

Birnbaum, Gary (Arizona)
Profile: p.156
Litigation **Band** 2
Table: p.152

Birnbaum, Sheila L
(New York)
Profile: p.1267
Insurance **Band** 3

Table: p.1213

Biron, Thomas
(Pennsylvania)
Profile: p.1519
Bankruptcy **Band** 2
Table: p.1494

Bishop, Bruce (Virginia)
Profile: p.1767
Litigation **Band** 3
Table: p.1763

Bishop, Doak (Texas)
Profile: p. 1672
Arbitration **Band** 2
Table: p.33
Energy **Band** 1
Table: p.1641

Bishop, Timothy S (Illinois)
Profile: p.719
Environment **Band** 2
Table: p.687

Bishop III, George W
(Tennessee)
Profile: p.1605
Corporate/M&A **Band** 2
Table: p.1594

Biskind, Neil (Arizona)
Profile: p.156
Real Estate **Band** 3
Table: p.154

Bissoon, Cathy
(Pennsylvania)
Profile: p.1519
Employment **Band** 4
Table: p.1500

Bithell, Walter (Idaho)
Profile: p.659
Litigation **Band** 1
Table: p.657

Bivens, Donald (Arizona)
Profile: p.156
Litigation **Band** 2
Table: p.152

Bizar, Steven E
(Pennsylvania)
Profile: p.1519
Antitrust **Band** 3
Table: p.1489

Black, Allen (Pennsylvania)
Profile: p.1519
Antitrust **Band** 2
Table: p.1489
Litigation **Band** 2
Table: p.1511

Black, Bruce (Colorado)
Profile: p.316
Antitrust **Band** 1
Table: p.311
Litigation **Band** 2
Table: p.311

Black, Kathryn (Alaska)
Profile: p.141
Corporate/M&A **Band** 1
Table: p.134

Black, Kenneth (Utah)
Profile: p.1736
Litigation **Band** 2
Table: p.1732

Black, Margaret (New
Jersey)
Profile: p.1137
Real Estate **Band** 3

Table: p.1134

Black, Roy (Florida)
Profile: p.535
Litigation **Band** 1
Table: p.522

Black Jr, Lewis S (Delaware)
Profile: p.351
Corporate/M&A ✪
Table: p.346

Black, Jr, Creed C
(Pennsylvania)
Profile: p.1520
Litigation **Band** 2
Table: p.1512

Blackburn, Frank D
(Louisiana)
Profile: p.869
Gaming & Licensing **Band** 2
Table: p.864

Blackburn, Thomas
(District of Columbia)
Profile: p.434
Energy **Band** 5
Table: p.386

Blackhurst, Steven
(Oregon)
Profile: p.1481
Litigation **Band** 3
Table: p.1477

Blackman, Jana Cohen
(Illinois)
Profile: p.719
Real Estate **Band** 4
Table: p.706

Blackmer, Jill
(New Hampshire)
Profile: p.1116
Employment **Band** 3
Table: p.1109

Blackstock, Jerry (Georgia)
Profile: p.606
Intellectual Property **Band** 2
Table: p.596
Litigation **Band** 3
Table: p.598

Blackstone, Robert A
(Washington)
Profile: p.1790
Employment **Band** 2
Table: p.1780

Blain, Russell (Florida)
Profile: p.535
Bankruptcy **Band** 2
Table: p.503

Blair, Andrew (Colorado)
Profile: p.316
Corporate/M&A **Band** 3
Table: p.303

Blair, Mitchell G (Ohio)
Profile: p.1437
Litigation **Band** 4
Table: p.1431

Blake, Jonathan D
(District of Columbia)
Profile: p.434
Telecom, Broadcast & Satellite
Band 1
Table: p.427

Blake Jr, Joseph
(South Carolina)
Profile: p.1579

Corporate/M&A **Band** 3
Table: p.1572

Blanchard, Kimberly S
(New York)
Profile: p.1267
Tax **Band** 3
Table: p.1255

Blanchard, Timothy P
(California)
Profile: p.245
Healthcare **Band** 3
Table: p.209

Bland, Douglas S (Texas)
Profile: p.1672
Energy **Band** 4
Table: p.1637
Projects **Band** 2
Table: p.1659

Blashek, Robert D
(California)
Profile: p.245
Tax **Band** 4
Table: p.241

Blassberg, Franci J
(New York)
Profile: p.1267
Private Equity **Band** 1
Table: p.1237

Blaszak, James S
(District of Columbia)
Profile: p.434
Telecom, Broadcast & Satellite
Band 4
Table: p.427

Blattner, J Wray (Ohio)
Profile: p.1438
Environment **Band** 3
Table: p.1425

Blau, Michael L
(Massachusetts)
Profile: p.963
Healthcare **Band** 2
Table: p.946

Blauch, Kevin C (National)
Profile: p.76
Capital Markets **Band** 4
Table: p.19

Blecha, Kirk (Nebraska)
Profile: p.1087
Insurance **Band** 2
Table: p.1085

Blecher, Maxwell M
(California)
Profile: p.246
Antitrust **Band** 1
Table: p.184
Litigation **Band** 3
Table: p.224

Blechman, Bill (Florida)
Profile: p.535
Antitrust **Band** 1
Table: p.498

Bleck, Daniel
(Massachusetts)
Profile: p.963
Bankruptcy **Band** 3
Table: p.935

Blessing, Peter H
(New York)
Profile: p.1267
Tax **Band** 2
Table: p.1255

B

Bley, Kenneth B (California)
Profile: p.246
Real Estate **Band** 2
Table: p.238

Blittner, David (New York)
Profile: p.1267
Private Equity **Up and coming**
Table: p.1237

Bloch, Robert E
(District of Columbia)
Profile: p.434
Antitrust **Band** 5
Table: p.367

Bloch, Thomas P
(Massachusetts)
Profile: p.963
Real Estate **Band** 2
Table: p.956

Block, Bruce (Wisconsin)
Profile: p.1824
Real Estate **Band** 1
Table: p.1822

Block, David (Florida)
Profile: p.535
Employment **Band** 4
Table: p.513

Block, Dennis (New York)
Profile: p.1268
Corporate/M&A **Band** 1
Table: p.1189

Block, Joseph G
(District of Columbia)
Profile: p.435
Environment **Band** 4
Table: p.392

Block, William (Washington)
Profile: p.1790
Real Estate **Band** 1
Table: p.1788

Bloodworth, Darryl (Florida)
Profile: p.535
Litigation **Band** 3
Table: p.521

Bloom, Herschel (Georgia)
Profile: p.606
Tax **Band** 1
Table: p.603

Bloom, Jacob A (California)
Profile: p.246
Media & Entertainment **Band** 2
Table: p.233

Bloom, Jerry (California)
Profile: p.246
Energy **Band** 1
Table: p.204

Bloom, Mark D (Florida)
Profile: p.535
Bankruptcy **Band** 1
Table: p.503

Bloom, Michael
(Pennsylvania)
Profile: p.1520
Bankruptcy **Band** 3
Table: p.1494

Bloom, Myron A
(Pennsylvania)
Profile: p.1520
Bankruptcy **Band** 2
Table: p.1494

Blue Jr, William A
(Tennessee)
Profile: p.1606
Employment **Band** 3
Table: p.1596

Bluedorn II, Donald C
(Pennsylvania)
Profile: p.1520
Environment **Band** 4
Table: p.1505

Blume, Fred (Pennsylvania)
Profile: p.1520
Corporate/M&A **Band** 3
Table: p.1497

Blumen, Rick D (Georgia)
Profile: p.606
Banking & Finance
Up and coming
Table: p.580

Blumenfeld, Chuck
(Washington)
Profile: p.1790
Environment **Band** 1
Table: p.1782

Blumenfeld, Jack B
(Delaware)
Profile: p.351
Intellectual Property **Band** 1
Table: p.348

Blumkin, Linda R (New York)
Profile: p.1268
Antitrust **Band** 4
Table: p.1170

Blumstein, Phil (Alaska)
Profile: p.142
Native Law **Band** 1
Table: p.140

Blumstein, Philip (Alaska)
Profile: p.142
Corporate/M&A **Band** 2
Table: p.134

Boardman, Richard (Idaho)
Profile: p.660
Litigation **Band** 2
Table: p.657

Boast, Molly S (New York)
Profile: p.1268
Antitrust **Band** 3
Table: p.1170

Bobber, Bernard J
(Wisconsin)
Profile: p.1824
Employment **Band** 1
Table: p.1819

Bobo Jr, William (South
Carolina)
Profile: p.1579
Real Estate **Band** 3
Table: p.1577

Bocock, Joseph (Oklahoma)
Profile: p.1464
Litigation **Band** 3
Table: p.1462

Bodine, Brian (Washington)
Profile: p.1790
Intellectual Property **Band** 1
Table: p.1784

Boe, Kathleen M (Vermont)
Profile: p.1748
Corporate/M&A **Band** 1
Table: p.1743

Boe, Tim (Arkansas)
Profile: p.175
Employment **Band** 1
Table: p.170

Boeglin, Daniel L (Indiana)
Profile: p.791
Corporate/M&A **Band** 2
Table: p.781

Boehnen, Daniel A (Illinois)
Profile: p.719
Intellectual Property **Band** 2
Table: p.696

Boehrer, Charles (Illinois)
Profile: p.719
Banking & Finance **Band** 3
Table: p.665

Bogaard, Jonathan H.
(National)
Profile: p.76
Aviation **Band** 3
Table: p.58

Bogdanoff, Lee R
(California)
Profile: p.246
Bankruptcy **Band** 3
Table: p.191

Bogdanow, Alan J (Texas)
Profile: p.1672
Corporate/M&A **Band** 4
Table: p.1631

Bogen, Andy (California)
Profile: p.246
Corporate/M&A **Band** 1
Table: p.197

Boggs, Jack (Florida)
Profile: p.535
Tax **Band** s
Table: p.531

Bogue, Stevenson
(Nebraska)
Profile: p.1087
Employment **Band** 2
Table: p.1084

Bohannon, Paul (Texas)
Profile: p.1672
Environment **Band** 3
Table: p.1643

Bohm, Richard D (New York)
Profile: p.1268
Media & Entertainment **Band** 1
Table: p.1235
Private Equity **Band** 2
Table: p.1237

Boice, William (Georgia)
Profile: p.607
Employment **Band** 2
Table: p.589
Litigation **Band** 2
Table: p.598

Boies, Bill (Illinois)
Profile: p.719
Employee Benefits **Band** 2
Table: p.681

Boies, David (New York)
Profile: p.1268
Antitrust **Band** 2
Table: p.1170
Litigation **Band** 1
Table: p.1222

Boise, April V (Ohio)
Profile: p.1438
Corporate/M&A
Up and coming
Table: p.1419

Boisseau, Richard (Georgia)
Profile: p.607
Employment **Band** 2
Table: p.589

Bokor, Bruce (Florida)
Profile: p.535
Tax **Band** 3
Table: p.531

Bolding, Grady (California)
Profile: p.246
Tax **Band** 3
Table: p.241

Boldt, Michael (Indiana)
Profile: p.791
Employment **Band** 2
Table: p.783

Bolen, Richard J
(West Virginia)
Profile: p.1808
Real Estate **Band** 3
Table: p.1806

Boles, H Hampton
(Alabama)
Profile: p.121
Real Estate **Band** 3
Table: p.119

Bolstein, Joel (Pennsylvania)
Profile: p.1520
Environment **Band** 3
Table: p.1505

Bolton, Richard (Michigan)
Profile: p.998
Corporate/M&A **Band** 3
Table: p.989

Bomse, Stephen (California)
Profile: p.246
Antitrust **Band** 2
Table: p.184
Litigation **Band** 4
Table: p.224

Bond, Thomas J (Texas)
Profile: p.1672
Insurance **Band** 2
Table: p.1648

Bond, W Michael (New York)
Profile: p.1268
Real Estate **Band** 5
Table: p.1248

Bondurant, Emmet J
(Georgia)
Profile: p.607
Antitrust **Band** 1
Table: p.578
Litigation **Band** 1
Table: p.598

Bonham, Mark E (Utah)
Profile: p.1736
Corporate/M&A **Band** 2
Table: p.1727

Bonifay, Cecelia (Florida)
Profile: p.535
Real Estate **Band** 3
Table: p.528

Bonner, Michael J (Nevada)
Profile: p.1101
Corporate/M&A **Band** 2
Table: p.1089

Booe, Mike (North Carolina)
Profile: p.1394
Bankruptcy **Band** 1
Table: p.1383

Booker, Daniel I
(Pennsylvania)
Profile: p.1520
Antitrust **Band** 2
Table: p.1489

Booker, William
(West Virginia)
Profile: p.1808
Corporate/M&A **Band** 1
Table: p.1798

Bookin, Daniel (California)
Profile: p.246
Litigation **Band** 1
Table: p.225

Bookman, Lloyd A
(California)
Profile: p.246
Healthcare **Band** 2
Table: p.209

Boone, Michael (Texas)
Profile: p.1672
Corporate/M&A **Band** 2
Table: p.1631

Boone, Thomas (Montana)
Profile: p.1079
Corporate/M&A **Band** 2
Table: p.1072
Real Estate **Band** 2
Table: p.1078

Boone Jr, Sidney (South
Carolina)
Profile: p.1579
Real Estate **Band** 1
Table: p.1577

Booth, Brian (Oregon)
Profile: p.1481
Corporate/M&A **Band** S
Table: p.1471

Booth, William (California)
Profile: p.246
Energy **Band** 3
Table: p.204

Boothby, Colleen
(District of Columbia)
Profile: p.435
Telecom, Broadcast & Satellite
Band 4
Table: p.427

Bopp III, Fred W (Maine)
Profile: p.897
Bankruptcy **Band** 2
Table: p.888

Bor, Andrew (Washington)
Profile: p.1790
Corporate/M&A **Band** 2
Table: p.1778

Borden, Mark
(Massachusetts)
Profile: p.963
Corporate/M&A **Band** 1
Table: p.937
Private Equity **Band** 1
Table: p.953

Borders, Sarah (Georgia)
Profile: p.607
Bankruptcy **Band** 1
Table: p.582

Borders, Thomas (Illinois)
Profile: p.720
Tax Band 3
Table: p.710

Born II, Samuel (Indiana)
Profile: p.791
Employment Band 1
Table: p.783

Borowitz, Peter L
(New York)
Profile: p.1268
Bankruptcy Band 3
Table: p.1179

Borun, Michael F (Illinois)
Profile: p.720
Intellectual Property Band 3
Table: p.696

Boshkoff, Ellen (Indiana)
Profile: p.791
Employment Band 3
Table: p.783

Bossert, Terry
(Pennsylvania)
Profile: p.1520
Environment Band 4
Table: p.1505

Bostelman, John T
(National)
Profile: p.76
Capital Markets Band 2
Table: p.14

Boston, Robert E
(Tennessee)
Profile: p.1606
Employment Band 1
Table: p.1596

Bostwick, Gary (California)
Profile: p.246
Media & Entertainment Band 3
Table: p.230

Bothwick, Jay
(Massachusetts)
Profile: p.963
Corporate/M&A Band 3
Table: p.937

Botica, Matthew J (Illinois)
Profile: p.720
Bankruptcy Band 3
Table: p.669

Bottrell, Lowell (North Dakota)
Profile: p.1410
Corporate/M&A Band 2
Table: p.1403

Bouchard, Andre G
(Delaware)
Profile: p.351
Chancery Band 3
Table: p.344

Bouknight, J A
(District of Columbia)
Profile: p.435
Energy Band 1
Table: p.386

Boulden, Michael R (Texas)
Profile: p.1672
Real Estate Band 2
Table: p.1662

Boulet, Virginia (Louisiana)
Profile: p.869
Corporate/M&A Band 4
Table: p.859

Boulware, Margaret (Texas)
Profile: p.1672
Intellectual Property Band 3
Table: p.1651

Bouma, John J (Arizona)
Profile: p.157
Litigation Band 2
Table: p.152

Bourdeau, Karl S
(District of Columbia)
Profile: p.435
Environment Band 3
Table: p.392

Boutin, Michelle (Alaska)
Profile: p.142
Bankruptcy Band 2
Table: p.133

Boutrous Jr, Theodore
(California)
Profile: p.246
Media & Entertainment Band 3
Table: p.230

Bowden, William P
(Delaware)
Profile: p.351
Bankruptcy Band 4
Table: p.341

Bowe Jr, James F
(District of Columbia)
Profile: p.435
Energy Band 5
Table: p.382

Bowen, Jay (Tennessee)
Profile: p.1606
Litigation Band 3
Table: p.1599

Bowen, Michael A
(Wisconsin)
Profile: p.1824
Litigation Band 2
Table: p.1821

Bowen, Stephen S (Illinois)
Profile: p.720
Tax Band 1
Table: p.710

Bowers, James (Missouri)
Profile: p.1055
Real Estate Band 2
Table: p.1053

Bowers, William (Texas)
Profile: p.1673
Tax Band 2
Table: p.1665

Bowers, William C
(National)
Profile: p.76
Aviation Band 3
Table: p.58

Bowie, Scott O (New York)
Profile: p.1268
Private Equity Band 3
Table: p.1241

Bowman, Everett J (North Carolina)
Profile: p.1394
Antitrust Band 1
Table: p.1390

Bowman, John (Texas)
Profile: p. 1673
Arbitration Band 3
Table: p.33
Energy Band 1
Table: p.1641

Bowman, Philip L (Kansas)
Profile: p.823
Real Estate Band S
Table: p.821

Bowman, William
(District of Columbia)
Profile: p.435
Insurance Band 1
Table: p.400
Litigation Band 3
Table: p.410

Bowser, William W
(Delaware)
Profile: p.351
Employment Band 3
Table: p.347

Boxer, Leonard (New York)
Profile: p.1268
Real Estate Band S
Table: p.1248

Boyajian, Victor
(New Jersey)
Profile: p.1137
Corporate/M&A Band 1
Table: p.1123

Boyce, William J (Texas)
Profile: p.1673
Litigation Band 2
Table: p.1656

Boyd, David R (Alabama)
Profile: p.121
Litigation Band 3
Table: p.116

Boyd, Eric E (Illinois)
Profile: p.720
Environment Band 4
Table: p.687

Boyd, Paul (Idaho)
Profile: p.660
Corporate/M&A Band 1
Table: p.655

Boyd, William (South Carolina)
Profile: p.1579
Corporate/M&A Band 3
Table: p.1572
Real Estate Band 2
Table: p.1577

Boyken, Quentin (Iowa)
Profile: p.812
Corporate/M&A Band 4
Table: p.802

Bozarth, Stephen J (Florida)
Profile: p.535
Real Estate Band 1
Table: p.526

Brach, Richard (New York)
Profile: p. 1268
Projects Band 2
Table: p.52
Projects Band 2
Table: p.1244

Bradbury, Steve (Idaho)
Profile: p.660
Real Estate Band 2
Table: p.658

Braddock, James D (Texas)
Profile: p.1673
Environment Band 2
Table: p.1643

Braden, Gregory C
(National)
Profile: p.77
Litigation Band 2
Table: p.25

Bradford, Donald E
(Louisiana)
Profile: p.870
Real Estate Band 1
Table: p.867

Bradley, Craig C (Illinois)
Profile: p.720
Private Equity Band 2
Table: p.676

Bradley, Wayne N (Georgia)
Profile: p.607
Corporate/M&A Band 4
Table: p.587

Bradley Jr, Craig C
(Kentucky)
Profile: p.839
Corporate/M&A Band 2
Table: p.827

Bradshaw, Penni Pearson
(North Carolina)
Profile: p.1394
Employment Band 2
Table: p.1386

Bradshaw II, Jean Paul
(Missouri)
Profile: p.1055
Litigation Band 1
Table: p.1049

Brady, Christopher J
(North Carolina)
Profile: p. 1394
Capital Markets Band 2
Table: p.22

Brady, Francis (Connecticut)
Profile: p.336
Litigation Band 1
Table: p.331

Brady, Robert S (Delaware)
Profile: p.351
Bankruptcy Band 2
Table: p.341

Braemer, Richard J
(Pennsylvania)
Profile: p.1520
Corporate/M&A Band 4
Table: p.1497

Brakke, Jon (North Dakota)
Profile: p.1410
Bankruptcy Band 1
Table: p.1403

Bramlett, Jeffrey (Georgia)
Profile: p.607
Litigation Band 3
Table: p.598

Bramnick, James (Florida)
Profile: p.535
Employment Band 3
Table: p.513

Branca, John G (California)
Profile: p.246
Media & Entertainment Band 2
Table: p.233

Brandes, Lawrence
(New York)
Profile: p.1268
Insurance Band 2
Table: p.1213

Brandow, John M (National)
Profile: p.77
Capital Markets Band 1
Table: p.16

Brands, Henk
(District of Columbia)
Profile: p.435
Telecom, Broadcast & Satellite Band 4
Table: p.427

Brandt, A Peter (Florida)
Profile: p.535
Construction Band 2
Table: p.507

Brann, Richard (Texas)
Profile: p.1673
Employment Band 1
Table: p.1634

Brannan, William (New York)
Profile: p.1268
Tax Band 3
Table: p.1255

Brannon, Jeanna (Georgia)
Profile: p.607
Real Estate Band 2
Table: p.601

Brasher, Lance
(District of Columbia)
Profile: p.435
Projects Band 3
Table: p.415

Brault, Albert (Maryland)
Profile: p.919
Litigation Band 2
Table: p.914

Braun, Lawrence M
(California)
Profile: p.246
Corporate/M&A Band 5

Braun, Peter
(Massachusetts)
Profile: p.963
Healthcare Band 2
Table: p.946

Braun, Stephen T
(Tennessee)
Profile: p.1606
Corporate/M&A Band 2
Table: p.1594

Bray, John
(District of Columbia)
Profile: p.435
Litigation Band 1
Table: p.410

Breaux, Ronald W (Texas)
Profile: p.1673
Antitrust Band 3
Table: p.1622

Breay, James (Michigan)
Profile: p.998
Banking & Finance Band 2
Table: p.987

Bredehoft, John M (Virginia)
Profile: p.1767
Employment Band 2
Table: p.1755

B

Breedlove, Gregory B
(Alabama)
Profile: p.121
Litigation Band 3
Table: p.116

Breglio, John F (New York)
Profile: p.1268
Media & Entertainment Band 1
Table: p.1235

Brenna, Nathan (Minnesota)
Profile: p.1017
Litigation Up and coming
Table: p.1011

Brennan, Daniel (Illinois)
Profile: p.720
Construction Band 3
Table: p.672

Brennan, James C (Virginia)
Profile: p.1767
Real Estate Band 3
Table: p.1765

Brennan, Matthew J
(New York)
Profile: p.1268
Environment Band 2
Table: p.1206

Brennan Jr, John T
(District of Columbia)
Profile: p.435
Healthcare Band 1
Table: p.398

Breslow, Stephanie
(New York)
Profile: p.1268
Private Equity Band 2
Table: p.1241

Bretschneider, Barry E
(Virginia)
Profile: p.1767
Intellectual Property Band 1
Table: p.1759

Bretz, Daniel J (Michigan)
Profile: p.998
Employment Band 2
Table: p.991

Breuning, Jonathan
(Nebraska)
Profile: p.1087
Employment Band 3
Table: p.1084

Brewer, Susan Slenker
(West Virginia)
Profile: p.1808
Litigation Band 2
Table: p.1803

Brewer Jr, Robert S
(California)
Profile: p.246
Litigation Band 2
Table: p.225

Brewster, William (Georgia)
Profile: p.607
Intellectual Property Band 4
Table: p.596

Breyfogle, Jon W
(District of Columbia)
Profile: p.436
Employee Benefits Band 3
Table: p.378

Brian, Brad (California)
Profile: p.246

Litigation Band 1
Table: p.224
Litigation Band 1
Table: p.225

Bricklemyer, Keith (Florida)
Profile: p.535
Real Estate Band 3
Table: p.528

Brickman, Steven A
(Alabama)
Profile: p.121
Real Estate Band 3
Table: p.119

Bridge, Catherine (Indiana)
Profile: p.791
Corporate/M&A Band 2
Table: p.781

Bridges, Andrew (California)
Profile: p.246
Intellectual Property Band 4
Table: p.216

Bridgesmith, Larry W
(Tennessee)
Profile: p.1606
Employment Band 2
Table: p.1596

Briggs, Heather (Vermont)
Profile: p.1748
Employment Band 2
Table: p.1745

Brigham, Johan V
(Massachusetts)
Profile: p.963
Corporate/M&A Band 3
Table: p.937

Bright Jr, William H
(Connecticut)
Profile: p.336
Litigation Band 2
Table: p.331

Brignone, Andrew (Nevada)
Profile: p.1101
Employment Band 1
Table: p.1091

Brindell, James (Florida)
Profile: p.535
Real Estate Band 3
Table: p.528

Brinkerhoff, Jeffrey C
(Wyoming)
Profile: p.1838
Litigation Band 2
Table: p.1835

Brinkman, David (Ohio)
Profile: p.1438
Intellectual Property Band 2
Table: p.1428

Brinkmann, Beth (District of
Columbia)
Profile: p.436
Litigation Band 2
Table: p.408

Bristow, Daryl (Texas)
Profile: p.1673
Litigation Band 1
Table: p.1656

Brittain, Max (Illinois)
Profile: p.720
Employment Band 1
Table: p.681

Brittenham, Harry M
(California)
Profile: p.246
Media & Entertainment Band 1
Table: p.233

Bro, Ruth Hill (Illinois)
Profile: p.720
Technology Band 2
Table: p.713

Broadbent, David K (Utah)
Profile: p.1736
Real Estate Band 3
Table: p.1733

Broaddus, William (Virginia)
Profile: p.1767
Litigation Band 2
Table: p.1763

Broadfoot, Alexander L
(Arizona)
Profile: p.157
Real Estate Band 3
Table: p.154

Broccolo, Bernadette
(Illinois)
Profile: p.720
Healthcare Band 2
Table: p.690

Brockelman, Kent (Arizona)
Profile: p.157
Employment Band 4
Table: p.148

Brockman, Richard J
(Alabama)
Profile: p.121
Corporate/M&A Band 2
Table: p.111

Broderick, JJ (Pennsylvania)
Profile: p.1520
Real Estate Band 3
Table: p.1516

Broders, John J (Louisiana)
Profile: p.870
Energy Band 1
Table: p.863

Brodsky, David M
(New York)
Profile: p.1269
Litigation Band 3
Table: p.1223
Litigation Band 3
Table: p.1224

Brody, Sara (California)
Profile: p.247
Litigation Band 4
Table: p.224

Brogan, James P (Colorado)
Profile: p.316
Intellectual Property Band 2
Table: p.309

Brogan, Stephen J
(District of Columbia)
Profile: p.436
Litigation Band 3
Table: p.410

Broglio, Dennis
(West Virginia)
Profile: p.1808
Real Estate Band 1
Table: p.1806

Bromberg, Lisa (New Jersey)
Profile: p.1137

Environment Band 2
Table: p.1129

Bromberg, Stephen A
(Michigan)
Profile: p.998
Real Estate Band 1
Table: p.996

Bromley, James L
(New York)
Profile: p.1269
Bankruptcy Band 4
Table: p.1179

Bronis, Stephen (Florida)
Profile: p.535
Litigation Band 2
Table: p.522

Bronstein, Joel (Florida)
Profile: p.535
Tax Band 3
Table: p.531

Brooke, Robert (Virginia)
Profile: p.1767
Intellectual Property Band 2
Table: p.1761

Brookner, Jason S (Texas)
Profile: p.1673
Bankruptcy Up and coming
Table: p.1627

Brooks, Robert (Rhode
Island)
Profile: p.1569
Employment Band 1
Table: p.1565

Brooman, David
(Pennsylvania)
Profile: p.1520
Environment Band 2
Table: p.1505

Brophy, James E (Arizona)
Profile: p.157
Corporate/M&A Band 4
Table: p.146

Brophy, Michael J (Arizona)
Profile: p.157
Environment Band 1
Table: p.150

Brose, Steven
(District of Columbia)
Profile: p.436
Energy Band 1
Table: p.382

Brosnahan, James
(California)
Profile: p.247
Litigation Band 2
Table: p.224
Litigation Band 1
Table: p.225

Broth, Mark T
(New Hampshire)
Profile: p.1116
Employment Band 1
Table: p.1109

Broude, Mark A (New York)
Profile: p.1269
Bankruptcy Band 4
Table: p.1179

Brower, Charles (National)
Profile: p.77
Arbitration Band 1
Table: p.34

Brown, Alan (Indiana)
Profile: p.791
Litigation Band 2
Table: p.785

Brown, Arthur
(District of Columbia)
Profile: p.436
Investment Management
Band 2
Table: p.406

Brown, Barbara B
(District of Columbia)
Profile: p.436
Employment Band 1
Table: p.380

Brown, Bowman (Florida)
Profile: p.535
Banking & Finance Band 1
Table: p.500

Brown, Christopher
(Florida)
Profile: p.535
Litigation Band 2
Table: p.522

Brown, Daniel (Florida)
Profile: p.535
Insurance Band 1
Table: p.519

Brown, Daryl J (Florida)
Profile: p.535
Construction Band 3
Table: p.507

Brown, David (Iowa)
Profile: p.812
Litigation Band 2
Table: p.807

Brown, David C (Kentucky)
Profile: p.839
Environment Band 2
Table: p.832

Brown, David H (Texas)
Profile: p.1674
Insurance Band 2
Table: p.1648

Brown, Dickson G
(New York)
Profile: p.1269
Tax Band 1
Table: p.1256

Brown, Donald J (Iowa)
Profile: p.812
Corporate/M&A Band 3
Table: p.802

Brown, Donald W
(California)
Profile: p.247
Insurance Band 1
Table: p.212

Brown, Duane (New Mexico)
Profile: p.1163
Corporate/M&A Band 2
Table: p.1155

Brown, Elliot H (New York)
Profile: p.1269
Media & Entertainment Band 1
Table: p.1235

Brown, Frank (Florida)
Profile: p.535
Employment Band 4
Table: p.513

Brown, Harald A (California)
Profile: p.247
Media & Entertainment Band 3
Table: p.233

Brown, J Jeffrey (Indiana)
Profile: p.791
Corporate/M&A Band 2
Table: p.781

Brown, James (Florida)
Profile: p.536
Employment Band 4
Table: p.513

Brown, James (Louisiana)
Profile: p.870
Litigation Band 2
Table: p.865

Brown, James B
(Pennsylvania)
Profile: p.1520
Employment Band 2
Table: p.1500

Brown, Jay Ward
(District of Columbia)
Profile: p.436
Media & Entertainment Band 3
Table: p.413

Brown, Jeffrey H (Illinois)
Profile: p.720
Media & Entertainment Band 2
Table: p.704

Brown, John S
(Massachusetts)
Profile: p.963
Tax Band 1
Table: p.959

Brown, Kim (Tennessee)
Profile: p.1606
Real Estate Band 2
Table: p.1603

Brown, Margaret A
(Massachusetts)
Profile: p.963
Corporate/M&A Band 3
Table: p.937

Brown, Reagan (Texas)
Profile: p.1674
Insurance Band 1
Table: p.1648
Litigation Band 2
Table: p.1656

Brown, Ricklin
(West Virginia)
Profile: p.1808
Employment Band 1
Table: p.1801

Brown, Robert (Colorado)
Profile: p.316
Real Estate Band 1
Table: p.313

Brown, Spencer (Missouri)
Profile: p.1055
Litigation Band 2
Table: p.1049

Brown, Stanley (Virginia)
Profile: p.1767
Employment Band 3
Table: p.1755

Brown, Stephen (Alabama)
Profile: p.121
Employment Band 3
Table: p.113

Brown, Stephen D
(Pennsylvania)
Profile: p.1520
Antitrust Band 3
Table: p.1489

Brown, Stephen Ross
(Montana)
Profile: p.1079
Corporate/M&A Band 2
Table: p.1072
Natural Resources Band 1
Table: p.1077

Brown, Ted (Florida)
Profile: p.536
Real Estate Band 3
Table: p.528

Brown, Walt (California)
Profile: p.247
Litigation Band 2
Table: p.225

Brown, William (Iowa)
Profile: p.812
Corporate/M&A Band 4
Table: p.802

Brown II, C David (Florida)
Profile: p.536
Real Estate Band 2
Table: p.526

Brown, Jr. Rodney L.
(Washington)
Profile: p.1790
Environment Band 1
Table: p.1782

Browne, Juliet T (Maine)
Profile: p.897
Environment Band 2
Table: p.892

Browne, Steven C
(Massachusetts)
Profile: p.963
Corporate/M&A Band 3
Table: p.937

Brownell, Thomas (Virginia)
Profile: p.1767
Construction Band 2
Table: p.1750

Brownell, William
(District of Columbia)
Profile: p.436
Environment Band 2
Table: p.392

Brownrigg, John (Nebraska)
Profile: p.1087
Litigation Band 3
Table: p.1085

Brownstein, Andrew R
(New York)
Profile: p.1269
Corporate/M&A Band 2
Table: p.1189

Brozman, Tina L (New York)
Profile: p.1269
Bankruptcy Band 4
Table: p.1179

Brubaker, Robert (Ohio)
Profile: p.1438
Environment Band 1
Table: p.1425

Bruen, James (California)
Profile: p.247
Environment Band 2

Brown, Stephen D
Table: p.207

Brumbaugh, John M
(Florida)
Profile: p.536
Litigation Band 3
Table: p.521

Brunner, Thomas W
(District of Columbia)
Profile: p.436
Insurance Band 3
Table: p.400

Bruns, Phillip T (Texas)
Profile: p.1674
Energy Band 2
Table: p.1640
Litigation Band 2
Table: p.1656

Bryan, Charles E (National)
Profile: p.77
Capital Markets Band 4
Table: p.19

Bryan, Karen (California)
Profile: p.247
Tax Band 3
Table: p.241

Bryant, David (Illinois)
Profile: p.720
Real Estate Band 4
Table: p.706

Bryant, John (Tennessee)
Profile: p.1606
Litigation Band 1
Table: p.1599
Litigation Band 3
Table: p.1599

Bryant, L Edward (Illinois)
Profile: p.720
Healthcare Band 1
Table: p.690

Bryant, Timothy (Illinois)
Profile: p.721
Private Equity Band 3
Table: p.676

Bryson, Susan (Connecticut)
Profile: p.336
Real Estate Band 1
Table: p.334

Buchanan, John
(District of Columbia)
Profile: p.436
Insurance Band 2
Table: p.402

Buchanan, Paul (Oregon)
Profile: p.1481
Employment Band 2
Table: p.1474

Buchanan Jr, Robert
(Massachusetts)
Profile: p.963
Antitrust Band 2
Table: p.930

Buchenroth, Stephen
(Ohio)
Profile: p.1438
Real Estate Band 1
Table: p.1434

Buchholtz, David
(New Mexico)
Profile: p.1163
Corporate/M&A Band 1
Table: p.1155

Buck, Frank W (Ohio)
Profile: p.1438
Employment Band 3
Table: p.1422

Buck, Gurdon (Connecticut)
Profile: p.336
Real Estate Band 2
Table: p.334

Buck, Peter (Washington)
Profile: p.1790
Real Estate Band 1
Table: p.1789

Buck, Peter (North Carolina)
Profile: p.1394
Banking & Finance Band 2
Table: p.1381
Corporate/M&A Band 1
Table: p.1384

Buck, Willis (Illinois)
Profile: p.77
Capital Markets Band 2
Table: p.21

Buckholz, Jr, Robert E
(National)
Profile: p.77
Capital Markets Band 3
Table: p.14

Bucking, James W
(Massachusetts)
Profile: p.963
Employment Band 3
Table: p.940

Buckler, Robert H (Georgia)
Profile: p.607
Employment Band 2
Table: p.589

Buckley, Christopher
(District of Columbia)
Profile: p.436
Environment Band 2
Table: p.392

Buckley, Daniel J (Ohio)
Profile: p.1438
Litigation Band 4
Table: p.1431

Buckley, Kevin J (Virginia)
Profile: p. 1768
Capital Markets Band 4
Table: p.19
Corporate/M&A Band 1
Table: p.1752

Buckley, Mert (Kansas)
Profile: p.823
Real Estate Band 1
Table: p.821

Buckley, Michael (Nevada)
Profile: p.1101
Real Estate Band 1
Table: p.1099

Bucy, Rhea (Tennessee)
Profile: p.1606
Litigation Band 2
Table: p.1599

Budny, Terrence (Illinois)
Profile: p.721
Real Estate Band 4
Table: p.706

Budoff, Marc (Arizona)
Profile: p.157
Litigation Band 3
Table: p.153

Budofsky, Daniel (National)
Profile: p.77
Capital Markets Band 3
Table: p.16

Budwick, Michael (Florida)
Profile: p.536
Bankruptcy Band 3
Table: p.503

Bueide, Daniel (North
Dakota)
Profile: p.1410
Real Estate Band 2
Table: p.1409

Buente, David
(District of Columbia)
Profile: p.436
Environment Band 1
Table: p.392

Buffington, Teresa
(Wyoming)
Profile: p.1838
Corporate/M&A Band 2
Table: p.1832

Buford, Douglas (Arkansas)
Profile: p.175
Corporate/M&A Band 1
Table: p.168

Buhle, Warren (New York)
Profile: p.1269
Banking & Finance Band 4
Table: p.1174

Bulchis, Ed (Washington)
Profile: p.1790
Intellectual Property Band 1
Table: p.1784

Bulger, Brian (Illinois)
Profile: p.721
Employment Band 2
Table: p.681

Bull, Edwin (Arizona)
Profile: p.157
Real Estate Band 2
Table: p.155

Bullen, Linda M (Nevada)
Profile: p.1101
Environment Band 3
Table: p.1093

Bullock, Brentley (Oregon)
Profile: p.1481
Corporate/M&A Band 3
Table: p.1471

Bumpass, T Merritt (Ohio)
Profile: p.1438
Employment Band 3
Table: p.1422

Bumpers, Heidi
(District of Columbia)
Profile: p.437
Environment Band 4
Table: p.392

Bumpers, William
(District of Columbia)
Profile: p.437
Environment Band 3
Table: p.392

Bundy, David H (Alaska)
Profile: p.142
Bankruptcy Band 1
Table: p.133

B

Bundy, Robert C (Alaska)
Profile: p.142
Litigation **Band 1**
Table: p.138

Buniva, Brian L (Virginia)
Profile: p.1768
Environment **Band 3**
Table: p.1757

Bunsow, Henry (California)
Profile: p.247
Intellectual Property **Band 3**
Table: p.216

Buoncristiani, David
(California)
Profile: p.247
Construction **Band 1**
Table: p.194

Buono, Kathryn M
(Wisconsin)
Profile: p.1824
Corporate/M&A **Band 1**
Table: p.1817

Burbidge, Richard D (Utah)
Profile: p.1736
Litigation **Band 1**
Table: p.1732

Burch Jr, Francis B
(Maryland)
Profile: p.919
Litigation **Band 2**
Table: p.914

**Burchett, Angela
Stinebruner** (Kentucky)
Profile: p.839
Real Estate **Band 2**
Table: p.838

Burchfield, Bobby R
(District of Columbia)
Profile: p.437
Litigation **Band 2**
Table: p.410

Buresh, James (New York)
Profile: p.1269
Banking & Finance **Band 4**
Table: p.1174

Burger, Peter
(New Hampshire)
Profile: p.1116
Corporate/M&A **Band 3**
Table: p.1107

Burger, Sharon
(Massachusetts)
Profile: p.963
Employment **Band 2**
Table: p.940

Burgess, Rick (Florida)
Profile: p.536
Environment **Band 3**
Table: p.516

Burgin, Sara (Texas)
Profile: p.1674
Environment **Band 2**
Table: p.1643

Burke, Carl (Idaho)
Profile: p.660
Litigation **Band S**
Table: p.657

Burke, David (Florida)
Profile: p.536
Tax **Band 3**
Table: p.531

Burke, James (Ohio)
Profile: p.1438
Litigation **Band 4**
Table: p.1431

Burke, Kim (Ohio)
Profile: p.1438
Environment **Band 3**
Table: p.1425

Burke, P John (California)
Profile: p.247
Media & Entertainment **Band 3**
Table: p.233

Burke, Robert
(Massachusetts)
Profile: p.964
Tax **Band 3**
Table: p.959

Burke, Steven M
(New Hampshire)
Profile: p.1116
Corporate/M&A **Band 3**
Table: p.1107
Tax **Band 2**
Table: p.1107

Burke, Ted (New York)
Profile: p. 1269
Projects **Band 2**
Table: p.52
Projects **Band 2**
Table: p.1244

Burke, Thomas (California)
Profile: p.247
Media & Entertainment **Band 3**
Table: p.230

Burke Jr, John K (Virginia)
Profile: p.1768
Litigation **Band 3**
Table: p.1763

Burke Jr, Raymond J (New York)
Profile: p.77
Shipping **Band 2**
Table: p.67

Burleigh, Jennifer
(New York)
Profile: p.1269
Private Equity **Band 3**
Table: p.1241

Burling, James
(Massachusetts)
Profile: p.964
Antitrust **Band 1**
Table: p.930

Burman, David J
(Washington)
Profile: p.1790
Litigation **Band 1**
Table: p.1786

Burner, Burnie (Texas)
Profile: p.1674
Insurance **Band 3**
Table: p.1648

Burnham, Beckey (Arizona)
Profile: p.157
Real Estate **Band 4**
Table: p.154

Burns, David (Texas)
Profile: p.1674
Banking & Finance **Band 2**
Table: p.1625

Burns, Stephen (National)
Profile: p.77
Capital Markets **Band 4**
Table: p.14

Burnstein, Richard
(Michigan)
Profile: p.998
Real Estate **Band 3**
Table: p.996

Burrage, Michael
(Oklahoma)
Profile: p.1465
Litigation **Band 3**
Table: p.1462

Burrell, Lizabeth (New York)
Profile: p.77
Shipping **Band 3**
Table: p.67

Burruezo, Carlos (Florida)
Profile: p.536
Employment **Band 4**
Table: p.513

Burrus, Robert (Virginia)
Profile: p.1768
Corporate/M&A **Band 1**
Table: p.1752

Burt, Antony (Illinois)
Profile: p.721
Insurance **Band 3**
Table: p.694

Burt, Donald (Nebraska)
Profile: p.1087
Corporate/M&A **Band 2**
Table: p.1082

Burt, Laurie (Massachusetts)
Profile: p.964
Environment **Band 1**
Table: p.943

Busch, John (Wisconsin)
Profile: p.1824
Litigation **Band 2**
Table: p.1821

Busch, William (Minnesota)
Profile: p.1017
Corporate/M&A **Band 3**
Table: p.1005

Buser, James D (Nebraska)
Profile: p.1087
Real Estate **Band 2**
Table: p.1086

Busey, Roxane C (Illinois)
Profile: p.721
Antitrust **Band 2**
Table: p.662

Busey, Stephen D (Florida)
Profile: p.536
Bankruptcy **Band 1**
Table: p.503

Bush, Christine K
(Rhode Island)
Profile: p.1569
Litigation **Up and coming**
Table: p.1567

Bush, Gayle (Washington)
Profile: p.1790
Bankruptcy **Band 1**
Table: p.1776

Bush, John K (Kentucky)
Profile: p.839
Litigation **Band 4**
Table: p.835

Bush III, F M (Mississippi)
Profile: p.1032
Corporate/M&A **Band 2**
Table: p.1024

Bussard, Donald A
(Delaware)
Profile: p.351
Corporate/M&A **Band 1**
Table: p.346

Busto, Mark (Washington)
Profile: p.1790
Employment **Band 1**
Table: p.1780

Butcher, David (Indiana)
Profile: p.791
Corporate/M&A **Band 3**
Table: p.781

Butler, Brian (Wisconsin)
Profile: p.1824
Litigation **Band 2**
Table: p.1821

Butler, James (Georgia)
Profile: p.607
Litigation **Band 3**
Table: p.598

Butler, James (Georgia)
Profile: p.607
Construction **Band 2**
Table: p.584

Butler, JoAnn (Idaho)
Profile: p.660
Real Estate **Band 1**
Table: p.658

Butler III, A Bates (Arizona)
Profile: p.157
Litigation **Band 2**
Table: p.153

Butler Jr, John Wm (Jack)
(Illinois)
Profile: p.721
Bankruptcy **Band 1**
Table: p.669

Butler Jr, Patrick J
(Louisiana)
Profile: p.870
Corporate/M&A **Band 3**
Table: p.859

Byowitz, Michael H
(New York)
Profile: p.1269
Antitrust **Band 3**
Table: p.1170

Byrd, Robert A (Mississippi)
Profile: p.1032
Bankruptcy **Band 1**
Table: p.1024

Byrne, Richard L
(Pennsylvania)
Profile: p.1521
Intellectual Property **Band 3**
Table: p.1508

Byrnes, Peter (Washington)
Profile: p.1790
Litigation **Band 1**
Table: p.1786

Cable, Franklin (Oregon)
Profile: p.1481
Corporate/M&A **Band 3**
Table: p.1471

Cable, Stuart M
(Massachusetts)
Profile: p.964
Corporate/M&A **Band 2**
Table: p.937

Cabot, Anthony (Nevada)
Profile: p.1101
Gaming & Licensing **Band 2**
Table: p.1094

Cabot, Howard Ross
(Arizona)
Profile: p.157
Litigation **Band 2**
Table: p.152

Cacciabeve, Charles
(Florida)
Profile: p.536
Construction **Band 2**
Table: p.507

Cacciatore, Ronald K
(Florida)
Profile: p.536
Litigation **Band 2**
Table: p.522

Cadwallader, John I (Ohio)
Profile: p.1438
Real Estate **Band 4**
Table: p.1434

Caen, Melissa (Georgia)
Profile: p.607
Energy **Up and coming**
Table: p.592

Cagle, Molly (Texas)
Profile: p.1674
Environment **Band 1**
Table: p.1643
Litigation **Band 1**
Table: p.1643

Cagney, Lawrence K
(New York)
Profile: p.1269
Employee Benefits **Band 2**
Table: p.1197

Cahan, James N (Illinois)
Profile: p.721
Environment **Band 4**
Table: p.687

Cahill Jr, Elwood (Louisiana)
Profile: p.870
Real Estate **Band 2**
Table: p.867

Cahoon, Susan (Georgia)
Profile: p.607
Litigation **Band 3**
Table: p.598

Cairns, Carolyn
(Washington)
Profile: p.1790
Employment **Band 1**
Table: p.1780

Cairns, James (California)
Profile: p.247
Banking & Finance **Band 3**
Table: p.187

Calamita, Paul (Virginia)
Profile: p.1768
Environment **Band 3**
Table: p.1757

Caldwell, Charles (Texas)
Profile: p.1674
Energy **Band 2**
Table: p.1641

Caldwell, Stokely
(North Carolina)
Profile: p.1394
Banking & Finance **Band 3**
Table: p.1381

Callahan, Michael R
(New Hampshire)
Profile: p.1116
Litigation **Band 2**
Table: p.1111

Callahan, Michael R
(Illinois)
Profile: p.721
Healthcare **Band 2**
Table: p.690

Calland, Dean (Pennsylvania)
Profile: p.1521
Environment **Band 1**
Table: p.1505

Calvin, Charles (Colorado)
Profile: p.316
Hotels and Resorts **Band 2**
Table: p.314

Calzone, David B (Michigan)
Profile: p.998
Employment **Band 2**
Table: p.991

Camahort, Steve (California)
Profile: p.247
Corporate/M&A **Band 2**
Table: p.197

Cameron, Streetar (Iowa)
Profile: p.813
Real Estate **Band 4**
Table: p.810

Cameron Jr, Donald B
(National)
Profile: p.77
International Trade **Band 2**
Table: p.40

Camp, Leo (Kentucky)
Profile: p.840
Real Estate **Band 2**
Table: p.838

Campbell, Andrew (Texas)
Profile: p.1674
Real Estate **Band 3**
Table: p.1662

Campbell, Charles E
(Georgia)
Profile: p.608
Bankruptcy **Band 2**
Table: p.582

Campbell, Christopher C
(Virginia)
Profile: p.1768
Intellectual Property **Band 2**
Table: p.1759

Campbell, Craig (North
Dakota)
Profile: p.1410
Litigation **Band 1**
Table: p.1406

Campbell, Daniel (Virginia)
Profile: p.1768
Real Estate **Band 3**
Table: p.1765

Campbell, David (Indiana)
Profile: p.791
Litigation **Band 1**
Table: p.785

Campbell, David S
(New Mexico)
Profile: p.1163
Real Estate **Band 1**
Table: p.1161

Campbell, Donald (Nevada)
Profile: p.1101
Litigation **Band 1**
Table: p.1096

Campbell, Lawrence
(Michigan)
Profile: p.998
Litigation **Band 1**
Table: p.994

Campbell, Margaret H
(Georgia)
Profile: p.608
Employment **Band 4**
Table: p.589

Campbell, Michael
(New Mexico)
Profile: p.1163
Environment **Band 1**
Table: p.1158

Campbell, Rhett (Texas)
Profile: p.1674
Bankruptcy **Band 4**
Table: p.1627

Campbell, Roy (Mississippi)
Profile: p.1032
Litigation **Band 3**
Table: p.1028

Campbell, Thomas (Illinois)
Profile: p.721
Antitrust **Band 3**
Table: p.662

Campbell, William (Oregon)
Profile: p.1481
Corporate/M&A **Band 1**
Table: p.1471

Campbell, William J
(Colorado)
Profile: p.317
Corporate/M&A **Band 3**
Table: p.303

Campbell II, L Webb
(Tennessee)
Profile: p.1606
Litigation **Band 3**
Table: p.1599

Campbell Jr, Boyd (North
Carolina)
Profile: p.1394
Banking & Finance **Band 3**
Table: p.1381
Corporate/M&A **Band 3**
Table: p.1384

Campbell Jr, John
(Louisiana)
Profile: p.870
Corporate/M&A **Band 4**
Table: p.859

Campbell Jr, Robert R
(Tennessee)
Profile: p.1606
Real Estate **Band 3**
Table: p.1603

Campbell Jr, Robert S
(Utah)
Profile: p.1736
Litigation **Band 2**
Table: p.1732

Campbell Jr, Woodrow W
(New York)
Profile: p.1269
Private Equity **Band S**
Table: p.1241

Campion, Thomas (New
Jersey)
Profile: p.1137
Litigation **Band 1**
Table: p.1131

Candler, James (Michigan)
Profile: p.998
Real Estate **Band 2**
Table: p.996

Cane, Paul (California)
Profile: p.247
Employment **Band 3**
Table: p.202

Canellos, Peter C
(New York)
Profile: p.1270
Tax **Band 1**
Table: p.1255

Cannada, Barry (Mississippi)
Profile: p.1032
Corporate/M&A **Band 1**
Table: p.1024

Cannada, Don (Mississippi)
Profile: p.1032
Real Estate **Band 1**
Table: p.1031

Cannon, Kim D. (Wyoming)
Profile: p.1838
Litigation **Band 2**
Table: p.1835

Cannon, Kinder (Florida)
Profile: p.536
Corporate/M&A **Band S**
Table: p.509

Canoni, John (New York)
Profile: p.1270
Employment **Band 3**
Table: p.1200

Canterbury Jr, Joe F (Texas)
Profile: p.1674
Construction **Band 1**
Table: p.1629

Cantlin, Richard (Oregon)
Profile: p.1481
Real Estate **Band 1**
Table: p.1479

Cantor, Matthew (New York)
Profile: p.1270
Bankruptcy **Band 3**
Table: p.1179

Capers, John (Georgia)
Profile: p.608
Corporate/M&A **Band 3**
Table: p.587

Caplan, David L (New York)
Profile: p.1270
Corporate/M&A **Band 4**
Table: p.1189

Caplan, Gordon (New York)
Profile: p.1270
Technology **Band 3**
Table: p.1259

Caplan, Sherri G (New York)
Profile: p.1270
Private Equity **Band 3**
Table: p.1241

Cappellanti, Ellen
(West Virginia)
Profile: p.1808
Corporate/M&A **Band 1**
Table: p.1798
Real Estate **Band 2**
Table: p.1806

Capraro Jr, Joseph A
(Massachusetts)
Profile: p.964
Intellectual Property **Band 3**
Table: p.948

**Carder-Thompson,
Elizabeth**
(District of Columbia)
Profile: p.437
Healthcare **Band 1**
Table: p.398

Cardwell, J Thomas
(Florida)
Profile: p.536
Banking & Finance **Band 1**
Table: p.500

Carey, Michael
(West Virginia)
Profile: p.1808
Litigation **Band 2**
Table: p.1803

Carey, Michael R (Florida)
Profile: p.536
Construction **Band 3**
Table: p.507

Carey, Stevens (California)
Profile: p.247
Real Estate **Band 2**
Table: p.238

Cargile, Ann Peldo
(Tennessee)
Profile: p.1606
Real Estate **Band 2**
Table: p.1603

Carleen, Donald P
(New York)
Profile: p.1270
Employee Benefits **Band 2**
Table: p.1197

Carlino, James (Indiana)
Profile: p.791
Real Estate **Band 2**
Table: p.788

Carlotti, Stephen
(Rhode Island)
Profile: p.1569
Corporate/M&A **Band 1**
Table: p.1564

Carlson, Alan (Minnesota)
Profile: p.1017
Litigation **Band 1**
Table: p.1012

Carlson, Bruce (North
Dakota)
Profile: p.1410
Litigation **Band 1**
Table: p.1406

Carlson, James (Ohio)
Profile: p.1438
Corporate/M&A **Band 2**
Table: p.1419

Carlson, Kent (Washington)
Profile: p.1790
Corporate/M&A **Band 1**
Table: p.1778

Carlson, Walter (Illinois)
Profile: p.722
Litigation **Band 4**
Table: p.700

Carlson, Wayne
(North Dakota)
Profile: p.1410
Litigation **Band 2**
Table: p.1407

Carmagnola, Domenick
(New Jersey)
Profile: p.1137
Employment **Band 1**
Table: p.1126

Carman, Steven F
(Missouri)
Profile: p.1055
Corporate/M&A **Band 3**
Table: p.1043

Carneal, George U
(National)
Profile: p.78
Aviation **Band 3**
Table: p.58

Carney, Thomas M
(Missouri)
Profile: p.1055
Litigation **Band 3**
Table: p.1049

Caron, David D (National)
Profile: p.78
Arbitration **Band 1**
Table: p.34

Carpenter, Bill (New Mexico)
Profile: p.1163
Litigation **Band S**
Table: p.1159

Carpenter, David (Illinois)
Profile: p.722
Telecom, Broadcast & Satellite
Band 1
Table: p.715

Carpenter, Edward
(South Dakota)
Profile: p.1592
Litigation **Band 2**
Table: p.1590

Carpenter, Michael (Ohio)
Profile: p.1438
Litigation **Band 4**
Table: p.1431

Carpenter, Willis (Colorado)
Profile: p.317
Real Estate **Band S**
Table: p.313

C

Carr, Don
(District of Columbia)
Profile: p.437
Environment Band 4
Table: p.392

Carr, Kevin L (West Virginia)
Profile: p.1808
Employment Up and coming
Table: p.1801

Carr, William E (Missouri)
Profile: p.1055
Real Estate Band 1
Table: p.1052

Carrell, Richard (Texas)
Profile: p.1674
Antitrust Band 2
Table: p.1622

Carrier, William (Maryland)
Profile: p.919
Employment Band 3
Table: p.912

Carroll, Frank (Iowa)
Profile: p.813
Corporate/M&A Band 2
Table: p.802

Carroll, James P (North Carolina)
Profile: p. 1394
Capital Markets Band 1
Table: p.22

Carroll, John (New York)
Profile: p.1270
Litigation Band 2
Table: p.1224

Carroll, Michael (California)
Profile: p.247
Environment Band 4
Table: p.207

Carroll, Michael P
(New York)
Profile: p.1270
Litigation Band 3
Table: p.1222

Carroll, Priscilla (Maryland)
Profile: p.919
Real Estate Band 4
Table: p.917

Carroll, Tom (New Jersey)
Profile: p.1137
Real Estate Band 2
Table: p.1135

Carron, Reid (Minnesota)
Profile: p.1017
Employment Band 2
Table: p.1008

Carrouth, Michael (South Carolina)
Profile: p.1579
Employment Band 3
Table: p.1574

Carruthers, Thomas Neely
(Alabama)
Profile: p.121
Corporate/M&A Band 1
Table: p.111

Carson, Christopher L
(Georgia)
Profile: p.608
Banking & Finance Band 1
Table: p.580

Carson, Van (Ohio)
Profile: p.1438
Environment Band 1
Table: p.1425

Carson II, William A
(Tennessee)
Profile: p.1606
Real Estate Band 3
Table: p.1603

Carssow, Tim (Georgia)
Profile: p.608
Real Estate Band 2
Table: p.601

Carter, Don G (Oregon)
Profile: p.1481
Real Estate Band 3
Table: p.1479

Carter, Eugenia (Wisconsin)
Profile: p.1824
Litigation Band 3
Table: p.1821

Carter, Francis (Florida)
Profile: p.536
Bankruptcy Band S
Table: p.503

Carter, James H (National)
Profile: p.78
Arbitration Band 1
Table: p.33

Carter, Mark (West Virginia)
Profile: p.1808
Employment Band 1
Table: p.1801

Carvin, Michael A
(District of Columbia)
Profile: p.437
Litigation Band 2
Table: p.408

Cary, George S
(District of Columbia)
Profile: p.437
Antitrust Band 2
Table: p.367

Cary, William (North Carolina)
Profile: p.1394
Employment Band 2
Table: p.1386

Caryl, Michael
(West Virginia)
Profile: p.1808
Corporate/M&A Band 2
Table: p.1798

Cascarilla, Ralph (Ohio)
Profile: p.1438
Environment Band 3
Table: p.1425
Litigation Band 2
Table: p.1432

Case, Charles D (North Carolina)
Profile: p.1394
Environment Band 1
Table: p.1388

Case, Daniel H (Hawaii)
Profile: p.648
Corporate/M&A Band S
Table: p.641

Case, David (Alaska)
Profile: p.142
Native Law Band 1
Table: p.140

Case, James H (Hawaii)
Profile: p.648
Corporate/M&A Band S
Table: p.641

Casey, David
(Massachusetts)
Profile: p.964
Employment Band 1
Table: p.940

Casey, Kevin (Pennsylvania)
Profile: p.1521
Intellectual Property Band 3
Table: p.1508

Casey, Michael (Florida)
Profile: p.536
Employment Band 1
Table: p.513

Casey, Esq, Warren J (New Jersey)
Profile: p.1137
Corporate/M&A Band 3
Table: p.1123

Cashdan, Jeffrey (Georgia)
Profile: p.608
Antitrust Band 2
Table: p.578

Cason, Len (Oklahoma)
Profile: p.1465
Tax Band 2
Table: p.1459

Casper Jr, Paul W (Ohio)
Profile: p.1438
Environment Band 1
Table: p.1425

Cassanos, Robert
(New York)
Profile: p.1270
Tax Band 4
Table: p.1255

Cassidy, Bart (Pennsylvania)
Profile: p.1521
Environment Band 3
Table: p.1505

Cassis, Charles (Kentucky)
Profile: p.840
Litigation Band 4
Table: p.835

Castaldo, Neil
(New Hampshire)
Profile: p.1116
Corporate/M&A Band 2
Table: p.1107

Caster, Lauren (Arizona)
Profile: p.157
Environment Band 3
Table: p.150

Cates, C Thomas
(Tennessee)
Profile: p.1606
Real Estate Band 2
Table: p.1603

Cathcart, Patrick
(California)
Profile: p.247
Insurance Band 1
Table: p.212

Caulkins, Charles (Florida)
Profile: p.536
Employment Band 3
Table: p.513

Cavalieri, Nick V (Ohio)
Profile: p.1439
Bankruptcy Band 2
Table: p.1414

Cavanagh Jr, Joseph V
(Rhode Island)
Profile: p.1569
Litigation Band 1
Table: p.1567

Cave, Bradley (Wyoming)
Profile: p.1838
Employment Band 2
Table: p.1833

Caverly, Joseph L
(Louisiana)
Profile: p.870
Corporate/M&A Band 3
Table: p.859

Cawley, Douglas (Texas)
Profile: p.1674
Intellectual Property Band 3
Table: p.1651

Cederoth, Richard A
(Illinois)
Profile: p.722
Intellectual Property Band 2
Table: p.696

Cendali, Dale (New York)
Profile: p.1270
Intellectual Property Band 2
Table: p.1217
Media & Entertainment Band 2
Table: p.1232

Cerabino, Thomas M
(New York)
Profile: p.1271
Corporate/M&A Band 4
Table: p.1189

Cerasia, Edward
(New Jersey)
Profile: p.1137
Employment Up and coming
Table: p.1126

Ceriani, Gary (Colorado)
Profile: p.317
Litigation Band 2
Table: p.311

Cerone, Rudy (Louisiana)
Profile: p.870
Corporate/M&A Band 2
Table: p.859

Chadakoff, Richard
(New York)
Profile: p.1271
Real Estate Band 5
Table: p.1248

Chadwick, James
(California)
Profile: p.248
Media & Entertainment Band 4
Table: p.230

Chaffetz, Peter (New York)
Profile: p.1271
Insurance Band 2
Table: p.1213

Chambers, Robert C
(Georgia)
Profile: p.608
Construction Band 2
Table: p.584

Champoux, David (Maine)
Profile: p.897
Corporate/M&A Band 2
Table: p.888

Chandler, Harry S (Idaho)
Profile: p.660
Employment Band 1
Table: p.656

Chandler, John A (Georgia)
Profile: p.608
Litigation Band 1
Table: p.598

Chang, Corlis J (Hawaii)
Profile: p.648
Litigation Band 1
Table: p.644

Chang, Leo (New York)
Profile: p.78
Shipping Band
Table: p.67
Shipping Band 2
Table: p.67

Chapin, David C
(Massachusetts)
Profile: p.964
Corporate/M&A Band 2
Table: p.937
Private Equity Band 1
Table: p.953

Chapman, William
(Washington)
Profile: p.1790
Environment Band 2
Table: p.1782

Chapman, William L
(New Hampshire)
Profile: p.1116
Litigation Band 2
Table: p.1111

Charbonneau, Robert
(Florida)
Profile: p.536
Bankruptcy Band 3
Table: p.503

Charkoudian , Stephen G
(Massachusetts)
Profile: p.964
Intellectual Property Band 3
Table: p.948

Charles, Scott K (New York)
Profile: p.1271
Bankruptcy Band 4
Table: p.1179

Charness, Michael
(National)
Profile: p.78
Government Contracts Band 3
Table: p.27

Charney, Steven M
(New York)
Profile: p.1271
Construction Band 3
Table: p.1186

Chase, Jeffrey (Colorado)
Profile: p.317
Litigation Band 1
Table: p.311

Chase III, Lee James
(Tennessee)
Profile: p.1606
Litigation Band 3
Table: p.1599

Chason, Craig (Virginia)
Profile: p.1768
Corporate/M&A Band 3
Table: p.1752

Chason, James R.
(Maryland)
Profile: p.919
Litigation Band 3
Table: p.914

Chatham, Henry
(Mississippi)
Profile: p.1032
Corporate/M&A Band 1
Table: p.1024

Chatilovicz, Peter
(District of Columbia)
Profile: p.437
Employment Band 2
Table: p.380

Chatzinoff, Howard
(New York)
Profile: p.1271
Corporate/M&A Band 4
Table: p.1189

Chaykin, Steven E (Florida)
Profile: p.536
Litigation Band 2
Table: p.522

Cheatham, Richard R
(Georgia)
Profile: p.608
Banking & Finance Band 2
Table: p.581

Cheatwood, Roy C
(Louisiana)
Profile: p.870
Litigation Band 2
Table: p.865

Cheavens, Joseph (Texas)
Profile: p.1674
Litigation Band 2
Table: p.1656

Checov, Martin S
(California)
Profile: p.248
Insurance Band 2
Table: p.212

Cheek III, James
(Tennessee)
Profile: p.1606
Corporate/M&A Band 1
Table: p.1594

Chefitz, Joel (Illinois)
Profile: p.722
Antitrust Band 2
Table: p.662

Chehi, Mark S (Delaware)
Profile: p.352
Bankruptcy Band 2
Table: p.341

Chepiga, Michael J
(New York)
Profile: p.1271
Litigation Band 1
Table: p.1223

Chernof, Steve (Wisconsin)
Profile: p.1824
Real Estate Band 1
Table: p.1822

Cherot, Suzanne (Alaska)
Profile: p.142

Real Estate Band 2
Table: p.141

Chertok, Mark (New York)
Profile: p.1272
Environment Band 3
Table: p.1205

Chesler, Evan (New York)
Profile: p.1272
Antitrust Band 4
Table: p.1170
Intellectual Property Band 2
Table: p.1217
Litigation Band 2
Table: p.1222

Chestler, Stuart (Oregon)
Profile: p.1481
Corporate/M&A Band 3
Table: p.1471

Chida, Junaid H (New York)
Profile: p.1272
Projects Band 4
Table: p.1244

Chierichella, John W
(National)
Profile: p.78
Government Contracts
Band 2
Table: p.27

Child, Ralph (Massachusetts)
Profile: p.964
Environment Band 1
Table: p.943

Chiles IV, EB (Chip)
(Arkansas)
Profile: p.175
Litigation Up & Coming

Chilton, Fred (California)
Profile: p.248
Tax Band 3
Table: p.241

Chinn, Adam D (New York)
Profile: p.1272
Employee Benefits Band 2
Table: p.1197

Chisholm, David (Montana)
Profile: p.1079
Corporate/M&A Band 1
Table: p.1072

Choi, Paul (Illinois)
Profile: p.722
Corporate/M&A Band 4
Table: p.675

Chory, John (Massachusetts)
Profile: p.964
Private Equity Band 3
Table: p.953

Chriss, Timothy (Maryland)
Profile: p.920
Real Estate Band 2
Table: p.917

Christensen, Amy D
(Montana)
Profile: p.1079
Employment Up and coming
Table: p.1073

Christensen, Dana
(Montana)
Profile: p.1079
Litigation Band 1
Table: p.1075

Christensen, Douglas
(North Dakota)
Profile: p.1410
Corporate/M&A Band 3
Table: p.1403

Christensen, Douglas R
(Minnesota)
Profile: p.1017
Employment Band 2
Table: p.1008

Christian, Betty Jo
(National)
Profile: p.78
Transport Band 2
Table: p.62

Christian, Joseph J
(Massachusetts)
Profile: p.964
Real Estate Band 3
Table: p.956

Christian, Thomas W
(Alabama)
Profile: p.121
Litigation Band 3
Table: p.116

Christiansen, Jon P
(Wisconsin)
Profile: p.1824
Litigation Band 2
Table: p.1821

Christianson, Cabot
(Alaska)
Profile: p.142
Bankruptcy Band 1
Table: p.133

Christy, Angela (Minnesota)
Profile: p.1017
Real Estate Band 2
Table: p.1014

Chu, Morgan (California)
Profile: p.248
Intellectual Property ✪
Table: p.216

Chumrau, Gary B (Montana)
Profile: p.1080
Corporate/M&A Band 2
Table: p.1072

Chun, Deborah (Hawaii)
Profile: p.648
Real Estate Band 1
Table: p.646

Churchill, David (National)
Profile: p.78
Government Contracts
Band 2
Table: p.27

Churchill, Stanley (Kansas)
Profile: p.823
Employment Band 2
Table: p.818

Chused, Wesley S.
(National)
Profile: p.78
Transport Band 2
Table: p.64

Cicarella, Thomas (Ohio)
Profile: p.1439
Banking & Finance Band 2
Table: p.1411

Cicero Jr, Frank (Illinois)
Profile: p.722

Antitrust Band 3
Table: p.662
Litigation Band 3
Table: p.700

Cieri, Richard (New York)
Profile: p.1272
Bankruptcy Band 1
Table: p.1179

Cifelli, James (Georgia)
Profile: p.608
Bankruptcy Band 2
Table: p.582

Cimino, Michael
(West Virginia)
Profile: p.1808
Litigation Band u
Table: p.1803

Ciresi, Michael (Minnesota)
Profile: p.1017
Litigation Band 1
Table: p.1011
Litigation Band 1
Table: p.1012

Citron, Diane (National)
Profile: p.78
Capital Markets Band 3
Table: p.19

Civins, Jeff (Texas)
Profile: p.1675
Environment Band 1
Table: p.1643

Clair, John (California)
Profile: p.248
Tax Band 1
Table: p.241

Clancy, Patrick L (Maryland)
Profile: p.920
Employment Band 3
Table: p.912

Clarence, Nanci L
(California)
Profile: p.248
Litigation Band 2
Table: p.225

Clark, Anthony W
(Delaware)
Profile: p.352
Bankruptcy Band 3
Table: p.341
Chancery Band 3
Table: p.344

Clark, Donald (Mississippi)
Profile: p.1032
Corporate/M&A Band 3
Table: p.1024

Clark, Glenn A (New Jersey)
Profile: p.1138
Litigation Band 2
Table: p.1131

Clark, James (National)
Profile: p.79
Capital Markets Band 3
Table: p.14

Clark, James (Illinois)
Profile: p.722
Banking & Finance Band 1
Table: p.665

Clark, James R (Wisconsin)
Profile: p.1824
Litigation Band 2
Table: p.1821

Clark, John (California)
Profile: p.248
Construction Band 1
Table: p.194

Clark, Kenneth (California)
Profile: p.248
Corporate/M&A Band 4
Table: p.197
IT Outsourcing Band 3
Table: p.221

Clark, Matthew J (National)
Profile: p.79
International Trade Band 3
Table: p.40

Clark, Merlyn (Idaho)
Profile: p.660
Litigation Band 2
Table: p.657

Clark, Peter (Pennsylvania)
Profile: p.1521
Bankruptcy Band 3
Table: p.1494

Clark, Peter D (New York)
Profile: p.79
Shipping Band 3
Table: p.67

Clark, Reginald J (Georgia)
Profile: p.608
Tax Band 4
Table: p.603

Clark, Reuben G
(North Carolina)
Profile: p.1394
Real Estate Band 3
Table: p.1392

Clark, Robert (Utah)
Profile: p.1736
Litigation Band 2
Table: p.1732

Clark, Ronald (Arkansas)
Profile: p.175
Corporate/M&A Band 1
Table: p.168
Corporate/M&A Band 2
Table: p.168

Clark Jr, Jude (Kentucky)
Profile: p.840
Real Estate Band 2
Table: p.838

Clarke, Donald
(District of Columbia)
Profile: p.437
Energy Band 5
Table: p.386

Clarke, Jennifer R
(Pennsylvania)
Profile: p.1521
Antitrust Band 3
Table: p.1489

Clary, Richard W (New York)
Profile: p.1272
Litigation Band 2
Table: p.1222

Claster, William (California)
Profile: p.248
Employment Band 4
Table: p.202

Claverie Sr, Philip deV
(Louisiana)
Profile: p.870
Banking & Finance Band 1

Table: p.857
Real Estate **Band 1**
Table: p.867

Clawson, Carol (Utah)
Profile: p.1736
Employment **Band 3**
Table: p.1730

Clay, Richard H C
(Kentucky)
Profile: p.840
Litigation **Band 4**
Table: p.835

Clay, Stephens (Georgia)
Profile: p.608
Litigation **Band 3**
Table: p.598

Cleary, David L (Vermont)
Profile: p.1748
Litigation **Band 2**
Table: p.1746

Cleary, John (Massachusetts)
Profile: p.964
Tax **Band 1**
Table: p.959

Cleary, Richard S
(Kentucky)
Profile: p.840
Employment **Band 1**
Table: p.830

Clees, Joseph (Arizona)
Profile: p.157
Employment **Band 2**
Table: p.148

Cleland, A Craig (Georgia)
Profile: p.609
Employment Up and coming
Table: p.589

Clement, Rodney
(Mississippi)
Profile: p.1032
Real Estate **Band 2**
Table: p.1031

Clement Jr, Roger A
(Maine)
Profile: p.897
Bankruptcy **Band 1**
Table: p.888

Clements, William L
(National)
Profile: p.79
International Trade **Band 2**
Table: p.41

Clemow, Brian (Connecticut)
Profile: p.336
Employment **Band 2**
Table: p.329

Cleveland, Christopher
(Minnesota)
Profile: p.1017
Corporate/M&A **Band 3**
Table: p.1005

Cleveland III, William
(South Carolina)
Profile: p.1579
Litigation **Band 3**
Table: p.1576

Climan, Richard (California)
Profile: p.248
Corporate/M&A **Band 2**
Table: p.197

Clineburg, William (Georgia)
Profile: p.609
Employment **Band 4**
Table: p.589

Clinton, William J (National)
Profile: p.79
International Trade **Band 4**
Table: p.40

Cloherty, Thomas
(Connecticut)
Profile: p.336
Employment **Band 1**
Table: p.329

Clonts, David (Texas)
Profile: p.1675
Intellectual Property **Band 2**
Table: p.1651

Closson, Tom
(New Hampshire)
Profile: p.1116
Employment **Band 3**
Table: p.1109

Clowdus, Michael W
(Colorado)
Profile: p.317
Hotels and Resorts **Band 1**
Table: p.314

Coalson Jr, John L (Georgia)
Profile: p.609
Tax **Band 1**
Table: p.603

Coats, William M (Texas)
Profile: p.1675
Construction **Band 2**
Table: p.1629

Coben, Jerome L (California)
Profile: p.248
Corporate/M&A **Band 2**
Table: p.197

Cochran, Eric L (New York)
Profile: p.1272
Corporate/M&A **Band 4**
Table: p.1189

Cockrell, Dale R (Montana)
Profile: p.1080
Natural Resources **Band 1**
Table: p.1077

Cockrill, Donald A
(South Carolina)
Profile: p.1579
Litigation **Band 3**
Table: p.1576

Cockrum, James (Kentucky)
Profile: p.840
Employment **Band 1**
Table: p.830

Cody, W J Michael
(Tennessee)
Profile: p.1606
Litigation **Band 3**
Table: p.1599

Coffey, Peter L (Wisconsin)
Profile: p.1824
Corporate/M&A **Band 3**
Table: p.1817

Cogan, J Kevin (Ohio)
Profile: p.1439
Litigation **Band 4**
Table: p.1431

Cogan Jr, John (Texas)
Profile: p.1675
Energy **Band 1**
Table: p.1637
Projects **Band 1**
Table: p.52
Projects **Band 1**
Table: p.1659

Cogbill III, John V (Virginia)
Profile: p. 1768
Real Estate **Band 1**
Table: p.1765
Transport **Band 2**
Table: p.64

Coggeshall, Christopher J W (Maine)
Profile: p.897
Real Estate **Band 2**
Table: p.895

Coglianese, Matthew
(Florida)
Profile: p.536
Environment **Band 3**
Table: p.516

Cogut, Charles 'Casey'
(New York)
Profile: p.1272
Corporate/M&A **Band 1**
Table: p.1189
Private Equity **Band 1**
Table: p.1237

Cohen, Abbi L (Pennsylvania)
Profile: p.1521
Environment **Band 4**
Table: p.1505

Cohen, Ben (New York)
Profile: p.1273
Tax **Band 3**
Table: p.1255

Cohen, Bret A
(Massachusetts)
Profile: p.964
Employment **Band 3**
Table: p.940

Cohen, Charles
(District of Columbia)
Profile: p.437
Employment **Band 3**
Table: p.380

Cohen, David (Maryland)
Profile: p.920
Real Estate **Band 4**
Table: p.917

Cohen, David
(District of Columbia)
Profile: p.437
Energy **Band 5**
Table: p.382

Cohen, Ezra H (Georgia)
Profile: p.609
Bankruptcy **Band 1**
Table: p.582

Cohen, H Rodgin (New York)
Profile: p.1273
Banking & Finance **Band 1**
Table: p.1174
Corporate/M&A **Band 1**
Table: p.1189

Cohen, Jerold (Georgia)
Profile: p.609
Tax **Band 1**
Table: p.603

Cohen, Joel M (New York)
Profile: p.1273
Antitrust **Band 4**
Table: p.1170

Cohen, Jon (Arizona)
Profile: p.157
Corporate/M&A **Band 2**
Table: p.146

Cohen, Jules (Florida)
Profile: p.537
Bankruptcy **Band 2**
Table: p.503

Cohen, Matthew
(Washington)
Profile: p.1790
Environment **Band 2**
Table: p.1782

Cohen, Michael Marks
(New York)
Profile: p.79
Shipping **Band 3**
Table: p.67

Cohen, Nancy (California)
Profile: p.248
Insurance **Band 3**
Table: p.212

Cohen, R Scott (Texas)
Profile: p.1675
Corporate/M&A **Band 4**
Table: p.1631

Cohen, Richard (Arizona)
Profile: p.157
Employment **Band 1**
Table: p.148

Cohen, Stanley H
(Pennsylvania)
Profile: p.1521
Intellectual Property **Band 2**
Table: p.1508

Cohen, Steven (New Jersey)
Profile: p.1138
Corporate/M&A **Band 2**
Table: p.1123

Cohen, Steven
(New Hampshire)
Profile: p.1116
Corporate/M&A **Band 2**
Table: p.1107
Tax **Band 1**
Table: p.1114

Cohen, Steven N
(North Carolina)
Profile: p. 1394
Capital Markets **Band 1**
Table: p.22

Cohn, Daniel
(Massachusetts)
Profile: p.964
Bankruptcy **Band 1**
Table: p.935

Cohn, Joshua (National)
Profile: p.79
Capital Markets **Band 2**
Table: p.16

Cohn, Robert (National)
Profile: p.79
Aviation **Band 3**
Table: p.58

Coil, James (Georgia)
Profile: p.609
Employment **Band 3**

Table: p.589

Cokeley, Bryan
(West Virginia)
Profile: p.1808
Employment **Band 1**
Table: p.1801

Cokinos, Gregory (Texas)
Profile: p.1675
Construction **Band 2**
Table: p.1629

Colacino, Antonio (Iowa)
Profile: p.813
Real Estate **Band 2**
Table: p.810

Colbo, Kimberlee A (Alaska)
Profile: p.142
Employment **Band 2**
Table: p.135

Cole, Alexandra (Illinois)
Profile: p.722
Construction **Band 3**
Table: p.672

Cole, Dan (Minnesota)
Profile: p.1017
Real Estate **Band 3**
Table: p.1014

Cole, Howard (Nevada)
Profile: p.1101
Employment **Band 1**
Table: p.1091

Cole, J Chase (Tennessee)
Profile: p.1606
Corporate/M&A **Band 1**
Table: p.1594

Cole, Terry (Florida)
Profile: p.537
Environment **Band 2**
Table: p.516

Cole, Thomas A (Illinois)
Profile: p.722
Corporate/M&A **Band 1**
Table: p.675

Cole III, Kenneth M
(Maine)
Profile: p.897
Real Estate **Band 2**
Table: p.895

Coleman, Aubrey L
(Georgia)
Profile: p.609
Construction **Band 2**
Table: p.584

Coleman, Chris (Oklahoma)
Profile: p.1465
Corporate/M&A **Band 2**
Table: p.1459

Coleman, Ira (Florida)
Profile: p.537
Healthcare **Band 1**
Table: p.518

Coleman, James (Texas)
Profile: p.1675
Litigation **Band 2**
Table: p.1656

Coleman, John (Alabama)
Profile: p.122
Employment **Band 3**
Table: p.113

Coleman, Kathryn A
(California)
Profile: p.248
Bankruptcy **Band** 4
Table: p.191

Coleman, Leonard
(West Virginia)
Profile: p.1808
Corporate/M&A **Band** 2
Table: p.1798

Coleman, Lynn R
(District of Columbia)
Profile: p.437
Energy **Band** 3
Table: p.386

Coleman, Patrick (Florida)
Profile: p.537
Employment **Band** s
Table: p.513

Coleman, Payson (National)
Profile: p.79
Aviation **Band** 3
Table: p.58

Coleman, Thomas
(California)
Profile: p.248
Banking & Finance **Band** 3
Table: p.187

Colen, Frederick
(Pennsylvania)
Profile: p.1521
Intellectual Property **Band** 2
Table: p.1508

Colletta, Anthony J
(New York)
Profile: p.1273
Real Estate **Band** 5
Table: p.1248

Collier, Philip W (Kentucky)
Profile: p.840
Litigation **Band** 2
Table: p.835

Collings, Robert L
(Pennsylvania)
Profile: p.1521
Environment **Band** 4
Table: p.1505

Collins, Brendan K
(Pennsylvania)
Profile: p.1521
Environment **Band** 4
Table: p.1505

Collins, Dennis G (Missouri)
Profile: p.1056
Employment **Band** 3
Table: p.1046

Collins, Joseph P (Illinois)
Profile: p.722
Capital Markets **Band**
Table: p.21
Capital Markets **Band** 1
Table: p.21

Collins, Kevin H (Iowa)
Profile: p.813
Litigation **Band** 2
Table: p.807

Collins, Mark (Delaware)
Profile: p.352
Bankruptcy **Band** 2
Table: p.341

Collins, W Dale (New York)
Profile: p.1273
Antitrust **Band** 2
Table: p.1170

Colson, Dean (Florida)
Profile: p.537
Litigation **Band** 3
Table: p.521

Colton, Neal (Pennsylvania)
Profile: p.1522
Bankruptcy **Band** 3
Table: p.1494

Colton, Roberta (Florida)
Profile: p.537
Bankruptcy **Band** 1
Table: p.503

Colvin, R Keith (Louisiana)
Profile: p.870
Real Estate **Band** 2
Table: p.867

Comiter, Richard (Florida)
Profile: p.537
Tax **Band** 3
Table: p.531

Commander III, Charles E
(Florida)
Profile: p.537
Real Estate **Band** 3
Table: p.526

Compton, Charles T
(California)
Profile: p.248
Antitrust **Band** 3
Table: p.184

Conard, David (Vermont)
Profile: p.1748
Real Estate **Band** 2
Table: p.1747

Conde, Kathryn Keough
(Massachusetts)
Profile: p.964
Antitrust **Up and coming**
Table: p.930

Condlin, Andrew (Virginia)
Profile: p.1768

Condo, James (Arizona)
Profile: p.157
Litigation **Band** 4
Table: p.152

Condon, Creighton
(New York)
Profile: p.1273
Corporate/M&A **Band** 1
Table: p.1189

Conklin, Robert (New
Mexico)
Profile: p.1163
Employment **Band** 1
Table: p.1157

Conlan, James F (Illinois)
Profile: p.723
Bankruptcy **Band** 3
Table: p.669

Conlon, Michael W (Texas)
Profile: p.1675
Corporate/M&A **Band** 2
Table: p.1631

Conlon, William (Illinois)
Profile: p.723
Litigation **Band** 3

Table: p.700

Connelly, Michael (Texas)
Profile: p.1675
Litigation **Band** 2
Table: p.1643

Connelly, Vincent J (Illinois)
Profile: p.723
Litigation **Band** 1
Table: p.700

Connelly, Warren E
(National)
Profile: p.79
International Trade **Band** 2
Table: p.40

Conner, Stewart (Kentucky)
Profile: p.840
Corporate/M&A **Band** 1
Table: p.827

Connery, Robert T
(Colorado)
Profile: p.317
Environment **Band** 2
Table: p.307

Connolly, Annemargaret
(District of Columbia)
Profile: p.438
Environment **Band** 2
Table: p.393

Connolly, Dennis J (Georgia)
Profile: p.609
Bankruptcy **Band** 1
Table: p.582

Connolly, Michael J
(New Hampshire)
Profile: p.1116
Litigation **Band** 3
Table: p.1111

Connolly, Robert M
(Kentucky)
Profile: p.840
Litigation **Band** 3
Table: p.835

Connolly, Theresa (Virginia)
Profile: p.1768
Employment **Band**
Table: p.1755
Employment **Band** 3
Table: p.1755

Connolly Jr, Arthur
(Delaware)
Profile: p.352
Intellectual Property **Band** 3
Table: p.348

Connor, Terence (Florida)
Profile: p.537
Employment **Band** 2
Table: p.513

Connors, Eugene
(Pennsylvania)
Profile: p.1522
Employment **Band** 2
Table: p.1500

Conrad, Albert H (Georgia)
Profile: p.609
Banking & Finance **Band** 1
Table: p.580

Conrad, David (Ohio)
Profile: p.1439
Real Estate **Band** 2
Table: p.1434

Conrad, Walter (Texas)
Profile: p.1675
Litigation **Band** 1
Table: p.1643

Conrad Jr, Winthrop B
(National)
Profile: p.79
Capital Markets **Band** 3
Table: p.14

Conroy, Joseph W (Virginia)
Profile: p.1768
Corporate/M&A **Band** 3
Table: p.1752

Constantine, Lloyd
(New York)
Profile: p.1273
Antitrust **Band** 2
Table: p.1170

Constine III, David E
(Virginia)
Profile: p.1768
Employment **Band** 3
Table: p.1755

Contratto, Dana
(District of Columbia)
Profile: p.438
Energy **Band** 4
Table: p.386

Conway, Gregory B
(Wisconsin)
Profile: p.1824
Litigation **Band** 3
Table: p.1821

Conway, Michael M
(Illinois)
Profile: p.723
Media & Entertainment **Band** 2
Table: p.703

Conway, Susan (Texas)
Profile: p.1675
Insurance **Band** 3
Table: p.1648

Conway, Timothy R (Illinois)
Profile: p.723
Construction **Band** 3
Table: p.672

Coogan, Peter
(Massachusetts)
Profile: p.964
Banking & Finance **Band** 1
Table: p.932
Corporate/M&A **Band** 3
Table: p.937

Cook, Bryson (Maryland)
Profile: p.920
Corporate/M&A **Band** 1
Table: p.909

Cook, Guy (Iowa)
Profile: p.813
Litigation **Band** 3
Table: p.807

Cook, James G
(New Hampshire)
Profile: p.1116
Corporate/M&A **Band** 2
Table: p.1107

Cook, Jay (Minnesota)
Profile: p.1017
Real Estate **Band** 1
Table: p.1014

Cook, Melanie K (California)
Profile: p.248
Media & Entertainment **Band** 3
Table: p.233

Cook, Michael L (New York)
Profile: p.1273
Bankruptcy **Band** 4
Table: p.1179

Cook, Philip C (Georgia)
Profile: p.609
Tax **Band** 2
Table: p.603

Cook, Philip E (California)
Profile: p.248
Litigation **Band** 4
Table: p.224

Cook, Rand (Utah)
Profile: p.1736
Real Estate **Band** 2
Table: p.1733

Cook Bush, Antoinette
(District of Columbia)
Profile: p.438
Telecom, Broadcast & Satellite **Band** 4
Table: p.427

Cooke, Gregg (Texas)
Profile: p.1675
Environment **Band** 4
Table: p.1643

Cooke, Susan
(Massachusetts)
Profile: p.964
Environment **Band** 1
Table: p.943

Cooney, James (North
Carolina)
Profile: p.1395
Litigation **Band** 2
Table: p.1390

Cooney, John R (New
Mexico)
Profile: p.1163
Environment **Band** 1
Table: p.1158

Cooney Jr, Robert L
(Pennsylvania)
Profile: p.1522

Coonrod, Stephan
(Washington)
Profile: p.1790
Corporate/M&A **Band** 2
Table: p.1778

Cooper, Brent (Texas)
Profile: p.1675
Insurance **Band** 1
Table: p.1648

Cooper, James (New York)
Profile: p.1273
Banking & Finance **Band** 1
Table: p.1174

Cooper, James (Texas)
Profile: p.1675
Insurance **Band** 3
Table: p.1648

Cooper, Jay L (California)
Profile: p.249
Media & Entertainment **Band** 2
Table: p.233

C

Cooper, John H (Alabama)
Profile: p.122
Corporate/M&A Band 2
Table: p.111

Cooper, Marc (Florida)
Profile: p.537
Litigation Band 2
Table: p.525

Cooper, Robert (California)
Profile: p.249
Antitrust Band 1
Table: p.184
Litigation Band 2
Table: p.224

Cooper, Ronald
(District of Columbia)
Profile: p.438
Employment Band 3
Table: p.380

Cooperman, Harriet E
(Maryland)
Profile: p.920
Employment Band 3
Table: p.912

Copeland, Gregory (Texas)
Profile: p.1675
Energy Band 2
Table: p.1640

Copenhaver, W Andrew
(North Carolina)
Profile: p.1395
Antitrust Band 1
Table: p.1390
Litigation Band 3
Table: p.1390

Corash, Michèle B
(California)
Profile: p.249
Environment Band 1
Table: p.207

Corbin, Robert L (California)
Profile: p.249
Litigation Band 2
Table: p.225

Corbyn, George (Oklahoma)
Profile: p.1465
Litigation Band 1
Table: p.1462

Corcoran, William
(New York)
Profile: p.965
Tax Band 3
Table: p.959

Cordell, David R (Oklahoma)
Profile: p.1465
Employment Band 2
Table: p.1461

Cordell, Ruffin
(District of Columbia)
Profile: p.438
Intellectual Property Band 3
Table: p.403

Cordero, Frank (Florida)
Profile: p.537
Tax Band u
Table: p.531

Corgan, Brian (Georgia)
Profile: p.609
Construction Band 2
Table: p.584

Corlew, John (Mississippi)
Profile: p.1033
Litigation Band 1
Table: p.1028

Corn-Revere, Robert
(District of Columbia)
Profile: p.438
Media & Entertainment Band 2
Table: p.413

Corr, Christopher F
(National)
Profile: p.79
International Trade Band 5
Table: p.40

Corr, Kelly (Washington)
Profile: p.1790
Litigation Band 2
Table: p.1786

Corrales, Carmen Amalia
(National)
Profile: p.80
Capital Markets
Up and coming
Table: p.14

Correro, Anthony J
(Louisiana)
Profile: p.870
Corporate/M&A Band 1
Table: p.859

Corretti, Douglas (Alabama)
Profile: p.122
Real Estate Band 2
Table: p.119

Cortesio, John (Iowa)
Profile: p.813
Corporate/M&A Band 3
Table: p.802

Coruzzi, Laura (New York)
Profile: p.1273
Intellectual Property Band 2
Table: p.1217

Coryell II, Cornelius E
(Kentucky)
Profile: p.840
Litigation Band 3
Table: p.835

Costello, Joseph J
(Pennsylvania)
Profile: p.1522
Employment Band 3
Table: p.1500

Costello Slovak, Patricia
(Illinois)
Profile: p.723
Employment Band 2
Table: p.681

Costley, Kevin (Minnesota)
Profile: p.1017
Corporate/M&A Band 3
Table: p.1005

Cotchett, Joseph
(California)
Profile: p.249
Litigation Band 2
Table: p.224

Cotropia, Charles S (Texas)
Profile: p.1675
Intellectual Property Band 3
Table: p.1651

Cottam, Dale (Wyoming)
Profile: p.1838
Corporate/M&A Band 2
Table: p.1832

Cotton, Stuart (New York)
Profile: p.1273
Insurance Band 2
Table: p.1213
Insurance Band 2
Table: p.1213

Cottrell III, Frederick
(Delaware)
Profile: p.352
Intellectual Property Band 4
Table: p.348

Coughlin, Jennifer (Alaska)
Profile: p.142
Litigation Band 3
Table: p.138

Coukos, Stephen J
(Massachusetts)
Profile: p.965
Banking & Finance Band 2
Table: p.932

Court, Leonard (Oklahoma)
Profile: p.1465
Employment Band 1
Table: p.1461

Courtnage, Michael S
(Washington)
Profile: p.1790
Real Estate Band 2
Table: p.1788

Couser, Richard B
(New Hampshire)
Profile: p.1116
Litigation Band 3
Table: p.1111

Cousins, Scott (Delaware)
Profile: p.352
Bankruptcy Band 4
Table: p.341

Coutroulis, Chris (Florida)
Profile: p.537
Antitrust Band 1
Table: p.498

Covey, Tyson J (Illinois)
Profile: p.723
Telecom, Broadcast & Satellite
Band 3
Table: p.715

Covington, George C
(North Carolina)
Profile: p.1395
Litigation Band 2
Table: p.1390

Covington, Peter J
(North Carolina)
Profile: p.1395
Litigation Band 2
Table: p.1390

Cowan, Cameron (National)
Profile: p.80
Capital Markets Band 1
Table: p.19

Cowan, J Donald
(North Carolina)
Profile: p.1395
Litigation Band 1
Table: p.1390

Cowan, Kevin (Florida)
Profile: p.537
Real Estate Band 3
Table: p.526

Cowart, Richard
(Tennessee)
Profile: p.1606
Corporate/M&A Band 2
Table: p.1594

Cowen, Stephen (Georgia)
Profile: p.609
Litigation Band 1
Table: p.599

Cox, Donald (Kentucky)
Profile: p.840
Litigation Band 1
Table: p.835

Cox, Randy (Montana)
Profile: p.1080
Litigation Band 1
Table: p.1075

Cox, Robert (Virginia)
Profile: p.1768
Construction Band 3
Table: p.1750

Cox, W Donald (Florida)
Profile: p.537
Insurance Band 2
Table: p.519

Cox Jr, Robert D
(Massachusetts)
Profile: p.965
Environment Band 3
Table: p.943

Coxe, Henry M (Florida)
Profile: p.537
Litigation Band 2
Table: p.522

Coyne, Thomas (Ohio)
Profile: p.1439
Real Estate Band 3
Table: p.1434

Crabb, Joseph (Arizona)
Profile: p.157
Corporate/M&A Band 4
Table: p.146

Craig, L Clifford (Ohio)
Profile: p.1439
Litigation Band 3
Table: p.1431

Craig III, Allen (Texas)
Profile: p.1675
Tax Band 3
Table: p.1665

Cramer, Eric (Pennsylvania)
Profile: p.1522
Antitrust Up and coming
Table: p.1489

Crane, Steven (California)
Profile: p.249
Insurance Band 3
Table: p.212

Cranmer, Thomas W
(Michigan)
Profile: p.998
Litigation Band 1
Table: p.994

Crass, Kevin (Arkansas)
Profile: p.175
Litigation Band 1

Table: p.172

Craven, Erica L (California)
Profile: p.249
Media & Entertainment
Up and coming
Table: p.230

Craven, George W (Illinois)
Profile: p.723
Tax Band 3
Table: p.710

Creamer Jr, Ronald E
(New York)
Profile: p.1273
Tax Band 4
Table: p.1255

Creel, Thomas (New York)
Profile: p.1273
Intellectual Property Band 3
Table: p.1217

Crement, Anthony (Illinois)
Profile: p.724
Employment Band 2
Table: p.681

Cremin, Pat (Oklahoma)
Profile: p.1465
Employment Band 1
Table: p.1461

Crenshaw Jr, Waverly D
(Tennessee)
Profile: p.1606
Employment Band 3
Table: p.1596

Crew, Eugene (California)
Profile: p.249
Antitrust Band 3
Table: p.184

Crewdson, Robert (Georgia)
Profile: p.610
Construction Band 2
Table: p.584

Cribley, James M (Hawaii)
Profile: p.648
Corporate/M&A Band 2
Table: p.641
Real Estate Band 2
Table: p.646

Crisafi, Frank A (Georgia)
Profile: p.610
Tax Band 3
Table: p.603

Crisman Jr, C Benjamin
(District of Columbia)
Profile: p.438
Antitrust Band 5
Table: p.367

Crist, Paul (California)
Profile: p.249
Litigation Band
Table: p.224
Litigation Band 4
Table: p.224

Critchley, Michael
(New Jersey)
Profile: p.1138
Litigation Band 1
Table: p.1133

Critchlow, Richard H
(Florida)
Profile: p.537
Litigation Band 2
Table: p.521

Critelli Jr, Nicholas (Iowa)
Profile: p.813
Litigation Band 3
Table: p.807

Crochet, Vicki (Louisiana)
Profile: p.870
Employment Band 3
Table: p.861

Cromer, Brian A (Kentucky)
Profile: p.840
Corporate/M&A Band 3
Table: p.827

Cromwell, David (Louisiana)
Profile: p.870
Banking & Finance Band 2
Table: p.857

Cronan IV, Charles J
(Kentucky)
Profile: p.840
Litigation Band 1
Table: p.835

Crone, Tom (Wisconsin)
Profile: p.1824
Employment Band 3
Table: p.1819

Cronin, William
(Washington)
Profile: p.1790
Litigation Band 2
Table: p.1786

Crosby, E Howell (Louisiana)
Profile: p.871
Real Estate Band 2
Table: p.867

Cross, Bruce Michael
(Washington)
Profile: p.1790
Employment Band 2
Table: p.1780

Cross, J Bruce (Arkansas)
Profile: p.175
Employment Band 3
Table: p.170

Cross, James (New York)
Profile: p.1273
Banking & Finance Band 4
Table: p.1174

Cross, Patrick (Indiana)
Profile: p.791
Corporate/M&A Band 3
Table: p.781

Crost, Katharine I
(National)
Profile: p.80
Capital Markets Band 4
Table: p.19

Crough, Maureen
(New York)
Profile: p.1274
Environment Band 3
Table: p.1206

Crow, Carter (Texas)
Profile: p.1676
Employment Up and coming
Table: p.1634

Crow, William (Oregon)
Profile: p.1481
Litigation Band 2
Table: p.1477

Crowe, Austin (Oregon)
Profile: p.1481
Litigation Band 2
Table: p.1477

Crowley, Frank (Montana)
Profile: p.1080
Natural Resources Band 1
Table: p.1077

Crowley, Lisanne
(District of Columbia)
Profile: p.438
Energy Band 4
Table: p.382

Croysdale, David
(Wisconsin)
Profile: p.1825
Employment Band 3
Table: p.1819

Crumbaugh, David G
(Illinois)
Profile: p.724
Banking & Finance Band 1
Table: p.665

Crutcher Jr, Pepper
(Mississippi)
Profile: p.1033
Employment Band 2
Table: p.1026

Cryder, Bruce E (Kentucky)
Profile: p.840
Environment Band 2
Table: p.832

Crystal, Jules I (Illinois)
Profile: p.724
Employment Band 3
Table: p.681

Cubell, Howard
(Massachusetts)
Profile: p.965
Tax Band 1
Table: p.959

Cuclis, James (Texas)
Profile: p.1676
Energy Band 5
Table: p.1637

Cudney, Kevin (Colorado)
Profile: p.317
Corporate/M&A Band 3
Table: p.303

Cuff, Terence (California)
Profile: p.249
Tax Band 2
Table: p.241

Culbertson, Robert
(District of Columbia)
Profile: p.438
Tax Band 3
Table: p.422

Culhane, James (Colorado)
Profile: p.317
Real Estate Band 2
Table: p.313

Culhane, Stephen
(New York)
Profile: p.1274
Private Equity Band 3
Table: p.1241

Culhane, Thomas
(Nebraska)
Profile: p.1087
Litigation Band 2

Table: p.1085

Cullen, Gary P (Illinois)
Profile: p.724
Corporate/M&A Band 3
Table: p.675

Cullen, Jack (Washington)
Profile: p.1790
Bankruptcy Band 1
Table: p.1776

Cullen, Richard (Virginia)
Profile: p.1768
Litigation Band 3
Table: p.1763

Cullen, William J (National)
Profile: p.80
Capital Markets Band 4
Table: p.19

Culley, Peter (Maine)
Profile: p.897
Litigation Band 2
Table: p.893

Culotta, Ken (Texas)
Profile: p.1676
Energy Band 2
Table: p.1637
Projects Band 2
Table: p.1659

Culpepper, Bruce (Florida)
Profile: p.537
Insurance Band 2
Table: p.519

Culwell, Todd (Texas)
Profile: p.1676
Projects Band 4
Table: p.1659

Cummings, Stephen
(Montana)
Profile: p.1080
Real Estate Band 1
Table: p.1078

Cummings, William
(Alaska)
Profile: p.142
Real Estate Band 2
Table: p.141

Cummins, Guylyn
(California)
Profile: p.249
Media & Entertainment Band 3
Table: p.230

Cunningham, Daniel P
(National)
Profile: p.80
Capital Markets Band 1
Table: p.16

Cunningham, Malcolm
(Florida)
Profile: p.537
Construction Band 3
Table: p.507

Cunningham, Peter C
(Florida)
Profile: p.537
Environment Band 3
Table: p.516

Cunningham, Richard
(National)
Profile: p.80
International Trade Band 1
Table: p.40

Cunningham, Robert
(Alabama)
Profile: p.122
Litigation Band 1
Table: p.116

Cunningham, Thomas
(Iowa)
Profile: p.813
Employment Band 3
Table: p.805

Cupps, David (Ohio)
Profile: p.1439
Litigation Band 1
Table: p.1431

Curley, Michael (New York)
Profile: p.1274
Employment Band 1
Table: p.1200

Curnin, Paul C (New York)
Profile: p.1274
Litigation Band 2
Table: p.1223

Curran, Bob (Maryland)
Profile: p.920
Corporate/M&A Band 3
Table: p.909

Curran, Denis A
(District of Columbia)
Profile: p.438

Curran, Gregory (Alabama)
Profile: p.122
Corporate/M&A Band 1
Table: p.111

Curran, William P (Nevada)
Profile: p.1101
Gaming & Licensing Band 3
Table: p.1094

Currault II, Douglas N
(Louisiana)
Profile: p.871
Corporate/M&A
Up and coming
Table: p.859

Currie, John Withers (South Carolina)
Profile: p.1579
Corporate/M&A Band 1
Table: p.1572

Currie, Michael (Ohio)
Profile: p.1439
Construction Band 2
Table: p.1417

Currier, Douglas P (Maine)
Profile: p.897
Employment Band 3
Table: p.890

Currier, Maria (Florida)
Profile: p.538
Healthcare Band 2
Table: p.518

Curry, Michael (Nebraska)
Profile: p.1087
Real Estate Band 2
Table: p.1086

Curry, Stanton (Arizona)
Profile: p.157
Environment Band 2
Table: p.150

Curtin, John (Jack)
(Massachusetts)
Profile: p.965
Antitrust Band S
Table: p.930

Curtin, Lawrence (Florida)
Profile: p.538
Environment Band 2
Table: p.516

Curtin, Neal (Massachusetts)
Profile: p.965
Banking & Finance Band 1
Table: p.932

Curtis, Charles G
(Wisconsin)
Profile: p.1825
Litigation Band 3
Table: p.1821

Curtis, George B (Colorado)
Profile: p.317
Litigation Band 4
Table: p.311

Curtis, J Vaughan (Georgia)
Profile: p.610
Corporate/M&A Band 4
Table: p.587

Curtis, Patricia (Nevada)
Profile: p.1101
Real Estate Band 2
Table: p.1099

Curtis, Susan M (National)
Profile: p.80
Capital Markets Band 2
Table: p.19

Curtiss, Catherine
(National)
Profile: p.80
International Trade Band 5
Table: p.40

Curtiss, James
(District of Columbia)
Profile: p.438
Energy Band 2
Table: p.390

Curtz, Chauncey SR
(Kentucky)
Profile: p.841
Environment Band 3
Table: p.832

Curzon, Thomas H (Arizona)
Profile: p.157
Corporate/M&A Band 1
Table: p.146

Cushing, Paul M (Georgia)
Profile: p.610
Banking & Finance Band 3
Table: p.580

Cusick, Michael (New York)
Profile: p.1274
Energy Band 3
Table: p.1202

Cusumano, Robert F (New York)
Profile: p.1274
Insurance Band 3
Table: p.1213

Cutchins IV, Clifford A
(Virginia)
Profile: p.1768
Corporate/M&A Band 1
Table: p.1752

C

Cutler, Kenneth (Minnesota)
Profile: p.1017
Corporate/M&A **Band 2**
Table: p.1005

Cutler, Richard A
(South Dakota)
Profile: p.1592
Corporate/M&A **Band 2**
Table: p.1587
Real Estate **Band 1**
Table: p.1592

Cuva, Anthony J (National)
Profile: p.80
Shipping **Band 1**
Table: p.71

Cyphers, Christopher
(Alaska)
Profile: p.142
Corporate/M&A **Band 2**
Table: p.134

Cyphert, Michael (Ohio)
Profile: p.1439
Environment **Band 3**
Table: p.1425

Czarniak, Julia (New York)
Profile: p.1274
Projects **Up and coming**
Table: p.1244

D

Dabney, James W
(New York)
Profile: p.1274
Intellectual Property **Band 3**
Table: p.1217

Dagenais, Don F (Missouri)
Profile: p.1056
Real Estate **Band 2**
Table: p.1052

Dagenhart, Larry (North
Carolina)
Profile: p.1395
Corporate/M&A **Band 3**
Table: p.1384

Dahlk, Thomas (Nebraska)
Profile: p.1087
Litigation **Band 2**
Table: p.1085

Dailey, Anna M
(West Virginia)
Profile: p.1808
Employment **Band 2**
Table: p.1801

Dale, James (Idaho)
Profile: p.660
Employment **Band 1**
Table: p.656

Dale III, Charles A
(Massachusetts)
Profile: p.965
Bankruptcy **Band 3**
Table: p.935

Daley, Paul (Massachusetts)
Profile: p.965
Bankruptcy **Band 2**
Table: p.935

Dalgleish, Douglas
(Missouri)
Profile: p.1056

Litigation Band 2
Table: p.1049

Dallas, Bruce (California)
Profile: p.80
Capital Markets **Band 1**
Table: p.23

Dalton, John (Georgia)
Profile: p.610
Litigation **Band 1**
Table: p.598

Dalton, Larry (Wisconsin)
Profile: p.1825
Real Estate **Band 2**
Table: p.1822

Daly, Lawrence (Montana)
Profile: p.1080
Litigation **Band 3**
Table: p.1075

D'Amante, Raymond
(New Hampshire)
Profile: p.1116
Real Estate **Band 2**
Table: p.1114

Damgaard, Roger
(South Dakota)
Profile: p.1592
Bankruptcy **Band 1**
Table: p.1587
Corporate/M&A **Band 1**
Table: p.1587

Damm, Jacqueline (Oregon)
Profile: p.1482
Employment **Up and coming**
Table: p.1474

Damon, Lisa (Massachusetts)
Profile: p.965
Employment **Band 2**
Table: p.940

Damschroder, Timothy R
(Michigan)
Profile: p.998
Corporate/M&A **Band 2**
Table: p.989

Danenbarger, Wright
(New Hampshire)
Profile: p.1116
Litigation **Band 3**
Table: p.1111

D'Angelo Jr, Alfred J
(Pennsylvania)
Profile: p.1522
Employment **Band 3**
Table: p.1500

Daniel, Harold T (Georgia)
Profile: p.610
Litigation **Band 3**
Table: p.598

Daniel, Josiah (Texas)
Profile: p.1676
Bankruptcy **Band 3**
Table: p.1627

Daniel, Laurie Webb
(Georgia)
Profile: p.610
Litigation **Band 3**
Table: p.598

Daniel, Thomas M (Alaska)
Profile: p.142
Employment **Band 1**
Table: p.135

Daniel II, John W (Virginia)
Profile: p.1768
Environment **Band 2**
Table: p.1757

Daniels Jr, John W
(Wisconsin)
Profile: p.1825
Real Estate **Band 2**
Table: p.1822

Dankner, Donald
(District of Columbia)
Profile: p.438
Energy **Band 5**
Table: p.386

Dannay, Richard (New York)
Profile: p.1274
Media & Entertainment **Band 3**
Table: p.1232

Danneman, Dale (Arizona)
Profile: p.158
Litigation **Band 4**
Table: p.152

D'Aquila, Barbara
(Minnesota)
Profile: p.1017
Employment **Band 2**
Table: p.1008

Darden, Michael (Texas)
Profile: p.1676
Energy **Band 5**
Table: p.1637

Dare, Mark (Virginia)
Profile: p.1768
Employment **Band 3**
Table: p.1755

Darling, William Duane
(Texas)
Profile: p.1676
Healthcare **Band 2**
Table: p.1646

D'Armond, William
(Louisiana)
Profile: p.871
Employment **Band S**
Table: p.861

Dash, James (Illinois)
Profile: p.724
Construction **Band 3**
Table: p.672

Daugherty, Patrick D
(Michigan)
Profile: p.998
Corporate/M&A **Band 2**
Table: p.989

Davenport, Kirk A
(National)
Profile: p.80
Capital Markets **Band 2**
Table: p.14

Davenport, Margaret A
(New York)
Profile: p.1274
Private Equity **Band 1**
Table: p.1237

David, Henry S (California)
Profile: p.249
Bankruptcy **Band 4**
Table: p.191

David, Todd R (Georgia)
Profile: p.610
Litigation **Band 3**

Table: p.598

Davidson, Barry (Florida)
Profile: p.538
Antitrust **Band 3**
Table: p.498
Litigation **Band 3**
Table: p.521

Davidson, Bruce C
(Wisconsin)
Profile: p.1825
Corporate/M&A **Band 2**
Table: p.1817

Davidson, Gordon
(California)
Profile: p.249
Corporate/M&A **Band 1**
Table: p.197

Davidson, Joshua (Texas)
Profile: p.1676
Corporate/M&A **Band 3**
Table: p.1631

Davies, Scott (Minnesota)
Profile: p.1017
Employment **Band 1**
Table: p.1008

Davis, Alan E (New Jersey)
Profile: p.1138
Corporate/M&A **Band 2**
Table: p.1123

Davis, Alan J (Pennsylvania)
Profile: p.1522
Litigation **Band 1**
Table: p.1511
Litigation **Band 2**
Table: p.1512

Davis, Alvin B (Florida)
Profile: p.538
Litigation **Band 3**
Table: p.521

Davis, Ames (Tennessee)
Profile: p.1606
Litigation **Band 2**
Table: p.1599

Davis, Christopher P
(Massachusetts)
Profile: p.965
Environment **Band 1**
Table: p.943

Davis, Doreen (Pennsylvania)
Profile: p.1522
Employment **Band 3**
Table: p.1500

Davis, Fred (New York)
Profile: p. 1274
Arbitration **Band 3**
Table: p.33
Litigation **Band 3**
Table: p.1222

Davis, Gardner F (Florida)
Profile: p.538
Corporate/M&A **Band 3**
Table: p.509

Davis, Gary (Oklahoma)
Profile: p.1465
Litigation **Band 2**
Table: p.1462

Davis, Gary Scott (Florida)
Profile: p.538
Healthcare **Band 1**
Table: p.518

Davis, George A (New York)
Profile: p.1274
Bankruptcy **Up and coming**
Table: p.1179

Davis, Grant L (Missouri)
Profile: p.1056
Litigation **Band 3**
Table: p.1049

Davis, James
(District of Columbia)
Profile: p.438
Intellectual Property **Band 2**
Table: p.403

Davis, Jefferson
(New Hampshire)
Profile: p.1116
Real Estate **Band 1**
Table: p.1114

Davis, Jeffrey J (North
Carolina)
Profile: p.1395
Litigation **Band 2**
Table: p.1390

Davis, Kirk S (Florida)
Profile: p.538
Healthcare **Band 1**
Table: p.518

Davis, Lee (Georgia)
Profile: p.610
Construction **Band 2**
Table: p.584

Davis, Mark (Mississippi)
Profile: p.1033
Real Estate **Band 2**
Table: p.1031

Davis, Michael
(Massachusetts)
Profile: p.965
Tax **Band 3**
Table: p.959

Davis, Michael (Wyoming)
Profile: p.1838
Employment **Band 1**
Table: p.1833

Davis, Oscar (Arkansas)
Profile: p.175
Employment **Band 3**
Table: p.170

Davis, Platt W (Texas)
Profile: p. 1676
Arbitration **Band 4**
Table: p.33
Energy **Band 1**
Table: p.1641

Davis, R Eberley (Kentucky)
Profile: p.841
Environment **Band 2**
Table: p.832

Davis, Robert P
(District of Columbia)
Profile: p.438
Employee Benefits **Band 3**
Table: p.378
Employment **Band 3**
Table: p.380

Davis, Scott J (Illinois)
Profile: p.724
Corporate/M&A **Band 2**
Table: p.675

Davis, Steven C (Oklahoma)
Profile: p.1465
Tax **Band** 2
Table: p.1459

Davis, Steven H (New York)
Profile: p.1275
Energy **Band** 2
Table: p.1202

Davis, Thomas (Alabama)
Profile: p.122
Employment **Band** 3
Table: p.113

Davis, Will (Texas)
Profile: p.1676
Insurance **Band** 3
Table: p.1648

Davis, William
(North Carolina)
Profile: p.1395
Litigation **Band** 1
Table: p.1390

Davis Jones, Laura
(Delaware)
Profile: p.352
Bankruptcy **Band** 2
Table: p.341

Davis Jr, Edward P
(California)
Profile: p.249
Media & Entertainment **Band** 4
Table: p.230

Davis Jr, Richard M
(Wyoming)
Profile: p.1838
Real Estate **Band** 2
Table: p.1836

Dawahare, Debra
(Kentucky)
Profile: p.841
Employment **Band** 3
Table: p.830

Dawda, Edward (Michigan)
Profile: p.998
Real Estate **Band** 1
Table: p.996

Dawson, Alistair (Texas)
Profile: p.1676

Dawson, Amos C (North
Carolina)
Profile: p.1395
Environment **Band** 2
Table: p.1388

Dawson, James (Minnesota)
Profile: p.1017
Employment **Band** 2
Table: p.1008

Dawson, Jon S (Alaska)
Profile: p.142
Bankruptcy **Band** 2
Table: p.133
Corporate/M&A **Band** 1
Table: p.134

Dawson, Stephen E
(Michigan)
Profile: p.998
Real Estate **Band** 2
Table: p.996

Dawson, William B (Texas)
Profile: p.1676
Litigation **Band** 3
Table: p.1656

Dax, John (New York)
Profile: p.1275
Energy **Band** 1
Table: p.1204

Day, Barton (Arizona)
Profile: p.158
Environment **Band** 3
Table: p.150

Day, Lloyd (California)
Profile: p.249
Intellectual Property **Band** 2
Table: p.216

Day, Michael (California)
Profile: p.249
Energy **Band** 2
Table: p.204

Day, Richard (Wyoming)
Profile: p.1838
Litigation **Band** S
Table: p.1835

Dayan, Michael D (National)
Profile: p.80
Capital Markets **Band** 2
Table: p.16

Dayanim, Behnam
(National)
Profile: p.80
International Trade
Up and coming
Table: p.41

de Armas, Luis (Florida)
Profile: p.538
Corporate/M&A **Band** 3
Table: p.509

de Bernardo, Mark
(District of Columbia)
Profile: p.438
Employment **Band** 3
Table: p.380

De Buys Jr, John (Alabama)
Profile: p.122
Real Estate **Band** 2
Table: p.119

De Chiara, Michael
(New York)
Profile: p.1275
Construction **Band** 4
Table: p.1186

de Lipkau, Ross (Nevada)
Profile: p.1101
Environment **Band** 1
Table: p.1093

De Meules, James H
(California)
Profile: p.249
Banking & Finance **Band** S
Table: p.187

De Sear, Edward (National)
Profile: p.81
Capital Markets **Band** 1
Table: p.19

De Vore, Bradford A (North
Carolina)
Profile: p.1395
Environment **Band** 2
Table: p.1388

de Wied, Warren (New York)
Profile: p.1275
Corporate/M&A
Up and coming
Table: p.1189

Deakins Jr, Homer L
(Georgia)
Profile: p.610
Employment **Band** 2
Table: p.589

Dean, Cathy (Missouri)
Profile: p.1056
Litigation **Band** 2
Table: p.1049

Deane, Richard (Georgia)
Profile: p.610
Litigation **Band** 1
Table: p.599

Deatherage, Scott (Texas)
Profile: p.1676
Litigation **Band** 2
Table: p.1643

deBeers, Kimberly A
(Illinois)
Profile: p.724
Private Equity **Band** 3
Table: p.676

Debruge, Marcel (Alabama)
Profile: p.122
Employment **Band** 3
Table: p.113

Dee, David (Florida)
Profile: p.538
Environment **Band** 2
Table: p.516

Dee, Francis X (New Jersey)
Profile: p.1138
Employment **Band** 1
Table: p.1126

Deem, Patrick D
(West Virginia)
Profile: p.1808
Corporate/M&A **Band** 2
Table: p.1798
Real Estate **Band** 1
Table: p.1806

Deeny, Raymond (Colorado)
Profile: p.317
Employment **Band** 2
Table: p.306

Dees, Stanley C (National)
Profile: p.81
Government Contracts
Band S
Table: p.27

DeFranceschi, Daniel
(Delaware)
Profile: p.352
Bankruptcy **Band** 4
Table: p.341

Degnan, Peter (Georgia)
Profile: p.610
Energy **Band** 2
Table: p.592

DeHihns III, Lee A (Georgia)
Profile: p.611
Environment **Band** 1
Table: p.593

Dehney, Robert J (Delaware)
Profile: p.352
Bankruptcy **Band** 3
Table: p.341

Deitch, Laurence B
(Michigan)
Profile: p.998
Corporate/M&A **Band** 3

Table: p.989

del Calvo, Jorge (California)
Profile: p.249
Corporate/M&A **Band** 2
Table: p.197

Delaney, John (New York)
Profile: p.1275
Technology **Band** 2
Table: p.1259

Delegal, Mark (Florida)
Profile: p.538
Insurance **Band** 2
Table: p.519

Delegal, Susan (Florida)
Profile: p.538
Real Estate **Band** 2
Table: p.528

Delikat, Michael (New York)
Profile: p.1275
Employment **Band** 1
Table: p.1200

Dellinger, Walter
(District of Columbia)
Profile: p.439
Litigation **Band** 1
Table: p.408

DeLucia, Richard L
(New York)
Profile: p.1275
Intellectual Property **Band** 3
Table: p.1217

DeMarco, Daniel A (Ohio)
Profile: p.1439
Bankruptcy **Band** 3
Table: p.1414

DeMaria, Gerald C
(Rhode Island)
Profile: p.1569
Litigation **Band** 2
Table: p.1567

DeMars, David
(North Dakota)
Profile: p.1410
Bankruptcy **Band** 2
Table: p.1403

DeMarte, Luke W (Illinois)
Profile: p.724
Media & Entertainment
Up and coming
Table: p.704

DeMeo, Ralph (Florida)
Profile: p.538
Environment **Band** 3
Table: p.516

Demerath, Jeffrey (Missouri)
Profile: p.1056
Litigation **Band** 1
Table: p.1049

Demetriou, Andrew James
(California)
Profile: p.250
Healthcare **Band** 1
Table: p.209

deMeza, Willliam (Florida)
Profile: p.538
Employment **Band** 2
Table: p.513

Dempsey, Kevin M
(National)
Profile: p.81

International Trade **Band** 4
Table: p.40

Dempster, Hazen H
(Georgia)
Profile: p.611
Banking & Finance **Band** 3
Table: p.580

DeMuro, Paul R (California)
Profile: p.250
Healthcare **Band** 2
Table: p.209

Denenberg, Alan (California)
Profile: p.81
Capital Markets **Band** 2
Table: p.23

Denger, Michael L
(District of Columbia)
Profile: p.439
Antitrust **Band** 3
Table: p.367

Denham, Robert E
(California)
Profile: p.250
Corporate/M&A **Band** 4
Table: p.197

DeNinno, David L
(Pennsylvania)
Profile: p.1522
Corporate/M&A **Band** 4
Table: p.1497

Denis, Paul T
(District of Columbia)
Profile: p.439
Antitrust **Band** 5
Table: p.367

Dennis, Patrick W
(California)
Profile: p.250
Environment **Band** 2
Table: p.207

Dennison, Karen D
(Nevada)
Profile: p.1101
Real Estate **Band** 1
Table: p.1099

Denny, Otway (Texas)
Profile: p.1677
Litigation **Band** 3
Table: p.1656

Densborn, Donald (Indiana)
Profile: p.791
Corporate/M&A **Band** 3
Table: p.781

Dent, Leslie (Georgia)
Profile: p.611
Employment **Band** 4
Table: p.589

DeOrchis, Vincent M
(New York)
Profile: p.81
Shipping **Band** 3
Table: p.67

DePaoli, Gordon (Nevada)
Profile: p.1101
Environment **Band** 1
Table: p.1093

DePrez, Anne (Indiana)
Profile: p.791
Litigation **Band** 2
Table: p.785

D

DeRosa, Franca L
(Connecticut)
Profile: p.336
Real Estate Band 2
Table: p.334

DeRosa, Frank J (New York)
Profile: p.1275
Intellectual Property Band 3
Table: p.1217

Derosby, Anthony R
(Maine)
Profile: p.897
Employment Band 3
Table: p.890

Derouin, James (Arizona)
Profile: p.158
Environment Band 2
Table: p.150

Derrick, Gary (Oklahoma)
Profile: p.1465
Corporate/M&A Band 2
Table: p.1459

DeSanctis, Michael
(District of Columbia)
Profile: p.439
Telecom, Broadcast & Satellite
Band 4
Table: p.427

DeSantis, Victor J
(District of Columbia)
Profile: p. 439
Projects Band 1
Table: p.52
Projects Band 1
Table: p.415

Desmarais, John M
(New York)
Profile: p.1275
Intellectual Property Band 1
Table: p.1217

Despins, Luc A (New York)
Profile: p.1275
Bankruptcy Band 1
Table: p.1179

Detherage, Andrew
(Indiana)
Profile: p.791
Litigation Band 3
Table: p.785

DeTroy, Peter (Maine)
Profile: p.897
Litigation Band 1
Table: p.893

Dettmann, David (Iowa)
Profile: p.813
Real Estate Band 1
Table: p.810

Dettmer, Scott (California)
Profile: p.250
Corporate/M&A Band 5
Table: p.197

Deutsch, Edward B (New
Jersey)
Profile: p.1138
Litigation Band 3
Table: p.1131

DeVault, John (Florida)
Profile: p.539
Litigation Band 1
Table: p.521

DeVecchio, Jay W (National)
Profile: p.81
Government Contracts
Band 3
Table: p.27

Devlin, Patricia (Hawaii)
Profile: p.648
Real Estate Band 2
Table: p.646

DeWald, Scott (Arizona)
Profile: p.158
Corporate/M&A Band 4
Table: p.146

Di Croce, Camille Holton
(New Hampshire)
Profile: p.1116
Corporate/M&A Band 3
Table: p.1107

Di Rosa, Paolo (National)
Profile: p.81
Arbitration Up and coming
Table: p.33

Dial, David (Georgia)
Profile: p.611
Construction Band 2
Table: p.584

Dial, Ellen (Washington)
Profile: p.1790
Real Estate Band 2
Table: p.1788

Diamond, Brian (New York)
Profile: p.1275
Real Estate Band 4
Table: p.1248

Diamond, Ivan M (Kentucky)
Profile: p.841
Corporate/M&A Band 3
Table: p.827

Diamond, Kenneth J
(Washington)
Profile: p.1790
Employment Band 3
Table: p.1780

DiAngelo, Christopher
(National)
Profile: p.81
Capital Markets Band 3
Table: p.19

Diaz Jr, Victor (Florida)
Profile: p.539
Litigation Band 3
Table: p.521

DiBlasi, Gandolfo V
(New York)
Profile: p.1275
Litigation Band 1
Table: p.1223

Dichiara, Peter M
(Massachusetts)
Profile: p.965
Intellectual Property Band 2
Table: p.948

Dichter, Mark (Pennsylvania)
Profile: p.1522
Employment Band 1
Table: p.1500

Dick, David (West Virginia)
Profile: p.1808
Employment Band 2
Table: p.1801

Dickens, John A (Wisconsin)
Profile: p.1825
Corporate/M&A Band 3
Table: p.1817

Dickinson, Christopher C
(Illinois)
Profile: p.724
Insurance Band 3
Table: p.695

Dickinson, John (Florida)
Profile: p.539
Employment Band 1
Table: p.513

Dickinson, Mark (Iowa)
Profile: p.813
Corporate/M&A Band 3
Table: p.802

Dickson, Andrea Roumell
(Michigan)
Profile: p.998
Employment Band 2
Table: p.991

Dickson, Robert J (Alaska)
Profile: p.142
Litigation Band 1
Table: p.138
Litigation Band 3
Table: p.138

Dickson, Roger W
(Tennessee)
Profile: p.1606
Litigation Band 3
Table: p.1599

Diehl Jr, Robert J (Michigan)
Profile: p.998
Banking & Finance Band 2
Table: p.987

Diekmann, Gilmore
(California)
Profile: p.250
Employment Band 3
Table: p.202

Diercks, Robert J
(Washington)
Profile: p.1791
Corporate/M&A Band 2
Table: p.1778

Dietz, Wallace W
(Tennessee)
Profile: p.1607
Litigation Band 2
Table: p.1599

DiGiovanni, Nick (Illinois)
Profile: p.724
Insurance Band 1
Table: p.694

DiGiovanni, Peter (Missouri)
Profile: p.1056
Real Estate Band 1
Table: p.1052

DiLeo, Anthony M
(Louisiana)
Profile: p.871
Corporate/M&A Band 3
Table: p.859

Dilg, Joseph C (Texas)
Profile: p.1677
Energy ✪
Table: p.1637

Dillard, Steve (Texas)
Profile: p.1677
Litigation Band 3
Table: p.1656

Dilloff, Neil (Maryland)
Profile: p.920
Litigation Band 2
Table: p.914

Dillon, Andrew J (Texas)
Profile: p.1677
Intellectual Property Band 2
Table: p.1651

DiLorenzo, Louis (New York)
Profile: p.1275
Employment Band 3
Table: p.1200

Dilworth, Lee C (Tennessee)
Profile: p.1607
Corporate/M&A Band 3
Table: p.1594

DiMatteo, John (New York)
Profile: p.1276
Intellectual Property Band 3
Table: p.1217

DiMichael, Nicholas
(National)
Profile: p.81
Transport Band 3
Table: p.62
Transport Band 2
Table: p.64

Dimling, Robert A (Ohio)
Profile: p.1439
Employment Band 3
Table: p.1422

Dimon, Samuel (New York)
Profile: p.1276
Tax Band 1
Table: p.1256

Dingel, Allyn (Idaho)
Profile: p.660
Litigation Band 1
Table: p.657

Dinkins, Carol (DC & Texas)
Profile: p. 1677
Environment Band 3
Table: p.392
Environment Band 1
Table: p.1643

Dinsmore, Robert
(West Virginia)
Profile: p.1808
Real Estate Band 3
Table: p.1806

Dinwiddie, Thomas
(Indiana)
Profile: p.791
Real Estate Band 3
Table: p.788

DiPrinzio, Eugene A
(Delaware)
Profile: p.352
Real Estate Band 2
Table: p.350

DiSalvatore, William P
(New York)
Profile: p.1276
Intellectual Property Band 2
Table: p.1217

Diskant, Gregory (New York)
Profile: p.1276
Intellectual Property Band 3
Table: p.1217

DiStefano, Joseph R
(Rhode Island)
Profile: p.1569
Real Estate Band 3
Table: p.1568

Dittmar, James S
(Massachusetts)
Profile: p.965
Litigation Band 1
Table: p.951

Dittrick, William (Nebraska)
Profile: p.1088
Litigation Band 2
Table: p.1085

Diviney, Craig (Minnesota)
Profile: p.1017
Litigation Band 1
Table: p.1012

DiVita, Robert R
(New Jersey)
Profile: p.1138
Real Estate Band 3
Table: p.1134

Divola, Julie (California)
Profile: p.250
Tax Band 2
Table: p.241

Dixon, Augustus M
(South Carolina)
Profile: p.1579
Corporate/M&A Band 2
Table: p.1572

Dixon, Brett W (Connecticut)
Profile: p.336
Corporate/M&A Band 2
Table: p.327

Dixon, Gary
(District of Columbia)
Profile: p.439
Insurance Band 3
Table: p.400

Dixon, Joyce A (Nebraska)
Profile: p.1088
Corporate/M&A Band 1
Table: p.1082

Dixon, Sharon Quinn
(Florida)
Profile: p.539
Tax Band 1
Table: p.531

Dobbs, C Edward (Georgia)
Profile: p.611
Banking & Finance Band 1
Table: p.580
Bankruptcy Band 1
Table: p.582

Dobbs, Tammy L (Alabama)
Profile: p.122
Employment Band 3
Table: p.113

Dockery, Michael (Montana)
Profile: p.1080
Real Estate Band 1
Table: p.1078

D

Docksey, Ross (Illinois)
Profile: p. 724
Business Process
Outsourcing: National **Band 1**
Table: p.10
Technology **Band 2**
Table: p.713

Dockstader, Kim (Idaho)
Profile: p.660
Employment **Band 2**
Table: p.656

Dodd, Jeff (Texas)
Profile: p.1677
Technology **Band 2**
Table: p.1668

Dodd, Richard (Washington)
Profile: p.1791
Corporate/M&A **Band 2**
Table: p.1778

Dodson, Gerald (California)
Profile: p.250
Intellectual Property **Band 3**
Table: p.216

Doerr, Brian (Kansas)
Profile: p.823
Real Estate **Band 2**
Table: p.821

Doetsch, Douglas A
(Illinois)
Profile: p.724
Banking & Finance **Band 2**
Table: p.665

Dogali, Andy (Florida)
Profile: p.539
Construction **Band 3**
Table: p.507

Doheny Jr, Frank P
(Kentucky)
Profile: p.841
Litigation **Band 4**
Table: p.835

Doke Jr, Marshall J
(National)
Profile: p.81
Government Contracts
Band 1
Table: p.27

Dokos, Daniel S (New York)
Profile: p.1276
Banking & Finance **Band 3**
Table: p.1174

Dolan, Edward
(District of Columbia)
Profile: p.439
Bankruptcy **Band 3**
Table: p.372

Dolin, Kenneth R (Illinois)
Profile: p.724
Employment **Band 3**
Table: p.681

Dolin, Mitchell F
(District of Columbia)
Profile: p.439
Insurance **Band 1**
Table: p.402

Doliner, Nathaniel (Florida)
Profile: p.539
Corporate/M&A **Band 2**
Table: p.509
Tax **Band 4**
Table: p.531

Dollinger, Martin E
(New Jersey)
Profile: p.1138
Real Estate **Band 1**
Table: p.1134

Dollison, Charles
(West Virginia)
Profile: p.1808
Real Estate **Band 2**
Table: p.1806
Real Estate **Band 2**
Table: p.1806

Dolson, Scott (Kentucky)
Profile: p.841
Corporate/M&A **Band 3**
Table: p.827

Domby, Arthur H (Georgia)
Profile: p.611
Environment **Band 3**
Table: p.593

Domike, Julie
(District of Columbia)
Profile: p.439
Environment **Band 4**
Table: p.392

Domina, David A (Nebraska)
Profile: p.1088
Litigation **Band 1**
Table: p.1085

Donadio, Donald
(North Carolina)
Profile: p.1395
Real Estate **Band 2**
Table: p.1392

Donarski, Michelle
(North Dakota)
Profile: p.1410
Employment **Band 2**
Table: p.1405

Donati, Donna J (Michigan)
Profile: p.998
Employment **Band 3**
Table: p.991

Donnelly, Dennis C
(Missouri)
Profile: p.1056
Employment **Band 3**
Table: p.1046

Donnelly, Paul (Missouri)
Profile: p.1056
Employment **Band 2**
Table: p.1046

Donohue, John
(Pennsylvania)
Profile: p.1522
Intellectual Property **Band 2**
Table: p.1508

Donohue, P Daniel
(South Dakota)
Profile: p.1592
Real Estate **Band 1**
Table: p.1592

Donovan, David (Virginia)
Profile: p.1768
Litigation **Band 3**
Table: p.1763

Donovan, Donald Francis
(National)
Profile: p.81
Arbitration **Band 1**
Table: p.33

Donovan, John
(Massachusetts)
Profile: p.965
Litigation **Band 1**
Table: p.951
Litigation **Band 1**
Table: p.951

Donovan, Joseph E (Illinois)
Profile: p.724
Telecom, Broadcast & Satellite
Up and coming
Table: p.715

Donovan, Richard T
(Arkansas)
Profile: p.175
Litigation **Band 3**
Table: p.172

Donovan, Thomas J
(New Hampshire)
Profile: p.1116
Litigation **Band 3**
Table: p.1111

Donovan Jr, Lawrence
(Colorado)
Profile: p.317
Real Estate **Band 3**
Table: p.313

Doran, James (Illinois)
Profile: p.724
Banking & Finance **Band 2**
Table: p.665

Doran, John Alan (Arizona)
Profile: p.158
Employment **Band 4**
Table: p.148

Doran, Scott (Ohio)
Profile: p.1439
Environment **Band 2**
Table: p.1425

Dore, Michael (New Jersey)
Profile: p.1138
Environment **Band 2**
Table: p.1129

Dorn, Joseph W (National)
Profile: p.82
International Trade **Band 3**
Table: p.40

Dorris, William (Georgia)
Profile: p.611
Construction **Band 1**
Table: p.584

Dorsey, Rufus Thomas
(Georgia)
Profile: p.611
Bankruptcy **Band 2**
Table: p.582

Dorton, David
(North Carolina)
Profile: p.1395
Real Estate **Band 3**
Table: p.1392

Dougherty, Charles R
(Massachusetts)
Profile: p.965
Bankruptcy **Band 3**
Table: p.935

Dougherty, Lucia (Florida)
Profile: p.539
Real Estate **Band 3**
Table: p.528

Douglas, Charles W
(Illinois)
Profile: p.724
Antitrust **Band 2**
Table: p.662
Litigation **Band 3**
Table: p.700

Douglas, James M
(New York)
Profile: p.1276
Banking & Finance **Band 2**
Table: p.1174

Douglas, John L (Georgia)
Profile: p.611
Banking & Finance **Band 1**
Table: p.581

Douglas, Robert J (Iowa)
Profile: p.813
Real Estate **Band 2**
Table: p.810

Dove, Luke (Mississippi)
Profile: p.1033
Litigation **Band 3**
Table: p.1028

Dover, Darrell (Arkansas)
Profile: p.175
Real Estate **Band 2**
Table: p.174

Dow, Melvin (Texas)
Profile: p.1677
Real Estate **Band 1**
Table: p.1662

Dow, T Andrew (Texas)
Profile: p.1677
Real Estate **Band 2**
Table: p.1662

Dow Jr, Robert M (Illinois)
Profile: p.725
Telecom, Broadcast & Satellite
Band 2
Table: p.715

Dowd, Martin F (New Jersey)
Profile: p.1138
Real Estate **Band 2**
Table: p.1134

Dowd Jr, Edward (Missouri)
Profile: p.1056
Litigation **Band 1**
Table: p.1049

Dowdy, L Craig (Georgia)
Profile: p.611
Energy **Band 2**
Table: p.592

Downer, Robert (Iowa)
Profile: p.813
Real Estate **Band 4**
Table: p.810

Downey, Alicia L
(Massachusetts)
Profile: p.965
Antitrust Up and coming
Table: p.930

Downey III, Charles J
(Connecticut)
Profile: p.336
Corporate/M&A **Band 2**
Table: p.327

Downs, Clark Evans
(District of Columbia)
Profile: p.439
Energy **Band 1**

Table: p.386

Downs, J Anthony
(Massachusetts)
Profile: p.966
Intellectual Property **Band 2**
Table: p.948
Litigation **Band 3**
Table: p.951

Downs, Joe (Florida)
Profile: p.539
Construction **Band 1**
Table: p.507

Dowsley III, Felix R
(Tennessee)
Profile: p.1607
Real Estate **Band 3**
Table: p.1603

Doyle, Scott (Virginia)
Profile: p.1769
Intellectual Property **Band 2**
Table: p.1759

Doyle, Thomas R (Maine)
Profile: p.898
Environment **Band 1**
Table: p.892

Doyle Jr, John
(North Carolina)
Profile: p.1395
Employment **Band 1**
Table: p.1386

Dozeman, Douglas A.
(Michigan)
Profile: p.998
Litigation **Band 3**
Table: p.994

Dragna, James J (California)
Profile: p.250
Environment **Band 4**
Table: p.207

Drake, Stephen R (Idaho)
Profile: p.660
Corporate/M&A **Band 3**
Table: p.655

Drake, Stuart
(District of Columbia)
Profile: p.439
Environment **Band 4**
Table: p.392

Dranoff, David (Illinois)
Profile: p.725
Banking & Finance **Band 3**
Table: p.665

Draper, Douglas S
(Louisiana)
Profile: p.871
Corporate/M&A **Band 1**
Table: p.859

Draper, Hayward L (Iowa)
Profile: p.813
Litigation **Band 3**
Table: p.807

Draper, John B (New Mexico)
Profile: p.1163
Natural Resources **Band 1**
Table: p.1158
Litigation ✪
Table: p.1158

D

Draper, Thomas B
(Massachusetts)
Profile: p.966
Banking & Finance **Band** 2
Table: p.932

Drapkin, Steven (California)
Profile: p.250
Employment **Band** 4
Table: p.202

Drasco, Dennis J
(New Jersey)
Profile: p.1138
Litigation **Band** 3
Table: p.1131

Dray, Mark S (Virginia)
Profile: p.1769
Employee Benefits **Band** 1
Table: p.1755

Dray, W Perry (Wyoming)
Profile: p.1838
Corporate/M&A **Band** 1
Table: p.1832
Real Estate **Band** 2
Table: p.1836

Dreher, Nicholas C (Hawaii)
Profile: p.648
Bankruptcy **Band** 1
Table: p.640

Dreitler, Joseph (Ohio)
Profile: p.1439
Intellectual Property **Band** 2
Table: p.1428

Dresher, J David (Alabama)
Profile: p.122
Real Estate **Band** 3
Table: p.119

Drew, Mark (Alabama)
Profile: p.122
Corporate/M&A **Band** 2
Table: p.111

Dreyfus, James K
(New York)
Profile: p.1276
Tax **Band** 4
Table: p.1255

Driggs, J Douglas (Nevada)
Profile: p.1101
Real Estate **Band** 3
Table: p.1099

Driker, Eugene (Michigan)
Profile: p.999
Litigation ✪
Table: p.994

Drinkwater, Robert
(Mississippi)
Profile: p.1033
Corporate/M&A **Band** 1
Table: p.1024

Drinkwater, Wayne
(Mississippi)
Profile: p.1033
Litigation ✪
Table: p.1028
Litigation **Band** 1
Table: p.1028

Drivas, Dimitrios (New York)
Profile: p.1276
Intellectual Property **Band** 1
Table: p.1217

Drooff, Michael J
(New Hampshire)
Profile: p.1116
Corporate/M&A **Band** 3
Table: p.1107

Dryden, William (Idaho)
Profile: p.660
Litigation **Band** 2
Table: p.657

Dubberly, David E
(South Carolina)
Profile: p.1579
Employment **Band** 2
Table: p.1574

Dube, Monte I (Illinois)
Profile: p.725
Healthcare **Band** 1
Table: p.690

Duffell, David K
(Rhode Island)
Profile: p.1569
Corporate/M&A **Band** 2
Table: p.1564

Duffy, Daniel F
(South Dakota)
Profile: p.1592
Litigation **Band** 2
Table: p.1590

Duffy, Don (Florida)
Profile: p.539
Tax **Band** 3
Table: p.531

Duffy, Pamela S (California)
Profile: p.250
Real Estate **Band** 1
Table: p.238

Duffy, Robert (Rhode Island)
Profile: p.1569
Litigation **Band** 2
Table: p.1567

Duffy, Robert H (Wisconsin)
Profile: p.1825
Employment **Band** 2
Table: p.1819

Dukes, David E
(South Carolina)
Profile: p.1579
Litigation **Band** 1
Table: p.1576

Dulcich, Thomas (Oregon)
Profile: p.1482
Litigation **Band** 2
Table: p.1477

DuMouchel, David F
(Michigan)
Profile: p.999
Litigation **Band** 1
Table: p.994

Dunbar, Charles
(West Virginia)
Profile: p.1808
Corporate/M&A **Band** 2
Table: p.1798

Duncan, J Kelly (Louisiana)
Profile: p.871
Gaming & Licensing **Band** 1
Table: p.864

Duncan, Margaret M
(Illinois)
Profile: p.725
Intellectual Property **Band** 3

Table: p.696

Duncan III, Brooke
(Louisiana)
Profile: p.871
Employment **Band** 2
Table: p.861

Dunham, Edward Wood
(Connecticut)
Profile: p.336
Litigation **Band** 1
Table: p.331

Dunham Jr, Wolcott B
(New York)
Profile: p.1276
Insurance ✪
Table: p.1213

Dunlay, Jon (Texas)
Profile: p.1678
Real Estate **Band** 2
Table: p.1662

Dunlevie, Steven S
(Georgia)
Profile: p.611
Banking & Finance **Band** 3
Table: p.581

Dunlop, Fred (Texas)
Profile: p.1678
Real Estate **Band** 1
Table: p.1662

Dunn, Christopher A
(National)
Profile: p.82
International Trade **Band** 4
Table: p.40

Dunn, Daniel (Colorado)
Profile: p.317
Environment **Band** 2
Table: p.307

Dunn, Daniel J (North
Dakota)
Profile: p.1410
Litigation **Band** 2
Table: p.1406

Dunn, Glenn H
(North Carolina)
Profile: p.1395
Environment **Band** 2
Table: p.1388

Dunn, Loren R (Washington)
Profile: p.1791
Environment **Band** 2
Table: p.1782

Dunn, M Douglas
(New York)
Profile: p.1276
Energy **Band** 1
Table: p.1202

Dunn, William (Michigan)
Profile: p.999
Real Estate **Band** 1
Table: p.996

Dunn Jr, J Thomas (North
Carolina)
Profile: p.1395
Banking & Finance **Band** 3
Table: p.1381

Dunne, Carey R (New York)
Profile: p.1276
Litigation **Band** 2
Table: p.1224

Dunne, Daniel J
(Washington)
Profile: p.1791
Litigation **Band** 3
Table: p.1786

Dunne, Dennis (New York)
Profile: p.1276
Bankruptcy **Band** 2
Table: p.1179

Dunner, Donald
(District of Columbia)
Profile: p.440
Intellectual Property **Band** 1
Table: p.403

Dunning, Elizabeth (Utah)
Profile: p.1736
Employment **Band** 2
Table: p.1730

Dunwoody, Stuart R
(Washington)
Profile: p.1791
Intellectual Property **Band** 2
Table: p.1784

Duplantis, BJ (Louisiana)
Profile: p.871
Energy **Band** 1
Table: p.863

Durant, E Terry
(Connecticut)
Profile: p.336
Employment **Band** 2
Table: p.329

Durchslag, Stephen
(Illinois)
Profile: p.725
Media & Entertainment **Band** 1
Table: p.704

Durham, Matthew M (Utah)
Profile: p.1736
Employment **Band** 3
Table: p.1730

Durick, Patrick (North
Dakota)
Profile: p.1410
Litigation **Band** 1
Table: p.1406

Durie, Daralyn J (California)
Profile: p.250
Intellectual Property **Band** 4
Table: p.216

Durkin, Denis (Florida)
Profile: p.539
Construction **Band** 3
Table: p.507

Durkin, Thomas M (Illinois)
Profile: p.725
Litigation **Band** 4
Table: p.700

Durling, James P (National)
Profile: p.82
International Trade **Band** 3
Table: p.40

Durrell, Brian (Alaska)
Profile: p.142
Corporate/M&A **Band** 1
Table: p.134

Dutton, David J (Iowa)
Profile: p.813
Litigation **Band** 1
Table: p.807

Dutton, Diana C (Texas)
Profile: p.1678
Environment **Band** 2
Table: p.1643

Duvin, Robert P (Ohio)
Profile: p.1439
Employment **Band** S
Table: p.1422

Dworetzky, Joseph A
(Pennsylvania)
Profile: p.1522
Bankruptcy **Band** 1
Table: p.1494

Dwyer, Jeffry
(District of Columbia)
Profile: p.440
Real Estate **Band** 3
Table: p.418

Dwyer, Maureen
(District of Columbia)
Profile: p.440
Real Estate **Band** 2
Table: p.418

Dwyer, Michael
(Washington)
Profile: p.1791
Corporate/M&A **Band** 3
Table: p.1778

Dwyer, Michael (Wisconsin)
Profile: p.1825
Real Estate **Band** 2
Table: p.1822

Dye, Alan L
(District of Columbia)
Profile: p.440
Corporate/Commercial **Band** 1
Table: p.376

Dye, Alexander M
(New York)
Profile: p.1276
Insurance **Band** 1
Table: p.1213

Dye, Phillip (Texas)
Profile: p.1678
Energy **Band** 3
Table: p.1640
Litigation **Band** 3
Table: p.1656

Dye, Scott (Nebraska)
Profile: p.1088
Real Estate **Band** 1
Table: p.1086
Real Estate **Band** 2
Table: p.1086

Dyekman, Gregory C
(Wyoming)
Profile: p.1838
Corporate/M&A **Band** 2
Table: p.1832
Real Estate **Band** 1
Table: p.1836

Dyer, Richard (New York)
Profile: p.1277
Construction **Band** 4
Table: p.1186

Dykes, Jeff (Texas)
Profile: p.1678
Energy **Band** 2
Table: p.1640

Dyleski-Najjar, Debra
(New Hampshire)
Profile: p.1116
Employment Band 3
Table: p.1109

Eades, David L
(North Carolina)
Profile: p.1395
Bankruptcy Band 1
Table: p.1383

Eagan, Ewell (Louisiana)
Profile: p.871
Litigation Band 3
Table: p.865

Eakeley, Douglas S
(New Jersey)
Profile: p.1138
Litigation Band 3
Table: p.1131

Earl, Stephen (Arizona)
Profile: p.158
Real Estate Band 2
Table: p.155

Earle, Jacqueline L (Hawaii)
Profile: p.648
Litigation Band 3
Table: p.644

Earp, Stephen W
(North Carolina)
Profile: p.1395
Environment Band 2
Table: p.1388

Earthman, Douglas
(Tennessee)
Profile: p.1607
Real Estate Band 3
Table: p.1603

Eastment, Thomas
(District of Columbia)
Profile: p.440
Energy Band 2
Table: p.382

Easton, Richard L
(Delaware)
Profile: p.352
Corporate/M&A Band 3
Table: p.346

Eatman, Louis P (California)
Profile: p.250
Real Estate Band 1
Table: p.238

Eaton, Joel (Florida)
Profile: p.539
Litigation Band 2
Table: p.525

Eaton II, George F (Maine)
Profile: p.898
Corporate/M&A Band 2
Table: p.888

Eaves, John M (New Mexico)
Profile: p.1163
Litigation Band 4
Table: p.1159

Ebby, David A (Pennsylvania)
Profile: p.1523
Real Estate Band 3
Table: p.1516

Ebby, Stuart F
(Pennsylvania)
Profile: p.1523
Real Estate Band 2
Table: p.1516

Ebel, Walter (Arkansas)
Profile: p.175
Corporate/M&A Band 1
Table: p.168

Ebert, Kim F (Indiana)
Profile: p.791
Employment Band 1
Table: p.783

Ebling, Louis K (Ohio)
Profile: p.1439
Intellectual Property Band 2
Table: p.1428

Eccles, Bob
(District of Columbia)
Profile: p. 440
Employee Benefits Band 1
Table: p.378
Litigation Band 1
Table: p.25

Eckstein, Kenneth H
(New York)
Profile: p.1277
Bankruptcy Band 3
Table: p.1179

Eckstein, Paul F (Arizona)
Profile: p.158
Litigation Band 1
Table: p.152

Eddy, Ronald M (Colorado)
Profile: p.317
Environment Band 2
Table: p.307

Edelman, Marty (New York)
Profile: p.1277
Real Estate Band 1
Table: p.1248

Edelman, Scott (New York)
Profile: p.1277
Litigation Band 3
Table: p.1224

Edelman, Scott (California)
Profile: p.250
Media & Entertainment Band 3
Table: p.230

Edgar, George
(District of Columbia)
Profile: p.440
Energy Band 1
Table: p.390

Edgar, Kenneth C (New York)
Profile: p.1277
Employee Benefits Band 1
Table: p.1197

Edison-Smith, Lisa (North Dakota)
Profile: p.1410
Employment Band 2
Table: p.1405

Edmonson, Tracy K
(California)
Profile: p.82
Capital Markets Band 2
Table: p.23

Edwards, A Clifford
(Montana)
Profile: p.1080
Litigation Band 2
Table: p.1075

Edwards, Charles L (Illinois)
Profile: p.725
Real Estate Band S
Table: p.706

Edwards, Mark
(Pennsylvania)
Profile: p.1523
Antitrust Band 3
Table: p.1489

Edwards, Michael
(Alabama)
Profile: p.122
Litigation Band 2
Table: p.116

Efflandt, Charles (Kansas)
Profile: p.823
Litigation Band 1
Table: p.819

Efron, Stanley (Minnesota)
Profile: p.1017
Corporate/M&A Band 3
Table: p.1005

Efroymson, Kevin (Nevada)
Profile: p.1101
Employment Band S
Table: p.1091

Eftimoff, Katerina M (Ohio)
Profile: p.1440
Environment Up and coming
Table: p.1425

Egan, Michael (Georgia)
Profile: p.611
Corporate/M&A Band 1
Table: p.587

Egan III, John J
(Massachusetts)
Profile: p.966
Private Equity Band 2
Table: p.953

Egan Jr, James C
(District of Columbia)
Profile: p.440
Antitrust Band 5
Table: p.367

Egerton, Charles (Florida)
Profile: p.539
Tax Band 2
Table: p.531

Eggert, Russell R (Illinois)
Profile: p.725
Environment Band 2
Table: p.687

Eggleston, Jon R (Vermont)
Profile: p.1748
Corporate/M&A Band 2
Table: p.1743

Eggleston, W Neil
(District of Columbia)
Profile: p.440
Litigation Band 2
Table: p.410

Ehrenberg, Peter H
(New Jersey)
Profile: p.1139
Corporate/M&A Band 1
Table: p.1123

Ehrlich, Kenneth
(Massachusetts)
Profile: p.966
Banking & Finance Band 2
Table: p.932

Ehrmann, Mark T
(Wisconsin)
Profile: p.1825
Corporate/M&A Band 3
Table: p.1817

Eid, Troy A (Colorado)
Profile: p.317
Environment Band 2
Table: p.307

Eide, David (Minnesota)
Profile: p.1017
Real Estate Band 1
Table: p.1014

Eidelman, Gary B
(Maryland)
Profile: p.920
Employment Band 3
Table: p.912

Eiland, Gary (Texas)
Profile: p.1678
Healthcare Band 1
Table: p.1646

Eimer, Nathan P (Illinois)
Profile: p.725
Antitrust Band 1
Table: p.662

Einhorn, David M (New York)
Profile: p.1277
Tax Band 4
Table: p.1255

Eisdorfer, Stephen M
(New Jersey)
Profile: p.1139
Real Estate Band 2
Table: p.1135

Eiseman, Byron (Arkansas)
Profile: p.175
Corporate/M&A Band S
Table: p.168

Eisen, Rebecca (California)
Profile: p.251
Employment Band 4
Table: p.202

Eisenberg, David (National)
Profile: p.82
Capital Markets Band 3
Table: p.19

Eisenberg, Susan (Florida)
Profile: p.539
Employment Band 3
Table: p.513

Eisenbrandt, James
(Missouri)
Profile: p.1056
Litigation Band 1
Table: p.1049

Eisenhofer, Jay W
(Delaware)
Profile: p.352
Chancery Band 3
Table: p.344

Eisenstat, Larry
(District of Columbia)
Profile: p.440
Energy Band 2
Table: p.386

Eisner, Rebecca (Illinois)
Profile: p. 725
Business Process
Outsourcing: National Band 3
Table: p.10
Technology Band 2
Table: p.713

Eizenstat, Stuart (National)
Profile: p.82
International Trade Band 3
Table: p.40

Ek, Dale (New Mexico)
Profile: p.1163
Real Estate Band 2
Table: p.1161

Ekberg, Charles
(Washington)
Profile: p.1791
Bankruptcy Band 1
Table: p.1776

Elacqua, James (California)
Profile: p.251
Intellectual Property Band 3
Table: p.216

Elam, Theodore M
(Oklahoma)
Profile: p.1465
Corporate/M&A Band 1
Table: p.1459

Elberger, Ronald (Indiana)
Profile: p.792
Litigation Band 2
Table: p.785

Elder, James (Oklahoma)
Profile: p.1465
Real Estate Band 1
Table: p.1464

Elderkin, David M (Iowa)
Profile: p.813
Litigation Band S
Table: p.807

Elderkin, Dianne
(Pennsylvania)
Profile: p.1523
Intellectual Property Band 3
Table: p.1508

Eldred Jr, Marshall Polk
(Kentucky)
Profile: p.841
Real Estate Band 2
Table: p.838

Eldridge, John R (Texas)
Profile: p.1678
Litigation Band 2
Table: p.1643

Elento-Sneed, Anna
(Hawaii)
Profile: p.648
Employment Band 2
Table: p.642

Elerding, Gene R (California)
Profile: p.251
Banking & Finance Band 2
Table: p.188

Elfman, Eric M
(Massachusetts)
Profile: p.966
Tax Band 2
Table: p.959

Elgison, Martin J (Georgia)
Profile: p.611
Intellectual Property Band 3
Table: p.596

Ellefson, Anne (South Carolina)
Profile: p.1580
Real Estate Band 3
Table: p.1577

Ellingson, Mae Nan (Montana)
Profile: p.1080
Corporate/M&A Band 1
Table: p.1072

Elliott, E Donald (District of Columbia)
Profile: p.440
Environment Band 3
Table: p.392

Elliott, Richard W (Washington)
Profile: p.1791
Environment Band 2
Table: p.1782

Ellis, Barnes (Oregon)
Profile: p.1482
Litigation ✪
Table: p.1477

Ellis, Emmett N (New York)
Profile: p.1277
Energy Band 2
Table: p.1202

Ellis, Karen (Tennessee)
Profile: p.1607
Employment Band 2
Table: p.1596

Ellis, Richard W (North Carolina)
Profile: p.1395
Litigation Band 3
Table: p.1390

Ellis, William (Virginia)
Profile: p.1769
Environment Band 2
Table: p.1757

Ellison, Christopher (California)
Profile: p.251
Energy Band 2
Table: p.204

Ellison, Morris (South Carolina)
Profile: p.1580
Real Estate Band 3
Table: p.1577

Ellison, Scott W (New Hampshire)
Profile: p.1116
Corporate/M&A Band 3
Table: p.1107

Ellison, Thomas (Utah)
Profile: p.1736
Real Estate Band 1
Table: p.1733

Ellman, Howard (California)
Profile: p.251
Real Estate Band 3
Table: p.238

Ellman, Jeffrey B (Georgia)
Profile: p.611
Bankruptcy Band 3

Table: p.582

Ellzey, Daniel (South Carolina)
Profile: p.1580
Employment Band 1
Table: p.1574

Elrod, Eugene R (District of Columbia)
Profile: p.441
Energy Band 1
Table: p.382

Elson, Vera M (California)
Profile: p.251
Intellectual Property
Up and coming
Table: p.216

Ely III, Hiram (Kentucky)
Profile: p.841
Litigation Band 3
Table: p.835

Emanuel, William J (California)
Profile: p.251
Employment Band 4
Table: p.202

Emch, A L (West Virginia)
Profile: p.1808
Litigation Band 1
Table: p.1803

Emerick, Steven P (Arizona)
Profile: p.158
Corporate/M&A Band 4
Table: p.146

Emerson, Carter W (Illinois)
Profile: p.726
Corporate/M&A Band 3
Table: p.675

Emerson, Daniel (Indiana)
Profile: p.792
Employment Band 3
Table: p.783

Emerson, Eric (National)
Profile: p.82
International Trade Up and coming
Table: p.40

Emmanuel, John (Florida)
Profile: p.539
Bankruptcy Band 3
Table: p.503

Emmerich, Adam O (New York)
Profile: p.1277
Corporate/M&A Band 4
Table: p.1189

Enderle Jr, Louis (West Virginia)
Profile: p.1808
Real Estate Band 3
Table: p.1806

Eng, Holly (Minnesota)
Profile: p.1017
Employment Up and coming
Table: p.1008

Engel, David (Massachusetts)
Profile: p.966
Corporate/M&A Band 2
Table: p.937

Engel, John (District of Columbia)
Profile: p.441
Real Estate Band 3
Table: p.418

Engh, Anna (District of Columbia)
Profile: p.441
Insurance Band 3
Table: p.402

England, Arthur J (Florida)
Profile: p.539
Litigation Band 2
Table: p.525

Englander, John (Massachusetts)
Profile: p.966
Intellectual Property Band 3
Table: p.948

Engler, Bruce (Minnesota)
Profile: p.1017
Corporate/M&A Band 2
Table: p.1005

Englert Jr, Roy (District of Columbia)
Profile: p.441
Litigation Band 1
Table: p.408

English, Craig (New York)
Profile: p.82
Shipping Band 4
Table: p.67

English, Stephen (Oregon)
Profile: p.1482
Litigation Band 1
Table: p.1477

Englund, Rudy A (Washington)
Profile: p.1791
Litigation Band 3
Table: p.1786

Engstrom, Eric (Kansas)
Profile: p.823
Corporate/M&A Band 1
Table: p.816

Enns, Rodrick (North Carolina)
Profile: p.1395
Antitrust Band 1
Table: p.1390

Ensor, R Steve (Georgia)
Profile: p.611
Employment Band 3
Table: p.589

Entwistle, Frederick M (South Dakota)
Profile: p.1592
Bankruptcy Band 2
Table: p.1587

Epstein, Gary (District of Columbia)
Profile: p.441
Telecom, Broadcast & Satellite Band 1
Table: p.427

Epstein, Gary (Florida)
Profile: p.539
Corporate/M&A Band 1
Table: p.509

Epstein, Jon David (Texas)
Profile: p.1678

Engel, John (District of Columbia)
Healthcare Band 2
Table: p.1646

Epstein, Michael (New York)
Profile: p.1277
Technology Band 3
Table: p.1259

Epstein, Roger H (Hawaii)
Profile: p.648
Tax Band 1
Table: p.641

Epstien, Jay (District of Columbia)
Profile: p.441
Real Estate Band 1
Table: p.418

Epting, Andrew K (South Carolina)
Profile: p.1580
Litigation Band 2
Table: p.1576

Erf, Stephen (Illinois)
Profile: p.726
Employment Band 3
Table: p.681

Erickson, David (Iowa)
Profile: p.813
Real Estate Band 2
Table: p.810

Erickson, David (Missouri)
Profile: p.823
Litigation Band 1
Table: p.819

Erly, Peter (Vermont)
Profile: p.1748
Corporate/M&A Band 2
Table: p.1743

Ernst, Andrew (Georgia)
Profile: p.612
Environment Band 2
Table: p.593

Ernst, David A. (Oregon)
Profile: p.1482
Litigation Band 3
Table: p.1477

Erspamer, Gordon (California)
Profile: p.251
Energy Band 3
Table: p.204

Ervin, James M (Florida)
Profile: p.539
Tax Band 3
Table: p.531

Erwin, Greg (Texas)
Profile: p.1678
Real Estate Band 2
Table: p.1662

Erwin, James R (Maine)
Profile: p.898
Employment Band 2
Table: p.890

Erwin, Martin (North Carolina)
Profile: p.1395
Employment Band 1
Table: p.1386

Eschels, Philip (Kentucky)
Profile: p.841
Employment Band 3
Table: p.830

Esserman, Susan (National)
Profile: p.82
International Trade Band 2
Table: p.40

Essig, Leonard (Missouri)
Profile: p.1056
Corporate/M&A Band 3
Table: p.1043

Estes III, John N (District of Columbia)
Profile: p.441
Energy Band 1
Table: p.386

Estrada, Miguel (District of Columbia)
Profile: p.441
Litigation Band 1
Table: p.408

Estridge, Larry D (South Carolina)
Profile: p.1580
Real Estate Band 1
Table: p.1577

Etcheverry, Raymond J (Utah)
Profile: p.1736
Litigation Band 2
Table: p.1732

Eth, Jordan (California)
Profile: p.251
Litigation Band 4
Table: p.224

Ettelson, Bruce (Illinois)
Profile: p.726
Private Equity Band 1
Table: p.676

Ettinger, John R (New York)
Profile: p.1278
Private Equity Band S
Table: p.1237

Eurich, Gregory (Colorado)
Profile: p.317
Employment Band 1
Table: p.306

Evanich, Kevin R (Illinois)
Profile: p.726
Corporate/M&A Band 2
Table: p.675
Private Equity Band 1
Table: p.676

Evans, Brian P (North Carolina)
Profile: p.1395
Real Estate Band 3
Table: p.1392

Evans, Craig (Missouri)
Profile: p.1056
Corporate/M&A Band 3
Table: p.1043

Evans, David E (Virginia)
Profile: p.1769
Environment Band 1
Table: p.1757

Evans, Edwin E (South Dakota)
Profile: p.1592
Litigation Band 1
Table: p.1590
Litigation Band 1
Table: p.1590

Evans, Kevin D (Colorado)
Profile: p.317
Litigation Band 1
Table: p.311

Evans, Mark
(District of Columbia)
Profile: p.441
Telecom, Broadcast & Satellite
Band 4
Table: p.427

Evans, Mark C (Texas)
Profile: p.1678
Banking & Finance Band 2
Table: p.1625
Projects Band 4
Table: p.1659

Evans, William J (Alaska)
Profile: p.142
Employment Band 2
Table: p.135

Evans III, Robert (National)
Profile: p.82
Capital Markets Band 3
Table: p.14

Evanusa, Michel S
(New York)
Profile: p.1278
Real Estate Band 5
Table: p.1248

Everett, Carl B
(Pennsylvania)
Profile: p.1523
Environment Band 4
Table: p.1505

Everett, John (Arkansas)
Profile: p.176
Litigation Band 2
Table: p.172

Everroad, John (Arizona)
Profile: p.158
Litigation Band 3
Table: p.152

Everson, David (Missouri)
Profile: p.1056
Litigation Band 1
Table: p.1049

Ewart, Lani (Hawaii)
Profile: p.648
Real Estate Band 1
Table: p.646

Ewing, Jim (Georgia)
Profile: p.612
Intellectual Property Band 2
Table: p.596

Ey Jr, Douglas W
(North Carolina)
Profile: p.1395
Litigation Band 3
Table: p.1390

F

Fabiano, John G
(Massachusetts)
Profile: p.966
Litigation Band 3
Table: p.951

Fadil, Adeeb (New York)
Profile: p.1278
Environment Band 2
Table: p.1206

Fagan, Christopher (Ohio)
Profile: p.1440
Intellectual Property Band 2
Table: p.1428

Fagen, Leslie (New York)
Profile: p.1278
Litigation Band 3
Table: p.1222

Fagin, Allen (New York)
Profile: p.1278
Employment Band 1
Table: p.1200

Fahey, Richard (Ohio)
Profile: p.1440
Environment Band 2
Table: p.1425

Fahey, Thomas M (Illinois)
Profile: p.726
Healthcare Band 2
Table: p.690

Fair, George (Mississippi)
Profile: p.1033
Corporate/M&A Band 2
Table: p.1024

Faiss, Robert D (Nevada)
Profile: p.1101
Gaming & Licensing Band 1
Table: p.1094

Fala, Herman C
(Pennsylvania)
Profile: p.1523
Real Estate Band 1
Table: p.1516

Falck, David (New York)
Profile: p.1278
Energy Band 1
Table: p.1202
Energy Band 2
Table: p.1202

Falk, R Scott (Illinois)
Profile: p.726
Corporate/M&A Band 3
Table: p.675

Fantaci, James (Louisiana)
Profile: p.871
Corporate/M&A Band 4
Table: p.859

Fanter, Robert (Iowa)
Profile: p.813
Litigation Band 2
Table: p.807

Farabow, Ford F
(District of Columbia)
Profile: p.441
Intellectual Property Band 2
Table: p.403

Fardon, D Alexander
(Tennessee)
Profile: p.1607
Litigation Band 2
Table: p.1599

Farer, David (New Jersey)
Profile: p.1139
Environment Band 2
Table: p.1129

Fargotstein, Phillip F
(Arizona)
Profile: p.158
Environment Band 2
Table: p.150

Farkas, Michelle (Vermont)
Profile: p.1748
Real Estate Band 3
Table: p.1747

Farmer, Guy (Florida)
Profile: p.539
Employment Band 1
Table: p.513

Farmer, John B (Virginia)
Profile: p.1769
Intellectual Property Band 2
Table: p.1761

Farmer, Scott
(District of Columbia)
Profile: p.441
Tax Band 4
Table: p.422

Farmer, Stephen
(West Virginia)
Profile: p.1808
Litigation Band 1
Table: p.1803

Farnham, James (Virginia)
Profile: p.1769
Litigation Band 3
Table: p.1763

Farolino, Shane (Ohio)
Profile: p.1440
Environment Band 3
Table: p.1425

Farr, Bartow
(District of Columbia)
Profile: p.441
Litigation Band 1
Table: p.408

Farr, Thomas A
(North Carolina)
Profile: p.1395
Employment Band 2
Table: p.1386

Farrar, Stanley F (California)
Profile: p.251
Banking & Finance Band S
Table: p.187
Banking & Finance Band S
Table: p.188

Farrell, Margaret
(Rhode Island)
Profile: p.1569
Corporate/M&A Band 2
Table: p.1564

Farris Jr, James G (Georgia)
Profile: p.612
Real Estate Band 3
Table: p.601

Faruki, Charles (Ohio)
Profile: p.1440
Litigation Band 2
Table: p.1431

Fasman, Zachary D
(New York)
Profile: p.1278
Employment Band 3
Table: p.1200

Fastow, Jay N (New York)
Profile: p.1278
Antitrust Band 4
Table: p.1170

Fatell, Bonnie Glantz
(Delaware)
Profile: p. 1523

Bankruptcy Band 3
Table: p.341
Bankruptcy Band 3
Table: p.1494

Fathe, Fred C (Arizona)
Profile: p.158
Real Estate Band 2
Table: p.154

Faulk, Richard (Texas)
Profile: p.1678
Litigation Band 2
Table: p.1643

Faulkner, Andrew M
(National)
Profile: p.83
Capital Markets Band 3
Table: p.19

Favretto, Richard J
(District of Columbia)
Profile: p.441
Antitrust Band 5
Table: p.367

Fay, Richard E
(North Carolina)
Profile: p.1395
Environment Band 2
Table: p.1388

Fay, Terrence M (Ohio)
Profile: p.1440
Environment Band 3
Table: p.1425

Fayne, Steve (California)
Profile: p.251
Media & Entertainment Band 3
Table: p.233

Feder, Philip (California)
Profile: p.251
Real Estate Band 1
Table: p.238

Federhar, Andrew M
(Arizona)
Profile: p.158
Litigation Band 4
Table: p.152

Fee, Michael K
(Massachusetts)
Profile: p.966
Litigation Band 1
Table: p.951

Feeney, James (Michigan)
Profile: p.999
Litigation Band 3
Table: p.994

Feeney, Matthew (Arizona)
Profile: p.158
Corporate/M&A Band 2
Table: p.146

Feese, Suzanne (Georgia)
Profile: p.612
Tax Band 3
Table: p.603

Feheley, Lawrence F (Ohio)
Profile: p.1440
Employment Band 3
Table: p.1422

Feher, David G (National)
Profile: p.83
Sport Band 2
Table: p.55

Feibelman, Jef (Tennessee)
Profile: p.1607
Litigation Band 2
Table: p.1599

Feinstein, Deborah
(District of Columbia)
Profile: p.442
Antitrust Band 4
Table: p.367

Feinstein, Fred I (Illinois)
Profile: p.726
Real Estate Band 4
Table: p.706

Feirson, Steven B
(Pennsylvania)
Profile: p.1523
Litigation Band 3
Table: p.1511

Felch, Patricia (Illinois)
Profile: p.726
Media & Entertainment Band 2
Table: p.703

Feldman, Boris (California)
Profile: p.251
Corporate/M&A Band 4
Table: p.197
Litigation Band 3
Table: p.224

Feldman, Jeffrey M (Alaska)
Profile: p.142
Litigation Band 1
Table: p.138

Feldman, Larry (California)
Profile: p.251
Litigation Band 3
Table: p.224
Media & Entertainment Band 3
Table: p.230

Feldman, Matthew A
(New York)
Profile: p.1278
Bankruptcy Band 3
Table: p.1179

Feldman, Robert (California)
Profile: p.252
Intellectual Property Band 4
Table: p.216
Litigation Band 4
Table: p.224

Feldman, Robert C (Texas)
Profile: p.1679
Real Estate Band 2
Table: p.1662

Feldman, Roger D
(Massachusetts)
Profile: p.966
Corporate/M&A Band 3
Table: p.937

Feldstein, Hydee R
(California)
Profile: p.252
Banking & Finance Band 2
Table: p.187
Bankruptcy Band 3
Table: p.191

Feldt, Harrell (Texas)
Profile: p.1679
Energy Band 2
Table: p.1640

Felger, Mark E. (Delaware)
Profile: p.353
Bankruptcy Band 4

Table: p.341

Felger, Thomas (Texas)
Profile: p.1679
Intellectual Property Band 3
Table: p.1651

Felix II, H Thomas
(Pennsylvania)
Profile: p.1523
Employment Band 2
Table: p.1500

Fellas, John (National)
Profile: p.83
Arbitration Band 4
Table: p.33

Fellner, Baruch
(District of Columbia)
Profile: p.442
Employment Band 3
Table: p.380

Felman, David (Florida)
Profile: p.539
Corporate/M&A Band 3
Table: p.509

Felmly, Bruce W
(New Hampshire)
Profile: p.1117
Litigation Band 1
Table: p.1111

Feltenstein, Martha
(New York)
Profile: p.1278
Real Estate Band 3
Table: p.1248

Felter, John Kenneth
(Massachusetts)
Profile: p.966
Litigation Band 2
Table: p.951

Felton, W Raymond (New Jersey)
Profile: p.1139
Corporate/M&A Band 3
Table: p.1123

Fenley, David A (Missouri)
Profile: p.1056
Real Estate Band 1
Table: p.1053

Fenton, Kathryn M
(District of Columbia)
Profile: p.442
Antitrust Band 5
Table: p.367

Fenzel, Mark S (Kentucky)
Profile: p.841
Litigation Band 4
Table: p.835

Feo, Edwin (California)
Profile: p. 252
Energy Band 1
Table: p.204
Projects Band 1 (National)
Table: p.52
Projects Band 1 (National)
Table: p.236
Transport Band 1 (National)
Table: p.64

Feola, Phil
(District of Columbia)
Profile: p.442
Real Estate Band 2
Table: p.418

Ferdinands, Paul (Georgia)
Profile: p.612
Bankruptcy Band 2
Table: p.582

Ferenbach, Cam (Nevada)
Profile: p.1101
Litigation Band 2
Table: p.1096

Ferencik, Robert (Florida)
Profile: p.539
Construction Band 2
Table: p.507

Ferguson, James (Illinois)
Profile: p.726
Litigation Band 4
Table: p.700

Ferland, Roger (Arizona)
Profile: p.158
Environment Band 1
Table: p.150

Ferrazzano, Dennis (Illinois)
Profile: p.726
Real Estate Band 2
Table: p.706

Ferrell, Charles (Minnesota)
Profile: p.1017
Real Estate Band 1
Table: p.1014

Ferrera, Tess
(District of Columbia)
Profile: p.442
Employee Benefits Band 3
Table: p.378

Ferretti, David P
(West Virginia)
Profile: p.1808
Corporate/M&A Band 3
Table: p.1798

Ferrin, Shawn (Utah)
Profile: p.1736
Real Estate Band 2
Table: p.1733

Ferris, Charles
(District of Columbia)
Profile: p.442
Telecom, Broadcast & Satellite Band 4
Table: p.427

Ferron Jr, William O
(Washington)
Profile: p.1791
Intellectual Property Band 2
Table: p.1784

Fersko, Jack (New Jersey)
Profile: p.1139
Real Estate Band 1
Table: p.1135

Fessler, Daniel (California)
Profile: p.252
Energy Band 3
Table: p.204

Fetscher, Candace
(Montana)
Profile: p.1080
Employment Band 1
Table: p.1073

Feuerstein, Howard
(Oregon)
Profile: p.1482
Real Estate Band 1
Table: p.1479

Few, Richard (South Carolina)
Profile: p.1580
Corporate/M&A Band 3
Table: p.1572

Fickle, Stanley (Indiana)
Profile: p.792
Litigation ✪
Table: p.785

Field, Andrea Bear
(District of Columbia)
Profile: p.442
Environment Band 2
Table: p.392

Field, Lawrence (Minnesota)
Profile: p.1017
Litigation Band 3
Table: p.1011

Fields, Bertram (California)
Profile: p.252
Media & Entertainment Band 1
Table: p.230

Fields, Henry M (California)
Profile: p.252
Banking & Finance Band 1
Table: p.188

Fields, Jack (Texas)
Profile: p.1679
Real Estate Band 2
Table: p.1662

Fields, Leslie (Colorado)
Profile: p.318
Real Estate Band 2
Table: p.313

Fields, Richard W
(New York)
Profile: p.1279
Insurance Band 3
Table: p.1213

Fife, Lori R (New York)
Profile: p.1279
Bankruptcy Band 3
Table: p.1179

Fifer, Sam (Illinois)
Profile: p.726
Media & Entertainment Band 1
Table: p.703

Figenshaw, Michael H
(Iowa)
Profile: p.813
Litigation Band 2
Table: p.807

Fijolek, Richard M (Texas)
Profile: p.1679
Tax Band 4
Table: p.1665

Fikso, Robert (Washington)
Profile: p.1791
Real Estate Band 3
Table: p.1788

Filardi, Edward V (New York)
Profile: p.1279
Intellectual Property Band 2
Table: p.1217

Fildes, Richard J (Florida)
Profile: p.539
Hotels and Resorts Band 1
Table: p.526

Fileti, Thomas (California)
Profile: p.252
Real Estate Band 3
Table: p.238

Fine, Drew S. (National)
Profile: p.83
Aviation Band 3
Table: p.58

Finke, Robert F (Illinois)
Profile: p.727
Antitrust Band 3
Table: p.662

Finkel, Robert (National)
Profile: p.83
Business Process
Outsourcing: National Band 3
Table: p.10

Finkelman, Daniel P
(Massachusetts)
Profile: p.966
Private Equity Band 2
Table: p.955

Finkelson, Allen (New York)
Profile: p.1279
Corporate/M&A Band 1
Table: p.1189

Finkelstein, Jesse A
(Delaware)
Profile: p.353
Chancery Band 1
Table: p.344
Corporate/M&A Band 2
Table: p.346

Finley, John G (New York)
Profile: p.1279
Corporate/M&A Band 2
Table: p.1189

Finley, Joseph (Minnesota)
Profile: p.1017
Real Estate Band 2
Table: p.1014

Finley, Thomas A (Iowa)
Profile: p.813
Litigation Band 2
Table: p.807

Finn Braddock, Patricia
(Texas)
Profile: p.1679
Environment Band 1
Table: p.1643

Finn III, Harold B
(Connecticut)
Profile: p.336
Corporate/M&A Band 1
Table: p.327

Finnegan, Sheila (Illinois)
Profile: p.727
Litigation Band 4
Table: p.700

Finnegan, IV, William N
(Texas)
Profile: p.1679
Corporate/M&A Band 4
Table: p.1631

Finto, Kevin J (Virginia)
Profile: p.1769
Environment Band 1
Table: p.1757

Finucane, Brian J (Missouri)
Profile: p.1056
Employment Band 2

Table: p.1046

Fiorentino, Mark H
(Nevada)
Profile: p.1101
Real Estate Band 1
Table: p.1099

Fischer, Gordon (Iowa)
Profile: p.813
Employment Band 3
Table: p.805

Fischer, Rebecca (Colorado)
Profile: p.318
Hotels and Resorts Band 1
Table: p.314

Fischer, Ronald (North Dakota)
Profile: p.1410
Litigation Band 1
Table: p.1406

Fischer, Samuel N
(California)
Profile: p.252
Media & Entertainment Band 2
Table: p.233

Fish, Ronald (Maryland)
Profile: p.920
Real Estate Band 2
Table: p.917

Fishbein, Matthew E
(New York)
Profile: p.1279
Litigation Band 3
Table: p.1224

Fisher, Morton (Maryland)
Profile: p.920
Real Estate Band 1
Table: p.917

Fisher, Robert (Missouri)
Profile: p.1057
Corporate/M&A Band 2
Table: p.1043

Fishman, David (Maryland)
Profile: p.920
Real Estate Band 1
Table: p.917

Fishman, Louis Y
(Louisiana)
Profile: p.871
Corporate/M&A Band 1
Table: p.859

Fishman, Michael T
(Illinois)
Profile: p.727
Real Estate Up & Coming

Fishman, Robert A
(Massachusetts)
Profile: p.966
Real Estate Band 1
Table: p.956
Real Estate Band 1
Table: p.957

Fisk, Hollye (Texas)
Profile: p.1679
Construction Band 2
Table: p.1629

Fiske, Robert (New York)
Profile: p.1279
Litigation Band 1
Table: p.1222
Litigation ✪
Table: p.1224

Fitch, Stephen (Ohio)
Profile: p.1440
Litigation **Band** 4
Table: p.1431

Fitzgerald, Anthony
(Connecticut)
Profile: p.336
Litigation **Band** 1
Table: p.331

FitzGerald, Brian T
(New York)
Profile: p.1279
Energy **Band** 1
Table: p.1204

FitzGerald, Edmond
(New York)
Profile: p.1279
Employee Benefits **Band** 3
Table: p.1197

Fitzgerald, James
(Nebraska)
Profile: p.1088
Litigation **Band** 2
Table: p.1085

Fitzgerald, Kevin M
(New Hampshire)
Profile: p.1117
Litigation **Band** 3
Table: p.1111

Fitzgerald, Miranda
(Florida)
Profile: p.539
Real Estate **Band** 1
Table: p.528

Fitzgerald, Peter
(District of Columbia)
Profile: p. 442
Projects **Band** 1
Table: p.52
Projects **Band** 1
Table: p.415

Fitzgerald, Robert (Virginia)
Profile: p.1769
Construction **Band** 1
Table: p.1750

Fitzgerald Jr, Robert E
(Missouri)
Profile: p.1057
Corporate/M&A **Band** 2
Table: p.1043
Real Estate **Band** 2
Table: p.1052

FitzMaurice, Daniel L
(Connecticut)
Profile: p.336
Litigation **Band** 3
Table: p.331

FitzPatrick Jr, James A
(New York)
Profile: p.1279
Insurance **Band** 3
Table: p.1213

Fjelstad, Eric B (Alaska)
Profile: p.142
Environment **Band** 1
Table: p.137

Flagel, Mark A (California)
Profile: p.252
Intellectual Property **Band** 3
Table: p.216

Flaherty, Thomas
(West Virginia)
Profile: p.1808
Litigation **Band** 1
Table: p.1803

Flaherty, Thomas (Virginia)
Profile: p.1769
Employment **Band** 3
Table: p.1755

Flake, Richard (Texas)
Profile: p.1679
Construction **Band** 3
Table: p.1629

Flanagan, Peter L (National)
Profile: p.83
International Trade **Band** 2
Table: p.41

Flanders Jr, Robert G
(Rhode Island)
Profile: p.1569
Litigation **Band** 3
Table: p.1567

Flanigan, Daniel (Missouri)
Profile: p.1057
Real Estate **Band** 2
Table: p.1052

Flaschen, Evan D
(Connecticut)
Profile: p.336
Corporate/M&A **Band** 2
Table: p.327

Flaum, Keith (California)
Profile: p.252
Corporate/M&A **Band** 5
Table: p.197

Fleder, Robert (New York)
Profile: p.1279
Employee Benefits **Band** 3
Table: p.1197

Fleischaker, Jon (Kentucky)
Profile: p.841
Employment **Band** 2
Table: p.830

Fleischer Jr, Arthur
(New York)
Profile: p.1280
Corporate/M&A **Band** S
Table: p.1189

Fleming, John H (Georgia)
Profile: p.612
Litigation **Band** 2
Table: p.598

Fleming, Joseph (Florida)
Profile: p.539
Employment **Band** 2
Table: p.513

Fleming, Terrence
(Minnesota)
Profile: p.1017
Litigation **Band** 2
Table: p.1011

Fleming Jr, Peter (New York)
Profile: p.1280
Litigation **Band** 2
Table: p.1224

Flesher, Gail (New York)
Profile: p.1280
Environment **Band** 1
Table: p.1206

Fletcher, Jennifer (Georgia)
Profile: p.612
Construction **Band** 1
Table: p.584

Fletcher, John (Arkansas)
Profile: p.176
Corporate/M&A **Band** 2
Table: p.168

Flexner, Donald L
(District of Columbia)
Profile: p.442
Antitrust **Band** 3
Table: p.367

Flick II, Lawrence
(Pennsylvania)
Profile: p.1524
Banking & Finance **Band** 1
Table: p.1493

Flinn, Patrick J (Georgia)
Profile: p.612
Intellectual Property **Band** 2
Table: p.596

Flint, Henry (North Carolina)
Profile: p.1395
Banking & Finance **Band** 2
Table: p.1381
Corporate/M&A **Band** 3
Table: p.1384

Flom, Joseph H (New York)
Profile: p.1280
Corporate/M&A **Band** S
Table: p.1189

Florack, James A (New York)
Profile: p.1280
Banking & Finance **Band** 4
Table: p.1174

Flowe Jr, Benjamin H
(National)
Profile: p.83
International Trade **Band** 1
Table: p.41

Floyd, Adam (Texas)
Profile: p.1679
Intellectual Property **Band** 3
Table: p.1651

Floyd, John (Georgia)
Profile: p.612
Litigation **Band** 3
Table: p.598

Fluharty, Robert
(West Virginia)
Profile: p.1808
Real Estate **Band** 2
Table: p.1806

Fluhrer, Gary (Washington)
Profile: p.1791
Real Estate **Band** 2
Table: p.1788

Flygare, Thomas
(New Hampshire)
Profile: p.1117
Employment **Band** 1
Table: p.1109

Flynn, Christopher (Illinois)
Profile: p.727
Energy **Band** 2
Table: p.685

Focht, Jack (Kansas)
Profile: p.823
Litigation **Band** 2
Table: p.819

Fodor, Susanna (New York)
Profile: p.1280
Construction **Band** 2
Table: p.1186

Fogarty, James
(Connecticut)
Profile: p.336
Litigation **Band** 2
Table: p.331

Foggan, Laura
(District of Columbia)
Profile: p.442
Insurance **Band** 1
Table: p.400

Fogler, Murray (Texas)
Profile: p.1679
Energy **Band** 3
Table: p.1640
Litigation **Band** 2
Table: p.1656

Fognani, John D (Colorado)
Profile: p.318
Environment **Band** 2
Table: p.307

Foley, Mark (Pennsylvania)
Profile: p.1524
Employment **Band** 2
Table: p.1500

Foley, Thomas (Iowa)
Profile: p.813
Employment **Band** 2
Table: p.805

Foltyn, David (Michigan)
Profile: p.999
Corporate/M&A **Band** 1
Table: p.989

Fontaine, Mary C (Illinois)
Profile: p.83
Capital Markets **Band** 2
Table: p.21

Fontana, Angela (Texas)
Profile: p.1679
Banking & Finance **Band** 3
Table: p.1625

Fontham, Michael R
(Louisiana)
Profile: p.872
Energy **Band** 1
Table: p.863

Foradas, Michael P (Illinois)
Profile: p.727
Insurance **Band** 1
Table: p.695

Forbush III, William B
(Massachusetts)
Profile: p.966
Real Estate **Band** 3
Table: p.956

Forcade, Bill S (Illinois)
Profile: p.727
Environment **Band** 3
Table: p.687

Ford, Barry (Mississippi)
Profile: p.1033
Litigation **Band** 2
Table: p.1028

Ford, Christopher D
(National)
Profile: p.83
Business Process
Outsourcing: National **Band** 2
Table: p.10

Ford, Debra Weiss
(New Hampshire)
Profile: p.1117
Employment **Band** 2
Table: p.1109

Ford, Gary M
(District of Columbia)
Profile: p.442
Employee Benefits **Band** 2
Table: p.378

Ford, Jeffrey (Texas)
Profile: p.1679
Construction **Band** 2
Table: p.1629

Ford, John M
(District of Columbia)
Profile: p.442
Investment Management
Up and coming
Table: p.406

Ford, Paul (National)
Profile: p.83
Capital Markets **Band** 2
Table: p.14

Ford Jacob, Valerie
(National)
Profile: p.83
Capital Markets **Band** 4
Table: p.14

Fore, John (California)
Profile: p.84
Capital Markets **Band** 2
Table: p.23

Foreman, Lee (Colorado)
Profile: p.318
Litigation **Band** 1
Table: p.311

Forman, Adam
(Massachusetts)
Profile: p.966
Employment **Band** 2
Table: p.940

Forman, Wayne F (Colorado)
Profile: p.318
Real Estate **Band** 1
Table: p.314

Fornaris, Carl A (Florida)
Profile: p.540
Banking & Finance **Band** 2
Table: p.500

Forrest, Katherine B
(New York)
Profile: p.1280
Antitrust **Band** 4
Table: p.1170
Intellectual Property **Band** 3
Table: p.1217

Forrester, J Paul (Illinois)
Profile: p.727
Banking & Finance **Band** 2
Table: p.665

Forry, Robert H (Georgia)
Profile: p.612
Energy **Band** 1
Table: p.592

F

Forst, David (California)
Profile: p.252
Tax Up and coming
Table: p.241

Forsten, Richard (Delaware)
Profile: p.353
Real Estate Band 2
Table: p.350

Forsyth, David (Louisiana)
Profile: p.872
Corporate/M&A Band 1
Table: p.859

Fort, Jeffrey (Illinois)
Profile: p.727
Environment Band 1
Table: p.687

Forte, Joseph Philip
(New York)
Profile: p.1280
Real Estate Band 3
Table: p.1248

Forte, Stephen M (Georgia)
Profile: p.612
Litigation Band 3
Table: p.598

Forti, David W
(Pennsylvania)
Profile: p.1524
Real Estate Band 3
Table: p.1516

Fortino, Paul (Oregon)
Profile: p.1482
Litigation Band 1
Table: p.1477

Fortney, David
(District of Columbia)
Profile: p.442
Employment Band 2
Table: p.380

Foss, Marilyn (North Dakota)
Profile: p.1410
Corporate/M&A Band 3
Table: p.1403

Foster, John (North Dakota)
Profile: p.1410
Bankruptcy Band 1
Table: p.1403

Foster, Murphy (Louisiana)
Profile: p.872
Employment Band 3
Table: p.861

Foster, Stephen H
(Montana)
Profile: p.1080
Natural Resources Band 1
Table: p.1077

Fournier, David M.
(Delaware)
Profile: p.353
Bankruptcy Band 4
Table: p.341

Foust, Lawrence L (Texas)
Profile: p.1679
Healthcare Band 2
Table: p.1646

Fowler, Jay (Kansas)
Profile: p.823
Litigation Band 2
Table: p.819

Fowler, John (Nevada)
Profile: p.1102
Corporate/M&A Band 1
Table: p.1089

Fox, David (New York)
Profile: p.1280
Corporate/M&A Band 4
Table: p.1189

Fox, J Nixon (Texas)
Profile: p.1679
Technology Band 3
Table: p.1668

Fox, Kate (Wyoming)
Profile: p.1838
Employment Band 1
Table: p.1833
Litigation Band 2
Table: p.1835

Fox, Michael W (Texas)
Profile: p.1679
Employment Band 3
Table: p.1634

Fox, Robert (Pennsylvania)
Profile: p.1524
Environment Band 2
Table: p.1505

Fox, Steven F (Georgia)
Profile: p.612
Corporate/M&A Band 4
Table: p.587

Foye, Thomas H
(South Dakota)
Profile: p.1592
Real Estate Band 1
Table: p.1592

Frackman, Russell
(California)
Profile: p.252
Media & Entertainment Band 2
Table: p.230

Fraidin, Stephen (New York)
Profile: p.1280
Corporate/M&A Band 3
Table: p.1189
Private Equity Band 1
Table: p.1237

Fram, Robert (California)
Profile: p.252
Intellectual Property Band 4
Table: p.216

France, Lucy T (Montana)
Profile: p.1080
Employment Up and coming
Table: p.1073

France, Thomas W
(Virginia)
Profile: p.1769
Corporate/M&A Band 4
Table: p.1752

France II, William N
(New York)
Profile: p.84
Shipping Band 4
Table: p.67

Francescani, David
(New York)
Profile: p.1280
Intellectual Property Band 3
Table: p.1217

Franchina, David A (North Carolina)
Profile: p.1395
Environment Band 2
Table: p.1388

Franczek, James (Illinois)
Profile: p.727
Employment Band 1
Table: p.681

Frank, Robert
(Massachusetts)
Profile: p.966
Intellectual Property Band 1
Table: p.948

Frank, Robert (Maine)
Profile: p.898
Litigation Band 1
Table: p.893

Frank, Steven J
(Massachusetts)
Profile: p.966
Intellectual Property Band 3
Table: p.948

Frankel, Roger L
(District of Columbia)
Profile: p.442
Bankruptcy Band 1
Table: p.372

Frankenheimer, John T
(California)
Profile: p.252
Media & Entertainment Band 3
Table: p.233

Franklin, Samuel (Alabama)
Profile: p.122
Litigation Band 1
Table: p.116

Frankovich, John (Nevada)
Profile: p.1102
Real Estate Band 3
Table: p.1099

Franse, R Nelson
(New Mexico)
Profile: p.1163
Litigation Band 2
Table: p.1159

Franson, Marc (Illinois)
Profile: p.728
Banking & Finance Band 3
Table: p.665

Frantz, Mary Ann (Oregon)
Profile: p.1482
Corporate/M&A Band 3
Table: p.1471

Frantz, Michael (Ohio)
Profile: p.1440
Employment Band 1
Table: p.1422

Frantz, Steven
(District of Columbia)
Profile: p.442
Energy Band 3
Table: p.390

Frantz, Thomas R (Virginia)
Profile: p.1769
Corporate/M&A Band 2
Table: p.1752

Frantze, David (Missouri)
Profile: p.1057
Real Estate Band 1
Table: p.1052

Franze, Laura M (Texas)
Profile: p.1680
Employment Band 2
Table: p.1634

Franzetti, Susan M (Illinois)
Profile: p.728
Environment Band 2
Table: p.687

Fraser, Thomas (Minnesota)
Profile: p.1018
Litigation Band 1
Table: p.1011

Fratianni, Constance A
(New York)
Profile: p.1280
Bankruptcy Band 4
Table: p.1179

Frazen, Laurence (Missouri)
Profile: p.1057
Litigation Band 3
Table: p.1049

Frazier, Keith D (Tennessee)
Profile: p.1607
Employment Band 3
Table: p.1596

Frazier, Randy (Arkansas)
Profile: p.176
Real Estate Band 1
Table: p.174

Frazier, Sydney (Alabama)
Profile: p.122
Employment Band 3
Table: p.113

Frederick, Jennifer
(New York)
Profile: p.1280
Projects Up and coming
Table: p.1244

Fredman, Stuart A (Utah)
Profile: p.1736
Corporate/M&A Band 3
Table: p.1727

Freed, Amy Bowerman
(Maryland)
Profile: p.920
Corporate/M&A
Up and coming
Table: p.909

Freed, Joel
(District of Columbia)
Profile: p.443
Intellectual Property Band 2
Table: p.403

Freed, Michael (Illinois)
Profile: p.728
Antitrust Band 2
Table: p.662

Freel, Mark (Rhode Island)
Profile: p.1569
Litigation Band 2
Table: p.1567

Freeland, Byron (Arkansas)
Profile: p.176
Employment Band 2
Table: p.170

Freeman, Louis S (Illinois)
Profile: p.728
Tax Band 1
Table: p.710

Freeman, Robert
(Nebraska)
Profile: p.1088
Corporate/M&A Band 1
Table: p.1082

Freeman Jr, Lee (Illinois)
Profile: p.728
Antitrust Band 1
Table: p.662

Frei, Donald (Ohio)
Profile: p.1440
Intellectual Property Band 3
Table: p.1428

Freidus, Harris B (New York)
Profile: p.1280
Real Estate Band 5
Table: p.1248

Freier, Elliot (California)
Profile: p.252
Tax Band 2
Table: p.241

Freilich, Robert (Missouri)
Profile: p.1057
Real Estate Band 2
Table: p.1053

Fremuth, Michael
(District of Columbia)
Profile: p.443
Energy Band 4
Table: p.382

French, Marilyn
(Massachusetts)
Profile: p.967
Private Equity Up and coming
Table: p.953

Frenkil, Steven (Maryland)
Profile: p.920
Employment Band 3
Table: p.912

Fretwell, Norman (Missouri)
Profile: p.1057
Corporate/M&A Band 2
Table: p.1043

Freund, Neil (Ohio)
Profile: p.1440
Litigation Band 4
Table: p.1431

Freyer, Dana H (National)
Profile: p.84
Arbitration Band
Table: p.33
Arbitration Band 2
Table: p.33

Friberg Sr, John E
(New Hampshire)
Profile: p.1117
Litigation Band 1
Table: p.1111

Frick, Ann (Colorado)
Profile: p.318
Litigation Band 4
Table: p.311

Fridy, Carl H (Pennsylvania)
Profile: p.1524
Banking & Finance Band 1
Table: p.1493

Friedland, Paul (National)
Profile: p.84
Arbitration Band 3
Table: p.33

Friedlander, Mark C
(Illinois)
Profile: p.728
Construction Band 1
Table: p.672

Friedli, Helen R (Illinois)
Profile: p.728
Corporate/M&A Band 4
Table: p.675

Friedman, Alan (California)
Profile: p.252
Employment Band 3
Table: p.202

Friedman, Andrew
(National)
Profile: p.84
Sport Band 2
Table: p.55

Friedman, Bruce A
(California)
Profile: p.252
Insurance Band 4
Table: p.212

Friedman, David (New York)
Profile: p.1281
Bankruptcy Band 3
Table: p.1179

Friedman, Dennis G
(Illinois)
Profile: p.728
Telecom, Broadcast & Satellite
Band 2
Table: p.715

Friedman, Dennis J
(New York)
Profile: p.1281
Corporate/M&A Band 4
Table: p.1189

Friedman, Edward (Texas)
Profile: p.1680
Employment Band 3
Table: p.1634

Friedman, Eric J (New York)
Profile: p.1281
Corporate/M&A Band 4
Table: p.1189

Friedman, Gary (New York)
Profile: p.1281
Employment Band 3
Table: p.1200

Friedman, Gary E
(Mississippi)
Profile: p.1033
Employment Band 2
Table: p.1026

Friedman, Gary M
(New York)
Profile: p.1281
Tax Band 3
Table: p.1255

Friedman, Lawrence B
(National)
Profile: p.84
Arbitration Band 3
Table: p.33

Friedman, Marc (New
Jersey)
Profile: p.1139
Litigation Band 2
Table: p.1133

Friedman, Michael H
(Pennsylvania)
Profile: p.1524
Corporate/M&A Band 3
Table: p.1497

Friedman, Steven A (Ohio)
Profile: p.1440
Construction Band 4
Table: p.1417

Friedrich, William R
(California)
Profile: p.252
Insurance Band 3
Table: p.212

Fries, Joseph
(District of Columbia)
Profile: p.443
Real Estate Band 1
Table: p.418

Frilot, George (Louisiana)
Profile: p.872
Litigation Band 3
Table: p.865

Frisbie Jr, Curtis L (Texas)
Profile: p.1680
Antitrust Band 3
Table: p.1622

Frisch, John B (Maryland)
Profile: p.920
Corporate/M&A Band 2
Table: p.909

Fritton, Karl (Pennsylvania)
Profile: p.1524
Employment Band 2
Table: p.1500

Fritz, Thomas G
(South Dakota)
Profile: p.1592
Litigation Band 2
Table: p.1590

Fritze, Daniel J (South
Carolina)
Profile: p.1580
Corporate/M&A Band 3
Table: p.1572

Frizell, Edward E (Missouri)
Profile: p.1057
Corporate/M&A Band 3
Table: p.1043

Frizzell, Jean C (Texas)
Profile: p.1680
Litigation Band 3
Table: p.1656

Fromm O'Brien, Eva (Texas)
Profile: p.1680
Environment Band 1
Table: p.1643
Litigation Band 2
Table: p.1643

Frost, Claudia Wilson
(Texas)
Profile: p.1680
Litigation Band 1
Table: p.1656

Frost II, John W (Florida)
Profile: p.540
Litigation Band 2
Table: p.521

Frost Jr, Don J
(District of Columbia)
Profile: p.443

Environment Band 4
Table: p.392
Environment Band 2
Table: p.393

Froy, Michael M (Illinois)
Profile: p.728
Corporate/M&A Band 4
Table: p.675

Frumkin, Joseph B
(New York)
Profile: p.1281
Corporate/M&A Band 4
Table: p.1189
Energy Band 2
Table: p.1202

Fruth, Terence (Minnesota)
Profile: p.1018
Litigation Band 3
Table: p.1011

Fry, Roger (Ohio)
Profile: p.1440
Litigation Band 4
Table: p.1431

Frye, B Michael (Vermont)
Profile: p.1748
Corporate/M&A Band 1
Table: p.1743

Fryer, Gregory (Maine)
Profile: p.898
Corporate/M&A Band 1
Table: p.888

Fryer, William (Georgia)
Profile: p.612
Real Estate Band 3
Table: p.601

Fuhr, Edward J (Virginia)
Profile: p.1769
Litigation Band 3
Table: p.1763

Fuhrman, Steven M
(New York)
Profile: p.1281
Bankruptcy Band 3
Table: p.1179

Fulkerson, Sam (Oklahoma)
Profile: p.1465
Employment Band 2
Table: p.1461

Fullenkamp, John
(Nebraska)
Profile: p.1088
Real Estate Band 1
Table: p.1086
Real Estate Band 1
Table: p.1086

Fuller, Gary (Oklahoma)
Profile: p.1465
Tax Band 1
Table: p.1459

Fuller, James (California)
Profile: p.252
Tax Band 1
Table: p.241

Fuller, William
(South Dakota)
Profile: p.1592
Litigation Band 1
Table: p.1590

Fuller III, William H (North
Carolina)
Profile: p.1396

Banking & Finance Band 3
Table: p.1381

Fullmer, Mark A (Louisiana)
Profile: p.872
Corporate/M&A Band 2
Table: p.859

Fulton, Charles
(North Carolina)
Profile: p.1396
Real Estate Band S
Table: p.1392

Funk, John A (Texas)
Profile: p. 1680
Business Process
Outsourcing: National Band 1
Table: p.10
Technology Band 1
Table: p.1668

Furci, Peter (New York)
Profile: p.1281
Tax Up and coming
Table: p.1255

Furey, Michael K
(New Jersey)
Profile: p.1139
Employment Band 2
Table: p.1126

Furr, Jeffrey (North Carolina)
Profile: p.1396
Litigation Band 3
Table: p.1390

G

Gabay, Donald (New York)
Profile: p.1281
Insurance Band 2
Table: p.1213

Gabbert Jr, Craig V
(Tennessee)
Profile: p.1607
Litigation Band 1
Table: p.1599
Litigation Band 2
Table: p.1599

Gabric, Ralph J (Illinois)
Profile: p.728
Intellectual Property Band 3
Table: p.696

Gabrio, Gino L (Hawaii)
Profile: p.648
Real Estate Band 2
Table: p.646

Gade, Mary A (Illinois)
Profile: p.728
Environment Band 4
Table: p.687

Gaffney, John (New York)
Profile: p.1281
Media & Entertainment Band 1
Table: p.1235

Gaffney, Todd (Iowa)
Profile: p.813
Litigation Band 3
Table: p.807

Gage, Robert
(District of Columbia)
Profile: p.443
Real Estate Band 4
Table: p.418

Gagliano, Bill (Ohio)
Profile: p.1440
Real Estate Band 4
Table: p.1434

Gagliardo, Joseph M
(Illinois)
Profile: p.728
Employment Band 2
Table: p.681

Gagnon, Bruce (Alaska)
Profile: p.142
Litigation Band 1
Table: p.138

Gaillard, Foster
(South Carolina)
Profile: p.1580
Real Estate Band 1
Table: p.1577

Galainena, David (Illinois)
Profile: p.84
Capital Markets Band 2
Table: p.21

Galardi, Gregg M
(Delaware)
Profile: p.353
Bankruptcy Band 1
Table: p.341

Galchus, Donna Smith
(Arkansas)
Profile: p.176
Employment Band 3
Table: p.170

Gale, Kelley (California)
Profile: p.253
Projects Band 3
Table: p.236

Galeota, William
(West Virginia)
Profile: p.1808
Litigation Band 2
Table: p.1803

Gall, John R (Ohio)
Profile: p.1440
Litigation Band 3
Table: p.1431

Gallagher, James J
(National)
Profile: p.84
Government Contracts Band 3
Table: p.27

Gallagher, Patrick C
(New York)
Profile: p.1281
Tax Band 3
Table: p.1255

Gallagher, Robert
(District of Columbia)
Profile: p. 443
Employee Benefits Band 1
Table: p.378
(National)
Litigation Band 2
Table: p.25

Gallagher, Sean (Colorado)
Profile: p.318
Employment Band 2
Table: p.306

Gallegos, J E (New Mexico)
Profile: p.1163
Environment Band 1
Table: p.1158
Litigation Band 3

G

Table: p.1159

Gallinger, John (Wyoming)
Profile: p.1838
Real Estate **Band 2**
Table: p.1836

Gallion, Theresa M (Florida)
Profile: p.540
Employment **Band 2**
Table: p.513

Gallo, Barbara (Georgia)
Profile: p.613
Environment **Band 3**
Table: p.593

Gallo, Greg (California)
Profile: p.253
Corporate/M&A **Band 1**
Table: p.197

Gallo, John N (Illinois)
Profile: p.728
Litigation **Band 4**
Table: p.700

Gallo, Joie Marie (California)
Profile: p.253
Media & Entertainment **Band 4**
Table: p.230

Gallo, Kenneth A
(District of Columbia)
Profile: p.443
Antitrust **Band 5**
Table: p.367

Galloway, Robert
(Mississippi)
Profile: p.1033
Litigation **Band 2**
Table: p.1028

Galvan, Hilda (Texas)
Profile: p.1680
Intellectual Property **Band 3**
Table: p.1651

Galvani, Paul
(Massachusetts)
Profile: p.967
Litigation **Band 2**
Table: p.951

Galvis, Sergio J (New York)
Profile: p. 1281
Projects **Band 2** (National)
Table: p.52
Projects **Band 2**
Table: p.1244

Gamboli, Michael
(Rhode Island)
Profile: p.1569
Employment **Band 1**
Table: p.1565

Gambro, Michael S
(National)
Profile: p.84
Capital Markets **Band 4**
Table: p.19

Gammage Jr, Grady
(Arizona)
Profile: p.158
Real Estate **Band 1**
Table: p.155

Gandhi, Samir A (National)
Profile: p.84
Capital Markets
Up and coming
Table: p.16

Gangemi, Columbus
(Illinois)
Profile: p.729
Employment **Band 1**
Table: p.681

Gannett, William B
(National)
Profile: p.85
Capital Markets **Band 4**
Table: p.14

Gannon, Christopher R
(Vermont)
Profile: p.1748
Corporate/M&A **Band 2**
Table: p.1743

Gansberg, Andrew
(New York)
Profile: p.1281
Energy **Band 1**
Table: p.1204

Ganske, Lyle (Ohio)
Profile: p.1440
Corporate/M&A **Band 1**
Table: p.1419

Ganz, Howard (New York)
Profile: p. 1282
Employment **Band 2**
Table: p.1200
Sport **Band 1**
Table: p.55

Garber, Kevin J
(Pennsylvania)
Profile: p.1524
Environment **Band 2**
Table: p.1505

Garcia, David A (Nevada)
Profile: p.1102
Corporate/M&A **Band 1**
Table: p.1089

Gardill, James (West Virginia)
Profile: p.1808
Corporate/M&A **Band 2**
Table: p.1798

Gardiner, John L (National)
Profile: p.85
Arbitration **Band 4**
Table: p.33

Gardner, Price (Arkansas)
Profile: p.176
Corporate/M&A **Band 2**
Table: p.168

Gardner, Russell H
(Maryland)
Profile: p.921
Employment **Band 2**
Table: p.912

Gardner, Stephen D
(New York)
Profile: p.1282
Tax **Band 4**
Table: p.1255

Gardner, William (Alabama)
Profile: p.122
Employment **Band 1**
Table: p.113

Garfinkel, Barry H
(National)
Profile: p.85
Arbitration **Band**
Table: p.33
Arbitration **Band 2**
Table: p.33

Garibaldi, Oscar M
(National)
Profile: p.85
Arbitration **Band 3**
Table: p.33

Garland, David (New Jersey)
Profile: p.1139
Employment **Band 2**
Table: p.1126

Garmer III, Benjamin F
(Wisconsin)
Profile: p.1825
Corporate/M&A **Band 1**
Table: p.1817

Garner, James (Louisiana)
Profile: p.872
Litigation **Band 3**
Table: p.865

Garnsey Jr, Walter W
(Colorado)
Profile: p.318
Litigation **Band 4**
Table: p.311

Garofalo, Gary B (National)
Profile: p.85
Aviation **Band 3**
Table: p.58

Garon, Philip S (Minnesota)
Profile: p.1018
Corporate/M&A **Band 1**
Table: p.1005

Garone, Michael (Oregon)
Profile: p.1482
Employment **Band 3**
Table: p.1474

Garre, Gregory G
(District of Columbia)
Profile: p.443
Litigation **Band 2**
Table: p.408

Garretson, Thomas P
(Kansas)
Profile: p.823
Corporate/M&A **Band 1**
Table: p.816

Garrett, G Lee (Georgia)
Profile: p.613
Litigation **Band 3**
Table: p.598

Garrett, Theodore
(District of Columbia)
Profile: p.443
Environment **Band S**
Table: p.392

Garrett, Tim K (Tennessee)
Profile: p.1607
Employment **Band 2**
Table: p.1596

Garrity, James (New York)
Profile: p.1282
Bankruptcy **Band 4**
Table: p.1179

Garrity Jr, Vincent F
(Pennsylvania)
Profile: p.1524
Corporate/M&A **Band 3**
Table: p.1497

Garry, William C
(South Dakota)
Profile: p.1592
Litigation **Band 2**

Table: p.1590

Gart, Brian (Florida)
Profile: p.540
Bankruptcy **Band 2**
Table: p.503

Gartman, John (California)
Profile: p.253
Intellectual Property **Band 3**
Table: p.216

Gartner, Steven (New York)
Profile: p.1282
Private Equity **Band 2**
Table: p.1237

Gartrell, Donald E
(New Hampshire)
Profile: p.1117
Real Estate **Band 2**
Table: p.1114

Garvin, Anthony O
(California)
Profile: p.253
Environment **Band 4**
Table: p.207

Garvin, Michele M
(Massachusetts)
Profile: p.967
Healthcare **Band 1**
Table: p.946

Garwood, Thomas (Florida)
Profile: p.540
Employment **Band 1**
Table: p.513

Garza, Deborah
(District of Columbia)
Profile: p.443
Antitrust **Band 5**
Table: p.367

Gasch Jr, Manning (Virginia)
Profile: p.1769
Environment **Band 2**
Table: p.1757

Gaskins, Richard C (North Carolina)
Profile: p.1396
Environment **Band 2**
Table: p.1388

Gately, Mark (Maryland)
Profile: p.921
Litigation **Band 2**
Table: p.914

Gates, Allan (Arkansas)
Profile: p.176
Litigation **Band 1**
Table: p.172
Litigation **Band 3**
Table: p.172

Gates, Martin S (Ohio)
Profile: p.1440
Banking & Finance **Band 2**
Table: p.1411

Gathright Jr, Joseph R
(Kentucky)
Profile: p.841
Real Estate **Band 2**
Table: p.838

Gatto, James (Virginia)
Profile: p.1769
Intellectual Property **Band 2**
Table: p.1759

Gauer, Keith A
(South Dakota)
Profile: p.1592
Bankruptcy **Band 2**
Table: p.1587

Gault, Robert M
(Massachusetts)
Profile: p.967
Employment **Band 3**
Table: p.940

Gavin, John N (Illinois)
Profile: p.729
Insurance **Band 2**
Table: p.692

Gavin, Tim (Texas)
Profile: p.1680
Antitrust **Band 3**
Table: p.1622

Gay, Faith Elizabeth
(Florida)
Profile: p.540
Litigation **Band 1**
Table: p.522

Gaynor, Bruce (Ohio)
Profile: p.1440
Real Estate **Band 3**
Table: p.1434

Gaynor, Kevin
(District of Columbia)
Profile: p.444
Environment **Band 3**
Table: p.392

Gearen, John J (Illinois)
Profile: p.729
Real Estate **Band 1**
Table: p.706

Geary, Sean (New York)
Profile: p.1282
Banking & Finance **Band 3**
Table: p.1174

Geary Jr, Francis B (Florida)
Profile: p.540
Healthcare **Band 2**
Table: p.518

Gee, David E (Utah)
Profile: p.1736
Real Estate **Band 1**
Table: p.1733

Gee, William S (Delaware)
Profile: p.353
Real Estate **Band 3**
Table: p.350

Gehring, Stephen
(Nebraska)
Profile: p.1088
Corporate/M&A **Band 2**
Table: p.1082

Geiger, Glenn C (New Jersey)
Profile: p.1139
Real Estate **Band 1**
Table: p.1135

Geiger, Kathleen (Delaware)
Profile: p.353
Intellectual Property **Band 3**
Table: p.348

Geiger, Richard S (Texas)
Profile: p.1680
Insurance **Band 3**
Table: p.1648

Gelband, Scott L
(Washington)
Profile: p.1791
Corporate/M&A Band 2
Table: p.1778

Gelber, Don (Hawaii)
Profile: p.648
Bankruptcy Band 1
Table: p.640

Gelber, Stephen M (Hawaii)
Profile: p.648
Corporate/M&A Band 2
Table: p.641
Tax Band 1
Table: p.641

Gelblum, Seth D (New York)
Profile: p.1282
Media & Entertainment Band 1
Table: p.1235

Gelfand, David I
(District of Columbia)
Profile: p.444
Antitrust Band 5
Table: p.367

Gelinas, Julia B (Indiana)
Profile: p.792
Litigation Band 3
Table: p.785

Geller, Kenneth S
(District of Columbia)
Profile: p.444
Litigation Band 1
Table: p.408

Gellman, Nancy
(Pennsylvania)
Profile: p.1524
Litigation Band 2
Table: p.1511

Gelman, Bruce L (Illinois)
Profile: p.729
Tax Up and coming
Table: p.710

Gelston, Philip (New York)
Profile: p.1282
Corporate/M&A Band 3
Table: p.1189

Genberg, Ira (Georgia)
Profile: p.613
Construction Band 2
Table: p.584

Genet, Chava (Florida)
Profile: p.540
Hotels and Resorts Band 1
Table: p.526

Geno, Craig M (Mississippi)
Profile: p.1033
Bankruptcy Band 1
Table: p.1024

Genova, Angelo
(New Jersey)
Profile: p.1139
Employment Band 2
Table: p.1126

Genovese, John H (Florida)
Profile: p.540
Bankruptcy Band 2
Table: p.503

Gentile, Carmen
(District of Columbia)
Profile: p.444
Energy Band 4

Gentile, Mark (Delaware)
Profile: p.353
Corporate/M&A Band 3
Table: p.346

Gentner, Joshua D.
(National)
Profile: p.85
Aviation Up and coming
Table: p.58

Genz, Peter (Georgia)
Profile: p.613
Tax Band 4
Table: p.603

Geoghegan, Patricia
(New York)
Profile: p.1282
Tax Band 4
Table: p.1255

George, Peter (Illinois)
Profile: p.729
Technology Band 3
Table: p.713

George, Peter E (Florida)
Profile: p.540
Litigation Band 2
Table: p.522

George, Shawn P
(West Virginia)
Profile: p.1808
Litigation Band 2
Table: p.1803

**Gerachis, George
Matthew** (Texas)
Profile: p.1680
Litigation Band 2
Table: p.1665

Gerakitis, Richard (Georgia)
Profile: p.613
Employment Band 3
Table: p.589

Gerber, Dean N (Illinois)
Profile: p. 729
Aviation Band 1 (National)
Table: p.58
Banking & Finance Band 3
Table: p.665

Gerber, Toby L (Texas)
Profile: p.1681
Bankruptcy Band 4
Table: p.1627

Gergen, Michael
(District of Columbia)
Profile: p.444
Energy Band 4
Table: p.386

Germain, Kenneth (Ohio)
Profile: p.1440
Intellectual Property Band 1
Table: p.1428

German, Charles (Missouri)
Profile: p.1057
Litigation Band 1
Table: p.1049
Litigation Band 1
Table: p.1049

Germann, Hans (Illinois)
Profile: p.729
Telecom, Broadcast & Satellite
Up and coming
Table: p.715

Gerrard, Michael (New York)
Profile: p.1282
Environment Band 1
Table: p.1205

Gersch, David P
(District of Columbia)
Profile: p.444
Litigation Band 3
Table: p.410

Gerson, Herb (Tennessee)
Profile: p.1607
Employment Band 3
Table: p.1596

Gerstein, Mark D (Illinois)
Profile: p.729
Corporate/M&A Band 2
Table: p.675
Private Equity Band 3
Table: p.676

Gerstell, Glenn
(District of Columbia)
Profile: p.444
Telecom, Broadcast & Satellite
Band 1
Table: p.429

Gerstenzang, Michael A
(New York)
Profile: p.1282
Private Equity Band 3
Table: p.1241

Gewin, James (Alabama)
Profile: p.122
Litigation Band 1
Table: p.116

Gewirtz, Elliot (National)
Profile: p.85
Aviation Band 1
Table: p.58

Gherlein, John M (Ohio)
Profile: p.1441
Corporate/M&A Band 3
Table: p.1419

Gholz, Charles (Virginia)
Profile: p.1769
Intellectual Property Band 1
Table: p.1759

Gianoulakis, John (Missouri)
Profile: p.1057
Litigation Band 3
Table: p.1049

Gibbons, John J (New Jersey)
Profile: p.1139
Litigation Band S
Table: p.1131

Gibbons, Robert J
(New York)
Profile: p.1282
Projects Band 4
Table: p.1244

Gibbs, Charles R (Texas)
Profile: p.1681
Bankruptcy Band 2
Table: p.1627

Gibbs, Kenneth C
(California)
Profile: p.253
Construction Band 2
Table: p.194

Gibbs, Lawrence
(District of Columbia)
Profile: p.444

Gerrard, Michael Tax Band 4
Table: p.422

Gibbs, Robert (Mississippi)
Profile: p.1033
Litigation Band 3
Table: p.1028

Gibbs, Robin C (Texas)
Profile: p.1681
Energy Band 1
Table: p.1640
Litigation Band 1
Table: p.1656

Gibby, Darin (Colorado)
Profile: p.318
Intellectual Property Band 1
Table: p.309

Giblin, Pamela (Texas)
Profile: p.1681
Environment Band 1
Table: p.1643

Gideon, Kenneth W
(District of Columbia)
Profile: p.444
Tax Band 2
Table: p.422

Gidley, J Mark
(District of Columbia)
Profile: p.444
Antitrust Band 4
Table: p.367

Gidley, James (Oregon)
Profile: p.1482
Litigation Band 2
Table: p.1477

Giesel, James A (Kentucky)
Profile: p.841
Corporate/M&A Band 3
Table: p.827

Gifford, David (Pennsylvania)
Profile: p.1525
Real Estate Band 3
Table: p.1516

Gifford, Mark (Wyoming)
Profile: p.1838
Litigation Band 2
Table: p.1835

Gigot, Thomas S
(District of Columbia)
Profile: p.444
Employee Benefits Band 3
Table: p.378

Gilberg, David J (National)
Profile: p.85
Capital Markets Band 2
Table: p.16

Gilbert, Donald R (Arizona)
Profile: p.158
Employment Band 4
Table: p.148

Gilbert, Leonard (Florida)
Profile: p.540
Bankruptcy Band 2
Table: p.503

Gilbert, Paul D (Tennessee)
Profile: p.1607
Corporate/M&A Band 3
Table: p.1594

Gilbert, Paul E (Arizona)
Profile: p.158
Real Estate Band 1

Table: p.155

Gilbert, Richard (California)
Profile: p.1282
Employee Benefits Band 2
Table: p.1197

Gilbert, Robert (Florida)
Profile: p.540
Bankruptcy Band 3
Table: p.503

Gilbert, Scott
(District of Columbia)
Profile: p.444
Insurance Band 1
Table: p.402

Gilford, Steven R (Illinois)
Profile: p.729
Insurance Band 1
Table: p.695

Gilkey, Duane C
(New Mexico)
Profile: p.1163
Employment Band 1
Table: p.1157

Gill, Richard (Alabama)
Profile: p.122
Litigation Band 3
Table: p.116

Gillece Jr, James (Maryland)
Profile: p.921
Employment Band 3
Table: p.912

Gillen, Craig A (Georgia)
Profile: p.613
Litigation Band 1
Table: p.599

Gillespie, Michael J
(New York)
Profile: p.1283
Media & Entertainment Band 1
Table: p.1235

Gillespie, Thomas (Texas)
Profile: p.1681
Banking & Finance Band 4
Table: p.1625

Gillette, Patricia (California)
Profile: p.253
Employment Band 3
Table: p.202

Gillies Jr, John J
(Connecticut)
Profile: p.336
Real Estate Band 2
Table: p.334

Gillis, Theresa (New York)
Profile: p.1283
Intellectual Property Band 3
Table: p.1217

Gilmore, Patrick (Alaska)
Profile: p.142
Litigation Band 2
Table: p.138

Gilpin, Thomas
(West Virginia)
Profile: p.1809
Real Estate Band 2
Table: p.1806

Gilson, Gary (Missouri)
Profile: p.1057
Corporate/M&A Band 1
Table: p.1043

G

Gilson, Jerome (Illinois)
Profile: p.729
Intellectual Property Band 2
Table: p.696

Ginos, Geoffrey (New York)
Profile: p.85
Shipping Band 4
Table: p.67

Ginsberg, Beth (Washington)
Profile: p.1791
Environment Band 2

Ginsburg, Dennis (Florida)
Profile: p.540
Tax Band 3
Table: p.531

Ginsburg, Roy (Minnesota)
Profile: p.1018
Employment Band 3
Table: p.1008

Giordano, P Gregory
(Nevada)
Profile: p.1102
Gaming & Licensing Band 3
Table: p.1094

Giotto, Thomas
(Pennsylvania)
Profile: p.1525
Employment Band 1
Table: p.1500

Girard, Robert D.
(California)
Profile: p.253
Healthcare Band 2
Table: p.209

Gisvold, Dean P (Oregon)
Profile: p.1482
Real Estate Band 2
Table: p.1479

Gitomer, Deborah (Texas)
Profile: p.1681
Energy Band 4
Table: p.1637

Gitter, Max (New York)
Profile: p.1283
Litigation Band 3
Table: p.1222

Gittes, Franklin M
(New York)
Profile: p.1283
Corporate/M&A Band 3
Table: p.1189

Gittler, Amy J (Arizona)
Profile: p.158
Employment Band 4
Table: p.148

Giuffra, Robert J (New York)
Profile: p.1283
Litigation Band 3
Table: p.1223
Litigation Band 3
Table: p.1224

Giuliani, Richard
(Massachusetts)
Profile: p.967
Tax Band 3
Table: p.959

Giunco Jr, John A
(New Jersey)
Profile: p.1140
Real Estate Band 2
Table: p.1135

Giunta, Joseph J (California)
Profile: p.253
Corporate/M&A Band 5
Table: p.197

Givens, Leonard D
(Michigan)
Profile: p.999
Employment Band 2
Table: p.991

Glad, Paul E B (California)
Profile: p.253
Insurance Band 1
Table: p.212

Glade, Peter (Oregon)
Profile: p.1482
Litigation Band 2
Table: p.1477

Glahn III, Wilbur A
(New Hampshire)
Profile: p.1117
Litigation Band 1
Table: p.1111

Glascock, Thomas B
(California)
Profile: p.253
Projects Band 3
Table: p.236

Glaser, D Louis (Illinois)
Profile: p.729
Healthcare Band 3
Table: p.690

Glaser, Kenneth (Texas)
Profile: p.1681
Intellectual Property Band 3
Table: p.1651

Glaser, Patricia (California)
Profile: p.253
Media & Entertainment Band 1
Table: p.230

Glasgow, Jr, Norman
(District of Columbia)
Profile: p.444
Real Estate Band 2
Table: p.418

Glass, Adam W (National)
Profile: p.85
Capital Markets Band 4
Table: p.19

Glasscock, Ed (Kentucky)
Profile: p.841
Corporate/M&A Band 1
Table: p.827

Glasser, Brian (West Virginia)
Profile: p.1809

Glazer, Dennis (New York)
Profile: p.1283
Litigation Band 3
Table: p.1222

Glazer, Michael
(Massachusetts)
Profile: p.967
Real Estate Band 1
Table: p.956

Glazer, Ronald B
(Pennsylvania)
Profile: p.1525
Real Estate Band 3
Table: p.1516

Glazer, Steven D (New York)
Profile: p.1283

Intellectual Property Band 3
Table: p.1217

Glazier, Robert (Florida)
Profile: p.540
Litigation Band 2
Table: p.525

Glenn, Robert (Florida)
Profile: p.540
Bankruptcy Band 2
Table: p.503

Glerum, Charles L
(Massachusetts)
Profile: p.967
Bankruptcy Band 2
Table: p.935

Glick, Anna (National)
Profile: p.85
Capital Markets Band 2
Table: p.19

Glickstein, David (Illinois)
Profile: p.730
Real Estate Band 3
Table: p.706

Glosband, Daniel
(Massachusetts)
Profile: p.967
Bankruptcy Band 1
Table: p.935

Glover, Stephen I
(District of Columbia)
Profile: p.444
Corporate/Commercial Band 1
Table: p.376

Godfrey, Lee (Texas)
Profile: p.1681
Antitrust Band 1
Table: p.1622
Energy Band 1
Table: p.1640
Litigation Band 1
Table: p.1656

Godfrey, Richard C (Illinois)
Profile: p.730
Litigation Band 2
Table: p.700

Godiner, Clifford A
(Missouri)
Profile: p.1057
Employment Band 3
Table: p.1046

Godshall, Brad (California)
Profile: p.253
Bankruptcy Band 4
Table: p.191

Goebel, Monica (Arizona)
Profile: p.158
Employment Band 2
Table: p.148

Goeltz, Thomas
(Washington)
Profile: p.1791
Real Estate Band 2
Table: p.1789

Goering, Gail (Illinois)
Profile: p.730
Insurance Band 3
Table: p.694

Goering, Kevin (New York)
Profile: p.1283
Media & Entertainment Band 2
Table: p.1232

Goetz, James (Montana)
Profile: p.1080
Litigation Band 1
Table: p.1075

Goetz, Peter (New York)
Profile: p.1283
Construction Band 3
Table: p.1186

Goetzinger, Patrick
(South Dakota)
Profile: p.1593
Corporate/M&A Band 2
Table: p.1587
Real Estate Band 2
Table: p.1592

Gold, Brian J (Illinois)
Profile: p.730
Employment Band 3
Table: p.681

Gold, Marc (Pennsylvania)
Profile: p.1525
Environment Band 2
Table: p.1505

Gold, Michael (Illinois)
Profile: p.730
Banking & Finance Band 2
Table: p.665

Gold, Ronald (Ohio)
Profile: p.1441
Bankruptcy Band 3
Table: p.1414

Goldammer, Vance
(South Dakota)
Profile: p.1593
Corporate/M&A Band 1
Table: p.1587

Goldberg, Catherine
(New Mexico)
Profile: p.1163
Real Estate Band 2
Table: p.1161

Goldberg, Charles
(Colorado)
Profile: p.318
Litigation Band 4
Table: p.311

Goldberg, Daniel
(Massachusetts)
Profile: p. 967
Antitrust Band 1
Table: p.930
Sport Band 2
Table: p.55

Goldberg, Donald J
(Pennsylvania)
Profile: p.1525
Litigation Band 1
Table: p.1512

Goldberg, Joseph
(New Mexico)
Profile: p.1163
Litigation Band 3
Table: p.1159

Goldberg, Louis L
(New York)
Profile: p.1283
Private Equity Band 3
Table: p.1237

Goldberg, Michael (Florida)
Profile: p.540
Bankruptcy Band 2
Table: p.503

Goldberg, Phillip (California)
Profile: p.253
Healthcare Band 3
Table: p.209

Goldberg, Richard R
(Pennsylvania)
Profile: p.1525
Real Estate Band 1
Table: p.1516

Goldberg, Stephen
(California)
Profile: p.253
Insurance Band 2
Table: p.212

Goldberg Jr, Fred T
(District of Columbia)
Profile: p.444
Tax Band 1
Table: p.422

Goldblatt, Craig
(District of Columbia)
Profile: p.445
Bankruptcy Up and coming
Table: p.372

Goldblatt, Stanford J
(Illinois)
Profile: p.730
Private Equity Band 2
Table: p.676

Golden, Arthur F (New York)
Profile: p.1283
Antitrust Band 3
Table: p.1170

Golden, Daniel H (New York)
Profile: p.1283
Bankruptcy Band 1
Table: p.1179

Golden, Gerald (Illinois)
Profile: p.730
Employment Band 2
Table: p.681

Golden, H Bruce (Texas)
Profile: p.1681
Litigation Band 3
Table: p.1656

Golden, Jonathan (Georgia)
Profile: p.613
Corporate/M&A Band 3
Table: p.587

Goldfein, Shepard
(New York)
Profile: p. 1284
Antitrust Band 3
Table: p.1170
Sport Band 1
Table: p.55

Goldman, Donald (California)
Profile: p.253
Healthcare Band 2
Table: p.209

Goldman, Joel K (Missouri)
Profile: p.1057
Litigation Band 3
Table: p.1049

Goldman, Matthew (Ohio)
Profile: p.1441
Bankruptcy Band 3
Table: p.1414

Goldman, Melvin (California)
Profile: p.253
Antitrust Band 3

G

Table: p.184
Litigation Band 3
Table: p.224

Goldman, Michael
(New York)
Profile: p.1284
Banking & Finance Band 3
Table: p.1174

Goldman, Michael
(Delaware)
Profile: p.353
Chancery Band 3
Table: p.344
Corporate/M&A Band 3
Table: p.346

Goldman, Michael P
(Illinois)
Profile: p.730
Insurance Band 2
Table: p.692

Goldman, Robert J
(California)
Profile: p.254
Intellectual Property Band 4
Table: p.216

Goldman, Robert S (Florida)
Profile: p.540
Tax Band 3
Table: p.531

Goldring, Stuart (New York)
Profile: p.1284
Tax Band 3
Table: p.1255

Goldschmidt, David J
(National)
Profile: p.85
Capital Markets Band 4
Table: p.14

Goldsmith, Willis J
(District of Columbia)
Profile: p.445
Employment Band 1
Table: p.380

Goldstein, Andrew (Illinois)
Profile: p.730
Media & Entertainment Band 2
Table: p.704

Goldstein, Bruce
(New Jersey)
Profile: p.1140
Litigation Band 2
Table: p.1131

Goldstein, Bruce
(District of Columbia)
Profile: p.445
Bankruptcy Band 3
Table: p.372

Goldstein, Joseph (Florida)
Profile: p.540
Real Estate Band 3
Table: p.528

Goldstein, Marcia
(New York)
Profile: p.1284
Bankruptcy Band 1
Table: p.1179

Goldstein, Mark (Nevada)
Profile: p.1102
Corporate/M&A Band 3
Table: p.1089

Goldstein, Marvin (National)
Profile: p.85
Capital Markets Band 3
Table: p.16

Goldstein, Marvin M (New Jersey)
Profile: p.1140
Employment Band 3
Table: p.1126

Goldstein, Steven J (Ohio)
Profile: p.1441
Intellectual Property Band 1
Table: p.1428

Goldstein, Stuart N (North Carolina)
Profile: p. 1396
Capital Markets Band 2
Table: p.22

Golemon, Kinnan (Texas)
Profile: p.1681
Environment Band S
Table: p.1643

Gonchar, Meryl A G
(New Jersey)
Profile: p.1140
Real Estate Band 2
Table: p.1135

Gonzalez, Daniel E
(National)
Profile: p.85
Arbitration Band 4
Table: p.33

Gonzalez, Ervin (Florida)
Profile: p.541
Litigation Band 2
Table: p.521

Gonzalez, Thomas M
(Florida)
Profile: p.541
Employment Band 2
Table: p.513

Gooch, W Kyle (Texas)
Profile: p.1681
Construction Band 3
Table: p.1629

Goodell, Gerald (Kansas)
Profile: p.823
Real Estate Band 3
Table: p.821

Goodheart, Lisa
(Massachusetts)
Profile: p.967
Environment Band 2
Table: p.943

Gooding, Douglas R
(Massachusetts)
Profile: p.967
Bankruptcy Band 3
Table: p.935

Goodkind, Conrad G
(Wisconsin)
Profile: p.1825
Corporate/M&A Band 3
Table: p.1817

Goodkind, Jim (California)
Profile: p.254
Media & Entertainment Band 4
Table: p.230

Goodling, Jonathon L
(Oregon)
Profile: p.1482
Real Estate Band 3
Table: p.1479

Goodman, Lisa (Delaware)
Profile: p.353
Real Estate Band 1
Table: p.350

Goodman, Louis A
(Massachusetts)
Profile: p.967
Corporate/M&A Band 2
Table: p.937

Goodman, Mark (Illinois)
Profile: p.730
Insurance Band 1
Table: p.692

Goodman, Ronald (National)
Profile: p.86
Arbitration Band 3
Table: p.33

Goodman, Saul
(District of Columbia)
Profile: p.445
Insurance Band 3
Table: p.402

Goodman, Stephen
(Pennsylvania)
Profile: p.1525
Corporate/M&A Band 1
Table: p.1497

Goodman, Stuart (Illinois)
Profile: p.730
Corporate/M&A Band 4
Table: p.675

Goodman, William M
(California)
Profile: p.254
Litigation Band 2
Table: p.225

Goodman Jr, William F
(Mississippi)
Profile: p.1033
Litigation Band 2
Table: p.1028

Goodnight, David R
(Washington)
Profile: p.1791
Litigation Band 3
Table: p.1786

Goodsell, Verne
(South Dakota)
Profile: p.1593
Litigation Band 2
Table: p.1590
Litigation Band 2
Table: p.1590

Goodwin, David B
(California)
Profile: p.254
Insurance Band 1
Table: p.212

Goodwin, Michael
(District of Columbia)
Profile: p.445
Real Estate Band 2
Table: p.418

Goodwin, Thomas
(West Virginia)
Profile: p.1809
Litigation Band 2

Table: p.1803

Goold, Barry (Nevada)
Profile: p.1102
Real Estate Band 1
Table: p.1099

Goolsby, Allen (Virginia)
Profile: p.1769
Corporate/M&A Band 1
Table: p.1752

Goolsby, George (Texas)
Profile: p.1681
Energy Band 2
Table: p.1637
Projects Band 2
Table: p.1659

Gordon, Andrew P (Nevada)
Profile: p.1102
Litigation Band 3
Table: p.1096

Gordon, Avron (Minnesota)
Profile: p.1018
Corporate/M&A Band 3
Table: p.1005

Gordon, Charles (Washington)
Profile: p.1791
Litigation Band 2
Table: p.1786

Gordon, Corbett (Oregon)
Profile: p.1482
Employment Band 1
Table: p.1474

Gordon, David A (New York)
Profile: p. 1284
Projects Band 1 (National)
Table: p.52
Projects Band 1
Table: p.1244

Gordon, David S
(New Jersey)
Profile: p.1140
Real Estate Band 3
Table: p.1134

Gordon, George G
(Pennsylvania)
Profile: p.1525
Antitrust Band 2
Table: p.1489

Gordon, Mark L (Illinois)
Profile: p.730
Technology Band 2
Table: p.713

Gordon, Nicholas (New York)
Profile: p.1284
Media & Entertainment Band 2
Table: p.1235

Gordon, R Kenneth (Texas)
Profile: p.1682
Healthcare Band 2
Table: p.1646

Gordon, Robert B
(Massachusetts)
Profile: p.967
Employment Band 1
Table: p.940

Gordon, Scott (New Mexico)
Profile: p.1163
Employment Band 2
Table: p.1157

Gordon, Stephen (New York)
Profile: p.1284
Tax Band 2
Table: p.1255

Gore, George (Ohio)
Profile: p.1441
Litigation Band 4
Table: p.1431

Gorelick, Jamie
(District of Columbia)
Profile: p.445
Litigation Band 3
Table: p.410

Goren, Samuel (Florida)
Profile: p.541
Real Estate Band 3
Table: p.528

Gorrell Jr, J Warren
(District of Columbia)
Profile: p.445
Corporate/Commercial Band 1
Table: p.376

Gorson, Matthew (Florida)
Profile: p.541
Real Estate Band 1
Table: p.526

Gorton, William T
(Kentucky)
Profile: p.841
Environment Band 3
Table: p.832

Gosfield, Gregory G
(Pennsylvania)
Profile: p.1525
Real Estate Band 3
Table: p.1516

Gosselink, Paul (Texas)
Profile: p.1682
Environment Band 4
Table: p.1643

Gossett, David
(South Carolina)
Profile: p.1580
Real Estate Band 3
Table: p.1577

Gottlieb, Joel E
(South Carolina)
Profile: p.1580
Real Estate Band 1
Table: p.1577

Gotts, Ilene Knable
(New York)
Profile: p.1284
Antitrust Band 1
Table: p.1170

Gotts, Lawrence J
(District of Columbia)
Profile: p. 1769
Intellectual Property Band 3
Table: p.403
Intellectual Property Band 2
Table: p.1759
(Virginia)

Gottschalk, Hugh
(Colorado)
Profile: p.318
Litigation Band 4
Table: p.311

Gottschalk, Steve
(Minnesota)
Profile: p.1018
Employment Band 3

Table: p.1008

Govett, Brett C (Texas)
Profile: p.1682
Intellectual Property Band 3
Table: p.1651

Gowland, Kimbal (Idaho)
Profile: p.660
Real Estate Band 3
Table: p.658

Goyne, Roderick (Texas)
Profile: p.1682
Banking & Finance Band 2
Table: p.1625

Grady, Kevin E (Georgia)
Profile: p.613
Antitrust Band 1
Table: p.578

Grady, Timothy (Ohio)
Profile: p.1441
Banking & Finance Band 2
Table: p.1411

Graev, Lawrence (New York)
Profile: p.1284
Private Equity Band 3
Table: p.1237

Graff Jr, F Thomas
(West Virginia)
Profile: p.1809
Corporate/M&A Band 2
Table: p.1798

Gragg, Lawrence (Florida)
Profile: p.541
Tax Band 1
Table: p.531

Graham, Andrew Jay
(Maryland)
Profile: p.921
Litigation ✪
Table: p.914

Graham, Bruce (Hawaii)
Profile: p.648
Real Estate Band 1
Table: p.646

Graham, Christopher
(Rhode Island)
Profile: p.1569
Corporate/M&A Band 2
Table: p.1564

Graham, D Collier
(Mississippi)
Profile: p.1033

Graham, Gary (Montana)
Profile: p.1080
Litigation Band 1
Table: p.1075

Graham, Lawrence
(Washington)
Profile: p.1791
Intellectual Property Band 2
Table: p.1784

Graham, Mary B (Delaware)
Profile: p.353
Intellectual Property Band 3
Table: p.348

Graham, Max (Hawaii)
Profile: p.648
Land Use Band 1
Table: p.643

Graham, Stephen M
(Washington)
Profile: p.1791
Corporate/M&A Band 3
Table: p.1778

Grahame, Heather H
(Alaska)
Profile: p.142
Environment Band 1
Table: p.137
Regulated Industries Band 1
Table: p.137

Grais, David J (New York)
Profile: p.1284
Insurance Band 3
Table: p.1213

Grala, Bronislaw (New York)
Profile: p.1284
Employee Benefits Band 2
Table: p.1197

Grammig, Robert (Florida)
Profile: p.541
Corporate/M&A Band 1
Table: p.509

Granda, John A (Missouri)
Profile: p.1057
Corporate/M&A Band 1
Table: p.1043

Grandis, Leslie (Virginia)
Profile: p.1770
Corporate/M&A Band 2
Table: p.1752

Grandison, W George
(National)
Profile: p.86
International Trade Band 3
Table: p.40

Grandoff, J Bert (Florida)
Profile: p.541
Construction Band S
Table: p.507

Granfield, Lindsee P
(New York)
Profile: p.1285
Bankruptcy Band 4
Table: p.1179

Grant, Elizabeth (Vermont)
Profile: p.1748
Employment Band 2
Table: p.1745

Grant, Eugene L (Oregon)
Profile: p.1482
Real Estate Band 2
Table: p.1479

Granwell, Alan Winston
(District of Columbia)
Profile: p.445
Tax Band 3
Table: p.422

Graves, Judson (Georgia)
Profile: p.613
Litigation Band 1
Table: p.598

Graves, Kathlyn (Arkansas)
Profile: p.176
Employment Band 1
Table: p.170

Gray, James (Maryland)
Profile: p.921
Litigation Band 3
Table: p.914

Gray, Robert F (Texas)
Profile: p.1682
Technology Band 1
Table: p.1668

Gray Jr, Marvin L
(Washington)
Profile: p.1791
Litigation Band 2
Table: p.1786

Grayson, E Lynn (Illinois)
Profile: p.730
Environment Band 3
Table: p.687

Grayson, Neil E
(South Carolina)
Profile: p.1580
Corporate/M&A Band 3
Table: p.1572

Greaney, William
(District of Columbia)
Profile: p.445
Insurance Band 2
Table: p.402

Greeley, Jack (Florida)
Profile: p.541
Banking & Finance Band 2
Table: p.500

Green, Barry D
(Massachusetts)
Profile: p.967
Real Estate Band 3
Table: p.956

Green, David W (Oregon)
Profile: p.1482
Real Estate Band 2
Table: p.1479

Green, Doug
(District of Columbia)
Profile: p.445
Energy Band 2
Table: p.386

Green, Frederick (New York)
Profile: p.1285
Corporate/M&A Band 4
Table: p.1189

Green, Jonathan (New York)
Profile: p.1285
Projects Band 1
Table: p.52
Projects Band 1
Table: p.1244

Green, Jordan (Arizona)
Profile: p.158
Litigation Band 1
Table: p.153

Green, Josh (California)
Profile: p.254
Corporate/M&A Band 5
Table: p.197

Green, Karen F
(Massachusetts)
Profile: p.967
Litigation Band 1
Table: p.951

Green, Mike (Iowa)
Profile: p.813
Real Estate Band 4
Table: p.810

Green, Ronald (New York)
Profile: p.1285
Employment Band 3
Table: p.1200

Green, Thomas C
(District of Columbia)
Profile: p.445
Litigation Band 1
Table: p.410

Green, William (Florida)
Profile: p.541
Environment Band 1
Table: p.516

Green, William (Washington)
Profile: p.1792
Real Estate Band 3
Table: p.1788

Greenbaum, Jack A
(New York)
Profile: p.86
Shipping Band 3
Table: p.67

Greenberg, Barry C.
(Maryland)
Profile: p.921
Real Estate Band 4
Table: p.917

Greenberg, Gordon A
(California)
Profile: p.254
Litigation Band 1
Table: p.225

Greenberg, Jeffrey
(California)
Profile: p. 1285
Projects Up and coming
Table: p.236
Projects Up and coming
Table: p.1244

Greenberg, Joel (New York)
Profile: p.1285
Corporate/M&A Band 4
Table: p.1189

Greenberg, Marilynn R
(New Jersey)
Profile: p.1140
Environment Band 2
Table: p.1129

Greenburg, Scott G
(Washington)
Profile: p.1792
Corporate/M&A Band 2
Table: p.1778

Greene, Kenneth (North
Carolina)
Profile: p.1396
Banking & Finance Band 2
Table: p.1381

Greene, Kevin C (Georgia)
Profile: p.613
Energy Band 1
Table: p.592

Greener, Richard (Idaho)
Profile: p.660
Litigation Band 1
Table: p.657

Greenfield, Gregg S
(South Dakota)
Profile: p.1593
Corporate/M&A Band 3
Table: p.1587

Greenfield, Robert A
(California)
Profile: p.254
Bankruptcy Band 2
Table: p.191

Greenfield, Russell R
(South Dakota)
Profile: p.1593
Real Estate Band S
Table: p.1592

Greengrass, Lawrence S
(New York)
Profile: p.1285
Insurance Band 3
Table: p.1213
Insurance Band 3
Table: p.1213

Greenman, Ronald L
(Oregon)
Profile: p.1482
Corporate/M&A Band 2
Table: p.1471

Greenspan, Eric (California)
Profile: p.254
Media & Entertainment Band 4
Table: p.230

Greenspan, Steven
(Connecticut)
Profile: p.337
Litigation Band 2
Table: p.331

Greenstein, Abraham
(District of Columbia)
Profile: p.446
Real Estate Band 2
Table: p.418

Greenthal, John (New York)
Profile: p.1285
Environment Band 3
Table: p.1205

Greenwald, John D
(National)
Profile: p.86
International Trade Band 2
Table: p.40

Greenwald, Steven
(California)
Profile: p.254
Energy Band 2
Table: p.204

Greenwell, Charles D
(Kentucky)
Profile: p.842
Litigation Band 4
Table: p.835

Greenwood, David (Utah)
Profile: p.1736
Litigation Band 2
Table: p.1732

Greer, Alan (Florida)
Profile: p.541
Litigation Band 2
Table: p.521

Greer, David (Ohio)
Profile: p.1441
Litigation Band 3
Table: p.1431

Greer, George E
(Washington)
Profile: p.1792
Litigation Band 3
Table: p.1786

G

Greer, Scott (Georgia)
Profile: p.613
Construction **Band 2**
Table: p.584

Gregory, Donald (Ohio)
Profile: p.1441
Construction **Band 2**
Table: p.1417

Gregory, H Watt (Arkansas)
Profile: p.176
Corporate/M&A **Band 1**
Table: p.168

Greig, Brian (Texas)
Profile: p.1682
Employment **Band 1**
Table: p.1634

Greising, Robert (Indiana)
Profile: p.792
Corporate/M&A **Band 3**
Table: p.781

Gremillion, L Todd (Texas)
Profile: p.1682
Energy **Band 4**
Table: p.1637

Grenier, John B (Alabama)
Profile: p.122
Corporate/M&A **Band 1**
Table: p.111

Grice, Richard (Georgia)
Profile: p.613
Banking & Finance **Band 2**
Table: p.580

Grier, Joseph L (New York)
Profile: p.1285
Media & Entertainment **Band 2**
Table: p.1235

Griffin, James (Missouri)
Profile: p.1057
Litigation **Band 1**
Table: p.1049

Griffin, John W (Georgia)
Profile: p.613
Real Estate **Band 2**
Table: p.601

Griffin III, Thomas N (North
Carolina)
Profile: p.1396
Environment **Band 2**
Table: p.1388

Griffinger, Michael R
(New Jersey)
Profile: p.1140
Litigation **Band 1**
Table: p.1131

Griffith, Richard (Kentucky)
Profile: p.842
Employment **Band 1**
Table: p.830

Griffith, Scott (Texas)
Profile: p.1682
Construction **Band 3**
Table: p.1629

Griffith, Spencer S
(National)
Profile: p.86
International Trade **Band 4**
Table: p.40

Grigera Naón, Horacio
(National)
Profile: p.86

Arbitration **Band 1**
Table: p.34

Grimes, Dale (Tennessee)
Profile: p.1607
Litigation **Band 3**
Table: p.1599

Grimm, William R (Rhode
Island)
Profile: p.1569
Litigation **Band 3**
Table: p.1567

Grimmer, Gary (Hawaii)
Profile: p.648
Litigation **Band 3**
Table: p.644

Grimshaw, Thomas T
(Colorado)
Profile: p.318
Real Estate **Band 1**
Table: p.314

Grindstaff, Michael J
(Florida)
Profile: p.541
Real Estate **Band 3**
Table: p.528

Grinfas, Dan (Washington)
Profile: p.1482
Employment **Up and coming**
Table: p.1474

Grishman, David
(Mississippi)
Profile: p.1033
Corporate/M&A **Band 2**
Table: p.1024

Groark Jr, Thomas
(Connecticut)
Profile: p.337
Litigation **Band S**
Table: p.331

Grogan, Michael (Florida)
Profile: p.541
Employment **Band 2**
Table: p.513

Grohman, Thomas
(Washington)
Profile: p.1792
Corporate/M&A **Band 3**
Table: p.1778

Groll, Michael (New York)
Profile: p.1285
Insurance **Band 3**
Table: p.1213

Gromacki, Joseph P
(Illinois)
Profile: p.731
Corporate/M&A
Up and coming
Table: p.675

Grooms, Timothy (Arkansas)
Profile: p.176
Real Estate **Band 1**
Table: p.174

Groskaufmanis, Karl
(District of Columbia)
Profile: p.446
Corporate/Commercial **Band 1**
Table: p.376

Gross, David (Minnesota)
Profile: p.1018
Litigation **Band 1**
Table: p.1012

Gross, Doug (Iowa)
Profile: p.813
Corporate/M&A **Band 4**
Table: p.802

Gross, Jefferson W (Utah)
Profile: p.1736
Litigation **Up and coming**
Table: p.1732

Gross, John (New York)
Profile: p.1285
Insurance **Band 2**
Table: p.1213

Gross, Michael J
(New Jersey)
Profile: p.1140
Environment **Band 1**
Table: p.1129

Gross, Steven F (New
Jersey)
Profile: p.1140
Corporate/M&A **Band 3**
Table: p.1123

Gross, Steven R (New York)
Profile: p.1285
Bankruptcy **Band 3**
Table: p.1179

Grossenburg, Bradley C
(South Dakota)
Profile: p.1593
Corporate/M&A **Band 1**
Table: p.1587

Grosser, Theodore D (Ohio)
Profile: p.1441
Corporate/M&A **Band 3**
Table: p.1419

Grosshandler, Seth
(National)
Profile: p.86
Capital Markets **Band 2**
Table: p.16

Grossman, Marshall
(California)
Profile: p.255
Litigation **Band 1**
Table: p.224
Media & Entertainment **Band 2**
Table: p.230

Grossman, Paul (California)
Profile: p.255
Employment **Band 1**
Table: p.202

Grossman, Shukie
(New York)
Profile: p.1285
Private Equity **Up and coming**
Table: p.1241

Grossman, Theodore (Ohio)
Profile: p.1441
Litigation **Band 2**
Table: p.1431

Groten, Eric (Texas)
Profile: p.1682
Environment **Band 4**
Table: p.1643

Grout, Robert W (Georgia)
Profile: p.613
Corporate/M&A **Band 4**
Table: p.587

Grove, Barry (New York)
Profile: p.1286
Construction **Band 2**

Table: p.1186

Grover, Parry (Alaska)
Profile: p.142
Employment **Band 1**
Table: p.135

Grovier, Tina M (Alaska)
Profile: p.143
Environment **Band 3**
Table: p.137
Regulated Industries **Band 2**
Table: p.137

Grubbs, R Howard (North
Carolina)
Profile: p.1396
Environment **Band 2**
Table: p.1388

Grubman, Allen (New York)
Profile: p.1286
Media & Entertainment **Band 1**
Table: p.1235

Grundfest, Jack (Arkansas)
Profile: p.176
Corporate/M&A **Band 1**
Table: p.168

Guariglia, Michael A
(New Jersey)
Profile: p.1140
Corporate/M&A **Band 3**
Table: p.1123

Guattery, Peter (Maryland)
Profile: p.921
Employment **Band 3**
Table: p.912

Guedry, David (Texas)
Profile: p.1682
Business Process
Outsourcing: National **Band 2**
Table: p.10
Technology **Band 1**
Table: p.1668

Guinasso, John (Oregon)
Profile: p.1482
Real Estate **Band 3**
Table: p.1479

Guinn, Guy (Ohio)
Profile: p.1441
Banking & Finance **Band 1**
Table: p.1411

Gulland, Eugene D
(National)
Profile: p.86
Arbitration **Band**
Table: p.33
Arbitration **Band 3**
Table: p.33

Gullickson, Charles D
(South Dakota)
Profile: p.1593
Corporate/M&A **Band 2**
Table: p.1587

Gullikson, Rosemary L
(National)
Profile: p.86
Business Process
Outsourcing: National **Band 3**
Table: p.10

Gundersen, Glenn A
(Pennsylvania)
Profile: p.1525
Intellectual Property **Band 4**
Table: p.1508

Gunderson, Bob (California)
Profile: p.255
Corporate/M&A **Band 3**
Table: p.197

Gunderson, Joseph R
(Iowa)
Profile: p.813
Litigation **Band 3**
Table: p.807

Gunn, David M (Texas)
Profile: p.1682
Litigation **Band 2**
Table: p.1656

Gunn, Paul (Mississippi)
Profile: p.1034
Real Estate **Band 2**
Table: p.1031

Gunsett, Daniel (Ohio)
Profile: p.1441
Environment **Band 2**
Table: p.1425

Gunter, Clifford (Texas)
Profile: p.1682
Energy **Band 2**
Table: p.1640

Gunter, Russell (Arkansas)
Profile: p.176
Employment **Band 1**
Table: p.170

Gupta, Paul (New York)
Profile: p.1286
Intellectual Property **Band 3**
Table: p.1217

Gupta, Shilpi (Illinois)
Profile: p.731
Corporate/M&A
Up and coming
Table: p.675

Gupton, John (Tennessee)
Profile: p.1608
Real Estate **Band 3**
Table: p.1603

Gurley, David (Florida)
Profile: p.541
Construction **Band 3**
Table: p.507

Gurney, Scott (Ohio)
Profile: p.1441
Construction **Band 4**
Table: p.1417

Guso, Jordi (Florida)
Profile: p.541
Bankruptcy **Band 2**
Table: p.503

Gustafson, Karna R
(Oregon)
Profile: p.1482
Real Estate **Up and coming**
Table: p.1479

Guthman, Jack (Illinois)
Profile: p.731
Real Estate **Band 1**
Table: p.706

Gutierrez, Jay
(District of Columbia)
Profile: p.446
Energy **Band 2**
Table: p.390

Gutmacher, Norman (Ohio)
Profile: p.1441
Real Estate Band 4
Table: p.1434

Gutowski, Peter (New York)
Profile: p.86
Shipping Band 2
Table: p.67

Gutter, Marvin (Florida)
Profile: p.541
Tax Band 2
Table: p.531

Guy III, G Hopkins
(California)
Profile: p.255
Intellectual Property Band 3
Table: p.216

Guynn, Randall (New York)
Profile: p.1286
Banking & Finance Band 3
Table: p.1174

Gwynne, Kurt F (Delaware)
Profile: p.353
Bankruptcy Band 4
Table: p.341

H

Haab, Eric (Illinois)
Profile: p.731
Insurance Band 3
Table: p.694

Haarlow, John (Illinois)
Profile: p.731
Insurance Band 1
Table: p.695

Haas, Karl P (Indiana)
Profile: p.792
Real Estate Band 1
Table: p.788

Hable, Kevin J (Kentucky)
Profile: p.842
Corporate/M&A Band 3
Table: p.827

Hack, Randall A (Illinois)
Profile: p.731
Antitrust Band 3
Table: p.662

Hackett, Robert J (Arizona)
Profile: p.159
Corporate/M&A Band 4
Table: p.146

Hackman, Stephen
(Indiana)
Profile: p.792
Corporate/M&A Band 3
Table: p.781

Hackney, Hamilton
(Massachusetts)
Profile: p.968
Environment Band 3
Table: p.943

Haddon, Harold (Colorado)
Profile: p.318
Litigation Band 1
Table: p.311

Haden Jr, William H
(Kentucky)
Profile: p.842
Real Estate Band 1
Table: p.838

Hadjis, Alex
(District of Columbia)
Profile: p.446
Intellectual Property Band 3
Table: p.403

Hadley, Joseph P (New York)
Profile: p.1286
Projects Band 3
Table: p.1244

Haefner, Gail (Vermont)
Profile: p.1748
Corporate/M&A Band 2
Table: p.1743

Hafer, Randall F (Georgia)
Profile: p.613
Construction Band 2
Table: p.584

Hafets, Richard J
(Maryland)
Profile: p.921
Employment Band 1
Table: p.912

Hafetz, Fred (New York)
Profile: p.1286
Litigation Band 3
Table: p.1224

Haffey, Dennis (Michigan)
Profile: p.999
Litigation Band 2
Table: p.994

Hafter, Jerome C
(Mississippi)
Profile: p.1034
Corporate/M&A Band 2
Table: p.1024

Hagen, Paul
(District of Columbia)
Profile: p.446
Environment Band 2
Table: p.392

Hagerott, Edward C
(California)
Profile: p.255
Real Estate Band 3
Table: p.238

Haggerty, John J (Ohio)
Profile: p.1441
Litigation Up and coming
Table: p.1431

Haglund, Michael E
(Oregon)
Profile: p.1482
Litigation Band 3
Table: p.1477

Hagy, James C (Illinois)
Profile: p.731
Real Estate Band 4
Table: p.706

Hahn, Arthur (Illinois)
Profile: p.731
Corporate/M&A Band 4
Table: p.675

Hahn, James H (Rhode
Island)
Profile: p.1569
Corporate/M&A Band 2

Table: p.1564

Hahn, Richard (New York)
Profile: p.1286
Bankruptcy Band 3
Table: p.1179

Hahn, Robert J
(North Carolina)
Profile: p.1396
Capital Markets Band 2
Table: p.22

Haigh, Mark W
(South Dakota)
Profile: p.1593
Litigation Band 2
Table: p.1590

Haims, Bruce D (New York)
Profile: p.1286
Tax Band 4
Table: p.1255

Haines, Lisa (Missouri)
Profile: p.1057
Real Estate Band 2
Table: p.1052

Hainline Jr, Theodore
(Florida)
Profile: p.541
Real Estate Band 3
Table: p.528

Hajek, Douglas J
(South Dakota)
Profile: p.1593
Corporate/M&A Band 2
Table: p.1587

Halbreich, David M
(California)
Profile: p.255
Insurance Band 2
Table: p.212

Hale, David J (Kentucky)
Profile: p.842
Litigation Band 4
Table: p.835

Hale, Russell (Florida)
Profile: p.542
Tax Band 3
Table: p.531

Halevy, Amy Karff (Texas)
Profile: p.1682
Employment Band 3
Table: p.1634

Haley, George M (Utah)
Profile: p.1736
Litigation Band 1
Table: p.1732

Haley, James F (New York)
Profile: p.1286
Intellectual Property Band 3
Table: p.1217

Haley, Joseph
(Massachusetts)
Profile: p.968
Real Estate Band 1
Table: p.957

Haley III, Raymond
(Kentucky)
Profile: p.842
Employment Band 3
Table: p.830

Hall, Alan (New Mexico)
Profile: p.1163
Corporate/M&A Band 2
Table: p.1155

Hall, Bruce (New Mexico)
Profile: p.1163
Litigation Band 1
Table: p.1159

Hall, Donald (Florida)
Profile: p.542
Real Estate Band 2
Table: p.528

Hall, Helena (Alaska)
Profile: p.143
Employment Band 2
Table: p.135

Hall, Kevin A
(South Carolina)
Profile: p.1580
Litigation Up and coming
Table: p.1576

Hall, Mark (Vermont)
Profile: p.1748
Real Estate Band 2
Table: p.1747

Hall, Michael W (California)
Profile: p.255
Corporate/M&A Band 5
Table: p.197

Hall, Richard (New York)
Profile: p.1286
Corporate/M&A Band 3
Table: p.1189

Hall, Thomas (New Jersey)
Profile: p.1140
Real Estate Band 2
Table: p.1135

Hall Jr, Cary (South Carolina)
Profile: p.1581
Corporate/M&A Band 2
Table: p.1572

Haller, Anthony
(Pennsylvania)
Profile: p.1525
Employment Band 3
Table: p.1500

Haller, Diane (Arizona)
Profile: p.159
Real Estate Band 2
Table: p.154

Halliday, Joseph W
(New York)
Profile: p.1286
Banking & Finance Band 4
Table: p.1174

Halling, Gary L (California)
Profile: p.255
Antitrust Band 3
Table: p.184

Hallman, Robert (New York)
Profile: p.1286
Environment Band 3
Table: p.1206

Hallos, Jeffrey L (Kentucky)
Profile: p.842
Corporate/M&A Band 3
Table: p.827

Halpern, Marcelo (Illinois)
Profile: p.731
Technology Band 3

Table: p.713

Halsey, Douglas (Florida)
Profile: p.542
Environment Band 1
Table: p.516

Halston, Daniel W
(Massachusetts)
Profile: p.968
Litigation Band 3
Table: p.951

Halverson, Jan (Minnesota)
Profile: p.1018
Employment Band 2
Table: p.1008

Halvey, John K (New York)
Profile: p. 1286
Business Process
Outsourcing: National ✪
Table: p.10
Technology Band 1
Table: p.1259

Hamann, Lee (Nebraska)
Profile: p.1088
Real Estate Band 1
Table: p.1086

Hamel, Douglas (Texas)
Profile: p.1682
Employment Band 1
Table: p.1634

Hamel, Mark (Minnesota)
Profile: p.1018
Real Estate Band 1
Table: p.1014

Hamill, John J (Illinois)
Profile: p.731
Telecom, Broadcast & Satellite
Band 2
Table: p.715

Hamilton, John W (Indiana)
Profile: p.792
Real Estate Band 3
Table: p.788

Hamilton, P Andrew
(Maine)
Profile: p.898
Environment Band 1
Table: p.892

Hamilton, Russell (Florida)
Profile: p.542
Employment Band 1
Table: p.513
Employment Band 1
Table: p.513

Hamlin, Harold (Arkansas)
Profile: p.176
Real Estate Band 3
Table: p.174

Hamm, Leisa (Illinois)
Profile: p.731
Insurance Band 2
Table: p.695

Hammer, Stuart (New York)
Profile: p.1286
Environment Band 3
Table: p.1206

Hammes, Jeffrey C (Illinois)
Profile: p.731
Corporate/M&A Band 4
Table: p.675
Private Equity Band 2
Table: p.676

Hammond, David
(West Virginia)
Profile: p.1809
Real Estate **Band 2**
Table: p.1806

Hammond, Herbert (Texas)
Profile: p.1683
Intellectual Property **Band 3**
Table: p.1651

Hammond, Larry (Arizona)
Profile: p.159
Litigation **Band 1**
Table: p.153

Hammond, Steven A
(National)
Profile: p.86
Arbitration **Band 4**
Table: p.33

Hampton, Joe M (Oklahoma)
Profile: p.1465
Litigation **Band 3**
Table: p.1462

Hamular, James (Arizona)
Profile: p.159
Environment **Band 3**
Table: p.150

Hancock, William K
(Alabama)
Profile: p.123
Employment **Band 3**
Table: p.113

Hancock Jr, John P
(Michigan)
Profile: p.999
Employment **Band 2**
Table: p.991

Handelsman, Lawrence
(New York)
Profile: p.1286
Bankruptcy **Band 3**
Table: p.1179

Handlos, Bryan G
(Nebraska)
Profile: p.1088
Corporate/M&A **Band 3**
Table: p.1082

Handly, Kevin
(Massachusetts)
Profile: p.968
Banking & Finance **Band 2**
Table: p.932

Handman, Laura R
(District of Columbia)
Profile: p.446
Media & Entertainment **Band 1**
Table: p.413

Handzlik, Jan (California)
Profile: p.255
Litigation **Band 1**
Table: p.225

Hangley, William
(Pennsylvania)
Profile: p.1526
Litigation **Band 1**
Table: p.1511

Hankins, Stuart (Arkansas)
Profile: p.176
Real Estate **Band 2**
Table: p.174

Hanks, James (Maryland)
Profile: p.921

Corporate/M&A **Band 1**
Table: p.909

Hanlon, Michael J
(Pennsylvania)
Profile: p.1526
Employment **Band 4**
Table: p.1500

Hanlon-Leh, Natalie
(Colorado)
Profile: p.318
Intellectual Property **Band 1**
Table: p.309

Hanna III, George V (North
Carolina)
Profile: p.1396
Litigation **Band 3**
Table: p.1390

Hanrahan, Marc P
(New York)
Profile: p.1286
Banking & Finance **Band 2**
Table: p.1174

Hanschen, Peter (California)
Profile: p.255
Energy **Band 2**
Table: p.204

Hansell, Edgar (Iowa)
Profile: p.813
Corporate/M&A **Band 1**
Table: p.802

Hansen, Edward J
(New York)
Profile: p.1286
Technology **Band 3**
Table: p.1259

Hansen, Kenneth
(District of Columbia)
Profile: p.446
Projects **Band 3**
Table: p.415

Hansen, Scott W
(Wisconsin)
Profile: p.1825
Litigation **Band 2**
Table: p.1821

Hansen, Tom (California)
Profile: p.255
Media & Entertainment **Band 1**
Table: p.233

Hanson Jr, Karl B (Florida)
Profile: p.542
Real Estate **Band 2**
Table: p.526

Hanzlik, Paul F (Illinois)
Profile: p.731
Energy **Band S**
Table: p.685

Haraldson, Comet
(South Dakota)
Profile: p.1593
Employment **Band 1**
Table: p.1589

Harbison, William L
(Tennessee)
Profile: p.1608
Litigation **Band 3**
Table: p.1599

Hardcastle, Jay (Tennessee)
Profile: p.1608
Corporate/M&A **Band 3**
Table: p.1594

Hardesty, Stephen (Idaho)
Profile: p.660
Corporate/M&A **Band 3**
Table: p.655

Hardie, Thornton (Texas)
Profile: p.1683
Tax **Band 2**
Table: p.1665

Hardiman, John L
(New York)
Profile: p.1286
Litigation **Band 3**
Table: p.1223

Hardin, Edward J (Georgia)
Profile: p.613
Corporate/M&A **Band 2**
Table: p.587

Hardin, Lloyd (Oklahoma)
Profile: p.1465
Real Estate **Band 1**
Table: p.1464

Hardin, Steven D (Indiana)
Profile: p.792
Real Estate **Up and coming**
Table: p.788

Hardin, William (Arizona)
Profile: p.159
Corporate/M&A **Band 3**
Table: p.146

Hardin III, Harry S
(Louisiana)
Profile: p.872
Litigation **Band 3**
Table: p.865

Harding, William (Nebraska)
Profile: p.1088
Employment **Band 2**
Table: p.1084

Hardy, Elizabeth P
(Michigan)
Profile: p.999
Employment **Band 2**
Table: p.991

Hardy, Michael (Ohio)
Profile: p.1441
Environment **Band 1**
Table: p.1425

Hardymon, Glen (North
Carolina)
Profile: p.1396
Real Estate **Band 3**
Table: p.1392

Hariton, David P (New York)
Profile: p.1286
Tax **Band 1**
Table: p.1256

Harkavy, Ronald
(Tennessee)
Profile: p.1608
Real Estate **Band 2**
Table: p.1603

Harkins, Deborah
(Louisiana)
Profile: p.872
Gaming & Licensing **Band 2**
Table: p.864

Harkins Jr, John G
(Pennsylvania)
Profile: p.1526
Litigation **Band S**
Table: p.1511

Harkrider, John D (New York)
Profile: p.1286
Antitrust **Up and coming**
Table: p.1170

Harless, Warren David
(Virginia)
Profile: p.1770
Litigation **Band 2**
Table: p.1763

Harman, Thomas
(District of Columbia)
Profile: p.446
Investment Management
Band 2
Table: p.406

Harmon, Christopher B
(Alabama)
Profile: p.123
Corporate/M&A **Band 2**
Table: p.111

Harmon, T Craig (Virginia)
Profile: p.1770
Real Estate **Band 3**
Table: p.1765

Harms, David B (National)
Profile: p.87
Capital Markets **Band 3**
Table: p.14

Harnden, Edwin (Oregon)
Profile: p.1482
Employment **Band 2**
Table: p.1474

Harnden, Ronald (Kansas)
Profile: p.823
Real Estate **Band 1**
Table: p.821

Harner, Paul E (Illinois)
Profile: p.731
Bankruptcy **Band**
Table: p.669
Bankruptcy **Band 3**
Table: p.669

Haroz, Michael
(Massachusetts)
Profile: p.968
Real Estate **Band 2**
Table: p.956

Harper, A J (Texas)
Profile: p.1683
Employment **Band 2**
Table: p.1634

Harper, Sue Erwin (South
Carolina)
Profile: p.1581
Employment **Band 2**
Table: p.1574

Harrell, Michael P
(New York)
Profile: p.1286
Private Equity **Band 1**
Table: p.1241

Harrigan, Kenneth (New
Mexico)
Profile: p.1163
Litigation **Band 1**
Table: p.1159

Harrigan Jr, Arthur W
(Washington)
Profile: p.1792
Litigation **Band 1**
Table: p.1786

Harrington, C Michael
(Texas)
Profile: p.1683
Corporate/M&A **Band 4**
Table: p.1631

Harrington, James (Illinois)
Profile: p.732
Environment **Band 3**
Table: p.687

Harrington, John R (Illinois)
Profile: p.732
Telecom, Broadcast & Satellite
Band 2
Table: p.715

Harrington, Michael C
(Connecticut)
Profile: p.337
Litigation **Up and coming**
Table: p.331

Harris, Adam (New York)
Profile: p.1287
Bankruptcy **Band 4**
Table: p.1179

Harris, Alan (California)
Profile: p.255
Construction **Band 1**
Table: p.194

Harris, Dale (Colorado)
Profile: p.318
Antitrust **Band 1**
Table: p.311
Litigation **Band 3**
Table: p.311

Harris, David L (New Jersey)
Profile: p.1140
Litigation **Band 1**
Table: p.1131
Litigation **Band 2**
Table: p.1133

Harris, Edward W (Indiana)
Profile: p.792
Litigation **Band 3**
Table: p.785

Harris, James (Texas)
Profile: p.1683
Environment **Band 3**
Table: p.1643
Litigation **Band 2**
Table: p.1643

Harris, Judith E
(Pennsylvania)
Profile: p.1526
Employment **Band 4**
Table: p.1500

Harris, L Douglas (New York)
Profile: p. 1287
Projects **Band 2**
Table: p.52
Projects **Band 2**
Table: p.1244

Harris, Larry D
(District of Columbia)
Profile: p.447
Construction **Band 2**
Table: p.374

Harris, Matthew T
(Tennessee)
Profile: p.1608
Real Estate **Band 2**
Table: p.1603

Harris, Morton A (Georgia)
Profile: p.613
Tax **Band 4**
Table: p.603

Harris, Robert J (Illinois)
Profile: p.732
Construction **Band 3**
Table: p.672

Harris, Scott
(District of Columbia)
Profile: p.447
Telecom, Broadcast & Satellite
Band 2
Table: p.427

Harris Jr, H Stephen
(Georgia)
Profile: p.613
Antitrust **Band 2**
Table: p.578

Harrison, Bruce S
(Maryland)
Profile: p.921
Employment **Band 3**
Table: p.912

Harrison, Joseph H (Illinois)
Profile: p.732
Capital Markets **Band 1**
Table: p.21

Harrison, Kirk R (Nevada)
Profile: p.1102
Litigation **Band 2**
Table: p.1096

Harrison, Lauren (Texas)
Profile: p.1683
Antitrust **Up and coming**
Table: p.1622

Harrison, Mark (Arizona)
Profile: p.159
Litigation **Band 4**
Table: p.152

Harrison, Sylvia (Nevada)
Profile: p.1102
Environment **Band 3**
Table: p.1093

Hart, Austin (Vermont)
Profile: p.1749
Real Estate **Band 3**
Table: p.1747

Hart, Gordon E (California)
Profile: p.255
Environment **Band 4**
Table: p.207

Hart, John (New York)
Profile: p.1287
Tax **Band 3**
Table: p.1255

Harter, Elizabeth
(West Virginia)
Profile: p.1809
Employment **Band 2**
Table: p.1801

Harth, David J (Wisconsin)
Profile: p.1825
Litigation **Band 3**
Table: p.1821

Hartig, Lawrence (Alaska)
Profile: p.143
Environment **Band 2**
Table: p.137

Hartle Munsch, Martha
(Pennsylvania)
Profile: p.1526
Employment **Band 1**
Table: p.1500

Hartley, James E (Colorado)
Profile: p.318
Antitrust **Band 1**
Table: p.311

Hartmann, H Michael
(Illinois)
Profile: p.732
Intellectual Property **Band 2**
Table: p.696

Hartmann, James
(Oklahoma)
Profile: p.1465
Real Estate **Band 1**
Table: p.1464

Hartmann, Melanie
(Louisiana)
Profile: p.872
Employment **Band 3**
Table: p.861

Hartnett, William M
(National)
Profile: p.87
Capital Markets **Band 1**
Table: p.14

Hartquist, David A
(National)
Profile: p.87
International Trade **Band 3**
Table: p.40

Hartsfield, Dan (Texas)
Profile: p.1683
Employment **Band 3**
Table: p.1634

Hartstein, Barry (Illinois)
Profile: p.732
Employment **Band 1**
Table: p.681

Harty, Frank (Iowa)
Profile: p.813
Employment **Band 1**
Table: p.805

Harty, Ronan P (New York)
Profile: p.1287
Antitrust **Band 1**
Table: p.1170

Harvell, Michael
(New Hampshire)
Profile: p.1117
Litigation **Band 1**
Table: p.1111

Harvey, Charles (Maine)
Profile: p.898
Litigation **Band 1**
Table: p.893

Harvey, Dean William
(Texas)
Profile: p.1683
Technology **Band 2**
Table: p.1668

Harvey, James (National)
Profile: p.87
Business Process
Outsourcing: National **Band 3**
Table: p.10

Harvin, David (Texas)
Profile: p.1683
Energy **Band 2**
Table: p.1640
Litigation **Band 2**
Table: p.1656

Harwell Jr, Aubrey B
(Tennessee)
Profile: p.1608
Litigation **Band 3**
Table: p.1599

Haskell, Mark
(District of Columbia)
Profile: p.447
Energy **Band 3**
Table: p.382

Haslam, Robert (California)
Profile: p.255
Intellectual Property **Band 4**
Table: p.216

Hasson Jr, James K
(Georgia)
Profile: p.614
Tax **Band 4**
Table: p.603

Hastie, John (Oklahoma)
Profile: p.1465
Real Estate **Band S**
Table: p.1464

Hastings, Douglas
(District of Columbia)
Profile: p.447
Healthcare **Band 1**
Table: p.398

Hastings, Susan C (Ohio)
Profile: p.1441
Employment **Band 3**
Table: p.1422

Hatch, Michael W
(Wisconsin)
Profile: p.1825
Real Estate **Band 1**
Table: p.1822

Hatchell, Mike A (Texas)
Profile: p.1683
Litigation **Band 2**
Table: p.1656

Hatcher, Julia
(District of Columbia)
Profile: p.447
Environment **Band 3**
Table: p.392

Hatfield, C Kent (Kentucky)
Profile: p.842
Environment **Band 2**
Table: p.832

Hathaway, Thomas MJ
(Michigan)
Profile: p.999
Employment **Band 3**
Table: p.991

Hatley, Joseph (Kansas)
Profile: p.823
Litigation **Band 2**
Table: p.819

Hatmaker, J Chadwick
(Tennessee)
Profile: p.1608

Hattersley III, Thomas
(Montana)
Profile: p.1080

Employment **Up & Coming**
Table: p.1073

Hauck, Terry (Oregon)
Profile: p.1482
Real Estate **Band 1**
Table: p.1479

Haughey, Stephen N (Ohio)
Profile: p.1441
Environment **Band 3**
Table: p.1425

Hauser III, Wade (Iowa)
Profile: p.813
Litigation **Band 3**
Table: p.807

Havel, Richard W
(California)
Profile: p.255
Bankruptcy **Band 3**
Table: p.191

Havlick, Scott (Colorado)
Profile: p.318
Intellectual Property **Band 2**
Table: p.309

Hawk, Barry E (New York)
Profile: p.1287
Antitrust **Band S**
Table: p.1170

Hawkins, Barry
(Connecticut)
Profile: p.337
Real Estate **Band 1**
Table: p.334

Hawkins, Holmes (Georgia)
Profile: p.614
Intellectual Property **Band 3**
Table: p.596

Hawkins, Michael (Ohio)
Profile: p.1442
Employment **Band 2**
Table: p.1422

Hawks, Christopher H.
(Wyoming)
Profile: p.1838
Real Estate **Band 2**
Table: p.1836

Hayden, Joe (New Jersey)
Profile: p.1140
Litigation **Band 1**
Table: p.1133

Hayden, Raymond P
(New York)
Profile: p.87
Shipping **Band 2**
Table: p.67

Hayden, William (Arizona)
Profile: p.159
Employment **Band 3**
Table: p.148

Hayes, David (California)
Profile: p.255
Intellectual Property **Band 3**
Table: p.216

Hayes, David
(District of Columbia)
Profile: p.447
Environment **Band 1**
Table: p.392

Hayes, James P (Iowa)
Profile: p.813
Litigation **Band 2**

Table: p.807

Hayes, Robert E
(South Dakota)
Profile: p.1593
Bankruptcy **Band 1**
Table: p.1587
Corporate/M&A **Band 1**
Table: p.1587
Real Estate **Band 2**
Table: p.1592

Hayes, Timothy G (Virginia)
Profile: p.1770
Environment **Band 1**
Table: p.1757

Hayes, William (Texas)
Profile: p.1683
Banking & Finance **Band 1**
Table: p.1625

Hayes, William (Ohio)
Profile: p.1442
Environment **Band 2**
Table: p.1425

Haygood, Paul (Louisiana)
Profile: p.872
Corporate/M&A **Band 2**
Table: p.859

Haynam, Douglas (Ohio)
Profile: p.1442
Environment **Band 2**
Table: p.1425

Haynes, Greg (Kentucky)
Profile: p.842
Litigation **Band 1**
Table: p.835

Haynes, John (Tennessee)
Profile: p.1608
Real Estate **Band 3**
Table: p.1603

Haynes, Joseph B (Georgia)
Profile: p.614
Litigation **Band 3**
Table: p.598

Haynor, Charles (Minnesota)
Profile: p.1018
Real Estate **Band 2**
Table: p.1014

Hazan, Scott L (New York)
Profile: p.1287
Bankruptcy **Band 3**
Table: p.1179

Hazlett, Mark (Hawaii)
Profile: p.648
Real Estate **Band 1**
Table: p.646

Hazlett, Richard (North
Carolina)
Profile: p.1396
Banking & Finance **Band 1**
Table: p.1381
Corporate/M&A **Band 3**
Table: p.1384

Head, J D (Texas)
Profile: p.1684
Environment **Band 3**
Table: p.1643

Headley, Linda (Texas)
Profile: p.1684
Employment **Band 2**
Table: p.1634

Healy, Kevin (New York)
Profile: p.1287
Environment **Band** 2
Table: p.1205

Healy, Martin
(Massachusetts)
Profile: p.968
Real Estate **Band** 1
Table: p.957

Heaphey, Christopher
(Alaska)
Profile: p.143
Real Estate **Band** 2
Table: p.141

Heard, Keith (New York)
Profile: p.87
Shipping **Band** 3
Table: p.67

Heard, Richard W
(Montana)
Profile: p.1080
Real Estate **Band** 2
Table: p.1078

Hearn, Curtis R (Louisiana)
Profile: p.872
Corporate/M&A **Band** 2
Table: p.859

Heath, Marc (Vermont)
Profile: p.1749
Litigation **Band** 3
Table: p.1746

Heaven Jr, Lewis (Kansas)
Profile: p.823
Real Estate **Band** 1
Table: p.821

Heckler, Douglas (Indiana)
Profile: p.792
Employment **Band** 3
Table: p.783

Hedican, Chris (Nebraska)
Profile: p.1088
Employment **Band** 1
Table: p.1084

Heeter, James (Missouri)
Profile: p.1057
Corporate/M&A **Band** 2
Table: p.1043

Heffernan, Barbara
(District of Columbia)
Profile: p.447
Energy **Band** 5
Table: p.382

Hefflinger, David (Nebraska)
Profile: p.1088
Corporate/M&A **Band** 1
Table: p.1082

Heftler, Thomas E (National)
Profile: p.87
Capital Markets **Band** 2
Table: p.16

Heidelberger, Brian L
(Illinois)
Profile: p.732
Media & Entertainment
Up and coming
Table: p.704

Heidt, Jeffrey L
(Massachusetts)
Profile: p.968
Healthcare **Band** 1
Table: p.946

Heihre, Michael (Hawaii)
Profile: p.648
Litigation **Band** 2
Table: p.644

Heim, Mike (Texas)
Profile: p.1684
Intellectual Property **Band** 3
Table: p.1651

Heim, Robert C
(Pennsylvania)
Profile: p.1526
Litigation **Band** 1
Table: p.1511

Heiman, David G (Ohio)
Profile: p.1442
Bankruptcy **Band** 1
Table: p.1414

Hein, Laura (Minnesota)
Profile: p.1018
Litigation **Band** 1
Table: p.1012

Heinke, Rex S (California)
Profile: p.256
Media & Entertainment **Band** 2
Table: p.230

Heintz, John
(District of Columbia)
Profile: p.447
Insurance **Band** 2
Table: p.402

Heinz, Von S (Nevada)
Profile: p.1102
Litigation **Band** 2
Table: p.1096

Heinzelman, Kris (National)
Profile: p.87
Capital Markets **Band** 1
Table: p.14

Heiss, Howard E (New York)
Profile: p.1287
Litigation **Band** 3
Table: p.1224

Heisse II, John R (California)
Profile: p.256
Construction **Band** 2
Table: p.194

Heist, Dale (Pennsylvania)
Profile: p.1526
Intellectual Property **Band** 2
Table: p.1508

Heitner, Kenneth H
(New York)
Profile: p.1287
Tax **Band** 2
Table: p.1255

Hejmanowski, Paul
(Nevada)
Profile: p.1102
Litigation **Band** 2
Table: p.1096

Held, Jerry (Alabama)
Profile: p.123
Real Estate **Band** 3
Table: p.119

Heleniak, David (New York)
Profile: p.1287
Corporate/M&A **Band** S
Table: p.1189

Helfand, Thomas (Texas)
Profile: p.1684
Tax **Band** 2
Table: p.1665

Heller, David (Illinois)
Profile: p.732
Bankruptcy **Band** 2
Table: p.669

Heller, Richard B (New York)
Profile: p.1287
Media & Entertainment **Band** 1
Table: p.1235

Heller, Ron (Hawaii)
Profile: p.648
Tax **Band** 1
Table: p.641

Heller, William J
(New Jersey)
Profile: p.1140
Litigation **Band** 1
Table: p.1133

Hellewell, Read (Utah)
Profile: p.1736
Real Estate **Band** 3
Table: p.1733

Hellow, John R (California)
Profile: p.256
Healthcare **Band** 1
Table: p.209

Helm, Robert W
(District of Columbia)
Profile: p.447
Investment Management
Band 1
Table: p.406

Helm III, Kennedy
(Kentucky)
Profile: p.842
Corporate/M&A **Band** 2
Table: p.827

Helman, Robert A (Illinois)
Profile: p.732
Corporate/M&A **Band** S
Table: p.675

Helmsing, Frederick
(Alabama)
Profile: p.123
Litigation **Band** 3
Table: p.116

Hemley, Robert (Vermont)
Profile: p.1749
Litigation **Band** 1
Table: p.1746

Hemminger, Pamela L
(California)
Profile: p.256
Employment **Band** 3
Table: p.202

Hemminger, Steven D
(California)
Profile: p.256
Intellectual Property **Band** 4
Table: p.216

Henderson, Douglas A
(Georgia)
Profile: p.614
Environment Up and coming
Table: p.593

Henderson, Richard (North
Dakota)
Profile: p.1410
Litigation **Band** 2

Table: p.1406

Henderson, Scott K
(Ontario)
Profile: p.159
Real Estate **Band** 4
Table: p.154

Henderson, Thomas
(Florida)
Profile: p.542
Real Estate **Band** 2
Table: p.526

Henderson Jr, Donald B
(New York)
Profile: p.1287
Insurance **Band** 2
Table: p.1213

Hendler, Clifford B
(District of Columbia)
Profile: p.447
Insurance **Band** 3
Table: p.400

Hendrick Esq, David R
(Georgia)
Profile: p.614
Construction **Band** 1
Table: p.584

Hendricks Jr, Ed (Arizona)
Profile: p.159
Litigation **Band** 3
Table: p.152

Hendrickson, David
(West Virginia)
Profile: p.1809
Litigation **Band** 2
Table: p.1803

Henegan, John (Mississippi)
Profile: p.1034
Litigation **Band** 2
Table: p.1028
Litigation **Band** 2
Table: p.1028

Hengen, Nancy (New York)
Profile: p.87
Shipping **Band** 1
Table: p.67

Henlein, Carl (Kentucky)
Profile: p.842
Litigation **Band** 2
Table: p.835

Henneburg, Frank H
(District of Columbia)
Profile: p.447
Real Estate **Band** 3
Table: p.418

Hennessey, Gilbert
(Massachusetts)
Profile: p.968
Intellectual Property **Band** 2
Table: p.948

Henney, Raymond
(Michigan)
Profile: p.999
Litigation **Band** 3
Table: p.994

Hennigan, Brian J
(California)
Profile: p.256
Litigation **Band** 1
Table: p.225

Hennigan, J Michael
(California)
Profile: p.256
Litigation **Band** 2
Table: p.224

Henning, Mark G (Illinois)
Profile: p.732
Real Estate **Band** 4
Table: p.706

Henry, Roxann E
(District of Columbia)
Profile: p.447
Antitrust **Band** 5
Table: p.367

Hensel, Donald (Georgia)
Profile: p.614
Tax **Band** 4
Table: p.603

Hensler, David
(District of Columbia)
Profile: p.447
Insurance **Band** 3
Table: p.400
Litigation **Band** 1
Table: p.410

Hensley Jr, Harold (Texas)
Profile: p.1163

Henze, Tom (Arizona)
Profile: p.159
Litigation **Band** 1
Table: p.153

Henze II, William F
(New York)
Profile: p.1287
Energy **Band** 2
Table: p.1202

Herald, J Patrick (Illinois)
Profile: p.732
Litigation **Band** 4
Table: p.700

Herbert, John (New York)
Profile: p.1287
Private Equity **Band** 3
Table: p.1237

Herdzina, John W
(Nebraska)
Profile: p.1088
Corporate/M&A **Band** 3
Table: p.1082

Herf, Charles (Arizona)
Profile: p.159
Employment **Band** 3
Table: p.148

Hering, Louis G (Delaware)
Profile: p.353
Corporate/M&A **Band** 3
Table: p.346

Heringer, Michael
(Montana)
Profile: p.1080
Employment **Band** 2
Table: p.1073

Herlihy, Edward D
(New York)
Profile: p.1287
Corporate/M&A **Band** 1
Table: p.1189

Herling, Michael J
(Connecticut)
Profile: p.337
Corporate/M&A **Band** 2

H

Table: p.327

Herman, John (Minnesota)
Profile: p.1018
Real Estate Band 1
Table: p.1015

Herman, Philip
(Massachusetts)
Profile: p.968
Banking & Finance Band 3
Table: p.932

Herman, Russ M (Louisiana)
Profile: p.872
Litigation Band 2
Table: p.865

Herman, Sarah Andrews
(North Dakota)
Profile: p.1410
Employment Band 1
Table: p.1405

Hermes, John N (Oklahoma)
Profile: p.1465
Litigation Band 1
Table: p.1462

Hermes, Robert N (Illinois)
Profile: p.732
Insurance Band 3
Table: p.694

Hermle, Lynne (California)
Profile: p.256
Employment Band 2
Table: p.202

Hernandez, Gary A
(California)
Profile: p.256
Insurance Band 3
Table: p.212

Hernandez, Jennifer
(California)
Profile: p.257
Environment Band 2
Table: p.207

Herr, David (Minnesota)
Profile: p.1018
Litigation Band 1
Table: p.1012

Herr, Robert (California)
Profile: p.257
Real Estate Band 3
Table: p.238

Herrington, Daniel
(Arkansas)
Profile: p.176
Employment Up and coming
Table: p.170

Hersch, Dennis S
(New York)
Profile: p.1288
Corporate/M&A Band 1
Table: p.1189
Media & Entertainment Band 1
Table: p.1235

Heryford, Craig
(Pennsylvania)
Profile: p.1526
Banking & Finance Band 2
Table: p.1493

Herzberg, Esq, Peter J
(New Jersey)
Profile: p.1141
Environment Band 2
Table: p.1129

Herzog, David K (Indiana)
Profile: p.792
Litigation Band 3
Table: p.785

Hess, Adam R (Virginia)
Profile: p.1770
Intellectual Property Band 2
Table: p.1759

Hession, John
(Massachusetts)
Profile: p.968
Private Equity Band 2
Table: p.953

Hester, Tracy (Texas)
Profile: p.1684
Environment Band 2
Table: p.1643

Heston, Mary Jo
(Washington)
Profile: p.1792
Bankruptcy Band 2
Table: p.1776

Heusel, Cornelius
(Louisiana)
Profile: p.872
Employment Band 3
Table: p.861

Hewey, Melissa (Maine)
Profile: p.898
Employment Band 3
Table: p.890

Hewitt, Henry (Oregon)
Profile: p.1482
Corporate/M&A Band S
Table: p.1471

Hewitt, Lester (Texas)
Profile: p.1684
Intellectual Property Band 2
Table: p.1651

Hewitt, William J (New York)
Profile: p.1288
Private Equity Band 2
Table: p.1241

Heyman, Kurt M (Delaware)
Profile: p.354
Chancery Band 4
Table: p.344

Heyman, Robert
(New Mexico)
Profile: p.1163
Corporate/M&A Band 2
Table: p.1155

Heywood, Thomas
(West Virginia)
Profile: p.1809
Corporate/M&A Band 1
Table: p.1798

Hibbs, Carol (Oregon)
Profile: p.1482
Corporate/M&A Band 3
Table: p.1471

Hickey, Michael
(South Dakota)
Profile: p.1593
Litigation Band 2
Table: p.1590

Hickey, Nicole Vickroy
(Ohio)
Profile: p.1442
Intellectual Property Band 3
Table: p.1428

Hickey, Paul (Wyoming)
Profile: p.1838
Litigation Band 2
Table: p.1835

Hickey Jr, John T (Illinois)
Profile: p.732
Litigation Band 3
Table: p.700

Hickok, Arthur (National)
Profile: p.87
Capital Markets
Up and coming
Table: p.19

Hickok, Robert L
(Pennsylvania)
Profile: p.1526
Litigation Band 3
Table: p.1511

Hicks, Alvin J (Nevada)
Profile: p.1102
Gaming & Licensing Band 2
Table: p.1094

Hicks, John (Tennessee)
Profile: p.1608
Litigation Band 3
Table: p.1599

Hicks, Patrick H (Nevada)
Profile: p.1102
Employment Band 3
Table: p.1091

Hicks, Robert J (Indiana)
Profile: p.792
Corporate/M&A Band 2
Table: p.781

Higer, Dale G (Idaho)
Profile: p.660
Real Estate Band S
Table: p.658

Higgins, Daniel B.
(California)
Profile: p.257
Healthcare Band 2
Table: p.209

Higgins, David K
(West Virginia)
Profile: p.1809
Corporate/M&A Band 3
Table: p.1798

Higgins, James E
(New Hampshire)
Profile: p.1117
Litigation Band 2
Table: p.1111

Higgins, Keith
(Massachusetts)
Profile: p.968
Corporate/M&A Band 1
Table: p.937

Higgins, Roger (Texas)
Profile: p.1684
Insurance Band 2
Table: p.1648

Higgins Jr, James R
(Kentucky)
Profile: p.842
Litigation Band 1
Table: p.835

High, Michael E (Maine)
Profile: p.898
Corporate/M&A Band 1
Table: p.888

High Jr, Charles (Texas)
Profile: p.1684
Employment Band 2
Table: p.1634

Hilgers, David W (Texas)
Profile: p.1684
Healthcare Band 2
Table: p.1646

Hill, Donald (Kansas)
Profile: p.824
Employment Band 3
Table: p.818

Hill, Douglas P
(New Hampshire)
Profile: p.1117
Real Estate Band 2
Table: p.1114

Hill, Earl (Nevada)
Profile: p.1102
Environment Band 2
Table: p.1093

Hill, Frank (Oklahoma)
Profile: p.1465
Real Estate Band 1
Table: p.1464

Hill, Henry (New Jersey)
Profile: p.1141
Real Estate Band 2
Table: p.1135

Hill, J Reginald (Tennessee)
Profile: p.1608
Corporate/M&A Band 2
Table: p.1594

Hill, James (North Dakota)
Profile: p.1410
Litigation Band 1
Table: p.1406

Hill, Richard (Washington)
Profile: p.1792
Real Estate Band 2
Table: p.1789

Hill, Robert F (Colorado)
Profile: p.319
Antitrust Band 1
Table: p.311
Litigation Band 1
Table: p.311

Hill, Thomas (Ohio)
Profile: p.1442
Litigation Band 3
Table: p.1431

Hill III, Benjamin (Florida)
Profile: p.542
Litigation Band 1
Table: p.521

Hill Jr, B Harvey (Georgia)
Profile: p.614
Banking & Finance Band 2
Table: p.580

Hill Noto, Margaret
(Oregon)
Profile: p.1482
Corporate/M&A Band 2
Table: p.1471

Hillenbrand, Hyman
(National)
Profile: p.87
Shipping Band 1
Table: p.71
Transport Band 3
Table: p.62

Transport Band 2
Table: p.64

Hiller, David P (Ohio)
Profile: p.1442
Employment Band 3
Table: p.1422

Hilliard, David (Illinois)
Profile: p.732
Intellectual Property Band 2
Table: p.696

Hilliard, Michael (Texas)
Profile: p.1684
Banking & Finance Band 3
Table: p.1625

Hilliard, Russell
(New Hampshire)
Profile: p.1117
Litigation Band 1
Table: p.1111

Hillman, Robert
(Massachusetts)
Profile: p.968
Intellectual Property Band 1
Table: p.948

Hilmes, Jack (Iowa)
Profile: p.813
Litigation Band 3
Table: p.807

Hilson, John (California)
Profile: p.257
Banking & Finance Band 1
Table: p.187

Hilton, Paul (Colorado)
Profile: p.319
Corporate/M&A Band 1
Table: p.303

Hilyard, Chad S (Colorado)
Profile: p.319
Intellectual Property Band 2
Table: p.309

Himeles, Martin (Maryland)
Profile: p.921
Litigation Band 2
Table: p.914

Himmel, Michael B (New
Jersey)
Profile: p.1141
Litigation Band 1
Table: p.1133

Hinchey, John (Georgia)
Profile: p.614
Construction Band 1
Table: p.584

Hinderks, Mark (Kansas)
Profile: p.824
Litigation Band 1
Table: p.819

Hinerman, Philip L
(Pennsylvania)
Profile: p.1527
Environment Band 4
Table: p.1505

Hines, Barry A (Kentucky)
Profile: p.842
Real Estate Band 2
Table: p.838

Hingle, Charles (Montana)
Profile: p.1080
Corporate/M&A Band 2
Table: p.1072

H

Litigation Band 3
Table: p.1075

Hink, John (Arizona)
Profile: p.159
Real Estate Band 4
Table: p.154

Hinkle IV, Samuel
(Kentucky)
Profile: p.843
Litigation Band 2
Table: p.835

Hinkley, Gerry (California)
Profile: p.257
Healthcare Band 2
Table: p.209

Hinman Jr, William
(California)
Profile: p.87
Capital Markets Band 1
Table: p.23

Hinson, Robin L
(North Carolina)
Profile: p.1396
Corporate/M&A Band 2
Table: p.1384

Hintze, John (Iowa)
Profile: p.813
Corporate/M&A Band 4
Table: p.802

Hipp, Ken (Hawaii)
Profile: p.648
Employment Band 1
Table: p.642

Hirsch, Barry (California)
Profile: p.257
Media & Entertainment Band 2
Table: p.233

Hirsch, Jeffrey L
(Massachusetts)
Profile: p.968
Employment Band 3
Table: p.940

Hirsch, Reece (California)
Profile: p.257
Healthcare Up and coming
Table: p.209

Hirsch, Stephen (Arizona)
Profile: p.159
Real Estate Band 2
Table: p.155

Hirschberg, William E
(New York)
Profile: p.1288
Banking & Finance Band 1
Table: p.1174

Hirschfeld, Michael (Ohio)
Profile: p.1442
Corporate/M&A Band 3
Table: p.1419

Hirschman, John (Indiana)
Profile: p.792
Real Estate Up and coming
Table: p.788

Hise, Daniel G (Mississippi)
Profile: p.1034
Corporate/M&A Band 1
Table: p.1024
Gaming & Licensing Band 1
Table: p.1024

Hisert, George A (California)
Profile: p.257
Banking & Finance Band 2
Table: p.187

Hishon, Robert H (Georgia)
Profile: p.614
Tax Band 4
Table: p.603

Hite, Richard (Kansas)
Profile: p.824
Litigation Band 1
Table: p.819

Hitselberger, Carol A
(Illinois)
Profile: p.87
Capital Markets Band 1
Table: p.21

Hitt, Jeffrey (Texas)
Profile: p.1684
Corporate/M&A Band 4
Table: p.1631

Hixon III, Samuel W
(Virginia)
Profile: p.1770
Litigation Band 2
Table: p.1763

Hluchan, Richard M
(New Jersey)
Profile: p.1141
Environment Band 1
Table: p.1129

Hobbins, Robert
(Minnesota)
Profile: p.1018
Employment Band 1
Table: p.1008

Hobbs, James R (Missouri)
Profile: p.1057
Litigation Band 1
Table: p.1049

Hobby, Scott M (National)
Profile: p.87
Business Process
Outsourcing: National Band 3
Table: p.10

Hobel, Lawrence (California)
Profile: p.257
Insurance Band 2
Table: p.212

Hoberg, Timothy E (Ohio)
Profile: p.1442
Corporate/M&A Band 2
Table: p.1419

Hochberg, Jeffrey D
(New York)
Profile: p.1288
Tax Up and coming
Table: p.1256

Hochberg, Kevin J (Illinois)
Profile: p.88
Capital Markets Band 2
Table: p.21

Hochberg, Sheldon
(National)
Profile: p.88
International Trade Band 4
Table: p.40

Hockett, Christopher
(California)
Profile: p.257
Antitrust Band 2

Table: p.184

Hodara, Fred S (New York)
Profile: p.1288
Bankruptcy Band 3
Table: p.1179

Hodes, Scott (Illinois)
Profile: p.732
Media & Entertainment Band 1
Table: p.704

Hodess, Ronald E
(Michigan)
Profile: p.999
Real Estate Band 3
Table: p.996

Hodge, Katherine D
(Illinois)
Profile: p.732
Environment Band 4
Table: p.687

Hodge Jr, E Clifton
(Mississippi)
Profile: p.1034
Corporate/M&A Band 2
Table: p.1024
Litigation Band 2
Table: p.1028

Hodges, Charles (Georgia)
Profile: p.614
Tax Up and coming
Table: p.603

Hodges Taylor, Laura
(Massachusetts)
Profile: p.968
Private Equity Band 2
Table: p.953

Hodgson Jr, Clark C
(Pennsylvania)
Profile: p.1527
Litigation Band 3
Table: p.1511

Hodson, Jerry B. (Oregon)
Profile: p.1482
Litigation Band 3
Table: p.1477

Hoeflich, Adam (Illinois)
Profile: p.733
Litigation Band 4
Table: p.700

Hofer, Roy (Illinois)
Profile: p.733
Intellectual Property Band 1
Table: p.696

Hoffar, Julian (Virginia)
Profile: p.1770
Construction Band 1
Table: p.1750

Hoffman, Daniel (Colorado)
Profile: p.319
Litigation Band S
Table: p.311

Hoffman, Jerome (Florida)
Profile: p.542
Antitrust Band 2
Table: p.498

Hoffman, Mark F
(Washington)
Profile: p.1792
Corporate/M&A Band 3
Table: p.1778

Hoffman, Robert J
(Missouri)
Profile: p.1057
Litigation Band 3
Table: p.1049

Hoffman, William (National)
Profile: p.88
International Trade Band 1
Table: p.41

Hoffmann, Christian
(Arizona)
Profile: p.159
Corporate/M&A Band 3
Table: p.146

Hoffmann, Warren
(Kentucky)
Profile: p.843
Environment Band 3
Table: p.832

Hofstetter, Richard
(New York)
Profile: p.1288
Media & Entertainment Band 2
Table: p.1235

Hogan, Edward (New Jersey)
Profile: p.1141
Environment Band 2
Table: p.1129

Hogan, John M (Florida)
Profile: p.542
Litigation Band 1
Table: p.522

Hogan, Patricia B (Ohio)
Profile: p.1442
Intellectual Property Band 3
Table: p.1428

Hogan III, Dennis P
(Nebraska)
Profile: p.1088
Real Estate Band 1
Table: p.1086

Hogfoss, Robert (Georgia)
Profile: p.614
Environment Band 2
Table: p.593

Hogue Jr, P Mason (South
Carolina)
Profile: p.1581
Corporate/M&A Band 2
Table: p.1572

Hokanson, Jeffrey (Indiana)
Profile: p.792
Litigation Band 3
Table: p.785

Holbreich, Curt (National)
Profile: p.88
Sport Band 2
Table: p.55

Holcomb, James M (Iowa)
Profile: p.813
Real Estate Band 2
Table: p.810

Holcomb, Mark E (Florida)
Profile: p.542
Tax Band 2
Table: p.531

Holden Jr, Frederick D
(California)
Profile: p.257
Bankruptcy Band 4
Table: p.191

Holder, Eric
(District of Columbia)
Profile: p.447
Litigation Band 3
Table: p.410

Holewinski, Kevin
(District of Columbia)
Profile: p.447
Environment Band 4
Table: p.392

Holifield, Marilyn (Florida)
Profile: p.542
Employment Band 4
Table: p.513

Holland, Mark (New York)
Profile: p.1288
Litigation Band 3
Table: p.1223

Holliday, Thomas E
(California)
Profile: p.257
Litigation Band 1
Table: p.225

Hollister, Timothy S
(Connecticut)
Profile: p.337
Real Estate Band 2
Table: p.334

Holloman Jr, James H
(Oklahoma)
Profile: p.1465
Tax Band 1
Table: p.1459

Hollyfield, John S (Texas)
Profile: p.1684
Real Estate Band 3
Table: p.1662

Holm, Kristi Geisler
(South Dakota)
Profile: p.1593
Employment Band 2
Table: p.1589

Holman, Michael (Ohio)
Profile: p.1442
Construction Band 2
Table: p.1417

Holmes, Ervin (Utah)
Profile: p.1736
Real Estate Band 3
Table: p.1733

Holmes, Jacqueline M
(District of Columbia)
Profile: p.447
Employment Up and coming
Table: p.380

Holmes, Robert (Colorado)
Profile: p.319
Real Estate Band 3
Table: p.313

Holmes, Whitney (Colorado)
Profile: p.319
Corporate/M&A Band 2
Table: p.303

Holscher, Mark (California)
Profile: p.257
Litigation Band 2
Table: p.225

Holshouser, Eric (Florida)
Profile: p.542
Employment Band 2
Table: p.513

h

Holt, Scott (Delaware)
Profile: p.354
Employment **Up and coming**
Table: p.347

Holt III, Berry (Tennessee)
Profile: p.1608
Corporate/M&A **Band 3**
Table: p.1594

Homburger, Thomas C
(Illinois)
Profile: p.733
Real Estate **Band 3**
Table: p.706

Honan III, William J
(New York)
Profile: p.88
Shipping **Band 2**
Table: p.67

Honeyman, Richard
(Kansas)
Profile: p.824
Litigation **Band 2**
Table: p.819

Hong, Ji Hoon (National)
Profile: p.88
Aviation **Band 1**
Table: p.58

Hood, James
(New Hampshire)
Profile: p.1117
Corporate/M&A **Band 2**
Table: p.1107

Hood, Thomas R (New York)
Profile: p.1288
Tax **Band 2**
Table: p.1256

Hood, Vicki V (Illinois)
Profile: p.733
Employee Benefits **Band 2**
Table: p.681

Hooker, David J (Ohio)
Profile: p.1442
Litigation **Band 2**
Table: p.1431

Hooper, Chester D
(New York)
Profile: p.88
Shipping **Band 2**
Table: p.67

Hooper, Patric (California)
Profile: p.257
Healthcare **Band 1**
Table: p.209

Hooper, Samuel E (Texas)
Profile: p.1684
Employment **Band 3**
Table: p.1634

Hope, Stephen D
(North Carolina)
Profile: p.1396
Corporate/M&A **Band 3**
Table: p.1384

Hopkins, Edward J (Florida)
Profile: p.542
Healthcare **Band 1**
Table: p.518

Hopkinson, R Ronald
(New York)
Profile: p.1288
Private Equity **Band 3**
Table: p.1237

Hopping, Wade (Florida)
Profile: p.542
Environment **Band S**
Table: p.516
Real Estate **Band S**
Table: p.528

Hopson, Edwin (Kentucky)
Profile: p.843
Employment **Band 1**
Table: p.830

Hopson, Keith (Texas)
Profile: p.1684
Environment **Band 3**
Table: p.1643

Horan, Richard (Virginia)
Profile: p.1770
Corporate/M&A **Band 3**
Table: p.1752

Horder, Richard (Georgia)
Profile: p.614
Environment **Band 1**
Table: p.593

Horkovich, Robert M
(New York)
Profile: p.1288
Insurance **Band 3**
Table: p.1213

Horlick, Gary N (National)
Profile: p.88
International Trade **Band 1**
Table: p.40

Hornak, Mark (Pennsylvania)
Profile: p.1527
Employment **Band 2**
Table: p.1500

Hornick, Robert (National)
Profile: p.88
Arbitration **Band 3**
Table: p.33

Hornreich, Michael (Florida)
Profile: p.542
Construction **Band 1**
Table: p.507

Horoschak, Mark J
(North Carolina)
Profile: p.1396
Antitrust **Band 1**
Table: p.1390

Horowitz, Mitchell (Florida)
Profile: p.542
Tax **Band 3**
Table: p.531

Horowitz, Philip
(District of Columbia)
Profile: p.448
Real Estate **Band 3**
Table: p.418

Horowitz, Richard M
(National)
Profile: p.88
Capital Markets **Band 4**
Table: p.19

Horowitz, Steven G
(New York)
Profile: p.1288
Real Estate **Band 3**
Table: p.1248

Horsch, Richard (New York)
Profile: p.1288
Environment **Band 3**
Table: p.1206

Horstmann, John F
(Pennsylvania)
Profile: p.1527
Bankruptcy **Band 2**
Table: p.1494

Horwitz, Richard L
(Delaware)
Profile: p.354
Intellectual Property **Band 3**
Table: p.348

Houghton, Robert (Iowa)
Profile: p.813
Litigation **Band 2**
Table: p.807

House, George W
(North Carolina)
Profile: p.1396
Environment **Band 2**
Table: p.1388

House, Michael (National)
Profile: p.88
International Trade **Band 4**
Table: p.40

Houser, Douglas (Oregon)
Profile: p.1483
Litigation **Band 1**
Table: p.1477

Hovious, R Gregg
(Kentucky)
Profile: p.843
Litigation **Band 3**
Table: p.835

Hovis, James W
(North Carolina)
Profile: p.1396
Banking & Finance **Band 1**
Table: p.1381

Howard, David M
(Pennsylvania)
Profile: p.1527
Litigation **Band 2**
Table: p.1512

Howard, Douglas D
(Montana)
Profile: p.1080
Real Estate **Band 2**
Table: p.1078

Howard, Linda Edell
(Tennessee)
Profile: p.1608
Media & Entertainment **Band 1**
Table: p.1602

Howard, Lindsay
(Pennsylvania)
Profile: p.1527
Environment **Band 4**
Table: p.1505

Howard, Nigel (New York)
Profile: p. 1288
Business Process
Outsourcing: National **Band 3**
Table: p.10
Technology **Band 3**
Table: p.1259

Howard, Theodore A
(District of Columbia)
Profile: p.448
Insurance **Band 3**
Table: p.400

Howard Jr, George S
(California)
Profile: p.257
Employment **Band 3**
Table: p.202

Howard, Jr, John L (Texas)
Profile: p.1684
Environment **Band 4**
Table: p.1643

Howe Jr, Gedney M
(South Carolina)
Profile: p.1581
Litigation **Band 2**
Table: p.1576

Howell, Geoffrey A
(Massachusetts)
Profile: p.968
Real Estate **Up and coming**
Table: p.956

Howell, John E (Texas)
Profile: p. 1684
Business Process
Outsourcing: National **Band 1**
Table: p.10
Technology **Band 1**
Table: p.1668

Howitt, John P (National)
Profile: p.88
Aviation **Band 3**
Table: p.58

Howlett, Timothy (Michigan)
Profile: p.999
Employment **Band 2**
Table: p.991

Hoye, Maria P (California)
Profile: p.258
Environment **Band 3**
Table: p.207

Hoyt, Scott (Texas)
Profile: p.1684
Insurance **Band 3**
Table: p.1648

Hubbard, Paul
(North Dakota)
Profile: p.1410
Real Estate **Band 1**
Table: p.1409

Huber, John
(District of Columbia)
Profile: p.448
Corporate/Commercial **Band 1**
Table: p.376

Huber, Karen A. (Maine)
Profile: p.898
Real Estate **Band 3**
Table: p.895

Huck, L Francis (New York)
Profile: p.1289
Banking & Finance **Band 1**
Table: p.1174

Huck, Robert (Nebraska)
Profile: p.1088
Real Estate **Band 2**
Table: p.1086
Real Estate **Band 2**
Table: p.1086

Hudanish, David (New York)
Profile: p. 1289
Business Process
Outsourcing: National **Band 2**
Table: p.10
Technology **Band 2**

Table: p.1259

Huddleston, Michael
(Texas)
Profile: p.1685
Insurance **Band 1**
Table: p.1648

Hudson, Paul (Georgia)
Profile: p.615
Corporate/M&A **Band 4**
Table: p.587
Healthcare **Band 2**
Table: p.594

Hudson, Robert (Florida)
Profile: p.542
Tax **Band 1**
Table: p.531

Huebner, Marshall S
(New York)
Profile: p.1289
Bankruptcy **Band 3**
Table: p.1179

Huffman, Fordham (Ohio)
Profile: p.1442
Litigation **Band 3**
Table: p.1431

Huffman, Gregory (Texas)
Profile: p.1685
Antitrust **Band 3**
Table: p.1622

Hugg, Joseph A
(Massachusetts)
Profile: p.968
Tax **Band 1**
Table: p.959

Hughes, Christopher
(New York)
Profile: p.1289
Intellectual Property **Band 3**
Table: p.1217

Hughes, Frank J (California)
Profile: p.258
Construction **Band 3**
Table: p.194

Hughes, Randall (Georgia)
Profile: p.615
Healthcare **Band 1**
Table: p.594

Hughes III, Hunter R
(Georgia)
Profile: p.615
Employment **Band 1**
Table: p.589

Hughes Jr, William H
(Georgia)
Profile: p.615
Construction **Band 2**
Table: p.584

Hughey, Roger (Kansas)
Profile: p.824
Real Estate **Band 3**
Table: p.821

Hughey Jr, James F
(Alabama)
Profile: p.123
Corporate/M&A **Band 1**
Table: p.111

Hugi, Robert F (Illinois)
Profile: p.89
Capital Markets ✪
Table: p.21

Hull, Robert J (Texas)
Profile: p.1685
Tax Band 4
Table: p.1665

Hull Jr, Gerald (New Jersey)
Profile: p.1141
Real Estate Band 1
Table: p.1134

Humes, Gary
(District of Columbia)
Profile: p.448
Real Estate Band 2
Table: p.418

Humke, Steven (Indiana)
Profile: p.792
Corporate/M&A Band 1
Table: p.781

Humphrey, Andrew
(Minnesota)
Profile: p.1018
Corporate/M&A Band 2
Table: p.1005

Humphrey, Lawton
(Washington)
Profile: p.1792
Employment Band 3
Table: p.1780

Humphreys, Hunter
(Tennessee)
Profile: p.1608
Real Estate Band 2
Table: p.1603

Humphreys, Ivan (California)
Profile: p.258
Tax Band 2
Table: p.241

Hunt, Gordon (California)
Profile: p.258
Construction Band 3
Table: p.194

Hunt, James L (California)
Profile: p.258
Antitrust Band 3
Table: p.184

Hunt, Jeffrey (Missouri)
Profile: p.1057
Litigation Band 3
Table: p.1049

Hunt, Jeffrey (Utah)
Profile: p.1737
Litigation Up and coming
Table: p.1732

Hunt, Paul
(District of Columbia)
Profile: p.448
Projects Up and coming
Table: p.415

Hunt, William S (Hawaii)
Profile: p.648
Litigation Band 3
Table: p.644

Hunter, Jerry (Missouri)
Profile: p.1058
Employment Band 2
Table: p.1046

Hunter, Jonathon
(Louisiana)
Profile: p.873
Energy Band 1
Table: p.863

Hunter, Robert (Missouri)
Profile: p.1058
Corporate/M&A Band 2
Table: p.1043

Huntrods, Ann (Minnesota)
Profile: p.1018
Employment Band 1
Table: p.1008

Hupfer, Kyle J (Indiana)
Profile: p.792
Corporate/M&A
Up and coming
Table: p.781

Hurley, Cynthia A (Iowa)
Profile: p.813
Real Estate Up and coming
Table: p.810

Hurley, Patrick W (New Mexico)
Profile: p.1163
Real Estate Band 1
Table: p.1161

Hurley, Timothy J (Ohio)
Profile: p.1442
Bankruptcy Band 3
Table: p.1414

Hurney Jr, Thomas J
(West Virginia)
Profile: p.1809
Litigation Band 2
Table: p.1803

Husband, John (Colorado)
Profile: p.319
Employment Band 1
Table: p.306

Husid, Douglas M
(Massachusetts)
Profile: p.969
Real Estate Band 1
Table: p.957

Hutcheon, Peter (New Jersey)
Profile: p.1141
Corporate/M&A Band 3
Table: p.1123

Hutcheson, Mark A
(Washington)
Profile: p.1792
Employment Band 1
Table: p.1780

Hutchings, Stephen H
(Alaska)
Profile: p.143
Litigation Band 1
Table: p.138
Litigation Band 3
Table: p.138

Hutchings Reed, Mary
(Illinois)
Profile: p.733
Media & Entertainment Band 1
Table: p.704

Hutchinson Jr, Joseph
(Ohio)
Profile: p.1442
Bankruptcy Band 4
Table: p.1414

Hutson, Benne C (North Carolina)
Profile: p.1396
Environment Band 2
Table: p.1388

Hutt, Peter Barton
(District of Columbia)
Profile: p.448
Healthcare Band 1
Table: p.398

Hutz, Rudolf E (Delaware)
Profile: p.354
Intellectual Property Band 2
Table: p.348

Hyatt, William (New Jersey)
Profile: p.1141
Environment Band 1
Table: p.1129

Hyde, Kevin E (Florida)
Profile: p.543
Employment Band 2
Table: p.513

Hyde, Robert C (Utah)
Profile: p.1737
Real Estate Band 2
Table: p.1733

Hyde, Terrill
(District of Columbia)
Profile: p.448
Tax Band 4
Table: p.422

Hylton, Hartwell (New York)
Profile: p.1289
Banking & Finance Band 3
Table: p.1174

Hyman, Alan (New York)
Profile: p.1290
Bankruptcy Band 3
Table: p.1179

Hyman, Milt (California)
Profile: p.258
Tax Band 1
Table: p.241

Hyne, Ernest E (Tennessee)
Profile: p.1608
Corporate/M&A Band 2
Table: p.1594

Icard, Thomas (Florida)
Profile: p.543
Construction Band 3
Table: p.507

Ichel, David (New York)
Profile: p.1290
Litigation Band 3
Table: p.1223

Ihrig, Richard (Minnesota)
Profile: p.1018
Litigation Band 3
Table: p.1011

Ilvedson, Duane
(North Dakota)
Profile: p.1410
Litigation Band 2
Table: p.1406

Immelt, Stephen (Maryland)
Profile: p.921
Litigation Band 2
Table: p.914

Imperato, Gabriel L
(Florida)
Profile: p.543
Healthcare Band 1
Table: p.518

Imse, Peter
(New Hampshire)
Profile: p.1117
Real Estate Band 1
Table: p.1114

Imus, Neil W
(District of Columbia)
Profile: p.448
Antitrust Band 5
Table: p.367

Indoe, William F (New York)
Profile: p.1290
Tax Band 4
Table: p.1255

Ing, J Douglas (Hawaii)
Profile: p.648
Land Use Band 1
Table: p.643

Ingersoll, Josy W (Delaware)
Profile: p.354
Intellectual Property Band 4
Table: p.348

Ingersoll, Richard K
(Hawaii)
Profile: p.648
Corporate/M&A Band 2
Table: p.641
Tax Band 1
Table: p.641

Inglima, Thomas (Virginia)
Profile: p.1770
Corporate/M&A Band 4
Table: p.1752

Ingram, Fredric (Alabama)
Profile: p.123
Employment Band 2
Table: p.113

Ingram Jr, Lindsey W
(Kentucky)
Profile: p.843
Environment Band 3
Table: p.832

Insolia, Robert (New York)
Profile: p.1290
Private Equity Band 3
Table: p.1241

Intihar, Steve (Ohio)
Profile: p.1442
Real Estate Band 4
Table: p.1434

Inveiss, Roberts E (Indiana)
Profile: p.792
Corporate/M&A Band 3
Table: p.781

Ippolito, Peter J (California)
Profile: p.258
Construction Band 2
Table: p.194

Irby, Peyton (Mississippi)
Profile: p.1034
Employment Band 3
Table: p.1026

Iredale, Nancy L (California)
Profile: p.258
Tax Band 3
Table: p.241

Ireland, D Jeffrey (Ohio)
Profile: p.1442
Litigation Band 4
Table: p.1431

Irmscher, David (Indiana)
Profile: p.792
Litigation Band 2
Table: p.785

Irvin, Michael P (Texas)
Profile: p.1685
Energy Band 4
Table: p.1637

Irwin, Kevin (Ohio)
Profile: p.1443
Bankruptcy Band 3
Table: p.1414

Isaacson, Andrew
(Maryland)
Profile: p.922
Real Estate Band 4
Table: p.917

Isaacson, Laurence B
(National)
Profile: p.89
Capital Markets Band 2
Table: p.19

Isaacson, William (National)
Profile: p.89
Arbitration Band 4
Table: p.33

Isackson, Robert M
(New York)
Profile: p.1290
Intellectual Property Band 3
Table: p.1217

Isaia, Russell
(Massachusetts)
Profile: p.969
Tax Band 1
Table: p.959

Iseman, Robert H
(New York)
Profile: p.1290
Healthcare Band 3
Table: p.1209

Ishikawa, Jesse S
(Wisconsin)
Profile: p.1825
Real Estate Band 2
Table: p.1822

Isicoff, Laurel M (Florida)
Profile: p.543
Bankruptcy Band 2
Table: p.503

Isken, Donald N (Delaware)
Profile: p.354
Real Estate Band 2
Table: p.350

Iskra, Eric W (West Virginia)
Profile: p.1809
Employment Band 2
Table: p.1801

Isler, Edward (Virginia)
Profile: p.1770
Employment Band 2
Table: p.1755

Isom, Chervis (Alabama)
Profile: p.123
Real Estate Band 2
Table: p.119

I

Ison, Eric (Kentucky)
Profile: p.843
Litigation **Band** 3
Table: p.835

Israel, Allen (Washington)
Profile: p.1792
Corporate/M&A **Band** 2
Table: p.1778

Israel, Sharon (Texas)
Profile: p.1685
Intellectual Property **Band** 3
Table: p.1651

Ivanhoe, Robert (New York)
Profile: p.1290
Real Estate **Band** 5
Table: p.1248

Ivester, Eric (Illinois)
Profile: p.733
Bankruptcy **Band** 3
Table: p.669

Iwamoto, Raymond S
(Hawaii)
Profile: p.648
Real Estate **Band** 2
Table: p.646

J

Jack, Andrew
(District of Columbia)
Profile: p.448
Corporate/Commercial **Band** 3
Table: p.376

Jack Jr, Donald (Arkansas)
Profile: p.176
Corporate/M&A **Band** 2
Table: p.168

Jackoway, James R
(California)
Profile: p.258
Media & Entertainment **Band** 2
Table: p.233

Jackson, Charles C (Illinois)
Profile: p.733
Employment **Band** 2
Table: p.681

Jackson, Reginald W (Ohio)
Profile: p.1443
Bankruptcy **Band** 3
Table: p.1414

Jackson, Thomas C
(District of Columbia)
Profile: p.448
Environment **Band** 4
Table: p.392

Jackson, William Stuart
(Arkansas)
Profile: p.176
Employment **Up and coming**
Table: p.170

Jacob, Clyde (Louisiana)
Profile: p.873
Employment **Band** 2
Table: p.861

Jacob, Cynthia (New Jersey)
Profile: p.1141
Employment **Band** 1
Table: p.1126

Jacobs, Gina (Mississippi)
Profile: p.1034
Corporate/M&A **Band** 3
Table: p.1024

Jacobs, Michael A
(California)
Profile: p.258
Intellectual Property **Band** 2
Table: p.216

Jacobs, Neil (Massachusetts)
Profile: p.969
Employment **Band** 3
Table: p.940

Jacobs, Paul (Colorado)
Profile: p.319
Real Estate **Band** 2
Table: p.313

Jacobs, Paul (New York)
Profile: p.1290
Private Equity **Band** 3
Table: p.1237

Jacobs, Peter (Maine)
Profile: p.898
Employment **Band** 3
Table: p.890

Jacobs, Stephen C (Texas)
Profile: p.1685
Real Estate **Band** 3
Table: p.1662

Jacobsen, Ray
(District of Columbia)
Profile: p.448
Antitrust **Band** 5
Table: p.367

Jacobs-Meadway, Roberta
(Pennsylvania)
Profile: p.1527
Intellectual Property **Band** 1
Table: p.1508

Jacobson, Fruman (Illinois)
Profile: p.733
Bankruptcy **Band** 2
Table: p.669

Jacobson, John R
(Tennessee)
Profile: p.1608
Litigation **Band** 3
Table: p.1599

Jacobson, Kenneth M
(Illinois)
Profile: p.733
Real Estate **Band** 3
Table: p.706

Jacobson, Marc (New York)
Profile: p.1290
Media & Entertainment **Band** 2
Table: p.1235

Jacobson, Martin D
(New York)
Profile: p. 1290
Aviation **Band** 3
Table: p.58
Projects **Band** 3
Table: p.1244

Jacobson, Michael A
(Illinois)
Profile: p.733
Banking & Finance
Up and coming
Table: p.665

Jacobson, Ronald H
(Illinois)
Profile: p.733
Banking & Finance **Band** 3
Table: p.665

Jacover, Jerold A (Illinois)
Profile: p.733
Intellectual Property **Band** 3
Table: p.696

Jaffe, Helene D (New York)
Profile: p.1290
Antitrust **Band** 4
Table: p.1170

Jaffe, Ira (Michigan)
Profile: p.999
Corporate/M&A **Band** 3
Table: p.989

Jaffe, Kenneth
(District of Columbia)
Profile: p.448
Energy **Band** 2
Table: p.386

Jaffe, Marc D (National)
Profile: p.89
Capital Markets **Band** 4
Table: p.14

Jaffe, Michael E
(District of Columbia)
Profile: p.448
Construction **Band** 2
Table: p.374

Jaffe, Seth D
(Massachusetts)
Profile: p.969
Environment **Band** 1
Table: p.943

Jahn, Paul E (California)
Profile: p.258
IT Outsourcing **Band** 3
Table: p.221

Jahnke, Mark J (Ohio)
Profile: p.1443
Corporate/M&A **Band** 3
Table: p.1419

Jakubowicz, Janet P
(Kentucky)
Profile: p.843
Litigation **Band** 3
Table: p.835

Jakubowski, Paul
(Massachusetts)
Profile: p.969
Real Estate **Band** 3
Table: p.956

James, Bruce A (Colorado)
Profile: p.319
Hotels and Resorts **Band** 2
Table: p.314

James, Dwight W (Iowa)
Profile: p.813
Litigation **Band** S
Table: p.807

Jamieson, Brewster
(Alaska)
Profile: p.143
Litigation **Band** 3
Table: p.138

Janik, Stephen (Oregon)
Profile: p.1483
Real Estate **Band** 1
Table: p.1479

Real Estate **Band** 1
Table: p.1479

Janis, Ronald H (New Jersey)
Profile: p.1141
Corporate/M&A **Band** 2
Table: p.1123

Janke, Ronald R (Ohio)
Profile: p.1443
Environment **Band** 2
Table: p.1425

Janove, Jathan (Utah)
Profile: p.1737
Employment **Band** 2
Table: p.1730

Janowitz, Robert (Missouri)
Profile: p.1058
Employment **Band** 2
Table: p.1046

Jansonius, John V (Texas)
Profile: p.1685
Employment **Band** 2
Table: p.1634

Jardine, James S (Utah)
Profile: p.1737
Litigation **Band** 1
Table: p.1732

Jarin, Kenneth M
(Pennsylvania)
Profile: p.1527
Employment **Band** 3
Table: p.1500

Jarman, William (Louisiana)
Profile: p.873
Litigation **Band** 3
Table: p.865

Jarrell, Brenda H
(Massachusetts)
Profile: p.969
Intellectual Property **Band** 3
Table: p.948

Jaubert, Lisa (Louisiana)
Profile: p.873
Energy **Band** 1
Table: p.863

Jaudes, Richard E
(Missouri)
Profile: p.1058
Employment **Band** 3
Table: p.1046

Jedrey, Christopher M
(Massachusetts)
Profile: p.969
Healthcare **Band** 1
Table: p.946

Jeffcoat III, Otis Allen
(South Carolina)
Profile: p.1581
Real Estate **Band** 3
Table: p.1577

Jeffress, William
(District of Columbia)
Profile: p.448
Litigation **Band** 1
Table: p.410
Litigation **Band** 1
Table: p.410

Jeffrey, Sheri (California)
Profile: p.258
Media & Entertainment **Band** 3
Table: p.233

Jeffries, M Hill (Georgia)
Profile: p.615
Corporate/M&A **Band** 2
Table: p.587

Jenett, Bruce (California)
Profile: p.258
Corporate/M&A **Band** 4
Table: p.197

Jenkins, Stephen E
(Delaware)
Profile: p.354
Chancery **Band** 4
Table: p.344

Jenkins, Steve (Texas)
Profile: p.1685
Real Estate **Band** 3
Table: p.1662

Jenkins III, Robert M
(National)
Profile: p.89
Transport **Band** 2
Table: p.62

Jenner, Jesse J (New York)
Profile: p.1291
Intellectual Property **Band** 2
Table: p.1217

Jennings, Paul G
(Tennessee)
Profile: p.1608
Litigation **Band** 2
Table: p.1599

Jennings Jr, James W
(Virginia)
Profile: p.1770
Litigation **Band** 2
Table: p.1763

Jensen, Curtis S
(South Dakota)
Profile: p.1593
Real Estate **Band** 2
Table: p.1592

Jensen, Garth (Colorado)
Profile: p.319
Corporate/M&A **Band** 2
Table: p.303

Jepson, Edward (Illinois)
Profile: p.734
Employment **Band** 1
Table: p.681

Jernigan, John L (North
Carolina)
Profile: p.1396
Corporate/M&A **Band** 1
Table: p.1384

Jernigan, Stacey G.C.
(Texas)
Profile: p.1685
Bankruptcy **Band** 4
Table: p.1627

Jernigan Jr, W Henry
(West Virginia)
Profile: p.1809
Litigation **Band** 1
Table: p.1803
Litigation **Band** 1
Table: p.1803

Jernstedt, Kenneth
(Oregon)
Profile: p.1483
Employment **Band** 2
Table: p.1474

Jessen, Paul (Nebraska)
Profile: p.1088
Corporate/M&A Band 2
Table: p.1082

Jewell, Robert V (Texas)
Profile: p.1685
Corporate/M&A Band 1
Table: p.1631
Technology Band 2
Table: p.1668

Jewell, Ronald R (New York)
Profile: p.1291
Corporate/M&A Band 4
Table: p.1189

Jewett, Steve (Colorado)
Profile: p.319
Intellectual Property Band 2
Table: p.309

Jobeun, Larry (Nebraska)
Profile: p.1088
Real Estate Band 2
Table: p.1086

Jocelyn, Richard L E
(Rhode Island)
Profile: p.1569
Employment Band 1
Table: p.1565

Joffe, Robert (New York)
Profile: p.1291
Antitrust Band 1
Table: p.1170

John, Philip (Texas)
Profile: p.1685
Antitrust Band 3
Table: p.1622

Johnson, Carmen (Florida)
Profile: p.543

Johnson, Charles E
(North Carolina)
Profile: p.1396
Employment Band 3
Table: p.1386

Johnson, Christopher D
(Arizona)
Profile: p.159
Corporate/M&A Band 1
Table: p.146

Johnson, Craig W
(California)
Profile: p.258
Corporate/M&A Band 3
Table: p.197

Johnson, David L (North
Dakota)
Profile: p.1410
Corporate/M&A Band 2
Table: p.1403

Johnson, David R (National)
Profile: p.89
International Trade Band 2
Table: p.41

Johnson, Dennis (Indiana)
Profile: p.792
Real Estate Band 3
Table: p.788

Johnson, Donald (Michigan)
Profile: p.999
Banking & Finance Band 2
Table: p.987
Corporate/M&A Band 3
Table: p.989

Johnson, E Barry (Alabama)
Profile: p.123
Employment Band 3
Table: p.113

Johnson, Garrett B (Illinois)
Profile: p.734
Litigation Band 4
Table: p.700

Johnson, James (Georgia)
Profile: p.615
Intellectual Property Band 4
Table: p.596

Johnson, Linda S
(New Hampshire)
Profile: p.1117
Employment Band 2
Table: p.1109

Johnson, Philip
(North Dakota)
Profile: p.1410
Real Estate Band 3
Table: p.1409

Johnson, Philip McBride
(National)
Profile: p.89
Capital Markets Band 3
Table: p.16

Johnson, Randal A.
(Oregon)
Profile: p.1483
Real Estate Band 3
Table: p.1479

Johnson, Richard (Indiana)
Profile: p.792
Real Estate Band 2
Table: p.788

Johnson, Steven
(North Dakota)
Profile: p.1410
Corporate/M&A Band 2
Table: p.1403

Johnson, Steven
(South Dakota)
Profile: p.1593
Litigation Band 2
Table: p.1590

Johnson, Thomas
(Nebraska)
Profile: p.1088
Insurance Band 2
Table: p.1085

Johnson, V Duncan (Rhode
Island)
Profile: p.1569
Corporate/M&A Band 1
Table: p.1564

Johnson, W Stanfield
(National)
Profile: p.89
Government Contracts
Band 1
Table: p.27

Johnson, Weyman (Georgia)
Profile: p.615
Employment Band 3
Table: p.589

Johnson Jr, John H (Georgia)
Profile: p.615
Environment Band 1
Table: p.593

Johnson Jr. O Thomas
(National)
Profile: p.89
Arbitration Band 4
Table: p.33

Johnston, George
(Maryland)
Profile: p.922
Employment Band 3
Table: p.912

Johnston, Jay (Virginia)
Profile: p.1770
Corporate/M&A Band 1
Table: p.1752

Johnston, John F (Delaware)
Profile: p.354
Corporate/M&A Band 2
Table: p.346

Johnston, M Elaine
(New York)
Profile: p.1291
Antitrust Band 4
Table: p.1170

Johnston, Mark G
(District of Columbia)
Profile: p.449
Telecom, Broadcast & Satellite
Band 4
Table: p.427

Johnston, Mike (Georgia)
Profile: p.615
Employment Band 2
Table: p.589

Johnston, Ronald L
(California)
Profile: p.258
Intellectual Property Band 3
Table: p.216

Johnston, Susan A
(Massachusetts)
Profile: p.969
Tax Band 3
Table: p.959

Johnston, Thomas (Maine)
Profile: p.898
Employment Band 2
Table: p.890

Johnstone, Andrea
(New Hampshire)
Profile: p.1117
Employment Band 1
Table: p.1109

Johnstone, Debbi M (Texas)
Profile: p.1685
Healthcare Band 2
Table: p.1646

Jolley, R Gardner (Nevada)
Profile: p.1102
Litigation Band 3
Table: p.1096

Jones, Barbara
(Massachusetts)
Profile: p.969
Corporate/M&A Band 3
Table: p.937

Jones, Cary (Utah)
Profile: p.1737
Real Estate Band 2
Table: p.1733

Jones, Celeste
(South Carolina)
Profile: p.1581
Litigation Band 3
Table: p.1576

Jones, Christy (Mississippi)
Profile: p.1034
Litigation Band 3
Table: p.1028

Jones, David F
(Pennsylvania)
Profile: p.1527
Employee Benefits Band 2
Table: p.1501

Jones, Erika (National)
Profile: p.89
Transport Band 2
Table: p.62
Transport Band 2
Table: p.64

Jones, Frank G (Texas)
Profile: p.1685
Litigation Band 2
Table: p.1656

Jones, J Randall (Nevada)
Profile: p.1102
Litigation Band 1
Table: p.1096

Jones, John (Montana)
Profile: p.1080
Real Estate Band 2
Table: p.1078

Jones, Karen (Washington)
Profile: p.1792
Employment Band 2
Table: p.1780

Jones, Leslie Terry (Nevada)
Profile: p.1102
Corporate/M&A Band 2
Table: p.1089
Real Estate Band 3
Table: p.1099

Jones, Michael R (Arkansas)
Profile: p.177
Employment Band 2
Table: p.170

Jones, Nancy S (Tennessee)
Profile: p.1608
Litigation Band 3
Table: p.1599

Jones, Philip (Tennessee)
Profile: p.1608
Real Estate Band 3
Table: p.1603

Jones, Richard D
(Pennsylvania)
Profile: p.1527
Real Estate Band 2
Table: p.1516

Jones, Robert (California)
Profile: p.259
Corporate/M&A Band 4
Table: p.197

Jones, Rod (Florida)
Profile: p.543
Banking & Finance Band 2
Table: p.500

Jones, Roger J (Illinois)
Profile: p.734
Tax Band 3
Table: p.710

Jones, Russell (Tennessee)
Profile: p.1608
Media & Entertainment Band 1
Table: p.1602

Jones, Steve (Missouri)
Profile: p.1058
Corporate/M&A Band 3
Table: p.1043

Jones, Thomas J (Florida)
Profile: p.543
Insurance Band 2
Table: p.519

Jones, Walker (Mississippi)
Profile: p.1034
Litigation Band 2
Table: p.1028

Jones, William Evan
(Montana)
Profile: p.1080
Litigation Band S
Table: p.1075

Jones Jr, Philip K
(Louisiana)
Profile: p.873
Corporate/M&A Band 2
Table: p.859

Jones Van Buren, Carolyn
(North Carolina)
Profile: p.1396
Environment Band 2
Table: p.1388

Jontz, Dennis (New Mexico)
Profile: p.1163
Corporate/M&A Band 3
Table: p.1155

Jordan, Carey (Texas)
Profile: p.1686
Intellectual Property
Up and coming
Table: p.1651

Jordan, Carl (Texas)
Profile: p.1686
Employment Band 1
Table: p.1634

Jordan, David J (Utah)
Profile: p.1737
Litigation Band 1
Table: p.1732

Jordan, Hilary P (Georgia)
Profile: p.615
Banking & Finance Band 2
Table: p.580

Jordan, J Phillip
(District of Columbia)
Profile: p.449
Energy Band 3
Table: p.386

Jordan, James B (Georgia)
Profile: p.615
Real Estate Band 2
Table: p.601

Jordan, Nora (New York)
Profile: p.1291
Private Equity Band 3
Table: p.1241

Jorgenson, Larry (Wyoming)
Profile: p.1838
Real Estate Band 2
Table: p.1836

J

Jorgenson, Mary Ann
(Ohio)
Profile: p.1443
Corporate/M&A Band 2
Table: p.1419

Joscelyn, Alan L (Montana)
Profile: p.1080
Natural Resources Band 1
Table: p.1077

Josefsberg, Robert (Florida)
Profile: p.543
Litigation Band 1
Table: p.521
Litigation Band 1
Table: p.522

Joseph, Allan J (National)
Profile: p.90
Government Contracts
Band 1
Table: p.27

Joseph, Gregory P
(New York)
Profile: p.1291
Litigation Band 2
Table: p.1222

Joseph, Robert (Illinois)
Profile: p.734
Antitrust Band 3
Table: p.662

Joseph III, Alfred S
(Kentucky)
Profile: p.843
Real Estate Band S
Table: p.838

Josepher, Richard (Florida)
Profile: p.543
Tax Band 3
Table: p.531

Joslin, Peter B (Vermont)
Profile: p.1749
Litigation Band 3
Table: p.1746

Jospin, Walter (Georgia)
Profile: p.615
Corporate/M&A Band 3
Table: p.587

Jost, Lawrence J
(Wisconsin)
Profile: p.1825
Real Estate Band 1
Table: p.1822

Joswick, David D (Michigan)
Profile: p.999
Corporate/M&A Band 1
Table: p.989

Joy, Robert (Massachusetts)
Profile: p.969
Employment Band 2
Table: p.940

Joy, William (Massachusetts)
Profile: p.969
Employment Band 3
Table: p.940

Judge, John P (Pennsylvania)
Profile: p.1528
Environment Band 3
Table: p.1505

Juliussen, James H (Alaska)
Profile: p.143
Employment Band 2
Table: p.135

Junewicz, James J (Illinois)
Profile: p.734
Corporate/M&A Band 3
Table: p.675

Jung, William F (Florida)
Profile: p.543
Litigation Band 2
Table: p.522

Jurgensmeyer, Randy R
(Texas)
Profile: p.1686
Real Estate Band 2
Table: p.1662

Justice, Gary (California)
Profile: p.259
Insurance Band 4
Table: p.212

K

Kaden, Alan
(District of Columbia)
Profile: p.449
Tax Band 4
Table: p.422

Kadet, Samuel (New York)
Profile: p.1291
Litigation Band 3
Table: p.1223

Kadlick, Richard F
(National)
Profile: p.90
Capital Markets Band 4
Table: p.19

Kadue, David (California)
Profile: p.259
Employment Band 4
Table: p.202

Kadzielski, Mark A
(California)
Profile: p.259
Healthcare Band 1
Table: p.209

Kaempfer, Christopher
(Nevada)
Profile: p.1102
Real Estate Band 1
Table: p.1099

Kafin, Robert (New York)
Profile: p.1291
Environment Band 2
Table: p.1205
Environment Band 2
Table: p.1206

Kafka, Gerald A
(District of Columbia)
Profile: p.449
Tax Band 4
Table: p.422

Kahn, Adam (Massachusetts)
Profile: p.969
Environment Band 2
Table: p.943

Kahn, David S
(District of Columbia)
Profile: p.449
Real Estate Band 3
Table: p.418

Kahn, Henry (Maryland)
Profile: p.922
Corporate/M&A Band 2
Table: p.909

Kahn, Richard R (New
Jersey)
Profile: p.1141
Real Estate Band 3
Table: p.1134

Kahnke, Randall
(Minnesota)
Profile: p.1018

Kaim, Henry (Texas)
Profile: p.1686
Bankruptcy Band 2
Table: p.1627

Kaiser Jr, Gordon S (Ohio)
Profile: p.1443
Corporate/M&A Band 2
Table: p.1419

Kaleczyc, Stanley
(Montana)
Profile: p.1080
Litigation Band 3
Table: p.1075

Kalish, Paul W
(District of Columbia)
Profile: p.449
Insurance Band 2
Table: p.400

Kalkines, George (New York)
Profile: p.1291
Healthcare Band 1
Table: p.1209

Kallas, Hani R (Ohio)
Profile: p.1443
Banking & Finance Band 2
Table: p.1411

Kallstrom, D. Ward
(National)
Profile: p.90
Litigation Band 2
Table: p.25

Kalteyer, Ronald (Texas)
Profile: p.1686
Tax Band 1
Table: p.1665

Kamer, Gregory (Nevada)
Profile: p.1102
Employment Band 1
Table: p.1091

Kamikawa, Ray K (Hawaii)
Profile: p.648
Corporate/M&A Band 2
Table: p.641
Tax Band 1
Table: p.641

Kamp, David (Ohio)
Profile: p.1443
Litigation Band 4
Table: p.1431

Kanan, Gregory B
(Colorado)
Profile: p.319
Antitrust Band 1
Table: p.311

Kane, Ivan P (Illinois)
Profile: p.734
Real Estate Band 2
Table: p.706

Kane, Jonathan
(Pennsylvania)
Profile: p.1528
Employment Band 3
Table: p.1500

Kane, Meredith (New York)
Profile: p.1291
Real Estate Band 5
Table: p.1248

Kannel, William
(Massachusetts)
Profile: p.969
Bankruptcy Band 3
Table: p.935

Kant, Robert (Arizona)
Profile: p.159
Corporate/M&A Band 2
Table: p.146

Kanter, Jane A
(District of Columbia)
Profile: p.449
Investment Management
Band 2
Table: p.406

Kanter, Stacy J (National)
Profile: p.90
Capital Markets Band 4
Table: p.14

Kantor, Hal (Florida)
Profile: p.543
Real Estate Band 1
Table: p.528

Kantor, Michael (National)
Profile: p.90
International Trade Band 2
Table: p.40

Kantrow, Lee (Louisiana)
Profile: p.873
Corporate/M&A Band 2
Table: p.859

Kaplan, Arthur M
(Pennsylvania)
Profile: p.1528
Antitrust Band 3
Table: p.1489

Kaplan, Barry M
(Washington)
Profile: p.1792
Litigation Band 3
Table: p.1786

Kaplan, Cathy (National)
Profile: p.90
Capital Markets Band 3
Table: p.19

Kaplan, David (Kentucky)
Profile: p.843
Litigation Up and coming
Table: p.835

Kaplan, Edward
(New Hampshire)
Profile: p.1118
Employment Band 2
Table: p.1109

Kaplan, Frank (California)
Profile: p.259
Insurance Band 3
Table: p.212

Kaplan, Gilbert (National)
Profile: p.90
International Trade Band 3
Table: p.40

Kaplan, H Deen (National)
Profile: p.90
International Trade Band 4
Table: p.40

Kaplan, Harvey (Missouri)
Profile: p.1058
Litigation Band 2
Table: p.1049

Kaplan, Jared (Illinois)
Profile: p.734
Employee Benefits Band 1
Table: p.681

Kaplan, Joel (Illinois)
Profile: p.734
Employment Band 2
Table: p.681

Kaplan, Jonathan E
(Tennessee)
Profile: p.1608
Employment Band 2
Table: p.1596

Kaplan, Philip (Arkansas)
Profile: p.177
Employment Band 1
Table: p.170
Litigation Band 1
Table: p.172

Kaplan, Robert D
(Washington)
Profile: p.1792
Corporate/M&A Band 2
Table: p.1778

Kaplan, Samuel (Minnesota)
Profile: p.1018
Corporate/M&A Band 2
Table: p.1005

Kaplan, Stephen H
(Colorado)
Profile: p.319
Real Estate Band 1
Table: p.314

Kaplan, Steven
(District of Columbia)
Profile: p.449
Corporate/Commercial Band 3
Table: p.376

Karaganis, Joseph (Illinois)
Profile: p.734
Environment Band 3
Table: p.687

Karell, Allan L (Montana)
Profile: p.1080
Real Estate Band 2
Table: p.1078

Karig, Adele M (New York)
Profile: p.1291
Private Equity Band 3
Table: p.1241
Tax Up and coming
Table: p.1255

Karmel, Philip E (New York)
Profile: p.1291
Environment Band 3
Table: p.1205

Karotkin, Stephen
(New York)
Profile: p.1291
Bankruptcy Band 2
Table: p.1179

Karp, Brad (New York)
Profile: p.1292
Litigation Band 2
Table: p.1223

Karp, Joel (Florida)
Profile: p.543
Tax Band s
Table: p.531

Karp, Joseph (California)
Profile: p.259
Energy Band 2
Table: p.204

Karp, Marvin (Ohio)
Profile: p.1443
Litigation Band 4
Table: p.1431

Karrenberg, Thomas (Utah)
Profile: p.1737
Litigation Band 2
Table: p.1732

Kasle, Jeffrey (Rhode Island)
Profile: p.1569
Employment Band 2
Table: p.1565

Kaslow, Howard (Nebraska)
Profile: p.1088
Corporate/M&A Band 1
Table: p.1082

Kasner, Jay B (New York)
Profile: p.1292
Litigation Band 1
Table: p.1223

Kasner, Stewart (Florida)
Profile: p.543
Tax Band u
Table: p.531

Kasper, David (Indiana)
Profile: p.793
Litigation Band 3
Table: p.785

Kass, Stephen (New York)
Profile: p.1292
Environment Band 3
Table: p.1205

Kassel, John B (Vermont)
Profile: p.1749
Real Estate Band 2
Table: p.1747

Kassin, Thomas (Georgia)
Profile: p.615
Employment Band 4
Table: p.589

Kassner, Andrew C
(Pennsylvania)
Profile: p.1528
Bankruptcy Band 3
Table: p.1494

Kastner, Ken
(District of Columbia)
Profile: p.449
Environment Band 4
Table: p.392

Katcher, Bruce S
(Pennsylvania)
Profile: p.1528
Environment Band 4
Table: p.1505

Katcher, Richard D
(New York)
Profile: p.1292

Corporate/M&A Band 1
Table: p.1189

Katelman, John (Nebraska)
Profile: p.1088
Real Estate Band 2
Table: p.1086

Katsh, Salem (New York)
Profile: p.1292
Intellectual Property Band 3
Table: p.1217

Kattan, Joseph
(District of Columbia)
Profile: p.450
Antitrust Band 3
Table: p.367

Katz, Allan J (Florida)
Profile: p.543
Insurance Band 1
Table: p.519

Katz, Alvin Charles (Illinois)
Profile: p.734
Real Estate Band 2
Table: p.706

Katz, Carole S
(Pennsylvania)
Profile: p.1528
Employment Band 2
Table: p.1500

Katz, David A (New York)
Profile: p.1292
Corporate/M&A Band 2
Table: p.1189

Katz, Donald L (National)
Profile: p.90
Aviation Band 2
Table: p.58

Katz, Lawrence (Arizona)
Profile: p.159
Employment Band 1
Table: p.148

Katz, M Marvin (Texas)
Profile: p.1686
Real Estate Band 1
Table: p.1662

Katz, Robert S (Hawaii)
Profile: p.648
Employment Band 1
Table: p.642

Katzke, Michael S (New York)
Profile: p.1292
Employee Benefits Band 3
Table: p.1197

Kauffman, Fred (Nebraska)
Profile: p.1088
Litigation Band 3
Table: p.1085

Kaufman, Andrew M
(Illinois)
Profile: p.734
Banking & Finance Band 3
Table: p.665

Kaufman, Christopher
(California)
Profile: p.259
Corporate/M&A Band 1
Table: p.197

Kaufman, D William
(Minnesota)
Profile: p.1018

Corporate/M&A Band 3
Table: p.1005

Kaufman, David (Mississippi)
Profile: p.1034
Litigation Band 2
Table: p.1028

Kaufman, Kenneth M
(District of Columbia)
Profile: p.450
Intellectual Property Band 3
Table: p.403

Kaufman, Mark D (Georgia)
Profile: p.616
Corporate/M&A Band 4
Table: p.587

Kaufman, Mark S (Georgia)
Profile: p.616
Bankruptcy Band 2
Table: p.582

Kaufman, Stephen E
(New York)
Profile: p.1292
Litigation Band 2
Table: p.1224

Kauss, Andrew (Georgia)
Profile: p.616
Real Estate Band 3
Table: p.601

Kavaler, Thomas (New York)
Profile: p.1292
Litigation Band 2
Table: p.1222

Kawashima, James (Hawaii)
Profile: p.648
Litigation Band 2
Table: p.644

Kawata, Yukako (New York)
Profile: p.1292
Private Equity Band 1
Table: p.1241

Kay, Craig (West Virginia)
Profile: p.1809
Corporate/M&A Band 2
Table: p.1798

Kay, Minta E
(Massachusetts)
Profile: p.969
Real Estate Band 3
Table: p.956

Kay, Richard A (Michigan)
Profile: p.999
Litigation Band 3
Table: p.994

Kayatta Jr, William (Maine)
Profile: p.898
Litigation Band 1
Table: p.893

Kayle, Bruce E (New York)
Profile: p.1292
Tax Band 2
Table: p.1256

Kaywood, Sam K (Georgia)
Profile: p.616
Tax Band 4
Table: p.603

Kazmarek, Edward 'Skip'
(Georgia)
Profile: p.616
Environment Band 2
Table: p.593

Keach, Robert J (Maine)
Profile: p.898
Bankruptcy Band 1
Table: p.888

Keane, Jennifer (Texas)
Profile: p.1686
Environment Up and coming
Table: p.1643

Keane, Paul (New York)
Profile: p.90
Shipping Band 3
Table: p.67

Kearfott, Joseph C
(Virginia)
Profile: p.1770
Litigation Band 3
Table: p.1763

Kearney, Esq, Dennis T
(New Jersey)
Profile: p.1141
Litigation Band 2
Table: p.1133

Keating, Geoffrey T
(District of Columbia)
Profile: p.450
Construction Band 2
Table: p.374

Keating, Michael
(Massachusetts)
Profile: p.969
Litigation Band 1
Table: p.951

Kee, Conrad (Connecticut)
Profile: p.337
Employment Band 3
Table: p.329

Keefe, Robert D
(Massachusetts)
Profile: p.969
Litigation Band 1
Table: p.951

Keehnel, Stellman
(Washington)
Profile: p.1792
Litigation Band 3
Table: p.1786

Keeler, Dennis C (Maine)
Profile: p.898
Real Estate Band 1
Table: p.895

Keen, C Matthew (North
Carolina)
Profile: p.1396
Employment Band 2
Table: p.1386

Keenan, Robert (Georgia)
Profile: p.616
Healthcare Up and coming
Table: p.594

Keene, Thomas (Alabama)
Profile: p.123
Litigation Band 1
Table: p.116

Keeney, Regina
(District of Columbia)
Profile: p.450
Telecom, Broadcast & Satellite
Band 4
Table: p.427

Keesal Jr, Samuel A
(National)
Profile: p.90
Shipping Band 1
Table: p.71

Keeton, Charles R
(Kentucky)
Profile: p.843
Corporate/M&A Band 3
Table: p.827

Keim, Robert (Missouri)
Profile: p.1058
Corporate/M&A Band 3
Table: p.1043

Keiner, Jeffrey (Florida)
Profile: p.543
Construction Band 3
Table: p.507

Keiner, Jr, R. Bruce
(National)
Profile: p.90
Aviation Band 3
Table: p.58

Keith, Calvin L (Oregon)
Profile: p.1483
Employment Band 2
Table: p.1474

Keithley, Brad (Texas)
Profile: p.1686
Energy Band 2
Table: p.1641

Keker, John (California)
Profile: p.259
Intellectual Property Band 2
Table: p.216
Litigation Band 1
Table: p.224
Litigation Band 1
Table: p.225

Keleher, William (New
Mexico)
Profile: p.1163
Real Estate Band 3
Table: p.1161

Kelleher, Thomas (Georgia)
Profile: p.616
Construction Band 1
Table: p.584

Keller, Brad (Washington)
Profile: p.1792
Litigation Band 1
Table: p.1786

Keller, Bruce P (New York)
Profile: p.1292
Intellectual Property Band 3
Table: p.1217
Media & Entertainment Band 2
Table: p.1232

Keller, Don (California)
Profile: p.259
Corporate/M&A Band 5
Table: p.197

Keller, Edwin A (Nevada)
Profile: p.1102

Keller, Kent (California)
Profile: p.259
Insurance Band 2
Table: p.212

Keller, Mary (Texas)
Profile: p.1686
Insurance Band 2

K

Table: p.1648

Keller, Stanley
(Massachusetts)
Profile: p.969
Corporate/M&A Band 2
Table: p.937

Kelley, David (Minnesota)
Profile: p.1018
Real Estate Band 2
Table: p.1014

Kelley, James J
(District of Columbia)
Profile: p.450
Employment Band 3
Table: p.380

Kelley, James R (Tennessee)
Profile: p.1609
Litigation Band 2
Table: p.1599

Kelley, Jay D (Texas)
Profile: p.1686
Energy Band 3
Table: p.1637
Projects Band 2
Table: p.1659

Kelley, Jeffrey (Georgia)
Profile: p.616
Bankruptcy Band 3
Table: p.582

Kelley, John (Georgia)
Profile: p.616
Corporate/M&A Band 4
Table: p.587

Kelley, Kevin (Texas)
Profile: p.1686
Real Estate Band 3
Table: p.1662

Kelley, Timothy (Illinois)
Profile: p.735
Media & Entertainment Band 1
Table: p.704

Kellner, Leon B
(District of Columbia)
Profile: p.450
Insurance Band 2
Table: p.402

Kellner, Robert (Maryland)
Profile: p.922
Employment Band 2
Table: p.912

Kellner, Stuart (Montana)
Profile: p.1080
Litigation Band 2
Table: p.1075

Kellogg, Michael
(District of Columbia)
Profile: p.450
Telecom, Broadcast & Satellite
Band 1
Table: p.427

Kelly, Christopher (Ohio)
Profile: p.1443
Corporate/M&A Band 3
Table: p.1419

Kelly, Deborah
(District of Columbia)
Profile: p.450
Employment Band 3
Table: p.380

Kelly, Henry (Illinois)
Profile: p.735
Telecom, Broadcast & Satellite
Band 2
Table: p.715

Kelly, Joseph A
(Rhode Island)
Profile: p.1569
Litigation Band 3
Table: p.1567

Kelly, Mark T (Texas)
Profile: p.1686
Corporate/M&A Band 1
Table: p.1631

Kelly, Michael J (New York)
Profile: p.1292
Bankruptcy Band 4
Table: p.1179

Kelly, Thomas M (New York)
Profile: p.1293
Insurance Band 2
Table: p.1213

Kelly, Timothy (Minnesota)
Profile: p.1018
Litigation Band 1
Table: p.1011

Kelso, Linda Y (Florida)
Profile: p.543
Corporate/M&A Band 3
Table: p.509

Kemp, Hal (Arkansas)
Profile: p.177
Real Estate Band 1
Table: p.174

Kendall, David
(District of Columbia)
Profile: p.450
Litigation Band 3
Table: p.410
Media & Entertainment Band 2
Table: p.413

Kendall, Michael J
(Massachusetts)
Profile: p.970
Private Equity Up and coming
Table: p.953

Kendall, Richard B
(California)
Profile: p.259
Media & Entertainment Band 2
Table: p.230

Kendig-Schrader, Julie
(Florida)
Profile: p.543
Real Estate Band 3
Table: p.528

Kendrick, Edmund H (New
Mexico)
Profile: p.1163
Environment Band 1
Table: p.1158

Kenlan, Jay (Vermont)
Profile: p.1749
Real Estate Band 1
Table: p.1747

Kennard, Wayne M
(Massachusetts)
Profile: p.970
Intellectual Property Band 3
Table: p.948

Kennedy, Dennis (Nevada)
Profile: p.1102
Litigation Band 1
Table: p.1096

Kennedy, Donald G
(Missouri)
Profile: p.1058
Real Estate Band 2
Table: p.1052

Kennedy, Donald J
(New York)
Profile: p.90
Shipping Band 3
Table: p.67

Kennedy, Elizabeth Gregg
(Iowa)
Profile: p.813
Employment Band 1
Table: p.805

Kennedy, John (Texas)
Profile: p.1687
Energy Band 2
Table: p.1641

Kennedy, John B (New York)
Profile: p.1293
Technology Band 3
Table: p.1259

Kennedy, Michael (Arizona)
Profile: p.160
Litigation Band 4
Table: p.152

Kennedy, Mike (California)
Profile: p.259
Corporate/M&A Band 3
Table: p.197

Kennedy, Robert (New York)
Profile: p.1293
Private Equity Band 3
Table: p.1237

Kennedy, Thomas H
(New York)
Profile: p.1293
Corporate/M&A Band 3
Table: p.1189

Kennedy III, James J
(Florida)
Profile: p.543
Healthcare Band 2
Table: p.518

Kenney, John A (Oklahoma)
Profile: p.1465
Litigation Band 2
Table: p.1462

Kent, Christopher H
(Oregon)
Profile: p.1483
Litigation Band 3
Table: p.1477

Kent, Ronald D (California)
Profile: p.259
Insurance Band 3
Table: p.212

Kenyon, Charity (California)
Profile: p.259
Media & Entertainment Band 3
Table: p.230

Kenyon, Douglas W (North
Carolina)
Profile: p.1396
Antitrust Band 1
Table: p.1390

Kepple, Lloyd (Minnesota)
Profile: p.1018
Real Estate Band 2
Table: p.1014

Kerger, Richard (Ohio)
Profile: p.1443
Litigation Band 4
Table: p.1431

Kern, David B (Wisconsin)
Profile: p.1825
Employment Band 1
Table: p.1819

Kerr, John (National)
Profile: p.90
Arbitration Band
Table: p.33
Arbitration Band 2
Table: p.33

Kerrick, Robert (Arizona)
Profile: p.160
Real Estate Band 2
Table: p.155

Kessler, Jeffrey L (New York)
Profile: p. 1293
Antitrust Band 4
Table: p.1170
Sport Band 1
Table: p.55

Kessler, Mark K
(Pennsylvania)
Profile: p.1528
Corporate/M&A Band 4
Table: p.1497

Kessler, Philip J (Michigan)
Profile: p.999
Litigation Band 1
Table: p.994

Kestner, Steven (Ohio)
Profile: p.1443
Corporate/M&A Band 3
Table: p.1419

Keyes, David (Texas)
Profile: p.1687
Banking & Finance Band 2
Table: p.1625

Keyes, Jeffrey (Minnesota)
Profile: p.1018
Litigation Band 2
Table: p.1011

Keyes, Judith Droz
(California)
Profile: p.259
Employment Band 4
Table: p.202

Keyser, Denise M (New
Jersey)
Profile: p.1142
Employment Band 2
Table: p.1126

Khorey, David (Michigan)
Profile: p.999
Employment Band 3
Table: p.991

Kiefer, Matthew J
(Massachusetts)
Profile: p.970
Real Estate Band 1
Table: p.957

Kiely, Bruce
(District of Columbia)
Profile: p.450
Energy Band 3
Table: p.382

Kienbaum, Thomas
(Michigan)
Profile: p.999
Employment Band 1
Table: p.991

Kiernan, John S (New York)
Profile: p.1293
Litigation Band 3
Table: p.1222

Kieselstein, Marc (Illinois)
Profile: p.735
Bankruptcy Band 3
Table: p.669

Kiesewetter, Jay W
(Tennessee)
Profile: p.1609
Employment Band 2
Table: p.1596

Kiessling, B Robbins
(New York)
Profile: p.1293
Banking & Finance Band 1
Table: p.1174

Kiggans, Thomas H
(Louisiana)
Profile: p.873
Employment Band 2
Table: p.861

Kikoler, Stephen P (Illinois)
Profile: p.735
Construction Band 2
Table: p.672

Kilb, Brian (California)
Profile: p.91
Banking & Finance Band 2
Table: p.187
Capital Markets Band 3
Table: p.23

Kilbane, Thomas S (Ohio)
Profile: p.1443
Litigation Band 1
Table: p.1431

Kilberg, William J
(District of Columbia)
Profile: p.450
Employee Benefits Band 3
Table: p.378
Employment Band 1
Table: p.380

Kilbreth, James (Maine)
Profile: p.899
Environment Band 2
Table: p.892
Litigation Band 3
Table: p.893

Kilgore III, Cada T (Georgia)
Profile: p.616
Energy Band 1
Table: p.592

Killworth, Richard (Ohio)
Profile: p.1443
Intellectual Property Band S
Table: p.1428

Kilmer, Jeffrey (Oregon)
Profile: p.1483
Litigation Band 3
Table: p.1477

Kilpatrick, J Thomas
(Georgia)
Profile: p.616
Employment Band 4
Table: p.589

Kim, Gregory R (Hawaii)
Profile: p.648
Corporate/M&A Band 1
Table: p.641

Kim, Robert C (Nevada)
Profile: p.1102
Corporate/M&A Band 3
Table: p.1089

Kimball, Albert (Texas)
Profile: p.1687
Intellectual Property Band 2
Table: p.1651

Kimball, Christian (Illinois)
Profile: p.735
Tax Band 3
Table: p.710

Kimball, David (Arizona)
Profile: p.160
Environment Band 1
Table: p.150

Kimball, George (California)
Profile: p. 260
Business Process
Outsourcing: National Band 2
Table: p.10
IT Outsourcing Band 2
Table: p.221

Kimball, John D (New York)
Profile: p.91
Shipping Band 1
Table: p.67

Kimerer, Mike (Arizona)
Profile: p.160
Litigation Band 3
Table: p.153

Kimmell, Kenneth L
(Massachusetts)
Profile: p.970
Environment Band 3
Table: p.943

Kimmelman, Louis B
(National)
Profile: p.91
Arbitration Band 4
Table: p.33

Kinder, Daniel K (Rhode Island)
Profile: p.1569
Employment Band 2
Table: p.1565

King, Bruce (Florida)
Profile: p.544
Construction Band 2
Table: p.507

King, Carol Weld
(District of Columbia)
Profile: p.450
Real Estate Band 4
Table: p.418

King, Chad W (Texas)
Profile: p.1687
Technology Band 3
Table: p.1668

King, David (Florida)
Profile: p.544
Litigation Band 2

Table: p.521

King, David C. (Maine)
Profile: p.899
Litigation Band 3
Table: p.893

King, G Roger (Ohio)
Profile: p.1443
Employment Band 2
Table: p.1422

King, June N (Kentucky)
Profile: p.843
Corporate/M&A Band 3
Table: p.827

King, Katherine (Louisiana)
Profile: p.873
Energy Band 1
Table: p.863

King, Kenton J (California)
Profile: p. 260
Capital Markets Band 3
Table: p.23
Corporate/M&A Band 1
Table: p.197

King, Kimberly (Florida)
Profile: p.544
Antitrust Band 3
Table: p.498

King, Richard A (Missouri)
Profile: p.1058
Real Estate Band 1
Table: p.1052
Real Estate Band 1
Table: p.1053

King, W Gregory (Kentucky)
Profile: p.843
Litigation Band 2
Table: p.835

King, William (Virginia)
Profile: p.1770
Litigation Band 1
Table: p.1763

King Jr, Evans (West Virginia)
Profile: p.1809
Corporate/M&A Band 2
Table: p.1798

King Jr, George S (South Carolina)
Profile: p.1581
Corporate/M&A Band 1
Table: p.1572

Kinney, Michael F
(Nebraska)
Profile: p.1088
Insurance Band 2
Table: p.1085

Kinsella, Peter (Colorado)
Profile: p.319
Intellectual Property Band 2
Table: p.309

Kinsolving, Ruth Barnes
(Florida)
Profile: p.544
Real Estate Band 2
Table: p.526

Kinzie, Jack L (Texas)
Profile: p.1687
Bankruptcy Band 2
Table: p.1627

Kipnees, Robert J
(New Jersey)
Profile: p.1142
Litigation Band 2
Table: p.1133

Kirby, Matthew T
(California)
Profile: p.260
Banking & Finance Band 1
Table: p.187

Kirchhoefer, Gregg (Illinois)
Profile: p. 735
Business Process
Outsourcing: National Band 3
Table: p.10
Technology Band 1
Table: p.713

Kiriakos, Thomas S (Illinois)
Profile: p.735
Bankruptcy Band 3
Table: p.669

Kirk, James (Oklahoma)
Profile: p.1465
Litigation Band 3
Table: p.1462

Kirk, Michael K (Kentucky)
Profile: p.843
Employment Band 3
Table: p.830

Kirkham, Steven
(Tennessee)
Profile: p.1609
Real Estate Band 3
Table: p.1603

Kirkland, Byron B (North Carolina)
Profile: p.1397
Corporate/M&A Band 2
Table: p.1384

Kirkland, David (Texas)
Profile: p.1687
Corporate/M&A Band 2
Table: p.1631

Kirkwood, Martin
(District of Columbia)
Profile: p.450
Energy Band 5
Table: p.386

Kirkwood, Peter (Florida)
Profile: p.544
Tax Band 4
Table: p.531

Kirmis, Lyle (North Dakota)
Profile: p.1410
Litigation Band 2
Table: p.1406

Kirpalani, Susheel (New York)
Profile: p.1293
Bankruptcy Band 3
Table: p.1179

Kirsch, Robert
(Massachusetts)
Profile: p.970
Environment Band 2
Table: p.943

Kirschbaum, Howard
(Illinois)
Profile: p.735
Real Estate Band 3
Table: p.706

Kirschner, Kenneth (Florida)
Profile: p.544
Corporate/M&A Band 3
Table: p.509

Kirshman, Norman H
(Nevada)
Profile: p.1102
Employment Band 2
Table: p.1091

Kirwan, BJ (California)
Profile: p.260
Environment Band 2
Table: p.207

Kirwin, Brian P (Florida)
Profile: p.544
Construction Band 3
Table: p.507

Kisch, Victor (Oregon)
Profile: p.1483
Employment Band 2
Table: p.1474

Kissel, Richard J (Illinois)
Profile: p.735
Environment Band S
Table: p.687

Kitchel, Chris (Oregon)
Profile: p.1483
Employment Band 2
Table: p.1474

Kitslaar, Libby (Illinois)
Profile: p.735
Corporate/M&A Band 4
Table: p.675

Klaas, Paul B (Minnesota)
Profile: p.1018
Litigation Band 3
Table: p.1011

Klaper, Martin (Indiana)
Profile: p.793
Employment Band 3
Table: p.783

Klawiter, Donald
(District of Columbia)
Profile: p.450
Antitrust Band 3
Table: p.367

Kleban, Barry (Pennsylvania)
Profile: p.1528
Bankruptcy Band 2
Table: p.1494

Klee, Kenneth N (California)
Profile: p.260
Bankruptcy Band 1
Table: p.191

Klein, Allen (National)
Profile: p.91
Business Process
Outsourcing: National Band 3
Table: p.10

Klein, Anthony (California)
Profile: p.260
IT Outsourcing Band 2
Table: p.221

Klein, Daniel (Delaware)
Profile: p.354
Real Estate Band 3
Table: p.350

Klein, David F
(District of Columbia)
Profile: p.451

Insurance Band 3
Table: p.402

Klein, Frederick
(District of Columbia)
Profile: p.451
Real Estate Band 1
Table: p.418

Klein, Jeffrey (New York)
Profile: p.1293
Employment Band 3
Table: p.1200

Klein, Justin P
(Pennsylvania)
Profile: p.1528
Corporate/M&A Band 2
Table: p.1497

Klein, Kenneth
(District of Columbia)
Profile: p.451
Tax Band 4
Table: p.422

Klein, Michael
(District of Columbia)
Profile: p.451
Litigation Band 3
Table: p.410

Klein, Randall (Illinois)
Profile: p.735
Bankruptcy Up and coming
Table: p.669

Klein, Steven (Louisiana)
Profile: p.873
Corporate/M&A Band 4
Table: p.859

Klein, Steven D (New York)
Profile: p.1293
Real Estate Band 4
Table: p.1248

Klein III, Otto G
(Washington)
Profile: p.1792
Employment Band 2
Table: p.1780

Kleinbard, Edward D
(New York)
Profile: p.1293
Tax Band 1
Table: p.1256

Kleinberg, Kenneth A
(California)
Profile: p.260
Media & Entertainment Band 2
Table: p.233

Kleinkopf, David (Colorado)
Profile: p.319
Hotels and Resorts Band 1
Table: p.314

Klenk, James (Illinois)
Profile: p.735
Media & Entertainment Band 1
Table: p.703

Klenk, Timothy C (Illinois)
Profile: p.735
Employment Band 3
Table: p.681

Klepper, Martin
(District of Columbia)
Profile: p. 451
Projects Band 2
Table: p.52
Projects Band 2

K

Table: p.415

Klevansky, Simon (Hawaii)
Profile: p.648
Litigation Band 3
Table: p.644

Klevorn, Andrew G (Illinois)
Profile: p.735
Antitrust Band 3
Table: p.662

Klimko, Justin (Michigan)
Profile: p.999
Corporate/M&A Band 2
Table: p.989

Kline, Douglas J
(Massachusetts)
Profile: p.970
Intellectual Property Band 2
Table: p.948

Kline, Eric (Pennsylvania)
Profile: p.1528
Banking & Finance Band 2
Table: p.1493

Kline, Scot (Vermont)
Profile: p.1749
Litigation Band 3
Table: p.1746

Kline, Thomas R
(Pennsylvania)
Profile: p.1528
Litigation Band 3
Table: p.1511

Kling, Lou R (New York)
Profile: p.1294
Corporate/M&A Band 2
Table: p.1189

Kling, Neal (Louisiana)
Profile: p.873
Real Estate Band 2
Table: p.867

Klinger, Edward (North
Dakota)
Profile: p.1410
Litigation Band 2
Table: p.1406

Klinghoffer, Teddy D
(Florida)
Profile: p.544
Corporate/M&A Band 2
Table: p.509

Kluttz, Joseph B C (North
Carolina)
Profile: p.1397
Banking & Finance Band 3
Table: p.1381
Bankruptcy Band 1
Table: p.1383

Klyman, Robert (California)
Profile: p.260
Bankruptcy Band 4
Table: p.191

Knapp, Spencer (Vermont)
Profile: p.1749
Corporate/M&A Band 1
Table: p.1743

Knauer, Thomas E (Virginia)
Profile: p.1770
Environment Band 2
Table: p.1757

Knauss, Charles
(District of Columbia)
Profile: p.451
Environment Band 2
Table: p.392

Knauss, Robert B
(California)
Profile: p.260
Corporate/M&A Band 5
Table: p.197

Knebel, Donald (Indiana)
Profile: p.793
Litigation Band 1
Table: p.785

Knee, Stephen H
(New Jersey)
Profile: p.1142
Corporate/M&A Band 3
Table: p.1123

Kneip, Frederick (New York)
Profile: p.1294
Employee Benefits Band 2
Table: p.1197

Knetsch, Jeffrey (Colorado)
Profile: p.319
Corporate/M&A Band 3
Table: p.303

Knickrehm, Donald (Idaho)
Profile: p.660
Real Estate Band S
Table: p.658

Knight, G Marcus (South
Carolina)
Profile: p.1581
Corporate/M&A Band 2
Table: p.1572

Knight, James T (New York)
Profile: p.1294
Banking & Finance Band 2
Table: p.1174

Knight, John H. (Delaware)
Profile: p.354
Bankruptcy Band 4
Table: p.341

Knight, Michael (Alabama)
Profile: p.123
Litigation Band 3
Table: p.116

Knight, Robert (Montana)
Profile: p.1080
Real Estate Band 1
Table: p.1078

Knipe, Quentin M (Idaho)
Profile: p.660
Real Estate Band 2
Table: p.658

Knoll, Susan (Texas)
Profile: p.1687
Intellectual Property Band 2
Table: p.1651

Knorek, John (Hawaii)
Profile: p.648
Employment Band 2
Table: p.642

Knowles, Leo (Nebraska)
Profile: p.1088
Litigation Band 3
Table: p.1085

Knowlton, William A
(Massachusetts)
Profile: p.970
Healthcare Band 2
Table: p.946

Knox, Daniel (Oregon)
Profile: p.1483
Litigation Band 3
Table: p.1477

Knudsen, Eric (Vermont)
Profile: p.1749
Real Estate Band 3
Table: p.1747

Knudson, David L
(South Dakota)
Profile: p.1593
Corporate/M&A Band 1
Table: p.1587

Knudson, Kathryn L
(Georgia)
Profile: p.616
Banking & Finance Band 2
Table: p.581

Knull III, William H (Texas)
Profile: p.1687
Litigation Band 3
Table: p.1656

Kobak, Scott M (New York)
Profile: p.1294
Real Estate Band 5
Table: p.1248

Kobayashi Jr, Bert T
(Hawaii)
Profile: p.648
Litigation Band 2
Table: p.644

Kobert, Roy (Florida)
Profile: p.544
Bankruptcy Band 3
Table: p.503

Kochanski, David
(Maryland)
Profile: p.922
Real Estate Band 3
Table: p.917

Kocher, Gary J (Washington)
Profile: p.1793
Corporate/M&A Band 3
Table: p.1778

Kociubes, Joseph L
(Massachusetts)
Profile: p.970
Litigation Band 2
Table: p.951

Koenigsberg, I Fred
(New York)
Profile: p.1294
Intellectual Property Band 2
Table: p.1217

Koffel, William B
(Massachusetts)
Profile: p.970
Employment Band 2
Table: p.940

Kofman, Robert (Florida)
Profile: p.544
Employment Band 3
Table: p.513

Kohn, Alan C (Missouri)
Profile: p.1058
Litigation Band 2
Table: p.1049

Kohn, Arthur H (New York)
Profile: p.1294
Employee Benefits Band 3
Table: p.1197

Kohn, Jeffrey (New York)
Profile: p.1294
Employment Band 3
Table: p.1200

Kohn, Joseph (Pennsylvania)
Profile: p.1528
Antitrust Band 2
Table: p.1489

Kohn, Richard (Illinois)
Profile: p.735
Banking & Finance Band 2
Table: p.665

Kokoruda, Thomas G
(Missouri)
Profile: p.1058
Litigation Band 3
Table: p.1049

Kolasky, William J
(District of Columbia)
Profile: p.451
Antitrust Band 3
Table: p.367

Kolb, Daniel (New York)
Profile: p.1294
Litigation Band 2
Table: p.1223

Kolb, William R
(Massachusetts)
Profile: p.970
Corporate/M&A Band 3
Table: p.937

Kolesar, Andrew (Ohio)
Profile: p.1443
Environment Band 3
Table: p.1425

Koltun, Timothy (Michigan)
Profile: p.1000
Real Estate Band 3
Table: p.996

Komeiji, John T (Hawaii)
Profile: p.648
Litigation Band 2
Table: p.644

Koneck, John (Minnesota)
Profile: p.1018
Real Estate Band 1
Table: p.1014

Konrad, Daniel J
(West Virginia)
Profile: p.1809

Koob, Charles E (New York)
Profile: p.1294
Antitrust Band 3
Table: p.1170
Litigation Band 2
Table: p.1222

Koons, Warren (Washington)
Profile: p.1793
Real Estate Band 3
Table: p.1788

Koons Jr, Robert A
(Pennsylvania)
Profile: p.1528
Intellectual Property Band 4
Table: p.1508

Korando, Kimberly J
(North Carolina)
Profile: p.1397
Employment Band 3
Table: p.1386

Korb, Philip (Pennsylvania)
Profile: p.1529
Real Estate Band 1
Table: p.1516

Korby, Mary (Texas)
Profile: p.1687
Corporate/M&A Band 4
Table: p.1631

Korff, Phyllis G (National)
Profile: p.91
Capital Markets Band 3
Table: p.14

Korman, Marty (California)
Profile: p.260
Corporate/M&A Band 4
Table: p.197

Kornberg, Alan (New York)
Profile: p.1294
Bankruptcy Band 2
Table: p.1179

Kornfeld, Armand J
(Washington)
Profile: p.1793
Bankruptcy Band 2
Table: p.1776

Kornreich, David (Florida)
Profile: p.544
Employment Band 3
Table: p.513

Kornreich, Edward S
(New York)
Profile: p.1294
Healthcare Band 2
Table: p.1209

Kornstein, Alan F (New
Jersey)
Profile: p.1142
Corporate/M&A Band 3
Table: p.1123

Kosacz, Barbara (California)
Profile: p.260
Corporate/M&A Band 4
Table: p.197

Koschik, David N (New York)
Profile: p.1294
Banking & Finance Band 4
Table: p.1174

Kotchka, Malani (Nevada)
Profile: p.1102
Employment Band 3
Table: p.1091

Kotran, Stephen M
(New York)
Profile: p.1294
Corporate/M&A
Up and coming
Table: p.1189

Kovner, Victor A (New York)
Profile: p.1295
Media & Entertainment Band 1
Table: p.1232

Kozachok, Steve
(Minnesota)
Profile: p.1018
Corporate/M&A
Up and coming
Table: p.1005

Kozak, John (Illinois)
Profile: p.736
Intellectual Property **Band 2**
Table: p.696

Kozyak, John W (Florida)
Profile: p.544
Bankruptcy **Band 1**
Table: p.503

Kraft, Barbara Simpson
(Alaska)
Profile: p.143
Corporate/M&A **Band 1**
Table: p.134

Kraftson, Daniel (Virginia)
Profile: p.1770
Construction **Band 3**
Table: p.1750

Krambeck, James (Iowa)
Profile: p.813
Corporate/M&A **Band 2**
Table: p.802

Kramer, Andrew
(District of Columbia)
Profile: p.451
Employment **Band 2**
Table: p.380

Kramer, Daniel (New York)
Profile: p.1295
Litigation **Band 3**
Table: p.1223

Kramer, J Scott
(Pennsylvania)
Profile: p.1529
Intellectual Property **Band 4**
Table: p.1508

Kramer, Jay (Arizona)
Profile: p.160
Real Estate **Band 3**
Table: p.154

Kramer, Kenneth M
(New York)
Profile: p.1295
Antitrust **Band 4**
Table: p.1170

Kramer, Merrill
(District of Columbia)
Profile: p.451
Energy **Band 5**
Table: p.386

Kramer, Morris J (New York)
Profile: p.1295
Corporate/M&A **Band 1**
Table: p.1189

Kramer, Samuel (Illinois)
Profile: p.736
Technology **Band 3**
Table: p.713

Kramer, Steven E
(Tennessee)
Profile: p.1609
Employment **Band 3**
Table: p.1596

Kramer, Thomas I (Oregon)
Profile: p.1483
Employment **Band 3**
Table: p.1474

Krapf, Robert J (Delaware)
Profile: p.354
Real Estate **Band 1**
Table: p.350

Krasnow, Jordan
(Massachusetts)
Profile: p.970
Real Estate **Band 1**
Table: p.956

Krasnow, Richard P
(New York)
Profile: p.1295
Bankruptcy **Band 4**
Table: p.1179

Krasow, Herbert
(Connecticut)
Profile: p.337
Real Estate **Band 2**
Table: p.334

Krauland, Edward (National)
Profile: p.91
International Trade **Band 1**
Table: p.41

Kraus, Alan E (New Jersey)
Profile: p.1142
Litigation **Band 2**
Table: p.1131

Kraus, Bruce R (New York)
Profile: p.1295
Technology **Band 1**
Table: p.1259

Kraus, Kenneth L
(Tennessee)
Profile: p.1609
Media & Entertainment **Band 1**
Table: p.1602

Krauss, Joseph G
(District of Columbia)
Profile: p.451
Antitrust **Band 5**
Table: p.367

Kravitt, Jason H P
(National)
Profile: p.91
Capital Markets **Band S**
Table: p.19

Krebs, Arno (Texas)
Profile: p.1687
Insurance **Band 3**
Table: p.1648

Krebs, Michael
(Massachusetts)
Profile: p.970
Banking & Finance **Band 3**
Table: p.932

Krebs, Stephen (Texas)
Profile: p.1687
Projects **Band 3**
Table: p.1659

Kreger, Michael E (Alaska)
Profile: p.143
Litigation **Band 1**
Table: p.138

Kreider, Gary (Ohio)
Profile: p.1443
Corporate/M&A **Band S**
Table: p.1419

Kreiger, Arthur
(Massachusetts)
Profile: p.970
Environment **Band 3**
Table: p.943

Kreller, Thomas R
(California)
Profile: p.260
Bankruptcy **Band 4**
Table: p.191

Krendl, Cathy S (Colorado)
Profile: p.319
Corporate/M&A **Band 3**
Table: p.303

Kress, Alan (New York)
Profile: p.1295
Media & Entertainment **Band 1**
Table: p.1235

Kreusler-Walsh, Jane
(Florida)
Profile: p.544
Litigation **Band 2**
Table: p.525

Krieger, Paul (Texas)
Profile: p.1687
Intellectual Property **Band 3**
Table: p.1651

Krieger, Thomas
(West Virginia)
Profile: p.1809
Employment **Band 2**
Table: p.1801

Krieser, Jason D (Texas)
Profile: p.1688
Technology **Band 3**
Table: p.1668

Krischer, Gordon (California)
Profile: p.260
Employment **Band 4**
Table: p.202

Kristol, Daniel (Delaware)
Profile: p.354
Real Estate **Band 3**
Table: p.350

Kritenbrink, Lawrence E
(Nebraska)
Profile: p.1088
Real Estate **Band 2**
Table: p.1086

Krizan, Lisa M (Virginia)
Profile: p.1770
Intellectual Property **Band 2**
Table: p.1761

Kroesche, Guy (Utah)
Profile: p.1737
Real Estate **Band 2**
Table: p.1733

Kronk, Catherine (Vermont)
Profile: p.1749
Real Estate **Band 2**
Table: p.1747

Kronk, Edward M
(Michigan)
Profile: p.1000
Litigation **Band 3**
Table: p.994

Kroon, David
(South Dakota)
Profile: p.1593
Corporate/M&A **Band 3**
Table: p.1587

Krouse Jr, George R
(National)
Profile: p.91
Capital Markets **Band 4**
Table: p.14

Krovatin, Gerald
(New Jersey)
Profile: p.1142
Litigation **Band 1**
Table: p.1133

Krueger, Herbert W (Illinois)
Profile: p.736
Employee Benefits **Band 1**
Table: p.681
Private Equity **Band 3**
Table: p.676

Krueger, Karen G (New York)
Profile: p.1295
Employee Benefits **Band 1**
Table: p.1197

Krugman, Edward P
(New York)
Profile: p.1295
Insurance **Band 2**
Table: p.1213

Krumholz, Dennis J (New Jersey)
Profile: p.1142
Environment **Band 1**
Table: p.1129

Krupka, Robert G
(California)
Profile: p.260
Intellectual Property **Band 1**
Table: p.216

Krupp, Peter C (Illinois)
Profile: p.736
Private Equity **Band 2**
Table: p.676

Kruse, Layne (Texas)
Profile: p.1688
Antitrust **Band 2**
Table: p.1622

Kubetz, Bernard J (Maine)
Profile: p.899
Litigation **Band 3**
Table: p.893

Kubicek, David W (Iowa)
Profile: p.813
Real Estate **Band 1**
Table: p.810

Kudenholdt, Stephen S
(National)
Profile: p.91
Capital Markets **Band 3**
Table: p.19

Kudlac, Kevin (Texas)
Profile: p.1688
Intellectual Property **Band 3**
Table: p.1651

Kudo, Benjamin (Hawaii)
Profile: p.648
Land Use **Band 1**
Table: p.643

Kuehne, Benedict P
(Florida)
Profile: p.544
Litigation **Band 2**
Table: p.522

Kuehnle, Kenton (Ohio)
Profile: p.1443

Real Estate **Band 4**
Table: p.1434

Kuester, Jeffrey R (Georgia)
Profile: p.617
Intellectual Property **Band 4**
Table: p.596

Kuhn, Michael (Texas)
Profile: p.1688
Real Estate **Band 3**
Table: p.1662

Kummer, Thomas F
(Nevada)
Profile: p.1102
Litigation **Band 3**
Table: p.1096

Kumpe, Peter (Arkansas)
Profile: p.177
Litigation **Band 2**
Table: p.172

Kuney, David
(District of Columbia)
Profile: p.452
Bankruptcy **Band 2**
Table: p.372

Kunkel, Daniel H (Florida)
Profile: p.544
Employment **Band 3**
Table: p.513

Kunkel, William R (Illinois)
Profile: p.736
Corporate/M&A **Band 2**
Table: p.675

Kuntz, Michael (Washington)
Profile: p.1793
Real Estate **Band 1**
Table: p.1788

Kunz, C Thomas (National)
Profile: p.92
Capital Markets **Band 1**
Table: p.19

Kunz, Donald (Michigan)
Profile: p.1000
Corporate/M&A **Band 1**
Table: p.989

Kupec, Christopher C
(North Carolina)
Profile: p.1397
Banking & Finance **Band 1**
Table: p.1381

Kurtzon, Michael S (Illinois)
Profile: p.736
Real Estate **Band 3**
Table: p.706

Kuryla, Matthew (Texas)
Profile: p.1688
Environment **Up and coming**
Table: p.1643

Kurzweil, David (Georgia)
Profile: p.617
Bankruptcy **Band 3**
Table: p.582

Kurzweil, Harvey (New York)
Profile: p.1295
Litigation **Band 3**
Table: p.1222

Kushner, Harold (Alabama)
Profile: p.123
Corporate/M&A **Band 1**
Table: p.111

K

Kutler, Marilyn
(Pennsylvania)
Profile: p.1529
Real Estate **Band 2**
Table: p.1516

Kutzman, John (Montana)
Profile: p.1080
Employment **Band 2**
Table: p.1073

Kutzschbach, George
(Texas)
Profile: p.1688
Energy **Band 2**
Table: p.1637

Kwasnick, Raymond
(Massachusetts)
Profile: p.970
Real Estate **Band 3**
Table: p.956

Kyle, Amy L (Massachusetts)
Profile: p.970
Banking & Finance **Band 2**
Table: p.932

Kyper, James R
(Pennsylvania)
Profile: p.1529
Intellectual Property **Band 4**
Table: p.1508

L

La Suer, Gene (Iowa)
Profile: p.813
Employment **Band 2**
Table: p.805

Labate, Robert (Illinois)
Profile: p.736
Media & Entertainment **Band 1**
Table: p.704

LaCagnin, Stephen
(West Virginia)
Profile: p.1809
Litigation **Band 2**
Table: p.1803

Lacy, John (Hawaii)
Profile: p.648
Litigation **Band 3**
Table: p.644

Lacy, Jr, Peyton (Alabama)
Profile: p.123
Employment **Band 3**
Table: p.113

Ladd, Jeffrey R (Illinois)
Profile: p.736
Healthcare **Band 2**
Table: p.690

Ladov, Donald (Pennsylvania)
Profile: p.1529
Employment **Band 2**
Table: p.1500

Lafferty, William M
(Delaware)
Profile: p.354
Chancery **Band 4**
Table: p.344

Lafiandra, Aldo L (Georgia)
Profile: p.617
Banking & Finance
Up and coming
Table: p.580

Lafitte, Gene W (Louisiana)
Profile: p.873
Litigation **Band 2**
Table: p.865

LaFollette, Christine B
(Texas)
Profile: p.1688
Corporate/M&A **Band 3**
Table: p.1631

LaFuze, William L (Texas)
Profile: p.1688
Intellectual Property **Band 1**
Table: p.1651

Laird, Michael S (Oklahoma)
Profile: p.1465
Real Estate **Band 1**
Table: p.1464

Lake, William T
(District of Columbia)
Profile: p.452
Telecom, Broadcast & Satellite
Band 2
Table: p.427

Lalle, Wayne (Virginia)
Profile: p.1770
Construction **Band 1**
Table: p.1750

Lamar III, Howard H
(Tennessee)
Profile: p.1609
Corporate/M&A **Band 3**
Table: p.1594

Lamb, Christopher J
(Delaware)
Profile: p.354
Real Estate **Band 3**
Table: p.350

Lamb, William S (New York)
Profile: p.1295
Energy **Band 1**
Table: p.1202
Energy **Band 1**
Table: p.1202

Lambert, LeRoy (New York)
Profile: p.92
Shipping **Band 3**
Table: p.67

Lamdin III, William
(Montana)
Profile: p.1080
Corporate/M&A **Band 1**
Table: p.1072

Lamken, Jeffrey A
(District of Columbia)
Profile: p.452
Litigation **Band 2**
Table: p.408

Lamm, Carolyn (National)
Profile: p.92
Arbitration **Band**
Table: p.33
Arbitration **Band 2**
Table: p.33

Lamon, Bruce (Hawaii)
Profile: p.649
Litigation **Band 2**
Table: p.644

Lampert, James
(Massachusetts)
Profile: p.970
Intellectual Property **Band 3**
Table: p.948

Lamson, Jeffrey (Iowa)
Profile: p.813
Corporate/M&A **Band 4**
Table: p.802

Lamson, William (Nebraska)
Profile: p.1088
Insurance **Band 1**
Table: p.1085

Landa, Leor (New York)
Profile: p.1296
Private Equity **Up and coming**
Table: p.1241

Landefeld, Stewart
(Washington)
Profile: p.1793
Corporate/M&A **Band 1**
Table: p.1778

Landis, Adam G. (Delaware)
Profile: p.354
Bankruptcy **Band 3**
Table: p.341

Landis, James M (Florida)
Profile: p.544
Antitrust **Band 3**
Table: p.498

Landon, Stephen
(South Dakota)
Profile: p.1593
Litigation **Band 2**
Table: p.1590

Landry, Charles (Louisiana)
Profile: p.873
Real Estate **Band 2**
Table: p.867

Landsberg, Barry S
(California)
Profile: p.260
Healthcare **Band 2**
Table: p.209

Lane, David (Virginia)
Profile: p.1770
Construction **Band 1**
Table: p.1750

Lane, Joe (Florida)
Profile: p.544
Construction **Band 3**
Table: p.507

Lane, Robert (Pennsylvania)
Profile: p.1529
Real Estate **Band 2**
Table: p.1516
Real Estate **Band 2**
Table: p.1516

Lane, Roger (Massachusetts)
Profile: p.970
Litigation **Band 3**
Table: p.951

Lane, Thomas (West Virginia)
Profile: p.1809
Real Estate **Band 1**
Table: p.1806

Langan, J Andrew (Illinois)
Profile: p.736
Antitrust **Band 2**
Table: p.662

Langdon, Larry R (California)
Profile: p.260
Tax **Band 4**
Table: p.241

Langel, John B
(Pennsylvania)
Profile: p.1529
Employment **Band 3**
Table: p.1500

Langer, Howard
(Pennsylvania)
Profile: p.1529
Antitrust **Band 3**
Table: p.1489

Langevin, Judith Bevis
(Minnesota)
Profile: p.1018
Employment **Band 2**
Table: p.1008

Langlois, Jack J (Texas)
Profile: p.1688
Energy **Band 4**
Table: p.1637

Laniado, Sam (New York)
Profile: p.1296
Energy **Band 1**
Table: p.1204

Lanier, Randolph (Alabama)
Profile: p.123
Real Estate **Band 2**
Table: p.119

Lansky, David (Arizona)
Profile: p.160
Real Estate **Band 1**
Table: p.154

Lapidus, Steve (Florida)
Profile: p.544
Tax **Band 1**
Table: p.531

Laporte, Claire
(Massachusetts)
Profile: p.970
Intellectual Property **Band 3**
Table: p.948

LaPorte, Dale C (Ohio)
Profile: p.1443
Corporate/M&A **Band 3**
Table: p.1419

Lapowsky, Robert
(Pennsylvania)
Profile: p.1529
Bankruptcy **Band 3**
Table: p.1494

Larsen, Tracy (Michigan)
Profile: p.1000
Corporate/M&A **Band 1**
Table: p.989

Larson, David (Wyoming)
Profile: p.1838
Real Estate **Band 1**
Table: p.1836

Larson, John (California)
Profile: p.260
Corporate/M&A **Band 3**
Table: p.197

Larson, Joseph D (New York)
Profile: p.
Antitrust **Up and coming**
Table: p.1170

LaRue, James D (Idaho)
Profile: p.660
Litigation **Band 2**
Table: p.657

Lasater Jr, W Robert
(New Mexico)
Profile: p.1163
Litigation **Band 1**
Table: p.1160

Lascher, Alan (New York)
Profile: p.1296
Real Estate **Band 4**
Table: p.1248

Laseter, Scott (Georgia)
Profile: p.617
Environment **Up and coming**
Table: p.593

Lassar, Scott R (Illinois)
Profile: p.736
Litigation **Band 3**
Table: p.700

Lassiter, Donnell
(North Carolina)
Profile: p.1397
Banking & Finance **Band 3**
Table: p.1381

Laster, J Travis (Delaware)
Profile: p.354
Chancery **Band 3**
Table: p.344

Latham, William Larry
(Mississippi)
Profile: p.1034
Litigation **Band 3**
Table: p.1028

Lathrop, Alex
(District of Columbia)
Profile: p.452
Insurance **Up and coming**
Table: p.402

Latimer, Kenneth A (Illinois)
Profile: p.736
Banking & Finance **Band 3**
Table: p.665

LaTour, Randall D (Ohio)
Profile: p.1443
Bankruptcy **Band 4**
Table: p.1414

Latza, William (New York)
Profile: p.1296
Insurance **Band 3**
Table: p.1213

Lauer, Eliot (New York)
Profile: p.1296
Litigation **Band 3**
Table: p.1222

Laupheimer, Ann Blair
(Pennsylvania)
Profile: p.1529
Litigation **Band 3**
Table: p.1511

Lauria, Thomas (Florida)
Profile: p.544
Bankruptcy **Band 3**
Table: p.503

Laurie, Ty D (Illinois)
Profile: p.736
Construction **Band 2**
Table: p.672

Lause, Michael F (Missouri)
Profile: p.1058
Corporate/M&A **Band 2**
Table: p.1043

Lavely Jr, John H (California)
Profile: p.261
Media & Entertainment **Band 2**
Table: p.230

Lavey, Stewart (New Jersey)
Profile: p.1142
Corporate/M&A **Band 3**
Table: p.1123

Lavey, Wendlene M (Ohio)
Profile: p.1443
Environment **Up and coming**
Table: p.1425

LaVine, Jordan A
(Pennsylvania)
Profile: p.1529
Intellectual Property
Up and coming
Table: p.1508

Lavorgna, Gregory J
(Pennsylvania)
Profile: p.1530
Intellectual Property **Band 2**
Table: p.1508

Law, David M
(New Hampshire)
Profile: p.1118
Tax **Band 2**
Table: p.1107

Law, Rhea (Florida)
Profile: p.544
Real Estate **Band 2**
Table: p.528

Lawall, Francis J
(Pennsylvania)
Profile: p.1530
Bankruptcy **Band 3**
Table: p.1494

Lawler, Andrew (New York)
Profile: p.1296
Litigation **Band 3**
Table: p.1224

Lawless, J Mark (Texas)
Profile: p.1688
Insurance **Band 2**
Table: p.1648

Lawlor, William G
(Pennsylvania)
Profile: p.1530
Corporate/M&A **Band 2**
Table: p.1497

Lawniczak, James (Ohio)
Profile: p.1443
Bankruptcy **Band 3**
Table: p.1414

Lawrence, Adam (Florida)
Profile: p.544
Litigation **Band 2**
Table: p.525

Lawrence, James K L
(Ohio)
Profile: p.1444
Employment **Band 2**
Table: p.1422

Lawrence, Robert
(Colorado)
Profile: p.320
Environment **Band 1**
Table: p.307

Lawson, David
(District of Columbia)
Profile: p.452

Telecom, Broadcast & Satellite
Band 4
Table: p.427

LeClaire, John R
(Massachusetts)
Profile: p.970
Private Equity **Band 2**
Table: p.953

Ledbetter, Cheryl
(West Virginia)
Profile: p.1809
Employment **Band 2**
Table: p.1801

Leddy, Mark
(District of Columbia)
Profile: p.452
Antitrust **Band 1**
Table: p.367

Lederer, Gregory (Iowa)
Profile: p.813
Litigation **Band 2**
Table: p.807

Lederman, Alan (Florida)
Profile: p.544
Tax **Band 1**
Table: p.531

LeDuc, André (Illinois)
Profile: p.737
Tax **Band 3**
Table: p.710

Lee, Carl B (Texas)
Profile: p.1688
Real Estate **Band 3**
Table: p.1662

Lee, Carolyn Joy (New York)
Profile: p.1296
Tax **Band 3**
Table: p.1255

Lee, Charlie (Virginia)
Profile: p.1770
Construction **Band 2**
Table: p.1750

Lee, James J (Texas)
Profile: p.1688
Bankruptcy **Band 2**
Table: p.1627

Lee, Jeffrey (Alabama)
Profile: p.123
Employment **Band 2**
Table: p.113

Lee, Jessica (Colorado)
Profile: p.320
Employment **Band 3**
Table: p.306

Lee, John (Texas)
Profile: p.1689
Bankruptcy **Band 1**
Table: p.1627

Lee, John R (Montana)
Profile: p.1080
Natural Resources **Band 2**
Table: p.1077

Lee, Robert C (Illinois)
Profile: p.737
Real Estate **Band 3**
Table: p.706

Lee, Stephen (Indiana)
Profile: p.793
Real Estate **Band 3**
Table: p.788

Layne, Jonathan (California)
Profile: p.261
Corporate/M&A **Band 5**
Table: p.197

Layson, Frank (Georgia)
Profile: p.617
Corporate/M&A **Band 4**
Table: p.587

Lazarow, Warren T
(California)
Profile: p.261
Corporate/M&A **Band 4**
Table: p.197

Lazarus, Larry (Arizona)
Profile: p.160
Real Estate **Band 2**
Table: p.155

Lazarus, Lewis H (Delaware)
Profile: p.354
Chancery **Band 4**
Table: p.344

Lazarus, Robert
(Mississippi)
Profile: p.1034
Corporate/M&A **Band 2**
Table: p.1024

Leach, Donald (Ohio)
Profile: p.1444
Construction **Band 3**
Table: p.1417

Leach, John (Alabama)
Profile: p.123
Litigation **Band 3**
Table: p.116

Leahy, James R (Texas)
Profile: p.1688
Litigation **Band 3**
Table: p.1656

Leake, Paul (New York)
Profile: p.1296
Bankruptcy **Band 4**
Table: p.1179

Leaverton, Bruce
(Washington)
Profile: p.1793
Bankruptcy **Band 2**
Table: p.1776

Lebowitz, Molly (Vermont)
Profile: p.1749
Real Estate **Band 1**
Table: p.1747

Leccese, Joseph M
(National)
Profile: p.92
Sport **Band 1**
Table: p.55

LeClair, Gary D (Virginia)
Profile: p.1770
Corporate/M&A **Band 2**

Table: p.1752

Lee, Steven J (New York)
Profile: p.1296
Intellectual Property **Band 2**
Table: p.1217

Lee, William F
(Massachusetts)
Profile: p.971
Intellectual Property ✪
Table: p.948

Lee, William S (Texas)
Profile: p.1689
Litigation **Band 2**
Table: p.1665

Leech, Sidney (Maryland)
Profile: p.922
Litigation **Band 3**
Table: p.914

Lefeber, Peter (Connecticut)
Profile: p.337
Employment **Band 2**
Table: p.329

Leff, Neil M (New York)
Profile: p.1296
Employee Benefits **Band 3**
Table: p.1197

Leff, Philip (Iowa)
Profile: p.813
Real Estate **Band 3**
Table: p.810

Lefkowitz, David (National)
Profile: p.92
Capital Markets **Band 4**
Table: p.14

Lefkowitz, Ken (New York)
Profile: p.1296
Corporate/M&A **Band 4**
Table: p.1189

Lefkowitz, Stephen
(New York)
Profile: p.1296
Real Estate **Band 1**
Table: p.1248

Leggette, Poe
(District of Columbia)
Profile: p.452
Energy **Band 3**
Table: p.382

Legler, Mitchell (Florida)
Profile: p.544
Corporate/M&A **Band 2**
Table: p.509

Lehman, Michael P
(New Hampshire)
Profile: p.1118
Litigation **Band 1**
Table: p.1111

Lehman, Steven (Montana)
Profile: p.1080
Employment **Band 1**
Table: p.1073

Lehr, Richard (Alabama)
Profile: p.123
Employment **Band 3**
Table: p.113

Leibensperger, Edward P
(Massachusetts)
Profile: p.971
Litigation **Band 3**
Table: p.951

Leibowitz, Lewis E
(National)
Profile: p.92
International Trade **Band 2**
Table: p.40

Leiby, Larry R (Florida)
Profile: p.544
Construction **Band 1**
Table: p.507

Leich, Christopher M
(Massachusetts)
Profile: p.971
Tax **Band 3**
Table: p.959

Leichtling, Ely A (Wisconsin)
Profile: p.1825
Employment **Band 2**
Table: p.1819

Leisner, Richard (Florida)
Profile: p.544
Corporate/M&A **Band 3**
Table: p.509

Lelong, Rivers (Louisiana)
Profile: p.873
Banking & Finance
Up and coming
Table: p.857

Lemein, Gregg D (Illinois)
Profile: p.737
Tax **Band**
Table: p.710
Tax **Band 2**
Table: p.710

Lemly, Thomas A
(Washington)
Profile: p.1793
Employment **Band 1**
Table: p.1780

Lenhard, Kirk (Nevada)
Profile: p.1103
Litigation **Band 2**
Table: p.1096

Lennon, Daniel
(District of Columbia)
Profile: p.452
Corporate/Commercial **Band 2**
Table: p.376

Lennon, Maureen (Montana)
Profile: p.1080
Employment **Band 2**
Table: p.1073

Lennox, Heather (Ohio)
Profile: p.1444
Bankruptcy **Band 3**
Table: p.1414

Lents, Donald (Missouri)
Profile: p.1058
Corporate/M&A **Band 1**
Table: p.1043

Leo, Thomas Glen
(California)
Profile: p.261
Media & Entertainment **Band 3**
Table: p.233

Leon, Christopher (North
Carolina)
Profile: p.1397
Banking & Finance **Band 3**
Table: p.1381

Laxalt, Bruce (Nevada)
Profile: p.1103
Litigation **Band 2**
Table: p.1096

Lawson, Jack (Indiana)
Profile: p.793
Real Estate **Band 3**
Table: p.788

Leon, Michael
(Massachusetts)
Profile: p.971
Environment **Band 2**
Table: p.943

Leonard, Stephen
(Massachusetts)
Profile: p.971
Environment **Band 2**
Table: p.943

Leonard III, Edward D
(Maine)
Profile: p.899
Real Estate **Band 2**
Table: p.895

Leonetti, Kenneth
(Massachusetts)
Profile: p.971
Bankruptcy **Band 3**
Table: p.935

Leong, Alvin K. (National)
Profile: p.92
Aviation **Up and coming**
Table: p.58

Leong, Donna Y L (Hawaii)
Profile: p.649
Land Use **Band 1**
Table: p.643
Real Estate **Band 1**
Table: p.646

Leong, Ronald Y K (Hawaii)
Profile: p.649
Employment **Band 2**
Table: p.642

Leonhardt, Frederick
(Florida)
Profile: p.544
Real Estate **Band 3**
Table: p.528

LePatner, Barry (New York)
Profile: p.1296
Construction **Band 4**
Table: p.1186

Lepene, Alan (Ohio)
Profile: p.1444
Bankruptcy **Band 1**
Table: p.1414

Leppo, Jeffery W.
(Washington)
Profile: p.1793
Environment **Band 1**
Table: p.1782

Lerach, William S
(California)
Profile: p.261
Litigation **Band 2**
Table: p.224

Lerman, Bradley (Illinois)
Profile: p.737
Litigation **Band 4**
Table: p.700

Lerman, Cary (California)
Profile: p.261
Insurance **Band 2**
Table: p.212

Lerman, Steven A
(District of Columbia)
Profile: p.452
Telecom, Broadcast & Satellite
Band 4
Table: p.427

Lerner, Jonathan J
(New York)
Profile: p.1296
Litigation **Band 2**
Table: p.1222
Litigation **Band 2**
Table: p.1223

Lerner, Stephen D (Ohio)
Profile: p.1444
Bankruptcy **Band 1**
Table: p.1414

Lesser, Bruce (Pennsylvania)
Profile: p.1530
Banking & Finance **Band 2**
Table: p.1493

Lesser, Henry (California)
Profile: p.261
Corporate/M&A **Band 3**
Table: p.197

Lesser, Steven (Florida)
Profile: p.545
Construction **Band 2**
Table: p.507

Lester, David (Kentucky)
Profile: p.843
Corporate/M&A **Band 2**
Table: p.827

Letscher, Tom (Minnesota)
Profile: p.1018
Corporate/M&A **Band 3**
Table: p.1005

Letzler, Kenneth
(District of Columbia)
Profile: p.452
Antitrust **Band 4**
Table: p.367

Leukart, Barbara (Ohio)
Profile: p.1444
Employment **Band 2**
Table: p.1422

Leukart II, Richard (Ohio)
Profile: p.1444
Employment **Band 3**
Table: p.1422

Levander, Andrew J
(New York)
Profile: p.1296
Litigation **Band 3**
Table: p.1224

LeVee, Jeffrey A (California)
Profile: p.261
Antitrust **Band 3**
Table: p.184

Leveille, Michael G
(Georgia)
Profile: p.617
Banking & Finance
Up and coming
Table: p.580

Leventhal, Robert A
(Florida)
Profile: p.545
Litigation **Band 2**
Table: p.522

Levi, Stuart D (New York)
Profile: p.1297
Technology **Band 2**
Table: p.1259

Levin, Ali (Utah)
Profile: p.1737
Employment **Up and coming**

Table: p.1730

Levin, Barry S (California)
Profile: p.261
Insurance **Band 3**
Table: p.212

Levin, Benjamin D
(Wisconsin)
Profile: p.1825
Real Estate **Band 2**
Table: p.1822

Levin, Christine C
(Pennsylvania)
Profile: p.1530
Antitrust **Band 3**
Table: p.1489
Litigation **Band 3**
Table: p.1512

Levin, Edward J (Maryland)
Profile: p.922
Real Estate **Band 1**
Table: p.917

Levin, Jack S (Illinois)
Profile: p.737
Corporate/M&A **Band S**
Table: p.675
Private Equity **Band S**
Table: p.676
Tax **Band S**
Table: p.710

Levin, Jay J (Georgia)
Profile: p.617
Real Estate **Band 3**
Table: p.601

Levin, Jim (Wisconsin)
Profile: p.1825
Real Estate **Band 2**
Table: p.1822

Levin, Matthew W (Georgia)
Profile: p.617
Bankruptcy **Band 3**
Table: p.582

Levin, Peter (New York)
Profile: p.1297
Banking & Finance **Band 2**
Table: p.1174

Levin, Richard B (California)
Profile: p.261
Bankruptcy **Band 2**
Table: p.191

Levine, Alan (New York)
Profile: p.1297
Litigation **Band 3**
Table: p.1222
Litigation **Band 3**
Table: p.1224

Levine, David J (National)
Profile: p.92
International Trade **Band 4**
Table: p.40
International Trade **Band 2**
Table: p.41

Levine, Harvey R (California)
Profile: p.261
Insurance **Band 2**
Table: p.212

Levine, Henry D
(District of Columbia)
Profile: p.452
Telecom, Broadcast & Satellite
Band 3
Table: p.427

Levine, Janet (California)
Profile: p.261
Litigation **Band 1**
Table: p.225

Levine, Lee
(District of Columbia)
Profile: p.452
Media & Entertainment **Band 1**
Table: p.413

Levine, Richard
(Massachusetts)
Profile: p.971
Bankruptcy **Band 3**
Table: p.935

Levine, Richard A
(Delaware)
Profile: p.355
Real Estate **Band 3**
Table: p.350

Levine, Richard E
(Maryland)
Profile: p.922
Real Estate **Band 3**
Table: p.917

Levine, Ronald (Colorado)
Profile: p.320
Corporate/M&A **Band 1**
Table: p.303

Levitas, Steven J
(North Carolina)
Profile: p.1397
Environment **Band 2**
Table: p.1388

Levy, Charles S (National)
Profile: p.93
International Trade **Band 4**
Table: p.40

Levy, Gregg (National)
Profile: p.93
Sport **Band 1**
Table: p.55

Levy, Jay M (Florida)
Profile: p.545
Litigation **Band 2**
Table: p.525

Levy, Lisa (New York)
Profile: p.1297
Tax **Band 4**
Table: p.1255

Levy, Mark (Colorado)
Profile: p.320
Corporate/M&A **Band 2**
Table: p.303

Levy, Mark P (Ohio)
Profile: p.1444
Intellectual Property **Band 3**
Table: p.1428

Levy, William A (Illinois)
Profile: p.737
Tax **Band 2**
Table: p.710

Lewin, Robert (New York)
Profile: p.1297
Insurance **Band 3**
Table: p.1213

Lewis, Charles (Illinois)
Profile: p.737
Construction **Band 3**
Table: p.672

Lewis, Daniel
(District of Columbia)
Profile: p.453
Bankruptcy **Band 1**
Table: p.372

Lewis, David
(District of Columbia)
Profile: p.453
Energy **Band 2**
Table: p.390

Lewis, Denise (Michigan)
Profile: p.1000
Real Estate **Band 3**
Table: p.996

Lewis, Frederick
(Tennessee)
Profile: p.1609
Employment **Band 3**
Table: p.1596

Lewis, Jack (Virginia)
Profile: p.1770
Corporate/M&A **Band 3**
Table: p.1752

Lewis, John (Ohio)
Profile: p.1444
Employment **Band 2**
Table: p.1422

Lewis, Kim Martin (Ohio)
Profile: p.1444
Bankruptcy **Band 2**
Table: p.1414

Lewis, Sidney (Louisiana)
Profile: p.873
Employment **Band 3**
Table: p.861

Lewis, Steve (Florida)
Profile: p.545
Environment **Band 3**
Table: p.516

Lewis, Terry (Florida)
Profile: p.545
Environment **Band 1**
Table: p.516

Lewis, Thomas B (Maryland)
Profile: p.922
Real Estate **Band 4**
Table: p.917

Lewis, Tom (Montana)
Profile: p.1080
Litigation **Band 1**
Table: p.1075

Lewis, William
(District of Columbia)
Profile: p.453
Environment **Band 2**
Table: p.392

Lewkow, Victor I (New York)
Profile: p.1297
Corporate/M&A **Band 1**
Table: p.1189

Lian Jr, Robert G
(District of Columbia)
Profile: p.453
Employment **Up and coming**
Table: p.380

Libanoff, Ira (Florida)
Profile: p.545
Construction **Band 3**
Table: p.507

L

Libbey, Keith (Minnesota)
Profile: p.1018
Corporate/M&A Band 2
Table: p.1005

Libin, Jerome
(District of Columbia)
Profile: p.453
Tax Band 2
Table: p.422

Lichtenbaum, Greta
(National)
Profile: p.93
International Trade Band 2
Table: p.41

Lichtenstein, Robert J
(Pennsylvania)
Profile: p.1530
Employee Benefits Band 1
Table: p.1501

Lichter, Linda (California)
Profile: p.261
Media & Entertainment Band 2
Table: p.233

Licko, Carol A (Florida)
Profile: p.545
Litigation Band 3
Table: p.521

Liddon, Rob (Tennessee)
Profile: p.1609
Real Estate Band 1
Table: p.1603

Liebenberg, Roberta
(Pennsylvania)
Profile: p.1530
Antitrust Band 2
Table: p.1489

Lieberman, David
(New York)
Profile: p.1297
Projects Band 4
Table: p.1244

Lieberman, Richard E
(Illinois)
Profile: p.737
Employment Band 1
Table: p.681

Liebman, Kenneth A
(Minnesota)
Profile: p.1018
Litigation Band 1
Table: p.1012

Liebman, Richard (Oregon)
Profile: p.1483
Employment Band 1
Table: p.1474

Liebmann, Jeff S (New York)
Profile: p.1297
Insurance Band 1
Table: p.1213

Liever, Michael H
(California)
Profile: p.261
Real Estate Band 2
Table: p.238

Liggett, Luther (Ohio)
Profile: p.1444
Construction Band 4
Table: p.1417

Lightfoot, Michael J
(California)
Profile: p.261
Litigation Band 2
Table: p.225

Lightfoot, Warren (Alabama)
Profile: p.123
Litigation Band 1
Table: p.116

Lighthizer, Robert E
(National)
Profile: p.93
International Trade Band 3
Table: p.40

Lightsey, Wallace
(South Carolina)
Profile: p.1581
Litigation Band 2
Table: p.1576

Lile, John G (Arkansas)
Profile: p.177
Employment Band 3
Table: p.170
Litigation Band 3
Table: p.172

Liles, Rutledge R (Florida)
Profile: p.545
Litigation Band 3
Table: p.521

Lilien, Warren (New York)
Profile: p.1297
Projects Band 4
Table: p.1244

Lillis, William (Iowa)
Profile: p.813
Real Estate Band 1
Table: p.810

Liloia, Gerald A (New Jersey)
Profile: p.1142
Litigation Band 2
Table: p.1131

Liman, Lewis J (New York)
Profile: p.1297
Litigation Band 3
Table: p.1224

Limeres, Amy (Alaska)
Profile: p.143
Employment Band 2
Table: p.135

Lincenberg, Gary (California)
Profile: p.261
Litigation Band 2
Table: p.225

Lincoln, Michael (Virginia)
Profile: p.1770
Corporate/M&A Band 2
Table: p.1752

Lindauer, Erik D (New York)
Profile: p.1297
Banking & Finance Band 3
Table: p.1174

Lindberg, Lawrence (Ohio)
Profile: p.1444
Real Estate Band 3
Table: p.1434

Lindefjeld, Robert O
(Pennsylvania)
Profile: p.1530
Intellectual Property Band 4
Table: p.1508

Lindenbaum, Samuel H
(New York)
Profile: p.1297
Real Estate Band 1
Table: p.1248

Lindgren, Jay (Minnesota)
Profile: p.1019
Real Estate Band 1
Table: p.1015

Lindley, Greg (Utah)
Profile: p.1737
Corporate/M&A Band 3
Table: p.1727

Lindquist, Shawn J (Utah)
Profile: p.1737
Corporate/M&A
Up and coming
Table: p.1727

Lindsey, David (National)
Profile: p.93
Arbitration Band 3
Table: p.33

Linfield, James (Colorado)
Profile: p.320
Corporate/M&A Band 1
Table: p.303

Linklater, William J (Joe)
(Illinois)
Profile: p.737
Litigation Band 3
Table: p.700

Linquanti, Richard C
(Colorado)
Profile: p.320
Hotels and Resorts Band 2
Table: p.314
Real Estate Band 3
Table: p.313

Linstroth, Tod (Wisconsin)
Profile: p.1825
Corporate/M&A Band 2
Table: p.1817

Linton, John (South Carolina)
Profile: p.1581
Litigation Band 1
Table: p.1576

Linxwiler, James (Alaska)
Profile: p.143
Environment Band 3
Table: p.137
Native Law Band 1
Table: p.140

Linzy, Howard S (Louisiana)
Profile: p.874
Employment Band 2
Table: p.861

Lipe, Guy (Texas)
Profile: p.1689
Energy Band 3
Table: p.1640

Lipke, Doug (Illinois)
Profile: p.737
Bankruptcy Band 3
Table: p.669

Lipman, Andrew D
(District of Columbia)
Profile: p.453
Telecom, Broadcast & Satellite
Band 3
Table: p.427

Lipman, Frederick
(Pennsylvania)
Profile: p.1530
Corporate/M&A Band 4
Table: p.1497

Lipsey, Charles
(District of Columbia)
Profile: p.453
Intellectual Property Band 3
Table: p.403

Lipshie, Samuel D
(Tennessee)
Profile: p.1609
Litigation Band 3
Table: p.1599

Lipsky, Abbott (Tad)
(District of Columbia)
Profile: p.453
Antitrust Band 5
Table: p.367

Lipson, Kevin J
(District of Columbia)
Profile: p.453
Energy Band 3
Table: p.382

Lipson, Lawrence
(New York)
Profile: p.1298
Real Estate Band 3
Table: p.1248

Lipton, M Steven
(California)
Profile: p.261
Healthcare Band 2
Table: p.209

Lipton, Martin (New York)
Profile: p.1298
Corporate/M&A Band S
Table: p.1189

Lipton, Richard (Illinois)
Profile: p.737
Tax Band
Table: p.710
Tax Band 2
Table: p.710

Lischer, Dale (Georgia)
Profile: p.617
Intellectual Property Band 4
Table: p.596

Liscio, Mark F (New York)
Profile: p.1298
Bankruptcy Band 4
Table: p.1179

Lisher, Mary (Indiana)
Profile: p.793
Real Estate Band 2
Table: p.788

Lisicky, Joseph G
(Delaware)
Profile: p.355
Real Estate Band 3
Table: p.350

Lisker, Steven (Arizona)
Profile: p.160
Real Estate Band 2
Table: p.154

Lisman, Carl H (Vermont)
Profile: p.1749
Real Estate Band 2
Table: p.1747

Litchford, Hal (Florida)
Profile: p.545
Antitrust Band 3
Table: p.498

Litt, Daniel
(District of Columbia)
Profile: p.453
Bankruptcy Band 2
Table: p.372

Littenberg, Joseph
(New Jersey)
Profile: p.1142
Litigation Band 1
Table: p.1133

Little, Catherine (Georgia)
Profile: p.617
Environment Band 3
Table: p.593

Little, David (Utah)
Profile: p.1737
Corporate/M&A Band 3
Table: p.1727

Little, Kathleen C (National)
Profile: p.93
International Trade Band 1
Table: p.41

Little, Nancy (Virginia)
Profile: p.1770
Real Estate Band 2
Table: p.1765

Little Jr, Curtis
(New Hampshire)
Profile: p.1118
Corporate/M&A Band 2
Table: p.1107

Littman, Bernice (Hawaii)
Profile: p.649
Real Estate Band 2
Table: p.646

Litwak, Lawrence B
(Massachusetts)
Profile: p.971
Healthcare Band 2
Table: p.946

Litwin, Stuart M (Illinois)
Profile: p.93
Capital Markets Band 1
Table: p.21

Litz, Thomas A (Missouri)
Profile: p.1058
Corporate/M&A Band 2
Table: p.1043

Livingston, Donald R
(District of Columbia)
Profile: p.453
Employment Band 2
Table: p.380

Livingston, Louis (Oregon)
Profile: p.1483
Employment Band S
Table: p.1474

Livingston, Theodore A
(Illinois)
Profile: p.737
Telecom, Broadcast & Satellite
Band 1
Table: p.715

Lloyd, Brian (Utah)
Profile: p.1737
Corporate/M&A Band 1
Table: p.1727

L

Lobo, Glyndwr P (New York)
Profile: p.1298
Corporate/M&A
Up and coming
Table: p.1189

Lobrano, John D (National)
Profile: p.93
Capital Markets Band 4
Table: p.14

Lockett, Laurel (Florida)
Profile: p.545
Environment Band 3
Table: p.516

Loeb, Christopher
(North Carolina)
Profile: p.1397
Real Estate Band 3
Table: p.1392

Loeb Jr, Charles W
(West Virginia)
Profile: p.1809
Real Estate Band 3
Table: p.1806

Loftis, James (National)
Profile: p.93
Arbitration Band 3
Table: p.33

Loftis III, James R
(District of Columbia)
Profile: p.454
Antitrust Band 3
Table: p.367

Loftis Jr, W Randolph
(North Carolina)
Profile: p.1397
Employment Band 1
Table: p.1386

Loftus, C Michael (National)
Profile: p.93
Transport Band 2
Table: p.62

Logan, Kenneth (New York)
Profile: p.1298
Antitrust Band 2
Table: p.1170

Logan III, Ben H (California)
Profile: p.261
Bankruptcy Band 3
Table: p.191

LoGuidice, Susan E (Maine)
Profile: p.899
Corporate/M&A Band 3
Table: p.888

Lohmann, Walter H
(District of Columbia)
Profile: p.454
Environment Band 4
Table: p.392
Environment Band 2
Table: p.393

Lohr Jr, Walter (Maryland)
Profile: p.922
Corporate/M&A Band 1
Table: p.909

Lokey Jr, James (Georgia)
Profile: p.617
Tax Band 3
Table: p.603

Lombardi, Dennis (Hawaii)
Profile: p.649
Real Estate Band 1

Table: p.646

Londa, Jeffrey C (Texas)
Profile: p.1689
Employment Band 1
Table: p.1634

London, Eric (West Virginia)
Profile: p.1809
Real Estate Band 3
Table: p.1806

London, Martin (New York)
Profile: p.1298
Litigation Band 1
Table: p.1222

Lonergan, James (California)
Profile: p.261
Real Estate Band 2
Table: p.238

Lonergan, Matthew
(Tennessee)
Profile: p.1609
Employment Band 3
Table: p.1596

Long, Clay C (Georgia)
Profile: p.617
Corporate/M&A Band 2
Table: p.587

Long, Scott (West Virginia)
Profile: p.1809
Litigation Band 2
Table: p.1803

Long, Thomas (Wyoming)
Profile: p.1838
Corporate/M&A Band 1
Table: p.1832

Long Jr, Robert A
(District of Columbia)
Profile: p.454
Litigation Band 2
Table: p.408

Looman, James (Illinois)
Profile: p.737
Banking & Finance Band 3
Table: p.665

Lopatka, Kenneth T
(Illinois)
Profile: p.738
Employment Band 2
Table: p.681

Lopes, James (California)
Profile: p.261
Bankruptcy Band 3
Table: p.191

Lopez-Castro, Corali
(Florida)
Profile: p.545
Bankruptcy Up and coming
Table: p.503

Lord, Craig (Pennsylvania)
Profile: p.1530
Real Estate Band 3
Table: p.1516

Lord, Elizabeth Osenton
(West Virginia)
Profile: p.1809
Corporate/M&A Band 3
Table: p.1798

Lorensen, Charles
(West Virginia)
Profile: p.1809
Corporate/M&A Band 1

Table: p.1798

Lorig, Frederick (California)
Profile: p.261
Intellectual Property Band 3
Table: p.216

Lotstein, James I
(Connecticut)
Profile: p.337
Corporate/M&A Band 1
Table: p.327

Lott, Marley (Texas)
Profile: p.1689
Real Estate Band 3
Table: p.1662

Lottner, Alan B (Colorado)
Profile: p.320
Real Estate Band 3
Table: p.313

Louden, Karen Jacobs
(Delaware)
Profile: p.355
Intellectual Property
Up and coming
Table: p.348

Loudon, Timothy D
(Nebraska)
Profile: p.1088
Employment Band 2
Table: p.1084

Loulakis, Michael (Virginia)
Profile: p.1770
Construction Band 2
Table: p.1750

Loumiet, Carlos (Florida)
Profile: p.545
Banking & Finance Band 2
Table: p.500

Love, Jane M (New York)
Profile: p.1298
Intellectual Property Band 3
Table: p.1217

Love III, Charles M
(West Virginia)
Profile: p.1809
Litigation Band 1
Table: p.1803

Loveland, Joseph (Georgia)
Profile: p.617
Litigation Band 3
Table: p.598

Loveless, Scott (Utah)
Profile: p.1737
Corporate/M&A Band 2
Table: p.1727

Lovett, John T (Kentucky)
Profile: p.843
Employment Band 3
Table: p.830

Lowe, Richard (Tennessee)
Profile: p.1609
Employment Band 3
Table: p.1596

Lowenthal, Mitchell A
(New York)
Profile: p.1298
Litigation Band 3
Table: p.1223

Lowinger, Frederick C
(Illinois)
Profile: p.738

Corporate/M&A Band 1
Table: p.675

Lowry, Patricia E (Florida)
Profile: p.545
Employment Band 4
Table: p.513

Lowther Jr, Edwin L
(Arkansas)
Profile: p.177
Litigation Band 2
Table: p.172

Lozow, Gary (Colorado)
Profile: p.320
Litigation Band 1
Table: p.311

Lubin, Andrew R
(Connecticut)
Profile: p.337
Real Estate Band 2
Table: p.334

Lubin, Donald G (Illinois)
Profile: p.738
Corporate/M&A Band 2
Table: p.675

Lucas, Edwin F
(North Carolina)
Profile: p.1397
Banking & Finance Band 3
Table: p.1381

Lucas, Roger S (Illinois)
Profile: p.738
Tax Band 3
Table: p.710

Luce, Gregory
(District of Columbia)
Profile: p.454
Healthcare Band 1
Table: p.398

Luce, Michael L
(South Dakota)
Profile: p.1593
Litigation Band 1
Table: p.1590

Lucero, Gene (California)
Profile: p.261
Environment Band 1
Table: p.207

Luchs, Richard W
(District of Columbia)
Profile: p.454
Real Estate Band 4
Table: p.418

Ludwiszewski, Raymond
(District of Columbia)
Profile: p.454
Environment Band 3
Table: p.392

Lueck, Martin (Minnesota)
Profile: p.1019
Litigation Band 1
Table: p.1012

Luepker, Wayne R (Illinois)
Profile: p.738
Employee Benefits Band 1
Table: p.681

Luger, Andrew (Minnesota)
Profile: p.1019
Litigation Band 1
Table: p.1011

Lukey, Joan (Massachusetts)
Profile: p.971
Employment Band 1
Table: p.940
Litigation Band 1
Table: p.951

Lukin, Mitch (Texas)
Profile: p.1689
Intellectual Property Band 3
Table: p.1651

Lund, Daniel (Louisiana)
Profile: p.874
Litigation Band 3
Table: p.865

Lundberg, G Andrew
(California)
Profile: p.261
Insurance Band 2
Table: p.212

Lundgren, K Thor
(Wisconsin)
Profile: p.1825
Corporate/M&A Band 3
Table: p.1817

Lundy, Robert W (California)
Profile: p.261
Healthcare Band 3
Table: p.209

Lunn, Gregory (Ohio)
Profile: p.1444
Intellectual Property Band 3
Table: p.1428

Lunsford III, Rodgers
(Georgia)
Profile: p.617
Intellectual Property Band 3
Table: p.596

Lupo, Raphael
(District of Columbia)
Profile: p.454
Intellectual Property Band 2
Table: p.403

Lurey, Alfred (Georgia)
Profile: p.617
Bankruptcy Band 2
Table: p.582

Lurey, Michael (California)
Profile: p.261
Bankruptcy Band 2
Table: p.191

Lurie, Paul (Illinois)
Profile: p.738
Construction Band 1
Table: p.672

Luscombe II, George A
(Illinois)
Profile: p.738
Tax Band 3
Table: p.710

Lusk, Neva (West Virginia)
Profile: p.1809
Litigation Band 2
Table: p.1803

Luskin, Michael (New York)
Profile: p.1298
Bankruptcy Band 4
Table: p.1179

Lust, David E
(South Dakota)
Profile: p.1593

Lustberg, Lawrence S
(New Jersey)
Profile: p.1142
Litigation Band 1
Table: p.1133

Luxton, Jane
(District of Columbia)
Profile: p.454
Environment Band 3
Table: p.392

Lybecker, Martin E
(District of Columbia)
Profile: p.454
Investment Management
Band 3
Table: p.406

Lyle, George R (Alaska)
Profile: p.143
Environment Band 3
Table: p.137

Lyman, Beverly (Ohio)
Profile: p.1444
Intellectual Property Band 3
Table: p.1428

Lyman, Bill (Illinois)
Profile: p.738
Construction Band 1
Table: p.672

Lyman, R Jeffrey
(Massachusetts)
Profile: p.971
Real Estate Band 1
Table: p.957

Lynch, Christine D
(Massachusetts)
Profile: p.971
Bankruptcy Up and coming
Table: p.935

Lynch, James M (Illinois)
Profile: p.738
Tax Band 2
Table: p.710

Lynch, John (Texas)
Profile: p.1689
Intellectual Property Band 2
Table: p.1651

Lynch, Lawrence T
(Wisconsin)
Profile: p.1825
Employment Band 3
Table: p.1819

Lynch, Patrick (California)
Profile: p.261
Antitrust Band S
Table: p.184

Lynch, Stephen M
(North Carolina)
Profile: p.1397
Corporate/M&A Band 3
Table: p.1384

Lyndrup, Peggy B
(Kentucky)
Profile: p.844
Corporate/M&A Band 2
Table: p.827

Lyon, Charles (Ohio)
Profile: p.1444
Intellectual Property Band 1
Table: p.1428

Lyon, Fred (Florida)
Profile: p.545
Construction Band 3
Table: p.507

Lyons, Francis X (Illinois)
Profile: p.738
Environment Band 4
Table: p.687

Lyons, Gregory
(Massachusetts)
Profile: p.971
Banking & Finance Band 2
Table: p.932

Lyons, James M (Colorado)
Profile: p.320
Litigation Band 1
Table: p.311

Lyons, Peter D (New York)
Profile: p.1298
Corporate/M&A Band 2
Table: p.1189

M

Maak, Charles (Utah)
Profile: p.1737
Real Estate Band s
Table: p.1733

Maberry, John Scott
(National)
Profile: p.93

Macbeth, Angus
(District of Columbia)
Profile: p.454
Environment Band 1
Table: p.392

MacBride, Owen (Illinois)
Profile: p.738
Energy Band 2
Table: p.685
Telecom, Broadcast & Satellite
Band 2
Table: p.715

MacCarthy, John L (Illinois)
Profile: p.739
Corporate/M&A Band 4
Table: p.675

MacDonald, Alan (Kentucky)
Profile: p.844
Corporate/M&A Band 2
Table: p.827

MacDonald, Elizabeth A
(Colorado)
Profile: p.320
Employment Band 3
Table: p.306

MacDonald, Terry J
(Montana)
Profile: p.1080
Litigation Band 3
Table: p.1075

Macdonald, Thomas
(Colorado)
Profile: p.320
Real Estate Band 1
Table: p.314

MacDonald III, Ralph F
(Georgia)
Profile: p.617
Banking & Finance Band 3

Table: p.581

Mace, Damond R (Ohio)
Profile: p.1444
Litigation Band 4
Table: p.1431

Mace, James (Nevada)
Profile: p.1103
Real Estate Band 2
Table: p.1099

MacEwan, Alan D (Maine)
Profile: p.899
Corporate/M&A Band 3
Table: p.888

MacGill, Robert (Indiana)
Profile: p.793
Litigation Band 2
Table: p.785

Machen, John (Maryland)
Profile: p.922
Real Estate Band 3
Table: p.917

Machlin, Barry N (Illinois)
Profile: p.454
Projects Band 2
Table: p.415

Machmeier, Bruce
(Minnesota)
Profile: p.1019
Corporate/M&A Band 2
Table: p.1005

Mack, J Frederick (Idaho)
Profile: p.660
Corporate/M&A Band 2
Table: p.655

Mack, Joel (California)
Profile: p.261
Energy Band 3
Table: p.204

Mack, Wayne (Pennsylvania)
Profile: p.1531
Antitrust Up and coming
Table: p.1489

Mackay, Douglas (Kansas)
Profile: p.824
Employment Band 3
Table: p.818

Mackey, Pamela (Colorado)
Profile: p.320
Litigation Band 1
Table: p.311

Mackey, Terry (Wyoming)
Profile: p.1838
Litigation Band 2
Table: p.1835

Mackie, Thomas
(Massachusetts)
Profile: p.971
Environment Band 2
Table: p.943

MacKinnon, D Scott
(Hawaii)
Profile: p.649
Real Estate Band 1
Table: p.646

MacMurray, John C
(New York)
Profile: p.1298
Private Equity Band 3
Table: p.1241

MacPherson, John
(Wyoming)
Profile: p.1838
Real Estate Band 2
Table: p.1836

Macpherson, Robert J
(New York)
Profile: p.1299
Construction Band 4
Table: p.1186

Madden, John J (New York)
Profile: p.1299
Corporate/M&A Band 2
Table: p.1189

Madden, Patrick M
(Washington)
Profile: p.1793
Employment Band 3
Table: p.1780

Madden, Thomas J
(National)
Profile: p.93
Government Contracts
Band 1
Table: p.27

Madden, William
(District of Columbia)
Profile: p.455
Energy Band 5
Table: p.386

Maddin, Michael (Michigan)
Profile: p.1000
Real Estate Band 2
Table: p.996

Madison, William
(New Mexico)
Profile: p.1163
Litigation Band 4
Table: p.1159

Madsen, Marcia (National)
Profile: p.93
Government Contracts
Band 2
Table: p.27

Magee, John B
(District of Columbia)
Profile: p.455
Tax Band 2
Table: p.422

Magnuson, Lee A
(South Dakota)
Profile: p.1593
Corporate/M&A Band 3
Table: p.1587

Magnuson, Roger
(Minnesota)
Profile: p.1019
Litigation Band 1
Table: p.1011

Maguire Jr, Charles D
(Colorado)
Profile: p.320
Corporate/M&A Band 3
Table: p.303

Mahoney, Colleen P
(District of Columbia)
Profile: p.455
Litigation Band 2
Table: p.410

Mahoney, Maureen
(District of Columbia)
Profile: p.455
Litigation Band 1
Table: p.408

Mahoney, Sean (Maine)
Profile: p.899
Environment Band 2
Table: p.892

Mahony, Gael
(Massachusetts)
Profile: p.971
Litigation Band 3
Table: p.951

Maida, Thomas J (Florida)
Profile: p.545
Insurance Band 2
Table: p.519

Maitland, Johan W E
(Vermont)
Profile: p.1749
Employment Band 2
Table: p.1745

Maizel, Jonathan
(District of Columbia)
Profile: p.455
Projects Band 3
Table: p.415

Major, Joseph E
(South Carolina)
Profile: p.1581
Litigation Band 3
Table: p.1576

Makens, Hugh (Michigan)
Profile: p.1000
Corporate/M&A Band 3
Table: p.989

Makley, Roger (Ohio)
Profile: p.1444
Litigation Band 2
Table: p.1432

Maledon, William (Arizona)
Profile: p.160
Litigation Band 1
Table: p.152

Malefatto, Alfred J (Florida)
Profile: p.545
Environment Band 2
Table: p.516

Malester, Ann
(District of Columbia)
Profile: p.455
Antitrust Band 4
Table: p.367

Malheiro, Sharon (Iowa)
Profile: p.813
Employment Band 3
Table: p.805

Malkerson, Bruce
(Minnesota)
Profile: p.1019
Real Estate Band 1
Table: p.1015

Malkin, Joseph (California)
Profile: p.261
Energy Band 1
Table: p.204

Mallery, Mark (Louisiana)
Profile: p.874
Employment Band 3
Table: p.861

M

Mallory, Richard C
(California)
Profile: p.262
Real Estate Band 2
Table: p.238

Mallow, Matthew J
(National)
Profile: p.94
Capital Markets Band S
Table: p.14

Malloy, Elizabeth A
(Pennsylvania)
Profile: p.1531
Employment Band 4
Table: p.1500

Malloy, Timothy J (Illinois)
Profile: p.739
Intellectual Property Band 1
Table: p.696

Malone, Gayle (Tennessee)
Profile: p.1609
Litigation Band 3
Table: p.1599

Malone, Judith
(Massachusetts)
Profile: p.971
Employment Band 2
Table: p.940

Malone Jr, Ernest
(Louisiana)
Profile: p.874
Employment Band 1
Table: p.861

Maloney, Marilyn (Texas)
Profile: p.1689
Banking & Finance Band 4
Table: p.1625

Maloy, Bruce (Georgia)
Profile: p.618
Litigation Band 1
Table: p.599

Malt, R Bradford
(Massachusetts)
Profile: p.972
Corporate/M&A Band 2
Table: p.937
Private Equity Band 2
Table: p.953
Private Equity Band 1
Table: p.955

Maltz, Gerald (Arizona)
Profile: p.160
Litigation Band 2
Table: p.152

Manchester, Susan A
(New Hampshire)
Profile: p.1118
Real Estate Band 1
Table: p.1114

Mancini, Paul (Hawaii)
Profile: p.649
Land Use Band 1
Table: p.643
Real Estate Band 2
Table: p.646

Mancino, Douglas M
(California)
Profile: p.262
Healthcare Band 1
Table: p.209

Mandel, David S (Florida)
Profile: p.545
Litigation Band 2
Table: p.522

Mandel, Reid A (Illinois)
Profile: p.739
Tax Band 3
Table: p.710

Mandelbaum, David G
(Pennsylvania)
Profile: p.1531
Environment Band 1
Table: p.1505

Mandell, Floyd A (Illinois)
Profile: p.739
Intellectual Property Band 3
Table: p.696

Manford III, Thomas D
(Texas)
Profile: p.1689
Technology Band 3
Table: p.1668

Mangan, John J (National)
Profile: p.94
International Trade Band 4
Table: p.40

Mangum, Geoffrey W
(Utah)
Profile: p.1737
Corporate/M&A Band 3
Table: p.1727

Manheimer, Jacob A
(Maine)
Profile: p.899
Bankruptcy Band 1
Table: p.888

Manitsky, Andrew D
(Vermont)
Profile: p.1749
Litigation Band 3
Table: p.1746

Manko, Joseph M
(Pennsylvania)
Profile: p.1531
Environment Band 1
Table: p.1505

Mann, Christopher L
(New York)
Profile: p.1299
Projects Band 3
Table: p.1244

Mann, Phillip L
(District of Columbia)
Profile: p.455
Tax Band 4
Table: p.422

Mann, Terry (Kansas)
Profile: p.824
Employment Band 1
Table: p.818

Manne, Neal (Texas)
Profile: p.1689
Litigation Band 2
Table: p.1656

Manner, Mark (Tennessee)
Profile: p.1609
Corporate/M&A Band 1
Table: p.1594

Manning, John (Montana)
Profile: p.1080
Corporate/M&A Band 1
Table: p.1072

Manning, William E
(Delaware)
Profile: p.355
Real Estate Band 2
Table: p.350

Mannino, Edward F
(Pennsylvania)
Profile: p.1531
Litigation Band 2
Table: p.1511

Manolopoulos, Lynn T
(Washington)
Profile: p.1793
Environment Band 2
Table: p.1782

Mansfield, Edward (Iowa)
Profile: p.813
Litigation Band 3
Table: p.807

Manson, Tom
(New Hampshire)
Profile: p.1118
Corporate/M&A Band 3
Table: p.1107

Manthey, Ron (Texas)
Profile: p.1689
Employment Band 3
Table: p.1634

Manulik, Mark (Oregon)
Profile: p.1483
Real Estate Band 3
Table: p.1479

March, Aaron (Missouri)
Profile: p.1058
Real Estate Band 2
Table: p.1053

March, Jon G (Michigan)
Profile: p.1000
Employment Band 2
Table: p.991

Marchetta, Anthony J
(New Jersey)
Profile: p.1142
Litigation Band 3
Table: p.1131

Marcil, Jack (North Dakota)
Profile: p.1410
Litigation Band 2
Table: p.1407

Marco, Frank J (Connecticut)
Profile: p.337
Corporate/M&A Band 2
Table: p.327

Marcu, Aaron R (New York)
Profile: p.1299
Litigation Band 3
Table: p.1224

Marcus, Benjamin E
(Maine)
Profile: p.899
Bankruptcy Band 2
Table: p.888

Marcus, Courtney (Texas)
Profile: p.1689
Banking & Finance
Up and coming
Table: p.1625

Marcus, George J (Maine)
Profile: p.899
Bankruptcy Band 1
Table: p.888

Marcy, Donald (Washington)
Profile: p.1793
Real Estate Band 2
Table: p.1789

Marella, Vincent J
(California)
Profile: p.262
Litigation Band 1
Table: p.225

Marenberg, Steven
(California)
Profile: p.262
Media & Entertainment Band 4
Table: p.230

Marett, Louis J
(Massachusetts)
Profile: p.972
Tax Band 3
Table: p.959

Mariani, Richard C
(New Jersey)
Profile: p.1142
Employment Band 2
Table: p.1126

Maring, David
(North Dakota)
Profile: p.1410
Litigation Band 1
Table: p.1406

Marino, Kevin (New Jersey)
Profile: p.1142
Litigation Band 2
Table: p.1133

Marion, David H
(Pennsylvania)
Profile: p.1531
Litigation Band 2
Table: p.1511

Mark, Richard G
(Minnesota)
Profile: p.1019
Litigation Band 3
Table: p.1011

Mark, Wayne J (Nebraska)
Profile: p.1088
Litigation Band 3
Table: p.1085

Markel, Gregory (New York)
Profile: p.1299
Litigation Band 2
Table: p.1223

Markham, Jesse W
(California)
Profile: p.262
Antitrust Band 2
Table: p.184

Markowitz, David (Oregon)
Profile: p.1483
Litigation ✪
Table: p.1477

Marks, Allan (California)
Profile: p. 262
Projects Band 3
Table: p.236
Transport Band 2
Table: p.64

Marks, Jeffrey A (Ohio)
Profile: p.1444
Bankruptcy Band 4
Table: p.1414

Marks, Kenneth S (Texas)
Profile: p.1690
Litigation Band 3
Table: p.1656

Marmaduke, Don H
(Oregon)
Profile: p.1483
Litigation Band S
Table: p.1477

Marmaro, Richard
(California)
Profile: p.262
Litigation Band 2
Table: p.225

Marmorstein, Vicki E
(California)
Profile: p.262
Banking & Finance Band 3
Table: p.187

Marovitz, Andrew (Illinois)
Profile: p.739
Antitrust Band 2
Table: p.662

Marr, Barry (Hawaii)
Profile: p.649
Employment Band 1
Table: p.642

Marren, John P (Illinois)
Profile: p.739
Healthcare Band 3
Table: p.690

Marrinson, Thomas A
(Illinois)
Profile: p.739
Insurance Band 3
Table: p.695

Marsack, Gary (Wisconsin)
Profile: p.1825
Employment Band 3
Table: p.1819

Marsden Jr, William
(Delaware)
Profile: p.355
Intellectual Property Band 2
Table: p.348

Marsh, David (Alabama)
Profile: p.123
Litigation Band 2
Table: p.116

Marsh, Gary W (Georgia)
Profile: p.618
Bankruptcy Band 3
Table: p.582

Marshall, Alison
(District of Columbia)
Profile: p.455
Employment Band 3
Table: p.380

Marshall, Gary (Virginia)
Profile: p.1770
Employment Band 3
Table: p.1755

Marshall, John
(Pennsylvania)
Profile: p.1531
Intellectual Property Band 4
Table: p.1508

Marshall, John T (Georgia)
Profile: p.618
Antitrust **Band** 3
Table: p.578
Litigation **Band** 2
Table: p.598

Marshall Cox, LeeAnne
(Tennessee)
Profile: p.1610
Real Estate **Band** 3
Table: p.1603

Marso, Lisa Hansen
(South Dakota)
Profile: p.1593
Employment **Band** 2
Table: p.1589

Marston, Edgar (Texas)
Profile: p.1690
Corporate/M&A **Band** 4
Table: p.1631

Martens, Don (California)
Profile: p.262
Intellectual Property **Band** 3
Table: p.216

Martin, Brian (Texas)
Profile: p.1690
Insurance **Band** 1
Table: p.1648

Martin, Channing J
(Virginia)
Profile: p.1770
Environment **Band** 2
Table: p.1757

Martin, Christopher W
(Texas)
Profile: p.1690
Insurance **Band** 1
Table: p.1648

Martin, Chrys (Oregon)
Profile: p.1483
Employment **Band** 2
Table: p.1474

Martin, Clark (Texas)
Profile: p.1690
Intellectual Property **Band** 2
Table: p.1651

Martin, Dave (Arkansas)
Profile: p.177
Employment **Band** 3
Table: p.170

Martin, David L (Mississippi)
Profile: p.1034
Corporate/M&A **Band** 3
Table: p.1024

Martin, Ernest (Texas)
Profile: p.1690
Insurance **Band** 1
Table: p.1648

Martin, Gerard P.
(Maryland)
Profile: p.922
Litigation **Band** 3
Table: p.914

Martin, Gregory S (Florida)
Profile: p.545
Construction **Band** 3
Table: p.507

Martin, John (Texas)
Profile: p. 1690
Business Process
Outsourcing: National **Band** 2

Table: p.10
Technology **Band** 1
Table: p.1668

Martin, Keith
(District of Columbia)
Profile: p. 455
Projects **Band** 2
Table: p.52
Projects **Band** 2
Table: p.415

Martin, Laura Keidan
(Illinois)
Profile: p.739
Healthcare **Band** 3
Table: p.690

Martin, Paul (Texas)
Profile: p.1690
Real Estate **Up and coming**
Table: p.1662

Martin, Renwick (National)
Profile: p.94
Capital Markets **Band** 1
Table: p.19

Martin, Timothy (Kentucky)
Profile: p.844
Real Estate **Band** 1
Table: p.838

Martinez, Roberto (Florida)
Profile: p.545
Litigation **Band** 2
Table: p.521
Litigation **Band** 1
Table: p.522

**Martinez de Andino, J
Michael** (Virginia)
Profile: p.1770
Intellectual Property **Band** 1
Table: p.1761

Martinez-Fraga, Pedro J
(National)
Profile: p.94
Arbitration **Band**
Table: p.33
Arbitration **Band** 4
Table: p.33

Martson Jr, William F
(Oregon)
Profile: p.1483
Litigation **Band** 3
Table: p.1477

Martucci, William
(Missouri)
Profile: p.1058
Employment **Band** 1
Table: p.1046

Martzell, Jack (Louisiana)
Profile: p.874
Litigation **Band** 3
Table: p.865

Marvin, Jack (Kansas)
Profile: p.824
Corporate/M&A **Band** 1
Table: p.816
Real Estate **Band** 2
Table: p.821

Marvin, John (Missouri)
Profile: p.1058
Corporate/M&A **Band** 3
Table: p.1043

Marx, David (Illinois)
Profile: p.739
Antitrust **Band** 2

Table: p.662

Marzetti, Phil (Georgia)
Profile: p.618
Tax **Band** 4
Table: p.603

Mascherin, Terri (Illinois)
Profile: p.740
Telecom, Broadcast & Satellite
Band 3
Table: p.715

Maser, Joel (Florida)
Profile: p.546
Tax **Band** 2
Table: p.531

Mashburn, Randal
(Tennessee)
Profile: p.1610
Litigation **Band** 2
Table: p.1599

Maslanka, Michael (Texas)
Profile: p.1690
Employment **Band** 2
Table: p.1634

Mason, Andrew S
(New York)
Profile: p.1299
Tax **Band** 4
Table: p.1255

Mason, C Steven
(North Carolina)
Profile: p.1397
Real Estate **Band** 3
Table: p.1392

Mason, David (Illinois)
Profile: p.740
Banking & Finance **Band** 2
Table: p.665

Mason, David (New York)
Profile: p.1299
Employee Benefits **Band** 3
Table: p.1197

Mason, Gerald (Wyoming)
Profile: p.1838
Litigation **Band** 2
Table: p.1835

Mason, J Cheney (Florida)
Profile: p.546
Litigation **Band** 2
Table: p.522

Mason, Richard G
(New York)
Profile: p.1299
Bankruptcy **Band** 3
Table: p.1179

Mason III, Julian L (Alaska)
Profile: p.143
Environment **Band** S
Table: p.137
Regulated Industries **Band** S
Table: p.137

Massad, Stephen A (Texas)
Profile: p.1690
Corporate/M&A **Band** 1
Table: p.1631

Massey, Raymond L
(Missouri)
Profile: p.1059
Litigation **Band** 3
Table: p.1049

Massopust, Richard
(Minnesota)
Profile: p.1019
Real Estate **Band** 2
Table: p.1014

Mast, Gregory (Arizona)
Profile: p.160
Real Estate **Band** 1
Table: p.154

Masters, Lori
(District of Columbia)
Profile: p.455
Insurance **Band** 3
Table: p.402

Masters, William B
(Louisiana)
Profile: p.874
Corporate/M&A **Band** 4
Table: p.859

Mastracco, Vincent
(Virginia)
Profile: p.1771
Corporate/M&A **Band** 2
Table: p.1752

Mastro, Randy (New York)
Profile: p.1299
Litigation **Band** 3
Table: p.1223

Masur, Daniel A
(District of Columbia)
Profile: p. 455
Business Process
Outsourcing: National **Band** 1
Table: p.10
IT Outsourcing **Band** 1
Table: p.430

Matchett, Sam (Georgia)
Profile: p.618
Employment **Band** 4
Table: p.589

Mather, Barbara W
(Pennsylvania)
Profile: p.1531
Antitrust **Band** 1
Table: p.1489
Litigation **Band** 1
Table: p.1511

Matheson, David S.
(Oregon)
Profile: p.1483
Corporate/M&A
Up and coming
Table: p.1471

Mathews, Daniel A
(National)
Profile: p.94
Transport **Band** 1
Table: p.64

Mathias, Robert (Maryland)
Profile: p.922
Litigation **Band** 1
Table: p.914

Mathias Jr, John H (Illinois)
Profile: p.740
Insurance **Band** 2
Table: p.695

Mathiason, Garry
(California)
Profile: p.262
Employment **Band** 3
Table: p.202

Matichak, Jill (California)
Profile: p.262
Banking & Finance **Band** 2
Table: p.187

Matis, Nina (Illinois)
Profile: p.740
Real Estate **Band** 1
Table: p.706

Matkins, Michael L
(California)
Profile: p.262
Real Estate **Band** 1
Table: p.238

Matkov, George (Illinois)
Profile: p.740
Employment **Band** S
Table: p.681

Mattei, Andrew (New York)
Profile: p.1299
Banking & Finance **Band** 3
Table: p.1174

Matthews, Christopher T
(Oregon)
Profile: p.1483
Real Estate **Band** 3
Table: p.1479

Matthews, Frank (Florida)
Profile: p.546
Environment **Band** 1
Table: p.516

Matthews, Joseph M
(Florida)
Profile: p.546
Litigation **Band** 3
Table: p.521

Matthews, Philip (California)
Profile: p.262
Insurance **Band** 2
Table: p.212

Mattingly, Patrick W
(Kentucky)
Profile: p.844
Corporate/M&A **Band** 2
Table: p.827

Mattox, Sharon (Texas)
Profile: p.1690
Environment **Band** 2
Table: p.1643
Litigation **Band** 2
Table: p.1643

Mauel, John (Texas)
Profile: p.1690
Projects **Band** 3
Table: p.1659

Maxey, JoAnn (Arkansas)
Profile: p.177
Employment **Band** 2
Table: p.170

May, Arnold P
(Massachusetts)
Profile: p.972
Tax **Band** 3
Table: p.959

May, Bruce (Arizona)
Profile: p.160
Real Estate **Band** 2
Table: p.154

M

May, Gregory
(District of Columbia)
Profile: p.456
Tax Band 3
Table: p.422

May, James (Alabama)
Profile: p.123
Employment Band 2
Table: p.113

May, Jr, Henry S (Texas)
Profile: p.1690
Energy Band 1
Table: p.1641

Mayer, Patricia V
(California)
Profile: p.263
Media & Entertainment Band 4
Table: p.230

Mayer, Thomas Moers
(New York)
Profile: p.1300
Bankruptcy Band 3
Table: p.1179

Mayer, William
(Massachusetts)
Profile: p.972
Banking & Finance Band 1
Table: p.932

Mayerle, Thomas M
(Minnesota)
Profile: p.1019
Real Estate Band 2
Table: p.1014

Mayerson, Michael A
(California)
Profile: p.263
Media & Entertainment Band 3
Table: p.233

Maynard Jr, Joe (Montana)
Profile: p.1080
Litigation Band 2
Table: p.1075

Maynes, Todd F (Illinois)
Profile: p.740
Tax Band 3
Table: p.710

Mayo, David (New York)
Profile: p.1300
Tax Band 4
Table: p.1255

Mayol, Juan (Florida)
Profile: p.546
Real Estate Band 3
Table: p.528

Mazo, Mark
(District of Columbia)
Profile: p.456
Corporate/Commercial Band 3
Table: p.376

Mazur, Sayward (New York)
Profile: p.1300
Construction Band 2
Table: p.1186

McAlpine, Fraser A (Texas)
Profile: p.1690
Employment Band 3
Table: p.1634

McAndrew, Karen (Vermont)
Profile: p.1749
Employment Band 2
Table: p.1745

Litigation Band 2
Table: p.1746

McAndrews, George P
(Illinois)
Profile: p.740
Intellectual Property Band 1
Table: p.696

McAughan Jr, Robert J
(Texas)
Profile: p.1691
Intellectual Property Band 2
Table: p.1651

McBride, David (Delaware)
Profile: p.355
Chancery Band 2
Table: p.344
Corporate/M&A Band 3
Table: p.346

McBride, Michael F
(National)
Profile: p.94
Transport Band 3
Table: p.62

McCabe, F Barry (Georgia)
Profile: p.618
Construction Band 2
Table: p.584

McCaffrey, John F (Ohio)
Profile: p.1444
Litigation Band 3
Table: p.1432

McCahill, Jane K (Illinois)
Profile: p.740
Healthcare Band 2
Table: p.690

McCall, Donn (Wyoming)
Profile: p.1839
Corporate/M&A Band 2
Table: p.1832

McCalla, Robert (Louisiana)
Profile: p.874
Employment Band 1
Table: p.861

McCallum, Charles
(Michigan)
Profile: p.1000
Corporate/M&A Band 3
Table: p.989

McCareins, Mark (Illinois)
Profile: p.740
Antitrust Band 2
Table: p.662

McCartan, Patrick F (Ohio)
Profile: p.1444
Litigation Band S
Table: p.1431

McCarthy, Brian J
(California)
Profile: p.263
Corporate/M&A Band 1
Table: p.197

McCarthy, John W (Maine)
Profile: p.899
Litigation Band 3
Table: p.893

McCarthy, Michael S
(Colorado)
Profile: p.320
Litigation Band 4
Table: p.311

McCarthy, Thomas
(Missouri)
Profile: p.1059
Employment Band 2
Table: p.1046

McCarthy, William
(Massachusetts)
Profile: p.972
Bankruptcy Band 1
Table: p.935

McCaw, Robert M
(New York)
Profile: p.1300
Litigation Band 2
Table: p.1223

McClard, Jack E (Virginia)
Profile: p.1771
Litigation Band 3
Table: p.1763

McClellan, Roger (Kansas)
Profile: p.824
Employment Band 3
Table: p.818

McClenahan, David
(Pennsylvania)
Profile: p.1531
Litigation Band 3
Table: p.1511

McClintock, Donald
(Alaska)
Profile: p.143
Real Estate Band 1
Table: p.141

McClintock, John (Iowa)
Profile: p.813
Litigation Band S
Table: p.807

McClosky, Donald (Florida)
Profile: p.546
Real Estate Band S
Table: p.528

McCollam, Andrew (Texas)
Profile: p.1691
Energy Band 3
Table: p.1640

McCollam, John B
(Louisiana)
Profile: p.874
Energy Band 1
Table: p.863
Litigation Band 2
Table: p.865

McCollum, James (Alaska)
Profile: p.143
Real Estate Band 2
Table: p.141

McCombs, David (Texas)
Profile: p.1691
Intellectual Property Band 2
Table: p.1651

McConaughy, Stewart
(Vermont)
Profile: p.1749
Corporate/M&A Band 1
Table: p.1743

McConnell, Alan (North
Carolina)
Profile: p.1397
Environment Band 2
Table: p.1388

McConnell, Karen C
(Arizona)
Profile: p.160
Corporate/M&A Band 1
Table: p.146

McConnell, Laura Haag
(Oklahoma)
Profile: p.1465
Litigation Band 3
Table: p.1462

McConnell, Mark S
(National)
Profile: p.94
International Trade Band 2
Table: p.40

McConnell, Mike (Texas)
Profile: p.1691
Bankruptcy Band 3
Table: p.1627

McCormack, William
(Texas)
Profile: p.1691
Corporate/M&A Band 4
Table: p.1631

McCormack, William F
(New York)
Profile: p.1300
Private Equity Band 3
Table: p.1241

McCormick, Mark (Iowa)
Profile: p.813
Litigation Band 2
Table: p.807

McCorriston, William C
(Hawaii)
Profile: p.649
Litigation ✪
Table: p.644

McCowan, Charles
(Louisiana)
Profile: p.874
Litigation Band 2
Table: p.865

McCown, Steven R (Texas)
Profile: p.1691
Employment Band 2
Table: p.1634

McCrea, Richard (Florida)
Profile: p.546
Employment Band 1
Table: p.513

McCreary, Charles (Ohio)
Profile: p.1444
Real Estate Band 2
Table: p.1434

McCue, Mark S
(New Hampshire)
Profile: p.1118
Corporate/M&A Band 3
Table: p.1107

McCullough, Jack
(Washington)
Profile: p.1793
Real Estate Band 1
Table: p.1789

McCullough, James
(National)
Profile: p.94
Government Contracts
Band 2
Table: p.27

McCullough, Joe (Illinois)
Profile: p.740
Insurance Band 2
Table: p.694

McCutcheon, Mary E
(California)
Profile: p.263
Insurance Band 4
Table: p.212

McDade, Thomas (Texas)
Profile: p.1691
Energy Band 2
Table: p.1640

McDaniel Jr, Dan M
(Mississippi)
Profile: p.1035
Gaming & Licensing Band 1
Table: p.1024

McDaniels, William
(District of Columbia)
Profile: p.456
Litigation Band 2
Table: p.410

McDavid, Janet L
(District of Columbia)
Profile: p.456
Antitrust Band 2
Table: p.367

McDermett Jr, Don J
(Texas)
Profile: p.1691

McDermott, Brian L
(Indiana)
Profile: p.793
Employment Band 3
Table: p.783

McDonald, Daniel
(Minnesota)
Profile: p.1019
Litigation Band 1
Table: p.1012

McDonald, David
(Washington)
Profile: p.1793
Litigation Band 3
Table: p.1786

McDonald, Derek (Texas)
Profile: p.1691
Environment Up and coming
Table: p.1643

McDonald, John (Ohio)
Profile: p.1444
Litigation Band 3
Table: p.1431

McDonald, Randall (New
Mexico)
Profile: p.1163
Corporate/M&A Band 3
Table: p.1155

McDonald, Scott (Texas)
Profile: p.1691
Employment Band 3
Table: p.1634

McDonnell, Brendan
(Oregon)
Profile: p.1483
Corporate/M&A Band 3
Table: p.1471

McDonnell, John J (Illinois)
Profile: p.740
Intellectual Property **Band** 2
Table: p.696

McDonough, Kathleen Furey (Delaware)
Profile: p.355
Employment **Band** 2
Table: p.347

McDowell, Jerry (Alabama)
Profile: p.124
Litigation **Band** 3
Table: p.116

McElhinny, Harold
(California)
Profile: p.263
Intellectual Property **Band** 2
Table: p.216

McElwee, Douglas
(West Virginia)
Profile: p.1810
Real Estate **Band** 3
Table: p.1806

McElyea, Russell (Montana)
Profile: p.1080
Real Estate **Band** 2
Table: p.1078

McEnroe, John T (Illinois)
Profile: p.740
Banking & Finance **Band** 3
Table: p.665

McFadden II, W Clark
(National)
Profile: p.95
International Trade **Band** 2
Table: p.41

McFalls, Michael
(District of Columbia)
Profile: p.456
Antitrust **Up and coming**
Table: p.367

McGee II, Richard H (North Dakota)
Profile: p.1410
Litigation **Band** 2
Table: p.1406

McGee Jr, Emmett F
(Maryland)
Profile: p.922
Employment **Band** 3
Table: p.912

McGill, Linda D (Maine)
Profile: p.899
Employment **Band** 1
Table: p.890

McGinn, Daniel
(North Carolina)
Profile: p.1397
Employment **Band** 1
Table: p.1386

McGivaren, Crawford
(Alabama)
Profile: p.124
Litigation **Band** 1
Table: p.116

McGlone, William M
(National)
Profile: p.95
International Trade **Band** 1
Table: p.41

McGlynn, Casey (California)
Profile: p.263
Corporate/M&A **Band** 5
Table: p.197

McGough Jr, W Thomas
(Pennsylvania)
Profile: p.1532
Litigation **Band** 3
Table: p.1511
Litigation **Band** 2
Table: p.1512

McGrane, John
(District of Columbia)
Profile: p.456
Energy **Band** 3
Table: p.386

McGrath, Brian (Nebraska)
Profile: p.1088
Employment **Band** 3
Table: p.1084

McGrath, Brian W
(Wisconsin)
Profile: p.1825
Litigation **Band** 3
Table: p.1821

McGrath, Kathryn
(District of Columbia)
Profile: p.456
Investment Management
Band 1
Table: p.406

McGrath, Robin L (Georgia)
Profile: p.618
Intellectual Property **Band** 4
Table: p.596

McGrory, John F (Oregon)
Profile: p.1483
Litigation **Band** 3
Table: p.1477

McGuigan, Thomas R
(Florida)
Profile: p.546
Corporate/M&A **Band** 1
Table: p.509

McGuire, Frank (Maine)
Profile: p.899
Employment **Band** 2
Table: p.890

McGuire, J Michael
(Maryland)
Profile: p.922
Employment **Band** 2
Table: p.912

McGuire, Robin (Louisiana)
Profile: p.874
Energy **Band** 1
Table: p.863

McGuire, W John
(District of Columbia)
Profile: p.456
Investment Management
Band 3
Table: p.406

McInerney, Denis
(New York)
Profile: p.1300
Litigation **Band** 1
Table: p.1224

McInnis, Judith
(South Carolina)
Profile: p.1581
Real Estate **Band** 3

Table: p.1577

McIntosh, Ian (Montana)
Profile: p.1080
Litigation **Up and coming**
Table: p.1075

McIsaac, Christopher
(District of Columbia)
Profile: p.456
Projects **Band** 2
Table: p.415

McKay, Daniel G (Maine)
Profile: p.899
Corporate/M&A **Band** 2
Table: p.888

McKearin, Robert (Vermont)
Profile: p.1749
Employment **Band** 2
Table: p.1745

McKee, T Braxton (Virginia)
Profile: p.1771
Corporate/M&A **Band** 3
Table: p.1752

McKee, William
(District of Columbia)
Profile: p.456
Tax **Band** 2
Table: p.422

McKeithen, Ward
(North Carolina)
Profile: p.1397
Litigation **Band** 1
Table: p.1390

McKenna, Susan (Florida)
Profile: p.546
Employment **Band** 2
Table: p.513

McKenzie, Diana (Illinois)
Profile: p.741
Technology **Band** 3
Table: p.713

McKenzie, Donald I N
(Tennessee)
Profile: p.1610
Corporate/M&A **Band** 3
Table: p.1594

McKenzie, James
(Pennsylvania)
Profile: p.1532
Corporate/M&A **Band** 4
Table: p.1497

McKibben, Michael D
(Alabama)
Profile: p.124
Litigation **Band** 2
Table: p.116

McKinney, Kenneth
(Oklahoma)
Profile: p.1465
Litigation **Band** 2
Table: p.1462

McKnight, Frederick (Rick) (California)
Profile: p.263
Litigation **Band** 4
Table: p.224

McKnight, Michael S
(South Dakota)
Profile: p.1593
Employment **Band** 1
Table: p.1589

McKool Jr, Mike (Texas)
Profile: p.1691
Intellectual Property **Band** 3
Table: p.1651
Litigation **Band** 3
Table: p.1656

McLaughlin, Ellen E
(Illinois)
Profile: p.741
Employment **Band** 3
Table: p.681

McLaughlin, Lawrence
(Michigan)
Profile: p.1000
Real Estate **⊙**
Table: p.996

McLaughlin, Mark (Illinois)
Profile: p.741
Antitrust **Band** 2
Table: p.662

McLaughlin, Patrick (Ohio)
Profile: p.1444
Litigation **Band** 1
Table: p.1432

McLean, Dennis E
(Washington)
Profile: p.1793
Real Estate **Band** 3
Table: p.1788

McLean, Michael
(Pennsylvania)
Profile: p.1532
Corporate/M&A **Band** 4
Table: p.1497

McLean, Ronald (North Dakota)
Profile: p.1410
Litigation **Band** 1
Table: p.1406

McLeay, Bart (Nebraska)
Profile: p.1088
Litigation **Band** 3
Table: p.1085

McLeod, David (Michigan)
Profile: p.1000
Banking & Finance **Band** 2
Table: p.987

McLucas, William
(District of Columbia)
Profile: p.456
Litigation **Band** 1
Table: p.410
Litigation **Band** 1
Table: p.410

McMahan, Jeffrey J
(Vermont)
Profile: p.1749
Corporate/M&A **Band** 2
Table: p.1743

McMahon, Louis L (Ohio)
Profile: p.1444
Environment **Up and coming**
Table: p.1425

McMahon, Michael (Ohio)
Profile: p.1444
Environment **Band** 2
Table: p.1425

McMahon, Terry (California)
Profile: p.263
Intellectual Property **Band** 1
Table: p.216

McManus, Randolph
(District of Columbia)
Profile: p.456
Energy **Band** 4
Table: p.382
Energy **Band** 2
Table: p.386

McManus Jr, Joseph A
(District of Columbia)
Profile: p.457
Construction **Band** 3
Table: p.374

McMenamin, J Robert
(Illinois)
Profile: p.741
Banking & Finance **Band** 2
Table: p.665

McMenimen, Dennis (Iowa)
Profile: p.813
Real Estate **Band** 4
Table: p.810

McMichael, Lawrence
(Pennsylvania)
Profile: p.1532
Bankruptcy **Band** 2
Table: p.1494

McMillan, Daniel D
(California)
Profile: p.263
Construction **Band** 3
Table: p.194

McMillan, Karen
(District of Columbia)
Profile: p.457
Investment Management
Band 3
Table: p.406

McMillan II, L Richards
(Louisiana)
Profile: p.874
Corporate/M&A **Band** 1
Table: p.859

McMurray, Kevin N (Ohio)
Profile: p.1445
Environment **Band** 3
Table: p.1425

McNally, Edward M
(Delaware)
Profile: p.355
Chancery **Band** 4
Table: p.344

McNamara, Elizabeth A
(New York)
Profile: p.1300
Media & Entertainment **Band** 3
Table: p.1232

McNamara, Lawrence J
(Texas)
Profile: p.1691
Employment **Band** 3
Table: p.1634

McNamara, Mary
(California)
Profile: p.263
Litigation **Band** 2
Table: p.225

McNamara, Neal
(Rhode Island)
Profile: p.1569
Employment **Band** 2
Table: p.1565
Litigation **Band** 3
Table: p.1567

M

McNamara, Rosalee M
(Missouri)
Profile: p.1059
Employment **Band 3**
Table: p.1046

McNealey, J Jeffrey (Ohio)
Profile: p.1445
Environment **Band S**
Table: p.1425

McNearney, John (Missouri)
Profile: p.1059
Real Estate **Band 2**
Table: p.1052

McNeil, Barry (Texas)
Profile: p.1691
Antitrust **Band 1**
Table: p.1622

McNeive, Lynda A
(Colorado)
Profile: p.320
Real Estate **Band 3**
Table: p.313

McNichol Jr, William
(Pennsylvania)
Profile: p.1532
Intellectual Property **Band 3**
Table: p.1508

McNiel, D Ferguson (Texas)
Profile: p.1691
Litigation **Band 3**
Table: p.1656

McPhee, Joan
(Massachusetts)
Profile: p.972
Litigation **Band 1**
Table: p.951

McQuaid, Janet (Texas)
Profile: p.1691
Environment **Up and coming**
Table: p.1643

McShea, David F
(Washington)
Profile: p.1793
Corporate/M&A **Band 3**
Table: p.1778

McSweeney, Maurice J
(Wisconsin)
Profile: p.1825
Litigation **Band S**
Table: p.1821

McTiernan, Edward F
(New Jersey)
Profile: p.1142
Environment **Band 2**
Table: p.1129

McTurnan, Lee B (Indiana)
Profile: p.793
Litigation **Band 1**
Table: p.785

McVeigh, John P (Maine)
Profile: p.899
Bankruptcy **Band 2**
Table: p.888

McWhorter, Hobart
(Alabama)
Profile: p.124
Litigation **Band 3**
Table: p.116

McWhorter, Val (Virginia)
Profile: p.1771
Construction **Band 2**

Table: p.1750

McWilliams, Susan (Susi)
(South Carolina)
Profile: p.1581
Employment **Band 3**
Table: p.1574
Litigation **Band 3**
Table: p.1576

Meadows, Charles (Texas)
Profile: p.1691
Litigation **Band 2**
Table: p.1665

Meadows, Craig (Idaho)
Profile: p.660
Litigation **Band 1**
Table: p.657

Meadows, Robert E (Texas)
Profile: p.1691
Energy **Band 3**
Table: p.1640
Litigation **Band 2**
Table: p.1656

Meadows, Stanley (Illinois)
Profile: p.741
Corporate/M&A **Band 4**
Table: p.675

Meadway, Jay K
(Pennsylvania)
Profile: p.1532
Intellectual Property **Band 4**
Table: p.1508

Meath, James (Virginia)
Profile: p.1771
Employment **Band 1**
Table: p.1755

Mechanic, Jonathan
(New York)
Profile: p.1300
Real Estate **Band 1**
Table: p.1248

Medaglia, Anthony
(Massachusetts)
Profile: p.972
Private Equity **Band 3**
Table: p.953

Mede, William (Alaska)
Profile: p.143
Employment **Band 2**
Table: p.135

Medlock, Bryan (Texas)
Profile: p.1692
Intellectual Property **Band 1**
Table: p.1651

Medved, Joseph W
(Missouri)
Profile: p.1059
Corporate/M&A **Band 1**
Table: p.1043

Meehan, Michael (Arizona)
Profile: p.160
Litigation **Band 3**
Table: p.152

Meehan, Wayne D
(New York)
Profile: p.95
Shipping **Band 3**
Table: p.67

Meeks, Thomas (Florida)
Profile: p.546
Litigation **Band 3**
Table: p.521

Meeks, William (Ohio)
Profile: p.1445
Litigation **Band 1**
Table: p.1432

Mehlman, Mark (Illinois)
Profile: p.741
Real Estate **Band 3**
Table: p.706

Meiklejohn, Paul
(Washington)
Profile: p.1793
Intellectual Property **Band 1**
Table: p.1784

Meir, Dennis (Georgia)
Profile: p.618
Bankruptcy **Band 2**
Table: p.582

Meiser, Kenneth E (New Jersey)
Profile: p.1143
Real Estate **Band 2**
Table: p.1135

Meisinger, Louis M
(California)
Profile: p.263
Media & Entertainment **Band 3**
Table: p.230

Meister, Margaret L
(New Mexico)
Profile: p.1163
Real Estate **Up and coming**
Table: p.1161

Melamed, Doug
(District of Columbia)
Profile: p.457
Antitrust **Band 2**
Table: p.367

Meland, Creighton (Illinois)
Profile: p.741
Banking & Finance **Band 3**
Table: p.665

Melby, Barbara Murphy
(National)
Profile: p.95
Business Process
Outsourcing: National **Band 2**
Table: p.10

Mele, Dennis (Florida)
Profile: p.546
Real Estate **Band 2**
Table: p.528

Melo, Thomas M (Texas)
Profile: p.1692
Employment **Band 1**
Table: p.1634

Meloy, Michael M
(Pennsylvania)
Profile: p.1532
Environment **Band 3**
Table: p.1505

Meltzer, Steven (Virginia)
Profile: p.1771
Corporate/M&A **Band 4**
Table: p.1752

Melwani, Vivek (New York)
Profile: p.1301
Bankruptcy **Up and coming**
Table: p.1179

Memel, Sherwin L
(California)
Profile: p.263

Healthcare **Band S**
Table: p.209

Mendeloff, Scott T (Illinois)
Profile: p.741
Litigation **Band 4**
Table: p.700

Mendelsohn, David (Illinois)
Profile: p.741
Insurance **Band 2**
Table: p.692

Mendelson, Alan C
(California)
Profile: p.263
Corporate/M&A **Band 1**
Table: p.197

Mendelson, Richard C
(California)
Profile: p.263
Real Estate **Band 3**
Table: p.238

Mendenhall, William
(Mississippi)
Profile: p.1035
Corporate/M&A **Band 3**
Table: p.1024

Mendez, John E (California)
Profile: p.263
Banking & Finance **Band 3**
Table: p.187

Mendoza, Julie C (National)
Profile: p.95
International Trade **Band 3**
Table: p.40

Menna, Gilbert
(Massachusetts)
Profile: p.972
Corporate/M&A **Band 2**
Table: p.937

Menotti, David E
(District of Columbia)
Profile: p.457
Environment **Band 3**
Table: p.392

Mensch, Linda (Illinois)
Profile: p.741
Media & Entertainment **Band 1**
Table: p.704

Mensik, Michael S (Illinois)
Profile: p.741
Business Process
Outsourcing: National **Band 3**
Table: p.10
Technology **Band 1**
Table: p.713

Menson, Richard L (Illinois)
Profile: p.741
Employee Benefits **Band 1**
Table: p.681

Mentlik, William (New Jersey)
Profile: p.1143
Litigation **Band 1**
Table: p.1133

Menzie, Edward G (South Carolina)
Profile: p.1581
Corporate/M&A **Band 1**
Table: p.1572
Real Estate **✪**
Table: p.1577

Mercer, John T W (Georgia)
Profile: p.618
Energy **Band 2**
Table: p.592

Meredith, Steven
(Massachusetts)
Profile: p.972
Private Equity **Band 3**
Table: p.953

Merkle, Craig (Maryland)
Profile: p.922
Litigation **Band 3**
Table: p.914

Merley, Dennis (Minnesota)
Profile: p.1019
Employment **Band 3**
Table: p.1008

Mermelstein, Joshua
(New York)
Profile: p.1301
Real Estate **Band 2**
Table: p.1248

Merriam, Dwight
(Connecticut)
Profile: p.337
Real Estate **Band 1**
Table: p.334

Merritt, Mark (North Carolina)
Profile: p.1397
Litigation **Band 2**
Table: p.1390

Mersol, Greg (Ohio)
Profile: p.1445
Employment **Band 2**
Table: p.1422

Merwin, Bruce (Texas)
Profile: p.1692
Construction **Band 3**
Table: p.1629

Messerman, Gerald (Ohio)
Profile: p.1445
Litigation **✪**
Table: p.1432

Messerschmidt, Michael
(Maine)
Profile: p.900
Employment **Band 2**
Table: p.890

Metcalf, Slade R (New York)
Profile: p.1301
Media & Entertainment **Band 2**
Table: p.1232

Metropoulos, Demetrios
(Illinois)
Profile: p.742
Telecom, Broadcast & Satellite **Band 3**
Table: p.715

Metropoulos, Jon (Montana)
Profile: p.1080
Natural Resources **Band 2**
Table: p.1077

Metzger, Richard
(District of Columbia)
Profile: p.457
Telecom, Broadcast & Satellite **Band 2**
Table: p.427

Metzke, John (Wyoming)
Profile: p.1839

Corporate/M&A Band 2
Table: p.1832

Meunier, Gerald E
(Louisiana)
Profile: p.875
Litigation Band 2
Table: p.865

Meusey, Joseph K
(Nebraska)
Profile: p.1088
Litigation Band 1
Table: p.1085

Meyer, Andrew C (Ohio)
Profile: p.1445
Employment Band 3
Table: p.1422

Meyer, David L (National)
Profile: p.95
Transport Band 3
Table: p.62

Meyer, G Christopher
(Ohio)
Profile: p.1445
Bankruptcy Band 1
Table: p.1414

Meyer, George (Florida)
Profile: p.546
Construction Band 1
Table: p.507

Meyer, Michael (California)
Profile: p.263
Real Estate Band 1
Table: p.238

Meyer, Paul (New York)
Profile: p.1301
Insurance Band 3
Table: p.1213

Meyer, Richard S (Virginia)
Profile: p.1771
Intellectual Property Band 2
Table: p.1759

Meyer, Theodore D (Texas)
Profile: p.1692
Employment Band 3
Table: p.1634

Meyers, Kent (Oklahoma)
Profile: p.1465
Litigation Band 2
Table: p.1462

Meyers, Michael (New York)
Profile: p.1301
Projects Band 4
Table: p.1244

Meyers, Todd (Georgia)
Profile: p.618
Bankruptcy Band 3
Table: p.582

Meyers III, Robert L (Texas)
Profile: p.1692
Construction Band 2
Table: p.1629

Meyerson, Lee (New York)
Profile: p.1301
Corporate/M&A Band 4
Table: p.1189

Miano, Steven T
(Pennsylvania)
Profile: p.1532
Environment Band 3
Table: p.1505

Micciche, Daniel J (Texas)
Profile: p.1692
Tax Band 3
Table: p.1665

Michaels, Jane (Colorado)
Profile: p.320
Intellectual Property Band 1
Table: p.309

Michaels, Joel
(District of Columbia)
Profile: p.457
Healthcare Band 1
Table: p.398

**Michel, Lisa
Wintersheimer** (Ohio)
Profile: p.1445
Employment Up and coming
Table: p.1422

Middlebrooks, David J
(Alabama)
Profile: p.124
Employment Band 2
Table: p.113

Middleton, Jack B
(New Hampshire)
Profile: p.1118
Litigation Band S
Table: p.1111

Mihlsten, George
(California)
Profile: p.264
Real Estate Band 1
Table: p.238

Mikels, Richard
(Massachusetts)
Profile: p.972
Bankruptcy Band 1
Table: p.935

Milam, Kenneth
(Mississippi)
Profile: p.1035
Employment Band 1
Table: p.1026

Milch, Thomas
(District of Columbia)
Profile: p.457
Environment Band 2
Table: p.392

Miles, Robin J (Texas)
Profile: p.1692
Banking & Finance Band 3
Table: p.1625

Miles, Steven
(District of Columbia)
Profile: p.457
Projects Band 3
Table: p.415

Milkman, Ruth
(District of Columbia)
Profile: p.457
Telecom, Broadcast & Satellite
Band 4
Table: p.427

Millard, David (Indiana)
Profile: p.793
Corporate/M&A Band 3
Table: p.781

Millard, John A (New York)
Profile: p.1301
Banking & Finance Band 4
Table: p.1174

Millen, Pressly M (North
Carolina)
Profile: p.1397
Litigation Band 2
Table: p.1390

Miller, Alan B (New York)
Profile: p.1301
Bankruptcy Band 3
Table: p.1179

Miller, Alan S (Pennsylvania)
Profile: p.1533
Environment Band 3
Table: p.1505

Miller, Barry (Ohio)
Profile: p.1445
Construction Band 2
Table: p.1417

Miller, Barry (Texas)
Profile: p.1692
Tax Band 3
Table: p.1665

Miller, Bradley (Oregon)
Profile: p.1483
Real Estate Band 2
Table: p.1479

Miller, Brian P (Florida)
Profile: p.546
Litigation Up and coming
Table: p.521

Miller, Charles E (Maine)
Profile: p.900
Real Estate Band 1
Table: p.895

Miller, Charles F (Missouri)
Profile: p.1059
Real Estate Band 1
Table: p.1052

Miller, Clifford (Hawaii)
Profile: p.649
Real Estate Band 1
Table: p.646

Miller, Craig (Washington)
Profile: p.1793
Litigation Band 3
Table: p.1786

Miller, Craig (Ohio)
Profile: p.1445
Real Estate Band 4
Table: p.1434

Miller, David S (New York)
Profile: p.1301
Tax Band 2
Table: p.1256

Miller, David W (Indiana)
Profile: p.793
Employment Band 1
Table: p.783

Miller, Elizabeth H
(Vermont)
Profile: p.1749
Litigation Band 3
Table: p.1746

Miller, Evan
(District of Columbia)
Profile: p.457
Employee Benefits Band 3
Table: p.378

Miller, Gale T (Colorado)
Profile: p.321
Antitrust Band 1

Table: p.311

Miller, Henry (Pennsylvania)
Profile: p.1533
Real Estate Band 1
Table: p.1516

Miller, J Gregg
(Pennsylvania)
Profile: p.1533
Bankruptcy Band 3
Table: p.1494

Miller, Kenneth W (Illinois)
Profile: p.742
Private Equity Band 3
Table: p.676

Miller, L Edward (Idaho)
Profile: p.660
Real Estate Band 3
Table: p.658

Miller, Laura B (Illinois)
Profile: p.742
Intellectual Property Band 3
Table: p.696

Miller, Lawrence
(District of Columbia)
Profile: p.458
Energy Band 5
Table: p.382

Miller, Lawrence A
(District of Columbia)
Profile: p.458
Real Estate Band 4
Table: p.418

Miller, Lee I (Illinois)
Profile: p.742
Real Estate Band 4
Table: p.706

Miller, Lloyd (Alaska)
Profile: p.143
Native Law Band 1
Table: p.140

Miller, Michelle
(Massachusetts)
Profile: p.972
Antitrust Band 1
Table: p.930

Miller, Morris (Florida)
Profile: p.546
Healthcare Band 1
Table: p.518

Miller, Nicholas (Idaho)
Profile: p.660
Corporate/M&A Band 1
Table: p.655

Miller, O'Malley (California)
Profile: p.264
Real Estate Band 2
Table: p.238

Miller, Peter A (New York)
Profile: p.1301
Real Estate Band 4
Table: p.1248

Miller, Ralph I (Texas)
Profile: p.1692
Litigation Band 3
Table: p.1656

Miller, Ranne B
(New Mexico)
Profile: p.1163
Litigation Band S
Table: p.1160

Miller, Rick (Georgia)
Profile: p.618
Corporate/M&A Band 4
Table: p.587

Miller, Robert (Idaho)
Profile: p.660
Real Estate Band S
Table: p.658

Miller, Robert (California)
Profile: p.264
Corporate/M&A Band 5
Table: p.197

Miller, Roger (Nebraska)
Profile: p.1088
Employment Band 2
Table: p.1084

Miller, Stephen D
(California)
Profile: p.264
Litigation Band 2
Table: p.225

Miller, Walter (Texas)
Profile: p.1692
Real Estate Up and coming
Table: p.1662

Miller, Winston (Kentucky)
Profile: p.844
Litigation Band 2
Table: p.835

Miller, Zach (Colorado)
Profile: p.321
Environment Band 2
Table: p.307

Miller Jr, Ben R (Louisiana)
Profile: p.875
Corporate/M&A Band 3
Table: p.859

Millet, Craig (California)
Profile: p.264
Bankruptcy Band 4
Table: p.191

Milliman, James (Kentucky)
Profile: p.844
Litigation Band 3
Table: p.835

Millisor, Kenneth (Ohio)
Profile: p.1445
Employment Band 1
Table: p.1422

Millner, Robert (Illinois)
Profile: p.742
Bankruptcy Band 2
Table: p.669

Millock, Peter J (New York)
Profile: p.1302
Healthcare Band 3
Table: p.1209

Mills, Gail L (Alabama)
Profile: p.124
Real Estate Band 3
Table: p.119

Mills, Jerry (Texas)
Profile: p.1692
Intellectual Property Band 2
Table: p.1651

Mills, Michael (Alaska)
Profile: p.143
Bankruptcy Band 1
Table: p.133

M

M

Mills, Phillip R (New York)
Profile: p.1302
Corporate/M&A Band 4
Table: p.1189

Mills Jr, Osborne (Ohio)
Profile: p.1445
Banking & Finance Band 1
Table: p.1411

Millspaugh, Thomas E D
(Maryland)
Profile: p.922
Real Estate Band 3
Table: p.917

Millstein, Julian (New York)
Profile: p. 1302
Business Process
Outsourcing: National Band 2
Table: p.10
Technology Band 3
Table: p.1259

Millstone, David J (Ohio)
Profile: p.1445
Employment Band 3
Table: p.1422

Milmed, Paul K (New York)
Profile: p.1302
Environment Band 3
Table: p.1206

Milmoe, J Gregory
(New York)
Profile: p.1302
Bankruptcy Band 1
Table: p.1179

Milom, W Michael
(Tennessee)
Profile: p.1610
Media & Entertainment Band 1
Table: p.1602

Minch, Roger J (North
Dakota)
Profile: p.1410
Bankruptcy Band 1
Table: p.1403

Minchella, Michael F
(California)
Profile: p.264
Construction Band 2
Table: p.194

Mindlin, Philip (New York)
Profile: p.1302
Bankruptcy Band 4
Table: p.1179

Minion, Robert G
(New Jersey)
Profile: p.1143
Corporate/M&A Band 2
Table: p.1123

Minisman, B G (Alabama)
Profile: p.124
Corporate/M&A Band 2
Table: p.111

Minkus, Daniel (Michigan)
Profile: p.1000
Corporate/M&A Band 3
Table: p.989

Minogue, Thomas J
(Missouri)
Profile: p.1059
Corporate/M&A Band 3
Table: p.1043

Miraldi, Leslee (Ohio)
Profile: p.1445
Banking & Finance Band 2
Table: p.1411

Mirvis, Theodore N
(New York)
Profile: p.1302
Litigation Band 2
Table: p.1223

Miscimarra, Philip A
(Illinois)
Profile: p.742
Employment Band 2
Table: p.681

Mishkin, Jeffrey A
(National)
Profile: p.95
Sport Band 1
Table: p.55

Missner, David (Illinois)
Profile: p.742
Bankruptcy Band 2
Table: p.669

Mitchell, Barry D (Arizona)
Profile: p.160
Litigation Band 4
Table: p.152

Mitchell, Beth H
(Massachusetts)
Profile: p.972
Real Estate Band 2
Table: p.956

Mitchell, Chris (Alabama)
Profile: p.124
Employment Band 2
Table: p.113

Mitchell, David S (National)
Profile: p.95

Mitchell, E Marlee
(Tennessee)
Profile: p.1610
Corporate/M&A Band 3
Table: p.1594

Mitchell, H Maurice
(Arkansas)
Profile: p.177
Real Estate Band S
Table: p.174

Mitchell, Marvin (Indiana)
Profile: p.793
Litigation Band 3
Table: p.785

Mitchell, Michael
(New York)
Profile: p.1302
Litigation Band 3
Table: p.1223

Mitchell, Nancy (Illinois)
Profile: p.742
Bankruptcy Band 3
Table: p.669

Mitchell, Stephen J
(Florida)
Profile: p.546
Real Estate Band 2
Table: p.526

**Mitchelson Jr, William
(Mitch) R** (Georgia)
Profile: p.618
Litigation Band 1
Table: p.599

Mixson, Dwight (Alabama)
Profile: p.124
Real Estate Band 2
Table: p.119

Mixson, H Lamar (Georgia)
Profile: p.618
Litigation Band 2
Table: p.598

Moates, G Paul (National)
Profile: p.95
Transport Band 1
Table: p.62

Moberly, Michael D
(Arizona)
Profile: p.160
Employment Band 3
Table: p.148

Mock, Randall D
(Oklahoma)
Profile: p.1465
Tax Band 2
Table: p.1459

Mockbee, David
(Mississippi)
Profile: p.1035
Litigation Band 1
Table: p.1028

Moeckel, Jennifer Shea
(New Hampshire)
Profile: p.1118
Employment Band 3
Table: p.1109

Moeling, Walter G (Georgia)
Profile: p.618
Banking & Finance Band 1
Table: p.581

Moellenberg, Dalva
(Arizona)
Profile: p.160
Environment Band 3
Table: p.150

Moeller Jr, Armin J
(Mississippi)
Profile: p.1035
Employment Band 2
Table: p.1026

Moffatt, Maura Griffith
(Massachusetts)
Profile: p.972
Real Estate Band 3
Table: p.956

Moffitt, Ronald (Utah)
Profile: p.1737
Corporate/M&A Band 2
Table: p.1727

Molavi, Kamyar (Georgia)
Profile: p.618
Construction Band 2
Table: p.584

Molen, Chris D (Georgia)
Profile: p.618
Banking & Finance Band 1
Table: p.580

Mollen, Neal D
(District of Columbia)
Profile: p.458
Employment Band 3
Table: p.380

Mollerup, Richard (Idaho)
Profile: p.660
Real Estate Band 3

Table: p.658

Molo, Steven (New York)
Profile: p.742
Litigation Band 3
Table: p.700

Moltenbrey, MJ
(District of Columbia)
Profile: p.458
Antitrust Band 5
Table: p.367

Monaco, Daniel A
(Pennsylvania)
Profile: p.1533
Intellectual Property Band 4
Table: p.1508

Monaco, Stephanie
(District of Columbia)
Profile: p.458
Investment Management
Band 3
Table: p.406

Monaghan, John J
(Massachusetts)
Profile: p.972
Bankruptcy Band 3
Table: p.935

Monahan Jr, John (Vermont)
Profile: p.1749
Litigation Band 3
Table: p.1746

Monk, Stephen (Alabama)
Profile: p.124
Real Estate Band 2
Table: p.119

Monk II, Charles O
(Maryland)
Profile: p.922
Litigation Band 2
Table: p.914

Monnheimer, Donald (New
Mexico)
Profile: p.1163
Corporate/M&A Band 3
Table: p.1155

Monohan, David (Kentucky)
Profile: p.844
Litigation Band 4
Table: p.835

Monroe, C Robert
(Missouri)
Profile: p.1059
Corporate/M&A Band 2
Table: p.1043

Monson, Terry (Iowa)
Profile: p.813
Real Estate Band 4
Table: p.810

Montague Jr, H Laddie
(Pennsylvania)
Profile: p.1533
Antitrust Band 2
Table: p.1489

Montgomery, Andrew S
(New Mexico)
Profile: p.1163
Litigation Band 4
Table: p.1159

Montgomery, Bruce
(District of Columbia)
Profile: p.458
Antitrust Band 4

Table: p.367

Montgomery, David
(New York)
Profile: p.1302
Construction Band 3
Table: p.1186

Montgomery, John T
(Massachusetts)
Profile: p.973
Litigation Band 3
Table: p.951

Montgomery, Margaret
(Vermont)
Profile: p.1749
Corporate/M&A Band 2
Table: p.1743

Moody, Christopher M
(New Mexico)
Profile: p.1163
Employment Band 2
Table: p.1157

Moody, Thomas H (Vermont)
Profile: p.1749
Corporate/M&A Band 2
Table: p.1743

Moody III, James H (Texas)
Profile: p.1692
Insurance Band 2
Table: p.1648

Moon, Richard G (Maine)
Profile: p.900
Employment Band 1
Table: p.890

Mooney, Ann M (California)
Profile: p.264
Insurance Band 4
Table: p.212

Mooney, Douglas G
(Washington)
Profile: p.1793
Employment Band 2
Table: p.1780

Moore, Charles A (Texas)
Profile: p.1692
Energy Band 1
Table: p.1641

Moore, Charles L
(New Mexico)
Profile: p.1163
Corporate/M&A Band 1
Table: p.1155

Moore, Dan (Iowa)
Profile: p.813
Real Estate Band 2
Table: p.810

Moore, Gary H (California)
Profile: p.264
IT Outsourcing Band 3
Table: p.221

Moore, George
(New Hampshire)
Profile: p.1118
Litigation Band 3
Table: p.1111

Moore, Harold F (New York)
Profile: p. 1302
Projects Band 1
Table: p.52
Projects Band 1
Table: p.1244

Moore, James E
(South Dakota)
Profile: p.1593
Litigation Band 2
Table: p.1590

Moore, Justin (Virginia)
Profile: p.1771
Corporate/M&A Band 3
Table: p.1752

Moore, Larry (Utah)
Profile: p.1737
Real Estate Band 3
Table: p.1733

Moore, Lynnwood
(Oklahoma)
Profile: p.1465
Corporate/M&A Band 1
Table: p.1459

Moore, Margaret
(District of Columbia)
Profile: p.458
Energy Band 4
Table: p.386

Moore, Michael (Arkansas)
Profile: p.177
Employment Band 1
Table: p.170

Moore, Mikel L (Montana)
Profile: p.1080
Litigation Band 2
Table: p.1075

Moore, Paul D
(Massachusetts)
Profile: p.973
Bankruptcy Band 2
Table: p.935

Moore, Robert (DC)
Profile: p.458
Tax Band 3
Table: p.422

Moore, Robert (California)
Profile: p.264
Bankruptcy Band 4
Table: p.191

Moore, Robert (Virginia)
Profile: p.1771
Construction Band 2
Table: p.1750

Moore, Scott S (Nebraska)
Profile: p.1088
Employment Band 3
Table: p.1084

Moore, Thomas J (Texas)
Profile: p.1693
Energy Band 5
Table: p.1637

Moore, Thurston R
(Virginia)
Profile: p.1771
Corporate/M&A Band 3
Table: p.1752

Moorefield, G Crawford
(Texas)
Profile: p.1693
Tax Band 4
Table: p.1665

Moorefield Jr, Harold
(Florida)
Profile: p.546
Bankruptcy Band 2
Table: p.503

Moorhead, Bruce W
(Georgia)
Profile: p.619
Banking & Finance Band 3
Table: p.580

Moorman, Robert (Oregon)
Profile: p.1483
Corporate/M&A Band 2
Table: p.1471

Moorse, Charles
(Minnesota)
Profile: p.1019
Corporate/M&A Band 3
Table: p.1005

Moot, John S
(District of Columbia)
Profile: p.458
Energy Band 2
Table: p.386

Mora, Mindy A (Florida)
Profile: p.546
Bankruptcy Band 2
Table: p.503

Morales, Gerard (Arizona)
Profile: p.160
Employment Band 4
Table: p.148

Moran, Joseph (Alaska)
Profile: p.143
Environment Band 3
Table: p.137
Regulated Industries Band 2
Table: p.137

Moran, Mark (National)
Profile: p.96
International Trade Band 2
Table: p.40

Moran, Patrick G (Illinois)
Profile: p.742
Real Estate Band 1
Table: p.706

Morgan, Ann (Nevada)
Profile: p.1103
Employment Band 3
Table: p.1091

Morgan, Charles (New York)
Profile: p.1302
Tax Band 2
Table: p.1256

Morgan, Kevan (Washington)
Profile: p.1793
Intellectual Property Band 2
Table: p.1784

Morgan, Linda (National)
Profile: p.96
Transport Band 1
Table: p.62

Morgan, Michael
(Washington)
Profile: p.1793
Corporate/M&A Band 1
Table: p.1778

Morgan, Pauline (Delaware)
Profile: p.355
Bankruptcy Band 4
Table: p.341

Morgan, Robert C
(New York)
Profile: p.1302
Intellectual Property Band 3
Table: p.1217

Morgenstern, Saul P
(New York)
Profile: p.1303
Antitrust Band 4
Table: p.1170

Morhouse, Sanford W
(New York)
Profile: p.1303
Private Equity Band 3
Table: p.1241

Moritz, Louis P (Illinois)
Profile: p.742
Real Estate Band 4
Table: p.706

Morley, Patrick R (North
Dakota)
Profile: p.1410
Litigation Band 2
Table: p.1406

Morphy, James C (New York)
Profile: p.1303
Corporate/M&A Band 1
Table: p.1189

Morreale, Justin P
(Massachusetts)
Profile: p.973
Private Equity Band 3
Table: p.953

Morreli, Stephen G (Maine)
Profile: p.900
Bankruptcy Band 2
Table: p.888

Morris, Ralph A (Illinois)
Profile: p.743
Employment Band 2
Table: p.681

Morris, Steve (Nevada)
Profile: p.1103
Litigation Band 2
Table: p.1096

Morris III, James W
(Virginia)
Profile: p.1771
Litigation Band 1
Table: p.1763

Morrison, David
(West Virginia)
Profile: p.1810
Employment Band 1
Table: p.1801

Morrison, Francis
(Connecticut)
Profile: p.337
Litigation Band 3
Table: p.331

Morrison, John (North
Dakota)
Profile: p.1410
Energy Band 1
Table: p.1407

Morrison, Kenneth P
(Illinois)
Profile: p.96
Capital Markets Band 1
Table: p.21

Morrison, Portia Owen
(Illinois)
Profile: p.743
Real Estate Band 2
Table: p.706

Morrison, Stephen G
(South Carolina)
Profile: p.1581
Litigation Band 1
Table: p.1576

Morrison, Victoria A
(New Jersey)
Profile: p.1143
Real Estate Band 2
Table: p.1134

Morriss, James (Texas)
Profile: p.1693
Environment Band 2
Table: p.1643

Morrow, Bill (California)
Profile: p.264
Tax Band 4
Table: p.241

Morrow, John H (Alabama)
Profile: p.124
Litigation Band 2
Table: p.116

Morse, Clinton S (Virginia)
Profile: p.1771
Employment Band 3
Table: p.1755

Morse, Robert (Texas)
Profile: p.1693
Litigation Band 2
Table: p.1643

Morvillo, Robert G
(New York)
Profile: p.1303
Litigation ✪
Table: p.1224

Moscarino, George (Ohio)
Profile: p.1445
Litigation Band S
Table: p.1432

Moscow, Cyril (Michigan)
Profile: p.1000
Corporate/M&A Band S
Table: p.989

Moscowitz, Jane (Florida)
Profile: p.546
Litigation Band 1
Table: p.522

Moscowitz, Norman A
(Florida)
Profile: p.546
Litigation Band 1
Table: p.522

Moseley, James F (National)
Profile: p.96
Shipping Band 1
Table: p.71

Moser, Kenneth A (North
Carolina)
Profile: p.1397
Banking & Finance Band 3
Table: p.1381

Moss, Edward (Florida)
Profile: p.546
Litigation Band 3
Table: p.521

Moss, Gary (Nevada)
Profile: p.1103
Employment Band 1
Table: p.1091

Moss, Steven M. (Ohio)
Profile: p.1445
Employment Up and coming
Table: p.1422

Mosseau, Peter
(New Hampshire)
Profile: p.1118
Litigation Band 1
Table: p.1111
Litigation Band 3
Table: p.1111

Motenko, Neil
(Massachusetts)
Profile: p.973
Antitrust Band 1
Table: p.930

Mottesi, Marcello A
(California)
Profile: p. 264
Capital Markets Band 3
Table: p.23

Moulthrop, Samuel P
(New Jersey)
Profile: p.1143
Environment Band 2
Table: p.1129

Mowe, Gregory (Oregon)
Profile: p.1483
Litigation Band 2
Table: p.1477

Mowrey, Robert (Georgia)
Profile: p.619
Environment Band 3
Table: p.593

Moye, James E (Florida)
Profile: p.546
Construction Band 1
Table: p.507

Moye, John (Colorado)
Profile: p.321
Corporate/M&A Band 3
Table: p.303

Moyer, Dennis K
(District of Columbia)
Profile: p.458
Real Estate Band 4
Table: p.418

Moyer Jr. E Homer M
(National)
Profile: p.96
International Trade Band 4
Table: p.40

Moyes, Jay (Arizona)
Profile: p.160
Environment Band 3
Table: p.150

Mrkonich, Marko
(Minnesota)
Profile: p.1019
Employment Band 3
Table: p.1008

Mrowiec, John S (Illinois)
Profile: p.743
Construction Band 3
Table: p.672

Muchmore, Clyde A
(Oklahoma)
Profile: p.1465
Litigation Band 2
Table: p.1462

M

Muchmore, Iris (Iowa)
Profile: p.813
Employment Band 2
Table: p.805

Mueller, Kathleen T
(Missouri)
Profile: p.1059
Real Estate Band 2
Table: p.1052

Muench, John E (Illinois)
Profile: p.743
Telecom, Broadcast & Satellite
Band 3
Table: p.715

Mugel, Christopher J
(Virginia)
Profile: p.1771
Intellectual Property Band 1
Table: p.1761

Mulaney Jr, Charles W
(Illinois)
Profile: p.743
Corporate/M&A Band 1
Table: p.675

Mulcahy, Michael
(Michigan)
Profile: p.1000
Real Estate Band 3
Table: p.996

Muldoon Jr, Robert J
(Massachusetts)
Profile: p.973
Litigation Band 2
Table: p.951

Mullen, Thomas A.
(Delaware)
Profile: p.355
Corporate/M&A Band 3
Table: p.346

Mulliken, David (California)
Profile: p.264
Insurance Band 3
Table: p.212

Mullin, Joel A (Oregon)
Profile: p.1483
Litigation Band 2
Table: p.1477

Mullis, Carl W (Georgia)
Profile: p.619
Antitrust Band 3
Table: p.578

Mumaugh, Brian (Colorado)
Profile: p.321
Employment Band 3
Table: p.306

Mummery, Dan (California)
Profile: p. 264
Business Process
Outsourcing: National Band 2
Table: p.10
IT Outsourcing Band 1
Table: p.221

Munck, William A (Texas)
Profile: p.1693
Intellectual Property Band 3
Table: p.1651

Muncy, Dennis (Illinois)
Profile: p.743
Telecom, Broadcast & Satellite
Band 2
Table: p.715

Munford, Luther T
(Mississippi)
Profile: p.1035
Litigation Band 1
Table: p.1028

Munger, Lisa Woods
(Hawaii)
Profile: p.649
Land Use Band 1
Table: p.643
Litigation Band 2
Table: p.644

Munitz, Gerald (Illinois)
Profile: p.743
Bankruptcy Band S
Table: p.669

Munsch, Russell (Texas)
Profile: p.1693
Bankruptcy Band 4
Table: p.1627

Munson, Myra (Alaska)
Profile: p.143
Native Law Band 1
Table: p.140

Munther, Merrily (Idaho)
Profile: p.660
Employment Band 2
Table: p.656

Murchison, John M (North
Carolina)
Profile: p.1397
Antitrust Band 1
Table: p.1390

Murdock Jr, Grady (Illinois)
Profile: p.743
Employment Band 3
Table: p.681

Muris, Timothy J
(District of Columbia)
Profile: p.458
Antitrust Band 4
Table: p.367

Murnane, Don P (New York)
Profile: p.96
Shipping Band 4
Table: p.67

Murphy, Brian R (Vermont)
Profile: p.1749
Corporate/M&A Band 2
Table: p.1743

Murphy, Harold B
(Massachusetts)
Profile: p.973
Bankruptcy Band 1
Table: p.935

Murphy, J Andrew
(District of Columbia)
Profile: p.458
Projects Band 3
Table: p.415

Murphy, Jack W
(District of Columbia)
Profile: p.458
Investment Management
Band 3
Table: p.406

Murphy, Joseph (Illinois)
Profile: p.743
Telecom, Broadcast & Satellite
Band 2
Table: p.715

Murphy, Lawrence
(Michigan)
Profile: p.1000
Employment Band 3
Table: p.991

Murphy, Liam (Vermont)
Profile: p.1749
Real Estate Band 1
Table: p.1747
Real Estate Band 1
Table: p.1747

Murphy, Marc S (Kentucky)
Profile: p.844
Litigation Band 4
Table: p.835

Murphy, Mary (California)
Profile: p.264
Real Estate Band 2
Table: p.238

Murphy, Michael (California)
Profile: p. 264
Business Process
Outsourcing: National Band 3
Table: p.10
IT Outsourcing Band 2
Table: p.221

Murphy, Patrick A
(California)
Profile: p.264
Bankruptcy Band S
Table: p.191

Murphy, Patrick J.
(Wyoming)
Profile: p.1839
Litigation Band 2
Table: p.1835

Murphy, Paul B (Georgia)
Profile: p.619
Litigation Band 3
Table: p.598

Murphy, Paul G (North
Carolina)
Profile: p. 1397
Capital Markets Band 2
Table: p.22

Murphy, Sandra
(West Virginia)
Profile: p.1810
Corporate/M&A Band 1
Table: p.1798

Murphy, Terrence
(Pennsylvania)
Profile: p.1533
Employment Band 3
Table: p.1500

Murphy, Thomas P (Virginia)
Profile: p.1771
Employment Band 3
Table: p.1755

Murphy, William (Maryland)
Profile: p.923
Litigation Band 2
Table: p.914

Murphy Jr, Charles C
(Georgia)
Profile: p.619
Antitrust Band 2
Table: p.578

Murray, Christopher
(California)
Profile: p.264
Media & Entertainment Band 2
Table: p.233

Murray, Craig (Texas)
Profile: p.1693
Banking & Finance Band 4
Table: p.1625

Murray, George (Missouri)
Profile: p.1059
Real Estate Band 2
Table: p.1052

Murray, Gregory (Illinois)
Profile: p.743
Banking & Finance Band 1
Table: p.665

Murray, Gregory (Michigan)
Profile: p.1000
Employment Band 2
Table: p.991

Murray, Thomas
(West Virginia)
Profile: p.1810
Corporate/M&A Band 2
Table: p.1798

Murray, William
(Pennsylvania)
Profile: p.1533
Intellectual Property Band 1
Table: p.1508

Murray Jr, William G
(California)
Profile: p.264
Real Estate Band 3
Table: p.238

Murtaugh, Christopher D
(Illinois)
Profile: p.743
Real Estate Band 3
Table: p.706

Musil, Greg L (Kansas)
Profile: p.824
Litigation Band 2
Table: p.819

Musser, William (South
Carolina)
Profile: p.1582
Corporate/M&A Band 3
Table: p.1572

Mutchnik, James (Illinois)
Profile: p.743
Antitrust Band 2
Table: p.662

Muth, Jon R (Michigan)
Profile: p.1000
Litigation Band 3
Table: p.994

Muto, Fred (California)
Profile: p.264
Corporate/M&A Band 5
Table: p.197

Mutryn, William
(District of Columbia)
Profile: p.458
Corporate/Commercial Band 3
Table: p.376

Muzzi, Christopher (Hawaii)
Profile: p.649
Bankruptcy Band u
Table: p.640

Myers, Donald J
(District of Columbia)
Profile: p.458
Employee Benefits Band 3
Table: p.378

Myers, John (New Mexico)
Profile: p.1163
Real Estate Band 1
Table: p.1161

Myers, Marlee
(Pennsylvania)
Profile: p.1533
Corporate/M&A Band 2
Table: p.1497

Myers, Roger (California)
Profile: p.264
Media & Entertainment Band 4
Table: p.230

Mytelka, Craig L (Virginia)
Profile: p.1771
Intellectual Property Band 2
Table: p.1761

N

Nachbar, Kenneth J
(Delaware)
Profile: p.355
Chancery Band 2
Table: p.344

Nachwalter, Michael
(Florida)
Profile: p.547
Litigation Band 1
Table: p.521

Nadel, Alan S (Pennsylvania)
Profile: p.1533
Intellectual Property Band 2
Table: p.1508

Nadel, Peter F (New York)
Profile: p.1303
Healthcare Band 1
Table: p.1209

Naeve, Clifford M
(District of Columbia)
Profile: p.458
Energy Band 1
Table: p.382
Energy ✪
Table: p.386

Naftalis, Gary P (New York)
Profile: p.1303
Litigation Band 2
Table: p.1222
Litigation Band 2
Table: p.1224

Nagel, Trevor (National)
Profile: p.96
Business Process
Outsourcing: National Band 3
Table: p.10

Nagelberg, Howard (Illinois)
Profile: p.743
Real Estate Band 3
Table: p.706

Nager, Glen
(District of Columbia)
Profile: p.459
Litigation Band 1
Table: p.408

Nagin, Stephen (Florida)
Profile: p.547
Antitrust **Band 2**
Table: p.498

Nagle, David E (Virginia)
Profile: p.1771
Employment **Band 2**
Table: p.1755

Nagle, James
(Massachusetts)
Profile: p.973
Employment **Band 2**
Table: p.940

Nakahata, John
(District of Columbia)
Profile: p.459
Telecom, Broadcast & Satellite
Band 3
Table: p.427

Nakashima, Steve (Hawaii)
Profile: p.649
Employment **Band 2**
Table: p.642

Nannes, John M
(District of Columbia)
Profile: p.459
Antitrust **Band 3**
Table: p.367

Napolitano, Steven (Illinois)
Profile: p.743
Corporate/M&A **Band 4**
Table: p.675
Private Equity **Band 2**
Table: p.676

Narducci, Lucas (Arizona)
Profile: p.160
Environment **Band 2**
Table: p.150

Nash, David (Ohio)
Profile: p.1445
Environment **Band 2**
Table: p.1425

Nash, Glenn (California)
Profile: p.264
Corporate/M&A **Band 5**
Table: p.197
IT Outsourcing **Band 2**
Table: p.221

Nasi, Michael (Texas)
Profile: p.1693

Nassau, Henry N
(Pennsylvania)
Profile: p.1533
Corporate/M&A **Band 2**
Table: p.1497

Natale, Andrew (Ohio)
Profile: p.1446
Construction **Band 2**
Table: p.1417

Nathan, Charles (New York)
Profile: p.1303
Corporate/M&A **Band 3**
Table: p.1189

Nathan, Irvin
(District of Columbia)
Profile: p.459
Litigation **Band 2**
Table: p.410

Nation, Floyd (Texas)
Profile: p.1693
Intellectual Property **Band 3**

Table: p.1651

Natsis, Anton N (California)
Profile: p.264
Real Estate **Band 2**
Table: p.238

Naugle, Louis (Pennsylvania)
Profile: p.1533
Environment **Band 3**
Table: p.1505

Navarro Baysinger, Kara S
(California)
Profile: p.265
Insurance **Band 4**
Table: p.212

Nayler, Greg (Iowa)
Profile: p.813
Employment **Band 3**
Table: p.805

Neaher, Edward
(District of Columbia)
Profile: p.459
Projects **Band 2**
Table: p.415

Neal, James F (Tennessee)
Profile: p.1610
Litigation **Band 3**
Table: p.1599

Neal, Kathy R (Oklahoma)
Profile: p.1465
Employment **Band 2**
Table: p.1461

Neal, Steve (California)
Profile: p.265
Litigation **Band 2**
Table: p.224

Neckles, Peter J (New York)
Profile: p.1303
Banking & Finance **Band 4**
Table: p.1174

Nedzbala, Michael
(North Carolina)
Profile: p.1397
Capital Markets **Band 2**
Table: p.22

Needell, Benjamin F
(New York)
Profile: p.1303
Real Estate **Band 1**
Table: p.1248

Needle, William (Georgia)
Profile: p.619
Intellectual Property **Band 1**
Table: p.596

Neel, James M (Texas)
Profile: p.1693
Employment **Band 3**
Table: p.1634

Neely, Sally S (California)
Profile: p.265
Bankruptcy **Band 3**
Table: p.191

Neff, Daniel A (New York)
Profile: p.1304
Corporate/M&A **Band 3**
Table: p.1189

Neighbours, John T
(Indiana)
Profile: p.793
Employment **Band 2**
Table: p.783

Neill, David S (New York)
Profile: p.1304
Antitrust **Band 4**
Table: p.1170

Neligan Jr, Patrick (Texas)
Profile: p.1693
Bankruptcy **Band 2**
Table: p.1627

Nellis, Noel W (California)
Profile: p.265
Real Estate **Band 1**
Table: p.238

Nelson, Carol Sue
(Alabama)
Profile: p.124
Employment **Band 2**
Table: p.113

Nelson, Marshall J
(Washington)
Profile: p.1793
Intellectual Property **Band 2**
Table: p.1784

Nelson, Stephen (Iowa)
Profile: p.814
Real Estate **Band 3**
Table: p.810

Nelson, William F
(District of Columbia)
Profile: p.459
Tax **Band 2**
Table: p.422

Neppl, William (Iowa)
Profile: p.814
Real Estate **Band 4**
Table: p.810

Nesgos, Peter (New York)
Profile: p.1304
Space, Satellite & Technology
Band 1
Table: p.1259

Ness, Andrew D
(District of Columbia)
Profile: p.459
Construction **Band 1**
Table: p.374

Nessim, Ronald J
(California)
Profile: p.265
Litigation **Band 2**
Table: p.225

Nester, Daniel C (Missouri)
Profile: p.1059
Real Estate **Band 2**
Table: p.1053

Nestrud, Charles (Arkansas)
Profile: p.177
Litigation **Band 1**
Table: p.172

Nettles, Larry (Texas)
Profile: p.1693
Environment **Band 3**
Table: p.1643

Neugebauer, Robert
(Washington)
Profile: p.1794
Real Estate **Band 3**
Table: p.1788

Neuhaus, Joseph E
(National)
Profile: p.96
Arbitration **Band**

Table: p.33
Arbitration **Band 3**
Table: p.33

Neumann, Gordon (Iowa)
Profile: p.814
Corporate/M&A **Band 2**
Table: p.802

Neuner, Robert (New York)
Profile: p.1304
Intellectual Property **Band 3**
Table: p.1217

Neupert, John (Oregon)
Profile: p.1483
Litigation **Band 3**
Table: p.1477

Neustadt, Arthur I (Virginia)
Profile: p.1771
Intellectual Property **Band 1**
Table: p.1759

Neveloff, Jay A (New York)
Profile: p.1304
Real Estate **Band 3**
Table: p.1248

Neville, Drew (Oklahoma)
Profile: p.1466
Litigation **Band 1**
Table: p.1462

Neville, Frank D (Wyoming)
Profile: p.1839
Litigation **Band 2**
Table: p.1835

Nevins, Patrick
(District of Columbia)
Profile: p.459
Energy **Up and coming**
Table: p.382

Newbold, J William
(Missouri)
Profile: p.1059
Litigation **Band 3**
Table: p.1049

Newborn, Steve A
(District of Columbia)
Profile: p.459
Antitrust **Band 2**
Table: p.367

Newcom, Charles W
(Colorado)
Profile: p.321
Employment **Band 3**
Table: p.306

Newcombe, George
(California)
Profile: p.265
Intellectual Property **Band 3**
Table: p.216

Newell, Francis Patrick
(Pennsylvania)
Profile: p.1533
Antitrust **Band 2**
Table: p.1489

Newell, Robert D (Oregon)
Profile: p.1483
Litigation **Band 2**
Table: p.1477

Newman, James (Nevada)
Profile: p.1103
Corporate/M&A
Up and coming
Table: p.1089

Newman, Jeanne (California)
Profile: p.265
Media & Entertainment **Band 3**
Table: p.233

Newman, Jeffrey H (New
Jersey)
Profile: p.1143
Real Estate **Band 2**
Table: p.1134

Newman, Karol Lyn
(District of Columbia)
Profile: p.459
Energy **Band 4**
Table: p.382

Newman, Lawrence W
(National)
Profile: p. 1305
Arbitration **Band**
Table: p.33

Newman, Margery (Illinois)
Profile: p.744
Construction **Band 3**
Table: p.672

Newman, Richard
(District of Columbia)
Profile: p.459
Real Estate **Band 3**
Table: p.418

Newman, Thomas R
(New York)
Profile: p.1305
Insurance **Band 2**
Table: p.1213

Newman Jr, John (Jack) M
(Ohio)
Profile: p.1446
Litigation **Band 1**
Table: p.1431

Newsome, J Kent (Texas)
Profile: p.1693
Real Estate **Band 2**
Table: p.1662

Newton, Robert O (Maine)
Profile: p.900
Litigation **Band 3**
Table: p.893

Newton, Trammell (Georgia)
Profile: p.619
Antitrust **Band 2**
Table: p.578

Nibert, Gregory J (New
Mexico)
Profile: p.1163
Environment **Band 1**
Table: p.1158

Nicely, Matthew R
(National)
Profile: p.97
International Trade
Up and coming
Table: p.40

Nicely, Philip (Indiana)
Profile: p.793
Real Estate **Band 2**
Table: p.788

Nicholas, Thomas
(Wyoming)
Profile: p.1839
Litigation **Band 1**
Table: p.1835

N

Nicholls III, Malcolm B
(Massachusetts)
Profile: p.973
Private Equity **Up and coming**
Table: p.955

Nichols, Phillip (California)
Profile: p.265
Real Estate **Band 2**
Table: p.238

Nichols, Tracy A (Florida)
Profile: p.547
Litigation **Band 3**
Table: p.521

Nicholson, Penn (Georgia)
Profile: p.619
Bankruptcy **Band 3**
Table: p.582

Nicholson, Phillip R
(California)
Profile: p.265
Real Estate **Band S**
Table: p.238

Nickel, Henry (DC)
Profile: p.459
Environment **Band 2**
Table: p.392

Nicklin, Emily (Illinois)
Profile: p.744
Litigation **Band 4**
Table: p.700

Niebruegge, Michael E
(Texas)
Profile: p.1693
Banking & Finance **Band 1**
Table: p.1625

Niehoff, Leonard M
(Michigan)
Profile: p.1000
Employment **Band 3**
Table: p.991

Nields, John W (DC)
Profile: p.459
Litigation **Band 3**
Table: p.410

Niemuth, Nathan R
(Arizona)
Profile: p.160
Employment **Band 4**
Table: p.148

Nierman, Todd (Indiana)
Profile: p.793
Employment **Band 3**
Table: p.783

Nigon, Kenneth
(Pennsylvania)
Profile: p.1533
Intellectual Property **Band 4**
Table: p.1508

Nijenhuis, Erika W
(New York)
Profile: p.1305
Tax **Band 2**
Table: p.1256

Nijman, Jennifer (Illinois)
Profile: p.744
Environment **Band 3**
Table: p.687

Nilson, George (Maryland)
Profile: p.923
Litigation **Band 3**
Table: p.914

Nims, Barbara (New York)
Profile: p.1305
Employee Benefits **Band 3**
Table: p.1197

Ninneman, Mary Pat
(Wisconsin)
Profile: p.1825
Employment **Band 3**
Table: p.1819

Nirenberg, David Z
(New York)
Profile: p.1305
Tax **Band 1**
Table: p.1256

Niro, Raymond (Illinois)
Profile: p.744
Intellectual Property **Band 1**
Table: p.696

Nisbet, A Wyckliff
(Arkansas)
Profile: p.177
Employee Benefits **Band 1**
Table: p.170

Nishimoto, John S (Hawaii)
Profile: p.649
Litigation **Band 3**
Table: p.644

Nix II, Robert (Michigan)
Profile: p.1000
Real Estate **Band 3**
Table: p.996

Nixon, Larry S (Virginia)
Profile: p.1771
Intellectual Property **Band 2**
Table: p.1759

Nixon, Richard (Missouri)
Profile: p.1060
Corporate/M&A **Band S**
Table: p.1043

Nobil, Steven (Ohio)
Profile: p.1446
Employment **Band 3**
Table: p.1422

Noble, Ron (Florida)
Profile: p.547
Environment **Band 3**
Table: p.516

Nocco, Frank (National)
Profile: p.97
Capital Markets **Band 3**
Table: p.19

Nodine, Larry (Georgia)
Profile: p.619
Intellectual Property **Band 2**
Table: p.596

Noecker, Kathlyn E
(Minnesota)
Profile: p.1019
Employment **Band 3**
Table: p.1008

Noel, Randall D (Tennessee)
Profile: p.1610
Litigation **Band 3**
Table: p.1599

Noell Jr, John W (Illinois)
Profile: p.744
Private Equity **Band 3**
Table: p.676

Nokes, Gregory
(Connecticut)
Profile: p.337
Employment **Band 3**
Table: p.329

Nolan, Thomas J (California)
Profile: p.265
Antitrust **Band 3**
Table: p.184
Litigation **Band 2**
Table: p.224

Nolan, William (Ohio)
Profile: p.1446
Employment **Band 3**
Table: p.1422

Nondorf, Kurt (Texas)
Profile: p.1694
Real Estate **Band 3**
Table: p.1662

Nonna, John M (New York)
Profile: p.1305
Insurance **Band 2**
Table: p.1213

Noona, Stephen E (Virginia)
Profile: p.1771
Intellectual Property **Band 1**
Table: p.1761

Noonan, Elizabeth (Rhode
Island)
Profile: p.1569
Real Estate **Band 3**
Table: p.1568

Nordhaus, Robert
(District of Columbia)
Profile: p.459
Energy **Band 3**
Table: p.386

Noreika, Maryellen
(Delaware)
Profile: p.355
Intellectual Property **Band 3**
Table: p.348

Norman, Mark A (Ohio)
Profile: p.1446
Environment **Band 3**
Table: p.1425

Norris, John (Texas)
Profile: p.1694
Intellectual Property **Band 2**
Table: p.1651

Norris, Megan P (Michigan)
Profile: p.1000
Employment **Band 2**
Table: p.991

Norris, Trenton H
(California)
Profile: p.265
Environment **Up and coming**
Table: p.207

North, John L (Georgia)
Profile: p.619
Intellectual Property **Band 4**
Table: p.596

Northam, Patrick
(Kentucky)
Profile: p.844
Corporate/M&A **Band 2**
Table: p.827
Environment **Band 2**
Table: p.832

Northup, Stephen A
(Virginia)
Profile: p.1771
Litigation **Band 3**
Table: p.1763

Norton, Bill (Tennessee)
Profile: p.1610
Litigation **Band 1**
Table: p.1599

Norton IV, Floyd L
(District of Columbia)
Profile: p.459
Energy **Band 3**
Table: p.386

Norwich, Donald
(Minnesota)
Profile: p.1019
Real Estate **Band 2**
Table: p.1014

Noteboom, Todd
(Minnesota)
Profile: p.1019
Litigation **Band 3**
Table: p.1011

Nourse, David A (New York)
Profile: p.97
Shipping **Band 2**
Table: p.67

Nouss, James (Missouri)
Profile: p.1060
Corporate/M&A **Band 1**
Table: p.1043

Novacek, Stephen V
(Nevada)
Profile: p.1103
Real Estate **Band 3**
Table: p.1099

Novak, Edward F (Arizona)
Profile: p.160
Litigation **Band 3**
Table: p.153

Novak, Tabor (Alabama)
Profile: p.124
Litigation **Band 3**
Table: p.116

Novak, Theodore (Illinois)
Profile: p.744
Real Estate **Band 1**
Table: p.706

Novick, Robert T (National)
Profile: p.97
International Trade **Band 1**
Table: p.40

Novikoff, Harold S
(New York)
Profile: p.1305
Bankruptcy **Band 1**
Table: p.1179

Nuechterlein, Jonathan
(District of Columbia)
Profile: p.460
Telecom, Broadcast & Satellite
Band 4
Table: p.427

Nuechterlein, Mike (Florida)
Profile: p.547
Construction **Band 1**
Table: p.507

Nurkin, Sidney J (Georgia)
Profile: p.619
Corporate/M&A **Band 1**
Table: p.587

Nusbaum, Jack H
(New York)
Profile: p.1305
Corporate/M&A **Band S**
Table: p.1189

Nussbaum, Bernard W
(New York)
Profile: p.1306
Litigation **Band 1**
Table: p.1222

Nussdorf, Melanie
(District of Columbia)
Profile: p.460
Employee Benefits **Band 1**
Table: p.378

Nutt, Robert L
(Massachusetts)
Profile: p.973
Corporate/M&A **Band 2**
Table: p.937

Nyhan, Christopher D
(Maine)
Profile: p.900
Litigation **Band 3**
Table: p.893

Nyhan, Lawrence (Illinois)
Profile: p.744
Bankruptcy **Band 2**
Table: p.669

Nylen Jr, Richard A
(Massachusetts)
Profile: p.973
Real Estate **Band 1**
Table: p.957

O

Oade, K Preston (Colorado)
Profile: p.321
Employment **Band 1**
Table: p.306

Oakes, Leslie (Georgia)
Profile: p.619
Environment **Band 3**
Table: p.593

Oakes, Royal (California)
Profile: p.265
Insurance **Band 4**
Table: p.212

Oakley, Mary Ann (Georgia)
Profile: p.619
Employment **Band 3**
Table: p.589

Oates, J Christopher
(North Carolina)
Profile: p.1398
Real Estate **Band 2**
Table: p.1392

Oberkfell, Keith F
(North Carolina)
Profile: p. 1398
Capital Markets **Band 2**
Table: p.22

O'Brien, Clare (New York)
Profile: p.1306
Corporate/M&A **Band 3**
Table: p.1189

O

O'Brien, George
(Connecticut)
Profile: p.337
Employment **Band 1**
Table: p.329

O'Brien, Michael (Utah)
Profile: p.1737
Employment **Band 1**
Table: p.1730

O'Brien, Richard (Illinois)
Profile: p.744
Media & Entertainment **Band 1**
Table: p.703

O'Brien, William
(Pennsylvania)
Profile: p.1534
Litigation **Band 1**
Table: p.1511

O'Bryan, Rory (Indiana)
Profile: p.793
Real Estate **Band 2**
Table: p.788

O'Connell, Barry G
(Montana)
Profile: p.1080
Litigation **Band 3**
Table: p.1075

O'Connell, George L
(California)
Profile: p.265
Litigation **Band 1**
Table: p.225

O'Connell, Mary Anne
(Missouri)
Profile: p.1060
Corporate/M&A **Band 2**
Table: p.1043

O'Connell, Timothy
(Washington)
Profile: p.1794
Employment **Band 3**
Table: p.1780

O'Connor, Karen (Illinois)
Profile: p.744
Technology **Up and coming**
Table: p.713

O'Connor, Robert (Utah)
Profile: p.1737
Corporate/M&A **Band 1**
Table: p.1727

O'Connor III, Charles A
(District of Columbia)
Profile: p.460
Environment **Band 4**
Table: p.392

O'Day, Stephen (Georgia)
Profile: p.619
Environment **Band 2**
Table: p.593

Ode, Paul (Vermont)
Profile: p.1749
Corporate/M&A **Band 1**
Table: p.1743

O'Dea, Jr, Joseph F
(Pennsylvania)
Profile: p.1534
Environment **Band 4**
Table: p.1505

O'Dear, Craig (Missouri)
Profile: p.1060
Litigation **Band 2**

Table: p.1049

Odlaug, Bruce (Minnesota)
Profile: p.1019
Real Estate **Band 2**
Table: p.1014

O'Donnell, Earle
(District of Columbia)
Profile: p.460
Energy **Band 1**
Table: p.386

O'Donnell, G Daniel
(Pennsylvania)
Profile: p.1534
Corporate/M&A **Band 2**
Table: p.1497

O'Donnell, Laura E (Texas)
Profile: p.1694
Employment **Up and coming**
Table: p.1634

O'Donnell, Matthew
(Ontario)
Profile: p.1143
Real Estate **Band 3**
Table: p.1134

O'Donnell, Neil (National)
Profile: p.97
Government Contracts
Band 3
Table: p.27

O'Donnell, Patricia (Ohio)
Profile: p.1446
Real Estate **Band 3**
Table: p.1434

Odorizzi, Michele L (Illinois)
Profile: p.744
Litigation **Band 4**
Table: p.700

Odsen, Frederick (Alaska)
Profile: p.143
Corporate/M&A **Band 2**
Table: p.134

Oelman, David (Texas)
Profile: p.1694
Corporate/M&A
Up and coming
Table: p.1631

Oesting, David W (Alaska)
Profile: p.143
Bankruptcy **Band 2**
Table: p.133
Litigation **Band 2**
Table: p.138

Oestreicher, Charles R
(Maine)
Profile: p.900
Real Estate **Band 2**
Table: p.895

Offer, Stuart J (California)
Profile: p.265
Tax **Band 1**
Table: p.241

Ofsa, Joyce (West Virginia)
Profile: p.1810
Real Estate **Band 3**
Table: p.1806

Ogilby, Anne Phillips
(Massachusetts)
Profile: p.973
Healthcare **Band 2**
Table: p.946

Ohnegian, Scott A
(New Jersey)
Profile: p.1143
Employment **Band 3**
Table: p.1126

Okeson, Nils (Georgia)
Profile: p.619
Corporate/M&A
Up and coming
Table: p.587

Okumura, Miki (Hawaii)
Profile: p.649
Tax **Band 1**
Table: p.641

Oland, Mark (Connecticut)
Profile: p.337
Real Estate **Band 2**
Table: p.334

Old, William (Virginia)
Profile: p.1771
Corporate/M&A **Band 4**
Table: p.1752

Oldham, Dudley (Texas)
Profile: p.1694
Litigation **Band 3**
Table: p.1656

Oldham, Joseph C
(Kentucky)
Profile: p.844
Employment **Band 3**
Table: p.830

O'Leary, Daniel (Oregon)
Profile: p.1483
Litigation **Band 3**
Table: p.1477

O'Leary, Michael (Texas)
Profile: p.1694
Corporate/M&A **Band 1**
Table: p.1631

Oleynik, Jeffrey E
(North Carolina)
Profile: p.1398
Antitrust **Band 1**
Table: p.1390
Litigation **Band 3**
Table: p.1390

Olian, Robert (Illinois)
Profile: p.744
Environment **Band 2**
Table: p.687

Oliff, James A (Virginia)
Profile: p.1771
Intellectual Property **Band 2**
Table: p.1759

Oliver, Craig (Tennessee)
Profile: p.1610
Employment **Up and coming**
Table: p.1596

Oliver, David (Missouri)
Profile: p.1060
Litigation **Band 2**
Table: p.1049

Oliver, James (Maryland)
Profile: p.923
Real Estate **Band 2**
Table: p.917

Oliver III, Rufus W (Texas)
Profile: p.1694
Antitrust **Band 2**
Table: p.1622

Oliver Jr, Samuel
(North Carolina)
Profile: p.1398
Real Estate **Band 1**
Table: p.1392

Olivier, Jeanne (New York)
Profile: p.1306
Projects **Band 4**
Table: p.1244

Olsen, Christine (California)
Profile: p.265
Banking & Finance **Band 3**
Table: p.187

Olson, Camille A (Illinois)
Profile: p.745
Employment **Band 3**
Table: p.681

Olson, John (Florida)
Profile: p.547
Bankruptcy **Band 3**
Table: p.503

Olson, Karl (California)
Profile: p.265
Media & Entertainment **Band 4**
Table: p.230

Olson, Pamela F
(District of Columbia)
Profile: p.460
Tax **Band 3**
Table: p.422

Olson, Richard (North
Dakota)
Profile: p.1410
Corporate/M&A **Band 1**
Table: p.1403

Olson, Ronald (California)
Profile: p.265
Litigation **Band 2**
Table: p.224
Media & Entertainment **Band 2**
Table: p.230

Olson, Stephen
(Pennsylvania)
Profile: p.1534
Employment **Band 2**
Table: p.1500

Olson, Theodore
(District of Columbia)
Profile: p.460
Litigation **Band 1**
Table: p.408

O'Malley, Kevin E (Arizona)
Profile: p.160
Litigation **Band 4**
Table: p.152

O'Malley Jr, Joseph M
(New York)
Profile: p.1306
Intellectual Property **Band 3**
Table: p.1217

O'Mara, James W
(Mississippi)
Profile: p.1035
Bankruptcy **Band 1**
Table: p.1024

Ominsky, Harris
(Pennsylvania)
Profile: p.1534
Real Estate **Band S**
Table: p.1516

Oncidi, Anthony J
(California)
Profile: p.265
Employment **Band 4**
Table: p.202

Ondrasik, Paul
(District of Columbia)
Profile: p. 460
Employee Benefits **Band 2**
Table: p.378
Litigation **Band 1**
Table: p.25

O'Neal, Stephen V
(California)
Profile: p.266
Construction **Band 2**
Table: p.194

O'Neal-Coble, Leslie
(Florida)
Profile: p.547
Construction **Band 1**
Table: p.507

O'Neil, Holland (Texas)
Profile: p.1694
Bankruptcy **Band 4**
Table: p.1627

O'Neil, Terry (New York)
Profile: p.1306
Employment **Band 3**
Table: p.1200

O'Neill, Brian (California)
Profile: p.266
Litigation **Band 1**
Table: p.225

O'Neill, Brian B (Minnesota)
Profile: p.1019
Litigation **Band 3**
Table: p.1011

O'Neill, Brian D
(District of Columbia)
Profile: p.460
Energy **Band 2**
Table: p.382

O'Neill, Edward (California)
Profile: p.266
Energy **Band 3**
Table: p.204

O'Neill, Robert (Vermont)
Profile: p.1749
Litigation **Band 2**
Table: p.1746

O'Neill Jr, John H
(District of Columbia)
Profile: p.460
Energy **Band 3**
Table: p.390

Oosterhouse, Carl
(Michigan)
Profile: p.1000
Corporate/M&A **Band 3**
Table: p.989

Oosterhuis, Paul W
(District of Columbia)
Profile: p.460
Tax **Band 1**
Table: p.422

Ordway, Eric (National)
Profile: p.97
Arbitration **Band 4**
Table: p.33

O

P

O'Reilly, Peter (Illinois)
Profile: p.745
Media & Entertainment **Band 2**
Table: p.704

O'Reilly, Timothy
(Pennsylvania)
Profile: p.1534
Employment **Band 4**
Table: p.1500

O'Reilly Jr, William R
(Massachusetts)
Profile: p.973
Real Estate **Band 3**
Table: p.956

Oringer, Andrew (New York)
Profile: p.1306
Employee Benefits **Band 3**
Table: p.1197

Orlansky, Susan (Alaska)
Profile: p.143
Litigation **Band 2**
Table: p.138

Orloff, Laurence B (New Jersey)
Profile: p.1143
Litigation **Band 1**
Table: p.1131

Ormseth, Kris J (Idaho)
Profile: p.660
Corporate/M&A **Band 3**
Table: p.655

Orr, Dennis P (New York)
Profile: p.1306
Antitrust **Band 4**
Table: p.1170

Orr, Rick W
(South Dakota)
Profile: p.1593
Employment **Band 1**
Table: p.1589

Orshefsky, Debbie (Florida)
Profile: p.547
Real Estate **Band 2**
Table: p.528

Ortbals, Mary Beth
(Missouri)
Profile: p.1060
Employment **Band 3**
Table: p.1046

Ortiz, Scott (Wyoming)
Profile: p.1839
Employment **Band 1**
Table: p.1833

Ortner, Charles (New York)
Profile: p.1306
Media & Entertainment **Band 3**
Table: p.1232

Osborn, John W (National)
Profile: p.97
Capital Markets **Band 1**
Table: p.16

Osborn II, Jones (Arizona)
Profile: p.160
Real Estate **Band 4**
Table: p.154

Osborne, Robert Stephen
(Illinois)
Profile: p.745
Corporate/M&A **Band 3**
Table: p.675

Osborne, Scott (Washington)
Profile: p.1794
Real Estate **Band 1**
Table: p.1788

Oscar, Lawrence E (Ohio)
Profile: p.1446
Bankruptcy **Band 4**
Table: p.1414

Osenbaugh, Kim
(Washington)
Profile: p.1794
Bankruptcy **Band 1**
Table: p.1776

Oshinsky, Jerold
(District of Columbia)
Profile: p.461
Insurance **Band 1**
Table: p.402

Osnos, David
(District of Columbia)
Profile: p.461
Real Estate **Band 2**
Table: p.418

Ossip, Michael J
(Pennsylvania)
Profile: p.1534
Employment **Band 3**
Table: p.1500

Ossola, Charles
(District of Columbia)
Profile: p.1771
Intellectual Property **Band 2**
Table: p.1759

Osterberg, Edward (Texas)
Profile: p.1694
Tax **Band 1**
Table: p.1665

Ostermeyer, Michael J
(Wisconsin)
Profile: p.1825
Real Estate **Band 2**
Table: p.1822

Ostlund, Richard
(Minnesota)
Profile: p.1019
Litigation **Band 3**
Table: p.1011

Ostrager, Barry R
(New York)
Profile: p.1306
Insurance **Band 1**
Table: p.1213
Litigation **Band 1**
Table: p.1222

O'Sullivan, John
(District of Columbia)
Profile: p.461
Energy **Band 4**
Table: p.386

O'Toole, Matthew J
(Delaware)
Profile: p.356
Corporate/M&A **Band 3**
Table: p.346

Overberg, Nathan (Iowa)
Profile: p.814
Employment **Up and coming**
Table: p.805

Overman, Robert (Kansas)
Profile: p.824
Employment **Band 2**
Table: p.818

Overstreet, Mark R
(Kentucky)
Profile: p.844
Environment **Band 3**
Table: p.832

Owendoff, Michael (Ohio)
Profile: p.1446
Real Estate **Up and coming**
Table: p.1434

Oxford, Terrell (Texas)
Profile: p.1694
Antitrust **Band 3**
Table: p.1622

Oxner, Dewey
(South Carolina)
Profile: p.1582
Litigation **Band S**
Table: p.1576

Ozier, William (Tennessee)
Profile: p.1610
Employment **Band 1**
Table: p.1596

P

Pace, Stanley Dan (Ohio)
Profile: p.1446
Employment **Band 2**
Table: p.1422

Pachulski, Isaac M
(California)
Profile: p.266
Bankruptcy **Band 2**
Table: p.191

Pachulski, Richard M
(California)
Profile: p.266
Bankruptcy **Band 1**
Table: p.191

Paci, Victor J
(Massachusetts)
Profile: p.973
Private Equity **Band 3**
Table: p.953

Page, Adele (North Dakota)
Profile: p.1410
Employment **Band 2**
Table: p.1405

Page, Marshall (Louisiana)
Profile: p.875
Banking & Finance **Band 2**
Table: p.857

Page, Michael (California)
Profile: p.266
Intellectual Property **Band 3**
Table: p.216

Page, Rosewell (Virginia)
Profile: p.1772
Litigation **Band 2**
Table: p.1763

Page, Thomas (Oregon)
Profile: p.1483
Real Estate **Band 1**
Table: p.1479

**Pagel Serebransky,
Elizabeth** (New York)
Profile: p.1307
Employee Benefits **Band 3**
Table: p.1197

Paget, David (New York)
Profile: p.1307
Environment **Band 2**
Table: p.1205

Painter, Robin A
(Massachusetts)
Profile: p.973
Private Equity **Band 1**
Table: p.955

Painter, William
(Mississippi)
Profile: p.1035
Corporate/M&A **Band 2**
Table: p.1024

Paisley, Bonnie
(New Mexico)
Profile: p.1163
Corporate/M&A **Band 2**
Table: p.1155

Pakenham, Timothy J
(Georgia)
Profile: p.620
Real Estate **Band 3**
Table: p.601

Palenchar, James (Colorado)
Profile: p.321
Corporate/M&A **Band 1**
Table: p.303

Paley, Alan (New York)
Profile: p.1307
Corporate/M&A **Band 4**
Table: p.1189

Palma, Laura (National)
Profile: p.97
Capital Markets **Band 3**
Table: p.19

Palmer, Crisman
(South Dakota)
Profile: p.1593
Litigation **Band 1**
Table: p.1590
Litigation **Band 1**
Table: p.1590

Palmer, Scott (Florida)
Profile: p.547
Antitrust **Band 2**
Table: p.498

Palmer, Thomas (Oregon)
Profile: p.1483
Corporate/M&A **Band 3**
Table: p.1471

Paltell, Eric (Maryland)
Profile: p.923
Employment **Band 2**
Table: p.912

Palumbo, Ralph H
(Washington)
Profile: p.1794
Environment **Band 1**
Table: p.1782
Litigation **Band 2**
Table: p.1786

Panagakis, George N
(Illinois)
Profile: p.745
Bankruptcy **Band 3**
Table: p.669

Panitch, Ronald L
(Pennsylvania)
Profile: p.1534
Intellectual Property **Band 1**
Table: p.1508

Pannell, H Gary (Georgia)
Profile: p.620
Banking & Finance **Band 3**
Table: p.581

Pannone, Gary R (Rhode Island)
Profile: p.1570
Corporate/M&A **Band 2**
Table: p.1564

Panoff, Robert (Florida)
Profile: p.547
Tax **Band 2**
Table: p.531

Panovka, Robin (New York)
Profile: p.1307
Real Estate **Band 4**
Table: p.1248

Pantaleo, Peter (New York)
Profile: p.1307
Bankruptcy **Band 1**
Table: p.1179

Pantel, Glenn S (New Jersey)
Profile: p.1143
Real Estate **Band 1**
Table: p.1135

Papavizas, Constantine G
(National)
Profile: p.98
Shipping **Band 1**
Table: p.71

Papel, Laurence
(Tennessee)
Profile: p.1610
Real Estate **Band 3**
Table: p.1603

Pappas, Edward H
(Michigan)
Profile: p.1000
Litigation **Band 3**
Table: p.994

Pappas, Lynn (Florida)
Profile: p.547
Real Estate **Band 1**
Table: p.528

Pappone, Michael
(Massachusetts)
Profile: p.973
Bankruptcy **Band 1**
Table: p.935

Paradee, John W (Delaware)
Profile: p.356
Real Estate **Band 2**
Table: p.350

Pardo Jr, James (Georgia)
Profile: p.620
Bankruptcy **Band 1**
Table: p.582

Paré, Jay (New York)
Profile: p.98
Shipping **Band 3**
Table: p.67

Pari, Joseph
(District of Columbia)
Profile: p.461
Tax **Band 3**
Table: p.422

Paris, Theodore W (Texas)
Profile: p.1694
Corporate/M&A **Band 4**
Table: p.1631

Paris, Zachary (Ohio)
Profile: p.1446
Real Estate Band 2
Table: p.1434

Parise, Michael J (Alaska)
Profile: p.144
Bankruptcy Band 1
Table: p.133

Park, William W (National)
Profile: p.98
Arbitration Band 1
Table: p.34

Parker, C Allen (New York)
Profile: p.1307
Banking & Finance Band 1
Table: p.1174

Parker, Dallas (Texas)
Profile: p.1694
Technology Band 1
Table: p.1668

Parker, David (Texas)
Profile: p.1695
Intellectual Property Band 3
Table: p.1651

Parker, Douglas S (Alaska)
Profile: p.144
Employment Band 1
Table: p.135

Parker, Gilbert E (Oregon)
Profile: p.1483
Real Estate Band 2
Table: p.1479

Parker, James (New Mexico)
Profile: p.1164
Corporate/M&A Band 3
Table: p.1155
Employment Band 2
Table: p.1157

Parker, John (Georgia)
Profile: p.620
Healthcare Band 1
Table: p.594

Parker, Richard G
(District of Columbia)
Profile: p.461
Antitrust Band 2
Table: p.367

Parks, John R (Georgia)
Profile: p.620
Real Estate Band 3
Table: p.601

Parks, Randall S (Virginia)
Profile: p.1772
Corporate/M&A Band 4
Table: p.1752

Parks, Timothy M (Oregon)
Profile: p.1484
Real Estate Up and coming
Table: p.1479

Parliman, Gregory C
(New Jersey)
Profile: p.1143
Employment Band 2
Table: p.1126

Parmley, Bruce
(District of Columbia)
Profile: p.461
Real Estate Band 2
Table: p.418

Parobek, Drew (Ohio)
Profile: p.1446
Bankruptcy Band 3
Table: p.1414

Parrino, Richard (Virginia)
Profile: p.1772
Corporate/M&A Band 4
Table: p.1752

Parsigian, Kenneth
(Massachusetts)
Profile: p.974
Litigation Band 3
Table: p.951

Parsons, Chuck (Minnesota)
Profile: p.1019
Real Estate Band 3
Table: p.1014

Parsons, David (Illinois)
Profile: p.745
Employment Band 3
Table: p.681

Parsons, Philip S (Florida)
Profile: p.547
Environment Band 1
Table: p.516

Parsons, W Stuart
(Wisconsin)
Profile: p.1825
Litigation Band S
Table: p.1821

Partridge, John J (Rhode
Island)
Profile: p.1570
Corporate/M&A Band 2
Table: p.1564

Partridge, Scott (Texas)
Profile: p.1695
Intellectual Property Band 1
Table: p.1651

Pasahow, Lynn (California)
Profile: p.266
Intellectual Property Band 3
Table: p.216

Pasano, Michael S (Florida)
Profile: p.547
Litigation Band 1
Table: p.522

Pascual, Rey (Georgia)
Profile: p.620
Corporate/M&A Band 4
Table: p.587

Pashby, Gary
(South Dakota)
Profile: p.1593
Litigation Band 1
Table: p.1590

Pasich, Kirk (California)
Profile: p.267
Insurance Band 1
Table: p.212

Passarelli, John (Nebraska)
Profile: p.1088
Litigation Band 1
Table: p.1085

Passman, Donald
(California)
Profile: p.267
Media & Entertainment Band 1
Table: p.233

Pasternack, Sam
(Massachusetts)
Profile: p.974
Intellectual Property Band 2
Table: p.948

Pastroff, Sanford (Illinois)
Profile: p.745
Antitrust Band 3
Table: p.662

Pastuszenski, Brian
(Massachusetts)
Profile: p.974
Litigation Band 1
Table: p.951

Pasulka-Brown, Kathleen
(Illinois)
Profile: p.745
Telecom, Broadcast & Satellite
Band 3
Table: p.715

Patberg, William L (Ohio)
Profile: p.1446
Environment Band 3
Table: p.1425

Pate, Stephen (Texas)
Profile: p.1695
Insurance Band 3
Table: p.1648

Paterson, Nancy (Texas)
Profile: p.1695
Employment Band 3
Table: p.1634

Patin, Douglas L
(District of Columbia)
Profile: p.461
Construction Band 2
Table: p.374

Patrick, Elizabeth (Georgia)
Profile: p.620
Construction Band 2
Table: p.584

Patrick III, William H
(Louisiana)
Profile: p.875
Corporate/M&A Band 2
Table: p.859

Patterson, Anne M (New
Jersey)
Profile: p.1143
Litigation Band 3
Table: p.1131

Patterson, Carl N
(North Carolina)
Profile: p.1398
Litigation Band 2
Table: p.1390

Patterson, Jeffrey (Nevada)
Profile: p.1103
Real Estate Band 3
Table: p.1099

Patterson, John
(New Mexico)
Profile: p.1164
Real Estate Band 2
Table: p.1161

Patterson, Robert S
(Tennessee)
Profile: p.1610
Litigation Band 3
Table: p.1599

Patterson, Thomas E
(California)
Profile: p.267
Bankruptcy Band 4
Table: p.191

Patterson, Jr, J A 'Tony'
(Texas)
Profile: p.1695
Healthcare Band 2
Table: p.1646

Patton, David (Texas)
Profile: p.1695
Energy Band 5
Table: p.1637

Patton, Stephen (Illinois)
Profile: p.745
Litigation Band 4
Table: p.700

Patton, William
(Massachusetts)
Profile: p.974
Antitrust Band 2
Table: p.930

Patton Jr, James L
(Delaware)
Profile: p.356
Bankruptcy Band 1
Table: p.341

Paul, Deborah L (New York)
Profile: p.1307
Tax Band 4
Table: p.1255

Paul, James T (Hawaii)
Profile: p.649
Litigation Band 3
Table: p.644

Paul, Marcia B (New York)
Profile: p.1307
Media & Entertainment Band 3
Table: p.1232

Paul, Niall (West Virginia)
Profile: p.1810
Employment Band 2
Table: p.1801

Paulson, Mark
(District of Columbia)
Profile: p.461
Intellectual Property Band 3
Table: p.403

Paustian, Kathleen M
(Nevada)
Profile: p.1103
Employment Band 3
Table: p.1091

Payne, Clare (Maine)
Profile: p.900
Employment Band 2
Table: p.890

Payne, William (Minnesota)
Profile: p.1019
Corporate/M&A Band 3
Table: p.1005

Payson, Robert (Delaware)
Profile: p.356
Chancery Band 2
Table: p.344

Pear, Charles (Hawaii)
Profile: p.649
Real Estate Band 1
Table: p.646

Pearce, John (Arizona)
Profile: p.161
Environment Band 3
Table: p.150

Pearlman, Samuel (Ohio)
Profile: p.1446
Real Estate Band 2
Table: p.1434

Pearlstein, Debra J
(New York)
Profile: p.1308
Antitrust Band 4
Table: p.1170

Pearlstein, Mark W
(Massachusetts)
Profile: p.974
Litigation Band 1
Table: p.951
Litigation Band 2
Table: p.951

Pearson, John R (Texas)
Profile: p.1695
Insurance Band 3
Table: p.1648

Pearson, Jonathan
(South Carolina)
Profile: p.1582
Employment Band 2
Table: p.1574

Pearson, Nick (New York)
Profile: p.1308
Insurance Band 3
Table: p.1213

Pearson Jr, John Y (Virginia)
Profile: p.1772
Litigation Band 3
Table: p.1763

Peaslee, James M
(New York)
Profile: p.1308
Tax Band 1
Table: p.1256

Pecht, Gerald (Texas)
Profile: p.1695
Energy Band 3
Table: p.1640

Peck, Kathy A (Oregon)
Profile: p.1484
Employment Band 2
Table: p.1474

Peck, Rodney (California)
Profile: p.267
Banking & Finance Band 1
Table: p.188

Peck, S Michael (Illinois)
Profile: p.745
Private Equity Band 3
Table: p.676

Peckar, Robert S (New York)
Profile: p.1308
Construction Band 1
Table: p.1186

Pecoulas, George A
(Illinois)
Profile: p.98
Capital Markets Band 1
Table: p.21

Peden, David (Texas)
Profile: p.1695
Construction Band 2
Table: p.1629

P

Pedersen, Luke (Texas)
Profile: p.1695
Intellectual Property
Up and coming
Table: p.1651

Pedlar, Alan (California)
Profile: p.267
Bankruptcy Band 3
Table: p.191

Pedowitz, Lawrence B
(New York)
Profile: p.1308
Litigation Band 1
Table: p.1224

Peek, J Stephen (Nevada)
Profile: p.1103
Litigation Band 2
Table: p.1096

Peifer, Charles (New Mexico)
Profile: p.1164
Litigation Band 3
Table: p.1159

Peirano, John (New Jersey)
Profile: p.1143
Employment Band 3
Table: p.1126

Peirce, Richard
(Pennsylvania)
Profile: p.1534
Intellectual Property
Up and coming
Table: p.1508

Peitzman, Lawrence
(California)
Profile: p.267
Bankruptcy Band 4
Table: p.191

Pelczarski, Karen A
(Rhode Island)
Profile: p.1570
Litigation Band 3
Table: p.1567

Pelfrey, D Patton (Kentucky)
Profile: p.844
Employment Band 1
Table: p.830

Pelham, Thomas (Florida)
Profile: p.547
Real Estate Band 2
Table: p.528

Pels, Gerald (Texas)
Profile: p.1695
Environment Band 3
Table: p.1643

Pence, Linda L (Indiana)
Profile: p.793
Litigation Band 1
Table: p.785

Pence, Thomas C
(Wisconsin)
Profile: p.1825
Employment Band 3
Table: p.1819

Pender, Bob
(District of Columbia)
Profile: p.461
Projects Band 3
Table: p.415

Pendleton, Lea B
(Massachusetts)
Profile: p.974

Private Equity Band 3
Table: p.953

Penna, Richard A
(District of Columbia)
Profile: p.461
Environment Band 4
Table: p.392

Pentelovitch, William
(Minnesota)
Profile: p.1019
Litigation Band 1
Table: p.1011

Pentz, Martin C
(Massachusetts)
Profile: p.974
Environment Band 3
Table: p.943

Penzer, Michèle (New York)
Profile: p.1308
Projects Band 4
Table: p.1244

Pepke, Michael T
(Wisconsin)
Profile: p.1826
Corporate/M&A Band 3
Table: p.1817

Pepple, Daniel P
(Washington)
Profile: p.1794
Real Estate Band 3
Table: p.1788

Peregrine, Michael W
(Illinois)
Profile: p.745
Healthcare Band 1
Table: p.690

Perellis, Andrew H (Illinois)
Profile: p.745
Environment Band 3
Table: p.687

Perez, Alfredo R (Texas)
Profile: p.1696
Bankruptcy Band 1
Table: p.1627

Perez, Luis (Florida)
Profile: p.547
Corporate/M&A Band 3
Table: p.509

Perich, Thomas J (Texas)
Profile: p.1696
Banking & Finance Band 3
Table: p.1625

Perisho, Russell
(Washington)
Profile: p.1794
Employment Band 1
Table: p.1780

Perkins, Alan (Arkansas)
Profile: p.177

Perkins, Harriet
(Pennsylvania)
Profile: p.1534
Intellectual Property Band 4
Table: p.1508

Perkins, Joseph J (Alaska)
Profile: p.144
Environment Band 3
Table: p.137

Perl, Sanford E (Illinois)
Profile: p.745
Private Equity Band 2
Table: p.676

Perlis, Mark
(District of Columbia)
Profile: p.461
Energy Band 4
Table: p.386

Perlman, Daniel J (Illinois)
Profile: p.746
Real Estate Band 4
Table: p.706

Perlstein, William J
(District of Columbia)
Profile: p.461
Bankruptcy Band 1
Table: p.372

Permut, Barry (Colorado)
Profile: p.321
Real Estate Band 2
Table: p.313

Pernick, Norman L
(Delaware)
Profile: p.356
Bankruptcy Band 2
Table: p.341

Perrenoud, Scott
(South Dakota)
Profile: p.1593
Corporate/M&A Band 3
Table: p.1587

Perry, Alan W (Mississippi)
Profile: p.1035
Litigation Band 1
Table: p.1028
Litigation Band 2
Table: p.1028

Perry, Charles (Georgia)
Profile: p.620
Environment Band 3
Table: p.593

Perry, Christopher
(Massachusetts)
Profile: p.974
Employment Band 3
Table: p.940

Perry, Donna (Kentucky)
Profile: p.845
Employment Band 2
Table: p.830

Persons, Oscar N (Georgia)
Profile: p.620
Litigation Band 2
Table: p.598

Persons, Ray (Georgia)
Profile: p.620
Litigation Band 3
Table: p.598

Perwin, Joel (Florida)
Profile: p.547
Litigation Band 1
Table: p.525

Perwin, Scott (Florida)
Profile: p.547
Antitrust Band 1
Table: p.498

Perzek, Philip (Illinois)
Profile: p.746
Banking & Finance Band 3
Table: p.665

Peterman, David (Texas)
Profile: p.1696
Technology Band 2
Table: p.1668

Peters, Gerald (California)
Profile: p.267
Healthcare Band 1
Table: p.209

Peters, Karen (Arizona)
Profile: p.161
Environment Band 2
Table: p.150

Peters, William (California)
Profile: p. 267
Business Process
Outsourcing: National Band 3
Table: p.10
IT Outsourcing Band 2
Table: p.221

Petersen, John (Kansas)
Profile: p.824
Real Estate Band 1
Table: p.821

Petersen, Larry (Montana)
Profile: p.1080
Corporate/M&A Band 2
Table: p.1072

Peterson, Alan (Nebraska)
Profile: p.1088
Litigation Band 1
Table: p.1085

Peterson, Brad L (Illinois)
Profile: p. 746
Business Process
Outsourcing: National Band 2
Table: p.10
Technology Band 1
Table: p.713

Peterson, Charles
(District of Columbia)
Profile: p.462
Energy Band 3
Table: p.390

Peterson, Edward (Texas)
Profile: p.1696
Real Estate Band 3
Table: p.1662

Peterson, Gale R (Texas)
Profile: p.1696
Intellectual Property Band 1
Table: p.1651

Peterson, Karen (Nevada)
Profile: p.1103
Environment Band 3
Table: p.1093

Peterson, Ken (Kansas)
Profile: p.824
Employment Band 2
Table: p.818

Peterson, Ralph (Florida)
Profile: p.547
Employment Band 4
Table: p.513

Peterson, Ronald R (Illinois)
Profile: p.746
Bankruptcy Band 3
Table: p.669

Peterson Jr, John M
(California)
Profile: p.267
Tax Band 2

Table: p.241

Petrich, Louis P (California)
Profile: p.267
Media & Entertainment Band 2
Table: p.230

Petrik, Michael T (Georgia)
Profile: p.620
Tax Band 3
Table: p.603

Petrikin, Ronald (Oklahoma)
Profile: p.1466
Employment Band 1
Table: p.1461

Petro, John J (Ohio)
Profile: p.1446
Construction Band 1
Table: p.1417

Petrocelli, Daniel
(California)
Profile: p.267
Litigation Band 3
Table: p.224

Petros, Gerald J
(Rhode Island)
Profile: p.1570
Litigation Band 1
Table: p.1567

Petruccelli, Gerald (Maine)
Profile: p.900
Litigation Band 2
Table: p.893

Petrus, Barbara (Hawaii)
Profile: p.649
Employment Band 2
Table: p.642

Petti, Fred (Arizona)
Profile: p.161

Pettibone, Jon (Arizona)
Profile: p.161
Employment Band 2
Table: p.148

Pettit, Ted N (Hawaii)
Profile: p.649
Bankruptcy Band 1
Table: p.640

Petumenos, Timothy J
(Alaska)
Profile: p.144
Litigation Band 2
Table: p.138

Pfefferle, Ben L (Ohio)
Profile: p.1446
Environment Band 3
Table: p.1425

Pfeiffer, Philip J (Texas)
Profile: p.1696
Employment Band 2
Table: p.1634

Pfeiffer, Steven L (Oregon)
Profile: p.1484
Real Estate Band 1
Table: p.1479

Pfennigs, Robert B
(Montana)
Profile: p.1080
Litigation Band 3
Table: p.1075

KEY TO RANKINGS: ✪ = STAR INDIVIDUAL   S = SENIOR STATESMAN

Pfister, Thomas (California)
Profile: p.267
Employment Band 1
Table: p.202

Phalen, Michael (Arizona)
Profile: p.161
Real Estate Band 2
Table: p.155

Phalin, Lawrence J (Florida)
Profile: p.547
Construction Band 3
Table: p.507

Pharis, Michael (Louisiana)
Profile: p.875
Employment Band 3
Table: p.861

Pharris, Charles A (New Mexico)
Profile: p.1164
Litigation Band 4
Table: p.1159

Phelan, Jeanne (Maryland)
Profile: p.923
Employment Band 2
Table: p.912

Phelan, Robin (Texas)
Profile: p.1696
Bankruptcy Band 1
Table: p.1627

Phelan, Rod (Texas)
Profile: p.1697
Litigation Band 2
Table: p.1656

Phibbs, Henry (Wyoming)
Profile: p.1839
Real Estate Band 2
Table: p.1836

Philips, Harry (Louisiana)
Profile: p.875
Litigation Band 3
Table: p.865

Phillips, Bradley S (California)
Profile: p.267
Antitrust Band 3
Table: p.184

Phillips, Carter (District of Columbia)
Profile: p.462
Litigation Band 1
Table: p.408

Phillips, Edward G (Tennessee)
Profile: p.1610
Employment Band 2
Table: p.1596

Phillips, Greer L (New York)
Profile: p.1308
Tax Band 4
Table: p.1255

Phillips, James E (Ohio)
Profile: p.1446
Litigation Band 3
Table: p.1432

Phillips, Jim W (North Carolina)
Profile: p.1398
Litigation Band 3
Table: p.1390

Phillips, John R (Missouri)
Profile: p.1060
Employment Band 1
Table: p.1046

Phillips, Lee (California)
Profile: p.267
Media & Entertainment Band 2
Table: p.233

Phillips, Paul D (Colorado)
Profile: p.321
Environment Band 1
Table: p.307

Phillips, Penny (Minnesota)
Profile: p.1019
Employment Band 3
Table: p.1008

Phillips, Stephen (Georgia)
Profile: p.620
Construction Band 2
Table: p.584

Phillips, William M (Ohio)
Profile: p.1446
Real Estate Band 4
Table: p.1434

Phillips IV, Barnet (New York)
Profile: p.1308
Tax Band 3
Table: p.1255

Phillips Jr, John (Tennessee)
Profile: p.1610
Employment Band 2
Table: p.1596

Phipps, David (Iowa)
Profile: p.814
Litigation Band 2
Table: p.807

Piccarreta, Michael L (Arizona)
Profile: p.161
Litigation Band 2
Table: p.153

Pickens, Scott E (Illinois)
Profile: p.746
Banking & Finance Band 3
Table: p.665

Pickert, Stephen W (Florida)
Profile: p.547
Construction Band 3
Table: p.507

Pickett, Andrew (Massachusetts)
Profile: p.974
Employment Band 3
Table: p.940

Pickett, Donn (California)
Profile: p.267
Antitrust Band 2
Table: p.184

Pidgeon, Steven (Arizona)
Profile: p.161
Corporate/M&A Band 1
Table: p.146

Piels, William (National)
Profile: p.98
Aviation Band 2
Table: p.58

Pieper, Nathaniel GW (National)
Profile: p.98
Shipping Band 1
Table: p.71

Pierce, John V H (National)
Profile: p.98
Arbitration Up and coming
Table: p.33

Pierce, Kenneth J (National)
Profile: p.98
International Trade Band 3
Table: p.40

Pierce, Morton A (New York)
Profile: p.1308
Corporate/M&A Band 3
Table: p.1189

Pierce, Robert (Florida)
Profile: p.547
Tax Band 3
Table: p.531

Pierce, Rudolph (Massachusetts)
Profile: p.974
Litigation Band 2
Table: p.951

Pierson, George J (New York)
Profile: p.1309
Construction Band 4
Table: p.1186

Pietropaoli, Paul D (Maine)
Profile: p.900
Real Estate Band 3
Table: p.895

Pietrzak, Robert (New York)
Profile: p.1309
Litigation Band 3
Table: p.1223

Piggott, Cameron (Michigan)
Profile: p.1000
Real Estate Band 3
Table: p.996

Pigman, Jack R (Ohio)
Profile: p.1446
Bankruptcy Band 2
Table: p.1414

Pignatelli, Michael A (New Hampshire)
Profile: p.1118
Litigation Band 1
Table: p.1111

Pill, Richard (West Virginia)
Profile: p.1810
Real Estate Band 2
Table: p.1806

Pillans III, Charles P (Florida)
Profile: p.547
Litigation Band 3
Table: p.521

Pimstone, Gregory N (California)
Profile: p.267
Healthcare Band 3
Table: p.209

Pincus, Robert B (Delaware)
Profile: p.356
Corporate/M&A Band 3
Table: p.346

Pinkerton, Glenn (Texas)
Profile: p.1697
Projects Band 3
Table: p.1659

Pinney Jr, Willard F (Connecticut)
Profile: p.337
Corporate/M&A Band 2
Table: p.327

Pinover, Eugene (New York)
Profile: p.1309
Real Estate Band 2
Table: p.1248

Piper, Jeffrey Scott (Hawaii)
Profile: p.649
Tax Up and coming
Table: p.641

Piper, Jonathan S (Maine)
Profile: p.900
Litigation Band 3
Table: p.893

Pircher, Leo (California)
Profile: p.267
Real Estate Band S
Table: p.238

Pirkey, Louis (Texas)
Profile: p.1697
Intellectual Property Band 1
Table: p.1651

Pisa, Regina M (Massachusetts)
Profile: p.974
Banking & Finance Band 2
Table: p.932
Corporate/M&A Band 2
Table: p.937

Pisanelli, James (Nevada)
Profile: p.1103
Litigation Band 2
Table: p.1096

Pisano, Vincent (National)
Profile: p.98
Capital Markets Band 3
Table: p.14

Piscitelli, Michael A (Florida)
Profile: p.547
Construction Band 3
Table: p.507

Piskorski, Thomas (Illinois)
Profile: p.746
Employment Band 2
Table: p.681

Pitcairn Jr, Robert (Ohio)
Profile: p.1446
Litigation Band 3
Table: p.1431

Pitt, M Stephen (Kentucky)
Profile: p.845
Litigation Band 3
Table: p.835

Pittman, Alisa (Georgia)
Profile: p.620
Employment Band 4
Table: p.589

Placenti, Frank (Arizona)
Profile: p.161
Corporate/M&A Band 2
Table: p.146

Plaine, Daniel (National)
Profile: p.98
International Trade Band 3
Table: p.40

Plambeck, Stephen (North Dakota)
Profile: p.1410
Litigation Band 2
Table: p.1406

Planning, Anne K (District of Columbia)
Profile: p.462
Real Estate Band 3
Table: p.418

Plevan, Bettina (New York)
Profile: p.1309
Employment Band 1
Table: p.1200

Plevin, Mark (District of Columbia)
Profile: p.462
Bankruptcy Band 3
Table: p.372

Ploor, Pamela M (Wisconsin)
Profile: p.1826
Employment Up and coming
Table: p.1819

Plum, Bernard (New York)
Profile: p.1309
Employment Band 3
Table: p.1200

Plumb, Charles (Oklahoma)
Profile: p.1466
Employment Band 2
Table: p.1461

Plumer, Mark J (District of Columbia)
Profile: p.462
Insurance Band 2
Table: p.402

Plumridge, Richard (Colorado)
Profile: p.321
Corporate/M&A Band 2
Table: p.303

Plybon, Christopher (West Virginia)
Profile: p.1810
Real Estate Band 2
Table: p.1806

Podhurst, Aaron (Florida)
Profile: p.547
Litigation Band 2
Table: p.521

Poelman, Ronald (Utah)
Profile: p.1737
Corporate/M&A Band 2
Table: p.1727

Poff, Joe (Texas)
Profile: p.1697
Corporate/M&A Band 3
Table: p.1631

Poff, William (Virginia)
Profile: p.1772
Litigation Band 1
Table: p.1763

P

Pogue, Mark (Rhode Island)
Profile: p.1570
Employment **Band 2**
Table: p.1565
Litigation **Band 2**
Table: p.1567

Pohl, Timothy R (Illinois)
Profile: p.746
Bankruptcy **Band 3**
Table: p.669

Pokempner, Joseph
(Maryland)
Profile: p.923
Employment **Band 3**
Table: p.912

Pokorski, Jody (Arizona)
Profile: p.161
Real Estate **Band 1**
Table: p.154

Pokotilow, Manny D
(Pennsylvania)
Profile: p.1534
Intellectual Property **Band 1**
Table: p.1508

Polebaum, Elliot E
(National)
Profile: p.98
Arbitration **Band 4**
Table: p.33

Polebaum, Mark
(Massachusetts)
Profile: p.974
Bankruptcy **Band 1**
Table: p.935

Polevoy, Martin D
(New York)
Profile: p.1309
Real Estate **Band 4**
Table: p.1248

Poliakoff, Abba (Maryland)
Profile: p.923
Corporate/M&A **Band 3**
Table: p.909

Policastro, Marc D
(New Jersey)
Profile: p.1143
Real Estate **Up and coming**
Table: p.1135

Pollack, Martin (New York)
Profile: p.1309
Tax **Band 3**
Table: p.1255

Pollak, Mark (Maryland)
Profile: p.923
Real Estate **Band 1**
Table: p.917

Polon, Ira H
(District of Columbia)
Profile: p.462
Corporate/Commercial **Band 3**
Table: p.376

Polsinelli, James (Missouri)
Profile: p.1060
Corporate/M&A **Band 2**
Table: p.1043

Pomerantz, Alan J
(New York)
Profile: p.1309
Real Estate **Band 4**
Table: p.1248

Pomerantz, Glenn D
(California)
Profile: p.267
Antitrust **Band 3**
Table: p.184
Media & Entertainment **Band 3**
Table: p.230

Pomerantz, Harold B
(Illinois)
Profile: p.746
Real Estate **Band 4**
Table: p.706

Pomerantz, Mark (New York)
Profile: p.1310
Litigation **Band 1**
Table: p.1224

Ponader, Erick (Indiana)
Profile: p.794
Real Estate **Band 3**
Table: p.788

Ponsetto, John (Vermont)
Profile: p.1749
Real Estate **Band 2**
Table: p.1747

Pontone, Kathleen
(Maryland)
Profile: p.923
Employment **Band 1**
Table: p.912

Pooley, James (California)
Profile: p.267
Intellectual Property **Band 3**
Table: p.216

Pope, David (Georgia)
Profile: p.620
Environment **Band 3**
Table: p.593

Pope, Michael (Illinois)
Profile: p.746
Litigation **Band 4**
Table: p.700

Pope, Nicholas A (Florida)
Profile: p.547
Hotels and Resorts **Band 1**
Table: p.526

Popeo, R Robert
(Massachusetts)
Profile: p.974
Litigation **Band s**
Table: p.951

Popofsky, Laurence
(California)
Profile: p.267
Antitrust **Band 1**
Table: p.184
Litigation **Band 2**
Table: p.224

Popofsky, Mark
(District of Columbia)
Profile: p.462
Antitrust **Up and coming**
Table: p.367

Porcelli, Frank P
(Massachusetts)
Profile: p.974
Intellectual Property **Band 1**
Table: p.948

Porges, Amelia (National)
Profile: p.99
International Trade **Band 5**
Table: p.40

Port, Alan D (Vermont)
Profile: p.1749
Corporate/M&A **Band 2**
Table: p.1743

Port, Gail (New York)
Profile: p.1310
Environment **Band 3**
Table: p.1206

Porter, Amy (Arizona)
Profile: p.161
Environment **Band 1**
Table: p.150

Porter, Daniel L (National)
Profile: p.99
International Trade **Band 4**
Table: p.40

Porter, David (Ohio)
Profile: p.1446
Corporate/M&A **Band 1**
Table: p.1419

Porter, Jeffrey R
(Massachusetts)
Profile: p.974
Environment **Band 2**
Table: p.943

Porter, Philip (Virginia)
Profile: p.1772
Intellectual Property **Band 2**
Table: p.1759

Porter, R Clay (National)
Profile: p.99
Transport **Band 2**
Table: p.64

Porter, Stephen
(District of Columbia)
Profile: p.462
Real Estate **Band 3**
Table: p.418

Portnoy, Jeffrey (Hawaii)
Profile: p.649
Litigation **Band 1**
Table: p.644

Pose, Christopher (Iowa)
Profile: p.814
Real Estate **Band 3**
Table: p.810

Posen, Richard (New York)
Profile: p.1310
Litigation **Band 3**
Table: p.1223

Positan, Wayne J
(New Jersey)
Profile: p.1144
Employment **Band 1**
Table: p.1126

Poss, Stephen D
(Massachusetts)
Profile: p.974
Litigation **Band 1**
Table: p.951
Litigation **Band 3**
Table: p.951

Poster, Robert (New York)
Profile: p.99
Shipping **Band 2**
Table: p.67

Postner, William J (New York)
Profile: p.1310
Construction **Band 2**
Table: p.1186

Potenza, Joseph
(District of Columbia)
Profile: p.463
Intellectual Property **Band 3**
Table: p.403

Potter, John (California)
Profile: p.267
Litigation **Band 2**
Table: p.225

Potter, Nicholas F
(New York)
Profile: p.1310
Insurance **Band 3**
Table: p.1213

Poulos, Denise A
(New Hampshire)
Profile: p.1118
Real Estate **Band 2**
Table: p.1114

Pouncey, Gerald (Georgia)
Profile: p.620
Environment **Band 3**
Table: p.593

Powar, Lee (Ohio)
Profile: p.1446
Bankruptcy **Band 3**
Table: p.1414

Powell, Bryan E (Oregon)
Profile: p.1484
Real Estate **Band 3**
Table: p.1479

Powell, Charles (Alabama)
Profile: p.124
Employment **Band 2**
Table: p.113

Powell, Charles D (Texas)
Profile: p.1697
Technology **Band 1**
Table: p.1668

Powell, David M (Arkansas)
Profile: p.177
Litigation **Band 3**
Table: p.172

Powell, Fred (Alabama)
Profile: p.124
Real Estate **Band 1**
Table: p.119

Powell, Kurt (Georgia)
Profile: p.621
Employment **Band 4**
Table: p.589

Powell, Thomas O (Georgia)
Profile: p.621
Banking & Finance **Band 2**
Table: p.581

Powell Jr, David D
(Colorado)
Profile: p.321
Employment **Band 1**
Table: p.306

Powers, John (Illinois)
Profile: p.746
Employment **Band 3**
Table: p.681

Powers, Matthew D
(California)
Profile: p.268
Intellectual Property **Band 1**
Table: p.216

Powers, Ragan (Washington)
Profile: p.1794
Bankruptcy **Band 2**
Table: p.1776

Powers, Tony G (Georgia)
Profile: p.621
Antitrust **Band 1**
Table: p.578

Powers, Victoria E (Ohio)
Profile: p.1447
Bankruptcy **Band 3**
Table: p.1414

Powers, Werner (Texas)
Profile: p.1697
Insurance **Band 3**
Table: p.1648

Powers Jr, George E
(Wyoming)
Profile: p.1839
Litigation **Band 2**
Table: p.1835

Pozza Jr, Clarence L
(Michigan)
Profile: p.1000
Litigation **Band 2**
Table: p.994

Prather, Paul E (Tennessee)
Profile: p.1610
Employment **Band 2**
Table: p.1596

Pratt, Carol Hempfling
(Massachusetts)
Profile: p.974
Banking & Finance **Band 2**
Table: p.932

Pratt, Don (Texas)
Profile: p.1697
Construction **Band 3**
Table: p.1629

Pratt, John (Georgia)
Profile: p.621
Intellectual Property **Band 4**
Table: p.596

Preis Jr, E Fredrick
(Louisiana)
Profile: p.875
Employment **Band 3**
Table: p.861

Preovolos, Penelope A
(California)
Profile: p.268
Antitrust **Band 3**
Table: p.184

Press, Martin (Florida)
Profile: p.547
Tax **Band 4**
Table: p.531

Pressman, Stewart (Hawaii)
Profile: p.649
Corporate/M&A **Band 1**
Table: p.641

Prestia, Paul (Pennsylvania)
Profile: p.1534
Intellectual Property **Band 1**
Table: p.1508

Preston, Richard
(District of Columbia)
Profile: p.463
Construction **Band 3**
Table: p.374

Preston, William D (Florida)
Profile: p.547
Environment **Band 1**
Table: p.516

Pretty, Laurence (California)
Profile: p.268
Intellectual Property **Band 4**
Table: p.216

Price, Charles (New Mexico)
Profile: p.1164
Real Estate **Band 1**
Table: p.1161

Price, Daniel M (National)
Profile: p.99
Arbitration **Band 2**
Table: p.33
International Trade **Band 2**
Table: p.40

Price, Gene (Alabama)
Profile: p.124
Corporate/M&A **Band 1**
Table: p.111

Price, Glenn (Kentucky)
Profile: p.845
Real Estate **Band 2**
Table: p.838

Price, James (Missouri)
Profile: p.1060
Litigation **Band 2**
Table: p.1049

Price, Joseph (West Virginia)
Profile: p.1810
Employment **Band 2**
Table: p.1801

Price, Joseph (National)
Profile: p.99
International Trade **Band 5**
Table: p.40

Price, Stanley B (Florida)
Profile: p.547
Real Estate **Band 1**
Table: p.528

Prichard, Allen (North
Carolina)
Profile: p.1398
Real Estate **Band 1**
Table: p.1392

Priest, Jim (Oklahoma)
Profile: p.1466
Employment **Band 2**
Table: p.1461

Prillaman, Fred C (Illinois)
Profile: p.746
Environment **Band 4**
Table: p.687

Primavera, Carl
(Pennsylvania)
Profile: p.1535
Real Estate **Band 2**
Table: p.1516

Prince, Aian (Georgia)
Profile: p.621
Corporate/M&A **Band 4**
Table: p.587

Prince, Allison
(District of Columbia)
Profile: p.463
Real Estate **Band 2**
Table: p.418

Prince, Kenneth S (New
York)
Profile: p.1310
Antitrust **Band 4**
Table: p.1170

Prince, Larry E (Idaho)
Profile: p.660
Corporate/M&A **Band 2**
Table: p.655

Pringle, Harry R (Maine)
Profile: p.900
Employment **Band 2**
Table: p.890

Pringle, Paul C (California)
Profile: p. 268
Capital Markets **Band 3**
Table: p.23

Pritchard, John (National)
Profile: p.99
Aviation **Band 2**
Table: p.58

Pritikin, David T (Illinois)
Profile: p.746
Intellectual Property **Band 3**
Table: p.696

Profusek, Robert A
(New York)
Profile: p.1310
Corporate/M&A **Band 3**
Table: p.1189

Proger, Phillip A
(District of Columbia)
Profile: p.463
Antitrust **Band 2**
Table: p.367

Prounis, Othon (New York)
Profile: p.1310
Private Equity **Band 3**
Table: p.1237

Prowell, William (Iowa)
Profile: p.814
Real Estate **Band 3**
Table: p.810

Pruden III, J Norfleet
(North Carolina)
Profile: p.1398
Corporate/M&A **Band 1**
Table: p.1384

Pruellage, John K (Missouri)
Profile: p.1060
Corporate/M&A **Band 2**
Table: p.1043

Pruetz, Adrian (California)
Profile: p.268
Intellectual Property **Band 4**
Table: p.216

Pruzinsky, Anthony J
(New York)
Profile: p.99
Shipping **Band 4**
Table: p.67

Pryor, Robert H (North
Carolina)
Profile: p.1398
Bankruptcy **Band 1**
Table: p.1383

Puchner, Joseph E
(Wisconsin)
Profile: p.1826
Real Estate **Band 2**
Table: p.1822

Puckett, Laura Treadgold
(Washington)
Profile: p.1794
Corporate/M&A **Band 3**
Table: p.1778

Pugliese, Frank A
(New York)
Profile: p.1310
Intellectual Property **Band 3**
Table: p.1217

Puig, Yvonne Karen (Texas)
Profile: p.1697
Healthcare **Band 2**
Table: p.1646

Puleo, Frank (New York)
Profile: p.1310
Banking & Finance **Band 2**
Table: p.1174

Pulley III, J Waverly
(Virginia)
Profile: p. 1772
Real Estate **Band 2**
Table: p.1765
Transport **Band 2**
Table: p.64

Puretz, Jeffrey S
(District of Columbia)
Profile: p.463
Investment Management
Band 2
Table: p.406

Putman, Frank (Texas)
Profile: p.1697
Technology **Band 2**
Table: p.1668

Putziger, Myrna
(Massachusetts)
Profile: p.974
Real Estate **Band 1**
Table: p.957

Pyburn Jr, Keith M
(Louisiana)
Profile: p.875
Employment **Band 2**
Table: p.861

Qasim, Imad (Illinois)
Profile: p.747
Corporate/M&A **Band 3**
Table: p.675

Quail, Beverly J (Colorado)
Profile: p.321
Real Estate **Band 2**
Table: p.313

Quale, John C
(District of Columbia)
Profile: p.463
Telecom, Broadcast & Satellite
Band 3
Table: p.427

Quander, Don (Montana)
Profile: p.1080
Natural Resources **Band 1**
Table: p.1077

Quarles, John
(District of Columbia)
Profile: p.463
Environment **Band 2**
Table: p.392

Quattlebaum, Marvin
(South Carolina)
Profile: p.1582
Real Estate **Band 3**
Table: p.1577

Quattlebaum, Steven
(Arkansas)
Profile: p.177
Litigation **Band 1**
Table: p.172

Quesenberry, Kathryn A
(Kentucky)
Profile: p.845
Employment Up and coming
Table: p.830

Quick, Patrick G
(Wisconsin)
Profile: p.1826
Corporate/M&A
Up and coming
Table: p.1817

Quin, Whayne
(District of Columbia)
Profile: p.463
Real Estate **Band 1**
Table: p.418

Quinn, James W (New York)
Profile: p. 1310
Litigation **Band 3**
Table: p.1222
Sport **Band 2**
Table: p.55

Quinn, John (California)
Profile: p.268
Litigation **Band 3**
Table: p.224

Quinn, John B (California)
Profile: p.268
Litigation **Band 2**
Table: p.224
Media & Entertainment **Band 3**
Table: p.230

Quinn, Yvonne S (New York)
Profile: p.1311
Antitrust **Band 4**
Table: p.1170

Quiñon, Jose (Florida)
Profile: p.548
Litigation **Band 2**
Table: p.522

Quint, Arnold
(District of Columbia)
Profile: p.463
Energy **Band 4**
Table: p.386

Raattama, Henry (Florida)
Profile: p.548
Tax **Band 2**
Table: p.531

Rabalais, Robert René
(Texas)
Profile: p.1697
Banking & Finance
Up and coming
Table: p.1625

Rabinovitz, Joel (California)
Profile: p.269
Tax **Band 2**
Table: p.241

Rabinowitz, David
(New Jersey)
Profile: p.1144
Real Estate **Band 3**
Table: p.1134

Rabinowitz, Mark I
(Pennsylvania)
Profile: p.1535
Banking & Finance **Band 2**
Table: p.1493

Rabinowitz, Stephen S
(New York)
Profile: p.1311
Intellectual Property **Band 3**
Table: p.1217

Rachlin, Robert (Vermont)
Profile: p.1749
Litigation **Band S**
Table: p.1746

Racioppi Jr, Nicholas
(New Jersey)
Profile: p.1144
Real Estate **Band 3**
Table: p.1134

Raciti-Knapp, Melissa
(New York)
Profile: p.1311
Projects **Band 4**
Table: p.1244

Rackow, Julian
(Pennsylvania)
Profile: p.1535
Real Estate **Band 2**
Table: p.1516

Radcliffe, Mark F
(California)
Profile: p.269
IT Outsourcing **Band 2**
Table: p.221

Rademaker, Randall J
(Illinois)
Profile: p.747
Banking & Finance **Band 3**
Table: p.665

Rader, Kermit L
(Pennsylvania)
Profile: p.1535
Environment **Band 4**
Table: p.1505

Radke, Kirk (New York)
Profile: p.1311
Private Equity **Band 2**
Table: p.1237

Radler, Barbara (Oregon)
Profile: p.1484
Real Estate **Band 2**
Table: p.1479

Radolinski, Anne M
(Minnesota)
Profile: p.1019
Employment **Band 3**
Table: p.1008

Radovich, Scott D (Hawaii)
Profile: p.649
Real Estate **Band 2**
Table: p.646

Radzely, Edward S
(New Jersey)
Profile: p.1144
Real Estate **Band 2**
Table: p.1134

R

Radzik, Edward C
(New York)
Profile: p.100
Shipping **Band 4**
Table: p.67

Raff, Joshua E (National)
Profile: p.100
Capital Markets **Band 3**
Table: p.19

Rafferty, Thomas G
(New York)
Profile: p.1311
Intellectual Property **Band 3**
Table: p.1217

Rafte, Alan (Texas)
Profile: p.1697
Energy **Band 4**
Table: p.1637
Projects **Band 4**
Table: p.1659

Rafuse, Nancy (Georgia)
Profile: p.621
Employment **Band 4**
Table: p.589

Ragalevsky, Stanley V
(Massachusetts)
Profile: p.974
Banking & Finance **Band 3**
Table: p.932

Ragland Jr, William M
(Georgia)
Profile: p.621
Intellectual Property **Band 3**
Table: p.596

Ragonetti, Thomas
(Colorado)
Profile: p.321
Real Estate **Band 1**
Table: p.313
Real Estate **Band 1**
Table: p.314

Ragosta, John A (National)
Profile: p.100
International Trade **Band 5**
Table: p.40

Raher, Patrick M
(District of Columbia)
Profile: p.463
Environment **Band 3**
Table: p.392

Raim, David
(District of Columbia)
Profile: p.463
Insurance **Band 2**
Table: p.400

Rain, John W (Texas)
Profile: p.1697
Banking & Finance **Band 4**
Table: p.1625

Rainey, Richard L
(North Carolina)
Profile: p.1398
Employment **Band 2**
Table: p.1386

Rainey Jr, Gordon F
(Virginia)
Profile: p.1772
Corporate/M&A **Band 3**
Table: p.1752

Raisch, Jerry W (Colorado)
Profile: p.321
Environment **Band 2**
Table: p.307

Raisler, Kenneth M
(National)
Profile: p.100
Capital Markets **Band 1**
Table: p.16

Rakay Nelson, Jane
(Washington)
Profile: p.1794
Real Estate **Band 3**
Table: p.1788

Rakusin, Steve (Florida)
Profile: p.548
Construction **Band 2**
Table: p.507

Ramer, Bruce (California)
Profile: p.269
Media & Entertainment **Band 1**
Table: p.233

Ramirez, John (Maryland)
Profile: p.923
Corporate/M&A **Band u**
Table: p.909

Ramirez, Kenneth (Texas)
Profile: p.1697
Environment **Band 2**
Table: p.1643

Ramis, Timothy V (Oregon)
Profile: p.1484
Real Estate **Band 1**
Table: p.1479

Ramos, Carey R (New York)
Profile: p.1311
Media & Entertainment **Band 2**
Table: p.1235

Rand, Richard M (Hawaii)
Profile: p.650
Employment **Band 2**
Table: p.642

Randall, Benjamin J
(Illinois)
Profile: p.747
Real Estate **Band 2**
Table: p.706

Randall, Jeff G (California)
Profile: p.269
Intellectual Property **Band 4**
Table: p.216

Raper, William (North
Carolina)
Profile: p.1398
Litigation **Band 2**
Table: p.1390

Raphael, Bruce W
(Massachusetts)
Profile: p.975
Banking & Finance **Band 3**
Table: p.932

Raphan, Melissa
(Minnesota)
Profile: p.1019
Employment **Band 3**
Table: p.1008

Rapisardi, John (New York)
Profile: p.1311
Bankruptcy **Band 4**
Table: p.1179

Rappaport, Linda E
(New York)
Profile: p.1311
Employee Benefits **Band 2**
Table: p.1197

Rasile, Craig (Florida)
Profile: p.548
Bankruptcy **Band 2**
Table: p.503

Raskin, David
(District of Columbia)
Profile: p.463
Energy **Band 3**
Table: p.386

Raskin, Jane (Florida)
Profile: p.548
Litigation **Band 1**
Table: p.522

Raskin, Kenneth A
(New York)
Profile: p.1311
Employee Benefits **Band 3**
Table: p.1197

Raskin, Martin R (Florida)
Profile: p.548
Litigation **Band 1**
Table: p.522

Raskopf, Robert (New York)
Profile: p.1311
Media & Entertainment **Band 3**
Table: p.1232

Rasmussen, Robert
(Florida)
Profile: p.548
Corporate/M&A **Band 2**
Table: p.509

Rassel, Richard E
(Michigan)
Profile: p.1000
Litigation **Band 2**
Table: p.994

Rath, Thomas D
(New Hampshire)
Profile: p.1118
Government Relations **Band 1**
Table: p.1107

Rather Jr, Gordon S
(Arkansas)
Profile: p.177
Litigation **Band 2**
Table: p.172

Ratliff, Reeder E
(Oklahoma)
Profile: p.1466
Tax **Band 2**
Table: p.1459

Ratner, Randall M (Texas)
Profile: p.1697
Real Estate **Band 3**
Table: p.1662

Rattigan, John
(Massachusetts)
Profile: p.975
Real Estate **Band 2**
Table: p.956

Rauch, David (Arizona)
Profile: p.161
Litigation **Band 4**
Table: p.152

Rauh, Carl S
(District of Columbia)
Profile: p.464
Litigation **Band 2**
Table: p.410

Ravich, Paul (Minnesota)
Profile: p.1019
Real Estate **Band 3**
Table: p.1014

Ravikoff, Ronald B (Florida)
Profile: p.548
Antitrust **Band 3**
Table: p.498

Rawlinson, Dennis P
(Oregon)
Profile: p.1484
Litigation **Band 3**
Table: p.1477

Rawson, Rachel (Ohio)
Profile: p.1447
Banking & Finance **Band 1**
Table: p.1411

Ray, Hugh M (Texas)
Profile: p.1697
Bankruptcy **Band 3**
Table: p.1627

Ray, Stephen E (Illinois)
Profile: p.747
Construction **Band 3**
Table: p.672

Raymond, James F
(New Hampshire)
Profile: p.1118
Real Estate **Band 2**
Table: p.1114

Raymond, Robert J
(New York)
Profile: p.1311
Employee Benefits **Band 3**
Table: p.1197

Raymond III, F Douglas
(Pennsylvania)
Profile: p.1535
Corporate/M&A **Band 3**
Table: p.1497

Raysman, Richard
(New York)
Profile: p. 1311
Business Process
Outsourcing: National **Band 3**
Table: p.10

Read, Sarah (Illinois)
Profile: p.747
Energy **Band S**
Table: p.685

Reade, Claire E (National)
Profile: p.100
International Trade **Band 3**
Table: p.40

Reamer, David C (California)
Profile: p.269
Banking & Finance **Band 3**
Table: p.187

Reardon, Roy (New York)
Profile: p.1312
Litigation **Band 1**
Table: p.1222

Reasoner, Carroll J (Iowa)
Profile: p.814
Corporate/M&A **Band 2**
Table: p.802

Reasoner, Harry (Texas)
Profile: p.1698
Antitrust **Band 2**
Table: p.1622
Energy **Band 1**
Table: p.1640
Litigation **Band 1**
Table: p.1656

Rebein, David (Kansas)
Profile: p.824
Litigation **Band 1**
Table: p.819

Rebein, Joseph (Missouri)
Profile: p.1060
Litigation **Band 3**
Table: p.1049

Reber, David J (Hawaii)
Profile: p.650
Corporate/M&A **Band 1**
Table: p.641

Reck, Joel M
(Massachusetts)
Profile: p.975
Real Estate **Band 3**
Table: p.956

Reck, Michael (Iowa)
Profile: p.814
Employment **Band 3**
Table: p.805

Reckmeyer, Peter R
(Alaska)
Profile: p.144
Corporate/M&A **Band 2**
Table: p.134

Rector, Richard (National)
Profile: p.100
Government Contracts
Band 3
Table: p.27

Redden, Joe (Texas)
Profile: p.1698
Litigation **Band 2**
Table: p.1656

Reddin, Jane E (Arizona)
Profile: p.161
Employment **Band 4**
Table: p.148

Redlick, David
(Massachusetts)
Profile: p.975
Corporate/M&A **Band 2**
Table: p.937

Redmond, Patricia (Florida)
Profile: p.548
Bankruptcy **Band 2**
Table: p.503

Reece, Joseph (Alaska)
Profile: p.144
Corporate/M&A **Band 2**
Table: p.134
Real Estate **Band 2**
Table: p.141

Reed, Glen (Georgia)
Profile: p.621
Healthcare **Band 1**
Table: p.594

Reed, John L (Delaware)
Profile: p.356
Chancery **Band 4**
Table: p.344

Reed, John S (Kentucky)
Profile: p.845
Litigation **Band 1**
Table: p.835

Reed, Kevin
(District of Columbia)
Profile: p.464
Telecom, Broadcast & Satellite
Band 4
Table: p.427

Reed, Kevin A (Texas)
Profile: p.1698
Healthcare **Band 2**
Table: p.1646

Reed, Lucy (National)
Profile: p.100
Arbitration **Band 1**
Table: p.33

Reed, Margery N
(Pennsylvania)
Profile: p.1535
Bankruptcy **Band 3**
Table: p.1494

Reed, Matthew (Maryland)
Profile: p.923
Real Estate **Band 4**
Table: p.917

Reed, Michael H
(Pennsylvania)
Profile: p.1535
Bankruptcy **Band 3**
Table: p.1494

Reed, Randall B (Wyoming)
Profile: p.1839
Corporate/M&A **Band 2**
Table: p.1832

Reed, Steven
(District of Columbia)
Profile: p.464
Energy **Band 3**
Table: p.382

Reed, Wendy
(District of Columbia)
Profile: p.464
Energy **Up and coming**
Table: p.386

Reed, William (Mississippi)
Profile: p.1035
Litigation **Band 2**
Table: p.1028

Reeder, Robert W (National)
Profile: p.100
Capital Markets **Band 3**
Table: p.16

Reese, Cathy L (Delaware)
Profile: p.356
Chancery **Band 4**
Table: p.344

Reeves, Edward (Oregon)
Profile: p.1484
Employment **Band 3**
Table: p.1474

Reeves, James N (Alaska)
Profile: p.144
Environment **Band 1**
Table: p.137

Reeves, Susan (Alaska)
Profile: p.144
Environment **Band 2**
Table: p.137

Reeves, Weston (Wyoming)
Profile: p.1839
Litigation **Band 1**
Table: p.1835

Reger, Robert (New York)
Profile: p.1312
Energy **Band 2**
Table: p.1202

Reges, Robert (Alaska)
Profile: p.144
Environment **Band 3**
Table: p.137

Reich, Yaron Z (New York)
Profile: p.1312
Tax **Band 3**
Table: p.1255

Reich Esq, Abraham C
(Pennsylvania)
Profile: p.1535
Litigation **Band 3**
Table: p.1511

Reid, Benjamine (Florida)
Profile: p.548
Litigation **Band 3**
Table: p.521

Reid, Spencer (New Mexico)
Profile: p.1164
Litigation **Band 4**
Table: p.1159

Reid Jr, Russell L (Texas)
Profile: p.1698
Bankruptcy **Band 3**
Table: p.1627

Reid, Jr, Glen G (Tennessee)
Profile: p.1611

Reidy, Daniel (Illinois)
Profile: p.747
Litigation **Band 2**
Table: p.700

Reidy, James P
(New Hampshire)
Profile: p.1118
Employment **Band 2**
Table: p.1109

Reidy, Joseph M (Ohio)
Profile: p.1447
Environment **Band 3**
Table: p.1425

Reilly, D Michael
(Washington)
Profile: p.1794
Employment **Band 3**
Table: p.1780

Reilly, Daniel (Colorado)
Profile: p.321
Litigation **Band 2**
Table: p.311

Reilly, Gregory B (New
Jersey)
Profile: p.1144
Litigation **Band 2**
Table: p.1131

Reilly, Kenneth J (Missouri)
Profile: p.548
Litigation **Band 3**
Table: p.521

Reimer, Eric R (California)
Profile: p.269
Banking & Finance **Band 3**
Table: p.187

Reines, Edward R
(California)
Profile: p.269
Intellectual Property **Band 4**
Table: p.216

Reinhardt, Daniel S
(Georgia)
Profile: p.621
Litigation **Band 3**
Table: p.598

Reinhart, Joe (Pennsylvania)
Profile: p.1535
Environment **Band 4**
Table: p.1505

Reinhart, Robert
(Minnesota)
Profile: p.1019
Employment **Band 1**
Table: p.1008

Reinhold, Richard L
(New York)
Profile: p.1312
Tax **Band 2**
Table: p.1255

Reisch, Scott H (Colorado)
Profile: p.321
Environment **Band 2**
Table: p.307

Reische, Alan L
(New Hampshire)
Profile: p.1118
Corporate/M&A **Band 1**
Table: p.1107

Reisman, Sharyl (New York)
Profile: p.1312
Environment **Band 3**
Table: p.1205

Reisman, Stephen H
(Florida)
Profile: p.548
Construction **Band 1**
Table: p.507

Reisman, W Michael
(National)
Profile: p.100
Arbitration **Band 1**
Table: p.34

Reisner, Lorin L (New York)
Profile: p.1312
Media & Entertainment **Band 3**
Table: p.1232

Reiss, John (New York)
Profile: p.1312
Corporate/M&A **Band 4**
Table: p.1189
Private Equity **Band 3**
Table: p.1237

Reiss, Michael (Washington)
Profile: p.1794
Employment **Band 1**
Table: p.1780

Reiter, Glenn M (National)
Profile: p.100
Capital Markets **Band 3**
Table: p.14

Remar, Robert (Georgia)
Profile: p.621
Litigation **Band 3**
Table: p.598

Remele Jr, Lewis A
(Minnesota)
Profile: p.1019
Litigation **Band 1**
Table: p.1011

Remington, Royce (Ohio)
Profile: p.1447
Construction **Band 3**
Table: p.1417

Remis, Shepard M
(Massachusetts)
Profile: p.975
Intellectual Property **Band 3**
Table: p.948

Remsburg, Edward W
(Iowa)
Profile: p.814
Litigation **Band 2**
Table: p.807

Renbarger, Robert (Texas)
Profile: p.1698
Environment **Band 4**
Table: p.1643

Renehan, Richard
(Massachusetts)
Profile: p.975
Litigation **Band 1**
Table: p.951

Renfert, Blaine (Wisconsin)
Profile: p.1826
Litigation **Band 3**
Table: p.1821

Renfrew, Charles B
(National)
Profile: p.100
Arbitration **Band 1**
Table: p.34

Renfroe, Tracie (Texas)
Profile: p.1698
Litigation **Band 2**
Table: p.1643

Reno, Russell (Maryland)
Profile: p.923
Real Estate **Band 2**
Table: p.917

Rentenbach, Paul
(Michigan)
Profile: p.1000
Corporate/M&A **Band 3**
Table: p.989

Repka, David A
(District of Columbia)
Profile: p.464
Energy **Band 3**
Table: p.390

Reppert, Richard L (Ohio)
Profile: p.1447
Real Estate **Band 1**
Table: p.1434

Reschly, Jason (Missouri)
Profile: p.1060
Corporate/M&A **Band 3**
Table: p.1043

Resnick, Donald I (Illinois)
Profile: p.747
Real Estate **Band 4**
Table: p.706

Ressler, Alison S (California)
Profile: p. 269
Capital Markets **Band 2**
Table: p.23

Reymond Jr, Leon J
(Louisiana)
Profile: p.875
Real Estate **Band 2**
Table: p.867

Reynolds, Chris (Texas)
Profile: p.1698
Energy **Band 3**
Table: p.1640
Litigation **Band 3**
Table: p.1656

Reynolds, Christopher
(New York)
Profile: p.1312
Employment **Band 3**
Table: p.1200

Reynolds, Nicholas S
(District of Columbia)
Profile: p.464
Energy **Band 1**
Table: p.390

Reynolds, Robert C
(National)
Profile: p.101
Business Process
Outsourcing: National **Band 3**
Table: p.10

Reynolds, Timothy G
(New York)
Profile: p.1312
Insurance **Band 3**
Table: p.1213

Reynolds III, John B
(National)
Profile: p.101
International Trade **Band 2**
Table: p.41

Reznicsek, Rick M (Florida)
Profile: p.548
Healthcare **Band 2**
Table: p.518

Rheaume, Warren J
(Washington)
Profile: p.1794
Intellectual Property **Band 2**
Table: p.1784

Rhodes, Thomas (Georgia)
Profile: p.621
Antitrust **Band 2**
Table: p.578

Rhorer, John R (Kentucky)
Profile: p.845
Environment **Band 3**
Table: p.832

Rhyne, Katherine L
(District of Columbia)
Profile: p.464
Environment **Band 3**
Table: p.392

Riback, Ronald (Michigan)
Profile: p.1000
Banking & Finance **Band 2**
Table: p.987

Ricciardi, Mark J (Nevada)
Profile: p.1103
Employment **Band 2**
Table: p.1091

R

Rice, Emily G
(New Hampshire)
Profile: p.1118
Employment **Band 2**
Table: p.1109
Litigation **Band 2**
Table: p.1111

Rice, Gary (New York)
Profile: p.1312
Banking & Finance **Band 3**
Table: p.1174

Rice, Glenn (New York)
Profile: p.1312
Bankruptcy **Band 4**
Table: p.1179

Rice, Stephen M (Nevada)
Profile: p.1103
Real Estate **Band 2**
Table: p.1099

Rich, Frederic C (New York)
Profile: p. 1312
Projects **Band 1**
Table: p.52
Projects **Band 1**
Table: p.1244

Rich, R Bruce (New York)
Profile: p.1312
Media & Entertainment **Band 3**
Table: p.1232

Richard, Andrea Leah
(Wyoming)
Profile: p.1839
Real Estate **Band 2**
Table: p.1836

Richard, Barry (Florida)
Profile: p.548
Litigation **Band 2**
Table: p.521
Litigation **Band 1**
Table: p.525

Richard, Molly (Texas)
Profile: p.1698
Intellectual Property **Band 2**
Table: p.1651

Richards, Russell (Georgia)
Profile: p.621
Corporate/M&A **Band 2**
Table: p.587

Richards III, Lee S
(New York)
Profile: p.1313
Litigation **Band 3**
Table: p.1224

Richardson, Joseph
(Arizona)
Profile: p.161
Corporate/M&A **Band 3**
Table: p.146

Richardson, Julia (DC)
Profile: p.464
Energy **Band 5**
Table: p.382

Richardson, Susan
(Georgia)
Profile: p.621
Environment **Up and coming**
Table: p.593

Richardson, Todd
(Nebraska)
Profile: p.1088
Corporate/M&A **Band 2**
Table: p.1082

Richey, P Jerome
(Pennsylvania)
Profile: p.1535
Employment **Band 4**
Table: p.1500

Richilano, John M
(Colorado)
Profile: p.321
Litigation **Band 1**
Table: p.311

Richman, Gerald (Florida)
Profile: p.548
Litigation **Band 3**
Table: p.521

Richman, Hershel J
(Pennsylvania)
Profile: p.1535
Environment **Band 2**
Table: p.1505

Richter, Peter (Oregon)
Profile: p.1484
Litigation **Band 2**
Table: p.1477

Riddell, Stephen (Georgia)
Profile: p.622
Employment **Band 4**
Table: p.589

Ridgley, Thomas (Ohio)
Profile: p.1447
Litigation **Band 4**
Table: p.1431

Ridley, Fred S (Florida)
Profile: p.548
Real Estate **Band 3**
Table: p.526

Ridley, John (New Jersey)
Profile: p.1144
Employment **Band 2**
Table: p.1126

Riedel, Harley (Florida)
Profile: p.548
Bankruptcy ✪
Table: p.503

Riedinger, Jerry
(Washington)
Profile: p.1794
Intellectual Property **Band 1**
Table: p.1784

Riedy, James
(District of Columbia)
Profile: p.464
Tax **Band 4**
Table: p.422

Rieke, Robert (Nebraska)
Profile: p.1088
Real Estate **Band 1**
Table: p.1086

Riesel, Daniel (New York)
Profile: p.1313
Environment **Band 1**
Table: p.1205

Riffel, Jerome (Missouri)
Profile: p.1060
Real Estate **Band 2**
Table: p.1053

Riggs, Kendrick R
(Kentucky)
Profile: p.845
Environment **Band 1**
Table: p.832

Riggs, Richard (Oklahoma)
Profile: p.1466
Real Estate **Band 1**
Table: p.1464

Rigot, Joseph M (Ohio)
Profile: p.1447
Corporate/M&A **Band 3**
Table: p.1419

Rikard, William L (North
Carolina)
Profile: p.1398
Litigation **Band 3**
Table: p.1390

Rikleen, Lauren Stiller
(Massachusetts)
Profile: p.975
Environment **Band 3**
Table: p.943

Riley, Byron (Iowa)
Profile: p.814
Corporate/M&A **Band 4**
Table: p.802

Riley, Richard A (Idaho)
Profile: p.660
Corporate/M&A **Band 3**
Table: p.655

Riley, Shawn (Ohio)
Profile: p.1447
Bankruptcy **Band 2**
Table: p.1414

Riley, Steven (Tennessee)
Profile: p.1611
Litigation **Band 1**
Table: p.1599

Riley Jr, James B (Illinois)
Profile: p.747
Healthcare **Band 3**
Table: p.690

Rill, James F
(District of Columbia)
Profile: p.464
Antitrust **Band 2**
Table: p.367

Rillstone, Douglas (Florida)
Profile: p.548
Environment **Band 3**
Table: p.516

Rindy, Dean (North Dakota)
Profile: p.1410
Real Estate **Band 3**
Table: p.1409

Ringel, Dean (New York)
Profile: p.1313
Media & Entertainment **Band 3**
Table: p.1232

Riopelle, Brian C (Virginia)
Profile: p.1772
Intellectual Property **Band 2**
Table: p.1761

Rios Rodriguez, Denise
(California)
Profile: p.269
Healthcare **Band 3**
Table: p.209

Rippie, E Glenn (Illinois)
Profile: p.747
Energy **Band 1**
Table: p.685

Rishwain, James (California)
Profile: p.269
Real Estate **Band 3**
Table: p.238

Riter, Charles
(South Dakota)
Profile: p.1593
Real Estate **Band 1**
Table: p.1592

Ritok, Joseph (Michigan)
Profile: p.1000
Employment **Band 1**
Table: p.991

Ritt, Roger M
(Massachusetts)
Profile: p.975
Tax **Band 2**
Table: p.959

Ritts, Leslie Sue
(District of Columbia)
Profile: p.464
Environment **Band 3**
Table: p.392

Rivkin, David W (National)
Profile: p.101
Arbitration **Band**
Table: p.33
Arbitration **Band 1**
Table: p.33

Rizzi, Robert
(District of Columbia)
Profile: p.269
Tax **Band 4**
Table: p.241

Rizzotti, Anthony
(Massachusetts)
Profile: p.975
Employment **Band 2**
Table: p.940

Roach, Gerald F (North
Carolina)
Profile: p.1398
Corporate/M&A **Band 2**
Table: p.1384

Roach Jr, William H
(Illinois)
Profile: p.747
Healthcare **Band 3**
Table: p.690

Roady, Celia
(District of Columbia)
Profile: p.464
Tax **Band 4**
Table: p.422

Robb, Peter (Vermont)
Profile: p.1749
Employment **Band 1**
Table: p.1745

Robbins, Lawrence
(District of Columbia)
Profile: p.464
Litigation **Band 1**
Table: p.408

Robbins, Robert B
(District of Columbia)
Profile: p.464
Corporate/Commercial **Band 2**
Table: p.376

Robeck, Mark (Texas)
Profile: p.1698
Energy **Band 3**
Table: p.1640

Robenalt, James (Ohio)
Profile: p.1447
Construction **Band 4**
Table: p.1417
Litigation **Band 4**
Table: p.1431

Roberson, Richard (Texas)
Profile: p.1698
Bankruptcy **Band 1**
Table: p.1627

Roberson, Jr, Thomas Y
(Louisiana)
Profile: p.875
Banking & Finance **Band 2**
Table: p.857

Roberts, Harry (Texas)
Profile: p.1699
Real Estate **Band 2**
Table: p.1662

Roberts, James (Virginia)
Profile: p.1772
Litigation **Band 1**
Table: p.1763

Roberts, Kenneth M
(Illinois)
Profile: p.747
Construction **Band 3**
Table: p.672

Roberts, Lee (Georgia)
Profile: p.622
Construction **Band 2**
Table: p.584

Roberts, Michele
(District of Columbia)
Profile: p.465
Litigation **Band 2**
Table: p.410

Roberts, Richard
(District of Columbia)
Profile: p.465
Energy **Band 2**
Table: p.386

Roberts, Thomas A
(New York)
Profile: p.1313
Corporate/M&A **Band 4**
Table: p.1189
Private Equity **Band 2**
Table: p.1237

Robertson, Allen K (North
Carolina)
Profile: p.1398
Banking & Finance **Band 3**
Table: p.1381

Robertson, Elihu (National)
Profile: p.101
Aviation **Band 3**
Table: p.58

Robertson, Eric (Illinois)
Profile: p.747
Energy **Band 2**
Table: p.685

Robertson, Gregory
(Virginia)
Profile: p.1772
Employment **Band 1**
Table: p.1755

Robertson, Jean R (Ohio)
Profile: p.1447
Bankruptcy **Band 4**
Table: p.1414

R

Robertson, Robert (Illinois)
Profile: p.747
Antitrust **Band** 2
Table: p.662

Robertson Jr, James K
(Connecticut)
Profile: p.337
Litigation **Band** 2
Table: p.331

Robfogel, Susan S
(New York)
Profile: p.1313
Healthcare **Band** 2
Table: p.1209

Robiner, Susan (Minnesota)
Profile: p.1019
Employment **Band** 3
Table: p.1008

Robins, Andrew S (Florida)
Profile: p.549
Hotels and Resorts **Band** 1
Table: p.526

Robins, Charles W
(Massachusetts)
Profile: p.975
Private Equity **Band** 2
Table: p.955

Robinson, Donald C
(Montana)
Profile: p.1081
Litigation **Band** 1
Table: p.1075

Robinson, Frank (Colorado)
Profile: p.321
Real Estate **Band** 1
Table: p.313

Robinson, Frederick
(District of Columbia)
Profile: p.465
Healthcare **Band** 1
Table: p.398

Robinson, John (Florida)
Profile: p.549
Employment **Band** 1
Table: p.513

Robinson, Marcia C
(Massachusetts)
Profile: p.975
Real Estate **Band** 3
Table: p.956

Robinson, Robert P
(Arizona)
Profile: p.161
Real Estate **Band** 3
Table: p.154

Robinson, Spencer
(Arkansas)
Profile: p.177
Employment **Band** 1
Table: p.170

Robinson, Stephen W
(Virginia)
Profile: p.1772
Employment **Band** 2
Table: p.1755

Robinson II, Russell M
(North Carolina)
Profile: p.1398
Corporate/M&A **Band** 1
Table: p.1384

Robinson III, Wm T
(Kentucky)
Profile: p.845
Litigation **Band** 4
Table: p.835

Robinson Jr, Neil C
(South Carolina)
Profile: p.1582
Real Estate **Band** 2
Table: p.1577

Robison, John (Wisconsin)
Profile: p.1826
Corporate/M&A **Band** 3
Table: p.1817

Robison, Kent (Nevada)
Profile: p.1103
Litigation **Band** 3
Table: p.1096

Robison, Reid (Oklahoma)
Profile: p.1466
Litigation **Band** 3
Table: p.1462

Robitzek, William (Maine)
Profile: p.901
Litigation **Band** 2
Table: p.893

Roble, Daniel T
(Massachusetts)
Profile: p.975
Healthcare **Band** 1
Table: p.946

Roby, Patrick M (Iowa)
Profile: p.814
Litigation **Band** 1
Table: p.807

Roby, Jr, Joseph J
(Minnesota)
Profile: p.1019
Employment **Band** 3
Table: p.1008

Rocap, Donald (Illinois)
Profile: p.748
Tax **Band** 2
Table: p.710

Rocap III, James
(District of Columbia)
Profile: p.465
Insurance **Band** 1
Table: p.400

Rocci, Steven (Pennsylvania)
Profile: p.1536
Intellectual Property **Band** 4
Table: p.1508

Rocha, Patricia (Rhode
Island)
Profile: p.1570
Litigation **Band** 2
Table: p.1567

Roche, William G (National)
Profile: p.101
Business Process
Outsourcing: National **Band** 3
Table: p.10

Rochelle, Michael (Texas)
Profile: p.1699
Bankruptcy **Band** 4
Table: p.1627

Rock, Neil L (New York)
Profile: p.1313
Real Estate **Band** 5
Table: p.1248

Rockett, James M
(California)
Profile: p.269
Banking & Finance **Band** 1
Table: p.188

Rockman, Jeffrey
(Maryland)
Profile: p.923
Employment **Band** 3
Table: p.912

Rockwell, David
(Washington)
Profile: p.1794
Real Estate **Band** 2
Table: p.1788

Rockwell, Sarah M
(Colorado)
Profile: p.321
Real Estate **Band** 1
Table: p.314

Rockwood, Linda (Colorado)
Profile: p.321
Environment **Band** 1
Table: p.307

Rod, Jonathan (New York)
Profile: p. 1313
Projects **Band** 2
Table: p.52
Projects **Band** 2
Table: p.1244

Rodburg, Michael L
(New Jersey)
Profile: p.1144
Environment **Band** 1
Table: p.1129

Roddenberry, Stephen
(Florida)
Profile: p.549
Corporate/M&A **Band** 1
Table: p.509

Rodgers, Stanley (Alabama)
Profile: p.124
Litigation **Band** 3
Table: p.116

Rodriguez, Cristina (Texas)
Profile: p.1699
Employment **Up and coming**
Table: p.1634

Rodriguez, Wilfredo A
(National)
Profile: p.101
Arbitration **Band** 4
Table: p.33

Roe Jr, Clifford A (Ohio)
Profile: p.1447
Corporate/M&A **Band** 3
Table: p.1419

Roeder, Kim H (Georgia)
Profile: p.622
Healthcare **Band** 2
Table: p.594

Roesch, Lynda E (Ohio)
Profile: p.1447
Intellectual Property **Band** 3
Table: p.1428

Rogers, Alan T (Alabama)
Profile: p.124
Litigation **Band** 3
Table: p.116

Rogers, Bruce F (Alabama)
Profile: p.125
Litigation **Band** 3
Table: p.116

Rogers, CB (Georgia)
Profile: p.622
Antitrust **Band** 3
Table: p.578
Litigation **Band** 1
Table: p.598

Rogers, Daniel (Texas)
Profile: p.1699
Energy **Band** 5
Table: p.1637
Projects **Band** 4
Table: p.1659

Rogers, E Mabry (Alabama)
Profile: p.125
Litigation ⚙
Table: p.116

Rogers, Ed
(District of Columbia)
Profile: p.465
Real Estate **Band** 4
Table: p.418

Rogers III, John L (Illinois)
Profile: p.748
Energy **Band** 3
Table: p.685

Rogers Jr, Charles F
(Rhode Island)
Profile: p.1570
Real Estate **Band** 2
Table: p.1568

Rogers Jr, Theodore O
(New York)
Profile: p.1313
Employment **Band** 1
Table: p.1200

Rogow, Bruce (Florida)
Profile: p.549
Litigation **Band** 2
Table: p.525

Roh, Charles E (National)
Profile: p.101
International Trade **Band** 4
Table: p.40

Rohback, Thomas G
(Connecticut)
Profile: p.337
Employment **Band** 3
Table: p.329

Rohlf, Joan (Alaska)
Profile: p.144
Employment **Band** 2
Table: p.135

Rohn, Frederick (New York)
Profile: p.1313
Construction **Band** 4
Table: p.1186

Rohrbach, Peter
(District of Columbia)
Profile: p.465
Telecom, Broadcast & Satellite
Band 2
Table: p.427

Rohyans, John (Ohio)
Profile: p.1447
Real Estate **Band** 2
Table: p.1434

Rokosz, Ronald (Illinois)
Profile: p.748
Banking & Finance **Band** 2
Table: p.665

Rolapp, Todd J (Tennessee)
Profile: p.1611
Corporate/M&A
Up and coming
Table: p.1594

Roles, Forrest (West Virginia)
Profile: p.1810
Employment **Band** 1
Table: p.1801

Rolfe, Ronald (New York)
Profile: p.1313
Antitrust **Band** 4
Table: p.1170

Rolnick, Lawrence M
(New Jersey)
Profile: p.1144
Litigation **Band** 1
Table: p.1131

Rom, Rebecca L
(Minnesota)
Profile: p.1020
Real Estate **Band** 1
Table: p.1015

Roman, Marissa J
(California)
Profile: p.269
Media & Entertainment **Up
and coming**
Table: p.233

Roman, Terry (Arizona)
Profile: p.161
Corporate/M&A **Band** 4
Table: p.146

Romano, Carmen J
(Pennsylvania)
Profile: p.1536
Corporate/M&A **Band** 2
Table: p.1497

Rondeau, Patrick J
(Massachusetts)
Profile: p.975
Corporate/M&A **Band** 3
Table: p.937
Private Equity **Band** 3
Table: p.953

Rooney, John E (Illinois)
Profile: p.748
Energy **Band** 3
Table: p.685
Telecom, Broadcast & Satellite
Band 3
Table: p.715

Rooney, William H
(New York)
Profile: p.1313
Antitrust **Band** 3
Table: p.1170

Root Jr, George L
(California)
Profile: p.270
Healthcare **Band** 1
Table: p.209

Roper, Harry J (Illinois)
Profile: p.748
Intellectual Property **Band** 3
Table: p.696

R

Ropski, Gary (Illinois)
Profile: p.748
Intellectual Property Band 1
Table: p.696

Rosati, Jack (Ohio)
Profile: p.1447
Construction Band 2
Table: p.1417

Rosati, Mario (California)
Profile: p.270
Corporate/M&A Band 3
Table: p.197

Rosch, Tom (California)
Profile: p.270
Antitrust Band 1
Table: p.184

Rose, Crystal K (Hawaii)
Profile: p.650
Litigation Band 2
Table: p.644

Rose, David A (Texas)
Profile: p.1699
Intellectual Property Band 3
Table: p.1651

Rose, Glenn B (Tennessee)
Profile: p.1611
Litigation Band 3
Table: p.1599

Rose, Stephen (California)
Profile: p.270
Tax Band 3
Table: p.241

Rose Jr, J William
(Alabama)
Profile: p.125
Corporate/M&A Band 2
Table: p.111

Rosegay, Margaret
(California)
Profile: p.270
Environment Band 4
Table: p.207

Rosen, Arthur R (New York)
Profile: p.1314
Tax Band 4
Table: p.1255

Rosen, Burt (New York)
Profile: p.1314
Tax Band 4
Table: p.1255

Rosen, Edward J (National)
Profile: p.101
Capital Markets Band 1
Table: p.16

Rosen, J Philip (New York)
Profile: p.1314
Real Estate Band 3
Table: p.1248

Rosen, Jeffrey J (New York)
Profile: p.1314
Corporate/M&A Band 3
Table: p.1189

Rosen, Matthew A (New York)
Profile: p.1314
Tax Band 1
Table: p.1255

Rosen, Peter K (California)
Profile: p.270
Insurance Band 3

Table: p.212

Rosen, Richard (New York)
Profile: p.1314
Litigation Band 2
Table: p.1223

Rosen, Richard L
(District of Columbia)
Profile: p.465
Antitrust Band 4
Table: p.367

Rosen , Seth (New York)
Profile: p.1314
Tax Band 4
Table: p.1255

Rosen, Stuart M (National)
Profile: p.101
International Trade Band 3
Table: p.40

Rosenbaum, David (Arizona)
Profile: p.161
Litigation Band 3
Table: p.152

Rosenbaum, Gary B
(California)
Profile: p.270
Banking & Finance Band 3
Table: p.187

Rosenbaum, Lois O
(Oregon)
Profile: p.1484
Litigation Band 2
Table: p.1477

Rosenbaum, Michael D
(Illinois)
Profile: p.748
Employee Benefits Band 2
Table: p.681

Rosenbaum, Robert
(Minnesota)
Profile: p.1020
Corporate/M&A Band 1
Table: p.1005

Rosenberg, Ben (Maryland)
Profile: p.923
Litigation Band 2
Table: p.914

Rosenberg, Harry
(Louisiana)
Profile: p.875
Litigation Band 3
Table: p.865

Rosenberg, Kenneth
(Pennsylvania)
Profile: p.1536
Real Estate Band 3
Table: p.1516

Rosenberg, Marc (National)
Profile: p.101
Capital Markets Band 4
Table: p.14

Rosenberg, Mark F (New York)
Profile: p.1314
Environment Band 3
Table: p.1205
Environment Band 3
Table: p.1206

Rosenberg, Michael
(Florida)
Profile: p.549
Tax Band 3

Table: p.531

Rosenberg, Robert
(New York)
Profile: p.1314
Bankruptcy Band 2
Table: p.1179

Rosenberg, Sumner
(Georgia)
Profile: p.622
Intellectual Property Band 4
Table: p.596

Rosenberg, Thomas (Ohio)
Profile: p.1447
Construction Band 3
Table: p.1417

Rosenblatt, Arnold
(New Hampshire)
Profile: p.1118

Rosenblatt, Paul M
(Georgia)
Profile: p.622
Bankruptcy Band 3
Table: p.582

Rosenblatt, Stephen W
(Mississippi)
Profile: p.1035
Bankruptcy Band 1
Table: p.1024

Rosenblatt, William
(New York)
Profile: p.1314
Insurance Band 1
Table: p.1213

Rosenbloom, David
(District of Columbia)
Profile: p.465
Tax Band 1
Table: p.422

Rosenbloom, David (Illinois)
Profile: p.748
Litigation Band 4
Table: p.700

Rosenbloom, James B
(Illinois)
Profile: p.749
Real Estate Band 3
Table: p.706

Rosenbloum, Robert
(Georgia)
Profile: p.622
Intellectual Property Band 4
Table: p.596

Rosenblum, Carl D
(Louisiana)
Profile: p.875
Energy Band 1
Table: p.863

Rosenblum, Jay (New Mexico)
Profile: p.1164
Corporate/M&A Band 2
Table: p.1155

Rosenblum, Peter
(Massachusetts)
Profile: p.975
Corporate/M&A Band 2
Table: p.937
Private Equity Band 1
Table: p.953

Rosenblum, Steve A
(New York)
Profile: p.1314
Corporate/M&A Band 4
Table: p.1189

Rosenfeld, Lawrence
(Arizona)
Profile: p.161
Employment Band 4
Table: p.148

Rosenfeld, Robert
(California)
Profile: p.270
Antitrust Band 3
Table: p.184

Rosenstein, Tony P (Texas)
Profile: p.1699
Employment Band 2
Table: p.1634

Rosenthal, Barry
(District of Columbia)
Profile: p.465
Real Estate Band 1
Table: p.418

Rosenthal, Daniel G (Ohio)
Profile: p.1447
Employment Band 3
Table: p.1422

Rosenthal, Michael D
(Illinois)
Profile: p.749
Private Equity Band 3
Table: p.676

Rosenthal, Paul C
(National)
Profile: p.101
International Trade Band 2
Table: p.40

Rosenwasser, Michael
(New York)
Profile: p.1314
Energy Band 3
Table: p.1202

Rosini, Neil (New York)
Profile: p.1314
Media & Entertainment Band 2
Table: p.1235

Rosner, David S (New York)
Profile: p.1314
Bankruptcy Band 4
Table: p.1179

Rosner, Douglas
(Massachusetts)
Profile: p.975
Bankruptcy Band 3
Table: p.935

Rosner, Richard (Ohio)
Profile: p.1447
Real Estate Band 1
Table: p.1434

Ross, Allen (New York)
Profile: p.1314
Construction Band 2
Table: p.1186

Ross, Barry (New York)
Profile: p.1314
Real Estate Band 4
Table: p.1248

Ross, David L (Florida)
Profile: p.549
Litigation Band 3
Table: p.521

Ross, Jerry W (California)
Profile: p.270
Environment Band 4
Table: p.207

Ross, John Walker
(Montana)
Profile: p.1081
Natural Resources Band 2
Table: p.1077

Ross, Judith (Texas)
Profile: p.1699
Bankruptcy Band 3
Table: p.1627

Ross, Lauri (Florida)
Profile: p.549
Litigation Band 1
Table: p.525

Ross, Nancy (Illinois)
Profile: p. 749
Employee Benefits Band 2
Table: p.681
Litigation Band 2
Table: p.25

Ross, Nelson G
(Massachusetts)
Profile: p.975
Employment Band 1
Table: p.940

Ross, Richard (Minnesota)
Profile: p.1020
Employment Band 1
Table: p.1008

Rossiter, Robert (Nebraska)
Profile: p.1088
Employment Band 1
Table: p.1084

Rosston, Richard (Alaska)
Profile: p.144
Corporate/M&A Band 1
Table: p.134
Real Estate Band 1
Table: p.141

Rotatori, Robert (Ohio)
Profile: p.1447
Litigation Band 2
Table: p.1432

Rotch, Peter B
(New Hampshire)
Profile: p.1118
Real Estate Band 1
Table: p.1114

Roth, Andrew B (New York)
Profile: p.1314
Healthcare Band 2
Table: p.1209

Roth, Stephen E
(District of Columbia)
Profile: p.465
Investment Management Band 3
Table: p.406

Rothenberg, Charles
(Virginia)
Profile: p.1772
Real Estate Band 3
Table: p.1765

Rothenberg, Laraine S
(New York)
Profile: p.1315
Employee Benefits Band 3
Table: p.1197

Rothermel, Sarah
(Massachusetts)
Profile: p.976
Private Equity Band 2
Table: p.955

Rothman, Jay O (Wisconsin)
Profile: p.1826
Corporate/M&A
Up and coming
Table: p.1817

Rothpletz Jr, Michael E
(New Jersey)
Profile: p.1144
Real Estate Band 3
Table: p.1134

Rothschild, Gita F
(New Jersey)
Profile: p.1144
Litigation Band 3
Table: p.1131

Rothwell, James T
(National)
Profile: p.101
Capital Markets Band 3
Table: p.16

Rottenberg, Alan
(Massachusetts)
Profile: p.976
Real Estate Band 1
Table: p.956

Rounsaville, Keith (Florida)
Profile: p.549
Antitrust Band 1
Table: p.498

Rousseau, Dionne M
(Louisiana)
Profile: p.875

Roussel, James H
(Louisiana)
Profile: p.875
Energy Band 1
Table: p.863

Roussel, Randy P.
(Louisiana)
Profile: p.876
Real Estate Band 2
Table: p.867

Rovine, Arthur (National)
Profile: p.101
Arbitration Band
Table: p.33
Arbitration Band 3
Table: p.33

Rovner, Philip (Delaware)
Profile: p.356
Intellectual Property Band 4
Table: p.348

Rowe, Jack D (Missouri)
Profile: p.1060
Employment Band 1
Table: p.1046

Rowe, Keven (Utah)
Profile: p.1737
Real Estate Band 2
Table: p.1733

Rowe, Larry Jordan
(Massachusetts)
Profile: p.976
Private Equity Band 1
Table: p.955

Rowe, Paul A (New Jersey)
Profile: p.1145
Litigation Band 1
Table: p.1131

Rowen, Andrew S
(New York)
Profile: p.1315
Insurance Band 2
Table: p.1213

Roy, Paul J N (Illinois)
Profile: p.749
Business Process
Outsourcing: National Band 3
Table: p.10
Technology Band 1
Table: p.713

Royall, M Sean (Texas)
Profile: p.1699
Antitrust Band 3
Table: p.1622

Royse, David T (Kentucky)
Profile: p.
Litigation Band 4
Table: p.835

Royse, David T (Kentucky)
Profile: p.845

Rozell, William (Alaska)
Profile: p.144
Environment Band 2
Table: p.137

Rozmarin, George
(Nebraska)
Profile: p.1088
Employment Band 1
Table: p.1084

Rubalcava, Sharon
(California)
Profile: p.270
Environment Band 2
Table: p.207

Rubin, David (Rhode Island)
Profile: p.1570
Real Estate Band 2
Table: p.1568

Rubin, Howard (Oregon)
Profile: p.1484
Employment Band 3
Table: p.1474

Rubin, James (Illinois)
Profile: p.749
Insurance Band 1
Table: p.694

Rubin, Jerome L
(Washington)
Profile: p.1794
Employment Band 2
Table: p.1780

Rubin, Joel D (Illinois)
Profile: p.749
Real Estate Band 2
Table: p.706

Rubin, Peter J (Maine)
Profile: p.901
Litigation Band 2
Table: p.893

Rubin, Robert (New York)
Profile: p.1315
Construction Band 1
Table: p.1186

Rubinfeld, Ira B (Utah)
Profile: p.1738
Real Estate Band 3
Table: p.1733

Rubinoff, Edward L
(National)
Profile: p.101
International Trade Band 1
Table: p.41

Rubinstein, Javier H
(National)
Profile: p.102
Arbitration Band 4
Table: p.33

Rubinstein, Joel S
(District of Columbia)
Profile: p.465
Construction Band 3
Table: p.374

Ruby, Allen (California)
Profile: p.270
Litigation Band 4
Table: p.224
Litigation Band 1
Table: p.225

Ruck, Charles K (California)
Profile: p.270
Corporate/M&A Band 4
Table: p.197

Ruckman, Deirdre (Texas)
Profile: p.1699
Bankruptcy Band 2
Table: p.1627

Rudd, David R (Utah)
Profile: p.1738
Corporate/M&A Band 2
Table: p.1727

Rudell, Michael (New York)
Profile: p.1315
Media & Entertainment Band 1
Table: p.1235

Rudlin, D Alan (Virginia)
Profile: p.1772
Litigation Band 2
Table: p.1763

Rudman, Jeffrey
(Massachusetts)
Profile: p.976
Litigation Band 1
Table: p.951

Rudman, Richard
(Massachusetts)
Profile: p.976
Real Estate Band 2
Table: p.956

Rudnick, Robert
(District of Columbia)
Profile: p.465
Tax Band 4
Table: p.422

Rudolph, Andrew J
(Pennsylvania)
Profile: p.1536
Employee Benefits Band 1
Table: p.1501

Ruegger, Philip T (New York)
Profile: p.1315
Corporate/M&A Band 3
Table: p.1189
Private Equity Band 1
Table: p.1237

Ruff, Randolph E (Illinois)
Profile: p.749
Construction Band 3
Table: p.672

Ruffatto, Steven R
(Montana)
Profile: p.1081
Natural Resources Band 1
Table: p.1077

Rugg, Joseph W (Florida)
Profile: p.549
Healthcare Band 2
Table: p.518

Ruggeri, James
(District of Columbia)
Profile: p.466
Insurance Up and coming
Table: p.400

Rule, Charles F (Rick)
(District of Columbia)
Profile: p.466
Antitrust Band 2
Table: p.367

Rummage, Stephen M
(Washington)
Profile: p.1794
Litigation Band 2
Table: p.1786

Running, Andrew R (Illinois)
Profile: p.749
Environment Band 4
Table: p.687

Runstad, Judith M
(Washington)
Profile: p.1794
Real Estate Band 1
Table: p.1789

Rupe, Alan L (Kansas)
Profile: p.824
Employment Band 1
Table: p.818

Rupert, Anton (Oklahoma)
Profile: p.1466
Litigation Band 3
Table: p.1462

Ruppert, John L (Colorado)
Profile: p.321
Corporate/M&A Band 3
Table: p.303

Rusche, Mark C (Georgia)
Profile: p.622
Real Estate Band 2
Table: p.601

Rush, Jeffery (Ohio)
Profile: p.1447
Banking & Finance Band 2
Table: p.1411

Rush, Stephen (Tennessee)
Profile: p.1611
Media & Entertainment Band 1
Table: p.1602

Rushford, Robert (Vermont)
Profile: p.1749
Real Estate Band 1
Table: p.1747

Rusing, Michael J (Arizona)
Profile: p.161
Litigation Band 4
Table: p.152

Ruskin, Bradley I (National)
Profile: p.102
Sport Band 2
Table: p.55

Rusman, Jared M
(New York)
Profile: p.1315
Tax Up and coming
Table: p.1255

Russ, Michael (Georgia)
Profile: p.622
Antitrust Band 3
Table: p.578
Litigation Band 2
Table: p.598

Russell, James (Illinois)
Profile: p.749
Environment Band 4
Table: p.687

Russell, James
(West Virginia)
Profile: p.1810
Real Estate Band 2
Table: p.1806

Russell, William (National)
Profile: p.102
Arbitration Up and coming
Table: p.33

Russell III, P Stephen
(Oregon)
Profile: p.1484
Real Estate Band 3
Table: p.1479

Russin, Peter (Florida)
Profile: p.549
Bankruptcy Band 3
Table: p.503

Russo, Richard (Colorado)
Profile: p.322
Corporate/M&A Band 3
Table: p.303

Rust, Dana (Virginia)
Profile: p.1772
Employment Band 3
Table: p.1755

Rust, Neil (California)
Profile: p.270
Banking & Finance Band 2
Table: p.187

Ruthberg, Miles (California)
Profile: p.270
Litigation Band 4
Table: p.224

Rutkowski, Joanne
(District of Columbia)
Profile: p.466
Energy Band 5
Table: p.386

Rutkowski, Larry (New York)
Profile: p.102
Shipping Band 1
Table: p.67

Rutledge, Kent (Wyoming)
Profile: p.1839
Litigation Band 2
Table: p.1835

R

Rutledge, Thomas E
(Kentucky)
Profile: p.845
Corporate/M&A Band 3
Table: p.827

Rutter, David (Tennessee)
Profile: p.1611
Real Estate Band 3
Table: p.1603

Rutter, Paul S (California)
Profile: p.270
Real Estate Band 3
Table: p.238

Ruxin, Paul (Illinois)
Profile: p.749
Energy Band S
Table: p.685

Ruzow, Daniel (New York)
Profile: p.1315
Environment Band 2
Table: p.1205

Ryan, Mary K
(Massachusetts)
Profile: p.976
Environment Band 2
Table: p.943

Ryan, Michael (Florida)
Profile: p.549
Real Estate Band 1
Table: p.526

Ryan, Michael L (New York)
Profile: p.1315
Corporate/M&A Band 3
Table: p.1189

Ryan, Patrick (Oklahoma)
Profile: p.1466
Litigation Band 1
Table: p.1462

Ryan, Patrick M (Wisconsin)
Profile: p.1826
Corporate/M&A Band 2
Table: p.1817

Ryan, Priscilla E (Illinois)
Profile: p.749
Employee Benefits Band 1
Table: p.681

Ryan, Thomas F (Illinois)
Profile: p.749
Antitrust Band 2
Table: p.662
Litigation Band 4
Table: p.700

Ryan Jr, James 'Jim' E
(Virginia)
Profile: p.1772
Environment Band 2
Table: p.1757

Ryan Jr, William F.
(Maryland)
Profile: p.923
Litigation Band 3
Table: p.914

Rydzel, James (Ohio)
Profile: p.1447
Employment Band 3
Table: p.1422

S

Saad, Michael D (Ohio)
Profile: p.1447
Real Estate Band 3
Table: p.1434

Saathoff, Dwight (Florida)
Profile: p.549
Real Estate Band 2
Table: p.528

Sabalis, Patricia (Vermont)
Profile: p.1749
Employment Band 1
Table: p.1745

Sabel, Bradley K (New York)
Profile: p.1315
Banking & Finance Band 2
Table: p.1174

Sabo, Roger (Ohio)
Profile: p.1448
Construction Band 3
Table: p.1417

Sacher, Steven
(District of Columbia)
Profile: p.466
Employee Benefits Band 2
Table: p.378

Sachs, John
(District of Columbia)
Profile: p. 466
Projects Band 1
Table: p.52
Projects Band 1
Table: p.415

Sacks, Robert A (California)
Profile: p.270
Litigation Band 3
Table: p.224

Sacks, Seymour (Arizona)
Profile: p.161
Real Estate Band 4
Table: p.154

Sacks, Stephen
(District of Columbia)
Profile: p.466
Litigation Band 3
Table: p.410

Sacripanti, Peter (New York)
Profile: p.1315
Environment Band 3
Table: p.1205

Saeed, Faiza (New York)
Profile: p.1316
Corporate/M&A Band 3
Table: p.1189

Saegert, Ann (Texas)
Profile: p.1699
Real Estate Band 3
Table: p.1662

Saferstein, Jeffrey D (New York)
Profile: p.1316
Bankruptcy Band 4
Table: p.1179

Saffer, David (Kentucky)
Profile: p.845
Real Estate Band 2
Table: p.838

Sagarin, Daniel
(Connecticut)
Profile: p.337
Litigation Band 2
Table: p.331

Sage, Michael (New York)
Profile: p.1316
Bankruptcy Band 3
Table: p.1179

Sager, Kelli L (California)
Profile: p.270
Media & Entertainment Band 1
Table: p.230

Saggese, Nicholas P
(California)
Profile: p. 271
Capital Markets Band 1
Table: p.23
Corporate/M&A Band 2
Table: p.197

Saint-Antoine, Paul
(Pennsylvania)
Profile: p.1536
Antitrust Band 3
Table: p.1489

Sakumoto, Randall (Hawaii)
Profile: p.650
Real Estate Band 2
Table: p.646

Salazar, John (New Mexico)
Profile: p.1164
Real Estate Band 1
Table: p.1161
Real Estate Band 2
Table: p.1161

Salch, Steven (Texas)
Profile: p.1699
Tax Band 3
Table: p.1665

Sale, Jon A (Florida)
Profile: p.549
Litigation Band 2
Table: p.522

Sales, Bruce (New Jersey)
Profile: p.1145
Litigation Band 2
Table: p.1133

Sales, Walter L (Kentucky)
Profile: p.845
Employment Band 2
Table: p.830

Salesin, Lowell (Michigan)
Profile: p.1000
Real Estate Band 2
Table: p.996

Salpeter, Alan N (Illinois)
Profile: p.750
Litigation Band 2
Table: p.700

Salter, Dean (Colorado)
Profile: p.322
Corporate/M&A Band 1
Table: p.303

Saltiel, David M (Illinois)
Profile: p.750
Media & Entertainment Band 1
Table: p.704

Salvatore, Paul (New York)
Profile: p.1316
Employment Band 2
Table: p.1200

Salyers, Douglas D
(Georgia)
Profile: p.622
Intellectual Property Band 4
Table: p.596

Salzman, Jerrold E (Illinois)
Profile: p.750
Capital Markets Band 1
Table: p.21

Salzman, Martin (Georgia)
Profile: p.622
Construction Band 2
Table: p.584

Samet, Andrew J (National)
Profile: p.102
International Trade Band 5
Table: p.40

Samorajczyk, Stanley J
(District of Columbia)
Profile: p.466
Bankruptcy Band 2
Table: p.372

Sampson, William
(Missouri)
Profile: p.1060
Litigation Band 1
Table: p.1049

Sams, Gary (Florida)
Profile: p.549
Environment Band 2
Table: p.516

Sams Jr, L F (Mississippi)
Profile: p.1035
Litigation Band 2
Table: p.1028

Samson, Russell (Iowa)
Profile: p.814
Employment Band 2
Table: p.805

Samuels, Jeffrey B
(New York)
Profile: p.1316
Tax Band 4
Table: p.1255

Samuels, Leslie B
(New York)
Profile: p.1316
Tax Band 3
Table: p.1255

Samuels, Mark (California)
Profile: p.271
Intellectual Property Band 4
Table: p.216

Samuels, Richard A
(New Hampshire)
Profile: p.1118
Corporate/M&A Band 1
Table: p.1107

Samuels, Stanley (Oregon)
Profile: p.1484
Real Estate Band S
Table: p.1479

Samuels, Stephen P (Ohio)
Profile: p.1448
Environment Band 3
Table: p.1425

Samuels Jones, Karen
(Colorado)
Profile: p.322
Real Estate Band 3
Table: p.313

Samuelson, Jaki (Iowa)
Profile: p.814
Employment Band 2
Table: p.805

Sanchez, Carl R (California)
Profile: p.271
Corporate/M&A Band 5
Table: p.197

Sanchez, Vincent (Illinois)
Profile: p.750
Technology Band 3
Table: p.713

Sand, Thomas C (Oregon)
Profile: p.1484
Litigation Band 3
Table: p.1477

Sandak, Lawrence (New Jersey)
Profile: p.1145
Employment Band 3
Table: p.1126

Sanders, David P (Illinois)
Profile: p.750
Media & Entertainment Band 1
Table: p.703

Sanders, James F
(Tennessee)
Profile: p.1611
Litigation Band 3
Table: p.1599

Sandler, David B (Kentucky)
Profile: p.845
Employment Band 3
Table: p.830

Sandler, Richard J
(National)
Profile: p.102
Capital Markets Band 1
Table: p.14

Sandler, Sheldon N
(Delaware)
Profile: p.356
Employment Band 1
Table: p.347

Sanford, Bruce W
(District of Columbia)
Profile: p.466
Media & Entertainment Band 3
Table: p.413

Sanford, Steven
(South Dakota)
Profile: p.1593
Litigation Band 1
Table: p.1590

Sankbeil, William
(Michigan)
Profile: p.1000
Litigation Band 3
Table: p.994

Sanker, Robert (Ohio)
Profile: p.1448
Bankruptcy Band 3
Table: p.1414

Sanoff, Robert
(Massachusetts)
Profile: p.976
Environment **Band 3**
Table: p.943

Sanseverino, Raymond
(New York)
Profile: p.1316
Real Estate **Band 5**
Table: p.1248

Sanson, Paul (Connecticut)
Profile: p.337
Litigation **Band 3**
Table: p.331

Santi, Richard G (Iowa)
Profile: p.814
Litigation **Band 1**
Table: p.807

Santoro, Nicholas J
(Nevada)
Profile: p.1103
Litigation **Band 2**
Table: p.1096

Saper, Jeff (California)
Profile: p.271
Capital Markets **Band 3**
Table: p.23
Corporate/M&A **Band 1**
Table: p.197

Sapp, Richard (Iowa)
Profile: p.814
Litigation **Band 1**
Table: p.807

Sarachan, Ronald A
(Pennsylvania)
Profile: p.1536
Environment **Band 4**
Table: p.1505

Sarasek, Peter A (Illinois)
Profile: p.750
Real Estate **Band 4**
Table: p.706

Sarchio, John J (New York)
Profile: p.1316
Insurance **Band 3**
Table: p.1213

Sarcone, James (Iowa)
Profile: p.814
Real Estate **Band 3**
Table: p.810

Sargeant, Richard T (Ohio)
Profile: p.1448
Environment **Band 3**
Table: p.1425

Sarno, Glenn (New York)
Profile: p.1316
Private Equity **Up and coming**
Table: p.1241

Sarosdy, Randall (Texas)
Profile: p.1699
Intellectual Property **Band 3**
Table: p.1651

Sartore, John T (Vermont)
Profile: p.1749
Litigation **Band 2**
Table: p.1746

Sarver, Richard E
(Louisiana)
Profile: p.876
Litigation **Band 3**
Table: p.865

Saslaw, Michael A. (Texas)
Profile: p.1699
Corporate/M&A **Band 4**
Table: p.1631

Sathy, Anup (Illinois)
Profile: p.750
Bankruptcy **Up and coming**
Table: p.669

Satriana, Daniel (Colorado)
Profile: p.322
Employment **Band 3**
Table: p.306

Satterfield, Jr, Andreas N
(South Carolina)
Profile: p.1582
Employment **Band 3**
Table: p.1574

Sauer, Jane (Alaska)
Profile: p.144
Corporate/M&A **Band 2**
Table: p.134

Saul, Gary (Florida)
Profile: p.549
Real Estate **Band 2**
Table: p.526

Saunders, Eric F (Maine)
Profile: p.901

Saunders, Paul (New York)
Profile: p.1316
Litigation **Band 3**
Table: p.1222

Saunders, Robert S
(Delaware)
Profile: p.356
Chancery **Band 4**
Table: p.344

Sauntry, June Ann (Georgia)
Profile: p.622
Antitrust **Band 2**
Table: p.578

Saupe, A William (Alaska)
Profile: p.144
Environment **Band 2**
Table: p.137
Regulated Industries **Band 1**
Table: p.137

Savage, Janet (Colorado)
Profile: p.322
Employment **Band 3**
Table: p.306

Savage, Joseph
(Massachusetts)
Profile: p.976

Savage Nelson, Elizabeth
(Nevada)
Profile: p.1103
Corporate/M&A
Up and coming
Table: p.1089

Savarese, John F (New York)
Profile: p.1316
Litigation **Band 2**
Table: p.1224

Savarise, Jeffrey A
(Kentucky)
Profile: p.845
Employment **Band 2**
Table: p.830

Savely, Carl D (Nevada)
Profile: p.1103

Environment Band 2
Table: p.1093

Savikas, Victor G
(California)
Profile: p.271
Intellectual Property **Band 4**
Table: p.216

Savitz, Stephen
(South Carolina)
Profile: p.1582
Employment **Band 3**
Table: p.1574

Savrin, Daniel S
(Massachusetts)
Profile: p.976
Antitrust **Band 2**
Table: p.930

Sawchak, Matthew W
(North Carolina)
Profile: p.1398
Antitrust **Band 1**
Table: p.1390

Sawyer, Ed (Florida)
Profile: p.549
Tax **Band 3**
Table: p.531

Sawyier, David R (Illinois)
Profile: p.750
Capital Markets **Band 1**
Table: p.21

Sax, Paul (California)
Profile: p.271
Tax **Band 2**
Table: p.241

Saxbe, Charles (Ohio)
Profile: p.1448
Litigation **Band 3**
Table: p.1431

Saxe, Deborah C (California)
Profile: p.271
Employment **Band 4**
Table: p.202

Saxton, James (Arkansas)
Profile: p.177
Real Estate **Band 3**
Table: p.174

Sayler, Robert
(District of Columbia)
Profile: p.466
Insurance **Band 1**
Table: p.402
Litigation **Band 2**
Table: p.410

Scalia, Eugene
(District of Columbia)
Profile: p.466
Employment **Band 1**
Table: p.380

Scallen, Timothy
(Minnesota)
Profile: p.1020
Corporate/M&A **Band 1**
Table: p.1005

Scanlon, Chris (Indiana)
Profile: p.794
Litigation **Band 1**
Table: p.785

Scannell, Gordon J (Maine)
Profile: p.901
Real Estate **Band 3**
Table: p.895

Scarborough, Robert
(New York)
Profile: p.1317
Tax **Band 1**
Table: p.1256

Scarr, Thomas
(West Virginia)
Profile: p.1810
Litigation **Band 2**
Table: p.1803

Scavone, Arthur (New York)
Profile: p.1317
Projects **Band 1**
Table: p.52
Projects **Band 1**
Table: p.1244

Schachter, Robert C
(New Jersey)
Profile: p.1145
Real Estate **Band 2**
Table: p.1134

Schacter, Ira (National)
Profile: p.102
Capital Markets **Band 4**
Table: p.19

Schaeffer, Fiona A
(New York)
Profile: p.1317
Antitrust **Up and coming**
Table: p.1170

Schaffer, Eric A
(Pennsylvania)
Profile: p.1536
Bankruptcy **Band 2**
Table: p.1494

Schaffer, Michael
(South Dakota)
Profile: p.1593
Litigation **Band 1**
Table: p.1590

Schaffran, Andrew
(New York)
Profile: p.1317
Employment **Band 2**
Table: p.1200

Schaffzin, Jonathan
(National)
Profile: p.103
Capital Markets **Band 4**
Table: p.14

Schagrin, Roger (National)
Profile: p.103
International Trade **Band 5**
Table: p.40

Schallhorn, Scott
(Arkansas)
Profile: p.177
Real Estate **Band 2**
Table: p.174

Scharfstein, Joel (New York)
Profile: p.1317
Tax **Band 3**
Table: p.1255

Schatzow, Michael
(Maryland)
Profile: p.923
Litigation **Band 3**
Table: p.914

Schechter, Lori (California)
Profile: p.271
Litigation **Band 4**
Table: p.224

Schechter, Mark
(District of Columbia)
Profile: p.466
Antitrust **Band 3**
Table: p.367

Schechtman, Paul
(New York)
Profile: p.1317
Litigation **Band 3**
Table: p.1224

Scheck, Stephanie
(Kansas)
Profile: p.824
Employment **Band 2**
Table: p.818

Scheeler, Charles P
(Maryland)
Profile: p.923
Litigation **Band 3**
Table: p.914

Scheibe, Robert H
(New York)
Profile: p.1317
Bankruptcy **Band 4**
Table: p.1179

Scheinberg, Ronald
(National)
Profile: p.103
Aviation **Band 1**
Table: p.58

Scheinfeld, Robert
(New York)
Profile: p.1317
Intellectual Property **Band 3**
Table: p.1217

Scheler, Brad Eric
(New York)
Profile: p.1317
Bankruptcy **Band 2**
Table: p.1179

Schell, Ivan J (Kentucky)
Profile: p.845
Corporate/M&A **Band 3**
Table: p.827

Schell, J Michael (New York)
Profile: p.1317
Corporate/M&A **Band 3**
Table: p.1189

Scher, Howard
(Pennsylvania)
Profile: p.1536
Litigation **Band 3**
Table: p.1511

Scher, Irving (New York)
Profile: p.1318
Antitrust **Band 2**
Table: p.1170

Scher, Peter L (National)
Profile: p.103
International Trade **Band 2**
Table: p.40

Scherkenbach, Frank E
(Massachusetts)
Profile: p.976
Intellectual Property **Band 3**
Table: p.948

Scherker, Elliot (Florida)
Profile: p.549
Litigation **Band 1**
Table: p.525

S

Scherman, William S
(District of Columbia)
Profile: p.466
Energy **Band 2**
Table: p.382
Energy **Band 1**
Table: p.386

Schetman, Richard
(National)
Profile: p.103
Capital Markets **Band 2**
Table: p.19

Scheu, William (Florida)
Profile: p.549
Real Estate **Band 3**
Table: p.526

Schick, Robert M (Texas)
Profile: p.1699
Litigation **Band 3**
Table: p.1656

Schifani, Ruth M
(New Mexico)
Profile: p.1164
Real Estate **Band 3**
Table: p.1161

Schiffer, Adam (Texas)
Profile: p.1700
Energy **Band 3**
Table: p.1640
Litigation **Band 3**
Table: p.1656

Schildhorn, Gary M
(Pennsylvania)
Profile: p.1536
Bankruptcy **Band 3**
Table: p.1494

Schildkraut, Marc
(District of Columbia)
Profile: p.466
Antitrust **Band 3**
Table: p.367

Schiller, Eric M (Illinois)
Profile: p.750
Real Estate **Band 2**
Table: p.706

Schiller, Jonathan D
(National)
Profile: p.103
Arbitration **Band**
Table: p.33
Arbitration **Band 2**
Table: p.33

Schiller, Lisa (Florida)
Profile: p.549
Bankruptcy **Band 3**
Table: p.503

Schilli, David (North
Carolina)
Profile: p.1398
Bankruptcy **Band 1**
Table: p.1383

Schindler, Ozzie (Florida)
Profile: p.549

Schlack, Carl J (Hawaii)
Profile: p.650
Real Estate **Band 2**
Table: p.646

Schler, Michael (New York)
Profile: p.1318
Tax **Band 1**
Table: p.1255

Schlickman, J Andrew
(Illinois)
Profile: p.750
Environment **Band 3**
Table: p.687

Schloemer, Jeffrey S (Ohio)
Profile: p.1448
Banking & Finance **Band 2**
Table: p.1411

Schlossberg, Bob
(District of Columbia)
Profile: p.466
Antitrust **Band 5**
Table: p.367

Schlossman, William
(North Dakota)
Profile: p.1410
Corporate/M&A **Band 2**
Table: p.1403

Schmall, Deborah J
(California)
Profile: p.271
Environment **Band 3**
Table: p.207

Schmidt, Don (Florida)
Profile: p.550
Healthcare **Band 1**
Table: p.518

Schmidt, Justin B
(Louisiana)
Profile: p.876
Real Estate **Up and coming**
Table: p.867

Schmidt, Kevin (New York)
Profile: p.1318
Private Equity **Up and coming**
Table: p.1237

Schmidt, William
(District of Columbia)
Profile: p.467
Employee Benefits **Band 2**
Table: p.378

Schmidt, William
(Massachusetts)
Profile: p.976
Tax **Band 1**
Table: p.959

Schmit, David E (Ohio)
Profile: p.1448
Intellectual Property **Band 1**
Table: p.1428

Schnabel, David H
(New York)
Profile: p.1318
Tax **Band 4**
Table: p.1255

Schnabl, Marco E (National)
Profile: p.103
Arbitration **Band 4**
Table: p.33

Schnadig, Richard H
(Illinois)
Profile: p.750
Employment **Band 2**
Table: p.681

Schnall, Matthew D
(Massachusetts)
Profile: p.976
Tax **Band 3**
Table: p.959

Schnapp, Karlyn (Ohio)
Profile: p.1448
Intellectual Property **Band 2**
Table: p.1428

Schnapp, Mark (Florida)
Profile: p.550
Litigation **Band 1**
Table: p.522

Schneebeck, Douglas G
(New Mexico)
Profile: p.1164
Litigation **Band 3**
Table: p.1159

Schneider, Jeffrey G
(New York)
Profile: p.1318
Healthcare **Band 3**
Table: p.1209

Schneider, Jon
(Massachusetts)
Profile: p.976
Bankruptcy **Band 3**
Table: p.935

Schneider, Lawrence
(National)
Profile: p.103
International Trade **Band 4**
Table: p.40

Schneider, Leslie
(District of Columbia)
Profile: p.467
Tax **Band 2**
Table: p.422

Schneider, Mark
(Washington)
Profile: p.1794
Environment **Band 1**
Table: p.1782

Schneider, Michael R
(Louisiana)
Profile: p.876
Real Estate **Band 2**
Table: p.867

Schneider, Robert F
(Hawaii)
Profile: p.650
Real Estate **Band 2**
Table: p.646

Schneider Jr, Harry H
(Washington)
Profile: p.1794
Litigation **Band 2**
Table: p.1786

Schneidman, Edward J
(Illinois)
Profile: p.750
Corporate/M&A **Band 4**
Table: p.675

Schneidman, Leonard
(Massachusetts)
Profile: p.976
Tax **Band 3**
Table: p.959

Schnell, Paul T (New York)
Profile: p.1318
Corporate/M&A **Band 4**
Table: p.1189

Schnoor, William
(Massachusetts)
Profile: p.976
Private Equity **Band 2**
Table: p.953

Schoenberg, Clifford H
(New York)
Profile: p.1318
Insurance **Band 3**
Table: p.1213

Schoenberg, Robert J
(New Jersey)
Profile: p.1145
Litigation **Band 2**
Table: p.1133

Schoenbrun, Larry (Texas)
Profile: p.1700
Corporate/M&A **Band 2**
Table: p.1631

Schonholtz, Margot
(New York)
Profile: p.1318
Bankruptcy **Band 2**
Table: p.1179

Schopf, Willam G (Illinois)
Profile: p.750
Antitrust **Band 3**
Table: p.662

Schor, Laurence
(District of Columbia)
Profile: p.467
Construction **Band 3**
Table: p.374

Schorling, William H
(Pennsylvania)
Profile: p.1536
Bankruptcy **Band 2**
Table: p.1494

Schraff, Christopher (Ohio)
Profile: p.1448
Environment **Band 1**
Table: p.1425

Schrag, Donald E (Kansas)
Profile: p.824
Real Estate **Band 2**
Table: p.821

Schrage, Russell (Iowa)
Profile: p.814
Real Estate **Band 3**
Table: p.810

Schrank, Charles E (Illinois)
Profile: p.751
Real Estate **Band 3**
Table: p.706

Schreck, Frank (Nevada)
Profile: p.1103
Gaming & Licensing **Band 1**
Table: p.1094

Schreiber, Rodd M (Illinois)
Profile: p.751
Corporate/M&A **Band 3**
Table: p.675

Schroder, Jack (Georgia)
Profile: p.622
Healthcare **Band 1**
Table: p.594

Schroeder, Jeffrey P
(District of Columbia)
Profile: p.467
Projects **Band 3**
Table: p.415

Schroeder, William
(Vermont)
Profile: p.1749
Real Estate **Band 1**
Table: p.1747

Schubart, Lawrence
(Arizona)
Profile: p.161
Real Estate **Band 2**
Table: p.155

Schuchard, Robert L
(California)
Profile: p.271
Healthcare **Band 3**
Table: p.209

Schuck, Edwin (California)
Profile: p.271
Tax **Band 4**
Table: p.241

Schuhmacher, Kenneth
(District of Columbia)
Profile: p.467
Projects **Up and coming**
Table: p.415

Schuler, Alison (New Mexico)
Profile: p.1164
Corporate/M&A **Band 3**
Table: p.1155

Schulhofer, Ellen (Nevada)
Profile: p.1103
Corporate/M&A **Band 1**
Table: p.1089

Schull, E Gunner (Hawaii)
Profile: p.650
Corporate/M&A **Band 1**
Table: p.641

Schulman, Clifford (Florida)
Profile: p.550
Real Estate **Band 1**
Table: p.528

Schultheis, Patrick J
(Washington)
Profile: p.1794
Corporate/M&A **Band 1**
Table: p.1778

Schultz, Andrew G (New
Mexico)
Profile: p.1164
Litigation **Band 2**
Table: p.1159

Schultz, Donald I (Wyoming)
Profile: p.1839
Litigation **Band 2**
Table: p.1835

Schultz, Robert J (North
Dakota)
Profile: p.1410
Employment **Band 3**
Table: p.1405

Schulz, David A (New York)
Profile: p.1318
Media & Entertainment **Band 2**
Table: p.1232

Schumer, Robert B
(New York)
Profile: p.1318
Corporate/M&A **Band 3**
Table: p.1189
Media & Entertainment **Band 2**
Table: p.1235

Schutz, Ron (Minnesota)
Profile: p.1020
Litigation **Band 1**
Table: p.1012

Schuurman, Willem (Texas)
Profile: p.1700
Intellectual Property **Band 1**
Table: p.1651

Schwab, Evan L
(Washington)
Profile: p.1794
Litigation **Band 3**
Table: p.1786

Schwab, Stephen W
(Illinois)
Profile: p.751
Insurance **Band 1**
Table: p.692
Insurance **Band 1**
Table: p.694

Schwartz, Alan (Michigan)
Profile: p.1000
Corporate/M&A **Band 3**
Table: p.989

Schwartz, Alan (New York)
Profile: p.1318
Private Equity **Band 3**
Table: p.1237

Schwartz, Andrew
(Massachusetts)
Profile: p.976
Bankruptcy **Band 2**
Table: p.935

Schwartz, Daniel L
(Connecticut)
Profile: p.337
Employment **Band 3**
Table: p.329

Schwartz, David
(District of Columbia)
Profile: p.467
Energy **Band 2**
Table: p.386

Schwartz, Donald (Illinois)
Profile: p.751
Banking & Finance **Band 2**
Table: p.665

Schwartz, Herbert (New
York)
Profile: p.1318
Intellectual Property **Band S**
Table: p.1217

Schwartz, Jaimie Paul
(Maine)
Profile: p.901
Real Estate **Band 2**
Table: p.895

Schwartz, James R
(California)
Profile: p.271
Healthcare **Band 1**
Table: p.209

Schwartz, Jeffrey (Ohio)
Profile: p.1448
Bankruptcy **Band 2**
Table: p.1414

Schwartz, Jodi J (New York)
Profile: p.1319
Tax **Band 2**
Table: p.1255

Schwartz, Jordan (National)
Profile: p.103
Capital Markets **Band 4**
Table: p.19

Schwartz, Max (New York)
Profile: p.1319
Employee Benefits **Band 1**
Table: p.1197

Schwartz, Michele P
(Texas)
Profile: p.1700
Intellectual Property **Band 3**
Table: p.1651

Schwartz, Niki (Ohio)
Profile: p.1448
Litigation **Band 1**
Table: p.1432

Schwartz, Paul D
(Massachusetts)
Profile: p.976
Real Estate **Band 3**
Table: p.956

Schwartz, Robert
(California)
Profile: p.271
Media & Entertainment **Band 3**
Table: p.230

Schwartz, Robert C
(Georgia)
Profile: p.622
Banking & Finance **Band 3**
Table: p.581

Schwartz, Steven
(New York)
Profile: p.1319
Insurance **Band 3**
Table: p.1213

Schwartz, William J
(New York)
Profile: p.1319
Litigation **Band 3**
Table: p.1224

Schwarz, James (Indiana)
Profile: p.794
Real Estate **Band 3**
Table: p.788

Schwebel, Judge Stephen
(National)
Profile: p.103
Arbitration **Band 1**
Table: p.34

Schwed, Robert (New York)
Profile: p.1319
Private Equity **Band 3**
Table: p.1237

Scimia, Joseph (Indiana)
Profile: p.794
Real Estate **Band 1**
Table: p.788

Scott, Craig M (Rhode
Island)
Profile: p.1570
Litigation **Band 2**
Table: p.1567

Scott, Donald E (Colorado)
Profile: p.322
Litigation **Band 3**
Table: p.311

Scott, Gary (Wyoming)
Profile: p.1839
Employment **Band 1**
Table: p.1833

Scott, John (Michigan)
Profile: p.1000
Litigation **Band 2**

Table: p.994

Scott, Pamela J (Delaware)
Profile: p.357
Real Estate **Band 2**
Table: p.350

Scott, Thane
(Massachusetts)
Profile: p.977
Antitrust **Band 1**
Table: p.930

Scott, W Rowlett
(Tennessee)
Profile: p.1611
Real Estate **Band 3**
Table: p.1603

Scott, William C (New
Mexico)
Profile: p.1164
Environment **Band 1**
Table: p.1158
Native Law **Band 1**
Table: p.1159

Scott IV, William M
(California)
Profile: p.271
Banking & Finance **Band 3**
Table: p.187

Scrivner, Tom (Wisconsin)
Profile: p.1826
Employment **Band 2**
Table: p.1819

Scullen, Sean M (Wisconsin)
Profile: p.1826
Employment **Up and coming**
Table: p.1819

Sczudlo, Paul (California)
Profile: p.272
Tax **Band 4**
Table: p.241

Seabaugh, William F
(Missouri)
Profile: p.1060
Corporate/M&A **Band 3**
Table: p.1043

Seabolt, Richard (California)
Profile: p.272
Insurance **Band 2**
Table: p.212

Seals, Paul (Texas)
Profile: p.1700
Environment **Band 2**
Table: p.1643

Sears, Barbara (Maryland)
Profile: p.923
Real Estate **Band 4**
Table: p.917

Seaton, Doug (Minnesota)
Profile: p.1020
Employment **Band 3**
Table: p.1008

Seay, James (Florida)
Profile: p.550
Real Estate **Band 2**
Table: p.526

Sebris, Robert (Washington)
Profile: p.1795
Employment **Band 2**
Table: p.1780

Seka, J Georg (California)
Profile: p.272
Intellectual Property **Band 4**
Table: p.216

Secrest III, Lawrence W
(District of Columbia)
Profile: p.467
Telecom, Broadcast & Satellite
Band 4
Table: p.427

Sederstrom, Charles
(Nebraska)
Profile: p.1088
Corporate/M&A **Band 3**
Table: p.1082

Sedran, Howard
(Pennsylvania)
Profile: p.1536
Antitrust **Band 3**
Table: p.1489

Seegull, Larry (Maryland)
Profile: p.924
Employment **Up and coming**
Table: p.912

Segal, Earl L
(District of Columbia)
Profile: p.467
Real Estate **Band 2**
Table: p.418

Segal, Michael (New York)
Profile: p.1319
Employee Benefits **Band 3**
Table: p.1197

Segal, Mike (Florida)
Profile: p.550
Healthcare **Band 2**
Table: p.518

Segall, Wynn H (National)
Profile: p.103
International Trade **Band 2**
Table: p.41

Segel, Alvin G (California)
Profile: p.272
Corporate/M&A **Band 5**
Table: p.197

Seide, Rochelle (New York)
Profile: p.1319
Intellectual Property **Band 3**
Table: p.1217

Seidel, Arthur (Pennsylvania)
Profile: p.1536
Intellectual Property **Band s**
Table: p.1508

Seiden, Richard (California)
Profile: p.272
Healthcare **Band 3**
Table: p.209

Seidenstricker, Paul W
(Wisconsin)
Profile: p.1826
Corporate/M&A **Band 3**
Table: p.1817

Seidman, Steven (New York)
Profile: p.1319
Corporate/M&A **Band 4**
Table: p.1189

Seiffert, James C
(Kentucky)
Profile: p.845
Corporate/M&A **Band 2**
Table: p.827

Selber Silverstein, Laurie
(Delaware)
Profile: p.357
Bankruptcy **Band 3**
Table: p.341
Chancery **Band 2**
Table: p.344

Selbo, Gregory B (North
Dakota)
Profile: p.1410

Selden, David (Arizona)
Profile: p.161
Employment **Band 2**
Table: p.148

Self, Shannon (Oklahoma)
Profile: p.1466
Corporate/M&A **Band 2**
Table: p.1459

Selig, John S (Arkansas)
Profile: p.177
Corporate/M&A **Band 1**
Table: p.168

Selinger, Jerry (Texas)
Profile: p.1700
Intellectual Property **Band 3**
Table: p.1651

Sellergren, David
(Minnesota)
Profile: p.1020
Real Estate **Band 1**
Table: p.1015

Sellers, Lawrence (Florida)
Profile: p.550
Environment **Band 1**
Table: p.516

Sellers, Randal H (Alabama)
Profile: p.125
Litigation **Band 3**
Table: p.116

Selman, Russell (Illinois)
Profile: p.751
Environment **Band 4**
Table: p.687

Seltzer, Martin S (Ohio)
Profile: p.1448
Environment **Band 2**
Table: p.1425

Selver, Paul D (New York)
Profile: p.1319
Real Estate **Band 1**
Table: p.1248

Selwyn, Mark D
(Massachusetts)
Profile: p.977
Intellectual Property **Band 3**
Table: p.948

Semple, Lloyd (Michigan)
Profile: p.1000
Corporate/M&A **Band S**
Table: p.989

Seneker, Carl (Kim)
(California)
Profile: p.272
Real Estate **Band 1**
Table: p.238

Senn, Mark (Colorado)
Profile: p.322
Real Estate **Band 2**
Table: p.313

S

Sennett, Michael (Illinois)
Profile: p.751
Antitrust Band 3
Table: p.662

Sennett, Nancy J
(Wisconsin)
Profile: p.1826
Litigation Band 3
Table: p.1821

Sensabaugh, Don
(West Virginia)
Profile: p.1810
Litigation Band 2
Table: p.1803

Sentilles III, Irwin F (Texas)
Profile: p.1700
Corporate/M&A Band 3
Table: p.1631

Serbaroli, Francis J
(New York)
Profile: p.1319
Healthcare Band 2
Table: p.1209

Serdahely, Douglas J
(Alaska)
Profile: p.144
Environment Band 3
Table: p.137
Litigation Band 3
Table: p.138

Sernau, Ronald D
(New York)
Profile: p.1319
Real Estate Band 5
Table: p.1248

Serota, Susan P (New York)
Profile: p.1320
Employee Benefits Band 1
Table: p.1197

Serotte, Neal (Maryland)
Profile: p.924
Employment Band 2
Table: p.912

Seryak, Richard J
(Michigan)
Profile: p.1000
Employment Band 3
Table: p.991

Settelmayer, Daniel K
(California)
Profile: p.272
Healthcare Band 2
Table: p.209

Setty, Nagendra (Georgia)
Profile: p.622
Intellectual Property Band 4
Table: p.596

Sexton, Robert (Alabama)
Profile: p.125
Real Estate Band 2
Table: p.119

Seyfer, Greg (Iowa)
Profile: p.814
Real Estate Band 3
Table: p.810

Seymon, Pamela S
(New York)
Profile: p.1320
Corporate/M&A Band 3
Table: p.1189

Seymour, Samuel W
(New York)
Profile: p.1320
Litigation Band 3
Table: p.1224

Sfregola, Michael F
(California)
Profile: p.272
Real Estate Band 2
Table: p.238

Shachar, Avishai (New York)
Profile: p.1320
Tax Band 2
Table: p.1255

Shackelford, Richard L
(Georgia)
Profile: p.622
Healthcare Band 1
Table: p.594

Shaft, Grant (North Dakota)
Profile: p.1410
Real Estate Band 2
Table: p.1409

Shalton, Lonnie (Missouri)
Profile: p.1060
Real Estate Band 2
Table: p.1052

Shank, Mark (Texas)
Profile: p.1700
Employment Band 3
Table: p.1634

Shanks, Patricia L
(California)
Profile: p.272
Environment Band 3
Table: p.207

**Shannon, Brendan
Linehan** (Delaware)
Profile: p.357
Bankruptcy Band 4
Table: p.341

Shannon, Kevin (Delaware)
Profile: p.357
Chancery Band 4
Table: p.344

Shanor, Stuart D
(New Mexico)
Profile: p.1164
Litigation Band 2
Table: p.1159

Shapiro, Clifford J (Illinois)
Profile: p.751
Construction Band 3
Table: p.672

Shapiro, Hal (National)
Profile: p.103
International Trade
Up and coming
Table: p.40

Shapiro, Howard (National)
Profile: p.103
Litigation Band 1
Table: p.25

Shapiro, Howard
(District of Columbia)
Profile: p.467
Litigation Band 2
Table: p.410

Shapiro, Howard
(District of Columbia)
Profile: p.467

Energy Band 3
Table: p.386

Shapiro, J Ben (Georgia)
Profile: p.622
Construction Band 1
Table: p.584

Shapiro, Jonathan (Maine)
Profile: p.901
Employment Band 2
Table: p.890

Shapiro, Keith (Illinois)
Profile: p.751
Bankruptcy Band 3
Table: p.669

Shapiro, Raymond
(Pennsylvania)
Profile: p.1537
Bankruptcy Band 1
Table: p.1494

Shapiro, Robert
(District of Columbia)
Profile: p.467
Energy Band 4
Table: p.386

Shapiro, Stephen R (Illinois)
Profile: p.751
Litigation Band 3
Table: p.700

Shapiro, Stuart (New York)
Profile: p.1320
Litigation Band 3
Table: p.1223

Shapley, Christopher
(Mississippi)
Profile: p.1035
Litigation Band 1
Table: p.1028

Sharbaugh, Charles
(Georgia)
Profile: p.622
Real Estate Band 3
Table: p.601

Sharer, Paul
(District of Columbia)
Profile: p.467
Intellectual Property Band 3
Table: p.403

Sharf, Jesse (California)
Profile: p.272
Real Estate Band 1
Table: p.238

Sharp, F DeArmond
(Nevada)
Profile: p.1103
Real Estate Band 3
Table: p.1099

Sharpe, Jeremy (Iowa)
Profile: p.814
Real Estate Band 1
Table: p.810

Sharpe, W Smith "Kris"
(Minnesota)
Profile: p.1020
Corporate/M&A Band 1
Table: p.1005

Sharrow, Regina (Indiana)
Profile: p.794
Corporate/M&A
Up and coming
Table: p.781

Shaughnessy, Kevin
(Florida)
Profile: p.550
Employment Band 2
Table: p.513

Shaw, John (Delaware)
Profile: p.357
Intellectual Property Band 3
Table: p.348

Shawe, Stephen D
(Maryland)
Profile: p.924
Employment Band 2
Table: p.912

Shay, Stephen
(Massachusetts)
Profile: p.977
Tax Band 1
Table: p.959

Shea, Daniel (Colorado)
Profile: p.322
Litigation Band 1
Table: p.311

Shea, James (Maryland)
Profile: p.924
Litigation Band 2
Table: p.914

Shea, John (Massachusetts)
Profile: p.977
Environment Band 3
Table: p.943

Shea, Kevin (Colorado)
Profile: p.322
Litigation Band 1
Table: p.311

Shearin, James T
(Connecticut)
Profile: p.337
Litigation Band 3
Table: p.331

Sheeder, Robert E (Texas)
Profile: p.1700
Employment Band 1
Table: p.1634

Sheeran, Timothy J (Ohio)
Profile: p.1448
Employment Band 3
Table: p.1422

Sheets, Mark (Tennessee)
Profile: p.1611
Real Estate Band 3
Table: p.1603

Sheffield, Jeffrey (Illinois)
Profile: p.751
Tax Band 1
Table: p.710

Sheinfeld, Myron M (Texas)
Profile: p.1700
Bankruptcy Band 4
Table: p.1627

Sheley, Raymond (Georgia)
Profile: p.622
Real Estate Band 3
Table: p.601

Sheller, John (Kentucky)
Profile: p.845
Employment Band 2
Table: p.830

Shelley, Patrick M
(Maryland)
Profile: p.924
Real Estate Band 4
Table: p.917

Shemin, Kenneth (Arkansas)
Profile: p.177
Litigation Band 1
Table: p.172

Sheneman, Margaret
(California)
Profile: p.272
Bankruptcy Band 4
Table: p.191

Shenker, Joseph C
(New York)
Profile: p.1320
Real Estate Band 1
Table: p.1248

Shepherd, Jay
(Massachusetts)
Profile: p.977
Employment Band 3
Table: p.940

Shepherd, Kevin (Maryland)
Profile: p.924
Real Estate Band 1
Table: p.917

Shepherd III, Thomas B
(Mississippi)
Profile: p.1036

Sheppard, Ben (Texas)
Profile: p. 1700
Arbitration Band 2
Table: p.33

Sheppard, William J
(Florida)
Profile: p.550
Litigation Band 2
Table: p.522

Shepro, Richard Warren
(Illinois)
Profile: p.751
Corporate/M&A Band 2
Table: p.675
Insurance Band 2
Table: p.692

Sher, Leopold (Louisiana)
Profile: p.876
Real Estate Band 1
Table: p.867

Sher, Stanley O. (National)
Profile: p.103
Shipping Band 1
Table: p.71

Sherck, Timothy C (Illinois)
Profile: p.752
Tax Band 2
Table: p.710

Sheridan, Robert E
(Montana)
Profile: p.1081
Litigation Band 2
Table: p.1075

Sherk, Kenneth J (Arizona)
Profile: p.162
Litigation Band 2
Table: p.152

Sherman, Craig E
(Washington)
Profile: p.1795

Corporate/M&A Band 3
Table: p.1778

Sherman, Morris
(Minnesota)
Profile: p.1020
Corporate/M&A Band 2
Table: p.1005

Sherman, Robert L
(New York)
Profile: p.1320
Intellectual Property Band 3
Table: p.1217

Sherman, Steven E
(California)
Profile: p.272
Banking & Finance Band 3
Table: p.187

Shernoff, William M
(California)
Profile: p.272
Insurance Band 2
Table: p.212

Sherrard III, Thomas J
(Tennessee)
Profile: p.1611
Corporate/M&A Band 3
Table: p.1594

Shevnock, Colleen M
(Michigan)
Profile: p.1000
Banking & Finance Band 2
Table: p.987

Shidlofsky, Lee H (Texas)
Profile: p.1700
Insurance Up and coming
Table: p.1648

Shiekman, Laurence Z
(Pennsylvania)
Profile: p.1537
Antitrust Band 2
Table: p.1489

Shield, William (Michigan)
Profile: p.1000
Banking & Finance Band 1
Table: p.987

Shiff, Adam L (New York)
Profile: p.1320
Bankruptcy Up and coming
Table: p.1179

Shim, Paul J (New York)
Profile: p.1320
Corporate/M&A Band 4
Table: p.1189

Shimshak, Stephen (New York)
Profile: p.1320
Bankruptcy Band 3
Table: p.1179

Shinay, Richard (Maine)
Profile: p.901
Real Estate Band 3
Table: p.895

Shipley, Ann (New York)
Profile: p.1320
Real Estate Band 4
Table: p.1248

Shipley III, Benjamin H
(Arkansas)
Profile: p.177

Shirley, James (New York)
Profile: p.103
Shipping Band 4
Table: p.67

Shivel Jr, Charles (Kentucky)
Profile: p.846
Litigation Band 4
Table: p.835

Shively, John D (Colorado)
Profile: p.322

Shlachter, Robert A
(Oregon)
Profile: p.1484
Litigation Band 3
Table: p.1477

Shockley, Steven C
(Indiana)
Profile: p.794
Litigation Band 2
Table: p.785

Shockro, Michael J
(California)
Profile: p. 272
Business Process
Outsourcing: National Band 3
Table: p.10
IT Outsourcing Band 2
Table: p.221

Shoemaker, Andrew
(Colorado)
Profile: p.322
Litigation Band 1
Table: p.311

Shoemaker Jr, James M
(South Carolina)
Profile: p.1582
Corporate/M&A Band 2
Table: p.1572

Shoemate, Steven R
(New York)
Profile: p.1320
Corporate/M&A
Up and coming
Table: p.1189

Shohat, Edward R (Florida)
Profile: p.550
Litigation Band 2
Table: p.522

Shoneman, Charles H
(District of Columbia)
Profile: p.467
Energy Band 4
Table: p.382

Shor, Michael T (National)
Profile: p.104
International Trade Band 4
Table: p.40

Shors, John (Iowa)
Profile: p.814
Corporate/M&A Band 3
Table: p.802

Short, Andrew (New York)
Profile: p.1321
Tax Band 4
Table: p.1255

Short, Barry (Missouri)
Profile: p.1060
Litigation Band 1
Table: p.1049
Litigation Band 2
Table: p.1049

Short Jr, Herbert J (Georgia)
Profile: p.622
Energy Band 2
Table: p.592

Short Jr, William B (Texas)
Profile: p.1700
Construction Band 3
Table: p.1629

Shortlidge, Neil (Kansas)
Profile: p.824
Real Estate Band 3
Table: p.821

Shortz, Richard (California)
Profile: p.272
Projects Band 2
Table: p.236

Shoss, Cynthia R (New York)
Profile: p.1321
Insurance Band 3
Table: p.1213

Showalter, Barton E (Texas)
Profile: p.1700
Intellectual Property Band 3
Table: p.1651

Shoyer, Andrew W
(National)
Profile: p.104
International Trade Band 3
Table: p.40

Shriner Jr, Thomas L
(Wisconsin)
Profile: p.1826
Litigation Band 1
Table: p.1821

Shteamer, Michael B
(Missouri)
Profile: p.1060
Real Estate Band 2
Table: p.1052

Shubin, John (Florida)
Profile: p.550
Real Estate Band 3
Table: p.528

Shugrue, John (Illinois)
Profile: p.752
Insurance Band 2
Table: p.695

Shuker, R Scott (Florida)
Profile: p.550
Bankruptcy Band 3
Table: p.503

Shulman, Larry R (Michigan)
Profile: p.1000
Banking & Finance Band 1
Table: p.987

Shulman, Lawrence A
(Maryland)
Profile: p.924
Real Estate Band 1
Table: p.917

Shulman, Robert
(District of Columbia)
Profile: p.467
Insurance Band 2
Table: p.402

Shulman, Ron (California)
Profile: p.272
Intellectual Property Band 3
Table: p.216

Shulruff, Stuart P (Illinois)
Profile: p.752
Banking & Finance Band 2
Table: p.665

Shults, Robert (Arkansas)
Profile: p.177
Litigation Band 1
Table: p.172

Shultz, Jack L (Nebraska)
Profile: p.1088
Employment Band 3
Table: p.1084

Shultz, Jeff
(South Dakota)
Profile: p.1593
Employment Band 2
Table: p.1589

Shumadine, Conrad
(Virginia)
Profile: p.1772
Litigation Band 2
Table: p.1763

Shuman, Robert
(West Virginia)
Profile: p.1810

Shuman, Stephen
(West Virginia)
Profile: p.1810
Real Estate Band 2
Table: p.1806

Shumate, Roger (Wyoming)
Profile: p.1839
Employment Band 2
Table: p.1833

Shuster, Michael (New York)
Profile: p.1321
Litigation Band 3
Table: p.1222

Shutran, Richard (New York)
Profile: p. 1321
Projects Band 1
Table: p.52
Projects Band 1
Table: p.1244

Sicalides , Barbara T
(Pennsylvania)
Profile: p.1537
Antitrust Band 3
Table: p.1489

Sicilian, James (Connecticut)
Profile: p.337
Litigation Band 2
Table: p.331

Sickle, David B (Illinois)
Profile: p.752
Real Estate Band 4
Table: p.706

Sicular, David (New York)
Profile: p.1321
Tax Band 4
Table: p.1255

Sidman, Robert (Ohio)
Profile: p.1448
Bankruptcy Band 2
Table: p.1414

Siebert, W Bernie
(Colorado)
Profile: p.322
Employment Band 3
Table: p.306

Siefert, Richard C
(Washington)
Profile: p.1795
Intellectual Property Band 2
Table: p.1784
Litigation Band 3
Table: p.1786

Siegal, Bradley (Alabama)
Profile: p.125
Real Estate Band 3
Table: p.119

Siegal, Don (Alabama)
Profile: p.125
Real Estate Band 2
Table: p.119

Siegel, Bradd N (Ohio)
Profile: p.1448
Employment Band 1
Table: p.1422

Siegel, David (California)
Profile: p.272
Litigation Band 4
Table: p.224

Siegel, Nathan E
(District of Columbia)
Profile: p.467
Media & Entertainment Band 3
Table: p.413

Siegel, Robert (California)
Profile: p.273
Employment Band 4
Table: p.202

Siegel, Stephen H (Florida)
Profile: p.550
Healthcare Band 2
Table: p.518

Siegel, Steven (Colorado)
Profile: p.322
Corporate/M&A Band 2
Table: p.303

Siegfried, Steven (Florida)
Profile: p.550
Construction Band 1
Table: p.507

Siemers, John C (Alaska)
Profile: p.144
Bankruptcy Band 1
Table: p.133

Siemon, Charles L (Florida)
Profile: p.550
Real Estate Band S
Table: p.528

Siffert, John S (New York)
Profile: p.1321
Litigation Band 3
Table: p.1224

Sigel, John (Massachusetts)
Profile: p.977
Bankruptcy Band 2
Table: p.935

Sikora, Clifford S
(District of Columbia)
Profile: p.467
Energy Band 4
Table: p.386

Silberberg, Marc L
(New York)
Profile: p.1321
Tax Band 4
Table: p.1255

S

Silberg, Jay
(District of Columbia)
Profile: p.467
Energy Band 1
Table: p.390

Silberman, Alan (Illinois)
Profile: p.752
Antitrust Band 2
Table: p.662

Silberstein, Rebecca F
(New York)
Profile: p.1321
Private Equity Band 3
Table: p.1241

Silbert, Earl
(District of Columbia)
Profile: p.468
Litigation Band 1
Table: p.410

Siler Jr, W Thomas
(Mississippi)
Profile: p.1036
Employment Band 1
Table: p.1026

Silliman, (Georgia)
Profile: p.623
Environment Band 3
Table: p.593

Silver, Jeffrey (Nevada)
Profile: p.1103
Gaming & Licensing Band 2
Table: p.1094

Silver, Michael J (Maryland)
Profile: p.924
Corporate/M&A Band 1
Table: p.909

Silverman, Eric (New York)
Profile: p.1321
Projects Band 3
Table: p.1244

Silverman, Lawrence
(Florida)
Profile: p.550
Antitrust Band 2
Table: p.498

Silverman, Leslie N
(National)
Profile: p.104
Capital Markets Band 2
Table: p.14

Silverman, Mark
(District of Columbia)
Profile: p.468
Tax Band 2
Table: p.422

Silverstein, Bruce L
(Delaware)
Profile: p.357
Chancery Band 3
Table: p.344

Silvestri, Stephen
(Maryland)
Profile: p.924
Employment Band 1
Table: p.912

Silvestri Jr, Frank J
(Connecticut)
Profile: p.337
Litigation Band 3
Table: p.331

Simkin, Steven (New York)
Profile: p.1321
Real Estate Band 2
Table: p.1248

Simmons, Richard
(California)
Profile: p.273
Employment Band 4
Table: p.202

Simmons, Sherwin (Florida)
Profile: p.550
Tax Band s
Table: p.531

Simms, Marsha E
(New York)
Profile: p.1321
Banking & Finance Band 4
Table: p.1174

Simon, Marc (Arizona)
Profile: p.162
Real Estate Band 2
Table: p.155

Simon, Mark C (Illinois)
Profile: p.752
Real Estate Band 3
Table: p.706

Simon, Michael H (Oregon)
Profile: p.1484
Litigation Band 3
Table: p.1477

Simons, Joseph
(District of Columbia)
Profile: p.468
Antitrust Band 5
Table: p.367

Simons, Laird (California)
Profile: p.273
Corporate/M&A Band 5
Table: p.197

Simons, Susan Brunick
(South Dakota)
Profile: p.1593
Employment Band 1
Table: p.1589

Simonson, James S
(Minnesota)
Profile: p.1020
Litigation Band 2
Table: p.1011

Simpler, Gary (Maryland)
Profile: p.924
Employment Band 3
Table: p.912

Simpson, James (Michigan)
Profile: p.1000
Real Estate Band 3
Table: p.996

Simpson, Patrick (Oregon)
Profile: p.1484
Corporate/M&A Band 2
Table: p.1471

Simpson, Reagan (Texas)
Profile: p.1700
Litigation Band 1
Table: p.1656

Simpson, Robert R
(Connecticut)
Profile: p.338
Litigation Up and coming
Table: p.331

Sims, Charles (New York)
Profile: p.1321
Media & Entertainment Band 2
Table: p.1232

Sims, Hunter (Virginia)
Profile: p.1772
Litigation Band 2
Table: p.1763

Sims, Joe
(District of Columbia)
Profile: p.468
Antitrust Band 1
Table: p.367

Sims, Luke E (Wisconsin)
Profile: p.1826
Corporate/M&A Band 2
Table: p.1817

Sims, Roger (Florida)
Profile: p.550
Environment Band 2
Table: p.516

Sinak, David (Texas)
Profile: p.1701
Tax Band 4
Table: p.1665

Sinatra, Geraldine A
(Pennsylvania)
Profile: p.1537
Corporate/M&A
Up and coming
Table: p.1497

Sinclair, Brad (North Dakota)
Profile: p.1410
Litigation Band 2
Table: p.1406

Sinclair, J Walter (Idaho)
Profile: p.660
Litigation Band 2
Table: p.657

Sinel, Norman
(District of Columbia)
Profile: p.468
Telecom, Broadcast & Satellite
Band 4
Table: p.427

Singer, Alan (Pennsylvania)
Profile: p.1537
Corporate/M&A Band 2
Table: p.1497

Singer, Andrew (California,
New York & National)
Profile: p. 1321
Projects Band 1
Table: p.52
Table: p.236
Table: p.1244

Singer, Eric L (Illinois)
Profile: p.752
Construction Band 3
Table: p.672

Singer, Fern (Alabama)
Profile: p.125
Employment Band 3
Table: p.113

Singer, Gary (California)
Profile: p.273
Corporate/M&A Band 5
Table: p.197

Singer, Leonard (New York)
Profile: p.1321
Energy Band 1

Table: p.1204

Singer, Louis (New York)
Profile: p.1321
Private Equity Band 3
Table: p.1241

Singer, Martin D (California)
Profile: p.273
Media & Entertainment Band 2
Table: p.230

Singer, Paul (Pennsylvania)
Profile: p.1537
Bankruptcy Band 1
Table: p.1494

Singer, Robert A (North
Carolina)
Profile: p.1398
Corporate/M&A Band 3
Table: p.1384

Singer, Steven
(Massachusetts)
Profile: p.977
Corporate/M&A Band 1
Table: p.937

Singer, Stuart (Florida)
Profile: p.550
Antitrust Band 2
Table: p.498

Singerman, Paul (Florida)
Profile: p.550
Bankruptcy ✪
Table: p.503

Singleton, Sarah M (New
Mexico)
Profile: p.1164
Environment Band 1
Table: p.1158

Siniscalco, Gary (California)
Profile: p.273
Employment Band 2
Table: p.202

Sink, Charles (California)
Profile: p.273
Construction Band 1
Table: p.194

Sinkfield, Richard H
(Georgia)
Profile: p.623
Litigation Band 1
Table: p.598

Sipe Jr. Samuel (National)
Profile: p.104
Transport Band 1
Table: p.62

Sipiora, David E (Colorado)
Profile: p.322
Intellectual Property Band 2
Table: p.309

Sirkin, Joel (Massachusetts)
Profile: p.977
Real Estate Band 2
Table: p.956

Sirkin, Michael (New York)
Profile: p.1322
Employee Benefits Band 2
Table: p.1197

Siske, Roger C (Illinois)
Profile: p.752
Employee Benefits Band 1
Table: p.681

Sit, Po (New York)
Profile: p.1322
Tax Band 2
Table: p.1256

Sitarchuk, Eric W
(Pennsylvania)
Profile: p.1537
Litigation Band 3
Table: p.1511

Sitton, Larry (North Carolina)
Profile: p.1398
Antitrust Band 1
Table: p.1390
Litigation Band 2
Table: p.1390

Skeffington, James
(Rhode Island)
Profile: p.1570
Corporate/M&A Band 2
Table: p.1564

Skelly, Paul
(District of Columbia)
Profile: p.468
Employment Band 3
Table: p.380

Skerritt, Daniel (Oregon)
Profile: p.1484
Litigation Band 1
Table: p.1477

Skilton, John (Wisconsin)
Profile: p.1826
Litigation Band 2
Table: p.1821

Skindrud, Michael
(Wisconsin)
Profile: p.1826
Corporate/M&A Band 2
Table: p.1817

Skinner, Honey J (Illinois)
Profile: p.752
Healthcare Band 3
Table: p.690

Skinner, Shannon
(Washington)
Profile: p.1795
Real Estate Band 3
Table: p.1788

Skinner, William P
(District of Columbia)
Profile: p.468
Insurance Band 2
Table: p.402

Sklar, Daniel W
(New Hampshire)
Profile: p.1118
Corporate/M&A Band 3
Table: p.1107

Sklar, Stanley P (Illinois)
Profile: p.752
Construction Band 2
Table: p.672

Sklaroff, Michael
(Pennsylvania)
Profile: p.1537
Real Estate Band 1
Table: p.1516
Real Estate Band 1
Table: p.1516

Sklarsky, Charles (Illinois)
Profile: p.752
Litigation Band 4
Table: p.700

Skolnick, Holly (Florida)
Profile: p.550
Litigation Band 1
Table: p.522

Slade, Lynn H (New Mexico)
Profile: p.1164
Environment Band 1
Table: p.1158
Native Law Band 1
Table: p.1159

Slater, James (Florida)
Profile: p.551
Real Estate Band 3
Table: p.526

Slater, Paul (Illinois)
Profile: p.752
Antitrust Band 3
Table: p.662

Slater, Thomas (Virginia)
Profile: p.1772
Litigation Band 1
Table: p.1763

Slater, Valerie A (National)
Profile: p.104
International Trade Band 3
Table: p.40

Slaughter Jr, Harrison T
(Florida)
Profile: p.551
Litigation Band 2
Table: p.522

Slavich, John (Texas)
Profile: p.1701
Environment Band 3
Table: p.1643

Sleeth, Tim E (Florida)
Profile: p.551
Environment Band 3
Table: p.516

Slonaker, Norman (National)
Profile: p.104
Capital Markets Band 3
Table: p.14

Slone, Daniel K (Virginia)
Profile: p.1772
Environment Band 2
Table: p.1757

Slotnick, Barry I (New York)
Profile: p.1322
Media & Entertainment Band 3
Table: p.1232

Slusky, Jerry (Nebraska)
Profile: p.1088
Real Estate Band 2
Table: p.1086

Slusser, William C (Texas)
Profile: p.1701
Intellectual Property Band 1
Table: p.1651

Small, Andrew (Illinois)
Profile: p.752
Real Estate Band 3
Table: p.706

Small, Jeffrey (National)
Profile: p.104
Capital Markets Band 2
Table: p.14

Small, John H (Delaware)
Profile: p.357
Corporate/M&A Band 3

Table: p.346

Small, Michael
(District of Columbia)
Profile: p.468
Energy Band 3
Table: p.386

Smallwood, Mary F
(Florida)
Profile: p.551
Environment Band 1
Table: p.516

Smedinghoff, Thomas J
(Illinois)
Profile: p.753
Technology Band 2
Table: p.713

Smilan, Laurie B (Virginia)
Profile: p.1772
Litigation Band 3
Table: p.1763

Smit, Robert (National)
Profile: p.104
Arbitration Band
Table: p.33
Arbitration Band 2
Table: p.33

Smith, Alison (Texas)
Profile: p.1701
Antitrust Band 3
Table: p.1622

Smith, Bradley Y (New York)
Profile: p.1322
Banking & Finance Band 1
Table: p.1174

Smith, Brian D (California)
Profile: p.273
Real Estate Band 2
Table: p.238

Smith, Brooks (Virginia)
Profile: p.1772
Environment Up and coming
Table: p.1757

Smith, Chris M (New York)
Profile: p.1322
Real Estate Band 2
Table: p.1248

Smith, David (Alabama)
Profile: p.125
Employment Band 3
Table: p.113

Smith, David S (Virginia)
Profile: p.1773
Employment Band 3
Table: p.1755

Smith, Douglas
(District of Columbia)
Profile: p.468
Energy Band 5
Table: p.386

Smith, Douglas D
(California)
Profile: p.273
Corporate/M&A Band 5
Table: p.197

Smith, Edwin
(Massachusetts)
Profile: p.977
Banking & Finance Band 1
Table: p.932

Smith, Felton (Alabama)
Profile: p.125
Real Estate Band 2
Table: p.119

Smith, George Anthony
(Georgia)
Profile: p.623
Construction Band 2
Table: p.584

Smith, Gordon (Georgia)
Profile: p.623
Litigation Band 3
Table: p.598

Smith, Gregory (Nevada)
Profile: p.1103
Employment Band 2
Table: p.1091

Smith, Gregory C
(California)
Profile: p.273
Corporate/M&A Band 3
Table: p.197

Smith, James (Georgia)
Profile: p.623
Corporate/M&A Band 4
Table: p.587

Smith, James E (Texas)
Profile: p.1701
Litigation Band 1
Table: p.1643

Smith, Janet Hugie (Utah)
Profile: p.1738
Employment Band 1
Table: p.1730

Smith, Jason (National)
Profile: p.105
Capital Markets
Up and coming
Table: p.19

Smith, Jeffrey (New York)
Profile: p.1322
Environment Band 1
Table: p.1206

Smith, Jeffrey Q (New York)
Profile: p.1322
Litigation Band 3
Table: p.1223

Smith, Jerry (Georgia)
Profile: p.623
Tax Band 4
Table: p.603

Smith, Joseph A (New York)
Profile: p.1322
Private Equity Band 3
Table: p.1241

Smith, Julious (Virginia)
Profile: p.1773
Corporate/M&A Band 2
Table: p.1752

Smith, Kevin (Kentucky)
Profile: p.846
Employment Band 2
Table: p.830

Smith, Laura (Arkansas)
Profile: p.177
Litigation Band 1
Table: p.172

Smith, Mark C (National)
Profile: p.105
Capital Markets Band 4

Table: p.14

Smith, Michael (Virginia)
Profile: p.1773
Litigation Band 1
Table: p.1763

Smith, Nathan H (Maine)
Profile: p.901
Real Estate Band 2
Table: p.895

Smith, Neil (California)
Profile: p.273
Intellectual Property Band 4
Table: p.216

Smith, Paul
(District of Columbia)
Profile: p.468
Litigation Band 1
Table: p.408
Media & Entertainment Band 1
Table: p.413

Smith, Paul T (California)
Profile: p.273
Healthcare Band 3
Table: p.209

Smith, Philip
(Massachusetts)
Profile: p.977
Banking & Finance Band 2
Table: p.932

Smith, Robert H (Florida)
Profile: p.551
Hotels and Resorts Band 1
Table: p.526

Smith, Roger
(District of Columbia)
Profile: p.468
Energy Band 3
Table: p.386

Smith, Sean (North Dakota)
Profile: p.1410
Corporate/M&A Band 1
Table: p.1403

Smith, Taylor (Mississippi)
Profile: p.1036
Employment Band 1
Table: p.1026

Smith, Ted (Ohio)
Profile: p.1448
Real Estate Band 4
Table: p.1434

Smith, Tefft W
(District of Columbia)
Profile: p.469
Antitrust Band
Table: p.367
Antitrust Band 5
Table: p.367

Smith, Wim Randolph
(District of Columbia)
Profile: p.469
Antitrust Band 4
Table: p.367

Smith III, Frank G (Georgia)
Profile: p.623
Intellectual Property Band 4
Table: p.596

Smith III, James (Kentucky)
Profile: p.846
Employment Band 1
Table: p.830

Smith III, William C
(Mississippi)
Profile: p.1036
Real Estate Band 2
Table: p.1031

Smith Jr, Robert (Jay) W
(Maryland)
Profile: p.924
Corporate/M&A ✪
Table: p.909

Smith, Jr, Turner T
(District of Columbia)
Profile: p.469
Environment Band 3
Table: p.392

Smits, Anthony J
(Connecticut)
Profile: p.338
Corporate/M&A
Up and coming
Table: p.327

Smoak, Lewis T
(South Carolina)
Profile: p.1582
Employment Band 3
Table: p.1574

Smolen, Lee M (Illinois)
Profile: p.753
Real Estate Band 3
Table: p.706

Smoyer, Divonne
(District of Columbia)
Profile: p.469
Insurance Band 3
Table: p.402

Smulian, Andrew (Florida)
Profile: p.551
Real Estate Band 2
Table: p.526

Smutny, Abby Cohen
(National)
Profile: p.105
Arbitration Band 2
Table: p.33

Smythe, Marianne
(District of Columbia)
Profile: p.469
Investment Management Band 1
Table: p.406

Smythe, Susan
(South Carolina)
Profile: p.1582
Real Estate Band 3
Table: p.1577

Sneed, Spencer (Alaska)
Profile: p.144
Bankruptcy Band 1
Table: p.133
Litigation Band 2
Table: p.138

Sneed, William M (Illinois)
Profile: p.753
Insurance Band 2
Table: p.694

Sneirson, Marilyn
(New Jersey)
Profile: p.1145
Employment Band 3
Table: p.1126

S

Snell, Virginia (Kentucky)
Profile: p.846
Litigation Band 3
Table: p.835

Snider, Jerry W (Minnesota)
Profile: p.1020
Litigation Band 1
Table: p.1011

Snow, Ronald
(New Hampshire)
Profile: p.1119
Litigation ✪
Table: p.1111
Litigation Band 1
Table: p.1111

Snow, Stephen E
(Rhode Island)
Profile: p.1570
Litigation Band 1
Table: p.1567

Snyder, Charles (Louisiana)
Profile: p.876
Corporate/M&A Band 4
Table: p.859

Snyder, David R (California)
Profile: p.273
Corporate/M&A Band 5
Table: p.197

Snyder, Jeffrey L (National)
Profile: p.105
International Trade Band 1
Table: p.41

Snyder, Sheryl (Kentucky)
Profile: p.846
Litigation Band 2
Table: p.835

Snyder, Stephen J
(Minnesota)
Profile: p.1020
Employment Band 3
Table: p.1008

Sobel, Gerald (New York)
Profile: p.1322
Intellectual Property Band 2
Table: p.1217

Sogn, Jon C
(South Dakota)
Profile: p.1593
Employment Band 2
Table: p.1589

Sohn, Michael N (DC)
Profile: p.469
Antitrust Band 2
Table: p.367

Solada, Mary (Indiana)
Profile: p.794
Real Estate Band 2
Table: p.788

Sollner, Richard (Florida)
Profile: p.551
Real Estate Band 3
Table: p.526

Solomon, Andrew P (New
York)
Profile: p.1322
Tax Band 2
Table: p.1255

Solomon, Randall (Ohio)
Profile: p.1448
Litigation Band 3
Table: p.1431

Solovy, Jerold S (Illinois)
Profile: p.753
Litigation Band 3
Table: p.700

Solow, Alan P (Illinois)
Profile: p.753
Bankruptcy Band 3
Table: p.669

Solow, Michael (Illinois)
Profile: p.753
Bankruptcy Band 2
Table: p.669

Solt, Christine G
(Massachusetts)
Profile: p.977
Healthcare Band 2
Table: p.946

Solum, Richard (Minnesota)
Profile: p.1020
Litigation Band 2
Table: p.1011

Somers, George W
(Indiana)
Profile: p.794
Real Estate Band 1
Table: p.788

Somerstein, Barry (Florida)
Profile: p.551
Real Estate Band 1
Table: p.526

Sommer, Dean (New York)
Profile: p.1323
Environment Band 2
Table: p.1205

Sommerhauser, Peter
(Wisconsin)
Profile: p.1826
Corporate/M&A Band 1
Table: p.1817

Sonberg, Steven (Florida)
Profile: p.551
Corporate/M&A Band 2
Table: p.509

Sonnenfeld, Marc
(Pennsylvania)
Profile: p.1538
Litigation Band 2
Table: p.1511

Sonsini, Larry W (California)
Profile: p.273
Corporate/M&A ✪
Table: p.197

Sopher, Edward (New York)
Profile: p.1323
Private Equity Band 3
Table: p.1241

Sorensen, Harvey (Kansas)
Profile: p.824
Corporate/M&A Band 1
Table: p.816

Sorensen, Sharp (Illinois)
Profile: p.753
Tax Band 3
Table: p.710

Sorenson, Derek L (Arizona)
Profile: p.162
Real Estate Band 4
Table: p.154

Soriano, Robert (Florida)
Profile: p.551
Bankruptcy Band 2
Table: p.503

Sorin, David (New Jersey)
Profile: p.1145
Corporate/M&A Band 1
Table: p.1123

Sorin, Robert J (New York)
Profile: p.1323
Real Estate Band 5
Table: p.1248

Sorkin, David (New York)
Profile: p.1323
Corporate/M&A Band 4
Table: p.1189

Sorondo, Rodolfo (Florida)
Profile: p.551
Litigation Band 1
Table: p.525

Sosland, Martin (Texas)
Profile: p.1701
Bankruptcy Band 1
Table: p.1627

Sosnick, Fredric (New York)
Profile: p.1323
Bankruptcy Band 4
Table: p.1179

Sostek, Bruce (Texas)
Profile: p.1701
Intellectual Property Band 3
Table: p.1651

Soto, Edward (Florida)
Profile: p.551
Litigation Band 3
Table: p.521

Sottile, James
(District of Columbia)
Profile: p.469
Insurance Band 2
Table: p.400

Soubly, Diane (Michigan)
Profile: p.1000
Employment Band 3
Table: p.991

Soussloff, Andrew D
(National)
Profile: p.105
Capital Markets Band 4
Table: p.14

Southworth II, Louis S
(West Virginia)
Profile: p.1810
Corporate/M&A Band 1
Table: p.1798
Corporate/M&A Band 1
Table: p.1798

Sowell, Thornwell F (South
Carolina)
Profile: p.1582
Litigation Band 2
Table: p.1576

Sozio, Steven (Ohio)
Profile: p.1448
Litigation Band 1
Table: p.1432

Spaan, Michael (Alaska)
Profile: p.144
Litigation Band 2
Table: p.138

Spaanstra, James R
(Colorado)
Profile: p.322
Environment Band 1
Table: p.307

Spak, Gregory J (National)
Profile: p.105
International Trade Band 5
Table: p.40

Spak, Walter J (National)
Profile: p.105
International Trade Band 3
Table: p.40

Spalding, William (Georgia)
Profile: p.623
Corporate/M&A Band 3
Table: p.587

Spangler, Nancy A (Virginia)
Profile: p.1773
Corporate/M&A Band 4
Table: p.1752

Spangler III, John I
(Georgia)
Profile: p.623
Construction Band 1
Table: p.584

Sparkman, Jon B
(New Hampshire)
Profile: p.1119

Sparks, Stephen S
(Missouri)
Profile: p.1060
Real Estate Band 2
Table: p.1052

Sparks III, A Gilchrist
(Delaware)
Profile: p.357
Chancery Band 1
Table: p.344
Corporate/M&A Band 2
Table: p.346

Sparks Jr, Robert R
(Virginia)
Profile: p.1773
Employment Band 3
Table: p.1755

Spartin, Debbie B
(District of Columbia)
Profile: p.469
Real Estate Band 3
Table: p.418

Spatt, Robert E (New York)
Profile: p.1323
Corporate/M&A Band 2
Table: p.1189

Spearman, Robert (North
Carolina)
Profile: p.1398

Spears, Berry (Texas)
Profile: p.1701
Bankruptcy Band 3
Table: p.1627

Spector, Arthur (Florida)
Profile: p.551
Bankruptcy Band 3
Table: p.503

Spector, Barry
(District of Columbia)
Profile: p.469
Energy Band 3
Table: p.386

Spector, Brian F (Florida)
Profile: p.551
Litigation Band 3
Table: p.521

Spector, David (Illinois)
Profile: p.753
Insurance Band 1
Table: p.694

Spector, Phillip
(District of Columbia)
Profile: p.469
Telecom, Broadcast & Satellite
Band 2
Table: p.427

Spencer, Bob (Louisiana)
Profile: p.876
Employment Band 3
Table: p.861

Spencer, Steven D
(National)
Profile: p.105
Litigation Band 2
Table: p.25

Sperling, Allan G (National)
Profile: p.105
Capital Markets Band 2
Table: p.14

Sperling, Robert (Illinois)
Profile: p.753
Litigation Band 3
Table: p.700

Speth II, Charles T (South
Carolina)
Profile: p.1582
Employment Band 1
Table: p.1574

Spiegel, John (California)
Profile: p.273
Litigation Band 2
Table: p.224

Spielberg, David (California)
Profile: p.273
Projects Band 2
Table: p.236

Spink, James W (Vermont)
Profile: p.1749
Litigation Band 3
Table: p.1746

Spink, Michael (Idaho)
Profile: p.660
Real Estate Band 2
Table: p.658

Spivak, Mark
(District of Columbia)
Profile: p.469
Projects Band 3
Table: p.415

Spivey, James K (Texas)
Profile: p.1701
Antitrust Band 3
Table: p.1622

Spivey III, John William
(Arkansas)
Profile: p.177
Real Estate Band 2
Table: p.174

Spradling, T Scott
(Oklahoma)
Profile: p.1466
Real Estate Band 1
Table: p.1464

KEY TO RANKINGS: ✪ = STAR INDIVIDUAL   S = SENIOR STATESMAN

Sprague, Richard
(Pennsylvania)
Profile: p.1538
Litigation **Band** 2
Table: p.1512

Spraker, Gary (Alaska)
Profile: p.144
Bankruptcy **Band** 2
Table: p.133

Spratling, Gary (California)
Profile: p.273
Antitrust **Band** 1
Table: p.184

Sprayregen, James HM
(Illinois)
Profile: p.754
Bankruptcy **Band** 1
Table: p.669

Springer, Claudia
(Pennsylvania)
Profile: p.1538
Bankruptcy **Band** 2
Table: p.1494

Springer, Felix (Connecticut)
Profile: p.338
Employment **Band** 1
Table: p.329

Squires III, William R
(Washington)
Profile: p.1795
Litigation **Band** 3
Table: p.1786

Squyres, Newal (Idaho)
Profile: p.660
Litigation **Band** 2
Table: p.657

Srebnick, Howard M
(Florida)
Profile: p.551
Litigation **Band** 2
Table: p.522

Sroufe, Evelyn Cruz
(Washington)
Profile: p.1795
Corporate/M&A **Band** 2
Table: p.1778

St Clair, Jay D (Alabama)
Profile: p.125
Employment **Band** 3
Table: p.113

St Peter, Gary (Rhode
Island)
Profile: p.1570
Employment **Band** 2
Table: p.1565

Stabler, Wendie C
(Delaware)
Profile: p.357
Real Estate **Band** 1
Table: p.350

Stack Jr, Stephen A
(Pennsylvania)
Profile: p.1538
Antitrust **Band** 3
Table: p.1489

Stacy, David (Colorado)
Profile: p.322
Employment **Band** 3
Table: p.306

Staffaroni, Robert J
(New York)
Profile: p.1323
Tax **Band** 3
Table: p.1255

Stage, Jon (Florida)
Profile: p.551
Employment **Band** 4
Table: p.513

Stageberg, Roger
(Minnesota)
Profile: p.1020
Corporate/M&A **Band** 3
Table: p.1005

Stahl, David M (Illinois)
Profile: p.754
Energy **Band** 3
Table: p.685

Stahl, Thomas (Missouri)
Profile: p.1060
Corporate/M&A **Band** 2
Table: p.1043

Stair, Kent (Georgia)
Profile: p.623
Construction **Band** 2
Table: p.584

Stallings, John (Kansas)
Profile: p.824
Real Estate **Band** 2
Table: p.821

Stamas, George
(District of Columbia)
Profile: p.469
Corporate/Commercial **Band** 2
Table: p.376

Stamelman, Andrew J
(New Jersey)
Profile: p.1145
Corporate/M&A **Band** 3
Table: p.1123

Stamp, Vincent B (Ohio)
Profile: p.1448
Environment **Band** 3
Table: p.1425

Stanchfield, Mike
(Minnesota)
Profile: p.1020
Corporate/M&A
Up and coming
Table: p.1005

Standish, Daniel J
(District of Columbia)
Profile: p.469
Insurance **Band** 2
Table: p.400

Stanford, Douglas (Florida)
Profile: p.551
Real Estate **Band** 3
Table: p.526

Stanley, Douglas (Kansas)
Profile: p.824
Employment **Band** 1
Table: p.818

Stanley, Hugh (Ohio)
Profile: p.1449
Litigation **Band** 4
Table: p.1431

Stanley, James T (Alaska)
Profile: p.144
Real Estate **Band** 2
Table: p.141

Stanley, Robert K (Indiana)
Profile: p.794
Litigation **Band** 2
Table: p.785

Stanton, Patrick M (New
Jersey)
Profile: p.1145
Employment **Band** 1
Table: p.1126

Stanton, Roger (Missouri)
Profile: p.1060
Litigation **Band** 2
Table: p.1049

Stanton, W Clark
(California)
Profile: p.274
Healthcare **Band** 3
Table: p.209

Stapleton, Benjamin F
(New York)
Profile: p.1323
Corporate/M&A **Band** 2
Table: p.1189

Stapleton, James F
(Connecticut)
Profile: p.338
Litigation **Band** S
Table: p.331

Starer, Brian (New York)
Profile: p.105
Shipping **Band** 4
Table: p.67

Stark, Stephen (Kansas)
Profile: p.824
Real Estate **Band** 2
Table: p.821

Starnes, Stancil (Alabama)
Profile: p.125
Litigation **Band** 1
Table: p.116

Starr, Judson
(District of Columbia)
Profile: p.469
Environment **Band** 2
Table: p.392

Starr, Kenneth W
(California)
Profile: p.470
Litigation **Band** S
Table: p.408

Starr, Michael (New York)
Profile: p.1323
Employment **Band** 3
Table: p.1200

Stearns, Eugene (Florida)
Profile: p.551
Litigation **Band** 2
Table: p.521

Steeg, Robert M (Louisiana)
Profile: p.876
Real Estate **Band** 1
Table: p.867

Steel, John M (Washington)
Profile: p.1795
Corporate/M&A **Band** 1
Table: p.1778

Steel, Michael J (California)
Profile: p.274
Environment **Band** 3
Table: p.207

Steenrod, Ralston W
(Kentucky)
Profile: p.846
Corporate/M&A **Band** 3
Table: p.827

Stefani, Randall (Iowa)
Profile: p.814
Litigation **Band** 2
Table: p.807

Stein, Grant T (Georgia)
Profile: p.623
Bankruptcy **Band** 1
Table: p.582

Stein, Jeffrey (Georgia)
Profile: p.623
Corporate/M&A **Band** 3
Table: p.587

Stein, Joshua (New York)
Profile: p.1324
Real Estate **Band** 3
Table: p.1248

Stein, Laurence (California)
Profile: p.274
Tax **Band** 4
Table: p.241

Stein, Lee (Arizona)
Profile: p.162
Litigation **Band** 3
Table: p.153

Stein, Mark (New York)
Profile: p.1324
Litigation **Band** 3
Table: p.1224

Stein, Stanton 'Larry'
(California)
Profile: p.274
Media & Entertainment **Band** 1
Table: p.230

Stein, Steven GM (Illinois)
Profile: p.754
Construction **Band** 1
Table: p.672

Steinberg, Donald R
(Massachusetts)
Profile: p.977
Intellectual Property **Band** 3
Table: p.948

Steinberg, Jonathan H
(California)
Profile: p.274
Intellectual Property **Band** 3
Table: p.216

Steinberg, Marty (Florida)
Profile: p.551
Antitrust **Band** 3
Table: p.498
Litigation **Band** 2
Table: p.521

Steinberg, Michael W
(District of Columbia)
Profile: p.470
Environment **Band** 2
Table: p.392

Steindler, Howard (Ohio)
Profile: p.1449
Real Estate **Band** 3
Table: p.1434

Steiner, Beat (Colorado)
Profile: p.322
Hotels and Resorts **Band** 1
Table: p.314

Steiner, Edward (Ohio)
Profile: p.1449
Corporate/M&A **Band** 2
Table: p.1419

Steiner, Jeffrey (New York)
Profile: p.1324

Steinthal, Kenneth (New
York)
Profile: p.1324
Media & Entertainment **Band** 3
Table: p.1232

Stemmler, John A
(Tennessee)
Profile: p.1611
Real Estate **Band** 3
Table: p.1603

Stempel, James A (Illinois)
Profile: p.754
Bankruptcy **Band** 3
Table: p.669

Stenmoe, Gregory
(Minnesota)
Profile: p.1020
Employment **Band** 3
Table: p.1008

Stensland, Dean (Montana)
Profile: p.1081
Real Estate **Band** 2
Table: p.1078

Stepaniak, Mark J (Ohio)
Profile: p.1449
Employment **Band** 3
Table: p.1422

Stephen, John M (Ohio)
Profile: p.1449
Employment **Band** 3
Table: p.1422

Stephens, Kenneth
(Oregon)
Profile: p.1484
Corporate/M&A **Band** 2
Table: p.1471

Stephens, Robert (Texas)
Profile: p.1701
Energy Up and coming
Table: p.1637

Stephens, Thomas
(Colorado)
Profile: p.322
Corporate/M&A **Band** 3
Table: p.303

Stephens, Thomas M
(Illinois)
Profile: p.754
Tax **Band** 3
Table: p.710

Stephenson, Alan
(New York)
Profile: p.1324
Corporate/M&A **Band** 2
Table: p.1189

Stephenson, Andrew
(District of Columbia)
Profile: p.470
Construction **Band** 2
Table: p.374

Stephenson, Barbara G
(New Mexico)
Profile: p.1164
Employment **Band** 2
Table: p.1157

Stephenson, Jack
(Alabama)
Profile: p.125
Corporate/M&A Band 2
Table: p.111

Stephenson, Mason W
(Georgia)
Profile: p.624
Real Estate Band 1
Table: p.601

Stephenson, Thomas
(South Carolina)
Profile: p.1583
Litigation Band 2
Table: p.1576

Stephenson III, Paul H
(Mississippi)
Profile: p.1036

Stepleton, James V
(Missouri)
Profile: p.1060
Corporate/M&A Band 3
Table: p.1043

Steptoe Jr, Robert M
(West Virginia)
Profile: p.1810
Employment Band 1
Table: p.1801

Stern, Akiba (New York)
Profile: p. 1324
Business Process
Outsourcing: National Band 3
Table: p.10
Technology Band 2
Table: p.1259

Stern, Claude M (California)
Profile: p.274
Intellectual Property Band 3
Table: p.216

Stern, Eric L (Pennsylvania)
Profile: p.1538
Real Estate Band 3
Table: p.1516

Stern, Gary (Illinois)
Profile: p.105
Capital Markets Band 1
Table: p.21

Stern, Joan N (Pennsylvania)
Profile: p.1538
Banking & Finance Band 2
Table: p.1493

Stern, Richard (New York)
Profile: p.1324
Bankruptcy Band 4
Table: p.1179

Stern, William E
(Massachusetts)
Profile: p.978
Banking & Finance
Up and coming
Table: p.932

Stern III, Walter E
(New Mexico)
Profile: p.1164
Native Law Band 1
Table: p.1159

Sternberg, Daniel S
(New York)
Profile: p.1324
Corporate/M&A Band 4
Table: p.1189

Sternberg, John (Colorado)
Profile: p.322
Real Estate Band 1
Table: p.313

Sterne, Robert
(District of Columbia)
Profile: p.470
Intellectual Property Band 3
Table: p.403

Stetson, Jim (Illinois)
Profile: p.754
Technology Band 3
Table: p.713

Steuber, David (California)
Profile: p.274
Insurance Band 2
Table: p.212

Steuer, Richard M
(New York)
Profile: p.1324
Antitrust Band 4
Table: p.1170

Stevens, C Eric (Tennessee)
Profile: p.1611
Employment Band 2
Table: p.1596

Stevens, Charles J
(California)
Profile: p.274
Litigation Band 1
Table: p.225

Stevens, Charles P
(Wisconsin)
Profile: p.1826
Employment Band 3
Table: p.1819

Stevens, Mark A
(Pennsylvania)
Profile: p.1538
Environment Band 4
Table: p.1505

Stevens, Mark C (California)
Profile: p.274
Corporate/M&A Band 3
Table: p.197

Stevens, William (Georgia)
Profile: p.624
Real Estate Band 3
Table: p.601

Stevens, Winfred (Maine)
Profile: p.901
Real Estate Band 3
Table: p.895

Stevenson, Brent (Utah)
Profile: p.1738
Corporate/M&A Band 3
Table: p.1727

Stevenson, Randy
(Nebraska)
Profile: p.1088
Employment Band 3
Table: p.1084

Stever, Donald W
(New York)
Profile: p.1325
Environment Band 2
Table: p.1205
Environment Band 3
Table: p.1206

Steverson, Randall (Hawaii)
Profile: p.650
Real Estate Band 1
Table: p.646

Stewart, Carol (Alabama)
Profile: p.125
Real Estate Band 3
Table: p.119

Stewart, Dan (Texas)
Profile: p.1701
Bankruptcy Band 1
Table: p.1627

Stewart, Mike (Oklahoma)
Profile: p.1466
Corporate/M&A Band 1
Table: p.1459

Stewart, Robert (Texas)
Profile: p.1701
Environment Band 2
Table: p.1643
Litigation Band 2
Table: p.1643

Stewart, Robert K (Alaska)
Profile: p.144
Employment Band 2
Table: p.135

Stewart, Terence P
(National)
Profile: p.105
International Trade Band 3
Table: p.40

Stewart III, J Hamilton
(South Carolina)
Profile: p.1583
Employment Band 3
Table: p.1574

Stichter, Don (Florida)
Profile: p.551
Bankruptcy Band S
Table: p.503

Still, Charles (Texas)
Profile: p.1701
Corporate/M&A Band 2
Table: p.1631

Stillman, Charles (New York)
Profile: p.1325
Litigation Band 1
Table: p.1224

Stillman, Gregory (Virginia)
Profile: p.1773
Litigation Band 1
Table: p.1763

Stillman, Nina G (Illinois)
Profile: p.754
Employment Band 1
Table: p.681

Stillwell, R Newcomb
(Massachusetts)
Profile: p.978
Private Equity Band 3
Table: p.953

Stinson, James R (Illinois)
Profile: p.754
Insurance Band 1
Table: p.692
Insurance Band 1
Table: p.694

Stiver, Charles (Florida)
Profile: p.551
Tax Band 4
Table: p.531

Stockbridge, Edward T
(Texas)
Profile: p.1702
Technology Band 2
Table: p.1668

Stocks, Bruce (Colorado)
Profile: p.322
Corporate/M&A Band 3
Table: p.303

Stockton, David (Georgia)
Profile: p.624
Corporate/M&A Band 4
Table: p.587

Stoddard III, John E (New
Jersey)
Profile: p.1145
Corporate/M&A Band 3
Table: p.1123

Stokes, Christopher S
(National)
Profile: p.105
International Trade Band 4
Table: p.40

Stokes, James S (Georgia)
Profile: p.624
Environment Band 2
Table: p.593

Stokes, Randall (Arizona)
Profile: p.162
Real Estate Band 3
Table: p.154

Stolkin, Ronald J (Arizona)
Profile: p.162
Employment Band 1
Table: p.148

Stoll, Neal R (New York)
Profile: p.1325
Antitrust Band 3
Table: p.1170

Stoll, Richard G
(District of Columbia)
Profile: p.470
Environment Band 4
Table: p.392

Stoll, Robert (Oregon)
Profile: p.1484
Litigation Band 2
Table: p.1477

Stoller, Robert (Alaska)
Profile: p.144
Environment Band 2
Table: p.137
Regulated Industries Band 1
Table: p.137

Stolzman, Robert (Rhode
Island)
Profile: p.1570
Real Estate Band 3
Table: p.1568

Stone, Alan J (Delaware)
Profile: p.357
Chancery Band 3
Table: p.344

Stone, Jeffrey (Illinois)
Profile: p.754
Litigation Band 3
Table: p.700

Stone, Steven W
(District of Columbia)
Profile: p.470
Investment Management

Band 3
Table: p.406

Stone, Susan (Texas)
Profile: p.1702

Stone, Susan (Illinois)
Profile: p.754
Insurance Band 2
Table: p.694

Stoner, Wayne L
(Massachusetts)
Profile: p.978
Intellectual Property Band 3
Table: p.948

Stopher, Edward H
(Kentucky)
Profile: p.846
Litigation Band 2
Table: p.835

Storey, Anne-Marie L
(Maine)
Profile: p.901
Employment Up and coming
Table: p.890

Storey, Lee (Arizona)
Profile: p.162
Environment Band 3
Table: p.150

Storey, Lesa J (Arizona)
Profile: p.162
Real Estate Band 2
Table: p.154

Stork, Anita (California)
Profile: p.274
Antitrust Band 3
Table: p.184

Storslee, Steven (North
Dakota)
Profile: p.1410
Litigation Band 1
Table: p.1406

Stout, Mikel (Kansas)
Profile: p.825
Litigation Band 1
Table: p.819

Stoviak, John F
(Pennsylvania)
Profile: p.1538
Environment Band 4
Table: p.1505

Stowers, Gerard
(West Virginia)
Profile: p.1810
Litigation Band 2
Table: p.1803

Strafer, Richard (Florida)
Profile: p.551
Litigation Band 1
Table: p.525

Strain, James A (Indiana)
Profile: p.794
Corporate/M&A Band 1
Table: p.781

Strain, Paul (Maryland)
Profile: p.924
Litigation Band 3
Table: p.914

Strama, Brenda (Texas)
Profile: p.1702
Healthcare Band 2
Table: p.1646

Strand, Margaret
(District of Columbia)
Profile: p.470
Environment Band 4
Table: p.392

Strand, Peter (Illinois)
Profile: p.754
Media & Entertainment Band 1
Table: p.704

Strand, Robert (Hawaii)
Profile: p.650
Real Estate Band 2
Table: p.646

Strangis, Ralph (Minnesota)
Profile: p.1020
Corporate/M&A Band 1
Table: p.1005

Strasheim, Jerrold
(Nebraska)
Profile: p.1088
Corporate/M&A Band 3
Table: p.1082

Strassberg, Richard
(New York)
Profile: p.1325
Litigation Band 3
Table: p.1224

Stratton, David B
(Delaware)
Profile: p.357
Bankruptcy Band 3
Table: p.341

Stratton, Wayne T (Kansas)
Profile: p.825
Litigation Band 2
Table: p.819

Strauch, John L (Ohio)
Profile: p.1449
Litigation Band 1
Table: p.1431

Straus, R James (Kentucky)
Profile: p.846
Corporate/M&A Band 2
Table: p.827

Strauss, Audrey (New York)
Profile: p.1325
Litigation Band 1
Table: p.1224

Strauss, David (Ohio)
Profile: p.1449
Real Estate Band 3
Table: p.1434

Strauss, Robert D (Georgia)
Profile: p.624
Banking & Finance Band 3
Table: p.580

Strecker, David (Oklahoma)
Profile: p.1466
Employment Band 2
Table: p.1461

Street, Phillip (Georgia)
Profile: p.624
Healthcare Band 2
Table: p.594

Streeter, Jon (California)
Profile: p.274
Intellectual Property Band 4
Table: p.216

Streff Jr, William A (Illinois)
Profile: p.1795
Intellectual Property Band 2
Table: p.696

Streicker, James R (Illinois)
Profile: p.755
Litigation Band 4
Table: p.700

Streit, Gary J (Iowa)
Profile: p.814
Corporate/M&A Band 2
Table: p.802

Strench, William G
(Kentucky)
Profile: p.846
Corporate/M&A Band 3
Table: p.827

Strickland, Tom (Colorado)
Profile: p.322
Environment Band 1
Table: p.307

Stricklin, Samuel M (Texas)
Profile: p.1702
Bankruptcy Band 4
Table: p.1627

Striefsky, Linda (Ohio)
Profile: p.1449
Real Estate Band 1
Table: p.1434

Strimbu Jr, Victor (Ohio)
Profile: p.1449
Employment Band 3
Table: p.1422

Strinden, Jon E (North
Dakota)
Profile: p.1410
Corporate/M&A Band 2
Table: p.1403

Stringer, Martin (Oklahoma)
Profile: p.1466
Corporate/M&A Band 2
Table: p.1459

Stringfellow, James S
(National)
Profile: p.106
Capital Markets Band 3
Table: p.19

Strober, Frederick D
(Pennsylvania)
Profile: p.1538
Real Estate Band 2
Table: p.1516

Strock, William (Texas)
Profile: p.1702
Employment Band 2
Table: p.1634

Stromberg, Ross E
(California)
Profile: p.274
Healthcare Band 1
Table: p.209

Stromfeld, Lary (National)
Profile: p.106
Capital Markets Band 3
Table: p.16

Strong, Keith (Montana)
Profile: p.1081
Litigation Band 1
Table: p.1075

Strother, Jack (Washington)
Profile: p.1795
Corporate/M&A Band 3
Table: p.1778

Stroube III, H Rey (Texas)
Profile: p.1702
Bankruptcy Band 4
Table: p.1627

Stroup, Robert (North
Dakota)
Profile: p.1410
Real Estate Band 1
Table: p.1409

Strubeck, Lou (Texas)
Profile: p.1702
Bankruptcy Band 2
Table: p.1627

Strunk, Sarah A (Arizona)
Profile: p.162
Corporate/M&A Band 4
Table: p.146

Struxness, Gregory E
(Oregon)
Profile: p.1484
Corporate/M&A Band 3
Table: p.1471

Stuart, Glen R
(Pennsylvania)
Profile: p.1538
Environment Band 4
Table: p.1505

Stubbs, Sidney (Florida)
Profile: p.551
Litigation Band 3
Table: p.521

Stucker, Robert J (Illinois)
Profile: p.755
Employee Benefits Band 2
Table: p.681

Stuckey, James A
(Louisiana)
Profile: p.876
Banking & Finance Band 1
Table: p.857

Studer, Judith (Wyoming)
Profile: p.1839
Employment Band 2
Table: p.1833
Litigation Band 2
Table: p.1835

Stumo, Mary (Minnesota)
Profile: p.1020
Employment Band 2
Table: p.1008

Stump, John C
(West Virginia)
Profile: p.1810
Corporate/M&A Band 3
Table: p.1798

Sturdivant, James
(Oklahoma)
Profile: p.1466
Litigation Band 1
Table: p.1462

Sturtz, Craig A (Ohio)
Profile: p.1449
Environment Up and coming
Table: p.1425

Stutts, Charles (Florida)
Profile: p.552
Banking & Finance Band 2

Table: p.500

Styles, Mark (New Mexico)
Profile: p.1164
Real Estate Band 2
Table: p.1161

Subin, Ben (Florida)
Profile: p.552
Construction Band 3
Table: p.507

Sudbeck, Roger
(South Dakota)
Profile: p.1593
Litigation Band 2
Table: p.1590

Sudell Jr, William H
(Delaware)
Profile: p.358
Bankruptcy Band 2
Table: p.341

Suflas, Steven W
(New Jersey)
Profile: p.1145
Employment Band 1
Table: p.1126

Sugarman, Robert
(New York)
Profile: p.1325
Media & Entertainment Band 3
Table: p.1232

Suggs Jr, Fred W
(South Carolina)
Profile: p.1583
Employment Band 3
Table: p.1574

Sukin, Michael (New York)
Profile: p.1325
Media & Entertainment Band 1
Table: p.1235

Sulkin, Robert M
(Washington)
Profile: p.1795
Litigation Band 3
Table: p.1786

Sullivan, Alan (Utah)
Profile: p.1738
Litigation Band 1
Table: p.1732

Sullivan, Barry (Illinois)
Profile: p.755
Litigation Band 4
Table: p.700

Sullivan, Brendan V
(District of Columbia)
Profile: p.470
Litigation Band 1
Table: p.410

Sullivan, Brian (Vermont)
Profile: p.1749
Real Estate Band 2
Table: p.1747

Sullivan, John (Montana)
Profile: p.1081
Employment Band 1
Table: p.1073

Sullivan, John L
(Massachusetts)
Profile: p.978
Real Estate Band 2
Table: p.956

Sullivan, Jon (Iowa)
Profile: p.814
Real Estate Band 3
Table: p.810

Sullivan, Kevin
(District of Columbia)
Profile: p.470
Antitrust Band 4
Table: p.367

Sullivan, Marcia W (Illinois)
Profile: p.755
Real Estate Band 4
Table: p.706

Sullivan, Mary Anne
(District of Columbia)
Profile: p.470
Energy Band 5
Table: p.386

Sullivan, Michael (Florida)
Profile: p.552
Hotels and Resorts Band 1
Table: p.526

Sullivan, Michael D
(District of Columbia)
Profile: p.470
Media & Entertainment Band 2
Table: p.413

Sullivan, Patrick W (New
Mexico)
Profile: p.1164

Sullivan, Peter (California)
Profile: p.275
Antitrust Band 3
Table: p.184

Sullivan, Robert (Montana)
Profile: p.1081
Litigation Band 3
Table: p.1075

Sullivan, Robert J
(New York)
Profile: p.1325
Insurance Band 1
Table: p.1213

Sullivan, Robert L
(Tennessee)
Profile: p.1611
Media & Entertainment Band 1
Table: p.1602

Sullivan, Shaun
(Connecticut)
Profile: p.338
Litigation Band 1
Table: p.331

Sullivan, T J
(District of Columbia)
Profile: p.470
Healthcare Band 1
Table: p.398

Sullivan, Thomas (Illinois)
Profile: p.755
Litigation Band S
Table: p.700

Sullivan, William (Illinois)
Profile: p.755
Employment Band 1
Table: p.681

Sullivan, Zane (Montana)
Profile: p.1081
Real Estate Band 1
Table: p.1078

S

Sullivan Jr, James J
(Pennsylvania)
Profile: p.1538
Employment **Band** 4
Table: p.1500

Sumberg, John C (Florida)
Profile: p.552
Real Estate **Band** 3
Table: p.526

Sun, Brian A (California)
Profile: p.275
Litigation **Band** 1
Table: p.225

Sundahl, John Alan
(Wyoming)
Profile: p.1839
Litigation **Band** 2
Table: p.1835

Sundback, Mark
(District of Columbia)
Profile: p.471
Energy **Band** 4
Table: p.382

Sung, Audrey L (National)
Profile: p.106
Shipping **Band** 1
Table: p.71

Sunshine, Ilene Robinson
(Massachusetts)
Profile: p.978
Employment **Band** 3
Table: p.940

Sunshine, Steven C
(District of Columbia)
Profile: p.471
Antitrust **Band** 4
Table: p.367

Suplee, Dennis R
(Pennsylvania)
Profile: p.1538
Litigation **Band** 2
Table: p.1511

Surkin, Elliot
(Massachusetts)
Profile: p.978
Real Estate **Band** 1
Table: p.956

Susko, A Richard
(New York)
Profile: p.1325
Employee Benefits ✪
Table: p.1197

Susman, Harry (Texas)
Profile: p.1702
Antitrust **Up and coming**
Table: p.1622

Susman, Stephen (Texas)
Profile: p.1702
Antitrust **Band** 1
Table: p.1622
Litigation **Band** 1
Table: p.1656

Sussman, Robert M
(District of Columbia)
Profile: p.471
Environment **Band** 2
Table: p.392

Sutherland, Mike (Texas)
Profile: p.1702
Bankruptcy **Band** 4
Table: p.1627

Sutherland, Susan J
(National)
Profile: p.106
Capital Markets **Band** 4
Table: p.14

Sutton, William (Arkansas)
Profile: p.178
Litigation **Band** S
Table: p.172

Suydam, John J (New York)
Profile: p.1325
Corporate/M&A **Band** 4
Table: p.1189

Svonkin, Mark (Connecticut)
Profile: p.338
Real Estate **Band** 2
Table: p.334

Swafford, T Anthony
(Tennessee)
Profile: p.1611
Employment **Band** 3
Table: p.1596

Swaim, Hall (Massachusetts)
Profile: p.978
Bankruptcy **Band** 2
Table: p.935

Swain, Lawrence A
(Kansas)
Profile: p.825
Corporate/M&A **Band** 1
Table: p.816

Swanger, James R (Iowa)
Profile: p.814
Employment **Band** 1
Table: p.805

Swann, Jerre (Georgia)
Profile: p.624
Intellectual Property **Band** 3
Table: p.596

Swanson, Daniel G
(California)
Profile: p.275
Antitrust **Band** 2
Table: p.184

Swanson, David M (South
Carolina)
Profile: p.1583
Real Estate **Band** 2
Table: p.1577

Swanson, James R
(Louisiana)
Profile: p.876
Litigation **Band** 3
Table: p.865

Swanson, Joel (Texas)
Profile: p.1702
Corporate/M&A **Band** 1
Table: p.1631

Swartz, Linda Z (New York)
Profile: p.1325
Tax **Band** 3
Table: p.1255

Sweeney, John (New York)
Profile: p.1325
Intellectual Property **Band** 2
Table: p.1217

Sweeney, Matthew
(Tennessee)
Profile: p.1611
Litigation **Band** 3
Table: p.1599

Sweeney, Neal (Georgia)
Profile: p.624
Construction **Band** 2
Table: p.584

Sweeney, Robert
(West Virginia)
Profile: p.1810
Litigation **Band** 2
Table: p.1803

Sweeney III, James F
(New York)
Profile: p.106
Shipping **Band** 4
Table: p.67

Sweet, Charles A
(District of Columbia)
Profile: p.650
Corporate/M&A **Band** 2
Table: p.641

Sweet, William J
(District of Columbia)
Profile: p.1326
Banking & Finance **Band** 2
Table: p.1174

Swenson, David
(District of Columbia)
Profile: p.471
Tax **Band** 3
Table: p.422

Swenson, Erik (Georgia)
Profile: p.624
Energy **Band** 2
Table: p.592

Swhier, Claudia (Indiana)
Profile: p.794
Corporate/M&A **Band** 2
Table: p.781

Swider, David (Indiana)
Profile: p.794
Employment **Band** 2
Table: p.783

Swift, Phelps (Wyoming)
Profile: p.1839
Real Estate **Band** 2
Table: p.1836

Swinton, David (Iowa)
Profile: p.814
Litigation **Band** 3
Table: p.807

Swirsky, Sherry A
(Pennsylvania)
Profile: p.1538
Antitrust **Band** 3
Table: p.1489

Sykes, David (Pennsylvania)
Profile: p.1539
Bankruptcy **Band** S
Table: p.1494

Sylvester, David (Virginia)
Profile: p.1773
Corporate/M&A **Band** 3
Table: p.1752

Sylvester, William
(Alabama)
Profile: p.125
Real Estate **Band** 3
Table: p.119

Symonds Jr, Robert L
(Delaware)
Profile: p.358
Corporate/M&A **Band** 3

Table: p.346

Symons, Howard
(District of Columbia)
Profile: p.471
Telecom, Broadcast & Satellite
Band 3
Table: p.427

Synnott, Aidan (New York)
Profile: p.1326
Antitrust **Band** 4
Table: p.1170

Szabo, Paul (Ohio)
Profile: p.1449
Intellectual Property **Band** 3
Table: p.1428

Szalkowski, Charles (Texas)
Profile: p.1702
Corporate/M&A **Band** 3
Table: p.1631
Technology **Band** 1
Table: p.1668

Tabachnick, Gene
(Pennsylvania)
Profile: p.1539
Intellectual Property **Band** 4
Table: p.1508

Tabak, Jeffrey E (New York)
Profile: p.1326
Private Equity **Band** 2
Table: p.1241

Tabor, Bert (Texas)
Profile: p.1702
Energy **Band** 1
Table: p.1641

Tabor, Jay (Texas)
Profile: p.1702
Corporate/M&A
Up and coming
Table: p.1631

Tachau, David Brandeis
(Kentucky)
Profile: p.846
Litigation **Band** 3
Table: p.835

Tager, Evan
(District of Columbia)
Profile: p.471
Litigation **Band** 2
Table: p.408

Tague, Brian (Florida)
Profile: p.552
Real Estate **Band** 1
Table: p.526

Taladay, John
(District of Columbia)
Profile: p.471
Antitrust **Up and coming**
Table: p.367

Taleff, Ward E (Montana)
Profile: p.1081
Litigation **Band** 2
Table: p.1075

Talley, Susan G (Louisiana)
Profile: p.876
Real Estate **Band** 1
Table: p.867

Tanenbaum, Jeffrey L
(New York)
Profile: p.1326
Bankruptcy **Band** 4
Table: p.1179

Tanenbaum, William A
(New York)
Profile: p.1326
Technology **Band** 2
Table: p.1259

Tank, David (Iowa)
Profile: p.814
Litigation **Band** 3
Table: p.807

Tanner, Gordon W
(Washington)
Profile: p.1795
Real Estate **Band** 3
Table: p.1788

Tanoury, Mark (California)
Profile: p.275
Corporate/M&A **Band** 3
Table: p.197

Tapscott, Andrew (Virginia)
Profile: p.1773
Real Estate **Band** 3
Table: p.1765

Tarabicos, Larry J
(Delaware)
Profile: p.358
Real Estate **Band** 2
Table: p.350

Tarantino, John (Rhode
Island)
Profile: p.1570
Litigation **Band** 1
Table: p.1567

Taranto, Richard
(District of Columbia)
Profile: p.471
Litigation **Band** 1
Table: p.408

Tarbe, Susan J (Florida)
Profile: p.552
Litigation **Band** 2
Table: p.522

Tarolli, Thomas (Ohio)
Profile: p.1449
Intellectual Property **Band** 2
Table: p.1428

Tarullo, Michael (Ohio)
Profile: p.1449
Construction **Band** 2
Table: p.1417

Tarun, Robert (Illinois)
Profile: p.755
Litigation **Band** 3
Table: p.700

Tata, Robert M (Virginia)
Profile: p.1773
Intellectual Property **Band** 2
Table: p.1761

Tate, Joseph A
(Pennsylvania)
Profile: p.1539
Antitrust **Band** 1
Table: p.1489
Litigation **Band** 1
Table: p.1511

Tate, Simmons (South Carolina)
Profile: p.1583
Litigation Band 3
Table: p.1576

Tate Jr, James S
(Tennessee)
Profile: p.1611
Real Estate Band 3
Table: p.1603

Taub, Kathy S
(District of Columbia)
Profile: p.471
Construction Band 2
Table: p.374

Taub, Philip B
(New Hampshire)
Profile: p.1119

Tavss, John (New York)
Profile: p.1326
Private Equity Band 3
Table: p.1241

Taylor, Allan B (Connecticut)
Profile: p.338
Litigation Band 3
Table: p.331

Taylor, Daniel (North Carolina)
Profile: p.1398
Litigation Band 2
Table: p.1390

Taylor, Jasper (Texas)
Profile: p.1703
Litigation Band 1
Table: p.1665

Taylor, Jay (Arkansas)
Profile: p.178

Taylor, John (Illinois)
Profile: p.471

Taylor, Karrin (Arizona)
Profile: p.162
Real Estate Band 2
Table: p.155

Taylor, Lyndon C (Texas)
Profile: p.1703
Energy Band 3
Table: p.1637
Projects Band 2
Table: p.1659

Taylor, Nolan S (Utah)
Profile: p.1738
Corporate/M&A Band 1
Table: p.1727

Taylor, Robert (California)
Profile: p.275
Antitrust Band 2
Table: p.184

Taylor, Roger (Georgia)
Profile: p.624
Intellectual Property Band 4
Table: p.596

Taylor, Ronald W (Maryland)
Profile: p.924
Employment Band 1
Table: p.912

Taylor, Tom (Utah)
Profile: p.1738
Corporate/M&A Band 3
Table: p.1727

Taylor, Willard B (New York)
Profile: p.1327
Tax Band 2
Table: p.1255

Taylor, William E (Maine)
Profile: p.901
Environment Band 1
Table: p.892

Taylor, Zachary (Mississippi)
Profile: p.1036

Teblum, Gary (Florida)
Profile: p.552
Corporate/M&A Band 2
Table: p.509

Tecson, Andrew P (Illinois)
Profile: p.755
Healthcare Band 3
Table: p.690

Tegeler, David W
(Massachusetts)
Profile: p.978
Private Equity Band 2
Table: p.955

Tehan, John (National)
Profile: p.106
Capital Markets Band 3
Table: p.14

Tein, Michael (Florida)
Profile: p.552
Litigation Up and coming
Table: p.522

Telegen, Arthur
(Massachusetts)
Profile: p.978
Employment Band 1
Table: p.940

Tell, Gary
(District of Columbia)
Profile: p.471
Employee Benefits
Up and coming
Table: p.378

Temin, Michael
(Pennsylvania)
Profile: p.1539
Bankruptcy Band S
Table: p.1494

Temkin, Elizabeth H
(Colorado)
Profile: p.323
Environment Band 1
Table: p.307

Temkin, Harvey L
(Wisconsin)
Profile: p.1826
Real Estate Band 2
Table: p.1822

Tempel, Angela E (Indiana)
Profile: p.794
Real Estate Up and coming
Table: p.788

Templin, Donald (Texas)
Profile: p.1703
Intellectual Property Band 3
Table: p.1651

Tenev, Jovi (New York)
Profile: p.106
Shipping Band 2
Table: p.67

Teplin, Lawrence (California)
Profile: p.275
Construction Band 2
Table: p.194

Ter Molen, Mark R (Illinois)
Profile: p.755
Environment Band 4
Table: p.687

Terp, Thomas T (Ohio)
Profile: p.1449
Environment Band 3
Table: p.1425

Terr, Leonard
(District of Columbia)
Profile: p.471
Tax Band 2
Table: p.422

Terrell, Anthony (New York)
Profile: p.1327

Terrell, Irvin (Texas)
Profile: p.1703
Litigation Band 1
Table: p.1656

Terry, Mike (Virginia)
Profile: p.1773
Real Estate Band 2
Table: p.1765

Tescher, Donald (Florida)
Profile: p.552
Tax Band 3
Table: p.531

Tessier, Frank (Louisiana)
Profile: p.877
Banking & Finance Band 1
Table: p.857

Tessier, Troy (South Carolina)
Profile: p.1583
Litigation Up and coming
Table: p.1576

Thaler, Jeffrey A (Maine)
Profile: p.902
Environment Band 2
Table: p.892

Thane, Jeremy (Montana)
Profile: p.1081
Employment Band 2
Table: p.1073

Tharnish, Deborah (Iowa)
Profile: p.814
Employment Band 2
Table: p.805
Litigation Band 3
Table: p.807

Theiss, Paul W (Illinois)
Profile: p.755
Corporate/M&A Band 4
Table: p.675

Theobald, James (Virginia)
Profile: p.1773
Real Estate Band 1
Table: p.1765
Real Estate Band 2
Table: p.1765

Thiel, John W (Minnesota)
Profile: p.1020
Real Estate Band 2
Table: p.1014

Thiem, Rebecca
(North Dakota)
Profile: p.1410
Litigation Band 1
Table: p.1406

Thieman, Frederick W
(Pennsylvania)
Profile: p.1539
Litigation Band 2
Table: p.1512

Thimsen, Gary
(South Dakota)
Profile: p.1593
Litigation Band 1
Table: p.1590

Thomas, Benjamin
(North Dakota)
Profile: p.1410
Employment Band 2
Table: p.1405

Thomas, Bill (Virginia)
Profile: p.1773
Real Estate Band 1
Table: p.1765

Thomas, Christopher
(Arizona)
Profile: p.162
Environment Band 2
Table: p.150

Thomas, Cynthia
(Washington)
Profile: p.1795
Real Estate Band 2
Table: p.1788

Thomas, Dale E (Illinois)
Profile: p.755
Energy Band 3
Table: p.685

Thomas, David
(West Virginia)
Profile: p.1810
Litigation Band 1
Table: p.1803

Thomas, Frederick B
(Illinois)
Profile: p.755
Corporate/M&A Band 2
Table: p.675

Thomas, Harry O (Florida)
Profile: p.552
Insurance Band 2
Table: p.519

Thomas, John (Oregon)
Profile: p.1484
Corporate/M&A Band 3
Table: p.1471

Thomas, Lizanne (Georgia)
Profile: p.624
Corporate/M&A Band 4
Table: p.587

Thomas, Michael (North Dakota)
Profile: p.1410
Corporate/M&A Band 2
Table: p.1403

Thomasch, Daniel J
(New York)
Profile: p.1327
Intellectual Property Band 3
Table: p.1217

Thomasch, Roger
(Colorado)
Profile: p.323
Litigation Band 2
Table: p.311

Thompson, B Todd
(Kentucky)
Profile: p.846
Litigation Band 4
Table: p.835

Thompson, Bob F
(Tennessee)
Profile: p.1611
Corporate/M&A Band 3
Table: p.1594

Thompson, Carolyn
(District of Columbia)
Profile: p.471
Energy Band 5
Table: p.382

Thompson, Dahl (Texas)
Profile: p.1703
Energy Band 5
Table: p.1637
Projects Band 4
Table: p.1659

Thompson, Gary (Virginia)
Profile: p.1773
Corporate/M&A Band 4
Table: p.1752

Thompson, Gary
(District of Columbia)
Profile: p.471
Insurance Up and coming
Table: p.402

Thompson, Jay (Texas)
Profile: p.1703
Insurance Band 3
Table: p.1648

Thompson, Jocelyn Niebur
(California)
Profile: p.275
Environment Band 4
Table: p.207

Thompson, John (Minnesota)
Profile: p.1020
Employment Band 3
Table: p.1008

Thompson, Kenneth E
(New Jersey)
Profile: p.1146
Corporate/M&A Band 2
Table: p.1123

Thompson, Mark (New York)
Profile: p.1327
Bankruptcy Band 4
Table: p.1179

Thompson, Michael
(District of Columbia)
Profile: p.471
Energy Band 5
Table: p.382

Thompson, Robert
(California)
Profile: p.275
Real Estate Band 1
Table: p.238

Thompson, Thomas M
(Pennsylvania)
Profile: p.1539
Corporate/M&A Band 4
Table: p.1497

Thompson, Tracy (California)
Profile: p.275
Employment Band 4
Table: p.202

Thompson III, Overton
(Tennessee)
Profile: p.1612
Litigation Band 3
Table: p.1599

Thompson, Jr, Clark (Texas)
Profile: p.1703
Real Estate Band 3
Table: p.1662

Thomson, Don (Iowa)
Profile: p.814
Litigation Band 3
Table: p.807

Thomson, Parker (Florida)
Profile: p.552
Litigation Band 3
Table: p.521

Thomte, Dennis L
(Nebraska)
Profile: p.1088
Litigation Band 1
Table: p.1085

Thornburgh, John (Indiana)
Profile: p.794
Corporate/M&A Band 2
Table: p.781

Thornhill, James (Virginia)
Profile: p.1773
Environment Band 3
Table: p.1757

Thornton, Charles
(California)
Profile: p.275
Real Estate Band 2
Table: p.238

Thorp, Michael (Washington)
Profile: p.1795
Environment Band 2
Table: p.1782

Thorpe, William L (Arizona)
Profile: p.162
Litigation Band 4
Table: p.152

Thoyer, Judith R (New York)
Profile: p.1327
Corporate/M&A Band 4
Table: p.1189

Thrapp, Richard (Indiana)
Profile: p.794
Corporate/M&A Band 2
Table: p.781

Throckmorton, Charles
(Florida)
Profile: p.552
Bankruptcy Band 1
Table: p.503

Throckmorton, Rex
(New Mexico)
Profile: p.1164
Litigation Band 4
Table: p.1159

Thrower, Randolph W
(Georgia)
Profile: p.624
Tax Band 4
Table: p.603

Thum, Robert B (California)
Profile: p.275
Construction Band 2
Table: p.194

Thumann, Henry (California)
Profile: p.275
Antitrust Band 3
Table: p.184

Thurber, Mark (Texas)
Profile: p.1703
Energy Band 4
Table: p.1637
Projects Band 3
Table: p.1659

Thurston, Sally A (New York)
Profile: p.1327
Tax Band 4
Table: p.1255

Thuston, Lee (Alabama)
Profile: p.125
Corporate/M&A Band 1
Table: p.111

Ticknor, George
(Massachusetts)
Profile: p.978
Banking & Finance Band 2
Table: p.932

Tieder, John (Virginia)
Profile: p.1773
Construction Band 1
Table: p.1750

Tilghman Jr, Richard
(Maryland)
Profile: p.924
Corporate/M&A Band 1
Table: p.909

Tillman, Eugene
(District of Columbia)
Profile: p.471
Healthcare Band 1
Table: p.398

Tilson, Joseph (Illinois)
Profile: p.756
Employment Band 2
Table: p.681

Tindall, John H (Alaska)
Profile: p.144
Real Estate Band 2
Table: p.141

Tinkham, Thomas
(Minnesota)
Profile: p.1020
Litigation Band 2
Table: p.1011

Tinney, John (West Virginia)
Profile: p.1810
Litigation Band 1
Table: p.1803

Tinnin Jr, Robert P
(New Mexico)
Profile: p.1164
Employment Band 2
Table: p.1157

Tinsley, Nancy (Indiana)
Profile: p.794
Litigation Band 2
Table: p.785

Tippens, Terry (Oklahoma)
Profile: p.1466
Litigation Band 3
Table: p.1462

Tipps, Maynard (North
Carolina)
Profile: p.1398
Real Estate Band 3
Table: p.1392

Tisdale, John R (Arkansas)
Profile: p.178

Tisdale Jr, Charles H
(Georgia)
Profile: p.624
Environment Band 2
Table: p.593

Tisdale Jr, Thomas S
(South Carolina)
Profile: p.1583
Litigation Band 3
Table: p.1576

Titley, Ian D (Virginia)
Profile: p.1773
Intellectual Property Band 1
Table: p.1761

Tittle, David (Indiana)
Profile: p.795
Litigation Band 2
Table: p.785

Tius, Susan (Hawaii)
Profile: p.650
Bankruptcy Band 1
Table: p.640

Tobey, Margaret
(District of Columbia)
Profile: p.472
Telecom, Broadcast & Satellite
Band 4
Table: p.427

Tobin, Charles D
(District of Columbia)
Profile: p.472
Media & Entertainment Band 2
Table: p.413

Tobor, Ben D (Texas)
Profile: p.1703
Intellectual Property Band 2
Table: p.1651

Todd, Owen (Massachusetts)
Profile: p.978
Litigation Band 1
Table: p.951

Toder, Richard (New York)
Profile: p.1327
Bankruptcy Band 2
Table: p.1179

Todrys, Steven C (New York)
Profile: p.1327
Tax Band 2
Table: p.1255

Toelke, Richard A
(Massachusetts)
Profile: p.978
Real Estate Band 3
Table: p.956

Tohill, Jim (Mississippi)
Profile: p.1036
Real Estate Band 2
Table: p.1031

Tolchinsky, Harold N
(New Jersey)
Profile: p.1146
Real Estate Band 3
Table: p.1134

Toll, Curtis (Pennsylvania)
Profile: p.1539
Environment Band 4
Table: p.1505

Tolles, Stephen (California)
Profile: p.275
Tax Band 3
Table: p.241

Tolley III, Edward P
(National)
Profile: p.106
Capital Markets Band 4
Table: p.14

Tomaso, Robert (Missouri)
Profile: p.1061
Employment Band 2
Table: p.1046

Tomlinson PC, Stephen G
(Illinois)
Profile: p.756
Real Estate Band 3
Table: p.706

Toner, Tom (Wyoming)
Profile: p.1839
Litigation Band 1
Table: p.1835
Real Estate Band 1
Table: p.1836

Tonery, Lisa (New York)
Profile: p.1327
Energy Band 2
Table: p.1202

Tongue, Thomas H (Oregon)
Profile: p.1484
Litigation Band 1
Table: p.1477

Tonsfeldt, Steven
(California)
Profile: p.275
Corporate/M&A Band 4
Table: p.197

Toole, William W (North
Carolina)
Profile: p.1399
Environment Band 2
Table: p.1388

Topham, Reed W (Utah)
Profile: p.1738
Corporate/M&A
Up and coming
Table: p.1727

Topolski, Douglas
(Maryland)
Profile: p.924
Employment Band 2
Table: p.912

Torgerson, James (Alaska)
Profile: p.144
Environment Band 1
Table: p.137

Torres, Joseph J (Illinois)
Profile: p.756

Torstrick, Brent
(North Carolina)
Profile: p.1399
Real Estate Band 1
Table: p.1392

Tortoriello, Robert L
(New York)
Profile: p.1327
Banking & Finance Band 1

Table: p.1174

Tosetti, Paul (California)
Profile: p.275
Corporate/M&A Band 1
Table: p.197

Tosi, Louis (Ohio)
Profile: p.1449
Environment Band 1
Table: p.1425

Toth, Bruce (Illinois)
Profile: p.756
Corporate/M&A Band 4
Table: p.675

Toulme, Nill V (Georgia)
Profile: p.624
Environment Band 3
Table: p.593

Toulon, Rik (California)
Profile: p.275
Media & Entertainment Band 3
Table: p.233

Towbin, Steven B (Illinois)
Profile: p.756
Bankruptcy Band 2
Table: p.669

Townsend, Christopher
(Illinois)
Profile: p.756
Energy Band 3
Table: p.685

Townsend, John (Texas)
Profile: p.1703
Litigation Band 2
Table: p.1665

Townsend, John M
(National)
Profile: p.106
Arbitration Band
Table: p.33
Arbitration Band 1
Table: p.33

Townsend, Robert
(New York)
Profile: p.1328
Corporate/M&A Band 4
Table: p.1189

Townsend, William D
(Florida)
Profile: p.552
Tax Band 1
Table: p.531

Tozzi, Rik S (Alabama)
Profile: p.126

Tracy, David (Rhode Island)
Profile: p.1570
Real Estate Band 1
Table: p.1568

Tracy, Timothy J (Alabama)
Profile: p.126
Corporate/M&A Band 2
Table: p.111

Trafford, Robert W (Ohio)
Profile: p.1449
Litigation Band 2
Table: p.1431

Trager, Michael D
(District of Columbia)
Profile: p.472
Corporate/Commercial Band 1
Table: p.376

T

Traurig, Robert (Florida)
Profile: p.552
Real Estate Band S
Table: p.528

Travis, Norton L (New York)
Profile: p.1328
Healthcare Band 3
Table: p.1209

Travostino, Joan (Alaska)
Profile: p.144
Bankruptcy Band 2
Table: p.133
Real Estate Band 2
Table: p.141

Treece, John (Illinois)
Profile: p.756
Antitrust Band 2
Table: p.662

Trenkle, William (Kansas)
Profile: p.825
Corporate/M&A Band 2
Table: p.816

Trent, Tom (Tennessee)
Profile: p.1612
Real Estate Band 1
Table: p.1603

Trepper, Myron (New York)
Profile: p.1328
Bankruptcy Band 1
Table: p.1179

Tribush, Bruce
(Massachusetts)
Profile: p.978
Real Estate Up and coming
Table: p.956

Trier, Dana L (New York)
Profile: p.1328
Tax Band 1
Table: p.1255

Tringali, Joseph (New York)
Profile: p.1328
Antitrust Band 4
Table: p.1170

Triplett, Thomas C (Kansas)
Profile: p.825
Corporate/M&A Band 2
Table: p.816

Triplett, Thomas M
(Oregon)
Profile: p.1484
Employment Band 3
Table: p.1474

Tripp, David (Missouri)
Profile: p. 1061
Litigation Band 1
Table: p.819
Table: p.1049

Tripp, Mark (Iowa)
Profile: p.814
Litigation Band 3
Table: p.807

Tritt, Cheryl
(District of Columbia)
Profile: p.472
Telecom, Broadcast & Satellite
Band 2
Table: p.427

Trombley, Gary (Florida)
Profile: p.553
Litigation Band 2
Table: p.522

Trooboff, Peter D (National)
Profile: p.106
International Trade Band 1
Table: p.41

Tropin, Harley S (Florida)
Profile: p.553
Litigation Band 1
Table: p.521

Troupe, Warren (Colorado)
Profile: p.323
Corporate/M&A Band 3
Table: p.303

Troupis, James R
(Wisconsin)
Profile: p.1826
Litigation Band 3
Table: p.1821

Truax, Tim (California)
Profile: p.275
Construction Band 3
Table: p.194

Truitt, Raymond (Maryland)
Profile: p.924
Real Estate Band 2
Table: p.917

Tsatalis, Marina (California)
Profile: p.275
Employment Up and coming
Table: p.202

Tsukazaki, Ben (Hawaii)
Profile: p.650
Land Use Band 1
Table: p.643

Tubach, Michael (California)
Profile: p.276
Antitrust Band 3
Table: p.184

Tubman, Lloyd H
(New Jersey)
Profile: p.1146
Environment Band 2
Table: p.1129

Tuchin, Michael L
(California)
Profile: p.276
Bankruptcy Band 3
Table: p.191

Tucker, Robert (Ohio)
Profile: p.1449
Litigation Band 4
Table: p.1431

Tucker, Roy (Oregon)
Profile: p.1484
Corporate/M&A Band 1
Table: p.1471

Tucker, Stefan
(District of Columbia)
Profile: p.472
Real Estate Band 3
Table: p.418

Tucker, William
(New Hampshire)
Profile: p.1119
Real Estate Band 1
Table: p.1114

Tull III, John E (Arkansas)
Profile: p.178
Litigation Band 2
Table: p.172

Tully, W Bradley (California)
Profile: p.276
Healthcare Band 3
Table: p.209

Tune, James F (Washington)
Profile: p.1795
Corporate/M&A Band 2
Table: p.1778

Tuohey, Mark H
(District of Columbia)
Profile: p.472
Litigation Band 2
Table: p.410

Turano, Thomas A
(Massachusetts)
Profile: p.978
Intellectual Property Band 3
Table: p.948

Turk, Robert (Florida)
Profile: p.553
Employment Band 1
Table: p.513

Turnbull, Kenneth J
(New York)
Profile: p.1328
Employment Band 3
Table: p.1200

Turner, Jonathan M
(California)
Profile: p.276
Employment Band 4
Table: p.202

Turner, Mark A. (Oregon)
Profile: p.1484
Litigation Band 3
Table: p.1477

Turner, Robert (Texas)
Profile: p.1704
Intellectual Property Band 2
Table: p.1651

Turner, Scott M (New York)
Profile: p.1328
Environment Band 3
Table: p.1205

Turner, Steven C (Nebraska)
Profile: p.1088
Corporate/M&A Band 3
Table: p.1082

Turner, Wayne C (Indiana)
Profile: p.795
Litigation Band 2
Table: p.785

Turner III, Glenn E
(California)
Profile: p.276
Construction Band 3
Table: p.194

Tussing, James D (National)
Profile: p.107
Aviation Band 2
Table: p.58

Tuteur, Michael
(Massachusetts)
Profile: p.978

Tuthill, Walter C (Delaware)
Profile: p.358
Corporate/M&A Band 3
Table: p.346

Tweel, Robert (West Virginia)
Profile: p.1810

Twohig, John E
(Massachusetts)
Profile: p.979
Real Estate Band 1
Table: p.957

Tyle, Craig
(District of Columbia)
Profile: p.472
Investment Management
Band 3
Table: p.406

Tyler, Paul (Iowa)
Profile: p.814
Real Estate Band 2
Table: p.810

Tyson Jr, Joseph B
(Wisconsin)
Profile: p.1826
Corporate/M&A Band 2
Table: p.1817

U

Ubell, Donald P (North
Carolina)
Profile: p.1399
Banking & Finance Band 2
Table: p.1381

Ubinger Jr, John
(Pennsylvania)
Profile: p.1539
Environment Band 4
Table: p.1505

Udolf, Bruce (Florida)
Profile: p.553
Litigation Band 2
Table: p.522

Ugrin, Neil (Montana)
Profile: p.1081
Litigation Band 3
Table: p.1075

Ullman, Samuel C (Florida)
Profile: p.553
Tax Band 1
Table: p.531

Ulman, Lawrence
(California)
Profile: p.276
Media & Entertainment Band 3
Table: p.233

Ulmer, Michael (Mississippi)
Profile: p.1036
Litigation Band 1
Table: p.1028

Ulterino, Eugene D.
(National)
Profile: p.107
Litigation Band 2
Table: p.25

Ulwick, James P (Maryland)
Profile: p.925
Litigation Band 1
Table: p.914

Undercofler, J Clayton
(Pennsylvania)
Profile: p.1539
Litigation Band 3
Table: p.1512

Underkofler, Paul (Texas)
Profile: p.1704
Construction Band 3
Table: p.1629

Unger, Timothy (Texas)
Profile: p. 1704
Energy Band 3
Table: p.1637
Projects Band 2
Table: p.52
Table: p.1659

Untereiner, Alan E
(District of Columbia)
Profile: p.472
Litigation Band 2
Table: p.408

Upton II, Robert W
(New Hampshire)
Profile: p.1119
Real Estate Band 2
Table: p.1114

Urda Kassis, Cynthia
(New York)
Profile: p.1328
Projects Band 2
Table: p.1244

Urga, William R (Nevada)
Profile: p.1103
Litigation Band 3
Table: p.1096

Uris, Harvey R (New York)
Profile: p.1328
Real Estate Band 3
Table: p.1248

Urness, Thor (Tennessee)
Profile: p.1612

Urowsky, Richard J
(New York)
Profile: p.1328
Antitrust Band 4
Table: p.1170

Urquhart, A William
(California)
Profile: p.276
Litigation Band 3
Table: p.224

Usdin, Steven W (Louisiana)
Profile: p.877
Litigation Band 3
Table: p.865

Utken, Gregory (Indiana)
Profile: p.795
Employment Band 2
Table: p.783

Utzschneider, John R
(Massachusetts)
Profile: p.979
Corporate/M&A Band 3
Table: p.937

U

V

Vacketta, Carl Lee
(National)
Profile: p.107
Government Contracts
Band 1
Table: p.27

Valderrama, Teresa S
(Texas)
Profile: p.1704
Employment Band 3
Table: p.1634

Valukas, Anton (Illinois)
Profile: p.756
Litigation Band 2
Table: p.700

Van Deventer, Kenneth M
(New Jersey)
Profile: p.1146
Litigation Band 3
Table: p.1131

Van Dyke, Peter (Oklahoma)
Profile: p.1466
Employment Band 1
Table: p.1461

Van Dyke, Thomas W
(Missouri)
Profile: p.1061
Corporate/M&A Band 1
Table: p.1043

Van Fleet, Allan (Texas)
Profile: p.1704
Antitrust Band 3
Table: p.1622

Van Gorp, Jon D (Illinois)
Profile: p.107

Van Hoy, Philip M (North
Carolina)
Profile: p.1399
Employment Band 1
Table: p.1386

Van Kirk, Mark (Texas)
Profile: p.1704
Real Estate Band 3
Table: p.1662

Van Kley, Jack A (Ohio)
Profile: p.1449
Environment Band 3
Table: p.1425

Van Nest, Robert
(California)
Profile: p.276
Intellectual Property Band 3
Table: p.216
Litigation Band 4
Table: p.224

Van Oot, Martha
(New Hampshire)
Profile: p.1119
Litigation Band 1
Table: p.1111

Van Slyke, David (Maine)
Profile: p.902
Environment Band 2
Table: p.892

van Westrum, Anthony
(Colorado)
Profile: p.323
Corporate/M&A Band 3
Table: p.303

Van Winkle, J Thomas
(Hawaii)
Profile: p.650

Van Winkle, Kenneth
(Arizona)
Profile: p.162
Real Estate Band 2
Table: p.154

Vance, R Patrick
(Louisiana)
Profile: p.877
Corporate/M&A Band 1
Table: p.859
Litigation Band 2
Table: p.865

VanCleave, Richard
(Oregon)
Profile: p.1484
Employment Band 3
Table: p.1474

Vander Haar, David
(Minnesota)
Profile: p.1020
Corporate/M&A Band 3
Table: p.1005

VanDeusen, Darrell R.
(Maryland)
Profile: p.925
Employment Band 3
Table: p.912

Vandevelde, John
(California)
Profile: p.276
Litigation Band 1
Table: p.225

Vanyo, Bruce (California)
Profile: p.277
Litigation Band 4
Table: p.224

Vardaman, John
(District of Columbia)
Profile: p.472
Litigation Band 2
Table: p.410

Vardell, James C (New York)
Profile: p.1329
Banking & Finance Band 2
Table: p.1174

Varela, Paul (Virginia)
Profile: p.1773
Construction Up and coming
Table: p.1750

Varner, Carlton A
(California)
Profile: p.277
Antitrust Band 3
Table: p.184

Varner, Chilton (Georgia)
Profile: p.625
Litigation Band 1
Table: p.598

Varney, Christine
(District of Columbia)
Profile: p.472
Antitrust Band 5
Table: p.367

Vasile, James
(District of Columbia)
Profile: p.472
Energy Band 5
Table: p.386

Vaughan, C David (Georgia)
Profile: p.625
Antitrust Band 3
Table: p.578

Vaughan, Keith W (North
Carolina)
Profile: p.1399
Litigation Band 1
Table: p.1390

Vaughan III, C Porter
(Virginia)
Profile: p.1773
Corporate/M&A Band 4
Table: p.1752

Vaughn, Scott (North
Carolina)
Profile: p.1399
Bankruptcy Band 1
Table: p.1383

Vay, John (Texas)
Profile: p.1704
Environment Band 4
Table: p.1643

Vazquez-Bello, Clemente
(Florida)
Profile: p.553
Banking & Finance Band 1
Table: p.500

Veerman, Louis R (Alaska)
Profile: p.144
Regulated Industries Band 2
Table: p.137

Venesy, Bryan (Ohio)
Profile: p.1449
Real Estate Band 4
Table: p.1434

Ventola, John F
(Massachusetts)
Profile: p.979
Bankruptcy Up and coming
Table: p.935

Vercruysse, Robert
(Michigan)
Profile: p.1000
Employment Band 1
Table: p.991

Verhoeven, Charles K
(California)
Profile: p.277
Intellectual Property Band 4
Table: p.216

Vering III, John (Missouri)
Profile: p.1061
Employment Band 2
Table: p.1046

Vermeys, Sonia Church
(Nevada)
Profile: p.1103
Corporate/M&A Band 3
Table: p.1089

Verrill Jr, Charles Owen
(National)
Profile: p.107
International Trade Band 4
Table: p.40

Verrilli, Donald B
(District of Columbia)
Profile: p.472
Litigation Band 1
Table: p.408
Telecom, Broadcast & Satellite
Band 4

Table: p.427

Verveer, Philip L
(District of Columbia)
Profile: p.473
Telecom, Broadcast & Satellite
Band 1
Table: p.427

Vetter, Jeff (California)
Profile: p.277
Corporate/M&A Band 5
Table: p.197

Vetter, Mark F (Wisconsin)
Profile: p.1826
Employment Band 3
Table: p.1819

Vezeau, Timothy (Illinois)
Profile: p.756
Intellectual Property Band 3
Table: p.696

Vezina, Rob (Florida)
Profile: p.553
Construction Band 2
Table: p.507

Vice, Robert B (Kentucky)
Profile: p.846
Real Estate Band 2
Table: p.838

Vicinanzo, David
(Massachusetts)
Profile: p.1119
Litigation Band 2
Table: p.1111

Vickers, Cass (Florida)
Profile: p.553
Tax Band 2
Table: p.531

Vickers, F Thomas (Ohio)
Profile: p.1449
Construction Band 4
Table: p.1417

Vickery, Ann Morgan
(District of Columbia)
Profile: p.473
Healthcare Band 1
Table: p.398

Victor, A Paul (New York)
Profile: p.1329
Antitrust Band 4
Table: p.1170

Vidmar, Jacqueline M
(Illinois)
Profile: p.756
Environment Band 4
Table: p.687

Vilardo, Terry Otero (Texas)
Profile: p.1704
Banking & Finance Band 4
Table: p.1625

Villa, John K
(District of Columbia)
Profile: p.473
Litigation Band 3
Table: p.410

Villeneuve, Tom (California)
Profile: p.277
Corporate/M&A Band 3
Table: p.197
IT Outsourcing Band 3
Table: p.221

Vincent, George H (Ohio)
Profile: p.1449
Corporate/M&A Band 2
Table: p.1419

Vincenti, Michael
(Kentucky)
Profile: p.846
Real Estate Band 1
Table: p.838

Vine, Stephen M (New York)
Profile: p.1329
Private Equity Band 2
Table: p.1241

Vines, Monte (Kansas)
Profile: p.825
Real Estate Band 3
Table: p.821

Virtel, James (Missouri)
Profile: p.1061
Litigation Band 2
Table: p.1049

Vishneski, John S (Illinois)
Profile: p.757
Insurance Band 3
Table: p.695

Vitale, Robert L (New York)
Profile: p.1329
Projects Band 4
Table: p.1244

Vitkowsky, Vincent J
(New York)
Profile: p.1329
Insurance Band 3
Table: p.1213

Vizcarrondo Jr, Paul
(New York)
Profile: p.1329
Litigation Band 2
Table: p.1223

Vlahakis, Patricia A
(New York)
Profile: p.1329
Corporate/M&A Band 4
Table: p.1189

Voboril, Joseph (Oregon)
Profile: p.1484
Real Estate Band 2
Table: p.1479

Vodra, William
(District of Columbia)
Profile: p.473
Healthcare Band 1
Table: p.398

Voge, William (New York)
Profile: p. 1329
Projects Band 1
Table: p.52
Projects Band 1
Table: p.1244

Vogel, Peter (Texas)
Profile: p.1704
Technology Band 2
Table: p.1668

Voigt, John (Tennessee)
Profile: p.1612
Corporate/M&A Band 3
Table: p.1594

Voigt, Richard (Connecticut)
Profile: p.338
Employment Band 3
Table: p.329

Voigts, Gene (Missouri)
Profile: p.1061
Litigation **Band 1**
Table: p.1049

Volling, James (Minnesota)
Profile: p.1020
Litigation **Band 3**
Table: p.1011

Vollmann, Alan
(District of Columbia)
Profile: p.473
Real Estate **Band 2**
Table: p.418

Volpert, Richard (California)
Profile: p.277

von Ende, Carl H (Michigan)
Profile: p.1000
Litigation **Band 1**
Table: p.994

Von Mehren, Robert B
(National)
Profile: p.107
Arbitration **Band 1**
Table: p.34

Voyles, Robb L (Texas)
Profile: p.1704
Litigation **Band 3**
Table: p.1656

Vreeland, Albert L
(Alabama)
Profile: p.126
Employment **Band 3**
Table: p.113

Vroman, James A (Illinois)
Profile: p.757
Environment **Band 3**
Table: p.687

Vyskocil, Mary Kay
(New York)
Profile: p.1329
Insurance **Band 2**
Table: p.1213

W

Wachsberger, Chaim
(New York)
Profile: p. 1329
Projects **Band 2**
Table: p.52
Projects **Band 2**
Table: p.1244

Wachtell, Herbert M
(New York)
Profile: p.1330
Litigation **Band 1**
Table: p.1222

Wachter, Charles (Florida)
Profile: p.553
Insurance **Band 2**
Table: p.519

Waddell Jr, William A
(Arkansas)
Profile: p.178
Litigation **Band 3**
Table: p.172

Waddoups, Clark (Utah)
Profile: p.1738
Litigation **Band 2**
Table: p.1732

Wade, James A
(Connecticut)
Profile: p.338
Litigation **Band S**
Table: p.331

Wade, Steven T (Montana)
Profile: p.1081
Natural Resources
Up and coming
Table: p.1077

Wadlow, R Clark
(District of Columbia)
Profile: p.473
Telecom, Broadcast & Satellite
Band 4
Table: p.427

Wagahoff Dale, Candy
(Idaho)
Profile: p.660
Employment **Band 1**
Table: p.656

Wagenbach, Jeffrey B
(New Jersey)
Profile: p.1146
Environment **Band 2**
Table: p.1129

Wagner, James (Hawaii)
Profile: p.650
Bankruptcy **Band 1**
Table: p.640

Wagner, William (Montana)
Profile: p.1081
Real Estate **Band 1**
Table: p.1078

Wahl, Nicholas P
(Wisconsin)
Profile: p.1826
Corporate/M&A **Band 3**
Table: p.1817

Wahle, Karen
(District of Columbia)
Profile: p.473
Employee Benefits
Up and coming
Table: p.378

Waks, Jay W (New York)
Profile: p.1330
Employment **Band 1**
Table: p.1200

Wakshlag, Stanley (Florida)
Profile: p.553
Litigation **Band 2**
Table: p.521

Walbolt, Sylvia (Florida)
Profile: p.553
Litigation **Band 1**
Table: p.525

Walch, Greg (Nevada)
Profile: p.1103
Environment **Band 2**
Table: p.1093

Wald, Douglas
(District of Columbia)
Profile: p.473
Antitrust **Band 5**
Table: p.367

Walden, S Calvin (New York)
Profile: p.1330
Intellectual Property **Up and
coming**
Table: p.1217

Walder, Justin (New Jersey)
Profile: p.1146
Litigation **Band 1**
Table: p.1133

Waldman, Ira J (California)
Profile: p.277
Real Estate **Band 2**
Table: p.238

Walker, Clarence W
(North Carolina)
Profile: p.1399
Corporate/M&A **Band 2**
Table: p.1384

Walker, Homer Lee
(Georgia)
Profile: p.625
Real Estate **Band 3**
Table: p.601

Walker, Jeffrey A
(Mississippi)
Profile: p.1036
Employment **Band 3**
Table: p.1026

Walker, John (New York)
Profile: p.1330
Banking & Finance **Band 3**
Table: p.1174

Walker, Mitchell
(Tennessee)
Profile: p.1612
Corporate/M&A **Band 2**
Table: p.1594

Walker, Paul (California)
Profile: p.277
Real Estate **Band 1**
Table: p.238

Walker, Robert (Tennessee)
Profile: p.1612
Litigation **Band 1**
Table: p.1599

Walker, Steve (Florida)
Profile: p.553
Environment **Band 2**
Table: p.516

Walker, Trenholm G
(South Carolina)
Profile: p.1583
Litigation **Band 3**
Table: p.1576

Walker, Jr, H William
(Florida)
Profile: p.553
Real Estate **Band 1**
Table: p.526

Wall, Christopher (National)
Profile: p.107
International Trade **Band 1**
Table: p.41

Wall, Daniel (California)
Profile: p.277
Antitrust **Band 1**
Table: p.184

Wall, Robert (Illinois)
Profile: p.757
Corporate/M&A **Band 1**
Table: p.675

Wall, Steven R
(Pennsylvania)
Profile: p.1539
Employment **Band 1**
Table: p.1500

Wallace, Barbara
(Mississippi)
Profile: p.1036
Employment **Band 3**
Table: p.1026

Wallace, Brian D (Louisiana)
Profile: p.877
Gaming & Licensing **Band 2**
Table: p.864

Wallace, Michael B
(Mississippi)
Profile: p.1036
Litigation **Band 2**
Table: p.1028

Wallace, W Kirk (New York)
Profile: p.1330
Tax **Band 2**
Table: p.1256

Wallack, Barry Z (Indiana)
Profile: p.795
Real Estate **Band 1**
Table: p.788

Wallack, James F
(Massachusetts)
Profile: p.979
Bankruptcy **Band 2**
Table: p.935

Wallander, William (Texas)
Profile: p.1704
Bankruptcy **Band 2**
Table: p.1627

Wallenstein, Jim (Texas)
Profile: p.1704
Real Estate **Band 1**
Table: p.1662

Waller Jr, Edward M
(Florida)
Profile: p.553
Healthcare **Band 2**
Table: p.518

Walmsley, Robert
(Louisiana)
Profile: p.877
Corporate/M&A **Band 4**
Table: p.859

Walsh, Brian C (Georgia)
Profile: p.625
Bankruptcy **Up and coming**
Table: p.582

Walsh, Christopher J
(Colorado)
Profile: p.323
Corporate/M&A **Band 2**
Table: p.303

Walsh, David G (Wisconsin)
Profile: p.1827
Corporate/M&A **Band 3**
Table: p.1817

Walsh, John (Colorado)
Profile: p.323
Litigation **Band 1**
Table: p.311

Walsh, Kathleen (New York)
Profile: p.1330
Private Equity **Band 3**
Table: p.1241

Walsh, Linda
(District of Columbia)
Profile: p.473
Energy **Band 5**
Table: p.386

Walsh, Michael F
(New York)
Profile: p.1330
Bankruptcy **Band 4**
Table: p.1179

Walsh, Thomas (Missouri)
Profile: p.1061
Litigation **Band 2**
Table: p.1049

Walsh, William (Virginia)
Profile: p.1773
Real Estate **Band 1**
Table: p.1765

Walsh Jr, Peter J (Delaware)
Profile: p.358
Chancery **Band 2**
Table: p.344

Walter, Brian P (California)
Profile: p.277
Employment **Band 4**
Table: p.202

Walter, Priscilla A (Pam)
(Illinois)
Profile: p.757
Technology **Band 3**
Table: p.713

Walters, Martha (Oregon)
Profile: p.1484
Litigation **Band 2**
Table: p.1477

Walters, Robert (Texas)
Profile: p.1705
Antitrust **Band 2**
Table: p.1622

Walters, Stephen (Oregon)
Profile: p.1484
Litigation **Band 2**
Table: p.1477

Walton, Gibson (Texas)
Profile: p.1705
Litigation **Band 3**
Table: p.1656

Walton, Leigh (Tennessee)
Profile: p.1612
Corporate/M&A **Band 1**
Table: p.1594

Wampler, Samuel (Ohio)
Profile: p.1449
Construction **Band 4**
Table: p.1417

Wamsley, James (Ohio)
Profile: p.1449
Intellectual Property **Band 3**
Table: p.1428

Wander, Herbert S (Illinois)
Profile: p.757
Corporate/M&A **Band 1**
Table: p.675

Wang, Sarah O (Hawaii)
Profile: p.650
Employment **Band 2**
Table: p.642

Wanner, David
(North Dakota)
Profile: p.1410
Real Estate **Band 3**
Table: p.1409

W

Ward, Bradford L (National)
Profile: p.107
International Trade **Band** 4
Table: p.40

Ward, Daniel (Ohio)
Profile: p.1449
Employment **Band** 2
Table: p.1422

Ward, Erica A
(District of Columbia)
Profile: p.474
Projects **Band** 2
Table: p.415

Ward, Patrick (North Dakota)
Profile: p.1410
Employment **Band** 2
Table: p.1405

Ward, R Lawrence
(Missouri)
Profile: p.1061
Litigation ✪
Table: p.1049

Ward, Richard
(Massachusetts)
Profile: p.979
Employment **Band** 1
Table: p.940

Ward, Richard C (Kentucky)
Profile: p.846
Environment **Band** 3
Table: p.832

Ward, Sarah M (New York)
Profile: p.1330
Projects **Band** 4
Table: p.1244

Ward Jr, Frank
(North Carolina)
Profile: p.1399
Employment **Band** 2
Table: p.1386

Warden, John L (New York)
Profile: p.1330
Antitrust **Band** 3
Table: p.1170

Wardle, Geoffrey (Idaho)
Profile: p.660
Real Estate **Band** 2
Table: p.658

Ware, Donald
(Massachusetts)
Profile: p.979
Intellectual Property **Band** 1
Table: p.948

Ware, Paul (Massachusetts)
Profile: p.979
Intellectual Property **Band** 2
Table: p.948
Litigation **Band** 1
Table: p.951

Ware, Rex D (Florida)
Profile: p.553
Tax **Band** 4
Table: p.531

Warin, Roger
(District of Columbia)
Profile: p.474
Insurance **Band** 1
Table: p.400

Warnecke, Michael O
(Illinois)
Profile: p.757

Intellectual Property Band 1
Table: p.696

Warner, Charles C (Ohio)
Profile: p.1449
Employment **Band** 2
Table: p.1422

Warner, Douglas (New York)
Profile: p.1331
Private Equity **Band** 3
Table: p.1237

Warner, Jonathan (Florida)
Profile: p.553
Tax **Band** 4
Table: p.531

Warner, Michael (Illinois)
Profile: p.757
Employment **Band** S
Table: p.681

Warner, Whitney
(New Mexico)
Profile: p.1164
Employment **Band** 2
Table: p.1157

Warner Jr, E Waide
(New York)
Profile: p.1331
Projects **Band** 3
Table: p.1244

Warnke, Stephen A
(New York)
Profile: p.1331
Healthcare **Band** 3
Table: p.1209

Warren, Charles (New York)
Profile: p.1331
Environment **Band** 3
Table: p.1205

Warren, Edward W
(District of Columbia)
Profile: p.474
Environment **Band** S
Table: p.392

Warren, J Steve (South
Carolina)
Profile: p.1583
Employment **Band** 3
Table: p.1574

Warren, Jerry (Oklahoma)
Profile: p.1466

Warren, Kenneth
(Pennsylvania)
Profile: p.1539
Environment **Band** 2
Table: p.1505

Warren III, John (South
Carolina)
Profile: p.1583
Corporate/M&A **Band** 1
Table: p.1572
Real Estate **Band** 1
Table: p.1577

Warshauer, David (Indiana)
Profile: p.795
Real Estate **Band** 1
Table: p.788

Warta, Darrell (Kansas)
Profile: p.825
Litigation **Band** 2
Table: p.819

Washburne, Thomas
(Maryland)
Profile: p.925
Corporate/M&A **Band** 2
Table: p.909

Wasserman, Craig M
(New York)
Profile: p.1331
Corporate/M&A **Band** 2
Table: p.1189

Wasserman, Michael G
(Georgia)
Profile: p.625
Tax **Band** 4
Table: p.603

Waterman, Ronald
(Montana)
Profile: p.1081
Litigation **Band** 2
Table: p.1075

Waterman, Thomas D
(Iowa)
Profile: p.814
Litigation **Band** 1
Table: p.807

Waterman III, Dana (Iowa)
Profile: p.814
Corporate/M&A **Band** 2
Table: p.802

Waterman Jr, Robert (Iowa)
Profile: p.814
Litigation **Band** 1
Table: p.807

Waters, Barry J
(Connecticut)
Profile: p.338
Employment **Band** 3
Table: p.329

Waters, Jennifer N
(District of Columbia)
Profile: p.474
Energy **Band** 5
Table: p.382

Waters, Paige D (Illinois)
Profile: p.757
Insurance **Band** 2
Table: p.692

Watkins, John (Maryland)
Profile: p.925
Corporate/M&A **Band** 2
Table: p.909

Watson, David
(Massachusetts)
Profile: p.979
Private Equity **Band** 2
Table: p.955

Watson, Jerome R
(Michigan)
Profile: p.1000
Employment **Band** 3
Table: p.991

Watson, Rom P
(Massachusetts)
Profile: p.979
Tax **Band** 2
Table: p.959

Watt, Dick (Texas)
Profile: p.1705
Energy **Band** 3
Table: p.1640

Watt, Robert (Virginia)
Profile: p.1773
Construction **Band** 1
Table: p.1750

Watt, Robert M (Kentucky)
Profile: p.846
Environment **Band** 1
Table: p.832

Watts, Grant (Alaska)
Profile: p.144
Litigation **Band** 1
Table: p.138

Wawro, Mark (Texas)
Profile: p.1705
Litigation **Band** 3
Table: p.1656

Waxman, Scott (Delaware)
Profile: p.358
Corporate/M&A **Band** 3
Table: p.346

Waxman, Seth
(District of Columbia)
Profile: p.474
Litigation **Band** 1
Table: p.408

Wayland, R Eddie
(Tennessee)
Profile: p.1612
Employment **Band** 2
Table: p.1596

Wayte, Alan (California)
Profile: p.277
Real Estate **Band** S
Table: p.238

Weathersby, Woods
(Tennessee)
Profile: p.1612
Real Estate **Band** 2
Table: p.1603

Weaver, Ronald (Florida)
Profile: p.553
Real Estate **Band** 2
Table: p.528

Weaver, William N (Illinois)
Profile: p.758
Private Equity **Band** 3
Table: p.676

Webb, Dan (Illinois)
Profile: p.758
Litigation ✪
Table: p.700

Webb, Eugene (Virginia)
Profile: p.1773
Employment **Band** 1
Table: p.1755

Webb, Thompson
(Maryland)
Profile: p.925
Corporate/M&A **Band** 2
Table: p.909

Webber, Charles F
(Minnesota)
Profile: p.1020
Litigation **Band** 3
Table: p.1011

Webber, Walter E (Maine)
Profile: p.902
Real Estate **Band** S
Table: p.895

Weber, Robert (Ohio)
Profile: p.1450
Litigation **Band** 1
Table: p.1431

Weber, Roger A (Ohio)
Profile: p.1450
Employment **Band** 2
Table: p.1422

Weber, Victoria (Florida)
Profile: p.553
Tax **Band** 1
Table: p.531

Weber III, Louis J (Illinois)
Profile: p.758
Tax **Band** 3
Table: p.710

Webster, Robert (New York)
Profile: p.1331
Banking & Finance **Band** 2
Table: p.1174

Weddington, Keith M
(North Carolina)
Profile: p.1399
Employment **Band** 3
Table: p.1386

Weems, Philip (Texas)
Profile: p.1705
Energy **Band** 2
Table: p.1637
Projects **Band** 2
Table: p.1659

Weems, Walter S
(Mississippi)
Profile: p.1036
Corporate/M&A **Band** 2
Table: p.1024

Weerasinghe, Rohan
(National)
Profile: p.107
Capital Markets **Band** 3
Table: p.14

Weese, Charles W
(Colorado)
Profile: p.323
Employment **Band** 3
Table: p.306

Weg, Howard J (California)
Profile: p.277
Bankruptcy **Band** 4
Table: p.191

Weible, Robert A (Ohio)
Profile: p.1450
Corporate/M&A **Band** 3
Table: p.1419

Weil, Thomas E (Texas)
Profile: p.1705
Projects **Band** 3
Table: p.1659

Wein, Howard (Pennsylvania)
Profile: p.1540
Environment **Band** 3
Table: p.1505

Weinberg, David B
(District of Columbia)
Profile: p.474
Environment **Band** 4
Table: p.392

Weinberg, Jay (Virginia)
Profile: p.1773
Real Estate **Band** S
Table: p.1765

W

Weinberg, Walter S (Illinois)
Profile: p.758

Weinberg Jr, Morris
(Florida)
Profile: p.553
Litigation Band 2
Table: p.522

Weinberger, Michael
(New York)
Profile: p.1331
Real Estate Band 3
Table: p.1248

Weinberger, Seth J (Illinois)
Profile: p.758
Technology Band 2
Table: p.713

Weiner, Arnold M.
(Maryland)
Profile: p.925
Litigation Band 3
Table: p.914

Weiner, Daniel H (National)
Profile: p.107
Arbitration Band 4
Table: p.33

Weiner, Michael L
(New York)
Profile: p.1331
Antitrust Band 3
Table: p.1170

Weiner, Peter (California)
Profile: p.277
Environment Band 3
Table: p.207

Weiner, Samuel (Ohio)
Profile: p.1450
Litigation Band 3
Table: p.1432

Weiner, Samuel (California)
Profile: p.277
Tax Band 4
Table: p.241

Weiner, Sanford A (Texas)
Profile: p.1705
Real Estate Band 1
Table: p.1662

Weiner, Stephen M
(Massachusetts)
Profile: p.979
Healthcare Band 1
Table: p.946

Weingarten, Reid
(District of Columbia)
Profile: p.474
Litigation Band 1
Table: p.410

Weinhardt, Mark (Iowa)
Profile: p.814
Litigation Band 3
Table: p.807

Weinstein, Andrew (Florida)
Profile: p.553
Tax Band 2
Table: p.531

Weinstein, Jerome
(Massachusetts)
Profile: p.979
Employment Band 3
Table: p.940

Weinstein, Joseph D
(Washington)
Profile: p.1795
Corporate/M&A Band 2
Table: p.1778

Weinstein, Ken
(District of Columbia)
Profile: p.474
Environment Band 3
Table: p.392

Weinstine, Robert
(Minnesota)
Profile: p.1020
Litigation Band 3
Table: p.1011

Weintraub, Lee (Florida)
Profile: p.553
Construction Band 2
Table: p.507

Weir, Bill (Ohio)
Profile: p.1450
Real Estate Band 3
Table: p.1434

Weir, H Patrick
(North Dakota)
Profile: p.1410
Litigation Band 1
Table: p.1407

Weirich, Geoff (Georgia)
Profile: p.625
Employment Band 2
Table: p.589

Weisberg, Mark S (Illinois)
Profile: p.758
Employee Benefits Band 2
Table: p.681

Weisburg, Henry (National)
Profile: p.107
Arbitration Band 2
Table: p.33

Weisel, Sheldon
(District of Columbia)
Profile: p.474
Real Estate Band 2
Table: p.418

Weisfelner, Edward
(New York)
Profile: p.1331
Bankruptcy Band 4
Table: p.1179

Weiss, Christopher (Florida)
Profile: p.553
Construction Band 1
Table: p.507

Weiss, Erica H
(District of Columbia)
Profile: p.474
Real Estate Band 3
Table: p.418

Weiss, Gregory A
(New York)
Profile: p.1331
Banking & Finance Band 4
Table: p.1174

Weiss, Harry J
(District of Columbia)
Profile: p.474
Corporate/Commercial Band 1
Table: p.376

Weiss, Jack (New York)
Profile: p.1331
Media & Entertainment Band 2
Table: p.1232

Weiss, Judith K (Arizona)
Profile: p.162
Corporate/M&A Band 4
Table: p.146

Weiss, Mark A (Ohio)
Profile: p.1450
Corporate/M&A
Up and coming
Table: p.1419

Weiss, Stephen M (Arizona)
Profile: p.162

Weiss, Zeff (Indiana)
Profile: p.795
Real Estate Band 1
Table: p.788

Weissler, Robert I (Florida)
Profile: p.553
Hotels and Resorts Band 1
Table: p.526

Weissman, Ellen V
(New York)
Profile: p.1331
Healthcare Band 3
Table: p.1209

Weissmann, Eric (California)
Profile: p.277
Media & Entertainment Band 2
Table: p.233

Weissmann, Henry
(California)
Profile: p.277
Energy Band 3
Table: p.204

Weitkamp, Gary R
(Kentucky)
Profile: p.846
Corporate/M&A Band 3
Table: p.827

Weitz, Mark (Minnesota)
Profile: p.1020
Corporate/M&A Band 3
Table: p.1005

Weitzel, Mark P (California)
Profile: p.277
Projects Band 2
Table: p.236

Welbaum, Earl (Florida)
Profile: p.553
Construction Band S
Table: p.507

Welch, Brian (Indiana)
Profile: p.795
Litigation Band 3
Table: p.785

Welch, Edward P (Delaware)
Profile: p.358
Chancery Band 4
Table: p.344

Welch, Thomas (Hawaii)
Profile: p.650
Real Estate Band 2
Table: p.646

Welch, W Scott (Mississippi)
Profile: p.1036
Litigation Band 2
Table: p.1028

Welin, Peter (Ohio)
Profile: p.1450
Construction Band 2
Table: p.1417

Welk, Thomas
(South Dakota)
Profile: p.1593
Litigation Band 2
Table: p.1590
Litigation Band 2
Table: p.1590

Welke, William R (Illinois)
Profile: p.758
Tax Band 3
Table: p.710

Wellen, Robert H
(District of Columbia)
Profile: p.474
Tax Band 3
Table: p.422

Weller, Phillip (Texas)
Profile: p.1705
Real Estate Band 1
Table: p.1662

Wellford, Hill (Virginia)
Profile: p.1774
Employment Band 1
Table: p.1755

Wells, Benjamin (Texas)
Profile: p.1705
Tax Band 1
Table: p.1665

Wells, Della Wager
(Georgia)
Profile: p.625
Energy Band 2
Table: p.592

Wells, Lawrence
(New Mexico)
Profile: p.1164
Real Estate Band 3
Table: p.1161

Wells, Stephen E
(District of Columbia)
Profile: p.474
Tax Band 4
Table: p.422

Wells, Theodore (New York)
Profile: p.1331
Litigation Band 2
Table: p.1222
Litigation Band 1
Table: p.1224

Welsch, Thomas M
(Montana)
Profile: p.1081
Litigation Band 2
Table: p.1075

Welsh, John F
(Massachusetts)
Profile: p.979
Employment Band 2
Table: p.940

Welsh, Russell (Missouri)
Profile: p.1061
Litigation Band 3
Table: p.1049

Wenner, Adam
(District of Columbia)
Profile: p.474
Energy Band 4
Table: p.386

Werner, John (Louisiana)
Profile: p.877
Corporate/M&A Band 4
Table: p.859

Werner, Philip (New York)
Profile: p.1332
Private Equity Band 3
Table: p.1237

Wertheimer, Robert J
(New York)
Profile: p.1332
Real Estate Band 4
Table: p.1248

Werther, Barbara G
(District of Columbia)
Profile: p.475
Construction Band 3
Table: p.374

Werts, Dale A (Missouri)
Profile: p.1061
Corporate/M&A Band 3
Table: p.1043

Wesely, Marissa C
(New York)
Profile: p.1332
Banking & Finance Band 4
Table: p.1174

West, Glenn D (Texas)
Profile: p.1705
Corporate/M&A Band 2
Table: p.1631

West, Joseph D
(District of Columbia)
Profile: p. 475
Construction Band 1
Table: p.374
Government Contracts
Band 3
Table: p.27

West, Paul (Louisiana)
Profile: p.877
Gaming & Licensing Band 1
Table: p.864

West, Philip
(District of Columbia)
Profile: p.475
Tax Band 3
Table: p.422

West, Ronald (Pennsylvania)
Profile: p.1540
Corporate/M&A Band 4
Table: p.1497

Wester, John (North Carolina)
Profile: p.1399
Employment Band 3
Table: p.1386
Litigation Band 1
Table: p.1390

Westesen, Neil G (Montana)
Profile: p.1081
Litigation Up and coming
Table: p.1075

Westgate, J Bradford
(New Hampshire)
Profile: p.1119
Real Estate Band 2
Table: p.1114

Weston, John (Utah)
Profile: p.1738
Corporate/M&A Band 3
Table: p.1727

W

Weston, Timothy
(Pennsylvania)
Profile: p.1540
Environment **Band 1**
Table: p.1505

Westover, Michael
(Colorado)
Profile: p.323

Westra, James
(Massachusetts)
Profile: p.979
Corporate/M&A **Band 2**
Table: p.937
Private Equity **Band 1**
Table: p.953

Westra, Mark W
(Minnesota)
Profile: p.1020
Real Estate **Band 2**
Table: p.1014

Wettach, Thomas
(Pennsylvania)
Profile: p.1540
Intellectual Property **Band 4**
Table: p.1508

Wexler, Kenneth A (Illinois)
Profile: p.758
Antitrust **Band 3**
Table: p.662

Whalen, Thomas J
(New York)
Profile: p.108
Shipping **Band 1**
Table: p.67

Wheat, David (Texas)
Profile: p.1705
Tax **Band 3**
Table: p.1665

Wheat, Jack A (Kentucky)
Profile: p.846
Litigation **Band 1**
Table: p.835

Wheat, James C
(New Hampshire)
Profile: p.1119
Litigation **Band 2**
Table: p.1111

Wheaton, James J
(Virginia)
Profile: p.1774
Corporate/M&A **Band 3**
Table: p.1752

Wheaton, John (Minnesota)
Profile: p.1021
Real Estate **Band 1**
Table: p.1014

Wheeler, Francis (Colorado)
Profile: p.323
Corporate/M&A **Band 1**
Table: p.303

Wheeler, Malcolm
(Colorado)
Profile: p.323
Litigation **Band 3**
Table: p.311

Wheeler, Raymond
(California)
Profile: p.277
Employment **Band 4**
Table: p.202

Wheelwright, Neil (Vermont)
Profile: p.1749
Real Estate **Band 3**
Table: p.1747

Whelan, Joseph D
(Rhode Island)
Profile: p.1570
Employment **Band 2**
Table: p.1565

Whelan, William (National)
Profile: p.108
Capital Markets **Band 4**
Table: p.14

Whistler, Philip (Indiana)
Profile: p.795
Litigation **Band 1**
Table: p.785

Whitaker, Glenn (Ohio)
Profile: p.1450
Litigation **Band 3**
Table: p.1432

White, Algird (New York)
Profile: p.1332
Energy **Band 1**
Table: p.1204

White, Andrew M
(California)
Profile: p.277
Media & Entertainment **Band 3**
Table: p.230

White, Benjamin T
(Georgia)
Profile: p.625
Tax **Band 3**
Table: p.603

White, Bruce (Illinois)
Profile: p.758
Environment **Band 3**
Table: p.687

White, Christen (Oregon)
Profile: p.1485
Real Estate **Band 1**
Table: p.1479

White, Ira (New York)
Profile: p.1332
Private Equity **Band 3**
Table: p.1237

White, Jeffrey M (Maine)
Profile: p.902
Litigation **Band 3**
Table: p.893

White, Jere (Alabama)
Profile: p.126
Litigation **Band 2**
Table: p.116

White, John (National)
Profile: p.108
Capital Markets **Band 1**
Table: p.14

White, Mary Jo (New York)
Profile: p.1332
Litigation **Band 2**
Table: p.1222
Litigation **Band 1**
Table: p.1224

White, Michael (Missouri)
Profile: p.1061
Real Estate **Band 1**
Table: p.1053

White, Pamela (Maryland)
Profile: p.925
Employment **Band 2**
Table: p.912

White, Robert B (Idaho)
Profile: p.660
Employment **Band 2**
Table: p.656

White, Robert J (California)
Profile: p.277
Bankruptcy **Band 4**
Table: p.191

White, T Gordon (Texas)
Profile: p.1705
Intellectual Property **Band 3**
Table: p.1651

White, W Christopher
(New York)
Profile: p.1332
Real Estate **Band 3**
Table: p.1248

Whitford, Joseph P
(Washington)
Profile: p.1795
Corporate/M&A **Band 3**
Table: p.1778

Whitledge, William H
(Massachusetts)
Profile: p.979
Tax **Band 3**
Table: p.959

Whitt, Burt (Virginia)
Profile: p.1774

Whittaker, Scott T
(Louisiana)
Profile: p.877
Corporate/M&A **Band 3**
Table: p.859

Whittemore, Anne Marie
(Virginia)
Profile: p.1774
Litigation **Band 2**
Table: p.1763

Whittemore, David
(Nevada)
Profile: p.1103
Real Estate **Band 2**
Table: p.1099

Whittemore, Richard J.
(Oregon)
Profile: p.1485
Litigation **Band 3**
Table: p.1477

Wiacek, Raymond
(District of Columbia)
Profile: p.475
Tax **Band 4**
Table: p.422

Wickers IV, Alonzo
(California)
Profile: p.277
Media & Entertainment **Band 4**
Table: p.230

Wickwire, Jon (Virginia)
Profile: p.1774
Construction **Band 1**
Table: p.1750

Wiederrich, James
(South Dakota)
Profile: p.1593
Corporate/M&A **Band 2**

Table: p.1587

Wielebinski, Joseph (Texas)
Profile: p.1705
Bankruptcy **Band 4**
Table: p.1627

Wieman, Lawrence E
(New York)
Profile: p.1332
Banking & Finance **Band 2**
Table: p.1174

Wiesen, Jeffrey M
(Massachusetts)
Profile: p.979
Corporate/M&A **Band 2**
Table: p.937

Wight, Richard J (New York)
Profile: p.1332
Banking & Finance **Band 4**
Table: p.1174

Wikstrom, Francis M
(Utah)
Profile: p.1738
Litigation **Band 2**
Table: p.1732

Wilbur, Brent A
(South Dakota)
Profile: p.1593

Wilcox, Gary B
(Pennsylvania)
Profile: p.475
Tax **Band 3**
Table: p.422

Wilcox, Kirby (California)
Profile: p.277
Employment **Band 1**
Table: p.202

Wild, Robert Andrew
(New York)
Profile: p.1332
Healthcare **Band 1**
Table: p.1209

Wilder, Richard
(District of Columbia)
Profile: p.475
Intellectual Property **Band 3**
Table: p.403

Wildman, Robert (Indiana)
Profile: p.795
Corporate/M&A **Band 3**
Table: p.781

Wildung, Wendy J
(Minnesota)
Profile: p.1021
Litigation **Band 3**
Table: p.1011

Wiley, Jay (Arizona)
Profile: p.162
Real Estate **Band 4**
Table: p.154

Wiley, Richard E
(District of Columbia)
Profile: p.475
Telecom, Broadcast
& Satellite ✪
Table: p.427

Wilhelmy, Thomas R
(Minnesota)
Profile: p.1021

Wilkins, Michael (Indiana)
Profile: p.795

Wilkinson, Beth
(District of Columbia)
Profile: p.475
Litigation **Band 2**
Table: p.410

Wilkinson, William (Ohio)
Profile: p.1450
Litigation **Band 2**
Table: p.1431

Wille, Karin (Minnesota)
Profile: p.1021
Employment **Band 3**
Table: p.1008

Willenzik, David S
(Louisiana)
Profile: p.877
Banking & Finance **Band 2**
Table: p.857

Williams, B John
(District of Columbia)
Profile: p.475
Tax **Band 3**
Table: p.422

Williams, David H
(Delaware)
Profile: p.358
Employment **Band 3**
Table: p.347

Williams, Douglas H
(Illinois)
Profile: p.758
Banking & Finance **Band 2**
Table: p.665

Williams, Ernest W
(Kentucky)
Profile: p.846
Corporate/M&A **Band 2**
Table: p.827

Williams, Gregory (Utah)
Profile: p.1738
Real Estate **Band 3**
Table: p.1733

Williams, Gregory P
(Delaware)
Profile: p.358
Chancery **Band 3**
Table: p.344

Williams, J Colby (Nevada)
Profile: p.1103
Litigation **Band 2**
Table: p.1096

Williams, James
(Pennsylvania)
Profile: p.1540
Real Estate **Band 3**
Table: p.1516

Williams, Jim
(North Carolina)
Profile: p.1399
Litigation **Band 1**
Table: p.1390

Williams, Nancy
(Washington)
Profile: p.1795
Employment **Band 1**
Table: p.1780

Williams, Nicholas R
(New York)
Profile: p.1332

Williams, Quinn (Arizona)
Profile: p.162
Corporate/M&A Band 3
Table: p.146

Williams, Samuel
(Massachusetts)
Profile: p.979
Corporate/M&A Band 3
Table: p.937

Williams, Steven R
(Virginia)
Profile: p.1774
Litigation Band 3
Table: p.1763

Williams, Thomas M
(Kentucky)
Profile: p.847
Employment Band 1
Table: p.830

Williams, William
(District of Columbia)
Profile: p.475
Energy Band 2
Table: p.382

Williams Jr, Lonnie (Arizona)
Profile: p.162
Employment Band 2
Table: p.148
Litigation Band 3
Table: p.152

Williams Jr, William J
(New York)
Profile: p. 1332
Capital Markets Band S
Table: p.14
Capital Markets Band S
Table: p.14

Williamson, Deborah
(Texas)
Profile: p.1706
Bankruptcy Band 3
Table: p.1627

Williamson, Holly H (Texas)
Profile: p.1706
Employment Band 3
Table: p.1634

Williamson, Joel V (Illinois)
Profile: p.758
Tax Band 1
Table: p.710

Williamson, Robert
(Georgia)
Profile: p.625
Bankruptcy Band 3
Table: p.582

Willis, Jane E
(Massachusetts)
Profile: p.979
Antitrust Up and coming
Table: p.930

Willis, Sterling Scott
(Louisiana)
Profile: p.877
Banking & Finance Band 2
Table: p.857

Willner, Keith
(District of Columbia)
Profile: p.475
Real Estate Band 2
Table: p.418

Willoughby, Barry M
(Delaware)
Profile: p.358
Employment Band 2
Table: p.347

Wilson, Anita
(District of Columbia)
Profile: p.476
Energy Up and coming
Table: p.382

Wilson, Brent (Georgia)
Profile: p.625
Employment Band 4
Table: p.589

Wilson, David H. (Oregon)
Profile: p.1485
Employment Band 3
Table: p.1474

Wilson, Michael (Florida)
Profile: p.553
Construction Band 2
Table: p.507

Wilson, Randon W (Utah)
Profile: p.1738
Corporate/M&A Band 3
Table: p.1727

Wilson, Robert (Texas)
Profile: p.1706
Real Estate Band 1
Table: p.1662

Wilson, Stanford (Georgia)
Profile: p.625
Employment Band 3
Table: p.589

Wilson III, Harry M (Florida)
Profile: p.553

Wiltshire, William M
(District of Columbia)
Profile: p.476
Telecom, Broadcast & Satellite
Band 4
Table: p.427

Wincek, Mark D
(District of Columbia)
Profile: p.476
Employee Benefits Band 3
Table: p.378

Wine, James C (Iowa)
Profile: p.814
Real Estate Band 4
Table: p.810

Wing, David (Missouri)
Profile: p.1061
Employment Band 3
Table: p.1046

Wing, John (New York)
Profile: p.1332
Litigation Band 2
Table: p.1224

Wing, Michael R (Georgia)
Profile: p.625
Bankruptcy Up and coming
Table: p.582

Winger, Gary (Utah)
Profile: p.1738
Corporate/M&A Band 3
Table: p.1727

Winkler, Peter (Arizona)
Profile: p.162
Real Estate Band 3

Table: p.154

Winn, Larry (Kansas)
Profile: p.825
Real Estate Band 3
Table: p.821

Winning Jr, William J
(Pennsylvania)
Profile: p.1540
Litigation Band 3
Table: p.1512

Winokur, Barton J
(Pennsylvania)
Profile: p.1540
Corporate/M&A Band 1
Table: p.1497

Winokur, Laurence
(Michigan)
Profile: p.1000
Real Estate Band 3
Table: p.996

Winslow III, Edward
(North Carolina)
Profile: p.1399
Corporate/M&A Band 3
Table: p.1384

Winston, Richard L
(Florida)
Profile: p.554
Tax Band 4
Table: p.531

Winston, Roger (Maryland)
Profile: p.925
Real Estate Band 2
Table: p.917

Winterbauer, Steven
(Washington)
Profile: p.1795
Employment Band 2
Table: p.1780

Winters, Karen A (Ohio)
Profile: p.1450
Environment Band 3
Table: p.1425

Winterscheidt, Rebecca
(Arizona)
Profile: p.163
Employment Band 3
Table: p.148

Wipperman, Robert
(National)
Profile: p.108
Capital Markets Band 3
Table: p.19

Wiseman, Michael M
(New York)
Profile: p.1332
Banking & Finance Band 3
Table: p.1174

Wiseman III, Thomas A
(Tennessee)
Profile: p.1612
Litigation Band 1
Table: p.1599

Witcoff, David L (Illinois)
Profile: p.758
Intellectual Property Band 2
Table: p.696

Witherspoon, Carolyn B
(Arkansas)
Profile: p.178
Employment Band 1

Table: p.170

Withey, Michael (Arizona)
Profile: p.163
Real Estate Band 2
Table: p.155

Witthoefft, Charles
(Virginia)
Profile: p.1774
Litigation Band 2
Table: p.1763

Wittmann, Phillip A
(Louisiana)
Profile: p.878
Litigation Band 1
Table: p.865

Woelfling, Maxine
(Pennsylvania)
Profile: p.1540
Environment Band 3
Table: p.1505

Wogan, John D (Louisiana)
Profile: p.878
Banking & Finance Band 2
Table: p.857

Wohl, Frank (New York)
Profile: p.1332
Litigation Band 3
Table: p.1224

Wohl, Jeffrey D (California)
Profile: p.278
Employment Band 4
Table: p.202

Wojciechowski, Mark S
(New York)
Profile: p.1332
Corporate/M&A Band 4
Table: p.1189

Wolenty, Barbara (Indiana)
Profile: p.795
Real Estate Band 3
Table: p.788

Wolf, Alan C (Louisiana)
Profile: p.878

Wolf, Barry M (New York)
Profile: p.1333
Private Equity Band 1
Table: p.1241

Wolf, Charles B (Illinois)
Profile: p. 758
Employee Benefits Band 2
Table: p.681

Wolf, Jerome (Missouri)
Profile: p.1061
Litigation Band 2
Table: p.1049

Wolf, Larry (Maryland)
Profile: p.925
Employment Band 2
Table: p.912

Wolf, Robert M
(Massachusetts)
Profile: p.979
Private Equity Band 2
Table: p.953

Wolf, Van (Arizona)
Profile: p.163
Environment Band 3
Table: p.150

Wolf, Wayne (New Mexico)
Profile: p.1164
Litigation Band 3
Table: p.1159

Wolfe, David L (Illinois)
Profile: p.758
Employee Benefits Band 2
Table: p.681

Wolfe, Gary (New York)
Profile: p.108
Shipping Band 1
Table: p.67

Wolfe, Richard (Louisiana)
Profile: p.878
Corporate/M&A Band 2
Table: p.859

Wolfe, Roger (West Virginia)
Profile: p.1810
Employment Band 2
Table: p.1801

Wolfe III, Frank B
(Oklahoma)
Profile: p.1466
Employment Band 2
Table: p.1461

Wolfe Jr, Donald (Delaware)
Profile: p.358
Chancery Band 2
Table: p.344

Wolff, Alan (National)
Profile: p.108
International Trade Band 2
Table: p.40

Wolff, Paul
(District of Columbia)
Profile: p.476

Wolff, Robert M (Ohio)
Profile: p.1450
Employment Band 3
Table: p.1422

Wolfson, Mark J (Florida)
Profile: p.554
Bankruptcy Band 2
Table: p.503

Wolfstone, Jeffrey (Oregon)
Profile: p.1485
Corporate/M&A Band 3
Table: p.1471

Wolitzer, Michael (New York)
Profile: p.1333
Private Equity Band 1
Table: p.1241

Wollin, David A
(Rhode Island)
Profile: p.1570
Litigation Band 2
Table: p.1567

Wollman, Diana L
(New York)
Profile: p.1333
Tax Band 4
Table: p.1255

Woloson, Kenneth (Nevada)
Profile: p.1103
Corporate/M&A Band 2
Table: p.1089

Wolowitz, David
(New Hampshire)
Profile: p.1119
Litigation Band 2

W

Table: p.1111

Wong, Danton S (Hawaii)
Profile: p.650
Real Estate Band 2
Table: p.646

Wong, David W (Hawaii)
Profile: p.650
Tax Band 1
Table: p.641

Wood, Lisa C
(Massachusetts)
Profile: p.979
Antitrust Band 2
Table: p.930

Wood, Mark (California)
Profile: p.278
Insurance Band 4
Table: p.212

Wood, Robert (Tennessee)
Profile: p.1612
Real Estate Band 3
Table: p.1603

Wood, William (Kansas)
Profile: p.825
Corporate/M&A Band 2
Table: p.816
Real Estate Band 3
Table: p.821

Wood, William (Texas)
Profile: p.1706
Energy Band 2
Table: p.1640

Woodbury, Judith Fletcher
(Maine)
Profile: p.902
Real Estate Band 3
Table: p.895

Woods, John (New York)
Profile: p.108

Woods, Sharon (Michigan)
Profile: p.1000
Litigation Band 2
Table: p.994

Woodson, R Duke (Florida)
Profile: p.554
Real Estate Band 2
Table: p.528

Woodward, Robert
(Georgia)
Profile: p.625
Tax Band 1
Table: p.603

Woodworth, Stanley
(Kansas)
Profile: p.825
Real Estate Band 2
Table: p.821

Woody, Charles
(West Virginia)
Profile: p.1810
Employment Band 1
Table: p.1801

Wooley, James (Ohio)
Profile: p.1450
Litigation Band 2
Table: p.1432

Wootton, Robert R (Illinois)
Profile: p.759
Tax Band 2
Table: p.710

Word, Terry (New Mexico)
Profile: p.1164
Litigation Band 3
Table: p.1159

Worrell, Danny (Texas)
Profile: p.1706
Environment Band 4
Table: p.1643

Worrell, David (Indiana)
Profile: p.795
Corporate/M&A Band 2
Table: p.781

Worsham, Lee (Florida)
Profile: p.554
Environment Band 3
Table: p.516

Worth, Diane (Kansas)
Profile: p.825
Employment Band 2
Table: p.818

Wortley, Michael (Texas)
Profile: p.1706
Corporate/M&A Band 1
Table: p.1631

Wovsaniker, Alan
(New Jersey)
Profile: p.1146
Corporate/M&A Band 2
Table: p.1123

Wren, Elizabeth
(North Carolina)
Profile: p.1399
Corporate/M&A Band 3
Table: p.1384

Wright, Douglas R
(Colorado)
Profile: p.323
Corporate/M&A Band 2
Table: p.303

Wright, James (Maryland)
Profile: p.925
Real Estate Band 3
Table: p.917

Wright, Jefferson V
(Maryland)
Profile: p.925
Litigation Band 2
Table: p.914

Wright, Joyce (Arizona)
Profile: p.163
Real Estate Band 3
Table: p.154

Wright, Murray (Virginia)
Profile: p.1774
Construction Band 2
Table: p.1750

Wright, Robert (Texas)
Profile: p.1706
Real Estate Band 2
Table: p.1662

Wright, Thomas (Kansas)
Profile: p.825
Litigation Band 2
Table: p.819

Wrobley, Ralph (Missouri)
Profile: p.1061
Corporate/M&A Band 1
Table: p.1043

Wulfe, Scott (Texas)
Profile: p.1706
Corporate/M&A Band 2
Table: p.1631

Wycoff, William
(Pennsylvania)
Profile: p.1540
Litigation Band 2
Table: p.1511

Wyld, Robert (Connecticut)
Profile: p.338
Litigation Band 3
Table: p.331

Wylie, Kenneth R (Illinois)
Profile: p.759
Insurance Band 1
Table: p.692
Insurance Band 2
Table: p.694

Wyman, Kenneth (New York)
Profile: p.1333
Projects Band 4
Table: p.1244

Wyman Jr, Robert
(California)
Profile: p.278
Environment Band 1
Table: p.207

Wymer, John (Georgia)
Profile: p.625
Employment Band 1
Table: p.589

Wyron, Richard H
(District of Columbia)
Profile: p.476
Bankruptcy Band 3
Table: p.372

Wyrsch, James R (Missouri)
Profile: p.1061
Litigation Band 1
Table: p.1049

Y

Yadley, Gregory (Florida)
Profile: p.554
Corporate/M&A Band 3
Table: p.509

Yance, James (Alabama)
Profile: p.126
Litigation Band 2
Table: p.116

Yang, John C
(District of Columbia)
Profile: p.476
Insurance Up and coming
Table: p.400

Yannucci, Thomas D
(District of Columbia)
Profile: p.476
Litigation Band 1
Table: p.410

Yastrow, Joseph (Illinois)
Profile: p.759
Employment Band 1
Table: p.681

Yates, Jack (Missouri)
Profile: p.1061
Employment Band 3
Table: p.1046

Yde, Paul
(District of Columbia)
Profile: p.476
Antitrust Band 3
Table: p.367

Yeager, Jay (Indiana)
Profile: p.795
Litigation Band 1
Table: p.785

Yeager, Robert
(Pennsylvania)
Profile: p.1540
Intellectual Property Band 4
Table: p.1508

Yeates, Marie (Texas)
Profile: p.1706
Litigation Band 1
Table: p.1656

Yelnosky, Maryann (Oregon)
Profile: p.1485
Employment Band 3
Table: p.1474

Yentzer, Steven R
(Washington)
Profile: p.1795
Corporate/M&A Band 3
Table: p.1778

Yerkes, Kenneth (Indiana)
Profile: p.795
Employment Band 1
Table: p.783

Yoder, Lowell D (Illinois)
Profile: p.759
Tax Band 2
Table: p.710

Yodowitz, Edward J
(New York)
Profile: p.1333
Litigation Band 3
Table: p.1223

Yohay, Stephen
(District of Columbia)
Profile: p.476
Employment Band 3
Table: p.380

Yoken, Stephen (Nevada)
Profile: p.1103

Yon, David A (Florida)
Profile: p.554
Insurance Band 2
Table: p.519

Yood, Kenneth J (California)
Profile: p.278
Healthcare Band 3
Table: p.209

York, Larry (Texas)
Profile: p.1706
Insurance Band 2
Table: p.1648

Youchah, Elayna (Nevada)
Profile: p.1103
Employment Band 2
Table: p.1091

Young, Cynthia (Kentucky)
Profile: p.847
Corporate/M&A Band 2
Table: p.827

Young, David J (Ohio)
Profile: p.1450
Litigation Band 1

Young, Douglas R
(California)
Profile: p.278
Litigation Band 2
Table: p.224
Litigation Band 2
Table: p.225

Young, Howard (Utah)
Profile: p.1738
Corporate/M&A Band 3
Table: p.1727

Young, Jeffrey E (Georgia)
Profile: p.625
Intellectual Property Band 4
Table: p.596

Young, Kenneth E
(South Carolina)
Profile: p.1583
Employment Band 3
Table: p.1574

Young, Kevin (New York)
Profile: p.1333
Environment Band 3
Table: p.1205

Young, Maureen A
(California)
Profile: p.278
Banking & Finance Band 2
Table: p.188

Young, Michael (New York)
Profile: p.1333
Litigation Band 2
Table: p.1223

Young, Rodger (Michigan)
Profile: p.1000
Litigation Band 2
Table: p.994

Young, William (Texas)
Profile: p.1706
Banking & Finance Band 4
Table: p.1625

Young Jr, Rutledge
(South Carolina)
Profile: p.1583
Litigation Band 3
Table: p.1576

Youngblood, Juliette
(California)
Profile: p.278
Media & Entertainment Band 3
Table: p.233

Younger, Carter (Virginia)
Profile: p.1774
Employment Band 2
Table: p.1755

Youngren, Nancy (Hawaii)
Profile: p.650
Real Estate Band 2
Table: p.646

Youngwood, Alfred D
(New York)
Profile: p.1333
Tax Band 2
Table: p.1255

Yuen, Leighton (Hawaii)
Profile: p.650
Real Estate Band 2
Table: p.646

Y

Yuffee, Michael
(District of Columbia)
Profile: p.476
Energy Band 5
Table: p.386

Yund, George (Ohio)
Profile: p.1450
Employment Band 2
Table: p.1422

Yungblut, Stephen (Texas)
Profile: p.1706
Construction Band 3
Table: p.1629

Yura, Mark (Illinois)
Profile: p.759
Real Estate Band 3
Table: p.706

Zabel, Sheldon (Illinois)
Profile: p.759
Environment Band 1
Table: p.687

Zabrowski, Patrick M
(Wisconsin)
Profile: p.1827
Real Estate Band 2
Table: p.1822

Zadick, Gary M (Montana)
Profile: p.1081
Employment Band 1
Table: p.1073

Zagore, David A (Ohio)
Profile: p.1450
Corporate/M&A Band 3
Table: p.1419

Zahler, Robert
(District of Columbia)
Profile: p. 476
Business Process
Outsourcing: National Band 1
Table: p.10
IT Outsourcing Band 1
Table: p.430

Zaiger, Mark L (Iowa)
Profile: p.814
Employment Band 1
Table: p.805

Zakarian, Albert
(Connecticut)
Profile: p.338
Employment Band 1
Table: p.329

Zandy, John C (Connecticut)
Profile: p.338
Employment Band 2
Table: p.329

Zangari, Ted (New Jersey)
Profile: p.1146

Zarov, Herbert (Illinois)
Profile: p.759
Litigation Band 4
Table: p.700

Zax, Leonard A
(District of Columbia)
Profile: p.476

Zazove, Daniel A (Illinois)
Profile: p.759
Bankruptcy Band 3
Table: p.669

Zech, Paul (Minnesota)
Profile: p.1021
Employment Band 2
Table: p.1008

Zeglovitch, Robert
(Minnesota)
Profile: p.1021
Employment Band 3
Table: p.1008

Zeiger, John W (Ohio)
Profile: p.1450
Litigation Band 2
Table: p.1431

Zeilinger, John S (Nebraska)
Profile: p.1088
Corporate/M&A Band 2
Table: p.1082

Zelek, Eugene (Illinois)
Profile: p.759
Antitrust Band 3
Table: p.662
Media & Entertainment Band 2
Table: p.704

Zelenock, Katheryne L
(Michigan)
Profile: p.1000
Real Estate Up and coming
Table: p.996

Zetlin, Michael (New York)
Profile: p.1334
Construction Band 3
Table: p.1186

Zewadski, William Knight
(Florida)
Profile: p.554
Bankruptcy Band 3
Table: p.503

Ziffren, Kenneth (California)
Profile: p.278
Media & Entertainment Band 1
Table: p.233

Ziman, Kenneth S
(New York)
Profile: p.1334
Bankruptcy Band 4
Table: p.1179

Zimbler, Jay (Illinois)
Profile: p.759
Tax Band 2
Table: p.710

Zimet, Bruce A (Florida)
Profile: p.554
Litigation Band 1
Table: p.522

Zimmerman, Edward M
(New Jersey)
Profile: p.1146
Corporate/M&A Band 2
Table: p.1123

Zimmerman, Todd E
(North Dakota)
Profile: p.1410
Litigation Band 2
Table: p.1406

Zimpritch, James B (Maine)
Profile: p.902
Corporate/M&A Band 1
Table: p.888

Zinober, Peter (Florida)
Profile: p.554
Employment ✪
Table: p.513

Zirinsky, Bruce (New York)
Profile: p.1334

Zischke, Michael H
(California)
Profile: p.278
Environment Band 2
Table: p.207
Real Estate Band 1
Table: p.238

Zisser, David A (Colorado)
Profile: p.323
Litigation Band 1
Table: p.311

Zody, Michael A (Utah)
Profile: p.1738
Employment Band 3
Table: p.1730

Zoli, Elise (Massachusetts)
Profile: p.979
Environment Band 3
Table: p.943

Zonn, Sidney (Pennsylvania)
Profile: p.1540
Employment Band 4
Table: p.1500

Zorn, Jonathan
(Massachusetts)
Profile: p.979
Tax Band 1
Table: p.959

Zornow, David M (New York)
Profile: p.1334
Litigation Band 2
Table: p.1224

Zovickian, Stephen
(California)
Profile: p.278
Construction Band 3
Table: p.194

Zucker, Carol (Nevada)
Profile: p.1103
Employment Band 1
Table: p.1091

Zucker, Jeffrey (Nevada)
Profile: p.1103
Corporate/M&A Band 1
Table: p.1089
Real Estate Band 1
Table: p.1099

Zuckerman, Richard
(Michigan)
Profile: p.1000
Litigation Band 1
Table: p.994

Zumbach, Steven E (Iowa)
Profile: p.814
Corporate/M&A Band 1
Table: p.802

Zussman, Richard
(Michigan)
Profile: p.1000
Real Estate Band 2
Table: p.996

Zutz, Robert
(District of Columbia)
Profile: p.476
Investment Management
Band 3
Table: p.406

Zweifach, Gerson
(District of Columbia)
Profile: p.476
Media & Entertainment Band 2
Table: p.413

Z

OTHER RECOMMENDED FIRMS

Abrahams Kaslow & Cassman LLP
8712 West Dodge Road, Suite 300, Omaha, NE 68114

Adams & Jones Chartered
600 Market Centre, 155 North Market, PO Box 1034, Wichita, KS 67201-1034

Adelman Lavine Gold & Levin
Suite 900, Four Penn Center, Philadelphia, PA 19103-2808

Ahlers & Cooney PC
100 Court Avenue, Suite 600, Des Moines, IA 50309

Allen & Allen Attorneys at Law, PC
The Federal Reserbe Bank Building, 701 East Byrd Street, PO Box 610, Richmond, VA 23218-0610

Allen Guthrie McHugh & Thomas, PLLC
500 Lee Street East, ste. 800, P.O. Box 3394, Charleston, WV 25333

Allensworth and Porter, L.L.P
620 Congress Avenue, Suite 100, Austin, TX 78701 -3229

Allison, MacKenzie, Russell, Pavlakis, Wright & Fagan, Ltd
402 North Division Street, Carson City, NV 89702

Alston Courtnage & Bassetti LLP
1000 Second Avenue, Suite 3900, Seattle, WA 98104-1045

Amburgey & Rubin PC
Riverplace Office Building, 1750 SW Harbor Way, Suite 450, Portland, OR 97201-0104

Anderson & Bottrell
State Bank Center, Suite 302, 3100 13th Avenue Southwest, PO Box 10247, Fargo, ND 58106-0247

Anderson & Kreiger LLP
43 Thorndike Street, Cambridge, MA 02141

Andrew M Lawler PC
641 Lexington Avenue, 27th Floor, New York, NY 10022

Andrews Myers Coulter & Cohen PC
2900 Weslayan, Suite 375, Houston, TX 77027-5109

Anthony Ostlund & Baer
90 South Seventh Street, Suite 3600, Minneapolis, MN 55402

Arent Fox PLLC
1050 Connecticut Avenue NW, Washington, DC 20036

Arguedas, Cassman & Headley, LLP
5900 Hollis Street, Suite N, Emeryville, CA 94608

Armstrong Allen PLLC
Brinkley Plaza, Suite 700, 80 Monroe Avenue, Memphis, TN 38103

Armstrong Hirsch Jackoway Tyerman & Wertheimer
Suite 1800, 1888 Century Park East, Century City, Los Angeles, CA 90067

Armstrong Teasdale LLP
One Metropolitan Square, Suite 2600, St Louis, MO 63102-2740

Ashburn & Mason, PC
1130 West 6th Avenue, Suite 100, Anchorage, AK 99501

Ashford & Wriston
Alii Place, Suite 1400, 1099 Alakea Street, Honolulu, HI 96810

Ater Wynne LLP
222 South West Columbia Street, Suite 1800, Portland, OR 97201

Atkinson, Conway & Gagnon
420 L Street, Suite 500, Anchorage, AK 99501-1989

August, Kulunas & Dawson, PA
250 Australian Avenue South, Suite 1100, West Palm Beach, FL 33401

Ausley & McMullen
Washington Square Building, 227 South Calhoun Street, PO Box 391, Tallahassee, FL 32302

Axinn Veltrop & Harkrider LLP
1370 Avenue of Americas, New York, NY 10019-6708

Ayabe, Chong, Nishimoto, Sia & Nakamura
Pauahi Tower, 1001 Bishop Street, Suite 2500, Honolulu, HI 96813

Baach Robinson & Lewis PLLC
One Thomas Circle NW, Suite 200, Washington, DC 20005-5803

Babst, Calland, Clements and Zomnir, A Professional Corporation
Two Gateway Center, Pittsburgh, PA 15222

Badiak Will & Ruddy
Suite 1040, 120 Broadway, New York, NY 10271

Bailey Cavalieri
10 West Broad Street, Columbus, OH 43215

Baird, Holm, McEachen, Pedersen, Hamann & Strasheim LLP
1500 Woodmen Tower, Omaha, NE 68102

Baker & Hostetler LLP
Washington Square, Suite 1100, 1050 Conneticut Avenue, Washington, DC 20036-5304

Ball Janik LLP
One Main Place, 101 SW Main Street, Suite 1100, Portland, OR 97204

Ball, Ball, Matthews & Novak
2000 Interstate Park, Suite 204, PO Box 2148, Montgomery, AL 36102

Bangs, McCullen, Butler, Foye & Simmons, LLP
818 St Joseph Street, PO Box 2670, Rapid City, SD 57709

Bankston, Gronning, O'Hara, PC
550 West 7th Avenue, Suite 1800, Anchorage, AK 99501

Banner & Witcoff Ltd
Ten South Wacker Drive, Chicago, IL 60606-7407

Barack Ferrazzano Kirschbaum Perlman & Nagelberg
333 West Wacker, Suite 2700, Chicago, IL 60606-1227

Barger & Wolen
515 South Flower Street, 34th Floor, Los Angeles, CA 90071

Barlow & Wilcox PA
201 Third Street North West, Suite 1130, Albuquerque, NM 87102

Barnes & Thornburg
1401 Eye Street NW, Suite 500, Washington, DC 20005

Barnett, Bolt, Kirkwood, Long & McBride
601 Bayshore Bouldevard, Suite 700, Tampa, FL 33606

Barris, Sott, Denn & Driker, PLLC
211 West Fort Street, Fifteenth Floor, Detroit, MI 48226-3281

Bartlit Beck Herman Palenchar & Scott
Courthouse Place, 54 West Hubbard Street, Chicago, IL 60610

Bassford Remele, A Professional Association
33 South Sixth Street, Suite 3800, Minneapolis, MN 55402-3707

Bastianelli, Brown & Kelley
1133 Twenty First Street NW, Suite 500, Washington, DC 20036

Bates & Carey
333 West Wacker Drive, Suite 900, Chicago, IL 60606

Bays Deaver Lung Rose Baba
Ali'i Place 1099 Alakea Street, Suite 1600, Honolulu, HI 96813

Beasley, Allen, Crow, Methvin, Portis & Miles, PC
218 Commerce Street, PO Box 4160, Montgomery, AL 36104

Beck, Redden & Secrest L.L.P
One Houston Center, 1221 McKinney Street, Suite 4500, Houston, TX 77010-2010

Becker & Poliakoff PA
Emerald Lake Corporate Park, 3111 Stirling Road, Fort Lauderdale, FL 33312

Beckman Lawson, LLP
800 Standard Federal Plaza, Fort Wayne, IN 46802

Bedell, Dittmar, DeVault, Pillans & Coxe
The Bedell Building, 101 East Adams Street, Jacksonville, FL 32202

Bedrava & Lyman
1301 W 22nd Street, Suite 914, Oak Brook, IL 60523-2018

Beggs & Lane
501 Commendencia Street, PO Box 12950, Pensacola, FL 32591-2950

Belin Lamson McCormick Zumbach Flynn, PC
The Financial Center, 666 Walnut Street, Suite 2000, Des Moines, IA 50309

Bell, Boyd & Lloyd LLC
Three First National Plaza, Suite 3300, 70 West Madison Street, Chicago, IL 60602-4027

Bell, Davis & Pitt, P.A.
Century Plaza, Suite 600, 100 North Cherry Street, Winston-Salem, NC 27101

Benesch, Friedlander, Coplan & Aronoff LLP
2300 BP Tower, 200 Public Square, Cleveland, OH 44114

Berens & Tate PC
10050 Regency Circle, Suite 400, Omaha, NE 68114

Berenstein, Moore, Berenstein, Heffernan & Moeller
300 Firstarbank Building, 501 Pierce Street, PO Box 3207, Sioux City, IA 51102

Berger & Montague PC
1622 Locust Street, Philadelphia, PA 19103

Berkes Crane Robinson & Seal, LLP
515 South Figueroa Street, Suite 1500, Los Angeles, CA 90071

Berkowitz Stanton Brandt Williams & Shaw LLP
2 Emanuel Cleaver II Boulevard, Suite 500, Kansas City, MO 64112

Berman & Simmons
85 Exchange Street, Portland, ME 04101

Berman DeValerio Pease Tabacco Burt & Pucillo
Northbridge Centre Suite 1701, West Palm Beach, FL 33401

Betzer Roybal & Eisenberg PC
4900 Lang Avenue NE, Suite 202, Albuquerque, NM 87109-4303

Beus Gilbert PLLC
4800 North Scottsdale Road, Suite 6000, Scottsdale, AZ 85251-7630

Bierman, Shohat, Loewy & Klein PA
Penthouse Two, 800 Brickell Avenue, Miami, FL 33131-2914

Bieser, Greer, & Landis LLP
400 National City Center, 6 North Main Street, Dayton, OH 45402-1908

Bingham McCutchen LLP
150 Federal Street, Boston, MA 02110

Bingham McHale LLP
2700 Market Tower, 10 West Market Street, Indianapolis, IN 46204

Bird, Marella, Boxer & Wolpert PC
1875 Century Park East, 23rd Floor, Los Angeles, CA 90067-2561

Biskind, Hunt & Taylor plc
11201 N Tatum Boulevard, Phoenix, AZ 85028

Black, Srebnick, Kornspan & Stumpf PA
201 South Biscayne Boulevard, Suite 1300, Miami, FL 33131

Blish & Cavanagh, LLP
Commerce Center, 30 Exchange Terrace, Providence, RI 02903

B

Bloom, Hergott and Diemer LLP
150 South Rodeo Drive, Third Floor,
Beverly Hills, CA 90212

Bodman LLP
100 Renaissance Center, 34th Floor, Detroit,
MI 48243

Bond, Schoeneck & King, PLLC
One Lincoln Center, Syracuse,
NY 13202-1355

Boone, Karlberg PC
201 West Main Street, Suite 300, PO Box
9199, Missoula, MT 59807-9199

**Boose Casey Ciklin Lubitz
Martens McBane & O'Connell**
Northbridge Tower 1, Nineteenth Floor, 515
North Flagler Drive, West Palm Beach,
FL 33401

Bose McKinney & Evans LLP
2700 First Indiana Plaza, 135 North
Pennsylvania Street, Indianapolis, IN 46204

**Bouchard Margules &
Friedlander PA**
222 Delaware Avenue, Suite 1400,
Wilmington, DE 19801

**Boult, Cummings, Conners &
Berry, PLC**
414 Union Street, Suite 1600, PO Box
198062, Nashville, TN 37219

Bowditch & Dewey LLP
311 Main Street, PO Box 15156, Worcester,
MA 01615-0156

**Bowles Rice McDavid Graff &
Love LLP**
600 Quarrier Street, PO Box 1386,
Charleston, WV 25325-1386

**Boyce, Greenfield, Pashby & Welk
LLP**
101 North Phillips Avenue, Suite 600, PO
Box 5015, Sioux Falls, SD 57117-5015

Bradley & Riley, PC
2007 First Avenue SE, PO Box 2804, Cedar
Rapids, IA 52406

**Bradshaw, Fowler, Proctor &
Fairgrave, PC**
801 Grand Avenue, Suite 3700, Des Moines,
IA 50309

Brault Graham Scott & Brault LLC
101 Washington Street, Rockville, MD 20850

Breazeale, Sachse & Wilson, LLP
One American Place, Twenty-Third Floor,
PO Box 3197, Baton Rouge, LA 70821

Bricker & Eckler LLP
100 South Third Street, Columbus,
OH 43215

**Briggs and Morgan, Professional
Association**
2200 IDS Center, 80 South Eighth Street,
Minneapolis, MN 55402

Bright & Lorig
633 West Fifth Street, Suite 3330, Los
Angeles, CA 90071

Broad and Cassel
Miami Center, Suite 3000, 201 South
Biscayne Boulevard, Miami, FL 33131

Brockelman Fatica PLC
21 East Sixth Street, No. 110, Tempe,
AZ 85281

**Bronstein, Carlson, Gleim &
Smith, PA**
Suite 1100, 150 Second Avenue North, St
Petersburg, FL 33701

**Brooks, Pierce, McLendon,
Humphrey & Leonard LLP**
2000 Renaissance Plaza, 230 North Elm
Street (27401), Greensboro, NC 27420

Brown Clark DeMay & Froman PA
1819 Main Street, Suite 1100, Sarasota,
FL 34236-5999

Brown Law Firm PC
315 North 24th Street, PO Drawer 849,
Billings, MT 59101

Brown McCarroll LLP
111 Congress Avenue, Suite 1400, Austin,
TX 78701-4043

**Brown Rudnick Berlack
Israels LLP**
One Financial Center, Boston, MA 02111

Bruce A Zimet PA
Suite 2612 One Financial Plaza, Fort
Lauderdale, FL 33394

Bruce S. Rogow, P.A.
500 East Broward Blvd, Suite 1930, Fort
Lauderdale, FL 33394

Bruder Gentile & Marcoux LLP
1701 Pennsylvania Avenue, Suite 900,
Washington, DC 20005-5805

Bryan Cave LLP
One Metropolitan Square, 211 North
Broadway, Suite 3600, St Louis,
MO 63102-2750

Buck & Gordon LLP
2025 First Avenue, Suite 500, Seattle,
WA 98121-3140

Buckingham Doolittle & Burroughs
191 West Nationwide Boulevard, Suite 300,
PO Box 151120, Columbus,
OH 43215-8120

Buist, Moore, Smythe, McGee P.A.
Five Exchange Street, PO Box 999,
Charleston, SC 29402

Bullard Smith Jernstedt Wilson
1000 SW Broadway, Suite 1900, Portland,
OR 97205

Bullivant Houser Bailey PC
300 Pioneer Tower, 888 SW Fifth Avenue,
Portland, OR 97204

Burch & Cracchiolo
702 East Osborn, Suite 200, Phoenix,
AZ 85011

Burch, Porter & Johnson PLLC
130 North Court, Memphis, TN 38103

Burke & Parsons
100 Park Avenue, 30th Floor, New York,
NY 10017-5533

Burr, Pease & Kurtz, PC
810 N Street, Anchorage, AK 99501

Butler Rubin Saltarelli & Boyd
70 West Madison, Suite 1800, Chicago,
IL 60602

**Butler, Wooten, Fryhofer,
Daughtery & Sullivan, LLP**
1500 Second Avenue, PO Box 2766,
Columbus, GA 31902

Byrnes & Keller
1000 Second Avenue, 38th Floor, Seattle,
WA 98104

C Michael Abbott PC
75 Fourteenth Street, Suite 2500, Atlanta,
GA 30309-3644

**Cabaniss, Johnston, Gardner,
Dumas & O'Neal**
2001 Park Place North, Suite 700,
Birmingham, AL 35203

Cades Schutte
Cades Schutte Building, 1000 Bishop Street,
Suite 1200, PO Box 939, Honolulu,
HI 96808

**Cadwell Sanford Deibert &
Garry LLP**
River Center, 200 East 10th Street, Suite 200,
PO Box, Sioux Falls, SD 57101-1157

Cahill Gordon & Reindel
80 Pine Street, New York, NY 10005-1702

Campbell & Williams
700 South 7th Street, Las Vegas,
NV 89101-6908

Campbell and Wells PA
2155 Louisiana Boulevard NE, Suite 10300,
Albuquerque, NM 87110

Caplin & Drysdale
One Thomas Circle NW, Suite 1100,
Washington, DC 20005-5802

**Carey, O'Malley, Whitaker &
Manson PA**
712 South Oregon Avenue, Tampa, FL
33606

Carey, Scott & Douglas, PLLC
1701 Bank One Center, 707 Virginia Street,
East Charleston, WV 25301

**Carlock Copeland Semler
& Stair, LLP**
2600 Marquis Two Tower, 285 Peachtree
Center Avenue, Atlanta, GA 30303

Carlsmith Ball LLP
Pacific Tower, Suite 2200, 1001 Bishop
Street, PO Box 656, Honolulu,
HI 96809-3402

Carmody & Torrance LLP
50 Leavenworth Street, PO Box 1110,
Waterbury, CT 06721

Carpenter & Klatskin
1500 Denver Club Building, Denver,
CO 80202

Carpenter & Lipps LLP
280 Plaza, Suite 1300, 280 North High
Street, Columbus, OH 43215

Carpenter & Stout Ltd
1600 University Boulevard NE, Suite A,
Albuquerque, NM 87102-1724

Carr, Tabb, Pope & Freeman, LLP
10 North Parkway Square, Atlanta,
GA 30327

**Carrington, Coleman, Sloman &
Blumenthal, LLP**
200 Crescent Court, Suite 1500, Dallas,
TX 75201

Carroll, Kelly & Murphy
One Turks Head Place, Suite 400,
Providence, RI 02903

Carruthers & Roth PA
235 North Edgeworth Street, PO Box 540,
Greensboro, NC 27402

**Carver Darden Koretzky Tessier
Finn Blossman & Areaux LLC**
Attorneys and Counselors at Law, Energy
Centre, 1100 Poydras Street, Suite 2700,
New Orleans, LA 70163

**Chamberlain, Hrdlicka, White,
Williams & Martin**
1200 Smith Street, Suite 1400, Houston,
TX 77002

Chambliss, Bahner & Stophel, P.C.
1000 Tallan Building, Two Union Square,
Chattanooga, TN 37402

**Charles L Siemon - Sole
Practitioner**
433 Real, Boca Ratón, FL 33428

Chester, Willcox & Saxbe LLP
65 East State Street, Suite 1000, Columbus,
OH 43215

Chisenhall, Nestrud & Julian, PA
400 West Capitol, Suite 2840, Little Rock,
AR 72201

Choate Hall & Stewart
Exchange Place, 53 State Street, Boston,
MA 02109-2891

**Christensen, Miller, Fink, Jacobs,
Glaser, Weil & Shapiro, LLP**
2121 Avenue of the Stars, 18th Floor, Los
Angeles, CA 90067

**Christensen, Moore, Cockrell,
Cummings & Axelberg PC**
Two Medicine Building, 160 Heritage Way,
PO Box 7370, Kalispell, MT 59904-0370

Christian & Barton LLP
909 East Main Street, Suite 1200,
Richmond, VA 23219

**Christian, Samson, Jones &
Chisholm, PLLC**
310 West Spruce, POBox 8479, Missoula,
MT 59807

**Chun, Kerr, Dodd, Beaman
& Wong**
745 Fort Street Mall, Suite 900, Honolulu,
HI 96813

**Cichanowicz, Callan, Keane,
Vengrow & Textor LLP**
61 Broadway, 30th Floor, Suite 3000, New
York, NY 10006-2802

Clark Hill PLC
500 Woodward Avenue, Suite 3500, Detroit,
MI 48226

Clark, Atcheson & Reisert
230 Park Avenue, New York, NY 10169

**Cleary Shahi Associates, A
Professional Corporation**
110 Merchants Row, Suite 7, PO Box 6740,
Rutland, VT 05702-6740

**Cline, Williams, Wright, Johnson &
Oldfather LLP**
1900 US Bank Building, 233 South 13th
Street, Lincoln, NE 68508

Coats Rose Yale Ryman Lee
800 First City Tower, 1001 Fannin, Houston,
TX 77002-6707

Coblentz, Patch, Duffy & Bass LLP
222 Kearny Street, Seventh Floor, San
Francisco, CA 94108

Coffman, Coleman, Andrews & Grogan
2065 Herschel Street, PO Box 40089, Jacksonville, FL 32203

Cohen & Grigsby PC
11 Stanwix Street, 15th Floor, Pittsburgh, PA 15222

Cohn & Whitesell LLP
101 Arch Street, Boston, MA 02110

Cokinos, Bosien and Young
2919 Allen Parkway, Suite 1500, Houston, TX 77019

Cole, Schotz, Meisel, Forman & Leonard PA
Court Plaza North, 25 Main Street, Hackensack, NJ 07602

Collier Shannon Scott
3050 K Street NW, Suite 400, Washington, DC 20007

Collier, Jacob & Mills
Corporate Park III, Third Floor, 580 Howard Avenue, Somerset, NJ 08873

Comiter, Singer & Baseman, LLP
3801 PGA Boulevard, Suite 802, Palm Beach Gardens, FL 33410

Commercial Law Group
2725 Oklahoma Tower, 210 Park Avenue, Oklahoma City, OK 73102-5643

Conley, Rose & Tayon
The Chase Building, 700 Lavaca, Suite 800, Austin, TX 78701-3102

Conmy Feste Ltd
200 Wells Fargo Center, 406 Main Avenue, PO Box 2686, Fargo, ND 58108-2686

Conner & Winters, PC
3700 First Place Tower, 15 East 5th Street, Tulsa, OK 74103-4344

Connolly, O'Malley, Lillis, Hansen & Olson LLP
317 Sixth Avenue, Suite 300, Bank of America Building, Des Moines, IA 50309

Constangy, Brooks & Smith, LLC
Suite 2400, 230 Peachtree Street North West, Atlanta, GA 30303-1557

Constantine & Partners (C&P)
477 Madison Avenue, 11th Floor, New York, NY 10022

Cook & Roach, L.L.P.
ChevronTexaco Heritage Plaza, 1111 Bagby, Suite 2650, Houston, TX 77002

Cook, Little, Rosenblatt & Manson PLLC
The Center of New Hampshire, 650 Elm Street, Manchester, NH 03101

Cooley Godward LLP
5 Palo Alto Square, 3000 El Camino Real, Palo Alto, CA 94306-2155

Coolidge, Wall, Womsley & Lombard
Suite 600, 33 West First Street, Dayton, OH 45402-1289

Copeland, Franco, Screws & Gill
444 South Perry Street, PO Box 347, Montgomery, AL 36101-0347

Corbyn Law Firm
Two Leadership Square, 211 North Robinson, Suite 1120, Oklahoma City, OK 73102

Corretti, Newsom & Hawkins
1804 7th Avenue North, Birmingham, AL 35203

Cosho, Humphrey, Greener & Welsh, PA
The Carnegie Building, 815 West Washington, Boise, ID 83702

Costello Porter Hill Heisterkamp Bushnell & Carpenter LLP
200 Security Building, 704 St Joseph Street, PO Box 290, Rapid City, SD 57709

Cotchett, Pitre, Simon & McCarthy
San Francisco Airport Office Center, 840 Malcolm Road, Suite 200, Burlingame, CA 94010

Cotsirilos Tighe & Streicker Ltd
Suite 600, 33 North Dearborn Street, Chicago, IL 60602

Coudert Brothers
The Grace Building, 1114 Avenue of the Americas, New York, NY 10036-7703

Cowan, Liebowitz & Latman
1133 Avenue of the Americas, New York, NY 10036-6799

Cox Castle & Nicholson LLP
2049 Century Park East, 28th Floor, Los Angeles, CA 90067

Cozen O'Connor
1900 Market Street, Philadelphia, PA 19103

Croker, Huck, Kasher, DeWitt, Anderson & Gonderinger, P.C.
The Omaha Tower, Suite 1250, 2120 South 72nd Street, Omaha, NE 68124

Cronin, Fried, Sekiya, Kekina & Fairbanks Attorneys At Law
1900 Davies Pacific Center, 841 Bishop Street, Honolulu, HI 96813-3908

Crowley, Haughey, Hanson, Toole & Dietrich, PLLP
490 North 31st Street, Suite 500, Billings, MT 59101-1288, PO Box 2529, Billings, MT 59103-2529

Cunningham Law Firm
400 Australian Avenue South, Suite 700, West Palm Beach, FL 33401

Cunningham, Bounds, Yance, Crowder & Brown, LLC
1601 Dauphin Street, PO Box 66705, Mobile, AL 36660

Cutler & Donahoe LLP
100 North Phillips Avenue, 9th Floor, Sioux Falls, SD 57104-6725

D'Amante Couser Steiner Pellerin, P.A.
9 Triangle Park Drive, PO Box 2650, Concord, NH 03302-2650

Daniels, Kashtan, Downs, Robertson & Magathan
3300 Ponce De Leon Boulevard, Miami, FL 33134

Danielson Harrigan Leyh & Tollefson, LLP
999 Third Avenue, Suite 4400, Seattle, WA 98104

Dann Pecar Newman & Kleiman, PC
One American Square, Suite 2300, Indianapolis, IN 46282

Davenport, Evans, Hurwitz & Smith LLP
206 West 14th Street, PO Box 1030, Sioux Falls, SD 57101-1030

Davis & Boghigian, PC
221 Main Street, Suite 301, PO Box 525, Nashua, NH 03061-0525

Davis & Cannon
40 South Main Street, PO Box 728, Sheridan, WY 82801

Davis & Ceriani
1350 17th Street, Denver, CO 80202

Davis & Kuelthau, S.C.
111 East Kilbourn Avenue, Suite 1400, Milwaukee, WI 53202

Davis Graham & Stubbs LLP
1550 Seventeenth Street, Suite 500, Denver, CO 80202

Davis, Brown, Koehn, Shors & Roberts, PC
The Financial Center, 666 Walnut Street, Suite 2500, Des Moines, IA 50309

Dawda, Mann, Mulcahy & Sadler PLC
39533 Woodward Ave, Suite 200, Bloomfield Hills, MI 48304-5103

Day Casebeer Madrid & Batchelder LLP
20300 Stevens Creek Boulevard, Suite 400, Cupertino, CA 95014

Day, Berry & Howard LLP
CityPlace I, Hartford, CT 06103-3499

Deacy & Deacy LLP
920 Main Street, Suite 1900, Kansas City, MO 64105

Dean, Mead, Egerton, Bloodworth, Capouano & Bozarth PA
800 North Magnolia Avenue, Suite 1500, Orlando, FL 32803

Deaner, Deaner, Scann, Malan & Larsen
720 South Fourth Street, Suite 300, Las Vegas, NV 89101

Demars & Turman Ltd
15 Broadway, Suite 510, PO Box 110, Fargo, ND 58107

DeOrchis & Partners, LLP
61 Broadway, 26th Floor, New York, NY 10006

Derrick & Briggs LLP
Bank One Center, 20th Floor, 100 North Broadway Avenue, Oklahoma City, OK 73102

Devine Millimet & Branch PA
PO Box 719, 111 Amherst Street, Manchester, NH 03105-0719

Dickinson Wright PLLC
500 Woodward, Suite 4000, Detroit, MI 48226-3425

Dickinson, Mackaman, Tyler & Hagen, P.C.
Suite 1600 Hub Tower, 699 Walnut Street, Des Moines, IA 50309

Dinse, Knapp & McAndrew PC
PO Box 988, 209 Battery Street, Burlington, VT 05402-0988

DiTrapano, Barrett & DiPiero, PLLC
604 Virginia Street East, Charleston, WV 25301

Doerner, Saunders, Daniel & Anderson, LLP
320 South Boston Avenue, Suite 500, Tulsa, OK 74103

Doffermyre, Shields, Canfield, Knowles & Devine
1355 Peachtree Street 1600, Atlanta, GA 30309 - 3269

Donovan Parry McDermott & Radzik
Wall Street Plaza, 88 Pine Street, New York, NY 10005-1801

Dorsey & Whitney LLP
50 South Sixth Street, Minneapolis, MN 55402-1498

Dover Dixon Horne
425 West Capitol, Suite 3700, Little Rock, AR 72201

Dow, Lohnes & Albertson, PLLC
1200 New Hampshire Avenue NW, Suite 800, Washington, DC 20036-6802

Downey, Brand, Seymour & Rohwer LLP
555 Capitol Mall, Suite 1050, Sacramento, CA 95814

Downs Rachlin Martin PLLC
90 Prospect Street, PO Box 99, St Johnsbury, VT 05819

Duffy, Sweeney & Scott Ltd
One Turks Head Place, Suite 1200, Providence, RI 02903

Duggan, Shadwick, Doerr & Kurlbaum, P.C.
11040 Oakmont Park, Overland Park, KS 66210

Durant, Nichols, Houston, Hodgson & Cortese-Costa, P.C.
1057 Broad Street, Bridgeport, CT 06604-4219

Durrell Law Group, PC
1400 West Benson Boulevard, Suite 370, Anchorage, AK 99503

Dutton, Braun, Staack & Hellman PLC
3151 Brockway Road, PO Box 810, Waterloo, IA 50704

Dykema Gossett PLLC
Third Floor West, Franklin Square, 1300 I Street NW, Washington, DC 20005

Eastman & Smith Ltd
One Seagate, Twenty-Fourth Floor, PO Box 10032, Toledo, OH 43699

Eaton Peabody
Fleet Center-Exchange Street, PO Box 1210, Bangor, ME 04402-1210

Eaves Bardacke Baugh Kierst & Kiernan PA
6400 Uptown Boulevard NE, Suite 110 - West (87110), PO Box 35670, Albuquerque, NM 87176

Eberle, Berlin, Kading, Turnbow & McKlveen, Chartered
Capitol Park Plaza, 300 North Sixth Street, Boise, ID 83701

Eckert Seamans Cherin & Mellott, LLC
600 Grant Street, 42nd Floor, Pittsburgh, PA 15219-2788

E

Edwards & Angell, LLP
101 Federal Street, Boston, MA 02110

Edwards Frickle Anner-Hughes & Cook
1601 Lewis Avenue, Suite206, PO Box 20039, Billings, MT 59104

Eggleston & Cramer, Ltd
150 South Champlain Street, PO Box 1489, Burlington, VT 05402

Elam & Burke PA
Key Financial Center, 702 West Idaho Street, Boise, ID 83701

Elarbee, Thompson, Sapp & Wilson, LLP
800 International Tower, 229 Peachtree Street NE, Atlanta, GA 30303

Elderkin & Pirnie PLC
115 First Avenue South East, PO Box 1968, Cedar Rapids, IA 52406

Eldridge Cooper Steichen & Leach PLLC
Suite 200, 110 West Seventh Street, Tulsa, OK 74119

Ellis & Winters LLP
1100 Crescent Green, Suite 200, Cary, NC 27511

Ellison Schneider & Harris
2015 H Street, Sacramento, CA 95814-3109

Ellman, Burke, Hoffman & Johnson
One Ecker Building, Suite 200, Ecker and Stevenson Streets, San Francisco, CA 94105

Epstein Becker & Green PC
250 Park Avenue, New York, NY 10177-1211

Erickson & Sederstrom, PC
Regency Westpointe, 10330 Regency Parkway Drive, Suite 100, Omaha, NE 68114

Everett Law Firm
1944 East Joyce Boulevard, Fayetteville, AR 72703

Fabian & Clendenin
215 South State Street, 12th Floor, PO Box 510210, Salt Lake City, UT 84111

Fabyanske, Westra & Hart PA
800 Lasalle Avenue, Suite 1900, Minneapolis, MN 55402-2037

Farella Braun & Martel LLP
Russ Building, 235 Montgomery Street, San Francisco, CA 94104

Farer Fersko
600 South Avenue, PO Box 580, Westfield, NJ 07091-0580

Farr & Taranto
Suite 800, 1220 19th Street, NW, Washington, DC 20036-2435

Faruki Ireland & Cox PLL
500 Courthouse Plaza SW, 10 North Ludlow Street, Dayton, OH 45402

Feldman & Orlansky
Suite 400, 500 L Street, Anchorage, AK 99501

Felhaber, Larson, Fenlon & Vogt, PC
220 South Sixth Street, Suite 2200, Minneapolis, MN 55402-4504

Ferencik, Libanoff, Brandt, Bustamante & Williams
150 South Pine Island Road, Suite 400, Fort Lauderdale, FL 33324

Ferrell Schultz Carter & Fertel PA
201 South Biscayne Bolevard, 34th Floor Miami Center, Miami, FL 33131-4325

Fine Kaplan & Black
Twenty Third Floor, 1845 Walnut Street, Philadelphia, PA 19103

Finley, Alt, Smith, Scharnberg, Craig, Hilmes & Gaffney PC
Equitable Building, 4th Floor, 604 Locust Street, Des Moines, IA 50309-3705

Finnegan Henderson Farabow Garrett & Dunner LLP
901 New York Avenue NW, Washington, DC 20001-4413

Fish & Neave IP Group of Ropes & Gray
1251 Avenue of the Americas, New York, NY 10020

Fish & Richardson
45 Rockefeller Plaza, Suite 2800, New York, NY 10111

Fisk & Fielder
2710 Stemmons Freeway, Suite 400, Dallas, TX 75207-2210

Flaherty, Sensabaugh & Bonasso PLLC
200 Capitaol Street, PO Box 3843, Charleston, WV 25301

Fleck, Mather & Strutz, Ltd.
Norwest Bank Building, Sixth Floor, 400 East Broadway, Bismarck, ND 58502

Fleeson, Gooing, Coulson & Kitch, LLC
125 North Market Street, Suite 1600, PO Box 997, Wichita, KS 67201

Flygare Schwarz & Closson PLLC
11 Court Street, PO Box 439, Exeter, NH 03833

Flynn, Gaskins & Bennett
2900 Metropolitan Center, Minneapolis, MN 55402

Fogarty, Cohen, Selby & Nemiroff LLC
88 Field Point Road, Greenwich, CT 06836-2508

Foley Hoag LLP
155 Seaport Boulevard, Boston, MA 02210-2600

Ford White & Nassen
1100 Highland Park Place, 4514 Cole Avenue, Dallas, TX 75205

Forizs and Dogali PL
4301 Anchor Plaza Parkway, Suite 300, Tampa, FL 33634

Foster Johnson McDonald Lucero Koinis LLP
40 First Plaza NW, Suite 735, Albuquerque, NM 87102

Foster Pepper & Shefelman PLLC
1111 Third Avenue, 34th Floor, Seattle, WA 98101

Fowler White Boggs Banker
501 East Kennedy Boulevard, Suite 1700, PO Box 1438, Tampa, FL 33602

Fowler, White, Burnett PA
Bank of America Tower, Seventeenth Floor, 100 SE Second Street, Miami, FL 33131

Franczek Sullivan
300 South Wacker Drive, Suite 3400, Chicago, IL 60606

Franklin, Weinrib, Rudell & Vassallo
488 Madison Avenue, New York, NY 10022

Frantz Ward LLP
55 Public Square Boulevard, 19th Floor, Cleveland, OH 44113

Fraser Stryker Law Firm
500 Energy Plaza, 409 South 17th Street, Omaha, NE 68102

Fredrikson & Byron PA
4000 Pillsbury Center, 200 South Sixth Street, Minneapolis, MN 55402-1425

Freeborn & Peters
311 South Wacker Drive, Suite 3000, Chicago, IL 60606

Freedman Boyd Daniels Hollander Goldberg & Cline PA
20 First Plaza, Suite 700, Albuquerque, NM 87102

Freehill Hogan & Mahar LLP
80 Pine Street, New York, NY 10005

Freeman, Freeman & Salzman
401 North Michigan Avenue, Suite 3200, Chicago, IL 60611-4207

Freilich, Leitner & Carlisle
1150 One Main Plaza, 4435 Main Street, Kansas City, MO 64111-7727

Freshfields Bruckhaus Deringer
520 Madison Ave, 34th Fl, New York, NY 10022

Friday, Eldredge & Clark
2000 Regions Center, 400 West Capitol Avenue, Little Rock, AR 72201

Frilot, Partridge, Kohnke & Clements LC
1100 Poydras Street, Suite 3600, New Orleans, LA 70163

Fritz, Byrne, Head & Harrison
2000 San Jacinto, 98 San Jacinto Boulevard, Austin, TX 78701

Fross Zelnick Lehrman & Zissu PC
866 UN Plaza, At First Avenue & 48th Street, New York, NY 10017

Fruth, Jamison & Elsass
80 South Eighth Street, Suite 3902, Minneapolis, MN 55402-2248

Fullenkamp, Doyle & Jobeun
11440 West Center Road, Omaha, NE 68144

G Richard Strafer PA
2400 South Dixie Highway, Suite 200, Miami, FL 33133

Gadsby Hannah LLP
225 Franklin Street, Boston, MA 02110-2811

Gainsburgh, Benjamin, David, Meunier & Warshauer
2800 Energy Centre, 1100 Poydras, New Orleans, LA 70163-2800

Gallagher & Kennedy PA
2575 East Camelback Road, Phoenix, AZ 85016-9225

Gallegos Law Firm PC
460 St Michael's Drive, Building 300, Santa Fe, NM 87505

Gallop, Johnson & Neuman LC
Interco Corporate Tower, 101 South Hanley, Suite 1600, St Louis, MO 63105

Gammage & Burnham, P.L.C.
One Renaissance Square, Two North Central Avenue, 18th Floor, Phoenix, AZ 85004

Gang Tyre Ramer & Brown
132 South Rodeo Drive, Beverly Hills, CA 90212

Garlington, Lohn & Robinson, PLLP
199 West Pine Street, PO Box 7909, Missoula, MT 59807

Gelber, Gelber, Ingersoll & Klevansky, A Law Corporation
Topa Financial Center, 745 Fort Street, Suite 1400, West Tower, Honolulu, HI 96813-3823

Genova, Burns & Vernoia
Eisenhower Plaza II, 354 Eisenhower Parkway, Livingston, NJ 07039

George & Lorensen
1526 Kanawhwa Boulevard E, Charleston, WV 25311-2413

George & Titus PA
100 South Ashley Drive, Suite 1290, Tampa, FL 33602-5360

Gignilliat, Savitz & Bettis LLP
900 Elmwood Avenue, Suite 100, Columbia, SC 29201

Gilbert Heintz & Randolph LLP
1100 New York Avenue, Suite 700, Washington, DC 20005

Gilchrist & Rutter Professional Corporation
1299 Ocean Avenue, Suite 900, Santa Monica, CA 90401-1000

Gilioli Alemani Bocchiola Tamburini e Partners in assoc with Curtis Mallet-Prevost Colt & Mosle LLP
Corso Venezia 5, Milan, 20121

Gilker and Jones PA
9222 North Highway 71, Mountainburg, AR 72946

Gilmartin, Poster & Shafto
845 Third Avenue, New York, NY 10012

Giordano Halleran & Ciesla PC
125 Half Mile Road, PO Box 190, Middletown, NJ 07748

Givens Pursley LLP
601 W Bannock, Boise, ID 83702

Glankler Brown, PLLC
One Commerce Square, Suite 1700, Memphis, TN 38103

Glenn Rasmussen Fogarty & Hooker
100 South Ashley Drive, Suite 1300, Tampa, FL 33601-3333

Godfrey & Kahn, SC
780 North Water Street, Milwaukee, WI 53202

If you can't find a firm here, see firm profiles at the end of every state

Goetz Fitzpatrick Most &
Bruckman LLP
One Penn Plaza, New York, NY 10119

Goetz, Gallik & Baldwin, PC
35 North Grand Avenue, PO Box 6580,
Bozeman, MT 59771-6580

Goins, Underkofler, Crawford &
Langdon LLP
1201 Elm Street, Suite 4800, Dallas,
TX 75270

Goldberg, Kohn, Bell, Black,
Rosenbloom & Moritz, Ltd
55 East Monroe Street, Suite 3700, Chicago,
IL 60603

Goodell, Stratton, Edmonds &
Palmer, LLP
515 South Kansas Avenue, Topeka,
KS 66603-3999

Goodin MacBride Squeri Ritchie
& Day LLP
Suite 900, 505 Sansome Street, San
Francisco, CA 94111

Goodsill Anderson Quinn & Stifel
Alii Place, Suite 1800, 1099 Alakea Street,
Honolulu, HI 96813

Goold Patterson Ales
Roadhouse & Day
4496 South Pecos Road, Las Vegas,
NV 89121

Gordon & Glickson
444 North Michigan Ave, Suite 3600,
Chicago, IL 60611-3903

Gordon & Silver Ltd
Ninth Floor, 3960 Howard Hughes Parkway,
Las Vegas, NV 89109

Gordon Murray Tilden
1325 Fourth Avenue, Suite 1800, Seattle,
WA 98101-2510

Gordon, Arata, McCollam,
Duplantis & Eagan LLP
201 St Charles Avenue, Suite 4000, New
Orleans, LA 70170-4000

Gordon, Feinblatt, Rothman,
Hoffberger & Hollander, LLC
The Garrett Building, 233 East Redwood
Street, Baltimore, MD 21202

Goren Cherof Doody & Ezrol PA
3099 East Commercial Boulevard, Suite 200,
Fort Lauderdale, FL 33308-4311

Gottlieb & Smith PA
Bank of America Plaza
Columbia, Suite 600, 1901 Main Street, PO
Box 51, Columbia, SC 29201

Gough, Shanahan, Johnson &
Waterman
33 South Last Chance Gulch, PO Box 1715,
Helena, MT 59601-1715

Goulston & Storrs
400 Atlantic Avenue, Boston, MA 02110

Gravel and Shea
Corporate Plaza, 76 St Paul Street, PO Box
369, Burlington, VT 05402-0369

Gray Robinson PA
301 East Pine Street, Suite 1400, Orlando,
FL 32802

Gray, Plant, Mooty, Mooty &
Bennett, PA
500 IDS Center, 80 South Eighth Street,
Minneapolis, MN 55402

Greenberg Glusker Fields Claman
Machtinger & Kinsella LLP
1900 Avenue of the Stars, 21st Floor,
Century City, Los Angeles, CA 90067

Greensfelder, Hemker & Gale, P.C.
2000 Equitable Building, 10 South
Broadway, St Louis, MO 63102

Greenstein Delorme & Luchs
1620 L Street Northwest, Suite 900,
Washington, DC 20036-5605

Gregory P Joseph Law
Offices LLC
805 Third Avenue, 31st Floor, New York,
NY 10022

Griffith & Nixon, P.C.
One Lincoln Centre, 5400 LBJ Freeway,
Suite 1025, Dallas, TX 75240

Gronek & Latham
390 North Orange Avenue, Suite 600, PO
Box 3353, Orlando, FL 32802

Groom Law Group
1701 Pennsylvania Avenue NW,
Washington, DC 20006

Gross & Welch, P.C.
2120 South 72nd Street, 800 Omaha Tower,
Omaha, NE 68124

Grossberg Yochelson Fox & Beyda
2000 L Street NW, Suite 675, Washington,
DC 20036-4907

Grotta, Glassman & Hoffman
75 Livingston Avenue, Roseland, NJ 07068

Guess & Rudd PC
510 L Street, Suite 700, Anchorage,
AK 99501

Gunderson Dettmer Stough
Villeneuve Franklin & Hachigian
155 Constitution Drive, Menlo Park,
CA 94025

Gunderson, Palmer, Goodsell
& Nelson LLP
440 Mount Rushmore Road, 3rd and 4th
Floors, Rapid City, SD 57709

Gunster, Yoakley & Stewart PA
Phillips Point, Suite 500 East, 777 South
Flagler Drive, West Palm Beach, FL 33401

Gurley Dramis
535 South Palm Avenue, Sarasota, FL 34236

Haddon, Morgan, Mueller, Jordan,
Mackey & Foreman PC
150 East Tenth Avenue, Denver, CO 80203

Hafetz & Necheles
500 Fifth Avenue, 29th Floor, New York,
NY 10110

Hahn Loeser & Parks LLP
3300 BP Tower, 200 Public Square,
Cleveland, OH 44114

Hale Lane Peek Dennison and
Howard
5441 Kietzke Lane, Second Floor, Reno,
NV 89511

Hall, Estill, Hardwick, Gable,
Golden & Nelson, PC
320 South Boston Avenue, Suite 400, Tulsa,
OK 74103

Hall, Farley, Oberrecht &
Blanton, PA
Key Financial Center, 702 West Idaho Street,
Suite 700, Boise, ID 83701

Hall, Render, Killian, Heath &
Lyman Professional Services
Corporation
One American Square, Suite 2000, Box
82064, Indianapolis, IN 46282

Hamilton Gaskins Fay & Moon
2020 Charlotte Plaza, 201 South College
Street, Charlotte, NC 28244-2020

Haney, Woloson & Mullins
1117 South Rancho Drive, Las Vegas,
NV 89102

Hankins & Hicks
800 West Fourth Street, PO Box 5670, Little
Rock, AR 72119

Hansen Jacobson Teller
Hoberman Newman, Warren,
Sloane & Richman, LLP
450 North Roxbury Drive, 8th Floor,
Beverly Hills, CA 90210-4222

Hansen, McClintock & Riley
Fleming Building, 8th Floor, 218 6th
Avenue, Des Moines, IA 50309-4092

Haralson, Miller, Pitt &
McAnally PLC
One South Church Avenue, Suite 900,
Tucson, AZ 85701-1620

Harding Shultz & Downs
800 Lincoln Square, 121 South 13th Street,
PO Box 82028, Lincoln, NE 68501-2028

Hare, Wynn, Newell & Newton LLP
The Historic Massey Building, 2025 Third
Avenue North, Suite 800, Birmingham,
AL 35203

Harris, Wiltshire & Grannis LLP
1200 Eighteenth Street NW, Suite 1200,
Washington, DC 20036-2560

Harrison & Moberly LLP
135 North Pennsylvania Street, Suite 2100,
Indianapolis, IN 46204

Harrison, Kemp & Jones, LLP
3800 Howard Hughes Parkway, Seventeenth
Floor, Las Vegas, NV 89109

Hartig Rhodes Hoge & Lekisch PC
717 K Street, Anchorage, AK 99501

Hartzog Conger Cason &
Neville, PC
1600 Bank of Oklahoma Plaza, 201 Robert S
Kerr, Oklahoma City, OK 73102

Harvey & Frank
Two City Center, PO Box 126, Portland, ME
04112-0126

Hatcher, Stubbs, Land, Hollis &
Rothschild, LLP
The Corporate Center, Suite 500,
Columbus, GA 31902

Hawley Troxell Ennis &
Hawley LLP
877 Main Street, Suite 1000, PO Box 1617,
Boise, ID 83702

Hayes Lorenzen Lawyers PLC
Plaza Centre One, Suite 580, 125 South
Dubuque Street, Iowa City, IA 52240

Haynes and Boone LLP
901 Main Street, Suite 3100, Dallas,
TX 75202

Haynsworth Sinkler Boyd PA
160 East Bay Street, PO Box 340,
Charleston, SC 29402-0340

Heard & Howard
219 North Fourth Street, PO Box 926,
Columbus, MT 59019-0926

Heath, Davis & McCalla
200 Perry-Brooks Building, 720 Brazous
Street, Austin, TX 78701

Helms Mulliss & Wicker PLLC
201 North Tryon Street, PO Box 31247,
Charlotte, NC 28202

Henderson Daily Withrow & DeVoe
One Indiana Square, Suite 2600,
Indianapolis, IN 46204-2071

Henson & Efron
220 South Sixth Street, Suite 1800,
Minneapolis, MN 55402-4503

Herge, Sparks & Christopher LLP
6862 Elm Street, Suite 360, McLean,
VA 22101

Herman, Herman, Katz &
Cotlar LLP
820 O'Keefe Avenue, New Orleans,
LA 70113-1116

Hickey&Mackey
1800 Carey Avenue, Suite 700, PO Drawer
467, Cheyenne, WY 82003

Higgins, Cavanagh & Cooney LLP
The Hay Building, Fourth Floor, 123 Dyer
Street, Providence, RI 02903

Hill & Robbins PC
1441 18th Street, 100 Blake Street Building,
Denver, CO 80202

Hill Gilstrap Perkins & Trotter, PC
1 Information Way, Suite 200, Little Rock,
AR 72202-2290

Hill Rivkins & Hayden LLP
45 Broadway, New York, NY 10006

Hill Wallack
202 Carnegie Center CN 5226, Princeton,
NJ 08543-5226

Hill, Ward & Henderson, PA
101 East Kennedy Boulevard, Suite 3700,
PO Box 2231, Tampa, FL 33601

Hinckley, Allen & Snyder LLP
28 State Street, 29th Floor, Boston, MA
02109 1775

Hinkle Elkouri Law Firm LLC
Suite 2000 Epic Center, 301 North Main
Street, Wichita, KS 67202

Hirschler Fleischer
The Federal Reserve Bank Building, 701
East Byrd Street, Richmond, VA 23218

Hirst & Applegate, PC
1720 Carey Avenue, Suite 200, PO Box 1083,
Cheyenne, WY 82003-1083

Hite, Fanning & Honeyman LLP
200 West Douglas Avenue, Suite 600,
Wichita, KS 67202-3089

Hodgson Russ LLP
One M & T Plaza, Suite 2000, Buffalo,
NY 14203

Hoffman Reilly Pozner &
Williamson
511 Sixteenth Street, Suite 700, Denver,
CO 80202

Holt Ney Zatcoff &
Wasserman, LLP
100 Galleria Parkway, Suite 600, Atlanta,
GA 30339

H

Honigman Miller Schwartz and Cohn
2290 First National Building, 660 Woodward Avenue, Detroit, MI 48226-3583

Hooper Lundy & Bookman Inc
1875 Century Park East, Suite 1600, Los Angeles, CA 90067

Howard, Rice, Nemerovski, Canady, Falk & Rabkin
Three Embarcadero Center, 7th Floor, San Francisco, CA 94111-4065

Howrey Simon Arnold & White
1299 Pennsylvania Avenue NW, Washington, DC 20004-2402

Huddleston Bolen LLP
611 Third Avenue, PO Box 2185, Huntington, WV 25722

Hughes & Luce LLP
1717 Main Street, Suite 2800, Dallas, TX 75201

Hughes Thorsness Powell Huddleston & Bauman LLC
550 West Seventh Avenue, Suite 1100, Anchorage, AK 99501

Hughes, Kellner, Sullivan & Alke
40 West Lawrence, PO Box 1166, Helena, MT 59624

Hunt, Ortmann, Blasco, Palffy & Rossell Inc
301 North Lake Avenue, 7th Floor, Pasedena, CA 91101

Hunter, Maclean, Exley & Dunn, PC
200 East Saint Julian Street, PO Box 9848, Savannah, GA 31412

Hurley Toevs Styles Hamblin & Panter PA
4155 Montgomery Boulevard NE, Albuquerque, NM 87109

Hurwitz & Sagarin LLC
PO Box 112, Milford, CT 06460

Husch & Eppenberger, LLC
1200 Main, Suite 1700, Kansas City, MO 63105

Hutchins, Wheeler & Dittmar
101 Federal Street, Boston, MA 02110

Icard, Merrill, Cullis, Timm, Furen & Ginsburg PA
2033 Main Street, Suite 600, Sarasota, FL 34237

Irell & Manella LLP
1800 Avenue of the Stars, Suite 900, Los Angeles, CA 90067-4276

Isaacson, Rosenbaum, Woods & Levy, PC
633 17th Street, Suite 2200, Denver, CO 80202

Ivins, Phillips & Barker
1700 Pennsylvania Avenue NW, Suite 600, Washington, DC 20006

J Cheney Mason PA
Bank of America Center, 390 North Orange Avenue, Suite 2100, Orlando, FL 32801

Jack, Lyon & Jones, PC
3400 TCBY Tower, 425 West Capitol Avenue, Little Rock, AR 72201

Jackson Lewis LLP
One Liberty Square, 55 Beattie Place, Suite 800, Greenville, DE 29601

Jackson Walker LLP
901 Main Street, Suite 6000, Dallas, TX 75202-3797

Jacobs, Chase, Frick, Kleinkopf & Kelley
1050 17th Street, Suite 1500, Denver, CO 80265

Jacobs, Grudberg, Belt & Dow PC
350 Orange Street, New Haven, CT 06503

Jaffe, Raitt, Heuer & Weiss, PC
One Woodward Avenue, Suite 2400, Detroit, MI 48226

Jane Kreusler-Walsh PA
Flagler Center, Suite 503, 501 South Flagler Drive, West Palm Beach, FL 33401

Janove Baar Associates
9 Exchange Place, Suite 1112, Salt Lake City, UT 84111

Jardine, Stephenson, Blewett and Weaver, P.C.
US Bank Building, Seventh Floor, 300 Central Avenue, Great Falls, MT 59403

Jay M Levy PA
Two Datran Center, Suite 1701, 9130 South Dadeland Boulevard, Miami, FL 33156

Jenkens & Gilchrist PC
1445 Ross Avenue, Suite 3200, Dallas, TX 75202-2799

Jenkins Fenstermaker, PLLC
401 Eleventh Street, 1100 Coal Exchange Building, PO Box 2688, Huntington, WV 25726-2688

Jennings, Strouss & Salmon, PLC
One Renaissance Square, Two North Central Avenue, Phoenix, AZ 85004-2385

Jensen Baird Gardner & Henry
Ten Free Street, PO Box 4510, Portland, ME 04112

Johnson, Pope, Bokor, Ruppel & Burns, PA
911 Chestnut Street, PO Box 1368, Clearwater, FL 33756

Johnston Barton Proctor & Powell LLP
2900 AmSouth/Harbert Plaza, 1901 Sixth Avenue North, Birmingham, AL 35203-2618

Jolley, Urga, Wirth & Woodbury
3800 Howard Hughes Parkway, 16th Floor, Las Vegas, NV 89109

Jones Vargas
3773 Howard Hughes Parkway, Third Floor South, Las Vegas, NV 89109

Jones Waldo Holbrook & McDonough PC
1500 Wells Fargo Plaza, 170 South Main Street, Salt Lake City, UT 84101

Jones, Foster, Johnston & Stubbs, P.A.
505 Flagler Drive, Suite 1100, West Palm Beach, FL 33401

Jorgenson Moffett LLC
10 Stormy Circle, P.O. Box 4978, Jackson, WY 83001

Jose M Quiñon - Sole Practitioner
2400 South Dixie Highway, Suite 200, Miami, FL 33133

Jung & Sisco
First Union Center, Suite 1240, 100 South Ashley Drive, Tampa, FL 33602

Kahn Kleinman
2600 Erieview Tower, 1301 East Ninth Street, Cleveland, OH 44114-1824

Kamer Zucker & Abbott
3000 West Charleston Boulevard, Suite 3, Las Vegas, NV 89102

Kantrow Spaht Weaver & Blitzer
Suite 300, City Plaza, 445 North Boulevard, PO Box 2997, Baton Rouge, LA 70821-2997

Kaplan, Brewer, Maxey & Haralson
415 Main Street, Little Rock, AR 72201

Kaplan, Strangis & Kaplan
5500 Wells Fargo Center, Minneapolis, MN 55402

Karaganis, White & Magel
414 North Orleans Street, Suite 810, Chicago, IL 60610

Karp & Genauer PA
2 Alhambra Plaza, Suite 1202, Coral Gables, FL 33134

Karp, Heurlin & Weiss PC
3060 North Swan Road, Suite 100, Tucson, AZ 85712-1225

Kasowitz Benson Torres & Friedman
1633 Broadway, New York, NY 10019

Katz, Teller, Brant & Hild
2400 Chemed Center, 255 East Fifth Street, Cincinnati, OH 45202-4724

Kaufman & Canoles
One Commercial Place, PO Box 3037, Norfolk, VA 23514

Kay Casto & Chaney PLLC
1600 Bank One Center, PO Box 2031, Charleston, WV 25327

Kean, Miller, Hawthorne, D'Armond, McCowan & Jarman, LLP
One American Place, 301 Main Street, 22nd Floor, Baton Rouge, LA 70821

Keating, Muething & Klekamp, PLL
1400 Provident Tower, One East Fourth Street, Cincinnati, OH 45202

Kegler, Brown, Hill & Ritter
Capitol Square, Suite 1800, 65 East State Street, Columbus, OH 43215-4294

Keleher & McLeod, PA
201 Third Street NW, Twelfth Floor, Albuquerque, NM 87103

Kelley Drye & Warren
101 Park Avenue, 30th Floor, New York, NY 10178

Kellogg, Huber, Hansen, Todd & Evans PLLC
1615 M Street NW, Suite 400, Washington, DC 20036

Kelly & Berens P.A.
Suite 3720 IDS Center, 80 South Eighth Street, Minneapolis, MN 55402

Kelly, Hart & Hallman, A Professional Corporation
201 Main Street, Suite 2500, Fort Worth, TX 76102

Kemp Smith LLP
221 North Kansas, Suite 1700, El Paso, TX 79901

Kenlan, Schwiebert & Facey, P.C.
71 Allen Street, PO Box 578, Rutland, VT 05702

Kennedy Covington Lobdell & Hickman LLP
Hearst Tower, 47th Floor, 214 North Tryon Street, Charlotte, NC 28202

Kennedy Lillis Schmidt & English
75 Maiden Lane, Suite 402, New York, NY 10038-4816

Kenyon & Kenyon
1500 K Street NW, Suite 700, Washington, DC 20005-1257

Kerr Russell & Weber
Detroit Center, 500 Woodward Avenue, Suite 2500, Detroit, MI 48226-3427

Kevin C Efroymson
2915 West Charleston Boulevard, Las Vegas, NV 89101

King & Ballow
1100 Union Street Plaza, 315 Union Street, Nashville, TN 37201

King, Blackwell & Downs PA
25 East Pine Street, Orlando, FL 32802-1631

Kirk & Chaney
101 Park Avenue, Suite 800, Oklahoma City, OK 73102

Kirschner & Legler
300-A Wharfside Way, Jacksonville, FL 32207

Kirshman Harris & Rosenthal
411 E Bonneville Avenue, Suite 300, Las Vegas, NV 89101

Klehr Harrison Harvey Branzberg & Ellers LLP
260 South Broad Street, Philadelphia, PA 19102-5003

Knobbe Martens Olson & Bear
2040 Main Street, 14th Floor, Irvine, CA 92614

Kohn Swift & Graf
One South Broad Street, Suite 2100, Philadelphia, PA 19107 3389

Kohn, Shands, Elbert, Gianoulakis & Giljum, LLP
One US Bank Plaza, Suite 2410, St Louis, MO 63101

Koley Jessen P.C.
One Pacific Place, 1125 South 103 Street, Suite 800, Omaha, NE 68124

Kollman & Saucier PA
Sun Life Building, 8th Floor, 20 South Charles Street, Baltimore, MD 21201-3225

Krasow, Garlick & Hadley LLC
One State Street, Hartford, CT 06103

Krieg DeVault LLP
One Indiana Square, Suite 2800, Indianapolis, IN 46204

If you can't find a firm here, see firm profiles at the end of every state

Kronish Lieb Weiner & Hellman LLP
1114 Avenue of the Americas, New York, NY 10036-7798

Krovatin & Associates LLC
744 Broad Street, Suite 1903, Newark, NJ 07102

Kutak Rock LLP
The Omaha Building, 1650 Farnam Street, Omaha, NE 68102-2186

Lamberth, Cifelli, Stokes & Stout, P.A.
Atlanta Financial Center, 3343 Peachtree Road, NE, East Tower, Suite 550, Atlanta, GA 30326-1022

Lamson, Dugan & Murray, LLP
Lamson Dugan & Murray Building, 10306 Regency Parkway Drive, Omaha, NE 68114

Landers & Parsons
310 West College Avenue, PO Box 271, Tallahassee, FL 32302

Lane & Waterman LLP
220 North Main Street, Suite 600, Davenport, IA 52801

Laner, Muchin, Dombrow, Becker, Levin, Tominberg
515 North State Suite, Suite 2800, Chicago, IL 60610

Langrock Sperry & Wool, LLP
111 South Pleasant Street, PO Drawer 351, Middlebury, VT 05753

Langsam Stevens & Silver LLP
1616 Walnut Street, Suite 1700, Philadelphia, PA 19103-5319

Lanier Ford Shaver & Payne
200 West Side Square, Suite 5000, Huntsville, AL 35804

Lankler Siffert & Wohl
33rd Floor, 500 Fifth Avenue, New York, NY 10110-3398

Latham & Burwell PLLC
447 Northpark Drive, Ridgeland, MS 39157

Latham & Watkins LLP
633 West Fifth Street, Suite 4000, Los Angeles, CA 90071-2007

Lathrop & Rutledge
1920 Thomes Avenue, Suite 500, PO Box 4068, Cheyenne, WY 82003

Lauri Waldman Ross - Sole Practitioner
Two Datran Center, Suite 1612, 9130 South Dadeland Boulevard, Miami, FL 33156

Lavely & Singer PC
2049 Century Park East, Suite 2400, Los Angeles, CA 90067-2906

Law Chambers Nicholas Critelli PC
317 Sixth Avenue, Suite 950, Des Moines, IA 50309-4128

Law Offices of GKRSE
1500 K Street NW, Suite 330, Washington, DC 20005

Law Offices of James McCollum LLC
510 L Street, Suite 540, Anchorage, AK 99501-1959

Law Offices of Jonathan H. (Jason) Warner, PA
9400 South Dadeland Boulevard, Suite 600, Miami, FL 33156

Law Offices of William H Booth
1500 Newell Avenue, 5th Floor, Walnut Creek, CA 94596

Lawler, Metzger, Milkman & Keeney, LLC
2001 K Street NW, Suite 802, Washington, DC 20006

Lawrence & Daniels
100 N Biscayne Boulevard, 21st Floor, Miami, FL 33132

Laxalt & Nomura
Bank of America Plaza, 50 West Liberty Street, Suite 700, Reno, NV 89501

Lea + O'Reilly
101 West Grand Avenue, Suite 200, Chicago, IL 60610

Leading-Edge Law Group, PLC
Three James Center, 1051 East Cary Street, Suite 1130, Richmond, VA 23219

Leatherwood Walker Todd & Mann PC
The Leatherwood Plaza, 300 East McBee Avenue, Suite 500, Greenville, SC 29601

LeClair Ryan, A Professional Corporation
707 East Main Street, 11th Floor, Richmond, VA 23219

Leff, Haupert, Traw & Willman LLP
222 South Linn Street, PO Box 2447, Iowa City, IA 52244 2447

Lehr Middlebrooks Price & Vreeland, P.C.
2021 Third Avenue North, Suite 300, Birmingham, AL 35203

Leitman, Siegal & Payne, PC
The Land Title Building, 600 North 20th Street, Suite 400, Birmingham, AL 35203

Lenrow, Kohn & Oliver
7 St Paul Street, Suite 940, Baltimore, MD 21202

Leonard, Street and Deinard Professional Association
150 South Fifth Street, Suite 2300, Minneapolis, MN 55402

Leopold, Petrich & Smith PA
2049 Century Park E, Suite 3110, Los Angeles, CA 90067

Leventhal & Slaughter PA
111 North Orange Avenue, Suite 700, Orlando, FL 32801

Levine Sullivan Koch & Schulz LLP
1050 17th Street NW, Suite 800, Washington, DC 20036

Levine, Steinberg, Miller & Huver
550 West Central Street, Suite 1810, San Diego, CA 92101-8596

Levy Phillips & Konigsberg LLP
800 Third Avenue, New York, NY 10022

Levy, Ram & Olson
639 Front Street, 4th Floor, San Francisco, CA 94111

Lewis & Slovak PC
725 Third Avenue North, PO Box 2325, Great Falls, MT 59403

Lewis and Roca
40 North Central Avenue, Phoenix, AZ 85004-4429

Lewis, Longman & Walker PA
1700 Palm Beach Lakes Boulevard, Suite 1000, West Palm Beach, FL 33401

Leydig, Voit & Mayer, Ltd
Two Prudential Plaza, 180 North Stetson Avenue, Suite 4900, Chicago, IL 60601-6780

Lightfoot, Franklin & White, LLC
The Clark Building, 400 20th Street North, Birmingham, AL 35203

Lightfoot, Vandevelde, Sadowsky, Medvene & Levine
655 South Hope Street, 13th Floor, Los Angeles, CA 90017

Liles, Gavin, Costantino & Murphy
One Enterprise Center, Suite 1500, 225 Water Street, Jacksonville, FL 32202

Linda S Mensch PC - Sole Practitioner
200 South Michigan Avenue, Suite 1240, Chicago, IL 60604

Lindner & Marsack, S.C.
411 East Wisconsin Avenue, Suite 1000, Milwaukee, WI 53202

Linowes and Blocher LLP
7200 Wisconsin Avenue, Suite 800, Bethesda, MD 20814

Lionel Sawyer & Collins
1700 Bank of America Plaza, 300 South Fourth Street, Las Vegas, NV 89101

Liskow & Lewis PLC
One Shell Square, 701 Poydras Street, Suite 5000, New Orleans, LA 70139-5099

Lisman, Webster, Kirkpatrick & Leckerling, P.C.
84 Pine Street, PO Box 728, Burlington, VT 05402

Litchford & Christopher
Bank of America Center, 390 North Orange Avenue, PO Box 1549, Orlando, FL 32802

Little, Medeiros, Kinder, Bulman & Whitney PC
72 Pine Street, Providence, RI 02903

Littler Mendelson PC
650 California Street, 20th Floor, San Francisco, CA 94108-2693

Lloyd, Gosselink, Blevins, Rochelle, Baldwin & Townsend, PC
111 Congress Avenue, Suite 1800, Austin, TX 78701

LMK PLC
1423 Park Avenue, Richmond, VA 23220

Locke Liddell & Sapp LLP
2200 Ross Avenue, Suite 2200, Dallas, TX 75201-6776

Loeb & Loeb LLP
10100 Santa Monica Boulevard, Suite 2200, Los Angeles, CA 90067-4164

Lommen, Nelson, Cole & Stageberg, P.A.
80 South 8th Street, Suite 2000, Minneapolis, MN 55402-2119

Long, Burner, Parks & DeLargy
515 Congress Avenue, Suite 1500, PO Box 2212, Austin, TX 78768-2212

Lord, Bissell & Brook
115 S LaSalle Street, Chicago, IL 60603

Lottner Rubin Fishman Brown & Saul, PC
633 Seventeenth Street, Suite 2700, Denver, CO 80202-3635

Lovells
One IBM Plaza Suite 1900, Chicago, IL 60611

Lowndes Drosdick Doster Kantor & Reed, PA
215 North Eola Drive, Orlando, FL 32801

Lueders, Robertson & Konzen
PO Box 725, 1939 Delmar Avenue, Granite City, IL 62040

Lynch, Cox, Gilman & Mahan, P.S.C.
Aegon Center, 400 West Market Street, Suite 2200, Louisville, KY 40202

MacPherson Kelly & Thompson
616 West Buffalo, PO Box 999, Rawlins, WY 82301

M

Maddin, Hauser, Wartell, Roth & Heller PC
28400 Northwestern Highway, Third Floor Essex Centre, Southfield, MI 48034-1839

Madison Harbour Mroz & Brennan PA
Suite 1600 Albuquerque Plaza, 201 Third Street North West, PO Box 25467, Albuquerque, NM 87102

Maloy & Jenkins
75 Fourteenth Street NW, 25th Floor, Atlanta, GA 30309

Manatt Phelps & Phillips LLP
11355 West Olymoic Boulevard, Los Angeles, CA 90064

Mancini Welch & Geiger LLP
The Kahului Building, 33 Lono Avenue, Suite 470, Kahului, HI 96732-1681

Manko, Gold, Katcher & Fox LLP
401 City Avenue, Suite 500, Bala Cynwyd, PA 19004

Manning Curtis Bradshaw & Bednar
Third Floor Newhouse Building, Salt Lake City, UT 84111

Manning Fulton & Skinner PA
PO Box 20389, Raleigh, NC 27619-0389

Maring Williams Law Office PC
1220 Main Avenue, Suite 105, PO Box 2103, Fargo, ND 58107-2103

Mariscal, Weeks, McIntyre & Friedlander PA
2901 North Central Avenue, Suite 200, Phoenix, AZ 85012

Mark W. Gifford
243 South Park Street, POBox 2508, Casper, WY 82602

Markowitz, Herbold, Glade & Mehlhaf PC
3000 Pacwest Center, 1211 South West Fifth Avenue, Portland, OR 97204-3730

Marr Hipp Jones & Wang
Pauahi Tower, 1001 Bishop Street, Suite 1550, Honolulu, HI 96813

Marsh, Rickard & Bryan P.C
800 Shades Creek Parkway, Suite 600, Birmingham, AL 35209-4532

Marshall Hill Cassas & De Lipkau
Holcomb Professional Center, Suite 300,
333 Holcomb Avenue, PO Box 2790, Reno,
NV 89505-2790

Marshall, Gerstein & Borun
6300 Sears Tower, 233 South Wacker Drive,
Chicago, IL 60606-6402

Martin & Churchill Chartered
8415 East 21st Street North, Wichita,
KS 67206-2954

**Martin, Pringle, Oliver, Wallace &
Bauer, L.L.P.**
100 North Broadway, Suite 500, Wichita,
KS 67202

Martzell & Bickford, APC
338 Lafayette Street, New Orleans,
LA 70130-3244

**Maslon Edelman Borman &
Brand, LLP**
3300 Wells Fargo Center, 90 South Seventh
Street, Minneapolis, MN 55402

Mason & Mason PC
Box 785, Pinedale, WY 82941

Matkov Salzman Madoff & Gunn
55 East Monroe Street, Suite 2900, Chicago,
IL 60603-5709

Maupin Taylor, P.A.
Highwoods Tower One, 3200 Beechleaf
Court, Suite 500, Raleigh, NC 27604

**May, Adam, Gerdes & Thompson,
L.L.P.**
503 South Pierre Street, PO Box 160,
Pierre, SD 57501

Maynard, Cooper & Gale PC
Harbert Plaza, 1901 Sixth Avenue North,
Suite 2400, Birmingham, AL 35203

Mazur, Carp & Rubin PC
1250 Broadway, Suite 3800, New York,
NY 10016

McConn & Rindy
31-37 3rd Avenue Southwest, Suite 212,
Fargo, ND 58103

**McCullough Hill Fikso
Kretschmer Smith**
2025 First Avenue, Suite 1130, Seattle,
WA 98121

McDade Fogler LLP
Two Houston Center, 909 Fannin, Suite
1200, Houston, TX 77010-1006

**McDonald Carano Wilson McCune
Bergin Frankovich & Hicks LLP**
241 Ridge Street, Reno, NV 89501

McDonald Hopkins Co
2100 Bank One Center, 600 Superior
Avenue East, Cleveland, OH 44114-2653

**McDowell Knight Roedder &
Sledge LLC**
63 South Royal Street, Suite 900, Mobile,
AL 36602

**McElroy, Deutsch, Mulvaney &
Carpenter, LLP**
Three Gateway Center, 17th Floor, 100
Mulberry Street, Newark, NJ 07102-4079

McEwen Gisvold LLP
Suite 1600, 1100 SW 6th Avenue, Portland,
OR 97204-1017

**McGee Hankla Backes &
Dobrovolny P.C.**
Suite 305 Wells Fargo Bank Center, 15
Second Avenue Southwest, Minot,
ND 58702

McGrath North Mullin & Kratz PC
Suite 3700 First National Tower, 1601
Dodge Street, Omaha, NE 68102-1627

McGuireWoods LLP
One James Center, 901 East Cary Street,
Richmond, VA 23219-4030

McKinney & Stringer, PC
Corporate Tower, 101 North Robinson,
Oklahoma City, OK 73102

McKool Smith
300 Crescent Court, Suite 1500, Dallas, TX
75201

McLaughlin & McCaffrey, LLP
Eaton Center, 1111 Superior Avenue East,
Suite 1350, Cleveland, OH 44114-2500

**McMahon, DeGulis, Hoffmann &
Lombardi LLP**
The Caxton Building, Suite 650, Cleveland,
OH 44115-1126

**McManus Schor Asmar &
Darden, L.L.P.**
1301 Conneticut Avenue, NW, Sixth Floor,
Washington, DC 20036

McNair Law Firm PA
1301 Gervais Street, PO Box 11390,
Columbia, SC 29211

McNair, Larson & Carlson Ltd
PO Box 2189, Fargo, ND 58108

**Meadows, Owens, Collier, Reed,
Cousins & Blau**
901 Main Street, Suite 3700, Dallas, TX
75202-3725

Meardon, Sueppel & Downer
122 South Linn Street, Iowa City, IA 52240

Meckler, Bulger & Tilson
8200 Sears Tower, 233 South Wacker Drive,
Chicago, IL 60606 6306

Meehan LLP
127 West Franklin Street, Tucson,
AZ 85702-1671

Melli Walker Pease & Ruhly S.C.
Ten East Doty, Suite 900, PO Box 1664,
Madison, WI 53701

Mendes & Mount LLP
750 Seventh Avenue, New York,
NY 10019-6829

Merchant & Gould PC
3200 IDS Centre, 80 South 8th Street,
Minneapolis, MN 55402

Messerman & Messerman Co, LPA
4100 Key Tower, 127 Public Square,
Cleveland, OH 44114

Meuleman Miller LLP
960 Broadway Avenue, Suite 400, Boise,
ID 83701

Meyer Capel, PC
Athenaeum Building, 306 West Church
Street, PO Box 6750, Champaign,
IL 61826-6750

Meyer, Hendricks & Bivens PA
3003 North Central Avenue, Suite 1200,
Phoenix, AZ 85012-2915

Milbank, Tweed, Hadley & McCloy
1 Chase Manhattan Plaza, 47th Floor, New
York, NY 10005

Miller & Chevalier Chartered
655 Fifteenth Street NW, Suite 900,
Washington, DC 20005-5701

**Miller Hamilton Snider &
Odom LLC**
254-256 State Street, PO Box 46, Mobile,
AL 36601

Miller Nash LLP
3400 US Bancorp Tower, 111 SW Fifth
Avenue, Portland, OR 97204

Miller Stratvert PA
500 Marquette Avenue, Suite 1100,
Albuquerque, NM 87102

Miller, Balis & O'Neil, PC
1140 Nineteenth Street NW, Suite 700,
Washington, DC 20036

**Miller, Johnson, Snell &
Cummiskey, P.L.C.**
250 Monroe Avenue NW, Suite 800, Grand
Rapids, MI 49503

Miller, Morton, Caillat & Nevis
25 Metro Drive, 7th Floor, San Jose,
CA 95110

Millisor & Nobil Co LPA
9150 South Hills Boulevard, Suite 300,
Cleveland, OH 44147-3599

**Mintz Levin Cohn Ferris Glovsky
and Popeo PC**
One Financial Center, Boston, MA 02111

Mitchell Hurst Jacobs & Dick
152 E Washington Street, Indianapolis,
IN 46204

Mitchell, McNutt & Sams PA
105 South Front Street, PO Box 7120,
Tupelo, MS 38802

Mitchell, Silberberg & Knupp LLP
11377 West Olympic Boulevard, Los
Angeles, CA 90064-1683

**Mock, Schwabe, Waldo, Elder,
Reeves & Bryant**
Fourteenth Floor, Two Leadership Square,
211 North Robinson Avenue, Oklahoma
City, OK 73102

**Modrall, Sperling, Roehl, Harris
& Sisk, PA**
500 Fourth Street NW, Bank of America
Centre, Suite 1000, Albuquerque,
NM 87103

Moehrke, Mackie & Shea, P.C.
137 Newbury Street, Boston, MA 02116

**Moffatt Thomas Barrett
Rock & Fields**
101 South Capitol Boulevard, 10th Floor,
PO Box 829, Boise, ID 83701

**Mohan, Alewelt, Prillaman
& Adami**
1 North Old Capitol Plaza, Suite 325,
Springfield, IL 62701-1323

Monteleone & McCrory, LLP
725 South Figueroa Street, Suite 3750, Los
Angeles, CA 90017-5402

**Montgomery, Barnett, Brown,
Read, Hammond & Mintz LLP**
3200 Energy Centre, 1100 Poydras Street,
New Orleans, LA 70163

**Montgomery, McCracken, Walker
& Rhoads, LLP**
123 South Broad Street, Philadelphia,
PA 19109

Moore & Lee LLP
1750 Tysons Boulevard, Suite 1450,
McLean, VA 22102-4208

Moore & Van Allen PLLC
40 Calhoun Street, Suite 300, Charleston,
SC 29401

Moore, O'Connell & Refling PC
601 Haggerty Lane, Suite 10, PO Box 1288,
Bozeman, MT 59771

Morris & Morris PC
1200 Wytestone Plaza, 801 East Main Street,
PO Box 30, Richmond, VA 23218-0030

Morris Pickering & Sanner
900 Bank of America Plaza, 300 South
Fourth Street, Las Vegas, NV 89101

**Morris, Laing, Evans, Brock &
Kennedy, Chartered**
300 North Mead, Suite 200, Wichita, KS
67202-2745

**Morse, Barnes-Brown &
Pendleton PC**
Reservoir Place, 1601 Trapelo Road, Suite
205, Waltham, MA 02451

**Morvillo, Abramowitz, Grand,
Iason & Silberberg, PC**
565 Fifth Avenue, New York, NY 10017

**Moscowitz, Moscowitz &
Magolnick PA**
Barclays Financial Center, 1111 Brickell
Avenue, Suite 2050, Miami, FL 33131

**Moulton, Bellingham, Longo &
Mather, PC**
Suite 1900 Sheraton Plaza, 27 North 27th
Street, Billings, MT 59103

**Moye, Giles, O'Keefe, Vermeire &
Gorrell LLP**
1225 Seventeenth Street, 29th Floor, Denver,
CO 80202

Moyer & Bergman, PLC
2720 First Avenue NE, Cedar Rapids,
IA 52406

**Much Shelist Freed Denenberg
Ament & Rubenstein, P.C.**
191 North Wacker Drive, Suite 1800,
Chicago, IL 60606

Mullikin, Larson & Swift
155 East Pearl Street, Suite 200, PO Box
4099, Jackson, WY 83001

Munger, Tolles & Olson LLP
355 South Grand Avenue, 35th Floor, Los
Angeles, CA 90071-1560

Murane & Bostwick LLC
201 North Wolcott, Casper, WY 82601

Murphy & Shaffer
36 South Charles Street, Suite 1400,
Baltimore, MD 21201-3109

Murphy Sullivan Kronk
275 College Street, PO Box 4485,
Burlington, VT 05406-4485

**Murphy, Goldammer &
Prendergast**
101 North Phillips Avenue, Suite 604, PO
Box 5015, Sioux Falls, SD 57117-5015

Murtha Cullina LLP
CityPlace I, 29th Floor, 185 Asylum Street,
Hartford, CT 06103

Myers Oliver & Price
1401 Central North West, Albuquerque,
NM 87104

Nagin Gallop Figueredo PA
3225 Aviation Avenue, Suite 301, Coconut
Grove, FL 33133

Neal & Harwell, PLC
Suite 2000, One Nashville Place, 150 Fourth
Avenue North, Nashville, TN 37219

Neal, Gerber & Eisenberg LLP
Two North La Salle Street, Suite 2200,
Chicago, IL 60602

Needle & Rosenberg, P.C
Suite 1000, 999 Peachtree Street, Atlanta,
GA 30309

**Neligan Tarpley Andrews
& Foley LLP**
1700 Pacific Avenue, Suite 2600, Dallas, TX
75201-7322

**Nelson Kinder Mosseau &
Saturley PC**
99 Middle Street, Manchester, NH 03101

Neubert, Pepe & Monteith PC
195 Church Street, 13th Floor, New Haven,
CT 06510

**Nickens Keeton Lawless Farrell &
Flack LLP**
327 Congress Avenue, Suite 490, Austin,
TX 78701

**Nicoletti Hornig Campise and
Sweeney**
Wall Street Plaza, 88 Pine Street, New York,
NY 10005-1801

Nilles, Hansen & Davies Ltd
1800 Radisson Tower, PO Box 2626, Fargo,
ND 58108

Niro, Scavone, Haller & Niro
181 West Madison, Suite 4600, Chicago,
IL 60602-4515

Norman, Hanson & DeTroy, LLC
415 Congress Street, Fifth Floor, PO Box
4600, Portland, ME 04112

**Norris, McLaughlin & Marcus, P.A.,
A Professional Corporation**
721 Route 202-206, PO Box 1018,
Bridgewater, NJ 08876

Nourse & Bowles LLP
One Exchange Plaza at 55 Broadway, New
York, NY 10006

Nungesser & Hill
56 State Route 25, Meredith, NH 03253

Nutter, McClennen & Fish, LLP
World Trade Centre West, 155 Seaport
Boulevard, Boston, MA 02110-2604

**Nyemaster, Goode, West, Hansell,
and O'Brien**
700 Walnut, Suite 1600, Des Moines,
IA 50309

Ober Kaler Grimes & Shriver
120 East Baltimore Street, Suite 800,
Baltimore, MD 21202-1643

**Oblon, Spivak, McClelland, Maier
& Neustadt PC**
1940 Duke Street, Alexandria, VA 22314

**Oertel, Fernandez, Cole &
Bryant, P.A.**
301 South Bronough Street, Fifth Floor, PO
Box 1110, Tallahassee, FL 32301-1110

Ohnstad Twichell PC
901 Thirteenth Avenue East, Second Floor,
PO Box 458, Fargo, ND 58078

Olson Burns Lee PC
PO Box 1180, Minot, ND 58702

**Oppenheimer Wolff &
Donnelly LLP**
2029 Century Park East, Suite 3800, Los
Angeles, CA 90067

**Orloff, Lowenbach, Stifelman
& Siegel**
101 Eisenhower Parkway, Roseland,
NJ 07068

Orr & Reno PA
One Eagle Square, PO Box 3550, Concord,
NH 03302

Oshima, Chun, Fong & Chung
Davies Pacific Center, Fourth Floor, 841
Bishop Street, Honolulu, HI 96813

**Otten, Johnson, Robinson, Neff &
Ragonetti, PC**
950 Seventeenth Street, 16th Floor, Denver,
CO 80202

**Otterbourg, Steindler, Houston &
Rosen**
230 Park Avenue, New York, NY 10169

Packman, Neuwahl & Rosenberg
1500 San Remo Avenue, Suite 125, Coral
Gables, FL 33146

**Pansing Hogan Ernst &
Bachman LLP**
10250 Regency Circle, Suite 300, Omaha,
NE 68114

Pappas Metcalf Jenks and Miller
245 Riverside Avenue, Suite 400,
Jacksonville, FL 32202-4926

**Parker, Hudson, Rainer &
Dobbs LLP**
1500 Marquis Two Tower, 285 Peachtree
Center Avenue NE, Atlanta, GA 30303

**Parker, Poe, Adams &
Bernstein LLP**
Three Wachovia Center, 401 South Tryon
Street, Suite 3000, Charlotte, NC 28202

**Parr Waddoups Brown
Gee & Loveless**
Suite 1300, 185 South State Street, Salt Lake
City, UT 84111

Partridge Snow & Hahn LLP
180 South Main Street, Providence,
RI 02903

Pasich & Kornfeld, LLP
10866 Wilshire Boulevard, Suite 300, Los
Angeles, CA 90024

Patricia A Felch - Attorney at Law
1510 Main Street, Evanston, IL 60202-1617

**Patterson, Belknap, Webb &
Tyler LLP**
1133 Avenue of Americas, New York, NY
10036-6710

**Pattishall, McAuliffe, Newbury,
Hilliard & Geraldson**
311 South Wacker Drive, Suite 5000,
Chicago, IL 60606

Paul A. Beck & Associates, P.C.
157 McFarland Road, Suite 100, Pittsburgh,
PA 15216

**Paul, Frank + Collins, A
Professional Corporation**
One Church Street, PO Box 1307,
Burlington, VT 05402

**Paul, Johnson, Park & Niles,
Attorneys At Law, A Law
Corporation**
American Savings Bank Tower, Suite 1300,
1001 Bishop Street, Honolulu, HI 96813

Pearce & Durick
314 East Thayer Avenue, PO Box 400,
Bismarck, ND 58502

Pearson Christensen LLP
24 North Fourth Street, PO Box 5758,
Grand Forks, ND 58201

Peifer, Hanson & Mullins PA
20 First Plaza Center North West, Suite 725,
Albuquerque, NM 87102-3347

**Peitzman, Glassman, Weg &
Kempinski**
1801 Avenue of the Stars, Suite 1225, Los
Angeles, CA 90067

**Pennington, Moore, Wilkinson,
Bell & Dunbar, PA**
215 South Monroe Street, Second Floor,
Tallahassee, FL 32301

**Pepple Johnson Cantu &
Schmidt, PLLC**
1218 Third Avenue, Suite 1900, Seattle, WA
98101-3051

Perkins Coie LLP
1201 Third Avenue, Seattle, WA 98101-3099

**Perkins, Thompson, Hinckley
& Keddy, P.A.**
One Canal Plaza, PO Box 426, Portland,
ME 04112

Petruccelli Martin & Haddow LLP
50 Monument Square, PO Box 17555,
Portland, ME 04112-8555

**Pettiette, Armand, Dunkelman,
Woodley, Byrd & Cromwell LLP**
509 Market Street, Suite 200, PO Box 1786,
Shreveport, LA 71101

Phibbs Law Office PC
PO Box 1028, 330 East Snow King Avenue,
Jackson, WY 83001

**Phillips McFall McCaffrey McVay &
Murrah, P.C.**
One Leadership Square, 12th Floor, 211
North Robinson, Oklahoma City, OK 73102

Piccarreta & Davis PC
145 South Sixth Avenue, Tucson,
AZ 85701-2007

Pill & Pill
1444 Edwin Miller Boulevard, Martinsburg,
WV 25401

Pircher, Nichols & Meeks
1925 Century Park East, 17th Floor, Los
Angeles, CA 90067

Podhurst Orseck, P.A.
Suite 800 City National Bank Building, 25
West Flagler Street, Miami, FL 33130-1780

**Polsinelli Shalton Welte
Suelthaus (PSWS)**
700 West 47th Street, Suite 1000, Kansas
City, MO 64112

Poore, Roth & Robinson, P.C.
1341 Harrison Avenue, PO Box 2000, Butte,
MT 59702

Porter & Hedges, LLP
Bank of America Center, 700 Louisiana
Street, 35th Floor, Houston,
TX 7700277210-4744

Postner & Rubin
Suite 210, 17 Battery Place, New York,
NY 10004

Potter Anderson & Corroon LLP
Hercules Plaza, 1313 North Market Street,
Wilmington, DE 19899-0951

Powell Goldstein LLP
Third Floor, 901 New York Avenue, NW,
Washington, DC 20001-4413

Poyner & Spruill LLP
3600 Glenwood Avenue, PO Box 10096,
Raleigh, NC 27605

Preston Gates & Ellis LLP
701 Fifth Avenue, Suite 5000, Seattle, WA
98104-7078

Prickett, Jones & Elliott PA
1310 King Street, PO Box 1328,
Wilmington, DE 19899-1328

Quarles & Brady LLP
411 East Wisconsin Avenue, Suite 2040,
Milwaukee, WI 53202

**Quilling, Selander, Cummiskey &
Lownds, P.C.**
2001 Bryan Tower, Suite 1800, Dallas,
TX 75201

**R. William Meeks - Sole
Practitioner**
511 South High Street, Columbus,
OH 43215

**Ramis Crew Corrigan &
Bachrach LLP**
1727 NW Hoyt Street, Portland, OR 97209

**Ramsay, Bridgforth, Harrelson &
Starling LLP**
Simmons First National Building, Eleventh
Floor, 501 Main Street, Post Office Box
8509, Pine Bluff,
AR 71611-8509

Raskin & Raskin PA
2601 South Bayshore Drive, Suite 600,
Miami, FL 33133

**Rath, Young and Pignatelli,
Professional Association**
One Capital Plaza, PO Box 1500, Concord,
NH 03302

**Ravich Meyer Kirkman McGrath &
Nauman, PA**
4545 IDS Center, 80 South Eighth Street,
Minneapolis, MN 55402

Ray & Isler PC
8245 Boone Boulevard, Suite 402, Tysons
Corner, Vienna, VA 22182-3813

Ray, Quinney & Nebeker PC
36 South State Street, Suite 1400, Salt Lake
City, UT 84111

Rebein Bangerter PA
810 West Frontview, Dodge City, KS 67801

**Reed Weitkamp Schell &
Vice PLLC**
500 West Jefferson, Suite 2400, Louisville,
KY 40202

R

S

Reeder & Shuman
PO Box 842, Morgantown, WV 26507

Reeves & Miller
Park Street Law Office, 242 South Park Street, PO Box 530, Casper, WY 82602

Reges & Boone LLC
9095 Glacier Highway, Suite 103, Juneau, AK 99801

Rendings, Fry & Dennis, LLP
1 West Fourth Street, Suite 900, Cincinnati, OH 45202-3688

Richards Layton & Finger
One Rodney Place, PO Box 551, Wilmington, DE 19899-1328

Richilano & Ridley PC
1800 15th Street, Suite 101, Denver, CO 80202-1185

Riddell Williams PS
1001 Fourth Avenue Plaza, Suite 4500, Seattle, WA 98154

Rider, Bennett, Egan & Arundel, LLP
333 South Seventh Street, Suite 2000, Minneapolis, MN 55402

Riegels Campos & Kenyon
2500 Venture Oaks Way, Suite 220, Sacramento, CA 95833

Riemer & Braunstein LLP
Three Center Plaza, Boston, MA 02108

Robbins, Russell, Englert, Orseck & Untereiner LLP
1801 K Street NW, Suite 411, Washington, DC 20006

Robert E Panoff PA
9400 South Dadeland Boulevard, Suite 106, Miami, FL 33156

Robert M. Knight
526 East Front Street, PO Box 8899, Missoula, MT 59807-8899

Robert Stoller - Sole Practitioner
800 Dimond Boulevard, Suite 3-537, Anchorage, AK 99515

Roberts & Holland LLP
Worldwide Plaza, 825 Eighth Avenue, New York, NY 10019-7416

Robins Kaplan Miller & Ciresi
2800 LaSalle Plaza, 800 LaSalle Avenue, Minneapolis, MN 55402

Robinson & McElwee PLLC
600 United Center, 500 Virginia Street East, Charleston, WV 25326

Robinson, Bradshaw & Hinson PA
101 North Tryon Street, Suite 1900, Charlotte, NC 28246

Robison, Belaustegui, Sharp & Low
71 Washington Street, Reno, NV 89503

Rochelle, Hutcheson & McCullough, LLP
325 North St Paul, Suite 4500, Dallas, TX 75201

Rodey, Dickason, Sloan, Akin & Robb, PA
201 Third Street North West, Suite 2200, Albuquerque, NM 87102

Roetzel & Andress PA
222 South Main Street, Akron, OH 44308

Rogers, Towers, Bailey, Jones & Gay, PA
1301 Riverplace Boulevard, Suite 1500, Jacksonville, FL 32207

Ronald K Cacciatore PA
100 North Tampa Street, Suite 2835, Tampa, FL 33602

Rose Law Firm
120 East Fourth Street, Little Rock, AR 72201-2893

Rosenberg, Martin, Funk, Greenberg, LLP
25 South Charles Street, Suite 2115, Baltimore, MD 21201

Rothgerber Johnson & Lyons LLP
One Tabor Center, 1200 17th Street, Suite 3000, Denver, CO 80202

Rouse Hendricks German May PC
One Petticoat Lane Building, 1010 Walnut Street, Suite 400, Kansas City, MO 64106

Rubin and Rudman LLP
50 Rowes Wharf, Boston, MA 02110

Ruby & Schofield
125 South Market Street, Suite 1001, San José, CA 95113-2285

Ruden McClosky SC
200 East Broward Boulevard, PO Box 1900, Fort Lauderdale, FL 33302

Rudman & Winchell LLC
84 Harlow Street, PO Box 1401, Bangor, ME 04402-1401

Rushton, Stakely, Johnston & Garrett
184 Commerce Street, Montgomery, AL 36104

Rusing & Lopez PLLC
6262 North Swan Road, Suite 200, Tucson, AZ 85718

Ryan & Whaley
900 Robinson Renaissance, 119 North Robinson Avenue, Oklahoma City, OK 73102

Sachnoff & Weaver LTD
30 South Wacker Drive, 29th Floor, Chicago, IL 60606-7484

Sacks Montgomery PC
800 Third Avenue, New York, NY 10022

Sacks Tierney PA
4250 North Drinkwater Boulevard, 4th Floor, Scottsdale, AZ 85251

Saiber Schlesinger Satz & Goldstein, LLC
One Gateway Center, Thirteenth Floor, Newark, NJ 07102-5311

Sale & Kuehne PA
Bank of America Tower, Suite 3550, 100 Southeast Second Street, Miami, FL 33131-2154

Samuel B Weiner Co. LPA
743 South Front Street, Columbus, OH 43206

Santoro, Driggs, Walch, Kearney, Johnson & Thompson
400 South 4th Street, 3rd Floor, Las Vegas, NV 89101

Schaffer Law Office
311 East 14th Street, Sioux Falls, SD 57104-5022

Scheuer Yost & Patterson PC
125 Lincoln Avenue, Suite 223, PO Drawer 9570, Santa Fe, NM 87504-9570

Schlack Ito & Lockwood Piper & Elkind, LLC
Topa Financial Centre, Fort Street Tower, 745 Fort Street, Suite 1500, Honolulu, HI 96813

Schnader Harrison Segal & Lewis LLP
1600 Market Street, Suite 3600, Philadelphia, PA 19103-7286

Schneider Tanaka Radovich Andrew & Tanaka, LLLC
The Topa Financial Center, Bishop Street Tower, Suite 501, Honolulu, HI 96813

Schreck Brignone
300 South Fourth Street, Suite 1200, Las Vegas, NV 89101

Schuler, Messersmith, Daly & Lansdowne
2155 Louisiana Boulevard NE, Suite 8500, Albuquerque, NM 87110-1229

Schwabe Williamson & Wyatt PC
Suites 1600-1900 Pacwest Center, 1211 SW Fifth Avenue, Portland, OR 97204

Schwartz, Bon, Walker & Studer LLC
141 South Center, Suite 505, Casper, WY 82601

Schwartz, Kushner & Rendon Co, LPA
2860 BP Tower, 200 Public Square, Cleveland, OH 44114

Scroggins & Williamson
1500 The Candler Building, 127 Peachtree Street NE, Atlanta, GA 30303

Sebris Busto James
14205 SE 36th Street, Suite 325, Bellevue, WA 98006

Senn Lewis & Visciano
1801 California Street, Suite 4300, Denver, CO 80205

Serkland Law Firm, PC
10 Roberts Street, PO Box 6017, Fargo, \ ND 58108

Serotte, Rockman & Westcott
409 Washington Avenue, Suite 610, Baltimore, MD 21204-7913

Shaft, Reis & Shaft Ltd
Gate City Federal Building, PO Box 5116, Grand Forks, ND 58206-5116

Shannon, Gracey, Ratliff & Miller LLP
777 Main Street, Suite 3800, Fort Worth, TX 76102

Shapiro Fussell
One Midtown Plaza, Suite 1200, 1360 Peachtree Street, Atlanta, GA 30309-3214

Shaw Gussis Fishman Glantz Wolfson & Towbin LLC
321N Clark Street, Suite 800, Chicago, IL 60610

Sheehey Furlong & Behm PC
Gateway Square, 30 Main Street, Burlington, VT 05402

Shefsky & Froelich
444 North Michigan Avenue, Chicago, IL 60611

Shemin & Hendren, PLLC
One East Center Street, Suite 212, Bank of America Plaza, PO Box 3578, Fayetteville, AR 72702

Sheppard, Mullin, Richter & Hampton LLP
333 South Hope Street, Forty-Eighth Floor, Los Angeles, CA 90071

Sheppard, White & Thomas PA
215 Washington Street, Jacksonville, FL 32202

Sher Garner Cahill Richter Klein McAlister & Hilbert, LLC
909 Poydras Street, Twenty Eight Floor, New Orleans, LA 70112-1033

Sherin and Lodgen LLP
100 Summer Street, Boston, MA 02110

Sherman & Howard LLC
633 Seventeenth Street, Suite 3000, Denver, CO 80202

Shernoff, Bidart & Darras LLP
600 South Indian Hill Boulevard, Claremont, CA 91711

Sherrard & Roe PLC
SunTrust Center, 424 Church Street, Suite 2000, Nashville, TN 37219

Shipman & Goodwin LLP
One American Row, Hartford, CT 06103

Shulman, Rogers, Gandal, Pordy & Ecker, PA
11921 Rockville Pike, Third Floor, Rockville, MD 20852

Shults Law Firm, LLP
200 West Capitol Avenue, Suite 1600, Little Rock, AR 72201-3637

Shumacker Witt Gaither & Whitaker, P.C.
1100 SunTrust Bank Building, 736 Market Street, Chattanooga, TN 37402-4856

Shumaker Loop & Kendrick LLP
North Courthouse Square, 1000 Jackson, Toledo, OH 43624

Shuttleworth & Ingersoll PLC
115 Third Street South East, Suite 500, PO Box 2107, Cedar Rapids, IA 52406

Siegel, O'Connor, Zangari, O'Donnell & Beck PC
150 Trumbell Street, Hartford, CT 06103

Siegfried, Rivera, Lerner, De La Torre & Sobel, PA
Suite 1102, 201 Alhambra Circle, Miami, FL 33134

Sills Cummis Epstein & Gross PC
The Legal Center, One Riverfront Plaza, Newark, NJ 07102

Simmons Perrine Albright & Ellwood P.L.C.
115 Third Street SE, Suite 1200, Cedar Rapids, IA 52401

Sirote & Permutt PC
2311 Highland Avenue South, PO Box 55727, Birmingham, AL 35205

Slusser, Wilson & Partridge LLP
4720 Three Allen Center, 333 Clay Street, Houston, TX 77002

Smith & Kotchka Ltd
317 South Sixth Street, Las Vegas, NV 89101

If you can't find a firm here, see firm profiles at the end of every state

Smith Gambrell & Russell LLP
Promenade II, Suite 3100, 1230 Peachtree
Street NE, Atlanta, GA 30309

Smith Mackinnon PA
Suite 800 Citrus Center
(Orange Co), 255 South Orange Avenue,
Orlando, FL 32801

Smith Pachter McWhorter & Allen
8000 Towers Crescent Drive, Suite 900,
Vienna, VA 22182

Smith, Currie & Hancock LLP
2600 Harris Tower-Peachtree Center, 233
Peachtree Street NE, Atlanta, GA 30303

**Sommer, Udall, Hardwick, Ahern &
Hyatt LLP**
200 West Marcy Street
Santa Fe, New Mexico 87501, Suite 129,
Santa Fe, NM 87501

Spencer Fane Britt & Browne LLP
1000 Walnut Street, Suite 1400, Kansas City,
MO 64106

Sperling & Slater
55 West Monroe Street, Suite 3300, Chicago,
IL 60603-5010

**Spieth Bell McCurdy &
Newell Co LPA**
2000 Huntington Building, 925 Euclid
Avenue, Cleveland, OH 44115-1496

Spink Butler, LLP
PO Box 639, Boise, ID 83701

**Spradling, Kennedy &
McPhail LLP**
The Tower, 1601 NW Expressway, Suite
1750, 405-418-2700
Facsimile: 405-418-2705, Oklahoma City,
OK 73118

Sprague & Sprague
The Wellington Building, Suite 400, 135
South Nineteenth Street, Philadelphia,
PA 19103

Squire, Sanders & Dempsey L.L.P.
4900 Key Tower, 127 Public Square,
Cleveland, OH 44114-1304

Stafford Rosenbaum LLP
3 South Pinckney Street, Suite 1000, PO Box
1784, Madison, WI 53701

**Stearns Weaver Miller Weissler
Alhadeff & Sitterson, P.A.**
Suite 2200 Museum Tower, 150 West Flagler
Street, Miami, FL 33130

Stein, Ray & Harris LLP
222 West Adams Street, Suite 1800, Chicago,
IL 60606

Steiner, Darling & Hutchinson LLP
303 East 17th Avenue, Suite 850, Denver,
CO 80203

Stephen E Kaufman, PC
277 Park Avenue, 47th Floor, New York,
NY 10172

Stephen Rakusin PA
1 East Broward Bouleard, Suite 1111, Fort
Lauderdale, FL 33301-1843

Steptoe & Johnson PLLC
Bank One Center, Sixth Floor, PO Box 2190,
Clarksburg, WV 26302-2190

Stetler & Duffy Ltd
140 South Dearborn, Suite 400, Chicago,
IL 60603

Stevens & Lee, P. C.
111 North Sixth Street, Reading,
PA 19603-0679

Stevens & O'Connell LLP
400 Capitol Mall, Suite 1400, Sacramento,
CA 95814-4412

Stillman & Friedman
425 Park Avenue, New York, NY 10022

**Stokes Bartholomew Evans &
Petree, P.A.**
SunTrust Center, 424 Church Street, Suite
2800, Nashville, TN 37219

Stokes Lawrence, PS
800 Fifth Avenue, Suite 4000, Seattle,
WA 98104-3179

**Stoll Stoll Berne Lokting &
Shlachter**
209 Southwest Oak Street, Portland,
OR 97204

Stoll, Keenon & Park, LLP
300 W Vine Street, Suite 2100, Lexington,
KY 40507

Storey & Burnham PLC
3030 East Camelback Road, Suite 265,
Phoenix, AZ 85016

Storslee Law Firm
PO Box 4007, 1802 Allison Drive, Bismarck,
ND 58502-4007

Strasburger & Price LLP
4300 NationsBank Plaza, 901 Main Street,
Dallas, TX 75202

Strecker & Associates
2150 Mid-Continent Tower, 401 South
Boston Avenue, Tulsa, OK 74103-4009

Stroock & Stroock & Lavan LLP
180 Maiden Lane, New York,
NY 10038-4982

**Sugarman, Rogers, Barshak
& Cohen, PC**
101 Merrimac Street, Boston,
MA 02114-4737

Sullivan & Worcester
One Post Office Square, Boston, MA 02109

Sullivan Weinstein & McQuay
Two Park Plaza, Boston, MA 02116-3902

**Sullivan, Tabaracci and
Rhoades PC**
1821 South Avenue West, Third Floor,
Missoula, MT 59801

Sulloway & Hollis PLLC
9 Capitol Street, PO Box 1256, Concord,
NH 03302

Summit Law Group, PLLC
315 Fifth Avenue South, Suite 1000, Seattle,
WA 98104

Susman Godfrey LLP
Suite 5100, 1000 Louisiana Street, Houston,
TX 77002-5096

Taft, Stettinius & Hollister LLP
425 Walnut Street, Suite 1800, Cincinnati,
OH 45202

**Tarolli, Sundheim, Covell, &
Tummino LLP**
1111 Leader Building, 526 Superior Avenue,
Cleveland, OH 44114

**Taylor, Porter, Brooks &
Phillips, LLP**
Bank One Centre, 8th Floor, 451 Florida
Street, Baton Rouge, LA 70821

**Tescher Gutter Chaves Josepher
Rubin Ruffin & Forman PA**
Boca Corporate Center, 2101 Corporate
Boulevard, Suite 107, Boca Ratón, FL
33431-7343

Tew Cardenas LLP
Four Seasons Office Tower, 1441 Brickell
Avenue, 15th Floor, Miami, FL 33131

The James Law Firm PC
630 Equitable Building, 604 Locust Street,
Des Moines, IA 50309

**The Law Office of Mark J.
Svonkin P.C.**
18 North Main Street, West Hartford,
CT 06107

The Lyon Firm PA
1031 West morse Boulevard, Suite 170,
Winter Park, FL 32789

The Steeg Law Firm, LLC
201 St Charles Avenue, Suite 3201, New
Orleans, LA 70170

The Tinney Law Firm
Fourteenth Floor, 707 Virginia Street,
Charleston, WV 25301

Thieman & Farrell
Koppers Buildings 436, 7th Avenue,
Pittsburgh, PA 15219

**Thomas Kayden Horstemeyer &
Risley LLP**
100 Galleria Parkway North West, Suite
1750, Atlanta, GA 30339

Thomas N Long PC
American National Bank Building, Suite
406, Cheyenne, WY 82003-0087

Thorp Reed & Armstrong
One Oxford Centre, Fourteenth Floor,
Pittsburgh, PA 15219-1425

**Timothy S Kelley - Sole
Practitioner**
540 N Lake Shore Drive, Suite 204, Chicago,
IL 60611

Tindall Bennett & Shoup PC
508 West 2nd Avenue, Third Floor,
Anchorage, AK 99501

Todd & Weld LLP
28 State Street, Boston, MA 02109

Tonkon Torp LLP
1600 Pioneer Tower, 888 South West Fifth
Avenue, Portland, OR 97204

Topel & Goodman PC
4th Floor, 832 Sansome Street, San
Francisco, CA 94111

**Torkildson, Katz, Fonseca, Jaffe,
Moore & Hetherington Attorneys
At Law, A Law Corporation**
Amfac Building, 15th Floor, 700 Bishop
Street, Honolulu, HI 96813

Townsend & Jones
5615 Kirby Drive, Suite 830, Houston,
TX 77005

**Townsend and Townsend and
Crew LLP**
Two Embarcadero Center, Eighth Floor, San
Francisco, CA 94111-3834

**Trenam, Kemker, Scharf, Barkin,
Frye, O'Neill & Mullis PA**
2700 Bank of America Plaza, 101 East
Kennedy Boulevard, Tampa, FL 33602

Triplett, Woolf & Garretson LLC
2959 North Rock Road, Suite 300, Wichita,
KS 67226

Trombley & Hanes
10th Floor, 707 North Franklin Street, P.O.
Box 3356, Tampa, FL 33602

Troutman Sanders LLP
401 Ninth Street NW, Suite 1000,
Washington, DC 20004-2134

Tschider & Smith
Professional Building, Suite 200, 418 East
Rosser Avenue, Bismarck, ND 58501

Tucker Ellis & West LLP
1100 Huntingdon Building, 925 Euclid
Avenue, Cleveland, OH 44115-1475

Turner & Mede, PC
1500 West 33rd Avenue, Suite 200,
Anchorage, AK 99503-3502

Tyler Cooper & Alcorn LLP
205 Church Street, PO Box 1936, New
Haven, CT 06509

**Ugrin, Alexander, Zadick &
Higgins, PC**
2 Railroad Square, PO Box 1746, Great Falls,
MT 59403

Ulmer & Berne LLP
Penton Media Building, 1300 East Ninth
Street, Suite 900, Cleveland, OH 44114

Upton and Hatfield LLP
10 Centre Street, PO Box 1090, Concord,
NH 03302

**Van Cott, Bagley, Cornwall &
McCarthy**
50 South Main Street, Suite 1600, PO Box
45340, Salt Lake City, UT 84145

Van Hoy Reutlinger Adams & Dunn
737 East Boulevard, Charlotte, NC 28203

Van Ness Feldman PC
1050 Thomas Jefferson Street NW, Seventh
Floor, Washington, DC 20007

**Varnum, Riddering, Schmidt &
Howlett LLP**
Bridgewater Place, PO Box 352, Grand
Rapids, MI 49501

Vaughan & Murphy
260 Peachtree Street NW, Suite 1600,
Atlanta, GA 30303

**Vedder, Price, Kaufman &
Kammholz**
222 North LaSalle Street, Chicago, IL 60601

Vercruysse Murray & Calzone, PC
31780 Telegraph Road, Suite 200, Bingham
Farms, MI 48226-3602

Vezina Lawrence & Piscitelli PA
318 North Calhoun Street, Tallahassee,
FL 32301

Vickers Madsen & Goldman
1705 Metropolitan Boulevard, Suite 101,
Tallahassee, FL 32308-3765

Vogel Campbell Blueher & Castle
6100 Uptown Boulevard NE, Suite 500,
Albuquerque, NM 87110-4143

V

Vogel Law Firm
502 First Avenue North, PO Box 1389, Fargo, ND 58107

von Briesen & Roper SC
411 East Wisconsin Avenue, Suite 700, Milwaukee, WI 53202

Wadleigh, Starr & Peters PLLC
95 Market Street, Manchester, NH 03101

Walder, Hayden & Brogan P.A.
5 Becker Farm Road, PO Box 901, Roseland, NJ 07068

Wallace King Domike & Branson PLLC
1050 Thomas Jefferson Street NW, Washington, DC 20007

Walston, Wells, Anderson & Bains
One Federal Place, 1819 Fifth Ave North, Suite 1100, Birmingham, AL 35203

Walter & Haverfield LLP
The Tower at Erieview, 1301 East Ninth Street, Suite 3500, Cleveland, OH 44114-1821

Ward and Smith, PA
1001 College Court, PO Box 867, New Bern, NC 28563

Warner Norcross & Judd LLP
900 Old Kent Building, 111 Lyon Street North West, Grand Rapids, MI 49503

Warren & Sinkler LLP
171 Church Street, Suite 340, PO Box 1254, Charleston, SC 29402

Watanabe Ing Kawashima & Komeiji
First Hawaiian Center, 999 Bishop Street, Suite 2300, Honolulu, HI 96813

Watt, Tieder, Hoffar & Fitzgerald, L.L.P.
7929 Westpark Drive, Suite 400, McLean, VA 22102

Webb Ziesenheim Logsdon Orkin & Hanson, PC
700 Koppers Bldg, 436 Seventh Ave, Pittsburgh, PA 15219-1818

Weinberg Richmond LLP
333 West Wacker Drive, Suite 1800, Chicago, IL 60606

Weinberg, Wheeler, Hudgins, Gunn & Dial, LLC
999 Peachtree Street NE, Suite 2700, Atlanta, GA 30309

Weissmann, Wolff, Bergman, Coleman, Grodin & Evall, LLP
Suite 900, 9665 Wilshire Boulevard, Beverly Hills, CA 90212-2345

Welbaum, Guernsey, Hingston, Greenleaf & Gregory LLP
Penthouse Suite, 901 Ponce de Leon Boulevard, Miami, FL 33134-3009

Wheeler Trigg Kennedy LLP
1801 California Street, Suite 3600, Denver, CO 80202-2617

White Goss Bowers March Schulte & Weisenfels, A Professional Corporation
4510 Belleview Avenue, Suite 300, Kansas City, MO 64111

White O'Connor Curry & Avanzado LLP
10100 Santa Monica Boulevard, Twenty-Third Floor, Los Angeles, CA 90067

White, Getgey & Meyer Co. LPA
1700 Fourth & Vine Tower, 1 West Fourth Street, Cincinnati, OH 45202-3621

Whiteford, Taylor & Preston LLP
7 Saint Paul Street, Baltimore, MD 21202

Whiteman Osterman & Hanna LLP
One Commerce Plaza, Albany, NY 12260

Whitfield & Eddy, P.L.C
317 6th Avenue, Suite 1200, Des Moines, IA 50309

Whyte Hirschboeck Dudek S.C.
111 E Wisconsin Avenue, Suite 2100, Milwaukee, WI 53202

Wickwire Gavin
8100 Boone Boulevard, Suite 700, Vienna, VA 22182

Wiggin & Dana LLP
One Century Tower, New Haven, CT 06508

Wiggin & Nourie
20 Market Street, PO Box 808, Manchester, NH 03105-0808

Wildman, Harrold, Allen & Dixon
225 West Wacker Drive, 30th Floor, Chicago, IL 60606

Wilentz Goldman & Spitzer, P.C.
90 Woodbridge Center Drive, Suite 900, Box 10, Woodbridge, NJ 07095

Willcox & Savage
One Commercial Place, Suite 1800, Norfolk, VA 23510

William Aaron
Miami Center, Suite 850, 201 South Biscayne Boulevard, Miami, FL 33131

William Rozell - Sole Practitioner
617 Willoghby Avenue, Juneau, AK 99801

Williams & Anderson PLC
Twenty-Second Floor, 111 Center Street, Little Rock, AR 72201

Williams & Connolly LLP
725 Twelfth Street, Washington, DC 20005

Williams & Petro Co. LLC
338 South High Street, Columbus, OH 43215

Williams Mullen
Two James Center, 1021 East Cary Street, Richmond, VA 23218

Williams, Porter, Day & Neville PC
159 North Wolcott Street, Suite 400, Casper, WY 82602

Williams, Zografos & Peck
334 Third Street, Post Office Box 547, Lake Oswego, OR 97034

Wilson, Elser, Moskowitz, Edelman & Dicker LLP
150 East 42nd Street, New York, NY 10017-5639

Winer & Bennett LLP
111 Concord Street, POBox 488, Nashua, NH 03061-0488

Winn & Alexander LLP
820 Bay Avenue, Suite 109, Capitola, CA 95010

Winne Banta Hetherington Basralian & Kahn, P.C.
21 Main Street, P.O. Box 647, Hackensack, NJ 07602

Winterbauer & Diamond, P.L.L.C.
1200 Fifth Avenue, Suite 1910, Seattle, WA 98101

Winthrop & Weinstine, A Professional Association
225 South Sixth Street, Suite 3500, Minneapolis, MN 55402-4629

Wise Carter Child & Caraway, Professional Association
401 East Capitol Street, Suite 600, PO Box 651, Jackson, MS 39205

Wold Johnson PC
400 Gate City Building, POBox 1680, Fargo, ND 58107

Wood, Herron & Evans, LLP
2700 Carew Tower, Cincinnati, OH 45202

Woods & Aitken LLP
301 South 13th Street, Suite 500, Lincoln, NE 68508

Woods Rogers PLC
Wachovia Tower, Suite 1400, 10 South Jefferson Street, Roanoke, VA 24038

Woods, Fuller, Shultz & Smith PC
300 South Phillips Avenue, Suite 300, PO Box 5027, Sioux Falls, SD 57117

Woodward, Hobson & Fulton LLP
2500 National City Tower, 101 South Fifth Street, Louisville, KY 40202

Word & Bogardus
500 Tijeras NW, Albuquerque, NM 87102

Worden Thane PC
111 North Higgins, Suite 600, Missoula, MT 59806

Wright & Talisman PC
Suite 600, 1200 G Street NW, Washington, DC 20005-3802

Wright Robinson Osthimer & Tatum
411 East Franklin Street, Suite 400, Richmond, VA 23219

Wright, Henson, Somers, Clark & Bake
Commerce Bank Building, 100 Southeast Ninth Street, 2nd Floor, P.O. Box 3555, Topeka, KS 66601-3555

Wyche, Burgess, Freeman & Parham, PA
44 East Camperdown Way, PO Box 728, Greenville, SC 29601

Wyrsch Hobbs & Mirakian PC
1101 Walnut Suite, Kansas City, MO 64106

Yonkee & Toner LLP
319 West Dow Street, PO Box 6288, Sheridan, WY 82801

York, Keller & Field
1265 Frost Bank Plaza, 816 Congress Avenue, Austin, TX 78701

Young & Susser PC Attorneys and Counselors
Suite 305 Westview Office Center, 26200 American Drive, Southfield, MI 48034

Young, Clement & Rivers LLP
28 Broad Street, PO Box 993, Charleston, SC 29402

Young, Sommer, Ward, Ritzenberg, Wooley, Baker & Moore LLC
5 Palisades Drive, Executive Woods, Albany, NY 12205

Zetlin & De Chiara LLP
801 Second Avenue, New York, NY 10017

Ziffren Brittenham Branca Fischer Gilbert-Lurie & Stiffelman LLP
1801 Century Park West, Los Angeles, CA 90067-6406

Zimney, Foster, Johnson, Dittus & Flaten, Chartered
Bremer Financial Center, Suite 200, 3100 Soouth Columbia Road, PO Box 13417, Grand Forks, ND 58208 3417

Zinober & McCrea, P.A.
Southtrust Plaza, 201 East Kennedy Boulevard Suite 800, PO Box 1378, Tampa, FL 33602

Zuckerman Spaeder LLP
Miami Center, Suite 900, 201 Biscayne Boulevard, Miami, FL 33131

Zuger Kirmis & Smith
316 North Fifth Street, PO Box 1695, Bismarck, ND 58502

Z

If you can't find a firm here, see firm profiles at the end of every state